D1082345

SCOTT®

2017
STANDARD POSTAGE STAMP CATALOGUE

ONE HUNDRED AND SEVENTY-THIRD EDITION IN SIX VOLUMES

VOLUME 5

COUNTRIES OF THE WORLD

N-Sam

SENIOR E

ADMINISTRATIVE A
PRINT

PB 9-23-16
769.5697 124.99
SCO
2017
V. 5

Scott Standard Postage Stamp Catalogue

A
A

Includes New Stam ... ly Catalogue Update

GATES PUBLIC LIBRARY
902 ELMGROVE ROAD
ROCHESTER, N.Y. 14624

Publishers o ... *World Monthly.*

Table of Contents

See Volume 1 for United States, United Nations and Countries of the World A-B
See Volume 2, 3, 4, 6 for Countries of the World, C-M, San-Z

Volume 2: C-F
Volume 3: G-I
Volume 4: J-M
Volume 6: San-Z

Scott Catalogue Mission Statement

The Scott Catalogue Team exists to serve the recreational, educational and commercial hobby needs of stamp collectors and dealers.

We strive to set the industry standard for philatelic information and products by developing and providing goods that help collectors identify, value, organize and present their collections.

Quality customer service is, and will continue to be, our highest priority. We aspire toward achieving total customer satisfaction.

Copyright Notice

The contents of this book are owned exclusively by Amos Media Co. and all rights thereto are reserved under the Pan American and Universal Copyright Conventions.

Copyright @2016 by Amos Media Co., Sidney, OH. Printed in U.S.A.

COPYRIGHT NOTE

Permission is hereby given for the use of material in this book and covered by copyright if:

(a) The material is used in advertising matter, circulars or price lists for the purpose of offering stamps for sale or purchase at the prices listed therein; and

(b) Such use is incidental to the business of buying and selling stamps and is limited in scope and length, i.e., it does not cover a substantial portion of the total number of stamps issued by any country or of any special category of stamps of any country; and

(c) Such material is not used as part of any catalogue, stamp album or computerized or other system based upon the Scott catalogue numbers, or in any updated valuations of stamps not offered for sale or purchase; and

(d) Such use is not competitive with the business of the copyright owner; and

(e) Such use is for editorial purposes in publications in the form of articles or commentary, except for computer software or the serialization of books in such publications, for which separate written permission is required.

Any use of the material in this book which does not satisfy all the foregoing conditions is forbidden in any form unless permission in each instance is given in writing by the copyright owner.

Trademark Notice

The terms SCOTT, SCOTT'S, SCOTT CATALOGUE NUMBERING SYSTEM, SCOTT CATALOGUE NUMBER, SCOTT NUMBER and abbreviations thereof, are trademarks of Amos Media Co., used to identify its publications and its copyrighted system for identifying and classifying postage stamps for dealers and collectors. These trademarks are to be used only with the prior consent of Amos Media Co.

No part of this work may be reproduced in any form or by any means, electronic or mechanical, including photocopying, without permission in writing from Amos Media Co., P.O. Box 4129, Sidney, OH 45365-4129.

ISBN 0-89487-511-3

Library of Congress Card No. 2-3301

AMOS MEDIA

SCOTT 911 VANDEMARK ROAD, SIDNEY, OHIO 45365 937-498-0802

Greetings, Fellow Scott Catalog User:

Value changes for Nicaragua and Portugal reflect increases

More than 9,100 value changes are recorded for Vol. 5 of the 2017 Scott *Standard Postage Stamp Catalogue*. Vol. 5 spans countries of the world N-Sam (Samoa).

Almost 360 value changes for the Central American country of Nicaragua reflect a healthy upward movement for these stamps. The 5-centavos on 1-peso yellow surcharged in black with ornaments on each side of "1901" (Scott 146b) advances from $7 to $30 in unused condition. The double-surcharge variety of the 20c on 2p salmon of the same issue (147b) in used condition moves from $12.50 to $27.50. The 1919 5c on 20c surcharge with type I numerals (Scott 392) jumps from $40 in used condition to $50. The surcharge with type III numerals (392b) advances from $50 used to $55.

As is true for many countries, value changes for Nicaragua stamps issued from 1990 to present show a mix of increases and decreases. Among modern issues, the 1993 sheet of 16 1.50-cordoba stamps featuring butterflyfish (Scott 1962) slides from $10 mint to $8. Value changes also were made among the back-of-the-book issues. The 1980 International Year of the Child sheet of two airmail stamps (C970) has been given a value of $21 in italics, indicating that the sheet is difficult to value accurately. Among the revenue stamps surcharged in 1907 for official use, the 1p on 2c orange with inverted surcharge skyrockets from $2.50 both unused and used to $14 in both conditions.

Mostly increases occur among the 100 changes in Portugal. The 2001 set of six stamps commemorating the 200th anniversary of Security Services (Scott 2447-2452) rises slightly, from $10 to $12 in mint condition and from $5 to $6 in used condition. The 1898 5-reis Vasco da Gama postage due variety with value and "Continente" omitted (Scott J1a) increases from $30 mint to $50.

The editors gave the South American country of Paraguay a close inspection this year, focusing on the stamps issued from 1940 to present. This inspection yielded almost 3,800 value changes. From 1950 to 1999, most of these changes are in a downward direction. Values for stamps issued from 2000 to date remain steady or show some increases. Increases also are found among the Portugal stamps inscribed for use in Azores and Madeira. The Azores 2004 Worldwide Fund for Nature (World Wildlife Fund) horizontal strip of four (Scott 480) jumps from $3 mint to $5.

Many of the 48 value changes in Romania reflect increases. The 1945 set honoring posts and telegraphs (Scott 588-594) jumps from $20.80 both mint and used for the set of seven to $23.30.

A sprinkling of value changes can be found in New Zealand. Scott 78, the 1898 6-penny green Kiwi stamp, soars from $90 unused to $120. The used value remains at $55. The Ross Dependency 1998 Ice Formations stamps in a block of six (L54a) rise from $11 mint and used to $15 mint and used.

St. Vincent Grenadines received a full line-by-line review. Although most of the almost 1,400 value changes reflect decreases for stamps issued prior to 2002, increases are found among later issues. The 2007 sheet of four stamps issued for the Grenadines island of Bequia to honor Halley's comet (Scott 413) jumps from $6 mint and used to $6.50 both ways. The souvenir sheet from the set (414) rises from $4.50 mint and used to $4.75 in both conditions. Significant increases are found among the stamps of the island of Mustique. The 2000 $1 sheet of eight showing the Paintings type of 1999 (Scott 2) skyrockets from $6 mint and used to $17.50 in both conditions. The imperforate variety (Scott 2i) jumps from $6 mint and used to $27.50 both ways.

The more than 40 value changes in Northern Nigeria reflect increases.

Fifty-eight values are scattered throughout Palestinian Authority with mixed results.

More than 1,000 value changes occur in Pitcairn Islands, with a few scattered increases.

Among the value changes for St. Thomas and Prince Islands is an increase in the value of the 1977 sheet of four stamps featuring paintings by Peter Paul Rubens. The sheet (Scott 473a) goes from $27.50 mint and used to $40 in both conditions. The 2½-reis brown newspaper stamp (P13) issued in 1899 moves upward, from $25 unused to $30.

More than 65 value changes were made among the stamps of Pakistan. A mix of increases and decreases are found. The 15-rupee dark green and dark brown (Scott 18) climbs from $65 unused to $90, while the 25r dark violet and blue-violet stamp (19) from the same set is adjusted downward, from $87.50 unused and used to $70 in both conditions.

Almost 100 value changes are sprinkled throughout the Philippines. Most of these changes reflect increases, with a few decreases. Among the surcharged issues of 1879, the 8 centimos on 100 milesimas de peso (Scott 75) rises from $300 unused to $400. The used value for the 1985 3.50-peso on 4.20p rose, type III, soars from 90¢ to $3. Other used values within the modern period show increases, with only a few decreases.

A few changes were made to the values of Nyasaland Protectorate stamps. The 1918 4-shilling black and red stamp on chalky paper increases from $45 unused and $85 used to $50 and $90, respectively.

Editorial enhancements for Russia

Several new listings for Russia have been brought over to the 2017 Vol. 5 catalog from the 2016 Scott *Classic Specialized Catalogue of Stamps and Covers 1840-1940*. A center inverted variety of the 1884 3.50-ruble black and gray stamp is now listed as Scott 39b. Dashes are placed in the unused and used value columns, indicating that the stamp exists in both conditions, but there is insufficient information to establish a value. The 1909-12 1r with center inverted, previously listed as 87e, has been renumbered as 87f. No. 87e has been assigned to a new listing of a vertical pair, imperforate between, valued at $25 unused with a dash in the used column. The center-doubled variety is now listed as 87g.

A type II variety has been added for the 1927 8-kopeck on 7k stamp surcharged in black. Type I has a 2-millimeter space between the lines of the surcharge. Listed as 349c, the type II variety has a 0.7mm space and is valued at $2,750 unused and $140 used. The type II stamp also exists with the surcharge inverted and is listed as 349d and valued at $275 unused in italics. A type II variety also has been added to No. 350 as 350b, valued at $10,500 unused in italics. This stamp with surcharge inverted (350c) is valued at $275 unused (in italics).

As always, we encourage you to pay special attention to the Number Additions, Deletions & Changes found on page 1676 in this volume.

While you settle in with your stamp album and Scott catalog, relax and enjoy the world's greatest hobby.

Donna Houseman

Donna Houseman/Catalogue Editor

Acknowledgments

Our appreciation and gratitude go to the following individuals who have assisted us in preparing information included in this year's Scott Catalogues. Some helpers prefer anonymity. These individuals have generously shared their stamp knowledge with others through the medium of the Scott Catalogue.

Those who follow provided information that is in addition to the hundreds of dealer price lists and advertisements and scores of auction catalogues and realizations that were used in producing the catalogue values. It is from those noted here that we have been able to obtain information on items not normally seen in published lists and advertisements. Support from these people goes beyond data leading to catalogue values, for they also are key to editorial changes.

A special acknowledgment to Liane and Sergio Sismondo of The Classic Collector for their assistance and knowledge sharing that have aided in the preparation of this year's Standard and Classic Specialized Catalogues.

Roland Austin
Robert Ausubel (Great Britain Collectors Club)
James K Beck (Latin American Philatelic Society)
Vladimir Berrio-Lemm
John Birkinbine II
Keith & Margie Brown
Josh Buchsbayew (Cherrystone Auctions)
Peter Bylen
Tina & John Carlson (JET Stamps)
Richard A Champagne (Richard A. Champagne, Ltd.)
Henry Chlanda
Frank D. Correl
Christopher Dahle
Charles Deaton
Ubaldo Del Toro
Bob & Rita Dumaine (Sam Houston Duck Co.)
Sister Theresa Durand
Mark Eastzer (Markest Stamp Co.)
Paul G. Eckman
Craig A. Eggleston
George Epstein (Allkor Stamp Co.)
George Eveleth (Spink USA)
Jeffrey M. Forster
Ernest E. Fricks (France & Colonies Philatelic Society)
Michael Fuchs
Frank Geiger (Worldstamps.com)
Bob Genisol (Sultan Stamp Center)
Allan Grant (Rushstamps, Ltd.)
Daniel E. Grau
Fred F. Gregory
Jan E. Gronwall
Grosvenor Auctions
Chris Harmer (Harmer-Schau Auctions)
Bruce Hecht (Bruce L. Hecht Co.)
Peter Hoffman
Armen Hovsepian (Armenstamp)
Philip J. Hughes
Doug Iams
Eric Jackson
John Jamieson (Saskatoon Stamp and Coin)
N. M. Janoowalla
Peter Jeannopoulos
Stephen Joe (International Stamp Service)
William A. Jones
Sheikh Shafiqul Islam
Allan Katz (Ventura Stamp Co.)
Stanford M. Katz
Lewis Kaufman (The Philatelic Foundation)
Patricia A. Kaufmann (Confederate Stamp Alliance)
William V. Kriebel (Brazil Philatelic Association)
George Krieger
Frederick P. Lawrence
Ken Lawrence
John R. Lewis (The William Henry Stamp Co.)
Ulf Lindahl
Ignacio Llach (Filatelia Llach S.L.)
Marilyn R. Mattke
William K. McDaniel
Gary Morris (Pacific Midwest Co.)
Peter Mosiondz, Jr.
Bruce M. Moyer (Moyer Stamps & Collectibles)
Richard H. Muller
Scott Murphy (Professional Stamp Experts)
Robert P. Odenweller
Nik & Lisa Oquist
Dr. Everett Parker
John Pearson (Pittwater Philatelic Service)
Donald J. Peterson (International Philippine Philatelic Society)
Stanley M. Piller (Stanley M. Piller & Associates)
Virgil Pirvulescu
Todor Drumev Popov
Peter W. W. Powell
Ken Pugh
Siddique Mahmudur Rahman
Ghassan D. Riachi
Andrew Sader
Mehrdad Sadri (Persiphila)
Theodosios Sampson PhD
Alexander Schauss (Schauss Philatelics)
Jacques C. Schiff, Jr. (Jacques C. Schiff, Jr., Inc.)
Chuck & Joyce Schmidt
Michael Schreiber
Guy Shaw
Jeff Siddiqui
Sergio & Liane Sismondo (The Classic Collector)
Jay Smith
Frank J. Stanley, III
James F. Taff
Peter Thy
Scott R. Trepel (Siegel Auction Galleries)
Dan Undersander (United Postal Stationery Society)
Herbert R. Volin
Philip T. Wall
Giana Wayman
William R. Weiss, Jr. (Weiss Expertizing)
Don White (Dunedin Stamp Centre)
Ralph Yorio
Val Zabijaka (Zabijaka Auctions)
Michal Zika
Steven Zirinsky (Zirinsky Stamps)

Addresses, Telephone Numbers, Web Sites, E-Mail Addresses of General & Specialized Philatelic Societies

Collectors can contact the following groups for information about the philately of the areas within the scope of these societies, or inquire about membership in these groups. Aside from the general societies, we limit this list to groups that specialize in particular fields of philately, particular areas covered by the Scott Standard Postage Stamp Catalogue, and topical groups. Many more specialized philatelic society exist than those listed below. These addresses are updated yearly, and they are, to the best of our knowledge, correct and current. Groups should inform the editors of address changes whenever they occur. The editors also want to hear from other such specialized groups not listed. Unless otherwise noted all website addresses begin with http://

American Philatelic Society
100 Match Factory Place
Bellefonte PA 16823-1367
Ph: (814) 933-3803
www.stamps.org
E-mail: apsinfo@stamps.org

American Stamp Dealers Association, Inc.
P.O. Box 692
Leesport PA 19553
Ph: (800) 369-8207
www.americanstampdealer.com
E-mail: asda@americanstampdealer.com

National Stamp Dealers Association
Robert Klein, President
430 E. Southern Ave.
Tempe AZ 85282-5216
Ph: (800) 875-6635
www.nsdainc.org
E-mail: nsda@nsdainc.org

International Society of Worldwide Stamp Collectors
Joanne Berkowitz, MD
P.O. Box 19006
Sacramento CA 95819
www.iswsc.org
E-mail: executivedirector@iswsc.org

Royal Philatelic Society
41 Devonshire Place
London, W1G 6JY
UNITED KINGDOM
www.rpsl.org.uk
E-mail: secretary@rpsl.org.uk

Royal Philatelic Society of Canada
P.O. Box 929, Station Q
Toronto, ON, M4T 2P1
CANADA
Ph: (888) 285-4143
www.rpsc.org
E-mail: info@rpsc.org

Young Stamp Collectors of America
Janet Houser
100 Match Factory Place
Bellefonte PA 16823-1367
Ph: (814) 933-3820
www.stamps.org/ysca/intro.htm
E-mail: ysca@stamps.org

Philatelic Research Resources

(The Scott editors encourage any additional research organizations to submit data for inclusion in this listing category)

American Philatelic Research Library
Tara Murray
100 Match Factory Place
Bellefonte PA 16823
Ph: (814) 933-3803
www.stamplibrary.org
E-mail: aprl@stamps.org

Institute for Analytical Philately, Inc.
P.O. Box 8035
Holland MI 49422-8035
Ph: (616) 399-9299
www.analyticalphilately.org
E-mail: info@analyticalphilately.org

The Western Philatelic Library
P.O. Box 2219
1500 Partridge Ave.
Sunnyvale CA 94087
Ph: (408) 733-0336
www.fwpf.org

Groups focusing on fields or aspects found in worldwide philately (some might cover U.S. area only)

American Air Mail Society
Stephen Reinhard
P.O. Box 110
Mineola NY 11501
www.americanairmailsociety.org
E-mail: sreinhard1@optonline.net

American First Day Cover Society
Douglas Kelsey
P.O. Box 16277
Tucson AZ 85732-6277
Ph: (520) 321-0880
www.afdcs.org
E-mail: afdcs@afdcs.org

American Revenue Association
Eric Jackson
P.O. Box 728
Leesport PA 19533-0728
Ph: (610) 926-6200
www.revenuer.org
E-mail: eric@revenuer.com

American Topical Association
Vera Felts
P.O. Box 8
Carterville IL 62918-0008
Ph: (618) 985-5100
www.americantopicalassn.org
E-mail: americantopical@msn.com

Christmas Seal & Charity Stamp Society
John Denune
234 E. Broadway
Granville OH 43023
Ph: (740) 587-0276
www.seal-society.org
E-mail: jdenune@roadrunner.com

Errors, Freaks and Oddities Collectors Club
Scott Shaulis
P.O. Box 549
Murrysville PA 15668-0549
Ph: (724) 733-4134
www.efocc.org

First Issues Collectors Club
Kurt Streepy, Secretary
3128 E. Mattatha Drive
Bloomington IN 47401
www.firstissues.org
E-mail: secretary@firstissues.org

International Society of Reply Coupon Collectors
Peter Robin
P.O. Box 353
Bala Cynwyd PA 19004
E-mail: peterrobin@verizon.net

The Joint Stamp Issues Society
Richard Zimmermann
29A Rue Des Eviats
Lalaye F-67220
FRANCE
www.phiparz.net
E-mail: richard.zimmermann@club-internet.fr

National Duck Stamp Collectors Society
Anthony J. Monico
P.O. Box 43
Harleysville PA 19438-0043
www.ndscs.org
E-mail: ndscs@ndscs.org

No Value Identified Club
Albert Sauvanet
Le Clos Royal B, Boulevard des Pas Enchantes
St. Sebastien-sur Loire, 44230
FRANCE
E-mail: alain.vailly@irin.univ nantes.fr

The Perfins Club
Jerry Hejduk
P.O. Box 490450
Leesburg FL 34749-0450
www.perfins.org
Ph: (352) 326-2117
E-mail: flprepers@comcast.net

Postage Due Mail Study Group
John Rawlins
13, Longacre
Chelmsford, CM1 3BJ
UNITED KINGDOM
E-mail: john.rawlins2@ukonline.co.uk.

Post Mark Collectors Club
Bob Milligan
7014 Woodland Oaks
Magnolia TX 77354
Ph: (281) 359-2735
www.postmarks.org
E-mail: bob.milligan@gmail.net

Postal History Society
George McGowan
P.O. Box 482
East Schodack NY 12063-0482
www.postalhistorysociety.org
E-mail: geolotus2003@nycap.rr.com

Precancel Stamp Society
Rick Podwell
P.O. Box 85
Fawn Grove PA 17321
Ph: (717) 817-8807
www.precancels.com
E-mail: psspromosec@comcast.net

United Postal Stationery Society
Stuart Leven
P.O. Box 24764
San Jose CA 95154-4764
www.upss.org
E-mail: poststat@gmail.com

United States Possessions Philatelic Society
Daniel F. Ring
P.O. Box 113
Woodstock IL 60098
www.uspps.net
E-mail: danielfring@hotmail.com

Groups focusing on U.S. area philately as covered in the Standard Catalogue

Canal Zone Study Group
Tom Brougham
737 Neilson St.
Berkeley CA 94707
www.CanalZoneStudyGroup.com
E-mail: czsgsecretary@gmail.com

Carriers and Locals Society
Martin Richardson
P.O. Box 74
Grosse Ile MI 48138
www.pennypost.org
E-mail: martinr362@aol.com

Confederate Stamp Alliance
Patricia A. Kaufmann
10194 N. Old State Road
Lincoln DE 19960
Ph. (302) 422-2656
www.csalliance.org
E-mail: trishkauf@comcast.net

Hawaiian Philatelic Society
Kay H. Hoke
P.O. Box 10115
Honolulu HI 96816-0115
Ph: (808) 521-5721

Plate Number Coil Collectors Club
Gene Trinks
16415 W. Desert Wren Court
Surprise AZ 85374
Ph: (623) 322-4619
www.pnc3.org
E-mail: gctrinks@cox.net

Ryukyu Philatelic Specialist Society
Laura Edmonds, Secy.
P.O. Box 240177
Charlotte NC 28224-0177
Ph: (336) 509-3739
www.ryukyustamps.org
E-mail: secretary@ryukyustamps.org

United Nations Philatelists
Blanton Clement, Jr.
P.O. Box 146
Morrisville PA 19067-0146
www.unpi.com
E-mail: bclemjr@yahoo.com

United States Stamp Society
Executive Secretary
P.O. Box 6634
Katy TX 77491-6631
www.usstamps.org
E-mail: webmaster@usstamps.org

U.S. Cancellation Club
Joe Crosby
E-mail: joecrosby@cox.nat

U.S. Philatelic Classics Society
Rob Lund
2913 Fulton St.
Everett WA 98201-3733
www.uspcs.org
E-mail: membershipchairman@uspcs.org

Groups focusing on philately of foreign countries or regions

Aden & Somaliland Study Group
Gary Brown
P.O. Box 106
Briar Hill, Victoria, 3088
AUSTRALIA
E-mail: garyjohn951@optushome.com.au

American Society of Polar Philatelists (Antarctic areas)
Alan Warren
P.O. Box 39
Exton PA 19341-0039
www.polarphilatelists.org

Andorran Philatelic Study Circle
D. Hope
17 Hawthorn Drive
Stalybridge, Cheshire, SK15 1UE
UNITED KINGDOM
apsc.free.fr
E-mail: apsc@free.fr

Australian States Study Circle of The Royal Sydney Philatelic Club
Ben Palmer
GPO 1751
Sydney, N.S.W., 2001
AUSTRALIA
www.philas.org.au/states

Austria Philatelic Society
Ralph Schneider
P.O. Box 23049
Belleville IL 62223
Ph: (618) 277-6152
www.austriaphilatelicsociety.com
E-mail: rschneiderstamps@att.net

American Belgian Philatelic Society
Edward de Bary
11 Wakefield Drive Apt. 2105
Asheville NC 28803

Bechuanalands and Botswana Society
Neville Midwood
69 Porlock Lane
Furzton, Milton Keynes, MK4 1JY
UNITED KINGDOM
www.nevsoft.com
E-mail: bbsoc@nevsoft.com

Bermuda Collectors Society
John Pare
405 Perimeter Road
Mount Horeb WI 53572
www.bermudacollectorssociety.org
E-mail: pare16@mhtc.net

Brazil Philatelic Association
William V. Kriebel
1923 Manning St.
Philadelphia PA 19103-5728
www.brazilphilatelic.org
E-mail: info@brazilphilatelic.org

British Caribbean Philatelic Study Group
Duane Larson
2 Forest Blvd.
Park Forest IL 60466
www.bcpsg.com
E-mail: dlarson283@aol.com

The King George VI Collectors Society (British Commonwealth)
Brian Livingstone
21 York Mansions, Prince of Wales Drive
London, SW11 4DL
UNITED KINGDOM
www.kg6.info
E-mail: livingstone484@btinternet.com

British North America Philatelic Society (Canada & Provinces)
David G. Jones
184 Larkin Drive
Nepean, ON, K2J 1H9
CANADA
www.bnaps.org
E-mail: shibumi.management@gmail.com

British West Indies Study Circle
John Seidl
4324 Granby Way
Marietta GA 30062
Ph: (770) 642-6424
www.bwisc.org
E-mail: john.seidl@gmail.com

Burma Philatelic Study Circle
Michael Whittaker
1, Ecton Leys, Hillside
Rugby, Warwickshire, CV22 5SL
UNITED KINGDOM
www.burmastamps.homecall.co.uk
E-mail: manningham8@mypostoffice.co.uk

Cape and Natal Study Circle
Dr. Guy Dillaway
P.O. Box 181
Weston MA 02493
www.nzsc.demon.co.uk

Ceylon Study Circle
R. W. P. Frost
42 Lonsdale Road, Cannington
Bridgewater, Somerset, TA5 2JS
UNITED KINGDOM
www.ceylonsc.org
E-mail: rodney.frost@tiscali.co.uk

Channel Islands Specialists Society
Moira Edwards
86, Hall Lane, Sandon
Chelmsford, Essex, CM2 7RQ
UNITED KINGDOM
www.ciss1950.org.uk
E-mail: membership@ciss1950.org.uk

China Stamp Society
Paul H. Gault
P.O. Box 20711
Columbus OH 43220
www.chinastampsociety.org
E-mail: secretary@chinastampsociety.org

Colombia/Panama Philatelic Study Group (COPAPHIL)
Thomas P. Myers
P.O. Box 522
Gordonsville VA 22942
www.copaphil.org
E-mail: tpmphil@hotmail.com

Association Filatelic de Costa Rica
Giana Wayman
c/o Interlink 102, P.O. Box 52-6770
Miami FL 33152
E-mail: scotland@racsa.co.cr

Society for Costa Rica Collectors
Dr. Hector R. Mena
P.O. Box 14831
Baton Rouge LA 70808
www.socorico.org
E-mail: hrmena@aol.com

International Cuban Philatelic Society
Ernesto Cuesta
P.O. Box 34434
Bethesda MD 20827
www.cubafil.org
E-mail: ecuesta@philat.com

Cuban Philatelic Society of America ®
P.O. Box 141656
Coral Gables FL 33114-1656
www.cubapsa.com
E-mail: cpsa.usa@gmail.com

Cyprus Study Circle
Colin Dear
10 Marne Close, Wem
Shropshire, SY4 5YE
UNITED KINGDOM
www.cyprusstudycircle.org/index.htm
E-mail: colindear@talktalk.net

Society for Czechoslovak Philately
Tom Cassaboom
P.O. Box 4124
Prescott AZ 86302
www.csphilately.org
E-mail: klfck1@aol.com

Danish West Indies Study Unit of the Scandinavian Collectors Club
Arnold Sorensen
7666 Edgedale Drive
Newburgh IN 47630
Ph: (812) 480-6532
www.scc-online.org
E-mail: valbydwi@hotmail.com

East Africa Study Circle
Michael Vesey-Fitzgerald
Gambles Cottage, 18 Clarence Road
Lyndhurst, SO43 7AL
UNITED KINGDOM
www.easc.org.uk
E-mail: secretary@easc.org.uk

Egypt Study Circle
Mike Murphy
109 Chadwick Road
London, SE15 4PY
UNITED KINGDOM
Trent Ruebush: North American Agent
E-mail: truebrush@usaid.gov
egyptstudycircle.org.uk
E-mail: egyptstudycircle@hotmail.com

Estonian Philatelic Society
Juri Kirsimagi
29 Clifford Ave.
Pelham NY 10803
Ph: (914) 738-3713

Ethiopian Philatelic Society
Ulf Lindahl
21 Westview Place
Riverside CT 06878
Ph: (203) 722-0769
home.comcast.net/~fbheiser/ethiopia5.htm
E-mail: ulindahl@optonline.net

Falkland Islands Philatelic Study Group
Carl J. Faulkner
615 Taconic Trail
Williamstown MA 01267-2745
Ph: (413) 458-4421
www.fipsg.org.uk
E-mail: cfaulkner@taconicwilliamstown.com

Faroe Islands Study Circle
Norman Hudson
40 Queen's Road, Vicar's Cross
Chester, CH3 5HB
UNITED KINGDOM
www.faroeislandssc.org
E-mail: jntropics@hotmail.com

Former French Colonies Specialist Society
COLFRA
BP 628
75367 Paris, Cedex 08
FRANCE
www.colfra.org
E-mail: secretaire@colfra.org

France & Colonies Philatelic Society
Edward Grabowski
111 Prospect St., 4C
Westfield NJ 07090
www.franceandcolps.org
E-mail: edjjg@alum.mit.edu

Germany Philatelic Society
P.O. Box 6547
Chesterfield MO 63006
www.germanyphilatelicusa.org

Plebiscite-Memel-Saar Study Group of the German Philatelic Society
Clayton Wallace
100 Lark Court
Alamo CA 94507
E-mail: claytonwallace@comcast.net

Gibraltar Study Circle
David R. Stirrups
152 The Rowans, Milton
Cambridge, CB24 6YX
UNITED KINGDOM
www.gibraltarstudycircle.wordpress.com
E-mail: beggloops@gmail.com

Great Britain Collectors Club
Steve McGill
10309 Brookhollow Circle
Highlands Ranch CO 80129
www.gbstamps.com/gbcc
E-mail: steve.mcgill@comcast.net

International Society of Guatemala Collectors
Jaime Marckwordt
449 St. Francis Blvd.
Daly City CA 94015-2136
www.guatemalastamps.com
E-mail:
membership@guatamalastamps.com

Haiti Philatelic Society
Ubaldo Del Toro
5709 Marble Archway
Alexandria VA 22315
www.haitiphilately.org
E-mail: u007ubi@aol.com

Hong Kong Stamp Society
Ming W. Tsang
P.O. Box 206
Glenside PA 19038
www.hkss.org
E-mail: hkstamps@yahoo.com

Society for Hungarian Philately
Robert Morgan
2201 Roscomare Road
Los Angeles CA 90077-2222
Ph; (617) 645-4045
www.hungarianphilately.org
E-mail: alan@hungarianstamps.com

India Study Circle
John Warren
P.O. Box 7326
Washington DC 20044
Ph: (202) 564-6876
www.indiastudycircle.org
E-mail: warren.john@epa.gov

Indian Ocean Study Circle
E. S. Hutton
29 Patermoster Close
Waltham Abby, Essex, EN9 3JU
UNITED KINGDOM
www.indianoceanstudycircle.com
E-mail:
secretary@indianoceanstudycircle.com

Society of Indo-China Philatelists
Ron Bentley
2600 N. 24th St.
Arlington VA 22207
www.sicp-online.org
E-mail: ron.bentley@verizon.net

Iran Philatelic Study Circle
Mehdi Esmaili
P.O. Box 750096
Forest Hills NY 11375
www.iranphilatelic.org
E-mail: m.esmaili@earthlink.net

Eire Philatelic Association (Ireland)
David J. Brennan
P.O. Box 704
Bernardsville NJ 07924
www.eirephilatelicassoc.org
E-mail: brennan704@aol.com

Society of Israel Philatelists
Edwin Kroft
P.O. Box 507
Northfield OH 44067
www.israelstamps.com
E-mail: israelstamps@gmail.com

Italy and Colonies Study Circle
Richard Harlow
7 Duncombe House, 8 Manor Road
Teddington, TW11 8BE
UNITED KINGDOM
www.icsc.pwp.blueyonder.co.uk
E-mail: harlowr@gmail.com

International Society for Japanese Philately
William Eisenhauer
P.O. Box 230462
Tigard OR 97281
www.isjp.org
E-mail: secretary@isjp.org

Korea Stamp Society
John E. Talmage
P.O. Box 6889
Oak Ridge TN 37831
www.pennfamily.org/KSS-USA
E-mail: jtalmage@usit.net

Latin American Philatelic Society
Jules K. Beck
30½ St. #209
St. Louis Park MN 55426-3551

Liberian Philatelic Society
William Thomas Lockard
P.O. Box 106
Wellston OH 45692
Ph: (740) 384-2020
E-mail: tlockard@zoomnet.net

Liechtenstudy USA (Liechtenstein)
Paul Tremaine
410 SW Ninth St.
Dundee OR 97115
Ph: (503) 538-4500
www.liechtenstudy.org
E-mail: editor@liechtenstudy.org

Lithuania Philatelic Society
John Variakojis
8472 Carlisle Court.
Burr Ridge IL 60527
Ph: (630) 974-6525
www.lithuanianphilately.com/lps
E-mail: variakojis@sbcglobal.net

Luxembourg Collectors Club
Gary B. Little
7319 Beau Road
Sechelt, BC, VON 3A8
CANADA
lcc.luxcentral.com
E-mail: gary@luxcentral.com

Malaya Study Group
David Tett
P.O. Box 34
Wheathampstead, Herts, AL4 8JY
UNITED KINGDOM
www.m-s-g.org.uk
E-mail: davidtett@aol.com

Malta Study Circle
Alec Webster
50 Worcester Road
Sutton, Surrey, SM2 6QB
UNITED KINGDOM
www.maltastudycircle.org.uk
E-mail: alecwebster50@hotmail.com

Mexico-Elmhurst Philatelic Society International
Thurston Bland
50 Regato
Rancho Santa Margarita CA 92688-3003
www.mepsi.org

Asociacion Mexicana de Filatelia
AMEXFIL
Jose Maria Rico, 129, Col. Del Valle
Mexico City DF, 03100
MEXICO
www.amexfil.mx
E-mail: amexfil@gmail.com

Society for Moroccan and Tunisian Philately
S.P.L.M.
206, bld. Pereire
75017 Paris
FRANCE
splm-philatelie.org
E-mail: splm206@aol.com

Nepal & Tibet Philatelic Study Group
Roger D. Skinner
1020 Covington Road
Los Altos CA 94024-5003
Ph: (650) 968-4163
www.fuchs-online.com/ntpsc/
E-mail: colinhepper@hotmail.co.uk

American Society for Netherlands Philately
Hans Kremer
50 Rockport Court
Danville CA 94526
Ph: (925) 820-5841
www.asnp1975.com
E-mail: hkremer@usa.net

New Zealand Society of Great Britain
Michael Wilkinson
121 London Road
Sevenoaks, Kent, TN13 1BH
UNITED KINGDOM
www.nzsgb.org.uk
E-mail: mwilkin799@aol.com

Nicaragua Study Group
Erick Rodriguez
11817 SW 11th St.
Miami FL 33184-2501
clubs.yahoo.com/clubs/
nicaraguastudygroup
E-mail: nsgsec@yahoo.com

Society of Australasian Specialists/Oceania
David McNamee
P.O. Box 37
Alamo CA 94507
www.sasoceania.org
E-mail: dmcnamee@aol.com

Orange Free State Study Circle
J. R. Stroud
24 Hooper Close
Burnham-on-sea, Somerset, TA8 1JQ
UNITED KINGDOM
orangefreestatephilately.org.uk
E-mail: richardstroudph@gofast.co.uk

Pacific Islands Study Circle
John Ray
24 Woodvale Ave.
London, SE25 4AE
UNITED KINGDOM
www.pisc.org.uk
E-mail: info@pisc.org.uk

Pakistan Philatelic Study Circle
Jeff Siddiqui
P.O. Box 7002
Lynnwood WA 98046
E-mail: jeffsiddiqui@msn.com

Centro de Filatelistas Independientes de Panama
Vladimir Berrio-Lemm
Apartado 0823-02748
Plaza Concordia Panama
PANAMA
E-mail: panahistoria@gmail.com

Papuan Philatelic Society
Steven Zirinsky
P.O. Box 49, Ansonia Station
New York NY 10023
Ph: (718) 706-0616
www.communigate.co.uk/york/pps
E-mail: szirinsky@cs.com

International Philippine Philatelic Society
Donald J. Peterson
P.O. Box 122
Brunswick MD 21716
Ph: (301) 834-6419
www.theipps.info
E-mail: dpeterson4526@gmail.com

Pitcairn Islands Study Group
Dr. Everett L. Parker
117 Cedar Breeze South
Glenburn ME 04401-1734
Ph: (386) 688-1358
www.pisg.net
E-mail: eparker@hughes.net

Polonus Philatelic Society (Poland)
Daniel Lubelski
P.O. Box 60438
Rossford OH 43460-
Ph: (419) 410-9115
www.polonus.org
E-mail: rvo1937@gmail.com

International Society for Portuguese Philately
Clyde Homen
1491 Bonnie View Road
Hollister CA 95023-5117
www.portugalstamps.com
E-mail: ispp1962@sbcglobal.net

Rhodesian Study Circle
William R. Wallace
P.O. Box 16381
San Francisco CA 94116
www.rhodesianstudycircle.org.uk
E-mail: bwall8rscr@earthlink.net

Rossica Society of Russian Philately
Alexander Kolchinsky
1506 Country Lake Drive
Champaign IL 6821-6428
www.rossica.org
E-mail: alexander.kolchinsky@rossica.org

St. Helena, Ascension & Tristan Da Cunha Philatelic Society
Dr. Everett L. Parker
117 Cedar Breeze South
Glenburn ME 04401-1734
Ph: (386) 754-8524
www.atlanticislands.org
E-mail: eparker@hughes.net

St. Pierre & Miquelon Philatelic Society
James R. (Jim) Taylor
2335 Paliswood Road SW
Calgary, AB, T2V 3P6
CANADA
www.stamps.org/spm

Associated Collectors of El Salvador
Joseph D. Hahn
1015 Old Boalsburg Road Apt G-5
State College PA 16801-6149
www.elsalvadorphilately.org
E-mail: jdhahn2@gmail.com

Fellowship of Samoa Specialists
Donald Mee
23 Leo St.
Christchurch, 8051
NEW ZEALAND
www.samoaexpress.org
E-mail: donanm@xtra.co.nz

Sarawak Specialists' Society
Stephen Schumann
2417 Cabrillo Drive-
Hayward CA 94545
Ph: (510) 785-4794
www.britborneostamps.org.uk
E-mail: sdsch@earthlink.net

Scandinavian Collectors Club
Steve Lund
P.O. Box 16213
St. Paul MN 55116
www.scc-online.org
E-mail: steve88h@aol.com

Slovakia Stamp Society
Jack Benchik
P.O. Box 555
Notre Dame IN 46556

Philatelic Society for Greater Southern Africa
Alan Hanks
34 Seaton Drive
Aurora, ON, L4G 2KI
CANADA
Ph: (905) 727-6993
www.psgsa.thestampweb.com
Email: alan.hanks@sympatico.ca

South Sudan Philatelic Society
William Barclay
134A Spring Hill Road
South Londonerry VT 05155
E-mail: bill.barclay@wfp.org

Spanish Philatelic Society
Robert H. Penn
1108 Walnut Drive
Danielsville PA 18038
Ph: (610) 844-8963
E-mail: roberthpenn43@gmail.com

Sudan Study Group
David Sher
5 Ellis Park Road
Toronto, ON, M6S 2V2
CANADA
www.sudanstamps.org
E-mail: sh3603@hotmail.com

American Helvetia Philatelic Society (Switzerland, Liechtenstein)
Richard T. Hall
P.O. Box 15053
Asheville NC 28813-0053
www.swiss-stamps.org
E-mail: secretary2@swiss-stamps.org

Tannu Tuva Collectors Society
Ken R. Simon
P.O. Box 385
Lake Worth FL 33460-0385
Ph: (561) 588-5954
www.tuva.tk
E-mail: yurttuva@yahoo.com

Society for Thai Philately
H. R. Blakeney
P.O. Box 25644
Oklahoma City OK 73125
E-mail: HRBlakeney@aol.com

Transvaal Study Circle
Chris Board
36 Wakefield Gardens
London, SE19 2NR
UNITED KINGDOM
www.transvaalstamps.org.uk
E-mail: c.board@macace.net

Ottoman and Near East Philatelic Society (Turkey and related areas)
Bob Stuchell
193 Valley Stream Lane
Wayne PA 19087
www.oneps.org
E-mail: rstuchell@msn.com

Ukrainian Philatelic & Numismatic Society
Martin B. Tatuch
5117 8th Road N.
Arlington VA 22205-1201
www.upns.org
E-mail: treasurer@upns.org

Vatican Philatelic Society
Sal Quinonez
1 Aldersgate, Apt. 1002
Riverhead NY 11901-1830
Ph: (516) 727-6426
www.vaticanphilately.org

British Virgin Islands Philatelic Society
Giorgio Migliavacca
P.O. Box 7007
St. Thomas VI 00801-0007
www.islandsun.com/category/collectables/
E-mail: issun@candwbvi.net

West Africa Study Circle
Martin Bratzel
1233 Virginia Ave.
Windsor, ON, N8S 2Z1
CANADA
www.wasc.org.uk/
E-mail: marty_bratzel@yahoo.ca

Western Australia Study Group
Brian Pope
P.O. Box 423
Claremont, Western Australia, 6910
AUSTRALIA
www.wastudygroup.com
E-mail: black5swan@yahoo.com.au

Yugoslavia Study Group of the Croatian Philatelic Society
Michael Lenard
1514 N. Third Ave.
Wausau WI 54401
Ph: (715) 675-2833
E-mail: mjlenard@aol.com

Topical Groups

Americana Unit
Dennis Dengel
17 Peckham Road
Poughkeepsie NY 12603-2018
www.americanaunit.org
E-mail: ddengel@americanaunit.org

Astronomy Study Unit
John W. G. Budd
728 Sugar Camp Way
Brooksville FL 34604
Ph: (352) 345-4799
E-mail: jwgbudd@gmail.com

Bicycle Stamp Club
Steve Andreasen
2000 Alaskan Way, Unit 157
Seattle WA 98121
members.tripod.com/~bicyclestamps
E-mail: steven.w.andreasen@gmail.com

Biology Unit
Alan Hanks
34 Seaton Drive
Aurora, ON, L4G 2K1
CANADA
Ph: (905) 727-6993

Bird Stamp Society
S. A. H. (Tony) Statham
Ashlyns Lodge, Chesham Road,
Berkhamsted, Hertfordshire HP4 2ST
UNITED KINGDOM
www.bird-stamps.org/bss
E-mail: tony.statham@sky.com

Captain Cook Society
Jerry Yucht
8427 Leale Ave.
Stockton CA 95212
www.captaincooksociety.com
E-mail: US@captaincooksociety.com

The CartoPhilatelic Society
Marybeth Sulkowski
2885 Sanford Ave, SW, #32361
Grandville MI 49418-1342
www.mapsonstamps.org
E-mail: secretary@mapsonstamps.org

Casey Jones Railroad Unit
Roy W. Menninger MD
P.O. Box 5511
Topeka KS 66605
Ph: (785) 231-8366
www.uqp.de/cjr/index.htm
E-mail: roymenn85@gmail.com

Cats on Stamps Study Unit
Robert D. Jarvis
2731 Teton Lane
Fairfield CA 94533
www.catsonstamps.org
E-mail: bobmarci@aol.com

Chemistry & Physics on Stamps Study Unit
Dr. Roland Hirsch
20458 Water Point Lane
Germantown MD 20874
www.cpossu.org
E-mail: rfhirsch@cpossu.org

Chess on Stamps Study Unit
Ray C. Alexis
608 Emery St.
Longmont CO 80501
E-mail: chessstuff911459@aol.com

Christmas Philatelic Club
Jim Balog
P.O. Box 774
Geneva OH 44041
www.christmasphilatelicclub.org
E-mail: jpbstamps@windstream.net

Christopher Columbus Philatelic Society
Donald R. Ager
P.O. Box 71
Hillsboro NH 03244-0071
Ph: (603) 464-5379
ccps.maphist.nl/
E-mail: meganddon@tds.net

Collectors of Religion on Stamps
James Bailey
P.O. Box 937
Brownwood TX 76804
www.coros-society.org
E-mail: corosec@directtv.net

Cricket Philatelic Society
A.Melville-Brown, President
11 Weppons, Ravens Road
Shoreham-by-Sea
West Sussex, BN43 5AW
UNITED KINGDOM
www.cricketstamp.net
E-mail: mel.cricket.100@googlemail.com

Dogs on Stamps Study Unit
Morris Raskin
202A Newport Road
Monroe Township NJ 08831
Ph: (609) 655-7411
www.dossu.org
E-mail: mraskin@cellurian.com

Earth's Physical Features Study Group
Fred Klein
515 Magdalena Ave.
Los Altos CA 94024
epfsu.jeffhayward.com

Ebony Society of Philatelic Events and Reflections, Inc. (African-American topicals)
Manuel Gilyard
800 Riverside Drive, Suite 4H
New York NY 10032-7412
www.esperstamps.org
E-mail: gilyardmani@aol.com

Europa Study Unit
Tonny E. Van Loij
3002 S. Xanthia St.
Denver CO 80231-4237
www.europastudyunit.org/
E-mail: tvanloij@gmail.com

Fine & Performing Arts
Deborah L. Washington
6922 S. Jeffery Blvd., #7 - North
Chicago IL 60649
E-mail: brasslady@comcast.net

Fire Service in Philately
John Zaranek
81 Hillpine Road
Cheektowaga NY 14227-2259
Ph: (716) 668-3352
E-mail: jczaranek@roadrunner.com

Gay & Lesbian History on Stamps Club
Joe Petronie
P.O. Box 190842
Dallas TX 75219-0842
www.facebook.com/glhsc
E-mail: glhsc@aol.com

Gems, Minerals & Jewelry Study Unit
Mrs. Gilberte Proteau
138 Lafontaine
Beloeil QC J3G 2G7
CANADA
Ph: (978) 851-8283
E-mail: gilberte.ferland@sympatico.ca

Graphics Philately Association
Mark H. Winnegrad
P.O. Box 380
Bronx NY 10462-0380
www.graphics-stamps.org
E-mail: indybrucel@yahoo.com

Journalists, Authors & Poets on Stamps
Ms. Lee Straayer
P.O. Box 6808
Champaign IL 61826
E-mail: lstraayer@dcbnet.com

Lighthouse Stamp Society
Dalene Thomas
1805 S Balsam St. #106
Lakewood CO 80232
Ph: (303) 986-6620
www.lighthousestampsociety.org
E-mail: dalene@lighthousestampsociety.org

Lions International Stamp Club
John Bargus
108-2777 Barry Road RR 2
Mill Bay, BC, V0R 2P2
CANADA
Ph: (250) 743-5782

Mahatma Gandhi On Stamps Study Circle
Pramod Shivagunde
Pratik Clinic, Akluj
Solapur, Maharashtra, 413101
INDIA
E-mail: drnanda@bom6.vsnl.net.in

Masonic Study Unit
Stanley R. Longenecker
930 Wood St.
Mount Joy PA 17552-1926
Ph: (717) 669-9094
E-mail: natsco@usa.net

Mathematical Study Unit
Monty J. Strauss
4209 88th St.
Lubbock TX 79423-2041
www.mathstamps.org

Medical Subjects Unit
Dr. Frederick C. Skvara
P.O. Box 6228
Bridgewater NJ 08807
E-mail: fcskvara@optonline.net

Military Postal History Society
Ed Dubin
1 S. Wacker Drive, Suite 3500
Chicago IL 60606
www.militaryPHS.org
E-mail: dubine@comcast.net

Mourning Stamps and Covers Club
James Bailey, Jr.
P.O. Box 937
Brownwood TX 76804
E-mail: jamesbailey@wildblue.net

Napoleonic Age Philatelists
Ken Berry
4117 NW 146th St.
Oklahoma City OK 73134-1746
Ph: (405) 748-8646
www.nap-stamps.org
E-mail: krb4117@att.net

Old World Archeological Study Unit
Caroline Scannell
11 Dawn Drive
Smithtown NY 11787-1761
www.owasu.org
E-mail: editor@owasu.org

Petroleum Philatelic Society International
Dr. Chris Coggins
174 Old Bedford Road
Luton, England, LU2 7HW
UNITED KINGDOM
E-mail: WAMTECH@Luton174.fsnet.co.uk

Rotary on Stamps Unit
Gerald L. Fitzsimmons
105 Calla Ricardo
Victoria TX 77904
rotaryonstamps.org
E-mail: glfitz@suddenlink.net

Scouts on Stamps Society International
Lawrence Clay
P.O. Box 6228
Kennewick WA 99336
Ph: (509) 735-3731
www.sossi.org
E-mail: rfrank@sossi.org

Ships on Stamps Unit
Les Smith
302 Conklin Ave.
Penticton, BC, V2A 2T4
CANADA
Ph: (250) 493-7486
www.shipsonstamps.org
E-mail: lessmith440@shaw.ca

Space Unit
Carmine Torrisi
P.O. Box 780241
Maspeth NY 11378
Ph: (917) 620-5687
stargate.1usa.com/stamps/
E-mail: ctorrisi1@nyc.rr.com

Sports Philatelists International
Mark Maestrone
2824 Curie Place
San Diego CA 92122-4110
www.sportstamps.org
Email: president@sportstamps.org

Stamps on Stamps Collectors Club
Alf Jordan
156 W. Elm St.
Yarmouth ME 04096
www.stampsonstamps.org
E-mail: ajordan1@maine.rr.com

Windmill Study Unit
Walter J. Hollien
607 N. Porter St.
Watkins Glenn NY 14891-1345
Ph: (862) 812-0030
E-mail: whollien@earthlink.net

Wine On Stamps Study Unit
David Wolfersberger
768 Chain Ridge Road
St. Louis MO 63122-3259
Ph: (314) 961-5032
www.wine-on-stamps.org
E-mail: dewolf2@swbell.net

Women on Stamps Study Unit
Hugh Gottfried
2232 26th St.
Santa Monica CA 90405-1902
E-mail: hgottfried@adelphia.net

Expertizing Services

The following organizations will, for a fee, provide expert opinions about stamps submitted to them. Collectors should contact these organizations to find out about their fees and requirements before submiting philatelic material to them. The listing of these groups here is not intended as an endorsement by Amos Media Co.

General Expertizing Services

American Philatelic Expertizing Service (a service of the American Philatelic Society)
100 Match Factory Place
Bellefonte PA 16823-1367
Ph: (814) 237-3803
Fax: (814) 237-6128
www.stamps.org
E-mail: ambristo@stamps.org
Areas of Expertise: Worldwide

B. P. A. Expertising, Ltd.
P.O. Box 1141
Guildford, Surrey, GU5 0WR
UNITED KINGDOM
E-mail: sec@bpaexpertising.org
Areas of Expertise: British Commonwealth, Great Britain, Classics of Europe, South America and the Far East

Philatelic Foundation
341 W. 38th St., 5th Floor
New York NY 10018
Ph: (212) 221-6555
Fax: (212) 221-6208
www.philatelicfoundation.org
E-mail: philatelicfoundation@verizon.net
Areas of Expertise: U.S. & Worldwide

Philatelic Stamp Authentication and Grading, Inc.
P.O. Box 41-0880
Melbourne FL 32941-0880
Customer Service: (305) 345-9864
www.psaginc.com
E-mail: info@psaginc.com
Areas of Expertise: U.S., Canal Zone, Hawaii, Philippines, Canada & Provinces

Professional Stamp Experts
P.O. Box 6170
Newport Beach CA 92658
Ph: (877) STAMP-88
Fax: (949) 833-7955
www.collectors.com/pse
E-mail: pseinfo@collectors.com
Areas of Expertise: Stamps and covers of U.S., U.S. Possessions, British Commonwealth

Royal Philatelic Society Expert Committee
41 Devonshire Place
London, W1N 1PE
UNITED KINGDOM
www.rpsl.org.uk/experts.html
E-mail: experts@rpsl.org.uk
Areas of Expertise: Worldwide

Expertizing Services Covering Specific Fields Or Countries

China Stamp Society Expertizing Service
1050 W. Blue Ridge Blvd.
Kansas City MO 64145
Ph: (816) 942-6300
E-mail: hjmesq@aol.com
Areas of Expertise: China

Confederate Stamp Alliance Authentication Service
Gen. Frank Crown, Jr.
P.O. Box 278
Capshaw AL 35742-0396
Ph: (302) 422-2656
Fax: (302) 424-1990
www.csalliance.org
E-mail: csaas@knology.net
Areas of Expertise: Confederate stamps and postal history

Errors, Freaks and Oddities Collectors Club Expertizing Service
138 East Lakemont Drive
Kingsland GA 31548
Ph: (912) 729-1573
Areas of Expertise: U.S. errors, freaks and oddities

Estonian Philatelic Society Expertizing Service
39 Clafford Lane
Melville NY 11747
Ph: (516) 421-2078
E-mail: esto4@aol.com
Areas of Expertise: Estonia

Hawaiian Philatelic Society Expertizing Service
P.O. Box 10115
Honolulu HI 96816-0115
Areas of Expertise: Hawaii

Hong Kong Stamp Society Expertizing Service
P.O. Box 206
Glenside PA 19038
Fax: (215) 576-6850
Areas of Expertise: Hong Kong

International Association of Philatelic Experts United States Associate members:

Paul Buchsbayew
119 W. 57th St.
New York NY 10019
Ph: (212) 977-7734
Fax: (212) 977-8653
Areas of Expertise: Russia, Soviet Union

William T. Crowe
P.O. Box 2090
Danbury CT 06813-2090
E-mail: wtcrowe@aol.com
Areas of Expertise: United States

John Lievsay
(see American Philatelic Expertizing Service and Philatelic Foundation)
Areas of Expertise: France

Robert W. Lyman
P.O. Box 348
Irvington on Hudson NY 10533
Ph and Fax: (914) 591-6937
Areas of Expertise: British North America, New Zealand

Robert Odenweller
P.O. Box 401
Bernardsville NJ 07924-0401
Ph and Fax: (908) 766-5460
Areas of Expertise: New Zealand, Samoa to 1900

Sergio Sismondo
The Regency Tower, Suite 1109
770 James Street
Syracuse NY 13203
Ph: (315) 422-2331
Fax: (315) 422-2956
Areas of Expertise: British East Africa, Camerouns, Cape of Good Hope, Canada, British North America

International Society for Japanese Philately Expertizing Committee
132 North Pine Terrace
Staten Island NY 10312-4052
Ph: (718) 227-5229
Areas of Expertise: Japan and related areas, except WWII Japanese Occupation issues

International Society for Portuguese Philately Expertizing Service
P.O. Box 43146
Philadelphia PA 19129-3146
Ph and Fax: (215) 843-2106
E-mail: s.s.washburne@worldnet.att.net
Areas of Expertise: Portugal and Colonies

Mexico-Elmhurst Philatelic Society International Expert Committee
P.O. Box 1133
West Covina CA 91793
Areas of Expertise: Mexico

Ukrainian Philatelic & Numismatic Society Expertizing Service
30552 Dell Lane
Warren MI 48092-1862
Areas of Expertise: Ukraine, Western Ukraine

V. G. Greene Philatelic Research Foundation
P.O. Box 204, Station Q
Toronto, ON, M4T 2M1
CANADA
Ph: (416) 921-2073
Fax: (416) 921-1282
www.greenefoundation.ca
E-mail: vggfoundation@on.aibn.com
Areas of Expertise: British North America

Information on Catalogue Values, Grade and Condition

Catalogue Value

The Scott Catalogue value is a retail value; that is, an amount you could expect to pay for a stamp in the grade of Very Fine with no faults. Any exceptions to the grade valued will be noted in the text. The general introduction on the following pages and the individual section introductions further explain the type of material that is valued. The value listed for any given stamp is a reference that reflects recent actual dealer selling prices for that item.

Dealer retail price lists, public auction results, published prices in advertising and individual solicitation of retail prices from dealers, collectors and specialty organizations have been used in establishing the values found in this catalogue. Amos Media Co. values stamps, but Amos Media is not a company engaged in the business of buying and selling stamps as a dealer.

Use this catalogue as a guide for buying and selling. The actual price you pay for a stamp may be higher or lower than the catalogue value because of many different factors, including the amount of personal service a dealer offers, or increased or decreased interest in the country or topic represented by a stamp or set. An item may occasionally be offered at a lower price as a "loss leader," or as part of a special sale. You also may obtain an item inexpensively at public auction because of little interest at that time or as part of a large lot.

Stamps that are of a lesser grade than Very Fine, or those with condition problems, generally trade at lower prices than those given in this catalogue. Stamps of exceptional quality in both grade and condition often command higher prices than those listed.

Values for pre-1900 unused issues are for stamps with approximately half or more of their original gum. Stamps with most or all of their original gum may be expected to sell for more, and stamps with less than half of their original gum may be expected to sell for somewhat less than the values listed. On rarer stamps, it may be expected that the original gum will be somewhat more disturbed than it will be on more common issues. Post-1900 unused issues are assumed to have full original gum. From breakpoints in most countries' listings, stamps are valued as never hinged, due to the wide availability of stamps in that condition. These notations are prominently placed in the listings and in the country information preceding the listings. Some countries also feature listings with dual values for hinged and never-hinged stamps.

Grade

A stamp's grade and condition are crucial to its value. The accompanying illustrations show examples of Very Fine stamps from different time periods, along with examples of stamps in Fine to Very Fine and Extremely Fine grades as points of reference. When a stamp seller offers a stamp in any grade from fine to superb without further qualifying statements, that stamp should not only have the centering grade as defined, but it also should be free of faults or other condition problems.

FINE stamps (illustrations not shown) have designs that are quite off center, with the perforations on one or two sides very close to the design but not quite touching it. There is white space between the perforations and the design that is minimal but evident to the unaided eye. Imperforate stamps may have small margins, and earlier issues may show the design just touching one edge of the stamp design. Very early perforated issues normally will have the perforations slightly cutting into the design. Used stamps may have heavier than usual cancellations.

FINE-VERY FINE stamps will be somewhat off center on one side, or slightly off center on two sides. Imperforate stamps will have two margins of at least normal size, and the design will not touch any edge. For perforated stamps, the perfs are well clear of the design, but are still noticeably off center. *However, early issues of a country may be printed in such a way that the design naturally is very close to the edges. In these cases, the perforations may cut into the design very slightly.* Used stamps will not have a cancellation that detracts from the design.

VERY FINE stamps will be just slightly off center on one or two sides, but the design will be well clear of the edge. The stamp will present a nice, balanced appearance. Imperforate stamps will be well centered within normal-sized margins. *However, early issues of many countries may be printed in such a way that the perforations may touch the design on one or more sides. Where this is the case, a boxed note will be found defining the centering and margins of the stamps being valued.* Used stamps will have light or otherwise neat cancellations. This is the grade used to establish Scott Catalogue values.

EXTREMELY FINE stamps are close to being perfectly centered. Imperforate stamps will have even margins that are slightly larger than normal. Even the earliest perforated issues will have perforations clear of the design on all sides.

Amos Media Co. recognizes that there is no formally enforced grading scheme for postage stamps, and that the final price you pay or obtain for a stamp will be determined by individual agreement at the time of transaction.

Condition

Grade addresses only centering and (for used stamps) cancellation. *Condition* refers to factors other than grade that affect a stamp's desirability.

Factors that can increase the value of a stamp include exceptionally wide margins, particularly fresh color, the presence of selvage, and plate or die varieties. Unusual cancels on used stamps (particularly those of the 19th century) can greatly enhance their value as well.

Factors other than faults that decrease the value of a stamp include loss of original gum, regumming, a hinge remnant or foreign object adhering to the gum, natural inclusions, straight edges, and markings or notations applied by collectors or dealers.

Faults include missing pieces, tears, pin or other holes, surface scuffs, thin spots, creases, toning, short or pulled perforations, clipped perforations, oxidation or other forms of color changelings, soiling, stains, and such man-made changes as reperforations or the chemical removal or lightening of a cancellation.

Grading Illustrations

On the following two pages are illustrations of various stamps from countries appearing in this volume. These stamps are arranged by country, and they represent early or important issues that are often found in widely different grades in the marketplace. The editors believe the illustrations will prove useful in showing the margin size and centering that will be seen on the various issues.

In addition to the matters of margin size and centering, collectors are reminded that the very fine stamps valued in the Scott catalogues also will possess fresh color and intact perforations, and they will be free from defects.

Examples shown are computer-manipulated images made from single digitized master illustrations.

Stamp Illustrations Used in the Catalogue

It is important to note that the stamp images used for identification purposes in this catlaogue may not be indicative of the grade of stamp being valued. Refer to the written discussion of grades on this page and to the grading illustrations on the following two pages for grading information.

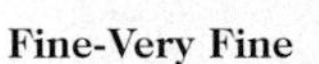

Fine-Very Fine

SCOTT CATALOGUES VALUE STAMPS IN THIS GRADE

Very Fine

Extremely Fine

Fine-Very Fine

SCOTT CATALOGUES VALUE STAMPS IN THIS GRADE

Very Fine

Extremely Fine

Fine-Very Fine

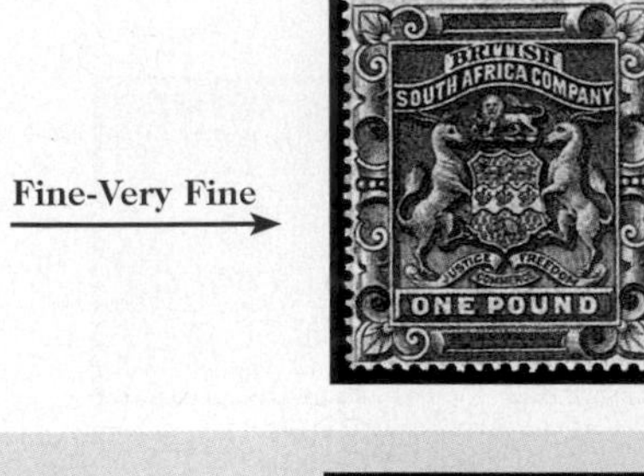

SCOTT CATALOGUES VALUE STAMPS IN THIS GRADE

Very Fine

Extremely Fine

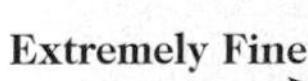

Fine-Very Fine

SCOTT CATALOGUES VALUE STAMPS IN THIS GRADE

Very Fine

Extremely Fine

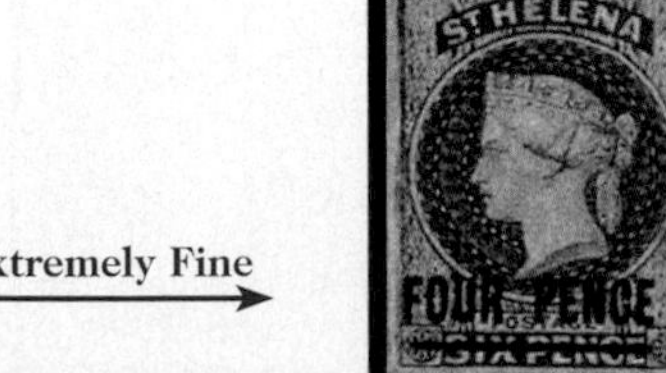

For purposes of helping to determine the gum condition and value of an unused stamp, Scott presents the following chart which details different gum conditions and indicates how the conditions correlate with the Scott values for unused stamps. Used together, the Illustrated Grading Chart on the previous pages and this Illustrated Gum Chart should allow catalogue users to better understand the grade and gum condition of stamps valued in the Scott catalogues.

Gum Categories:	MINT N.H.	ORIGINAL GUM (O.G.)				NO GUM
	 **Mint Never Hinged** *Free from any disturbance*	 **Lightly Hinged** *Faint impression of a removed hinge over a small area*	 **Hinge Mark or Remnant** *Prominent hinged spot with part or all of the hinge remaining*	 **Large part o.g.** *Approximately half or more of the gum intact*	**Small part o.g.** *Approximately less than half of the gum intact*	**No gum** *Only if issued with gum*
Commonly Used Symbol:	★★	★	★	★	★	(★)
Pre-1900 Issues (Pre-1881 for U.S.)	*Very fine pre-1900 stamps in these categories trade at a premium over Scott value*			Scott Value for "Unused"		Scott "No Gum" listings for selected unused classic stamps
From 1900 to breakpoints for listings of never-hinged stamps	Scott "Never Hinged" listings for selected unused stamps	Scott Value for "Unused" (Actual value will be affected by the degree of hinging of the full o.g.)				
From breakpoints noted for many countries	Scott Value for "Unused"					

Never Hinged (NH; ★★): A never-hinged stamp will have full original gum that will have no hinge mark or disturbance. The presence of an expertizer's mark does not disqualify a stamp from this designation.

Original Gum (OG; ★): Pre-1900 stamps should have approximately half or more of their original gum. On rarer stamps, it may be expected that the original gum will be somewhat more disturbed than it will be on more common issues. Post-1900 stamps should have full original gum. Original gum will show some disturbance caused by a previous hinge(s) which may be present or entirely removed. The actual value of a post-1900 stamp will be affected by the degree of hinging of the full original gum.

Disturbed Original Gum: Gum showing noticeable effects of humidity, climate or hinging over more than half of the gum. The significance of gum disturbance in valuing a stamp in any of the Original Gum categories depends on the degree of disturbance, the rarity and normal gum condition of the issue and other variables affecting quality.

Regummed (RG; (★)): A regummed stamp is a stamp without gum that has had some type of gum privately applied at a time after it was issued. This normally is done to deceive collectors and/or dealers into thinking that the stamp has original gum and therefore has a higher value. A regummed stamp is considered the same as a stamp with none of its original gum for purposes of grading.

Understanding the Listings

On the opposite page is an enlarged "typical" listing from this catalogue. Below are detailed explanations of each of the highlighted parts of the listing.

1 Scott number — Scott catalogue numbers are used to identify specific items when buying, selling or trading stamps. Each listed postage stamp from every country has a unique Scott catalogue number. Therefore, Germany Scott 99, for example, can only refer to a single stamp. Although the Scott catalogue usually lists stamps in chronological order by date of issue, there are exceptions. When a country has issued a set of stamps over a period of time, those stamps within the set are kept together without regard to date of issue. This follows the normal collecting approach of keeping stamps in their natural sets.

When a country issues a set of stamps over a period of time, a group of consecutive catalogue numbers is reserved for the stamps in that set, as issued. If that group of numbers proves to be too few, capital-letter suffixes, such as "A" or "B," may be added to existing numbers to create enough catalogue numbers to cover all items in the set. A capital-letter suffix indicates a major Scott catalogue number listing. Scott generally uses a suffix letter only once. Therefore, a catalogue number listing with a capital-letter suffix will seldom be found with the same letter (lower case) used as a minor-letter listing. If there is a Scott 16A in a set, for example, there will seldom be a Scott 16a. However, a minor-letter "a" listing may be added to a major number containing an "A" suffix (Scott 16Aa, for example).

Suffix letters are cumulative. A minor "b" variety of Scott 16A would be Scott 16Ab, not Scott 16b.

There are times when a reserved block of Scott catalogue numbers is too large for a set, leaving some numbers unused. Such gaps in the numbering sequence also occur when the catalogue editors move an item's listing elsewhere or have removed it entirely from the catalogue. Scott does not attempt to account for every possible number, but rather attempts to assure that each stamp is assigned its own number.

Scott numbers designating regular postage normally are only numerals. Scott numbers for other types of stamps, such as air post, semi-postal, postal tax, postage due, occupation and others have a prefix consisting of one or more capital letters or a combination of numerals and capital letters.

2 Illustration number — Illustration or design-type numbers are used to identify each catalogue illustration. For most sets, the lowest face-value stamp is shown. It then serves as an example of the basic design approach for other stamps not illustrated. Where more than one stamp use the same illustration number, but have differences in design, the design paragraph or the description line clearly indicates the design on each stamp not illustrated. Where there are both vertical and horizontal designs in a set, a single illustration may be used, with the exceptions noted in the design paragraph or description line.

When an illustration is followed by a lower-case letter in parentheses, such as "A2(b)," the trailing letter indicates which overprint or surcharge illustration applies.

Illustrations normally are 70 percent of the original size of the stamp. Oversized stamps, blocks and souvenir sheets are reduced even more. Overprints and surcharges are shown at 100 percent of their original size if shown alone, but are 70 percent of original size if shown on stamps. In some cases, the illustration will be placed above the set, between listings or omitted completely. Overprint and surcharge illustrations are not placed in this catalogue for purposes of expertizing stamps.

3 Paper color — The color of a stamp's paper is noted in italic type when the paper used is not white.

4 Listing styles — There are two principal types of catalogue listings: major and minor.

Major listings are in a larger type style than minor listings. The catalogue number is a numeral that can be found with or without a capital-letter suffix, and with or without a prefix.

Minor listings are in a smaller type style and have a small-letter suffix or (if the listing immediately follows that of the major number) may show only the letter. These listings identify a variety of the major item. Examples include perforation and shade differences, multiples (some souvenir sheets, booklet panes and se-tenant combinations), and singles of multiples.

Examples of major number listings include 16, 28A, B97, C13A, 10N5, and 10N6A. Examples of minor numbers are 16a and C13Ab.

5 Basic information about a stamp or set — Introducing each stamp issue is a small section (usually a line listing) of basic information about a stamp or set. This section normally includes the date of issue, method of printing, perforation, watermark and, sometimes, some additional information of note. *Printing method, perforation and watermark apply to the following sets until a change is noted.* Stamps created by overprinting or surcharging previous issues are assumed to have the same perforation, watermark, printing method and other production characteristics as the original. Dates of issue are as precise as Scott is able to confirm and often reflect the dates on first-day covers, rather than the actual date of release.

6 Denomination — This normally refers to the face value of the stamp; that is, the cost of the unused stamp at the post office at the time of issue. When a denomination is shown in parentheses, it does not appear on the stamp. This includes the non-denominated stamps of the United States, Brazil and Great Britain, for example.

7 Color or other description — This area provides information to solidify identification of a stamp. In many recent cases, a description of the stamp design appears in this space, rather than a listing of colors.

8 Year of issue — In stamp sets that have been released in a period that spans more than a year, the number shown in parentheses is the year that stamp first appeared. Stamps without a date appeared during the first year of the issue. Dates are not always given for minor varieties.

9 Value unused and Value used — The Scott catalogue values are based on stamps that are in a grade of Very Fine unless stated otherwise. Unused values refer to items that have not seen postal, revenue or any other duty for which they were intended. Pre-1900 unused stamps that were issued with gum must have at least most of their original gum. Later issues are assumed to have full original gum. From breakpoints specified in most countries' listings, stamps are valued as never hinged. Stamps issued without gum are noted. Modern issues with PVA or other synthetic adhesives may appear ungummed. Unused self-adhesive stamps are valued as appearing undisturbed on their original backing paper. Values for used self-adhesive stamps are for examples either on piece or off piece. For a more detailed explanation of these values, please see the "Catalogue Value," "Condition" and "Understanding Valuing Notations" sections elsewhere in this introduction.

In some cases, where used stamps are more valuable than unused stamps, the value is for an example with a contemporaneous cancel, rather than a modern cancel or a smudge or other unclear marking. For those stamps that were released for postal and fiscal purposes, the used value represents a postally used stamp. Stamps with revenue cancels generally sell for less.

Stamps separated from a complete se-tenant multiple usually will be worth less than a pro-rated portion of the se-tenant multiple, and stamps lacking the attached labels that are noted in the listings will be worth less than the values shown.

10 Changes in basic set information — Bold type is used to show any changes in the basic data given for a set of stamps. These basic data categories include perforation gauge measurement, paper type, printing method and watermark.

11 Total value of a set — The total value of sets of three or more stamps issued after 1900 are shown. The set line also notes the range of Scott numbers and total number of stamps included in the grouping. The actual value of a set consisting predominantly of stamps having the minimum value of 25 cents may be less than the total value shown. Similarly, the actual value or catalogue value of se-tenant pairs or of blocks consisting of stamps having the minimum value of 25 cents may be less than the catalogue values of the component parts.

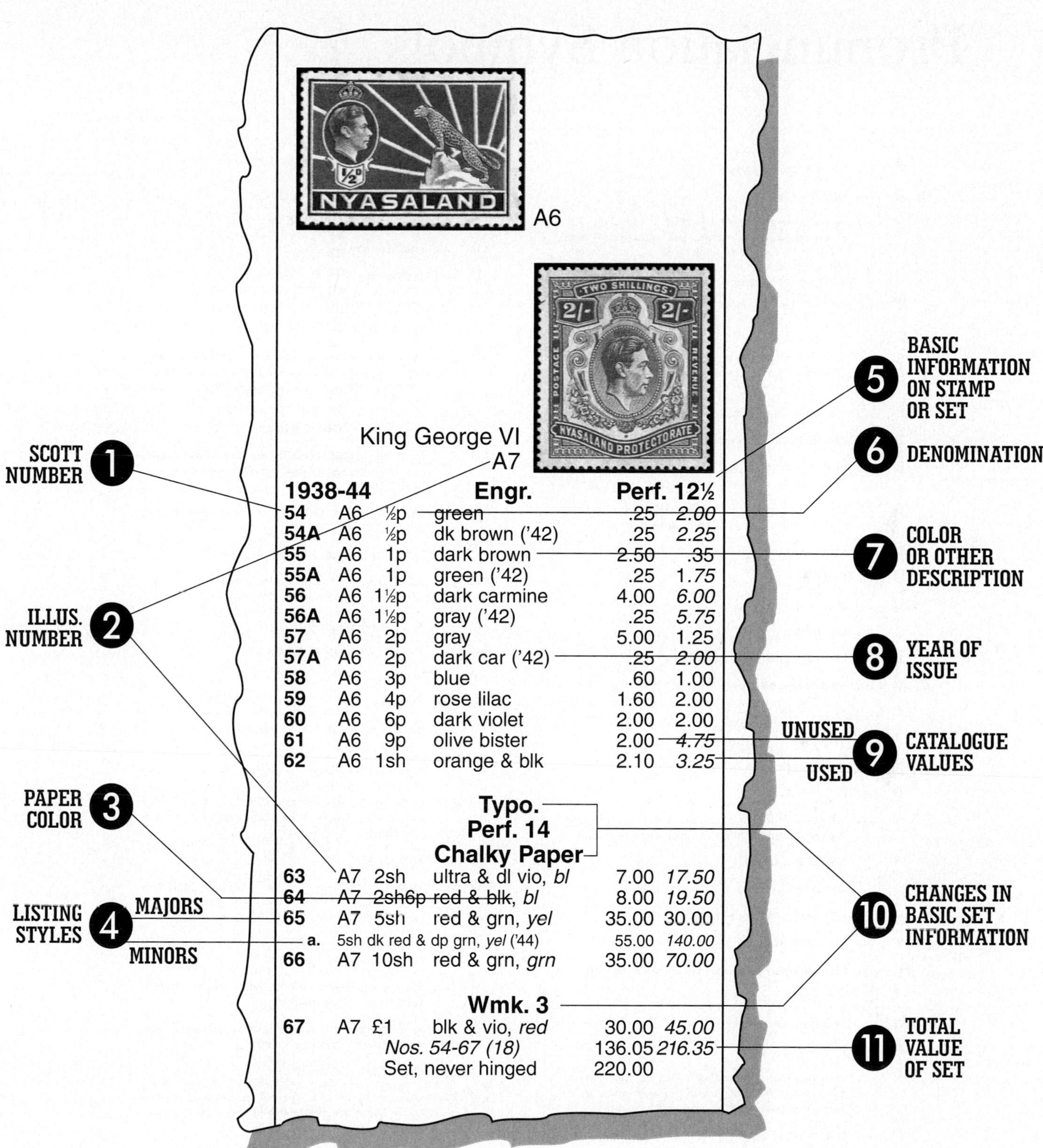
NYASALAND
A6
TWO SHILLINGS
2/- 2/-
POSTAGE REVENUE
NYASALAND PROTECTORATE
King George VI
A7
1938-44 Engr. Perf. 12½
54 A6 ½p green .25 2.00
54A A6 ½p dk brown ('42) .25 2.25
55 A6 1p dark brown 2.50 .35
55A A6 1p green ('42) .25 1.75
56 A6 1½p dark carmine 4.00 6.00
56A A6 1½p gray ('42) .25 5.75
57 A6 2p gray 5.00 1.25
57A A6 2p dark car ('42) .25 2.00
58 A6 3p blue .60 1.00
59 A6 4p rose lilac 1.60 2.00
60 A6 6p dark violet 2.00 2.00
61 A6 9p olive bister 2.00 4.75
62 A6 1sh orange & blk 2.10 3.25
Typo.
Perf. 14
Chalky Paper
63 A7 2sh ultra & dl vio, bl 7.00 17.50
64 A7 2sh6p red & blk, bl 8.00 19.50
65 A7 5sh red & grn, yel 35.00 30.00
a. 5sh dk red & dp grn, yel ('44) 55.00 140.00
66 A7 10sh red & grn, grn 35.00 70.00
Wmk. 3
67 A7 £1 blk & vio, red 30.00 45.00
Nos. 54-67 (18) 136.05 216.35
Set, never hinged 220.00
SCOTT NUMBER 1
ILLUS. NUMBER 2
PAPER COLOR 3
LISTING STYLES 4
MAJORS
MINORS
5 BASIC INFORMATION ON STAMP OR SET
6 DENOMINATION
7 COLOR OR OTHER DESCRIPTION
8 YEAR OF ISSUE
UNUSED
9 CATALOGUE VALUES
USED
10 CHANGES IN BASIC SET INFORMATION
11 TOTAL VALUE OF SET

Pronunciation Symbols

ə .... banana, collide, abut

ˈə, ˌə .... humdrum, abut

^{ə} .... immediately preceding \l\, \n\, \m\, \ŋ\, as in battle, mitten, eaten, and sometimes open \ˈō-p^{ə}m\, lock and key \-^{ə}ŋ-\; immediately following \l\, \m\, \r\, as often in French table, prisme, titre

ər .... further, merger, bird

ˈər-, ˈə-r .... as in two different pronunciations of hurry \ˈhər-ē, ˈhə-rē\

a .... mat, map, mad, gag, snap, patch

ā .... day, fade, date, aorta, drape, cape

ä .... bother, cot, and, with most American speakers, father, cart

ȧ .... father as pronounced by speakers who do not rhyme it with *bother*; French patte

au̇ .... now, loud, out

b .... baby, rib

ch .... chin, nature \ˈnā-chər\

d .... did, adder

e .... bet, bed, peck

ˈē, ˌē .... beat, nosebleed, evenly, easy

ē .... easy, mealy

f .... fifty, cuff

g .... go, big, gift

h .... hat, ahead

hw .... whale as pronounced by those who do not have the same pronunciation for both *whale* and *wail*

i .... tip, banish, active

ī .... site, side, buy, tripe

j .... job, gem, edge, join, judge

k .... kin, cook, ache

k̲ .... German ich, Buch; one pronunciation of loch

l .... lily, pool

m .... murmur, dim, nymph

n .... no, own

^{n} .... indicates that a preceding vowel or diphthong is pronounced with the nasal passages open, as in French *un bon vin blanc* \œ^{n} -bō^{n} -va^{n} -blä^{n}\

ŋ .... sing \ˈsiŋ\, singer \ˈsiŋ-ər\, finger \ˈfiŋ-gər\, ink \ˈiŋk \

ō .... bone, know, beau

ȯ .... saw, all, gnaw, caught

œ .... French boeuf, German Hölle

œ̄ .... French feu, German Höhle

ȯi .... coin, destroy

p .... pepper, lip

r .... red, car, rarity

s .... source, less

sh .... as in shy, mission, machine, special (actually, this is a single sound, not two); with a hyphen between, two sounds as in *grasshopper* \ˈgras-ˌhä-pər\

t .... tie, attack, late, later, latter

th .... as in thin, ether (actually, this is a single sound, not two); with a hyphen between, two sounds as in *knighthood* \ˈnīt-ˌhu̇d\

t̲h̲ .... then, either, this (actually, this is a single sound, not two)

ü .... rule, youth, union \ˈyün-yən\, few \ˈfyü\

u̇ .... pull, wood, book, curable \ˈkyu̇r-ə-bəl\, fury \ˈfyu̇r-ē\

ue .... German füllen, hübsch

ue̅ .... French rue, German fühlen

v .... vivid, give

w .... we, away

y .... yard, young, cue \ˈkyü\, mute \ˈmyüt\, union \ˈyün-yən\

^{y} .... indicates that during the articulation of the sound represented by the preceding character the front of the tongue has substantially the position it has for the articulation of the first sound of *yard*, as in French *digne* \dēn^{y}\

z .... zone, raise

zh .... as in vision, azure \ˈa-zhər\ (actually, this is a single sound, not two); with a hyphen between, two sounds as in *hogshead* \ˈhȯgz-ˌhed, ˈhägz-\

\ .... slant line used in pairs to mark the beginning and end of a transcription: \ˈpen\

ˈ .... mark preceding a syllable with primary (strongest) stress: \ˈpen-mən-ˌship\

ˌ .... mark preceding a syllable with secondary (medium) stress: \ˈpen-mən-ˌship\

\- .... mark of syllable division

( ) .... indicate that what is symbolized between is present in some utterances but not in others: *factory* \ˈfak-t(ə-)rē\

÷ .... indicates that many regard as unacceptable the pronunciation variant immediately following: *cupola* \ˈkyü-pə-lə, ÷-ˌlō\

The system of pronunciation is used by permission from Merriam-Webster's Collegiate® Dictionary, Tenth Edition ©1993 by Merrian-Webster Inc., publisher of the Merriam-Webster® dictionaries.

Catalogue Listing Policy

It is the intent of Amos Media Co. to list all postage stamps of the world in the *Scott Standard Postage Stamp Catalogue*. The only strict criteria for listing is that stamps be decreed legal for postage by the issuing country and that the issuing country actually have an operating postal system. Whether the primary intent of issuing a given stamp or set was for sale to postal patrons or to stamp collectors is not part of our listing criteria. Scott's role is to provide basic comprehensive postage stamp information. It is up to each stamp collector to choose which items to include in a collection.

It is Scott's objective to seek reasons why a stamp should be listed, rather than why it should not. Nevertheless, there are certain types of items that will not be listed. These include the following:

1. Unissued items that are not officially distributed or released by the issuing postal authority. If such items are officially issued at a later date by the country, they will be listed. Unissued items consist of those that have been printed and then held from sale for reasons such as change in government, errors found on stamps or something deemed objectionable about a stamp subject or design.

2. Stamps "issued" by non-existent postal entities or fantasy countries, such as Nagaland, Occusi-Ambeno, Staffa, Sedang, Torres Straits and others. Also, stamps "issued" in the names of legitimate, stamp-issuing countries that are not authorized by those countries.

3. Semi-official or unofficial items not required for postage. Examples include items issued by private agencies for their own express services. When such items are required for delivery, or are valid as prepayment of postage, they are listed.

4. Local stamps issued for local use only. Postage stamps issued by governments specifically for "domestic" use, such as Haiti Scott 219-228, or the United States non-denominated stamps, are not considered to be locals, since they are valid for postage throughout the country of origin.

5. Items not valid for postal use. For example, a few countries have issued souvenir sheets that are not valid for postage. This area also includes a number of worldwide charity labels (some denominated) that do not pay postage.

6. Egregiously exploitative issues such as stamps sold for far more than face value, stamps purposefully issued in artificially small quantities or only against advance orders, stamps awarded only to a selected audience such as a philatelic bureau's standing order customers, or stamps sold only in conjunction with other products. All of these kinds of items are usually controlled issues and/or are intended for speculation. These items normally will be included in a footnote.

7. Items distributed by the issuing government only to a limited group, club, philatelic exhibition or a single stamp dealer or other private company. These items normally will be included in a footnote.

8. Stamps not available to collectors. These generally are rare items, all of which are held by public institutions such as museums. The existence of such items often will be cited in footnotes.

The fact that a stamp has been used successfully as postage, even on international mail, is not in itself sufficient proof that it was legitimately issued. Numerous examples of so-called stamps from non-existent countries are known to have been used to post letters that have successfully passed through the international mail system.

There are certain items that are subject to interpretation. When a stamp falls outside our specifications, it may be listed along with a cautionary footnote.

A number of factors are considered in our approach to analyzing how a stamp is listed. The following list of factors is presented to share with you, the catalogue user, the complexity of the listing process.

Additional printings — "Additional printings" of a previously issued stamp may range from an item that is totally different to cases where it is impossible to differentiate from the original. At least a minor number (a small-letter suffix) is assigned if there is a distinct change in stamp shade, noticeably redrawn design, or a significantly different perforation measurement. A major number (numeral or numeral and capital-letter combination) is assigned if the editors feel the "additional printing" is sufficiently different from the original that it constitutes a different issue.

Commemoratives — Where practical, commemoratives with the same theme are placed in a set. For example, the U.S. Civil War Centennial set of 1961-65 and the Constitution Bicentennial series of 1989-90 appear as sets. Countries such as Japan and Korea issue such material on a regular basis, with an announced, or at least predictable, number of stamps known in advance. Occasionally, however, stamp sets that were released over a period of years have been separated. Appropriately placed footnotes will guide you to each set's continuation.

Definitive sets — Blocks of numbers generally have been reserved for definitive sets, based on previous experience with any given country. If a few more stamps were issued in a set than originally expected, they often have been inserted into the original set with a capital-letter suffix, such as U.S. Scott 1059A. If it appears that many more stamps than the originally allotted block will be released before the set is completed, a new block of numbers will be reserved, with the original one being closed off. In some cases, such as the U.S. Transportation and Great Americans series, several blocks of numbers exist. Appropriately placed footnotes will guide you to each set's continuation.

New country — Membership in the Universal Postal Union is not a consideration for listing status or order of placement within the catalogue. The index will tell you in what volume or page number the listings begin.

"No release date" items — The amount of information available for any given stamp issue varies greatly from country to country and even from time to time. Extremely comprehensive information about new stamps is available from some countries well before the stamps are released. By contrast some countries do not provide information about stamps or release dates. Most countries, however, fall between these extremes. A country may provide denominations or subjects of stamps from upcoming issues that are not issued as planned. Sometimes, philatelic agencies, those private firms hired to represent countries, add these later-issued items to sets well after the formal release date. This time period can range from weeks to years. If these items were officially released by the country, they will be added to the appropriate spot in the set. In many cases, the specific release date of a stamp or set of stamps may never be known.

Overprints — The color of an overprint is always noted if it is other than black. Where more than one color of ink has been used on overprints of a single set, the color used is noted. Early overprint and surcharge illustrations were altered to prevent their use by forgers.

Personalized Stamps — Since 1999, the special service of personalizing stamp vignettes, or labels attached to stamps, has been offered to customers by postal administrations of many countries. Sheets of these stamps are sold, singly or in quantity, only through special orders made by mail, in person, or through a sale on a computer website with the postal administrations or their agents for which an extra fee is charged, though some countries offer to collectors at face value personalized stamps having generic images in the vignettes or on the attached labels. It is impossible for any catalogue to know what images have been chosen by customers. Images can be 1) owned or created by the customer, 2) a generic image, or 3) an image pulled from a library of stock images on the stamp creation website. It is also impossible to know the quantity printed for any stamp having a particular image. So from a valuing standpoint, any image is equivalent to any other image for any personalized stamp having the same catalogue number. Illustrations of personalized stamps in the catalogue are not always those of stamps having generic images.

Personalized items are listed with some exceptions. These include:
1. Stamps or sheets that have attached labels that the customer cannot personalize, but which are nonetheless marketed as "personalized," and are sold for far more than the franking value.
2. Stamps or sheets that can be personalized by the customer, but where a portion of the print run must be ceded to the issuing country for sale to other customers.
3. Stamps or sheets that are created exclusively for a particular commercial client, or clients, including stamps that differ from any similar stamp that has been made available to the public.
4. Stamps or sheets that are deliberately conceived by the issuing authority that have been, or are likely to be, created with an excessive number of different face values, sizes, or other features that are changeable.
5. Stamps or sheets that are created by postal administrations using the same system of stamp personalization that has been put in place for use by the public that are printed in limited quantities and sold above face value.
6. Stamps or sheets that are created by licensees not directly affiliated or controlled by a postal administration.

Excluded items may or may not be footnoted.

Se-tenants — Connected stamps of differing features (se-tenants) will be listed in the format most commonly collected. This includes pairs, blocks or larger multiples. Se-tenant units are not always symmetrical. An example is Australia Scott 508, which is a block of seven stamps. If the stamps are primarily collected as a unit, the major number may be assigned to the multiple, with minors going to each component stamp. In cases where continuous-design or other unit se-tenants will receive significant postal use, each stamp is given a major Scott number listing. This includes issues from the United States, Canada, Germany and Great Britain, for example.

Special Notices

Classification of stamps

The *Scott Standard Postage Stamp Catalogue* lists stamps by country of issue. The next level of organization is a listing by section on the basis of the function of the stamps. The principal sections cover regular postage, semi-postal, air post, special delivery, registration, postage due and other categories. Except for regular postage, catalogue numbers for all sections include a prefix letter (or number-letter combination) denoting the class to which a given stamp belongs. When some countries issue sets containing stamps from more than one category, the catalogue will at times list all of the stamps in one category (such as air post stamps listed as part of a postage set).

The following is a listing of the most commonly used catalogue prefixes.

Prefix .... Category
C......... Air Post
M........ Military
P......... Newspaper
N......... Occupation - Regular Issues
O........ Official
Q........ Parcel Post
J.......... Postage Due
RA...... Postal Tax
B......... Semi-Postal
E......... Special Delivery
MR...... War Tax

Other prefixes used by more than one country include the following:
H......... Acknowledgment of Receipt
I.......... Late Fee
CO...... Air Post Official
CQ...... Air Post Parcel Post
RAC.... Air Post Postal Tax
CF...... Air Post Registration
CB...... Air Post Semi-Postal
CBO... Air Post Semi-Postal Official
CE...... Air Post Special Delivery
EY....... Authorized Delivery
S......... Franchise
G........ Insured Letter
GY...... Marine Insurance
MC..... Military Air Post
MQ..... Military Parcel Post
NC...... Occupation - Air Post
NO...... Occupation - Official
NJ........ Occupation - Postage Due
NRA.... Occupation - Postal Tax
NB...... Occupation - Semi-Postal
NE...... Occupation - Special Delivery
QY...... Parcel Post Authorized Delivery
AR...... Postal-fiscal
RAJ..... Postal Tax Due
RAB.... Postal Tax Semi-Postal
F......... Registration
EB....... Semi-Postal Special Delivery
EO...... Special Delivery Official
QE...... Special Handling

New issue listings

Updates to this catalogue appear each month in the *Linn's Stamp News* monthly magazine. Included in this update are additions to the listings of countries found in the *Scott Standard Postage Stamp Catalogue* and the *Specialized Catalogue of United States Stamps and Covers*, as well as corrections and updates to current editions of this catalogue.

From time to time there will be changes in the final listings of stamps from the *Linn's Stamp News* magazine to the next edition of the catalogue. This occurs as more information about certain stamps or sets becomes available.

The catalogue update section of the *Linn's Stamp News* magazine is the most timely presentation of this material available. Annual subscriptions to *Linn's Stamp News* are available from Linn's Stamp News, Box 926, Sidney, OH 45365-0926.

Number additions, deletions & changes

A listing of catalogue number additions, deletions and changes from the previous edition of the catalogue appears in each volume. See Catalogue Number Additions, Deletions & Changes in the table of contents for the location of this list.

Understanding valuing notations

The *minimum catalogue value* of an individual stamp or set is 25 cents. This represents a portion of the cost incurred by a dealer when he prepares an individual stamp for resale. As a point of philatelic-economic fact, the lower the value shown for an item in this catalogue, the greater the percentage of that value is attributed to dealer mark up and profit margin. In many cases, such as the 25-cent minimum value, that price does not cover the labor or other costs involved with stocking it as an individual stamp. The sum of minimum values in a set does not properly represent the value of a complete set primarily composed of a number of minimum-value stamps, nor does the sum represent the actual value of a packet made up of minimum-value stamps. Thus a packet of 1,000 different common stamps — each of which has a catalogue value of 25 cents — normally sells for considerably less than 250 dollars!

The *absence of a retail value* for a stamp does not necessarily suggest that a stamp is scarce or rare. A dash in the value column means that the stamp is known in a stated form or variety, but information is either lacking or insufficient for purposes of establishing a usable catalogue value.

Stamp values in *italics* generally refer to items that are difficult to value accurately. For expensive items, such as those priced at $1,000 or higher, a value in italics indicates that the affected item trades very seldom. For inexpensive items, a value in italics represents a warning. One example is a "blocked" issue where the issuing postal administration may have controlled one stamp in a set in an attempt to make the whole set more valuable. Another example is an item that sold at an extreme multiple of face value in the marketplace at the time of its issue.

One type of warning to collectors that appears in the catalogue is illustrated by a stamp that is valued considerably higher in used condition than it is as unused. In this case, collectors are cautioned to be certain the used version has a genuine and contemporaneous cancellation. The type of cancellation on a stamp can be an important factor in determining its sale price. Catalogue values do not apply to fiscal, telegraph or non-contemporaneous postal cancels, unless otherwise noted.

Some countries have released back issues of stamps in canceled-to-order form, sometimes covering as much as a 10-year period. The Scott Catalogue values for used stamps reflect canceled-to-order material when such stamps are found to predominate in the marketplace for the issue involved. Notes frequently appear in the stamp listings to specify which items are valued as canceled-to-order, or if there is a premium for postally used examples.

Many countries sell canceled-to-order stamps at a marked reduction of face value. Countries that sell or have sold canceled-to-order stamps at *full* face value include United Nations, Australia, Netherlands, France and Switzerland. It may be almost impossible to identify such stamps if the gum has been removed, because official government canceling devices are used. Postally used examples of these items on cover, however, are usually worth more than the canceled-to-order stamps with original gum.

Abbreviations

Scott uses a consistent set of abbreviations throughout this catalogue to conserve space, while still providing necessary information.

COLOR ABBREVIATIONS

amb. amber
anil.. aniline
ap.... apple
aqua aquamarine
az .... azure
bis ... bister
bl ..... blue
bld... blood
blk... black
bril... brilliant
brn... brown
brnsh brownish
brnz. bronze
brt.... bright
brnt . burnt
car... carmine
cer... cerise
chlky chalky
chamchamois
chnt. chestnut
choc chocolate
chr... chrome
cit .... citron
cl...... claret
cob.. cobalt
cop.. copper
crim. crimson
cr ..... cream
dk .... dark
dl ..... dull
dp .... deep
db .... drab
emer emerald
gldn. golden
gryshgrayish
grn... green
grnsh greenish
hel ... heliotrope
hn .... henna
ind ... indigo
int .... intense
lav ... lavender
lem .. lemon
lil ..... lilac
lt ...... light
mag. magenta
man. manila
mar.. maroon
mv ... mauve
multi multicolored
mlky milky
myr .. myrtle
ol ..... olive
olvn . olivine
org... orange
pck .. peacock
pnksh pinkish
Prus. Prussian
pur... purple
redsh reddish
res ... reseda
ros ... rosine
ryl .... royal
sal ... salmon
saph sapphire
scar. scarlet
sep .. sepia
sien . sienna
sil..... silver
sl...... slate
stl .... steel
turq.. turquoise
ultra ultramarine
Ven.. Venetian
ver ... vermilion
vio ... violet
yel ... yellow
yelsh yellowish

When no color is given for an overprint or surcharge, black is the color used. Abbreviations for colors used for overprints and surcharges include: "(B)" or "(Blk)," black; "(Bl)," blue; "(R)," red; and "(G)," green.

Additional abbreviations in this catalogue are shown below:

Adm. ....Administration
AFL................American Federation of Labor
Anniv. ....Anniversary
APS ....American Philatelic Society
Assoc. ....Association
ASSR. ....Autonomous Soviet Socialist Republic
b. ....Born
BEP...............Bureau of Engraving and Printing
Bicent. ....Bicentennial
Bklt. ....Booklet
Brit. ....British
btwn. ....Between
Bur. ....Bureau
c. or ca. ....Circa
Cat. ....Catalogue
Cent. ....Centennial, century, centenary
CIO ....Congress of Industrial Organizations
Conf. ....Conference
Cong. ....Congress
Cpl. ....Corporal
CTO ....Canceled to order
d. ....Died
Dbl. ....Double
EDU ....Earliest documented use
Engr. ....Engraved
Exhib. ....Exhibition
Expo. ....Exposition
Fed. ....Federation
GB ....Great Britain
Gen. ....General
GPO ....General post office
Horiz. ....Horizontal
Imperf. ....Imperforate
Impt. ....Imprint
Intl. ....International
Invtd. ....Inverted
L ....Left
Lieut., lt. ....Lieutenant
Litho. ....Lithographed
LL ....Lower left
LR ....Lower right
mm ....Millimeter
Ms. ....Manuscript
Natl. ....National
No. ....Number
NY ....New York
NYC ....New York City
Ovpt. ....Overprint
Ovptd. ....Overprinted
P ....Plate number
Perf. ....Perforated, perforation
Phil. ....Philatelic
Photo. ....Photogravure
PO ....Post office
Pr. ....Pair
P.R. ....Puerto Rico
Prec. ....Precancel, precanceled
Pres. ....President
PTT ....Post, Telephone and Telegraph
R ....Right
Rio ....Rio de Janeiro
Sgt. ....Sergeant
Soc. ....Society
Souv. ....Souvenir
SSR ....Soviet Socialist Republic, see ASSR
St. ....Saint, street
Surch. ....Surcharge
Typo. ....Typographed
UL ....Upper left
Unwmkd. ......Unwatermarked
UPU ....Universal Postal Union
UR ....Upper Right
US ....United States
USPOD ....United States Post Office Department
USSR ....Union of Soviet Socialist Republics
Vert. ....Vertical
VP ....Vice president
Wmk. ....Watermark
Wmkd. ....Watermarked
WWI ....World War I
WWII ....World War II

Examination

Amos Media Co. will not comment upon the genuineness, grade or condition of stamps, because of the time and responsibility involved. Rather, there are several expertizing groups that undertake this work for both collectors and dealers. Neither will Amos Media Co. appraise or identify philatelic material. The company cannot take responsibility for unsolicited stamps or covers sent by individuals.

All letters, E-mails, etc. are read attentively, but they are not always answered due to time considerations.

How to order from your dealer

When ordering stamps from a dealer, it is not necessary to write the full description of a stamp as listed in this catalogue. All you need is the name of the country, the Scott catalogue number and whether the desired item is unused or used. For example, 'Japan Scott 422 unused" is sufficient to identify the unused stamp of Japan listed as "422 A206 5y brown."

Basic Stamp Information

A stamp collector's knowledge of the combined elements that make a given stamp issue unique determines his or her ability to identify stamps. These elements include paper, watermark, method of separation, printing, design and gum. On the following pages each of these important areas is briefly described.

Paper

Paper is an organic material composed of a compacted weave of cellulose fibers and generally formed into sheets. Paper used to print stamps may be manufactured in sheets, or it may have been part of a large roll (called a web) before being cut to size. The fibers most often used to create paper on which stamps are printed include bark, wood, straw and certain grasses. In many cases, linen or cotton rags have been added for greater strength and durability. Grinding, bleaching, cooking and rinsing these raw fibers reduces them to a slushy pulp, referred to by paper makers as "stuff." Sizing and, sometimes, coloring matter is added to the pulp to make different types of finished paper.

After the stuff is prepared, it is poured onto sieve-like frames that allow the water to run off, while retaining the matted pulp. As fibers fall onto the screen and are held by gravity, they form a natural weave that will later hold the paper together. If the screen has metal bits that are formed into letters or images attached, it leaves slightly thinned areas on the paper. These are called watermarks.

When the stuff is almost dry, it is passed under pressure through smooth or engraved rollers - dandy rolls - or placed between cloth in a press to be flattened and dried.

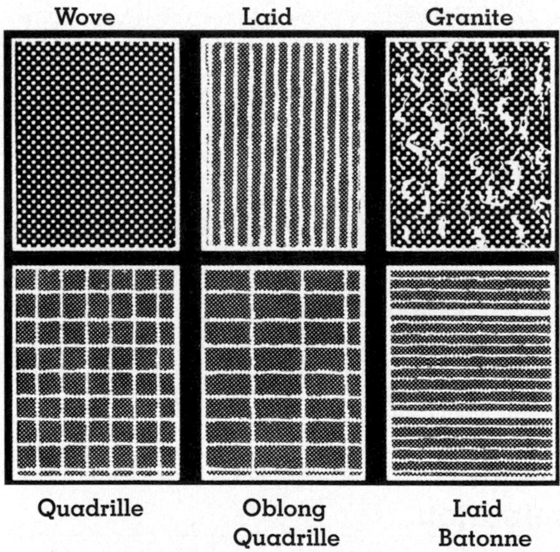

Stamp paper falls broadly into two types: wove and laid. The nature of the surface of the frame onto which the pulp is first deposited causes the differences in appearance between the two. If the surface is smooth and even, the paper will be of fairly uniform texture throughout. This is known as *wove paper*. Early papermaking machines poured the pulp onto a continuously circulating web of felt, but modern machines feed the pulp onto a cloth-like screen made of closely interwoven fine wires. This paper, when held to a light, will show little dots or points very close together. The proper name for this is "wire wove," but the type is still considered wove. Any U.S. or British stamp printed after 1880 will serve as an example of wire wove paper.

Closely spaced parallel wires, with cross wires at wider intervals, make up the frames used for what is known as *laid paper*. A greater thickness of the pulp will settle between the wires. The paper, when held to a light, will show alternate light and dark lines. The spacing and the thickness of the lines may vary, but on any one sheet of paper they are all alike. See Russia Scott 31-38 for examples of laid paper.

Batonne, from the French word meaning "a staff," is a term used if the lines in the paper are spaced quite far apart, like the printed ruling on a writing tablet. Batonne paper may be either wove or laid. If laid, fine laid lines can be seen between the batons.

Quadrille is the term used when the lines in the paper form little squares. *Oblong quadrille* is the term used when rectangles, rather than squares, are formed. Grid patterns vary from distinct to extremely faint. See Mexico-Guadalajara Scott 35-37 for examples of oblong quadrille paper.

Paper also is classified as thick or thin, hard or soft, and by color. Such colors may include yellowish, greenish, bluish and reddish.

Brief explanations of other types of paper used for printing stamps, as well as examples, follow.

Colored — Colored paper is created by the addition of dye in the paper-making process. Such colors may include shades of yellow, green, blue and red. *Surface-colored papers*, most commonly used for British colonial issues in 1913-14, are created when coloring is added only to the surface during the finishing process. Stamps printed on surface-colored paper have white or uncolored backs, while true colored papers are colored through. See Jamaica Scott 71-73.

Pelure — Pelure paper is a very thin, hard and often brittle paper that is sometimes bluish or grayish in appearance. See Serbia Scott 169-170.

Native — This is a term applied to handmade papers used to produce some of the early stamps of the Indian states. Stamps printed on native paper may be expected to display various natural inclusions that are normal and do not negatively affect value. Japanese paper, originally made of mulberry fibers and rice flour, is part of this group. See Japan Scott 1-18.

Manila — This type of paper is often used to make stamped envelopes and wrappers. It is a coarse-textured stock, usually smooth on one side and rough on the other. A variety of colors of manila paper exist, but the most common range is yellowish-brown.

Silk — Introduced by the British in 1847 as a safeguard against counterfeiting, silk paper contains bits of colored silk thread scattered throughout. The density of these fibers varies greatly and can include as few as one fiber per stamp or hundreds. U.S. revenue Scott R152 is a good example of an easy-to-identify silk paper stamp.

Silk-thread paper has uninterrupted threads of colored silk arranged so that one or more threads run through the stamp or postal stationery. See Great Britain Scott 5-6 and Switzerland Scott 14-19.

Granite — Filled with minute cloth or colored paper fibers of various colors and lengths, granite paper should not be confused with either type of silk paper. Austria Scott 172-175 and a number of Swiss stamps are examples of granite paper.

Chalky — A chalk-like substance coats the surface of chalky paper to discourage the cleaning and reuse of canceled stamps, as well as to provide a smoother, more acceptable printing surface. Because the designs of stamps printed on chalky paper are imprinted on what is often a water-soluble coating, any attempt to remove a cancellation will destroy the stamp. *Do not soak these stamps in any fluid.* To remove a stamp printed on chalky paper from an envelope, wet the paper from underneath the stamp until the gum dissolves enough to release the stamp from the paper. See St. Kitts-Nevis Scott 89-90 for examples of stamps printed on this type of chalky paper.

India — Another name for this paper, originally introduced from China about 1750, is "China Paper." It is a thin, opaque paper often used for plate and die proofs by many countries.

Double — In philately, the term double paper has two distinct meanings. The first is a two-ply paper, usually a combination of a thick and a thin sheet, joined during manufacture. This type was used experimentally as a means to discourage the reuse of stamps.

The design is printed on the thin paper. Any attempt to remove a cancellation would destroy the design. U.S. Scott 158 and other Banknote-era stamps exist on this form of double paper.

The second type of double paper occurs on a rotary press, when the end of one paper roll, or web, is affixed to the next roll to save time feeding the paper through the press. Stamp designs are printed over the joined paper and, if overlooked by inspectors, may get into post office stocks.

Goldbeater's Skin — This type of paper was used for the 1866 issue of Prussia, and was a tough, translucent paper. The design was printed in reverse on the back of the stamp, and the gum applied over the printing. It is impossible to remove stamps printed on this type of paper from the paper to which they are affixed without destroying the design.

Ribbed — Ribbed paper has an uneven, corrugated surface made by passing the paper through ridged rollers. This type exists on some copies of U.S. Scott 156-165.

Various other substances, or substrates, have been used for stamp manufacture, including wood, aluminum, copper, silver and gold foil, plastic, and silk and cotton fabrics.

Watermarks

Watermarks are an integral part of some papers. They are formed in the process of paper manufacture. Watermarks consist of small designs, formed of wire or cut from metal and soldered to the surface of the mold or, sometimes, on the dandy roll. The designs may be in the form of crowns, stars, anchors, letters or other characters or symbols. These pieces of metal - known in the paper-making industry as "bits" - impress a design into the paper. The design sometimes may be seen by holding the stamp to the light. Some are more easily seen with a watermark detector. This important tool is a small black tray into which a stamp is placed face down and dampened with a fast-evaporating watermark detection fluid that brings up the watermark image in the form of dark lines against a lighter background. These dark lines are the thinner areas of the paper known as the watermark. Some watermarks are extremely difficult to locate, due to either a faint impression, watermark location or the color of the stamp. There also are electric watermark detectors that come with plastic filter disks of various colors. The disks neutralize the color of the stamp, permitting the watermark to be seen more easily.

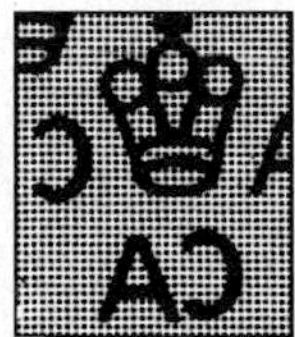

Multiple watermarks of Crown Agents and Burma

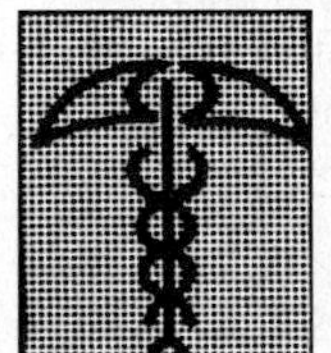

Watermarks of Uruguay, Vatican City and Jamaica

WARNING: Some inks used in the photogravure process dissolve in watermark fluids (Please see the section on Soluble Printing Inks). Also, see "chalky paper."

Watermarks may be found normal, reversed, inverted, reversed and inverted, sideways or diagonal, as seen from the back of the stamp. The relationship of watermark to stamp design depends on the position of the printing plates or how paper is fed through the press. On machine-made paper, watermarks normally are read from right to left. The design is repeated closely throughout the sheet in a "multiple-watermark design." In a "sheet watermark," the design appears only once on the sheet, but extends over many stamps. Individual stamps may carry only a small fraction or none of the watermark.

"Marginal watermarks" occur in the margins of sheets or panes of stamps. They occur on the outside border of paper (ostensibly outside the area where stamps are to be printed). A large row of letters may spell the name of the country or the manufacturer of the paper, or a border of lines may appear. Careless press feeding may cause parts of these letters and/or lines to show on stamps of the outer row of a pane.

Soluble Printing Inks

WARNING: Most stamp colors are permanent; that is, they are not seriously affected by short-term exposure to light or water. Many colors, especially of modern inks, fade from excessive exposure to light. There are stamps printed with inks that dissolve easily in water or in fluids used to detect watermarks. Use of these inks was intentional to prevent the removal of cancellations. Water affects all aniline inks, those on so-called safety paper and some photogravure printings - all such inks are known as fugitive colors. *Removal from paper of such stamps requires care and alternatives to traditional soaking.*

Separation

"Separation" is the general term used to describe methods used to separate stamps. The three standard forms currently in use are perforating, rouletting and die-cutting. These methods are done during the stamp production process, after printing. Sometimes these methods are done on-press or sometimes as a separate step. The earliest issues, such as the 1840 Penny Black of Great Britain (Scott 1), did not have any means provided for separation. It was expected the stamps would be cut apart with scissors or folded and torn. These are examples of imperforate stamps. Many stamps were first issued in imperforate formats and were later issued with perforations. Therefore, care must be observed in buying single imperforate stamps to be certain they were issued imperforate and are not perforated copies that have been altered by having the perforations trimmed away. Stamps issued imperforate usually are valued as singles. However, imperforate varieties of normally perforated stamps should be collected in pairs or larger pieces as indisputable evidence of their imperforate character.

PERFORATION

The chief style of separation of stamps, and the one that is in almost universal use today, is perforating. By this process, paper between the stamps is cut away in a line of holes, usually round, leaving little bridges of paper between the stamps to hold them together. Some types of perforation, such as hyphen-hole perfs, can be confused with roulettes, but a close visual inspection reveals that paper has been removed. The little perforation bridges, which project from the stamp when it is torn from the pane, are called the teeth of the perforation.

As the size of the perforation is sometimes the only way to differentiate between two otherwise identical stamps, it is necessary to be able to accurately measure and describe them. This is done with a perforation gauge, usually a ruler-like device that has dots or graduated lines to show how many perforations may be counted in the space of two centimeters. Two centimeters is the space universally adopted in which to measure perforations.

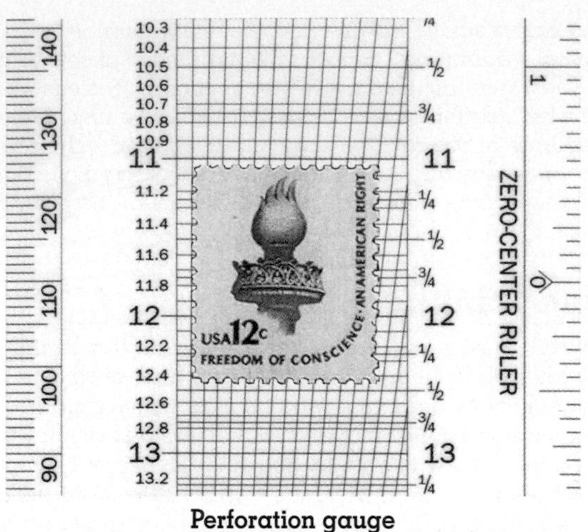

Perforation gauge

To measure a stamp, run it along the gauge until the dots on it fit exactly into the perforations of the stamp. If you are using a graduated-line perforation gauge, simply slide the stamp along the surface until the lines on the gauge perfectly project from the center of the bridges or holes. The number to the side of the line of dots or lines that fit the stamp's perforation is the measurement. For example, an "11" means that 11 perforations fit between two centimeters. The description of the stamp therefore is "perf. 11." If the gauge of the perforations on the top and bottom of a stamp differs from that on the sides, the result is what is known as *compound perforations*. In measuring compound perforations, the gauge at top and bottom is always given first, then the sides. Thus, a stamp that measures 11 at top and bottom and 10½ at the sides is "perf. 11 x 10½." See U.S. Scott 632-642 for examples of compound perforations.

Stamps also are known with perforations different on three or all four sides. Descriptions of such items are clockwise, beginning with the top of the stamp.

A perforation with small holes and teeth close together is a "fine perforation." One with large holes and teeth far apart is a "coarse perforation." Holes that are jagged, rather than clean-cut, are "rough perforations." *Blind perforations* are the slight impressions left by the perforating pins if they fail to puncture the paper. Multiples of stamps showing blind perforations may command a slight premium over normally perforated stamps.

The term *syncopated perfs* describes intentional irregularities in the perforations. The earliest form was used by the Netherlands from 1925-33, where holes were omitted to create distinctive patterns. Beginning in 1992, Great Britain has used an oval perforation to help prevent counterfeiting. Several other countries have started using the oval perfs or other syncopated perf patterns.

A new type of perforation, still primarily used for postal stationery, is known as microperfs. Microperfs are tiny perforations (in some cases hundreds of holes per two centimeters) that allows items to be intentionally separated very easily, while not accidentally breaking apart as easily as standard perforations. These are not currently measured or differentiated by size, as are standard perforations.

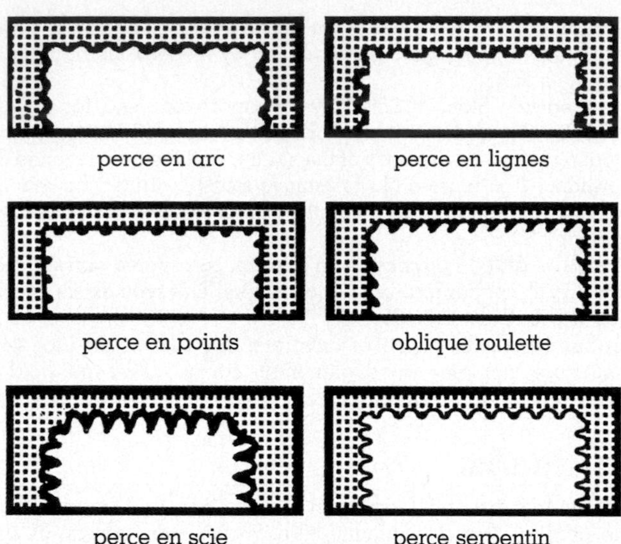

perce en arc — perce en lignes — perce en points — oblique roulette — perce en scie — perce serpentin

ROULETTING

In rouletting, the stamp paper is cut partly or wholly through, with no paper removed. In perforating, some paper is removed. Rouletting derives its name from the French roulette, a spur-like wheel. As the wheel is rolled over the paper, each point makes a small cut. The number of cuts made in a two-centimeter space determines the gauge of the roulette, just as the number of perforations in two centimeters determines the gauge of the perforation.

The shape and arrangement of the teeth on the wheels varies. Various roulette types generally carry French names:

Perce en lignes - rouletted in lines. The paper receives short, straight cuts in lines. This is the most common type of rouletting. See Mexico Scott 500.

Perce en points - pin-rouletted or pin-perfed. This differs from a small perforation because no paper is removed, although round, equidistant holes are pricked through the paper. See Mexico Scott 242-256.

Perce en arc and *perce en scie* - pierced in an arc or saw-toothed designs, forming half circles or small triangles. See Hanover (German States) Scott 25-29.

Perce en serpentin - serpentine roulettes. The cuts form a serpentine or wavy line. See Brunswick (German States) Scott 13-18.

Once again, no paper is removed by these processes, leaving the stamps easily separated, but closely attached.

DIE-CUTTING

The third major form of stamp separation is die-cutting. This is a method where a die in the pattern of separation is created that later cuts the stamp paper in a stroke motion. Although some standard stamps bear die-cut perforations, this process is primarily used for self-adhesive postage stamps. Die-cutting can appear in straight lines, such as U.S. Scott 2522, shapes, such as U.S. Scott 1551, or imitating the appearance of perforations, such as New Zealand Scott 935A and 935B.

Printing Processes

ENGRAVING (Intaglio, Line-engraving, Etching)

Master die — The initial operation in the process of line engraving is making the master die. The die is a small, flat block of softened steel upon which the stamp design is recess engraved in reverse.

Master die

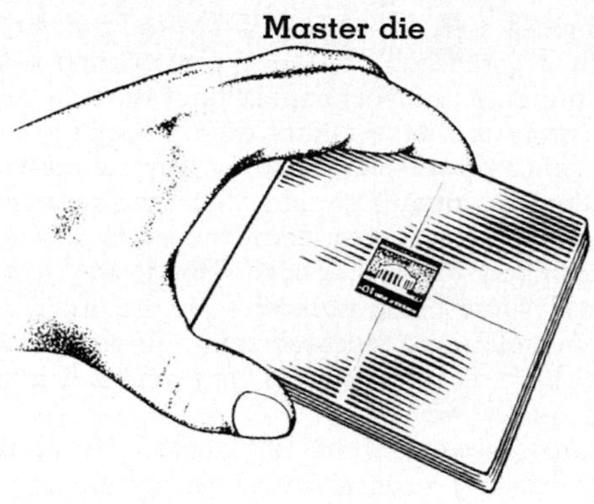

Photographic reduction of the original art is made to the appropriate size. It then serves as a tracing guide for the initial outline of the design. The engraver lightly traces the design on the steel with his graver, then slowly works the design until it is completed. At various points during the engraving process, the engraver hand-inks the die and makes an impression to check his progress. These are known as progressive die proofs. After completion of the engraving, the die is hardened to withstand the stress and pressures of later transfer operations.

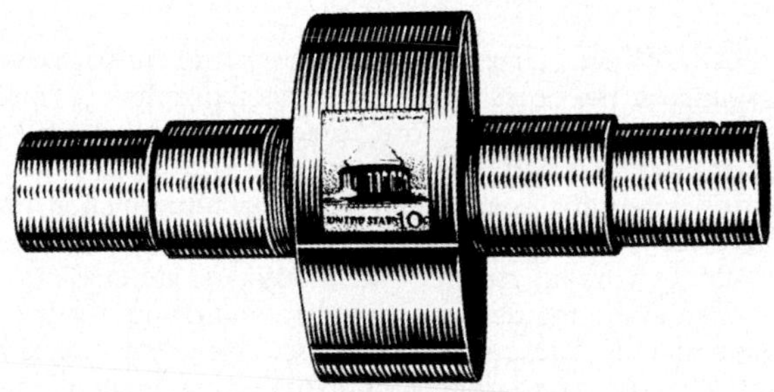

Transfer roll

Transfer roll — Next is production of the transfer roll that, as the name implies, is the medium used to transfer the subject from the master die to the printing plate. A blank roll of soft steel, mounted on a mandrel, is placed under the bearers of the transfer press to allow it to roll freely on its axis. The hardened die is placed on the bed of the press and the face of the transfer roll is applied to the die, under pressure. The bed or the roll is then rocked back and forth under increasing pressure, until the soft steel of the roll is forced into every engraved line of the die. The resulting impression on the roll is known as a "relief" or a "relief transfer." The engraved image is now positive in appearance and stands out from the steel. After the required number of reliefs are "rocked in," the soft steel transfer roll is hardened.

Different flaws may occur during the relief process. A defective relief may occur during the rocking in process because of a minute piece of foreign material lodging on the die, or some other cause. Imperfections in the steel of the transfer roll may result in a breaking away of parts of the design. This is known as a relief break, which will show up on finished stamps as small, unprinted areas. If a damaged relief remains in use, it will transfer a repeating defect to the plate. Deliberate alterations of reliefs sometimes occur. "Altered reliefs" designate these changed conditions.

Plate — The final step in pre-printing production is the making of the printing plate. A flat piece of soft steel replaces the die on the bed of the transfer press. One of the reliefs on the transfer roll is positioned over this soft steel. Position, or layout, dots determine the correct position on the plate. The dots have been lightly marked on the plate in advance. After the correct position of the relief is determined, the design is rocked in by following the same method used in making the transfer roll. The difference is that this time the image is being transferred from the transfer roll, rather than to it. Once the design is entered on the plate, it appears in reverse and is recessed. There are as many transfers entered on the plate as there are subjects printed on the sheet of stamps. It is during this process that double and shifted transfers occur, as well as re-entries. These are the result of improperly entered images that have not been properly burnished out prior to rocking in a new image.

Modern siderography processes, such as those used by the U.S. Bureau of Engraving and Printing, involve an automated form of rocking designs in on preformed cylindrical printing sleeves. The same process also allows for easier removal and re-entry of worn images right on the sleeve.

Transferring the design to the plate

Following the entering of the required transfers on the plate, the position dots, layout dots and lines, scratches and other markings generally are burnished out. Added at this time by the siderographer are any required *guide lines, plate numbers* or other *marginal markings.* The plate is then hand-inked and a proof impression is taken. This is known as a plate proof. If the impression is approved, the plate is machined for fitting onto the press, is hardened and sent to the plate vault ready for use.

On press, the plate is inked and the surface is automatically wiped clean, leaving ink only in the recessed lines. Paper is then forced under pressure into the engraved recessed lines, thereby receiving the ink. Thus, the ink lines on engraved stamps are slightly raised, and slight depressions (debossing) occur on the back of the stamp. Prior to the advent of modern high-speed presses and more advanced ink formulations, paper had to be dampened before receiving the ink. This sometimes led to uneven shrinkage by the time the stamps were perforated, resulting in improperly perforated stamps, or misperfs. Newer presses use drier paper, thus both *wet* and *dry printings* exist on some stamps.

Rotary Press — Until 1914, only flat plates were used to print engraved stamps. Rotary press printing was introduced in 1914, and slowly spread. Some countries still use flat-plate printing.

After approval of the plate proof, older *rotary press plates* require additional machining. They are curved to fit the press cylinder. "Gripper slots" are cut into the back of each plate to receive the "grippers," which hold the plate securely on the press. The plate is then hardened. Stamps printed from these bent rotary press plates are longer or wider than the same stamps printed from flat-plate presses. The stretching of the plate during the curving process is what causes this distortion.

Re-entry — To execute a re-entry on a flat plate, the transfer roll is re-applied to the plate, often at some time after its first use on the press. Worn-out designs can be resharpened by carefully burnishing out the original image and re-entering it from the transfer roll. If the original impression has not been sufficiently removed and the transfer roll is not precisely in line with the remaining impression, the resulting double transfer will make the re-entry obvious. If the registration is true, a re-entry may be difficult or impossible to distinguish. Sometimes a stamp printed from a successful re-entry is identified by having a much sharper and clearer impression than its neighbors. With the advent of rotary presses, post-press re-entries were not possible. After a plate was curved for the rotary press, it was impossible to make a re-entry. This is because the plate had already been bent once (with the design distorted).

However, with the introduction of the previously mentioned modern-style siderography machines, entries are made to the preformed cylindrical printing sleeve. Such sleeves are dechromed and softened. This allows individual images to be burnished out and re-entered on the curved sleeve. The sleeve is then rechromed, resulting in longer press life.

Double Transfer — This is a description of the condition of a transfer on a plate that shows evidence of a duplication of all, or a portion of the design. It usually is the result of the changing of the registration between the transfer roll and the plate during the rocking in of the original entry. Double transfers also occur when only a portion of the design has been rocked in and improper positioning is noted. If the worker elected not to burnish out the partial or completed design, a strong double transfer will occur for part or all of the design.

It sometimes is necessary to remove the original transfer from a plate and repeat the process a second time. If the finished re-worked image shows traces of the original impression, attributable to incomplete burnishing, the result is a partial double transfer.

With the modern automatic machines mentioned previously, double transfers are all but impossible to create. Those partially doubled images on stamps printed from such sleeves are more than likely re-entries, rather than true double transfers.

Re-engraved — Alterations to a stamp design are sometimes necessary after some stamps have been printed. In some cases, either the original die or the actual printing plate may have its "temper" drawn (softened), and the design will be re-cut. The resulting impressions from such a re-engraved die or plate may differ slightly from the original issue, and are known as "re-engraved." If the alteration was made to the master die, all future printings will be consistently different from the original. If alterations were made to the printing plate, each altered stamp on the plate will be slightly different from each other, allowing specialists to reconstruct a complete printing plate.

Dropped Transfers — If an impression from the transfer roll has not been properly placed, a dropped transfer may occur. The final stamp image will appear obviously out of line with its neighbors.

Short Transfer — Sometimes a transfer roll is not rocked its entire length when entering a transfer onto a plate. As a result, the finished transfer on the plate fails to show the complete design, and the finished stamp will have an incomplete design printed. This is known as a "short transfer." U.S. Scott No. 8 is a good example of a short transfer.

TYPOGRAPHY (Letterpress, Surface Printing, Flexography, Dry Offset, High Etch)

Although the word "Typography" is obsolete as a term describing a printing method, it was the accepted term throughout the first century of postage stamps. Therefore, appropriate Scott listings in this catalogue refer to typographed stamps. The current term for this form of printing, however, is "letterpress."

As it relates to the production of postage stamps, letterpress printing is the reverse of engraving. Rather than having recessed areas trap the ink and deposit it on paper, only the raised areas of the design are inked. This is comparable to the type of printing seen by inking and using an ordinary rubber stamp. Letterpress includes all printing where the design is above the surface area, whether it is wood, metal or, in some instances, hardened rubber or polymer plastic.

For most letterpress-printed stamps, the engraved master is made in much the same manner as for engraved stamps. In this instance, however, an additional step is needed. The design is transferred to another surface before being transferred to the transfer roll. In this way, the transfer roll has a recessed stamp design, rather than one done in relief. This makes the printing areas on the final plate raised, or relief areas.

For less-detailed stamps of the 19th century, the area on the die not used as a printing surface was cut away, leaving the surface area raised. The original die was then reproduced by stereotyping or electrotyping. The resulting electrotypes were assembled in the required number and format of the desired sheet of stamps. The plate used in printing the stamps was an electroplate of these assembled electrotypes.

Once the final letterpress plates are created, ink is applied to the raised surface and the pressure of the press transfers the ink impression to the paper. In contrast to engraving, the fine lines of letterpress are impressed on the surface of the stamp, leaving a debossed surface. When viewed from the back (as on a typewritten page), the corresponding line work on the stamp will be raised slightly (embossed) above the surface.

PHOTOGRAVURE (Gravure, Rotogravure, Heliogravure)

In this process, the basic principles of photography are applied to a chemically sensitized metal plate, rather than photographic paper. The design is transferred photographically to the plate through a halftone, or dot-matrix screen, breaking the reproduction into tiny dots. The plate is treated chemically and the dots form depressions, called cells, of varying depths and diameters, depending on the degrees of shade in the design. Then, like engraving, ink is applied to the plate and the surface is wiped clean. This leaves ink in the tiny cells that is lifted out and deposited on the paper when it is pressed against the plate.

Gravure is most often used for multicolored stamps, generally using the three primary colors (red, yellow and blue) and black. By varying the dot matrix pattern and density of these colors, virtually any color can be reproduced. A typical full-color gravure stamp will be created from four printing cylinders (one for each color). The original multicolored image will have been photographically separated into its component colors.

Modern gravure printing may use computer-generated dot-matrix screens, and modern plates may be of various types including metal-coated plastic. The catalogue designation of Photogravure (or "Photo") covers any of these older and more modern gravure methods of printing.

For examples of the first photogravure stamps printed (1914), see Bavaria Scott 94-114.

LITHOGRAPHY (Offset Lithography, Stone Lithography, Dilitho, Planography, Collotype)

The principle that oil and water do not mix is the basis for lithography. The stamp design is drawn by hand or transferred from engraving to the surface of a lithographic stone or metal plate in a greasy (oily) substance. This oily substance holds the ink, which will later be transferred to the paper. The stone (or plate) is wet with an acid fluid, causing it to repel the printing ink in all areas not covered by the greasy substance.

Transfer paper is used to transfer the design from the original stone or plate. A series of duplicate transfers are grouped and, in turn, transferred to the final printing plate.

Photolithography — The application of photographic processes to lithography. This process allows greater flexibility of design, related to use of halftone screens combined with line work. Unlike photogravure or engraving, this process can allow large, solid areas to be printed.

Offset — A refinement of the lithographic process. A rubber-covered blanket cylinder takes the impression from the inked lithographic plate. From the "blanket" the impression is *offset* or transferred to the paper. Greater flexibility and speed are the principal reasons offset printing has largely displaced lithography. The term "lithography" covers both processes, and results are almost identical.

EMBOSSED (Relief) Printing

Embossing, not considered one of the four main printing types, is a method in which the design first is sunk into the metal of the die. Printing is done against a yielding platen, such as leather or linoleum. The platen is forced into the depression of the die, thus forming the design on the paper in relief. This process is often used for metallic inks.

Embossing may be done without color (see Sardinia Scott 4-6); with color printed around the embossed area (see Great Britain Scott 5 and most U.S. envelopes); and with color in exact registration with the embossed subject (see Canada Scott 656-657).

HOLOGRAMS

For objects to appear as holograms on stamps, a model exactly the same size as it is to appear on the hologram must be created. Rather than using photographic film to capture the image, holography records an image on a photoresist material. In processing, chemicals eat away at certain exposed areas, leaving a pattern of constructive and destructive interference. When the photoresist is developed, the result is a pattern of uneven ridges that acts as a mold. This mold is then coated with metal, and the resulting form is used to press copies in much the same way phonograph records are produced.

A typical reflective hologram used for stamps consists of a reproduction of the uneven patterns on a plastic film that is applied to a reflective background, usually a silver or gold foil. Light is reflected off the background through the film, making the pattern present on the film visible. Because of the uneven pattern of the film, the viewer will perceive the objects in their proper three-dimensional relationships with appropriate brightness.

The first hologram on a stamp was produced by Austria in 1988 (Scott 1441).

FOIL APPLICATION

A modern technique of applying color to stamps involves the application of metallic foil to the stamp paper. A pattern of foil is applied to the stamp paper by use of a stamping die. The foil usually is flat, but it may be textured. Canada Scott 1735 has three different foil applications in pearl, bronze and gold. The gold foil was textured using a chemical-etch copper embossing die. The printing of this stamp also involved two-color offset lithography plus embossing.

THERMOGRAPHY

In the 1990s stamps began to be enhanced with thermographic printing. In this process, a powdered polymer is applied over a sheet that has just been printed. The powder adheres to ink that lacks drying or hardening agents and does not adhere to areas where the ink has these agents. The excess powder is removed and the sheet is briefly heated to melt the powder. The melted powder solidifies after cooling, producing a raised, shiny effect on the stamps. See Scott New Caledonia C239-C240.

COMBINATION PRINTINGS

Sometimes two or even three printing methods are combined in producing stamps. In these cases, such as Austria Scott 933 or Canada 1735 (described in the preceding paragraph), the multiple-printing technique can be determined by studying the individual characteristics of each printing type. A few stamps, such as Singapore Scott 684-684A, combine as many as three of the four major printing types (lithography, engraving and typography). When this is done it often indicates the incorporation of security devices against counterfeiting.

INK COLORS

Inks or colored papers used in stamp printing often are of mineral origin, although there are numerous examples of organic-based pigments. As a general rule, organic-based pigments are far more subject to varieties and change than those of mineral-based origin.

The appearance of any given color on a stamp may be affected by many aspects, including printing variations, light, color of paper, aging and chemical alterations.

Numerous printing variations may be observed. Heavier pressure or inking will cause a more intense color, while slight interruptions in the ink feed or lighter impressions will cause a lighter appearance. Stamps printed in the same color by water-based and solvent-based inks can differ significantly in appearance. This affects several stamps in the U.S. Prominent Americans series. Hand-mixed ink formulas (primarily from the 19th century) produced under different conditions (humidity and temperature) account for notable color variations in early printings of the same stamp (see U.S. Scott 248-250, 279B, for example). Different sources of pigment can also result in significant differences in color.

Light exposure and aging are closely related in the way they affect stamp color. Both eventually break down the ink and fade colors, so that a carefully kept stamp may differ significantly in color from an identical copy that has been exposed to light. If stamps are exposed to light either intentionally or accidentally, their colors can be faded or completely changed in some cases.

Papers of different quality and consistency used for the same stamp printing may affect color appearance. Most pelure papers, for example, show a richer color when compared with wove or laid papers. See Russia Scott 181a, for an example of this effect.

The very nature of the printing processes can cause a variety of differences in shades or hues of the same stamp. Some of these shades are scarcer than others, and are of particular interest to the advanced collector.

Luminescence

All forms of tagged stamps fall under the general category of luminescence. Within this broad category is fluorescence, dealing with forms of tagging visible under longwave ultraviolet light, and phosphorescence, which deals with tagging visible only under shortwave light. Phosphorescence leaves an afterglow and fluorescence does not. These treated stamps show up in a range of different colors when exposed to UV light. The differing wavelengths of the light activates the tagging material, making it glow in various colors that usually serve different mail processing purposes.

Intentional tagging is a post-World War II phenomenon, brought about by the increased literacy rate and rapidly growing mail volume. It was one of several answers to the problem of the need for more automated mail processes. Early tagged stamps served the purpose of triggering machines to separate different types of mail. A natural outgrowth was to also use the signal to trigger machines that faced all envelopes the same way and canceled them.

Tagged stamps come in many different forms. Some tagged stamps have luminescent shapes or images imprinted on them as a form of security device. Others have blocks (United States), stripes, frames (South Africa and Canada), overall coatings (United States), bars (Great Britain and Canada) and many other types. Some types of tagging are even mixed in with the pigmented printing ink (Australia Scott 366, Netherlands Scott 478 and U.S. Scott 1359 and 2443).

The means of applying taggant to stamps differs as much as the intended purposes for the stamps. The most common form of tagging is a coating applied to the surface of the printed stamp. Since the taggant ink is frequently invisible except under UV light, it does not interfere with the appearance of the stamp. Another common application is the use of phosphored papers. In this case the paper itself either has a coating of taggant applied before the stamp is printed, has taggant applied during the papermaking process (incorporating it into the fibers), or has the taggant mixed into the coating of the paper. The latter method, among others, is currently in use in the United States.

Many countries now use tagging in various forms to either expedite mail handling or to serve as a printing security device against counterfeiting. Following the introduction of tagged stamps for public use in 1959 by Great Britain, other countries have steadily joined the parade. Among those are Germany (1961); Canada and Denmark (1962); United States, Australia, France and Switzerland (1963); Belgium and Japan (1966); Sweden and Norway (1967); Italy (1968); and Russia (1969). Since then, many other countries have begun using forms of tagging, including Brazil, China, Czechoslovakia, Hong Kong, Guatemala, Indonesia, Israel, Lithuania, Luxembourg, Netherlands, Penrhyn Islands, Portugal, St. Vincent, Singapore, South Africa, Spain and Sweden to name a few.

In some cases, including United States, Canada, Great Britain and Switzerland, stamps were released both with and without tagging. Many of these were released during each country's experimental period. Tagged and untagged versions are listed for the aforementioned countries and are noted in some other countries' listings. For at least a few stamps, the experimentally tagged version is worth far more than its untagged counterpart, such as the 1963 experimental tagged version of France Scott 1024.

In some cases, luminescent varieties of stamps were inadvertently created. Several Russian stamps, for example, sport highly fluorescent ink that was not intended as a form of tagging. Older stamps, such as early U.S. postage dues, can be positively identified by the use of UV light, since the organic ink used has become slightly fluorescent over time. Other stamps, such as Austria Scott 70a-82a (varnish bars) and Obock Scott 46-64 (printed quadrille lines), have become fluorescent over time.

Various fluorescent substances have been added to paper to make it appear brighter. These optical brighteners, as they are known, greatly affect the appearance of the stamp under UV light. The brightest of these is known as Hi-Brite paper. These paper varieties are beyond the scope of the Scott Catalogue.

Shortwave UV light also is used extensively in expertizing, since each form of paper has its own fluorescent characteristics that are impossible to perfectly match. It is therefore a simple matter to detect filled thins, added perforation teeth and other alterations that involve the addition of paper. UV light also is used to examine stamps that have had cancels chemically removed and for other purposes as well.

Gum

The Illustrated Gum Chart in the first part of this introduction shows and defines various types of gum condition. Because gum condition has an important impact on the value of unused stamps, we recommend studying this chart and the accompanying text carefully.

The gum on the back of a stamp may be shiny, dull, smooth, rough, dark, white, colored or tinted. Most stamp gumming adhesives use gum arabic or dextrine as a base. Certain polymers such as polyvinyl alcohol (PVA) have been used extensively since World War II.

The *Scott Standard Postage Stamp Catalogue* does not list items by types of gum. The *Scott Specialized Catalogue of United States Stamps and Covers* does differentiate among some types of gum for certain issues.

Reprints of stamps may have gum differing from the original issues. In addition, some countries have used different gum formulas for different seasons. These adhesives have different properties that may become more apparent over time.

Many stamps have been issued without gum, and the catalogue will note this fact. See, for example, United States Scott 40-47. Sometimes, gum may have been removed to preserve the stamp. Germany Scott B68, for example, has a highly acidic gum that eventually destroys the stamps. This item is valued in the catalogue with gum removed.

Reprints and Reissues

These are impressions of stamps (usually obsolete) made from the original plates or stones. If they are valid for postage and reproduce obsolete issues (such as U.S. Scott 102-111), the stamps are *reissues.* If they are from current issues, they are designated as *second, third,* etc., *printing.* If designated for a particular purpose, they are called *special printings.*

When special printings are not valid for postage, but are made from original dies and plates by authorized persons, they are *official reprints. Private reprints* are made from the original plates and dies by private hands. An example of a private reprint is that of the 1871-1932 reprints made from the original die of the 1845 New Haven, Conn., postmaster's provisional. *Official reproductions* or imitations are made from new dies and plates by government authorization. Scott will list those reissues that are valid for postage if they differ significantly from the original printing.

The U.S. government made special printings of its first postage stamps in 1875. Produced were official imitations of the first two stamps (listed as Scott 3-4), reprints of the demonetized pre-1861 issues (Scott 40-47) and reissues of the 1861 stamps, the 1869 stamps and the then-current 1875 denominations. Even though the official imitations and the reprints were not valid for postage, Scott lists all of these U.S. special printings.

Most reprints or reissues differ slightly from the original stamp in some characteristic, such as gum, paper, perforation, color or watermark. Sometimes the details are followed so meticulously that only a student of that specific stamp is able to distinguish the reprint or reissue from the original.

Remainders and Canceled to Order

Some countries sell their stock of old stamps when a new issue replaces them. To avoid postal use, the *remainders* usually are canceled with a punch hole, a heavy line or bar, or a more-or-less regular-looking cancellation. The most famous merchant of remainders was Nicholas F. Seebeck. In the 1880s and 1890s, he arranged printing contracts between the Hamilton Bank Note Co., of which he was a director, and several Central and South American countries. The contracts provided that the plates and all remainders of the yearly issues became the property of Hamilton. Seebeck saw to it that ample stock remained. The "Seebecks," both remainders and reprints, were standard packet fillers for decades.

Some countries also issue stamps *canceled-to-order (CTO),* either in sheets with original gum or stuck onto pieces of paper or envelopes and canceled. Such CTO items generally are worth less than postally used stamps. In cases where the CTO material is far more prevalent in the marketplace than postally used examples, the catalogue value relates to the CTO examples, with postally used examples noted as premium items. Most CTOs can be detected by the presence of gum. However, as the CTO practice goes back at least to 1885, the gum inevitably has been soaked off some stamps so they could pass as postally used. The normally applied postmarks usually differ slightly from standard postmarks, and specialists are able to tell the difference. When applied individually to envelopes by philatelically minded persons, CTO material is known as *favor canceled* and generally sells at large discounts.

Cinderellas and Facsimiles

Cinderella is a catch-all term used by stamp collectors to describe phantoms, fantasies, bogus items, municipal issues, exhibition seals, local revenues, transportation stamps, labels, poster stamps and many other types of items. Some cinderella collectors include in their collections local postage issues, telegraph stamps, essays and proofs, forgeries and counterfeits.

A *fantasy* is an adhesive created for a nonexistent stamp-issuing authority. Fantasy items range from imaginary countries (Occusi-Ambeno, Kingdom of Sedang, Principality of Trinidad or Torres Straits), to non-existent locals (Winans City Post), or nonexistent transportation lines (McRobish & Co.'s Acapulco-San Francisco Line).

On the other hand, if the entity exists and could have issued stamps (but did not) or was known to have issued other stamps, the items are considered *bogus* stamps. These would include the Mormon postage stamps of Utah, S. Allan Taylor's Guatemala and Paraguay inventions, the propaganda issues for the South Moluccas and the adhesives of the Page & Keyes local post of Boston.

Phantoms is another term for both fantasy and bogus issues.

Facsimiles are copies or imitations made to represent original stamps, but which do not pretend to be originals. A catalogue illustration is such a facsimile. Illustrations from the Moens catalogue of the last century were occasionally colored and passed off as stamps. Since the beginning of stamp collecting, facsimiles have been made for collectors as space fillers or for reference. They often carry the word "facsimile," "falsch" (German), "sanko" or "mozo" (Japanese), or "faux" (French) overprinted on the face or stamped on the back. Unfortunately, over the years a number of these items have had fake cancels applied over the facsimile notation and have been passed off as genuine.

Forgeries and Counterfeits

Forgeries and counterfeits have been with philately virtually from the beginning of stamp production. Over time, the terminology for the two has been used interchangeably. Although both forgeries and counterfeits are reproductions of stamps, the purposes behind their creation differ considerably.

Among specialists there is an increasing movement to more specifically define such items. Although there is no universally accepted terminology, we feel the following definitions most closely mirror the items and their purposes as they are currently defined.

Forgeries (also often referred to as *Counterfeits*) are reproductions of genuine stamps that have been created to defraud collectors. Such spurious items first appeared on the market around 1860, and most old-time collections contain one or more. Many are crude and easily spotted, but some can deceive experts.

An important supplier of these early philatelic forgeries was the Hamburg printer Gebruder Spiro. Many others with reputations in this craft included S. Allan Taylor, George Hussey, James Chute, George Forune, Benjamin & Sarpy, Julius Goldner, E. Oneglia and L.H. Mercier. Among the noted 20th-century forgers were Francois Fournier, Jean Sperati and the prolific Raoul DeThuin.

Forgeries may be complete replications, or they may be genuine stamps altered to resemble a scarcer (and more valuable) type. Most forgeries, particularly those of rare stamps, are worth only a small fraction of the value of a genuine example, but a few types, created by some of the most notable forgers, such as Sperati, can be worth as much or more than the genuine. Fraudulently produced copies are known of most classic rarities and many medium-priced stamps.

In addition to rare stamps, large numbers of common 19th- and early 20th-century stamps were forged to supply stamps to the early packet trade. Many can still be easily found. Few new philatelic forgeries have appeared in recent decades. Successful imitation of well-engraved work is virtually impossible. It has proven far easier to produce a fake by altering a genuine stamp than to duplicate a stamp completely.

Counterfeit (also often referred to as *Postal Counterfeit* or *Postal Forgery*) is the term generally applied to reproductions of stamps that have been created to defraud the government of revenue. Such items usually are created at the time a stamp is current and, in some cases, are hard to detect. Because most counterfeits are seized when the perpetrator is captured, postal counterfeits, particularly used on cover, are usually worth much more than a genuine example to specialists. The first postal counterfeit was of Spain's 4-cuarto carmine of 1854 (the real one is Scott 25). Apparently, the counterfeiters were not satisfied with their first version, which is now very scarce, and they soon created an engraved counterfeit, which is common. Postal counterfeits quickly followed in Austria, Naples, Sardinia and the Roman States. They have since been created in many other countries as well, including the United States.

An infamous counterfeit to defraud the government is the 1-shilling Great Britain "Stock Exchange" forgery of 1872, used on telegraph forms at the exchange that year. The stamp escaped detection until a stamp dealer noticed it in 1898.

Fakes

Fakes are genuine stamps altered in some way to make them more desirable. One student of this part of stamp collecting has estimated that by the 1950s more than 30,000 varieties of fakes were known. That number has grown greatly since then. The widespread existence of fakes makes it important for stamp collectors to study their philatelic holdings and use relevant literature. Likewise, collectors should buy from reputable dealers who guarantee their stamps and make full and prompt refunds should a purchased item be declared faked or altered by some mutually agreed-upon authority. Because fakes always have some genuine characteristics, it is not always possible to obtain unanimous agreement among experts regarding specific items. These students may change their opinions as philatelic knowledge increases. More than 80 percent of all fakes on the philatelic market today are regummed, reperforated (or perforated for the first time), or bear forged overprints, surcharges or cancellations.

Stamps can be chemically treated to alter or eliminate colors. For example, a pale rose stamp can be re-colored to resemble a blue shade of high market value. In other cases, treated stamps can be made to resemble missing color varieties. Designs may be changed by painting, or a stroke or a dot added or bleached out to turn an ordinary variety into a seemingly scarcer stamp. Part of a stamp can be bleached and reprinted in a different version, achieving an inverted center or frame. Margins can be added or repairs done so deceptively that the stamps move from the "repaired" into the "fake" category.

Fakers have not left the backs of the stamps untouched either. They may create false watermarks, add fake grills or press out genuine grills. A thin India paper proof may be glued onto a thicker backing to create the appearance an issued stamp, or a proof printed on cardboard may be shaved down and perforated to resemble a stamp. Silk threads are impressed into paper and stamps have been split so that a rare paper variety is added to an otherwise inexpensive stamp. The most common treatment to the back of a stamp, however, is regumming.

Some in the business of faking stamps have openly advertised fool-proof application of "original gum" to stamps that lack it, although most publications now ban such ads from their pages. It is believed that very few early stamps have survived without being hinged. The large number of never-hinged examples of such earlier material offered for sale thus suggests the widespread extent of regumming activity. Regumming also may be used to hide repairs or thin spots. Dipping the stamp into watermark fluid, or examining it under longwave ultraviolet light often will reveal these flaws.

Fakers also tamper with separations. Ingenious ways to add margins are known. Perforated wide-margin stamps may be falsely represented as imperforate when trimmed. Reperforating is commonly done to create scarce coil or perforation varieties, and to eliminate the naturally occurring straight-edge stamps found in sheet margin positions of many earlier issues. Custom has made straight-edged stamps less desirable. Fakers have obliged by perforating straight-edged stamps so that many are now uncommon, if not rare.

Another fertile field for the faker is that of overprints, surcharges and cancellations. The forging of rare surcharges or overprints began in the 1880s or 1890s. These forgeries are sometimes difficult to detect, but experts have identified almost all. Occasionally, overprints or cancellations are removed to create non-overprinted stamps or seemingly unused items. This is most commonly done by removing a manuscript cancel to make a stamp resemble an unused example. "SPECIMEN" overprints may be removed by scraping and repainting to create non-overprinted varieties. Fakers use inexpensive revenues or pen-canceled stamps to generate unused stamps for further faking by adding other markings. The quartz lamp or UV lamp and a high-powered magnifying glass help to easily detect removed cancellations.

The bigger problem, however, is the addition of overprints, surcharges or cancellations - many with such precision that they are very difficult to ascertain. Plating of the stamps or the overprint can be an important method of detection.

Fake postmarks may range from many spurious fancy cancellations to a host of markings applied to transatlantic covers, to adding normally appearing postmarks to definitives of some countries with stamps that are valued far higher used than unused. With the increased popularity of cover collecting, and the widespread interest in postal history, a fertile new field for fakers has come about. Some have tried to create entire covers. Others specialize in adding stamps, tied by fake cancellations, to genuine stampless covers, or replacing less expensive or damaged stamps with more valuable ones. Detailed study of postal rates in effect at the time a cover in question was mailed, including the analysis of each handstamp used during the period, ink analysis and similar techniques, usually will unmask the fraud.

Restoration and Repairs

Scott bases its catalogue values on stamps that are free of defects and otherwise meet the standards set forth earlier in this introduction. Most stamp collectors desire to have the finest copy of an item possible. Even within given grading categories there are variances. This leads to a controversial practice that is not defined in any universal manner: stamp *restoration*.

There are broad differences of opinion about what is permissible when it comes to restoration. Carefully applying a soft eraser to a stamp or cover to remove light soiling is one form of restoration, as is washing a stamp in mild soap and water to clean it. These are fairly accepted forms of restoration. More severe forms of restoration include pressing out creases or removing stains caused by tape. To what degree each of these is acceptable is dependent upon the individual situation. Further along the spectrum is the freshening of a stamp's color by removing oxide build-up or the effects of wax paper left next to stamps shipped to the tropics.

At some point in this spectrum the concept of *repair* replaces that of restoration. Repairs include filling thin spots, mending tears by reweaving or adding a missing perforation tooth. Regumming stamps may have been acceptable as a restoration or repair technique many decades ago, but today it is considered a form of fakery.

Restored stamps may or may not sell at a discount, and it is possible that the value of individual restored items may be enhanced over that of their pre-restoration state. Specific situations dictate the resultant value of such an item. Repaired stamps sell at substantial discounts from the value of sound stamps.

Terminology

Booklets — Many countries have issued stamps in small booklets for the convenience of users. This idea continues to become increasingly popular in many countries. Booklets have been issued in many sizes and forms, often with advertising on the covers, the panes of stamps or on the interleaving.

The panes used in booklets may be printed from special plates or made from regular sheets. All panes from booklets issued by the United States and many from those of other countries contain stamps that are straight edged on the sides, but perforated between. Others are distinguished by orientation of watermark or other identifying features. Any stamp-like unit in the pane, either printed or blank, that is not a postage stamp, is considered to be a *label* in the catalogue listings.

Scott lists and values booklet panes. Modern complete booklets also are listed and valued. Individual booklet panes are listed only when they are not fashioned from existing sheet stamps and, therefore, are identifiable from their sheet stamp counterparts.

Panes usually do not have a used value assigned to them because there is little market activity for used booklet panes, even though many exist used and there is some demand for them.

Cancellations — The marks or obliterations put on stamps by postal authorities to show that they have performed service and to prevent their reuse are known as cancellations. If the marking is made with a pen, it is considered a "pen cancel." When the location of the post office appears in the marking, it is a "town cancellation." A "postmark" is technically any postal marking, but in practice the term generally is applied to a town cancellation with a date. When calling attention to a cause or celebration, the marking is known as a "slogan cancellation." Many other types and styles of cancellations exist, such as duplex, numerals, targets, fancy and others. See also "precancels," below.

Coil Stamps — These are stamps that are issued in rolls for use in dispensers, affixing and vending machines. Those coils of the United States, Canada, Sweden and some other countries are perforated horizontally or vertically only, with the outer edges imperforate. Coil stamps of some countries, such as Great Britain and Germany, are perforated on all four sides and may in some cases be distinguished from their sheet stamp counterparts by watermarks, counting numbers on the reverse or other means.

Covers — Entire envelopes, with or without adhesive postage stamps, that have passed through the mail and bear postal or other markings of philatelic interest are known as covers. Before the introduction of envelopes in about 1840, people folded letters and wrote the address on the outside. Some people covered their letters with an extra sheet of paper on the outside for the address, producing the term "cover." Used airletter sheets, stamped envelopes and other items of postal stationery also are considered covers.

Errors — Stamps that have some major, consistent, unintentional deviation from the normal are considered errors. Errors include, but are not limited to, missing or wrong colors, wrong paper, wrong watermarks, inverted centers or frames on multicolor printing, inverted or missing surcharges or overprints, double impressions, missing perforations, unintentionally omitted tagging and others. Factually wrong or misspelled information, if it appears on all examples of a stamp, are not considered errors in the true sense of the word. They are errors of design. Inconsistent or randomly appearing items, such as misperfs or color shifts, are classified as freaks.

Color-Omitted Errors — This term refers to stamps where a missing color is caused by the complete failure of the printing plate to deliver ink to the stamp paper or any other paper. Generally, this is caused by the printing plate not being engaged on the press or the ink station running dry of ink during printing.

Color-Missing Errors — This term refers to stamps where a color or colors were printed somewhere but do not appear on the finished stamp. There are four different classes of color-missing errors, and the catalog indicates with a two-letter code appended to each such listing what caused the color to be missing. These codes are used only for the United States' color-missing error listings.

FO = A *foldover* of the stamp sheet during printing may block ink from appearing on a stamp. Instead, the color will appear on the back of the foldover (where it might fall on the back of the selvage or perhaps on the back of the stamp or another stamp). FO also will be used in the case of foldunders, where the paper may fold underneath the other stamp paper and the color will print on the platen.

EP = A piece of *extraneous paper* falling across the plate or stamp paper will receive the printed ink. When the extraneous paper is removed, an unprinted portion of stamp paper remains and shows partially or totally missing colors.

CM = A misregistration of the printing plates during printing will result in a *color misregistration*, and such a misregistraion may result in a color not appearing on the finished stamp.

PS = *A perforation shift* after printing may remove a color from the finished stamp. Normally, this will occur on a row of stamps at the edge of the stamp pane.

Measurements - When measurements are given in the Scott catalogues for stamp size, grill size or any other reason, the first measurement given is always for the top and bottom dimension, while the second measurement will be for the sides (just as perforation gauges are measured). Thus, a stamp size of 15mm x 21mm will indicate a vertically oriented stamp 15mm wide at top and bottom, and 21mm tall at the sides. The same principle holds for measuring or counting items such as U.S. grills. A grill count of 22x18 points (B grill) indicates that there are 22 grill points across by 18 grill points down.

Overprints and Surcharges — Overprinting involves applying wording or design elements over an already existing stamp. Overprints can be used to alter the place of use (such as "Canal Zone" on U.S. stamps), to adapt them for a special purpose ("Porto" on Denmark's 1913-20 regular issues for use as postage due stamps, Scott J1-J7) or to commemorate a special occasion (United States Scott 647-648).

A *surcharge* is a form of overprint that changes or restates the face value of a stamp or piece of postal stationery.

Surcharges and overprints may be handstamped, typeset or, occasionally, lithographed or engraved. A few hand-written overprints and surcharges are known.

Personalized Stamps — In 1999, Australia issued stamps with se-tenant labels that could be personalized with pictures of the customer's choice. Other countries quickly followed suit, with some offering to print the selected picture on the stamp itself within a frame that was used exclusively for personalized issues. As the picture used on these stamps or labels vary, listings for such stamps are for any picture within the common frame (or any picture on a se-tenant label), be it a "generic" image or one produced especially for a customer, almost invariably at a premium price.

Precancels — Stamps that are canceled before they are placed in the mail are known as precancels. Precanceling usually is done to expedite the handling of large mailings and generally allow the affected mail pieces to skip certain phases of mail handling.

In the United States, precancellations generally identified the point of origin; that is, the city and state. This information appeared across the face of the stamp, usually centered between parallel lines. More recently, bureau precancels retained the parallel lines, but the city and state designations were dropped. Recent coils have a service inscription that is present on the original printing plate. These show the mail service paid for by the stamp. Since these stamps are not intended to receive further cancellations when used as intended, they are considered precancels. Such items often do not have parallel lines as part of the precancellation.

In France, the abbreviation *Affranchts* in a semicircle together with the word *Postes* is the general form of precancel in use. Belgian precancellations usually appear in a box in which the name of the city appears. Netherlands precancels have the name of the city enclosed between concentric circles, sometimes called a "lifesaver." Precancellations of other countries usually follow these patterns, but may be any arrangement of bars, boxes and city names.

Precancels are listed in the Scott catalogues only if the precancel changes the denomination (Belgium Scott 477-478); if the precanceled stamp is different from the non-precanceled version (such as untagged U.S. precancels); or if the stamp exists only precanceled (France Scott 1096-1099, U.S. Scott 2265).

Proofs and Essays — Proofs are impressions taken from an approved die, plate or stone in which the design and color are the same as the stamp issued to the public. Trial color proofs are impressions taken from approved dies, plates or stones in colors that vary from the final version. An essay is the impression of a design that differs in some way from the issued stamp. "Progressive die proofs" generally are considered to be essays.

Provisionals — These are stamps that are issued on short notice and intended for temporary use pending the arrival of regular issues. They usually are issued to meet such contingencies as changes in government or currency, shortage of necessary postage values or military occupation.

During the 1840s, postmasters in certain American cities issued stamps that were valid only at specific post offices. In 1861, postmasters of the Confederate States also issued stamps with limited validity. Both of these examples are known as "postmaster's provisionals."

Se-tenant — This term refers to an unsevered pair, strip or block of stamps that differ in design, denomination or overprint.

Unless the se-tenant item has a continuous design (see U.S. Scott 1451a, 1694a) the stamps do not have to be in the same order as shown in the catalogue (see U.S. Scott 2158a).

Specimens — The Universal Postal Union required member nations to send samples of all stamps they released into service to the International Bureau in Switzerland. Member nations of the UPU received these specimens as samples of what stamps were valid for postage. Many are overprinted, handstamped or initial-perforated "Specimen," "Canceled" or "Muestra." Some are marked with bars across the denominations (China-Taiwan), punched holes (Czechoslovakia) or back inscriptions (Mongolia).

Stamps distributed to government officials or for publicity purposes, and stamps submitted by private security printers for official approval, also may receive such defacements.

The previously described defacement markings prevent postal use, and all such items generally are known as "specimens."

Tete Beche — This term describes a pair of stamps in which one is upside down in relation to the other. Some of these are the result of intentional sheet arrangements, such as Morocco Scott B10-B11. Others occurred when one or more electrotypes accidentally were placed upside down on the plate, such as Colombia Scott 57a. Separation of the tete-beche stamps, of course, destroys the tete beche variety.

Currency Conversion

Country	Dollar	Pound	S Franc	Yen	HK $	Euro	Cdn $	Aus $
Australia	1.3849	1.9426	1.3860	0.0121	0.1781	1.5021	1.0277	—
Canada	1.3476	1.8903	1.3487	0.0118	0.1733	1.4616	—	0.9731
European Union	0.9220	1.2933	0.9227	0.0081	0.1186	—	0.6842	0.6658
Hong Kong	7.7758	10.907	7.7820	0.0681	—	8.4336	5.7701	5.6147
Japan	114.10	160.05	114.19	—	14.674	123.75	84.669	82.389
Switzerland	0.9992	1.4016	—	0.0088	0.1285	1.0837	0.7415	0.7215
United Kingdom	0.7129	—	0.7135	0.0062	0.0917	0.7732	0.5290	0.5148
United States	—	1.4027	1.0008	0.0088	0.1286	1.0846	0.7421	0.7221

Country	Currency	U.S. $ Equiv.
Jamaica	dollar	.0083
Japan	yen	.0088
Jordan	dinar	1.4104
Kazakhstan	tenge	.0029
Kenya	shilling	.0099
Kiribati	Australian dollar	.7221
Korea (South)	won	.0008
Korea (North)	won	.0077
Kosovo	euro	1.0846
Kuwait	dinar	3.3245
Kyrgyzstan	som	.0136
Laos	kip	.0001
Latvia	euro	1.0846
Lebanon	pound	.0007
Lesotho	maloti	.0637
Liberia	dollar	.0118
Libya	dinar	.7188
Liechtenstein	Swiss franc	1.0008
Lithuania	euro	1.0846
Luxembourg	euro	1.0846
Macao	pataca	.1249
Macedonia	denar	.0177
Malagasy Republic	ariary	.0003
Malawi	kwacha	.0014
Malaysia	ringgit (dollar)	.2405
Maldive Islands	rafiyaa	.0649
Mali	Community of French Africa (CFA) franc	.0017
Malta	euro	1.0846
Marshall Islands	U.S. dollar	1.000
Mauritania	ouguiya	.0032
Mauritius	rupee	.0278
Mexico	peso	.0557
Micronesia	U.S. dollar	1.000
Moldova	leu	.0502
Monaco	euro	1.0846
Mongolia	tugrik	.0005
Montenegro	euro	1.0846
Montserrat	East Caribbean dollar	.3704
Morocco	dirham	.1009
Mozambique	metical	.0206

Source: **xe.com** *Mar. 2, 2016. Figures reflect values as of Mar. 2, 2016.*

COMMON DESIGN TYPES

Pictured in this section are issues where one illustration has been used for a number of countries in the Catalogue. Not included in this section are overprinted stamps or those issues which are illustrated in each country. Because the location of Never Hinged breakpoints varies from country to country, some of the values in the listings below will be for unused stamps that were previously hinged.

EUROPA

Europa, 1956

The design symbolizing the cooperation among the six countries comprising the Coal and Steel Community is illustrated in each country.

Belgium.....*496-497*
France.....*805-806*
Germany.....*748-749*
Italy.....*715-716*
Luxembourg.....*318-320*
Netherlands.....*368-369*

Nos. 496-497 (2)	9.00	.70
Nos. 805-806 (2)	6.80	1.10
Nos. 748-749 (2)	7.30	1.20
Nos. 715-716 (2)	11.50	1.25
Nos. 318-320 (3)	73.00	50.00
Nos. 368-369 (2)	72.50	1.75
Set total (13) Stamps	180.10	56.00

Europa, 1958

"E" and Dove — CD1

European Postal Union at the service of European integration.

1958, Sept. 13

Belgium.....527-528
France.....889-890
Germany.....790-791
Italy.....750-751
Luxembourg.....341-343
Netherlands.....375-376
Saar.....317-318

Nos. 527-528 (2)	4.25	.60
Nos. 889-890 (2)	1.65	.55
Nos. 790-791 (2)	3.65	.65
Nos. 750-751 (2)	1.85	.60
Nos. 341-343 (3)	2.35	1.15
Nos. 375-376 (2)	2.50	.75
Nos. 317-318 (2)	1.05	2.30
Set total (15) Stamps	17.30	6.60

Europa, 1959

6-Link Enless Chain — CD2

1959, Sept. 19

Belgium.....536-537
France.....929-930
Germany.....805-806
Italy.....791-792
Luxembourg.....354-355
Netherlands.....379-380

Nos. 536-537 (2)	1.55	.60
Nos. 929-930 (2)	1.85	.90
Nos. 805-806 (2)	1.55	.65
Nos. 791-792 (2)	.80	.50
Nos. 354-355 (2)	3.50	1.40
Nos. 379-380 (2)	9.90	1.25
Set total (12) Stamps	19.15	5.30

Europa, 1960

19-Spoke Wheel CD3

First anniverary of the establishment of C.E.P.T. (Conference Europeenne des Administrations des Postes et des Telecommunications.) The spokes symbolize the 19 founding members of the Conference.

1960, Sept.

Belgium.....553-554
Denmark.....379
Finland.....376-377
France.....970-971
Germany.....818-820
Great Britain.....377-378
Greece.....688
Iceland.....327-328
Ireland.....175-176
Italy.....809-810
Luxembourg.....374-375
Netherlands.....385-386
Norway.....387
Portugal.....866-867
Spain.....941-942
Sweden.....562-563
Switzerland.....400-401
Turkey.....1493-1494

Nos. 553-554 (2)	1.25	.55
No. 379 (1)	.55	.50
Nos. 376-377 (2)	1.70	1.80
Nos. 970-971 (2)	.55	.50
Nos. 818-820 (3)	2.25	1.50
Nos. 377-378 (2)	9.00	5.00
No. 688 (1)	5.00	2.00
Nos. 327-328 (2)	1.30	1.30
Nos. 175-176 (2)	75.00	14.00
Nos. 809-810 (2)	.70	.50
Nos. 374-375 (2)	1.00	.80
Nos. 385-386 (2)	3.65	1.50
No. 387 (1)	1.25	1.25
Nos. 866-867 (2)	2.25	1.25
Nos. 941-942 (2)	1.50	.75
Nos. 562-563 (2)	1.05	.55
Nos. 400-401 (2)	1.25	.65
Nos. 1493-1494 (2)	2.10	1.35
Set total (34) Stamps	111.35	35.75

Europa, 1961

19 Doves Flying as One — CD4

The 19 doves represent the 19 members of the Conference of European Postal and Telecommunications Administrations C.E.P.T.

1961-62

Belgium.....572-573
Cyprus.....201-203
France.....1005-1006
Germany.....844-845
Great Britain.....382-384
Greece.....718-719
Iceland.....340-341
Italy.....845-846
Luxembourg.....382-383
Netherlands.....387-388
Spain.....1010-1011
Switzerland.....410-411
Turkey.....1518-1520

Nos. 572-573 (2)	.75	.50
Nos. 201-203 (3)	*2.10*	*1.20*
Nos. 1005-1006 (2)	.50	.50
Nos. 844-845 (2)	.60	.75
Nos. 382-384 (3)	.75	.90
Nos. 718-719 (2)	.80	.50
Nos. 340-341 (2)	.90	.90
Nos. 845-846 (2)	.55	.50
Nos. 382-383 (2)	.70	.70
Nos. 387-388 (2)	.55	.50
Nos. 1010-1011 (2)	.70	.55
Nos. 410-411 (2)	1.25	.60
Nos. 1518-1520 (3)	2.45	1.30
Set total (29) Stamps	12.60	9.40

Europa, 1962

Young Tree with 19 Leaves CD5

The 19 leaves represent the 19 original members of C.E.P.T.

1962-63

Belgium.....582-583
Cyprus.....219-221
France.....1045-1046
Germany.....852-853
Greece.....739-740
Iceland.....348-349
Ireland.....184-185
Italy.....860-861
Luxembourg.....386-387
Netherlands.....394-395
Norway.....414-415
Switzerland.....416-417
Turkey.....1553-1555

Nos. 582-583 (2)	.65	.65
Nos. 219-221 (3)	*76.25*	*4.40*
Nos. 1045-1046 (2)	.60	.50
Nos. 852-853 (2)	.70	.80
Nos. 739-740 (2)	2.25	1.15
Nos. 348-349 (2)	.85	.85
Nos. 184-185 (2)	2.00	1.50
Nos. 860-861 (2)	1.35	.55
Nos. 386-387 (2)	.85	.70
Nos. 394-395 (2)	1.40	.75
Nos. 414-415 (2)	2.25	2.25
Nos. 416-417 (2)	1.65	1.00
Nos. 1553-1555 (3)	*3.00*	1.55
Set total (28) Stamps	93.80	16.65

Europa, 1963

Stylized Links, Symbolizing Unity — CD6

1963, Sept.

Belgium.....598-599
Cyprus.....229-231
Finland.....419
France.....1074-1075
Germany.....867-868
Greece.....768-769
Iceland.....357-358
Ireland.....188-189
Italy.....880-881
Luxembourg.....403-404
Netherlands.....416-417
Norway.....441-442
Switzerland.....429
Turkey.....1602-1603

Nos. 598-599 (2)	1.60	.65
Nos. 229-231 (3)	*54.75*	*5.15*
No. 419 (1)	1.25	.55
Nos. 1074-1075 (2)	.60	.50
Nos. 867-868 (2)	.50	.55
Nos. 768-769 (2)	5.25	1.90
Nos. 357-358 (2)	1.50	1.50
Nos. 188-189 (2)	4.75	3.25
Nos. 880-881 (2)	.65	.50
Nos. 403-404 (2)	1.00	.80
Nos. 416-417 (2)	2.25	1.00
Nos. 441-442 (2)	4.75	3.00
No. 429 (1)	.90	.60
Nos. 1602-1603 (2)	1.40	.60
Set total (27) Stamps	81.15	20.45

Europa, 1964

Symbolic Daisy — CD7

5th anniversary of the establishment of C.E.P.T. The 22 petals of the flower symbolize the 22 members of the Conference.

1964, Sept.

Austria.....738
Belgium.....614-615
Cyprus.....244-246
France.....1109-1110
Germany.....897-898
Greece.....801-802
Iceland.....367-368
Ireland.....196-197
Italy.....894-895
Luxembourg.....411-412
Monaco.....590-591
Netherlands.....428-429
Norway.....458
Portugal.....931-933
Spain.....1262-1263
Switzerland.....438-439
Turkey.....1628-1629

No. 738 (1)	1.20	.80
Nos. 614-615 (2)	1.40	.60
Nos. 244-246 (3)	*35.75*	*3.45*
Nos. 1109-1110 (2)	.50	.50
Nos. 897-898 (2)	.50	.50
Nos. 801-802 (2)	5.00	1.90
Nos. 367-368 (2)	2.00	1.65
Nos. 196-197 (2)	20.00	4.25
Nos. 894-895 (2)	.55	.50
Nos. 411-412 (2)	.90	.55
Nos. 590-591 (2)	2.50	.70
Nos. 428-429 (2)	1.80	.60
No. 458 (1)	4.50	4.50
Nos. 931-933 (3)	*10.00*	*2.00*
Nos. 1262-1263 (2)	1.30	.80
Nos. 438-439 (2)	1.60	.50
Nos. 1628-1629 (2)	2.65	1.35
Set total (34) Stamps	92.15	25.15

Europa, 1965

Leaves and "Fruit" CD8

1965

Belgium.....636-637
Cyprus.....262-264
Finland.....437
France.....1131-1132
Germany.....934-935
Greece.....833-834
Iceland.....375-376
Ireland.....204-205
Italy.....915-916
Luxembourg.....432-433
Monaco.....616-617
Netherlands.....438-439
Norway.....475-476
Portugal.....958-960
Switzerland.....469
Turkey.....1665-1666

Nos. 636-637 (2)	.50	.50
Nos. 262-264 (3)	*25.35*	*3.80*
No. 437 (1)	1.25	.55
Nos. 1131-1132 (2)	.75	.80
Nos. 934-935 (2)	.50	.50
Nos. 833-834 (2)	2.25	1.15
Nos. 375-376 (2)	2.50	1.75
Nos. 204-205 (2)	20.00	3.35
Nos. 915-916 (2)	.50	.50
Nos. 432-433 (2)	.80	.60
Nos. 616-617 (2)	3.25	1.65
Nos. 438-439 (2)	.75	.55
Nos. 475-476 (2)	4.00	3.10
Nos. 958-960 (3)	*10.00*	*2.75*
No. 469 (1)	1.15	.25
Nos. 1665-1666 (2)	3.50	2.10
Set total (32) Stamps	77.05	23.90

Europa, 1966

Symbolic Sailboat — CD9

1966, Sept.

Andorra, French.....172
Belgium.....675-676
Cyprus.....275-277
France.....1163-1164
Germany.....963-964

Greece 862-863
Iceland 384-385
Ireland 216-217
Italy 942-943
Liechtenstein 415
Luxembourg 440-441
Monaco 639-640
Netherlands 441-442
Norway 496-497
Portugal 980-982
Switzerland 477-478
Turkey 1718-1719

No. 172 (1)	3.00	3.00
Nos. 675-676 (2)	.80	.50
Nos. 275-277 (3)	*4.75*	*1.90*
Nos. 1163-1164 (2)	.60	.50
Nos. 963-964 (2)	.50	.55
Nos. 862-863 (2)	2.25	1.05
Nos. 384-385 (2)	5.00	3.80
Nos. 216-217 (2)	7.00	2.00
Nos. 942-943 (2)	.50	.50
No. 415 (1)	.40	.35
Nos. 440-441 (2)	.80	.60
Nos. 639-640 (2)	2.00	.65
Nos. 441-442 (2)	1.50	.65
Nos. 496-497 (2)	5.00	3.00
Nos. 980-982 (3)	*9.75*	2.25
Nos. 477-478 (2)	1.60	.60
Nos. 1718-1719 (2)	3.35	1.75
Set total (34) Stamps	48.80	23.65

Europa, 1967

Cogwheels
CD10

1967

Andorra, French 174-175
Belgium 688-689
Cyprus 297-299
France 1178-1179
Germany 969-970
Greece 891-892
Iceland 389-390
Ireland 232-233
Italy 951-952
Liechtenstein 420
Luxembourg 449-450
Monaco 669-670
Netherlands 444-447
Norway 504-505
Portugal 994-996
Spain 1465-1466
Switzerland 482
Turkey B120-B121

Nos. 174-175 (2)	10.75	6.25
Nos. 688-689 (2)	1.05	.55
Nos. 297-299 (3)	*4.25*	*1.75*
Nos. 1178-1179 (2)	.80	.70
Nos. 969-970 (2)	.55	.55
Nos. 891-892 (2)	3.75	1.00
Nos. 389-390 (2)	3.00	2.00
Nos. 232-233 (2)	6.15	2.30
Nos. 951-952 (2)	.60	.50
No. 420 (1)	.45	.40
Nos. 449-450 (2)	1.00	.70
Nos. 669-670 (2)	2.75	.70
Nos. 444-447 (4)	5.00	1.85
Nos. 504-505 (2)	3.25	2.75
Nos. 994-996 (3)	*9.50*	1.85
Nos. 1465-1466 (2)	.50	.50
No. 482 (1)	.70	.25
Nos. B120-B121 (2)	3.50	2.75
Set total (38) Stamps	57.55	27.35

Europa, 1968

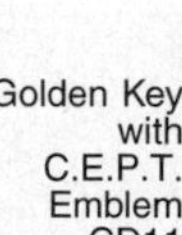

Golden Key
with
C.E.P.T.
Emblem
CD11

1968

Andorra, French 182-183
Belgium 705-706
Cyprus 314-316
France 1209-1210
Germany 983-984
Greece 916-917
Iceland 395-396
Ireland 242-243
Italy 979-980
Liechtenstein 442
Luxembourg 466-467
Monaco 689-691
Netherlands 452-453
Portugal 1019-1021
San Marino 687
Spain 1526
Switzerland 488
Turkey 1775-1776

Nos. 182-183 (2)	16.50	10.00
Nos. 705-706 (2)	1.25	.50
Nos. 314-316 (3)	*2.90*	*1.75*
Nos. 1209-1210 (2)	.90	.55
Nos. 983-984 (2)	.50	.55
Nos. 916-917 (2)	3.75	1.65
Nos. 395-396 (2)	3.00	2.50
Nos. 242-243 (2)	3.75	3.00
Nos. 979-980 (2)	.50	.50
No. 442 (1)	.45	.40
Nos. 466-467 (2)	.80	.70
Nos. 689-691 (3)	*5.40*	.95
Nos. 452-453 (2)	2.10	.70
Nos. 1019-1021 (3)	*9.75*	2.10
No. 687 (1)	.55	.35
No. 1526 (1)	.25	.25
No. 488 (1)	.45	.25
Nos. 1775-1776 (2)	5.00	2.00
Set total (35) Stamps	57.80	28.70

Europa, 1969

"EUROPA"
and "CEPT"
CD12

Tenth anniversary of C.E.P.T.

1969

Andorra, French 188-189
Austria 837
Belgium 718-719
Cyprus 326-328
Denmark 458
Finland 483
France 1245-1246
Germany 996-997
Great Britain 585
Greece 947-948
Iceland 406-407
Ireland 270-271
Italy 1000-1001
Liechtenstein 453
Luxembourg 475-476
Monaco 722-724
Netherlands 475-476
Norway 533-534
Portugal 1038-1040
San Marino 701-702
Spain 1567
Sweden 814-816
Switzerland 500-501
Turkey 1799-1800
Vatican 470-472
Yugoslavia 1003-1004

Nos. 188-189 (2)	18.50	12.00
No. 837 (1)	.65	.30
Nos. 718-719 (2)	.75	.50
Nos. 326-328 (3)	*3.00*	*1.35*
No. 458 (1)	.75	.75
No. 483 (1)	3.50	.75
Nos. 1245-1246 (2)	.55	.50
Nos. 996-997 (2)	.80	.50
No. 585 (1)	.25	.25
Nos. 947-948 (2)	5.00	1.50
Nos. 406-407 (2)	4.20	2.40
Nos. 270-271 (2)	4.00	2.00
Nos. 1000-1001 (2)	.70	.50
No. 453 (1)	.45	.45
Nos. 475-476 (2)	1.00	.70
Nos. 722-724 (3)	*10.50*	2.00
Nos. 475-476 (2)	2.60	1.15
Nos. 533-534 (2)	3.75	2.35
Nos. 1038-1040 (3)	17.85	2.40
Nos. 701-702 (2)	.90	.90
No. 1567 (1)	.25	.25
Nos. 814-816 (3)	4.00	2.85
Nos. 500-501 (2)	1.85	.60
Nos. 1799-1800 (2)	3.85	2.25
Nos. 470-472 (3)	.75	.75
Nos. 1003-1004 (2)	4.00	4.00
Set total (51) Stamps	94.40	43.95

Europa, 1970

Interwoven
Threads
CD13

1970

Andorra, French 196-197
Belgium 741-742
Cyprus 340-342
France 1271-1272
Germany 1018-1019
Greece 985, 987
Iceland 420-421
Ireland 279-281
Italy 1013-1014
Liechtenstein 470
Luxembourg 489-490
Monaco 768-770
Netherlands 483-484
Portugal 1060-1062
San Marino 729-730
Spain 1607
Switzerland 515-516
Turkey 1848-1849
Yugoslavia 1024-1025

Nos. 196-197 (2)	20.00	8.50
Nos. 741-742 (2)	1.10	.55
Nos. 340-342 (3)	*2.70*	*1.90*
Nos. 1271-1272 (2)	.65	.50
Nos. 1018-1019 (2)	.60	.50
Nos. 985,987 (2)	7.75	2.00
Nos. 420-421 (2)	6.00	4.00
Nos. 279-281 (3)	9.50	3.30
Nos. 1013-1014 (2)	.65	.50
No. 470 (1)	.45	.45
Nos. 489-490 (2)	.80	.80
Nos. 768-770 (3)	*6.35*	2.10
Nos. 483-484 (2)	2.50	1.15
Nos. 1060-1062 (3)	*9.85*	2.35
Nos. 729-730 (2)	.90	.55
No. 1607 (1)	.25	.25
Nos. 515-516 (2)	1.85	.60
Nos. 1848-1849 (2)	5.00	2.25
Nos. 1024-1025 (2)	.80	.80
Set total (40) Stamps	77.70	33.05

Europa, 1971

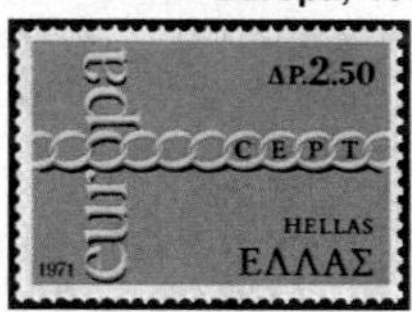

"Fraternity,
Cooperation,
Common
Effort"
CD14

1971

Andorra, French 205-206
Belgium 803-804
Cyprus 365-367
Finland 504
France 1304
Germany 1064-1065
Greece 1029-1030
Iceland 429-430
Ireland 305-306
Italy 1038-1039
Liechtenstein 485
Luxembourg 500-501
Malta 425-427
Monaco 797-799
Netherlands 488-489
Portugal 1094-1096
San Marino 749-750
Spain 1675-1676
Switzerland 531-532
Turkey 1876-1877
Yugoslavia 1052-1053

Nos. 205-206 (2)	20.00	7.75
Nos. 803-804 (2)	1.30	.55
Nos. 365-367 (3)	*2.60*	*1.75*
No. 504 (1)	5.00	.75
No. 1304 (1)	.45	.40
Nos. 1064-1065 (2)	.60	.50
Nos. 1029-1030 (2)	4.00	1.80
Nos. 429-430 (2)	5.00	3.75
Nos. 305-306 (2)	5.00	1.50
Nos. 1038-1039 (2)	.65	.50
No. 485 (1)	.45	.45
Nos. 500-501 (2)	1.00	.80
Nos. 425-427 (3)	*.80*	*.80*
Nos. 797-799 (3)	*15.00*	2.80
Nos. 488-489 (2)	2.50	1.15
Nos. 1094-1096 (3)	*9.75*	1.75
Nos. 749-750 (2)	.65	.55
Nos. 1675-1676 (2)	.75	.55
Nos. 531-532 (2)	1.85	.65
Nos. 1876-1877 (2)	5.60	2.50
Nos. 1052-1053 (2)	.50	.50
Set total (43) Stamps	83.45	31.75

Europa, 1972

Sparkles, Symbolic
of Communications
CD15

1972

Andorra, French 210-211
Andorra, Spanish 62
Belgium 825-826
Cyprus 380-382
Finland 512-513
France 1341
Germany 1089-1090
Greece 1049-1050
Iceland 439-440
Ireland 316-317
Italy 1065-1066
Liechtenstein 504
Luxembourg 512-513
Malta 450-453
Monaco 831-832
Netherlands 494-495
Portugal 1141-1143
San Marino 771-772
Spain 1718
Switzerland 544-545
Turkey 1907-1908
Yugoslavia 1100-1101

Nos. 210-211 (2)	21.00	7.00
No. 62 (1)	45.00	45.00
Nos. 825-826 (2)	.95	.55
Nos. 380-382 (3)	*5.95*	*2.45*
Nos. 512-513 (2)	7.00	1.40
No. 1341 (1)	.50	.35
Nos. 1089-1090 (2)	1.30	.50
Nos. 1049-1050 (2)	2.00	1.55
Nos. 439-440 (2)	2.90	2.65
Nos. 316-317 (2)	13.00	4.50
Nos. 1065-1066 (2)	.65	.50
No. 504 (1)	.45	.45
Nos. 512-513 (2)	1.00	.80
Nos. 450-453 (4)	1.05	1.40
Nos. 831-832 (2)	5.00	1.40
Nos. 494-495 (2)	3.25	1.15
Nos. 1141-1143 (3)	*9.85*	1.50
Nos. 771-772 (2)	.70	.50
No. 1718 (1)	.50	.40
Nos. 544-545 (2)	1.65	.60
Nos. 1907-1908 (2)	7.50	3.00
Nos. 1100-1101 (2)	1.20	1.20
Set total (44) Stamps	132.40	78.85

Europa, 1973

Post Horn
and Arrows
CD16

1973

Andorra, French 219-220
Andorra, Spanish 76
Belgium 839-840
Cyprus 396-398
Finland 526
France 1367
Germany 1114-1115
Greece 1090-1092
Iceland 447-448
Ireland 329-330
Italy 1108-1109
Liechtenstein 528-529
Luxembourg 523-524
Malta 469-471
Monaco 866-867
Netherlands 504-505
Norway 604-605
Portugal 1170-1172
San Marino 802-803
Spain 1753
Switzerland 580-581
Turkey 1935-1936
Yugoslavia 1138-1139

Nos. 219-220 (2)	20.00	11.00
No. 76 (1)	.65	.55
Nos. 839-840 (2)	1.00	.65
Nos. 396-398 (3)	*4.25*	*2.10*
No. 526 (1)	1.25	.55
No. 1367 (1)	1.60	.75
Nos. 1114-1115 (2)	.90	.50
Nos. 1090-1092 (3)	2.10	1.40
Nos. 447-448 (2)	7.00	4.05

Nos. 329-330 (2)	5.25	2.00
Nos. 1108-1109 (2)	.65	.50
Nos. 528-529 (2)	.60	.60
Nos. 523-524 (2)	.90	1.00
Nos. 469-471 (3)	.90	1.20
Nos. 866-867 (2)	15.00	2.40
Nos. 504-505 (2)	2.85	1.10
Nos. 604-605 (2)	6.25	2.40
Nos. 1170-1172 (3)	*13.00*	2.15
Nos. 802-803 (2)	*1.00*	.60
No. 1753 (1)	.35	.25
Nos. 580-581 (2)	1.55	.60
Nos. 1935-1936 (2)	10.00	4.50
Nos. 1138-1139 (2)	1.15	1.10
Set total (46) Stamps	98.20	41.95

Europa, 2000

CD17

2000

Albania....................2621-2622
Andorra, French....................522
Andorra, Spanish....................262
Armenia....................610-611
Austria....................1814
Azerbaijan....................698-699
Belarus....................350
Belgium....................1818
Bosnia & Herzegovina (Moslem)....358
Bosnia & Herzegovina (Serb)........111-112
Croatia....................428-429
Cyprus....................959
Czech Republic....................3120
Denmark....................1189
Estonia....................394
Faroe Islands....................376
Finland....................1129
Aland Islands....................166
France....................2771
Georgia....................228-229
Germany....................2086-2087
Gibraltar....................837-840
Great Britain (Jersey)....................935-936
Great Britain (Isle of Man)....................883
Greece....................1959
Greenland....................363
Hungary....................3699-3700
Iceland....................910
Ireland....................1230-1231
Italy....................2349
Latvia....................504
Liechtenstein....................1178
Lithuania....................668
Luxembourg....................1035
Macedonia....................187
Malta....................1011-1012
Moldova....................355
Monaco....................2161-2162
Poland....................3519
Portugal....................2358
Portugal (Azores)....................455
Portugal (Madeira)....................208
Romania....................4370
Russia....................6589
San Marino....................1480
Slovakia....................355
Slovenia....................424
Spain....................3036
Sweden....................2394
Switzerland....................1074
Turkey....................2762
Turkish Rep. of Northern Cyprus....500
Ukraine....................379
Vatican City....................1152

Nos. 2621-2622 (2)	11.00	11.00
No. 522 (1)	2.00	1.00
No. 262 (1)	1.60	.70
Nos. 610-611 (2)	9.00	9.00
No. 1814 (1)	1.40	1.40
Nos. 698-699 (2)	8.00	8.00
No. 350 (1)	1.75	1.75
No. 1818 (1)	1.40	.60
No. 358 (1)	4.75	4.75
Nos. 111-112 (2)	135.00	135.00
Nos. 428-429 (2)	6.25	6.25
No. 959 (1)	2.10	1.40
No. 3120 (1)	1.00	.40
No. 1189 (1)	3.50	2.25
No. 394 (1)	1.25	1.25
No. 376 (1)	3.00	3.00
No. 1129 (1)	2.00	.60
No. 166 (1)	2.00	1.10
No. 2771 (1)	1.40	.40
No. 228-229 (1)	9.00	9.00
Nos. 2086-2087 (2)	4.15	1.90
Nos. 837-840 (4)	5.50	5.30
Nos. 935-936 (2)	2.40	2.40
No. 883 (1)	1.50	1.50
No. 1959 (1)	3.00	3.00
No. 363 (1)	1.90	1.90
Nos. 3699-3700 (2)	6.50	2.50
No. 910 (1)	2.00	2.00
Nos. 1230-1231 (2)	4.75	4.75
No. 2349 (1)	1.50	.40
No. 504 (1)	5.00	2.40
No. 1178 (1)	2.25	1.75
No. 668 (1)	1.50	1.50
No. 1035 (1)	1.40	1.00
No. 187 (1)	3.25	3.25
Nos. 1011-1012 (2)	4.35	4.35
No. 355 (1)	3.50	3.50
Nos. 2161-2162 (2)	2.80	1.40
No. 3519 (1)	1.10	.50
No. 2358 (1)	1.25	.65
No. 455 (1)	1.25	.50
No. 208 (1)	1.25	.50
No. 4370 (1)	2.50	1.25
No. 6589 (1)	2.00	.85
No. 1480 (1)	1.00	1.00
No. 355 (1)	1.10	.55
No. 424 (1)	3.25	1.60
No. 3036 (1)	.75	.40
No. 2394 (1)	3.00	2.25
No. 1074 (1)	2.10	.75
No. 2762 (1)	2.00	2.00
No. 500 (1)	2.50	2.50
No. 379 (1)	4.50	3.00
No. 1152 (1)	1.25	1.25
Set total (68) Stamps	295.45	263.20

The Gibraltar stamps are similar to the stamp illustrated, but none have the design shown above. All other sets listed above include at least one stamp with the design shown, but some include stamps with entirely different designs. Bulgaria Nos. 4131-4132, Guernsey Nos. 802-803 and Yugoslavia Nos. 2485-2486 are Europa stamps with completely different designs.

PORTUGAL & COLONIES
Vasco da Gama

Fleet Departing CD20

Fleet Arriving at Calicut — CD21

Embarking at Rastello CD22

Muse of History CD23

San Gabriel, da Gama and Camoens CD24

Archangel Gabriel, the Patron Saint CD25

Flagship San Gabriel — CD26

Vasco da Gama — CD27

Fourth centenary of Vasco da Gama's discovery of the route to India.

1898

Azores....................93-100
Macao....................67-74
Madeira....................37-44
Portugal....................147-154
Port. Africa....................1-8
Port. Congo....................75-98
Port. India....................189-196
St. Thomas & Prince Islands...170-193
Timor....................45-52

Nos. 93-100 (8)	122.00	76.25
Nos. 67-74 (8)	136.00	96.75
Nos. 37-44 (8)	44.55	34.00
Nos. 147-154 (8)	169.30	43.45
Nos. 1-8 (8)	23.95	21.70
Nos. 75-98 (24)	41.15	34.45
Nos. 189-196 (8)	20.25	12.95
Nos. 170-193 (24)	38.75	34.30
Nos. 45-52 (8)	21.50	10.45
Set total (104) Stamps	617.45	364.30

Pombal
POSTAL TAX
POSTAL TAX DUES

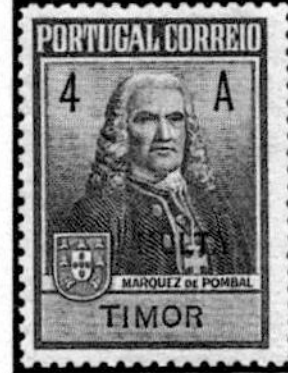

Marquis de Pombal — CD28

Planning Reconstruction of Lisbon, 1755 — CD29

Pombal Monument, Lisbon — CD30

Sebastiao Jose de Carvalho e Mello, Marquis de Pombal (1699-1782), statesman, rebuilt Lisbon after earthquake of 1755. Tax was for the erection of Pombal monument. Obligatory on all mail on certain days throughout the year. Postal Tax Dues are inscribed "Multa."

1925

Angola.......... RA1-RA3, RAJ1-RAJ3
Azores.......... RA9-RA11, RAJ2-RAJ4
Cape Verde...... RA1-RA3, RAJ1-RAJ3
Macao.......... RA1-RA3, RAJ1-RAJ3
Madeira.......... RA1-RA3, RAJ1-RAJ3
Mozambique..... RA1-RA3, RAJ1-RAJ3
Nyassa.......... RA1-RA3, RAJ1-RAJ3
Portugal........ RA11-RA13, RAJ2-RAJ4
Port. Guinea..... RA1-RA3, RAJ1-RAJ3
Port. India........ RA1-RA3, RAJ1-RAJ3
St. Thomas & Prince Islands.......... RA1-RA3, RAJ1-RAJ3
Timor.......... RA1-RA3, RAJ1-RAJ3

Nos. RA1-RA3,RAJ1-RAJ3 (6)	7.50	6.00
Nos. RA9-RA11,RAJ2-RAJ4 (6)	6.60	9.30
Nos. RA1-RA3,RAJ1-RAJ3 (6)	6.00	5.40
Nos. RA1-RA3,RAJ1-RAJ3 (6)	19.50	4.20
Nos. RA1-RA3,RAJ1-RAJ3 (6)	4.35	12.45
Nos. RA1-RA3,RAJ1-RAJ3 (6)	2.55	2.70
Nos. RA1-RA3,RAJ1-RAJ3 (6)	52.50	38.25
Nos. RA11-RA13,RAJ2-RAJ4 (6)	5.80	5.20
Nos. RA1-RA3,RAJ1-RAJ3 (6)	3.30	2.70
Nos. RA1-RA3,RAJ1-RAJ3 (6)	3.45	3.45
Nos. RA1-RA3,RAJ1-RAJ3 (6)	3.60	3.60
Nos. RA1-RA3,RAJ1-RAJ3 (6)	2.10	3.90
Set total (72) Stamps	117.25	97.15

Vasco da Gama CD34

Mousinho de Albuquerque CD35

Dam CD36

Prince Henry the Navigator CD37

Affonso de Albuquerque CD38

Plane over Globe CD39

1938-39

Angola....................274-291, C1-C9
Cape Verde....................234-251, C1-C9
Macao....................289-305, C7-C15
Mozambique....................270-287, C1-C9
Port. Guinea....................233-250, C1-C9
Port. India....................439-453, C1-C8
St. Thomas & Prince Islands... 302-319, 323-340, C1-C18
Timor....................223-239, C1-C9

Nos. 274-291,C1-C9 (27)	141.35	22.25
Nos. 234-251,C1-C9 (27)	100.00	31.20
Nos. 289-305,C7-C15 (26)	701.70	135.60
Nos. 270-287,C1-C9 (27)	63.45	11.20
Nos. 233-250,C1-C9 (27)	88.05	30.70
Nos. 439-453,C1-C8 (23)	74.75	25.50
Nos. 302-319,323-340,C1-C18 (54)	319.25	190.35
Nos. 223-239,C1-C9 (26)	149.25	73.15
Set total (237) Stamps	1,638.	519.95

Lady of Fatima

Our Lady of the Rosary, Fatima, Portugal — CD40

1948-49

Angola....................315-318
Cape Verde....................266
Macao....................336
Mozambique....................325-328
Port. Guinea....................271
Port. India....................480
St. Thomas & Prince Islands....................351
Timor....................254

Nos. 315-318 (4)	88.50	17.90
No. 266 (1)	8.50	4.50
No. 336 (1)	40.00	12.00
Nos. 325-328 (4)	20.00	4.50
No. 271 (1)	3.25	3.00
No. 480 (1)	2.50	2.25
No. 351 (1)	7.25	6.50
No. 254 (1)	3.00	3.00
Set total (14) Stamps	173.00	53.65

A souvenir sheet of 9 stamps was issued in 1951 to mark the extension of the 1950 Holy Year. The sheet contains: Angola No. 316, Cape Verde No. 266, Macao No. 336, Mozambique No. 325, Portuguese Guinea No. 271, Portuguese India Nos. 480, 485, St. Thomas & Prince Islands No. 351, Timor No. 254. The sheet also contains a portrait of Pope Pius XII and is inscribed "Encerramento do

Ano Santo, Fatima 1951." It was sold for 11 escudos.

Holy Year

Church Bells and Dove CD41

Angel Holding Candelabra CD42

Holy Year, 1950.

1950-51

Angola 331-332
Cape Verde 268-269
Macao 339-340
Mozambique 330-331
Port. Guinea 273-274
Port. India 490-491, 496-503
St. Thomas & Prince Islands 353-354
Timor 258-259

Nos. 331-332 (2)	7.60	1.35
Nos. 268-269 (2)	4.75	2.20
Nos. 339-340 (2)	55.00	12.50
Nos. 330-331 (2)	1.75	.85
Nos. 273-274 (2)	3.50	2.60
Nos. 490-491,496-503 (10)	12.80	5.40
Nos. 353-354 (2)	7.50	4.40
Nos. 258-259 (2)	3.75	3.25
Set total (24) Stamps	96.65	32.55

A souvenir sheet of 8 stamps was issued in 1951 to mark the extension of the Holy Year. The sheet contains: Angola No. 331, Cape Verde No. 269, Macao No. 340, Mozambique No. 331, Portuguese Guinea No. 275, Portuguese India No. 490, St. Thomas & Prince Islands No. 354, Timor No. 258, some with colors changed. The sheet contains doves and is inscribed 'Encerramento do Ano Santo, Fatima 1951.' It was sold for 17 escudos.

Holy Year Conclusion

Our Lady of Fatima — CD43

Conclusion of Holy Year. Sheets contain alternate vertical rows of stamps and labels bearing quotation from Pope Pius XII, different for each colony.

1951

Angola 357
Cape Verde 270
Macao 352
Mozambique 356
Port. Guinea 275
Port. India 506
St. Thomas & Prince Islands 355
Timor 270

No. 357 (1)	5.25	1.50
No. 270 (1)	1.50	1.25
No. 352 (1)	37.50	10.00
No. 356 (1)	2.25	1.00
No. 275 (1)	1.00	.65
No. 506 (1)	1.60	1.00
No. 355 (1)	2.50	2.00
No. 270 (1)	2.00	1.75
Set total (8) Stamps	53.60	19.15

Medical Congress

CD44

First National Congress of Tropical Medicine, Lisbon, 1952. Each stamp has a different design.

1952

Angola 358
Cape Verde 287
Macao 364
Mozambique 359
Port. Guinea 276
Port. India 516
St. Thomas & Prince Islands 356
Timor 271

No. 358 (1)	1.25	.45
No. 287 (1)	.70	.50
No. 364 (1)	9.75	4.25
No. 359 (1)	1.10	.55
No. 276 (1)	.45	.35
No. 516 (1)	4.75	2.00
No. 356 (1)	.30	.30
No. 271 (1)	1.00	1.00
Set total (8) Stamps	19.30	9.40

Postage Due Stamps

CD45

1952

Angola J37-J42
Cape Verde J31-J36
Macao J53-J58
Mozambique J51-J56
Port. Guinea J40-J45
Port. India J47-J52
St. Thomas & Prince Islands J52-J57
Timor J31-J36

Nos. J37-J42 (6)	4.05	3.15
Nos. J31-J36 (6)	2.80	2.30
Nos. J53-J58 (6)	17.45	6.85
Nos. J51-J56 (6)	1.80	1.55
Nos. J40-J45 (6)	2.55	2.55
Nos. J47-J52 (6)	6.10	6.10
Nos. J52-J57 (6)	4.15	4.15
Nos. J31-J36 (6)	3.50	3.50
Set total (48) Stamps	42.40	30.15

Sao Paulo

Father Manuel da Nobrega and View of Sao Paulo — CD46

Founding of Sao Paulo, Brazil, 400th anniv.

1954

Angola 385
Cape Verde 297
Macao 382
Mozambique 395
Port. Guinea 291
Port. India 530
St. Thomas & Prince Islands 369
Timor 279

No. 385 (1)	.80	.50
No. 297 (1)	.70	.60
No. 382 (1)	14.00	3.00
No. 395 (1)	.40	.30
No. 291 (1)	.35	.25
No. 530 (1)	.80	.40
No. 369 (1)	.80	.60
No. 279 (1)	.85	.70
Set total (8) Stamps	18.70	6.35

Tropical Medicine Congress

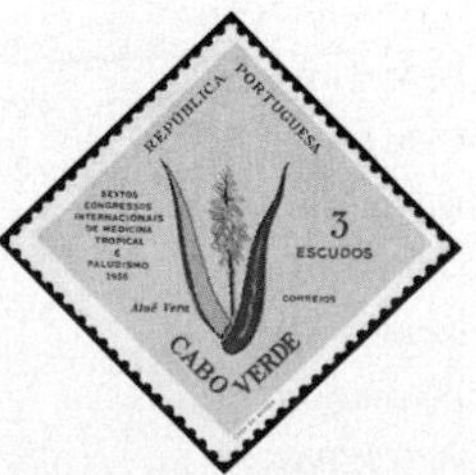

CD47

Sixth International Congress for Tropical Medicine and Malaria, Lisbon, Sept. 1958. Each stamp shows a different plant.

1958

Angola 409
Cape Verde 303
Macao 392
Mozambique 404
Port. Guinea 295
Port. India 569
St. Thomas & Prince Islands 371
Timor 289

No. 409 (1)	3.50	1.10
No. 303 (1)	5.50	2.10
No. 392 (1)	8.00	3.00
No. 404 (1)	4.00	.85
No. 295 (1)	2.75	1.10
No. 569 (1)	1.75	.75
No. 371 (1)	2.75	2.25
No. 289 (1)	3.00	2.75
Set total (8) Stamps	31.25	13.90

Sports

CD48

Each stamp shows a different sport.

1962

Angola 433-438
Cape Verde 320-325
Macao 394-399
Mozambique 424-429
Port. Guinea 299-304
St. Thomas & Prince Islands 374-379
Timor 313-318

Nos. 433-438 (6)	6.50	3.20
Nos. 320-325 (6)	15.25	5.20
Nos. 394-399 (6)	74.00	14.60
Nos. 424-429 (6)	5.70	2.45
Nos. 299-304 (6)	4.95	2.15
Nos. 374-379 (6)	6.75	3.20
Nos. 313-318 (6)	6.40	3.70
Set total (42) Stamps	119.55	34.50

Anti-Malaria

Anopheles Funestus and Malaria Eradication Symbol — CD49

World Health Organization drive to eradicate malaria.

1962

Angola 439
Cape Verde 326
Macao 400
Mozambique 430
Port. Guinea 305
St. Thomas & Prince Islands 380
Timor 319

No. 439 (1)	2.00	.90
No. 326 (1)	1.40	.90
No. 400 (1)	6.50	2.00
No. 430 (1)	1.40	.40
No. 305 (1)	1.25	.45
No. 380 (1)	2.00	1.50
No. 319 (1)	.75	.60
Set total (7) Stamps	15.30	6.75

Airline Anniversary

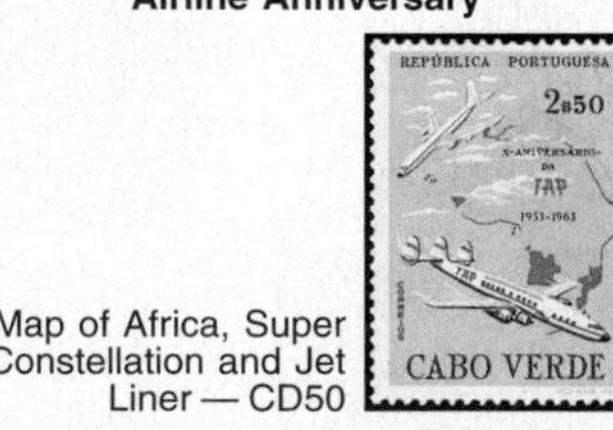

Map of Africa, Super Constellation and Jet Liner — CD50

Tenth anniversary of Transportes Aereos Portugueses (TAP).

1963

Angola 490
Cape Verde 327
Mozambique 434
Port. Guinea 318
St. Thomas & Prince Islands 381

No. 490 (1)	1.25	.50
No. 327 (1)	1.10	.70
No. 434 (1)	.40	.25
No. 318 (1)	.65	.35
No. 381 (1)	.70	.60
Set total (5) Stamps	4.10	2.40

National Overseas Bank

Antonio Teixeira de Sousa — CD51

Centenary of the National Overseas Bank of Portugal.

1964, May 16

Angola 509
Cape Verde 328
Port. Guinea 319
St. Thomas & Prince Islands 382
Timor 320

No. 509 (1)	.90	.30
No. 328 (1)	1.10	.75
No. 319 (1)	.65	.40
No. 382 (1)	.70	.50
No. 320 (1)	.75	.60
Set total (5) Stamps	4.10	2.55

ITU

ITU Emblem and the Archangel Gabriel — CD52

International Communications Union, Cent.

1965, May 17

Angola 511
Cape Verde 329
Macao 402
Mozambique 464
Port. Guinea 320
St. Thomas & Prince Islands 383
Timor 321

No. 511 (1)	1.25	.65
No. 329 (1)	2.10	1.40
No. 402 (1)	5.00	2.00
No. 464 (1)	.40	.25
No. 320 (1)	1.90	.75
No. 383 (1)	1.50	1.00
No. 321 (1)	1.50	.90
Set total (7) Stamps	13.65	6.95

National Revolution

CD53

40th anniv. of the National Revolution. Different buildings on each stamp.

1966, May 28

Angola 525
Cape Verde 338
Macao 403
Mozambique 465
Port. Guinea 329
St. Thomas & Prince Islands 392
Timor 322

No. 525 (1)	.45	.25
No. 338 (1)	.60	.45
No. 403 (1)	5.00	2.00
No. 465 (1)	.50	.30
No. 329 (1)	.55	.35
No. 392 (1)	.75	.50
No. 322 (1)	1.50	.90
Set total (7) Stamps	9.35	4.75

Navy Club

CD54

Centenary of Portugal's Navy Club. Each stamp has a different design.

1967, Jan. 31

Angola 527-528
Cape Verde 339-340
Macao.......................................412-413
Mozambique 478-479
Port. Guinea 330-331
St. Thomas & Prince Islands...393-394
Timor 323-324

Nos. 527-528 (2)	2.25	1.00
Nos. 339-340 (2)	2.00	1.40
Nos. 412-413 (2)	9.50	3.75
Nos. 478-479 (2)	1.20	.65
Nos. 330-331 (2)	1.20	.90
Nos. 393-394 (2)	3.20	1.25
Nos. 323-324 (2)	4.00	2.00
Set total (14) Stamps	23.35	10.95

Admiral Coutinho

CD55

Centenary of the birth of Admiral Carlos Viegas Gago Coutinho (1869-1959), explorer and aviation pioneer. Each stamp has a different design.

1969, Feb. 17

Angola 547
Cape Verde 355
Macao..417
Mozambique 484
Port. Guinea 335
St. Thomas & Prince Islands..........397
Timor 335

No. 547 (1)	1.00	.35
No. 355 (1)	.35	.25
No. 417 (1)	3.75	1.50
No. 484 (1)	.25	.25
No. 335 (1)	.35	.25
No. 397 (1)	.50	.35
No. 335 (1)	1.10	.85
Set total (7) Stamps	7.30	3.80

Administration Reform

Luiz Augusto Rebello da Silva — CD56

Centenary of the administration reforms of the overseas territories.

1969, Sept. 25

Angola 549
Cape Verde 357
Macao..419
Mozambique 491
Port. Guinea 337
St. Thomas & Prince Islands..........399
Timor 338

No. 549 (1)	.25	.25
No. 357 (1)	.35	.25
No. 419 (1)	5.00	1.00
No. 491 (1)	.25	.25
No. 337 (1)	.25	.25
No. 399 (1)	.45	.45
No. 338 (1)	.40	.25
Set total (7) Stamps	6.95	2.70

Marshal Carmona

CD57

Birth centenary of Marshal Antonio Oscar Carmona de Fragoso (1869-1951), President of Portugal. Each stamp has a different design.

1970, Nov. 15

Angola 563
Cape Verde 359
Macao..422
Mozambique 493
Port. Guinea 340
St. Thomas & Prince Islands..........403
Timor 341

No. 563 (1)	.45	.25
No. 359 (1)	.55	.35
No. 422 (1)	2.25	1.25
No. 493 (1)	.40	.25
No. 340 (1)	.35	.25
No. 403 (1)	.75	.45
No. 341 (1)	.25	.25
Set total (7) Stamps	5.00	3.05

Olympic Games

CD59

20th Olympic Games, Munich, Aug. 26-Sept. 11. Each stamp shows a different sport.

1972, June 20

Angola 569
Cape Verde 361
Macao..426
Mozambique 504
Port. Guinea 342
St. Thomas & Prince Islands..........408
Timor 343

No. 569 (1)	.65	.25
No. 361 (1)	.65	.30
No. 426 (1)	3.25	1.00
No. 504 (1)	.30	.25
No. 342 (1)	.45	.25
No. 408 (1)	.35	.25
No. 343 (1)	.50	.50
Set total (7) Stamps	6.15	2.80

Lisbon-Rio de Janeiro Flight

CD60

50th anniversary of the Lisbon to Rio de Janeiro flight by Arturo de Sacadura and Coutinho, March 30-June 5, 1922. Each stamp shows a different stage of the flight.

1972, Sept. 20

Angola 570
Cape Verde 362
Macao..427
Mozambique 505
Port. Guinea 343
St. Thomas & Prince Islands..........409
Timor 344

No. 570 (1)	.35	.25
No. 362 (1)	1.50	.30
No. 427 (1)	22.50	7.50
No. 505 (1)	.25	.25
No. 343 (1)	.25	.25
No. 409 (1)	.35	.25
No. 344 (1)	.25	.40
Set total (7) Stamps	25.45	9.20

WMO Centenary

WMO Emblem — CD61

Centenary of international meterological cooperation.

1973, Dec. 15

Angola 571
Cape Verde 363
Macao..429
Mozambique 509
Port. Guinea 344
St. Thomas & Prince Islands..........410
Timor 345

No. 571 (1)	.45	.25
No. 363 (1)	.65	.30
No. 429 (1)	6.25	1.75
No. 509 (1)	.30	.25
No. 344 (1)	.45	.35
No. 410 (1)	.60	.50
No. 345 (1)	1.75	2.00
Set total (7) Stamps	10.45	5.40

FRENCH COMMUNITY

Upper Volta can be found under Burkina Faso in Vol. 1
Madagascar can be found under Malagasy in Vol. 3

Colonial Exposition

People of French Empire CD70

Women's Heads CD71

France Showing Way to Civilization CD72

"Colonial Commerce" CD73

International Colonial Exposition, Paris.

1931

Cameroun...................................213-216
Chad 60-63
Dahomey 97-100
Fr. Guiana 152-155
Fr. Guinea 116-119
Fr. India 100-103
Fr. Polynesia.....................................76-79
Fr. Sudan.....................................102-105
Gabon...120-123
Guadeloupe 138-141
Indo-China....................................140-142
Ivory Coast 92-95
Madagascar..................................169-172
Martinique....................................129-132
Mauritania...65-68
Middle Congo 61-64
New Caledonia 176-179
Niger 73-76
Reunion 122-125
St. Pierre & Miquelon...................132-135
Senegal 138-141
Somali Coast.................................135-138
Togo..254-257
Ubangi-Shari 82-85
Upper Volta......................................66-69
Wallis & Futuna Isls. 85-88

Nos. 213-216 (4)	23.00	18.25
Nos. 60-63 (4)	22.00	22.00
Nos. 97-100 (4)	26.00	26.00
Nos. 152-155 (4)	22.00	22.00
Nos. 116-119 (4)	19.75	19.75
Nos. 100-103 (4)	18.00	*18.00*
Nos. 76-79 (4)	30.00	30.00
Nos. 102-105 (4)	19.00	19.00
Nos. 120-123 (4)	17.50	17.50
Nos. 138-141 (4)	19.00	19.00
Nos. 140-142 (3)	11.50	11.50
Nos. 92-95 (4)	22.50	22.50
Nos. 169-172 (4)	7.90	5.00
Nos. 129-132 (4)	21.00	21.00
Nos. 65-68 (4)	22.00	22.00
Nos. 61-64 (4)	20.50	20.50
Nos. 176-179 (4)	24.00	24.00
Nos. 73-76 (4)	21.50	21.50
Nos. 122-125 (4)	22.00	22.00
Nos. 132-135 (4)	24.00	24.00
Nos. 138-141 (4)	20.00	20.00
Nos. 135-138 (4)	22.00	22.00
Nos. 254-257 (4)	22.00	22.00
Nos. 82-85 (4)	21.00	21.00
Nos. 66-69 (4)	19.00	19.00
Nos. 85-88 (4)	35.00	35.00
Set total (103) Stamps	552.15	544.50

Paris International Exposition Colonial Arts Exposition

"Colonial Resources" CD74 CD77

Overseas Commerce CD75

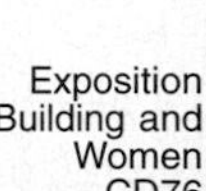

Exposition Building and Women CD76

"France and the Empire" CD78

Cultural Treasures of the Colonies CD79

Souvenir sheets contain one imperf. stamp.

1937

Cameroun...................................217-222A
Dahomey 101-107
Fr. Equatorial Africa 27-32, 73
Fr. Guiana 162-168
Fr. Guinea 120-126
Fr. India 104-110
Fr. Polynesia.................................117-123
Fr. Sudan.....................................106-112
Guadeloupe 148-154
Indo-China....................................193-199
Inini..41
Ivory Coast 152-158
Kwangchowan 132
Madagascar..................................191-197
Martinique....................................179-185
Mauritania...69-75
New Caledonia 208-214
Niger 73-83
Reunion 167-173
St. Pierre & Miquelon...................165-171
Senegal 172-178
Somali Coast.................................139-145
Togo..258-264
Wallis & Futuna Isls. 89

Nos. 217-222A (7)	18.80	20.30
Nos. 101-107 (7)	23.60	27.60
Nos. 27-32, 73 (7)	28.10	32.10
Nos. 162-168 (7)	22.50	24.50
Nos. 120-126 (7)	24.00	28.00
Nos. 104-110 (7)	21.15	30.50
Nos. 117-123 (7)	58.50	75.00
Nos. 106-112 (7)	23.60	27.60
Nos. 148-154 (7)	19.55	21.05
Nos. 193-199 (7)	17.70	19.70
No. 41 (1)	19.00	22.50
Nos. 152-158 (7)	22.20	26.20
No. 132 (1)	9.25	11.00
Nos. 191-197 (7)	19.25	21.75
Nos. 179-185 (7)	19.95	21.70
Nos. 69-75 (7)	20.50	24.50
Nos. 208-214 (7)	39.00	50.50
Nos. 73-83 (11)	42.70	46.70
Nos. 167-173 (7)	21.70	23.20
Nos. 165-171 (7)	49.60	64.00
Nos. 172-178 (7)	21.00	23.80
Nos. 139-145 (7)	25.60	32.60
Nos. 258-264 (7)	20.40	20.40
No. 89 (1)	28.50	37.50
Set total (154) Stamps	616.15	732.70

Curie

Pierre and Marie Curie CD80

40th anniversary of the discovery of radium. The surtax was for the benefit of the Intl. Union for the Control of Cancer.

1938

Cameroun	B1
Cuba	B1-B2
Dahomey	B2
France	B76
Fr. Equatorial Africa	B1
Fr. Guiana	B3
Fr. Guinea	B2
Fr. India	B6
Fr. Polynesia	B5
Fr. Sudan	B1
Guadeloupe	B3
Indo-China	B14
Ivory Coast	B2
Madagascar	B2
Martinique	B2
Mauritania	B3
New Caledonia	B4
Niger	B1
Reunion	B4
St. Pierre & Miquelon	B3
Senegal	B3
Somali Coast	B2
Togo	B1

No. B1 (1)	10.00	10.00
Nos. B1-B2 (2)	8.50	2.40
No. B2 (1)	9.50	9.50
No. B76 (1)	21.00	12.50
No. B1 (1)	24.00	24.00
No. B3 (1)	13.50	13.50
No. B2 (1)	8.75	8.75
No. B6 (1)	10.00	10.00
No. B5 (1)	20.00	20.00
No. B1 (1)	12.50	12.50
No. B3 (1)	11.00	10.50
No. B14 (1)	12.00	12.00
No. B2 (1)	11.00	7.50
No. B2 (1)	11.00	11.00
No. B2 (1)	13.00	13.00
No. B3 (1)	7.75	7.75
No. B4 (1)	16.50	17.50
No. B1 (1)	15.00	15.00
No. B4 (1)	14.00	14.00
No. B3 (1)	21.00	22.50
No. B3 (1)	10.50	10.50
No. B2 (1)	7.75	7.75
No. B1 (1)	20.00	20.00
Set total (24) Stamps	308.25	292.15

Caillie

Rene Caillie and Map of Northwestern Africa — CD81

Death centenary of Rene Caillie (1799-1838), French explorer. All three denominations exist with colony name omitted.

1939

Dahomey	108-110
Fr. Guinea	161-163
Fr. Sudan	113-115
Ivory Coast	160-162
Mauritania	109-111
Niger	84-86
Senegal	188-190
Togo	265-267

Nos. 108-110 (3)	1.20	3.60
Nos. 161-163 (3)	1.20	3.20
Nos. 113-115 (3)	1.20	3.20
Nos. 160-162 (3)	1.05	2.55
Nos. 109-111 (3)	1.05	3.80
Nos. 84-86 (3)	1.05	2.35
Nos. 188-190 (3)	1.05	2.90
Nos. 265-267 (3)	1.05	3.30
Set total (24) Stamps	8.85	24.90

New York World's Fair

Natives and New York Skyline CD82

1939

Cameroun	223-224
Dahomey	111-112
Fr. Equatorial Africa	78-79
Fr. Guiana	169-170
Fr. Guinea	164-165
Fr. India	111-112
Fr. Polynesia	124-125
Fr. Sudan	116-117
Guadeloupe	155-156
Indo-China	203-204
Inini	42-43
Ivory Coast	163-164
Kwangchowan	133-134
Madagascar	209-210
Martinique	186-187
Mauritania	112-113
New Caledonia	215-216
Niger	87-88
Reunion	174-175
St. Pierre & Miquelon	205-206
Senegal	191-192
Somali Coast	179-180
Togo	268-269
Wallis & Futuna Isls.	90-91

Nos. 223-224 (2)	2.80	2.40
Nos. 111-112 (2)	1.60	3.20
Nos. 78-79 (2)	1.60	3.20
Nos. 169-170 (2)	2.60	2.60
Nos. 164-165 (2)	1.60	3.20
Nos. 111-112 (2)	3.00	*6.00*
Nos. 124-125 (2)	4.80	4.80
Nos. 116-117 (2)	1.60	3.20
Nos. 155-156 (2)	2.50	2.50
Nos. 203-204 (2)	2.05	2.05
Nos. 42-43 (2)	7.50	9.00
Nos. 163-164 (2)	1.50	3.00
Nos. 133-134 (2)	2.50	2.50
Nos. 209-210 (2)	1.50	2.50
Nos. 186-187 (2)	2.35	2.35
Nos. 112-113 (2)	1.40	2.80
Nos. 215-216 (2)	3.35	3.35
Nos. 87-88 (2)	1.40	2.80
Nos. 174-175 (2)	2.80	2.80
Nos. 205-206 (2)	4.80	6.00
Nos. 191-192 (2)	1.40	2.80
Nos. 179-180 (2)	1.40	2.80
Nos. 268-269 (2)	1.40	2.80
Nos. 90-91 (2)	6.00	6.00
Set total (48) Stamps	63.45	84.65

French Revolution

Storming of the Bastille CD83

French Revolution, 150th anniv. The surtax was for the defense of the colonies.

1939

Cameroun	B2-B6
Dahomey	B3-B7
Fr. Equatorial Africa	B4-B8, CB1
Fr. Guiana	B4-B8, CB1
Fr. Guinea	B3-B7
Fr. India	B7-B11
Fr. Polynesia	B6-B10, CB1
Fr. Sudan	B2-B6
Guadeloupe	B4-B8
Indo-China	B15-B19, CB1
Inini	B1-B5
Ivory Coast	B3-B7
Kwangchowan	B1-B5
Madagascar	B3-B7, CB1
Martinique	B3-B7
Mauritania	B4-B8
New Caledonia	B5-B9, CB1
Niger	B2-B6
Reunion	B5-B9, CB1
St. Pierre & Miquelon	B4-B8
Senegal	B4-B8, CB1
Somali Coast	B3-B7
Togo	B2-B6
Wallis & Futuna Isls.	B1-B5

Nos. B2-B6 (5)	60.00	60.00
Nos. B3-B7 (5)	47.50	47.50
Nos. B4-B8,CB1 (6)	120.00	120.00
Nos. B4-B8,CB1 (6)	79.50	79.50
Nos. B3-B7 (5)	47.50	47.50
Nos. B7-B11 (5)	28.75	*32.50*
Nos. B6-B10,CB1 (6)	122.50	122.50
Nos. B2-B6 (5)	50.00	50.00
Nos. B4-B8 (5)	50.00	50.00
Nos. B15-B19,CB1 (6)	85.00	85.00
Nos. B1-B5 (5)	75.00	87.50
Nos. B3-B7 (5)	43.75	43.75
Nos. B1-B5 (5)	46.25	46.25
Nos. B3-B7,CB1 (6)	65.50	65.50
Nos. B3-B7 (5)	52.50	52.50
Nos. B4-B8 (5)	42.50	42.50
Nos. B5-B9,CB1 (6)	101.50	101.50
Nos. B2-B6 (5)	60.00	60.00
Nos. B5-B9,CB1 (6)	87.50	87.50
Nos. B4-B8 (5)	67.50	72.50
Nos. B4-B8,CB1 (6)	57.00	57.00
Nos. B3-B7 (5)	45.00	45.00
Nos. B2-B6 (5)	42.50	42.50
Nos. B1-B5 (5)	95.00	95.00
Set total (128) Stamps	1,572.	1,594.

Plane over Coastal Area CD85

All five denominations exist with colony name omitted.

1940

Dahomey	C1-C5
Fr. Guinea	C1-C5
Fr. Sudan	C1-C5
Ivory Coast	C1-C5
Mauritania	C1-C5
Niger	C1-C5
Senegal	C12-C16
Togo	C1-C5

Nos. C1-C5 (5)	4.00	4.00
Nos. C1-C5 (5)	4.00	4.00
Nos. C1-C5 (5)	4.00	4.00
Nos. C1-C5 (5)	3.80	3.80
Nos. C1-C5 (5)	3.50	3.50
Nos. C1-C5 (5)	3.50	3.50
Nos. C12-C16 (5)	3.50	3.50
Nos. C1-C5 (5)	3.15	3.15
Set total (40) Stamps	29.45	29.45

Defense of the Empire

Colonial Infantryman — CD86

1941

Cameroun	B13B
Dahomey	B13
Fr. Equatorial Africa	B8B
Fr. Guiana	B10
Fr. Guinea	B13
Fr. India	B13
Fr. Polynesia	B12
Fr. Sudan	B12
Guadeloupe	B10
Indo-China	B19B
Inini	B7
Ivory Coast	B13
Kwangchowan	B7
Madagascar	B9
Martinique	B9
Mauritania	B14
New Caledonia	B11
Niger	B12
Reunion	B11
St. Pierre & Miquelon	B8B
Senegal	B14
Somali Coast	B9
Togo	B10B
Wallis & Futuna Isls.	B7

No. B13B (1)	1.60
No. B13 (1)	1.20
No. B8B (1)	3.50
No. B10 (1)	1.40
No. B13 (1)	1.40
No. B13 (1)	1.25
No. B12 (1)	3.50
No. B12 (1)	1.40
No. B10 (1)	1.00
No. B19B (1)	1.60
No. B7 (1)	1.75
No. B13 (1)	1.25
No. B7 (1)	.85
No. B9 (1)	1.50
No. B9 (1)	1.40
No. B14 (1)	.95
No. B11 (1)	1.60
No. B12 (1)	1.40
No. B11 (1)	1.60
No. B8B (1)	3.75
No. B14 (1)	1.25
No. B9 (1)	1.60
No. B10B (1)	1.25
No. B7 (1)	2.40
Set total (24) Stamps	40.40

Each of the CD86 stamps listed above is part of a set of three stamps. The designs of the other two stamps in the set vary from country to country. Only the values of the Common Design stamps are listed here.

Colonial Education Fund

CD86a

1942

Cameroun	CB3
Dahomey	CB4
Fr. Equatorial Africa	CB5
Fr. Guiana	CB4
Fr. Guinea	CB4
Fr. India	CB3
Fr. Polynesia	CB4
Fr. Sudan	CB4
Guadeloupe	CB3
Indo-China	CB5
Inini	CB3
Ivory Coast	CB4
Kwangchowan	CB4
Malagasy	CB5
Martinique	CB3
Mauritania	CB4
New Caledonia	CB4
Niger	CB4
Reunion	CB4
St. Pierre & Miquelon	CB3
Senegal	CB5
Somali Coast	CB3
Togo	CB3
Wallis & Futuna	CB3

No. CB3 (1)	1.10	
No. CB4 (1)	.80	5.50
No. CB5 (1)	.80	
No. CB4 (1)	1.10	
No. CB4 (1)	.40	5.50
No. CB3 (1)	.90	
No. CB4 (1)	2.00	
No. CB4 (1)	.40	5.50
No. CB3 (1)	1.10	
No. CB5 (1)	1.10	
No. CB3 (1)	1.25	
No. CB4 (1)	1.00	5.50
No. CB4 (1)	1.00	
No. CB5 (1)	.65	
No. CB3 (1)	1.00	
No. CB4 (1)	.80	
No. CB4 (1)	1.60	
No. CB4 (1)	.35	
No. CB4 (1)	.90	
No. CB3 (1)	5.25	
No. CB5 (1)	.80	6.50
No. CB3 (1)	.70	
No. CB3 (1)	.35	
No. CB3 (1)	2.25	
Set total (24) Stamps	27.60	28.50

Cross of Lorraine & Four-motor Plane CD87

1941-5

Cameroun	C1-C7
Fr. Equatorial Africa	C17-C23
Fr. Guiana	C9-C10
Fr. India	C1-C6
Fr. Polynesia	C3-C9
Fr. West Africa	C1-C3
Guadeloupe	C1-C2
Madagascar	C37-C43

Martinique C1-C2
New Caledonia C7-C13
Reunion C18-C24
St. Pierre & Miquelon C1-C7
Somali Coast C1-C7

Nos. C1-C7 (7)	6.30	6.30
Nos. C17-C23 (7)	10.40	6.35
Nos. C9-C10 (2)	3.80	3.10
Nos. C1-C6 (6)	9.30	*15.00*
Nos. C3-C9 (7)	13.75	10.00
Nos. C1-C3 (3)	9.50	3.90
Nos. C1-C2 (2)	3.75	2.50
Nos. C37-C43 (7)	5.60	3.80
Nos. C1-C2 (2)	3.00	1.60
Nos. C7-C13 (7)	8.35	8.35
Nos. C18-C24 (7)	7.05	5.00
Nos. C1-C7 (7)	11.60	9.40
Nos. C1-C7 (7)	13.95	11.10
Set total (71) Stamps	106.35	86.40

Transport Plane CD88

Caravan and Plane CD89

1942

Dahomey C6-C13
Fr. Guinea C6-C13
Fr. Sudan C6-C13
Ivory Coast C6-C13
Mauritania C6-C13
Niger C6-C13
Senegal C17-C25
Togo C6-C13

Nos. C6-C13 (8)	7.15
Nos. C6-C13 (8)	5.75
Nos. C6-C13 (8)	8.00
Nos. C6-C13 (8)	11.15
Nos. C6-C13 (8)	9.75
Nos. C6-C13 (8)	6.90
Nos. C17-C25 (9)	9.45
Nos. C6-C13 (8)	6.75
Set total (65) Stamps	64.90

Red Cross

Marianne CD90

The surtax was for the French Red Cross and national relief.

1944

Cameroun B28
Fr. Equatorial Africa B38
Fr. Guiana B12
Fr. India B14
Fr. Polynesia B13
Fr. West Africa B1
Guadeloupe B12
Madagascar B15
Martinique B11
New Caledonia B13
Reunion B15
St. Pierre & Miquelon B13
Somali Coast B13
Wallis & Futuna Isls. B9

No. B28 (1)	2.00	1.60
No. B38 (1)	1.60	1.20
No. B12 (1)	1.75	1.25
No. B14 (1)	1.50	1.25
No. B13 (1)	2.00	1.60
No. B1 (1)	6.50	4.75
No. B12 (1)	1.40	1.00
No. B15 (1)	.90	.90
No. B11 (1)	1.20	1.20
No. B13 (1)	1.50	1.50
No. B15 (1)	1.60	1.10
No. B13 (1)	2.75	2.40
No. B13 (1)	1.75	2.00
No. B9 (1)	4.50	3.25
Set total (14) Stamps	30.95	25.00

Eboue

CD91

Felix Eboue, first French colonial administrator to proclaim resistance to Germany after French surrender in World War II.

1945

Cameroun 296-297
Fr. Equatorial Africa 156-157
Fr. Guiana 171-172
Fr. India 210-211
Fr. Polynesia 150-151
Fr. West Africa 15-16
Guadeloupe 187-188
Madagascar 259-260
Martinique 196-197
New Caledonia 274-275
Reunion 238-239
St. Pierre & Miquelon 322-323
Somali Coast 238-239

Nos. 296-297 (2)	2.40	1.95
Nos. 156-157 (2)	2.55	2.00
Nos. 171-172 (2)	2.45	2.00
Nos. 210-211 (2)	2.20	1.95
Nos. 150-151 (2)	3.60	2.85
Nos. 15-16 (2)	2.40	2.40
Nos. 187-188 (2)	2.05	1.60
Nos. 259-260 (2)	2.00	1.45
Nos. 196-197 (2)	2.05	1.55
Nos. 274-275 (2)	3.40	3.00
Nos. 238-239 (2)	2.40	2.00
Nos. 322-323 (2)	4.40	3.45
Nos. 238-239 (2)	2.45	2.10
Set total (26) Stamps	34.35	28.30

Victory

Victory — CD92

European victory of the Allied Nations in World War II.

1946, May 8

Cameroun C8
Fr. Equatorial Africa C24
Fr. Guiana C11
Fr. India C7
Fr. Polynesia C10
Fr. West Africa C4
Guadeloupe C3
Indo-China C19
Madagascar C44
Martinique C3
New Caledonia C14
Reunion C25
St. Pierre & Miquelon C8
Somali Coast C8
Wallis & Futuna Isls. C1

No. C8 (1)	1.60	1.20
No. C24 (1)	1.60	1.25
No. C11 (1)	1.75	1.25
No. C7 (1)	1.00	2.00
No. C10 (1)	2.75	2.00
No. C4 (1)	1.60	1.20
No. C3 (1)	1.25	1.00
No. C19 (1)	1.00	.55
No. C44 (1)	1.00	.35
No. C3 (1)	1.30	1.00
No. C14 (1)	2.25	1.25
No. C25 (1)	1.10	.90
No. C8 (1)	2.10	1.75
No. C8 (1)	1.75	1.40
No. C1 (1)	2.50	1.90
Set total (15) Stamps	24.55	19.00

Chad to Rhine

Leclerc's Departure from Chad — CD93

Battle at Cufra Oasis — CD94

Tanks in Action, Mareth — CD95

Normandy Invasion — CD96

Entering Paris — CD97

Liberation of Strasbourg — CD98

"Chad to the Rhine" march, 1942-44, by Gen. Jacques Leclerc's column, later French 2nd Armored Division.

1946, June 6

Cameroun C9-C14
Fr. Equatorial Africa C25-C30
Fr. Guiana C12-C17
Fr. India C8-C13
Fr. Polynesia C11-C16
Fr. West Africa C5-C10
Guadeloupe C4-C9
Indo-China C20-C25
Madagascar C45-C50
Martinique C4-C9
New Caledonia C15-C20
Reunion C26-C31
St. Pierre & Miquelon C9-C14
Somali Coast C9-C14
Wallis & Futuna Isls. C2-C7

Nos. C9-C14 (6)	12.05	9.70
Nos. C25-C30 (6)	14.70	10.80
Nos. C12-C17 (6)	12.65	10.35
Nos. C8-C13 (6)	12.80	*15.00*
Nos. C11-C16 (6)	17.55	13.40
Nos. C5-C10 (6)	16.05	11.95
Nos. C4-C9 (6)	12.00	9.60
Nos. C20-C25 (6)	6.40	6.40
Nos. C45-C50 (6)	10.30	8.40
Nos. C4-C9 (6)	8.85	7.30
Nos. C15-C20 (6)	13.40	11.90
Nos. C26-C31 (6)	10.25	6.55
Nos. C9-C14 (6)	17.30	14.35
Nos. C9-C14 (6)	18.10	12.65
Nos. C2-C7 (6)	13.75	10.45
Set total (90) Stamps	196.15	158.80

UPU

French Colonials, Globe and Plane — CD99

Universal Postal Union, 75th anniv.

1949, July 4

Cameroun C29
Fr. Equatorial Africa C34
Fr. India C17
Fr. Polynesia C20
Fr. West Africa C15
Indo-China C26
Madagascar C55
New Caledonia C24
St. Pierre & Miquelon C18
Somali Coast C18
Togo C18
Wallis & Futuna Isls. C10

No. C29 (1)	8.00	4.75
No. C34 (1)	16.00	12.00
No. C17 (1)	11.50	8.75
No. C20 (1)	20.00	15.00
No. C15 (1)	12.00	8.75
No. C26 (1)	4.75	4.00
No. C55 (1)	4.00	2.75
No. C24 (1)	8.25	5.25
No. C18 (1)	20.00	12.00
No. C18 (1)	14.00	10.50
No. C18 (1)	8.50	7.00
No. C10 (1)	12.50	8.25
Set total (12) Stamps	139.50	99.00

Tropical Medicine

Doctor Treating Infant CD100

The surtax was for charitable work.

1950

Cameroun B29
Fr. Equatorial Africa B39
Fr. India B15
Fr. Polynesia B14
Fr. West Africa B3
Madagascar B17
New Caledonia B14
St. Pierre & Miquelon B14
Somali Coast B14
Togo B11

No. B29 (1)	7.25	5.50
No. B39 (1)	7.25	5.50
No. B15 (1)	6.00	4.00
No. B14 (1)	10.50	8.00
No. B3 (1)	9.50	7.25
No. B17 (1)	5.50	5.50
No. B14 (1)	6.75	5.25
No. B14 (1)	17.00	13.00
No. B14 (1)	7.75	6.25
No. B11 (1)	5.00	3.50
Set total (10) Stamps	82.50	63.75

Military Medal

Medal, Early Marine and Colonial Soldier — CD101

Centenary of the creation of the French Military Medal.

1952

Cameroun 322
Comoro Isls. 39
Fr. Equatorial Africa 186

Fr. India 233
Fr. Polynesia 179
Fr. West Africa 57
Madagascar 286
New Caledonia 295
St. Pierre & Miquelon 345
Somali Coast 267
Togo 327
Wallis & Futuna Isls. 149

No. 322 (1)	7.25	3.25
No. 39 (1)	50.00	40.00
No. 186 (1)	8.00	5.50
No. 233 (1)	5.50	7.00
No. 179 (1)	13.50	10.00
No. 57 (1)	8.75	6.50
No. 286 (1)	3.75	2.50
No. 295 (1)	7.50	6.00
No. 345 (1)	17.00	13.00
No. 267 (1)	9.00	8.00
No. 327 (1)	5.50	4.75
No. 149 (1)	9.50	7.00
Set total (12) Stamps	145.25	113.50

Liberation

Allied Landing, Victory Sign and Cross of Lorraine — CD102

Liberation of France, 10th anniv.

1954, June 6

Cameroun C32
Comoro Isls. C4
Fr. Equatorial Africa C38
Fr. India C18
Fr. Polynesia C22
Fr. West Africa C17
Madagascar C57
New Caledonia C25
St. Pierre & Miquelon C19
Somali Coast C19
Togo C19
Wallis & Futuna Isls. C11

No. C32 (1)	7.25	4.75
No. C4 (1)	35.00	20.00
No. C38 (1)	12.00	8.00
No. C18 (1)	11.00	8.00
No. C22 (1)	10.00	8.00
No. C17 (1)	12.00	5.50
No. C57 (1)	3.25	2.00
No. C25 (1)	8.25	5.00
No. C19 (1)	18.00	12.00
No. C19 (1)	10.50	8.50
No. C19 (1)	7.00	5.50
No. C11 (1)	12.50	8.25
Set total (12) Stamps	146.75	95.50

FIDES

Plowmen CD103

Efforts of FIDES, the Economic and Social Development Fund for Overseas Possessions (Fonds d' Investissement pour le Developpement Economique et Social). Each stamp has a different design.

1956

Cameroun 326-329
Comoro Isls. 43
Fr. Equatorial Africa 189-192
Fr. Polynesia 181
Fr. West Africa 65-72
Madagascar 292-295
New Caledonia 303
St. Pierre & Miquelon 350
Somali Coast 268-269
Togo 331

Nos. 326-329 (4)	6.90	3.20
No. 43 (1)	2.25	1.60
Nos. 189-192 (4)	3.20	1.65
No. 181 (1)	4.00	2.00
Nos. 65-72 (8)	16.00	6.35
Nos. 292-295 (4)	2.25	1.20
No. 303 (1)	1.90	1.10
No. 350 (1)	6.50	3.50
Nos. 268-269 (2)	5.35	3.15
No. 331 (1)	4.25	2.10
Set total (27) Stamps	52.60	25.85

Flower

CD104

Each stamp shows a different flower.

1958-9

Cameroun 333
Comoro Isls. 45
Fr. Equatorial Africa 200-201
Fr. Polynesia 192
Fr. So. & Antarctic Terr. 11
Fr. West Africa 79-83
Madagascar 301-302
New Caledonia 304-305
St. Pierre & Miquelon 357
Somali Coast 270
Togo 348-349
Wallis & Futuna Isls. 152

No. 333 (1)	1.60	.80
No. 45 (1)	5.50	4.50
Nos. 200-201 (2)	3.60	1.60
No. 192 (1)	6.50	4.00
No. 11 (1)	10.00	8.00
Nos. 79-83 (5)	10.45	5.60
Nos. 301-302 (2)	1.60	.60
Nos. 304-305 (2)	9.25	3.00
No. 357 (1)	4.50	2.40
No. 270 (1)	4.25	1.40
Nos. 348-349 (2)	1.10	.50
No. 152 (1)	4.50	2.50
Set total (20) Stamps	62.85	34.90

Human Rights

Sun, Dove and U.N. Emblem CD105

10th anniversary of the signing of the Universal Declaration of Human Rights.

1958

Comoro Isls. 44
Fr. Equatorial Africa 202
Fr. Polynesia 191
Fr. West Africa 85
Madagascar 300
New Caledonia 306
St. Pierre & Miquelon 356
Somali Coast 274
Wallis & Futuna Isls. 153

No. 44 (1)	11.00	11.00
No. 202 (1)	2.40	1.25
No. 191 (1)	13.00	8.75
No. 85 (1)	2.40	2.00
No. 300 (1)	.80	.40
No. 306 (1)	3.00	1.50
No. 356 (1)	3.50	2.50
No. 274 (1)	3.50	2.10
No. 153 (1)	5.75	4.00
Set total (9) Stamps	45.35	33.50

C.C.T.A.

CD106

Commission for Technical Cooperation in Africa south of the Sahara, 10th anniv.

1960

Cameroun 339
Cent. Africa 3
Chad 66
Congo, P.R. 90
Dahomey 138
Gabon 150
Ivory Coast 180
Madagascar 317
Mali 9
Mauritania 117
Niger 104
Upper Volta 89

No. 339 (1)	1.60	.75
No. 3 (1)	1.90	.65
No. 66 (1)	1.90	.50
No. 90 (1)	1.00	1.00
No. 138 (1)	.50	.25
No. 150 (1)	1.40	1.10
No. 180 (1)	1.10	.50
No. 317 (1)	.60	.30
No. 9 (1)	1.40	.50
No. 117 (1)	.75	.40
No. 104 (1)	.85	.45
No. 89 (1)	.45	.40
Set total (12) Stamps	13.45	6.80

Air Afrique, 1961

Modern and Ancient Africa, Map and Planes — CD107

Founding of Air Afrique (African Airlines).

1961-62

Cameroun C37
Cent. Africa C5
Chad C7
Congo, P.R. C5
Dahomey C17
Gabon C5
Ivory Coast C18
Mauritania C17
Niger C22
Senegal C31
Upper Volta C4

No. C37 (1)	1.00	.50
No. C5 (1)	1.00	.55
No. C7 (1)	1.00	.25
No. C5 (1)	1.75	.90
No. C17 (1)	.80	.40
No. C5 (1)	11.00	6.00
No. C18 (1)	2.00	1.25
No. C17 (1)	2.50	1.25
No. C22 (1)	1.75	.90
No. C31 (1)	.80	.30
No. C4 (1)	.65	.45
Set total (11) Stamps	24.25	12.75

Anti-Malaria

CD108

World Health Organization drive to eradicate malaria.

1962, Apr. 7

Cameroun B36
Cent. Africa B1
Chad B1
Comoro Isls. B1
Congo, P.R. B3
Dahomey B15
Gabon B4
Ivory Coast B15
Madagascar B19
Mali B1
Mauritania B16
Niger B14
Senegal B16
Somali Coast B15
Upper Volta B1

No. B36 (1)	1.00	.45
No. B1 (1)	1.40	1.40
No. B1 (1)	1.25	.50
No. B1 (1)	4.00	4.00
No. B3 (1)	1.40	1.00
No. B15 (1)	.75	.75
No. B4 (1)	1.00	1.00
No. B15 (1)	1.25	1.25
No. B19 (1)	.75	.50
No. B1 (1)	1.25	.60
No. B16 (1)	.80	.80
No. B14 (1)	.60	.60
No. B16 (1)	1.10	.65
No. B15 (1)	7.00	7.00
No. B1 (1)	.95	.95
Set total (15) Stamps	24.50	21.45

Abidjan Games

CD109

Abidjan Games, Ivory Coast, Dec. 24-31, 1961. Each stamp shows a different sport.

1962

Cent. Africa 19-20, C6
Chad 83-84, C8
Congo, P.R. 103-104, C7
Gabon 163-164, C6
Niger 109-111
Upper Volta 103-105

Nos. 19-20,C6 (3)	3.90	2.60
Nos. 83-84,C8 (3)	6.30	1.55
Nos. 103-104,C7 (3)	3.85	1.80
Nos. 163-164,C6 (3)	5.00	3.00
Nos. 109-111 (3)	2.60	1.10
Nos. 103-105 (3)	3.15	1.80
Set total (18) Stamps	24.80	11.85

African and Malagasy Union

Flag of Union CD110

First anniversary of the Union.

1962, Sept. 8

Cameroun 373
Cent. Africa 21
Chad 85
Congo, P.R. 105
Dahomey 155
Gabon 165
Ivory Coast 198
Madagascar 332
Mauritania 170
Niger 112
Senegal 211
Upper Volta 106

No. 373 (1)	2.00	.75
No. 21 (1)	1.25	.60
No. 85 (1)	1.25	.25
No. 105 (1)	1.50	.50
No. 155 (1)	1.25	.90
No. 165 (1)	1.60	1.25
No. 198 (1)	2.10	.75
No. 332 (1)	.80	.80
No. 170 (1)	.75	.50
No. 112 (1)	.80	.40
No. 211 (1)	.80	.50
No. 106 (1)	1.50	.90
Set total (12) Stamps	15.60	8.10

Telstar

Telstar and Globe Showing Andover and Pleumeur-Bodou — CD111

First television connection of the United States and Europe through the Telstar satellite, July 11-12, 1962.

1962-63

Andorra, French 154
Comoro Isls. C7
Fr. Polynesia C29
Fr. So. & Antarctic Terr. C5
New Caledonia C33
St. Pierre & Miquelon C26
Somali Coast C31
Wallis & Futuna Isls. C17

No. 154 (1)	2.00	1.60
No. C7 (1)	5.00	3.00
No. C29 (1)	11.50	8.00

No. C5 (1)	29.00	21.00
No. C33 (1)	30.00	18.50
No. C26 (1)	7.25	5.50
No. C31 (1)	1.00	1.00
No. C17 (1)	3.50	3.50
Set total (8) Stamps	89.25	62.10

Freedom From Hunger

World Map and Wheat Emblem CD112

U.N. Food and Agriculture Organization's "Freedom from Hunger" campaign.

1963, Mar. 21

Cameroun................................B37-B38
Cent. Africa B2
Chad B2
Congo, P.R. B4
Dahomey B16
Gabon B5
Ivory Coast B16
Madagascar B21
Mauritania B17
Niger B15
Senegal B17
Upper Volta B2

Nos. B37-B38 (2)	2.25	.75
No. B2 (1)	1.25	1.25
No. B2 (1)	2.00	.50
No. B4 (1)	1.40	1.00
No. B16 (1)	.80	.80
No. B5 (1)	1.00	1.00
No. B16 (1)	1.50	1.50
No. B21 (1)	.60	.45
No. B17 (1)	.80	.80
No. B15 (1)	.60	.60
No. B17 (1)	.80	.50
No. B2 (1)	.95	.95
Set total (13) Stamps	13.95	10.10

Red Cross Centenary

CD113

Centenary of the International Red Cross.

1963, Sept. 2

Comoro Isls. 55
Fr. Polynesia 205
New Caledonia 328
St. Pierre & Miquelon 367
Somali Coast 297
Wallis & Futuna Isls. 165

No. 55 (1)	9.50	7.00
No. 205 (1)	15.00	12.00
No. 328 (1)	9.00	6.75
No. 367 (1)	12.00	6.75
No. 297 (1)	6.25	6.25
No. 165 (1)	4.00	3.50
Set total (6) Stamps	55.75	42.25

African Postal Union, 1963

UAMPT Emblem, Radio Masts, Plane and Mail CD114

Establishment of the African and Malagasy Posts and Telecommunications Union.

1963, Sept. 8

Cameroun C47
Cent. Africa C10
Chad C9
Congo, P.R. C13
Dahomey C19
Gabon C13
Ivory Coast C25
Madagascar C75
Mauritania C22
Niger C27
Rwanda 36
Senegal C32
Upper Volta C9

No. C47 (1)	2.25	1.00
No. C10 (1)	1.90	.85
No. C9 (1)	2.40	.60
No. C13 (1)	1.40	.75
No. C19 (1)	.75	.25
No. C13 (1)	1.90	.80
No. C25 (1)	2.50	1.50
No. C75 (1)	1.25	.80
No. C22 (1)	1.50	.60
No. C27 (1)	1.25	.60
No. 36 (1)	.90	.55
No. C32 (1)	1.75	.50
No. C9 (1)	1.50	.75
Set total (13) Stamps	21.25	9.55

Air Afrique, 1963

Symbols of Flight — CD115

First anniversary of Air Afrique and inauguration of DC-8 service.

1963, Nov. 19

Cameroun C48
Chad C10
Congo, P.R. C14
Gabon C18
Ivory Coast C26
Mauritania C26
Niger C35
Senegal C33

No. C48 (1)	1.25	.40
No. C10 (1)	2.40	.60
No. C14 (1)	1.60	.60
No. C18 (1)	1.40	.65
No. C26 (1)	1.00	.50
No. C26 (1)	.70	.25
No. C35 (1)	.90	.50
No. C33 (1)	2.00	.65
Set total (8) Stamps	11.25	4.15

Europafrica

Europe and Africa Linked — CD116

Signing of an economic agreement between the European Economic Community and the African and Malagasy Union, Yaounde, Cameroun, July 20, 1963.

1963-64

Cameroun 402
Cent. Africa C12
Chad C11
Congo, P.R. C16
Gabon C19
Ivory Coast 217
Niger C43
Upper Volta C11

No. 402 (1)	2.25	.60
No. C12 (1)	2.50	1.75
No. C11 (1)	2.00	.50
No. C16 (1)	1.60	1.00
No. C19 (1)	1.40	.75
No. 217 (1)	1.10	.35
No. C43 (1)	.85	.50
No. C11 (1)	1.50	.80
Set total (8) Stamps	13.20	6.25

Human Rights

Scales of Justice and Globe CD117

15th anniversary of the Universal Declaration of Human Rights.

1963, Dec. 10

Comoro Isls. 56
Fr. Polynesia 206
New Caledonia 329
St. Pierre & Miquelon 368
Somali Coast 300
Wallis & Futuna Isls. 166

No. 56 (1)	9.50	7.50
No. 205 (1)	15.00	12.00
No. 329 (1)	8.00	6.00
No. 368 (1)	6.50	3.50
No. 300 (1)	8.50	8.50
No. 166 (1)	8.00	7.50
Set total (6) Stamps	55.50	45.00

PHILATEC

Stamp Album, Champs Elysees Palace and Horses of Marly CD118

Intl. Philatelic and Postal Techniques Exhibition, Paris, June 5-21, 1964.

1963-64

Comoro Isls. 60
France 1078
Fr. Polynesia 207
New Caledonia 341
St. Pierre & Miquelon 369
Somali Coast 301
Wallis & Futuna Isls. 167

No. 60 (1)	4.50	4.00
No. 1078 (1)	.25	.25
No. 206 (1)	15.00	10.00
No. 341 (1)	8.50	6.75
No. 369 (1)	11.00	8.00
No. 301 (1)	7.75	7.75
No. 167 (1)	3.50	3.50
Set total (7) Stamps	50.50	40.25

Cooperation

CD119

Cooperation between France and the French-speaking countries of Africa and Madagascar.

1964

Cameroun 409-410
Cent. Africa 39
Chad 103
Congo, P.R. 121
Dahomey 193
France 1111
Gabon 175
Ivory Coast 221
Madagascar 360
Mauritania 181
Niger 143
Senegal 236
Togo 495

Nos. 409-410 (2)	2.50	.50
No. 39 (1)	1.00	.55
No. 103 (1)	1.00	.25
No. 121 (1)	.80	.35
No. 193 (1)	.80	.35
No. 1111 (1)	.25	.25
No. 175 (1)	.90	.60
No. 221 (1)	1.10	.35
No. 360 (1)	.60	.25
No. 181 (1)	.60	.35
No. 143 (1)	.80	.40
No. 236 (1)	1.60	.85
No. 495 (1)	.70	.25
Set total (14) Stamps	12.65	5.30

ITU

Telegraph, Syncom Satellite and ITU Emblem CD120

Intl. Telecommunication Union, Cent.

1965, May 17

Comoro Isls. C14
Fr. Polynesia C33
Fr. So. & Antarctic Terr. C8
New Caledonia C40
New Hebrides 124-125
St. Pierre & Miquelon C29
Somali Coast C36
Wallis & Futuna Isls. C20

No. C14 (1)	20.00	10.00
No. C33 (1)	80.00	52.50
No. C8 (1)	200.00	160.00
No. C40 (1)	12.00	9.00
Nos. 124-125 (2)	40.50	34.00
No. C29 (1)	24.00	11.00
No. C36 (1)	15.00	9.00
No. C20 (1)	21.00	15.00
Set total (9) Stamps	412.50	300.50

French Satellite A-1

Diamant Rocket and Launching Installation — CD121

Launching of France's first satellite, Nov. 26, 1965.

1965-66

Comoro Isls. C16a
France 1138a
Reunion 359a
Fr. Polynesia C41a
Fr. So. & Antarctic Terr. C10a
New Caledonia C45a
St. Pierre & Miquelon C31a
Somali Coast C40a
Wallis & Futuna Isls. C23a

No. C16a (1)	11.00	11.00
No. 1138a (1)	.65	.65
No. 359a (1)	3.50	3.00
No. C41a (1)	14.00	14.00
No. C10a (1)	29.00	24.00
No. C45a (1)	8.25	7.00
No. C31a (1)	15.00	15.00
No. C40a (1)	7.00	7.00
No. C23a (1)	9.25	9.25
Set total (9) Stamps	97.65	90.90

French Satellite D-1

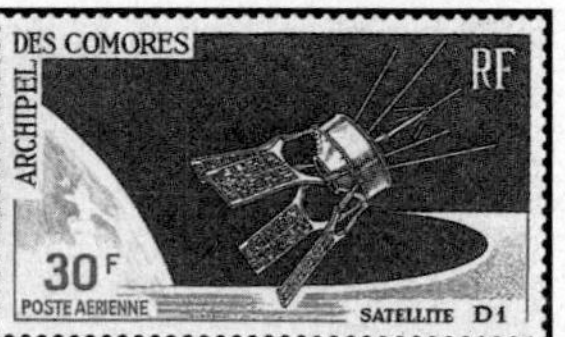

D-1 Satellite in Orbit — CD122

Launching of the D-1 satellite at Hammaguir, Algeria, Feb. 17, 1966.

1966

Comoro Isls. C17
France 1148

Fr. Polynesia C42
Fr. So. & Antarctic Terr. C11
New Caledonia C46
St. Pierre & Miquelon C32
Somali Coast C49
Wallis & Futuna Isls. C24

No. C17 (1)	4.00	4.00
No. 1148 (1)	.25	.25
No. C42 (1)	7.00	4.75
No. C11 (1)	57.50	40.00
No. C46 (1)	3.00	2.00
No. C32 (1)	10.50	6.50
No. C49 (1)	4.25	2.75
No. C24 (1)	3.50	3.50
Set total (8) Stamps	90.00	63.75

Air Afrique, 1966

Planes and Air Afrique Emblem — CD123

Introduction of DC-8F planes by Air Afrique.

1966

Cameroun C79
Cent. Africa C35
Chad C26
Congo, P.R. C42
Dahomey C42
Gabon C47
Ivory Coast C32
Mauritania C57
Niger C63
Senegal C47
Togo C54
Upper Volta C31

No. C79 (1)	.80	.25
No. C35 (1)	1.00	.40
No. C26 (1)	1.00	.25
No. C42 (1)	1.00	.25
No. C42 (1)	.75	.25
No. C47 (1)	.90	.35
No. C32 (1)	1.00	.60
No. C57 (1)	.80	.30
No. C63 (1)	.65	.35
No. C47 (1)	.80	.30
No. C54 (1)	.80	.25
No. C31 (1)	.75	.50
Set total (12) Stamps	10.25	4.05

African Postal Union, 1967

Telecommunications Symbols and Map of Africa — CD124

Fifth anniversary of the establishment of the African and Malagasy Union of Posts and Telecommunications, UAMPT.

1967

Cameroun C90
Cent. Africa C46
Chad C37
Congo, P.R. C57
Dahomey C61
Gabon C58
Ivory Coast C34
Madagascar C85
Mauritania C65
Niger C75
Rwanda C1-C3
Senegal C60
Togo C81
Upper Volta C50

No. C90 (1)	2.40	.65
No. C46 (1)	2.25	.85
No. C37 (1)	2.00	.60
No. C57 (1)	1.60	.60
No. C61 (1)	1.75	.95
No. C58 (1)	2.25	.95
No. C34 (1)	3.50	1.50
No. C85 (1)	1.25	.60
No. C65 (1)	1.25	.60
No. C75 (1)	1.40	.60
Nos. C1-C3 (3)	2.30	1.25
No. C60 (1)	1.75	.50
No. C81 (1)	1.90	.30
No. C50 (1)	1.80	.70
Set total (16) Stamps	27.40	10.65

Monetary Union

Gold Token of the Ashantis, 17-18th Centuries — CD125

West African Monetary Union, 5th anniv.

1967, Nov. 4

Dahomey 244
Ivory Coast 259
Mauritania 238
Niger 204
Senegal 294
Togo 623
Upper Volta 181

No. 244 (1)	.65	.65
No. 259 (1)	.85	.40
No. 238 (1)	.45	.25
No. 204 (1)	.45	.25
No. 294 (1)	.60	.25
No. 623 (1)	.60	.25
No. 181 (1)	.70	.35
Set total (7) Stamps	4.30	2.40

WHO Anniversary

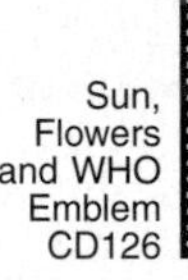

Sun, Flowers and WHO Emblem CD126

World Health Organization, 20th anniv.

1968, May 4

Afars & Issas 317
Comoro Isls. 73
Fr. Polynesia 241-242
Fr. So. & Antarctic Terr. 31
New Caledonia 367
St. Pierre & Miquelon 377
Wallis & Futuna Isls. 169

No. 317 (1)	3.00	3.00
No. 73 (1)	2.75	2.00
Nos. 241-242 (2)	22.00	12.75
No. 31 (1)	65.00	45.00
No. 367 (1)	4.50	2.25
No. 377 (1)	12.00	8.00
No. 169 (1)	6.50	4.50
Set total (8) Stamps	115.75	77.50

Human Rights Year

Human Rights Flame — CD127

1968, Aug. 10

Afars & Issas 322-323
Comoro Isls. 76
Fr. Polynesia 243-244
Fr. So. & Antarctic Terr. 32
New Caledonia 369
St. Pierre & Miquelon 382
Wallis & Futuna Isls. 170

Nos. 322-323 (2)	6.50	3.70
No. 76 (1)	3.50	3.50
Nos. 243-244 (2)	24.00	14.00
No. 32 (1)	60.00	45.00
No. 369 (1)	3.00	1.50
No. 382 (1)	10.00	5.50
No. 170 (1)	3.75	3.75
Set total (9) Stamps	110.75	76.95

2nd PHILEXAFRIQUE

CD128

Opening of PHILEXAFRIQUE, Abidjan, Feb. 14. Each stamp shows a local scene and stamp.

1969, Feb. 14

Cameroun C118
Cent. Africa C65
Chad C48
Congo, P.R. C77
Dahomey C94
Gabon C82
Ivory Coast C38-C40
Madagascar C92
Mali C65
Mauritania C80
Niger C104
Senegal C68
Togo C104
Upper Volta C62

No. C118 (1)	3.25	1.25
No. C65 (1)	1.90	1.90
No. C48 (1)	2.40	1.00
No. C77 (1)	2.00	1.75
No. C94 (1)	2.25	2.25
No. C82 (1)	2.25	2.25
Nos. C38-C40 (3)	14.50	14.50
No. C92 (1)	1.75	.85
No. C65 (1)	2.00	1.00
No. C80 (1)	1.90	.75
No. C104 (1)	2.75	1.90
No. C68 (1)	2.00	1.40
No. C104 (1)	2.25	.45
No. C62 (1)	4.00	3.75
Set total (16) Stamps	45.20	35.00

Concorde

Concorde in Flight CD129

First flight of the prototype Concorde supersonic plane at Toulouse, Mar. 1, 1969.

1969

Afars & Issas C56
Comoro Isls. C29
France C42
Fr. Polynesia C50
Fr. So. & Antarctic Terr. C18
New Caledonia C63
St. Pierre & Miquelon C40
Wallis & Futuna Isls. C30

No. C56 (1)	25.00	16.00
No. C29 (1)	24.00	16.00
No. C42 (1)	1.00	.35
No. C50 (1)	55.00	35.00
No. C18 (1)	55.00	37.50
No. C63 (1)	35.00	20.00
No. C40 (1)	32.50	12.00
No. C30 (1)	15.00	10.00
Set total (8) Stamps	242.50	146.85

Development Bank

Bank Emblem — CD130

African Development Bank, fifth anniv.

1969

Cameroun 499
Chad 217
Congo, P.R. 181-182
Ivory Coast 281
Mali 127-128
Mauritania 267
Niger 220
Senegal 317-318
Upper Volta 201

No. 499 (1)	.80	.25
No. 217 (1)	.70	.25
Nos. 181-182 (2)	.80	.50
No. 281 (1)	.70	.40
Nos. 127-128 (2)	1.25	.50
No. 267 (1)	.60	.25
No. 220 (1)	.60	.30
Nos. 317-318 (2)	1.55	.50
No. 201 (1)	.70	.30
Set total (12) Stamps	7.70	3.25

ILO

ILO Headquarters, Geneva, and Emblem — CD131

Intl. Labor Organization, 50th anniv.

1969-70

Afars & Issas 337
Comoro Isls. 83
Fr. Polynesia 251-252
Fr. So. & Antarctic Terr. 35
New Caledonia 379
St. Pierre & Miquelon 396
Wallis & Futuna Isls. 172

No. 337 (1)	2.75	2.00
No. 83 (1)	1.25	.75
Nos. 251-252 (2)	24.00	12.50
No. 35 (1)	18.50	11.00
No. 379 (1)	2.25	1.10
No. 396 (1)	10.00	5.50
No. 172 (1)	3.00	2.90
Set total (8) Stamps	61.75	35.75

ASECNA

Map of Africa, Plane and Airport CD132

10th anniversary of the Agency for the Security of Aerial Navigation in Africa and Madagascar (ASECNA, Agence pour la Securite de la Navigation Aerienne en Afrique et a Madagascar).

1969-70

Cameroun 500
Cent. Africa 119
Chad 222
Congo, P.R. 197
Dahomey 269
Gabon 260
Ivory Coast 287
Mali 130
Niger 221
Senegal 321
Upper Volta 204

No. 500 (1)	2.00	.60
No. 119 (1)	2.25	.80
No. 222 (1)	1.00	.25
No. 197 (1)	2.00	.40
No. 269 (1)	.90	.55
No. 260 (1)	1.75	.75
No. 287 (1)	.90	.40
No. 130 (1)	1.00	.40
No. 221 (1)	1.25	.70
No. 321 (1)	1.60	.50
No. 204 (1)	1.75	1.00
Set total (11) Stamps	16.40	6.35

U.P.U. Headquarters

CD133

New Universal Postal Union headquarters, Bern, Switzerland.

1970

Afars & Issas....342
Algeria....443
Cameroun....503-504
Cent. Africa....125
Chad....225
Comoro Isls....84
Congo, P.R....216
Fr. Polynesia....261-262
Fr. So. & Antarctic Terr....36
Gabon....258
Ivory Coast....295
Madagascar....444
Mali....134-135
Mauritania....283
New Caledonia....382
Niger....231-232
St. Pierre & Miquelon....397-398
Senegal....328-329
Tunisia....535
Wallis & Futuna Isls....173

No. 342 (1)	2.50	1.40
No. 443 (1)	1.10	.40
Nos. 503-504 (2)	2.60	.55
No. 125 (1)	1.90	.70
No. 225 (1)	1.00	.25
No. 84 (1)	5.50	2.00
No. 216 (1)	.80	.25
Nos. 261-262 (2)	20.00	10.00
No. 36 (1)	45.00	29.00
No. 258 (1)	.90	.55
No. 295 (1)	1.10	.50
No. 444 (1)	.55	.25
Nos. 134-135 (2)	1.25	.50
No. 283 (1)	.60	.30
No. 382 (1)	3.00	1.50
Nos. 231-232 (2)	1.20	.60
Nos. 397-398 (2)	34.00	17.50
Nos. 328-329 (2)	1.55	.55
No. 535 (1)	.60	.25
No. 173 (1)	4.00	4.00
Set total (26) Stamps	129.15	71.05

De Gaulle

CD134

First anniversary of the death of Charles de Gaulle, (1890-1970), President of France.

1971-72

Afars & Issas....356-357
Comoro Isls....104-105
France....1325a
Fr. Polynesia....270-271
Fr. So. & Antarctic Terr....52-53
New Caledonia....393-394
Reunion....380a
St. Pierre & Miquelon....417-418
Wallis & Futuna Isls....177-178

Nos. 356-357 (2)	14.50	9.50
Nos. 104-105 (2)	9.00	5.75
No. 1325a (1)	4.50	4.00
Nos. 270-271 (2)	51.50	29.50
Nos. 52-53 (2)	47.00	33.50
Nos. 393-394 (2)	25.00	11.75
No. 380a (1)	9.25	8.00
Nos. 417-418 (2)	57.50	30.00
Nos. 177-178 (2)	24.00	16.25
Set total (16) Stamps	242.25	148.25

African Postal Union, 1971

UAMPT Building, Brazzaville, Congo — CD135

10th anniversary of the establishment of the African and Malagasy Posts and Telecommunications Union, UAMPT. Each stamp has a different native design.

1971, Nov. 13

Cameroun....C177
Cent. Africa....C89
Chad....C94
Congo, P.R....C136
Dahomey....C146
Gabon....C120
Ivory Coast....C47
Mauritania....C113
Niger....C164
Rwanda....C8
Senegal....C105
Togo....C166
Upper Volta....C97

No. C177 (1)	2.00	.50
No. C89 (1)	2.25	.85
No. C94 (1)	1.50	.50
No. C136 (1)	1.60	.75
No. C146 (1)	1.75	.80
No. C120 (1)	1.75	.70
No. C47 (1)	2.00	1.00
No. C113 (1)	1.20	.65
No. C164 (1)	1.25	.60
No. C8 (1)	2.75	2.25
No. C105 (1)	1.60	.50
No. C166 (1)	1.25	.40
No. C97 (1)	1.50	.70
Set total (13) Stamps	22.40	10.20

West African Monetary Union

African Couple, City, Village and Commemorative Coin — CD136

West African Monetary Union, 10th anniv.

1972, Nov. 2

Dahomey....300
Ivory Coast....331
Mauritania....299
Niger....258
Senegal....374
Togo....825
Upper Volta....280

No. 300 (1)	.65	.25
No. 331 (1)	1.00	.50
No. 299 (1)	.75	.25
No. 258 (1)	.55	.30
No. 374 (1)	.50	.30
No. 825 (1)	.60	.25
No. 280 (1)	.60	.25
Set total (7) Stamps	4.65	2.10

African Postal Union, 1973

Telecommunications Symbols and Map of Africa — CD137

11th anniversary of the African and Malagasy Posts and Telecommunications Union (UAMPT).

1973, Sept. 12

Cameroun....574
Cent. Africa....194
Chad....294
Congo, P.R....289
Dahomey....311
Gabon....320
Ivory Coast....361
Madagascar....500
Mauritania....304
Niger....287
Rwanda....540
Senegal....393
Togo....849
Upper Volta....297

No. 574 (1)	1.75	.40
No. 194 (1)	1.25	.75
No. 294 (1)	1.75	.40
No. 289 (1)	1.60	.50
No. 311 (1)	1.25	.55
No. 320 (1)	1.40	.75
No. 361 (1)	2.50	1.00
No. 500 (1)	1.10	.35
No. 304 (1)	1.10	.40
No. 287 (1)	.90	.60
No. 540 (1)	3.75	2.00
No. 393 (1)	1.60	.50
No. 849 (1)	1.00	.35
No. 297 (1)	1.25	.70
Set total (14) Stamps	22.20	9.25

Philexafrique II — Essen

CD138

CD139

Designs: Indigenous fauna, local and German stamps. Types CD138-CD139 printed horizontally and vertically se-tenant in sheets of 10 (2x5). Label between horizontal pairs alternately commemoratives Philexafrique II, Libreville, Gabon, June 1978, and 2nd International Stamp Fair, Essen, Germany, Nov. 1-5.

1978-1979

Benin....C286a
Central Africa....C201a
Chad....C239a
Congo Republic....C246a
Djibouti....C122a
Gabon....C216a
Ivory Coast....C65a
Mali....C357a
Mauritania....C186a
Niger....C292a
Rwanda....C13a
Senegal....C141a
Togo....C364a

No. C286a (1)	9.00	8.50
No. C201a (1)	7.50	7.50
No. C239a (1)	8.00	4.00
No. C246a (1)	7.00	7.00
No. C122a (1)	8.50	8.50
No. C216a (1)	6.50	4.00
No. C65a (1)	9.00	9.00
No. C357a (1)	7.50	3.00
No. C186a (1)	4.50	4.00
No. C292a (1)	6.00	5.00
No. C13a (1)	4.00	4.00
No. C147a (1)	10.00	4.00
No. C364a (1)	3.00	1.50
Set total (13) Stamps	90.50	70.00

BRITISH COMMONWEALTH OF NATIONS

The listings follow established trade practices when these issues are offered as units by dealers. The Peace issue, for example, includes only one stamp from the Indian state of Hyderabad. The U.P.U. issue includes the Egypt set. Pairs are included for those varieties issued with bilingual designs se-tenant.

Silver Jubilee

Windsor Castle and King George V CD301

Reign of King George V, 25th anniv.

1935

Antigua....77-80
Ascension....33-36
Bahamas....92-95
Barbados....186-189
Basutoland....11-14
Bechuanaland Protectorate....117-120
Bermuda....100-103
British Guiana....223-226
British Honduras....108-111
Cayman Islands....81-84
Ceylon....260-263
Cyprus....136-139
Dominica....90-93
Falkland Islands....77-80
Fiji....110-113
Gambia....125-128
Gibraltar....100-103
Gilbert & Ellice Islands....33-36
Gold Coast....108-111
Grenada....124-127
Hong Kong....147-150
Jamaica....109-112
Kenya, Uganda, Tanzania....42-45
Leeward Islands....96-99
Malta....184-187
Mauritius....204-207
Montserrat....85-88
Newfoundland....226-229
Nigeria....34-37
Northern Rhodesia....18-21
Nyasaland Protectorate....47-50
St. Helena....111-114
St. Kitts-Nevis....72-75
St. Lucia....91-94
St. Vincent....134-137
Seychelles....118-121
Sierra Leone....166-169
Solomon Islands....60-63
Somaliland Protectorate....77-80
Straits Settlements....213-216
Swaziland....20-23
Trinidad & Tobago....43-46
Turks & Caicos Islands....71-74
Virgin Islands....69-72

The following have different designs but are included in the omnibus set:

Great Britain....226-229
Offices in Morocco (Sp. Curr.)....67-70
Offices in Morocco (Br. Curr.)....226-229
Offices in Morocco (Fr. Curr.)....422-425
Offices in Morocco (Tangier)....508-510
Australia....152-154
Canada....211-216
Cook Islands....98-100
India....142-148
Nauru....31-34
New Guinea....46-47
New Zealand....199-201
Niue....67-69
Papua....114-117
Samoa....163-165
South Africa....68-71
Southern Rhodesia....33-36
South-West Africa....121-124

Nos. 77-80 (4)	22.50	*21.95*
Nos. 33-36 (4)	69.00	*135.00*
Nos. 92-95 (4)	25.00	*43.00*
Nos. 186-189 (4)	30.15	49.30
Nos. 11-14 (4)	12.10	*23.00*
Nos. 117-120 (4)	17.00	*31.25*
Nos. 100-103 (4)	18.00	*58.25*
Nos. 223-226 (4)	18.35	35.50
Nos. 108-111 (4)	15.25	*15.35*
Nos. 81-84 (4)	16.95	17.75
Nos. 260-263 (4)	12.60	23.35
Nos. 136-139 (4)	39.75	*34.40*
Nos. 90-93 (4)	18.85	19.85
Nos. 77-80 (4)	51.00	13.75
Nos. 110-113 (4)	15.25	29.00
Nos. 125-128 (4)	12.65	*29.25*
Nos. 100-103 (4)	32.00	47.50
Nos. 33-36 (4)	34.50	*53.50*
Nos. 108-111 (4)	26.25	*62.85*
Nos. 124-127 (4)	18.60	*45.00*
Nos. 147-150 (4)	76.50	21.00
Nos. 109-112 (4)	19.70	39.00
Nos. 42-45 (4)	8.75	*11.00*
Nos. 96-99 (4)	35.75	49.60
Nos. 184-187 (4)	22.00	33.70
Nos. 204-207 (4)	47.60	58.25
Nos. 85-88 (4)	10.25	*30.25*
Nos. 226-229 (4)	17.50	12.05
Nos. 34-37 (4)	13.25	*59.75*
Nos. 18-21 (4)	16.75	16.25
Nos. 47-50 (4)	39.75	*80.25*
Nos. 111-114 (4)	31.15	*33.25*
Nos. 72-75 (4)	11.55	*18.50*
Nos. 91-94 (4)	16.00	*20.80*
Nos. 134-137 (4)	9.45	*21.25*
Nos. 118-121 (4)	17.50	*31.00*
Nos. 166-169 (4)	21.25	*56.00*
Nos. 60-63 (4)	30.00	38.00
Nos. 77-80 (4)	18.75	*50.75*
Nos. 213-216 (4)	15.00	*25.10*
Nos. 20-23 (4)	6.80	18.25
Nos. 43-46 (4)	12.30	27.75
Nos. 71-74 (4)	9.25	16.25
Nos. 69-72 (4)	22.20	47.50
Nos. 226-229 (4)	7.25	*7.45*

Nos. 67-70 (4)	14.35	26.10
Nos. 226-229 (4)	8.20	28.90
Nos. 422-425 (4)	3.90	2.00
Nos. 508-510 (3)	18.80	23.85
Nos. 152-154 (3)	45.75	60.35
Nos. 211-216 (6)	26.30	13.35
Nos. 98-100 (3)	9.90	14.00
Nos. 142-148 (7)	23.25	11.80
Nos. 31-34 (4)	12.60	13.85
Nos. 46-47 (2)	4.35	1.70
Nos. 199-201 (3)	21.75	31.75
Nos. 67-69 (3)	10.55	26.50
Nos. 114-117 (4)	9.20	17.00
Nos. 163-165 (3)	4.40	5.50
Nos. 68-71 (4)	57.00	155.00
Nos. 33-36 (4)	30.00	45.25
Nos. 121-124 (4)	14.50	36.10
Set total (245) Stamps	1,357.	2,125.

Coronation

Queen Elizabeth and King George VI CD302

1937

Aden 13-15
Antigua 81-83
Ascension 37-39
Bahamas 97-99
Barbados 190-192
Basutoland 15-17
Bechuanaland Protectorate 121-123
Bermuda 115-117
British Guiana 227-229
British Honduras 112-114
Cayman Islands 97-99
Ceylon 275-277
Cyprus 140-142
Dominica 94-96
Falkland Islands 81-83
Fiji 114-116
Gambia 129-131
Gibraltar 104-106
Gilbert & Ellice Islands 37-39
Gold Coast 112-114
Grenada 128-130
Hong Kong 151-153
Jamaica 113-115
Kenya, Uganda, Tanzania 60-62
Leeward Islands 100-102
Malta 188-190
Mauritius 208-210
Montserrat 89-91
Newfoundland 230-232
Nigeria 50-52
Northern Rhodesia 22-24
Nyasaland Protectorate 51-53
St. Helena 115-117
St. Kitts-Nevis 76-78
St. Lucia 107-109
St. Vincent 138-140
Seychelles 122-124
Sierra Leone 170-172
Solomon Islands 64-66
Somaliland Protectorate 81-83
Straits Settlements 235-237
Swaziland 24-26
Trinidad & Tobago 47-49
Turks & Caicos Islands 75-77
Virgin Islands 73-75

The following have different designs but are included in the omnibus set:

Great Britain 234
Offices in Morocco (Sp. Curr.) 82
Offices in Morocco (Fr. Curr.) 439
Offices in Morocco (Tangier) 514
Canada 237
Cook Islands 109-111
Nauru 35-38
Newfoundland 233-243
New Guinea 48-51
New Zealand 223-225
Niue 70-72
Papua 118-121
South Africa 74-78
Southern Rhodesia 38-41
South-West Africa 125-132

Nos. 13-15 (3)	3.00	5.75
Nos. 81-83 (3)	2.00	3.75
Nos. 37-39 (3)	2.75	2.75
Nos. 97-99 (3)	1.15	3.05
Nos. 190-192 (3)	1.10	1.05
Nos. 15-17 (3)	1.15	3.00
Nos. 121-123 (3)	.95	3.35
Nos. 115-117 (3)	1.25	5.00
Nos. 227-229 (3)	1.45	3.05
Nos. 112-114 (3)	1.20	2.35
Nos. 97-99 (3)	1.10	2.30
Nos. 275-277 (3)	8.25	10.35
Nos. 140-142 (3)	3.75	6.50
Nos. 94-96 (3)	.85	2.40
Nos. 81-83 (3)	2.90	2.30
Nos. 114-116 (3)	1.35	5.75
Nos. 129-131 (3)	1.00	4.70
Nos. 104-106 (3)	2.60	6.45
Nos. 37-39 (3)	.85	2.00
Nos. 112-114 (3)	3.10	10.00
Nos. 128-130 (3)	1.00	.85
Nos. 151-153 (3)	27.00	12.50
Nos. 113-115 (3)	1.35	1.25
Nos. 60-62 (3)	1.00	2.35
Nos. 100-102 (3)	1.55	4.00
Nos. 188-190 (3)	1.25	1.60
Nos. 208-210 (3)	2.05	3.75
Nos. 89-91 (3)	1.00	3.35
Nos. 230-232 (3)	7.00	2.80
Nos. 50-52 (3)	3.25	8.50
Nos. 22-24 (3)	.95	2.25
Nos. 51-53 (3)	1.05	1.30
Nos. 115-117 (3)	1.45	2.05
Nos. 76-78 (3)	.95	2.05
Nos. 107-109 (3)	1.05	2.05
Nos. 138-140 (3)	.80	4.75
Nos. 122-124 (3)	1.20	1.90
Nos. 170-172 (3)	1.95	5.65
Nos. 64-66 (3)	.90	2.00
Nos. 81-83 (3)	1.10	3.40
Nos. 235-237 (3)	3.25	1.60
Nos. 24-26 (3)	1.05	1.75
Nos. 47-49 (3)	1.00	1.00
Nos. 75-77 (3)	1.30	1.55
Nos. 73-75 (3)	1.20	5.00
No. 234 (1)	.25	.25
No. 82 (1)	.80	.80
No. 439 (1)	.35	.25
No. 514 (1)	.55	.55
No. 237 (1)	.35	.25
Nos. 109-111 (3)	.85	.80
Nos. 35-38 (4)	1.15	5.50
Nos. 233-243 (11)	34.50	30.40
Nos. 48-51 (4)	1.40	7.90
Nos. 223-225 (3)	1.40	2.75
Nos. 70-72 (3)	.80	2.05
Nos. 118-121 (4)	1.60	5.25
Nos. 74-78 (5)	9.25	10.80
Nos. 38-41 (4)	4.00	16.25
Nos. 125-132 (8)	5.50	8.45
Set total (189) Stamps	170.15	258.25

Peace

King George VI and Parliament Buildings, London CD303

Return to peace at the close of World War II.

1945-46

Aden 28-29
Antigua 96-97
Ascension 50-51
Bahamas 130-131
Barbados 207-208
Bermuda 131-132
British Guiana 242-243
British Honduras 127-128
Cayman Islands 112-113
Ceylon 293-294
Cyprus 156-157
Dominica 112-113
Falkland Islands 97-98
Falkland Islands Dep. 1L9-1L10
Fiji 137-138
Gambia 144-145
Gibraltar 119-120
Gilbert & Ellice Islands 52-53
Gold Coast 128-129
Grenada 143-144
Jamaica 136-137
Kenya, Uganda, Tanzania 90-91
Leeward Islands 116-117
Malta 206-207
Mauritius 223-224
Montserrat 104-105
Nigeria 71-72
Northern Rhodesia 46-47
Nyasaland Protectorate 82-83
Pitcairn Islands 9-10
St. Helena 128-129
St. Kitts-Nevis 91-92
St. Lucia 127-128
St. Vincent 152-153
Seychelles 149-150
Sierra Leone 186-187
Solomon Islands 80-81
Somaliland Protectorate 108-109
Trinidad & Tobago 62-63
Turks & Caicos Islands 90-91
Virgin Islands 88-89

The following have different designs but are included in the omnibus set:

Great Britain 264-265
Offices in Morocco (Tangier) 523-524
Aden
Kathiri State of Seiyun 12-13
Qu'aiti State of Shihr and Mukalla 12-13
Australia 200-202
Basutoland 29-31
Bechuanaland Protectorate 137-139
Burma 66-69
Cook Islands 127-130
Hong Kong 174-175
India 195-198
Hyderabad 51-53
New Zealand 247-257
Niue 90-93
Pakistan-Bahawalpur O16
Samoa 191-194
South Africa 100-102
Southern Rhodesia 67-70
South-West Africa 153-155
Swaziland 38-40
Zanzibar 222-223

Nos. 28-29 (2)	.55	2.15
Nos. 96-97 (2)	.50	.80
Nos. 50-51 (2)	.90	1.80
Nos. 130-131 (2)	.50	1.40
Nos. 207-208 (2)	.50	1.10
Nos. 131-132 (2)	.55	.55
Nos. 242-243 (2)	1.05	1.40
Nos. 127-128 (2)	.50	.50
Nos. 112-113 (2)	.60	.80
Nos. 293-294 (2)	.60	2.10
Nos. 156-157 (2)	1.00	.70
Nos. 112-113 (2)	.50	.50
Nos. 97-98 (2)	.90	1.35
Nos. 1L9-1L10 (2)	1.40	1.00
Nos. 137-138 (2)	.50	1.75
Nos. 144-145 (2)	.50	.95
Nos. 119-120 (2)	.75	1.00
Nos. 52-53 (2)	.50	.50
Nos. 128-129 (2)	1.85	3.75
Nos. 143-144 (2)	.50	.95
Nos. 136-137 (2)	.90	12.50
Nos. 90-91 (2)	.65	.65
Nos. 116-117 (2)	.50	1.50
Nos. 206-207 (2)	.65	2.00
Nos. 223-224 (2)	.50	1.05
Nos. 104-105 (2)	.50	.50
Nos. 71-72 (2)	.70	2.75
Nos. 46-47 (2)	1.25	2.00
Nos. 82-83 (2)	.50	.50
Nos. 9-10 (2)	1.40	1.40
Nos. 128-129 (2)	.65	.70
Nos. 91-92 (2)	.50	.50
Nos. 127-128 (2)	.50	.60
Nos. 152-153 (2)	.50	.50
Nos. 149-150 (2)	.55	.50
Nos. 186-187 (2)	.50	.50
Nos. 80-81 (2)	.50	1.30
Nos. 108-109 (2)	.70	.50
Nos. 62-63 (2)	.50	.50
Nos. 90-91 (2)	.50	.50
Nos. 88-89 (2)	.50	.50
Nos. 264-265 (2)	.50	.70
Nos. 523-524 (2)	1.50	3.00
Nos. 12-13 (2)	.50	.90
Nos. 12-13 (2)	.50	1.25
Nos. 200-202 (3)	1.60	3.00
Nos. 29-31 (3)	2.10	2.60
Nos. 137-139 (3)	2.05	4.75
Nos. 66-69 (4)	1.60	1.30
Nos. 127-130 (4)	2.20	2.00
Nos. 174-175 (2)	7.25	3.15
Nos. 195-198 (4)	4.75	3.60
Nos. 51-53 (3)	1.50	1.70
Nos. 247-257 (11)	3.95	3.90
Nos. 90-93 (4)	1.70	2.20
No. O16 (1)	5.50	7.00
Nos. 191-194 (4)	2.05	1.00
Nos. 100-102 (3)	1.20	4.00
Nos. 67-70 (4)	1.40	1.75
Nos. 153-155 (3)	2.55	3.50
Nos. 38-40 (3)	2.40	5.50
Nos. 222-223 (2)	.65	1.00
Set total (151) Stamps	75.55	114.30

Silver Wedding

King George VI and Queen Elizabeth

CD304 CD305

1948-49

Aden 30-31
Kathiri State of Seiyun 14-15
Qu'aiti State of Shihr and Mukalla 14-15
Antigua 98-99
Ascension 52-53
Bahamas 148-149
Barbados 210-211
Basutoland 39-40
Bechuanaland Protectorate 147-148
Bermuda 133-134
British Guiana 244-245
British Honduras 129-130
Cayman Islands 116-117
Cyprus 158-159
Dominica 114-115
Falkland Islands 99-100
Falkland Islands Dep. 1L11-1L12
Fiji 139-140
Gambia 146-147
Gibraltar 121-122
Gilbert & Ellice Islands 54-55
Gold Coast 142-143
Grenada 145-146
Hong Kong 178-179
Jamaica 138-139
Kenya, Uganda, Tanzania 92-93
Leeward Islands 118-119
Malaya
Johore 128-129
Kedah 55-56
Kelantan 44-45
Malacca 1-2
Negri Sembilan 36-37
Pahang 44-45
Penang 1-2
Perak 99-100
Perlis 1-2
Selangor 74-75
Trengganu 47-48
Malta 223-224
Mauritius 229-230
Montserrat 106-107
Nigeria 73-74
North Borneo 238-239
Northern Rhodesia 48-49
Nyasaland Protectorate 85-86
Pitcairn Islands 11-12
St. Helena 130-131
St. Kitts-Nevis 93-94
St. Lucia 129-130
St. Vincent 154-155
Sarawak 174-175
Seychelles 151-152
Sierra Leone 188-189
Singapore 21-22
Solomon Islands 82-83
Somaliland Protectorate 110-111
Swaziland 48-49
Trinidad & Tobago 64-65
Turks & Caicos Islands 92-93
Virgin Islands 90-91
Zanzibar 224-225

The following have different designs but are included in the omnibus set:

Great Britain 267-268
Offices in Morocco (Sp. Curr.) 93-94
Offices in Morocco (Tangier) 525-526
Bahrain 62-63
Kuwait 82-83
Oman 25-26
South Africa 106
South-West Africa 159

Nos. 30-31 (2)	30.40	42.00
Nos. 14-15 (2)	17.35	12.50
Nos. 14-15 (2)	17.55	14.75
Nos. 98-99 (2)	10.05	13.75
Nos. 52-53 (2)	60.55	57.95
Nos. 148-149 (2)	45.25	40.30
Nos. 210-211 (2)	18.35	13.05
Nos. 39-40 (2)	52.80	55.25
Nos. 147-148 (2)	45.35	50.25
Nos. 133-134 (2)	47.75	55.25
Nos. 244-245 (2)	24.25	28.45
Nos. 129-130 (2)	22.75	53.20
Nos. 116-117 (2)	22.75	28.50
Nos. 158-159 (2)	58.50	78.05
Nos. 114-115 (2)	25.25	32.75
Nos. 99-100 (2)	112.10	83.60
Nos. 1L11-1L12 (2)	4.25	6.00
Nos. 139-140 (2)	18.20	10.75
Nos. 146-147 (2)	22.75	25.25
Nos. 121-122 (2)	66.00	83.00
Nos. 54-55 (2)	16.25	24.25
Nos. 142-143 (2)	35.25	37.75
Nos. 145-146 (2)	25.25	25.25
Nos. 178-179 (2)	363.90	136.60
Nos. 138-139 (2)	30.35	72.75
Nos. 92-93 (2)	52.75	72.75
Nos. 118-119 (2)	7.00	8.25
Nos. 128-129 (2)	29.25	53.25
Nos. 55-56 (2)	35.25	50.25
Nos. 44-45 (2)	35.75	62.75
Nos. 1-2 (2)	35.40	49.75
Nos. 36-37 (2)	28.10	38.20
Nos. 44-45 (2)	28.00	38.05
Nos. 1-2 (2)	40.50	37.80

Nos. 99-100 (2)	27.80	*37.75*
Nos. 1-2 (2)	33.50	*58.00*
Nos. 74-75 (2)	30.25	25.30
Nos. 47-48 (2)	35.25	*62.75*
Nos. 223-224 (2)	40.55	45.25
Nos. 229-230 (2)	17.75	*45.25*
Nos. 106-107 (2)	9.25	*18.25*
Nos. 73-74 (2)	17.85	*22.80*
Nos. 238-239 (2)	35.30	*45.75*
Nos. 48-49 (2)	92.80	90.25
Nos. 85-86 (2)	19.25	*32.75*
Nos. 11-12 (2)	49.25	51.00
Nos. 130-131 (2)	32.80	*42.80*
Nos. 93-94 (2)	11.25	7.25
Nos. 129-130 (2)	22.25	*45.25*
Nos. 154-155 (2)	27.75	*30.25*
Nos. 174-175 (2)	55.40	*60.40*
Nos. 151-152 (2)	16.25	*45.75*
Nos. 188-189 (2)	24.75	*26.25*
Nos. 21-22 (2)	131.25	45.40
Nos. 82-83 (2)	13.40	13.40
Nos. 110-111 (2)	8.40	*8.75*
Nos. 48-49 (2)	40.30	*47.75*
Nos. 64-65 (2)	32.75	*38.25*
Nos. 92-93 (2)	15.25	*20.30*
Nos. 90-91 (2)	18.85	21.35
Nos. 224-225 (2)	29.60	38.00
Nos. 267-268 (2)	40.40	40.25
Nos. 93-94 (2)	20.10	25.35
Nos. 525-526 (2)	23.10	29.25
Nos. 62-63 (2)	38.45	*72.50*
Nos. 82-83 (2)	45.50	45.50
Nos. 25-26 (2)	46.00	*47.50*
No. 106 (1)	.90	1.25
No. 159 (1)	1.25	.35
Set total (136) Stamps	2,590.	2,780.

U.P.U.

Mercury and Symbols of Communications — CD306

Plane, Ship and Hemispheres — CD307

Mercury Scattering Letters over Globe CD308

U.P.U. Monument, Bern CD309

Universal Postal Union, 75th anniversary.

1949

Aden ...32-35
Kathiri State of Seiyun...16-19
Qu'aiti State of Shihr and Mukalla ...16-19
Antigua ...100-103
Ascension ...57-60
Bahamas ...150-153
Barbados ...212-215
Basutoland...41-44
Bechuanaland Protectorate...149-152
Bermuda...138-141
British Guiana...246-249
British Honduras...137-140
Brunei ...79-82
Cayman Islands...118-121
Cyprus ...160-163
Dominica...116-119
Falkland Islands ...103-106
Falkland Islands Dep...1L14-1L17
Fiji...141-144
Gambia ...148-151
Gibraltar...123-126
Gilbert & Ellice Islands...56-59
Gold Coast ...144-147
Grenada...147-150
Hong Kong ...180-183
Jamaica ...142-145
Kenya, Uganda, Tanzania ...94-97
Leeward Islands ...126-129
Malaya
Johore ...151-154
Kedah...57-60
Kelantan ...46-49
Malacca...18-21
Negri Sembilan ...59-62
Pahang...46-49
Penang...23-26
Perak...101-104
Perlis ...3-6
Selangor...76-79
Trengganu ...49-52
Malta...225-228
Mauritius...231-234
Montserrat ...108-111
New Hebrides, British ...62-65
New Hebrides, French ...79-82
Nigeria ...75-78
North Borneo...240-243
Northern Rhodesia...50-53
Nyasaland Protectorate...87-90
Pitcairn Islands...13-16
St. Helena ...132-135
St. Kitts-Nevis...95-98
St. Lucia ...131-134
St. Vincent...170-173
Sarawak...176-179
Seychelles ...153-156
Sierra Leone...190-193
Singapore ...23-26
Solomon Islands...84-87
Somaliland Protectorate...112-115
Southern Rhodesia ...71-72
Swaziland ...50-53
Tonga...87-90
Trinidad & Tobago ...66-69
Turks & Caicos Islands ...101-104
Virgin Islands...92-95
Zanzibar...226-229

The following have different designs but are included in the omnibus set:

Great Britain...276-279
Offices in Morocco (Tangier) ...546-549
Australia...223
Bahrain ...68-71
Burma...116-121
Ceylon ...304-306
Egypt ...281-283
India...223-226
Kuwait...89-92
Oman...31-34
Pakistan-Bahawalpur 26-29, O25-O28
South Africa...109-111
South-West Africa ...160-162

Nos. 32-35 (4)	5.50	*7.80*
Nos. 16-19 (4)	3.10	*3.60*
Nos. 16-19 (4)	2.75	2.55
Nos. 100-103 (4)	4.15	*6.85*
Nos. 57-60 (4)	12.40	10.00
Nos. 150-153 (4)	5.60	9.55
Nos. 212-215 (4)	4.40	14.15
Nos. 41-44 (4)	4.75	*10.00*
Nos. 149-152 (4)	3.35	*7.25*
Nos. 138-141 (4)	4.75	5.55
Nos. 246-249 (4)	2.65	4.20
Nos. 137-140 (4)	3.35	4.75
Nos. 79-82 (4)	7.75	6.75
Nos. 118-121 (4)	4.00	6.40
Nos. 160-163 (4)	4.60	8.30
Nos. 116-119 (4)	2.30	5.65
Nos. 103-106 (4)	14.90	17.10
Nos. 1L14-1L17 (4)	15.50	14.00
Nos. 141-144 (4)	3.35	14.00
Nos. 148-151 (4)	3.50	7.85
Nos. 123-126 (4)	6.25	9.50
Nos. 56-59 (4)	4.85	*8.75*
Nos. 144-147 (4)	3.05	*6.95*
Nos. 147-150 (4)	2.30	3.55
Nos. 180-183 (4)	74.25	23.60
Nos. 142-145 (4)	2.70	6.00
Nos. 94-97 (4)	2.90	3.40
Nos. 126-129 (4)	3.05	*9.60*
Nos. 151-154 (4)	4.70	8.90
Nos. 57-60 (4)	4.80	12.00
Nos. 46-49 (4)	4.25	12.65
Nos. 18-21 (4)	4.25	*17.30*
Nos. 59-62 (4)	3.50	10.75
Nos. 46-49 (4)	3.00	7.25
Nos. 23-26 (4)	5.10	11.75
Nos. 101-104 (4)	3.65	10.75
Nos. 3-6 (4)	3.95	14.25
Nos. 76-79 (4)	4.90	12.30
Nos. 49-52 (4)	4.95	9.75
Nos. 225-228 (4)	4.50	4.85
Nos. 231-234 (4)	4.35	6.70
Nos. 108-111 (4)	3.40	3.85
Nos. 62-65 (4)	1.60	*4.10*
Nos. 79-82 (4)	24.25	24.25
Nos. 75-78 (4)	2.80	*9.25*
Nos. 240-243 (4)	7.15	6.50
Nos. 50-53 (4)	5.00	*6.50*
Nos. 87-90 (4)	4.05	4.05
Nos. 13-16 (4)	18.50	16.50
Nos. 132-135 (4)	4.85	7.10
Nos. 95-98 (4)	3.35	4.70
Nos. 131-134 (4)	2.55	*3.85*
Nos. 170-173 (4)	2.20	*5.05*
Nos. 176-179 (4)	9.00	11.10
Nos. 153-156 (4)	3.25	4.10
Nos. 190-193 (4)	3.00	5.10
Nos. 23-26 (4)	20.75	14.20
Nos. 84-87 (4)	4.35	4.90
Nos. 112-115 (4)	3.95	8.70
Nos. 71-72 (2)	1.95	*2.25*
Nos. 50-53 (4)	2.80	4.65
Nos. 87-90 (4)	3.25	*5.25*
Nos. 66-69 (4)	3.15	3.15
Nos. 101-104 (4)	3.65	4.00
Nos. 92-95 (4)	2.60	4.60
Nos. 226-229 (4)	5.45	13.50
Nos. 276-279 (4)	1.35	*2.10*
Nos. 546-549 (4)	3.20	*10.15*
No. 223 (1)	.60	.55
Nos. 68-71 (4)	5.00	*16.75*
Nos. 116-121 (6)	7.15	5.30
Nos. 304-306 (3)	3.35	4.25
Nos. 281-283 (3)	5.75	2.70
Nos. 223-226 (4)	35.50	10.50
Nos. 89-92 (4)	6.10	10.25
Nos. 31-34 (4)	5.55	15.75
Nos. 26-29,O25-O28 (8)	2.00	*42.00*
Nos. 109-111 (3)	2.20	3.00
Nos. 160-162 (3)	3.95	6.00
Set total (313) Stamps	496.45	687.35

University

Arms of University College CD310

Alice, Princess of Athlone CD311

1948 opening of University College of the West Indies at Jamaica.

1951

Antigua ...104-105
Barbados ...228-229
British Guiana...250-251
British Honduras...141-142
Dominica...120-121
Grenada...164-165
Jamaica ...146-147
Leeward Islands ...130-131
Montserrat ...112-113
St. Kitts-Nevis...105-106
St. Lucia ...149-150
St. Vincent...174-175
Trinidad & Tobago ...70-71
Virgin Islands...96-97

Nos. 104-105 (2)	1.35	*3.25*
Nos. 228-229 (2)	1.85	1.55
Nos. 250-251 (2)	1.10	*1.25*
Nos. 141-142 (2)	1.40	2.15
Nos. 120-121 (2)	1.40	*1.75*
Nos. 164-165 (2)	1.20	*1.60*
Nos. 146-147 (2)	.95	.85
Nos. 130-131 (2)	1.35	4.00
Nos. 112-113 (2)	.85	*1.50*
Nos. 105-106 (2)	.90	1.50
Nos. 149-150 (2)	1.40	1.50
Nos. 174-175 (2)	1.00	*2.15*
Nos. 70-71 (2)	.75	.75
Nos. 96-97 (2)	1.50	*3.40*
Set total (28) Stamps	17.00	27.20

Coronation

Queen Elizabeth II — CD312

1953

Aden ...47
Kathiri State of Seiyun...28
Qu'aiti State of Shihr and Mukalla ...28
Antigua ...106
Ascension ...61
Bahamas ...157
Barbados ...234
Basutoland...45
Bechuanaland Protectorate...153
Bermuda...142
British Guiana...252
British Honduras...143
Cayman Islands...150
Cyprus...167
Dominica...141
Falkland Islands ...121
Falkland Islands Dependencies ...1L18
Fiji...145
Gambia...152
Gibraltar...131
Gilbert & Ellice Islands...60
Gold Coast ...160
Grenada...170
Hong Kong ...184
Jamaica ...153
Kenya, Uganda, Tanzania ...101
Leeward Islands ...132
Malaya
Johore ...155
Kedah...82
Kelantan ...71
Malacca...27
Negri Sembilan ...63
Pahang...71
Penang...27
Perak...126
Perlis ...28
Selangor...101
Trengganu ...74
Malta...241
Mauritius...250
Montserrat ...127
New Hebrides, British ...77
Nigeria ...79
North Borneo...260
Northern Rhodesia...60
Nyasaland Protectorate...96
Pitcairn Islands...19
St. Helena ...139
St. Kitts-Nevis...119
St. Lucia ...156
St. Vincent...185
Sarawak...196
Seychelles ...172
Sierra Leone...194
Singapore ...27
Solomon Islands...88
Somaliland Protectorate...127
Swaziland ...54
Trinidad & Tobago ...84
Tristan da Cunha...13
Turks & Caicos Islands ...118
Virgin Islands...114

The following have different designs but are included in the omnibus set:

Great Britain...313-316
Offices in Morocco (Tangier) ...579-582
Australia...259-261
Bahrain ...92-95
Canada ...330
Ceylon ...317
Cook Islands ...145-146
Kuwait...113-116
New Zealand ...280-284
Niue ...104-105
Oman...52-55
Samoa ...214-215
South Africa...192
Southern Rhodesia ...80
South-West Africa ...244-248
Tokelau Islands...4

No. 47 (1)	1.25	1.25
No. 28 (1)	.40	*1.50*
No. 28 (1)	1.10	.60
No. 106 (1)	.50	*.75*
No. 61 (1)	1.25	2.50
No. 157 (1)	1.25	.75
No. 234 (1)	1.00	.25
No. 45 (1)	.50	*.60*
No. 153 (1)	.75	.35
No. 142 (1)	.85	.40
No. 252 (1)	.45	.25
No. 143 (1)	.55	.40
No. 150 (1)	.40	*1.00*
No. 167 (1)	1.50	1.00
No. 141 (1)	.40	.40
No. 121 (1)	.90	1.50
No. 1L18 (1)	1.50	1.50
No. 145 (1)	1.75	.60
No. 152 (1)	.50	.50
No. 131 (1)	.50	.50
No. 60 (1)	.65	2.25
No. 160 (1)	.95	.25

No. 170 (1)	.30	.25
No. 184 (1)	7.00	.35
No. 153 (1)	.95	.25
No. 101 (1)	.40	.25
No. 132 (1)	1.00	2.25
No. 155 (1)	1.40	.30
No. 82 (1)	2.25	.60
No. 71 (1)	1.60	1.60
No. 27 (1)	1.10	1.50
No. 63 (1)	1.40	.65
No. 71 (1)	2.25	.25
No. 27 (1)	1.75	.30
No. 126 (1)	1.60	.25
No. 28 (1)	1.75	4.00
No. 101 (1)	1.75	.25
No. 74 (1)	1.50	1.00
No. 241 (1)	.50	.25
No. 250 (1)	1.00	.25
No. 127 (1)	.65	.50
No. 77 (1)	.75	.60
No. 79 (1)	.45	.25
No. 260 (1)	2.00	1.00
No. 60 (1)	.70	.25
No. 96 (1)	.75	.75
No. 19 (1)	2.25	2.25
No. 139 (1)	1.25	1.25
No. 119 (1)	.35	.25
No. 156 (1)	.70	.35
No. 185 (1)	.50	.30
No. 196 (1)	2.00	2.25
No. 172 (1)	.80	.80
No. 194 (1)	.40	.40
No. 27 (1)	2.50	.40
No. 88 (1)	1.10	1.10
No. 127 (1)	.40	.25
No. 54 (1)	.30	.25
No. 84 (1)	.25	.25
No. 13 (1)	1.00	1.75
No. 118 (1)	.40	1.10
No. 114 (1)	.40	1.00
Nos. 313-316 (4)	16.35	8.75
Nos. 579-582 (4)	7.40	5.20
Nos. 259-261 (3)	4.60	3.25
Nos. 92-95 (4)	15.25	12.75
No. 330 (1)	.25	.25
No. 317 (1)	1.50	.25
Nos. 145-146 (2)	2.90	2.90
Nos. 113-116 (4)	16.00	8.50
Nos. 280-284 (5)	5.65	6.85
Nos. 104-105 (2)	1.75	1.75
Nos. 52-55 (4)	15.25	6.50
Nos. 214-215 (2)	2.10	1.00
No. 192 (1)	.30	.25
No. 80 (1)	7.25	7.25
Nos. 244-248 (5)	4.90	3.50
No. 4 (1)	3.75	2.75
Set total (106) Stamps	173.50	122.65

Separate designs for each country for the visit of Queen Elizabeth II and the Duke of Edinburgh.

Royal Visit 1953

1953

Aden 62
Australia 267-269
Bermuda 163
Ceylon 318
Fiji 146
Gibraltar 146
Jamaica 154
Kenya, Uganda, Tanzania 102
Malta 242
New Zealand 286-287

No. 62 (1)	.65	2.00
Nos. 267-269 (3)	2.35	1.90
No. 163 (1)	.50	.25
No. 318 (1)	1.25	.25
No. 146 (1)	.65	.35
No. 146 (1)	.50	.30
No. 154 (1)	.50	.25
No. 102 (1)	.50	.25
No. 242 (1)	.35	.25
Nos. 286-287 (2)	.50	.50
Set total (13) Stamps	7.75	6.30

West Indies Federation

Map of the Caribbean CD313

Federation of the West Indies, April 22, 1958.

1958

Antigua 122-124
Barbados 248-250
Dominica 161-163
Grenada 184-186
Jamaica 175-177
Montserrat 143-145
St. Kitts-Nevis 136-138
St. Lucia 170-172
St. Vincent 198-200
Trinidad & Tobago 86-88

Nos. 122-124 (3)	5.80	3.80
Nos. 248-250 (3)	1.60	2.90
Nos. 161-163 (3)	1.95	1.85
Nos. 184-186 (3)	1.50	1.20
Nos. 175-177 (3)	3.10	4.20
Nos. 143-145 (3)	2.35	1.35
Nos. 136-138 (3)	3.00	1.85
Nos. 170-172 (3)	2.05	2.80
Nos. 198-200 (3)	1.50	1.75
Nos. 86-88 (3)	.75	.90
Set total (30) Stamps	23.60	22.60

Freedom from Hunger

Protein Food CD314

U.N. Food and Agricultural Organization's "Freedom from Hunger" campaign.

1963

Aden 65
Antigua 133
Ascension 89
Bahamas 180
Basutoland 83
Bechuanaland Protectorate 194
Bermuda 192
British Guiana 271
British Honduras 179
Brunei 100
Cayman Islands 168
Dominica 181
Falkland Islands 146
Fiji 198
Gambia 172
Gibraltar 161
Gilbert & Ellice Islands 76
Grenada 190
Hong Kong 218
Malta 291
Mauritius 270
Montserrat 150
New Hebrides, British 93
North Borneo 296
Pitcairn Islands 35
St. Helena 173
St. Lucia 179
St. Vincent 201
Sarawak 212
Seychelles 213
Solomon Islands 109
Swaziland 108
Tonga 127
Tristan da Cunha 68
Turks & Caicos Islands 138
Virgin Islands 140
Zanzibar 280

No. 65 (1)	1.75	1.75
No. 133 (1)	.35	.35
No. 89 (1)	1.00	1.00
No. 180 (1)	.65	.65
No. 83 (1)	.50	.25
No. 194 (1)	.50	.50
No. 192 (1)	1.00	.50
No. 271 (1)	.45	.25
No. 179 (1)	.65	.25
No. 100 (1)	3.25	2.25
No. 168 (1)	.50	.30
No. 181 (1)	.30	.30
No. 146 (1)	11.50	3.50
No. 198 (1)	5.25	2.75
No. 172 (1)	.50	.25
No. 161 (1)	4.00	2.25
No. 76 (1)	1.40	.40
No. 190 (1)	.30	.25
No. 218 (1)	57.50	8.75
No. 291 (1)	2.00	2.00
No. 270 (1)	.50	.50
No. 150 (1)	.55	.45
No. 93 (1)	.60	.25
No. 296 (1)	1.90	.75
No. 35 (1)	10.00	4.50
No. 173 (1)	2.25	1.10
No. 179 (1)	.40	.40
No. 201 (1)	.90	.50
No. 212 (1)	1.60	1.75
No. 213 (1)	.85	.35
No. 109 (1)	2.00	.85
No. 108 (1)	.50	.50
No. 127 (1)	.70	.35
No. 68 (1)	.90	.40
No. 138 (1)	.50	.50
No. 140 (1)	.50	.50
No. 280 (1)	1.50	.80
Set total (37) Stamps	119.50	42.95

Red Cross Centenary

Red Cross and Elizabeth II CD315

1963

Antigua 134-135
Ascension 90-91
Bahamas 183-184
Basutoland 84-85
Bechuanaland Protectorate 195-196
Bermuda 193-194
British Guiana 272-273
British Honduras 180-181
Cayman Islands 169-170
Dominica 182-183
Falkland Islands 147-148
Fiji 203-204
Gambia 173-174
Gibraltar 162-163
Gilbert & Ellice Islands 77-78
Grenada 191-192
Hong Kong 219-220
Jamaica 203-204
Malta 292-293
Mauritius 271-272
Montserrat 151-152
New Hebrides, British 94-95
Pitcairn Islands 36-37
St. Helena 174-175
St. Kitts-Nevis 143-144
St. Lucia 180-181
St. Vincent 202-203
Seychelles 214-215
Solomon Islands 110-111
South Arabia 1-2
Swaziland 109-110
Tonga 134-135
Tristan da Cunha 69-70
Turks & Caicos Islands 139-140
Virgin Islands 141-142

Nos. 134-135 (2)	1.10	1.50
Nos. 90-91 (2)	8.25	2.70
Nos. 183-184 (2)	2.30	2.55
Nos. 84-85 (2)	1.20	.90
Nos. 195-196 (2)	.95	.85
Nos. 193-194 (2)	2.75	2.55
Nos. 272-273 (2)	1.05	.80
Nos. 180-181 (2)	1.00	2.25
Nos. 169-170 (2)	.95	2.00
Nos. 182-183 (2)	.70	1.05
Nos. 147-148 (2)	19.75	6.00
Nos. 203-204 (2)	4.00	3.55
Nos. 173-174 (2)	.85	.85
Nos. 162-163 (2)	6.25	5.40
Nos. 77-78 (2)	2.25	3.25
Nos. 191-192 (2)	.80	.50
Nos. 219-220 (2)	39.50	8.85
Nos. 203-204 (2)	.75	1.65
Nos. 292-293 (2)	2.50	4.75
Nos. 271-272 (2)	.90	.90
Nos. 151-152 (2)	1.00	.80
Nos. 94-95 (2)	1.00	.50
Nos. 36-37 (2)	6.50	5.50
Nos. 174-175 (2)	1.70	2.30
Nos. 143-144 (2)	.90	.90
Nos. 180-181 (2)	1.25	1.25
Nos. 202-203 (2)	.90	.90
Nos. 214-215 (2)	1.10	.90
Nos. 110-111 (2)	1.25	1.15
Nos. 1-2 (2)	1.25	1.25
Nos. 109-110 (2)	1.10	1.10
Nos. 134-135 (2)	1.00	1.25
Nos. 69-70 (2)	1.50	1.00
Nos. 139-140 (2)	.95	1.10
Nos. 141-142 (2)	.80	.80
Set total (70) Stamps	120.00	73.55

Shakespeare

Shakespeare Memorial Theatre, Stratford-on-Avon — CD316

400th anniversary of the birth of William Shakespeare.

1964

Antigua 151
Bahamas 201
Bechuanaland Protectorate 197
Cayman Islands 171
Dominica 184
Falkland Islands 149
Gambia 192
Gibraltar 164
Montserrat 153
St. Lucia 196
Turks & Caicos Islands 141
Virgin Islands 143

No. 151 (1)	.40	.25
No. 201 (1)	.60	.35
No. 197 (1)	.35	.35
No. 171 (1)	.35	.30
No. 184 (1)	.35	.35
No. 149 (1)	1.75	.50
No. 192 (1)	.35	.25
No. 164 (1)	.65	.55
No. 153 (1)	.35	.25
No. 196 (1)	.45	.25
No. 141 (1)	.40	.40
No. 143 (1)	.45	.45
Set total (12) Stamps	6.45	4.25

ITU

ITU Emblem CD317

Intl. Telecommunication Union, cent.

1965

Antigua 153-154
Ascension 92-93
Bahamas 219-220
Barbados 265-266
Basutoland 101-102
Bechuanaland Protectorate 202-203
Bermuda 196-197
British Guiana 293-294
British Honduras 187-188
Brunei 116-117
Cayman Islands 172-173
Dominica 185-186
Falkland Islands 154-155
Fiji 211-212
Gibraltar 167-168
Gilbert & Ellice Islands 87-88
Grenada 205-206
Hong Kong 221-222
Mauritius 291-292
Montserrat 157-158
New Hebrides, British 108-109
Pitcairn Islands 52-53
St. Helena 180-181
St. Kitts-Nevis 163-164
St. Lucia 197-198
St. Vincent 224-225
Seychelles 218-219
Solomon Islands 126-127
Swaziland 115-116
Tristan da Cunha 85-86
Turks & Caicos Islands 142-143
Virgin Islands 159-160

Nos. 153-154 (2)	1.65	1.35
Nos. 92-93 (2)	1.90	1.50
Nos. 219-220 (2)	1.35	1.35
Nos. 265-266 (2)	1.50	1.25
Nos. 101-102 (2)	.85	.65
Nos. 202-203 (2)	1.10	.75
Nos. 196-197 (2)	2.15	2.25
Nos. 293-294 (2)	.60	.55
Nos. 187-188 (2)	.85	.85
Nos. 116-117 (2)	1.75	1.75
Nos. 172-173 (2)	1.00	1.00
Nos. 185-186 (2)	.55	.55
Nos. 154-155 (2)	7.75	3.65
Nos. 211-212 (2)	2.70	2.70
Nos. 167-168 (2)	9.00	5.95
Nos. 87-88 (2)	.95	.75
Nos. 205-206 (2)	.50	.50
Nos. 221-222 (2)	32.00	4.55
Nos. 291-292 (2)	1.20	.65
Nos. 157-158 (2)	1.25	1.15
Nos. 108-109 (2)	.65	.50
Nos. 52-53 (2)	6.25	4.30
Nos. 180-181 (2)	.80	.60
Nos. 163-164 (2)	.60	.60
Nos. 197-198 (2)	1.25	1.25
Nos. 224-225 (2)	.80	.90
Nos. 218-219 (2)	.90	.60
Nos. 126-127 (2)	.70	.55
Nos. 115-116 (2)	.75	.75
Nos. 85-86 (2)	1.15	.65
Nos. 142-143 (2)	.90	.90
Nos. 159-160 (2)	.95	.95
Set total (64) Stamps	86.30	46.25

Intl. Cooperation Year

ICY Emblem CD318

1965

Antigua	155-156
Ascension	94-95
Bahamas	222-223
Basutoland	103-104
Bechuanaland Protectorate	204-205
Bermuda	199-200
British Guiana	295-296
British Honduras	189-190
Brunei	118-119
Cayman Islands	174-175
Dominica	187-188
Falkland Islands	156-157
Fiji	213-214
Gibraltar	169-170
Gilbert & Ellice Islands	104-105
Grenada	207-208
Hong Kong	223-224
Mauritius	293-294
Montserrat	176-177
New Hebrides, British	110-111
New Hebrides, French	126-127
Pitcairn Islands	54-55
St. Helena	182-183
St. Kitts-Nevis	165-166
St. Lucia	199-200
Seychelles	220-221
Solomon Islands	143-144
South Arabia	17-18
Swaziland	117-118
Tristan da Cunha	87-88
Turks & Caicos Islands	144-145
Virgin Islands	161-162

Nos. 155-156 (2)	.60	.50
Nos. 94-95 (2)	1.30	1.50
Nos. 222-223 (2)	.65	1.40
Nos. 103-104 (2)	.75	.85
Nos. 204-205 (2)	.85	1.00
Nos. 199-200 (2)	2.25	1.25
Nos. 295-296 (2)	.65	.60
Nos. 189-190 (2)	.60	.55
Nos. 118-119 (2)	.85	.85
Nos. 174-175 (2)	1.00	.95
Nos. 187-188 (2)	.55	.55
Nos. 156-157 (2)	7.00	1.90
Nos. 213-214 (2)	2.60	2.35
Nos. 169-170 (2)	1.25	*2.75*
Nos. 104-105 (2)	.95	.60
Nos. 207-208 (2)	.50	.50
Nos. 223-224 (2)	26.00	4.10
Nos. 293-294 (2)	.70	.70
Nos. 176-177 (2)	.80	.65
Nos. 110-111 (2)	.50	.50
Nos. 126-127 (2)	12.00	12.00
Nos. 54-55 (2)	6.35	4.50
Nos. 182-183 (2)	.95	.50
Nos. 165-166 (2)	.70	.60
Nos. 199-200 (2)	.55	.55
Nos. 220-221 (2)	.90	.65
Nos. 143-144 (2)	.70	.60
Nos. 17-18 (2)	1.20	.50
Nos. 117-118 (2)	.75	.75
Nos. 87-88 (2)	1.35	.75
Nos. 144-145 (2)	.85	.85
Nos. 161-162 (2)	.80	.80
Set total (64) Stamps	77.45	47.10

Churchill Memorial

Winston Churchill and St. Paul's, London, During Air Attack CD319

1966

Antigua	157-160
Ascension	96-99
Bahamas	224-227
Barbados	281-284
Basutoland	105-108
Bechuanaland Protectorate	206-209
Bermuda	201-204
British Antarctic Territory	16-19
British Honduras	191-194
Brunei	120-123
Cayman Islands	176-179
Dominica	189-192
Falkland Islands	158-161
Fiji	215-218
Gibraltar	171-174
Gilbert & Ellice Islands	106-109
Grenada	209-212
Hong Kong	225-228
Mauritius	295-298
Montserrat	178-181
New Hebrides, British	112-115
New Hebrides, French	128-131
Pitcairn Islands	56-59
St. Helena	184-187
St. Kitts-Nevis	167-170
St. Lucia	201-204
St. Vincent	241-244
Seychelles	222-225
Solomon Islands	145-148
South Arabia	19-22
Swaziland	119-122
Tristan da Cunha	89-92
Turks & Caicos Islands	146-149
Virgin Islands	163-166

Nos. 157-160 (4)	3.05	2.55
Nos. 96-99 (4)	10.00	7.15
Nos. 224-227 (4)	2.30	*3.20*
Nos. 281-284 (4)	3.00	4.45
Nos. 105-108 (4)	2.80	3.25
Nos. 206-209 (4)	2.50	2.50
Nos. 201-204 (4)	4.00	4.00
Nos. 16-19 (4)	41.35	20.00
Nos. 191-194 (4)	2.55	1.80
Nos. 120-123 (4)	8.00	7.25
Nos. 176-179 (4)	3.40	3.55
Nos. 189-192 (4)	1.15	1.15
Nos. 158-161 (4)	12.75	7.80
Nos. 215-218 (4)	5.15	3.45
Nos. 171-174 (4)	3.05	5.30
Nos. 106-109 (4)	1.75	1.30
Nos. 209-212 (4)	1.10	1.10
Nos. 225-228 (4)	68.00	12.15
Nos. 295-298 (4)	4.05	4.05
Nos. 178-181 (4)	1.60	1.55
Nos. 112-115 (4)	2.30	1.00
Nos. 128-131 (4)	10.25	10.25
Nos. 56-59 (4)	11.00	6.75
Nos. 184-187 (4)	1.85	1.95
Nos. 167-170 (4)	1.70	1.70
Nos. 201-204 (4)	1.50	1.50
Nos. 241-244 (4)	1.50	1.75
Nos. 222-225 (4)	3.20	3.60
Nos. 145-148 (4)	1.75	1.75
Nos. 19-22 (4)	3.80	2.50
Nos. 119-122 (4)	1.70	2.55
Nos. 89-92 (4)	5.95	2.70
Nos. 146-149 (4)	1.60	1.75
Nos. 163-166 (4)	1.90	1.90
Set total (136) Stamps	231.55	139.20

Royal Visit, 1966

Queen Elizabeth II and Prince Philip CD320

Caribbean visit, Feb. 4 - Mar. 6, 1966.

1966

Antigua	161-162
Bahamas	228-229
Barbados	285-286
British Guiana	299-300
Cayman Islands	180-181
Dominica	193-194
Grenada	213-214
Montserrat	182-183
St. Kitts-Nevis	171-172
St. Lucia	205-206
St. Vincent	245-246
Turks & Caicos Islands	150-151
Virgin Islands	167-168

Nos. 161-162 (2)	3.80	2.60
Nos. 228-229 (2)	3.05	3.05
Nos. 285-286 (2)	3.00	2.00
Nos. 299-300 (2)	3.35	1.60
Nos. 180-181 (2)	3.45	1.80
Nos. 193-194 (2)	3.00	.60
Nos. 213-214 (2)	.90	.50
Nos. 182-183 (2)	1.70	1.00
Nos. 171-172 (2)	.80	.75
Nos. 205-206 (2)	1.50	1.35
Nos. 245-246 (2)	2.75	1.35
Nos. 150-151 (2)	1.20	.70
Nos. 167-168 (2)	2.25	2.25
Set total (26) Stamps	30.75	19.55

World Cup Soccer

Soccer Player and Jules Rimet Cup CD321

World Cup Soccer Championship, Wembley, England, July 11-30.

1966

Antigua	163-164
Ascension	100-101
Bahamas	245-246
Bermuda	205-206
Brunei	124-125
Cayman Islands	182-183
Dominica	195-196
Fiji	219-220
Gibraltar	175-176
Gilbert & Ellice Islands	125-126
Grenada	230-231
New Hebrides, British	116-117
New Hebrides, French	132-133
Pitcairn Islands	60-61
St. Helena	188-189
St. Kitts-Nevis	173-174
St. Lucia	207-208
Seychelles	226-227
Solomon Islands	167-168
South Arabia	23-24
Tristan da Cunha	93-94

Nos. 163-164 (2)	.85	.50
Nos. 100-101 (2)	2.50	1.80
Nos. 245-246 (2)	.65	.65
Nos. 205-206 (2)	1.75	1.75
Nos. 124-125 (2)	1.40	1.00
Nos. 182-183 (2)	.75	.75
Nos. 195-196 (2)	1.20	.75
Nos. 219-220 (2)	2.00	1.20
Nos. 175-176 (2)	1.85	1.75
Nos. 125-126 (2)	.80	.60
Nos. 230-231 (2)	.65	*.95*
Nos. 116-117 (2)	1.00	1.00
Nos. 132-133 (2)	7.00	7.00
Nos. 60-61 (2)	5.50	5.00
Nos. 188-189 (2)	1.25	.60
Nos. 173-174 (2)	.85	.80
Nos. 207-208 (2)	1.15	.90
Nos. 226-227 (2)	.85	.85
Nos. 167-168 (2)	.70	.70
Nos. 23-24 (2)	1.90	.55
Nos. 93-94 (2)	1.25	.80
Set total (42) Stamps	35.85	29.90

WHO Headquarters

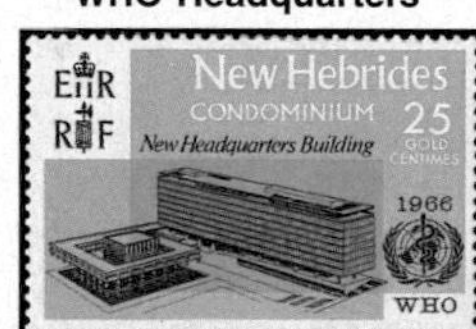

World Health Organization Headquarters, Geneva — CD322

1966

Antigua	165-166
Ascension	102-103
Bahamas	247-248
Brunei	126-127
Cayman Islands	184-185
Dominica	197-198
Fiji	224-225
Gibraltar	180-181
Gilbert & Ellice Islands	127-128
Grenada	232-233
Hong Kong	229-230
Montserrat	184-185
New Hebrides, British	118-119
New Hebrides, French	134-135
Pitcairn Islands	62-63
St. Helena	190-191
St. Kitts-Nevis	177-178
St. Lucia	209-210
St. Vincent	247-248
Seychelles	228-229
Solomon Islands	169-170
South Arabia	25-26
Tristan da Cunha	99-100

Nos. 165-166 (2)	1.05	.55
Nos. 102-103 (2)	6.60	3.50
Nos. 247-248 (2)	.80	.80
Nos. 126-127 (2)	1.35	1.00
Nos. 184-185 (2)	2.25	1.40
Nos. 197-198 (2)	.75	.75
Nos. 224-225 (2)	5.10	3.90
Nos. 180-181 (2)	6.50	4.50
Nos. 127-128 (2)	.80	.70
Nos. 232-233 (2)	.80	.50
Nos. 229-230 (2)	14.25	2.30
Nos. 184-185 (2)	1.00	1.00
Nos. 118-119 (2)	.75	.50
Nos. 134-135 (2)	8.75	8.75
Nos. 62-63 (2)	7.25	6.50
Nos. 190-191 (2)	3.50	1.50
Nos. 177-178 (2)	.65	.65
Nos. 209-210 (2)	.80	.80
Nos. 247-248 (2)	1.15	1.05
Nos. 228-229 (2)	1.25	.75
Nos. 169-170 (2)	.80	.80
Nos. 25-26 (2)	2.10	.70
Nos. 99-100 (2)	1.90	1.25
Set total (46) Stamps	70.15	44.15

UNESCO Anniversary

"Education" — CD323

"Science" (Wheat ears & flask enclosing globe). "Culture" (lyre & columns). 20th anniversary of the UNESCO.

1966-67

Antigua	183-185
Ascension	108-110
Bahamas	249-251
Barbados	287-289
Bermuda	207-209
Brunei	128-130
Cayman Islands	186-188
Dominica	199-201
Gibraltar	183-185
Gilbert & Ellice Islands	129-131
Grenada	234-236
Hong Kong	231-233
Mauritius	299-301
Montserrat	186-188
New Hebrides, British	120-122
New Hebrides, French	136-138
Pitcairn Islands	64-66
St. Helena	192-194
St. Kitts-Nevis	179-181
St. Lucia	211-213
St. Vincent	249-251
Seychelles	230-232
Solomon Islands	171-173
South Arabia	27-29
Swaziland	123-125
Tristan da Cunha	101-103
Turks & Caicos Islands	155-157
Virgin Islands	176-178

Nos. 183-185 (3)	1.90	*2.50*
Nos. 108-110 (3)	11.00	6.15
Nos. 249-251 (3)	2.35	2.35
Nos. 287-289 (3)	2.50	2.15
Nos. 207-209 (3)	4.30	3.90
Nos. 128-130 (3)	5.00	*7.40*
Nos. 186-188 (3)	2.50	1.70
Nos. 199-201 (3)	1.60	.75
Nos. 183-185 (3)	6.50	3.25
Nos. 129-131 (3)	2.50	1.65
Nos. 234-236 (3)	1.10	1.20
Nos. 231-233 (3)	89.00	20.00
Nos. 299-301 (3)	2.10	1.50
Nos. 186-188 (3)	2.40	2.40
Nos. 120-122 (3)	1.90	1.90
Nos. 136-138 (3)	7.75	7.75
Nos. 64-66 (3)	7.10	4.75
Nos. 192-194 (3)	5.25	3.65
Nos. 179-181 (3)	.90	.90
Nos. 211-213 (3)	1.15	1.15
Nos. 249-251 (3)	2.30	1.35
Nos. 230-232 (3)	2.40	2.40
Nos. 171-173 (3)	2.00	1.50
Nos. 27-29 (3)	5.90	3.05
Nos. 123-125 (3)	1.45	1.45
Nos. 101-103 (3)	2.00	1.40
Nos. 155-157 (3)	1.05	1.05
Nos. 176-178 (3)	1.30	1.30
Set total (84) Stamps	177.20	90.50

Silver Wedding, 1972

Queen Elizabeth II and Prince Philip — CD324

Designs: borders differ for each country.

1972

Anguilla	161-162
Antigua	295-296
Ascension	164-165
Bahamas	344-345
Bermuda	296-297
British Antarctic Territory	43-44
British Honduras	306-307
British Indian Ocean Territory	48-49

Brunei 186-187
Cayman Islands 304-305
Dominica 352-353
Falkland Islands 223-224
Fiji 328-329
Gibraltar 292-293
Gilbert & Ellice Islands 206-207
Grenada 466-467
Hong Kong 271-272
Montserrat 286-287
New Hebrides, British 169-170
Pitcairn Islands 127-128
St. Helena 271-272
St. Kitts-Nevis 257-258
St. Lucia 328-329
St.Vincent 344-345
Seychelles 309-310
Solomon Islands 248-249
South Georgia 35-36
Tristan da Cunha 178-179
Turks & Caicos Islands 257-258
Virgin Islands 241-242

Nos. 161-162 (2)	1.30	*1.50*
Nos. 295-296 (2)	.50	.50
Nos. 164-165 (2)	.80	.80
Nos. 344-345 (2)	.60	.60
Nos. 296-297 (2)	.50	.50
Nos. 43-44 (2)	7.75	6.10
Nos. 306-307 (2)	.90	.90
Nos. 48-49 (2)	2.30	1.00
Nos. 186-187 (2)	.65	.85
Nos. 304-305 (2)	.75	.75
Nos. 352-353 (2)	.65	.65
Nos. 223-224 (2)	1.10	1.10
Nos. 328-329 (2)	1.00	1.00
Nos. 292-293 (2)	.50	.50
Nos. 206-207 (2)	.50	.50
Nos. 466-467 (2)	.70	.70
Nos. 271-272 (2)	2.10	1.75
Nos. 286-287 (2)	.55	.55
Nos. 169-170 (2)	.50	.50
Nos. 127-128 (2)	.90	.85
Nos. 271-272 (2)	.70	1.20
Nos. 257-258 (2)	.65	.50
Nos. 328-329 (2)	.75	.75
Nos. 344-345 (2)	.55	.55
Nos. 309-310 (2)	.95	.95
Nos. 248-249 (2)	.60	.60
Nos. 35-36 (2)	1.40	1.40
Nos. 178-179 (2)	.70	.70
Nos. 257-258 (2)	.50	.50
Nos. 241-242 (2)	.50	.50
Set total (60) Stamps	31.85	29.25

Princess Anne's Wedding

Princess Anne and Mark Phillips — CD325

Wedding of Princess Anne and Mark Phillips, Nov. 14, 1973.

1973

Anguilla 179-180
Ascension 177-178
Belize 325-326
Bermuda 302-303
British Antarctic Territory 60-61
Cayman Islands 320-321
Falkland Islands 225-226
Gibraltar 305-306
Gilbert & Ellice Islands 216-217
Hong Kong 289-290
Montserrat 300-301
Pitcairn Islands 135-136
St. Helena 277-278
St. Kitts-Nevis 274-275
St. Lucia 349-350
St. Vincent 358-359
St. Vincent Grenadines 1-2
Seychelles 311-312
Solomon Islands 259-260
South Georgia 37-38
Tristan da Cunha 189-190
Turks & Caicos Islands 286-287
Virgin Islands 260-261

Nos. 179-180 (2)	.55	.55
Nos. 177-178 (2)	.65	.65
Nos. 325-326 (2)	.50	.50
Nos. 302-303 (2)	.50	.50
Nos. 60-61 (2)	1.10	1.10
Nos. 320-321 (2)	.55	.55
Nos. 225-226 (2)	.75	.75
Nos. 305-306 (2)	.55	.55
Nos. 216-217 (2)	.50	.50
Nos. 289-290 (2)	3.25	2.25
Nos. 300-301 (2)	.65	.65
Nos. 135-136 (2)	.70	.60
Nos. 277-278 (2)	.50	.50
Nos. 274-275 (2)	.50	.50
Nos. 349-350 (2)	.50	.50
Nos. 358-359 (2)	.50	.50
Nos. 1-2 (2)	.50	.50
Nos. 311-312 (2)	.70	.70
Nos. 259-260 (2)	.70	.70
Nos. 37-38 (2)	.75	.75
Nos. 189-190 (2)	.50	.50
Nos. 286-287 (2)	.50	.50
Nos. 260-261 (2)	.50	.50
Set total (46) Stamps	16.40	15.30

Elizabeth II Coronation Anniv.

CD326

CD327

CD328

Designs: Royal and local beasts in heraldic form and simulated stonework. Portrait of Elizabeth II by Peter Grugeon. 25th anniversary of coronation of Queen Elizabeth II.

1978

Ascension 229
Barbados 474
Belize 397
British Antarctic Territory 71
Cayman Islands 404
Christmas Island 87
Falkland Islands 275
Fiji 384
Gambia 380
Gilbert Islands 312
Mauritius 464
New Hebrides, British 258
St. Helena 317
St. Kitts-Nevis 354
Samoa 472
Solomon Islands 368
South Georgia 51
Swaziland 302
Tristan da Cunha 238
Virgin Islands 337

No. 229 (1)	2.25	2.25
No. 474 (1)	1.35	1.35
No. 397 (1)	1.75	1.75
No. 71 (1)	6.00	6.00
No. 404 (1)	2.00	2.50
No. 87 (1)	3.50	*4.00*
No. 275 (1)	4.00	4.00
No. 384 (1)	2.75	2.75
No. 380 (1)	1.50	1.50
No. 312 (1)	1.25	1.25
No. 464 (1)	2.75	2.75
No. 258 (1)	1.75	1.75
No. 317 (1)	1.75	1.75
No. 354 (1)	1.00	1.00
No. 472 (1)	2.00	2.00
No. 368 (1)	3.00	3.00
No. 51 (1)	3.00	3.00
No. 302 (1)	1.75	1.75
No. 238 (1)	1.50	1.50
No. 337 (1)	2.25	2.25
Set total (20) Stamps	47.10	48.10

Queen Mother Elizabeth's 80th Birthday

CD330

Designs: Photographs of Queen Mother Elizabeth. Falkland Islands issued in sheets of 50; others in sheets of 9.

1980

Ascension 261
Bermuda 401
Cayman Islands 443
Falkland Islands 305
Gambia 412
Gibraltar 393
Hong Kong 364
Pitcairn Islands 193
St. Helena 341
Samoa 532
Solomon Islands 426
Tristan da Cunha 277

No. 261 (1)	.50	.50
No. 401 (1)	.45	.45
No. 443 (1)	.45	.45
No. 305 (1)	.40	.40
No. 412 (1)	.40	.50
No. 393 (1)	.35	.35
No. 364 (1)	1.10	1.00
No. 193 (1)	.60	.60
No. 341 (1)	.50	.50
No. 532 (1)	.55	.55
No. 426 (1)	.50	.50
No. 277 (1)	.45	.45
Set total (12) Stamps	6.25	6.25

Royal Wedding, 1981

Prince Charles and Lady Diana — CD331

CD331a

Wedding of Charles, Prince of Wales, and Lady Diana Spencer, St. Paul's Cathedral, London, July 29, 1981.

1981

Antigua 623-627
Ascension 294-296
Barbados 547-549
Barbuda 497-501
Bermuda 412-414
Brunei 268-270
Cayman Islands 471-473
Dominica 701-705
Falkland Islands 324-326
Falkland Islands Dep. 1L59-1L61
Fiji 442-444
Gambia 426-428
Ghana 759-764
Grenada 1051-1055
Grenada Grenadines 440-443
Hong Kong 373-375
Jamaica 500-503
Lesotho 335-337
Maldive Islands 906-909
Mauritius 520-522
Norfolk Island 280-282
Pitcairn Islands 206-208
St. Helena 353-355
St. Lucia 543-549
Samoa 558-560
Sierra Leone 509-518
Solomon Islands 450-452
Swaziland 382-384
Tristan da Cunha 294-296
Turks & Caicos Islands 486-489
Caicos Island 8-11
Uganda 314-317
Vanuatu 308-310
Virgin Islands 406-408

Nos. 623-627 (5)	7.55	2.55
Nos. 294-296 (3)	1.10	1.10
Nos. 547-549 (3)	.90	.90
Nos. 497-501 (5)	10.95	10.95
Nos. 412-414 (3)	2.00	2.00
Nos. 268-270 (3)	2.15	*4.50*
Nos. 471-473 (3)	1.35	1.35
Nos. 701-705 (5)	8.35	2.35
Nos. 324-326 (3)	1.65	1.70
Nos. 1L59-1L61 (3)	1.45	1.45
Nos. 442-444 (3)	1.70	1.70
Nos. 426-428 (3)	.80	.80
Nos. 759-764 (9)	5.00	5.00
Nos. 1051-1055 (5)	9.85	1.85
Nos. 440-443 (4)	2.35	2.35
Nos. 373-375 (3)	3.30	3.10
Nos. 500-503 (4)	1.50	1.25
Nos. 335-337 (3)	1.10	1.10
Nos. 906-909 (4)	1.70	1.80
Nos. 520-522 (3)	2.75	2.75
Nos. 280-282 (3)	1.35	1.35
Nos. 206-208 (3)	1.10	1.10
Nos. 353-355 (3)	.85	.85
Nos. 543-549 (5)	8.50	8.50
Nos. 558-560 (3)	.85	.85
Nos. 509-518 (10)	15.50	15.50
Nos. 450-452 (3)	1.05	1.05
Nos. 382-384 (3)	1.30	1.25
Nos. 294-296 (3)	.90	.90
Nos. 486-489 (4)	2.20	2.20
Nos. 8-11 (4)	6.25	6.25
Nos. 314-317 (4)	3.30	3.00
Nos. 308-310 (3)	1.15	1.15
Nos. 406-408 (3)	1.30	1.30
Set total (131) Stamps	113.10	95.80

Princess Diana

CD332

CD333

Designs: Photographs and portrait of Princess Diana, wedding or honeymoon photographs, royal residences, arms of issuing country. Portrait photograph by Clive Friend. Souvenir sheet margins show family tree, various people related to the princess. 21st birthday of Princess Diana of Wales, July 1.

1982

Antigua 663-666
Ascension 313-316
Bahamas 510-513
Barbados 585-588
Barbuda 544-547
British Antarctic Territory 92-95
Cayman Islands 486-489
Dominica 773-776
Falkland Islands 348-351
Falkland Islands Dep. 1L72-1L75
Fiji 470-473
Gambia 447-450
Grenada 1101A-1105
Grenada Grenadines 485-491
Lesotho 372-375
Maldive Islands 952-955
Mauritius 548-551
Pitcairn Islands 213-216
St. Helena 372-375
St. Lucia 591-594
Sierra Leone 531-534
Solomon Islands 471-474
Swaziland 406-409
Tristan da Cunha 310-313
Turks and Caicos Islands 531-534
Virgin Islands 430-433

Nos. 663-666 (4)	9.70	9.70
Nos. 313-316 (4)	3.95	3.95
Nos. 510-513 (4)	6.00	3.85
Nos. 585-588 (4)	3.40	3.25
Nos. 544-547 (4)	9.75	7.70
Nos. 92-95 (4)	5.30	3.45
Nos. 486-489 (4)	*5.40*	*2.70*
Nos. 773-776 (4)	7.05	7.05
Nos. 348-351 (4)	3.10	3.10
Nos. 1L72-1L75 (4)	2.50	2.60
Nos. 470-473 (4)	4.50	4.50
Nos. 447-450 (4)	2.85	2.85
Nos. 1101A-1105 (7)	16.05	15.55
Nos. 485-491 (7)	17.65	17.65
Nos. 372-375 (4)	4.00	4.00
Nos. 952-955 (4)	7.25	7.25
Nos. 548-551 (4)	5.50	5.50
Nos. 213-216 (4)	2.15	2.15
Nos. 372-375 (4)	2.95	2.95
Nos. 591-594 (4)	9.90	9.90
Nos. 531-534 (4)	7.60	7.60
Nos. 471-474 (4)	2.90	2.90
Nos. 406-409 (4)	3.85	2.25
Nos. 310-313 (4)	3.65	1.45
Nos. 486-489 (4)	2.20	2.20
Nos. 430-433 (4)	3.55	3.55
Set total (110) Stamps	152.70	139.60

250th anniv. of first edition of Lloyd's List (shipping news publication) & of Lloyd's marine insurance.

CD335

Designs: First page of early edition of the list; historical ships, modern transportation or harbor scenes.

1984

Ascension	351-354
Bahamas	555-558
Barbados	627-630
Cayes of Belize	10-13
Cayman Islands	522-526
Falkland Islands	404-407
Fiji	509-512
Gambia	519-522
Mauritius	587-590
Nauru	280-283
St. Helena	412-415
Samoa	624-627
Seychelles	538-541
Solomon Islands	521-524
Vanuatu	368-371
Virgin Islands	466-469

Nos. 351-354 (4)	3.30	2.55
Nos. 555-558 (4)	4.55	2.95
Nos. 627-630 (4)	6.10	5.15
Nos. 10-13 (4)	3.05	3.05
Nos. 522-526 (5)	9.30	8.45
Nos. 404-407 (4)	3.65	4.00
Nos. 509-512 (4)	6.15	6.15
Nos. 519-522 (4)	4.20	4.30
Nos. 587-590 (4)	8.95	8.95
Nos. 280-283 (4)	2.40	2.35
Nos. 412-415 (4)	2.40	2.40
Nos. 624-627 (4)	2.75	2.55
Nos. 538-541 (4)	5.25	5.25
Nos. 521-524 (4)	4.65	3.95
Nos. 368-371 (4)	2.40	2.40
Nos. 466-469 (4)	5.00	5.00
Set total (65) Stamps	74.10	69.45

Queen Mother 85th Birthday

CD336

Designs: Photographs tracing the life of the Queen Mother, Elizabeth. The high value in each set pictures the same photograph taken of the Queen Mother holding the infant Prince Henry.

1985

Ascension	372-376
Bahamas	580-584
Barbados	660-664
Bermuda	469-473
Falkland Islands	420-424
Falkland Islands Dep.	1L92-1L96
Fiji	531-535
Hong Kong	447-450
Jamaica	599-603
Mauritius	604-608
Norfolk Island	364-368
Pitcairn Islands	253-257
St. Helena	428-432
Samoa	649-653
Seychelles	567-571
Zil Elwannyen Sesel	101-105
Solomon Islands	543-547
Swaziland	476-480
Tristan da Cunha	372-376
Vanuatu	392-396

Nos. 372-376 (5)	5.35	5.35
Nos. 580-584 (5)	7.95	6.45
Nos. 660-664 (5)	8.00	6.70
Nos. 469-473 (5)	9.90	9.90
Nos. 420-424 (5)	8.25	7.60
Nos. 1L92-1L96 (5)	8.25	8.25
Nos. 531-535 (5)	7.05	7.05
Nos. 447-450 (4)	10.25	8.50
Nos. 599-603 (5)	7.30	8.00
Nos. 604-608 (5)	11.80	11.80
Nos. 364-368 (5)	5.05	5.05
Nos. 253-257 (5)	5.25	5.95
Nos. 428-432 (5)	5.25	5.25
Nos. 649-653 (5)	8.65	7.80
Nos. 567-571 (5)	8.70	8.70
Nos. 101-105 (5)	7.15	7.15
Nos. 543-547 (5)	4.45	4.45
Nos. 476-480 (5)	8.00	7.50
Nos. 372-376 (5)	5.40	5.40
Nos. 392-396 (5)	5.25	5.25
Set total (99) Stamps	147.25	142.10

Queen Elizabeth II, 60th Birthday

CD337

1986, April 21

Ascension	389-393
Bahamas	592-596
Barbados	675-679
Bermuda	499-503
Cayman Islands	555-559
Falkland Islands	441-445
Fiji	544-548
Hong Kong	465-469
Jamaica	620-624
Kiribati	470-474
Mauritius	629-633
Papua New Guinea	640-644
Pitcairn Islands	270-274
St. Helena	451-455
Samoa	670-674
Seychelles	592-596
Zil Elwannyen Sesel	114-118
Solomon Islands	562-566
South Georgia	101-105
Swaziland	490-494
Tristan da Cunha	388-392
Vanuatu	414-418
Zambia	343-347

Nos. 389-393 (5)	2.80	2.80
Nos. 592-596 (5)	2.75	3.70
Nos. 675-679 (5)	3.35	3.20
Nos. 499-503 (5)	4.90	4.90
Nos. 555-559 (5)	4.55	4.45
Nos. 441-445 (5)	3.95	4.95
Nos. 544-548 (5)	4.05	4.05
Nos. 465-469 (5)	9.60	6.85
Nos. 620-624 (5)	2.95	3.05
Nos. 470-474 (5)	2.10	2.10
Nos. 629-633 (5)	3.70	3.70
Nos. 640-644 (5)	4.50	4.50
Nos. 270-274 (5)	2.70	2.70
Nos. 451-455 (5)	3.05	3.05
Nos. 670-674 (5)	2.90	2.90
Nos. 592-596 (5)	2.70	2.70
Nos. 114-118 (5)	2.25	2.25
Nos. 562-566 (5)	2.50	2.50
Nos. 101-105 (5)	3.55	3.55
Nos. 490-494 (5)	2.30	2.30
Nos. 388-392 (5)	3.00	3.00
Nos. 414-418 (5)	3.10	3.10
Nos. 343-347 (5)	1.75	1.75
Set total (115) Stamps	79.00	78.05

Royal Wedding

Marriage of Prince Andrew and Sarah Ferguson
CD338

1986, July 23

Ascension	399-400
Bahamas	602-603
Barbados	687-688
Cayman Islands	560-561
Jamaica	629-630
Pitcairn Islands	275-276
St. Helena	460-461
St. Kitts	181-182
Seychelles	602-603
Zil Elwannyen Sesel	119-120
Solomon Islands	567-568
Tristan da Cunha	397-398
Zambia	348-349

Nos. 399-400 (2)	1.60	1.60
Nos. 602-603 (2)	2.75	2.75
Nos. 687-688 (2)	2.25	1.25
Nos. 560-561 (2)	1.50	2.15
Nos. 629-630 (2)	1.75	1.75
Nos. 275-276 (2)	2.40	2.40
Nos. 460-461 (2)	1.05	1.05
Nos. 181-182 (2)	1.50	1.50
Nos. 602-603 (2)	2.50	2.50
Nos. 119-120 (2)	2.30	2.30
Nos. 567-568 (2)	1.00	1.00
Nos. 397-398 (2)	1.40	1.40
Nos. 348-349 (2)	1.10	1.30
Set total (26) Stamps	23.10	22.95

Queen Elizabeth II, 60th Birthday

Queen Elizabeth II & Prince Philip, 1947 Wedding Portrait — CD339

Designs: Photographs tracing the life of Queen Elizabeth II.

1986

Anguilla	674-677
Antigua	925-928
Barbuda	783-786
Dominica	950-953
Gambia	611-614
Grenada	1371-1374
Grenada Grenadines	749-752
Lesotho	531-534
Maldive Islands	1172-1175
Sierra Leone	760-763
Uganda	495-498

Nos. 674-677 (4)	8.00	8.00
Nos. 925-928 (4)	6.75	6.75
Nos. 783-786 (4)	25.60	25.60
Nos. 950-953 (4)	7.25	7.25
Nos. 611-614 (4)	8.25	7.90
Nos. 1371-1374 (4)	6.80	6.80
Nos. 749-752 (4)	6.75	6.75
Nos. 531-534 (4)	5.50	5.50
Nos. 1172-1175 (4)	7.00	7.00
Nos. 760-763 (4)	6.30	6.30
Nos. 495-498 (4)	8.50	8.50
Set total (44) Stamps	96.70	96.35

Royal Wedding, 1986

CD340

Designs: Photographs of Prince Andrew and Sarah Ferguson during courtship, engagement and marriage.

1986

Antigua	939-942
Barbuda	809-812
Dominica	970-973
Gambia	635-638
Grenada	1385-1388
Grenada Grenadines	758-761
Lesotho	545-548
Maldive Islands	1181-1184
Sierra Leone	769-772
Uganda	510-513

Nos. 939-942 (4)	8.25	8.25
Nos. 809-812 (4)	15.90	15.80
Nos. 970-973 (4)	7.25	7.25
Nos. 635-638 (4)	8.55	8.55
Nos. 1385-1388 (4)	8.30	8.30
Nos. 758-761 (4)	9.00	9.00
Nos. 545-548 (4)	7.95	7.95
Nos. 1181-1184 (4)	10.20	10.20
Nos. 769-772 (4)	5.55	5.55
Nos. 510-513 (4)	9.50	10.25
Set total (40) Stamps	90.45	91.10

Lloyds of London, 300th Anniv.

CD341

Designs: 17th century aspects of Lloyds, representations of each country's individual connections with Lloyds and publicized disasters insured by the organization.

1986

Ascension	454-457
Bahamas	655-658
Barbados	731-734
Bermuda	541-544
Falkland Islands	481-484
Liberia	1101-1104
Malawi	534-537
Nevis	571-574
St. Helena	501-504
St. Lucia	923-926
Seychelles	649-652
Zil Elwannyen Sesel	146-149
Solomon Islands	627-630
South Georgia	131-134
Trinidad & Tobago	484-487
Tristan da Cunha	439-442
Vanuatu	485-488

Nos. 454-457 (4)	5.00	5.00
Nos. 655-658 (4)	8.90	4.95
Nos. 731-734 (4)	12.50	8.35
Nos. 541-544 (4)	8.25	5.60
Nos. 481-484 (4)	6.30	4.55
Nos. 1101-1104 (4)	4.25	4.25
Nos. 534-537 (4)	11.00	7.85
Nos. 571-574 (4)	8.35	8.35
Nos. 501-504 (4)	8.70	7.15
Nos. 923-926 (4)	9.40	9.40
Nos. 649-652 (4)	13.10	13.10
Nos. 146-149 (4)	11.25	11.25
Nos. 627-630 (4)	7.90	4.45
Nos. 131-134 (4)	6.30	3.70
Nos. 484-487 (4)	11.85	8.50
Nos. 439-442 (4)	7.60	7.60
Nos. 485-488 (4)	5.90	5.90
Set total (68) Stamps	146.55	119.95

Moon Landing, 20th Anniv.

CD342

Designs: Equipment, crew photographs, spacecraft, official emblems and report profiles created for the Apollo Missions. Two stamps in each set are square in format rather than like the stamp shown; see individual country listings for more information.

1989

Ascension	468-472
Bahamas	674-678
Belize	916-920
Kiribati	517-521
Liberia	1125-1129
Nevis	586-590
St. Kitts	248-252
Samoa	760-764
Seychelles	676-680
Zil Elwannyen Sesel	154-158
Solomon Islands	643-647
Vanuatu	507-511

Nos. 468-472 (5)	9.40	8.60
Nos. 674-678 (5)	23.00	19.70
Nos. 916-920 (5)	27.40	23.50
Nos. 517-521 (5)	12.50	12.50
Nos. 1125-1129 (5)	8.50	8.50
Nos. 586-590 (5)	7.50	7.50
Nos. 248-252 (5)	8.00	8.00
Nos. 760-764 (5)	9.60	9.05
Nos. 676-680 (5)	16.65	16.65
Nos. 154-158 (5)	26.85	26.85

Nos. 643-647 (5)	12.75	11.60
Nos. 507-511 (5)	9.90	9.90
Set total (60) Stamps	172.05	162.35

Queen Mother, 90th Birthday

CD343

CD344

Designs: Portraits of Queen Elizabeth, the Queen Mother. See individual country listings for more information.

1990

Ascension....................491-492
Bahamas....................698-699
Barbados....................782-783
British Antarctic Territory..........170-171
British Indian Ocean Territory........106-107
Cayman Islands....................622-623
Falkland Islands....................524-525
Kenya....................527-528
Kiribati....................555-556
Liberia....................1145-1146
Pitcairn Islands....................336-337
St. Helena....................532-533
St. Lucia....................969-970
Seychelles....................710-711
Zil Elwannyen Sesel....................171-172
Solomon Islands....................671-672
South Georgia....................143-144
Swaziland....................565-566
Tristan da Cunha....................480-481

Nos. 491-492 (2)	4.75	5.65
Nos. 698-699 (2)	5.65	5.65
Nos. 782-783 (2)	4.00	3.70
Nos. 170-171 (2)	6.75	6.75
Nos. 106-107 (2)	20.75	21.25
Nos. 622-623 (2)	5.10	*6.75*
Nos. 524-525 (2)	5.25	5.25
Nos. 527-528 (2)	7.00	7.00
Nos. 555-556 (2)	5.60	5.60
Nos. 1145-1146 (2)	3.25	3.25
Nos. 336-337 (2)	4.25	4.25
Nos. 532-533 (2)	5.25	5.25
Nos. 969-970 (2)	5.25	5.25
Nos. 710-711 (2)	6.60	6.60
Nos. 171-172 (2)	8.25	8.25
Nos. 671-672 (2)	6.50	*6.40*
Nos. 143-144 (2)	5.75	5.75
Nos. 565-566 (2)	4.35	4.35
Nos. 480-481 (2)	5.60	5.60
Set total (38) Stamps	119.90	122.55

Queen Elizabeth II, 65th Birthday, and Prince Philip, 70th Birthday

CD345

CD346

Designs: Portraits of Queen Elizabeth II and Prince Philip differ for each country. Printed in sheets of 10 + 5 labels (3 different) between. Stamps alternate, producing 5 different triptychs.

1991

Ascension....................506a
Bahamas....................731a
Belize....................970a
Bermuda....................618a
Kiribati....................572a
Mauritius....................734a
Pitcairn Islands....................349a
St. Helena....................555a
St. Kitts....................319a
Samoa....................791a
Seychelles....................724a
Zil Elwannyen Sesel....................178a
Solomon Islands....................689a
South Georgia....................150a
Swaziland....................587a
Vanuatu....................541a

No. 506a (1)	3.50	3.75
No. 731a (1)	4.00	4.00
No. 970a (1)	3.75	3.75
No. 618a (1)	4.00	4.00
No. 572a (1)	4.00	4.00
No. 734a (1)	3.75	3.75
No. 349a (1)	3.25	3.25
No. 555a (1)	2.75	2.75
No. 319a (1)	3.00	3.00
No. 791a (1)	4.25	4.25
No. 724a (1)	5.00	5.00
No. 178a (1)	6.50	6.50
No. 689a (1)	4.50	4.50
No. 150a (1)	7.00	7.00
No. 587a (1)	4.25	4.25
No. 541a (1)	2.50	2.50
Set total (16) Stamps	66.00	66.25

Royal Family Birthday, Anniversary

CD347

Queen Elizabeth II, 65th birthday, Charles and Diana, 10th wedding anniversary: Various photographs of Queen Elizabeth II, Prince Philip, Prince Charles, Princess Diana and their sons William and Henry.

1991

Antigua....................1446-1455
Barbuda....................1229-1238
Dominica....................1328-1337
Gambia....................1080-1089
Grenada....................2006-2015
Grenada Grenadines....................1331-1340
Guyana....................2440-2451
Lesotho....................871-875
Maldive Islands....................1533-1542
Nevis....................666-675
St. Vincent....................1485-1494
St. Vincent Grenadines....................769-778
Sierra Leone....................1387-1396
Turks & Caicos Islands....................913-922
Uganda....................918-927

Nos. 1446-1455 (10)	21.95	20.30
Nos. 1229-1238 (10)	146.25	139.90
Nos. 1328-1337 (10)	30.20	30.20
Nos. 1080-1089 (10)	24.65	24.40
Nos. 2006-2015 (10)	25.45	22.10
Nos. 1331-1340 (10)	23.85	23.35
Nos. 2440-2451 (12)	21.40	21.15
Nos. 871-875 (5)	13.55	13.55
Nos. 1533-1542 (10)	29.60	29.60
Nos. 666-675 (10)	25.65	25.65
Nos. 1485-1494 (10)	26.75	25.90
Nos. 769-778 (10)	25.40	25.40
Nos. 1387-1396 (10)	26.55	26.55
Nos. 913-922 (10)	31.65	30.00
Nos. 918-927 (10)	26.60	26.60
Set total (147) Stamps	499.50	484.65

Queen Elizabeth II's Accession to the Throne, 40th Anniv.

CD348

Various photographs of Queen Elizabeth II with local Scenes.

1992

Antigua....................1513-1518
Barbuda....................1306-1311
Dominica....................1414-1419
Gambia....................1172-1177
Grenada....................2047-2052
Grenada Grenadines....................1368-1373
Lesotho....................881-885
Maldive Islands....................1637-1642
Nevis....................702-707
St. Vincent....................1582-1587
St. Vincent Grenadines....................829-834
Sierra Leone....................1482-1487
Turks and Caicos Islands....................978-987
Uganda....................990-995
Virgin Islands....................742-746

Nos. 1513-1518 (6)	16.00	14.10
Nos. 1306-1311 (6)	144.50	98.75
Nos. 1414-1419 (6)	12.50	12.50
Nos. 1172-1177 (6)	16.60	16.35
Nos. 2047-2052 (6)	15.95	15.95
Nos. 1368-1373 (6)	17.00	15.35
Nos. 881-885 (5)	11.90	11.90
Nos. 1637-1642 (6)	17.55	17.55
Nos. 702-707 (6)	13.80	13.80
Nos. 1582-1587 (6)	14.40	14.40
Nos. 829-834 (6)	19.65	19.65
Nos. 1482-1487 (6)	22.50	22.50
Nos. 913-922 (10)	31.65	30.00
Nos. 990-995 (6)	19.50	19.50
Nos. 742-746 (5)	15.50	15.50
Set total (92) Stamps	389.00	337.80

CD349

1992

Ascension....................531-535
Bahamas....................744-748
Bermuda....................623-627
British Indian Ocean Territory........119-123
Cayman Islands....................648-652
Falkland Islands....................549-553
Gibraltar....................605-609
Hong Kong....................619-623
Kenya....................563-567
Kiribati....................582-586
Pitcairn Islands....................362-366
St. Helena....................570-574
St. Kitts....................332-336
Samoa....................805-809
Seychelles....................734-738
Zil Elwannyen Sesel....................183-187
Solomon Islands....................708-712
South Georgia....................157-161
Tristan da Cunha....................508-512
Vanuatu....................555-559
Zambia....................561-565

Nos. 531-535 (5)	6.35	6.35
Nos. 744-748 (5)	6.90	4.70
Nos. 623-627 (5)	8.20	7.30
Nos. 119-123 (5)	24.75	*21.00*
Nos. 648-652 (5)	7.60	7.10
Nos. 549-553 (5)	6.80	8.20
Nos. 605-609 (5)	5.15	*5.50*
Nos. 619-623 (5)	5.65	2.65
Nos. 563-567 (5)	9.10	9.10
Nos. 582-586 (5)	3.85	3.85
Nos. 362-366 (5)	5.35	5.35
Nos. 570-574 (5)	5.70	5.70
Nos. 332-336 (5)	6.60	5.50
Nos. 805-809 (5)	8.10	6.15
Nos. 734-738 (5)	10.80	10.80
Nos. 183-187 (5)	9.40	9.40
Nos. 708-712 (5)	7.95	7.30
Nos. 157-161 (5)	5.85	5.75
Nos. 508-512 (5)	8.75	8.30
Nos. 555-559 (5)	3.65	3.65
Nos. 561-565 (5)	5.60	5.60
Set total (105) Stamps	162.10	149.25

Royal Air Force, 75th Anniversary

CD350

1993

Ascension....................557-561
Bahamas....................771-775
Barbados....................842-846
Belize....................1003-1008
Bermuda....................648-651
British Indian Ocean Territory........136-140
Falkland Is.....................573-577
Fiji....................687-691
Montserrat....................830-834
St. Kitts....................351-355

Nos. 557-561 (5)	16.70	14.85
Nos. 771-775 (5)	26.00	22.20
Nos. 842-846 (5)	13.65	12.35
Nos. 1003-1008 (6)	19.40	18.70
Nos. 648-651 (4)	10.50	9.95
Nos. 136-140 (5)	17.50	17.50
Nos. 573-577 (5)	11.25	11.25
Nos. 687-691 (5)	18.95	18.95
Nos. 830-834 (5)	14.35	14.35
Nos. 351-355 (5)	24.45	23.95
Set total (50) Stamps	172.75	164.05

Royal Air Force, 80th Anniv.

Design CD350 Re-inscribed

1998

Ascension....................697-701
Bahamas....................907-911
British Indian Ocean Terr....................198-202
Cayman Islands....................754-758
Fiji....................814-818
Gibraltar....................755-759
Samoa....................957-961
Turks & Caicos Islands....................1258-1265
Tuvalu....................763-767
Virgin Islands....................879-883

Nos. 697-701 (5)	17.35	17.35
Nos. 907-911 (5)	14.25	13.55
Nos. 136-140 (5)	17.50	17.50
Nos. 754-758 (5)	15.75	15.75
Nos. 814-818 (5)	15.50	15.50
Nos. 755-759 (5)	9.70	9.70
Nos. 957-961 (5)	16.70	15.90
Nos. 1258-1265 (2)	32.00	32.00
Nos. 763-767 (5)	9.75	9.75
Nos. 879-883 (5)	17.00	17.00
Set total (47) Stamps	165.50	164.00

End of World War II, 50th Anniv.

CD351

CD352

1995

Ascension....................613-617
Bahamas....................824-828
Barbados....................891-895
Belize....................1047-1050
British Indian Ocean Territory........163-167
Cayman Islands....................704-708
Falkland Islands....................634-638
Fiji....................720-724
Kiribati....................662-668
Liberia....................1175-1179
Mauritius....................803-805
St. Helena....................646-654
St. Kitts....................389-393
St. Lucia....................1018-1022
Samoa....................890-894
Solomon Islands....................799-803
South Georgia....................198-200
Tristan da Cunha....................562-566

Nos. 613-617 (5)	21.50	21.50
Nos. 824-828 (5)	22.00	18.70
Nos. 891-895 (5)	14.20	11.90
Nos. 1047-1050 (4)	7.45	6.75
Nos. 163-167 (5)	16.25	16.25

Nos. 704-708 (5)	18.15	14.45
Nos. 634-638 (5)	17.90	17.40
Nos. 720-724 (5)	21.35	21.35
Nos. 662-668 (7)	16.30	16.30
Nos. 1175-1179 (5)	15.25	11.15
Nos. 803-805 (3)	7.50	7.50
Nos. 646-654 (9)	26.10	26.10
Nos. 389-393 (5)	13.60	13.60
Nos. 1018-1022 (5)	14.25	11.15
Nos. 890-894 (5)	14.25	13.50
Nos. 799-803 (5)	17.50	17.50
Nos. 198-200 (3)	14.00	14.00
Nos. 562-566 (5)	20.10	20.10
Set total (91) Stamps	297.65	279.20

UN, 50th Anniv.

CD353

1995

Bahamas	839-842
Barbados	901-904
Belize	1055-1058
Jamaica	847-851
Liberia	1187-1190
Mauritius	813-816
Pitcairn Islands	436-439
St. Kitts	398-401
St. Lucia	1023-1026
Samoa	900-903
Tristan da Cunha	568-571
Virgin Islands	807-810

Nos. 839-842 (4)	8.00	7.05
Nos. 901-904 (4)	7.00	5.75
Nos. 1055-1058 (4)	5.70	5.60
Nos. 847-851 (5)	6.50	5.95
Nos. 1187-1190 (4)	9.65	9.65
Nos. 813-816 (4)	3.90	3.90
Nos. 436-439 (4)	8.15	8.15
Nos. 398-401 (4)	6.15	6.15
Nos. 1023-1026 (4)	7.50	7.25
Nos. 900-903 (4)	9.35	8.20
Nos. 568-571 (4)	13.50	13.50
Nos. 807-810 (4)	9.45	9.45
Set total (49) Stamps	94.85	90.60

Queen Elizabeth, 70th Birthday

CD354

1996

Ascension	632-635
British Antarctic Territory	240-243
British Indian Ocean Territory	176-180
Falkland Islands	653-657
Pitcairn Islands	446-449
St. Helena	672-676
Samoa	912-916
Tokelau	223-227
Tristan da Cunha	576-579
Virgin Islands	824-828

Nos. 632-635 (4)	5.90	5.90
Nos. 240-243 (4)	10.50	8.90
Nos. 176-180 (5)	11.50	11.50
Nos. 653-657 (5)	14.35	11.90
Nos. 446-449 (4)	8.60	8.60
Nos. 672-676 (5)	12.70	12.70
Nos. 912-916 (5)	11.50	11.50
Nos. 223-227 (5)	11.35	11.35
Nos. 576-579 (4)	8.35	8.35
Nos. 824-828 (5)	11.80	11.80
Set total (46) Stamps	106.55	102.50

Diana, Princess of Wales (1961-97)

CD355

1998

Ascension	696
Bahamas	901A-902
Barbados	950
Belize	1091
Bermuda	753
Botswana	659-663
British Antarctic Territory	258
British Indian Ocean Terr.	197
Cayman Islands	752A-753
Falkland Islands	694
Fiji	819-820
Gibraltar	754
Kiribati	719A-720
Namibia	909
Niue	706
Norfolk Island	644-645
Papua New Guinea	937
Pitcairn Islands	487
St. Helena	711
St. Kitts	437A-438
Samoa	955A-956
Seycelles	802
Solomon Islands	866-867
South Georgia	220
Tokelau	252B-253
Tonga	980
Niuafo'ou	201
Tristan da Cunha	618
Tuvalu	762
Vanuatu	718A-719
Virgin Islands	878

No. 696 (1)	5.50	5.50
Nos. 901A-902 (2)	5.30	5.30
No. 950 (1)	5.00	5.00
No. 1091 (1)	5.50	5.50
No. 753 (1)	5.50	5.50
Nos. 659-663 (5)	10.25	10.10
No. 258 (1)	6.25	6.25
No. 197 (1)	6.50	6.50
Nos. 752A-753 (3)	7.75	7.75
No. 694 (1)	4.75	4.75
Nos. 819-820 (2)	6.00	6.00
No. 754 (1)	4.75	4.75
Nos. 719A-720 (2)	4.85	4.85
No. 909 (1)	1.90	1.90
No. 706 (1)	5.50	5.50
Nos. 644-645 (2)	5.25	5.25
No. 937 (1)	6.50	6.50
No. 487 (1)	4.75	4.75
No. 711 (1)	4.25	4.25
Nos. 437A-438 (2)	5.15	5.15
Nos. 955A-956 (2)	7.00	7.00
No. 802 (1)	6.25	6.25
Nos. 866-867 (2)	6.90	6.90
No. 220 (1)	5.25	5.25
Nos. 252B-253 (2)	6.75	6.75
No. 980 (1)	5.75	5.75
No. 201 (1)	7.75	7.75
No. 618 (1)	5.00	5.00
No. 762 (1)	4.00	4.00
Nos. 718A-719 (2)	8.00	8.00
No. 878 (1)	5.50	5.50
Set total (46) Stamps	179.35	179.20

Wedding of Prince Edward and Sophie Rhys-Jones

CD356

1999

Ascension	729-730
Cayman Islands	775-776
Falkland Islands	729-730
Pitcairn Islands	505-506
St. Helena	733-734
Samoa	971-972
Tristan da Cunha	636-637
Virgin Islands	908-909

Nos. 729-730 (2)	5.90	5.90
Nos. 775-776 (2)	5.50	5.50
Nos. 729-730 (2)	15.00	15.00
Nos. 505-506 (2)	7.00	7.00
Nos. 733-734 (2)	5.00	5.00
Nos. 971-972 (2)	5.00	5.00
Nos. 636-637 (2)	7.50	7.50
Nos. 908-909 (2)	8.30	8.30
Set total (16) Stamps	59.20	59.20

1st Manned Moon Landing, 30th Anniv.

CD357

1999

Ascension	731-735
Bahamas	942-946
Barbados	967-971
Bermuda	778
Cayman Islands	777-781
Fiji	853-857
Jamaica	889-893
Kirbati	746-750
Nauru	465-469
St. Kitts	460-464
Samoa	973-977
Solomon Islands	875-879
Tuvalu	800-804
Virgin Islands	910-914

Nos. 731-735 (5)	13.90	13.90
Nos. 942-946 (5)	14.10	14.10
Nos. 967-971 (5)	8.65	7.75
No. 778 (1)	8.00	8.00
Nos. 777-781 (5)	10.30	10.30
Nos. 853-857 (5)	10.40	10.40
Nos. 889-893 (5)	10.20	10.00
Nos. 746-750 (5)	8.85	8.85
Nos. 465-469 (5)	8.90	10.15
Nos. 460-464 (5)	12.00	12.00
Nos. 973-977 (5)	13.45	13.30
Nos. 875-879 (5)	10.00	9.85
Nos. 800-804 (5)	7.45	7.45
Nos. 910-914 (5)	15.00	15.00
Set total (66) Stamps	151.20	151.05

Queen Mother's Century

CD358

1999

Ascension	736-740
Bahamas	951-955
Cayman Islands	782-786
Falkland Islands	734-738
Fiji	858-862
Norfolk Island	688-692
St. Helena	740-744
Samoa	978-982
Solomon Islands	880-884
South Georgia	231-235
Tristan da Cunha	638-642
Tuvalu	805-809

Nos. 736-740 (5)	17.00	17.00
Nos. 951-955 (5)	14.00	12.90
Nos. 782-786 (5)	9.15	9.15
Nos. 734-738 (5)	30.75	27.75
Nos. 858-862 (5)	15.00	15.00
Nos. 688-692 (5)	10.30	10.30
Nos. 740-744 (5)	16.15	16.15
Nos. 978-982 (5)	12.50	12.10
Nos. 880-884 (5)	10.00	9.45
Nos. 231-235 (5)	30.25	29.75
Nos. 638-642 (5)	18.00	18.00
Nos. 805-809 (5)	8.65	8.65
Set total (60) Stamps	191.75	186.20

Prince William, 18th Birthday

CD359

2000

Ascension	755-759
Cayman Islands	797-801
Falkland Islands	762-766
Fiji	889-893
South Georgia	257-261
Tristan da Cunha	664-668
Virgin Islands	925-929

Nos. 755-759 (5)	17.75	17.75
Nos. 797-801 (5)	13.05	12.75
Nos. 762-766 (5)	27.15	23.75
Nos. 889-893 (5)	14.00	14.00
Nos. 257-261 (5)	29.00	29.00
Nos. 664-668 (5)	21.50	21.50
Nos. 925-929 (5)	14.75	14.75
Set total (35) Stamps	137.20	133.50

Reign of Queen Elizabeth II, 50th Anniv.

CD360

2002

Ascension	790-794
Bahamas	1033-1037
Barbados	1019-1023
Belize	1152-1156
Bermuda	822-826
British Antarctic Territory	307-311
British Indian Ocean Territory	239-243
Cayman Islands	844-848
Falkland Islands	804-808
Gibraltar	896-900
Jamaica	952-956
Nauru	491-495
Norfolk Island	758-762
Papua New Guinea	1019-1023
Pitcairn Islands	552
St. Helena	788-792
St. Lucia	1146-1150
Solomon Islands	931-935
South Georgia	274-278
Swaziland	706-710
Tokelau	302-306
Tonga	1059
Niuafo'ou	239
Tristan da Cunha	706-710
Virgin Islands	967-971

Nos. 790-794 (5)	16.25	16.25
Nos. 1033-1037 (5)	15.75	15.75
Nos. 1019-1023 (5)	13.15	13.15
Nos. 1152-1156 (5)	15.50	15.15
Nos. 822-826 (5)	18.50	18.50
Nos. 307-311 (5)	25.00	25.00
Nos. 239-243 (5)	22.00	22.00
Nos. 844-848 (5)	14.25	14.25
Nos. 804-808 (5)	23.50	22.50
Nos. 896-900 (5)	6.65	6.65
Nos. 952-956 (5)	18.25	18.25
Nos. 491-495 (5)	18.75	18.75
Nos. 758-762 (5)	19.50	19.50
Nos. 1019-1023 (5)	14.50	14.50
No. 552 (1)	9.25	9.25
Nos. 788-792 (5)	19.75	19.75
Nos. 1146-1150 (5)	12.25	12.25
Nos. 931-935 (5)	16.00	16.00
Nos. 274-278 (5)	28.50	28.50
Nos. 706-710 (5)	12.75	12.75
Nos. 302-306 (5)	17.00	17.00
No. 1059 (1)	8.00	8.00
No. 239 (1)	7.00	7.00
Nos. 706-710 (5)	18.50	18.50
Nos. 967-971 (5)	19.00	19.00
Set total (113) Stamps	409.55	408.20

Queen Mother Elizabeth (1900-2002)

CD361

2002

Ascension	799-801
Bahamas	1044-1046
Bermuda	834-836
British Antarctic Territory	312-314
British Indian Ocean Territory	245-247
Cayman Islands	857-861
Falkland Islands	812-816
Nauru	499-501
Pitcairn Islands	561-565
St. Helena	808-812
St. Lucia	1155-1159
Seychelles	830
Solomon Islands	945-947
South Georgia	281-285
Tokelau	312-314
Tristan da Cunha	715-717
Virgin Islands	979-983

Nos. 799-801 (3)	9.75	9.75
Nos. 1044-1046 (3)	9.35	9.35
Nos. 834-836 (3)	12.50	12.50
Nos. 312-314 (3)	19.25	19.25
Nos. 245-247 (3)	19.50	19.50
Nos. 857-861 (5)	15.00	15.00
Nos. 812-816 (5)	31.50	31.50
Nos. 499-501 (3)	16.00	16.00
Nos. 561-565 (5)	15.25	15.25
Nos. 808-812 (5)	12.00	12.00
Nos. 1155-1159 (5)	13.00	13.00
No. 830 (1)	6.50	6.50
Nos. 945-947 (3)	11.00	11.00
Nos. 281-285 (5)	20.00	20.00
Nos. 312-314 (3)	14.25	13.75
Nos. 715-717 (3)	16.25	16.25
Nos. 979-983 (5)	26.50	26.50
Set total (63) Stamps	267.60	267.10

Head of Queen Elizabeth II

CD362

2003

Ascension	822
Bermuda	865
British Antarctic Territory	322
British Indian Ocean Territory	261
Cayman Islands	878
Falkland Islands	828
St. Helena	820
South Georgia	294
Tristan da Cunha	731
Virgin Islands	1003

No. 822 (1)	13.50	13.50
No. 865 (1)	55.00	55.00
No. 322 (1)	10.00	10.00
No. 261 (1)	12.50	12.50
No. 878 (1)	17.00	17.00
No. 828 (1)	10.00	10.00
No. 820 (1)	9.00	9.00
No. 294 (1)	9.00	9.00
No. 731 (1)	10.00	10.00
No. 1003 (1)	10.00	10.00
Set total (10) Stamps	156.00	156.00

Coronation of Queen Elizabeth II, 50th Anniv.

CD363

2003

Ascension	823-825
Bahamas	1073-1075
Bermuda	866-868
British Antarctic Territory	323-325
British Indian Ocean Territory	262-264
Cayman Islands	879-881
Jamaica	970-972
Kiribati	825-827
Pitcairn Islands	577-581
St. Helena	821-823
St. Lucia	1171-1173
Tokelau	320-322
Tristan da Cunha	732-734
Virgin Islands	1004-1006

Nos. 823-825 (3)	13.50	13.50
Nos. 1073-1075 (3)	13.00	13.00
Nos. 866-868 (3)	14.25	14.25
Nos. 323-325 (3)	26.00	26.00
Nos. 262-264 (3)	31.00	31.00
Nos. 879-881 (3)	20.25	20.25
Nos. 970-972 (3)	11.75	11.75
Nos. 825-827 (3)	13.50	13.50
Nos. 577-581 (5)	14.40	14.40
Nos. 821-823 (3)	7.25	7.25
Nos. 1171-1173 (3)	8.75	8.75
Nos. 320-322 (3)	20.00	20.00
Nos. 732-734 (3)	16.75	16.75
Nos. 1004-1006 (3)	25.00	25.00
Set total (44) Stamps	235.40	235.40

Prince William, 21st Birthday

CD364

2003

Ascension	826
British Indian Ocean Territory	265
Cayman Islands	882-884
Falkland Islands	829
South Georgia	295
Tokelau	323
Tristan da Cunha	735
Virgin Islands	1007-1009

No. 826 (1)	7.50	7.50
No. 265 (1)	9.00	9.00
Nos. 882-884 (3)	7.65	7.65
No. 829 (1)	14.50	14.50
No. 295 (1)	9.00	9.00
No. 323 (1)	7.25	7.25
No. 735 (1)	6.00	6.00
Nos. 1007-1009 (3)	10.00	10.00
Set total (12) Stamps	70.90	70.90

Scott International Album

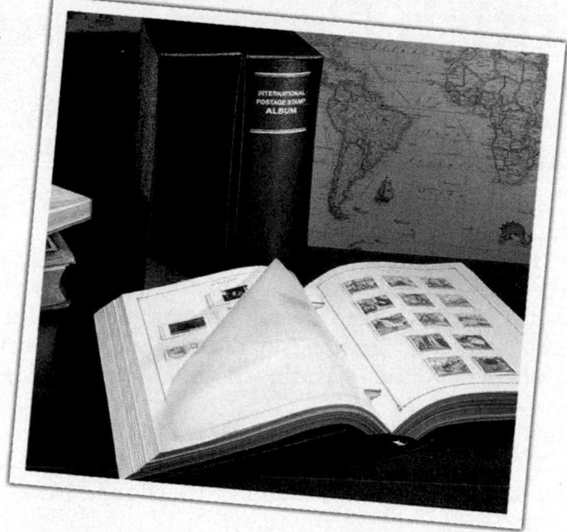

Prices have never been so low on selected album parts. It is a wonderful opportunity to collect internationally. The Ultimate Album for Worldwide Collectors! Pick a period in history and embark on a philatelic adventure. With the International Album, the whole world is divided chronologically into more than 50 parts. From the classic era of philately to present day, the International is one of the broadest and far reaching worldwide albums available. ***Binders are sold separately.***

- More than 16,000 pages with spaces for over 220,000 stamps.
- Pages printed on 2 sides.

Item	*Part*	*Binder*		*Retail*	*AA**
801A140	1A1	(1840-1940)	Regular	$150.00	$120.00
801A240	1A2	(1840-1940)	Regular	$150.00	$120.00
801B140	1B1	(1840-1940)	Regular	$150.00	$120.00
801B240	1B2	(1840-1940)	Regular	$150.00	$120.00
802P149	2A	(1940-49)	Regular	$150.00	$120.00
802P249	2B	(1940-49)	Regular	$150.00	$120.00
803P155	3A	(1949-55)	Regular	$150.00	$120.00
803P255	3B	(1949-55)	Regular	$150.00	$120.00
804P159	4A	(1956-60)	Regular	$150.00	$120.00
804P259	4B	(1956-60)	Regular	$150.00	$120.00
805P063	5	(1960-63)	Jumbo	$150.00	$120.00
805P165	5A	(1963-65)	Jumbo	$150.00	$120.00
806P066	6	(1965-66)	Jumbo	$150.00	$120.00
806P168	6A	(1966-68)	Jumbo	$150.00	$120.00
807P171	7A	(1968-71)	Jumbo	$150.00	$120.00
807P271	7B	(1968-71)	Jumbo	$150.00	$120.00
808P173	8A	(1971-73)	Regular	$150.00	$120.00
808P273	8B	(1971-73)	Regular	$150.00	$120.00
809P074	9	(1973-74)	Regular	$150.00	$120.00
810P075	10	(1974-75)	Jumbo	$150.00	$120.00
811P076	11	(1975-76)	Jumbo	$150.00	$120.00
812P077	12	(1976-77)	Jumbo	$150.00	$120.00
813P078	13	(1977-78)	Jumbo	$150.00	$120.00
814P078	14	(1978)	Regular	$150.00	$120.00
815P079	15	(1979)	Regular	$150.00	$120.00
816P080	16	(1980)	Jumbo	$150.00	$120.00
817P081	17	(1981)	Regular	$150.00	$120.00
818P082	18	(1982)	Regular	$150.00	$120.00
819P083	19	(1983)	Regular	$150.00	$120.00
820P084	20	(1984)	Jumbo	$150.00	$120.00
821P085	21	(1985)	Jumbo	$150.00	$120.00
822P186	22A	(1986)	Regular	**$60.00**	**$44.00**
822P286	22B	(1986)	Regular	$150.00	$120.00
823P187	23A	(1987)	Regular	**$60.00**	**$44.00**
823P287	23B	(1987)	Regular	$150.00	$120.00
824P188	24A	(1988)	Regular	**$60.00**	**$44.00**
824P288	24B	(1988)	Regular	**$60.00**	**$44.00**
825P189	25A	(1989)	Regular	**$60.00**	**$44.00**
825P289	25B	(1989)	Regular	**$60.00**	**$44.00**
826P190	26A	(1990)	Regular	$150.00	$120.00
826P290	26B	(1990)	Regular	**$60.00**	**$44.00**
827P191	27A	(1991)	Regular	**$60.00**	**$44.00**
827P291	27B	(1991)	Regular	**$60.00**	**$44.00**
828P192	28A	(1992)	Regular	**$60.00**	**$44.00**
828P292	28B	(1992)	Regular	**$60.00**	**$44.00**
829P193	29A	(1993)	Regular	**$60.00**	**$44.00**
829P293	29B	(1993)	Regular	**$60.00**	**$44.00**
830P194	30A	(1994)	Regular	**$60.00**	**$44.00**
830P294	30B	(1994)	Regular	**$60.00**	**$44.00**
831P195	31A	(1995)	Regular	**$60.00**	**$44.00**
831P295	31B	(1995)	Regular	**$60.00**	**$44.00**
832P196	32A	(1996)	Regular	**$60.00**	**$44.00**
832P296	32B	(1996)	Regular	**$60.00**	**$44.00**
833P197	33A	(1997)	Regular	**$60.00**	**$44.00**
833P297	33B	(1997)	Regular	**$60.00**	**$44.00**
834P198	34A	(1998)	Regular	$150.00	$120.00
834P298	34B	(1998)	Regular	**$60.00**	**$44.00**
835P199	35A	(1999)	Regular	$150.00	$120.00
835P299	35B	(1999)	Regular	$150.00	$120.00
836P100	36A	(2000)	Regular	$150.00	$120.00
836P200	36B	(2000)	Regular	$150.00	$120.00
837P101	37A	(2001)	Regular	$150.00	$120.00
837P201	37B	(2001)	Regular	$150.00	$120.00
838P102	38A	(2002)	Regular	**$60.00**	**$44.00**
838P202	38B	(2002)	Regular	**$60.00**	**$44.00**
839P103	39A	(2003)	Regular	**$60.00**	**$44.00**
839P203	39B	(2003)	Regular	**$60.00**	**$44.00**
840P104	40A	(2004)	Regular	**$60.00**	**$44.00**
840P204	40B	(2004)	Regular	**$60.00**	**$44.00**
841P105	41A	(2005)	Regular	**$60.00**	**$44.00**
841P205	41B	(2005)	Regular	**$60.00**	**$44.00**
842P106	42A	(2006)	Regular	$135.00	$99.99
842P206	42B	(2006)	Regular	$135.00	$99.99
843P107	43A	(2007)	Regular	$99.99	$72.50
843P207	43B	(2007)	Regular	$99.99	$72.50
844P108	44A	(2008)	Jumbo	$135.00	$99.99
844P208	44B	(2008)	Jumbo	$135.00	$99.99
845P109	45A	(2009)	Jumbo	$135.00	$99.99
845P209	45B	(2009)	Jumbo	$135.00	$99.99
846P110	46A	(2010)	Regular	$135.00	$99.99
846P210	46B	(2010)	Regular	$135.00	$99.99
847P111	47A	(2011)	Regular	$135.00	$99.99
847P211	47B	(2011)	Regular	$135.00	$99.99
848P112	48A	(2012)	Regular	$135.00	$99.99
848P212	48B	(2012)	Regular	$135.00	$99.99
849P113	49A	(2013)	Regular	$135.00	$99.99
849P213	49B	(2013)	Regular	$135.00	$99.99
850P114	50A	(2014)	Regular	$135.00	$99.99
850P214	50B	(2014)	Regular	$135.00	$99.99
800PC72	People's Republic of China			$49.99	$39.99
800BOH	Bosnia & Herzegovina 1879-2007			$49.99	$39.99

INTERNATIONAL SERIES BINDERS AND SLIPCASES

Attractive, blue two-post binder is available in two sizes. Features distinctive silver embossed spine. **Binder will hold International pages only.** Labels available for all parts. For a complete list see AmosAdvantage.com

Item		*Retail*	*AA**
800B001	Regular Binder Holds 300 pages	$52.99	$40.99
800B002	Jumbo Binder Holds 400 pages.	$52.99	$40.99
800BC01	Regular Binder Slipcase	$32.99	$26.99
800BC02	Jumbo Binder Slipcase	$32.99	$26.99
8__LB01	International Label(s)	$2.29	$1.69

Ordering Information: *AA prices apply to paid subscribers of Amos Media publications, or orders placed online. Prices, terms and product availability subject to change. Taxes will apply in CA, OH & IL.
Shipping & Handling: United States: Orders under $10 are only $3.99 - 10% of order total. Minimum charge $7.99 Maximum Charge $45.00. **Canada:** 20% of order total. Minimum charge $19.99 Maximum charge $200.00. **Foreign** orders are shipped via FedExl Intl. or USPS and billed actual freight.

AMOS ADVANTAGE

Call **1-800-572-6885**

Outside U.S. & Canada Call: **(937) 498-0800**

Visit **AmosAdvantage.com**

P.O. Box 4129, Sidney, Ohio 45365-4129

British Commonwealth of Nations

Dominions, Colonies, Territories, Offices and Independent Members

Comprising stamps of the British Commonwealth and associated nations.

A strict observance of technicalities would bar some or all of the stamps listed under Burma, Ireland, Kuwait, Nepal, New Republic, Orange Free State, Samoa, South Africa, South-West Africa, Stellaland, Sudan, Swaziland, the two Transvaal Republics and others but these are included for the convenience of collectors.

1. Great Britain

Great Britain: Including England, Scotland, Wales and Northern Ireland.

2. The Dominions, Present and Past

AUSTRALIA

The Commonwealth of Australia was proclaimed on January 1, 1901. It consists of six former colonies as follows:

New South Wales
Victoria
Queensland
Tasmania
South Australia
Western Australia

The following islands and territories are, or have been, administered by Australia: Australian Antarctic Territory, Christmas Island, Cocos (Keeling) Islands, Nauru, New Guinea, Norfolk Island, Papua.

CANADA

The Dominion of Canada was created by the British North America Act in 1867. The following provinces were former sepa- rate colonies and issued postage stamps:

British Columbia and Vancouver Island
Newfoundland
New Brunswick
Nova Scotia
Prince Edward Island

FIJI

The colony of Fiji became an independent nation with dominion status on Oct. 10, 1970.

GHANA

This state came into existence Mar. 6, 1957, with dominion status. It consists of the former colony of the Gold Coast and the Trusteeship Territory of Togoland. Ghana became a republic July 1, 1960.

INDIA

The Republic of India was inaugurated on January 26, 1950. It succeeded the Dominion of India which was proclaimed August 15, 1947, when the former Empire of India was divided into Pakistan and the Union of India. The Republic is composed of about 40 predominantly Hindu states of three classes: governor's provinces, chief commissioner's provinces and princely states. India also has various territories, such as the Andaman and Nicobar Islands.

The old Empire of India was a federation of British India and the native states. The more important princely states were autonomous. Of the more than 700 Indian states, these 43 are familiar names to philatelists because of their postage stamps.

CONVENTION STATES

Chamba
Faridkot
Gwalior
Jhind
Nabha
Patiala

FEUDATORY STATES

Alwar
Bahawalpur
Bamra
Barwani
Bhopal
Bhor
Bijawar
Bundi
Bussahir
Charkhari
Cochin
Dhar
Dungarpur
Duttia
Faridkot (1879-85)
Hyderabad
Idar
Indore
Jaipur
Jammu
Jammu and Kashmir
Jasdan
Jhalawar
Jhind (1875-76)
Kashmir
Kishangarh
Kotah
Las Bela
Morvi
Nandgaon
Nowanuggur
Orchha
Poonch
Rajasthan
Rajpeepla
Sirmur
Soruth
Tonk
Travancore
Wadhwan

NEW ZEALAND

Became a dominion on September 26, 1907. The following islands and territories are, or have been, administered by New Zealand:

Aitutaki
Cook Islands (Rarotonga)
Niue
Penrhyn
Ross Dependency
Samoa (Western Samoa)
Tokelau Islands

PAKISTAN

The Republic of Pakistan was proclaimed March 23, 1956. It succeeded the Dominion which was proclaimed August 15, 1947. It is made up of all or part of several Moslem provinces and various districts of the former Empire of India, including Bahawalpur and Las Bela. Pakistan withdrew from the Commonwealth in 1972.

SOUTH AFRICA

Under the terms of the South African Act (1909) the self-governing colonies of Cape of Good Hope, Natal, Orange River Colony and Transvaal united on May 31, 1910, to form the Union of South Africa. It became an independent republic May 3, 1961.

Under the terms of the Treaty of Versailles, South-West Africa, formerly German South-West Africa, was mandated to the Union of South Africa.

SRI LANKA (CEYLON)

The Dominion of Ceylon was proclaimed February 4, 1948. The island had been a Crown Colony from 1802 until then. On May 22, 1972, Ceylon became the Republic of Sri Lanka.

3. Colonies, Past and Present; Controlled Territory and Independent Members of the Commonwealth

Aden
Aitutaki
Anguilla
Antigua
Ascension
Bahamas
Bahrain
Bangladesh
Barbados
Barbuda
Basutoland
Batum
Bechuanaland
Bechuanaland Prot.
Belize
Bermuda
Botswana
British Antarctic Territory
British Central Africa
British Columbia and Vancouver Island
British East Africa
British Guiana

British Honduras
British Indian Ocean Territory
British New Guinea
British Solomon Islands
British Somaliland
Brunei
Burma
Bushire
Cameroons
Cape of Good Hope
Cayman Islands
Christmas Island
Cocos (Keeling) Islands
Cook Islands
Crete,
British Administration
Cyprus
Dominica
East Africa & Uganda
Protectorates
Egypt
Falkland Islands
Fiji
Gambia
German East Africa
Gibraltar
Gilbert Islands
Gilbert & Ellice Islands
Gold Coast
Grenada
Griqualand West
Guernsey
Guyana
Heligoland
Hong Kong
Indian Native States
(see India)
Ionian Islands
Jamaica
Jersey
Kenya
Kenya, Uganda & Tanzania
Kuwait
Labuan
Lagos
Leeward Islands
Lesotho
Madagascar
Malawi
Malaya
Federated Malay States
Johore
Kedah
Kelantan
Malacca
Negri Sembilan
Pahang
Penang
Perak
Perlis
Selangor
Singapore
Sungei Ujong
Trengganu
Malaysia
Maldive Islands
Malta
Man, Isle of
Mauritius
Mesopotamia
Montserrat
Muscat
Namibia
Natal
Nauru
Nevis
New Britain
New Brunswick
Newfoundland
New Guinea
New Hebrides
New Republic
New South Wales
Niger Coast Protectorate
Nigeria
Niue
Norfolk Island
North Borneo
Northern Nigeria
Northern Rhodesia
North West Pacific Islands
Nova Scotia
Nyasaland Protectorate
Oman
Orange River Colony
Palestine
Papua New Guinea
Penrhyn Island
Pitcairn Islands
Prince Edward Island
Queensland
Rhodesia
Rhodesia & Nyasaland
Ross Dependency
Sabah
St. Christopher
St. Helena
St. Kitts
St. Kitts-Nevis-Anguilla
St. Lucia
St. Vincent
Samoa
Sarawak
Seychelles
Sierra Leone
Solomon Islands
Somaliland Protectorate
South Arabia
South Australia
South Georgia
Southern Nigeria
Southern Rhodesia
South-West Africa
Stellaland
Straits Settlements
Sudan
Swaziland
Tanganyika
Tanzania
Tasmania
Tobago
Togo
Tokelau Islands
Tonga
Transvaal
Trinidad
Trinidad and Tobago
Tristan da Cunha
Trucial States
Turks and Caicos
Turks Islands
Tuvalu
Uganda
United Arab Emirates
Victoria
Virgin Islands
Western Australia
Zambia
Zanzibar
Zululand

POST OFFICES IN FOREIGN COUNTRIES

Africa
East Africa Forces
Middle East Forces
Bangkok
China
Morocco
Turkish Empire

Make Collecting Easy with Scott Specialty Series Albums

Scott Albums Feature:

- High quality chemically neutral paper printed on one side
- All spaces identified by Scott numbers with either illustrations or descriptions.
- All pages have matching borders
- Pages contain general postage issues, as well as complete back-of-the-book materials
- Albums supplemented annually

For a complete list of Scott Specialty Series Pages available, visit us at AmosAdvantage.com or call 800-572-6885. We would be glad to help!

Colonies, Former Colonies, Offices, Territories Controlled by Parent States

Belgium

Belgian Congo
Ruanda-Urundi

Denmark

Danish West Indies
Faroe Islands
Greenland
Iceland

Finland

Aland Islands

France

COLONIES PAST AND PRESENT, CONTROLLED TERRITORIES

Afars & Issas, Territory of
Alaouites
Alexandretta
Algeria
Alsace & Lorraine
Anjouan
Annam & Tonkin
Benin
Cambodia (Khmer)
Cameroun
Castellorizo
Chad
Cilicia
Cochin China
Comoro Islands
Dahomey
Diego Suarez
Djibouti (Somali Coast)
Fezzan
French Congo
French Equatorial Africa
French Guiana
French Guinea
French India
French Morocco
French Polynesia (Oceania)
French Southern & Antarctic Territories
French Sudan
French West Africa
Gabon
Germany
Ghadames
Grand Comoro
Guadeloupe
Indo-China
Inini
Ivory Coast
Laos
Latakia
Lebanon
Madagascar
Martinique
Mauritania
Mayotte
Memel
Middle Congo
Moheli
New Caledonia
New Hebrides
Niger Territory
Nossi-Be
Obock
Reunion
Rouad, Ile
Ste.-Marie de Madagascar
St. Pierre & Miquelon
Senegal
Senegambia & Niger
Somali Coast
Syria
Tahiti
Togo
Tunisia
Ubangi-Shari
Upper Senegal & Niger
Upper Volta
Viet Nam
Wallis & Futuna Islands

POST OFFICES IN FOREIGN COUNTRIES

China
Crete
Egypt
Turkish Empire
Zanzibar

Germany

EARLY STATES

Baden
Bavaria
Bergedorf
Bremen
Brunswick
Hamburg
Hanover
Lubeck
Mecklenburg-Schwerin
Mecklenburg-Strelitz
Oldenburg
Prussia
Saxony
Schleswig-Holstein
Wurttemberg

FORMER COLONIES

Cameroun (Kamerun)
Caroline Islands
German East Africa
German New Guinea
German South-West Africa
Kiauchau
Mariana Islands
Marshall Islands
Samoa
Togo

Italy

EARLY STATES

Modena
Parma
Romagna
Roman States
Sardinia
Tuscany
Two Sicilies
  Naples
  Neapolitan Provinces
  Sicily

FORMER COLONIES, CONTROLLED TERRITORIES, OCCUPATION AREAS

Aegean Islands
  Calimno (Calino)
  Caso
  Cos (Coo)
  Karki (Carchi)
  Leros (Lero)
  Lipso
  Nisiros (Nisiro)
  Patmos (Patmo)
  Piscopi
  Rodi (Rhodes)
  Scarpanto
  Simi
  Stampalia
Castellorizo
Corfu
Cyrenaica
Eritrea
Ethiopia (Abyssinia)
Fiume
Ionian Islands
  Cephalonia
  Ithaca
  Paxos
Italian East Africa
Libya
Oltre Giuba
Saseno
Somalia (Italian Somaliland)
Tripolitania

POST OFFICES IN FOREIGN COUNTRIES

"ESTERO"*
Austria
China
  Peking
  Tientsin
Crete
Tripoli
Turkish Empire
  Constantinople
  Durazzo
  Janina
Jerusalem
Salonika
Scutari
Smyrna
Valona

*Stamps overprinted "ESTERO" were used in various parts of the world.

Netherlands

Aruba
Caribbean Netherlands
Curacao
Netherlands Antilles (Curacao)
Netherlands Indies
Netherlands New Guinea
St. Martin
Surinam (Dutch Guiana)

Portugal

COLONIES PAST AND PRESENT, CONTROLLED TERRITORIES

Angola
Angra
Azores
Cape Verde
Funchal
Horta
Inhambane
Kionga
Lourenco Marques
Macao
Madeira
Mozambique
Mozambique Co.
Nyassa
Ponta Delgada
Portuguese Africa
Portuguese Congo
Portuguese Guinea
Portuguese India
Quelimane
St. Thomas & Prince Islands
Tete
Timor
Zambezia

Russia

ALLIED TERRITORIES AND REPUBLICS, OCCUPATION AREAS

Armenia
Aunus (Olonets)
Azerbaijan
Batum
Estonia
Far Eastern Republic
Georgia
Karelia
Latvia
Lithuania
North Ingermanland
Ostland
Russian Turkestan
Siberia
South Russia
Tannu Tuva
Transcaucasian Fed. Republics
Ukraine
Wenden (Livonia)
Western Ukraine

Spain

COLONIES PAST AND PRESENT, CONTROLLED TERRITORIES

Aguera, La
Cape Juby
Cuba
Elobey, Annobon & Corisco
Fernando Po
Ifni
Mariana Islands
Philippines
Puerto Rico
Rio de Oro
Rio Muni
Spanish Guinea
Spanish Morocco
Spanish Sahara
Spanish West Africa

POST OFFICES IN FOREIGN COUNTRIES

Morocco
Tangier
Tetuan

Dies of British Colonial Stamps

DIE A:

1. The lines in the groundwork vary in thickness and are not uniformly straight.

2. The seventh and eighth lines from the top, in the groundwork, converge where they meet the head.

3. There is a small dash in the upper part of the second jewel in the band of the crown.

4. The vertical color line in front of the throat stops at the sixth line of shading on the neck.

DIE B:

1. The lines in the groundwork are all thin and straight.

2. All the lines of the background are parallel.

3. There is no dash in the upper part of the second jewel in the band of the crown.

4. The vertical color line in front of the throat stops at the eighth line of shading on the neck.

DIE I:

1. The base of the crown is well below the level of the inner white line around the vignette.

2. The labels inscribed "POSTAGE" and "REVENUE" are cut square at the top.

3. There is a white "bud" on the outer side of the main stem of the curved ornaments in each lower corner.

4. The second (thick) line below the country name has the ends next to the crown cut diagonally.

DIE Ia.	DIE Ib.
1 as die II.	1 and 3 as die II.
2 and 3 as die I.	2 as die I.

DIE II:

1. The base of the crown is aligned with the underside of the white line around the vignette.

2. The labels curve inward at the top inner corners.

3. The "bud" has been removed from the outer curve of the ornaments in each corner.

4. The second line below the country name has the ends next to the crown cut vertically.

Wmk. 1
Crown and C C

Wmk. 2
Crown and C A

Wmk. 3
Multiple Crown and C A

Wmk. 4
Multiple Crown and Script C A

Wmk. 4a

Wmk. 314
St. Edward's Crown and C A Multiple

Wmk. 373

Wmk. 384

Wmk. 406

British Colonial and Crown Agents Watermarks

Watermarks 1 to 4, 314, 373, 384 and 406, common to many British territories, are illustrated here to avoid duplication.

The letters "CC" of Wmk. 1 identify the paper as having been made for the use of the Crown Colonies, while the letters "CA" of the others stand for "Crown Agents." Both Wmks. 1 and 2 were used on stamps printed by De La Rue & Co.

Wmk. 3 was adopted in 1904; Wmk. 4 in 1921; Wmk. 314 in 1957; Wmk. 373 in 1974; Wmk. 384 in 1985; Wmk 406 in 2008.

In Wmk. 4a, a non-matching crown of the general St. Edwards type (bulging on both sides at top) was substituted for one of the Wmk. 4 crowns which fell off the dandy roll. The non-matching crown occurs in 1950-52 printings in a horizontal row of crowns on certain regular stamps of Johore and Seychelles, and on various postage due stamps of Barbados, Basutoland, British Guiana, Gold Coast, Grenada, Northern Rhodesia, St. Lucia, Swaziland and Trinidad and Tobago. A variation of Wmk. 4a, with the non-matching crown in a horizontal row of crown-CA-crown, occurs on regular stamps of Bahamas, St. Kitts-Nevis and Singapore.

Wmk. 314 was intentionally used sideways, starting in 1966. When a stamp was issued with Wmk. 314 both upright and sideways, the sideways varieties usually are listed also – with minor numbers. In many of the later issues, Wmk. 314 is slightly visible.

Wmk. 373 is usually only faintly visible.

A GRAND COLLECTION

2017 SCOTT CATALOGUE VOLUME 5 IS NOW AVAILABLE!

The Scott Catalogues are the most trusted resource to help stamp collectors and dealers identify and value their stamps. Hundreds of new listings and thousands of value changes in each 2017 volume will allow you to stay on the cutting edge of the stamp market.

ITEM#	DESCRIPTION	RETAIL	AA	RELEASE DATES
C171	2017 Scott Volume 1 (US and Countries A-B)	124.99	94.99	Now Available
C172	2017 Scott Volume 2 (Countries C-F)	124.99	94.99	Now Available
C173	2017 Scott Volume 3 (Countries G-I)	124.99	94.99	Now Available
C174	2017 Scott Volume 4 (Countries J-M)	124.99	94.99	Now Available
C175	2017 Scott Volume 5 (Countries N-SAM)	124.99	94.99	Now Available
C176	2017 Scott Volume 6 (Countries SAN-Z)	124.99	94.99	9/1/16
C17S	2017 Scott US Specialized	124.99	94.99	10/1/16
C17C	2017 Scott Classic	174.99	154.99	11/1/16

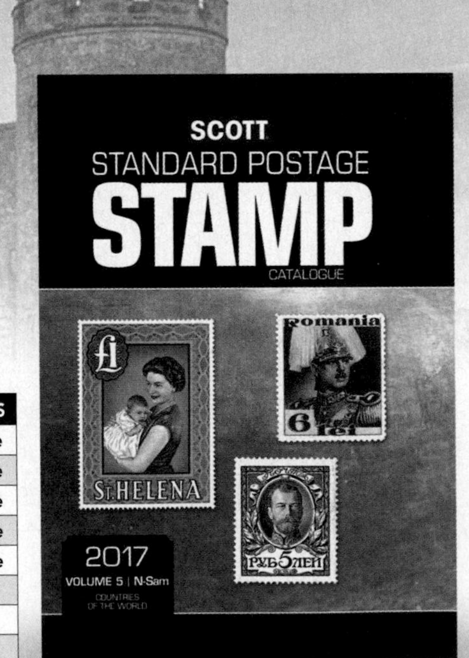

Get yours today by visiting **AmosAdvantage.com**

Or call 1-800-572-6885 | Outside U.S. & Canada Call: 1-937-498-0800

P.O. Box 4129, Sidney, OH 45365

ORDERING INFORMATION: *AA prices apply to paid subscribers of Amos Media titles, or for orders placed online. Prices, terms and product availability subject to change. Shipping & Handling – United States: Orders under $10 are only $3.99 - 10% of order total. Minimum charge $7.99 Maximum Charge $45.00. Canada: 20% of order total. Minimum charge $19.99 Maximum charge $200.00. Foreign orders are shipped via FedEx Intl. or USPS and billed actual freight. Taxes will apply in CA, OH, & IL.

NAMIBIA

nə-'mi-bē-ə

LOCATION — In southwestern Africa between Angola and South Africa, bordering on the Atlantic Ocean
GOVT. — Republic
AREA — 318,261 sq. mi.
POP. — 1,648,270 (1999 est.)
CAPITAL — Windhoek

Formerly South West Africa.

100 Cents = 1 Rand
100 Cents = 1 Dollar (1993)

Catalogue values for unused stamps in this country are for Never Hinged items.

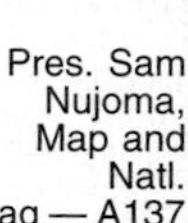

Pres. Sam Nujoma, Map and Natl. Flag — A137

Perf. 14½x14, 14x14½

1990, Mar. 21 Litho. Unwmk.

659	A137	18c	shown	.30	.25
660	A137	45c	Dove, map, hands unchained, vert.	1.00	1.00
661	A137	60c	Flag, map	1.60	1.50
			Nos. 659-661 (3)	2.90	2.75

Independence from South Africa.

Sights of Namibia A138

1990, Apr. 26 ***Perf. 14½x14***

662	A138	18c	Fish River Canyon	.50	.40
663	A138	35c	Quiver-tree Forest	.70	.60
664	A138	45c	Tsaris Mountains	.90	.80
665	A138	60c	Dolerite Hills	1.25	1.00
a.			Souvenir sheet of 1	4.75	4.75
			Nos. 662-665 (4)	3.35	2.80

No. 665a publicizes the 150th anniv. of the Penny Black. Sold for 1.50r.

Architectural Development of Windhoek A139

Designs: 18c, Early central business area. 35c, Modern central business area. 45c, First municipal building. 60c, Current municipal building.

1990, July 26 ***Perf. 14½x14***

666	A139	18c	multicolored	.35	.40
667	A139	35c	multicolored	.55	.50
668	A139	45c	multicolored	.70	.70
669	A139	60c	multicolored	.90	.90
			Nos. 666-669 (4)	2.50	2.50

Farming and Ranching A140

1990, Oct. 11 ***Perf. 14½x14***

670	A140	20c	Cornfields	.30	.30
671	A140	35c	Sanga cattle	.55	.50
672	A140	50c	Damara sheep	.90	.75
673	A140	65c	Irrigation	1.00	.90
			Nos. 670-673 (4)	2.75	2.45

Gypsum — A141

Oranjemund Alluvial Diamond Mine A142

1991, Jan. 2 ***Perf. 14½x14***

674	A141	1c	shown	.25	.25
675	A141	2c	Fluorite	.25	.25
676	A141	5c	Mimetite	.25	.25
677	A141	10c	Azurite	.35	.25
679	A141	20c	Dioptase	.40	.25
680	A142	25c	shown	.40	.30
681	A142	30c	Tsumeb mine	.50	.35
682	A142	35c	Rosh Pinah mine	.60	.40
683	A141	40c	Diamond	.75	.45
684	A142	50c	Uis mine	.75	.45
685	A141	65c	Boltwoodite	.85	.65
686	A142	1r	Rossing mine	1.25	.90
687	A141	1.50r	Wulfenite	2.00	1.25
688	A141	2r	Gold	2.50	2.00
689	A141	5r	Willemite	6.25	3.00
			Nos. 674-689 (15)	17.35	11.00

Nos. 676, 677 were reprinted in 1992 on phosphorescent paper.

Namibian Weather Service, Cent. A143

20c, Weather balloon. 35c, Sunshine recorder. 50c, Measuring equipment. 65c, Gobabeb weather station.

1991, Feb. 2 ***Perf. 14½x14***

690	A143	20c	multicolored	.30	.25
691	A143	35c	multicolored	.45	.45
692	A143	50c	multicolored	.65	.55
693	A143	65c	multicolored	.75	.65
			Nos. 690-693 (4)	2.15	1.90

Mountain Zebra A144

1991, Apr. 18 ***Perf. 14½x14***

694	A144	20c	Four zebras	*1.25*	*.70*
695	A144	25c	Mother suckling foal	*1.75*	*.90*
696	A144	45c	Three zebras	*2.25*	*1.75*
697	A144	60c	Two zebras	*2.75*	*3.00*
			Nos. 694-697 (4)	*8.00*	*6.35*

A souvenir sheet of 1 #696 was sold for 1.50r by the Philatelic Foundation of South Africa. Value $7.

Mountains A145

1991, July 18 ***Perf. 14½x14***

698	A145	20c	Karas	.35	.35
699	A145	25c	Gamsberg	.45	.45
700	A145	45c	Brukkaros	.65	.65
701	A145	60c	Erongo	.75	.75
			Nos. 698-701 (4)	2.20	2.20

Tourist Camps A146

Designs: 20c, Bernabe De la Bat Tourist Camp, Waterberg. 25c, Von Bach Recreation Resort. 45c, Gross Barmen Hot Springs. 60c, Namutoni Rest Camp.

1991, Oct. 24 ***Perf. 14½x14***

702	A146	20c	multicolored	.40	.25
703	A146	25c	multicolored	.50	.35
704	A146	45c	multicolored	.80	.65
705	A146	60c	multicolored	1.10	1.00
			Nos. 702-705 (4)	2.80	2.25

Windhoek Conservatoir, 21st Anniv. — A147

Designs: 20c, Artist's palette, brushes. 25c, French horn, neck of violin. 45c, Pan pipes, masks of Comedy and Tragedy, lyre. 60c, Ballet pas de deux.

1992, Jan. 30 ***Perf. 14x14½***

706	A147	20c	multicolored	.30	.25
707	A147	25c	multicolored	.35	.25
708	A147	45c	multicolored	.65	.55
709	A147	60c	multicolored	.85	.85
			Nos. 706-709 (4)	2.15	1.90

Freshwater Fish — A148

1992, Apr. 16 ***Perf. 14½x14***

710	A148	20c	Blue kurper	.45	.30
711	A148	25c	Yellow fish	.55	.35
712	A148	45c	Carp	.90	.60
713	A148	60c	Catfish	1.00	.80
			Nos. 710-713 (4)	2.90	2.05

A souvenir sheet of 1 No. 712 was sold by the Philatelic Foundation of South Africa. Value, $6.50.

Views of Swakopmund — A149

1992, July 2 ***Perf. 14½x14***

714	A149	20c	Jetty	.40	.30
715	A149	25c	Swimming pool	.50	.40
716	A149	45c	State House, lighthouse	.75	.60
717	A149	60c	Palm beach	1.00	.75
a.			Souvenir sheet of 4, #714-717	3.50	3.50
			Nos. 714-717 (4)	2.65	2.05

1992 Summer Olympics, Barcelona A150

1992, July 24 ***Perf. 14½x14***

718	A150	20c	Runners	.35	.25
719	A150	25c	Flag, emblem	.45	.35
720	A150	45c	Swimmers	.80	.60
721	A150	60c	Olympic stadium	.90	.75
a.			Souvenir sheet of 4, #718-721	3.00	3.00
			Nos. 718-721 (4)	2.50	1.95

No. 721a sold for 2r.

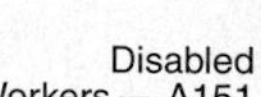

Disabled Workers — A151

Designs: 20c, Wrapping cucumbers. 25c, Finishing a woven mat. 45c, At a spinning wheel. 60c, Cleaning potted plants.

1992, Sept. 10 ***Perf. 14x14½***

722	A151	20c	multicolored	.30	.25
723	A151	25c	multicolored	.35	.25
724	A151	45c	multicolored	.60	.50
725	A151	60c	multicolored	.70	.55
			Nos. 722-725 (4)	1.95	1.55

Endangered Animals A152

1993, Feb. 25 ***Perf. 14½x14***

726	A152	20c	Loxodonta africana	.60	.40
727	A152	25c	Tragelaphus spekei	.70	.50
728	A152	45c	Diceros bicornis	1.10	.80
729	A152	60c	Lycaon pictus	1.40	1.00
a.			Souvenir sheet of 4, #726-729	5.00	5.00
			Nos. 726-729 (4)	3.80	2.70

Namibia Nature Foundation. No. 729a sold for 2.10r.

Arrival of Simmentaler Cattle in Namibia, Cent. A153

1993, Apr. 16 ***Perf. 14½x14***

730	A153	20c	Cows and calves	.30	.25
731	A153	25c	Cow and calf	.35	.25
732	A153	45c	Head of stud bull	.60	.40
733	A153	60c	Arrival on boat, 1893	.85	.75
			Nos. 730-733 (4)	2.10	1.65

A souvenir sheet of one No. 732 has inscription for National Philatelic Exhibition. Sold for 3r. Value, $4.

Namib Desert A154

1993, June 4 ***Perf. 14½x14***

734	A154	30c	Sossusvlei	.35	.30
735	A154	40c	Blutkuppe	.45	.10
736	A154	65c	Homeb	.65	.65
737	A154	85c	Moon landscape	.80	.80
			Nos. 734-737 (4)	2.25	2.15

SOS Children's Village A155

1993, Aug. 6 Litho. ***Perf. 14***

738	A155	30c	Happiness	.30	.25
739	A155	40c	A loving family	.40	.30
740	A155	65c	Home sweet home	.65	.60
741	A155	85c	My village	.85	.80
			Nos. 738-741 (4)	2.20	1.95

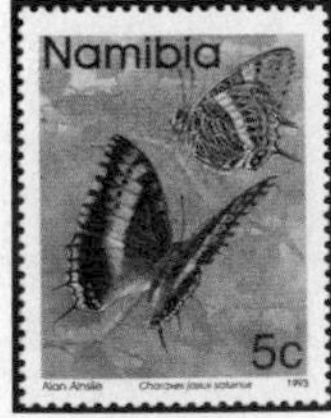

A156

Butterflies: 5c, Charaxes jasius saturnus. 10c, Acraea anemosa. 20c, Papilio nireus lyaeus. 30c, Junonia octavia sesamus. (35c), Graphium antheus. 40c, Hypolimnas misippus. 50c, Physcaeneura panda. 65c, Charaxes candiope. 85c, Junonia hierta cebrene. 90c, Colotis celimene pholoe. $1, Cacyreus dicksoni. $2, Charaxes bohemani. $2.50, Stugeta bowkeri tearei. $5, Byblia anvatara acheloia.

1993-94 *Perf. 14x14½*

742	A156	5c	multicolored	.25	.25
743	A156	10c	multicolored	.25	.25
744	A156	20c	multicolored	.25	.25
745	A156	30c	multicolored	.25	.25
745A	A156	(35c)	multicolored	.45	.25
746	A156	40c	multicolored	.25	.25
747	A156	50c	multicolored	.30	.30
748	A156	65c	multicolored	.40	.40
749	A156	85c	multicolored	.50	.50
750	A156	90c	multicolored	.55	.55
751	A156	$1	multicolored	.60	.60
752	A156	$2	multicolored	1.25	1.25
753	A156	$2.50	multicolored	1.50	1.50
754	A156	$5	multicolored	3.25	3.25
			Nos. 742-754 (14)	10.05	9.85

No. 745A is inscribed "STANDARDISED MAIL" and sold for 35c when issued.

Issued: No. 745A, 4/8/94; others, 10/1/93.

Perf. 14½x15 Syncopated Type A

1997

742a	A156	5c	multicolored	.35	.35
747a	A156	50c	multicolored	1.25	1.00

Issued: Nos. 742a, 747a, 3/3/97.

Coastal Angling A157

1994, Feb. 4 **Litho.** *Perf. 14*

755	A157	30c	Blacktail	.25	.25
756	A157	40c	Kob	.35	.30
757	A157	65c	Steenbras	.60	.55
758	A157	85c	Galjoen	.80	.75
a.			Souvenir sheet of 4, #755-758	2.75	2.75
			Nos. 755-758 (4)	2.00	1.85

Incorporation of Walvis Bay into Namibia A158

1994, Mar. 1

759	A158	30c	Quay	.45	.40
760	A158	65c	Aerial view	.70	.70
761	A158	85c	Map of Namibia	1.10	1.10
			Nos. 759-761 (3)	2.25	2.20

A159

Flowers: 35c, Adenolobus pechuelii. 40c, Hibiscus elliottiae. 65c, Pelargonium cortusifolium. 85c, Hoodia macrantha.

1994, Apr. 8 **Litho.** *Perf. 14*

762	A159	35c	multicolored	.30	.25
763	A159	40c	multicolored	.35	.30
764	A159	65c	multicolored	.60	.50
765	A159	85c	multicolored	.75	.65
			Nos. 762-765 (4)	2.00	1.70

A160

Storks of Etosha.

1994, June 3 **Litho.** *Perf. 14*

766	A160	35c	Yellowbilled	.40	.25
767	A160	40c	Abdim's	.50	.30
768	A160	80c	Openbilled	.75	.60
769	A160	$1.10	White	1.00	.85
			Nos. 766-769 (4)	2.65	2.00

Trains A161

1994, Aug. 5 **Litho.** *Perf. 13½x14*

770	A161	35c	Steam railcar	.45	.30
771	A161	70c	Class Krauss	.80	.55
772	A161	80c	Class 24	.90	.75
773	A161	$1.10	Class 7C	1.40	1.00
			Nos. 770-773 (4)	3.55	2.60

A souvenir sheet of 1 #772 was sold for 3r by the Philatelic Foundation of South Africa. Value $2.75.

Railways in Namibia, Cent. A162

Locomotives: 35c, Prince Edward, 1st in service. 70c, Ex-German SWA 2-8-0 tank. 80c, Class 8. $1.10, Class 33 400 diesel electric.

1995, Mar. 8 **Litho.** *Perf. 14*

774	A162	35c	multicolored	.40	.25
775	A162	70c	multicolored	.70	.35
776	A162	80c	multicolored	.80	.60
777	A162	$1.10	multicolored	1.20	.90
a.			Souvenir sheet of 4, #774-777	3.75	3.75
			Nos. 774-777 (4)	3.10	2.10

No. 777a sold for $3.50.

No. 777a exists inscribed "Reprint November 1996." Value $4.75.

A163

1995, Mar. 21 **Litho.** *Perf. 14*

778	A163	(35c)	multicolored	.50	.50

Independence, 5th anniv. No. 778 is inscribed "STANDARDISED MAIL" and sold for 35c on day of issue.

A164

Fossils: 40c, Geochelone stromeri. 80c, Diamantornis wardi. 90c, Prohyrax hendeyi. $1.20, Crocodylus lloydi.

1995, May 24 **Litho.** *Perf. 14*

779	A164	40c	multicolored	.65	.35
780	A164	80c	multicolored	1.00	.55
781	A164	90c	multicolored	1.10	.60
782	A164	$1.20	multicolored	1.50	2.00
			Nos. 779-782 (4)	4.25	3.50

A souvenir sheet of 1 #780 was sold for 3r by the Philatelic Foundation of South Africa. Value $3.

Finnish Mission, 125th Anniv. A165

Designs: 40c, Mission church, Martti Rautanen (1845-1926). 80c, Albin Savola (1867-1934), Oniipa printing press. 90c, Oxwagon, Karl Emanuel August Weikkolin (1842-91). $1.20, Dr. Selma Raino (1873-1939), Onandjokwe Hospital.

1995, July 10 **Litho.** *Perf. 14*

783	A165	40c	multicolored	.45	.25
784	A165	80c	multicolored	.70	.70
785	A165	90c	multicolored	.75	.70
786	A165	$1.20	multicolored	.90	.90
			Nos. 783-786 (4)	2.80	2.55

Traditional Adornments — A166

1995, Aug. 16 **Litho.** *Perf. 14½x14*

787	A166	40c	Ivory buttons	.35	.25
788	A166	80c	Conus shell	.60	.45
789	A166	90c	Cowrie shells	.70	.50
790	A166	$1.20	Shell button	.85	.65
			Nos. 787-790 (4)	2.50	1.85

Souvenir Sheet

Singapore '95 — A167

1995, Sept. 10 **Litho.** *Perf. 14*

791	A167	$1.20	Phacochoerus aethiopicus	1.75	1.75

UN, 50th Anniv. A168

1995, Oct. 24

792	A168	40c	blue & black	.45	.45

Tourism A169

1996, Apr. 1 **Litho.** *Perf. 15x14*

793	A169	(45c)	Bogenfels Arch	.25	.25
794	A169	90c	Ruacana Falls	.35	.35
795	A169	$1	Epupa Falls	.40	.40
796	A169	$1.30	Wild horses	.60	.60
			Nos. 793-796 (4)	1.60	1.60

No. 793 is inscribed "Standardised Mail" and sold for 45c on day of issue.

Catholic Missions in Namibia A170

50c, Döbra Education and Training Centre. 95c, Heirachabis. $1, Windhoek St. Mary's Cathedral. $1.30, Ovamboland Old Church & School.

1996, May 27 **Litho.** *Perf. 15x14*

797	A170	50c	multicolored	.25	.25
798	A170	95c	multicolored	.40	.40
799	A170	$1	multicolored	.45	.45
800	A170	$1.30	multicolored	.55	.55
			Nos. 797-800 (4)	1.65	1.65

Souvenir Sheet

CAPEX 96 — A171

1996, June 8 **Litho.** *Perf. 14½x14*

801	A171	$1.30	African lynx	1.50	1.50

UNICEF, 50th Anniv. A172

Designs: (45c), Children have rights. $1.30, Educate the girl.

1996, June 14 **Litho.** *Perf. 15x14*

802	A172	(45c)	multicolored	.25	.25
803	A172	$1.30	multicolored	.70	.60

No. 802 is inscribed "Standard Postage" and sold for 45c on day of issue.

1996 Summer Olympic Games, Atlanta A173

1996, June 27

804	A173	(45c)	Boxing	.25	.25
805	A173	90c	Cycling	.40	.40
806	A173	$1	Swimming	.45	.45
807	A173	$1.30	Running	.50	.50
			Nos. 804-807 (4)	1.60	1.60

No. 804 is inscribed "Standard Postage" and sold for 45c on day of issue.

Constellations — A174

Designs: (45c), Scorpio. 90c, Sagittarius. $1, Southern Cross. $1.30, Orion.

1996, Sept. 12 Litho. ***Perf. 15x14***

808 A174 (45c) multicolored .25 .25
809 A174 90c multicolored .35 .35
810 A174 $1 multicolored .45 .45
a. Souvenir sheet of 1 2.00 2.00
811 A174 $1.30 multicolored .55 .55
Nos. 808-811 (4) 1.60 1.60

No. 808 is inscribed "Standard Postage" and sold for 45c on day of issue.

No. 810a sold for $3.50. No. 810a exists inscribed "Reprint February 17, 1997. Sold in aid of organized philately N$3.50."

Early Pastoral Pottery — A175

Designs: (45c), Urn-shaped storage vessel. 90c, Bag-shaped cooking vessel. $1, Reconstructed pot. $1.30, Large storage vessel.

1996, Oct. 17 ***Perf. 14x15***

812 A175 (45c) multicolored .25 .25
813 A175 90c multicolored .40 .40
814 A175 $1 multicolored .45 .45
815 A175 $1.30 multicolored .50 .50
Nos. 812-815 (4) 1.60 1.60

No. 812 is inscribed "Standard Postage" and sold for 45c on day of issue.

Ancient //Khauxa!nas Ruins, near Karasburg — A176

Various views of stone wall.

1997, Feb. 6 Litho. ***Perf. 15x14***

816 A176 (50c) multicolored .35 .30
817 A176 $1 multicolored .75 .60
818 A176 $1.10 multicolored .85 .70
819 A176 $1.50 multicolored 1.50 1.50
Nos. 816-819 (4) 3.45 3.10

No. 816 is inscribed "Standard Postage" and sold for 45c on day of issue.

Souvenir Sheet

Hong Kong '97, Intl. Stamp Exhibition — A176a

1997, Feb. 12 Litho. ***Perf. 14½x14***

819A A176a $1.30 Sanga bull *2.00 2.00*

No. 819A sold for $3.50. An inscription, "REPRINT 1 APRIL 1997," was added to a later printing of this sheet. Value $3.

A177

1997, Apr. 8 Litho. ***Perf. 14x14½***

820 A177 $2 multicolored 1.00 1.00

Heinrich von Stephan (1831-97), founder of UPU.

A178

Jackass Penguins.

1997, May 15 Litho. ***Perf. 14x14½***

821 A178 (50c) shown .35 .35
822 A178 $1 Nesting .55 .40
823 A178 $1.10 With young .75 .65
824 A178 $1.50 Swimming .90 .80
Nos. 821-824 (4) 2.55 2.20

Souvenir Sheet

824A A178 Sheet of 4, #b.-e. 3.00 3.00

World Wildlife Fund. No. 821 is inscribed "Standard Postage" and sold for 45c on day of issue.

Nos. 824Ab-824Ae are like Nos. 821-824 but do not have the WWF emblem. No. 824A sold for $5.

Wild Cats A179

1997, June 12 Litho. ***Perf. 14½x14***

825 A179 (45c) Felis caracal .25 .25
826 A179 $1 Felis lybica .40 .40
827 A179 $1.10 Felis serval .50 .50
828 A179 $1.50 Felis nigripes .60 .60
Nos. 825-828 (4) 1.75 1.75

No. 825 is inscribed "Standard Postage" and sold for 45c on day of issue. A souvenir sheet containing a $5 stamp like #828 exists. Value $2.25.

See Nos. 878-881.

Helmeted Guineafowl A180

1997, June 5 ***Perf. 14½x14***

829 A180 $1.20 multicolored 1.10 1.10

A181

Baskets: 50c, Collecting bag. 90c, Powder basket. $1.20, Fruit basket. $2, Grain basket.

1997, July 8 Litho. ***Perf. 14x14½***

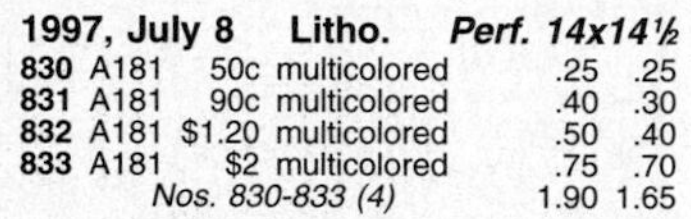

830 A181 50c multicolored .25 .25
831 A181 90c multicolored .40 .30
832 A181 $1.20 multicolored .50 .40
833 A181 $2 multicolored .75 .70
Nos. 830-833 (4) 1.90 1.65

Cinderella Waxbill — A182

60c, Blackchecked waxbill.

Perf. 14x14½ Syncopated Type A

1997, May 5 Booklet Stamps

834 A182 50c shown .25 .25
835 A182 60c multicolored .30 .30
a. Booklet pane, 5 each #834-835 3.00
Complete booklet, #835a 3.00

A183

Greetings Stamps A184

Flowers: No. 836, Catophractes alexandri. No. 837, Crinun paludosum. No. 838, Gloriosa superba. No. 839, Tribulus zeyheri. No. 840, Aptosimum pubescens.

Helmeted guineafowl: No. 841, In bed. No. 842, Holding flowers. No. 843, As music conductor. No. 844, Prepared to travel. No. 845, Wearing heart necklace.

1997, July 11 Litho. ***Perf. 14x13½***

Booklet Stamps

836 A183 (50c) multicolored .50 .50
837 A183 (50c) multicolored .50 .50
838 A183 (50c) multicolored .50 .50
839 A183 (50c) multicolored .50 .50
840 A183 (50c) multicolored .50 .50
a. Booklet pane, 2 each #836-840 + 10 labels 5.00
Complete booklet, #840a 5.00
841 A184 50c multicolored .50 .50
842 A184 50c multicolored .50 .50
843 A184 50c multicolored .50 .50
844 A184 $1 multicolored .90 .90
845 A184 $1 multicolored .90 .90
a. Booklet pane, 2 each #841-845 + 10 labels 6.25
Complete booklet, #845a 6.25

Nos. 836-840 are inscribed "Standard Postage" and sold for 45c on day of issued.

Namibian Veterinary Assoc., 50th Anniv. — A185

1997, Sept. 12 ***Perf. 14***

846 A185 $1.50 multicolored .70 .70

Souvenir Sheet

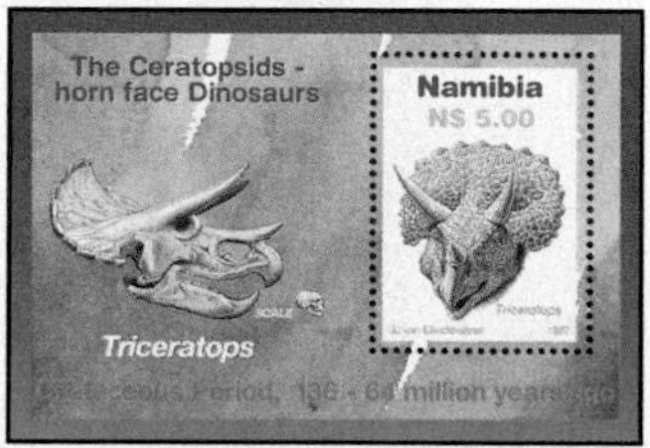

Triceratops — A186

1997, Sept. 27 Litho. ***Perf. 13***

847 A186 $5 multicolored 2.25 2.25

World Post Day — A187

1997, Oct. 9 Litho. ***Perf. 14x15***

848 A187 (45c) multicolored .60 .40

No. 848 is inscribed "Standard Postage" and sold for 45c on day of issue.

Trees — A188

1997, Oct. 10

849 A188 (50c) False mopane .25 .25
850 A188 $1 Ana tree .40 .40
851 A188 $1.10 Shepherd's tree .45 .55
852 A188 $1.50 Kiaat .55 .70
Nos. 849-852 (4) 1.65 1.90

No. 849 is inscribed "Standard Postage" and sold for 45c on day of issue.

Fauna and Flora — A189

5c, Flame lily. 10c, Bushman poison. 20c, Camel's foot. 30c, Western rhigozum. 40c, Bluecheeked bee-eater. (50c), Rosyfaced lovebird. 50c, Laughing dove. 60c, Lappetfaced vulture. 90c, Yellowbilled hornbill. $1, Lilacbreasted roller. $1.10, Hippopotamus. ($1.20), Leopard. $1.20, Giraffe. $1.50, Elephant. $2, Lion. $4, Buffalo. $5, Black rhinoceros. $10, Cheetah.

1997, Nov. 3 Litho. ***Perf. 13½***

853 A189 5c multi .25 .25
854 A189 10c multi .25 .25
855 A189 20c multi .25 .25
856 A189 30c multi .25 .25
857 A189 40c multi .25 .25
858 A189 (50c) multi .25 .25
a. Booklet pane of 10, perf 14x13½ 2.50
Complete booklet, #858a 2.50
859 A189 50c multi .25 .25
860 A189 60c multi .30 .25
861 A189 90c multi .40 .35
862 A189 $1 multi .45 .40
863 A189 $1.10 multi .50 .40
864 A189 ($1.20) multi .55 .45
a. Booklet pane of 10, perf 14x13½ 5.50
Complete booklet, #864a 5.50
865 A189 $1.20 multi .45 .40
866 A189 $1.50 multi .50 .45
867 A189 $2 multi .65 .60
868 A189 $4 multi 1.00 1.00
869 A189 $5 multi 1.25 1.25
870 A189 $10 multi 2.25 2.25
a. Bklt. pane, 1 ea #853-870, perf 14x13½ 9.75
Complete booklet, #870a 9.75
Nos. 853-870 (18) 10.05 9.55

Self-Adhesive

Die Cut Perf. 12x12½

870B A189 (45c) like #858 .25 .25
870C A189 $1 like #862 .45 .45
870D A189 ($1.20) like #864 .60 .60
Nos. 870B-870D (3) 1.30 1.30

No. 858 is inscribed "Standard Postage" and sold for 50c on day issue. No. 864 is inscribed "Postcard Rate" and sold for $1.20 on day of issue.

For surcharges see #959-962, 1060-1063, 1071-1080, 1132-1040.

Christmas A190

Various pictures of a helmeted guineafowl.

1997, Nov. 3 ***Perf. 13x12½***

871 A190 (50c) multicolored .25 .25
872 A190 $1 multicolored .45 .45
873 A190 $1.10 multicolored .45 .45
874 A190 $1.50 multicolored .55 .55
Nos. 871-874 (4) 1.70 1.70

Souvenir Sheet

875 A190 $5 multi, vert. 2.50 2.50

No. 871 is inscribed "Standard Postage" and sold for 50c on day of issue.

A191

1997, Nov. 27 ***Perf. 14x15***

876 A191 (50c) multicolored .50 .50

John Muafangejo (1943-87), artist. No. 876 is inscribed "Standard Postage" and sold for 50c on day of issue.

A192

1998, Jan. 15

877 A192 (50c) brown & gray .35 .35

Gabriel B. Taapopi (1911-85). No. 877 is inscribed "Standard Postage" and sold for 50c on day of issue.

Wild Cats Type of 1997

Designs: $1.20, Panthera pardus. $1.90, Panthera leo, female carrying young. $2, Panthera leo, male. $2.50, Acinonyx jubatus.

1998, Jan. 26 ***Perf. 13x12½***

878 A179 $1.20 multicolored .60 .60
879 A179 $1.90 multicolored .70 .70
880 A179 $2 multicolored .80 .80
881 A179 $2.50 multicolored 1.00 1.00
a. Souvenir sheet, #878-881 3.75 3.75
Nos. 878-881 (4) 3.10 3.10

Narra Plant — A194

1998, Feb. 9 ***Perf. 12½x13***

882 A194 $2.40 multicolored .80 .80

Water Awareness A195

1998, Mar. 23 **Litho.** ***Perf. 14x15***

883 A195 (50c) multicolored .35 .35

No. 883 is inscribed "Standard Postage" and sold for 50c on date of issue.

Nos. 885-895 were initially not available in Namibia. They were issued Nov. 23, 1997, at a Shanghai, China, stamp exhibition by a Chinese stamp dealer acting for the Namibia Post Office. There is some question whether they were sold in Namibia, but if they were, it was not until early 1998.

A197

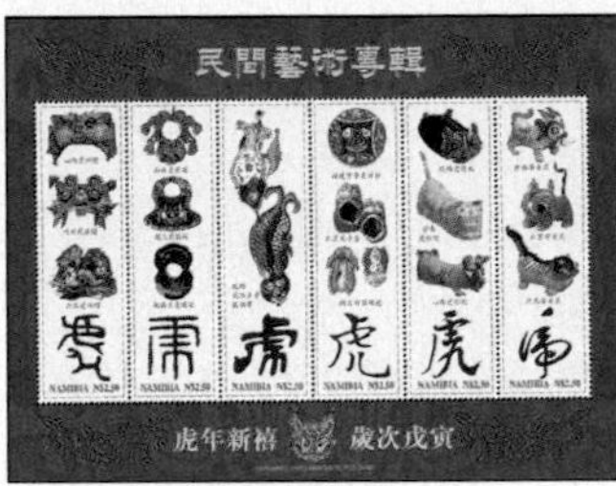

Lunar New Year — A198

Chinese inscriptions, wood cut images of a tiger, stylized drawings of tiger in — #885: a, orange. b, light green. c, yellow. d, blue. e, dark green. f, lilac.

No. 886: Various tiger figures, Chinese inscriptions.

No. 887, Chinese inscriptions, stylized tigers.

Perf. 13½x12½

1997, Nov. 23 **Litho.**

885 A197 $2.50 Sheet of 6, #a.-f. 6.50 6.50

Perf. 14x13½

886 A198 $2.50 Sheet of 6, #a.-f. 6.50 6.50

Souvenir Sheets

Perf. 12½

887 A197 $6 multicolored 3.00 3.00
888 A198 $6 multicolored 3.00 3.00

Nos. 887-888 each contain one 69x38mm stamp.

Macau Returns to China in 1999 A199

Designs: No. 890, Flag, building. No. 892, Flag, Deng Xiaoping, building.

1997, Nov. 23 ***Perf. 13½***

889 A199 $4.50 multicolored 2.60 2.60

Size: 59x27mm

Perf. 13½x13

890 A199 $4.50 multicolored 3.50 3.50

Souvenir Sheets

Perf. 13½x12½

891 A199 $6 multicolored 3.25 3.25

Perf. 12½

892 A199 $6 multicolored 3.25 3.25

Nos. 889-890 issued in sheets of 3. No. 891 contains one 62x33mm stamp, No. 892 one 69x33mm stamp.

Return of Hong Kong to China — A200

Chinese landmarks — #892A: b, Beijing, Natl. Capital of China. c, Return of Hong Kong, 1997. d, Return of Macao, 1999. e, The Taiwan Region.

1997, Nov. 17 **Litho.** ***Perf. 14x13½***

892A A200 $3.50 Sheet of 4, #b.-e. 7.50 7.50

Souvenir Sheet

Perf. 12½

893 A200 $6 Chinese landmarks 2.75 2.75

No. 893 contains one 72x41mm stamp.

Shanghai Communique, 25th Anniv. — A201

No. 894: a, Pres. Nixon, Mao Zedong, 1972. b, Pres. Carter, Deng Xiaoping, 1979. c, Pres. Reagan, Deng Xiaoping, 1984. d, Pres. Bush, Deng Xiaoping, 1989.

$6, Nixon, Zhou Enlai, 1972.

1997, Nov. 17 ***Perf. 13½x12½***

894 A201 $3.50 Sheet of 4, #a.-d. 5.50 5.50

Souvenir Sheet

Perf. 14x13½

895 A201 $6 multicolored 3.00 3.00

No. 895 contains one 67x33mm stamp.

Owls — A204

1998, Apr. 1 **Litho.** ***Perf. 13½x13***

Booklet Stamps

898 A204 55c Rat (prey) .45 .45

Size: 38x23mm

899 A204 $1.50 Whitefaced owl .80 .80
900 A204 $1.50 Barred owl .80 .80
901 A204 $1.90 Spotted eagle owl 1.10 1.10

Size: 61x21mm

902 A204 $1.90 Barn owl 1.10 1.10
a. Booklet pane, #898-902 4.25
Complete booklet, #902a 4.25

See No. 950.

Shells A205

Designs: (55c), Patella granatina. $1.10, Cymatium cutaceum africanum. $1.50, Conus mozambicus. $6, Venus verrucosa.

1998, May 14 **Litho.** ***Perf. 12½***

903 A205 (55c) multicolored .30 .30
904 A205 $1.10 multicolored .50 .50
905 A205 $1.50 multicolored .65 .65
906 A205 $6 multicolored 2.50 2.50
a. Souvenir sheet, #903-906 4.50 4.50
Nos. 903-906 (4) 3.95 3.95

No. 903 inscribed "Standard Postage."

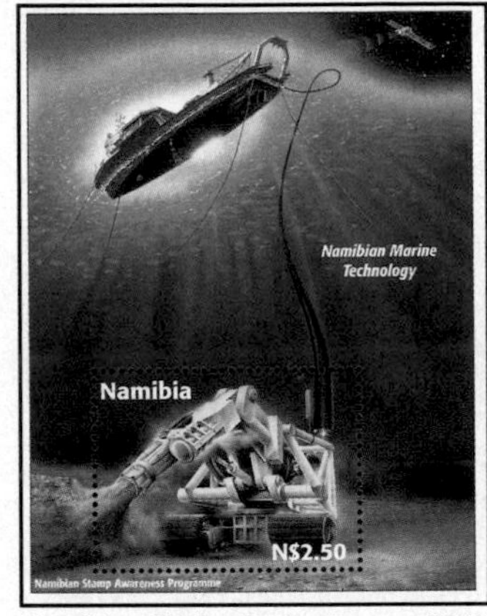

Namibian Marine Technology — A206

1998, May 18 **Litho.** ***Perf. 14½x14***

908 A206 $2.50 multicolored 2.00 2.00

Diana, Princess of Wales (1961-97)

Common Design Type

Working for removal of land mines: a, Wearing face shield. b, Wearing Red Cross shirt. c, In white blouse. d, With child.

1998, May 18 **Litho.** ***Perf. 14½x14***

909 CD355 $1 Sheet of 4, #a.-d. 1.90 1.90

World Environment Day — A207

(55c), Namibian coast. $1.10, Okavango sunset. $1.50, Sossusvlei. $1.90, African moringo.

1998, June 5 **Litho.** ***Perf. 13x13½***

910 A207 (55c) multicolored .30 .30
911 A207 $1.10 multicolored .50 .50
912 A207 $1.50 multicolored .55 .55
913 A207 $1.90 multicolored .60 .60
Nos. 910-913 (4) 1.95 1.95

No. 910 is inscribed "Standard Postage."

Souvenir Sheet

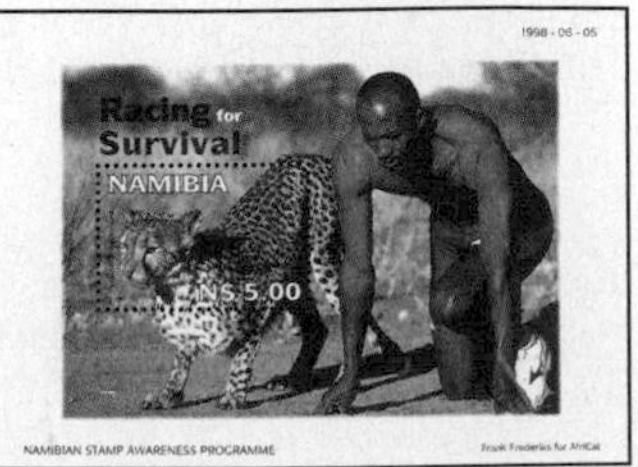

Racing for Survival — A208

1998, June 5 ***Perf. 13***

914 A208 $5 Acinonyx jubatus 2.25 2.25

Animals and Their Young — A209

a, Chacma baboon. b, Blue wildebeest. c, Suricate. d, Elephant. e, Burchell's zebra.

1998, June 18 ***Perf. 13½x13***
915 A209 $1.50 Sheet of 5, #a.-e. 3.25 3.25

Souvenir Sheet

1998 World Cup Soccer Championships, France — A210

1998, July 1 **Litho.** ***Perf. 14***
916 A210 $5 multicolored 2.00 2.00

Flora and Fauna of the Caprivi Strip — A211

Designs: a, Carmine bee-eater. b, Sable antelope. c, Lechwe. d, Woodland waterberry. e, Nile monitor. f, African jacana. g, African fish eagle. h, Woodland kingfisher. i, Nile crocodile. j, Black mamba.

1998, Sept. 26 **Litho.** ***Perf. 12½***
917 A211 60c Sheet of 10, #a.-j. *10.00 10.00*

#917b-917c, 917e are 40x40mm, #917i is 54x30mm, #917j is 32x30mm.

Souvenir Sheet

Black Rhinoceros — A212

1998, Oct. 20 **Litho.** ***Perf. 13***
918 A212 $5 multicolored 2.25 2.25

Ilsapex '98, Intl. Philatelic Exhibition, Johannesburg.

Souvenir Sheet

Whales — A213

1998, Oct. 9 **Litho.** ***Perf. 13½x14***
919 A213 $5 multicolored 2.50 2.50

See Norfolk Island No. 665, South Africa No. 1095.

Damara Dik Dik — A214

Striped Tree Squirrel — A215

1999, Jan. 18 **Litho.** ***Perf. 13½***
920 A214 $1.80 multi 2.75 2.75
921 A215 $2.65 multi 4.50 4.50

"Yoka" the Snake — A216

"Yoka" the Snake A217

Cartoon pictures of Yoka: No. 922, Turning head. No. 923, Wrapped around tree branch. No. 924, Tail wrapped around branch and female snake. No. 925, With female snake and mouse. No. 926, In love. No. 927, Yoka tied up in knots. No. 928, Smashed with footprint. No. 929, Female snake's tail, Yoka's head. No. 930, Female snake singing to dazed Yoka. No. 931, Lying with tail over nose.

Serpentine Die Cut
1999, Feb. 1 **Self-Adhesive** **Litho.**
Booklet Stamps

922 A216 $1.60 multicolored .55 .55
923 A217 $1.60 multicolored .55 .55
924 A216 $1.60 multicolored .55 .55
925 A217 $1.60 multicolored .55 .55
926 A216 $1.60 multicolored .55 .55
927 A217 $1.60 multicolored .55 .55
928 A216 $1.60 multicolored .55 .55
929 A216 $1.60 multicolored .55 .55
930 A216 $1.60 multicolored .55 .55
931 A217 $1.60 multicolored .55 .55
a. Bklt. pane of 10, #922-931 5.50

The peelable paper backing serves as a booklet cover.

Souvenir Sheet

Passenger Liner "Windhuk" — A218

1999, Mar. 18 ***Perf. 14***
932 A218 $5.50 multicolored 2.25 2.25

Gliders A219

1999, Apr. 13 **Litho.** ***Perf. 13***
933 A219 $1.60 Zögling, 1928 1.00 1.00
934 A219 $1.80 Schleicher, 1998 1.25 1.25

Souvenir Sheet

IBRA '99, Nuremberg, Germany — A220

1999, Apr. 27 **Litho.** ***Perf. 14x14¼***
935 A220 $5.50 multi 2.10 2.10

Falcons — A221

60c, Greater kestrel. $1.60, Rock kestrel. $1.80, Red-necked falcon. $2.65, Lanner falcon.

1999, May 18 **Litho.** ***Perf. 13¼x13½***
936 A221 60c multicolored .70 .40
937 A221 $1.60 multicolored 1.00 .90
938 A221 $1.80 multicolored 1.10 1.00
939 A221 $2.65 multicolored 1.75 2.00
Nos. 936-939 (4) 4.55 4.30

Souvenir Sheet

Termitomyces Schimperi — A222

1999, June 19 **Litho.** ***Perf. 13¾***
940 A222 $5.50 multicolored 2.25 2.25

PhilexFrance '99 World Philatelic Exhibition.

Wetland Birds A223

Designs: $1.60, Wattled crane. $1.80, Burchell's sand grouse. $1.90, Rock pratincole. $2.65, Eastern white pelican.

1999, June 28 ***Perf. 12¾***
941 A223 $1.60 multicolored .80 .40
942 A223 $1.80 multicolored 1.00 .90
943 A223 $1.90 multicolored 1.25 1.00
944 A223 $2.65 multicolored 1.75 1.60
Nos. 941-944 (4) 4.80 3.90

Orchids A224

Designs: $1.60, Eulophia hereroensis. $1.80, Ansellia africana. $2.65, Eulophia leachii. $3.90, Eulophia speciosa. $5.50, Eulophia walleri.

Litho. & Embossed
1999, Aug. 21 ***Perf. 12¾***
945 A224 $1.60 multicolored .80 .80
946 A224 $1.80 multicolored .90 .90
947 A224 $2.65 multicolored 1.25 1.25
948 A224 $3.90 multicolored 1.75 1.75
Nos. 945-948 (4) 4.70 4.70

Souvenir Sheet

949 A224 $5.50 multicolored 2.75 2.75

Embossing is found only on the margin of No. 949. China 1999 World Philatelic Exhibition (No. 949).

Owl Type of 1998
Souvenir Sheet

Perf. 13½x12¾
1999, Sept. 30 **Litho.**
950 A204 $11 Like #902 6.00 6.00

Selection of stamp design as "most beautiful," 5th Stamp World Cup.

Urieta Kazahendike (Johanna Gertze) (1836-1935) A225

1999, Oct. 1 **Litho.** ***Perf. 12¾***
951 A225 $20 multicolored 5.75 5.75

Souvenir Sheet

Turn of the Millennium — A226

Perf. 13¾x13¼
1999, Dec. 31 **Litho.**
952 A226 $9 multi 4.25 4.25

No. 952 has a holographic image. Soaking in water may affect the hologram.

Sunset Over Namibia — A227

1999-2000 ***Perf. 13¼x13¾***
953 A227 $2.20 shown 1.50 1.50
954 A227 $2.40 Sunrise 1.75 1.75

Issued: $2.20, 12/31; $2.40, 1/1/00.

Ducks A228

Designs: $2, South African shelduck. $2.40, Whitefaced duck. $3, Knobbilled duck. $7, Cape shoveller.

2000, Feb. 18 **Litho.** ***Perf. 13***
955 A228 $2 multi 1.10 1.10
956 A228 $2.40 multi 1.25 1.25
957 A228 $3 multi 1.50 1.50
958 A228 $7 multi 3.25 3.25
Nos. 955-958 (4) 7.10 7.10

Nos. 853-856 Surcharged

2000, Mar. 1 Litho. *Perf. 13½*

959 A189 (65c) on 5c multi .40 .40
960 A189 $1.80 on 30c multi .90 .90
961 A189 $3 on 10c multi 1.50 1.50
962 A189 $6 on 20c multi 3.00 3.00
Nos. 959-962 (4) 5.80 5.80

See No. 1000.

Independence, 10th Anniv. — A229

2000, Mar. 21 *Perf. 13¼x13¾*

963 A229 65c Children .75 .40
964 A229 $3 Flag 2.00 2.00

Passion Play — A230

Designs: $2.10, Jesus with crown of thorns. $2.40, Carrying cross.

2000, Apr. 1 *Perf. 13¾*

965 A230 $2.10 multi .80 .80
966 A230 $2.40 multi .95 .95

Fauna of the Namib Desert — A231

Designs: a, $2, Tenebrionid beetle. b, $2 Brown hyena. c, $2, Namib golden mole. d, $2, Shovel-snouted lizard. e, $2, Dune lark. f, $6, Namib side-winding adder.

2000, May 22 *Perf. 14½*

967 A231 Sheet of 6, #a-f 9.00 9.00

The Stamp Show 2000, London.

Sizes of stamps: Nos. 967a-967c, 30x25mm; No. 967d, 30x50mm; Nos. 967e-967f, 26x37mm. Portions of the design were applied by a thermographic process, producing a shiny raised effect.

Welwitschia Mirabilis — A232

Various views of Welwitschia plants. Denominations: (65c), $2.20, $3, $4.

2000, June 21 Litho. *Perf. 13¾*

968-971 A232 Set of 4 5.25 5.25

No. 968 is inscribed "Standard inland mail."

Souvenir Sheet

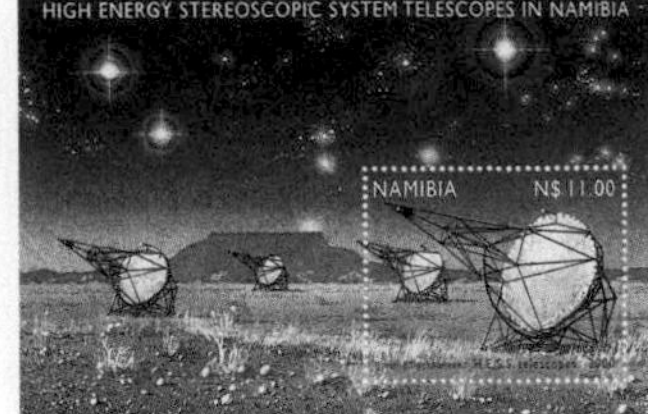

High Energy Stereoscopic Sytem Telescopes — A233

2000, July 7 *Perf. 13¼x13¾*

972 A233 $11 multi 6.75 6.75

Fruit Trees — A234

Designs: (65c), Jackalberry. $2, Sycamore fig. $2.20, Bird plum. $7, Marula.

2000, Aug. 16 Litho. *Perf. 13¼x14*

973-976 A234 Set of 4 5.50 5.50

No. 973 is inscribed "Standard inland mail."

Souvenir Sheet

Yoka in Etosha — A235

2000, Sept. 1 *Perf. 13¼x13*

977 A235 $11 multi 5.75 5.75

Coelenterates A236

Designs: ($1), Anthothoe stimpsoni. $2.45, Bundosoma capensis. $3.50, Anthopleura stephensoni. $6.60, Pseudactinia flagellifera.

2001, Apr. 18 Litho. *Perf. 13¾*

978-981 A236 Set of 4 5.00 5.00

No. 978 is inscribed "Standard inland mail."

Civil Aviation A237

Designs: ($1), Cessna 210 Turbo. $2.20, Douglas DC-6B. $2.50, Pitts 52A. $13.20, Bell 407 helicopter.

2001, May 9 *Perf. 13¼x13¾*

982-985 A237 Set of 4 11.00 11.00

No. 982 is inscribed "Standard inland mail."

Renewable Energy Resources — A238

No. 986: a, Wood efficient stove. b, Biogas digester. c, Solar cooker. d, Repair, reuse, recycle. e, Solar water pump. f, Solar home system. g, Solar street light. h, Solar water heater. i, Solar telecommunication. j, Wind water pump.

2001, Aug. 15 *Perf. 13½x14*

986 A238 Sheet of 10 11.00 11.00
a.-e. ($1) Any single .45 .45
f.-j. $3.50 Any single 1.40 1.40

Nos. 986a-986e are inscribed "Standard Mail."

Central Highlands Flora and Fauna — A239

No. 987: a, ($1.00), Ruppell's parrot (31x29mm). b, $3.50, Camel thorn (54x29mm). c, ($1.00), Flap-necked chameleon (39x29mm). d, ($1.00), Klipspringer (39x29mm). e, $3.50, Berg aloe (39x29mm). f, $3.50, Kudu (39x39mm). g, ($1.00), Rockrunner (39x29mm). h, $3.50, Namibian rock agama (39x39mm). i, ($1.00), Pangolin (39x39mm). j, $3.50, Armored ground cricket (39x29mm).

2001, Sept. 5 *Perf. 12½x12¾*

987 A239 Sheet of 10, #a-j 13.50 13.50

Nos. 987a, 987c, 987d, 987g, 987i are inscribed "Standard Mail."

Tribal Women — A240

No. 988, ($1.30): a, Mbalantu. b, Damara. c, Herero (leather headdress). d, San. e, Mafue. f, Baster.

No. 989, ($1.30): a, Mbukushu. b, Herero (flowered headdress). c, Himba. d, Kwanyama. e, Nama. f, Ngandjera/Kwaluudhi.

2002, Apr. 20 Litho. *Perf. 13¼x13*
Sheets of 6, #a-f

988-989 A240 Set of 2 9.50 9.50
988g Sheet of 6 with incorrect back inscriptions 9.00 9.00
989g Sheet of 6 with incorrect back inscriptions 9.00 9.00

Stamps are inscribed "Standard Mail."

The back inscriptions on Nos. 988g and 989g are placed incorrectly so that the inscriptions for the stamps on the left side of the sheet have the back inscriptions of the stamps on the right side of the sheet, and vice versa.

The Mbukushu stamp on No. 989g reads "Standard Maiil."

Birds — A241

Designs: ($1.30), African hoopoe. $2.20, Paradise flycatchers. $2.60, Swallowtailed bee-eaters. $2.80, Malachite kingfisher.

2002, May 15 *Perf. 13¾x13¼*

990-993 A241 Set of 4 6.00 6.00

No. 990 is inscribed "Standard Mail."

Ephemeral Rivers A242

Designs: ($1.30), Kuiseb River floods halting movement of sand dunes, vert. (36x48mm). $2.20, Bird flying over lake of Tsauchab River flood water. $2.60, Elephants in dry bed of Hoarusib River (86x22mm). $2.80, Birds near Nossob River flood water. $3.50, Birds near Fish River, vert. (55x21mm).

2002, July 1 *Perf. 13x13¼,13¼x13*

994-998 A242 Set of 5 7.50 7.50

See No. 1023.

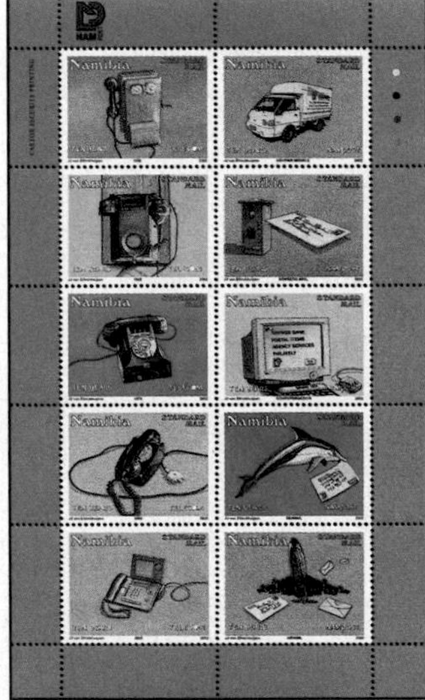

Namibia Post and Telecommunications, 10th Anniv. — A243

No. 999: a, Telephone, blue background. b, Telephone, yellow background. c, Telephone, green background. d, Telephone, lilac background. e, Picturephone, brown background. f, Mail van. g, Pillar box and letter. h, Computer. i, Dolphin with letter. j, Airplane and letters.

2002, Aug. 1 Litho. *Perf. 13¼x13*

999 A243 ($1.30) Sheet of 10, #a-j 7.00 7.00
k. Sheet of 10, 2 each #a-e 7.00 7.00
l. Sheet of 10, 2 each #f-j 7.00 7.00

Stamps are inscribed "Standard Mail."

Nos. 853-854 Surcharged

2002, Oct. 21 Litho. *Perf. 13½*

1000 A189 ($1.45) on 5c #853 .75 .75
1001 A189 ($1.45) on 10c #854 .75 .75

Surcharge on No. 1000 has letters that lean more to the right than those on No. 959. The two "d's" have tops that curve to the right on No. 1000, but have serifs that point left on No. 959. The cross line of the "t's" are lower on No. 1000 than on No. 959.

Prevention of AIDS — A244

Designs: ($1.45), Cross. $2.45, Condom. $2.85, Man and hand. $11.50, Test tubes.

2002, Dec. 1 *Perf. 13½x13*

1002-1005 A244 Set of 4 7.50 7.50

No. 1002 is inscribed "Standard Mail."

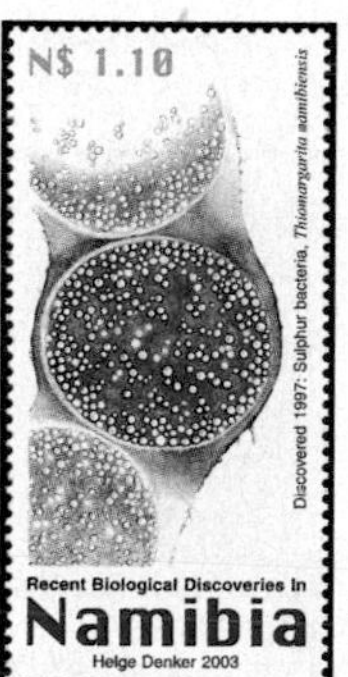

Recent Biological Discoveries A245

Designs: $1.10, Sulphur bacteria. $2.45, Whiteheadia etesionamibensis. $2.85, Cunene flathead (catfish), horiz. $3.85, Zebra racer, horiz. $20, Gladiator (insect).

Perf. 13¾x13¼, 13¼x13¾

2003, Feb. 24

1006-1010 A245 Set of 5 9.25 9.25

Rural Development — A246

Designs: $1.45, Water and electricity supply. ($2.75), Conservancy formation and land use diversification. $4.40, Education and health services. ($11.50), Communication and road infrastructure.

2003, Apr. 17 Litho. *Perf. 13¼x13¾*

1011-1014 A246 Set of 4 6.75 6.75

No. 1012 is inscribed "Postcard Rate" and No. 1014 is inscribed "Registered Mail."

Wetlands — A247

Designs: $1.10, Women and cattle near oshana. $2.85, Birds at Omadhiya Lakes. ($3.85), Cuvelai Drainage.

2003, June 6

1015-1017 A247 Set of 3 5.75 5.75

No. 1017 is inscribed "Non-Standard Mail."

Heroes Acre Monuments — A248

Various monuments with inscriprions: ($1.45), Standard Mail. ($2.75), Postcard Rate. ($3.85), Non-Standard Mail.

2003, Aug. 27 *Perf. 13¼*

1018-1020 A248 Set of 3 4.50 4.50

Souvenir Sheet

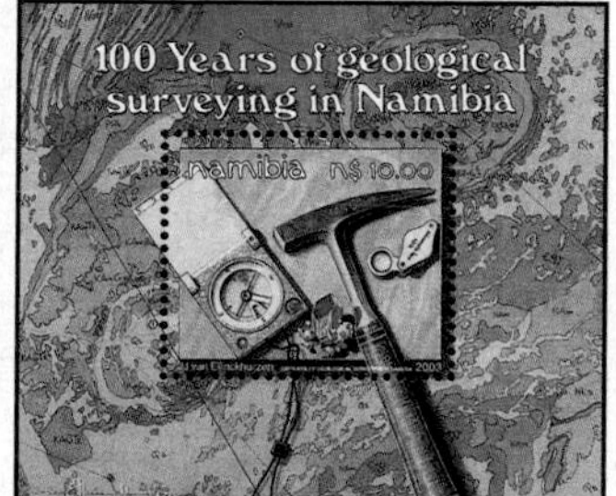

Geological Surveying in Namibia, Cent. — A249

2003, Sept. 10 *Perf. 13¼x13¾*

1021 A249 $10 multi 8.75 8.75

Souvenir Sheet

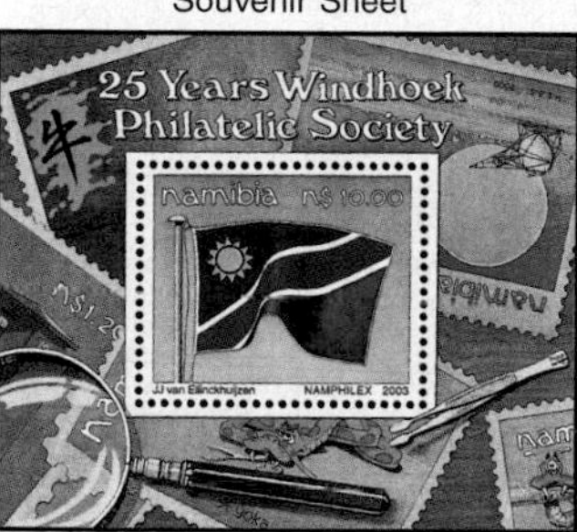

Windhoek Philatelic Society, 25th Anniv. — A250

2003, Sept. 10

1022 A250 $10 multi 7.00 7.00

Ephemeral Rivers Type of 2002

Souvenir Sheet

2003, Dec. 8 *Perf. 13¼x13*

1023 A242 $3.15 Like #996 3.75 3.75

Design voted "most beautiful stamp" at 8th Stamp World Cup, Paris.

Vervet Monkeys — A251

Designs: $1.60, Adult holding fruit. $3.15, Two monkeys on tree branches. $3.40, Adult and young. ($14.25), Adult chewing on twig. $4.85, Like #1024.

2004, Jan. 30 *Perf. 13*

1024-1027 A251 Set of 4 9.50 9.50

Souvenir Sheet

1028 A251 $4.85 multi 3.25 3.25

No. 1027 is inscribed "Inland Registered Mail Paid." 2004 Hong Kong Stamp Expo (#1028).

Honeybees on Flowers A252

Honeybees on: ($1.60), Sickle bush. $2.70, Daisy. ($3.05), Aloe. $3.15, Cat's claw. ($14.25), Edging senecio. $4.85, Pretty lady.

2004, Feb. 2 *Perf. 13x13¼*

1029-1033 A252 Set of 5 8.75 8.75

Souvenir Sheet

1034 A252 $4.85 multi 3.00 3.00

No. 1029 is inscribed "Standard mail;" No. 1031, "Post card rate;" No. 1033, "Inland registered mail paid."

Anti-Colonial Resistance, Cent. — A253

2004, Mar. 23 Litho. *Perf. 13¼*

1035 A253 ($1.60) multi 1.60 1.60

Souvenir Sheet

1036 A253 $5 multi 2.50 2.50

No. 1035 is inscribed "Standard Mail."

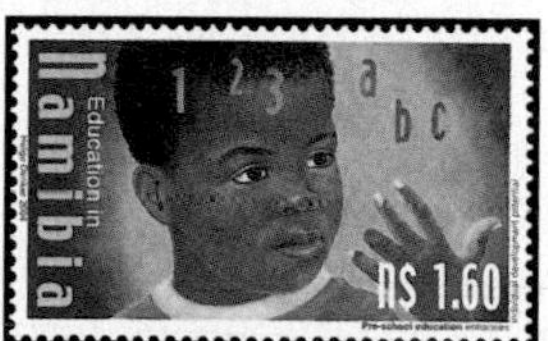

Education in Namibia — A254

Designs: $1.60, Pre-school education enhances individual development potential. $2.75, Primary and secondary school education for all lays the foundation for equal opportunity. $4.40, Advanced learning and vocational training provide career options. ($12.65), Lifelong learning encourages personal growth and the capacity for leadership.

2004, Apr. 19 *Perf. 13¼x13¾*

1037-1040 A254 Set of 4 8.00 8.00

No. 1040 is inscribed "Registered Mail."

Fishing Industry — A255

Fish and: $1.60, Ship and dockworkers. $2.75, Ship. $4.85, Workers at processing plant.

Perf. 13¼x13¾

2004, June 22 Litho.

1041-1043 A255 Set of 3 6.50 6.50

Historic Buildings in Bethanie A256

Designs: ($1.60), Joseph Ferdericks House. ($3.05), Schmelen House. ($4.40), Rhenish Mission Church. ($12.65), Stone Church.

2004, July 7 *Perf. 14x13½*

1044-1047 A256 Set of 4 9.00 9.00

No. 1044 is inscribed "Standard Mail;" No. 1045, "Postcard rate;" No. 1046, "Non-Standard Mail," No. 1047, "Registered Mail."

2004 Summer Olympics, Athens A257

Designs: ($1.60), Wrestling. $2.90, Boxing, vert. $3.40, Pistol shooting. $3.70, Mountain biking, vert.

Perf. 14x13¼, 13¼x14

2004, Aug. 3 Litho.

1048-1051 A257 Set of 4 9.75 9.75
1051a Inscribed "XXVIII Olympiad" 5.00 5.00

No. 1048 is inscribed "Standard Mail."
No. 1051 has incorrect inscription "XVIII Olympiad."
No. 1051a issued 9/14.

Miniature Sheet

Birds — A258

No. 1052: a, African fish eagles, national bird of Namibia. b, African fish eagles, national bird of Zimbabwe. c, Peregrine falcons, national bird of Angola. d, Cattle egrets, national bird of Botswana. e, Purple-crested louries, national bird of Swaziland. f, Blue cranes, national bird of South Africa. g, Bat-tailed trogons. h, African fish eagles, national bird of Zambia.

2004, Oct. 11 Litho. *Perf. 14*

1052 A258 $3.40 Sheet of 8, #a-h 19.00 19.00

See Botswana Nos. 792-793, South Africa No. 1342, Swaziland Nos. 727-735, Zambia No. 1033, and Zimbabwe No. 975.

Rotary International, Cent. — A259

2005, Feb. 23 Litho. *Perf. 13x13¼*

1053 A259 $3.70 multi 3.00 3.00

Pres. Hifikepunye Pohamba A260

2005, Mar. 21 *Perf. 13¼x14*

1054 A260 ($1.70) multi 2.50 2.50

Inscribed "Standard Mail."

Sunbirds
A261

Designs: $2.90, Marico sunbird. $3.40, Dusky sunbird. ($4.80), White-bellied sunbird. ($15.40), Scarlet-chested sunbird.
$10, Amethyst sunbird, horiz.

2005, Apr. 14 Litho. *Perf. 13¼x14*
1055-1058 A261 Set of 4 13.00 13.00

Souvenir Sheet

Perf. 14x13¼

1059 A261 $10 multi 5.50 5.50

No. 1057 is inscribed "Non-Standard Mail"; No. 1058, "Registered Inland Postage Paid."

Nos. 855, 859, 861 and 868 Surcharged

a

b

c

2005, June 7 Litho. *Perf. 13½*

1060	A189(a)	($1.70)	on 50c #859	1.00	1.00
1061	A189(b)	$2.90	on 20c #855	45.00	25.00
1062	A189(c)	($4.80)	on $4 #868	3.25	3.25
1063	A189(b)	$5.20	on 90c #861	3.75	3.75
	Nos. 1060-1063 (4)			53.00	33.00

Medicinal
Plants
A262

Designs: ($1.70), Nara. $2.90, Devil's claw. ($3.10), Hoodia. ($4.80), Tsamma.

2005, July 22 *Perf. 14x13¼*
1064-1067 A262 Set of 4 6.50 6.50

No. 1064 is inscribed "Standard Mail"; No. 1066, "Postcard Rate"; No. 1067, "Non-Standard Mail".

Crops — A263

Designs: $2.90, Vegetables. $3.40, Pearl millet. ($13.70), Corn.

2005, Aug. 2 *Perf. 13¼x13¾*
1068-1070 A263 Set of 3 9.50 9.50

No. 1070 is inscribed "Registered Mail."

Nos. 855, 861, 862, 866, 868-870 Surcharged Type "b" and

d

e

f

g

2005, Aug. 10 Litho. *Perf. 13½*

1070A	A189(a)	($1.70)	on 10c #854	*200.00*	*75.00*
1071	A189(d)	($1.70)	on 20c #855	1.00	.75
1072	A189(d)	($1.70)	on 90c #861	1.00	.75
1073	A189(d)	($1.70)	on $1 #862	.75	.75
1074	A189(b)	$2.90	on 90c #861	3.50	3.50
1075	A189(e)	($4.80)	on $1.50 #866	2.50	2.50
1076	A189(b)	$5.20	on 20c #855	3.50	3.50
1077	A189(f)	($15.40)	on $4 #868	4.00	4.00
1078	A189(g)	($18.50)	on $10 #870	7.50	7.50
1079	A189(b)	$25	on $5 #869	10.00	10.00
1080	A189(b)	$50	on $10 #870	20.00	20.00
	Nos. 1070A-1080 (11)			253.75	128.25

Gulls
A264

Designs: $3.10, Cape gulls. $4, Hartlaub's gulls. $5.50, Sabine's gull. ($16.20), Gray-headed gulls.

2006, Feb. 28 Litho. *Perf. 14x13¼*
1081-1084 A264 Set of 4 13.00 13.00

No. 1084 is inscribed "Inland Registered Mail Paid."

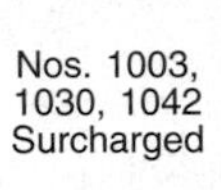

Nos. 1003,
1030, 1042
Surcharged

Methods and Perfs As Before

2006, Apr. 13

1085	A244	$3.10	on $2.45 #1003	2.25	2.25
1086	A252	$3.10	on $2.70 #1030	2.25	2.25
1087	A255	$3.10	on $2.75 #1042	2.25	2.25
	Nos. 1085-1087 (3)			6.75	6.75

Size, location and fonts of surcharges differ.

Dolphins
A265

Designs: ($1.80), Risso's dolphin. $3.10, Southern right-whale dolphins, vert. $3.70, Benguela dolphin. $4, Common dolphins. $5.50, Bottlenose dolphins, vert.

Perf. 13x13¼, 13¼x13

2006, Apr. 26 Litho.
1088-1092 A265 Set of 5 9.00 9.00

No. 1088 is inscribed "Standard Mail."

Miniature Sheets

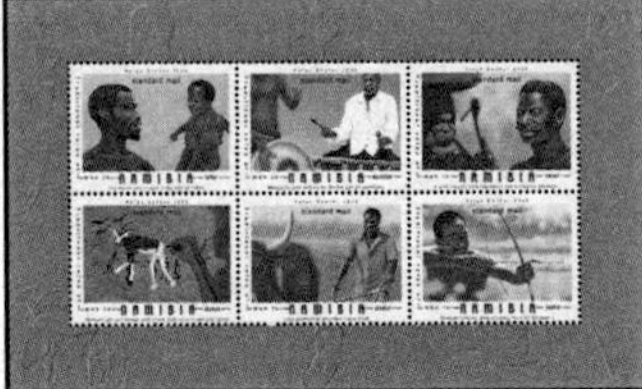

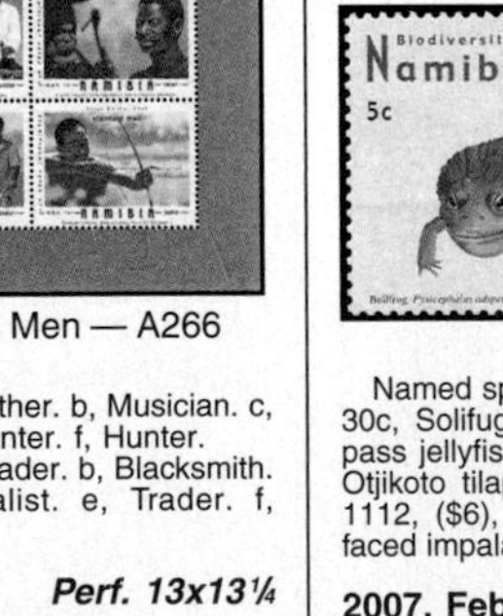

Traditional Roles of Men — A266

No. 1093, ($1.80): a, Father. b, Musician. c, Carver. d, Shaman. e, Planter. f, Hunter.
No. 1094, ($1.80): a, Leader. b, Blacksmith. c, Protector. d, Pastoralist. e, Trader. f, Storyteller.

2006, May 24 *Perf. 13x13¼*

Sheets of 6, #a-f

1093-1094 A266 Set of 2 7.50 7.50

Nos. 862, 865
Surcharged

2006, June 20 Litho. *Perf. 13½*

1095	A189	($3.30)	on $1 #862	2.50	2.50
1096	A189	($3.30)	on $1.20 #865	2.50	2.50

Nos. 1095-1096 are inscribed "Postcard Rate." Location of surcharges differs.

Perennial
Rivers
A267

Designs: $3.10, Orange River. $5.50, Kumene River, vert. (21x55mm). ($19.90), Zambezi River (87x22mm).

Perf. 14x13¼, 13½ ($5.50)

2006, July 24
1097-1099 A267 Set of 3 13.00 13.00

No. 1099 is inscribed "Registered Non Standard Mail."

Otavi Mines and Railway Company (OMEG) Rail Line, Cent
A268

Designs: $3.10, Construction of the rail line. $3.70, Henschel Class NG15 locomotive No. 41. $5.50, Narrow gauge Class Jung tank locomotive No. 9.

2006, Aug. 9 *Perf. 14¾x14*
1100-1102 A268 Set of 3 7.00 7.00

Otjiwarongo,
Cent. — A269

2006, Nov. 17 *Perf. 14*
1103 A269 $1.90 multi 1.40 1.40

Printed in sheets of 10.

Flora and
Fauna
A270

Named species: 5c, Bullfrog. 10c, Mesemb. 30c, Solifuge. 40c, Jewel beetle. 60c, Compass jellyfish. ($1.90), Web-footed gecko. $2, Otjikoto tilapia. No. 1111, $6, Milkbush. No. 1112, ($6), African hawk eagle. $10, Black-faced impala. $25, Lichens. $50, Baobab tree.

2007, Feb. 15 Litho. *Perf. 14x13¼*

1104	A270	5c	multi	.25	.25
1105	A270	10c	multi	.25	.25
1106	A270	30c	multi	.25	.25
1107	A270	40c	multi	.25	.25
1108	A270	60c	multi	.25	.25
1109	A270	($1.90)	multi	.65	.35
a.	Perf. 14			.80	.80
1110	A270	$2	multi	.75	.50
1111	A270	$6	multi	2.00	1.00
1112	A270	($6)	multi	2.00	1.00
1113	A270	$10	multi	3.25	1.75
1114	A270	$25	multi	7.00	7.00
1115	A270	$50	multi	14.00	14.00
	Nos. 1104-1115 (12)			30.90	26.85

No. 1109 is inscribed "Standard Mail." No. 1112 is inscribed "Non-standard Mail."
See Nos. 1165-1168.

A271

Etosha National Park, Cent. — A272

Designs: ($1.90), Otjovasandu Wilderness Area. $3.40, Okaukuejo Waterhole. ($17.20), Scientist conducting anthrax research.

No. 1119: a, Gabar goshawk (30x30mm). b, Umbrella thorn tree (50x30mm). c, Red-billed queleas (40x30mm). d, Burchell's zebras (40x30mm). e, Elephant (40x30mm). f, Blue wildebeest (40x30mm). g, Mustard tree (40x30mm). h, Black emperor dragonfly (40x40mm). i, Springbok (40x40mm). j, Ground agama (40x40mm).

Litho. With Foil Application

2007, Mar. 22 ***Perf. 14x13¼***

1116-1118 A271 Set of 3 12.50 12.50

Miniature Sheet

Litho.

1119 A272 ($2.25) Sheet of 10, #a-j 13.50 13.50

No. 1116 is inscribed "Standard Mail"; No. 1118, "Inland Registered Mail Paid"; Nos. 1119a-1119j, "Postcard Rate."

Dragonflies A273

Designs: ($1.90), Blue emperor dragonfly. $3.90, Rock dropwing dragonfly. $4.40, Red-veined dropwing dragonfly. ($6), Jaunty dropwing dragonfly.

$6, Blue basker dragonfly.

2007, Apr. 16 Litho. ***Perf. 12¾x14***

1120-1123 A273 Set of 4 7.75 7.75

Souvenir Sheet

Perf. 14x13¼

1124 A273 $6 multi 3.50 3.50

No. 1120 is inscribed "Standard Mail"; No. 1123, "Non Standard Mail Paid."

Trees A274

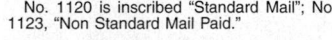

Designs: ($1.90), Commiphora kraeuseliana. $3.40, Commiphora wildii. $3.90, Commiphora glaucescens. ($6), Commiphora dinteri.

2007, July 20 Litho. ***Perf. 13¼x13¾***

1125-1128 A274 Set of 4 7.00 7.00

No. 1125 is inscribed "Standard Mail"; No. 1128, "Non-standard Mail."

Flowers — A275

Designs: ($1.90), Cheiridopsis caroli-schmidtii. ($6), Namibia ponderosa. ($17.20), Fenestraria rhopalophylla.

2007, Aug. 31

1129-1131 A275 Set of 3 11.50 11.50

No. 1129 is inscribed "Standard Mail"; No. 1130, "Non-standard Mail"; No. 1131, "Inland Registered Mail Paid."

Nos. 1129-1131 were each printed in sheets of 10 + 5 labels.

Nos. 861, 865, 866 and 868 Surcharged

h

i

j

k

2007, Oct. 1 Litho. ***Perf. 13½***

1132 A189(h) ($2) on 90c #861 .90 .65

1133 A189(h) ($2) on $1.20 #865 .90 .65

1134 A189(h) ($2) on $1.50 #866 .90 .65

1135 A189(h) ($2) on $4 #868 .90 .65

1136 A189(i) $3.70 on $1.20 #865 1.50 1.25

1137 A189(i) $4.20 on $1.20 #865 1.50 1.40

1138 A189(i) $4.85 on $1.20 #865 1.75 1.60

1139 A189(j) ($6.50) on $1.20 #865 2.50 2.25

1140 A189(k) ($16.45) on $1.20 #865 7.50 *9.00*

Nos. 1132-1140 (9) 18.35 18.10

Location of surcharge varies.

Miniature Sheets

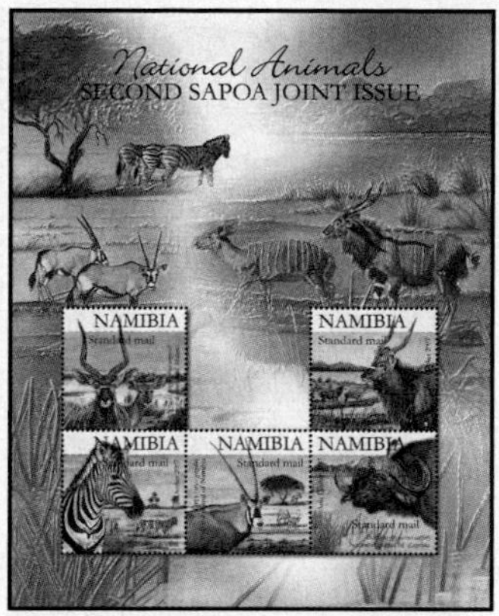
National Animals — A276

Nos. 1141 and 1142: a, Nyala (Malawi). b, Nyala (Zimbabwe). c, Burchell's zebra (Botswana). d, Oryx (Namibia). e, Buffalo (Zambia).

2007, Oct. 9 Litho. ***Perf. 13¾***

Granite Paper (#1141)

Country Name in Black

1141 A276 ($2) Sheet of 5, #a-e 4.75 4.75

Litho. With Foil Application

Country Name in Silver

1142 A276 ($2) Sheet of 5, #a-e 4.75 4.75

Nos. 1141a-1141e, 1142a-1142e are inscribed "Standard mail."

See Botswana No. 838, Malawi No. 752, Zambia Nos. 1097-1101, Zimbabwe Nos. 1064-1068.

Weaver Birds — A277

Designs: ($2), Southern masked weaver. $3.70, Red-headed weaver. ($3.90), White-browed sparrow weaver. $4.20, Sociable weaver. ($18.45), Thick-billed weaver.

2008, Feb. 28 Litho. ***Perf. 13½x14***

1143-1147 A277 Set of 5 11.00 11.00

No. 1143 is inscribed "Standard Mail"; No. 1145, "Postcard Rate"; No. 1147, "Inland Registered Mail Paid."

Euphorbia Flowers — A278

Designs: ($3.90), Euphorbia virosa. $6.45, Euphorbia dregeana. ($22.95), Euphorbia damarana.

$6.45 — Type I: "E" over "I" in Latin inscription. Type II: Corrected version, no "I".

2008

1148 A278 ($3.90) multi 1.25 1.25

1149 A278 $6.45 multi, Type I 1.60 1.60

a. Type II 2.50 2.50

1150 A278 ($22.95) multi 6.25 6.25

Nos. 1148-1150 (3) 9.10 9.10

Issued: Nos. 1148-1150, 3/3; No. 1149a, 5/27. No. 1148 inscribed "Postcard Rate"; No. 1150, "Registered Non-Standard Mail."

Miniature Sheet

Discovery of Diamonds in Namibia, Cent. — A279

No. 1151: a, Uncut diamonds. b, Land mining. c, Marine mining. d, Diamond jewelry.

Litho. With Foil Application

2008, Apr. 15 ***Perf. 14x13½***

1151 A279 $2 Sheet of 4, #a-d 5.00 5.00

Miniature Sheet

Traditional Houses — A280

No. 1152: a, Herero. b, Kavango. c, Owambo. d, Nama. e, Caprivi. f, San.

2008, May 27 Litho.

1152 A280 ($2.20) Sheet of 6, #a-f 4.00 4.00

Nos. 1152a-1152f are each inscribed "Standard Mail."

Twyfelfontein UNESCO World Heritage Site — A281

Rock drawings: No. 1153, ($7.20), No. 1156a ($2.20), Lion man. No. 1154, ($7.20), No. 1156b ($2.20), Giraffe, Dancing kudu. No. 1155, ($7.20), No. 1156c ($2.20), Elephant.

2008, June 27 ***Perf. 13½x13¾***

1153-1155 A281 Set of 3 7.00 7.00

Souvenir Sheet

1156 A281 ($2.20) Sheet of 3, #a-c 3.00 3.00

Nos. 1153-1155 are each inscribed "Non-Standard Mail"; Nos. 1156a-1156c, "Standard Mail."

Ediacaran Fossils — A282

Designs: ($2), Rangea. ($3.90), Swartpuntia. ($18.45), Pteridinium. ($22.95), Ernietta.

Litho. & Embossed

2008, Aug. 8 ***Perf. 13¼x14***

1157-1160 A282 Set of 4 14.00 14.00

No. 1157 is inscribed "Standard Mail"; No. 1158, "Postcard Rate"; No. 1159, "Registered Non-standard Mail"; No. 1160, "Registered Inland Mail Paid."

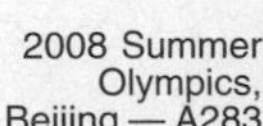

2008 Summer Olympics, Beijing — A283

Designs: $2, Female runner, sun and Earth. $3.70, Athlete with arms raised. $3.90, Athlete at finish line. $4.20, Female runner with arms extended.

2008, Aug. 15 Litho. ***Perf. 13¼x13***
1161-1164 A283 Set of 4 3.75 3.75

Flora and Fauna Type of 2007

Designs: $4.10, Thimble grass. $4.60, Bronze whaler shark. $5.30, Deep sea red crab. ($18.20), False ink cap mushroom.

2008, Oct. 1 Litho. ***Perf. 14x13¼***
1165 A270 $4.10 multi 1.10 1.10
1166 A270 $4.60 multi 1.25 1.25
1167 A270 $5.30 multi 1.50 1.50
1168 A270 ($18.20) multi 5.00 5.00
Nos. 1165-1168 (4) 8.85 8.85

No. 1168 is inscribed "Registered Mail."

Eagles — A284

Designs: $4.10, Martial eagle. ($4.30), Bataleur eagle. $4.60, Verreaux's eagle. ($25.40), Tawny eagle.

2009, Feb. 2 Litho. ***Perf. 13¼x13¾***
1169-1172 A284 Set of 4 13.50 13.50

No. 1170 is inscribed "Postcard Rate"; No. 1172, "Registered Non-Standard Mail."

New Year 2009 (Year of the Ox) A285

Litho. With Foil Application
2009, Apr. 10 ***Perf. 14x13¼***
1173 A285 $2.20 multi 1.00 1.00

Miniature Sheet

Flora and Fauna of the Brandberg — A286

No. 1174: a, Augur buzzard (30x30mm). b, Numasfels Peak (50x30mm). c, Quiver tree (40x30mm). d, CMR beetle (40x30mm). e, Leopard (40x30mm). f, Kobas (40x30mm). g, Bokmakiri (40x30mm). h, Jameson's red rock rabbit (40x40mm). i, Brandberg halfmens (40x40mm). j, Jordan's girdled lizard (40x40mm).

2009, Apr. 10 Litho. ***Perf. 14x13¼***
1174 A286 ($4.30) Sheet of 10, #a-j 11.00 11.00

Nos. 1174a-1174j are each inscribed "Postcard Rate."

Souvenir Sheet

First Crossing of Africa by Automobile, Cent. — A287

2009, May 1 ***Perf. 13¾x14¼***
1175 A287 $7.10 multi 2.50 2.50

Wild Horses — A288

Designs: $5.30, Two horses. $8, Three horses. ($20.40), Four horses.

2009, July 3 ***Perf. 13¾x14***
1176-1178 A288 Set of 3 10.00 10.00

No. 1178 is inscribed "Inland Registered Mail Paid." See No. 1185.

Souvenir Sheet

German Higher Private School, Cent. — A289

2009, Aug. 21 Litho. ***Perf. 13½***
1179 A289 $4.60 multi 2.00 2.00

Geckos A290

Designs: $4.40, Festive gecko. $5, Koch's barking gecko. $6, Giant ground gecko. $7.70, Velvety thick-toed gecko. ($18.20), Bradfield's Namib day gecko.

2009, Sept. 30 ***Perf. 13¾***
1180-1184 A290 Set of 5 11.00 11.00

No. 1184 is inscribed "Registered Mail."

Horses Type of 2009

Design: Four horses in desert.

2009, Nov. 2 ***Perf. 13¾x14***
1185 A288 ($4.60) multi 1.50 1.50

No. 1185 is inscribed "Postcard Rate."

Miniature Sheet

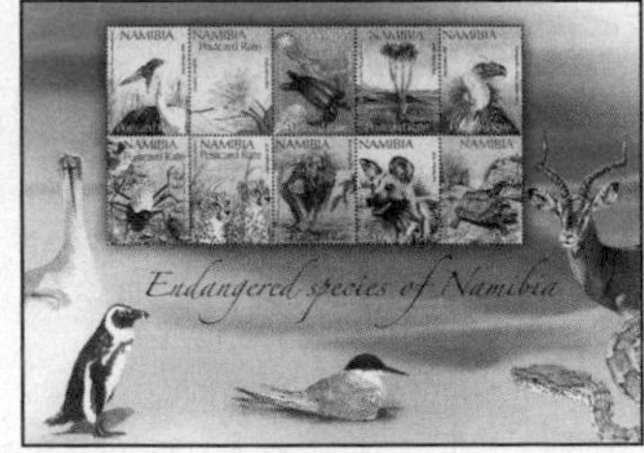

Endangered Species — A291

No. 1186: a, Wattled crane. b, Gazania thermalis. c, Leatherback turtle. d, Giant quiver tree. e, Cape vulture. f, White Namib toktokkie. g, Cheetah. h, Hook-lipped rhinoceros. i, wild dog. j, Nama-padloper tortoise.

2010, Feb. 8 ***Perf. 13¼x13***
1186 A291 ($4.60) Sheet of 10, #a-j 12.00 12.00

Nos. 1186a-1186j are inscribed "Postcard Rate."

Independence, 20th Anniv. — A292

Perf. 13¼x13¾
2010, Mar. 21 Litho.
1187 A292 ($2.50) multi .70 .70

No. 1187 is inscribed "Standard mail."

Miniature Sheet

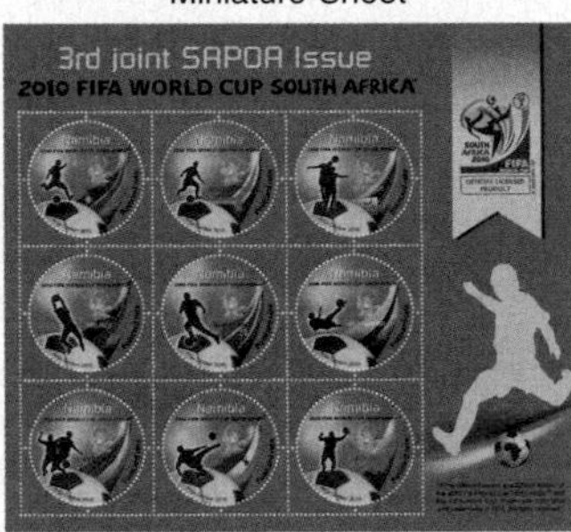

2010 World Cup Soccer Championships, South Africa — A293

No. 1188 — Soccer players, ball, 2010 World Cup mascot and flag of: a, Namibia. b, South Africa. c, Zimbabwe. d, Malawi. e, Swaziland. f, Botswana. g, Mauritius. h, Lesotho. i, Zambia.

2010, Apr. 9 Litho. ***Perf. 13½***
1188 A293 ($4.60) Sheet of 9, #a-i 12.50 12.50

Nos. 1188a-1188i are inscribed "Postcard rate." A miniature sheet containing No. 1188a and stamps from South Africa, Zimbabwe, Malawi, Swaziland, Botswana, Mauritius, Lesotho and Zambia was sold by Namibia Post for $40. The sheet apparently was not sold by any other country. See Botswana Nos. 896-905, Lesotho No. , Malawi No. 753, Mauritius No. , South Africa No. 1403, Swaziland Nos. 794-803, Zambia Nos. 1115-1118, and Zimbabwe Nos. 1112-1121.

Miniature Sheet

Birds — A294

No. 1189: a, Northern black korhaan. b, Red-crested korhaan. c, Black-bellied bustard. d, Rüppell's korhaan. e, Ludwig's bustard. f, Kori bustard.

2010, Apr. 14 ***Perf. 13½x14***
1189 A294 ($4.60) Sheet of 6, #a-f 9.00 9.00

Nos. 1189a-1189f are inscribed "Postcard rate."

Lighthouses A295

Designs: $4.40, Swakopmund Lighthouse. ($9.50), Diaz Point Lighthouse, Lüderitzbucht. ($18.20), Pelican Point Lighthouse, Walvis Bay.

2010, June 18 ***Perf. 13½x13¾***
1190-1192 A295 Set of 3 8.50 8.50

No. 1191 is inscribed "Non-standard mail." No. 1192 is inscribed "Registered Mail."

Souvenir Sheet

Christuskirche, Windhoek, Cent. — A296

2010, Aug. 6 ***Perf. 14***
1193 A296 $5 multi 1.75 1.75

Oryx — A296a

2010, Sept. 18 *Perf. 13¾*

1193A A296a ($2.50) multi	2.00	2.00

No. 1193A was printed in sheets of 5 that sold for $25. The lower half of the stamp, as shown, is a generic image that could be personalized.

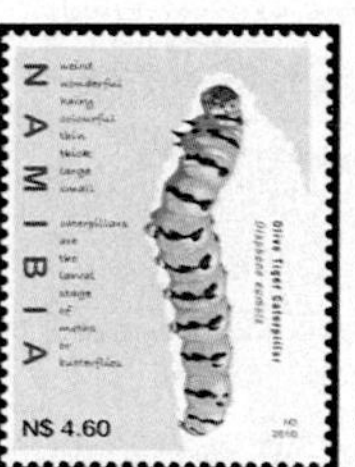

Caterpillars A297

Designs: $4.60, Olive tiger caterpillar. $5.30, African armyworm. $6.40, Wild silk caterpillar. ($29.40), Mopane caterpillar.

2010, Oct. 1 **Litho.**

1194-1197 A297 Set of 4	13.50	13.50

Souvenir Sheet

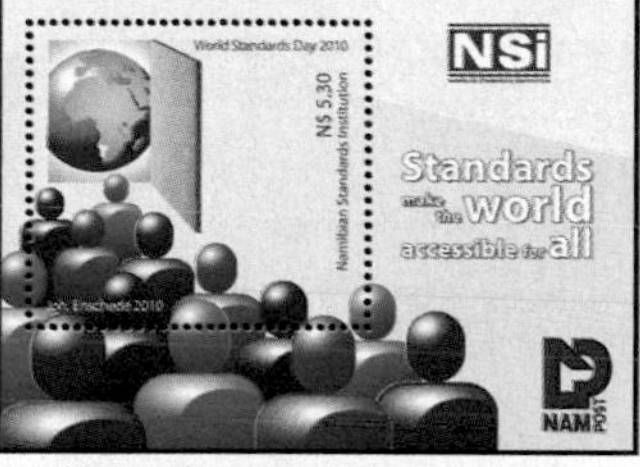

World Standards Day — A298

2010, Oct. 18 *Perf. 14x13½*

1198 A298 $5.30 multi	1.60	1.60

Wildlife A299

Designs: $4.60, Leopard. ($5), African elephant, vert. $5.30, Black rhinoceros. $6.40, African buffalo. ($8.50), Lion, vert.

2011, Jan. 28 *Perf. 14x13¼, 13¼x14*

1199-1203 A299 Set of 5	8.25	8.25

No. 1200 is inscribed "Postcard Rate." No. 1203 is inscribed "Non-standard Mail."

Miniature Sheet

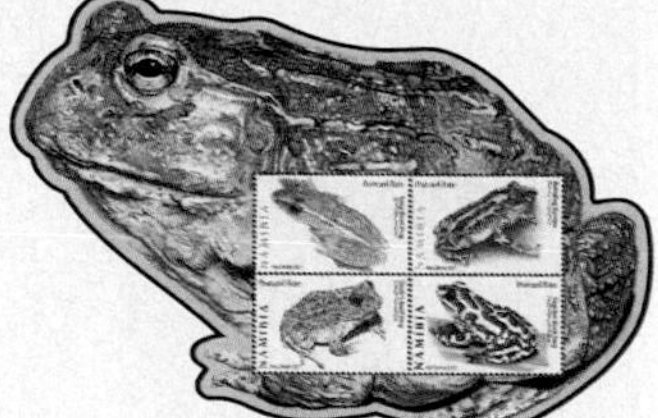

Frogs — A300

No. 1204: a, Long reed frog. b, Bubbling kassina. c, Tandy's sand frog. d, Angolan reed frog.

2011, Mar. 23 *Perf. 13¼x14*

1204 A300 ($5) Sheet of 4, #a-d	6.00	6.00

Nos. 1204a-1204d each were inscribed "Postcard Rate."

Souvenir Sheet

Road Safety Campaign — A301

2011, May 11 *Perf. 13x13¼*

1205 A301 $5.30 multi	1.60	1.60

Miniature Sheet

Endangered Marine Life — A302

No. 1206: a, Cape gannet (30x30mm). b, Atlantic yellow-nosed albatross (50x30mm). c, African penguin (40x30mm). d, Southern right whale (40x30mm). e, Bank cormorant (40x30mm). f, West coast steenbras (40x30mm). g, Split-fan kelp (40x40mm). h, Cape rock lobster (40x40mm).

2011, May 16 *Perf. 14x13¼*

1206 A302 $4.60 Sheet of 8, #a-h	12.00	12.00

Personalized Stamps — A303

Designs: No. 1207, Oryx. elephant and leopard, Etosha National Park. No. 1208, Lizard and rock paintings, Twyfelfontein UNESCO World Heritage Site. No. 1209, Bird over Fish River Canyon. No. 1210, Antelope, Sossusvlei Region. No. 1211, Rhinoceros in Community Conservation Area.

2011, June 7 *Perf. 13¼x13*

1207 A303 ($5) multi + label	2.50	2.50
1208 A303 ($5) multi + label	2.50	2.50
1209 A303 ($5) multi + label	2.50	2.50
1210 A303 ($5) multi + label	2.50	2.50
1211 A303 ($5) multi + label	2.50	2.50
a. Sheet of 5, #1207-1211, + 5 labels	12.50	12.50
Nos. 1207-1211 (5)	12.50	12.50

Nos. 1207-1211, each inscribed "Postcard rate," were printed in sheets of 5 stamps + 5 labels that could be personalized. Label shown is a generic image. Sheets of 5, including No. 1211a, each sold for $35.

Aloes — A304

Designs: ($5), Aloe gariepensis. ($8.50), Aloe variegata. ($20.90), Aloe striata ssp. karasbergensis.

2011, June 21 *Perf. 13¼x14*

1212-1214 A304 Set of 3	10.50	10.50

No. 1212 is inscribed "Postcard Rate." No. 1213 is inscribed "Non Standard Mail." No. 1214 is inscribed "Registered Mail."

Grebes — A305

Designs: No. 1215, ($2.70), Little grebe. No. 1216, ($2.70), Great crested grebe. ($23.60), Black-necked grebe, horiz.

2011, July 18 *Perf. 13¼x14, 14x13¼*

1215-1217 A305 Set of 3	9.00	9.00

Nos. 1215-1216 are each inscribed "Standard Mail." No. 1217 is inscribed "Inland Registered Mail."

Grasses — A306

Designs: ($2.70), Natal red top. $4.80, Feather-top chloris. $5.40, Urochloa brachyura. $6.50, Nine-awned grass. ($8.50), Foxtail buffalo grass.

2011, Sept. 30 **Litho.** *Perf. 13½x14*

1218-1222 A306 Set of 5	8.00	8.00

No. 1218 is inscribed "Standard mail"; No. 1222, "Non-standard mail."

Birds — A308

Designs: 5c, Carp's tit. 10c, Hartlaub's spurfowl. 20c, Herero chat.30c, Rüppell's parrot. 50c, Rüppell's korhaan. ($2.90), White-tailed shrike. $5, Rockrunner. ($5.30), Dune lark. ($8.90), Damara hornbill. $20, Damara tern. ($21.90), Violet wood hoopoe. $100, Bare-cheeked babbler.

2012, Feb. 15 **Litho.** *Perf. 13¼*

1224 A308	5c multi	.25	.25
1225 A308	10c multi	.25	.25
1226 A308	20c multi	.25	.25
1227 A308	30c multi	.25	.25
1228 A308	50c multi	.25	.25
1229 A308	($2.90) multi	.80	.80
1230 A308	$5 multi	1.40	1.40
1231 A308	($5.30) multi	1.40	1.40
1232 A308	($8.90) multi	2.40	2.40
1233 A308	$20 multi	5.50	5.50
1234 A308	($21.90) multi	6.00	6.00
1235 A308	$100 multi	27.00	27.00
	Nos. 1224-1235 (12)	45.75	45.75

No. 1229 is inscribed "Standard mail"; No. 1231, "Postcard rate"; No. 1232, "Non-standard mail"; No. 1234, "Registered mail."

See Nos. 1254-1258.

Bats A309

Designs: No. 1236, ($5.30), Straw-colored fruit bats. No. 1237, ($5.30), Egyptian slit-faced bats. No. 1238, ($5.30), Angolan epauletted fruit bats.

2012, Apr. 9 *Perf. 13¼*

Stamps + Labels

1236-1238 A309 Set of 3	5.00	5.00

Nos. 1236-1238 are inscribed "Postcard rate."

2012 Summer Olympics and Paralympics, London — A310

Designs: $2.90, Shooting. $4.80, Running, vert. $5.40, Cycling. $6.50, Wheelchair racer, vert.

2012, Apr. 16 *Perf. 13x13¼, 13¼x13*

1239-1242 A310 Set of 4	5.75	5.75

Scorpions — A311

Designs: $4.80, Parabuthus villosus. ($5.30), Parabuthus namibensis. $5.40, Opistophthalmus carinatus. $6.50, Hottentotta arenaceus.

2012, June 11 *Perf. 14x13¾*

1243-1246 A311 Set of 4	6.50	6.50

Souvenir Sheets

Telecom Namibia, 20th Anniv. — A312

Nampost, 20th Anniv. — A313

No. 1247: a, Satellite dishes. b, Fiber-optic cable strands.

No. 1248: a, Postman in bush. b, Mail truck.

2012, July 31 ***Perf. 12½***

1247 A312 $2.90 Sheet of 2, #a-b 2.00 2.00
1248 A313 $2.90 Sheet of 2, #a-b 2.00 2.00

Souvenir Sheet

Gobabeb Research and Training Center, 50th Anniv. — A314

No. 1249: a, ($3.10), Namaqua chameleon. b, $5.10, Dune grass. c, $5.80, Flying saucer beetle.

2012, Sept. 22 ***Perf. 13¼x14***

1249 A314 Sheet of 3, #a-c 4.00 4.00

No. 1249a is inscribed "Standard Mail."

Mongooses A315

Designs: $5.10, Black mongoose. ($5.60), Yellow mongoose, vert. $5.80, Banded mongoose. $6.90, Dwarf mongoose.

Perf. 14¾x14¼, 14¼x14¾

2012, Oct. 1

1250-1253 A315 Set of 4 6.50 6.50

No. 1251 is inscribed "Postcard Rate."

Birds Type of 2012

Designs: 90c, Benguela long-billed lark. $1, Barlow's lark. $3, Rosy-faced lovebirds. $10, Gray's larks. $12, Monteiro's hornbill.

2013, Mar. 1 ***Perf. 13¼***

1254 A308 90c multi .30 .30
1255 A308 $1 multi .30 .30
1256 A308 $3 multi .90 .90
1257 A308 $10 multi 3.25 3.25
1258 A308 $12 multi 3.75 3.75
Nos. 1254-1258 (5) 6.15 6.15

Beetles A316

Designs: ($3.10), Glittering jewel beetle. $5.10, Red-spotted lily weevil. $5.50, Garden fruit chafer. $6.90, Lunate ladybird. ($26.50), Two-spotted ground beetle.

2013, Apr. 5

1259-1263 A316 Set of 5 14.50 14.50

No. 1259 is inscribed "Standard mail;" No. 1263, "Inland registered mail."

Miniature Sheets

Children — A317

No. 1264, ($3.10) — Inscriptions: a, Right to family, shelter & a healthy environment. b, Faith & joy. c, Right to health, nutrition & safety. d, Freedom from neglect, fear, abuse & violence. e, Love & trust. f, Freedom of identity, traditions & beliefs.

No. 1265, ($3.10) — Inscriptions: a, Right to early development support, education & information. b, Aspirations & dreams. c, Right to special care & support. d, Freedom of expression, association & participation. e, Play & creativity. f, Freedom from discrimination & exploitation.

2013, June 17 Litho. ***Perf. 13x13¼***
Sheets of 6, #a-f

1264-1265 A317 Set of 2 12.00 12.00

Nos. 1264a-1264f and 1265a-1265f are each inscribed "Standard mail."

Souvenir Sheet

Environmental Education — A318

2013, June 20 Litho. ***Perf. 13¼x13***

1266 A318 $5.10 multi 1.75 1.75

Souvenir Sheet

Man and Woman Riding in Donkey Cart — A319

2013, July 12 Litho. ***Perf. 13x13¼***

1267 A319 $5.80 multi 1.75 1.75

Johanna Benson, Gold Medalist at 2012 Paralympics A320

2013, Aug. 21 Litho. ***Perf. 13¼x13***

1268 A320 ($3.10) multi .65 .65
1269 A320 ($6) multi + label — —

No. 1268 is inscribed "Standard mail" and was printed in sheets of 10.

No. 1269 is inscribed "Postcard rate" and was printed in sheets that sold for $40 containing 5 stamps + 5 labels that could be personalized.

Antelopes — A321

Designs: $5.40, Elands. No. 1271, ($6), Greater kudus. No. 1272, ($6), Gemsboks. $6.20, Sables. $7.30, Blue wildebeests.

2013, Sept. 30 Litho. ***Perf. 12½***

1270-1274 A321 Set of 5 6.25 6.25

Nos. 1271 and 1272 are both inscribed "Postcard Rate."

Wooden Vessels A322

Designs: ($3.30), HaMbukushu. $5.40, BaSubiya. ($6), Naman. $6.20, AaWambo. $7.30, OvaHerero.

2014, Feb. 10 Litho. ***Perf. 14x13¼***

1275-1279 A322 Set of 5 5.25 5.25

No. 1275 is inscribed "Standard Mail;" No. 1277; "Postcard Rate."

Miniature Sheet

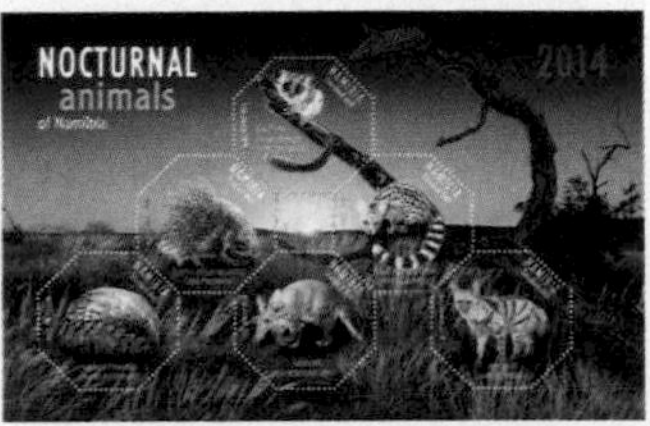

Nocturnal Animals — A323

No. 1280: a, Southern lesser galago. b, Cape porcupine. c, Small-spotted genet. d, Ground pangolin. e, Aardvark. f, Aardwolf.

2014, Mar. 14 Litho. ***Perf. 13¼***

1280 A323 ($3.30) Sheet of 6, #a-f, + label 3.75 3.75

Nos. 1280a-1280f are each inscribed "Standard Mail."

Namibian Flag on Map of Namibia A324

2014, May 21 Litho. ***Perf. 14x13¼***

1281 A324 ($3.30) multi .65 .65

Souvenir Sheet

1282 A324 ($27.20) multi 5.25 5.25

No. 1281 is inscribed "Standard Mail;" No. 1282, "Inland Registered Mail."

Antelopes — A325

Designs: No. 1283, ($6), Red lechwes. No. 1284, ($6), Bushbucks. No. 1285, ($6), Red hartebeests. No. 1286, ($6), Springboks.

2014, May 27 Litho. ***Perf. 13¼x13½***

1283-1286 A325 Set of 4 4.50 4.50

Nos. 1283-1286 are each inscribed "Postcard Rate."

Snakes A326

Designs: $5.40, Black mamba. ($6), Boomslang. $6.20, Puff adder. $7.30, Zebra snake.

2014, June 4 Litho. ***Perf. 13¾***

1287-1290 A326 Set of 4 4.75 4.75

No. 1288 is inscribed "Postcard Rate."

First Visit of Chinese Navy to Namibia A327

Designs: No. 1291, $3.30, Taihu. No. 1292, $3.30, Yancheng.

2014, June 11 Litho. ***Perf. 13x13¼***

1291-1292 A327 Set of 2 1.25 1.25

A souvenir sheet containing two $3.30 stamps depicting Walvis Bay harbor and the Luoyang sold for $15.

Miniature Sheet

Flora and Fauna of the Kalahari Desert — A328

No. 1293: a, Peregrine falcon (30x30mm). b, Cape turtle doves (50x30mm). c, Shepherd's tree (40x30mm). d, Giraffe (40x30mm). e, African monarch butterfly (40x30mm). f, Cheetah (40x30mm). g, Gemsbok cucumbers (40x30mm). h, Suricates (40x40mm). i, Trumpet-thorn (40x40mm). j, Spotted sandveld lizard (40x40mm).

2014, July 28 Litho. *Perf. 14x13½*
1293 A328 ($6) Sheet of 10, #a-j 11.50 11.50

Nos. 1293a-1293j are each inscribed "Postcard Rate."

In 2014 and 2015, Namibia postal officials declared as "illegal" souvenir sheets with a $5 denomination depicting various dogs and other wildlife, and a stamp inscribed "Postage Paid" depicting a dog and cat.

Kingfishers — A329

Designs: ($5.70), Pied kingfishers. ($6.40), Half-collared kingfishers. ($6.60), Woodland kingfishers. ($7.70), Malachite kingfishers. ($28.30), Giant kingfishers.

2014, Oct. 1 Litho. *Perf. 13¼x14*
1294-1298 A329 Set of 5 9.75 9.75

No. 1294 is inscribed "Zone A;" No. 1295, "Postcard Rate;" No. 1296, "Zone B;" No. 1297, "Zone C;" No. 1298, "Inland Registered Mail."

Souvenir Sheet

Namib Sand Sea UNESCO World Heritage Site — A330

No. 1299: a, Sossusvlei/Deadvlei. b, Comicus spp. c, Sandwich Harbor.

2015, Feb. 6 Litho. *Perf. 13¼*
1299 A330 ($6.40) Sheet of 3, #a-c 3.25 3.25

Nos. 1299a-1299c are each inscribed "Postcard Rate."

Presidents of Namibia — A331

Designs: ($3.50), Pres. Hage Geingob. $30, Presidents Sam Nujoma, Hifikepunye Pohamba, Hage Geingob, map and flag of Namibia, horiz.

Litho. With Foil Application

2015, Mar. 21 *Perf. 13¼x13¾*
1300 A331 ($3.50) multi .60 .60

Litho., Sheet Margin Litho. With Foil Application

Souvenir Sheet

Perf. 14½x14

1301 A331 $30 multi 5.25 5.25

Inauguration of Pres. Geingob, Independence, 25th anniv. (No. 1301). No. 1301 contains one 75x26mm stamp.

Bee-Eaters A332

Designs: ($3.50), White-fronted bee-eater. $5.70, Southern carmine bee-eater, horiz. $6.60, Swallow-tailed bee-eater, horiz. $7.70, Little bee-eaters, horiz. ($28.30), European bee-eater.

Perf. 14x14¼, 14¼x14

2015, May 15 Litho.
1302-1306 A332 Set of 5 8.50 8.50

No. 1302 is inscribed "Standard Mail;" No. 1306, "Inland Registered Mail."

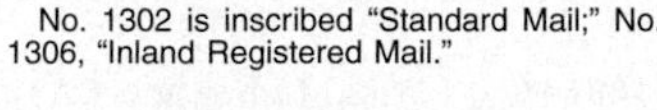

Sharks — A335

Designs: $5.70, Bronze whaler shark. ($6.80), Broadnose sevengill shark. $6.60, Great white shark. $7.70, Smooth hammerhead shark.

2015, Aug. 19 Litho. *Perf. 14½x14*
1316-1319 A335 Set of 4 4.00 4.00

No. 1317 is inscribed "Postcard Rate."

Coursers — A336

Designs: ($6.05), Burchell's courser. ($6.80), Three-banded courser. ($7), Double-banded courser. ($8.20), Bronze-winged courser.

2015, Oct. 1 Litho. *Perf. 13½*
1320-1323 A336 Set of 4 4.25 4.25

No. 1320 is inscribed "Zone A;" No. 1321, "Postcard Rate:" No. 1322, "Zone B;" No. 1323, "Zone C."

NATAL

nə-'tal

LOCATION — Southern coast of Africa, bordering on the Indian Ocean
GOVT. — British Crown Colony
AREA — 35,284 sq. mi.
POP. — 1,206,386 (1908)
CAPITAL — Pietermaritzburg

Natal united with Cape of Good Hope, Orange Free State and the Transvaal in 1910 to form the Union of South Africa.

12 Pence = 1 Shilling
20 Shillings = 1 Pound

Values for Nos. 1-7 are for examples with complete margins and free from damage. Unused values for No. 8 on are for stamps with original gum as defined in the catalogue introduction. Very fine examples of Nos. 8-49, 61-63 and 79 will have perforations touching the design on one or more sides due to the narrow spacing of the stamps on the plates. Stamps with perfs clear of the design on all four sides are scarce and will command higher prices.

Watermark

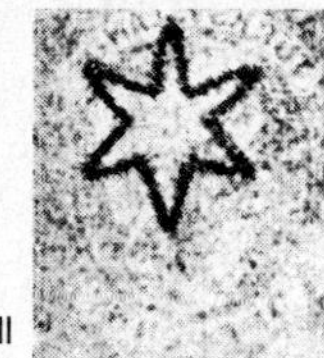
Wmk. 5 — Small Star

Crown and V R (Victoria Regina) — A1

Crown and V R (Victoria Regina) — A2

Crown and Laurel — A3

A4

A5

Colorless Embossing

1857 Unwmk. *Imperf.*
1 A1 3p *rose* 725.
a. Tete beche pair 55,000.
2 A2 6p *green* 2,000.
a. Diagonal half used as 3p on cover 16,500.
3 A3 9p *blue* 65,000. 13,000.
4 A4 1sh *buff* 10,500.

1858
5 A5 1p *blue* 1,400.
6 A5 1p *rose* 2,200.
a. No. 1 embossed over No. 6 —
7 A5 1p *buff* 1,450.

Reprints: The paper is slightly glazed, the embossing sharper and the colors as follows: 1p pale blue, deep blue, carmine rose or yellow; 3p pale rose or carmine rose; 6p bright green or yellow green; 1sh pale buff or pale yellow. Bogus cancellations are found on the reprints.

The stamps printed on surface-colored paper are revenue stamps with trimmed perforations.

Listings of shades will be found in the *Scott Classic Specialized Catalogue.*

Queen Victoria — A6

1860 Engr. *Perf. 14*
8 A6 1p rose 190.00 95.00
9 A6 3p blue 225.00 60.00
a. Vert. pair, imperf betwn. 13,000.

1863 *Perf. 13*
10 A6 1p red 130.00 35.00

1861 *Clean-cut Perf. 14 to 16*
11 A6 3p blue 350.00 82.50

1862 *Rough Perf. 14 to 16*
12 A6 3p blue 175.00 45.00
a. Imperf., pair 4,500.
b. Imperf. horiz. or vert., pair 6,500.
13 A6 6p gray 275.00 75.00

1862 Wmk. 5
14 A6 1p rose 180.00 82.50

Imperforate stamps of the 1p and 3p on paper watermarked small star are proofs.

1864 Wmk. 1 *Perf. 12½*
15 A6 1p carmine red 140.00 50.00
16 A6 6p violet 90.00 37.50

No. 15 imperf is a proof.

Queen Victoria — A7

1867 Typo. *Perf. 14*
17 A7 1sh green 275.00 52.50

For types A6 and A7 overprinted or surcharged see Nos. 18-50, 61-63, 76, 79.

Stamps of 1860-67 Overprinted

1869 Overprint 12¾mm
18 A6 1p carmine red (#15) 525.00 100.00
b. Double overprint — —
19 A6 3p blue (#12) 700.00 110.00
19A A6 3p blue (#9) — 550.00
19B A6 3p blue (#11) 1,050. 325.00
20 A6 6p violet (#16) 650.00 110.00
21 A7 1sh green (#17) *30,000.* 2,100.

Same Overprint 13¾mm
22 A6 1p rose (#15b) 1,200. 325.00
23 A6 3p blue (#12) 2,800. 550.00
a. Inverted overprint
23B A6 3p blue (#9) — —
23C A6 3p blue (#11) — 1,100.
24 A6 6p violet (#16) 2,750. 225.00
25 A7 1sh green (#17) *35,000.* *3,250.*

Same Overprint 14½ to 15½mm
26 A6 1p rose (#15b) 1,050. 250.00
27 A6 3p blue (#12) — 450.00
27A A6 3p blue (#11) — 775.00
27B A6 3p blue (#9) — —
28 A6 6p violet (#16) 2,100. 140.00
29 A7 1sh green (#17) *32,000.* *2,750.*

Overprinted

30 A6 1p rose (#15b) 150.00 55.00
b. Inverted overprint
31 A6 3p blue (#12) 250.00 55.00
a. Double overprint 1,800.

31B A6 3p blue (#11) 225.00 62.50
31C A6 3p blue (#9) 400.00 95.00
32 A6 6p violet (#16) 210.00 77.50
33 A7 1sh green (#17) 350.00 87.50

Overprinted

34 A6 1p rose (#15b) 650.00 120.00
35 A6 3p blue (#12) 825.00 120.00
35A A6 3p blue (#11) 1,200. 375.00
35B A6 3p blue (#9) *4,250. 925.00*
36 A6 6p violet (#16) 825.00 120.00
b. Inverted overprint
37 A7 1sh green (#17) *37,500. 2,000.*

Overprinted in Black or Red

1870-73 Wmk. 1 *Perf. 12½*

38 A6 1p red 120.00 16.50
39 A6 3p ultra (R) ('72) 130.00 16.50
40 A6 6p lilac ('73) 250.00 45.00
Nos. 38-40 (3) 500.00 78.00

Overprinted in Red, Black or Green — g

1870 *Perf. 14*

41 A7 1sh green (R) — *9,500.*
42 A7 1sh green (Bk) — *1,750.*
a. Double overprint *3,900.*
43 A7 1sh green (G) 150.00 13.00

See No. 76.

Type of 1867 Overprinted

1873

44 A7 1sh brown lilac 425.00 30.00

No. 44 without overprint is a revenue.

Type of 1864 Overprinted

1874 *Perf. 12½*

45 A6 1p rose red 400.00 95.00
a. Double overprint

Overprinted

1875

46 A6 1p rose red 185.00 70.00
b. Double overprint 1,900. 650.00

Overprinted

1875 Overprint 14½mm *Perf. 12½*

47 A6 1p yellow 100.00 100.00
a. Double overprint, one albino 275.00 —

48 A6 1p rose red 140.00 87.50
a. Inverted overprint 2,250. 575.00
49 A6 6p violet 95.00 10.00
a. Inverted overprint 900.00 190.00
b. Double overprint 1,050.

Perf. 14

50 A7 1sh green 140.00 9.00
a. Double overprint 425.00
Nos. 47-50 (4) 475.00 206.50

The 1p yellow without overprint is a revenue.

A8 A9

A10 A11

Queen Victoria — A12

1874-78 Typo. Wmk. 1 *Perf. 14*

51 A8 1p dull rose 55.00 8.50
52 A9 3p ultramarine 190.00 40.00
a. Perf. 14x12½ 2,500. 1,100.
53 A10 4p brown ('78) 210.00 18.00
54 A11 6p violet 110.00 9.00

Perf. 15½x15

55 A12 5sh claret 525.00 120.00

Perf. 14

56 A12 5sh claret ('78) 450.00 120.00
57 A12 5sh carmine 120.00 42.50

Perf. 12½

58 A10 4p brown ('78) 400.00 82.50

See Nos. 65-71. For types A8-A10 surcharged see Nos. 59-60, 72-73, 77, 80.

Surcharged in Black

n

No. 60

o

1877 *Perf. 14*

59 A8(n) ½p on 1p rose 45.00 *82.50*
a. Double surcharge "1/2"
60 A8(n) ½p on 1p rose 110.00 —

Surcharge "n" exists in 3 or more types each of the large "1/2" (No. 59) and the small "1/2" (No. 60).

"HALF" and "½" were overprinted separately; "½" may be above, below or overlapping.

Perf. 12½

61 A6(o) ½p on 1p yel 13.00 *25.00*
a. Double surcharge 400.00 230.00
b. Inverted surcharge 400.00 240.00
c. Pair, one without surcharge 4,750. 3,000.
d. "POTAGE" 350.00 250.00
e. "POSAGE" 350.00 325.00
f. "POSTAGE" omitted 2,500. —
62 A6(o) 1p on 6p vio 82.50 13.00
a. "POSTAGE" omitted
b. "POTAGE" 650.00 190.00
63 A6(o) 1p on 6p rose 150.00 60.00
a. Inverted surcharge 1,750. 600.00
b. Double surcharge — 350.00
c. Dbl. srch., one inverted 400.00 250.00
d. Triple srch., one invtd.
e. Quadruple surcharge 550.00 300.00
f. "POTAGE" 1,000. 390.00
Nos. 61-63 (3) 245.50 98.00

No. 63 without overprint is a revenue.

A14

1880 Typo. *Perf. 14*

64 A14 ½p blue green 27.50 32.50
a. Vertical pair, imperf. between

1882-89 Wmk. Crown and CA (2)

65 A14 ½p blue green ('84) 120.00 20.00
66 A14 ½p gray green ('84) 6.00 1.40
67 A8 1p rose ('84) 7.50 .30
68 A9 3p ultra ('84) 170.00 22.00
69 A9 3p gray ('89) 10.00 5.25
70 A10 4p brown 15.00 1.90
71 A11 6p violet 12.00 2.75
Nos. 65-71 (7) 340.50 53.60

Surcharged in Black

p q

1885-86

72 A8(p) ½p on 1p rose 24.00 14.00
73 A9(q) 2p on 3p gray ('86) 35.00 7.00

A17

1887

74 A17 2p olive green, die B ('89) 6.00 1.75
a. Die A 60.00 3.00

For explanation of dies A and B see "Dies of British Colonial Stamps" in the catalogue introduction.

Type of 1867 Overprinted Type "g" in Red

1888

76 A7 1sh orange 11.00 1.90
a. Double overprint *3,250.*

Surcharged in Black

1891

77 A10 2½p on 4p brown 17.50 17.50
a. "PENGE" 77.50
b. "PENN" 325.00 275.00
c. Double surcharge 400.00 350.00
d. As "c," in vert. pair with normal stamp 650.00 *750.00*
e. Inverted surcharge 550.00 475.00
f. Vert. pair, surcharge tete-beche 2,250. *3,000.*

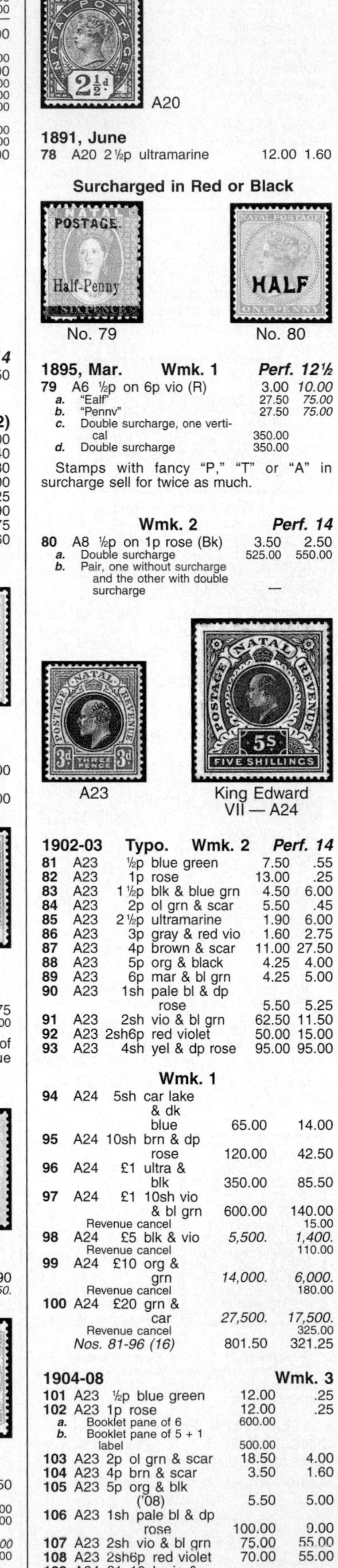

A20

1891, June

78 A20 2½p ultramarine 12.00 1.60

Surcharged in Red or Black

No. 79 No. 80

1895, Mar. Wmk. 1 *Perf. 12½*

79 A6 ½p on 6p vio (R) 3.00 *10.00*
a. "Ealf" 27.50 *75.00*
b. "Penny" 27.50 *75.00*
c. Double surcharge, one vertical 350.00
d. Double surcharge 350.00

Stamps with fancy "P," "T" or "A" in surcharge sell for twice as much.

Wmk. 2 *Perf. 14*

80 A8 ½p on 1p rose (Bk) 3.50 2.50
a. Double surcharge 525.00 550.00
b. Pair, one without surcharge and the other with double surcharge —

A23 King Edward VII — A24

1902-03 Typo. Wmk. 2 *Perf. 14*

81 A23 ½p blue green 7.50 .55
82 A23 1p rose 13.00 .25
83 A23 1½p blk & blue grn 4.50 6.00
84 A23 2p ol grn & scar 5.50 .45
85 A23 2½p ultramarine 1.90 6.00
86 A23 3p gray & red vio 1.60 2.75
87 A23 4p brown & scar 11.00 27.50
88 A23 5p org & black 4.25 4.00
89 A23 6p mar & bl grn 4.25 5.00
90 A23 1sh pale bl & dp rose 5.50 5.25
91 A23 2sh vio & bl grn 62.50 11.50
92 A23 2sh6p red violet 50.00 15.00
93 A23 4sh yel & dp rose 95.00 95.00

Wmk. 1

94 A24 5sh car lake & dk blue 65.00 14.00
95 A24 10sh brn & dp rose 120.00 42.50
96 A24 £1 ultra & blk 350.00 85.50
97 A24 £1 10sh vio & bl grn 600.00 140.00
Revenue cancel 15.00
98 A24 £5 blk & vio *5,500. 1,400.*
Revenue cancel 110.00
99 A24 £10 org & grn *14,000. 6,000.*
Revenue cancel 180.00
100 A24 £20 grn & car *27,500. 17,500.*
Revenue cancel 325.00
Nos. 81-96 (16) 801.50 321.25

1904-08 Wmk. 3

101 A23 ½p blue green 12.00 .25
102 A23 1p rose 12.00 .25
a. Booklet pane of 6 600.00
b. Booklet pane of 5 + 1 label 500.00
103 A23 2p ol grn & scar 18.50 4.00
104 A23 4p brn & scar 3.50 1.60
105 A23 5p org & blk ('08) 5.50 5.00
106 A23 1sh pale bl & dp rose 100.00 9.00
107 A23 2sh vio & bl grn 75.00 55.00
108 A23 2sh6p red violet 70.00 55.00
109 A24 £1 10sh vio & org brn, chalky paper 1,900. *5,000.*
Revenue cancel 55.00
Nos. 101-108 (8) 296.50 130.10

A25

A26

1908-09

110 A25 6p red violet 5.75 3.50
111 A25 1sh blk, *grn* 7.75 3.25
112 A25 2sh bl & vio, *bl* 19.00 3.75
113 A25 2sh6p red & blk, *bl* 32.00 3.75
114 A26 5sh red & grn, *yell* 30.00 45.00
115 A26 10sh red & grn, *grn* 135.00 135.00
116 A26 £1 blk & vio, *red* 440.00 400.00
Nos. 110-116 (7) 669.50 594.25

OFFICIAL STAMPS

Nos. 101-103, 106 and Type A23 Overprinted

1904 **Wmk. 3** ***Perf. 14***

O1 A23 ½p blue green 3.75 .45
O2 A23 1p rose 13.00 1.10
O3 A23 2p ol grn & scar 45.00 22.50
O4 A23 3p gray & red vio 25.00 *5.50*
O5 A23 6p mar & bl grn 87.50 82.50
O6 A23 1sh pale bl & dp rose 250.00 *275.00*
Nos. O1-O6 (6) 424.25 *387.05*

Stamps of Natal were replaced by those of the Union of South Africa.

NAURU

nä-'ü-ˌrü

LOCATION — An island on the Equator in the west central Pacific Ocean, midway between the Marshall and Solomon Islands.
GOVT. — Republic
AREA — 8½ sq. mi.
POP. — 10,605 (1999 est.)
CAPITAL — None. Parliament House is in Yaren District.

The island, a German possession, was captured by Australian forces in 1914 and, following World War I, was mandated to the British Empire. It was administered jointly by Great Britain, Australia and New Zealand.

In 1947 Nauru was placed under United Nations trusteeship, administered by Australia. On January 31, 1968, Nauru became a republic.

See North West Pacific Islands.

12 Pence = 1 Shilling
100 Cents = 1 Dollar (1966)

Catalogue values for unused stamps in this country are for Never Hinged items, beginning with Scott 39.

Watermarks

Wmk. 388 — Multiple "SPM"

Great Britain Stamps of 1912-13 Overprinted at Bottom of Stamp

1916-23 **Wmk. 33** ***Perf. 14½x14***

1 A82 ½p green 3.50 *10.00*
2 A83 1p scarlet 2.50 *13.00*
3 A84 1½p red brn ('23) 57.50 *85.00*
4 A85 2p org (die I) 3.00 *15.00*
c. 2p deep orange (die II) ('23) 75.00 *110.00*
6 A86 2½p ultra 5.00 *12.00*
7 A87 3p violet 3.00 *11.00*
8 A88 4p slate green 3.00 *14.50*
a. Double ovpt 260.00
9 A89 5p yel brown 4.50 *15.00*
10 A89 6p dull violet 10.00 *17.00*
11 A90 9p blk brn 14.00 *24.00*
12 A90 1sh bister 13.00 *22.50*
Nos. 1-12 (11) 119.00 *239.00*

Great Britain Stamps of 1915 Overprinted

Wmk. 34 ***Perf. 11x12***

13 A91 2sh6p lt brn 90.00 *125.00*
a. 2sh6p black brown 625.00 *1,600.*
14 A91 5sh carmine 150.00 *200.00*
b. 5sh rose carmine 3,000. 2,750.
15 A91 10sh lt blue (R) 375.00 *400.00*
c. 10sh indigo blue *12,500.* 6,000.

Same Ovpt. on Great Britain No. 179a and 179b

1920

16 A91 2sh6p gray brown 92.50 *160.00*
Nos. 13-16 (4) 707.50 *885.00*
Nos. 1-16 (15) 826.25 *1,109.*

Double and triple overprints, with one overprint albino, exist for most of the 1-16 overprints. Additional color shades exist for No. 13-16, and values given are for the most common varieties. For detailed listings, see *Scott Classic Specialized Catalogue.*

1923 **Overprint Centered**

1b A82 ½p 8.00 *55.00*
2c A83 1p 22.50 *42.50*
3a A84 1½p 35.00 *57.50*
4d A85 2p As No. 4a 40.00 *80.00*
Nos. 1b-4d (4) 105.50 *235.00*

On Nos. 1-12 "NAURU" is usually 12¾mm wide and at the foot of the stamp. In 1923 four values were overprinted with the word 13½mm wide and across the middle of the stamp.

Forged overprints exist.

Freighter — A1

1924-48 **Unwmk.** **Engr.** ***Perf. 11***

17 A1 ½p orange brown 2.25 *3.00*
b. Perf. 14 ('47) 1.40 *10.00*
18a A1 1p green 2.50 *4.00*
19a A1 1½p red 1.10 *2.00*
20a A1 2p orange 4.50 *8.00*
21a A1 2½p blue ('48) 4.00 *4.00*
c. Horiz. pair, imperf between *17,000.* *22,500.*
d. Vert. pair, imperf between *17,000.* *22,500.*
22a A1 3p grnsh gray ('47) 5.50 *19.00*
23a A1 4p olive green 5.00 *15.00*
24 A1 5p dk brown 4.50 *7.50*
25 A1 6p dark violet 5.25 *19.00*
26 A1 9p brown olive 10.50 *21.00*
27a A1 1sh brown red 11.00 4.50
28a A1 2sh6p slate green 32.00 *40.00*
29a A1 5sh claret 37.50 *60.00*
30a A1 10sh yellow 85.00 *125.00*
Nos. 17-30a (14) 204.85 323.00

Two printings were made of Nos. 17-30, the first (1924-34) on unsurfaced, grayish paper (Nos. 17-30), the second (1937-48) on glazed surfaced white paper (Nos. 17a-30a). Values are for the most common type. For detailed listings, see *Scott Classic Specialized Catalogue.*

Stamps of Type A1 Overprinted in Black

1935, July 12 ***Perf. 11***

Glazed Paper

31 A1 1½p red 1.10 *1.10*
32 A1 2p orange 2.50 *6.00*
33 A1 2½p blue 2.50 *1.75*
34 A1 1sh brown red 6.50 *5.00*
Nos. 31-34 (4) 12.60 *13.85*
Set, never hinged 20.00

25th anniv. of the reign of George V.

George VI — A2

1937, May 10 **Engr.**

35 A2 1½p salmon rose .25 *1.00*
36 A2 2p dull orange .25 *2.00*
37 A2 2½p blue .25 *1.25*
38 A2 1sh brown violet .40 *1.25*
Nos. 35-38 (4) 1.15 *5.50*
Set, never hinged 2.25

Coronation of George VI & Elizabeth.

Catalogue values for unused stamps in this section, from this point to the end of the section, are for Never Hinged items.

Casting Throw-net — A3

Anibare Bay — A4

3½p, Loading phosphate. 4p, Frigate bird. 6p, Nauruan canoe. 9p, Meeting house (domaneab). 1sh, Palms. 2sh6p, Buada lagoon. 5sh, Map.

1954, Feb. 6 ***Perf. 14½x14, 14x14½***

39 A3 ½p purple .25 .50
40 A4 1p green .25 .30
41 A3 3½p red 1.75 .75
42 A3 4p deep blue 2.25 2.00
43 A3 6p orange .70 .30
44 A3 9p brown lake .65 .25
45 A4 1sh dk rose violet .50 .35
46 A3 2sh6p dk gray green 3.00 1.00
47 A4 5sh lilac rose 8.00 2.50
Nos. 39-47 (9) 17.35 7.95

See Nos. 58-71.

Balsam — A5

Black Lizard — A6

Capparis — A7

Coral Pinnacles — A8

White Tern — A9

2p, Micronesian pigeon, vert. 3p, Poison nut flower. 3sh3p, Nightingale reed warbler.

Perf. 13½, Perf. 14½x13½ (10p), Perf. 14½ (2sh3p)

Photo.; Engraved (10p, 2sh3p)

1963-65 **Unwmk.**

49 A9 2p multi ('65) .75 2.00
50 A6 3p red org, sl grn & yel ('64) .40 .30
51 A5 5p gray, bl grn & yellow .40 .65
52 A6 8p green & black 1.75 .75
53 A7 10p black ('64) .60 .50
54 A9 1sh3p ap grn, blk & Prus bl ('65) 1.25 *4.75*
55 A8 2sh3p vio blue ('64) 2.25 .65
56 A6 3sh3p lt yel, bl, brn & blk ('65) 1.50 3.75
Nos. 49-56 (8) 8.90 13.35

Issue dates: 5p, Apr. 22. 8p, July 1. 3p, 10p, 2sh3p, Apr. 16. 2p, 1sh3p, 3sh3p, May 3.

"Simpson and His Donkey" by Wallace Anderson — A9a

Perf. 13½x13

1965, Apr. 14 **Photo.** **Unwmk.**

57 A9a 5p brt green, sepia & blk .35 .35

See note after Australia No. 387.

Types of 1954-65
Values in Cents and Dollars

Designs: 1c, Anibare Bay. 2c, Casting throw-net. 3c, Loading phosphate. 4c, Balsam. 5c, Palms. 7c, Black lizard. 8c, Capparis. 10c, Frigate bird. 15c, White tern. 25c, Coral pinnacles. 30c, Poison nut flower. 35c, Reed warbler. 50c, Micronesian pigeon, vert. $1, Map.

Engr.; Photo. (4c, 7c, 15c, 30c-50c)

1966 ***Perf. 14½x14, 14x14½***

58 A4 1c dark blue .25 .25
59 A3 2c claret .25 .50
60 A3 3c green .30 *1.50*
61 A5 4c lilac, grn & yel .25 .25
62 A4 5c violet blue .25 .75
63 A6 7c fawn & black .35 .25
64 A7 8c olive green .25 .25
65 A3 10c dark red .40 .25
66 A9 15c ap grn, blk & Prus blue .75 2.25
67 A3 25c sepia .45 *3.00*
68 A6 30c brick red, sl grn, & yellow .45 .35
69 A6 35c lt yel, bl, brn & black .90 .40
70 A9 50c yel, bluish blk & brown 1.50 1.00
71 A4 $1 claret 1.50 1.00
Nos. 58-71 (14) 7.85 12.00

The engraved stamps are luminescent.

Issued: 2c, 3c, 5c, 15c, 25c, 35c, 5/25; others, 2/14.

Republic

Nos. 58-71 Overprinted in Red, Black or Orange "REPUBLIC / OF / NAURU"

1968

72 A4 1c dark blue (R) .25 .35
73 A3 2c claret .25 .25
74 A3 3c green .25 .25
75 A5 4c lilac, grn & yel .25 .25
76 A4 5c violet blue (O) .25 .25
77 A6 7c fawn & blk (R) .25 .25
78 A7 8c olive green (R) .25 .25
79 A3 10c dark red .70 .30
80 A9 15c ap grn, blk & Prus blue 1.50 *3.25*
81 A3 25c sepia (R) .40 .30
82 A6 30c brick red, sl grn & yellow .75 .30
83 A6 35c multicolored 1.25 .50
84 A9 50c yel, bluish blk & brown 1.50 .60
85 A4 $1 claret 1.75 .70
Nos. 72-85 (14) 9.60 7.80

Issued: 4c, 7c, 30c, 35c, 5/15; others, 1/31.

Nauru Woman Watching Rising Sun — A10

Planting Seedling and Map of Nauru — A11

Perf. 13x13½

1968, Sept. 11 Photo. Unwmk.

86 A10 5c multicolored .30 .25
87 A11 10c brt blue, blk & green .30 .25

Independence of Nauru.

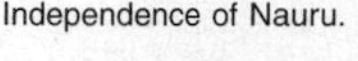

Flag of Nauru — A12

1969, Jan. 31 Litho. *Perf. 13½*

88 A12 15c dk vio blue, yel & org .60 .55

For overprint see No. 90.

Commission Emblem and Nauru A13

1972, Feb. 7 Litho. *Perf. 14½x14*

89 A13 25c blue, yellow & black .55 .55

South Pacific Commission, 25th anniv.

No. 88 Ovptd. in Gold

1973, Jan. 31 *Perf. 13½*

90 A12 15c multicolored .35 .35

Fifth anniversary of independence.

Lotus (Ekwenababae) A14 — Map of Nauru, Artifacts A15

Catching Flyingfish A16

Designs: 2c, Kauwe iud. 3c, Rimone. 4c, Denea. 5c, Beach morning-glory. 7c, Golden butterflyfish. 10c, Nauruan ball game (itsibweb). 15c, Nauruan wrestling. 20c, Snaring frigate birds. 25c, Nauruan girl with flower garland. 30c, Men catching noddies. 50c, Frigate birds.

1973 Litho. *Perf. 13½x14*

91 A14 1c pale yellow & multi .25 .25
92 A14 2c pale ocher & multi .30 .25
93 A14 3c pale violet & multi .30 .25
94 A14 4c pale green & multi .30 .30
95 A14 5c pale blue & multi .30 .30

Perf. 14½x14, 14x14½

96 A16 7c blue & multi .40 *.80*
97 A16 8c black & multi .30 .25
98 A16 10c multicolored .30 .25
99 A15 15c green & multi .35 .25
100 A15 20c blue & multi .50 .50
101 A15 25c yellow & multi .45 .45
102 A16 30c multicolored .50 .50
103 A16 50c multicolored .80 .75
104 A15 $1 blue & multi 1.40 .75
Nos. 91-104 (14) 6.45 5.85

Issue dates: Nos. 97-100, May 23; Nos. 96, 101-103, July 25; others Mar. 28, 1973.

Cooperative Store — A17 — Eigigu, the Girl in the Moon — A18

Design: 25c, Timothy Detudamo and cooperative store emblem.

1973, Dec. 20 Litho. *Perf. 14½x14*

105 A17 5c multicolored .65 .65
106 A17 25c multicolored .65 .65
107 A18 50c multicolored 1.20 1.20
Nos. 105-107 (3) 2.50 2.50

50th anniversary of Nauru Cooperative Society, founded by Timothy Detudamo.

"Eigamoiya" — A19

10c, Phosphate mining. 15c, "Nauru Chief" plane over Nauru. 25c, Nauru chieftain with frigate-bird headdress. 35c, Capt. J. Fearn, sailing ship "Hunter" & map of Nauru. 50c, "Hunter" off Nauru.

Perf. 13x13½, 13½x13

1974, May 21 Litho.

Sizes: 70x22mm (7c, 35c, 50c); 33x20mm (10c, 15c, 25c)

108 A19 7c multicolored .60 *.90*
109 A19 10c multicolored .50 .25
110 A19 15c multicolored .65 .45
111 A19 25c multicolored 1.00 1.00
112 A19 35c multicolored 3.50 3.50
113 A19 50c multicolored 2.50 2.50
Nos. 108-113 (6) 8.75 8.60

175th anniversary of Nauru's first contact with the outside world.

Map of Nauru A20 — Post Office A21

UPU Emblem and: 20c, Mailman on motorcycle. $1, Flag of Nauru and UPU Building, Bern, vert.

1974, July 23 Litho. *Perf. 14*

114 A20 5c multicolored .25 .25

Perf. 13½x13, 13x13½

115 A21 8c multicolored .25 .25
116 A21 20c multicolored .25 .25
117 A21 $1 multicolored 1.50 1.50
a. Souv. sheet of 4, #114-117, imperf. 4.00 4.00
Nos. 114-117 (4) 2.25 2.25

Cent. of the UPU.

Rev. P. A. Delaporte — A22

1974, Dec. 10 Litho. *Perf. 14½*

118 A22 15c brt pink & multi .30 .30
119 A22 20c blue & multi .60 .60

Christmas 1974. Delaporte, a German-born American missionary, took Christianity to Nauru and translated the New Testament into Nauruan.

Nauru, Grain, Albert Ellis, Phosphate Rock — A23

Designs: 7c, Phosphate mining and coolie carrying load. 15c, Electric freight train, tugs and ship. 25c, Excavator, cantilever and truck.

1975, July 23 Litho. *Perf. 14½x14*

120 A23 5c multicolored .30 .30
121 A23 7c multicolored .40 .40
122 A23 15c multicolored 1.10 1.10
123 A23 25c multicolored 1.50 1.50
Nos. 120-123 (4) 3.30 3.30

75th anniv. of discovery of phosphate (5c); 70th anniv. of Pacific Phosphate Co. Mining Agreement (7c); 50th anniv. of British Phosphate Commissioners (15c); 5th anniv. of Nauru Phosphate Corp. (25c).

Melanesian Outrigger and Map of SPC's Area — A24

No. 124, Micronesian outrigger. No. 125, Polynesian double hull. No. 127, Polynesian outrigger.

1975, Sept. 1 Litho. *Perf. 14x14½*

124 A24 20c multicolored .85 .85
125 A24 20c multicolored .85 .85
126 A24 20c shown .85 .85
127 A24 20c multicolored .85 .85
a. Block of 4, #124-127 3.75 3.75
Nos. 124-127 (4) 3.40 3.40

South Pacific Commission Conference, Nauru, Sept. 29-Oct. 10.

New Civic Center A25

Design: 50c, "Domaneab" (meeting house) and flags of participating nations.

1975, Sept. 29 Litho. *Perf. 14½*

128 A25 30c multicolored .30 .30
129 A25 50c multicolored .55 .55

South Pacific Commission Conference, Nauru, Sept. 29-Oct. 10.
Nos. 128-129 exist imperf. Value, set $12.

Virgin Mary, Stained-glass Window — A26

Christmas: 7c, 15c, "Suffer little children to come unto me," stained-glass window, Orro Protestant Church. 25c, like 5c, Yaren Catholic Church.

1975, Nov. 7 Litho. *Perf. 14½*

130 A26 5c gray blue & multi .25 .25
131 A26 7c green & multi .25 .25
132 A26 15c brown & multi .25 .55
133 A26 25c lilac & multi .25 .75
Nos. 130-133 (4) 1.00 1.80

Frangipani Forming Lei Around Nauru A27

14c, Hand crowning Nauru with lei. 25c, Reed warbler, birds flying from Truk to Nauru. 40c, Reunion of islanders in Boar Harbor.

1976, Jan. 31 Litho. *Perf. 14½*

134 A27 10c green & multi .25 .25
135 A27 14c violet & multi .25 .25
136 A27 25c red & multi .25 .25
137 A27 40c blue & multi .30 .30
Nos. 134-137 (4) 1.05 1.05

30th anniversary of the return of the islanders from Japanese internment on Truk.
Nos. 134-137 exist imperf. Value, set $20.

Nauru Nos. 7 and 11 A28

15c, Nauru Nos. 10, 12. 25c, Nauru No. 13. 50c, Nauru No. 14, "Specimen."

1976, May 6 Litho. *Perf. 13½x14*

138 A28 10c multicolored .25 .25
139 A28 15c multicolored .25 .25
140 A28 25c multicolored .25 .25
141 A28 50c multicolored .40 .40
Nos. 138-141 (4) 1.15 1.15

60th anniv. of Nauru's 1st postage stamps.
Nos. 138-141 exist imperf. Value, set $17.50.

Nauru Shipping and Pandanus — A29

Designs: 20c, Air Nauru Boeing 737 and Fokker F28, and tournefortia argentea. 30c, Earth satellite station and thespesia populnea. 40c, Area produce and cordia subcordata.

1976, July 26 Litho. *Perf. 13½x14*

142 A29 10c multicolored .25 .25
143 A29 20c multicolored .25 .25
144 A29 30c multicolored .25 .25
145 A29 40c multicolored .45 .45
Nos. 142-145 (4) 1.20 1.20

7th South Pacific Forum, Nauru, July 1976.
Nos. 142-145 exist imperf. Value, set $35.

Nauruan Children's Choir — A30

20c, Angels. #146, 148, denominations at lower right. #147, 149, denominations at lower left.

1976, Nov. Litho. *Perf. 14x13½*

146 15c multicolored .25 .25
147 15c multicolored .25 .25
a. A30 Pair, #146-147 .55 .55

148 20c multicolored .25 .25
149 20c multicolored .25 .25
a. A30 Pair, #148-149 .55 .55
Nos. 146-149 (4) 1.00 1.00

Christmas.

Nos. 146-149 exist imperf. Value, set of two se-tenant pairs $65.

Nauru House, Melbourne, and Coral Pinnacles — A32

30c, Nauru House and Melbourne skyline.

1977, Apr. 14 Photo. *Perf. 14½*
150 A32 15c multicolored .25 .25
151 A32 30c multicolored .40 .40

Opening of Nauru House in Melbourne, Australia.

For surcharges see Nos. 161-164.

Cable-laying Ship Anglia, 1902 — A33

Designs: 15c, Nauru radar station. 20c, Stern of Anglia. 25c, Radar antenna.

1977, Sept. 7 Photo. *Perf. 14½*
152 A33 7c multicolored .25 .25
153 A33 15c multicolored .25 .25
154 A33 20c multicolored .30 .30
155 A33 25c multicolored .40 .40
Nos. 152-155 (4) 1.20 1.20

1st transpacific cable, 75th anniv., and 1st artificial earth satellite, 20th anniv.

Catholic Church, Yaren, and Father Kayser — A34

Designs: 25c, Congregational Church, Orro. 30c, Catholic Church, Arubo.

1977, Oct. Photo. *Perf. 14½*
156 A34 15c multicolored .25 .25
157 A34 25c multicolored .25 .25
158 A34 30c multicolored .25 .25
Nos. 156-158 (3) .75 .75

Christmas, and 55th anniversary of first Roman Catholic Church on Nauru.

Coat of Arms of Nauru — A35

1978, Jan. 31 Litho. *Perf. 14½*
159 A35 15c blue & multi .25 .25
160 A35 60c emerald & multi .35 .35

10th anniversary of independence.

Nos. 150-151 Surcharged with New Value and Two Bars

1978, Apr. Photo. *Perf. 14½*
161 A32 4c on 15c multi 1.10 1.75
162 A32 5c on 15c multi 1.10 1.75
163 A32 8c on 30c multi 1.10 1.75
164 A32 10c on 30c multi 1.10 1.75
Nos. 161-164 (4) 4.40 7.00

Girls Catching Fish in Buada Lagoon A36

Designs: 1c, Fisherman and family collecting shellfish. 2c, Pigs foraging near coral reef. 3c, Gnarled tree and birds. 4c, Girl catching fish with hands. 5c, Bird catching fish. 10c, Ijuw Lagoon. 15c, Young girl and coral formation. 20c, Reef pinnacles, Anibare Bay. 25c, Pinnacles, Meneng shore. 30c, Frigate bird. 32c, Coconut palm and noddies. 40c, Iwiyi, wading bird. 50c, Frigate birds. $1, Pinnacles, Topside. $2, Newly uncovered pinnacles, Topside. $5, Old pinnacles, Topside.

1978-79 Photo. *Perf. 14½*
165 A36 1c multicolored .35 .25
166 A36 2c multicolored .35 .25
167 A36 3c multicolored 1.00 .75
168 A36 4c multicolored .40 .25
169 A36 5c multicolored 1.00 .80
170 A36 7c multicolored .25 *1.00*
171 A36 10c multicolored .25 .25
172 A36 15c multicolored .25 .25
173 A36 20c multicolored .30 .30
174 A36 25c multicolored .35 .35
175 A36 30c multicolored 1.00 .45
176 A36 32c multicolored 1.50 1.00
177 A36 40c multicolored 1.25 1.25
178 A36 50c multicolored 1.25 1.25
179 A36 $1 multicolored 1.00 1.00
180 A36 $2 multicolored .75 .75
181 A36 $5 multicolored 3.50 2.00
Nos. 165-181 (17) 14.75 12.15

Issued: #166-169, 6/6/79; others, 5/1978.

"APU" — A37

1978, Aug. 28 Litho. *Perf. 13½*
182 A37 15c multicolored .40 .90
183 A37 20c gold, blk & dk blue .60 1.10

14th General Assembly of Asian Parliamentary Union, Nauru, Aug. 28-Sept. 1. On sale during conference only.

Mother and Child — A38

Christmas: 15c, 20c, Angel over the Pacific, horiz. 30c, like 7c.

1978, Nov. 1 Litho. *Perf. 14*
184 A38 7c multicolored .25 .25
185 A38 15c multicolored .25 .25
186 A38 20c multicolored .25 .25
187 A38 30c multicolored .25 .25
Nos. 184-187 (4) 1.00 1.00

Lord Baden-Powell and Cub Scout — A39

30c, Boy Scout. 50c, Explorer.

1978, Dec. 1 Litho. *Perf. 14*
188 A39 20c multicolored .25 .25
189 A39 30c multicolored .25 .25
190 A39 50c multicolored .40 .40
Nos. 188-190 (3) .90 .90

70th anniversary of 1st Scout Troop.

Flyer A over Nauru Airfield A40

Designs: No. 192, "Southern Cross" and Boeing 727. No. 193, "Southern Cross" and Boeing 737. 30c, Wright Flyer over Nauru.

1979, Jan. *Perf. 14½*
191 A40 10c multicolored .30 .30
192 A40 15c multicolored .35 .35
193 A40 15c multicolored .35 .35
a. Pair, #192-193 .90 .90
194 A40 30c multicolored .60 .60
Nos. 191-194 (4) 1.60 1.60

1st powered flight, 75th anniv. and Kingsford Smith's US-Australia and Australia-New Zealand flights, 50th anniv.

Nos. 192-193 printed checkerwise.

Nos. 191-194 exist imperf. Value, set of two singles (Nos. 191, 194) and pair (193a), $65.

Rowland Hill, Marshall Islands No. 15 with Nauru Cancel A41

1979, Feb. 27 Litho. *Perf. 14½*
195 A41 5c shown .25 .25
196 A41 15c Nauru No. 15 .25 .25
197 A41 60c Nauru No. 160 .40 .60
a. Souvenir sheet of 3, #195-197 .90 1.25
Nos. 195-197 (3) .90 1.10

Sir Rowland Hill (1795-1879), originator of penny postage.

Dish Antenna, Earth Station, ITU Emblem — A42

ITU Emblem and: 32c, Woman operating Telex machine. 40c, Radio beacon operator.

1979, Aug. Litho. *Perf. 14½*
198 A42 7c multicolored .25 .25
199 A42 32c multicolored .30 .30
200 A42 40c multicolored .40 .35
Nos. 198-200 (3) .95 .90

Intl. Radio Consultative Committee (CCIR) of the ITU, 50th anniv.

Nos. 198-200 exist imperf. Value, set $20.

Nauruan Girl — A43

IYC Emblem, Nauruan Children: 15c, Boy. 25c, 32c, 50c, Girls, diff.

1979, Oct. 3 Litho. *Perf. 14½*
201 A43 8c multicolored .25 .25
202 A43 15c multicolored .25 .25
203 A43 25c multicolored .25 .25
204 A43 32c multicolored .25 .25
205 A43 50c multicolored .25 .25
a. Strip of 5, #201-205 1.25 1.25

International Year of the Child.

Star, Scroll, Ekwenababa Flower — A44

Star and Flowers: 15c, Milos. 20c, Denea. 30c, Morning glories.

1979, Nov. 14 Litho. *Perf. 14½*
206 A44 7c multicolored .25 .25
207 A44 15c multicolored .25 .25
208 A44 20c multicolored .25 .25
209 A44 30c multicolored .25 .25
Nos. 206-209 (4) 1.00 1.00

Christmas.

Nos. 206-209 exist imperf. Value, set $65.

Nauruan Plane over Melbourne — A45

Air Nauru, 10th Anniversary (Plane Over): 20c, Tarawa. 25c, Hong Kong. 30c, Auckland.

1980, Feb. 28 Litho. *Perf. 14½*
210 A45 15c multicolored .35 .25
211 A45 20c multicolored .35 .25
212 A45 25c multicolored .45 .30
213 A45 30c multicolored .55 .40
Nos. 210-213 (4) 1.70 1.20

Early Steam Locomotive A46

32c, Electric locomotive. 60c, Clyde diesel-hydraulic locomotive.

1980, May 6 Litho. *Perf. 15*
214 A46 8c shown .25 .25
215 A46 32c multicolored .30 .30
216 A46 60c multicolored .45 .45
a. Souvenir sheet of 3, #214-216 1.75 2.25
Nos. 214-216 (3) 1.00 1.00

Nauru Phosphate Corp., 10th anniv. No. 216a also for London 1980 Intl. Stamp Exhibition, May 6-14; Penny Black, 140th anniv.

Christmas 1980 — A47

Designs: 30c, "Glory to God in the Highest . . ." in English and Nauruan.

1980, Sept. 24 Litho. *Perf. 15*
217 20c English .25 .25
218 20c Nauruese .25 .25
a. A47 Pair, #217-218 .55 .55
219 30c English .25 .25
220 30c Nauruese .25 .25
a. A47 Pair, #219-220 .55 .55
Nos. 217-220 (4) 1.00 1.00

See Nos. 236-239.

Flags of Nauru, Australia, Gt. Britain and New Zealand, UN Emblem — A49

30c, UN Trusteeship Council. 50c, 1968 independence ceremony.

1980, Dec. 20 Litho. *Perf. 14½*
221 A49 25c shown .25 .25

Size: 72x22mm

Perf. 14

222 A49 30c multicolored .30 .30
223 A49 50c multicolored .40 .40
Nos. 221-223 (3) .95 .95

UN de-colonization declaration, 20th anniv.
No. 222 printed se-tenant with label showing flags of UN and Nauru, issued Feb. 11, 1981.

Timothy Detudamo (Former Head Chief), Domaneab (Meeting House) — A50

1981, Feb. Litho. *Perf. 14½*
224 A50 20c shown .25 .25
225 A50 30c Raymond Gadabu .30 .25
226 A50 50c Hammer DeRoburt .45 .35
Nos. 224-226 (3) 1.00 .85

Legislative Council, 30th anniversary.

Casting Net by Hand A51

1981 Litho. *Perf. 12*
227 A51 8c shown .25 .25
228 A51 20c Ancient canoe .25 .25
229 A51 32c Powered boat .25 .25
230 A51 40c Fishing vessel .25 .25
a. Souvenir sheet of 4, #230 2.00 2.00
Nos. 227-230 (4) 1.00 1.00

Bank of Nauru, 5th Anniv. A52

1981, July 21 Litho. *Perf. 14x14½*
231 A52 $1 multicolored 1.00 1.00

ESCAP Secy. Maramis Delivering Inaugural Speech — A53

20c, Maramis, Pres. de Robert. 25c, Plaque. 30c, Raising UN flag.

1981, Oct. 24 Litho. *Perf. 14½*
232 A53 15c shown .25 .25
233 A53 20c multicolored .25 .25
234 A53 25c multicolored .25 .25
235 A53 30c multicolored .25 .25
Nos. 232-235 (4) 1.00 1.00

UN Day and first anniv. of Economic and Social Commission for Asia and Pacific (ESCAP) liaison office in Nauru.

Christmas Type of 1980

Christmas (Biblical Scriptures in English and Nauruan): 20c, "His Name Shall Be Called Emmanuel." 30c, "To You is Born This Day . . ."

1981, Nov. 14 Litho. *Perf. 14½*
236 A47 20c multicolored .25 .25
237 A48 20c multicolored .25 .25
a. Pair, #236-237 .50 .50
238 A47 30c multicolored .25 .25
239 A48 30c multicolored .25 .25
a. Pair, #238-239 .50 .50
Nos. 236-239 (4) 1.00 1.00

10th Anniv. of South Pacific Forum A54

1981, Dec. 9 Litho. *Perf. 13½x14*
240 A54 10c Globe, dish antenna .25 .25
241 A54 20c Ship .25 .25
242 A54 30c Jet .35 .35
243 A54 40c Produce .40 .40
Nos. 240-243 (4) 1.25 1.25

Scouting Year — A55

7c, Carrying packages. 8c, Scouts, life preserver, vert. 15c, Pottery making, vert. 20c, Inspection. 25c, Scout, cub. 40c, Troop.

1982, Feb. 23 Litho. *Perf. 14*
244 A55 7c multicolored .25 .25
245 A55 8c multicolored .25 .25
246 A55 15c multicolored .25 .25
247 A55 20c multicolored .25 .25
248 A55 25c multicolored .30 .30
249 A55 40c multicolored .45 .45
a. Souv. sheet of 6, #244-249, imperf. 1.75 1.75
Nos. 244-249 (6) 1.75 1.75

A56

Ocean Thermal Energy Conversion — A57

Designs: No. 250, Plant under construction. No. 251, Completed plant.

1982, June 10 Litho. *Perf. 13½*
250 Pair + 2 labels 1.00 1.00
a.-b. A56 25c any single .45 .45
251 Pair + 2 labels 1.50 1.50
a.-b. A57 40c any single .70 .70

75th Anniv. of Phosphate Industry A58

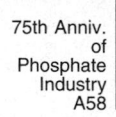

5c, Freighter Fido, 1907. 10c, Locomotive Nellie, 1907. 30c, Modern Clyde diesel train, 1982. 60c, Flagship Eigamoiya, 1969.
$1, Freighters.

1982, Oct. 11 Litho. *Perf. 14*
252 A58 5c multicolored .30 .25
253 A58 10c multicolored .50 .30
254 A58 30c multicolored .90 .60
255 A58 60c multicolored 1.50 1.10
Nos. 252-255 (4) 3.20 2.25

Souvenir Sheet

256 A58 $1 multicolored 1.75 1.75

ANPEX '82 Natl. Stamp Exhibition, Brisbane, Australia, Nos. 252-255 se-tenant with labels describing stamp. No. 256 contains one 68x27mm stamp.

Visit of Queen Elizabeth II and Prince Philip A59

1982, Oct. 21 *Perf. 14½*
257 A59 20c Elizabeth, vert. .25 .25
258 A59 50c Philip, vert. .65 .55
259 A59 $1 Couple 1.10 1.00
Nos. 257-259 (3) 2.00 1.80

Christmas A60

Clergymen: 20c, Father Bernard Lahn, Catholic Mission Church. 30c, Rev. Itubwa Amram, Orro Central Church. 40c, Pastor James Aingimea, Tsiminita Memorial Church, Denigomodu. 50c, Bishop Paul Mea, Diocese of Tarawa-Nauru-Tuvalu.

1982, Nov. 17
260 A60 20c multicolored .25 .30
261 A60 30c multicolored .30 .40
262 A60 40c multicolored .40 .60
263 A60 50c multicolored .55 .80
Nos. 260-263 (4) 1.50 2.10

15th Anniv. of Independence — A61

15c, Speaker of Parliament, vert. 20c, People's Court, vert. 30c, Law Courts. 50c, Parliament.

1983, Mar. 23 Wmk. 373 *Perf. 14½*
264 A61 15c multicolored .25 .25
265 A61 20c multicolored .25 .25
266 A61 30c multicolored .30 .30
267 A61 50c multicolored .55 .55
Nos. 264-267 (4) 1.35 1.35

World Communications Year — A62

5c, Earth Satellite Staion NZ. 10c, Omni-directional Range Installation. 20c, Fixed-station ambulance driver. 25c, Radio Nauru broadcaster. 40c, Air mail service.

1983, May. 11 Litho. *Perf. 14*
268 A62 5c multicolored .25 .25
269 A62 10c multicolored .25 .25
270 A62 20c multicolored .30 .30
271 A62 25c multicolored .40 .40
272 A62 40c multicolored .60 .60
Nos. 268-272 (5) 1.80 1.80

Angam Day (Homecoming) — A63

Perf. 14x13½

1983, Sept. 14 Litho. Wmk. 373
273 A63 15c MV Trinza arriving .25 .25

Size: 25x40mm

Perf. 14

274 A63 20c Elsie Agio in exile .25 .25
275 A63 30c Baby on scale .35 .35
276 A63 40c Children .40 .40
Nos. 273-276 (4) 1.25 1.25

Christmas A64

Designs: 5c, The Holy Virgin, the Holy Child and St. John, School of Raphael. 15c, The Mystical Betrothal of St. Catherine with Jesus, School of Paolo Veronese. 50c, Madonna on the Throne Surrounded by Angels, School of Seville.

Perf. 14½x14, 14x14½

1983, Nov. 16 Litho. Wmk. 373
277 A64 5c multi, vert. .25 .25
278 A64 15c multi, vert. .25 .25
279 A64 50c multicolored .50 .50
Nos. 277-279 (3) 1.00 1.00

Common Design Types pictured following the introduction.

Lloyd's List Issue

Common Design Type

20c, Ocean Queen. 25c, Enna G. 30c, Baron Minto loading phosphate. 40c, Triadic, 1940.

1984, May 23 Litho. *Perf. 14½x14*
280 CD335 20c multicolored .40 .35
281 CD335 25c multicolored .50 .50
282 CD335 30c multicolored .70 .70
283 CD335 40c multicolored .80 .80
Nos. 280-283 (4) 2.40 2.35

1984 UPU Congress — A65

1984, June 4 Wmk. 373 *Perf. 14*
284 A65 $1 No. 117 1.10 1.40

Coastal Scene A66

Perf. 13½x14, 14x13½

1984, Sept. 21
285 A66 1c shown .30 *.60*
286 A66 3c Woman, vert. .30 .30
287 A66 5c Fishing vessel .40 .40
288 A66 10c Golfer .90 .60
289 A66 15c Phosphate excavation, vert. .90 .60
290 A66 20c Surveyor, vert. .65 .50
291 A66 25c Air Nauru jet .90 .50
292 A66 30c Elderly man, vert. .60 .50
293 A66 40c Social service 1.00 1.00
294 A66 50c Fishing, vert. 1.25 1.25
295 A66 $1 Tennis, vert. 2.50 2.50
296 A66 $2 Lagoon Anabar 3.25 3.25
Nos. 285-296 (12) 12.95 12.00

For surcharges see Nos. 425-427.

Local Butterflies A67

25c, Common eggfly (female). 30c, Common eggfly (male). 50c, Wanderer (female).

1984, July 24 *Perf. 14*
297 A67 25c multicolored .50 .50
298 A67 30c multicolored .60 .60
299 A67 50c multicolored 1.00 1.00
Nos. 297-299 (3) 2.10 2.10

Christmas A68

30c, Buada Chapel, vert. 40c, Detudamo Memorial Church, vert. 50c, Candle-light service.

1984, Nov. 14

300 A68 30c multicolored .45 .45
301 A68 40c multicolored .55 .55
302 A68 50c multicolored .75 .75
Nos. 300-302 (3) 1.75 1.75

Air Nauru, 15th Anniv. A69

20c, Jet. 30c, Crew, vert. 40c, Fokker F28 over Nauru. 50c, Cargo handling, vert.

1985, Feb. 26 Wmk. 373 *Perf. 14*

303 A69 20c multicolored .50 .40
304 A69 30c multicolored .70 .60
305 A69 40c multicolored .90 .90
306 A69 50c multicolored 1.25 1.25
Nos. 303-306 (4) 3.35 3.15

Nauru Phosphate Corp., 15th Anniv. A70

20c, Open-cut mining. 25c, Rail transport. 30c, Phosphate drying plant. 50c, Early steam engine.

1985, July 31

307 A70 20c multicolored .90 .60
308 A70 25c multicolored 1.75 .90
309 A70 30c multicolored 1.50 .90
310 A70 50c multicolored 2.50 1.50
Nos. 307-310 (4) 6.65 3.90

Christmas — A71

1985, Oct.

311 50c Canoe 1.25 1.25
312 50c Mother and child 1.25 1.25
a. A71 Pair, #311-312 2.50 2.50

No. 312a has a continuous design.

Audubon Birth Bicentenary A72

Illustrations of the brown noddy by John J. Audubon.

1985, Dec. 31

313 A72 10c Adult and young .40 .40
314 A72 20c Flying .60 .60
315 A72 30c Two adults .75 .75
316 A72 50c Adult 1.10 1.10
Nos. 313-316 (4) 2.85 2.85

Early Transportation — A73

15c, Douglas motorcycle. 20c, Truck. 30c, German steam locomotive, 1910. 40c, Baby Austin.

1986, Mar. 5 Wmk. 384

317 A73 15c multicolored 1.00 .80
318 A73 20c multicolored 1.25 .90
319 A73 30c multicolored 1.50 1.50
320 A73 40c multicolored 1.90 1.90
Nos. 317-320 (4) 5.65 5.10

Bank of Nauru, 10th Anniv. A74

Winning drawings of children's competition.

1986, July 21 Litho. *Perf. 14*

321 A74 20c multicolored .25 .25
322 A74 25c multicolored .30 .30
323 A74 30c multicolored .35 .35
324 A74 40c multicolored .45 .45
Nos. 321-324 (4) 1.35 1.35

Flowers A75

20c, Plumeria rubra. 25c, Tristellateia australis. 30c, Bougainvillea cultivar. 40c, Delonix regia.

1986, Sept. 30 Wmk. 384

325 A75 20c multicolored .50 .40
326 A75 25c multicolored .75 .60
327 A75 30c multicolored .85 .75
328 A75 40c multicolored 1.10 1.10
Nos. 325-328 (4) 3.20 2.85

Christmas A76

1986, Dec. 8 Wmk. 373

329 A76 20c Men caroling .60 .50
330 A76 $1 Carolers, invalid 2.25 2.25

Tribal Dances — A77

1987, Jan. 31

331 A77 20c Girls .75 .75
332 A77 30c Men and women 1.00 1.00
333 A77 50c Boy, vert. 2.00 2.00
Nos. 331-333 (3) 3.75 3.75

Artifacts A78

25c, Hibiscus-fiber skirt. 30c, Headband, necklaces. 45c, Necklaces. 60c, Pandanus-leaf fan.

1987, July 30 *Perf. 14*

334 A78 25c multicolored .80 .80
335 A78 30c multicolored .95 .95
336 A78 45c multicolored 1.25 1.25
337 A78 60c multicolored 1.75 1.75
Nos. 334-337 (4) 4.75 4.75

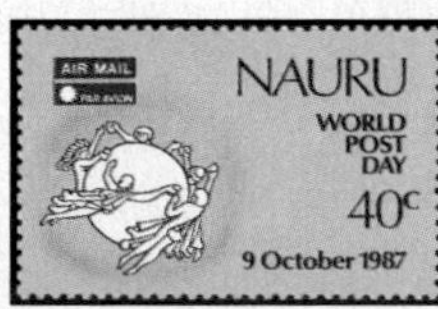

World Post Day — A79

40c, UPU emblem, airmail label.

Perf. 14½x14

1987, Oct. 9 Litho. Wmk. 384

338 A79 40c multicolored 1.60 1.60

Souvenir Sheet

1987, Oct. 20 *Imperf.*

339 A79 $1 Emblem, vert. 4.00 4.00

Nauru Congregational Church, Cent. — A80

Perf. 13x13½

1987, Nov. 5 Wmk. 373

340 A80 40c multicolored 1.50 1.50

Island Christmas Celebration — A81

1987, Nov. 27 Wmk. 384 *Perf. 14*

341 A81 20c shown .75 .50
342 A81 $1 Sign on building 3.00 3.00

A82

Natl. Independence, 20th Anniv. — A83

Heraldic elements independent of or as part of the natl. arms: 25c, Phosphate mining and shipping. 40c, Tomano flower, vert. 55c, Frigate bird, vert. $1, Natl. arms.

Perf. 13½x14, 14x13½

1988, May 16 Unwmk.

343 A82 25c multicolored 1.25 1.25
344 A82 40c multicolored 1.50 1.50
345 A82 55c multicolored 2.25 2.25

Perf. 13

346 A83 $1 multicolored 3.75 3.75
Nos. 343-346 (4) 8.75 8.75

Nauru Post Office, 80th Anniv. A84

30c, Nauru highlighted on German map of the Marshall Islands, & canceled Marshall Islands #25. 50c, Letter mailed from Nauru to Dresden & post office, 1908. 70c, Post office, 1988, & Nauru #348 canceled on airmail cover.

1988, July 14 Wmk. 384 *Perf. 14*

347 A84 30c multicolored .75 .75
348 A84 50c multicolored 1.10 1.10
349 A84 70c multicolored 1.75 1.75
Nos. 347-349 (3) 3.60 3.60

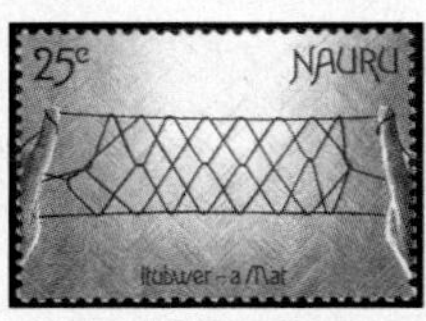

String Games A85

1988, Aug. 1 Unwmk. *Perf. 13½x14*

350 A85 25c Mat .35 .35
351 A85 40c The Pursuer .55 .55
352 A85 55c Holding Up the Sky .85 .85
353 A85 80c Manujie's Sword 1.25 1.25
Nos. 350-353 (4) 3.00 3.00

UPU, Cent. — A86

1988, Oct. 1 *Perf. 13½x14*

354 A86 $1 multicolored 1.50 1.50

Hark! The Herald Angels Sing, by Charles Wesley (1703-91) A87

1988, Nov. 28 *Perf. 13½*

355 A87 20c "Hark..." .65 .65
356 A87 60c "Glory to..." 1.50 1.50
357 A87 $1 "Peace on Earth" 2.25 2.25
Nos. 355-357 (3) 4.40 4.40

A88

15c, NIC emblem. 50c, APT, ITU emblems. $1, Mounted photograph. $2, UPU emblem, US Capitol.

1989, Nov. 19 *Perf. 14x15*

358 A88 15c multicolored .50 .50
359 A88 50c multicolored 1.00 1.00
360 A88 $1 multicolored 2.25 2.25
361 A88 $2 multicolored 3.50 3.50
Nos. 358-361 (4) 7.25 7.25

Annivs. and events: Nauru Insurance Corp., 15th Anniv. (15c). World Telecommunications Day and 10th anniv of the Asia-Pacific Telecommunity (50c); Photography 150th anniv. ($1); and 20th UPU Congress, Washington, DC ($2).

Christmas — A89

1989, Dec. 15 Litho. *Perf. 14x15*

362 A89 20c shown .60 .60
363 A89 $1 Children opening gifts 2.50 2.50

A90

Legend of Eigigu, The Girl in the Moon: 25c, Eigigu works while sisters play, rocket lift-off. 30c, Eigigu climbing tree, capsule in lunar orbit. 50c, Eigigu stealing from blind woman, lunar module on moon. $1, Eigigu with husband, Maramen (the moon), astronaut stepping on moon.

1989, Dec. 22 Litho. *Perf. 14x15*

364	A90 25c multicolored	*4.00*	*3.50*
365	A90 30c multicolored	*4.25*	*3.75*
366	A90 50c multicolored	*8.00*	*7.00*
367	A90 $1 multicolored	*11.00*	*9.00*
	Nos. 364-367 (4)	*27.25*	*23.25*

Limited supplies of Nos. 364-367 were available through agent.

A91

50c, Mining by hand. $1, Mechanized extraction.

1990, July 3 Litho. *Perf. 14x15*

368	A91 50c multicolored	1.10	1.10
369	A91 $1 multicolored	1.60	1.60

Nauru Phosphate Corp., 20th anniv.

Christmas — A92

No. 370, Children. No. 371, Telling Christmas story.

1990, Nov. 26 Litho. *Perf. 14*

370	25c multicolored	1.40	1.40
371	25c multicolored	1.40	1.40
a.	A92 Pair, #370-371	3.25	3.25

Legend of Eoiyepiang, Daughter of Thunder and Lightning — A93

1990, Dec. 24 Litho. *Perf. 14x15*

372	A93 25c Woman with baby	1.50	1.00
373	A93 30c Weaving flowers	1.75	1.00
374	A93 50c Listening to storm	2.25	2.25
375	A93 $1 Couple	3.25	3.25
	Nos. 372-375 (4)	8.75	7.50

Flowers A94

1991, July 15 Litho. *Perf. 14½*

380	A94 15c Oleander	.25	.25
381	A94 20c Lily	.25	.25
382	A94 25c Passion Flower	.30	.30
383	A94 30c Lily, diff.	.40	.40
384	A94 35c Caesalpinia	.45	.45
385	A94 40c Clerodendron	.50	.50
387	A94 45c Bauhina pinnata	.55	.55
388	A94 50c Hibiscus, vert.	.60	.60
389	A94 75c Apocynaceae	.85	.85
390	A94 $1 Bindweed, vert.	1.10	1.10
391	A94 $2 Tristellateia, vert.	2.25	2.25
392	A94 $3 Impala lily, vert.	3.00	*4.00*
	Nos. 380-392 (12)	10.50	11.50

Souvenir Sheet

Christmas — A95

$2, Stained glass window.

1991, Dec. 12 Litho. *Perf. 14*

395	A95 $2 multicolored	5.50	5.50

Asian Development Bank, 25th Meeting A96

1992, May 4 Litho. *Perf. 14x14½*

396	A96 $1.50 multicolored	2.75	2.75

Christmas A97

Children's drawings: 45c, Christmas trees, flags and balloons. 60c, Santa in sleigh, reindeer on flag.

1992, Nov. 23 Litho. *Perf. 14½x14*

397	A97 45c multicolored	1.25	1.25
398	A97 60c multicolored	1.60	1.60

Hammer DeRoburt (1922-1992) A98

1993, Jan. 31 Litho. *Perf. 14x14½*

399	A98 $1 multicolored	2.75	2.75

Independence, 25th anniv.

Constitution Day, 15th Anniv. — A99

1993, May 17 Litho. *Perf. 14x14½*

400	A99 70c Runners	1.40	1.40
401	A99 80c Declaration of Republic	1.50	1.50

24th South Pacific Forum — A100

1993, Aug. 9 Litho. *Perf. 14½x14*

402	A100 60c Seabirds	1.60	1.60
403	A100 60c Birds, dolphin	1.60	1.60
404	A100 60c Coral, fish	1.60	1.60
405	A100 60c Fish, coral, diff.	1.60	1.60
a.	Block of 4, #402-405	8.00	8.00
b.	Souvenir sheet of 4, #402-405	10.00	10.00

No. 405a is a continuous design.
No. 405b exists with SINGPEX '93 overprint, sold at the exhibition. Value, unused or used, $12.50.

Christmas — A101

Designs: 55c, "Peace on earth..." 65c, "Hark the Herald Angels Sing."

1993, Nov. 29 Litho. *Perf. 14½x14*

406	A101 55c multicolored	1.00	1.00
407	A101 65c multicolored	1.25	1.25

Child's Best Friend — A102

1994, Feb. 10 Litho. *Perf. 14*

408	$1 Girls, dogs	2.00	2.00
409	$1 Boys, dogs	2.00	2.00
a.	A102 Pair, #408-409	5.00	5.00
b.	Souvenir sheet of 2, #408-409	5.25	5.25
c.	As "b," ovptd. in sheet margin	6.00	6.00
d.	As "b," ovptd. in sheet margin	6.50	6.50

No. 409c ovptd. with Hong Kong '94 emblem. No. 409d ovptd. with SINGPEX '94 emblem in gold.
Issued: #409c, 2/18/94; #409d, 8/31/94.

15th Commonwealth Games, Victoria — A103

1994, Sept. 8 Litho. *Perf. 14x14½*

410	A103 $1.50 Weight lifting	2.25	2.25

ICAO, 50th Anniv. A104

55c, Emblems. 65c, Nauru Intl. Airport. 80c, DVOR navigational aid. $1, Airport fire engines.

1994, Dec. 14

411	A104 55c multicolored	.65	.65
412	A104 65c multicolored	.75	.75
413	A104 80c multicolored	.95	.95
414	A104 $1 multicolored	1.25	1.25
a.	Souvenir sheet of 4, #411-414	6.00	6.00
	Nos. 411-414 (4)	3.60	3.60

United Nations, 50th Anniv. A105

No. 415, National flag. No. 416, National coat of arms. No. 417, Canoe, UN emblem. No. 418, Jet, ship, UN emblem.

1995, Jan. 1 *Perf. 14x14½*

415	A105 75c multicolored	1.50	1.50
416	A105 75c multicolored	1.50	1.50
417	A105 75c multicolored	1.50	1.50
418	A105 75c multicolored	1.50	1.50
a.	Block of 4, #415-418	6.75	6.75
b.	Souvenir sheet of 4, #415-418	7.00	7.00

Nos. 417-418 are a continuous design.

Christmas — A106

75c, Star over Bethlehem.

1994, Nov. 20 Litho. *Perf. 14½x14*

419	A106 65c shown	1.25	1.10
420	A106 75c multicolored	1.40	1.30

Membership in Intl. Olympic Committee A107

1994, Dec. 27 *Perf. 14x14½*

421	A107 50c multicolored	.60	.60

Nauru Phosphate Corporation, 25th Anniv. A108

Designs: No. 422, Signing of Phosphate Agreement, June 15, 1967. No. 423, Nauru Pres. Bernard Dowiyogo, Australian Prime Minister Paul Keating at signing Nauru-Australia Compact of Settlement. $2, Mining phosphate.

1995, July 1 Litho. *Perf. 14x15*

422	A108 60c multicolored	1.40	1.40
423	A108 60c multicolored	1.40	1.40
a.	Pair, #422-423	3.75	3.75

Souvenir Sheet

424	A108 $2 multicolored	4.00	4.00

No. 291 Surcharged & Overprinted

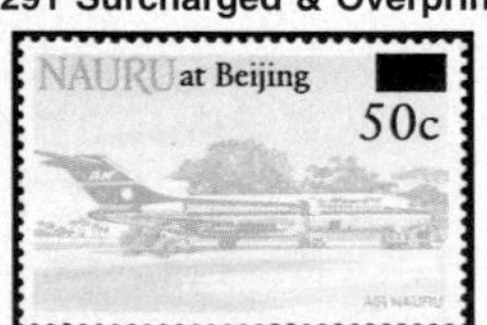

1995, Aug. 19 Litho. *Perf. 13½x14*

425	A66 50c on 25c "at Beijing"	1.75	1.75
426	A66 $1 on 25c "at Singapore"	2.25	2.25
427	A66 $1 on 25c "at Jakarta"	2.25	2.25
a.	Strip of 3, #425-427	8.50	8.50

UN, 50th Anniv. A109

Designs: 75c, Nauru coastline. $1.50, UN headquarters, US, aerial view of Nauru.

1995, Oct. 24 Litho. *Perf. 14*
428 A109 75c multicolored 1.40 1.40
429 A109 $1.50 multicolored 2.75 2.75

Christmas — A110

1995, Dec. 7 Litho. *Perf. 14*
430 60c Seeking the Way 1.00 1.00
431 70c Finding the Way 1.10 1.10
a. A110 Pair, #430-431 2.60 2.60

Return From Truk, 50th Anniv. A111

1996, Jan. 31 *Perf. 12*
432 A111 75c multicolored 1.40 1.40
433 A111 $1.25 multicolored 2.50 2.50
a. Souvenir sheet of 2, #432-433 4.50 4.50

Souvenir Sheet

Nanjing Stone Carving, Keeping off the Evils — A112

1996, Mar. 20 Litho. *Perf. 12*
434 A112 45c multicolored 1.40 1.40

CHINA '96, 9th Asian Intl. Philatelic Exhibition.

End of World War II, 50th Anniv. — A113

Designs: 75c, Children playing on old cannon. $1.50, Girls making flower leis in front of pillbox.

1995, Sept. 13 Litho. *Perf. 14x13½*
435 A113 75c multicolored 1.75 1.75
436 A113 $1.50 multicolored 3.25 3.25
a. Pair, Nos. 435-436 + label 7.50 *7.50*
b. As "a," ovptd. in gold on label *10.00 10.00*
c. As "a," ovptd. in gold on label *10.00 10.00*

No. 436a exists with two different labels: one showing a war memorial, the other a dove. Gold overprint on memorial label is Hongpex '96 Exhibition emblem (No. 436b); on dove label, a silhouette of a rat (No. 436c). Nos. 436a and 436b-436c may be collected as blocks of four.

Issued: Nos. 436b, 436c, 1996.

1996 Summer Olympic Games, Atlanta A114

Discobolus and: 40c, Running pictograph, vert. 50c, Weight lifting pictograph, vert. 60c, Weight lifter. $1, Runner.

Perf. 13½x14, 14x13½
1996, July 21 Litho.
437 A114 40c multicolored 1.00 1.00
438 A114 50c multicolored 1.25 1.25
439 A114 60c multicolored 1.50 1.50
440 A114 $1 multicolored 1.75 1.75
Nos. 437-440 (4) 5.50 5.50

Christmas A115

Designs: 50c, Candles, angel with trumpet, nativity. 70c, Angel, candles, map, fauna.

1996, Dec. 16 Litho. *Perf. 14*
441 A115 50c multicolored 1.00 1.00
442 A115 70c multicolored 1.25 1.25

World Wildlife Fund A116

Fish: a, 20c, Dolphinfish. b, 30c, Wahoo. c, 40c, Pacific sailfish. d, 50c, Yellowfin tuna.

1997, Feb. 12 Litho. *Perf. 11½*
443 A116 Strip of 4, #a.-d. 5.00 5.00

A117

Giant Buddha (various statues): a, 1c. b, 2c. c, 5c. d, 10c. e, 12c. f, 15c. g, 25c.

1997, Feb. 12 *Perf. 14*
444 A117 Sheet of 7, #a.-g. 3.00 3.00

Hong Kong '97, Hong Kong's return to China. No. 444g is 60x80mm.

A118

Designs: 80c, Engagement portrait. $1.20, 50th Wedding anniversary portrait.

1997, July 15 Litho. *Perf. 13½*
445 A118 80c multicolored 1.40 1.50
446 A118 $1.20 multicolored 2.00 2.25
a. Souvenir sheet, #445-446 4.25 4.25

Queen Elizabeth II and Prince Philip, 50th wedding anniv.

Christmas A119

1997, Nov. 5 Litho. *Perf. 13½*
447 A119 60c Monument .90 .55
448 A119 80c Church 1.40 1.40

Nauru Congregational Church, 110th anniv.

Souvenir Sheet

Commonwealth, Oceania and South Pacific Weight Lifting Championships — A120

Various contestants lifting weights: a, 40c. b, 60c. c, 80c. d, $1.20.

1998, Mar. 25 Litho. *Perf. 14*
449 A120 Sheet of 4, #a.-d. 4.00 4.00

Visit of Juan Antonio Samaranch, Pres. of Intl. Olympic Committee — A121

1998, May 4 *Perf. 13½*
450 A121 $2 multicolored 2.75 2.75

Souvenir Sheet

28th Parliamentary Conference — A122

1997, July 24 Litho. *Perf. 14*
451 A122 $2 multicolored 3.25 3.25

A123

Diana, Princess of Wales (1961-97): a, In yellow. b, White blouse. c, Wearing tiara. d, White & black outfit. e, Pink hat. f, White dress.

1998, Aug. 31
452 A123 70c Sheet of 6, #a.-f. 5.25 5.25

A125

1998 Commonwealth Games, Kuala Lumpur: 40c, Gymnast on pommel horse. 60c, Throwing discus. 70c, Runner. 80c, Weight lifter.

1998, Sept. 11 Litho. *Perf. 13½x14*
454 A125 40c multicolored .60 .60
455 A125 60c multicolored .90 .90
456 A125 70c multicolored 1.00 1.00
457 A125 80c multicolored 1.10 1.10
a. Souvenir sheet, #454-457 3.75 3.75
Nos. 454-457 (4) 3.60 3.60

Independence, 30th Anniv. — A126

Squadron Leader L.H. Hicks and: $1, Band. $2, National anthem.

1998, Oct. 26 Litho. *Perf. 14*
458 A126 $1 multicolored .90 .90
459 A126 $2 multicolored 3.00 3.00
a. Souvenir sheet, #458-459 4.25 4.25

Christmas — A127

Star, island scene and: 85c, Fish, candle, flowers. 95c, Flowers, fruits, Christmas present.

1998 *Perf. 13½x12½*
460 A127 85c multicolored 1.25 1.25
461 A127 95c multicolored 1.40 1.40

First Contact with Island, Bicent. — A128

Designs: No. 462, Sailing ship Snow Hunter. No. 463, Capt. John Fearn.

1998, Dec. 1 *Perf. 12*
462 A128 $1.50 multicolored 2.00 2.00
463 A128 $1.50 multicolored 2.00 2.00
a. Pair, #462-463 4.75 4.75
b. Souvenir sheet, #463a 5.50 5.50

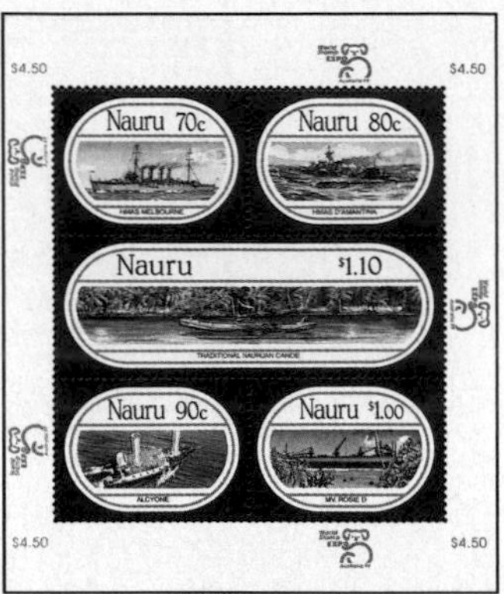

Ships — A129

Designs: a, 70c, HMAS Melbourne. b, 80c, HMAS D'Amantina. c, $1.10, Traditional Nauruan canoe. d, 90c, Alcyone. e, $1, MV Rosie D.

1999, Mar. 19 Litho. *Perf. 12*
464 A129 Sheet of 5, #a.-e. 6.75 6.75

Australia '99, World Stamp Expo. No. 464c is 80x30mm.

1st Manned Moon Landing, 30th Anniv.

Common Design Type

Designs: 70c, Neil Armstrong. 80c, Service module and lunar module fire towards moon. 90c, Aldrin deploying EASEP. $1, Command module enters earth atmosphere.
$2, Earth as seen from moon.

Perf. 14x13¾
1999, July 20 Litho. Wmk. 384
465 CD357 70c multicolored .90 .90
466 CD357 80c multicolored 1.25 1.25
467 CD357 90c multicolored 1.50 1.50
468 CD357 $1 multicolored 1.75 *3.00*
Nos. 465-468 (4) 5.40 6.65

Souvenir Sheet
Perf. 14
469 CD357 $2 multicolored 3.50 3.50

No. 469 contains one circular stamp 40mm in diameter.

China 1999 World Philatelic Exhibition — A130

a, Tursiops truncatus. b, Xiphias gladius.

Perf. 12¾x12½
1999, Aug. 21 Litho. Unwmk.
470 A130 50c Sheet of 2, #a.-b. 4.25 4.25

UPU, 125th Anniv. A131

1999, Aug. 23 Litho. *Perf. 11¾*
471 A131 $1 multicolored 1.75 1.75

Christmas — A132

Designs: 65c, Native woman. 70c, Christmas tree and candle.

Perf. 13½x13¾
1999, Nov. 10 Litho. Wmk. 388
472 A132 65c multi 1.10 1.10
473 A132 70c multi 1.25 1.25

Millennium A133

70c, Woman in native costume, fishermen on beach. $1.10, Satellite dish, runner, cross, airplane, crane, jeep and boat. $1.20, Man on computer, woman holding globe.

Perf. 11¾x12
2000, Jan. 1 Litho. Wmk. 388
474 A133 70c multi 1.75 2.00
475 A133 $1.10 multi 2.75 3.25
476 A133 $1.20 multi 3.25 3.50
a. Souvenir sheet of 3, #474-476 8.00 8.00
Nos. 474-476 (3) 7.75 8.75

Nauru Phosphate Corp. 30th Anniv. A134

Designs: $1.20, Power plant. $1.80, Phosphate train. $2, Albert Ellis.

2000, May 27 Litho. *Perf. 12½x12¾*
477-479 A134 Set of 3 7.75 7.75
479a Souv. sheet, #477-479, perf 12 7.50 7.50

No. 479a exists imperf. Value, $15.

Queen Mother, 100th Birthday A135

Designs: $1, Dark blue hat. $1.10, Lilac hat. $1.20, Waving, light blue hat. $1.40, Blue hat.

2000, Aug. 4 *Perf. 14¼*
480-483 A135 Set of 4 8.25 8.25
483a Souvenir sheet, #480-483, perf. 13¾x13½ 7.75 7.75

2000 Summer Olympics, Sydney — A136

Olympic rings, map of Australia, Sydney Opera House and: 90c, Running. $1, Basketball. $1.10, Weight lifting. $1.20, Olympic torch and runner.

2000 Photo. *Perf. 11¾*
484-487 A136 Set of 4 9.50 9.50

Christmas A137

Designs: 65c, Flower, girl decorating Christmas tree, star, decorated Christmas tree. 75c, Ornament, child on toy train, palm tree, gift.

2000 Litho. *Perf. 13¾x13½*
488-489 A137 Set of 2 3.00 3.00
489a Souvenir sheet, #488-489 3.25 3.25

Stamps from No. 489a are perf. 14¼x14¼x13¾x14¼.

32nd Pacific Islands Forum — A138

No. 490 — Island and: a, 90c, Yellow flowers, bird flying to right. b, $1, Red flowers, bird flying to left. c, $1.10, Yellow flowers, birds facing right. d, $2, Red flowers, bird facing left.

Perf. 14½x14
2001, Aug. 14 Litho. Unwmk.
490 A138 Block of 4, #a-d 12.50 12.50
e. Souvenir sheet, #490 13.00 13.00

Reign Of Queen Elizabeth II, 50th Anniv. Issue

Common Design Type

Designs: Nos. 491, 495a, 70c, Princess Elizabeth in uniform, 1946. Nos. 492, 495b, 80c, Wearing patterned hat. Nos. 493, 495c, 90c, Wearing hat, 1951. Nos. 494, 495d, $1, In 1997. No. 495e, $4, 1955 portrait by Annigoni (38x50mm).

Perf. 14¼x14½, 13¾ (#495e)
2002, Feb. 6 Litho. Wmk. 373
With Gold Frames
491 CD360 70c multicolored 1.75 1.75
492 CD360 80c multicolored 2.00 2.00
493 CD360 90c multicolored 2.10 2.10
494 CD360 $1 multicolored 2.40 2.40
Nos. 491-494 (4) 8.25 8.25

Souvenir Sheet
Without Gold Frames
495 CD360 Sheet of 5, #a-e 10.50 10.50

Miniature Sheet

In Remembrance of Sept. 11, 2001 Terrorist Attacks — A139

No. 496: a, 90c. b, $1. c, $1.10. d, $2.

Wmk. 373
2002, May 17 Litho. *Perf. 13¾*
496 A139 Sheet of 4, #a-d 8.75 8.75

Butterflies — A140

No. 497: a, Parthenos sylvia. b, Delias madetes. c, Danaus philene. d, Arhopala hercules. e, Papilio canopus. f, Danaus schenkii. g, Parthenos figrina. h, Mycalesis phidon. i, Vindula sapor.
$2, Graphium agamemnon.

2002, June 28 *Perf. 13¾x14¼*
497 A140 50c Sheet of 9, #a-i 12.00 12.00

Souvenir Sheet
498 A140 $2 multi 4.50 4.50

Queen Mother Elizabeth (1900-2002)

Common Design Type

Designs: Nos. 499, 501a, $1.50, Wearing hat (black and white photograph). Nos. 500, 501b, $1.50, Wearing blue hat.

Perf. 13¾x4¼
2002, Aug. 5 Litho. Wmk. 373
With Purple Frames
499 CD361 $1.50 multicolored 3.75 3.75
500 CD361 $1.50 multicolored 3.75 3.75

Souvenir Sheet
Without Purple Frames
Perf. 14½x14¼
501 CD361 Sheet of 2, #a-b 8.50 8.50

Fire Fighting A141

Designs: 20c, Building fire. 50c, Blaze at sea. 90c, Forest fire. $1, New and old fire helmets. $1.10, Modern ladder truck, old pump engine. $2, Modern and late 19th cent. firefighters.
$5, Modern fire engine and rescue vehicle.

Perf. 14x14¼
2002, Aug. 31 Litho. Wmk. 373
502-507 A141 Set of 6 12.00 12.00

Souvenir Sheet
508 A141 $5 multi 15.00 15.00

Roman Catholic Church in Nauru, Cent. — A142

No. 509: a, First church building, Arubo. b, Father Friedrich Gründl, first missionary. c, Sister Stanisla, first sister. d, Second church building, Ibwenape. e, Brother Kalixtus Bader, first lay brother. f, Father Alois Kayser, missionary.

Wmk. 373
2002, Dec. 8 Litho. *Perf. 13¾*
509 A142 $1.50 Sheet of 6, #a-f 19.00 19.00

Christmas — A143

Designs: 15c, The Holy Family with Dancing Angels, by Sir Anthony Van Dyck. $1, The Holy Virgin with the Child, by Luca Cangiasus. $1.20, The Holy Family with the Cat, by Rembrandt. $3, The Holy Family with St. John, by Raphael.

2002, Dec. 8
510-513 A143 Set of 4 10.00 10.00

Worldwide Fund For Nature (WWF) A144

Designs: 15c, Red-and-black anemone fish, Bubble tentacle sea anemone. $1, Orange-fin anemone fish, Leathery sea anemone. $1.20, Pink anemone fish, Magnificent sea anemone. $3, Clark's anemone fish, Merten's sea anemone.

Wmk. 373

2003, Apr. 29 Litho. ***Perf. 14***
514-517 A144 Set of 4 11.00 11.00
517a Miniature sheet, 4 each #514-517 45.00 45.00

Powered Flight, Cent. — A145

No. 518: a, Santos-Dumont wins the Deutsch Prize, Oct. 1901. b, USS Shenandoah at Lakehurst, NJ. c, R101 at Cardington Mast, U.K., Oct. 1929. d, R34 crossing Atlantic, July 1919. e, Zeppelin No. 1, 1900. f, USS Los Angeles moored to the USS Patoka. g, Goodyear C-71 airship. h, LZ-130 Graf Zeppelin II at Friedrichshafen, Germany. i, Zeppelin NT.

No. 519 — LZ-127 Graf Zeppelin: a, Over Mt. Fuji. b, Over San Francisco. c, Exchanging mail with Russian ice breaker, Franz Josef Land.

2003, Oct. 26
518 A145 50c Sheet of 9, #a-i 12.00 12.00
519 A145 $2 Sheet of 3, #a-c 14.00 14.00

Bird Life International A146

Nauru reed warbler: No. 520, Bird on reed. No. 521, Bird on branch with insect in beak, vert. No. 522a, Close-up of head. No. 522b, Bird with open beak, vert. No. 522c, Nest with chicks.

2003, Nov. 10 ***Perf. 14¼x13¾***
520 A146 $1.50 multi 4.75 4.75
a. Perf. 14¼x14½ 4.75 4.75

Perf. 13¾x14¼
521 A146 $1.50 multi 4.75 4.75
a. Perf. 14½x14¼ 4.75 4.75

Souvenir Sheet

Perf. 14¼x14½, 14½x14¼ (#522b)
522 Sheet, #520a, 521a, 522a-522c 17.00 17.00
a.-c. A146 $1.50 Any single 3.50 3.50

Battle of Trafalgar, Bicent. — A147

Designs: 25c, Aigle in action against HMS Defiance. 50c, French "Eprouvette." 75c, Santissima Trinidad in action against HMS Africa. $1, Emperor Napoleon Bonaparte, vert. $1.50, HMS Victory. No. 528, $2.50, Vice-Admiral Sir Horatio Nelson, vert.

No. 529, $2.50, vert.: a, Admiral Pierre Villeneuve. b, Formidable.

2005, Mar. 29 Litho. ***Perf. 13¼***
523-528 A147 Set of 6 13.00 13.00

Souvenir Sheet
529 A147 $2.50 Sheet of 2, #a-b 10.50 10.50

No. 527 has particles of wood from the HMS Victory embedded in the areas covered by a thermographic process that produces a shiny, raised effect.

End of World War II, 60th Anniv. — A148

No. 530: a, German raider Komet shells Nauru, 1940. b, French warship Le Triomphant assists in evacuation of civilians, 1942. c, Japanese forces occupy Nauru, 1942. d, US Air Force B-24 Liberator aircraft bombing missions, 1943. e, USS Paddle stationed off Nauru, 1943. f, B-25G Mitchell "Coral Princess" shot down over Nauru, 1944. g, Spitfires, Battle of Britain, 1940. h, HMAS Diamantine arrives at Nauru, 1945. i, D-Day landings, 1944. j, Union Jack is hoisted again, 1945.

$5, HMAS Manoora sinks Italian MV Romolo, 1940.

2005, Apr. 21 ***Perf. 13¾***
530 A148 75c Sheet of 10, #a-j 15.00 15.00

Souvenir Sheet
531 A148 $5 multi 9.75 9.75

Pacific Explorer 2005 World Stamp Expo, Sydney (No. 531).

Pope John Paul II (1920-2005) A149

2005, Aug. 18 Litho. ***Perf. 14x14¼***
532 A149 $1 multi 2.00 2.00

Rotary International, Cent. — A150

2005, Sept. 12 ***Perf. 14½x14¼***
533 A150 $2.50 multi 4.75 4.75

BirdLife International — A151

No. 534, 25c: a, Rota bridled white-eye. b, Faichuk white-eye. c, Samoan white-eye. d, Bridled white-eye. e, Long-billed white-eye. f, Golden white-eye.

No. 535, 50c: a, Kuhl's lorikeet. b, Masked shining parrot. c, Crimson shining parrot. d, Blue lorikeet. e, Henderson lorikeet. f, Ultramarine lorikeet.

No. 536, $1: a, Atoll fruit dove. b, Henderson fruit dove. c, Cook Islands fruit dove. d, Rapa fruit dove. e, Whistling dove. f, Mariana fruit dove.

Perf. 14¼x14½
2005, Sept. 12 Litho.

Sheets of 6, #a-f
534-536 A151 Set of 3 28.00 28.00

Christmas — A152

Stories by Hans Christian Andersen (1805-75): 25c, The Little Fir Tree. 50c, The Wild Swans. 75c, The Farmyard Cock and the Weather Cock. $1, The Storks. $2.50, The Toad. $5, The Ice Maiden.

2005, Oct. 10 ***Perf. 14***
537-542 A152 Set of 6 16.50 16.50

Battle of Trafalgar, Bicent. — A153

Designs: 50c, HMS Victory. $1, Ships in battle, horiz. $5, Admiral Horatio Nelson.

2005, Oct. 18 ***Perf. 13½***
543-545 A153 Set of 3 14.00 14.00

Anniversaries — A154

No. 546, 25c: a, Wolfgang Amadeus Mozart. b, Piano and violin.

No. 547, 50c: a, Isambard Kingdom Brunel. b, Chain and pulley.

No. 548, 75c: a, Edmond Halley. b, Halley's quadrant.

No. 549, $1: a, Charles Darwin. b, Early microscope.

No. 550, $1.25: a, Thomas Alva Edison. b, Light bulb.

No. 551, $1.50: a, Christopher Columbus. b, Astrolabe.

2006, May 27 Litho. ***Perf. 13¼x12½***

Horiz. Pairs, #a-b
546-551 A154 Set of 6 22.50 22.50

Birth of Mozart, 250th anniv., Birth of Brunel, bicent., Birth of Halley, 350th anniv., Darwin's voyage on the Beagle, 175th anniv., Death of Edison, 75th anniv., Death of Columbus, 500th anniv.

2006 World Cup Soccer Championships, Germany — A155

Scenes from championship matches won by: $1, Uruguay, 1950. $1.50, Argentina, 1978. $2, Italy, 1982. $3, Brazil, 2002.

2006, June 9 ***Perf. 14***
552-555 A155 Set of 4 15.00 15.00

Dinosaurs A156

Designs: 10c, Parasaurolophus. 25c, Quetzalcoatlus. 50c, Spinosaurus. 75c, Triceratops. $1, Tyrannosaurus rex. $1.50, Euoplocephalus. $2, Velociraptor. $2.50, Protoceratops.

2006, Aug. 14 ***Perf. 13¼x13½***
556-563 A156 Set of 8 17.50 17.50

Miniature Sheet

Victoria Cross, 150th Anniv. — A157

No. 564: a, Lt. Gerald Graham carrying wounded man. b, Pvt. Mac Gregor shooting rifle. c, Pvt. Alexander Wright repelling a sortie. d, Cpl. John Ross viewing evacuation of the Redan. e, Sgt. McWheeney digging with bayonet. f, Brevet Maj. G. L. Goodlake surprising enemy. Descriptions of vignettes are on labels below each stamp.

2006, Sept. 12 ***Perf. 13¼x12½***
564 A157 $1.50 Sheet of 6, #a-f, + 6 labels 18.00 18.00

Miniature Sheet

Inaugural Flight of the Concorde, 30th Anniv. — A158

No. 565: a, British Airways Concorde G-BOAF on ground. b, First flight of Concorde 002, 1969. c, Concorde landing. d, Queen's Golden Jubilee flypast, 2002. e, 50th anniv. of Battle of Britain, 1990. f, Concorde at 60,000 feet. g, Extreme condition testing. h, Concorde on runway. i, First commercial flight, 1976. j, Concorde above Earth. k, British Airways Concorde G-BOAF in flight. l, Two Concordes on ground.

2006, Oct. 10 ***Perf. 14¼x13¾***
565 A158 $1 Sheet of 12, #a-l, + 3 labels 26.00 26.00

Miniature Sheet

Year of Three Kings, 70th Anniv. — A159

No. 566: a, Queen Elizabeth II. b, King George V and Princess Elizabeth. c, King Edward VIII and Princess Elizabeth. d, King George VI and Princess Elizabeth.

2006, Oct. 17
566 A159 $1.50 Sheet of 4, #a-d 13.00 13.00

Wedding of Queen Elizabeth II and Prince Philip, 60th Anniv. — A160

Designs: $1, Couple. $1.50, Couple in coach. $2, At wedding ceremony. $3, Couple walking.
$5, Queen Elizabeth II in bridal gown.

2007, Jan. 31 Litho. *Perf. 13¾*
567-570 A160 Set of 4 14.00 14.00

Souvenir Sheet

Perf. 14¼

571 A160 $5 multi 9.75 9.75

No. 571 contains one 43x57mm stamp.

A161

Royal Air Force, 90th Anniv. — A162

Aviation pioneers: No. 572, 70c, Sir Douglas Bader (1910-82), World War II fighter ace. No. 573, 70c, R. J. Mitchell (1895-1937), designer of Spitfire airplane. No. 574, 70c, Sir Frank Whittle (1907-96), inventor of jet engine. No. 575, 70c, Sir Sydney Camm (1893-1966), designer of Hawker Hurricane airplane. No. 576, 70c, Air Vice Marshal James E. "Johnnie" Johnson (1915-2001), World War II fighter ace.
$3, Avro Vulcan.

Wmk. 373

2008, May 19 Litho. *Perf. 14*
572-576 A161 Set of 5 8.50 8.50

Souvenir Sheet

577 A162 $3 multi 7.50 7.50

Nos. 572-576 were each printed in sheets of 8 + central label.

2008 Summer Olympics, Beijing A163

Designs: 15c, Bamboo, badminton. 25c, Dragon, archery. 75c, Lanterns, weight lifting. $1, Fish, diving.

Perf. 13¼

2008, Aug. 8 Litho. Unwmk.
578-581 A163 Set of 4 5.00 5.00

A164

End of World War I, 90th Anniv. — A165

World War I recruitment posters inscribed: No. 582, $1, "A Happy New Year to our Gallant Soldiers." No. 583, $1, "The Empire Needs Men." No. 584, $1, "South Australians." No. 585, $1, "Your King and Country Need You." No. 586, $1, "Britons." No. 587, $1, "An Appeal to You."
$2, Queen's Wreath of Remembrance.

Wmk. 406

2008, Sept. 16 Litho. *Perf. 14*
582-587 A164 Set of 6 13.00 13.00

Souvenir Sheet

588 A165 $2 multi 4.25 4.25

Worldwide Fund for Nature (WWF) A166

Greater frigate bird: 25c, Adult and chick. 75c, Two in flight. $1, Landing. $2, One in flight.

Perf. 13¼x13

2008, Oct. 14 Unwmk.
589-592 A166 Set of 4 8.25 8.25
592a Sheet, 4 each #589-592, perf. 13 33.00 33.00

Naval Aviation, Cent. A167

Designs: No. 593, $1.50, Avro 504C. No. 594, $1.50, Fairey Flycatcher. No. 595, $1.50, Short Folder. No. 596, $1.50, De Havilland Sea Vixen.
$3, Grumman Avenger in Operation Meridian, 1945.

Wmk. 406

2009, Sept. 3 Litho. *Perf. 14*
593-596 A167 Set of 4 12.50 12.50

Souvenir Sheet

597 A167 $3 multi 6.25 6.25

Nos. 593-596 each were printed in sheets of 8 + central label.

Russian Space Program — A168

Flags of Russia and Nauru and: No. 598, 60c, Sputnik satellite, 1957. No. 599, 60c, Yuri Gagarin, first man in space, 1961. $1.20, Nauru Island from space. $2.25, Vostok 1. $3, International Space Station.

Perf. 14½x14

2011, Apr. 12 Unwmk.
598-602 A168 Set of 5 16.50 16.50

Souvenir Sheet

Wedding of Prince William and Catherine Middleton — A169

Perf. 14¾x14¼

2011, Apr. 29 Wmk. 406
603 A169 $5 multi 11.00 11.00

SEMI-POSTAL STAMP

Miniature Sheet of 4

1996 Summer Olympics, Atlanta — SP1

Designs: a, Birds, denomination UR. b. Birds, denomination UL. c, 4 dolphins. d, 2 dolphins.

1995, Sept. 1 Litho. *Perf. 12*
B1 SP1 60c +15c, #a.-d. 7.00 6.50

Surcharge for sports development in Nauru.

NEPAL

nə-'pol

LOCATION — In the Himalaya Mountains between India and Tibet
GOVT. — Republic
AREA — 56,136 sq. mi.
POP. — 24,302,653 (1999 est.)
CAPITAL — Kathmandu

Nepal stamps were valid only in Nepal and India until April 1959, when they became valid to all parts of the world.

4 Pice = 1 Anna
64 Pice = 16 Annas = 1 Rupee
100 Paisa = 1 Rupee (1958)

Catalogue values for unused stamps in this country are for Never Hinged items, beginning with Scott 103 in the regular postage section, Scott C1 in the air post section and Scott O1 in the officials section.

Nos. 1-24, 29A were issued without gum.

Sripech and Crossed Khukris — A1

1881 Typo. Unwmk. *Pin-perf.*

European Wove Paper

1 A1 1a ultramarine 300.00 *475.00*
2 A1 2a purple 375.00 500.00
a. Tete beche pair *1,400. 1,400.*
3 A1 4a green 500.00 *650.00*

Imperf

4 A1 1a blue 175.00 140.00
5 A1 2a purple 200.00 *200.00*
a. Tete beche pair *800.00 800.00*
6 A1 4a green 275.00 *500.00*

1886 Native Wove Paper *Imperf.*
7 A1 1a ultramarine 22.50 *32.50*
a. Tete beche pair *150.00 175.00*
8 A1 2a violet 37.50 37.50
a. Tete beche pair *200.00 200.00*
9 A1 4a green 55.00 55.00
a. Tete beche pair *300.00 250.00*
Nos. 7-9 (3) 115.00 125.00

Used values for Nos. 9-49 are for telegraph cancels.

Siva's Bow and Two Khukris — A2

1899-1917 *Imperf.*

Native Wove Paper

10 A2 ½a black 20.00 13.50
a. Tete beche pair *100.00* 55.00
11 A2 ½a red orange ('17) *1,750.* 400.00
a. Tete beche pair

Pin-perf.

12 A2 ½a black 30.00 17.50
a. Tete beche pair *225.00* 55.00

No. 11 is known postally used on six covers.

Type of 1881

1898-1917 *Imperf.*
13 A1 1a pale blue 60.00 60.00
a. 1a bluish green 75.00 75.00
b. Tete beche pair *150.00 150.00*
c. As "a," tete beche pair *300.00 300.00*
14 A1 2a gray violet 60.00 60.00
a. Tete beche pair *140.00 140.00*
15 A1 2a claret ('17) *100.00* 32.50
a. Tete beche pair *225.00 100.00*
16 A1 2a brown ('17) 25.00 12.00
a. Tete beche pair 55.00 42.50
17 A1 4a dull green 70.00 70.00
a. Tete beche pair 350.00 *350.00*
b. Cliche of 1a in plate of 4a ('04) *500.00 400.00*
c. As "b," pair — —
Nos. 13-17 (5) 315.00 234.50

#17b has the recut frame of the 1904 issue. #17b probably was used only on telegraph/telephone forms.

Pin-perf.

18 A1 1a pale blue 17.50 10.00
a. Tete beche pair *75.00 50.00*
19 A1 2a gray violet 90.00 90.00
a. Tete beche pair *300.00 300.00*
20 A1 2a claret ('17) 90.00 45.00
a. Tete beche pair 250.00 —

21	A1	2a brown ('17)	90.00	45.00
a.		Tete beche pair	*250.00*	—
22	A1	4a dull green	150.00	150.00
a.		Tete beche pair	*900.00*	*900.00*

Frame Recut on All Cliches, Fewer Lines

1903-04 Native Wove Paper *Imperf.*

23	A1	1a bright blue	20.00	13.00
a.		Tete beche pair	*60.00*	*42.50*

Pin-perf.

24	A1	1a bright blue	30.00	
a.		Tete beche pair	*120.00*	

European Wove Paper

23b	A1	1a blue	*950.00*	1,000.
23c		Tete beche pair	*1,750.*	

Pin-perf.

24b	A1	1a blue	650.00	—
24c		Tete beche pair	*2,750.*	

Siva Mahadeva — A3

1907 Engr. *Perf. 13½*

European Wove Paper

26	A3	2p brown	9.00	2.50
27	A3	4p green	10.00	2.50
28	A3	8p carmine	14.00	2.50
29	A3	16p violet	27.50	6.00
		Nos. 26-29 (4)	60.50	13.50

Type A3 has five characters in bottom panel, reading "Gurkha Sirkar." Date divided in lower corners is "1964." Outer side panels carry denomination (also on A5).

A4

1917-18 *Imperf.*

29A	A4	1a bright blue	12.00	5.00
b.		1a indigo	12.00	6.00
c.		Pin-perf.	17.50	15.00

No. 29A may not have been used postally.

In 1917 a telephone and telegraph system was started and remainder stocks and further printings of designs A1 and A2 were used to pay telegrams fees. Design A4 was designed for telegraph use but was valid for postal use. After 1929 design A3 was used for telegrams. The usual telegraph cancellation is crescent-shaped.

Type of 1907 Redrawn

A5

Nine characters in bottom panel reading "Nepal Sirkar"

1929 *Perf. 14, 14½*

Size: 24¾x18¾mm

30	A5	2p dark brown	12.00	1.00
31	A5	4p green	12.00	1.25
32	A5	8p deep red	45.00	3.00
33	A5	16p dark red vio	32.50	3.00
34	A5	24p orange yellow	27.50	4.00
35	A5	32p dark ultra	32.50	4.00

Size: 26x19½mm

36	A5	1r orange red	40.00	9.00

Size: 28x21mm

37	A5	5r brown & black	47.50	*30.00*
		Nos. 30-37 (8)	249.00	*55.25*

On Nos. 30-37 the date divided in lower corners is "1986."

Type of 1929 Redrawn

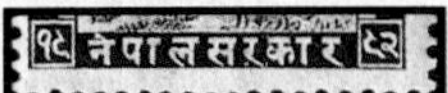

Date characters in Lower Corners read "1992"

1935 Unwmk. Engr. *Perf. 14*

38	A5	2p dark brown	6.00	1.50
39	A5	4p green	6.00	2.00
40	A5	8p bright red	150.00	10.00
41	A5	16p dk red violet	15.00	3.00
42	A5	24p orange yellow	15.00	4.50
43	A5	32p dark ultra	16.00	5.00
		Nos. 38-43 (6)	208.00	26.00

Redrawn Type of 1935

Perf. 11, 11x11½, 12x11½

1941-46 Typo.

44	A5	2p black brown	1.25	.70
a.		2p green (error)	13.00	
45	A5	4p bright green	2.50	1.25
46	A5	8p rose red	3.75	1.00
47	A5	16p chocolate ('42)	22.50	4.25
48	A5	24p orange ('46)	18.00	3.50
49	A5	32p deep blue ('46)	24.00	6.25

Size: 29x19½mm

50	A5	1r henna brown ('46)	47.50	30.00
		Nos. 44-50 (7)	119.50	46.95
		Set, never hinged	250.00	

Exist imperf. vert. or horiz. Full imperf. examples were not regularly issued.

Swayambhunath Stupa — A6

Temple of Krishna — A7

View of Kathmandu A8

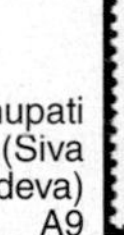

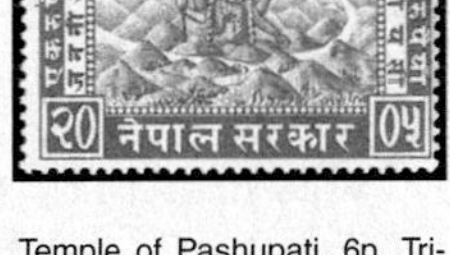

Pashupati (Siva Mahadeva) A9

Designs: 4p, Temple of Pashupati. 6p, Tri-Chundra College. 8p, Mahabuddha Temple. 24p, Guheswori Temple, Patan. 32p, The 22 Fountains, Balaju.

Perf. 13½x14, 13½, 14

1949, Oct. 1 Litho. Unwmk.

51	A6	2p brown	1.50	1.25
52	A6	4p green	1.50	1.25
53	A6	6p rose pink	2.75	1.25
54	A6	8p vermilion	3.00	2.00
55	A7	16p rose lake	3.00	2.00
56	A8	20p blue	6.25	3.25
57	A8	24p carmine	5.50	2.00
58	A8	32p ultramarine	10.00	3.25
59	A9	1r red orange	47.50	30.00
		Nos. 51-59 (9)	81.00	46.25
		Set, never hinged	150.00	

King Tribhuvana Bir Bikram — A10

1954, Apr. 15 Unwmk. *Perf. 14*

Size: 18x22mm

60	A10	2p chocolate	1.25	.65
61	A10	4p green	4.50	2.00
62	A10	6p rose	1.00	.65
63	A10	8p violet	.80	.65
64	A10	12p red orange	8.00	3.25

Size: 25½x29½mm

65	A10	16p red brown	1.00	.65
66	A10	20p car rose	2.25	2.00
67	A10	24p rose lake	1.75	2.00
68	A10	32p ultramarine	2.50	2.00
69	A10	50p rose pink	22.50	9.00
70	A10	1r vermilion	27.50	15.00
71	A10	2r orange	25.00	12.00
		Nos. 60-71 (12)	98.05	49.85
		Set, never hinged	225.00	

Map of Nepal A11

1954, Apr. 15 Size: 29½x17½mm

72	A11	2p chocolate	1.25	1.25
73	A11	4p green	4.50	2.00
74	A11	6p rose	12.50	3.25
75	A11	8p violet	.75	.40
76	A11	12p red orange	19.00	1.00

Size: 38x21½mm

77	A11	16p red brown	1.00	.45
78	A11	20p car rose	1.50	.45
79	A11	24p rose lake	1.50	.45
80	A11	32p ultramarine	2.00	.80
81	A11	50p rose pink	20.00	3.00
82	A11	1r vermilion	25.00	3.50
83	A11	2r orange	17.50	3.50
		Nos. 72-83 (12)	106.50	20.05
		Set, never hinged	235.00	

Planting Rice — A12

Throne — A13

Hanuman Gate — A14

King Mahendra Bir Bikram and Queen Ratna — A15

Design: 8p, Ceremonial arch and elephant.

Perf. 13½x14, 11½, 13½, 14

Litho., Photo. (6p)

1956 Granite Paper Unwmk.

84	A12	4p green	4.50	*9.00*
85	A13	6p crimson & org	2.75	*5.00*
86	A12	8p light violet	2.25	*2.50*
87	A14	24p carmine rose	4.75	*9.00*
88	A15	1r brown red	100.00	*110.00*
		Nos. 84-88 (5)	114.25	*135.50*
		Set, never hinged	180.00	

Coronation of King Mahendra Bir Bikram and Queen Ratna Rajya Lakshmi.

Mountain Village and UN Emblem — A16

1956, Dec. 14 Litho. *Perf. 13½*

89	A16	12p ultra & orange	3.75	*6.00*
		Never hinged	7.50	

1st anniv. of Nepal's admission to the UN.

Crown of Nepal — A17

Perf. 13½x14

1957, June 22 Unwmk.

Size: 18x22mm

90	A17	2p dull red brown	.50	*1.00*
91	A17	4p light green	.70	*1.00*
92	A17	6p pink	.50	*1.00*
93	A17	8p light violet	.50	*1.00*
94	A17	12p orange vermilion	2.75	*1.75*

Size: 25½x30mm

95	A17	16p red brown	4.00	2.75
96	A17	20p deep pink	6.00	3.75
97	A17	24p brt car rose	4.00	3.50
98	A17	32p ultramarine	5.50	3.75
99	A17	50p rose red	12.00	8.00
100	A17	1r brown orange	15.00	15.00
101	A17	2r orange	10.00	*11.00*
		Nos. 90-101 (12)	61.45	*53.50*
		Set, never hinged	110.00	

Lumbini Temple — A18

1958, Dec. 10 Typo. *Perf. 11*

Without Gum

102	A18	6p yellow	2.00	2.00

10th anniversary of Universal Declaration of Human Rights. Exists imperf.

Catalogue values for unused stamps in this section, from this point to the end of the section, are for Never Hinged items.

Map and Flag — A19

1959, Feb. 18 Engr. *Perf. 14½*

103	A19	6p carmine & light green	.85	.50

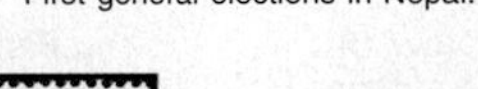

First general elections in Nepal.

Statue of Vishnu, Changu Narayan A20

Krishna Conquering Black Serpent A21

Designs: 4p, Nepalese glacier. 6p, Golden Gate, Bhaktapur. 8p, Nepalese musk deer. 12p, Rhinoceros. 16p, 20p, 24p, 32p, 50p, Nyatapola Temple, Bhatgaon. 1r, 2r, Himalayan impeyan pheasant. 5r, Satyr tragopan.

Perf. 13½x14, 14x13½

1959-60 Litho. Unwmk.

Size: 18x22mm

104	A20	1p chocolate	.25	.25
105	A21	2p gray violet	.25	.25
106	A20	4p light ultra	.55	.40
107	A20	6p vermilion	.55	.25
108	A21	8p sepia	.40	.25
109	A21	12p greenish gray	.55	.25

Size: 25½x30mm

110	A20	16p brown & lt vio	.55	.25
111	A20	20p blue & dull rose	2.00	1.00
112	A20	24p green & pink	2.00	1.00
113	A20	32p brt vio & ultra	1.20	1.00
114	A20	50p rose red & grn	2.00	1.00
115	A20	1r redsh brn & bl	24.00	8.50

116 A20 2r rose lil & ultra 16.00 9.00
117 A20 5r vio & rose red ('60) 100.00 80.00
Nos. 104-117 (14) 150.30 103.40

Nepal's admission to the UPU.

Spinning Wheel — A22

1959, Apr. 10 Typo. *Perf. 11*
118 A22 2p dark red brown .55 .35

Issued to promote development of cottage industries.
Exists imperf. Value $26.

King Mahendra — A23

1959, Apr. 14
119 A23 12p bluish black .65 .50

Nepal's admission to UPU. Exists imperf. and ungummed. Value $200.
No. 119 exists with paper maker's watermark "LOVELY BOND / MADE IN SWEDEN". Value, unused or used, $12.

King Mahendra Opening Parliament — A24

1959, July 1 Unwmk. *Perf. 10½*
120 A24 6p deep carmine 1.20 1.20

First session of Parliament. Exists imperf. Value, pair $45.

Sri Pashupati Nath — A25

1959, Nov. 19 *Perf. 11*
Size: 18x24½mm
121 A25 4p dp yellow green .80 .80
Size: 20½x28mm
122 A25 8p carmine 1.60 1.00
Size: 24½x33mm
123 A25 1r light blue 11.00 8.00
Nos. 121-123 (3) 13.40 9.80

Renovation of Sri Pashupati Temple. Nos. 121-123 exist imperf. between.

King Mahendra — A26

1960, June 11 Photo. *Perf. 14*
Size: 25x30mm
124 A26 1r red lilac 2.40 1.40

King Mahendra's 40th birthday. See Nos. 147-151A. For overprint see No. O15.

Children, Temple and Mt. Everest — A27

1960 Typo. *Perf. 11*
125 A27 6p dark blue 27.50 14.00

1st Children's Day, Mar. 1, 1960. Printed in sheets of four. Exists imperf.; value $45 unused.

Mount Everest — A28

Himalaya mountain peaks: 5p, Machha Puchhre. 40p, Mansalu.

1960-61 Photo. *Perf. 14*
126 A28 5p claret & brown ('61) .50 .25
127 A28 10p ultra & rose lilac .70 .25
128 A28 40p vio & red brn ('61) 1.50 .85
Nos. 126-128 (3) 2.70 1.35

King Tribhuvana — A29

1961, Feb. 18 *Perf. 13x13½*
129 A29 10p red brown & orange .75 .25

Tenth Democracy Day.

King Mahendra — A30

1961, June 11 *Perf. 14x14½*
130 A30 6p emerald .50 .50
131 A30 12p ultramarine .65 .65
132 A30 50p carmine rose .90 .90
133 A30 1r brown 2.25 2.25
Nos. 130-133 (4) 4.30 4.30

King Mahendra's 41st birthday.

Prince Gyanendra Canceling Stamps — A31

1961 Typo. *Perf. 11*
134 A31 12p orange *40.00 40.00*

Children's Day, Mar. 1, 1961.
Exists imperf. Value, $75.

Malaria Eradication Emblem and Temple — A32

Design: 1r, Emblem and Nepalese flag.

1962, Apr. 7 Litho. *Perf. 13x13½*
135 A32 12p blue & lt blue .55 .50
136 A32 1r magenta & orange 1.75 1.50

WHO drive to eradicate malaria.

King Mahendra A33

1962, June 11 Unwmk. *Perf. 13*
137 A33 10p slate blue .30 .25
138 A33 15p brown .50 .40
139 A33 45p dull red brown .75 .75
140 A33 1r olive gray 1.40 1.10
Nos. 137-140 (4) 2.95 2.50

King Mahendra's 42nd birthday.

Bhanu Bhakta Acharya — A34

10p, Moti Ram Bhatta. 40p, Shambu Prasad.

1962 Photo. *Perf. 14x14½*
141 A34 5p orange brown .45 .45
142 A34 10p deep aqua .55 .45
143 A34 40p olive bister .70 .55
Nos. 141-143 (3) 1.70 1.45

Issued to honor Nepalese poets.

Mahendra Type of 1960 and

King Mahendra — A35

1962-66 *Perf. 14½x14*
144 A35 1p car rose .25 .25
145 A35 2p brt blue .25 .25
145A A35 3p gray ('66) .80 .40
146 A35 5p golden brown .25 .25

Perf. 14x14½
Size: 21½x38mm
147 A26 10p rose claret .25 .25
148 A26 40p brown .55 .55
149 A26 75p blue green 15.00 13.00

Perf. 14
Size: 25x30mm
150 A26 2r red orange 2.00 1.50
151 A26 5r gray green 4.00 3.00
151A A26 10r violet ('66) 13.00 10.00
Nos. 144-151A (10) 36.35 29.45

See No. 199. For overprints see Nos. O12-O14.

Blackboard, Book and UN Emblem — A36

1963, Jan. 6 *Perf. 14½x14*
152 A36 10p dark gray .50 .25
153 A36 15p brown .70 .45
154 A36 50p violet blue 1.50 .75
Nos. 152-154 (3) 2.70 1.45

UNESCO "Education for All" campaign.

Five-pointed Star and Hands Holding Lamps — A37

Unwmk.
1963, Feb. 19 Photo. *Perf. 13*
155 A37 5p blue .45 .25
156 A37 10p reddish brown .50 .25
157 A37 50p rose lilac 1.50 .25
158 A37 1r blue green 2.50 .25
Nos. 155-158 (4) 4.95 1.00

Panchayat System and National Day.

Man, Tractor and Wheat — A38

1963, Mar. 21 *Perf. 14x14½*
159 A38 10p orange .55 .25
160 A38 15p dark ultra 1.00 .40
161 A38 50p green 1.75 .80
162 A38 1r brown 4.00 .90
Nos. 159-162 (4) 7.30 2.35

FAO "Freedom from Hunger" campaign.

Map of Nepal and Hand A39

1963, Apr. 14 Unwmk. *Perf. 13*
163 A39 10p green .50 .25
164 A39 15p claret 1.00 .40
165 A39 50p slate 1.75 .55
166 A39 1r violet blue 4.00 .90
Nos. 163-166 (4) 7.25 2.10

Rastriya Panchayat system.

King Mahendra — A40

1963, June 11 *Perf. 13*
167 A40 5p violet .35 .25
168 A40 10p brown orange .60 .25
169 A40 15p dull green .80 .50
Nos. 167-169 (3) 1.75 1.00

King Mahendra's 43rd birthday.

East-West Highway on Map of Nepal and King Mahendra A41

1964, Feb. 19 Photo. *Perf. 13*

170	A41	10p blue & dp orange	.40	.25
171	A41	15p dk blue & dp org	.60	.25
172	A41	50p dk grn & redsh brn	1.25	.40
		Nos. 170-172 (3)	2.25	.90

Issued to publicize the East-West Highway as "The Prosperity of the Country."

King Mahendra Speaking Before Microphone — A42

1964, June 11 *Perf. 14*

173	A42	1p brown olive	.40	.25
174	A42	2p gray	.40	.25
175	A42	2r golden brown	2.00	1.20
		Nos. 173-175 (3)	2.80	1.70

King Mahendra's 44th birthday.

Crown Prince Birendra — A43

Perf. 14x14½

1964, Dec. 28 Photo. Unwmk.

176	A43	10p dark green	1.50	.95
177	A43	15p brown	1.40	.95

19th birthday (coming of age) of Crown Prince Birendra Bir Bikram Shah Deva.

Nepalese Flag and Swords, Olympic Emblem A44

1964, Dec. 31 Litho. *Perf. 13x13½*

178	A44	10p red & ultra	1.75	.80

18th Olympic Games, Tokyo, Oct. 10-25.

Farmer Plowing — A45 Family — A46

Designs: 5p, Grain. 10p, Chemical plant.

1965 Photo. *Perf. 13½*

179	A45	2p brt green & black	.40	.40
180	A45	5p pale yel green & brn	.50	.40
181	A45	10p gray & purple	.65	.40
182	A46	15p yellow & brown	1.00	.90
		Nos. 179-182 (4)	2.55	2.10

Issued to publicize land reform.

The 2p also exists on light green paper.

Issue dates: 15p, Feb. 10; others, Dec. 16.

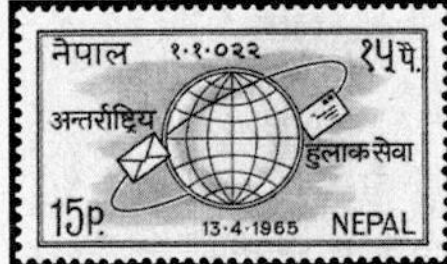

Mail Circling Globe A47

1965, Apr. 13 *Perf. 14½x14*

183	A47	15p rose lilac	.55	.40

Issued for Nepalese New Year.

King Mahendra — A48

Perf. 14x14½

1965, June 11 Photo. Unwmk.

184	A48	50p rose violet	1.25	.75

King Mahendra's 45th birthday.

Victims of Revolution, 1939-40 — A49

1965, June 11 *Perf. 13*

185	A49	15p bright green	.65	.40

The men executed by the Rana Government 1939-40 were: Shukra Raj Shastri, Dasharath Chand, Dharma Bhakta and Ganga Lal Shresta.

ITU Emblem — A50

1965, Sept. 15 Photo. *Perf. 13*

186	A50	15p deep plum & black	.70	.50

Cent. of the ITU.

Devkota — A51

1965, Oct. 14 *Perf. 14x14½*

187	A51	15p red brown	.55	.40

Lakshmi Prasad Devkota (1908-1959), poet.

ICY Emblem A52

Engr. and Litho.

1965, Oct. 24 *Perf. 11½x12*

188	A52	1r multicolored	1.40	1.00

International Cooperation Year.

Nepalese Flag and King A53

1966, Feb. 18 Photo. *Perf. 14½x14*

189	A53	15p deep blue & red	1.25	.60

Issued for Democracy Day.

Siva, Parvati and Pashupati Temple — A54

1966, Feb. 18 *Perf. 14*

190	A54	15p violet	.65	.55

Hindu festival Maha Sivaratri.

Emblem — A55

Perf. 14½x14

1966, June 10 Photo. Unwmk.

191	A55	15p dk green & orange	.80	.50

National Philatelic Exhib., June 10-16.

King Mahendra — A56

1966, June 11 *Perf. 13x13½*

192	A56	15p yellow & vio brown	.45	.30

Issued for King Mahendra's 46th birthday.

Kanti Rajya Lakshmi — A57

1966, July 5 Photo. *Perf. 14x14½*

193	A57	15p golden brown	.60	.45

60th birthday of Queen Mother Kanti Rajya Lakshmi.

Queen Ratna Rajya Lakshmi Devi Shah — A58

1966, Aug. 19 Photo. *Perf. 13*

194	A58	15p yellow & brown	.65	.50

Issued for Children's Day.

Krishna with Consort Radha and Flute — A59

1966, Sept. 7

195	A59	15p dk purple & yellow	.70	.50

Krishnastami 2023, the birthday of Krishna.

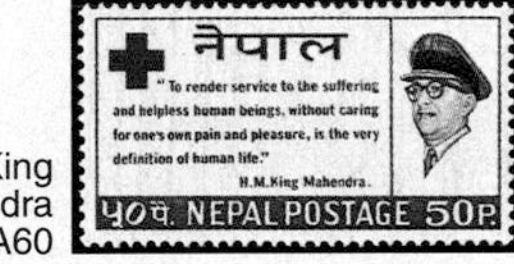

King Mahendra A60

1966, Oct. 1 Photo. *Perf. 14½x14*

196	A60	50p slate grn & dp car	5.50	2.00

Issued to commemorate the official recognition of the Nepalese Red Cross.

Opening of WHO Headquarters Building, Geneva — A61

1966, Nov. 11 Photo. *Perf. 14*

197	A61	1r purple	3.00	1.75

Lekhnath Paudyal — A62

1966, Dec. 29 Photo. *Perf. 14*

198	A62	15p dull violet blue	.60	.50

Lekhnath Paudyal (1884-1966), poet.

King Type of 1962

1967, Feb. 10 Photo. *Perf. 14½x14*

199	A35	75p blue green	1.60	.80

Rama and Sita — A63

1967, Apr. 18 Litho. *Perf. 14*

200	A63	15p brown & yellow	.75	.60

Rama Navami 2024, the birthday of Rama.

Buddha — A64

1967, May 23 Photo. ***Perf. 13½x13***
201 A64 75p orange & purple 1.40 1.10

2,511th birthday of Buddha.

King Mahendra Addressing Crowd and Himalayas — A65

1967, June 11 ***Perf. 13***
202 A65 15p dk brown & lt blue .70 .45

King Mahendra's 47th birthday.

Queen Ratna among Children A66

1967, Aug. 20 Photo. ***Perf. 13***
203 A66 15p pale yel & dp brown .60 .45

Issued for Children's Day on the birthday of Queen Ratna Rajya Lakshmi Devi Shah.

Durbar Square, Bhaktapur A67

5p, Ama Dablam Mountain, ITY emblem.

1967, Oct. 24 ***Perf. 13½x14***
Size: 29½x21mm
204 A67 5p violet .55 .45
Perf. 14½x14
Size: 37½x19½mm
205 A67 65p brown 1.00 .85

Intl. Tourist Year, 1967. See No. C2.

Official Reading Proclamation — A68

1967, Dec. 16 Litho. ***Perf. 13***
206 A68 15p multicolored .75 .50

"Back to the Villages" campaign.

Crown Prince Birendra, Boy Scouts and Scout Emblem — A69

1967, Dec. 29 Photo. ***Perf. 14½x14***
207 A69 15p ultramarine 1.25 .70

60th anniv. of Boy Scouts.

Prithvi Narayan — A70

1968, Jan. 11 ***Perf. 14x14½***
208 A70 15p blue & rose 1.25 .70

Rajah Prithvi Narayan (1779-1839), founder of modern Nepal.

Arms of Nepal — A71

1968, Feb. 19 Photo. ***Perf. 14x14½***
209 A71 15p crimson & dk blue 1.10 .70

Issued for National Day.

WHO Emblem and Flag of Nepal A72

1968, Apr. 7 ***Perf. 13***
210 A72 1.20r dull yel, red & ultra 4.50 2.50

World Health Day (UN WHO).

Goddess Sita and Shrine A73

1968, May 6 Photo. ***Perf. 14½x14***
211 A73 15p violet & org brown .80 .50

King Mahendra, Pheasant and Himalayas A74

1968, June 11 Photo. ***Perf. 13½***
212 A74 15p multicolored 4.50 .40

King Mahendra's 48th birthday.

Flag, Children and Queen Ratna — A75

1968, Aug. 19 Litho. ***Perf. 13x13½***
213 A75 5p blue grn, yel & ver .50 .30

Fourth National Children's Day.

Buddha and Human Rights Flame A76

1968, Dec. 10 Photo. ***Perf. 14½x14***
214 A76 1r dk green & red 4.50 2.75

International Human Rights Year.

Young People Dancing Around Flag A77

1968, Dec. 28 Photo. ***Perf. 14½x14***
215 A77 25p violet blue 1.25 .65

23rd birthday of Crown Prince Birendra, which is celebrated as Youth Festival.

UN Building, Nepalese and UN Flags — A78

1969, Jan. 1 ***Perf. 13½x13***
216 A78 1r multicolored 1.75 1.25

Issued to commemorate Nepal's admission to the UN Security Council for 1969-1970.

Amsu Varma — A79

Portraits: 25p, Ram Shah. 50p, Bhimsen Thapa.

1969, Apr. 13 Photo. ***Perf. 14x14½***
217 A79 15p green & purple .70 .60
218 A79 25p blue green .95 .75
219 A79 50p orange brown 1.25 1.75
Nos. 217-219 (3) 2.90 3.10

Amsu Varma, 7th cent. ruler and reformer; Ram Shah, 17th cent. ruler and reformer, and Bhimsen Thapa, 18-19th cent. administrator and reformer.

ILO Emblem A80

1969, May 1 Photo. ***Perf. 14½x14***
220 A80 1r car rose, blk & lt brown 7.00 4.00

50th anniv. of the ILO.

King Mahendra — A81

1969, June 20 ***Perf. 13½x13***
221 A81 25p gold & multi .75 .50

King Mahendra's 49th birthday (50th by Oriental count). Issuance delayed from June 11 to 20.

King Tribhuvana and Wives A82

1969, July 1 ***Perf. 14½x14***
222 A82 25p yellow & ol gray .75 .45

64th anniv. of the birth of King Tribhuvana.

Queen Ratna & Child Playing — A83

1969, Aug. 20 Photo. ***Perf. 14x14½***
223 A83 25p gray & rose car .70 .50

5th Natl. Children's Day and to for the 41st birthday of Queen Ratna Rajya Lakshmi Devi Shah.

Rhododendron & Himalayas — A84

Flowers: No. 225, Narcissus. No. 226, Marigold. No. 227, Poinsettia.

1969, Sept. 17 Photo. ***Perf. 13½***
224 A84 25p lt blue & multi 1.00 .65
225 A84 25p brown red & multi 1.00 .65
226 A84 25p black & multi 1.00 .65
227 A84 25p multicolored 1.00 .65
a. Block of 4, #224-227 4.50 4.50

Durga, Goddess of Victory — A85

1969, Oct. 17 Photo. ***Perf. 14x14½***
228 A85 15p black & orange .50 .40
229 A85 50p black, bis brn & vio 1.25 1.00

Issued to celebrate the Dasain Festival.

Crown Prince Birendra and Princess Aishwarya A86

1970, Feb. 27 Photo. ***Perf. 13½***
230 A86 25p multicolored .70 .40

Wedding of Crown Prince Birendra Bir Bikram Shah Deva and Crown Princess Aishwarya Rajya Lakshmi Devi Rana, Feb. 27-28.

Agricultural Products, Cow, Fish — A87

1970, Mar. 21 Litho. *Perf. 12½*
231 A87 25p multicolored .70 .50

Issued to publicize the Agricultural Year.

Bal Bhadra Kunwar A88

1970, Apr. 13 Photo. *Perf. 14½x14*
232 A88 1r ol bister & red lilac 1.75 1.00

Bal Bhadra Kunwar, leader in the 1814 battle of Kalanga against British forces.

King Mahendra, Mountain Peak and Crown — A89

1970, June 11 Litho. *Perf. 11½*
233 A89 50p gold & multi 1.25 .65

King Mahendra's 50th birthday.

Gosainkund A90

Lakes: 25p, Phewa Tal. 1r, Rara Daha.

1970, June 11 Photo. *Perf. 13½*
234 A90 5p dull yellow & multi .50 .40
235 A90 25p gray & multi .75 .60
236 A90 1r pink & multi 1.25 1.10
Nos. 234-236 (3) 2.50 2.10

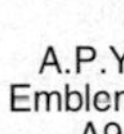

A.P.Y. Emblem A91

1970, July 1 *Perf. 14½x14*
237 A91 1r dark blue & blue 1.25 .90

Asian Productivity Year 1970.

Bal Mandir Building and Queen Ratna A92

1970, Aug. 20 Photo. *Perf. 14½x14*
238 A92 25p gray & bister brn .70 .40

Issued for Children's Day. The Bal Mandir Building in Taulihawa is the headquarters of the National Children's Organization.

New UPU Headquarters, Bern — A93

1970, Oct. 9 Photo. *Perf. 14½x14*
239 A93 2.50r ocher & sepia 2.50 1.75

UN Flag A94

1970, Oct. 24 Photo. *Perf. 14½x14*
240 A94 25p blue & brown .70 .50

25th anniversary of the United Nations.

Royal Palace and Square, Patan A95

25p, Bodhnath stupa, near Kathmandu, vert. 1r, Gauri Shankar, holy mountain.

Perf. 11x11½, 11½x11
1970, Dec. 28 Litho.
241 A95 15p multicolored .50 .25
242 A95 25p multicolored .75 .50
243 A95 1r multicolored 1.25 .80
Nos. 241-243 (3) 2.50 1.55

Crown Prince Birendra's 25th birthday.

Statue of Harihar (Vishnu-Siva) — A96

1971, Jan. 26 Photo. *Perf. 14x14½*
244 A96 25p bister brn & black .70 .45

Torch and Target A97

1971, Mar. 21 Photo. *Perf. 13½x13*
245 A97 1r bluish gray & dp org 1.75 1.00

Intl. year against racial discrimination.

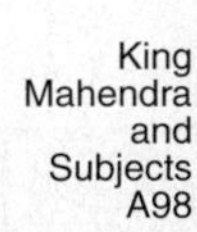

King Mahendra and Subjects A98

1971, June 11 Photo. *Perf. 14½x14*
246 A98 25p dull purple & blue .70 .30

King Mahendra's 51st birthday.

Sweta Bhairab (Siva) — A99

Sculptures of Siva: 25p, Manhankal Bhairab. 50p, Kal Bhairab.

1971, July 11 *Perf. 13x13½*
247 A99 15p org brn & blk .50 .40
248 A99 25p lt green & black .60 .50
249 A99 50p blue & black 1.25 .85
Nos. 247-249 (3) 2.35 1.75

Queen Ratna Receiving Garland A100

1971, Aug. 20 Photo. *Perf. 11½*
Granite Paper
250 A100 25p gray & multi .70 .35

Children's Day, Queen Ratna's birthday.

Map and Flag of Iran, Flag of Nepal A101

1971, Oct. 14 Granite Paper
251 A101 1r pink & multi 1.75 .75

2500th anniversary of the founding of the Persian empire by Cyrus the Great.

UNICEF Emblem, Mother and Child A102

1971, Dec. 11 *Perf. 14½x14*
252 A102 1r gray blue 1.75 1.00

25th anniversary of UNICEF.

Everest A103

Himalayan Peaks: 1r, Kangchenjunga. 1.80r, Annapurna I.

1971, Dec. 28 *Perf. 13½x13*
253 A103 25p blue & brown .50 .30
254 A103 1r dp blue & brown 2.00 .70
255 A103 1.80r blue & yel brown 2.25 1.25
Nos. 253-255 (3) 4.75 2.25

"Visit Nepal."

Royal Standard — A104

1972, Feb. 19 Photo. *Perf. 13*
256 A104 25p dark red & black .70 .35

National Day.

Araniko and White Dagoba, Peking — A105

1972, Apr. 13 Litho. *Perf. 13*
257 A105 15p lt blue & ol gray .40 .30

Araniko, a 14th century Nepalese architect, who built the White Dagoba at the Miaoying Monastery, Peking, 1348.

Book Year Emblem, Ancient Book A106

1972, Sept. 8 Photo. *Perf. 14½x14*
258 A106 2p ocher & brown .25 .25
259 A106 5p tan & black .30 .25
260 A106 1r blue & black 1.40 .90
Nos. 258-260 (3) 1.95 1.40

International Book Year.

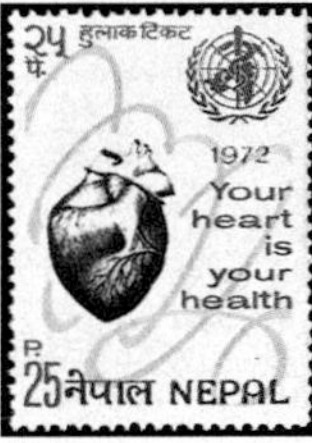

Heart and WHO Emblem — A107

1972, Nov. 6 Photo. *Perf. 13x13½*
261 A107 25p dull grn & claret .75 .40

"Your heart is your health," World Health Month.

King Mahendra (1920-1972) A108

1972, Dec. 15 Photo. *Perf. 13½x13*
262 A108 25p brown & black .70 .35

King Birendra — A109

1972, Dec. 28 Photo. *Perf. 13x13½*
263 A109 50p ocher & purple .75 .50

King Birendra's 27th birthday.

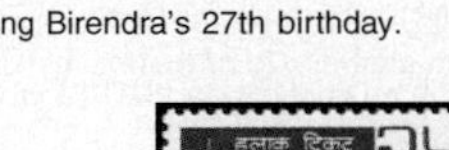

Northern Border Costume A110

Nepalese Costumes: 50p, Hill dwellers. 75p, Kathmandu Valley couple. 1r, Inner Terai couple.

1973, Feb. 18 Photo. *Perf. 13*

264	A110	25p dull lilac & multi	.50	.25
265	A110	50p lemon & multi	.70	.40
266	A110	75p multicolored	1.00	.65
267	A110	1r multicolored	1.50	.95
a.		Block of 4, #264-267	4.25	4.25

National Day.

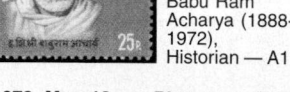

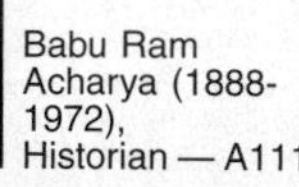

Babu Ram Acharya (1888-1972), Historian — A111

1973, Mar. 12 Photo. *Perf. 13*

268 A111 25p olive gray & car .60 .30

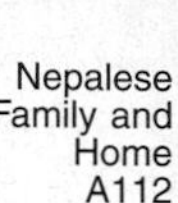

Nepalese Family and Home A112

1973, Apr. 7 Photo. *Perf. 14½x14*

269 A112 1r Prus blue & ocher 1.25 .85

25th anniv. of the WHO.

Lumbini Garden, Birthplace of Buddha — A113

1973, May 17 Photo. *Perf. 13x13½*

270	A113	25p shown	.50	.25
271	A113	75p Mt. Makalu	.75	.50
272	A113	1r Gorkha Village	1.25	.95
		Nos. 270-272 (3)	2.50	1.70

FAO Emblem, Women Farmers A114

1973, June 29 Photo. *Perf. 14½x14*

273 A114 10p dark gray & violet .50 .25

World food program, 10th anniversary.

INTERPOL Headquarters and Emblem — A115

1973, Sept. 3

274 A115 25p bister & blue .60 .30

50th anniversary of the International Criminal Police Organization (INTERPOL).

Shom Nath Sigdyal (1884-1972), Scholar — A116

1973, Oct. 5 Photo. *Perf. 13x13½*

275 A116 1.25r violet blue 1.25 .85

Cow A117

1973, Oct. 25 Photo. *Perf. 13½x13*

276	A117	2p shown	.30	.25
277	A117	3.25r Yak	2.25	1.50

Festival of Lights (Tihar).

King Birendra — A118

Perf. 13, 13½x14, 15x14½

1973-74 Photo.

278	A118	5p dark brown	.25	.25
279	A118	15p ol brn & dk brn ('74)	.30	.25
280	A118	1r reddish brn & dk brn ('74)	1.25	.70
		Nos. 278-280 (3)	1.80	1.20

King Birendra's 28th birthday.

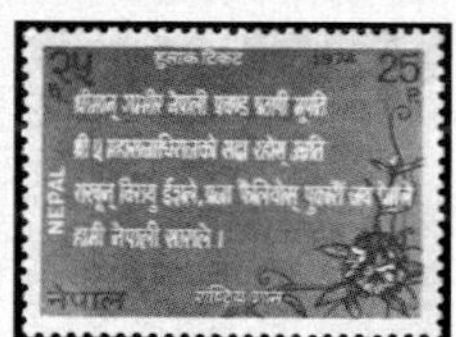

National Anthem A119

Natl. Day: 1r, Score of national anthem.

1974, Feb. 18 Photo. *Perf. 13½x13*

281	A119	25p rose carmine	.50	.25
282	A119	1r deep green	.80	.65

King Janak on Throne — A120

1974, Apr. 14 Litho. *Perf. 13½*

283 A120 2.50r multicolored 2.00 1.75

Children's Village and SOS Emblem — A121

1974, May 20 Litho. *Perf. 13½x13*

284 A121 25p ultra & red .65 .45

25th anniv. of SOS Children's Village Intl.

Baghchal A122

1974, July 1 Litho. *Perf. 13*

285	A122	2p Soccer	.25	.25
286	A122	2.75r shown	1.50	1.10

Popular Nepalese games.

WPY Emblem — A123

1974, Aug. 19 Litho. *Perf. 13*

287 A123 5p ocher & blue .50 .25

World Population Year.

UPU Monument, Bern — A124

1974, Oct. 9 Litho. *Perf. 13*

288 A124 1r olive & black 1.25 .60

Centenary of Universal Postal Union.

Butterfly A125

Designs: Nepalese butterflies.

1974, Oct. 16

289	A125	10p lt brown & multi	.25	.25
290	A125	15p lt blue & multi	.45	.30
291	A125	1.25r multicolored	1.75	1.00
292	A125	1.75r buff & multi	2.50	1.10
		Nos. 289-292 (4)	4.95	2.65

King Birendra — A126

1974, Dec. 28 Litho. *Perf. 13½x13*

293 A126 25p gray green & black .40 .25

King Birendra's 29th birthday.

Muktinath — A127

Peacock Window A128

1974, Dec. 31 *Perf. 13x13½, 13½x13*

294	A127	25p multicolored	.50	.25
295	A128	1r multicolored	1.10	.70

Tourist publicity.

Guheswari Temple — A129

Rara A130

Pashupati Temple — A131

King Birendra and Queen Aishwarya — A132

Designs: 1r, Throne. 1.25r, Royal Palace.

1975, Feb. 24 Litho. *Perf. 13x13½*

296 A129 25p multicolored .40 .25

Photo.

Perf. 14½x14

297 A130 50p multicolored .60 .25

Granite Paper

Perf. 11½, 11 (A131)

298	A132	1r olive & multi	.75	.70
299	A132	1.25r multicolored	1.50	.75
300	A131	1.75r multicolored	1.00	.95
301	A132	2.75r gold & multi	1.75	1.25
a.		Souvenir sheet of 3	6.75	6.75
		Nos. 296-301 (6)	6.00	4.15

Coronation of King Birendra, Feb. 24, 1975. No. 301a contains 3 imperf. stamps similar to Nos. 298-299, 301 and label with inscription.

Tourist Year Emblem A133

Swayambhunath Stupa, Kathmandu — A134

Perf. 12½x13½, 13½x12½

1975, May 25 Litho.

302	A133	2p yellow & multi	.25	.25
303	A134	25p violet & black	.50	.45

South Asia Tourism Year.

Tiger A135

1975, July 17 Litho. *Perf. 13*

304	A135	2p shown	.50	.45
305	A135	5p Deer, vert.	.50	.55
306	A135	1r Panda	1.25	1.10
		Nos. 304-306 (3)	2.25	2.10

Wildlife conservation.

Queen Aishwarya and IWY Emblem — A136

1975, Nov. 8 Litho. *Perf. 13*

307 A136 1r lt blue & multi .80 .40

International Women's Year.

Ganesh Peak — A137

Rupse Falls — A138

Kumari, Living Goddess of Nepal — A139

1975, Dec. 16 Litho. *Perf. 13½*

308	A137	2p multicolored	.25	.25
309	A138	25p multicolored	.35	.30
310	A139	50p multicolored	1.00	.50
		Nos. 308-310 (3)	1.60	1.05

Tourist publicity.

King Birendra — A140

1975, Dec. 28 Photo. *Perf. 13*

311 A140 25p rose lil & red lil .45 .25

King Birendra's 30th birthday.

Flag and Map of Nepal A141

1976, Feb. 19 Litho. *Perf. 13*

312 A141 2.50r dark blue & red 1.25 1.00

National or Democracy Day.

Rice Cultivation — A142

1976, Apr. 11 Litho. *Perf. 13*

313 A142 25p multicolored .40 .25

Agricultural development.

Flags of Nepal and Colombo Plan — A143

1976, July 1 Photo. *Perf. 13x13½*

314 A143 1r multicolored .80 .50

Colombo Plan, 25th anniversary.

Runner — A144

1976, July 31 Photo. *Perf. 13x13½*

315 A144 3.25r black & ultra 2.25 1.25

21st Olympic Games, Montreal, Canada, July 17-Aug. 1.

Dove and Map of South East Asia — A145

1976, Aug. 17 Litho. *Perf. 13½*

316 A145 5r bister, black & ultra 2.75 1.50

5th Summit Conference of Non-aligned Countries, Colombo, Sri Lanka, Aug. 9-19.

Folk Dances A146

1976, Sept. 27 Litho. *Perf. 13½x13*

317	A146	10p Lakha mask	.25	.25
318	A146	15p Maruni	.30	.25
319	A146	30p Jhangad	.50	.25
320	A146	1r Sebru	1.00	.40
		Nos. 317-320 (4)	2.05	1.15

Nepalese Lily — A147

Flowers: No. 322, Meconopsis grandis. No. 323, Cardiocrinum giganteum, horiz. No. 324, Megacodon stylophorus, horiz.

1976-77 Litho. *Perf. 13*

321	A147	30p lt ultra & multi	.80	.25
322	A147	30p brown & multi	.80	.25
323	A147	30p violet & multi	.80	.25
324	A147	30p violet & multi	.80	.25
		Nos. 321-324 (4)	3.20	1.00

Issue dates: Nov. 7, 1976, Jan. 24, 1977.

King Birendra — A148

1976, Dec. 28 Photo. *Perf. 14*

325	A148	5p green	.25	.25
326	A148	30p multicolored	.45	.25

King Birendra's 31st birthday.

Bell and American Bicentennial Emblem — A149

1976, Dec. 31 Litho. *Perf. 13½*

327 A149 10r multicolored 4.00 3.00

American Bicentennial.

Warrior Kazi Amar Singh Thapa, Natl. Hero A150

1977, Feb. 18 Photo. *Perf. 13x13½*

328 A150 10p multicolored .50 .25

Terracotta Figurine, Kapilavastu Excavations — A151

Asoka Pillar, Lumbini A152

1977, May 3 Photo. *Perf. 14½x14*

329	A151	30p dark violet	.30	.25
330	A152	5r green & brown	2.00	1.50

Tourist publicity.

Cheer Pheasant A153

Birds of Nepal: 5p, Great pied hornbill, vert. 1r, Green magpie. 2.30r, Nepalese laughing thrush, vert.

1977, Sept. 17 Photo. *Perf. 13*

331	A153	5p multicolored	.75	.30
332	A153	15p multicolored	1.25	.30
333	A153	1r multicolored	2.25	.65
334	A153	2.30r multicolored	3.75	1.25
		Nos. 331-334 (4)	8.00	2.50

Tukuche Peak, Nepalese Police Flag A154

1977, Oct. 2

335 A154 1.25r multicolored .85 .50

Ascent of Tukuche, Himalaya Mountains, by Nepalese police team, first anniversary.

Scout Emblem, Map of Nepal — A155

1977, Nov. 7 Litho. *Perf. 13½*

336 A155 3.50r multicolored 1.75 .85

Boy Scouts of Nepal, 25th anniversary.

Dhanwantari, Health Goddess — A156

1977, Nov. 9 Photo. *Perf. 13*

337 A156 30p bluish green .50 .25

Health Day.

Flags, Map of Nepal — A157

1977, Dec. 5 Photo. *Perf. 13½*

338 A157 1r multicolored .60 .30

Colombo Plan, 26th Consultative Meeting, Kathmandu, Nov. 29-Dec. 7.

King Birendra — A158

1977, Dec. 28

339	A158	5p olive	.25	.25
340	A158	1r red brown	.65	.50

King Birendra's 32nd birthday.

Post Office Seal, New Post Office A159

75p, Post Office date stamp & new Post Office.

1978, Apr. 14 Photo. *Perf. 14½x14*

341	A159	25p org brn & blk	.25	.25
342	A159	75p bister & black	.50	.40

Centenary of Nepalese postal service.

Mt. Everest
A160

Design: 4r, Mt. Everest, different view.

1978, May 29 Photo. *Perf. 13½x13*

343 A160 2.30r red brn & slate 1.25 .75

344 A160 4r grn & vio blue 2.25 1.75

1st ascent of Mt. Everest, 25th anniv.

Mountains, Trees, Environmental Emblem — A161

1978, June 5

345 A161 1r blue green & orange .70 .30

World Environment Day, June 5.

Queen Mother Ratna — A162

1978, Aug. 20 Photo. *Perf. 14*

346 A162 2.30r olive gray 1.25 .60

Queen Mother Ratna, 50th birthday.

Trisula River Rapids
A163

Tourist Publicity: 50p, Nepalese window. 1r, Dancer, Mahakali dance, vert.

1978, Sept. 15 Litho. *Perf. 14*

347 A163 10p multicolored .30 .25

348 A163 50p multicolored .50 .35

349 A163 1r multicolored 1.00 .55

Nos. 347-349 (3) 1.80 1.15

Human Rights Emblem — A164

1978, Oct. 10 Litho. *Perf. 13½*

350 A164 25p red brown & red .30 .25

351 A164 1r dark blue & red .70 .30

Universal Declaration of Human Rights, 30th anniversary.

Choerospondias Axillaris — A165

Designs: 1r, Castanopsis indica, vert. 1.25r, Elaeocarpus sphaericus.

1978, Oct. 31 Photo. *Perf. 13*

352 A165 5p multicolored .40 .25

353 A165 1r multicolored .60 .50

354 A165 1.25r multicolored 1.25 .60

Nos. 352-354 (3) 2.25 1.35

King Birendra — A166

1978, Dec. 17 *Perf. 13½x14*

355 A166 30p brown & indigo .30 .25

356 A166 2r violet & black .80 .65

King Birendra's 33rd birthday.

Kamroop and Patan Temples and Deity
A167

Red Machhindra Chariot — A168

Perf. 14½x14, 13½

1979 Photo., Litho.

357 A167 75p claret & olive .60 .30

358 A168 1.25r multicolored .70 .50

Red Machhindra Nath Festival, Lalitpur (Patan).

Issue dates: 75p, Apr. 27; 1.25r, July 25.

Bas-relief — A169

1979, May 12 Photo. *Perf. 13*

359 A169 1r yellow & brown .60 .30

Lumbini Year.

Tree Planting — A170

1979, June 29 Photo. *Perf. 13x13½*

360 A170 2.30r multicolored 1.50 .85

Afforestation campaign.

Children with Flag, IYC Emblem — A172

1979, Aug. 20 *Perf. 13½*

362 A172 1r light brown .75 .45

Intl. Year of the Child; Natl. Children's Day.

Mount Pabil
A173

Tourism: 50p, Swargadwari Temple. 1.25r, Altar with statues of Shiva and Parbati.

1979, Sept. 26 Photo. *Perf. 13½x13*

363 A173 30p dk blue green .30 .25

364 A173 50p multicolored .35 .25

365 A173 1.25r multicolored .65 .55

Nos. 363-365 (3) 1.30 1.05

Northern Shrike — A174

Perf. 14½x13½

1979, Nov. 22 Photo.

366 A174 10p shown .45 .25

367 A174 10r Aethopyga ignicauda 7.50 4.75

Intl. World Pheasant Assoc. Symposium, Kathmandu, Nov. 21-23. See No. C7.

Coin, Lichhavi Period, Obverse — A175

Malla Period, Obverse — A175a

Shaw Period, Obverse — A175b

Ancient Coins: No. 369, Lichhavi Period, reverse. No. 371, Malla Period, reverse. No. 373, Shah Period, reverse.

1979, Dec. 16 Photo. *Perf. 15*

368 A175 5p brn & brn org .25 .25

369 A175 5p brn & brn org .25 .25

a. Pair, #368-369 .55 .55

370 A175a 15p dark blue .30 .25

371 A175a 15p dark blue .30 .25

a. Pair, #370-371 .65 .65

372 A175b 1r slate blue .75 .50

373 A175b 1r slate blue .75 .50

a. Pair, #372-373 1.75 1.75

Nos. 368-373 (6) 2.60 2.00

King Birendra — A176

Ban-Ganga Dam — A177

1979, Dec. 28 Litho. *Perf. 14*

374 A176 25p multicolored .25 .25

375 A177 2.30r multicolored 1.00 .65

King Birendra's 34th birthday.

Samyak Pooja Festival
A178

1980, Jan. 15 *Perf. 13½*

376 A178 30p vio brn & gray .50 .25

Holy Basil — A179

30p, Himalayan valerian. 1r, Nepalese pepper. 2.30r, Himalayan rhubarb.

1980, Mar. 24 Photo. *Perf. 14x14½*

377 A179 5p shown .25 .25

378 A179 30p multicolored .30 .25

379 A179 1r multicolored .60 .30

380 A179 2.30r multicolored 1.25 .65

Nos. 377-380 (4) 2.40 1.45

Gyandil Das
A180

Nepalese Writers: 30p, Shddhi Das Amatya. 1r, Pahal Man Singh Snwar. 2.30r, Jay Prithibi Bahadur Singh.

1980, Apr. 13 *Perf. 13½x13*

381 A180 5p bister & rose lilac .25 .25

382 A180 30p vio brn & lt red brn .30 .25

383 A180 1r blue & olive gray .50 .30

384 A180 2.30r ol grn & dk blue 1.00 .65

Nos. 381-384 (4) 2.05 1.45

Jwalaji Dailekh (Temple), Holy Flame — A181

1980, Sept. 14 Litho. *Perf. 14½*

385 A181 10p shown .25 .25

386 A181 1r Godavari Pond .50 .30

387 A181 5r Mt. Dhaulagiri 2.25 1.25

Nos. 385-387 (3) 3.00 1.80

Temple Statue — A182

1980, Oct. 29 *Perf. 14x13½*
388 A182 25r multicolored 8.50 5.00

World Tourism Conf., Manila, Sept. 27.

King Birendra's 35th Birthday — A183

1980, Dec. 28 Litho. *Perf. 14*
389 A183 1r multicolored .60 .25

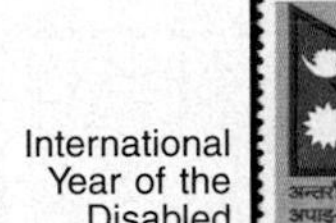

International Year of the Disabled A184

1981, Jan. 1
390 A184 5r multicolored 2.25 1.40

Nepal Rastra Bank, 25th Anniv. A185

1981, Apr. 26 Litho. *Perf. 14*
391 A185 1.75r multicolored .80 .50

A186

1981, July 16
392 A186 10p No. 1 .25 .25
393 A186 40p No. 2 .30 .25
394 A186 3.40r No. 3 1.75 1.25
a. Souvenir sheet of 3, #392-394 3.00 3.00
Nos. 392-394 (3) 2.30 1.75

Nepalese stamp cent.

A187

1981, Oct. 30 Litho. *Perf. 14*
395 A187 1.75r multicolored .50 .40

Intl. Hotel Assoc., 70th council meeting, Kathmandu.

Stamp Centenary — A188

1981, Dec. 27 Litho. *Perf. 14*
396 A188 40p multicolored .60 .25

Nepal '81 Stamp Exhibition, Kathmandu, Dec. 27-31.

King Birendra's 36th Birthday — A189

1981, Dec. 28
397 A189 1r multicolored .55 .30

Hrishikesh, Buddhist Stone Carving, Ridi — A190

25p, Tripurasundari Pavilion, Baitadi. 2r, Mt. Langtang Lirung.

1981, Dec. 30
398 A190 5p shown .25 .25
399 A190 25p multicolored .30 .25
400 A190 2r multicolored .75 .50
Nos. 398-400 (3) 1.30 1.00

Royal Nepal Academy, 25th Anniv. A191

1982, June 23 Litho. *Perf. 14*
401 A191 40p multicolored .40 .25

Balakrishna Sama — A192

1982, July 21 *Perf. 13½*
402 A192 1r multicolored .50 .30

Dish Antenna, Satellite — A193

1982, Nov. 7 Litho. *Perf. 14*
403 A193 5r multicolored 2.00 1.25

Mt. Nuptse — A194

Intl. Union of Alpinists Assoc., 50th Anniv. (Himalaya Peaks): b, Mt. Lhotse (31x31mm). c, Mt. Everest (40x31mm). Continuous design.

1982, Nov. 18 *Perf. 13½*
404 A194 Strip of 3 3.50 3.50
a. 25p multicolored .25 .25
b. 2r multicolored .75 .50
c. 3r multicolored 1.75 .90

9th Asian Games — A195

1982, Nov. 19 *Perf. 14*
405 A195 3.40r multicolored 1.50 1.00

Kulekhani Hydro-electric Plant — A196

1982, Dec. 2 *Perf. 13½*
406 A196 2r Lake, dam 1.00 .50

A197

1982, Dec. 28 *Perf. 12½*
407 A197 5p multicolored .40 .25

King Birendra's 37th birthday.

A198

1983, June 15 Litho. *Perf. 14*
408 A198 50p multicolored .50 .25

25th anniv. of Nepal Industrial Development Co.

25th Anniv. of Royal Nepal Airlines A199

1983, Aug. 1 *Perf. 13½*
409 A199 1r multicolored .90 .30

World Communications Year — A200

1983, Oct. 30 Litho. *Perf. 12*
410 A200 10p multicolored .60 .25

A201

Musical instruments.

1983, Nov. 3
411 A201 5p Sarangi .25 .25
412 A201 10p Kwota .30 .25
413 A201 50p Narashinga .35 .25
414 A201 1r Murchunga .65 .50
Nos. 411-414 (4) 1.55 1.25

A202

1983, Dec. 20
415 A202 4.50r multicolored 1.75 1.00

Chakrapani Chalise (1883-1957), national anthem composer and poet.

King Birendra's 38th Birthday A203

1983, Dec. 28 *Perf. 14*
416 A203 5r multicolored 2.00 1.00

Temple, Barahkshetra A204

2.20r, Triveni pilgrimage site. 6r, Mt. Cho-oyu.

1983, Dec. 30 *Perf. 14*
417 A204 1r shown .30 .25
418 A204 2.20r multicolored .80 .50
419 A204 6r multicolored 2.25 1.50
Nos. 417-419 (3) 3.35 2.25

Auditor General, 25th Anniv. A204a

1984, June 28 Litho. *Perf. 14*
419A A204a 25p Open ledger .80 .60

A205

1984, July 1 Litho. *Perf. 14*

420 A205 5r Transmission tower	2.00	1.25

Asia-Pacific Broadcasting Union, 20th anniv.

A206

1984, July 8

421 A206 50p University emblem .45 .25

Tribhuvan University, 25th anniv.

A207

1984, Aug. 5

422 A207 10r Boxing 3.75 2.10

1984 Summer Olympic Games, Los Angeles.

A208

1984, Sept. 18

423 A208 1r multicolored .45 .25

Family Planning Assoc., 25th anniv.

Social Services Day — A209

1984, Sept. 24

424 A209 5p multicolored .40 .25

Wildlife A210

10p, Gavialis gangeticus. 25p, Panthera uncia. 50p, Antilope cervicapra.

1984, Nov. 30

425 A210 10p multicolored .40 .30
426 A210 25p multicolored .60 .35
427 A210 50p multicolored 1.00 .45
Nos. 425-427 (3) 2.00 1.10

Chhinna Masta Bhagvati Temple and Goddess Sakhandeshwari Devi, Statue — A211

Designs: 10p, Lord Vishu the Giant, Yajna Ceremony on Bali, bas-relief, A. D. 467, vert. 5r, Mt. Api, Himalayas, vert.

1984, Dec. 21

428 A211 10p multicolored .25 .25
429 A211 1r multicolored .30 .30
430 A211 5r multicolored 2.00 1.25
Nos. 428-430 (3) 2.55 1.80

King Birendra, 39th Birthday A212

1984, Dec. 28

431 A212 1r multicolored .45 .25

Sagarmatha Natl. Park — A213

1985, May 6

432 A213 10r Mt. Everest, wildlife 6.00 2.25

King Mahendra Trust Congress for Nature Conservation, May 6-11.

Illustration from Shiva Dharma Purana, 13th Cent. Book — A214

Design: Maheshware, Lord Shiva, with brahma and vishnu. #433b, left person sitting on wall. #433d, left person on throne.

1985, May 30

433 Strip of 5 3.50 2.50
a.-e. A214 50p any single .40 .25
f. Strip of 5, imperf within 4.50

#433 has a continuous design. Sizes: #433a, 433e, 26x22mm; #433b, 433d, 24x22mm; #433c, 17x22mm.

UN, 40th Anniv. — A215

1985, Oct. 24 Litho. *Perf. 13½x14*

434 A215 5r multicolored 1.75 1.00

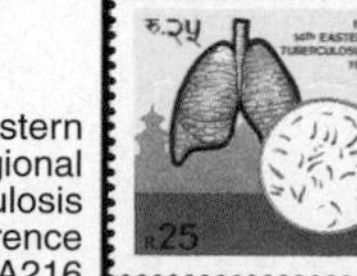

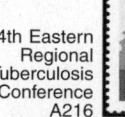

14th Eastern Regional Tuberculosis Conference A216

1985, Nov. 25

435 A216 25r multicolored 7.50 5.50

First South Asian Regional Cooperation Summit — A217

1985, Dec. 8 *Perf. 14*

436 A217 5r Flags 1.75 .75

Temple of Jaleshwar, Mohottary Underwater Project — A218

1r, Temple of Shaileshwari, Doti. 2r, Lake Phoksundo, Dolpa.

1985, Dec. 15 Litho. *Perf. 14x13½*

437 A218 10p shown .25 .25
438 A218 1r multicolored .45 .30
439 A218 2r multicolored .80 .40
Nos. 437-439 (3) 1.50 .95

Intl. Youth Year — A219

1985, Dec. 21 *Perf. 14*

440 A219 1r multicolored .45 .25

Devi Ghat Hydro-electric Dam Project A220

1985, Dec. 28 Litho. *Perf. 14*

441 A220 2r multicolored .80 .60

King Birendra, 40th Birthday — A221

1985, Dec. 28

442 A221 50p Portrait .45 .25

Panchayat System, 25th Anniv. — A222

1986, Apr. 10 *Perf. 13½*

443 A222 4r multicolored 1.50 1.00

Pharping Hydroelectric Station, 75th Anniv. — A223

1986, Oct. 9 Litho. *Perf. 14x13½*

444 A223 15p multicolored .50 .25

Architecture, Artifacts — A224

5p, Pashupati Temple. 10p, Lumbini Fort. 1r, Crown of Nepal.

1986, Oct. 9 Photo. *Perf. 13x13½*

445 A224 5p multicolored .25 .25
446 A224 10p multicolored .30 .25
446A A224 50p like 5p ('87) .40 .25
447 A224 1r multicolored .50 .25
Nos. 445-447 (4) 1.45 1.00

No. 446A issued Apr. 14.

Asian Productivity Org., 25th Anniv. A225

1986, Oct. 26 Litho. *Perf. 13½x14*

448 A225 1r multicolored .50 .25

Reclining Buddha, Kathmandu Valley — A226

Mt. Pumori, Khumbu Range A227

Perf. 14, 13½x13

1986, Oct. 26 Litho.

449 A226 60p multicolored .30 .25
450 A227 8r multicolored 2.75 1.25

King Birendra, 41st Birthday — A228

1986, Dec. 28 Litho. *Perf. 13x13½*

451 A228 1r multicolored .45 .25

Intl. Peace Year — A229

1986, Dec. 28 *Perf. 14*

452 A229 10r multicolored 2.50 1.75

Social Service Natl. Coordination Council, 10th Anniv. — A230

1987, Sept. 22 Litho. *Perf. 13½*
453 A230 1r Natl. flag, emblem .45 .25

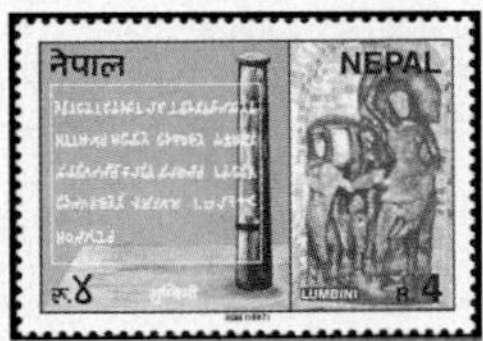
Birth of Buddha A231

Design: Asoka Pillar, enlargement of commemorative text and bas-relief of birth.

1987, Oct. 28 *Perf. 14*
454 A231 4r multicolored 1.25 .75

First Natl. Boy Scout Jamboree, Kathmandu — A232

1987, Oct. 28 Litho. *Perf. 14*
455 A232 1r multicolored .85 .40

A233

1987, Nov. 2
456 A233 60p gold & lake .30 .25

3rd SAARC (Southeast Asian Assoc. for Regional Cooperation) Summit Conference, Kathmandu.

A234

1987, Nov. 10
457 A234 4r multicolored 1.10 .75

Rastriya Samachar Samiti (Natl. news agency), 25th anniv.

Intl. Year of Shelter for the Homeless A235

1987, Dec. 21 Litho. *Perf. 14*
458 A235 5r multicolored 1.75 1.00

Kashthamandap Temple, Kathmandu A236

1987, Dec. 21 Photo. *Perf. 13½x13*
459 A236 25p multicolored .40 .25

Surya Bikram Gyawali (b. 1898), Historian — A237

1987, Dec. 21 *Perf. 13x13½*
460 A237 60p multicolored .50 .25

King Birendra, 42nd Birthday — A238

Perf. 14½x13½
1987, Dec. 28 Litho.
461 A238 25p multicolored .50 .25

Mount Kanjiroba A239

1987, Dec. 30 *Perf. 14*
462 A239 10r multicolored 3.00 1.75

Crown Prince Dipendra's 18th Birthday — A240

1988, Mar. 28 Litho. *Perf. 14*
463 A240 1r multicolored .50 .25

Nepal Bank, Ltd., 50th Anniv. — A241

1988, Apr. 8
464 A241 2r multicolored .50 .25

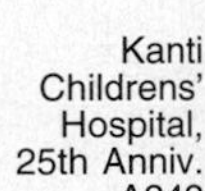

Kanti Childrens' Hospital, 25th Anniv. A242

1988, Apr. 8
465 A242 60p multicolored .50 .25

Royal Shuklaphanta Wildlife Reserve A243

1988, Apr. 8
466 A243 60p Swamp deer 1.25 .25

A244

1988, Aug. 20 Litho. *Perf. 14x13½*
467 A244 5r multicolored 1.75 1.25

Queen Mother Ratna Rajya Laxmi Devi Shah, 60th birthday.

Nepal Red Cross, 25th Anniv. — A245

1988, Sept. 12 Litho. *Perf. 14x13½*
468 A245 1r dull fawn & dark red .50 .25

Bindhyabasini, Pokhara — A246

1988, Oct. 16 Litho. *Perf. 14½*
469 A246 15p multicolored .50 .25

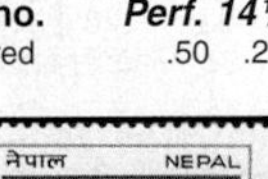

King Birendra, 43rd Birthday — A247

1988, Dec. 28 Litho. *Perf. 14*
470 A247 4r multicolored 1.25 .60

A248

1989, Mar. 3 Litho. *Perf. 13½x14*
471 A248 1r Temple .50 .25

Pashupati Area Development Trust.

SAARC Year — A249

1989, Dec. 8 *Perf. 13x13½*
472 A249 60p multicolored .50 .25

Combating Drug Abuse & Trafficking.

A250

1989, Oct. 5 *Perf. 14*
473 A250 4r vio, brt grn & blk .85 .45

Asia-Pacific Telecommunity, 10th anniv.

King Birendra, 44th Birthday A251

Perf. 13½x14½
1989, Dec. 28 Litho.
474 A251 2r multicolored .70 .25

Child Survival — A252

Design: Oral rehydration therapy, immunization, breast-feeding and growth monitoring.

1989, Dec. 31 *Perf. 13½*
475 A252 1r multicolored .50 .25

Rara Natl. Park — A253

1989, Dec. 31 *Perf. 14½x15*
476 A253 4r multicolored 1.00 .30

Mt. Ama Dablam A254

1989, Dec. 31 *Perf. 14*
477 A254 5r multicolored 1.25 .60

A255

1990, Jan. 3
478 A255 1r multicolored .50 .25

Crown Prince Dipendra investiture, Jan. 3.

Temple of the Goddess Manakamana, Gorkha — A256

1990, Apr. 12 **Litho.** *Perf. 14½*
479 A256 60p deep blue & black .65 .25

A257

1990, Aug. 20 **Litho.** *Perf. 14*
480 A257 1r multicolored .50 .25

Nepal Children's Organization, 25th anniv.

Bir Hospital, Cent. — A258

1990, Sept. 13 **Litho.** *Perf. 14x13½*
481 A258 60p orange, blue & red .50 .25

A259

1990, Oct. 9 *Perf. 14½*
482 A259 4r multicolored .80 .50

Asian-Pacific Postal Training Center, 20th anniv.

SAARC Year of the Girl Child A260

1990, Dec. 24 **Litho.** *Perf. 14½*
483 A260 4.60r multicolored 1.25 .65

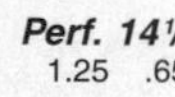

Bageshwori Temple, Nepalganj A261

Mt. Saipal A262

1990, Dec. 24 *Perf. 13½*
484 A261 1r multicolored .50 .25
485 A262 5r multicolored .75 .40

B.P. Koirala (1914-82) — A263

1990, Dec. 31 *Perf. 14*
486 A263 60p red, org brn & blk .50 .25

King Birendra, 45th Birthday A264

1990, Dec. 28
487 A264 2r multicolored .50 .25

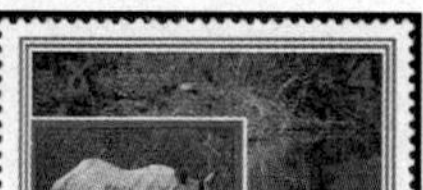

Royal Chitwan Natl. Park A265

1991, Feb. 10 **Litho.** *Perf. 14½*
488 A265 4r multicolored 1.50 .65

Restoration of Multiparty Democracy, 1st Anniv. — A266

1991, Apr. 9 **Litho.** *Perf. 14*
489 A266 1r multicolored .50 .25

Natl. Census — A267

1991, May 3 *Perf. 14x13½*
490 A267 60p multicolored .50 .25

A268

1991, Aug. 15 *Perf. 14½x13½*
491 A268 3r multicolored .50 .25

Federation of Nepalese Chambers of Commerce and Industry, 25th anniv.

A269

1991, Sept. 4 **Litho.** *Perf. 14*
492 A269 60p gray & red .50 .25

Nepal Junior Red Cross, 25th anniv.

Re-establishment of Parliament, 1st Session — A270

1991, Sept. 10 *Perf. 14½*
493 A270 1r multicolored .50 .25

Constitution Day — A271

1991, Nov. 9 **Litho.** *Perf. 15x14*
494 A271 50p multicolored .65 .25

Mt. Kumbhakarna — A272

1991, Oct. **Litho.** *Perf. 13½x14*
495 A272 4.60r multicolored .75 .30

Vivaha Mandap — A274

1991, Dec. 11 *Perf. 11½*
497 A274 1r multicolored .50 .25

SAARC Year of Shelter — A275

1991, Dec. 28 *Perf. 13½x14*
498 A275 9r multicolored 2.00 1.00

King Birendra, 46th Birthday — A276

1991, Dec. 28 *Perf. 14x13½*
499 A276 8r multicolored 1.00 .60

Nepal Philatelic Society, 25th Anniv. — A277

1992, July 11 **Litho.** *Perf. 13*
500 A277 4r multicolored .60 .30

Protect the Environment A278

1992, Oct. 24 **Litho.** *Perf. 12½x13*
501 A278 60p multicolored .65 .25

Rights of the Child A279

1992, Oct. 24 *Perf. 13½x13*
502 A279 1r multicolored .50 .25

Temples A280

75p, Thakurdwara. 1r, Namo Buddha. 2r, Narijhowa. 11r, Dantakali.

1992, Nov. 10 *Perf. 14*
503 A280 75p multicolored .30 .25
504 A280 1r multicolored .35 .25
505 A280 2r multicolored .45 .25
506 A280 11r multicolored 2.25 1.00
Nos. 503-506 (4) 3.35 1.75

No. 506 is airmail.

A281

1992, Dec. 20 Photo. *Perf. 13x13½*
507 A281 40p brown & green .50 .25

Agricultural Development Bank, 25th anniv.

Birds — A282

1r, Pin-tailed green pigeon. 3r, Bohemian waxwing. 25r, Rufous-tailed finch lark.

1992, Dec. 20 Litho. *Perf. 11½*
508 A282 1r multicolored .30 .25
509 A282 3r multicolored .60 .30
510 A282 25r multicolored 4.75 2.50
Nos. 508-510 (3) 5.65 3.05

King Birendra, 47th Birthday A283

1992, Dec. 28 *Perf. 12½x13*
511 A283 7r multicolored 1.10 .45

Poets — A284

Designs: No. 512, Pandit Kulchandra Gautam. No. 513, Chittadhar Hridaya. No. 514, Vidyapati. No. 515, Teongsi Sirijunga.

1992, Dec. 31 *Perf. 11½*
512 A284 1r blue & multi .80 .25
513 A284 1r brown & multi .80 .25
514 A284 1r tan & multi .80 .25
515 A284 1r gray & multi .80 .25
Nos. 512-515 (4) 3.20 1.00

1992 Summer Olympics, Barcelona — A285

1992, Dec. 31
516 A285 25r multicolored 4.50 2.50

Fish — A286

Designs: 25p, Tor putitora. 1r, Schizothorax plagiostomus. 5r, Anguilla bengalensis, temple of Chhabdi Barahi. 10r, Psilorhynchus pseudecheneis.

1993, Aug. 6 Litho. *Perf. 11½*
Granite Paper
517 A286 25p multicolored .50 .25
518 A286 1r multicolored .55 .40
519 A286 5r multicolored 1.25 .90
520 A286 10r multicolored 2.25 1.00
a. Souvenir sheet of 4, #517-520 7.00 7.00
Nos. 517-520 (4) 4.55 2.55

World AIDS Day — A287

1993, Dec. 1 Litho. *Perf. 13½x14½*
521 A287 1r multicolored .50 .25

Tanka Prasad Acharya — A288

1r, Sungdare Sherpa. 7r, Siddhi Charan Shrestha. 15r, Falgunand.

1993, Dec. 2 *Perf. 13½*
522 A288 25p shown .25 .25
523 A288 1r multicolored .30 .25
524 A288 7r multicolored 1.00 .40
525 A288 15r multicolored 2.00 1.25
Nos. 522-525 (4) 3.55 2.15

Holy Places A289

1.50r, Halesi Mahadev, Khotang. 5r, Devghat, Tanahun. 8r, Bagh Bhairab, Kirtipur.

Perf. 13½x14½
1993, Dec. 28 Litho.
526 A289 1.50r multicolored .25 .25
527 A289 5r multicolored .75 .50
528 A289 8r multicolored 1.25 .80
Nos. 526-528 (3) 2.25 1.55

Tourism A290

Designs: 5r, Tushahiti Sundari Chowk, Patan. 8r, White water rafting.

1993, Dec. 28
529 A290 5r multicolored .75 .40
530 A290 8r multicolored 1.25 .65

King Birendra, 48th Birthday — A291

1993, Dec. 28 *Perf. 14*
531 A291 10r multicolored 1.25 .75

Large Building, Courtyard A293

Pagoda, Courtyard A293a

Monument A294

Arms A295

Fort — A296

Mt. Everest — A299

Pagoda (Nyata Pola) — A300

Map of Nepal — A301

Design: 50p, Pagoda, vert.

Perf. 14½, 12, (#533A, 538, 540), 14¼x14
Photo., Litho. (#533A, 535A, 538, 540)

1994-96
533 A293 10p green .45 .25
533A A293a 10p claret & black .45 .25
534 A294 20p violet brown .45 .25
535 A295 25p carmine, 21x23mm .45 .25
535A A295 25p carmine, 21x26mm .75 .25
536 A296 30p slate .45 .25
537 A293 50p dark blue .45 .25
538 A293a 50p black & claret .45 .25
539 A299 1r multicolored 1.00 .25
539A A300 1r blue & claret .75 .25

Perf. 14½x13½
540 A301 5r multicolored .75 .35
Nos. 533-540 (11) 6.40 2.85

Issued: 20p, No. 535, 30p, 5/17/94; No. 539, 7/6/94; 5r, 9/22/94; Nos. 533, 537, 1995; No. 535A, 8/2/96. Nos. 533A, 538, 539A, 10/9/96.

Pasang Lhamu Sherpa (1960-1993) A304

1994, Sept 2 Litho. *Perf. 14*
544 A304 10r multicolored 1.50 .75

Stop Smoking Campaign A305

1994, Sept. 26 *Perf. 13½x14*
545 A305 1r multicolored .75 .25

A306

Methods of transporting mail.

1994, Oct. 9 *Perf. 13x13½*
546 A306 1.50r multicolored .80 .25

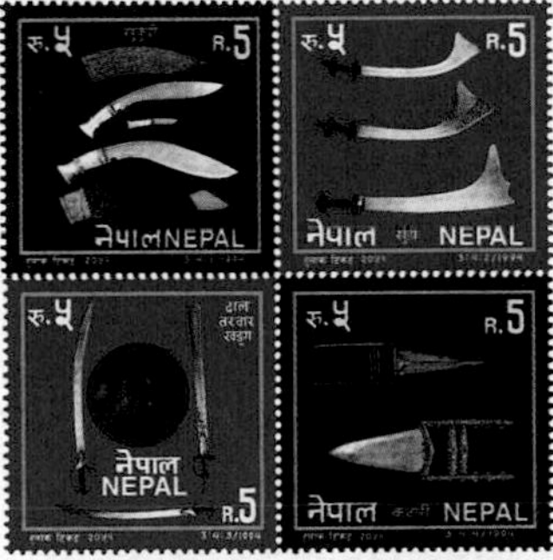
Traditional Weapons — A307

No. 547: a, Daggers, scabbards. b, Yataghans. c, Sabers, shield. d, Carved stone daggers.

1994, Oct. 9 *Perf. 14*
547 A307 5r Block of 4, #a.-d. 3.25 3.25

ILO, 75th Anniv. A308

1994, Oct. 9 *Perf. 13*
548 A308 15r blue & gold 2.00 1.25

World Food Day — A309

1994, Oct. 23 *Perf. 14*
549 A309 25r multicolored 3.00 2.00

Orchids — A310

a, Dendrobium densiflorum. b, Coelogyne flaccida. c, Cymbidium devonianum. d, Coelogyne corymbosa.

1994, Nov. 7 ***Perf. 14x13½***
550 A310 10r Block of 4, #a.-d. 6.00 6.00

Intl. Year of the Family — A311

1994, Dec. 5 ***Perf. 12½x13***
551 A311 9r green & red 1.25 .75

ICAO, 50th Anniv. — A312

1994, Dec. 7
552 A312 11r blue & gold 1.25 .80

Mushrooms — A313

1994, Dec. 20 ***Perf. 14***
553 A313 7r Cordyceps sinensis 1.10 .50
554 A313 7r Morchella conica 1.10 .50
555 A313 7r Amanita caesarea 1.10 .50
556 A313 7r Russula nepalensis 1.10 .50
Nos. 553-556 (4) 4.40 2.00

Famous Men — A314

Designs: 1r, Dharanidhar Koirala, poet. 2r, Narayan Gopal Guruwacharya, singer. 6r, Bahadur Shah, military leader, vert. 7r, Balaguru Shadananda, religious leader.

1994, Dec. 23 ***Perf. 13½x14, 14x13½***
557 A314 1r multicolored .35 .25
558 A314 2r multicolored .35 .25
559 A314 6r multicolored .90 .50
560 A314 7r multicolored 1.00 .55
Nos. 557-560 (4) 2.60 1.55

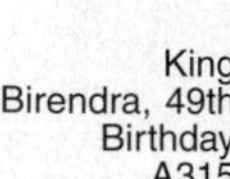

King Birendra, 49th Birthday A315

1994, Dec. 28 ***Perf. 14***
561 A315 9r multicolored 1.00 .70

Tilicho Lake, Manang A316

11r, Taleju Temple, Katmandou, vert.

1994, Dec. 28 ***Perf. 13½x14, 14x13½***
562 A316 9r multicolored .90 .70
563 A316 11r multicolored 1.10 .80

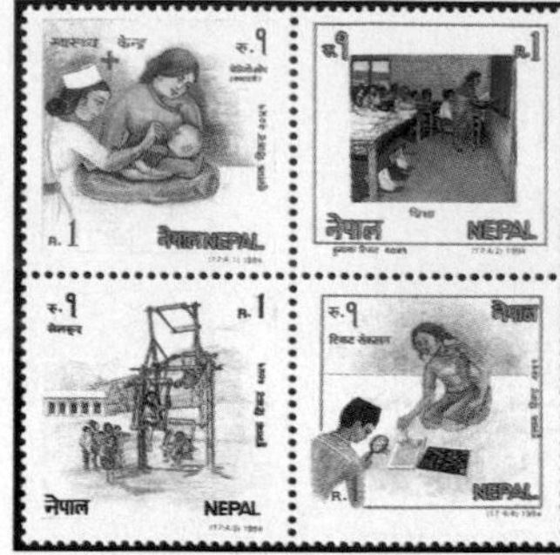

Care of Children — A317

No. 564: a, Vaccination. b, Education. c, Playground activities. d, Stamp collecting.

1994, Dec. 30 ***Perf. 14***
564 A317 1r Block of 4, #a.-d. .80 .80

Fight Against Cancer — A318

1995, June 23 Litho. ***Perf. 14x13½***
565 A318 2r red & black .50 .25

A319

Famous People: a, Bhim Nidhi Tiwari, writer. b, Yuddha Prasad Mishra, writer. c, Chandra Man Singh Maskey, artist. d, Parijat, writer.

1995, July 11 ***Perf. 14***
566 A319 3r Block of 4, #a.-d. 2.00 2.00

A320

Famous Men: 15p, Bhakti Thapa, warrior. 1r, Madan Bhandari, politician. 4r, Prakash Raj Kaphley, human rights activist.

1995, Sept. 1 Litho. ***Perf. 14x13½***
567 A320 15p multicolored .25 .25
568 A320 1r multicolored .25 .25
569 A320 4r multicolored .40 .30
Nos. 567-569 (3) .90 .80

Animals A321

Designs: a, Bos gaurus. b, Felis lynx. c, Macaca assamensis. d, Hyaena hyaena.

1995, Sept. 1 Litho. ***Perf. 12***
570 A321 10p Block of 4, #a.-d. 6.00 6.00

Tourism A322

1r, Bhimeshwor Temple, Dolakha, vert. 5r, Ugra Tara Temple, Dadeldhura. 7r, Mt. Nampa. 18r, Thanka art, Nrity Aswora, vert.

Perf. 14x13½, 13½x14
1995, Nov. 8 **Litho.**
574 A322 1r multicolored .25 .25
575 A322 5r multicolored .60 .35
576 A322 7r multicolored 1.00 .50

Size: 26x39mm

577 A322 18r multicolored 2.50 1.25
Nos. 574-577 (4) 4.35 2.35

FAO, 50th Anniv. A323

1995, Oct. 16 Litho. ***Perf. 13½x14***
578 A323 7r multicolored .90 .45

UN, 50th Anniv. A324

1995, Oct. 22 Litho. ***Perf. 11½***
Granite Paper
579 A324 50r multicolored 6.00 3.50

Lumbini, Birth Place of Gautama Buddha — A325

1995, Dec. 23 Litho. ***Perf. 14***
580 A325 20r multicolored 3.00 1.50

King Birendra, 50th Birthday
A326 A327

1995, Dec. 28 ***Perf. 12***
Granite Paper (No. 581)
581 A326 1r multicolored .50 .25
Perf. 13x13½
582 A327 12r multicolored 1.50 .95

SAARC, 10th Anniv. A328

1995, Dec. 28 ***Perf. 13½***
583 A328 10r multicolored 1.50 .70

Karnali Bridge — A329

1996, May 13 Litho. ***Perf. 14***
584 A329 7r multicolored 1.00 .50

1996 Summer Olympic Games, Atlanta — A330

1996, Oct. 9 Photo. ***Perf. 12***
Granite Paper
585 A330 7r multicolored 1.00 .45

Kaji Kalu Pande A331

Hem Raj Sharma, Grammarian A332

#587, Pushpa Lal Shrestha. #589, Padma Prasad Bhattarai, scholar, philosopher. #590, Suvarna Shamsher Rana. #591, Bhawani Bhikshu, novelist, writer.

Perf. 13½x14, 14x13½
1996, Aug. 6 **Litho.**
586 A331 75p multicolored .35 .25
587 A331 1r multicolored .35 .25
588 A332 1r multicolored .35 .25
589 A332 3r multicolored .35 .25
590 A331 5r multicolored .60 .30
591 A332 5r multicolored .60 .30
Nos. 586-591 (6) 2.60 1.60

See Nos. 614-615.

Asoka Pillar, Lumbini — A333

1996, Dec. 1 Litho. ***Perf. 11½***
592 A333 12r multicolored 2.00 1.00

Tourism A334

Designs: 1r, Arjun Dhara, Jhapa. 2r, Palace of Nuwakot. 8r, Traditional Gaijatra, Bhaktapur. 10r, Begnash Lake, Kaski.

1996, Nov. 20 Litho. *Perf. 14*

593 A334	1r multicolored	.35	.25
594 A334	2r multicolored	.35	.25
595 A334	8r multicolored	1.25	.60
596 A334	10r multicolored	1.50	.90
	Nos. 593-596 (4)	3.45	2.00

Butterflies and Birds — A335

Designs: a, Krishna pea-cock butterfly. b, Great Himalayan barbet. c, Sarus crane. d, Northern junglequeen butterfly.

1996, Nov. 20 Litho. *Perf. 14*

597 A335 5r Block of 4, #a.-d. 4.25 4.25

Annapurna Mountain Range — A336

Designs: a, Annapurna South, Annapurna I. b, Machhapuchhre, Annapurna III. c, Annapurna IV, Annapurna II.

1996, Dec. 28 Litho. *Perf. 14*

601 A336 18r Strip of 3, #a.-c. 7.00 7.00

King Birendra, 51st Birthday — A337

1996, Dec. 28 Photo. *Perf. 12*
Granite Paper

602 A337 10r multicolored 1.00 .65

Accession of King Birendra to Throne, 25th Anniv. A338

1997, Feb. 1 Litho. *Perf. 14*

603 A338 2r multicolored 1.00 .25

Nepal Postal Service — A339

1997, Apr. 12 Litho. *Perf. 14*

604 A339 2r brown & red .60 .25

Nepalese-Japanese Diplomatic Relations, 40th Anniv. — A340

1997, Apr. 6 Photo. *Perf. 12*

605 A340 18r multicolored 2.50 1.25

Visit Nepal '98 — A341

2r, Emblem. 10r, Upper Mustang. 18r, Rafting Sunkoshi. 20r, Changunarayan (Bhaktapur), vert.

1997, July 6 Litho. *Perf. 14*

606 A341	2r multicolored	.25	.25
607 A341	10r multicolored	1.10	.75
608 A341	18r multicolored	2.00	1.25
609 A341	20r multicolored	2.25	1.40
	Nos. 606-609 (4)	5.60	3.65

A342

Traditional costumes.

1997, Sept. 30 Litho. *Perf. 14*

610 A342	5r Rana Tharu	.50	.30
611 A342	5r Gurung	.50	.30
612 A342	5r Chepang	.50	.30
	Nos. 610-612 (3)	1.50	.90

A343

1997, Sept. 30 *Perf. 11½*

613 A343 20r multicolored 2.25 1.50

Diplomatic relations between Nepal and US, 50th anniv.

Personality Type of 1996

Designs: No. 614, Riddhi Bahadur Malla, writer. No. 615, Dr. K.I. Singh, political leader.

1997, Nov. 6 Litho. *Perf. 11½*

614 A332	2r multicolored	.45	.25
615 A332	2r multicolored	.45	.25

A344

Traditional Technology A345

#616, Janto (grinder), horiz. #617, Dhiki, horiz. #618, Okhal. #619, Kol (oil mill).

1997, Dec. 29 Litho. *Perf. 14*

616 A344	5r multicolored	.60	.35
617 A344	5r multicolored	.60	.35
618 A344	5r multicolored	.60	.35
619 A345	5r multicolored	.60	.35
	Nos. 616-619 (4)	2.40	1.40

Flowers A346

40p, Jasminum gracile. 1r, Callistephus chinensis. 2r, Manglietia insignis. 15r, Luculia gratissima.

1997, Dec. 11

620 A346	40p multicolored	.25	.25
621 A346	1r multicolored	.25	.25
622 A346	2r multicolored	.35	.25
623 A346	15r multicolored	2.00	.90
	Nos. 620-623 (4)	2.85	1.65

King Birendra, 52nd Birthday — A347

1997, Dec. 29 Photo. *Perf. 11½*

624 A347 10r multicolored 1.10 .75

Visit Nepal '98 — A348

Designs: 2r, Sunrise, Shree Antudanda, Ilam. 10r, Maitidevi Temple, Kathmandu. 18r, Great Reunification Gate, Kapilavastu. 20r, Mt. Cholatse, Solukhumbu, vert.

1998, May 8 Photo. *Perf. 11½*

625 A348	2r multicolored	.25	.25
626 A348	10r multicolored	1.10	.65
627 A348	18r multicolored	2.00	1.25
628 A348	20r multicolored	2.25	1.40
	Nos. 625-628 (4)	5.60	3.55

Famous People — A349

Designs: 75p, Ram Prasad Rai, freedom fighter. 1r, Imansingh Chemjong, philologist. No. 631, Tulsi Meher Shrestha, social worker. No. 632, Dadhi Ram Marasini, Sanskrit expert. 5.40r, Mahananda Sapkota, linguist.

1998, June 26 Litho. *Perf. 14x13½*

629 A349	75p brown & black	.25	.25
630 A349	1r rose lilac & black	.25	.25
631 A349	2r blue & black	.30	.25
632 A349	2r olive & black	.30	.25
633 A349	5.40r red & black	.65	.30
	Nos. 629-633 (5)	1.75	1.30

1998 World Cup Soccer Championships, France — A350

1998, June 26 *Perf. 14*

634 A350 12r multicolored 1.50 .85

Ganesh Man Singh (1915-97), Senior Democratic Leader A351

1998, Sept. 18 Photo. *Perf. 11½*

635 A351 5r multicolored .60 .35

Peace Keeping Mission of the Royal Nepalese Army, 40th Anniv. A352

1998, Oct. 9 Litho. *Perf. 13½x13*

636 A352 10r multicolored 1.25 .70

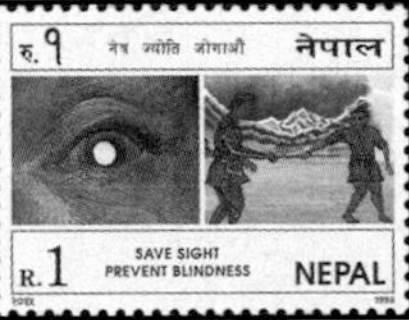

Save Sight, Prevent Blindness A353

1998, Nov. 29 Photo. *Perf. 12*
Granite Paper

637 A353 1r multicolored .40 .25

Snakes A354

1.70r, King cobra. 2r, Golden tree snake. 5r, Asiatic rock python. 10r, Karan's pit viper.

1998, Nov. 29 Litho. *Perf. 14*

638 A354	1.70r multicolored	.30	.25
639 A354	2r multicolored	.35	.25
640 A354	5r multicolored	.90	.30
641 A354	10r multicolored	1.75	.75
	Nos. 638-641 (4)	3.30	1.55

Universal Declaration of Human Rights, 50th Anniv. A355

1998, Dec. 10 Litho. *Perf. 14*

642 A355 10r multicolored 1.10 .65

A356

1998, Dec. 27 *Perf. 14x13½*

643 A356 10r multicolored 1.10 .60

Asian and Pacific Decade of Disabled Persons, 1993-2002.

A357

1998, Dec. 29 *Perf. 13x13½*
644 A357 2r multicolored .40 .25

King Birendra, 53rd birthday.

Marsyangdi Dam and Hydro-Electric Power Station — A358

1998, Dec. 29 *Perf. 11½*
Granite Paper
645 A358 12r multicolored 1.35 .85

Nepal Eye Hospital, 25th Anniv. A359

1999, Apr. 8 Litho. *Perf. 14*
646 A359 2r multicolored .50 .40

Tourism A360

Designs: No. 647, Kalika Bhagawati Temple, Baglung. No. 648, Chandan Nath Temple, vert. 12r, Bajra Yogini Temple, Sankhu, vert. No. 650, Mt. Everest. No. 651, Lumbini Pillar Script translated into English.

1999, June 7 *Perf. 13½x13, 13x13½*
647 A360 2r multicolored .35 .25
648 A360 2r multicolored .35 .25
649 A360 12r multicolored 1.75 1.10
650 A360 15r multicolored 2.00 1.25
651 A360 15r multicolored 2.00 1.25
Nos. 647-651 (5) 6.45 4.10

Tetracerus Quadricornis A361

No. 653, Ovis ammon hodgsonii.

Granite Paper

1999, June 7 Photo. *Perf. 11¾*
652 A361 10r shown 1.40 .85
653 A361 10r multicolored 1.40 .85

8th SAF Games, Kathmandu A362

Perf. 13½x14¼
1999, Sept. 30 Litho.
654 A362 10r multicolored 1.40 .85

UPU, 125th Anniv. — A363

1999, Oct. 9 *Perf. 13½*
655 A363 15r multicolored 1.60 1.60

Famous People A364

Designs: No. 656, Ram Narayan Mishra (1922-67), freedom fighter. No. 657, Bhupi Sherchan (1935-89), poet. No. 658, Master Mitrasen (1895-1946), writer. No. 659, Rudra Raj Pandey (1901-87), writer. No. 660, Gopal Prasad Rimal (1917-73), writer. No. 661, Mangaladevi Singh (1924-96), politician.

1999, Nov. 20 Litho. *Perf. 13¾*
656 A364 1r multicolored .30 .25
657 A364 1r multicolored .30 .25
658 A364 1r multicolored .30 .25
659 A364 2r multicolored .35 .25
660 A364 2r multicolored .35 .25
661 A364 2r multicolored .35 .25
Nos. 656-661 (6) 1.95 1.50

Dances A365

1999, Dec. 26 Litho. *Perf. 11¾x12*
662 A365 5r Sorathi .75 .45
663 A365 5r Bhairav .75 .45
664 A365 5r Jhijhiya .75 .45
Nos. 662-664 (3) 2.25 1.35

Intl. Labor Organization's Campaign Against Child Labor — A366

1999, Dec. 29 *Perf. 13½x14¼*
665 A366 12r multi 1.60 1.00

A367

1999, Dec. 29 *Perf. 14¼x13½*
666 A367 5r multi .70 .50

King Birendra's 54th birthday.

A368

2000, Apr. 2 Photo. *Perf. 12x11¾*
Granite Paper
667 A368 15r multi 2.00 1.75

Queen Aishwarya Rajya Laxmi Devi Shah, 50th birthday (in 1999).

Radio Nepal, 50th Anniv. A369

2000, Apr. 2 Litho. *Perf. 13½x14¼*
668 A369 2r multi .45 .25

Gorkhapatra Newspaper, Cent. — A370

2000, May 5 *Perf. 14*
669 A370 10r multi 1.25 1.25

Tourism A371

Designs: 12r, Tchorolpa Glacial Lake, Dolakha. 15r, Dakshinkali Temple, Kathmandu. 18r, Annapurna.

2000, June 30 Litho. *Perf. 13¾x14*
670-672 A371 Set of 3 5.75 5.75

First ascent of Annapurna, 50th anniv. (No. 672).

Rani Pokhari and Temple, Kathmandu A372

Frame color: 50p, Orange. 1r, Blue. 2r, Brown.

2000, July 7 Photo. *Perf. 11½*
673-675 A372 Set of 3 .70 .70

Geneva Conventions, 50th Anniv. A373

2000, Sept. 7 Litho. *Perf. 13½x14¼*
676 A373 5r multi .75 .70

2000 Summer Olympics, Sydney A374

2000, Sept. 7 Photo. *Perf. 11¾x12*
Granite Paper
677 A374 25r multi 3.75 3.25

Famous People — A375

Designs: No. 678, 2r, Hridayachandra Singh Pradhan, writer (olive green frame). No. 679, 2r, Thir Bam Malla, revolutionary (brown frame). No. 680, 5r, Krishna Prasad Koirala, social reformer (indigo frame). No. 681, 5r, Manamohan Adhikari, politician (red frame).

2000, Sept. 7 Litho. *Perf. 14*
678-681 A375 Set of 4 1.70 1.70

Worldwide Fund for Nature (WWF) A376

#682, Bengal florican. #683, Lesser adjutant stork. #684, Female greater one-horned rhinoceros and calf. #685, Male greater one-horned rhinoceros.

2000, Nov. 14 Photo. *Perf. 11¾*
Granite Paper
682-685 A376 10r Set of 4 5.75 5.25

King Birendra's 55th Birthday — A377

2000, Dec. 28 Photo. *Perf. 12x11¾*
Granite Paper
686 A377 5r multi .80 .65

Flowers A378

Designs: No. 687, Talauma hodgsonii. No. 688, Mahonia napaulensis. No. 689, Dactylorhiza hatagirea, vert.

2000, Dec. 28 *Perf. 11¾x12, 12x11¾*
Granite Paper
687-689 A378 5r Set of 3 2.60 2.10

Establishment of Democracy, 50th Anniv. A379

Perf. 11¾x11½

2001, Feb. 16 **Photo.**

Granite Paper

690 A379 5r King Tribhuvan .80 .65

2001 Census A380

2001, Apr. 17 **Photo.** ***Perf. 11¾***

Granite Paper

691 A380 2r multi .50 .25

Famous Nepalese — A381

Designs: No. 692, 2r, Khaptad Baba (bright pink background, white Nepalese numeral at UR), ascetic. No. 693, 2r, Bhikkhu Pragyananada Mahathera (red violet background), religious teacher. No. 694, 2r, Guru Prasad Mainali (pink background, red Nepalese numeral at UR), writer. No. 695, 2r, Tulsi Lal Amatya (brown violet background), politician. No. 696, 2r, Madan Lal Agrawal (light blue background), industrialist.

Perf. 14¼x13½

2001, June 29 **Litho.**

692-696 A381 Set of 5 1.25 1.25

Ficus Religiosa — A382

2001, Nov. 2 **Litho.** ***Perf. 14¼x13½***

697 A382 10r multi 1.40 1.40

UN High Commissioner for Refugees, 50th Anniv. — A383

2001, Nov. 2 ***Perf. 14***

698 A383 20r multi 2.75 2.50

Herbs — A384

Designs: 5r, Water pennywort. 15r, Rockfoil. 30r, Himalayan yew.

2001, Nov. 2 ***Perf. 13¾***

699-701 A384 Set of 3 7.50 7.50

Nepalese Flag — A385

2001, Nov. 28 ***Perf. 14***

702 A385 10r multi .50 .40

King Birendra (1945-2001) A386

2001, Dec. 28 ***Perf. 14¼x13½***

703 A386 15r multi 2.25 1.75

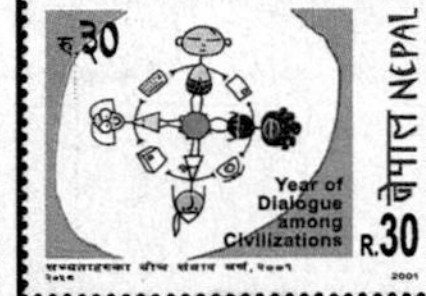

Year of Dialogue Among Civilizations A387

2001, Dec. 28 ***Perf. 14***

704 A387 30r multi 4.00 3.75

Tourism A388

Designs: 2r, Amargadi Fort. 5r, Hiranyavarna Mahavihar, vert. 15r, Jugal Mountain Range.

Perf. 13½x14¼, 14¼x13½

2001, Dec. 28

705-707 A388 Set of 3 3.00 3.00

Nepal Scouts, 50th Anniv. — A389

2002, Apr. 9 **Litho.** ***Perf. 14¼x13½***

708 A389 2r red brn & olive .50 .35

2002 World Cup Soccer Championships, Japan and Korea — A390

2002, May 31 **Litho.** ***Perf. 13½x12¾***

709 A390 15r multi 2.10 2.10

King Gyanendra's Accession to Throne, 1st Anniv. — A391

2002, June 5 ***Perf. 13¾***

710 A391 5r multi .70 .70

King Birendra (1945-2001) and Queen Aishwarya (1949-2001) A392

2002, June 5 ***Perf. 14***

711 A392 10r multi .80 .80

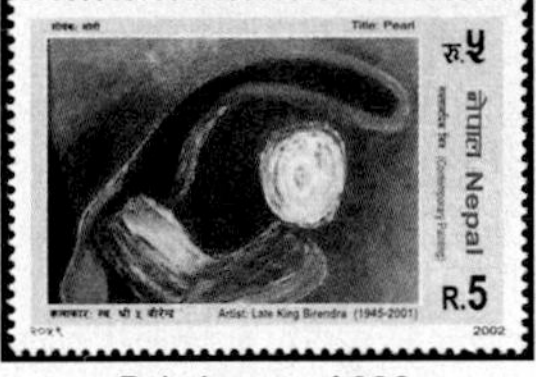

Paintings — A393

Designs: No. 712, 5r, Pearl, by King Birendra. No. 713, 5r, Aryabalokiteshwor, by Siddhimuni Shakya, vert.

Perf. 13½x13¾, 13¾x13½

2002, July 29

712-713 A393 Set of 2 1.40 1.40

Insects — A394

Designs: 3r, Leaf beetle. 5r, Locust.

2002, Sept. 6 ***Perf. 14***

714-715 A394 Set of 2 1.25 1.25

Societal Messages A395

Designs: 1r, Untouchable family behind barbed wire (untouchables should not be discriminated against). 2r, Children and parents waving (female children should not be discriminated against).

2002, Sept. 6 ***Perf. 14¼x14***

716-717 A395 Set of 2 .70 .70

Intl. Year of Mountains — A396

2002, Oct. 9 **Litho.** ***Perf. 14***

718 A396 5r multi .80 .65

Tourism A397

Designs: No. 719, 5r, Mt. Nilgiri, Mustang. No. 720, 5r, Pathibhara Devisthan, Taplejung. No. 721, 5r, Ramgram Stupa, Hawalparasi. No. 722, 5r, Galeshwor Mahadevsthan, Myagdi.

2002, Oct. 9

719-722 A397 Set of 4 3.25 2.75

South Asian Association for Regional Cooperation Charter Day — A398

2002, Dec. 8 ***Perf. 13½x12¾***

723 A398 15r multi 2.00 1.60

Famous Men — A399

Designs: 2r, Dava Bir Singh Kansakar, social worker. 25r, Rev, Ekai Kawaguchi (1866-1945), Buddhist scholar.

2002, Dec. 8 ***Perf. 13x13½***

724-725 A399 Set of 2 3.00 3.00

Nepal Chamber of Commerce, 50th Anniv. (in 2002) — A400

2003, Apr. 10 **Litho.** ***Perf. 14***

726 A400 5r multi .60 .60

Industry and Commerce Day — A401

2003, Apr. 11 ***Perf. 13½x12¾***

727 A401 5r multi .60 .60

First Ascent of Mt. Everest, 50th Anniv. A402

2003, May 29 **Litho.** ***Perf. 13½x14¼***

728 A402 25r multi 3.25 3.25

Babu Chiri Sherpa (1965-2001), Mountaineer — A403

2003, June 27 *Perf. 14*
729 A403 5r multi .75 .60

King Gyanendra, 56th Birthday A404

2003, July 7 *Perf. 13½x14¼*
730 A404 5r multi .75 .65

Tea Garden, Eastern Nepal A405

2003, July 7 *Perf. 14*
731 A405 25r multi 3.00 3.00

Dr. Dilli Raman Regmi (1913-2001), Politician and Historian — A406

2003, Aug. 31
732 A406 5r brown & blk .60 .60

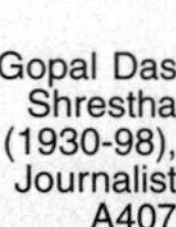

Gopal Das Shrestha (1930-98), Journalist A407

2003, Sept. 23 **Litho.** *Perf. 14*
733 A407 5r multi .60 .60

Export Year 2003 — A408

2003, Oct. 9 *Perf. 13½x14*
734 A408 25r multi 3.00 3.00

Sankhadhar Sakhwaa, Initiator of Nepalese Calendar A409

2003, Oct. 26 *Perf. 13½x12¾*
735 A409 5r multi .60 .60

Flowers — A410

No. 736: a, Lotus. b, Picrorhiza. c, Himalayan rhubarb. d, Night jasmine.

Perf. 14¼x13½

2003, Dec. 23 **Litho.**
736 A410 10r Block of 4, #a-d 4.25 4.25

Tourism A411

Designs: No. 737, 5r, Kali Gandaki "A" hydroelectric dam site. No. 738, 5r, Ganesh idol, Kageshwar, vert. 30r, Buddha icon, Swayambhunath.

2003, Dec. 23 *Perf. 14*
737-739 A411 Set of 3 4.50 4.50

Social Services of United Mission to Nepal, 50th Anniv. — A412

2004, Mar. 5 **Litho.** *Perf. 14*
740 A412 5r multi .60 .60

National Society of Comprehensive Eye Care, 25th Anniv. — A413

2004, Mar. 25
741 A413 5r multi .65 .65

Marwadi Sewa Samiti, 50th Anniv. A414

2004, Apr. 9
742 A414 5r multi .65 .65

King Gyanendra, 57th Birthday — A415

2004, July 7 **Litho.** *Perf. 14*
743 A415 5r multi .65 .65

Management Education, 50th Anniv. — A416

2004, Sept. 24 **Litho.** *Perf. 14*
744 A416 5r multi .60 .60

Asia-Pacific Telecommunity, 25th Anniv. — A417

2004, Sept. 24
745 A417 5r multi .65 .65

FIFA (Fédération Internationale de Football Association), Cent. — A418

2004, Sept. 24
746 A418 20r multi 2.00 2.00

Mountains — A419

No. 747: a, Mt. Everest. b, Mt. Kanchenjunga Main. c, Mt. Lhotse. d, Mt. Makalu I. e, Mt. Cho Oyu. f, Mt. Dhaulagiri. g, Mt. Manasalu. h, Mt. Annapurna I.

2004, Oct. 19 **Litho.** *Perf. 14*
747 A419 Block of 8 8.00 8.00
a.-h. 10r Any single 1.00 1.00

Famous Men — A420

Designs: No. 748, 5r, Nayaraj Panta (1913-2002), historian. No. 749, 5r, Narahari Nath (1914-2003), yogi.

2004, Nov. 3
748-749 A420 Set of 2 1.20 1.20

Flora and Fauna — A421

No. 750: a, Rufous piculet woodpecker. b, Giant atlas moth. c, Serma guru. d, High altitude rice.

2004, Nov. 3
750 A421 10r Block of 4, #a-d 4.00 4.00

Mayadevi Temple, Lumbini A422

Gadhimai Temples, Bara A423

2004, Nov. 30 *Perf. 13½x13*
751 A422 10r multi 1.40 1.00
752 A423 10r multi 1.40 1.00

Madan Puraskar Trust, 50th Anniv. — A424

2004, Dec. 13 *Perf. 14*
753 A424 5r multi .55 .55

Sculptures — A425

No. 754: a, Jayavarma. b, Umamaheshwar. c, Vishwarupa. d, Banshagopal.

2004, Dec. 27 *Perf. 13½*
754 A425 10r Block of 4, #a-d 3.75 3.75

Nepal Rastra Bank, 50th Anniv. (in 2006) A426

2005, Apr. 27 Litho. *Perf. 14*
755 A426 2r multi .60 .60

First Ascent of Mt. Makalu, 50th Anniv. — A427

2005, May 15
756 A427 10r multi 1.00 1.00

First Ascent of Mt. Kanchanjunga, 50th Anniv. — A428

2005, May 25
757 A428 12r multi 1.10 1.10

King Gyanendra, 58th Birthday — A429

2005, July 7 Litho. *Perf. 14*
758 A429 5r multi .55 .55

Life of Buddha A430

No. 759: a, Birth at Lumbini. b, Enlightenment at Bodhagaya. c, First Sermon at Sarnath. d, Mahaparinirvana at Kushinagar.

2005, July 21
759 Horiz. strip of 4, any background color 4.00 4.00
a.-d. A430 10r Any single, any background color 1.00 1.00
Sheet of 4 horiz. strips 16.00 —

The sheet has four horizontal strips with background colors of yellow, green, red and purple.

Queen Mother Ratna Rajya Laxmi Devi Shah A431

2005, Aug. 20
760 A431 20r multi 2.00 2.00

Fruits and Nuts — A432

No. 761: a, Indian gooseberry. b, Walnut. c, Wood apple. d, Golden evergreen raspberry.

2005, Aug. 20
761 A432 10r Block of 4, #a-d 4.00 4.00

Mammals A433

No. 762: a, Gangetic dolphin. b, Indian pangolin. c, Asiatic wild elephant. d, Clouded leopard.

2005, Aug. 31 Litho. *Perf. 14*
762 Horiz. strip of 4, any background color 4.00 4.00
a.-d. A433 10r Any single, any background color 1.00 1.00
Sheet of 4 horiz. strips 16.00 —

The sheet has four horizontal strips with background colors of yellow, green, red and purple.

Late Bhupalmansingh Karki, Social Worker — A434

2005, Sept. 24
763 A434 2r multi .60 .60

Tourism — A435

No. 764: a, Ghodaghodi Lake, Kailali. b, Budhasubba, Sunasari. c, Kalinchok Bhagawati, Dolakha. d, Panauti City, Kabhrepalanchok.

2005, Oct. 9
764 A435 5r Block of 4, #a-d 2.00 2.00

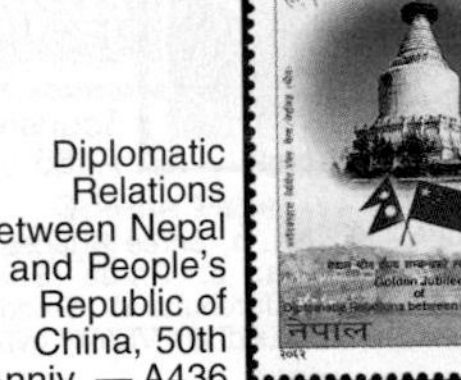
Diplomatic Relations Between Nepal and People's Republic of China, 50th Anniv. — A436

2005, Dec. 26
765 A436 30r multi 3.25 3.25

Admission to United Nations, 50th Anniv. A437

2005, Dec. 26
766 A437 50r multi 5.50 5.50

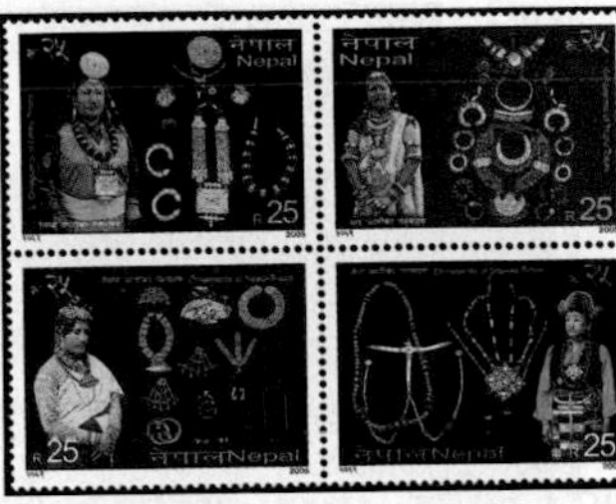
Tribal Ornaments — A438

No. 767 — Ornaments of: a, Limbu tribes. b, Tharu tribes. c, Newar tribes. d, Sherpa tribes.

2005, Dec. 26
767 A438 25r Block of 4, #a-d 11.00 11.00

King Tribhuvan (1906-55) A439

2006, Feb. 17 Litho. *Perf. 13¼x13*
768 A439 5r multi .55 .55

Democracy Day.

Queen Komal Rayja Laxmi Devi Shah — A440

2006, Mar. 8
769 A440 5r multi .55 .55

Intl. Women's Day.

World Hindu Federation, 25th Anniv. — A441

2006, Apr. 6 *Perf. 12¾*
770 A441 2r multi .35 .35

First Ascent of Mt. Lhotse, 50th Anniv. A442

First Ascent of Mt. Manaslu, 50th Anniv. A443

2006, May 9 *Perf. 13x13¼*
771 A442 25r multi 2.50 2.50
772 A443 25r multi 2.50 2.50

Supreme Court, 50th Anniv. A444

2006, May 21
773 A444 5r multi .65 .65

Fauna, Flora and Mushrooms A445

Designs: No. 774, Imperial butterfly. No. 774A, Nepalese primrose. No., 774B, Chaffer beetle. No. 774C, Beautiful stream frog. No. 774D, White pine mushroom.

2006, June 12 *Perf. 12¾*
774-774D Set of 5 5.50 5.50
e. Horiz. strip of 5, #774-774D 7.00 7.00

Nos. 774-774D were printed in sheets of 50 stamps, containing ten of each stamp, but containing only two horizontal strips of the stamps.

Diplomatic Relations Between Nepal and Russia, 50th Anniv. — A446

2006, Aug. 22 *Perf. 13¼x13*
775 A446 30r multi 1.75 1.75

Diplomatic Relations Between Nepal and Japan, 50th Anniv. A447

2006, Sept. 1 *Perf. 13x13¼*
776 A447 30r multi 1.75 1.75

Mt. Everest — A448

Stag Beetle — A449

2006, Sept. 19 *Perf. 14¼x14*
777 A448 1r blk & bl grn .25 .25
778 A449 2r black .35 .35

Perf. 14x13¾
Size: 29x25mm

779 A448 5r blk, pink & blue .55 .35
Nos. 777-779 (3) 1.15 .95

Khagendra Bahadur Basnet, Activist for Rights of the Disabled — A540

Perf. 13¾x13½

2012, Dec. 31 Litho.

Granite Paper

890 A540 10r multi .50 .50

Kishore and Kumar Narsingh Rama, Architects A541

Perf. 13¾x13½

2012, Dec. 31 Litho.

Granite Paper

891 A541 10r multi .50 .50

Karuna (1920-2008) and Lupau Ratna Tuladhar (1918-93), Operators of First Public Bus Service in Nepal — A542

Perf. 13¾x13½

2012, Dec. 31 Litho.

Granite Paper

892 A542 10r multi .50 .50

Visit Lumbini Year A543

Perf. 13¾x13½

2012, Dec. 31 Litho.

Granite Paper

893 A543 20r multi 1.00 1.00

Rajmansingh Chitrakar (1797-1865), Painter — A544

No. 894 — Chitrakar and his paintings of: a, Tibetan antelopes. b, Birds.

Perf. 13¾x13½

2012, Dec. 31 Litho.

Granite Paper

894 A544 10r Horiz. pair, #a-b 1.00 1.00

Pandit Ramakanta Jha, Politician — A545

2013, Jan. 18 Litho. *Perf. 13¾x13½*

895 A545 10r multi .55 .55

Nepalese Partnership With World Bank Group, 50th Anniv. — A546

Perf. 13¾x13½

2013, Mar. 18 Litho.

Granite Paper

896 A546 10r multi .60 .60

Melwa Devi Gurung (1898-1955), Singer — A547

Perf. 13¾x13½

2013, June 10 Litho.

Granite Paper

897 A547 5r multi .50 .50

Lake Salpa A548

Lomanthang Durbar — A549

Salhes Garden, Lok Nayak Raja Salhes A550

Sahashra Dhara Jatra Festival — A551

Perf. 13¾x13½

2013, June 10 Litho.

Granite Paper

898 A548 10r multi .60 .60
899 A549 10r multi .60 .60
900 A550 10r multi .60 .60

Perf. 13½x13¾

901 A551 10r multi .60 .60
Nos. 898-901 (4) 2.40 2.40

Ramraja Prasad Singh (1935-2012), Politician — A552

Moti Kaji Shakya (1913-97), Sculptor A553

Bhimbahadur Tamang (1933-2012), Politician — A554

Basudev Prasad Dhungana (1933-2012), Advocate for Senior Citizens — A555

Harihar Gautam (1901-65), Social Worker — A556

Gopal Pande (1913-78), Writer — A557

2013, Oct. 9 Litho. *Perf. 13¾x13½*

Granite Paper

902 A552 10r multi .55 .55
903 A553 10r multi .55 .55
904 A554 10r multi .55 .55
905 A555 10r multi .55 .55

Perf. 13½x13¾

906 A556 10r multi .55 .55
907 A557 10r multi .55 .55
Nos. 902-907 (6) 3.30 3.30

Nepal Red Cross Society, 50th Anniv. A558

2013, Oct. 9 Litho. *Perf. 13¾x13½*

Granite Paper

908 A558 50r multi 2.25 2.25

Batsaladevi Bhagawali, Dhadhing — A559

2013, Oct. 30 Litho. *Perf. 13¾x13½*

909 A559 1r multi .65 .65

Rupchandra Bista (1933-99), Politician — A560

Kewalpure Kisan (1926-2011), Poet — A561

Rupak Raj Sharma (1954-92), Soccer Player A562

Ram Sharan Darnal (1937-2011), Music Researcher — A563

Diamond Shumsher Rana (1919-2011), Writer — A564

2013, Oct. 30 Litho. *Perf. 13¾x13½*

910 A560 5r multi .40 .40

Granite Paper

911 A561 5r multi .40 .40
912 A562 10r multi .65 .65
913 A563 10r multi .65 .65
914 A564 20r multi 1.25 1.25
Nos. 910-914 (5) 3.35 3.35

Bagalamukhi Devi, Lalitpur — A565

Rajdevi Temple, Saptari A566

Ivory Window, Hanumandhoka Palace, Kathmandu — A567

Kakre Bihar, Surkhet A568

Argha Bhagawati, Arghakhanchi — A569

2013, Dec. 31 Litho. *Perf. 13¼*
Granite Paper

915	A565	1r multi	.50	.50
916	A566	1r multi	.50	.50
917	A567	5r multi	.50	.50
918	A568	5r multi	.50	.50
919	A569	5r multi	.50	.50
		Nos. 915-919 (5)	2.50	2.50

Shankar Koirala (1930-97), Writer — A570

Ramhari Sharma (1916-2012), Politician A571

Bhanubhakta Acharya (1814-68), Poet — A572

Dr. Dilliraman Regmi (1913-2001), Historian — A573

2013, Dec. 31 Litho. *Perf. 13¼*
Granite Paper

920	A570	3r multi	.50	.50
921	A571	3r multi	.50	.50
922	A572	10r multi	.60	.60
923	A573	10r multi	.60	.60
		Nos. 920-923 (4)	2.20	2.20

Museums A574

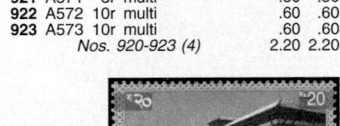

Designs: No. 924, 20r, National Art Museum, Bhaktapur. No. 925, 20r, International Mountain Museum, Kaski. No. 926, 20r, Patan Museum, Patan. 35r, National Museum, Chhauni.

2013, Dec. 31 Litho. *Perf. 13¼*
Granite Paper

924-927 A574 Set of 4 5.25 5.25

Kathmandu Valley World Heritage Property — A575

Designs: No. 928, 25r, Bhaktapur Durbar Square Monument Zone. No. 929, 25r, Bauddhanath Monument Zone. No. 930, 25r, Changu Narayan Monument Zone. No. 931, 30r, Swayambhu Monument Zone. No. 932, 30r, Hanumandhoka Durbar Square Monument Zone. No. 933, 30r, Pashupati Monument Zone. No. 934, 30r, Patan Durbar Square Monument Zone.

2013, Dec. 31 Litho. *Perf. 13¼*
Granite Paper

928-934 A575 Set of 7 10.00 10.00

Rara Lake, Mugu A576

2013, Dec. 31 Litho. *Perf. 13¼*
Granite Paper

935 A576 40r multi 2.25 2.25

Flora A577

Designs: No. 936, 40r, Wild asparagus. No. 937, 40r, Chireta. No. 938, 40r, Long pepper. No. 939, 40r, Fragrant wintergreen.

2013, Dec. 31 Litho. *Perf. 13¼*
Granite Paper

936-939 A577 Set of 4 9.00 9.00

Extinct Animals and Their Fossils A578

Designs: No. 940, 50r, Giraffa punjabensis and fossil molar teeth. No. 941, 50r, Ramapithecus sivalensis and fossil molar teeth. No. 942, 50r, Hexaprotodon sivalensis and fossil skull. No. 943, 50r, Archidiskidon planifrons and fossil skull.

2013, Dec. 31 Litho. *Perf. 13¼*
Granite Paper

940-943 A578 Set of 4 10.00 10.00

Ascent of Mt. Everest, 60th Anniv, A579

2013, Dec. 31 Litho. *Perf. 13¼*
Granite Paper

944 A579 100r multi 5.50 5.50

Rishikesh Temple, Ridi A580

2014, Oct. 9 Litho. *Perf. 13¼*
Granite Paper

945 A580 5r multi .50 .50

Narayanhiti Palace Museum, Kathmandu — A581

2014, Oct. 9 Litho. *Perf. 13¼*
Granite Paper

946 A581 20r multi 1.00 1.00

Scouting in Nepal, 60th Anniv. — A582

2014, Oct. 9 Litho. *Perf. 13¼*
Granite Paper

947 A582 30r multi 2.00 2.00

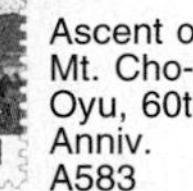

Ascent of Mt. Cho-Oyu, 60th Anniv. A583

2014, Oct. 9 Litho. *Perf. 13¼*
Granite Paper

948 A583 100r multi 5.50 5.50

Manakamana Cable Car — A584

2014, Oct. 30 Litho. *Perf. 13¼*
Granite Paper

949 A584 50r multi 3.00 3.00

Junior Chamber International of Nepal, 50th Anniv. — A585

2014, Nov. 11 Litho. *Perf. 13¼*
Granite Paper

950 A585 10r multi .50 .50

Kathmandu Buildings A586

Designs: 1r, Shivaparbati Temple. 2r, Kumari Ghar.

2014, Dec. 9 Litho. *Perf. 13¼*
Granite Paper

951-952 A586 Set of 2 .80 .80

Natural History Museum, Kathmandu A587

2014, Dec. 9 Litho. *Perf. 13¼*
Granite Paper

953 A587 1r multi .35 .35

Aadeshwor Mahadev, Kathmandu A588

2014, Dec. 9 Litho. *Perf. 13¼*
Granite Paper

954 A588 1r multi .35 .35

2014 International Cricket Council World Twenty 20 Competition, Bangladesh A589

2014, Dec. 9 Litho. *Perf. 13¼*
Granite Paper

955 A589 2r multi .35 .35

Female Community Health Volunteers Program, 25th Anniv. (in 2013) — A590

2014, Dec. 9 Litho. *Perf. 13¼*
Granite Paper

956 A590 3r multi .35 .35

Koteshwor Mahadev, Kathmandu A591

2014, Dec. 9 Litho. *Perf. 13¼*
Granite Paper

957 A591 4r multi .45 .45

Prem Bahadur Kansakar (1917-91), Social Worker — A592

2014, Dec. 9 Litho. *Perf. 13¼*
Granite Paper

958 A592 5r multi .50 .50

Paragliding, Kaski — A593

2014, Dec. 9 Litho. *Perf. 13¼*
Granite Paper

959 A593 10r multi .55 .55

Miniature Sheets

Moths — A594

No. 960, 10r: a, Acherontia lachesis. b, Asota producta. c, Argina argus. d, Biston contectaria.

No. 961, 10r: a, Brahmaea wallichii. b, Campylotes histrionicus. c, Dermaleipa (Lagoptera) juno. d, Episteme adulatrix.

No. 962, 10r: a, Erasmia pulchella. b, Eterusia aedea edocla. c, Eudocima salaminia. d, Gynautocera papilionaria.

2014, Dec. 9 Litho. *Perf. 13¼*
Granite Paper
Sheets of 4, #a-d

960-962 A594 Set of 3 6.75 6.75

Miniature Sheet

Birthplace of Buddha — A595

No. 963: a, Birthplace of Lord Buddha, Lumbini. b, Ashoka Pillar, Lumbini. c, Ramagrama, Nawalparasi. d, Tilaurakot, Kapilavastu.

2014, Dec. 9 Litho. *Perf. 13¼*
Granite Paper

963 A595 20r Sheet of 4, #a-d 4.00 4.00

2014 Winter Olympics, Sochi, Russia — A596

2014, Dec. 10 Litho. *Perf. 13¼*
Granite Paper

964 A596 2r multi .50 .50

Tenzing-Hillary Everest Marathon A597

2014, Dec. 19 Litho. *Perf. 13¼*
Granite Paper

965 A597 3r multi .40 .40

B. P. Koirala (1914-82), Prime Minister — A598

2014, Dec. 31 Litho. *Perf. 13¼*
Granite Paper

966 A598 10r multi .40 .40

Dwarika Bhakta Mathema (1902-68), Musician — A599

2015, July 1 Litho. *Perf. 13¼*
Granite Paper

967 A599 1r multi .25 .25

Chandeshwori Temple, Banepa — A600

Makwanpur Gadhi, Makwanpur — A601

Lamjung Durbar, Lamjung A602

Siddha Pokhari, Bhaktapur A603

Doleshwor Mahadev, Bhaktapur — A604

Sindhuli Gadhi, Sindhuli A605

Kaliyadaman, Sundari Chowk, Hanumandhoka — A606

Mohankali Dhungedhara, Hanumandhoka — A607

Taleju Temple, Nuwakot A608

Bulbule Lake, Surkhet A609

2015, July 1 Litho. *Perf. 13¼*
Granite Paper

968 A600 1r multi .25 .25
969 A601 1r multi .25 .25
970 A602 2r multi .25 .25
971 A603 2r multi .25 .25
972 A604 5r multi .25 .25
973 A605 5r multi .25 .25
974 A606 5r multi .25 .25
975 A607 8r multi .25 .25
976 A608 10r multi .25 .25
977 A609 10r multi .25 .25
Nos. 968-977 (10) 2.50 2.50

Fewa Lake and Machhapuchchhre, Kaski — A610

Serpentine Die Cut 12¼
2015, July 1 Litho.
Self-Adhesive

978 A610 60r multi 1.25 1.25

A611

A612

A613

B.P. Koirala Highway, Flags of Nepal and Japan A614

2015, July 1 Litho. *Perf. 13¼*
Granite Paper

979 Strip of 4 1.00 1.00
a. A611 10r multi .25 .25
b. A612 10r multi .25 .25
c. A613 10r multi .25 .25
d. A614 10r multi .25 .25

Nepal-Japan cooperation.

Prehistoric Elephants — A615

Emblem of Tribhuvan University Natural History Museum and: No. 980, 10r, Deinotherium indicum. No. 981, 10r, Elephas hysudricus. No. 982, 10r, Elephas namadicus. No. 983, 10r, Gomphotherium sp. No. 984, 10r, Stegodon bombifrons. No. 985, 10r, Stegodon ganesa.

2015, July 7 Litho. *Perf. 13¼*
Granite Paper

980-985 A615 Set of 6 1.25 1.25

Diplomatic Relations Between Nepal and People's Republic of China, 60th Anniv. — A616

2015, Aug. 1 Litho. *Perf. 13¼*
Granite Paper

986 A616 20r multi .40 .40

Narasimha, Hanumandhoka A617

Nautale Durbar, Hanumandhoka — A618

Rani Mahal, Palpa A619

Gaddi Baithak, Hanumandhoka — A620

2015, Aug. 11 Litho. *Perf. 14x13½*
Granite Paper

987 A617 10r multi .25 .25

Perf. 13½x14

988 A618 10r multi .25 .25
989 A619 25r multi .50 .50
990 A620 35r multi .70 .70
Nos. 987-990 (4) 1.70 1.70

Miniature Sheet

Ascent of Mounts Kanchenjunga and Makalu, 60th Anniv. — A621

No. 991: a, Mt. Kanchenjunga. b, Mt. Makalu. c, Airplane over mountains. d, Unnamed mountains. e, Hillary Peak. f, Tenzing Peak.

Perf. 13½x13¼
2015, Aug. 11 Litho.
Granite Paper

991 A621 10r Sheet of 6, #a-f 1.25 1.25

Non-Violence, Harmony, Morality and Freedom From Addiction A622

2015, Aug. 16 Litho. *Perf. 13¼*
Granite Paper

992 A622 25r multi .50 .50

Wildlife Reserves and National Parks A623

Designs: 1r, Koshi Tappu Wildlife Reserve. No. 994, 2r, Sagarmatha National Park. No. 995, 2r, Chitwan National Park. No. 996, 5r, Shuklaphanta Wildlife Reserve. No. 997, 5r, Lamtang National Park.

2015, Oct. 2 Litho. *Perf. 13¼*
Granite Paper

993-997 A623 Set of 5 .30 .30

Flora A624

Designs: No. 998, 10r, Abies spectabilis. No. 999, 10r, Gentiana robusta. No. 1000, 10r, Lilium nepalense. No. 1001, 10r, Maharanga emodi. No. 1002, 10r, Paris polyphylla. No. 1003, 10r, Saussurea gossipiphora.

2015, Oct. 2 Litho. *Perf. 13¼*
Granite Paper

998-1003 A624 Set of 6 1.25 1.25

Sarbeshwor Mahadev, Lalitpur — A625

2015, Oct. 9 Litho. *Perf. 13¼*
Granite Paper

1004 A625 3r multi .25 .25

Earthquake Survival Techniques — A626

2015, Oct. 9 Litho. *Perf. 13¼*
Granite Paper

1005 A626 5r multi .25 .25

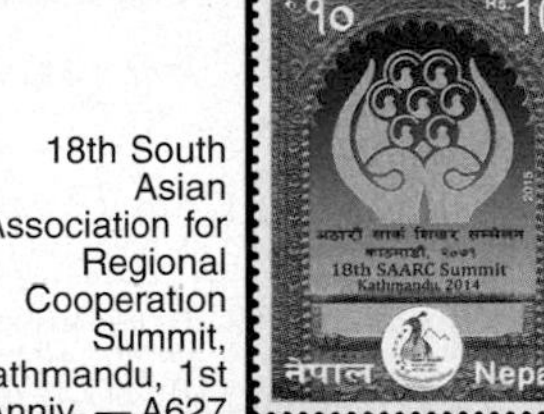

18th South Asian Association for Regional Cooperation Summit, Kathmandu, 1st Anniv. — A627

2015, Oct. 9 Litho. *Perf. 13¼*
Granite Paper

1006 A627 10r multi .25 .25

Famous Men A628

Designs: No. 1007, 8r, Deviprasad Uprety (1912-92), social worker. No. 1008, 8r, Nagendra Prasad Rijal (1927-94), politician. No. 1009, 8r, Yadav Prasad Pant (1915-2007), economist. No. 1010, 8r, Shreeprasad Parajuli (1911-62), martyr. No. 1011, 8r, Ganeshman Singh (1915-97), politician. No. 1012, 8r, Siddhi Charan Shrestha (1912-92), poet, vert.

2015, Dec. 31 Litho. *Perf. 13¼*
Granite Paper

1007-1012 A628 Set of 6 .95 .95

AIR POST STAMPS

Catalogue values for unused stamps in this section are for Never Hinged items.

Bird over Kathmandu AP1

Rough Perf 11½
1958, Oct. 16 Typo. Unwmk.
Without Gum

C1 AP1 10p dark blue 2.40 2.00

Plane over Kathmandu AP2

1967, Oct. 24 Photo. *Perf. 13½x13*

C2 AP2 1.80r multicolored 2.00 1.50

International Tourist Year.

God Akash Bhairab and Nepal Airlines Emblem AP3

Map of Nepal with Airlines Network AP4

Design: 2.50r, Plane over Himalayas.

Perf. 14½x14, 13 (65p)
1968, July 1 Photo.

C3 AP3 15p blue & bis brn .50 .50
C4 AP4 65p violet blue 1.25 1.00
C5 AP3 2.50r dp blue & scar 3.75 2.75
Nos. C3-C5 (3) 5.50 4.25

10th anniv. of the Royal Nepal Airlines Corp.

Flyer and Jet — AP5

1978, Dec. 12 Photo. *Perf. 13*

C6 AP5 2.30r blue & ocher 1.40 .80

75th anniversary of 1st powered flight.

Pheasant Type of 1979

3.50r, Impeyan pheasant, horiz.

1979, Nov. 22 Photo. *Perf. 14½x14*

C7 A174 3.50r multicolored 3.25 2.00

OFFICIAL STAMPS

Catalogue values for unused stamps in this section are for Never Hinged items.

Soldiers and Arms of Nepal — O1

Perf. 13½
1959, Nov. 1 Litho. Unwmk.
Size: 29x17½mm

O1 O1 2p reddish brown .25 .25
O2 O1 4p yel green .25 .25
O3 O1 6p salmon pink .25 .25
O4 O1 8p brt violet .30 .25
O5 O1 12p red orange .35 .25

Size: 37½x21½mm

O6 O1 16p red brown .50 .35
O7 O1 24p carmine .60 .50
O8 O1 32p rose car 1.00 .70
O9 O1 50p ultramarine 1.75 1.25
O10 O1 1r rose red 3.25 2.25
O11 O1 2r orange 6.50 5.00
Nos. O1-O11 (11) 15.00 11.30

Nos. 144-146 and 124 Overprinted in Black

1960-62 Photo. *Perf. 14½x14*

Overprint 12½mm Long

O12	A35	1p carmine rose ('62)	.25	.25
O13	A35	2p bright blue ('62)	.25	.25
O14	A35	5p golden brown ('62)	.35	.35
		Nos. O12-O14 (3)	.85	.85

Perf. 14

Overprint 14½mm Long

O15	A26	1r red lilac	1.50	1.50

The overprint, "Kaj Sarkari" in Devanagari characters means "Service." Five other denominations, 10p, 40p, 75p, 2r and 5r, were similarly overprinted but not issued. Value, 5 values $3. A few exist on 1960 first day covers.

In 1983 substantial quantities of the set of nine values were sold as remainders by the Post Office at face value (under $1 for the set).

The existence of covers from 1985-86 indicate that some of these may have been used as regular postage stamps.

NETHERLANDS

'ne-t͟hər-lən‚d‚z

(Holland)

LOCATION — Northwestern Europe, bordering on the North Sea
GOVT. — Kingdom
AREA — 16,029 sq. mi.
POP. — 15,807,641 (1999 est.)
CAPITAL — Amsterdam

100 Cents = 1 Gulden (Guilder or Florin)
100 Cents = 1 Euro (2002)

Catalogue values for unused stamps in this country are for Never Hinged items, beginning with Scott 216 in the regular postage section, Scott B123 in the semi-postal section, Scott C13 in the airpost section, Scott J80 in the postage due section, and Scott O44 in the official section.

Values for unused stamps are for examples with original gum as defined in the catalogue introduction. Very fine examples of Nos. 4-12 will have perforations touching the frameline on one or more sides due to the narrow spacing of the stamps on the plates. Stamps with perfs clear on all four sides are very scarce and command higher prices.

Watermarks

Wmk. 158

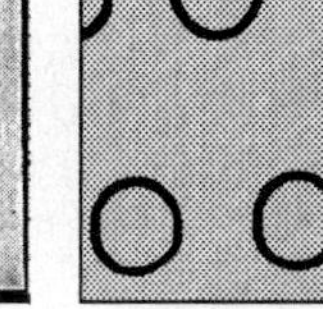

Wmk. 202 — Circles

King William III — A1

Wmk. 158

1852, Jan. 1 Engr. *Imperf.*

1	A1	5c blue	400.00	35.00
a.		5c light blue	450.00	40.00
b.		5c steel blue	750.00	100.00
c.		5c dark blue	450.00	35.00
2	A1	10c lake	450.00	27.50
3	A1	15c orange yellow	775.00	130.00

In 1895 the 10c was privately reprinted in several colors on unwatermarked paper by Joh. A. Moesman, whose name appears on the back.

King William III — A2

1864 Unwmk. *Perf. 12½x12*

4	A2	5c blue	300.00	16.00
5	A2	10c lake	425.00	8.00
6	A2	15c orange	1,050.	100.00
a.		15c yellow	1,350.	115.00

The paper varies considerably in thickness. It is sometimes slightly bluish, also vertically ribbed.

William III — A3

1867 *Perf. 12¾x11¾*

7	A3	5c ultra	115.00	2.75
8	A3	10c lake	225.00	4.75
9	A3	15c orange brn	640.00	35.00
10	A3	20c dk green	625.00	24.00
11	A3	25c dk violet	2,100.	110.00
12	A3	50c gold	2,500.	160.00

The paper of Nos. 7-22 sometimes has an accidental bluish tinge of varying strength. During its manufacture a chemical whitener (bluing agent) was added in varying quantities. No particular printing was made on bluish paper.

Two varieties of numerals in each value, differing chiefly in the thickness.

Oxidized copies of the 50c are worth much less.

Imperforate varieties of Nos. 7-12 are proofs.

See the *Scott Specialized Catalogue* for listings by perforations.

1869

Perf. 10½x10

7c	A3	5c ultra	225.00	11.50
8c	A3	10c lake	230.00	7.75
9c	A3	15c orange brown	2,700.	1,150.
10c	A3	20c dark green	1,550.	155.00

Coat of Arms — A4

1869-71 Typo. *Perf. 13¼, 14*

17	A4	½c red brown ('71)	24.00	3.75
c.		Perf. 14	*2,300.*	875.00
18	A4	1c black	210.00	70.00
19	A4	1c green	15.50	2.25
c.		Perf. 14	27.50	5.50
20	A4	1½c rose	150.00	77.50
b.		Perf. 14	175.00	97.50
21	A4	2c buff	60.00	15.00
c.		Perf. 14	55.00	14.00
22	A4	2½c violet ('70)	475.00	70.00
c.		Perf. 14	775.00	425.00

Imperforate varieties are proofs.

A5

A6

Perf. 12½, 13, 13½, 13x14, 14, 12½x12 and 11½x12

1872-88

23	A5	5c blue	11.50	.30
a.		5c ultra	14.00	1.25
24	A5	7½c red brn ('88)	35.00	18.00
25	A5	10c rose	57.50	1.60
26	A5	12½c gray ('75)	62.50	2.40
27	A5	15c brn org	350.00	5.25
28	A5	20c green	425.00	5.00
29	A5	22½c dk grn ('88)	77.50	42.50
30	A5	25c dull vio	525.00	4.00
31	A5	50c bister	650.00	11.00
32	A5	1g gray vio ('88)	480.00	40.00
33	A6	2g50c rose & ultra	900.00	105.00

Imperforate varieties are proofs.

Numeral of Value — A7

HALF CENT:

Type I — Fraction bar 8 to 8½mm long.

Type II — Fraction bar 9mm long and thinner.

Perf. 12½, 13½, 14, 12½x12, 11½x12

1876-94

34	A7	½c rose (II)	11.50	.30
a.		½c rose (I)	15.00	.50
c.		Laid paper		60.00
d.		Perf. 14 (I)	1,950.	575.00
35	A7	1c emer grn ('94)	2.75	.25
b.		As "c," laid paper	70.00	7.25
c.		1c green	8.00	.25
36	A7	2c olive yel ('94)	32.50	2.75
a.		2c yellow	65.00	3.50
37	A7	2½c violet ('94)	14.00	.30
b.		2½c dark violet ('94)	17.50	.45
c.		2½c lilac	100.00	.80
d.		Laid paper	—	—
		Nos. 34-37 (4)	60.75	3.60

Imperforate varieties are proofs.

Princess Wilhelmina — A8

1891-94 *Perf. 12½*

40	A8	3c orange ('94)	8.00	2.30
a.		3c orange yellow ('92)	11.50	2.75
41	A8	5c lt ultra ('94)	4.00	.25
a.		5c dull blue	5.00	.25
42	A8	7½c brown ('94)	15.00	6.25
a.		7½c red brown	27.50	6.25
43	A8	10c brt rose ('94)	23.50	1.60
a.		10c brick red	45.00	2.40
44	A8	12½c bluish gray ('94)	23.50	1.60
a.		12½c gray	40.00	1.75
45	A8	15c yel brn ('94)	60.00	5.00
a.		15c orange brown	80.00	5.50
46	A8	20c green ('94)	70.00	3.00
a.		20c yellow green	80.00	3.00
47	A8	22½c dk grn ('94)	32.50	13.50
a.		22½c deep blue green	55.00	13.50
48	A8	25c dl vio ('94)	110.00	6.00
a.		25c dark violet	110.00	6.00
49	A8	50c yel brn ('94)	550.00	20.00
a.		50c bister	575.00	27.50
50	A8	1g gray vio	625.00	77.50

The paper used in 1891-93 was white, rough and somewhat opaque. In 1894, a thinner, smooth and sometimes transparent paper was introduced.

The 5c orange was privately produced.

Princess Wilhelmina — A9

1893-96 *Perf. 11½x11*

51	A9	50c emer & yel brn ('96)	80.00	15.00
a.		Perf. 11	*2,500.*	200.00
52	A9	1g brn & ol grn ('96)	200.00	22.50
a.		Perf. 11	225.00	60.00
53	A9	2g 50c brt rose & ultra	400.00	130.00
a.		2g 50c lil rose & ultra, perf. 11	475.00	130.00
b.		Perf. 11½	500.00	140.00

Perf. 11

54	A9	5g brnz grn & red brn ('96)	700.00	425.00

A10

Queen Wilhelmina — A11

Perf. 12½ (#70, 73, 75-77, 81-82), 11½, 11½x11, 11x11½

1898-1924

55	A10	½c violet	.45	.25
56	A10	1c red	.90	.25
b.		Imperf., pair	*2,000.*	—
57	A10	1½c ultra ('08)	6.00	.85
58	A10	1½c dp blue ('13)	3.00	.35
59	A10	2c yellow brn	3.75	.25
60	A10	2½c deep green	3.25	.25
b.		Imperf., pair	*6,250.*	
61	A11	3c orange	16.50	3.25
62	A11	3c pale ol grn ('01)	1.10	.25
63	A11	4c claret ('21)	1.60	1.10
64	A11	4½c violet ('19)	3.75	3.75
65	A11	5c car rose	1.60	.25
66	A11	7½c brown	.75	.25
a.		Tête bêche pair ('24)	80.00	72.50
67	A11	10c gray lilac	6.25	.25
68	A11	12½c blue	3.25	.30
69	A11	15c yellow brn	100.00	3.25
70	A11	15c bl & car ('08)	6.25	.25
71	A11	17½c vio ('06)	50.00	12.00
73	A11	17½c ultra & brn ('10)	15.00	.90
74	A11	20c yellow green	150.00	.75
75	A11	20c ol grn & gray ('08)	10.00	.50
76	A11	22½c brn & ol grn	9.25	.60
77	A11	25c car & blue	9.25	.45
78	A11	30c lil & vio brn ('17)	24.00	.50
79	A11	40c grn & org ('20)	34.00	1.10
80	A11	50c brnz grn & red brn	110.00	1.10
81	A11	50c gray & vio ('14)	70.00	1.10
a.		Perf 11½x11	70.00	16.50
82	A11	60c ol grn & grn ('20)	34.00	1.10
a.		Perf 11½	200.00	20.00
		Nos. 55-82 (27)	673.90	35.20
		Set, never hinged	3,000.	

See Nos. 107-112. For overprints and surcharges see Nos. 102-103, 106, 117-123, 135-136, O1-O8.

A12

I II

Type I — The figure "1" is 3¾mm high and 2¾mm wide.

Type II — The figure "1" is 3½mm high and 2½mm wide, it is also thinner than in type I.

Perf. 11, 11x11½, 11½, 11½x11

1898-1905 Engr.

83	A12	1g dk grn, II ('99)	52.50	.75
a.		1g dark green, I ('98)	190.00	110.00
84	A12	2½g brn lil ('99)	100.00	3.25
85	A12	5g claret ('99)	225.00	6.00
86	A12	10g orange ('05)	775.00	675.00
		Set, never hinged	2,975.	

For surcharge see No. 104.

Admiral M. A. de Ruyter and Fleet — A13

1907, Mar. 23 Typo. *Perf. 12x12½*

87	A13	½c blue	2.00	1.25
88	A13	1c claret	3.50	2.25
89	A13	2½c vermilion	6.00	2.25
		Nos. 87-89 (3)	11.50	5.75
		Set, never hinged	37.00	

De Ruyter (1607-1676), naval hero.

For surcharges see Nos. J29-J41.

King William I — A14

Designs: 2½c, 12½c, 1g, King William I. 3c, 20c, 2½g, King William II. 5c, 25c, 5g, King William III. 10c, 50c, 10g, Queen Wilhelmina.

Perf. 11½x11, 11½ (#97, 100-101)

1913, Nov. 29 **Engr.**

90	A14	2½c green, *grn*	.80	.80
91	A14	3c buff, *straw*	1.80	1.50
92	A14	5c rose red, *sal*	1.25	.90
93	A14	10c gray blk	4.25	2.40
94	A14	12½c dp blue, *bl*	3.00	1.90
95	A14	20c orange brn	13.00	11.00
96	A14	25c pale blue	15.00	8.75
97	A14	50c yel grn	32.50	27.50
98	A14	1g claret	47.50	20.00
a.		Perf. 11½	60.00	20.00
99	A14	2½g dull violet	120.00	50.00
100	A14	5g yel, *straw*	225.00	40.00
101	A14	10g red, *straw*	800.00	725.00
		Nos. 90-101 (12)	1,264.	889.75
		Set, never hinged	2,285.	

Centenary of Dutch independence.
For surcharge see No. 105.

No. 78 Surcharged in Red or Black

a

b

1919, Dec. 1 ***Perf. 12½***

102	A11	(a) 40c on 30c (R)	22.50	3.25
103	A11	(b) 60c on 30c (Bk)	25.00	3.75
		Set, never hinged	140.00	

Nos. 86 and 101 Surcharged in Black

1920, Aug. 17 ***Perf. 11, 11½***

104	A12	2.50g on 10g	145.00	110.00
		Never hinged	300.00	
105	A14	2.50g on 10g	160.00	100.00
		Never hinged	325.00	
		Set, never hinged	625.00	

No. 64 Surcharged in Red

1921, Mar. 1 **Typo.** ***Perf. 12½***

106	A11	4c on 4½c vio	4.00	1.60
		Never hinged	8.00	

A17

1921-22 **Typo.** ***Perf. 12½***

107	A17	5c green ('22)	11.00	.25
108	A17	12½c vermilion ('22)	18.00	1.75
109	A17	20c blue	27.50	.25
		Nos. 107-109 (3)	56.50	2.25
		Set, never hinged	215.00	

Queen Type of 1898-99, 10c Redrawn

1922 ***Perf. 12½***

110	A11	10c gray	29.00	.25
		Never hinged	75.00	

Imperf

111	A11	5c car rose	7.25	7.25
		Never hinged	13.50	
112	A11	10c gray	7.25	7.25
		Never hinged	14.00	
		Nos. 110-112 (3)	43.50	14.75

In redrawn 10c the horizontal lines behind the Queen's head are wider apart.

Orange Tree and Lion of Brabant
A18

Post Horn and Lion
A19

Numeral of Value — A20

1923, Mar. 9 ***Perf. 12½***

113	A18	1c dark violet	.55	.60
		Never hinged	1.75	
114	A18	2c orange	6.00	.25
		Never hinged	9.00	
115	A19	2½c bluish green	1.75	.65
		Never hinged	3.50	
116	A20	4c deep blue	1.25	.60
		Never hinged	2.75	
		Nos. 113-116 (4)	9.55	2.10
		Set, never hinged	17.00	

Nos. 56, 58, 62, 65, 68, 73, 76 Surcharged in Various Colors

c

d

1923, July ***Perf. 12½***

117	A10(c)	2c on 1c (Bl)	.45	.25
		Never hinged	.90	
118	A10(c)	2c on 1½c (Bk)	.45	.25
		Never hinged	.90	
119	A11(d)	10c on 3c (Br)	4.25	.25
		Never hinged	10.00	
120	A11(d)	10c on 5c (Bk)	8.00	.50
		Never hinged	17.50	
121	A11(d)	10c on 12½c (R)	7.25	.90
		Never hinged	19.00	

Perf. 11½x11

122	A11(d)	10c on 17½c (R)	4.00	4.00
		Never hinged	8.00	
a.		Perf. 11½	*1,600.*	*800.00*
b.		Perf. 12½	4.00	4.00
		Never hinged	8.00	
123	A11(d)	10c on 22½c (R)	4.00	4.00
		Never hinged	6.50	
a.		Perf. 11½	3.00	3.50
		Never hinged	6.50	
b.		Perf. 12½	4.00	4.00
		Never hinged	8.00	
		Nos. 117-123 (7)	28.40	10.15
		Set, never hinged	62.50	

Queen Wilhelmina
A21 A22

Perf. 11½x12½, 11½x12 (5c)

1923, Oct. **Engr.**

124	A22	2c myrtle green	.25	.25
		Never hinged	1.10	
a.		Vert. pair, imperf. between	*2,400.*	
125	A21	5c green	.35	.25
		Never hinged	1.10	
a.		Vert. pair, imperf. between	*1,800.*	
126	A22	7½c carmine	.50	.25
		Never hinged	2.00	
127	A22	10c vermilion	.40	.25
		Never hinged	1.50	
a.		Vert. pair, imperf. between	*550.00*	*575.00*
128	A22	20c ultra	3.50	1.00
		Never hinged	1.50	
129	A22	25c yellow	5.50	1.10
		Never hinged	15.00	

Perf. 11½

130	A22	35c orange	5.00	3.00
		Never hinged	15.00	
131	A22	50c black	17.00	.50
		Never hinged	45.00	
132	A21	1g red	30.00	7.25
		Never hinged	60.00	
133	A21	2½g black	210.00	200.00
		Never hinged	450.00	
134	A21	5g dark blue	200.00	175.00
		Never hinged	375.00	
		Nos. 124-134 (11)	472.50	388.85
		Set, never hinged	975.00	

25th anniv. of the assumption as monarch of the Netherlands by Queen Wilhelmina at the age of 18.

No. 119 Overprinted in Red

No. 73 With Additional Surcharge in Blue

1923 **Typo.** ***Perf. 12½***

135	A11	10c on 3c	1.10	1.00
		Never hinged	8.00	
136	A11	1g on 17½c	62.50	15.00
		Never hinged	160.00	
a.		Perf. 11½	95.00	40.00
b.		Perf. 11½x11	80.00	30.00

Stamps with red surcharge were prepared for use as Officials but were not issued.

Queen Wilhelmina — A23

1924, Sept. 6 **Photo.** ***Perf. 12½***

137	A23	10c slate green	32.50	35.00
		Never hinged	55.00	
138	A23	15c gray black	42.50	45.00
		Never hinged	80.00	
139	A23	35c brown orange	32.50	35.00
		Never hinged	60.00	
		Nos. 137-139 (3)	107.50	115.00

These stamps were available solely to visitors to the International Philatelic Exhibition at The Hague and were not obtainable at regular post offices. Set of three on international philatelic exhibition cover dataed Sept. 6-12, 15-17, 1924, value, $110. Set of three on Netherland Philatelic Exhibition cover dated Sept. 13-14, value, $150.

See Nos. 147-160, 172-193. For overprints and surcharge see Nos. 194, O11, O13-O15.

Ship in Distress — A23a

Lifeboat — A23b

1924, Sept. 15 **Litho.** ***Perf. 11½***

140	A23a	2c black brn	3.75	2.50
		Never hinged	7.25	
141	A23b	10c orange brn	6.50	2.00
		Never hinged	13.00	

Centenary of Royal Dutch Lifeboat Society.

Type A23 and

Gull — A24

1924-26 **Unwmk.** ***Perf. 12½***

142	A24	1c deep red	.75	.90
		Never hinged	.90	
143	A24	2c red orange	2.50	.25
		Never hinged	3.75	
144	A24	2½c deep green	3.00	.80
		Never hinged	5.00	
145	A24	3c yel grn ('25)	15.00	1.00
		Never hinged	50.00	
146	A24	4c dp ultra	3.00	.70
		Never hinged	15.00	

Photo.

147	A23	5c dull green	3.50	.75
		Never hinged	8.00	
148	A23	6c org brn ('25)	.75	.50
		Never hinged	1.40	
149	A23	7½c orange ('25)	.35	.25
		Never hinged	1.10	
150	A23	9c org red & blk ('26)	1.50	1.25
		Never hinged	3.00	
151	A23	10c red, *shades*	1.50	.25
		Never hinged	5.50	
152	A23	12½c deep rose	1.60	.35
		Never hinged	4.50	
153	A23	15c ultra	6.00	.45
		Never hinged	15.00	
154	A23	20c dp blue ('25)	10.00	.60
		Never hinged	22.00	
155	A23	25c olive bis ('25)	22.50	.85
		Never hinged	40.00	
156	A23	30c violet	13.00	.65
		Never hinged	40.00	
157	A23	35c olive brn ('25)	30.00	6.00
		Never hinged	80.00	
158	A23	40c dp brown	35.00	.75
		Never hinged	200.00	
159	A23	50c blue grn ('25)	60.00	.60
		Never hinged	275.00	
160	A23	60c dk violet ('25)	27.50	.80
		Never hinged	100.00	
		Nos. 142-160 (19)	237.45	17.70
		Set, never hinged	725.00	

See Nos. 164-171, 243A-243Q. For overprints and surcharges see Nos. 226-243, O9-O10.

NETHERLANDS

Classics, Singles, Sets, Year Sets - 1958 to date

B-O-B including Court of Justice, Covers & Specialized

Great stock of Netherlands Colonies available by want list!

We Buy!!! Netherlands, U.S. & Worldwide

1-800-94-STAMP
(1-800-947-8267)

HENRY GITNER PHILATELISTS, INC.
HGPI

P.O. Box 3077-S, Middletown, NY 10940
Tel: 845-343-5151 Fax: 845-343-0068
PayPal Toll Free: 1-800-947-8267
E-mail: hgitner@hgitner.com

PHILATELY - THE QUIET EXCITEMENT!

Syncopated Perforations

Type A

Type B

Type C

These special "syncopated" or "interrupted" perforations, devised for coil stamps, are found on Nos. 142-156, 158-160, 164-166, 168-185, 187-193 and certain semipostals of 1925-33, between Nos. B9 and B69. There are four types:

A (1st stamp is #142a). On two shorter sides, groups of four holes separated by blank spaces equal in width to two or three holes.

B (1st stamp is #164a). As "A," but on all four sides.

C (1st stamp is #164b). On two shorter sides, end holes are omitted.

D (1st stamp is #174c). Four-hole sequence on horiz. sides, three-hole on vert. sides.

Syncopated, Type A (2 Sides)

1925-26

142a A24 1c deep red .75 .80
Never hinged 1.45
143a A24 2c red orange 2.75 2.50
Never hinged 4.50
144a A24 2½c deep green 2.75 1.25
Never hinged 4.50
145a A24 3c yellow green 18.00 20.00
Never hinged 40.00
146a A24 4c deep ultra 2.75 1.90
Never hinged 7.00
147a A23 5c dull green 5.50 2.50
Never hinged 10.00
148a A23 6c orange brown 110.00 100.00
Never hinged 190.00
149a A23 7½c orange 1.10 1.00
Never hinged 1.50
150a A23 9c org red & blk 1.75 1.25
Never hinged 2.50
151a A23 10c red 11.00 2.75
Never hinged 17.00
152a A23 12½c deep rose 1.75 1.50
Never hinged 3.50
153a A23 15c ultra 67.50 6.00
Never hinged 145.00
154a A23 20c deep blue 10.00 4.00
Never hinged 20.00
155a A23 25c olive bister 42.50 45.00
Never hinged 90.00
156a A23 30c violet 14.50 10.50
Never hinged 27.50
158a A23 40c deep brown 45.00 36.00
Never hinged 160.00
159a A23 50c blue green 55.00 20.00
Never hinged 240.00
160a A23 60c dark violet 27.50 11.00
Never hinged 70.00
Nos. 142a-160a (18) 420.10 267.95
Set, never hinged 1,035.

A25

1925-30 Engr. *Perf. 11½*

161 A25 1g ultra 8.00 .65
Never hinged 25.00
162 A25 2½g car ('27) 90.00 3.00
Never hinged 175.00
163 A25 5g gray blk 160.00 2.50
Never hinged 300.00
Nos. 161-163 (3) 258.00 6.15

Types of 1924-26 Issue

Perf. 12½, 13½x12½, 12½x13½

1926-39 Wmk. 202 Litho.

164 A24 ½c gray ('28) .90 1.00
165 A24 1c dp red ('27) .25 .25
166 A24 1½c red vio ('28) 1.10 .25
c. "CEN" for "CENT" 165.00 275.00
d. "GENT" for "CENT" 120.00 115.00
167 A24 1½c gray ('35) .25 .25
a. 1½c dark gray .25 .25
168 A24 2c dp org .25 .25
a. 2c red orange .25 .25
169 A24 2½c green ('27) 2.75 .25
170 A24 3c yel grn ('27) .25 .25
171 A24 4c dp ultra ('27) .25 .25

Photo.

172 A23 5c dp green .25 .25
173 A23 6c org brn ('27) .25 .25
174 A23 7½c dk vio ('27) 3.25 .25
175 A23 7½c red ('28) .35 .25
176 A23 9c org red & blk ('28) 11.00 12.00
b. Value omitted *14,500.*
177 A23 10c red 1.30 .25
178 A23 10c dl vio ('29) 2.50 .25
179 A23 12½c dp rose ('27) 42.50 4.50
180 A23 12½c ultra ('28) .25 .25
181 A23 15c ultra 7.25 .25
182 A23 15c orange ('29) 1.30 .25
183 A23 20c dp blue ('28) 7.25 .25
184 A23 21c ol brn ('31) 25.00 .90
185 A23 22½c ol brn ('27) 7.25 3.00
186 A23 22½c dp org ('39) 15.50 16.00
187 A23 25c ol bis ('27) 4.50 .25
188 A23 27½c gray ('28) 4.50 .90
189 A23 30c violet 5.00 .25
190 A23 35c olive brn 62.50 12.50
191 A23 40c dp brown 9.00 .25
192 A23 50c blue grn 5.00 .25
193 A23 60c black ('29) 57.50 .90
Nos. 164-193 (30) 279.20 56.95
Set, never hinged 640.00

Syncopated, Type A (2 Sides), 12½

1926-27

168b A24 2c deep orange .40 .40
170a A24 3c yellow green .60 .60
171a A24 4c deep ultra .60 .60
172a A23 5c deep green .70 .60
173a A23 6c orange brown .40 .45
174a A23 7½c dark violet 4.50 2.00
177a A23 10c red 1.00 .85
181a A23 15c ultra 7.00 3.00
185a A23 22½c olive brown 7.00 2.50
187a A23 25c olive bister 20.00 18.00
189a A23 30c violet 19.00 12.00
190a A23 35c olive brown 77.50 22.50
191a A23 40c deep brown 50.00 40.00
Nos. 168b-191a (13) 188.70 103.50
Set, never hinged 360.00

1928 *Syncopated, Type B (4 Sides)*

164a A24 ½c gray .80 .65
165a A24 1c deep red .30 .30
166a A24 1½c red violet .80 .25
168c A24 2c deep orange 1.00 .60
169a A24 2½c green 2.75 .25
170b A24 3c yellow green .75 .75
171b A24 4c deep ultra .75 .65
172b A23 5c deep green 1.00 .75
173b A23 6c orange brown .75 .50
174b A23 7½c dark violet 4.25 2.00
175a A23 7½c red .25 .25
176a A23 9c org red & blk 10.00 12.50
178a A23 10c dull violet 5.25 5.00
179a A23 12½c deep rose 80.00 80.00
180a A23 12½c ultra 1.40 .40
181b A23 15c ultra 9.00 2.00
182a A23 15c orange .75 .30
183a A23 20c deep blue 7.00 3.00
187b A23 25c olive bister 17.00 10.00
188a A23 27½c gray 4.50 2.00
189b A23 30c violet 15.00 8.00
191b A23 40c deep brown 35.00 22.50
192a A23 50c blue green 55.00 45.00
193a A23 60c black 45.00 22.50
Nos. 164a-193a (24) 298.30 220.15
Set, never hinged 600.00

Syncopated, Type C (2 Sides, Corners Only)

1930

164b A24 ½c gray 1.00 .70
165b A24 1c deep red 1.00 .40
166b A24 1½c red violet .90 .25
168d A24 2c deep orange .80 .70
169b A24 2½c green 2.75 .25
170c A24 3c yellow green 1.10 .50
171c A24 4c deep ultra .50 .25
172c A23 5c deep green .70 .70
173c A23 6c orange brown .70 .70
178b A23 10c dull violet 8.00 7.00
183b A23 20c deep blue 7.75 3.75
184a A23 21c olive brown 25.00 9.00
189c A23 30c violet 12.00 7.00
192b A23 50c blue green 45.00 45.00
Nos. 164b-192b (14) 107.20 76.20
Set, never hinged 225.00

Syncopated, Type D (3 Holes Vert., 4 Holes Horiz.)

1927

174c A23 7½c dark violet *2,750.* *2,100.*
Never hinged *3,750.*

No. 185 Surcharged in Red

1929, Nov. 11 *Perf. 12½*

194 A23 21c on 22½c ol brn 21.00 1.50
Never hinged 47.50

Queen Wilhelmina — A26

1931, Oct. Photo. *Perf. 12½*

195 A26 70c dk bl & red 30.00 .80
Never hinged 120.00
a. Perf. 14½x13½ ('39) 36.00 8.00
Never hinged 140.00

See No. 201.

Arms of the House of Orange — A27

William I — A28

Designs: 5c, William I, Portrait by Goltzius. 6c, Portrait of William I by Van Key. 12½c, Portrait attributed to Moro.

1933, Apr. 1 Unwmk. Engr.

196 A27 1½c black .55 .40
197 A28 5c dark green 1.75 .40
198 A28 6c dull violet 2.75 .30
199 A28 12½c deep blue 17.00 3.50
Nos. 196-199 (4) 22.05 4.60
Set, never hinged 55.00

400th anniv. of the birth of William I, Count of Nassau and Prince of Orange, frequently referred to as William the Silent.

Star, Dove and Sword — A31

1933, May 18 Photo. Wmk. 202

200 A31 12½c dp ultra 9.00 .75
Never hinged 27.50

For overprint see No. O12.

Queen Wilhelmina Design of 1931

Queen Wilhelmina and ships.

Perf. 14½x13½

1933, July 26 Wmk. 202

201 A26 80c Prus bl & red 110.00 3.25
Never hinged 350.00

Willemstad Harbor — A33

Van Walbeeck's Ship — A34

Perf. 14x12½

1934, July 2 Engr. Unwmk.

202 A33 6c violet blk 3.50 .25
203 A34 12½c dull blue 22.00 3.00
Set, never hinged 77.50

Tercentenary of Curacao.

Minerva — A35

Design: 12½c, Gisbertus Voetius.

Wmk. 202

1936, May 15 Photo. *Perf. 12½*

204 A35 6c brown lake 2.50 .25
205 A35 12½c indigo 4.50 4.50
Set, never hinged 16.00

300th anniversary of the founding of the University at Utrecht.

Boy Scout Emblem A37

"Assembly" A38

Mercury — A39

1937, Apr. 1 *Perf. 14½x13½*

206 A37 1½c multicolored .40 .25
207 A38 6c multicolored 1.25 .25
208 A39 12½c multicolored 4.00 1.40
Nos. 206-208 (3) 5.65 1.90
Set, never hinged 12.00

Fifth Boy Scout World Jamboree, Vogelenzang, Netherlands, 7/31-8/13/37.

Wilhelmina — A40

1938, Aug. 27 *Perf. 12½x12*

209 A40 1½c black .25 .25
210 A40 5c red orange .30 .25
211 A40 12½c royal blue 4.00 1.60
Nos. 209-211 (3) 4.55 2.10
Set, never hinged 13.50

Reign of Queen Wilhelmina, 40th anniv.

St. Willibrord — A41

Design: 12½c, St. Willibrord as older man.

Perf. 12½x14

1939, June 15 Engr. Unwmk.

212 A41 5c dk slate grn .75 .25
213 A41 12½c slate blue 5.00 2.75
Set, never hinged 14.00

12th centenary of the death of St. Willibrord.

Woodburning Engine — A43

Design: 12½c, Streamlined electric car.

Perf. 14½x13½

1939, Sept. 1 Photo. Wmk. 202

No.	Type	Value	Color	Unused	Used
214	A43	5c	dk slate grn	.80	.25
215	A43	12½c	dark blue	8.00	4.00
			Set, never hinged	22.50	

Centenary of Dutch Railroads.

Catalogue values for unused stamps in this section, from this point to the end of the section, are for Never Hinged items.

Queen Wilhelmina — A45

1940-47 *Perf. 13½x12½*

No.	Type	Value	Color	Unused	Used
216	A45	5c	dk green	.25	.25
216B	A45	6c	hn brn ('47)	.55	.25
217	A45	7½c	brt red	.25	.25
218	A45	10c	brt red vio	.25	.25
219	A45	12½c	sapphire	.25	.25
220	A45	15c	light blue	.25	.25
220B	A45	17½c	slate bl ('46)	1.25	.70
221	A45	20c	purple	.35	.25
222	A45	22½c	olive grn	1.25	.85
223	A45	25c	rose brn	.35	.25
224	A45	30c	bister	.80	.35
225	A45	40c	brt green	1.25	.60
225A	A45	50c	orange ('46)	9.50	.60
225B	A45	60c	pur brn ('46)	8.50	2.00
			Nos. 216-225B (14)	25.05	7.10

Imperf. examples of Nos. 216, 218-220 were released through philatelic channels during the German occupation, but were never issued at any post office. Value, set, $1.

For overprints see Nos. O16-O24.

Type of 1924-26 Surcharged in Black or Blue

Perf. 12½x13½

1940, Oct. Photo. Wmk. 202

No.	Type	Value	Color	Unused	Used
226	A24	2½c	on 3c ver	2.00	.25
227	A24	5c	on 3c lt grn	.25	.25
228	A24	7½c	on 3c ver	.25	.25
a.			Pair, #226, 228	4.00	1.50
229	A24	10c	on 3c lt grn	.25	.25
230	A24	12½c	on 3c lt bl (Bl)	.30	.25
231	A24	17½c	on 3c lt grn	.60	.65
232	A24	20c	on 3c lt grn	.40	.25
233	A24	22½c	on 3c lt grn	.80	.85
234	A24	25c	on 3c lt grn	.50	.25
235	A24	30c	on 3c lt grn	.65	.30
236	A24	40c	on 3c lt grn	.80	.60
237	A24	50c	on 3c lt grn	.70	.40
238	A24	60c	on 3c lt grn	1.60	.85
239	A24	70c	on 3c lt grn	3.75	1.75
240	A24	80c	on 3c lt grn	5.50	4.00
241	A24	1g	on 3c lt grn	35.00	32.50
242	A24	2.50g	on 3c lt grn	40.00	37.50
243	A24	5g	on 3c lt grn	37.50	35.00
			Nos. 226-243 (18)	130.85	116.15
			Set, hinged	70.00	

No. 228a is from coils.

Gull Type of 1924-26

1941

No.	Type	Value	Color	Unused	Used
243A	A24	2½c	dk green	1.25	.35
b.			Booklet pane of 6	10.00	
243C	A24	5c	brt green	.25	.25
243E	A24	7½c	henna	.25	.25
r.			Pair, #243A, 243E	1.00	1.00
243G	A24	10c	brt violet	.25	.25
243H	A24	12½c	ultra	.25	.25
243J	A24	15c	lt blue	.25	.25
243K	A24	17½c	red org	.25	.25
243L	A24	20c	lt violet	.25	.25
243M	A24	22½c	dk ol grn	.25	.25
243N	A24	25c	lake	.25	.25
243O	A24	30c	olive	3.50	.25

No.	Type	Value	Color	Unused	Used
243P	A24	40c	emerald	.25	.25
243Q	A24	50c	orange brn	.25	.25
			Nos. 243A-243Q (13)	7.50	3.35

No. 243Er is from coils.

Post Horn and Lion — A46

Gold Surcharge

1943, Jan. 15 Photo. *Perf. 12½x12*

No.	Type	Value	Color	Unused	Used
244	A46	10c	on 2½c yel	.25	.25
a.			Surcharge omitted	*6,000.*	*6,500.*

Founding of the European Union of Posts and Telegraphs at Vienna, Oct. 19, 1942.

Sea Horse — A47

Triple-crown Tree — A48

Admiral M. A. de Ruyter — A54

Designs: 2c, Swans. 2½c, Tree of Life. 3c, Tree with snake roots. 4c, Man on horseback. 5c, Rearing white horses. 10c, Johan Evertsen. 12½c, Martin Tromp. 15c, Piet Hein. 17½c, Willem van Ghent. 20c, Witte de With. 22½c, Cornelis Evertsen. 25c, Tjerk de Vries. 30c, Cornelis Tromp. 40c, Cornelis Evertsen De Jongste.

Perf. 12x12½, 12½x12

1943-44 Photo. Wmk. 202

No.	Type	Value	Color	Unused	Used
245	A47	1c	black	.25	.25
246	A48	1½c	rose lake	.25	.25
247	A47	2c	dk blue	.25	.25
248	A48	2½c	dk blue grn	.25	.25
249	A47	3c	copper red	.25	.25
250	A48	4c	black brown	.25	.25
251	A47	5c	dull yel grn	.25	.25
			Unwmk.		
252	A54	7½c	henna brn	.25	.25
a.			Thinner numerals and letters ('44)	.25	.25
253	A54	10c	dk green	.25	.25
254	A54	12½c	blue	.25	.25
255	A54	15c	dull lilac	.25	.25
256	A54	17½c	slate ('44)	.25	.25
257	A54	20c	dull brown	.25	.25
258	A54	22½c	org red	.25	.25
259	A54	25c	vio rose ('44)	.35	.55
260	A54	30c	cobalt bl ('44)	.25	.25
			Engr.		
261	A54	40c	bluish blk	.25	.25
			Nos. 245-261 (17)	4.35	4.55

In 1944, 200,000 examples of No. 247 were privately punched with a cross and printed on the back with a number and the words "Prijs 15 Cent toeslag ten bate Ned. Roode Kruis." These were sold at an exhibition, the surtax going to the Red Cross. The Dutch post office tolerated these stamps.

Soldier — A64

S. S. "Nieuw Amsterdam" — A65

Pilot — A66

Cruiser "De Ruyter" — A67

Queen Wilhelmina — A68

Perf. 12, 12½

1944-46 Unwmk. Engr.

No.	Type	Value	Color	Unused	Used
262	A64	1½c	black	.25	.25
263	A65	2½c	yellow grn	.25	.25
264	A66	3c	dull red brn	.25	.25
265	A67	5c	dk blue	.25	.25
266	A68	7½c	vermilion	.25	.25
267	A68	10c	yellow org	.25	.25
268	A68	12½c	ultra	.25	.25
269	A68	15c	dl red brn ('46)	1.40	1.00
270	A68	17½c	gray grn ('46)	1.00	1.00
271	A68	20c	violet	.35	.25
272	A68	22½c	rose red ('46)	.55	.80
273	A68	25c	brn org ('46)	2.00	1.40
274	A68	30c	blue grn	.25	.25
275	A68	40c	dk vio brn ('46)	2.00	1.90
276	A68	50c	red vio ('46)	1.10	1.00
			Nos. 262-276 (15)	10.40	9.35

These stamps were used on board Dutch war and merchant ships until Netherlands' liberation.

Lion and Dragon — A69

1945, July 14 *Perf. 12½x14*

No.	Type	Value	Color	Unused	Used
277	A69	7½c	red orange	.25	.25

Netherlands' liberation or "rising again."

Queen Wilhelmina — A70

1946 Engr. *Perf. 13½x14*

No.	Type	Value	Color	Unused	Used
278	A70	1g	dark blue	1.00	.40
279	A70	2½g	brick red	125.00	7.00
280	A70	5g	dk olive grn	125.00	21.00
281	A70	10g	dk purple	125.00	21.00
			Nos. 278-281 (4)	376.00	49.40
			Set, hinged	200.00	

A71

Perf. 12½x13½

1946-47 Wmk. 202 Photo.

No.	Type	Value	Color	Unused	Used
282	A71	1c	dark red	.25	.25
283	A71	2c	ultra	.25	.25
284	A71	2½c	dp orange ('47)	7.00	1.40
285	A71	4c	olive green	.35	.25
			Nos. 282-285 (4)	7.85	2.15

The 1c was reissued in 1969 on phosphorescent paper in booklet pane No. 345b. The 4c was reissued on fluorescent paper in 1962.

The 2c was issued in coils in 1972. Every fifth stamp has black control number on back.

See Nos. 340-343A, 404-406.

Queen Wilhelmina
A72 A73

1947-48 *Perf. 13½x12½*

No.	Type	Value	Color	Unused	Used
286	A72	5c	olive grn ('48)	.90	.25
287	A72	6c	brown black	.30	.25
288	A72	7½c	dp red brn ('48)	.30	.25
289	A72	10c	brt red vio	.55	.25
290	A72	12½c	scarlet ('48)	.55	.30
291	A72	15c	purple	6.50	.25
292	A72	20c	deep blue	7.00	.25
293	A72	22½c	ol brn ('48)	.55	.55
294	A72	25c	ultra	13.00	.25
295	A72	30c	dp orange	13.00	.25
296	A72	35c	dk blue grn	13.00	.50
297	A72	40c	henna brown	16.00	.50
			Engr.		
298	A73	45c	dp bl ('48)	17.50	10.00
299	A73	50c	brown ('48)	11.50	.25
300	A73	60c	red ('48)	14.50	1.75
			Nos. 286-300 (15)	115.15	15.85
			Set, hinged	60.00	

For surcharge see No. 330.

Type of 1947

1948 Photo.

No.	Type	Value	Color	Unused	Used
301	A72	6c	gray blue	.45	.25

Queen Wilhelmina — A74

Perf. 12½x14

1948, Aug. 30 Engr. Unwmk.

No.	Type	Value	Color	Unused	Used
302	A74	10c	vermilion	.25	.25
303	A74	20c	deep blue	1.50	1.40

Reign of Queen Wilhelmina, 50th anniv.

Queen Juliana — A75

Perf. 14x13

1948, Sept. 7 Photo. Wmk. 202

No.	Type	Value	Color	Unused	Used
304	A75	10c	dark brown	1.10	.25
305	A75	20c	ultra	1.40	.45

Investiture of Queen Juliana, Sept. 6, 1948.

Queen Juliana — A76

1949 *Perf. 13½x12½*

No.	Type	Value	Color	Unused	Used
306	A76	5c	olive green	.55	.25
307	A76	6c	gray blue	.30	.25
308	A76	10c	deep orange	.30	.25
309	A76	12c	orange red	1.50	1.50
310	A76	15c	olive brown	3.25	.25
311	A76	20c	brt blue	3.00	.25
312	A76	25c	orange brn	9.50	.25
313	A76	30c	violet	7.50	.25
314	A76	35c	gray	13.00	.25
315	A76	40c	red violet	27.50	.25
316	A76	45c	red orange	1.40	.80
317	A76	50c	blue green	7.50	.25
318	A76	60c	red brown	11.00	.25
			Nos. 306-318 (13)	86.30	5.05

See No. 325-327. For surcharge see No. B248.

Queen Juliana — A77

1949 Unwmk. Engr. *Perf. 12½x12*

319	A77	1g rose red		3.50	.25
320	A77	2½g black brn		240.00	1.00
321	A77	5g orange brn		375.00	2.50
322	A77	10g dk vio brn		275.00	12.00
		Nos. 319-322 (4)		893.50	15.75
		Set, hinged		400.00	

Two types exist of No. 321.

Post Horns Entwined — A78

Perf. 11½x12½

1949, Oct. 1 Photo. Wmk. 202

323 A78 10c brown red .75 .25
324 A78 20c dull blue 6.75 2.00

75th anniversary of the UPU.

Juliana Type of 1949

1950-51 *Perf. 13½x12½*

325 A76 12c scarlet ('51) 6.00 .60
326 A76 45c violet brn 42.50 .30
327 A76 75c car rose ('51) 85.00 1.25
Nos. 325-327 (3) 133.50 2.15

Janus Dousa — A79

Design: 20c, Jan van Hout.

1950, Oct. 3 *Perf. 11½x13*

328 A79 10c olive brown 3.75 .25
329 A79 20c deep blue 4.25 1.60

375th anniversary of the founding of the University of Leyden.

No. 288 Surcharged with New Value

1950, May *Perf. 13½x12½*

330 A72 6c on 7½c dp red brn 2.00 .25

Miner — A80

Perf. 12x12½

1952, Apr. 16 Engr. Unwmk.

331 A80 10c dark blue 2.50 .25

50th anniversary of the founding of Netherlands' mining and chemical industry.

Telegraph Poles and Train of 1852 — A81

Designs: 6c, Radio towers. 10c, Mail Delivery 1852. 20c, Modern postman.

1952, June 28 *Perf. 13x14*

332 A81 2c gray violet .45 .25
333 A81 6c vermilion .45 .25
334 A81 10c green .45 .25
335 A81 20c gray blue 8.25 2.00
Nos. 332-335 (4) 9.60 2.75

Centenary of Dutch postage stamps and of the telegraph service.

1952, June 28

336 A81 2c chocolate 22.50 15.00
337 A81 6c dk bluish grn 22.50 15.00
338 A81 10c brown carmine 22.50 15.00
339 A81 20c violet blue 22.50 15.00
Nos. 336-339 (4) 90.00 60.00

Nos. 336 to 339 sold for 1.38g, which included the price of admission to the International Postage Stamp Centenary Exhibition, Utrecht.

Numeral Type of 1946-47

Perf. 12½x13½

1953-57 Wmk. 202 Photo.

340 A71 3c dp org brn .25 .25
341 A71 5c orange .25 .25
342 A71 6c gray ('54) .25 .25
343 A71 7c red org .25 .25
343A A71 8c brt lilac ('57) .25 .25
Nos. 340-343A (5) 1.25 1.25

The 5c and 7c perf. on 3 sides, and with watermark vertical, are from booklet panes Nos. 346a-346b. The 5c perf. on 3 sides, with wmk. horiz., is from No. 349a.

In 1972 the 5c was printed on phosphorescent paper.

A82

1953-71 Wmk. 202 *Perf. 13½x12½*

344 A82 10c dk red brn .25 .25
a. Bklt. pane of 6 (1 #344 + 5 #346C)('65) 5.00
345 A82 12c dk Prus grn ('54) .25 .25
a. Bklt. pane of 7 + label (5 #345 + 2 #347)('67) 5.50
b. Bklt. pane, 4 #282 + 8 #345 ('69) 12.50
346 A82 15c dp carmine .25 .25
a. Bklt. pane of 8 (2 #341 in vert. pair + 6 #346)('64) 17.00
b. Bklt. pane of 12 (10 #343 + 2 #346)('64) 12.50
e. Bklt. pane of 8 (2 #341 in horiz. pair + 6 #346)('70) 9.00
346C A82 18c dull bl ('65) .30 .25
d. Bklt. pane of 10 (8 #343A + 2 #346C)('65) 4.50
347 A82 20c dk gray .25 .25
b. Bklt. pane of 5 + label ('66) 4.00
347A A82 24c olive ('63) .30 .25
348 A82 25c deep blue .25 .25
349 A82 30c deep orange .40 .25
a. Bklt. pane of 5 + label (2 #341 + 3 #349)('71) 22.50
350 A82 35c dk ol brn ('54) .95 .25
351 A82 37c aqua ('58) .55 .25
352 A82 40c dk slate .25 .25
353 A82 45c scarlet .40 .25
354 A82 50c dk bl grn .30 .25
355 A82 60c brown bister .30 .25
356 A82 62c dl red lil ('58) 4.50 4.00
357 A82 70c blue ('57) .45 .25
358 A82 75c deep plum .45 .25
359 A82 80c brt vio ('58) .50 .25
360 A82 85c brt bl grn ('56) .70 .25
360A A82 95c org brn ('67) 1.40 .25
Nos. 344-360A (20) 13.00 8.75

Coils of the 12, 15, 20, 25, 30, 40, 45, 50, 60, 70, 75 and 80c were issued in 1972. Black control number on back of every fifth stamp.

Watermark is vertical on some stamps from booklet panes.

Some booklet panes, Nos. 344a, 347b, 349a, etc., have a large selvage the size of four or six stamps, with printed inscription and sometimes illustration.

Phosphorescent paper was introduced in 1967 for the 12, 15, 20 and 45c; in 1969 for the 25c, and in 1971 for the 30, 40, 50, 60, 70, 75 and 80c.

Of the booklet panes, Nos. 345a, 345b, 346d, 346e and 347b were issued on both ordinary and phosphorescent paper, and No. 349a only on phosphorescent paper.

See No. 407. For surcharge see No. 374.

Queen Juliana — A83

Perf. 12½x12

1954-57 Unwmk. Engr.

361 A83 1g vermilion 2.75 .25
362 A83 2½g dk green ('55) 9.00 .25
363 A83 5g black ('55) 3.00 .25
364 A83 10g vio bl ('57) 16.00 1.50
Nos. 361-364 (4) 30.75 2.25

St. Boniface — A84

1954, June 16

365 A84 10c blue 2.40 .25

1200th anniv. of the death of St. Boniface.

Queen Juliana — A84a

Wmk. 202

1954, Dec. 15 Photo. *Perf. 13½*

366 A84a 10c scarlet .80 .25

Issued to publicize the Charter of the Kingdom, adopted December 15, 1954.

See Netherlands Antilles No. 232, Surinam No. 264.

Flaming Sword — A85

1955, May 4 *Perf. 12½x12*

367 A85 10c crimson 1.50 .25

10th anniv. of Netherlands' liberation.

"Rebuilding Europe" — A86

1956, Sept. 15 Unwmk. *Perf. 13x14*

368 A86 10c rose brn & blk *2.50* .25
369 A86 25c brt bl & blk *70.00 1.50*

Europa. Issued to symbolize the cooperation among the six countries comprising the Coal and Steel Community.

Admiral M. A. de Ruyter — A87

30c, Flagship "De Zeven Provincien."

1957, July 2 Engr. *Perf. 12½x12*

370 A87 10c orange .75 .25
371 A87 30c dk blue 4.00 1.75

Adm. M. A. de Ruyter (1607-1676).

"United Europe" — A88

1957, Sept. 16 Photo. *Perf. 13x14*

372 A88 10c blk, gray & ultra *1.00* .25
373 A88 30c dull grn & ultra *9.50 1.25*

United Europe for peace and prosperity.

No. 344 Surcharged in Silver with New Value and Bars

Perf. 13½x12½

1958, May 16 Photo. Wmk. 202

374 A82 12c on 10c 1.10 .25
a. Double surcharge 400.00 400.00
b. Inverted surcharge 400.00 400.00

Common Design Types pictured following the introduction.

Europa Issue, 1958

Common Design Type

Perf. 13x14

1958, Sept. 13 Litho. Unwmk.

Size: 22x33mm

375 CD1 12c org ver & blue *.50* .25
376 CD1 30c blue & red *2.00 .50*

NATO Emblem — A89

1959, Apr. 3 *Perf. 12½x12*

377 A89 12c yel org & blue .25 .25
378 A89 30c red & blue 1.00 .45

10th anniversary of NATO.

Europa Issue, 1959.

Common Design Type

1959, Sept. 19 *Perf. 13x14*

Size: 22x33mm

379 CD2 12c crimson *.90* .25
380 CD2 30c yellow grn *9.00 1.00*

Douglas DC-8 and World Map — A90

Design: 30c, Douglas DC-8 in flight.

1959, Oct. 5 Engr. *Perf. 14x13*

381 A90 12c carmine & ultra .25 .25
382 A90 30c dp blue & dp grn 1.50 .90

40th anniversary of the founding of KLM, Royal Dutch Airlines.

J. C. Schroeder van der Kolk — A91

Design: 30c, Johannes Wier.

Perf. 12½x12

1960, July 18 Unwmk.

383 A91 12c red .70 .25
384 A91 30c dark blue 5.50 1.50

Issued to publicize Mental Health Year and to honor Schroeder van der Kolk and Johannes Wier, pioneers of mental health.

Europa Issue, 1960

Common Design Type

1960, Sept. 19 Photo. *Perf. 12x12½*

Size: 27x21mm

385 CD3 12c car rose & org *.40* .25
386 CD3 30c dk blue & yel *3.25 1.25*

1st anniv. of CEPT. Spokes symbolize 19 founding members of Conference.

Europa Issue, 1961
Common Design Type

1961, Sept. 18 ***Perf. 14x13***
Size: 32½x21½mm

387 CD4 12c golden brown .25 .25
388 CD4 30c Prus blue *.30 .25*

Queen Juliana and Prince Bernhard
A92

Perf. 14x13

1962, Jan. 5 **Unwmk.** **Photo.**

389 A92 12c dk red .25 .25
390 A92 30c dk green 1.25 1.00

Silver wedding anniversary of Queen Juliana and Prince Bernhard.

Telephone Dial — A93

Designs: 12c, Map showing telephone network. 30c, Arch and dial, horiz.

1962, May 22 ***Perf. 13x14, 14x13***

391 A93 4c brown red & blk .25 .25
392 A93 12c brown ol & blk .60 .25
393 A93 30c black, bis & Prus bl 1.90 1.25
Nos. 391-393 (3) 2.75 1.75

Completion of the automation of the Netherlands telephone network.

Europa Issue, 1962
Common Design Type

1962, Sept. 17 ***Perf. 14x13***
Size: 33x22mm

394 CD5 12c lemon, yel & blk *.30 .25*
395 CD5 30c blue, yel & blk *1.10 .50*

Polder with Canals and Windmills — A94

Design: 4c, Cooling towers, Limburg State Coal Mines. 10c, Dredging in Delta.

Perf. 12½x13½

1962-66 **Wmk. 202** **Photo.**

399 A94 4c dk blue ('63) .25 .25
401 A94 6c grn & dk grn .70 .25
403 A94 10c dp claret ('63) .25 .25
a. Booklet pane of 10 ('66) 4.00
Nos. 399-403 (3) 1.20 .75

The 10c was issued in coils in 1972. Every fifth stamp has black control number on back.
See No. 461Ab.

Types of 1946 and 1953

1962-73 **Unwmk.**
Phosphorescent Paper

404 A71 4c olive green .60 .25
405 A71 5c orange ('73) .40 .25
406 A71 8c bright lilac 13.00 12.00
407 A82 12c dk Prus green .75 .40
Nos. 404-407 (4) 14.75 12.90

The 5c is from booklets and has the phosphor on the front only.
Issue dates: 5c, Jan. 12; others Aug. 27.
See Nos. 460d, 461c, 461d and 463a.

Wheat Emblem and Globe — A95

1963, Mar. 21 **Photo.** ***Perf. 14x13***

413 A95 12c dl bl, dk bl & yel .25 .25
414 A95 30c dl car, rose & yel 1.10 .95

FAO "Freedom from Hunger" campaign.

Inscription in Circle — A96

Perf. 13x14

1963, May 7 **Unwmk.** **Litho.**

415 A96 30c brt blue, blk & grn 1.40 1.00

1st Intl. Postal Conf., Paris, cent.

Europa Issue, 1963
Common Design Type

1963, Sept. 16 **Photo.** ***Perf. 14x13***
Size: 33x22mm

416 CD6 12c red brown & yel *.50 .25*
417 CD6 30c Prus green & yel *1.75 .75*

Prince William of Orange Landing at Scheveningen
A97

Designs: 12c, G. K. van Hogendorp, A. F. J. A. Graaf van der Duyn van Maasdam and L. Graaf van Limburg Stirum, Dutch leaders, 1813. 30c, Prince William taking oath of allegiance.

1963, Nov. 18 **Photo.** ***Perf. 12x12½***
Size: 27½x27½mm

418 A97 4c dull bl, blk & brn .25 .25
419 A97 5c dk grn, blk & red .25 .25
420 A97 12c olive & blk .25 .25
421 A97 30c maroon & blk .50 .50
Nos. 418-421 (4) 1.25 1.25

150th anniversary of the founding of the Kingdom of the Netherlands.

Knights' Hall, The Hague — A98

1964, Jan. 9 ***Perf. 14x13***

422 A98 12c olive & blk .25 .25

500th anniversary of the meeting of the States-General (Parliament).

Arms of Groningen University — A99

Design: 30c, Initials "AG" and crown.

1964, June 16 **Engr.** ***Perf. 12½x12***

423 A99 12c slate .25 .25
424 A99 30c yellow brown .25 .25

350th anniv. of the University of Groningen.

Railroad Light Signal
A100

Design: 40c, Electric locomotive.

1964, July 28 **Photo.** ***Perf. 14x13***

425 A100 15c black & brt grn .25 .25
426 A100 40c black & yellow .80 .55

125th anniv. of the Netherlands railroads.

Bible, Chrismon and Dove — A101

1964, Aug. 25 **Unwmk.**

427 A101 15c brown red .25 .25

150th anniversary of the founding of the Netherlands Bible Society.

Europa Issue, 1964
Common Design Type

1964, Sept. 14 **Photo.** ***Perf. 13x14***
Size: 22x33mm

428 CD7 15c dp olive grn *.40 .25*
429 CD7 20c yellow brown *1.40 .35*

Benelux Issue

King Baudouin, Queen Juliana and Grand Duchess Charlotte
A101a

1964, Oct. 12 ***Perf. 14x13***
Size: 33x22mm

430 A101a 15c purple & buff .25 .25

20th anniversary of the signing of the customs union of Belgium, Netherlands and Luxembourg.

Queen Juliana — A102

1964, Dec. 15 **Photo.** ***Perf. 13x14***

431 A102 15c green .25 .25

10th anniversary of the Charter of the Kingdom of the Netherlands.

"Killed in Action" and "Destroyed Town" — A103

Statues: 15c, "Docker" Amsterdam, and "Killed in Action" Waalwijk. 40c, "Destroyed Town" Rotterdam, and "Docker" Amsterdam.

1965, Apr. 6 **Photo.** ***Perf. 12x12½***

432 A103 7c black & dk red .25 .25
433 A103 15c black & dk olive .25 .25
434 A103 40c black & dk red .75 .60
Nos. 432-434 (3) 1.25 1.10

Resistance movement of World War II.

Knight Class IV, Order of William — A104

1965, Apr. 29 ***Perf. 13x14***

435 A104 1g gray .90 .75

150th anniversary of the establishment of the Military Order of William.

ITU Emblem
A105

1965, May 17 **Litho.** ***Perf. 14x13***

436 A105 20c dull bl & tan .25 .25
437 A105 40c tan & dull bl .40 .30

Centenary of the International Telecommunication Union.

Europa Issue, 1965
Common Design Type

1965, Sept. 27 **Photo.**
Size: 33x22mm

438 CD8 18c org brn, dk red & blk *.25 .25*
439 CD8 20c sapphire, brn & blk *.50 .30*

Marines of 1665 and 1965 — A106

1965, Dec. 10 **Engr.** ***Perf. 13x14***

440 A106 18c dk vio bl & car .25 .25

Netherlands Marine Corps, 300th anniv.

Europa Issue, 1966
Common Design Type

1966, Sept. 26 **Photo.** ***Perf. 13x14***
Size: 22x33mm

441 CD9 20c citron *.50 .25*
442 CD9 40c dull blue *1.00 .40*

Assembly Hall, Delft University
A107

1967, Jan. 5 **Litho.** ***Perf. 14x13***

443 A107 20c dl sage grn & sepia .25 .25

125th anniversary of the founding of the Delft University of Technology.

Europa Issue, 1967
Common Design Type

Perf. 13x14

1967, May 2 **Unwmk.** **Photo.**
Ordinary Paper
Size: 22x32½mm

444 CD10 20c dull blue *.75 .25*
445 CD10 45c dull vio brn *1.75 .60*

Wmk. 202

446 CD10 20c dull blue *.75 .40*
447 CD10 45c dull vio brn *1.75 .60*
Nos. 444-447 (4) 5.00 1.85

Nos. 446-447 are on phosphorescent paper.

Stamp of 1852, #1 — A108

1967, May 8 **Engr.** **Unwmk.**

448 A108 20c shown 3.25 2.25
449 A108 25c No. 5 3.25 2.25
450 A108 75c No. 10 3.25 2.25
Nos. 448-450 (3) 9.75 6.75

AMPHILEX 67, Amsterdam, May 11-21. Sold only in complete sets together with a 2.50g admission ticket to Amsterdam Philatelic Exhibition. Issued in sheets of 10 (5x2).

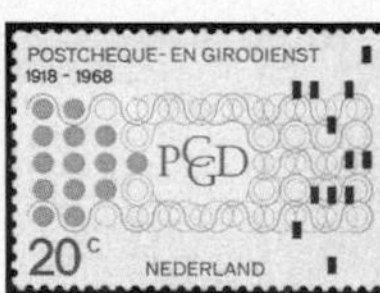

Coins and Punched Card — A109

1968, Jan. 16 Photo. *Perf. 14x13*
451 A109 20c ver, blk & dl yel .25 .25

50th anniversary of the postal checking service.

Luminescence

All commemorative issues from No. 451 to No. 511 are printed on phosphorescent paper except No. 478 which is printed with phosphorescent ink, and Nos. 490-492. Some later issues are tagged.

Europa Issue, 1968

Common Design Type

1968, Apr. 29 Photo. *Perf. 14x13*

Size: 32½x22mm

452 CD11 20c deep blue .50 .25
453 CD11 45c crimson 1.60 *.45*

National Anthem — A110

1968, Aug. 27 Litho. *Perf. 13x14*
454 A110 20c gray, org, car & dk bl .25 .25

400th anniversary of the national anthem "Wilhelmus van Nassouwe."

Fokker F.2, 1919, and Friendship F.29 — A111

Planes: 12c, Wright A, 1909, and Cessna sports plane. 45c, De Havilland DH-9, 1919, and Douglas DC-9.

1968, Oct. 1 Photo. *Perf. 14x13*
455 A111 12c crim, pink & blk .25 .25
456 A111 20c brt grn, bl grn & blk .25 .25
457 A111 45c brt bl, lt grn & blk 1.40 1.10
Nos. 455-457 (3) 1.90 1.60

50th anniv. of the founding in 1919 of Royal Dutch Airlines and the Royal Netherlands Aircraft Factories Fokker, and the 60th anniv. in 1967 of the Royal Netherlands Aeronautical Assoc.

"iao" — A112

Design is made up of 28 minute lines, each reading "1919 internationale arbeids-organisatie 1969".

1969, Feb. 25 Engr. *Perf. 14x13*
458 A112 25c brick red & blk .45 .25
459 A112 45c ultra & blue 1.00 .65

International Labor Organization, 50th anniv.

A113

Queen Juliana — A114

Perf. 13½ horiz. x 12½ on one vert. side

1969-75 Photo.

460 A113 25c orange ver .95 .25
a. Bklt. pane of 4 + 2 labels 12.50
460B A113 25c dull red ('73) .45 .25
c. Booklet pane of 6 (#460B + 5 #461A) 27.50
d. Booklet pane of 12 (5 #405 + 7 #460B) 16.00

Perf. 13x12½

461 A113 30c choc ('72) .25 .25
d. Bklt. pane of 10 (4 #405 + 6 #461 + 2 labels)('74) 6.50
Complete booklet, #461d 6.50
461A A113 35c grnsh bl ('72) .25 .25
b. Bklt. pane of 5 (3 #403, 2 #461A + label)('72) 25.00
c. Bklt. pane of 10 (5 #405 + 5 #461A + 2 labels)('75) 4.50
Complete booklet, #461c 4.50
462 A113 40c car rose ('72) .25 .25
a. Bklt. pane of 5 + label ('73) 7.50
463 A113 45c ultra ('72) .25 .25
a. Bklt. pane of 8 (4 #405 + 4 #463) ('74) 4.00
Complete booklet, #463a 4.00
464 A113 50c lilac ('72) .25 .25
a. Bklt. pane of 4 + 2 labels ('75) 3.00
Complete booklet, #464a 3.00
465 A113 60c slate bl ('72) .30 .25
a. Bklt. pane of 5 + label ('80) 3.00
466 A113 70c bister ('72) .35 .25
467 A113 75c green ('72) .35 .25
468 A113 80c red org ('72) .40 .25
468A A113 90c gray ('75) .50 .25

Perf. 13x14

469 A114 1g yel green .45 .25
470 A114 1.25g maroon .60 .25
471 A114 1.50g yel bis ('71) .75 .25
471A A114 2g dp rose lil ('72) .95 .25
472 A114 2.50g grnsh bl 1.25 .25
473 A114 5g gray ('70) 2.40 .25
474 A114 10g vio bl ('70) 4.75 .85
Nos. 460-474 (19) 15.70 5.35

Both 25c stamps issued only in booklets.

Printings were both ordinary and phosphorescent paper for Nos. 460, 460a, 469, 471-474.

Coil printings were issued later for Nos. 461, 462-472. Black control number on back of every fifth stamp.

Booklet panes have a large selvage the size of 4 or 6 stamps, with printed inscription.

See No. 542.

Europa Issue, 1969

Common Design Type

1969, Apr. 28 Photo. *Perf. 14x13*

Size: 33½x22mm

475 CD12 25c dark blue *.60* .25
476 CD12 45c red *2.00* *.90*

A114a

Möbius strip in Benelux colors.

1969, Sept. 8 Photo. *Perf. 13x14*
477 A114a 25c multicolored .25 .25

25th anniversary of the signing of the customs union of Belgium, Netherlands and Luxembourg.

A115

Photo. & Engr.

1969, Sept. 30 *Perf. 13x14*
478 A115 25c yellow grn & maroon .25 .25

Desiderius Erasmus (1469-1536), scholar.

Queen Juliana and Rising Sun — A116

1969, Dec. 15 Photo. *Perf. 14x13*
479 A116 25c blue & multi .25 .25

15th anniversary of the Charter of the Kingdom of the Netherlands.

Prof. E. M. Meijers A117

1970, Jan. 13 Photo. *Perf. 14x13*
480 A117 25c blue, vio bl & grn .25 .25

Issued to publicize the new Civil Code and to honor Prof. Meijers, who prepared it.

Dutch Pavilion, EXPO '70 — A118

1970, Mar. 10 Photo. *Perf. 14x13*
481 A118 25c multicolored .25 .25

EXPO '70 International Exposition, Osaka, Japan, Mar. 15-Sept. 13.

"V" for Victory — A119

1970, Apr. 21 Photo. *Perf. 13x14*
482 A119 12c red, ultra, brn ol & lt bl .25 .25

25th anniv. of liberation from the Germans.

Europa Issue, 1970

Common Design Type

1970, May 4 Photo. *Perf. 14x13*

Size: 32½x21½mm

483 CD13 25c carmine *.50* .25
484 CD13 45c dk blue *2.00* *.90*

Panels — A120

Globe — A121

1970, June 23 Photo. *Perf. 13x14*
485 A120 25c gray, blk & brt yel grn .30 .25
486 A121 45c ultra, blk & pur .60 .50

#485 publicizes the meeting of the interparliamentary Union; #486 the UN 25th anniv.

Punch Cards — A122

1971, Feb. 16 Photo. *Perf. 14x13*
487 A122 15c dp rose lilac .25 .25

14th national census, 1971.

Europa Issue, 1971

Common Design Type

1971, May 3 Photo. *Perf. 14x13*

Size: 33x22mm

488 CD14 25c lil rose, yel & blk *.50* .25
489 CD14 45c ultra, yel & blk *2.00* *.90*

No. 488 was issued in coils and sheets. In the coils every fifth stamp has a black control number on the back.

Prince Bernhard, Fokker F27, Boeing 747 B — A123

Designs: 15c, Stylized carnation (Prince Bernhard Fund). 20c, Giant Panda (World Wildlife Fund). 15c, 20c horiz.

Photo., Litho. (20c)

1971, June 29 *Perf. 13x14*
490 A123 15c black & yellow .25 .25
491 A123 20c multicolored 4.00 2.50
492 A123 25c multicolored .30 .25
Nos. 490-492,B475 (4) 6.80 5.25

60th birthday of Prince Bernhard. See No. B475.

DELTAPLAN
20 C NEDERLAND
Map of Delta — A124

1972, Feb. 15 Photo. *Perf. 14x13*
493 A124 20c bl, grn, blk & red .25 .25

Publicity for the Delta plan, a project to shorten the coastline and to build roads.

Europa Issue 1972

Common Design Type

1972, May 5 Photo. *Perf. 13x14*

Size: 22x33mm

494 CD15 30c blue & bis *1.25* .25
495 CD15 45c orange & bis *2.00* *.90*

No. 494 was issued in coils and sheets. In the coils every fifth stamp has a black control number on the back.

Thorbecke Quotation A126

1972, June 2 Photo. *Perf. 14x13*
496 A126 30c lt ultra & blk .25 .25

Jan Rudolf Thorbecke (1798-1872), statesman, who said: "There is more to be done in the world than ever before."

Dutch Flag — A127

1972 ***Perf. 13x14***
497 A127 20c blue & multi .30 .25
498 A127 25c blue & multi .70 .25

400th anniversary of the Dutch flag.
Issue dates: 20c, July 4; 25c, Nov. 1.

Woman Hurdler A128

30c, Woman swimmer. 45c, Bicycling.

1972, July 11 ***Perf. 14x13***
499 A128 20c multicolored .25 .25
500 A128 30c crimson & multi .35 .25
501 A128 45c violet & multi .60 .60
Nos. 499-501 (3) 1.20 1.10

20th Olympic Games, Munich, 8/26-9/11.

Red Cross — A129

1972, Aug. 15 Photo. ***Perf. 13x14***
502 A129 5c red .25 .25
Nos. 502,B485-B488 (5) 3.00 2.55

Netherlands Red Cross.

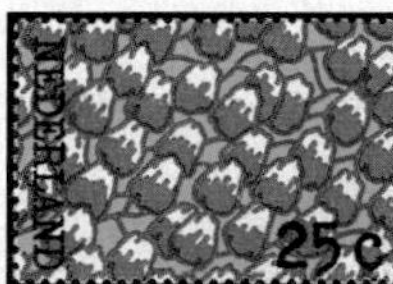

Tulips — A130

1973, Mar. 20 Photo. ***Perf. 14x13***
503 A130 25c rose, brt grn & blk .40 .25

Dutch flower and bulb exports.

Europa Issue 1973
Common Design Type

1973, May 1 Photo. ***Perf. 14x13***
Size: 32½x22mm
504 CD16 35c bright blue *1.10* .25
505 CD16 50c purple *1.75* *.85*

Hockey A132

Woman Gymnast A133

Antenna, Burum A134

Rainbow, Measures A135

Photo. (25c, 35c); Litho. (30c, 50c)
1973, July 31 ***Perf. 13x14, 14x13***
506 A132 25c black & green .30 .25
507 A133 30c gray & multi 1.10 .35
508 A134 35c blue & multi .40 .25
509 A135 50c blue & multi .55 .45
Nos. 506-509 (4) 2.35 1.30

Netherlands Hockey Assoc., 75th anniv. (25c); Rhythmical Gymnastics World Championship, Rotterdam (30c); inauguration of satellite ground station at Burum (35c); cent. of intl. meteorological cooperation (50c).

Queen Juliana, Dutch and House of Orange Colors A136

Engr. & Photo.
1973, Sept. 4 ***Perf. 13x12***
510 A136 40c silver & multi .45 .25

25th anniversary of reign of Queen Juliana.

Chain with Open Link — A137

1973, Oct. 16 Photo. ***Perf. 13x14***
511 A137 40c grn, blk, gold & sil .75 .25

Development Corporation.

Nature and Environment — A138

1974, Feb. 19 Photo. ***Perf. 13x14***
512 A138 Strip of 3 2.10 1.75
a. 25c Bird of prey .70 .35
b. 25c Tree .70 .35
c. 25c Fisherman in boat and frog .70 .35

75th anniv. of the Netherlands Assoc. for the Protection of Birds and of the State Forestry Service.

Soccer Ball — A139

Tennis Ball — A140

Perf. 14x13, 13x14
1974, June 5 **Photo.**
513 A139 25c multicolored .30 .25
514 A140 40c multicolored .45 .25

World Cup Soccer Championship, Munich, June 13-July 7 (25c) and 75th anniversary of the Royal Dutch Lawn Tennis Association (40c).

Cattle — A141

Pierced Crab under Lens — A142

Shipwreck Seen Through Binoculars — A143

1974, July 30 ***Perf. 13x14***
515 A141 25c multicolored 5.50 1.40
516 A142 25c sal pink & multi .50 .25
517 A143 40c dk violet & multi .45 .25
Nos. 515-517 (3) 6.45 1.90

Cent. of the Netherlands Cattle Herdbook Soc. (#515); 25th anniv. of Queen Wilhelmina Fund (for cancer research) (#516); sesquicentennial of Royal Dutch Lifeboat Soc. (#517).

BENELUX Issue

"BENELUX" A143a

1974, Sept. 10 Photo. ***Perf. 14x13***
518 A143a 30c bl grn, dk grn & lt bl .35 .25

30th anniv. of the signing of the customs union of Belgium, Netherlands and Luxembourg.

Council of Europe Emblem A144

NATO Emblem and Sea Gull A145

1974, Sept. 10 ***Perf. 13x14***
519 A144 45c black, bl & yel .50 .25
520 A145 45c dk blue & silver .50 .25

25th anniv. of Council of Europe (No. 519) and of North Atlantic Treaty Organization (No. 520).

Letters and Hands, Papier-maché Sculpture — A146

1974, Oct. 9
521 A146 60c purple & multi .35 .25

Centenary of Universal Postal Union.

People and Map of Dam Square A147

Brain with Window Symbolizing Free Thought A148

Design: No. 523, Portuguese Synagogue and map of Mr. Visser Square. 35c, No. 526, like No. 522.

1975 Photo. ***Perf. 13x14***
522 A147 30c multicolored .35 .25
523 A147 30c multicolored .35 .25
524 A147 35c multicolored .40 .25
525 A148 45c dp blue & multi .50 .25
Nos. 522-525 (4) 1.60 1.00

Coil Stamps
Perf. 13 Horiz.
526 A147 30c multicolored .35 .25
527 A147 35c multicolored .40 .25

700th anniv. of Amsterdam (No. 522); 300th anniv. of the Portuguese Synagogue in Amsterdam (No. 523) and 400th anniv. of the founding of the University of Leyden and the beginning of higher education in the Netherlands (No. 525).

Issue dates: Nos. 522-523, 525-526, Feb. 26; Nos. 524, 527, Apr. 1.

Eye Looking over Barbed Wire — A149

1975, Apr. 29 Photo. ***Perf. 13x14***
528 A149 35c black & carmine .40 .25

Liberation of the Netherlands from Nazi occupation, 30th anniversary.

Company Emblem and "Stad Middelburg" A150

1975, May 21 Photo. ***Perf. 14x13***
529 A150 35c multicolored .40 .25

Zeeland Steamship Company, centenary.

Albert Schweitzer in Boat — A151

1975, May 21
530 A151 50c multicolored .55 .25

Albert Schweitzer (1875-1965), medical missionary.

Symbolic Metric Scale — A152

1975, July 29 Litho. ***Perf. 14x13***
531 A152 50c multicolored .55 .25

Cent. of Intl. Meter Convention, Paris, 1875.

Playing Card with Woman, Man, Pigeons, Pens — A153

1975, July 29 ***Perf. 13x14***

532 A153 35c multicolored .40 .25

International Women's Year 1975.

Fingers Reading Braille — A154

1975, Oct. 7 **Photo.** ***Perf. 13x14***

533 A154 35c multicolored .40 .25

Sesquicentennial of the invention of Braille system of writing for the blind by Louis Braille (1809-1852).

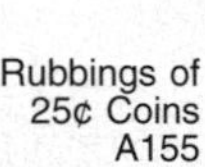

Rubbings of 25¢ Coins A155

1975, Oct. 7 ***Perf. 14x13***

534 A155 50c green, blk & bl .55 .25

To publicize the importance of saving.

Lottery Ticket, 18th Century A156

1976, Feb. 3 **Photo.** ***Perf. 14x13***

535 A156 35c multicolored .40 .25

250th anniversary of National Lottery.

Queen Type of 1969 and

A157

1976-86 **Photo.** ***Perf. 12½x13½***

536 A157 5c gray .25 .25

Booklet Panes

- *a.* (3 #536, 2 #537, 3 #542) 3.00
  - Complete booklet, #536a 3.50
- *b.* (4 #536, 2 #537, 4 #539 + 2 labels) 3.25
  - Complete booklet, #536b 3.50
- *c.* (#536, 2 #537, 5 #542) 3.00
  - Complete booklet, #536c 3.50
- *d.* (4 #536, 7 #539 + label) 3.00
  - Complete booklet, #536d 3.50
- *e.* (2 #536, 2 #540, 4 #541) 3.00
- *f.* (5 #536, 2 #537, 2 #540, 3 #542) + 2 labels 4.00
  - Complete booklet, #536f 4.00
- *g.* (1 #536, 2 #537, 5 #543) ('86) 3.00
  - Complete booklet, #536g 3.50

537 A157 10c ultra .25 .25
538 A157 25c violet .30 .25
539 A157 40c sepia .45 .25
540 A157 45c brt blue .50 .25
541 A157 50c lil rose ('80) .55 .25

- *a.* Bklt. pane, 5 each #537, 541 + 2 labels 2.75
  - Complete booklet, #541a 3.25

542 A113 55c carmine .60 .25
543 A157 55c brt grn ('81) .60 .25
544 A157 60c apple grn ('81) .65 .25
545 A157 65c dk red brn ('86) .70 .25
Nos. 536-545 (10) 4.85 2.50

Compare No. 544 with No. 791. No. 542 also issued in coils with control number on the back of every 5th stamp.

See Nos. 903-905.

Coil Stamps

1976-86 ***Perf. 13½ Vert.***

546 A157 5c slate gray .25 .25
547 A157 10c ultra .25 .25
548 A157 25c violet .30 .25
549 A157 40c sepia ('77) .45 .25
550 A157 45c brt blue .50 .25
551 A157 50c brt rose ('79) .55 .25
552 A157 55c brt grn ('81) .60 .25
553 A157 60c apple grn ('81) .65 .25
554 A157 65c dk red brn ('86) .70 .25
Nos. 546-554 (9) 4.25 2.25

See Nos. 772, 774, 786, 788, 791.

De Ruyter Statue, Flushing A158

1976, Apr. 22 **Photo.** ***Perf. 14x13***

555 A158 55c multicolored .60 .25

Adm. Michiel Adriaenszon de Ruyter (1607-1676), Dutch naval hero, 300th death anniversary.

Van Prinsterer and Page — A159

1976, May 19 **Photo.** ***Perf. 14x13***

556 A159 55c multicolored .60 .25

Guillaume Groen van Prinsterer (1801-1876), statesman and historian.

Women Waving American Flags — A160

Design is from a 220-year old permanent wooden calendar from Ameland Island.

1976, May 25 **Litho.**

557 A160 75c multicolored .80 .25

American Bicentennial.

Marchers A161

1976, June 15 **Photo.** ***Perf. 14x13***

558 A161 40c multicolored .45 .25

Nijmegen 4-day march, 60th anniversary.

A number of stamps issued from 1970 on appear to have parts of the designs misregistered, blurry, or look off-center. These stamps are deliberately designed that way. Most prominent examples are Nos. 559, 582, 602, 656, 711-712, 721, B638-B640, B662-B667.

Runners A162

1976, June 15 **Litho.** **Tagged**

559 A162 55c multicolored .60 .25

Royal Dutch Athletic Soc., 75th anniv.

Printing: One Communicating with Many — A163

1976, Sept. 2 **Photo.** ***Perf. 13x14***

560 A163 45c blue & red .50 .25

Netherlands Printers Organization, 75th anniv.

Sailing Ship and City — A164

Design: 75c, Sea gull over coast.

1976, Sept. 2 **Litho.** ***Perf. 14x13***

Tagged

561 A164 40c bister, red & bl .45 .25
562 A164 75c ultra, yel & red .80 .30

Zuider Zee Project, the conversion of water areas into land.

Radiation of Heat and Light — A165

Ballot and Pencil A166

Perf. 13x14, 14x13

1977, Jan. 25 **Photo.**

563 A165 40c multicolored .45 .25
564 A166 45c black, red & ocher .50 .25

Coil Stamps

Perf. 13 Horiz.

565 A165 40c multicolored .45 .25

Perf. 13 Vert.

566 A166 45c multicolored .50 .25

Publicity for wise use of energy (40c) and forthcoming elections (45c). Nos. 565-566 have black control number on back of every 5th stamp.

For overprint see No. 569.

Spinoza — A167

1977, Feb. 21 **Photo.** ***Perf. 13x14***

567 A167 75c multicolored .80 .25

Baruch Spinoza (1632-1677), philosopher, 300th death anniversary.

Delft Bible Text, Old Type, Electronic "a" — A168

1977, Mar. 8 ***Perf. 14x13***

568 A168 55c ocher & black .60 .25

Delft Bible (Old Testament), oldest book printed in Dutch, 500th anniversary. Printed in sheets of 50 se-tenant with label inscribed with description of stamp design and purpose.

No. 564 Overprinted in Blue

1977, Apr. 15 **Photo.** ***Perf. 14x13***

569 A166 45c multicolored .50 .25

Elections of May 25.

Kaleidoscope of Activities — A169

1977, June 9 **Litho.** ***Perf. 13x14***

570 A169 55c multicolored .60 .25

Netherlands Society for Industry and Commerce, bicentenary.

Man in Wheelchair Looking at Obstacles A170

Engineer's Diagram of Water Currents A171

Teeth, Dentist's Mirror — A172

1977, Sept. 6 **Photo.** ***Perf. 14x13***

571 A170 40c multicolored .45 .25

Litho.

572 A171 45c multicolored .50 .25

Perf. 13x14

573 A172 55c multicolored .60 .25
Nos. 571-573 (3) 1.55 .75

50th anniversaries of AVO (Actio vincit omnia), an organization to help the handicapped (40c), and of Delft Hydraulic Laboratory (45c); centenary of Dentists' Training in the Netherlands (55c).

"Postcode" A173

1978, Mar. 14 Photo. ***Perf. 14x13***
574 A173 40c dk blue & red .45 .25
575 A173 45c red, dk & lt bl .50 .25

Introduction of new postal code.

European Human Rights Treaty — A174

1978, May 2 Photo. ***Perf. 13x14***
576 A174 45c gray, blue & blk .50 .25

European Treaty of Human Rights, 25th anniv.

Europa Issue

Haarlem City Hall — A175

1978, May 2
577 A175 55c multicolored *1.00* .25

Chess Board and Move Diagram A176

Korfball A177

1978, June 1 Photo. ***Perf. 13x14***
578 A176 40c multicolored .45 .25
Litho.
579 A177 45c red & vio bl .50 .25

18th IBM Chess Tournament, Amsterdam, July 12, and 75th anniversary of korfball in the Netherlands.

Man Pointing to his Kidney — A178

Heart, Torch, Gauge and Clouds — A179

1978, Aug. 22 Photo. ***Perf. 13x13½***
580 A178 40c multicolored .45 .25
Perf. 13x14
581 A179 45c multicolored .50 .25

Importance of kidney transplants and drive against hypertension.

Epaulettes, Military Academy — A180

1978, Sept. 12 Photo. ***Perf. 13x14***
582 A180 55c multicolored .60 .25

Royal Military Academy, sesquicentennial. Printed in continuous design in sheets of 100 (10x10).

Verkade as Hamlet A181

1978, Oct. 17 Photo. ***Perf. 14x13***
583 A181 45c multicolored .50 .25

Eduard Rutger Verkade (1878-1961), actor and producer.

Clasped Hands and Arrows — A182

1979, Jan. 23 Engr. ***Perf. 13x14***
584 A182 55c blue .60 .25

Union of Utrecht, 400th anniversary.

European Parliament A183

1979, Feb. 20 Litho. ***Perf. 13½x13***
585 A183 45c blue, blk & red .50 .25

European Parliament, first direct elections, June 7-10.

Queen Juliana A184

1979, Mar. 13 Photo. ***Perf. 13½x14***
586 A184 55c multicolored .60 .25

70th birthday of Queen Juliana.

A185

Europa: 55c, Dutch Stamps and magnifying glass. 75c, Hand on Morse key, and ship at sea.

1979, May 2 Litho. ***Perf. 13x13½***
587 A185 55c multicolored *.50* .25
588 A185 75c multicolored *1.25* *.30*

A186

Map of Netherlands with chamber locations.

1979, June 5 Litho. ***Perf. 13x14***
589 A186 45c multicolored .50 .25

Netherlands Chambers of Commerce and 175th anniversary of Maastricht Chamber.

Soccer A187

1979, Aug. 28 Litho. ***Perf. 14x13***
590 A187 45c multicolored .50 .25

Centenary of soccer in the Netherlands.

Suffragettes — A188

1979, Aug. 28 Photo. ***Perf. 13x14***
591 A188 55c multicolored .60 .25

Voting right for women, 60th anniversary.

Inscribed Tympanum and Architrave A189

1979, Oct. 2 Photo. ***Perf. 14x13***
592 A189 40c multicolored .45 .25

Joost van den Vondel (1587-1679), Dutch poet and dramatist.

"Gay Company," Tile Floor — A190

1979, Oct. 2
593 A190 45c multicolored .50 .25

Jan Steen (1626-1679), Dutch painter.

Alexander de Savornin Lohman (1837-1924) — A191

Politicians: 50c, Pieter Jelles Troelstra (1860-1930), Social Democratic Workmen's Party leader. 60c, Pieter Jacobus Oud (1886-1968), mayor of Rotterdam.

1980, Mar. 4 Photo. ***Perf. 13x13½***
594 A191 45c multicolored .50 .25
595 A191 50c multicolored .55 .25
596 A191 60c multicolored .65 .25
Nos. 594-596 (3) 1.70 .75

British Bomber Dropping Food, Dutch Flag — A192

Anne Frank — A193

Perf. 13x14, 14x13
1980, Apr. 25 Photo.
597 A192 45c multicolored .50 .25
598 A193 60c multicolored .65 .25

35th anniv. of liberation from the Germans.

Queen Beatrix, Palace — A194

1980, Apr. 30 ***Perf. 13x14, 13x13½***
599 A194 60c multicolored .65 .25

Installation of Queen Beatrix.
See No. 608.

Boy and Girl Inspecting Stamp — A195

1980, May 1 ***Perf. 14x13***
600 A195 50c multicolored .55 .25

Youth philately; NVPH Stamp Show, s'Gravenhagen, May 1-3 and JUPOSTEX Stamp Exhibition, Eindhoven, May 23-27. No. 600 printed se-tenant with label.

Bridge Players, "Netherlands" Hand — A196

1980, June 3 Litho. ***Perf. 13x14***
601 A196 50c multicolored .55 .25

6th Bridge Olympiad, Valkenburg, 9/27-10/11.

Truck Transport A197

60c, Two-axle railway hopper truck. 80c, Inland navigation barge.

1980, Aug. 26 Photo. ***Perf. 13½x13***
602 A197 50c shown .55 .25
603 A197 60c multicolored .65 .25
604 A197 80c multicolored .90 .25
Nos. 602-604 (3) 2.10 .75

Queen Wilhelmina, Excerpt from Speech, Netherlands Flag — A198

1980, Sept. 23 Litho. *Perf. 13½x13*
605 A198 60c shown *.50* .25
606 A198 80c Winston Churchill, British flag *1.00* *.30*

Europa.

Abraham Kuyper, University Emblem, "100" — A199

1980, Oct. 14 Litho. *Perf. 13½x13*
607 A199 50c multicolored .55 .25

Free University centennial (founded by Kuyper).

Queen Beatrix Type of 1980
Perf. 13x13½, 13x14
1981, Jan. 6 Photo.
608 A194 65c multicolored .70 .25

Parcel A200

Designs: 55c, Dish antenna and telephone. 65c, Bank books.

1981, May 19 Litho. *Perf. 13½x13*
609 A200 45c multicolored .50 .25
610 A200 55c multicolored .60 .25
611 A200 65c multicolored .70 .25
a. Souvenir sheet of 3, #609-611 2.75 2.75

Centenaries: Parcel Post Service (45c); Public telephone service (55c); National Savings Bank (65c).

Huis ten Bosch (Royal Palace), The Hague A201

1981, June 16 Litho. *Perf. 13½x13*
612 A201 55c multicolored .60 .25

Europa Issue

Carillon A202

1981, Sept. 1 Litho. *Perf. 13½x13*
613 A202 45c shown *.50* .25
614 A202 65c Barrel organ *.65* *.25*

450th Anniv. of Council of State — A203

1981, Oct. 1 Photo. *Perf. 13½x13*
615 A203 65c multi .70 .25

Excavator and Ship's Screw (Exports) A204

1981, Oct. 20 Photo. *Perf. 13½x13*
616 A204 45c shown .50 .25
617 A204 55c Cast iron component, scale .60 .25
618 A204 60c Tomato, lettuce .65 .25
619 A204 65c Egg, cheese .70 .25
Nos. 616-619 (4) 2.45 1.00

Queen Beatrix — A205

Black Vignette

1981-86 Photo. *Perf. 13½x12½*
620 A205 65c tan .70 .25
621 A205 70c lt vio ('82) .75 .25
a. Bklt. pane, 4 #536, 4 #621 4.00
Complete booklet, #621a 4.00
622 A205 75c pale pink ('82) .85 .25
a. Bklt. pane of 4 ('86) 3.25
623 A205 90c lt grn('82) 1.00 .25
624 A205 1g lt vio('82) 1.10 .25
625 A205 1.40g pale grn('82) 1.50 .25
626 A205 2g lem ('82) 2.25 .25
627 A205 3g pale vio ('82) 3.25 .25
628 A205 4g brt yel grn ('82) 4.50 .25
629 A205 5g lt grnsh bl ('82) 5.50 .25
630 A205 6.50g lt lil rose ('82) 7.25 .25
631 A205 7g pale bl ('86) 7.75 .25
Nos. 620-631 (12) 36.40 3.00

Coil Stamps
Perf. 13½ Horiz.
632 A205 70c lt vio ('82) 1.10 .25
633 A205 75c pale pink ('86) .80 .25
634 A205 1g lt vio ('82) 1.10 .25
635 A205 2g lem ('82) 2.25 .25
636 A205 6.50g lt lil rose ('82) 7.25 .25
637 A205 7g pale bl ('86) 7.75 .25
Nos. 632-637 (6) 20.25 1.50

See Nos. 685-699.

University of Amsterdam, 350th Anniv. A206

1982, Jan. 14 Litho. *Perf. 13½x13*
638 A206 65c multi .70 .25

Royal Dutch Skating Assoc. Centenary — A207

1982, Feb. 26 Litho. *Perf. 13x13½*
639 A207 45c multi .50 .25

Bicentenary of US-Netherlands Diplomatic Relations — A208

1982, Apr. 20 Photo. *Perf. 13½x13*
640 A208 50c multi .55 .25
641 A208 65c multi .70 .25

See US No. 2003.

Sandwich Tern and Eider Duck, Waddenzee A209

1982, June 8 Litho. *Perf. 13½x13*
642 A209 50c shown .55 .25
643 A209 70c Barnacle geese .75 .25

Dutch Road Safety Assoc, 50th Anniv. — A210

1982, Aug. 24 Photo. *Perf. 13x14*
644 A210 60c multi .65 .25

Europa 1982 — A211

Fortification Layouts.

1982, Sept. 16 Litho. *Perf. 13x13½*
645 A211 50c Enkhuizen, 1590 *.60* .25
646 A211 70c Coevorden, 1680 *.75* *.25*

Royal Palace, Dam Square, Amsterdam — A212

1982, Oct. 5 Litho. *Perf. 13x13½*
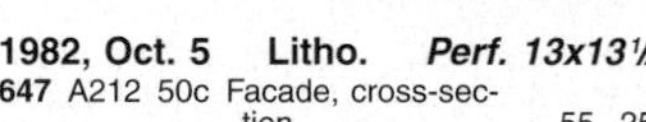
647 A212 50c Facade, cross-section .55 .25
648 A212 60c Aerial view .65 .25

Royal Dutch Touring Club Centenary A213

1983, Mar. 1 Litho. *Perf. 13½x13*
649 A213 70c multi .75 .25

A214

Europa: 50c, Netherlands Newspaper Publishers Assoc., 75th anniv. 70c, Launching of European Telecommunication Satellite Org. ECS F-1 rocket, June 3.

1983, May 17 Litho. *Perf. 13x13½*
650 A214 50c multi *.85* .25
651 A214 70c multi *1.00* *.25*

A215

De Stijl ("The Style") Modern Art Movement, 1917-31: 50c, Composition 1922, by P. Mondriaan. 65c, Maison Particuliere contra Construction, by C. van Eesteren and T. van Doesburg.

1983, June 21 Litho. *Perf. 13x13½*
652 A215 50c multi .55 .25
653 A215 65c multi .70 .25

Symbolic Separation of Church — A216

1983, Oct. 11 Litho. *Perf. 13x13½*
654 A216 70c multi .75 .25

Martin Luther (1483-1546).

2nd European Parliament Election, June 14 — A217

1984, Mar. 13 Litho. *Perf. 13½x13*
655 A217 70c multicolored .75 .25

St. Servatius (d. 384) — A218

1984, May 8 Photo. *Perf. 13x14*
656 A218 60c Statue, 1732 .65 .25

Europa (1959-84) A219

1984, May 22 *Perf. 13½x13*
657 A219 50c blue *.85* *.25*
a. Perf. 14x13 *3.00* *2.50*
658 A219 70c yellow green *1.50* *.30*
a. Perf. 14x13 *3.00* *2.50*

Perf. 14x13 stamps are coils. Every fifth stamp has a control number on the back.

William of Orange (1533-84) A220

1984, July 10 Photo. *Perf. 14x13*
659 A220 70c multicolored .75 .25

World Wildlife Fund — A221

1984, Sept. 18 Litho. *Perf. 14x13*
660 A221 70c Pandas, globe 2.75 .40

11th Intl. Small Business Congress, Amsterdam, Oct. 24-26 — A222

1984, Oct. 23 Litho. *Perf. 13x13½*
661 A222 60c Graph, leaf .65 .25

Guide Dog Fund — A223

Photogravure and Engraved

1985, Jan. 22 ***Perf. 14x13***
662 A223 60c Sunny, first guide dog .65 .25

A224

Tourism A224a

1985, Feb. 26 **Photo.**
663 A224 50c multicolored .55 .25
664 A224a 70c multicolored .75 .25

Cent. of the Tourist office "Geuldal," and 50th anniv. of the Natl. Park "De Hoge Veluwe."

Liberation from German Forces, 40th Anniv. A225

Designs: 50c, Jewish star, mastheads of underground newspapers, resistance fighter. 60c, Allied supply air drop, masthead of The Flying Dutchman, Polish soldier at Arnhem. 65c, Liberation Day in Amsterdam, masthead, first edition of Het Parool (underground newspaper), American cemetery at Margraten. 70c, Dutch women in Japanese prison camp, Japanese occupation currency, building of the Burma Railway.

1985, May 5 **Photo.** ***Perf. 14x13***
665 A225 50c blk, buff & red .55 .25
666 A225 60c blk, buff & brt bl .65 .25
667 A225 65c blk, buff & org .70 .30
668 A225 70c blk, buff & brt grn .75 .25
Nos. 665-668 (4) 2.65 1.05

WWII resistance effort (1940-1945) and liberation of Europe, 1945.

Europa '85 — A226

1985, June 4 **Litho.** ***Perf. 13x13½***
669 A226 50c Piano keyboard *1.00 .25*
670 A226 70c Stylized organ pipes *1.25 .30*

Natl. Museum of Fine Arts, Amsterdam, Cent. — A227

Anniversaries and events: 50c, Museum in 1885, 1985. 60c, Nautical College, Amsterdam, bicent.: Students training. 70c, SAIL-85, Amsterdam: Sailboat rigging.

1985, July 2 **Photo.** ***Perf. 13½x13***
671 A227 50c multicolored .55 .25
672 A227 60c multicolored .65 .25

Perf. 14x13
673 A227 70c multicolored .75 .25
Nos. 671-673 (3) 1.95 .75

Wildlife Conservation A228

Designs: 50c, Porpoise, statistical graph. 70c, Seal, molecular structure models.

1985, Sept. 10 **Litho.** ***Perf. 13½x13***
674 A228 50c multicolored .55 .25
675 A228 70c multicolored .75 .25

Penal Code, Cent. — A229

Amsterdam Datum Ordinance, 300th Anniv. A230

Lithographed, Photogravure (60c)

1986, Jan. 21 ***Perf. 14x13***
676 A229 50c Text .55 .25
677 A230 60c Elevation gauge .65 .25

Sexbierum Windmill Test Station Inauguration A231

1986, Mar. 4 **Litho.** ***Perf. 14x13***
678 A231 70c multicolored .75 .25

Het Loo Palace Gardens, Apeldoorn — A232

1986, May 13 **Litho.** ***Perf. 13x14***
679 A232 50c shown *.75 .25*

Photo.
680 A232 70c Air and soil pollution *1.00 .30*

Europa 1986.

Utrecht Cathedral — A233

60c, German House, c.1350. 70c, Utrecht University charter, horiz.

1986, June 10 **Photo.** ***Perf. 13x14***
681 A233 50c shown .55 .25
682 A233 60c multicolored .65 .25

Perf. 14x13
683 A233 70c multicolored .75 .25
Nos. 681-683 (3) 1.95 .75

Cathedral restoration, 1986. Heemschut Conservation. Soc., 75th anniv. Utrecht University, 350th anniv.

Willem Drees (1886-1988), Statesman — A234

1986, July 1 **Litho.** ***Perf. 13x13½***
684 A234 55c multicolored .60 .25

Queen Type of 1981

1986-90 **Photo.** ***Perf. 13½x12½***
685 A205 1.20g citron & blk 1.40 .25
686 A205 1.50g lt rose vio & blk 1.60 .25
688 A205 2.50g tan & blk 2.75 .25
694 A205 7.50g lt grn & blk 8.25 1.00
Nos. 685-694 (4) 14.00 1.75

Coil Stamps

Perf. 13½ Horiz.
697 A205 1.50g lt rose vio & blk 1.60 .25
699 A205 2.50g tan & blk 2.75 .25

Issue dates: Nos. 685, 688, 699, 9/23. Nos. 686, 697, 8/19. 7.50g, 5/29/90.

Billiards A235

Perf. 14x13, 13x14

1986, Sept. 9 **Photo.**
705 A235 75c shown .80 .35
706 A235 75c Checkers, vert. .80 .35

Royal Dutch Billiards Assoc., Checkers Association, 75th annivs.

Delta Project Completion A236

65c, Storm-surge barrier. 75c, Barrier withstanding flood.

1986, Oct. 7 **Photo.** ***Perf. 14x13***
708 A236 65c multicolored .70 .25
709 A236 75c multicolored .80 .25

Princess Juliana and Prince Bernhard, 50th Wedding Anniv. — A237

1987, Jan. 6 **Photo.** ***Perf. 13x14***
710 A237 75c multicolored .80 .25

Intl. Year of Shelter for the Homeless A238

Designs: 75c, Salvation Army, cent.

1987, Feb. 10 **Photo.** ***Perf. 14x13***
711 A238 65c multicolored .70 .25
712 A238 75c multicolored .80 .25

Dutch Literature A239

Authors: 55c, Eduard Douwes Dekker (1820-1887) and De Harmonie Club, Batavia. 75c, Constantijn Huygens (1596-1687) and Scheveningseweg, The Hague.

1987, Mar. 10 **Litho.** ***Perf. 13½x13***
713 A239 55c multicolored .60 .25
714 A239 75c multicolored .80 .25

Europa 1987 — A240

Modern architecture: 55c, Scheveningen Dance Theater, designed by Rem Koolhaas. 75c, Montessori School, Amsterdam, designed by Herman Hertzberger.

1987, May 12 **Litho.** ***Perf. 14x13***
715 A240 55c multicolored *1.00 .30*
716 A240 75c multicolored *1.25 .35*

Produce Auction at Broeck op Langedijk, 1887 — A241

Designs: 65c, Field in Groningen Province, signatures of society founders. 75c, Auction, bidding, price indicator, 1987.

1987, June 16 **Photo.** ***Perf. 14x13***
717 A241 55c shown .60 .25
718 A241 65c multicolored .70 .25
719 A241 75c multicolored .80 .25
Nos. 717-719 (3) 2.10 .75

Sale of produce by auction in the Netherlands, cent., and Groningen Agricultural Society, 150th anniv. (No. 718).

Union of the Netherlands Municipalities, 75th Anniv. — A242

1987, Oct. 6 **Litho.** ***Perf. 13x14***
720 A242 75c multicolored .80 .25

Noordeinde Palace, The Hague A243

1987, Oct. 27 **Photo.** ***Perf. 14x13***
721 A243 65c multicolored .70 .25

A244

Booklet Stamps

Perf. 13½x13 on 3 Sides

1987, Dec. 1 **Photo.**
722 A244 50c dk ultra, emer & dk red .55 .25
723 A244 50c dk red, dk ultra & yel .45 .25
724 A244 50c dk ultra, yel & dk red .45 .25
725 A244 50c dk red, emer & yel .45 .25
726 A244 50c emer, dk red & dk ultra .45 .25
a. Bklt. pane, 4 each #722-726 12.00
Complete booklet #726a 16.00
Nos. 722-726 (5) 2.35 1.25

Netherlands Cancer Institute, 75th Anniv. A246

1988, Apr. 19 Litho. ***Perf. 13½x13***

728 A246 75c multicolored .80 .25

Europa 1988 — A247

Modern transportation meeting ecological requirements: 55c, Cyclist, rural scenery, chemical formulas, vert. 75c, Cyclists seen through car-door mirror.

1988, May 17 Litho. ***Perf. 13x13½***

729 A247 55c multicolored *1.25* .25

Perf. 13½x13

730 A247 75c multicolored *1.50* .25

Coronation of William III and Mary Stuart, King and Queen of England, 300th Anniv. (in 1989) — A248

Designs: 65c, Prism splitting light as discovered by Sir Isaac Newton, planet Saturn as observed by Christian Huygens, and pendulum clock, c. 1688. 75c, William of Orange (1650-1702) and Mary II (1662-1694).

1988, June 14 ***Perf. 14x13***

731 A248 65c multicolored .70 .25

732 A248 75c multicolored .80 .25

Arrival of Dutch William in England, 300th anniv.

Modern Art — A249

Paintings by artists belonging to Cobra: 55c, *Cobra Cat,* 1950, by Appel. 65c, *Stag Beetle,* 1948, by Corneille. 75c, *Fallen Horse,* 1950, by Constant.

1988, July 5 Litho. ***Perf. 13½x13***

733 A249 55c multicolored .60 .35

734 A249 65c multicolored .70 .35

735 A249 75c multicolored .80 .25

Nos. 733-735 (3) 2.10 .95

Each stamp printed se-tenant with label picturing the featured artist's signature.

Cobra, an intl. organization established in 1948 by expressionist artists from Copenhagen, Brussels and Amsterdam.

Australia Bicentennial — A250

1988, Aug. 30 Photo. ***Perf. 13x14***

736 A250 75c multicolored .80 .25

A251

A252

1988, Sept. 27 Litho. ***Perf. 13x13½***

737 A251 75c dk green & green .80 .25

738 A252 75c bright violet .80 .25

Erasmus University, Rotterdam, 75th anniv. (#737), Amsterdam Concertgebouw & Orchestra, cent. (#738).

Holiday Greetings — A253

1988, Dec. 1 Photo. ***Perf. 13½x12½***

739 A253 50c multicolored .55 .25

"Holland," etc.

Stamps inscribed "Holland," "Stadspost," etc., are private issues. In some cases overprints or surcharges on Netherlands stamps may be created.

Privatization of the Netherlands Postal Service — A254

Mailbox, sorting machine, mailbag, mailman, telephone key pad, fiber optics cable, microwave transmitter & telephone handset.

Litho. & Engr.

1989, Jan. 3 ***Perf. 13x13½***

740 A254 75c multicolored .80 .25

Dutch Trade Unions — A255

1989, Feb. 7 Litho. ***Perf. 13x13½***

741 A255 55c shown .60 .25

Photo.

Perf. 13x14

742 A255 75c Hands, mouths .80 .25

NATO, 40th Anniv. A256

1989, Mar. 14 Litho. ***Perf. 14x13***

743 A256 75c multicolored .80 .25

Europa 1989 — A257

Children's games (string telephone): 55c, Boy. 75c Girl.

1989, May 9 Litho. ***Perf. 13½x13***

744 A257 55c multicolored 1.00 *.25*

745 A257 75c multicolored 1.25 *.30*

Dutch Railways, 150th Anniv. A258

1989, June 20 Litho. ***Perf. 13½x13***

746 A258 55c Rails .60 .25

747 A258 65c Trains .70 .25

Perf. 14x13

748 A258 75c Passengers .80 .25

Nos. 746-748 (3) 2.10 .75

Royal Dutch Soccer Assoc., Cent. — A259

1989, Sept. 5 Photo. ***Perf. 13x14***

749 A259 75c multicolored .80 .25

Treaty of London, 150th Anniv. — A260

Map of Limburg Provinces

1989, Oct. 2 Litho. ***Perf. 13x14***

750 A260 75c multicolored .80 .25

See Belgium No. 1327.

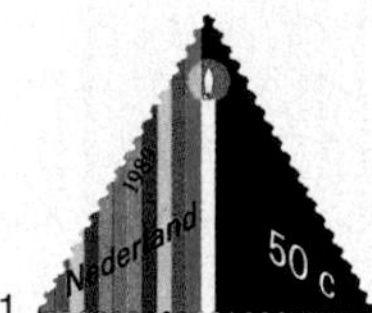

A261

Perf. 13x13x13½

1989, Nov. 30 Photo.

751 A261 50c multicolored .55 .25

Sold only in sheets of 20.

Anniversaries A262

Designs: 65c, Leiden coat of arms (tulip), and layout of the Hortus Botanicus in 1601. 75c, Assessing work conditions (clock, sky, wooden floor), horiz.

1990, Feb. 6 Litho. ***Perf. 13x13½***

752 A262 65c multicolored .70 .25

Perf. 13½x13

753 A262 75c multicolored .80 .25

Hortus Botanicus, Leiden, 400th anniv. (65c); Labor Inspectorate, cent. (75c).

Vincent van Gogh (1853-1890) — A263

Details of works by van Gogh: 55c, *Self-portrait,* pencil sketch, 1886-87. 75c, *The Green Vineyard,* painting, 1888.

1990, Mar. 6 ***Perf. 13x13½***

754 A263 55c multicolored .60 .25

755 A263 75c multicolored .80 .25

Rotterdam Reconstruction — A264

1990, May 8 Litho. ***Perf. 13½x13***

756 A264 55c shown .60 .25

757 A264 65c Diagram .70 .25

758 A264 75c Modern bldgs. .80 .25

Nos. 756-758 (3) 2.10 .75

Europa A264a

Post offices.

1990, June 12

759 A264a 55c Veere *1.25* *.30*

760 A264a 75c Groningen *1.40* *.35*

Dutch East India Co. Ships — A265

Sail '90 — A266

1990, July 3 ***Perf. 13x13½***

761 A265 65c multicolored .70 .25

762 A266 75c multicolored .80 .25

Queens of the House of Orange A267

1990, Sept. 5 Litho. ***Perf. 13½***

763 A267 150c multicolored 1.60 .50

Century of rule by Queens Emma, Wilhelmina, Juliana and Beatrix.

A268

1990, Oct. 9 Photo. *Perf. 13x14*

764 A268 65c multicolored .70 .25

Natl. emergency phone number.

A269

1990, Nov. 29 Photo. *Perf. 14*

765 A269 50c multicolored .55 .25
a. Tete-beche pair 1.10 .40

All pairs in sheet are tete-beche.

Threats to the Environment A270

1991, Jan. 30 Litho. *Perf. 13½x13*

766 A270 55c Air pollution .60 .25
767 A270 65c Water pollution .70 .25
768 A270 75c Soil pollution .80 .25
Nos. 766-768 (3) 2.10 .75

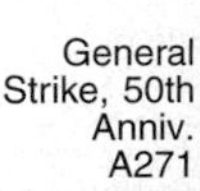

General Strike, 50th Anniv. A271

1991, Feb. 25 Photo. *Perf. 14x13*

769 A271 75c multicolored .80 .25

Queen Beatrix and Prince Claus, 25th Wedding Anniv. A272

1991, Mar. 11 Litho. *Perf. 13½x13*

770 A272 75c shown .80 .25
771 A272 75c Riding horses .80 .25
a. Pair, #770-771 1.60 1.60

Numeral Type of 1976 and

Queen Beatrix — A273

Perf. 12½x13½, 13½x12½

1991-94 Photo.

772 A157 70c gray violet .75 .25
a. Booklet pane, 5 each #537, 772 5.00
773 A273 75c green .80 .25
a. Bklt. pane of 4 + 2 labels 3.50
Complete booklet, #773a 6.00
774 A157 80c red lilac .90 .25
774A A273 80c red brown .90 .25
b. Booklet pane of 5 + label 4.75
Complete booklet, #774Ab 4.75
775 A273 90c blue 1.00 .25
776 A273 1g purple 1.10 .25
777 A273 1.30g gray blue 1.40 .30
778 A273 1.40g gray olive 1.50 .30
779 A273 1.60g magenta 1.75 .30
780 A273 2g yel brown 2.75 .35
781 A273 2.50g red lilac 3.25 .60
782 A273 3g blue 5.50 .40
783 A273 5g brown red 4.00 .75

Perf. 14x13, Syncopated

784 A273 7.50g purple 8.25 2.00
785 A273 10g green 11.00 1.25
Nos. 772-785 (15) 44.85 7.75

Coil Stamps

Perf. 13½ Vert. (A157), Horiz. (A273)

786 A157 70c gray violet .75 .25
787 A273 75c green .80 .80
788 A157 80c red lilac .90 .25
789 A273 80c red brown .90 .25
790 A273 1.60g magenta 1.75 .30
Nos. 786-790 (5) 5.10 1.85

Booklet Stamp

Perf. 12½x13½

791 A157 60c lemon .65 .25
a. Bklt. pane, 2 #791, 4 #772 4.50

Issued: 75c, 3/14/91; 60c, 70c, #774, 1.60g, 6/25/91; #774A, 789, 1.30g, 1.40g, 9/3/91; 1g, 2g, 3g, 5g, 11/11/92; 90c, 2/2/93; 2.50g, 9/7/93; 10g, 11/29/93; 7.50g, 11/28/94.

See #902, 906-913, 1091-1104, 1216, 1218-1221, 1223.

A274

A275

Designs: 55c, Gerard Philips, carbon filament experiments, 1890. 65c, Electrical wiring. 75c, Laser video disk experiment.

Perf. 13x14, 14x13

1991, May 15 Photo.

792 A274 55c multicolored .60 .25
793 A275 65c multicolored .70 .25
794 A274 75c multicolored .80 .25
Nos. 792-794 (3) 2.10 .75

Philips Electronics, cent. (Nos. 792, 794). Netherlands Normalization Institute, 75th anniv. (No. 793).

A276

Europa: 75c, Ladders to another world.

1991, June 11 Litho. *Perf. 13x13½*

795 A276 55c multicolored *1.00* .30
796 A276 75c multicolored *1.25* .35

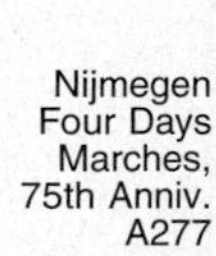

Nijmegen Four Days Marches, 75th Anniv. A277

1991, July 9 Photo. *Perf. 14x13*

797 A277 80c multicolored .90 .25

Dutch Nobel Prize Winners A278

Designs: 60c, Jacobus H. Van't Hoff, chemistry, 1901. 70c, Pieter Zeeman, physics, 1902. 80c, Tobias M. C. Asser, peace, 1911.

1991, Sept. 3 *Perf. 14x13*

798 A278 60c multicolored .65 .25
799 A278 70c multicolored .75 .25
800 A278 80c multicolored .90 .25
Nos. 798-800 (3) 2.30 .75

Public Libraries, Cent. — A279

1991, Oct. 1 Litho. *Perf. 13½x13*

801 A279 70c Children reading .75 .25
802 A279 80c Books .90 .25

A280

1991, Nov. 28 Photo. *Perf. 14*

803 A280 55c multicolored .60 .25

Delft University of Technology, Sesquicent. A281

New Civil Code — A282

1992, Jan. 7 Litho. *Perf. 13½x13*

804 A281 60c multicolored .65 .25
805 A282 80c multicolored .90 .25

Souvenir Sheet

A283

1992 Olympics, Albertville and Barcelona: No. 806a, Volleyball, rowing. b, Shotput, rowing. c, Speedskating, rowing. d, Field hockey.

1992, Feb. 4 Litho. *Perf. 13x14*

806 A283 80c Sheet of 4, #a.-d. 3.75 3.75

Tulips — A284

Map — A284a

1992, Feb. 25 Litho. *Perf. 13x12½*

807 A284 70c multicolored .75 .25

Photo.

Perf. 13x14

808 A284a 80c multicolored .90 .25

Expo '92, Seville.

Discovery of New Zealand and Tasmania by Abel Tasman, 350th Anniv. A285

1992, Mar. 12 Photo. *Perf. 14x13*

809 A285 70c multicolored .75 .25

A286 A287

1992, Apr. 28 Litho. *Perf. 13x13½*

810 A286 60c multicolored .65 .25
811 A287 80c multicolored .90 .25

Royal Assoc. of Netherlands Architects, 150th Anniv. (#810). Opening of Building for Lower House of States General (#811).

Discovery of America, 500th Anniv. A288

Perf. 13½x13, 13x13½

1992, May 12 Litho.

812 A288 60c Globe, Columbus *1.25* .35
813 A288 80c Sailing ship, vert. *1.75* .35

Europa. On normally centered stamps the white border appears at the left side of No. 813.

Royal Netherlands Numismatics Society, Cent. — A289

1992, May 19 Photo. *Perf. 13x14*

814 A289 70c multicolored .75 .25

Netherlands Pediatrics Society, Cent. — A290

1992, June 16 Litho. *Perf. 13½x13*

815 A290 80c multicolored .90 .25

First Deportation Train from Westerbork Concentration Camp, 50th Anniv. — A291

1992, Aug. 25 *Perf. 13x13½*

816 A291 70c multicolored .75 .25

Single European Market A292

1992, Oct. 6 *Perf. 13½x13*

817 A292 80c multicolored .90 .25

Queen Beatrix, 12½Years Since Investiture — A293

1992, Oct. 30 *Perf. 13x13½*

818 A293 80c multicolored 1.00 .25

Christmas Rose — A294

1992, Nov. 30 **Photo.** *Perf. 14*

819 55c Red flower .60 .25
820 55c Silver flower .60 .25
a. A294 Pair, #819-820 1.25 .25

Netherlands Cycle and Motor Industry Assoc. (RAI), Cent. — A295

Designs: 70c, Couple riding bicycle. 80c, Early automobile.

1993, Jan. 5 **Litho.** *Perf. 13½x13*

821 A295 70c multicolored .80 .25
822 A295 80c black & yellow .90 .25

A296

Greeting Stamps — A296a

Geometric shapes.

1993, Feb. 2 **Photo.** *Perf. 14x13½*

823 A296 70c multi .80 .25
824 A296a 70c multi, diff. .80 .25
a. Tete-beche pair, #823-824 1.60 .25

Mouth-to-mouth Resuscitation A297

Royal Horse Artillery Lead Driver, Horses A298

Leaf, Insect Pests — A299

1993, Feb. 16 **Litho.** *Perf. 13x13½*

825 A297 70c multicolored .80 .25
826 A298 80c multicolored .90 .25
827 A299 80c multicolored .90 .25
Nos. 825-827 (3) 2.60 .75

Royal Netherlands First Aid Assoc., cent. (#825). Royal Horse Artillery, bicent. (#826). University of Agriculture, 75th anniv. (#827).

On No. 826, normally centered stamps show design extending to top and right sides only.

Royal Dutch Notaries' Assoc., 150th Anniv. — A300

Litho. & Engr.

1993, Mar. 2 *Perf. 14x13*

828 80c Top half of emblem .90 .25
829 80c Bottom half of emblem .90 .25
a. A300 Pair, #828-829 1.80 .35

No. 829a has continuous design.

Butterflies A301

Designs: 70c, Pearl-bordered fritillary (Zilvervlek). 80c, Large tortoiseshell (Grote vos). 90c, Large white (Koolwitje). 160c, Polyommatus icarus.

1993, Mar. 23 **Photo.**

830 A301 70c black & multi .80 .25
831 A301 80c yellow & multi .90 .25
832 A301 90c green & multi 1.00 .25
Nos. 830-832 (3) 2.70 .75

Souvenir Sheet

833 A301 160c red & multi 1.75 1.75

On normally centered stamps the white border appears at the right side.

Radio Orange — A302

Designs: No. 834, Woman broadcasting. No. 835, Man listening.

1993, May 5 **Photo.** *Perf. 14x13*

834 80c orange red & purple .95 .25
835 80c purple & orange red .95 .25
a. A302 Pair, #834-835 1.90 .40

European Youth Olympic Days — A303

Symbols of Olympic sports.

1993, June 1 *Perf. 13x14*

836 A303 70c blue & multi .85 .25
837 A303 80c yellow & multi .95 .25

Europa A304

Contemporary sculpture by: 70c, Wessel Couzijn. 80c, Per Kirkeby. 160c, Naum Gabo, vert.

Perf. 13½x13, 13x13½

1993, July 6 **Litho.**

838 A304 70c blk, blue & grn 1.00 *.50*
839 A304 80c black, red & yel 1.25 *.30*
840 A304 160c black, blue & pur 1.40 *.90*
Nos. 838-840 (3) 3.65 1.70

Dutch Nobel Prize Winners — A305

Designs: 70c, J.D. van der Waals, physics, 1910. 80c, Willem Einthoven, medicine, 1924. 90c, Christiaan Eijkman, medicine, 1929.

1993, Sept. 7 **Litho.** *Perf. 13x13½*

841 A305 70c multicolored .85 .25
842 A305 80c multicolored .95 .25
843 A305 90c multicolored 1.10 .25
Nos. 841-843 (3) 2.90 .75

Letter Writing Day — A306

1993, Sept. 14 **Photo.** *Perf. 14x13*

844 80c Pencils, pen .95 .25
845 80c Envelope, contents .95 .25
a. A306 Pair, #844-845 1.90 .50

Stamp Day — A307

1993, Oct. 8 **Litho.** *Perf. 13½x13*

846 A307 70c shown .80 .25
847 A307 80c Dove with envelope .95 .25

December Stamps — A308

Clock hand pointing to "12:" and: No. 848, Star, candle, Christmas tree. No. 849, Fireworks.

1993, Nov. 29 **Photo.** *Perf. 12*

848 A308 55c blue & multi .60 .25
849 A308 55c red & multi .60 .25
a. Pair, #848-849 1.25 .25

Issued in sheets of 20, 10 each #848-849 + label. Each stamp contains perforations placed within the design to resemble snowflakes.

Piet Mondrian (1872-1944), Painter A309

Details from paintings: 70c, The Red Mill. 80c, Rhomboid with Yellow Lines. 90c, Broadway Boogie Woogie.

1994, Feb. 1 **Litho.** *Perf. 13½x13*

850 A309 70c multicolored .80 .25
851 A309 80c multicolored .95 .25
852 A309 90c multicolored 1.10 .25
Nos. 850-852 (3) 2.85 .75

Wild Flowers A310

1994, Mar. 15 **Photo.** *Perf. 14½x13*

853 A310 70c Downy rose .80 .25
854 A310 80c Daisy .95 .25
855 A310 90c Woods forget-me-not 1.10 .25
Nos. 853-855 (3) 2.85 .75

Souvenir Sheet

856 A310 160c Fire lily croceum 3.00 2.25

Dutch Aviation, 75th Anniv. A311

1994, Apr. 6 **Litho.** *Perf. 13½x13*

857 A311 80c KLM .95 .25
858 A311 80c Fokker .95 .25
859 A311 80c NLR .95 .25
Nos. 857-859 (3) 2.85 .75

Planetarium, Designed by Eise Eisinga — A312

Design: 90c, Television image of moon landing, footprint on moon.

1994, May 5 **Photo.** *Perf. 13x14*

860 A312 80c multicolored .90 .25
861 A312 90c multicolored 1.00 .25

First manned moon landing, 25th anniv. (#861).

1994 World Cup Soccer Championships, U.S. — A313

1994, June 1

862 A313 80c multicolored .90 .25

No. 862 printed with se-tenant label.

Stock Exchange Floor, Initials KPN A314

1994, June 13 **Litho.** *Perf. 13½*

863 A314 80c multicolored .90 .25

Offering of shares in Royal PTT Netherlands NV (KPN).

Bicycle, Car, Road Sign — A315

80c, Silhouettes of horses, riders, carriage.

1994, June 14 Photo. *Perf. 14x13*

864 A315 70c multicolored	.85	.25

Litho.

Perf. 13½x13

865 A315 80c multicolored	.90	.25

First road signs placed by Dutch motoring assoc. (ANWB), cent. (#864). World Equestrian Games, The Hague (#865).

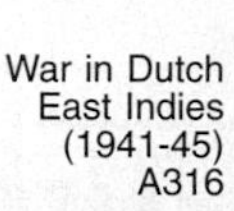

War in Dutch East Indies (1941-45) A316

Operation Market Garden (1944) — A316a

Perf. 14x13, 13x14

1994, Aug. 15 Photo.

866 A316 80c multicolored	1.00	.25
867 A316a 90c multicolored	1.10	.30

Lighthouses A317

Designs: 70c, Brandaris, Terschelling Island. 80c, Ameland Island, vert. 90c, Vlieland Island, vert.

Perf. 13½x13, 13x13½

1994, Sept. 13 Litho.

868 A317 70c multicolored	.90	.25
869 A317 80c multicolored	1.00	.25
870 A317 90c multicolored	1.10	.30
Nos. 868-870 (3)	3.00	.80

December Stamps — A318

1994, Nov. 28 Photo. *Perf. 13½*

871 A318 55c Snowflake, tree	.65	.25
872 A318 55c Candle, star	.65	.25
a. Pair, #871-872	1.30	.30
b. Min. sheet, 10 #872a + label	13.00	

One stamp in #872a is rotated 90 degrees to the other stamp.

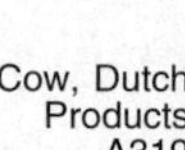

Cow, Dutch Products A319

1995, Jan 2 Photo. *Perf. 14x13½*

873 A319 100c multicolored	1.25	.30

Hendrik Nicolaas Werkman (1882-1945), Printer — A320

Mesdag Museum Restoration A321

Mauritius No. 2 — A322

1995, Jan. 17 Litho. *Perf. 14x13½*

874 A320 80c multicolored	1.00	.25
875 A321 80c multicolored	1.00	.25

Litho. & Engr.

Perf. 13½x14

876 A322 80c multicolored	1.00	.25
Nos. 874-876 (3)	3.00	.75

Acquisition of Mauritius No. 2 by Netherlands PTT Museum (#876).

Motion Pictures, Cent. — A323

70c, Joris Iven, documentary film maker. 80c, Scene from film, "Turkish Delight," 1972.

1995, Feb. 28 Photo. *Perf. 14x13*

877 A323 70c multicolored	.90	.25
878 A323 80c multicolored	1.00	.25

Mahler Festival A324

Design: 80c, Gustav Mahler, (1860-1911), composer, 7th Symphony score.

1995, Mar. 21 Litho. *Perf. 13½x13*

879 A324 80c blue & black	1.00	.25

Institute of Registered Accountants, Cent. — A325

Assoc. of Building Contractors, Cent. — A326

1995, Mar. 28

880 A325 80c multicolored	1.00	.25
881 A326 80c multicolored	1.00	.25

50th Anniversaries A327

Designs: No. 882, End of World War II, "45, 95" No. 883, Liberation of the Netherlands, "40, 45." No. 884, Founding of the UN, "50."

1995, May 3 Litho. *Perf. 13x13½*

882 A327 80c multicolored	1.00	.25
883 A327 80c multicolored	1.00	.25
884 A327 80c multicolored	1.00	.25
Nos. 882-884 (3)	3.00	.75

Signs of the Zodiac, Birthday Cake — A328

1995, May 22 Photo. *Perf. 14x13½*

885 A328 70c multicolored	1.10	.25

18th World Boy Scout Jamboree — A329

Sail Amsterdam '95 — A330

Perf. 13x13½, 13½x13

1995, June 6 Litho.

886 A329 70c multicolored	.90	.25
887 A330 80c multicolored	1.00	.25

Birds of Prey A330a

Perf. 13x14, 14x13

1995, Sept. 5 Photo.

888 A330a 70c Kestrel, vert.	.90	.25
889 A330a 80c Hen harrier	1.00	.25
890 A330a 100c Red kite	1.25	.25
Nos. 888-890 (3)	3.15	.75

Souvenir Sheet

891 A330a 160c Honey buzzard	2.00	2.00

Nobel Prize Winners A331

No. 892, F. Zernike, physics, 1953. No. 893, P.J.W. Debye, chemistry, 1936. No. 894, J. Tinbergen, economics, 1969.

1995, Sept. 26 Litho. *Perf. 13½x13*

892 A331 80c green & multi	1.00	.25
893 A331 80c blue & multi	1.00	.25
894 A331 80c red & multi	1.00	.25
Nos. 892-894 (3)	3.00	.75

Dutch Cabaret, Cent. A332

Designs: 70c, Eduard Jacobs (1868-1914), Jean-Louis Pisuisse (1880-1927). 80c, Wim Kan (1911-83), Freek de Jonge (b. 1944).

1995, Oct. 17 Litho. *Perf. 13½x14*

895 A332 70c multicolored	.90	.25
896 A332 80c multicolored	1.00	.25

Numeral Type of 1976 and Queen Type of 1991

1995-2001 Photo. *Perf. 13½x12½*

902 A273 1.50g green	1.50	.40

Self-Adhesive (Nos. 903-911)

Booklet Stamps

Die Cut Perf. 14¼

903 A157 5c gray	.25	.25
a. Double-sided pane of 10	.45	
904 A157 10c ultramarine	.25	.25
a. Double-sided pane of 10	.85	
905 A157 25c violet	.30	.25
a. Double sided pane of 10	3.00	
906 A273 85c blue green	.95	.25
a. Booklet pane of 5	5.00	
907 A273 1g purple	1.10	.25
a. Booklet pane of 5	5.50	
908 A273 1.10g blue	1.25	.25
a. Booklet pane of 5	6.25	
909 A273 1.45g green	1.60	.30
a. Booklet pane of 5	8.00	
910 A273 2.50g red lilac	2.75	.55
a. Booklet pane of 5	14.00	
911 A273 5g brown red	5.50	1.10
a. Booklet pane of 5	27.50	
Nos. 903-911 (9)	13.95	3.45

Coil Stamps

Perf. 13½ Horiz.

912 A273 1g gray violet	1.10	.25
913 A273 1.10g blue	1.25	.25

Issued: No. 912, 10/5; 1.50g, 3/17/98, No. 913, 8/1/00; 5c, 10c, 25c, 6/18/01; 85c, 1.45g, 7/2/01; Nos. 907, 908, 2.50g, 5g, 9/3/01. 85c has added euro denomination.

December Stamps — A333

Serpentine Die Cut 12½x13

1995, Nov. 27 Self-Adhesive

916 A333 55c Children, star	.70	.25
917 A333 55c Children, stars	.70	.25
a. Pair, Nos. 916-917	1.40	

Issued in sheets of 20, checkerboard style.

Paintings by Johannes Vermeer (1632-75) — A334

Entire paintings or details: 70c, A Lady Writing a Letter, with Her Maid. 80c, The Love Letter. 100c, A Woman in Blue Reading a Letter.

1996, Feb. 27 Litho. *Perf. 13x13½*

918 A334 70c multicolored	.80	.25
919 A334 80c multicolored	.95	.25
920 A334 100c multicolored	1.25	.25
a. Souvenir sheet, Nos. 918-920	3.00	.60
Nos. 918-920 (3)	3.00	.75

Spring Flowers A335

Designs: 70c, Daffodil bulb, garden tools. 80c, Closeup of woman, tulip. 100c, Snake's head (fritillaria). 160c, Crocuses.

1996, Mar. 21 Litho. ***Perf. 13½x13***

No.	Type	Description	Unused	Used
921	A335	70c multicolored	.80	.25
922	A335	80c multicolored	.95	.25
923	A335	100c multicolored	1.25	.25
		Nos. 921-923 (3)	3.00	.75

Souvenir Sheet

No.	Type	Description	Unused	Used
924	A335	160c multicolored	1.90	.40

A336

1996, Apr. 1 ***Perf. 13x13½***

No.	Type	Description	Unused	Used
925	A336	70c Moving stamp	.85	.25

No. 925 was sold in sheets of 20. See #951.

Comic Strips, Cent. — A337

Mr. Olivier B. Bommel, by Marten Toonder: a, O.B. Bommel goes on holiday. b, O.B. Bommel receives letter.

1996, May 14 Litho. ***Perf. 13½x13***

No.	Type	Description	Unused	Used
926		Sheet of 2 + 2 labels	1.75	1.75
a.		A337 70c multicolored	.80	.80
b.		A337 80c multicolored	.95	.95

Vacations A338

Scene, flower: No. 927, Beach, sunflower. No. 928, Cyclists, gerbera. 80c, Gables in Amsterdam, cornflower. 100c, Windmills at "Zaanse Schans"' open air museum, anemone.

1996, May 31

No.	Type	Description	Unused	Used
927	A338	70c multicolored	.85	.25
928	A338	70c multicolored	.85	.25
929	A338	80c multicolored	.95	.25
930	A338	100c multicolored	1.25	.25
		Nos. 927-930 (4)	3.90	1.00

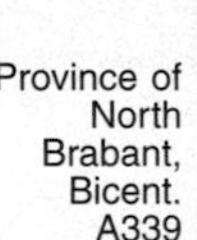

Province of North Brabant, Bicent. A339

1996, June 13 Litho. ***Perf. 13½x13***

No.	Type	Description	Unused	Used
931	A339	80c multicolored	.90	.25

Sporting Events A340

Designs: 70c, Lighting the Olympic Torch, 1996 Summer Olympic Games, Atlanta. 80c, Tour de France cycling race. 100c, Euro '96 Soccer Championships, Wembley Stadium, England. 160c, Olympic rings, track sports, Atlanta stadium.

1996, June 25

No.	Type	Description	Unused	Used
932	A340	70c multicolored	.80	.25
933	A340	80c multicolored	.90	.25
934	A340	100c multicolored	1.10	.30
935	A340	160c multicolored	1.75	.45
		Nos. 932-935 (4)	4.55	1.25

Erasmus Bridge, Rotterdam — A341

Designs: No. 936, Martinus Nijhoff Bridge over Waal River, horiz. No. 938, Wijker Tunnel under North Sea Canal, horiz.

1996, Aug. 6 ***Perf. 13½x13, 13x13½***

No.	Type	Description	Unused	Used
936	A341	80c multicolored	.90	.25
937	A341	80c shown	.90	.25
938	A341	80c multicolored	.90	.25
		Nos. 936-938 (3)	2.70	.75

UNICEF, 50th Anniv. — A342

Designs: 70c, School children from Ghana. 80c, Girl from Ghana with tray on head.

1996, Sept. 3 ***Perf. 13x13½***

No.	Type	Description	Unused	Used
939	A342	70c multicolored	.80	.25
940	A342	80c multicolored	.90	.25

Sesame Street in Netherlands, 20th Anniv. A343

70c, Bert & Ernie. 80c, Pino, Ieiemienie & Tommie.

1996, Sept. 3 ***Perf. 13½x13***

No.	Type	Description	Unused	Used
941	A343	70c multicolored	.80	.25
942	A343	80c multicolored	.90	.25

Voyages of Discovery A344

Voyages of: 70c, Petrus Plancius (1552-1622), cartographer. #944, Willem Barents (d. 1597). #945, Cornelis de Houtman (1540-99). 100c, Mahu en De Cordes (1598-1600).

1996, Oct. 1

No.	Type	Description	Unused	Used
943	A344	70c multicolored	.80	.25
944	A344	80c multicolored	.90	.25
945	A344	80c multicolored	.90	.25
946	A344	100c multicolored	1.10	.30
		Nos. 943-946 (4)	3.70	1.05

December Stamps — A345

Collage of faces, hands: No. 947, Wing, ear, hands. No. 948, Mouth, two faces. No. 949, Woman with eyes closed, hand. No. 950, Eyes, face with mouth open.

Serpentine Die Cut 9 Horiz.

1996, Nov. 26 Self-Adhesive

No.	Type	Description	Unused	Used
947	A345	55c multicolored	.65	.25
948	A345	55c multicolored	.65	.25
949	A345	55c red violet & multi	.65	.25
950	A345	55c blue & multi	.65	.25
a.		Block or strip of 4, #947-950	2.60	

Issued in sheets of 20.

Moving Stamp Type of 1996

Die Cut Perf. 13

1997, Jan. 2 Photo.

Self-Adhesive

No.	Type	Description	Unused	Used
951	A336	80c like No. 925	.90	.25

No. 951 sold in panes of 20.

Business Stamps A346

Geometric designs.

Coil Stamps

Sawtooth Die Cut 13½, Syncopated (on 1 Side)

1997, Jan. 2 Self-Adhesive

No.	Type	Description	Unused	Used
952	A346	80c pink & multi	.90	.25
953	A346	160c green & multi	1.75	.50

Cross-Country Skating Championships — A347

1997, Jan. 4 Photo. ***Perf. 14x13***

No.	Type	Description	Unused	Used
954	A347	80c multicolored	.90	.25

Surprise Stamps A348

Inscriptions beneath scratch-off heart-shaped panels: b, Schrijf me. c, Groetjes. d, Ik hou van je. e, Tot gauw. f, Ik denk aan je. g, XXX-jes. h, Ik mis je. i, Geintje. j, Zomaar. k, Wanneer?

1997, Jan. 21 ***Perf. 14x13½***

No.	Type	Description	Unused	Used
955		Sheet of 10	9.00	2.50
a.		A348 80c Any single, unscratched heart	.90	.25
b.-k.		A348 80c Any single, scratched heart		.25

Unused value for #955a is with attached selvage. Inscriptions are shown in selvage beside each stamp.

Nature and Environment A349

1997, Feb. 25 Litho. ***Perf. 13½x13***

No.	Type	Description	Unused	Used
956	A349	80c Pony	.90	.90
957	A349	100c Sheep	1.10	1.10

Souvenir Sheet

No.	Type	Description	Unused	Used
958	A349	160c Sheep, diff.	2.75	2.75

Suske & Wiske Comic Strip Characters A350

#959, Suske, Wiske, Tante Sidonia, & Lambik. #960a, Jerome making exclamation.

Perf. 13½x12½

1997, Mar. 18 Litho.

No.	Type	Description	Unused	Used
959	A350	80c multicolored	.90	.25

Souvenir Sheet

No.	Type	Description	Unused	Used
960		Sheet of 2, #959, 960a	1.90	1.00
a.		A350 80c violet & red	.90	.25

A351

Greetings Stamps A352

#961, Birthday cake. #962, Amaryllis surrounded by cup of coffee, two glasses of wine, hand writing card, candlelight.

1997, May 6 Photo. ***Perf. 14x13½***

No.	Type	Description	Unused	Used
961	A351	80c multicolored	.90	.25
962	A352	80c multicolored	.90	.25

See No. 1035.

Marshall Plan, 50th Anniv. — A353

Designs: No. 963, Map of Europe. No. 964, Flag, quotation from George C. Marshall.

1997, May 27 Litho. ***Perf. 13½x13***

No.	Type	Description	Unused	Used
963		80c multicolored	.90	.35
964		80c multicolored	.90	.35
a.		A353 Pair, #963-964	2.25	2.25

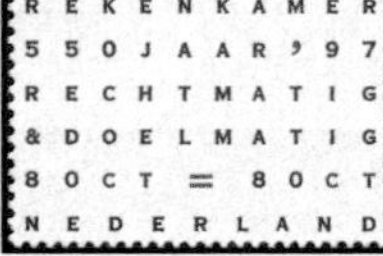

Court of Audit, 550th Anniv. A354

1997, May 27 ***Perf. 13½x13***

No.	Type	Description	Unused	Used
965	A354	80c multicolored	.90	.25

European Council of Ministers Meeting, Amsterdam A355

1997, June 17 Litho. ***Perf. 13½***

No.	Type	Description	Unused	Used
966	A355	100c multicolored	1.25	1.00

Water Recreation A356

80c, Swimming, row boat. 1g, Sailboats.

1997, July 1 ***Perf. 13½x13***

No.	Type	Description	Unused	Used
967	A356	80c multicolored	1.00	.25
968	A356	1g multicolored	1.25	.30

Royal Institute of Engineers, 150th Anniv. A357

1997, Aug. 5

No.	Type	Description	Unused	Used
969	A357	80c multicolored	1.00	.25

Netherlands Asthma Center, Cent. — A358

1997, Aug. 5

970 A358 80c multicolored 1.00 .25

Horticultural Education at Florens College, Aalsmeer, Cent. — A359

1997, Aug. 5

971 A359 80c multicolored 1.00 1.00

Franz Schubert (1797-1828), Composer A360

1997, Aug. 5

972 A360 80c multicolored 1.00 .25

A361

Youth Stamps A362

1997, Sept. 2

973 A361 80c multicolored 1.00 .25
a. Bklt. pane of 5 + 2 labels 5.00
Complete booklet, #973a 5.00
974 A362 80c multicolored 1.00 .25

Issued: No. 973a, 7/6/99.

Birth Announcement Stamp — A363

Die Cut Perf. 13½x13

1997, Oct. 7 **Photo.**

Self-Adhesive

975 A363 80c multicolored .90 .25

See Nos. 1033, 1071, 1109, 1260.

A364

December Stamps: Stylized people head to head showing either a star or heart in the center.

Serpentine Die Cut

1997, Nov. 25 **Photo.**

Self-Adhesive

Background Colors

976 A364 55c yellow .60 .25
977 A364 55c blue .60 .25
978 A364 55c orange .60 .25
979 A364 55c red .60 .25
980 A364 55c yellow green .60 .25
981 A364 55c green .60 .25
a. Sheet, 3 ea #976, 978-979, 981, 4 ea #977, 980 12.50 12.50

A365

1998, Jan. 2 **Litho.** ***Perf. 13½***

982 A365 80c gray blue .90 .25

Death announcement stamp.
See Nos. 1059, 1072, 1110, 1261

Delftware A366

100c, Cow, tiles with pictures of sailing ships. 160c, Tiles, one picturing boy standing on head.

1998, Jan. 2 **Photo.** ***Die Cut***

Self-Adhesive

983 A366 100c multicolored 1.10 1.10
984 A366 160c multicolored 1.75 1.75

Issued in both coil strips and sheets with priority labels.

A368

Growing Fruit in the Four Seasons: No. 986, Orchard in bloom, spring. No. 987, Strawberries, summer. No. 988, Harvesting, autumn. No. 989, Pruning, winter.

1998, Feb. 17 **Litho.** ***Perf. 13x13½***

Booklet Stamps

986 A368 80c multicolored .90 .90
987 A368 80c multicolored .90 .90
988 A368 80c multicolored .90 .90
989 A368 80c multicolored .90 .90
a. Booklet pane, #986-989 3.75
Complete booklet, #989a 3.75

A369

Die Cut Perf. 13½

1998, Mar. 17 **Photo.**

Self-Adhesive

990 A369 80c multicolored .90 .25

Marriage and wedding anniversaries. No. 990 was issued in sheets of 10.
See No. 1034.

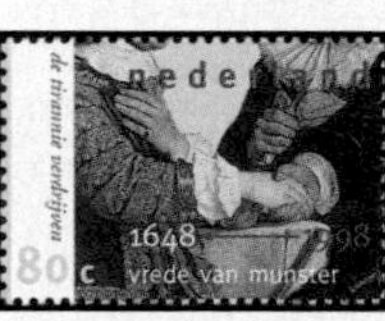
Anniversaries A370

#991, Men shaking hands, Treaty of Munster, 350th anniv. #992, Statue of John Rudolf Thorbecke, Dutch constitution, 150th anniv. #993, Child on swing, Universal Declaration of Human Rights, 50th anniv.

1998, Mar. 17 **Litho.** ***Perf. 13½x13***

991 A370 80c multicolored .90 .25
992 A370 80c multicolored .90 .25
993 A370 80c multicolored .90 .25
a. Strip of 3, #991-993 2.75 2.75

Letter Writing Day A371

1998, May 8 **Litho.** ***Perf. 13½***

994 A371 80c multicolored .90 .25

1998 World Cup Soccer Championships, France — A372

1998, May 19 **Litho.** ***Perf. 13½***

995 A372 80c multicolored .90 .25

Rabo Bank, Cent. — A373

1998, May 19 ***Perf. 13½x13***

996 A373 80c multicolored .90 .25

Royal Netherlands Field Hockey Federation, Cent. — A374

1998, May 19

997 A374 80c multicolored .90 .25

Central Administration in Friesland, 500th Anniv. A375

1998, June 9 **Litho.** ***Perf. 13½x13***

998 A375 80c multicolored .90 .25

Water Management A375a

1998, June 9

999 A375a 80c shown .90 .50
1000 A375a 1g Aerial view 1.10 1.10

Split of Royal Netherlands PTT — A376

#1001, TNT Post Groep. #1002, KPN NV.

1998, June 29

1001 80c red, black & blue .90 .25
1002 80c blue, blk & grn .90 .25
a. A376 Vert. pair, #1001-1002 1.90 1.90

No. 1002a is a continuous design.

Natl. Library of the Netherlands, Bicent. A377

1998, July 7

1003 A377 80c multicolored .90 .25

A378

No. 1004, Maurits Cornelis Escher (1898-1972), Graphic Artist. No. 1005, Simon Vestdijk (1898-1971), writer.

1998, July 7 ***Perf. 13x13½***

1004 A378 80c multicolored .90 .25
1005 A378 80c multicolored .90 .25
a. Pair, #1004-1005 1.90 1.90

Souvenir Sheet

A379

Inauguration of Queen Wilhelmina, Cent.: a, Queen Wilhelmina. b, Gilded Coach.

1998, Sept. 1 **Litho.** ***Perf. 13x13½***

1006 A379 80c Sheet of 2, #a.-b. 1.90 1.90

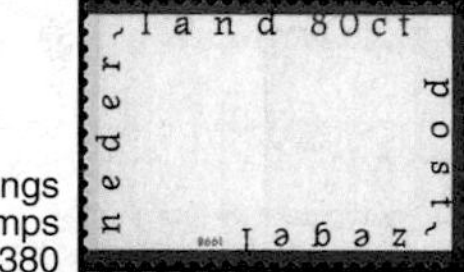
Greetings Stamps A380

Colors of stamp edges, clockwise from side adjacent to "Neder:" No. 1007: a, yellow, orange, red, red. b, red, orange, pink, yellow orange. c, red, orange, rose, orange. d, orange, red, light orange, yellow orange. e, yellow, orange, pink, red.

Serpentine Die Cut Perf. 13½x13

1998, Sept. 1 **Litho.**

Self-Adhesive

1007 80c Sheet of 10, 2 each #a.-e. 9.00
a.-e. A380 any single .90 .25

Each side of No. 1007 contains a pane of 1 each #1007a-1007e and 10 different self-adhesive labels.

Nos. 1008-1011 are unassigned.

Pets — A381

1998, Sept. 22 ***Perf. 13½x13***

1012 A381 80c Dog .90 .70
a. Bklt. pane of 5 + 2 labels 4.75
Complete booklet, #1012a 4.75
1013 A381 80c Kittens .90 .70
1014 A381 80c Rabbits .90 .90
Nos. 1012-1014 (3) 2.70 2.30

Issued: No. 1012a, 7/6/99.

Jan, Jans en de Kinderen Comic Strip, by Jan Kruis — A382

Characters: No. 1015, Writing letters. No. 1016, In automobile, mailing letter.

1998, Oct. 6 Litho. *Perf. 13½x13*

1015 A382 80c multicolored .90 .25
a. Booklet pane, 10 #1015 + 20 labels 9.00
Complete booklet, #1015a 9.00
1016 A382 80c multicolored .90 .25
a. Sheet of 2, #1015-1016 + 3 labels 1.90 .40

December Stamps — A383

25c, Stylized tree, house on top of earth.
No. 1018:
Silhouetted against moon: a, Rabbit. b, House. c, Bird. d, Tree. e, Deer.
Silhouetted against horizon: f, Rabbit. g, House. h, Bird. i, Tree. j, Deer.
House with: k, Rabbit. l, Heart. m. Bird. n, Tree. o, Deer.
Tree with: p, Rabbit. q, House. r, Bird. s, Heart. t, Deer.

1998-99 Litho. *Perf. 13*

1017 A383 25c multicolored .30 .25

Self-Adhesive

Die Cut Perf. 9

1018 A383 55c Sheet of 20, #a.-t. 12.50 3.25

Issued: #1018, 11/24; #1017, 1/5/99.

Introduction of the Euro — A384

1999, Jan. 5 Litho. *Perf. 13x12½*

1019 A384 80c multicolored .90 .25

Netherlands Postal Services, Bicent. — A385

1999, Jan. 15 Litho. *Perf. 13½x14*

1020 A385 80c multi + label .90 .80

See No. 1039

A386

1999, Feb. 2 Litho. *Perf. 12¾x13¼*

1021 A386 80c Spoonbill .90 .25
1022 A386 80c Globe, tern .90 .25

Protection of birds and migrating waterfowl. Netherlands Society for Protection of Birds, cent (#1021). African-Eurasian Waterbird Agreement (#1022).

A387

1999, Feb. 2 *Perf. 12¾x13¼*

Booklet Stamp

1023 A387 80c multicolored .90 .25
a. Booklet pane of 4 3.75
Complete booklet, #1023a 3.75

Royal Dutch Lawn Tennis Assoc., cent.

Views During the Four Seasons A388

Designs: a, Haarlemmerhout in fall. b, Sonsbeek in winter. c, Weerribben in spring. d, Keukenhof in summer.

1999, Mar. 2 Litho. *Perf. 13¼x12¾*

1024 Booklet pane of 4, #a.-d. 4.00 4.00
a.-d. A388 80c Any single .90 .90
Complete booklet, #1024 4.25

I Love Stamps A389

1999, May 6 Litho. *Perf. 13¼x12¾*

1025 A389 80c I Love Stamps .90 .75
1026 A389 80c Stamps Love Me .90 .75
a. Booklet pane, 3 #1025, 2 #1026 + 2 labels 4.50
Complete booklet, #1026a 4.50

Nos. 1025-1026 each contain a hologram. Soaking may affect the hologram.

Maritime Anniversaries A390

1999, May 6 Litho. *Perf. 12¾x13¼*

1027 A390 80c Freighters .90 .25
1028 A390 80c Lifeboats .90 .25

Schuttevaer Ship Masters Assoc., 150th anniv. (#1027). Netherlands Lifeboat Assoc., 175th anniv. (#1028).

Paintings A391

No. 1029: a, The Goldfinch, by Carel Fabritius. b, Self-portrait, by Rembrandt. c, Self-portrait, by Judith Leyster. d, St. Sebastian, by Hendrick Ter Brugghen. e, Beware of Luxury, by Jan Steen. f, The Sick Child, by Gabriel Metsu. g, Gooseberries, by Adriaen Coorte. h, View of Haarlem, by Jacob van Ruisdael. i, Mariaplaats Utrecht, by Pieter Saenredam. j, Danae, by Rembrandt.
1g, The Jewish Bride, by Rembrandt.

1999, June 8 Litho. *Perf. 13¼x13¾*

1029 Sheet of 10, #a.-j. 10.00 10.00
a.-j. A391 80c any single .90 .90

Self-Adhesive

Die Cut Syncopated

1030 A391 1g multicolored 1.10 1.10

No. 1030 issued in sheets of 5 stamps and blue priority mail etiquettes.

A392

1999, July 6 Litho. *Perf. 13¼x12¾*

1031 A392 80c multicolored .90 .25

Self-Adhesive

Die Cut 13½ Syncopated

1032 A392 80c multicolored .90 .25

Birth Announcement Type of 1997 and Marriage Type of 1998

1999, July 6 Litho. *Perf. 13¼x12¾*

Booklet Stamps

1033 A363 80c multicolored .90 .25
a. Booklet pane of 5 + 2 labels 4.50
Complete booklet, #1033a 4.50

Perf. 13¼

1034 A369 80c multicolored .90 .25
a. Booklet pane of 5 + 2 labels 4.50
Complete booklet, #1034a 4.50

Greetings Type of 1997

Die Cut 13½ Syncopated

1999, July 6 Litho.

Self-Adhesive

1035 A352 80c multicolored .90 .25

VNO-NCW Employer Organization, Cent. A392a

1999, Sept. 7 Litho. *Perf. 13¼x12¾*

1036 A392a 80c multicolored .90 .25

Tintin — A393

#1037, Tintin, Snowy in space suits. #1038a, Tintin, Snowy, Capt. Haddock in spacecraft.

1999, Oct. 8 *Perf. 13¼x12¾*

1037 A393 80c multicolored .90 .25
a. Booklet pane of 5 + 2 labels 4.50
Complete booklet, #1037a 4.50

Souvenir Sheet

1038 Sheet of 2, #1037, 1038a 1.90 1.90
a. A393 80c multicolored .90 .25

Postal Service Bicentennial Type

Souvenir Sheet

1999, Oct. 15 Litho. *Perf. 13¼x13¾*

1039 A385 5g multicolored 5.50 5.50

The numeral in the denomination is made up of perforations.

Millennium A394

Highlights of the 20th Century: a, Construction of barrier dam, 1932. b, Satellite. c, Amsterdam Bourse, 1903, designed by H. P. Berlage. d, Empty highway, 1973-74 oil crisis. e, Prime Minister Willem Drees's social welfare programs, 1947. f, Flood control projects 1953-97. g, European soccer champions, 1988. h, Liberation, 1945. i, Woman suffrage. j, Eleven-city skating race.

1999, Oct. 25 Litho. *Perf. 13¼x12¾*

1040 Sheet of 10 10.00 10.00
a.-j. A394 80c any single .90 .90

December Stamps — A395

Designs: a, Santa's head. b, Angel, musical notes, vert. c, Ornaments in box. d, Crescent-shaped Santa's head, vert. e, Santa, four trees. f, Clock, vert. g, Skater. h, Tree of people holding candles, vert. i, Man and woman. j, Woman, tree, star, vert. k, Angel, musical score. l, Hand, vert. m, Tree. n, Cat with crown, vert. o, Bird, house. p, Baby as angel, vert. q, Dog with cap. r, Angel with halo, vert. s, Family in house. t, Tree with presents, vert.

Serpentine Die Cut 7

1999, Nov. 30 Photo.

Self-Adhesive

1041 A395 Sheet of 20, #a-t 12.00
a.-t. 55c any single .60 .25

A396

2000, Jan. 4 Litho. *Perf. 13x12¾*

1042 A396 25c multi .30 .25

Souvenir Sheet

Holy Roman Emperor Charles V (1500-58) — A397

Designs: a, Gulden coin, Charles' aunt and guardian, Margaret of Austria, Charles V on Horseback in Bologna, by Juan de la Corte. b, Map of the Netherlands, Charles V on Horseback at the Battle of Mühlberg, by Titian, Charles' daughter, Margaret of Parma.

2000, Jan. 4 *Perf. 13¼*

1043 A397 Sheet of 2 + label 1.90 1.90
a.-b. 80c Any single .90 .25

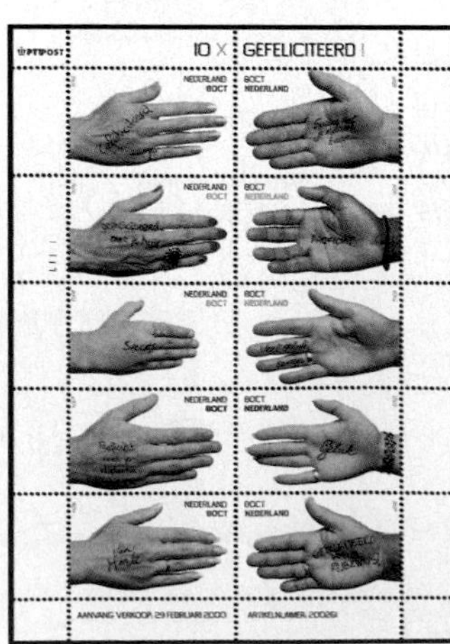

Greetings — A398

Color of denomination or country name and hands (back or palm) with written messages: a, Pink, back. b, Pink, palm. c, Orange, back. d, Orange, palm. e, Green, back. f, Green, palm. g, Blue, back. h, Blue, palm. i, Red, back. j, Red, palm.

Perf. 13¼x13¾

2000, Feb. 29 **Litho.**

1044 A398 Sheet of 10, #a-j 9.00 9.00
a.-j. 80c any single .90 .25

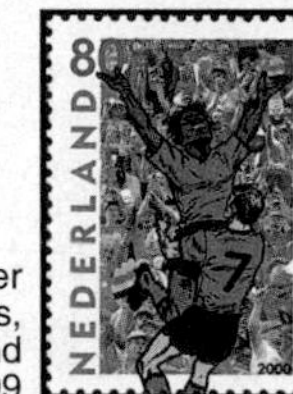

European Soccer Championships, Netherlands and Belgium — A399

2000, Mar. 25 *Perf. 12¾x13¼*

Booklet Stamps

1045 A399 80c Crowd, players .90 .25
1046 A399 80c Crowd, ball .90 .25
a. Booklet pane, 3 #1045, 2 #1046 + 2 labels 4.50
Booklet, #1046a 4.50

See Belgium No. 1796.

Items in Rijksmuseum — A400

a, Feigned Sorrow (woman wiping eye), by Cornelis Troost. b, Harlequin and Colombine, Meissen porcelain piece, by J. J. Kändler. c, Kabuki Actor Ebizo Ichikawa IV, by Sharaku. d, Apsara from India. e, Carved head of St. Vitus. f, Woman in Turkish Costume, by Jean Etienne Liotard. g, J. van Speyk (man with epaulet), by J. Schoemaker Doyer. h, Engraving of King Saul, by Lucas van Leyden. i, Statue, L'Amour Menacant, by E. M. Falconet. j, Photograph of two men, by C. Ariens.
100c, The Night Watch, by Rembrandt.

2000, Apr. 14 *Perf. 13¼x13¾*

1047 A400 Sheet of 10, #a-j 9.00 9.00
a.-j. 80c any single .90 .25

Die Cut Syncopated

Self-Adhesive

1048 A400 100c multi 1.10 .30

#1048 issued in sheets of 5 + 5 priority mail etiquettes.
See Nos. 1051, 1053.

Doe Maar, Popular Musical Group A401

2000, May 2 Litho. *Perf. 13¼x12¾*

1049 A401 80c Song titles .90 .25
1050 A401 80c Album cover .90 .25
a. Booklet pane, 2 #1049, 3 #1050, + 2 labels 4.50
Booklet, #1050a 4.50

Rijksmuseum Type of 2000 with Priority Mail Emblem Added and

Dutch Landscape, by Jeroen Krabbé — A402

Designs: Nos. 1051, 1053, The Night Watch, by Rembrandt.
Die cut perf. 4 on right side and right parts of top and bottom sides.

Die Cut Similar to Sync.

2000, Aug. 1 **Litho.**

Self-Adhesive

1051 A400 110c pur & multi 1.20 .30

Die Cut Sync.

1052 A402 110c multi 1.20 .30

Coil Stamp

Die Cut Similar to Sync.

1053 A400 110c blue & multi 1.20 .30
Nos. 1051-1053 (3) 3.60 .90

Nos. 1051-1052 issued in sheets of 5. No. 1051 lacks die cut "holes" on left side and at upper left. No. 1053 lacks die cut "holes" on left side, but has only two at upper left.

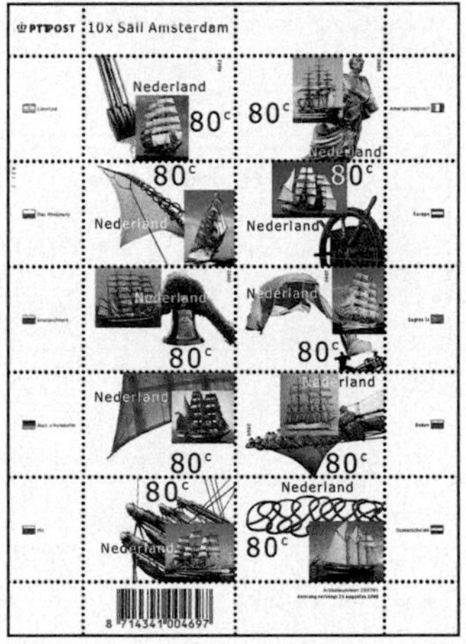

Sail 2000, Amsterdam Harbor — A403

No. 1054: a, Block and Libertad, Argentina. b, Figurehead and Amerigo Vespucci, Italy. c, Unfurled white sail, Dar Mlodziezy, Poland. d, Ship's wheel, Europa, Netherlands. e, Bell, Kruzenshtern, Russia. f, Deckhand adjusting sail, Sagres II, Portugal. g, Green sail, Alexander von Humboldt, Germany. h, Crewmen on bowsprit, Sedov, Russia. i. Spreaders, furled sails and ropes, Mir, Russia. j, Rope, Oosterschelde, Netherlands.

Perf. 13¼x12¾

2000, Aug. 21 **Litho.**

1054 A403 Sheet of 10 9.00 9.00
a.-j. 80c Any single .90 .25

Sjors and Sjimmie A404

Comic strip characters: No. 1055, Rollerblading. No. 1056, In go-kart. No. 1057, Wearing headphones. No. 1058, Hanging on rope.

2000, Sept. 23

1055 A404 80c multi .90 .25
1056 A404 80c multi .90 .25
a. Pair, #1055-1056 1.90 1.90
1057 A404 80c multi .90 .25
a. Souvenir sheet, #1056-1057 1.90 1.90

Booklet Stamp

1058 A404 80c multi .90 .25
a. Booklet pane, 3 #1057, 2 #1058 + 2 labels 4.50
Booklet, #1058a 4.50
Nos. 1055-1058 (4) 3.60 1.00

Death Announcement Type of 1998

Die Cut Perf. 13¼

2000, Oct. 10 **Photo.**

1059 A365 80c gray blue .90 .25

Endangered Species A405

Designs: No. 1060, Aeshna viridis (Groene glazenmaker). No. 1061, Misgurnus fossilis (Grote modderkruiper).

2000, Oct. 10 Litho. *Perf. 13¼x12¾*

Booklet Stamps

1060 A405 80c multi .90 .25
1061 A405 80c multi .90 .25
a. Booklet pane, 3 #1060, 2 #1061 + 2 labels 4.50
Booklet, #1061a 4.50

Souvenir Sheet

Amphilex 2002 Intl. Stamp Show, Amsterdam — A406

No. 1062: a, Boat. b, Carriage.

2000, Oct. 10

1062 A406 Sheet of 2 1.90 1.90
a.-b. 80c Any single .90 .25

Christmas — A407

No. 1063: a, Woman, man with tree on shoulder. b, Woman, child decorating tree. c, Couple dancing. d, Tuba player. e, Man carrying hat and tree. f, Man with child on shoulder. g, Woman reading. h, Couple kissing. i, Piano player. j, Woman at window. k, Woman in chair. l, Santa by fire. m, Snowman. n, Couple in front of house. o, Violin player. p, Children on sled. q, Man writing letter. r, Woman with food tray. s, Four people. t, Woman asleep.

Serpentine Die Cut 14½x15

2000, Nov. 28 **Photo.**

Self-Adhesive

1063 A407 Sheet of 20 13.00
a.-t. 60c Any single .65 .25

A408

2001, Jan. 2 Litho. *Perf. 12¾x13¼*

1064 A408 20c multi .25 .25

Royal Dutch Nature Society, Cent. — A409

No. 1065: a, Whinchat thrush. b, People in rowboat. c, Fox. d, People with binoculars. e, Scotch rose and June beetles.

2001, Jan. 26 Litho. *Perf. 13½x12¾*

1065 Booklet pane of 5, #a-e, +2 labels 4.50 —
a.-e. A409 80c Any single .90 .25
Booklet, #1065 4.50

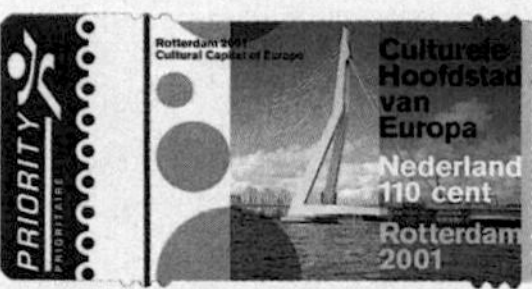

Rotterdam, 2001 European Cultural Capital — A410

Die Cut Similar to Sync.

2001, Mar. 14 **Litho.**

Self- Adhesive

1066 A410 110c multi 1.25 .30

Printed in sheets of 5. Die cutting has no "holes" at left, but has "holes" at top and bottom at the thin vertical line.

Book Week — A411

No. 1067: a, Quote by Edgar du Perron. b, Photograph by Ulay. c, Quote by Hafid Bouazza. d, Photograph by Ed van der Elsken. e, Quote by Adriaan van Dis. f, Photograph by Anton Corbijn. g, Quote by Kader Abdolah. h, Photographs by Celine van Balen. i, Quote by Ellen Ombre. j, Photograph by Cas Oorthuys.

2001, Mar. 14 *Perf. 13¼x13¾*

1067 A411 Sheet of 10 9.00 9.00
a.-j. 80c Any single .90 .25

Souvenir Sheet

Max Euwe (1901-81), Chess Champion — A412

No. 1068: a, Chessboard. b, Euwe, chess pieces.

2001, Apr. 3 *Perf. 13¼x12¾*

1068 A412 Sheet of 2 1.90 1.90
a.-b. 80c Any single .90 .25

Souvenir Sheet

Intl. Volunteers Year — A413

No. 1069: a, Rescue workers. b, People with animal cages.

2001, Apr. 3

1069 A413 Sheet of 2 1.90 1.90
a.-b. 80c Any single .90 .25

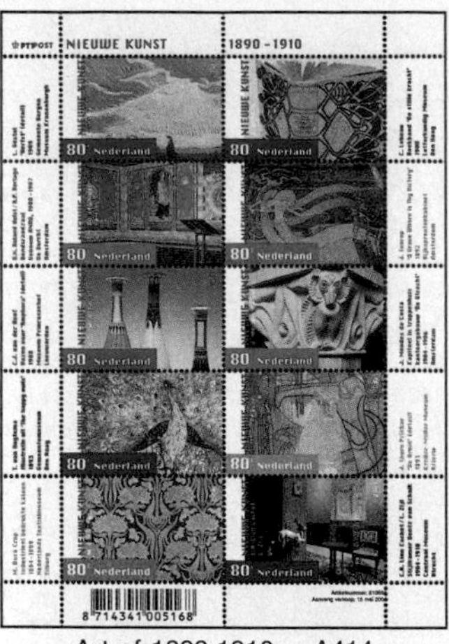
Art of 1892-1910 — A414

Art: a, "Autumn," L. Gestel. b, Book cover for "De Stille Kracht," C. Lebeau. c, Burcht Federal Council Hall, R. N. Roland Holst and H. P. Berlage. d, "O grave, where is thy victory?," J. Toorop. e, Vases from "Amphoras," C. J. van der Hoef. f, De Utrecht office building capital, J. Mendes da Costa. g, Illustration from "The Happy Owls," T. van Hoytema. h, "The Bride," J. Thorn Prikker. i, Printed fabric, M. Duco Crop. j, Dentz van Schaik period room, Central Museum, Utrecht, C. A. Lion Cachet and L. Zijl.

2001, May 15 *Perf. 14¾*

1070 A414 Sheet of 10 9.00 9.00
a.-j. 80c Any single .90 .25

Birth Announcement Type of 1997 with Added Euro Denomination

Die Cut Perf. 13¼x12¾

2001, July 2 **Litho.**

Booklet Stamp

Self-Adhesive

1071 A363 85c multi .95 .25
a. Booklet pane of 5 4.75

Death Announcement Type of 1998 with Added Euro Denomination

Die Cut Perf. 13¼

2001, July 2 **Litho.**

Self-Adhesive

1072 A365 85c gray blue .95 .25

Wedding Stamp — A415

Die Cut Perf. 13¼x12¾

2001, July 2 **Photo.**

Booklet Stamp

Self-Adhesive

1073 A415 85c multi .95 .25
a. Booklet pane of 5 4.75

See No. 1111.

A416

2001, July 2 **Booklet Stamp**

Self-Adhesive

1074 A416 85c multi .95 .25
a. Booklet pane of 10 9.50

See No. 1112.

Arrows A417

Serpentine Die Cut 14x13½

2001, July 2 **Coil Stamp** **Photo.**

Self-Adhesive

1075 A417 85c pur & silver .95 .25

See Nos. 1105-1106.

Change of Address Stamp — A418

Die Cut Perf. 14½x14

2001, July 2 **Photo.**

Self-Adhesive

1076 A418 85c orange & blk .95 .25

See No. 1113.

Polder — A419

Coast at Zandvoort — A420

Design: 1.65g, Cyclists on Java Island, Amsterdam.

2001, July 2 *Die Cut Perf. 13¼x12¾*

Booklet Stamps

Self-Adhesive

1077 A419 85c multi .95 .25
a. Booklet pane of 5 4.75

Serpentine Die Cut 12¾ Syncopated

1078 A420 1.20g multi 1.25 .25
a. Booklet pane of 5 6.25
1079 A420 1.65g multi 1.75 .35
a. Booklet pane of 5 8.75

Nos. 1078 and 1079 have rouletting between stamp and etiquette.

See Nos. 1114-1116.

Cartoon Network Cartoons — A421

No. 1080: a, Tom and Jerry. b, The Flintstones. c, Johnny Bravo. d, Dexter's Laboratory. e, The Powerpuff Girls.

Perf. 13½x12¾

2001, Aug. 28 **Litho.**

1080 A421 Booklet pane of 5, #a-e, + 2 labels 4.75 —
a.-e. 85c Any single .95 .25
Booklet, #1080 4.75

Greetings — A422

No. 1081: a, Veel Geluk (9 times). b, Gefeliciteerd! (11 times). c, Veel Geluk (4 times), horiz. d, Gefeliciteerd! (5 times), horiz. e, Proficiat (7 times). f, Succes! (7 times). g, Van Harte. . . (9 times). h, Proficiat (3 times), horiz. i, Succes! (3 times), horiz. j, Van Harte. . . (4 times), horiz.

Die Cut Perf. 13x13¼, 13¼x13

2001, Sept. 3 **Photo.**

Self-Adhesive

1081 Booklet of 10 9.50
a.-j. A422 85c Any single .95 .25

See No. 1117.

Change From Guilder to Euro Currency — A423

Etched on Silver Foil

2001, Sept. 25 *Die Cut Perf. 12¾*

Self-Adhesive

1082 A423 12.75g Guilder coins 12.50 —

Cancels can be easily removed from these stamps.

Souvenir Sheet

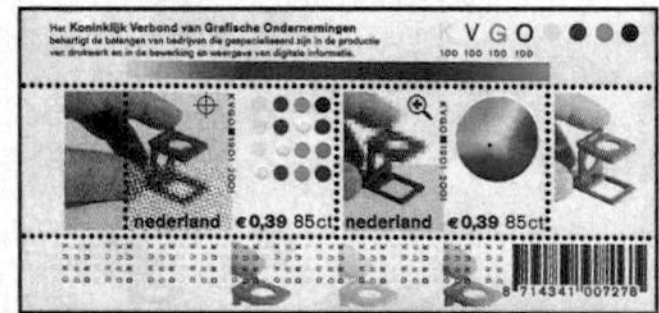
Royal Dutch Association of Printers, Cent. — A424

No. 1083 — Magnifying glass and: a, Color dots. b, Spectrum.

Photo. & Embossed

2001, Oct. 12 *Perf. 14x13½*

1083 A424 Sheet of 2 1.90 1.90
a.-b. 85c Any single .95 .25

Souvenir Sheet

Dutch Stamps, 150th Anniv. (in 2002) — A425

No. 1084: a, Waigaat Canal and ramparts, Williamstad, Curacao. b, Pangka sugar refinery, Java Island, Netherlands Indies.

2001, Oct. 12 **Photo.** *Perf. 14x13½*

1084 A425 Sheet of 2 1.90 1.90
a.-b. 85c Any single .95 .25

Amphilex 2002 Intl. Stamp Show, Amsterdam.

December Stamps — A426

No. 1085: a, Clock, grapes. b, Grapes, stars, doughnut balls. c, Doughnut balls, spire of church tower. d, Cherub. e, Champagne bottle. f, Wreath, roof. g, Windows of church tower. h, Ornament on Christmas tree. i, Christmas tree on sign. j, Cake in window. k, Christmas tree with ornaments, church tower. l, Santa Claus. m, Mug of hot chocolate on sign, snowman's head. n, Candles in window. o, Church tower, decorated market stalls. p, Reindeer. q, Snowman. r, Wrapped gift. s, Bonfire. t, Children on sled.

Serpentine Die Cut 13¼x13

2001, Nov. 27 **Photo.**

Self-Adhesive

1085 Sheet of 20 13.00
a.-t. A426 60c Any single .65 .25

100 Cents = 1 Euro (€)

Queen Type of 1991, Arrows Type of 2001 With Euro Denominations Only and

A427

Die Cut Perf. 14¼, Serpentine Die Cut 14 (#1086, 12c), Serpentine Die Cut 14¼ (55c, 57c 70c, 72c), Perf 14¼x13½ (#1087, 5c, 10c)

Photo, Litho (5c, 12c)

2002, Jan. 2 **Self-Adhesive**

1086 A427 2c red .25 .25
a. Booklet pane of 5 .20

Water-Activated Gum

1087 A427 2c red .25 .25
1088 A427 5c red violet .25 .25
1089 A427 10c blue .25 .25

Self-Adhesive Booklet Stamps

1090 A427 12c green .30 .25
a. Booklet pane of 5 1.50
1091 A273 25c brn & dk grn .60 .25
a. Booklet pane of 5 3.00
1092 A273 39c bl grn & red .95 .25
a. Booklet pane of 5 4.75
b. Booklet pane of 10 9.50
1093 A273 40c bl & brn .95 .25
a. Booklet pane of 5 4.75
1094 A273 50c fawn & emer 1.25 .25
a. Booklet pane of 5 6.25
1095 A273 55c lilac & brown 1.40 .25
a. Booklet pane of 5 7.00
1096 A273 57c brn & blue grn 1.50 .30
a. Booklet pane of 5 7.50
1097 A273 61c pur & red brn 1.60 .30
a. Booklet pane of 5 8.00
1098 A273 65c grn & pur 1.60 .30
a. Booklet pane of 5 8.00
1099 A273 70c ol grn & bl grn 1.75 .30
a. Booklet pane of 5 8.75
1100 A273 72c blue & brt vio 1.90 .30
a. Booklet pane of 5 9.50
1101 A273 76c olive & grn 2.00 .30
a. Booklet pane of 5 10.00
1102 A273 78c bl & ol brn 1.90 .30
a. Booklet pane of 5 9.50
1103 A273 €1 grn & blue 2.40 .40
a. Booklet pane of 5 12.00
1104 A273 €3 red vio & grn 7.25 1.25
a. Booklet pane of 5 37.50
Nos. 1086-1104 (19) 28.35 6.25

Coil Stamps

Self-Adhesive

Serpentine Die Cut Perf. 14x13½

1105 A417 39c pur & silver .95 .25
1106 A417 78c blue & gold 1.90 .30

Issued: 12c, 25c, 39c, 40c, 50c, 65c, 78c, €1, €3, 1/2/02; 2c (#1086), 1/28/02; 2c (#1087), 9/2/02; 10c, 11/26/02; 5c, 55c, 70c, 1/2/03; 57c, 72c, 1/2/04; 61c, 76c, 1/3/05.

See No. 1259.

Souvenir Sheet

Wedding of Prince Willem-Alexander and Máxima Zorreguieta — A428

No. 1108: a, Portraits. b, Names.

2002, Jan. 10 **Photo.** *Perf. 14*

1108 A428 Sheet of 2 1.90 1.90
a.-b. 39c Either single .95 .25

Types of 1998-2001 With Euro Denominations Only

Die Cut Perf. 13¼x12¾

Photo., Litho. (#1110)

2002, Jan. 28 **Self-Adhesive**

1109 A363 39c multi .95 .25
a. Booklet pane of 5 4.75

Die Cut Perf. 13¼

1110 A365 39c gray blue .95 .25

Die Cut Perf. 13¼x12¾

1111 A415 39c multi .95 .25
a. Booklet pane of 5 4.75
1112 A416 39c multi .95 .25
a. Booklet pane of 10 9.50

Die Cut Perf. 14½x14

1113 A418 39c orange & blk .95 .25

Die Cut Perf. 13¼x12¾

1114 A419 39c multi .95 .25
a. Booklet pane of 5 4.75

Serpentine Die Cut 12¾ Syncopated

1115 A420 54c Like #1078 1.25 .25
a. Booklet pane of 5 6.25
1116 A420 75c Like #1079 1.75 .35
a. Booklet pane of 5 8.75
Nos. 1109-1116 (8) 8.70 2.10

Nos. 1115-1116 have rouletting between stamp and etiquette.

Greetings Type of 2001 with Euro Denominations Only

No. 1117: a, Veel Geluk (9 times). b, Gefeliciteerd! (11 times). c, Veel Geluk (4 times), horiz. d, Gefeliciteerd! (5 times), horiz. e, Proficiat (7 times). f, Succes! (7 times). g, Van Harte. . . (9 times). h, Proficiat (3 times), horiz. i, Succes! (3 times), horiz. j, Van Harte. . . (4 times), horiz.

Die Cut Perf. 13x13¼, 13¼x13

2002, Jan. 28 **Photo.**

Self-Adhesive

1117 Booklet of 10 9.50
a.-j. A422 39c Any single .95 .25

Provinces A429

2002 **Litho.** *Perf. 14½x14¾*

1118 A429 39c Friesland .95 .95
1119 A429 39c Drenthe .95 .95
1120 A429 39c Noord-Holland .95 .95
1121 A429 39c Gelderland .95 .95
1122 A429 39c Noord-Brabant .95 .95
1123 A429 39c Groningen .95 .95
1124 A429 39c Zuid-Holland .95 .95
1125 A429 39c Utrecht .95 .95
1126 A429 39c Limburg .95 .95
1127 A429 39c Overijssel .95 .95
1128 A429 39c Zeeland .95 .95
1129 A429 39c Flevoland .95 .95
a. Souvenir sheet of 12, #1118-1129 11.40
Nos. 1118-1129 (12) 11.40 11.40

Nos. 1118-1129 each were issued in sheets of 12 + 6 labels.

Issued: No. 1118, 3/12; No. 1119, 3/26; No. 1120, 4/9; No. 1121, 4/23. No. 1122, 5/7; No. 1123, 5/21. No. 1124, 6/4; No. 1125, 6/18; No. 1126, 7/2. No. 1127, 7/16; No. 1128, 7/30; No. 1129, 8/13.

Efteling Theme Park, 50th Anniv. A430

Characters: a, Bald man. b, Jester. c, Fairy. d, Man with thumb extended. e, Man with mouth open.

Serpentine Die Cut 13¼x12¾

2002, May 14 **Photo.**

Self-Adhesive

1130 Booklet pane of 5 4.75
a.-e. A430 39c Any single .95 .25

Europa A431

Designs: No. 1131, Lions and circus tent. No. 1132, Acrobats, juggler, animal acts.

Perf. 14½x14¾

2002, June 11 **Litho.**

1131 A431 54c multi 1.50 .75
1132 A431 54c multi 1.50 .75
a. Tete-beche pair, #1131-1132 3.50 3.25

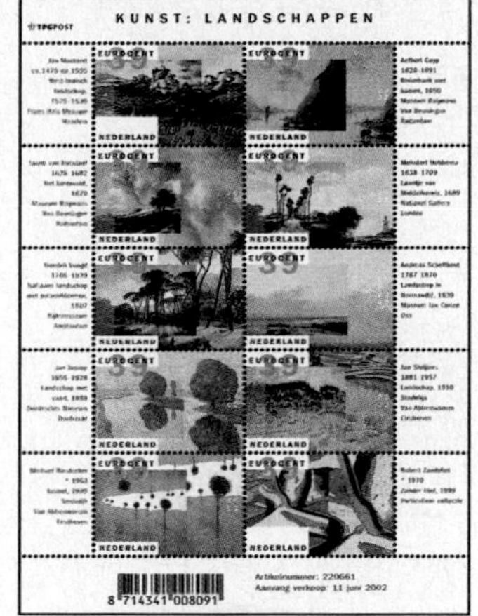

Landscape Paintings — A432

No. 1133: a, West Indian Landscape, by Jan Mostaert. b, Landscape with Cows, by Aelbert Cuyp. c, Grain Field, by Jacob van Ruisdael. d, Path in Middelharnis, by Meindert Hobbema. e, Italian Landscape, by Hendrik Vogel. f, Normandy Landscape, by Andreas Schelfhout. g, Landscape with Canal, by Jan Toorop. h, Landscape, by Jan Sluijters. i, Kismet, by Michael Raedecker. j, Untitled painting, by Robert Zandvliet. Names of artwork and artist are on sheet margins adjacent to stamps.

2002, June 11 **Photo.** *Perf. 14½*

1133 A432 Sheet of 10 9.50 2.50
a.-j. 39c Any single .95 .25

A433

Die Cut Perf. 14¼

2002, July **Coil Stamps** **Photo.**

1134 A433 39c blue & red .95 .25
1135 A433 78c green & red 1.90 .30

See Nos. 1157, 1173.

Souvenir Sheet

Amphilex 2002 Intl. Stamp Exhibition, Amsterdam — A434

No. 1136: a, One ship. b, Two ships.

2002, Aug. 30 **Litho.** *Perf. 14x13½*

1136 A434 Sheet of 2 1.90 1.90
a.-b. 39c Either single .95 .25

Dutch stamps, 150th anniv.; Dutch East India Company, 400th anniv.

Industrial Heritage — A435

No. 1137: a, Spakenberg shipyard, 1696. b, Dedemsvaart lime kilns, 1820. c, Cruquius steam pumping station, 1849. d, Heerlen coal mine shaft, 1898. e, Hengelo salt pumping tower, 1918. f, Weidum windmotor, 1920. g, Zevenaar brick oven, 1925. h, Breda brewery, 1926. i, Water works, Tilburg, 1927. j, Schoonebeck oil well pump, 1947.

2002, Sept. 24 *Perf. 14½x14¾*

1137 A435 Sheet of 10 9.50 9.50
a.-j. 39c Any single .95 .25

December Stamps — A436

No. 1138: a, Person, child, fence and trees. b, Man seated, trees. c, Head facing left. d, Red tree, person in black. e, Woman with white hair, tree. f, Person standing in grass. g, Man standing with legs crossed. h, Woman, windmill. i, Man on stool. j, Face with black lips. k, Man standing near tree, with bent knee. l, Man standing near trees, both hands in pockets. m, Two people seated. n, Person with black hair. o, Man with child on shoulders. p, Face, with black hair and eye looking right. q, Person with gold lips looking left. r, Head of person near shore. s, Person with sunglasses standing near shore. t, Woman with arms extended.

Serpentine Die Cut 13

2002, Nov. 26 **Photo.**

Self-Adhesive

1138 A436 Sheet of 20 14.00
a.-t. 29c Any single .70 .25

Paintings by Vincent Van Gogh — A437

Designs: 39c, Self-portrait, 1886. 59c, Sunflowers, 1887. 75c, The Sower, 1888.

Die Cut Perf. 14¼

2003, Jan. 2 **Photo.**

Booklet Stamps

Self-Adhesive

1139 A437 39c multi .95 .25
a. Booklet pane of 10 9.50

Serpentine Die Cut 13¼ Syncopated

1140 A437 59c multi + etiquette 1.40 .30
a. Booklet pane of 5+5 etiquettes 7.00
1141 A437 75c multi + etiquette 1.75 .30
a. Booklet pane of 5+5 etiquettes 8.75

A row of rouletting separates stamps from the etiquettes.

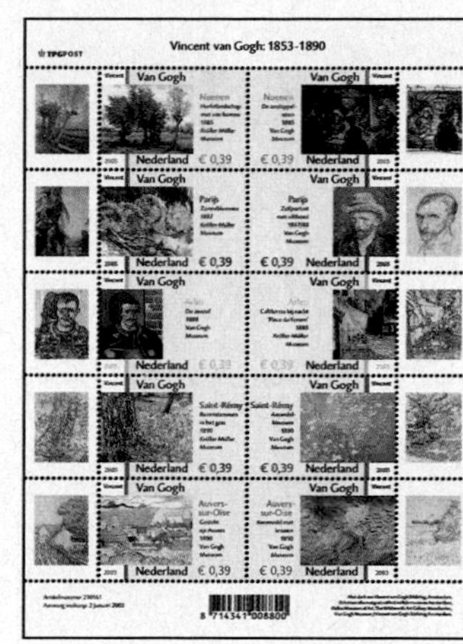

Paintings by Vincent Van Gogh — A438

No. 1142: a, Autumn Landscape with Four Trees, 1885. b, The Potato Eaters, 1885. c, Four Cut Sunflowers, 1887. d, Self-portrait with Gray Felt Hat, 1887-88. e, The Zouave, 1888. f, The Cafe Terrace on the Place du Forum, at Night, 1888. g, Pine Trees and Dandelions in the Garden of Saint-Paul Hospital, 1890. h, Blossoming Almond Tree, 1890. i, View of Auvers, 1890. j, Wheat Field with Crows, 1890.

2003, Jan. 2 **Litho.** *Perf. 14½*

1142 A438 Sheet of 10 8.25 8.25
a.-j. 39c Any single .80 .25

Water Control — A439

No. 1143: a, North Pier, Ijmuiden, 1869. b, Hanseweert Lock, 1865. c, Damming of the Wieringermeer, 1929. d, Ijsselmeer Dam (no date). e, Water breaching dike at Willemstad, 1953. f, Repairing dike at Stavenisse, 1953. g, Damming of the Zandkreek, 1960. h, Damming of the Grevelingen, 1964. i, Oosterschelde flood barrier, 1995. j, High water in Roermond, 1993.

2003, Feb. 1 **Photo.**

1143 A439 Sheet of 10 8.50 8.50
a.-j. 39c Any single .85 .25

Johann Enschedé and Sons, Printers, 300th Anniv. — A440

No. 1144: a, Binary code, mathematics symbols. b, Fleischman's musical notation symbols.

Litho. & Embossed

2003, Mar. 4 *Perf. 14x12¾*
1144 A440 Horiz. pair 1.75 1.75
a.-b. 39c Either single .85 .25

No. 1144a has photogravure back printing that can be seen through blank triangle on face of stamp.

Souvenir Sheets

Island Fauna — A441

No. 1145: a, Eurasian oyster catcher and pilings. b, Spoonbill, horiz. c, Eider. d, Harbor seal, horiz.
No. 1146: a, Sea gull. b, Stone curlew, horiz. c, Gull and seals. d, Crab, horiz.

2003, May 6 **Litho.** *Perf. 14½*
1145 A441 Sheet of 4 3.75 3.75
a.-d. 39c Any single .90 .25
1146 A441 Sheet of 4 5.75 5.75
a.-d. 59c Any single 1.40 .30

A442

Personalized Stamps — A443

No. 1147: a, Flowers. b, Flag. c, Gift. d, Martini glass. e, Medal. f, Guitar. g, Balloons. h, Paper cut-outs. i, Cake. j, Party hat.
No. 1148 — Numeral color: a, Bright blue. b, Dull green. c, Lilac. d, Red violet. e, Dull orange. f, Yellow green. g, Olive. h, Dull blue. i, Red. j, Orange brown.

Perf. 13½x12¾

2003, May 20 **Photo.**
1147 A442 Sheet of 10 + 10 labels 9.25 9.25
a.-j. 39c Any single .90 .25
1148 A443 Sheet of 10 + 10 labels 9.25 9.25
a.-j. 39c Any single .90 .25

Labels could be personalized for an additional fee.

Douwe Egberts Co., 250th Anniv. — A444

2003, June 3 **Litho.** *Perf. 14½x14¾*
1149 39c Spotted cup .90 .25
1150 39c White cup .90 .25
a. A444 Horiz. pair, #1149-1150 1.80 .50

Land, Air and Water — A445

2003, June 24
1151 A445 39c Airplate at UL .90 .25
1152 A445 39c Fish at LR .90 .25
a. Horiz. pair, #1151-1152 1.80 .50

Nelson Mandela, 85th Birthday, and Nelson Mandela Children's Fund — A446

2003, July 18
1153 A446 39c Mandela .90 .25
1154 A446 39c Children's Fund .90 .25
a. Horiz. pair, #1153-1154 1.80 .50

"From Me to You" — A447

Die Cut Perf. 14¼x14½

2003, Sept. 1 **Photo.**

Booklet Stamp

Self-Adhesive

1155 A447 39c multi .90 .25
a. Booklet pane of 5 4.50

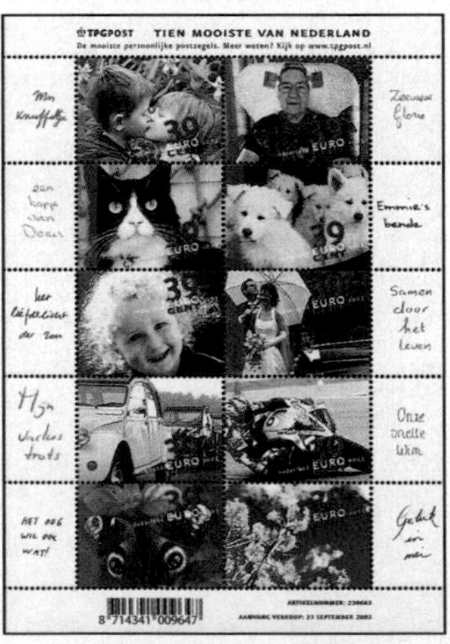

Photographs — A448

No. 1156: a, Children kissing. b, Woman. c, Cat. d, Puppies. e, Girl. f, Bride and groom. g, Automobiles. h, Motorcycle race. i, Butterfly. j, Flowers and sky.

Perf. 14½x14¾

2003, Sept. 23 **Litho.**
1156 A448 Sheet of 10 9.25 9.25
a.-j. 39c Any single .90 .25

Numeral Type of 2002

Die Cut Perf. 13½

2003, Oct. 2 **Photo.**

Self-Adhesive

Stamp + Label

1157 A433 39c Prus bl & red .90 .25

No. 1157 has "2003" year date and was printed in sheets of 50 stamps + 50 labels. Labels could be personalized for an additional fee.

Stamp Collecting A449

2003, Oct. 20 **Litho.** *Perf. 14½x14¾*
1158 A449 39c multi .90 .25

A booklet containing 2 booklet panes of 4 #1158 and three different imperf incomplete progressive proofs of these panes sold for €9.95.

A450

December Stamps — A451

Designs: No. 1159, Five-pointed star.
No. 1160: a, Family. b, Open gift box. c, Cat and dog. d, Christmas tree. e, Toast. f, Bell. g, Hand with pencil. h, Head of reindeer. i, Hand with flower. j, Holly leaf and berries. k, Candle. l, Eight-pointed star. m, Man and woman. n, Snowman. o, Fireplace. p, Angel. q, Man and woman dancing. r, Round Christmas ornament. s, Mother and child. t, Treetop ornament.

Perf. 13½x12¾

2003, Nov. 25 **Litho.**
1159 A450 29c multi + label .70 .25

Photo.

Self-Adhesive

Serpentine Die Cut 13

1160 A451 Sheet of 20 14.00
a.-t. 29c Any single .70 .25

No. 1159 was printed in sheets of 10 stamps + 10 labels. Labels could be personalized. No. 1160 is printed with panel of thermochromic ink which reveals a message when warmed.

Queen Beatrix and Family — A452

No. 1161: a, Princess Beatrix as infant with Queen Juliana and Prince Bernhard, 1938. b, Princess Beatrix playing on swings with Princess Irene, 1943. c, Princess Beatrix with horse, 1951. d, Princess Beatrix reading book, 1964. e, Princess Beatrix talking with Prince Claus, 1965. f, Princess Beatrix, Prince Claus and infant Prince Willem-Alexander, 1967. g, Princess Beatrix, Prince Claus and three young sons, 1975. h, Queen Beatrix and Prince Claus dancing, 1998. i, Royal Family, 1999. j, Queen at art exhibition, 2000.

2003, Dec. 9 **Photo.** *Perf. 14¼*
1161 A452 Sheet of 10 9.50 9.50
a.-j. 39c Any single .95 .25

A booklet containing five panes each with two horizontally adjacent stamps from Nos. 1161a-1161j, in perf 13½x13¾, sold for €9.95.

Souvenir Sheet

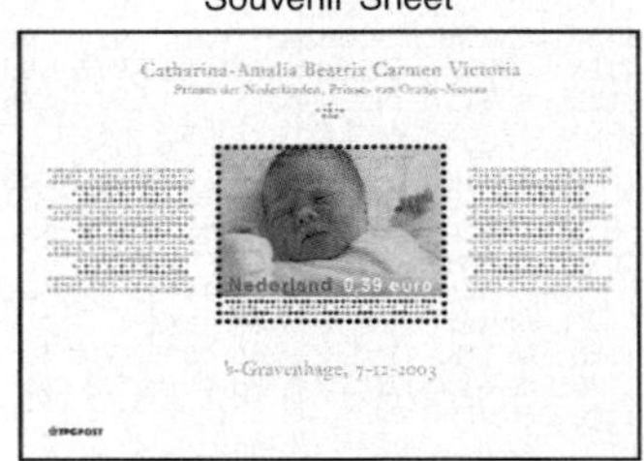

Birth of Princess Catharina-Amalia — A453

2003, Dec. 16 **Litho.** *Perf. 13¾*
1162 A453 39c multi 1.00 .25

See footnote below No. 1174.

Paintings — A454

Designs: 61c, Woman Reading a Letter, by Gabriel Metsu. 77c, The Letter, by Jan Vermeer.

Serpentine Die Cut 13 Horiz. Syncopated

2004, Jan. 2 **Photo.**

Booklet Stamps

Stamp + Detachable Etiquette

1163 A454 61c multi 1.60 .35
a. Booklet pane of 5 8.00
1164 A454 77c multi 2.00 .40
a. Booklet pane of 5 10.00

Royal Netherlands Meteorological Institute, 150th Anniv. — A455

Designs: No. 1165, Rain (rainbow at left. No. 1166, Sun (rainbow at right).

2004, Jan. 31 Litho. *Perf. 14½x14¾*

1165	39c multi	1.00	.25
1166	39c multi	1.00	.25
a.	A455 Horiz. pair, #1165-1166	2.00	.50

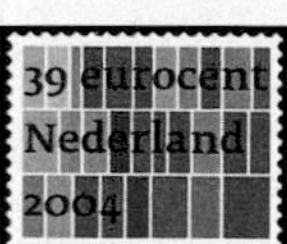

Retangles — A456

Die Cut Perf. 14¼

2004, Mar. 2 Photo.

Self-Adhesive

1167	A456 39c red & multi	1.00	.25
1168	A456 78c green & multi	2.00	.50

See Nos. 1263-1264.

Spyker Automobiles — A457

Designs: No. 1169, 1922 Spyker. No. 1170, 2003 Spyker C8 Double 12 R.

2004, May 10 Litho. *Perf. 14½*

1169	39c multi	.95	.25
1170	39c multi	.95	.25
a.	A457 Horiz. pair, #1169-1170	1.90	.50

A booklet containing four panes of perf 13¼x13 stamps (one pane of two No. 1169, one pane of two No. 1170, two panes containing two each of Nos. 1169-1170) sold for €9.95.

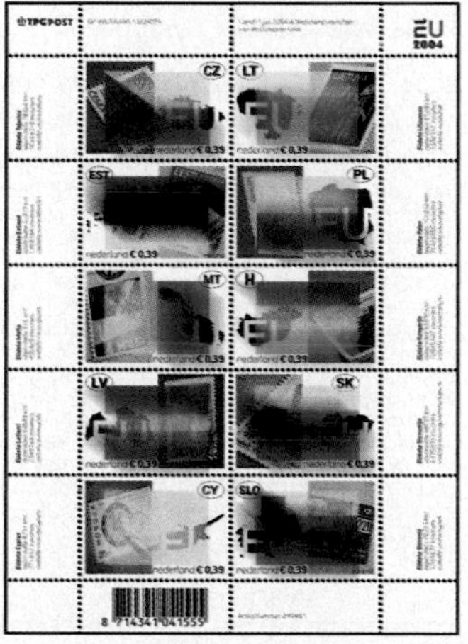

Expansion of European Union — A458

No. 1171 — Map, flag and stamps of new European Union members: a, Czech Republic. b, Lithuania. c, Estonia. d, Poland. e, Malta. f, Hungary. g, Latvia. h, Slovakia. i, Cyprus. j, Slovenia.

2004, May 10 *Perf. 14½*

1171	A458	Sheet of 10	9.50	9.50
a.-j.		39c Any single	.95	.25

Numeral — A459

Perf. 13½x12¾

2004, June 1 Photo.

1172	A459 39c multi + label	.95	.25

Labels could be personalized.

Numeral Type of 2002

2004, June 23 *Die Cut Perf. 13½*

Self-Adhesive

Stamp + Label

1173	A433 39c org red & blue	1.00	.25

No. 1173 has "2004" year date and has Olympic Torch Relay label.

Miniature Sheet

Prince Willem-Alexander, Princess Máxima and Princess Catharina-Amalia — A460

No. 1174: a, Prince Willem-Alexander and Princess Máxima announcing engagement. b, Princess Máxima showing engagement ring. c, Prince Willem-Alexander (without hat) and Princess Máxima looking at each other at wedding ceremony. d, Prince Willem-Alexander and Princess Máxima looking ahead at wedding ceremony. e, Prince Willem-Alexander and Princess Máxima kissing. f, Prince Willem-Alexander (with hat) looking at Princess Máxima. g, Prince Willem-Alexander and Princess Máxima looking at Princess Catharina-Amalia. h, Prince Willem-Alexander and Princess Máxima looking at book, Princess Máxima holding Princess Catharina-Amalia. i, Baptism of Princess Catharina-Amalia. j, Clergyman holding ceremony notes and touching head of Princess Catharina-Amalia at baptism.

2004, June 23 Litho. *Perf. 13¾*

1174	A460	Sheet of 10	10.00	10.00
a.-j.		39c Any single	1.00	.25

A booklet containing five panes, each with two horizontally adjacent stamps of Nos. 1174a-1174j, and a booklet pane of No. 1162, sold for €9.95.

Veluwe Nature Park — A461

No. 1175: a, Rabbit. b, Bird. c, Doe. d, Boar.
No. 1176: a, Fox. b, Woodpecker. c, Buck. d, Ram.

2004, July 6 Photo. *Perf. 13¼x12¾*

1175	A461	Sheet of 4	4.00	4.00
a.-d.		39c Any single	1.00	.25
1176	A461	Sheet of 4 + 4 etiquettes	6.00	6.00
a.-d.		61c Any single	1.50	.35

Souvenir Sheet

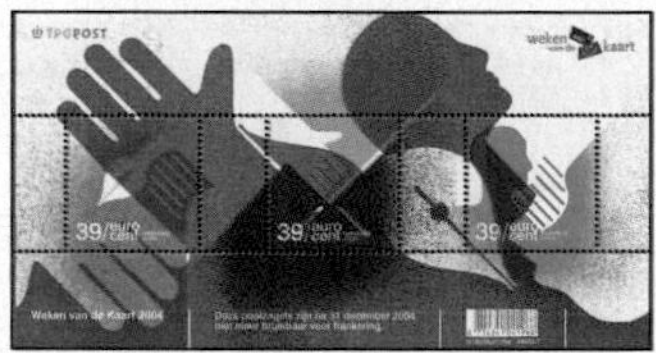

Greeting Card Week — A462

No. 1177: a, Pen nib. b, Hand. c, Head.

Perf. 13¼x13¾

2004, Sept. 1 Photo.

1177	A462	Sheet of 3 + 2 labels	3.00	3.00
a.-c.		39c Any single	1.00	.25

Paintings by Carel Fabritius (1622-54) — A463

No. 1178: a, Mercurius en Argus, c. 1645-47. b, Self-portrait, c. 1645. c, Mercurius en Aglauros, c. 1645-47. d, Abraham de Potter, 1649. e, Hagar en de Engel, c. 1643-45. f, De Schildwacht, c. 1654. g, Hera, c. 1643. h, Self-portrait, 1654. i, Self-portrait, c. 1647-48. j, Het Puttertje, 1654.

2004, Sept. 24 Litho. *Perf. 14½*

1178	A463	Sheet of 10	13.50	13.50
a.-f.		39c Any single	.95	.25
g.-j.		78c Any single	1.90	.30

Snowman — A464

December Stamps — A465

No. 1180: a, Shadows. b, People with gifts. c, Girl and dog. d, Children. e, Sheep. f, Polar bears. g, Children making snowman. h, People dragging Christmas tree. i, Man and woman in water. j, People around Christmas tree.

Perf. 13½x12¾

2004, Nov. 25 Litho.

1179	A464 29c multi + label	.80	.25

Photo.

Self-Adhesive

Serpentine Die Cut 12¾x13¼

1180	Block of 10	8.00	
a.-j.	A465 29c Any single	.80	.25

Hearts — A466

Serpentine Die Cut 14¼

2005, Jan. 3 Photo.

Self-Adhesive

1181	A466 39c multi	1.00	.25
a.	Booklet pane of 10	10.00	

See No. 1262.

Building Silhouettes — A467

Designs: 39c, Windmill and field. 65c, House and brick wall. 81c, Greenhouse and field.

Serpentine Die Cut 14¼

2005, Jan. 3 Self-Adhesive

1182	A467 39c multi	1.00	.25
a.	Booklet pane of 10	10.00	

Serpentine Die Cut 13¼ Horiz. Syncopated

1183	A467 65c multi + etiquette	1.75	.45
a.	Booklet pane of 5	8.75	
1184	A467 81c multi + etiquette	2.10	.50
a.	Booklet pane of 5	10.50	
	Nos. 1182-1184 (3)	4.85	1.20

On Nos. 1183 and 1184 a row of rouletting separates stamp from etiquette.

Netherlands Views — A468

2005 Litho. *Perf. 14¼*

1185	A468 39c shown	1.00	.25
1186	A468 39c Nijmegen	1.00	.25
1187	A468 39c Rotterdam	1.00	.25
1188	A468 39c Weesp	1.00	.25
1189	A468 39c Monnickendam	.95	.25
1190	A468 39c Goes	.95	.25
1191	A468 39c Boalsert	1.00	.25
1192	A468 39c Amsterdam	1.00	.25
1193	A468 39c Roermond	.95	.25
a.	Souvenir sheet, #1186, 1187, 1190, 1192, 1193	5.00	5.00
1194	A468 39c Papendrecht	.95	.25
a.	Souvenir sheet, #1185, 1188, 1189, 1191, 1194	5.00	5.00
	Nos. 1185-1194 (10)	9.80	2.50

Issued: Nos. 1185-1186, 2/8; Nos. 1187-1188, 4/12; Nos. 1189-1190, 6/14. Nos. 1191-1192, 8/9; Nos. 1193-1194, 1193a, 1194a, 10/14.

A booklet containing five panes, each with the two stamps issued on the same day with perf. 13½x12¾, sold for €9.95.

Art — A469

No. 1195: a, Trying, by Liza May Post. b, Emilie, by Sidi El Karchi. c, ZT, by Koen Vermeule. d, Het Bedrijf, by Lieshout Studio. e, Me Kissing Vinoodh (Passionately), by Inez van Lamsweerde. f, Lena, by Carla van de Puttelaar. g, Nr. 13, by Tom Claasen. h, Untitled, by Pieter Kusters. i, Witte Roos, by Ed van der Kooy. j, Portrait of a Boy (Grand Prix), bu Tiong Ang.

2005, Feb. 25 Litho. *Perf. 14½*

1195	A469	Sheet of 10	10.50	10.50
a.-j.		39c Any single	1.00	.25

Business Symbols — A470

Die Cut Perf. 14¼

2005, Mar. 22 Litho.

Self-Adhesive

1196	A470 39c multi	1.00	.25

Souvenir Sheets

Natuurmonumenten, Cent. — A471

No. 1197: a, Cormorant. b, Dragonfly. c, Water lily. d, Fish.

No. 1198: a, Bird. b, Butterfly. c, Lizard. d, Sheep.

2005, Mar. 22 Photo. *Perf. 13¼x13*

1197 A471 Sheet of 4 4.00 4.00
a.-d. 39c Any single 1.00 .25
1198 A471 Sheet of 4 + 4 etiquettes 6.75 6.75
a.-d. 65c Any single 1.60 .40

A booklet containing four panes, each with two litho., perf 14x13¾ stamps like Nos. 1197a-1197d and 1198a-1198d, sold for €9.95.

Souvenir Sheet

Queen Beatrix, 25th Anniv. of Reign — A472

Photos: a, Coronation, 1980. b, Giving speech, 1991. c, With Nelson Mandela, 1999. d, Visiting colonies, 1999. e, At European Parliament, 2004.

2005, Apr. 30 Litho. *Perf. 13¼x13¾*

1199 A472 Sheet of 5 16.00 16.00
a. 39c multi 1.00 .25
b. 78c multi 2.00 .50
c. 117c multi 3.00 .75
d. 156c multi 4.00 1.00
e. 225c multi 6.00 1.50
f. Booklet pane of 1, #1199a 1.75 —
g. Booklet pane of 1, #1199b 3.25 —
h. Booklet pane of 1, #1199c 5.00 —
i. Booklet pane of 1, #1199d 6.50 —
j. Booklet pane of 1, #1199e 9.50 —
Complete booklet, #1199f-1199j 26.00

Complete booklet sold for €9.95.

Numerals — A473

Die Cut Perf. 14¼

2005, May 24 Photo.

Coil Stamps

Self-Adhesive

1200 A473 39c bronze .95 .25
1201 A473 78c silver 1.90 .50

Souvenir Sheet

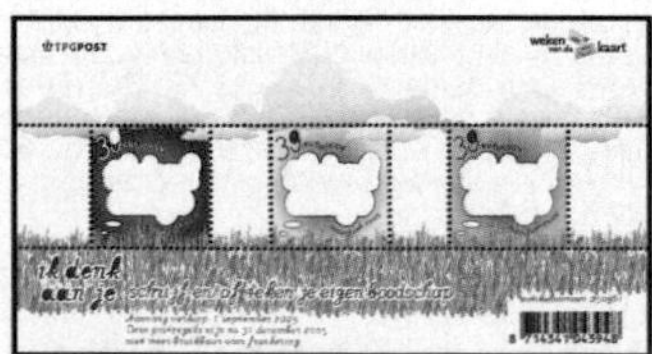

Greeting Card Week — A474

No. 1202: a, Red background, denomination in white. b, Yellow background, denomination in red. c, Blue background, denomination in red.

2005, Sept. 1 Litho. *Perf. 13½x13¾*

1202 A474 Sheet of 3 + 2 labels 3.00 3.00
a.-c. 39c Any single 1.00 .25

Farm Technology — A475

Sheep and: No. 1203, Dutch windmills. No. 1204, Chinese water wheel.

2005, Sept. 22 Litho. *Perf. 14½*

1203 81c multi 2.00 .50
1204 81c multi 2.00 .50
a. A475 Horiz. pair, #1203-1204 4.00 1.00

See People's Republic of China Nos. 3452-3453.

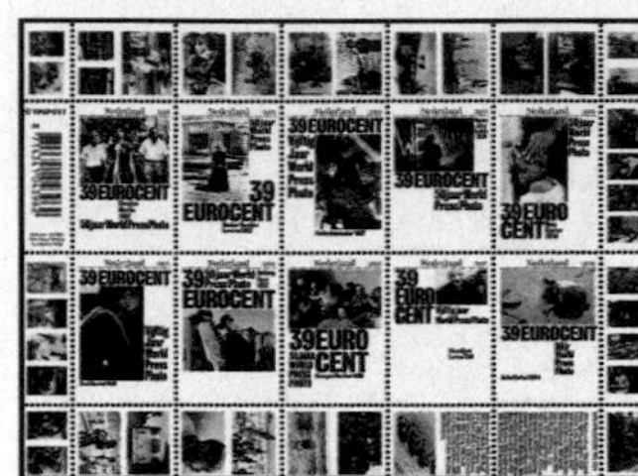

World Press Photo, 50th Anniv. — A476

No. 1205 — Silver Camera award-winning news photographs by: a, Douglas Martin, 1957. b, Héctor Rondón Lovera, 1962. c, Co Rentmeester, 1967. d, Hanns-Jörg Anders, 1969. e, Ovie Carter, 1974. f, David Burnett, 1979. g, Anthony Suau, 1987. h, Georges Merillon, 1990. i, Claus Bjorn Larsen, 1999. j, Arko Datta, 2004.

2005, Oct. 8 Litho.

1205 A476 Sheet of 10 9.50 9.50
a.-j. 39c Any single .95 .25

Trains — A477

Designs: No. 1206, Blue Angel. No. 1207, Locomotive 3737. No. 1208, ICE. No. 1209, Koploper.

2005, Oct. 14 Litho.

1206 A477 39c blue & multi .95 .25
1207 A477 39c green & multi .95 .25
1208 A477 39c red & multi .95 .25
1209 A477 39c yel & multi .95 .25
a. Block of 4, #1206-1209 3.80 1.00

A478

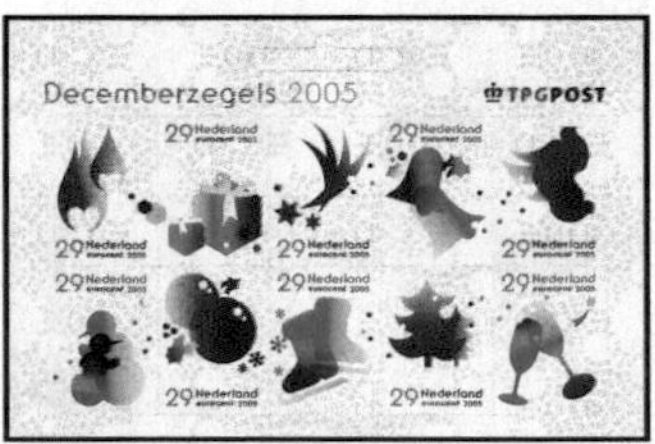

December Stamps — A479

No. 1211: a, Flames and hearts. b, Gifts. c, Comets. d, Bells. e, Doves. f, Snowmen. g, Ornaments. h, Ice skates. i, Christmas trees. j, Champagne flutes.

Perf. 13½x12¾

2005, Nov. 24 Litho.

1210 A478 29c multi + label .70 .25

Photo.

1211 A479 Sheet of 10 7.00 7.00
a.-j. 29c Any single .70 .25

Labels on No. 1210 could be personalized for a fee.

Modern Art — A480

No. 1212: a, Koe in de Optrekkende Avondmist, by Ed van der Elsken. b, Double Dutch, by Berend Strik. c, Hollandse Velden, by Hans van der Meer. d, Tomorrow, by Marijke van Warmerdam. e, A Day in Holland/Holland in a Day, by Barbara Visser. f, Composite mit Rode Ruit, by Daan van Golden. g, Untitled work, by J. C. J. Vanderhayden. h, De Groene Kathedraal, by Mariana Boozem. i, Hollandpan, by John Körmerling. j, Drijfbeeld, by Atelier Van Lieshout.

No. 1213: a, Study for Horizon, by Sigurdur Gudmundsson. b, Lost Luggage Depot, by Jeff Wall. c, 11,000 Tulipes, by Daniel Buren. d, Flets & Stal, by FAT. e, Double Sunset, by Olafur Ellasson.

No. 1214: a, Untitled, by Dustin Larson. b, Working Progress, by Tadashi Kawamata. c, Boerderijgezichten, by Sean Snyder. d, Toc Toc, by Amalia Pica. e, Freude, by Rosemarie Trockel.

Serpentine Die Cut 14¼

2006, Jan. 2 Litho.

Self-Adhesive

1212 Booklet pane of 10 9.50
a.-j. A480 39c Any single .95 .25

Serpentine Die Cut 13 Vert. Syncopated

1213 Booklet pane of 5 + 5 etiquettes 8.50
a.-e. A480 69c Any single + etiquette 1.60 .40
1214 Booklet pane of 5 + 5 etiquettes 10.50
a.-e. A480 85c Any single + etiquette 2.00 .50

On Nos. 1213 and 1214, a row of microrouletting separates stamps from etiquettes.

Queen Type of 1991

Die Cut Perf. 14¼ Syncopated

2006-09 Photo.

Self-Adhesive

Booklet Stamps

1216 A273 44c rose & ol grn 1.25 .25
a. Booklet pane of 10 12.50

Die Cut Perf. 14¼

1218 A273 44c rose & ol grn 1.25 .25
a. Booklet pane of 10 12.50
1219 A273 67c bl grn & blue 1.75 .30
a. Booklet pane of 5 8.75
1220 A273 74c gray grn & pur 2.10 .50
a. Booklet pane of 5 10.50
1221 A273 80c blue & red vio 2.00 .50
a. Booklet pane of 5 10.00
1223 A273 88c lilac & gray grn 2.40 .40
a. Booklet pane of 5 12.00
Nos. 1216-1223 (6) 10.75 2.20

Issued: 80c, 1/2; 44c, 67c, 88c, 12/11; 74c, 1/2/09.

Netherlands Tourism Areas — A481

2006 Litho. *Perf. 14½x14¼*

1240 A481 39c Leiden .95 .25
1241 A481 39c Sittard .95 .25
1242 A481 39c Vlieland 1.00 .25
1243 A481 39c Woudrichem 1.00 .25
1244 A481 39c Enkhuizen 1.00 .25
a. Souvenir sheet, #1240-1244 5.00 5.00
1245 A481 39c Schoonhoven 1.00 .25
1246 A481 39c Zutphen 1.00 .25
1247 A481 39c Deventer 1.00 .25
1248 A481 39c Zwolle 1.00 .25
1249 A481 39c Kampen 1.00 .25
a. Souvenir sheet, #1245-1249 5.00 5.00
Nos. 1240-1249 (10) 9.90 2.50

Issued: No. 1240, 2/1; No. 1241, 2/3; No. 1242, 4/28; No. 1243, 5/24; Nos. 1244-1245, 6/2; Nos. 1246-1247, 8/4; Nos. 1248-1249, 9/1. Nos. 1244a, 1249a, 10/10.

A booklet containing five panes of one each of Nos. 1240-1241, 1242-1243, 1244-1245, 1246-1247, and 1248-1249 sold for €9.95.

Souvenir Sheet

Dutch Speed Skating Gold Medalists in the Winter Olympics — A482

No. 1250: a, Ard Schenk. b, Yvonne van Gennip.

Litho. With Three-Dimensional Plastic

2006, Feb. 10 *Serpentine Die Cut 9*

Self-Adhesive

1250 A482 Sheet of 2 1.90
a.-b. 39c Either single .95 .50

The two stamps and a top and bottom sheet margin are affixed to a sheet of backing paper. A booklet containing five examples of No. 1250 sold for €9.95.

Personalized Stamp — A483

2006, May 1 Litho. *Perf. 13½x14*

1251 A483 39c multi 1.00 .25

No. 1251, showing Dutch soccer player Dirk Kuyt, sold for face value to the public and is the generic image for this stamp. Stamps depicting twenty other Dutch soccer players (Edwin van der Sar, Arjen Robben, Mark van Bommel, Ron Vlaar, Giovanni van Bronckhorst, Khalid Boulahrouz, Romeo Castelen, Jan Vennegoor of Hesselink, Urby Emanuelson, Ruud van Nistelrooy, Henk Timmer, Rafael van der Vaart, Hedwiges Maduro, Wesley Sneijder, Robin van Persie, Nigel de Jong, Barry Opdam, Joris Mathijsen, Denny Landzaat, and Phillip Cocu) were produced by postal authorities to sell as a special set for €12.95 per sheet of 10 different players. Examples of No. 1251 with other images are personalized stamps that sold for €12.95 per sheet of 10 stamps.

Miniature Sheet

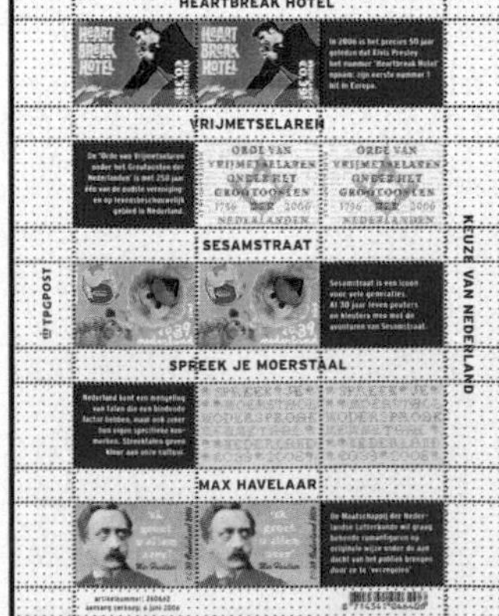

Stamps Chosen By the Public — A484

No. 1252: a, Elvis Presley. b, Masonic emblem. c, Muppets Purk and Pino. d, Needlepoint design of sayings in languages used in Twente, Limburg and Friesland. e, Max Havelaar, fictional character.

2006, June 10 ***Perf. 14½***

1252 A484 Sheet of 10, 2 each #a-e, + 17 labels 10.00 10.00
a.-e. 39c Any single 1.00 .25

Heartbreak Hotel, by Presley, 50th anniv., Dutch Grand Masonic Lodge, 250th anniv.; Dutch version of Sesame Street. 30th anniv.

Rembrandt (1606-69), Painter — A485

No. 1253: a, Bearded Man in Oriental Cape and Robe. b, Old Woman Seated at a Table. c, Saskia van Uylenburgh. d, Rembrandt's Son, Titus. e, Portrait of a Woman at the Window. €6.45, Self-portrait with Saskia.

2006, June 15 **Litho.** ***Perf. 13¾***

1253 A485 Block of 5 + label 5.00 5.00
a.-e. 39c Any single 1.00 .25

Souvenir Sheet

Litho. & Engr.

On Thin Card

1254 A485 €6.45 tan & black 17.00 17.00

See Germany No. 2387. A booklet containing two panes, each containing Nos. 1253a, 1253b, and 1253d, one pane of No. 1253c and Germany No. 2387, and one pane containing two No. 1253e, sold for €9.95. The booklet was withdrawn from sale after it was discovered that the German stamp in the booklet was printed with perforations and tagging without the authorization of German postal authorities, but most of the booklets produced had already been distributed. Value, $80.

Drawing by Karel Appel (1921-2006) A486

2006, Sept. 1 **Litho.** ***Perf. 13¼x14***

1255 A486 39c multi 1.00 .25

A booklet containing five panes of 2 No. 1255 sold for €9.95.

Miniature Sheet

Endangered Animals — A487

No. 1256: a, Giraffe. b, Butterfly. c, Manchurian crane. d, Francois' leaf monkey. e, Blue poison dart frog. f, Red panda. g, Lowland gorilla. h, Sumatran tiger. i, Asian lion. j, Indian rhinoceros. k, Asian elephant. l, Pygmy hippopotamus.

2006, Oct. 4 ***Perf. 13¾***

1256 A487 Sheet of 12 12.00 12.00
a.-l. 39c Any single 1.00 .25

A booklet containing one pane each of Nos. 1256a-1256c, 1256d-1256f, 1256g-1256i, and 1256j-1256l sold for €9.95.

Renaming of Postal Corporation as TNT Post — A488

2006, Oct. 16 **Litho.** ***Perf. 14½***

1257 A488 39c multi 1.00 .25

Snowflakes — A489

No. 1258: a, Small blue green, large dark blue flakes. b, Large pink, small red flakes. c, Small pink, large brown flakes. d, Large blue, small red flakes. e, Small blue green, large brown flakes. f, Small blue, large red flakes. g, Large green, small brown flakes. h, Small blue, large pink flakes. i, Large red, small brown flakes. j, Small pink, large blue green flakes.

Serpentine Die Cut 12¾x13¼

2006, Nov. 23 **Photo.**

Self-Adhesive

1258 Block of 10 7.75
a.-j. A489 29c Any single .75 .25

Numeral and "NL" Type of 2002

Perf. 14¼x13½

2006, Dec. 11 **Photo.**

1259 A427 3c brown .25 .25

Birth Announcement Type of 1997

Serpentine Die Cut 13¼x12¾

2006, Dec. 11 **Photo.**

Self-Adhesive

1260 A363 44c multi 1.25 .30

Death Announcement Type of 1997

Serpentine Die Cut 13¼

2006, Dec. 11 **Photo.**

Self-Adhesive

1261 A365 44c multi 1.25 .30

Hearts Type of 2005

Serpentine Die Cut 14½x14¼

2006, Dec. 11 **Litho.**

Self-Adhesive

1262 A466 44c multi 1.25 .30
a. Booklet pane of 10 12.50

Rectangles Type of 2004

Die Cut Perf. 14¼x14½

2006, Dec. 11 **Photo.**

Self-Adhesive

1263 A456 44c multi 1.25 .30
1264 A456 88c multi 2.40 .40

Dutch Products — A490

No. 1265: a, Glide glass goblet. b, Revolt chair. c, Heineken beer bottle. d, Bugaboo stroller. e, Lapin kettle. f, Milk bottle lamp. g, Carrier bicycle. h, Fluorescent screw-bottom lightbulb. i, Unox smoked sausage. j, Tulip. 72c, Clap skates. 89c, Cheese slicer.

Die Cut Perf. 14¼

2006, Dec. 11 **Photo.**

Self-Adhesive

1265 Booklet pane of 10 12.50
a.-j. A490 44c Any single 1.25 .25

Serpentine Die Cut 11

1266 A490 72c multi + etiquette 1.90 .30
a. Booklet pane of 5 + 5 etiquettes 9.50
1267 A490 89c multi + etiquette 2.40 .40
a. Booklet pane of 5 + 5 etiquettes 12.00

On Nos. 1266-1267, a row of microrouletting separates stamps from etiquettes.

Numerals — A491

2007, Jan. 2 ***Die Cut Perf. 14¼x14½***

Self-Adhesive

1268 A491 44c multi 1.25 .30
a. Serpentine die cut 13½ + label 1.25 .30
1269 A491 88c multi, vert. 2.40 .40

The generic label on No. 1268a depicts a mailbox. These labels could be personalized for an additional fee.

A492

Personalized Stamps — A493

2007 **Litho.** ***Perf. 14x13½***

1270 A492 44c multi 1.25 .30

Self-Adhesive

Serpentine Die Cut 13¼x13

1271 A493 44c multi 1.25 .30

Issued: No. 1270, 1/2; No. 1271, 9/21. The generic vignettes of Nos. 1270 (Royal Dutch Mint), and 1271 (Mathematician L. E. J. Brouwer), which sold for face value, are shown. These stamps, printed in sheets of 10, could be personalized with horizontal or vertical images for an additional fee.

Netherlands Tourism Areas — A494

2007 **Litho.** ***Perf. 14½x14¼***

1272 A494 44c Gouda 1.25 .30
1273 A494 44c Groningen 1.25 .30
1274 A494 44c Vlissingen 1.25 .30
1275 A494 44c Hoorn 1.25 .30
1276 A494 44c Leerdam 1.25 .30
1277 A494 44c Den Helder 1.25 .30
1278 A494 44c Lelystad 1.25 .30
1279 A494 44c Den Haag (The Hague) 1.25 .30
a. Souvenir sheet, #1274-1275, 1277-1279 6.25 6.25
1280 A494 44c Utrecht 1.25 .30
1281 A494 44c Edam 1.25 .30
a. Souvenir sheet, #1272-1273, 1276, 1280-1281 6.25 6.25
Nos. 1272-1281 (10) 12.50 3.00

Issued: Nos. 1272-1273, 2/7; No. 1274, 3/23; No. 1275, 3/26; No. 1276, 4/13; No. 1277, 7/24; No. 1278, 8/8; No. 1279, 8/15. Nos. 1279a, 1281a, 10/17; No. 1280, 10/3; No. 1281, 10/10. A booklet containing five panes of one each of Nos. 1272-1273, 1274-1275, 1276-1277, 1278-1279, and 1280-1281 in perf. 13½x12½ sold for €9.95.

Trees in Spring — A495

Trees in Summer — A496

Trees in Autumn — A497

Trees in Winter — A498

Designs: No. 1282, Lime tree. No. 1283, Horse chestnut bud. No. 1284, Bark of plane tree. No. 1285, Oak tree. No. 1286, Maple samaras. No. 1287, Trunk and branches of beech tree. No. 1288, Black alder tree. No. 1289, White willow tree in water.

2007 **Litho.** ***Perf. 14½***

1282 44c multi 1.25 .30
1283 44c multi 1.25 .30
a. A495 Horiz. pair, #1282-1283 2.50 .60
1284 44c multi 1.25 .30
1285 44c multi 1.25 .30
a. A496 Horiz. pair, #1284-1285 2.50 .60
1286 44c multi 1.25 .30
1287 44c multi 1.25 .30
a. A497 Horiz. pair, #1286-1287 2.50 .60
1288 44c multi 1.25 .30
1289 44c multi 1.25 .30
a. A498 Horiz. pair, #1288-1289 2.50 .60
Nos. 1282-1289 (8) 10.00 2.40

Issued: Nos. 1282-1283, 3/23; Nos. 1284-1285, 6/21; Nos. 1286-1287, 9/21; Nos. 1288-1289, 11/12.

Miniature Sheet

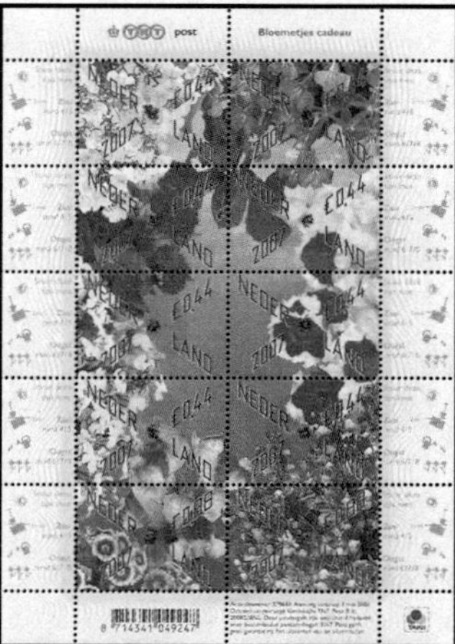

Flowers — A499

No. 1290: a, Yellow and white toadflax at L, blue lobelia at R, red pinks at LR. b, Blue lobelias and white petunia. c, Yellow and white toadflax at UL, red pinks at UR and LL, sky at LR. d, Red snapdragon at UL, blue lobelia at top, white petunias at UR, red and white petunias at bottom, sky at LL. e, Red pinks at top, white toadflax at UL and LL, sky at R. f, Red and white petunias at R, sky at left. g, White toadflax at L, pink snapdragons at LR, sky at UR. h, Red and white petunia at top, pink snapdragons at LL, red violet toadflax at LR, sky at UL. i, White toadflax at UL, red and white snapdragons at UR, white and red pinks at LL. j, Red violet toadflax.

Litho & Embossed

2007, May 1 ***Perf. 13½***

1290 A499 Sheet of 10 12.50 12.50
a.-j. 44c Any single 1.25 .30

Flower seeds are sealed under a round piece of adhesive tape in the embossed circle in the center of the stamps. The left and right sheet selvage contains instructions on planting the stamps and seeds. A booklet containing five panes, each containing one of the five horizontal pairs of stamps from the sheet and the adjacent selvage, sold for €9.95.

Europa — A500

2007, July 26 Litho. *Perf. 13½*

1291	72c Moon	2.00	.50
1292	72c Sun	2.00	.50
a.	A500 Pair, #1291-1292	4.00	1.00

Scouting, cent. Printed in sheets of 10. Sheet margins inscribed "Priority" serve as etiquettes. A booklet containing three different panes, each containing a horizontal pair and two etiquettes, sold for €9.95.

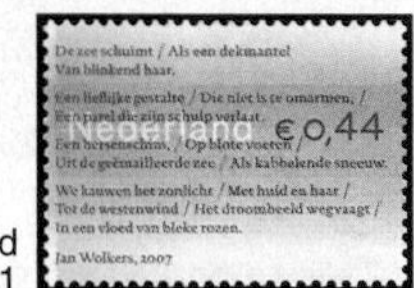

Greeting Card Weeks — A501

2007, Sept. 3 *Perf. 13¾*

1293	A501 44c multi	1.25	.30

Printed in sheets of 3.

Kingdom of the Netherlands, Bicent. A502

Litho. & Embossed

2007, Sept. 11 *Perf. 13¼*

Booklet Stamp

1294	A502 €6.45 multi	29.00	15.00
	Complete booklet	29.00	

No. 1294 was sold only in a booklet pane of one stamp in a booklet containing one pane, which sold for €9.95.

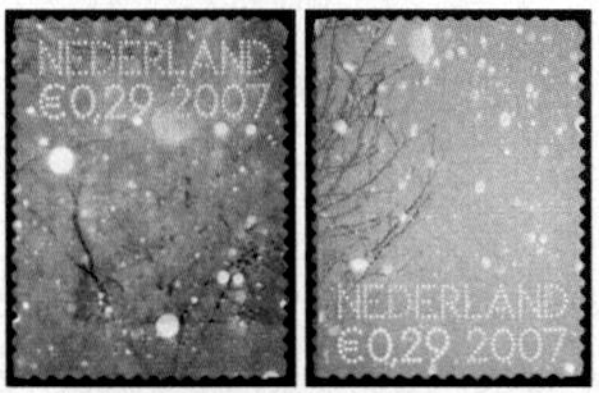

A503 A504

A505 A506

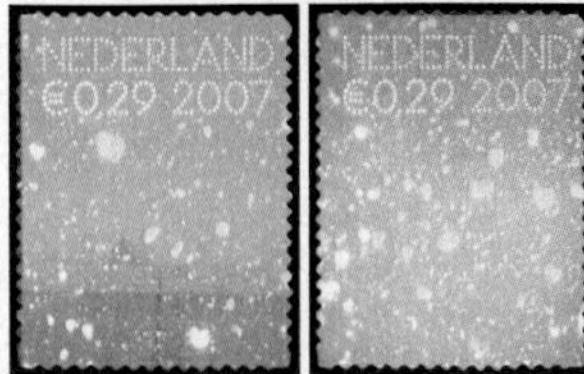

A507 A508

A509 A510

Snowflakes and Trees
A511 A512

A513 A514

A515 A516

A517 A518

A519 A520

Fireworks
A521 A522

Serpentine Die Cut 12¾x13¼

2007, Nov. 22 Photo.

Self-Adhesive

1295	Block of 10	8.50	
a.	A503 29c multi	.85	.25
b.	A504 29c multi	.85	.25
c.	A505 29c multi	.85	.25
d.	A506 29c multi	.85	.25
e.	A507 29c multi	.85	.25
f.	A508 29c multi	.85	.25
g.	A509 29c multi	.85	.25
h.	A510 29c multi	.85	.25
i.	A511 29c multi	.85	.25
j.	A512 29c multi	.85	.25

Litho.

Serpentine Die Cut 12¾

1296	Block of 10	13.00	
a.	A513 29c multi, unscratched panel	1.25	.30
b.	A514 29c multi, unscratched panel	1.25	.30
c.	A515 29c multi, unscratched panel	1.25	.30
d.	A516 29c multi, unscratched panel	1.25	.30
e.	A517 29c multi, unscratched panel	1.25	.30
f.	A518 29c multi, unscratched panel	1.25	.30
g.	A519 29c multi, unscratched panel	1.25	.30
h.	A520 29c multi, unscratched panel	1.25	.30
i.	A521 29c multi, unscratched panel	1.25	.30
j.	A522 29c multi, unscratched panel	1.25	.30
k.-t.	As #1296a-1296j, any single, scratched panel		.30

No. 1296 sold for €4.40, with €1.50 of the total going towards lottery prizes awarded to the sender of and mail recipient of stamps with prizes found under the scratch-off panel at the bottom of the stamps. Scratch-off panels are separated from the stamps by a row of rouletting.

Ecology — A523

No. 1297: a, Hybrid vehicle with electric plug. b, House and sun (solar energy). c, Cow with electric plug (biofuels). d, Wind generators. e, Trees. f, Flowers, carpoolers in automobile. g, "Groen" with electric plug. h, Truck (soot filters). i, Birds and envelope (green mail). j, Insulated house.

75c, Bicycle with globe hemispheres as wheels. 92c, Heart-shaped globe.

Die Cut Perf. 14¼

2008, Jan. 2 Litho.

Self-Adhesive

1297	Booklet pane of 10	13.00	
a.-j.	A523 44c Any single	1.25	.30

Photo.

Serpentine Die Cut 11

1298	A523 75c multi + etiquette	2.25	.55
1299	A523 92c multi + etiquette	2.75	.70

On Nos. 1298-1299 a row of microrouletting separates stamps from etiquettes.

See Nos. 1324-1325.

A524

A525

A526

A527

A528

A529

Personalized Stamps — A530

2008 Litho. *Perf. 14x13½*

1300	A524 44c multi	1.25	.30

Perf. 13½x14

1301	A525 44c multi	1.25	.30

Perf. 13½x13, 13x13½

1302	Horiz. strip of 5	6.50	3.25
a.	A526 44c multi	1.25	.30
b.	A527 44c multi	1.25	.30
c.	A528 44c multi	1.25	.30
d.	A529 44c multi	1.25	.30
e.	A530 44c multi	1.25	.30

Issued: Nos. 1300-1301, 1/2; No. 1302, 3/18. The generic vignettes of Nos. 1300 (Netherlands Federation of Philatelic Associations, cent.), 1301 (Netherlands Association of Stamp Dealers, 80th anniv.), and 1302 (winning art for personalized stamp design contest), which sold for face value, are shown. These stamps, printed in sheets of 10, could be personalized for an additional fee. A booklet containing 5 panes of Nos. 1300-1301, each with different pane margins, sold for € 9.95. Other booklets containing panes of Nos. 1300 or 1301 with different vignettes exist. These booklets usually sold for €9.95, and may contain fewer than ten stamps.

Netherlands Tourism Areas — A531

2008 Litho. *Perf. 14½x14¼*

1303	A531 44c Sneek	1.40	.35
1304	A531 44c Coevorden	1.40	.35
1305	A531 44c Heusden	1.40	.35
1306	A531 44c Amersfoort	1.40	.35
1307	A531 44c Zoetermeer	1.40	.35
a.	Souvenir sheet of 5, #1303-1307	7.00	3.50
	Nos. 1303-1307 (5)	7.00	1.75

Issued: Nos. 1303-1304, 3/25; Nos. 1305-1306, 4/22; No. 1307, 6/3; No. 1307a, 6/12. A booklet containing five panes, with each pane containing two perf. 13½x12¾ examples of each stamp, sold for €9.95.

Europa A532

2008, May 20 Litho. *Perf. 13½x12¾*

1308	A532 75c multi	2.40	.60
a.	Tete-beche pair	4.80	1.25

Sheet margins, inscribed "Priority," served as etiquettes.

Royal Netherlands Academy of Arts and Sciences, 200th Anniv. A533

European Central Bank, 10th Anniv. A534

AEX Stock Index, 25th Anniv. A535

Bruna Bookshop Chain, 140th Anniv. A536

Royal Dutch Tourist Board, 125th Anniv. A537

2008, May 20 ***Perf. 13¼x12¾***

1309	Vert. strip of 5	7.00	3.50
a.	A533 44c multi	1.40	.35
b.	A534 44c multi	1.40	.35
c.	A535 44c multi	1.40	.35
d.	A536 44c multi	1.40	.35
e.	A537 44c multi	1.40	.35

Souvenir Sheet

Rembrandt Association, 125th Anniv. — A538

2008, June 12 ***Perf. 13¾***

1310	A538 €6.65 multi	21.00	10.50

Dutch Food Products A539

Designs: No. 1311, Container of adobo seasoning mix, Madame Jeannette peppers, Edam cheese. No. 1312, Peas, can of condensed milk, papaya, vert. No. 1313, Ham, plantain, bottle of Ponche Pistachio liqueur, vert.

2008, July 8 ***Perf. 13¾***

1311	A539 92c multi	3.00	.75
1312	A539 92c multi	3.00	.75
1313	A539 92c multi	3.00	.75
a.	Souvenir sheet of 5, #1311-1313, Aruba #330, Netherlands Antilles #1187, + 3 etiquettes, 144x75mm	9.00	4.50
b.	Booklet pane, as "a," 150x102mm	15.50	—
	Complete booklet, 2 #1313b	31.00	
	Nos. 1311-1313 (3)	9.00	2.25

No. 1313a sold for €2.76. Complete booklet sold for €9.95. Nos. 1312-1313 were available only in Nos. 1313a and 1313b. No. 1311 was available in Nos. 1313a, 1313b, Aruba No. 332a, and Netherlands Antilles No. 1189a.

Miniature Sheet

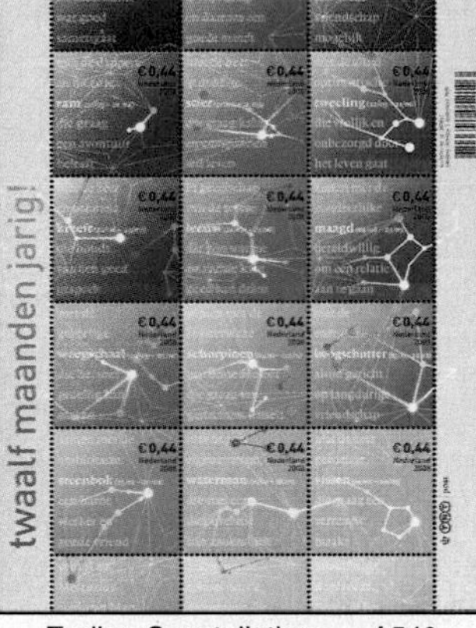

Zodiac Constellations — A540

No. 1314: a, Ram (Aries). b, Stier (Taurus). c, Tweeling (Gemini). d, Kreeft (Cancer). e, Leeuw (Leo). f, Maagd (Virgo). g, Weegschaal (Libra). h, Schorpioen (Scorpio). i, Boogschutter (Sagittarius). j, Steenbok (Capricorn). k, Waterman (Aquarius). l, Vissen (Pisces).

2008, Sept. 1 **Litho.** ***Perf. 13¾***

1314	A540 Sheet of 12	15.00	15.00
a.-l.	44c Any single	1.25	.30

Greeting Card Weeks A541

2008, Sept. 1 ***Perf. 14½***

1315	A541 44c multi	1.25	.30

Printed in sheets of 3.

Gnomes A542

Designs: No. 1316, Pinkeltje. No. 1317, Wipneus en Pim. No. 1318, Piggelmee. No. 1319, Paulus de boskabouter. No. 1320, De Kabouter.

2008, Oct. 1 ***Perf. 13½x12¾***

1316	A542 75c multi	2.10	.50
1317	A542 75c multi	2.10	.50
1318	A542 75c multi	2.10	.50
1319	A542 75c multi	2.10	.50
1320	A542 75c multi	2.10	.50
a.	Vert. strip of 5, #1316-1320	10.50	2.50

Nos. 1316-1320 were printed in sheets of 10, containing two of each stamp. The other strip in the sheet is in a different stamp order and the two strips in the sheet are tete-beche.

Miniature Sheet

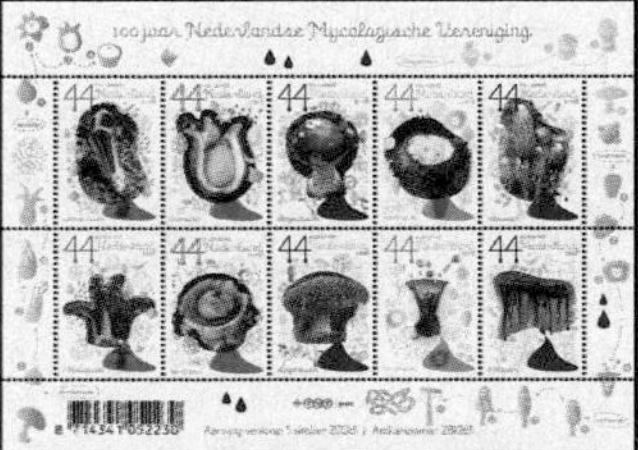

Mushrooms — A543

No. 1321 — Early and late stages of mushroom's life: a, Inktviszwam (early). b, Aardater (early). c, Vliegenzwam (early). d, Nestzwam (early). e, Inktzwam (early). f, Inktviszwam (late). g, Aardater (late). h, Vliegenzwam (late). i, Nestzwam (late). j, Inktzwam (late).

2008, Oct. 1 ***Perf. 14½***

1321	A543 Sheet of 10	12.50	12.50
a.-j.	44c Any single	1.25	.30

A booklet containing 5 panes, each showing a vertical pair from the sheet (same mushroom in different stages), sold for €9.95.

A544

December Stamps — A545

No. 1323: a, Building with large clock face and gift. b, Three dark envelopes, left half of Christmas tree. c, Right half of Christmas tree, top of ladder. d, Bell, Christmas tree. e, Building, gifts. f, Christmas tree, building with people on roof. g, Building, knife, fork and candle. h, House, bottom of ladder. i, Postcard, left side of fireplace. j, Right side of fireplace, fork and spoon.

Serpentine Die Cut 12

2008, Nov. 18 **Self-Adhesive**

1322	A544 34c multi	.90	.25
1323	A545 Block of 10	9.00	
a.-j.	34c Any single	.90	.25

The vignette of No. 1322 could be personalized for a fee.

Ecology Types of 2008

Designs: 77c, Bicycle with globe hemispheres as wheels. 95c, Heart-shaped globe.

Serpentine Die Cut 11

2009, Jan. 2 **Photo.**

Booklet Stamps

Self-Adhesive

1324	A523 77c multi + etiquette	2.25	.55
a.	Booklet pane of 5	11.50	
1325	A523 95c multi + etiquette	2.75	.70
a.	Booklet pane of 5	14.00	

On Nos. 1324-1325 a row of microrouletting separates stamps from etiquettes.

Miniature Sheet

Braille Alphabet, 180th Anniv. — A546

No. 1326 — Letters (on front and back), and in Braille: a, Hulde roem mythe. b, Adres komst thuis. c, Uniek zelfs dank. d, Super zodra adieu. e, Hevig dwars naief. f, Moed extra kans. g, Begin marge exact. h, Afijn bekaf kus. i, Geluk wens bravo. j, Fabel credo liefs. k, Quasi niets ophef. l, Brief vurig hart.

Litho., Photo & Embossed

2009, Jan. 10 ***Perf. 13¾***

1326	A546 Sheet of 12	14.00	14.00
a.-l.	44c Any single	1.10	.30
m.	Booklet pane of 3, #1326a-1326c	6.50	—
n.	Booklet pane of 3, #1326d-1326f	6.50	—
o.	Booklet pane of 3, #1326g-1326i	6.50	—
p.	Booklet pane of 3, #1326j-1326l	6.50	—
	Complete booklet, #1326m-13326p	26.00	

Louis Braille (1809-52), educator of the blind. Complete booklet sold for €9.95.

A547

Personalized Stamps — A548

Serpentine Die Cut 12

2009, Mar. 10 **Litho.**

Self-Adhesive

1327	A547 44c multi	1.25	.30
1328	A548 44c multi	1.25	.30

The generic vignettes of Nos. 1327 (Dutch Golf Federation) and 1328 (Dutch Stamp Collectors' Association), which sold at face value, are shown. These stamps, printed in sheets of 10, could be personalized for an additional fee. See Nos. 1300-1301 for perforated stamps having these frames.

Netherlands Tourism Areas — A549

2009 **Litho.** ***Perf. 14½x14¼***

1329	A549 44c Assen	1.25	.30
1330	A549 44c Tilburg	1.25	.30
1331	A549 44c Oosterhout	1.25	.30
1332	A549 44c Roosendaal	1.25	.30
1333	A549 44c Delfzijl	1.25	.30
a.	Souvenir sheet of 5, #1329-1333	6.25	3.25
	Nos. 1329-1333 (5)	6.25	1.50

Issued: Nos. 1329-1330, 3/10; Nos. 1331-1332, 4/28; No. 1333, 6/16; No. 1333a, 6/12. A booklet containing five panes, with each pane containing two perf. 13½x12¾ examples of each stamp, sold for €9.95.

Europa — A550

Designs: No. 1334, Map of low frequency array radio telescopes superimposed on map of Europe. No. 1335, Sketch of Saturn and Titan, telescope lens of Christiaan Huygens.

2009, Apr. 7 **Litho.** ***Perf. 13¼x12¾***

1334	77c multi	2.10	.50
1335	77c multi	2.10	.50
a.	A550 Horiz. pair, #1334-1335	4.20	1.00

Intl. Year of Astronomy. Sheet margins serve as etiquettes. No. 1335 is upside-down in relation to No. 1334.

Souvenir Sheet

Queens Wilhelmina, Juliana and Beatrix — A551

Litho. & Engr.

2009, Apr. 28 *Perf. 13¾*

1336 A551 €7 multi 19.00 9.50
a. Booklet pane of 1 27.00 —
Complete booklet, #1336a 27.00

Size of No. 1336a: 145x102mm. Complete booklet sold for €9.95.

Flasks, Artist's Mannequin, Party Streamer A552

Window, Egg, Binoculars A553

Atlas Sheltering Figurines A554

Coffee Service A555

Blocks, Pictures of Children A556

2009, May 12 Photo. *Perf. 14½*

1337 Vert. strip of 5 6.25 3.25
a. A552 44c multi 1.25 .30
b. A553 44c multi 1.25 .30
c. A554 44c multi 1.25 .30
d. A555 44c multi 1.25 .30
e. A556 44c multi 1.25 .30

Dutch Cancer Society, 60th anniv. (No. 1337a); Netherlands Bird Protection Society, 110th anniv. (No. 1337b); Cordaid Mensen in Nood (Men in Need), 95th anniv. (No. 1337c); National Sunflower Society, 60th anniv. (No. 1337d); SOS Children's Village, 60th anniv. (No. 1337e).

Music — A557

No. 1338: a, Tuba, trumpet and saxophone players. b, "When you sing you begin with Do Re Mi." c, Baton twirlers. d, "Jauchzet, frohlocket." e, Sousaphone players. f, "Para bailar la bamba."

2009, July 14 Litho. *Perf. 13½*

1338 A557 Block of 6 13.50 6.75
a.-f. 77c Any single 2.25 .60

World Music Contest, Kerkrade and Europa Cantat, Utrecht. Printed in sheets of 10 containing Nos. 1338e, 1338f, and 2 each Nos. 1338a-1338d. Sheet margins served as etiquettes. Stamps showing text are upside-down in relation to stamps showing people.

Miniature Sheet

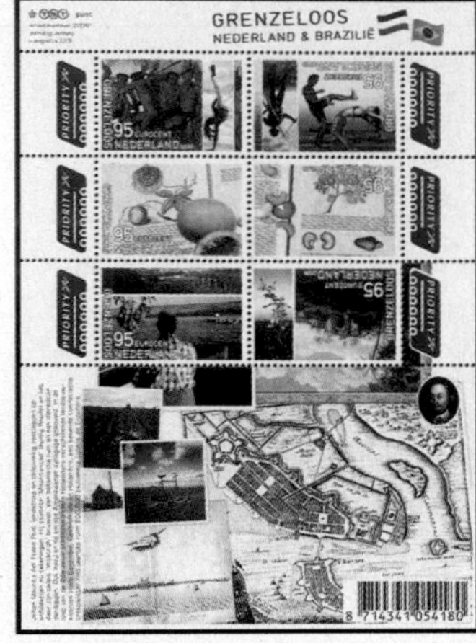

Dutch Connections With Brazil — A558

No. 1339: a, Tarairu Tribe War Dance, painting by Albert Eckhout, man standing on one hand. b, Capoeira performers, Tarairu tribesman. c, Passion fruit, and scientific book picturing passion fruit blossom. d, Cashews and scientific book picturing cashew tree. e, Sugar Plantation, painting by Frans Post; farmer looking at livestock. f, Church, Olinda, painting by Post; rose bush.

2009, Aug. 4 *Perf. 13½x12¾*

1339 A558 Sheet of 6 16.50 8.25
a.-f. 95c Any single 2.75 .70

No. 1339 was printed with three different illustrations in the bottom sheet margin, with each sheet having a different arrangement of stamps. Sheet margins at left and right served as etiquettes.

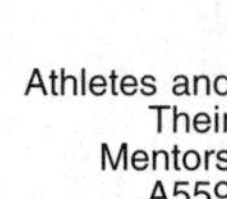

Athletes and Their Mentors A559

No. 1340: a, Anthony van Assche, gymnast, and mentor Jochem Uytdehaage. b, Leon Commandeur, cyclist, and mentor Johan Kenkhuis. c, Mike Marissen, swimmer, and mentor Bas van de Goor. d, Maureen Groefsema, judoist, and mentor Lobke Berkhout. e, Aniek van Koot, wheelchair tennis player, and mentor Marko Koers.

2009, Aug. 25 Photo. *Perf. 14½*

1340 Vert. strip of 5 6.25 3.25
a.-e. A559 44c Any single 1.25 .30

Stichting Sporttop, Olympic athlete development organization.

Greeting Card Week — A560

2009, Sept. 7 Litho. *Perf. 14½*

1341 A560 44c multi 1.40 .35

Miniature Sheets

Birthday Greetings — A561

"88" and: Nos. 1342a, 1343e, "Gefeliciteerd!" Nos. 1342b, 1343b, "Hoera!" Nos. 1342c, 1343c, "Proficiat!" Nos. 1342d, 1343d, "Nog Vele Jaren!" Nos. 1342e, 1343a, "Van Harte!"

2009, Sept. 22 Litho. *Perf. 13½*

1342 A561 Sheet of 5 7.00 3.50
a.-e. 44c Any single 1.40 .35

Self-Adhesive

Serpentine Die Cut 13¼x13

Stamp Size: 20x25mm

1343 A561 Sheet of 5 7.00
a.-e. 44c Any single 1.40 .35

Lines in the "88" on each stamp could be colored in to create all ten digits. Unused values are for stamps without any such alterations. Used values are for stamps with or without alterations.

A562

Personalized Stamps A563

2009-10 *Perf. 13¼*

1344 A562 44c multi 1.40 .35

Self-Adhesive

Serpentine Die Cut 12½

1345 A563 44c multi 1.25 .30

Issued: No. 1344, 10/1; No. 1345, 1/12/10. The generic vignettes for Nos. 1344 (Stamp Day) and 1345 (Wadden Sea Society), which sold at face value, are shown. These stamps, printed in sheets of 10, could be personalized for an additional fee. A booklet containing five panes, each with two examples of No. 1344 with the Stamp Day vignette sold for €9.95.

Miniature Sheet

Powered Flight in the Netherlands, Cent. — A564

No. 1346: a, Medical helicopter. b, Boeing 747. c, Apache helicopter. d, Terminal B, Schiphol Airport. e, Fokker F-27. f, Lockheed Super Constellation. g, Fokker F-18 "Pelikaan." h, Douglas DC-2 "Uiver" in Melbourne race. i, Wright Flyer. j, Fokker Spin, piloted by Anthony Fokker.

2009, Oct. 1 *Perf. 13½*

1346 A564 Sheet of 10 14.00 7.00
a.-j. 44c Any single 1.40 .35

A booklet containing five panes, each with a different horizontal pair from No. 1346, sold for €9.95.

December Stamps — A565

No. 1347: a, Green gift, pink ribbon, red background. b, Candelabra on yellow gift, blue background. c, Christmas tree on light blue gift, bright yellow green background. d, Light pink gift, red ribbon, gray background. e, Woman holding glass on yellow gift, pink background. f, Man holding glass on yellow gift, gray background. g, Christmas tree on blue gift, pink background. h, Red violet gift, red ribbon, carmine background. i, Christmas tree on yellow gift, blue background. j, Christmas tree on blue gift, red background.

Serpentine Die Cut 12¾x13¼

2009, Nov. 19 **Self-Adhesive**

1347 Block of 10 10.00
a.-j. A565 34c Any single 1.00 .25

Netherlands Tourism Areas — A566

2010 Litho. *Perf. 14½x14¼*

1348 A566 44c Haarlem 1.25 .35
1349 A566 44c Middelburg 1.25 .35
1350 A566 44c Maastricht 1.25 .35
1351 A566 44c Arnhem 1.25 .35
1352 A566 44c Leeuwarden 1.10 .30
a. Souvenir sheet of 5, #1348-1352 6.25 3.25

Issued: Nos. 1348-1349, 1/12. Nos. 1350-1351, 3/29; Nos. 1352, 1352a, 6/22. A booklet containing five panes, with each pane containing two perf. 13½x12¾ examples of each stamp, sold for €9.95.

Miniature Sheet

Dutch Patent Act, Cent. — A567

No. 1353: a, Submarine invented by Cornelis Drebbel, 1620. b, Light-emitting diode lighting invented by Philips, 2007. c, Artificial kidney invented by Willem Kolff, 1943. d, VacuVin vacuum sealer for wine bottles invented by Bernd Schneider. e, Milking robot invented by Van der Lely, 1987. f, Bicycle chain case invented by Wilhelmine J. van der Woerd. g, Automated handwriting recognition invented by TNT Post, 1980. h, Solar-powered vehicle invented by Solar Team Twente. i, Dyneema fiber invented by DSM, 1979. j, Telescope invented by Hans Lipperhey, 1608.

2010, Feb. 9 Litho. *Perf. 13¼x12¾*

1353 A567 Sheet of 10 12.50 6.25
a.-j. 44c Any single 1.25 .35

A booklet containing five panes, with each pane containing a horizontal pair from the sheet, sold for €9.95.

75th Book Week — A568

2010, Mar. 9 Litho. *Imperf.*

1354 A568 €2.20 multi 6.00 3.00

No. 1354 is printed as a miniature book made up of two pieces of paper of different sizes. Both pieces of paper are printed on both sides, and are glued together. The cover of the book is the longer of the two pieces of paper, and is folded into three parts. The stamp, the front cover of the book, is the middle part of this piece of paper. The gum, applied to the left of the stamp, becomes the book's back cover when the longer piece of paper is folded. A photograph of a man holding a book, is to the right of the stamp, and is the book's first page. Text appears on the reverse of this picture and the stamp, and another picture depicting a man reading a book is printed on the back of the gum. The second piece of paper, folded in half to constitute four pages of the book, has text only, and is glued to the back of longer sheet where the fold between the stamp and the photo is found. Values are for the complete item.

VVV, Dutch Tourist Information Office, 125th Anniv. A569

Royal Tropical Institute, Cent. A570

Duinrell Amusement Park, Wassenaar, 75th Anniv. A571

Euromast Tower, Rotterdam, 50th Anniv. A572

Djoser Travel, 25th Anniv. A573

2010, Mar. 23 Photo. *Perf. 14½*

1355 Vert. strip of 5 6.25 3.25
- *a.* A569 44c multi 1.25 .35
- *b.* A570 44c multi 1.25 .35
- *c.* A571 44c multi 1.25 .35
- *d.* A572 44c multi 1.25 .35
- *e.* A573 44c multi 1.25 .35

Greeting Card Weeks A574

2010, Mar. 29 Litho.

1356 A574 44c multi 1.25 .35

Printed in sheets of 3.

Souvenir Sheet

Breskens Lighthouse — A575

2010, Apr. 27 *Perf. 13¾*

1357 A575 €7 multi 19.00 9.50

Personalized Stamp — A576

2010, July 1 Litho. *Perf. 13½x14*

1358 A576 1 gray & black 1.10 .30

The generic vignette of No. 1358, which sold for the franking value of 44c, and was printed in sheets of 10, is shown. The vignette part of the stamp could be personalized for an additional fee. Booklets containing stamps showing different vignettes that could not be personalized sold for €9.95.

Rectangles — A577

2010, July 1 *Die Cut Perf. 14¼*

Self-Adhesive

1359 A577 1 multi 1.10 .30

Sold for 44c on day of issue. Compare with type A456.

Birth Announcement Stamp — A578

2010, July 1 *Die Cut Perf. 14¼*

Self-Adhesive

1360 A578 1 multi 1.10 .30

Sold for 44c on day of issue.

Hearts — A579

2010, July 1 *Die Cut Perf. 14¼*

Self-Adhesive

1361 A579 1 multi 1.10 .30
- *a.* Booklet pane of 10 11.00

Sold for 44c on day of issue. Compare with type A466.

Death Announcement Stamp — A580

Serpentine Die Cut 11¾

2010, July 1 Photo.

Self-Adhesive

1362 A580 1 multi 1.10 .30

Sold for 44c on day of issue. Compare with type A365.

Numerals
A581 A582

Serpentine Die Cut 13½

2010, July 1 Litho.

Self-Adhesive

1363 A581 1 multi + label 1.10 .30

Coil Stamps

Photo.

Die Cut Perf. 14¼

1364 A581 1 multi 1.10 .30

1365 A582 2 multi 2.25 .60

On day of issue Nos. 1363-1364 each sold for 44c, and No. 1365 sold for 88c. Label on No. 1363 could be personalized. Compare with type A491.

Queen Beatrix With Large Numeral — A583

Die Cut Perf. 14¼ Syncopated

2010, July 1 Photo.

Booklet Stamps

Self-Adhesive

1366 A583 1 metallic blue & lil 1.10 .30
- *a.* Booklet pane of 10 11.00

Die Cut Perf. 14¼

1367 A583 2 gold & metallic grn 2.25 .60
- *a.* Booklet pane of 5 11.50

On day of issue, No. 1366 sold for 44c and No. 1367 sold for 88c. Compare with Type A273.

A584

A585

Ecology — A586

No. 1368: a, Hybrid vehicle with electric plug. b, House and sun (solar energy). c, Cow with electric plug (biofuels). d, Wind generators. e, Trees. f, Flowers, carpoolers in automobile. g, "Groen" with electric plug. h, Truck (soot filters). i, Birds and envelope (green mail). j, Insulated house.

Die Cut Perf. 14¼

2010, July 1 Litho.

Booklet Stamps

Self-Adhesive

1368 Booklet pane of 10 11.00
- *a.-j.* A584 1 Any single 1.10 .30

Photo.

Serpentine Die Cut 11

1369 A585 1 Europa multi + etiquette 2.00 .50
- *a.* Booklet pane of 5 + 5 etiquettes 10.00

1370 A586 1 Wereld multi + etiquette 2.40 .60
- *a.* Booklet pane of 5 + 5 etiquettes 12.00

On Nos. 1369-1370 a row of microrouletting separates stamps from etiquettes. On day of issue, Nos. 1368a-1368j each sold for 44c; No. 1369, for 77c; No. 1370, for 95c. Compare with type A523.

Miniature Sheet

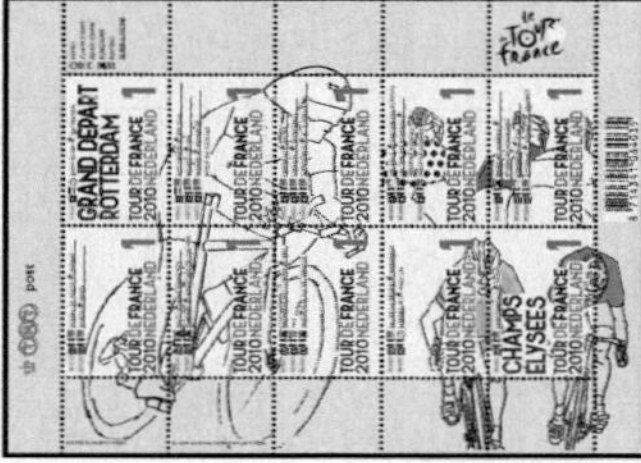

Start of 2010 Tour de France in Rotterdam — A587

No. 1371 — Dates and stages of the Tour de France: a, July 3 (preliminary stage). b, July 4-6 (stages 1-3). c, July 7-9 (stages 4-6). d, July 10-12 (stages 7-8). e, July 13-15 (stages 9-11). f, July 16-17 (stages 12-13). g, July 18-19 (stages 14-15). h, July 20-22 (stages 16-17). i, July 23-24 (stages 18-19). j, July 25 (stage 20).

2010, July 1 Photo. *Perf. 14½*

1371 A587 Sheet of 10 11.00 5.50
- *a.-j.* 1 Any single 1.10 .30

On day of issue, Nos. 1371a-1371j each sold for 44c.

Miniature Sheet

Royal Dutch Forestry Association, Cent. — A588

No. 1372: a, Maple leaves, forest canopy, tip of jay's wing, "1" in white at LR. b, Maple leaves, forest canopy, "1" in brown at UL. c, Jay, forest canopy, "1" in brown at LR. d, Forest canopy, rose leaves, "1" in white at UL. e, Rose hips and leaves, "1" in white at LR. f, Rose leaves, tree trunks, "1" in brown at UL. g, Rose hips, logs, bracken leaves, "1" in brown at LR. h, Bracken leaves, logs, "1" in white at UL. i, Tree roots, moss, "1" in white at LR. j, Tree roots, mushrooms, "1" in brown at UL.

Perf. 13¼x12¾

2010, Aug. 17 Litho.

1372 A588 Sheet of 10 12.50 6.25
- *a.-j.* 1 Any single 1.25 .35

On day of issue, Nos. 1372a-1372j each sold for 44c. A booklet containing five panes, each showing a horizontal pair from the sheet, sold for €9.95.

Miniature Sheet

Dutch Connections With Surinam — A589

No. 1373: a, Building with balconies and dormers, lamp. b, Building with stairway, hand rail. c, Women in native dress. d, Two women, one upside-down. e, Wood, feathers, achiote seeds. f, Onions, achiote fruit, tobacco.

2010, Aug. 17 Litho. ***Perf. 13½x13***

1373 A589 Sheet of 6 15.00 7.50
a.-f. 1 Wereld Any single 2.50 .65

No. 1373 was printed with three different illustrations in the bottom sheet margin, with each sheet having a different arrangement of stamps. Sheet margins at left and right served as etiquettes. On day of issue Nos. 1373a-1373f each sold for 95c.

Personalized Stamp — A590

2010, Sept. 14 Litho. ***Perf. 13½x14***

1374 A590 1 multi 1.25 .35

The generic vignette shown on this stamp, commemorating Stamp Day, sold for 44c on day of issue. This stamp, printed in sheets of 10, could be personalized for an additional fee. A booklet containing five panes, each with two examples of No. 1374 with the generic vignette, sold for €9.95.

Woman and Windmill — A591

Litho. With 3-Dimensional Plastic Affixed

Serpentine Die Cut 9x8¾

2010, Sept. 29 Self-Adhesive

1375 A591 5 multi 6.25 1.60

Sold for €2.20 on day of issue.

Stop AIDS Campaign — A592

No. 1376: a, African woman with "Stop AIDS Now!" poster on head. b, African woman, ribbon. c, Hand holding pill, ribbon. d, African woman pointing to ribbon. e, Ribbon, heads of African man and woman. f, African woman wearing headdress.

2010, Oct. 12 Litho. ***Perf. 14½***

1376 A592 Block of 6 7.50 3.75
a.-f. 1 Any single 1.25 .35

Nos. 1376a-1376f each sold for 44c on day of issue.

Personalized Stamp — A593

2010, Nov. 23 Litho. ***Perf. 13½x14***

1377 A593 (34c) multi .95 .25

The generic vignette shown on this stamp depicts Snoopy. This stamp, printed in sheets of 10, could be personalized for an additional fee.

December Stamps — A594

No. 1378: a, Santa Claus carrying tree. b, Bell and ribbon. c, Rocking horse and flowers. d, Embroidered heart. e, Deer, flower and candle on Christmas card. f, Deer and ribbon. g, Santa Claus. h, Handshake and flowers on Christmas card. i, Angel with flowers. j, Gingerbread house.

Serpentine Die Cut 12¾

2010, Nov. 23 Self-Adhesive

1378 Block of 10 9.50
a.-j. A594 (34c) Any single .95 .25
k. Booklet pane of 10, #1378a-1378j 13.50
Complete booklet, 2 #1378k 27.00

Complete booklet sold for €9.95.

Personalized Stamp — A595

Die Cut Perf. 13x13¼

2011, Jan. 10 Litho.

Self-Adhesive

1379 A595 1 black 1.25 .35

The generic vignette of No. 1379 depicting St. John's Cathedral, 's Hertogenbosch, which sold for the franking value of 46c and printed in sheets of 10, is shown. The vignette part of the stamp could be personalized for an additional fee.

Netherlands Tourism Areas — A596

2011 ***Perf. 14½x14¼***

1380 A596 1 Almere 1.25 .35
1381 A596 1 Eindhoven 1.25 .35
1382 A596 1 Apeldoorn 1.40 .45
1383 A596 1 Breda 1.40 .45
1384 A596 1 Enschede 1.40 .45
a. Souvenir sheet of 5, #1380-1384 6.75 3.50
Nos. 1380-1384 (5) 6.70 2.05

Issued: Nos. 1380-1381, 1/10; Nos. 1382-1383, 4/11; Nos. 1384, 1384a, 5/23. On day of issue, Nos, 1380-1384 each sold for 46c. A booklet containing five panes, with each pane containing two perf. 13½x12¾ examples of each stamp, sold for €9.95.

Personalized Stamp A597

2011, Jan. 31 ***Perf. 13¾***

1385 A597 1 multi 1.25 .35

The generic vignette of No. 1385 depicting a great tit, which sold for the franking value of 46c and printed in sheets of 10, is shown. The vignette part of the stamp could be personalized for an additional fee. Numerous stamps depicting different birds in the vignette were created after Jan. 31 by postal authorities. An electronic audio pen which sold for €39.95 would play the song of the bird when placed near the stamp. Numerous stamps depicting recording artists in the vignette began appearing in 2012.

Miniature Sheet

Utrecht University, 375th Anniv. — A598

No. 1386 — Various anniversaries at Utrecht University: a, 90th anniv. of psychology studies (brain). b, 100th anniv. of Unitas Student Society (owl). c, 65th birthday of Gerard t'Hooft. 1999 Nobel Physics laureate (t'Hooft). d, 125th anniv. of Utrecht University Foundation (globe). e, 50th anniv. of Utrecht Science Park de Uithof (aerial view of park). f, 190th anniv. of veterinary medicine program (horse). g, 45th anniv. of Institute of Theater Studies (theater spotlight). h, 250th anniv. of death of Petrus van Musschenbroek, professor of mathematics and philosophy (van Musschenbroek). i, 25th anniv. of Mebiose Student Association for the Biological Sciences (stylized DNA molecule). j, 325th anniv. of Senaatzaal Portrait Gallery (Senaatzaal).

2011, Mar. 28 ***Perf. 13¼x12¾***

1386 A598 Sheet of 10 14.00 7.00
a.-j. 1 Any single 1.40 .45

Nos. 1386a-1386j each sold for 46c on day of issue. A booklet containing 5 panes, each containing a horizontal pair of stamps on the sheet, sold for €9.95.

Miniature Sheet

City of the Netherlands — A599

No. 1387 — Inscriptions in bold type: a, Kenniscluster, Arnhem (black-framed code box). b, Kenniscluster, Arnhem (building). c, Parkeertoren Nederland (black-framed code box). d, Parkeertoren Nederland (building). e, De Boekenberg, Spijkenisse (black-framed code box). f, Skytower, Amsterdam (building). g, Skytower, Amsterdam (black-framed code box). h, De Boekenberg, Spijkenisse (building). i, Windpost, Maasvlakte (black-framed code box). j, Windpost, Maasvlakte (building). k, Map of the Netherlands.

2011, Mar. 28 ***Perf. 13¼***

1387 A599 Sheet of 12, #1387a-1387j, 2 #1387k 17.00 8.50

On day of issue, Nos. 1387a-1387k each sold for 46c. The code boxes activate an augmented reality application when scanned by a webcam when visting the www.toekomstinbeweging.nl website.

Greeting Card Week A600

2011, Apr. 18 ***Perf. 14½***

1388 A600 1 multi 1.40 .45

No. 1388 sold for 46c on day of issue. Printed in sheets of 3.

Organization for Economic Cooperation and Development, 50th Anniv. — A601

Royal Dutch Billiards Federation, Cent. A602

Royal Dutch Checkers Federation, Cent. A603

Loevenstein Castle, 650th Anniv. A604

Association of Dutch Composers, Cent. A605

2011, May 2 *Perf. 13¼x12¾*

1389 Vert. strip of 5 7.00 3.50
a. A601 1 multi 1.40 .45
b. A602 1 multi 1.40 .45
c. A603 1 multi 1.40 .45
d. A604 1 multi 1.40 .45
e. A605 1 multi 1.40 .45

Nos. 1389a-1389e each sold for 46c on day of issue.

Miniature Sheet

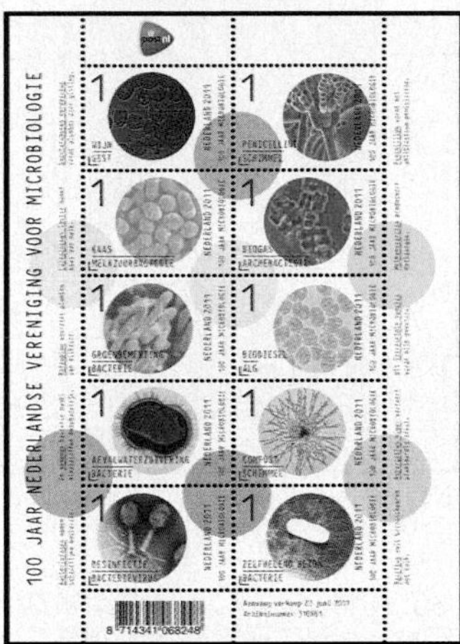
Netherlands Society for Microbiology, Cent. — A606

No. 1390 — Various microorganisms and inscription: a, Wijn / Gist (wine / yeast). b, Penicilline / Schimmel (penicillin / mold). c, Kaas / Melkzuurbacterie (cheese / lactic bacteria). d, Biogas / Archebacterie (biogas / archaea). e, Groenbemesting / Bacterie (green manure / bacteria). f, Biodiesel / Alg. (biodiesel / algae). g, Afvalwaterzuivering / Bacterie (waste water purification / bacteria). h, Compost / Schimmel (compost / mold). i, Desinfectie / Bacterievirus (disinfectant / bacteriophage). j, Zelfhelend beton / bacterie (self-curing concrete / bacteria).

2011, May 27

1390 A606 Sheet of 10 14.00 7.00
a.-j. 1 Any single 1.40 .45

Nos. 1390a-1390j each sold for 46c on day of issue. A booklet containing 5 panes, each containing a horizontal pair of stamps on the sheet, sold for €9.95.

Initial Public Offering of Royal Post NL Stock A607

2011, May 31 **Litho.**

1391 A607 1 multi 1.40 .45

No. 1391 sold for 46c on day of issue.

Miniature Sheet

Dutch Connections With South Africa — A608

No. 1392: a, Dutch-style South African houses in elephant (olifant). b, Poem by Ingrid Jonker in leopard (luipaard). c, Grapes in buffalo (buffel). d, South African house in rhinoceros (neushoorn). e, Painting of Jan van Riebeeck arriving at Cape of Good Hope in lion (leeuw). f, Dutch East India Company pottery in penguin (pinguin).

2011, July 25 *Perf. 13¼x12¾*

1392 A608 Sheet of 6 16.50 8.25
a.-f. 1 Wereld Any single 2.75 .85

No. 1392 was printed with three different illustrations in the bottom sheet margin, with each sheet having a different arrangement of stamps. Sheet margins at left and right served as etiquettes. On day of issue Nos. 1392a-1392f each sold for 95c.

De Bond Heemschut Historical Preservation Society, Cent. — A609

No. 1393: a, American Embassy, The Hague. b, Amerongen Castle. c, Tricot factory, Winterswijk. d, Noord-Zuid-Hollands Coffee House, Amsterdam. e, St. Servatius Bridge, Maastricht. f, Synagogue, Groningen.

2011, Aug. 22 *Perf. 13¼x12¾*

1393 A609 Block of 6 7.50 3.75
a.-f. 1 Any single 1.25 .35

Nos. 1393a-1393f each sold for 46c on day of issue.

A610

A611

Ecology — A612

No. 1394: a, Shirt on clothesline. b, Stylized plant. c, Bird. d, Hen. e, Kites. f, House. g, Laptop computer. h, Suitcase and leaf, horiz. i, Butterfly, horiz. j, Electric vehicle and plug, horiz.

Die Cut Perf. 14¼

2011, Sept. 1 **Litho.**

Booklet Stamps Self-Adhesive

1394 Booklet pane of 10 12.50
a.-j. A610 1 Any single 1.25 .35

Photo.

Serpentine Die Cut 11

1395 A611 1 Europa multi + etiquette 2.25 .60
a. Booklet pane of 5 11.50
1396 A612 1 Wereld multi + etiquette 2.60 .80
a. Booklet pane of 5 13.00

On Nos. 1395-1396 a row of microrouletting separates stamps from etiquettes. On day of issue, Nos. 1394a-1394j each sold for 46c,; No. 139, for 79c; No. 1396, for 95c.

Miniature Sheet

Herman Renz Circus, Cent. — A613

No. 1397: a, Fire eater. b, Snake handler. c, Clown. d, Trained horse. e, Man balancing hat on nose. f, Tumbling act. g, Lion. h, Acrobat lifting another acrobat. i, Elephant. j, Unicyclist on tightrope.

Perf. 12¾x13¼

2011, Sept. 19 **Litho.**

1397 A613 Sheet of 10 12.50 6.25
a.-j. A613 1 Any single 1.25 .30

On day of issue, Nos. 1397a-1397j each sold for 46c.

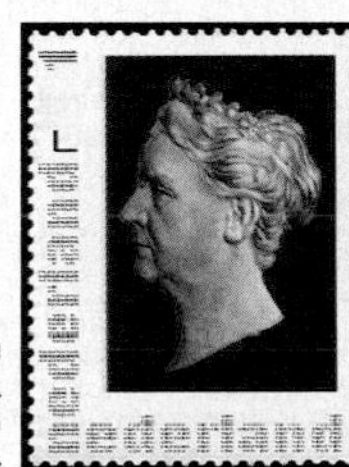
Queen Wilhelmina (1880-1962) A614

2011, Oct. 14 *Perf. 13¼x13½*

1398 A614 1 multi 1.25 .30

Stamp Day. No. 1398 sold for 46c on day of issue. A booklet containing five panes, each containing two No. 1398, sold for €9.95.

Postcrossing.com — A615

No. 1399 — Postcards depicting: a, Sunset, man and woman kissing under umbrella, donkey and house, puppies, nesting dolls, Eiffel Tower, Asian woman, beach in Rio. b, Baby surrounded by sunflower petals, sheep, beach, bull fight, Sphinx and Pyramid, Cuban car, building in Finland. c, Bridge, fish and coral, building in Antwerp, Belgium, Taj Mahal, Asian woman, soccer players, tower and Arabic text. d, Flamingo in Miami, beach in Rio, Petronas Towers, Kuala Lumpur, Acropolis, buildings in Warsaw, Big Ben and statue, London, woman, and China Central Television Building, Beijing. e, Boat and building in Finland, Prague and Hradcany Castle, tulips, chimpanzee wearing cowboy hat, Hong Kong skyline, Asian woman, bird, comic strip. f, Cat, windmill and tulips, Netherlands, Cliffs of Moher, Ireland, Calgary skyline, churches, St. Petersburg, Russia, Great Wall of China, woman praying, two boys.

2011, Oct. 14 *Perf. 13¼x12¾*

1399 A615 Block of 6 + 6 etiquettes 15.00 7.50
a.-c. 1 Europa Any single 2.25 .60
d.-f. 1 Wereld Any single 2.60 .80

On day of issue Nos. 1399a-1399c each sold for 79c, and Nos. 1399d-1399f each sold for 95c.

December Stamps — A616

No. 1400: a, Candle. b, Reindeer, bird and fir trees. c, Bird on heart. d, Three Christmas ornaments. e, Church and houses. f, Reindeer with Christmas ornament, birds and candles on antlers. g, Angel with candles. h, Bird, holding Christmas ornament on fir branch. i, Snowman. j, Squirrel and Christmas ornament.

Serpentine Die Cut 12½

2011, Nov. 22 **Litho.**

Self-Adhesive

1400 Block of 10 10.00
a.-j. A616 (36c) Any single 1.00 .30

Personalized Stamp — A617

2011, Nov. 22 *Die Cut Perf. 13x13¼*

Self-Adhesive

1401 A617 (36c) multi 1.00 .30

The generic vignette shown on this stamp depicts two birds under mistletoe. This stamp could be personalized for an additional fee.

A618

Personalized Stamps — A619

2012, Jan. 2 **Litho.** *Perf. 13½x14*

1402 A618 1 Europa black 2.25 .55
1403 A619 1 Wereld black 2.50 .65

The generic vignettes of Nos. 1402 and 1403, which are shown, sold for the franking value of 85c and 95c, respectively. Nos. 1402 and 1403 each were printed in sheets of 10. The vignette parts of the stamp could be personalized for an additional fee.

Country Houses — A620

Country houses in: No. 1404, Mattemburgh. No. 1405, Amstenrade. No. 1406, Trompenburg. No. 1407, Vollenhoven. No. 1408, Middachten.

2012 ***Perf. 14½x14¼***

1404 A620 1 multi 1.40 .35
a. Perf. 13½x12¾ 2.50 2.50
b. Booklet pane of 2 #1404a 5.00 5.00
1405 A620 1 multi 1.40 .35
a. Perf. 13½x12¾ 2.50 2.50
b. Booklet pane of 2 #1405a 5.00 5.00
1406 A620 1 multi 1.40 .35
a. Perf. 13½x12¾ 2.50 2.50
b. Booklet pane of 2 #1406a 5.00 5.00
1407 A620 1 multi 1.40 .35
a. Perf. 13½x12¾ 2.50 2.50
b. Booklet pane of 2 #1407a 5.00 5.00
1408 A620 1 multi 1.25 .35
a. Perf. 13½x12¾ 2.50 2.50
b. Booklet pane of 2 #1408a 5.00 5.00
Complete booklet, #1404b, 1405b, 1406b, 1407b, 1408b 25.00
c. Souvenir sheet of 5, #1404-1408 7.00 3.50
Nos. 1404-1408 (5) 6.85 1.75

Issued: Nos. 1404-1405, 1/30; Nos. 1406-1407, 2/27; Nos. 1404a, 1404b, 1405a, 1405b, 1406a, 1406b, 1407a, 1407b, 1408, 1408a, 1408b, 1408c, 5/21. Nos. 1404-1408 each sold for 50c on day of issue. Complete booklet sold for €9.95 on day of issue.

Dutch Salvation Army, 125th Anniv. A621

2012, Feb. 27 ***Perf. 13¼x13½***

1409 A621 1 multi 1.40 .35

No. 1409 sold for 50c on day of issue.

Albert Heijn Grocery Stores, 125th Anniv. — A622

Designs: No. 1410, Original store, employee with first delivery bicycle. No. 1411, Coffee beans, coffee plant workers. No. 1412, Hamster, shoppers in grocery store. No. 1413, Shopper with child in shopping cart, store employees.

Serpentine Die Cut 13¼x13

2012, Feb. 27 **Self-Adhesive**

1410 A622 1 multi 1.40 .35
1411 A622 1 multi 1.40 .35
1412 A622 1 multi 1.40 .35
1413 A622 1 multi 1.40 .35
Nos. 1410-1413 (4) 5.60 1.40

Nos. 1410-1413 each sold for 50c on day of issue.

Greeting Card Week — A623

2012, Mar. 26 ***Perf. 13¼x13½***

1414 A623 1 multi 1.40 .35

No. 1414 sold for 50c on day of issue. Printed in sheets of 3.

A624

Tourism — A625

No. 1415: a, National Maritime Museum, Dutch East Indiaman "The Amsterdam," country name in white. b, Muziekgebouw Concert Hall, cruise ship "MSC Lirica," country name in gold.

No. 1416: a, The Bend in the Herengracht Canal, painting by Gerrit Berckheyde, country name in white. b, Skinny Bridge over Amstel River, country name in gold.

2012, Mar. 26 **Litho.**

1415 A624 Horiz. pair 2.80 1.40
a.-b. 1 Either single 1.40 .35
1416 A625 Pair 4.50 2.25
a.-b. 1 Europa Either single 2.25 .60

Europa (#1416b). On day of issue, Nos. 1415a-1415b each sold for 50c and Nos. 1416a-1416b each sold for 85c.

Netherlands Open Air Museum, Cent. — A626

Historical photographs: Nos. 1417a, 1417k, Women cleaning (green, at left), Marketplace (black, at right). Nos. 1417b, 1417l, Marketplace (black, at left). Woman sewing (purple, at right). Nos. 1417c, 1417m, Children with smartphone (rose, at left), Children crossing street (blue, at right). Nos. 1417d, 1417n, Children crossing street (blue, at left), Children playing (black, at right). Nos. 1417e, 1417o, Cots and worker at migrant worker's lodging (blue, at left), Sod hut (purple at right). Nos. 1417f, 1417p, Sod hut (purple, at left), Children watching television (rose, at right). Nos. 1417g, 1417q, Campers and van (purple, at left), Children with tablet and camp light (green, at right). Nos. 1417h, 1417r, Children with tablet and camp light (green, at left), Hockey players at Netherlands Open Air Museum (blue, at right). Nos. 1417i, 1417s, People boarding airplane at Schiphol Airport (black, at left), Car at gas station (rose, at right). Nos. 1417j, 1417t, Car at gas station (rose, at left), Hay cart (green, at right).

2012, Apr. 23 ***Perf. 13¼x12¾***

1417 A626 Sheet of 10 14.00 7.00
a.-j. 1 Any single 1.40 .35
k.-t. Any single, perf. 14½ 2.60 2.60
u. Booklet pane of 2, #1417k-1417l 5.25 —
v. Booklet pane of 2, #1417m-1417n 5.25 —
w. Booklet pane of 2, #1417o-1417p 5.25 —
x. Booklet pane of 2, #1417q-1417r 5.25 —
y. Booklet pane of 2, #1417s-1417t 5.25 —
Complete booklet, #1417u, 1417v, 1417w, 1417x, 1417y 26.50

Nos. 1417a-1417t each sold for 50c on day of issue.

Miniature Sheet

Madurodam Miniature Park, 60th Anniv. — A627

No. 1418 — Miniatures of: a, Dutch East India ship. b, Windmills and building. c, Cheese market (crowd in plaza in front of building). d, Port of Rotterdam and tanker ships. e, Field of flowers. f, Rijksmuseum. g, Schiphol Airport. h, Delta Works (people near white conneted pipes). i, Maasvlakte 2 port project (dredger). j, Binnenhof, horses and carriages.

2012, May 21 ***Perf. 13¼x13½***

1418 A627 Sheet of 10 12.50 6.25
a.-j. 1 Any single 1.25 .35

Nos. 1418a-1418j each sold for 50c on day of issue.

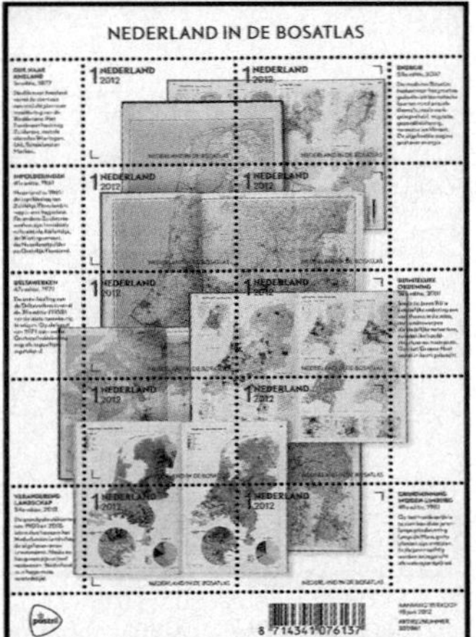

Maps of the Netherlands from the Bosatlas — A628

Designs: Nos. 1419a, 1419k, Upper left section of map from 1877 atlas, upper part of page 62 from 2007 atlas. Nos. 1419b, 1419l, Upper right section of map from 1877 atlas, upper sections of pages 62 and 63 from 2007 atlas. Nos. 1419c, 1419m, Section of map from 1877 atlas, upper left section of page 60 from 1961 atlas. Nos. 1419d, 1419n, Section of map from 1877 atlas, lower section of page 63 from 2007 atlas, upper right section of page 61 from 1961 atlas. Nos. 1419e, 1419o, Section of map from page 60 of 1961 atlas, sections of pages depicting South Netherlands (Zuid-Nederland) from 1971 atlas, upper left section of page 60 from 2001 atlas. Nos. 1419f, 1419p, Section of page 61 from 1961 atlas, upper right section of pages 60 and upper left section of 61 from 2001 atlas. Nos. 1419g, 1419q, Lower section of South Netherlands map from 1971 atlas, lower section of page 60 from 2001 atlas, upper sections of pages 39 from 2012 atlas. Nos. 1419h, 1419r, Lower sections of pages 60 and 61 from 2001 atlas, upper right section of page 39 from 2012 atlas, section of page from 1981 atlas. Nos. 1419i, 1419s, Lower sections of pages 38 and 39 from 2012 atlas. Nos. 1419j, 1419t, Lower right section of page 39 from 2012 atlas, lower right section of page from 1981 atlas.

2012, June 18 ***Perf. 13¼x12¾***

1419 A628 Sheet of 10 12.50 6.25
a.-j. 1 Any single 1.25 .35
k.-t. Any single, perf. 14½ 2.50 2.50
u. Booklet pane of 2, #1419k-1419l 5.00 —
v. Booklet pane of 2, #1419m-1419n 5.00 —
w. Booklet pane of 2, #1419o-1419p 5.00 —
x. Booklet pane of 2, #1419q-1419r 5.00 —
y. Booklet pane of 2, #1419s-1419t 5.00 —
Complete booklet, #1419u, 1419v, 1419w, 1419x, 1419y 25.00

Nos. 1419a-1419j each sold for 50c on day of issue. Complete booklet sold for €9.95.

Miniature Sheet

Netherlands Olympic Committee and Netherlands Sports Federation, Cent. — A629

No. 1420 — Athletes: a, Sjoukje Dijkstra, figure skater. b, Anton Geesink, judoka. c, Nico Rienks, rower. d, Ellen van Langen, runner. e, Field hockey player. f, Leontien Zijlaard-van Moorsel, cyclist. g, Esther Vergeer, Paralympian tennis player. h, Maarten van der Weijden, swimmer. i, Anky van Grunsven, dressage. j, Nicolien Sauerbreij, snowboarder.

2012, July 4 ***Perf. 13¼x13½***

1420 A629 Sheet of 10 12.50 6.25
a.-j. 1 Any single 1.25 .35

Nos. 1420a-1420j each sold for 50c on day of issue.

Miniature Sheet

Seasons Magazine, 20th Anniv. — A630

No. 1422 — Photography from magazine with inscription at LR: a, Esdoorn (maple leaves). b, IJsbloem (frost flower). c, Peul (snow peas). d, Dahlia. e, Kievitsbloem (fritillaries). f, Lijsterbes (rowanberries). g, Rode zonnehoed (Purple coneflower). h, Rimpelroos, Rozenbottel, Rozengeranium (Rugosa rose, rose hips, rose geranium). i, Tulp (tulips). j, Blauwe bes (blueberries).

2012, July 16 ***Perf. 13½x13¼***

1421 A630 Sheet of 10 12.50 6.25
a.-j. 1 Any single 1.25 .35

Nos. 1421a-1421j each sold for 50c on day of issue.

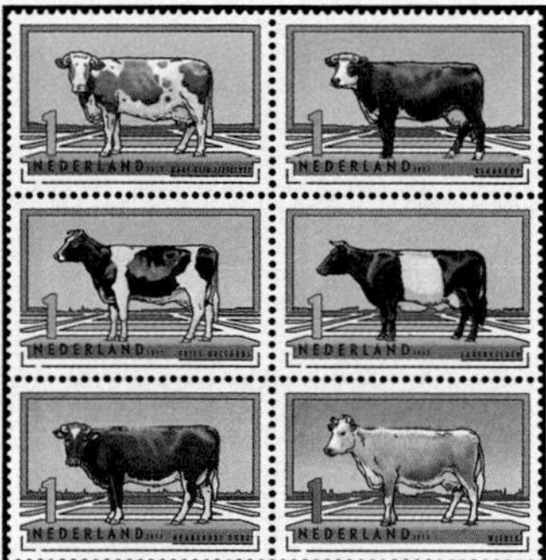

Cattle Breeds — A631

Designs: Nos. 1422a, 1422g, Maas-Rijn-Ijsselvee (Meuse-Rhine-Issel). Nos. 1422b, 1422h, Blaarkop. Nos. 1422c, 1422i, Fries-Hollands (Dutch Friesian). Nos. 1422d, 1422j, Lakenvelder (Dutch Belted). Nos. 1422e, 1422k, Brandrode Rund. Nos. 1422f, 1422l, Witrik.

2012, Aug. 13 *Perf. 13¼x12¾*

1422 A631 Block of 6 8.50 4.25
a.-f. 1 Any single 1.40 .35
g.-l. 1 Any single, perf. 14½ 2.60 2.60
m. Booklet pane of 2 #1422g 5.25 —
n. Booklet pane of 2 #1422h 5.25 —
o. Booklet pane of 2 #1422i 5.25 —
p. Booklet pane of 2 #1422j 5.25 —
q. Booklet pane of 2, #1422k, 1422l 5.25 —
Complete booklet, #1422m, 1422n, 1422o, 1422p, 1422q 26.50

Nos. 1422a-1422f each sold for 50c on day of issue. Complete booklet sold for €9.95 on day of issue.

Miniature Sheet

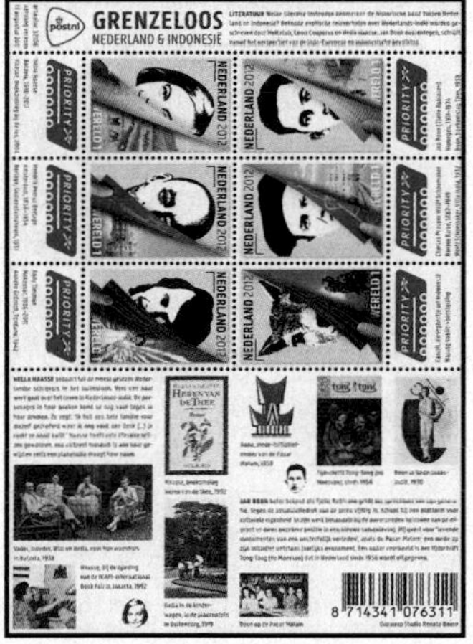

Dutch Connections With Indonesia — A632

No. 1423: a, Hella Haasse (1918-2011), writer, cattle and tea planters. b, Tjalie Robinson (1911-74), writer, dog on chain. c, Hendrik Petrus Berlage (1856-1934), architect, Gemeentemuseum, The Hague. d, Charles Prosper Wolff Schoemaker (1882-1949), architect, (wearing hat), Villa Isola, Bandung, Indonesia. e, Andy Tielman (1936-2011), musician, Anneke Grönloh, singer. f, Chevrotain, Indonesian shadow puppet.

2012, Aug. 13 *Perf. 13½x13¼*

1423 A632 Sheet of 6 15.00 7.50
a.-f. 1 Wereld Any single 2.50 .65

No. 1423 was printed with three different illustrations in the bottom sheet margin, with each sheet having a different arrangement of stamps. Sheet margins at left and right served as etiquettes. On day of issue, Nos. 1423a-1423f each sold for 95c.

Royal Carré Theater, Amsterdam, 125th Anniv. — A633

No. 1424: a, Theater. b, Toon Hermans, microphone, balloons. c, Oscar Carré's circus horses. d, Two male ballet dancers. e, Guitarist and lights. f, Two dancers from *Cats*. g, Tightrope artist with unicycle. h, Ballerina. i, Circus elephants. j, Chandeliers and "125.".

2012, Sept. 10 *Perf. 12¾x13¼*

1424 A633 Sheet of 10 14.00 7.00
a.-j. 1 Any single 1.40 .35
k. Booklet pane of 2, #1424a, 1424c 5.25 —
l. Booklet pane of 2, #1424b, 1424j 5.25 —
m. Booklet pane of 2, #1424e, 1424f 5.25 —
n. Booklet pane of 2, #1424d, 1424h 5.25 —
o. Booklet pane of 2, #1424g, 1424i 5.25 —
Complete booklet, #1424k, 1424l, 1424m, 1424n, 1424o 26.50

On day of issue, Nos. 1424a-1424j each sold for 50c and complete booklet sold for €9.95.

Miniature Sheet

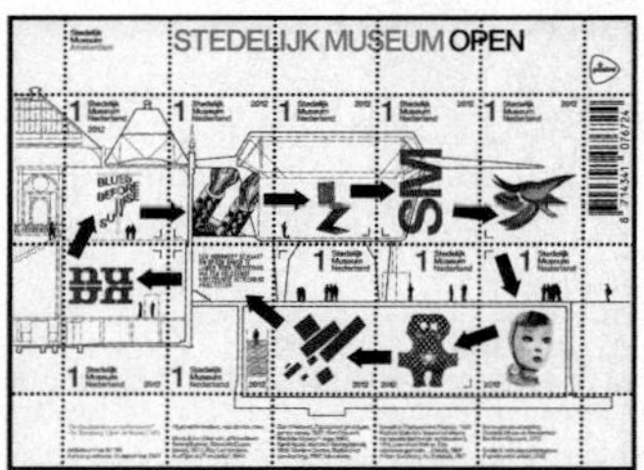

Reopening of Stedelijk Museum, Amsterdam — A634

No. 1425 — Arrows and: a, Blues Before Sunrise poster, by Mevis & Van Deursen. b, As I Opened Fire, by Roy Lichtenstein (cannons). c, Zig-zag chair prototype, by Gerrit Rietveld. d, Musuem logo (SM), by Wim Crouwel. e, Mural, by Karel Appel. f, Now 2, by Willem Sandberg (nu). g, An Object Made. . ., by Lawrence Weiner (text, man on staircase). h, Suprematist Composition (Eight Red Rectangles), by Kazimir Malevich. i, Empathy Displacement 7, by Mike Kelley (polka-dotted object). j, Barbie (With Pearl Necklace), by Marlene Dumas (doll's head).

2012, Sept. 24 *Perf. 13½x13¼*

1425 A634 Sheet of 10 14.00 7.00
a.-j. 1 Any single 1.40 .35

Nos. 1425a-1425j each sold for 50c on day of issue.

Souvenir Sheet

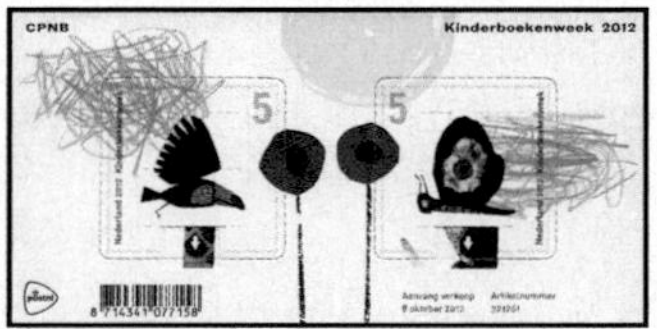

Children's Book Week — A635

No. 1426: a, Bird. b, Butterfly.

2012, Oct. 8 ***Rouletted***

On Cardboard

1426 A635 Sheet of 2 13.00 6.50
a.-b. 5 Either single 6.50 3.25

Nos. 1426a-1426b each sold for €2.50. Parts of the stamps pop up when the cardboard slide on each stamp is pulled out.

Queen Juliana — A636

2012, Oct. 19 *Perf. 13¼x14*

1427 A636 1 multi 1.25 .35
a. Booklet pane of 2 5.00 —
Complete booket, 5 #1427a 25.00

Stamp Day. No. 1427 sold for 50c on day of issue. Complete booklet sold for €9.95 and contains five examples of No. 1427a, each with a different pane margin.

December Stamps — A637

No. 1428 — Christmas knitting patterns featuring: a, Christmas trees and red violet hearts. b, Candles. c, Christmas trees and green hearts. d, Reindeer. e, Snowmen. f, Angels with horns. g, Red reindeer and heart. h, Poinsettias. i, Christmas ornaments and poinsettias. j, Angels and musical notes.

Serpentine Die Cut 12¾x12½

2012, Nov. 20 **Self-Adhesive**

1428 A637 Block of 10 11.00
a.-j. (40c) Any single 1.10 .30

A638

Personalized Stamps — A639

2013, Jan. 2 **Litho.** *Perf. 13¼x14*

1429 A638 1 multi 1.50 1.50

Self-Adhesive

1430 A639 1 multi 1.50 1.50

Nos. 1429-1430 each sold for 54c on day of issue. Vignettes shown are the generic images available on the day of issue. Vignettes could be personalized for a fee.

Traditional Women's Head Coverings — A640

Head covering from: No. 1431, Bunschoten-Spakenburg. No. 1432, Staphorst. No. 1433, Marken. No. 1434, Walcheren. No. 1435, Noordwest-Veluwe.

2013 **Litho.** *Perf. 14½x14¼*

1431 A640 1 multi 1.50 1.50
a. Perf. 13½x12½ 2.75 2.75
b. Booklet pane of 2 #1431a 5.50 —
1432 A640 1 multi 1.50 1.50
a. Perf. 13½x12½ 2.75 2.75
b. Booklet pane of 2 #1432a 5.50 —
1433 A640 1 multi 1.40 1.40
a. Perf. 13½x12½ 2.75 2.75
b. Booklet pane of 2 #1433a 5.50 —
1434 A640 1 multi 1.40 1.40
a. Perf. 13½x12½ 2.75 2.75
b. Booklet pane of 2 #1434a 5.50 —
1435 A640 1 multi 1.50 1.50
a. Perf. 13½x12½ 2.75 2.75
b. Booklet pane of 2 #1435a 5.50 —
Complete booklet, #1431b, 1432b, 1433b, 1434b, 1435b 27.50
c. Souvenir sheet of 5, #1431-1435 7.50 7.50
Nos. 1431-1435 (5) 7.30 7.30

Issued: Nos. 1431-1432, 1/2; Nos. 1433-1434, 2/25; Nos. 1431a-1431b, 1432a-1432b, 1433a-1433b, 1434a-1434b, 1435-1435c, 5/21. Nos. 1431-1435 each sold for 54c on day of issue. Complete booklet sold for €9.95.

Miniature Sheet

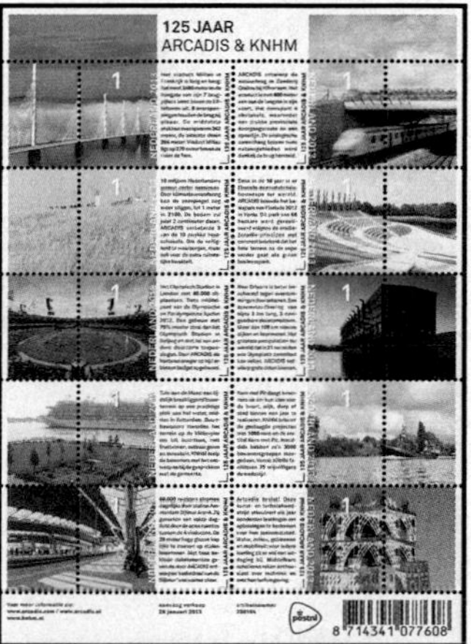

Netherlands Land Development Society, 125th Anniv. — A641

No. 1436 — Construction projects developed by Arcadis and KNHM: a, Millau Viaduct, France. b, Train under Zanderij Crailoo Wildlife Crossing Bridge. c, Lighthouse, flags and grass-covered dunes. d, Floriade (terraced garden), Venlo. e, Olympic Stadium, London. f, Storm barrier, New Orleans, Louisiana. g, Garden on Meuse River, Rotterdam. h, Water, trees and tower in distance (Kern met Pit Contest). i, Amsterdam Bijlmer ArenA railway station. j, Model constructed for Artcadia children's art and technology contest.

2013, Jan. 28 **Litho.** *Perf. 13¼x13½*

1436 A641 Sheet of 10 15.00 15.00
a.-j. 1 Any single 1.50 1.50

Nos. 1436a-1436j each sold for 54c on day of issue.

Miniature Sheet

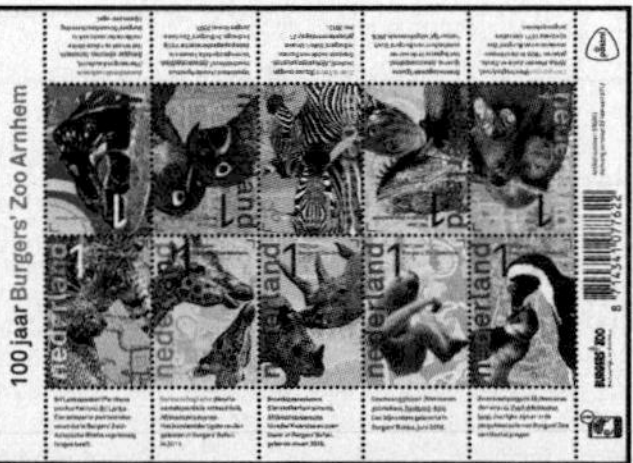

Animals in Burgers' Zoo, Arnhem — A642

No. 1437: a, Panthera pardus kotiya (Sri Lankan leopards). b, Pterapogon kauderni (Banggai cardinalfish) witheggs in mouth. c,

Giraffa camelopardalis rothschildi (giraffes). d, Anodorhynchus hyacinthinus (hyacinth macaws). e, Ceratotherium simum (white rhinoceroses). f, Equus quagga boehmi (Grant's zebras). g, Nomascus gabriellae (yellow-cheeked gibbons). h, Iguana iguana (green iguanas). i, Spheniscus demersus (jackass penguins). j, Pan troglodytes (chimpanzees).

Perf. 13¼x12¾

2013, Feb. 25 Litho.

1437	A642	Sheet of 10	14.00	14.00
a.-j.		1 Any single	1.40	1.40
k.		Booklet pane of 2, #1437a-1437b	5.25	—
l.		Booklet pane of 2, #1437c-1437d	5.25	—
m.		Booklet pane of 2, #1437e-1437f	5.25	—
n.		Booklet pane of 2, #1437g-1437h	5.25	—
o.		Booklet pane of 2, #1437i-1437j	5.25	—
		Complete booklet, #1437k, 1437l, 1437m, 1437n, 1437o	26.50	

Nos. 1437a-1437j each sold for 54c on day of issue. Complete booklet sold for €9.95.

Famous Women — A643

No. 1438: a, Alexandrine Tinne (1835-69), explorer of Sahara region. b, Belle van Zuylen (1740-1805), writer. c, Trijn van Leemput (c. 1530-1607), heroine in Eighty Years' War. d, Maria van Oosterwijck (1630-93), painter. e, Mary, Duchess of Burgundy (1457-82). f, Anna Zernike (1887-1972), theologian, first female minister in Netherlands.

Perf. 13¼x12¾

2013, Mar. 25 Litho.

1438	A643	Block of 6	8.50	8.50
a.-f.		1 Any single	1.40	1.40

Nos. 1438a-1438f each sold for 54c on day of issue.

Miniature Sheet

Reopening of Main Building of Rijksmuseum — A644

No. 1439: a, Right part of *The Gallant Conversation,* by Gerard ter Borch, left part of *Interior of the Church of St. Odulphus in Assendelft,* by Pieter Jansz. b, Right part of *Interior of the Church of St. Odolphus in Assendelft, Mary Magdalene,* by Jan van Scorel. c, *Still Life of Fruits and Flowers,* by Balthasar van der Ast, left part of *Still Life with Flowers,* by Hans Bollongier. d, Right part of *Still Life with Flowers,* left part of *Vivi in a Red Dress in a Forest,* by Jacob Olie, Jr. e, Right edge of *Sheet with Five Butterflies a Wasp and Two Flies,* by Pieter Withoos, Bunya no Yasuhide from *Modern Parody on the Six Poets and Six Flowers,* by Kunisada Utagawa, left edge of *Italian Landscape with Stone Pines,* by Hendrik Voogd. f, Right part of *Italian Landscape with Stone Pines,* left part of *The Threatened Swan,* by Jan Asselijn. g, Right part of *Still Life with Gilded Cup,* by Willem Claesz, *The Milkmaid,* by Johannes Vermeer. h, *Still Life with Cheeses,* by Floris Claesz van Dijck, left part of tile from Sommelsdijk Orphanage. i, Right part of *Gerard Andriesz Bicker,* by Bartholomeus van der Helst, left part of *Portrait of Giuliano da Sangallo,* by Piero di Cosomo. j, Right part of *Portrait of Giuliano da Sangallo,* left part of *The Night Watch,* by Rembrandt.

Perf. 13¼x12¾

2013, Mar. 25 Litho.

1439	A644	Sheet of 10	14.00	14.00
a.-j.		1 Any single	1.40	1.40

Nos. 1439a-1439j each sold for 54c on day of issue.

Abdication of Queen Beatrix A645

2013, Mar. 25 Litho. ***Perf. 14x13½***

1440	A645	1 blue & blk	1.40	1.40

No. 1440 sold for 54c on day of issue.

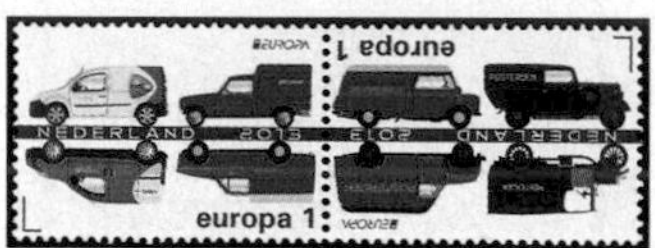

Europa — A646

No. 1441: a and c, Modern mail vans (2013 Renault Kangoo, 1976 Simca 1100 VF, 2010 Fiat Fiorino, 1974 Daf 33). b and d, Old mail vans (1960 Bedford CA, 1936, Opel P4, 1956 Opel Blitz, 1918 GMC).

2013, Apr. 22 Litho. ***Perf. 13¼x12¾***

1441	A646	Pair	4.80	4.80
a.-b.		1 Europa Either single	2.40	2.40
c.-d.		1 Europa Either single, perf. 14½	4.25	4.25
e.		Booklet pane of 2, #1441c-1441d	8.75	—
		Complete booklet, 3 #1441e	26.50	

Nos. 1441a-1441b each sold for 90c on day of issue. Complete booklet sold for €9.95, and contains three panes of No. 1441e with different orientations of the stamps.

Ascension to Throne of King Willem-Alexander A647

Perf. 14¼x14 Syncopated

2013, Apr. 30 Litho.

Booklet Stamps Self-Adhesive

1442	A647	1 blk, red & bl	1.40	1.40
a.		Booklet pane of 10	14.00	
1443	A647	2 blk, bl & grn	3.00	3.00
a.		Booklet pane of 5	15.00	

On day of issue, No. 1442 sold for 54c and No. 1443 sold for €1.08.

King Willem-Alexander — A648

2013, May 21 Litho. ***Perf. 14x13½***

1444	A648	1 red & blk	1.50	1.50

No. 1444 sold for 54c on day of issue.

Writers — A649

No. 1445: a, Simon Carmiggelt (1913-87). b, Gerrit Kouwenaar. c, Louis Couperus (1863-1923). d, Adriaan Roland Holst (1888-1976). e, Godfried Bomans (1913-71).

2013, May 21 Litho. ***Perf. 14½***

1445		Horiz. strip of 5	7.50	7.50
a.-e.	A649	1 Any single	1.50	1.50

Nos. 1445a-1445e each sold for 54c on day of issue. Printed in sheets containing 2 each of Nos. 1445a-1445e + 5 central labels.

World Blood Donor Day — A650

No. 1446: a, Queen, "1" in red. b, King, "1" in white.

2013, June 17 Litho. ***Perf. 14½***

1446	A650	Pair	3.00	3.00
a.-b.		1 Either single	1.50	1.50

On day of issue Nos. 1446a-1446b each sold for 54c.

Miniature Sheet

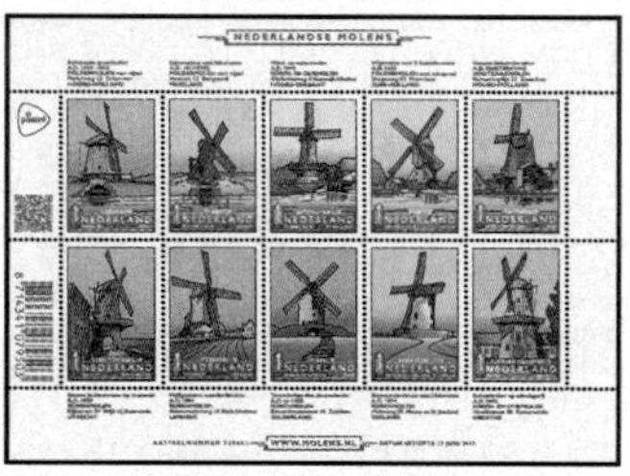

Windmills — A651

No. 1447 — Various windmill types located in: a and k, Schermer. b and l, Burgwerd. c and m, Heeswijk-Dinther. d and n, Hoornaar. e and o, Zaandam. f and p, Wijk bij Duurstede. g and q, Klein Genhout. h and r, Zeddam. i and s, Nieuw- en Sint Joosland. j and t, Roderwolde.

2013, June 17 Litho. ***Perf. 14½***

1447	A651	Sheet of 10	15.00	15.00
a.-j.		1 Any single	1.50	1.50
k.-t.		1 Any single, perf. 12¾x13¼	2.75	2.75
u.		Booklet pane of 2, #1447k, 1447p	5.50	—
v.		Booklet pane of 2, #1447l, 1447q	5.50	—
w.		Booklet pane of 2, #1447m, 1447r	5.50	—
x.		Booklet pane of 2, #1447n, 1447s	5.50	—
y.		Booklet pane of 2, #1447o, 1447t	5.50	—
		Complete booklet, #1447u, 1447v, 1447w, 1447x, 1447y	27.50	

Nos. 1447a-1447j each sold for 54c on day of issue. Complete booklet sold for €9.95.

Miniature Sheet

Royal Dutch Swimming Association, 125th Anniv. — A652

No. 1448: a, People standing at edge of pool. b, Two synchronized divers. c, Water polo player. d, Diver about to enter water. e, People standing at edge of pool, people lined up on diving platform. f, Two synchronized swimmers. g, Swimmer and lane barriers. h, Teacher and children learning how to swim. i, Swimmer's head near edge of pool. j, Swimmer bent over ready to start race.

2013, Aug. 12 Litho. ***Perf. 14½***

1448	A652	Sheet of 10	16.00	16.00
a.-j.		1 Any single	1.60	1.60

Nos. 1448a-1448j each sold for 60c on day of issue.

Miniature Sheet

Dutch Connections With Belgium — A653

No. 1449: a, Museum aan de Stroom, Antwerp, Belgium, designed by Neutelings Riedijk Architectural Agency. b, Design for Hoenderloo Museum, by Henry van de Velde. c, Twelve books, country name at left. d, Thirteen books, country name at right. e, Après-midi à Amsterdam, by Rik Wouters. f, De Vlakte, by Jakob Smits.

Perf. 13¼x12¾

2013, Aug. 12 Litho.

1449	A653	Sheet of 6	16.50	16.50
a.-f.		1 Wereld Any single	2.75	2.75

Nos. 1449a-1449f each sold for €1 on day of issue. No. 1449 was printed with three different illustrations in the bottom sheet margin, with each sheet having a different arrangement of stamps. Sheet margins at left and right served as etiquettes.

Greeting Card Week — A654

2013, Sept. 9 Litho. ***Perf. 14½***

1450	A654	1 multi	1.60	1.60

No. 1450 sold for 60c on day of issue and was printed in sheets of 3.

Miniature Sheet

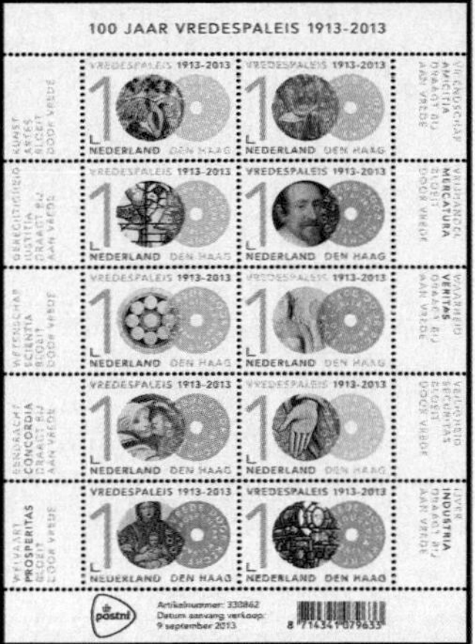

Peace Palace, The Hague, Cent. — A655

No. 1451 — Details of architectural or artistic items of the Peace Palace in circle at left, word at top in inner ring of words in circle at right: a and k, Detail of wall tile, Artes. b and l, Bronze medallion on entrance gates, Amicitia. c and m, Stained-glass window in Central Hall, Iustitia. d and n, Portrait of Hugo de Groot, by Michiel Jansz.van Mierevelt, Mercatura. e and o, Marble floor in Entrance Hall, Scientia. f and p, Relief sculpture by Toon Dupuis, Veritas. g and q, Prestudy for unmade tapestry, Concordia. h and r, Tile panel, Securitas. i and s, Peace Goddess with Child, by Herman Rosse, Prosperitas. j and t, Stained-glass window depicting locomotive, Industria.

2013, Sept. 9 Litho. ***Perf. 13¼x12¾***

1451 A655 Sheet of 10 16.00 16.00
a.-j. 1 Any single 1.60 1.60
k.-t. 1 Any single, perf. 14½ 2.75 2.75
u. Booklet pane of 2, #1451k-1451l 5.50 —
v. Booklet pane of 2, #1451m-1451n 5.50 —
w. Booklet pane of 2, #1451o-1451p 5.50 —
x. Booklet pane of 2, #1451q-1451r 5.50 —
y. Booklet pane of 2, #1451s-1451t 5.50 —
Complete booklet, #1451u, 1451v, 1451w, 1451x, 1451y 27.50

Nos. 1451a-1451j each sold for 60c on day of issue. Complete booklet sold for €9.95.

Airplanes and Queen Wilhelmina From Type AP5 A656

2013, Oct. 18 Litho. ***Perf. 14x13½***

1452 A656 1 multi 1.60 1.60
a. Booklet pane of 2 5.50 —
Complete booklet, 5 #1452a 27.50

Stamp Day. No. 1452 sold for 60c on day of issue. Complete booklet sold for €9.95.

Legend of St. Nicholas (Santa Claus) — A657

No. 1453: a, St. Nicholas on horse, Black Peter, and Moon. b, Black Peter with gift. c, Moon, tree and house. d, St. Nicholas with crozier. e, Shoe filled with gifts.

2013, Nov. 4 Litho. ***Perf. 13¾x13¼***

1453 Horiz. strip of 5 8.00 8.00
a.-e. A657 1 Any single 1.60 1.60

Nos. 1453a-1453e sold for 60c on day of issue and emit a spice scent when scratched.

Miniature Sheet

December Stamps — A658

No. 1454: a, Buildings at night, comet in sky over Christmas tree. b, Buildings at night, Christmas tree. c, Buildings at night, people viewing fireworks. d, Buildings at night, Christmas tree, large star at left, Moon over top of tower. e, Buildings at night, large star at left, Christmas trees. f, Buildings at night, people viewing large star at right. g, Buildings at night, Christmas tree, man running. h, Buildings at night, clock on tower at right. i, Girl on ice skates looking at bird in tree. j, Boy in sled on ice, man ice skating. k, Two ice skaters, windmill. l, Boy in sled on ice, tower at right. m, Snowman, star and top of Christmas tree. n, Man pulling Christmas tree on cart. o, Dog looking at postman on bicycle. p, Woman holding dog's leash, tower at right. q, Man and woman under mistletoe. r, Birds under bridge, Christmas tree. s, Buildings in day, Christmas tree. t, Buidlings in day, tower at right.

Serpentine Die Cut 12½x12¼

2013, Nov. 19 Litho.

Self-Adhesive

1454 A658 Sheet of 20 30.00
a.-t. (55c) Any single 1.50 1.50

Kingdom of the Netherlands, 200th Anniv. — A659

No. 1455: a, Landing of Willem I, 1813, King Willem I, flag of the Netherlands. b, List of monarchs.

2013, Nov. 30 Litho. ***Perf. 14½***

1455 A659 Pair, #a-b 7.00 7.00
a.-b. 2 Either single 3.50 3.50

On day of issue Nos. 1455a-1455b both sold for €1.28.

King Willem-Alexander
A660 A661

Die Cut Perf. 14¼ Syncopated

2013, Nov. 30 Photo.

Booklet Stamps

Self-Adhesive

1456 A660 1 blue & blk 1.75 1.75
a. Booklet pane of 10 17.50
d. Dated "2015" 1.60 1.60
e. Booklet pane of 10 #1456d 16.00

Serpentine Die Cut 11¼

1457 A661 1 International gray & blk 3.00 3.00
a. Booklet pane of 5 15.00
d. Dated "2015" 2.60 2.60
e. Booklet pane of 5 #1457d 13.00

Die Cut Perf. 14¼

1458 A660 2 ver & blk 3.50 3.50
a. Booklet pane of 5 17.50
d. Dated "2015" 3.25 3.25
e. Booklet pane of 5 #1458d 16.50
Nos. 1456-1458 (3) 8.25 8.25

On day of issue, No. 1456 sold for 64c; No. 1457, for €1.05; No. 1458, for €1.28.

Issued: Nos. 1456d, 1456e, 1457d, 1457e, 1458d, 1458e, 1/5/15. On day of issue, No. 1456d sold for 69c; No. 1457d, €1.15; No. 1458d, €1.38.

Numerals
A662 A663

Die Cut Perf. 13½ Syncopated

2014, Jan. 2 Coil Stamps Litho.

Self-Adhesive

1459 A662 1 multi 1.75 1.75
1460 A663 2 multi 3.50 3.50

On day of issue, No. 1459 sold for 64c; No. 1460, for €1.28.

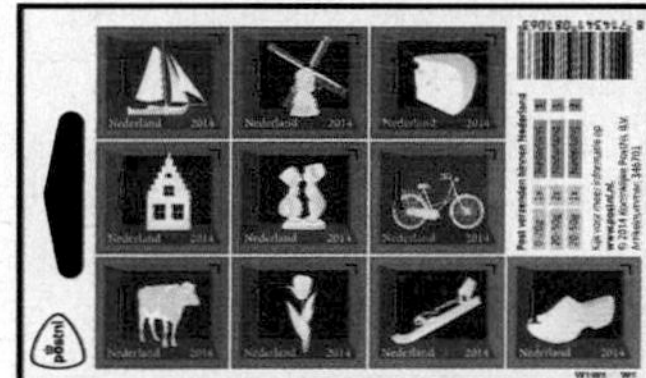

A664

Dutch Items — A665

Designs: No. 1461a, Frisian flat-bottomed boat. Nos. 1461b, 1462a, Windmill. No. 1461c, Wedge of Gouda cheese. Nos. 1461d, 1462d, House with step-gable roof. No. 1461e, Boy and girl in Dutch costumes kissing. Nos. 1461f, 1462b, Bicycle. Nos. 1461g, 1462c, Holstein-Frisian cow. Nos. 1461h, 1462e, Tulip. No. 1461i, Ice skate. No. 1461j, Wooden shoe.

Die Cut Perf. 14¼

2014, Jan. 2 Litho.

Self-Adhesive

1461 A664 Booklet pane of 10 17.50
a.-j. 1 Any single 1.75 1.75

Serpentine Die Cut 11¼

1462 A665 Booklet pane of 5 15.00
a.-e. 1 International Any single 3.00 3.00

On day of issue, Nos. 1461a-1461j each sold for 64c; Nos. 1462a-1462 each sold for €1.05.

Miniature Sheet

Automobiles in Louwman Museum Collection — A666

No. 1463: a, 1887 De Dion-Bouton & Trépardoux. b, 1910 Brooke Swan Car. c, 1912 Eysink. d, 1912 Spyker. e, 1932, Bugatti. f, 1935 Duesenberg. g, 1936 Toyota. h, 1960 Porsce race car. i, 1964 Aston Martin. j, 1965 Ferrari.

2014, Jan. 27 Litho. ***Perf. 13¼x13½***

1463 A666 Sheet of 10 17.50 17.50
a.-j. 1 Any single 1.75 1.75
k. Booklet pane of 2, #1463a-1463b 6.75 —
l. Booklet pane of 2, #1463c-1463d 6.75 —
m. Booklet pane of 2, #1463e-1463f 6.75 —
n. Booklet pane of 2, #1463g-1463h 6.75 —
o. Booklet pane of 2, #1463i-1463j 6.75 —
Complete booklet, #1463k-1463o 34.00

On day of issue, Nos. 1463a-1463j each sold for 64c. Complete booklet sold for €12.45.

Ceramics — A667

Ceramics from: No. 1464, Loosdrecht. No. 1465, Tegelen. No. 1466, Harlingen. No. 1467, Makkum. No. 1468, Delft.

2014 Litho. ***Perf. 14½x14¼***

1464 A667 1 multi 1.75 1.75
a. Perf. 13½x12½ 3.25 3.25
b. Booklet pane of 2 #1464a 6.75 —
1465 A667 1 multi 1.75 1.75
a. Perf. 13½x12½ 3.25 3.25
b. Booklet pane of 2 #1465a 6.75 —
1466 A667 1 multi 1.75 1.75
a. Perf. 13½x12½ 3.25 3.25
b. Booklet pane of 2 #1466a 6.75 —
1467 A667 1 multi 1.75 1.75
a. Perf. 13½x12½ 3.25 3.25
b. Booklet pane of 2 #1467a 6.75 —
1468 A667 1 multi 1.75 1.75
a. Perf. 13½x12½ 3.25 3.25
b. Booklet pane of 2 #1468a 6.75 —
Complete booklet, #1464b, 1465b, 1466b, 1467b, 1468b 34.00
c. Souvenir sheet of 5, #1464-1468 8.75 8.75

Issued: Nos. 1464, 1465, 1/27; Nos. 1466, 1467, 2/24; Nos. 1464a, 1464b, 1465a, 1465b, 1466a, 1466b, 1467a, 1467b, 1468, 1468a, 1468b, 1468c, 5/19. On day of issue, Nos. 1464-1468 each sold for 64c. Complete booklet sold for €12.45.

Youth Philately Day — A668

No. 1469: a, Carrier pigeon (duif). b, Hedgehog (egel).

2014, Mar. 24 Litho. *Die Cut*
Self-Adhesive

1469 A668 Pair, #a-b 3.50
a.-b. 1 Either single 1.75 1.75

Printed in sheets of 10 containing five each Nos. 1469a-1469b, with adjacent stamps at different distances from each other. On day of issue, Nos. 1469a-1469b each sold for 64c.

Constitution of the Kingdom of the Netherlands, 200th Anniv. — A669

No. 1470: a, King Willem-Alexander, text from coronation oath, blue panel. b, Statue of King Willem I, text from oath to the Constitution, red panel.

Perf. 13½x13¼

2014, Mar. 29 Litho.

1470 A669 Pair, #a-b 7.00 7.00
a.-b. 2 Either single 3.50 3.50

On day of issue, Nos. 1470a-1470b each sold for €1.28.

Europa — A670

No. 1471 — Drie Pruiken Barrel Organ: a, Internal machinery. b, Front of organ with figurines and builder's name.

2014, Apr. 22 Litho. *Perf. 13¼x13½*

1471 A670 Horiz. pair 6.00 6.00
a.-b. 1 International Either single 3.00 3.00

On day of issue, Nos. 1471a-1471b each sold for €1.05.

Miniature Sheet

Orchids — A671

No. 1472: a, Gymnadenia conopsea. b, Orchis militaris. c, Orchis anthropophora. d, Anacamptis pyramidalis. e, Dactylorhiza maculata. f, Orchis purpurea. g, Platanthera bifolia. h, Orchis mascula. i, Coeloglossum viride. j, Orchis simia.

2014, Apr. 22 Litho. *Perf. 13½x13¼*

1472 A671 Sheet of 10 17.50 17.50
a.-j. 1 Any single 1.75 1.75
k. Booklet pane of 2, #1472a, 1472f 7.00 —
l. Booklet pane of 2, #1472b, 1472g 7.00 —
m. Booklet pane of 2, #1472c, 1472h 7.00 —
n. Booklet pane of 2, #1472d, 1472i 7.00 —
o. Booklet pane of 2, #1472e, 1472j 7.00 —
Complete booklet, #1472k-1472o 35.00

On day of issue, Nos. 1472a-1472j each sold for 64c. Complete booklet sold for €12.45.

Miniature Sheet

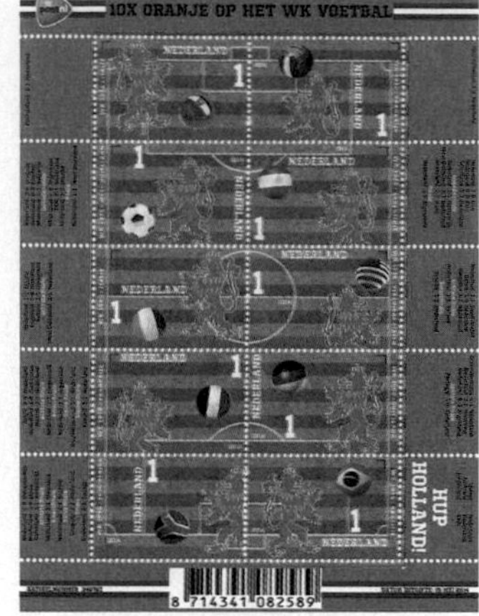

2014 World Cup Soccer Championships, Brazil — A672

No. 1473 — Dutch lion, soccer ball with host county flag and year: a, Italy, 1934. b, France, 1938. c, West Germany, 1974. d, Argentina, 1978. e, Italy, 1990. f, United States, 1994. g, France, 1998. h, Germany, 2006. i, South Africa, 2010, j, Brazil, 2014.

2014, May 19 Litho. *Perf. 13¼x13½*

1473 A672 Sheet of 10 17.50 17.50
a.-j. 1 Any single 1.75 1.75

On day of issue, Nos. 1473a-1473j each sold for 64c.

Personalized Stamp — A673

2014, July 1 Litho. *Perf. 13½x14*

1474 A673 1 International multi 3.00 3.00

No. 1474 sold for €1.05 on day of issue. The vignette shown is the generic image available on the day of issue. Vignettes could be personalized for a fee.

Miniature Sheet

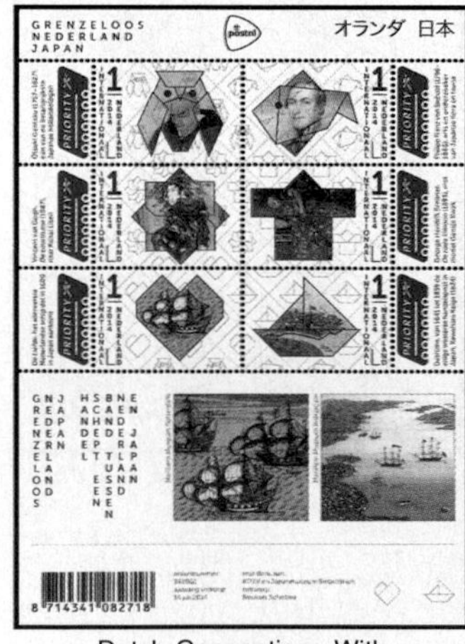

Dutch Connections With Japan — A674

No. 1475: a, Gentaku Otsuki (1757-1827), Japanese expert on the Dutch ("1" at UL). b, Philipp Franz von Siebold (1796-1866), physician in Japan ("1" at UR). c, The Courtesan, by Vincent van Gogh ("1" at UL). d, The Red Kimono, by George Hendrik Breitner ("1" at UR). e, Dutch ship Liefde ("1" at UL). f, Dejima Island, detail of painting by Keiga Kawahara ("1" at UR).

2014, July 14 Litho. *Perf. 13¼x13½*

1475 A674 Sheet of 6 18.00 18.00
a.-f. 1 International Any single 3.00 3.00

Nos. 1475a-1475f each sold for €1.05 on day of issue. No. 1475 was printed with three different illustrations in the bottom sheet margin, with each sheet having a different arrangement of stamps. Sheet margins at left and right served as etiquettes.

Royal Family Riding Bicycles A675

King Willem-Alexander and Queen Máxima at 2014 Winter Olympics — A676

King Willem-Alexander and Queen Máxima — A677

2001 Announcement of Engagement — A678

Royal Family in New York City — A679

2014, Aug. 2 Litho. *Perf. 13¼x13½*

1476 Vert. strip of 5 8.75 8.75
a. A675 1 multi 1.75 1.75
b. A676 1 multi 1.75 1.75
c. A677 1 multi 1.75 1.75
d. A678 1 multi 1.75 1.75
e. A679 1 multi 1.75 1.75

12½ year anniv. of marriage of King Willem-Alexander and Queen Máxima. Printed in sheets containing two vertical strips. Nos. 1476a-1476e each sold for 64c on day of sale.

Miniature Sheet

UNESCO World Heritage Sites in the Netherlands — A680

No. 1477: a, Beemster Polder, 1999. b, Wadden Sea, 2009. c, Schokland and Surroundings, 1995. d, Windmill Network at Kinderdijk-Elshout, 1997. e, Rietveld Schröder House, 2000. f, D.F. Wouda Steam Pumping Station, 1998. g, Canal Ring of Amsterdam, 2010. h, Willemstad, Curaçao, 1997. i, Fort near Spijkerboor, Defense Ring of Amsterdam, 1996. j, Pampus Island Fort, Defense Ring of Amsterdam, 1996.

Perf. 13¼x13½

2014, Aug. 11 Litho.

1477 A680 Sheet of 10 17.50 17.50
a.-j. 1 Any single 1.75 1.75
k. Booklet pane of 2, #1477a-1477b 6.75 —
l. Booklet pane of 2, #1477c-1477d 6.75 —
m. Booklet pane of 2, #1477e-1477f 6.75 —
n. Booklet pane of 2, #1477g-1477h 6.75 —
o. Booklet pane of 2, #1477i-1477j 6.75 —
Complete booklet, #1477k-1477o 34.00

On day of issue, Nos. 1477a-1477j each sold for 64c. Complete booklet sold for €12.45.

Miniature Sheet

Railways in the Netherlands, 175th Anniv. — A681

No. 1478: a, Locomotives and electric cable towers. b, Locomotive, clock with second hand, Arnhem train station stairway and escalator. c, Tile work and Haarlem station. d, Electric locomotive and map of railway line stations. e, Vertical lift railway bridge, green track signal. f, Emblem for Tienertoer reduced rate program, winged wheel emblem. g, Locomotive and red track signal. h, Clock without second hand, Rotterdam train station. i, New and old symbols for Netherlands Railways, track network. j, Locomotive, Netherlands #215.

2014, Sept. 8 Litho. *Perf. 13¼x13½*

1478 A681 Sheet of 10 16.00 16.00
a.-j. 1 Any single 1.60 1.60
k. Booklet pane of 2, #1478a-1478b 6.50 —
l. Booklet pane of 2, #1478c-1478d 6.50 —
m. Booklet pane of 2, #1478e-1478f 6.50 —
n. Booklet pane of 2, #1478g-1478h 6.50 —
o. Booklet pane of 2, #1478i-1478j 6.50 —
Complete booklet, #1478k-1478o 32.50

On day of issue, Nos. 1478a-1478j each sold for 64c. Complete booklet sold for €12.45.

Hardwell, Disk Jockey — A682

Tiesto, Disk Jockey — A683

Afrojack, Disk Jockey — A684

Dash Berlin, Disk Jockey — A685

Armin Van Buuren, Disk Jockey — A686

2014, Oct. 6 Litho. *Perf. 13½x13¼*

1479 Horiz. strip of 5 8.00 8.00
a. A682 1 multi 1.60 1.60
b. A683 1 multi 1.60 1.60
c. A684 1 multi 1.60 1.60
d. A685 1 multi 1.60 1.60
e. A686 1 multi 1.60 1.60

Printed in sheets containing two strips. On day of issue, Nos. 1479a-1479e each sold for 64c.

Stamp Day A687

2014, Oct. 17 Litho. *Perf. 13x13¼*

1480 A687 1 multi 1.60 1.60
a. Booklet pane of 2 6.25 —
Complete booklet, 5 #1480a 31.50

On day of issue No. 1480 sold for 64c. Complete booklet sold for €12.45. The five examples of No. 1480a in the complete booklet have different margins.

December Stamps — A688

No. 1481: a, Mittens. b, Two round Christmas ornaments. c, Owl, Santa's sleigh in flight. d, People kissing under mistletoe. e, Champagne flutes. f, Plate of Christmas pastries. g, Snowman. h, Christmas tree. i, Hand placing ornament on Christmas tree. j, House, envelope, mailbox. k, Fondue pot and Christmas ornament. l, Bells. m, Candle. n, Candy cane and Christmas ornament. o, Reindeer and sleigh. p, Ice skates. q, Stockings. r, Birds. s, Wrapped gifts. t, Rockets and fireworks.

Serpentine Die Cut 12½

2014, Nov. 17 Photo.

Self-Adhesive

1481 A688 Booklet pane of 20 30.00
a.-t. (59c) Any single 1.50 1.50

Miniature Sheet

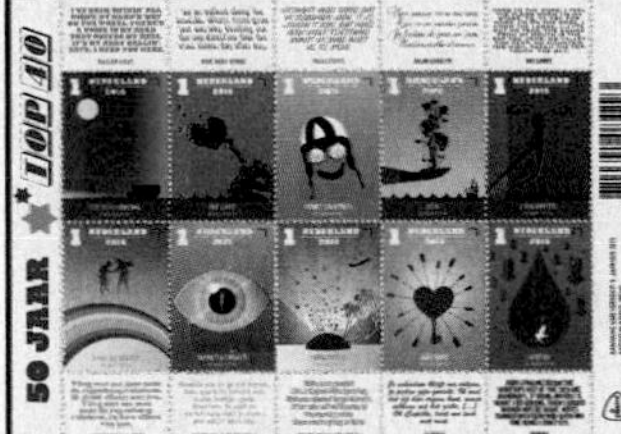

Dutch Top 40 Music Rankings, 50th Anniv. — A689

No. 1482: a, "Radar Love," by Golden Earring. b, "One Way Wind," by The Cats. c, "Willempie," by André van Duin. d, "Mon Amour," by BZN. e, "No Limit," by 2 Unlimited. f, "Vlieg Met Me Mee," by Paul de Leeuw. g, "Dromen Zijn Bedrog," by Marco Borsato. h, "We're Going to Ibiza!" by Vengaboys. i, "Cupido," by Jan Smit. j, "Birds," by Anouk.

2015, Jan. 5 Litho. *Perf. 13½x13¼*

1482 A689 Sheet of 10 16.00 16.00
a.-j. 1 Any single 1.60 1.60

On day of issue, Nos. 1482a-1482j each sold for 69c.

Fortified Towns — A690

Fortifications of: No. 1483, Bourtange. No. 1484, Elburg. No. 1485, Naarden. No. 1486, Willemstad. No. 1487, Hulst.

2015 Litho. *Perf. 14½x14¼*

1483 A690 1 multi 1.60 1.60
a. Perf. 13½x12¾ 2.75 2.75
b. Booklet pane of 2 #1483a 5.50 —
1484 A690 1 multi 1.60 1.60
a. Perf. 13½x12¾ 2.75 2.75
b. Booklet pane of 2 #1484a 5.50 —
1485 A690 1 multi 1.60 1.60
a. Perf. 13½x12¾ 2.75 2.75
b. Booklet pane of 2 #1485a 5.50 —
1486 A690 1 multi 1.60 1.60
a. Perf. 13½x12¾ 2.75 2.75
b. Booklet pane of 2 #1486a 5.50 —
1487 A690 1 multi 1.60 1.60
a. Perf. 13½x12¾ 2.75 2.75
b. Booklet pane of 2 #1487a 5.50 —
Complete booklet, #148b, 1484b, 1485b, 1486b, 1487b 27.50
c. Souvenir sheet of 5, #1483-1487 8.00 8.00
Nos. 1483-1487 (5) 8.00 8.00

Issued: Nos. 1483, 1484, 1485, 2/2/15. Nos. 1483a, 1484a, 1485a, 1486, 1486a, 1487, 1487b, 1487c, 5/26/15. Nos. 1483-1487 each sold for 69c on day of issue. Complete booklet sold for €12.45.

Baby Carriage, Baby Bottle, Rocking Horse and Baby Toys — A691

Die Cut Perf. 14¼x14½

2015, Mar. 2 Photo.

Self-Adhesive

1488 A691 1 multi 1.60 1.60

No. 1488 sold for 69c on day of issue.

Map of Netherlands and Royal Items — A692

No. 1489 — Map and: a, Royal arms, inscription "Koning Willem-Alexander / 2013." b, Signature of King William I. inscription "Koning Willem I / 1815."

2015, Mar. 2 Litho. *Perf. 13½x13¼*

1489 A692 Pair, #a-b 6.50 6.50
a.-b. 2 Either single 3.25 3.25

On day of issue, Nos. 1489a and 1489b each sold for €1.38.

Bridges — A693

No. 1490: a and k, High speed railroad Bridge, Moerdijk, 2006. b and l, Ehzer Bridge, Almen, 1946. c and m, Kolenhaven Bridge, Delft, 2004. d and n, Cable-stayed bridge, Heusden, 1989. e and o, Zouthaven Bridge, Amsterdam, 2005. f and p, Jan Waaijer Bridge, Zoetermeer, 2013. g and q, De Oversteek Bridge, Nijmegen, 2013. h and r, Zeeland Bridge, Oosterschelde, 1965. i and s, Hanzeboog Bridge, Zwolle, 2011. j and t, Nescio Bridge, Amsterdam, 2006.

Perf. 13½x12¾

2015, Mar. 30 Litho.

1490 A693 Sheet of 10 16.00 16.00
a.-j. 1 Any single 1.60 1.60
k.-t. 1 Any single, perf. 14½x14¼ 2.75 2.75
u. Booklet pane of 2, #1490k-1490l 5.50 —
v. Booklet pane of 2, #1490m-1490n 5.50 —
w. Booklet pane of 2, #1490o-1490p 5.50 —
x. Booklet pane of 2, #1490q-1490r 5.50 —
y. Booklet pane of 2, #1490s-1490t 5.50 —
Complete booklet, #1490u, 1490v, 1490w, 1490x, 1490y 27.50

On day of issue, Nos. 1490a-1490j each sold for 69c. Complete booklet sold for €12.45. Descriptions of the bridges shown are found on the adjacent sheet selvage.

Hearts and Dots — A694

Die Cut Perf. 14¼x14½

2015, Apr. 28 Photo.

Booklet Stamp

Self-Adhesive

1491 A694 1 multi 1.60 1.60
a. Booklet pane of 10 16.00

No. 1491 sold for 69c on day of issue.

Toys and Games — A695

No. 1492: a, Video game equipment. b, Rubik's cube.

No. 1493: a, Robot and wind-up key. b, Board game.

2015, Apr. 28 Litho. *Perf. 13¼x13½*

1492 A695 Horiz. pair 3.25 3.25
a.-b. 1 Either single 1.60 1.60
1493 A695 Horiz. pair 5.25 5.25
a.-b. 1 International Either single 2.60 2.60

Europa (No. 1493). On day of issue, Nos. 1492a-1492b each sold for 69c; Nos. 1493a-1493b, €1.15.

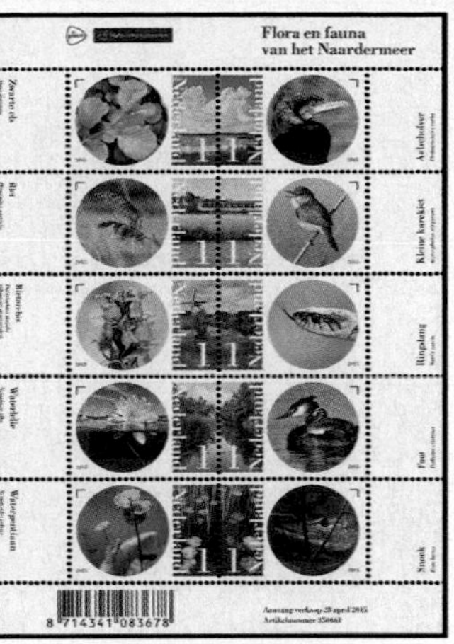

Flora and Fauna — A696

No. 1494: a and k, Alnus glutinosa. b and l, Phalacrocorax carbo. c and m, Phragmites australis. d and n, Acrocephalus scirpaceus. e and o, Dactylorhiza majalis subspecies praetermissa. f and p, Natrix natrix. g and q, Nymphaea alba. h and r, Podiceps cristatus. i and s, Nymphoides peltata. j and t, Esox lucius.

2015, Apr. 28 Litho. *Perf. 13¼x12¾*

1494 A696 Sheet of 10 16.00 16.00
a.-j. 1 Any single 1.60 1.60
k.-t. 1 Any single, perf. 14½x14¼ 2.75 2.75
u. Booklet pane of 2, #1494s-1494t 5.50 —
v. Booklet pane of 2, #1494q-1494r 5.50 —
w. Booklet pane of 2, #1494o-1494p 5.50 —
x. Booklet pane of 2, #1494m-1494n 5.50 —
y. Booklet pane of 2, #1494k-1494l 5.50 —
Complete booklet, #1494u, 1494v, 1494w, 1494x, 1494y 27.50

On day of issue, Nos. 1494a-1494j each sold for 69c. Complete booklet sold for €12.45.

Volvo Ocean Race — A697

No. 1495: a, Three crewmembers on boat. b, Wave crashing against sailboat with Volvo Ocean Race emblem on bow. c, Sailboats in harbor. d, Four crewmembers in protective gear. e, View from mast of crew on deck. f, Boat with sail inscribed "Vestas."

2015, May 26 Litho. *Perf. 13¼x13¾*

1495 A697 Block of 6 9.75 9.75
a.-f. 1 Any single 1.60 1.60

On day of issue, Nos. 1495a-1495f each sold for 69c.

King William II (1792-1849) — A698

Perf. 13½x13¼

2015, June 22 Litho.

1496 A698 1 International multi 2.60 2.60

Battle of Waterloo, 200th anniv. No. 1496 sold for €1.15 on day of issue.

Simple Science Experiments — A699

No. 1497: a, Match under egg passing through neck of bottle. b, Water in heated balloon. c, Battery made of lemons. d, Optical illusion of pencil behind glass of water. e, Lightbulb and positively and negatively charged balloons.

2015, July 20 Litho. *Perf. 13½x13¼*

1497	Horiz. strip of 5	7.50	7.50
a.-e.	A699 1 Any single	1.50	1.50

On day of issue, Nos. 1497a-1497e each sold for 69c.

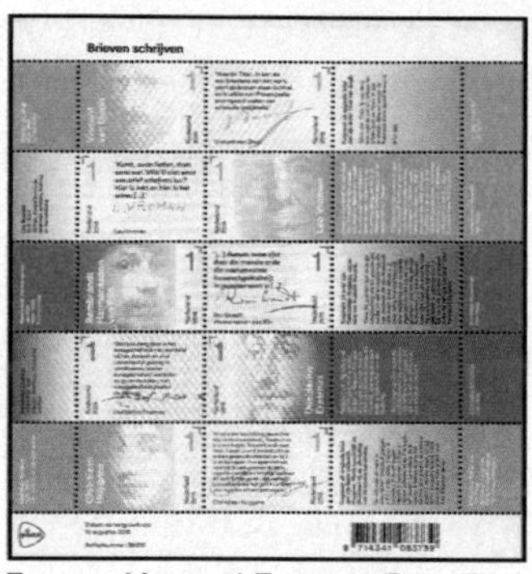

Famous Men and Excerpts From Their Letters — A700

No. 1498: a and k, Vincent van Gogh (1853-90), painter. b and l, Signature and excerpt from letter by van Gogh. c and m, Signature and excerpt from letter by Leo Vroman (1915-2014), poet. d and n, Vroman. e and o, Rembrandt van Rijn (1606-69), painter. f and p, Signature and excerpt from letter by Rembrandt. g and q, Signature and excerpt from letter by Desiderius Erasmus (1466-1536), theologian. h and r, Erasmus. i and s, Christiaan Huygens (1629-95), scientist. j and t, Signature and excerpt of letter by Huygens.

Perf. 13½x12¾

2015, Aug. 17 Litho.

1498	A700 Sheet of 10 + 5 labels	16.00	16.00
a.-j.	1 Any single	1.60	1.60
k.-t.	1 Any single, perf. 14½	2.75	2.75
u.	Booklet pane of 2, #1498k-1498l	5.50	—
v.	Booklet pane of 2, #1498m-1498n	5.50	—
w.	Booklet pane of 2, #1498o-1498p	5.50	—
x.	Booklet pane of 2, #1498q-1498r	5.50	—
y.	Booklet pane of 2, #1498s-1498t	5.50	—
	Complete booklet, #1498u, 1498v, 1498w, 1498x, 1498y	27.50	

On day of issue, Nos. 1498a-1498j each sold for 69c. Complete booklet sold for €12.45.

Miniature Sheet

Photographs of Animals by Charlotte Dumas — A701

No. 1499 — Title of photograph: a, Retrieved (retriever named Guinness and trailer in background), 2011. b, Day is Done, 2004 (horse named Isolde, white wall behind horse), 2004. c, Reverie (wolf named Taza sleeping), 2005. d, Tiger Tiger (tiger named Zeus), 2007. e, Heart Shaped Hole (dog named Tom Tom standing next to wall), 2008. f, Retrieved (dog named Moxie sitting on dock), 2011. g, Randagi (street dog laying on step), 2006. h, Anima (horse named Ringo in darkened stall), 2012. i, The Widest Prairies (horse named Rocky Road standing in field), 2013. j, Casa Voyageurs (cat named Kat), 2012.

Perf. 13¼x13½

2015, Sept. 14 Litho.

1499	A701 Sheet of 10	16.00	16.00
a.-j.	1 Any single	1.60	1.60

On day of issue Nos. 1499a-1499j each sold for 69c. Titles of photographs are in sheet selvage adjacent to each stamp.

Miniature Sheet

Dutch Connections With the United States of America — A702

No. 1500: a, "Jan Kees" on pinstriped uniform in script of New York Yankees emblem. b, New York City subway signs using Dutch spellings of Harlem and Brooklyn. c, City Hall, The Hague, designed by Richard Meier. d, High Line Linear Park, New York City. e, Hotdog USA, by Jan Cremer. f, Photograph of breakedancer Kid Freeze holding boom box, by Jamel Shabazz.

Perf. 13¼x13½

2015, Sept. 14 Litho.

1500	A702 Sheet of 6	16.00	16.00
a.-f.	1 International Any single	2.60	2.60

Nos. 1500a-1500f each sold for €1.15 on day of issue. No. 1500 was printed with three different illustrations in the bottom sheet margin, with each sheet having a different arrangement of stamps. Sheet margins at left and right served as etiquettes.

Miniature Sheet

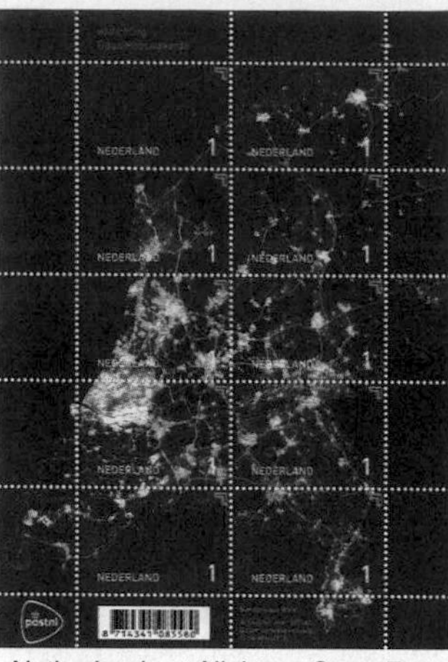

Netherlands at Night as Seen From Space — A703

No. 1501: a, West Frisian Islands. b, Northern Netherlands (area around Groningen and Leeuwarden). c, North Holland Province (area around Alkmaar). d, Drenthe and Overijssel Provinces (area around Hoogeveen and Meppel). e, Area around Amsterdam and Utrecht. f, Flevoland Province (area around Deventer and Apeldoorn). g, Area around Rotterdam. h, Area around Nijmegen and 's Hertogenbosch. i, Zeeland Province and North Brabant Province area north of Belgian border. j, Southeastern Netherlands (area around Eindhoven and Echt).

2015, Oct. 12 Litho. *Perf. 13¼x13½*

1501	A703 Sheet of 10	16.00	16.00
a.-j.	1 Any single	1.60	1.60

Ship Models at Rotterdam Maritime Museum — A704

No. 1502: a and k, Aegir. b and l, Bomschuit. c and m, Trio. d and n, Sindoro. e and o, Sultan van Koetei. f and p, Fairmount Expedition. g and q, Mataró. h and r, Assahan. i and s, Nedlloyd Houtman. j and t, Padmos/Blijdorp.

2015, Oct. 12 Litho. *Perf. 13½x12¾*

1502	A704 Sheet of 10	16.00	16.00
a.-j.	1 Any single	1.60	1.60
k.-t.	1 Any single, perf. 14½	2.75	2.75
u.	Booklet pane of 2, #1502q, 1502t	5.50	—
v.	Booklet pane of 2, #1502l, 1502m	5.50	—
w.	Booklet pane of 2, #1502n, 1502o	5.50	—
x.	Booklet pane of 2, #1502r, 1502s	5.50	—
y.	Booklet pane of 2, #1502k, 1502p	5.50	—
	Complete booklet, #1502u, 1502v, 1502w, 1502x, 1502y	27.50	

On day of issue Nos. 1502a-1502j each sold for 69c. Complete booklet sold for €12.45.

Netherlands No. 266 — A705

2015, Oct. 16 Litho. *Perf. 13½x14*

1503	A705 1 multi	1.60	1.60
a.	Booklet pane of 2	5.50	—
	Complete booklet, 5 #1503a	27.50	

No. 1503 sold for 69c on day of issue. Complete booklet sold for €12.45. The five examples of No. 1503a in the complete booklet have different margins.

December Stamps — A706

No. 1504 — Snowflakes and: a, Fox in den, deer and bird. b, Woman and deer. c, Bird on woman's hand. d, Swans. e, Polar bear and bird. f, Rabbits. g, Squirrels. h, Birds in flight. i, Woman and dog. j, Rabbit, bird, fawn, and deer.

Serpentine Die Cut 12½x12¾

2015, Nov. 24 Photo.

Self-Adhesive

1504	A706 Block of 10	14.00	
a.-j.	(64c) Any single	1.40	1.40

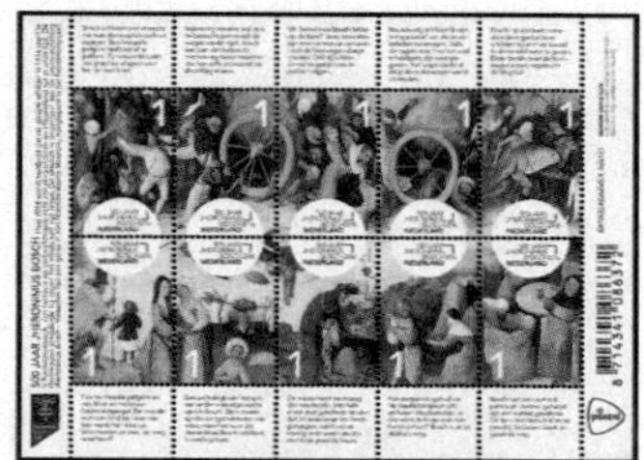

The Hay Wagon, by Hieronymus Bosch (c. 1450-1516) — A707

No. 1505 — Painting details: a and k, Man holding stick, woman holding infant. b and l, Wagon wheel, woman holding stick. c and m, Man in blue with lifted arms at side of wagon. d and n, Man in red looking at wagon wheel from behind. e and o, People with heads of animals. f and p, Man holding stick and carrying infant on back, child. g and q, Bird roasting on a spit. h and r, Man looking in woman's mouth. i and s, Bagpipe player and nun holding hay. j and t, Woman reaching in bag of hay, monk holding glass.

2016, Jan. 4 Litho. *Perf. 13½x13¼*

1505	A707 Sheet of 10	16.00	16.00
a.-j.	1 Any single	1.60	1.60
k.	Booklet pane of 2, #1505a, 1505f	5.50	—
l.	Booklet pane of 2, #1505b, 1505g	5.50	—
m.	Booklet pane of 2, #1505c, 1505h	5.50	—
n.	Booklet pane of 2, #1505d, 1505i	5.50	—
o.	Booklet pane of 2, #1505e, 1505j	5.50	—
	Complete booklet, #1505k, 1505l, 1505m, 1505n, 1505o	27.50	

On day of issue, Nos. 1505a-1505j each sold for 73c. Complete booklet sold for €12.45.

SEMI-POSTAL STAMPS

Design Symbolical of the Four Chief Means for Combating Tuberculosis: Light, Water, Air and Food — SP1

Perf. 12½

1906, Dec. 21 Typo. Unwmk.

B1 SP1 1c (+1c) rose red 20.00 11.00
B2 SP1 3c (+3c) pale ol grn 30.00 26.00
B3 SP1 5c (+5c) gray 30.00 15.00
Nos. B1-B3 (3) 80.00 *52.00*
Set, never hinged 475.00

Surtax aided the Society for the Prevention of Tuberculosis.

Nos. B1-B3 canceled-to-order "AMSTERDAM 31.07 10-12 N," sell at $3 a set.

Symbolical of Charity SP2

SP3

1923, Dec. 15 ***Perf. 11½***

B4 SP2 2c (+5c) vio bl 17.00 17.00
B5 SP3 10c (+5c) org red 17.00 17.00
Set, never hinged 75.00

The surtax was for the benefit of charity.

Allegory, Charity Protecting Child — SP6

1924, Dec. 15 Photo. ***Perf. 12½***

B6 SP6 2c (+2c) emer 1.80 1.80
B7 SP6 7½c (+3½c) dk brn 6.75 8.00
B8 SP6 10c (+2½c) vermilion 4.00 1.80
Nos. B6-B8 (3) 12.55 11.60
Set, never hinged 26.00

These stamps were sold at a premium over face value for the benefit of Child Welfare Societies.

Arms of North Brabant SP7

Arms of Gelderland SP8

Arms of South Holland — SP9

1925, Dec. 17 ***Perf. 12½***

B9 SP7 2c (+2c) grn & org .85 .75
B10 SP8 7½c (+3½c) vio & bl 4.25 4.50
B11 SP9 10c (+2½c) red & org 3.50 .45
Nos. B9-B11 (3) 8.60 5.70
Set, never hinged 18.50

Surtax went to Child Welfare Societies.

Syncopated Perfs., Type A

B9a SP7 2c (+2c) 18.50 22.00
B10a SP8 7½c (+3½c) 37.50 37.50
B11a SP9 10c (+2½c) 65.00 52.00
Nos. B9a-B11a (3) 121.00 111.50
Set, never hinged 250.00

Arms of Utrecht SP10

Arms of Zeeland SP11

Arms of North Holland SP12

Arms of Friesland SP13

1926, Dec. 1 Wmk. 202 ***Perf. 12½***

B12 SP10 2c (+2c) sil & red .50 .40
B13 SP11 5c (+3c) grn & gray bl 1.40 1.10
B14 SP12 10c (+3c) red & gold 2.10 .25
B15 SP13 15c (+3c) ultra & yel 5.50 4.25
Nos. B12-B15 (4) 9.50 6.00
Set, never hinged 25.00

The surtax on these stamps was devoted to Child Welfare Societies.

Syncopated Perfs., Type A

B12a SP10 2c (+2c) 4.75 4.75
B13a SP11 5c (+3c) 7.25 7.25
B14a SP12 10c (+3c) 13.50 13.50
B15a SP13 15c (+3c) 14.50 14.50
Nos. B12a-B15a (4) 40.00 40.00
Set, never hinged 95.00

King William III — SP14

Red Cross and Doves — SP18

Designs: 3c, Queen Emma. 5c, Prince Consort Henry. 7½c, Queen Wilhelmina.

Perf. 11½, 11½x12 B

1927, June Photo. Unwmk.

B16 SP14 2c (+2c) scar 2.50 2.25

Engr.

B17 SP14 3c (+2c) dp grn 5.75 *8.00*
B18 SP14 5c (+3c) slate bl 1.00 1.00

Photo.

B19 SP14 7½c (+3½c) ultra 4.50 1.50
B20 SP18 15c (+5c) ultra & red 8.75 8.00
Nos. B16-B20 (5) 22.50 20.75
Set, never hinged 52.50

60th anniversary of the Netherlands Red Cross Society. The surtaxes in parentheses were for the benefit of the Society.

Arms of Drenthe SP19

Arms of Groningen SP20

Arms of Limburg SP21

Arms of Overijssel SP22

1927, Dec. 15 Wmk. 202 ***Perf. 12½***

B21 SP19 2c (+2c) dp rose & vio .35 .30
B22 SP20 5c (+3c) ol grn & yel 1.50 1.25
B23 SP21 7½c (+3½c) red & blk 3.25 .35
B24 SP22 15c (+3c) ultra & org brn 4.75 4.25
Nos. B21-B24 (4) 9.85 6.15
Set, never hinged 26.00

The surtax on these stamps was for the benefit of Child Welfare Societies.

Syncopated Perfs., Type A

B21a SP19 2c (+2c) 1.90 1.40
B22a SP20 5c (+3c) 3.50 1.75
B23a SP21 7½c (+3½c) 4.25 1.75
B24a SP22 15c (+3c) 12.50 9.00
Nos. B21a-B24a (4) 22.15 13.90
Set, never hinged 57.50

Rowing — SP23

Fencing — SP24

Soccer SP25

Yachting SP26

Putting the Shot SP27

Running SP28

Riding SP29

Boxing SP30

Perf. 11½, 12, 11½x12, 12x11½

1928, Mar. 27 Litho.

B25 SP23 1½c (+1c) dk grn 1.90 1.40
B26 SP24 2c (+1c) red vio 2.40 1.75
B27 SP25 3c (+1c) green 2.40 2.00
B28 SP26 5c (+1c) lt bl 3.00 1.40
B29 SP27 7½c (+2½c) org 3.00 1.75
B30 SP28 10c (+2c) scarlet 6.75 5.25
B31 SP29 15c (+2c) dk bl 6.75 3.75
B32 SP30 30c (+3c) dk brn 20.00 17.50
Nos. B25-B32 (8) 46.20 34.80
Set, never hinged 150.00

The surtax on these stamps was used to help defray the expenses of the Olympic Games of 1928.

Jean Pierre Minckelers — SP31

5c, Hermann Boerhaave. 7½c, Hendrik Antoon Lorentz. 12½c, Christian Huygens.

1928, Dec. 10 Photo. ***Perf. 12x12½***

B33 SP31 1½c (+1½c) vio .55 .40
B34 SP31 5c (+3c) grn 1.75 .60

Perf. 12

B35 SP31 7½c (+2½c) ver 3.50 .25
a. Perf. 12x12½ 4.75 .70
B36 SP31 12½c (+3½c) ultra 9.75 7.50
a. Perf. 12x12½ 77.50 7.75
Nos. B33-B36 (4) 15.55 8.75
Set, never hinged 37.50

The surtax on these stamps was for the benefit of Child Welfare Societies.

Child on Dolphin — SP35

1929, Dec. 10 Litho. ***Perf. 12½***

B37 SP35 1½c (+1½c) gray 2.10 .45
B38 SP35 5c (+3c) blue grn 3.50 .75
B39 SP35 6c (+4c) scarlet 2.10 .35
B40 SP35 12½c (+3½c) dk bl 13.50 11.00
Nos. B37-B40 (4) 21.20 12.55
Set, never hinged 62.50

Surtax for child welfare.

Syncopated Perfs., Type B

B37a SP35 1½c (+1½c) 3.00 1.25
B38a SP35 5c (+3c) 4.50 1.25
B39a SP35 6c (+4c) 3.25 1.25
B40a SP35 12½c (+3½c) 25.00 14.00
Nos. B37a-B40a (4) 35.75 17.75
Set, never hinged 72.50

Rembrandt and His "Cloth Merchants of Amsterdam" SP36

Perf. 11½

1930, Feb. 15 Engr. Unwmk.

B41 SP36 5c (+5c) bl grn 6.75 6.00
B42 SP36 6c (+5c) gray blk 5.25 3.50
B43 SP36 12½c (+5c) dp bl 9.00 8.00
Nos. B41-B43 (3) 21.00 17.50
Set, never hinged 52.50

Surtax for the benefit of the Rembrandt Soc.

"Spring" — SP37

5c, Summer. 6c, Autumn. 12½c, Winter.

1930, Dec. 10 ***Perf. 12½***

B44 SP37 1½c (+1½c) lt red 1.50 .45
B45 SP37 5c (+3c) gray grn 2.25 .60
B46 SP37 6c (+4c) claret 2.00 .45
B47 SP37 12½c (+3½c) lt ultra 16.00 8.50
Nos. B44-B47 (4) 21.75 10.00
Set, never hinged 52.50

Surtax was for Child Welfare work.

Syncopated Perfs., Type C

B44a SP37 1½c (+1½c) 2.40 1.25
B45a SP37 5c (+3c) 3.50 1.25
B46a SP37 6c (+4c) 2.40 1.25
B47a SP37 12½c (+3½c) 19.00 12.50
Nos. B44a-B47a (4) 27.30 16.25
Set, never hinged 55.00

Stained Glass Window and Detail of Repair Method — SP41

6c, Gouda Church and repair of window frame.

Wmk. 202

1931, Oct. 1 Photo. ***Perf. 12½***

B48 SP41 1½c (+1½c) bl grn 17.00 15.00
B49 SP41 6c (+4c) car rose 20.00 17.00
Set, never hinged 75.00

Deaf Mute Learning Lip Reading — SP43

Designs: 5c, Mentally retarded child. 6c, Blind girl learning to read Braille. 12½c, Child victim of malnutrition.

1931, Dec. 10 *Perf. 12½*

B50 SP43 1½c (+1½c) ver & ultra 1.90 1.25
B51 SP43 5c (+3c) Prus bl & vio 5.25 1.25
B52 SP43 6c (+4c) vio & grn 5.25 1.25
B53 SP43 12½c (+3½c) ultra & dp org 29.00 21.00
Nos. B50-B53 (4) 41.40 24.75
Set, never hinged 95.00

The surtax was for Child Welfare work.

Syncopated Perfs., Type C

B50a SP43 1½c (+1½c) 1.90 1.25
B51a SP43 5c (+3c) 5.25 1.25
B52a SP43 6c (+4c) 5.50 1.25
B53a SP43 12½c (+3½c) 30.00 22.50
Nos. B50a-B53a (4) 42.65 26.25
Set, never hinged 105.00

Drawbridge — SP47

Designs: 2½c, Windmill and Dikes. 6c, Council House, Zierikzee. 12½c, Flower fields.

1932, May 23 *Perf. 12½*

B54 SP47 2½c (+1½c) turq grn & blk 7.00 5.00
B55 SP47 6c (+4c) gray blk & blk 10.50 5.00
B56 SP47 7½c (+3½c) brt red & blk 30.00 12.50
B57 SP47 12½c (+2½c) ultra & blk 32.50 19.00
Nos. B54-B57 (4) 80.00 41.50
Set, never hinged 190.00

The surtax was for the benefit of the National Tourist Association.

Furze and Boy — SP51

Designs (Heads of children and flowers typifying the seasons): 5c, Cornflower. 6c, Sunflower. 12½c, Christmas rose.

1932, Dec. 10 *Perf. 12½*

B58 SP51 1½c (+1½c) brn & yel 2.10 .45
B59 SP51 5c (+3c) red org & ultra 2.75 .75
B60 SP51 6c (+4c) dk grn & ocher 2.10 .35
B61 SP51 12½c (+3½c) ocher & ultra 27.50 18.00
Nos. B58-B61 (4) 34.45 19.55
Set, never hinged 90.00

The surtax aided Child Welfare Societies.

Syncopated Perfs., Type C

B58a SP51 1½c (+1½c) 2.75 1.60
B59a SP51 5c (+3c) 3.50 1.60
B60a SP51 6c (+4c) 3.50 1.60
B61a SP51 12½c (+3½c) 35.00 22.50
Nos. B58a-B61a (4) 44.75 27.30
Set, never hinged 100.00

Monument at Den Helder SP55

The "Hope," A Church and Hospital Ship SP56

Lifeboat in a Storm SP57

Dutch Sailor and Sailors' Home SP58

1933, June 10 *Perf. 14½x13½*

B62 SP55 1½c (+1½c) dp red 3.50 1.60
B63 SP56 5c (+3c) bl grn & red org 10.50 3.00
B64 SP57 6c (+4c) dp grn 16.00 2.50
B65 SP58 12½c (+3½c) ultra 24.00 17.50
Nos. B62-B65 (4) 54.00 24.60
Set, never hinged 125.00

The surtax was for the aid of Sailors' Homes.

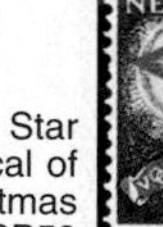

Child Carrying the Star of Hope, Symbolical of Christmas Cheer — SP59

1933, Dec. 11 *Perf. 12½*

B66 SP59 1½c (+1½c) sl & org brn 1.50 .55
B67 SP59 5c (+3c) dk brn & ocher 2.00 .65
B68 SP59 6c (+4c) bl grn & gold 2.50 .55
B69 SP59 12½c (+3½c) dk bl & sil 25.00 18.00
Nos. B66-B69 (4) 31.00 19.75
Set, never hinged 75.00

The surtax aided Child Welfare Societies.

Syncopated Perfs., Type C

B66a SP59 1½c (+1½c) 1.90 .70
B67a SP59 5c (+3c) 2.60 .90
B68a SP59 6c (+4c) 3.25 .90
B69a SP59 12½c (+3½c) 26.00 20.00
Nos. B66a-B69a (4) 33.75 22.50
Set, never hinged 87.50

Queen Wilhelmina SP60

Princess Juliana SP61

Perf. 12½

1934, Apr. 28 **Engr.** **Unwmk.**

B70 SP60 5c (+4c) dk vio 11.50 3.25
B71 SP61 6c (+5c) blue 10.50 4.25
Set, never hinged 52.50

The surtax was for the benefit of the Anti-Depression Committee.

Dowager Queen Emma — SP62

1934, Oct. 1 *Perf. 13x14*

B72 SP62 6c (+2c) blue 11.50 1.40
Never hinged 27.50

Surtax for the Fight Tuberculosis Society.

Poor Child — SP63

Perf. 13½x13

1934, Dec. 10 **Photo.** **Wmk. 202**

B73 SP63 1½c (+1½c) olive 1.40 .45
B74 SP63 5c (+3c) rose red 2.40 1.00
B75 SP63 6c (+4c) bl grn 2.40 .25
B76 SP63 12½c (+3½c) ultra 22.50 16.00
Nos. B73-B76 (4) 28.70 17.70
Set, never hinged 75.00

The surtax aided child welfare.

Henri D. Guyot SP64

A. J. M. Diepenbrock SP65

F. C. Donders SP66

J. P. Sweelinck SP67

Perf. 12½ x 12, 12

1935, June 17 **Engr.** **Unwmk.**

B77 SP64 1½c (+1½c) dk car 1.50 1.25
B78 SP65 5c (+3c) blk brn 4.00 3.50
B79 SP66 6c (+4c) myr grn 4.50 .70
B80 SP67 12½c (+3½c) dp bl 24.00 4.00
Nos. B77-B80 (4) 34.00 9.45
Set, never hinged 87.50

Surtax for social and cultural projects.

Netherlands Map, DC-3 Planes' Shadows SP68

Perf. 14x13

1935, Oct. 16 **Photo.** **Wmk. 202**

B81 SP68 6c (+4c) brn 24.00 7.50

Surtax for Natl. Aviation.

Girl Picking Apple — SP69

1935, Dec. 4 *Perf. 14½x13½*

B82 SP69 1½c (+1½c) crim .50 .30
B83 SP69 5c (+3c) dk yel grn 1.40 1.10
B84 SP69 6c (+4c) blk brn 1.25 .30
B85 SP69 12½c (+3½c) ultra 20.00 7.00
Nos. B82-B85 (4) 23.15 8.70
Set, never hinged 80.00

The surtax aided child welfare.

H. Kamerlingh Onnes — SP70

Dr. A. S. Talma — SP71

Msgr. H. J. A. M. Schaepman SP72

Desiderius Erasmus SP73

Perf. 12½x12

1936, May 1 **Engr.** **Unwmk.**

B86 SP70 1½c (+1½c) brn blk .80 .75
B87 SP71 5c (+3c) dl grn .80 *3.25*
B88 SP72 6c (+4c) dk red 3.50 .50
B89 SP73 12½c (+3½c) dl bl 13.00 2.50
Nos. B86-B89 (4) 18.10 7.00
Set, never hinged 60.00

Surtax for social and cultural projects.

Cherub — SP74

Perf. 14½x13½

1936, Dec. 1 **Photo.** **Wmk. 202**

B90 SP74 1½c (+1½c) lil gray .50 .30
B91 SP74 5c (+3c) turq grn 2.00 .75
B92 SP74 6c (+4c) dp red brn 1.90 .25
B93 SP74 12½c (+3½c) ind 14.00 4.75
Nos. B90-B93 (4) 18.40 6.05
Set, never hinged 45.00

The surtax aided child welfare.

Jacob Maris — SP75

Franciscus de la Boe Sylvius — SP76

Joost van den Vondel SP77

Anthony van Leeuwenhoek SP78

Perf. 12½x12

1937, June 1 **Engr.** **Unwmk.**

B94 SP75 1½c (+1½c) blk brn .50 .40
B95 SP76 5c (+3c) dl grn 4.00 2.75
B96 SP77 6c (+4c) brn vio 1.00 .25
B97 SP78 12½c (+3½c) dl bl 7.00 .85
Nos. B94-B97 (4) 12.50 4.25
Set, never hinged 35.00

Surtax for social and cultural projects.

"The Laughing Child" after Frans Hals — SP79

Perf. 14½x13½

1937, Dec. 1 Photo. Wmk. 202

B98 SP79 1½c (+1½c) blk .25 .25
B99 SP79 3c (+2c) grn 1.50 1.00
B100 SP79 4c (+2c) hn brn .60 .45
B101 SP79 5c (+3c) bl grn .50 .25
B102 SP79 12½c (+3½c) dk bl 7.25 1.40
Nos. B98-B102 (5) 10.10 3.35
Set, never hinged 32.50

The surtax aided child welfare.

Marnix van Sint Aldegonde SP80

Otto Gerhard Heldring SP81

Maria Tesselschade SP82

Hermann Boerhaave SP84

Harmenszoon Rembrandt van Rijn — SP83

Perf. 12½x12

1938, May 16 Engr. Unwmk.

B103 SP80 1½c (+1½c) sep .30 .50
B104 SP81 3c (+2c) dk grn .55 .30
B105 SP82 4c (+2c) rose lake 1.75 1.50
B106 SP83 5c (+3c) dk sl grn 2.25 .30
B107 SP84 12½c (+3½c) dl bl 7.75 1.10
Nos. B103-B107 (5) 12.60 3.70
Set, never hinged 32.50

The surtax was for the benefit of cultural and social relief.

Child with Flowers, Bird and Fish — SP85

Perf. 14½x13½

1938, Dec. 1 Photo. Wmk. 202

B108 SP85 1½c (+1½c) blk .25 .25
B109 SP85 3c (+2c) mar .30 .25
B110 SP85 4c (+2c) dk bl grn .60 .80
B111 SP85 5c (+3c) hn brn .25 .25
B112 SP85 12½c (+3½c) dp bl 9.00 1.75
Nos. B108-B112 (5) 10.40 3.30
Set, never hinged 35.00

The surtax aided child welfare.

Matthijs Maris — SP86

Anton Mauve — SP87

Gerard van Swieten SP88

Nikolaas Beets SP89

Peter Stuyvesant — SP90

Perf. 12½x12

1939, May 1 Engr. Unwmk.

B113 SP86 1½c (+1½c) sepia .60 .60
B114 SP87 2½c (+2½c) gray grn 3.00 2.75
B115 SP88 3c (+3c) ver .80 1.00
B116 SP89 5c (+3c) dk sl grn 2.00 .30
B117 SP90 12½c (+3½c) indigo 5.00 .85
Nos. B113-B117 (5) 11.40 5.50
Set, never hinged 40.00

The surtax was for the benefit of cultural and social relief.

Child Carrying Cornucopia — SP91

Perf. 14½x13½

1939, Dec. 1 Photo. Wmk. 202

B118 SP91 1½c (+1½c) blk .25 .25
B119 SP91 2½c (+2½c) dk ol grn 3.75 2.00
B120 SP91 3c (+3c) hn brn .40 .25
B121 SP91 5c (+3c) dk grn .85 .25
B122 SP91 12½c (+3½c) dk bl 4.00 1.00
Nos. B118-B122 (5) 9.25 3.75
Set, never hinged 40.00

The surtax was used for destitute children.

Catalogue values for unused stamps in this section, from this point to the end of the section, are for Never Hinged items.

Vincent van Gogh SP92

E. J. Potgieter SP93

Petrus Camper SP94

Jan Steen SP95

Joseph Scaliger — SP96

Perf. 12½x12

1940, May 11 Engr. Wmk. 202

B123 SP92 1½c +1½c brn blk 1.90 .25
B124 SP93 2½c +2½c dk grn 6.00 1.40
B125 SP94 3c +3c car 3.75 1.10
B126 SP95 5c +3c dp grn 7.75 .25
a. Booklet pane of 4 250.00
B127 SP96 12½c +3½c dp bl 6.75 .80

Surtax for social and cultural projects.

Type of 1940 Surcharged in Black

1940, Sept. 7

B128 SP95 7½c +2½c on 5c +3c dk red .50 .25
Nos. B123-B128 (6) 26.65 4.05

Child with Flowers and Doll — SP97

Perf. 14½x13½

1940, Dec. 2 Photo. Wmk. 202

B129 SP97 1½c +1½c dl bl gray .65 .25
B130 SP97 2½c +2½c dp ol 2.50 .50
B131 SP97 4c +3c royal bl 2.50 .65
B132 SP97 5c +3c dk bl grn 2.50 .25
B133 SP97 7½c +3½c hn .65 .25
Nos. B129-B133 (5) 8.80 1.90

The surtax was used for destitute children.

Dr. Antonius Mathijsen SP98

Dr. Jan Ingenhousz SP99

Aagje Deken SP100

Johannes Bosboom SP101

A. C. W. Staring — SP102

Perf. 12½x12

1941, May 29 Engr. Wmk. 202

B134 SP98 1½c +1½c blk brn .80 .25
B135 SP99 2½c +2½c dk sl grn .80 .25
B136 SP100 4c +3c red .80 .25
B137 SP101 5c +3c slate grn .80 .25
B138 SP102 7½c +3½c rose vio .80 .25
Nos. B134-B138 (5) 4.00 1.25

The surtax was for cultural and social relief.

Rembrandt's Painting of Titus, His Son — SP103

Perf. 14½x13½

1941, Dec. 1 Photo. Wmk. 202

B139 SP103 1½c +1½c vio blk .30 .25
B140 SP103 2½c +2½c dk ol .30 .25
B141 SP103 4c +3c royal blue .30 .25
B142 SP103 5c +3c dp grn .30 .25
B143 SP103 7½c +3½c dp henna brn .30 .25
Nos. B139-B143 (5) 1.50 1.25

The surtax aided child welfare.

Legionary

SP104 SP105

1942, Nov. 1 *Perf. 12½x12, 12x12½*

B144 SP104 7½c +2½c dk red 1.00 1.00
a. Sheet of 10 90.00 100.00
B145 SP105 12½c +87½c ultra 7.00 10.00
a. Sheet of 4 75.00 125.00

The surtax aided the Netherlands Legion.

#B144a, B145a measure 155x111mm and 94x94mm respectively.

19th Century Mail Cart — SP108

1943, Oct. 9 Unwmk. *Perf. 12x12½*

B148 SP108 7½c +7½c henna brn .25 .25

Issued to commemorate Stamp Day.

Child and House — SP109

#B150, Mother & Child. #B151, Mother $ Children. #B152, Child Carrying Sheaf of Wheat. #B153, Mother & Children, diff.

Perf. 12½x12

1944, Mar. 6 Wmk. 202

B149 SP109 1½c +3½c dl blk .25 .25
B150 SP109 4c +3½ rose lake .25 .25
B151 SP109 5c +5c dk bl grn .25 .25

No.	Design	Value	Unused	Used
B152	SP109	7½c +7½c dp hn brn	.25	.25
B153	SP109	10c +40c royal blue	.25	.25
		Nos. B149-B153 (5)	1.25	1.25

The surtax aided National Social Service and winter relief.

Child — SP114

1945, Dec. 1 Photo. *Perf. 14½x13½*

No.	Design	Value	Unused	Used
B154	SP114	1½c +2½c gray	.25	.25
B155	SP114	2½c +3½c dk bl grn	.25	.25
B156	SP114	5c +5c brn red	.25	.25
B157	SP114	7½c +4½c red	.25	.25
B158	SP114	12½c +5½c brt bl	.25	.25
		Nos. B154-B158 (5)	1.25	1.25

The surtax was for Child Welfare.

Fortuna — SP115

Perf. 12½x12

1946, May 1 Engr. Unwmk.

No.	Design	Value	Unused	Used
B159	SP115	1½c +3½c brn blk	.45	.25
B160	SP115	2½c +5c dl grn	.60	.30
B161	SP115	5c +10c dk vio	.65	.40
B162	SP115	7½c +15c car lake	.45	.25
B163	SP115	12½c +37½c dk bl	.75	.30
		Nos. B159-B163 (5)	2.90	1.50

The surtax was for victims of World War II.

Princess Irene — SP116

Designs: Nos. B165, B167, Princess Margriet. Nos. B168-B169, Princess Beatrix.

1946, Sept. 16

No.	Design	Value	Unused	Used
B164	SP116	1½c +1½c blk brn	.50	.40
B165	SP116	2½c +1½c bl grn	.50	.40
B166	SP116	4c +2c magenta	.50	.40
B167	SP116	5c +2c brown	.50	.40
B168	SP116	7½c +2½c red	.50	.25
B169	SP116	12½c +7½c dk bl	.50	.40
		Nos. B164-B169 (6)	3.00	2.25

The surtax was for child welfare and anti-tuberculosis work.

Child on Merry-go-round SP119

1946, Dec. 2 Photo. Wmk. 202

No.	Design	Value	Unused	Used
B170	SP119	2c +2c lil gray	.40	.25
B171	SP119	4c +2c dk grn	.40	.25
B172	SP119	7½c +2½c brt red	.40	.25
B173	SP119	10c +5c dp plum	.40	.25
B174	SP119	20c +5c dp bl	.40	.30
		Nos. B170-B174 (5)	2.00	1.30

The surtax was for child welfare.

Dr. Hendrik van Deventer SP120

Peter Cornelisz Hooft SP121

Johan de Witt SP122

Jean F. van Royen SP123

Hugo de Groot — SP124

1947, Aug. 1 Engr. Unwmk.

No.	Design	Value	Unused	Used
B175	SP120	2c +2c dark red	.60	.25
B176	SP121	4c +2c dk green	1.25	.40
B177	SP122	7½c +2½c dk pur brn	1.90	.40
B178	SP123	10c +5c brown	1.40	.25
B179	SP124	20c +5c dk blue	1.10	.40
		Nos. B175-B179 (5)	6.25	1.70

The surtax was for social and cultural purposes.

Children SP125

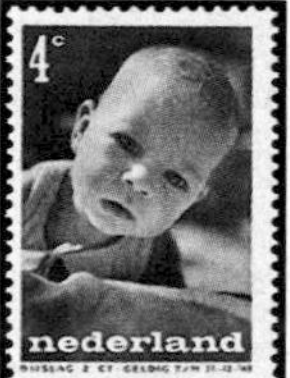

Infant SP126

1947, Dec. 1 Photo. *Perf. 13x14*

No.	Design	Value	Unused	Used
B180	SP125	2c +2c red brn	.25	.25
B181	SP126	4c +2c bl grn	1.25	.40
B182	SP126	7½c +2½c sepia	1.25	.55
B183	SP126	10c +5c dk red	.75	.25
B184	SP125	20c +5c blue	1.25	.65
		Nos. B180-B184 (5)	4.75	2.10

The surtax was for child welfare.

Hall of Knights, The Hague — SP127

Designs: 6c+4c, Royal Palace, Amsterdam. 10c+5c, Kneuterdyk Palace, The Hague. 20c+5c, New Church, Amsterdam.

1948, June 17 Engr. *Perf. 13½x14*

No.	Design	Value	Unused	Used
B185	SP127	2c +2c dk brn	1.50	.25
B186	SP127	6c +4c grn	1.50	.25
B187	SP127	10c +5c brt red	1.25	.25
B188	SP127	20c +5c deep blue	1.50	.65
		Nos. B185-B188 (4)	5.75	1.40

The surtax was for cultural and social purposes.

Boy in Kayak — SP128

5c+3c, Swimming. 6c+4c, Sledding. 10c+5c, Swinging. 20c+8c, Figure skating.

1948, Nov. 15 Photo. *Perf. 13x14*

No.	Design	Value	Unused	Used
B189	SP128	2c +2c yel grn	.25	.25
B190	SP128	5c +3c dk bl grn	2.00	.65
B191	SP128	6c +4c gray	.85	.25
B192	SP128	10c +5c red	.25	.25
B193	SP128	20c +8c blue	2.25	.65
		Nos. B189-B193 (5)	5.60	2.05

The surtax was for child welfare.

Beach Terrace SP129

Boy and Girl Hikers SP130

Campers SP131

Reaping SP132

Sailboats SP133

1949, May 2 Wmk. 202 *Perf. 14x13*

No.	Design	Value	Unused	Used
B194	SP129	2c +2c bl & org yel	.90	.25
B195	SP130	5c +3c bl & yel	1.50	1.00
B196	SP131	6c +4c dk bl grn	1.50	.35
B197	SP132	10c +5c bl & org yel	2.50	.25
B198	SP133	20c +5c blue	1.75	1.25
		Nos. B194-B198 (5)	8.15	3.10

The surtax was for cultural and social purposes.

Hands Reaching for Sunflower — SP134

Perf. 14½x13½

1949, Aug. 1 Photo. Unwmk.

Flower in Yellow

No.	Design	Value	Unused	Used
B199	SP134	2c +3c gray	1.10	.25
B200	SP134	6c +4c red brown	.70	.30
B201	SP134	10c +5c brt blue	2.25	.25
B202	SP134	30c +10c dk brown	6.25	2.00
		Nos. B199-B202 (4)	10.30	2.80

The surtax was for the Red Cross and for Indonesia Relief work.

"Autumn" — SP135

5c+3c, "Summer." 6c+4c, "Spring." 10c+5c, "Winter." 20c+7c, "New Year."

1949, Nov. 14 Engr. *Perf. 13x14*

No.	Design	Value	Unused	Used
B203	SP135	2c +3c brown	.25	.25
B204	SP135	5c +3c red	3.25	.95
B205	SP135	6c +4c dull green	1.10	.25
B206	SP135	10c +5c gray	.25	.25
B207	SP135	20c +7c blue	3.50	.85
		Nos. B203-B207 (5)	8.35	2.55

The surtax was for child welfare.

Figure from PTT Monument, The Hague SP136

Grain Binder SP137

Designs: 4c+2c, Dike repairs. 5c+3c, Apartment House, Rotterdam. 10c+5c, Bridge section being towed. 20c+5c, Canal freighter.

1950, May 2 *Perf. 12½x12, 12x12½*

No.	Design	Value	Unused	Used
B208	SP136	2c +2c dk brown	1.50	.75
B209	SP136	4c +2c dk green	13.00	8.00
B210	SP136	5c +3c sepia	6.75	2.50
B211	SP137	6c +4c purple	3.00	.70
B212	SP137	10c +5c blue gray	3.00	.25
B213	SP137	20c +5c deep blue	13.00	9.50
		Nos. B208-B213 (6)	40.25	21.70

The surtax was for social and cultural works.

Church Ruins and Good Samaritan — SP138

1950, July 17 Photo. *Perf. 12½x12*

No.	Design	Value	Unused	Used
B214	SP138	2c +2c ol brn	3.00	1.25
B215	SP138	5c +3c brn red	16.00	*13.00*
B216	SP138	6c +4c dp grn	9.50	1.50
B217	SP138	10c +5c brt lil rose	10.00	.30
B218	SP138	20c +5c ultra	22.50	*24.00*
		Nos. B214-B218 (5)	61.00	*40.05*

The surtax was for the restoration of ruined churches.

Baby and Bees — SP139

Designs: 5c+3c, Boy and rooster. 6c+4c, Girl feeding birds. 10c+5c, Boy and fish. 20c+7c, Girl, butterfly and toad.

1950, Nov. 13 *Perf. 13x12*

No.	Design	Value	Unused	Used
B219	SP139	2c +3c car	.25	.25
B220	SP139	5c +3c ol grn	7.00	3.00
B221	SP139	6c +4c dk bl grn	2.00	.65
B222	SP139	10c +5c lilac	.25	.25
B223	SP139	20c +7c blue	13.00	8.00
		Nos. B219-B223 (5)	22.50	12.15

The surtax was to aid needy children.

Hillenraad Castle SP140

Bergh Castle SP141

Castles: 6c+4c, Hernen. 10c+5c, Rechteren. 20c+5c, Moermond.

Perf. 12x12½, 12½x12

1951, May 15 Engr. Unwmk.

B224 SP140 2c +2c purple 3.00 1.50
B225 SP141 5c +3c dk red 8.00 7.75
B226 SP140 6c +4c dk brown 1.40 1.25
B227 SP141 10c +5c dk green 3.00 .60
B228 SP141 20c +5c dp blue 7.00 *7.75*
Nos. B224-B228 (5) 22.40 *18.85*

The surtax was for cultural, medical and social purposes.

Girl and Windmill — SP142

Designs: 5c+3c, Boy and building construction. 6c+4c, Fisherboy and net. 10c+5c, Boy, chimneys and steelwork. 20c+7c, Girl and apartment house.

1951, Nov. 12 Photo. *Perf. 13x14*

B229 SP142 2c +3c dp green .60 .25
B230 SP142 5c +3c sl vio 8.50 3.00
B231 SP142 6c +4c dk brown 6.00 .50
B232 SP142 10c +5c red brown .40 .25
B233 SP142 20c +7c dp bl 8.50 *6.00*
Nos. B229-B233 (5) 24.00 *10.00*

The surtax was for child welfare.

Jan van Riebeeck — SP143

1952, Mar. *Perf. 12½x12*

B234 SP143 2c +3c dk gray 5.50 3.50
B235 SP143 6c +4c dk bl grn 7.25 3.50
B236 SP143 10c +5c brt red 9.00 3.50
B237 SP143 20c +5c brt blue 5.25 3.50
Nos. B234-B237 (4) 27.00 14.00

Tercentenary of Van Riebeeck's landing in South Africa. Surtax was for Van Riebeeck monument fund.

Scotch Rose — SP144

Designs: 5c+3c, Marsh marigold. 6c+4c, Tulip. 10c+5c, Ox-eye daisy. 20c+5c, Cornflower.

1952, May 1

B238 SP144 2c +2c cer & dl grn .85 .50
B239 SP144 5c +3c dp grn & yel 3.25 3.25
B240 SP144 6c +4c red & dl grn 2.75 1.00
B241 SP144 10c +5c org yel & dl grn 2.75 .35
B242 SP144 20c +5c bl & dl grn 17.00 8.00
Nos. B238-B242 (5) 26.60 13.10

The surtax was for social, cultural and medical purposes.

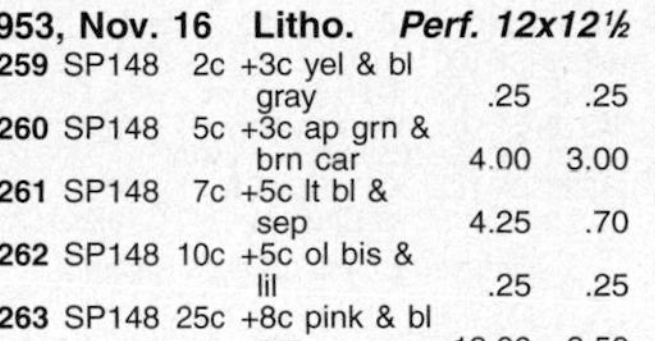

Girl and Dog — SP145

2c+3c, Boy & goat. 5c+3c, Girl on donkey. 10c+5c, Boy & kitten. 20c+7c, Boy & rabbit.

Design in Black

Perf. 12x12½

1952, Nov. 17 Unwmk.

B243 SP145 2c +3c olive .25 .25
B244 SP145 5c +3c dp rose 3.25 .90
B245 SP145 6c +4c aqua 2.75 .30
B246 SP145 10c +5c org yel .25 .25
B247 SP145 20c +7c blue 8.00 5.00
Nos. B243-B247 (5) 14.50 6.70

The surtax was for child welfare.

No. 308 Surcharged in Black

Perf. 13½x13

1953, Feb. 10 Wmk. 202

B248 A76 10c +10c org yel .55 .25

The surtax was for flood relief.

Hyacinth — SP146

Designs: 5c+3c, African Marigold. 6c+4c, Daffodil. 10c+5c, Anemone. 20c+5c, Iris.

1953, May 1 Unwmk. *Perf. 12½x12*

B249 SP146 2c +2c vio & grn .85 .30
B250 SP146 5c +3c dp org & grn 4.50 3.25
B251 SP146 6c +4c grn & yel 2.10 .40
B252 SP146 10c +5c dk red & grn 3.25 .30
B253 SP146 20c +5c dp ultra & grn 14.50 10.50
Nos. B249-B253 (5) 25.20 14.75

The surtax was for social, cultural and medical purposes.

Red Cross on Shield — SP147

Designs: 6c+4c, Man holding lantern. 7c+5c, Worker and ambulance at flood. 10c+5c, Nurse giving blood transfusion. 25c+8c, Red Cross flags.

Cross in Red

1953, Aug. 24 Engr.

B254 SP147 2c +3c dk ol .80 .30
B255 SP147 6c +4c dk vio brn 5.00 2.75
B256 SP147 7c +5c dk gray grn 1.25 .40
B257 SP147 10c +5c red .85 .25
B258 SP147 25c +8c dp bl 8.25 4.00
Nos. B254-B258 (5) 16.15 7.70

The surtax was for the Red Cross.

Spade, Flag, Bucket and Girl's Head — SP148

Head of child and: 5c+3c, Apple. 7c+5c, Pigeon. 10c+5c, Sailboat. 25c+8c, Tulip.

1953, Nov. 16 Litho. *Perf. 12x12½*

B259 SP148 2c +3c yel & bl gray .25 .25
B260 SP148 5c +3c ap grn & brn car 4.00 3.00
B261 SP148 7c +5c lt bl & sep 4.25 .70
B262 SP148 10c +5c ol bis & lil .25 .25
B263 SP148 25c +8c pink & bl grn 12.00 8.50
Nos. B259-B263 (5) 20.75 12.70

The surtax was for child welfare.

Martinus Nijhoff, Poet — SP149

5c+3c, Willem Pijper, composer. 7c+5c, H. P. Berlage, architect. 10c+5c, Johan Huizinga, historian. 25c+8c, Vincent van Gogh, painter.

1954, May 1 Photo. *Perf. 12½x12*

B264 SP149 2c +3c dp bl 1.75 1.25
B265 SP149 5c +3c ol brn 3.25 2.40
B266 SP149 7c +5c dk red 3.50 .95
B267 SP149 10c +5c dl grn 7.75 .60
B268 SP149 25c +8c plum 13.50 9.50
Nos. B264-B268 (5) 29.75 14.70

The surtax was for social and cultural purposes.

Boy Flying Model Plane — SP150

Portrait: 10c+4c, Albert E. Plesman.

1954, Aug. 23 *Perf. 12½x12*

B269 SP150 2c +2c ol grn 1.25 .75
B270 SP150 10c +4c dk gray bl 3.50 .50

The surtax was for the Netherlands Aviation Foundation.

Children Making Paper Chains — SP151

Girl Brushing Teeth — SP152

7c+5c, Boy sailing toy boat. 10c+5c, Nurse drying child. 25c+8c, Young convalescent, drawing.

Perf. 12x12½, 12½x12

1954, Nov. 15

B271 SP151 2c +3c brn .25 .25
B272 SP152 5c +3c ol grn 4.25 2.75
B273 SP152 7c +5c gray bl 1.75 .40
B274 SP152 10c +5c brn red .25 .25
B275 SP151 25c +8c dp bl 10.00 4.50
Nos. B271-B275 (5) 16.50 8.15

The surtax was for child welfare.

Factory, Rotterdam SP153

Amsterdam Stock Exchange SP154

5c+3c, Post office, The Hague. 10c+5c, Town hall, Hilversum. 25c+8c, Office building, The Hague.

1955, Apr. 25 Engr.

B276 SP153 2c +3c brnsh bis 1.25 .95
B277 SP153 5c +3c bl grn 3.00 2.00
B278 SP154 7c +5c rose brn 1.25 .80
B279 SP153 10c +5c steel bl 2.00 .25
B280 SP153 25c +8c choc 12.00 *7.50*
Nos. B276-B280 (5) 19.50 *11.50*

The surtax was for social and cultural purposes.

Microscope and Crab — SP155

1955, Aug. 15 Photo. *Perf. 12½x12*

Crab in Red

B281 SP155 2c +3c dk gray .60 .35
B282 SP155 5c +3c dk grn 2.75 1.60
B283 SP155 7c +5c dk vio 1.50 .45
B284 SP155 10c +5c dk bl .95 .25
B285 SP155 25c +8c olive 7.50 4.00
Nos. B281-B285 (5) 13.30 6.65

The surtax was for cancer research.

Willem van Loon by Dirck Santvoort — SP156

Portraits: 5+3c, Boy by Jacob Adriaanszoon Backer. 7+5c, Girl by unknown artist. 10+5c, Philips Huygens by Adriaan Hanneman. 25+8c, Constantijn Huygens by Adriaan Hanneman.

1955, Nov. 14 Unwmk.

B286 SP156 2c +3c dk grn .35 .25
B287 SP156 5c +3c dp car 3.75 1.75
B288 SP156 7c +5c dl red brn 4.00 .50
B289 SP156 10c +5c dp bl .35 .25
B290 SP156 25c +8c purple 9.50 5.75
Nos. B286-B290 (5) 17.95 8.50

The surtax was for child welfare.

Farmer Wearing High Cap — SP157

Rembrandt Etchings: 5c+3c, Young Tobias with Angel. 7c+5c, Persian Wearing Fur Cap. 10c+5c, Old Blind Tobias. 25c+8c, Self-portrait of 1639.

1956, Apr. 23 Engr. *Perf. 13½x14*

B291 SP157 2c +3c bluish blk 3.00 1.75
B292 SP157 5c +3c ol grn 3.00 1.75
B293 SP157 7c +5c brown 4.50 3.00
B294 SP157 10c +5c dk grn 13.00 .25
B295 SP157 25c +8c redsh brn 18.00 12.00
Nos. B291-B295 (5) 41.50 18.75

350th anniv. of the birth of Rembrandt van Rijn.

Surtax for social and cultural purposes.

Sailboat — SP158

Designs: 5c+3c, Woman runner. 7c+5c, Amphora depicting runners. 10c+5c, Field hockey. 25c+8c, Waterpolo player.

1956, Aug. 27 Litho. *Perf. 12½x12*

B296	SP158	2c +3c brt bl & blk	.90	.55
B297	SP158	5c +3c dl yel & blk	1.25	.85
B298	SP158	7c +5c red brn & blk	1.60	.85
B299	SP158	10c +5c gray & blk	3.00	.45
B300	SP158	25c +8c brt grn & blk	6.25	*4.50*
		Nos. B296-B300 (5)	13.00	*7.20*

16th Olympic Games at Melbourne, Nov. 22-Dec. 8, 1956.
The surtax was for the benefit of the Netherlands Olympic Committee.

Boy by Jan van Scorel — SP159

Children's Portraits: 5c+3c, Boy, 1563. 7c+5c, Girl, 1563. 10c+5c, Girl, 1590. 25c+8c, Eechie Pieters, 1592.

1956, Nov. 12 Photo. Unwmk.

B301	SP159	2c +3c blk vio	.35	.25
B302	SP159	5c +3c ol grn	1.25	.90
B303	SP159	7c +5c brn vio	3.75	1.25
B304	SP159	10c +5c dp red	.40	.25
B305	SP159	25c +8c dk bl	7.50	3.50
		Nos. B301-B305 (5)	13.25	6.15

The surtax was for child welfare.

Motor Freighter SP160

Ships: 6c+4c, Coaster. 7c+5c, "Willem Barendsz." 10c+8c, Trawler. 30c+8c, S. S. "Nieuw Amsterdam."

1957, May 13 Photo. *Perf. 14x13*

B306	SP160	4c +3c brt bl	1.25	.75
B307	SP160	6c +4c brt vio	3.25	2.00
B308	SP160	7c +5c dk car rose	2.00	.90
B309	SP160	10c +8c grn	4.00	.25
B310	SP160	30c +8c choc	5.00	*2.75*
		Nos. B306-B310 (5)	15.50	*6.65*

The surtax was for social and cultural purposes.

White Pelican Feeding Young — SP161

Designs: 6c+4c, Vacation ship, "Castle of Staverden." 7c+5c, Cross and dates: 1867-1957. 10c+8c, Cross and laurel wreath. 30c+8c, Globe and Cross.

1957, Aug. 19 Litho. *Perf. 12x12½*
Cross in Red

B311	SP161	4c +3c bl & red	1.25	.70
B312	SP161	6c +4c dk grn	1.60	.80
B313	SP161	7c +5c dk grn & pink	1.60	.80
B314	SP161	10c +8c yel org	1.40	.25
B315	SP161	30c +8c vio bl	3.00	*1.60*
		Nos. B311-B315 (5)	8.85	*4.15*

90th anniversary of the founding of the Netherlands Red Cross.

Girl by B. J. Blommers — SP162

Girls' Portraits by: 6c+4c, William B. Tholen. 8c+4c, Jan Sluyters. 12c+9c, Matthijs Maris. 30c+9c, Cornelis Kruseman.

1957, Nov. 18 Photo. *Perf. 12½x12*

B316	SP162	4c +4c dp car	.35	.25
B317	SP162	6c +4c ol grn	3.75	2.25
B318	SP162	8c +4c gray	3.25	1.25
B319	SP162	12c +9c dp claret	.35	.25
B320	SP162	30c +9c dk bl	8.50	4.50
		Nos. B316-B320 (5)	16.20	8.50

The surtax was for child welfare.

Woman from Walcheren, Zeeland — SP163

Regional Costumes: 6c+4c, Marken. 8c+4c, Scheveningen. 12c+9c, Friesland. 30c+9c, Volendam.

1958, Apr. 28 Photo. Unwmk.

B321	SP163	4c +4c blue	.70	.40
B322	SP163	6c +4c bister	2.75	1.75
B323	SP163	8c +4c dk car rose	4.50	1.10
B324	SP163	12c +9c org brn	1.60	.25
B325	SP163	30c +9c vio	7.25	*4.50*
		Nos. B321-B325 (5)	16.80	*8.00*

Surtax for social and cultural purposes.

Girl on Stilts and Boy on Tricycle — SP164

Children's Games: 6c+4c, Boy and girl on scooters. 8c+4c, Leapfrog. 12c+9c, Roller skating. 30c+9c, Boy in toy car and girl jumping rope.

1958, Nov. 17 Litho.

B326	SP164	4c +4c lt bl	.25	.25
B327	SP164	6c +4c dp red	3.00	1.75
B328	SP164	8c +4c brt bl grn	1.75	.65
B329	SP164	12c +9c red org	.25	.25
B330	SP164	30c +9c dk bl	6.25	3.00
		Nos. B326-B330 (5)	11.50	5.90

The surtax was for child welfare.

Tugs and Caisson SP165

Designs: 6c+4c, Dredger. 8c+4c, Laborers making fascine mattresses. 12c+9c, Grab cranes. 30c+9c, Sand spouter.

1959, May 11 *Perf. 14x13*

B331	SP165	4c +4c dk bl, *bl grn*	1.50	.90
B332	SP165	6c +4c red org, *gray*	1.60	1.00
B333	SP165	8c +4c bl vio, *lt bl*	2.25	1.00
B334	SP165	12c +9c bl grn, *brt yel*	4.00	.25
B335	SP165	30c +9c dk brn, *brick red*	6.75	*4.25*
		Nos. B331-B335 (5)	16.10	*7.40*

Issued to publicize the endless struggle to keep the sea out and the land dry.
The surtax was for social and cultural purposes.

Child in Playpen — SP166

Designs: 6c+4c, Playing Indian. 8c+4c, Child feeding geese. 12c+9c, Children crossing street. 30c+9c, Doing homework.

1959, Nov. 16 *Perf. 12½x12*

B336	SP166	4c +4c dp rose & dk bl	.25	.25
B337	SP166	6c +4c red brn & emer	1.90	.85
B338	SP166	8c +4c red & bl	3.00	1.10
B339	SP166	12c +9c grnsh bl, org & gray	.25	.25
B340	SP166	30c +9c yel & bl	4.50	2.75
		Nos. B336-B340 (5)	9.90	5.20

The surtax was for child welfare.

Refugee Woman — SP167

1960, Apr. 7 Photo. *Perf. 13x14*

B341	SP167	12c +8c dp claret	.50	.30
B342	SP167	30c +10c dk ol grn	2.50	1.75

Issued to publicize World Refugee Year, July 1, 1959-June 30, 1960. The surtax was for aid to refugees.

Tulip — SP168

Flowers: 6c+4c, Gorse. 8c+4c, White waterlily, horiz. 12c+8c, Red poppy. 30c+10c, Blue sea holly.

Perf. 12½x12, 12x12½
1960, May 23 Unwmk.

B343	SP168	4c +4c gray, grn & red	.80	.40
B344	SP168	6c +4c sal, grn & yel	.60	.30
B345	SP168	8c +4c multi	1.75	.85
B346	SP168	12c +8c dl org, red & grn	1.75	.30
B347	SP168	30c +10c yel, grn & ultra	6.25	4.50
		Nos. B343-B347 (5)	11.15	6.35

The surtax was for child welfare.

Girl from Marken — SP169

Regional Costumes: 6c+4c, Volendam. 8c+4c, Bunschoten. 12c+9c, Hindeloopen. 30c+9c, Huizen.

1960, Nov. 14 *Perf. 12½x12*

B348	SP169	4c +4c multi	.25	.25
B349	SP169	6c +4c multi	1.10	.80
B350	SP169	8c +4c multi	3.50	1.10
B351	SP169	12c +9c multi	.25	.25
B352	SP169	30c +9c multi	6.00	3.50
		Nos. B348-B352 (5)	11.10	5.90

The surtax was for child welfare.

Herring Gull — SP170

Birds: 6c+4c, Oystercatcher, horiz. 8c+4c, Curlew. 12c+8c, Avocet, horiz. 30c+10c, Lapwing.

Perf. 12½x12, 12x12½
1961, Apr. 24 Litho. Unwmk.

B353	SP170	4c +4c yel & grnsh gray	.85	.85
B354	SP170	6c +4c fawn & blk	.40	.25
B355	SP170	8c +4c ol & red brn	.85	.70
B356	SP170	12c +8c lt bl & gray	1.75	.25
B357	SP170	30c +10c grn & blk	3.50	2.75
		Nos. B353-B357 (5)	7.35	4.80

The surtax was for social and cultural purposes.

St. Nicholas on his Horse — SP171

Holiday folklore: 6c+4c, Epiphany. 8c+4c, Palm Sunday. 12c+9c, Whitsun bride, Pentecost. 30c+9c, Martinmas.

1961, Nov. 13 *Perf. 12½x12*

B358	SP171	4c +4c brt red	.25	.25
B359	SP171	6c +4c brt bl	1.10	.85
B360	SP171	8c +4c olive	1.10	.85
B361	SP171	12c +9c dp grn	.25	.25
B362	SP171	30c +9c dp org	3.00	2.00
		Nos. B358-B362 (5)	5.70	4.20

The surtax was for child welfare.

Christian Huygens' Pendulum Clock by van Ceulen — SP172

Designs: 4c+4c, Cat, Roman sculpture, horiz. 6c+4c, Fossil Ammonite. 12c+ 8c, Figurehead from admiralty ship model. 30c+10c, Guardsmen Hendrick van Berckenrode and Jacob van Lourensz, by Frans Hals, horiz.

Perf. 14x13, 13x14
1962, Apr. 27 Photo.

B363	SP172	4c +4c ol grn	1.00	.85
B364	SP172	6c +4c gray	.50	.40
B365	SP172	8c +4c dp claret	1.10	.85
B366	SP172	12c +8c olive bis	1.10	.25
B367	SP172	30c +10c bl blk	1.25	1.25
		Nos. B363-B367 (5)	4.95	3.60

The surtax was for social and cultural purposes. Issued to publicize the International Congress of Museum Experts, July 4-11.

Children Cooking — SP173

Children's Activities: 6c+4c, Bicycling. 8c+4c, Watering flowers. 12c+9c, Feeding chickens. 30c+9c, Music making.

1962, Nov. 12 *Perf. 12½x12*

B368	SP173	4c +4c red	.25	.25
B369	SP173	6c +4c yel bis	1.25	.30
B370	SP173	8c +4c ultra	1.50	.85
B371	SP173	12c +9c dp grn	.25	.25
B372	SP173	30c +9c dk car rose	2.50	1.90
		Nos. B368-B372 (5)	5.75	3.55

The surtax was for child welfare.

Gallery Windmill — SP174

Windmills: 6c+4c, North Holland polder mill. 8c+4c, South Holland polder mill, horiz. 12c+8c, Post mill. 30c+10c, Wip mill.

Perf. 13x14, 14x13

1963, Apr. 24 Litho. Unwmk.

B373 SP174 4c +4c dk bl 1.00 .75
B374 SP174 6c +4c dk pur 1.00 .75
B375 SP174 8c +4c dk grn 1.25 .90
B376 SP174 12c +8c blk 2.00 .25
B377 SP174 30c +10c dk car 2.00 1.75
Nos. B373-B377 (5) 7.25 4.40

The surtax was for social and cultural purposes.

Roadside First Aid Station SP175

Designs: 6c+4c, Book collection box. 8c+4c, Crosses. 12c+9c, International aid to Africans. 30c+9c, First aid team.

1963, Aug. 20 ***Perf. 14x13***

B378 SP175 4c +4c dk bl & red .35 .25
B379 SP175 6c +4c dl pur & red .25 .25
B380 SP175 8c +4c blk & red .85 .50
B381 SP175 12c +9c red brn & red .50 .25
B382 SP175 30c +9c yel grn & red 1.50 1.00
Nos. B378-B382 (5) 3.45 2.25

Centenary of the Intl. Red Cross. The surtax went to the Netherlands Red Cross.

"Aunt Lucy Sat on a Goosey" — SP176

Nursery Rhymes: 6c+4c, "In the Hague there lives a count." 8c+4c, "One day I passed a puppet's fair." 12c+9c, "Storky, storky, Billy Spoon." 30c+9c, "Ride on in a little buggy."

1963, Nov. 12 Litho. ***Perf. 13x14***

B383 SP176 4c +4c grnsh bl & dk bl .25 .25
B384 SP176 6c +4c org red & sl grn .70 .45
B385 SP176 8c +4c dl grn & dk brn 1.00 .45
B386 SP176 12c +9c yel & dk pur .25 .25
B387 SP176 30c +9c rose & dk bl 1.75 1.25
Nos. B383-B387 (5) 3.95 2.65

The surtax was for mentally and physically handicapped children.

Seeing-Eye Dog — SP177

8c+5c, Three red deer. 12c+9c, Three kittens. 30c+9c, European bison and young.

1964, Apr. 21 ***Perf. 12x12½***

B388 SP177 5c +5c gray ol, red & blk .35 .25
B389 SP177 8c +5c dk red, pale brn & blk .35 .25
B390 SP177 12c +9c dl yel, blk & gray .35 .25
B391 SP177 30c +9c bl, gray & blk .55 .40
Nos. B388-B391 (4) 1.60 1.15

The surtax was for social and cultural purposes.

Child Painting — SP178

"Artistic and Creative Activities of Children": 10c+5c, Ballet dancing. 15c+10c, Girl playing the flute. 20c+10c, Little Red Riding Hood (masquerading children). 40c+15c, Boy with hammer at work bench.

Perf. 13x14

1964, Nov. 17 Photo. Unwmk.

B392 SP178 7c +3c lt ol grn & bl .45 .30
B393 SP178 10c +5c red, brt pink & grn .35 .25
B394 SP178 15c +10c yel bis, blk & yel .25 .25
B395 SP178 20c +10c brt pink, brn & red .45 .25
B396 SP178 40c +15c bl & yel grn .75 .50
Nos. B392-B396 (5) 2.25 1.55

The surtax was for child welfare.

View of Veere SP179

Views: 10c+6c, Thorn. 18c+12c, Dordrecht. 20c+10c, Staveren. 40c+10c, Medemblik.

1965, June 1 Litho. ***Perf. 14x13***

B397 SP179 8c +6c yel & blk .35 .25
B398 SP179 10c +6c grnsh bl & blk .35 .25
B399 SP179 18c +12c sal & blk .35 .25
B400 SP179 20c +10c bl & blk .35 .25
B401 SP179 40c +10c ap grn & blk .60 .40
Nos. B397-B401 (5) 2.00 1.40

The surtax was for social and cultural purposes.

Child SP180

Designs by Children: 10c+6c, Ship. 18c+12c, Woman, vert. 20c+10c, Child, lake and swan. 40c+10c, Tractor.

Perf. 14x13, 13x14

1965, Nov. 16 Photo.

B402 SP180 8c +6c multi .25 .25
B403 SP180 10c +6c multi .45 .40
B404 SP180 18c +12c multi .25 .25
a. Min. sheet of 11, 5 #B402, 6 #B404 + label 20.00 18.00
B405 SP180 20c +10c multi .50 .40
B406 SP180 40c +10c multi .80 .45
Nos. B402-B406 (5) 2.25 1.75

The surtax was for child welfare.

"Help them to a safe haven" SP181

1966, Jan. 31 Photo. ***Perf. 14x13***

B407 SP181 18c +7c blk & org yel .40 .25
B408 SP181 40c +20c blk & red .40 .25
a. Min. sheet of 3, #B407, 2 #B408 4.00 3.00

The surtax was for the Intergovernmental Committee for European Migration (ICEM). The message on the stamps was given and signed by Queen Juliana.

Inkwell, Goose Quill and Book — SP182

Designs: 12c+8c, Fragment of Gysbert Japicx manuscript. 20c+10c, Knight on horseback, miniature from "Roman van Walewein" manuscript, 1350. 25c+10c, Initial "D" from "Ferguut" manuscript, 1350. 40c+20c, Print shop, 16th century woodcut.

1966, May 3 ***Perf. 13x14***

B409 SP182 10c +5c multi .30 .30
B410 SP182 12c +8c multi .35 .30
B411 SP182 20c +10c multi .45 .40
B412 SP182 25c +10c multi .50 .40
B413 SP182 40c +20c multi .55 .50
Nos. B409-B413 (5) 2.15 1.90

Gysbert Japicx (1603-1666), Friesian poet, and the 200th anniversary of the founding of the Netherlands Literary Society.
The surtax was for social and cultural purposes.

Infant SP183

Designs: 12c+8c, Daughter of the painter S. C. Lixenberg. 20c+10c, Boy swimming. 25c+10c, Dominga Blazer, daughter of Carel Blazer, photographer of this set. 40c+20c, Boy and horse.

1966, Nov. 15 Photo. ***Perf. 14x13***

B414 SP183 10c +5c dp org & bl .25 .25
B415 SP183 12c +8c ap grn & red .25 .25
B416 SP183 20c +10c brt bl & red .25 .25
a. Min. sheet of 12, 4 #B414, 5 #B415, 3 #B416 3.00 3.00
B417 SP183 25c +10c brt rose lil & dk bl .80 .75
B418 SP183 40c +20c dp car & dk grn .70 .65
Nos. B414-B418 (5) 2.25 2.15

The surtax was for child welfare.

Whelk Eggs SP184

15c+10c, Whelk. 20c+10c, Mussel with acorn shells. 25c+10c, Jellyfish. 45c+20c, Crab.

1967, Apr. 11 Unwmk. Litho.

B419 SP184 12c +8c ol grn & tan .30 .25
B420 SP184 15c +10c lt bl, ultra & blk .30 .25
B421 SP184 20c +10c gray, blk & red .30 .25
B422 SP184 25c +10c brn car, plum & ol brn .55 .50
B423 SP184 45c +20c multi .70 .65
Nos. B419-B423 (5) 2.15 1.90

Red Cross and Dates Forming Cross SP185

15c+10c, Crosses. 20c+10c, Initials "NRK" forming cross. 25c+10c, Maltese cross and crosses. 45c+20c, "100" forming cross.

1967, Aug. 8 ***Perf. 14x13***

B424 SP185 12c +8c dl bl & red .30 .25
B425 SP185 15c +10c red .40 .35
B426 SP185 20c +10c ol & red .30 .25
B427 SP185 25c +10c ol grn & red .40 .35
B428 SP185 45c +20c gray & red .70 .50
Nos. B424-B428 (5) 2.10 1.70

Centenary of the Dutch Red Cross.

"Lullaby for the Little Porcupine" — SP186

Nursery Rhymes: 15c+10c, "Little Whistling Kettle." 20c+10c, "Dikkertje Dap and the Giraffe." 25c+10c, "The Nicest Flowers." 45c+20c, "Pippeljoentje, the Little Bear."

1967, Nov. 7 Litho. ***Perf. 13x14***

B429 SP186 12c +8c multi .25 .25
B430 SP186 15c +10c multi .25 .25
B431 SP186 20c +10c multi .25 .25
a. Min. sheet of 10, 3 #B429, 4 #B430, 3 #B431 4.25 4.25
B432 SP186 25c +10c multi .85 .75
B433 SP186 45c +20c multi 1.00 .75
Nos. B429-B433 (5) 2.60 2.25

The surtax was for child welfare.

St. Servatius Bridge, Maastricht SP187

Bridges: 15c+10c, Narrow Bridge, Amsterdam. 20c+10c, Railroad Bridge, Culenborg. 25c+10c, Van Brienenoord Bridge, Rotterdam. 45c+20c, Zeeland Bridge, Schelde Estuary.

1968, Apr. 9 Photo. ***Perf. 14x13***

B434 SP187 12c +8c green .65 .85
B435 SP187 15c +10c ol brn .75 .90
B436 SP187 20c +10c rose red .65 .25
B437 SP187 25c +10c gray .65 .85
B438 SP187 45c +20c ultra 1.00 1.25
Nos. B434-B438 (5) 3.70 4.10

Goblin SP188

Fairy Tale Characters: 15c+10c, Giant. 20c+10c, Witch. 25c+10c, Dragon. 45c+20c, Magician.

1968, Nov. 12 Photo. ***Perf. 14x13***

B439 SP188 12c +8c grn, pink & blk .25 .25
B440 SP188 15c +10c bl, pink & blk .25 .25
B441 SP188 20c +10c bl, emer & blk .25 .25
a. Min. sheet of 10, 3 #B439, 4 #B440, 3 #B441 8.00 8.00
B442 SP188 25c +10c org red, org & blk 2.00 1.90
B443 SP188 45c +20c yel, org & blk 1.90 1.90
Nos. B439-B443 (5) 4.65 4.55

The surtax was for child welfare.

Villa Huis ter Heide, 1915 SP189

Contemporary Architecture: 15c+10c, House, Utrecht, 1924. 20c+10c, First open-air school, Amsterdam, 1960. 25c+10c, Burgweeshuis (orphanage), Amsterdam, 1960. 45c+20c, Netherlands Congress Building, The Hague, 1969.

1969, Apr. 15 Photo. ***Perf. 14x13***

B444 SP189 12c +8c lt brn & sl .85 .85
B445 SP189 15c +10c bl, gray & red .85 1.10
B446 SP189 20c +10c vio & blk .85 1.10
B447 SP189 25c +10c grn & gray 1.00 .52
B448 SP189 45c +20c gray, bl & yel 1.10 1.25
Nos. B444-B448 (5) 4.65 4.82

Surtax for social and cultural purposes.

Stylized Crab — SP190

1969, Aug. 12 Photo. *Perf. 13x14*

B449 SP190 12c +8c vio 1.00 1.10
B450 SP190 25c +10c org 1.40 .55
B451 SP190 45c +20c bl grn 1.75 2.50
Nos. B449-B451 (3) 4.15 4.15

20th anniv. of the Queen Wilhelmina Fund. The surtax was for cancer research.

Child with Violin — SP191

12c+8c, Child with flute. 20c+10c, Child with drum. 25c+10c, Three children singing, horiz. 45c+20c, Two girls dancing, horiz.

1969, Nov. 11 *Perf. 13x14, 14x13*

B452 SP191 12c +8c ultra, blk & yel .25 .25
B453 SP191 15c +10c blk & red .25 .25
B454 SP191 20c +10c red, blk & yel 2.00 1.75
B455 SP191 25c +10c yel, blk & red .30 .25
a. Min. sheet of 10, 4 #B452, 4 #B453, 2 #B455 8.75 7.25
B456 SP191 45c +20c grn, blk & red 2.75 2.75
Nos. B452-B456 (5) 5.55 5.25

The surtax was for child welfare.

Isometric Projection from Circle to Square — SP192

Designs made by Computer: 15c+10c, Parallel planes in a cube. 20c+10c, Two overlapping scales. 25c+10c, Transition phases of concentric circles with increasing diameters. 45c+20c, Four spirals.

Lithographed and Engraved

1970, Apr. 7 *Perf. 13x14*

B457 SP192 12c +8c yel & blk .90 .90
B458 SP192 15c +10c sil & blk .90 .90
B459 SP192 20c +10c blk .90 .90
B460 SP192 25c +10c brt bl & blk .90 .60
B461 SP192 45c +20c sil & white .90 .90
Nos. B457-B461 (5) 4.50 4.20

Surtax for social and cultural purposes.

Bleeding Heart — SP193

1970, July 28 Photo. *Perf. 13x14*

B462 SP193 12c +8c org yel, red & blk .65 .75
B463 SP193 25c +10c pink, red & blk .65 .40
B464 SP193 45c +20c brt grn, red & blk .70 .75
Nos. B462-B464 (3) 2.00 1.90

The surtax was for the Netherlands Heart Foundation.

Toy Block — SP194

1970, Nov. 10 Photo. *Perf. 13x14*

B465 SP194 12c +8c bl, vio bl & grn .25 .25
B466 SP194 15c +10c grn, bl & yel 1.25 1.25
B467 SP194 20c +10c lil rose, red & vio bl 1.25 1.25
B468 SP194 25c +10c red, yel & lil rose .40 .25
a. Min. sheet of 11, 9 #B465, 2 #B468 + label 12.00 11.00
B469 SP194 45c +20c gray & blk 1.60 1.50
Nos. B465-B469 (5) 4.75 4.50

The surtax was for child welfare.

St. Paul — SP195

Designs: 15c+10c, "50" and people. 25c+10c, Joachim and Ann. 30c+15c, John the Baptist and the Scribes. 45c+20c, St. Anne. The sculptures are wood, 15th century, and in Dutch museums.

1971, Apr. 20 Litho. *Perf. 13x14*

B470 SP195 15c +10c multi 1.25 1.25

Lithographed and Photogravure

B471 SP195 20c +10c gray, grn & blk 1.00 1.00
B472 SP195 25c +10c buff, org & blk 1.10 .50
B473 SP195 30c +15c gray, bl & blk 1.25 1.25
B474 SP195 45c +20c pink, ver & blk 1.25 1.25
Nos. B470-B474 (5) 5.85 5.25

50th anniversary of the Federation of Netherlands Universities for Adult Education.

Detail from Borobudur — SP196

1971, June 29 Litho. *Perf. 13x14*

B475 SP196 45c +20c pur, yel & blk 2.25 2.25

60th birthday of Prince Bernhard. Surtax for Save Borobudur Temple Fund.

"Earth" — SP197

Designs: 20c+10c, "Air" (butterfly). 25c+10c, "Sun," horiz. 30c+15c, "Moon," horiz. 45c+20c, "Water" (child looking at reflection).

Perf. 13x14, 14x13

1971, Nov. 9 Photo.

B476 SP197 15c +10c blk, lil & org .30 .25
B477 SP197 20c +10c yel, blk & rose lil .35 .25
B478 SP197 25c +10c multi .40 .25
a. Min. sheet of 9, 6 #B476, #B477, 2 #B478 9.00 8.75
B479 SP197 30c +15c bl, blk & pur 1.00 .40
B480 SP197 45c +20c grn, blk & bl 1.75 1.60
Nos. B476-B480 (5) 3.80 2.75

The surtax was for child welfare.

Luminescence

Some semipostal issues from Nos. B481-B484 onward are on phosphorescent paper.

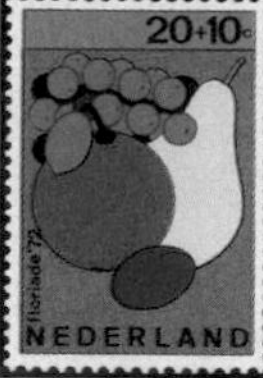

Stylized Fruits — SP198

1972, Apr. 11 Litho. *Perf. 13x14*

B481 SP198 20c +10c shown .90 .80
B482 SP198 25c +10c Flower .90 .80
B483 SP198 30c +15c "Sunlit Landscape" .90 .55
B484 SP198 45c +25c "Music" .90 .80
Nos. B481-B484 (4) 3.60 2.95

Summer festivals: Nos. B481-B482 publicize the Floriade, flower festival; Nos. B483-B484 the Holland Festival of Arts.

Red Cross, First Aid — SP199

Red Cross and: 25c+10c, Blood bank. 30c+15c, Disaster relief. 45c+25c, Child care.

1972, Aug. 15 *Perf. 13x14*

B485 SP199 20c +10c brt pink & red .55 .45
B486 SP199 25c +10c org & red .70 .80
B487 SP199 30c +15c blk & red .70 .25
B488 SP199 45c +25c ultra & red .80 .80
Nos. B485-B488 (4) 2.75 2.30

Surtax for the Netherlands Red Cross.

Prince Willem-Alexander SP200

Photographs of Dutch Princes: 30c+10c, Johan Friso. 35c+15c, Constantijn. 50c+20c, Johan Friso, Constantijn and Willem-Alexander. All are horizontal.

Perf. 13x14, 14x13

1972, Nov. 7 Photo.

B489 SP200 25c +15c multi .45 .25
B490 SP200 30c +10c multi .75 .75
B491 SP200 35c +15c multi .75 .25
a. Min. sheet of 7, 4 #B489, #B490, 2 #B491 + label 6.00 5.25
B492 SP200 50c +20c multi 1.90 2.00
Nos. B489-B492 (4) 3.85 3.25

Surtax was for child welfare.

"W. A. Scholten," 1874 SP201

Ships: 25c+15c, Flagship "De Seven Provincien," 1673, vert. 35c+15c, "Veendam," 1923. 50c+20c, Zuider Zee fish well boat, 17th century, vert.

1973, Apr. 10 Litho.

B493 SP201 25c +15c multi 1.10 1.10
B494 SP201 30c +10c multi 1.10 1.10
B495 SP201 35c +15c multi 1.25 .65
B496 SP201 50c +20c multi 1.25 1.25
Nos. B493-B496 (4) 4.70 4.10

Tercentenary of the Battle of Kijkduin and centenary of the Holland-America Line.
Surtax for social and cultural purposes.

Chessboard SP202

Games: 30c+10c, Tick-tack-toe. 40c+20c, Maze. 50c+20c, Dominoes.

1973, Nov. 13 Photo. *Perf. 13x14*

B497 SP202 25c +15c multi .45 .25
B498 SP202 30c +10c multi .75 .35
B499 SP202 40c +20c multi .60 .25
a. Min. sheet of 6, 2 #B497, #B498, 3 #B499 8.25 7.50
B500 SP202 50c +20c multi 1.60 1.50
Nos. B497-B500 (4) 3.40 2.35

Surtax was for child welfare.

Music Bands SP203

Herman Heijermans SP204

Designs: 30c+10c, Ballet dancers and traffic lights. 50c+20c, Kniertje, the fisher woman, from play by Heijermans.

1974, Apr. 23 Litho. *Perf. 13x14*

B501 SP203 25c +15c multi .70 .70
B502 SP203 30c +10c multi .70 .70

Photo.

B503 SP204 40c +20c multi .70 .40
B504 SP204 50c +20c multi .75 .75
Nos. B501-B504 (4) 2.85 2.55

Surtax was for various social and cultural institutions.

Boy with Hoop — SP205

Designs: 35c+20c, Girl and infant. 45c+20c, Two girls. 60c+20c, Girl sitting on balustrade. Designs are from turn-of-the-century photographs.

1974, Nov. 12 Photo. *Perf. 13x14*

B505 SP205 30c +15c brown .50 .25
B506 SP205 35c +20c maroon .60 .40
B507 SP205 45c +20c black brn .70 .25
a. Min. sheet of 6, 4 #B505, #B506, #B507 3.50 3.25
B508 SP205 60c +20c indigo 1.00 1.10
Nos. B505-B508 (4) 2.80 2.00

Surtax was for child welfare.

Beguinage, Amsterdam SP206

Cooper's Gate, Middelburg SP207

Designs: 35c+20c, St. Hubertus Hunting Lodge, horiz. 60c+20c, Orvelte Village, horiz.

Perf. 14x13, 13x14

1975, Apr. 4 **Litho.**

B509 SP206 35c +20c multi .60 .60
B510 SP206 40c +15c multi .60 .60
B511 SP207 50c +20c multi .75 .75
B512 SP207 60c +20c multi .90 .90
Nos. B509-B512 (4) 2.85 2.85

European Architectural Heritage Year 1975. Surtax was for various social and cultural institutions.

Orphans, Sculpture, 1785
SP208

40c+15c, Milkmaid, 17th cent. 50c+25c, Aymon's 4 sons on steed Bayard, 17th cent. 60c+25c, Life at orphanage, 1557. All designs are after ornamental stones from various buildings.

1975, Nov. 11 **Photo.** ***Perf. 14x13***

B513 SP208 35c +15c multi .55 .55
B514 SP208 40c +15c multi .60 .60
B515 SP208 50c +25c multi .80 .80
a. Min. sheet of 5, 3 #B513, 2 #B515 + label 3.00 3.00
B516 SP208 60c +25c multi .95 .95
Nos. B513-B516 (4) 2.90 2.90

Surtax was for child welfare.

Hedgehog
SP209

Book with "ABC" and Grain; Open Field
SP210

Green Frog and Spawn
SP212

People and Initials of Social Security Acts
SP211

Perf. 14x13, 13x14

1976, Apr. 6 **Litho.**

B517 SP209 40c +20c multi .65 .65
B518 SP210 45c +20c multi .65 .65

Photo.

B519 SP211 55c +20c multi .80 .80
B520 SP212 75c +25c multi 1.10 1.10
Nos. B517-B520 (4) 3.20 3.20

Surtax for various social and cultural institutions. #B517, B520 for wildlife protection; #B518 cent. of agricultural education and 175th anniv. of elementary education legislation; #B519 75th anniv. of social legislation and the Social Insurance Bank.

Patient Surrounded by Caring Hands — SP213

1976, Sept. 2 **Litho.** ***Perf. 13x14***

B521 SP213 55c +25c multi .90 .90

Dutch Anti-Rheumatism Assoc., 50th anniv.

Netherlands No. 41 — SP214

Designs: No. B523, #64. No. B524, #155. No. B525, #294. No. B526, #220.

1976, Oct. 8 **Litho.** ***Perf. 13x14***

B522 SP214 55c +55c multi 1.25 1.25
B523 SP214 55c +55c multi 1.25 1.25
B524 SP214 55c +55c multi 1.25 1.25
a. Strip of 3, #B522-B524 3.75 3.75

Photo.

B525 SP214 75c +75c multi 1.60 1.60
B526 SP214 75c +75c multi 1.60 1.60
a. Pair, #B525-B526 3.25 3.25
Nos. B522-B526 (5) 6.95 6.95

Amphilex 77 Philatelic Exhibition, Amsterdam, May 26-June 5, 1977. No. B526a printed checkerwise.
See Nos. B535-B538.

Soccer
SP215

Children's Drawings: 45c+20c, Sailboat. 55c+20c, Elephant. 75c+25c, Mobile home.

1976, Nov. 16 **Photo.** ***Perf. 14x13***

B527 SP215 40c +20c multi .65 .65
B528 SP215 45c +20c multi .65 .65
B529 SP215 55c +20c multi .80 .80
a. Min. sheet of 6, 2 each #B527-B529 4.25 4.25
B530 SP215 75c +25c multi 1.10 1.10
Nos. B527-B530 (4) 3.20 3.20

Surtax was for child welfare.

Hot Room, Thermal Bath, Heerlen
SP216

45c+20c, Altar of Goddess Nehalennia, 200 A.D., Eastern Scheldt. 55c+20c, Part of oaken ship, Zwammerdam. 75c+25c, Helmet with face, Waal River at Nijmegen.

1977, Apr. 19 **Photo.** ***Perf. 14x13***

B531 SP216 40c +20c multi .65 .65
B532 SP216 45c +20c multi .70 .70
B533 SP216 55c +20c multi .80 .80
B534 SP216 75c +25c multi 1.10 1.10
Nos. B531-B534 (4) 3.25 3.25

Archaeological finds of Roman period.
Surtax for various social and cultural institutions.

Type of 1976

Designs: No. B535, Netherlands #83. No. B536, Netherlands #128. No. B537, Netherlands #211. No. B538, Netherlands #302.

1977, May 26 **Litho.** ***Perf. 13x14***

B535 SP214 55c +45c multi 1.10 1.10
B536 SP214 55c +45c multi 1.10 1.10
a. Pair, #B535-B536 2.25 2.25
B537 SP214 55c +45c multi 1.10 1.10
B538 SP214 55c +45c multi 1.10 1.10
a. Souv. sheet of 2, #B535, B538 2.25 2.25
b. Pair, #B537-B538 2.25 2.25
Nos. B535-B538 (4) 4.40 4.40

Amphilex 77 International Philatelic Exhibition, Amsterdam May 26-June 5. No. B538a sold at Exhibition only.

Risk of Drowning — SP217

Childhood Dangers: 45c+20c, Poisoning. 55c+20c, Following ball into street. 75c+25c, Playing with matches.

1977, Nov. 15 **Photo.** ***Perf. 13x14***

B539 SP217 40c +20c multi .65 .65
B540 SP217 45c +20c multi .70 .70
B541 SP217 55c +20c multi .80 .80
a. Min. sheet of 6, 2 each #B539-B541 4.50 4.50
B542 SP217 75c +25c multi 1.10 1.10
Nos. B539-B542 (4) 3.25 3.25

Surtax was for child welfare.

Anna Maria van Schuurman
SP218

Delft Plate
SP219

Designs: 45c+20c, Part of letter written by author Belle van Zuylen (1740-1805). 75c+25c, Makkum dish with dog.

1978, Apr. 11 **Litho.** ***Perf. 13x14***

B543 SP218 40c +20c multi .65 .65
B544 SP218 45c +20c multi .70 .70

Photo.

B545 SP219 55c +20c multi .80 .80
B546 SP219 75c +25c multi 1.10 1.10
Nos. B543-B546 (4) 3.25 3.25

Dutch authors and pottery products.

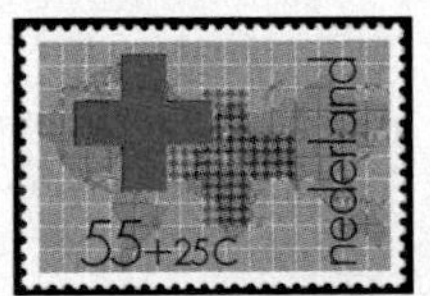

Red Cross and World Map
SP220

1978, Aug. 22 **Photo.** ***Perf. 14x13***

B547 SP220 55c +25c multi .90 .90
a. Souvenir sheet of 3 2.75 2.75

Surtax was for Dutch Red Cross.

Boy Ringing Doorbell
SP221

Designs: 45c+20c, Child reading book. 55c+20c, Boy writing "30x Children for Children," vert. 75c+25c, Girl at blackboard, arithmetic lesson.

Perf. 14x13, 13x14

1978, Nov. 14 **Photo.**

B548 SP221 40c +20c multi .65 .65
B549 SP221 45c +20c multi .70 .70
B550 SP221 55c +20c multi .80 .80
a. Min. sheet of 6, 2 each #B548-B550 4.50 4.50
B551 SP221 75c +25c multi 1.10 1.10
Nos. B548-B551 (4) 3.25 3.25

Surtax was for child welfare.

Psalm Trilogy, by Jurriaan Andriessen
SP222

Birth of Christ (detail) Stained-glass Window
SP223

Designs: 45c+20c, Amsterdam Toonkunst Choir. 75c+25c, William of Orange, stained-glass window, 1603. Windows from St. John's Church, Gouda.

1979, Apr. 3 **Photo.** ***Perf. 13x14***

B552 SP222 40c +20c multi .25 .25
B553 SP222 45c +20c multi .40 .25
B554 SP223 55c +20c multi .40 .25
B555 SP223 75c +25c multi .55 .40
Nos. B552-B555 (4) 1.60 1.15

Surtax for social and cultural purposes.

Child Sleeping Under Blanket
SP224

Designs: 45c+20c, Infant. 55c+20c, African boy, vert. 75c+25c, Children, vert.

1979, Nov. 13 ***Perf. 14x13, 13x14***

B556 SP224 40c +20c blk, red & yel .65 .65
B557 SP224 45c +20c blk & red .70 .70
B558 SP224 55c +20c blk & yel .80 .80
a. Min. sheet, 2 each #B556-B558 4.50 4.50
B559 SP224 75c +25c blk, ultra & red 1.10 1.10
Nos. B556-B559 (4) 3.25 3.25

Surtax was for child welfare (in conjuction with International Year of the Child).

Roads Through Sand Dunes
SP225

50c+20c, Park mansion vert. 60c+25c, Sailing. 80c+35c, Bicycling, moorlands.

Perf. 14x13, 13x14

1980, Apr. 15 **Litho.**

B560 SP225 45c +20c multi .70 .70
B561 SP225 50c +20c multi .75 .75
B562 SP225 60c +25c multi .95 .95
B563 SP225 80c +35c multi 1.25 1.25
Nos. B560-B563 (4) 3.65 3.65

Society for the Promotion of Nature Preserves, 75th anniv. Surtax for social and cultural purposes.

Wheelchair Basketball — SP226

1980, June 3 **Litho.** ***Perf. 13x14***

B564 SP226 60c +25c multi .95 .95

Olympics for the Disabled, Arnhem and Veenendaal, June 21-July 5. Surtax was for National Sports for the Handicapped Fund.

Harlequin and Girl Standing in Open Book
SP227

Designs: 50c+20c, Boy on flying book, vert. 60c+30c, Boy reading King of Frogs, vert. 80c+30c, Boy "engrossed" in book.

Perf. 14x13, 13x14

1980, Nov. 11 **Photo.**

B565 SP227 45c +20c multi .70 .70
B566 SP227 50c +20c multi .75 .75
B567 SP227 60c +30c multi 1.00 1.00
a. Min. sheet of 5, 2 #B565, 3 #B567 + label 4.50 4.50
B568 SP227 80c +30c multi 1.25 1.25
Nos. B565-B568 (4) 3.70 3.70

Surtax was for child welfare.

Salt Marsh with Outlet Ditch at Low Tide — SP228

Designs: 55c+25c, Dike. 60c+25c, Land drainage. 65c+30c, Cultivated land.

1981, Apr. 7 Photo. *Perf. 13x14*

B569 SP228 45c +20c multi .70 .70
B570 SP228 55c +25c multi .90 .90
B571 SP228 60c +25c multi .95 .95
B572 SP228 65c +30c multi 1.00 1.00
Nos. B569-B572 (4) 3.55 3.55

Intl. Year of the Disabled SP229

Various people.

Perf. 14x13, 13x14

1981, Nov. 10 Photo.

B573 SP229 45c +25c multi .75 .75
B574 SP229 55c +20c multi, vert .80 .80
B575 SP229 60c +25c multi, vert. .95 .95
B576 SP229 65c +30c multi 1.00 1.00
a. Min. sheet of 5, 3 #B573, 2 #B576 + label 4.50 4.50
Nos. B573-B576 (4) 3.50 3.50

Surtax was for child welfare.

Floriade '82, Amsterdam, Apr. — SP230

1982, Apr. 7 Litho. *Perf. 13½x13*

B577 SP230 50c +20c shown .75 .75
B578 SP230 60c +25c Anemones .95 .95
B579 SP230 65c +25c Roses 1.00 1.00
B580 SP230 70c +30c African violets 1.10 1.10
Nos. B577-B580 (4) 3.80 3.80

Surtax was for culture and social welfare institutions.

Birds on Child's Head — SP231

Children and Animals: 60c+20c, Boy and cat. 65c+20c, Boy and rabbit. 70c+30c, Boy and bird.

1982, Nov. 16 Photo. *Perf. 13x14*

B581 SP231 50c +30c multi .90 .90
B582 SP231 60c +20c multi .90 .90
a. Min. sheet of 5, 4 #B581, #B582 4.50 4.50
B583 SP231 65c +20c multi .95 .95
B584 SP231 70c +30c multi 1.10 1.10
Nos. B581-B584 (4) 3.85 3.85

Surtax was for child welfare.

Johan van Oldenbarneveldt (1547-1619), Statesman, by J. Houbraken — SP232

Paintings: 60c+25c, Willem Jansz Blaeu (1571-1638), cartographer, by Thomas de Keijser. 65c+25c, Hugo de Groot (1583-1645), statesman, by J. van Ravesteyn. 70c+30c, Portrait of Saskia van Uylenburch, by Rembrandt (1606-1669).

1983, Apr. 19 Photo. *Perf. 14x13*

B585 SP232 50c +20c multi .75 .75
B586 SP232 60c +25c multi .95 .95
B587 SP232 65c +25c multi 1.00 1.00
B588 SP232 70c +30c multi 1.10 1.10
Nos. B585-B588 (4) 3.80 3.80

Surtax was for cultural and social welfare institutions.

Red Cross Workers — SP233

Designs: 60c+20c, Principles. 65c+25c, Sociomedical work. 70c+30c, Peace.

1983, Aug. 30 Photo. *Perf. 13x14*

B589 SP233 50c +25c multi .80 .80
B590 SP233 60c +20c multi .90 .90
B591 SP233 65c +25c multi 1.00 1.00
B592 SP233 70c +30c multi 1.10 1.10
a. Bklt. pane, 4 #B589, 2 #B592 5.50 5.50
Complete booklet, #B592a 5.50
Nos. B589-B592 (4) 3.80 3.80

Surtax was for Red Cross.

Children's Christmas SP235

1983, Nov. 16 Photo. *Perf. 14x13*

B596 SP235 50c +10c Ox & donkey .65 .65
B597 SP235 50c +25c Snowman .80 .80
B598 SP235 60c +30c Stars 1.00 1.00
B599 SP235 70c +30c Epiphany 1.10 1.10
a. Min. sheet, 4 #B597, 2 #B599 5.00 5.00
Nos. B596-B599 (4) 3.55 3.55

Surtax was for Child Welfare.

Eurasian Lapwings SP236

Birds: 60c+25c, Ruffs. 65c+25c, Redshanks, vert. 70c+30c, Black-tailed godwits, vert.

1984, Apr. 3 *Perf. 14x13, 13x14*

B600 SP236 50c +20c multi .75 .75
B601 SP236 60c +25c multi .95 .95
B602 SP236 65c +25c multi 1.00 1.00
B603 SP236 70c +30c multi 1.10 1.10
a. Bklt. pane, 2 #B600, 2 #B603 3.75 3.75
Complete booklet, #B603a 3.75
Nos. B600-B603 (4) 3.80 3.80

Surtax for cultural and social welfare institutions.

FILACENTO '84 — SP237

Centenary of Organized Philately: 50c+20c, Eye, magnifying glass (36x25mm). 60c+25c, Cover, 1909 (34½x25mm). 70c+30c, Stamp club meeting, 1949 (34½x24mm).

1984, June 13 Litho. *Perf. 14x13*

B604 SP237 50c +20c multi .75 .75
B605 SP237 60c +25c multi .95 .95
B606 SP237 70c +30c multi 1.10 1.10
a. Souv. sheet of 3, #B604-B606 3.00 3.00
Nos. B604-B606 (3) 2.80 2.80

No. B606a issued Sept. 5, 1984.

Comic Strips — SP238

1984, Nov. 14 Litho. *Perf. 13x13½*

B607 SP238 50c +25c Music lesson .80 .80
B608 SP238 60c +20c Dentist .90 .90
B609 SP238 65c +20c Plumber 1.00 1.00
B610 SP238 70c +30c King 1.10 1.10
a. Min. sheet, 4 #B607, 2 #B610 5.50 5.50
Nos. B607-B610 (4) 3.80 3.80

Surtax was for child welfare.

Winterswijk Synagogue, Holy Arc — SP239

Religious architecture: 50+20c, St. Martin's Church, Zaltbommel, vert. 65+25c, Village Congregational Church, Bolsward, vert. 70+30c, St. John's Cathedral, 'S-Hertogenbosch, detail of buttress.

Perf. 13x14, 14x13

1985, Mar. 26 Photo.

B611 SP239 50c +20c gray & brt bl .75 .75
B612 SP239 60c +25c dk red brn, Prus bl & pck bl .95 .95
B613 SP239 65c +25c sl bl, red brn & gray ol 1.00 1.00
B614 SP239 70c +30c gray, brt bl & bis 1.10 1.10
a. Bklt. pane, 2 #B611, 2 #B614 4.00 4.00
Complete booklet, #B614a 4.00
Nos. B611-B614 (4) 3.80 3.80

Surtax for social and cultural purposes.

Traffic Safety SP240

No B615, Photograph, lock, key. No. B616, Boy, target. No. B617, Girl, hazard triangle. No. B618, Boy, traffic sign.

1985, Nov. 13 Photo. *Perf. 13x14*

B615 SP240 50c +25c multi .80 .80
B616 SP240 60c +20c multi .90 .90
B617 SP240 65c +20c multi .95 .95
B618 SP240 70c +30c multi 1.10 1.10
a. Souv. sheet, 4 #B615, 2 #B618 5.50 5.50
Nos. B615-B618 (4) 3.75 3.75

Surtax was for child welfare organizations.

Antique Measuring Instruments SP241

No. B619, Balance. No. B620, Clock mechanism. No. B621, Barometer. No. B622, Jacob's staff.

Perf. 13½x13, 13x13½

1986, Apr. 8 Litho.

B619 SP241 50c +20c multi .75 .75
B620 SP241 60c +25c multi .95 .95
B621 SP241 65c +25c multi 1.00 1.00
B622 SP241 70c +30c multi 1.10 1.10
a. Bklt. pane, 2 each #B619, B622 4.00 4.00
Complete booklet, #B622a 4.00
Nos. B619-B622 (4) 3.80 3.80

Nos. B620-B621 vert.

Youth and Culture SP242

1986, Nov. 12 Litho. *Perf. 14x13*

B623 SP242 55c +25c Music .90 .90

Perf. 13½x13

B624 SP242 65c +35c Visual arts 1.10 1.10
B625 SP242 75c +35c Theater 1.25 1.25
a. Min. sheet of 5, #B623, 2 each #B624-B625, perf. 14x13 5.75 5.75
Nos. B623-B625 (3) 3.25 3.25

Surtax for child welfare organizations.

Traditional Industries SP243

Designs: 55c+30c, Steam pumping station, Nijkerk. 65c+35c, Water tower, Deventer. 75c+35c, Brass foundry, Joure.

1987, Apr. 7 Photo. *Perf. 14x13*

B626 SP243 55c +30c multi .95 .95
B627 SP243 65c +35c multi 1.10 1.10
B628 SP243 75c +35c multi 1.25 1.25
a. Bklt. pane, 2 #B626, 2 #B628 4.50 4.50
Complete booklet, #B628a 4.50
Nos. B626-B628 (3) 3.30 3.30

Surtax for social and cultural welfare organizations.

Red Cross SP244

1987, Sept. 1 Photo. *Perf. 14x13*

B629 SP244 55c +30c multi .95 .95
B630 SP244 65c +35c multi, diff. 1.10 1.10
B631 SP244 75c +35c multi, diff. 1.25 1.25
a. Bklt. pane, 2 #B629, 2 #B631 4.50 4.50
Complete booklet, #B631a 4.50
Nos. B629-B631 (3) 3.30 3.30

Surtax for nat'l. Red Cross.

Youth and Professions SP245

Perf. 13x14, 14x13

1987, Nov. 11 Photo.

B632 SP245 55c +25c Woodcutter, vert. .90 .90
B633 SP245 65c +35c Sailor 1.10 1.10
B634 SP245 75c +35c Pilot 1.25 1.25
a. Miniature sheet of 5, #B632, 2 #B633, 2 #B634 5.75 5.75
Nos. B632-B634 (3) 3.25 3.25

Surtax for child welfare organizations.

FILACEPT '88, October 18, The Hague SP246

Designs: 55c +55c, Narcissus cyclamineus and poem "I call you flowers," by Jan Hanlo. No. B636, Rosa gallica versicolor. No. B637, Eryngium maritimum and map of The Hague from 1270.

1988, Feb. 23 Litho. *Perf. 13½x13*

B635 SP246 55c +55c multi 1.25 1.25
B636 SP246 75c +70c multi 1.60 1.60
B637 SP246 75c +70c multi 1.60 1.60
a. Min. sheet of 3 + 3 labels, #B635-B637 4.50 4.50
Nos. B635-B637 (3) 4.45 4.45

Surtax helped finance exhibition.
No. B637a issued Oct. 18, 1988.

Man and the Zoo — SP247

No B638, Equus quagga quagga. No. B639, Carribean sea cow. No. B640, Sam the orangutan, vert.

Perf. 14x13, 13x14

1988, Mar. 22 **Photo.**

B638	SP247 55c +30c multi	.95	.95
B639	SP247 65c +35c multi	1.10	1.10
B640	SP247 75c +35c multi	1.25	1.25
a.	Bklt. pane, 2 #B638, 2 #B640	4.50	4.50
	Complete booklet, #B640a	4.00	
	Nos. B638-B640 (3)	3.30	3.30

Natural Artis Magistra zoological soc., 150th anniv. Surtax for social and cultural welfare organizations.

Royal Dutch Swimming Federation, Cent. SP248

Children's drawings on the theme "Children and Water." No. B641, Rain. No. B642, Getting Ready for the Race. No. B643, Swimming Test.

1988, Nov. 16 **Photo.** ***Perf. 14x13***

B641	SP248 55c +25c multi	.90	.90
B642	SP248 65c +35c multi	1.10	1.10
B643	SP248 75c +35c multi	1.25	1.25
a.	Min. sheet of 5, #B641, 2 each #B642-B643	5.75	5.75
	Nos. B641-B643 (3)	3.25	3.25

Surtax to benefit child welfare organizations.

Ships SP249

Designs: No. B644, Pleasure yacht (boyer), vert. No. B645, Zuiderzee fishing boat (smack). No. B646, Clipper.

Perf. 13x14, 14x13

1989, Apr. 11 **Photo.**

B644	SP249 55c +30c multi	.95	.95
B645	SP249 65c +35c multi	1.10	1.10
B646	SP249 75c +35c multi	1.25	1.25
a.	Bklt. pane, #B644-B645, 2 #B646	4.75	4.75
	Complete booklet, #B646a	4.75	
	Nos. B644-B646 (3)	3.30	3.30

Surtax for social and cultural organizations.

Children's Rights SP250

1989, Nov. 8 **Litho.** ***Perf. 13½x13***

B647	SP250 55c +25c Housing	.90	.90
B648	SP250 65c +35c Food	1.10	1.10
B649	SP250 75c +35c Education	1.25	1.25
a.	Min. sheet of 5, #B647, 2 each #B648-B649	5.75	5.75
	Nos. B647-B649 (3)	3.25	3.25

UN Declaration of Children's Rights, 30th anniv. Surtax for child welfare.

Summer Weather SP251

No. B650, Girl, flowers. No. B651, Clouds, isobars, vert. No. B652, Weather map, vert.

Perf. 14x13, 13x14

1990, Apr. 3 **Photo.**

B650	SP251 55c +30c multi	.95	.95
B651	SP251 65c +35c multi	1.10	1.10
B652	SP251 75c +35c multi	1.25	1.25
a.	Bklt. pane, #B650-B651, 2 #B652	4.75	4.75
	Complete booklet, #B652a	4.75	
	Nos. B650-B652 (3)	3.30	3.30

Surtax for social & cultural welfare organizations.

Children's Hobbies SP252

1990, Nov. 7 **Litho.** ***Perf. 13½x13***

B653	SP252 55c +25c Riding	.90	.90
B654	SP252 65c +35c Computers	1.10	1.10
B655	SP252 75c +35c Philately	1.25	1.25
a.	Souv. sheet of 5, #B653, 2 each #B654-B655	5.75	5.75
	Nos. B653-B655 (3)	3.25	3.25

Surtax for child welfare.

Dutch Farms SP253

55c+30c, Frisian farm, Wartena. 65c+35c, Guelders T-style farm, Kesteren. 75c+35c, Closed construction farm, Nuth (Limburg).

1991, Apr. 16 **Litho.** ***Perf. 13½x13***

B656	SP253 55c +30c multi	.95	.95
a.	Photo.	.95	.95
B657	SP253 65c +35c multi	1.10	1.10
B658	SP253 75c +35c multi	1.25	1.25
a.	Photo.	1.25	1.25
b.	Bklt. pane, 2 #B656a, 3 #B658a	5.75	5.75
	Complete booklet, #B658b	5.75	
	Nos. B656-B658 (3)	3.30	3.30

Surtax for social and cultural welfare organizations.

Children Playing SP254

No. B659, Doll, robot. No. B660, Cycle race. No. B661, Hide and seek.

1991, Nov. 6 **Litho.** ***Perf. 13½x13***

B659	SP254 60c +30c multi	1.00	1.00
a.	Photo., perf. 14x13½	1.00	1.00
B660	SP254 70c +35c multi	1.25	1.25
B661	SP254 80c +40c multi	1.40	1.40
a.	Photo., perf. 14x13½	1.40	1.40
b.	Min. sheet, 4 #B659a, 2 #B661a	7.00	7.00
	Nos. B659-B661 (3)	3.65	3.65

Floriade 1992, World Horticultural Exhibition SP255

Various plants and flowers.

1992, Apr. 7 **Litho.** ***Perf. 13½x13***

B662	SP255 60c +30c multi	1.10	1.10
a.	Photo., perf. 14x13½	1.10	1.10
B663	SP255 70c +35c multi	1.25	1.25
a.	Photo., perf. 14x13½	1.25	1.25
B664	SP255 80c +40c multi	1.50	1.50
a.	Photo., perf. 14x13½	1.50	1.50
b.	Booklet pane of 6, 3 #B662a, 2 #B663a, #B664a	7.50	
	Complete booklet, #B664b	7.50	
	Nos. B662-B664 (3)	3.85	3.85

Surtax for social and cultural welfare organizations.

Stamps in No. 664b are tete-beche (1 pair of B662a, 1 pair of B663a, 1 pair of B662a and B664a).

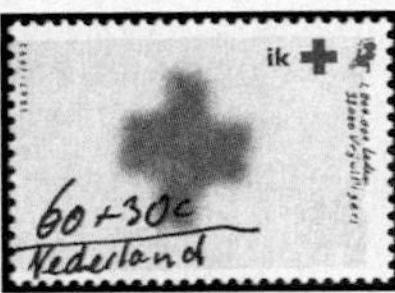

Netherlands Red Cross, 125th Anniv. SP256

No. B665, Shadow of cross. No B666, Aiding victim. No. B667, Red cross on bandage.

1992, Sept. 8 **Litho.** ***Perf. 13½x13***

B665	SP256 60c +30c multi	1.10	1.10
a.	Photo., perf. 14 on 3 sides	1.10	1.10
B666	SP256 70c +35c multi	1.25	1.25
a.	Photo., perf. 14 on 3 sides	1.25	1.25
B667	SP256 80c +40c multi	1.40	1.40
a.	Photo., perf. 14 on 3 sides	1.40	1.40
b.	Bklt. pane, 3 #B665a, 2 #B666a, 1 #B667a	7.25	
	Complete booklet, #B667b	7.50	
	Nos. B665-B667 (3)	3.75	3.75

On normally centered stamps, the white border appears on the top, bottom and right sides only.

Children Making Music — SP257

No. B668, Saxophone player. No. B669, Piano player. No. B670, Bass player.

1992, Nov. 11 **Litho.** ***Perf. 13x13½***

B668	SP257 60c +30c multi	1.00	1.00
a.	Photo., perf. 13½x14	1.00	1.00
B669	SP257 70c +35c multi	1.25	1.25
a.	Photo., perf. 13½x14	1.25	1.25
B670	SP257 80c +40c multi	1.40	1.40
a.	Photo., perf. 13½x14	1.40	1.40
b.	Min. sheet, 3 #B668a, 2 #B669a, #B670a	7.00	
	Nos. B668-B670 (3)	3.65	3.65

Senior Citizens — SP258

1993, Apr. 20 **Litho.** ***Perf. 13x13½***

B671	SP258 70c +35c shown	1.25	1.25
a.	Photo., perf. 13½x14	1.25	1.25
B672	SP258 70c +35c couple	1.25	1.25
a.	Photo., perf. 13½x14	1.25	1.25
B673	SP258 80c +40c woman	1.40	1.40
a.	Photo., perf. 13½x14	1.40	1.40
b.	Booklet pane, 1 #B671a, 2 #B672a, 3 #B673a	9.25	
	Complete booklet, #B673b	9.25	
	Nos. B671-B673 (3)	3.90	3.90

Children and the Media SP259

Designs: No. B674, Child wearing newspaper hat. No. B675, Elephant wearing earphones. 80c + 40c, Television, child's legs.

1993, Nov. 17 **Litho.** ***Perf. 13½x13***

B674	SP259 70c +35c multi	1.25	1.25
a.	Photo., perf. 14x13½	1.25	1.25
B675	SP259 70c +35c multi	1.25	1.25
a.	Photo., perf. 14x13½	1.25	1.25
B676	SP259 80c +40c multi	1.40	1.40
a.	Photo., perf. 14x13½	1.40	1.40
b.	Min. sheet, 2 each #B674a-B676a	8.00	
	Nos. B674-B676 (3)	3.90	3.90

FEPAPOST '94 — SP260

Birds: 70c+60c, Branta leucopsis. 80c+70c, Luscinia svecica. 90c+80c, Anas querquedula.

1994, Feb. 22 **Litho.** ***Perf. 14x13***

B677	SP260 70c +60c multi	1.50	1.50
B678	SP260 80c +70c multi	1.75	1.75
B679	SP260 90c +80c multi	2.00	2.00
a.	Min. sheet, #B677-B679 + 3 labels, perf. 13½x13	5.25	
	Nos. B677-B679 (3)	5.25	5.25

Issued: No. B679a, 10/17/94.

Senior Citizens — SP261

Designs: 80c+40c, Man talking on telephone seen from behind. 90c+35c, Man in suit talking on telephone.

1994, Apr. 26 **Litho.** ***Perf. 13x13½***

B680	SP261 70c +35c shown	1.25	1.25
a.	Photo., perf. 13½x14	1.25	1.25
B681	SP261 80c +40c multi	1.40	1.40
a.	Photo., perf. 13½x14	1.40	1.40
B682	SP261 90c +35c multi	1.50	1.50
a.	Photo., perf. 13½x14	1.50	1.50
b.	Booklet pane, 2 #B680a, 3 #B681a, #B682a	8.25	
	Nos. B680-B682 (3)	4.15	4.15

Child Welfare Stamps SP262

Designs: 70c+35c, Holding ladder for woman painting. 80c+40c, Helping to balance woman picking cherries, vert. 90c+35c, Supporting boy on top of play house, vert.

Perf. 13½x13, 13x13½

1994, Nov. 9 **Litho.**

B683	SP262 70c +35c multi	1.25	1.25
B684	SP262 80c +40c multi	1.40	1.40
B685	SP262 90c +35c multi	1.50	1.50
a.	SP262 Miniature sheet, 2 #B683, 3 #B684, 1 #B685, perf. 13x14	9.00	
	Nos. B683-B685 (3)	4.15	4.15

Senior Citizens SP263

Designs: 70c+35c, Indonesia #1422 on postcard. 80c+40c, Couple seen in bus mirror. 100c+45c, Grandparents, child at zoo.

1995, Apr. 11 **Litho.** ***Perf. 13½x13***

B686	SP263 70c +35c multi	1.40	1.40
B687	SP263 80c +40c multi	1.50	1.50
B688	SP263 100c +45c multi	1.90	1.90
a.	Miniature sheet, 2 #B686, 3 #B687, 1 #B688	9.50	
	Nos. B686-B688 (3)	4.80	4.80

Child Welfare Stamps SP264

Computer drawings by children: 70c+35c, Dino, by S. Stegeman. 80c+40c, The School Teacher, by L. Ensing, vert. 100c+50c, Children and Colors, by M. Jansen.

Perf. 13½x13, 13x13½

1995, Nov. 15 **Litho.**

B689	SP264 70c +35c multi	1.25	1.25
B690	SP264 80c +40c multi	1.50	1.50
B691	SP264 100c +50c multi	1.90	1.90
a.	Min. sheet of 6, 2 #B689, 3 #B690, 1 #B691	9.75	9.75
	Nos. B689-B691 (3)	4.65	4.65

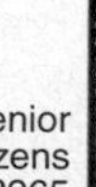
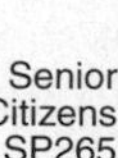

Senior Citizens SP265

No. B692, Swimming. No. B693, Babysitting. No. B694, Playing piano.

1996, Apr. 23 Litho. *Perf. 13¼x12¾*

B692 SP265 70c +35c multi 1.25 1.25
B693 SP265 80c +40c multi 1.40 1.40
B694 SP265 100c +50c multi 1.75 1.75
a. Sheet of 6, 2 #B692, 3 #B693, 1 #B694, perf. 13x12½ 8.00 8.00
Nos. B692-B694 (3) 4.40 4.40

Child Welfare Stamps — SP266

Designs: 70c+35c, Baby, books. No. B696, Boy, toys. No. B697, Girl, tools.

Perf. 12¾x13¼

1996, Nov. 6 Litho.

B695 SP266 70c +35 multi 1.10 1.10
B696 SP266 80c +40c multi 1.40 1.40
B697 SP266 80c +40c multi 1.40 1.40
a. Sheet of 2 each, #B695-B697 8.00 8.00
Nos. B695-B697 (3) 3.90 3.90

Senior Citizens SP267

Designs: No. B698, Rose in full bloom. No. B699, Stem of rose. No. B700, Rose bud.

1997, Apr. 15 Litho. *Perf. 13¼x12¾*

B698 SP267 80c +40c multi 1.40 1.40
B699 SP267 80c +40c multi 1.40 1.40
B700 SP267 80c +40c multi 1.40 1.40
a. Min. sheet, 2 each #B698-B700 8.50 8.50
Nos. B698-B700 (3) 4.20 4.20

Netherlands Red Cross — SP268

1997, May 27 Litho. *Perf. 12¾x13¼*

B701 SP268 80c +40c multi 1.40 1.40

Child Welfare Stamps SP269

Children's Fairy Tales: No. B702, Hunter with wolf, from "Little Red Riding Hood." No. B703, Dropping loaves of bread, from "Tom Thumb." No. B704, Man opening bottle, from "Genie in the Bottle."

Perf. 13¼x12¾

1997, Nov. 12 Litho.

B702 SP269 80c +40c multi 1.40 1.40
B703 SP269 80c +40c multi 1.40 1.40
B704 SP269 80c +40c multi 1.40 1.40
a. Min. sheet of 2 each, #B702-B704 8.50 8.50
Nos. B702-B704 (3) 4.20 4.20

Senior Citizens SP270

#B705, Sports shoe. #B706, Note on paper. #B707, Wrapped piece of candy.

1998, Apr. 21 Litho. *Perf. 13¼x12¾*

B705 SP270 80c +40c multi 1.40 1.40
B706 SP270 80c +40c multi 1.40 1.40
B707 SP270 80c +40c multi 1.40 1.40
a. Sheet, 2 each #B705-B707 8.50 8.50
Nos. B705-B707 (3) 4.20 4.20

Child Welfare Stamps SP271

#B708, Elephant riding horse. #B709, Pig, rabbit decorating cake. #B710, Pig, goose, rabbit carrying flower, frog carrying flag.

Perf. 13¼x12¾

1998, Nov. 11 Litho.

B708 SP271 80c +40c multi 1.40 1.40
B709 SP271 80c +40c multi 1.40 1.40
B710 SP271 80c +40c multi 1.40 1.40
a. Sheet, 2 each #B708-B710 8.50 8.50
Nos. B708-B710 (3) 4.20 4.20

Intl. Year of Older Persons SP272

1999, Apr. 13 Litho. *Perf. 13¼x12¾*

B711 SP272 80c +40c Woman 1.40 1.40
B712 SP272 80c +40c Black man 1.40 1.40
B713 SP272 80c +40c Caucasian man 1.40 1.40
a. Min. sheet, 2 ea #B711-B713 8.50 8.50
Nos. B711-B713 (3) 4.20 4.20

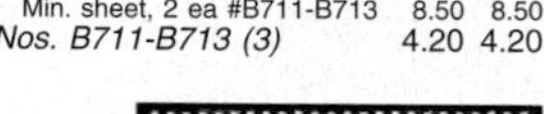

Child Welfare Stamps SP273

Designs: No. B714, Boy on tow truck. No. B715, Girl and chef. No. B716, Children stamping envelope.

Perf. 13¼x12¾

1999, Nov. 10 Litho.

B714 SP273 80c +40c multi 1.40 1.40
B715 SP273 80c +40c multi 1.40 1.40
B716 SP273 80c +40c multi 1.40 1.40
a. Sheet, 2 each #B714-B716 8.50 8.50
Nos. B714-B716 (3) 4.20 4.20

Senior Citizens SP274

2000, Apr. 4 Litho. *Perf. 13¼x12¾*

B717 SP274 80c +40c Swimmers 1.40 1.40
B718 SP274 80c +40c Bowlers 1.40 1.40
B719 SP274 80c +40c Fruit picker 1.40 1.40
a. Souvenir sheet, 2 each #B717-B719 8.50 8.50
Nos. B717-B719 (3) 4.20 4.20

Souvenir Sheet

Child Welfare — SP275

Designs: Nos. B720a, B721, Children with masks. No. B720b, Child with ghost costume. No. B720c, Child on alligator. Nos. B720d, B722, Child in boat. Nos. B720e, B723, Children cooking. No. B720f, Children in dragon costume.

2000, Nov. 8 Litho. *Perf. 13¼x12¾*

B720 SP275 Sheet of 6 8.50 8.50
a.-f. 80c +40c Any single 1.40 1.40

Self-Adhesive

Serpentine Die Cut 15

B721 SP275 80c +40c multi 1.40 1.40
B722 SP275 80c +40c multi 1.40 1.40
B723 SP275 80c +40c multi 1.40 1.40
Nos. B721-B723 (3) 4.20 4.20

Flowers SP276

Designs: No. B724a, Caryopteris. Nos. B724b, B725, Helenium. Nos. B724c, B726, Alcea rugosa. No. B724d, Euphorbia schillingii. No. B724e, B727, Centaurea dealbata. No. B724f, Inula hookeri.

2001, Apr. 24 Litho. *Perf. 13¼x12¾*

B724 Sheet of 6 6.00 6.00
a.-f. SP276 80c+40c Any single 1.00 1.00

Serpentine Die Cut 14¾x15

Self-Adhesive

B725 SP276 80c +40c multi 1.40 1.40
B726 SP276 80c +40c multi 1.40 1.40
B727 SP276 80c +40c multi 1.40 1.40
a. Booklet, 10 each #B725-727 42.50
Nos. B725-B727 (3) 4.20 4.20

Children and Computers SP277

Black figure: No. B728a, Retrieving letter from printer. No. B728b, Crossing road with letter. No. B728c, Sliding down green vine. No. B728d, Posting letter. Nos. B728e, B729, Crossing river on log. No. B728f, Swinging on rope.

2001, Nov. 6 Photo. *Perf. 14x13½*

B728 Sheet of 6 8.50 8.50
a.-f. SP277 85c +40c Any single 1.40 1.40

Self-Adhesive

Die Cut Perf. 13¼x13

B729 SP277 85c +40c multi 1.10 1.10

Surtax for Dutch Children's Stamp Foundation.

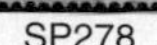

SP278

SP279

SP280

SP281

SP282

Floriade 2002 — SP283

2002, Apr. 2 Litho. *Perf. 14¾x14½*

B730 SP278 39c +19c multi 1.40 1.40
B731 SP279 39c +19c multi 1.40 1.40
B732 SP280 39c +19c multi 1.40 1.40
B733 SP281 39c +19c multi 1.40 1.40
B734 SP282 39c +19c multi 1.40 1.40
B735 SP283 39c +19c multi 1.40 1.40
a. Block of 6, #B730-B735 8.50 8.50

Nos. B730-B735 are impregnated with a floral scent.

Surtax for National Help the Aged Fund.

Blossom Walk, 10th Anniv. — SP284

2002, Apr. 27 Litho. *Perf. 14¾x14½*

B736 SP284 39c +19c multi 1.40 1.40

Surtax for Red Cross.

Children — SP285

No. B737: a, Child with red head, red cat. b, Child with green head, blue father. c, Child with red head, blue ball. d, Child with yellow head, green pet dish. e, Child with brown head, legs of child. f, Child with yellow head, blue dog.

2002, Nov. 5 Photo. *Perf. 14x13½*

B737 SP285 Sheet of 6 8.50 8.50
a.-f. 39c +19c Any single 1.40 1.40

Surtax for Dutch Children's Stamp Foundation.

Flowers — SP286

No. B738: a, Orange yellow lilies of the Incas. b, Lilac sweet peas. c, Pansies. d, Red orange and yellow trumpet creepers. e, Red campions. f, Purple, white and yellow irises.

2003, Apr. 8 Photo. *Perf. 14½x14¾*

B738	SP286	Block of 6	7.50	7.50
a.-f.		39c +19c Any single	1.25	1.25

Souvenir Sheet

Items in a Child's Life — SP287

No. B739: a, Note pad, radio, ballet shoes. b, Theater masks, book. c, Microphone, musical staff, paintbrush. d, Violin, soccer ball, television. e, Television, drum, light bulbs. f, Light bulbs, trombone, hat, headphones.

2003, Nov. 4 *Perf. 14x13½*

B739	SP287	Sheet of 6	8.00	8.00
a.-f.		39c +19c Any single	1.25	1.25

Flowers — SP288

No. B740 — Various flowers with background color of: a, Lilac. b, Pink. c, Brownish gray. d, Ocher. e, Blue gray. f, Olive.

2004, Apr. 6 Photo. *Perf. 14¾x14½*

B740	SP288	Block of 6	8.50	8.50
a.-f.		39c + 19c any single	1.40	1.40

Souvenir Sheet

Fruit and Sports — SP289

No. B741: a, Watermelon, soccer. b, Lemon, rope jumping. c, Orange, cycling. d, Pear, skateboarding. e, Banana, sit-ups. f, Strawberry, weight lifting.

2004, Nov. 9 Photo. *Perf. 14½*

B741	SP289	Sheet of 6	9.00	9.00
a.-f.		39c +19c Any single	1.50	1.50

December Stamps — SP290

No. B742 — Inscriptions: a, Novib. b, Stop AIDS Now. c, Natuurmonumenten. d, KWF Kankerbestrijding. e, UNICEF. f, Plan Nederland. g, Tros Helpt. h, Greenpeace. i, Artsen Zonder Grenzen (Doctors Without Borders). j, World Food Program.

Serpentine Die Cut 8¾x9

2004, Nov. 25 Self-Adhesive

B742		Block of 10	10.50	10.50
a.-j.		SP290 29c +10c Any single	1.00	1.00

The surtax went to the various organizations named on the stamps.

Souvenir Sheets

SP291

Summer Stamps — SP292

No. B743 — Illustrations for children's stories and silhouette of: a, Children and barrel. b, Two children. c, Frying pan.

No. B744 — Illustrations for children's stories and silhouette of: a, Monkey. b, Cup, saucer and spoon. c, Cat playing with ball.

2005, Apr. 5 Litho. *Perf. 13¼x13¾*

B743	SP291	Sheet of 3 + 2 labels	4.50	4.50
a.-c.		39c +19c Any single	1.50	1.50
B744	SP292	Sheet of 3 + 2 labels	4.50	4.50
a.-c.		39c +19c Any single	1.50	1.50

Miniature Sheet

Miffy the Bunny, by Dick Bruna — SP293

No. B745: a, Bunny and dog. b, Four bunnies. c, Bunny holding teddy bear. d, Bunny writing letter. e, White and brown bunnies. f, Six bunnies.

2005, Nov. 8 Photo. *Perf. 14½*

B745	SP293	Sheet of 6	8.50	8.50
a.-f.		39c+19c Any single	1.40	1.40

The surtax went to the Foundation for Children's Welfare Stamps. A booklet containing four panes of two stamps sold for €9.95.

SP294 SP295

SP296 SP297

SP298 SP299

SP300 SP301

Religious Art from Museum Catharijnconvent, Utrecht
SP302 SP303

Serpentine Die Cut 8¾x9

2005, Nov. 24 Litho.

B746		Booklet pane of 10	9.50	
a.		SP294 29c+10c multi	.95	.95
b.		SP295 29c+10c multi	.95	.95
c.		SP296 29c+10c multi	.95	.95
d.		SP297 29c+10c multi	.95	.95
e.		SP298 29c+10c multi	.95	.95
f.		SP299 29c+10c multi	.95	.95
g.		SP300 29c+10c multi	.95	.95
h.		SP301 29c+10c multi	.95	.95
i.		SP302 29c+10c multi	.95	.95
j.		SP303 29c+10c multi	.95	.95

The surtax went to the various organizations named on the margin and backing paper of the booklet pane.

Souvenir Sheets

SP304

Illustrations From Reading Boards — SP305

No. B747: a, Monkey and birds. b, Walnut. c, Cat.

No. B748: a, Boy playing with game. b, Girl holding rattle. c, Girl playing with doll.

2006, Apr. 4 Litho. *Perf. 13½x13¾*

B747	SP304	Sheet of 3 + 2 labels	4.25	4.25
a.-c.		39c +19c Any single	1.40	1.40
B748	SP305	Sheet of 3 + 2 labels	4.25	4.25
a.-c.		39c +19c Any single	1.40	1.40

Surtax for National Fund for Care of the Elderly.

Souvenir Sheet

Children — SP306

No. B749: a, Six children, boy in orange shirt with hands up and with foot on ball. b, Eight children, girl in red shirt with hands in air. c, Six children, girl at right standing. d, Six children, boy in orange shirt with hands down and kicking ball. e, Eight children, girl in red shirt with hands at waist. f, Six children, girl at right seated.

2006, Nov. 7 Photo. *Perf. 14½*

B749	SP306	Sheet of 6	9.25	9.25
a.-f.		39c +19c Any single	1.50	1.50

Surtax for Dutch Children's Stamp Foundation.

SP307

SP308

SP309

SP310

SP311

SP312

SP313

SP314

SP315

Children Wearing Angel Costumes — SP316

Serpentine Die Cut 8¾x9

2006, Nov. 23 Litho.

Self-Adhesive

B750		Block of 10	10.50	10.50
a.		SP307 29c +10c multi	1.00	1.00
b.		SP308 29c +10c multi	1.00	1.00
c.		SP309 29c +10c multi	1.00	1.00
d.		SP310 29c +10c multi	1.00	1.00
e.		SP311 29c +10c multi	1.00	1.00
f.		SP312 29c +10c multi	1.00	1.00
g.		SP313 29c +10c multi	1.00	1.00
h.		SP314 29c +10c multi	1.00	1.00
i.		SP315 29c +10c multi	1.00	1.00
j.		SP316 29c +10c multi	1.00	1.00

The surtax went to the various organizations named in the sheet selvage.

Souvenir Sheets

Beach Activities — SP317

No. B751: a, Woman pulling dress up in surf, boy in water. b, Woman standing in surf, children on ponies on beach. c, Children on ponies on beach, children playing on beach.

No. B752: a, Children playing on beach, family posing for photograph on beach. b, Boy waving, people in large beach chair. c, Boy on sail-powered beach cart, family digging sand at shore.

2007, Apr. 4 Litho. *Perf. 13¼x12¾*

B751 SP317	Sheet of 3	5.50	5.50
a.-c.	44c +22c Any single	1.75	1.75
B752 SP317	Sheet of 3	5.50	5.50
a.-c.	44c +22c Any single	1.75	1.75

Surtax for Natiional Fund for Senior Citizen's Help.

Netherlands Red Cross, 140th Anniv. SP318

2007, July 19 *Perf. 13¼*

B753 SP318	44c +22c multi	1.90	1.90

Surtax for Netherlands Red Cross. Printed in sheets of 3.

Miniature Sheet

Children and Safety — SP319

No. B754 — Child: a, Watching television. b, And building at night. c, In bed. d, And computer. e, And kitten. f, Reading book.

2007, Nov. 6 Litho. *Perf. 14½*

B754 SP319	Sheet of 6	12.00	12.00
a.-f.	44c +22c any single	2.00	2.00

Surtax for Foundation for Children's Welfare Stamps.

SP320

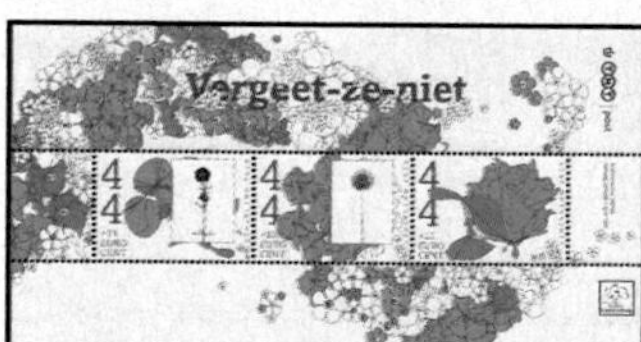

Forget-me-nots — SP321

No. B755: a, Forget-me-not, head-on view. b, Purple crane's bill geranium. c, Pink Japanese anemone.

No. B756: a, Purple larkspur. b, Globe thistle. c, Forget-me-not, side view.

2008, Apr. 1 Litho. *Perf. 14½*

B755 SP320	Sheet of 3	6.25	6.25
a.-c.	44c+22c Any single	2.00	2.00
B756 SP321	Sheet of 3	6.25	6.25
a.-c.	44c+22c Any single	2.00	2.00

Surtax for National Fund for Elderly Assistance.

Miniature Sheet

Children's Education — SP322

No. B757 — Letters of word "Onderwijs" (education): a, "O." b, "ND." c, "ER." d, "W." e, "IJ." f, "S."

2008, Nov. 4 Photo. *Perf. 14½*

B757 SP322	Sheet of 6	10.00	10.00
a.-f.	44c +22c Any single	1.60	1.60

Surtax for Foundation for Children's Welfare Stamps.

Miniature Sheet

Elder Care — SP323

No. B758: a, Couple dancing. b, Woman with bag cart. c, Ballet dancer. d, Woman with guide dog. e, Man playing trumpet. f, Woman holding diploma.

2009, Apr. 7 Litho. *Perf. 14½*

B758 SP323	Sheet of 6	10.50	10.50
a.-f.	44c +22c Any single	1.75	1.75

Surtax for National Fund for Elderly Assistance.

Miniature Sheet

Children's Activities — SP324

No. B759 — Stylized children: a, With pencil. b, With magnifying glasses. c, Watching falling star. d, Playing. e, Reading newspaper. f, With stylized Pegasus.

2009, Nov. 3 Photo. *Perf. 14½*

B759 SP324	Sheet of 6	12.00	12.00
a.-f.	44c+22c Any single	2.00	2.00

Surtax for Foundation for Children's Welfare Stamps.

Miniature Sheet

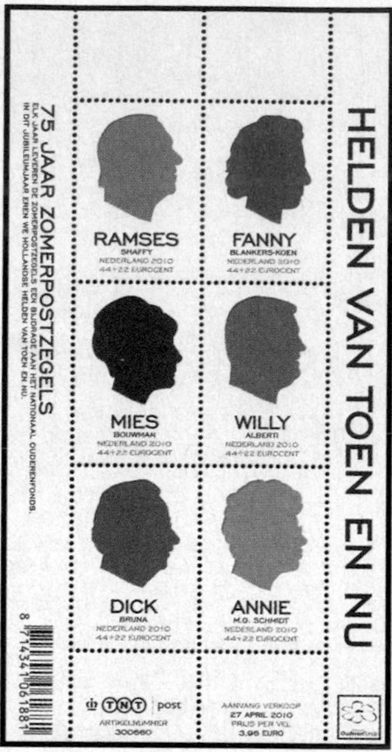

Famous People — SP325

No. B760 — Silhouettes of: a, Ramses Shaffy (1933-2009), singer and actor. b, Fanny Blankers-Koen (1918-2004), Olympic gold medalist. c, Mies Bouwman, television personality. d, Willy Alberti (1926-85), singer. e, Dick Bruna, writer and illustrator. f, Annie M. G. Schmidt (1911-95), writer.

2010, Apr. 27 Litho. *Perf. 14½*

B760 SP325	Sheet of 6	10.50	10.50
a.-f.	44c + 22c Any single	1.75	1.75

Surtax for National Fund for Elderly Assistance.

Miniature Sheet

Children and Mathematical Symbols — SP326

No. B761: a, Boy with red shirt. b, Boy with dark gray shirt, hand near head. c, Boy with gray shirt, hand in front of chest. d, Girl with red and orange dress. e, Girl with arms clasped behind head. f, Girl with arm raised.

2010, Nov. 9 *Perf. 14x13¾*

B761 SP326	Sheet of 6	11.00	11.00
a.-f.	1 + 22c Any single	1.75	1.75

Nos. B761a-B761f each had a franking value of 44c, with the 22c surtax going to the Foundation for Children's Welfare Stamps.

Miniature Sheet

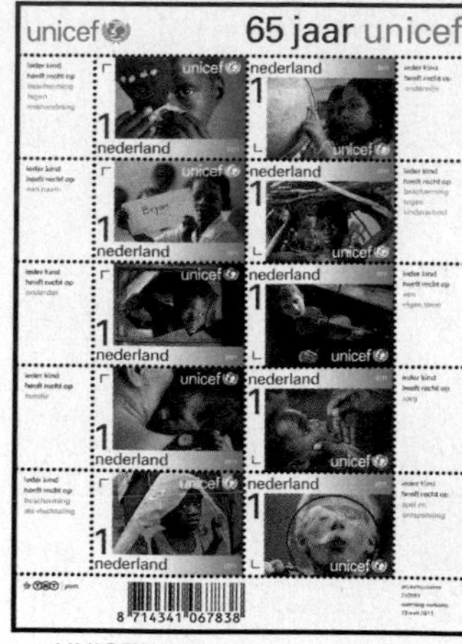

UNICEF, 65th Anniv. — SP327

No. B762: a, Child holding doll. b, Children touching globe. c, Boy holding card showing his name. d, Boy carrying branches. e, Boy looking out of broken window. f, Boy playing violin. g, Mother holding child. h, Child receiving medicine. i, Child using dog food bag as hood. j, Child blowing bubbles.

2011, May 23 *Perf. 13¼x12¾*

B762 SP327	Sheet of 10	19.00	19.00
a.-j.	1 + (20c) Any single	1.90	1.90
k.	Booklet pane of 2, #B762a-B762b	5.75	—
l.	Booklet pane of 2, #B762c-B762d	5.75	—
m.	Booklet pane of 2, #B762e-B762f	5.75	—
n.	Booklet pane of 2, #B762g-B762h	5.75	—
o.	Booklet pane of 2, #B762i-B762j	5.75	—
	Complete booklet, #B762k-B762o	29.00	

Nos. B762a-B762j each had a franking value of 46c, with the 20c surtax going to UNICEF. Complete booklet sold for €9.95.

Miniature Sheet

Children at Play — SP328

No. B763 — Child wearing: a, Orange shirt. b, Light green shirt. c, Pink shirt. d, Purple shirt. e, Blue green shirt. f, White shirt.

2011, Oct. 29 Photo. *Perf. 14½*

B763 SP328	Sheet of 6	11.50	11.50
a.-f.	1 + 23c Any single	1.90	1.90

Nos. B763a-B763f each had a franking value of 46c, with the 23c surtax going to the Foundation for Children's Welfare Stamps.

Red Cross — SP329

No. B764: a, Cross in red, text "Eerste Hulp bij ongellukken." b, Woman in cross, text "Eerste Hulp dóór iedereen." c, Hand and child's head in cross, text "Eerste Hulp vóór iedereen."

2012, Jan. 30 Litho. *Perf. 13¼x13½*

B764 SP329	Horiz. strip of 3	6.00	6.00
a.-c.	1 +25c any single	2.00	2.00

Nos. B764a-B764c each had a franking value of 50c, with the 25c surtax going to the Dutch Red Cross. No. B764 was printed in sheets containing two strips.

Miniature Sheet

Princesses — SP330

No. B765: a, Princess Catharina- Amalia. b, Princesses Alexia, Ariane and Catharina-Amalia (five buttons on blouse of Princess Ariane visible). c, Princess Ariane. d, Princesses Catharina-Amalia, Alexia and Ariane (Catharina-Amalia at left). e, Princess Alexia. f, Princesses Alexia, Ariane and Catharina-Amalia (three buttons on blouse of Princess Ariane visible).

2012, Nov. 6 Photo. *Perf. 14½*

B765 SP330 Sheet of 6 11.50 11.50
a.-f. 1 + 25c Any single 1.90 1.90

Nos. B765a-B765f each had a franking value of 50c, with the 23c surtax going to the Foundation for Children's Welfare Stamps.

Miniature Sheet

Ethiopian Children — SP331

No. B766: a, Boy, multiplication table. b, Boy holding bundle of sticks. c, Girl carrying young boy on her back. d, Girl, letters of Amharic alphabet. e, Boy, poster with pictures and English words. f, Boy carrying goat.

2013, Nov. 4 Litho. *Perf. 14½*

B766 SP331 Sheet of 6 14.50 14.50
a.-f. 1+30c Any single 2.40 2.40

Nos. B766a-B766f each had a franking value of 60c on the day of issue, with the 30c surtax going to th Foundation for Children's Welfare Stamps.

Miniature Sheet

Children in Works from the Rijksmuseum — SP332

No. B767: a, Children at the beach (36x25mm). b, Children riding donkey (36x25mm). c, Girl wearing kimono (36x25mm). d, Girl and boys near piano (36x25mm). e, Boy on skateboard (36x50mm).

2014, Nov. 3 Litho. *Perf. 14½*

B767 SP332 Sheet of 5 12.00 12.00
a.-e. 1+32c Any single 2.40 2.40

Nos. B767a-B767b had a franking value of 64c on the day of issue, with the 32c surtax going to the Foundation for Children's Welfare Stamps.

Miniature Sheet

Illustrations From Little Golden Books Series of Children's Books — SP333

No. B768: a, Sofa, toys strung together with cart containing dog and cat. b, Bird chasing cat in tree away from nest. c, Child pulling toys strung together. d, Duck, goose and house. e, Cat on mitten. f, Duck, goose, cat and pig.

2015, Nov. 2 Litho. *Perf. 13¼*

B768 SP333 Sheet of 6 13.50 13.50
a.-f. 1+34c Any single 2.25 2.25

Nos. B768a-B768f each had a franking value of 69c on the day of issue, with the 34c surcharge going to the Foundation for Children's Welfare Stamps.

AIR POST STAMPS

Stylized Seagull — AP1

Perf. 12½

1921, May 1 Unwmk. Typo.

C1	AP1	10c red	1.50	1.25
C2	AP1	15c yellow grn	6.25	2.50
C3	AP1	60c dp blue	19.00	.50
		Nos. C1-C3 (3)	26.75	4.25
		Set, never hinged	190.00	

Nos. C1-C3 were used to pay airmail fee charged by the carrier, KLM.

Lt. G. A. Koppen — AP2

Capt. Jan van der Hoop — AP3

Wmk. Circles (202)

1928, Aug. 20 Litho. *Perf. 12*

C4	AP2	40c orange red	.25	.25
C5	AP3	75c blue green	.25	.25
		Set, never hinged	1.25	

Mercury — AP4

Perf. 11½

1929, July 16 Unwmk. Engr.

C6	AP4	1½g gray	2.50	1.65
C7	AP4	4½g carmine	1.75	3.00
C8	AP4	7½g blue green	24.00	4.50
		Nos. C6-C8 (3)	28.25	9.15
		Set, never hinged	70.00	

Queen Wilhelmina — AP5

Perf. 12½, 14x13

1931, Sept. 24 Photo. Wmk. 202

C9 AP5 36c org red & dk bl 10.00 .60
Never hinged 70.00

Fokker Pander AP6

1933, Oct. 9 *Perf. 12½*

C10 AP6 30c dark green .40 .60
Never hinged .80

Nos. C10-C12 were issued for use on special flights.

Crow in Flight AP7

1938-53 *Perf. 13x14*

C11	AP7	12½c dk blue & gray	.35	.25
C12	AP7	25c dk bl & gray ('53)	1.50	1.50
		Set, never hinged	4.25	

Catalogue values for unused stamps in this section, from this point to the end of the section, are for Never Hinged items.

Seagull — AP8

Perf. 13x14

1951, Nov. 12 Engr. Unwmk.

C13	AP8	15g gray	230.00	85.00
C14	AP8	25g blue gray	230.00	85.00
		Set, hinged	260.00	

Airplane AP9

1966, Sept. 2 Litho. *Perf. 14x13*

C15 AP9 25c gray, blk & bl .35 .35

Issued for use on special flights.

AP10

1980, May 13 Photo. *Perf. 13x14*

C16 AP10 1g multicolored .90 .90

REGISTRATION STAMPS

Personalized Stamp — R1

Die Cut Perf. 12¾x12½

Etched on Silver Foil

2011, Oct. 10 Self-Adhesive

F1 R1 (€7) silver 19.00 19.00

The vignette portion of No. F1 could be personalized for €34.95. The image shown, depicting Piet Hein and a warship, is a generic image.

Queen Beatrix and King William-Alexander R2

With Embossed Crown and Date

Die Cut Perf. 12¾x12½

Etched on Silver Foil

2013, Apr. 30 Self-Adhesive

F2 R2 (€7.70) silver 20.00 20.00

MARINE INSURANCE STAMPS

Floating Safe Attracting Gulls — MI1

Floating Safe with Night Flare — MI2

Fantasy of Floating Safe — MI3

Perf. 11½

1921, Feb. 2 Unwmk. Engr.

GY1	MI1	15c slate grn	11.00	*75.00*
GY2	MI1	60c car rose	15.00	*75.00*
GY3	MI1	75c gray brn	18.50	*75.00*
GY4	MI2	1.50g dk blue	65.00	*425.00*
GY5	MI2	2.25g org brn	110.00	*550.00*
GY6	MI3	4½g black	165.00	*675.00*
GY7	MI3	7½g red	250.00	*925.00*
		Nos. GY1-GY7 (7)	634.50	*2,800.*
		Set, never hinged	1,500.	

POSTAGE DUE STAMPS

Postage due types of Netherlands were also used for Netherlands Antilles, Netherlands Indies and Surinam in different colors.

D1

Unwmk.

1870, May 15 **Typo.** ***Perf. 13***

J1	D1	5c brown, *org*	72.50	15.00
J2	D1	10c violet, *bl*	150.00	20.00
a.		Perf 12½x12	300.00	32.50

D2

Type I — 34 loops. "T" of "BETALEN" over center of loop; top branch of "E" of "TE" shorter than lower branch.

Type II — 33 loops. "T" of "BETALEN" between two loops.

Type III — 32 loops. "T" of "BETALEN" slightly to the left of loop; top branch of first "E" of "BETALEN" shorter than lower branch.

Type IV — 37 loops. Letters of "PORT" larger than in the other three types.

Imperforate varieties are proofs.

Perf. 11½x12, 12½x12, 12½, 13½

1881-87 **Value in Black**

J3	D2	1c lt blue (III)	11.00	11.00
a.		Type I	15.00	18.00
b.		Type II	20.00	20.00
c.		Type IV	47.50	52.50
J4	D2	1½c lt blue (III)	15.00	15.00
a.		Type I	18.00	18.00
b.		Type II	24.00	24.00
c.		Type IV	75.00	75.00
J5	D2	2½c lt blue (III)	37.50	5.00
a.		Type I	45.00	5.50
b.		Type II	50.00	6.00
c.		Type IV	210.00	125.00
J6	D2	5c lt blue (III) ('87)	140.00	3.50
a.		Type I	50.00	5.00
b.		Type II	130.00	5.25
c.		Type IV	1,250.	350.00
J7	D2	10c lt blue (III) ('87)	92.50	4.00
a.		Type I	115.00	4.50
b.		Type II	125.00	5.00
c.		Type IV	2,500.	375.00
J8	D2	12½c lt blue (III)	95.00	25.00
a.		Type I	165.00	40.00
b.		Type II	130.00	45.00
c.		Type IV	350.00	100.00
J9	D2	15c lt blue (III)	90.00	4.00
a.		Type I	105.00	4.50
b.		Type II	120.00	5.00
c.		Type IV	130.00	25.00
J10	D2	20c lt blue (III)	35.00	4.00
a.		Type I	47.50	4.25
b.		Type II	50.00	5.50
c.		Type IV	137.50	27.50
J11	D2	25c lt blue (III)	210.00	3.50
a.		Type I	230.00	3.00
b.		Type II	275.00	4.50
c.		Type IV	425.00	170.00

Value in Red

J12	D2	1g lt blue (III)	85.00	30.00
a.		Type I	85.00	37.50
b.		Type II	100.00	40.00
c.		Type IV	175.00	75.00
		Nos. J3-J12 (10)	811.00	105.00

See Nos. J13-J26, J44-J60. For surcharges see Nos. J27-J28, J42-J43, J72-J75.

1896-1910 ***Perf. 12½***

Value in Black

J13	D2	½c dk bl (I) ('01)	.40	.35
J14	D2	1c dk blue (I)	1.65	.35
a.		Type III	2.50	3.25
J15	D2	1½c dk blue (I)	.75	.35
a.		Type III	2.50	2.50
J16	D2	2½c dk blue (I)	1.50	.75
a.		Type III	3.25	.55
J17	D2	3c dk bl (I) ('10)	1.65	1.10
J18	D2	4c dk bl (I) ('09)	1.65	2.25
J19	D2	5c dk blue (I)	13.00	.35
a.		Type III	16.00	.55
J20	D2	6½c dk bl (I) ('07)	45.00	45.00
J21	D2	7½c dk bl (I) ('04)	1.75	.55
J22	D2	10c dk blue (I)	35.00	.55
a.		Type III	52.50	1.50
J23	D2	12½c dk blue (I)	30.00	1.10
a.		Type III	45.00	3.50
J24	D2	15c dk blue (I)	35.00	.90
a.		Type III	55.00	1.00
J25	D2	20c dk blue (I)	20.00	8.00
a.		Type III	20.00	8.75
J26	D2	25c dk blue (I)	45.00	.75
a.		Type III	50.00	1.00
		Nos. J13-J26 (14)	232.35	62.35

Surcharged in Black

1906, Jan. 10 ***Perf. 12½***

J27	D2	50c on 1g lt bl (III)	125.00	110.00
a.		50c on 1g light blue (I)	165.00	140.00
b.		50c on 1g light blue (II)	175.00	150.00

Surcharged in Red

1906, Oct. 6

J28	D2	6½c on 20c dk bl (I)	5.50	5.00

Nos. 87-89 Surcharged

1907, Nov. 1

J29	A13	½c on 1c claret	1.25	1.25
J30	A13	1c on 1c claret	.50	.50
J31	A13	1½c on 1c claret	.50	.50
J32	A13	2½c on 1c claret	1.25	1.25
J33	A13	5c on 2½c ver	1.40	.40
J34	A13	6½c on 2½c ver	3.50	3.50
J35	A13	7½c on ½c blue	2.00	1.25
J36	A13	10c on ½c blue	1.75	.75
J37	A13	12½c on ½c blue	5.00	4.75
J38	A13	15c on 2½c ver	6.00	4.00
J39	A13	25c on ½c blue	9.00	8.50
J40	A13	50c on ½c blue	42.50	40.00
J41	A13	1g on ½c blue	60.00	55.00
		Nos. J29-J41 (13)	134.65	121.65

Two printings of the above surcharges were made. Some values show differences in the setting of the fractions; others are practically impossible to distinguish.

No. J20 Surcharged in Red

1909, June

J42	D2	4c on 6½c dark blue	5.50	5.00
		Never hinged	20.00	

No. J12 Surcharged in Black

1910, July 11

J43	D2	3c on 1g lt bl, type III	30.00	27.50
		Never hinged	100.00	
a.		Type I	37.50	40.00
		Never hinged	110.00	
b.		Type II	40.00	40.00
		Never hinged	125.00	

Type I

1912-21 ***Perf. 12½, 13½x13***

Value in Color of Stamp

J44	D2	½c pale ultra	.25	.25
J45	D2	1c pale ultra ('13)	.25	.25
J46	D2	1½c pale ultra ('15)	1.90	1.50
J47	D2	2½c pale ultra	.25	.25
J48	D2	3c pale ultra	.40	.40
J49	D2	4c pale ultra ('13)	.25	.25
J50	D2	4½c pale ultra ('16)	5.25	5.00
J51	D2	5c pale ultra	.25	.25
J52	D2	5½c pale ultra ('16)	5.00	5.00
J53	D2	7c pale ultra ('21)	2.25	2.25
J54	D2	7½c pale ultra ('13)	2.50	1.00
J55	D2	10c pale ultra ('13)	.40	.40
J56	D2	12½c pale ultra ('13)	.40	.40
J57	D2	15c pale ultra ('13)	.40	.40
J58	D2	20c pale ultra ('20)	.40	.25
J59	D2	25c pale ultra ('17)	80.00	.60
J60	D2	50c pale ultra ('20)	.40	.25
		Nos. J44-J60 (17)	100.55	18.70
		Set, never hinged	450.00	

D3

1921-38 **Typo.** ***Perf. 12½, 13½x12½***

J61	D3	3c pale ultra ('28)	.25	.25
J62	D3	6c pale ultra ('27)	.25	.25
J63	D3	7c pale ultra ('28)	.40	.40
J64	D3	7½c pale ultra ('26)	.40	.40
J65	D3	8c pale ultra ('38)	.40	.40
J66	D3	9c pale ultra ('30)	.40	.40
J67	D3	11c ultra ('21)	13.00	3.50
J68	D3	12c pale ultra ('28)	.40	.25
J69	D3	25c pale ultra ('25)	.40	.25
J70	D3	30c pale ultra ('35)	.40	.25
J71	D3	1g ver ('21)	.50	.25
		Nos. J61-J71 (11)	16.80	6.60
		Set, never hinged	50.00	

Stamps of 1912-21 Surcharged

1923, Dec. ***Perf. 12½***

J72	D2	1c on 3c ultra	.75	.50
J73	D2	2½c on 7c ultra	1.20	.50
J74	D2	25c on 1½c ultra	8.00	.50
J75	D2	25c on 7½c ultra	10.00	.50
		Nos. J72-J75 (4)	19.95	2.00
		Set, never hinged	45.00	

Nos. 56, 58, 62, 65 Surcharged

1924, Aug.

J76	A11	4c on 3c olive grn	1.50	1.10
J77	A10	5c on 1c red	.75	.40
a.		Surcharge reading down	500.00	450.00
J78	A10	10c on 1½c blue	.95	.40
a.		Tête bêche pair	8.50	8.50
J79	A11	12½c on 5c carmine	.95	.50
a.		Tête bêche pair	10.00	10.00
		Nos. J76-J79 (4)	4.15	2.40

The 11c on 22½c and 15c on 17½c exist. These were used by the postal service for accounting of parcel post fees.

Catalogue values for unused stamps in this section, from this point to the end of the section, are for Never Hinged items.

D5

Perf. 13½x12½

1947-58 **Wmk. 202** **Photo.**

J80	D5	1c light blue ('48)	.25	.25
J81	D5	3c light blue ('48)	.40	.25
J82	D5	4c light blue	12.00	.90
J83	D5	5c light blue ('48)	.45	.25
J84	D5	6c light blue ('50)	.30	.35
J85	D5	7c light blue	.25	.25
J86	D5	8c light blue ('48)	.25	.25
J87	D5	10c light blue	.25	.25
J88	D5	11c light blue	.35	.45
J89	D5	12c light blue ('48)	.55	1.10
J90	D5	14c light blue ('53)	.90	.90
J91	D5	15c light blue	.35	.25
J92	D5	16c light blue	.80	1.25
J93	D5	20c light blue	.35	.25
J94	D5	24c light blue ('57)	1.25	1.40
J95	D5	25c light blue ('48)	.45	.25
J96	D5	26c light blue ('58)	1.90	1.75
J97	D5	30c light blue ('48)	.60	.25
J98	D5	35c light blue	.65	.25
J99	D5	40c light blue	.75	.25
J100	D5	50c light blue ('48)	.80	.25
J101	D5	60c light blue ('58)	1.00	.45
J102	D5	85c light blue ('50)	17.00	.45
J103	D5	90c light blue ('56)	2.75	.45
J104	D5	95c light blue ('57)	2.75	.60
J105	D5	1g carmine ('48)	2.50	.25
J106	D5	1.75g carmine ('57)	5.50	.40
		Nos. J80-J106 (27)	55.35	13.95

OFFICIAL STAMPS

Regular Issues of 1898-1908 Overprinted

1913 **Typo.** **Unwmk.** ***Perf. 12½***

O1	A10	1c red	4.00	2.75
O2	A10	1½c ultra	1.00	2.25
O3	A10	2c yellow brn	7.00	7.00
O4	A10	2½c dp green	16.00	12.00
O5	A11	3c olive grn	4.00	1.00
O6	A11	5c carmine rose	4.00	4.50
O7	A11	10c gray lilac	35.00	37.50
		Nos. O1-O7 (7)	71.00	67.00

Same Overprint in Red on No. 58

1919

O8	A10	1½c deep blue (R)	100.00	110.00

Nos. O1 to O8 were used to defray the postage on matter relating to the Poor Laws.

Counterfeit overprints exist.

For the International Court of Justice

Regular Issue of 1926-33 Overprinted in Gold

1934 **Wmk. 202** ***Perf. 12½***

O9	A24	1½c red violet	1.50
O10	A24	2½c deep green	1.50
O11	A23	7½c red	2.25
O12	A31	12½c deep ultra	22.50
O13	A23	15c orange	2.00
O14	A23	30c violet	2.25
a.		Perf. 13½x12½	2.25
		Nos. O9-O14 (6)	32.00

Same Overprint on No. 180 in Gold

1937 ***Perf. 13½x12½***

O15	A23	12½c ultra	16.00

"Mint" Officials

Nos. O9-O15, O20-O43 were sold to the public only canceled. Uncanceled, they were obtainable only by favor of an official or from UPU specimen stamps.

Same on Regular Issue of 1940 Overprinted in Gold

1940 ***Perf. 13½x12½***

O16	A45	7½c bright red	22.50	8.75
O17	A45	12½c sapphire	22.50	8.75
O18	A45	15c lt blue	22.50	8.75
O19	A45	30c bister	22.50	8.75
		Nos. O16-O19 (4)	90.00	35.00

Nos. 217 to 219, 221 and 223 Overprinted in Gold

1947

O20	A45	7½c bright red	1.10
O21	A45	10c brt red violet	1.10
O22	A45	12½c sapphire	1.10
O23	A45	20c purple	1.10
O24	A45	25c rose brown	1.10
		Nos. O20-O24 (5)	5.50

O1

Perf. 14½x13½

1950 **Unwmk.** **Photo.**

O25	O1	2c ultra	8.75
O26	O1	4c olive green	8.75

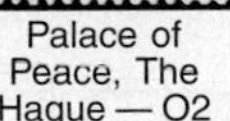

Palace of Peace, The Hague — O2

Queen Juliana — O3

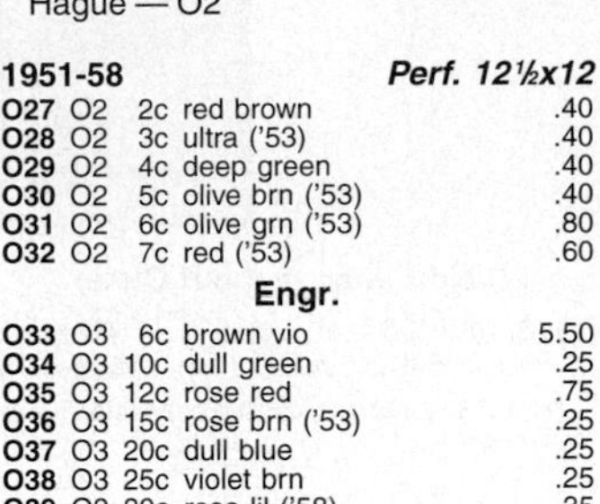

1951-58 *Perf. 12½x12*

O27	O2	2c	red brown	.40
O28	O2	3c	ultra ('53)	.40
O29	O2	4c	deep green	.40
O30	O2	5c	olive brn ('53)	.40
O31	O2	6c	olive grn ('53)	.80
O32	O2	7c	red ('53)	.60

Engr.

O33	O3	6c	brown vio	5.50
O34	O3	10c	dull green	.25
O35	O3	12c	rose red	.75
O36	O3	15c	rose brn ('53)	.25
O37	O3	20c	dull blue	.25
O38	O3	25c	violet brn	.25
O39	O3	30c	rose lil ('58)	.35
O40	O3	1g	slate gray	.80
			Nos. O27-O40 (14)	11.40

1977, May **Photo.** *Perf. 12½x12*

O41	O2	40c	brt grnsh blue	.50
O42	O2	45c	brick red	.50
O43	O2	50c	brt rose lilac	.50
			Nos. O41-O43 (3)	1.50

Catalogue values for unused stamps in this section, from this point to the end of the section, are for Never Hinged items.

Peace Palace, The Hague — O4

Palm, Sun and Column — O4a

1989-94 **Litho.**

O44	O4	5c	black & org yel	.25	.25
O45	O4	10c	black & blue	.25	.25
O46	O4	25c	black & red	.30	.30
O47	O4	50c	black & yel grn	.60	.60
O48	O4	55c	black & pink	.55	.55
O49	O4	60c	black & bister	.75	.75
O50	O4	65c	black & bl grn	.75	.75
O51	O4	70c	blk & gray bl	.90	.90
O52	O4	75c	black & yellow	.70	.70
O53	O4	80c	black & gray grn	1.00	1.00
O54	O4	1g	black & orange	1.10	1.10
O55	O4	1.50g	blk & blue	1.60	1.60
O56	O4	1.60g	blk & rose brn	2.00	2.00

Litho. & Engr.

O57	O4a	5g	multicolored	5.50	5.50
O58	O4a	7g	multicolored	6.50	6.50
			Nos. O44-O58 (15)	22.75	22.75

Issued: 55c, 75c, 7g, 10/24/89; 65c, 1g, 1.50g, 5g, 10/23/90; 5c, 10c, 25c, 50c, 60c, 70c, 80c, 10/22/91; 1.60g, 11/28/94.

Intl. Court of Justice — O5

Emblem of Intl. Court of Justice — O6

2004, Jan. 2 **Litho.** *Perf. 14¾x14½*

O59	O5	39c	multi	1.00	1.00
O60	O6	61c	multi	1.60	1.60

Intl. Court of Justice — O7

Emblem of Intl. Court of Justice — O8

Doves — O9

2011, Apr. 11 *Perf. 13½x13¼*

O61	O7	1	multi	1.40	1.40
O62	O8	1	Europa multi	2.40	2.40
O63	O9	1	Wereld multi	2.75	2.75
			Nos. O61-O63 (3)	6.55	6.55

On day of issue, Nos. O61-O63 each sold for 46c, 79c, and 95c, respectively.

VARIO STOCK SHEETS

Vario stock sheets offer unparalleled quality and versatility.

They're a convenient and easy way to store and organize stamps. Vario stock sheets are carefully manufactured to be free of harmful plasticized PVC, and softeners. Vario stock will fit all standard 3-ring binders and are available in a variety of sizes.

NOTE: Black sheets have pockets on both sides. Clear sheets have pockets on one side only. "S" in item number denotes black page. "C" in item number denotes clear page.

Sold in packages of 5. Retail $5.25 **AA* $4.25**

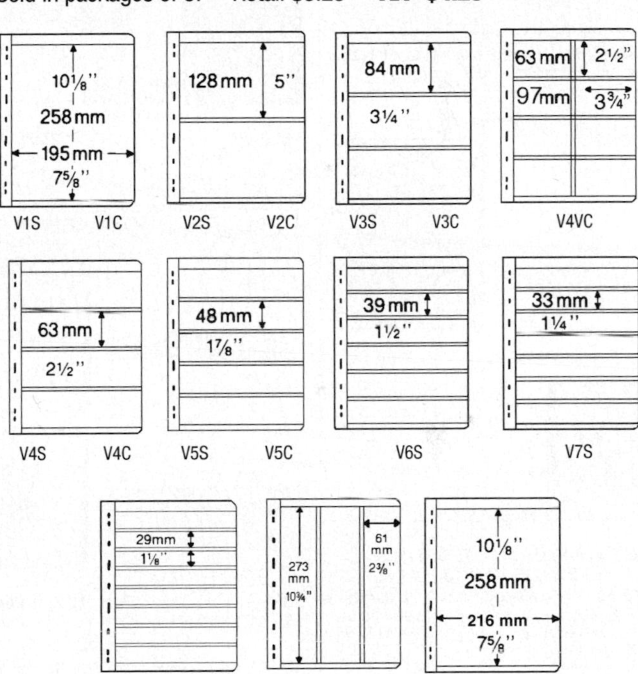

THREE-RING BINDERS

We have the binders for you! Take a look at our handsome matching binder & slipcase sets. These great sets are available in blue or black. If you prefer a heavy duty binder, check out our metal-hinged, thick panel binder. What are you waiting for?

Item	*Description*	*Retail*	*AA**
SSBSBL	Blue 3-Ring Binder and Slipcase	$21.99	**$17.99**
SSBSBK	Black 3-Ring Binder and Slipcase	$21.99	**$17.99**
SSBMBK	Black Metal Hinged 3-Ring Binder	$24.99	**$19.99**

1-800-572-6885

Outside U.S. & Canada

(937) 498-0800

AmosAdvantage.com

Ordering Information: *AA prices apply to paid subscribers of Amos Media publications, or orders placed online. Prices, terms and product availability subject to change. Taxes will apply in CA, OH & IL.

Shipping & Handling: United States: Orders under $10 are only $3.99. 10% of order over $10 total. Minimum Freight Charge $7.99; Maximum Freight Charge $45.00. Canada: 20% of order total. Minimum Freight Charge $19.99; Maximum Freight Charge $200.00. Foreign: Orders are shipped via FedEx Economy International or USPS and billed actual freight.

Mail Orders To: Amos Media Co., P.O. Box 4129, Sidney OH 45365

NETHERLANDS ANTILLES

'ne-thər-lən dz an-'ti-lēz

(Curaçao)

LOCATION — Two groups of islands about 500 miles apart in the West Indies, north of Venezuela
AREA — 383 sq. mi.
POP. — 207,333 (1995)
CAPITAL — Willemstad

Formerly a colony, Curaçao, Netherlands Antilles became an integral part of the Kingdom of the Netherlands under the Constitution of 1954. On Jan. 1, 1986, the island of Aruba achieved a separate status within the Kingdom and began issuing its own stamps.

100 Cents = 1 Gulden

Catalogue values for unused stamps in this country are for Never Hinged items, beginning with Scott 164 in the regular postage section, Scott B1 in the semi-postal section, Scott C18 in the airpost section, Scott CB9 in the airpost semi-postal section, and Scott J41 in the postage due section.

Values for unused examples of Nos. 1-44 are for stamps without gum.

Watermark

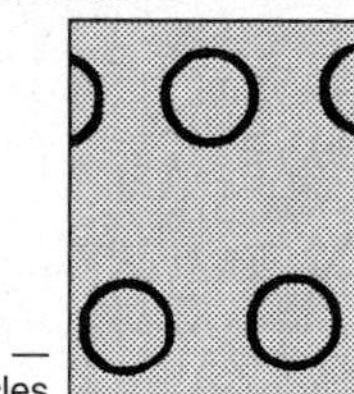

Wmk. 202 — Circles

King William III — A1

Regular Perf. 11½, 12½, 11½x12, 12½x12, 13½x13, 14

1873-79 Typo. Unwmk.

1	A1	2½c green	5.00	8.00
2	A1	3c bister	55.00	*110.00*
3	A1	5c rose	10.00	12.00
4	A1	10c ultra	60.00	17.00
5	A1	25c brown orange	45.00	10.00
6	A1	50c violet	1.75	2.50
7	A1	2.50g bis & pur ('79)	37.50	37.50
		Nos. 1-7 (7)	214.25	*197.00*

See bluish paper note with Netherlands #7-22.

The gulden denominations, Nos. 7 and 12, are of larger size.

See 8-12. For surcharges see #18, 25-26.

Perf. 14, Small Holes

1b	A1	2½c	12.00	15.00
2b	A1	3c	60.00	*140.00*
3b	A1	5c	14.50	21.00
4b	A1	10c	72.50	80.00
5b	A1	25c	65.00	45.00
6b	A1	50c	26.00	30.00
		Nos. 1b-6b (6)	250.00	*331.00*

"Small hole" varieties have the spaces between the holes wider than the diameter of the holes.

1886-89 *Perf. 11½, 12½, 12½x12*

8	A1	12½c yellow	95.00	52.50
9	A1	15c olive ('89)	27.50	19.00
10	A1	30c pearl gray ('89)	35.00	50.00
11	A1	60c olive bis ('89)	42.50	17.00
12	A1	1.50g lt & dk bl ('89)	100.00	80.00
		Nos. 8-12 (5)	300.00	218.50

Nos. 1-12 were issued without gum until 1890. Imperfs. are proofs.

Numeral — A2

1889 *Perf. 12½*

13	A2	1c gray	.85	1.00
14	A2	2c violet	.65	1.25
15	A2	2½c green	4.50	3.00
16	A2	3c bister	5.00	4.50
17	A2	5c rose	21.00	1.75
		Nos. 13-17 (5)	32.00	11.50

Black Handstamped Surcharge

1891 *Perf. 12½x12*

Without Gum

18	A1	25c on 30c pearl gray	15.00	14.00

No. 18 exists with double surcharge, value $225, and with inverted surcharge, value $275.

Queen Wilhelmina — A4

1892-96 *Perf. 12½*

19	A4	10c ultra ('95)	1.25	1.25
20	A4	12½c green	26.00	6.25
21	A4	15c rose ('93)	2.50	2.50
22	A4	25c brown orange	100.00	5.50
23	A4	30c gray ('96)	2.50	*5.50*
		Nos. 19-23 (5)	132.25	21.00

No. 4 Handstamped Surcharge in Magenta

No. 10 Handstamped Surcharge in Black

1895 *Perf. 12½, 13½x13*

25	A1	2½c on 10c ultra	13.00	8.00

Perf. 12½x12

26	A1	2½c on 30c gray	125.00	6.00

Nos. 25-26 exist with surcharge double or inverted.

No. 26 and No. 25, perf. 13½x13, were issued without gum.

Netherlands Nos. 77, 68 Surcharged in Black

1902, Jan. 1 *Perf. 12½*

27	A11	25c on 25c car & bl	2.00	2.00

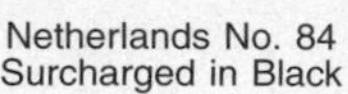

Netherlands No. 84 Surcharged in Black

1901, May 1 Engr. *Perf. 11½x11*

28	A12	1.50g on 2.50g brn lil	20.00	21.00

1902, Mar. 1 Typo. *Perf. 12½*

29	A11	12½c on 12½c blue	25.00	7.00

A9

A10

1904-08

30	A9	1c olive green	1.40	.90
31	A9	2c yellow brown	12.00	3.00
32	A9	2½c blue green	4.00	.35
33	A9	3c orange	7.50	4.00
34	A9	5c rose red	7.00	.35
35	A9	7½c gray ('08)	27.50	6.00
36	A10	10c slate	11.00	3.00
37	A10	12½c deep blue	1.25	.50
38	A10	15c brown	14.00	10.00
39	A10	22½c brn & ol ('08)	14.00	8.50
40	A10	25c violet	14.00	1.90
41	A10	30c brown orange	32.50	13.00
42	A10	50c red brown	27.50	8.25
		Nos. 30-42 (13)	173.65	59.75

Queen Wilhelmina — A11

1906, Nov. 1 Engr. *Perf. 11½*

Without Gum

43	A11	1½g red brown	35.00	25.00
44	A11	2½g slate blue	35.00	24.00

A12

Queen Wilhelmina

A13 A14

Perf. 12½, 11, 11½, 11x11½

1915-33 Typo.

45	A12	½c lilac ('20)	1.60	1.10
46	A12	1c olive green	.25	.25
47	A12	1½c blue ('20)	.25	.25
48	A12	2c yellow brn	1.25	1.40
49	A12	2½c green	.90	.25
50	A12	3c yellow	2.25	1.50
51	A12	3c green ('26)	2.60	2.50
52	A12	5c rose	2.00	.25
53	A12	5c green ('22)	3.75	2.75
54	A12	5c lilac ('26)	2.00	.25
55	A12	7½c drab	1.10	.30
56	A12	7½c bister ('20)	1.10	.25
57	A12	10c lilac ('22)	5.00	4.50
58	A12	10c rose ('26)	4.25	1.25
59	A13	10c car rose	13.00	3.00
60	A13	12½c blue	2.25	.50
61	A13	12½c red ('22)	2.00	1.60
62	A13	15c olive grn	.65	.65
63	A13	15c lt blue ('26)	4.00	2.50
64	A13	20c blue ('22)	6.50	3.00
65	A13	20c olive grn ('26)	2.50	2.25
66	A13	22½c orange	2.50	2.25
67	A13	25c red violet	3.25	.90
68	A13	30c slate	3.25	.65
69	A13	35c sl & red ('22)	3.25	4.25

Perf. 11½x11, 11½, 12½, 11

Engr.

70	A14	50c green	4.00	.25
71	A14	1½g violet	13.00	11.00
72	A14	2½g carmine	21.00	20.00
a.		Perf. 12½ ('33)	140.00	*300.00*
		Nos. 45-72 (28)	109.45	69.60

Some stamps of 1915 were also issued without gum.

For surcharges see #74, 107-108, C1-C3.

A15

Laid Paper, without Gum

1918, July 16 Typo. *Perf. 12*

73	A15	1c black, *buff*	6.75	3.75

"HAW" are the initials of Postmaster H. A. Willemsen.

No. 60 Surcharged in Black

1918, Sept. 1 *Perf. 12½*

74	A13	5c on 12½c blue	3.75	2.00
a.		"5" 2½mm wide	60.00	32.50
b.		Double surcharge		700.00

The "5" of No. 74 is 3mm wide. Illustration shows No. 74a surcharge.

Queen Wilhelmina — A16

1923 Engr. *Perf. 11½, 11x11½*

75	A16	5c green	1.00	2.00
76	A16	7½c olive grn	1.25	1.60
77	A16	10c car rose	1.75	2.00
78	A16	20c indigo	2.50	3.50
a.		Perf. 11x11½	3.25	4.25
79	A16	1g brown vio	30.00	19.00
80	A16	2½g gray black	70.00	*170.00*
81	A16	5g brown	90.00	*200.00*
a.		Perf. 11x11½	625.00	
		Nos. 75-81 (7)	196.50	*398.10*

25th anniv. of the assumption of the government of the Netherlands by Queen Wilhelmina, at the age of 18.

Nos. 80-81 with clear cancel between Aug. 1, 1923 and Apr. 30, 1924, sell for considerably more.

Types of Netherlands Marine Insurance Stamps, Inscribed "CURACAO" Surcharged in Black

1927, Oct. 3

87	MI1	3c on 15c dk green	.25	.30
88	MI1	10c on 60c car rose	.25	.45
89	MI1	12½c on 75c gray brn	.25	.45
90	MI2	15c on 1.50g dk bl	3.00	2.50
a.		Double surcharge	*500.00*	
91	MI2	25c on 2.25g org brn	6.50	6.25
92	MI3	30c on 4½g black	13.00	11.00
93	MI3	50c on 7½g red	7.50	7.25
		Nos. 87-93 (7)	30.75	28.20

Nos. 90, 91 and 92 have "FRANKEER-ZEGEL" in one line of small capitals. Nos. 90 and 91 have a heavy bar across the top of the stamp.

Queen Wilhelmina — A17

1928-30 Engr. *Perf. 11½, 12½*

No.	Type	Description	Unused	Used
95	A17	6c orange red ('30)	1.50	.40
a.		Booklet pane of 6		
96	A17	7½c orange red	.60	.45
97	A17	10c carmine	1.50	.35
98	A17	12½c red brown	1.50	1.00
a.		Booklet pane of 6		
99	A17	15c dark blue	1.50	.35
a.		Booklet pane of 6		
100	A17	20c blue black	5.75	.55
101	A17	21c yellow grn ('30)	9.25	14.00
102	A17	25c brown vio	3.50	1.40
103	A17	27½c black ('30)	12.00	14.00
104	A17	30c deep green	5.75	.55
105	A17	35c brnsh black	2.00	1.75
		Nos. 95-105 (11)	44.85	34.80

No. 96 Surcharged in Black with Bars over Original Value

1929, Nov. 1

No.	Type	Description	Unused	Used
106	A17	6c on 7½c org red	1.40	1.00
a.		Inverted surcharge	275.00	260.00

No. 51 Surcharged in Red

1931, Mar. 1 Typo. *Perf. 12½*

No.	Type	Description	Unused	Used
107	A12	2½c on 3c green	1.10	1.10

No. 49 Surcharged in Red

1932, Oct. 29

No.	Type	Description	Unused	Used
108	A12	1½c on 2½c grn	3.50	3.50

Prince William I, Portrait by Van Key — A18

1933 Photo. *Perf. 12½*

No.	Type	Description	Unused	Used
109	A18	6c deep orange	1.75	1.40

400th birth anniv. of Prince William I, Count of Nassau and Prince of Orange, frequently referred to as William the Silent.

Willem Usselinx — A19

Van Walbeeck's Ship — A22

Designs: 2½c, 5c, 6c, Frederik Hendrik. 10c, 12½c, 15c, Jacob Binckes. 27½c, 30c, 50c, Cornelis Evertsen the Younger. 1.50g, 2.50g, Louis Brion.

1934, Jan. 1 Engr. *Perf. 12½*

No.	Type	Description	Unused	Used
110	A19	1c black	1.00	1.25
111	A19	1½c dull violet	.75	.30
112	A19	2c orange	1.00	1.25
113	A19	2½c dull green	.85	1.25
114	A19	5c black brn	.85	.85
115	A19	6c violet bl	.75	.25
116	A19	10c lake	2.00	1.00
117	A19	12½c bister brn	6.50	7.00
118	A19	15c blue	1.60	1.00
119	A22	20c black	3.00	2.00
120	A22	21c brown	11.00	13.00
121	A22	25c dull green	11.00	11.00
122	A19	27½c brown vio	14.00	16.00
123	A19	30c scarlet	11.00	5.25
124	A19	50c orange	11.00	8.25
125	A19	1.50g indigo	47.50	50.00
126	A19	2.50g yellow grn	52.50	47.50
		Nos. 110-126 (17)	176.30	167.15

3rd centenary of the founding of the colony.

Numeral A25

Queen Wilhelmina A26

1936, Aug. 1 Litho. *Perf. 13½x13*

Size: 18x22mm

No.	Type	Description	Unused	Used
127	A25	1c brown black	.25	.25
128	A25	1½c deep ultra	.25	.25
129	A25	2c orange	.25	.25
130	A25	2½c green	.25	.25
131	A25	5c scarlet	.35	.25

Engr.

Perf. 12½

Size: 20¼x30½mm

No.	Type	Description	Unused	Used
132	A26	6c brown vio	.45	.25
133	A26	10c orange red	.85	.25
134	A26	12½c dk bl grn	1.50	.95
135	A26	15c dark blue	1.25	.60
136	A26	20c orange yel	1.25	.60
137	A26	21c dk gray	2.25	2.25
138	A26	25c brown lake	1.50	.75
139	A26	27½c violet brn	2.50	2.75
140	A26	30c olive brn	.60	.25

Perf. 13x14

Size: 22x33mm

No.	Type	Description	Unused	Used
141	A26	50c dull yel grn	3.00	.25
a.		Perf. 14	50.00	.25
142	A26	1.50g black brn	18.00	13.00
a.		Perf. 14	40.00	20.00
143	A26	2.50g rose lake	16.00	11.00
a.		Perf. 14	16.00	11.00
		Nos. 127-143 (17)	50.50	34.15

See Nos. 147-151. For surcharges see Nos. B1-B3.

Queen Wilhelmina — A27

Perf. 12½x12

1938, Aug. 27 Photo. Wmk. 202

No.	Type	Description	Unused	Used
144	A27	1½c dull purple	.25	.25
145	A27	6c red orange	.80	.75
146	A27	15c royal blue	1.50	1.25
		Nos. 144-146 (3)	2.55	2.25

Reign of Queen Wilhelmina, 40th anniv.

Numeral Type of 1936 and

Queen Wilhelmina — A28

1941-42 Unwmk. Litho. *Perf. 12½*

Thick Paper

Size: 17¾x22mm

No.	Type	Description	Unused	Used
147	A25	1c gray brn ('42)	1.50	1.25
148	A25	1½c dull blue ('42)	9.00	.25
149	A25	2c lt orange ('42)	8.00	4.00
150	A25	2½c green ('42)	1.00	.25
151	A25	5c crimson ('42)	1.00	.25

Photo.

Perf. 12½, 13

Size: 18½x23mm

No.	Type	Description	Unused	Used
152	A28	6c rose violet	2.00	2.00
153	A28	10c red orange	1.50	1.00
154	A28	12½c lt green	2.00	.90
155	A28	15c brt ultra	4.00	2.00
156	A28	20c orange	1.10	.55
157	A28	21c gray	2.25	1.75
158	A28	25c brown lake	2.25	1.60
159	A28	27½c deep brown	3.25	3.25
160	A28	30c olive bis	9.00	3.00

Size: 21x26½mm

No.	Type	Description	Unused	Used
161	A28	50c olive grn ('42)	12.00	.25
162	A28	1½g gray ol ('42)	17.00	1.75
163	A28	2½g rose lake ('42)	16.00	1.25
		Nos. 147-163 (17)	92.85	25.30

Imperfs. are proofs.

See Nos. 174-187.

Catalogue values for unused stamps in this section, from this point to the end of the section, are for Never Hinged items.

Bonaire A29

St. Eustatius — A30

Designs: 2c, View of Saba. 2½c, St. Maarten. 5c, Aruba. 6c, Curaçao.

Perf. 13x13½, 13½x13

1943, Feb. 1 Engr. Unwmk.

No.	Type	Description	Unused	Used
164	A29	1c rose vio & org brn	.25	.25
165	A30	1½c dp bl & yel grn	.25	.25
166	A29	2c sl blk & org brn	.60	.25
167	A29	2½c grn & org	.30	.25
168	A29	5c red & slate blk	1.25	.25
169	A29	6c rose lil & lt bl	.75	.60
		Nos. 164-169 (6)	3.40	1.85

Royal Family — A35

1943, Nov. 8 *Perf. 13½x13*

No.	Type	Description	Unused	Used
170	A35	1½c deep orange	.30	.30
171	A35	2½c red	.30	.30
172	A35	6c black	1.40	.70
173	A35	10c deep blue	1.40	1.25
		Nos. 170-173 (4)	3.40	2.55

Princess Margriet Francisca of the Netherlands.

Wilhelmina Type of 1941

1947 Photo. *Perf. 13½x13*

Size: 18x22mm

No.	Type	Description	Unused	Used
174	A28	6c brown vio	1.75	*2.25*
175	A28	10c orange red	1.75	*2.25*
176	A28	12½c dk blue grn	1.75	*2.25*
177	A28	15c dark blue	1.75	*3.00*
178	A28	20c orange yel	1.75	*3.75*
179	A28	21c dark gray	2.50	*3.75*
180	A28	25c brown lake	.25	.25
181	A28	27½c chocolate	2.25	3.00
182	A28	30c olive bister	2.00	1.25
183	A28	50c dull yel grn	2.10	.25

Perf. 13½x14

Engr.

Size: 25x31¼mm

No.	Type	Description	Unused	Used
184	A28	1½g dark brown	3.25	1.50
185	A28	2½g rose lake	60.00	27.50
186	A28	5g olive green	125.00	*200.00*
187	A28	10g red orange	160.00	*300.00*
		Nos. 174-187 (14)	366.10	551.00

Used values for Nos. 186-187 are for genuinely canceled copies clearly dated before the end of 1949.

A36

Queen Wilhelmina — A37

1948 Unwmk. Photo. *Perf. 13½x13*

No.	Type	Description	Unused	Used
188	A36	6c dk vio brn	1.10	1.25
189	A36	10c scarlet	1.10	*1.60*
190	A36	12½c dk blue grn	1.10	1.10
191	A36	15c deep blue	1.10	*1.25*
192	A36	20c red orange	1.10	*2.50*
193	A36	21c black	1.10	*2.50*
194	A36	25c brt red vio	.50	.25
195	A36	27½c henna brn	22.50	23.50
196	A36	30c olive brown	20.00	1.50
197	A36	50c olive green	19.00	.35

Perf. 12½x12

Engr.

No.	Type	Description	Unused	Used
198	A37	1.50g chocolate	37.50	8.50
		Nos. 188-198 (11)	106.10	44.30

Queen Wilhelmina — A38

1948, Aug. 30 *Perf. 13x14*

No.	Type	Description	Unused	Used
199	A38	6c vermilion	.75	.60
200	A38	12½c deep blue	.75	.60

Reign of Queen Wilhelmina, 50th anniv.

Queen Juliana — A39

Perf. 14x13½

1948, Oct. 18 Photo. Wmk. 202

No.	Type	Description	Unused	Used
201	A39	6c red brown	.75	.60
202	A39	12½c dark green	.75	.60

Investiture of Queen Juliana, Sept. 6, 1948. Nos. 201-202 were issued in Netherlands Sept. 6.

Ship of Ojeda — A40

Alonso de Ojeda — A41

Perf. 14x13, 13x14

1949, July 26 Photo. Unwmk.

203	A40	6c olive green	3.50	2.75
204	A41	12½c brown red	4.25	3.75
205	A40	15c ultra	4.75	3.75
		Nos. 203-205 (3)	12.50	10.25

450th anniversary of the discovery of Curaçao by Alonso de Ojeda, 1499.

Post Horns Entwined — A42

1949, Oct. 3 ***Perf. 12x12½***

206	A42	6c brown red	4.50	3.00
207	A42	25c dull blue	4.50	1.50

UPU, 75th anniversary.

A43

A44

Queen Juliana — A45

1950-79 Photo. ***Perf. 13x13½***

208	A43	1c red brown	.25	.25
209	A43	1½c blue	.25	.25
210	A43	2c orange	.25	.25
211	A43	2½c green	1.25	.25
212	A43	3c purple	.30	.25
212A	A43	4c yel grn ('59)	.80	.45
213	A43	5c dark red	.25	.25
		Perf. 13½x13		
214	A44	6c deep plum	1.50	.25
215	A44	7½c red brn ('54)	6.00	.25
216	A44	10c red	2.25	.25
a.		Redrawn ('79)	.25	.25
217	A44	12½c dk green	2.75	.25
218	A44	15c deep blue	2.75	.25
a.		Redrawn ('79)	.25	.25
219	A44	20c orange	3.00	.25
a.		Redrawn ('79)	.25	.25
220	A44	21c black	3.00	2.00
221	A44	22½c blue grn ('54)	6.75	.25
222	A44	25c violet	5.00	.25
a.		Redrawn ('79)	.25	.25
223	A44	27½c henna brn	7.50	2.50
224	A44	30c olive brown	13.50	.25
225	A44	50c olive green	14.00	.25
		Perf. 12½x12		
		Engr.		
226	A45	1½g slate grn	50.00	.35
227	A45	2½g black brn	60.00	2.00
228	A45	5g rose red	75.00	12.00
229	A45	10g dk vio brn	225.00	75.00
		Nos. 208-229 (23)	481.35	98.30

Nos. 216a, 218a, 219a and 222a are from booklets Nos. 427a and 428a. Background design is sharper and stamps have one or two straight edges.

See Nos. 427-429. For surcharge see No. B20.

Fort Beekenburg A46

Perf. 13½x12½

1953, June 16 Photo.

230	A46	22½c olive brown	7.00	.75

Founding of Fort Beekenburg, 250th anniv.

Beach at Aruba A47

1954, May 1 ***Perf. 11x11½***

231	A47	15c dk bl, sal & dp bl	5.00	3.00

3rd congress of the Caribbean Tourist Assoc., Aruba, May 3-6.

Queen Juliana — A48

1954, Dec. 15 ***Perf. 13½***

232	A48	7½c olive green	1.00	.75

Charter of the Kingdom, adopted Dec. 15, 1954. See Netherlands No. 366, Surinam No. 264.

Beach A49

Petroleum Refinery, Aruba — A50

1955, Dec. 5 Litho. ***Perf. 12***

233	A49	15c chnt, bl & emer	3.00	2.00
234	A50	25c chnt, bl & emer	4.00	2.75

Caribbean Commission, 21st meeting, Aruba.

St. Annabaai Harbor and Flags — A51

1956, Dec. 6 Unwmk. ***Perf. 14x13***

235	A51	15c lt bl, blk & red	.40	.30

Caribbean Commission, 10th anniversary.

Man Watching Rising Sun — A52

1957, Mar. 14 Photo. ***Perf. 11x11½***

236	A52	15c black & yellow	.30	.30

1st Caribbean Mental Health Conference, Aruba, Mar. 14-19.

Tourism A53

1957, July 1 Litho. ***Perf. 14x13***

237	A53	7½c Saba	.35	.30
238	A53	15c St. Maarten	.35	.30
239	A53	25c St. Eustatius	.35	.30
		Nos. 237-239 (3)	1.05	.90

Curaçao Intercontinental Hotel — A54

1957, Oct. 12 ***Perf. 14x13***

240	A54	15c lt ultra	.25	.25

Intercontinental Hotel, Willemstad, opening.

Map of Curaçao A55

1957, Dec. 10 ***Perf. 14x13½***

241	A55	15c indigo & lt bl	.55	.55

International Geophysical Year.

Flamingoes, Bonaire A56

Designs: 7½c, 8c, 25c, 1½g, Old buildings, Curaçao. 10c, 5g, Extinct volcano and palms, Saba. 15c, 30c, 1g, Fort Willem III, Aruba. 20c, 35c, De Ruyter obelisk, St. Eustatius. 12c, 40c, 2½g, Town Hall, St. Maarten.

1958-59 Litho. ***Perf. 14x13***

Size: 33x22mm

242	A56	6c lt ol grn & pink	2.00	.25
243	A56	7½c red brn & org	.25	.25
244	A56	8c dk bl & org ('59)	.25	.25
245	A56	10c gray & org yel	.25	.25
246	A56	12c bluish grn & gray ('59)	.25	.25
247	A56	15c grn & lt ultra	.25	.25
a.		15c green & lilac	.25	.25
248	A56	20c crim & gray	.25	.25
249	A56	25c Prus bl & yel grn	.25	.25
250	A56	30c brn & bl grn	.25	.25
251	A56	35c gray & rose ('59)	.30	.25
252	A56	40c mag & grn	.30	.25
253	A56	50c grysh brn & pink	.35	.25
254	A56	1g brt red & gray	.75	.25
255	A56	1½g rose vio & pale brn	1.10	.25
256	A56	2½g blue & citron	1.25	.30
257	A56	5g lt red brn & rose lil	3.75	.60
		Nos. 242-257 (16)	11.80	4.40

See Nos. 340-348, 400-403. For surcharge see No. B58.

Globe A57

1958, Oct. 16 ***Perf. 11x11½***

258	A57	7½c blue & lake	.25	.25
259	A57	15c red & ultra	.25	.25

50th anniv. of the Netherlands Antilles Radio and Telegraph Administration.

Hotel Aruba Caribbean A58

1959, July 18 ***Perf. 14x13***

260	A58	15c multi	.30	.30

Opening of the Hotel Aruba Caribbean, Aruba.

Sea Water Distillation Plant — A59

1959, Oct. 16 Photo. ***Perf. 14x13***

261	A59	20c bright blue	.35	.35

Opening of sea water distillation plant at Balashi, Aruba.

Netherlands Antilles Flag — A60

1959, Dec. 14 Litho. ***Perf. 13½***

262	A60	10c ultra & red	.30	.30
263	A60	20c ultra, yel & red	.30	.30
264	A60	25c ultra, grn & red	.30	.30
		Nos. 262-264 (3)	.90	.90

5th anniv. of the new constitution (Charter of the Kingdom).

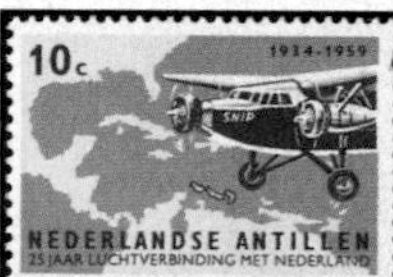

Fokker "Snip" and Map of Caribbean A61

Designs: 20c, Globe showing route flown, and plane. 25c, Map of Atlantic ocean and view of Willemstad. 35c, Map of Atlantic ocean and plane on Aruba airfield.

1959, Dec. 22 Unwmk. ***Perf. 14x13***

265	A61	10c yel, lt & dk bl	.30	.25
266	A61	20c yel, lt & dk bl	.30	.25
267	A61	25c yel, lt & dk bl	.30	.25
268	A61	35c yel, lt & dk bl	.30	.35
		Nos. 265-268 (4)	1.20	1.10

25th anniv. of Netherlands-Curaçao air service.

Msgr. Martinus J. Niewindt — A62

1960, Jan. 12 Photo. ***Perf. 13½***

269	A62	10c deep claret	.30	.25
270	A62	20c deep violet	.40	.40
271	A62	25c olive green	.40	.40
		Nos. 269-271 (3)	1.10	1.05

Death centenary of Monsignor Niewindt, first apostolic vicar for Curaçao.

Worker, Flag and Factories — A63

1960, Apr. 29 ***Perf. 12½x13½***
272 A63 20c multi .30 .30

Issued for Labor Day, May 1, 1960.

US Brig "Andrea Doria" and Gun at Fort Orange, St. Eustatius A64

1961, Nov. 16 **Litho.** ***Perf. 14x13½***
273 A64 20c bl, red, grn & blk .50 .50

185th anniv. of 1st salute by a foreign power to the US flag flown by an American ship.

Queen Juliana and Prince Bernhard A64a

1962, Jan. 31 **Photo.** ***Perf. 14x13***
274 A64a 10c deep orange .25 .25
275 A64a 25c deep blue .25 .25

Silver wedding anniversary of Queen Juliana and Prince Bernhard.

Benta Player — A65

6c, Corn masher. 20c, Petji kerchief. 25c, "Jaja" (nurse) with child, sculpture.

Perf. 12½x13½

1962, Mar. 14 **Photo.**

276 A65 6c red brn & yel	.25	.25
277 A65 10c shown	.25	.25
278 A65 20c crim, ind & brt grn	.30	.30
279 A65 25c brt grn, brn & gray	.30	.30
a. Souvenir sheet of 4, #276-279	1.25	1.25
Nos. 276-279 (4)	1.10	1.10

Emblem of Family Relationship A66

25c, Emblem of mental health (cross).

1963, Apr. 17 **Litho.** ***Perf. 14x13½***
280 A66 20c dk blue & ocher .30 .30
281 A66 25c blue & red .30 .30

Fourth Caribbean Conference for Mental Health, Curaçao, Apr. 17-23.

Dove with Olive Branch A67

1963, July 1 **Unwmk.** ***Perf. 14x13***
282 A67 25c org yel & dk brn .25 .25

Centenary of emancipation of the slaves.

Hotel Bonaire A68

1963, Aug. 31 ***Perf. 14x13***
283 A68 20c dk red brown .25 .25

Opening of Hotel Bonaire on Bonaire.

Prince William of Orange Taking Oath of Allegiance — A69

1963, Nov. 21 **Photo.** ***Perf. 13½x14***
284 A69 25c green, blk & rose .25 .25

150th anniversary of the founding of the Kingdom of the Netherlands.

Chemical Equipment A70

1963, Dec. 10 **Litho.** ***Perf. 14x13½***
285 A70 20c bl grn, brt yel grn & red .35 .35

Opening of chemical factories on Aruba.

Airmail Letter and Wings A71

Design: 25c, Map of Caribbean, Miami-Curaçao route and planes of 1929 and 1964.

1964, June 22 **Photo.** ***Perf. 11x11½***
286 A71 20c lt bl, red & ultra .25 .25
287 A71 25c lt grn, bl, red & blk .25 .25

35th anniversary of the first regular Curaçao airmail service.

Map of the Caribbean A72

1964, Nov. 30 **Litho.** **Unwmk.**
288 A72 20c ultra, org & dk red .25 .25

5th meeting of the Caribbean Council, Curaçao, Nov. 30-Dec. 4.

Netherlands Antilles Flags, Map of Curaçao and Crest — A73

1964, Dec. 14 **Litho.** ***Perf. 11½x11***
289 A73 25c lt bl & multi .25 .25

10th anniversary of the Charter of the Kingdom of the Netherlands. The flags, shaped like seagulls, represent the six islands comprising the Netherlands Antilles.

Princess Beatrix — A74

1965, Feb. 22 **Photo.** ***Perf. 13½x14***
290 A74 25c brick red .25 .25

Visit of Princess Beatrix of Netherlands.

ITU Emblem, Old and New Communication Equipment — A75

1965, May 17 **Litho.** ***Perf. 13½***
291 A75 10c brt bl & dk bl .25 .25

ITU, centenary.

Shell Refinery, Curaçao A76

10c, Catalytic cracking installation, vert. 25c, Workers operating manifold, primary distillation plant, vert.

Perf. 13½x14, 14x13½

1965, June 22 **Photo.**

292 A76 10c blk, red & yel	.25	.25
293 A76 20c multi	.25	.25
294 A76 25c multi	.25	.25
Nos. 292-294 (3)	.75	.75

50th anniv. of the oil industry in Curaçao.

Floating Market, Curaçao A77

Designs (flag and): 2c, Divi-divi tree and Haystack Mountain, Aruba. 3c, Laco, Saba. 4c, Flamingoes, Bonaire. 5c, Church ruins, St. Eustatius. 6c, Lobster, St. Maarten.

1965, Aug. 25 **Litho.** ***Perf. 14x13***

295 A77 1c lt grn, ultra & red	.25	.25
296 A77 2c yel, ultra & red	.25	.25
297 A77 3c chlky bl, ultra & red	.25	.25
298 A77 4c org, ultra & red	.25	.25
299 A77 5c lt bl, ultra & red	.25	.25
300 A77 6c pink, ultra & red	.25	.25
Nos. 295-300 (6)	1.50	1.50

Budgerigars, Wedding Rings and Initials — A79

1966, Mar. 10 **Photo.** ***Perf. 13½x14***
302 A79 25c gray & multi .25 .25

Issued to commemorate the marriage of Princess Beatrix and Claus van Amsberg.

M. A. de Ruyter and Map of St. Eustatius — A80

1966, June 19 **Photo.** ***Perf. 13½***
303 A80 25c vio, ocher & lt bl .25 .25

Visit of Adm. Michiel Adriaanszoon de Ruyter (1607-1676) to St. Eustatius, 1666.

Liberal Arts and Grammar A81

10c, Rhetoric and dialectic. 20c, Arithmetic and geometry. 25c, Astronomy and music.

Perf. 13½x12½

1966, Sept. 19 **Litho.** **Unwmk.**

304 A81 6c yel, bl & blk	.25	.25
305 A81 10c yel grn, red & blk	.25	.25
306 A81 20c bl, yel & blk	.25	.25
307 A81 25c red, yel grn & blk	.25	.25
Nos. 304-307 (4)	1.00	1.00

25th anniversary of secondary education.

Cruiser A82

Ships: 10c, Sailing ship. 20c, Tanker. 25c, Passenger ship.

Perf. 13½x14

1967, Mar. 29 **Litho.** **Unwmk.**

308 A82 6c lt & dk grn	.25	.25
309 A82 10c org & brn	.25	.25
310 A82 20c sep & brn	.25	.25
311 A82 25c chlky bl & dk bl	.25	.25
Nos. 308-311 (4)	1.00	1.00

60th anniv. of *Onze Vloot* (Our Fleet), an organization which publicizes the Dutch navy and merchant marine and helps seamen.

Manuel Carlos Piar (1777-1817), Independence Hero — A83

1967, Apr. 26 **Photo.** ***Perf. 14x13***
312 A83 20c red & blk .25 .25

Marine Guarding Beach — A78

1965, Dec. 10 **Photo.** ***Perf. 13x10½***
301 A78 25c multi .25 .25

Netherlands Marine Corps, 300th anniv.

Discobolus after Myron — A84

10c, Hand holding torch, & Olympic rings. 25c, Stadium, doves & Olympic rings.

1968, Feb. 19 Litho. *Perf. 13x14*

313 A84 10c multi .25 .25
314 A84 20c dk brn, ol & yel .25 .25
315 A84 25c bl, dk bl & brt yel grn .25 .25
Nos. 313-315 (3) .75 .75

19th Olympic Games, Mexico City, 10/12-27.

Friendship 500 — A84a

Designs: 20c, Beechcraft Queen Air. 25c, Friendship and DC-9.

1968, Dec. 3 Litho. *Perf. 14x13*

315A A84a 10c dl yel, blk & brt bl .25 .25
315B A84a 20c tan, blk & brt bl .25 .25
315C A84a 25c sal pink, blk & brt bl .25 .25
Nos. 315A-315C (3) .75 .75

Dutch Antillean Airlines (ALM).

Map of Bonaire, Radio Mast and Waves — A85

1969, Mar. 6 *Perf. 14x13½*

316 A85 25c bl, emer & blk .25 .25

Opening of the relay station of the Dutch World Broadcasting System on Bonaire.

Code of Law — A86

Designs: 25c, Scales of Justice.

Perf. 12½x13½

1969, May 19 Photo.

317 A86 20c dk grn, yel grn & gold .25 .25
318 A86 25c vio bl, bl & gold .25 .25

Court of Justice, centenary.

ILO Emblem, Cactus and House — A87

1969, Aug. 25 Litho. *Perf. 14x13*

319 A87 10c bl & blk .25 .25
320 A87 25c dk red & blk .25 .25

ILO, 50th anniversary.

Queen Juliana and Rising Sun — A87a

1969, Dec. 12 Photo. *Perf. 14x13*

321 A87a 25c bl & multi .25 .25

15th anniv. of the Charter of the Kingdom of the Netherlands. Phosphorescent paper.

Radio Bonaire Studio and Transmitter — A88

Design: 15c, Radio waves and cross set against land, sea and air.

1970, Feb. 5 Photo. *Perf. 12½x13½*

322 A88 10c multi .25 .25
323 A88 15c multi .25 .25

5th anniv. of the opening of the Trans World Missionary Radio Station, Bonaire.

Altar, St. Anna's Church, Otraband 1752 — A89

20c, Interior, Synagogue at Punda, 1732, horiz. 25c, Pulpit, Fort Church, Fort Amsterdam, 1769.

Perf. 13½x14, 14x13½

1970, May 12 Photo.

324 A89 10c gold & multi .25 .25
325 A89 20c gold & multi .25 .25
326 A89 25c gold & multi .25 .25
Nos. 324-326 (3) .75 .75

St. Theresia Church, St. Nicolaas A90

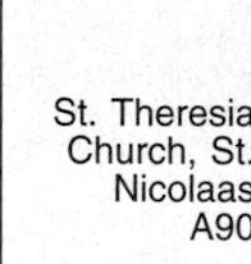

1971, Feb. 9 Litho. *Perf. 14x13½*

327 A90 20c dl bl, gray & rose .25 .25

40th anniversary of the Parish of St. Theresia at St. Nicolaas, Aruba.

A91

1971, Feb. 24 *Perf. 13½x14*

328 A91 25c Lions emblem .25 .25

Lions Club in the Netherlands Antilles, 25th anniversary.

A91a

Prince Bernhard, Fokker F27, Boeing 747B.

1971, June 29 Photo. *Perf. 13x14*

329 A91a 45c multi .40 .40

60th birthday of Prince Bernhard.

Pedro Luis Brion (1782-1821), Naval Commander in Fight for South American Independence A92

1971, Sept. 27 Photo. *Perf. 13x12½*

330 A92 40c multi .25 .25

Flamingoes, Bonaire A93

Designs: 1c, Queen Emma Bridge, Curaçao. 2c, The Bottom, Saba. 4c, Water tower, Aruba. 5c, Fort Amsterdam, St. Maarten. 6c, Fort Orange, St. Eustatius.

1972, Jan. 17 Litho. *Perf. 13½x14*

331 A93 1c yel & multi .25 .25
332 A93 2c yel grn & multi .25 .25
333 A93 3c dp org & multi .25 .25
334 A93 4c brt bl & multi .25 .25
335 A93 5c red org & multi .25 .25
336 A93 6c lil rose & multi .25 .25
Nos. 331-336 (6) 1.50 1.50

Ship in Dry Dock — A94

1972, Apr. 7 *Perf. 14x13½*

337 A94 30c bl gray & multi .25 .25

Inauguration of large dry dock facilities in Willemstad.

Juan Enrique Irausquin — A95

1972, June 20 Photo. *Perf. 13x14*

338 A95 30c deep orange .25 .25

Irausquin (1904-1962), financier and patriot.

Costa Gomez — A96

1972, Oct. 27 Litho.

339 A96 30c yel grn & blk .25 .25

Moises Frumencio da Costa Gomez (1907-1966), lawyer, legislator, patriot.

Island Series Type of 1958-59

Designs: 45c, 85c, Extinct volcano and palms, Saba. 55c, 90c, De Ruyter obelisk, St. Eustatius. 65c, 75c, 10g, Flamingoes, Bonaire. 70c, Fort Willem III, Aruba. 95c, Town Hall, St. Maarten.

1973, Feb. 12 Litho. *Perf. 14x13*

Size: 33x22mm

340 A56 45c vio bl & lt bl .35 .25
341 A56 55c dk car rose & emer .40 .25
342 A56 65c green & pink .45 .25
343 A56 70c gray vio & org 1.00 .25
344 A56 75c brt lilac & salmon .50 .30
345 A56 85c brn ol & apple grn .60 .30
346 A56 90c blue & ocher .65 .35
347 A56 95c orange & yellow .80 .40
348 A56 10g brt ultra & sal 6.50 3.75
Nos. 340-348 (9) 11.25 6.10

Mailman — A97

Designs: 15c, King William III from 1873 issue. 30c, Emblem of Netherlands Antilles postal service.

1973, May 23 Photo. *Perf. 13x14*

349 A97 15c lil, gold & vio .25 .25
350 A97 20c dk grn & multi .30 .25
351 A97 30c org & multi .30 .25
Nos. 349-351 (3) .85 .75

Centenary of first stamps of Netherlands Antilles.

Cable Linking Aruba, Curaçao and Bonaire A98

30c, 6 stars symbolizing the islands, cable. 45c, Saba, St. Maarten and St. Eustatius linked by cable.

1973, June 20 Litho. *Perf. 14x13*

352 A98 15c multi .30 .30
353 A98 30c multi .35 .30
354 A98 45c multi .35 .30
a. Souvenir sheet of 3, #352-354 1.75 1.50
Nos. 352-354 (3) 1.00 .90

Inauguration of the inter-island submarine cable.

Queen Juliana, Netherlands Antilles and House of Orange Colors — A99a

Engr. & Photo.

1973, Sept. 4 *Perf. 12½x12*

355 A99a 15c silver & multi .40 .40

25th anniversary of reign of Queen Juliana.

Jan Hendrik Albert Eman — A99

1973, Oct. 17 Litho. *Perf. 13x14*

356 A99 30c lt yel grn & blk .25 .25

Eman (1888-1957), founder of the People's Party in Aruba, member of Antillean Parliament.

Lionel Bernard Scott — A100

1974, Jan. 28

357 A100 30c lt bl & multi .25 .25

Scott (1897-1966), architect and statesman.

Family at Supper — A101

Designs: 12c, Parents watching children at play. 15c, Mother and daughter sewing, father and son gardening.

1974, Feb. 18 Litho. *Perf. 13x14*

358 A101 6c bl & multi .25 .25
359 A101 12c bis & multi .25 .25
360 A101 15c grn & multi .25 .25
Nos. 358-360 (3) .75 .75

Planned parenthood and World Population Year.

Desulphurization Plant, Lago — A102

Designs: 30c, Distillation plant. 45c, Lago refinery at night.

1974, Aug. 12 Litho. *Perf. 14x13*

361 A102 15c lt bl, blk & yel .25 .25
362 A102 30c lt bl, blk & yel .30 .30
363 A102 45c dk brn & multi .40 .40
Nos. 361-363 (3) .95 .95

Oil industry in Aruba, 50th anniversary.

UPU Emblem — A103

1974, Oct. 9 Litho. *Perf. 13x14*

364 A103 15c yel grn, blk & gold .35 .30
365 A103 30c bl, blk & gold .35 .30

Centenary of Universal Postal Union.

Queen Emma Bridge A104

Willemstad Bridges: 30c, Queen Juliana Bridge. 40c, Queen Wilhelmina Bridge.

1975, Feb. 5 Litho. *Perf. 14x13*

366 A104 20c ultra & multi .30 .25
367 A104 30c ultra & multi .30 .30
368 A104 40c ultra & multi .40 .40
Nos. 366-368 (3) 1.00 .95

Dedication of new Queen Juliana Bridge spanning Curaçao Harbor.

Salt Crystals A105

Designs: 20c, Solar salt pond. 40c, Map of Bonaire and location of solar salt pond, vert.

Perf. 14x13, 13x14

1975, Apr. 24 Litho.

369 A105 15c multi .30 .25
370 A105 20c multi .30 .30
371 A105 40c multi .40 .30
Nos. 369-371 (3) 1.00 .85

Bonaire's salt industry.

Aruba Airport, 1935 and Fokker F-18 — A106

30c, Aruba Airport, 1950, & Douglas DC-9. 40c, New Princess Beatrix Airport & Boeing 727.

1975, June 19 Litho. *Perf. 14x13*

372 A106 15c vio & multi .25 .25
373 A106 30c blk & multi .35 .30
374 A106 40c yel & multi .35 .30
Nos. 372-374 (3) .95 .85

40th anniversary of Aruba Airport.

International Women's Year Emblem A107

12c, "Women's role in social development." 20c, Embryos within female & male symbols.

1975, Aug. 1 Photo. *Perf. 14x13*

375 A107 6c multi .25 .25
376 A107 12c multi .25 .25
377 A107 20c multi .30 .30
Nos. 375-377 (3) .80 .80

International Women's Year 1975.

Beach, Aruba A108

Tourist Publicity: No. 379, Beach pavilion and boat, Bonaire. No. 380, Table Mountain and Spanish Water, Curaçao.

1976, June 21 Litho. *Perf. 14x13*

378 A108 40c blue & multi .40 .40
379 A108 40c blue & multi .40 .40
380 A108 40c blue & multi .40 .40
Nos. 378-380 (3) 1.20 1.20

Julio Antonio Abraham — A109

1976, Aug. 10 Photo. *Perf. 13x14*

381 A109 30c tan & claret .30 .30

Julio Antonio Abraham (1909-1960), founder of Democratic Party of Bonaire.

Dike and Produce — A110

1976, Sept. 21 Litho.

382 A110 15c shown .30 .25
383 A110 35c Cattle .40 .35
384 A110 45c Fish .40 .40
Nos. 382-384 (3) 1.10 1.00

Agriculture, husbandry and fishing in Netherlands Antilles.

Plaque, Fort Oranje Memorial A111

Designs: 40c, Andrea Doria in St. Eustatius harbor receiving salute. 55c, Johannes de Graaff, Governor of St. Eustatius, holding Declaration of Independence.

1976, Nov. 16 Litho. *Perf. 14x13*

385 A111 25c multi .50 .30
386 A111 40c multi .50 .30
387 A111 55c multi .50 .50
Nos. 385-387 (3) 1.50 1.10

First gun salute to US flag, St. Eustatius, Nov. 16, 1776.

See. No. 619.

Dancer with Cactus Headdress — A112

Carnival: 35c, Woman in feather costume. 40c, Woman in pompadour costume.

1977, Jan. 20 Litho. *Perf. 13x14*

388 A112 25c multi .40 .30
389 A112 35c multi .40 .30
390 A112 40c multi .40 .30
Nos. 388-390 (3) 1.20 .90

Bird Petroglyph, Aruba — A113

Indian Petroglyphs: 35c, Loops and spiral, Savonet Plantation, Curaçao. 40c, Tortoise, Onima, Bonaire.

1977, Mar. 29

391 A113 25c red & multi .35 .30
392 A113 35c brn & multi .35 .30
393 A113 40c yel & multi .45 .30
Nos. 391-393 (3) 1.15 .90

A114

Tropical Trees: 25c, Cordia Sebestena. 40c, East Indian walnut, vert. 55c, Tamarind.

1977, July 20 *Perf. 14x13, 13x14*

394 A114 25c blk & multi .30 .30
395 A114 40c blk & multi .40 .30
396 A114 55c blk & multi .50 .50
Nos. 394-396 (3) 1.20 1.10

A115

Designs: 20c, Chimes, Spritzer & Fuhrmann Building. 40c, Globe with Western Hemisphere and sun over Curaçao. 55c, Diamond ring and flag of Netherlands Antilles.

1977, Sept. 27 Litho. *Perf. 13x14*

397 A115 20c brt grn & multi .30 .25
398 A115 40c yel & multi .40 .35
399 A115 55c bl & multi .50 .50
Nos. 397-399 (3) 1.20 1.10

Spritzer & Fuhrmann, jewelers of Netherlands Antilles, 50th anniversary.

Island Series Type of 1958-59

Designs: 20c, 35c, 55c, De Ruyter obelisk, St. Eustatius. 40c, Town Hall, St. Maarten.

Perf. 13½ Horiz.

1977, Nov. 30 Photo.

Size: 39x22mm

400 A56 20c crim & gray .70 .50
a. Bklt. pane of 6 (2 #400, 4 #402) 5.25
401 A56 35c gray & rose 1.10 .80
a. Bklt. pane of 4 (1 #401, 3 #403) 6.00
402 A56 40c magenta & grn .70 .50
403 A56 55c dk car rose & emer 1.10 1.10
Nos. 400-403 (4) 3.60 2.90

Nos. 400-403 issued in booklets only. No. 400a has label with red inscription in size of 3 stamps; No. 401a has label with dark carmine rose inscription in size of 2 stamps.

Winding Road, Map of Saba — A116

Tourism: 35c, Ruins of Synagogue, map of St. Eustatius. 40c, Greatbay, Map of St. Maarten.

1977, Nov. 30 Litho. *Perf. 14x13*

404 A116 25c multi .25 .25
405 A116 35c multi .25 .25
406 A116 40c multi .25 .25
Nos. 404-406 (3) .75 .75

Tete-beche gutter pairs exist.

Treasure Chest A117

Designs: 20c, Logo of Netherlands Antilles Bank. 40c, Safe deposit door.

1978, Feb. 7 Litho. *Perf. 14x13*

407 A117 15c brt & dk bl .25 .25
408 A117 20c org & gold .25 .25
409 A117 40c brt & dk grn .25 .25
Nos. 407-409 (3) .75 .75

Bank of Netherlands Antilles, 150th anniv. Tete-beche gutter pairs exist.

Flamboyant — A118

Flowers: 25c, Erythrina velutina. 40c, Guaiacum officinale, horiz. 55c, Gliricidia sepium, horiz.

Perf. 13x14, 14x13

1978, May 31 **Litho.**

410 A118 15c multi .25 .25
411 A118 25c multi .25 .25
412 A118 40c multi .30 .25
413 A118 55c multi .35 .35
Nos. 410-413 (4) 1.15 1.10

Polythysana Rubrescens — A119

Butterflies: 25c, Caligo eurilochus. 35c, Prepona omphale amesis. 40c, Morpho aega.

1978, June 20 ***Perf. 13x14***

414 A119 15c multi .25 .25
415 A119 25c multi .25 .25
416 A119 35c multi .30 .25
417 A119 40c multi .35 .35
Nos. 414-417 (4) 1.15 1.10

"Conserve Energy" — A120

1978, Aug. 31 **Litho.** ***Perf. 13x14***

418 A120 15c org & blk .25 .25
419 A120 20c dp grn & blk .25 .25
420 A120 40c dk red & blk .30 .30
Nos. 418-420 (3) .80 .80

Morse Ship-to-Shore Service A121

Designs: 40c, Ship-to-shore telex service. 55c, Future radar-satellite service, vert.

Perf. 14x13, 13x14

1978, Oct. 16 **Litho.**

421 A121 20c multi .25 .25
422 A121 40c multi .30 .30
423 A121 55c multi .45 .45
Nos. 421-423 (3) 1.00 1.00

Ship-to-shore communications, 70th anniv.

Villa Maria Waterworks A122

35c, Leonard B. Smith, vert. 40c, Opening of Queen Emma Bridge, Willemstadt, 1888.

1978, Dec. 13

424 A122 25c multi .25 .25
425 A122 35c multi .25 .25
426 A122 40c multi .30 .25
Nos. 424-426 (3) .80 .75

L. B. Smith, engineer, 80th death anniv.

Queen Juliana Type of 1950

1979, Jan. 11 **Photo.** ***Perf. 13½x13***

427 A44 5c dp yel .25 .25
a. Bklt. pane of 10 (4 #427, 1 #216a, 2 #222a, 3 #429) 3.00
428 A44 30c brown .25 .25
a. Bklt. pane of 10 (1 #428, 4 #218a, 3 #219a, 2 #222a) 3.00
429 A44 40c brt bl .30 .25
Nos. 427-429 (3) .80 .75

Nos. 427-429 issued in booklets only. Nos. 427a-428a have 2 labels and selvages the size of 6 stamps. Background design of booklet stamps sharper than 1950 issue. All stamps have 1 or 2 straight edges.

Goat and Conference Emblem A123

75c, Horse & map of Curaçao. 150c, Cattle, Netherlands Antilles flag, UN & Conf. emblems.

1979, Apr. 18 **Litho.** ***Perf. 14x13***

437 A123 50c multi .30 .30
438 A123 75c multi .40 .40
439 A123 150c multi .75 .75
a. Souv. sheet of 3, perf. 13½x13 1.50 1.50
Nos. 437-439 (3) 1.45 1.45

12th Inter-American Meeting at Ministerial Level on Foot and Mouth Disease and Zoonosis Control, Curaçao, Apr. 17-20. No. 439a contains Nos. 437-439 in changed colors.

Dutch Colonial Soldier, Emblem — A124

1979, July 4 **Litho.** ***Perf. 13x14***

440 A124 1g multi .55 .50
Nos. 440,B166-B167 (3) 1.20 1.10

Netherlands Antilles Volunteer Corps, 50th anniv.

A125

Flowering Trees: 25c, Casearia Tremula. 40c, Cordia cylindro-stachya. 1.50g, Melochia tomentosa.

1979, Sept. 3 **Litho.** ***Perf. 13x14***

441 A125 25c multi .25 .25
442 A125 40c multi .30 .30
443 A125 1.50g multi .75 .75
Nos. 441-443 (3) 1.30 1.30

A126

Designs: 65c, Dove and Netherlands flag. 1.50g, Dove and Netherlands Antilles flag.

1979, Dec. 6 **Litho.** ***Perf. 13x14***

444 A126 65c multi .50 .40
445 A126 1.50g multi .80 .80

Constitution, 25th anniversary.

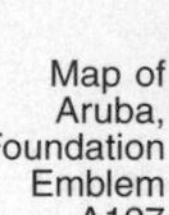

Map of Aruba, Foundation Emblem A127

1g, Foundation headquarters, Aruba.

1979, Dec. 18 ***Perf. 14x13***

446 A127 95c multi .60 .60
447 A127 1g multi .70 .70

Cultural Foundation Center, Aruba, 30th anniv.

Cupola, 1910, Fort Church — A128

1980, Jan. 9 ***Perf. 13x14***

448 A128 100c multi .60 .60
Nos. 448,B172-B173 (3) 1.30 1.30

Fort Church, Curaçao, 210th anniv. (1979).

Rotary Emblem A129

Designs: 50c, Globe and cogwheels. 85c, Cogwheel and Rotary emblem.

1980, Feb. 22 **Litho.** ***Perf. 14x13***

449 A129 45c multi .25 .25
450 A129 50c multi .30 .30
451 A129 85c multi .50 .50
a. Souvenir sheet of 3, #449-451, perf. 13½x13 1.10 1.10
b. Strip of 3, #449-451 1.10 1.10

Rotary Intl., 75th anniv. No. 451a has continuous design.

Coin Box, 1905 — A130

Post Office Savings Bank of Netherlands Antilles, 75th Anniv.: 150c, Coin box, 1980.

1980, Apr. 2 **Litho.** ***Perf. 14x13***

452 A130 25c multi .25 .25
453 A130 150c multi .90 .90

Netherlands Antilles No. 200, Arms — A131

60c, No. 290, royal crown.

1980, Apr. 29 **Photo.**

454 A131 25c shown .25 .25
455 A131 60c multicolored .30 .30
a. Bklt. pane of 5 + 3 labels (#428, 2 #454, 2 #455) 3.00

Abdication of Queen Juliana of the Netherlands.

Tete-beche gutter pairs exist.

Sir Rowland Hill (1795-1879), Originator of Penny Postage A132

60c, London 1980 emblem. 1g, Airmail label.

1980, May 6 **Litho.**

456 A132 45c shown .30 .30
457 A132 60c multicolored .30 .30
458 A132 1g multicolored .70 .70
a. Souv. sheet of 3, perf. 13½x14 1.40 1.40
Nos. 456-458 (3) 1.30 1.30

London 1980 Intl. Stamp Exhibition, May 6-14. No. 458a contains Nos. 456-458 in changed colors.

Leptotila Verreauxi A133

1980, Sept. 3 **Litho.** ***Perf. 14x13***

459 A133 25c shown .30 .25
460 A133 60c Mockingbird .55 .55
461 A133 85c Coereba flaveola .75 .75
Nos. 459-461 (3) 1.60 1.55

Rudolf Theodorus Palm — A134

1g, Score, hand playing piano.

1981, Jan. 27 **Litho.** ***Perf. 13x14***

462 A134 60c shown .40 .40
463 A134 1g multicolored .75 .70

Palm, composer, birth centenary.

Alliance Mission Emblem, Map of Aruba A135

1981, Mar. 24 ***Perf. 14x13***

464 A135 30c shown .25 .25
465 A135 50c Curaçao .40 .30
466 A135 1g Bonaire map .75 .70
Nos. 464-466 (3) 1.40 1.25

Evangelical Alliance Mission anniversaries: 35th in Aruba, 50th in Curaçao, 30th in Bonaire.

St. Elisabeth's Hospital, 125th Anniv. A136

1981, June 24 **Litho.** ***Perf. 14x13***

467 A136 60c Gateway .40 .40
468 A136 1.50g shown 1.00 1.00

Oregano Blossom — A137

1981, Nov. 24 **Litho.** ***Perf. 13x14***

469 A137 45c shown .30 .30
470 A137 70c Flaira .50 .50
471 A137 100c Welisali .70 .70
Nos. 469-471 (3) 1.50 1.50

Ship Pilot Service Cent. — A138

Designs: Various ships.

1982, Jan. 13 Litho. *Perf. 13x14*
472 A138 70c multi .55 .55
473 A138 85c multi .60 .60
474 A138 1g multi .70 .70
Nos. 472-474 (3) 1.85 1.85

A139

1982, Mar. 15 Litho. *Perf. 13x14*
475 A139 75c Altar .60 .60
476 A139 85c Building .60 .60
477 A139 150c Pulpit 1.00 1.00
Nos. 475-477 (3) 2.20 2.20

Community Mikve Israel-Emanuel Synagogue, 250th anniv.

A140

75c, Flags, Peter Stuyvesant.

1982, Apr. 21 Litho. *Perf. 13x14*
478 A140 75c multicolored .70 .70
a. Souvenir sheet .75 .75

US-Netherlands diplomatic relations bicentenary.
See. No. 619b.

A141

1982, May 5
479 A141 35c Radar screen .30 .30
480 A141 75c Control tower .60 .60
481 A141 150c Antenna 1.00 1.00
Nos. 479-481 (3) 1.90 1.90

Intl. Air Traffic Controllers' Year.

A142

1982, June 9 Litho. *Perf. 13x14*
482 A142 45c Emblem .30 .30
483 A142 85c Mail bag .60 .60
484 A142 150c Flags of France, Neth. Ant. 1.10 1.00
a. Souvenir sheet of 3, #482-484 2.25 2.25
Nos. 482-484 (3) 2.00 1.90

PHILEXFRANCE '82 Stamp Exhibition, Paris, June 11-21.

Brown Chromis A143

1982, Sept. 15 Litho. *Perf. 14x13*
485 A143 35c shown .50 .50
486 A143 75c Spotted trunkfish 1.00 1.00
487 A143 85c Blue tang 1.10 1.10
488 A143 100c French angelfish 1.40 1.40
Nos. 485-488 (4) 4.00 4.00

Natural Bridge, Aruba A144

1983, Apr. 12 Litho. *Perf. 14x13*
489 A144 35c shown .30 .30
490 A144 45c Lac-Bay, Bonaire .40 .40
491 A144 100c Willemstad, Curaçao .90 .90
Nos. 489-491 (3) 1.60 1.60

World Communications Year — A145

1983, May 17 Litho. *Perf. 13x14*
492 A145 1g multi .90 .90
a. Souvenir sheet .95 .95

BRASILIANA '83 — A146

45c, Ship, postal building, Waalgat. 55c, Flags, emblem. 100c, Governor's Palace, Sugar Loaf Mt.

1983, June 29 Litho. *Perf. 13x14*
493 A146 45c multi .50 .50
494 A146 55c multi .55 .55
495 A146 100c multi .95 .95
a. Souvenir sheet of 3, #493-495 2.25 2.25
Nos. 493-495 (3) 2.00 2.00

Fruit Tree — A147

45c, Mangifera indica. 55c, Malpighia punicifolia. 100c, Citrus aurantifolia.

1983, Sept. 13 Litho. *Perf. 13x14*
496 A147 45c multicolored .70 .70
497 A147 55c multicolored .80 .80
498 A147 100c multicolored 1.40 1.40
Nos. 496-498 (3) 2.90 2.90

Local Government Buildings A148

1983, Dec. 20 Litho. *Perf. 14x13*
499 A148 20c Saba .25 .25
500 A148 25c St. Eustatius .25 .25
501 A148 30c St. Maarten .30 .30
502 A148 35c Aruba *.30* *.30*
503 A148 45c Bonaire .40 .40
a. Perf. 13½ horiz. ('86) .25 .25
504 A148 55c Curaçao .50 .50
a. Perf. 13½ horiz. ('86) .25 .25
b. Bklt. pane of 4 + label (2 #503a, 504a) ('86) 1.75
Nos. 499-504 (6) 2.00 2.00

See Nos. 515-520, 543A-555.

Amigoe di Curaçao Newspaper Centenary A149

45c, Copy programming. 55c, Printing press. 85c, Man reading newspaper.

1984, Jan. 5 Litho.
505 A149 45c multicolored .40 .40
506 A149 55c multicolored .50 .50
507 A149 85c multicolored .90 .90
Nos. 505-507 (3) 1.80 1.80

40th Anniv. of Intl. Civil Aviation Org. — A150

Various emblems.

1984, Feb. 28 Litho. *Perf. 14x13*
508 A150 25c Winair .25 .25
509 A150 45c ICAO .40 .40
510 A150 55c ALM .50 .50
511 A150 100c Plane .90 .90
Nos. 508-511 (4) 2.05 2.05

Chamber of Commerce and Industry Centenary — A151

45c, Bonnet maker. 55c, Emblem. 100c, River, bridge, boat.

1984, May 29 Litho. *Perf. 13½*
512 A151 45c multicolored .60 .60
513 A151 55c multicolored .60 .60
514 A151 100c multicolored .95 .95
Nos. 512-514 (3) 2.15 2.15

Govt. Building Type of 1983

1984, June 26 Litho. *Perf. 14x13*
515 A148 60c like 20c .55 .55
516 A148 65c like 25c .60 .60
517 A148 75c like 30c .75 .75
518 A148 85c like 35c .85 .85
519 A148 90c like 45c .90 .90
520 A148 95c like 55c 1.00 1.00
Nos. 515-520 (6) 4.65 4.65

For surcharges see Nos. B306-B307.

Local Birds — A152

45c, Tiaris bicolor. 55c, Zonotrichia capensis. 150c, Chlorostilbon mellisugus.

1984, Sept. 18 Litho. *Perf. 14x13*
521 A152 45c multi .85 .85
522 A152 55c multi 1.10 1.10
523 A152 150c multi 2.25 2.25
Nos. 521-523 (3) 4.20 4.20

Eleanor Roosevelt (1884-1962) — A153

1984, Oct. 11 Litho. *Perf. 13x14*
524 A153 45c At Hyde Park .50 .50
525 A153 85c Portrait .80 .80
526 A153 100c Reading to children .90 .90
Nos. 524-526 (3) 2.20 2.20

Tete-beche gutter pairs exist.

Flamingos A154

1985, Jan. 9 Litho. *Perf. 14x13*
527 A154 25c Adult pullets .55 .55
528 A154 45c Juveniles .90 .90
529 A154 55c Adults wading 1.10 1.10
530 A154 100c Adults flying 1.60 1.60
Nos. 527-530 (4) 4.15 4.15

Curaçao Masonic Lodge Bicent. — A155

45c, Compass, sun, moon and stars. 55c, Doorway, columns and 5 steps. 100c, Star, 7 steps.

1985, Feb. 21 Litho. *Perf. 13x14*
531 A155 45c multi .50 .50
532 A155 55c multi .70 .70
533 A155 100c multi 1.10 1.10
Nos. 531-533 (3) 2.30 2.30

UN, 40th Anniv. A156

1985, June 5 Litho. *Perf. 14x13*
534 A156 55c multi .60 .60
535 A156 1g multi 1.00 1.00

Papiamentu, Language of the Antilles A157

45c, Pierre Lauffer (1920-1981), author and poem Patria. 55c, Waves of Papiamentu.

1985, Sept. 4 Litho. *Perf. 14x13*
536 A157 45c multi .45 .45
537 A157 55c multi .60 .60

Tete-beche gutter pairs exist.

Flora — A158

5c, Calotropis procera. 10c, Capparis flexuosa. 20c, Mimosa distachya. 45c, Ipomoea nil. 55c, Heliotropium ternatum. 1.50g, Ipomoea incarnata.

1985, Nov. 6 *Perf. 13x14*

538 A158 5c multi .30 .25
539 A158 10c multi .30 .25
540 A158 20c multi .45 .30
541 A158 45c multi .70 .50
542 A158 55c multi .85 .55
543 A158 1.50g multi 1.40 1.25
Nos. 538-543 (6) 4.00 3.10

Govt. Building Type of 1983

1985-89 *Perf. 14x13*

543A A148 70c like 20c ('88) .50 .40
543B A148 85c like 45c ('88) .60 .55
544 A148 1g like 20c 1.00 1.00
545 A148 1.50g like 25c 1.25 1.25
546 A148 2.50g like 30c ('86) 2.10 1.75
551 A148 5g like 45c ('86) 4.25 3.50
554 A148 10g like 55c ('87) 7.25 5.75
555 A148 15g like 20c ('89) 10.50 9.25
Nos. 543A-555 (8) 27.45 23.45

Issued: 70c, 85c, 3/16; 1g, 1.50g, 12/4; 2.50g, 1/8; 5g, 12/3; 10g, 5/20; 15g, 2/8.

For surcharge see No. B308.

Curaçao Town Hall, 125th Anniv. A159

1986, Jan. 8 *Perf. 14x13, 13x14*

561 A159 5c Town Hall .25 .25
562 A159 15c State room, vert. .25 .25
563 A159 25c Court room .25 .25
564 A159 55c Entrance, vert. .50 .50
Nos. 561-564 (4) 1.25 1.25

Amnesty Intl., 25th Anniv. A160

45c, Prisoner chained. 55c, Peace bird imprisoned. 100c, Prisoner behind bars.

1986, May 28 Litho. *Perf. 14x13*

565 A160 45c multi .40 .40
566 A160 55c multi .50 .50
567 A160 100c multi .90 .90
Nos. 565-567 (3) 1.80 1.80

Mailboxes A161

Perf. 14x13, 13x14

1986, Sept. 3 **Litho.**

568 A161 10c PO mailbox .25 .25
569 A161 25c Steel mailbox .25 .25
570 A161 45c Mailbox on brick wall .35 .35
571 A161 55c Pillar box .40 .40
Nos. 568-571 (4) 1.25 1.25

Nos. 569-571 vert.

Friars of Tilburg in the Antilles, Cent. — A162

10c, Brother Mauritius Vliegendehond, residence, 1886. 45c, Monsignor Ferdinand Kieckens, St. Thomas College, Roodeweg. 55c, Father F.S. de Beer, 1st general-superior, & college courtyard.

1986, Nov. 13 Litho. *Perf. 13x14*

572 A162 10c multi .25 .25
573 A162 45c multi .35 .35
574 A162 55c multi .45 .45
Nos. 572-574 (3) 1.05 1.05

Princess Juliana & Prince Bernhard, 50th Wedding Anniv. — A163

1987, Jan. 7 Litho. *Perf. 13x14*

575 A163 1.35g multi 1.10 1.10
a. Souvenir sheet 1.25 1.25

Maduro Holding, Inc., Sesquicent. — A164

70c, Expansion map. 85c, Corporate divisions. 1.55g, S.E.L. Maduro, founder.

1987, Jan. 26

576 A164 70c multi .50 .50
577 A164 85c multi .60 .60
578 A164 1.55g multi 1.10 1.10
Nos. 576-578 (3) 2.20 2.20

Curaçao Rotary Club, 50th Anniv. A165

15c, Map of the Antilles. 50c, Rotary headquarters. 65c, Map of Curaçao.

1987, Apr. 2 Litho. *Perf. 14x13*

579 A165 15c multicolored .25 .25
580 A165 50c multicolored .40 .40
581 A165 65c multicolored .50 .50
Nos. 579-581 (3) 1.15 1.15

Bolivar-Curaçao Friendship, 175th Anniv. — A166

60c, Octagon, residence of Simon Bolivar in Curaçao. 70c, Bolivarian Soc. Headquarters, 1949, Willemstad. 80c, Octagon interior (bedroom). 90c, Manual Carlos Piar, Simon Bolivar (1783-1830) & Pedro Luis Brion.

1987, July 24 Litho. *Perf. 14x13*

582 A166 60c multi .40 .40
583 A166 70c multi .50 .50
584 A166 80c multi .55 .55
585 A166 90c multi .65 .65
Nos. 582-585 (4) 2.10 2.10

Bolivarian Society, 50th anniv. (70c, 90c).

Antilles Natl. Parks Foundation, 25th Anniv. A167

70c, Phaethon lepturus. 85c, Odocoileus virginianus curassavicus. 1.55g, Iguana iguana.

1987, Dec. 1 Litho. *Perf. 14x13*

586 A167 70c multi .70 .70
587 A167 85c multi .80 .80
588 A167 1.55g multi 1.50 1.50
Nos. 586-588 (3) 3.00 3.00

The Curaçao Courant, 175th Anniv. A168

Designs: 55c, 19th Cent. printing press, lead type. 70c, Keyboard, modern press.

1987, Dec. 11

589 A168 55c multi .50 .50
590 A168 70c multi .60 .60

Mijnmaatschappij Phosphate Mining Co., Curaçao, 75th Anniv. — A169

40c, William Godden, founder. 105c, Processing plant. 155c, Tafelberg.

1988, Jan. 21

591 A169 40c multicolored .30 .30
592 A169 105c multicolored .80 .80
593 A169 155c multicolored 1.25 1.25
Nos. 591-593 (3) 2.35 2.35

States of the Netherlands Antilles, 50th Anniv. A170

Designs: 65c, John Horris Sprockel, 1st president, and natl. colors, crest. 70c, Development of state elections, women's suffrage. 155c, Natl. colors, crest, constellation representing the 5 islands and separation of Aruba.

1988, Apr. 5 **Litho.**

594 A170 65c multi .50 .50
595 A170 70c multi .50 .50
596 A170 155c multi 1.10 1.10
Nos. 594-596 (3) 2.10 2.10

Abolition of Slavery, 125th Anniv. A171

1988, July 1 Litho. *Perf. 14x13*

597 A171 155c shown 1.25 1.25
598 A171 190c Slave Wall, Curaçao 1.40 1.40

3rd Conference for Great Cities of the Americas, Curaçao, Aug. 24-27 A172

1988, Aug. 24 **Litho.**

599 A172 80c shown .60 .60
600 A172 155c Bridge, globe 1.25 1.25

Interamerican Foundation of Cities conference on building bridges between peoples.

Charles Ernst Barend Hellmund (1896-1952) — A173

Men and women who initiated community development: 65c, Atthelo Maud Edwards Jackson (1901-1970). 90c, Nicolaas Debrot (1902-1981). 120c, William Charles De La Try Ellis (1881-1977).

1988, Sept. 20 *Perf. 13x14*

601 A173 55c multi .40 .40
602 A173 65c multi .50 .50
603 A173 90c multi .65 .65
604 A173 120c multi .85 .85
Nos. 601-604 (4) 2.40 2.40

Tete-beche gutter pairs exist.

Cacti — A174

1988, Dec. 13 Litho. *Perf. 13x14*

605 A174 55c Cereus hexagonus .55 .55
606 A174 115c Melocactus 1.10 1.10
607 A174 125c Opuntia wentiana 1.25 1.25
Nos. 605-607 (3) 2.90 2.90

Wildlife Protection and Curaçao Foundation for the Prevention of Cruelty to Animals A175

1989, Mar. 9 Litho. *Perf. 14x13*

608 A175 65c Crested quail .65 .65
609 A175 115c Dogs, cats 1.10 1.10

Cruise Ships at St. Maarten and Curaçao A176

1989, May 8 **Litho.**

610 A176 70c Great Bay Harbor .55 .55
611 A176 155c St. Annabay 1.25 1.25

Tourism.

A177

Social and Political Figures: 40c, Paula Clementina Dorner (1901-1969), teacher. 55c, John Aniceto de Jongh (1885-1951), pharmacist, Parliament member. 90c, Jacobo Palm (1887-1982), composer. 120c, Abraham Mendes Chumaceiro (1841-1902), political reformer.

1989, Sept. 20 Litho. *Perf. 13x14*

612 A177 40c multi .35 .35
613 A177 55c multi .45 .45
614 A177 90c multi .80 .80
615 A177 120c multi 1.10 1.10
Nos. 612-615 (4) 2.70 2.70

A178

30c, 7 Symptoms of cancer. 60c, Radiation treatment. 80c, Fund emblem, healthy person.

1989, Nov. 7 Litho.

616 A178 30c multi .30 .30
617 A178 60c multi .60 .60
618 A178 80c multi .75 .75
Nos. 616-618 (3) 1.65 1.65

Queen Wilhelmina Fund, 40th anniv. Nos. 616-618 printed se-tenant with inscribed labels.

Souvenir Sheet

World Stamp Expo '89 and 20th UPU Congress, Washington, DC — A179

Designs: 70c, Monument, St. Eustatius, where the sovereignty of the US was 1st recognized by a foreign officer, Nov. 16, 1776. 155c, Peter Stuyvesant, flags representing bicent. of US-Antilles diplomatic relations, vert. 250c, 9-Gun salute of the *Andrea Doria*.

1989, Nov. 17 Litho. *Perf. 13*

619 Sheet of 3 3.75 3.25
a. A179 70c multicolored .55 .50
b. A179 155c multicolored 1.25 1.10
c. A179 250c multicolored 1.75 1.50

A180

1989, Dec. 1 *Perf. 13½x14*

620 A180 30c Fireworks .25 .25
621 A180 100c Ornaments on tree .75 .75

Christmas 1989 and New Year 1990. Nos. 620-621 printed se-tenant with labels inscribed "Merry X-mas and Happy New Year" in four languages.

Flowering plants — A181

30c, Tephrosia cinerea. 55c, Erithalis fruticosa. 65c, Evolvulus antillanus. 70c, Jacquinia arborea. 125c, Tournefortia gnaphalodes. 155c, Sesuvium portulacastrum.

1990, Jan. 31 Litho. *Perf. 13x14*

622 A181 30c multi .25 .25
623 A181 55c multi .40 .40
624 A181 65c multi .50 .50
625 A181 70c multi .55 .55
626 A181 125c multi 1.00 1.00
627 A181 155c multi 1.10 1.10
Nos. 622-627 (6) 3.80 3.80

Dominican Nuns in the Netherlands Antilles, Cent. A182

10c, Nurse, flag, map. 55c, St. Rose Hospital and St. Martin's Home. 60c, St. Joseph School.

1990, May 7 Litho. *Perf. 14x13*

628 A182 10c multicolored .25 .25
629 A182 55c multicolored .60 .60
630 A182 60c multicolored .70 .70
Nos. 628-630 (3) 1.55 1.55

A183

Poets: 40c, Carlos Alberto Nicolaas-Perez (1915-1989). 60c, Evert Stephanus Jordanus Kruythoff (1893-1967). 80c, John De Pool (1873-1947). 150c, Joseph Sickman Corsen (1853-1911).

1990, Aug. 8 Litho. *Perf. 13x14*

631 A183 40c multicolored .45 .45
632 A183 60c multicolored .70 .70
633 A183 80c multicolored .95 .95
634 A183 150c multicolored 1.75 1.75
Nos. 631-634 (4) 3.85 3.85

A184

Netherlands queens.

1990, Sept. 5 *Perf. 13x14*

635 A184 100c Emma 1.10 1.00
636 A184 100c Wilhelmina 1.10 1.00
637 A184 100c Juliana 1.10 1.00
638 A184 100c Beatrix 1.10 1.00
Nos. 635-638 (4) 4.40 4.00

Souvenir Sheet

Perf. 14x13

639 A184 250c Four Queens, horiz. 3.50 2.25

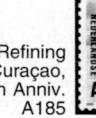

Oil Refining in Curaçao, 75th Anniv. A185

1990, Oct. 1 Litho. *Perf. 14x13*

640 A185 100c multicolored 1.10 1.00

Christmas A186

1990, Dec. 5 Litho. *Perf. 13½x14*

641 A186 30c Gifts .35 .30
642 A186 100c shown 1.10 1.00

25th anniv. of Bon Bisina Project (No. 641). Nos. 641-642 each printed with se-tenant label showing holiday greetings.

Express Mail Service, 5th Anniv. A187

1991, Jan. 16 Litho. *Perf. 14x13*

643 A187 20g multicolored 20.00 20.00

Fish — A188

Designs: 10c, Scuba diver, French grunt. 40c, Spotted trunkfish. 55c, Coppersweeper. 75c, Skindiver, yellow goatfish. 100c, Blackbar soldierfish.

1991, Mar. 13 *Perf. 13x14*

644 A188 10c multicolored .25 .25
645 A188 40c multicolored .50 .50
646 A188 55c multicolored .65 .65
647 A188 75c multicolored .90 .90
648 A188 100c multicolored 1.25 1.25
Nos. 644-648 (5) 3.55 3.55

Greetings A189

1991, May 8 *Perf. 14x13*

649 A189 30c Good luck .35 .35
650 A189 30c Thank you .35 .35
651 A189 30c Love you .35 .35
652 A189 30c Happy day .35 .35
653 A189 30c Get well soon .35 .35
654 A189 30c Happy birthday .35 .35
Nos. 649-654 (6) 2.10 2.10

Lighthouses — A190

30c, Westpoint, Curaçao. 70c, Willem's Tower, Bonaire. 115c, Little Curaçao, Curaçao.

1991, June 19 Litho. *Perf. 13x14*

655 A190 30c multicolored .35 .35
656 A190 70c multicolored .85 .85
657 A190 115c multicolored 1.40 1.40
Nos. 655-657 (3) 2.60 2.60

Peter Stuyvesant College, 50th Anniv. A191

Espamer '91 — A192

1991, July 5 *Perf. 14x13, 13x14*

658 A191 65c multicolored .80 .80
659 A192 125c multicolored 1.50 1.50

Christmas A193

1991, Dec. 2 Litho. *Perf. 13½x14*

660 A193 30c shown .35 .35
661 A193 100c Angel, shepherds 1.10 1.10

Nos. 660-661 printed with se-tenant labels.

A194

Litho. & Typo.

1991, Dec. 16 *Perf. 13x14*

662 A194 30c J. A. Correa .35 .35
663 A194 70c "75," coat of arms .90 .90
664 A194 155c I. H. Capriles 1.75 1.75
a. Strip of 3, #662-664 3.05 3.05

Maduro and Curiel's Bank NV, 75th anniv.

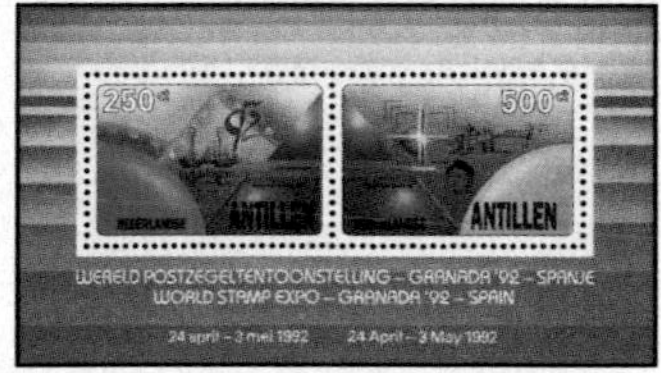

Odocoileus Virginianus A195

1992, Jan. 29 Litho. *Perf. 14x13*

666 A195 5c Fawn 2.00 1.25
667 A195 10c Two does 2.00 1.25
668 A195 30c Buck 2.00 1.25
669 A195 40c Buck & doe in water 2.00 1.25
670 A195 200c Buck drinking 2.50 2.25
671 A195 355c Buck, diff. 4.00 4.00
Nos. 666-671 (6) 14.50 11.25

World Wildlife Fund. Nos. 670-671 are airmail and do not have the WWF emblem. Nos. 670-671 are airmail.

Souvenir Sheet

Discovery of America, 500th Anniv. — A196

Designs: a, 250c, Alhambra, Granada, Spain. b, 500c, Carthusian Monastery, Seville, Spain.

1992, Apr. 1 Litho. *Perf. 14x13*

672 A196 Sheet of 2, #a.-b. 9.00 8.00

#672a, Granada '92. #672b, Expo '92, Seville.

Discovery of America, 500th Anniv. A197

250c, Sailing ship. 500c, Map, Columbus.

1992, May 13 Litho. *Perf. 14x13*

673 A197 250c multicolored 3.00 3.00
674 A197 500c multicolored 6.00 6.00

World Columbian Stamp Expo '92, Chicago.

Container Terminal, Curaçao A198

1992, June 26

675 A198 80c multi .95 .95
676 A198 125c multi, diff. 1.50 1.50

Famous People — A199

Designs: 30c, Angela Altagracia de Lannoy-Willems (1913-1983), politician and social activist. 40c, Lodewijk Daniel Gerharts (1901-1983), politician and promoter of tourism for Bonaire. 55c, Cyrus Wilberforce Wathey (1901-1969), businessman and philanthropist. 70c, Christiaan Winkel (1899-1962), deputy governor of Netherlands Antilles. 100c, Franciscan Nuns of Roosendaal, educational and charitable group, 150th anniversary of arrival in Curaçao.

1992, Sept. 1 Litho. *Perf. 13x14*

677 A199 30c grn & blk, *tan* .40 .40
678 A199 40c blue & blk, *tan* .50 .50
679 A199 55c yel org & blk, *tan* .65 .65
680 A199 70c lake & blk, *tan* .85 .85
681 A199 100c blue & blk, *tan* 1.25 1.25
Nos. 677-681 (5) 3.65 3.65

Queen Beatrix's 1992 Visit — A200

Designs: 70c, Queen in white hat, Prince Claus. 100c, Queen signing jubilee register. 175c, Queen in black hat, Prince Claus, native girl.

1992, Nov. 9 Litho. *Perf. 14x13*

682 A200 70c multicolored .90 .90
683 A200 100c multicolored 1.25 1.25
684 A200 175c multicolored 2.25 2.25
Nos. 682-684 (3) 4.40 4.40

Queen Beatrix's accession to the throne, 12½ year anniv. (#683).

Christmas A201

Perf. 14x13½, 13½x14

1992, Dec. 1 Litho.

685 A201 30c Nativity scene .35 .35
686 A201 100c Mary, Joseph, vert. 1.25 1.25

No. 686 printed with se-tenant label.

Flowers — A202

1993, Feb. 3 Litho. *Perf. 13x14*

687 A202 75c Hibiscus .95 .95
688 A202 90c Helianthus annuus 1.10 1.10
689 A202 175c Ixora 2.25 2.25
690 A202 195c Rosea 2.50 2.50
Nos. 687-690 (4) 6.80 6.80

Anniversaries A203

Map of islands and: 65c, Airplane, air routes. 75c, Natl. Laboratory, scientist using microscope. 90c, Airplane at Princess Juliana Intl. Airport. 175c, Yellow and white crosses.

1993, Mar. 9 *Perf. 14x13*

691 A203 65c multicolored .80 .80
692 A203 75c multicolored .95 .95
693 A203 90c multicolored 1.25 1.25
694 A203 175c multicolored 2.25 2.25
Nos. 691-694 (4) 5.25 5.25

Princess Juliana Intl. Airport, 50th anniv. (#691, 693). Natl. Laboratory, 75th anniv. (#692). Princess Margaret White/Yellow Cross Foundation for District Nursing, 50th anniv. (#694).

Dogs — A204

1993, May 26 Litho. *Perf. 13x14*

695 A204 65c Pekingese .80 .80
696 A204 90c Poodle 1.10 1.10
697 A204 100c Pomeranian 1.25 1.25
698 A204 175c Papillon 2.25 2.25
Nos. 695-698 (4) 5.40 5.40

Entry of Netherlands Antilles into UPAEP A205

Designs: 150c, Indian cave painting, Bonaire. 200c, Emblem of Brasiliana '93, flag of Netherlands Antilles. 250c, Map of Central and South America, Netherlands Antilles, Spain, and Portugal, document being signed.

1993, July 15 Litho. *Perf. 14x13*

699 A205 150c multicolored 1.90 1.90
700 A205 200c multicolored 2.50 2.50
701 A205 250c multicolored 3.25 3.25
Nos. 699-701 (3) 7.65 7.65

Brasiliana '93 (#700).

Contemporary Art — A206

1993, July 23 Litho. *Perf. 13x14*

702 A206 90c silver & multi 1.10 1.10
703 A206 150c gold & multi 1.90 1.90

US Consulate General in Netherlands Antilles, Bicent. A207

1993, Nov. 16 Litho. *Perf. 14x13*

704 A207 65c American Consulate .80 .80
705 A207 90c Coats of Arms 1.10 1.10
706 A207 175c Eagle in flight 2.25 2.25
Nos. 704-706 (3) 4.15 4.15

Christmas — A208

Designs: 30c, Mosaic of mother and child. 115c, Painting of Mary holding Christ.

1993, Dec. 1 *Perf. 13x14*

707 A208 30c multicolored .35 .35
708 A208 115c multicolored 1.40 1.40

Dogs — A209

1994, Feb. 2 Litho. *Perf. 14x13*

709 A209 65c Basset .80 .80
710 A209 75c Pit bull terrier .95 .95
711 A209 90c Cocker spaniel 1.10 1.10
712 A209 175c Chow 2.25 2.25
Nos. 709-712 (4) 5.10 5.10

Birds — A210

1994, Mar. 2 Litho. *Perf. 13x14*

713 A210 50c Polyborus plancus .60 .60
714 A210 95c Pavo muticus 1.10 1.10
715 A210 100c Ara macao 1.25 1.25
716 A210 125c Icterus icterus 1.50 1.50
Nos. 713-716 (4) 4.45 4.45

A211

Famous People: 65c, Joseph Husurell Lake (1925-76), politician, journalist. 75c, Efrain Jonckheer (1917-87), diplomat. 100c, Michiel Martinus Romer (1865-1937), educator. 175c, Carel Nicolaas Winkel (1882-1973), public official, social worker.

1994, Apr. 8

717 A211 65c olive & blk, *grn* .80 .80
718 A211 75c brn & blk, *lt brn* .95 .95
719 A211 100c grn & blk, *bl* 1.25 1.25
720 A211 175c brn & blk, *tan* 2.25 2.25
Nos. 717-720 (4) 5.25 5.25

A212

1994 World Cup Soccer Championships, US: 90c, Socks, soccer shoes, horiz. 150c, Shoe, ball. 175c, Whistle, horiz.

Perf. 14x13, 13x14

1994, May 4 Litho.

721 A212 90c multicolored 1.10 1.10
722 A212 150c multicolored 1.90 1.90
723 A212 175c multicolored 2.25 2.25
Nos. 721-723 (3) 5.25 5.25

A213

ILO, 75th Anniv.: 90c, Declaration, chair, gavel. 110c, "75" over heart. 200c, Wind-blown tree.

1994, June 1 Litho. *Perf. 13x14*

724 A213 90c multicolored 1.10 1.10
725 A213 110c multicolored 1.40 1.40
726 A213 200c multicolored 2.50 2.50
Nos. 724-726 (3) 5.00 5.00

Wildlife A214

Designs: 10c, Ware-wara, blenchi, parakeet, dolphin. 35c, Dolphin, pelican, troupial. 50c, Iguana, fish, lobster, sea hedgehog. 125c, Sea hedgehog, sea apple, fish, turtle, flamingos, ducks.

1994, Aug. 4 Litho. *Perf. 14x13*

727 A214 10c multicolored .25 .25
728 A214 35c multicolored .45 .45
729 A214 50c multicolored .65 .65
730 A214 125c multicolored 1.60 1.60
a. Souvenir sheet, #727-730 2.75 2.75
Nos. 727-730 (4) 2.95 2.95

PHILAKOREA '94 (#730a).

FEPAPOST '94 — A215

2.50g, Netherlands #277. 5g, #109.

1994, Oct. 5 Litho. *Perf. 14x13*

731 A215 2.50g multicolored 2.75 2.75
732 A215 5g multicolored 5.50 5.50
a. Souv. sheet of 2, #731-732, perf. 13½x13 8.25 8.25

Christmas A216

1994, Dec. 1 Litho. *Perf. 14x13*

733 A216 30c shown .30 .30
734 A216 115c Hands holding earth 1.25 1.25

Curaçao Carnivals A217

Carnival scene and: 125c, Buildings, Willemstad. 175c, Floating market. 250c, House with thatched roof.

1995, Jan. 19 Litho. *Perf. 14x13*

735 A217 125c multicolored 1.40 1.40
736 A217 175c multicolored 2.00 2.00
737 A217 250c multicolored 2.75 2.75
Nos. 735-737 (3) 6.15 6.15

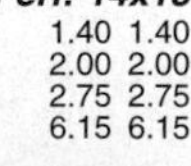
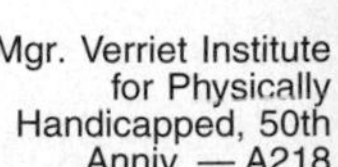

Mgr. Verriet Institute for Physically Handicapped, 50th Anniv. — A218

Design: 90c, Cedric Virginie, handicapped worker at Public Library.

1995, Feb. 2 Litho. *Perf. 13x14*

738 A218 65c multicolored .75 .75
739 A218 90c multicolored 1.00 1.00

Dogs — A219

1995, Mar. 29 Litho. *Perf. 14x13*
740 A219 75c Doberman .85 .85
741 A219 85c Shepherd .95 .95
742 A219 100c Bouvier 1.10 1.10
743 A219 175c St. Bernard 2.00 2.00
Nos. 740-743 (4) 4.90 4.90

Flags, Coats of Arms of Island Territories A220

10c, Bonaire. 35c, Curaçao. 50c, St. Maarten. 65c, Saba. 75c, St. Eustatius, natl. flag, coat of arms. 90c, Flags of territories, natl. coat of arms.

1995, June 30 Litho. *Perf. 14x13*
744 A220 10c multicolored .25 .25
745 A220 35c multicolored .40 .40
746 A220 50c multicolored .55 .55
747 A220 65c multicolored .75 .75
748 A220 75c multicolored .85 .85
749 A220 90c multicolored 1.00 1.00
Nos. 744-749 (6) 3.80 3.80

Domestic Cats — A221

Designs: 25c, Siamese sealpoint. 60c, Maine coon. 65c, Egyptian silver mau. 90c, Angora. 150c, Persian blue smoke.

1995, Sept. 29 Litho. *Perf. 13x14*
750 A221 25c multicolored .30 .30
751 A221 60c multicolored .65 .65
752 A221 65c multicolored .75 .75
753 A221 90c multicolored 1.00 1.00
754 A221 150c multicolored 1.60 1.60
Nos. 750-754 (5) 4.30 4.30

Christmas and New Year — A222

Designs: 30c, Three Magi following star. 115c, Fireworks above houses, Handelskade.

1995, Dec. 1 Litho. *Perf. 13½x13*
755 A222 30c multicolored .35 .35
756 A222 115c multicolored 1.25 1.25

Nos. 755-756 each printed with se-tenant label.

A223

Curaçao Lions Club, 50th Anniv.: 75c, List of services to community. 105c, Seal. 250c, Hands clasp.

1996, Feb. 26 Litho. *Perf. 13x14*
757 A223 75c multicolored .85 .85
758 A223 105c multicolored 1.25 1.25
759 A223 250c multicolored 2.75 2.75
Nos. 757-759 (3) 4.85 4.85

A224

1996, Apr. 12 Litho. *Perf. 13x14*
760 A224 85c shown .95 .95
761 A224 175c Telegraph key 2.00 2.00

Radio, cent.

A225

1996, Apr. 12
762 A225 60c shown .70 .70
763 A225 75c Tornado, sun .80 .80

Dr. David Ricardo Capriles Clinic, 60th anniv.

A226

1996, May 8 Litho. *Perf. 13x14*
764 A226 85c shown .95 .95
765 A226 225c Bible 2.50 2.50

Translation of the Bible into Papiamentu.

CAPEX '96 — A227

Butterflies: 5c, Agraulis vanillae. 110c, Callithea philotima. 300c, Parthenos sylvia. 750c, Euphaedra francina.

1996, June 5 Litho. *Perf. 14x13*
766 A227 5c multicolored .25 .25
767 A227 110c multicolored 1.25 1.25
768 A227 300c multicolored 3.50 3.50
a. Souvenir sheet of 2, #767-768 4.75 4.75
769 A227 750c multicolored 8.50 8.50
Nos. 766-769 (4) 13.50 13.50

Famous Antillean Personalities A228

Designs: 40c, Mary Gertrude Johnson Hassel (1853-1939), introduced drawn thread (Spanish work) to Saba. 50c, Cornelis Marten (Papa Cornes) (1749-1852), spiritual care giver on Bonaire. 75c, Phelippi Benito Chakutoe (1891-1967), union leader. 85c, Christiaan Josef Hendrikus Engels (1907-80), physician, painter, pianist, poet.

1996, Aug. 21 Litho. *Perf. 14x13*
770 A228 40c orange & black .45 .45
771 A228 50c green & black .55 .55
772 A228 75c brown & black .85 .85
773 A228 85c blue & black .95 .95
Nos. 770-773 (4) 2.80 2.80

Horses A229

1996, Sept. 26 Litho. *Perf. 14x13*
774 A229 110c Shire 1.25 1.25
775 A229 225c Shetland pony 2.50 2.50
776 A229 275c Thoroughbred 3.00 3.00
777 A229 350c Przewalski 4.00 4.00
Nos. 774-777 (4) 10.75 10.75

Christmas — A230

35c, Money bag, straw hat, candy cane, gifts, poinsettias, star. 150c, Santa Claus.

Serpentine Die Cut 13x13½
1996, Dec. 2 Litho.
Self-Adhesive
778 A230 35c multicolored .40 .40
779 A230 150c multicolored 1.70 1.70

Mushrooms A231

40c, Galerina autumnalis. 50c, Amanita virosa. 75c, Boletus edulis. 175c, Amanita muscaria.

1997, Feb. 19 Litho. *Perf. 14x13*
780 A231 40c multicolored .45 .45
781 A231 50c multicolored .55 .55
782 A231 75c multicolored .85 .85
783 A231 175c multicolored 2.00 2.00
Nos. 780-783 (4) 3.85 3.85

Birds — A232

5c, Melopsittacus undulatus. 25c, Cacatua leadbeateri leadbeateri. 50c, Amazona barbadensis. 75c, Ardea purpurea. 85c, Chrysolampis mosquitus. 100c, Balearica pavonina. 110c, Pyrocephalus rubinus. 125c, Phoenicopteurus ruber. 200c, Pandion haliaetus. 225c, Ramphastos sulfuratus.

1997, Mar. 26 Litho. *Perf. 13x14*
784 A232 5c multicolored .25 .25
785 A232 25c multicolored .30 .30
786 A232 50c multicolored .55 .55
787 A232 75c multicolored .90 .90
788 A232 85c multicolored .95 .95
789 A232 100c multicolored 1.10 1.10
790 A232 110c multicolored 1.25 1.25
791 A232 125c multicolored 1.40 1.40
792 A232 200c multicolored 2.25 2.25
793 A232 225c multicolored 2.50 2.50
Nos. 784-793 (10) 11.45 11.45

Greetings Stamps — A233

#799A, like #794. #799B, Correspondence in 3 languages. #799C, Positivism, flower, sun. #799D, like #795. #799E, Success, rising sun. 85c, like #796. 100c, like #797. #799H, like #798. #799I, Love, silhouette of couple. 225c, like #799.

1997, Apr. 16
794 A233 40c Love .45 .45
795 A233 75c Positivism .85 .85
796 A233 85c Mother's Day .95 .95
797 A233 100c Correspondence 1.10 1.10
798 A233 110c Success 1.25 1.25
799 A233 225c Congratulations 2.75 2.75
Nos. 794-799 (6) 7.35 7.35

Booklet Stamps
Size: 21x25mm
Perf. 13x14 on 3 Sides
799A A233 40c multicolored .50 .50
799B A233 40c multicolored .50 .50
799C A233 75c multicolored .95 .95
799D A233 75c multicolored .95 .95
799E A233 75c multicolored .95 .95
799F A233 85c multicolored 1.10 1.10
799G A233 100c multicolored 1.25 1.25
799H A233 110c multicolored 1.40 1.40
799I A233 110c multicolored 1.40 1.40
799J A233 225c multicolored 2.75 2.75
k. Booklet pane of 10, #799A-799J + label 11.75
Complete booklet, #799k 11.75

Stamps arranged in booklet out of Scott order.

Signs of the Chinese Calendar A234

Stylized designs.

1997, May 19 Litho. *Perf. 14x13*
800 A234 5c Rat .25 .25
801 A234 5c Ox .25 .25
802 A234 5c Tiger .25 .25
803 A234 40c Rabbit .45 .45
804 A234 40c Dragon .45 .45
805 A234 40c Snake .45 .45
806 A234 75c Horse .85 .85
807 A234 75c Goat .85 .85
808 A234 75c Monkey .85 .85
809 A234 100c Rooster 1.10 1.10
810 A234 100c Dog 1.10 1.10
811 A234 100c Pig 1.10 1.10
a. Souvenir sheet of 12, #800-811 7.75 7.75
Nos. 800-811 (12) 7.95 7.95

No. 811a for PACIFIC 97. Issued: 5/19/97.

Coins — A235

1997, Aug. 6 *Perf. 13x14*
812 A235 85c Plaka, 2½ cent 1.10 1.10
813 A235 175c Stuiver, 5 cent 2.25 2.25
814 A235 225c Fuèrtè, 2½ gulden 2.75 2.75
Nos. 812-814 (3) 6.10 6.10

A236

Shanghai '97, Intl. Stamp Exhibition — A237

15c, Nampu Grand Bridge, Shanghai. 40c, Giant panda, horiz. 75c, Tiger, New Year 1998.

90c, Buildings in downtown Shanghai.

Perf. 14x13, 13x14

1997, Nov. 19 **Litho.**

815 A236 15c multicolored .25 .25
816 A237 40c multicolored .45 .45
817 A237 75c multicolored .85 .85
Nos. 815-817 (3) 1.55 1.55

Souvenir Sheet

818 A236 90c multicolored 1.00 1.00

A238

Christmas and New Year: 35c, Left panel of triptych from Roman Catholic Church, Willemstad. 150c, Champagne bottle being opened, calendar.

1997, Dec. 1 *Perf. 13x14*

819 A238 35c multicolored .40 .40
820 A238 150c multicolored 1.75 1.75

A239

Total Solar Eclipse, Curacao: 85c, Sun partially covered by moon's shadow. 110c, Outer edge of sun showing beyond moon's shadow. 225c, Total solar eclipse.
750c, Hologram of the eclipse.

1998, Feb. 26 **Litho.** *Perf. 13x14*

821 A239 85c multicolored .95 .95
822 A239 110c multicolored 1.25 1.25
823 A239 225c multicolored 2.50 2.50
Nos. 821-823 (3) 4.70 4.70

Souvenir Sheet

824 A239 750c multicolored 9.00 9.00

No. 824 contains a hologram which may be damaged by soaking.

ISRAEL '98 World Stamp Exhibition — A240

Designs: 40c, Dead Sea. 75c, Zion Gate, Jerusalem. 110c, Masada.
225c, Mikvé Israel-Emanuel Synagogue, Curacao.

1998, Apr. 29 **Litho.** *Perf. 13x14*

825 A240 40c multicolored .45 .45
826 A240 75c multicolored .85 .85
827 A240 110c multicolored 1.25 1.25
Nos. 825-827 (3) 2.55 2.55

Souvenir Sheet

828 A240 225c multicolored 2.50 2.50

Elias Moreno Brandao & Sons, Car Dealership, 75th Anniv. A241

Chevrolet automobiles: 40c, 1923 Superior, Elias Moreno Brandao. 55c, 1934 Roadster. 75c, 1949 Styleline Deluxe. 110c, 1957 Bel Air Convertible. 225c, 1963 Corvette "Stingray." 500c, 1970 Chevelle SS-454.

1998, May 4 *Perf. 14x13*

829 A241 40c multicolored .45 .45
830 A241 55c multicolored .60 .60
831 A241 75c multicolored .85 .85
832 A241 110c multicolored 1.25 1.25
833 A241 225c multicolored 2.50 2.50
834 A241 500c multicolored 5.50 5.50
Nos. 829-834 (6) 11.15 11.15

A242

Advisory Council, 50th Anniv.: 75c, Natl. flag, natl. arms. 85c, Gavel, stars, natl. arms.

1998, June 1 **Litho.** *Perf. 13x14*

835 A242 75c multicolored .85 .85
836 A242 85c multicolored .95 .95

A243

Famous People: 40c, Christina Elizabeth Flanders (1908-96). 75c, Abraham Jesurun Dz. (1839-1918). 85c, Gerrit Simeon Newton (1884-1949). 110c, Eduardo Adriana (1925-97).

1998, June 24 *Perf. 13*

837 A243 40c multicolored .45 .45
838 A243 75c multicolored .85 .85
839 A243 85c multicolored .95 .95
840 A243 110c multicolored 1.25 1.25
Nos. 837-840 (4) 3.50 3.50

Mailboxes — A244

1998, July 29 **Litho.** *Perf. 13x14*

841 A244 15c Ireland .25 .25
842 A244 40c Nepal .45 .45
843 A244 75c Uruguay .85 .85
844 A244 85c Curacao .95 .95
Nos. 841-844 (4) 2.50 2.50

See Nos. 932-935.

A245

Privatization of Natl. Postal Service: 75c, Globe, map of North and South America, horiz. 110c, Numbers and tree on screen. 225c, #207 and #846, horiz.

1998, Aug. 5 *Perf. 13*

845 A245 75c multicolored .85 .85
846 A245 110c multicolored 1.25 1.25
847 A245 225c multicolored 2.50 2.50
Nos. 845-847 (3) 4.60 4.60

A246

Endangered Species: 5c, Black rhinoceros, horiz. 75c, White-tailed hawk. 125c, White-tailed deer, horiz. 250c, Tiger.

1998, Aug. 26 *Perf. 13½*

848 A246 5c multicolored .25 .25
849 A246 75c multicolored .85 .85
850 A246 125c multicolored 1.50 1.50
851 A246 250c multicolored 2.75 2.75
Nos. 848-851 (4) 5.35 5.35

Intl. Year of the Ocean A247

1998, Sept. 30 **Litho.** *Perf. 13*

852 A247 275c Mako shark 3.00 3.00
853 A247 350c Manta ray 4.00 4.00

1998 Philatelic Exhibition, The Hague, Netherlands A248

1998, Oct. 8 *Perf. 14x13*

854 A248 225c No. 213 2.50 2.50
855 A248 500c No. 218 5.75 5.75

Souvenir Sheet

856 A248 500c Nos. 61, 218 6.25 6.25

Price Waterhouse Coopers in Netherlands Antilles, 60th Anniv. — A249

Emblems, company buildings in Julianaplein, minerals: 75c, Lapis lazuli. 225c, Pyrite.

1998, Nov. 13 *Perf. 13½*

857 75c multicolored .85 .85
858 225c multicolored 2.50 2.50
a. A249 Pair, #857-858 3.50 3.50

Christmas A250

Children's drawings: 35c, Christmas tree, vert. 150c, Mail box at Christmas.

Perf. 13x14, 14x13

1998, Dec. 1 **Litho.**

859 A250 35c multicolored .40 .40
860 A250 150c multicolored 1.75 1.75

Avila Beach Hotel, 50th Anniv. A251

Designs: 75c, Exterior view of hotel, Dr. Pieter Hendrik Maal. 110c, Beach, delonix regia. 225c, Mesquite tree, porposis juliflora.

1999, Feb. 3 **Litho.** *Perf. 14x13*

861 A251 75c multicolored .85 .85
862 A251 110c multicolored 1.25 1.25
863 A251 225c multicolored 2.50 2.50
Nos. 861-863 (3) 4.60 4.60

New Year 1999 (Year of the Rabbit) and China '99, World Stamp Exhibition, Beijing A252

Designs: 75c, Rabbit, Great Wall of China. No. 865, Rabbit, Jade Pagoda, Beijing, vert. No. 866, Rabbit, landscape, vert.

Perf. 14x13, 13x14

1999, Mar. 30 **Litho.**

864 A252 75c multicolored .85 .85
865 A252 225c multicolored 2.50 2.50

Souvenir Sheet

Perf. 13x13½

866 A252 225c multicolored 2.50 2.50

Government Correctional Institute (GOG) for Youth, 50th Anniv. A253

Design, traditional musical instrument: 40c, Couple dancing, wiri. 75c, Building, bamba. 85c, Man using file and vise, triangle.

Perf. 13x14, 14x13

1999, Apr. 28 **Litho.**

867 A253 40c multi, vert. .45 .45
868 A253 75c multi, vert. .85 .85
869 A253 85c multi .95 .95
Nos. 867-869 (3) 2.25 2.25

Recorded History of Curacao, 500th Anniv. A254

Curacao 500 emblem and: 75c, Ship launching. 110c, Houses on Rifwater, Otrobanda, Pasa Kontrami Bridge. 175c, #870-871. 225c, Fort Beeckenburg. 500c, #204, sailing ship.

1999, May 19 *Perf. 14x13*

870 A254 75c multicolored .85 .85
871 A254 110c multicolored 1.25 1.25
872 A254 175c multicolored 1.90 1.90
873 A254 225c multicolored 2.50 2.50
874 A254 500c multicolored 5.75 5.75
Nos. 870-874 (5) 12.25 12.25

Wilson "Papa" Godett (1932-95), Politician — A255

1999, May 28 *Perf. 13x14*

875 A255 75c multicolored .85 .85

Millennium A256

Designs: 5c, Indians, map. 10c, Indian, ship, armored horseman. 40c, Flags of islands, Autonomy monument, Curacao, autonomy document. 75c, Telephone, #5. 85c, Airplane. 100c, Oil refinery. 110c, Satellite dish, underwater cable. 125c, Tourist ship, bridge. 225c, Island residents, music box. 350c, Birds, cacti.

1999, Aug. 4 Litho. *Perf. 13½*

876 A256 5c multicolored .25 .25
877 A256 10c multicolored .25 .25
878 A256 40c multicolored .40 .40
879 A256 75c multicolored .75 .75
880 A256 85c multicolored .85 .85
881 A256 100c multicolored 1.00 1.00
882 A256 110c multicolored 1.10 1.10
883 A256 125c multicolored 1.25 1.25
884 A256 225c multicolored 2.25 2.25
885 A256 350c multicolored 3.50 3.50

Size: 31x31mm

Self-Adhesive

Serpentine Die Cut 8

886 A256 5c multicolored .25 .25
887 A256 10c multicolored .25 .25
888 A256 40c multicolored .40 .40
889 A256 75c multicolored .75 .75
890 A256 85c multicolored .85 .85
891 A256 100c multicolored 1.00 1.00
892 A256 110c multicolored 1.10 1.10
893 A256 125c multicolored 1.25 1.25
894 A256 225c multicolored 2.25 2.25
895 A256 350c multicolored 3.50 3.50
Nos. 876-895 (20) 23.20 23.20

A257

Designs: 150c, Church of the Conversion of St. Paul, Saba. 250c, Flamingo, Bonaire. 500c, Courthouse of Philipsburg, St. Martin.

1999, Oct. 1 Litho. *Perf. 14x13*

896 A257 150c multicolored 1.60 1.60
897 A257 250c multicolored 2.75 2.75
898 A257 500c multicolored 5.50 5.50
Nos. 896-898 (3) 9.85 9.85

Flowers — A258

Designs: No. 899, Allamanda. No. 900, Bougainvillea. No. 901, Gardenia jasminoides. No. 902, Saintpaulia ionantha. No. 903, Cymbidium. No. 904, Strelitzia. No. 905, Cassia fistula. No. 906, Phalaenopsis. No. 907, Doritaenopsis. No. 908, Guzmania. No. 909, Caralluma hexagona. No. 910, Catharanthus roseus.

1999, Nov. 15 *Perf. 13½*

899 A258 40c multicolored .90 .90
900 A258 40c multicolored .90 .90
a. Pair, #899-900 2.00 2.00
901 A258 40c multicolored .90 .90
902 A258 40c multicolored .90 .90
a. Pair, #901-902 2.00 2.00
903 A258 75c multicolored 1.25 1.25
904 A258 75c multicolored 1.25 1.25
a. Pair, #903-904 2.75 2.75
905 A258 75c multicolored 1.25 1.25
906 A258 75c multicolored 1.25 1.25
a. Pair, #905-906 2.75 2.75
907 A258 110c multicolored 2.00 2.00
908 A258 110c multicolored 2.00 2.00
a. Pair, #907-908 5.00 5.00
909 A258 225c multicolored 3.50 3.50
910 A258 225c multicolored 3.50 3.50
a. Pair, #909-910 8.00 8.00
Nos. 899-910 (12) 19.60 19.60

Christmas A259

Year 2000 A260

1999, Dec. 1 Litho. *Perf. 13x14*

911 A259 35c multi .90 .50
912 A260 150c multi 2.25 1.75

Greetings Stamps — A261

#913, 40c, #918, 150c, Hearts, roses. #914, 40c, #919, 150c, Mothers, globe. #915, 40c, Father, baby, blocks. #916, 75c, Dog in gift box. #917, 110c, Butterfly, flowers in vase. #920, 225c, Hands, rings.

2000, Jan. 27 Litho. *Perf. 13x14*

913-920 A261 Set of 8 14.00 12.00

New Year 2000 (Year of the Dragon) A262

2000, Feb. 28 *Perf. 14x13*

921 A262 110c shown 2.25 1.75

Souvenir Sheet

922 A262 225c Two dragons 5.00 5.00

Fauna A263

Designs: 40c, Red eye tree toad. 75c, King penguin, vert. 85c, Killer whale, vert. 100c, African elephant, vert. 110c, Chimpanzee, vert. 225c, Indian tiger.

2000, Mar. 29 *Perf. 14x13, 13x14*

923-928 A263 Set of 6 15.00 11.00

Space — A264

Designs: 75c, Space Shuttle. No. 930, 225c, Astronaut, flag, space station.

2000, June 21 Litho. *Perf. 13x14*

929-930 A264 Set of 2 6.00 5.00

Souvenir Sheet

Perf. 13x13¼

931 A264 225c Colonized planet 5.00 5.00

World Stamp Expo 2000, Anaheim.

Mailbox Type of 1998

Mailboxes from: 110c, Mexico. 175c, Dubai. 350c, England. 500c, United States.

2000, Aug. 8 *Perf. 13x14*

932-935 A244 Set of 4 16.50 16.50

2000 Summer Olympics, Sydney — A265

75c, Cycling. No. 937, 225c, Running.

2000, Aug. 8 Litho. *Perf. 13x14*

936-937 A265 Set of 2 5.75 5.00

Souvenir Sheet

938 A265 225c Swimming 5.00 5.00

Social Insurance Bank, 40th Anniv. A266

Designs: 75c, People, islands, vert. 110c, Hands. 225c, Emblem, vert.

2000, Sept. 1 *Perf. 13x14, 14x13*

939-941 A266 Set of 3 6.00 6.00

Christmas A267

Songs: 40c, Jingle Bells, vert. 150c, We Wish You a Merry Christmas.

2000, Nov. 15 *Perf. 13x14, 14x13*

942-943 A267 Set of 2 3.50 3.50

New Year 2001 (Year of the Snake) A268

Designs: 110c, Red milk snake. 225c, Indian cobra, vert.

2001, Jan. 17 Litho. *Perf. 14x13*

944 A268 110c multi 2.25 1.75

Souvenir Sheet

Perf. 13x14

945 A268 225c multi 5.00 5.00

Hong Kong 2001 Stamp Exhibition — A269

Designs: 25c, Birds in forest. 40c, Palm trees and waterfall. 110c, Spinner dolphins.

2001, Feb. 1 *Perf. 13x14*

946-948 A269 Set of 3 4.00 3.00

Cats and Dogs — A270

Designs: 55c, Persian shaded golden. 75c, Burmese bluepoint. 110c, Beagle and American wirehair. 175c, Golden retriever. 225c, German shepherd. 750c, British shorthair black-silver marble.

2001, Mar. 7 Litho. *Perf. 13x14*

949-954 A270 Set of 6 25.00 22.50

Ships — A271

Designs: 110c, Z. M. Mars. 275c, Z. M. Alphen. 350c, Z. M. Curaçao, horiz. 500c, Schooner Pioneer, horiz.

2001, Apr. 26 *Perf. 13x14, 14x13*

955-958 A271 Set of 4 22.50 20.00

Fedjai the Postal Worker — A272

Fedjai: 5c, On bicycle. 40c, With children. 75c, Looking at nest in mailbox. 85c, Talking with woman. 100c, Chased atop mailbox by dog. 110c, Looking at boy's stamp album.

2001, June 5 Litho. *Perf. 13x14*

959-964 A272 Set of 6 5.00 5.00

See No. 1012.

Cave Bats — A273

Designs: 85c, Map of bat species in Kueba Bosá. 110c, Leptonycteris nivalis curasaoe. 225c, Glosophaga elongata.

2001, Aug. 20 Litho. *Perf. 14x13*

965-967 A273 Set of 3 5.00 5.00

Birds — A274

No. 968: a, 10c, Trochilus polytmus. b, 85c, Pelecanus onocrotalus. c, 110c, Erythrura gouldiae. d, 175c, Passerina ciris. e, 250c, Fratercula arctica. f, 375c, Anhinga anhinga.

2001, Sept. 28 *Perf. 12¾x13½*

968 A274 Block of 6, #a-f 20.00 17.50

Philipsburg Methodist Church, 150th Anniv. A275

Map of St. Maarten and: 75c, Church building. 110c, Bibles.

2001, Oct. 19 *Perf. 14x13*

969-970 A275 Set of 2 2.25 2.25

Christmas and New Year's Day — A276

Designs: 40c, Clock, people from 8 countries. 150c, Dove, poinsettias, baby Jesus, and people from 4 countries, vert.

Perf. 13½x12¾, 12¾x13½

2001, Nov. 15 Litho.

971-972 A276 Set of 2 2.25 2.25

Wedding of Prince Willem-Alexander and Máxima Zorreguieta — A277

Designs: 75c, Prince. 110c, Máxima.
No. 975: a, 2.25f, Prince. b, 2.75f, Máxima.

2002, Feb. 2 Litho. *Perf. 12¾x14*
973-974 A277 Set of 2 2.10 2.10

Souvenir Sheet
Perf. 12¾x13½

975 A277 Sheet of 2, #a-b 5.75 5.75

New Year 2002 (Year of the Horse) — A278

Designs: 25c, Horse rearing. 95c, Horse's head.

2002, Mar. 1 *Perf. 12¾x14*
976 A278 25c multi .30 .30

Souvenir Sheet
Perf. 12¾x13½

977 A278 95c multi 1.10 1.10

Flora & Fauna A279

Designs: 50c, Chlorostilbon mellisugus and Passiflora foetida, vert. 95c, Anolis lineatus and Cordia sebestena. 120c, Odonata. 145c, Coenobita clypeatus. 285c, Polistes versicolor, vert.

Perf. 12¾x13½, 13½x12¾
2002, Mar. 27 Litho.
978-982 A279 Set of 5 8.00 8.00

Butterflies — A280

Designs: 25c, Dryas iulia, vert. 145c, Danaus plexippus. 400c, Mechanitis polymnia. 500c, Pyrhapygopsis socrates.

Perf. 12¾x13½, 13½x12¾
2002, May 22 Litho.
983-986 A280 Set of 4 12.50 12.50

Fedjai the Postal Worker Type of 2001

Fedjai: 10c, Jumping rope with children, horiz. 55c, Scolding dog. 95c, Delivering letter to child. 240c, Helping elderly lady across street.

Perf. 13¾x12¾, 12¾x13¾
2002, July 31
987-990 A272 Set of 4 4.50 4.50

Amphilex 2002 Intl. Stamp Exhibition, Amsterdam — A281

Details from the 1885 version of "The Potato Eaters," by Vincent Van Gogh: 70c, 95c, 145c, 240c.
550c, Entire painting, horiz.

Perf. 12¾x13½
2002, Aug. 26 Litho.
991-994 A281 Set of 4 6.25 6.25

Souvenir Sheet
Perf. 14x12¾

995 A281 550c multi 6.25 6.25

Orchids — A282

Designs: 95c, Wingfieldara casseta. 285c, Cymbidium Magna Charta. 380c, Brassolaeliocattleya. 750c, Miltonia spectabilis.

2002, Sept. 27 *Perf. 12¾x14*
996-999 A282 Set of 4 17.00 17.00

Christmas and New Year — A283

Designs: 95c, Christmas tree decorations. 240c, Lanterns.

2002, Nov. 15 *Perf. 14x12¾*
1000-1001 A283 Set of 2 3.75 3.75

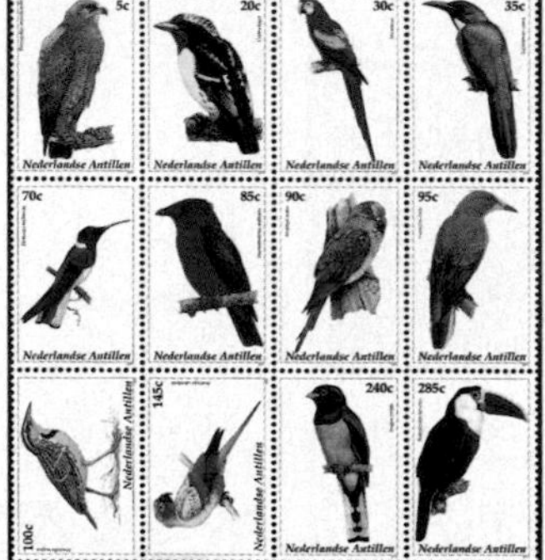

Birds — A284

No. 1002: a, 5c, Buteogallus meridionalis. b, 20c, Capito niger. c, 30c, Ara macao. d, 35c, Jacamerops aurea. e, 70c, Florisuga mellivora. f, 85c, Haematoderus militaris. g, 90c, Aratinga aurea. h, 95c, Psarocolius viridis. i, 100c, Sturnella magna, horiz. j, 145c, Aratinga solstitialis, horiz. k, 240c, Trogon viridis. l, 285c, Rhamphastos tucanus.

2002, Dec. 11 Litho. *Perf. 13x14*
1002 A284 Block of 12, #a-l 13.50 13.50

New Year 2003 (Year of the Ram) — A285

Chinese character and: 25c, Ram's head. 95c, Ram.

2003, Feb. 3
1003 A285 25c multi .30 .30

Souvenir Sheet

1004 A285 95c multi 1.10 1.10

Butterflies — A286

No. 1005: a, 5c, Rhetus arcius, vert. b, 10c, Evenus teresina. c, 25c, Bhutanitis thaidina. d, 30c, Semomesia capanea. e, 45c, Papilio machaon. f, 55c, Papilio multicaudata, vert. g, 65c, Graphium weiskei, vert. h, 95c, Ancyluris formosissima venabalis, vert. i, 100c, Euphaedra neophron. j, 145c, Ornithoptera goliath samson. k, 275c, Ancyluris colubra, vert. l, 350c, Papilio lorquinianus, vert.

Perf. 12¾x14 (vert. stamps), 14x12¾
2003, Apr. 23 Litho.
1005 A286 Block of 12, #a-l 13.50 13.50

Printed in sheets of 2 blocks separated by a central gutter.

Miniature Sheet

Musical Instruments — A287

No. 1006: a, 20c, Trumpet. b, 75c, Percussion instruments. c, 145c, Tenor saxophone. d, 285c, Double bass.

2003, May 28 *Perf. 12¾x14*
1006 A287 Sheet of 4, #a-d 6.00 6.00

Johann Enschedé and Sons, Printers, 300th Anniv. — A288

No. 1007: a, 70c, 25-florin bank note, 1827. b, 95c, #4. c, 145c, Revenue stamp. d, 240c, Portion of 1967 bank note.
550c, Enschedé headquarters, Netherlands.

2003, June 3
1007 A288 Sheet of 4, #a-d 6.25 6.25

Souvenir Sheet

1008 A288 550c multi 6.25 6.25

Bank of the Netherlands Antilles, 175th Anniv. A289

Designs: 95c, Portion of 10-guilder banknote with serial number magnified. 145c, Road map, Bank headquarters. 285c, Early bank document, vert.

Perf. 14x12¾, 12¾x14
2003, June 26
1009-1011 A289 Set of 3 6.00 6.00

Fedjai, the Postal Worker Type of 2001
Miniature Sheet

No. 1012: a, 30c, Fedjai giving gift to Angelina. b, 95c, Fedjai and Angelina at wedding. c, 145c, Fedjai taking pregnant wife on bicycle, horiz. d, 240c, Fedjai shows son to coworkers.

Perf. 12¾x14, 14x12¾ (#1012c)
2003, June 31
1012 A272 Sheet of 4, #a-d 5.75 5.75

Ships — A290

No. 1013: a, 5c, Egyptian boat, 15th cent. B.C. b, 5c, Ship of King Tutankhamen. c, 35c, Picture from Greek vase depicting Ulysses and the Sirens. d, 35c, Egyptian river boat. e, 40c, Greek dromond. f, 40c, Illustration from 15th cent. edition of Virgil's Aeneid. g, 60c, Javanese fusta. h, 60c, Greek trade ship. i, 75c, Venetian cog, 16th cent. j, 75c, Mora from Bayeux Tapestry. k, 85c, HMS Pembroke, ship of Capt. James Cook, vert. l, 85c, Savannah, first transatlantic steamship, 1819, vert.
Illustration reduced.

Perf. 14x12¾, 12¾x14 (vert. stamps)
2003, Aug. 7
1013 A290 Block of 12, #a-l 6.75 6.75

Miniature Sheets

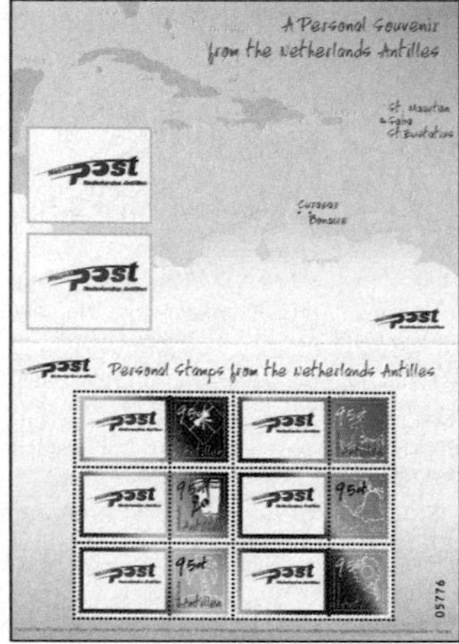

Personalized Stamps — A291

Designs: Nos. 1014a, 1015a, Gift. Nos. 1014b, 1015b, Rocking horse. Nos. 1014c, 1015c, Conga drums. Nos. 1014d, 1015d, Bells. Nos. 1014e, 1015e, Palm tree. Nos. 1014f, 1015f, Flower.

2003, Sept. 17 Litho. *Perf. 13¼x14*
1014 A291 95c Sheet of 6, #a-f, + 6 labels 12.00 12.00
1015 A291 145c Sheet of 6, #a-f, + 6 labels 17.00 17.00

Labels could be personalized. Nos. 1014-1015 each sold for $6 and $8.50 respectively in US funds.

Cats — A292

No. 1016: a, 5c, Bombay. b, 20c, Persian sealpoint. c, 25c, British shorthair blotchy. d, 50c, British blue. e, 65c, Persian chinchilla. f, 75c, Tonkinese red point. g, 85c, Balinese lilac tabbypoint. h, 95c, Persian shaded cameo. i, 100c, Burmilla. j, 145c, Chocolate tortie shaded silver eastern shorthair. k, 150c, Devon Rex silver tabby. l, 285c, Persian black tabby.

2003, Sept. 29 ***Perf. 12¾x14***
1016 A292 Block of 12, #a-l 12.50 12.50

Souvenir Sheet

Christmas and New Year's Day — A293

No. 1017 — Cacti with faces and Christmas lights and: a, 75c, Star. b, 240c, Clock.

2003, Nov. 17 Litho. ***Perf. 13x14***
1017 A293 Sheet of 2, #a-b 3.50 3.50

Airport Code and Local Attraction A294

Curves and Lines — A295

Designs: 50c, BON (Bonaire), slave hut. 75c, CUR (Curaçao), Handelskade, Willemstad. 95c, SAB (Saba), Holy Rosary Roman Catholic Church, Hell's Gate, Anglican Church, Valley. 120c, EUX (St. Eustatius), Simon Docker House, Fort Orange. 145c, SXM (St. Maarten), bird at sunset. 240c, CUR, Queen Emma Bridge. 285c, SXM, Simpson Bay.

2003, Nov. 27 ***Perf. 13½x12¾***

1018	A294	50c multi	.55	.55
1019	A294	75c multi	.85	.85
1020	A294	95c multi	1.10	1.10
1021	A294	120c multi	1.40	1.40
1022	A294	145c multi	1.60	1.60
1023	A294	240c multi	2.75	2.75
1024	A294	285c multi	3.25	3.25
1025	A295	380c multi	4.25	4.25
		Nos. 1018-1025 (8)	15.75	15.75

Birth of Princess Catharina-Amalia, Dec. 7, 2003 — A296

No. 1026: a, 145c, Princess Catharina-Amalia. b, 380c, Prince Willem-Alexander and Princess Catharina-Amalia.

2004, Jan. 16 ***Perf. 13½x13¾***
1026 A296 Horiz. pair, #a-b 6.00 6.00
c. Miniature sheet, #1026a, 1026b + central label 6.00 6.00

New Year 2004 (Year of the Monkey) — A297

Designs: 95c, Golden snub-nosed monkey. 145c, Monkey holding peach, on fan.

2004, Jan. 21 ***Perf. 13x13½***
1027 A297 95c multi 1.10 1.10

Souvenir Sheet

1028 A297 145c multi + 2 labels 1.60 1.60

Houses and Mansions — A298

No. 1029: a, 10c, Belvedère, L. B Smithplein 3. b, 25c, Hoogstraat 27. c, 35c, Landhuis Brievengat. d, 65c, Scharlooweg 102. e, 95c, Hoogstraat 21-25. f, 145c, Villa Maria, Van den Brandhofstraat 3 t/m 6. g, 275c, Werfstraat 6. h, 350c, Landhuis Ronde Klip.

2004, Feb. 20 ***Perf. 13½x13***
1029 A298 Block of 8, #a-h 11.50 11.50

See No. 1066.

Wild Animals — A299

No. 1030: a, 5c, Loxodonta africana. b, 10c, Loxodonta africana, diff. c, 25c, Loxodonta africana, diff. d, 35c, Pan troglodytes. e, 45c, Pan troglodytes, diff. f, 55c, Pan troglodytes, diff. g, 65c, Ursus maritimus. h, 95c, Ursus maritimus, diff. i, 100c, Ursus maritimus, diff. j, 145c, Panthera leo. k, 275c, Panthera leo, diff. l, 350c, Panthera leo, diff.

2004, Mar. 31
1030 A299 Block of 12, #a-l 13.50 13.50

Transportation — A300

No. 1031: a, 10c, Diesel locomotive, 1977. b, 55c, Water dealer and cart, 1900. c, 75c, 1903 Ford Model A. d, 85c, Oil tanker, 2004. e, 95c, 1903 Wright Flyer. f, 145c Penny Farthing bicycles, 1871.

2004, Apr. 27
1031 A300 Block of 6, #a-f 5.25 5.25

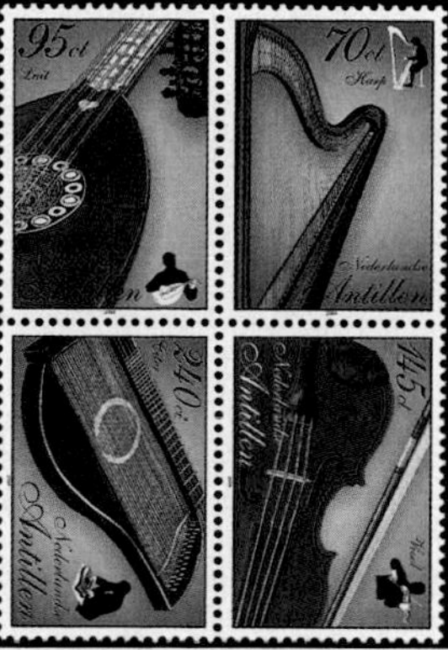

String Instruments — A301

No. 1032: a, 70c, Harp. b, 95c, Lute. c, 145c, Violin, horiz. d, 240c, Zither, horiz.

2004, May 26 ***Perf. 13x13½, 13½x13***
1032 A301 Block of 4, #a-d 6.25 6.25

Dogs — A302

No. 1033: a, 5c, Miniature pinscher. b, 5c, Pomeranian. c, 35c, Longhaired teckel. d, 35c, Shih tzu. e, 40c, Boxer. f, 40c, Jack Russell terrier. g, 60c, Basset hound. h, 60c, Braque de l'Ariege. i, 75c, Afghan hound. j, 75c, Old English sheepdog (bobtail). k, 85c, Entelbucher Sennen. l, 85c, Mastiff.

2004, June 22 ***Perf. 13x13½***
1033 A302 Block of 12, #a-l 6.75 6.75

World Stamp Championship 2004, Singapore — A303

No. 1034: a, 95c, Ship in St. Annabay Harbor, Curaçao, dragon. b, 95c, Flags of Singapore and Netherlands Antilles, lion. c, 145c, Brionplein houses, Curaçao, dragon. d, 145c, Ships at Dr. A. C. Wathey Cruise and Cargo Facility, St. Maarten, lion.
500c, Like No. 1034b.

2004, Aug. 23 ***Perf. 13½x13***
1034 A303 Block of 4, #a-d 5.50 5.50

Souvenir Sheet

1035 A303 500c multi 5.75 5.75

Fish and Ducks A304

No. 1036: a, Pomacanthus paru. b, Epinephelus guttatus. c, Mycteroperca interstitialis. d, Holacanthus isabelita. e, Epinephelus itajara. f, Holacanthus ciliaris. g, Anas americana, Sphyreana barracuda. h, Anas discors. i, Anas bahamensis. j, Aythya affinis.

2004, Sept. 28

1036		Block of 10	13.50	13.50
a.	A304	30c multi	.35	.35
b.	A304	65c multi	.75	.75
c.	A304	70c multi	.80	.80
d.	A304	75c multi	.85	.85
e.	A304	85c multi	.95	.95
f.	A304	95c multi	1.00	1.00
g.	A304	100c multi	1.10	1.10
h.	A304	145c multi	1.60	1.60
i.	A304	250c multi	2.75	2.75
j.	A304	285c multi	3.25	3.25

Birds — A305

Designs: 10c, Icterus icterus. 95c, Coereba flaveola. 100c, Zonotrichia capensis. 145c, Sterna hirundo. 250c, Phoenicopterus ruber. 500c, Buteo albicaudatus.

2004, Oct. 8
1037-1042 A305 Set of 6 12.50 12.50

Miniature Sheets

Coats of Arms and Flags — A306

Nos. 1043 and 1044 — Arms of: a, Bonaire. b, Curacao. c, Saba. d, St. Eustatius. e, St. Maarten. f, Flags of Islands of Netherlands Antilles.

2004, Oct. Litho. ***Perf. 13½x13¾***
1043 A306 95c Sheet of 6, #a-f, + 6 labels *13.00 13.00*
1044 A306 145c Sheet of 6, #a-f, + 6 labels *19.00 19.00*

Labels on Nos. 1043-1044 could be personalized. The two sheets together sold for €12.42.

Turtles A307

Designs: 100c, Loggerhead turtle. 145c, Kemp's Ridley turtle. 240c, Green turtle. 285c, Olive Ridley turtle. 380c, Hawksbill turtle. 500c, Leatherback turtle.

2004, Dec. 10 Litho. ***Perf. 13½x13***
1045-1050 A307 Set of 6 18.50 18.50

Buildings — A308

Beach Scene — A309

Self-Adhesive

2004 Litho. *Die Cut*

1051	A308 145c multi		4.00	4.00
1052	A309 145c multi		4.00	4.00
a.	Horiz. pair, #1051-1052		8.00	

Nos. 1051-1052 were printed in sheets of 10 containing five of each stamp at the right of the sheet. At the left of the sheet are three stamp-like vignettes lacking die cutting that were not valid for postage. The spaces at the right of the stamps where the birds are shown in the illustration was intended for personalization by customers on cruise ships that came to St. Maarten or Curacao. The three stamp-like vignettes at the left of the sheet also show the same personalized picture. Four different sheets, each depicting different birds in the space for personalization on each stamp and the three vignettes at the left of the sheet, were created as exemplars. The sheets, depicting birds or a personalized image, sold for $20 in US currency. The stamps were for postage for postcards mailed anywhere in the world.

Flowers A310

Designs: 65c, Hibiscus rosa sinensis. 76c, Plumbago auriculata. 97c, Tecoma stans. 100c, Ixora coccinea. 122c, Catharanthus roseus. 148c, Lantana camara. 240c, Tradescantia pallida. 270c, Nerium oleander. 285c, Plumeria obtusa. 350c, Bougainvillea spectabilis.

2005, Jan. 3 Litho. *Perf. 13½x13*

1053	A310 65c multi	.75	.75
1054	A310 76c multi	.85	.85
1055	A310 97c multi	1.10	1.10
1056	A310 100c multi	1.10	1.10
1057	A310 122c multi	1.40	1.40
1058	A310 148c multi	1.75	1.75
1059	A310 240c multi	2.75	2.75
1060	A310 270c multi	3.00	3.00
1061	A310 285c multi	3.25	3.25
1062	A310 350c multi	4.00	4.00
	Nos. 1053-1062 (10)	19.95	19.95

New Year 2005 (Year of the Rooster) — A311

Designs: 145c, Rooster and Chinese character. 500c, Two roosters.

2005, Feb. 9 *Perf. 13x13½*

1063 A311 145c multi 1.60 1.60

Souvenir Sheet

1064 A311 500c multi 5.75 5.75

Souvenir Sheet

Queen Beatrix, 25th Anniv. of Reign — A312

Photos: a, Coronation, 1980. b, Giving speech, 1991. c, With Nelson Mandela, 1999. d, Visiting colonies, 1999. e, At European Parliament, 2004.

2005, Apr. 30 *Perf. 13¼x13¾*

1065	A312 Sheet of 5	13.00	13.00
a.	50c multi	.60	.60
b.	97c multi	1.10	1.10
c.	145c multi	1.60	1.60
d.	285c multi	3.25	3.25
e.	550c multi	6.25	6.25

Houses & Mansions Type of 2004

No. 1066: a, 10c, Scharlooweg 76. b, 21c, Landhuis Zeelandia. c, 25c, Berg Altena. d, 35c, Landhuis Dokterstuin. e, 97c, Landhuis Santa Martha. f, 148c, Landhuis Seri Papaya. g, 270c, Landhuis Rooi Katooje. h, 300c, Plaza Horacio Hoyer 19.

2005, May 31 *Perf. 13½x13*

1066 A298 Block of 8, #a-h 10.50 10.50

Paintings by Vincent van Gogh — A313

No. 1067: a, 10c, Vase with Fourteen Sunflowers, detail. b, 65c, Sunflowers, detail. c, 80c, Self-portrait. d, 120c, Sunflowers, detail, diff. e, 150c, Vase with Fourteen Sunflowers. f, 175c, Joseph Roulin.

500c, Sunflowers, detail, diff.

2005, June 16 *Perf. 13x13½*

1067 A313 Block of 6, #a-f 10.00 10.00

Souvenir Sheet

1068 A313 500c multi 8.00 8.00

Otrobanda Section of Willemstad, 300th Anniv. (in 2007) — A314

No. 1069: a, 100c, Breedestraat. b, 150c, Wharf area. c, 285c, Rifwater. d, 500c, Brionplein bus stop.

2005, July 28 *Perf. 13½x13*

1069 A314 Block of 4, #a-d 12.00 12.00

See Nos. 1108-1111, 1157-1160.

Fruit — A315

2005, Aug. 31

1070	Block of 10	15.00	15.00
a.	A315 25c Papaya	.30	.30
b.	A315 45c Pomegranates	.50	.50
c.	A315 70c Mango	.80	.80
d.	A315 75c Bananas	.85	.85
e.	A315 85c Cashews	.95	.95
f.	A315 97c Soursops	1.10	1.10
g.	A315 145c Tamarinds	1.60	1.60
h.	A315 193c Watermelons	2.25	2.25
i.	A315 270c Gennips	3.00	3.00
j.	A315 300c Sea grapes	3.50	3.50

See Nos. 1247-1256.

Worldwide Fund for Nature (WWF) — A316

No. 1071: a, 51c, Blushing star coral. b, 148c, Rose coral. c, 270c, Smooth flower coral. d, 750c, Symmetrical brain coral.

2005, Sept. 29

1071 A316 Block of 4, #a-d 14.00 14.00

Musical Instruments A317

Designs: 55c, Bandoneon. 97c, Bagpipe, vert. 145c, Vina. 195c, Samisen, vert. 240c, Shofar. 285c, Kaha di òrgel, vert.

2005, Nov. 8 *Perf. 13½x13, 13x13½*

1072-1077 A317 Set of 6 11.50 11.50

A318

Santa Claus and: 10c, Children's hands. 97c, Children, horiz. 148c, Ornament, horiz. 580c, Chair.

Perf. 13x13½, 13½x13

2005, Nov. 17

1078-1081 A318 Set of 4 9.50 9.50

Christmas.

A319

Designs: 97c, Aerial view of St. Elizabeth Hospital, Willemstad. 145c, Stained glass window in hospital chapel. 300c, Entrance to first community hospital.

2005, Dec. 2 *Perf. 13x13½*

1082-1084 A319 Set of 3 6.25 6.25

St. Elizabeth Hospital, 150th anniv.

New Year 2006 (Year of the Dog) — A320

Chinese character and: 100c, Porcelain dogs. 149c, Various dog breeds.

500c, Dog and zodiac animals.

2006, Jan. 30 *Perf. 13½x13*

1085-1086 A320 Set of 2 2.75 2.75

Souvenir Sheet

1087 A320 500c multi 5.75 5.75

Equines A321

No. 1088: a, Turkmenian Kulan. b, Rhineland heavy draft horse. c, Donkey. d, Mule. e, Hanoverian and Arabian horses.

Perf. 13¼x12¾

2006, Feb. 24 Litho.

1088	Horiz. strip of 5	13.00	13.00
a.	A321 50c multi	.55	.55
b.	A321 100c multi	1.10	1.10
c.	A321 149c multi	1.75	1.75
d.	A321 285c multi	3.25	3.25
e.	A321 550c multi	6.25	6.25

Frogs — A322

Designs: 55c, Hyla cinerea. 100c, Dendrobates tinctorius. 149c, Dendrobates azureus. 405c, Epipedobates tricolor.

2006, Mar. 10 *Perf. 13¼x12¾*

1089-1092 A322 Set of 4 8.00 8.00

Butterflies A323

Designs: 24c, Danaus chrysippus. 53c, Prepona praeneste. 100c, Caligo uranus. 149c, Ituna lamirus. 285c, Euphaedra gausape. 335c, Morpho hecuba.

2006, Apr. 7

1093-1098 A323 Set of 6 11.00 11.00

Orchids A324

No. 1099: a, Brassolaeliocattleya Susan Harry M. G. R. b, Miltoniopsis Jean Sabourin. c, Promenaea xanthina Sylvan Sprite. d, Paphiopedilum Streathamense Wedgewood, vert. e, Cattleya chocoensis Linden, vert. f, Disa kewensis Rita Helen, vert.

Perf. 13¼x12¾, 12¾x13¼ (vert. stamps)

2006, Apr. 26

1099	Block of 6	21.00	21.00
a.	A324 153c multi	1.75	1.75
b.	A324 240c multi	2.75	2.75
c.	A324 285c multi	3.25	3.25
d.	A324 295c multi	3.25	3.25
e.	A324 380c multi	4.25	4.25
f.	A324 500c multi	5.75	5.75

Automobiles A325

Designs: 51c, 1976 MGB. 100c, 1963 Studebaker Avanti. 149c, 1953 Pegaso Cabriolet. 153c, 1939 Delage Aerosport. 195c, 1924 Hispano-Suiza Boulogne. 750c, 1903 Pierce Arrow Motorette.

2006, May 10 ***Perf. 13¼x12¾***
1100-1105 A325 Set of 6 16.00 16.00

Washington 2006 World Philatelic Exhibition — A326

No. 1106: a, 100c, Mailboxes of United States and Netherlands Antilles. b, 100c, Queen Emma Bridge, Curaçao, George Washington Bridge, New York and New Jersey. c, 149c, UPU emblem. d, 149c, Fokker F18-Snip, Fokker F4 airplanes.
405c, U.S. Capitol, Palace of the Governor of the Netherlands Antilles.

2006, May 26
1106 A326 Block of 4, #a-d 5.75 5.75

Souvenir Sheet

1107 A326 405c multi 4.75 4.75

Otrobanda Type of 2005

Designs: 100c, Hoogstraat. 149c, Emmabrug. 335c, Pasa Kontrami. 500c, Seaman's Home.

2006, June 16
1108-1111 A314 Set of 4 12.50 12.50

Greetings A327

Designs: 52c, Bless you. 55c, Love. 77c, All the best. 95c, Regards. 1.00g, Go for it. 1.49g, Tolerance. 1.53g, Positivism. 2.85g, Keep on going. 3.35g, Success. 4.05g, Be good.

2006, July 31
1112-1121 A327 Set of 10 19.00 19.00

See No. 1239-1245.

Birds — A328

No. 1122: a, Taeniopygia guttata. b, Parus caeruleus, vert. c, Pitta genus. d, Pyrrhula pyrrhula, vert. e, Calospiza fastuosa. f, Cosmopsarus regius, vert. g, Coracias caudatus, vert. h, Merops apiaster, vert. i, Icterus nigrogularis. j, Dendrocopus major, vert. k, Amazona barbadensis. l, Alcedo atthis, vert.

Perf. 13¼x12¾, 12¾x13¼ (vert. stamps)

2006, Aug. 18

1122	Block of 12	8.25	8.25
a.-b.	A328 5c Either single	.25	.25
c.-d.	A328 35c Either single	.35	.35
e.-f.	A328 60c Either single	.65	.65
g.-h.	A328 75c Either single	.85	.85
i.-j.	A328 85c Either single	.95	.95
k.-l.	A328 100c Either single	1.10	1.10

Miniature Sheets

Personalized Stamps — A329

Nos. 1123 and 1124: a, Dog, "Thank you." b, Flower, "Missing you." c, Hearts, "Love you." d, Cat, "Hello." e, Teddy bear, "Hugs & kisses." f, Dolphin, "Wish you were here."

Perf. 13¼x13¾

2006, Aug. 26 **Litho.**

Stamps Inscribed "Local Mail"

1123 A329 (1g) Sheet of 6, #a-f, + 6 labels 11.50 11.50

Stamps Inscribed "International Mail"

1124 A329 (1.49g) Sheet of 6, #a-f, + 6 labels 17.00 17.00

On day of issue, No. 1123 sold for 10g, and No. 1124 sold for 15g. Labels could be personalized. Labels shown are generic.

Rembrandt (1606-69), Painter — A330

No. 1125: a, 70c, The Nightwatch (detail of girl). b, 100c, De Staalmeesters. c, 153c, The Jewish Bride (detail). d, 285c, Self-portrait.
550c, The Nightwatch (detail of men).

Perf. 12¾x13¼

2006, Sept. 28 **Litho.**
1125 A330 Block of 4, #a-d 7.00 7.00

Souvenir Sheet

1126 A330 550c multi 6.25 6.25

Souvenir Sheet

Royal Visit of Queen Beatrix — A331

No. 1127 — Various photos of Queen Beatrix with background colors of: a, 149c, Red. b, 285c, Blue. c, 335c, Yellow. d, 750c, Orange.

2006, Nov. 13 ***Perf. 13¼x12¾***
1127 A331 Sheet of 4, #a-d 17.00 17.00

Christmas A332

Designs: 45c, Candles. 100c, Bells. 149c, Candles. 215c, Bells. 285c, Steeple. 380c, Flower.

2006, Nov. 15
1128-1133 A332 Set of 6 13.50 13.50

Fauna — A333

No. 1134: a, Cacatua leadbeateri leadbeateri. b, Aptenocytes patagonica. c, Pan troglodytes. d, Stenella longirostris. e, Anolis lineatus and Cordia sebestina, horiz. f, Passerina ciris. g, Dryas lulia. h, Bombay cat. i, Epinephelus guttatus, horiz. j, Panthera leo, horiz. k, Pomeranian dog. l, Hawksbill turtle, horiz.

Perf. 12¾x13¼, 13¼x12¾

2007, Jan. 26 **Litho.**

1134	Block of 12	14.00	14.00
a.	A333 3c multi	.25	.25
b.	A333 25c multi	.30	.30
c.	A333 53c multi	.60	.60
d.	A333 60c multi	.65	.65
e.	A333 80c multi	.90	.90
f.	A333 81c multi	.90	.90
g.	A333 95c multi	1.10	1.10
h.	A333 106c multi	1.25	1.25
i.	A333 145c multi	1.60	1.60
j.	A333 157c multi	1.75	1.75
k.	A333 161c multi	1.90	1.90
l.	A333 240c multi	2.75	2.75

New Year 2007 (Year of the Pig) — A334

Designs: 104c, Berkshire pig. 155c, Wart hog.
500c, Pig, vert.

2007, Feb. 20 ***Perf. 13¼x12¾***
1135-1136 A334 Set of 2 3.00 3.00

Souvenir Sheet

Perf. 12¾x13¼

1137 A334 500c multi 5.75 5.75

Islands — A335

Designs: 1c, Flag of Bonaire, divers and marine life. 2c, Flag of Curaçao, royal poinciana flowers. 3c, Flag of Saba, The Bottom. 4c, Flag of Statia (St. Eustatius), cannons at Fort Orange. 5c, Flag of St. Maarten, cruise ship and pier. 104c, Map of Bonaire, flamingos, horiz. 285c, Map of Curaçao, Chobolobo Landhouse, laraha tree, horiz. 335c, Map of Saba, houses, horiz. 405c, Map of Statia, oil storage tanks, horiz. 500c, Map of St. Maarten, Guavaberry Emporium, horiz.

Perf. 12¾x13¼, 13¼x12¾

2007, Mar. 1

1138	A335	1c multi	.25	.25
1139	A335	2c multi	.25	.25
1140	A335	3c multi	.25	.25
1141	A335	4c multi	.25	.25
1142	A335	5c multi	.25	.25
1143	A335	104c multi	1.25	1.25
1144	A335	285c multi	3.25	3.25
1145	A335	335c multi	3.75	3.75
1146	A335	405c multi	4.75	4.75
1147	A335	500c multi	5.75	5.75
	Nos. 1138-1147 (10)		20.00	20.00

See Nos. 1221-1226.

Ananzi the Spider A336

No. 1148 — Ananzi with: a, Turtle. b, Shark. c, Parrot. d, Cow. e, Dog. f, Goat. g, Chicken. h, Donkey.

2007, Mar. 21 ***Perf. 13¼x12¾***
1148 Block of 8 10.00 10.00
a.-h. A336 104c Any single 1.25 1.25

Saba Lace Designs — A337

Various lace designs with background colors of: 59c, Red. 80c, Green. 95c, Blue. 104c, Red. 155c, Green. 159c, Blue.

2007, Apr. 20 ***Perf. 12¾x13¼***
1149-1154 A337 Set of 6 7.50 7.50

Marine Life — A338

No. 1155: a, School of fish and sea floor. b, Portuguese man-of-war. c, Coral reef. d, Sea turtle. e, Sea anemones. f, Fish.

2007, May 22

1155	Block of 6	20.00	20.00
a.	A338 104c multi	1.25	1.25
b.	A338 155c multi	1.75	1.75
c.	A338 195c multi	2.25	2.25
d.	A338 335c multi	3.75	3.75
e.	A338 405c multi	4.75	4.75
f.	A338 525c multi	6.00	6.00

Fruits and Vegetables — A339

No. 1156: a, Grapes, Brussels sprouts, tomatoes, peppers and bananas. b, Pumpkins. c, Cucumber, tomatoes, corn, leeks. d, Strawberries, orange, peaches, pineapple. e, Avocados, horiz. f, Lemons, horiz. g, Peppers, corn, potato, mushrooms, horiz. h, Mangos, horiz.

Perf. 12¾x13¼, 13¼x12¾

2007, June 19

1156	Block of 8	11.50	11.50
a.	A339 10c multi	.25	.25
b.	A339 25c multi	.30	.30
c.	A339 35c multi	.40	.40
d.	A339 65c multi	.75	.75
e.	A339 95c multi	1.10	1.10
f.	A339 145c multi	1.60	1.60
g.	A339 275c multi	3.00	3.00
h.	A339 350c multi	4.00	4.00

Otrabanda Type of 2005

Designs: 104c, Brionplein Square. 155c, Jopi Building and Hotel Otrabanda. 285c, Kura Hulanda. 380c, Luna Blou.

2007, July 26 ***Perf. 13¼x12¾***
1157-1160 A314 Set of 4 10.50 10.50

Nature — A340

No. 1161: a, 30c, Nautilus shell. b, 65c, Turtles on beach. c, 70c, Grasshopper. d, 75c, Cactus. e, 85c, Swamp. f, 95c, Bird on cactus. g, 104c, Surf spray at rocks. h, 145c, Plants near water. i, 250c, Rainbow in rainforest. j, 285c, Sun on horizon.

Perf. 12¾x 13¼

2007, Aug. 22 Litho.

1161 A340 Block of 10, #a-j 13.50 13.50

Paintings by Dutch Artists — A341

No. 1162: a, 104c, Portrait of a Man (probably Nicolaes Hasselaer), by Frans Hals. b, 104c, Wedding of Isaak Abrahamsz Massa and Beatrix van der Lean, by Hals. c, 155c, The Merry Drinker, by Hals. d, 155c, Serenade, by Judith Leyster.

550c, The Meagre Company, by Hals, horiz.

2007, Sept. 20 ***Perf. 12¾x13¼***

1162 A341 Block of 4, #a-d 6.00 6.00

Souvenir Sheet

Perf. 13¼x12¾

1163 A341 550c multi 6.25 6.25

Dutch Royalty — A342

No. 1164: a, 50c, Queen Emma (1858-1934). b, 104c, Queen Wilhelmina (1880-1962). c, 155c, Queen Juliana (1909-2004). d, 285c, Queen Beatrix. e, 380c, Princess Máxima. f, 550c, Princess Catharina-Amalia.

2007, Oct. 10 ***Perf. 12¾x13¼***

1164 A342 Block of 6, #a-f 17.50 17.50

Christmas and New Year — A343

Designs: 48c, Candle. 104c, Gifts under Christmas tree. 155c, Musical notes and song lyrics, horiz. 215c, "2008" above "2007," horiz.

Perf. 12¾x13¼, 13¼x12¾

2007, Nov. 15 Litho.

1165-1168 A343 Set of 4 6.00 6.00

Mailboxes — A344

No. 1169 — Various mailboxes with panel color of: a, 20c, Yellow. b, 104c, Green. c, 240c, Light blue. d, 285c, Lilac. e, 380c, Orange. f, 500c, Brown.

2007, Dec. 3 ***Perf. 12¾x13¼***

1169 A344 Block of 6, #a-f 17.50 17.50

Lighthouses — A345

No. 1170: a, Fort Oranje, Bonaire. b, Malmok, Bonaire. c, Noordpunt, Curaçao. d, Klein Curaçao. e, Willemstoren, Bonaire. f, Bullenbaai, Curaçao.

2008, Jan. 21

1170 A345 158c Block of 6, #a-f 11.00 11.00

New Year 2008 (Year of the Rat) — A346

Designs: 106c, Stylized rat. 158c, Rat. 500c, Rat on branch, horiz.

2008, Feb. 7 ***Perf. 12¾x13¼***

1171-1172 A346 Set of 2 3.00 3.00

Souvenir Sheet

Perf. 13¼x12¾

1173 A346 500c multi 5.75 5.75

Dutch Royalty — A347

No. 1174: a, 75c, Princess Catharina-Amalia. b, 100c, Princess, diff. c, 125c, Crown Prince Willem-Alexander. d, 250c, Crown Prince, diff. e, 375c, Queen Beatrix. f, 500c, Queen, diff.

2008, Feb. 28 ***Perf. 12¾x13¼***

1174 A347 Block of 6, #a-f 16.00 16.00

Global Warming — A348

No. 1175: a, 50c, Smokestacks. b, 75c, Polar bear. c, 125c, Windmills. d, 250c, Beach and lighthouse.

2008, Mar. 20 ***Perf. 13¼x12¾***

1175 A348 Block of 4, #a-d 5.75 5.75

2008 Summer Olympics, Beijing — A349

No. 1176: a, 25c, Runner. b, 35c, Gymnast on rings. c, 75c, Swimmer. d, 215c, Cyclist.

2008, Apr. 1 ***Perf. 12¾x13¼***

1176 A349 Block of 4, #a-d 4.00 4.00

Stamp Passion Philatelic Exhibition, the Netherlands — A350

No. 1177: a, 75c, Netherlands Antilles #C14. b, 100c, Netherlands Antilles #29. c, 125c, Netherlands Antilles #CB19. d, 250c, Netherlands #O32. e, 375c, Netherlands #134. f, 500c, Netherlands Antilles #187.

2008, Apr. 11

1177 A350 Block of 6, #a-f 16.00 16.00

Images of stamps shown on Nos. 1177a, 1177c and 1177e are distorted.

Catholic Diocese of Netherlands Antilles and Aruba, 50th Anniv. — A351

Designs: 59c, Chapel of Alto Vista, Aruba. 106c, Cross at Seru Largu, Bonaire. 158c, St. Ann Church, Curaçao. 240c, Sacred Heart Church, Saba. 285c, Roman Catholic Church of Oranjestad, St. Eustatius. 335c, Mary Star of the Sea Church, St. Maarten.

2008, Apr. 28
1178-1183 A351 Set of 6 13.50 13.50

Dolls Depicting Women Doing Work — A352

No. 1184: a, 145c, Pounding corn (Batidó di maíshi den pilon). b, 145c, Selling fish (Bendedó di piská). c, 145c, Baking fish (Hasadó di masbangu riba bleki). d, 145c, Roasting coffee beans (Totadó di kòfi). e, 155c, Scrubbing clothes on scrub board (Labadera). f, 155c, Carrying basket of clothes (Labadó di paña na laman). g, 155c, Grinding corn on coral (Muladó di maíshi chikí riba pieda). h, 155c, Weaving hat (Trahadó di sombré).

2008, May 15
1184 A352 Block of 8, #a-h 13.50 13.50

Paintings by Johannes Vermeer (1632-75) — A353

No. 1185: a, 145c, Little Street. b, 145c, Girl with Pearl Earring. c, 155c, Woman in Blue Reading Letter. d, 155c, The Love Letter. 500c, The Milkmaid.

2008, June 23
1185 A353 Sheet of 4, #a-d, + 2 labels 6.75 6.75

Souvenir Sheet

1186 A353 500c multi 5.75 5.75

Windows A354

Various windows.

2008, July 8 ***Perf. 13¾***
1187 A354 5c multi .25 .25
1188 A354 106c multi, vert. 1.25 1.25
1189 A354 285c multi, vert., diff. 3.25 3.25
a. Souvenir sheet of 5, # 1187-1189, Aruba #330, Netherlands #1311, + etiquette 4.75 4.75

Nos. 1188-1189 were only available in No. 1189a. No. 1187 also was available in Aruba No. 332a and in Netherlands Nos. 1313a and 1313b.

Shells A355

Designs: 20c, Cypraea zebra. 40c, Charonia variegata. 65c, Calliostoma armillata. 106c, Strombus gigas. 158c, Pina carnea. 285c, Olivia sayana. 335c, Natica canrena. 405c, Voluta musica.

Perf. 13¼x12¾

2008, Sept. 19 **Litho.**
1190 A355 20c multi .25 .25
1191 A355 40c multi .45 .45
1192 A355 65c multi .75 .75
1193 A355 106c multi 1.25 1.25
1194 A355 158c multi 1.75 1.75
1195 A355 285c multi 3.25 3.25
1196 A355 335c multi 3.75 3.75
1197 A355 405c multi 4.75 4.75
Nos. 1190-1197 (8) 16.20 16.20

African Animals — A356

No. 1198: a, 75c, Giraffes, vert. b, 150c, Elephants. c, 175c, Cheetahs. d, 250c, Zebras.
No. 1199, Impalas, vert.

Perf. 13¼x12¾, 12¾x13¼ (vert. stamps)

2008, Oct. 2
1198 A356 Block of 4, #a-d 7.50 7.50

Souvenir Sheet

1199 A356 250c multi 3.00 3.00

Christmas and New Year's Day — A357

Designs: 50c, Plate of basil. 106c, Flowers. 158c, Fishermen in boat. 215c, Dock.

Perf. 13¼x12¾

2008, Nov. 14 **Litho.**
1200-1203 A357 Set of 4 6.00 6.00

Traditional Costumes — A358

No. 1204: a, 100c, Antillean girl. b, 104c, Dutch boy. c, 155c, Japanese girl.

2008, Nov. 27 ***Perf. 12¾x13¼***
1204 A358 Horiz. strip of 3, #a-c 4.00 4.00

Birds A359

No. 1205: a, Kasuaris (cassowary). b, Struisvogel (ostrich). c, Pinguin (penguin). d, Kalkoen (wild turkey). e, Aalscholver (cormorant), horiz. f, Mandarijneend (Mandarin duck), horiz. g, Putter-distelvink (goldfinch), horiz. h, Groene reiger (green heron), horiz.

Perf. 12¾x13¼, 13¼x12¾ (horiz. stamps)

2008, Dec. 12
1205 A359 158c Block of 8, #a-h 22.00 22.00

Flowers A360

No. 1206: a, Nelumbo nucifera. b, Chrysanthemum leucanthemum. c, Hepatica nobilis. d, Cistus incanus. e, Alamanda. f, Wise portia.

2009, Jan. 26 **Litho.** ***Perf. 13¼x12¾***
1206 Block of 6 17.00 17.00
a. A360 75c multi .85 .85
b. A360 150c multi 1.75 1.75
c. A360 200c multi 2.25 2.25
d. A360 225c multi 2.50 2.50
e. A360 350c multi 4.00 4.00
f. A360 500c multi 5.50 5.50

New Year 2009 (Year of the Ox) — A361

Chinese character and: 110c, Outline of ox. 168c, Ox, horiz.

Perf. 12¾x13¼, 13¼x12¾

2009, Feb. 19
1207-1208 A361 Set of 2 3.25 3.25

Butterflies — A362

No. 1209: a, 25c, Lycaena phlaeas. b, 35c, danaus plexippus. c, 50c, Nymphalis antiopa. d, 105c, Carterocephalus palaemon. e, 115c, Inachis io. f, 155c, Phyciodes tharos. g, 185c, Papilio glaucus. h, 240c, Dryas iulia. i, 315c, Libytheana carinenta. j, 375c, Melanis pixe. k, 400c, Asterocampa celtis. l, 1000c, Historis acheronta.

2009, Mar. 2 ***Perf. 13¼x12¾***
1209 A362 Block of 12, #a-l 34.00 34.00

Birds — A363

No. 1210: a, 10c, Daptrius americanus. b, 45c, Amazona amazonica. c, 80c, Querula purpurata. d, 145c, Aratinga leucophthalmus. e, 190c, Xipholena punicea. f, 235c, Celeus torquatus. g, 285c, Lamprospiza melanoleuca. h, 300c, Selenidera culik. i, 335c, Amazila viridigaster. j, 425c, Tangara gyrola. k, 450c, Nyctibius grandis. l, 500c, Galbula leucogastra.

2009, Apr. 20 *Perf. 12¾x13¼*

1210 A363 Block of 12, #a-l 35.00 35.00

Telecommunications and Posts Department, Cent. — A364

Designs: 59c, Ship, telegraph operator. 110c, Person on telephone, room with radio and television. 164c, Person at computer, satellite dish, street scene.

2009, May 18 *Perf. 13¼x12¾*

1211-1213 A364 Set of 3 3.75 3.75

Pianos A365

Pianos manufactured by: 175c, J. B. & Sons, 1796. 225c, J. Schantz, 1818, vert. 250c, Steinway-Welt, 1927, vert. 350c, Yamaha, 2007.

Perf. 13¼x12¾, 12¾x13¼

2009, June 1

1214-1217 A365 Set of 4 11.50 11.50

Nos. 1214-1217 were printed in a sheet of 8 containing two of each stamp, with a central label.

Miniature Sheets

A366

A367

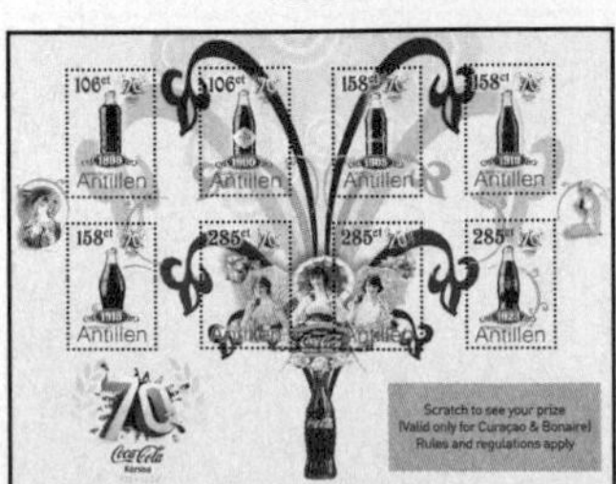

Coca-Cola Bottling on Curaçao, 70th Anniv. — A368

No. 1218 — Fria soft drinks: a, No bottle shown. b, Bottle with pink drink, parts of blue balls at UL and bottom. c, Bottle with purple drink, parts of red ball at UL and purple ball at right. d, Bottle with yellow drink, parts of green ball at UL and purple ball at LR. e, Bottle with orange drink, parts of purple ball at UL and red ball at LL. f, Bottle with red drink, parts of purple ball at UL, blue ball at LR. g, Bottle with pale pink drink, part of red ball at LR. h, Bottle with yellow-green drink, part of orange ball at LR.

No. 1219: a, Coca-Cola advertisement showing couple on beach and bottle. b, Women around counter with two Coca-Cola advertisements. c, Coca-Cola building with awning at left. d, Man at vending machine. e, Man and automobile in front of building with Coca-Cola advertisement, vert. f, Two men holding bottles of Coca-Cola. g, Men and women around a counter. h, Delivery truck.

No. 1220: a, 106c, 1899 Coca-Cola bottle. b, 106c, 1900 Coca-Cola bottle. c, 158c, 1905 Coca-Cola bottle. d, 158c, 1913 Coca-Cola bottle. e, 158c, 1915 Coca-Cola bottle. f, 285c, Woman holding glass of Coca-Cola and blue-striped umbrella. g, 285c, Woman holding glass of Coca-Cola and yellow umbrella. h, 285c, 1923 Coca-Cola bottle.

Perf. 12¾x13¼, 13¼x12¾

2008, Dec. 23 **Litho.**

1218	A366	106c Sheet of 8, #a-h	9.50	9.50
1219	A367	158c Sheet of 8, #a-h	14.50	14.50
1220	A368	Sheet of 8, #a-h	17.50	17.50
		Nos. 1218-1220 (3)	41.50	41.50

Islands Type of 2007

Designs: 30c, Flag of Bonaire, divers and marine life. 59c, Map of Statia, oil storage tanks, horiz. 110c, Flag of Curaçao, royal poinciana flowers. 164c, Flag of St. Maarten, cruise ship and pier. 168c, Map of bonaire, flamingos, horiz. 285c, Map of Saba, houses, horiz.

Perf. 12¾x13¼, 13¼x12¾

2009, Jan.

1221	A335	30c multi	.35	.35
1222	A335	59c multi	.70	.70
1223	A335	110c multi	1.25	1.25
1224	A335	164c multi	1.90	1.90
1225	A335	168c multi	1.90	1.90
1226	A335	285c multi	3.25	3.25
		Nos. 1221-1226 (6)	9.35	9.35

Souvenir Sheet

Birds — A369

No. 1227: a, 5g, Celeus undatus. b, 10g, Todopleura fusca.

2009, July 20 *Perf. 13¼x12¾*

1227 A369 Sheet of 2, #a-b 17.00 17.00

Sailing Ships — A370

No. 1228: a, 1c, Merchantman, 200. b, 2c, Caravel, 1490. c, 3c, Naos, 1492. d, 4c, Constant, 1605. e, 5c, Merchant ship, 1620. f, 80c, Vasa, 1628. g, 220c, Hoys, 1730. h, 275c, Bark, 1750. i, 385c, Schooner, 1838. j, 475c, Sailing rig, 1884. k, 500c, Fifie, 1903. l, 750c, Junk, 1938.

2009, Aug. 31

1228 A370 Block of 12, #a-l 31.00 31.00

Snakes — A371

No. 1229: a, 275c, Bothriopsis bilineata. b, 325c, Bothriechis schlegelii. c, 340c, Agkistrodeon piscivorous. d, 390c, Erythrolamprus aesculapii. e, 420c, Atropoides mexicanus. f, 450c, Bothriechis nigroviridis.

2009, Oct. 5

1229 A371 Block of 6, #a-f 26.00 26.00

Aviation Pioneers A372

Designs: 59c, Freddy Johnson (1932-2001). 110c, Norman Chester Wathey (1925-2001). 164c, José Dormoy (1925-2007).

Perf. 13¼x12¾

2009, Nov. 10 **Litho.**

1230-1232 A372 Set of 3 3.75 3.75

Airplanes A373

No. 1233: a, Wright Flyer, 1903. b, DST Skysleeper, 1935. c, Cessna 170, 1948. d, Lockheed Constellation, 1943. e, De Havilland Comet, 1949. f, BAC Super VC10, 1962.

2009, Nov. 16

1233	Block of 6	25.00	25.00
a.	A373 55c multi	.65	.65
b.	A373 100c multi	1.10	1.10
c.	A373 205c multi	2.40	2.40
d.	A373 395c multi	4.50	4.50
e.	A373 645c multi	7.25	7.25
f.	A373 800c multi	9.00	9.00

Hanukkah A374

Christmas A375

Kwanzaa A376

New Year's Day A377

2009, Nov. 30 *Perf. 12¾x13¼*

1234	A374	50c multi	.60	.60
1235	A375	110c multi	1.25	1.25
1236	A376	168c multi	1.90	1.90
1237	A377	215c multi	2.50	2.50
		Nos. 1234-1237 (4)	6.25	6.25

Fruit — A378

2009, Dec. 28 **Litho.**

1238	Block of 8 + label	23.00	23.00
a.	A378 20c Sapodilla	.25	.25
b.	A378 45c Pineapple	.50	.50
c.	A378 125c Mamey sapote	1.40	1.40
d.	A378 145c Avocado	1.60	1.60
e.	A378 160c Mangosteen	1.75	1.75
f.	A378 210c Rambutan	2.40	2.40
g.	A378 295c Pomelo	3.50	3.50
h.	A378 1000c Watermelon	11.50	11.50

Greetings Type of 2006

Designs: 32c, Bless you. 60c, Love. 81c, All the best. 87c, Regards. 1.06g, Go for it. 1.57g, Tolerance. 1.61g, Positivism.

2009 *Perf. 13¼x12¾*

1239-1245 A327 Set of 7 7.75 7.75

Flowers — A379

No. 1246: a, 50c, Opuntia basilaris. b, 75c, Aristolochiaceae. c, 125c, Protea cynaroides. d, 175c, Louisiana iris. e, 200c, Spontaneous frangipani. f, 250c, Red azaleas. g, 300c, English Heritage rose. h, 350c, Aquilegia. i, 475c, Octavia Hill rose. j, 500c, Tea rose.

2010, Jan. 25 **Litho.** *Perf. 13¼x12¾*

1246 A379 Block of 10, #a-j 29.00 29.00

Fruit Type of 2005

2010, Feb. 1 **Litho.** *Perf. 13¼x12¾*

1247	A315	1c	Papaya	.25	.25
1248	A315	5c	Pomegranates	.25	.25
1249	A315	30c	Mangos	.35	.35
1250	A315	59c	Bananas	.70	.70
1251	A315	79c	Cashews	.90	.90
1252	A315	111c	Soursops	1.25	1.25
1253	A315	164c	Tamarinds	1.90	1.90
1254	A315	170c	Watermelons	2.00	2.00
1255	A315	199c	Gennips	2.25	2.25
1256	A315	285c	Sea grapes	3.25	3.25
			Nos. 1247-1256 (10)	13.10	13.10

New Year 2010 (Year of the Tiger) — A380

Designs: 111c, Tiger cub. 164c, Tiger and cub. 170c, White tiger.

2010, Feb. 1 *Perf. 12¾x13¼*

1257-1259 A380 Set of 3 5.00 5.00

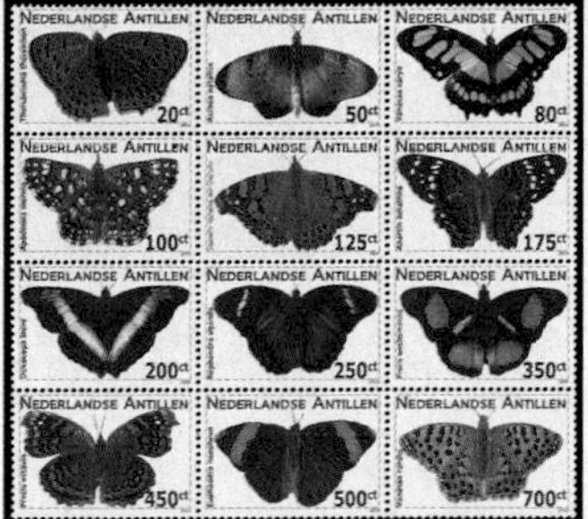
Butterflies — A381

No. 1260: a, 20c, Thersamonia thersamon. b, 50c, Acraea natalica. c, 80c, Vanessa carye. d, 100c, Apodemia mormo. e, 125c, Siproeta stelenes meridionalis. f, 175c, Anartia amathea. g, 200c, Doxocopa laure. h, 250c, Euphaedra uganda. i, 350c, Precis westermannii. j, 450c, Precis octavia. k, 500c, Euphaedra neophron. l, 700c, Vanessa cardui.

2010, Mar. 1 ***Perf. 13¼x12¾***
1260 A381 Block of 12, #a-l 34.00 34.00

Paintings by Vincent Van Gogh — A382

Designs: 200c, Self-portrait, 1888. 400c, Agostina Segatori, 1887. 500c, Arlesian Woman, 1888. 700c, Emperor Moth, 1889.

2010, Apr. 7 ***Perf. 12¾x13¼***
1261 A382 200c multi 2.25 2.25
1262 A382 400c multi 4.50 4.50
1263 A382 500c multi 5.75 5.75
1264 A382 700c multi 8.00 8.00
Nos. 1261-1264 (4) 20.50 20.50

Nos. 1261-1264 were printed in sheets of 8 containing two of each stamp with a central label.

Birds A383

No. 1265: a, 75c, Pipra aureola. b, 150c, Neopelma chrysocephalum. c, 200c, Oxyruncus cristatus. d, 225c, Automolus rufipileatus. e, 350c, Empidonomus varius. f, 500c, Veniliornis sanguineus.

2010, May 10
1265 A383 Block of 6, #a-f 17.00 17.00

Ships — A384

No. 1266 — Inscriptions: a, 100c, Osberg, 800. b, 125c, Dromon, 910. c, 175c, Cocca, 1500. d, 200c, Mary, 1661. e, 250c, Houtport, 1700. f, 300c, Santissima Trinidad, 1769. g, 350c, Vrachtschip, 1800. h, 400c, Amistad, 1839. i, 450c, Oorlogsschip, 1840. j, 650c, Nederlands schip, 1850.

Perf. 13¼x12¾
2010, June 14 **Litho.**
1266 A384 Block of 10, #a-j 34.00 34.00

Netherlands Antilles Stamps — A385

No. 1267: a, 25c, #109. b, 50c, #140. c, 100c, #77. d, 250c, #144. e, 275c, #290. f, 300c, #75. g, 400c, #C34. h, 600c, #200.
No. 1268: a, 700c, #204. b, 800c, #141.

2010, July 19 ***Perf. 12¾x13¼***
1267 A385 Block of 8, #a-h 22.50 22.50

Souvenir Sheet

1268 A385 Sheet of 2, #a-b 17.00 17.00

Image of stamp on No. 1267d is distorted.

TeleCuraçao, 50th Anniv. A386

Television showing: 59c, Cameraman. 111c, Transmission tower. 164c, 50th anniversary emblem.

2010, Aug. 2 Litho. ***Perf. 13¼x12¾***
1269-1271 A386 Set of 3 3.75 3.75

Pocket Watches — A387

No. 1272 — Watches made by: a, Ulysse, 1890. b, Hampden, 1910. c, Elgin, 1924. d, Illinois, 1928. e, Vacheron, 1955.

2010, Sept. 6 ***Perf. 12¾x13¼***
1272 Horiz. strip of 5 14.00 14.00
a. A387 125c multi 1.40 1.40
b. A387 175c multi 2.00 2.00
c. A387 250c multi 3.00 3.00
d. A387 300c multi 3.50 3.50
e. A387 350c multi 4.00 4.00

On Oct. 10, 2010, the Netherlands Antilles was dissolved, being replaced by three entities: Caribbean Netherlands, Curaçao and St. Martin.

SEMI-POSTAL STAMPS

Catalogue values for unused stamps in this section are for Never Hinged items.

Nos. 132, 133 and 135 Surcharged in Black

1947, Dec. 1 Unwmk. ***Perf. 12½***
B1 A26 1½c + 2½c on 6c .90 .80
B2 A26 2½c + 5c on 10c .90 .80
B3 A26 5c + 7½c on 15c .90 .80
Nos. B1-B3 (3) 2.70 2.40

The surtax was for the National Inspanning Welzijnszorg in Nederlandsch Indie, relief organization for Netherlands Indies.

Curaçao Children
SP1 SP2

Design: Nos. B6, B9, Girl.

1948, Nov. 3 Photo. ***Perf. 12½x12***
B4 SP1 6c + 10c ol brn 2.25 1.75
B5 SP2 10c + 15c brt red 2.25 1.75
B6 SP2 12½c + 20c Prus grn 2.25 1.75
B7 SP1 15c + 25c brt bl 2.25 1.75
B8 SP2 20c + 30c red brn 2.25 1.75
B9 SP2 25c + 35c purple 2.25 1.75
Nos. B4-B9 (6) 13.50 10.50

The surtax was for child welfare and the White/Yellow Cross Foundation.

Leapfrog — SP4

Designs: 5c+2½c, Flying kite. 6c+2½c, Girls swinging. 12½c+5c, "London Bridge." 25c+10c, Rolling hoops.

Perf. 14½x13½
1951, Aug. 16 **Unwmk.**
B10 SP4 1½c + 1c pur 1.75 2.10
B11 SP4 5c + 2½c brn 10.00 4.50
B12 SP4 6c + 2½c blue 10.00 4.50
B13 SP4 12½c + 5c red 10.00 4.50
B14 SP4 25c + 10c dl grn 10.00 4.00
Nos. B10-B14 (5) 41.75 19.60

The surtax was for child welfare.

Ship and Gull — SP5

Designs: 6c+4c, Sailor and lighthouse. 12½c+7c, Prow of sailboat. 15c+10c, Ships. 25c+15c, Ship, compass and anchor.

1952, July 16 ***Perf. 13x14***
B15 SP5 1½c + 1c dk grn 1.00 1.10
B16 SP5 6c + 4c choc 8.00 3.25
B17 SP5 12½c + 7c red vio 8.00 3.50
B18 SP5 15c + 10c dp bl 10.00 4.25
B19 SP5 25c + 15c red 9.00 3.25
Nos. B15-B19 (5) 36.00 15.35

The surtax was for the seamen's welfare fund.

No. 226 Surcharged in Black

1953, Feb. 21
B20 A45 22½c + 7½c on 1½g .90 1.00

The surtax was for flood relief in the Netherlands.

Tribulus Cistoides SP6

Flowers: 7½c+5c, Yellow hibiscus. 15c+5c, Oleander. 22½c+7½c, Cactus. 25c+10c, Red hibiscus.

1955, May 17 Photo. ***Perf. 14x13***
Flowers in Natural Colors
B21 SP6 1½c + 1c bl grn & dk bl .30 .35
B22 SP6 7½c + 5c dp ultra 2.50 1.75
B23 SP6 15c + 5c ol grn 2.50 1.90
B24 SP6 22½c + 7½c dk bl 2.50 1.75
B25 SP6 25c + 10c ind & gray 2.50 1.90
Nos. B21-B25 (5) 10.30 7.65

The surtax was for child welfare.

Prince Bernhard and Queen Juliana SP7

1955, Oct. 19 ***Perf. 11x12***
B26 SP7 7½c + 2½c rose brn .25 .25
B27 SP7 22½c + 7½c dp bl .80 .80

Royal visit to the Netherlands Antilles, Oct. 1955.
Surtax paid for a gift.

Lord Baden-Powell — SP8

1957, Feb. 22 ***Perf. 14x13½***
B28 SP8 6c + 1½c org yel .40 .40
B29 SP8 7½c + 2½c dp grn .40 .40
B30 SP8 15c + 5c red .40 .40
Nos. B28-B30 (3) 1.20 1.20

50th anniv. of the Boy Scout movement.

Soccer Player — SP9

Map of Central America and the Caribbean SP10

Designs: 15c+5c, Goalkeeper catching ball. 22½c+7½c, Men playing soccer.

1957, Aug. 6 ***Perf. 12x11, 11x12***

B31 SP9 6c + 2½c org .40 .50
B32 SP10 7½c + 5c dk red .80 .90
B33 SP9 15c + 5c brt bl grn .90 .90
B34 SP9 22½c + 7½c brt bl .90 .70
Nos. B31-B34 (4) 3.00 3.00

8th Central American and Caribbean Soccer Championships, Aug. 11-25.
Surtax was for organizing costs.

American Kestrel — SP11

Birds: 7½+1½c, Yellow oriole. 15+2½c, Common ground doves. 22½+2½c, Brown-throated parakeet.

1958, Apr. 15 **Photo.** ***Perf. 13½x14***

B35 SP11 2½c + 1c multi .25 .25
B36 SP11 7½c + 1½c multi .70 .60
B37 SP11 15c + 2½c multi .80 .80
B38 SP11 22½c + 2½c multi .90 .70
Nos. B35-B38 (4) 2.65 2.35

The surtax was for child welfare.

Flag and Map — SP12

1958, Dec. 1 **Litho.** ***Perf. 13½***
Cross in Red

B39 SP12 6c + 2c red brn .30 .30
B40 SP12 7½c + 2½c bl grn .40 .40
B41 SP12 15c + 5c org yel .40 .40
B42 SP12 22½c + 7½c blue .40 .40
Nos. B39-B42 (4) 1.50 1.50

The surtax was for the Red Cross.

Community House, Zeeland SP13

Historic buildings: 7½c+2½c, Molenplein. 15c+5c, Saba, vert. 22½c+7½c, Scharlooburg. 25c+7½c, Community House, Brievengat.

Perf. 14x13½, 13½x14
1959, Sept. 16 **Litho.**

B43 SP13 6c + 1½c multi .80 .70
B44 SP13 7½c + 2½c multi .80 .80
B45 SP13 15c + 5c multi .80 .80
B46 SP13 22½c + 7½c multi .80 .80
B47 SP13 25c + 7½c multi .80 .80
Nos. B43-B47 (5) 4.00 3.90

The surtax went to the Foundation for the Preservation of Historical Monuments.

Fish — SP14

Designs. 10c+2c, SCUBA diver with spear gun, vert. 25c+5c, Two fish.

1960, Aug. 24 **Photo.** ***Perf. 13½***

B48 SP14 10c + 2c sapphire .80 .80
B49 SP14 20c + 3c multi 1.10 1.10
B50 SP14 25c + 5c blk, brt pink & dk bl 1.10 1.10
Nos. B48-B50 (3) 3.00 3.00

The surtax was for the fight against cancer.

Infant — SP15

Designs: 10c+3c, Girl and doll. 20c+6c, Boy on beach. 25c+8c, Children in school.

1961, July 24 **Litho.** ***Perf. 13½x14***
Designs in Black

B51 SP15 6c + 2c lt yel grn .25 .25
B52 SP15 10c + 3c rose red .25 .25
B53 SP15 20c + 6c yellow .25 .25
B54 SP15 25c + 8c orange .25 .25
Nos. B51-B54 (4) 1.00 1.00

The surtax was for child welfare.

Globe and Knight SP16

1962, May 2 ***Perf. 13½x14½***

B55 SP16 10c + 5c green .60 .55
B56 SP16 20c + 10c carmine .60 .55
B57 SP16 25c + 10c dk bl .60 .55
Nos. B55-B57 (3) 1.80 1.65

Intl. Candidates Chess Tournament, Willemstad, May-June.

No. 248 Surcharged

1963, Mar. 21

B58 A56 20c + 10c crimson & gray .40 .40

FAO "Freedom from Hunger" campaign.

Child and Flowers — SP17

Designs: 6c+3c, Three girls and flowers, horiz. 10c+5c, Girl with ball and trees, horiz. 20c+10c, Three boys with flags, horiz. 25c+12c, Singing boy.

Perf. 14½x13½, 13½x14½
1963, Oct. 23 **Photo.** **Unwmk.**

B59 SP17 5c + 2c multi .25 .25
B60 SP17 6c + 3c multi .25 .25
B61 SP17 10c + 5c multi .25 .25
B62 SP17 20c + 10c multi .25 .25
B63 SP17 25c + 12c multi .25 .25
Nos. B59-B63 (5) 1.25 1.25

Surtax for child welfare.

Bougainvillea SP18

Designs: 10c+5c, Wild rose. 20c+10c, Chalice flower. 25c+11c, Bellisima.

1964, Oct. 21 ***Perf. 14x13***
Flowers in Natural Colors

B64 SP18 6c + 3c bl vio & blk .25 .25
B65 SP18 10c + 5c yel brn, yel & blk .25 .25
B66 SP18 20c + 10c dull red & blk .25 .25
B67 SP18 25c + 11c citron & brn .25 .25
Nos. B64-B67 (4) 1.00 1.00

The surtax was for child welfare.

Sea Anemones and Star Coral SP19

Corals: 6c+3c, Blue cup sponges. 10c+5c, Green cup sponges. 25c+11c, Basket sponge, knobbed brain coral and reef fish.

1965, Nov. 10 **Photo.** ***Perf. 14x13½***

B68 SP19 6c + 3c multi .25 .25
B69 SP19 10c + 5c multi .25 .25
B70 SP19 20c + 10c multi .25 .25
B71 SP19 25c + 11c multi .25 .25
Nos. B68-B71 (4) 1.00 1.00

The surtax was for child welfare.

ICEM Type of Netherlands

1966, Jan. 31 **Photo.** ***Perf. 14x13***

B72 SP181 35c + 15c brn & dl yel .25 .25

The surtax was for the Intergovernmental Committee for European Migration (ICEM). The message on the stamps was given and signed by Queen Juliana.

Girl Cooking — SP20

Youth at Work: 10c+5c, Nurse's aide with infant. 20c+10c, Young metalworker. 25c+11c, Girl ironing.

1966, Nov. 15 ***Perf. 13½***

B73 SP20 6c + 3c multi .25 .25
B74 SP20 10c + 5c multi .25 .25
B75 SP20 20c + 10c multi .25 .25
B76 SP20 25c + 11c multi .25 .25
Nos. B73-B76 (4) 1.00 1.00

The surtax was for child welfare.

Helping Hands Supporting Women — SP21

1967, July 4 **Litho.** ***Perf. 13x14***

B77 SP21 6c + 3c bl & blk .25 .25
B78 SP21 10c + 5c brt pink & blk .25 .25
B79 SP21 20c + 10c lilac .25 .25
B80 SP21 25c + 11c dk bl .25 .25
Nos. B77-B80 (4) 1.00 1.00

The surtax was for various social and cultural institutions.

Nanzi the Spider and the Tiger — SP22

Nanzi Stories (Folklore): 6c+3c, Princess Longnose, vert. 10c+5c, The Turtle and the Monkey. 25c+11c, Adventure of Shon Arey, vert.

Perf. 14x13, 13x14
1967, Nov. 15 **Photo.**

B81 SP22 6c + 3c dk red, pink & org .25 .25
B82 SP22 10c + 5c vio bl & org .25 .25
B83 SP22 20c + 10c grn & org .25 .25
B84 SP22 25c + 11c brt bl & org .25 .25
Nos. B81-B84 (4) 1.00 1.00

The surtax was for child welfare.

Lintendans (Dance) and Koeoekoe House SP23

1968, May 29 **Litho.** ***Perf. 14x13***

B85 SP23 10c + 5c multi .25 .25
B86 SP23 15c + 5c multi .25 .25
B87 SP23 20c + 10c multi .25 .25
B88 SP23 25c + 10c multi .25 .25
Nos. B85-B88 (4) 1.00 1.00

The surtax was for various social and cultural institutions.

Boy and Pet Cat — SP24

Designs: 6c+3c, Boy and goat. 10c+5c, Girl and poodle. 25c+11c, Girl and duckling.

1968, Nov. 13 **Photo.** ***Perf. 13½***

B89 SP24 6c + 3c multi .25 .25
B90 SP24 10c + 5c multi .25 .25
B91 SP24 20c + 10c multi .25 .25
B92 SP24 25c + 11c multi .25 .25
Nos. B89-B92 (4) 1.00 1.00

The surtax was for child welfare.

Carnival Headpiece SP25

Folklore: 15c+5c, Harvest-home festival. 20c+10c, Feast of St. John (dancers & cock). 25c+10c, "Dande" New Year's celebration.

1969, July 23 **Litho.** ***Perf. 13½***

B93 SP25 10c + 5c multi .25 .25
B94 SP25 15c + 5c multi .25 .25
B95 SP25 20c + 10c multi .30 .30
B96 SP25 25c + 10c multi .30 .30
Nos. B93-B96 (4) 1.10 1.10

The surtax was for various social and cultural institutions.

Boy Playing Guitar SP26

Designs: 10c+5c, Girl with English flute. 20c+10c, Boy playing the marimula. 25c+11c, Girl playing the piano.

1969, Nov. 3 Litho. *Perf. 14x13*

B97 SP26 6c + 3c org & vio .25 .25
B98 SP26 10c + 5c yel & brt grn .30 .30
B99 SP26 20c + 10c bl & car .30 .30
B100 SP26 25c + 11c pink & brn .30 .30
Nos. B97-B100 (4) 1.15 1.15

The surtax was for child welfare.

Printing Press and Quill — SP27

Mass Media: 15c+5c, Filmstrip and reels. 20c+10c, Horn and radio mast. 25c+10c, Television antenna and eye focused on globe.

1970, July 14 Litho. *Perf. 13½*

B101 SP27 10c + 5c multi .30 .30
B102 SP27 15c + 5c multi .30 .30
B103 SP27 20c + 10c multi .30 .30
B104 SP27 25c + 10c multi .30 .30
Nos. B101-B104 (4) 1.20 1.20

The surtax was for various social and cultural institutions.

Mother and Child — SP28

Designs: 10c+5c, Girl holding piggy bank. 20c+10c, Boys wrestling (Judokas). 25c+11c, Youth carrying small boy on his shoulders.

1970, Nov. 16 *Perf. 13½x14*

B105 SP28 6c + 3c multi .50 .50
B106 SP28 10c + 5c multi .50 .50
B107 SP28 20c + 10c multi .50 .50
B108 SP28 25c + 11c multi .50 .50
Nos. B105-B108 (4) 2.00 2.00

The surtax was for child welfare.

Charcoal Burner SP29

Kitchen Utensils: 15c+5c, Earthenware vessel for water. 20c+10c, Baking oven. 25c+10c, Soup plate, stirrer and kneading stick.

1971, May 12 *Perf. 14x13½*

B109 SP29 10c + 5c multi .40 .40
B110 SP29 15c + 5c multi .40 .40
B111 SP29 20c + 10c multi .40 .40
B112 SP29 25c + 10c multi .40 .40
Nos. B109-B112 (4) 1.60 1.60

Surtax was for various social and cultural institutions.

Homemade Dolls and Comb — SP30

Homemade Toys: 20c+10c, Carts. 30c+15c, Musical top made from calabash.

1971, Nov. 16 *Perf. 13½x14*

B113 SP30 15c + 5c multi .50 .50
B114 SP30 20c + 10c multi .50 .50
B115 SP30 30c + 15c multi .50 .50
Nos. B113-B115 (3) 1.50 1.50

Surtax was for child welfare.

Steel Band SP31

Designs: 20c+10c, Harvest festival (Seu). 30c+15c, Tambu dancers.

1972, May 16

B116 SP31 15c + 5c multi .60 .60
B117 SP31 20c + 10c multi .60 .60
B118 SP31 30c + 15c multi .60 .60
Nos. B116-B118 (3) 1.80 1.80

Surtax was for various social and cultural institutions.

Child at Play on Ground SP32

Designs: 20c+10c, Child playing in water. 30c+15c, Child throwing ball into air.

1972, Nov. 14 Litho. *Perf. 14x13*

B119 SP32 15c + 5c multi .70 .70
B120 SP32 20c + 10c multi .70 .70
B121 SP32 30c + 15c multi .70 .70
Nos. B119-B121 (3) 2.10 2.10

Surtax was for child welfare.

Pedestrian Crossing, Traffic Sign — SP33

Designs: 15c+7c, School crossing. 40c+20c, Traffic light, road and car.

1973, Apr. 9 Litho. *Perf. 13x14*

B122 SP33 12c + 6c multi .60 .60
B123 SP33 15c + 7c multi .60 .60
B124 SP33 40c + 20c multi .60 .60
Nos. B122-B124 (3) 1.80 1.80

Surtax was for various social and cultural institutions.

"1948-73" SP34

20c+10c, Children. 30c+15c, Mother & child.

1973, Nov. 19 Litho. *Perf. 14x13*

B125 SP34 15c + 5c multi .70 .70
B126 SP34 20c + 10c multi .70 .70
a. Min. sheet, 2 ea #B125-B126 3.00 3.00
B127 SP34 30c + 15c multi 1.10 1.10
Nos. B125-B127 (3) 2.50 2.50

Child Welfare semi-postal stamps, 25th anniv.

Girl Combing her Hair — SP35

15c+7c, Young people listening to rock music. 40c+20c, Drummer, symbolizing rock music.

1974, Apr. 9 Litho. *Perf. 14x13*

B128 SP35 12c + 6c multi .80 .80
B129 SP35 15c + 7c multi .80 .80
B130 SP35 40c + 20c multi .80 .80
Nos. B128-B130 (3) 2.40 2.40

Surtax was for various social and cultural institutions.

Child, Saw and Score — SP36

Designs: 20c+10c, Footprints in circle. 30c+15c, Moon and sun. Each design includes score of a children's song.

1974, Nov. 12 Litho. *Perf. 13x14*

B131 SP36 15c + 5c multi .60 .60
B132 SP36 20c + 10c multi .60 .60
B133 SP36 30c + 15c multi .60 .60
Nos. B131-B133 (3) 1.80 1.80

Surtax was for child welfare.

Carved Stone Grid, Flower Pot SP37

Jewish Tombstone, Mordecai's Procession SP38

Design: 40c+20c, Ornamental stone from facade of Jewish House, 1728.

1975, Mar. 21 Litho. *Perf. 13x14*

B134 SP37 12c + 6c multi .60 .60
B135 SP38 15c + 7c multi .60 .60
B136 SP37 40c + 20c multi .60 .60
Nos. B134-B136 (3) 1.80 1.80

Surtax was for various social and cultural institutions.

Children Building Curaçao Windmill SP39

Designs: 20c+10c, Girl molding clay animal. 30c+15c, Children drawing picture.

1975, Nov. 12 Litho. *Perf. 14x13*

B137 SP39 15c + 5c multi .55 .55
B138 SP39 20c + 10c multi .55 .55
B139 SP39 30c + 15c multi .55 .55
Nos. B137-B139 (3) 1.65 1.65

Surtax was for child welfare.

Carrying a Child — SP40

Designs: Different ways of carrying a child. 40c+18c is vertical.

Perf. 14x13, 13x14

1976, Oct. 4 Litho.

B140 SP40 20c + 10c multi .45 .45
B141 SP40 25c + 12c multi .45 .45
B142 SP40 40c + 18c multi .45 .45
Nos. B140-B142 (3) 1.35 1.35

Surtax was for child welfare.

Composite: Aces of Hearts, Clubs, Diamonds and Spades — SP41

Designs: 25c+12c, "King" and inscription. 40c+18c, Hand holding cards; map of Aruba as ace of hearts, horiz.

Perf. 13x14, 14x13

1977, May 6 Litho.

B143 SP41 20c + 10c red & blk .30 .30
B144 SP41 25c + 12c multi .30 .30
a. Min. sheet, 2 ea #B143-B144 1.40 1.10
B145 SP41 40c + 18c multi .50 .50
Nos. B143-B145 (3) 1.10 1.10

Central American and Caribbean Bridge Championships, Aruba.

Souvenir Sheet

1977, May 26 *Perf. 13½x14*

B146 SP41 Sheet of 3 2.75 2.50

Amphilex 77 International Philatelic Exhibition, Amsterdam, May 26-June 5. No. B146 contains 3 stamps similar to Nos. B143-B145 with bright green background.

Children and Toys — SP42

Children playing with fantasy animals.

1977, Oct. 25 Litho. *Perf. 14x13*

B147 SP42 15c + 5c multi .30 .25
B148 SP42 20c + 10c multi .30 .30
B149 SP42 25c + 12c multi .40 .40
B150 SP42 40c + 18c multi .50 .40
a. Min. sheet, 2 ea #B148, B150 1.75 1.60
Nos. B147-B150 (4) 1.50 1.35

Surtax was for child welfare.

Water Skiing — SP43

Designs: 20c+10c, Sailing. 25c+12c, Soccer. 40c+18c, Baseball.

1978, Mar. 31 Litho. *Perf. 13x14*

B151 SP43 15c + 5c multi .25 .25
B152 SP43 20c + 10c multi .25 .25
B153 SP43 25c + 12c multi .25 .25
B154 SP43 40c + 18c multi .25 .25
Nos. B151-B154 (4) 1.00 1.00

Surtax was for sports. Tete-beche gutter pairs exist.

Red Cross SP44

1978, Sept. 19 Litho. *Perf. 14x13*

B155 SP44 55c + 25c red & blk .25 .25
a. Souv. sheet of 3, perf. 13½x13 1.60 1.60

Henri Dunant (1828-1910), founder of Red Cross. Surtax for the Red Cross.

Tete-beche gutter pairs exist.

Roller Skating — SP45

Children's Activities: 20c+10c, Kite flying. 25c+12c, Playing marbles. 40c+ 18c, Bicycling.

1978, Nov. 7 Litho. *Perf. 13x14*

B156 SP45 15c + 5c multi .30 .30
B157 SP45 20c + 10c multi .40 .30
a. Min. sheet, 2 ea #B156-B157 1.75 1.50
B158 SP45 25c + 12c multi .40 .40
B159 SP45 40c + 18c multi .50 .45
Nos. B156-B159 (4) 1.60 1.45

Surtax was for child welfare.

Carnival King — SP46

25th Aruba Carnival: 75c+20c, Carnival Queen and coat of arms.

1979, Feb. 20 Litho. *Perf. 13x14*

B160 SP46 40c + 10c multi .40 .30
B161 SP46 75c + 20c multi .55 .50

Regatta Emblem — SP47

Designs: 35c+10c, Race. 40c+15c, Globe and yacht, horiz. 55c+25c, Yacht, birds and sun.

Perf. 13x14, 14x13

1979, May 16 Litho.

B162 SP47 15c + 5c multi .25 .25
B163 SP47 35c + 10c multi .25 .25
B164 SP47 40c + 15c multi .30 .30
B165 SP47 55c + 25c multi .40 .40
a. Souv. sheet of 4, #B162-B165 1.10 1.10
Nos. B162-B165 (4) 1.20 1.20

12th International Sailing Regatta, Bonaire. #B164 in souvenir sheet is perf 13x14.

Volunteer Corps Type, 1979

15c+10c, Soldiers, 1929 and 1979. 40c+20c, Soldier guarding oil refinery, Guard emblem.

1979, July 4 Litho. *Perf. 13x14*

B166 A124 15c + 10c multi .25 .25
B167 A124 40c + 20c multi .40 .35

Girls Reading Book, IYC Emblem — SP48

IYC Emblem and Children's Drawings: 25c+12c, Infant and cat. 35c+15c, Girls walking under palm trees. 50c+20c, Children wearing adult clothing.

1979, Oct. 24 Litho. *Perf. 13x14*

B168 SP48 20c + 10c multi .25 .25
B169 SP48 25c + 12c multi .30 .30
B170 SP48 35c + 15c multi .40 .30
a. Souv. sheet, 2 ea #B168, B170 1.25 1.25
B171 SP48 50c + 20c multi .50 .50
Nos. B168-B171 (4) 1.45 1.35

International Year of the Child. Surtax for child welfare.

Fort Church Type of 1980

Designs: 20c+10c, Brass chandelier, 1909, horiz. 50c+25c, Pipe organ.

Perf. 14x13, 13x14

1980, Jan. 9 Litho.

B172 A128 20c + 10c multi .25 .25
B173 A128 50c + 25c multi .45 .45

Volleyball, Olympic Rings — SP49

Designs: 25c+10c, Woman gymnast. 30c+15c, Male gymnast. 60c+25c, Basketball.

1980, June 25 Litho. *Perf. 13x14*

B174 SP49 25c + 10c multi .25 .25
B175 SP49 30c + 15c multi .30 .30
B176 SP49 45c + 20c multi .40 .35
B177 SP49 60c + 25c multi .50 .45
a. Souvenir sheet of 6, 3 each #B174, B177, perf. 14x13½ 2.25 1.90
Nos. B174-B177 (4) 1.45 1.35

22nd Summer Olympic Games, Moscow, July 19-Aug. 3.

St. Maarten Landscape SP50

Children's Drawings: 30c+15c, House in Bonaire. 40c+20c, Child at blackboard. 60c+25c, Dancers, vert.

Perf. 14x13, 13x14

1980, Oct. 22 Litho.

B178 SP50 25c + 10c multi .30 .25
B179 SP50 30c + 15c multi .35 .30
B180 SP50 40c + 20c multi .40 .40
B181 SP50 60c + 25c multi .50 .50
a. Souvenir sheet of 6+ 4 labels, 3 each #B178, B181 2.50 2.25
Nos. B178-B181 (4) 1.55 1.45

Surtax was for child welfare. #B178 in souvenir sheet is perf 13x14.

Girl Using Sign Language — SP51

Designs: 25c+10c, Blind woman. 30c+15c, Man in wheelchair. 45c+20c, Infant in walker.

1981, Apr. 7 Litho. *Perf. 13x14*

B182 SP51 25c + 10c multi .25 .25
B183 SP51 30c + 15c multi .30 .30
B184 SP51 45c + 20c multi .55 .55
B185 SP51 60c + 25c multi .60 .60
Nos. B182-B185 (4) 1.70 1.70

International Year of the Disabled. Surtax was for handicapped children.

Tennis Player — SP52

1981, May 27 Litho. *Perf. 13x14*

B186 SP52 30c + 15c shown .35 .35
B187 SP52 50c + 20c Diving .55 .55
B188 SP52 70c + 25c Boxing .75 .75
a. Min. sheet of 3, #B186-B188 1.75 1.75
Nos. B186-B188 (3) 1.65 1.65

Surtax was for sporting events.

Den Mother and Cub Scout SP53

Scouting in Netherlands Antilles, 50th Anniv.: 70c+25c, van der Maarel, national founder. 1g+50c, Ronde Klip (headquarters).

1981, Sept. 16 Litho. *Perf. 14x13*

B189 SP53 45c + 20c multi .60 .60
B190 SP53 70c + 25c multi .80 .80
B191 SP53 1g + 50c multi 1.25 1.25
a. Min. sheet of 3, #B189-B191, perf. 13½x13 2.75 2.50
Nos. B189-B191 (3) 2.65 2.65

Surtax was for various social and cultural institutions.

Girl and Teddy Bear — SP54

Designs: 35c+15c, Mother and child. 45c+20c, Two children. 55c+25c, Boy and cat.

1981, Oct. 21 Litho. *Perf. 13x14*

B192 SP54 35c + 15c multi .30 .30
B193 SP54 45c + 20c multi .50 .50
B194 SP54 55c + 25c multi .60 .60
a. Min. sheet, 2 ea #B192, B194 2.00 2.00
B195 SP54 85c + 40c multi .90 .90
Nos. B192-B195 (4) 2.30 2.30

Surtax for child welfare.

Fencing SP55

1982, Feb. 17 Litho. *Perf. 14x13*

B196 SP55 35c + 15c shown .30 .30
B197 SP55 45c + 20c Judo .50 .50
B198 SP55 70c + 35c Soccer .80 .80
a. Miniature sheet of 2 + label 1.75 1.75
B199 SP55 85c + 40c Bicycling .90 .90
Nos. B196-B199 (4) 2.50 2.50

Surtax was for sporting events.

Girl Playing Accordion SP56

1982, Oct. 20 Litho.

B200 SP56 35c + 15c shown .40 .40
B201 SP56 75c + 35c Guitar .90 .90
B202 SP56 85c + 40c Violin 1.00 1.00
a. Min. sheet of 3, #B200-B202 2.50 2.50
Nos. B200-B202 (3) 2.30 2.30

Surtax for child welfare.

Traditional House, Saba SP57

1982, Nov. 17 Litho.

B203 SP57 35c + 15c shown .40 .40
B204 SP57 75c + 35c Aruba .90 .90
B205 SP57 85c + 40c Curaçao 1.00 1.00
a. Souv. sheet of 3, #B203-B205 2.50 2.50
Nos. B203-B205 (3) 2.30 2.30

Surtax was for various social and cultural institutions.

High Jump SP58

No. B207, Weight lifting. No. B208, Wind surfing.

1983, Feb. 22 Litho.

B206 SP58 35c + 15c shown .30 .30
B207 SP58 45c + 20c multi .60 .60
B208 SP58 85c + 40c multi 1.00 1.00
Nos. B206-B208 (3) 1.90 1.90

Surtax was for sporting events.

Child with Lizard — SP59

No. B210, Child with insects. No. B211, Child with animal.

1983, Oct. 18 Litho. *Perf. 13x14*

B209 SP59 45c + 20c shown .60 .60
B210 SP59 55c + 25c multi .75 .75
B211 SP59 100c + 50c multi 1.40 1.40
a. Souv. sheet of 3, #B209-B211 2.75 2.75
Nos. B209-B211 (3) 2.75 2.75

Surtax was for Childrens' Charity.

Pre-Columbian Artifacts — SP60

1983, Nov. 22 Litho. *Perf. 13x14*

B212 SP60 45c + 20c multi .70 .70
B213 SP60 55c + 25c multi .80 .80
B214 SP60 85c + 40c multi 1.00 1.00
B215 SP60 100c + 50c multi 1.40 1.40
Nos. B212-B215 (4) 3.90 3.90

Curaçao Baseball Federation, 50th Anniv. SP61

1984, Mar. 27 Litho. *Perf. 14x13*

B216 SP61 25c + 10c Catching .65 .65
B217 SP61 45c + 20c Batting 1.25 1.25
B218 SP61 55c + 25c Pitching 1.60 1.60

B219 SP61 85c + 40c Running 1.90 1.90
a. Min. sheet of 3, #B217-B219 5.00 5.00
Nos. B216-B219 (4) 5.40 5.40

Surtax was for baseball fed., 1984 Olympics.

Microphones, Radio SP62

Designs: 55c+25c, Radio, record player. 100c+50c, Record players.

1984, Apr. 24 Litho. *Perf. 14x13*

B220 SP62 45c + 20c multi .75 .75
B221 SP62 55c + 25c multi 1.00 1.00
B222 SP62 100c + 50c multi 1.25 1.25
Nos. B220-B222 (3) 3.00 3.00

Surtax was for social and cultural institutions.

Boy Reading — SP63

Designs: 55c+25c, Parents reading to children. 100c+50c, Family worship.

1984, Nov. 7 Litho. *Perf. 13x14*

B223 SP63 45c + 20c multi .75 .75
B224 SP63 55c + 25c multi 1.00 1.00
B225 SP63 100c + 50c multi 1.25 1.25
a. Souv. sheet of 3, #B223-B225 3.25 3.25
Nos. B223-B225 (3) 3.00 3.00

Surtax was for children's charity.

Soccer Players SP64

1985, Mar. 27 Litho. *Perf. 14x13*

B226 SP64 10c + 5c multi .25 .25
B227 SP64 15c + 5c multi .25 .25
B228 SP64 45c + 20c multi .70 .70
B229 SP64 55c + 25c multi .90 .90
B230 SP64 85c + 40c multi 1.25 1.25
Nos. B226-B230 (5) 3.35 3.35

The surtax was for sporting events.

Intl. Youth Year — SP65

No. B231, Youth, computer keyboard. No. B232, Girl listening to music. No. B233, Youth breakdancing.

1985, Apr. 29 Litho.

B231 SP65 45c + 20c multi .75 .75
B232 SP65 55c + 25c multi 1.00 1.00
B233 SP65 100c + 50c multi 1.50 1.50
Nos. B231-B233 (3) 3.25 3.25

Surtax for youth, social and cultural organizations.

Children — SP66

1985, Oct. 16 Litho. *Perf. 13x14*

B234 SP66 5c + 5c Eskimo .25 .25
B235 SP66 10c + 5c African .25 .25
B236 SP66 25c + 10c Asian .40 .40
B237 SP66 45c + 20c Dutch .70 .70
B238 SP66 55c + 25c American Indian .80 .80
a. Souv. sheet of 3, #B236-B238 2.00 2.00
Nos. B234-B238 (5) 2.40 2.40

Surtax for child welfare.

Sports — SP67

1986, Feb. 19 Litho. *Perf. 13x14*

B239 SP67 15c + 5c Running .25 .25
B240 SP67 25c + 10c Horse racing .40 .40
B241 SP67 45c + 20c Car racing .65 .65
B242 SP67 55c + 25c Soccer .75 .75
Nos. B239-B242 (4) 2.05 2.05

Surtax for the natl. Sports Federation.

Handicrafts — SP68

1986, Apr. 29

B243 SP68 30c + 15c Painting .40 .40
B244 SP68 45c + 20c Sculpting .55 .55
B245 SP68 55c + 25c Ceramics .70 .70
Nos. B243-B245 (3) 1.65 1.65

Surtax for Curaçao Social & Cultural Care.

Sports — SP69

1986, Oct. 15 Litho. *Perf. 13x14*

B246 SP69 20c + 10c Soccer .25 .25
B247 SP69 25c + 15c Tennis .35 .35
B248 SP69 45c + 20c Judo .50 .50
B249 SP69 55c + 25c Baseball .65 .65
a. Min. sheet of 2, #B248-B249 1.25 1.25
Nos. B246-B249 (4) 1.75 1.75

Surtax for the natl. Sports Foundation.

Social and Cultural Programs — SP70

1987, Mar. 11 Litho.

B250 SP70 35c + 15c Musicians .40 .40
B251 SP70 45c + 25c Handicapped .50 .50
B252 SP70 85c + 40c Pavilion .95 .95
Nos. B250-B252 (3) 1.85 1.85

Surtax for the Jong Wacht (Youth Guard) and the natl. Red Cross.

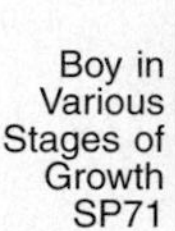

Boy in Various Stages of Growth SP71

1987, Oct. 21 Litho. *Perf. 14x13*

B253 SP71 40c +15c Infant .45 .45
B254 SP71 55c +25c Toddler .60 .60
B255 SP71 115c +50c Boy 1.25 1.25
a. Souv. sheet of 3, #B253-B255 2.50 2.50
Nos. B253-B255 (3) 2.30 2.30

Surtax benefited Child Care programs.

Queen Emma Bridge, Cent. — SP72

55c+25c, Bridge, vert. 115c+55c, View of Willemstad Harbor and quay. 190c+60c, Flags of the Netherlands, Antilles and US, Leonard B. Smith, engineer.

1988, May 9 *Perf. 13x14, 14x13*

B256 SP72 55c +25c multi .60 .60
B257 SP72 115c +55c multi 1.25 1.25
B258 SP72 190c +60c multi 1.75 1.75
Nos. B256-B258 (3) 3.60 3.60

Surtax for social and cultural purposes.

Youth Care Campaign SP73

No. B259, Girl, television. No. B260, Boy, portable stereo. No. B261, Girl, computer.

1988, Oct. 26 Litho. *Perf. 14x13*

B259 SP73 55c +25c multi .60 .60
B260 SP73 65c +30c multi .70 .70
B261 SP73 115c +55c multi 1.25 1.25
a. Souv. sheet of 3, #B259-B261 2.60 2.50
Nos. B259-B261 (3) 2.55 2.55

Surtax for child welfare.

Curaçao Stamp Assoc., 50th Anniv. — SP75

Designs: 30c+10c, Type A25 and No. 461 under magnifying glass. 55c+20c, Simulated stamp (learning to use tongs). 80c+30c, Barn owl, album, magnifying glass, tongs.

1989, Jan. 18 Litho. *Perf. 13x14*

B264 30c +10c multi .30 .30
B265 55c +20c multi .55 .55
B266 80c +30c multi .75 .75
a. SP75 Strip of 3, #B264-B266 1.60 1.60

No. B266a has a continuous design. Surtaxed for welfare organizations.

Child and Nature SP76

No. B267, Girl, boy, tree. No. B268, Playing on beach. No. B269, Father and child.
No. B270, At the beach, diff.

1989, Oct. 25 Litho. *Perf. 14x13*

B267 SP76 40c +15c multi .35 .35
B268 SP76 65c +30c multi .70 .70
B269 SP76 115c +55c multi 1.25 1.25
Nos. B267-B269 (3) 2.30 2.30

Souvenir Sheet

B270 SP76 155c +75c multi 1.60 1.60

Surtax for child welfare.

Natl. Girl Scout Movement, 60th Anniv. — SP77

Totolika, 60th Anniv. — SP78

Natl. Boy Scout Movement, 60th Anniv. — SP79

1990, Mar. 7 Litho. *Perf. 13x14*

B271 SP77 30c +10c multi .35 .35
B272 SP78 40c +15c multi .45 .45
B273 SP79 155c +65c multi 1.75 1.75
Nos. B271-B273 (3) 2.55 2.55

Parents' and Friends Association of Persons with a Mental Handicap (Totolika).
Surtax for social and cultural purposes.

SP80

1990, June 13 Litho. *Perf. 13x14*

B274 SP80 65c +30c multi .90 .90

Sport Unie Brion Trappers Soccer Club. Exists in tete-beche gutter pairs.

SP81

1990, June 13

B275 SP81 115c +55c multi 1.60 1.60

Anti-drug campaign. Exists in tete-beche gutter pairs.

Youth Care Campaign SP82

No. B276, Bees, flowers. No. B277, Dolphins. No. B278, Donkey, bicycle. No. B279, Goat, house. No. B280, Rabbit. No. B281, Lizard, moon.

1990, Oct. 31 Litho. *Perf. 14x13*

B276 SP82 30c +5c multi .40 .40
B277 SP82 55c +10c multi .70 .70
B278 SP82 65c +15c multi .90 .90
B279 SP82 100c +20c multi 1.40 1.40
B280 SP82 115c +25c multi 1.60 1.60
B281 SP82 155c +55c multi 2.25 2.25
Nos. B276-B281 (6) 7.25 7.25

Surtax for child welfare.
See Nos. B285-B288.

Social and Cultural Care — SP83

Designs: 30c+10c, Youth philately. 65c+25c, St. Vincentius Brass Band, 50th anniv. 155c+55c, Curaçao Community Center Federation.

1991, Apr. 3 Litho. *Perf. 14x13*

B282	SP83 30c +10c multi	.50	.50
B283	SP83 65c +25c multi	1.10	1.10
B284	SP83 155c +55c multi	2.50	2.50
	Nos. B282-B284 (3)	4.10	4.10

Youth Care Campaign Type of 1990

Fight illiteracy: 40c+15c, Octopus holding numbers and letters. 65c+30c, Birds, blackboard. 155c+65c, Turtle telling time. No. B288a, Owl, flag. b, Books, bookworms. c, Seahorse.

1991, Oct. 31 Litho. *Perf. 14x13*

B285	SP82 40c +15c multi	.60	.60
B286	SP82 65c +30c multi	1.00	1.00
B287	SP82 155c +65c multi	2.40	2.40
	Nos. B285-B287 (3)	4.00	4.00

Souvenir Sheet

Imperf

B288	Sheet of 3	4.25	4.25
a.	SP82 55c +25c multi	.90	.90
b.	SP82 100c +35c multi	1.50	1.50
c.	SP82 115c +50c multi	1.75	1.75

Surtax for child welfare.

SP84

1992 Summer Olympics, Barcelona: a, 30c + 10c, Triangle and oval. b, 55c + 25c, Globe showing location of Netherland Antilles, flag. c, 115c + 55c, Emblem of Netherlands Antilles Olympic Committee.

1992, Mar. 4 Litho. *Perf. 13x14*

B289	SP84 Strip of 3, #a.-c.	3.50	3.50

Netherlands Antilles Olympic Committee, 60th Anniv.

SP85

No. B290, Spaceship. No. B291, Robot. No. B292, Extraterrestrial.
No. B293, Extraterrestrial, diff.

1992, Oct. 28 Litho. *Perf. 13x14*

B290	SP85 30c +10c multi	.50	.50
B291	SP85 70c +30c multi	1.25	1.25
B292	SP85 100c +40c multi	1.75	1.75
	Nos. B290-B292 (3)	3.50	3.50

Souvenir Sheet

B293	SP85 155c +70c multi	2.75	2.75

Surtax for child welfare.

SP86

Designs: 65c+25c, Fire safety, child playing with blocks. 90c+35c, Child fastening auto safety belt, vert. 175c+75c, Child wearing flotation equipment while swimming. 35c+15c, Alert child studying.

Perf. 14x13, 13x14

1993, Oct. 27 Litho.

B294	SP86 65c +25c multi	1.10	1.10
B295	SP86 90c +35c multi	1.50	1.50
B296	SP86 175c +75c multi	3.00	3.00
	Nos. B294-B296 (3)	5.60	5.60

Souvenir Sheet

Perf. 13½x13

B297	SP86 35c +15c Sheet of 5 + label	3.00	3.00

Surtax for child welfare.

Intl. Year of the Family — SP87

No. B298, Woman, baby. No. B299, Daughter, father. No. B300, Grandparents.
No. B301, Intl. emblem.

1994, Oct. 26 Litho. *Perf. 13x14*

B298	SP87 35c +15c multi	.60	.60
B299	SP87 65c +25c multi	1.00	1.00
B300	SP87 90c +35c multi	1.40	1.40
	Nos. B298-B300 (3)	3.00	3.00

Souvenir Sheet

B301	SP87 175c +75c multi	2.75	2.75

Surtax for the benefit of the Antillean Youth Care Federation.

Slave Rebellion in Curaçao, Bicent. SP88

Designs: 30c+10c, Monument, bird with outstretched wings. 45c+15c, Bird, bell tower.

1995, Aug. 17 Litho. *Perf. 14x13*

B302	SP88 30c +10c multi	.45	.45
B303	SP88 45c +15c multi	.65	.65

Youth Philately SP89

Stamp drawings by children from: 65c+25c, Curaçao, Bonaire. 75c+35c, St. Maarten, St. Eustatius, Saba.

1995, Aug. 17

B304	SP89 65c +25c multi	1.00	1.00
B305	SP89 75c +35c multi	1.25	1.25

Nos. 516-517, 544 Surcharged in Red Brown

1995, Sept. 22 Litho. *Perf. 14x13*

B306	A148 65c +65c on #516	1.60	1.60
B307	A148 75c +75c on #517	1.90	1.90
B308	A148 1g +1g on #544	2.50	2.50
	Nos. B306-B308 (3)	6.00	6.00

Surcharge for hurricane relief.

Child Welfare Stamps SP91

Promotion of Children's Good Deeds: 35c+15c, Helping elderly across street. 65c+25c, Reading newspaper to blind person. 90c+35c, Caring for younger sibling. 175c+75c, Giving flowers to sick person.

1995, Oct. 25 Litho. *Perf. 14x13*

B309	SP91 35c +15c multi	.55	.55
B310	SP91 65c +25c multi	1.00	1.00
B311	SP91 90c +35c multi	1.40	1.40
B312	SP91 175c +75c multi	2.75	2.75
	Nos. B309-B312 (4)	5.70	5.70

Surtax for various youth organizations.

Child Welfare Stamps SP92

UNICEF, 50th anniv.: 40c+15c, Child wandering streets. 75c+25c, Child labor in Asia. 110c+45c, Child in wartime (former Yugoslavia), vert. 225c+100c, Caribbean poverty, vert.

Perf. 14x13, 13x14

1996, Oct. 23 Litho.

B313	SP92 40c +15c multi	.65	.65
B314	SP92 75c +25c multi	1.10	1.10
B315	SP92 110c +45c multi	1.75	1.75
B316	SP92 225c +100c multi	3.50	3.50
	Nos. B313-B316 (4)	7.00	7.00

Social and Cultural Care Stamps — SP93

Designs: 40c+15c, Curaçao Foundation for the cure and resettlement of ex-prisoners, 50th anniv. 75c+30c, ABVO (General Union of Public Servants), 60th anniv. 85+40c, 110c+50c, Red Cross Corps section, Curaçao, 65th anniv.

1997, Jan. 16 Litho. *Perf. 13x14*

B317	SP93 40c +15c multi	.60	.60
B318	SP93 75c +30c multi	.25	.25
B319	SP93 85c +40c multi	1.40	1.40
B320	SP93 110 +50c multi	1.60	1.60
	Nos. B317-B320 (4)	3.85	3.85

Child Welfare Stamps SP94

Musical notes, musical instruments: 40c+15c, Drums. 75c+25c, Piano. 110c+45c, Flute. 225c+100c, Guitar.

1997, Oct. 22 Litho. *Perf. 14x13*

B321	SP94 40c +15c multi	.65	.65
B322	SP94 75c +25c multi	1.10	1.10
B323	SP94 110c +45c multi	1.75	1.75
B324	SP94 225c +100c multi	3.50	3.50
	Nos. B321-B324 (4)	7.00	7.00

Social and Cultural Care — SP95

No. B325, Curacao Museum, 50th anniv. No. B326, Seawater Desalination, 70th anniv. 75c+25c, Water area, Lac Cai Bonaire, vert. 85c+40c, Water area, Klein-Bonaire, vert.

Perf. 14x13, 13x14

1998, Mar. 9 Litho.

B325	SP95 40c +15c multi	.60	.60
B326	SP95 40c +15c multi	.60	.60
B327	SP95 75c +25c multi	1.10	1.10
B328	SP95 85c +40c multi	1.40	1.40
	Nos. B325-B328 (4)	3.70	3.70

Child Welfare Stamps — SP96

Universal Rights of the Child: 40c+15c, Child holding cutouts representing family. 75c+25c, Children eating watermelon. 110c+45c, Handicapped children drawing pictures. 225c+100c, Children holding cans with string to play telephone.

1998, Oct. 28 Litho. *Perf. 13x14*

B329	SP96 40c +15c multi	.60	.60
B330	SP96 75c +25c multi	1.10	1.10
B331	SP96 110c +45c multi	1.75	1.75
B332	SP96 225c +100c multi	3.75	3.75
	Nos. B329-B332 (4)	7.20	7.20

Buildings — SP97

Willemstad buildings on World Heritage List: 40c+15c, Houses, Ijzerstraat neighborhood, horiz. 75c+30c, Postal Museum. 110c+50c, "Bridal Cake" building, Scharloo area, horiz.

Perf. 14x13, 13x14

1999, Sept. 28 Litho.

B333	SP97 40c +15c multi	.60	.60
B334	SP97 75c +30c multi	1.25	1.25
B335	SP97 110c +50c multi	1.75	1.75
	Nos. B333-B335 (3)	3.60	3.60

Sports — SP98

1999, Oct. 27 *Perf. 13x14*

B336	SP98 40c +15c Basketball	.60	.60
B337	SP98 75c +25c Golf	1.10	1.10
B338	SP98 110c +45c Fencing	1.75	1.75
B339	SP98 225c +100c Tennis	3.75	3.75
	Nos. B336-B339 (4)	7.20	7.20

Social and Cultural Care — SP99

Designs: 75c+30c, Children playing. 110c+50c, Chemistry lesson. 225c+100c, Arithmetic lesson, vert.

Perf. 14x13, 13x14

2000, Apr. 28 Litho.

B340-B342	SP99 Set of 3	6.75	6.75

Youth Care SP100

Designs: 40c+15c, Child reaching up, vert. 75c+25c, Children learning with computers. 110c+45c, Children playing with toy boat. 225c+100c, Children and map, vert.

Perf. 13x14, 14x13

2000, Oct. 25 Litho.

B343-B346	SP100 Set of 4	7.50	7.50

Caribbean Postal Union, 5th Anniv. — SP101

Designs: 75c+25c, Pen, emblem. 110c+45c, Emblem. 225c+100c, Globe, emblem.

2001, May 21 Litho. ***Perf. 13¼x13¾***

B347-B349 SP101 Set of 3 6.50 6.50

Youth Care SP102

Designs: 40c+15c, Boy feeding baby. 75c+25c, Girls dancing, vert. 110c+45c, Boy pushing woman in wheelchair, vert.

Perf. 13½x12¾, 12¾x13½

2001, Oct. 24 Litho.

B350-B352 SP102 Set of 3 3.75 3.75

2002 World Cup Soccer Championships, Japan and Korea — SP103

Soccer player with: 95c+35c, Ball of flags. 145c+55c, Ball with map. 240c+110c, Ball.

2002, June 25 Litho. ***Perf. 12¾x14***

B353-B355 SP103 Set of 3 7.75 7.75

Youth Care SP104

"Dialogue among civilizations:" 50c+15c, Lion and fish. 95c+35c, Kangaroo and iguana. 145c+55c, Goat and penguin. 240c+110c, Lizard and toucan.

2002, Oct. 24 ***Perf. 14x12¾***

B356-B359 SP104 Set of 4 8.50 8.50

Miniature Sheet

Maps of the Netherlands Antilles — SP105

No. B360: a, 25c+10c, Portion of 1688 map by Hendrick Doncker showing Curaçao and Bonaire. b, 30c+15c, Portion of Doncker map showing St. Maarten, Saba and St. Eustatius, vert. c, 55c+25c, Modern map of Curaçao and Bonaire. d, 85c+35c, Modern map of St. Maarten, Saba and St. Eustatius, vert. e, 95c+40c, Modern map of Caribbean Islands.

Perf. 14x12¾, 12¾x14 (vert. stamps)

2003, Mar. 19 Litho.

B360 SP105 Sheet of 5, #a-e 4.75 4.75

Miniature Sheet

Youth Care — SP106

No. B361: a, 50c+15c, Boy taking shower. b, 95c+35c, Girl with umbrella. c, 145c+55c, Boy with watering can. d, 240c+110c, Hands in water from open faucet.

2003, Oct. 22 Litho. ***Perf. 13x14***

B361 SP106 Sheet of 4, #a-d 8.50 8.50

Intl. Year of Fresh Water.

Youth Care SP107

No. B362: a, Boy, girl, slave huts. b, Girl, Autonomy Monument. c, Boy, girl, broken stone walls built by slaves. d, Boy, girl, wall of plantation house. e, Boy, preamble of Netherlands Constitution.

2004, Oct. 20 ***Perf. 13½x13***

B362	Horiz. strip of 5	8.25	8.25
a.	SP107 50c +15c multi	.75	.75
b.-c.	SP107 95c +35c either single	1.50	1.50
d.-e.	SP107 145c +55c either single	2.25	2.25

Autonomy of the Netherlands Antilles, 50th anniv. (Nos. B362b, B362e), Intl. Year Commemorating the Struggle Against Slavery and its Abolition (Nos. B362a, B362c, B362d).

Intl. Year of Sports and Physical Education — SP108

Designs: 55c+20c, Soccer. 97c+36c, Table tennis. 148c+56c, Tennis. 240c+110c, Baseball.

2005, Dec. 24 Litho. ***Perf. 13x13½***

B363-B366 SP108 Set of 4 8.75 8.75

Youth Care — SP109

Hatted globes showing: 55c+20c, North and South America. 100c+45c, Africa. 149c+61c, Europe, Africa and Asia. 285c+125c, Africa and Asia.

2006, Oct. 23 Litho. ***Perf. 12¾x13¼***

B367-B370 SP109 Set of 4 9.50 9.50

Youth Care SP110

Family: 59c+26c, Praying at dinner table. 104c+46c, Respecting flag. 155c+65c, As baseball team. 285c+125c, Studying together.

2007, Oct. 24 Litho. ***Perf. 13¼x12¾***

B371-B374 SP110 Set of 4 9.75 9.75

Youth Care — SP111

Potato: 59c+26c, As potato farmer. 1.06g+46c, Peeling potatoes. 1.58g+65c, Eating French fries. 2.85g+1.25g, Family.

2008, Oct. 23 Litho. ***Perf. 12¾x13¼***

B375-B378 SP111 Set of 4 9.75 9.75

Intl. Year of the Potato.

Youth Care — SP112

Designs: 59c+26c, Galileo Galilei and silhouette of boy. 110c+45c, Silhouettes of stargazers and telescope. 168c+75c, Silhouettes of children watching space shuttle. 285c+125c, Men walking on Moon.

2009, Oct. 26 Litho. ***Perf. 12¾x13¼***

B379-B382 SP112 Set of 4 10.50 10.50

Intl. Year of Astronomy.

AIR POST STAMPS

Regular Issues of 1915-22 Surcharged in Black

Perf. 12½

1929, July 6 Typo. Unwmk.

C1	A13	50c on 12½c red	13.00	13.00
C2	A13	1g on 20c blue	13.00	13.00
C3	A13	2g on 15c ol grn	42.50	47.50
		Nos. C1-C3 (3)	68.50	73.50

Excellent forgeries exist.

Allegory, "Flight" — AP1

1931-39 Engr.

C4	AP1	10c Prus grn ('34)	.25	.25
C5	AP1	15c dull blue ('38)	.25	.25
C6	AP1	20c red	.75	.25
C7	AP1	25c gray ('38)	.75	.60
C8	AP1	30c yellow ('39)	.30	.30
C9	AP1	35c dull blue	.80	.90
C10	AP1	40c green	.60	.40
C11	AP1	45c orange	2.25	2.25
C12	AP1	50c lake ('38)	.75	.50
C13	AP1	60c brown vio	.60	.35
C14	AP1	70c black	6.50	2.50
C15	AP1	1.40g brown	4.25	5.25
C16	AP1	2.80g bister	5.00	5.50
		Nos. C4-C16 (13)	23.05	19.30

No. C6 Surcharged in Black

1934, Aug. 25

C17 AP1 10c on 20c red 19.00 17.00

Catalogue values for unused stamps in this section, from this point to the end of the section, are for Never Hinged items.

Map of the Atlantic AP2

Plane over Islands AP3

Map of Curaçao, Aruba and Bonaire AP4

Planes — AP5

Plane — AP6

1942, Oct. 20 *Perf. 13x13½*

C18	AP2	10c grn & bl	.25	.25
C19	AP3	15c rose car & yel grn	.25	.25
C20	AP4	20c red brn & grn	.25	.35
C21	AP5	25c dp ultra & org brn	.25	.25
C22	AP6	30c red & lt vio	.30	.30
C23	AP2	35c dk vio & ol grn	.45	.30
C24	AP3	40c gray ol & chnt	.50	.40
C25	AP4	45c dk red & blk	.35	.35
C26	AP5	50c vio & blk	.85	.25
C27	AP6	60c lt yel brn & dl bl	.85	.60
C28	AP2	70c red brn & Prus bl	1.10	.60
C29	AP3	1.40g bl vio & sl grn	6.75	1.40
C30	AP4	2.80g int bl & lt bl	8.50	3.00
C31	AP5	5g rose lake & sl grn	15.00	10.50
C32	AP6	10g grn & red brn	20.00	18.00
		Nos. C18-C32 (15)	55.65	36.80

For surcharges see Nos. CB9-CB12.

Plane and Post Horn — AP7

DC-4 above Waves — AP8

1947 **Photo.** *Perf. 12½x12*

C32A	AP7	6c gray blk	.25	.25
C33	AP7	10c deep red	.25	.25
C33A	AP7	12½c plum	.30	.25
C34	AP7	15c deep blue	.30	.25
C35	AP7	20c dl yel grn	.35	.25
C36	AP7	25c org yel	.35	.25
C37	AP7	30c lilac gray	.50	.35
C38	AP7	35c org red	.60	.50
C39	AP7	40c blue grn	.70	.60
C40	AP7	45c brt violet	.85	.75
C41	AP7	50c carmine	1.25	.65
C42	AP7	60c brt blue	2.50	1.00
C43	AP7	70c brown	2.50	1.00

Engr.

Perf. 12x12½

C44	AP8	1.50g black	1.25	.50
C45	AP8	2.50g dk car	10.00	2.75
C46	AP8	5g green	20.00	6.50
C47	AP8	7.50g dk blue	60.00	50.00
C48	AP8	10g dk red vio	45.00	12.00
C49	AP8	15g red org	72.50	60.00
C50	AP8	25g chocolate	60.00	50.00
		Nos. C32A-C50 (20)	279.45	188.10

AIR POST SEMI-POSTAL STAMPS

Flags of the Netherlands and the House of Orange with Inscription "Netherlands Shall Rise Again" — SPAP1

Engr. & Photo.

1941, Dec. 11 **Unwmk.** *Perf. 12*

CB1	SPAP1	10c + 10c multi	5.25	5.25
CB2	SPAP1	15c + 25c multi	19.00	19.00
CB3	SPAP1	20c + 25c multi	19.00	19.00
CB4	SPAP1	25c + 25c multi	19.00	19.00
CB5	SPAP1	30c + 50c multi	19.00	19.00
CB6	SPAP1	35c + 50c multi	19.00	19.00
CB7	SPAP1	40c + 50c multi	19.00	19.00
CB8	SPAP1	50c +100c multi	19.00	19.00
		Nos. CB1-CB8 (8)	138.25	138.25

The surtax was used by the Prince Bernhard Committee to purchase war material for the Netherlands' fighting forces in Great Britain.

Catalogue values for unused stamps in this section, from this point to the end of the section, are for Never Hinged items.

Nos. C29-C32 Surcharged in Black

1943, Dec. 1 *Perf. 13x13½*

CB9	AP3	40c + 50c on 1.40g	5.25	4.25
CB10	AP4	45c + 50c on 2.80g	5.25	4.25
CB11	AP5	50c + 75c on 5g	5.25	4.25
CB12	AP6	60c + 100c on 10g	5.25	4.25
		Nos. CB9-CB12 (4)	21.00	17.00

The surtax was for the benefit of prisoners of war. These stamps were not sold to the public in the normal manner. All were sold in sets by advance subscription, the majority to philatelic speculators.

On No. CB9 overprint reads: "Voor / Krijgsgevangenen."

Princess Juliana — SPAP2

Engr. & Photo.

1944, Aug. 16 *Perf. 12*

Frame in carmine & deep blue, cross in carmine

CB13	SPAP2	10c + 10c lt brn	1.90	1.50
CB14	SPAP2	15c + 25c turq grn	1.75	1.50
CB15	SPAP2	20c + 25c dk ol gray	1.75	1.50
CB16	SPAP2	25c + 25c slate	1.75	1.50
CB17	SPAP2	30c + 50c sepia	1.75	1.50
CB18	SPAP2	35c + 50c chnt	1.75	1.50
CB19	SPAP2	40c + 50c grn	1.75	1.50
CB20	SPAP2	50c + 100c dk vio	1.90	1.60
		Nos. CB13-CB20 (8)	14.30	12.10

The surtax was for the Red Cross.

Map of Netherlands Indies — SPAP3

Map of Netherlands — SPAP4

Photo. & Typo.

1946, July 1 *Perf. 11x11½*

CB21	SPAP3	10c + 10c	.75	.75
CB22	SPAP3	15c + 25c	.85	.75
CB23	SPAP3	20c + 25c	.85	.75
CB24	SPAP3	25c + 25c	.85	.75
CB25	SPAP3	30c + 50c	.85	1.00
a.		Double impression of denomination	400.00	400.00
CB26	SPAP3	35c + 50c	.85	1.00
CB27	SPAP3	40c + 75c	.85	1.10
CB28	SPAP3	50c + 100c	.85	1.10
CB29	SPAP4	10c + 10c	.75	.75
CB30	SPAP4	15c + 25c	.85	.75
CB31	SPAP4	20c + 25c	.85	.75
CB32	SPAP4	25c + 25c	.85	.75
CB33	SPAP4	30c + 50c	.85	1.00
CB34	SPAP4	35c + 50c	.85	1.00
CB35	SPAP4	40c + 75c	.85	1.10
CB36	SPAP4	50c + 100c	.85	1.10
		Nos. CB21-CB36 (16)	13.40	14.40

The surtax on Nos. CB21 to CB36 was for the National Relief Fund.

POSTAGE DUE STAMPS

D1

Type I — 34 loops. "T" of *"BETALEN"* over center of loop, top branch of "E" of *"TE"* shorter than lower branch.

Type II — 33 loops. "T" of *"BETALEN"* over center of two loops.

Type III — 32 loops. "T" of *"BETALEN"* slightly to the left of loop, top of first "E" of *"BETALEN"* shorter than lower branch.

Value in Black

1889 **Unwmk.** **Typo.** *Perf. 12½*

Type III

J1	D1	2½c green	3.00	3.25
J2	D1	5c green	2.00	1.75
J3	D1	10c green	32.50	27.50
J4	D1	12½c green	375.00	200.00
J5	D1	15c green	20.00	17.00
J6	D1	20c green	9.00	9.00
J7	D1	25c green	190.00	150.00
J8	D1	30c green	10.00	9.00
J9	D1	40c green	10.00	9.00
J10	D1	50c green	40.00	37.50

Nos. J1-J10 were issued without gum.

Type I

J1a	D1	2½c	3.00	4.00
J2a	D1	5c	40.00	35.00
J3a	D1	10c	35.00	35.00
J4a	D1	12½c	375.00	200.00
J5a	D1	15c	21.00	19.00
J6a	D1	20c	65.00	65.00
J7a	D1	25c	600.00	350.00
J8a	D1	30c	75.00	75.00
J9a	D1	40c	75.00	75.00
J10a	D1	50c	45.00	40.00

Type II

J1b	D1	2½c	5.00	4.75
J2b	D1	5c	200.00	150.00
J3b	D1	10c	40.00	37.50
J4b	D1	12½c	400.00	250.00
J5b	D1	15c	25.00	20.00
J6b	D1	20c	425.00	425.00
J7b	D1	25c	*1,600.*	*1,600.*
J8b	D1	30c	400.00	400.00
J9b	D1	40c	400.00	400.00
10b	D1	50c	47.50	45.00

D2

1892-98 **Value in Black** *Perf. 12½*

J11	D2	2½c green (III)	.25	.25
J12	D2	5c green (III)	.60	.45
J13	D2	10c green (III)	1.50	.40
J14	D2	12½c green (III)	1.60	.60
J15	D2	15c green (III) ('95)	2.50	1.10
J17	D2	25c green (III)	1.25	.95
		Nos. J11-J17 (6)	7.70	3.75

Type I

J11a	D2	2½c	.50	.50
J12a	D2	5c	2.50	2.50
J13a	D2	10c	2.75	2.00
J14a	D2	12½c	2.00	1.40
J16	D2	20c green ('95)	3.50	1.40
J17a	D2	25c	1.50	1.50
J18	D2	30c green ('95)	25.00	13.00
J19	D2	40c green ('95)	25.00	15.00
J20	D2	50c green ('95)	30.00	15.00

Type II

J11b	D2	2½c	20.00	20.00
J12b	D2	5c	1.00	1.00
J13b	D2	10c	1.75	1.10
J14b	D2	12½c	9.00	8.00
J17b	D2	25c	*12.50*	*12.50*
		Nos. J11b-J17b (5)	44.25	42.60

Type I

On Yellowish or White Paper

Value in Color of Stamp

1915 *Perf. 12½, 13½x12½*

J21	D2	2½c green	1.00	.95
J22	D2	5c green	1.00	.95
J23	D2	10c green	.90	.80
J24	D2	12½c green	1.25	1.10
J25	D2	15c green	1.90	2.00
J26	D2	20c green	1.00	1.75
J27	D2	25c green	.35	.25
J28	D2	30c green	3.00	3.25
J29	D2	40c green	3.00	3.25
J30	D2	50c green	2.50	3.00
		Nos. J21-J30 (10)	15.90	17.30

1944 *Perf. 11½*

J23a	D2	10c yellow green	20.00	18.00
J24a	D2	12½c yellow green	20.00	10.00
J27a	D2	25c yellow green	40.00	1.00
		Nos. J23a-J27a (3)	80.00	29.00

Type of 1915

Type I

Value in Color of Stamp

Perf. 13½x13

1948-49 **Unwmk.** **Photo.**

J31	D2	2½c bl grn ('48)	1.75	1.10
J32	D2	5c bl grn ('48)	1.75	1.10
J33	D2	10c blue green	15.00	10.00
J34	D2	12½c blue green	16.00	1.75
J35	D2	15c blue green	27.50	16.00
J36	D2	20c blue green	25.00	16.00
J37	D2	25c blue green	1.75	.35
J38	D2	30c blue green	27.50	21.00
J39	D2	40c blue green	27.50	21.00
J40	D2	50c blue green	27.50	16.00
		Nos. J31-J40 (10)	171.25	104.30

Catalogue values for unused stamps in this section, from this point to the end of the section, are for Never Hinged items.

D3

1953-59 **Photo.**

J41	D3	1c dk blue grn ('59)	.25	.25
J42	D3	2½c dk blue grn	.50	.45
J43	D3	5c dk blue grn	.25	.25
J44	D3	6c dk blue grn ('59)	.45	.30
J45	D3	7c dk blue grn ('59)	.45	.30
J46	D3	8c dk blue grn ('59)	.45	.30
J47	D3	9c dk blue grn ('59)	.45	.30
J48	D3	10c dk blue grn	.25	.25
J49	D3	12½c dk blue grn	.25	.25
J50	D3	15c dk blue grn	.30	.25
J51	D3	20c dk blue grn	.30	.30
J52	D3	25c dk blue grn	.45	.25
J53	D3	30c dk blue grn	1.10	.90
J54	D3	35c dk blue grn ('59)	1.25	.90
J55	D3	40c dk blue grn	1.10	.90
J56	D3	45c dk blue grn ('59)	1.25	.90
J57	D3	50c dk blue grn	1.10	.65
		Nos. J41-J57 (17)	10.15	7.70

NETHERLANDS INDIES

'ne-thər-lən,d,z 'in-dēs

(Dutch Indies, Indonesia)

LOCATION — East Indies
GOVT. — Dutch colony
AREA — 735,268 sq. mi.
POP. — 76,000,000 (estimated 1949)
CAPITAL — Jakarta (formerly Batavia)

Netherlands Indies consisted of the islands of Sumatra, Java, the Lesser Sundas, Madura, two thirds of Borneo, Celebes, the Moluccas, western New Guinea and many small islands.

Netherlands Indies changed its name to Indonesia in 1948. The Netherlands transferred sovereignty on Dec. 28, 1949, to the Republic of the United States of Indonesia (see "Indonesia"), except for the western part of New Guinea (see "Netherlands New Guinea"). The Republic of Indonesia was proclaimed Aug. 15, 1950.

100 Cents = 1 Gulden
100 Sen = 1 Rupiah (1949)

Catalogue values for unused stamps in this country are for Never Hinged items, beginning with Scott 250 in the regular postage section, Scott B57 in the semi-postal section, and Scott J43 in the postage due section.

Values for unused stamps are for examples with original gum as defined in the catalogue introduction. Very fine examples of No. 2 will have perforations touching the frameline on one or more sides due to the narrow spacing of the stamps on the plates. Stamps with perfs clear of the framelines on all four sides are scarce and will command higher prices.

Watermarks

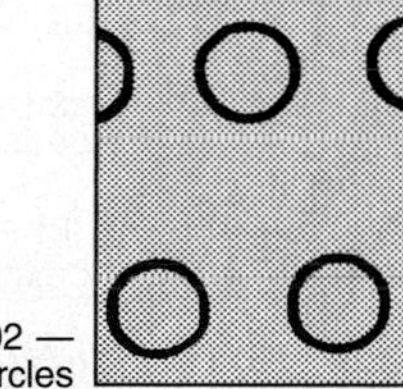

Wmk. 202 — Circles

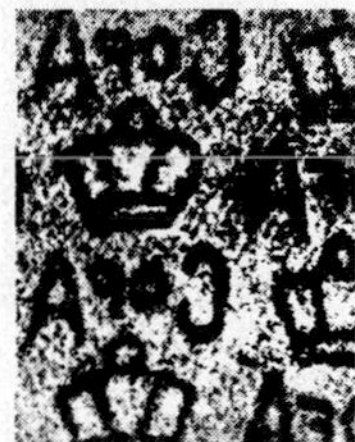

Wmk. 228 — Small Crown and C of A Multiple

King William III — A1

Unwmk.

1864, Apr. 1 **Engr.** ***Imperf.***

1	A1	10c lake	450.00	100.00

1868 ***Perf. 12½x12***

2	A1	10c lake	1,250.	150.00

Privately perforated examples of No. 1 sometimes are mistaken for No. 2.

King William III — A2

ONE CENT:
Type I — "CENT" 6mm long.
Type II — "CENT" 7½mm long.

Perf. 11½x12, 12½, 12½x12, 13x14, 13½, 14, 13½x14

1870-88 **Typo.**

3	A2	1c sl grn, type I	6.00	4.50
a.		Perf. 13x14, small holes	10.00	8.00
4	A2	1c sl grn, type II	2.75	1.75
5	A2	2c red brown	6.00	4.00
a.		2c fawn	6.00	4.00
6	A2	2c violet brn	110.00	95.00
7	A2	2½c orange	35.00	20.00
8	A2	5c pale green	50.00	3.50
a.		Perf. 14, small holes	60.00	4.00
b.		Perf. 13x14, small holes	50.00	5.00
9	A2	10c orange brn	13.00	.25
a.		Perf. 14, small holes	24.00	.80
b.		Perf. 13x14, small holes	35.00	.80
10	A2	12½c gray	3.50	1.50
a.		Perf. 12½x12		1,000.
11	A2	15c bister	17.00	1.50
a.		Perf. 13x14, small holes	27.50	1.75
12	A2	20c ultra	100.00	5.00
a.		Perf. 14, small holes	100.00	5.00
b.		Perf. 13x14, small holes	100.00	5.25
13	A2	25c dk violet	14.00	.55
b.		Perf. 13x14, small holes	25.00	2.50
c.		Perf. 14, large holes	450.00	100.00
14	A2	30c green	27.50	3.25
15	A2	50c carmine	17.00	1.50
a.		Perf. 14, small holes	22.50	1.50
b.		Perf. 13x14, small holes	17.00	1.50
c.		Perf. 14, large holes	25.00	2.50
16	A2	2.50g green & vio	100.00	17.50
b.		Perf. 14, small holes	100.00	17.50
c.		Perf. 14, large holes	110.00	17.50
		Nos. 3-16 (14)	501.75	159.80

Imperforate examples of Nos. 3-16 are proofs. The 1c red brown and 2c yellow are believed to be bogus.

"Small hole" varieties have the spaces between the holes wider than the diameter of the holes.

Numeral of Value — A3

1883-90 ***Perf. 12½***

17	A3	1c slate grn ('88)	.75	.25
a.		Perf. 12½x12	1.10	.65
18	A3	2c brown ('84)	.75	.25
a.		Perf. 12½x12	.75	.30
b.		Perf. 11½x12	65.00	22.50
19	A3	2½c yellow	.75	.65
a.		Perf. 12½x12	1.25	.75
b.		Perf. 11½x12	20.00	7.50
20	A3	3c lilac ('90)	.85	.25
21	A3	5c green ('87)	45.00	27.50
22	A3	5c ultra ('90)	9.00	.25
		Nos. 17-22 (6)	57.10	29.15

For surcharges and overprint see Nos. 46-47, O4.

Queen Wilhelmina — A4

1892-97 ***Perf. 12½***

23	A4	10c orange brn ('95)	5.00	.30
24	A4	12½c gray ('97)	9.00	*12.50*
25	A4	15c bister ('95)	15.00	1.75
26	A4	20c ultra ('93)	35.00	1.60
27	A4	25c violet	35.00	1.60
28	A4	30c green ('94)	42.50	2.00
29	A4	50c carmine ('93)	30.00	1.40
30	A4	2.50g org brn & ultra	165.00	40.00
		Nos. 23-30 (8)	336.50	61.15

For overprints see Nos. O21-O27.

Netherlands Nos. 67-69, 74, 77, 80, 84 Surcharged in Black

1900, July 1

31	A11	10c on 10c gray lil	1.40	.25
32	A11	12½c on 12½c blue	2.25	.55
33	A11	15c on 15c yel brn	2.50	.30
34	A11	20c on 20c yel grn	13.00	.60
35	A11	25c on 25c car & bl	13.00	.70
36	A11	50c on 50c brnz grn & red brn	22.50	.90

1902 ***Perf. 11½x11***

37	A12	2.50g on 2½g brn lil	45.00	11.00
a.		Perf. 11	50.00	12.50
		Nos. 31-37 (7)	99.65	14.30

A6

1902-09 ***Perf. 12½***

38	A6	½c violet	.35	.25
39	A6	1c olive grn	.35	.25
a.		Booklet pane of 6		
40	A6	2c yellow brn	2.75	.25
41	A6	2½c green	1.75	.25
a.		Booklet pane of 6		
42	A6	3c orange	1.75	1.10
43	A6	4c ultra ('09)	11.00	9.00
44	A6	5c rose red	4.25	.25
a.		Booklet pane of 6		
45	A6	7½c gray ('08)	2.25	.30
		Nos. 38-45 (8)	24.45	11.65

For overprints see Nos. 63-69, 81-87, O1-O9.

Nos. 18, 20 Surcharged

1902

46	A3	½c on 2c yel brn	.25	.25
a.		Double surcharge	175.00	150.00
47	A3	2½c on 3c violet	.25	.25

Queen Wilhelmina — A9

1903-08

48	A9	10c slate	1.00	.25
a.		Booklet pane of 6		
49	A9	12½c deep blue ('06)	1.50	.25
a.		Booklet pane of 6		
50	A9	15c chocolate ('06)	7.25	2.00
a.		Ovptd. with 2 horiz. bars	2.50	1.00
51	A9	17½c bister ('08)	3.00	.25
52	A9	20c grnsh slate	1.50	1.50
53	A9	20c olive grn ('05)	30.00	.25
54	A9	22½c brn & ol grn ('08)	3.75	.25
55	A9	25c violet ('04)	12.50	.25
56	A9	30c orange brn	32.50	.30
57	A9	50c red brown ('04)	25.00	.30
		Nos. 48-57 (10)	118.00	5.60

For overprints and surcharges see Nos. 58, 70-78, 88-96, 139, O10-O18.

No. 52 Surcharged in Black

1905, July 6

58	A9	10c on 20c grnsh slate	3.75	1.90

Queen Wilhelmina — A10

1905-12 **Engr.** ***Perf. 11x11½***

59	A10	1g dull lilac ('06)	60.00	.40
a.		Perf. 11½x11	60.00	.50
b.		Perf. 11	70.00	11.00
60	A10	1g dl lil, *bl* ('12)	60.00	6.50
a.		Perf. 11	70.00	*75.00*
61	A10	2½g slate bl ('05)	82.50	3.00
a.		Perf. 11½	82.50	3.50
b.		Perf. 11½x11	90.00	3.50
c.		Perf. 11	675.00	
62	A10	2½g sl bl, *bl* ('12)	90.00	40.00
a.		Perf. 11	100.00	100.00
		Nos. 59-62 (4)	292.50	49.90

Sheets of Nos. 60 & 62 were soaked in an indigo solution.

For overprints and surcharge see Nos. 79-80, 97-98, 140, O19-O20.

Previous Issues Overprinted

1908, July 1

63	A6	½c violet	.25	.25
64	A6	1c olive grn	.35	.25
65	A6	2c yellow brn	1.50	2.00
66	A6	2½c green	.75	.25
67	A6	3c orange	.65	1.10
68	A6	5c rose red	2.25	.40
69	A6	7½c gray	2.50	2.25
70	A9	10c slate	.55	.25
71	A9	12½c dp blue	12.00	3.50
72	A9	15c choc (#50a)	3.75	2.00
73	A9	17½c bister	1.40	.95
74	A9	20c olive grn	7.50	1.40
75	A9	22½c brn & ol grn	5.75	3.50
76	A9	25c violet	5.75	.30
77	A9	30c orange brn	20.00	3.25
78	A9	50c red brown	10.00	1.00
79	A10	1g dull lilac	90.00	4.50
80	A10	2½g slate blue	100.00	65.00
		Nos. 63-80 (18)	264.95	92.15

The above stamps were overprinted for use in the territory outside of Java and Madura, stamps overprinted "Java" being used in these latter places.

The 15c is overprinted, in addition, with two horizontal lines, 2½mm apart.

The overprint also exists on Nos. 59a-59b. Same values.

Overprint Reading Down

63a	A6	½c	.55	*3.25*
64a	A6	1c	.55	*2.50*
65a	A6	2c	2.25	*4.50*
66a	A6	2½c	.95	*3.00*
67a	A6	3c	15.00	*40.00*
68a	A6	5c	2.25	*2.50*
70a	A9	10c	.65	*1.90*
71a	A9	12½c	4.50	*8.00*
72a	A9	15c	32.50	*75.00*
74a	A9	20c	7.25	8.00
75a	A9	22½c	*1,400*	*1,400.*
76a	A9	25c	5.50	7.25
77a	A9	30c	11.00	15.00
78a	A9	50c	7.50	9.00
79a	A10	1g	175.00	225.00
80a	A10	2½g	*2,250.*	*2,500.*

Overprinted

1908, July 1

81	A6	½c violet	.25	.25
b.		Double overprint	550.00	
82	A6	1c olive grn	.30	.30
83	A6	2c yellow brn	2.10	2.10
84	A6	2½c green	1.10	.25
85	A6	3c orange	.90	.90
86	A6	5c rose red	2.75	.25
87	A6	7½c gray	2.25	2.10

88 A9 10c slate .75 .25
89 A9 12½c deep blue 2.50 .70
b. Dbl. ovpt., one inverted 150.00 150.00
90 A9 15c choc (on No. 50a) 3.50 3.00
91 A9 17½c bister 1.90 .80
92 A9 20c olive grn 11.00 .90
93 A9 22½c brn & ol grn 4.75 2.50
94 A9 25c violet 4.75 .40
95 A9 30c orange brn 29.00 2.50
96 A9 50c red brown 18.00 .70
97 A10 1g dull lilac 45.00 3.00
b. Perf. 11 57.50 5.00
98 A10 2½g slate blue 70.00 47.50
Nos. 81-98 (18) 200.80 68.40

Inverted Overprint

81a A6 ½c 1.00 *2.75*
82a A6 1c 1.00 *3.25*
83a A6 2c 3.50 *7.25*
84a A6 2½c 3.00 *4.00*
85a A6 3c 20.00 27.50
86a A6 5c 3.00 3.75
88a A9 10c 2.00 *2.50*
89a A9 12½c 3.25 5.75
90a A9 15c 3.50 *11.00*
92a A9 20c 11.00 12.00
94a A9 25c 6.00 *11.00*
95a A9 30c 29.00 29.00
96a A9 50c 18.00 22.50
97a A10 1g 180.00 180.00
98a A10 2½g *2,750.* *3,000.*

A11

Queen Wilhelmina
A12 A13

Typo., Litho. (#114A)

1912-40 ***Perf. 12½***

101 A11 ½c lt vio .25 .25
102 A11 1c olive grn .25 .25
103 A11 2c yellow brn .50 .25
104 A11 2c gray blk ('30) .50 .25
105 A11 2½c green 1.40 .25
106 A11 2½c lt red ('22) .30 .25
107 A11 3c yellow .50 .25
108 A11 3c green ('29) .80 .25
109 A11 4c ultra .75 .30
110 A11 4c dp grn ('28) 1.40 .25
111 A11 4c yellow ('30) 10.00 4.50
112 A11 5c rose 1.25 .25
113 A11 5c green ('22) 1.05 .25
114 A11 5c chlky bl ('28) .65 .25
114A A11 5c ultra ('40) 1.00 .25
115 A11 7½c bister .45 .25
116 A11 10c lilac ('22) 1.10 .25
117 A12 10c car rose ('14) .85 .25
118 A12 12½c dull bl ('14) 1.10 .25
119 A12 12½c red ('22) 1.10 .25
120 A12 15c blue ('29) 10.00 .30
121 A12 17½c red brn ('15) 1.10 .30
122 A12 20c green ('15) 2.00 .30
123 A12 20c blue ('22) 2.00 .30
124 A12 20c orange ('32) 17.00 .30
125 A12 22½c orange ('15) 2.00 .50
126 A12 25c red vio ('15) 2.00 .25
127 A12 30c slate ('15) 2.25 .25
128 A12 32½c vio & red ('22) 2.25 .25
129 A12 35c org brn ('29) 10.00 .70
130 A12 40c green ('22) 2.25 .25

Perf. 11½

Engr.

131 A13 50c green ('13) 4.75 .25
a. Perf. 11x11½ 5.00 .35
b. Perf. 12½ 5.00 .35
132 A13 60c dp blue ('22) 5.50 .25
133 A13 80c orange ('22) 4.75 .25
134 A13 1g brown ('13) 3.50 .25
a. Perf. 11x11½ 4.00 .25
135 A13 1.75g dk vio, p. 12½ ('31) 17.50 2.40
136 A13 2½g car ('13) 14.50 .50
a. Perf. 11x11½ 15.00 .75
b. Perf. 12½ 16.00 .70
Nos. 101-136 (37) 128.55 16.90

For surcharges and overprints see Nos. 137-138, 144-150, 102a-123a, 158, 194-195, B1-B3, C1-C5.

Water Soluble Ink

Some values of types A11 and A12 and late printings of types A6 and A9 are in soluble ink. The design disappears when immersed in water.

Nos. 105, 109, 54, 59 Surcharged

1917-18 **Typo.** ***Perf. 12½***

137 A11 ½c on 2½c .30 .30
138 A11 1c on 4c ('18) .55 .55
139 A9 17½c on 22½c ('18) 1.25 .55
a. Inverted surcharge 350.00 425.00

Perf. 11x11½

140 A10 30c on 1g ('18) 10.00 2.25
a. Perf. 11½x11 140.00 55.00
Nos. 137-140 (4) 12.10 3.65

Nos. 121, 125, 131, 134 Surcharged in Red or Blue

On A12

On A13

Two types of 32½c on 50c:
I — Surcharge bars spaced as in illustration.
II — Bars more closely spaced.

1922, Jan. ***Perf. 12½***

144 A12 12½c on 17½c (R) .30 .25
145 A12 12½c on 22½c (R) .40 .25
146 A12 20c on 22½c (Bl) .40 .25

Perf. 11½, 11x11½

147 A13 32½c on 50c (Bl) (I, perf. 11½) 1.25 .25
a. Type II, perf. 11½ 10.00 .25
b. Type I, perf. 11x11½ 1,000. 6.00
c. Type II, perf. 11x11½ 19.00 1.00
148 A13 40c on 50c (R) 3.75 .45
149 A13 60c on 1g (Bl) 6.00 .40
150 A13 80c on 1g (R) 6.75 .90
Nos. 144-150 (7) 18.85 2.75

Stamps of 1912-22 Overprinted in Red, Blue, Green or Black

a

b

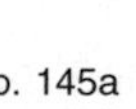

No. 145a

1922, Sept. 18 **Typo.** ***Perf. 12½***

102a A11(a) 1c ol grn (R) 7.00 5.75
103a A11(a) 2c yel brn (Bl) 7.00 5.75
106a A11(a) 2½c lt red (G) 65.00 *72.50*
107a A11(a) 3c yellow (R) 7.00 7.00
109a A11(a) 4c ultra (R) 38.50 36.00
113a A11(a) 5c green (R) 13.00 10.00
115a A11(a) 7½c drab (Bl) 9.00 5.75
116a A11(a) 10c lilac (Bk) 70.00 80.00
145a A12(b) 12½c on 22½c org (Bl) 7.00 7.00
121a A12(b) 17½c red brn (Bk) 7.00 5.75
123a A12(b) 20c blue (Bk) 7.00 5.75
Nos. 102a-123a (11) 237.50 241.25

Issued to publicize the 3rd Netherlands Indies Industrial Fair at Bandoeng, Java.

Nos. 102a-123a were sold at a premium for 3, 4, 5, 6, 8, 9, 10, 12½, 15, 20 and 22½ cents respectively.

Queen Wilhelmina — A15

1923, Aug. 31 **Engr.** ***Perf. 11½***

151 A15 5c myrtle green .25 .25
a. Perf. 11½x11 400.00 140.00
b. Perf. 11x11½ 4.50 .55
152 A15 12½c rose .25 .25
a. Perf. 11x11½ 1.25 .25
b. Perf. 11½x11 1.75 .25
153 A15 20c dark blue .35 .25
a. Perf. 11½x11 3.25 .40
154 A15 50c red orange 1.40 .60
a. Perf. 11x11½ 6.50 1.25
b. Perf. 11½x11 2.00 .90
c. Perf. 11 4.50 .85
155 A15 1g brown vio 2.75 .40
a. Perf. 11½x11 7.50 .80
156 A15 2½g gray black 35.00 12.00
157 A15 5g orange brown 135.00 125.00
Nos. 151-157 (7) 175.00 138.75

25th anniversary of the assumption of the government of the Netherlands by Queen Wilhelmina, at the age of 18.

No. 123 Surcharged

1930, Dec. 13 **Typo.** ***Perf. 12½***

158 A12 12½c on 20c bl (R) .30 .25
a. Inverted surcharge 375.00 475.00

Prince William I, Portrait by Van Key — A16

1933, Apr. 18 **Photo.**

163 A16 12½c deep orange 1.25 .25

400th anniv. of the birth of Prince William I, Count of Nassau and Prince of Orange, frequently referred to as William the Silent.

Rice Field Scene
A17

Queen Wilhelmina
A18

Queen Wilhelmina
A19

1933-37 **Unwmk.** ***Perf. 11½x12½***

164 A17 1c lilac gray ('34) .25 .25
165 A17 2c plum ('34) .25 .25
166 A17 2½c bister ('34) .25 .25
167 A17 3c yellow grn ('34) .25 .25
168 A17 3½c dark gray ('37) .25 .25
169 A17 4c dk olive ('34) 1.00 .25
170 A17 5c ultra ('34) .25 .25
171 A17 7½c violet ('34) 1.50 .25
172 A17 10c ver ('34) 2.10 .25
173 A18 10c ver ('37) .30 .25
174 A18 12½c dp org ('34) .30 .25
a. 12½c light orange, perf. 12½ ('33) 7.50 .40
175 A18 15c ultra ('34) .30 .25
176 A18 20c plum ('34) .50 .25
177 A18 25c blue grn ('34) 2.10 .25
178 A18 30c lilac gray ('34) 3.25 .25
179 A18 32½c bister ('34) 9.00 *10.00*
180 A18 35c violet ('34) 5.00 1.25
181 A18 40c yel grn ('34) 3.00 .25
182 A18 42½c yellow ('34) 3.00 .25

1934, Jan 16 ***Perf. 12½***

183 A19 50c lilac gray 5.00 .25
184 A19 60c ultra 6.00 .50
185 A19 80c vermilion 6.00 .60
186 A19 1g violet 6.25 .40
187 A19 1.75g yellow grn 20.00 15.00
188 A19 2.50g plum 22.50 2.00
Nos. 164-188 (25) 98.60 34.25

See Nos. 200-225. For overprints and surcharges see Nos. 271-275, B48, B57.

Water Soluble Ink

Nos. 164-188 and the first printing of No. 163 have soluble ink and the design disappears when immersed in water.

Nos. C6-C7, C14, C9-C10 Surcharged in Black

a

b

1934 **Typo.** ***Perf. 12½x11½, 12½***

189 AP1(a) 2c on 10c .30 .45
190 AP1(a) 2c on 20c .25 .25
191 AP3(b) 2c on 30c .40 .60
192 AP1(a) 42½c on 75c 4.25 .25
193 AP1(a) 42½c on 1.50g 4.25 .40
Nos. 189-193 (5) 9.45 1.95

Nos. 127-128 Surcharged with New Value in Red or Black

1937, Sept. ***Perf. 12½***

194 A12 10c on 30c (R) 2.50 .25
a. Double surcharge *675.00*
195 A12 10c on 32½c (Bk) 2.75 .30

Wilhelmina — A20

Perf. 12½x12

1938, Aug. 30 **Photo.** **Wmk. 202**

196 A20 2c dull purple .25 .25
197 A20 10c car lake .25 .25
198 A20 15c royal blue 1.25 .75
199 A20 20c red orange .50 .30
Nos. 196-199 (4) 2.25 1.55

40th anniv. of the reign of Queen Wilhelmina.

Types of 1933-37

1938-40 **Photo.** ***Perf. 12½x12***

200 A17 1c lilac gray ('39) .30 *.80*
201 A17 2c plum ('39) .25 .25
202 A17 2½c bister ('39) .50 .50
203 A17 3c yellow grn ('39) 1.50 1.25
205 A17 4c gray ol ('39) 1.50 1.25
206 A17 5c ultra ('39) .25 .25
a. Perf. 12x12½ 1.25 .25
207 A17 7½c violet ('39) 2.50 1.00
208 A18 10c ver ('39) .25 .25
210 A18 15c ultra ('39) .25 .25
211 A18 20c plum ('39) .25 .25
a. Perf. 12x12½ 1.25 .25
212 A18 25c blue grn ('39) 25.00 24.00
213 A18 30c lilac gray ('39) 6.50 .80
215 A18 35c violet ('39) 2.75 .65
216 A18 40c dp yel grn ('40) 5.00 .25

Perf. 12½

218 A19 50c lilac gray ('40) 275.00
219 A19 60c ultra ('39) 10.50 1.25
220 A19 80c ver ('39) 62.50 26.00
221 A19 1g violet ('39) 27.50 .85
223 A19 2g Prus green 27.50 14.00
225 A19 5g yellow brn 25.00 6.00
Nos. 200-216,219-225 (19) 199.80 79.85

The note following No. 188 applies also to this issue.

The 50c was sold only at the philatelic window in Amsterdam.

War Dance of Nias Island — A23

Legong Dancer of Bali — A24

Wayang Wong Dancer of Java A25

Padjogé Dancer, Southern Celebes A26

Dyak Dancer of Borneo — A27

1941 **Unwmk.** ***Perf. 12½***

228 A23 2½c rose violet .25 .25
229 A24 3c green .25 .50
230 A25 4c olive green .25 .45
231 A26 5c blue .25 .25
232 A27 7½c dark violet .50 .25
Nos. 228-232 (5) 1.50 1.70

See Nos. 279-280, 293, N38.
Imperfs. are printers waste.

A28

Queen Wilhelmina A28a

1941 ***Perf. 12½***

Size: 18x22¾mm

234 A28 10c red orange .25 .25
a. Perf. 13½ .40 .40
235 A28 15c ultra 1.50 1.25
236 A28 17½c orange .40 .60
237 A28 20c plum 21.00 35.00
238 A28 25c Prus green 30.00 47.50
239 A28 30c olive bis 1.90 1.10
240 A28 35c purple 95.00 *325.00*
241 A28 40c yellow grn 8.00 2.50

Perf. 13½

Size: 20½x26mm

242 A28 50c car lake 2.00 .70
243 A28 60c ultra 1.60 .60
244 A28 80c red orange 1.90 .95
245 A28 1g purple 2.00 .30
246 A28 2g Prus green 10.00 1.10
247 A28 5g bis, perf. 12½ 350.00 *700.00*
248 A28 10g green 30.00 15.00

Size: 26x32mm

249 A28a 25g orange 250.00 140.00
Nos. 234-249 (16) 805.55 *1,271.*

Nos. 242-246 come with pin-perf 13½.

The 10c comes in two types: 1¼mm between "10" and "CENT," and 1¾mm.

For overprints and surcharge see Nos. 276-278, J43-J46.

Catalogue values for unused stamps in this section, from this point to the end of the section, are for Never Hinged items.

Rice Fields — A29

Barge on Java Lake — A30

University of Medicine, Batavia A31

Palms on Shore — A32

Plane over Bromo Volcano A33

Queen Wilhelmina
A34 A35

1945-46, Oct. 1 **Engr.** ***Perf. 12***

250 A29 1c green .25 .25
251 A30 2c rose lilac .25 .30
252 A31 2½c dull lilac .25 .25
253 A32 5c blue .25 .25
254 A33 7½c olive gray .50 .25
255 A34 10c red brown .25 .25
256 A34 15c dark blue .25 .25
257 A34 17½c rose lake .25 .25
258 A34 20c sepia .25 .25
259 A34 30c slate gray .30 .25
260 A35 60c gray black .65 .25
261 A35 1g blue green 1.10 .25
262 A35 2½g red orange 3.75 .50
Nos. 250-262 (13) 8.30 3.55

For surcharge see No. 304.
Issued: 15c, 1946, others 10/1/45.

Railway Viaduct Near Soekaboemi A36

Dam and Power Station A37

Palm Tree and Menangkabau House — A38

Huts on Piles A39

Buddhist Stupas A40

Perf. 14½x14

1946 **Typo.** **Wmk. 228**

263 A36 1c dark green .25 .25
264 A37 2c black brown .25 .25
265 A38 2½c scarlet .25 .25
266 A39 5c indigo .25 .25
267 A40 7½c ultra .25 .25
Nos. 263-267 (5) 1.25 1.25

Nos. 265, 267, 263 Surcharged

1947, Sept. 25

268 A38 3c on 2½c scar .25 .25
269 A40 3c on 7½c ultra .25 .25
a. Double surcharge 200.00 200.00
270 A36 4c on 1c dk green .25 .25
Nos. 268-270 (3) .75 .75

No. 219 Surcharged with New Value and Bars in Red

1947, Sept. 25 **Wmk. 202** ***Perf. 12½***

271 A19 45c on 60c ultra 1.25 1.25

Nos. 212, 218 and 220 Overprinted "1947" in Red or Black

1947, Sept. 25 ***Perf. 12½x12, 12½***

272 A18 25c blue green (R) .25 .25
a. Unwmkd. 125.00
273 A19 50c lilac gray (R) .70 .25
274 A19 80c vermilion 1.10 .75
a. Unwmkd. 500.00 140.00
Nos. 272-274 (3) 2.05 1.25

Bar above "1947" on No. 274.

Nos. 174, 241, 247 and Type of 1941 Overprinted "1947" in Black

Perf. 12½, 12½x12 (2g)

1947, Sept. 25 **Unwmk.**

275 A18 12½c deep orange .25 .25
276 A28 40c yellow green .40 .25
277 A28 2g Prus green 3.75 .50
278 A28 5g bister 11.00 7.50
Nos. 275-278 (4) 15.40 8.50

The overprint is vertical on Nos. 276-278.

Dancer Types of 1941, 1945

1948, May 13 **Litho.** ***Perf. 12½***

279 OS21 3c rose red .25 .25
280 A24 4c dull olive grn .25 .25

Queen Wilhelmina — A41

1948 **Photo.** ***Perf. 12½***

Size: 18x22mm

281 A41 15c red orange .60 .80
282 A41 20c brt blue .25 .25
283 A41 25c dk green .25 .25
284 A41 40c dp yellow grn .25 .25
285 A41 45c plum .40 .60
286 A41 50c red brown .25 .25
287 A41 80c brt red .30 .25

Perf. 13

Size: 20½x26mm

288 A41 1g deep violet .25 .25
a. Perf. 12½ x 12 .75 .40
289 A41 10g green 30.00 8.25
290 A41 25g orange 67.50 50.00
Nos. 281-290 (10) 100.05 61.15

See Nos. 291-292. For overprints see Nos. 294-303.

Wilhelmina Type of 1948 Inscribed "1898-1948"

1948, Aug. 31 ***Perf. 12½x12***

Size: 21x26½mm

291 A41 15c orange .30 .25
292 A41 20c ultra .30 .25

Reign of Queen Wilhelmina, 50th anniv.

Dancer Type of 1941

1948, Sept. **Photo.** ***Perf. 12½***

293 A27 7½c olive bister .70 .80

Juliana Type of Netherlands 1948

Perf. 14½x13½

1948, Sept. 25 **Wmk. 202**

293A A75 15c red orange .30 .25
293B A75 20c deep ultra .30 .25

Investiture of Queen Juliana, Sept. 6, 1948.

Indonesia

Nos. 281 to 287 Overprinted in Black

Two types of overprint:
I — Shiny ink, bar 1.8mm wide. By G. C. T. van Dorp & Co.
II — Dull ink, bar 2.2mm. By G. Kolff & Co.

1948 ***Perf. 12½***

294 A41 15c red orange (I) .60 .25
a. Type II .55 .25
295 A41 20c bright blue (I) .25 .25
a. Type II .25 .25
296 A41 25c dark green (I) .25 .25
a. Type II .25 .25
297 A41 40c dp yel grn (I) .25 .25
298 A41 45c plum ('49) (II) .80 .70
299 A41 50c red brn ('49) (II) .25 .25
300 A41 80c bright red (I) .65 .25
a. Type II .65 .25

Nos. 288-290 Overprinted in Black

Two or Three Bars

Perf. 12½x12

301 A41 1g deep violet .90 .25
a. Perf. 13 1.50 .25

Perf. 13

302 A41 10g green 72.50 9.00
303 A41 25g orange 90.00 62.50
Nos. 294-303 (10) 166.45 73.95

Same Overprint in Black on No. 262

1949 **Engr.** ***Perf. 12***

Bars 28½mm long

304 A35 2½g red orange 20.00 7.25

A42

Tjandi Puntadewa Temple Entrance, East Java — A43

Detail, Temple of the Dead, Bedjuning, Bali A44

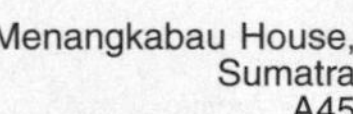

Menangkabau House, Sumatra
A45

Toradja House, Celebes — A46

Designs: 5r, 10r, 25r, Temple entrance.

Perf. 12½, 11½

1949 Unwmk. Photo.

No.	Type	Value	Color	Unused	Used
307	A42	1s	gray	.25	.25
a.	Perf. 11½			.40	.25
308	A42	2s	claret	.25	.25
a.	Perf. 11½			5.00	*14.00*
309	A42	2½s	olive brown	.25	.25
a.	Perf. 11½			.25	.25
310	A42	3s	rose pink	.25	.25
a.	Perf. 11½			1.10	.75
311	A42	4s	green	.30	.50
312	A42	5s	blue	.25	.25
a.	Perf. 11½			1.00	.25
313	A42	7½s	dark green	.40	.25
a.	Perf. 11½			1.00	.75
314	A42	10s	violet	.25	.25
a.	Perf. 11½				*375.00*
315	A42	12½s	brt red	.30	.25
a.	Perf. 11½			4.00	4.00
316	A43	15s	rose red	.25	.25
a.	Perf. 12½			.30	.25
317	A43	20s	gray black	.25	.25
a.	Perf. 12½			.30	.75
318	A43	25s	ultra	.30	.25
319	A44	30s	brt red	.30	.25
320	A44	40s	gray green	.30	.25
321	A44	45s	claret	.30	.25
a.	Perf. 12½			2.75	.50
322	A45	50s	orange brn	.30	.25
323	A45	60s	brown	.40	.25
324	A45	80s	scarlet	.30	.25
a.	Perf. 12½			4.00	.25

The 4s is perf. 12½. The 25s, 30s, 40s, 50s, 60s come both 12½ and 11½, same values.

Perf. 12½

No.	Type	Value	Color	Unused	Used
325	A46	1r	purple	.30	.25
326	A46	2r	gray green	2.25	.25
327	A46	3r	red violet	24.00	.25
328	A46	5r	dk brown	24.00	.25
329	A46	10r	gray	57.50	.50
330	A46	25r	orange brn	.30	.25
	Nos. 307-330 (24)			113.55	6.50

Nos. 307-330 remained on sale in Indonesia Republic post offices until May 23, 1958, and were valid for postage until June 30, 1958.

For surcharge, see Indonesia Nos. 335-358.

Globe and Arms of Bern — A48

1949, Oct. 1 *Perf. 12½*

No.	Type	Value	Color	Unused	Used
331	A48	15s	bright red	.70	.35
332	A48	25s	ultra	.70	.25

Nos. 307-330 remained on sale in Indonesia Republic post offices until May 23, 1958, and were valid for postage until June 30, 1958. 75th anniv. of UPU.

See Indonesia (republic) for subsequent listings.

SEMI-POSTAL STAMPS

Regular Issue of 1912-14 Surcharged in Carmine

1915, June 10 Unwmk. *Perf. 12½*

No.	Type	Value	Color	Unused	Used
B1	A11	1c + 5c	ol grn	4.50	4.50
B2	A11	5c + 5c	rose	4.50	4.50
B3	A12	10c + 5c	rose	7.25	7.25
	Nos. B1-B3 (3)			16.25	16.25

Surtax for the Red Cross.

Bali Temple
SP1

Watchtower
SP2

Menangkabau Compound — SP3

Borobudur Temple, Java
SP4

Perf. 11½x11, 11x11½

1930, Dec. 1 Photo.

No.	Type	Value	Color	Unused	Used
B4	SP1	2c (+ 1c)	vio & brn	1.00	.80
B5	SP2	5c (+ 2½c)	dk grn & brn	4.75	2.50
B6	SP3	12½c (+ 2½c)	dp red & brn	3.25	.50
B7	SP4	15c (+ 5c)	ultra & brn	5.75	5.75
	Nos. B4-B7 (4)			14.75	9.55

Surtax for youth care.

Farmer and Carabao
SP5

5c, Fishermen. 12½c, Dancers. 15c, Musicians.

1931, Dec. 1 Engr. *Perf. 12½*

No.	Type	Value	Color	Unused	Used
B8	SP5	2c (+ 1c)	olive bis	3.00	2.00
B9	SP5	5c (+ 2½c)	bl grn	4.25	3.75
B10	SP5	12½c (+ 2½c)	dp red	3.25	.55
B11	SP5	15c (+ 5c)	dl bl	8.25	7.00
	Nos. B8-B11 (4)			18.75	13.30

The surtax was for the aid of the Leper Colony at Salatiga.

Weaving
SP9

5c, Plaiting rattan. 12½c, Woman batik dyer. 15c, Coppersmith.

1932, Dec. 1 Photo. *Perf. 12½*

No.	Type	Value	Color	Unused	Used
B12	SP9	2c (+ 1c)	dp vio & bis	.40	.40
B13	SP9	5c (+ 2½c)	dp grn & bis	2.50	2.00
B14	SP9	12½c (+ 2½c)	brt rose & bis	.85	.30
B15	SP9	15c (+ 5c)	bl & bis	3.25	3.00
	Nos. B12-B15 (4)			7.00	5.70

The surtax was donated to the Salvation Army.

Woman and Lotus — SP13

Designs: 5c, "The Light that Shows the Way." 12½c, YMCA emblem. 15c, Jobless man.

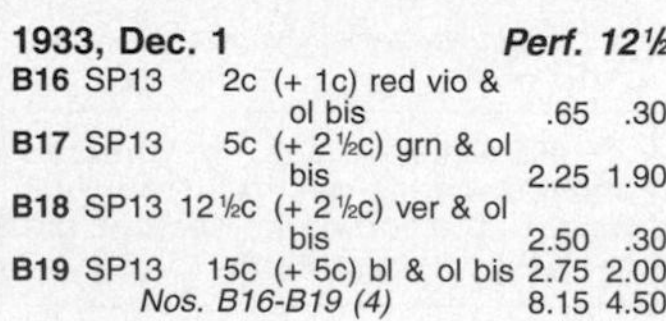

1933, Dec. 1 *Perf. 12½*

No.	Type	Value	Color	Unused	Used
B16	SP13	2c (+ 1c)	red vio & ol bis	.65	.30
B17	SP13	5c (+ 2½c)	grn & ol bis	2.25	1.90
B18	SP13	12½c (+ 2½c)	ver & ol bis	2.50	.30
B19	SP13	15c (+ 5c)	bl & ol bis	2.75	2.00
	Nos. B16-B19 (4)			8.15	4.50

The surtax was for the Amsterdam Young Men's Society for Relief of the Poor in Netherlands Indies.

Dowager Queen Emma — SP17

1934, Sept. 15 *Perf. 13x14*

No.	Type	Value	Color	Unused	Used
B20	SP17	12½c (+ 2½c)	blk brn	1.25	.45

Issued in memory of the late Dowager Queen Emma of Netherlands. The surtax was for the Anti-Tuberculosis Society.

A Pioneer at Work — SP18

Designs: 5c, Cavalryman rescuing wounded native. 12½c, Artilleryman under fire. 15c, Bugler.

1935 *Perf. 12½*

No.	Type	Value	Color	Unused	Used
B21	SP18	2c (+ 1c)	plum & ol bis	1.25	1.00
B22	SP18	5c (+ 2½c)	grn & ol bis	3.25	2.25
B23	SP18	12½c (+ 2½c)	red org & ol bis	3.25	.25
B24	SP18	15c (+ 5c)	brt bl & ol bis	4.50	4.50
	Nos. B21-B24 (4)			12.25	8.00

The surtax was for the Indies Committee of the Christian Military Association for the East and West Indies.

Child Welfare Work — SP22

1936, Dec. 1 Size: 23x20mm

No.	Type	Value	Color	Unused	Used
B25	SP22	2c (+ 1c)	plum	1.00	.60

Size: 30x26½mm

No.	Type	Value	Color	Unused	Used
B26	SP22	5c (+ 2½c)	gray vio	1.25	1.10
B27	SP22	7½c (+ 2½c)	dk vio	1.25	1.25
B28	SP22	12½c (+ 2½c)	red org	1.25	.30
B29	SP22	15c (+5c)	brt bl	2.00	1.75
	Nos. B25-B29 (5)			6.75	5.00

Surtax for Salvation Army.

Boy Scouts — SP23

1937, May 1

No.	Type	Value	Color	Unused	Used
B30	SP23	7½c + 2½c	dk ol brn	1.25	1.00
B31	SP23	12½c + 2½c	rose car	1.25	.50

Fifth Boy Scout World Jamboree, Vogelenzang, Netherlands, July 31-Aug. 13, 1937. Surtax for Netherlands Indies Scout Association.

Sifting Rice — SP24

Designs: 3½c, Mother and children. 7½c, Plowing with carabao team. 10c, Carabao team and cart. 20c, Native couple.

1937, Dec. 1

No.	Type	Value	Color	Unused	Used
B32	SP24	2c (+ 1c)	dk brn & org	1.10	.80
B33	SP24	3½c (+ 1½c)	gray	1.10	.80
B34	SP24	7½c (+ 2½c)	Prus grn & org	1.25	.95
B35	SP24	10c (+ 2½c)	car & org	1.25	.25
B36	SP24	20c (+ 5c)	brt bl	1.25	1.10
	Nos. B32-B36 (5)			5.95	3.90

Surtax for the Public Relief Fund for indigenous poor.

Modern Plane — SP28

Design: 20c, Plane nose facing left.

Wmk. 202

1938, Oct. 15 Photo. *Perf. 12½*

No.	Type	Value	Color	Unused	Used
B36A	SP28	17½c (+5c)	olive brn	.85	.85
B36B	SP28	20c (+5c)	slate	.85	.55

10th anniversary of the Dutch East Indies Royal Air Lines (K. N. I. L. M.).

Surtax for the Aviation Fund in the Netherlands Indies.

Nun and Child
SP29 SP30

Designs: 7½c, Nurse examining child's arm. 10c, Nurse bathing baby. 20c, Nun bandaging child's head.

1938, Dec. 1 Wmk. 202 *Perf. 12½*

No.	Type	Value	Color	Unused	Used
B37	SP29	2c (+ 1c)	vio	.60	.45

Perf. 11½x12

No.	Type	Value	Color	Unused	Used
B38	SP30	3½c (+ 1½c)	brt grn	1.00	.90

Perf. 12x11½

No.	Type	Value	Color	Unused	Used
B39	SP30	7½c (+ 2½c)	cop red	.80	.85
B40	SP30	10c (+ 2½c)	ver	.90	.25
B41	SP30	20c (+ 5c)	brt ultra	1.00	.95
	Nos. B37-B41 (5)			4.30	3.40

The surtax was for the Central Mission Bureau in Batavia.

Social Workers
SP34

Indonesian Nurse Tending Patient
SP35

European Nurse Tending Patient — SP36

Perf. 13x11½, 11½x13

1939, Dec. 1 Photo.

No.	Type	Value	Color	Unused	Used
B42	SP34	2c (+ 1c)	purple	.25	.25
B43	SP35	3½c (+ 1½c)	bl grn & pale bl grn	.30	.25
B44	SP34	7½c (+ 2½c)	cop brn	.25	.25
B45	SP35	10c (+ 2½c)	scar & pink	1.40	.80

B46 SP36 10c (+ 2½c) scar 1.40 .80
B47 SP36 20c (+ 5c) dk bl .40 .35
Nos. B42-B47 (6) 4.00 2.70

No. B44 shows native social workers.
Nos. B45 and B46 were issued se-tenant vertically and horizontally. The surtax was used for the Bureau of Social Service.

No. 174 Surcharged in Brown

1940, Dec. 2 Unwmk. ***Perf. 12x12½***
B48 A18 10c + 5c on 12½c dp org 1.10 .40

SP37

Netherlands coat of arms and inscription "Netherlands Shall Rise Again"

1941, May 10 Litho. ***Perf. 12½***
B49 SP37 5c + 5c multi .25 .25
B50 SP37 10c + 10c multi .25 .25
B51 SP37 1g + 1g multi 9.00 6.75
Nos. B49-B51 (3) 9.50 7.25

The surtax was used to purchase fighter planes for Dutch pilots fighting with the Royal Air Force in Great Britain.

SP38

Designs: 2c, Doctor and child, 3½c, Rice eater. 7½c, Nurse and patient. 10c, Nurse and children. 15c, Basket weaver.

1941, Sept. 22 **Photo.**
B52 SP38 2c (+ 1c) yel grn .60 .55
B53 SP38 3½c (+ 1½c) vio brn 4.00 3.50
B54 SP38 7½c (+ 2½c) vio 3.25 2.75
B55 SP38 10c (+ 2½c) dk red .90 .25
B56 SP38 15c (+ 5c) saph 9.50 6.00
Nos. B52-B56 (5) 18.25 13.05

The surtax was used for various charities.

Catalogue values for unused stamps in this section, from this point to the end of the section, are for Never Hinged items.

Indonesia

No. 208 Surcharged in Black

Perf. 12½x12
1948, Feb. 2 **Wmk. 202**
B57 A18 15c + 10c on 10c .25 .25
a. Inverted surcharge 210.00 210.00

The surtax was for war victims and other charitable purposes.

AIR POST STAMPS

Regular Issues of 1913-1923 Surcharged in Black or Blue

Nos. 119 & 126 Surcharged

No. 133 Surcharged

No. 134 Surcharged

No. 136 Surcharged

Perf. 12½, 11½
1928, Sept. 20 **Unwmk.**
C1 A12 10c on 12½c red 1.00 1.00
C2 A12 20c on 25c red vio 2.25 2.25
C3 A13 40c on 80c org 1.90 1.50
C4 A13 75c on 1g brn (Bl) .90 .55
C5 A13 1½g on 2½g car 6.25 5.50
Nos. C1-C5 (5) 12.30 10.80

On Nos. C4 and C5 there are stars over the original values and the airplane is of different shape. On No. C3 there are no bars under "OST."

Planes over Temple AP1

1928, Dec. 1 Litho. ***Perf. 12½x11½***
C6 AP1 10c red violet .30 .25
C7 AP1 20c brown .85 .55
C8 AP1 40c rose 1.00 .55
C9 AP1 75c green 2.25 .25
C10 AP1 1.50g orange 4.00 .50
Nos. C6-C10 (5) 8.40 2.10

For surcharges see Nos. 189-190, 192-193, C11-C12, C17.

No. C8 Surcharged in Black or Green

1930-32
C11 AP1 30c on 40c rose .90 .25
C12 AP1 30c on 40c rose (G) ('32) 1.25 .25

Pilot at Controls of Plane AP2

1931, Apr. 1 Photo. ***Perf. 12½***
C13 AP2 1g blue & brown 11.00 11.00

Issued for the first air mail flight from Java to Australia.

Landscape and Garudas AP3

1931, May
C14 AP3 30c red violet 2.25 .25
C15 AP3 4½g bright blue 8.00 3.00
C16 AP3 7½g yellow green 10.00 3.25
Nos. C14-C16 (3) 20.25 6.50

For surcharge see No. 191.

No. C10 Surcharged in Blue

1932, July 21 ***Perf. 12½x11½***
C17 AP1 50c on 1.50g org 2.50 .40
a. Inverted surcharge 1,800. 2,000.

Airplane AP4

1933, Oct. 18 Photo. ***Perf. 12½***
C18 AP4 30c deep blue 2.10 1.75

MARINE INSURANCE STAMPS

Floating Safe Attracting Gulls — MI1

Floating Safe with Night Flare — MI2

Artistic Fantasy of Floating Safe — MI3

Perf. 11½
1921, Nov. 1 Unwmk. Engr.
GY1 MI1 15c slate green 2.25 *40.00*
GY2 MI1 60c rose 4.00 *50.00*
GY3 MI1 75c gray brn 4.00 *55.00*
GY4 MI2 1.50g dark blue 25.00 *250.00*
GY5 MI2 2.25g org brn 32.50 *350.00*
GY6 MI3 4½g black 65.00 *600.00*
GY7 MI3 7½g red 80.00 *700.00*
Nos. GY1-GY7 (7) 212.75 *2,045.*

POSTAGE DUE STAMPS

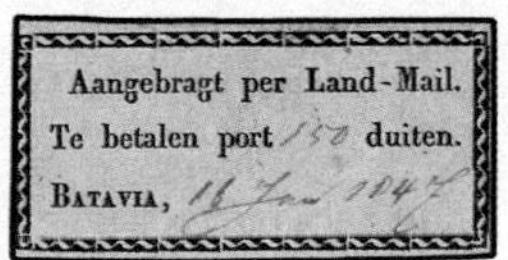
Aangebragt per Land-Mail.
Te betalen port 150 duiten.
Batavia, 18 Jan 1847
D1

Aangebragt per Land-Mail.
Te betalen port f 2.16 koper.
Batavia, 13 aug 1846
D2

1845-46 Unwmk. Typeset ***Imperf.***
Bluish Paper
J1 D1 black ('46) *1,650.*
J2 D2 black *2,000.*
a. "Maill" instead of "Mail" *3,200.*

D3

Perf. 12½x12, 13x14, 10½x12
1874 **Typo.**
J3 D3 5c ocher 300.00 275.00
J4 D3 10c green, *yel* 120.00 100.00
J5 D3 15c ocher, *org* 25.00 20.00
a. Perf. 11½x12 40.00 40.00
J6 D3 20c green, *blue* 40.00 17.50
a. Perf. 11½x12 80.00 25.00
Nos. J3-J6 (4) 485.00 412.50

D4

Type I — 34 loops. "T" of "Betalen" over center of loop, top branch of "E" of "Te" shorter than lower branch.
Type II — 33 loops. "T" of "Betalen" over center of two loops.
Type III — 32 loops. "T" of "Betalen" slightly to the left of loop, top branch of first "E" of "Betalen" shorter than lower branch.
Type IV — 37 loops and letters of "PORT" larger than in the other three types.

Value in Black

Perf. 11½x12, 12½, 12½x12, 13½
1882-88 **Type III**
J7 D4 2½c carmine .40 1.10
J8 D4 5c carmine .25 .40
J9 D4 10c carmine 2.50 3.00
J10 D4 15c carmine 3.00 3.00
J11 D4 20c carmine 135.00 1.00
J12 D4 30c carmine 1.75 2.50
J13 D4 40c carmine 1.25 2.00
J14 D4 50c deep salmon .75 .60
J15 D4 75c carmine .45 .50
Nos. J7-J15 (9) 145.35 14.10

Type I

J7a D4 2½c carmine .40 1.10
J8a D4 5c carmine .25 .45
J9a D4 10c carmine 3.25 4.00
J10a D4 15c carmine 3.25 3.50
J11a D4 20c carmine 95.00 .50
J12a D4 30c carmine 3.25 4.00
J13a D4 40c carmine 1.40 2.00
J14a D4 50c deep salmon .80 .60
J15a D4 75c carmine .50 .60
Nos. J7a-J15a (9) 108.10 16.75

Type II

J7b D4 2½c carmine .50 1.40
J8b D4 5c carmine .25 .50
J9b D4 10c carmine 3.50 4.50
J10b D4 15c carmine 3.75 4.00
J11b D4 20c carmine 165.00 1.00
J12b D4 30c carmine 7.00 7.50
J13b D4 40c carmine 1.50 2.50
J14b D4 50c deep salmon .85 .75
J15b D4 75c carmine .65 .85
Nos. J7b-J15b (9) 183.00 23.00

Type IV

J7c D4 2½c carmine 2.25 3.00
J8c D4 5c carmine 1.00 1.75
J9c D4 10c carmine 20.00 24.00
J10c D4 15c carmine 13.00 14.00
J11c D4 20c carmine 250.00 9.00
J13c D4 40c carmine 2.50 3.50
J14c D4 50c deep salmon 15.00 *20.00*
J15c D4 75c carmine 1.25 2.50
Nos. J7c-J15c (8) 305.00 77.75

D5

1892-95 Type I ***Perf. 12½***
J16 D5 10c carmine 2.25 .30
J17 D5 15c carmine ('95) 12.00 1.75
J18 D5 20c carmine 2.00 .25
Nos. J16-J18 (3) 16.25 2.30

Type III

J16a D5 10c dull red 2.75 2.00
J18a D5 20c dull red 3.75 1.40

Type II

J16b D5 10c dull red 13.00 13.00
J18b D5 20c dull red 18.00 6.50

1906-09 **Type I**
J19 D5 2½c carmine ('08) .50 .30
J20 D5 5c carmine ('09) 2.25 .25
J21 D5 30c carmine 17.50 5.75
J22 D5 40c carmine ('09) 12.50 1.50
J23 D5 50c carmine ('09) 8.50 .90
J24 D5 75c carmine ('09) 17.00 4.00
Nos. J19-J24 (6) 58.25 12.70

Value in Color of Stamp

1913-39 ***Perf. 12½***
J25 D5 1c salmon ('39) .25 *1.25*
J26 D5 2½c salmon .25 .25
J27 D5 3½c salmon ('39) .25 *1.25*
J28 D5 5c salmon .25 .25
J29 D5 7½c salmon ('22) .25 .25
J30 D5 10c salmon .25 .25
J31 D5 12½c salmon ('22) 2.75 .25
J32 D5 15c salmon 2.75 .25
J33 D5 20c salmon .25 .25
J34 D5 25c salmon ('22) .25 .25
J35 D5 30c salmon .25 .25
J36 D5 37½c salmon ('30) 22.50 22.50
J37 D5 40c salmon .25 .25
J38 D5 50c salmon 1.40 .25
J39 D5 75c salmon 2.50 .25
Nos. J25-J39 (15) 34.40 28.00

Thick White Paper Invisible Gum Numerals Slightly Larger

1941 **Litho.** ***Perf. 12½***
J25a D5 1c light red .60 *2.00*
J28a D5 5c light red .65 1.00
J30a D5 10c light red 10.50 10.00
J32a D5 15c light red 1.00 1.00
J33a D5 20c light red .80 .80
J35a D5 30c light red 1.25 1.00
J37a D5 40c light red 1.00 .80
Nos. J25a-J37a (7) 15.80 16.60

No. J36 Surcharged with New Value

1937, Oct. 1 **Unwmk.** ***Perf. 12½***
J40 D5 20c on 37½c salmon .25 .30

D6

1939-40
J41 D6 1g salmon 5.00 7.50
J42 D6 1g blue ('40) .30 *4.50*
a. 1g lt bl, thick paper, invisible gum .90 *1.00*

Catalogue values for unused stamps in this section, from this point to the end of the section, are for Never Hinged items.

Nos. 234, 237 and 241 Surcharged or Overprinted in Black

1946, Mar. 11 **Photo.**
J43 A28 2½c on 10c red org .60 .55
J44 A28 10c red orange 1.25 1.10
J45 A28 20c plum 6.25 3.50
J46 A28 40c yellow green 60.00 45.00
Nos. J43-J46 (4) 68.10 50.15

D7

Perf. 14½x14
1946, Aug. 14 **Wmk. 228** **Typo.**
J47 D7 1c purple 1.00 1.40
J48 D7 2½c brn org 3.50 2.00
J49 D7 3½c ultra 1.00 1.40
J50 D7 5c red orange 1.00 1.40
J51 D7 7½c Prus green 1.00 1.40
J52 D7 10c deep magenta 1.00 1.40
J53 D7 20c light ultra 1.00 1.40
J54 D7 25c olive 1.50 2.00
J55 D7 30c red brown 1.50 2.00
J56 D7 40c yellow grn 2.25 1.50
J57 D7 50c yellow 2.25 1.50
J58 D7 75c aqua 2.25 1.50
J59 D7 100c apple green 2.25 1.50
Nos. J47-J59 (13) 21.50 20.40

1948 **Litho.** **Unwmk.** ***Perf. 12½***
J59A D7 2½c brown orange .90 *2.00*

OFFICIAL STAMPS

Regular Issues of 1883-1909 Overprinted

Perf. 12½
1911, Oct. 1 **Typo.** **Unwmk.**
O1 A6 ½c violet .25 .30
O2 A6 1c olive grn .25 .25
O3 A6 2c yellow brn .25 .25
O4 A3 2½c yellow .75 .75
O5 A6 2½c blue grn 1.40 1.25
O6 A6 3c orange .40 .40
O7 A6 4c ultra .25 .25
O8 A6 5c rose red .80 .80
b. Double overprint *325.00*
O9 A6 7½c gray 2.75 2.75
O10 A9 10c slate .25 .25
O11 A9 12½c deep blue 2.00 2.25
O12 A9 15c chocolate .65 .65
a. Overprinted with two bars 32.50
b. As "a," "Dienst" inverted 52.50
O13 A9 17½c bister 2.75 2.50
O14 A9 20c olive grn .60 .50
O15 A9 22½c brn & ol grn 3.50 3.00
O16 A9 25c violet 2.00 2.00
O17 A9 30c orange brn .90 .60
O18 A9 50c red brown 12.00 7.00
O19 A10 1g dull lilac 3.00 1.25
O20 A10 2½g slate blue 27.50 30.00
Nos. O1-O20 (20) 62.25 57.00

The overprint reads diagonally downward on Nos. O1-O3 and O5-O9.

Overprint Inverted

O1a A6 ½c 45.00 *125.00*
O2a A6 1c 3.00 *19.00*
O3a A6 2c 3.00 *20.00*
O5a A6 2½c 9.00 *30.00*
O6a A6 3c 110.00 *40.00*
O8a A6 5c 3.00 *20.00*
O10a A9 10c 3.00 *7.00*
O11a A9 12½c 32.50 *55.00*
O14a A9 20c 175.00 70.00
O16a A9 25c *1,250.* *1,000.*
O17a A9 30c 225.00 140.00
O18a A9 50c 32.50 32.50
O19a A10 1g *525.00* 850.00
O20a A10 2½g 225.00 *625.00*

Regular Issue of 1892-1894 Overprinted

1911, Oct. 1
O21 A4 10c orange brn 1.25 .60
O22 A4 12½c gray 3.00 *5.50*
O23 A4 15c bister 3.00 3.00
O24 A4 20c blue 3.00 1.00
O25 A4 25c lilac 12.00 10.00
O26 A4 50c carmine 2.50 1.25
O27 A4 2.50g org brn & bl 55.00 55.00
Nos. O21-O27 (7) 79.75 76.35

Inverted Overprints

O21a A4 10c 15.00 *50.00*
O22a A4 12½c 425.00 *400.00*
O23a A4 15c 425.00 *325.00*
O24a A4 20c 165.00 *175.00*
O25a A4 25c 800.00 *900.00*
O26a A4 50c 15.00 *75.00*
O27a A4 2.50g 1,150. *1,450.*

OCCUPATION STAMPS

Issued under Japanese Occupation

During the Japanese occupation of the Netherlands Indies, 1942-45, the occupation forces applied a great variety of overprints to supplies of Netherlands Indies stamps of 1933-42. A few typical examples are shown above.

Most of these overprinted stamps were for use in limited areas, such as Java, Sumatra, Bangka and Billiton, etc. The anchor overprints were applied by the Japanese naval authorities for areas under their control.

For a time, stamps of Straits Settlements and some of the Malayan states, with Japanese overprints, were used in Sumatra and the Riouw archipelago. Stamps of Japan without overprint were also used in the Netherlands Indies during the occupation.

For Use in Java and Sumatra

100 Sen (Cents) = 1 Rupee (Gulden)

Globe Showing Japanese Empire — OS1

Farmer Plowing Rice Field — OS2

Mt. Semeru, Java's Highest Active Volcano — OS3

Bantam Bay, Northwest Java — OS4

Values in Sen

Perf. 12½
1943, Mar. 9 **Unwmk.** **Litho.**
N1 OS1 2s red brown 1.25 4.25
N2 OS2 3½s carmine 1.25 1.25
N3 OS3 5s green 1.25 1.25
N4 OS4 10s light blue 14.00 2.50
Nos. N1-N4 (4) 17.75 9.25

Issued to mark the anniversary of Japan's "Victory" in Java.

For Use in Java (also Sumatra, Borneo and Malaya)

Javanese Dancer OS5

Javanese Puppet OS6

Buddha Statue, Borobudur OS7

Map of Java OS8

Sacred Dancer of Djokja Palace, and Borobudur OS9

Bird of Vishnu, Map of Java and Mt. Semeru OS10

Plowing with Carabao OS11

Terraced Rice Fields OS12

Values in Cents, Sen or Rupees

1943-44 **Unwmk.** ***Perf. 12½***
N5 OS5 3½c rose red 1.10 .80
N6 OS6 5s yellow grn 1.10 .80
N7 OS7 10c dk blue 1.10 .60
N8 OS8 20c gray olive 1.40 1.40
N9 OS9 40c rose lilac 3.50 3.25
N10 OS10 60c red orange 5.00 1.60
N11 OS11 80s fawn ('44) 11.00 5.50
N12 OS12 1r violet ('44) 42.50 11.50
Nos. N5-N12 (8) 66.70 25.45

Indies Soldier — OS13

1943, Apr.
N13 OS13 3½c rose 11.00 15.00
N14 OS13 10c blue 55.00 9.50

Issued to commemorate reaching the postal savings goal of 5,000,000 gulden.

For Use in Sumatra

Batta Tribal House OS14

Menangkabau House OS15

Plowing with Carabao OS16

Nias Island Scene OS17

Carabao Canyon — OS18

1943 **Unwmk.** ***Perf. 12½***
N15 OS14 1c olive green .55 .30
N16 OS14 2c brt yel brn .55 .30
N17 OS14 3c bluish green .55 .30
N18 OS15 3½c rose red 2.50 .30
N19 OS15 4c ultra 2.75 .55
N20 OS15 5c red orange .80 .30

N21 OS16 10c blue gray .80 .30
N22 OS16 20c orange brn 1.10 .40
N23 OS17 30c red violet 1.10 .75
N24 OS17 40c dull brown 10.00 2.50
N25 OS18 50c bister brn 10.00 2.50
N26 OS18 1r lt blue vio 52.50 10.50
Nos. N15-N26 (12) 83.20 19.00

For Use in the Lesser Sunda Islands, Molucca Archipelago and Districts of Celebes and South Borneo Controlled by the Japanese Navy

Japanese Flag, Island Scene
OS19

Mt. Fuji, Kite, Flag, Map of East Indies
OS20

Values in Cents and Gulden

1943 Wmk. 257 Typo. ***Perf. 13***
N27 OS19 2c brown .40 *15.00*
N28 OS19 3c yellow grn .40 *15.00*
N29 OS19 3½c brown org 3.25 *15.00*
N30 OS19 5c blue .40 *15.00*
N31 OS19 10c carmine .40 *15.00*
N32 OS19 15c ultra .60 *15.00*
N33 OS19 20c dull violet .80 *15.00*

Engr.

N34 OS20 25c orange 8.25 *18.00*
N35 OS20 30c blue 9.00 *13.00*
N36 OS20 50c slate green 12.00 *30.00*
N37 OS20 1g brown lilac 65.00 *65.00*
Nos. N27-N37 (11) 100.50 *231.00*

Issued under Nationalist Occupation

Menari Dancer of Amboina — OS21

Perf. 12½
1945, Aug. Photo. Unwmk.
N38 OS21 2c carmine .25 .35

This stamp was prepared in 1941 or 1942 by Netherlands Indies authorities as an addition to the 1941 "dancers" set, but was issued in 1945 by the Nationalists (Indonesian Republic). It was not recognized by the Dutch. Exists imperforate.

NETHERLANDS NEW GUINEA

'ne-thər-lən,d,z 'nü 'gi-nē

(Dutch New Guinea)

LOCATION — Western half of New Guinea, southwest Pacific Ocean
GOVT. — Former Overseas Territory of the Netherlands
AREA — 151,789 sq. mi.
POP. — 730,000 (est. 1958)
CAPITAL — Hollandia

Netherlands New Guinea came under temporary United Nations administration Oct. 1, 1962, when stamps of this territory overprinted "UNTEA" were introduced to replace issues of Netherlands New Guinea. See West New Guinea (West Irian) in Vol. 6.

100 Cents = 1 Gulden

Catalogue values for all unused stamps in this country are for Never Hinged items.

A1

A2

Queen Juliana — A3

Perf. 12½x13½
1950-52 Unwmk. Photo.
1 A1 1c slate blue .40 .25
2 A1 2c deep org .40 .25
3 A1 2½c olive brn .55 .25
4 A1 3c deep plum 1.75 1.50
5 A1 4c blue grn 1.75 1.25
6 A1 5c ultra 3.50 .25
7 A1 7½c org brown .55 .25
8 A1 10c purple 1.75 .25
9 A1 12½c crimson 1.75 1.40

Perf. 13½x12½
10 A2 15c brown org 2.00 .75
11 A2 20c blue 1.00 .25
12 A2 25c orange red 1.00 .25
13 A2 30c dp blue ('52) 11.00 .30
14 A2 40c blue grn 1.75 .25
15 A2 45c brown ('52) 5.50 .50
16 A2 50c deep orange 1.50 .25
17 A2 55c brown blk ('52) 10.00 .40
18 A2 80c purple 12.00 3.25

Engr. ***Perf. 12½x12***
19 A3 1g red 17.50 .50
20 A3 2g yellow brn ('52) 12.00 1.10
21 A3 5g dk olive grn 20.00 2.00
Nos. 1-21 (21) 107.65 15.45

For surcharges see Nos. B1-B3.

Bird of Paradise — A4

Queen Victoria Crowned Pigeon — A5

Queen Juliana — A6

10c, 15c, 20c, Bird of Paradise with raised wings.

Photo.; Litho. (Nos. 24, 26, 28)
1954-60 ***Perf. 12½x12***
22 A4 1c ver & yel ('58) .25 .25
23 A4 5c choc & yel .25 .25
24 A5 7c org red, bl & brn vio ('59) .40 .25
25 A4 10c aqua & red brn .25 .25
26 A5 12c grn, bl & brn vio ('59) .40 .25
27 A4 15c dp yel & red brn .25 .25
28 A5 17c brn vio & bl ('59) .40 .25
29 A4 20c lt bl grn & red brn ('56) 1.00 .60
30 A6 25c red .25 .25
31 A6 30c deep blue .55 .25
32 A6 40c dp orange ('60) 2.50 2.25
33 A6 45c dk olive ('58) 1.00 1.25
34 A6 55c dk blue grn .75 .25
35 A6 80c dl gray vio 1.75 .30
36 A6 85c dk vio brn ('56) 1.75 .55
37 A6 1g plum ('59) 5.75 2.50
Nos. 22-37 (16) 17.50 9.95

Stamps overprinted "UNTEA" are listed under West Irian in Vol. 6.
For surcharges see Nos. B4-B6.

Papuan Watching Helicopter — A7

1959, Apr. 10 Photo. ***Perf. 11½x11***
38 A7 55c red brown & blue 1.75 1.25

1959 expedition to the Star Mountains of New Guinea.

Mourning Woman — A8

1960, Apr. 7 Unwmk. ***Perf. 13x14***
39 A8 25c blue .70 .60
40 A8 30c yellow bister .70 .60

World Refugee Year, 7/1/59-6/30/60.

Council Building
A9

1961, Apr. 5 Litho. ***Perf. 11x11½***
41 A9 25c bluish green .30 *.40*
42 A9 30c rose .30 *.40*

Inauguration of the New Council.

School Children Crossing Street — A10

Design: 30c, Men looking at traffic sign.

1962, Mar. 16 Photo. ***Perf. 14x13***
43 A10 25c dp blue & red .40 .40
44 A10 30c brt green & red .40 .40

Need for road safety.

Queen Juliana and Prince Bernhard
A11

1962, Apr. 28 Unwmk. ***Perf. 14x13***
45 A11 55c olive brown .45 *.50*

Silver wedding anniv.

Tropical Beach
A12

Design: 30c, Palm trees on beach.

1962, July 18 ***Perf. 14x13***
46 A12 25c multicolored .30 *.40*
47 A12 30c multicolored .30 *.40*

5th So. Pacific Conf., Pago Pago, July 1962.

SEMI-POSTAL STAMPS

Regular Issue of 1950-52 Surcharged in Black

Perf. 12½x13½
1953, Feb. 9 Unwmk. Photo.
B1 A1 5c + 5c ultra 10.00 8.00

Perf. 13½x12½
B2 A2 15c + 10c brn org 12.00 10.00
B3 A2 25c + 10c org red 12.00 10.00
Nos. B1-B3 (3) 34.00 28.00

The tax was for flood relief work in the Netherlands.

Nos. 23, 25, 27 Surcharged in Red

1955, Nov. 1 ***Perf. 12½x12***
B4 A4 5c + 5c 2.00 2.00
B5 A4 10c + 10c 2.00 2.00
B6 A4 15c + 10c 2.00 2.00
Nos. B4-B6 (3) 6.00 6.00

The surtax was for the Red Cross.

Leprosarium
SP1

10c+5c, 30c+10c, Young Papuan and huts.

Perf. 12x12½
1956, Dec. 15 Unwmk. Photo.
B7 SP1 5c + 5c dk slate grn 1.25 .80
B8 SP1 10c + 5c brn violet 1.25 .80
B9 SP1 25c + 10c brt blue 1.25 .80
B10 SP1 30c + 10c ocher 1.25 .80
Nos. B7-B10 (4) 5.00 3.20

The surtax was for the fight against leprosy.

Papuan Girl and Beach Scene — SP2

10c+5c, 30c+10c, Papuan boy and pile dwelling.

1957, Oct. 1 ***Perf. 12½x12***
B11 SP2 5c + 5c maroon 1.10 .90
B12 SP2 10c + 5c slate grn 1.10 .90
B13 SP2 25c + 10c brown 1.10 .90
B14 SP2 30c + 10c dark blue 1.10 .90
Nos. B11-B14 (4) 4.40 3.60

The surtax was to fight infant mortality.

Ancestral Image, North Coast New Guinea — SP3

Design: 10c+5c, 30c+10c, Bowl in form of human figure, Asmat-Papua.

1958, Oct. 1 Litho. ***Perf. 12½x12***
B15 SP3 5c + 5c bl, blk & red 1.00 1.00
B16 SP3 10c + 5c rose lake, blk, red & yel 1.00 1.00
B17 SP3 25c + 10c bl grn, blk & red 1.00 1.00

B18 SP3 30c + 10c ol gray, blk, red & yel 1.00 1.00
Nos. B15-B18 (4) 4.00 4.00

The surtax was for the Red Cross.

Bignonia — SP4

Flowers: 10c+5c, Orchid. 25c+10c, Rhododendron. 30c+10c, Gesneriacea.

1959, Nov. 16 Photo. *Perf. 12½x13*

B19 SP4 5c + 5c car rose & grn .75 .75
B20 SP4 10c + 5c ol, yel & lil .75 .75
B21 SP4 25c + 10c red, org & grn .75 .75
B22 SP4 30c + 10c vio & grn .75 .75
Nos. B19-B22 (4) 3.00 3.00

Birdwing SP5

Various Butterflies.

Perf. 13x12½

1960, Sept. 1 Unwmk. Litho.

B23 SP5 5c + 5c lt bl, blk, emer & yel 1.75 1.00
B24 SP5 10c + 5c sal, blk & bl 1.75 1.00
B25 SP5 25c + 10c yel, blk & org red 2.25 2.00
B26 SP5 30c + 10c lt grn, brn & yel 2.25 2.00
Nos. B23-B26 (4) 8.00 6.00

Surtax for social care.

Rhinoceros Beetle and Coconut Palm Leaf — SP6

Beetles & leaves of host plants: 10c+5c, Ectocemus 10-maculatus Montri, a primitive weevil. 25c+10c, Stag beetle. 30c+10c, Tortoise beetle.

1961, Sept. 15 *Perf. 13x12½*

Beetles in Natural Colors

B27 SP6 5c + 5c deep org .60 .60
B28 SP6 10c + 5c lt ultra .60 .60
B29 SP6 25c + 10c citron .60 .60
B30 SP6 30c + 10c green .60 .60
Nos. B27-B30 (4) 2.40 2.40

Surtax for social care.

Crab — SP7

Designs: 10c+5c, Lobster, vert. 25c+10c, Spiny lobster, vert. 30c+10c, Shrimp.

Perf. 14x13, 13x14

1962, Sept. 17 Unwmk.

B31 SP7 5c + 5c red, grn, brn & yel .25 .25
B32 SP7 10c + 5c Prus bl & yel .25 .25
B33 SP7 25c + 10c multicolored .25 .25
B34 SP7 30c + 10c bl, org red & yel .25 .25
Nos. B31-B34 (4) 1.00 1.00

The surtax on Nos. B19-B34 went to various social works organizations.

POSTAGE DUE STAMPS

D1

Perf. 13½x12½

1957 Photo. Unwmk.

J1 D1 1c vermilion .50 .30
J2 D1 5c vermilion 1.25 *1.50*
J3 D1 10c vermilion 3.00 *3.50*
J4 D1 25c vermilion 4.25 2.50
J5 D1 40c vermilion 4.25 2.50
J6 D1 1g blue 7.50 *15.00*
Nos. J1-J6 (6) 20.75 25.30

NEVIS

ˈnē-vəs

LOCATION — West Indies, southeast of Puerto Rico
GOVT. — A former presidency of the Leeward Islands Colony (British)
AREA — 36 sq. mi.
POP. — 8,794 (1991)

Nevis stamps were discontinued in 1890 and replaced by those of the Leeward Islands. From 1903 to 1956 stamps of St. Kitts-Nevis and Leeward Islands were used concurrently. From 1956 to 1980 stamps of St. Kitts-Nevis were used. While still a part of St. Kitts-Nevis, Nevis started issuing stamps in 1980.

See Leeward Islands and St. Kitts-Nevis.

12 Pence = 1 Shilling
100 Cents = 1 Dollar

Catalogue values for unused stamps in this country are for Never Hinged items, beginning with Scott 100 in the regular postage section and Scott O1 in the officials section.

Unused examples of Nos. 1-8 almost always have no original gum, and they are valued without gum. These stamps with original gum are worth more. Other issues are valued with original gum as defined in the catalogue introduction. Very fine examples of Nos. 1-8, will have perforations touching the design on at least one side due to the narrow spacing of the stamps on the plates. Stamps with perfs clear of the design on all four sides are scarce and will command higher prices.

Medicinal Spring
A1 A2

A3 A4

1861 Unwmk. Engr. *Perf. 13*

Bluish Wove Paper

1 A1 1p lake rose 325.00 140.00
2 A2 4p dull rose 950.00 200.00
3 A3 6p gray 775.00 260.00
4 A4 1sh green 1,100. 250.00

Grayish Wove Paper

5 A1 1p lake rose 110.00 60.00
6 A2 4p dull rose 175.00 80.00
7 A3 6p lilac gray 175.00 65.00
8 A4 1sh green 400.00 95.00

1867 White Wove Paper *Perf. 15*

9 A1 1p red 65.00 55.00
10 A2 4p orange 155.00 25.00
11 A4 1sh yellow green 925.00 125.00
12 A4 1sh blue green 325.00 45.00

Laid Paper

13 A4 1sh yel green *25,000.* 6,750.
Manuscript cancel 3,000.

No. 13 values are for stamps with design cut into on one or two sides.

1876 Wove Paper Litho.

14 A1 1p rose 32.50 25.00
14A A1 1p red 45.00 30.00
b. 1p vermilion 45.00 45.00
c. Imperf., pair *1,900.*
d. Half used as ½p on cover *4,500.*
15 A2 4p orange 190.00 45.00
a. Imperf.
b. Vert. pair, imperf. between *12,750.*
16 A3 6p olive gray 250.00 250.00
17 A4 1sh gray green 100.00 *125.00*
a. 1sh dark green 135.00 *175.00*
b. Horiz. strip of 3, perf. all around & imperf. btwn. *20,000.*

Perf. 11½

18 A1 1p vermilion 65.00 60.00
a. Horiz. pair, imperf. btwn.
b. Half used as ½p on cover *4,500.*
c. Imperf., pair 1,000.
Nos. 14-18 (6) 682.50 535.00

Queen Victoria — A5

1879-80 Typo. Wmk. 1 *Perf. 14*

19 A5 1p violet ('80) 90.00 55.00
a. Diagonal half used as ½p on cover *1,500.*
20 A5 2½p red brown 175.00 100.00

1882-90 Wmk. Crown and CA (2)

21 A5 ½p green ('83) 14.00 *27.50*
22 A5 1p violet 125.00 47.50
a. Half used as ½p on cover 900.00
23a A5 1p carmine ('84) 20.00 20.00
24 A5 2½p red brown 140.00 55.00
25 A5 2½p ultra ('84) 24.00 27.50
26 A5 4p blue 400.00 55.00
27 A5 4p gray ('84) 25.00 10.00
28 A5 6p green ('83) 500.00 400.00
29 A5 6p brown org ('86) 27.50 *77.50*
30 A5 1sh violet ('90) 125.00 *225.00*
Nos. 21-30 (10) 1,400. *945.00*

Half of No. 22 Surcharged in Black or Violet

1883

31 A5 ½p on half of 1p 1,100. 60.00
a. Double surcharge 450.00
b. Unsevered pair *7,500.*
c. Surcharged on half of 1p revenue stamp 600.00
32 A5 ½p on half of 1p (V) 1,250. 55.00
a. Double surcharge 450.00
b. Unsevered pair *7,500.* 850.00
c. Surcharged on half of 1p revenue stamp 600.00

Surcharge reads up or down.

Catalogue values for unused stamps in this section, from this point to the end of the section, are for Never Hinged items.

St. Kitts-Nevis Nos. 357-369 Ovptd.

Perf. 14½x14

1980, June 23 Litho. Wmk. 373

100 A61 5c multicolored .25 .25
101 A61 10c multicolored .25 .25
102 A61 12c multicolored .25 .30
103 A61 15c multicolored .25 .25
104 A61 25c multicolored .25 .25
a. Unwatermarked .80 *1.50*
105 A61 30c multicolored .25 .25
106 A61 40c multicolored .30 .30
107 A61 45c multicolored .75 .50
108 A61 50c multicolored .30 .30
109 A61 55c multicolored .40 .25
110 A61 $1 multicolored .30 .30
a. Unwatermarked 2.50 *5.00*
111 A61 $5 multicolored 1.50 1.00
112 A61 $10 multicolored 2.50 1.50
Nos. 100-112 (13) 7.55 5.70

The bars cover "St. Christopher" and "Anguilla."

80th Birthday of Queen Mother Elizabeth — A6

1980, Sept. 4 *Perf. 14*

113 A6 $2 multicolored .40 .50

Ships and Boats — A6a

5c, Nevis lighter. 30c, Local fishing boat. 55c, *Caona.* $3, Windjammer's S.V. *Polynesia.*

1980, Oct. 8

114 A6a 5c multicolored .25 .25
115 A6a 30c multicolored .25 .25
116 A6a 55c multicolored .25 .25

Size: 38x52mm

117 A6a $3 multicolored .65 .65
a. Perf. 12½x12 .65 .65
b. Booklet pane of 3 #117a 2.00
Nos. 114-117 (4) 1.40 1.40

No. 117b separated into three parts by roulettes running vert. through the margin surrounding the stamps. For overprint see No. 538.

Christmas — A7

1980, Nov. 20 *Perf. 14*

118 A7 5c Mother and child .30 .30
119 A7 30c Heralding angel .30 .30
120 A7 $2.50 Three kings .60 .60
Nos. 118-120 (3) 1.20 1.20

Landmarks — A8

A9

5c, Charlestown Pier. 10c, Court House & Library. 15c, New River Mill. 20c, Nelson Museum. 25c, St. James' Parish Church. 30c, Nevis Lane. 40c, Zetland Plantation. 45c, Nisbet Plantation. 50c, Pinney's Beach. 55c, Eva Wilkin's Studio. $1, Nevis at dawn. $2.50, Ft. Charles ruins. $5, Old Bath House. $10, Nisbet's Beach.

1981, Feb. 5

No Date Imprint Below Design

121 A8 5c multicolored .25 .25
122 A8 10c multicolored .25 .25
123 A9 15c multicolored .25 .25
124 A9 20c multicolored .25 .25
125 A9 25c multicolored .25 .25
126 A9 30c multicolored .25 .25
127 A9 40c multicolored .25 .25
128 A9 45c multicolored .25 .25
129 A9 50c multicolored .25 .25
130 A9 55c multicolored .30 .30
131 A9 $1 multicolored .55 .55
132 A9 $2.50 multicolored .75 .75
133 A9 $5 multicolored 1.50 1.50
134 A9 $10 multicolored 3.00 3.00
Nos. 121-134 (14) 8.35 8.35

For surcharges see Nos. 169-181.

1982, June 9

Inscribed "1982" Below Design

121a A8 5c multicolored .30 .30
122a A8 10c multicolored .30 .30
123a A9 15c multicolored .25 .25
124a A9 20c multicolored .25 .25
125a A9 25c multicolored .25 .25
126a A9 30c multicolored .25 .25
127a A9 40c multicolored .25 .25
128a A9 45c multicolored .25 .25
129a A9 50c multicolored .25 .25
130a A9 55c multicolored .30 .30
131a A9 $1 multicolored .55 .55
132a A9 $2.50 multicolored .75 .75
133a A9 $5 multicolored 1.50 1.50
134a A9 $10 multicolored 3.00 3.00
Nos. 121a-134a (14) 8.45 8.45

1983

Inscribed "1983" Below Design

124b A9 20c multicolored .50 .25
125b A9 25c multicolored .50 .25
126b A9 30c multicolored .50 .25
127b A9 40c multicolored .50 .25
128b A9 45c multicolored .50 .25
129b A9 50c multicolored .50 .25
130b A9 55c multicolored .50 .25
132b A9 $2.50 multicolored 1.50 1.25
Nos. 124b-132b (8) 5.00 3.00

Prince Charles, Lady Diana, Royal Yacht Charlotte A9a

Prince Charles and Lady Diana — A9b

No. 135, Couple, *Royal Caroline*. No. 136, Couple. No. 137, Couple, *Royal Sovereign*. No. 139, Couple, HMY *Britannia*.

1981, June 23 Wmk. 373 ***Perf. 14***

135 A9a 55c multicolored .25 .25
a. Bklt. pane of 4, perf. 12, unwmkd. 1.10 1.10
136 A9b 55c multicolored .25 .25
137 A9a $2 multicolored .65 .65
138 A9b $2 like No. 136 .65 .65
a. Bklt. pane of 2, perf. 12, unwmkd. 1.75 1.75
139 A9a $5 multicolored 1.25 1.25
140 A9b $5 like No. 136 1.25 1.25
Nos. 135-140 (6) 4.30 4.30

Souvenir Sheet

1981, Dec. 14 ***Perf. 12***

141 A9b $4.50 like No. 136 2.00 2.00

Stamps of the same denomination issued in sheets of 7 (6 type A9a and 1 type A9b).

For surcharges see Nos. 453-454.

Butterflies A10

5c, Zebra. 30c, Malachite. 55c, Southern dagger tail. $2, Large orange sulphur.

1982, Feb. 16 ***Perf. 14***

142 A10 5c multicolored .25 .25
143 A10 30c multicolored .25 .25
144 A10 55c multicolored .25 .25
145 A10 $2 multicolored 1.25 1.25
Nos. 142-145 (4) 2.00 2.00

For overprint see No. 452.

1983, June 8

30c, Tropical chequered skipper. 55c, Caribbean buckeye, vert. $1.10, Common long-tailed skipper, vert. $2, Mimic.

146 A10 30c multicolored .45 .45
147 A10 55c multicolored .45 .45
148 A10 $1.10 multicolored .65 .65
149 A10 $2 multicolored .90 .90
Nos. 146-149 (4) 2.45 2.45

21st Birthday of Princess Diana, July 1 — A11

1982, June 22 ***Perf. 13½x14***

150 A11 30c Caroline of Brunswick .25 .25
151 A11 55c Brunswick arms .30 .30
152 A11 $5 Diana 1.20 1.20
Nos. 150-152 (3) 1.75 1.75

For surcharge see No. 449.

Nos. 150-152 Overprinted "ROYAL BABY"

1982, July 12

153 A11 30c multicolored .25 .25
154 A11 55c multicolored .35 .35
155 A11 $5 multicolored 1.40 1.40
Nos. 153-155 (3) 2.00 2.00

Birth of Prince William of Wales, June 21.

Scouting, 75th Anniv. — A12

1982, Aug. 18

156 A12 5c Cycling .35 .35
157 A12 30c Running .45 .45
158 A12 $2.50 Building campfire .90 .90
Nos. 156-158 (3) 1.70 1.70

For overprints see Nos. 447, 455.

Christmas — A13

Illustrations by youths — 15c, Eugene Seabrookes. 30c, Kharenzabeth Glasgow. $1.50, David Grant. $2.50, Leonard Huggins. Nos. 159-160 vert.

1982, Oct. 20 ***Perf. 13½x14, 14x13½***

159 A13 15c multicolored .30 .30
160 A13 30c multicolored .30 .30
161 A13 $1.50 multicolored .40 .40
162 A13 $2.50 multicolored .75 .75
Nos. 159-162 (4) 1.75 1.75

Coral — A14

15c, Tube sponge. 30c, Stinging coral. 55c, Flower coral. $3, Sea rod, red fire sponge.

1983, Jan. 12 ***Perf. 14***

163 A14 15c multicolored .25 .25
164 A14 30c multicolored .40 .40
165 A14 55c multicolored .40 .40
166 A14 $3 multicolored 1.20 1.20
a. Souvenir sheet of 4, #163-166 2.40 2.40
Nos. 163-166 (4) 2.25 2.25

For overprints see Nos. 446, 448.

Commonwealth Day — A15

55c, HMS *Boreas* off Nevis. $2, Lord Nelson, *Boreas*.

1983, Mar. 14

167 A15 55c multicolored .25 .25
168 A15 $2 multicolored .65 .65

Nos. 121a and 123a-134a Ovptd.

No. 169

No. 170-181

1983, Sept. 19

169 A8 5c multicolored .25 .25
c. Overprint larger with serifed letters 1.25 *2.25*
170 A9 15c multicolored .25 .25
171 A9 20c multicolored .25 .25
172 A9 25c multicolored .25 .25
173 A9 30c multicolored .25 .25
174 A9 40c multicolored .25 .30
175 A9 45c multicolored .30 .40
176 A9 50c multicolored .30 .40
177 A9 55c multicolored .35 .45
178 A9 $1 multicolored .45 .45
179 A9 $2.50 multicolored .45 .70
180 A9 $5 multicolored .55 .85
181 A9 $10 multicolored .75 1.10
Nos. 169-181 (13) 4.65 5.90

The overprints on Nos. 169a and 169c were applied locally.

Nos. 121, 123-127, 130-134 Ovptd.

1983

169a A8 5c multicolored, larger ovpt. 15.00 12.00
170a A9 15c multicolored 42.50 42.50
171a A9 20c multicolored 6.00 6.00
172a A9 25c multicolored 6.00 6.00
173a A9 30c multicolored 1.10 1.10
174a A9 40c multicolored 1.00 1.00
177a A9 55c multicolored 1.00 1.00
178a A9 $1 multicolored 1.00 1.00
179a A9 $2.50 multicolored 1.40 1.40
180a A9 $5 multicolored 2.50 2.50
181a A9 $10 multicolored 4.50 4.50
Nos. 169a-181a (11) 82.00 79.00

Nos. 124b-132b and Additional values inscribed "1983" Ovptd.

1983

170b A9 15c multicolored 1.75 1.00
171b A9 20c multicolored 1.75 1.00
172b A9 25c multicolored 1.75 1.00
173b A9 30c multicolored 1.75 1.00
174b A9 40c multicolored 1.75 1.00
175b A9 45c multicolored 1.75 1.00
176b A9 50c multicolored 1.75 1.00
177b A9 55c multicolored 1.75 1.00
178b A9 $1 multicolored 2.25 1.25
179b A9 $2.50 multicolored 1.75 1.00
180b A9 $5 multicolored 3.00 3.00
181b A9 $10 multicolored 6.00 6.00
Nos. 170b-181b (12) 27.00 19.25

1st Manned Flight, Bicent. A16

10c, Montgolfier Balloon, 1783, vert. 45c, Lindbergh's Sikorsky S-38 carrying mail, 1929. 50c, Beechcraft Twin Bonanza. $2.50, Sea Harrier, 1st operational V/STOL fighter.

1983, Sept. 28 **Wmk. 380**

182 A16 10c multicolored .25 .25
183 A16 45c multicolored .25 .25
184 A16 50c multicolored .25 .25
185 A16 $2.50 multicolored .50 .50
a. Souvenir sheet of 4, #182-185 1.75 1.75
Nos. 182-185 (4) 1.25 1.25

Christmas A17

1983, Nov. 7

186 A17 5c Nativity .25 .25
187 A17 30c Shepherds, flock .25 .25
188 A17 55c Angels .25 .25
189 A17 $3 Youths .90 .90
a. Souvenir sheet of 4, #186-189 1.50 1.50
Nos. 186-189 (4) 1.65 1.65

Leaders of the World

Large quantities of some Leaders of the World issues were sold at a fraction of face value when the printer was liquidated.

A18

Leaders of the World: Locomotives — No. 190, 1882 Class Wee Bogie, UK. No. 191, 1968 JNR Class EF81, Japan. No. 192, 1878 Snowdon Ranger, UK. No. 193, 1927 P.O. Class 5500, France. No. 194, 1859 Connor Single Class. No. 195, 1904 Large Belpaire Passenger, UK. No. 196, 1829 Stourbridge Lion, US. No. 197, 1934 Cock O' The North. No. 198, 1945 County of Oxford, GB. No. 199, 1940 SNCF Class 240P, France. No. 200, 1851 Comet, UK. No. 201, 1904 County Class, UK. No. 202, 1926 JNR Class 7000, Japan. No. 203, 1877 Nord L'Outrance, France. No. 204, 1919 CM St.P&P Bipolar, US. No. 205, 1897 Palatinate Railway Class P3, Germany. No. 206, 1908 Class 8H, UK. No. 207, 1927 King George V. No. 208, 1951 Britannia. No. 209, 1924 Pendennis Castle. No. 210, 1960 Evening Star. No. 211, 1934 Stanier Class 5, GB. No. 212, 1946 Winston Churchill Battle of Britain. No. 213, 1935 Mallard A4. No. 214, 1899 Q.R. Class PB-15, Australia. No. 215, 1836 C&St.L Dorchester, Canada. No. 216, 1953 U.P. Gas Turbine, US. No. 217, 1969 U.P. Centennial Class, US. No. 218, 1866 No. 23 Class A, UK. No. 219, 1955 NY, NH & HR FL9, US. No. 220, 1837 B&O

Lafayette, US. No. 221, 1964 JNR Shin-Kansen, Japan. No. 222, 1928 DRG Class 64, Germany. No. 223, 1882 D&RGR Class C-16, US.

1983-86 Litho. Unwmk. *Perf. 12½*

Se-tenant Pairs, #a.-b.

a. — Side and front views.

b. — Action scene.

No.	Type	Denom.	Description	Unused	Used
190	A18	1c	multicolored	.25	.25
191	A18	5c	multicolored	.25	.25
192	A18	5c	multicolored	.25	.25
193	A18	10c	multicolored	.25	.25
194	A18	15c	multicolored	.25	.25
195	A18	30c	multicolored	.25	.25
196	A18	30c	multicolored	.25	.25
197	A18	45c	multicolored	.25	.25
198	A18	55c	multicolored	.25	.25
199	A18	60c	multicolored	.25	.25
200	A18	60c	multicolored	.25	.25
201	A18	60c	multicolored	.25	.25
202	A18	60c	multicolored	.25	.25
203	A18	75c	multicolored	.30	.30
204	A18	75c	multicolored	.30	.30
205	A18	75c	multicolored	.30	.30
206	A18	90c	multicolored	.30	.30
207	A18	$1	multicolored	.35	.35
208	A18	$1	multicolored	.35	.35
209	A18	$1	multicolored	.35	.35
210	A18	$1	multicolored	.35	.35
211	A18	$1	multicolored	.35	.35
212	A18	$1	multicolored	.35	.35
213	A18	$1	multicolored	.35	.35
214	A18	$1	multicolored	.35	.35
215	A18	$1	multicolored	.35	.35
216	A18	$1.50	multicolored	.50	.50
217	A18	$1.50	multicolored	.50	.50
218	A18	$2	multicolored	.70	.70
219	A18	$2	multicolored	.70	.70
220	A18	$2	multicolored	.70	.70
221	A18	$2.50	multicolored	1.00	1.00
222	A18	$2.50	multicolored	1.00	1.00
223	A18	$3	multicolored	1.00	1.00
			Nos. 190-223 (34)	13.70	13.70

Issued: #190, 200, 218, 4/26/85; #191, 193, 199, 221, 10/29/84; #192, 195, 201, 203, 214, 222, 7/26/85; #194, 197, 202, 204, 215, 217, 220, 223, 10/1/86; #196, 205, 216, 219, 1/30/86; #198, 206-213, 11/10/83.

British Monarchs, Scenes from History — A20

#258a, Boer War. #258b, Queen Victoria. #259a, Signing of the Magna Carta. #259b, King John. #260a, Victoria, diff. #260b, Osborne House. #261a, John, diff. #261b, Newark Castle, Nottinghamshire. #262a, Battle of Dettingen. #262b, King George II. #263a, George II, diff. #263b, Bank of England, 1732. #264a, George II's coat of arms. #264b, George II, diff. #265a, John's coat of arms. #265b, John, diff. #266a, Victoria's coat of arms. #266b, Victoria, diff.

1984

No.	Type	Denom.	Description	Unused	Used
258	A20	5c	Pair, #a.-b.	.25	.25
259	A20	5c	Pair, #a.-b.	.25	.25
260	A20	50c	Pair, #a.-b.	.25	.25
261	A20	55c	Pair, #a.-b.	.25	.25
262	A20	60c	Pair, #a.-b.	.25	.25
263	A20	75c	Pair, #a.-b.	.25	.25
264	A20	$1	Pair, #a.-b.	.25	.25
265	A20	$2	Pair, #a.-b.	.60	.60
266	A20	$3	Pair, #a.-b.	.50	.50
			Nos. 258-266 (9)	2.85	2.85

Issued: #258, 260, 262-264, 266, 4/11; others, 11/20.

Tourism A22

No. 276, Golden Rock Inn. No. 277, Rest Haven Inn. No. 278, Cliffdwellers Hotel. No. 279, Pinney's Beach Hotel.

1984, May 16 Wmk. 380 *Perf. 14*

No.	Type	Denom.	Description	Unused	Used
276	A22	55c	multicolored	.40	.40
277	A22	55c	multicolored	.40	.40
278	A22	55c	multicolored	.40	.40
279	A22	55c	multicolored	.40	.40
			Nos. 276-279 (4)	1.60	1.60

Seal of the Colony — A22a 279A

1984, June 8 Wmk. 380 *Perf. 14*

No.	Type	Denom.	Description	Unused	Used
279A	A22a	$15	dull red	1.60	5.25

Tourism Type of 1984

No. 280, Croney's Old Manor Hotel. No. 281, Montpelier Plantation Inn. No. 282, Nisbet's Plantation Inn. No. 283, Zetland Plantation Inn.

1985, Feb. 12

No.	Type	Denom.	Description	Unused	Used
280	A22	$1.20	multicolored	.60	.60
281	A22	$1.20	multicolored	.60	.60
282	A22	$1.20	multicolored	.60	.60
283	A22	$1.20	multicolored	.60	.60
			Nos. 280-283 (4)	2.40	2.40

A23

Leaders of the World: Classic cars — No. 285, 1932 Cadillac V16 Fleetwood Convertible, US. No. 286, 1935 Delahaye Type 35 Cabriolet, France. No. 287, 1916 Packard Twin Six Touring Car, US. No. 288, 1929 Lagonda Speed Model Touring Car, GB. No. 289, 1958 Ferrari Testarossa, Italy. No. 290, 1934 Voisin Aerodyne, France. No. 291, 1912 Sunbeam Coupe De L'Auto, GB. No. 292, 1936 Adler Trumpf, Germany. No. 293, 1886 Daimler 2-Cylinder, Germany. No. 294, 1930 Riley Brooklands Nine, UK. No. 295, 1967 Jaguar E-Type 4.2 Liter, GB. No. 296, 1970 Porsche 911 S Targa, Germany. No. 297, 1948 Cisitalia Pinnifarina Coupe, Italy. No. 298, 1885 Benz Three-wheeler, Germany. No. 299, 1966 Alfa Romeo GTA, Italy. No. 300, 1947 Volkswagen Beetle, Germany. No. 301, 1963 Buick Riviera. No. 302, 1947 MG TC, GB. No. 303, 1960 Cooper Climax, UK. No. 304, 1957 Maserati Tipo 250F, Italy. No. 305, 1913 Pierce Arrow Type 66, US. No. 306, 1904 Ford 999, US. No. 307, 1980 Porsche 928S, Germany. No. 308, 1910 Oldsmobile Limited, US. No. 309, 1951 Jaguar C-Type, UK. No. 310, 1928 Willys-Knight 66A, US. No. 311, 1933 MG K3 Magnette, GB. No. 312, 1937 Lincoln Zephyr, US. No. 313, 1937 ERA 1.5 I B Type, UK. No. 314, 1953 Studebaker Starliner, US. No. 315, 1926 Pontiac 2-door, US. No. 316, 1966 Cobra Roadster 289, US. No. 317, 1930 MG M-Type Midget, UK. No. 318, 1966 Aston Martin DB6 Hardtop, GB. No. 319, 1932 Pierce Arrow V12, US. No. 320, 1971 Rolls Royce Corniche, UK. No. 321, 1953 Chevrolet Corvette, US. No. 322, 1919 Cunningham V-8, US.

1984-86 Unwmk. *Perf. 12½*

Se-tenant Pairs, #a.-b.

a. — Side and front views.

b. — Action scene.

No.	Type	Denom.	Description	Unused	Used
285	A23	1c	multicolored	.25	.25
286	A23	1c	multicolored	.25	.25
287	A23	5c	multicolored	.25	.25
288	A23	5c	multicolored	.25	.25
289	A23	5c	multicolored	.25	.25
290	A23	10c	multicolored	.25	.25
291	A23	10c	multicolored	.25	.25
292	A23	10c	multicolored	.25	.25
293	A23	15c	multicolored	.25	.25
294	A23	15c	multicolored	.25	.25
295	A23	30c	multicolored	.25	.25
296	A23	35c	multicolored	.25	.25
297	A23	35c	multicolored	.25	.25
298	A23	45c	multicolored	.25	.25
299	A23	45c	multicolored	.25	.25
300	A23	50c	multicolored	.25	.25
301	A23	50c	multicolored	.25	.25
302	A23	55c	multicolored	.25	.25
303	A23	60c	multicolored	.25	.25
304	A23	60c	multicolored	.25	.25
305	A23	60c	multicolored	.25	.25
306	A23	75c	multicolored	.25	.25
307	A23	75c	multicolored	.25	.25
308	A23	75c	multicolored	.25	.25
309	A23	$1	multicolored	.30	.30
310	A23	$1	multicolored	.30	.30
311	A23	$1.15	multicolored	.35	.35
312	A23	$1.50	multicolored	.40	.40
313	A23	$1.50	multicolored	.40	.40
314	A23	$1.75	multicolored	.45	.45
315	A23	$2	multicolored	.55	.55
316	A23	$2.50	multicolored	.70	.70
317	A23	$2.50	multicolored	.70	.70
318	A23	$3	multicolored	.75	.75
319	A23	$3	multicolored	.75	.75
320	A23	$3	multicolored	.75	.75
321	A23	$3	multicolored	.75	.75
322	A23	$3	multicolored	.75	.75
			Nos. 285-322 (38)	13.90	13.90

Issued: #285, 287, 293, 296, 298, 302, 316, 318, 7/25/84; #286, 289-290, 301, 303, 306, 317, 320, 2/20/85; #288, 295, 300, 319, 10/23/84; #291, 297, 307, 311-312, 315, 10/4/85; #292, 303, 308-309, 313, 321, 1/30/86; #294, 299, 305, 310, 314, 322, 8/15/86.

Culturama Carnival, 10th Anniv. A24a

30c, Carpentry. 55c, Weaving mats and baskets. $1, Ceramics. $3, Carnival queen, folk dancers.

Wmk. 380

1984, Aug. 1 Litho. *Perf. 14*

No.	Type	Denom.	Description	Unused	Used
361	A24a	30c	multicolored	.25	.25
362	A24a	55c	multicolored	.25	.25
363	A24a	$1	multicolored	.25	.25
364	A24a	$3	multicolored	.65	.65
			Nos. 361-364 (4)	1.40	1.40

Flowers — A24b

1984, Aug. 8

No Date Imprint Below Design

No.	Type	Denom.	Description	Unused	Used
365	A24b	5c	Yellow bell	.25	.25
366	A24b	10c	Plumbago	.25	.25
367	A24b	15c	Flamboyant	.25	.25
368	A24b	20c	Eyelash orchid	.25	.25
a.			Inscribed "1986"	.55	.35
369	A24b	30c	Bougainvillea	.25	.25
370	A24b	40c	Hibiscus	.25	.25
a.			Inscribed "1986"	.40	.35
371	A24b	50c	Night-blooming cereus	.25	.25
372	A24b	55c	Yellow mahoe	.25	.25
373	A24b	60c	Spider lily	.30	.30
374	A24b	75c	Scarlet cordia	.35	.35
375	A24b	$1	Shell ginger	.30	.40
376	A24b	$3	Blue petrea	.60	1.10
377	A24b	$5	Coral hibiscus	1.10	2.00
378	A24b	$10	Passion flower	2.25	3.50
			Nos. 365-378 (14)	6.90	9.65

Nos. 368a and 370a issued 7/23/86.

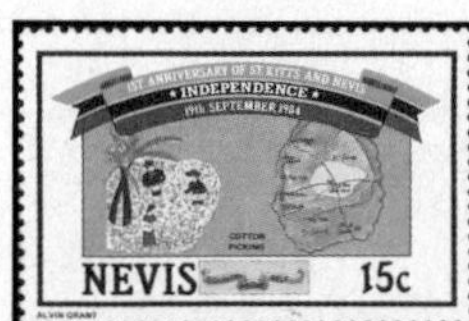

Independence of St. Kitts and Nevis, 1st Anniv. — A26

1984, Sept. 18

No.	Type	Denom.	Description	Unused	Used
379	A26	15c	Picking cotton	.25	.25
380	A26	55c	Hamilton House	.25	.25
381	A26	$1.10	Self-sufficiency in food production	.35	.35
382	A26	$3	Pinney's Beach	.60	1.00
			Nos. 379-382 (4)	1.45	1.85

Leaders of the World — A27

Cricket players and team emblems and match scenes: No. 383, C.P. Mead, England. No. 384, J.D. Love, Yorkshire. No. 385, S.J. Dennis, Yorkshire. No. 386, J.B. Statham, England. No. 387, Sir Learie Constantine, West Indies. No. 388, B.W. Luckhurst, Kent. No. 389, Sir Leonard Hutton, England. No. 390, B.L. D'Oliveira, England.

Pairs, #a.-b.

1984 Unwmk. *Perf. 12½*

No.	Type	Denom.	Description	Unused	Used
383	A27	5c	multicolored	.25	.25
384	A27	5c	multicolored	.25	.25
385	A27	15c	multicolored	.25	.25
386	A27	25c	multicolored	.25	.25
387	A27	55c	multicolored	.25	.25
388	A27	55c	multicolored	.25	.25
389	A27	$2.50	multicolored	.50	1.25
390	A27	$2.50	multicolored	.50	1.25
			Nos. 383-390 (8)	2.50	4.00

Issued: #383, 386, 389, 10/23; others, 11/20.

Christmas A29

Musicians from local bands: 15c, Flutist and drummer of the Honeybees Band. 40c, Guitar and barhow players of the Canary Birds Band. 60c, Shell All Stars steel band. $3, Choir, organist, St. John's Church, Fig Tree.

1984, Nov. 2 Wmk. 380 *Perf. 14*

No.	Type	Description	Unused	Used
399-402	A29	Set of 4	2.25	2.25

Birds A30

1985, Mar. 19

No.	Type	Denom.	Description	Unused	Used
403	A30	20c	Broad-winged hawk	1.10	.25
404	A30	40c	Red-tailed hawk	1.25	.35
405	A30	60c	Little blue heron	1.25	.45
406	A30	$3	Great white heron	2.75	2.25
			Nos. 403-406 (4)	6.35	3.30

Leaders of the World — A31

Birds: #407a, Painted bunting. #407b, Golden-crowned kinglet. #408a, Eastern bluebird. #408b, Northern cardinal. #409a, Common flicker. #409b, Western tanager. #410a, Belted kingfisher. #410b, Mangrove cuckoo. #411a, Yellow warbler. #411b, Cerulean warbler. #412a, Sage thrasher. #412b, Evening grosbeak. #413a, Burrowing owl. #413b, Long-eared owl. #414a, Blackburnian warbler. #414b, Northern oriole.

1985 Unwmk. *Perf. 12½*

No.	Type	Denom.	Description	Unused	Used
407	A31	1c	Pair, #a.-b.	.25	.25
408	A31	5c	Pair, #a.-b.	.25	.25
409	A31	40c	Pair, #a.-b.	.35	.35
410	A31	55c	Pair, #a.-b.	.40	.40
411	A31	60c	Pair, #a.-b.	.45	.45
412	A31	60c	Pair, #a.-b.	.45	.45

413 A31 $2 Pair, #a.-b. 1.25 1.25
414 A31 $2.50 Pair, #a.-b. 1.50 1.50
Nos. 407-414 (8) 4.90 4.90

John J. Audubon, ornithologist, birth bicent.
Issued: 1c, 40c, #412, $2.50, 6/3; others, 3/25.

Girl Guides, 75th Anniv. — A32

15c, Troop, horiz. 60c, Uniforms, 1910, 1985. $1, Lord and Lady Baden-Powell. $3, Princess Margaret.

1985, June 17 Wmk. 380 *Perf. 14*
423 A32 15c multicolored .25 .25
424 A32 60c multicolored .25 .25
425 A32 $1 multicolored .30 .30
426 A32 $3 multicolored .80 1.25
Nos. 423-426 (4) 1.60 2.05

Queen Mother Elizabeth — A33

#427a, 432a, Black hat, white plume. #427b, 432b, Blue hat, pink feathers. #428a, Blue hat. #428b, Tiara. #429a, Violet & blue hat. #429b, Blue hat. #430a, 433a, Light blue hat. #430b, 433b, Black hat. #431a, As a child, c. 1910. #431b, Queen consort, c. 1945.

1985, July 31 Unwmk. *Perf. 12½*
427 A33 45c Pair, #a.-b. .25 .25
428 A33 75c Pair, #a.-b. .30 .30
429 A33 $1.20 Pair, #a.-b. .55 .55
430 A33 $1.50 Pair, #a.-b. .70 .70
Nos. 427-430 (4) 1.80 1.80

Souvenir Sheets

431 A33 $2 Sheet of 2, #a.-b. 2.00 2.00
432 A33 $3.50 Sheet of 2, #a.-b. 2.00 2.00
433 A33 $6 Sheet of 2, #a.-b. 4.00 4.00

Issued: #432-433, 12/27; others, 7/31.
For overprints see No. 450.

Great Western Railway, 150th Anniv. — A34

Railway engineers and their achievements: #438a, Isambard Brunel. #438b, Royal Albert Bridge, 1859. #439a, William Dean. #439b, *Lord of the Isles,* 1895. #440a, *Lode Star,* 1907. #440b, G.J. Churchward. #441a, Pendennis Castle Class, 1924. #441b, C.B. Collett.

1985, Aug. 31
438 A34 25c Pair, #a.-b. .25 .25
439 A34 50c Pair, #a.-b. .30 .30
440 A34 $1 Pair, #a.-b. .50 .50
441 A34 $2.50 Pair, #a.-b. 1.30 1.30
Nos. 438-441 (4) 2.35 2.35

Nos. 163, 157, 164, 151, 427, 144, 139-140 and 158 Ovptd. or Srchd. "CARIBBEAN ROYAL VISIT 1985" in 2 or 3 Lines

Perf. 14, 12½ (45c)

1985, Oct. 23 Wmk. as Before
446 A14 15c No. 163 1.00 1.00
447 A12 30c No. 157 2.00 2.00
448 A14 30c No. 164 1.00 1.00
449 A11 40c on 55c No. 151 2.25 2.25
450 A33 45c Pair, #a.-b. 3.00 3.00
452 A10 55c No. 144 2.25 2.25
453 A9a $1.50 on $5 No. 139 3.75 3.75
454 A9b $1.50 on $5 No. 140 13.00 *15.00*
455 A12 $2.50 No. 158 4.00 4.00
Nos. 446-455 (9) 32.25 34.25

Christmas A36

Anglican, Roman Catholic and Methodist churches — 10c, St. Paul's, Charlestown. 40c, St. Theresa, Charlestown. 60c, Methodist Church, Gingerland. $3, St. Thomas, Lowland.

1985, Nov. 5 Wmk. 380 *Perf. 15*
456 A36 10c multicolored .25 .25
457 A36 40c multicolored .30 .30
458 A36 60c multicolored .40 .40
459 A36 $3 multicolored 1.25 1.25
Nos. 456-459 (4) 2.20 2.20

Spitfire Fighter Plane, 50th Anniv. — A37

1986, Mar. 24 Unwmk. *Perf. 12½*
460 A37 $1 Prototype K.5054, 1936 .30 .30
461 A37 $2.50 Mk.1A, 1940 .70 .70
462 A37 $3 Mk.XII, 1944 .80 .80
463 A37 $4 Mk.XXIV, 1948 1.20 1.20
Nos. 460-463 (4) 3.00 3.00

Souvenir Sheet

464 A37 $6 Seafire Mk.III 3.00 3.00

No. 464 exists imperf. Value, $12.50 unused.

Discovery of America, 500th Anniv. (in 1992) — A38

#465a, American Indian. #465b, Columbus trading with Indians. #466a, Columbus's coat of arms. #466b, Breadfruit. #467a, Galleons. #467b, Columbus.

1986, Apr. 11
465 A38 75c Pair, #a.-b. .90 .90
466 A38 $1.75 Pair, #a.-b. 2.25 2.25
467 A38 $2.50 Pair, #a.-b. 3.25 3.25
Nos. 465-467 (3) 6.40 6.40

Souvenir Sheet

468 A38 $6 Columbus, diff. 6.50 6.50

Printed in continuous designs picturing various maps of Columbus's voyages.

Queen Elizabeth II, 60th Birthday — A39

Various portraits.

1986, Apr. 21
472 A39 5c multicolored .25 .25
473 A39 75c multicolored .25 .25
474 A39 $2 multicolored .50 .50
475 A39 $8 multi, vert. 2.00 2.00
Nos. 472-475 (4) 3.00 3.00

Souvenir Sheet

476 A39 $10 multicolored 6.00 6.00

1986 World Cup Soccer Championships, Mexico — A40

1c, Character trademark. 2c, Brazilian player. 5c, Danish player. 10c, Brazilian, diff. 20c, Denmark vs. Spain. 30c, Paraguay vs. Chile. 60c, Italy vs. W. Germany. 75c, Danish team. $1, Paraguayan team. $1.75, Brazilian team. $3, Italy vs. England. $6, Italian team.

Size of 75c, $1, $1.75, $6: 56x35½mm

Perf. 15, 12½ (75c, $1, $1.75, $6)

1986, May 16
477 A40 1c multicolored .25 .25
478 A40 2c multicolored .25 .25
479 A40 5c multicolored .25 .25
480 A40 10c multicolored .25 .25
481 A40 20c multicolored .25 .25
482 A40 30c multicolored .25 .25
483 A40 60c multicolored .35 .35
484 A40 75c multicolored .50 .50
485 A40 $1 multicolored .70 .70
486 A40 $1.75 multicolored .80 .80
487 A40 $3 multicolored 1.30 1.30
488 A40 $6 multicolored 2.50 2.50
Nos. 477-488 (12) 7.65 7.65

Souvenir Sheets

Perf. 12½

489 A40 $1.50 like $1.75 1.90 1.90
490 A40 $2 like $6 2.10 2.10

Perf. 15

491 A40 $2 like 20c 2.10 2.10
492 A40 $2.50 like 60c 2.50 2.50
493 A40 $4 like 30c 3.50 3.50

Nos. 478-483 and 487 vert.

Local Industry A41

1986, July 18 Wmk. 380 *Perf. 14*
494 A41 15c Textile .35 .35
495 A41 40c Carpentry .50 .50
496 A41 $1.20 Agriculture 1.40 1.40
497 A41 $3 Fishing 3.25 3.25
Nos. 494-497 (4) 5.50 5.50

A42

Wedding of Prince Andrew and Sarah Ferguson — A43

#498a, Andrew. #498b, Sarah. #499a, Andrew at the races, horiz. #499b, Andrew in Africa, horiz.

1986, July 23 Unwmk. *Perf. 12½*
498 A42 60c Pair, #a.-b. .40 .40
499 A42 $2 Pair, #a.-b. 1.25 1.25

Souvenir Sheet

500 A43 $10 Couple on Balcony 4.25 4.25

Printed in vert. and horiz. pairs.
For overprints see Nos. 521-522.

Coral — A44

1986, Sept. 8 Wmk. 380 *Perf. 15*
503 A44 15c Gorgonia .25 .25
504 A44 60c Fire coral .30 .30
505 A44 $2 Elkhorn coral 1.00 1.00
506 A44 $3 Feather star 1.30 1.30
Nos. 503-506 (4) 2.85 2.85

A45

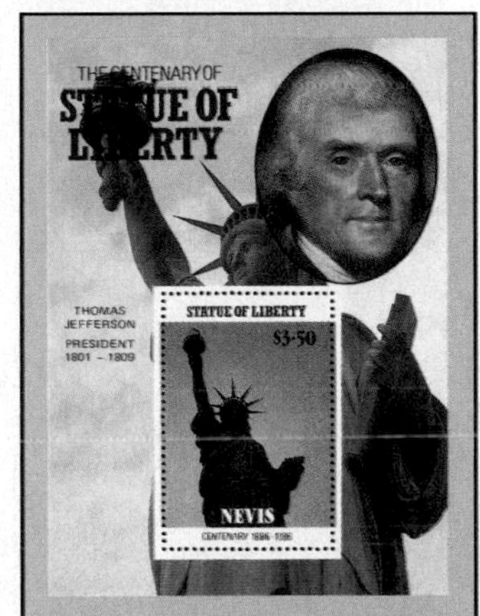

Statue of Liberty, Cent. — A46

15c, Statue, World Trade Center. 25c, Statue, tall ship. 40c, Under renovation (front). 60c, Renovation (side). 75c, Statue, Operation Sail. $1, Tall ship. $1.50, Renovation (arm, head). $2, Ship flying Liberty flag. $2.50, Statue, Manhattan. $3, Workers on scaffold.
$3.50, Statue at dusk. $4, Head. $4.50, Torch struck by lightning. $5, Torch, blazing sun.
All stamps are vertical except the $1 & $2.

1986, Oct. 28 Unwmk. *Perf. 14*
507 A45 15c multicolored .25 .25
508 A45 25c multicolored .25 .25
509 A45 40c multicolored .25 .25
510 A45 60c multicolored .40 .40
511 A45 75c multicolored .50 .50
512 A45 $1 multicolored .65 .65
513 A45 $1.50 multicolored .85 .85
514 A45 $2 multicolored 1.10 1.10
515 A45 $2.50 multicolored 1.25 1.25
516 A45 $3 multicolored 1.60 1.60
Nos. 507-516 (10) 7.10 7.10

Souvenir Sheets

517 A46 $3.50 multicolored 2.10 2.10
518 A46 $4 multicolored 2.25 2.25
519 A46 $4.50 multicolored 2.50 2.50
520 A46 $5 multicolored 2.75 2.75

Nos. 498-499 Ovptd. "Congratulations to T.R.H. The Duke & Duchess of York"

1986, Nov. 17 *Perf. 12½*
521 A42 60c Pair, #a.-b. .45 .45
522 A42 $2 Pair, #a.-b. 1.50 1.50

Sports A47

1986, Nov. 21 *Perf. 14*
525 A47 10c Sailing .30 .30
526 A47 25c Netball .30 .30
527 A47 $2 Cricket 2.10 2.10
528 A47 $3 Basketball 3.25 3.25
Nos. 525-528 (4) 5.95 5.95

Christmas — A48

Churches: 10c, St. George's Anglican Church, Gingerland. 40c, Methodist Church, Fountain. $1, Charlestown Methodist Church. $5, Wesleyan Holiness Church, Brown Hill.

1986, Dec. 8
529 A48 10c multicolored .25 .25
530 A48 40c multicolored .30 .30
531 A48 $1 multicolored .75 .75
532 A48 $5 multicolored 3.25 3.25
Nos. 529-532 (4) 4.55 4.55

US Constitution — A49

Christening of the Hamilton, 1788 — A50

US Constitution, bicent. and 230th anniv. of the birth of Alexander Hamilton: 40c, Alexander Hamilton, Hamilton House. 60c, Hamilton. $2, George Washington and members of the 1st presidential cabinet.

1987, Jan. 11
533 A49 15c shown .25 .25
534 A49 40c multicolored .30 .30
535 A49 60c multicolored .45 .45
536 A49 $2 multicolored 1.10 1.10
Nos. 533-536 (4) 2.10 2.10

Souvenir Sheet

537 A50 $5 shown 8.50 8.50

No. 117 Overprinted

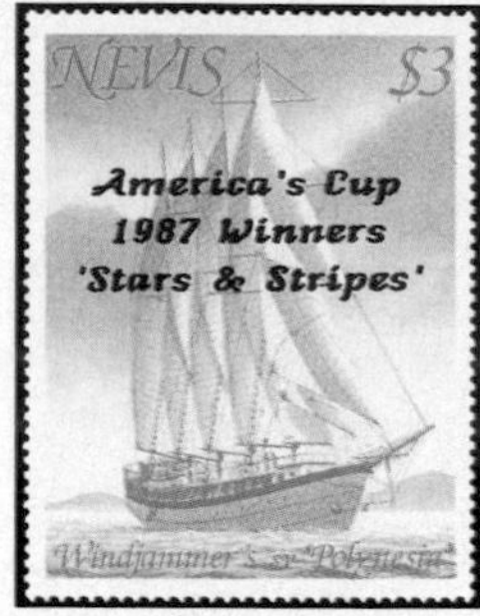

1987, Feb. 20 **Wmk. 373**
538 A6a $3 multicolored 1.60 1.60

Wedding of Capt. Horatio Nelson and Frances Nisbet, Bicent.
A51

1987, Mar. 11 **Wmk. 380**
539 A51 15c Fig Tree Church .35 .35
540 A51 60c Frances Nisbet .85 .85
541 A51 $1 HMS *Boreas* 1.40 1.40
542 A51 $3 Capt. Nelson 3.25 3.25
Nos. 539-542 (4) 5.85 5.85

Souvenir Sheet

543 Sheet of 2, #542, 543a 6.00 6.00
a. A51 $3 like No. 540 3.50 3.50

A52

#544a, Queen angelfish. #544b, Blue angelfish. #545a, Blue thum. #545b, Red thum. #546a, Red hind. #546b, Rock hind. #547a, Coney Butterfish. #547b, Coney butterfish, diff.

1987, July 22 **Unwmk.** *Perf. 15*
544 A52 60c Pair, #a.-b. .70 .70
545 A52 $1 Pair, #a.-b. 1.25 1.25
546 A52 $1.50 Pair, #a.-b. 1.75 1.75
547 A52 $2.50 Pair, #a.-b. 3.00 3.00
Nos. 544-547 (4) 6.70 6.70

Mushrooms — A53

15c, Panaeolus antillarum. 50c, Pycnoporus sanguineus. $2, Gymnopilus chrysopellus. $3, Cantharellus cinnabarinus.

1987, Oct. 16 **Wmk. 384** *Perf. 14*
552 A53 15c multicolored .40 .40
553 A53 50c multicolored 1.00 1.00
554 A53 $2 multicolored 3.00 3.00
555 A53 $3 multicolored 3.50 3.50
Nos. 552-555 (4) 7.90 7.90

Christmas — A54

1987, Dec. 4 *Perf. 14½*
556 A54 10c Rag doll .25 .25
557 A54 40c Coconut boat .25 .25
558 A54 $1.20 Sandbox cart .70 .70
559 A54 $5 Two-wheeled cart 2.25 2.25
Nos. 556-559 (4) 3.45 3.45

Sea Shells — A55

1988, Feb. 15 *Perf. 14x14½*
560 A55 15c Hawk-wing conch .30 .30
561 A55 40c Roostertail conch .45 .45
562 A55 60c Emperor helmet .60 .60
563 A55 $2 Queen conch 1.60 1.60
564 A55 $3 King helmet 2.10 2.10
Nos. 560-564 (5) 5.05 5.05

Intl. Red Cross and Red Crescent Organizations, 125th Annivs. — A56

Activities: 15c, Visiting the sick and the elderly. 40c, First aid training. 60c, Wheelchairs for the disabled. $5, Disaster relief.

1988, June 20 *Perf. 14½x14*
565 A56 15c multicolored .25 .25
566 A56 40c multicolored .30 .30
567 A56 60c multicolored .45 .45
568 A56 $5 multicolored 3.00 3.00
Nos. 565-568 (4) 4.00 4.00

A57

1988, Aug. 26 *Perf. 14*
569 Strip of 4 3.75 3.75
a. A57 10c Runner at starting block .25 .25
b. A57 $1.20 Leaving block .70 .70
c. A57 $2 Full stride 1.20 1.20
d. A57 $3 Crossing finish line 1.75 1.75
e. Souvenir sheet of 4, #569a-569d 3.75 3.75

1988 Summer Olympics, Seoul. Printed se-tenant in a continuous design. Stamps in No. 569e are 23½x36½.

A58

1988, Sept. 19 **Wmk. 373** *Perf. 14½*
570 A58 $5 multicolored 3.25 3.25

Independence, 5th anniv.

Common Design Types pictured following the introduction.

Lloyds of London
Common Design Type

Designs: 15c, Act of Parliament incorporating Lloyds, 1871. 60c, *Cunard Countess* in Nevis Harbor, horiz. $2.50, Space shuttle, deployment of satellite in space, horiz. $3, *Viking Princess* on fire in the Caribbean, 1966.

1988, Oct. 31 **Wmk. 384** *Perf. 14*
571 CD341 15c multicolored .45 .45
572 CD341 60c multicolored .90 .90
573 CD341 $2.50 multicolored 2.50 2.50
574 CD341 $3 multicolored 4.50 4.50
Nos. 571-574 (4) 8.35 8.35

Christmas Flowers — A59

1988, Nov. 7 *Perf. 14½*
575 A59 15c Poinsettia .25 .25
576 A59 40c Tiger claws .25 .25
577 A59 60c Sorrel flower .35 .35
578 A59 $1 Christmas candle .60 .60
579 A59 $5 Snow bush 2.40 2.40
Nos. 575-579 (5) 3.85 3.85

Battle of Frigate Bay, 1782 — A60

Exhibition emblem & maps. #580a-580c in a continuous design.

1989, Apr. 17 *Perf. 14*
580 A60 Strip of 3 3.75 3.75
a. 50c multicolored .30 .30
b. $1.20 multicolored .80 .80
c. $2 multicolored 1.40 1.40

Size: 34x47mm
Perf. 14x13½

581 A60 $3 Map of Nevis, 1764 3.25 3.25

French revolution bicent., PHILEXFRANCE '89.

Nocturnal Insects and Frogs — A61

1989, May 15
582 A61 10c Cicada .30 .30
583 A61 40c Grasshopper .50 .50
584 A61 60c Cricket .85 .85
585 A61 $5 Tree frog 4.50 4.50
a. Souvenir sheet of 4, #582-585 7.50 7.50
Nos. 582-585 (4) 6.15 6.15

Moon Landing, 20th Anniv.
Common Design Type

Apollo 12: 15c, Vehicle Assembly Building, Kennedy Space Center. 40c, Crew members Charles Conrad Jr., Richard Gordon and Alan Bean. $2, Mission emblem. $3, Moon operation in the Sun's glare. $6, Buzz Aldrin deploying passive seismic experiment package on the lunar surface, Apollo 11 mission.

1989, July 20 *Perf. 14x13½*
Size of Nos. 587-588: 29x29mm
586 CD342 15c multicolored .25 .25
587 CD342 40c multicolored .25 .25
588 CD342 $2 multicolored 1.25 1.25
589 CD342 $3 multicolored 1.75 1.75
Nos. 586-589 (4) 3.50 3.50

Souvenir Sheet

590 CD342 $6 multicolored 4.00 4.00

Queen Conchs *(Strombus gigas)* A62

1990, Jan. 31

591 A62 10c shown .35 .35
592 A62 40c Conch, diff .65 .65
593 A62 60c Conch, diff 1.50 1.50
594 A62 $1 Conch, diff 2.25 2.25
Nos. 591-594 (4) 4.75 4.75

Souvenir Sheet

595 A62 $5 Fish and coral 5.75 5.75

World Wildlife Fund.

Wyon Portrait of Victoria — A63

40c, Engine-turned background. 60c, Heath's engraving. $4, Inscriptions added. $5, Completed design.

Perf. 14x15

1990, May 3 Litho. Unwmk.

596 A63 15c brn, blk, tan .25 .25
597 A63 40c grn, blk, lt grn .30 .30
598 A63 60c blk, gray .50 .50
599 A63 $4 blue, blk, lt blue 3.00 3.00
Nos. 596-599 (4) 4.05 4.05

Souvenir Sheet

600 A63 $5 multicolored 5.25 5.25

Penny Black, 150th anniv. No. 600 for Stamp World London '90.

A64

1990, May 3 ***Perf. 13½***

601 A64 15c brown .25 .25
602 A64 40c deep green .30 .30
603 A64 60c violet .50 .50
604 A64 $4 bright ultra 3.50 3.50
Nos. 601-604 (4) 4.55 4.55

Souvenir Sheet

605 A64 $5 gray, lake & buff 5.50 5.50

Penny Black 150th anniversary and commemoration of the Thurn & Taxis postal service.

Crabs A65

Designs include UPAE and discovery of America anniversary emblems.

1990, June 25 Litho. ***Perf. 14***

606 A65 5c Sand fiddler .25 .25
607 A65 15c Great land crab .25 .25
608 A65 20c Blue crab .30 .30
609 A65 40c Stone crab .40 .40
610 A65 60c Mountain crab .60 .60
611 A65 $2 Sargassum crab 1.40 1.40
612 A65 $3 Yellow box crab 2.00 2.00
613 A65 $4 Spiny spider crab 2.75 2.75
Nos. 606-613 (8) 7.95 7.95

Souvenir Sheets

614 A65 $5 Wharf crab 4.00 4.00
615 A65 $5 Sally lightfoot 4.00 4.00

Queen Mother 90th Birthday
A66 A67

1990, July 5

616 A66 $2 shown 1.50 1.50
617 A67 $2 shown 1.50 1.50
618 A66 $2 Queen Consort, diff. 1.50 1.50
a. Strip of 3, #616-618 4.50 4.50

Souvenir Sheet

619 A67 $6 Coronation Portrait, diff. 5.00 5.00

Nos. 616-618 printed in sheet of 9.

A68

Players from participating countries.

1990, Oct. 1 Litho. ***Perf. 14***

620 A68 10c Cameroun .25 .25
621 A68 25c Czechoslovakia .25 .25
622 A68 $2.50 England 2.25 2.25
623 A68 $5 West Germany 4.75 4.75
Nos. 620-623 (4) 7.50 7.50

Souvenir Sheets

624 A68 $5 Spain 4.00 4.00
625 A68 $5 Argentina 4.00 4.00

World Cup Soccer Championships, Italy.

A69

Christmas (Orchids): 10c, Cattleya deckeri. 15c, Epidendrum ciliare. 20c, Epidendrum fragrans. 40c, Epidendrum ibaguense. 60c, Epidendrum latifolium. $1.20, Maxillaria conferta. $2, Epidendrum strobiliferum. $3, Brassavola cucullata. $5, Rodriguezia lanceolata.

Unwmk.

1990, Nov. 19 Litho. ***Perf. 14***

626 A69 10c multicolored .30 .30
627 A69 15c multicolored .30 .30
628 A69 20c multicolored .30 .30
629 A69 40c multicolored .45 .45
630 A69 60c multicolored .70 .70
631 A69 $1.20 multicolored 1.30 1.30
632 A69 $2 multicolored 2.25 2.25
633 A69 $3 multicolored 3.50 3.50
Nos. 626-633 (8) 9.10 9.10

Souvenir Sheet

634 A69 $5 multicolored 8.00 8.00

Peter Paul Rubens (1577-1640), Painter A70

Details from The Feast of Achelous: 10c, Pitchers. 40c, Woman at table. 60c, Two women. $4, Achelous feasting. $5, Complete painting, horiz.

1991, Jan. 14 Litho. ***Perf. 13½***

635 A70 10c multicolored .30 .30
636 A70 40c multicolored .50 .50
637 A70 60c multicolored .80 .80
638 A70 $4 multicolored 4.25 4.25
Nos. 635-638 (4) 5.85 5.85

Souvenir Sheet

639 A70 $5 multicolored 6.25 6.25

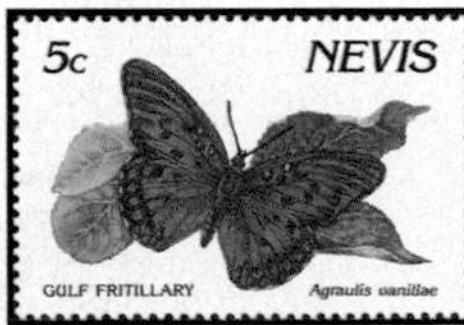

Butterflies A71

5c, Gulf fritillary. 10c, Orion. 15c, Dagger wing. 20c, Red anartia. 25c, Caribbean buckeye. 40c, Zebra. 50c, Southern dagger tail. 60c, Silver spot. 75c, Doris. $1, Mimic. $3, Monarch. $5, Small blue grecian. $10, Tiger. $20, Flambeau.

1991, Mar. ***Perf. 14***

No Date Imprint Below Design

640 A71 5c multicolored .25 .25
641 A71 10c multicolored .25 .25
642 A71 15c multicolored .25 .25
643 A71 20c multicolored .25 .25
644 A71 25c multicolored .25 .25
645 A71 40c multicolored .35 .35
646 A71 50c multicolored .50 .50
647 A71 60c multicolored .55 .55
648 A71 75c multicolored .65 .65
649 A71 $1 multicolored .90 .90
650 A71 $3 multicolored 2.75 2.75
651 A71 $5 multicolored 4.50 4.50
652 A71 $10 multicolored 9.00 9.00
653 A71 $20 multicolored 18.00 18.00
Nos. 640-653 (14) 38.45 38.45

For overprints see Nos. O41-O54.

1992, Mar. 1 "1992" Below Design

640a A71 5c multicolored .25 .25
641a A71 10c multicolored .25 .25
642a A71 15c multicolored .25 .25
643a A71 20c multicolored .25 .25
644a A71 25c multicolored .30 .25
645a A71 40c multicolored .40 .25
646a A71 50c multicolored .50 .50
648b A71 75c multicolored .65 .65
648A A71 80c multicolored 1.50 1.50
649a A71 $1 multicolored .90 .90
650a A71 $3 multicolored 2.75 2.75
651a A71 $5 multicolored 4.50 4.50
652a A71 $10 multicolored 9.00 9.00
653a A71 $20 multicolored 18.00 18.00
Nos. 640a-653a (14) 39.50 39.30

1994 "1994" Below Design

640b A71 5c multicolored .40 .40
641b A71 10c multicolored .40 .40
644b A71 25c multicolored .40 .40
646b A71 50c multicolored .40 .40
648Ab A71 80c multicolored 1.75 1.75
Nos. 640b-648Ab (5) 3.35 3.35

Space Exploration-Discovery Voyages — A72

1991, Apr. 22 Litho. ***Perf. 14***

654 A72 15c Viking Mars lander .25 .25
655 A72 40c Apollo 11 lift-off .30 .30
656 A72 60c Skylab .45 .45
657 A72 75c Salyut 6 .55 .55
658 A72 $1 Voyager 1 .75 .75
659 A72 $2 Venera 7 1.25 1.25
660 A72 $4 Gemini 4 2.50 2.50
661 A72 $5 Luna 3 3.25 3.25
Nos. 654-661 (8) 9.30 9.30

Souvenir Sheet

662 A72 $6 Sailing ship, vert. 5.50 5.50
663 A72 $6 Columbus' landfall 5.50 5.50

Discovery of America, 500th anniv. (in 1992) (No. 663).

Miniature Sheet

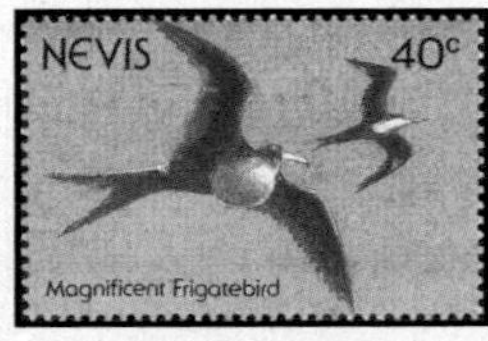

Birds A73

Designs: a, Magnificent frigatebird. b, Roseate tern. c, Red-tailed hawk. d, Zenaida dove. e, Bananaquit. f, American kestrel. g, Grey kingbird. h, Prothonotary warbler. i, Blue-hooded euphonia. j, Antillean crested hummingbird. k, White-tailed tropicbird. l, Yellow-bellied sapsucker. m, Green-throated carib. n, Purple-throated carib. o, Black-bellied tree duck. p, Ringed kingfisher. q, Burrowing owl. r, Ruddy turnstone. s, Great white heron. t, Yellow-crowned night heron.

1991, May 28

664 A73 40c Sheet of 20, #a.-t. 16.00 16.00

Souvenir Sheet

665 A73 $6 Great egret 11.00 11.00

Royal Family Birthday, Anniversary

Common Design Type

No. 674, Elizabeth, Philip. No. 675, Charles, Diana & family.

1991, July 5 Litho. ***Perf. 14***

666 CD347 10c multicolored .30 .30
667 CD347 15c multicolored .30 .30
668 CD347 40c multicolored .45 .45
669 CD347 50c multicolored .60 .60
670 CD347 $1 multicolored 1.00 1.00
671 CD347 $2 multicolored 2.00 2.00
672 CD347 $4 multicolored 4.00 4.00
673 CD347 $5 multicolored 5.00 5.00
Nos. 666-673 (8) 13.65 13.65

Souvenir Sheets

674 CD347 $5 multicolored 6.00 6.00
675 CD347 $5 multicolored 6.00 6.00

10c, 50c, $1, Nos. 673, 675, Charles and Diana, 10th Wedding Anniv. Others, Queen Elizabeth II 65th birthday.

Japanese Trains A74

Locomotives: 10c, C62 Steam, vert. 15c, C56 Steam. 40c, Streamlined C55, steam. 60c, Class 1400 Steam. $1, Class 485 bonnet type rail diesel car, vert. $2, C61 Steam, vert. $3, Class 485 express train. $4, Class 7000 electric train. No. 684, D51 Steam. No. 685, Hikari bullet train.

1991, Aug. 12

676-683 A74 Set of 8 14.00 14.00

Souvenir Sheets

684-685 A74 $5 Set of 2 11.00 11.00

Phila Nippon '91.

Christmas A75

Paintings by Albrecht Durer: 10c, Mary Being Crowned by an Angel. 40c, Mary with the Pear. 60c, Mary in a Halo. $3, Mary with the Crown of Stars and Scepter. No. 690, The Holy Family. No. 691, Mary at the Yard Gate.

1991, Dec. 20 Litho. *Perf. 13½*

686 A75 10c yel green & blk .25 .25
687 A75 40c org brown & blk .30 .30
688 A75 60c blue & black .45 .45
689 A75 $3 brt magenta & blk 1.90 1.90
Nos. 686-689 (4) 2.90 2.90

Souvenir Sheets

690 A75 $6 black 8.00 8.00
691 A75 $6 black 8.00 8.00

A76

Mushrooms: 15c, Marasmius haematocephalus. 40c, Psilocybe cubensis. 60c, Hygrocybe acutoconica. 75c, Hygrocybe occidentalis. $1, Boletellus cubensis. $2, Gymnopilus chrysopellus. $4, Cantharellus cinnabarinus. $5, Chlorophyllum molybdites. No. 700, Our Lady of the Snows (8 mushrooms). No. 701, Our Lady of the Snows (4 mushrooms), diff.

1991, Dec. 20 Litho. *Perf. 14*

692-699 A76 Set of 8 10.00 10.00

Souvenir Sheet

700-701 A76 $6 Set of 2 10.00 10.00

Queen Elizabeth II's Accession to the Throne, 40th Anniv.

Common Design Type

1992, Feb. 26 Litho. *Perf. 14*

702 CD348 10c multicolored .25 .25
703 CD348 40c multicolored .30 .30
704 CD348 $1 multicolored .75 .75
705 CD348 $5 multicolored 3.50 3.50
Nos. 702-705 (4) 4.80 4.80

Souvenir Sheets

706 CD348 $6 Queen, people on beach 4.50 4.50
707 CD348 $6 Queen, seashell 4.50 4.50

A77

Gold medalists: 20c, Monique Knol, France, cycling. 25c, Roger Kingdom, US, 110-meter hurdles. 50c, Yugoslavia, water polo. 80c, Anja Fichtel, West Germany, foil. $1, Said Aouita, Morocco, 5000-meters. $1.50, Yuri Sedykh, USSR, hammer throw. $3, Yelena Shushunova, USSR, gymnastics. $5, Vladimir Artemov, USSR, gymnastics. No. 716, Florence Griffith-Joyner, US, 100-meter dash. No. 717, Naim Suleymanoglu, Turkey, weight lifting.

1992, May 7 Litho. *Perf. 14*

708-715 A77 Set of 8 11.50 11.50

Souvenir Sheets

716-717 A77 $6 Set of 2 8.25 8.25

1992 Summer Olympics, Barcelona. All athletes except those on $1 and $1.50 won gold medals in 1988. No. 715 incorrectly spelled "Valimir."

Spanish Art — A78

Designs: 20c, Landscape, by Mariano Fortuny, vert. 25c, Dona Juana la Loca, by Francisco Pradilla Ortiz. 50c, Idyll, by Fortuny, vert. 80c, Old Man in the Sun, by Fortuny, vert. $1, $2, The Painter's Children in the Japanese Salon (different details), vert., by Fortuny. $3, Still Life (Sea Bream and Oranges), by Luis Eugenio Melendez. $5, Still Life (Box of Sweets, Pastry, and Other Objects), by Melendez, vert. No. 726, Moroccans by Fortuny. No. 727, Bullfight, by Fortuny.

Perf. 13x13½, 13½x13

1992, June 1 Litho.

718-725 A78 Set of 8 12.50 12.50

Size: 120x95mm

Imperf

726-727 A78 $6 Set of 2 8.25 8.25

Granada '92.

A79

1992, July 6 *Perf. 14*

728 A79 20c Early compass .30 .60
729 A79 50c Manatee .60 .60
730 A79 80c Green turtle .90 .90
731 A79 $1.50 Santa Maria 1.60 1.60
732 A79 $3 Queen Isabella 3.00 3.00
733 A79 $5 Pineapple 5.50 5.50
Nos. 728-733 (6) 11.90 12.20

Souvenir Sheets

734 A79 $6 Storm petrel, horiz. 5.50 5.50
735 A79 $6 Pepper, horiz. 5.50 5.50

Discovery of America, 500th anniv. World Columbian Stamp Expo '92, Chicago.

A80

1992, Aug. 24 *Perf. 14½*

736 A80 $1 Coming ashore .80 .80
737 A80 $2 Natives, ships 1.50 1.50

Discovery of America, 500th anniv. Organization of East Caribbean States.

Wolfgang Amadeus Mozart, Bicent. of Death (in 1991) — A81

1992, Oct. Litho. *Perf. 14*

738 A81 $3 multicolored 3.00 3.00

Souvenir Sheet

739 A81 $6 Don Giovanni 5.25 5.25

Mickey's Portrait Gallery A82

10c, Minnie Mouse, 1930. 15c, Mickey Mouse. 40c, Donald Duck. 80c, Mickey Mouse, 1930. $1, Daisy Duck. $2, Pluto. $4, Goofy. $5, Goofy, 1932.

No. 748, Plane Crazy. No. 749, Mickey, Home Sweet Home, horiz.

1992, Nov. 9 Litho. *Perf. 13½x14*

740 A82 10c multicolored .25 .25
741 A82 15c multicolored .35 .35
742 A82 40c multicolored .45 .45
743 A82 80c multicolored .75 .75
744 A82 $1 multicolored 1.00 1.00
745 A82 $2 multicolored 1.75 1.75
746 A82 $4 multicolored 3.50 3.50
747 A82 $5 multicolored 4.00 4.00
Nos. 740-747 (8) 12.05 12.05

Souvenir Sheet

Perf. 14x13½

748 A82 $6 multicolored 6.00 6.00
749 A82 $6 multicolored 6.00 6.00

Christmas A83

Details or entire paintings: 20c, The Virgin and Child Between Two Saints, by Giovanni Bellini. 40c, The Virgin and Child Surrounded by Four Angels, by Master of the Castello Nativity. 50c, Virgin and Child Surrounded by Angels with St. Frediano and St. Augustine, by Fra Filippo Lippi. 80c, The Virgin and Child Between St. Peter and St. Sebastian, by Giovanni Bellini. $1, The Virgin and Child with St. Julian and St. Nicholas of Myra, by Lorenzo Di Credi. $2, Saint Bernardino and a Female Saint Presenting a Donor to Virgin and Child, by Francesco Bissolo. $4, Madonna and Child with Four Cherubs, Ascribed to Barthel Bruyn. $5, The Virgin and Child, by Quentin Metsys. No. 758, The Virgin and Child Surrounded by Two Angels, by Perugino. No. 759, Madonna and Child with the Infant St. John and Archangel Gabriel, by Sandro Botticelli.

1992, Nov. 16 Litho. *Perf. 13½x14*

750-757 A83 Set of 8 11.00 11.00

Souvenir Sheet

758-759 A83 $6 Set of 2 10.00 10.00

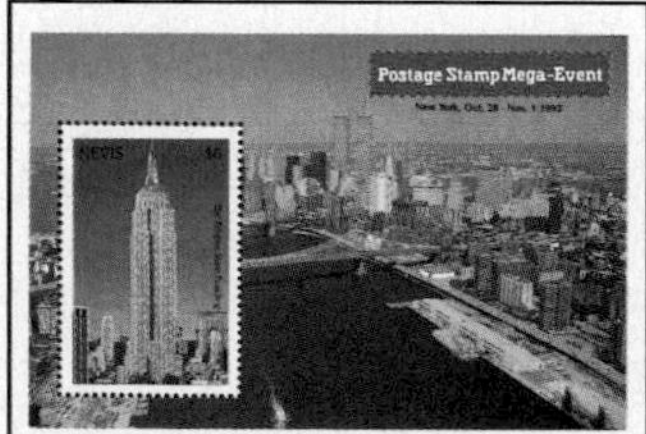

Empire State Building, New York City — A84

1992, Oct. 28 Litho. *Perf. 14*

760 A84 $6 multicolored 5.50 5.50

Postage Stamp Mega Event '92, New York City.

A85

A89

A86

A87

NEVIS 80¢

A88

A90

A92

A91

PAINTINGS FROM THE LOUVRE

BICENTENNIAL 1793 – 1993

Anniversaries and Events — A93

Designs: 15c, Japanese launch vehicle H-2. 50c, Hindenburg on fire, 1937. 75c, Charles de Gaulle, Konrad Adenauer. No. 764, Horatio Nelson Museum, Nevis. No. 765, Red Cross emblem, Nevis. No. 766, America's Cup yacht *Resolute*, 1920, vert. No. 767, St. Thomas Anglican Church. No. 768, Care Bear, butterfly and flower. No. 770, Blue whale. No. 771, WHO, ICN, FAO emblems, graph showing population growth. vert. No. 772, Lion, Lion's Intl. emblem. No. 773, John F. Kennedy, Adenauer. No. 774, Lebaudy, first flying machine with mechanical engine. No. 775, Soviet Energia launch vehicle SL-17.

Elvis Presley: No. 776a, Portrait. b, With guitar. c, With microphone.

Details or entire paintings, by Georges de La Tour: No. 777a, The Cheater (left). b, The Cheater (center). c, The Cheater (right). d, St. Joseph, the Carpenter. e, Saint Thomas. f, Adoration of the Shepherds (left). g, Adoration of the Shepherds (right). h, La Madeleine a La Veilleuse.

No. 778, Care Bear, palm tree, vert. No. 779, Manned maneuvering unit in space. No. 780, Count Zeppelin taking off from Goppingen for Friedrichshafen. No. 781, Adenauer. No. 782, America's Cup yacht. No. 783, The Angel Departing from the Family of Tobias, by Rembrandt.

1993 Litho. *Perf. 14*

761	A85	15c multicolored	.25	.25
762	A86	50c multicolored	.40	.40
763	A87	75c multicolored	.80	.80
764	A88	80c multicolored	.90	.90
765	A88	80c multicolored	.90	.90
766	A89	80c multicolored	.60	.60
767	A88	80c multicolored	.60	.60
768	A90	80c multicolored	.60	.60
770	A88	$1 multicolored	.75	.75
771	A91	$3 multicolored	3.50	3.50
772	A85	$3 multicolored	3.00	3.00
773	A87	$5 multicolored	3.00	3.00
774	A86	$5 multicolored	3.50	3.50
775	A85	$5 multicolored	3.50	3.50

Perf. 14

776	A92	$1 Strip of 3, #a.-c.	2.00	2.00
		Nos. 761-776 (15)	24.30	24.30

Miniature Sheet

Perf. 12

777	A93	$1 Sheet of 8, #a.-h. + label	8.00	8.00

Souvenir Sheets

Perf. 14

778	A90	$2 multicolored	1.25	1.25
779	A85	$6 multicolored	5.25	5.25
780	A86	$6 multicolored	5.25	5.25
781	A87	$6 multicolored	5.50	5.50
782	A89	$6 multicolored	4.00	4.00

Perf. 14½

783	A92	$6 multicolored	6.00	6.00

Intl. Space Year (#761, 775, 779). Count Zeppelin, 75th anniv. of death (#762, 774, 780). Konrad Adenauer, 25th anniv. of death (#763, 773, 781). Anglican Church in Nevis, 150th anniv. Opening of Horatio Nelson Museum (#764). Nevis and St. Kitts Red Cross, 50th anniv. (#765). America's Cup yacht race (#766, 782). (#767). Lions Intl., 75th anniv. (#772). Earth Summit, Rio de Janeiro (#768, 770, 778). Intl. Conference on Nutrition, Rome (#771). Elvis Presley, 15th death anniv. (in 1992) (#776). Louvre Art Museum, bicent. (#777, 783).

Nos. 779-781 have continuous designs.

No. 783 contains one 55x89mm stamp.

Issued: No. 767, Mar.; others, Jan. 14.

Tropical Flowers — A94

1993, Mar. 26 Litho. *Perf. 14*

784	A94	10c Frangipani	.25	.25
785	A94	25c Bougainvillea	.25	.25
786	A94	50c Allamanda	.50	.50
787	A94	80c Anthurium	.80	.80
788	A94	$1 Ixora	1.00	1.00
789	A94	$2 Hibiscus	2.00	2.00
790	A94	$4 Shrimp plant	4.00	4.00
791	A94	$5 Coral vine	5.00	5.00
		Nos. 784-791 (8)	13.80	13.80

Souvenir Sheets

792	A94	$6 Lantana	5.00	5.00
793	A94	$6 Petrea	5.00	5.00

Butterflies A95

10c, Antillean blue. 25c, Cuban crescent-spot. 50c, Ruddy daggerwing. 80c, Little yellow. $1, Atala. $1.50, Orange-barred giant sulphur. $4, Tropic queen. $5, Malachite.

No. 802, Polydamas swallowtail. No. 803, West Indian Buckeye.

1993, May 17 Litho. *Perf. 14*

794	A95	10c multicolored	.30	.30
795	A95	25c multicolored	.30	.30
796	A95	50c multicolored	.60	.60
797	A95	80c multicolored	.90	.90
798	A95	$1 multicolored	1.00	1.00
799	A95	$1.50 multicolored	1.40	1.40
800	A95	$4 multicolored	4.00	4.00
801	A95	$5 multicolored	5.00	5.00
		Nos. 794-801 (8)	13.50	13.50

Souvenir Sheets

802	A95	$6 multicolored	5.75	5.75
a.		Ovptd. in sheet margin	5.00	5.00
803	A95	$6 multicolored	5.75	5.75
a.		Ovptd. in sheet margin	5.00	5.00

Location of Hong Kong '94 emblem on Nos. 802a-803a varies.

Nos. 802a, 803a issued Feb. 18, 1994.

Miniature Sheet

Coronation of Queen Elizabeth II, 40th Anniv. A96

Designs: a, 10c, Official coronation photograph. b, 80c, Queen, wearing Imperial Crown of State. c, $2, Queen, sitting on throne during ceremony. d, $4, Prince Charles kissing mother's hand.

$6, Portrait, "Riding on Worcran in the Great Park at Windsor," by Susan Crawford, 1977.

1993, June 2 Litho. *Perf. 13½x14*

804	A96	Sheet, 2 ea #a.-d.	10.00	10.00

Souvenir Sheet

Perf. 14

805	A96	$6 multicolored	4.00	4.00

No. 805 contains one 28x42mm stamp.

Independence of St. Kitts and Nevis, 10th Anniv. — A97

Designs: 25c, Natl. flag, anthem. 80c, Brown pelican, map of St. Kitts and Nevis.

1993, Sept. 19 Litho. *Perf. 13½*

807	A97	25c multicolored	.50	.50
808	A97	80c multicolored	1.50	1.50

1994 World Cup Soccer Championships, US — A98

Soccer players: 10c, Garaba, Hungary; Platini, France. 25c, Maradona, Argentina; Bergomi, Italy. 50c, Fernandez, France; Rats, Russia. 80c, Munoz, Spain. $1, Elkjaer, Denmark; Goicoechea, Spain. $2, Coelho, Brazil; Tigana, France. $3, Troglio, Argentina; Alejnikov, Russia. No. 816, $5, Karas, Poland; Costa, Brazil.

Each $5: No. 817, Belloumi, Algeria. No. 818, Steven, England, vert.

1993, Nov. 9 Litho. *Perf. 14*

809-816	A98	Set of 8	14.00	14.00

Souvenir Sheets

817-818	A98	Set of 2	22.50	22.50

Christmas A99

Works by Albrecht Durer: 20c, Annunciation of Mary. 40c, The Nativity. 50c, Holy Family on a Grassy Bank. 80c, The Presentation of Christ in the Temple. $1, Virgin in Glory on the Crescent. $1.60, The Nativity, diff. $3, Madonna and Child. $5, The Presentation of Christ in the Temple (detail).

Each $6: No. 827, Mary with Child and the Long-Tailed Monkey, by Durer. No. 828, The Rest on the Flight into Egypt, by Fragonard, horiz.

1993, Nov. 30 *Perf. 13*

819-826	A99	Set of 8	12.50	12.50

Souvenir Sheets

827-828	A99	Set of 2	20.00	20.00

Tuff Mickey — A100

Disney's Mickey Mouse playing: 10c, Basketball. 50c, Volleyball. $1, Soccer. $5, Boxing.

No. 837, $6, Tug-of-war. No. 838, Ringing carnival bell with hammer, vert.

Disney's Minnie Mouse: 25c, Welcome to my island, vert. 80c, Sunny and snappy, vert. $1.50, Happy hoopin', vert. $4, Jumping for joy, vert.

Perf. 14x13½, 13½x14

1994, Mar. 15 Litho.

829	A100	10c multicolored	.25	.25
830	A100	25c multicolored	.25	.25
831	A100	50c multicolored	.55	.55
832	A100	80c multicolored	.80	.80
833	A100	$1 multicolored	.90	.90
834	A100	$1.50 multicolored	1.30	1.30
835	A100	$4 multicolored	3.50	3.50
836	A100	$5 multicolored	4.50	4.50
		Nos. 829-836 (8)	12.05	12.05

Souvenir Sheets

837	A100	$6 multicolored	12.00	12.00
838	A100	$6 multicolored	12.00	12.00

Hummel Figurines — A101

Designs: 5c, Umbrella Girl. 25c, For Father. 50c, Apple Tree Girl. 80c, March Winds. $1, Have the Sun in Your Heart. $1.60, Blue Belle. $2, Winter Fun. $5, Apple Tree Boy.

1994, Apr. 6 Litho. *Perf. 14*

839-846	A101	Set of 8	11.50	11.50
845a		Souv. sheet, #839, 843-845	4.00	4.00
846a		Souv. sheet, #840-842, 846	6.50	6.50

Beekeeping — A102

Designs: 50c, Beekeeper cutting wild nest of bees. 80c, Group of beekeepers, 1987. $1.60, Decapping frames of honey. $3, Queen bee rearing.

$6, Queen bee, worker bees, woman extracting honey.

1994, June 13 Litho. *Perf. 14*

847-850	A102	Set of 4	7.75	7.75

Souvenir Sheet

851	A102	$6 multicolored	7.50	7.50
a.		Ovptd. in sheet margin	5.50	5.50

No. 851a Overprinted "2nd Caribbean Beekeeping Congress / August 14-18, 2000" in sheet margin. Issued 8/14/00.

Issued: No. 851a, 8/17/00.

Miniature Sheet

Cats — A103

Designs: a, Blue point Himalayan. b, Black & white Persian. c, Cream Persian. d, Red Persian. e, Persian. f, Persian black smoke. g, Chocolate smoke Persian. h, Black Persian.

Each $6: No. 853, Brown tabby Persian. No. 854, Silver tabby Persian.

1994, July 20

852	A103	80c Sheet of 8, #a.-h.	7.00	7.00

Souvenir Sheets

853-854	A103	Set of 2	21.00	21.00

Marine Life A104

Marine Life A104a

Designs: 10c, Striped burrfish. 25c, Black coral, white & yellow, vert. 40c, Black coral, white & red, vert. 50c, Black coral, yellow & green, vert. 80c, Black coral, spiral-shaped, vert. $1, Blue-striped grunt. $1.60, Blue angelfish. $3, Cocoa damselfish.

No. 864a, Flameback angelfish. b, Reef bass. c, Honey gregory. d, Saddle squirrelfish. e, Cobalt chromis. f, Cleaner goby. g, Slendertail cardinalfish. h, Royal gramma.

Each $6: No. 865, Sailfish, vert. No. 866, Blue marlin.

1994, July 25 Litho. *Perf. 14*

856-863	A104	Set of 8	8.00	8.00
860a		Strip of 4, #857-860	4.00	4.00
860b		Min. sheet, 3 each #857-860	13.00	13.00

Miniature Sheet of 8

864	A104a	50c #a.-h.	9.50	9.50
i.		Ovptd. in sheet margin	4.00	4.00

Souvenir Sheets

865-866	A104a	Set of 2	24.00	24.00

Nos. 857-860, World Wildlife Fund. No. 864i overprinted in sheet margin with PHILAKOREA '94 emblem.

Issued: #864i, 8/16; #860b, 7/25.

Local Architecture — A105

Designs: 25c, Residence, Barnes Ghaut Village. 50c, House above grocery store, Newcastle. $1, Treasury Building, Charlestown. $5, House above supermarket, Charlestown. $6, Apartment houses.

1994, Aug. 22
867-870 A105 Set of 4 8.00 8.00

Souvenir Sheet

871 A105 $6 multicolored 5.25 5.25

Order of the Caribbean Community — A106

First award recipients: 25c, William Demas, economist, Trinidad and Tobago. 50c, Sir Shridath Ramphal, statesman, Guyana. $1, Derek Walcott, writer, Nobel Laureate, St. Lucia.

1994, Sept. 1
872-874 A106 Set of 3 3.25 3.25

Miniature Sheet of 8

PHILAKOREA '94 — A107

Folding screen, longevity symbols embroidered on silk, Late Choson Dynasty: a, #1. b, #2. c, #3. d, #4. e, #5. f, #6. g, #7. h, #8.

1994 Litho. *Perf. 14*
875 A107 50c #a.-h. 5.00 5.00

Christmas — A108

Different details from paintings: 20c, 40c, 50c, $5, The Virgin Mary as Queen of Heaven, by Jan Provost. 80c, $1, $1.60, $3, Adoration of the Magi, by Workshop of Hugo van der Goes.
No. 884, The Virgin Mary as Queen of Heaven (complete). $6, Adoration of the Magi (complete).

1994, Dec. 1 Litho. *Perf. 14*
876-883 A108 Set of 8 10.00 10.00

Souvenir Sheets

884 A108 $5 multicolored 5.25 5.25
885 A108 $6 multicolored 6.25 6.25

Disney Valentines — A109

Designs: 10c, Mickey, Minnie. 25c, Donald, Daisy. 50c, Pluto, Fifi. 80c, Clarabelle, Horace Horsecollar. $1, Pluto, Figaro. $1.50, Polly, Peter Penguin. $4, Prunella Pullet, Hick Rooster. $5, Jenny Wren, Cock Robin.
Each $6: No. 894, Minnie, vert. No. 895, Daisy, vert.

1995, Feb. 14 Litho. *Perf. 14x13½*
886-893 A109 Set of 8 11.50 11.50

Souvenir Sheets
Perf. 13½x14

894-895 A109 Set of 2 11.50 11.50

Birds — A110

Designs: 50c, Hooded merganser. 80c, Green-backed heron. $2, Double crested cormorant. $3, Ruddy duck.
Hummingbirds: No. 900a, Rufous-breasted hermit. b, Purple-throated carib. c, Green mango. d, Bahama woodstar. e, Hispaniolan emerald. f, Antillean crested. g, Green-throated carib. h, Antillean mango. i, Vervian. j, Jamaican mango. k, Cuban emerald. l, Blue-headed.
Each $6: No. 901, Black skimmer. No. 902, Snowy plover.

1995, Mar. 30 Litho. *Perf. 14*
896-899 A110 Set of 4 3.75 3.75

Miniature Sheet of 12

900 A110 50c #a.-l. 10.00 10.00

Souvenir Sheets

901-902 A110 Set of 2 10.00 10.00

Dogs A111

Designs: 25c, Pointer. 50c, Old Danish pointer. $1, German short-haired pointer. $2, English setter.
No. 907a, Irish setter. b, Weimaraner. c, Gordon setter. d, Britanny spaniel. e, American cocker spaniel. f, English cocker spaniel. g, Labrador retriever. h, Golden retriever. i, Flat-coated retriever.
Each $6: #908, Bloodhound. #909, German shepherd.

1995, May 23 Litho. *Perf. 14*
903-906 A111 Set of 4 2.75 2.75

Miniature Sheet of 9

907 A111 80c #a.-i. 11.00 11.00

Souvenir Sheets

908-909 A111 Set of 2 11.00 11.00

Cacti — A112

Designs: 40c, Schulumbergera truncata. 50c, Echinocereus pectinatus. 80c, Mammillaria zelmanniana alba. $1.60, Lobivia hertriehiana. $2, Hamatocatcus setispinus. $3, Astrophytum myriostigma.
Each $6: No. 916, Opuntia robusta. No. 917, Rhipsalidopsis gaertneri.

1995, June 20 Litho. *Perf. 14*
910-915 A112 Set of 6 6.50 6.50

Souvenir Sheets

916-917 A112 Set of 2 10.00 10.00

Miniature Sheets of 6 or 8

End of World War II, 50th Anniv. — A113

Famous World War II Personalities: No. 918: a, Clark Gable. b, Audie Murphy. c, Glenn Miller. d, Joe Louis. e, Jimmy Doolittle. f, John Hersey. g, John F. Kennedy. h, Jimmy Stewart.
Planes: No. 919: a, F4F Wildcat. b, F4U-1A Corsair. c, Vought SB2U Vindicator. d, F6-F Hellcat. e, SDB Dauntless. f, TBF-1 Avenger.
Each $6: No. 920, Jimmy Doolittle, vert. No. 921, Fighter plane landing on aircraft carrier.

1995, July 20
918 A113 $1.25 #a.-h. + label 10.00 10.00
919 A113 $2 #a.-f. + label 11.00 11.00

Souvenir Sheets

920-921 A113 Set of 2 15.00 15.00

UN, 50th Anniv. — A114

People of various races: No. 922a, $1.25, Two men, child. b, $1.60, Man wearing turban, man with beard, woman. c, $3, Two men in business suits, woman.
$6, Nelson Mandela.

1995, July 20 Litho. *Perf. 14*
922 A114 Strip of 3, #a.-c. 4.25 4.25

Souvenir Sheet

923 A114 $6 multicolored 4.50 4.50

No. 922 is a continuous design.

1995 Boy Scout Jamboree, Holland — A115

Scouts in various activities: No. 924a, $1, Two wearing backpacks. b, $2, One holding rope, one wearing backpack. c, $4, One crossing rope bridge, one looking at map, natl. flag.
$6, Scout in kayak.

1995, July 20
924 A115 Strip of 3, #a.-c. 5.50 5.50

Souvenir Sheet

925 A115 $6 multicolored 6.00 6.00

No. 924 is a continuous design.

Rotary Intl., 90th Anniv. A116

Designs: $5, Rotary emblem, natl. flag.
$6, Rotary emblem, beach.

1995, July 20
926 A116 $5 multicolored 4.00 4.00

Souvenir Sheet

927 A116 $6 multicolored 4.75 4.75

Queen Mother, 95th Birthday — A117

No. 928: a, Drawing. b, Pink hat. c, Formal portrait. d, Green blue hat.
$6, Wearing crown jewels.

1995, July 20 *Perf. 13½x14*
928 A117 $1.50 Block or strip of 4, #a.-d. 4.50 4.50

Souvenir Sheet

928E A117 $6 multicolored 4.75 4.75

No. 928 was issued in sheets of 2.
Sheets of Nos. 928 and 928E exist with margins overprinted with black border and text "In Memoriam 1900-2002."

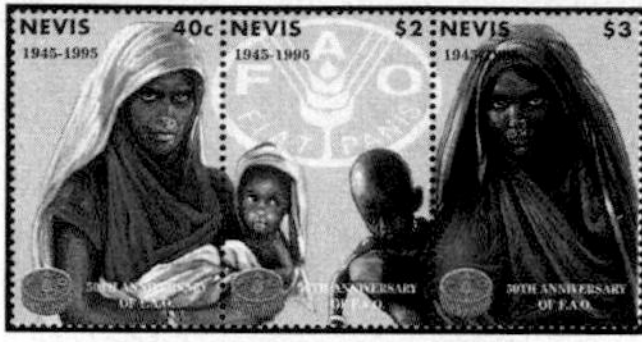

FAO, 50th anniv. — A118

No. 929a, 40c, Woman with tan sari over head. b, $2, FAO emblem, two infants. c, $3, Woman with blue sari over head.
$6, Man with hands around hoe handle.

1995, July 20 *Perf. 14*
929 A118 Strip of 3, #a.-c. 4.25 4.25

Souvenir Sheet

930 A118 $6 multicolored 4.75 4.75

No. 929 is a continuous design.

Miniature Sheet of 9

Nobel Prize Recipients — A119

No. 931: a, Emil A. von Behring, medicine, 1901. b, Wilhelm Roentgen, physics, 1901. c, Paul J.L. Heyse, literature, 1910. d, Le Duc Tho, peace, 1973. e, Yasunari Kawabata, 1968. f, Tsung-Dao Lee, physics, 1957. g, Werner Heisenberg, physics, 1932. h, Johannes Stark, physics, 1919. i, Wilhelm Wien, physics, 1911.
$6, Kenzaburo Oe, literature, 1994.

1995, July 20
931 A119 $1.25 #a.-i. 9.50 9.50

Souvenir Sheet

932 A119 $6 multicolored 4.75 4.75

Souvenir Sheet

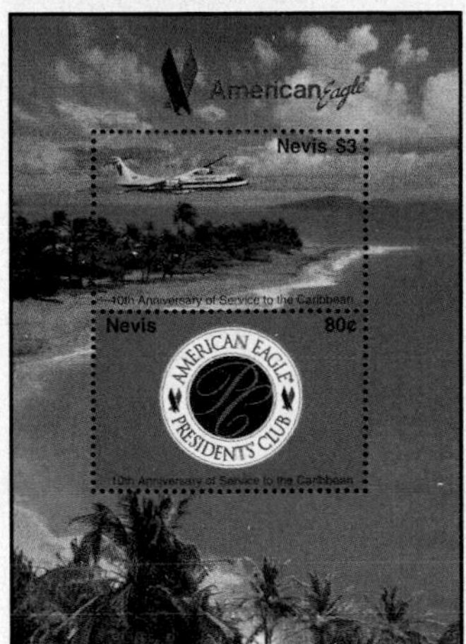

American Eagle Service, 10th Anniv. — A120

a, 80c, President's Club Emblem. b, $3, Airplane over beach.

1995, Aug. 28 Litho. *Perf. 14*
933 A120 Sheet of 2, #a.-b. 3.75 3.75

Miniature Sheet of 16

Marine Life — A121

No. 934: a, Great egrets. b, 17th cent. ship. c, Marlin. d, Herring gulls. e, Nassau groupers. f, Manta ray. g, Leopard shark, hammerhead shark. h, Hourglass dolphins. i, Spanish hogfish. j, Jellyfish, sea horses. k, Angel fish. l, Hawsbill turtle. m, Octopus vulgaris (i, j, m). n, Moray eel (o). o, Queen angelfish, butterflyfish. p, Ghost crab, sea star.
Each $6: No. 935, Nassau grouper. No. 936, Queen angelfish, vert.

1995, Sept. 1
934 A121 50c #a.-p. 8.00 8.00

Souvenir Sheets

935-936 A121 Set of 2 11.00 11.00

Singapore '95 (#935-936).

Natl. Telephone Co., SKANTEL Ltd., 10th Anniv. — A122

Designs: $1, Repairman working on telephone. $1.50, Company sign on building.
$5, Front of SKANTEL's Nevis office, horiz.

1995, Oct. 23 Litho. *Perf. 14*
937 A122 $1 multicolored .90 .90
938 A122 $1.50 multicolored 1.25 1.25

Souvenir Sheet

939 A122 $5 multicolored 4.50 4.50

Christmas Paintings, by Duccio di Buoninsegna (1250-1318) — A123

Details or entire paintings: 20c, Rucellai Madonna and Child. 50c, Border angel from Rucellai Madonna facing left. 80c, Madonna and Child. $1, The Annuniciation. $1.60, Madonna and Child. $3, Border angel from Rucellai Madonna facing right.
No. 946, Nativity with Prophets Isiah and Ezekiel. No. 947, Crevole Madonna.

1995, Dec. 1 Litho. *Perf. 13½x14*
940-945 A123 Set of 6 7.50 7.50

Souvenir Sheets

946 A123 $5 multicolored 4.75 4.75
947 A123 $6 multicolored 5.50 5.50

Four Seasons Resort, 5th Anniv. A124

Designs: 25c, Beach, resort buildings. 50c, Sailboats on beach. 80c, Golf course. $2, Premier Simeon Daniel laying cornerstone.
$6, Lounge chair on beach, sunset.

1996, Feb. 14 Litho. *Perf. 14*
948-951 A124 Set of 4 2.75 2.75

Souvenir Sheet

952 A124 $6 multicolored 4.75 4.75

New Year 1996 (Year of the Rat) — A125

Rat, various plant life, with olive margin: Nos. 953: a, Looking up at butterfly. b, Crawling left. c, Looking up at horsefly. d, Looking up at dragonfly.
Nos. 954a-954d: like Nos. 953a-953d, with yellow brown margin.
$3, Berries above rat.

1996, Feb, 28
953 A125 $1 Block of 4, #a.-d. 3.00 3.00

Miniature Sheet

954 A125 $1 Sheet of 4, #a.-d. 3.00 3.00

Souvenir Sheet

955 A125 $3 multicolored 3.00 3.00

No. 953 was issued in sheets of 16 stamps.

Pagodas of China A126

#956: a, Qian Qing Gong, 1420, Beijing. b, Qi Nian Dian, Temple of Heaven, Beijing. c, Zhongnanhai, Beijing. d, Da Zing Hall, Shenyang Palace. e, Temple of the Sleeping Buddha, Beijing. f, Huang Qiong Yu, Alter of Heaven, Beijing. g, Grand Bell Temple, Beijing. h, Imperial Palace, Beijing. i, Pu Tuo Temple.
$6, Summer Palace of emperor Wan Yanliang, 1153, Beijing, vert.

1996, May 15 Litho. *Perf. 14*
956 A126 $1 Sheet of 9, #a.-i. 6.75 6.75

Souvenir Sheet

957 A126 $6 multicolored 4.50 4.50

CHINA '96, 9th Asian Intl. Philatelic Exhibition (#956).

Queen Elizabeth II, 70th Birthday — A127

Queen wearing: a, Blue dress, pearls. b, Formal white dress. c, Purple dress, hat.
$6, In uniform at trooping of the color.

1996, May 15 Litho. *Perf. 13½x14*
958 A127 $2 Strip of 3, #a.-c. 3.75 3.75

Souvenir Sheet

959 A127 $6 multicolored 3.75 3.75

No. 958 was issued in sheets of 9 stamps with each strip in a different order.

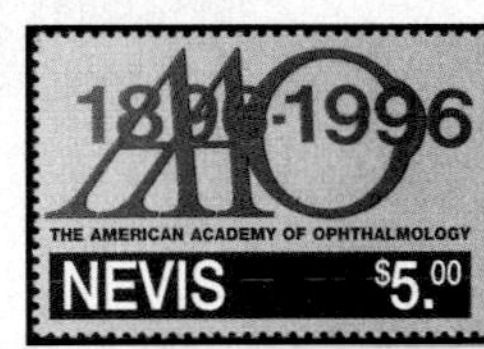

1996 Summer Olympic Games, Atlanta A128

Designs: 25c, Ancient Greek athletes boxing. 50c, Mark Spitz, gold medalist, swimming, 1972. 80c, Siegbert Horn, kayak singles gold medalist, 1972. $3, Slegestor Triumphal Arch, Munich, vert.
Pictures inside gold medals: No. 964, vert.: a, Jim Thorpe. b, Glenn Morris. c, Bob Mathias. d, Rafer Johnson. e, Bill Toomey. f, Nikolay Avilov. g, Bruce Jenner. h, Daley Thompson. i, Christian Schenk.
Each $5: No. 965, Willi Holdorf, vert. No. 966, Hans-Joachim Walde, silver medal, vert.

1996, May 28 *Perf. 14*
960-963 A128 Set of 4 3.75 3.75
964 A128 $1 Sheet of 9, #a.-i. 7.25 7.25

Souvenir Sheets

965-966 A128 Set of 2 15.00 15.00

Olymphilex '96 (#965).

UNESCO, 50th Anniv. — A129

25c, Cave paintings, Tassili N'Ajjer, Algeria. $2, Tikal Natl. Park, Guatemala, vert. $3, Temple of Hera at Samos, Greece.
$6, Pueblo, Taos, US.

1996, July 1 Litho. *Perf. 14*
967-969 A129 Set of 3 4.75 4.75

Souvenir Sheet

970 A129 $6 multicolored 4.50 4.50

UNICEF, 50th Anniv. A130

25c, Children reading book. 50c, Girl receiving innoculation. $4, Faces of young people.
$6, Girl, vert.

1996, July 1
971-973 A130 Set of 3 4.50 4.50

Souvenir Sheet

974 A130 $6 multicolored 4.50 4.50

Disney's Sweethearts — A131

Designs: a, Pocahontas, John Smith, Flit. b, Mowgli, The Girl, Kaa. c, Belle, Beast, Mrs. Potts, Chip. d, Cinderella, Prince Charming, Jaq. e, Pinocchio, Dutch Girl Marionette, Jiminy Cricket. f, Grace Martin, Henry Coy. g, Snow White, Prince. h, Aladdin, Jasmine, Abu. i, Pecos Bill, Slue Foot Sue.
Each $6: No. 977, Sleeping Beauty, Prince Phillip, vert. No. 978, Ariel, Eric.

Perf. 14x13½, 13½x14
1996, June 17 Litho.
975 A131 $2 Sheet of 9, #a.-i. 21.00 21.00

Souvenir Sheets

977-978 A131 Set of 2 13.00 13.00

A number has been reserved for an additional sheet with this set.

American Academy of Ophthalmology, Cent. — A132

1996, July 1 Litho. *Perf. 14*
979 A132 $5 multicolored 4.00 4.00

Flowers — A133

Designs: 25c, Rothmannia longiflora. 50c, Gloriosa simplex. $2, Catharanthus roseus. $3, Plumbago auriculata.
No. 984: a, Monodora myristica. b, Giraffa camelopardalis. c, Adansonia digitata. d, Ansellia gigantea. e, Geissorhiza rochensis. f, Arctotis venusta. g, Gladiohis cardinalis. h, Eucomis bicolor. i, Protea obtusifolia.
$5, Stelitzia reginae.

1996, Sept. 24 Litho. *Perf. 14*
980-983 A133 Set of 4 4.25 4.25
984 A133 $1 Sheet of 9, #a.-i. 6.75 6.75

Souvenir Sheet

985 A133 $5 multicolored 3.75 3.75

Christmas A134

Designs: 25c, Western meadowlark, vert. 50c, American goldfinch. 80c, Santa in sleigh, reindeer. $1, Western meadowlark, diff., vert. $1.60, Mockingbird, vert. $5, Yellow-rumped caleque.

Each $6: No. 992, Macaw. No. 993, Vermilion flycatcher.

1996, Dec. 2 Litho. *Perf. 14*

986-991 A134 Set of 6 7.25 7.25

Souvenir Sheets

992-993 A134 Set of 2 9.00 9.00

New Year 1997 (Year of the Ox) — A135

Painting, "Five Oxen," by Han Huang: a, 50c. b, 80c. c, $1.60. d, $2.

1997, Jan. 16 Litho. *Perf. 14x15*

994 A135 Sheet of 4, #a.-d. + label 4.25 4.25

A136

Pandas: a, Eating leaves on branch. b, Face, eating. c, Paws holding object. d, Hanging upside down. e, Lying between tree branch. f, Climbing tree.

$5, Mother, cub.

1997, Feb. 12 Litho. *Perf. 14*

995 A136 $1.60 Sheet of 6, #a.-f. 9.50 9.50

Souvenir Sheet

996 A136 $5 multicolored 3.75 3.75

Hong Kong '97.

A137

Cricket Players: 25c, Elquemedo Willet. 80c, Stuart Williams. $2, Keith Arthurton.

Each $5: No. 1000, Willet, Arthurton, Williams, 1990 Nevis team. No. 1001, Williams, Arthurton, 1994 West Indies team, vert.

1997, May 1 Litho. *Perf. 14*

997-999 A137 Set of 3 2.25 2.25

Souvenir Sheets

1000-1001 A137 Set of 2 7.50 7.50

Queen Elizabeth II, Prince Philip, 50th Wedding Anniv. A138

No. 1002: a, Queen Elizabeth II. b, Royal arms. c, Prince, Queen in red hat. d, Queen in blue coat, Prince. e, Caernarfon Castle. f, Prince Philip.

$5, Queen wearing crown.

1997, May 29 Litho. *Perf. 14*

1002 A138 $1 Sheet of 6, #a.-f. 5.00 5.00

Souvenir Sheet

1003 A138 $5 multicolored 4.00 4.00

Paintings by Hiroshige (1797-1858) A139

No. 1004: a, Scattered Pines, Tone River. b, Nakagawa River Mouth. c, Niijuku Ferry. d, Horie and Nekozane. e, View of Konodai and the Tone River. f, Maple Trees at Mama, Tekona Shrine & Bridge.

Each $6: No. 1005, Mitsumata Wakarenofuchi. No. 1006, Moto-Hachinan Shrine, Sunamura.

1997, May 29 *Perf. 13½x14*

1004 A139 $1.60 Sheet of 6, #a.-f. 8.00 8.00

Souvenir Sheets

1005-1006 A139 Set of 2 9.00 9.00

Paul Harris (1868-1947), Founder of Rotary Intl. — A140

$2, Literacy promotion, portrait of Harris.

$5, Rotary Village Corps coaching soccer for youths in Chile.

1997, May 29 *Perf. 14*

1007 A140 $2 multicolored 1.75 1.75

Souvenir Sheet

1008 A140 $5 multicolored 3.75 3.75

Heinrich von Stephan (1831-97) A141

No. 1009: a, Russian Reindeer Post, 1859. b, Von Stephan, UPU emblem. c, Steamboat, City of Cairo, 1800's.

$5, Portrait of Von Stephan, Bavarian postal messenger, 1640.

1997, May 29

1009 A141 $1.60 Sheet of 3, #a.-c. 3.50 3.50

Souvenir Sheet

1010 A141 $5 multicolored 3.75 3.75

PACIFIC 97.

Butterflies and Moths A142

10c, Crimson speckled. 25c, Purple emperor. 50c, Regent skipper. 80c, Provence burnet moth. $1, Common wall butterfly. $4, Cruiser butterfly.

No. 1017: a, Red-lined geometrid. b, Boisduval's autumnal moth. c, Blue pansy. d, Common clubtail. e, Tufted jungle queen. f, Lesser marbled fritillary. g, Peacock royal. h, Emperor gum moth. i, Orange swallow-tailed moth.

Each $5: No. 1018, Jersey tiger. No. 1019, Japanese emperor.

1997, May 12 Litho. *Perf. 14*

1011-1016 A142 Set of 6 5.50 5.50

1017 A142 $1 Sheet of 9, #a.-i. 7.25 7.25

Souvenir Sheets

1018-1019 A142 Set of 2 7.50 7.50

Souvenir Sheet

Mother Goose — A143

1997, May 29

1020 A143 $5 Boy, two pigeons 3.75 3.75

Golf Courses of the World A144

Designs: a, Augusta National, U.S. b, Cabo Del Sol, Mexico. c, Cypress Point, U.S. d, Lost City, South Africa. e, Moscow Country Club, Russia. f, New South Wales, Australia. g, Royal Montreal, Canada. h, St. Andrews, Scotland. i, Four Seasons Resort, Nevis.

1997, July 15

1021 A144 $1 Sheet of 9, #a.-i. 7.50 7.50

Mushrooms A145

Designs: 25c, Cantharellus cibarius. 50c, Stropharia aeruginosa. $3, Lactarius turpis. $4, Entoloma Jypeatum.

No. 1026: a, Suillus luteus. b, Amanita musearia. c, Lactarius rufus. d, Amanita rubescens. e, Armillaria mellea. f, Russula sardonia.

No. 1027: a, Boletus edulis. b, Pholiota lenta. c, Cortinarius bolaris. d, Coprinus picaceus. e, Amanita phalloides. f, Cystolepiota aspera.

Each $5: No. 1028, Gymnopilus junonius. No. 1029, Galerina mutabilis, philiota auriuella.

1997, Aug. 12 Litho. *Perf. 13*

1022-1025 A145 Set of 4 6.00 6.00

Sheets of 6

1026 A145 80c #a.-f. 3.75 3.75

1027 A145 $1 #a.-f. 4.50 4.50

Souvenir Sheets

1028-1029 A145 Set of 2 8.00 8.00

Diana, Princess of Wales (1961-97) — A146

Various portraits.

1997, Sept. 19 Litho. *Perf. 14*

1030 A146 $1 Sheet of 9, #a.-i. 7.50 7.50

Trains A147

Designs: 10c, New Pacific type, Victorian Government Railways, Australia. 50c, Express locomotive, Imperial Government Railways, Japan. 80c, Turbine driven locomotive, London, Midland & Scottish Railway. $1, Electric passenger & freight locomotive, Swiss Federal Railways. $2, 3 cylinder compound express locomotive, London, Midland, Scottish Railway. $3, Express locomotive Kestrel, Great Northern Railway, Ireland.

No. 1037: a, 2-8-2 Mikado, Sudan Government Railways. b, Mohammed Ali El Kebir locomotive, Egyptian State Railways. c, "Schools" class locomotive, Southern Railway. d, Drum Battery Train, Great Southern Railways, Ireland. e, "Pacific" express locomotive, German State Railways. f, Mixed traffic locomotive, Canton-Hankow Railway, China.

Each $5: No. 1038, "King" class express, Great Western Railway. No. 1039, High pressure locomotive, London, Midland and Scottish Railway.

1997, Sept. 29 Litho. *Perf. 14*

1031-1036 A147 Set of 6 6.25 6.25

1037 A147 $1.50 Sheet of 6, #a.-f. 7.25 7.25

Souvenir Sheets

1038-1039 A147 Set of 2 8.00 8.00

Christmas — A148

Entire paintings or details: 20c, 25c, Diff. details from Selection of Angels, by Durer. 50c, Andromeda and Perseus, by Rubens. 80c, $1.60, Diff. details from Astronomy, by Raphael. $5, Holy Trinity, by Raphael.

Each $5: No. 1046, Ezekiel's Vision, by Raphael, horiz. No. 1047, Justice, by Rapahel, horiz.

1997, Nov. 26 Litho. *Perf. 14*

1040-1045 A148 Set of 6 7.00 7.00

Souvenir Sheets

1046-1047 A148 Set of 2 7.50 7.50

New Year 1998 (Year of the Tiger) — A149

Tigers: No. 1048: a, Jumping right. b, Looking back over shoulder. c, Jumping left. d, Looking forward.
No. 1049, Tiger, vert.

1998, Jan. 19 Litho. *Perf. 14*
1048 A149 80c Sheet of 4, #a.-d. 4.00 4.00

Souvenir Sheet

1049 A149 $2 multicolored 2.25 2.25

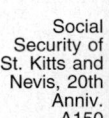

Social Security of St. Kitts and Nevis, 20th Anniv. A150

Designs: 30c, Logo, vert. $1.20, Front of Social Security building.
$6, Social Security staff, Charlestown, Nevis.

1998, Feb. 2 Litho. *Perf. 13*
1050 A150 30c multicolored .30 .30
1051 A150 $1.20 multicolored .90 .90

Souvenir Sheet
Perf. 13½x13

1052 A150 $6 multicolored 4.50 4.50

No. 1052 contains one 56x36mm stamp.

Fruit — A151

1998, Mar. 9 *Perf. 14*
No Year Imprint Below Design

1053 A151 5c Soursop .25 .25
1054 A151 10c Carambola .25 .25
1055 A151 25c Guava .25 .25
1056 A151 30c Papaya .25 .25
1057 A151 50c Mango .40 .40
1058 A151 60c Golden apple .45 .45
1059 A151 80c Pineapple .60 .60
1060 A151 90c Watermelon .70 .70
1061 A151 $1 Bananas .75 .75
1062 A151 $1.80 Orange 1.40 1.40
1063 A151 $3 Honeydew 2.25 2.25
1064 A151 $5 Cantaloupe 3.75 3.75
1065 A151 $10 Pomegranate 7.50 7.50
1066 A151 $20 Cashew 15.00 15.00
Nos. 1053-1066 (14) 33.80 33.80

For overprints see #O55-O66.

2000, Mar. 22
Inscribed "2000" Below Design

1054a A151 10c multicolored .25 .25
1056a A151 30c multicolored .40 .25
1059a A151 80c multicolored .90 .60
1062a A151 $1.80 multicolored 1.75 1.40
1064a A151 $5 multicolored 4.00 4.00
1065a A151 $10 multicolored 7.50 7.50
Nos. 1054a-1065a (6) 14.80 14.00

Endangered Species — A152

Designs: 30c, Fish eagle. 80c, Summer tangers. 90c, Orangutan. $1.20, Tiger. $2, Cape pangolin. $3, Moatzin.
No. 1073: a, Chimpanzee. b, Keel-billed toucan. c, Chaco peccary. d, Spadefoot toad. e, Howler monkey. f, Alaskan brown bear. g, Koala. h, Brown pelican. i, Iguana.
Each $5: No. 1074, Mandrill. No. 1075, Polar bear.

1998, Mar. 31 Litho. *Perf. 14*
1067-1072 A152 Set of 6 6.50 6.50
1073 A152 $1 Sheet of 9, #a.-i. 7.00 7.00

Souvenir Sheets

1074-1075 A152 Set of 2 8.50 8.50

Aircraft A153

Designs: 10c, Boeing 747 200B. 90c, Cessna 185 Skywagon. $1.80, McDonnell Douglas DC-9 SO. $5, Airbus A300 B4.
No. 1080: a, Northrop B-2A. b, Lockheed SR-71A. c, Beechcraft T-44A. d, Sukhoi Su-27UB. e, Hawker Siddeley (BAe) Harrier GR.MK1. f, Boeing E-3A Sentry. g, Convair B-36H. h, IAI Kfir C2.
Each $5: No. 1081, Lockheed F-117A. No. 1082, Concorde G-BOAA.

1998, May 19 Litho. *Perf. 14*
1076-1079 A153 Set of 4 6.25 6.25
1080 A153 $1 Sheet of 8, #a.-h. 6.50 6.50

Souvenir Sheets

1081-1082 A153 Set of 2 8.25 8.25

#1081-1082 each contain 1 57x42mm stamp.

Chaim Topol Portraying Tevye from "Fiddler on the Roof" — A154

1998, May 17 Litho. *Perf. 13½*
1083 A154 $1.60 multicolored 1.75 1.75

Israel '98. Issued in sheets of 6.

Voice of Nevis (VON) Radio, 10th Anniv. A155

20c, Logo of Nevis Broadcasting Co., vert. 30c, Evered "Webbo" Herbert, station manager at controls. $1.20, Exterior of offices and studios.
$5, Merritt Herbert, managing director, opening ceremony, 1988.

1998, June 18 *Perf. 14*
1084-1086 A155 Set of 3 1.60 1.60

Souvenir Sheet

1087 A155 $5 multicolored 4.00 4.00

Intl. Year of the Ocean A156

30c, Butterflyfish. 80c, Bicolor cherub. $1.20, Silver badgerfish. $2, Asfur angelfish.
No. 1092, vert: a, Copperbanded butterflyfish. b, Forcepsfish. c, Double-saddled butterflyfish. d, Blue surgeonfish. e, Orbiculate batfish. f, Undulated triggerfish. g, Rock beauty. h, Flamefish. i, Queen angelfish.
No. 1093: a, Pygama cardinal fish. b, Wimplefish. c, Long-nosed filefish. d, Oriental sweetlips. e, Blue spotted boxfish. f, Blue stripe angelfish. g, Goldrim tang. h, Royal gramma. i, Common clownfish.
Each $5: No. 1094, Longhorned cowfish, vert. No. 1095, Red-faced batfish, vert.

1998, Aug. 18 Litho. *Perf. 14*
1088-1091 A156 Set of 4 5.75 5.75
1092 A156 90c Sheet of 9, #a.-i. 6.00 6.00
1093 A156 $1 Sheet of 9, #a.-i. 6.75 6.75

Souvenir Sheets

1094-1095 A156 Set of 2 8.50 8.50

Diana, Princess of Wales (1961-97) A157

1998, Oct. 15 Litho. *Perf. 14*
1096 A157 $1 multicolored .80 .80

No. 1096 was issued in sheets of 6.

Mahatma Gandhi (1869-1948) A158

Portraits: No. 1097, In South Africa, 1914. No. 1098, At Downing Street, London.

1998, Oct. 15
1097 A158 $1 multicolored .90 .90
1098 A158 $1 multicolored .90 .90

Nos. 1097-1098 were each issued in sheets of 6.

Royal Air Force, 80th Anniv. A159

Aircraft — #1100: a, Panavia Tornado F3 ADV. b, Panavia Tornado F3 IDV. c, Tristar K Mk1 Tanker refueling Panavia Tornado. d, Panavia Tornado GRI.
Each $5: No. 1101, Wessex helicopter, fighter plane. No. 1102, Early aircraft, birds.

1998, Oct. 15 Litho. *Perf. 14*
1100 A159 $2 Sheet of 4, #a.-d. 7.00 7.00

Souvenir Sheets

1101-1102 A159 Set of 2 9.25 9.25

1998 World Scouting Jamboree, Chile — A160

Designs: a, Four Boy Scouts from around the world. b, Boy Scout accompanying Gettysburg veterans, 1913. c, First black troop, Virginia, 1928.

1998, Oct. 15
1103 A160 $3 Sheet of 3, #a.-c. 7.50 7.50

Independence, 15th Anniv. — A161

Design: Prime Minister Kennedy Simmonds receiving constitutional instruments from Princess Margaret, Countess of Snowden.

1998, Oct. 15 Litho. *Perf. 14*
1104 A161 $1 multicolored .95 .95

Organization of American States, 50th Anniv. A162

1998, Oct. 15 *Perf. 14*
1105 A162 $1 multicolored .75 .75

Enzo Ferrari (1898-1988), Automobile Manufacturer — A163

No. 1106: a, 365 California. b, Pininfarina's P6. c, 250 LM.
$5, 212 Export Spyder.

1998, Oct. 15
1106 A163 $2 Sheet of 3, #a.-c. 5.50 5.50

Souvenir Sheet

1107 A163 $5 multicolored 4.75 4.75

No. 1107 contains one 91x35mm stamp.

Christmas — A164

Designs: 25c, Kitten, Santa. 60c, Kitten, ornament. 80c, Kitten in sock, vert. 90c, Puppy, presents. $1, Cherub sleeping, birds. $3, Child making snowball, vert.
Each $5: No. 1114, Family, vert. No. 1115, Two dogs.

1998, Nov. 24 Litho. *Perf. 14*
1108-1113 A164 Set of 6 5.25 5.25

Souvenir Sheets

1114-1115 A164 Set of 2 7.75 7.75

New Year 1999 (Year of the Rabbit) — A165

Color of pairs of rabbits — #1116: a, brown & gray. b, brown & white. c, brown. d, white & black spotted.
$5, Adult white rabbit, 3 bunnies.

1999, Jan. 4 Litho. *Perf. 14*
1116 A165 $1.60 Sheet of 4, #a.-d. 5.25 5.25

Souvenir Sheet

1117 A165 $5 multicolored 4.50 4.50

No. 1117 contains one 58x47mm stamp.

Disney Characters Playing Basketball A166

Basketball in background — #1118, each $1: a, Mickey in green. b, Donald. c, Minnie. d, Goofy. e, One of Donald's nephews. f, Goofy, Mickey. g, Mickey in purple. h, Huey, Dewey, Louie.

Green & white background — #1119, each $1: a, Mickey in purple. b, Goofy. c, Minnie in puple. d, Mickey in yellow & gray. e, Minnie in yellow. f, Donald. g, Donald & Mickey. h, One of Donald's nephews.

No. 1120, $5, Minnie, green bow, horiz. No. 1121, $5, Minnie, purple bow, horiz. No. 1122, $6, Mickey in purple, horiz. No. 1123, $6, Mickey in yellow, horiz.

Perf. 13½x14, 14x13½

1998, Dec. 24 **Litho.**

Sheets of 8, #a-h

1118-1119 A166 Set of 2 17.00 17.00

Souvenir Sheets

1120-1121 A166 Set of 2 8.75 8.75
1122-1123 A166 Set of 2 11.00 11.00

Mickey Mouse, 70th anniv.

1998 World Cup Soccer Players — A167

No. 1124: a, Laurent Blanc, France. b, Dennis Bergkamp, Holland. c, David Sukor, Croatia. d, Ronaldo, Brazil. e, Didier Deschamps, France. f, Patrick Kluivert, Holland. g, Rivaldo, Brazil. h, Zinedine Zidane, France.

$5, Zinedine Zidane, close-up.

1999, Jan. 18 ***Perf. 13½***

1124 A167 $1 Sheet of 8, #a.-h. 6.25 6.25

Souvenir Sheet

1125 A167 $5 multicolored 4.00 4.00

Australia '99, World Stamp Expo A168

Dinosaurs: 30c, Kritosaurus. 60c, Oviraptor. 80c, Eustreptospondylus. $1.20, Tenontosaurus. $2, Ouranosaurus. $3, Muttaburrasaurus.

No. 1132, $1.20: a, Edmontosaurus. b, Avimimus. c, Minmi. d, Segnosaurus. e, Kentrosaurus. f, Deinonychus.

No. 1133, #1.20: a, Saltasaurus. b, Compsoganthus c, Hadrosaurus. d, Tuojiangosaurus. e, Euoplocephalus. f, Anchisaurus.

Each $5: #1134, Triceratops. #1135, Stegosaurus.

1999, Feb. 22 **Litho.** ***Perf. 14***

1126-1131 A168 Set of 6 6.50 6.50

Sheets of 6, #a-f

1132-1133 A168 Set of 2 11.50 11.50

Souvenir Sheets

1134-1135 A168 Set of 2 8.00 8.00

World Leaders of the 20th Century — A169

No. 1136: a, Emperor Haile Selassie (1892-1975), Ethiopia. b, Selassie, Ethiopian warriors, flag. c, David Ben-Gurion (1886-1973), Prime Minister of Israel. d, Ben-Gurion, Israeli flag. e, Pres. Franklin Roosevelt (1882-1945), Eleanor Roosevelt (1884-1962), UN emblem. f, Roosevelts campaigning, US GI in combat. g, Mao Tse-tung (1893-1976), Chinese leader, 1934 Long March. h, Poster of Mao, soldier.

Each $5: No. 1137, Gandhi. No. 1138, Nelson Mandela.

1999, Mar. 8

1136 A169 90c Sheet of 8, #a.-h. 6.75 6.75

Souvenir Sheets

1137-1138 A169 Set of 2 8.00 8.00

#1136b-1136c, 1136f-1136g are each 53x38mm.

Birds A170

No. 1139, each $1.60: a, Yellow warbler. b, Common yellowthroat. c, Painted bunting. d, Belted kingfisher. e, American kestrel. f, Northern oriole.

No. 1140, each $1.60: a, Malachite kingfisher. b, Lilac-breasted roller. c, Swallow-tailed bee-eater. d, Eurasian jay. e, Black-collared apalis. f, Gray-backed camaroptera.

Each $5: No. 1141, Banaquit. No. 1142, Ground scraper thrush, vert.

1999, May 10 **Litho.** ***Perf. 14***

Sheets of 6, #a-f

1139-1140 A170 Set of 2 15.00 15.00

Souvenir Sheets

1141-1142 A170 Set of 2 8.00 8.00

Orchids A171

Designs: 20c, Phaius hybrid, vert. 25c, Cuitlauzina pendula, vert. 50c, Bletilla striata, vert. 80c, Cymbidium "Showgirl," vert. $1.60, Zygopetalum crinitium. $3, Dendrobium nobile.

No. 1149, vert, each $1: a, Cattleya pumpernickel. b, Odontocidium Arthur Elle. c, Neostylis Lou Sneary. d, Phalaenopsis Aprodite. e, Arkundina graminieolia. f, Cymbidium Hunter's Point. g, Rynchoatylis coelestis. h, Cymbidium Elf's castle.

No. 1150, vert, each $1: a, Cattleya intermedia. b, Cattleya Sophia Martin. c, Phalaenopsis Little Hal. d, Laeliocattleya alisal "Rodeo." e, Laelia lucasiana fournieri. f, Cymbidium Red beauty. g, Sobralia sp. h, Promenaea xanthina.

Each $5: No. 1151, Philippine wind orchid. No. 1152, Dragon's mouth.

1999, June 15 **Litho.** ***Perf. 14***

1143-1148 A171 Set of 6 5.50 5.50

Sheets of 8, #a-h

1149-1150 A171 14.50 14.50

Souvenir Sheets

1151-1152 A171 Set of 2 8.00 8.00

Wedding of Prince Edward and Sophie Rhys-Jones A172

No. 1153, each $2: a, Sophie in checked suit. b, Couple walking across grass. c, Sophie in black hat, suit, d, Prince Edward in white shirt.

No. 1154, each $2: a, Couple standing in front of building. b, Sophie wearing large hat. c, Sophie in black dress. d, Edward in striped shirt.

Each $5: No. 1155, Couple posing for engagement photo, horiz. No. 1156, Edward kissing Sophie, horiz.

1999, June 19 **Litho.** ***Perf. 14¼***

Sheets of 4, #a-d

1153-1154 A172 Set of 2 12.50 12.50

Souvenir Sheets

1155-1156 A172 Set of 2 8.00 8.00

IBRA '99, World Stamp Exhibition, Nuremberg — A173

Beuth 2-2-2 locomotive and: 30c, Baden #1. 80c, Brunswick #1.

Sailing ship Kruzenshstern and: 90c, Bergedorf #2 & #1a. $1, Bremen #1.

$5, Regensburg air post label on cover.

1999, July 1 ***Perf. 14x14½***

1157-1160 A173 Set of 4 2.75 2.75

Souvenir Sheet

1161 A173 $5 multicolored 3.50 3.50

Souvenir Sheets

PhilexFrance '99, World Philatelic Exhibition — A174

Trains: No. 1162, $5: First Class Carriage, 1837. No. 1163, $5: 141.R Mixed Traffic 2-8-2, 1949.

1999, July 1 ***Perf. 14x13½***

1162-1163 A174 Set of 2 8.25 8.25

Paintings by Hokusai (1760-1849) A175

Details or entire paintings — #1164: a, (Five) Women Returning Home at Sunset. b, The Blind. c, (Four) Women Returning Home at Sunset. d, A Young Man on a White Horse. e, The Blind (man with beard). f, A Peasant Crossing a Bridge.

No. 1165: a, Poppies (one in bloom). b, The Blind (man with goatee). c, Poppies. d, Abe No Nakamaro Gazing at the Moon from a Terrace. e, The Blind. f, Cranes on a Snowy Pine.

Each $5: No. 1166, Carp in a Waterfall. No. 1167, A Rider in the Snow.

1999, July 1 ***Perf. 13½x14***

Sheets of 6

1164 A175 $1 #a.-f. 4.50 4.50
1165 A175 $1.60 #a.-f. 7.25 7.25

Souvenir Sheets

1166-1167 A175 Set of 2 8.25 8.25

Culturama Festival, 25th Anniv. — A176

Designs: 30c, Steel drummers. 80c, Clowns. $1.80, Masqueraders with "Big Drum." No. 1171, $5, String band.

No. 1172, Masquerade dancers.

1999, July 1 **Litho.** ***Perf. 14***

1168-1171 A176 Set of 4 6.25 6.25

Souvenir Sheet

1172 A176 $5 multicolored 4.00 4.00

No. 1172 contains one 51x38mm stamp.

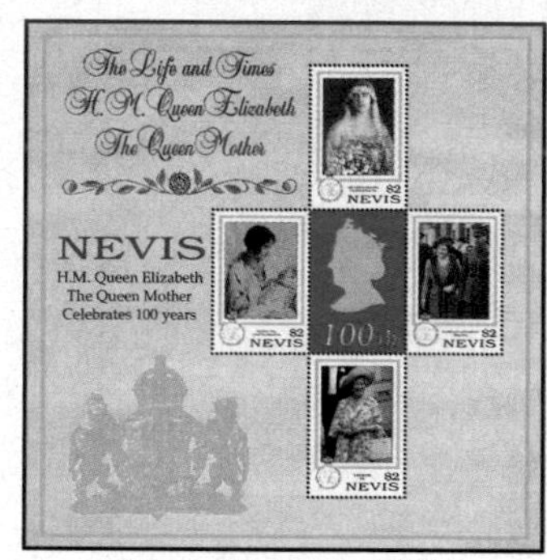

Queen Mother — A177

Queen Mother (b. 1900): No. 1173: a, In bridal gown, 1923. b, With Princess Elizabeth, 1926. c, With King George VI in World War II. d, Wearing hat, 1983.

$6, Wearing tiara, 1957.

Gold Frames

1999, Aug. 4 **Sheet of 4** ***Perf. 14***

1173 A177 $2 #a.-d., + label 6.25 6.25

Souvenir Sheet

Perf. 13¾

1174 A177 $6 multicolored 4.75 4.75

No. 1174 contains one 38x51mm stamp.

See Nos. 1287-1288.

Christmas — A178

30c, Adoration of the Magi, by Albrecht Durer. 90c, Canigiani Holy Family, by Raphael. $1.20, The Nativity, by Durer. $1.80, Madonna Surrounded by Angels, by Peter Paul Rubens. $3, Madonna Surrounded by Saints, by Rubens.

$5, Madonna and Child by a Window, by Durer, horiz.

1999, Nov. 12 **Litho.** ***Perf. 14***

1175-1179 A178 Set of 5 5.75 5.75

Souvenir Sheet

1180 A178 $5 multicolored 4.00 4.00

Millennium
A179

Scenes of Four Seasons Resort: a, Aerial view. b, Palm tree, beach. c, Golf course. d, Couple on beach.

1999 Litho. *Perf. 14¼x13¾*
1181 A179 30c Sheet of 4, #a.-d. .90 .90

Flowers
A180

Various flowers making up a photomosaic of Princess Diana.

1999, Dec. 31 Litho. *Perf. 13¾*
1182 A180 $1 Sheet of 8, #a.-h. 6.50 6.50

New Year 2000 (Year of the Dragon) — A181

No. 1183: a, Dragon showing 9 claws. b, Dragon showing 10 claws. c, Dragon showing 5 claws. d, Dragon showing 8 claws.
$5, Dragon, vert.

2000, Feb. 5 *Perf. 14*
1183 A181 $1.60 Sheet of 4, #a.-d. 4.75 4.75

Souvenir Sheet
Perf. 13¾
1184 A181 $5 multi 4.25 4.25

No. 1184 contains one 38x50mm stamp.

Millennium
A182

No. 1185 — Highlights of 1700-1750: a, Jonathan Swift writes "Gulliver's Travels." b, Manchu Dynasty flourishes in China. c, Bartolomeo Cristofori invents piano. d, Capt. William Kidd hanged for piracy. e, Astronomer William Herschel born. f, George I succeeds Queen Anne as British ruler. g, Russian treaty with China. h, Bubonic plague hits Austria and Germany. i, Kaigetsudo paints "Standing Woman." j, Queen Anne ascends to English throne. k, Anders Celsius invents centigrade scale for thermometer. l, Vitus Bering discovers Alaska and Aleutian Islands. m, Edmond Halley predicts return of comet. n, John and Charles Wesley found Methodism movement. o, Isaac Newton publishes "Opticks." p, England and Scotland form Great Britain (60x40mm). q, Johann Sebastian Bach composes "The Well-Tempered Clavier."

No. 1186 — Highlights of the 1990s: a, Boris Yeltsin becomes prime minister of Russian Federation. b, Gulf War begins. c, Civil War in Bosnia. d, Signing of the Oslo Accords. e, John Major, Albert Reynolds search for peace in Northern Ireland. f, F.W. De Klerk, Nelson Mandela end apartheid in South Africa. g, Cal Ripken, Jr. breaks record for most consecutive baseball games played. h, Kobe, Japan earthquake. i, Inca girl, believed to be 500 years old, found in ice. j, Sojourner beams back images from Mars. k, Dr. Ian Wilmot clones sheep "Dolly." l, Princess Diana dies in car crash. m, Hong Kong returned to China. n, Septuplets born and survive. o, Guggenheim Museum in Bilbao, Spain completed. p, Countdown to year 2000 (60x40mm). q, Pres. William J. Clinton impeached.

2000, Jan. 4 Litho. *Perf. 12¾x12½*
Sheets of 17
1185 A182 30c #a.-q., + label 5.00 5.00
1186 A182 50c #a.-q., + label 7.25 7.25

Misspellings and historical inaccuracies abound on Nos. 1185-1186.

Tropical Fish
A183

Designs: 30c, Spotted scat. 80c, Platy variatus. 90c, Emerald betta. $4, Cowfish.

No. 1191, each $1: a, Oriental sweetlips. b, Royal gramma. c, Threadfin butterflyfish. d, Yellow tang. e, Bicolor angelfish. f, Catalina goby. g, False cleanerfish. h, Powder blue surgeon.

No. 1192, each $1: a, Sailfin tang. b, Black-capped gramma. c, Majestic snapper. d, Purple firefish. e, Clown trigger. f, Yellow longnose. g, Clown wrasse. h, Yellow-headed jawfish.

Each $5: No. 1193, Clown coris. No. 1194, Clown killifish.

2000, Mar. 27 *Perf. 14*
1187-1190 A183 Set of 4 5.00 5.00

Sheets of 8, #a.-h.
1191-1192 A183 Set of 2 13.00 13.00

Souvenir Sheets
1193-1194 A183 Set of 2 8.00 8.00

Dogs — A184

Designs: 10c, Miniature pinscher. 20c, Pyrenean mountain dog. 30c, Welsh Springer spaniel. 80c, Alaskan malamute. $2, Bearded collie. $3, Amercian cocker spaniel.

No. 1201, horiz.: a, Beagle. b, Basset hound. c, St. Bernard. d, Rough collie. e, Shih tzu. f, American bulldog.

No. 1202, horiz.: a, Irish red and white setter. b, Dalmatian. c, Pomeranian. d, Chihuahua. e, English sheepdog. f, Samoyed.

Each $5: No. 1203, Leonberger. No. 1204, Longhaired miniature dachshund, horiz.

2000, May 1 Litho. *Perf. 14*
1195-1200 A184 Set of 6 5.25 5.25
1201 A184 90c Sheet of 6, #a-f 4.50 4.50
1202 A184 $1 Sheet of 6, #a-f 5.00 5.00

Souvenir Sheets
1203-1204 A184 Set of 2 8.50 8.50

100th Test Match at Lord's Ground — A185

Designs: $2, Elquemede Willett. $3, Keith Arthurton.
$5, Lord's Ground, horiz.

2000, June 10
1205-1206 A185 Set of 2 4.00 4.00

Souvenir Sheet
1207 A185 $5 multi 4.00 4.00

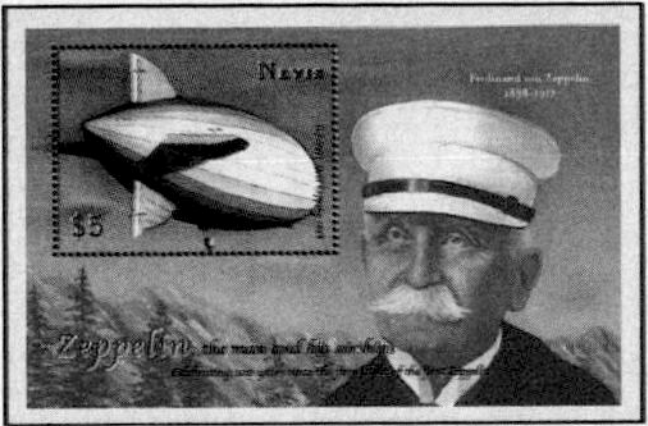
First Zeppelin Flight, Cent. — A186

No. 1208: a, LZ-129. b, LZ-1. c, LZ-11.
$5, LZ-127.

2000, June 10 *Perf. 14*
1208 A186 $3 Sheet of 3, #a-c 7.00 7.00

Souvenir Sheet
Perf. 14¼
1209 A186 $5 multi 4.25 4.25

No. 1208 contains three 38x25mm stamps.

Berlin Film Festival, 50th Anniv. — A187

No. 1210: a, Rani Radovi. b, Salvatore Giuliano. c, Schoenzeit für Füchse. d, Shirley MacLaine. e, Simone Signoret. f, Sohrab Shahid Saless.
$5, Komissar.

2000, June 10 *Perf. 14*
1210 A187 $1.60 Sheet of 6, #a-f 7.50 7.50

Souvenir Sheet
1211 A187 $5 multi 4.25 4.25

Spacecraft — A188

No. 1212, each $1.60: a, Mars IV probe. b, Mars Water. c, Mars 1. d, Viking. e, Mariner 7. f, Mars Surveyor.

No. 1213, each $1.60: a, Mariner 9. b, Mars 3. c, Mariner 4. d, Planet B. e, Mars Express Lander. f, Mars Express.

Each $5: No. 1214, Mars Observer. No. 1215, Mars Climate Observer, vert.

2000, June 10 Sheets of 6, #a-f
1212-1213 A188 Set of 2 15.00 15.00

Souvenir Sheets
1214-1215 A188 Set of 2 8.00 8.00

Souvenir Sheets

2000 Summer Olympics, Sydney — A189

No. 1216: a, Gisela Mauermeyer. b, Uneven bars. c, Wembley Stadium, London, and British flag. d, Ancient Greek horse racing.

2000, June 10
1216 A189 $2 Sheet of 4, #a-d 5.00 5.00

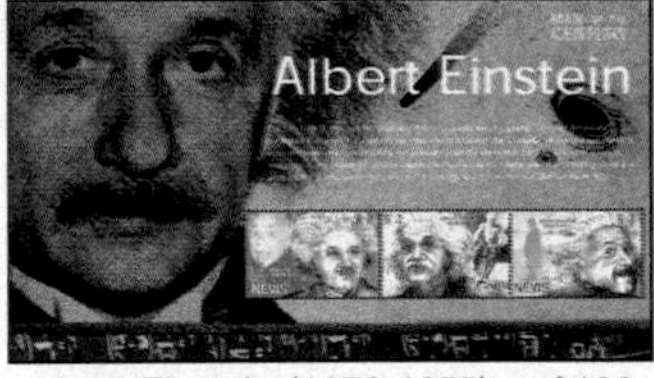

Albert Einstein (1879-1955) — A190

No. 1217: a, Sticking out tongue. b, Riding bicycle. c, Wearing hat.

2000, June 10
1217 A190 $2 Sheet of 3, #a-c 5.00 5.00

Public Railways, 175th Anniv. — A191

No. 1218: a, Locomotion No. 1, George Stephenson. b, Trevithick's 1804 drawing of locomotive.

2000, June 10
1218 A191 $3 Sheet of 2, #a-b 4.50 4.50

Johann Sebastian Bach (1685-1750) — A192

2000, June 10
1219 A192 $5 multi 4.25 4.25

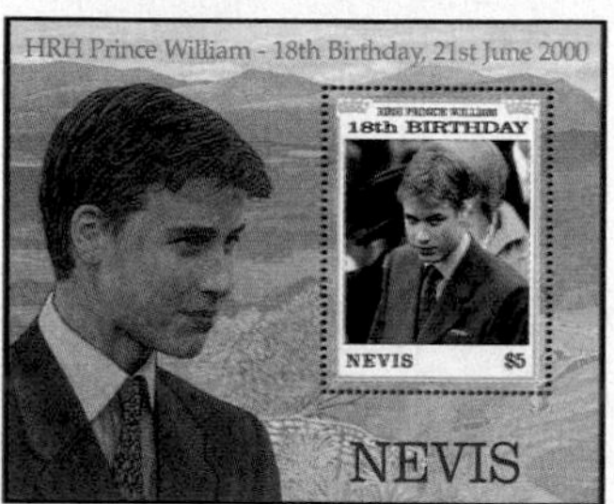

Prince William, 18th Birthday — A193

No. 1220: a, Reaching to shake hand. b, In ski gear. c, With jacket open. d, In sweater.
$5, In suit and tie.

2000, June 21 ***Perf. 14***
1220 A193 $1.60 Sheet of 4, #a-d 4.75 4.75

Souvenir Sheet
Perf. 13¾
1221 A193 $5 multi 4.00 4.00

No. 1220 contains four 28x42mm stamps.

Souvenir Sheets

Bob Hope, Entertainer — A194

No. 1222: a, Wearing Air Force Ranger uniform. b, With Sammy Davis, Jr. c, With wife, Dolores. d, On golf course. e, In suit behind microphone. f, Walking.

2000, July 10 ***Perf. 14***
1222 A194 $1 Sheet of 6, #a-f 5.25 5.25

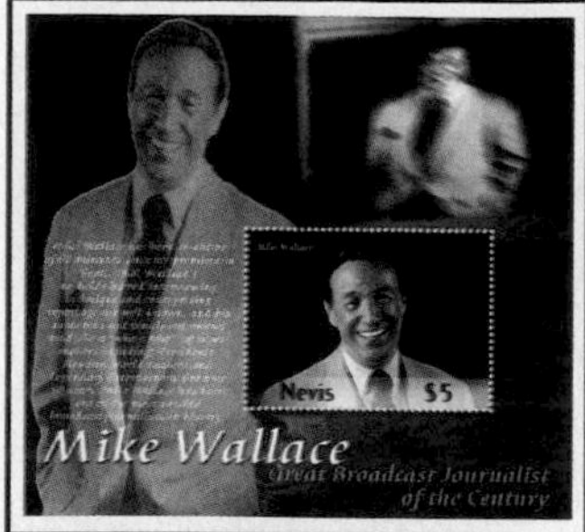

Mike Wallace, Broadcast Journalist — A195

2000, July 10 ***Perf. 13¾***
1223 A195 $5 multi 4.25 4.25

Carifesta VII — A196

Designs: 30c, Emblem. 90c, Festival participants. $1.20, Dancer.

2000, Aug. 17 ***Perf. 14***
1224-1226 A196 Set of 3 2.25 2.25

Monarchs — A197

No. 1227: a, King Edward III of England, 1327-77. b, Holy Roman Emperor Charles V (Charles I of Spain), 1520-56. c, Holy Roman Emperor Joseph II of Austria-Hungary, 1780-90. d, King Henry II of Germany, 1002-24. e, King Louis IV of France, 936-54. f, King Louis II of Bavaria, 1864-86.
$5, King Louis IX of France, 1226-70.

2000, Aug. 1 **Litho.** ***Perf. 13¾***
1227 A197 $1.60 Sheet of 6, #a-f 8.00 8.00

Souvenir Sheet
1228 A197 $5 multi 4.25 4.25

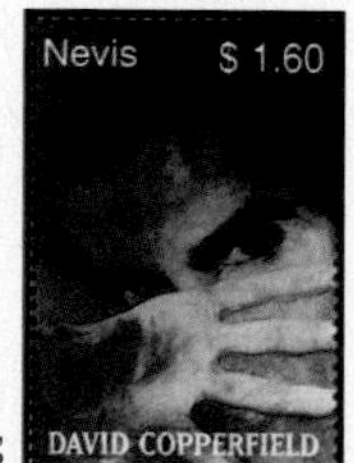

David Copperfield, Magician — A198

2000, Aug. 10 ***Perf. 14***
1229 A198 $1.60 multi 2.00 2.00

Printed in sheets of 4.

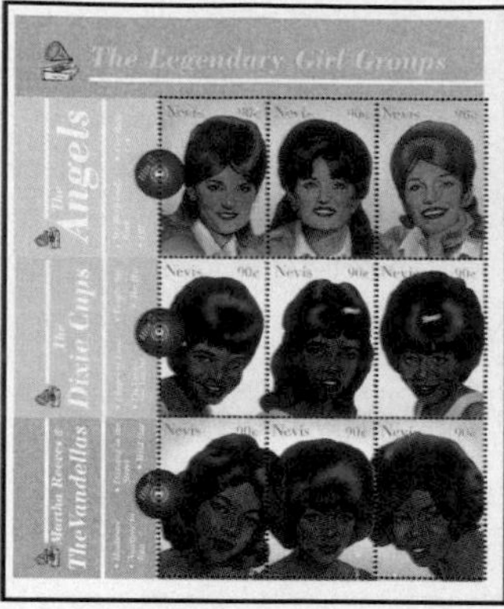

Female Singing Groups — A199

Singers from the Angels (a-c, blue background), Dixie Cups (d-f, yellow background) and Martha Reeves and the Vandellas (g-i, pink background): a, Record half. b, Woman with long hair. c, Woman with hand on chin. d, Record half. e, Woman with mole on cheek. f, Woman, no mole. g, Record half. h, Woman, not showing teeth. i, Woman showing teeth.

2000, Aug. 10
1230 A199 90c Sheet of 9, #a-i 6.75 6.75

Butterflies A200

Designs: 30c, Zebra. 80c, Julia. $1.60, Small flambeau. $5, Purple mort bleu.
No. 1235, $1: a, Ruddy dagger. b, Common morpho. c, Banded king shoemaker. d, Figure of eight. e, Grecian shoemaker. f, Mosaic.
No. 1236, $1: a, White peacock. b, Hewitson's blue hairstreak. c, Tiger pierid. d, Gold drop helicopsis. e, Cramer's mesene. f, Red-banded pereute.
No. 1237, $5, Common mechanitis. No. 1238, $5, Hewitson's pierella.

2001, Mar. 22
1231-1234 A200 Set of 4 6.00 6.00

Sheets of 6, #a-f
1235-1236 A200 Set of 2 9.50 9.50

Souvenir Sheets
1237-1238 A200 Set of 2 7.75 7.75

Flowers A201

Designs: 30c, Golden elegance oriental lily. 80c, Frangipani. $1.60, Garden zinnia. $5, Rose elegance lily.
No. 1243, 90c: a, Star of the march. b, Tiger lily. c, Mont Blanc lily. d, Torch ginger. e, Cattleya orchid. f, Saint John's wort.
No. 1244, $1: a, Culebra. b, Rubellum lily. c, Silver elegance oriental lily. d, Chinese hibiscus. e, Tiger lily. f, Royal poinciana.
No. 1245, $1.60: a, Epiphyte. b, Enchantment lily. c, Glory lily. d, Purple granadilla. e, Jacaranda. f, Shrimp plant.
No. 1246, $5, Dahlia. No. 1247, $5, Bird of Paradise.

2000, Oct. 30
1239-1242 A201 Set of 4 6.00 6.00

Sheets of 6, #a-f
1243-1245 A201 Set of 3 17.00 17.00

Souvenir Sheets
1246-1247 A201 Set of 2 7.75 7.75

The Stamp Show 2000, London (Nos. 1243-1247).

Christmas — A203

Designs: 30c, The Coronation of the Virgin, by Diego Velazquez, vert. 80c, The Immaculate Conception, by Velazquez, vert. 90c, Madonna and Child, by Titian. $1.20, Madonna and Child With St. John the Baptist and St. Catherine, by Titian.
$6, Madonna and Child With St. Catherine, by Titian.

2000, Dec. 4 **Litho.** ***Perf. 13½***
1249-1252 A203 Set of 4 2.40 2.40

Souvenir Sheet
1253 A203 $6 multi 4.50 4.50

New Year 2001 (Year of the Snake) — A204

No. 1254: a, Snake coiled on branch, facing right. b, Snake coiled on branch, facing left. c, Snake on ground, facing right. d, Snake on ground, facing left.
$5, Snake raising head.

2001, Jan. 4 ***Perf. 14***
1254 A204 $1.60 Sheet of 4, #a-d 4.75 4.75

Souvenir Sheet
1255 A204 $5 multi 3.75 3.75

195th Annual Leeward Islands Methodist Church District Conference — A205

Churches: a, Charlestown. b, Jessups. c, Clifton. d, Trinity. e, Combermere. f, Gingerland. g, New River.

2001, Jan. 23

1256 A205 50c Sheet of 7, #a-g 2.60 2.60

Garden of Eden — A206

No. 1257, $1.60: a, Red-crested woodpecker, unicorn. b, African elephant. c, Siberian tiger. d, Greater flamingo, Adam and Eve. e, Hippopotamus. f, Harlequin frog.

No. 1258, $1.60: a, Giraffe. b, Rainbow boa constrictor. c, Mountain cottontail rabbit. d, Bluebuck antelope. e, Red fox. f, Box turtle.

No. 1259, $5, Bald eagle. No. 1260, $5, Blue and gold macaw, vert. No. 1261, $5, Toucan, vert. No. 1262, $5, Koala, vert.

2001, Jan. 31 ***Perf. 14***

Sheets of 6, #a-f

1257-1258 A206 Set of 2 14.50 14.50

Souvenir Sheets

1259-1262 A206 Set of 4 15.00 15.00

Mushrooms A207

Designs: 20c, Clavulinopsis corniculata. 25c, Cantharellus cibarius. 50c, Chlorociboria aeruginascens. 80c, Auricularia auricula judae. $2, Peziza vesiculosa. $3, Mycena acicula.

No. 1269, $1: a, Entoloma incanum. b, Entoloma nitidum. c, Stropharia cyanea. d, Otidea onotica. e, Aleuria aurantia. f, Mitrula paludosa. g, Gyromitra esculenta. h, Helvella crispa. i, Morchella semilibera.

No. 1270, $5, Omphalotus olearius. No. 1271, $5, Russula sardonia.

2001, May 15 **Litho.** ***Perf. 14***

1263-1268 A207 Set of 6 5.25 5.25

1269 A207 $1 Sheet of 9, #a-i 7.00 7.00

Souvenir Sheets

1270-1271 A207 Set of 2 7.75 7.75

Tale of Prince Shotoku — A208

No. 1272, $2: a, Conception of Prince Shotoku. b, At six. c, At ten. d, At eleven.

No. 1273, $2: a, At sixteen (soldiers at gate). b, At sixteen (soldiers on horseback). c, At thirty-seven. d, At forty-four.

2001, May 31 ***Perf. 13¾***

Sheets of 4, #a-d

1272-1273 A208 Set of 2 12.00 12.00

Phila Nippon '01, Japan.

Queen Victoria (1819-1901) — A209

No. 1274: a, Prince Albert. b, Queen Victoria (flower in hair). c, Alexandrina Victoria. d, Duchess of Kent. e, Queen Victoria (as old woman). f, Prince of Wales.

$5, Queen Victoria (with tiara).

2001, July 9 **Litho.** ***Perf. 14***

1274 A209 $1.20 Sheet of 6, #a-f 5.50 5.50

Souvenir Sheet

1275 A209 $5 multi 3.75 3.75

Queen Elizabeth II, 75th Birthday — A210

No. 1276: a, Blue hat. b, Tiara. c, Yellow hat. d, Tan hat. e, Red hat. f, No hat.

$5, Blue hat, diff.

2001, July 9

1276 A210 90c Sheet of 6, #a-f 4.00 4.00

Souvenir Sheet

1277 A210 $5 multi 3.75 3.75

Flags of the Caribbean Community — A211

No. 1278: a, Antigua & Barbuda. b, Bahamas. c, Barbados. d, Belize. e, Dominica. f, Grenada. g, Guyana. h, Jamaica. i, Montserrat. j, St. Kitts & Nevis. k, St. Lucia. l, Surinam. m, St. Vincent & the Grenadines. n, Trinidad & Tobago.

2001, Dec. 3 **Litho.** ***Perf. 14***

1278 A211 90c Sheet of 14, #a-n 9.50 9.50

Christmas A212

Flowers: 30c, Christmas candle, vert. 90c, Poinsettia. $1.20, Snowbush. $3, Tiger claw, vert.

2001, Dec. 3

1279-1282 A212 Set of 4 4.00 4.00

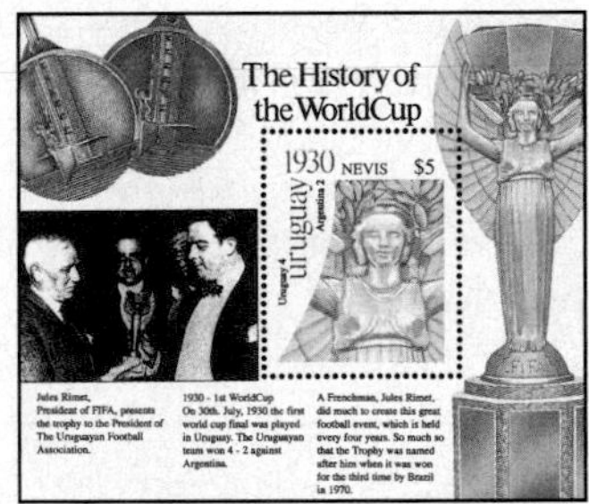

2002 World Cup Soccer Championships, Japan and Korea — A213

No. 1283, $1.60: a, Moracana Stadium, Brazil, 1950. b, Ferenc Puskas, 1954. c, Luis Bellini, 1958. d, Mauro, 1962. e, Cap, 1966. f, Banner, 1970.

No. 1284, $1.60: a, Passarella, 1978. b, Dino Zoff, 1982. c, Azteca Stadium, Mexico, 1986. d, San Siro Stadium, Italy, 1990. e, Dennis Bergkamp, Netherlands, 1994. f, Stade de France, 1998.

No. 1285, $5, Head from Jules Rimet Cup, 1930. No. 1286, $5, Head and globe from World Cup trophy, 2002.

2001, Dec. 10 ***Perf. 13¾x14¼***

Sheets of 6, #a-f

1283-1284 A213 Set of 2 14.50 14.50

Souvenir Sheets

Perf. 14½x14¼

1285-1286 A213 Set of 2 7.50 7.50

Queen Mother Type of 1999 Redrawn

No. 1287: a, In bridal gown, 1923. b, With Princess Elizabeth, 1926. c, With King George VI in World War II. d, Wearing hat, 1983.

$6, Wearing tiara, 1957.

2001, Dec. 13 ***Perf. 14***

Yellow Orange Frames

1287 A177 $2 Sheet of 4, #a-d, + label 6.00 6.00

Souvenir Sheet

Perf. 13¾

1288 A177 $6 multi 4.50 4.50

Queen Mother's 101st birthday. No. 1288 contains one 38x51mm stamp with a bluer background than that found on No. 1174. Sheet margins of Nos. 1287-1288 lack embossing and gold arms and frames found on Nos. 1173-1174.

Reign of Queen Elizabeth II, 50th Anniv. — A214

No. 1289: a, Queen with Prince Philip. b, Prince Philip. c, Queen with yellow dress. d, Queen touching horse.

$5, Queen with Prince Philip, diff.

2002, Feb. 6 ***Perf. 14¼***

1289 A214 $2 Sheet of 4, #a-d 6.00 6.00

Souvenir Sheet

1290 A214 $5 multi 3.75 3.75

New Year 2002 (Year of the Horse) — A215

Horse paintings by Ren Renfa: a, Brown and white horse. b, Horse with ribs showing. c, Horse with tassel under neck. d, Gray horse.

2002, Mar. 4 ***Perf. 13¼***

1291 A215 $1.60 Sheet of 4, #a-d 4.75 4.75

Insects, Birds and Whales — A216

No. 1292, $1.20: a, Beechey's bee. b, Banded king shoemaker butterfly. c, Streaked sphinx caterpillar. d, Hercules beetle. e, South American palm beetle. f, Giant katydid.

No. 1293, $1.60: a, Roseate spoonbill. b, White-tailed tropicbird. c, Ruby-throated tropicbird. d, Black skimmer. e, Black-necked stilt. f, Mourning dove.

No. 1294, $1.60: a, Sperm whale. b, Sperm and killer whales. c, Minke whales. d, Fin whale. e, Blainville's beaked whale. f, Pygmy sperm whale.

No. 1295, $5, Click beetle. No. 1296, $5, Royal tern. No. 1297, $5, Humpback whale, vert.

2002, Aug. 15 **Litho.** ***Perf. 14***

Sheets of 6, #a-f

1292-1294 A216 Set of 3 21.00 21.00

Souvenir Sheets

1295-1297 A216 Set of 3 12.00 12.00

APS Stampshow (#1293).

United We Stand — A217

2002, Aug. 26

1298 A217 $2 multi 1.50 1.50

Printed in sheets of 4.

2002 Winter Olympics, Salt Lake City — A218

Designs: No. 1299, $2, Figure skating. No. 1300, $2, Freestyle skiing.

2002, Aug. 26

1299-1300 A218 Set of 2 3.00 3.00

a. Souvenir sheet, #1299-1300 3.00 3.00

Intl. Year of Mountains — A219

No. 1301: a, Mt. Assiniboine, Canada. b, Mt. Atitlán, Guatemala. c, Mt. Adams, US. d, Matterhorn, Switzerland and Italy. e, Mt. Dhaulagiri, Nepal. f, Mt. Chamlang, Nepal.

$5, Mt. Kvaenangen, Norway.

2002, Aug. 26

1301 A219 $2 Sheet of 6, #a-f 9.00 9.00

Souvenir Sheet

1302 A219 $5 multi 3.75 3.75

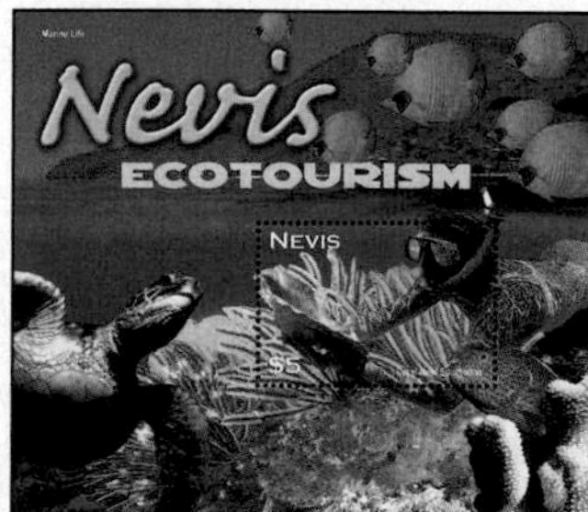

Ecotourism — A220

No. 1303: a, Horseback riding on beach. b, Windsurfing. c, Pinney's Beach. d, Cross-country hike. e, Robert T. Jones Golf Course. f, Scuba safaris.

$5, Coral reef snorkeling.

2002, Aug. 26

1303 A220 $1.60 Sheet of 6, #a-f 7.25 7.25

Souvenir Sheet

1304 A220 $5 multi 3.75 3.75

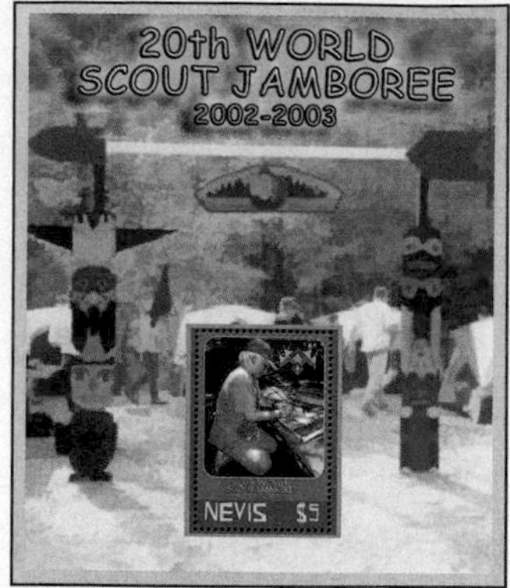

20th World Scout Jamboree, Thailand — A221

No. 1305: a, Scouts in two canoes. b, Scouts in one canoe. c, Scout on rope bridge. d, Scouts in inflatable rafts.

$5, Scout working on leatherwork project.

2002, Aug. 26

1305 A221 $2 Sheet of 4, #a-d 6.00 6.00

Souvenir Sheet

1306 A221 $5 multi 3.75 3.75

Souvenir Sheet

Artwork of Eva Wilkin (1898-1989) — A222

No. 1307: a, Unnamed painting of windmill. b, Nevis Peak (sepia toned). c, Fig Tree Church. d, Nevis Peak (full color).

2002, Sept. 23

1307 A222 $1.20 Sheet of 4, #a-d 3.75 3.75

Japanese Art — A223

No. 1308: a, Golden Pheasants and Loquat, by Shoei Kano. b, Flowers and Birds of the Four Seasons (snow-covered branches), by Koson Ikeda. c, Pheasants and Azaleas, by Kano. d, Flowers and Birds of the Four Seasons (tree and hill), by Ikeda.

No. 1309, $3: a, Flying bird from Birds and Flowers of Summer and Autumn, by Terutada Shikibu. b, Red flower, from Birds and Flowers of Summer and Autumn, by Shikibu

No. 1310, $3: a, White flower from Birds and Flowers of Summer and Autumn, by Shikibu. b, Perched bird from Birds and Flowers of Summer and Autumn, by Shikibu.

No. 1311, $3, horiz.: a, Bird facing right, from Two Birds on Willow and Peach Trees, by Buson Yosa. b, Bird facing left, from Two Birds on Willow and Peach Trees, by Yosa.

No. 1312, $5, Golden Pheasants Among Rhododendrons, by Baiitsu Yamamoto. No. 1313, $5, Muskrat and Camellias, by Neko Jako, horiz.

2002 ***Perf. 14x14¾***

1308 A223 $2 Sheet of 4, #a-d 6.00 6.00

Sheets of 2, #a-b

Perf. 13¾

1309-1311 A223 Set of 3 13.50 13.50

Souvenir Sheets

1312-1313 A223 Set of 2 7.50 7.50

No. 1308 contains four 29x80mm stamps.

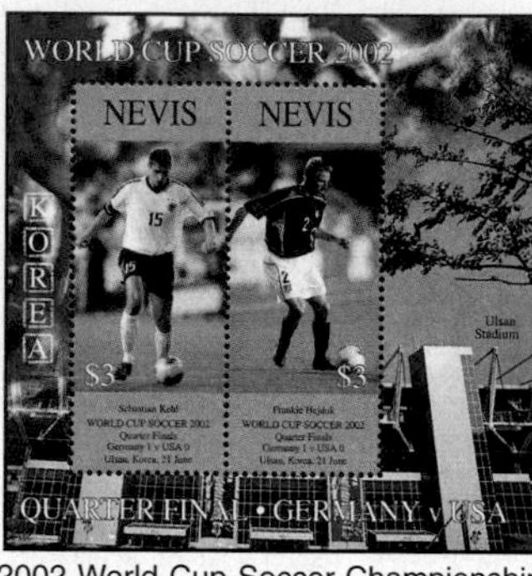

2002 World Cup Soccer Championship Quarterfinal Matches — A224

No. 1314, $1.20: a, Claudio Reyna and Torsten Frings. b, Michael Ballack and Eddie Pope. c, Sebastian Kehl and Brian McBride. d, Puyol and Eul Yong Lee. e, Jin Cheul Choi and Gaizka Mendieta. f, Juan Valeron and Jin Cheul Choi.

No. 1315, $1.60: a, Emile Heskey and Edmilson. b, Rivaldo and Sol Campbell. c, Ronaldinho and Nicky Butt. d, Ilhan Mansiz and Omar Daf. e, Hasan Sas and Papa Bouba Diop. f, Lamine Diatta and Hakan Sukur.

No. 1316, $3: a, Sebastian Kehl. b, Frankie Hejduk.

No. 1317, $3: a, Hong Myung Bo. b, Gaizka Mendieta.

No. 1318, $3: a, David Beckham and Roque Junior. b, Paul Scholes and Rivaldo.

No. 1319, $3: a, Alpay Ozalan. b, Khalilou Fadiga.

2002, Nov. 4 **Litho.** ***Perf. 13¼***

Sheets of 6, #a-f

1314-1315 A224 Set of 2 12.50 12.50

Souvenir Sheets of 2, #a-b

1316-1319 A224 Set of 4 18.00 18.00

Christmas — A225

Religious art: 30c, Madonna and Child Enthroned with Saints, by Perugino. 80c, Adoration of the Magi, by Domenico Ghirlandaio. 90c, San Zaccaria Altarpiece, by Giovanni Bellini. $1.20, Presentation at the Temple, by Bellini. $5, Madonna and Child, by Simone Martini.

$6, Maestà, by Martini.

2002, Nov. 4 ***Perf. 14¼***

1320-1324 A225 Set of 5 6.25 6.25

Souvenir Sheet

Perf. 14x14¼

1325 A225 $6 multi 4.50 4.50

New Year 2003 (Year of the Ram) — A226

2003, Feb. 10 ***Perf. 14x13¾***

1326 A226 $2 multi 2.00 2.00

Printed in sheets of 4.

Pres. John F. Kennedy (1917-63) — A227

No. 1327, $2: a, Robert and Edward Kennedy. b, John F. Kennedy. c, Joseph P., Jr., and John F. Kennedy as children. d, Robert and John F. Kennedy.

No. 1328, $2: a, Taking oath of office, 1961. b, At cabinet oath ceremony, 1961. c, With Russian foreign minister Andrei Gromyko, 1963. d, Cuban Missile Crisis, 1962.

2003, Mar. 10 **Litho.** ***Perf. 14***

Sheets of 4, #a-d

1327-1328 A227 Set of 2 12.00 12.00

Elvis Presley (1935-77) — A228

2003, Mar. 10 **Litho.** ***Perf. 14***

1329 A228 $1.60 multi 1.25 1.25

Printed in sheets of 6.

First Non-Stop Solo Transatlantic Flight, 75th Anniv. — A229

No. 1330, $2: a, Ryan Airlines crew attaches wing to fuselage of the Spirit of St. Louis. b, Charles Lindbergh, Donald Hall and President of Ryan Flying Co. c, Lindbergh planning flight. d, Hall designing Spirit of St. Louis.

No. 1331, $2: a, Hall. b, Lindbergh. c, Automobile towing Spirit of St. Louis from Ryan factory. d, Spirit of St. Louis being towed at Curtiss Field.

2003, Mar. 10 **Sheets of 4, #a-d**

1330-1331 A229 Set of 2 12.00 12.00

Princess Diana (1961-97) — A230

No. 1332: a, Wearing blue dress. b, Wearing blue dress, pearl necklace. c, Wearing black gown. d, Wearing hat.
$5, Wearing black dress and necklace.

2003, Mar. 10 *Perf. 12¼*
1332 A230 $2 Sheet of 4, #a-d 6.00 6.00

Souvenir Sheet

1333 A230 $5 multi 3.75 3.75

Marlene Dietrich (1901-92) — A231

No. 1334: a, With cigarette, country name at right. b, With cigarette, country name at left. c, Close-up. d, Wearing hat and white jacket.
$5, Wearing dress.

2003, Mar. 10 *Perf. 14*
1334 A231 $1.60 Sheet, #a-b, 2 each #c-d 7.25 7.25

Souvenir Sheet

1335 A231 $5 multi 3.75 3.75

Coronation of Queen Elizabeth II, 50th Anniv. — A232

No. 1336: a, Queen as young woman. b, Queen as older woman. c, Queen wearing glasses.
$5, Queen wearing tiara.

2003, May 13
1336 A232 $3 Sheet of 3, #a-c 6.75 6.75

Souvenir Sheet

1337 A232 $5 multi 3.75 3.75

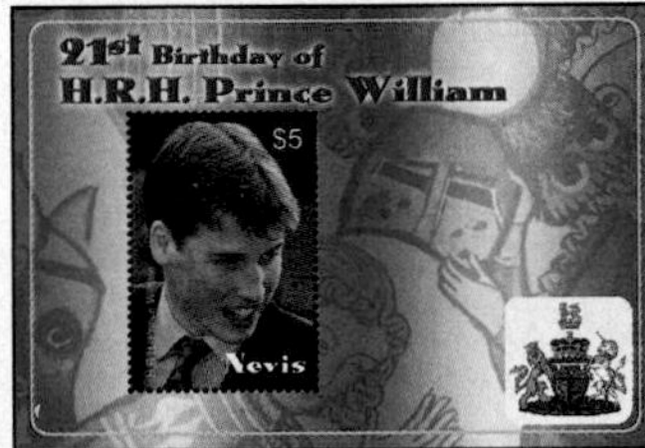

Prince William, 21st Birthday — A233

No. 1338: a, Wearing suit, showing teeth. b, Wearing suit. c, Wearing sweater.
$5, Wearing suit, diff.

2003, May 13
1338 A233 $3 Sheet of 3, #a-c 6.75 6.75

Souvenir Sheet

1339 A233 $5 multi 3.75 3.75

Powered Flight, Cent. — A234

No. 1340: a, A. V. Roe triplane. b, A. V. Roe Type D biplane. c, Avro Type F. d, Avro 504.
$5, Avro 561.

2003, May 13
1340 A234 $1.80 Sheet of 4, #a-d 5.75 5.75

Souvenir Sheet

1341 A234 $5 multi 4.00 4.00

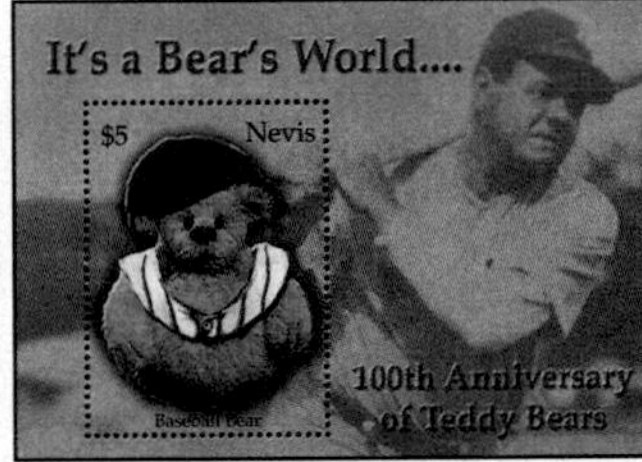

Teddy Bears, Cent. (in 2002) — A235

No. 1342: a, Abraham Lincoln bear. b, Napoleon bear. c, King Henry VIII bear. d, Charlie Chaplin bear.
$5, Baseball bear.

2003, May 13 *Perf. 13¼*
1342 A235 $2 Sheet of 4, #a-d 6.25 6.25

Souvenir Sheet

1343 A235 $5 multi 4.00 4.00

Tour de France Bicycle Race, Cent. — A236

No. 1344: a, Gustave Garrigou, 1911. b, Odile Defraye, 1912. c, Philippe Thys, 1913. d, Thys, 1914.
$5, François Faber.

2003, May 13
1344 A236 $2 Sheet of 4, #a-d 6.00 6.00

Souvenir Sheet

1345 A236 $5 multi 3.75 3.75

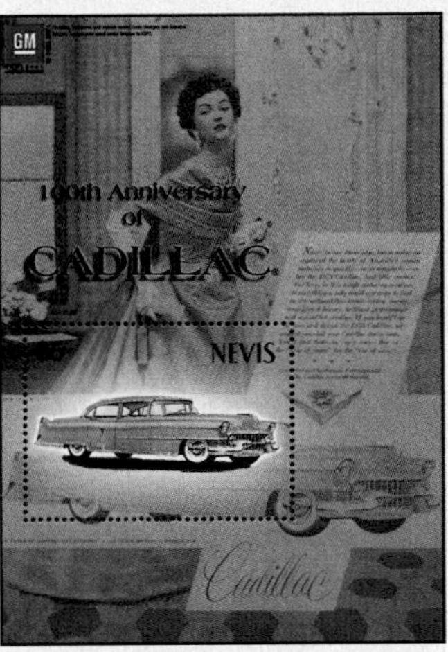

General Motors Automobiles — A237

No. 1346, $2 — Cadillacs: a, 1933 355-C V8 sedan. b, 1953 Eldorado. c, 1977 Coupe de Ville. d, 1980 Seville Elegante.
No. 1347, $2 — Corvettes: a, 1970. b, 1974. c, 1971. d, 1973.
No. 1348, $5, 1954 Cadillac. No. 1349, $5, 1997 C5 Corvette.

2003, May 13

Sheets of 4, #a-d

1346-1347 A237 Set of 2 12.00 12.00

Souvenir Sheets

1348-1349 A237 Set of 2 7.50 7.50

Orchids A238

Designs: 20c, Phalaenopsis joline, vert. $1.20, Vanda thonglor, vert. No. 1352, $2, Potinara. $3, Lycaste aquila.
No. 1354, $2: a, Brassolaelia cattleya. b, Cymbidium claricon. c, Calanthe vestita. d, Odontoglossum crispum.
$5, Odontioda brocade.

2003, Oct. 24 *Perf. 14*
1350-1353 A238 Set of 4 5.00 5.00
1354 A238 $2 Sheet of 4, #a-d 6.25 6.25

Souvenir Sheet

1355 A238 $5 multi 4.00 4.00

Butterflies A239

Designs: 30c, Perisama bonplandii. 90c, Danaus formosa. $1, Amauris vashti. $3, Lycorea ceres.
No. 1360: a, Kallima rumia. b, Nessaea ancaeus. c, Callicore cajetani. d, Hamadryas guatemalena.
$5, Euphaedra medon.

2003, Oct. 24
1356-1359 A239 Set of 4 4.25 4.25
1360 A239 $2 Sheet of 4, #a-d 6.25 6.25

Souvenir Sheet

1361 A239 $5 multi 4.00 4.00

Marine Life A240

Designs: 30c, Epinephelus striatus, vert. 80c, Acropora, vert. 90c, Myripristis hexagona. No. 1365, $5, Trichechus manatus.
No. 1366: a, Lioices latus. b, Chelmon rostratus. c, Epinephelus merra. d, Acanthurus coeruleus.
No. 1367, $5, Haemulon sciurus.

2003, Oct. 24
1362-1365 A240 Set of 4 5.50 5.50
1366 A240 $2 Sheet of 4, #a-d 6.25 6.25

Souvenir Sheet

1367 A240 $5 multi 4.00 4.00

Christmas A241

Designs: 30c, Madonna of the Magnificat, by Botticelli. 90c, Madonna with the Long Neck, by Il Parmigianino. $1.20, Virgin and Child With St. Anne, by Leonardo da Vinci. $5, Madonna and Child and Scenes from the Life of St. Anne, by Filippo Lippi.
$6, Conestabile Madonna, by Raphael.

2003, Nov. 5 *Perf. 14¼*
1368-1371 A241 Set of 4 5.50 5.50

Souvenir Sheet

1372 A241 $6 multi 4.50 4.50

World AIDS Day A242

National flag, AIDS ribbon and: 90c, Stylized men. $1.20, Map.

2003, Dec. 1 *Perf. 14*
1373-1374 A242 Set of 2 1.60 1.60

New Year 2004 (Year of the Monkey) A243

Designs: $1.60, Monkey King and Chinese text. $3, Monkey King.

2004, Feb. 16 **Litho.** *Perf. 13¼*
1375 A243 $1.60 red & black 1.50 1.50

Souvenir Sheet

Perf. 13¼x13

1376 A243 $3 multi 2.50 2.50

No. 1375 printed in sheets of 4. No. 1376 contains one 30x40mm stamp.

Girl Guides in Nevis, 50th Anniv. — A244

Designs: 30c, Badges. 90c, Guide and guide leader, horiz. $1.20, Lady Olave Baden-Powell. $5, Guides wearing t-shirts.

2004, Feb. 22 *Perf. 14*
1377-1380 A244 Set of 4 5.50 5.50

Paintings in the Hermitage, St. Petersburg, Russia — A245

Designs: 30c, Still Life with a Drapery, by Paul Cézanne. 90c, The Smoker, by Cézanne, vert. $2, Girl with a Fan, by Pierre Auguste Renoir, vert. No. 1384, $5, Grove, by André Derain, vert.

No. 1385, Lady in the Garden (Sainte Adresse), by Claude Monet.

2004, Mar. 4 ***Perf. 13¼***

1381-1384 A245 Set of 4 6.25 6.25

Imperf

Size: 94x74mm

1385 A245 $5 multi 3.75 3.75

Paintings by Norman Rockwell (1894-1978) — A246

No. 1386, vert.: a, The Morning After. b, Solitaire. c, Easter Morning. d, Walking to Church.

$5, The Graduate.

2004, Mar. 4 ***Perf. 13¼***

1386 A246 $2 Sheet of 4, #a-d 6.00 6.00

Souvenir Sheet

1387 A246 $5 multi 3.75 3.75

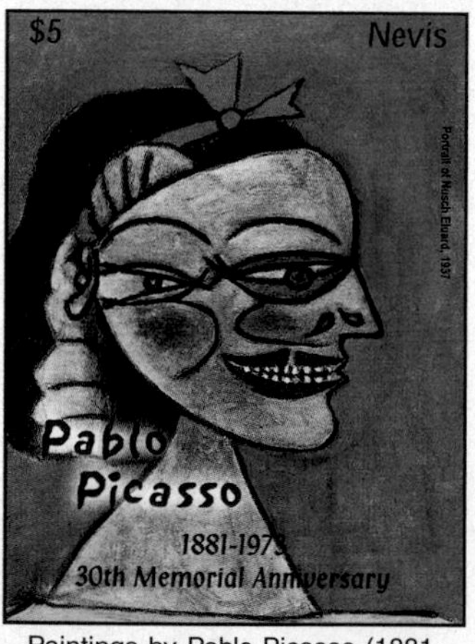

Paintings by Pablo Picasso (1881-1973) — A247

No. 1388, $2: a, Woman with a Hat. b, Seated Woman. c, Portrait of Nusch Eluard. d, Woman in a Straw Hat.

No. 1389, $2: a, L'Arlésienne. b, The Mirror. c, Repose. d, Portrait of Paul Eluard.

No. 1390, Portrait of Nusch Eluard, diff. No. 1391, Reclining Woman with a Book, horiz.

2004, Mar. 4 ***Perf. 13¼***

Sheets of 4, #a-d

1388-1389 A247 Set of 2 12.00 12.00

Imperf

1390 A247 $5 shown 3.75 3.75

Size: 100x75mm

1391 A247 $5 multi 3.75 3.75

ASDA Mega-Event, New York (#1389).

A248

Marilyn Monroe — A249

No. 1393 — Placement of stamp on sheet: a, UL. b, UR. c, LL. d, LR.

2004, June 17 ***Perf. 13½x13¼***

1392 A248 60c multi .45 .45

Perf. 13¼

1393 A249 $2 Sheet of 4, #a-d 6.00 6.00

John Denver (1943-97), Musician — A250

Placement of stamp on sheet: a, Top left. b, Top right. c, Bottom left. d, Bottom right.

2004, June 17 ***Perf. 13¾x13½***

1394 A250 $1.20 Sheet of 4, #a-d 3.75 3.75

2004 Summer Olympics, Athens A251

Designs: 30c, Commemorative medal, 1968 Mexico City Olympics. 90c, Pentathlon. $1.80, Avery Brundage, Intl. Olympic Committee President. $3, Women's tennis, 1920 Antwerp Olympics, horiz.

2004, Sept. 7 **Litho.** ***Perf. 14¼***

1395-1398 A251 Set of 4 4.50 4.50

Intl. Year of Peace — A252

No. 1399: a, Country name at right, dove's feet not visible. b, Country name at left. c, Country name at right, dove's feet visible.

2004, Sept. 7

1399 A252 $3 Sheet of 3, #a-c 6.75 6.75

Souvenir Sheet

Deng Xiaoping (1904-97), Chinese Leader — A253

2004, Sept. 7 ***Perf. 14***

1400 A253 $5 multi 3.75 3.75

D-Day, 60th Anniv. — A254

No. 1401: a, HMCS Penetang. b, Landing Craft Infantry (Large). c, LCT (6). d, Landing Craft Tank (Rocket). e, Landing Barge Kitchen. f, Battleship Texas.

$6, HMS Scorpion.

2004, Sept. 7

1401 A254 $1.20 Sheet of 6, #a-f 5.50 5.50

Souvenir Sheet

1402 A254 $6 multi 4.50 4.50

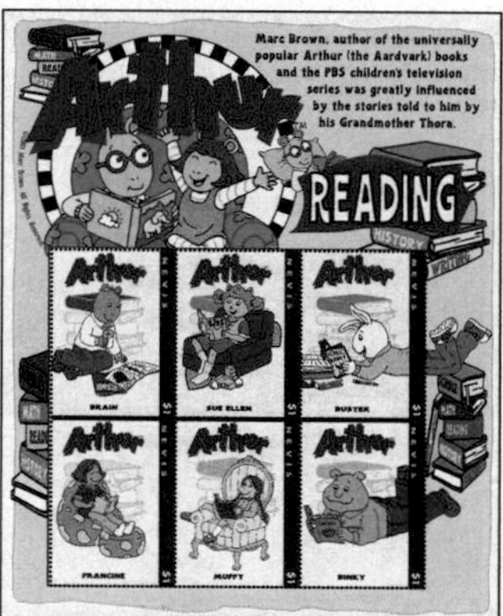

Arthur and Friends — A255

No. 1403 — Characters reading: a, Brain. b, Sue Ellen. c, Buster. d, Francine. e, Muffy. f, Binky.

No. 1404, $2 — Characters, with purple background: a, Arthur. b, D. W. c, Francine, looking right. d, Buster, diff.

No. 1405, $2 — Characters, with lilac background: a, Binky, diff. b, Sue Ellen, diff. c, Brain, diff. d, Francine, looking left.

2004, June 17 **Litho.** ***Perf. 14¼***

1403 A255 $1 Sheet of 6, #a-f 4.50 4.50

Sheets of 4, #a-d

1404-1405 A255 Set of 2 12.00 12.00

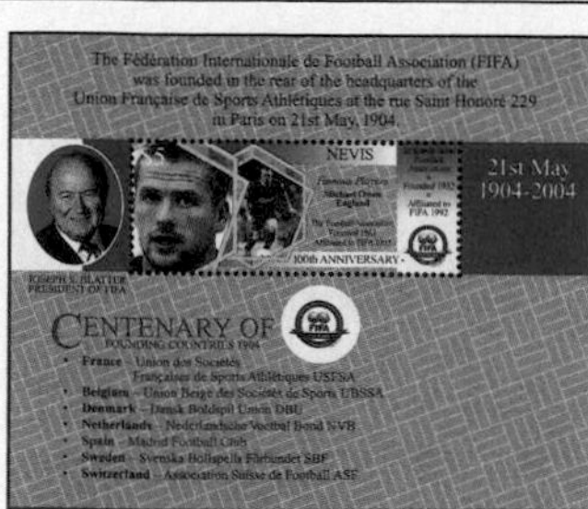

FIFA (Fédération Internationale de Football Association), Cent. — A256

Jason Berkley Joseph, Soccer Player — A257

No. 1406: a, Nery Pumpido. b, Gary Lineker. c, Thomas Hassler. d, Sol Campbell.

No. 1407, Michael Owen.

2004, Nov. 29 ***Perf. 12¾x12½***

1406 A256 $2 Sheet of 4, #a-d 6.00 6.00

Souvenir Sheets

1407 A256 $5 multi 3.75 3.75

1408 A257 $5 multi 3.75 3.75

Marginal inscription on No. 1408, "100th Anniversary World Cup Soccer" is incorrect as the first World Cup was held in 1930.

Elvis Presley (1935-77) A258

No. 1409 — Wearing checked shirt: a, Blue background. b, Bright red violet background.

No. 1410 — Color of sweater: a, Red. b, Orange yellow. c, Blue. d, Blue green. e, Red violet. f, Bright green.

2004, Nov. 29 ***Perf. 13½x13¼***

1409 A258 $1.20 Pair, #a-b 1.90 1.90

1410 A258 $1.20 Sheet of 6, #a-f 5.50 5.50

No. 1409 printed in sheets of 3 pairs.

Christmas A259

Paintings by Norman Rockwell: 25c, Santa's Good Boys. 30c, Ride 'em Cowboy. 90c, Christmas Sing Merrilie. No. 1414, $5, The Christmas Newsstand.
No. 1415, $5, Is He Coming.

2004, Dec. 1 ***Perf. 12***
1411-1414 A259 Set of 4 5.00 5.00
Imperf
Size: 63x73mm
1415 A259 $5 multi 3.75 3.75

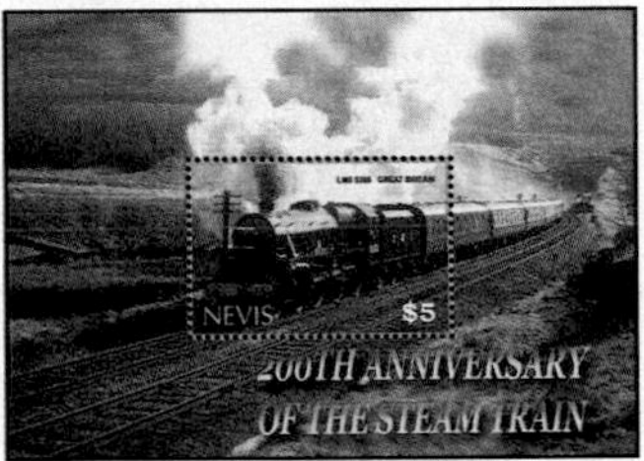

Locomotives, 200th Anniv. — A260

No. 1416: a, Steam Idyll, Indonesia. b, 2-8-2, Syria. c, Narrow gauge Mallet 0-4-4-0T, Portugal. d, Western Pacific Bo-Bo Road Switcher, US.
$5, LMS 5305, Great Britain.

2004, Dec. 13 ***Perf. 13¼x13½***
1416 A260 $3 Sheet of 4, #a-d 9.00 9.00
Souvenir Sheet
1417 A260 $5 multi 3.75 3.75

Reptiles and Amphibians — A261

No. 1418: a, Gekko gecko. b, Eyelash viper. c, Green iguana. d, Whistling frog.
$5, Hawksbill turtle.

2005, Jan. 10 ***Perf. 14***
1418 A261 $1.20 Sheet of 4, #a-d 4.00 4.00
Souvenir Sheet
1419 A261 $5 multi 4.00 4.00

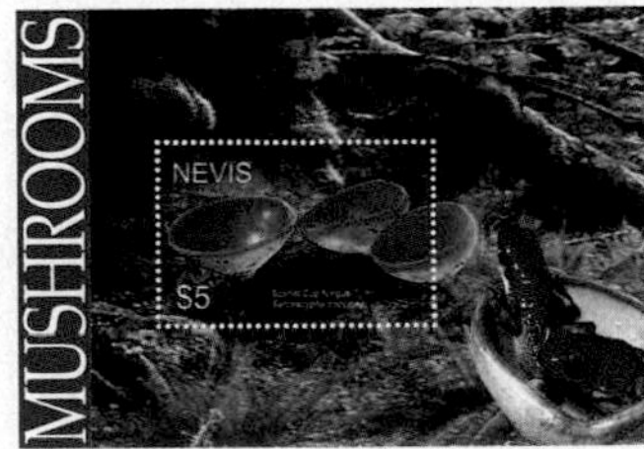

Mushrooms — A262

No. 1420: a, Xeromphalina campanella. b, Calvatia sculpta. c, Mitrula elegans. d, Aleuria aurantia.
$5, Scarlet cup.

2005, Jan. 10
1420 A262 $2 Sheet of 4, #a-d 6.25 6.25
Souvenir Sheet
1421 A262 $5 multi 4.00 4.00

Hummingbirds — A263

No. 1422: a, Rufous hummingbird. b, Green-crowned brilliant. c, Ruby-throated hummingbird. d, Purple-throated Carib.
$5, Magnificent hummingbird.

2005, Jan. 10 **Litho.** ***Perf. 14***
1422 A263 $2 Sheet of 4, #a-d 6.25 6.25
Souvenir Sheet
1423 A263 $5 multi 4.00 4.00

Sharks — A264

No. 1424: a, Zebra shark. b, Caribbean reef shark. c, Blue shark. d, Bronze whaler.
$5, Blacktip reef shark.

2005, Jan. 10
1424 A264 $2 Sheet of 4, #a-d 6.25 6.25
Souvenir Sheet
1425 A264 $5 multi 4.00 4.00

Artist's Depictions of Hawksbill Turtles — A265

Artist: 30c, Leon Silcott. 90c, Kris Liburd. $1.20, Alice Webber. $5, Jeuaunito Huggins.

2005, Jan. 10
1426-1429 A265 Set of 4 6.00 6.00

Souvenir Sheet

New Year 2005 (Year of the Rooster) — A266

No. 1430: a, Rooster, blue green background. b, Rooster silhouette, light green background. c, Rooster silhouette, blue background. d, Rooster, red violet background.

2005, Jan. 17 ***Perf. 12***
1430 A266 75c Sheet of 4, #a-d 2.50 2.50

Friedrich von Schiller (1759-1805), Writer — A267

No. 1431: a, Schiller, country name in pink. b, Schiller, country name in blue. c, Schiller's birthplace, Marbach, Germany.
$5, Statue of Schiller, Chicago.

2005, May 16 ***Perf. 12¾***
1431 A267 $3 Sheet of 3, #a-c 6.75 6.75
Souvenir Sheet
1432 A267 $5 multi 3.75 3.75

Rotary International, Cent. — A268

No. 1433, vert.: a, Barefoot child. b, Vaccination of child. c, Child with crutches and braces.
$5, Woman and children.

2005, May 16
1433 A268 $3 Sheet of 3, #a-c 6.75 6.75
Souvenir Sheet
1434 A268 $5 multi 3.75 3.75

Hans Christian Andersen (1805-75), Author — A269

No. 1435: a, The Little Mermaid. b, Thumbelina. c, The Snow Queen. d, The Emperor's New Clothes.
$6, Andersen.

2005, May 16
1435 A269 $2 Sheet of 4, #a-d 6.00 6.00
Souvenir Sheet
1436 A269 $6 multi 4.50 4.50

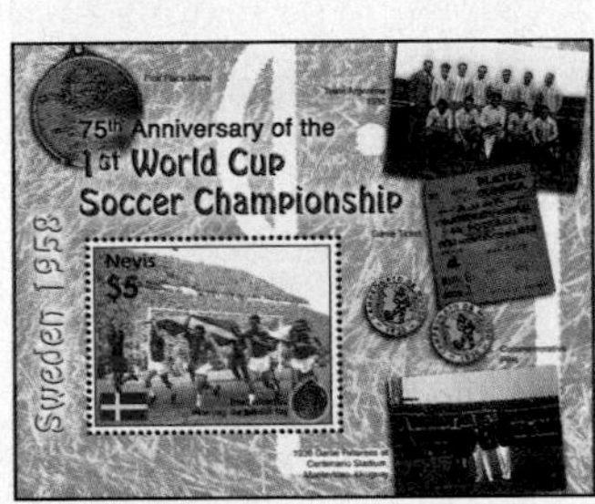

World Cup Soccer Championships, 75th Anniv. — A270

No. 1437: a, Brazil, 1958 champions. b, Scene from 1958 Brazil-Sweden final. c, Rasunda Stadium, Stockholm. d, Pele.
$5, 1958 Brazil team celebrating victory.

2005, May 16 **Litho.**
1437 A270 $2 Sheet of 4, #a-d 6.00 6.00
Souvenir Sheet
1438 A270 $5 multi 3.75 3.75

End of World War II, 60th Anniv. — A271

No. 1439, $2: a, Gen. Charles de Gaulle. b, Gen. George S. Patton. c, Field Marshal Bernard Montgomery. d, Liberation of concentration camps. e, Political cartoon about end of war.
No. 1440, $2, horiz.: a, Flight crew of the Enola Gay. b, Atomic bomb mushroom cloud. c, Souvenir of Japanese surrender ceremony. d, Japanese delegation on USS Missouri. e, Gen. Douglas MacArthur speaking at surrender ceremony.

2005, May 16 ***Perf. 12¾***
Sheets of 5, #a-e
1439-1440 A271 Set of 2 15.00 15.00

Battle of Trafalgar, Bicent. — A272

Various ships and: 30c, Admiral William Cornwallis. 90c, Capt. Maurice Suckling. $1.20, Fleet Admiral Earl Howe. $3, Sir John Jervis.
$5, Earl Howe on the quarterdeck of the Queen Charlotte.

2005, May 16 ***Perf. 12¾***
1441-1444 A272 Set of 4 4.25 4.25
Souvenir Sheet
Perf. 12
1445 A272 $5 multi 3.75 3.75

A273

Prehistoric Animals — A274

Designs: 30c, Tyrannosaurus rex. No. 1447, $5, Hadrosaur.
No. 1448, $1.20: a, Apatosaurus. b, Camarasaurus. c, Iguanodon. d, Edmontosaurus. e, Centrosaurus. f, Euoplocephalus.
No. 1449, $1.20: a, Ouranosaurus. b, Parasaurolophus. c, Psittacosaurus. d, Stegosaurus. e, Scelidosaurus. f, Hypsilophodon.
No. 1450, $1.20, vert.: a, Deinotherium. b, Platybelodon. c, Palaeoloxodon. d, Arsinotherium. e, Procoptodon. f, Macrauchenia.
No. 1451, $5, Brontotherium. No. 1452, $5, Daspletosaurus. No. 1453, $5, Pliosaur.

2005, June 7 *Perf. 12¾*
1446-1447 A273 Set of 2 4.00 4.00

Sheets of 6, #a-f

1448-1450 A274 Set of 3 16.50 16.50

Souvenir Sheets

1451-1453 A274 Set of 3 11.50 11.50

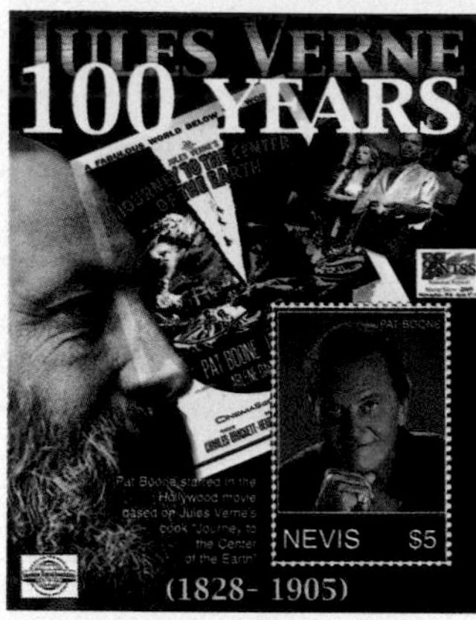

Jules Verne (1828-1905), Writer — A275

No. 1454 — Story characters: a, Captain Nemo, *20,000 Leagues Under the Sea.* b, Michael Strogoff, *Michael Strogoff.* c, Phileas Fogg, *Around the World in 80 Days.* d, Captain Cyrus Smith, *Mysterious Island.*
$5, Pat Boone, actor in movie, *Journey to the Center of the Earth.*

2005, June 17
1454 A275 $2 Sheet of 4, #a-d 6.00 6.00

Souvenir Sheet

1455 A275 $5 multi 3.75 3.75

2005 National Topical Stamp Show, Milwaukee (#1455).

Vatican City No. 66 — A276

Pope John Paul II (1920-2005) A277

2005, July 12 *Perf. 13x13¼*
1456 A276 90c multi .70 .70

Perf. 13½x13¼

1457 A277 $4 multi 3.00 3.00

National Basketball Association Players — A278

Designs: No. 1458, $1, Shareef-Abdur Rahim (shown), Portland Trail Blazers. No. 1459, $1, Shaun Livingston, Los Angeles Clippers. No. 1460, $1, Vince Carter, New Jersey Nets. No. 1461, $1, Rasheed Wallace, Detroit Pistons.
No. 1462: a, Theo Ratliff, Portland Trail Blazers. b, Portland Trail Blazers emblem.

2005, July 26 *Perf. 14*
1458-1461 A278 Set of 4 3.00 3.00
1462 A278 $1 Sheet, 10 #1462a, 2 #1462b 9.00 9.00

Souvenir Sheet

Sun Yat-sen (1866-1925), Chinese Leader — A279

No. 1463: a, Wearing blue suit, harbor in background. b, Wearing suit and tie. c, Wearing blue suit, statue in background. d, Wearing brown red suit.

2005, Aug. 19 **Litho.** *Perf. 14*
1463 A279 $2 Sheet of 4, #a-d 6.00 6.00

Taipei 2005 Intl. Stamp Exhibition.

Christmas — A280

Designs: 25c, Madonna and the Angels, by Fra Angelico. 30c, Madonna and the Child, by Fra Filippo Lippi. 90c, Madonna and Child, by Giotto. $4, Madonna of the Chair, by Raphael.
$5, Adoration of the Magi, by Giovanni Batista Tiepolo, horiz.

2005, Dec. 1 *Perf. 13½*
1464-1467 A280 Set of 4 4.25 4.25

Souvenir Sheet

1468 A280 $5 multi 3.75 3.75

U.S. Forest Service, Cent. (in 2005) — A281

No. 1469, vert.: a, Eldorado National Forest, California. b, Pisgah National Forest, North Carolina. c, Chattahoochee-Oconee National Forests, Georgia. d, Nantahala National Forest, North Carolina. e, Bridger-Teton National Forest, Wyoming. f, Mount Hood National Forest, Oregon.
No. 1470, $6, Klamath National Forest, California. No. 1471, $6, The Source Rain Forest Walk, Nevis, vert.

2006, Jan. 3
1469 A281 $1.60 Sheet of 6, #a-f 7.25 7.25

Souvenir Sheets

1470-1471 A281 Set of 2 9.00 9.00

A Dog, by Ren Xun — A282

2006, Jan. 3
1472 A282 75c multi .70 .70

New Year 2006 (Year of the Dog). Printed in sheets of 4.

Queen Elizabeth II, 80th Anniv. — A283

No. 1473 — Queen wearing: a, Black hat with feather. b, No hat. c, Tiara. d, White hat.
$5, As young woman.

2006, Mar. 20 **Litho.** *Perf. 13¼*
1473 A283 $2 Sheet of 4, #a-d 6.00 6.00

Souvenir Sheet

1474 A283 $5 multi 3.75 3.75

2006 Winter Olympics, Turin — A284

Designs: 25c, U.S. #1796. 30c, Italy #705. 90c, Italy #707. $1.20, Emblem of 1980 Lake Placid Winter Olympics, vert. $4, Italy #708. $5, Emblem of 1956 Cortina d'Ampezzo Winter Olympics.

Perf. 14¼ (25c, $1.20), 13¼

2006, Apr. 24
1475-1480 A284 Set of 6 8.75 8.75

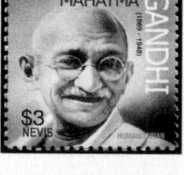

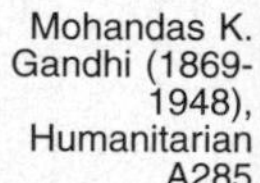

Mohandas K. Gandhi (1869-1948), Humanitarian A285

2006, May 27 *Perf. 12x11½*
1481 A285 $3 multi 2.25 2.25

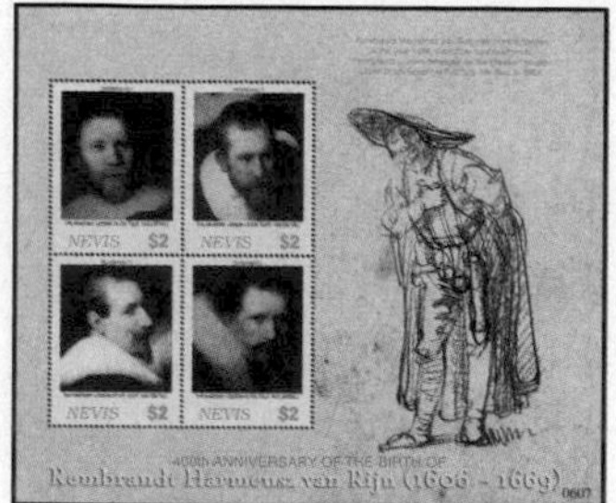

Rembrandt (1606-69), Painter — A286

No. 1482 — Various men from The Anatomy Lesson of Dr. Tulp.
$6, Bald-headed Old Man.

2006, June 23 *Perf. 13¼*
1482 A286 $2 Sheet of 4, a-d 6.00 6.00

Imperf

Size: 70x100mm

1483 A286 $6 multi 4.50 4.50

Miniature Sheets

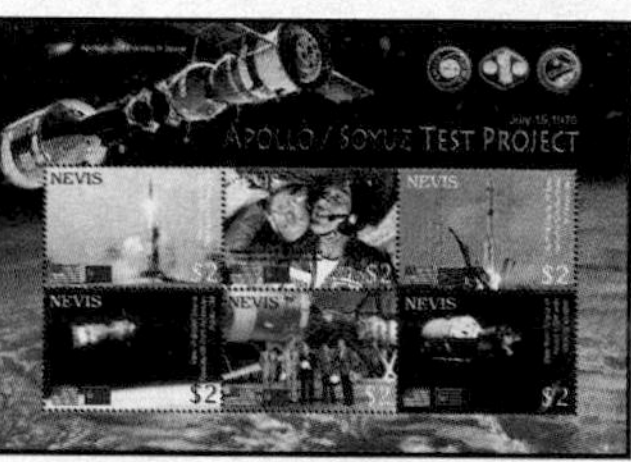

Space Achievements — A287

No. 1484 — Apollo-Soyuz: a, Liftoff of Saturn IB rocket . b, Astronaut Donald K. Slayton, Cosmonaut Aleksei A. Leonov. c, Liftoff of Soyuz 19. d, Soyuz in space. e, American and Soviet crews, model of docked spacecraft. f, Apollo in space.
No. 1485 — Viking I: a, Liftoff of Titan Centaur rocket. b, Viking I in flight. c, Model of Viking I on Mars. d, Mars.

2006, Sept. 11 *Perf. 13¼*
1484 A287 $2 Sheet of 6, #a-f 9.00 9.00
1485 A287 $3 Sheet of 4, #a-d 9.00 9.00

Christmas A288

Designs: 25c, Charlestown Christmas tree. 30c, Snowman decoration. 90c, Reindeer decorations. $4, Christmas tree and gifts, vert.
$6, Santa Claus and children.

2006, Dec. 8
1486-1489 A288 Set of 4 4.25 4.25

Souvenir Sheet

1490 A288 $6 multi 4.50 4.50

Scouting, Cent. A289

Designs: $3, Flags, Map of Great Britain and Ireland. $5, Flags, bird, map, horiz.

2007, Jan. 29 **Litho.** *Perf. 13¼*
1491 A289 $3 multi 2.25 2.25

Souvenir Sheet

1492 A289 $5 multi 3.75 3.75

No. 1491 printed in sheets of 4.

Miniature Sheet

Marilyn Monroe (1926-62), Actress — A290

No. 1493 — Monroe: a, With head tilted. b, Wearing necklace. c, With lips closed. d, Wearing sash.

2007, Jan. 29
1493 A290 $2 Sheet of 4, #a-d 6.00 6.00

Cricket World Cup — A291

Designs: 90c, Cricket World Cup emblem, flag of St. Kitts and Nevis, map of Nevis. $2, Emblem and Runako Morton.
$6, Emblem.

2007, May 1 ***Perf. 14***
1494-1495 A291 Set of 2 2.25 2.25

Souvenir Sheet

1496 A291 $6 multi 4.50 4.50

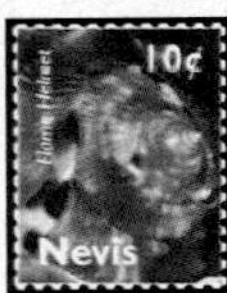

Shells — A292

Designs: 10c, Flame helmet. 25c, Rooster tail conch. 30c, Beaded periwinkle. 60c, Emperor helmet. 80c, Scotch bonnet. 90c Milk conch. $1, Beaded periwinkle, diff. $1.20, Alphabet cone. $1.80, Measled cowrie. $3, King helmet. $5, Atlantic hairy triton. $10, White-lined mitre. $20, Reticulated cowrie.

2007, July 5 ***Perf. 12½x13¼***

1497 A292	10c	multi	.25	.25
1498 A292	25c	multi	.25	.25
1499 A292	30c	multi	.30	.30
1500 A292	60c	multi	.50	.50
1501 A292	80c	multi	.65	.65
1502 A292	90c	multi	.75	.75
1503 A292	$1	multi	.80	.80
1504 A292	$1.20	multi	1.00	1.00
1505 A292	$1.80	multi	1.50	1.50
1506 A292	$3	multi	2.40	2.40
1507 A292	$5	multi	4.00	4.00
1508 A292	$10	multi	7.75	7.75
1509 A292	$20	multi	16.00	16.00
Nos. 1497-1509 (13)			36.15	36.15

Worldwide Fund for Nature (WWF) — A293

No. 1510 — Rainbow parrotfish: a, Facing left, white coral above fish. b, Two parrotfish. c, Facing left, ocean floor below fish. d, Facing right.

2007, July 23 ***Perf. 13½***

1510	Strip of 4	4.00	4.00
a.-d.	A293 $1.20 Any single	.95	.95
e.	Miniature sheet, 2 each #1510a-1510d	7.75	7.75

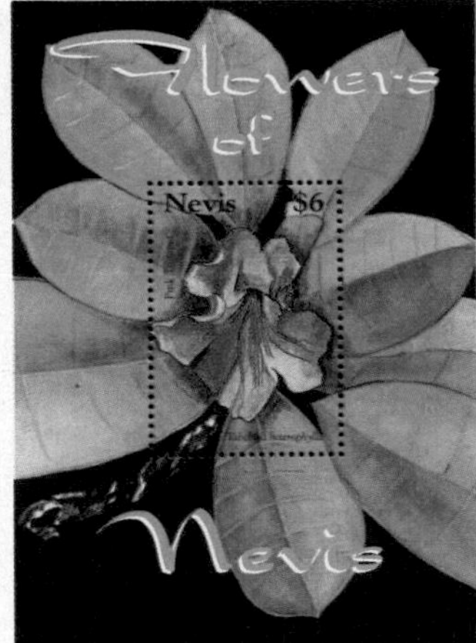

Flowers — A294

No. 1511: a, Wild cilliment. b, Jumbie beads. c, Wild sage. d, Blood flower.
$6, Pink trumpet.

2007, July 23 ***Perf. 13¼***
1511 A294 $2 Sheet of 4, #a-d 6.25 6.25

Souvenir Sheet

1512 A294 $6 multi 4.75 4.75

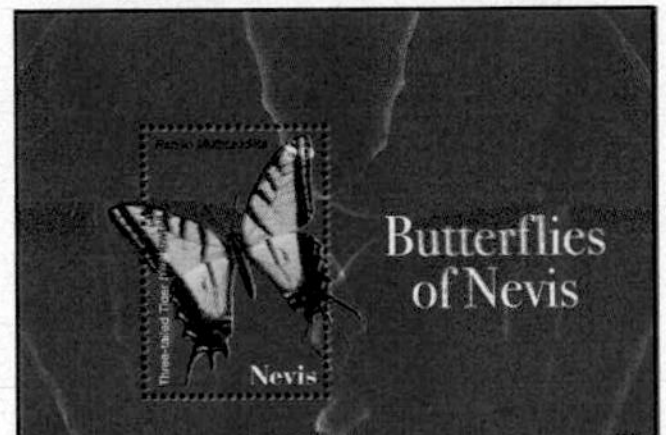

Butterflies — A295

No. 1513: a, Zetides swallowtail. b, Hahnel's Amazon swallowtail. c, Haitian mimic. d, Marbled white.
$6, Three-tailed tiger swallowtail.

2007, July 23
1513 A295 $2 Sheet of 4, #a-d 6.25 6.25

Souvenir Sheet

1514 A295 $6 multi 4.75 4.75

Miniature Sheet

Elvis Presley (1935-77) — A296

No. 1515 — Various photographs of Presley with: a, Denomination in white, country name in violet, laces showing on shirt. b, Denomination in blue. c, Denomination in bister. d, Denomination and country name in pink. e, Denomination in white, country name in pink. f, Denomination in white, country name in violet, laces not showing on shirt.

2007, Aug. 13
1515 A296 $1.20 Sheet of 6, #a-f 5.50 5.50

Princess Diana (1961-97) — A297

No. 1516: a, With head on hands. b, Wearing black dress. c, Wearing pink jacket. d, Wearing white dress.
$6, Wearing hat.

2007, Aug. 13
1516 A297 $2 Sheet of 4, #a-d 6.00 6.00

Souvenir Sheet

1517 A297 $6 multi 4.50 4.50

Miniature Sheets

Concorde — A298

No. 1518, $1.20 — Concorde with portions of globe in background: a, Western United States. b, Central United States. c, Atlantic Ocean and Eastern Canada. d, Central Pacific Ocean. e, Central America. f, Northeastern South America.

No. 1519, $1.20 — Concorde with: a, Green frame, white denomination. b, Red frame, blue denomination. c, Green frame, yellow denomination. d, Red frame, yellow denomination. e, Green frame, blue denomination. f, Red frame, white denomination.

2007, Aug. 13 **Litho.** ***Perf. 13¼***

Sheets of 6, #a-f

1518-1519 A298 Set of 2 11.00 11.00

Pope Benedict XVI — A299

2007, Oct. 24
1520 A299 $1 multi .75 .75

Printed in sheets of 8.

Miniature Sheet

Wedding of Queen Elizabeth II and Prince Philip, 60th Anniv. — A300

No. 1521 — Couple: a, Queen wearing tiara. b, Waving. c, Wearing feathered hats. d, In gilded coach, Queen in blue, waving. e, In coach, Queen with red hat, waving. f, On balcony, Queen waving.

2007, Oct. 24
1521 A300 $1.20 Sheet of 6, #a-f 5.50 5.50

Miniature Sheet

Inauguration of Pres. John F. Kennedy, 46th Anniv. — A301

No. 1522: a, Jacqueline Kennedy. b, John F. Kennedy, hands at side. c, John F. Kennedy, clapping. d, Vice president Lyndon B. Johnson.

2007, Nov. 28
1522 A301 $3 Sheet of 4, #a-d 9.00 9.00

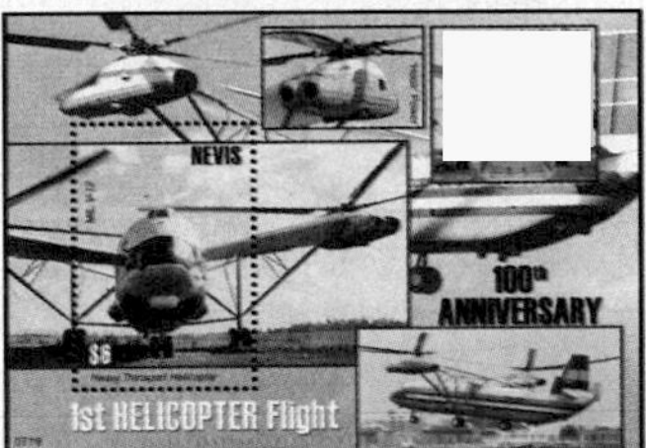

First Helicopter Flight, Cent. — A302

No. 1523, horiz.: a, Westland Sea King. b, Schweizer N330TT. c, Sikorsky R-4/R-5. d, PZL Swidnik.
$6, MIL V-12.

2007, Nov. 28
1523 A302 $3 Sheet of 4, #a-d 9.00 9.00

Souvenir Sheet

1524 A302 $6 multi 4.50 4.50

Paintings by Qi Baishi (1864-1957) — A303

No. 1525: a, Begonias and Rock. b, Mother and Child. c, Fish and Bait. d, Solitary Hero.
$6, Chrysanthemums and Insects.

2007, Nov. 28 ***Perf. 12½***
1525 A303 $3 Sheet of 4, #a-d 9.00 9.00

Souvenir Sheet

Perf. 13¼

1526 A303 $6 multi 4.50 4.50

No. 1525 contains four 32x80mm stamps.

Christmas A304

Paintings: 25c, The Rest on the Flight Into Egypt, by Federico Barocci. 30c, The Annunciation, by Barocci. 90c, The Annunciation, by Cavalier d'Arpino. $4, The Rest on the Flight Into Egypt, by Francesco Mancini.
$5, The Virgin and Child Between Saints Peter and Paul and the Twelve Magistrates of the Rota, by Antoniazzo Romano.

2007, Dec. 3 ***Perf. 11¼x11½***
1527-1530 A304 Set of 4 4.25 4.25

Souvenir Sheet
Perf. 13½
1531 A304 $5 multi 3.75 3.75

Miniature Sheet

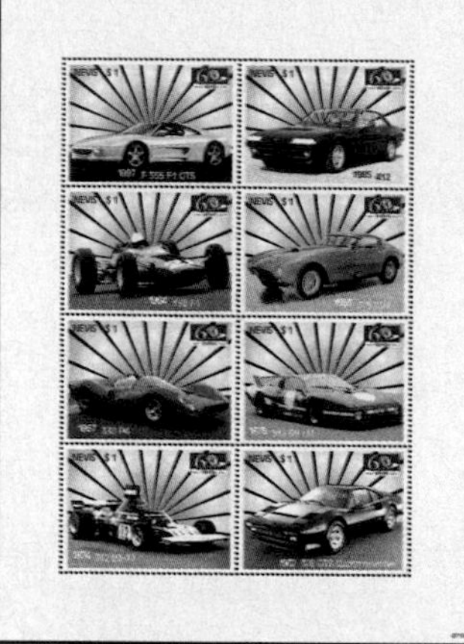

Ferrari Automobiles, 60th Anniv. — A305

No. 1532: a, 1997 F 355 F1 GTS. b, 1985 412. c, 1964 158 F1. d, 1953 375 MM. e, 1967 330 P4. f, 1978 512 BB LM. g, 1974 312 B3-74. h, 1982 308 GTB Quattrovalvole.

2007, Dec. 10 ***Perf. 13¼***
1532 A305 $1 Sheet of 8, #a-h 6.00 6.00

Miniature Sheet

2008 Summer Olympics, Beijing — A306

No. 1533: a, Cycling. b, Kayaking. c, Sailing. d, Equestrian.

2008, Mar. 8 **Litho.** ***Perf. 12¾***
1533 A306 $2 Sheet of 4, #a-d 6.00 6.00

Israel 2008 Intl. Philatelic Exhibition — A307

No. 1534 — Sites in Israel: a, Mt. Masada. b, Red Sea and mountains. c, Dead Sea. d, Sea of Galilee.
$5, Mt. Hermon.

2008, May 21 **Litho.** ***Perf. 11½x11¼***
1534 A307 $1.50 Sheet of 4, #a-d 4.50 4.50

Souvenir Sheet
1535 A307 $5 multi 3.75 3.75

32nd America's Cup Yacht Races — A308

No. 1536 — Various yachts: a, $1.20. b, $1.80. c, $3. d, $5.

2007, Dec. 31 **Litho.** ***Perf. 13½***
1536 A308 Block of 4, #a-d 8.25 8.25

No. 1536 was not made available until late 2008.

Miniature Sheets

A309

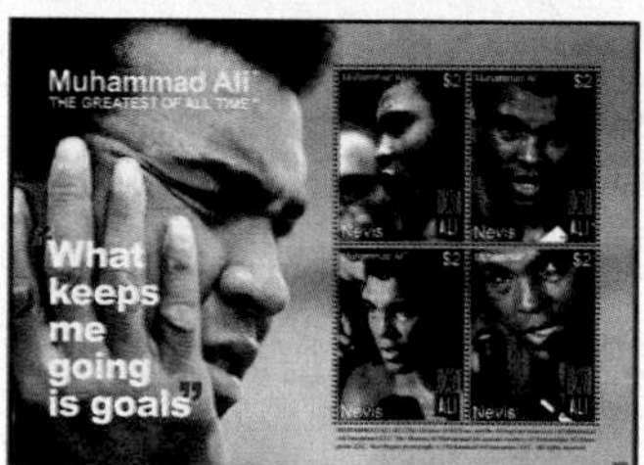

Muhammad Ali, Boxer — A310

No. 1537 — Ali: a, In ring with fists at side. b, In ring, opponent at right. c, In ring, opponent punching. d, With arm on ropes. e, With arms raised. f, Receiving trophy.
No. 1538 — Ali: a, Facing left, face in background. b, With microphones, at bottom. c, Facing left, with microphone at left. d, With large microphone at LL.

2008, Sept. 3 **Litho.** ***Perf. 11½x12***
1537 A309 $1.80 Sheet of 6, #a-f 8.25 8.25

Perf. 13¼
1538 A310 $2 Sheet of 4, #a-d 6.25 6.25

Miniature Sheet

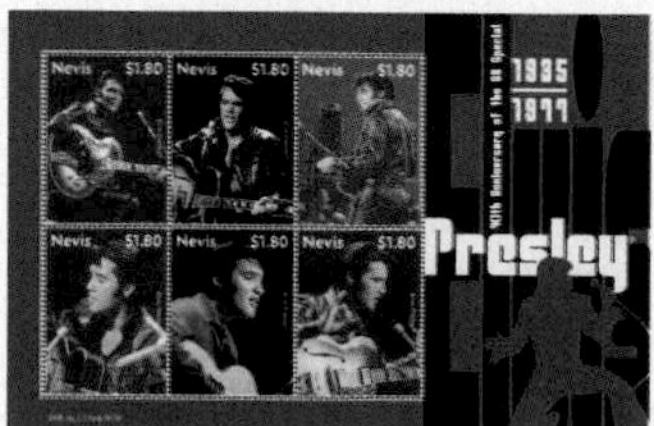

Elvis Presley (1935-77) — A311

No. 1539 — Presley with guitar: a, Microphone at right, both hands on guitar. b, Microphone at left, hand on neck of guitar. c, With audience at LL. d, Microphone at left, no hands shown. e, Wearing blue shirt. f, Microphone at right, with hands off guitar.

2008, Sept. 3 ***Perf. 13¼***
1539 A311 $1.80 Sheet of 6, #a-f 8.25 8.25

Miniature Sheet

Visit to New York of Pope Benedict XVI — A312

No. 1540 — Pope Benedict XVI and background with: a, Gray spot to left of "N" in "Nevis." b, Left half of United Nations emblem. c, Right half of United Nations Emblem. d, Gray spot between "E" and "V" in "Nevis."

2008, Sept. 17
1540 A312 $2 Sheet of 4, #a-d 6.25 6.25

Geothermal Well — A313

2008, Sept. 19 ***Perf. 11½***
1541 A313 $5 multi 4.00 4.00

Independence, 25th anniv.

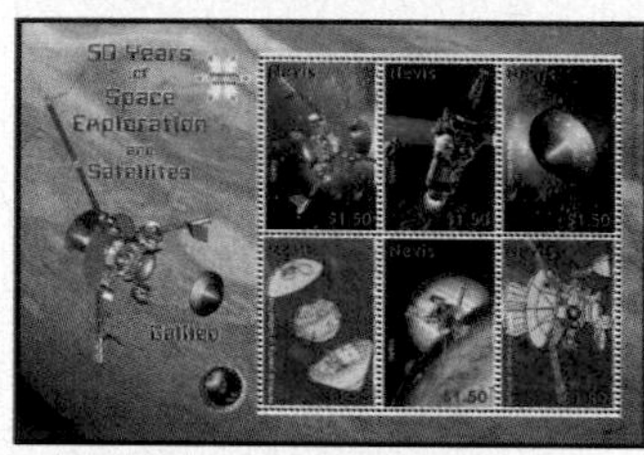

A314

Space Exploration, 50th Anniv. — A315

No. 1542: a, Galileo spacecraft with arms extended, stars in background. b, Galileo on booster rocket. c, Galileo probe. d, Technical drawing of Galileo probe. e, Galileo, planet and moon. f, Technical drawing of Galileo.
No. 1543: a, Voyager 1 and ring diagram. b, Io, Ganymede, Voyager 1 and Callisto. c, Ganymede, Europa, Callisto and Voyager 1. d, Voyager 1 and radiating line diagram. e, Voyager 1, Titan and Dione. f, Titan, Voyager 1 and Enceladus.
No. 1544: a, Technical drawing of Apollo 11 command module. b, Saturn V rocket on launch pad. c, Edwin E. Aldrin on Moon. d, Technical drawing of Apollo 11 lunar module.
No. 1545: a, Van Allen radiation belt. b, Technical drawing of Explorer 1. c, James Van Allen. d, Explorer 1 above Earth.

2008, Dec. 3 ***Perf. 13¼***
1542 A314 $1.50 Sheet of 6, #a-f 7.00 7.00
1543 A315 $1.50 Sheet of 6, #a-f 7.00 7.00
1544 A314 $2 Sheet of 4, #a-d 6.25 6.25
1545 A315 $2 Sheet of 4, #a-d 6.25 6.25

Christmas A316

Traditional holiday foods: 25c, Roast pig. 30c, Fruit cake. 80c, Pumpkin pie. 90c, Sorrel drink. $2, Fruit cake, diff.
$6, Baked ham and turkey, vert.

2008, Dec. 5 ***Perf. 11½***
1546-1550 A316 Set of 5 3.25 3.25

Souvenir Sheet
1551 A316 $6 multi 4.75 4.75

Miniature Sheet

Inauguration of U.S. President Barack Obama — A317

No. 1552 — Pres. Obama and, in background: a, Window. b, Flag and chair. c, White House and flowers. d, Chair.

2009, Jan. 20 **Litho.** ***Perf. 11½x12***
1552 A317 $3 Sheet of 4, #a-d 9.25 9.25

Agricultural Open Day, 15th Anniv. A318

Designs: 25c, Fruits and packaged foods. 30c, Fruits. 90c, Goats. $5, Workers propagating plants.
$6, Entertainment at fair.

2009, Mar. 26 ***Perf. 11½***
1553-1556 A318 Set of 4 5.00 5.00

Souvenir Sheet
Perf. 13½
1557 A318 $6 multi 4.75 4.75

No. 1557 contains one 51x37mm stamp.

Miniature Sheets

A319

China 2009 World Stamp Exhibition, Luoyang — A320

No. 1558 — Olympic Sports: a, Shooting. b, Field hockey. c, Taekwondo. d, Softball.
No. 1559 — Emperor Hsuan-yeh (Kangxi) (1654-1722): a, Wearing blue robe. b, Wearing Robe with blue sleeves. c, Wearing robe with yellow sleeves. d, At desk.

2009, Apr. 10 ***Perf. 14x14¾***

1558 A319 $1.40 Sheet of 4, #a-d 4.25 4.25

Perf. 12¾x12½

1559 A320 $1.40 Sheet of 4, #a-d 4.25 4.25

Charles Darwin (1809-82), Naturalist — A321

No. 1560, horiz.: a, Marine iguana. b, Statue of Darwin, Shrewsbury, England. c, Platypus. d, Vampire bat. e, Painting of Darwin by George Richmond. f, Large ground finch.
$6, 1881 colorized photograph of Darwin

2009, June 15		***Perf. 11½***
1560 A321 $2 Sheet of 6, #a-f	9.00	9.00

Souvenir Sheet

Perf. 13¼

1561 A321 $6 multi 4.50 4.50

No. 1560 contains six 40x30mm stamps.

Dolphins and Whales — A322

No. 1562: a, Amazon River dolphin. b, Indus river dolphin. c, Atlantic white-sided dolphin. d, La Plata dolphin. e, Peale's dolphin. f, White-beaked dolphin.
No. 1563: a, Long-finned pilot whale. b, Short-finned pilot whale.
No. 1564: a, Killer whale. b, Pygmy killer whale.

2009, June 15 ***Perf. 13¼***

1562 A322 $2 Sheet of 6, #a-f 9.00 9.00

Souvenir Sheets

1563 A322 $3 Sheet of 2, #a-b 4.50 4.50
1564 A322 $3 Sheet of 2, #a-b 4.50 4.50

Souvenir Sheets

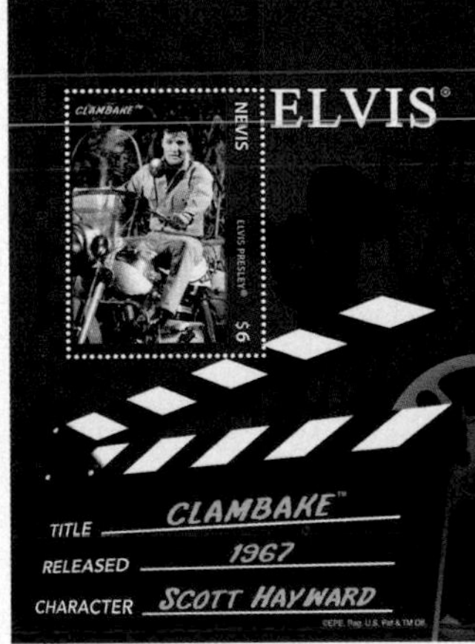

A323

A324

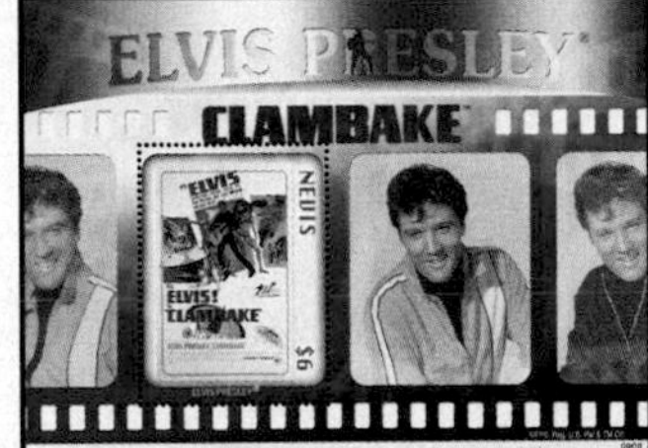

A325

Elvis Presley (1935-77) — A326

2009, June 15		***Perf. 13¼***
1565 A323 $6 multi	4.50	4.50
1566 A324 $6 multi	4.50	4.50
1567 A325 $6 multi	4.50	4.50
1568 A326 $6 multi	4.50	4.50
Nos. 1565-1568 (4)	18.00	18.00

Miniature Sheet

Pres. Abraham Lincoln (1809-65) — A327

No. 1569: a, Lincoln Memorial and Reflecting Pool. b, Front view of Lincoln sculpture in Lincoln Memorial. c, Head and hand of Lincoln sculpture. d, Aerial view of Lincoln Memorial.

2009, Aug. 20

1569 A327 $2.50 Sheet of 4, #a-d 7.50 7.50

Miniature Sheet

The Three Stooges — A328

No. 1570: a, Moe Howard, Curly Howard and Larry Fine. b, Curly Howard. c, Moe Howard. d, Larry Fine.

2009, Aug. 20 ***Perf. 11½***

1570 A328 $2.50 Sheet of 4, #a-d 7.50 7.50

Miniature Sheet

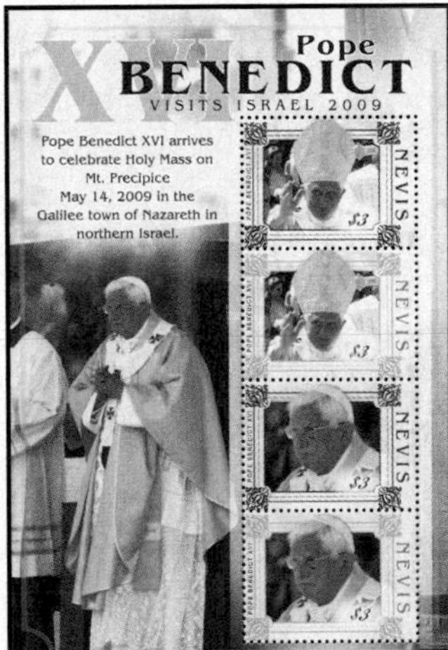

Pope Benedict XVI — A329

No. 1571 — Pope Benedict XVI: a, Wearing miter, brown frame. b, Wearing miter, bister frame. c, Wearing zucchetto and eyeglasses, brown frame. d, Wearing zucchetto and eyeglasses, bister frame.

2009, Aug. 20

1571 A329 $3 Sheet of 4, #a-d 9.00 9.00

Miniature Sheets

A330

Michael Jackson (1958-2009) — A331

No. 1572 — Jackson with country name in: a, Blue. b, Yellow. c, Lilac. d, Red.

No. 1573 — Jackson: a, With microphone near mouth, hands raised. b, With arms extended to side. c, Holding microphone. d, With people in background.

Perf. 11¼x11½

2009, Sept. 25 **Litho.**

1572 A330 $2 Sheet of 4, #a-d 6.00 6.00

Perf. 11½x12

1573 A331 $3 Sheet of 4, #a-d 9.00 9.00

Worldwide Fund for Nature (WWF) A332

No. 1574 — Caribbean reef squid with denomination in: a, Pink and blue. b, Pink. c, Orange and red. d, Green and blue.

2009, Dec. 1		***Perf. 13¼***
1574 Strip or block of 4	6.00	6.00
a.-d. A332 $2 Any single	1.50	1.50
e. Sheet of 8, 2 each #1574a-1574d	12.00	12.00

Flowers A333

Designs: 25c, Genipa americana. 50c, Clusia rosea. 80c, Browallia americana. 90c, Bidens alba. $1, Begonia odorata. $5, Jatropha gossypiifolia.
No. 1581: a, Crantzia cristata. b, Selaginella flabellata. c, Hibiscus tiliaceus. d, Heliconia psittacorum.

2009, Dec. 1 **Litho.** ***Perf. 13x13¼***

1575-1580 A333 Set of 6 6.25 6.25
1581 A333 $2.50 Sheet of 4, #a-d 7.50 7.50

Christmas A334

Designs: 25c, Magi on camels. 30c, Holy Family. 90c, Magus and camel in stars. $5, Holy Family and angels.

2009, Dec. 7 **Litho.** ***Perf. 14¾x14¼***

1582-1585 A334 Set of 4 5.00 5.00

First Man on the Moon, 40th Anniv. — A335

No. 1586: a, Astronaut Neil Armstrong, Saturn V rocket. b, Astronauts Edwin "Buzz" Aldrin and Michael Collins. c, Apollo 11 command module, Moon. d, Apollo 11 lunar module leaving Moon.
$6, Armstrong and lunar module.

2009, Dec. 30 **Litho.** ***Perf. 11½x12***

1586 A335 $2.50 Sheet of 4, #a-d 7.75 7.75

Souvenir Sheet

Perf. 11½x11¼

1587 A335 $6 multi 4.75 4.75

Intl. Year of Astronomy.

Miniature Sheet

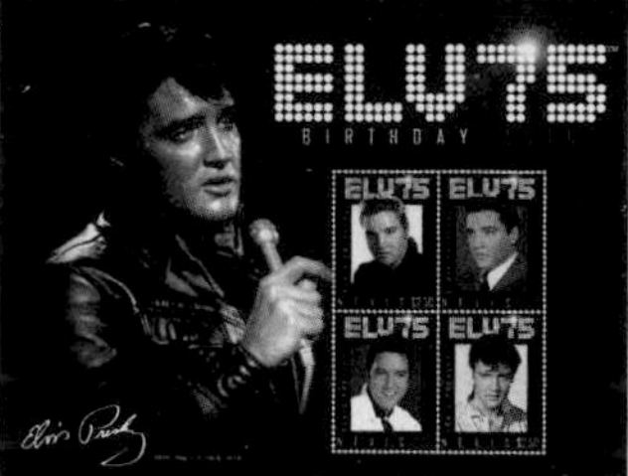

Elvis Presley (1935-77) — A336

No. 1588 — Presley wearing: a, Black jacket. b, Brown suit and blue shirt. c, White shirt with red neckerchief. d, Blue shirt.

2010, Mar. 2 Litho. ***Perf. 12x11½***
1588 A336 $2.50 Sheet of 4, #a-d 7.75 7.75

Ferrari Race Cars and Parts A337

No. 1589, $1.25: a, Engine diagram of 1947 125 S. b, 1947 125 S.
No. 1590, $1.25: a, Engine of 1951 500 F2. b, 1951 500 F2.
No. 1591, $1.25: a, Exhaust pipe of 1953 553 F2. b, 1953 553 F2.
No. 1592, $1.25: a, Engine of 1957 Dino 156 F2. b, 1957 Dino 156 F2.

2010, Mar. 2 ***Perf. 12***
Vert. Pairs, #a-b
1589-1592 A337 Set of 4 7.75 7.75

Mushrooms A338

Designs: 25c, Psilocybe guilartensis. 80c, Alboleptonia flavifolia. $1, Agaricus sp. $5, Psilocybe caerulescens.
No. 1597: a, Psilocybe portoricensis. b, Boletus ruborculus. c, Psilocybe plutonia (one). d, Alboleptonia largentii. e, Psilocybe plutonia (three). f, Collybia aurea.

2010, Mar. 24 Litho. ***Perf. 11½***
1593-1596 A338 Set of 4 5.25 5.25
1597 A338 $1.50 Sheet of 6, #a-f 6.75 6.75

A339

A340

Birds — A341

Designs: 30c, Great blue heron. 90c, Magnificent frigatebird. $1, Masked booby. $5, Great egret.
No. 1602: a, White-tailed tropicbird. b, Audubon's shearwater. c, Red-billed tropicbird. d, Leach's storm petrel.
No. 1603: a, Brown pelican. b, Brown booby.

2010, May 21 ***Perf. 11½***
1598-1601 A339 Set of 4 5.50 5.50
1602 A340 $2 Sheet of 4, #a-d 6.00 6.00
Souvenir Sheet
Perf. 11½x12
1603 A341 $3 Sheet of 2, #a-b 4.50 4.50

Miniature Sheets

A342

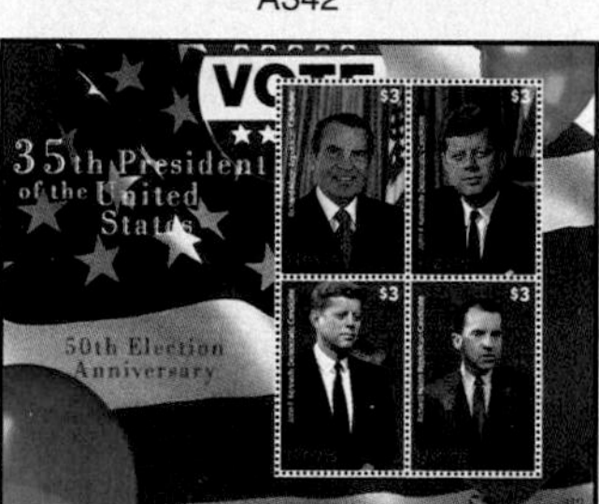

Election of Pres. John F. Kennedy, 50th Anniv. — A343

No. 1604 — Denomination in red: a, Kennedy. b, USSR Premier Nikita Khrushchev. c, Khrushchev on sofa. d, Kennedy on sofa.
No. 1605 — Denomination in white: a, Pres. Richard M. Nixon, color photograph. b, Kennedy, color photograph. c, Kennedy, black-and-white photograph. d, Nixon, black-and-white photograph.

2010, May 21 Litho. ***Perf. 13¼***
1604 A342 $3 Sheet of 4, #a-d 9.00 9.00
1605 A343 $3 Sheet of 4, #a-d 9.00 9.00

Girl Guides, Cent. — A344

No. 1606: a, Four Girl Guides and adult leader. b, Four Girl Guides. c, Girl Guide climbing rock. d, Three Girl Guides.
$6, Four Girl Guides, vert.

2010, May 21 ***Perf. 11½x12***
1606 A344 $3 Sheet of 4, #a-d 9.00 9.00
Souvenir Sheet
Perf. 11¼x11½
1607 A344 $6 multi 4.50 4.50

A345

Whales — A346

Designs: $1.20, Minke whale. $1.80, Northern right whale. $3, Fin whale. $5, Sei whale.
$6, Blue whale.

2010, July 14 ***Perf. 13x13¼***
1608-1611 A345 Set of 4 8.25 8.25
Souvenir Sheet
1612 A346 $6 multi 4.50 4.50

Souvenir Sheet

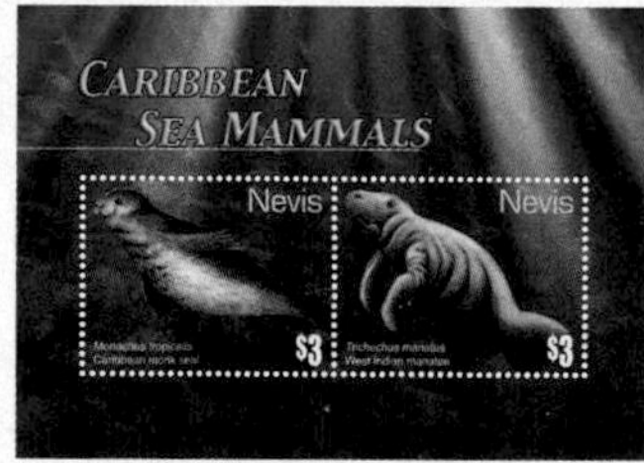

Sea Mammals — A347

No. 1613: a, Caribbean monk seal. b, West Indian manatee.

2010, July 14
1613 A347 $3 Sheet of 2, #a-b 4.50 4.50

Miniature Sheet

John F. Kennedy's 1960 US Presidential Campaign Buttons — A348

No. 1614: a, "Vote Kennedy for President." b, "For President John F. Kennedy." c, "Kennedy Johnson." d, "America Needs Kennedy Johnson."

2010, Sept. 8 ***Perf.***
1614 A348 $2 Sheet of 4, #a-d 6.00 6.00

Orchids — A349

No. 1615, horiz.: a, Heart-lipped brassavola. b, Waunakee Sunset. c, Moss-loving cranichis. d, Longclaw orchid. e, Golden yellow cattleya. f, Fat Cat.
$6, Von Martin's brassavola.

2010, Sept. 8 ***Perf. 11½x12***
1615 A349 $2 Sheet of 6, #a-f 9.00 9.00
Souvenir Sheet
Perf. 11½
1616 A349 $6 multi 4.50 4.50

Henri Dunant (1828-1910), Founder of Red Cross — A350

No. 1617 — Dunant and: a, Bertha von Suttner. b, Victor Hugo. c, Charles Dickens. d, Harriet Beecher Stowe.
$6, Dunant and scene of abolition of slavery in Washington, DC.

2010, Sept. 8 ***Perf. 13x13¼***
1617 A350 $2.50 Sheet of 4, #a-d 7.50 7.50
Souvenir Sheet
1618 A350 $6 multi 4.50 4.50

A351

Princess Diana (1961-97) — A352

No. 1619 — Princess Diana wearing: a, Black hat, black jacket. b, Black and white hat, white dress. c, Tiara.
$3, White dress, no hat.

2010, Dec. 6 ***Perf. 12***
1619 A351 $2 Vert. strip of 3, #a-c 4.50 4.50
1620 A352 $3 multi 2.25 2.25

No. 1619 was printed in sheets containing 2 of each stamp. No. 1620 was printed in sheets of 4.

Christmas A353

Paintings: 30c, Annunciation, by Paolo Uccello. 90c, The Altarpiece of the Rose Garlands, by Albrecht Dürer. $1.80, Like 30c. $2, Sistine Madonna, by Raphael. $2.30, Like $2. $3, The Adoration of the Magi, by Giotto di Bondone.

2010, Dec. 6 ***Perf. 12***
1621-1626 A353 Set of 6 7.75 7.75

A354

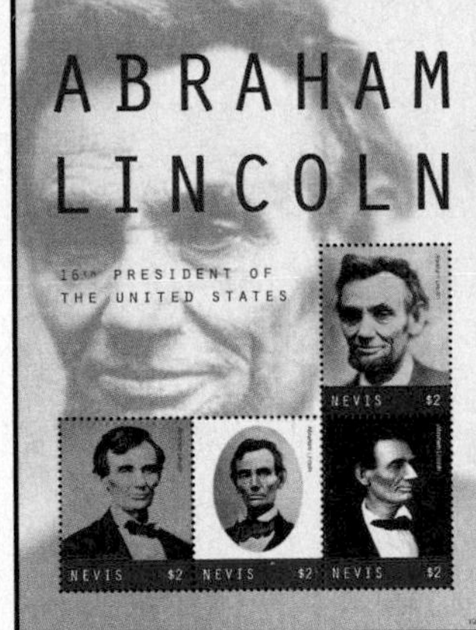

Pres. Abraham Lincoln (1809-65) — A355

No. 1628 — Lincoln: a, With buff background. b, With gray background. c, Oval photograph. d, With black background.

2010, Dec. 10 ***Perf. 11½***
1627 A354 $2 black 1.50 1.50
1628 A355 $2 Sheet of 4, #a-d 6.00 6.00

Bank of Nevis — A356

Designs: 30c, Old building. $5, New building.

2010, Dec. 9 Litho. ***Perf. 11¼x11½***
1629-1630 A356 Set of 2 4.00 4.00

Pope John Paul II (1920-2005) A357

Pope John Paul II wearing: $3, Miter. $4, Red hat.

2010, Dec. 10 ***Perf. 14x14¾***
1631-1632 A357 Set of 2 5.25 5.25

No. 1631 was printed in sheets of 4; No. 1632, in sheets of 3.

Elvis Presley (1935-77) A358

Presley wearing: No. 1633, $3, Black jacket, white shirt. No. 1634, $3, Red shirt.

2010, Dec. 10
1633-1634 A358 Set of 2 4.50 4.50

Nos. 1633-1634 each were printed in sheets of 4.

2010 World Cup Soccer Championships, South Africa — A359

No. 1635, $1.50: a, Marek Hamsik. b, Giovanni Van Bronckhorst. c, Robert Vittek. d, Eljero Elia. e, Miroslav Stoch. f, Dirk Kuyt.
No. 1636, $1.50: a, Lucio. b, Alexis Sanchez. c, Dani Alves. d, Arturo Vidal. e, Gilberto Silva. f, Rodrigo Tello.
No. 1637, $1.50: a, Liedson. b, Xavi Hernandez. c, Simao. d, Jasper Juinen. e, Cristiano Ronaldo. f, David Villa.
No. 1638, $1.50: a, Paulo Da Silva. b, Yoshito Okubo. c, Edgar Barreto. d, Yuichi Komano. e, Cristian Riveros. f, Yasuhito Endo.
No. 1639, $1.50: a, Netherlands coach Bert van Marwijk. b, Joris Mathijsen.
No. 1640, $1.50: a, Brazil coach Dunga. b, Kaka.
No. 1641, $1.50: a, Spain coach Vicente del Bosque. b, Sergio Ramos.
No. 1642, $1.50: a, Paraguay coach Gerardo Martino. b, Roque Santa Cruz.

2010, Dec. 10 ***Perf. 12***

Sheets of 6, #a-f

1635-1638 A359 Set of 4 27.00 27.00

Souvenir Sheets of 2, #a-b

1639-1642 A359 Set of 4 9.00 9.00

Trip to India of U.S. President Barack Obama — A360

No. 1643: a, Barack and Michelle Obama leaving Air Force One. b, Pres. Obama addressing Indian students in Mumbai. c, Pres. Obama signing Mumbai terrorist attacks condolence book. d, Pres. Obama and Indian Prime Minister Manmohan Singh. $6, Pres. Obama addressing Indian students in Mumbai, horiz.

2010, Dec. 10 ***Perf. 14¼x14¾***
1643 A360 $3 Sheet of 4, #a-d 9.00 9.00

Souvenir Sheet

Perf. 14¾x14¼

1644 A360 $6 multi 4.50 4.50

Indipex 2011, New Delhi.

Engagement of Prince William and Catherine Middleton — A361

No. 1645: a, Arms of Prince William (38mm diameter). b, Buckingham Palace (86x40mm arc-shaped). c, Catherine Middleton, black-and-white photo (86x40mm arc-shaped). d, Prince William, black-and-white photo (86x40mm arc-shaped).
No. 1646: a, Couple (86x40mm arc-shaped). b, Catherine Middleton, color photo (86x40mm arc-shaped). c, Prince William, color photo (86x40mm arc-shaped). $6, Couple, diff.

2010, Dec. 30 ***Perf. 13***
1645 A361 $3 Sheet of 4, #a-d 9.00 9.00
1646 A361 $3 Sheet of 4, #1645a, 1646a-1646c 9.00 9.00

Souvenir Sheet

Perf. 11½x11¼

1647 A361 $6 multi 4.50 4.50

No. 1647 contains one 40x30mm stamp.

Miniature Sheets

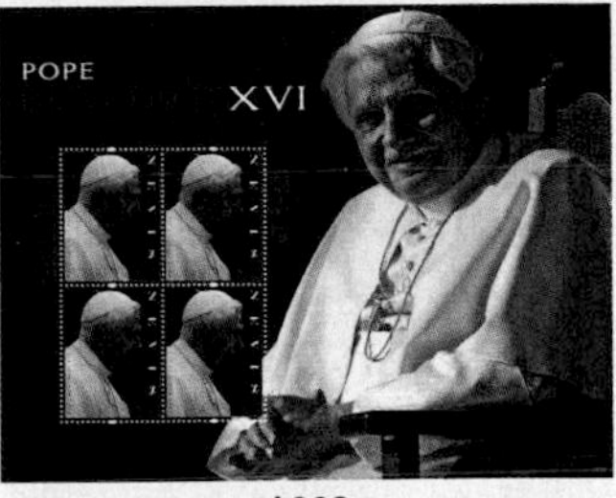

A362

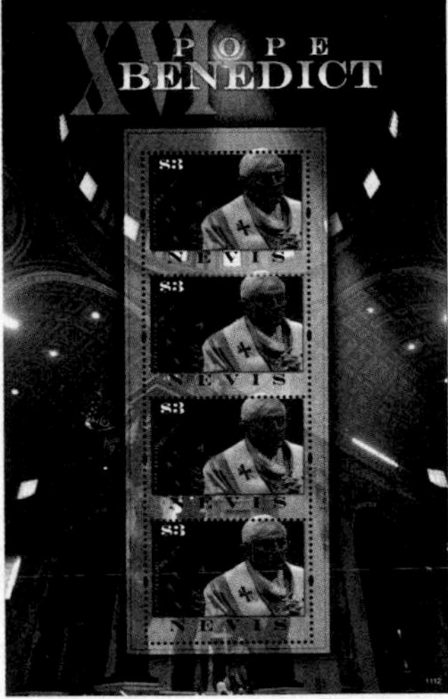

Pope Benedict XVI — A363

No. 1648 — Pope Benedict XVI with: a, Part of white stole outside frame line at LR. b, Black areas outside of frame line.
No. 1649 — Pope Benedict with: a, Windows under "N," "V" and "S" in country name. b, Protruding corner of ceiling to left of "N" in country name. c, White area under "N" in country name. d, Cross and head of statue under "V" of country name.

2011, Mar. 30 ***Perf. 13 Syncopated***
1648 A362 $3 Sheet of 4, #1648a, 3 #1648b 9.00 9.00
1649 A363 $3 Sheet of 4, #a-d 9.00 9.00

Mohandas K. Gandhi (1869-1948), Indian Nationalist A364

Gandhi and: No. 1650, $3, Orange panel at bottom. No. 1651, $3, Red brown panel at left.

2011, Mar. 30 ***Perf. 12***
1650-1651 A364 Set of 2 4.50 4.50

Nos. 1650-1651 each were printed in sheets of 4.

A365

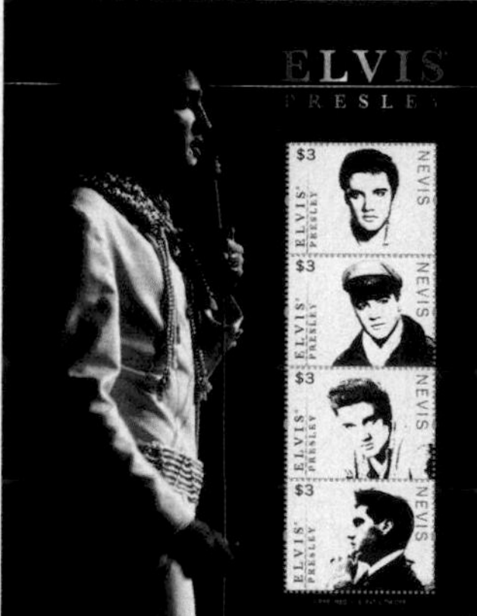

A366

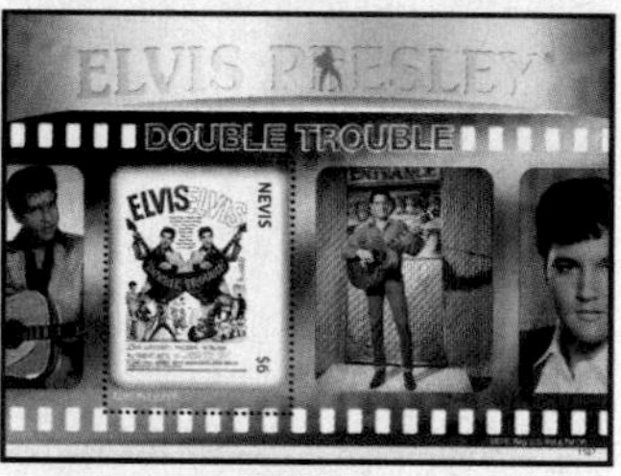

A367

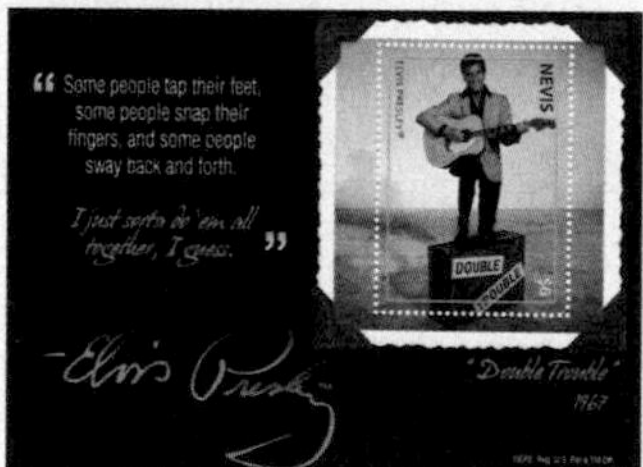

A368

A369

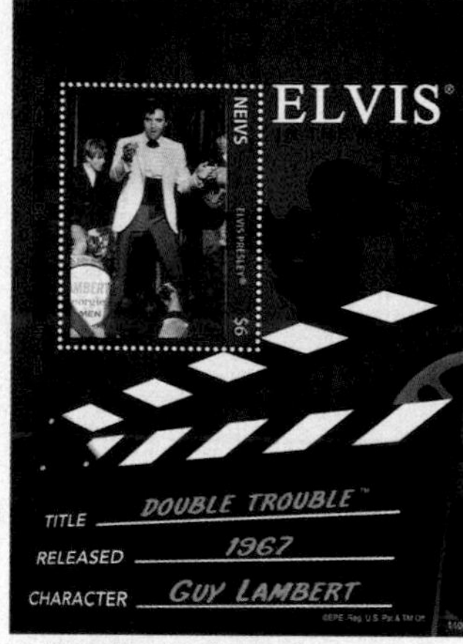

Elvis Presley (1935-77) — A370

No. 1652 — Presley and: a, Country name in white at UL. b, Country name in black at LR, Presley holding microphone. c, No country name. d, Country name in black at LL, no microphone shown.

No. 1653 — Presley: a, Head and neck only. b, Wearing hat. c, Wearing jacket. d, Touching his chin.

2011, Mar. 30 ***Perf. 13 Syncopated***

1652 A365 $3 Sheet of 4, #a-d 9.00 9.00
1653 A366 $3 Sheet of 4, #a-d 9.00 9.00

Souvenir Sheets

Perf. 12½

1654 A367 $6 multi 4.50 4.50
1655 A368 $6 multi 4.50 4.50
1656 A369 $6 multi 4.50 4.50
1657 A370 $6 multi 4.50 4.50
Nos. 1654-1657 (4) 18.00 18.00

Miniature Sheets

Cats — A371

No. 1658, $2.50: a, Maine Coon cat. b, Norwegian Forest cat. c, Ragdoll cat. d, Turkish Angora cat.

No. 1659: $2.50: a, Russian Blue cat. b, Siamese cat. c, Abyssinan cat. d, Bombay cat.

2011, Apr. 4 ***Perf. 12***

Sheets of 4, #a-d

1658-1659 A371 Set of 2 15.00 15.00

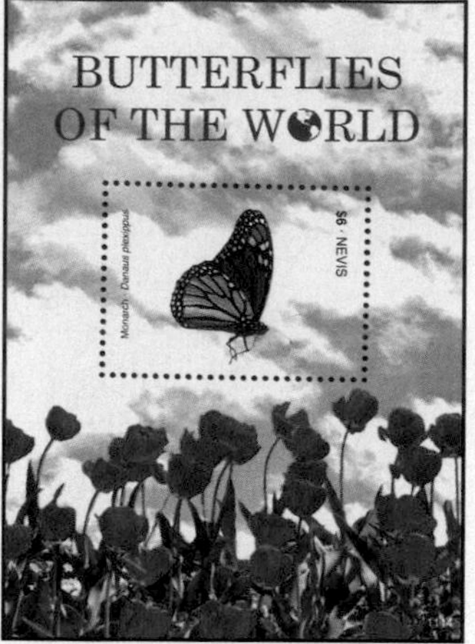

Butterflies — A372

No. 1660: a, Meadow argus. b, Gulf fritillary. c, Eastern tiger swallowtail. d, Gabb's checkerspot. e, Indian leafwing. f, Blue diadem. $6, Monarch butterfly.

2011, Apr. 4 ***Perf. 13 Syncopated***

1660 A372 $2 Sheet of 6, #a-f 9.00 9.00

Souvenir Sheet

Perf. 12

1661 A372 $6 multi 4.50 4.50

British Royalty — A373

Designs: No. 1662, Prince Philip.

No. 1663 — Queen Elizabeth II wearing: a, White dress. b, Lilac dress.

No. 1664, King George V. No. 1665, King George VI.

2011, Apr. 4 ***Perf. 13 Syncopated***

1662 A373 $2 multi 1.50 1.50
1663 A373 $2 Pair, #a-b 3.00 3.00
1664 A373 $3 multi 2.25 2.25
1665 A373 $3 multi 2.25 2.25
Nos. 1662-1665 (4) 9.00 9.00

Nos. 1662, 1664-1665 each were printed in sheets of 4. No. 1663 was printed in sheet containing two pairs.

Miniature Sheets

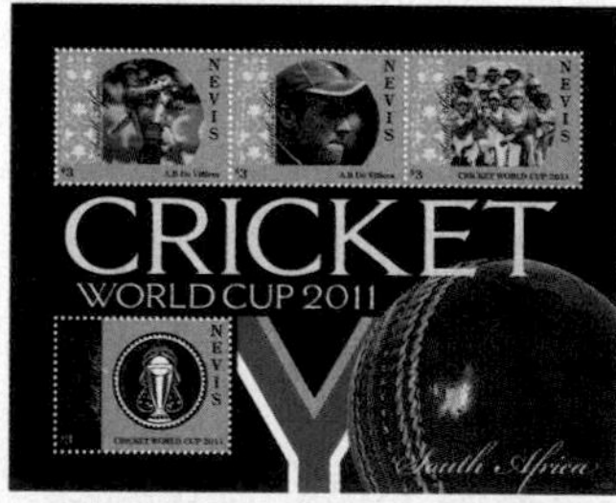

2011 Cricket World Cup, India, Bangladesh and Sri Lanka — A374

No. 1666 — Inscribed "South Africa," with dull orange background: a, A. B. De Villiers batting. b, Close-up of De Villiers. c, Posed photograph of South Africa team. d, Cricket World Cup.

No. 1667 — Inscribed "South Africa," with orange background: a, Like #1666a. b, Like #1666b. c, South Africa team celebrating. d, Like #1666d.

No. 1668 — Inscribed "Pakistan," with olive green background: a, Shoaib Akhtar running. b, Close-up of Akhtar. c, Pakistan team. d Like #1666d.

No. 1669 — Inscribed "Sri Lanka," with red brown background: a, Kumar Sangakkara on cricket pitch. b, Close-up of Sangakkara. c, Sri Lanka team. d, Like #1666d.

No. 1670 — Inscribed "West Indies," with dark red background: a, Chris Gayle holding on cricket bat. b, Close-up of Gayle. c, West Indies team. d, Like #1666d.

2011, Apr. 4 ***Perf. 12***

1666 A374 $3 Sheet of 4, #a-d 9.00 9.00
1667 A374 $3 Sheet of 4, #a-d 9.00 9.00
1668 A374 $3 Sheet of 4, #a-d 9.00 9.00
1669 A374 $3 Sheet of 4, #a-d 9.00 9.00
1670 A374 $3 Sheet of 4, #a-d 9.00 9.00
Nos. 1666-1670 (5) 45.00 45.00

Wedding of Prince William and Catherine Middleton — A375

No. 1671: a, Groom facing right. b, Bride waving.

No. 1672: a, Bride. b, Groom facing forward. c, Couple in coach, facing left, groom waving.

No. 1673: a, Couple standing. b, Couple in coach, facing right, groom waving.

2011, Apr. 29 **Litho.** ***Perf. 12***

1671 A375 $3 Pair, #a-b 4.50 4.50
1672 A375 $3 Sheet of 4, #1672a-1672b, 2 #1672c 9.00 9.00

Souvenir Sheet

1673 A375 $6 Sheet of 2, #a-b 9.00 9.00

No. 1671 was printed in sheets containing two pairs.

Miniature Sheets

Pres. Abraham Lincoln (1809-65) — A376

No. 1674, $2: a, Union soldier. b, Civil War era illustration with shield, books, wounded snake. c, Union soldiers in trenches. d, Lincoln.

No. 1675, $2 — Lincoln and quotes: a, "Government of the people, by the people, for the people shall not perish from the Earth." b, "The best way to destroy an enemy is to make him a friend." c, "A house divided against itself cannot stand." d, "Avoid popularity if you would have peace."

2011, June 20 ***Perf. 13 Syncopated***

Sheets of 4, #a-d

1674-1675 A376 Set of 2 12.00 12.00

U.S. Civil War, 150th anniv.

Miniature Sheets

Princess Diana (1961-97) — A377

No. 1676, $2 — Red panel, Princess Diana: a, Facing forward, wearing dress with dark collar. b, Wearing sailor's cap. c, Facing left, wearing striped blouse. d, Wearing maroon hat.

No. 1677, $2 — Yellow panel, Princess Diana wearing: a, Purple jacket. b, Black and white hat. c, Black jacket. d, Red dress.

2011, June 20 ***Perf. 12***

Sheets of 4, #a-d

1676-1677 A377 Set of 2 12.00 12.00

A378

A379

Marine Life — A380

Designs: 10c, Blue stripe grunt. 30c, Red hind. 40c, Red snapper. $5, Old wife.

No. 1682: a, Spotfin butterflyfish. b, Caribbean reef squid. c, Chubs. d, Surgeonfish. e, Blue-headed wrasse. f, Long-spine porcupinefish.

$6, Anemonefish.

2011, July 6 ***Perf. 12***

1678-1681 A378 Set of 4 4.25 4.25

1682 A379 $2 Sheet of 6, #a-f 9.00 9.00

Souvenir Sheet

1683 A380 $6 multi 4.50 4.50

Shells — A381

Designs: 20c, Scaphella junonia. 30c, Strombus gigas. $1.80, Busycon contrarium. $5, Arca zebra.

No. 1688: a, Charonia variegata. b, Cypraea aurantium. c, Cyphoma gibbosa. d, Chicoreus articulatus.

No. 1689, $6, Thais deltoidea. No. 1690, $6, Cittarium pica.

2011, July 25 ***Perf. 12***

1684-1687 A381 Set of 4 5.50 5.50

Perf. 13 Syncopated

1688 A381 $2.50 Sheet of 4, #a-d 7.50 7.50

Souvenir Sheets

1689-1690 A381 Set of 2 9.00 9.00

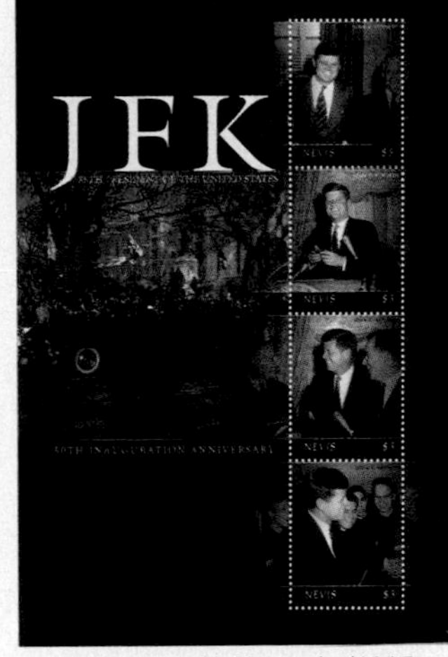

Pres. John F. Kennedy (1917-63) — A382

No. 1691 — Kennedy: a, In front of window next to other man. b, With lectern visible. c, With other man in front of microphones. d, Greeting youths.

$6, Kennedy on path shoveled in snow.

2011, Aug. 29 ***Perf. 12***

1691 A382 $3 Sheet of 4, #a-d 9.00 9.00

Souvenir Sheet

1692 A382 $6 multi 4.50 4.50

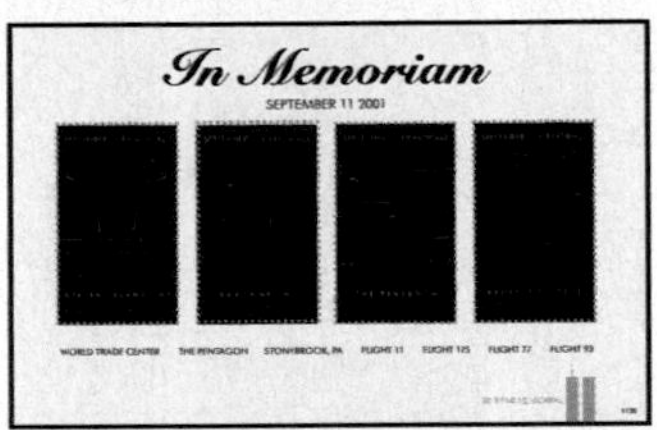

Sept. 11, 2001 Terrorist Attacks, 10th Anniv. — A383

No. 1693 — Memorials at: a, Staten Island, New York. b, Bayonne, New Jersey. c, Pentagon. d, Jerusalem, Israel.

$6, Ground Zero Reflecting Pools.

2011, Sept. 9 **Litho.**

1693 A383 $2.75 Sheet of 4, #a-d 8.25 8.25

Souvenir Sheet

1694 A383 $2.75 multi 4.50 4.50

Miniature Sheet

Inter Milan Soccer Team — A384

No. 1695: a, Team photo, 1910. b, Giorgio Muggiani, team founder. c, Angelo Moratti, past president of team. d, Heleno Herrera, coach. e, Team celebrating 2011 TIM Cup championship. f, Giacinto Facchetti, player and team president. g, Sandro Mazzola, player. h, Mario Corso, player. i, Luis Suarez, player.

2011, Sept. 13 ***Perf. 12¾***

1695 A384 $1.50 Sheet of 9, #a-i 10.00 10.00

A385

Dogs — A386

No. 1696: a, Alaskan malamute. b, Yorkshire terrier. c, Black Labrador retriever. d, Dachshund.

$6, Beagle.

2011, Oct. 14 ***Perf. 13 Syncopated***

1696 A385 $2.75 Sheet of 4, #a-d 8.25 8.25

Souvenir Sheet

1697 A386 $6 multi 4.50 4.50

Christmas A387

Paintings by Melchior Broederlam: 25c, Annunciation. 30c, Visitation. 90c, Presentation in the Temple. $5, Flight into Egypt.

2011, Nov. 7 ***Perf. 12***

1698-1701 A387 Set of 4 4.75 4.75

Reptiles — A388

No. 1702: a, Anegada ground iguana. b, Antilles racer. c, Brown anole. d, Lesser Antillean iguana.

$6, Anegada ground iguana, horiz.

2011, Nov. 14 **Litho.** ***Perf. 12***

1702 A388 $3 Sheet of 4, #a-d 9.00 9.00

Souvenir Sheet

Perf. 12½

1703 A388 $6 multi 4.50 4.50

No. 1703 contains one 51x38mm stamp.

Miniature Sheets

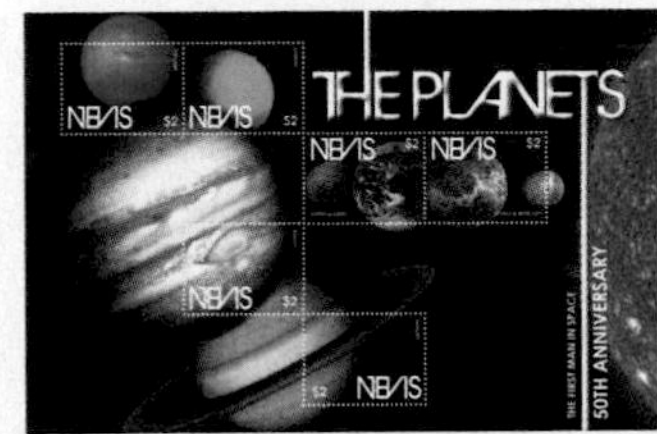

First Man in Space, 50th Anniv. — A389

No. 1704 — Planets: a, Neptune. b, Uranus. c, Earth and Mars. d, Venus and Mercury. e, Jupiter. f, Saturn.

No. 1705 — Phases of the Moon: a, Full (country name in black). b, Waxing gibbous ("N" of country name in white). c, First quarter ("NE" and part of "V" of country name in white). d, Waxing crescent (country name in white).

2011, Dec. 16 ***Perf. 12½x12***

1704 A389 $2 Sheet of 6, #a-f 9.00 9.00

Perf. 13

1705 A389 $3 Sheet of 4, #a-d 9.00 9.00

No. 1705 contains four 35mm diameter stamps.

Sinking of the Titanic, Cent. — A390

No. 1706: a, Stowaway on rope. b, Grand Staircase of the Olympic. c, Titanic at Southampton dock. d, Reading and writing room.

$6, Titanic sinking.

2012, Feb. 8 ***Perf. 13 Syncopated***

1706 A390 $3 Sheet of 4, #a-d 9.00 9.00

Souvenir Sheet

Perf. 12

1707 A390 $6 multi 4.50 4.50

Elvis Presley (1935-77) — A391

No. 1708 — Presley: a, With guitar and gray suit, no microphone. b, With guitar, gray suit, microphone on stand. c, With beige suit. d, With guitar, white suit, holding microphone.

$9, Presley in gray suit playing guitar.

2012, Mar. 26 ***Perf. 12***

1708 A391 $2.50 Sheet of 4, #a-d 7.50 7.50

Souvenir Sheet

Perf. 13¼

1709 A391 $9 multi 6.75 6.75

Medicinal Spring — A392

Nevis Coat of Arms — A393

2012, June 14 ***Perf. 11¼***

1710 A392 $100 multi 75.00 75.00
1711 A393 $150 multi 110.00 110.00

Reign of Queen Elizabeth II, 60th Anniv. — A394

No. 1712 — Various photographs of Queen Elizabeth II with denomination at: a, LR. b, LL. c, UR. d, UL.
$10, Queen Elizabeth II wearing tiara.

2012, July 25 ***Perf. 13¾***

1712 A394 $3 Sheet of 4, #a-d 9.00 9.00

Souvenir Sheet

1713 A394 $10 multi 7.50 7.50

Charles Dickens (1812-70), Writer — A395

Designs: $3.50, Dickens.
No. 1715: a, Books by Dickens. b, Dickens, diff.

2012, Aug. 7 **Litho.**

1714 A395 $3.50 multi 2.60 2.60

Souvenir Sheet

1715 A395 $4.50 Sheet of 2, #a-b 6.75 6.75

No. 1714 was printed in sheets of 4.

Miniature Sheet

Stingrays — A396

No. 1716: a, Caribbean whiptail. b, Lesseer electric ray. c, Giant manta ray. d, Southern stingray. e, Spotted eagle ray.

2012, Aug. 7 ***Perf. 12***

1716 A396 $3 Sheet of 5, #a-e 11.00 11.00

Illustrations From *Peter Pan,* by James M. Barrie (1860-1937) — A397

No. 1717 — Various illustrations with upper panel in: a, Green. b, Yellow green. c, Dull brown. d, Blue.
$6, Yellow green panel at right.

2012, Aug. 9 ***Perf. 13 Syncopated***

1717 A397 $3 Sheet of 4, #a-d 9.00 9.00

Souvenir Sheet

1718 A397 $6 multi 4.50 4.50

Miniature Sheet

Butterflies — A398

No. 1719: a, Hamadryas amphinome. b, Lycorea halia atergatis. c, Marpesia eleuchea bahamensis. d, Pyrisitia proterpia, with antennae. e, Pyrisitia proterpia, without antennae. f, Pyrrhocalles antiqua.

2012, Nov. 28 ***Perf. 12***

1719 A398 $2.50 Sheet of 6, #a-f 11.00 11.00

Beetles — A399

No. 1720: a, Lema biornata. b, Lema splendida. c, Lema minuta. d, Lema dorsalis.
No. 1721: a, Stilodes heydeni. b, Stilodes leoparda.

2012, Nov. 28 ***Perf. 13¾***

1720 A399 $2.50 Sheet of 4, #a-d 7.50 7.50

Souvenir Sheet

1721 A399 $4 Sheet of 2, #a-b 6.00 6.00

Painting of the Sistine Chapel Ceiling by Michelangelo, 500th Anniv. — A400

No. 1722 — Details from Ancestors of Christ: a, Man with hand at face. b, Woman, man and infant. c, Woman kissing child. d, Woman and naked child at right.
$9, The Creation of Adam, horiz.

2012, Nov. 28 ***Perf. 13¾***

1722 A400 $3.50 Sheet of 4, #a-d 10.50 10.50

Souvenir Sheet

Perf. 12

1723 A400 $9 multi 6.75 6.75

No. 1723 contains one 80x30mm stamp.

Souvenir Sheets

Elvis Presley (1935-77) — A401

Presley: No. 1724, $9, Playing guitar, purple frame, country name in red. No. 1725, $9, With two women, black frame and country name. No. 1726, $9, With band, playing guitar, red frame and country name. No. 1727, $9, Holding microphone, red frame and country name. No. 1728, $9, Holding microphone, gray frame and country name.

2012, Nov. 28 ***Perf. 12¾***

1724-1728 A401 Set of 5 34.00 34.00

Christmas A402

Paintings by Caravaggio: 25c, Adoration of the Shepherds. 30c, Annunciation. 90c, Holy Family with St. John the Baptist. $1, Nativity with St. Francis and St. Lawrence. $3, Rest on the Flight into Egypt. $5, Madonna of the Rosary.

2012, Nov. 28 **Litho.**

1729-1734 A402 Set of 6 7.75 7.75

Coronation of Queen Elizabeth II, 60th Anniv. — A403

No. 1735 — Queen Elizabeth II: a, Holding orb. b, Wearing blue hat. c, Wearing pink hat. d, Wearing sash.
$9, Queen Elizabeth II wearing crown, waving.

2013, Apr. 13 ***Perf. 13 Syncopated***
1735 A403 $3.25 Sheet of 4, #a-d 9.75 9.75

Souvenir Sheet

1736 A403 $9 multi 6.75 6,75

Miniature Sheets

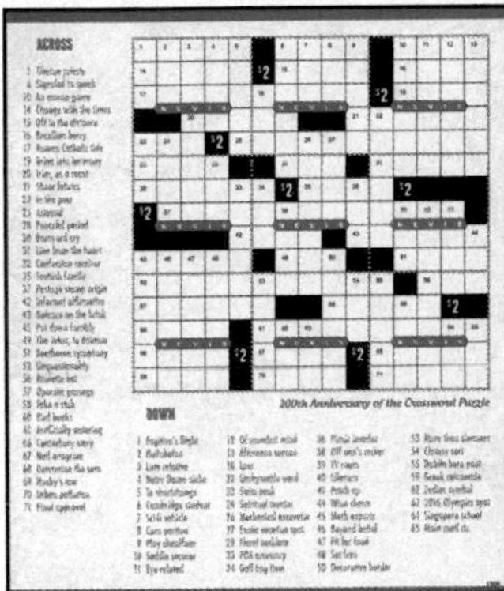

Crossword Puzzles, Cent. — A404

No. 1737, $2 — Stamps with green panels and numbered squares: a, 1-5, 14, 17, 20, 23-25. b, 6-9, 15, 18, 21, 26-27. c, 10-13, 16, 19, 22. d, 28-29, 32-33, 37, 42, 45-48. e, 30, 34-36, 38, 43, 49-50. f, 31, 39-41, 44, 51. g, 52, 57, 60, 66, 69. h, 53-54, 58, 61-63, 67, 70. i, 55-56, 59, 64-65, 68, 71.
No. 1738, $2 — Stamps with red panels and numbered squares: a, 1-5, 14, 17, 20, 22, 23. b, 6-9, 15, 18, 21, 24. c, 10-13, 16, 19. d, 25, 29, 32-33, 37, 40-43. e, 26-27, 30, 34, 44. f, 28, 31, 35-36, 38-39, 45. g, 46-47, 49, 52, 56, 59. h, 48, 50-51, 53, 57, 60. i, 54-55, 58, 61.

2013, Apr. 3 ***Perf. 13¾***

Sheets of 9, #a-i

1737-1738 A404 Set of 2 27.00 27.00

On Nos. 1737-1738, crossword puzzle clues are in sheet margins and puzzle answers are printed on the backs of the stamps.

Personalizable Stamp — A405

2013, Apr. 22 ***Perf. 14x14¾***
1739 A405 $3 multi 2.25 2.25

No. 1739 was printed in sheets of 9 and presumably could be personalized for an extra fee.

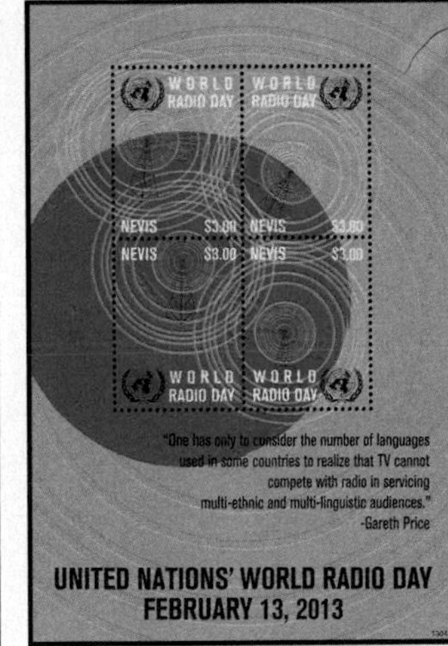

World Radio Day — A406

No. 1740 — Radio antennae and concentric circles with United Nations emblem at: a, UL. b, UR. c, LL. d, LR.
$8, Radio antenna, concentric circles, United Nations emblem at LL.

2013, Apr. 25 ***Perf. 12***
1740 A406 $3 Sheet of 4, #a-d 9.00 9.00

Souvenir Sheet

1741 A406 $8 multi 6.00 6.00

Bees — A408

No. 1744: a, Bicyrtes quadrifasciatus. b, Bembix americana. c, Ammophila apicalis. d, Ectemnius continuus.
$8, Bicyrtes quadrifasciatus, diff.

2013, Apr. 25 ***Perf. 12***
1744 A408 $4 Sheet of 4, #a-d 12.00 12.00

Souvenir Sheet

1745 A408 $8 multi 6.00 6.00

Fruit — A409

No. 1746: a, Lemon. b, Persimmons. c, Yellow plum. d, Oranges.
$9, Peach, vert.

2013, June 3 ***Perf. 13¾***
1746 A409 $3.25 Sheet of 4, #a-d 9.75 9.75

Souvenir Sheet

Perf. 12½

1747 A409 $9 multi 6.75 6.75

No. 1747 contains one 38x51mm stamp.

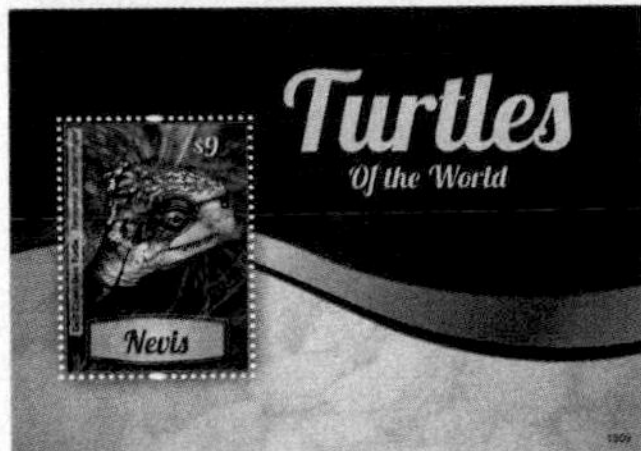

Turtles — A410

No. 1748: a, Desert tortoise. b, African helmeted turtle. c, Redbelly turtle. d, Red-eared slider.
$9, Gulf Coast box turtle.

2013, June 3 ***Perf. 13 Syncopated***
1748 A410 $3.25 Sheet of 4, #a-d 9.75 9.75

Souvenir Sheet

1749 A410 $9 multi 6.75 6.75

Parrots — A411

No. 1750: a, Imperial amazon. b, Cuban amazon. c, Hispanolian parrot. d, St. Vincent amazon.
$9, St. Lucia amazon, vert.

2013, June 3 ***Perf. 13¾***
1750 A411 $3.25 Sheet of 4, #a-d 9.75 9.75

Souvenir Sheet

Perf. 12½

1751 A411 $9 multi 6.75 6.75

No. 1751 contains one 38x51mm stamp.

Hummingbirds — A407

No. 1742: a, Antillean mango. b, Ruby-throated hummingbird. c, Purple-throated carib. d, Long-billed starthroat.
No. 1743: a, Green-throated carib. b, Tufted coquette.

2013, Apr. 25 ***Perf. 13¾***
1742 A407 $3.25 Sheet of 4, #a-d 9.75 9.75

Souvenir Sheet

1743 A407 $4.50 Sheet of 2, #a-b 6.75 6.75

Nos. 1742 and 1743 exist imperf. Value, set $25.

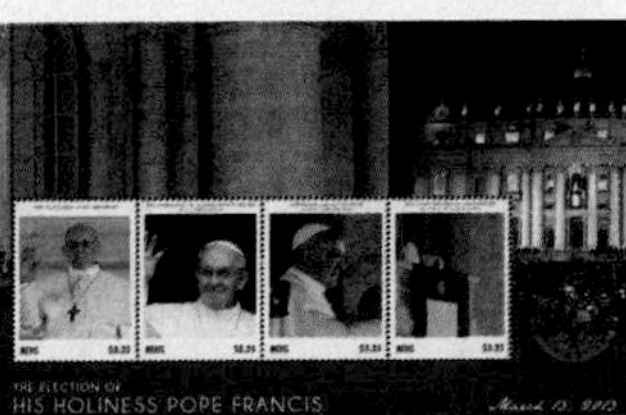

Election of Pope Francis — A412

No. 1752 — Pope Francis: a, Waving, orange background. b, Waving, black background. c, Facing right. d, On balcony with assistant.
$9, Pope Francis, assistant with microphone.

2013, June 3 ***Perf. 14***
1752 A412 $3.25 Sheet of 4, #a-d 9.75 9.75

Souvenir Sheet

Perf. 12½

1753 A412 $9 multi 6.75 6.75

No. 1753 contains one 38x51mm stamp.

Souvenir Sheet

Elvis Presley (1935-77) — A413

Litho., Margin Embossed

2013, July 8 ***Imperf.***

Without Gum

1754 A413 $20 black 15.00 15.00

Birth of Prince George of Cambridge — A414

No. 1755: a, Duke and Duchess of Cambridge, Prince George. b, Prince George. c, Duchess of Cambridge, Prince George. d, Duke of Cambridge, Prince George.
No. 1756: a, Duke and Duchess of Cambridge, Prince George, diff. b, Prince George, diff.

2013, Sept. 10 Litho. ***Perf. 12x12½***
1755 A414 $3.25 Sheet of 4, #a-d 9.75 9.75

Souvenir Sheet

1756 A414 $4.75 Sheet of 2, #a-b 7.00 7.00

Flora of Thailand — A415

No. 1757: a, Pineapple. b, Papayas. c, Red pineapple. d, Plumeria. e, Magnolia. f, Camellia.
$9, Bromeliad, vert.

2013, Aug. 26 Litho. *Perf. 13¾*

1757 A415 $2.50 Sheet of 6, #a-f 11.50 11.50

Souvenir Sheet

Perf. 12½

1758 A415 $9 multi 6.75 6.75

Thailand 2013 World Stamp Exhibition, Bangkok. No. 1758 contains one 38x51mm stamp.

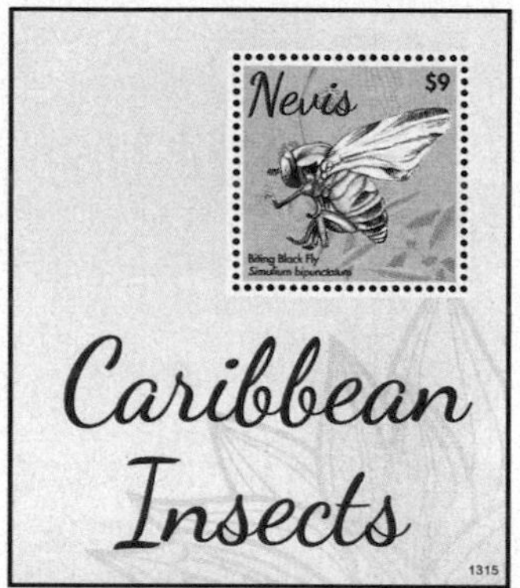

Insects — A416

No. 1759: a, Citrus root weevil. b, West Indian firetail. c, Catarina. d, Field cricket.
$9, Biting black fly.

2013, Sept. 17 Litho. *Perf. 12½*

1759 A416 $3.50 Sheet of 4, #a-d 10.50 10.50

Souvenir Sheet

1760 A416 $9 multi 6.75 6.75

Independence, 30th Anniv. — A417

Designs: 30c, Soldiers handling flag. $5, National anthem, vert. (30x50mm). $10, Soldiers on parade.
$9, Map of St. Kitts and Nevis, vert.

Perf. 12½x13¼, 12 ($5)

2013, Sept. 19 Litho.

1761-1763 A417 Set of 3 11.50 11.50

Souvenir Sheet

Perf. 13¼x12½

1764 A417 $9 multi 6.75 6.75

Christmas A418

Paintings by Carlo Crivelli: 30c, Adoration of the Shepherds. 90c, Christ Blessing. $2, Immaculate Conception. $5, Madonna d'Ancona.

2013, Dec. 2 Litho. *Perf. 12½*

1765-1768 A418 Set of 4 6.25 6.25

Fish — A419

Designs: 10c, Barred hogfish. 15c, Bluefaced angelfish (Pomacanthus xanthometopon). 20c, Comb grouper. 30c, Spotfin hogfish. 90c, Yellow jack. $1, Broadbarred firefish. $1.20, Queen angelfish. $2, Stoplight parrotfish. $3, Tiger grouper. $5, Titan triggerfish. $10, Blue-striped grunt. $20, Flameback angelfish.

2013, Dec. 4 Litho. *Perf. 13¾*

1769	A419	10c multi	.25	.25
1770	A419	15c multi	.25	.25
1771	A419	20c multi	.25	.25
1772	A419	30c multi	.25	.25
1773	A419	90c multi	.65	.65
1774	A419	$1 multi	.75	.75
1775	A419	$1.20 multi	.90	.90
1776	A419	$2 multi	1.50	1.50
1777	A419	$3 multi	2.25	2.25
1778	A419	$5 multi	3.75	3.75
1779	A419	$10 multi	7.50	7.50
1780	A419	$20 multi	15.00	15.00
		Nos. 1769-1780 (12)	33.30	33.30

A420

A421

A422

Nelson Mandela (1918-2013), President of South Africa — A423

No. 1782 — Mandela: a, Wearing blue and white shirt with AIDS ribbon below top button. b, Wearing black and white shirt, person in background. c, Waving. d, Wearing black and white shirt.

2013, Dec. 15 Litho. *Perf. 13¾*

1781 A420 $4 multi 3.00 3.00

1782 A421 $4 Sheet of 4, #a-d 12.00 12.00

Souvenir Sheets

1783 A422 $14 multi 10.50 10.50

1784 A423 $14 multi 10.50 10.50

No. 1781 was printed in sheets of 4.

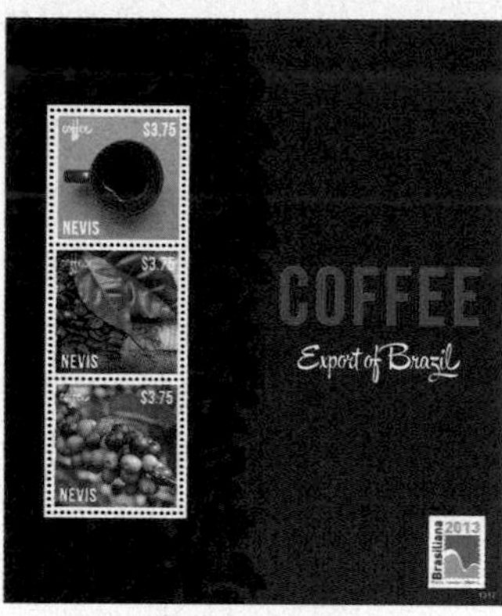

Coffee — A424

No. 1785: a, Cup of coffee. b, Leaves and roasted beans. c, Coffee berries.
$9, Roasted bean.

2013, Nov. 18 Litho. *Perf. 12½*

1785 A424 $3.75 Sheet of 3, #a-c 8.50 8.50

Souvenir Sheet

1786 A424 $9 multi 6.75 6.75

2013 Brasiliana Intl. Philatelic Exhibition, Rio de Janeiro.

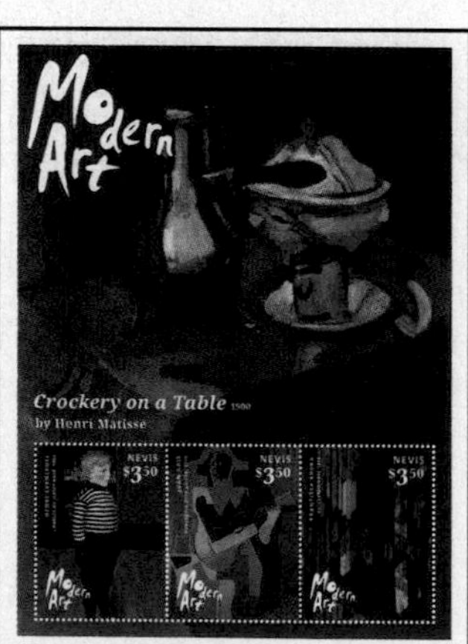

Modern Art — A425

No. 1787, $3.50: a, Charles au Jersey Rayé, by Henri Evenepoel. b, Harlequin with Guitar, by Juan Gris. c, Katedrala, by Frantisek Kupka.

No. 1788, $3.50: a, Madras Rouge, by Henri Matisse. b, Nude with a Parrot, by George Bellows. c, The Old Guitarist, by Pablo Picasso.

No. 1789, $9, Senecio, by Paul Klee. No. 1790, $9, Udnie, by Francis Picabia.

2014, Jan. 3 Litho. *Perf. 12¾*

Sheets of 3, #a-c

1787-1788 A425 Set of 2 15.50 15.50

Souvenir Sheets

1789-1790 A425 Set of 2 13.50 13.50

Alexander Hamilton (1755-1804), First U.S. Treasury Secretary — A426

Designs: 30c, Portrait of Hamilton. 90c, Statue of Hamilton, U.S. Treasury Building. $10, Parchment scrolls.
$9, Nevis Heritage Center, horiz.

2014, Jan. 11 Litho. *Perf. 14*

1791-1793 A426 Set of 3 8.50 8.50

Souvenir Sheet

Perf. 12

1794 A426 $9 multi 6.75 6.75

No. 1794 contains one 50x30mm stamp.

Miniature Sheets

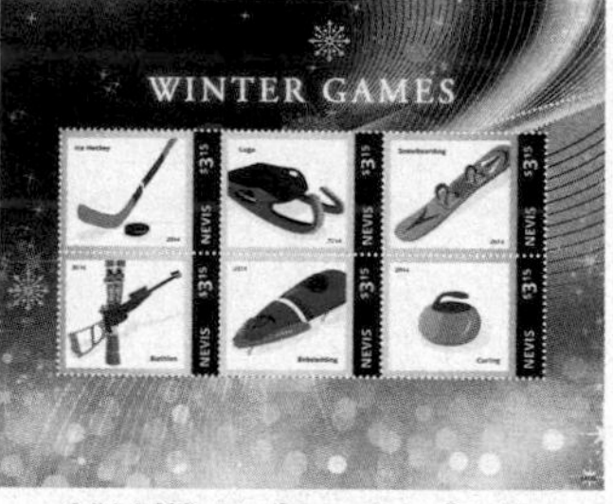

2014 Winter Olympics, Sochi, Russia — A427

No. 1795: a, Ice hockey stick and puck. b, Luge. c, Snowboard. d, Biathlon skis and rifle. e, Bobsled. f, Curling stone.
No. 1796, vert.: a, Ski jumping. b, Speed skating. c, Alpine skiing. d, Figure skating.

2014, Mar. 5 Litho. *Perf. 12*

1795 A427 $3.15 Sheet of 6, #a-f 14.00 14.00

1796 A427 $4.75 Sheet of 4, #a-d 14.00 14.00

No. 1796 contains four 30x50mm stamps.

World War I, Cent. — A428

No. 1797, $3.15: a, Recruitment station, Trafalgar Square, London, 1914. b, Man wearing body armor, 1915. c, French machine gunners take position, 1917. d, Fort Brady, 1915. e, World War I photographer, 1917. f, Medical officer in a gas mask, 1915.

No. 1798, $3.15 — War posters from: a, France, 1915. b, Great Britain, 1914. c, United States, 1914. d, Germany, 1914. e, Australia, 1914. f, Italy, 1914.

No. 1799, $5: a, French soldiers in a trench at Berry-au-Bac, 1914. b, French soldier standing in the entrance to a trench, 1914.

No. 1800, $5 — War recruitment posters from: a, Great Britain, 1914. b, United States, 1917.

2014, Mar. 5 Litho. *Perf. 12¾*

Sheets of 6, #a-f

1797-1798 A428 Set of 2 28.00 28.00

Souvenir Sheets of 2, #a-b

1799-1800 A428 Set of 2 15.00 15.00

Characters from *Downton Abbey* Television Series — A429

No. 1801: a, Anna. b, Ivy. c, Daisy. d, Alfred Nugent.
$9, Tom Branson and Lady Sybil Crawley, horiz.

2014, Mar. 5 Litho. *Perf. 14*

1801 A429 $3.25 Sheet of 4, #a-d 9.75 9.75

Souvenir Sheet

1802 A429 $9 multi 6.75 6.75

Worldwide Fund for Nature (WWF) — A430

Nos. 1803 and 1804 — Caribbean reef shark: a, One shark, nose pointing to UR. b, Two sharks and fish. c, One shark with nose pointing to UL and fish. d, One shark with nose pointing left and fish.

2014, Apr. 2 Litho. *Perf. 14*

1803 A430 $2.50 Block or vert. strip of 4, #a-d 7.50 7.50

1804 A430 $2.75 Block or vert. strip of 4, #a-d 8.25 8.25

Berlin Wall Graffiti Art — A431

No. 1805: a, Dove, ball and chain. b, Pink stylized face. c, Reproduction of inner left cover of Pink Floyd's *The Wall* album (Marching hammers and broken wall). d, Soldier and barbed wire. e, Hand with upraised, chained thumb. f, Hands at prison window, chain.
No. 1806: a, Two stylized heads. b, Reproduction of inner right cover of Pink Floyd's *The Wall* album (mother, teacher and creature).

2014, June 23 Litho. *Perf. 12¾*

1805 A431 $3 Sheet of 6, #a-f 13.50 13.50

Souvenir Sheet

1806 A431 $5 Sheet of 2, #a-b 7.50 7.50

Fall of Berlin Wall, 25th anniv.

Orchids — A432

No. 1807: a, Phalaenopsis. b, Phalaenopsis Sogo Yukidian. c, Aerides houlettiana. d, Zygopetalum crinitum.
No. 1808: a, Laelia gouldiana. b, Miltonia regnellii. c, Epidendrum fulgens. d, Cattleya alaorii.
No. 1809, vert.: a, Pink phalaenopsis, diff. b, Miltonia. No. 1810, vert.: a, Yellow phalaenopsis. b, Miltoniopsis.

2014, July 7 Litho. *Perf. 14*

1807 A432 $4 Sheet of 4, #a-d 12.00 12.00

1808 A432 $4 Sheet of 4, #a-d 12.00 12.00

Souvenir Sheet

1809 A432 $9 Sheet of 2, #a-b 13.50 13.50

1810 A432 $9 Sheet of 2, #a-b 13.50 13.50

Nevis Financial Services Department, 30th Anniv. A433

Background color: 30c, Purple. $2, Greenish blue. $5, Blue.

2014, June 20 Litho. *Perf. 13¼*

1811-1813 A433 Set of 3 5.50 5.50

Dogs — A434

No. 1814, $3.25: a, Great Dane. b, Komondor. c, Kuvasz. d, St. Bernard.
No. 1815, $3.25: a, Italian greyhound. b, Pomeranian. c, Chihuahua. d, Japanese chin.
No. 1816, $5: a, Newfoundland. b, Alaskan malamute.
No. 1817, $5: a, Mini pinshcer. b, Chinese crested.

2014, Aug. 14 Litho. *Perf. 14*

Sheets of 4, #a-d

1814-1815 A434 Set of 2 19.50 19.50

Souvenir Sheets of 2, #a-b

1816-1817 A434 Set of 2 15.00 15.00

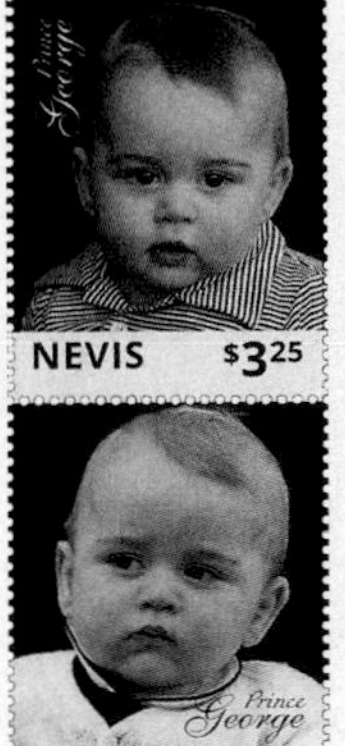

A435

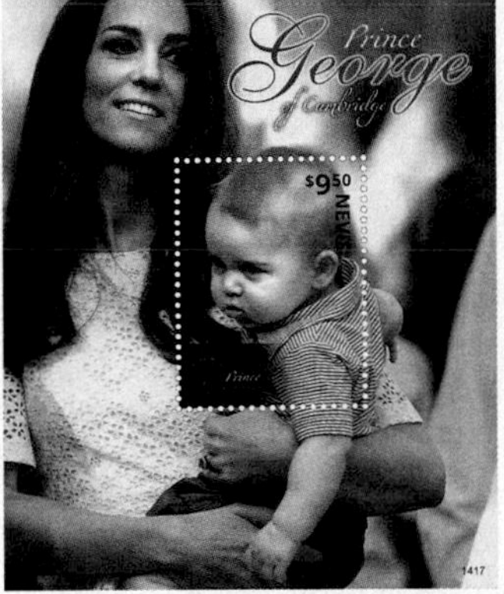

Prince George of Cambridge — A436

No. 1818 — Prince George wearing: a, Blue and white striped shirt. b, White shirt.
No. 1819, $9.50, Prince George (shown). No. 1820, $9.50, Prince George (close-up).

2014, Aug. 14 Litho. *Perf. 14*

1818 A435 $3.25 Vert. pair, #a-b 5.00 5.00

Souvenir Sheets

Perf. 12

1819-1820 A436 Set of 2 14.00 14.00

No. 1818 was printed in sheets containing three pairs. One example of No. 1818b has a different background, showing the shirt and tie of Prince William.

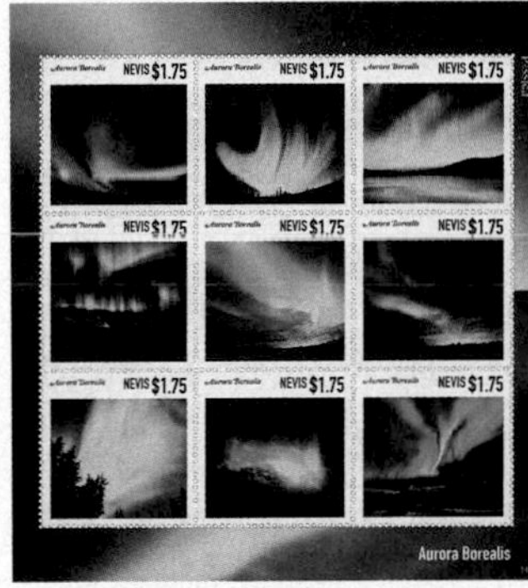

Aurora Borealis — A437

No. 1821, Various depictions of the Aurora Borealis, as shown.
$10, Aurora Borealis, diff.

2014, Sept. 3 Litho. *Perf. 13¾*

1821 A437 $1.75 Sheet of 9, #a-i 12.00 12.00

Souvenir Sheet

1822 A437 $10 multi 7.50 7.50

Macaws — A438

No. 1823, $3.25: a, Blue and yellow macaw. b, Red-shouldered macaw. c, Red-fronted macaw. d, Green-winged macaw.
No. 1824, $3.25: a, Indigo macaw. b, Hyacinth macaw. c, Blue-headed macaw. d, Great green macaw.
No. 1825, $5: a, Scarlet macaaw. b, Golden-collared macaw.
No. 1826, $5: a, Blue and yellow macaw, diff. b, Blue-throated macaw.

2014, Sept. 3 Litho. *Perf. 14*

Sheets of 4, #a-d

1823-1824 A438 Set of 2 19.50 19.50

Souvenir Sheets of 2, #a-b

1825-1826 A438 Set of 2 15.00 15.00

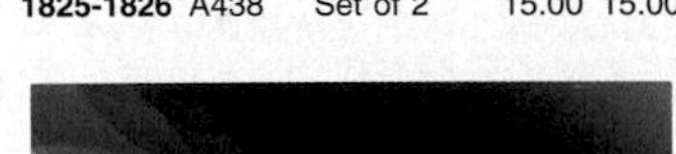

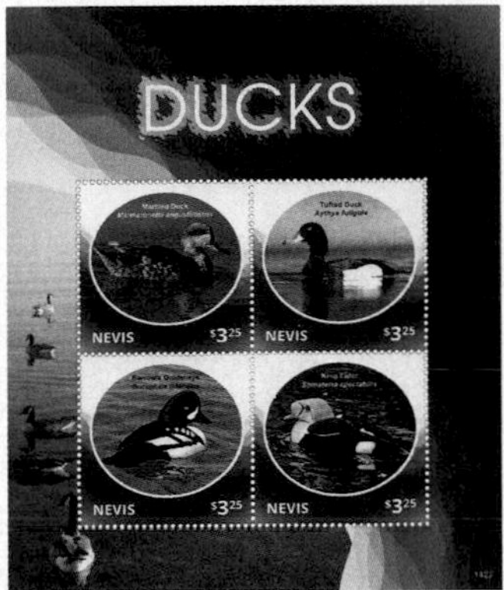

Ducks — A439

No. 1827, $3.25: a, Marbled duck. b, Tufted duck. c, Barrow's goldeneye. d, King eider.
No. 1828, $3.25: a, Wood duck. b, Rosy-billed pochard. c, Puna teal. d, Maned duck.
No. 1829, $10, Indian whistling ducks, vert. No. 1830, $10, Yellow-billed ducks, vert.

2014, Sept. 4 Litho. *Perf. 13¾*

Sheets of 4, #a-d

1827-1828 A439 Set of 2 19.50 19.50

Souvenir Sheets

Perf. 12

1829-1830 A439 Set of 2 15.00 15.00

Nos. 1829-1830 each contain one 30x40mm stamp.

A440

Coral Reefs — A441

Various corals and fish, as shown.

2014, Sept. 4 Litho. *Perf. 12*

1831 A440 $3.25 Sheet of 8. #a-h 19.50 19.50

Souvenir Sheet

1832 A441 $5 Sheet of 2, #a-b 7.50 7.50

Visit of Pope Francis to Israel A442

Designs: $1.25, Pope Francis seated with Israeli President Shimon Peres.

No. 1834 — Pope Francis: a, Standing at Church of the Holy Sepulchre. b, Kneeling at Church of the Holy Sepulchre. c, At Yad Vashem Holocaust Museum. d, At Dome of the Rock.

No. 1835, $9.50, Pope Francis facing left. and praying at Yad Vashem Holocaust Museum. No. 1836, $9.50, Pope Francis facing right and praying at the Wailing Wall.

2014, Oct. 14 Litho. *Perf. 14*

1833 A442 $1.25 multi .95 .95

Perf. 12

1834 A442 $3.25 Sheet of 4, #a-d 9.75 9.75

Souvenir Sheets

1835-1836 A442 Set of 2 14.00 14.00

Cicely Tyson, Actress — A443

2014, Jan. 1 Litho. *Perf. 14*

1837 A443 $3.25 multi 2.40 2.40

No. 1837 was printed in sheets of 4.

40th Culturama Festival — A444

Designs: $5, Crowd watching perfomers. No. 1839, $10, Dancers and crowd.

No. 1840, $10, King Meeko and King Dis and Dat, musicians.

2014, Aug. 1 Litho. *Perf. 13¼x12½*

1838-1839 A444 Set of 2 11.00 11.00

Souvenir Sheet

Perf. 12x12½

1840 A444 $10 multi 7.50 7.50

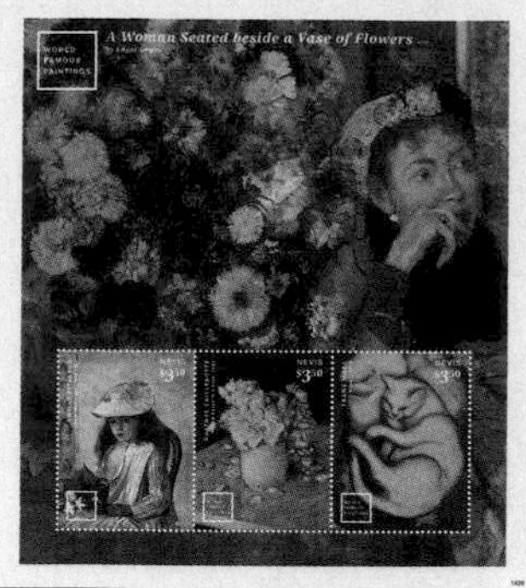

Paintings — A445

No. 1841, $3.50: a, The Artist's Daughter, by Camille Pissarro. b, Yellow Roses in a Vase, by Gustave Caillebotte. c, Kitten, by Franz Marc.

No. 1842, $3.50: a, Clump of Chrysanthemums, by Caillebotte. b, Woman Combing Her Hair, by Edgar Degas. c, Still Life with a Curtain, by Paul Gauguin.

No. 1843, $10, Road in Maine, by Edward Hopper. No. 1844, $10, Baby Reaching for an Apple, by Mary Cassatt.

2014, Oct. 14 Litho. *Perf. 12¾x12½*

Sheets of 3, #a-c

1841-1842 A445 Set of 2 15.50 15.50

Size:100x100mm

Imperf

1843-1844 A445 Set of 2 15.00 15.00

Christmas A446

Paintings by Raphael: 30c, Madonna of Foligno. 90c, The Transfiguration. $2, Madonna of Loreto. $5, Madonna del Baldacchino.

2014, Oct. 24 Litho. *Perf. 12½*

1845-1848 A446 Set of 4 6.00 6.00

Steam Locomotives of 1857 — A447

No. 1849, $3.25: a, Queen Class of Engines. b, Fourth and Fifth Lots Coupled. c, Eight Feet Passenger Engine. d, Third Lot Coupled.

No. 1850, $3.25: a, Five Feet Tank Engine. b, Sixth and Seventh Lots Coupled. c, Bogie Engine. d, Six Feet Tank Engine.

No. 1851, $10, Seven Feet Coupled Engine. No. 1852, $10, 6 Feet 6 Inches Coupled.

2014, Nov. 3 Litho. *Perf. 12*

Sheets of 4, #a-d

1849-1850 A447 Set of 2 19.50 19.50

Souvenir Sheets

1851-1852 A447 Set of 2 15.00 15.00

A448

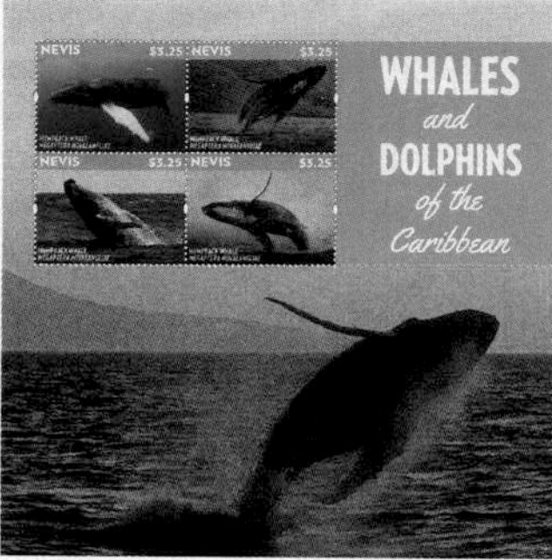

Whales and Dolphins — A449

No. 1853, Various photographs of killer whale, as shown.

No. 1854, Various photographs of humpback whale, as shown.

No. 1855, $10, Pygmy killer whale. No. 1856, $10, Sperm whale.

Perf. 13 Syncopated

2014, Dec. 16 Litho.

1853 A448 $3.15 Sheet of 6, #a-f 14.00 14.00

1854 A449 $3.25 Sheet of 4, #a-d 9.75 9.75

Souvenir Sheets

1855-1856 A449 Set of 2 15.00 15.00

Rosetta Mission — A450

No. 1857: a, Philae landing on Comet 67P. b, Philae passing Earth. c, Philae passing Mars. d, Philae break away.

$10, Philae's descent to Comet 67P.

2015, Jan. 1 Litho. *Perf. 13¾*

1857 A450 $3.25 Sheet of 4, #a-d 9.75 9.75

Souvenir Sheet

1858 A450 $10 multi 7.50 7.50

Prehistoric Mammals — A451

No. 1859, $3.25: a, Daeodon. b, Pseudaelurus. c, Stenomylus. d, Amebelodon.

No. 1860, $3.25: a, Megacerops. b, Synthetoceras. c, Merychyrus. d, Prosthennops.

No. 1861, $10, Saber-toothed cat. No. 1862, $10, Woolly mammoth.

2015, Jan. 21 Litho. *Perf. 14*

Sheets of 4, #a-d

1859-1860 A451 Set of 2 19.50 19.50

Souvenir Sheets

Perf. 12

1861-1862 A451 Set of 2 15.00 15.00

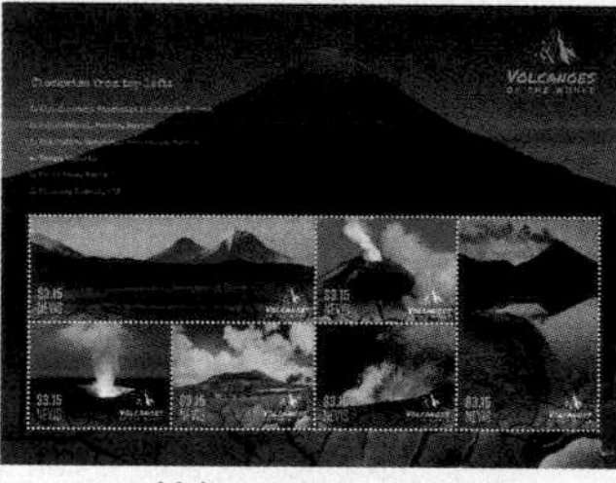

Volcanoes — A452

No. 1863: a, Klyuchevskoy Volcano, Russia (80x30mm). b, Popocatépetl Volcano, Mexico (40x30mm). c, Kamchatka Volcano, Russia (40x60mm). d, Kilauea Volcano, U.S. (40x30mm). e, Nevis Peak, Nevis (40x30mm). f, Yasur Volcano, Vanuatu (40x30mm).

$10, Mt. Fuji, Japan.

2015, Mar. 2 Litho. *Perf. 14*

1863 A452 $3.15 Sheet of 6, #a-f 14.00 14.00

Souvenir Sheet

Perf. 12

1864 A452 $10 multi 7.50 7.50

No. 1864 contains one 65x32mm triangular stamp.

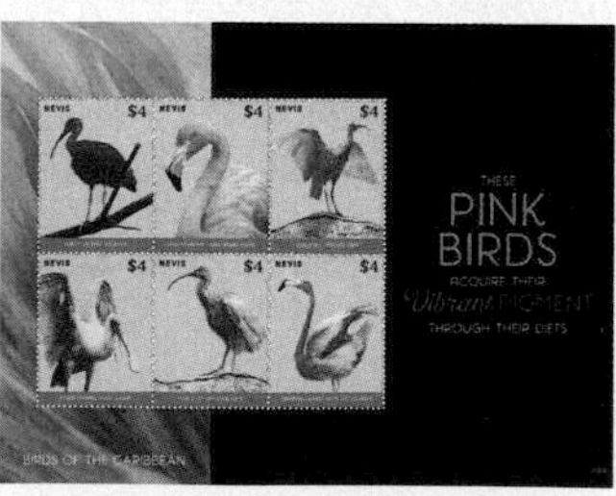

Birds — A453

No. 1865: a, Scarlet ibis on tree branch. b, Greater flamingo. c, Scarlet ibis on rock with wings extended. d, Roseate spoonbill. e, Scarlet ibis on rock looking left. f, Caribbean flamingo.

$10, Caribbean flamingo, diff.

2015, Mar. 2 Litho. *Perf. 14*

1865 A453 $4 Sheet of 6, #a-f 18.00 18.00

Souvenir Sheet

1866 A453 $10 multi 7.50 7.50

No. 1866 contains one 30x80mm stamp.

Loggerhead Sea Turtles — A454

No. 1867, Various photographs.
$10, Loggerhead sea turtle, diff.

2015, Mar. 24 Litho. *Perf. 14*

1867 A454 $3.15 Sheet of 6, #a-f 14.00 14.00

Souvenir Sheet

Perf. 12

1868 A454 $10 multi 7.50 7.50

Pope Benedict XVI — A455

No. 1869: a, Pope Benedict XVI on balcony with arms extended. b, Pope Benedict XVI wearing red zucchetto. c, Smoke announcing election of Pope Benedict XVI. d, Crowd at inauguration of Pope Benedict XVI. e, Pope Benedict XVI wearing miter. f, Pope Benedict XVI wearing white zucchetto.
$10, Pope Benedict XVI seated.

2015, Mar. 24 Litho. *Perf. 14*

1869 A455 $3.15 Sheet of 6, #a-f 14.00 14.00

Souvenir Sheet

Perf. 12

1870 A455 $10 multi 7.50 7.50

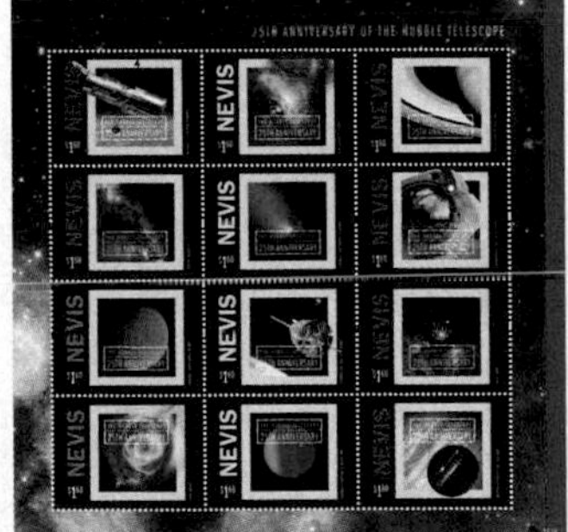

Hubble Space Telescope, 25th Anniv. — A456

No. 1871: a, Hubble Space Telescope above Earth. b, Crab Nebula. c, Rings of Saturn. d, Orion Nebula. e, Comet. f, Astronaut repairing telescope. g, Mars. h, Hubble Space Telescope, Earth at LL corner. i, NGC 3603. j, NGC 6543. k, Neptune. l, A moon in front of Jupiter.
$10, Hubble Space Telescope, diff.

2015, Mar. 24 Litho. *Perf. 14*

1871 A456 $1.60 Sheet of 12, #a-l 14.50 14.50

Souvenir Sheet

Perf. 12½

1872 A456 $10 multi 7.50 7.50

No. 1872 contains one 51x38mm stamp.

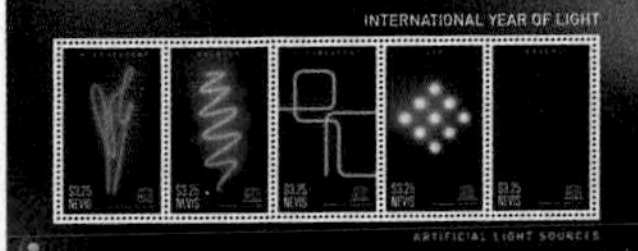

International Year of Light — A457

No. 1873 — UNESCO emblem, light and inscription: a, Incandescent. b, Halogen. c, Fluorescent. d, LED. e, Laser.
$10, UNESCO emblem and "2015 / International / Year of / Light."

2015, Apr. 15 Litho. *Perf. 12*

1873 A457 $3.25 Sheet of 5, #a-e 12.00 12.00

Souvenir Sheet

Perf. 12¾

1874 A457 $10 multi 7.50 7.50

No. 1874 contains one 38x51mm stamp.

English Lighthouses — A458

No. 1875: a, Roker Pier Lighthouse. b, Beachy Head Lighthouse. c, New Lighthouse at Dungeness. d, Smeaton's Tower. e, St. Catherine's Lighthouse. f, Flamborough Head Lighthouse.
$10, Needles Lighthouse.

2015, Apr. 15 Litho. *Perf. 14*

1875 A458 $3.15 Sheet of 6, #a-f 14.00 14.00

Souvenir Sheet

1876 A458 $10 multi 7.50 7.50

Europhilex Stamp Exhibition, London.

2015 Cricket World Cup, Australia and New Zealand A459

Designs: $4, Hagley Oval, Christchurch, New Zealand.
$10, Cricket World Cup, vert.

2015, May 4 Litho. *Perf. 14*

1877 A459 $4 multi 3.00 3.00

Souvenir Sheet

Perf. 12

1878 A459 $10 multi 7.50 7.50

First Battle of Ypres, Cent. (in 2014) — A460

No. 1879: a, Second Scots Guards testing trench, Ghent. b, Second Battalion Scots Guards. c, Sikh Regiment, Ypres. d, Naval armored car, Menin Road.
$10, British medics aid wounded comrade.

2015, Nov. 1 Litho. *Perf. 12*

1879 A460 $3.25 Sheet of 4, #a-d 9.75 9.75

Souvenir Sheet

Perf. 12½

1880 A460 $10 multi 7.50 7.50

No. 1880 contains one 51x38mm stamp.

Christmas — A461

Paintings by Bartolomé Esteban Murillo: 30c, The Annunciation. 90c, Nativity. $2, Madonna and Child. $5, Adoration of the Shepherds.

2015, Nov. 2 Litho. *Perf. 14*

1881-1884 A461 Set of 4 6.00 6.00

Queen Elizabeth II, Longest-Reigning British Monarch — A462

No. 1885 — Various photographs of Queen Elizabeth II with denomination in: a, Magenta. b, Turquoise green. c, Violet gray. d, Ochre, e, Black. f, Gray.
$10, Queen Elizabeth II wearing pink and white dress.

2015, Nov. 25 Litho. *Perf. 14*

1885 A462 $3.15 Sheet of 6, #a-f 14.00 14.00

Souvenir Sheet

Perf. 12¾

1886 A462 $10 multi 7.50 7.50

No. 1886 contains one 38x51mm stamp.

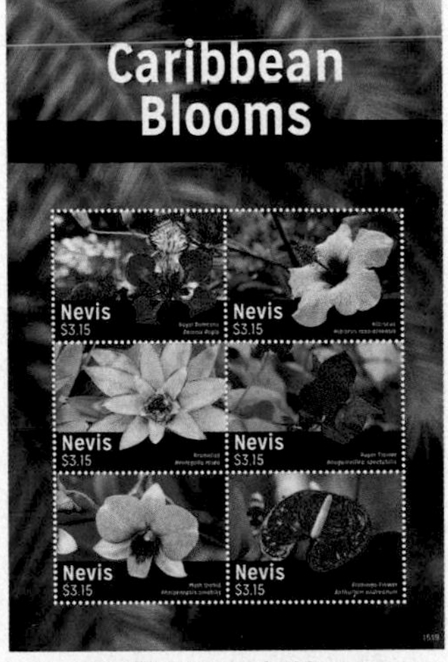

Flowers — A463

No. 1887: a, Royal poinciana. b, Hibiscus. c, Bromeliad. d, Paper flower. e, Moth orchid. f, Flamingo flower.
$10, Red palulu, vert.

2015, Dec. 7 Litho. *Perf. 14*

1887 A463 $3.15 Sheet of 6, #a-f 14.00 14.00

Souvenir Sheet

Perf. 12

1888 A463 $10 multi 7.50 7.50

No. 1888 contains one 30x50mm stamp.

Bank of Nevis Limited, 30th Anniv. A464

Designs: 30c, Bank building. 90c, Bank building, diff. $5, Sir Simeon Daniel (1934-2012), premier of Nevis, bank founder, vert.

2015, Dec. 9 Litho. *Perf. 14*

1889-1891 A464 Set of 3 4.75 4.75

Kingfishers — A465

No. 1892: a, Belted kingfisher. b, Ringed kingfisher. c, Green and rufous kingfisher. d, Green kingfisher, showing breast. e, Amazon kingfisher. f, Green kingfisher, showing back.
$10, Belted kingfisher in flight.

2015, Dec. 17 Litho. *Perf. 13¾*

1892 A465 $3.15 Sheet of 6, #a-f 14.00 14.00

Souvenir Sheet

1893 A465 $10 multi 7.50 7.50

Visit of Pope Francis to New York City — A466

No. 1894, Various photographs of Pope Francis, as shown.
$10, Pope Francis looking forward with left arm raised.

2015, Dec. 17 Litho. *Perf. 14*

1894 A466 $3.15 Sheet of 6, #a-f 14.00 14.00

Souvenir Sheet

Perf. 12

1895 A466 $10 multi 7.50 7.50

OFFICIAL STAMPS

Catalogue values for unused stamps in this section are for Never Hinged items.

Nos. 103-112 Ovptd. "OFFICIAL"

Perf. 14½x14

1980, July 30 Litho. Wmk. 373

O1	A61	15c multicolored	.25	.25
O2	A61	25c multicolored	.25	.25
O3	A61	30c multicolored	.25	.25
O4	A61	40c multicolored	.25	.25

O5 A61 45c multicolored .25 .25
O6 A61 50c multicolored .25 .25
O7 A61 55c multicolored .25 .25
O8 A61 $1 multicolored .30 .30
O9 A61 $5 multicolored 1.60 1.60
O10 A61 $10 multicolored 2.75 2.75
Nos. O1-O10 (10) 6.40 6.40

Inverted or double overprints exist on some denominations.

Nos. 123-134 Ovptd. "OFFICIAL"

1981, Mar. *Perf. 14*

O11 A9 15c multicolored .25 .25
O12 A9 20c multicolored .25 .25
O13 A9 25c multicolored .25 .25
O14 A9 30c multicolored .25 .25
O15 A9 40c multicolored .25 .25
O16 A9 45c multicolored .25 .25
O17 A9 50c multicolored .25 .25
O18 A9 55c multicolored .25 .25
O19 A9 $1 multicolored .35 .35
O20 A9 $2.50 multicolored .80 .80
O21 A9 $5 multicolored 1.60 1.60
O22 A9 $10 multicolored 2.75 2.75
Nos. O11-O22 (12) 7.50 7.50

Nos. 135-140 Ovptd. or Surcharged "OFFICIAL" in Blue or Black

1983, Feb. 2

O23 A9a 45c on $2 #137 .30 .30
O24 A9b 45c on $2 #138 .30 .30
O25 A9a 55c #135 .40 .40
O26 A9b 55c #136 .40 .40
O27 A9a $1.10 on $5 #139 (Bk) .80 .80
O28 A9b $1.10 on $5 #140 (Bk) .80 .80
Nos. O23-O28 (6) 3.00 3.00

Inverted or double overprints exist on some denominations.

Nos. 367-378 Ovptd. "OFFICIAL"

1985, Jan. 2 **Wmk. 380**

O29 A24b 15c multicolored .30 .30
O30 A24b 20c multicolored .30 .30
O31 A24b 30c multicolored .30 .30
O32 A24b 40c multicolored .30 .30
O33 A24b 50c multicolored .35 .35
O34 A24b 55c multicolored .35 .35
O35 A24b 60c multicolored .35 .35
O36 A24b 75c multicolored .45 .45
O37 A24b $1 multicolored .65 .65
O38 A24b $3 multicolored 1.90 1.90
O39 A24b $5 multicolored 3.25 3.25
O40 A24b $10 multicolored 6.50 6.50
Nos. O29-O40 (12) 15.00 15.00

Nos. 640-646, 648-653 Ovptd. "OFFICIAL"

1993 **Litho.** *Perf. 14*

O41 A71 5c multicolored .30 .30
O42 A71 10c multicolored .30 .30
O43 A71 15c multicolored .30 .30
O44 A71 20c multicolored .30 .30
O45 A71 25c multicolored .30 .30
O46 A71 40c multicolored .35 .35
O47 A71 50c multicolored .50 .50
O48 A71 75c multicolored .70 .70
O49 A71 80c multicolored .75 .75
O50 A71 $1 multicolored .95 .95
O51 A71 $3 multicolored 2.75 2.75
O52 A71 $5 multicolored 4.75 4.75
O53 A71 $10 multicolored 9.25 9.25
O54 A71 $20 multicolored 18.00 18.00
Nos. O41-O54 (14) 39.50 39.50

Dated "1992."

Nos. 1055-1066 Ovptd. "OFFICIAL"

1999, Mar. 22 **Litho.** *Perf. 14*

O55 A151 25c multicolored .25 .25
O56 A151 30c multicolored .25 .25
O57 A151 50c multicolored .40 .40
O58 A151 60c multicolored .45 .45
O59 A151 80c multicolored .60 .60
O60 A151 90c multicolored .70 .70
O61 A151 $1 multicolored .75 .75
O62 A151 $1.80 multicolored 1.40 1.40
O63 A151 $3 multicolored 2.25 2.25
O64 A151 $5 multicolored 3.75 3.75
O65 A151 $10 multicolored 7.50 7.50
O66 A151 $20 multicolored 15.00 15.00
Nos. O55-O66 (12) 33.30 33.30

NEW BRITAIN

'nü 'bri-tən

LOCATION — South Pacific Ocean, northeast of New Guinea
GOVT. — Australian military government
AREA — 13,000 sq. mi. (approx.)
POP. — 50,600 (approx.)
CAPITAL — Rabaul

The island Neu-Pommern, a part of former German New Guinea, was captured during World War I by Australian troops and named New Britain. Following the war it was mandated to Australia and designated a part of the Mandated Territory of New Guinea. See German New Guinea, North West Pacific Islands and New Guinea.

12 Pence = 1 Shilling

Stamps of German New Guinea, 1900, Surcharged

Kaiser's Yacht "The Hohenzollern"
A3 A4

First Setting

Surcharge lines spaced 6mm on 1p-8p, 4mm on 1sh-5sh

Perf. 14, 14½

1914, Oct. 17 **Unwmk.**

1 A3 1p on 3pf brown 750.00 *875.00*
2 A3 1p on 5pf green 95.00 *200.00*
3 A3 2p on 10pf car 100.00 *260.00*
4 A3 2p on 20pf ultra 100.00 *200.00*
a. "2d." dbl., "G.R.I." omitted 6,000.
b. Inverted surcharge 16,500.
5 A3 2½p on 10pf car 105.00 *220.00*
6 A3 2½p on 20pf ultra 120.00 *250.00*
a. Inverted surcharge
7 A3 3p on 25pf org & blk, *yel* 350.00 *475.00*
8 A3 3p on 30pf org & blk, *sal* 475.00 *525.00*
a. Double surcharge *15,000.* *15,000.*
b. Triple surcharge
9 A3 4p on 40pf lake & black 475.00 *625.00*
a. Double surcharge 4,100. *5,000.*
b. Inverted surcharge *16,250.*
c. "4d." omitted
10 A3 5p on 50pf pur & blk, *sal* 825.00 *1,100.*
a. Double surcharge *16,250.*
11 A3 8p on 80pf lake & blk, *rose* 1,050. *1,650.*
a. No period after "8d" *4,600.*
b. Surcharged "G.R.I. 4d" (error) *15,250.*
12 A4 1sh on 1m car 5,500. *4,750.*
13 A4 2sh on 2m blue 3,750. *4,500.*
a. Surcharged "G.R.I. 5s" (error) *45,000.*
b. Surcharged "G.R.I. 2d" corrected by hand-stamped "5" *55,000.*
14 A4 3sh on 3m blk vio 6,000. *7,750.*
a. No period after "I" 14,000. *14,000.*
15 A4 5sh on 5m slate & car 14,000. *16,500.*
a. No period after "I" 18,500. 21,000.
b. Surcharged "G.R.I. 1s" (error) *87,500.*

"G.R.I." stands for Georgius Rex Imperator.

Second Setting

Surcharge lines spaced 5mm on 1p-8p, 5½mm on 1sh-5sh

1914, Dec. 16

16 A3 1p on 3pf brown 75.00 *95.00*
a. Double surcharge 1,400. *1,850.*
b. "I" for "1" 825.00
c. "1" with straight top serif 135.00 165.00
d. Inverted surcharge 5,500. —
e. "4" for "1" *17,500.*
f. Small "1" 350.00
g. Double surcharge, one inverted *7,750.*
17 A3 1p on 5pf green 30.00 *55.00*
a. Double surcharge 5,250.
b. "G. I. R." *13,000.* *14,000.*
c. "d" inverted 3,500.
d. No periods after "G R I" *11,000.*
e. Small "1" 140.00 210.00
f. "1d" double —
g. No period after "1d"
h. Triple surcharge
18 A3 2p on 10pf car 45.00 *65.00*
a. Double surcharge *16,250.* *16,250.*
b. Dbl. surch., one inverted *13,000.*
c. Surcharged "G. I. R., 3d" *13,000.*
d. Surcharged "1d" *12,000.* *11,000.*
e. Period before "G" *11,000.*
f. No period after "2d" 200.00 *275.00*
g. Inverted surcharge
h. "2d" double, one inverted
j. Pair, #18, 20 *30,000.*
19 A3 2p on 20pf ultra 50.00 *75.00*
a. Double surcharge 3,500. *4,750.*
b. Double surch., one inverted 5,000. *6,500.*
c. "R" inverted *9,250.*
d. Surcharged "1d" *13,000.* *14,000.*
f. Inverted surcharge 10,500.
h. Pair, one without surcharge 25,000.
i. Vertical pair, #19, 21 20,000. 23,000.
20 A3 2½p on 10pf car 250.00 375.00
21 A3 2½p on 20pf ultra 2,100. 2,100.
a. Double surcharge, one invtd.
b. "2½" triple
c. Surcharged "3d" in pair with normal *42,500.*
22 A3 3p on 25pf org & blk, *yel* 185.00 *275.00*
a. Double surcharge *11,000.* *13,000.*
b. Inverted surcharge *11,000.* *13,000.*
c. "G. R. I." only
d. "G. I. R."
e. Pair, one without surcharge *15,000.*
f. Surcharged "G. I. R., 5d"
g. Surcharged "1d" *22,000.*
23 A3 3p on 30pf org & blk, *sal* 175.00 *220.00*
a. Double surcharge 4,000. *4,600.*
b. Double surcharge, one invtd. 4,400. *5,000.*
c. "d" inverted
d. Surcharged "1d" *12,000.* *14,000.*
e. Triple surcharge
g. Double inverted surcharge *13,000.* *14,000.*
h. Pair, one without surcharge *14,000.*
24 A3 4p on 40pf lake & blk 185.00 *300.00*
a. Double surcharge 3,500. —
b. Double surcharge, both invtd. *13,000.*
c. Double surcharge, one invtd. 5,250.
d. Inverted surcharge 9,250.
e. Surcharged "1d" 8,750.
f. "1" on "4"
g. As "e," inverted *20,000.*
h. Surcharge "G.R.I. 3d," double (error) *27,500.*
i. No period after "I" 3,500.
25 A3 5p on 50pf pur & blk, *sal* 350.00 *385.00*
a. Double surcharge 4,400.
b. Double surcharge, one invtd. *10,500.* *10,500.*
c. "5" omitted
d. Inverted surcharge 9,750. *9,750.*
e. Double inverted surcharge 13,000. *14,000.*
f. "G. I. R."
g. Surcharge "G.R.I. 3d" (error) *23,000.*
26 A3 8p on 80pf lake & blk, *rose* 475.00 *650.00*
a. Double surcharge 7,000. *8,250.*
b. Double surcharge, one invtd. 7,000. *8,250.*
c. Triple surcharge 8,750. *9,250.*
d. No period after "8d"
e. Inverted surcharge *14,000.* 14,000.
f. Surcharged "3d" *18,500.* *18,500.*
27 A4 1sh on 1m car 5,250. *7,750.*
a. No period after "I" *12,000.*
28 A4 2sh on 2m bl 5,500. *8,750.*
a. Surcharged "5s"
b. Double surcharge
c. No period after "I" *13,000.*
29 A4 3sh on 3m blk vio 9,750. *16,250.*
a. No periods after "R I"
b. "G.R.I." double *45,000.*
29C A4 5sh on 5m sl & car *42,500.* *45,000.*
d. No periods after "R I"
e. Surcharged "1s"

Nos. 18-19 Surcharged with Large "1"

1915, Jan.

29F A3 1(p) on 2p on 10pf carmine *32,500.* *30,000.*
29G A3 1(p) on 2p on 20pf ultramarine *30,000.* *17,500.*

Same Surcharge on Stamps of Marshall Islands

1914

30 A3 1p on 3pf brn 95.00 *150.00*
a. Inverted surcharge 9,250.
31 A3 1p on 5pf green 90.00 *130.00*
a. Double surcharge 3,800. *5,000.*
b. No period after "d"
c. Inverted surcharge 5,250.
32 A3 2p on 10pf car 27.50 *40.00*
a. Double surcharge 3,800.
b. Double surcharge, one invtd. 5,000.
c. Surcharge sideways 10,500.
d. No period after "2d"
e. No period after "G" 875.00
f. Inverted surcharge 7,000.
33 A3 2p on 20 pf ultra 30.00 *50.00*
a. No period after "d" 80.00 *150.00*
b. Double surcharge 4,000. 5,250.
c. Double surcharge, one invtd. *9,750.* *10,500.*
d. Inverted surcharge *10,500.* *10,500.*
e. "I" omitted
34 A3 3p on 25pf org & blk, *yel* 475.00 *600.00*
a. Double surcharge 4,100. *5,000.*
b. Double surcharge, one invtd. 4,250.
c. No period after "d" 925.00 1,250.
d. Inverted surcharge 13,000.
35 A3 3p on 30pf org & blk, *sal* 475.00 *600.00*
a. No period after "d" 925.00 *1,200.*
b. Inverted surcharge 8,750. 9,250.
c. Double surcharge 7,000.
d. Double surcharge, one invtd.
36 A3 4p on 40pf lake & blk 175.00 *250.00*
a. No period after "d" 475.00 *700.00*
b. Double surcharge 7,000. *8,000.*
c. "4d" omitted
d. "1d" on "4d"
e. No period after "R"
f. Inverted surcharge 9,750.
g. Surcharged "1d" *17,500.*
h. Surcharged "G.R.I. 3d" double
37 A3 5p on 50pf pur & blk, *sal* 275.00 *375.00*
a. "d" omitted 4,000.
b. Double surcharge *10,500.*
c. "5d" double
d. Inverted surcharge *16,500.*
38 A3 8p on 80pf lake & blk, *rose* 525.00 775.00
a. Inverted surcharge *10,500.*
b. Double surcharge *10,000.*
c. Double surcharge, one invtd.
d. Triple surcharge *16,500.*
e. Double surcharge, both inverted *13,250.* *14,000.*
39 A4 1sh on 1m car 4,100. *5,500.*
a. Double surcharge *45,000.*
b. Dbl. surch., one with "s1" for "1s"
c. No period after "I" 6,500. 9,250.
d. Additional surcharge "1d" *50,000.*
40 A4 2sh on 2m blue 2,000. 4,500.
a. Double surcharge, one invtd. *45,000.* *45,000.*
b. Double surcharge *45,000.*
c. Large "S"
d. No period after "I" 3,750. *6,500.*
41 A4 3sh on 3m blk vio 6,500. *9,750.*
a. Double surcharge *42,500.* *45,000.*
b. No period after "I" 8,750.
c. No period after "R I"
d. Inverted surcharge
42 A4 5sh on 5m sl & car *14,000.* *15,000.*
a. Double surcharge, one invtd. *75,000.*

See Nos. 44-45.

A5

Surcharged in Black on Registration Label

Town Name in Sans-Serif Letters

1914 *Perf. 12*

43 A5 3p black & red (Rabaul) 300.00 *350.00*
a. Double surcharge (Rabaul) 5,500. *7,000.*
44 A5 3p black & red (Friedrich Wilhelmshaven) 275.00 *875.00*
45 A5 3p black & red (Herbertshohe) 325.00 *825.00*
46 A5 3p black & red (Kawieng) 350.00 *700.00*
a. Double surcharge
47 A5 3p black & red (Kieta) 500.00 *875.00*
a. Pair, one without surcharge *16,500.*
48 A5 3p black & red (Manus) 325.00 *925.00*
a. Double surcharge *9,250.*
49 A5 3p black & red (Deulon) 27,500. *30,000.*
50 A5 3p black & red (Stephansort) *4,500.*

Nos. 44, 46 and 48 exist with town name in letters with serifs. The varieties Deutsch-Neuguinea, Deutsch Neu-Guinea, etc., are known. For detailed listings see the *Scott Classic Specialized Catalogue of Stamps and Covers.*

Nos. 32-33 Surcharged with Large "1"

1915

51 A3 1p on 2p on 10pf 275. 300.
a. "1" double *16,500.*
b. "1" inverted *20,000.* *20,000.*
52 A3 1p on 2p on 20pf 4,000. 2,750.
a. "1" inverted *20,000.* *20,000.*

The stamps of Marshall Islands surcharged "G. R. I." and new values in British currency were all used in New Britain and are therefore listed here.

Stamps of Marshall Islands Surcharged

Surcharge lines spaced 6mm apart

53 A3 1p on 3pf brown *3,750.*
a. Inverted surcharge *16,000.*
54 A3 1p on 5pf green *3,750.*
a. Inverted surcharge *16,500.*

55 A3 2p on 10pf car 4,750.
56 A3 2p on 20pf ultra 4,250.
a. Inverted surcharge 17,000.
57 A3 2½p on 10pf car 30,000.
58 A3 2½p on 20pf ultra 45,000.
59 A3 3p on 25pf org & blk, *yel* 7,000.
60 A3 3p on 30pf org & blk, *sal* 7,000.
61 A3 4p on 40pf lake & blk 7,000.
a. Inverted surcharge 18,000.
62 A3 5p on 50pf pur & blk, *sal* 6,500.
63 A3 8p on 80pf lake & blk, *rose* 7,500.
a. Inverted surcharge 20,000.

Surcharge lines spaced 5 ½mm apart

64 A4 1sh on 1m car 17,500.
a. Large "S" 22,500.
65 A4 2sh on 2m bl 14,500.
a. Large "S" 20,000.
66 A4 3sh on 3m blk vi-ol 30,000.
a. Large "S" 40,000.
67 A4 5sh on 5m sl & car 45,000.
a. Large "S" 52,500.

OFFICIAL STAMPS

O1

German New Guinea Nos. 7-8 Surcharged

1915 Unwmk. *Perf. 14*
O1 O1 1p on 3pf brown 35.00 *80.00*
a. Double surcharge 5,500.
O2 O1 1p on 5pf green 110.00 *150.00*

NEW CALEDONIA

ˈnü ˌka-lə-ˈdō-nyə

LOCATION — Island in the South Pacific Ocean, east of Queensland, Australia
GOVT. — French Overseas Territory
AREA — 7,172 sq. mi.
POP. — 197,361 (1999 est.)
CAPITAL — Noumea

Dependencies of New Caledonia are the Loyalty Islands, Isle of Pines, Huon Islands and Chesterfield Islands.

100 Centimes = 1 Franc

Catalogue values for unused stamps in this country are for Never Hinged items, beginning with Scott 252 in the regular postage section, Scott B13 in the semi-postal section, Scott C14 in the airpost section, Scott J32 in the postage due section, and Scott O1 in the official section.

Watermark

Wmk. 385

Napoleon III — A1

1859 Unwmk. Litho. *Imperf.*
Without Gum
1 A1 10c black 250.00 250.00

Fifty varieties. Counterfeits abound. See No. 315.

Type of French Colonies, 1877 Surcharged in Black

Nos. 2-5 Nos. 6-7

1881-83
2 A8 5c on 40c red, *straw* ('82) 425.00 425.00
a. Inverted surcharge 1,600. 1,600.
b. Double surcharge 1,350.
c. Double surcharge, both inverted 1,900. 1,900.
3 A8 05c on 40c red, *straw* ('83) 40.00 40.00
4 A8 25c on 35c dp vio, *yel* 300.00 300.00
a. Inverted surcharge 950.00 950.00
5 A8 25c on 75c rose car, *rose* ('82) 400.00 400.00
a. Inverted surcharge 1,250. 1,250.

1883-84
6 A8 5c on 40c red, *straw* ('84) 26.50 26.50
a. Inverted surcharge 26.50 26.50
7 A8 5c on 75c rose car, *rose* ('83) 52.50 52.50
a. Inverted surcharge 75.00 75.00

In type "a" surcharge, the narrower-spaced letters measure 14½mm, and an early printing of No. 4 measures 13½mm. Type "b" letters measure 18mm.

French Colonies No. 59 Surcharged in Black

No. 8

Nos. 9-10

1886 *Perf. 14x13½*
8 A9 5c on 1fr 32.50 26.50
a. Inverted surcharge 45.00 45.00
b. Double surcharge 200.00 200.00
c. Double surcharge, one inverted 225.00 225.00
9 A9 5c on 1fr 32.50 30.00
a. Inverted surcharge 60.00 60.00
b. Double surcharge 200.00 200.00
c. Double surcharge, one inverted 225.00 225.00

French Colonies No. 29 Surcharged *Imperf*
10 A8 5c on 1fr *10,000. 11,500.*

Types of French Colonies, 1877-86, Surcharged in Black

Nos. 11, 13

No. 12

1891-92 *Imperf.*
11 A8 10c on 40c red, *straw* ('92) 45.00 40.00
a. Inverted surcharge 42.50 37.50
b. Double surcharge 100.00 100.00
c. Double surcharge, one inverted 190.00 190.00
d. No period after "10c" 125.00 125.00

Perf. 14x13½
12 A9 10c on 30c brn, *bis* 25.00 22.50
a. Inverted surcharge 25.00 22.50
b. Double surcharge 67.50 67.50
c. Double surcharge, inverted 60.00 60.00
d. Double surcharge, one inverted 100.00 100.00
13 A9 10c on 40c red, *straw* ('92) 26.00 26.00
a. Inverted surcharge 26.00 26.00
b. No period after "10c" 60.00 60.00
c. Double surcharge 67.50 67.50
d. Double surcharge, one inverted 110.00 100.00
Nos. 11-13 (3) 96.00 88.50

Variety "double surcharge, one inverted" exists on Nos. 11-13. Value slightly higher than for "double surcharge."

Types of French Colonies, 1877-86, Handstamped in Black — g

1892 *Imperf.*
16 A8 20c red, *grn* 350.00 *400.00*
a. Inverted surcharge 850.00 900.00
17 A8 35c violet, *org* 75.00 75.00
a. Pair, one stamp without surcharge 950.00
18 A8 40c red, *straw* *1,500.*
19 A8 1fr bronz grn, *straw* 300.00 300.00

The 1c, 2c, 4c and 75c of type A8 are believed not to have been officially made or actually used.

1892 *Perf. 14x13½*
23 A9 5c green, *grnsh* 19.00 15.00
a. Pair, one stamp without overprint 600.00
24 A9 10c blk, *lavender* 140.00 82.50
25 A9 15c blue 110.00 60.00
a. Pair, one stamp without overprint 825.00
26 A9 20c red, *grn* 110.00 60.00
27 A9 25c yellow, *straw* 30.00 22.50
28 A9 25c black, *rose* 110.00 37.50
29 A9 30c brown, *bis* 90.00 75.00
30 A9 35c violet, *org* 240.00 190.00
a. Inverted overprint 650.00
b. Pair, one stamp without overprint 1,350.
32 A9 75c carmine, *rose* 225.00 190.00
a. Pair, one stamp without overprint 1,350.
33 A9 1fr bronz grn, *straw* 190.00 175.00
Nos. 23-33 (10) 1,264. 907.50

The note following No. 19 also applies to the 1c, 2c, 4c and 40c of type A9.

Surcharged in Blue or Black — h

1892-93 *Imperf.*
34 A8 10c on 1fr brnz grn, *straw* (Bl) *5,250. 4,500.*

Perf. 14x13½
35 A9 5c on 20c red, *grn* (Bk) 27.50 22.50
a. Inverted surcharge 125.00 125.00
b. Double surcharge 82.50 100.00
36 A9 5c on 75c car, *rose* (Bk) 22.50 16.50
a. Inverted surcharge 125.00 125.00
b. Double surcharge 82.50 82.50
37 A9 5c on 75c car, *rose* (Bl) 18.50 15.00
a. Inverted surcharge 125.00 125.00
b. Double surcharge 82.50 82.50
38 A9 10c on 1fr brnz grn, *straw* (Bk) 21.00 15.00
a. Inverted surcharge 600.00 600.00
39 A9 10c on 1fr brnz grn, *straw* (Bl) 22.50 21.00
a. Inverted surcharge 125.00 125.00
b. Double surcharge 85.00 85.00
Nos. 35-39 (5) 112.00 90.00

Navigation and Commerce — A12

1892-1904 Typo. *Perf. 14x13½*
Name of Colony in Blue or Carmine
40 A12 1c black, *blue* 1.10 1.10
41 A12 2c brown, *buff* 1.90 1.90
42 A12 4c claret, *lav* 2.50 2.25
43 A12 5c green, *grnsh* 4.00 1.90
44 A12 5c yellow green ('00) 2.25 1.50
45 A12 10c blk, *lavender* 9.00 5.25
46 A12 10c rose red ('00) 11.00 1.50
47 A12 15c bl, quadrille paper 30.00 3.50
48 A12 15c gray ('00) 20.00 1.50
49 A12 20c red, *grn* 20.00 10.50
50 A12 25c black, *rose* 25.00 6.75
51 A12 25c blue ('00) 22.00 10.50
52 A12 30c brown, *bis* 25.00 13.50
53 A12 40c red, *straw* 26.00 13.50
54 A12 50c carmine, *rose* 67.50 37.50
55 A12 50c brn, *az* (name in car) ('00) 125.00 85.00
56 A12 50c brn, *az* (name in bl) ('04) 65.00 42.50
57 A12 75c violet, *org* 37.50 26.50
58 A12 1fr bronz grn, *straw* 45.00 26.50
Nos. 40-58 (19) 539.75 293.15

Perf. 13½x14 stamps are counterfeits.
For overprints and surcharges see Nos. 59-87, 117-121.

Nos. 41-42, 52, 57-58, 53 Surcharged in Black

j

k

1900-01
59 A12 (h) 5c on 2c ('01) 22.50 19.00
a. Double surcharge 140.00 140.00
b. Inverted surcharge 125.00 125.00
Never hinged 210.00
60 A12 (h) 5c on 4c 4.50 4.50
a. Inverted surcharge 82.50 82.50
b. Double surcharge 87.50 87.50
61 A12 (j) 15c on 30c 5.25 4.50
a. Inverted surcharge 75.00 75.00
b. Double surcharge 67.50 67.50
62 A12 (j) 15c on 75c ('01) 20.00 17.50
a. Pair, one without surcharge —
b. Inverted surcharge 130.00 130.00
c. Double surcharge 140.00 140.00
63 A12 (j) 15c on 1fr ('01) 26.50 26.50
a. Double surcharge 175.00 175.00
b. Inverted surcharge 175.00 175.00
Nos. 59-63 (5) 78.75 72.00

1902
64 A12 (k) 5c on 30c 10.50 9.00
a. Inverted surcharge 52.50 52.50
65 A12 (k) 15c on 40c 10.50 8.25
a. Inverted surcharge 52.50 52.50

Jubilee Issue

Stamps of 1892-1900 Overprinted in Blue, Red, Black or Gold

1903
66 A12 1c blk, *lil bl* (Bl) 3.00 3.00
a. Inverted overprint *290.00 290.00*
67 A12 2c brown, *buff* (Bl) 5.25 4.50
68 A12 4c claret, *lav* (Bl) 7.50 6.00
a. Double overprint *375.00 375.00*
69 A12 5c dk grn, *grnsh* (R) 7.50 4.50
70 A12 5c yellow green (R) 10.00 9.00
71 A12 10c blk, *lav* (R) 19.00 16.00
72 A12 10c blk, *lav* (double G & Bk) 11.50 9.00
73 A12 15c gray (R) 15.00 11.50
74 A12 20c red, *grn* (Bl) 22.00 19.00
75 A12 25c blk, *rose* (Bl) 19.50 19.00
a. Double overprint 325.00
76 A12 30c brown, *bis* (R) 26.50 22.50
77 A12 40c red, *straw* (Bl) 34.00 30.00
78 A12 50c car, *rose* (Bl) 60.00 52.50
a. Pair, one without overprint *300.00*
79 A12 75c vio, *org* (Bk) 77.50 72.50
a. Dbl. ovpt. in blk and red *500.00*
80 A12 1fr brnz grn, *straw* (Bl) 120.00 115.00
a. Dbl. ovpt., one in red *525.00 525.00*
Nos. 66-80 (15) 438.25 394.00

With Additional Surcharge of New Value in Blue

(a)

(b)

(c)

No.	Description	Unused	Used
81	A12 (a) 1c on 2c #67	1.90	1.90
a.	Numeral double	*115.00*	*115.00*
b.	Numeral only	400.00	
82	A12 (b) 2c on 4c #68	3.50	3.50
83	A12 (a) 4c on 5c #69	2.25	2.25
a.	Small "4"	*650.00*	*650.00*
84	A12 (c) 4c on 5c #70	3.00	3.00
a.	Pair, one without numeral		
85	A12 (b) 10c on 15c #73	3.00	3.00
86	A12 (b) 15c on 20c #74	3.75	3.75
87	A12 (b) 20c on 25c #75	9.00	9.00
	Nos. 81-87 (7)	26.40	26.40

50 years of French occupation.

Surcharge on Nos. 81-83, 85-86 is horizontal, reading down.

There are three types of numeral on No. 83. The numeral on No. 84 is identical with that of No. 83a except that its position is upright.

Nos. 66-87 are known with "I" of "TENAIRE" missing.

Kagu
A16

Landscape
A17

Ship — A18

1905-28 Typo. *Perf. 14x13½*

No.	Description	Unused	Used
88	A16 1c blk, *green*	.30	.30
89	A16 2c red brown	.30	.30
90	A16 4c bl, *org*	.45	.45
91	A16 5c pale green	.55	.55
92	A16 5c dl bl ('21)	.40	.40
93	A16 10c carmine	1.90	1.25
94	A16 10c green ('21)	.75	.75
95	A16 10c red, *pink* ('25)	.85	.85
96	A16 15c violet	.90	.85
97	A17 20c brown	.55	.55
98	A17 25c blue, *grn*	1.05	.60
99	A17 25c red, *yel* ('21)	.75	.75
100	A17 30c brn, *org*	1.40	.85
101	A17 30c dp rose ('21)	2.50	2.50
102	A17 30c org ('25)	.60	.60
103	A17 35c blk, *yellow*	.75	.75
104	A17 40c car, *grn*	1.25	1.05
105	A17 45c vio brn, *lav*	.75	.75
106	A17 50c car, *org*	3.25	3.00
107	A17 50c dk bl ('21)	1.75	1.75
108	A17 50c gray ('25)	1.05	1.05
109	A17 65c dp bl ('28)	.90	.90
110	A17 75c ol grn, *straw*	.85	.70
111	A17 75c bl, *bluish* ('25)	.90	.90
112	A17 75c violet ('27)	1.15	1.15
113	A18 1fr bl, *yel grn*	1.30	1.05
114	A18 1fr dp bl ('25)	1.90	1.90
115	A18 2fr car, *bl*	3.50	2.25
116	A18 5fr blk, *straw*	6.75	6.75
	Nos. 88-116 (29)	39.30	35.50

See Nos. 311, 317a. For surcharges see Nos. 122-135, B1-B3, Q1-Q3.

Nos. 96, 98, 103, 106, 113 and 115, pasted on cardboard and handstamped "TRESORIER PAYEUR DE LA NOUVELLE CALEDONIE" were used as emergency currency in 1914.

Stamps of 1892-1904 Surcharged in Carmine or Black

1912

No.	Description	Unused	Used
117	A12 5c on 15c gray (C)	1.50	*1.90*
a.	Inverted surcharge	210.00	210.00
118	A12 5c on 20c red, *grn*	1.50	*1.90*
119	A12 5c on 30c brn, *bis* (C)	2.25	*3.00*
120	A12 10c on 40c red, *straw*	3.25	*3.25*
121	A12 10c on 50c brn, *az* (C)	3.25	*4.25*
	Nos. 117-121 (5)	11.75	14.30

Two spacings between the surcharged numerals are found on Nos. 117 to 121. For detailed listings, see the *Scott Classic Specialized Catalogue of Stamps and Covers.*

No. 96 Surcharged in Brown

1918

No.	Description	Unused	Used
122	A16 5c on 15c violet	1.90	1.90
a.	Double surcharge	75.00	75.00
b.	Inverted surcharge	45.00	45.00

The color of the surcharge on No. 122 varies from red to dark brown.

No. 96 Surcharged

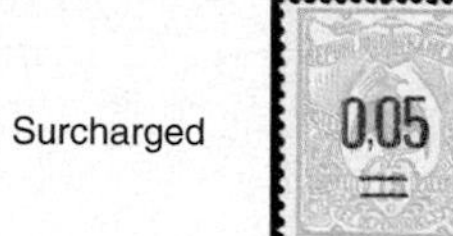

1922

No.	Description	Unused	Used
123	A16 5c on 15c vio (R)	.60	.60
a.	Double surcharge	75.00	75.00

Stamps and Types of 1905-28 Surcharged in Red or Black

1924-27

No.	Description	Unused	Used
124	A16 25c on 15c vio	.75	.75
a.	Double surcharge	75.00	
b.	Double surcharge, one inverted	110.00	
125	A18 25c on 2fr car, *bl*	.85	.85
126	A18 25c on 5fr blk, *straw*	.90	.90
a.	Double surcharge	125.00	125.00
b.	Triple surcharge	225.00	210.00
127	A17 60c on 75c bl grn (R)	.75	.75
128	A17 65c on 45c red brn	2.00	2.00
129	A17 85c on 45c red brn	2.00	2.00
130	A17 90c on 75c dp rose	1.05	1.05
131	A18 1.25fr on 1fr dp bl (R)	.90	.90
132	A18 1.50fr on 1fr dp bl, *bl*	1.60	1.60
133	A18 3fr on 5fr red vio	2.10	2.10
134	A18 10fr on 5fr ol, *lav* (R)	7.50	7.50
135	A18 20fr on 5fr vio rose, *org*	14.50	14.50
	Nos. 124-135 (12)	34.90	34.90

Issue years: Nos. 125-127, 1924. Nos. 124, 128-129, 1925. Nos. 131, 134, 1926. Nos. 130, 132-133, 135, 1927.

Bay of Palétuviers Point
A19

Landscape with Chief's House
A20

Admiral de Bougainville and Count de La Pérouse — A21

1928-40 Typo.

No.	Description	Unused	Used
136	A19 1c brn vio & ind	.25	.25
137	A19 2c dk brn & yel grn	.25	.25
137B	A19 3c brn vio & ind	.30	.30
138	A19 4c org & Prus grn	.25	.25
139	A19 5c Prus bl & dp ol	.45	.45
140	A19 10c gray lil & dk brn	.30	.30
141	A19 15c yel brn & dp bl	.55	.55
142	A19 20c brn red & dk brn	.55	.55
143	A19 25c dk grn & dk brn	.70	.55
144	A20 30c gray grn & bl grn	.60	.60
145	A20 35c blk & brt vio	.90	.90
146	A20 40c brt red & olvn	.55	.55
147	A20 45c dp bl & red org	1.60	1.30
147A	A20 45c bl grn & dl grn	1.05	1.05
148	A20 50c vio & brn	.85	.85
149	A20 55c vio bl & car	3.50	2.25
150	A20 60c vio bl & car	.75	.75
151	A20 65c org brn & bl	1.30	1.15
152	A20 70c dp rose & brn	.60	.60
153	A20 75c Prus bl & ol gray	1.40	1.15
154	A20 80c red brn & grn	1.15	1.00
155	A20 85c grn & brn	2.00	1.30
156	A20 90c dp red & brt red	1.30	.90
157	A20 90c ol grn & rose red	1.05	1.05
158	A21 1fr dp ol & sal red	7.25	4.25
159	A21 1fr rose red & dk car	2.25	1.75
160	A21 1fr brn red & grn	1.05	1.05
161	A21 1.10fr dp grn & brn	12.00	12.00
162	A21 1.25fr brn red & grn	1.20	1.20
163	A21 1.25fr rose red & dk car	1.15	1.15
164	A21 1.40fr dk bl & red org	1.20	1.20
165	A21 1.50fr dp bl & bl	.90	.90
166	A21 1.60fr dp grn & brn	1.35	1.35
167	A21 1.75fr dk bl & red org	1.05	1.05
168	A21 1.75fr violet bl	1.50	1.05
169	A21 2fr red org & brn	.90	.75
170	A21 2.25fr vio bl	1.20	1.20
171	A21 2.50fr brn & lt brn	1.75	1.75
172	A21 3fr mag & brn	.75	.75
173	A21 5fr dk bl & brn	1.15	1.15
174	A21 10fr vio & brn, *pnksh*	1.30	1.30
175	A21 20fr red & brn, *yel*	2.75	2.75
	Nos. 136-175 (42)	62.90	55.45

The 35c in Prussian green and dark green without overprint is listed as Wallis and Futuna No. 53a.

Issue years: 35c, 70c, 85c, #162, 167, 1933; 55c, 80c, #159, 168, 1938; #157, 163, 2.25fr, 1939; 3c, 60c, 1.40fr, 1.60fr, 2.50fr, 147A, 160, 1940; others, 1928.

For overprints see #180-207, 217-251, Q4-Q6.

Common Design Types pictured following the introduction.

Colonial Exposition Issue

Common Design Types

1931 Engr. *Perf. 12½*

Country Name Typo. in Black

No.	Description	Unused	Used
176	CD70 40c dp green	6.00	6.00
177	CD71 50c violet	6.00	6.00
178	CD72 90c red orange	6.00	6.00
179	CD73 1.50fr dull blue	6.00	6.00
	Nos. 176-179 (4)	24.00	24.00

Paris-Nouméa Flight Issue

Regular Issue of 1928 Overprinted

1932 *Perf. 14x13½*

No.	Description	Unused	Used
180	A20 40c brt red & olvn	475.00	*500.00*
181	A20 50c vio & brn	475.00	*500.00*

Arrival on Apr. 5, 1932 at Nouméa, of the French aviators, Verneilh, Dévé and Munch.

Excellent forgeries exist of #180-181.

Types of 1928-33 Overprinted in Black or Red

1933

No.	Description	Unused	Used
182	A19 1c red vio & dl bl	6.50	*7.00*
183	A19 2c dk brn & yel grn	6.50	*7.00*
184	A19 4c dl org & Prus bl	6.50	*7.00*
185	A19 5c Prus grn & ol (R)	6.50	*7.00*
186	A19 10c gray lil & dk brn (R)	6.50	*7.00*
187	A19 15c yel brn & dp bl (R)	6.50	*7.00*
188	A19 20c brn red & dk brn	6.50	*7.00*
189	A19 25c dk grn & dk brn (R)	6.50	*7.00*
190	A20 30c gray grn & bl grn (R)	6.75	*7.50*
191	A20 35c blk & lt vio	6.75	*7.50*
192	A20 40c brt red & olvn	6.75	*7.00*
193	A20 45c dp bl & red org	6.75	*7.50*
194	A20 50c vio & brn	6.75	*7.00*
195	A20 70c dp rose & brn	7.50	*8.00*
196	A20 75c Prus bl & ol gray (R)	7.50	*8.00*
197	A20 85c grn & brn	7.50	*8.00*
198	A20 90c dp red & brt red	9.50	*10.00*
199	A21 1fr dp ol & sal red	9.50	*10.00*
200	A21 1.25fr brn red & grn	9.50	*10.00*
201	A21 1.50fr dp bl & bl (R)	9.50	*10.00*
202	A21 1.75fr dk bl & red org	9.50	*10.00*
203	A21 2fr red org & brn	9.50	*10.00*
204	A21 3fr mag & brn	9.50	*10.00*
205	A21 5fr dk bl & brn (R)	9.50	*10.00*
206	A21 10fr vio & brn, *pnksh*	10.00	*11.00*
207	A21 20fr red & brn, *yel*	10.00	*11.00*
	Nos. 182-207 (26)	204.25	218.50

1st anniv., Paris-Noumea flight. Plane centered on Nos. 190-207.

Paris International Exposition Issue

Common Design Types

1937 Engr. *Perf. 13*

No.	Description	Unused	Used
208	CD74 20c dp vio	2.75	2.75
209	CD75 30c dk grn	2.75	2.75
210	CD76 40c car rose	2.75	2.75
211	CD77 50c dk brn & bl	2.75	2.75
212	CD78 90c red	2.75	2.75
213	CD79 1.50fr ultra	2.75	2.75
	Nos. 208-213 (6)	16.50	16.50

Colonial Arts Exhibition Issue

Souvenir Sheet

Common Design Type

1937 *Imperf.*

No.	Description	Unused	Used
214	CD78 3fr sepia	22.50	*34.00*

New York World's Fair Issue

Common Design Type

1939 *Perf. 12½x12*

No.	Description	Unused	Used
215	CD82 1.25fr car lake	1.60	1.60
216	CD82 2.25fr ultra	1.75	1.75

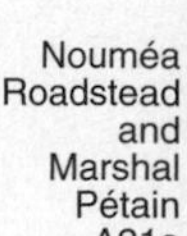

Nouméa Roadstead and Marshal Pétain
A21a

1941 Engr. *Perf. 12½x12*
216A A21a 1fr bluish green .75
216B A21a 2.50fr dark blue .75

Nos. 216A-216B were issued by the Vichy government in France, but were not placed on sale in the colony.
For surcharges, see Nos. B12A-B12B.

Types of 1928-40 Overprinted in Black

1941 *Perf. 14x13½*
217 A19 1c red vio & dl bl 13.50 13.50
218 A19 2c dk brn & yel grn 13.50 13.50
219 A19 3c brn vio & ind 13.50 13.50
220 A19 4c dl org & Prus bl 13.50 13.50
221 A19 5c Prus bl & dp ol 13.50 13.50
222 A19 10c gray lil & dk brn 13.50 13.50
223 A19 15c yel brn & dp bl 18.00 18.00
224 A19 20c brn red & dk brn 18.00 18.00
225 A19 25c dk grn & dk brn 18.00 18.00
226 A20 30c gray grn & bl grn 18.00 18.00
227 A20 35c blk & brt vio 18.00 18.00
228 A20 40c brt red & olvn 18.00 18.00
229 A20 45c bl grn & dl grn 18.00 18.00
230 A20 50c vio & brn 18.00 18.00
231 A20 55c vio bl & car 18.00 18.00
232 A20 60c vio bl & car 18.00 18.00
233 A20 65c org brn & bl 18.00 18.00
234 A20 70c dp rose & brn 18.00 18.00
235 A20 75c Prus bl & ol gray 18.00 18.00
236 A20 80c red brn & grn 18.00 18.00
237 A20 85c grn & brn 18.00 18.00
238 A20 90c dp red & brt red 18.00 18.00
239 A21 1fr rose red & dk car 18.00 18.00
240 A21 1.25fr brn red & grn 18.00 18.00
241 A21 1.40fr dk bl & red org 18.00 18.00
242 A21 1.50fr dp bl & bl 18.00 18.00
243 A21 1.60fr dp grn & brn 18.00 18.00
244 A21 1.75fr dk bl & red org 18.00 18.00
245 A21 2fr red org & brn 18.00 18.00
246 A21 2.25fr vio bl 18.00 18.00
247 A21 2.50fr brn & lt brn 22.00 19.50
248 A21 3fr mag & brn 22.00 19.50
249 A21 5fr dk bl & brn 22.00 19.50
250 A21 10fr vio & brn, *pnksh* 22.00 22.00
251 A21 20fr red & brn, *yel* 23.50 23.50
Nos. 217-251 (35) 624.50 617.00
Set, never hinged 875.00

Issued to note this colony's affiliation with the "Free France" movement.

Catalogue values for unused stamps in this section, from this point to the end of the section, are for Never Hinged items.

Kagu A22

1942 Photo. *Perf. 14½x14*
252 A22 5c brown .40 .25
253 A22 10c dk gray bl .45 .30
254 A22 25c emerald .70 .30
255 A22 30c red org .70 .45
256 A22 40c dk slate grn .70 .45
257 A22 80c dl red brn .70 .45
258 A22 1fr rose vio .90 .70
259 A22 1.50fr red .90 .70
260 A22 2fr gray blk 1.30 1.10
261 A22 2.50fr brt ultra 1.30 1.10
262 A22 4fr dl vio 1.30 1.10
263 A22 5fr bister 1.30 1.10
264 A22 10fr dp brn 1.60 1.50
265 A22 20fr dp grn 2.50 2.25
Nos. 252-265 (14) 14.75 11.75

Types of 1928 Without "RF"

1944 Typo. *Perf. 14x13½*
265A A19 10c gray lil & dk brn .75
265B A20 60c vio bl & car 1.50

Nos. 265A-265B were issued by the Vichy government in France, but were not placed on sale in the colony.

Stamps of 1942 Surcharged in Carmine or Black

1945-46 Unwmk. *Perf. 14½x14*
266 A22 50c on 5c (C) ('46) 1.60 1.50
267 A22 60c on 5c (C) 1.60 1.50
268 A22 70c on 5c (C) 1.60 1.50
269 A22 1.20fr on 5c (C) .85 .75
270 A22 2.40fr on 25c .85 .75
271 A22 3fr on 25c ('46) 1.00 .75
272 A22 4.50fr on 25c 1.90 1.10
273 A22 15fr on 2.50fr (C) 2.60 2.00
Nos. 266-273 (8) 12.00 9.85

Eboue Issue
Common Design Type

1945 Engr. *Perf. 13*
274 CD91 2fr black .90 .90
275 CD91 25fr Prus grn 2.50 2.10

Kagus A23

Ducos Sanatorium A24

Porcupine Isle — A25

Nickel Foundry A26

"Towers of Notre Dame" A27

Chieftain's House — A28

1948 Unwmk. Photo. *Perf. 13½x13*
276 A23 10c yel & brn .45 .30
277 A23 30c grn & brn .45 .30
278 A23 40c org & brn .45 .30
279 A24 50c pink & brn .60 .45
280 A24 60c yel & brn .85 .60
281 A24 80c lt grn & bl grn .85 .60
282 A25 1fr brn, pur & org .90 .70
283 A25 1.20fr pale gray, brn & bl .90 .70
284 A25 1.50fr cream, dk bl & yel .90 .70
285 A26 2fr pck grn & brn .90 .70
286 A26 2.40fr ver & dp rose 1.20 .85
287 A26 3fr org & pur 7.50 2.00
288 A26 4fr bl & dk bl 2.50 1.10
289 A27 5fr ver & pur 2.75 1.30
290 A27 6fr yel & brn 2.75 1.60
291 A27 10fr org & dk bl 2.75 1.60
292 A28 15fr brn & gray 4.00 1.75
293 A28 20fr pur & yel 4.00 2.25
294 A28 25fr dk bl & org 5.00 3.75
Nos. 276-294 (19) 39.70 21.55

Military Medal Issue
Common Design Type

1952 Engr. & Typo. *Perf. 13*
295 CD101 2fr multi 7.50 6.00

Admiral Bruni d'Entrecasteaux and his Two Frigates — A29

Designs: 2fr, Msgr. Douarre and Cathedral of Nouméa. 6fr, Admiral Dumont d'Urville and map. 13fr, Admiral Auguste Febvrier-Despointes and Nouméa roadstead.

1953, Sept. 24 Engr.
296 A29 1.50fr org brn & dp claret 7.50 6.75
297 A29 2fr ind & aqua 7.00 3.75
298 A29 6fr dk brn, bl & car 12.00 6.00
299 A29 13fr bl grn & dk grnsh bl 14.00 7.50
Nos. 296-299 (4) 40.50 24.00

Centenary of the presence of the French in New Caledonia.

"Towers of Notre Dame" — A30

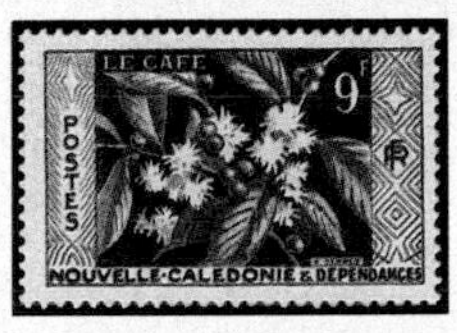

Coffee A31

1955, Nov. 21 Unwmk. *Perf. 13*
300 A30 2.50fr dk brn, ultra & grn 1.90 1.05
301 A30 3fr grn, ultra & red brn 8.25 4.00
302 A31 9fr vio bl & indigo 3.00 1.05
Nos. 300-302 (3) 13.15 6.10

FIDES Issue
Common Design Type

Design: Dumbea Dam.

1956, Oct. 22 Engr. *Perf. 13x12½*
303 CD103 3fr grn & bl 1.90 1.10

Flower Issue
Common Design Type

Designs: 4fr, Xanthostemon. 15fr, Hibiscus.

1958, July 7 Photo. *Perf. 12x12½*
304 CD104 4fr multi 3.50 1.25
305 CD104 15fr grn, red & yel 5.75 1.75

Imperforates
Most stamps of New Caledonia from 1958 onward exist imperforate, in trial colors, or in small presentation sheets in which the stamps are printed in changed colors.

Human Rights Issue
Common Design Type

1958, Dec. 10 Engr. *Perf. 13*
306 CD105 7fr car & dk bl 3.00 1.50

Brachyrus Zebra — A32

Lienardella Fasciata A33

Designs: 10fr, Claucus and Spirographe. 26fr, Fluorescent corals.

1959, Mar. 21 Engr. *Perf. 13*
307 A32 1fr lil gray & red brn 1.25 .55
308 A33 3fr bl, grn & red 1.75 .60
309 A32 10fr dk brn, Prus bl & org brn 4.00 1.40
310 A33 26fr multi 7.25 3.50
Nos. 307-310 (4) 14.25 6.05

Types of 1859, 1905 and

Girl Operating Check Writer A34

Telephone Receiver and Exchange A35

Port-de-France (Nouméa) in 1859 — A36

Designs: 9fr, Wayside mailbox and mail bus, vert. 33fr, like 19fr without stamps.

Perf. 13½x13, 13
1960, May 20 Unwmk.
311 A16 4fr red 1.00 .55
312 A34 5fr claret & org brn 1.20 .75
313 A36 9fr dk grn & brn 1.20 .75
314 A35 12fr bl & blk 1.50 .90
315 A1 13fr slate blue 4.00 2.00
316 A36 19fr bl grn, dl grn & red 4.25 1.25
317 A36 33fr Prus bl & dl red 4.50 2.75
a. Souv. sheet of 3, #315, 311, 317 + label 18.50 15.00
Nos. 311-317 (7) 17.65 8.95

Cent. of postal service and stamps in New Caledonia.
No. 317a has label between 4fr and 33fr stamps.

Melanesian Sailing Canoes A37

Designs: 4fr, Spear fisherman, vert. 5fr, Sail Rock and sailboats, Noumea.

1962, July 2 Engr. *Perf. 13*
318 A37 2fr slate grn, ultra & brn 1.10 .55
319 A37 4fr brn, car & grn 1.40 .55
320 A37 5fr sepia, grn & bl 1.75 .75
Nos. 318-320 (3) 4.25 1.85

See Nos. C29-C32.

Map of Australia and South Pacific — A37a

1962, July 18 **Photo.** ***Perf. 13x12***
321 A37a 15fr multi 3.50 1.90

Fifth South Pacific Conf., Pago Pago, 1962.

Air Currents over Map of New Caledonia and South Pacific, Barograph and Compass Rose — A38

1962, Nov. 5 ***Perf. 12x12½***
322 A38 50fr multi 9.75 6.00

3rd regional assembly of the World Meteorological Association, Noumea, November 1962.

Wheat Emblem and Globe A38a

1963, Mar. 21 **Engr.** ***Perf. 13***
323 A38a 17fr choc & dk bl 3.75 1.75

FAO "Freedom from Hunger" campaign.

Relay Race — A39

Perf. 12½

1963, Aug. 29 **Unwmk.** **Photo.**
324 A39 1fr shown .90 .60
325 A39 7fr Tennis 1.90 .90
326 A39 10fr Soccer 2.75 1.50
327 A39 27fr Javelin 4.50 2.70
Nos. 324-327 (4) 10.05 5.75

South Pacific Games, Suva, Aug. 29-Sept. 7.

Red Cross Centenary Issue

Common Design Type

1963 Sept. 2 **Engr.** ***Perf. 13***
328 CD113 37fr bl, gray & car 9.00 6.75

Human Rights Issue

Common Design Type

1963, Dec. 10 **Unwmk.** ***Perf. 13***
329 CD117 50fr sl grn & dp claret 8.00 6.00

Bikkia Fritillarioides — A40

Flowers: 1fr, Freycinettia Sp. 3fr, Xanthostemon Francii. 4fr, Psidiomyrtus locellatus. 5fr, Callistemon suberosum. 7fr, Montrouziera sphaeroidea, horiz. 10fr, Ixora collina, horiz. 17fr, Deplanchea speciosa.

Photogravure; Lithographed (2fr, 3fr)

1964-65 ***Perf. 13x12½***
330 A40 1fr multi .85 .55
331 A40 2fr multi .85 .60
332 A40 3fr multi 1.75 .75
333 A40 4fr multi ('65) 3.25 .90
334 A40 5fr multi ('65) 3.75 1.25
335 A40 7fr multi 5.25 1.60
336 A40 10fr multi 6.75 1.75
337 A40 17fr multi 9.50 4.25
Nos. 330-337 (8) 31.95 11.65

Sea Squirts — A41

Design: 10fr, Alcyonium catalai. 17fr, Shrimp (hymenocera elegans).

1964-65 **Engr.** ***Perf. 13***
338 A41 7fr dk bl, org & brn 1.75 1.00
339 A41 10fr dk red & dk vio bl ('65) 2.75 1.10
340 A41 17fr dk bl, mag & grn 4.75 2.50
Nos. 338-340 (3) 9.25 4.60

Nouméa Aquarium. See Nos. C41-C43.

Philatec Issue

Common Design Type

1964, Apr. 9 **Unwmk.** ***Perf. 13***
341 CD118 40fr dk vio, grn & choc 8.50 6.75

De Gaulle's 1940 Poster "A Tous les Francais" A42

1965, Sept. 20 **Engr.** ***Perf. 13***
342 A42 20fr red, bl & blk 12.50 8.25

25th anniv. of the rallying of the Free French.

Amedee Lighthouse — A43

1965, Nov. 25
343 A43 8fr dk vio bl, bis & grn 1.90 1.00

Centenary of the Amedee lighthouse.

Games' Emblem — A44

1966, Mar. 1 **Engr.** ***Perf. 13***
344 A44 8fr dk red, brt bl & blk 1.75 .90

2nd So. Pacific Games, Nouméa, Dec. 1966.

Red-throated Parrot Finch — A45

Design: 3fr, Giant imperial pigeon.

1966, Oct. 10 **Litho.** ***Perf. 13x12½***

Size: 22x37mm

345 A45 1fr green & multi 3.00 1.50
346 A45 3fr citron & multi 6.00 1.90

See #361-366, 380-381, C48-C49A, C70-C71.

Dancers and UNESCO Emblem A46

1966, Nov. 4 **Engr.** ***Perf. 13***
347 A46 16fr pur, ocher & grn 2.40 1.40

20th anniv. of UNESCO.

High Jump and Games' Emblem A47

1966, Dec. 8 **Engr.** ***Perf. 13***
348 A47 17fr shown 3.00 1.25
349 A47 20fr Hurdling 4.50 2.10
350 A47 40fr Running 5.75 2.40
351 A47 100fr Swimming 9.50 6.25
a. Souv. sheet of 4, #348-351 + label 32.50 32.50
Nos. 348-351 (4) 22.75 12.00

2nd So. Pacific Games, Nouméa, Dec. 8-18.

Lekine Cliffs A48

1967, Jan. 14 **Engr.** ***Perf. 13***
352 A48 17fr brt grn, ultra & sl grn 2.40 2.00

Magenta Stadium, Nouméa A49

Design: 20fr, Ouen Toro Municipal Swimming Pool, Nouméa.

1967, June 5 **Photo.** ***Perf. 12x13***
353 A49 10fr multi 1.50 .85
354 A49 20fr multi 3.50 1.60

ITY Emblem, Beach at Nouméa A50

1967, June 19 **Engr.** ***Perf. 13***
355 A50 30fr multi 4.75 2.60

Issued for International Tourist Year, 1967.

19th Century Mailman A51

1967, July 12
356 A51 7fr dk car, bl grn & brn 3.25 1.40

Issued for Stamp Day.

Papilio Montrouzieri — A52

Butterflies: 9fr, Polyura clitarchus. 13fr, 15fr, Hypolimnas bolina, male and female respectively.

1967-68 **Engr.** ***Perf. 13***

Size: 36x22mm

357 A52 7fr lt grn, blk & ultra 4.75 1.25
358 A52 9fr brn, lil & ind ('68) 5.75 1.50
359 A52 13fr vio bl, brn org & dk brn 7.00 2.50
360 A52 15fr dk brn, bl & yel 10.00 4.50
Nos. 357-360,C51-C53 (7) 65.50 27.75

Issued: 9fr, 3/26/68; others, 8/10/67.

Bird Type of 1966

Birds: 1fr, New Caledonian grass warbler. 2fr, New Caledonia whistler. 3fr, New Caledonia white-throated pigeon. 4fr, Kagus. 5fr, Crested parakeet. 10fr, Crow honey-eater.

1967-68 **Photo.** ***Perf. 13x12½***

Size: 22x37mm

361 A45 1fr multi 1.50 1.00
362 A45 2fr multi 3.25 1.25
363 A45 3fr multi 2.25 1.40
364 A45 4fr grn & multi 5.50 2.50
365 A45 5fr lt yel & multi 7.00 3.25
366 A45 10fr pink & multi 14.00 4.25
Nos. 361-366 (6) 33.50 13.65

Issued: #364-366, 12/16/67; others 5/14/68.

WHO Anniversary Issue

Common Design Type

1968, May 4 **Engr.** ***Perf. 13***
367 CD126 20fr mar, vio & dk bl grn 4.50 2.25

Ferrying Mail Truck Across Tontouta River, 1900 A53

1968, Sept. 2 **Engr.** ***Perf. 13***
368 A53 9fr dk red brn, grn & ultra 3.75 1.60

Issued for Stamp Day, 1968.

Human Rights Year Issue

Common Design Type

1968, Aug. 10 **Engr.** ***Perf. 13***
369 CD127 12fr sl grn, dp car & org yel 3.00 1.50

Conus Geographus — A54

1968, Nov. 9 Engr. *Perf. 13*
Size: 36x22mm

370 A54 10fr dk brn, brt bl & gray 4.25 2.25
Nos. 370,C58-C60 (4) 37.75 13.50

Car on Road A55

1968, Dec. 26 Engr. *Perf. 13*
371 A55 25fr dp bl, sl grn & hn brn 9.00 3.75

2nd Automobile Safari of New Caledonia.

Cattle Dip — A56

1969, May 10 Engr. *Perf. 13*
Size: 36x22mm

372 A56 9fr shown 1.50 1.00
373 A56 25fr Cattle branding 3.00 1.75
Nos. 372-373,C64 (3) 10.25 6.00

Cattle breeding in New Caledonia.

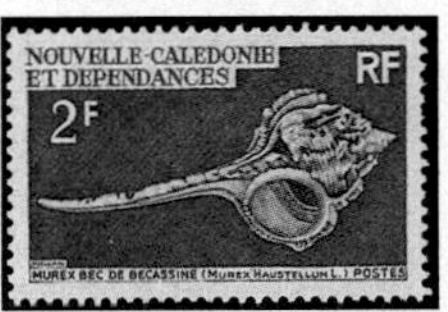

Murex Haustellum A57

Sea Shells: 5fr, Venus comb. 15fr, Murex ramosus.

1969, June 21 Engr. *Perf. 13*
Size: 35½x22mm

374 A57 2fr ver, bl & brn 1.75 .90
375 A57 5fr dl red, pur & beige 3.75 1.20
376 A57 15fr ver, dl grn & gray 6.00 2.40
Nos. 374-376,C65 (4) 39.00 16.00

Judo A58

1969, Aug. 7 Engr. *Perf. 13*
Size: 36x22mm

377 A58 19fr shown 3.75 1.90
378 A58 20fr Boxers 3.75 1.90
Nos. 377-378,C66-C67 (4) 19.50 8.80

3rd South Pacific Games, Port Moresby, Papua and New Guinea, Aug. 13-23.

ILO Issue
Common Design Type

1969, Nov. 24 Engr. *Perf. 13*
379 CD131 12fr org, brn vio & brn 2.25 1.10

Bird Type of 1966

15fr, Friarbird. 30fr, Sacred kingfisher.

1970, Feb. 19 Photo. *Perf. 13*
Size: 22x37mm

380 A45 15fr yel grn & multi 8.25 3.25
381 A45 30fr pale salmon & multi 12.00 5.50
Nos. 380-381,C70-C71 (4) 62.75 25.25

UPU Headquarters Issue
Common Design Type

1970, May 20 Engr. *Perf. 13*
382 CD133 12fr brn, gray & dk car 3.00 1.50

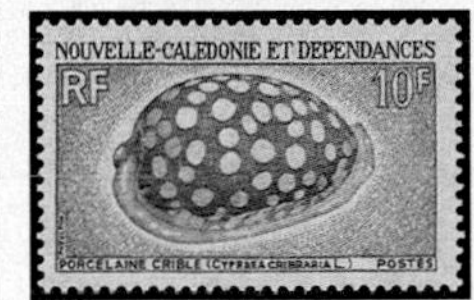

Porcelain Sieve Shell A59

Designs: 1fr, Strombus epidromis linne, vert. No. 385, Strombus variabilis swainson, vert. 21fr, Mole porcelain shell.

1970 Size: 22x36mm, 36x22mm

383 A59 1fr brt grn & multi 2.25 .75
384 A59 10fr rose & multi 5.25 1.50
385 A59 10fr blk & multi 6.75 2.40
386 A59 21fr bl grn, brn & dk brn 10.00 4.00
Nos. 383-386,C73-C76 (8) 68.25 28.90

See Nos. 395-396, C89-C90.

Packet Ship "Natal," 1883 A60

1970, July 23 Engr. *Perf. 13*
387 A60 9fr Prus bl, blk & brt grn 4.00 1.40

Issued for Stamp Day.

Dumbea Railroad Post Office A61

1971, Mar. 13 Engr. *Perf. 13*
388 A61 10fr red, slate grn & blk 5.00 2.00

Stamp Day, 1971.

Racing Yachts — A62

1971, Apr. 17 Engr. *Perf. 13*
389 A62 16fr bl, Prus bl & sl grn 5.00 3.00

Third sailing cruise from Whangarei, New Zealand, to Nouméa.

Morse Recorder, Communications Satellite — A63

1971, May 17 Engr. *Perf. 13*
390 A63 19fr red, lake & org 3.00 1.25

3rd World Telecommunications Day.

Weight Lifting — A64

1971, June 24 Engr. *Perf. 13*
391 A64 11fr shown 2.50 1.00
392 A64 23fr Basketball 3.75 1.50
Nos. 391-392,C82-C83 (4) 18.00 8.75

4th South Pacific Games, Papeete, French Polynesia, Sept. 8-19.

De Gaulle Issue
Common Design Type

Designs: 34fr, Pres. de Gaulle, 1970. 100fr, Gen. de Gaulle, 1940.

1971, Nov. 9
393 CD134 34fr dk pur & blk 9.00 3.75
394 CD134 100fr dk pur & blk 16.00 8.00

Sea Shell Type of 1970

Designs: 1fr, Scorpion conch, vert. 3fr, Common spider conch., vert.

1972, Mar. 4 Engr. *Perf. 13*
Size: 22x36mm

395 A59 1fr vio & dk brn 2.00 .70
396 A59 3fr grn & ocher 3.00 .80
Nos. 395-396,C89-C90 (4) 24.00 8.50

Carved Wooden Pillow — A66

1972-73 Photo. *Perf. 12½x13*
397 A66 1fr Doorpost, Goa ('73) 1.25 .40
398 A66 2fr shown 1.25 .65
399 A66 5fr Monstrance 1.75 .80
400 A66 12fr Tchamba mask 4.75 1.25
Nos. 397-400,C102-C103 (6) 15.25 6.10

Objects from Nouméa Museum.
Issued: 2fr-15fr, 8/5.

Chamber of Commerce Emblem — A67

1972, Dec. 16
401 A67 12fr blk, yel & brt bl 1.60 .90

Junior Chamber of Commerce, 10th anniv.

Tchamba Mask — A68

1973, Mar. 15 Engr. *Perf. 13*
402 A68 12fr lilac 8.25 2.00
a. Booklet pane of 5 200.00

No. 402 issued in booklets only.
See No. C99.

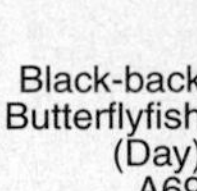

Black-back Butterflyfish (Day) A69

1973, June 23 Photo. *Perf. 13x12½*
403 A69 8fr shown 2.50 1.00
404 A69 14fr same fish (night) 3.75 1.50
Nos. 403-404,C105 (3) 11.75 4.50

Nouméa Aquarium.

Emblem A70

1973, July 21 *Perf. 13*
405 A70 20fr grn, yel & vio bl 2.25 .80

School Coordinating Office, 10th anniv.

"Nature Protection" — A72

1974, June 22 Photo. *Perf. 13x12½*
406 A72 7fr multi 1.40 .55

Scorched Landscape A73

1975, Feb. 7 Photo. *Perf. 13*
407 A73 20fr multi 2.25 1.10

"Prevent brush fires."

Calanthe Veratrifolia — A74

Design: 11fr, Liperanthus gigas.

1975, May 30 Photo. *Perf. 13*
408 A74 8fr pur & multi 3.00 1.00
409 A74 11fr dk bl & multi 3.50 1.00
Nos. 408-409,C125 (3) 14.00 4.25

Orchids. See Nos. 425-426.

Festival Emblem — A75

1975, Sept. 6 Photo. *Perf. 12½x13*
410 A75 12fr ultra, org & yel 1.10 .70

Melanesia 2000 Festival.

Birds in Flight — A76

1975, Oct. 18 Photo. *Perf. 13½x13*
411 A76 5fr ocher, yel & blk 1.10 .55

Nouméa Ornithological Society, 10th anniversary.

Georges Pompidou — A77

1975, Dec. 6 Engr. *Perf. 13*
412 A77 26fr dk grn, blk & sl 2.75 1.25

Pompidou (1911-74), president of France.

Sea Birds A78

Perf. 13x12½, 12½x13
1976, Feb. 26 Photo.
413 A78 1fr Brown booby .90 .45
414 A78 2fr Blue-faced booby 1.40 .70
415 A78 8fr Red-footed booby, vert. 2.00 1.10
Nos. 413-415 (3) 4.30 2.25

Festival Emblem A79

1976, Mar. 13 Litho. *Perf. 12½*
416 A79 27fr bl, org & blk 2.00 .90

Rotorua 1976, South Pacific Arts Festival, New Zealand.

Lion and Lions Emblem — A80

1976, Mar. 13 Photo. *Perf. 12½x13*
417 A80 49fr multi 4.25 2.00

Lions Club of Nouméa, 15th anniversary.

Music Pavilion — A81

Design: 30fr, Fountain, vert.

1976, July 3 Litho. *Perf. 12½*
418 A81 25fr multi 1.50 .70
419 A81 30fr blue & multi 1.75 1.00

Old Nouméa.

Polluted Shore — A82

1976, Aug. 21 Photo. *Perf. 13*
420 A82 20fr dp bl & multi 2.00 .90

Nature protection.

South Pacific People A83

1976, Oct. 23 Photo. *Perf. 13*
421 A83 20fr bl & multi 1.75 .90

16th South Pacific Commission Conference, Nouméa, Oct. 1976.

Giant Grasshopper — A84

1977, Feb. 21 Engr. *Perf. 13*
422 A84 26fr shown 1.90 1.25
423 A84 31fr Beetle and larvae 2.75 1.40

Ground Satellite Station, Nouméa — A85

1977, Apr. 16 Litho. *Perf. 13*
424 A85 29fr multi 2.10 1.10

Orchid Type of 1975

Designs: 22fr, Phajus daenikeri. 44fr, Dendrobium finetianum.

1977, May 23 Photo. *Perf. 13*
425 A74 22fr brn & multi 3.75 1.25
426 A74 44fr bl & multi 4.25 1.90

Mask, Palms, "Stamps" — A86

1977, June 25 Photo. *Perf. 13*
427 A86 35fr multi 1.75 1.00

Philately in school, Philatelic Exhibition, La Perouse Lyceum, Nouméa.

Trees A87

1977, July 23 Photo. *Perf. 13*
428 A87 20fr multi 1.50 .75

Nature protection.

Congress Emblem — A88

1977, Aug. 6 Photo. *Perf. 13*
429 A88 200fr multi 9.25 5.50

French Junior Economic Chambers Congress, Nouméa.

Young Frigate Bird — A89

22fr, Terns, horiz. 40fr, Sooty terns, horiz.

1977-78 Photo. *Perf. 13*
430 A89 16fr multi 5.75 1.00
431 A89 22fr multi 2.25 1.10
432 A89 40fr multi 3.75 1.50
Nos. 430-432,C138 (4) 17.75 5.20

Issued: 16fr, 9/17/77; 22fr, 40fr, 2/11/78.

Mare and Foal — A90

1977, Nov. 19 Engr. *Perf. 13*
433 A90 5fr multi 1.25 .55

10th anniversary of the Society for Promotion of Caledonian Horses.

Araucaria Montana — A91

1978, Mar. 17 Photo. *Perf. 12½x13*
434 A91 16fr multi 1.25 .55

See No. C149.

Halityle Regularis — A92

1978, May 20 Photo. *Perf. 13*
436 A92 10fr vio bl & multi 1.25 .45

Nouméa Aquarium.

Stylized Turtle and Globe A93

1978, May 20
437 A93 30fr multi 3.00 1.10

Protection of the turtle.

Flying Fox — A94

1978, June 10
438 A94 20fr multi 1.75 1.00

Nature protection.

Maurice Leenhardt — A95

1978, Aug. 12 Engr. *Perf. 13*
439 A95 37fr multi 2.00 1.25

Pastor Maurice Leenhardt (1878-1954).

Soccer Player, League Emblem — A96

1978, Nov. 4 Photo. *Perf. 13*
440 A96 26fr multi 2.00 .90

New Caledonia Soccer League, 50th anniversary.

Lifu Island A97

1978, Dec. 9 Litho. *Perf. 13*
441 A97 33fr multi 1.75 .90

Petroglyph, Mère — A98

1979, Jan. 27 Engr. *Perf. 13*
442 A98 10fr brick red 1.25 .55

Map of Ouvea — A99

Design: 31fr, Map of Mare Island, horiz.

Perf. 12½x13, 13x12½
1979, Feb. 17 Photo.
443 A99 11fr multi 1.25 .55
444 A99 31fr multi 1.75 .75

House at Artillery Point — A100

1979, Apr. 28 Photo. *Perf. 13*
445 A100 20fr multi 1.40 .70

Auguste Escoffier — A101

1979, July 21 Engr. *Perf. 12½x13*
446 A101 24fr multi 1.25 .70

Auguste Escoffier Hotel School.

Regatta and Games Emblem A102

1979, Aug. 11 Photo. *Perf. 13*
447 A102 16fr multi 1.50 .70

6th South Pacific Games, Suva, Fiji, Aug. 27-Sept. 8.

Agathis Ovata A103

1979, Oct. 20 Photo. *Perf. 13x12½*
448 A103 5fr shown 1.00 .35
449 A103 34fr Cyathea intermedia 2.00 .75

Pouembout Rodeo A104

1979, Oct. 27 Engr. *Perf. 13x12½*
450 A104 12fr multi 1.25 .55

Bantamia Merleti A105

1979, Dec. 1 Photo. *Perf. 13x11½*
451 A105 23fr multi 1.50 .70

Fluorescent corals from Nouméa Aquarium.

Map of Pine Tree Island, Fishermen with Nets A106

1980, Jan. 12 Photo. *Perf. 13x12½*
452 A106 23fr multi 1.50 .45

Hibbertia Virotii A107

1980, Apr. 19 Photo. *Perf. 13x12½*
453 A107 11fr shown 1.40 .65
454 A107 12fr Grevillea meisneri 1.40 .65

Philately at School — A108

1980, May 10 Litho. *Perf. 12½*
455 A108 30fr multi 1.10 .55

Prevention of Traffic Accidents A109

1980, July 5 Photo. *Perf. 13x12½*
456 A109 15fr multi .85 .35

Parribacus Caledonicus — A110

Noumea Aquarium Crustacea: 8fr, Panulirus versicolor.

1980, Aug. 23 Litho. *Perf. 13x13½*
457 A110 5fr multi .50 .35
458 A110 8fr multi .75 .55

Solar Energy A111

1980, Oct. 11 Photo. *Perf. 13x12½*
459 A111 23fr multi 1.40 .70

Manta Birostris A112

25fr, Carcharhinus amblyrhnchos.

1981, Feb. 18 Photo. *Perf. 13x12½*
460 A112 23fr shown 2.00 .90
461 A112 25fr multicolored 2.00 .90

Belep Islands A113

1981, Mar. 4
462 A113 26fr multi 1.25 .55

Cypraea Stolida A114

1fr, Cymbiola rossiniana, vert. 2fr, Connus floccatus, vert.

1981, June 17 Photo. *Perf. 13*
463 A114 1fr multicolored .50 .25
464 A114 2fr multicolored .70 .45
465 A114 13fr shown 1.10 .70
Nos. 463-465 (3) 2.30 1.40

See Nos. 470-471.

Corvette Constantine, 1854 — A115

25fr, Aviso le Phoque, 1853.

1981, July 22 Engr. *Perf. 13*
466 A115 10fr shown 1.25 .55
467 A115 25fr multicolored 1.75 1.10

See Nos. 476-477.

Intl. Year of the Disabled A116

1981, Sept. 2 Litho. *Perf. 12½*
468 A116 45fr multicolored 1.50 .75

Nature Preservation A117

1981, Nov. 7 Photo. *Perf. 13*
469 A117 28fr multicolored 2.00 .90

Marine Life Type of 1981

1982, Jan. 20 Photo. *Perf. 13x13½*
470 A114 13fr Calappa calappa 1.25 .70
471 A114 25fr Etisus splendidus 1.75 1.10

Chalcantite A118

1982, Mar. 17 Photo. *Perf. 13x13½*
472 A118 15fr shown 2.25 1.10
473 A118 30fr Anorthosite 3.00 1.10

Melaleuca Quinquenervia — A119

20fr, Savannah trees, vert.

1982, June 23 Photo. *Perf. 13*

474 A119 20fr multicolored 1.00 .70
475 A119 29fr shown 1.25 .70

Ship Type of 1981

44fr, Barque Le Cher. 59fr, Naval dispatch vessel Kersaint.

1982, July 7 Engr.

476 A115 44fr multicolored 1.75 .65
477 A115 59fr multicolored 2.50 1.00

Ateou Tribe Traditional House — A120

1982, Oct. 13 Photo. *Perf. 13½x13*

478 A120 52fr multicolored 1.60 .90

Grey's Ptilope — A121

1982, Nov. 6

479 A121 32fr shown 1.25 .70
480 A121 35fr Caledonian loriquet 2.00 .90

Central Education Coordination Office — A122

1982, Nov. 27 Litho. *Perf. 13½x13*

481 A122 48fr Boat 1.75 .75

Bernheim Library, Noumea — A123

1982, Dec. 15 Engr. *Perf. 13*

482 A123 36fr multicolored 1.10 .55

Caledonian Orchids A123a

10fr, Dendrobium oppositifolium. 15fr, Dendrobium munificum. 29fr, Dendrobium fractiflexum.

1983, Feb. 16 Photo. *Perf. 13x13½*

482A A123a 10fr multicolored .75 .35
482B A123a 15fr multicolored 1.10 .45
482C A123a 29fr multicolored 1.75 .90
Nos. 482A-482C (3) 3.60 1.70

Xanthostemon Aurantiacum — A124

1fr, Crinum asiaticum. 2fr, Xanthostemon aurantiacum. 4fr, Metrosideros demonstrans, vert.

1983, Mar. 23 Litho. *Perf. 13*

483 A124 1fr multicolored .30 .25
484 A124 2fr multicolored .30 .25
485 A124 4fr multicolored .30 .25
Nos. 483-485 (3) .90 .75

25th Anniv. of Posts and Telecommunications Dept. — A125

Telephones and post offices.

1983, Apr. 30 Litho. *Perf. 13*

486 A125 30fr multicolored .75 .35
487 A125 40fr multicolored .90 .45
488 A125 50fr multicolored 1.25 .55
a. Souvenir sheet of 3 11.00 10.00
b. Strip of 3, #486-488 3.75 2.00

No. 488a contains Nos. 486-488 with changed background colors.

Local Snakes A126

1983, June 22 Photo. *Perf. 13*

489 A126 31fr Laticauda laticauda 1.40 .55
490 A126 33fr Laticauda colubrina 1.75 .75

A127

1983, Aug. 10 Engr.

491 A127 16fr Volleyball .95 .55

7th South Pacific Games, Sept.

Nature Protection A128

1983, Oct. 12 Photo. *Perf. 12½*

492 A128 56fr multi 2.00 1.00

Birds of Prey A129

34fr, Tyto Alba Lifuensis, vert. 37fr, Pandion Haliaetus.

1983, Nov. 16 Litho. *Perf. 13*

493 A129 34fr multicolored 1.50 .70
494 A129 37fr multicolored 1.90 1.00

Local Shells — A130

5fr, Conus chenui. 15fr, Conus moluccensis. 20fr, Conus optimus.

1984, Jan. 11 Litho. & Engr.

495 A130 5fr multicolored .45 .25
496 A130 15fr multicolored .80 .55
497 A130 20fr multicolored 1.00 .70
Nos. 495-497 (3) 2.25 1.50

See Nos. 521-522.

Steamers A131

1984, Feb. 8 Engr.

498 A131 18fr St. Joseph .90 .65
499 A131 31fr St. Antoine 1.35 .70

Arms of Noumea — A132

1984, Apr. 11 Litho. *Perf. 12½x13*

500 A132 35fr multi 1.10 .50

See No. 546, 607, C214.

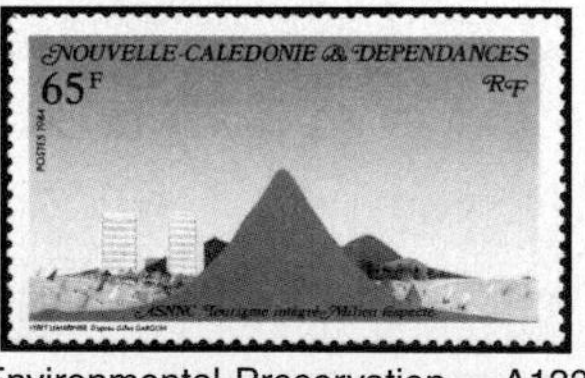

Environmental Preservation — A133

1984, May 23 *Perf. 13*

501 A133 65fr Island scene 2.00 .80

Orchids — A134

16fr, Diplocaulobium ou-hinnae. 38fr, Acianthus atepalus.

1984, July 18 Litho. *Perf. 12*

502 A134 16fr multicolored 1.25 .55
503 A134 38fr multicolored 1.75 1.10

Cent. of Public Schooling A135

1984, Oct. 11 Litho. *Perf. 13½x13*

504 A135 59fr Schoolhouse 1.75 .70

Kagu — A137

1985-86 Engr. *Perf. 13*

511 A137 1fr brt bl .25 .25
512 A137 2fr green .25 .25
513 A137 3fr brt org .25 .25
514 A137 4fr brt grn .25 .25
515 A137 5fr dp rose lil .25 .25
516 A137 35fr crimson 1.25 .35
517 A137 38fr vermilion 1.25 .55
518 A137 40fr brt rose ('86) 1.00 .55
Nos. 511-518 (8) 4.75 2.70

Issued: 1, 2, 5, 38fr, 5/22; 3, 4, 35fr, 2/13; 40fr, 7/30.

See types A179, A179a.

Sea Shell Type of 1984

Lithographed and Engraved

1985, Feb. 27 *Perf. 13*

521 A130 55fr Conus bullatus 1.50 .90
522 A130 72fr Conus lamberti 2.00 1.40

25th World Meteorological Day — A138

17fr, Radio communication, storm.

1985, Mar. 20 Litho.

523 A138 17fr multicolored .65 .35

Red Cross, Medicine Without Frontiers — A139

1985, Apr. 10 *Perf. 12½*

524 A139 41fr multi 1.25 .55

Telephone Switching Center Inauguration — A140

1985, Apr. 24

525 A140 70fr E 10 B installation 1.75 .90

Marguerite La Foa Suspension Bridge A141

1985, May 10 **Engr.** ***Perf. 13***
526 A141 44fr brt bl & red brn 1.25 .70

Historical Preservation Association.

Le Cagou Philatelic Society — A142

1985, June 15 **Litho.**
527 A142 220fr multi 5.75 3.25
a. Souvenir sheet, perf. 12½ 7.25 6.50

No. 527a sold for 230fr.

4th Pacific Arts Festival — A143

1985, July 3 ***Perf. 13½***
Black Overprint
528 A143 55fr multi 1.40 1.00
529 A143 75fr multi 2.00 1.25

Not issued without overprint. Festival was transferred to French Polynesia.

Intl. Youth Year — A144

1985, July 24 **Litho.** ***Perf. 13***
530 A144 59fr multi 1.75 .80

Amedee Lighthouse Electrification — A145

1985, Aug. 13
531 A145 89fr multi 2.25 1.10

Environmental Conservation A146

1985, Sept. 18
532 A146 100fr Planting trees 2.50 1.10

Birds A147

1985, Dec. 18 ***Perf. 12½***
533 A147 50fr Poule sultane 1.25 .80
534 A147 60fr Merle caledonien 1.75 1.00

Noumea Aquarium A148

10fr, Pomacanthus imperator. 17fr, Rhinopias aphanes.

1986, Feb. 19 **Litho.** ***Perf. 12½x13***
535 A148 10fr multicolored .45 .25
536 A148 17fr multicolored .65 .35

Kanumera Bay, Isle of Pines — A149

1986, Mar. 26 **Litho.** ***Perf. 12½***
537 A149 50fr shown 1.10 .55
538 A149 55fr Inland village 1.40 .80

See Nos. 547-548, 617-618.

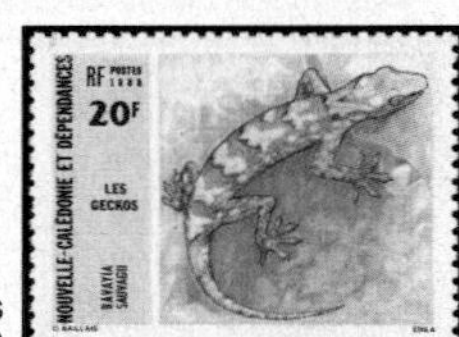
Geckos A150

20fr, Bavayia sauvagii. 45fr, Rhacodactylus leachianus.

1986, Apr. 16 ***Perf. 12½x13***
539 A150 20fr multicolored .65 .45
540 A150 45fr multicolored 1.40 .80

1986 World Cup Soccer Championships, Mexico — A151

1986, May 28 ***Perf. 13***
541 A151 60fr multi 1.50 1.00

1st Pharmacy in New Caledonia, 120th Anniv. — A152

1986, June 25 **Litho.** ***Perf. 13***
542 A152 80fr multi 1.75 1.10

Orchids A153

44fr, Coelogynae licastioides. 58fr, Calanthe langei.

1986, July 16 ***Perf. 12½x13***
543 A153 44fr multicolored 1.40 .80
544 A153 58fr multicolored 1.75 .90

STAMPEX '86, Adelaide — A154

1986, Aug. 4 ***Perf. 12½***
545 A154 110fr Bird 3.00 1.40

Arms Type of 1984

1986, Oct. 11 **Litho.** ***Perf. 13½***
546 A132 94fr Mont Dore 3.00 1.10

Landscape Type of 1986

40fr, West landscape, vert. 76fr, South Landscape.

1986, Oct. 29 **Litho.** ***Perf. 12½***
547 A149 40fr multicolored .90 .70
548 A149 76fr multicolored 1.60 .80

Flowers A156

Niponthes vieillardi, Syzygium ngayense, Archidendropsis Paivana, Scavola balansae.

1986, Nov. 12 ***Perf. 12½***
549 A156 73fr multi 1.75 .90

Nature Protection Assoc.

A157

1986, Nov. 26 ***Perf. 13x12½***
550 A157 350fr Emblem 7.50 4.25

Noumea Lions Club, 25th anniv.

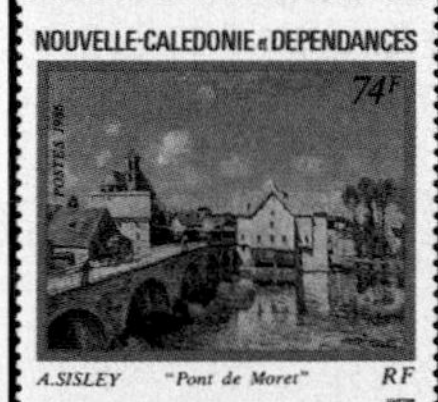
A158

Paintings: 74fr, Moret Point, by A. Sisley. 140fr, Butterfly Chase, by B. Morisot.

1986, Dec. 23 **Litho.** ***Perf. 13***
551 A158 74fr multi 2.25 1.40
552 A158 140fr multi 4.00 1.60

A159

1987, Jan. 28 ***Perf. 13½***
553 A159 30fr Challenge France 1.00 .55
554 A159 70fr French Kiss 2.00 1.10

America's Cup.

Plants, Butterflies A160

46fr, Anona squamosa, Graphium gelon. 54fr, Albizzia granulosa, Polyura gamma.

1987, Feb. 25 **Litho.** ***Perf. 13x12½***
555 A160 46fr multi 1.75 .80
556 A160 54fr multi 2.00 .90

Pirogues A161

1987, May 13 **Engr.** ***Perf. 13x12½***
557 A161 72fr from Isle of Pines 1.75 1.00
558 A161 90fr from Ouvea 2.25 1.25

New Town Hall, Mont Dore A162

1987, May 23 **Litho.** ***Perf. 12½x13***
559 A162 92fr multi 2.10 1.00

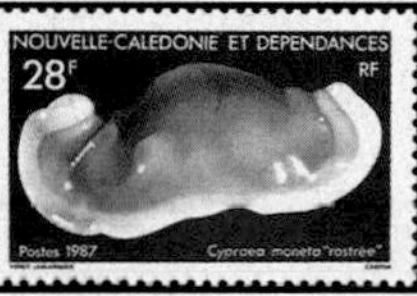
Seashells A163

1987, June 24 ***Perf. 13***
560 A163 28fr Cypraea moneta .75 .45
561 A163 36fr Cypraea martini 1.25 .70

8th South Pacific Games — A164

1987, July 8 ***Perf. 12½x13***
562 A164 40fr multi 1.00 .55

A165

1987, July 22 *Perf. 13½*
563 A165 270fr multi 5.75 2.75

Soroptimist Int'l. 13th Convention, Melbourne, July 26-31.

Birds A166

18fr, Zosterops xanthochroa. 21fr, Falco peregrinus nesiotes, vert.

1987, Aug. 26 *Perf. 13*
564 A166 18fr multicolored .90 .35
565 A166 21fr multicolored 1.10 .35

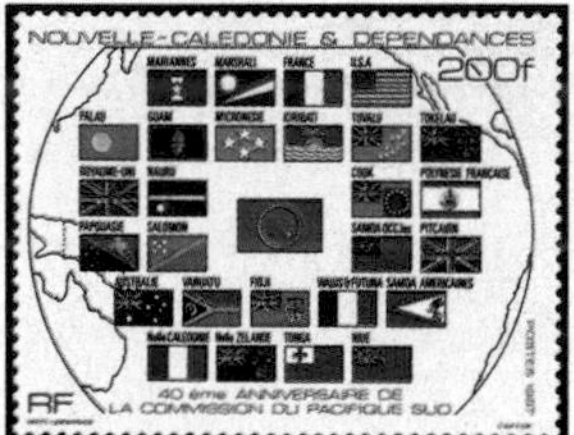

South Pacific Commission, 40th Anniv. — A167

1987, Oct. 14 **Litho.** *Perf. 13*
566 A167 200fr multi 5.00 2.50

Philately at School A168

1987, Oct. 21 *Perf. 12½*
567 A168 15fr multi .50 .35

8th South Pacific Games, Noumea — A169

1987, Dec. 8 **Litho.** *Perf. 12½*
568 A169 20fr Golf .75 .35
569 A169 30fr Rugby 9.00 1.00
570 A169 100fr Long jump 2.75 1.40
Nos. 568-570 (3) 12.50 2.75

Map, Ships, La Perouse — A170

1988, Feb. 10 **Engr.** *Perf. 13*
571 A170 36fr dark rose lil 1.40 .55

Disappearance of La Perouse expedition, 200th anniv., and Jean-Francois de Galaup (1741-1788), Comte de La Perouse.

French University of the South Pacific at Noumea and Papeete A171

1988, Feb. 24 **Litho.** *Perf. 13x12½*
572 A171 400fr multi 9.25 4.25

Tropical Fish A172

30fr, Pomacanthus semicirculatus. 46fr, Glyphidodontops cyaneus.

1988, Mar. 23 **Litho.** *Perf. 13*
573 A172 30fr multicolored 1.10 .55
574 A172 46fr multicolored 1.50 .80

Intl. Red Cross and Red Crescent Organizations, 125th Annivs. — A173

1988, Apr. 27
575 A173 300fr multi 7.50 3.75

Regional Housing A174

Designs: 19fr, Mwaringou, Canala Region, vert. 21fr, Nathalo, Lifou.

1988, Apr. 13 **Engr.** *Perf. 13*
576 A174 19fr emer grn, brt blue & red brn .45 .25
577 A174 21fr brt blue, emer grn & red brn .70 .25

Medicinal Plants A175

1988, May 18 **Litho.** *Perf. 13x12½*
578 A175 28fr Ochrosia elliptica .90 .55
579 A175 64fr Rauvolfia levenetii 1.90 1.10

No. 579 is airmail.

Living Fossils — A176

51fr, Gymnocrinus richeri.

1988, June 11 *Perf. 13*
580 A176 51fr multicolored 2.25 .90

Bourail Museum and Historical Soc. — A177

1988, June 25 **Litho.** *Perf. 13*
581 A177 120fr multi 3.00 1.60

Kagu — A179

1988-90 **Engr.** *Perf. 13*
584 A179 1fr bright blue .50 .25
585 A179 2fr green .50 .25
586 A179 3fr bright orange .75 .25
587 A179 4fr bright green .75 .25
588 A179 5fr deep rose lilac 1.00 .25
589 A179 28fr orange 1.00 .25
590 A179 40fr bright rose 1.10 .25
Nos. 584-590 (7) 5.60 1.75

Issued: 40fr, 8/10/88; 1fr, 4fr, 1/25/89; 2fr, 3fr, 5fr, 4/19/89; 28fr, 1/15/90.

See Type A137.

Kagu — A179a

1990-93 **Engr.** *Perf. 13*
591 A179a 1fr dark blue .25 .25
592 A179a 2fr bright green .25 .25
593 A179a 3fr brt yel org .30 .25
594 A179a 4fr dark green .30 .25
595 A179a 5fr bright violet .30 .25
596 A179a 9fr blue black .35 .25
597 A179a 12fr orange .40 .25
598 A179a 40fr lilac rose 1.00 .25
599 A179a 50fr red 1.40 .30
Nos. 591-599 (9) 4.55 2.30

Issued: 50fr, 9/5/90; 1fr-5fr, 1/9/91; 40fr, 1/15/92; 9fr, 12fr, 1/25/93.

See Type A137 and Nos. 675, 683. For surcharge see No. 685.

SYDPEX '88 — A178

Designs: No. 582, La Perouse aboard *La Boussole,* gazing through spyglass at the First Fleet in Botany Bay, Jan. 24, 1788. No. 583, Capt. Phillip and crew ashore on Botany Bay watching the approach of La Perouse's ships *La Boussole* and *L'Astrolabe.*

1988, July 30 **Litho.** *Perf. 13x12½*
582 A178 42fr multi 1.50 .90
583 A178 42fr multi 1.50 .90
a. Souvenir sheet of 2, #582-583, perf. 13x13½ 4.75 4.25
b. Strip of 2, #582-583 + label 3.50 3.00

No. 583a sold for 120fr.

1988 Summer Olympics, Seoul — A180

1988, Sept. 14 *Perf. 12½x12*
600 A180 150fr multi 3.75 2.00

Pasteur Institute, Noumea, Cent. A181

1988, Sept. 28 **Engr.** *Perf. 13*
601 A181 100fr blk, brt ultra & dark red 2.75 1.40

Writers — A182

72fr, Georges Baudoux (1870-1949). 73fr, Jean Mariotti (1901-1975).

1988, Oct. 15 **Engr.** *Perf. 13*
602 A182 72fr multicolored 1.60 .90
603 A182 73fr multicolored 1.60 .90

No. 603 is airmail.

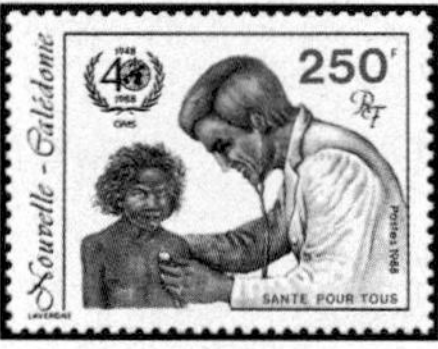

WHO, 40th Anniv. A183

1988, Nov. 16 **Litho.** *Perf. 13x12½*
604 A183 250fr multi 6.00 2.75

Art Type of 1984 Without "ET DEPENDANCES"

Paintings by artists of the Pacific: 54fr, *Land of Men,* by L. Bunckley. 92fr, *The Latin Quarter,* by Marik.

1988, Dec. 7
605 AP113 54fr multi 2.25 1.00
606 AP113 92fr multi 3.00 1.40

Arms Type of 1984 Without "ET DEPENDANCES"

1989, Feb. 22 **Litho.** *Perf. 13½*
607 A132 200fr Koumac 4.50 2.00

Indigenous Flora A184

80fr, Parasitaxus ustus, vert. 90fr, Tristaniopsis guillainii.

1989, Mar. 22 Litho. *Perf. 13½*

608	A184 80fr multicolored	2.00	1.10
609	A184 90fr multicolored	2.50	1.40

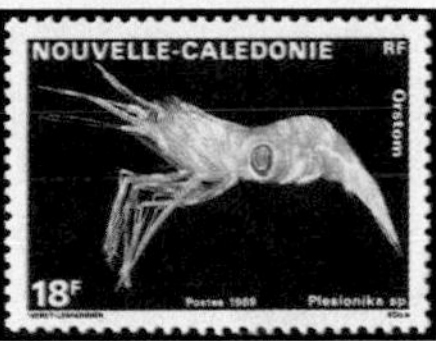

Marine Life A185

1989, May 17 Litho. *Perf. 12½x13*

610	A185 18fr Plesionika	.55	.35
611	A185 66fr Ocosia apia	1.50	1.00
612	A185 110fr Latiaxis	2.75	1.60
	Nos. 610-612 (3)	4.80	2.95

See Nos. 652-653.

French Revolution, Bicent. — A186

1989, July 7 Litho. *Perf. 13½*

613	A186 40fr Liberty	2.75	.85
614	A186 58fr Equality	2.75	1.25
615	A186 76fr Fraternity	2.75	1.40
	Nos. 613-615 (3)	8.25	3.50

Souvenir Sheet

616	A186 180fr Liberty, Equality, Fraternity	5.50	5.50

Nos. 614-616 are airmail.

Landscape Type of 1986 Without "ET DEPENDANCES"

64fr, La Poule rookery, Hienghene. 180fr, Ouaieme ferry.

1989, Aug. 23 Litho. *Perf. 13*

617	A149 64fr multicolored	1.50	.75
618	A149 180fr multicolored	4.00	1.60

No. 617 is airmail.

Carved Bamboo — A187

Litho. & Engr.

1989, Sept. 27 *Perf. 12½x13*

619	A187 70fr multicolored	1.75	.70

See No. C216.

A188

1989, Oct. 25 Litho. *Perf. 13*

620	A188 350fr multicolored	8.50	3.50

Hobie-Cat 14 10th World Championships, Nov. 3, Noumea.

Natl. Historical Soc., 20th Anniv. — A189

Cover of *Moeurs: Superstitions of New Caledonians,* cover of book on Melanesian oral literature and historians G. Pisier, R.P. Neyret and A. Surleau.

1989, Nov. 3 Engr.

621	A189 74fr brown & black	2.00	.80

Ft. Teremba — A190

1989, Nov. 18 Engr.

622	A190 100fr bl grn & dk org	2.50	1.40

Marguerite Historical Preservation Soc.

Impressionist Paintings — A191

Designs: 130fr, The Escape of Rochefort, by Manet. 270fr, Self-portrait, by Courbet.

1989, Dec. 6 Litho. *Perf. 13½*

623	A191 130fr multicolored	3.25	1.90
624	A191 270fr multicolored	7.50	4.00

Fr. Patrick O'Reilly (1900-1988), Writer — A192

1990, Jan. 24 Engr. *Perf. 13x13½*

625	A192 170fr blk & plum	4.75	1.90

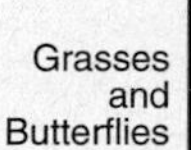

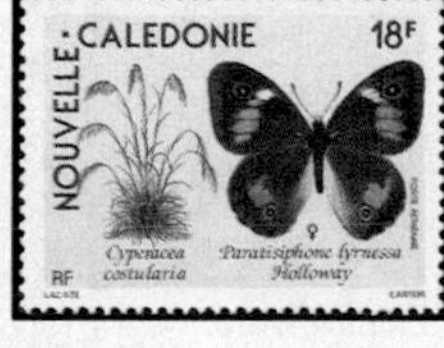

Grasses and Butterflies A193

Various Cyperacea costularia and Paratisiphone lyrnessa: 18fr, Female. 50fr, Female, diff. 94fr, Male.

1990, Feb. 21 Litho. *Perf. 13½*

626	A193 18fr shown	.60	.40
627	A193 50fr multicolored	1.50	.70
628	A193 94fr multicolored	2.10	1.25
	Nos. 626-628 (3)	4.20	2.35

Nos. 626 and 628 are airmail.

A194

1990, Mar. 16 Engr. *Perf. 12½x13*

629	A194 85fr Kanakan money	1.90	.80
630	A194 140fr money, diff.	3.00	1.40

A195

1990, Mar. 16 Litho. *Perf. 13x13½*

631	A195 230fr multicolored	6.25	2.75

Jade and mother of pearl exhibition, New Caledonian Museum.

Noumea Aquarium A196

10fr, Phyllidia ocellata. 42fr, Chromodoris kuniei, vert.

1990, Apr. 25 *Perf. 13x12½, 12½x13*

632	A196 10fr multicolored	.35	.25
633	A196 42fr multicolored	1.25	.70

Petroglyphs A197

1990, July 11 Engr. *Perf. 13*

634	A197 40fr Neounda	1.10	.55
635	A197 58fr Kassducou	1.60	.90

No. 635 is airmail.

Meeting Center of the Pacific — A198

1990, July 25 Litho. *Perf. 13*

636	A198 320fr multicolored	7.00	3.00

World Cup Soccer Championships, Italy — A199

1990, May 30 Litho. *Perf. 13*

637	A199 240fr multicolored	6.00	3.00

Flowers A200

105fr, Gardenia aubryi. 130fr, Hibbertia baudouinii.

1990, Nov. 7 *Perf. 13x12½*

638	A200 105fr multicolored	2.50	1.25
639	A200 130fr multicolored	3.00	2.00

La Maison Celieres by M. Petron A201

365fr, Le Mont-Dore de Jade by C. Degroiselle.

1990, Dec. 5 *Perf. 12½*

640	A201 110fr multicolored	3.50	1.50
641	A201 365fr multicolored	9.50	4.25

No. 640 is airmail.

Writers — A202

Designs: #642, Louise Michel (1830-1905). #643, Charles B. Nething (1867-1947).

1991, Mar. 20 Engr. *Perf. 13*

642	125fr rose lil & bl	3.00	1.50
643	125fr brn & bl	3.00	1.50
a.	A202 Pair, #642-643 + label	6.50	6.00

Native Huts — A203

1991, May 15 Litho. *Perf. 12*

644	A203 12fr Houailou	.25	.25
645	A203 35fr Hienghene	1.00	.50

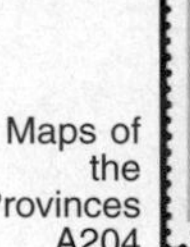

Maps of the Provinces A204

1991, June 17 Litho. *Perf. 13½*
646 A204 45fr Northern 1.00 .45
647 A204 45fr Island 1.00 .45
648 A204 45fr Southern 1.00 .45
a. Strip of 3, #646-648 3.50 3.25

Orchids — A205

55fr, Dendrobium biflorum. 70fr, Dendrobium closterium.

1991, July 24 Litho. *Perf. 13*
649 A205 55fr multicolored 1.60 .80
650 A205 70fr multicolored 2.10 1.00

French Institute of Scientific Research — A206

1991, Aug. 26
651 A206 170fr multicolored 3.75 1.75

Marine Life Type of 1989

60fr, Monocentris japonicus. 100fr, Tristigenys niphonia.

1991, Aug. 26 Litho. *Perf. 12*
652 A185 60fr multicolored 1.50 .80
653 A185 100fr multicolored 2.50 1.10

9th South Pacific Games, Papua New Guinea A207

1991, Sept. 6 *Perf. 12½*
654 A207 170fr multicolored 3.75 1.75

Vietnamese in New Caledonia, Cent. — A208

1991, Sept. 8 Engr. *Perf. 13x12½*
655 A208 300fr multicolored 7.50 2.75

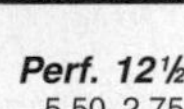

Lions Club of New Caledonia, 30th Anniv. — A209

1991, Oct. 5 Litho. *Perf. 12½*
656 A209 192fr multicolored 5.50 2.75

First Commercial Harvesting of Sandalwood, 150th Anniv. — A210

1991, Oct. 23 Engr. *Perf. 13*
657 A210 200fr multicolored 5.25 2.75

Phila Nippon '91 — A211

Plants and butterflies: 8fr, Phillantus, Eurema hecabe. 15fr, Pipturus incanus, Hypolimnas octocula. 20fr, Stachytarpheta urticaefolia, Precis villida. 26fr, Malaisia scandens, Cyrestis telamon.

Butterflies: No. 662a, Cyrestis telamon, vert. b, Hypolimnas octocula, vert. c, Eurema hecabe, vert. d, Precis villida, vert.

1991, Nov. 16 Litho. *Perf. 12½*
658 A211 8fr multicolored .25 .25
659 A211 15fr multicolored .35 .35
660 A211 20fr multicolored .45 .35
661 A211 26fr multicolored .70 .45
a. Strip of 4, #658-661 + label 2.75 2.50

Souvenir Sheet

662 A211 75fr Sheet of 4, #a.-d. 10.00 10.00

Central Bank for Economic Cooperation, 50th Anniv. — A212

Designs: No. 663, Nickel processing plant, dam. No. 664, Private home, tourist hotels.

1991, Dec. 2 Litho. *Perf. 13*
663 76fr multicolored 3.00 1.25
664 76fr multicolored 3.00 1.25
a. A212 Pair, #663-664 + label 7.00 7.00

Preservation of Nature — A213

15fr, Madeleine waterfalls.

1992, Mar. 25 Litho. *Perf. 13*
665 A213 15fr multicolored .75 .25
a. Souv. sheet, perf. 12½ 4.00 4.00

No. 665a sold for 150fr.

Immigration of First Japanese to New Caledonia, Cent. — A214

1992, June 11 Litho. *Perf. 13x12½*
666 95fr yellow & multi 2.50 1.25
667 95fr gray & multi 2.50 1.25
a. A214 Pair, #666-667 + label 6.25 6.25

Arrival of American Armed Forces, 50th Anniv. — A215

1992, Aug. 13
668 A215 50fr multicolored 1.50 .60

Lagoon Protection — A216

1993, Feb. 23 Litho. *Perf. 13*
669 A216 120fr multicolored 3.50 1.40

Kagu Type of 1990

1993-94 Engr. *Perf. 13*
675 A179a 55fr red 1.50 .25
676 A179a (60fr) claret 1.50 .35

Self-Adhesive
Litho.
Die Cut Perf. 10

681 A179a 5fr bright lilac .50 .25
a. Bklt. pane, 8+8, gutter btwn. 8.00
683 A179a 55fr red 2.00 .70
a. Bklt. pane, 8+8, gutter btwn. 32.50

Issued: Nos. 675, 683, 4/7/93; No. 676, 1/27/94; No. 681, 2/94.

No. 676 sold for 60fr on day of issue.

By their nature, Nos. 681a, 683a are complete booklets. The peelable paper backing serves as a booklet cover.

This is an expanding set. Numbers may change.

No. 599 Surcharged

1993 Engr. *Perf. 13*
685 A179a 55fr on 50fr red 1.40 .70

Philately in School — A217

1993, Apr. 7 Litho. *Perf. 13½*
686 A217 25fr multicolored .75 .30

For overprint see No. 690.

Miniature Sheet of 13

Town Coats of Arms A218

Designs: a, Bourail. b, Noumea. c, Canala. d, Kone. e, Paita. f, Dumbea. g, Koumac. h, Ponerhouen. i, Kaamoo Hyehen. j, Mont Dore. k, Thio. l, Kaala-Gomen. m, Touho.

1993, Dec. 10 Litho. *Perf. 13½*
687 A218 70fr #a.-m., + 2 labels 40.00 27.50

Souvenir Sheet

Hong Kong '94 — A219

Wildlife: a, Panda. b, Kagu.

1994, Feb. 18 Litho. *Perf. 13*
688 A219 105fr Sheet of 2, #a.-b. 8.25 8.25

First Postal Delivery Route, 50th Anniv. — A220

1994, Apr. 28 Engr. *Perf. 13*
689 A220 15fr multicolored .50 .25

No. 686 Ovptd. in Blue

1994, Apr. 22 Litho. *Perf. 13½*
690 A217 25fr multicolored .70 .35

Headquarters of New Caledonian Post Office — A222

1994, June 25 Litho. *Perf. 13½x13*
691 Strip of 4, #a.-d. 8.00 8.00
a. A222 30fr 1859 .75 .45
b. A222 60fr 1936 1.50 .80
c. A222 90fr 1967 2.10 1.40
d. A222 120fr 1993 3.00 1.75

Pacific Sculpture — A223

1994, June 25 Litho. *Perf. 13x13½*
693 A223 60fr multicolored 1.50 .70

Chambeyronia Macrocarpa A224

1994, July 7 Litho. *Perf. 13x13½*
694 A224 90fr multicolored 2.25 1.10

No. J46 Overprinted With Bar Over "Timbre Taxe"

1994, Aug. 8 Litho. *Perf. 13*
696 D5 5fr multicolored 13.50 3.25

Stag A227

1994, Aug. 14 Litho. *Perf. 13½*
697 A227 150fr multicolored 3.50 1.60

Jacques Nervat, Writer — A228

1994, Sept. 15 *Perf. 13x13½*
698 A228 175fr multicolored 4.00 1.90

Frigate Nivose A229

No. 699, 30fr, Ship at sea. No. 700, 30fr, Ship along shore. No. 701, 30fr, Ship docked. No. 702, 60fr, Painting of frigate, map of island, ship's crest. No. 703, 60fr, Ship's bell. No. 704, 60fr, Sailor looking at ship.

1994, Oct. 7 Litho. *Perf. 13½*

Booklet Stamps

699	A229 30fr multicolored	1.25	.45
700	A229 30fr multicolored	1.25	.45
701	A229 30fr multicolored	1.25	.35
702	A229 60fr multicolored	2.00	.80
703	A229 60fr multicolored	2.00	.80
704	A229 60fr multicolored	2.00	.80
a.	Booklet pane, #699-704	11.00	
	Booklet, 4 #704a	55.00	

Philately at School A230

1994, Nov. 4 Litho. *Perf. 13½*
705 A230 30fr multicolored .75 .35

For overprint see No. 749

Christmas A231

Top of bell starts below: a, Second "o." b, Third "e." c, "a." d, "C." e, Second "e."

1994, Dec. 17
706 Strip of 5 5.00 5.00
a.-e. A231 30fr Any single .85 .55

Nos. 706a-706e differ in location of the red ball, yellow bell and statue. No.706 is designed for stereoscopic viewing.

Le Monde Newspaper, 50th Anniv. — A232

1994, Dec. 17
707 A232 90fr multicolored 2.50 1.60

Louis Pasteur (1822-95) — A233

1995, Feb. 13 Litho. *Perf. 13*
708 A233 120fr No. 601 2.75 1.40

Charles de Gaulle (1890-1970) — A234

Litho. & Embossed

1995, Mar. 28 *Perf. 13*
709 A234 1000fr blue & gold 22.50 16.00

Teacher's Training College for the French Territories in the Pacific — A235

1995, Apr. 24 Litho. *Perf. 13*
710 A235 100fr multicolored 2.25 1.25

Sylviornis Neo-Caledonia, Fossil Bird — A236

1995, May 16 Litho. *Perf. 13x13½*
711 A236 60fr multicolored 1.75 .70

10th Sunshine Triathlon — A237

1995, May 26 Engr. *Perf. 13x12½*
712 A237 60fr multicolored 1.50 .90

Creation of the CFP Franc, 1945 A238

Top of tree at left points to: a, Second "e." b, Second "l." c, First "l." d, First "e."

1995, June 8 Litho. *Perf. 13x13½*
713 A238 10fr Strip of 4, #a.-d. 1.25 1.25

Nos. 713a-713d show coin rotating clockwise with trees, hut at different locations. No. 713 is designed for stereoscopic viewing.

1st New Caledonian Deputy in French Natl. Assembly, 50th Anniv. A239

1995, June 8 *Perf. 13½*
714 A239 60fr multicolored 1.50 .70

End of World War II, 50th Anniv. A240

1995, June 8 *Perf. 13x13½*
715 A240 90fr multicolored 2.00 1.10

UN, 50th Anniv. A241

1995, June 8
716 A241 90fr multicolored 2.00 1.10

Sebertia Acuminata A242

1995, July 28 Litho. *Perf. 13x13½*
717 A242 60fr multicolored 1.75 .80

Singapore '95 — A243

Sea birds: 5fr, Anous stolidus. 10fr, Larus novaehollandiae. 20fr, Sterna dougallii. 35fr, Pandion haliaetus. 65fr, Sula sula. 125fr, Fregata minor.

1995, Aug. 24 Litho. *Perf. 13x13½*

718	A243 5fr multicolored	.25	.25
719	A243 10fr multicolored	.25	.25
720	A243 20fr multicolored	.45	.25
721	A243 35fr multicolored	.90	.55
722	A243 65fr multicolored	1.60	1.10
723	A243 125fr multicolored	3.25	1.60
a.	Souvenir sheet, #718-723 + label	9.50	9.50
	Nos. 718-723 (6)	6.70	4.00

10th South Pacific Games A244

1995, Aug. 24
724 A244 90fr multicolored 2.50 1.25

Sculpture, The Lizard Man, by Dick Bone — A248

1995, Oct. 25 Litho. *Perf. 13*
730 A248 65fr multicolored 1.60 .90

Gargariscus Prionocephalus — A249

1995, Dec. 15 Litho. *Perf. 13*
731 A249 100fr multicolored 2.50 1.25

Francis Carco (1886-1958), Poet & Novelist — A250

1995, Nov. 15 Litho. *Perf. 13x13½*
732 A250 95fr multicolored 2.25 1.25

Ancient Pottery — A251

1996, Apr. 12 Litho. *Perf. 13*

733 A251 65fr multicolored 1.60 .90

Endemic Rubiaceous Plants — A252

Designs: 65fr, Captaincookia margaretae. 95fr, Ixora cauliflora.

1996, Apr. 17

734 A252 65fr multicolored 1.50 .80
735 A252 95fr multicolored 2.25 1.10

7th Va'a (Outrigger Canoe) World Championship, Noumea, New Caledonia — A253

Designs: a, 30fr, Islander standing on shore with early version of canoe. b, 65fr, Early single-hull canoe with islanders. c, 95fr, Early catamaran, people rowing. d, 125fr, Modern racing canoe.

1996, May 10 Litho. *Perf. 13*

736 A253 Strip of 4, #a.-d. 7.50 7.50

No. 736 is a continuous design.

CHINA '96 — A254

Marine life: 25fr, Halieutaea stellata. 40fr, Perotrochus deforgesi. 65fr, Mursia musorstomia. 125fr, Metacrinus levii.

1996, May 18

737 A254 25fr multicolored .55 .35
738 A254 40fr multicolored .85 .65
739 A254 65fr multicolored 1.50 .90
740 A254 125fr multicolored 2.75 1.60
Nos. 737-740 (4) 5.65 3.50

Nos. 737-740 were each issued in sheets of 10 + 5 labels.

On Nos. 737-740 portions of the design were applied by a thermographic process producing a shiny, raised effect.

737a Booklet pane of 6 5.00
738a Booklet pane of 6 6.50
739a Booklet pane of 6 12.50
740a Booklet pane of 6 25.00
Complete booklet, #737a-740a 49.00

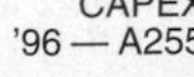

CAPEX '96 — A255

Orchids: 5fr, Sarcochilus koghiensis. 10fr, Phaius robertsii. 25fr, Megastylis montana. 65fr, Dendrobium macrophyllum. 95fr, Dendrobium virotii. 125fr, Ephemerantha comata.

1996, June 25 Litho. *Perf. 13*

741 A255 5fr multicolored .35 .25
742 A255 10fr multicolored .35 .25
743 A255 25fr multicolored .75 .35
744 A255 65fr multicolored 1.50 .65
745 A255 95fr multicolored 2.50 1.00
746 A255 125fr multicolored 2.50 1.25
a. Booklet pane of 6, #741-746 7.75
Souvenir booklet, 4 #746a 38.00
Nos. 741-746 (6) 7.95 3.75

Nos. 741-746 were each issued in sheets of 10 + 5 labels.

No. 705 Ovptd. with UNICEF Emblem in Blue

1996, Sept. 12 Litho. *Perf. 13½*

749 A230 30fr multicolored .85 .45

UNICEF, 50th anniv.

Ordination of the First Melanesian Priests A258

1996, Oct. 9 Litho. *Perf. 13*

750 A258 160fr multicolored 3.50 1.90

Portions of the design on No. 750 were applied by a thermographic process producing a shiny, raised effect.

7th Festival of South Pacific Arts A259

Designs: 100fr, Dancer, face carving. 105fr, Wood carvings of women. 200fr, Painting by Paula Boi. 500fr, Gaica Dance, Lifou.

1996, Oct. 9

751 A259 100fr multicolored 2.25 1.25
752 A259 105fr multicolored 2.25 1.25
753 A259 200fr multicolored 4.50 2.25
754 A259 500fr multicolored 11.00 5.75
Nos. 751-754 (4) 20.00 10.50

No. 751 is airmail.

French Pres. Francois Mitterrand (1916-96) — A260

1997, Mar. 14 Litho. *Perf. 13*

755 A260 1000fr multicolored 20.00 11.25

Alphonse Daudet (1840-97), Writer — A261

Designs: No. 756, "Letters from a Windmill." No. 757, "Le Petit Chose." No. 758, "Tartarin of Tarascon." No. 759, Daudet writing.

1997, May 14 *Perf. 13*

756 A261 65fr multicolored 1.50 1.50
757 A261 65fr multicolored 1.50 1.50
758 A261 65fr multicolored 1.50 1.50
759 A261 65fr multicolored 1.50 1.50
a. Souvenir sheet, #756-759 6.50 6.50

Henri La Fleur, First Senator of New Caledonia — A262

1997, June 12 Litho. *Perf. 13*

760 A262 105fr multicolored 2.40 1.25

Insects A263

Designs: a, Tectocoris diophthalmus. b, Kanakia gigas. c, Aenetus cohici.

1997, June 25 Litho. *Perf. 13x12½*

761 A263 65fr Strip of 3, #a.-c. 5.00 4.50

Jacques Iekawe (1946-92), First Melanesian Prefect — A264

1997, July 23 Litho. *Perf. 13*

762 A264 250fr multicolored 5.50 2.50

Kagu — A265

1997, Aug. 13 Engr. *Perf. 13*

763 A265 95fr blue 2.25 .35

See Nos. 772-773C, 878-879, 897.

Horse Racing A266

1997, Sept. 20 Litho. *Perf. 13*

764 A266 65fr Harness racing 1.75 .80
765 A266 65fr Thoroughbred racing 1.75 .80

Early Engraving of "View of Port de France" (Noumea) — A267

Photo. & Engr.

1997, Sept. 22 *Perf. 13x12½*

766 A267 95fr multicolored 2.25 1.25

See No. 802.

A268

1997, Sept. 22 Litho. *Perf. 13*

767 A268 150fr multicolored 3.00 1.75

First Melanesian election, 50th anniv.

Hippocampus Bargibanti A269

1997, Nov. 3 Litho. *Perf. 13½x13*

768 A269 100fr multicolored 4.50 1.50

5th World Conf. on Fish of the Indo-Pacific. Issued in sheets of 10+5 labels.

South Pacific Arts A270

Designs: a, Doka wood carvings. b, Beizam dance mask. c, Abstract painting of primative life by Yvette Bouquet.

1997, Nov. 3 *Perf. 13*

769 A270 100fr Strip of 3, #a.-c. 7.50 6.50

Christmas A271

Designs: 95fr, Santa on surfboard pulled by dolphins. 100fr, Dolphin with banner in mouth.

1997, Nov. 17

770 A271 95fr multicolored 4.00 1.00
771 A271 100fr multicolored 4.00 1.00

Nos. 770-771 issued in sheets of 10+5 labels.

Kagu Type of 1997

1997-98 Engr. *Perf. 13*

772 A265 30fr orange 1.00 .35
773 A265 (70fr) red 2.00 .35

Booklet Stamps
Self-Adhesive
Litho.
Serpentine Die Cut 11

773A A265 (70fr) red 2.00 .45
b. Booklet pane of 10 22.50

Engr.
Serpentine Die Cut 6¾ Vert.

773C A265 (70fr) red — —
d. Booklet pane of 10 —

The peelable paper backing of No. 773A serves as a booklet cover.

Issued: 30fr, 1997; No. 773A, 1/2/98; No. 773C, 2004.

A272

Mushrooms: #774, Lentinus tuber-regium. #775, Volvaria bombycina. #776, Morchella anteridiformis.

1998, Jan. 22 Litho. *Perf. 13*

774 A272 70fr multicolored 1.75 .80
775 A272 70fr multicolored 1.75 .80
776 A272 70fr multicolored 1.75 .80
Nos. 774-776 (3) 5.25 2.40

A273

Artifacts from Territorial Museum: 105fr, Mask, Northern Region. 110fr, "Dulon" door frame pillar, Central Region.

1998, Mar. 17 Litho. *Perf. 13*

777 A273 105fr multicolored 2.25 1.10
778 A273 110fr multicolored 2.40 1.10

Paul Gauguin (1848-1903) — A274

1998, May 15 Litho. *Perf. 13*

779 A274 405fr multicolored 9.75 5.00

1998 World Cup Soccer Championships, France — A280

1998, June 5 Photo. *Perf. 12½*

787 A280 100fr multicolored 2.25 1.25

A281

Jean-Marie Tjibaou Cultural Center — A282

Designs: 30fr, "Mitimitia," artwork by Fatu Feu'u. No. 789, Jean-Marie Tjibaou (1936-89), Melanesian political leader. No. 790, Exterior view of building, vert. 105fr, "Man Bird," painting by Mathias Kauage.

1998, June 21 Litho. *Perf. 13x13½*

788 A281 30fr multicolored 1.25 .35
a. Booklet pane of 6 7.50
789 A281 70fr multicolored 1.50 .85
a. Booklet pane of 6 9.00
790 A281 70fr multicolored 1.50 .85
a. Booklet pane of 6 9.00
791 A282 105fr multicolored 2.50 1.25
a. Booklet pane of 6 15.00
Complete booklet, #788a, 789a, 790a, 791a 42.50
Nos. 788-791 (4) 6.75 3.30

Abolition of Slavery, 150th Anniv. — A283

1998, July 21 Engr. *Perf. 13*

792 A283 130fr multicolored 2.75 1.50

Postman, Dogs A284

1998, Aug. 20 Litho. *Perf. 13*

793 A284 70fr multicolored 1.75 .85

Arab Presence in New Caledonia, Cent. A285

1998, Sept. 4

794 A285 80fr multicolored 1.75 1.00

A286

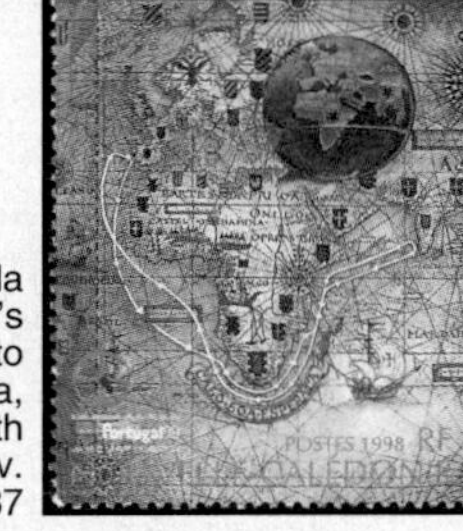
Vasco da Gama's Voyage to India, 500th Anniv. A287

No. 795: a, Port in India. b, Da Gama at Cape of Good Hope, ships at sea. c, Da Gama meeting with Indians. d, Da Gama's picture in crest.

No. 796: a, Map of route. b, Vasco da Gama. c, Ship at anchor.

1998, Sept. 4

795 A286 100fr Strip of 4, #a.-d. 9.00 9.00

Souvenir Sheet

796 A287 70fr Sheet of 3, #a.-c. 5.50 5.50

Portugal '98 Intl. Philatelic Exhibition.

A288

Litho. & Engr.

1998, Sept. 25 *Perf. 12½x13*

797 A288 110fr multicolored 2.25 2.25

Vincent Bouquet (1893-1971), High Chief.

A289

World Wildlife Fund — Kagu: 5fr, Male. 10fr, Female. 15fr, Two in grass. 70fr, Two in dirt, one ruffling feathers.

1998, Oct. 20 Litho. *Perf. 13*

798 A289 5fr multicolored .25 .25
799 A289 10fr multicolored .45 .45
800 A289 15fr multicolored .75 .65
801 A289 70fr multicolored 2.00 1.75
Nos. 798-801 (4) 3.45 3.10

Early Engraving Type of 1997

1998, Nov. 4 Engr. *Perf. 13x12½*

802 A267 155fr Nou Island 3.25 2.00

Universal Declaration of Human Rights, 50th Anniv. — A290

1998, Nov. 4 Engr. *Perf. 13*

803 A290 70fr blk, bl & bl grn 1.40 1.40

Columnar Pine A291

1998, Nov. 5 Litho. *Perf. 13x13½*

804 A291 100fr shown 2.25 2.00
805 A291 100fr Coast, forest 2.25 2.00

A292

Post and Telecommunications, 40th Anniv.: #806, Switchboard, bicycle, early post office. #807, Cell phone, microwave relay, motorcycle.

1998, Nov. 27 Litho. *Perf. 13½x13*

806 A292 70fr multicolored 1.60 1.60
807 A292 70fr multicolored 1.60 1.60
a. Pair, #806-807 + label 3.50 3.50

A293

Underwater scenes (Greetings Stamps): No. 808, Fish, coral forming flower, Happy Anniversary. No. 809, Fish up close, Happy New Year. No. 810, Open treasure chest, Best Wishes. No. 811, Fish, starfish forming Christmas tree, Merry Christmas.

1998, Dec. 1

808 A293 100fr multicolored 2.25 2.00
809 A293 100fr multicolored 2.25 2.00
810 A293 100fr multicolored 2.25 2.00
811 A293 100fr multicolored 2.25 2.00
Nos. 808-811 (4) 9.00 8.00

Monument to the Disappearance of the Ship Monique, 20th Anniv. — A294

1998, Dec. 1 *Perf. 13*

812 A294 130fr multicolored 3.00 2.50

Arachnids A295

Designs: No. 813, Argiope aetherea. No. 814, Barycheloides alluvviophilus. No. 815, Latrodectus hasselti. No. 816, Crytophora moluccensis.

1999, Mar. 19 Litho. ***Perf. 13x13½***

813	A295 70fr multicolored	1.60	1.40
814	A295 70fr multicolored	1.60	1.40
815	A295 70fr multicolored	1.60	1.40
816	A295 70fr multicolored	1.60	1.40
	Nos. 813-816 (4)	6.40	5.60

Carcharodon Megalodon — A296

Designs: 100fr, Fossil tooth of megalodon. No. 818: a, Shark swimming with mouth open, vert. b, Comparison of shark to man and carcharodon carcharias. c, Fossil tooth on bottom of ocean.

1999, Mar. 19 ***Perf. 12½***

817 A296 100fr multicolored 3.00 2.00

Souvenir Sheet

Perf. 13

818 A296 70fr Sheet of 3, #a.-c. 6.75 6.75

Nos. 818a is 30x40mm and 818b is 40x30mm.

Australia '99, World Stamp Expo (#818).

Paul Bloc (1883-1970), Writer — A297

1999, Apr. 23 Engr. ***Perf. 13x12½***

819 A297 105fr grn, bl grn & brn 2.50 2.25

Traditional Musical Instruments A298

1999, May 20 Litho. ***Perf. 13½x13***

820	A298 30fr Bwanjep	.75	.60
821	A298 70fr Sonnailles	1.50	1.40
822	A298 100fr Flutes	2.25	2.00
	Nos. 820-822 (3)	4.50	4.00

11th South Pacific Games, Guam A299

1999, May 20 ***Perf. 13x13¼***

823	A299 5fr Track & field	.25	.25
824	A299 10fr Tennis	.25	.25
825	A299 30fr Karate	.75	.60
826	A299 70fr Baseball	1.60	1.40
	Nos. 823-826 (4)	2.85	2.50

Overseas Transport Squadron 52, Humanitarian Missions — A300

1999, June 18 ***Perf. 13***

827 A300 135fr multicolored 3.25 2.75

Escoffier Hotel Catering and Business School, Noumea, 20th Anniv. — A301

1999, June 17 Litho. ***Perf. 13***

828	A301 70fr Building, computer	1.60	1.40
a.	Pair + central label	3.50	5.00
829	A301 70fr Building, chef's hat	1.60	1.40
a.	Pair + central label	3.50	5.00

New Caledonia's First Postage Stamp, 140th Anniv. — A302

Designs: No. 830, #1.

No. 831: a, Two #1. b, #1, diff. c, #1 up close. d, like #830. e, Design A265, image of Napolean III from #1, "1999."

1999, July 2 Photo. ***Perf. 13¼***

830 A302 70fr multicolored 1.75 1.40

Souvenir Sheet

Perf. 12

831	Sheet of 5	27.50	27.50
a.	A302 100fr Engraved	2.50	2.50
b.	A302 100fr Litho., thermograph	2.50	2.50
c.	A302 100fr Litho.	2.50	2.50
d.	A302 100fr Litho. & embossed	2.50	2.50
e.	A302 700fr Litho., hologram	15.00	15.00

Nos. 831a-831d are each 36x28mm. No. 831e is 44x35mm. Portions of the design on No. 831b were applied by a thermographic process producing a shiny, raised effect. No. 831e contains a holographic image. Soaking in water may affect the hologram.

PhilexFrance '99 (#831).

Tourism A303

1999, Sept. 28 Litho. ***Perf. 13¼***

832	A303 5fr Fish, vegetables	.25	.25
833	A303 30fr Lobster dish	.75	.55
834	A303 70fr Tourist huts	1.50	1.25
835	A303 100fr Hotel pool	2.25	1.90
	Nos. 832-835 (4)	4.75	3.95

Ratification of Noumea Accord, 1998 — A304

1999, Nov. 10 Litho. ***Perf. 13x13½***

836 A304 70fr multi 1.50 1.25

Aji Aboro Dance A305

1999, Nov. 10

837 A305 70fr multi 1.50 1.25

Château Hagen — A306

1999, Nov. 18 ***Perf. 13***

838 A306 155fr multi 3.50 2.75

Nature Protection — A307

1999, Dec. 7

839 A307 30fr multi .75 .50

Greetings — A308

Designs: No. 840, "Joyeux Noel." No. 841, "Félicitations." No. 842, "Bon Anniversaire." No. 843, "Meilleurs Voeux 2000."

1999, Dec. 20

840	A308 100fr multi	2.50	1.75
841	A308 100fr multi	2.50	1.75
842	A308 100fr multi	2.50	1.75
843	A308 100fr multi	2.50	1.75
	Nos. 840-843 (4)	10.00	7.00

Amédée Lighthouse A309

2000, Mar. 7 Litho. ***Perf. 13½x12***

844 A309 100fr multi 2.75 1.60

Ship Emile Renouf — A310

2000, Apr. 19 Engr. ***Perf. 13x13¼***

845 A310 135fr multi 3.50 2.25

Painting by Giles Subileau — A311

2000, June 15 Litho. ***Perf. 13***

846 A311 155fr multi 4.00 2.25

Souvenir Sheet

New Year 2000 (Year of the Dragon) — A312

Denomination: a, at R. b, at L.

2000, June 15

847 A312 105fr Sheet of 2, #a-b 5.00 4.50

Antoine de Saint-Exupéry (1900-44), Aviator, Writer — A313

2000, July 7

848 A313 130fr multi 3.00 2.75

World Stamp Expo 2000, Anaheim.

Noumea Aquarium A314

Designs: No. 849, Hymenocera elegans. No. 850, Fluorescent corals. No. 851, Chelinus undulatus.

2000, July 7 ***Perf. 13x13¼***

849-851 A314 70fr Set of 3 5.00 3.00

Mangrove Heart A315

2000, Aug. 10 Photo. *Perf. 13*
852 A315 100fr multi 2.50 1.40

Value is for copy with surrounding selvage.

2000 Summer Olympics, Sydney A316

Designs: 10fr, Archery. 30fr, Boxing. 80fr, Cycling. 100fr, Fencing.

2000, Sept. 15 Litho. *Perf. 13x13¼*
853-856 A316 Set of 4 5.00 4.50

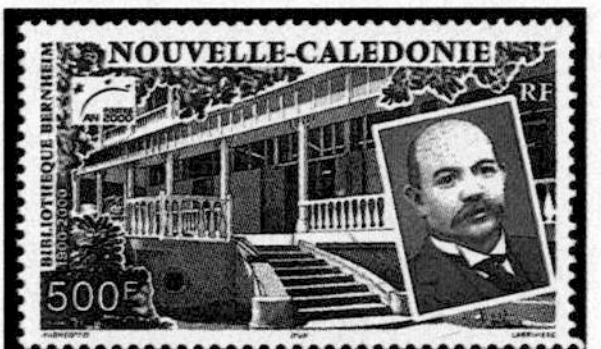
Lucien Bernheim (1856-1917), Library Founder, and Bernheim Library, Cent. — A317

2000, Oct. 24 Engr. *Perf. 13*
857 A317 500fr multi 11.00 7.25

A318

8th Pacific Arts Festival — A319

Kanak money and background colors of: 90fr, Orange. 105fr, Dark blue.

Festival emblem and works of art — No. 860: a, White denomination at UL, "RF" at UR. b, White denomination and "RF" at UL. c, Yellow denomination. d, White denomination at UR.

2000, Oct. 24 *Perf. 13x13¼*
858-859 A318 Set of 2 4.50 3.00

Souvenir Sheet

860 A319 70fr Sheet of 4, #a-d 6.25 6.25

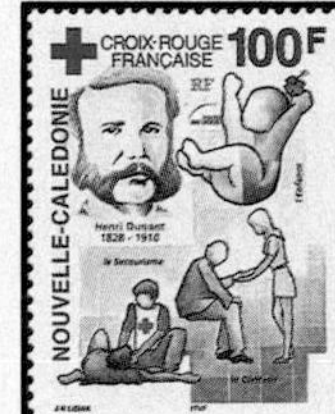
Red Cross — A320

2000, Nov. 9 Litho. *Perf. 13¼x13*
861 A320 100fr multi 2.25 2.00

Queen Hortense (1848-1900) A321

2000, Nov. 9 Engr. *Perf. 12½x13*
862 A321 110fr multi 2.50 2.25

Northern Province Landscapes — A322

a, Fisherman in canoe. b, Motorboat near beach and cliffs. c, Fisherman on raft.

2000, Nov. 9 Litho. *Perf. 13x13¼*
863 A322 Horiz. strip of 3 6.50 6.50
a.-c. 100fr Any single 2.00 1.50

Philately in School — A323

Children's art by: a, Kévyn Pamoiloun. b, Lise-Marie Samanich. c, Alexandre Mandin.

2000, Nov. 14 *Perf. 13¼x13*
864 A323 Horiz. strip of 3 4.50 3.50
a.-c. 70fr Any single 1.40 1.10

Christmas, Holy Year 2000 A324

2000, Dec. 19 *Perf. 13*
865 A324 100fr multi 2.00 1.60

Portions of the design were applied by a thermographic process producing a shiny, raised effect.

Greetings — A325

Kagu and: No. 866, "Meilleurs voeux de bonheur." No. 867, "Vive les vacances." No. 868, Félicitations.

2000, Dec. 19 *Perf. 13¼x13*
866-868 A325 100fr Set of 3 6.75 6.00

No. 868 printed se-tenant with two labels.

New Year 2001 (Year of the Snake) — A326

Designs: 100fr, Snake on beach, snake wearing robe.

No. 870: a, Snake in flowers. b, Snake in city.

2001, Feb. 15 Litho. *Perf. 13*
869 A326 100fr multi 2.50 2.00

Souvenir Sheet

Perf. 13½x13

870 A326 70fr Sheet of 2, #a-b 4.25 4.25

Size of Nos. 870a-870b: 30x40mm.

Sailing Ship France II — A327

2001, Apr. 18 Engr. *Perf. 13x13¼*
871 A327 110fr multi 2.50 2.25

Noumea Aquarium — A328

Nautilus macromphalus: a, Conjoined pair. b, Anatomical cross-section. c, Pair separated.

2001, May 22 Litho.
872 A328 Horiz. strip of 3 7.00 7.00
a.-c. 100fr Any single 2.25 1.50

Corvus Moneduliodes and Tools — A329

2001, June 14 *Perf. 13*
873 A329 70fr multi 1.60 1.50

Operation Cetacean — A330

No. 874: a, Pair of Megaptera novaeangliae underwater. b, Whales breaching surface.

2001, July 18 *Perf. 13x13¼*
874 A330 Horiz. pair with central label 5.00 5.00
a.-b. 100fr Any single 2.25 1.50

See Vanuatu Nos. 785-787.

The Keeper of Gaia, the Eden, by Ito Waia — A331

Vision From Oceania, by Jipé Le-Bars — A332

2001, Aug. 22 *Perf. 13*
875 A331 70fr multi 1.75 1.40
876 A332 110fr multi 2.50 2.25

Year of Dialogue Among Civilizations A333

2001, Sept. 19 Litho. *Perf. 13x13¼*
877 A333 265fr multi 6.50 5.50

Kagu Type of 1997

2001 Engr. *Perf. 13*
878 A265 100fr bright blue 2.75 1.50

Self-Adhesive

Litho.

Serpentine Die Cut 11

879 A265 100fr bright blue 2.75 1.50
a. Booklet pane of 10 32.50

Issued: No. 878, 9/23; No. 879, 9/20.

For surcharge see No. 972.

The Lonely Boatman, by Marik — A334

2001, Oct. 11 Litho. *Perf. 13*
880 A334 110fr multi 2.25 2.25

Underwater Observatory — A335

2001, Oct. 11
881 A335 135fr multi 3.75 2.75

Qanono Church, Lifou — A336

2001, Oct. 11
882 A336 500fr multi 12.00 10.00

Fernande Le Riche (1884-1967), Novelist — A337

2001, Nov. 8
883 A337 155fr brown & blue 3.50 3.25

First Olympic Gold Medal Won by a New Caledonian A338

2001, Nov. 8 *Perf. 13x13¼*
884 A338 265fr multi 6.25 5.25

Kitesurfing A339

2001, Nov. 16 *Perf. 13*
885 A339 100fr multi 2.50 2.00

"The Book, My Friend" Literacy Campaign A340

2001, Nov. 27 *Perf. 13x13¼*
886 A340 70fr multi 1.75 1.40

Lifou Scenes — A341

No. 887: a, Easo. b, Jokin.

2001, Nov. 27 *Perf. 13¼x13*
887 A341 100fr Vert. pair, #a-b 4.75 4.50

Greetings A342

Flying fox and: No. 888, 100fr, Joyeux Noel (Merry Christmas). No. 889, 100fr, Meilleurs voeux (Best wishes). No. 890, 100fr, Vive la fete (Long live the holiday).

2001, Dec. 7 *Perf. 13x13¼*
888-890 A342 Set of 3 6.50 6.00

New Year 2002 (Year of the Horse) — A343

Designs: 100fr, Horse, other zodiac animals.
No. 892, vert.: a, Horse. b, Seahorse.

2002, Feb. 7 *Perf. 13*
891 A343 100fr multi 2.50 2.25

Souvenir Sheet

892 A343 70fr Sheet of 2, #a-b 3.50 3.25

Love A344

2002, Feb. 13
893 A344 100fr multi 2.50 2.00

Value is for stamp with surrounding selvage.

Cricket — A345

2002, Mar. 20 **Litho.** *Perf. 13*
894 A345 100fr multi 2.50 2.00

Ancient Hatchet — A346

2002, Mar. 20 **Litho.**
895 A346 505fr multi 12.00 11.00

Portions of the design were applied by a thermographic process producing a shiny, raised effect.

Hobie Cat 16 World Championships — A347

2002, Apr. 1 **Litho.** *Perf. 13*
896 A347 70fr multi 1.60 1.40

Kagu Type of 1997

2002, Apr. 15 **Engr.** *Perf. 13*
897 A265 5fr purple .30 .25

2002 World Cup Soccer Championships, Japan and Korea — A348

2002, May 15 **Photo.**
898 A348 100fr multi 2.75 2.00

Values are for stamp with surrounding selvage.

Souvenir Sheet

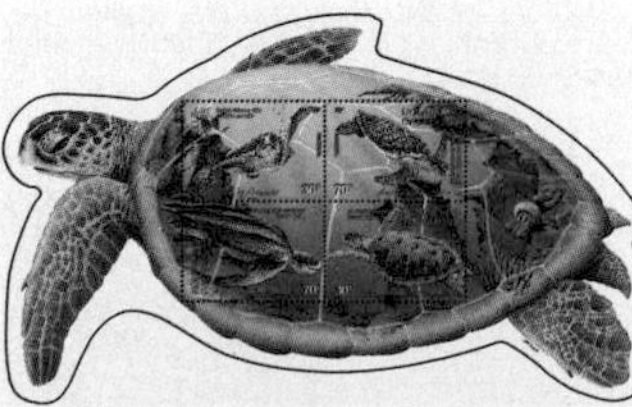
Turtles at Noumea Aquarium — A349

No. 899: a, 30fr, Caretta caretta. b, 70fr, Eretmochelys imbricat. c, 70fr, Dermochelys coriacea. d, 30fr, Chelonia mydas.

2002, May 15 **Litho.** *Perf. 13x13¼*
899 A349 Sheet of 4, #a-d 4.75 4.75
e. As #899, with inscription added in margin 4.75 4.75

Issued: No. 899e, 10/24/03. Inscription in margin of No. 899e reads "Coupe du monde 2003 / Champion du monde."

Corvette Alcmene and Map — A350

2002, June 13 **Engr.** *Perf. 13x13¼*
900 A350 210fr multi 5.00 4.25

Coffee — A351

No. 901: a, Coffee plant and beans. b, Bean roasters. c, Coffee makers, woman, cup of coffee.

2002, June 13 **Litho.**
901 A351 Horiz. strip of 3 5.00 5.00
a.-c. 70fr Any single 1.50 1.40

No. 901 was impregnated with coffee scent.

Edmond Caillard (1912-91), Astronomer — A352

2002, June 26 **Engr.**
902 A352 70fr multi 1.75 1.50

Statue of Emma Piffault (1861-77), by Michel Rocton — A353

2002, July 17 **Litho.** *Perf. 13¼x13*
903 A353 10fr multi .35 .25

Noumea Circus School — A354

2002, Aug. 30 *Perf. 13*
904 A354 70fr multi 1.60 1.40

Illustrations From Books by Jean Mariotti — A355

2002, Sept. 18
905 A355 70fr multi 1.60 1.40

Operation Cetacean — A356

No. 906: a, Adult and young of Physeter macrocephalus. b, Physeter macrocephalus and squid.

2002, Sept. 18 ***Perf. 13x13¼***
906 A356 Horiz. pair with central label 4.75 4.75
a.-b. 100fr Either single 2.25 2.00

See Norfolk Island No. 783.

Intl. Year of Mountains — A357

2002, Nov. 7 Litho. ***Perf. 13***
907 A357 100fr multi 2.50 2.00

Christmas and New Year's Day — A358

2002, Nov. 7
908 A358 100fr multi 2.00 2.00

Bourail Fort Powder Magazine — A359

2002, Nov. 7 Engr. ***Perf. 13x12½***
909 A359 1000fr multi 24.00 20.00

Mel Me Mec, by Adrien Trohmae — A360

2002, Nov. 28 Litho. ***Perf. 13***
910 A360 100fr multi 2.50 2.00

New Year 2003 (Year of the Ram) A361

2003, Jan. 29
911 A361 100fr multi 2.50 2.00

Printed in sheets of 10 + 2 labels.

Valentine's Day — A362

2003, Jan. 29 Photo. ***Perf. 13***
912 A362 100fr multi 2.50 2.00

Values are for stamps with surrounding selvage.

Jubilee Issue, Cent. — A363

2003 Litho. ***Perf. 13¼x13***
913 A363 70fr No. 77 1.75 1.40

Booklet Stamp

Size: 19x25mm

913A A363 70fr No. 77 1.40 1.40
b. Booklet pane of 10 14.00 —

Issued: No. 913, 2/7. No. 913A, 8/20.

Kagu — A364

2003 Engr. ***Perf. 13***
914 A364 10fr green .25 .25
915 A364 15fr brown .35 .25
916 A364 30fr orange .80 .60
917 A364 (70fr) red 1.60 1.40
Nos. 914-917 (4) 3.00 2.50

Booklet Stamps

Litho. & Embossed

Perf. 13¼x13¾

918 A364 70fr gray & silver 1.60 1.40
a. Booklet pane of 10 16.00 —
Complete booklet, #913Ab, 918a 30.00

Engr.

Serpentine Die Cut 6¾ Vert.

Self-Adhesive

919 A364 (70fr) red 1.90 1.40
a. Booklet pane of 10 20.00

Issued: Nos. 914-917, 2/7; No. 918, 8/20; No. 919, 5/15.

See Nos. 938, 965-966, 985-986, 1007, 1070.

Fish at Nouméa Aquarium — A365

No. 920: a, Epinephelus maculatus. b, Plectropomus leopardus. c, Cromileptes altivelis.

2003, Apr. 9 Photo. ***Perf. 12¾***
920 A365 70fr Horiz. strip of 3, #a-c 5.00 4.00

Greater Nouméa High School — A366

2003, May 14 Litho. ***Perf. 13***
921 A366 70fr multi 1.75 1.40

Operation Cetacean — A367

No. 922: a, Dugong swimming (79x29mm). b, Dugong feeding (40x29mm).

2003, June 11 ***Perf. 13x13¼***
922 A367 100fr Horiz. pair, #a-b 5.00 4.00

12th South Pacific Games, Suva, Fiji — A368

Designs: 5fr, Trapshooting. 30fr, Rugby. 70fr, Squash.

2003, June 11
923-925 A368 Set of 3 2.50 2.10

Man Picking Fruit From a Tree, by Paul Gauguin (1848-1903) A369

2003, June 25 Photo. ***Perf. 13***
926 A369 100fr multi 2.50 1.90

Aircalin, 20th Anniv. — A370

2003, July 9 **Litho.**
927 A370 100fr multi 2.50 1.90

Governor Paul Feillet (1857-1903) A371

2003, July 9 Engr. ***Perf. 12½x13***
928 A371 100fr bl grn & ol grn 2.50 1.90

Souvenir Sheet

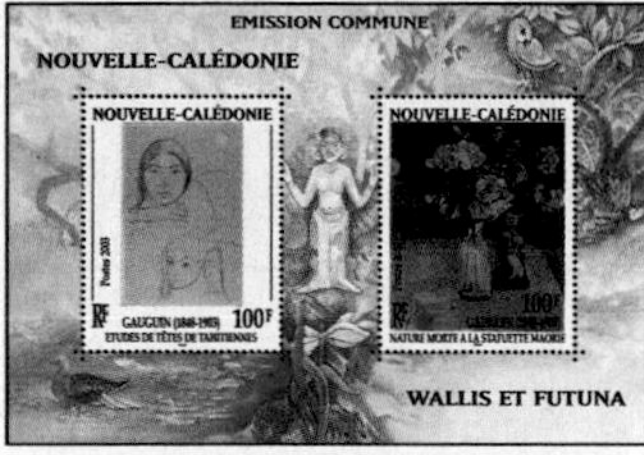

Paintings by Paul Gauguin — A372

No. 929: a, Study of Heads of Tahitian Women. b, Still Life with Maori Statuette.

2003, Aug. 20 Litho. ***Perf. 13***
929 A372 100fr Sheet of 2, #a-b 5.00 4.50

German Shepherd — A373

2003, Oct. 8
930 A373 105fr multi 2.50 2.10

Le Phoque, Le Prony and Le Catinat in Balade Roadstead, 1853 — A374

2003, Oct. 8 Engr. ***Perf. 13x12½***
931 A374 110fr multi 2.75 2.10

Robert Tatin d'Avesnières (1925-82), Painter — A375

2003, Oct. 8 Litho. ***Perf. 13***
932 A375 135fr multi 3.25 2.60

Souvenir Sheet

Geckos — A376

No. 933: a, 30fr, Bavayia cyclura. b, 30fr, Rhacodactylus chahoua. c, 70fr, Rhacodactylus ciliatus. d, 70fr, Eurydactylodes vieillardi.

2003, Oct. 8 ***Perf. 13x13¼***
933 A376 Sheet of 4, #a-d 5.50 5.50

Ouen Island — A377

2003, Nov. 6 ***Perf. 13***
934 A377 100fr multi 2.50 1.90

Merry Christmas and Happy New Year A378

2003, Nov. 6
935 A378 100fr multi 2.50 1.90

New Year 2004 (Year of the Monkey) — A379

Designs: 70fr, Monkeys, Hong Kong skyline. No. 937: a, Tiger and woman. b, Monkey on horse.

2004, Jan. 30 **Litho.** ***Perf. 13***
936 A379 70fr multi 1.75 1.50

Souvenir Sheet
Perf. 13¼x13
Litho. With Foil Application

937 A379 100fr Sheet of 2, #a-b 5.00 5.00

2004 Hong Kong Stamp Expo. No. 937 contains two 30x40mm stamps.

Kagu Type of 2003

2004, Feb. 11 **Engr.** ***Perf. 13***
938 A364 100fr blue 2.50 2.10

For surcharge see No. 973.

Love A380

2004, Feb. 11 **Photo.**
939 A380 100fr multi 2.50 2.10

Values are for stamps with surrounding selvage.

Stamp Day — A381

2004, May 15 **Litho.**
940 A381 105fr multi 2.60 2.10

Railroads in New Caledonia — A382

2004, May 15 **Engr.** ***Perf. 13x12½***
941 A382 155fr multi 3.75 3.25

Rays — A383

No. 942: a, Dasyatis kuhlii. b, Aetobatus narinari. c, Taeniura meyeni.

2004, May 15 **Litho.** ***Perf. 13x13¼***
942 A383 Horiz. strip of 3 7.25 7.25
a.-c. 100fr Any single 2.25 2.00

Souvenir Sheet

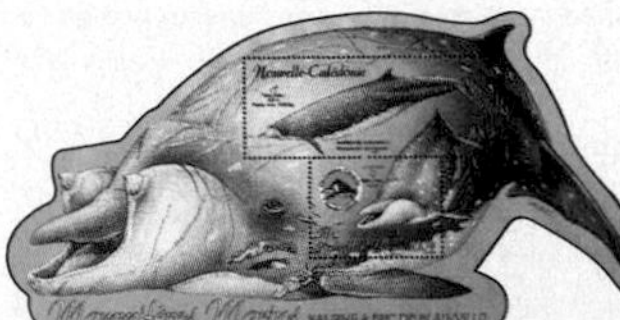
Mesoplodon Densirostris — A384

No. 943: a, Male (79x29mm). b, Female (40x29mm).

2004, May 15
943 A384 100fr Sheet of 2, #a-b 5.00 5.00

Operation Cetacean.

Flowers — A385

No. 944: a, Oxera sulfurea. b, Turbina inopinata. c, Gardenia urvillei.

2004, June 26
944 A385 Horiz. strip of 3 7.25 7.25
a.-c. 100fr Any single 2.25 2.00

Sandalwood — A386

Designs: 200fr, Sandalwood sculpture, house.
No. 946: a, Fruit and flowers. b, Sandalwood oil extraction machinery. c, Flowerpot.

2004, June 26 ***Perf. 13***
945 A386 200fr multi 4.75 4.25

Souvenir Sheet
Perf. 13x13¼

946 A386 100fr Sheet of 3, #a-c 7.25 7.25

No. 946 contains three 40x29mm stamps.

Noumea, 150th Anniv. — A387

2004, July 8 **Litho.** ***Perf. 13***
947 A387 70fr multi 1.60 1.50

Miniature Sheet

Cats — A388

No. 948: a, Mixed breed. b, Oriental. c, Persian. d, Birman. e, European. f, Abyssinian.

2004, July 25
948 A388 100fr Sheet of 6, #a-f 14.50 12.50

2004 Summer Olympics, Athens A389

Designs: No. 949, 70fr, Women's rhythmic gymnastics. No. 950, 70fr, Women's 4x400m relay. No. 951, 70fr, Beach volleyball.

2004, Aug. 5 ***Perf. 13x13¼***
949-951 A389 Set of 3 5.00 4.50

Symposium on French Research in the Pacific — A390

No. 952: a, Butterfly, hut. b, Dolphin, woman.

2004, Aug. 10 ***Perf. 13***
952 A390 Pair 4.75 4.75
a.-b. 100fr Either single 2.25 2.00

Belep Island and Walla Bay — A391

2004, Nov. 10
953 A391 100fr multi 2.50 2.25

Tradimodernition, by Nathalie Deschamps — A392

2004, Nov. 10
954 A392 505fr multi 12.00 11.00

Christmas — A393

2004, Dec. 8
955 A393 100fr multi 2.50 2.25

A394

New Year 2005 (Year of the Rooster) — A395

No. 957: a, Rooster. b, Monkey.

2005, Feb. 9 **Litho.** ***Perf. 13***
956 A394 100fr multi 2.50 2.25

Souvenir Sheet
Perf. 13¼x13

957 A395 100fr Sheet of 2, #a-b 4.75 4.50

Rotary International, Cent. A396

2005, Feb. 23 **Photo.** ***Perf. 12½***
958 A396 110fr multi 2.75 2.50

Values are for stamps with surrounding selvage.

Francophone Week — A397

2005, Mar. 17 Litho. *Perf. 13x13¼*
959 A397 135fr multi 3.25 3.00

Printed in sheets of 10 + 5 labels. See Wallis & Futuna Islands No. 600.

20th International Triathlon, Noumea — A398

2005, Apr. 22 Litho. *Perf. 13*
960 A398 80fr multi 2.00 1.75

Coastal Tour Ship — A399

2005, May 21
961 A399 75fr multi 1.90 1.60

New Caledonian Railways — A400

2005, May 21
962 A400 745fr multi 18.00 15.00

Dolphins — A401

No. 963: a, Stenella attenuata. b, Turciop truncatus. c, Stenella longirostris.

2005, May 21 *Perf. 13x13¼*
963 A401 Horiz. strip of 3 7.75 7.75
a.-c. 100fr Any single 2.25 2.00

For surcharge, see No. 971.

Souvenir Sheet

Sharks — A402

No. 964: a, Carcharinus melanopterus. b, Nebrius ferrugineus.

2005, July 20 *Perf. 13*
964 A402 110fr Sheet of 2, #a-b 5.25 4.50

Kagu Type of 2003

2005, Aug. 10 Engr. *Perf. 13*
965 A364 1fr sky blue .25 .25
966 A364 3fr brt yel green .60 .25

Luengoni Beach, Lifou — A403

2005, Aug. 24 Litho.
967 A403 85fr multi 2.00 1.75

Parakeets A404

Designs: No. 968, 75fr, Eunymphicus uvaeensis. No. 969, 75fr, Eunymphicus cornutus. No. 970, 75fr, Cyanoramphus saisseti.

2005, Aug. 24 *Perf. 13x13¼*
968-970 A404 Set of 3 5.50 4.75

No. 963 Surcharged in Silver

and Nos. 878 and 938 Surcharged

Methods and Perfs as Before

2005
971 Horiz. strip of 3 (#963) 7.00 7.00
a.-c. A401 100fr +10fr Any single 2.25 2.25
972 A265 100fr +10fr bright blue (#878) 2.25 2.25
973 A364 100fr +10fr blue (#938) 2.25 2.25
Nos. 971-973 (3) 11.50 11.50

Issued: No. 971, July. Nos. 972-973, Oct.

World Health Organization West Pacific Region Conference, Noumea — A405

2005, Sept. 14 Litho. *Perf. 13x13¼*
974 A405 150fr multi 3.75 3.00

World Peace Day — A406

2005, Sept. 21 *Perf. 13¼x13*
975 A406 85fr multi 2.00 1.75

Governor Eugène du Bouzet (1805-67) A407

2005, Nov. 10 Engr.
976 A407 500fr multi 12.50 10.00

Petroglyphs — A408

Designs: No. 977, 120fr, Enclosed crosses. No. 978, 120fr, Petroglyph, Balade. No. 979, 120fr, Ouaré Petroglyph, Hienghène.

2005, Nov. 10 *Perf. 13x12¾*
977-979 A408 Set of 3 8.75 7.25

Common Destiny, Artwork by Ito Waia and Adjé A409

2005, Dec. 7 Litho. *Perf. 13*
980 A409 190fr multi 4.75 4.00

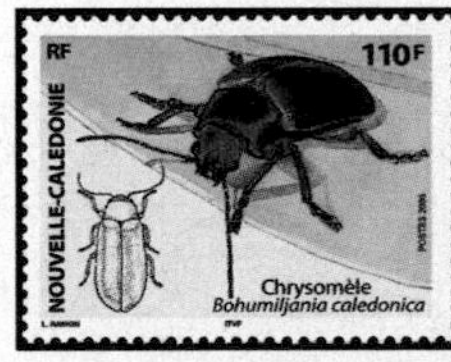

Insects A410

Designs: No. 981, 110fr, Bohumiljania caledonica. No. 982, 110fr, Bohumiljania humboldti. No. 983, 110fr, Cazeresia montana.

2005, Dec. 7 *Perf. 13x13¼*
981-983 A410 Set of 3 8.00 6.75

Christmas A411

2005, Dec. 8 *Perf. 13¼x13*
984 A411 110fr multi 2.75 2.25

Kagu Type of 2003

2006 Engr. *Perf. 13*
985 A364 110fr dk blue gray 2.75 2.25

Booklet Stamp
Self-Adhesive
Serpentine Die Cut 6¾ Vert.

986 A364 110fr dk blue gray 2.75 2.25
a. Booklet pane of 10 30.00

Issued: No. 985, 1/18. No. 986, June.

Nokanhoui Islet — A412

2006, Mar. 9 Litho. *Perf. 13*
987 A412 110fr multi 2.75 2.25

Automobiles — A413

No. 988: a, 1903 Georges Richard. b, 1925 Renault NN. c, 1925 Citroen Tréfle.

2006, Mar. 23 *Perf. 13x13¼*
988 A413 Horiz. strip of 3 8.00 8.00
a.-c. 110fr Any single 2.50 2.25

New Caledonian Red Cross, 60th Anniv. — A414

2006, Apr. 12 Litho. *Perf. 13¼x13*
989 A414 75fr red & black 1.90 1.60

Conus Geographus A415

2006, Apr. 12 Litho. *Perf. 13*
990 A415 150fr multi 3.75 3.25

11th World Congress on Pain, New Caledonia, 2005. Portions of the design were applied by a thermographic process producing a shiny, raised effect.

Arrival of French Colonists, 80th Anniv. — A416

2006, May 23 Engr. *Perf. 13x12¾*
991 A416 180fr multi 4.50 3.75

2006 World Cup Soccer Championships, Germany — A417

2006, June 8 Litho. *Perf. 13*
992 A417 110fr multi 2.75 2.25

BirdLife International A418

Designs: No. 993, 75fr, Charmosyna diadema. No. 994, 75fr, Aegotheles savesi. No. 995, 75fr, Gallirallus lafresnayanis.

2006, June 17 *Perf. 13¼x13*
993-995 A418 Set of 3 5.50 4.75

Souvenir Sheet

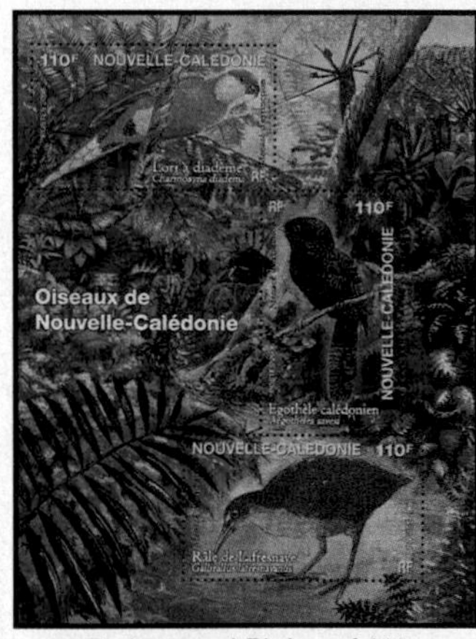

Endangered Birds — A419

No. 996: a, Charmosyna diadema. b, Aegotheles savesi, vert. c, Gallirallus lafresnayanis.

2006, June 17
996 A419 110fr Sheet of 3, #a-c 8.00 7.00

Creeper Flowers — A420

No. 997: a, Artia balansae. b, Oxera brevicalyx. c, Canavalia favieri.

2006, June 17 *Perf. 13x13¼*
997 A420 Horiz. strip of 3 8.00 8.00
a.-c. 110fr Any single 2.50 2.25

Mobile Post Office — A421

2006, Aug. 5 Engr. *Perf. 13x12¾*
998 A421 75fr multi 1.75 1.60

Stamp Day.

New Caledonian Evacuee Voluntary Aid Association, 25th Anniv. — A422

2006, Aug. 5 Litho. *Perf. 13¼x13*
999 A422 85fr multi 2.00 1.90

17th South Pacific Regional Environment Program Conference, Noumea — A423

2006, Sept. 11 Litho. *Perf. 13*
1000 A423 190fr multi 4.00 4.00

Nakale 7547 Locomotive of New Caledonia Railroad — A424

2006, Sept. 19 Engr. *Perf. 13x13¼*
1001 A424 320fr multi 6.75 6.75

Kaneka Music, 20th Anniv. A425

2006, Nov. 8 Litho. *Perf. 13x13½*
1002 A425 75fr multi 1.90 1.75

Mobilis Mobile Phone Service, 10th Anniv. — A426

2006, Nov. 8 *Perf. 13*
1003 A426 75fr multi 1.90 1.75

Wooden Players Puppet Theater, 30th Anniv. — A427

2006, Nov. 8
1004 A427 280fr multi 7.00 6.25

Christmas A428

Litho. & Engr.

2006, Nov. 9 *Perf. 13*
1005 A428 110fr multi 2.75 2.50

Lizard Man, Sculpture by Joseph Poukiou A429

2006, Dec. 13 Litho.
1006 A429 110fr multi 2.75 2.40

Kagu Type of 2003

2007, Jan. 25 Engr. *Perf. 13*
1007 A364 5fr purple .35 .25

New Year 2007 (Year of the Pig) A430

2007, Feb. 6 Litho. *Perf. 13*
1008 A430 110fr multi 2.50 2.50

Printed in sheets of 10 + central label.

General Secretariat of the South Pacific Community, 60th Anniv. — A431

2007, Feb. 6
1009 A431 120fr multi 2.75 2.75

Audit Office, Bicent. A432

2007, Mar. 17 Engr. *Perf. 13¼*
1010 A432 110fr multi 2.50 2.50

Treaty of Rome, 50th Anniv. A433

2007, May 10 Litho. *Perf. 13x13¼*
1011 A433 110fr multi 2.50 2.50

13th South Pacific Games, Samoa — A434

2007, June 13 Litho. *Perf. 13*
1012 A434 75fr multi 1.75 1.75

Submarine Cable Between Noumea and Sydney — A435

2007, June 13 Litho. & Engr.
1013 A435 280fr multi 6.50 6.50

Fish A436

Designs: 35fr, Siganus lineatus. 75fr, Lutianus adetii. 110fr, Naso unicornis.

2007, June 13 Litho. *Perf. 13x13½*
1014-1016 A436 Set of 3 5.00 5.00

Natl. Sea Rescue Society, 40th Anniv. — A437

2007, Aug. 3 *Perf. 13*
1017 A437 75fr multi 1.75 1.75

BirdLife International — A438

Endangered birds: 35fr, Gymnomyza aubryana. 75fr, Coracina analis. 110fr, Rhynochetos jubatus.

2007, Aug. 3 ***Perf. 13x13¼***
1018-1020 A438 Set of 3 5.00 5.00

A439

A440

A441

A442

A443

A444

A445

A446

A447

Mailboxes
A448

2007, Aug. 3 ***Perf. 13¼x13, 13x13¼***

1021	Booklet pane of 10	17.50	17.50
a.	A439 75fr multi	1.75	1.75
b.	A440 75fr multi	1.75	1.75
c.	A441 75fr multi	1.75	1.75
d.	A442 75fr multi	1.75	1.75
e.	A443 75fr multi	1.75	1.75
f.	A444 75fr multi	1.75	1.75
g.	A445 75fr multi	1.75	1.75
h.	A446 75fr multi	1.75	1.75
i.	A447 75fr multi	1.75	1.75
j.	A448 75fr multi	1.75	1.75
	Complete booklet, #1021	17.50	

Stamp Day.

Souvenir Sheet

Kagu Philatelic Club, 60th Anniv. — A449

No. 1022: a, Magnifying glass over New Caledonia #262 on cover. b, Kagu.

Litho. & Silk Screened

2007, Aug. 3 ***Perf. 13x13¼***
1022 A449 110fr Sheet of 2, #a-b 5.00 5.00

Season of New Hebrides Culture in New Zealand — A450

2007, Aug. 16 **Litho.** ***Perf. 13***
1023 A450 190fr multi 4.50 4.50

New Aquarium of New Caledonia — A451

No. 1024 — Entrance of new aquarium and: a, Gymnothorax polyranodon (40x30mm). b, Entrance of old aquarium. (80x30mm). c, Monodactylus argenteus (40x30mm). d, Negaprion brevirostris (40x30mm). e, Pseudanthias bicolor (40x30mm).

2007, Aug. 31 ***Perf. 13x13¼***
1024 A451 110fr Booklet pane of 5, #a-e 13.00 13.00
Complete booklet, 2 #1024 26.00

2007 Rugby World Cup, France
A452

2007, Sept. 5 **Photo.** ***Perf.***
1025 A452 110fr multi 2.60 2.60

Jules Repiquet (1874-1960), Governor of New Caledonia, 1914-23 — A453

2007, Oct. 10 **Engr.** ***Perf. 13x13¼***
1026 A453 320fr multi 7.75 7.75

Tropical Fruits
A454

Designs: 35fr, Bananas and passion fruits. 75fr, Vanilla beans, vert. 110fr, Pineapples and lychees.

Perf. 13x13¼, 13¼x13

2007, Nov. 8 **Litho.**
1027-1029 A454 Set of 3 5.50 5.50

The banana, vanilla bean and pineapple portions of these stamps are covered with scratch-and-sniff coatings having those fragrances.

La Montagnarde Locomotive, New Caledonian Railways — A455

2007, Nov. 8 **Engr.** ***Perf. 13x13¼***
1030 A455 400fr multi 10.00 10.00

Tao Waterfall
A456

2007, Nov. 8 **Litho.** ***Perf. 13***
1031 A456 110fr multi 2.75 2.75

The Damned, Performance by Najib Guerfi Dance Company — A457

2007, Nov. 8
1032 A457 110fr multi 2.75 2.75

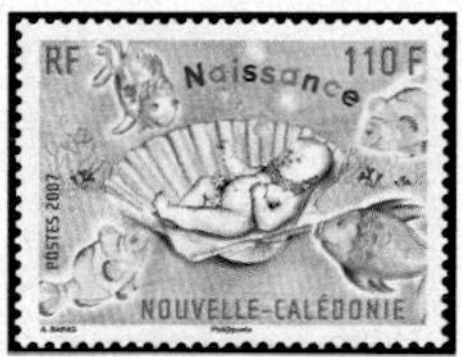
Birth Announcement — A458

2007, Nov. 8 ***Perf. 13x13¼***
1033 A458 110fr multi 2.75 2.75

New Year's Greetings
A459

2007, Nov. 8
1034 A459 110fr multi 2.75 2.75

Rooftop Totem — A460

2007, Dec. 5 **Litho.** ***Perf. 13***
1035 A460 110fr multi 2.75 2.75

New Year 2008 (Year of the Rat)
A461

2008, Feb. 6 **Litho.** ***Perf. 13***
1036 A461 110fr multi 3.00 3.00

Academic Palms, Bicent. — A462

Litho. & Embossed

2008, Mar. 17 ***Perf. 13x13¼***
1037 A462 110fr multi 3.00 3.00

Tjibaou Cultural Center, 10th Anniv. — A463

2008, June 14 **Litho.** ***Perf. 13***
1038 A463 120fr multi 3.25 3.25

Matignon Accords, 20th Anniv. — A464

2008, June 14
1039 A464 430fr multi 11.50 11.50

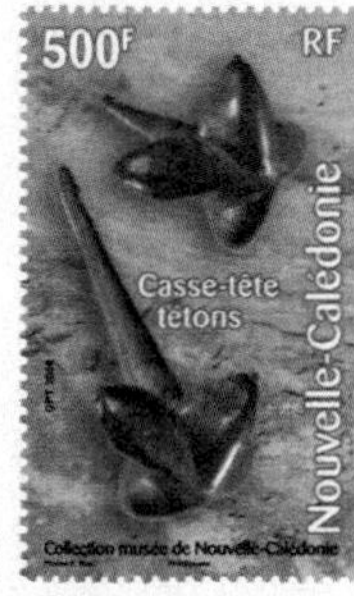
Kanak Ax — A465

2008, June 14
1040 A465 500fr multi 13.50 13.50

BirdLife International — A466

Endangered birds: No. 1041, 110fr, Pterodroma leucoptera. No. 1042, 110fr, Pseudobulweria rostrata. No. 1043, 110fr, Nesofregatta fuliginosa.

2008, June 14 ***Perf. 13x13¼***
1041-1043 A466 Set of 3 8.75 8.75

Fruit A467

Designs: No. 1044, 110fr, Citrus nobilis. No. 1045, 110fr, Mangifera indica. No. 1046, 110fr, Carica papaya.

2008, June 14
1044-1046 A467 Set of 3 8.75 8.75

2008 Summer Olympics, Beijing A468

Designs: No. 1047, 75fr, Weight lifting. No. 1048, 75fr, Table tennis. No. 1049, 75fr, Taekwondo.

2008, July 31
1047-1049 A468 Set of 3 5.75 5.75

Office of Posts and Telecommunications, 50th Anniv. — A469

Designs: No. 1050, 75fr, New Caledonia #314, dish antennas, cable, map of South Pacific. No. 1051, 75fr, New Caledonia #311, savings card, person at computer. No. 1052, 75fr, New Caledonia #C106, mailbox, mail sorter.

2008, July 31
1050-1052 A469 Set of 3 5.75 5.75

Miniature Sheet

Telecommunications History — A470

No. 1053: a, Telegraph. b, Radio telephone. c, Satellite and antenna. d, Fiber-optic cables and flowers.

2008, July 31 ***Perf. 13¼x13***
1053 A470 75fr Sheet of 4, #a-d 7.50 7.50

Kagu — A471

Serpentine Die Cut 6¾x7¾

2008 **Self-Adhesive** **Litho.**
1054 A471 (75fr) red & multi 4.50 4.50
1055 A471 110fr blue & multi 5.25 5.25

Nos. 1054 and 1055 each were issued in sheets of 20 and 25. Sheets of 20 of each stamp sold for 3800fr and 4500fr, respectively, and sheets of 25 sold for 4125fr and 5000fr, respectively. The left part of the stamp, which cannot be separated from the stamp, could be personalized if desired. The left part of the stamp shown has a generic image that was utilized if a customer did not provide an image for personalization.

Koné Fort — A472

2008, Oct. 3 **Engr.** ***Perf. 13x12¾***
1056 A472 220fr multi 5.00 5.00

Fifth French Republic, 50th Anniv. — A473

2008, Oct. 14 ***Perf. 13x13¼***
1057 A473 290fr blue & red 6.25 6.25

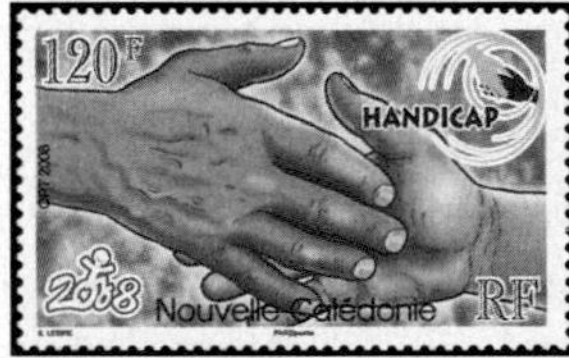
Handicap Awareness — A474

2008, Nov. 6 **Litho.** ***Perf. 13***
1058 A474 120fr multi 2.60 2.60

Diahot River — A475

No. 1059 — View of river with denomination color of: a, Green. b, Blue violet.

2008, Nov. 6
1059 A475 Horiz. pair + central label 5.00 5.00
a.-b. 110fr Either single 2.50 2.50

Christmas A476

2008, Nov. 6 ***Perf. 13¼x13***
1060 A476 110fr multi 2.50 2.50

14th Pacific Games, New Caledonia A477

2008, Dec. 12 ***Perf. 13***
1061 A477 110fr multi 2.50 2.50

Miniature Sheet

New Caledonia Lagoons UNESCO World Heritage Site — A478

No. 1062: a, Birds from Entrecasteaux Reefs Zone. b, Snake from Northeastern Coastal Zone, horiz. c, Sea turtles from Beautemps-Beaupré Zone, horiz. d, Fish from Great Northern Lagoon Zone. e, Dugong from Western Coastal Zone. f, Whale from Great Southern Lagoon Zone, horiz.

Perf. 13¼x13, 13x13¼ (horiz. stamps)

2008, Dec. 12
1062 A478 75fr Sheet of 6, #a-f 10.50 10.50

Fish — A479

No. 1063 — Fish sold at local fish markets: a, Lethrinus atkinsoni. b, Chlorurus microrhinos. c Lethrinus nebulosus.

2009, Mar. 25 **Litho.** ***Perf. 13x13¼***
1063 A479 Horiz. strip of 3 5.00 5.00
a.-c. 75fr Any single 1.60 1.60

New Year 2009 (Year of the Ox) A480

2009, Apr. 8 ***Perf. 13***
1064 A480 75fr multi 1.75 1.75

Souvenir Sheet

New Year 2009 (Year of the Ox) — A481

No. 1065 — Ox: a, Standing. b, Charging.

2009, Apr. 8 **Litho.** ***Perf. 13***
1065 A481 110fr Sheet of 2, #a-b 5.00 5.00

The Turtle Bearer, Sculpture by Tein Thavouvace — A482

2009, May 14 Litho. *Perf. 13*
1066 A482 180fr multi 4.25 4.25

BirdLife International — A483

No. 1067 — Terns: a, Sterna nereis. b, Sterna sumatrana. c, Sterna dougalli.

2009, June 10 *Perf. 13x13¼*
1067 A483 Horiz. strip of 3 5.25 5.25
a.-c. 75fr Any single 1.75 1.75

Jean-Pierre Jeunet Cinema, La Foa, 10th Anniv. — A484

2009, June 26 *Perf. 13*
1068 A484 75fr multi 1.75 1.75

Third France-Oceania Summit, Noumea — A485

No. 1069 — Earth in: a, Hands. b, Flower.

2009, July 16
1069 A485 110fr Pair, #a-b 5.25 5.25

Kagu Type of 2003
Serpentine Die Cut 7½ Vert.
2009, July Litho.
Booklet Stamp
Self-Adhesive

1070 A364 (75fr) red 1.75 1.75
a. Booklet pane of 10 17.50

A486

Kagu — A487

2009, Aug. 6 Engr. *Perf. 13*
1071 A486 5fr purple .25 .25
1072 A486 10fr green .25 .25
a. Dated "2014" .25 .25
1073 A486 (75fr) red 1.75 1.75
1074 A486 110fr dark blue 2.60 2.60

Litho. With Three-Dimensional Plastic Affixed
Perf. 16
Self-Adhesive

1075 A487 500fr multi 12.00 12.00

Litho.
Serpentine Die Cut 7½ Vert.
Booklet Stamp

1076 A486 (75fr) red 1.75 1.75
a. Booklet pane of 10 17.50
b. As #1076, serpentine die cut 6¾ vert., with "Phil@poste" printer's inscription at bottom 1.60 1.60
c. Booklet pane of 10 #1076b 16.00
d. As "b," dated "2014" 1.75 1.75
e. Booklet pane of 10 #1076d 17.50
Nos. 1071-1076 (6) 18.60 18.60

No. 1075 printed in sheets of 4.
Issued: Nos. 1076b, 1076c, June 2010; Nos. 1076d, 1076e, July 2014.
See No. 1131.

Intl. Year of Astronomy — A488

2009, Aug. 6 Litho. *Perf. 13*
1077 A488 110fr multi 2.60 2.60

Miniature Sheet

New Caledonia Postal Service, 150th Anniv. — A489

No. 1078 — Modes of mail delivery: a, Coach. b, Horse, vert. c, Automobile. d, Mail deliverer on foot, vert.

2009, Aug. 6 *Perf. 13¼*
1078 A489 110fr Sheet of 4, #a-d 10.50 10.50

Society for Historical Research, 40th Anniv. — A490

2009, Aug. 6 Engr. *Perf. 13x13¼*
1079 A490 75fr multi 1.75 1.75

Personalized Stamps — A490a

Serpentine Die Cut 6¾x8
2009, Sept. Litho.
Self-Adhesive

1079A A490a (75fr) red & multi — —
1079B A490a 110fr blue & multi — —

Nos. 1079A and 1079B were issued in sheets of 20 and 25. The personalized part of the stamp is at left. The illustration is that of a generic image used for both No. 1079A and 1079B. Sheets with other personalized images sold for more than the face value.

14th Pacific Games, New Caledonia A491

2009, Nov. 5 Litho. *Perf. 13*
1080 A491 75fr multi 1.90 1.90

Western Coastal Zone of Lagoons of New Caledonia UNESCO World Heritage Site — A492

2009, Nov. 5
1081 A492 75fr multi 1.90 1.90

Christmas A493

2009, Nov. 5 *Perf. 13x13¼*
1082 A493 110fr multi 2.75 2.75

Canala Barracks — A494

2009, Nov. 5 Engr.
1083 A494 120fr multi 3.00 3.00

Maritime History Museum, Noumea, 10th Anniv. — A495

No. 1084: a, Ships and museum. b, Ship and map.

2009, Nov. 5 Litho.
1084 A495 75fr Horiz. pair, #a-b 3.75 3.75

A496

Tontouta River — A497

2009, Nov. 5 *Perf. 13*
1085 Horiz. pair + central label 5.50 5.50
a. A496 110fr multi 2.75 2.75
b. A497 110fr multi 2.75 2.75

Women and Children, by Micheline Néporon A498

2010, Mar. 8 Litho. *Perf. 13*
1086 A498 110fr multi 2.50 2.50

Intl. Women's Day.

Champlain Alliance, 25th Anniv. A499

2010, Mar. 18 *Perf. 13x13¼*
1087 A499 110fr multi 2.50 2.50

Fish — A500

No. 1089 — Fish sold at local fish markets: a, Acanthocybium solandri. b, Thunnus albacares. c, Coryphaena hippurus.

2010, Mar. 18
1088 A500 Horiz. strip of 3 5.25 5.25
a.-c. 75fr multi 1.75 1.75

New Year 2010 (Year of the Tiger) A501

2010, Mar. 18 *Perf. 13*
1089 A501 110fr multi 2.50 2.50

Dumbea River — A502

No. 1090: a, River bends. b, Canoers on river, bridge.

2010, Mar. 18
1090 A502 Horiz. pair + central label 5.00 5.00
a.-b. 110fr Either single 2.50 2.50

14th Va'a (Outrigger Canoe) World Championships, Anse Vata Bay — A503

2010, May 3 Litho. *Perf. 13x13¼*
1091 A503 75fr multi 1.75 1.75

French Pavilion, Expo 2010, Shanghai — A504

2010, June 14 *Perf. 13*
1092 A504 110fr multi 2.40 2.40

Mueo Fort — A505

2010, Aug. 5 Engr. *Perf. 13x13¼*
1093 A505 75fr multi 1.75 1.75

2010 Youth Olympics, Singapore — A506

2010, Aug. 5 Litho. *Perf. 13*
1094 A506 75fr multi 1.75 1.75

St. Joseph's Cathedral, Noumea A507

2010, Aug. 5 Litho. & Engr.
1095 A507 1000fr multi 22.50 22.50

Nickel Mining — A508

No. 1096: a, Open-pit mine. b, Smelter. c, Ship transport.

Litho. With Foil Application

2010, Aug. 5 *Perf. 13x12¾*
1096 A508 75fr Horiz. strip of 3, #a-c 5.00 5.00

Miniature Sheet

Flora and Fauna of Grandes Fougères Park — A509

No. 1097: a, Pteropus ornatus. b, Ducula goliath. c, Cyathea sp. d, Calanthe langel.

2010, Aug. 5 Litho. *Perf. 13¼x13*
1097 A509 110fr Sheet of 4, #a-d 9.75 9.75

14th Pacific Games, New Caledonia — A510

2010, Aug. 27 *Perf. 13*
1098 A510 75fr multi 1.60 1.60

Fourth Melanesian Arts Festival — A511

2010, Sept. 8
1099 A511 180fr multi 4.00 4.00

Governor Henri Sautot (1885-1963) — A512

2010, Sept. 16 Engr. *Perf. 13x13¼*
1100 A512 250fr multi 6.00 6.00

New Caledonia's alliance with Free France, 70th anniv.

Road Safety A513

Designs: No. 1101, 75fr, Car with drunk driver. No. 1102, 75fr, Woman with baby stroller in crosswalk escaping speeding motorcyclist.

2010, Oct. 13 Litho. *Perf. 13x13¼*
1101-1102 A513 Set of 2 3.50 3.50

Great Northern Lagoon UNESCO World Heritage Site — A514

2010, Nov. 3 *Perf. 13*
1103 A514 75fr multi 1.75 1.75

New Caledonia House, Paris — A515

2010, Nov. 3
1104 A515 110fr multi 2.50 2.50

Intl. Year of Biodiversity A516

2010, Nov. 3 *Perf. 13¼*
1105 A516 110fr multi 2.50 2.50

Christmas A517

2010, Nov. 3 *Perf. 13x13¼*
1106 A517 110fr multi 2.50 2.50

New Year 2011 (Year of the Rabbit) A518

2011, Feb. 2 *Perf. 13*
1107 A518 110fr multi 2.50 2.50

Printed in sheets of 10 + central label.

Inauguration of Digital High Definition Television Transmission — A519

2011, Feb. 2 *Perf. 13x13¼*
1108 A519 75fr multi 1.75 1.75

14th Pacific Games, New Caledonia A520

2011, Mar. 17 *Perf. 13*
1109 A520 110fr multi 2.75 2.75

Rivers — A521

No. 1110: a, Pourina River. b, Ouinné River.

2011, Mar. 17 Litho.
1110 A521 Horiz. pair + central label 5.50 5.50
a.-b. 110fr Either single 2.75 2.75

Transcaledonian Adventure Race, 20th Anniv. — A522

2011, June 23 *Perf. 13x13¼*
1111 A522 75fr multi 1.75 1.75

Podoserpula Miranda — A523

2011, June 23 *Perf. 13¼x13*
1112 A523 110fr multi 2.60 2.60

Ouégoa Fort — A524

2011, Aug. 5 Engr. *Perf. 13x13¼*
1113 A524 75fr multi 1.90 1.90

Ouvea and Beautemps-Beaupré Lagoon Area UNESCO World Heritage Site — A525

2011, Aug. 5 Litho. *Perf. 13*
1114 A525 75fr multi 1.90 1.90

Intl. Year of Forests — A526

2011, Aug. 5
1115 A526 120fr multi 3.00 3.00

Miniature Sheet

Rivière Bleue Provincial Park — A527

No. 1116: a, Syzygium acre. b, Montrouziera gabriellae. c, Waterfall. d, Rhynochetos jubatus.

2011, Aug. 5 Photo. *Perf. 13¼x13*
1116 A527 110fr Sheet of 4, #a-d 11.00 11.00

Kanak Traditional Games A528

2011, Aug. 27 Litho. *Perf. 13x13¼*
1117 A528 75fr multi 1.75 1.75

Souvenir Sheet

14th Pacific Games, Noumea — A529

No. 1118 — Emblem and: a, Medal. b, Torch. c, Flame basin.

Photo. Photo & Embossed (#1118a)
2011, Aug. 27 *Perf. 13¼x13*
1118 A529 110fr Sheet of 3, #a-c 7.75 7.75

Ruins and Chimney of Nimba Sugar Factory, Dumbea — A530

2011, Nov. 3 Engr. *Perf. 13x13¼*
1119 A530 450fr multi 10.50 10.50

Animals and Scenery A531

Designs: No. 1120, 110fr, Cerf rusa (rusa deer). No. 1121, 110fr, Tricot rayé (striped jersey snake). No. 1122, 110fr, Lindéralique Cliffs. No. 1123, 110fr, Ilôt Canard, vert.

Perf. 13x13¼, 13¼x13
2011, Nov. 3 Litho.
1120-1123 A531 Set of 4 10.50 10.50

Christmas A532

2011, Nov. 3 *Perf. 13¼x13*
1124 A532 110fr multi 2.60 2.60

Jacques Lafleur (1932-2010), Politician — A533

2011, Dec. 1 Engr. *Perf. 12¼x13*
1125 A533 1000fr multi 22.50 22.50

New Year 2012 (Year of the Dragon) A534

2012, Jan. 23 Litho. *Perf. 13*
1126 A534 75fr multi 1.75 1.75

Printed in sheets of 10 + central label.

St. Valentine's Day — A535

2012, Jan. 23
1127 A535 110fr multi 2.50 2.50

Values are for stamps with surrounding selvage.

Voh, 120th Anniv. — A536

No. 1128: a, Coffee plantation. b, Mine.

2012, Jan. 23 *Perf. 13x13¼*
1128 A536 110fr Horiz. pair, #a-b 5.00 5.00

Southern Backpacking Trail — A537

2012, Mar. 5 *Perf. 13¼x13*
1129 A537 110fr multi 2.50 2.50

Ouaménie Sugar Works Chimney A538

2012, May 4 Engr. *Perf. 12¼x13*
1130 A538 750fr multi 16.00 16.00

Kagu Type of 2009

2012, June 5 Engr. *Perf. 13*
1131 A486 30fr orange .65 .65
a. Dated "2014" .60 .60

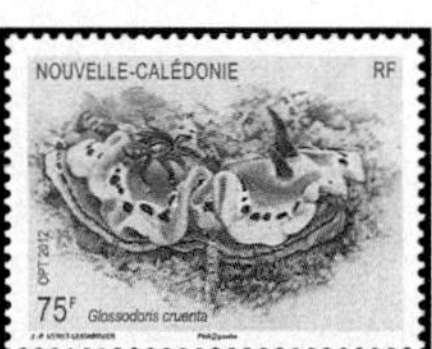

Nudibranchs — A539

Designs: 75fr, Glossodoris cruenta. 85fr, Halgerda sp., vert. 120fr, Noumea catalai.

Perf. 13x13¼, 13¼x13
2012, July 6 Litho.
1132-1134 A539 Set of 3 5.75 5.75

Souvenir Sheet

Japanese Presence on New Caledonia, 120th Anniv. — A540

No. 1135: a, Memorial. b, Nickel miner with pick, horiz. c, Mine worker with ore cart, horiz.

Perf. 13¼x13, 13x13¼
2012, July 6 Photo.
1135 A540 110fr Sheet of 3, #a-c 6.75 6.75

Amborella Trichopoda A541

2012, Aug. 6 Litho. *Perf. 13¼x13*
1136 A541 180fr multi 4.00 4.00

2012 Paralympics, London — A542

Designs: No. 1137, 75fr, Wheelchair race. No. 1138, 75fr, Shot put.

2012, Aug. 6 *Perf. 13x13¼*
1137-1138 A542 Set of 2 3.25 3.25

Local Scenes — A543

Designs: No. 1139, 110fr, Bonhomme de Bourail rock formation. No. 1140, 110fr, Hut made of coconut palm fronds, Maré. No. 1141, 110fr, Mouth of Koumac River. No. 1142, 110fr, Cowboys and cattle.

2012, Aug. 6 *Perf. 13*
1139-1142 A543 Set of 4 9.50 9.50

Souvenir Sheet

Michel Corbasson Zoo and Forest, Noumea, 50th Anniv. — A544

No. 1143: a, Rhacodactylus leachianus. b, Corvus moneduloides. c, Pittosporum tanianum.

2012, Sept. 25 *Perf. 13¼x13*
1143 A544 110fr Sheet of 3, #a-c 7.25 7.25

National Tree Planting Campaign A545

2012, Sept. 26 *Perf. 13*
1144 A545 75fr multi 1.60 1.60

3G Technology A546

2012, Sept. 26 ***Perf. 13x13¼***
1145 A546 280fr multi 6.00 6.00

Whales in Great Southern Lagoon Zone — A547

2012, Nov. 9 ***Perf. 13***
1146 A547 75fr multi 1.60 1.60

Mangrove Forest A548

2012, Nov. 9 **Litho.**
1147 A548 75fr multi 1.60 1.60

Christmas A549

2012, Nov. 9 ***Perf. 13x13¼***
1148 A549 110fr multi 2.40 2.40

New Year 2013 (Year of the Snake) A550

2013, Feb. 7 **Litho.** ***Perf. 13***
1149 A550 110fr multi 2.40 2.40

Encastreaux Reefs Area — A551

2013, Mar. 7
1150 A551 110fr multi 2.40 2.40

Opening of La Tontouta Intl. Airport, Noumea — A552

2013, Mar. 19
1151 A552 110fr multi 2.40 2.40

Bacouya Sugar Factory Chimney — A553

2013, May 13 **Engr.** ***Perf. 13x12¼***
1152 A553 120fr multi 2.75 2.75

Red Cross South Pacific Regional Intervention Platform — A554

2013, June 7 **Litho.** ***Perf. 13***
1153 A554 75fr multi 1.75 1.75

Opening of Calédoscope, New Philatelic Office — A555

2013, June 7 **Litho.** ***Perf. 14½***
1154 A555 75fr multi 1.75 1.75

Naso Unicornis — A556

2013, June 7 **Engr.** ***Perf. 13***
1155 A556 110fr blue 2.50 2.50

Marine Life in Lagoons A557

No. 1156: a, Plectorpomus leopardus, Epinephelus polyphekadion. b, Carcharhinus amblyrhynchos. c, Scomberomorus commerson. d, Chelonia mydas. e, Caranx melampygus. f, Tridacna maxima, Forcipiger flavissimus. g, Chromis viridis. h, Panulirus penicillatus. i, Myripristis berndti. j, Lutjanus kasmira.

Serpentine Die Cut 11
2013, June 8 **Litho.**
Self-Adhesive
1156 Booklet pane of 10 25.00
a.-j. A557 110fr Any single 2.50 2.50

Re-opening of Maritime History Museum — A558

2013, June 28 **Litho.** ***Perf. 13***
1157 A558 110fr multi 2.40 2.40

Opening of Nouville Penitentiary Museum — A559

2013, Aug. 7 **Litho.** ***Perf. 13***
1158 A559 280fr multi 6.25 6.25

Birth of a Girl — A560

Birth of a Boy — A561

2013, Aug. 8 **Litho.** ***Perf. 13¼x13***
1159 A560 110fr multi 2.50 2.50
1160 A561 110fr multi 2.50 2.50

World Swimming Championships for the Intellectually Disabled, Dumbea — A562

2013, Aug. 19 **Litho.** ***Perf. 13***
1161 A562 120fr multi 2.75 2.75

Captaincookia Tree — A563

2013, Sept. 9 **Litho.** ***Perf. 13¼x13***
1162 A563 85fr multi 1.90 1.90

Pouembout Dovecote — A564

2013, Sept. 9 **Litho.** ***Perf. 13¼x13***
1163 A564 180fr multi 4.00 4.00

Wildlife and Landscapes — A565

Designs: 85fr, Fruit bat and bougainvillea flowers. 110fr, 500-Franc Note Beach, Hienghène. 190fr, Warrior's Leap, Maré Island, vert. 250fr, Thio and Bota Méré, vert.

Perf. 13x13¼, 13¼x13
2013, Nov. 6 **Litho.**
1164-1167 A565 Set of 4 14.50 14.50

Beekeeping — A566

No. 1168: a, Jars of honey, honeydipper, flower, beekeeper checking hives. b, Bees and hives.

2013, Nov. 6 **Litho.** ***Perf. 13***
1168 A566 110fr Horiz. pair, #a-b 5.00 5.00

Miniature Sheet

Orchids — A567

No. 1169: a, Eria karicouyensis. b, Earina deplanchei, vert. c, Eriaxis rigida, vert. d, Dendrobium poissonianum.

Perf. 13x13¼, 13¼x13
2013, Sept. 10 **Litho.**
1169 A567 110fr Sheet of 4, #a-d 10.00 10.00

Christmas A568

2013, Nov. 6 **Litho.** ***Perf. 13x13¼***
1170 A568 110fr multi 2.50 2.50

Miniature Sheet

New Banknotes — A569

No. 1171: a, 75fr, 500-franc banknote. b, 75fr, 1000-franc banknote. c, 110fr, 5000-franc banknote. d, 110fr, 10,000-franc banknote.

Litho. & Silk-screened

2014, Jan. 20 *Perf. 13x12¾*
1171 A569 Sheet of 4, #a-d 8.50 8.50

New Year 2014 (Year of the Horse) A570

2014, Feb. 3 Litho. *Perf. 13*
1172 A570 110fr multi 2.50 2.50

No. 1172 was printed in sheets of 10 + central label.

Exhibition at Tjibaou Cultural Center of Kanak Art — A571

2014, Mar. 15 Litho. *Perf. 12¾x13*
1173 A571 110fr multi 2.60 2.60

North and East Coastal Zone UNESCO World Heritage Site — A572

2014, Apr. 22 Litho. *Perf. 13¼x13*
1174 A572 110fr multi 2.60 2.60

Veteran's Center, Noumea, 50th Anniv. A573

2014, May 16 Litho. *Perf. 13x13¼*
1175 A573 150fr multi 3.50 3.50

Cajoulle House, Koné — A574

2014, May 16 Engr. *Perf. 13x13¼*
1176 A574 750fr multi 17.00 17.00

World Blood Donor Day — A575

2014, June 6 Litho. *Perf. 13*
1177 A575 110fr multi 2.50 2.50

Landscapes and Wildlife — A576

Designs: 75fr, Koné Coral Reef. 110fr, Golden damselfish (poisson-demoiselle), horiz. 120fr, Horned parakeet (perruche), horiz. 190fr, Drowned Forest (La Fôret Noyée).

Perf. 13¼x13, 13x13¼

2014, June 6 Litho.
1178-1181 A576 Set of 4 11.50 11.50

Marine Rescue Service, 10th Anniv. — A577

Litho. & Engr.

2014, Sept. 8 *Perf. 13*
1182 A577 110fr multi 2.40 2.40

Souvenir Sheet

Flora and Fauna of the Mining Scrubland — A578

No. 1183: a, Red-throated parrotfinch (Diamant psittaculaire). b, Grevillea gillivrayi, vert. c, Deplanchea sessilifolia.

Perf. 13x13¼, 13¼x13

2014, Sept. 8 Photo.
1183 A578 110fr Sheet of 3, #a-c 7.00 7.00

Murraya Paniculata Bonsai, by Jean-Jacques Mahuteau A579

2014, Oct. 6 Litho. *Perf. 13¼x13*
1184 A579 150fr multi 3.25 3.25

Isle of Pines Penitentiary — A580

2014, Oct. 6 Engr. *Perf. 13x12½*
1185 A580 280fr multi 6.00 6.00

Papilio Montrouzieri A581

Litho. & Embossed With Foil Application

2014, Nov. 6 *Perf. 13½*
1186 A581 180fr multi 3.75 3.75

Niaouli Flowers and Oil Distillation — A582

2014, Nov. 6 Litho. *Perf. 13*
1187 A582 190fr multi 4.00 4.00

No. 1187 is impregnated with a niaouli scent.

Kanak Weaving A583

Litho. & Embossed

2014, Nov. 6 *Perf. 13*
1188 A583 250fr multi 5.25 5.25

Christmas A584

2014, Nov. 6 Litho. *Perf. 13x13¼*
1189 A584 110fr multi 2.40 2.40

New Year 2015 (Year of the Goat) A585

2015, Feb. 19 Litho. *Perf. 13*
1190 A585 110fr multi 2.10 2.10

No. 1190 was printed in sheets of 10 + central label.

Dick Ukeiwe (1928-2013), Senator — A586

2015, Feb. 19 Engr. *Perf. 13¼*
1191 A586 500fr dark blue & brown 9.25 9.25

Pittosporum Tanianum A587

2015, Mar. 19 Litho. *Perf. 13x13¼*
1192 A587 120fr multi 2.25 2.25

Kô Salt Marshes, Poingam — A588

2015, Apr. 22 Litho. *Perf. 13*
1193 A588 450fr multi 8.50 8.50

Children's Art — A589

Designs: No. 1194, Wildlife, by Eliot-Louis Hatterer.

No. 1195, horiz.: a, Building, tree and Sun, by Emmanuelle Hnawang. b, Flower and snake, by Thomas Bodeouarou.

2015, June 5 Litho. *Perf. 13¼x13*
1194 A589 75fr multi 1.40 1.40

Perf. 13x13¼

1195 Horiz. pair + central label 2.80 2.80
a.-b. A589 75fr Either single 1.40 1.40

World War I, Cent. A590

No. 1196 — Military medals and: a, Soldiers boarding the Sontay. b, Battle of the Serre. c, Soldiers returning home on the El Kantara.

2015, June 5 Litho. *Perf. 13x13¼*

1196 Horiz. strip of 3 2.00 2.00
a.-c. A590 35fr Any single .65 .65

Souvenir Sheet

Birds — A591

No. 1197: a, Nycticorax caledonicus. b, Egretta sacra albolineata, horiz. c, Egretta novaehollandiae nana.

Perf. 13¼x13, 13x13¼

2015, June 5 Litho.

1197 A591 110fr Sheet of 3, #a-c 6.25 6.25

Maxat, First Yam Farming Cycle — A592

2015, July 20 Litho. *Perf. 13*

1198 A592 110fr multi 2.10 2.10

New Caledonia Ornithological Society, 50th Anniv. — A593

2015, Aug. 5 Litho. *Perf. 13*

1199 A593 180fr multi 3.50 3.50

Château Escande, Poya — A594

2015, Sept. 15 Engr. *Perf. 13x12½*

1200 A594 750fr multi 14.00 14.00

First Lighting of Amédée Lighthouse, 150th Anniv. — A595

2015, Nov. 5 Litho. *Perf. 13*

1201 A595 110fr multi 2.00 2.00

Flowers A596

No. 1202: a, Arthroclianthus deplanchei. b, Thiollierea campanulata. c, Xanthostemon aurantiacus. d, Deplanchea speciosa. e, Xanthostemon sulfureus. f, Deplanchea sessifolia. g, Boronella pancheri. h, Artia balansae. i, Virotia angustifolia. j, Arthroclianthus microbotrys.

Serpentine Die Cut 11

2015, Nov. 5 Litho.

Self-Adhesive

1202 Booklet pane of 10 20.00
a.-j. A596 110fr Any single 2.00 2.00

Miniature Sheet

Turtles — A597

No. 1203 — Inscriptions: a, Tortue bonne écaille. b, Tortue grosse tête. c, Tortue verte, horiz. d, Tortue luth, horiz.

2015, Nov. 5 Photo. *Perf. 13½x13*

1203 A597 110fr Sheet of 4, #a-d 8.00 8.00

Christmas — A598

Litho. & Thermographed

2015, Nov. 5 *Perf. 13 on 3 Sides*

1204 A598 110fr multi 2.00 2.00

SEMI-POSTAL STAMPS

No. 93 Surcharged

1915 Unwmk. *Perf. 14x13½*

B1 A16 10c + 5c carmine 1.50 1.50
a. Inverted surcharge 75.00 75.00
b. Cross omitted 100.00 —
c. Double surcharge 160.00 160.00

Regular Issue of 1905 Surcharged

1917

B2 A16 10c + 5c rose 1.50 1.30
a. Double surcharge 130.00 —
B3 A16 15c + 5c violet 1.50 1.40

Curie Issue

Common Design Type

1938, Oct. 24 *Perf. 13*

B4 CD80 1.75fr + 50c brt ultra 16.50 17.50

French Revolution Issue

Common Design Type

1939, July 5 Photo.

Name and Value Typo. in Black

B5 CD83 45c + 25c green 13.50 13.50
B6 CD83 70c + 30c brown 13.50 13.50
B7 CD83 90c + 35c red org 13.50 13.50
B8 CD83 1.25fr + 1fr rose pink 13.50 13.50
B9 CD83 2.25fr + 2fr blue 13.50 13.50
Nos. B5-B9 (5) 67.50 67.50

Common Design Type and

Dumont d'Urville's ship, "Zélée" — SP2

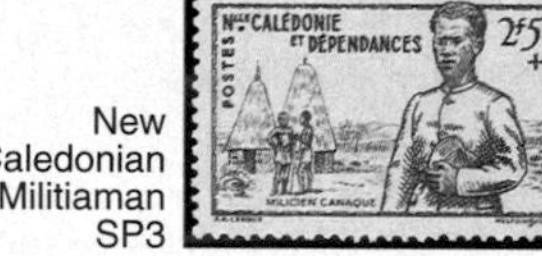

New Caledonian Militiaman SP3

1941 Photo. *Perf. 13½*

B10 SP2 1fr + 1fr red 1.60
B11 CD86 1.50fr + 3fr maroon 1.60
B12 SP3 2.50fr + 1fr dk blue 1.60
Nos. B10-B12 (3) 4.80

Nos. B10-B12 were issued by the Vichy government in France, but were not placed on sale in New Caledonia.

Nos. 216A-216B Srchd. in Black or Red

1944 Engr. *Perf. 12½x12*

B12A 50c + 1.50fr on 2.50fr deep blue (R) .90
B12B + 2.50fr on 1fr green 1.00

Colonial Development Fund.

Nos. B12A-B12B were issued by the Vichy government in France, but were not placed on sale in New Caledonia.

Catalogue values for unused stamps in this section, from this point to the end of the section, are for Never Hinged items.

Red Cross Issue

Common Design Type

1944 *Perf. 14½x14*

B13 CD90 5fr + 20fr brt scar 1.50 1.50

The surtax was for the French Red Cross and national relief.

Tropical Medicine Issue

Common Design Type

1950, May 15 Engr. *Perf. 13*

B14 CD100 10fr + 2fr red brn & sepia 6.75 5.25

The surtax was for charitable work.

AIR POST STAMPS

Seaplane Over Pacific Ocean AP1

1938-40 Unwmk. Engr. *Perf. 13*

C1 AP1 65c deep violet 1.00 1.00
a. "65c" omitted 225.00
C2 AP1 4.50fr red 1.60 1.60
C3 AP1 7fr dk bl grn ('40) 1.15 .85
C4 AP1 9fr ultra 3.00 2.60
C5 AP1 20fr dk orange ('40) 2.25 2.25
C6 AP1 50fr black ('40) 3.75 3.25
Nos. C1-C6 (6) 12.75 11.55

Type of 1938-40 Without "RF"

1942-43

C6A AP1 65c deep violet .30
C6B AP1 4.50fr red .30
C6C AP1 5fr yellow brown .55
C6D AP1 9fr ultramarine .45
C6E AP1 10fr brown lilaca 1.00
C6F AP1 20fr dark orange 1.60
C6G AP1 50fr black 1.75
Nos. C6A-C6G (7) 5.95

Nos. C6A-C6G were issued by the Vichy government in France, but were not placed on sale in New Caledonia.

Common Design Type

1942 Unwmk. *Perf. 14½x14*

C7 CD87 1fr dk orange .70 .70
C8 CD87 1.50fr brt red .70 .70
C9 CD87 5fr brown red .70 .70
C10 CD87 10fr black 1.00 1.00
C11 CD87 25fr ultra 1.40 1.40
C12 CD87 50fr dk green 1.75 1.75
C13 CD87 100fr plum 2.10 2.10
Nos. C7-C13 (7) 8.35 8.35

Eagle — AP1a

1944 *Perf. 13*

C13A AP1a 100fr gray green & blue green 1.50

No. C13A was issued by the Vichy government in France, but was not placed on sale in New Caledonia.

Catalogue values for unused stamps in this section, from this point to the end of the section, are for Never Hinged items.

Victory Issue

Common Design Type

1946, May 8 Engr. *Perf. 12½*

C14 CD92 8fr brt ultra 2.25 1.25

Chad to Rhine Issue

Common Design Types

1946, June 6

C15 CD93 5fr black 1.75 1.60
C16 CD94 10fr carmine 1.75 1.60
C17 CD95 15fr dk blue 1.75 1.60
C18 CD96 20fr orange brn 1.75 1.60
C19 CD97 25fr olive grn 2.40 2.00
C20 CD98 50fr dk rose vio 4.00 3.50
Nos. C15-C20 (6) 13.40 11.90

St. Vincent Bay — AP2

Planes over Islands — AP3

View of Nouméa — AP4

Perf. 13x12½, 12½x13

1948, Mar. 1 Photo. Unwmk.

C21	AP2 50fr org & rose vio	6.00	4.00
C22	AP3 100fr bl grn & sl bl	10.50	4.50
C23	AP4 200fr brown & yel	16.50	8.50
	Nos. C21-C23 (3)	33.00	17.00

UPU Issue

Common Design Type

1949, Nov. 21 Engr. *Perf. 13*

C24 CD99 10fr multicolored 8.25 5.25

Liberation Issue

Common Design Type

1954, June 6

C25 CD102 3fr indigo & ultra 8.25 5.00

Conveyor for Nickel Ore — AP5

1955, Nov. 21 Unwmk. *Perf. 13*

C26 AP5 14fr indigo & sepia 5.00 1.50

Rock Formations, Bourail — AP6

1959, Mar. 21

C27 AP6 200fr lt bl, brn & grn 34.00 15.00

Yaté Dam — AP7

1959, Sept. 21 Engr.

C28 AP7 50fr grn, brt bl & sepia 11.50 4.50

Dedication of Yaté Dam.

Fisherman with Throw-net — AP8

Skin Diver Shooting Bumphead Surgeonfish — AP9

20fr, Nautilus shell. 100fr, Yaté rock.

1962 Unwmk. *Perf. 13*

C29	AP8 15fr red, Prus grn & sep	6.00	2.25
C30	AP9 20fr dk sl grn & org ver	12.00	3.75
C31	AP9 25fr red brn, gray & bl	12.00	4.50
C32	AP9 100fr dk brn, dk bl & sl grn	20.00	11.50
	Nos. C29-C32 (4)	50.00	22.00

Telstar Issue

Common Design Type

1962, Dec. 4 Unwmk. *Perf. 13*

C33 CD111 200fr dk bl, choc & grnsh bl 30.00 18.50

Nickel Mining, Houailou — AP10

1964, May 14 Photo.

C34 AP10 30fr multi 4.00 2.50

Isle of Pines — AP11

1964, Dec. 7 Engr. *Perf. 13*

C35 AP11 50fr dk bl, sl grn & choc 5.75 2.60

Phyllobranchus — AP12

Design: 27fr, Paracanthurus teuthis (fish).

1964, Dec. 21 Photo.

C36	AP12 27fr red brn, yel, dp bl & blk	7.50	3.50
C37	AP12 37fr bl, brn & yel	9.00	5.00

Issued to publicize the Nouméa Aquarium.

Greco-Roman Wrestling — AP13

1964, Dec. 28 Engr.

C38 AP13 10fr brt grn, pink & blk 18.00 15.00

18th Olympic Games, Tokyo, Oct. 10-25.

Nimbus Weather Satellite over New Caledonia AP14

1965, Mar. 23 Photo. *Perf. 13x12½*

C39 AP14 9fr multi 4.25 3.25

Fifth World Meteorological Day.

ITU Issue

Common Design Type

1965, May 17 Engr. *Perf. 13*

C40 CD120 40fr lt bl, lil rose & lt brn 12.00 9.00

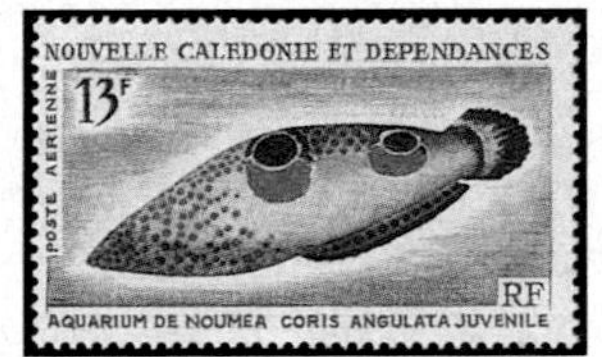
Coris Angulata (Young Fish) — AP15

15fr, Adolescent fish. 25fr, Adult fish.

1965, Dec. 6 Engr. *Perf. 13*

C41	AP15 13fr red org, ol bis & blk	4.50	1.90
C42	AP15 15fr ind, sl grn & bis	6.00	2.00
C43	AP15 25fr ind & yel grn	9.00	5.10
	Nos. C41-C43 (3)	19.50	9.00

Issued to publicize the Nouméa Aquarium.

French Satellite A-1 Issue

Common Design Type

Designs: 8fr, Diamant rocket and launching installations. 12fr, A-1 satellite.

1966, Jan. 10 Engr. *Perf. 13*

C44	CD121 8fr rose brn, ultra & Prus bl	3.50	1.60
C45	CD121 12fr ultra, Prus bl & rose brn	4.00	3.00
a.	Strip of 2, #C44-C45 + label	8.25	7.00

French Satellite D-1 Issue

Common Design Type

1966, May 16 Engr. *Perf. 13*

C46 CD122 10fr dl bl, ocher & sep 3.00 2.00

Port-de-France, 1866 — AP16

1966, June 2

C47 AP16 30fr dk red, bl & ind 5.25 3.50

Port-de-France changing name to Nouméa, cent.

Bird Type of Regular Issue

Designs: 27fr, Uvea crested parakeet. 37fr, Scarlet honey eater. 50fr, Two cloven-feathered doves.

1966-68 Photo. *Perf. 13*

Size: 26x46mm

C48	A45 27fr pink & multi	8.25	4.00
C49	A45 37fr grn & multi	12.00	6.25

Size: 27x48mm

C49A	A45 50fr multi ('68)	15.00	7.50
	Nos. C48-C49A (3)	35.25	17.75

Issued: 27fr, 37fr, Oct. 10; 50fr, May 14.

Sailboats and Map of New Caledonia-New Zealand Route — AP17

1967, Apr. 15 Engr. *Perf. 13*

C50 AP17 25fr brt grn, dp ultra & red 6.75 3.75

2nd sailboat race from Whangarei, New Zealand, to Nouméa, New Caledonia.

Butterfly Type of Regular Issue

Butterflies: 19fr, Danaus plexippus. 29fr, Hippotion celerio. 85fr, Delias elipsis.

1967-68 Engr. *Perf. 13*

Size: 48x27mm

C51	A52 19fr multi ('68)	8.00	4.00
C52	A52 29fr multi ('68)	10.00	5.00
C53	A52 85fr red, dk brn & yel	20.00	9.00
	Nos. C51-C53 (3)	38.00	18.00

Issued: 85fr, Aug. 10; others, Mar. 26.

Jules Garnier, Garnierite and Mine — AP18

1967, Oct. 9 Engr. *Perf. 13*

C54 AP18 70fr bl gray, brn & yel grn 9.00 5.25

Discovery of garnierite (nickel ore), cent.

Lifu Island — AP19

1967, Oct. 28 Photo. *Perf. 13*

C55 AP19 200fr multi 14.00 7.50

Skier, Snowflake and Olympic Emblem — AP20

1967, Nov. 16 Engr. *Perf. 13*

C56 AP20 100fr brn red, sl grn & brt bl 17.50 7.50

10th Winter Olympic Games, Grenoble, France, Feb. 6-18, 1968.

Sea Shell Type of Regular Issue

Designs: 39fr, Conus lienardi. 40fr, Conus cabriti. 70fr, Conus coccineus.

1968, Nov. 9 Engr. *Perf. 13*

C58 A54 39fr bl grn, brn & gray 8.25 2.75
C59 A54 40fr blk, brn red & ol 8.25 3.00
C60 A54 70fr brn, pur & gray 17.00 5.50
Nos. C58-C60 (3) 33.50 11.25

Maré Dancers — AP21

1968, Nov. 30 Engr. *Perf. 13*

C61 AP21 60fr grn, ultra & hn brn 7.50 5.00

World Map and Caudron C 600 "Aiglon" — AP22

1969, Mar. 24 Engr. *Perf. 13*

C62 AP22 29fr lil, dk bl & dk car 5.25 2.75

Stamp Day and honoring the 1st flight from Nouméa to Paris of Henri Martinet & Paul Klein, Mar. 24, 1939.

Concorde Issue

Common Design Type

1969, Apr. 17 Engr. *Perf. 13*

C63 CD129 100fr sl grn & brt grn 35.00 20.00

Cattle Type of Regular Issue

Design: 50fr, Cowboy and herd.

1969, May 10 Engr. *Perf. 13*
Size: 48x27mm

C64 A56 50fr sl grn, dk brn & red brn 5.75 3.25

Sea Shell Type of Regular Issue, 1969

Design: 100fr, Black murex.

1969, June 21 Engr. *Perf. 13*
Size: 48x27mm

C65 A57 100fr lake, bl & blk 27.50 11.50

Sports Type of 1969

30fr, Woman diver. 39fr, Shot put, vert.

1969, Aug. 7 Engr. *Perf. 13*
Size: 48x27mm, 27x48mm

C66 A58 30fr dk brn, bl & blk 5.25 2.00
C67 A58 39fr dk ol, brt grn & ol 6.75 3.00

Napoleon in Coronation Robes, by François P. Gerard AP23

1969, Oct. 2 Photo. *Perf. 12½x12*

C68 AP23 40fr lil & multi 16.50 10.00

200th birth anniv. of Napoleon Bonaparte (1769-1821).

Air France Plane over Outrigger Canoe — AP24

1969, Oct. 2 Engr. *Perf. 13*

C69 AP24 50fr slate grn, sky bl & choc 5.50 3.25

20th anniversary of the inauguration of the Nouméa to Paris airline.

Bird Type of Regular Issue

39fr, Emerald doves. 100fr, Whistling kite.

1970, Feb. 19 Photo. *Perf. 13*
Size: 27x48mm

C70 A45 39fr multi 15.00 5.00
C71 A45 100fr lt bl & multi 27.50 11.50

Planes Circling Globe and Paris-Nouméa Route — AP25

1970, May 6 Engr. *Perf. 13*

C72 AP25 200fr vio, org brn & grnsh bl 17.50 9.75

10th anniversary of the Paris to Nouméa flight: "French Wings Around the World."

Shell Type of Regular Issue, 1970

22fr, Strombus sinautus humphrey, vert. 33fr, Argus porcelain shell. 34fr, Strombus vomer, vert. 60fr, Card porcelain shell.

1970 Engr. *Perf. 13*
Size: 27x48mm, 48x27mm

C73 A59 22fr bl & multi 8.00 3.75
C74 A59 33fr brn & gray bl 10.00 5.00
C75 A59 34fr pur & multi 10.00 4.75
C76 A59 60fr lt grn & brn 16.00 6.75
Nos. C73-C76 (4) 44.00 20.25

See Nos. C89-C90.

Bicyclists on Map of New Caledonia — AP26

1970, Aug. 20 Engr. *Perf. 13*

C77 AP26 40fr bl, ultra & choc 6.75 3.25

The 4th Bicycling Race of New Caledonia.

Mt. Fuji and Monorail Train — AP27

45fr, Map of Japan and Buddha statue.

1970, Sept. 3 Photo. *Perf. 13x12½*

C78 AP27 20fr blk, bl & yel grn 5.00 1.90
C79 AP27 45fr mar, lt bl & ol 6.50 3.25

EXPO '70 International Exposition, Osaka, Japan, Mar. 15-Sept. 13.

Racing Yachts AP28

1971, Feb. 23 Engr. *Perf. 13*

C80 AP28 20fr grn, blk & ver 3.75 1.25

First challenge in New Zealand waters for the One Ton Cup ocean race.

Lt. Col. Broche and Map of Mediterranean — AP29

1971, May 5 Photo. *Perf. 12½*

C81 AP29 60fr multi 8.25 3.25

30th anniversary of Battalion of the Pacific.

Pole Vault — AP30

1971, June 24 Engr. *Perf. 13*

C82 AP30 25fr shown 3.75 2.00
C83 AP30 100fr Archery 8.00 4.25

4th South Pacific Games, Papeete, French Polynesia, Sept. 8-19.

Port de Plaisance, Nouméa — AP31

1971, Sept. 27 Photo. *Perf. 13*

C84 AP31 200fr multi 17.50 7.75

Golden Eagle and Pilot's Leaflet — AP32

1971, Nov. 20 Engr. *Perf. 13*

C85 AP32 90fr dk brn, org & indigo 8.25 3.75

1st flight New Caledonia — Australia with Victor Roffey piloting the Golden Eagle, 40th anniv.

Skiing and Sapporo '72 Emblem — AP33

1972, Jan. 22 Engr. *Perf. 13*

C86 AP33 50fr brt bl, car & sl grn 6.00 2.75

11th Winter Olympic Games, Sapporo, Japan, Feb. 3-13.

South Pacific Commission Headquarters, Nouméa — AP34

1972, Feb. 5 Photo.

C87 AP34 18fr bl & multi 2.25 .85

South Pacific Commission, 25th anniv.

St. Mark's Basilica, Venice — AP35

1972, Feb. 5 Engr.

C88 AP35 20fr lt grn, bl & grn 4.25 1.25

UNESCO campaign to save Venice.

Shell Type of Regular Issue, 1970

Designs: 25fr, Orange spider conch, vert. 50fr, Chiragra spider conch, vert.

1972, Mar. 4 Engr. *Perf. 13*
Size: 27x48mm

C89 A59 25fr dp car & dk brn 8.00 3.00
C90 A59 50fr grn, brn & rose car 11.00 4.00

Breguet F-ALMV and Globe — AP36

1972, Apr. 5 Engr. *Perf. 13*

C91 AP36 110fr brt rose lil, bl & grn 12.50 7.00

40th anniversary of the first Paris-Nouméa flight, Mar. 9-Apr. 5, 1932.

Round House and Festival Emblem — AP37

1972, May 13
C92 AP37 24fr org, bl & brn 3.00 1.50

So. Pacific Festival of Arts, Fiji, May 6-20.

Hurdles and Olympic Rings — AP38

1972, Sept. 2 Engr. *Perf. 13*
C93 AP38 72fr vio, bl & red lil 7.50 3.75

20th Olympic Games, Munich, Aug. 26-Sept. 11.

New Post Office, Noumea — AP39

1972, Nov. 25 Engr. *Perf. 13*
C94 AP39 23fr brn, brt bl & grn 2.25 1.00

Molière and Scenes from Plays — AP40

1973, Feb. 24 Engr. *Perf. 13*
C95 AP40 50fr multi 7.50 2.75

300th anniversary of the death of Molière (Jean Baptiste Poquelin, 1622-1673), French actor and playwright.

Woodlands — AP41

Designs: 18fr, Palm trees on coast, vert. 21fr, Waterfall, vert.

1973, Feb. 24 Photo.
C96 AP41 11fr gold & multi 2.00 1.00
C97 AP41 18fr gold & multi 3.00 1.50
C98 AP41 21fr gold & multi 4.00 1.50
Nos. C96-C98 (3) 9.00 4.00

Concorde — AP42

1973, Mar. 15 Engr. *Perf. 13*
C99 AP42 23fr blue 18.00 3.75
a. Booklet pane of 5 300.00

No. C99 issued in booklets only.

El Kantara in Panama Canal — AP43

1973, Mar. 24 Engr. *Perf. 13*
C100 AP43 60fr brn, yel grn & blk 7.50 3.25

50th anniversary of steamship connection Marseilles to Nouméa through Panama Canal.

Sun, Earth, Wind God and Satellite — AP44

1973, Mar. 24
C101 AP44 80fr multi 7.00 2.75

Centenary of intl. meteorological cooperation and 13th World Meteorological Day.

Museum Type of Regular Issue

Designs: 16fr, Carved arrows and arrowhead. 40fr, Carved entrance to chief's house.

1973, Apr. 30 Photo. *Perf. 12½x13*
C102 A66 16fr multi 2.25 1.00
C103 A66 40fr multi 4.00 2.00

DC-10 over Map of Route Paris to Nouméa — AP45

1973, May 26 Engr. *Perf. 13*
C104 AP45 100fr brn, ultra & sl grn 7.50 3.50

First direct flight by DC-10, Nouméa to Paris.

Fish Type of Regular Issue

32fr, Old and young olive surgeonfish.

1973, June 23 Photo. *Perf. 13x12½*
C105 A69 32fr multi 5.50 2.00

Coach, 1880 — AP46

1973, Sept. 22 Engr. *Perf. 13*
C106 AP46 15fr choc, bl & sl grn 2.25 1.00

Stamp Day 1973.

Landscape — AP47

West Coast Landscapes: 8fr, Rocky path, vert. 26fr, Trees on shore.

1974, Feb. 23 Photo. *Perf. 13*
C107 AP47 8fr gold & multi 1.60 .90
C108 AP47 22fr gold & multi 2.25 1.40
C109 AP47 26fr gold & multi 3.75 1.50
Nos. C107-C109 (3) 7.60 3.80

Anse-Vata, Scientific Center, Nouméa — AP48

1974, Mar. 23 Photo. *Perf. 13x12½*
C110 AP48 50fr multi 3.00 1.60

Ovula Ovum AP49

1974, Mar. 23
C111 AP49 3fr shown 1.50 .55
C112 AP49 32fr Hydatina 4.00 1.10
C113 AP49 37fr Dolium perdix 4.50 2.10
Nos. C111-C113 (3) 10.00 3.75

Nouméa Aquarium.

Capt. Cook, Map of Grande Terre and "Endeavour" — AP50

Designs: 25fr, Jean F. de la Perouse, his ship and map of Grande Terre. 28fr, French sailor, 18th century, on board ship, vert. 30fr, Antoine R. J. d'Entrecasteaux, ship and map. 36fr, Dumont d'Urville, ship and map of Loyalty Islands.

1974, Sept. 4 Engr. *Perf. 13*
C114 AP50 20fr multi 3.00 .90
C115 AP50 25fr multi 4.00 1.40
C116 AP50 28fr multi 5.00 1.40
C117 AP50 30fr multi 7.00 1.60
C118 AP50 36fr multi 8.00 3.00
Nos. C114-C118 (5) 27.00 8.30

Discovery and exploration of New Caledonia and Loyalty Islands.

UPU Emblem and Symbolic Design — AP51

1974, Oct. 9 Engr. *Perf. 13*
C119 AP51 95fr multi 6.00 2.75

Centenary of Universal Postal Union.

Abstract Design — AP52

1974, Oct. 26 Photo. *Perf. 13*
C120 AP52 80fr bl, blk & org 4.25 2.00

ARPHILA 75, Philatelic Exhibition, Paris, June 6-16, 1975.

Hôtel Chateau-Royal, Nouméa — AP53

1975, Jan. 20 Photo. *Perf. 13*
C121 AP53 22fr multi 2.00 .90

Cricket — AP54

Designs: 25fr, Bougna ceremony (food offering). 31fr, Pilou dance.

1975, Apr. 5 Photo. *Perf. 13*
C122 AP54 3fr bl & multi 1.25 .45
C123 AP54 25fr olive grn & multi 2.50 .70
C124 AP54 31fr yel grn & multi 3.00 1.10
Nos. C122-C124 (3) 6.75 2.25

Tourist publicity.

Orchid Type of 1975

Design: 42fr, Eriaxis rigida.

1975, May 30
C125 A74 42fr grn & multi 7.50 2.25

Globe as "Flower" with "Stamps" and leaves — AP55

1975, June 7 Engr. *Perf. 13*
C126 AP55 105fr multi 7.50 2.75

ARPHILA 75 International Philatelic Exhibition, Paris, June 6-16.

Discus and Games' Emblem — AP56

50fr, Volleyball and Games' emblem.

1975, Aug. 23 Photo. *Perf. 13x12½*
C127 AP56 24fr emer, pur & dk bl 2.00 1.00
C128 AP56 50fr multi 3.50 2.00

5th South Pacific Games, Guam, Aug. 1-10.

Concorde — AP57

1976, Jan. 21 Engr. *Perf. 13*
C129 AP57 147fr car & ultra 12.00 7.00

First commercial flight of supersonic jet Concorde, Paris-Rio de Janeiro, Jan. 21.
For surcharge see No. C141.

Telephones 1876 and 1976, Satellite — AP58

1976, Apr. 12 Photo. *Perf. 13*
C130 AP58 36fr multi 2.25 1.25

Centenary of first telephone call by Alexander Graham Bell, Mar. 10, 1876.

Battle Scene — AP59

1976, June 14 Engr. *Perf. 13*
C131 AP59 24fr red brn & ver 3.00 1.00

American Bicentennial.

Runners and Maple Leaf — AP60

1976, July 24 Engr. *Perf. 13*
C132 AP60 33fr car, vio & brn 1.75 1.00

21st Olympic Games, Montreal, Canada, July 17-Aug. 1.

Whimsical Bird as Student and Collector AP61

1976, Aug. 21 Photo.
C133 AP61 42fr multi 3.00 1.50

Philately in School, Philatelic Exhibition in La Perouse Lyceum, Nouméa.

Old City Hall, Nouméa — AP62

Design: 125fr, New City Hall, Nouméa.

1976, Oct. 22 Photo. *Perf. 13*
C134 AP62 75fr multi 5.00 2.75
C135 AP62 125fr multi 7.25 3.25

Lagoon, Women and Festival Symbols AP63

1977, Jan. 15 Photo. *Perf. 13x12½*
C136 AP63 11fr multi 1.25 .55

Summer Festival 1977, Nouméa.

Training Children in Toy Cars — AP64

1977, Mar. 12 Litho. *Perf. 13*
C137 AP64 50fr multi 3.00 1.60

Road safety training.

Bird Type of 1977

Design: 42fr, Male frigate bird, horiz.

1977, Sept. 17 Photo. *Perf. 13*
C138 A89 42fr multi 6.00 1.60

Magenta Airport and Routes — AP65

Design: 57fr, La Tontouta airport.

1977, Oct. 22 Litho. *Perf. 13*
C139 AP65 24fr multi 1.50 .90
C140 AP65 57fr multi 3.00 1.10

No. C129 Surcharged in Violet Blue: "22.11.77 PARIS NEW YORK"

1977, Nov. 22 Engr. *Perf. 13*
C141 AP57 147fr car & ultra 14.00 9.00

Concorde, 1st commercial flight Paris-NY.

Old Nouméa, by H. Didonna — AP66

Valley of the Settlers, by Jean Kreber — AP67

1977, Nov. 26 Photo. *Perf. 13*
C142 AP66 41fr gold & multi 3.00 1.50

Engr.

C143 AP67 42fr red brn & dk brn 3.00 1.50

"Underwater Carnival," Aubusson Tapestry — AP68

1978, June 17 Photo. *Perf. 13*
C144 AP68 105fr multi 5.50 2.25

"The Hare and the Tortoise" — AP69

1978, Aug. 19 Photo. *Perf. 13x13½*
C145 AP69 35fr multi 4.50 1.50

School philately.

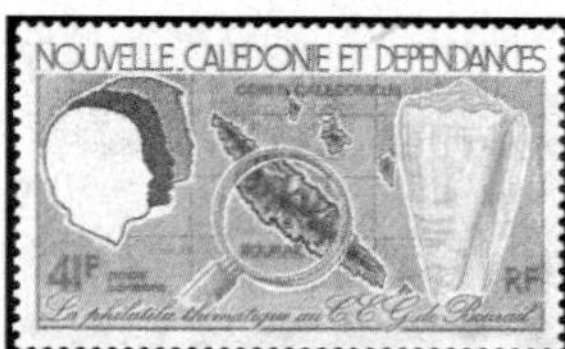

Bourail School Children, Map and Conus Shell — AP70

1978, Sept. 30 Engr. *Perf. 13*
C146 AP70 41fr multi 3.00 1.25

Promotion of topical philately in Bourail public schools.

Old and New Candles — AP71

1978, Oct. 28 Photo. *Perf. 13*
C147 AP71 36fr multi 2.00 .75

Third Caledonian Senior Citizens' Day.

Faubourg Blanchot, by Lacouture — AP72

1978, Nov. 25 Photo. *Perf. 13*
C148 AP72 24fr multi 1.50 1.00

Type of 1978

Design: 42fr, Amyema scandens, horiz.

1978, Mar. 17 *Perf. 13x12½*
C149 A91 42fr multi 3.50 1.60

Orbiting Weather Satellites, WMO Emblem AP73

1979, Mar. 24 Photo. *Perf. 13*
C150 AP73 53fr multi 2.00 1.00

First world-wide satellite system in the atmosphere.

Ships and Emblem — AP74

1979, Mar. 31 Engr.
C151 AP74 49fr multi 2.00 .80

Chamber of Commerce and Industry, centenary.

Child's Drawing, IYC Emblem AP75

1979, Apr. 21 Photo. *Perf. 13*
C152 AP75 35fr multi 2.00 .85

International Year of the Child.

Surf Casting AP76

Design: 30fr, Swordfish fishing.

1979, May 26 Litho. *Perf. 12½*
C153 AP76 29fr multi 2.00 1.00
C154 AP76 30fr multi 2.00 1.00

Port-de-France, 1854, and de Montravel — AP77

1979, June 16 **Engr.** ***Perf. 13***
C155 AP77 75fr multi 4.25 2.25

125th anniversary of Noumea, formerly Port-de-France, founded by L. Tardy de Montravel.

The Eel Queen, Kanaka Legend — AP78

1979, July 7 **Photo.** ***Perf. 13***
C156 AP78 42fr multi 3.00 1.75

Nature protection.

Map of New Caledonia, Postmark, Five Races — AP79

1979, Aug. 18 **Photo.** ***Perf. 13***
C157 AP79 27fr multi 1.50 .55

New Caledonian youth and philately.

Orstom Center, Noumea, Orstom Emblem — AP80

1979, Sept. 17 **Photo.** ***Perf. 13***
C158 AP80 25fr multi 1.50 .55

Old Post Office, Noumea, New Caledonia No. 1, Hill — AP81

1979, Nov. 17 **Engr.**
C159 AP81 150fr multi 5.25 2.00

Sir Rowland Hill (1795-1879), originator of penny postage.

Pirogue AP82

1980, Jan. 26 **Engr.** ***Perf. 13***
C160 AP82 45fr multi 2.00 1.10

Rotary Intl., 75th Anniv. — AP83

1980, Feb. 23 **Photo.** ***Perf. 13***
C161 AP83 100fr multi 4.00 1.60

Man Holding Dolphinfish AP84

1980, Mar. 29 **Photo.** ***Perf. 13x12½***
C162 AP84 34fr shown 1.75 1.00
C163 AP84 39fr Fishermen, sail fish, vert. 2.50 1.25

Coral Seas Air Rally — AP85

1980, June 7 **Engr.** ***Perf. 13***
C164 AP85 31fr multi 1.50 .75

Carved Alligator, Boat — AP86

1980, June 21 **Photo.**
C165 AP86 27fr multi 1.50 .55

South Pacific Arts Festival, Port Moresby, Papua New Guinea.

New Caledonian Kiwanis, 10th Anniversary — AP87

1980, Sept. 10 **Photo.** ***Perf. 13***
C166 AP87 50fr multi 1.90 .90

View of Old Noumea — AP88

1980, Oct. 25 **Photo.** ***Perf. 13½***
C167 AP88 33fr multi 1.50 .90

Charles de Gaulle, 10th Anniversary of Death — AP89

1980, Nov. 15 **Engr.** ***Perf. 13***
C168 AP89 120fr multi 7.00 3.50

Fluorescent Coral, Noumea Aquarium AP90

1980, Dec. 13 **Photo.** ***Perf. 13x13½***
C169 AP90 60fr multi 2.25 1.10

Xeronema Moorei AP91

51fr, Geissois pruinosa.

1981, Mar. 18 **Photo.** ***Perf. 13x12½***
C170 AP91 38fr shown 1.50 1.25
C171 AP91 51fr multicolored 2.00 1.40

Yuri Gagarin and Vostok I — AP92

20th Anniversary of First Space Flights: 155fr, Alan B. Shepard, Freedom 7.

1981, Apr. 8 **Engr.** ***Perf. 13***
C172 AP92 64fr multi 2.75 1.10
C173 AP92 155fr multi 4.50 2.10
a. Souv. sheet of 2, #C172-C173 15.00 15.00

No. C173a sold for 225fr.

40th Anniv. of Departure of Pacific Batallion — AP93

1981, May 5 **Photo.** ***Perf. 13***
C174 AP93 29fr multi 3.00 1.10

Ecinometra Mathaei AP94

51fr, Prionocidaris verticillata.

1981, Aug. 5 **Photo.** ***Perf. 13x13½***
C175 AP94 38fr shown 1.50 .80
C176 AP94 51fr multicolored 2.25 .95

No. 4, Post Office Building AP95

1981, Sept. 16 **Photo.** ***Perf. 13x13½***
C177 AP95 41fr multi 1.60 .75

Stamp Day.

Old Noumea Latin Quarter — AP96

1981, Oct. 14 **Photo.** ***Perf. 13½***
C178 AP96 43fr multi 1.60 .75

New Caledonia to Australia Airmail Flight by Victor Roffey, 50th Anniv. AP97

1981, Nov. 21 **Engr.** ***Perf. 13***
C179 AP97 37fr multi 1.25 .65

Rousette AP98

1982, Feb. 24 **Engr.** ***Perf. 13***
C180 AP98 38fr shown 1.25 .75
C181 AP98 51fr Kagu 1.75 .85

See Nos. C188B-C188C.

50th Anniv. of Paris-Noumea Flight — AP99

250fr, Pilots, map, plane.

1982, Apr. 5 Engr. *Perf. 13*
C182 AP99 250fr multi 7.00 3.50

Scouting Year — AP100

1982, Apr. 21 Photo. *Perf. 13½x13*
C183 AP100 40fr multi 1.40 .65

PHILEXFRANCE '82 Intl. Stamp Show, Paris, June 11-21 — AP101

1982, May 12 Engr. *Perf. 13*
C184 AP101 150fr multi 3.25 2.00

1982 World Cup AP102

1982, June 9 Photo. *Perf. 13x13½*
C185 AP102 74fr multi 2.10 1.00

French Overseas Possessions Week, Sept. 18-25 — AP103

100fr, Map, kagu, citizens.

1982, Sept. 17 *Perf. 13x12½*
C186 AP103 100fr multicolored 2.75 1.00

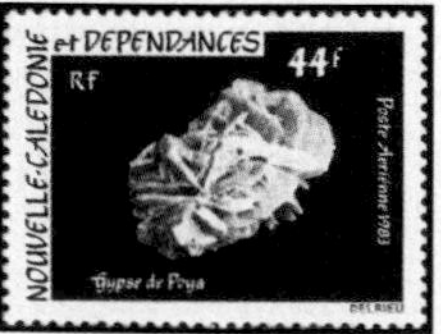

Gypsum, Poya Mines AP104

59fr, Silica gel, Kone mine.

1983, Jan. 15 Photo. *Perf. 13x13½*
C187 AP104 44fr shown 2.50 1.10
C188 AP104 59fr multicolored 3.50 1.40

World Communications Year — AP104a

Design: WCY emblem, map, globe.

1983, Mar. 9 Litho. *Perf. 13*
C188A AP104a 170fr multi 3.50 1.50

Aircraft Type of 1982

46fr, Pou-du-Ciel. 61fr, L'Aiglon Caudron.

1983, July 6 Engr. *Perf. 13*
C188B AP98 46fr multi 1.50 .75
C188C AP98 61fr multi 2.50 1.25

Temple and Dancers — AP105

1983, July 20 Litho. *Perf. 12½x12*
C189 AP105 47fr multi 1.50 .80

BANGKOK '83 Intl. Stamp Show, Aug. 4-13.

Oueholle Tribe, Straw Hut — AP106

1983, Sept. 7 Litho. *Perf. 13*
C190 AP106 76fr multi 2.00 1.10

Loyalty Islander by the Shore, by R. Mascart AP107

Paintings: 350fr, The Guitarist from Mare Island, by P. Neilly.

1983, Dec. 7 Photo. *Perf. 13*
C191 AP107 100fr multi 3.75 1.75
C192 AP107 350fr multi 9.00 5.25

Noumea Aquarium Fish AP108

46fr, Amphiprion clarkii. 61fr, Centropyge bicolor.

1984, Mar. 7 Photo. *Perf. 13*
C193 AP108 46fr multi 2.25 .90
C194 AP108 61fr multi 2.75 1.25

Local Plants — AP109

51fr, Araucaria columnaris. 67fr, Pritchardiopsis jeanneneyi.

1984, Apr. 25 Litho. *Perf. 12½x13*
C195 AP109 51fr multi 2.00 .90
C196 AP109 67fr multi 2.75 1.25

1984 Summer Olympics — AP110

1984, June 20 Photo. *Perf. 13½x13*
C197 AP110 50fr Swimming 1.75 1.10
C198 AP110 83fr Wind surfing 3.50 1.60
C199 AP110 200fr Running 6.00 2.75
Nos. C197-C199 (3) 11.25 5.45

Ausipex '84 — AP111

1984, Sept. 21 Engr. *Perf. 13*
C200 AP111 150fr Exhibition Hall 4.00 1.60
a. Souvenir sheet 6.00 6.00

Se-tenant with label showing exhibition emblem. No. C200a contains No. C200 in changed colors.

Army Day — AP112

1984, Oct. 27 Litho. *Perf. 13½x13*
C201 AP112 51fr multi 1.50 .70

Woman Fishing for Crabs, by Mme. Bonnet de Larbogne — AP113

Painting: 300fr, Cook Discovering New Caledonia, by Pilioko.

1984, Nov. 8 Litho. *Perf. 13x12½*
C202 AP113 120fr multi 3.50 1.75
C203 AP113 300fr multi 8.00 4.50

See Nos. 605-606.

Transpac Dragon Rapide, Map AP114

1985, Oct. 2 Litho. *Perf. 13½*
C204 AP114 80fr multi 1.75 1.25

Internal air services, 30th anniv.

UN, 40th Anniv. AP115

Perf. 12½x13
1985, Oct. 25 Wmk. 385
C205 AP115 250fr multi 5.50 2.00

Jules Garnier High School AP116

1985, Nov. 13 Unwmk. *Perf. 13*
C206 AP116 400fr multi 9.75 4.25

Paris-Noumea Scheduled Flights, 30th Anniv. — AP117

1986, Jan. 6
C207 AP117 72fr multi 2.00 1.25

Nou Island Livestock Warehouse — AP118

1986, June 14 Engr. *Perf. 13*
C208 AP118 230fr Prus bl, sep & brn 5.25 2.75

ATR-42 Inaugural Service AP119

1986, Aug. 13 Litho. *Perf. 12½x13*
C209 AP119 18fr multi .55 .45

STOCKHOLMIA '86 — AP120

1986, Aug. 29 Engr. *Perf. 13*
C210 AP120 108fr No. 1 2.75 1.25

Natl. Assoc. of Amateur Radio Operators, 25th Anniv. AP121

1987, Jan. 7 Litho. *Perf. 12½*
C211 AP121 64fr multi 1.75 .85

Nature Conservation, Fight Noise Pollution — AP122

1987, Mar. 25 Litho. *Perf. 13x12½*
C212 AP122 150fr multi 4.00 1.75

French Cricket Federation AP123

1987, Nov. 25 Litho. *Perf. 12½*
C213 AP123 94fr multi 2.25 1.75

Arms Type of 1984

1988, Jan. 13 *Perf. 12½x13*
C214 A132 76fr Dumbea 2.25 1.00

Rotary Intl. Anti-Polio Campaign — AP124

1988, Oct. 26 Litho. *Perf. 13½*
C215 AP124 220fr multi 5.25 2.75

Bamboo Type of 1989

Litho. & Engr.

1989, Sept. 27 *Perf. 12½x13*
C216 A187 44fr multi 1.25 .65

De Gaulle's Call For French Resistance, 50th Anniv. AP125

1990, June 20 Litho. *Perf. 12½*
C217 AP125 160fr multicolored 4.00 1.75

Military Cemetery, New Zealand — AP126

Auckland 1990: #C219, Brigadier William Walter Dove.

1990, Aug. 24 *Perf. 13*
C218 AP126 80fr multi 2.00 1.00
C219 AP126 80fr multi 2.00 1.00
a. Pair, #C218-C219 + label 4.75 4.75

Souvenir Sheet

New Zealand 1990 — AP126a

1990, Aug. 25 Litho. *Perf. 13x12½*
C219B AP126a 150fr multi 6.00 5.00

Crustaceans AP127

30fr, Munidopsis sp. Orstom. 60fr, Lyreidius tridentatus.

1990, Oct. 17 LItho. *Perf. 12½x13*
C220 AP127 30fr multi 1.00 .55
C221 AP127 60fr multi 2.00 1.10

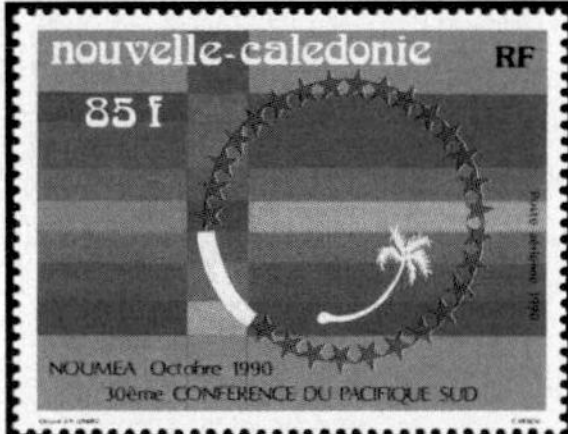
30th South Pacific Conference — AP128

1990, Oct. 29 Litho. *Perf. 13*
C222 AP128 85fr multicolored 2.10 1.10

Gen. Charles de Gaulle (1890-1970) AP129

1990, Nov. 21 Engr. *Perf. 13*
C223 AP129 410fr dk blue 10.00 5.00

Scenic Views — AP130

1991, Feb. 13 Litho. *Perf. 13*
C224 AP130 36fr Fayawa-Ouvea Bay .90 .50
C225 AP130 90fr shown 2.40 1.25

See No. C246.

New Caledonian Cricket Players by Marcel Moutouh — AP131

Design: 435fr, Saint Louis by Janine Goetz.

1991, Dec. 18 *Perf. 13x12½*
C226 AP131 130fr multicolored 3.00 2.00
C227 AP131 435fr multicolored 10.00 5.00

See Nos. C236, C242, C260.

Blue River Nature Park — AP132

1992, Feb. 6 Litho. *Perf. 12½*
C228 AP132 400fr multicolored 9.25 4.75
a. Souvenir sheet of 1 10.50 10.50

No. C228a sold for 450fr and was issued 2/5/92.

Native Pottery AP133

Photo. & Engr.

1992, Apr. 9 *Perf. 12½x13*
C229 AP133 25fr black & orange .75 .30

Expo '92, Seville AP134

1992, Apr. 25 Litho. *Perf. 13*
C230 AP134 10fr multicolored .35 .25

Discovery of America, 500th Anniv. AP135

#C234: a, Erik the Red, Viking longship. b, Columbus, coat of arms. c, Amerigo Vespucci.

1992, May 22 Litho. *Perf. 13½*
C231 AP135 80fr Pinta 2.00 1.00
C232 AP135 80fr Santa Maria 2.00 1.00
C233 AP135 80fr Nina 2.00 1.00
a. Strip of 3, #C231-C233 6.00 6.00
b. Bklt. pane of 3, #C231-C233 10.00 10.00

Souvenir Sheet

Perf. 12½

C234 AP135 110fr Sheet of 3, #a.-c. 10.00 10.00

World Columbian Stamp Expo '92, Chicago. No. C234 sold for 360fr.

1992 Summer Olympics, Barcelona — AP136

1992, July 25 *Perf. 13*
C235 AP136 260fr Synchronized swimming 6.75 3.25

Painters of the Pacific Type of 1991

Design: 205fr, Wahpa, by Paul Mascart

1992, Sept. 28 Litho. *Perf. 12½x13*
C236 AP131 205fr multicolored 5.00 2.50

Australian Bouvier — AP138

1992, Oct. 4 *Perf. 12*
C237 AP138 175fr multicolored 5.25 2.40

Exploration of New Caledonian Coast by Chevalier d'Entrecasteaux, Bicent. — AP139

1992, Nov. 18 Engr. *Perf. 13*
C238 AP139 110fr bl grn, ocher & olive grn 2.50 1.25

Shells — AP140

30fr, Amalda fuscolingua. 50fr, Cassis abbotti.

1992, Nov. 26 Litho. *Perf. 13½x13*
C239 AP140 30fr multi .75 .35
C240 AP140 50fr multi 1.25 .75

The vignettes on Nos. C239-C240 were applied by a thermographic process, producing a shiny, raised effect.

AP141

Comic Strip Characters from "La Brousse en Folie," by Bernard Berger: a, Dede. b. Torton Marcel in Mimine II. c, Tathan. d, Joinville.

1992, Dec. 9 Litho. *Perf. 13½*
C241 AP141 80fr Strip of 4, #a.-d. 8.50 8.50

Painters of the Pacific Type of 1991

Design: 150fr, Noumea, 1890, by Gaston Roullet (1847-1925).

1993, Mar. 25 Litho. *Perf. 13x12½*
C242 AP131 150fr multicolored 3.50 1.75

Extraction of Attar from Niaouli Flowers (Melaleuca Quinquenervia), Cent. — AP142

1993, Apr. 28 *Perf. 13*
C243 AP142 85fr multicolored 2.00 1.00

Nicolaus Copernicus (1473-1543) — AP143

1993, May 5 Engr. *Perf. 13*
C244 AP143 110fr multicolored 3.00 1.25

Polska '93.

Noumea Temple, Cent. AP144

1993, June 16 Litho. *Perf. 12½x13*
C245 AP144 400fr multicolored 9.00 4.50

Scenic Views Type of 1991

1993, July 8 Litho. *Perf. 13*
C246 AP130 85fr Malabou 2.00 1.00

Little Train of Thio — AP145

1993, July 24 Engr. *Perf. 13*
C247 AP145 115fr multicolored 2.75 1.40

AP146

1993, Aug. 18 Litho.
C248 AP146 100fr multicolored 2.50 1.10

Henri Rochefort (1831-1913), writer.

AP147

Bangkok '93: No. C249, Vanda coerulea. No. C250, Megastylis paradoxa. 140fr, Royal Palace, Bangkok, horiz.

1993, Oct. 1 *Perf. 13½*
C249 AP147 30fr multicolored 1.00 .35
C250 AP147 30fr multicolored 1.00 .35

Souvenir Sheet
Perf. 13

C251 AP147 140fr multicolored 3.50 3.50

No. C251 contains one 52x40mm stamp.

Air Caledonia, 10th Anniv. — AP148

1993, Oct. 9 *Perf. 13*
C252 AP148 85fr multicolored 2.25 1.10

New Caledonia-Australia Telephone Cable, Cent. — AP149

1993, Oct. 15 Engr. *Perf. 13x12½*
C253 AP149 200fr blue & black 4.75 2.25

Oxpleurodon Orbiculatus — AP150

1993, Oct. 15 Litho. *Perf. 13½*
C254 AP150 250fr multicolored 6.00 2.75

Portions of the design on No. C254 were applied by a thermographic process producing a shiny, raised effect.

Tontouta Airport, Noumea, 25th Anniv. — AP151

1993, Nov. 29 Litho. *Perf. 13*
C255 AP151 90fr multicolored 2.25 1.00

Christmas — AP152

1993, Dec. 9 Litho.
C256 AP152 120fr multicolored 3.00 1.25

Portions of the design on No. C256 were applied by a thermographic process producing a shiny, raised effect.

New Year 1994 (Year of the Dog) AP153

1994, Feb. 18 Litho. *Perf. 13*
C257 AP153 60fr multicolored 1.75 .85

Hong Kong '94.

First Airbus A340 Flight, Paris-Noumea — AP154

1994, Mar. 31 Litho. *Die Cut 8*
Self-Adhesive
C258 AP154 90fr multicolored 2.75 1.25

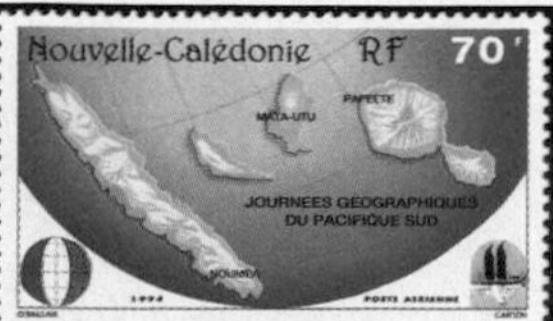
South Pacific Geography Day — AP155

1994, May 10 Litho. *Perf. 13*
C259 AP155 70fr multicolored 1.75 .85

See Wallis and Futuna No. C177.

Painters of the Pacific Type of 1991

Design: 120fr, Legende du Poulpe, by Micheline Neporon.

1994, June 24 Litho. *Perf. 13*
C260 AP131 120fr multicolored 3.00 1.40

Pottery, Museum of Noumea AP156

1994, July 6 Litho. *Perf. 12½x13*
C261 AP156 95fr multicolored 2.50 1.10

1994 World Cup Soccer Championships, U.S. — AP156a

1994, July 12 Litho. *Perf. 13*
C261A AP156a 105fr multicolored 2.50 1.50

Intl. Year of the Family AP157

PHILAKOREA '94 — AP158

Korean cuisine: No. C263a, Rice, celery, carrots, peppers. b, Lettuce, cabbage, garlic. c, Onions. d, Shrimp, oysters.

1994, Aug. 17 *Perf. 13½x13*
C262 AP157 60fr multicolored 3.00 1.00

Souvenir Sheet
Perf. 12½

C263 Sheet of 4 4.75 4.75
a.-d. AP158 35fr any single 1.10 1.00

Research Ship Atalante — AP159

1994, Aug. 26 ***Perf. 13***
C264 AP159 120fr multicolored 2.75 1.50

Masons in New Caledonia, 125th Anniv. — AP160

1994, Sept. 16 ***Perf. 13***
C265 AP160 350fr multicolored 8.00 3.75

Participation in First European Stamp Show — AP161

1994, Oct. 15 **Litho.** ***Perf. 13***
C266 AP161 90fr Island 2.00 1.00
C267 AP161 90fr Herding cattle 2.00 1.00
a. Pair, #C266-C267 + label 4.50 4.50

ORSTOM, 50th Anniv. — AP162

1994, Nov. 14 **Photo.** ***Perf. 13***
C268 AP162 95fr multicolored 2.50 1.25

Tiebaghi Mine — AP163

1994, Nov. 24 **Litho.**
C269 AP163 90fr multicolored 2.75 1.00

South Pacific Tourism Year AP164

1995, Mar. 15 **Litho.** ***Perf. 13½***
C270 AP164 90fr multicolored 2.50 1.00

35th South Pacific Conference, Noumea — AP165

1995, Oct. 25 **Litho.** ***Perf. 13***
C271 AP165 500fr multicolored 12.00 5.00

Kanak Dances AP166

1995, Dec. 8 **Litho.** ***Perf. 13x13½***
C272 AP166 95fr Ouaré 2.25 1.00
C273 AP166 100fr Pothé 2.50 1.00

Mekosuchus Inexpactatus — AP167

1996, Feb. 23 **Litho.** ***Perf. 13x13½***
C274 AP167 125fr multicolored 2.75 1.50

Indonesian Centenary AP168

1996, July 20
C275 AP168 130fr multicolored 3.00 3.00

Louis Brauquier (1900-76), Writer — AP169

1996, Aug. 7 **Litho.** ***Perf. 12½***
C276 AP169 95fr multicolored 2.25 1.10

Ile Nou Ground Station, 20th Anniv. AP170

125fr, Guglielmo Marconi, telegraph wires.

1996, Sept. 26 **Litho.** ***Perf. 13***
C277 AP170 95f multicolored 2.25 1.10
C278 AP170 125fr multicolored 2.75 1.50
a. Pair, #C277-C278 + label 5.00 5.00

Radio, cent. (#C278).

Regional Views — AP171

1996, Nov. 7 **Litho.** ***Perf. 13***
C279 AP171 95fr Great reef 2.25 1.10
C280 AP171 95fr Mount Koghi 2.25 1.10
a. Pair, #C279-C280 + label 4.75 4.75

50th Autumn Philatelic Salon.

Christmas AP172

1996, Nov. 25 ***Perf. 13½x13***
C281 AP172 95fr multicolored 2.25 1.10

Horned Turtle Meiolania AP173

1997, Jan. 8 **Litho.** ***Perf. 13***
C282 AP173 95fr multicolored 3.00 1.25

Portions of the design were applied by a thermographic process producing a shiny, raised effect.

South Pacific Commission, 50th Anniv. — AP174

1997, Feb. 7 **Litho.** ***Perf. 13X13½***
C283 AP174 100fr multicolored 2.25 1.10

Hong Kong '97 AP175

New Year 1997 (Year of the Ox) — #C285: a, Water buffalo pulling plow. b, Cattle in pasture.

1997, Feb. 12 ***Perf. 13***
C284 AP175 95fr multicolored 2.50 1.10

Sheet of 2
Perf. 13x13½

C285 AP175 75fr #a.-b. 3.50 3.25

No. C285 contains two 40x30mm stamps.

Melanesian Pottery — AP176

Lapita pottery c. 1200-1000 B.C.: No. C286, With stylized faces. No. C287, With labyrinth pattern.

1997, May 14 **Litho.** ***Perf. 13***
C286 AP176 95fr multicolored 2.25 2.25
C287 AP176 95fr multicolored 2.25 2.25

TRAPAS, French Airlines in the South Pacific, 1947-50 — AP177

Airplane, emblem, map showing: No. C288, Australia, New Herbrides, Suva, Tahiti, New Zealand. No. C289, Koumac, Poindimie, Noumea, Isle of Pines.

Photo. & Engr.

1997, Aug. 12 ***Perf. 13***
C288 AP177 95fr multicolored 2.10 2.10
C289 AP177 95fr multicolored 2.10 2.10
a. Pair, #C288-C289 4.25 4.25

Regular Paris-Noumea Air Service, 50th Anniv. — AP178

1999, Sept. 29 **Photo.** ***Perf. 13x12½***
C290 AP178 100fr multicolored 2.50 2.00

Inauguration of Noumea-Osaka Air Service — AP179

2001, Oct. 11 **Litho.** ***Perf. 13***
C291 AP179 110fr multi 2.25 2.25

AIR POST SEMI-POSTAL STAMPS

French Revolution Issue
Common Design Type
Unwmk.
1939, July 5 **Photo.** ***Perf. 13***
Name and Value Typo. in Orange
C B1 CD83 4.50fr + 4fr brn blk 34.00 34.00

Father & Child — SPAP1

1942, June 22	**Engr.**		***Perf. 13***
CB2 SPAP1	1.50fr + 3.50fr green	1.60	
CB3 SPAP1	2fr + 6fr yel brn	1.60	

Native children's welfare fund.

Nos. CB2-CB3 were issued by the Vichy government in France, but were not placed on sale in New Caledonia.

Colonial Education Fund

Common Design Type

1942, June 22		
CB4 CD86a	1.20fr + 1.80fr blue & red	1.60

No. CB4 was issued by the Vichy government in France, but was not placed on sale in New Caledonia.

POSTAGE DUE STAMPS

For a short time in 1894, 5, 10, 15, 20, 25 and 30c postage stamps (Nos. 43, 45, 47, 49, 50 and 52) were overprinted with a "T" in an inverted triangle and used as Postage Due stamps.

French Colonies Postage Due Stamps Overprinted in Carmine, Blue or Silver

1903	**Unwmk.**		***Imperf.***
J1 D1	5c blue (C)	3.75	3.75
J2 D1	10c brown (C)	11.50	11.50
J3 D1	15c yel grn (C)	22.50	11.50
J4 D1	30c carmine (Bl)	19.00	15.00
J5 D1	50c violet (Bl)	65.00	22.50
J6 D1	60c brn, *buff* (Bl)	260.00	95.00
J7 D1	1fr rose, *buff* (S)	42.50	26.00
b.	Double overprint	225.00	225.00
J8 D1	2fr red brn (Bl)	1,300.	1,300.
	Nos. J1-J8 (8)	1,724.	1,485.

Nos. J1 to J8 are known with the "I" in "TENAIRE" missing.

Fifty years of French occupation.

Men Poling Boat — D2

1906	**Typo.**	***Perf. 13½x14***	
J9 D2	5c ultra, *azure*	.70	*.75*
J10 D2	10c vio brn, *buff*	.70	*.75*
J11 D2	15c grn, *greenish*	1.00	*1.10*
J12 D2	20c blk, *yellow*	1.00	*1.10*
J13 D2	30c carmine	1.35	*1.50*
J14 D2	50c ultra, *buff*	2.25	2.25
J15 D2	60c brn, *azure*	1.50	*1.90*
J16 D2	1fr dk grn, *straw*	2.25	*2.75*
	Nos. J9-J16 (8)	10.75	*12.10*

Type of 1906 Issue Surcharged

1926-27			
J17 D2	2fr on 1fr vio	5.75	*6.25*
J18 D2	3fr on 1fr org brn	5.75	*6.25*

Malayan Sambar — D3

1928			**Typo.**
J19 D3	2c sl bl & dp brn	.25	*.40*
J20 D3	4c brn red & bl grn	.45	*.60*
J21 D3	5c red org & bl blk	.60	*.75*
J22 D3	10c mag & Prus bl	.60	*.75*
J23 D3	15c dl grn & scar	.60	*.75*
J24 D3	20c mar & ol grn	1.05	*1.10*
J25 D3	25c bis brn & sl bl	.75	*.90*
J26 D3	30c bl grn & ol grn	1.05	*1.10*
J27 D3	50c lt brn & dk red	1.35	*1.50*
J28 D3	60c mag & brt rose	1.35	*1.50*
J29 D3	1fr dl bl & Prus grn	1.75	*1.90*
J30 D3	2fr dk red & ol grn	1.90	*2.25*
J31 D3	3fr violet & brn	2.75	*3.00*
	Nos. J19-J31 (13)	14.45	*16.50*

Catalogue values for unused stamps in this section, from this point to the end of the section, are for Never Hinged items.

D4

1948	**Unwmk.**	**Photo.**	***Perf. 13***
J32 D4	10c violet	.30	.30
J33 D4	30c brown	.40	.40
J34 D4	50c blue green	.60	.60
J35 D4	1fr orange	.60	.60
J36 D4	2fr red violet	.75	.75
J37 D4	3fr red brown	.75	.75
J38 D4	4fr dull blue	1.10	1.10
J39 D4	5fr henna brown	1.10	1.10
J40 D4	10fr slate green	1.75	1.75
J41 D4	20fr violet blue	2.40	2.40
	Nos. J32-J41 (10)	9.75	9.75

Bat — D5

1983	**Litho.**	***Perf. 13***	
J42 D5	1fr multi	.25	.25
J43 D5	2fr multi	.30	.30
J44 D5	3fr multi	.30	.30
J45 D5	4fr multi	.45	.45
J46 D5	5fr multi	.55	.55
J47 D5	10fr multi	.75	.75
J48 D5	20fr multi	.90	.90
J49 D5	40fr multi	1.40	1.40
J50 D5	50fr multi	1.75	1.75
	Nos. J42-J50 (9)	6.65	6.65

For overprint see No. 696.

MILITARY STAMPS

Stamps of the above types, although issued by officials, were unauthorized and practically a private speculation.

OFFICIAL STAMPS

Catalogue values for unused stamps in this section are for Never Hinged items.

Ancestor Pole — O1

Various carved ancestor poles.

1959	**Unwmk.**	**Typo.**	***Perf. 14x13***
O1 O1	1fr org yel	.45	.45
O2 O1	3fr lt bl grn	.45	.45
O3 O1	4fr purple	.60	.60
O4 O1	5fr ultra	.75	.75
O5 O1	9fr black	1.00	1.00
O6 O1	10fr brt vio	1.40	1.40
O7 O1	13fr yel grn	1.50	1.50
O8 O1	15fr lt bl	2.00	2.00
O9 O1	24fr red lilac	2.40	2.40
O10 O1	26fr deep org	2.75	2.75
O11 O1	50fr green	5.75	5.75
O12 O1	100fr chocolate	11.00	11.00
O13 O1	200fr red	20.00	20.00
	Nos. O1-O13 (13)	50.05	50.05

Carved Wooden Pillow — O2

Vignette: Green, Red Brown (2, 29, 31, 35, 38, 65, 76fr), Brown (40fr), Blue (58fr)

1973-87	**Photo.**	***Perf. 13***	
O14 O2	1fr yellow	.30	.30
O14A O2	2fr green ('87)	.25	.25
O15 O2	3fr tan	.45	.45
O16 O2	4fr pale violet	.60	.60
O17 O2	5fr lilac rose	.60	.60
O18 O2	9fr light blue	1.00	1.00
O19 O2	10fr orange	1.10	1.10
O20 O2	11fr bright lilac ('76)	.60	.60
O21 O2	12fr bl grn ('73)	1.25	1.25
O22 O2	15fr green ('76)	.70	.70
O23 O2	20fr rose ('76)	.75	.75
O24 O2	23fr red ('80)	1.00	1.00
O25 O2	24fr Prus bl ('76)	1.00	1.00
O25A O2	25fr gray ('81)	1.30	1.30
O26 O2	26fr yellow ('76)	1.05	1.05
O26A O2	29fr dl grn ('83)	1.30	1.30
O26B O2	31fr yellow ('82)	1.40	1.40
O26C O2	35fr yellow ('84)	1.50	1.50
O27 O2	36fr dp lil rose ('76)	1.30	1.30
O27A O2	38fr tan	1.50	1.50
O27B O2	40fr blue ('87)	1.30	1.30
O28 O2	42fr bister ('76)	1.50	1.50
O29 O2	50fr blue ('76)	1.50	1.50
O29A O2	58fr blue grn ('87)	1.75	1.75
O29B O2	65fr lilac ('84)	1.90	1.90
O29C O2	76fr brt yel ('87)	2.25	2.25
O30 O2	100fr red ('76)	2.75	2.75
O31 O2	200fr orange ('76)	5.00	5.00
	Nos. O14-O31 (28)	36.90	36.90

PARCEL POST STAMPS

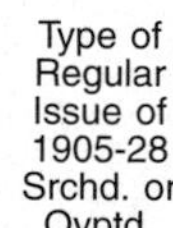
Type of Regular Issue of 1905-28 Srchd. or Ovptd.

1926	**Unwmk.**	***Perf. 14x13½***	
Q1 A18	50c on 5fr olive, *lav*	1.30	*1.90*
Q2 A18	1fr deep blue	1.75	*2.75*
Q3 A18	2fr car, *bluish*	2.10	*3.00*
	Nos. Q1-Q3 (3)	5.15	*7.65*

Regular Issue of 1928 Overprinted

1930			
Q4 A20	50c violet & brown	1.30	*1.90*
Q5 A21	1fr dp ol & sal red	1.75	*2.75*
Q6 A21	2fr red org & brn	2.10	*3.00*
	Nos. Q4-Q6 (3)	5.15	7.65

NEW GUINEA

'nü 'gi-nē

LOCATION — On an island of the same name in the South Pacific Ocean, north of Australia.

GOVT. — Mandate administered by Australia

AREA — 93,000 sq. mi.

POP. — 675,369 (1940)

CAPITAL — Rabaul

The territory occupies the northeastern part of the island and includes New Britain and other nearby islands. It was formerly a German possession and should not be confused with British New Guinea (Papua) which is in the southeastern part of the same island, nor Netherlands New Guinea (Vol. 4). For previous issues see German New Guinea, New Britain, North West Pacific Islands. Issues for 1952 and later are listed under Papua.

12 Pence = 1 Shilling

20 Shillings = 1 Pound

Native Huts — A1

1925-28	**Engr.**	***Perf. 11***	
1 A1	½p orange	2.75	*8.00*
2 A1	1p yellow green	2.75	*6.25*
3 A1	1½p vermilion ('26)	3.75	*3.00*
4 A1	2p claret	6.50	*5.00*
5 A1	3p deep blue	7.00	4.50
6 A1	4p olive green	15.00	*24.00*
7 A1	6p yel bister ('28)	6.50	*55.00*
a.	6p light brown	22.50	*55.00*
b.	6p olive bister ('27)	11.00	*52.50*
8 A1	9p deep violet	15.00	*50.00*
9 A1	1sh gray green	17.50	*30.00*
10 A1	2sh red brown	35.00	*55.00*
11 A1	5sh olive bister	55.00	75.00
12 A1	10sh dull rose	120.00	*200.00*
13 A1	£1 grnsh gray	210.00	*325.00*
	Nos. 1-13 (13)	496.75	840.75

For overprints see Nos. C1-C13, O1-O9.

Bird of Paradise — A2

1931, Aug. 2			
18 A2	1p light green	4.50	4.00
19 A2	1½p red	5.75	*11.50*
20 A2	2p violet brown	5.75	2.50
21 A2	3p deep blue	5.75	5.50
22 A2	4p olive green	7.50	*27.50*
23 A2	5p slate green	8.00	*22.50*
24 A2	6p bister	8.00	*25.00*
25 A2	9p dull violet	9.50	*21.00*
26 A2	1sh bluish gray	7.00	*17.00*
27 A2	2sh red brown	11.50	*47.50*
28 A2	5sh olive brown	47.50	*62.50*
29 A2	10sh rose red	120.00	*150.00*
30 A2	£1 gray	250.00	*300.00*
	Nos. 18-30 (13)	490.75	*696.50*

10th anniversary of Australian Mandate.

For overprints see #C14-C27, O12-O22.

Type of 1931 without date scrolls

1932-34		***Perf. 11***	
31 A2	1p light green	6.00	.25
32 A2	1½p violet brown	6.00	*17.00*
33 A2	2p red	5.50	.25
34 A2	2½p dp grn ('34)	7.50	*27.50*
35 A2	3p gray blue	6.00	1.25
36 A2	3½p magenta ('34)	15.00	*18.00*
37 A2	4p olive green	6.00	*7.00*
38 A2	5p slate green	7.00	.80
39 A2	6p bister	7.50	*4.00*
40 A2	9p dull violet	11.00	*25.00*
41 A2	1sh bluish gray	6.00	*11.50*
42 A2	2sh red brown	5.00	*19.00*
43 A2	5sh olive brown	30.00	*50.00*

44	A2	10sh rose red	60.00	*80.00*
45	A2	£1 gray	120.00	*110.00*
		Nos. 31-45 (15)	298.50	*371.55*

For overprints see #46-47, C28-C43, O23-O35. See footnote following C43.

Silver Jubilee Issue

Stamps of 1932-34 Overprinted

1935, June 27 **Glazed Paper**

46	A2	1p light green	1.10	.85
47	A2	2p red	3.25	.85
		Set, never hinged	6.50	

King George VI — A3

1937, May 18 **Engr.**

48	A3	2p salmon rose	.30	*1.60*
49	A3	3p blue	.30	*1.90*
50	A3	5p green	.35	*1.90*
51	A3	1sh brown violet	.45	*2.50*
		Nos. 48-51 (4)	1.40	*7.90*
		Set, never hinged	2.50	

Coronation of George VI and Queen Elizabeth.

AIR POST STAMPS

Regular Issues of 1925-28 Overprinted

1931, June ***Perf. 11***

C1	A1	½p orange	1.75	*8.50*
C2	A1	1p yellow green	1.75	*5.75*
C3	A1	1½p vermilion	1.40	*7.00*
C4	A1	2p claret	1.40	*8.00*
C5	A1	3p deep blue	2.00	*15.00*
C6	A1	4p olive green	1.40	*10.00*
C7	A1	6p light brown	2.00	*16.00*
C8	A1	9p deep violet	3.50	*19.00*
C9	A1	1sh gray green	3.50	*19.00*
C10	A1	2sh red brown	8.00	*47.50*
C11	A1	5sh ol bister	22.50	*75.00*
C12	A1	10sh light red	92.50	*120.00*
C13	A1	£1 grnsh gray	170.00	*290.00*
		Nos. C1-C13 (13)	311.70	*640.75*

Type of Regular Issue of 1931 and Nos. 18-30 Overprinted

1931, Aug.

C14	A2	½p orange	3.75	3.75
C15	A2	1p light green	4.50	*6.00*
C16	A2	1½p red	4.25	*11.50*
C17	A2	2p violet brown	4.25	3.50
C18	A2	3p deep blue	7.00	*7.00*
C19	A2	4p olive green	7.00	7.00
C20	A2	5p slate green	7.00	12.50
C21	A2	6p bister	8.00	*30.00*
C22	A2	9p dull violet	9.00	*17.00*
C23	A2	1sh bluish gray	8.50	*17.00*
C24	A2	2sh red brown	18.00	*55.00*
C25	A2	5sh olive brown	47.50	*80.00*
C26	A2	10sh rose red	87.50	*140.00*
C27	A2	£1 gray	150.00	*290.00*
		Nos. C14-C27 (14)	366.25	*680.25*

10th anniversary of Australian Mandate.

Same Overprint on Type of Regular Issue of 1932-34 and Nos. 31-45

1932-34 ***Perf. 11***

C28	A2	½p orange	.65	*1.75*
C29	A2	1p light green	1.40	*2.50*
C30	A2	1½p violet brown	2.00	*9.50*
C31	A2	2p red	2.00	*.35*
C32	A2	2½p dp grn ('34)	8.75	2.75
C33	A2	3p gray blue	3.75	3.50
C34	A2	3½p mag ('34)	5.25	*3.75*
C35	A2	4p olive green	5.00	*11.50*
C36	A2	5p slate green	8.00	*8.50*
C37	A2	6p bister	5.00	*17.00*
C38	A2	9p dull violet	7.00	*10.00*
C39	A2	1sh bluish gray	7.00	*10.00*
C40	A2	2sh red brown	11.50	*55.00*
C41	A2	5sh olive brown	55.00	*65.00*
C42	A2	10sh rose red	100.00	92.50
C43	A2	£1 gray	87.50	62.50
		Nos. C28-C43 (16)	309.80	*356.10*

No. C28 exists without overprint, but is believed not to have been issued in this condition. Value $200.

Plane over Bulolo Goldfield AP1

1935, May 1 **Engr.** **Unwmk.**

C44	AP1	£2 violet	350.00	160.00
C45	AP1	£5 green	750.00	550.00

AP2

1939, Mar. 1

C46	AP2	½p orange	2.50	*8.00*
C47	AP2	1p green	2.00	*5.00*
C48	AP2	1½p vio brown	2.25	*15.00*
C49	AP2	2p red orange	5.00	4.00
C50	AP2	3p dark blue	8.50	*21.00*
C51	AP2	4p ol bister	9.00	9.75
C52	AP2	5p slate grn	8.00	4.50
C53	AP2	6p bister brn	20.00	26.00
C54	AP2	9p dl violet	20.00	32.50
C55	AP2	1sh sage green	20.00	27.50
C56	AP2	2sh car lake	45.00	65.00
C57	AP2	5sh ol brown	85.00	130.00
C58	AP2	10sh rose red	325.00	350.00
C59	AP2	£1 grnsh gray	95.00	*130.00*
		Nos. C46-C59 (14)	647.25	828.25
		Set, never hinged	1,100.	

OFFICIAL STAMPS

Regular Issue of 1925 Overprinted

1925-29 **Unwmk.** ***Perf. 11***

O1	A1	1p yellow green	4.00	*5.00*
O2	A1	1½p vermilion ('29)	6.25	*19.00*
O3	A1	2p claret	2.75	*4.25*
O4	A1	3p deep blue	6.00	*10.00*
O5	A1	4p olive green	5.00	*9.75*
O6	A1	6p yel bister ('29)	8.00	*40.00*
a.		6p olive bister	25.00	*40.00*
O7	A1	9p deep violet	4.50	*40.00*
O8	A1	1sh gray green	6.25	*40.00*
O9	A1	2sh red brown	37.50	*70.00*
		Nos. O1-O9 (9)	80.25	*238.00*

Nos. 18-28 Overprinted

1931, Aug. 2

O12	A2	1p light green	12.00	*14.00*
O13	A2	1½p red	12.00	*13.50*
O14	A2	2p violet brown	12.00	*8.00*
O15	A2	3p deep blue	7.50	*7.00*
O16	A2	4p olive green	7.00	*9.75*
O17	A2	5p slate green	11.50	*13.50*
O18	A2	6p bister	16.00	*19.00*
O19	A2	9p dull violet	18.00	*32.50*
O20	A2	1sh bluish gray	18.00	*32.50*
O21	A2	2sh red brown	45.00	*80.00*
O22	A2	5sh olive brown	110.00	*200.00*
		Nos. O12-O22 (11)	269.00	*429.75*

10th anniversary of Australian Mandate.

Same Overprint on Nos. 31-43

1932-34

O23	A2	1p light green	17.00	*18.00*
O24	A2	1½p violet brown	18.00	*18.00*
O25	A2	2p red	18.00	*3.75*
O26	A2	2½p dp green ('34)	8.00	*8.25*
O27	A2	3p gray blue	11.00	*40.00*
O28	A2	3½p magenta ('34)	8.00	*10.00*
O29	A2	4p olive green	18.00	*30.00*
O30	A2	5p slate green	10.00	*30.00*
O31	A2	6p bister	22.50	*55.00*
O32	A2	9p dull violet	16.00	*47.50*
O33	A2	1sh bluish gray	17.50	*32.50*
O34	A2	2sh red brown	40.00	*85.00*
O35	A2	5sh olive brown	140.00	*190.00*
		Nos. O23-O35 (13)	344.00	*568.00*

NEW HEBRIDES, BRITISH

'nü 'he-brə-ˌdēz

LOCATION — A group of islands in the South Pacific Ocean northeast of New Caledonia

GOVT. — Condominium under the joint administration of Great Britain and France

AREA — 5,790 sq. mi.

POP. — 100,000 (est. 1976)

CAPITAL — Vila (Port-Vila)

Stamps were issued by both Great Britain and France. In 1911 a joint issue bore the coats of arms of both countries. The British stamps bore the arms of Great Britain and the value in British currency on the right and the French arms and value at the left. On the French stamps the positions were reversed. After World War II when the franc dropped in value, both series were sold for their value in francs.

New Hebrides became the independent state of Vanuatu in 1980.

12 Pence = 1 Shilling

100 Centimes = 1 Franc

100 Centimes = 1 Hebrides Franc (FNH) (1977)

French issues (inscribed "Nouvelles Hebrides") follow after No. J20.

Catalogue values for unused stamps in this country are for Never Hinged items, beginning with Scott 62 in the regular postage section, Scott J11 in the postage due section.

British Issues

Stamps of Fiji, 1903-06, Overprinted

1908-09 **Wmk. 2** ***Perf. 14***

Colored Bar Covers "FIJI" on #2-6, 9

1	A22	½p gray grn ('09)	60.00	*92.50*
2	A22	2p vio & orange	2.25	*2.50*
3	A22	2½p vio & ultra, *bl*	2.00	*2.50*
4	A22	5p vio & green	3.50	*4.00*
5	A22	6p vio & car rose	3.75	*3.50*
6	A22	1sh grn & car rose	145.00	*300.00*
		Nos. 1-6 (6)	216.50	*405.00*

Wmk. Multiple Crown and CA (3)

7	A22	½p gray green	1.00	*8.00*
8	A22	1p carmine	.60	*1.00*
a.		Pair, one without overprint	*10,000.*	
9	A22	1sh grn & car rose ('09)	27.50	*4.25*
		Nos. 7-9 (3)	29.10	*13.25*

Nos. 2-6, 9 are on chalk-surfaced paper.

Stamps of Fiji, 1904-11, Overprinted in Black or Red

1910, Dec. 15

10	A22	½p green	4.00	*30.00*
11	A22	1p carmine	11.00	*9.75*
12	A22	2p gray	.80	*3.50*
13	A22	2½p ultra	1.00	*6.00*
14	A22	5p violet & ol grn	2.25	*7.50*
15	A22	6p violet	4.00	*7.50*
16	A22	1sh black, *grn* (R)	6.00	*8.50*
		Nos. 10-16 (7)	29.05	*72.75*

Nos. 14-16 are on chalk-surfaced paper.

Native Idols — A1

1911, July 25 **Engr.** **Wmk. 3**

17	A1	½p pale green	1.00	*2.00*
18	A1	1p red	5.50	*2.25*
19	A1	2p gray	9.25	4.50
20	A1	2½p ultramarine	4.25	*6.25*
21	A1	5p olive green	5.00	*8.00*
22	A1	6p claret	3.50	*5.75*
23	A1	1sh black, *green*	3.00	*15.00*
24	A1	2sh violet, *blue*	40.00	*25.00*
25	A1	5sh green, *yel*	50.00	*55.00*
		Nos. 17-25 (9)	121.50	*123.75*

See Nos. 33-37. For surcharges see Nos. 26-29, 38-39, French Issues No. 36.

Surcharged

1920-21

26	A1	1p on 5p ol grn ('21)	10.00	*70.00*
a.		Inverted surcharge	4,500.	
27	A1	1p on 1sh blk, *grn*	4.00	*15.00*
28	A1	1p on 2sh vio, *blue*	1.75	*11.50*
29	A1	1p on 5sh grn, *yel*	1.75	*11.50*

On French Issue No. 16

30	A2	2p on 40c red, *yel* ('21)	2.00	*22.00*
		Nos. 26-30 (5)	19.50	*130.00*

French Issue No. 27

Wmk. R F in Sheet

31	A2	2p on 40c red, *yel* ('21)	145.00	*700.00*

The letters "R.F." are the initials of "Republique Francaise." They are large double-lined Roman capitals, about 120mm high. About one-fourth of the stamps in each sheet show portions of the watermark, the other stamps are without watermark.

No. 26a is considered by some to be printers' waste.

Type of 1911 Issue

1921, Oct. **Wmk. 4**

33	A1	1p rose red	3.00	*16.00*
34	A1	2p gray	5.00	*45.00*
37	A1	6p claret	16.00	*85.00*
		Nos. 33-37 (3)	24.00	*146.00*

For surcharge see No. 40.

Stamps of 1911-21 Surcharged with New Values as in 1920-21

1924, May 1 **Wmk. 3**

38 A1 1p on ½p pale green 4.50 *25.00*
39 A1 5p on 2½p ultra 8.50 *27.50*
a. Inverted surcharge 3,500.

Wmk. 4

40 A1 3p on 1p rose red 4.50 *12.50*
Nos. 38-40 (3) 17.50 *65.00*

No. 39a is considered by some to be printers' waste.

A3

The values at the lower right denote the currency and amount for which the stamps were to be sold. The English stamps could be bought at the French post office in French money.

1925 **Engr.**

41 A3 ½p (5c) black 1.40 *21.00*
42 A3 1p (10c) green 1.10 *19.00*
43 A3 2p (20c) grnsh gray 2.00 *3.00*
44 A3 2½p (25c) brown 1.10 *15.00*
45 A3 5p (50c) ultra 3.50 *3.00*
46 A3 6p (60c) claret 4.00 *16.00*
47 A3 1sh (1.25fr) blk, *grn* 3.75 *21.00*
48 A3 2sh (2.50fr) vio, *bl* 7.00 *25.00*
49 A3 5sh (6.25fr) grn, *yel* 7.00 *29.00*
Nos. 41-49 (9) 30.85 *152.00*

Beach Scene A5

1938, June 1 **Wmk. 4** ***Perf. 12***

50 A5 5c green 3.00 *4.50*
51 A5 10c dark orange 3.00 *2.25*
52 A5 15c violet 4.00 *4.50*
53 A5 20c rose red 3.75 *5.00*
54 A5 25c brown 1.90 *3.00*
55 A5 30c dark blue 4.50 *3.00*
56 A5 40c olive green 5.00 *7.00*
57 A5 50c brown vio 1.90 *3.00*
58 A5 1fr car, *emerald* 9.00 *9.75*
59 A5 2fr dk blue, *emer* 30.00 25.00
60 A5 5fr red, *yellow* 75.00 55.00
61 A5 10fr violet, *blue* 225.00 85.00
Nos. 50-61 (12) 366.05 207.00
Set, never hinged 500.00

Catalogue values for unused stamps in this section, from this point to the end of the section, are for Never Hinged items.

Common Design Types pictured following the introduction.

UPU Issue

Common Design Type

1949, Oct. 10 **Engr.** ***Perf. 13½***

62 CD309 10c red orange .30 *1.00*
63 CD309 15c violet .30 *1.00*
64 CD309 30c violet blue .40 *1.00*
65 CD309 50c rose violet .60 *1.10*
Nos. 62-65 (4) 1.60 *4.10*

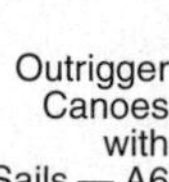

Outrigger Canoes with Sails — A6

Designs: 25c, 30c, 40c and 50c, Native Carving. 1fr, 2fr and 5fr, Island couple.

1953, Apr. 30 ***Perf. 12½***

66 A6 5c green 1.00 1.00
67 A6 10c red 1.00 .35
68 A6 15c yellow 1.00 .25
69 A6 20c ultramarine 1.00 .30
70 A6 25c olive 1.00 .40
71 A6 30c light brown 1.00 .50
72 A6 40c black brown 1.00 .80
73 A6 50c violet 1.25 .90
74 A6 1fr deep orange 6.25 1.75
75 A6 2fr red violet 6.25 *9.00*
76 A6 5fr scarlet 10.00 *22.50*
Nos. 66-76 (11) 30.75 *37.75*

Coronation Issue

Common Design Type

1953, June 2 ***Perf. 13½x13***

77 CD312 10c car & black .75 .60

Discovery of New Hebrides, 1606 — A7

20c, 50c, Britannia, Marianne, Flags & Mask.

Perf. 14½x14

1956, Oct. 20 **Photo.** **Wmk. 4**

78 A7 5c emerald .25 .25
79 A7 10c crimson .25 .25
80 A7 20c ultramarine .25 .25
81 A7 50c purple .25 .25
Nos. 78-81 (4) 1.00 1.00

50th anniv. of the establishment of the Anglo-French Condominium.

Port Vila and Iririki Islet — A8

Designs: 25c, 30c, 40c, 50c, Tropical river and spear fisherman. 1fr, 2fr, 5fr, Woman drinking from coconut (inscribed: "Franco-British Alliance 4th March 1947").

1957, Sept. 3 **Engr.** ***Perf. 13½x13***

82 A8 5c green .50 *1.25*
83 A8 10c red .35 .25
84 A8 15c orange yellow .60 *1.25*
85 A8 20c ultramarine .50 .25
86 A8 25c olive .60 .25
87 A8 30c light brown .60 .25
88 A8 40c sepia .60 .25
89 A8 50c violet .90 .25
90 A8 1fr orange 1.25 1.25
91 A8 2fr rose lilac 6.00 3.50
92 A8 5fr black 12.00 5.50
Nos. 82-92 (11) 23.90 14.25

Freedom from Hunger Issue

Common Design Type

Perf. 14x14½

1963, Sept. 2 **Photo.** **Wmk. 314**

93 CD314 60c green .60 .25

Red Cross Centenary Issue

Common Design Type with Royal Cipher and "RF" Replacing Queen's Portrait

1963, Sept. 2 **Litho.** ***Perf. 13***

94 CD315 15c black & red .40 .25
95 CD315 45c ultra & red .60 .25

Copra Industry A9

Designs: 5c, Manganese loading, Forari Wharf. 10c, Cacao. 20c, Map of New Hebrides, tuna, marlin, ships. 25c, Striped triggerfish. 30c, Pearly nautilus (mollusk). 40c, 60c, Turkeyfish. 50c, Lined tang (fish). 1fr, Cardinal honey-eater and hibiscus. 2fr, Buff-bellied flycatcher. 3fr, Thicket warbler. 5fr, White-collared kingfisher.

Wmk. 314 (10c, 20c, 40c, 60c, 3fr); Unwmkd. (others)

Perf. 12½ (10c, 20c, 40c, 60c); 14 (3fr); 13 (others)

Photo. (10c, 20c, 40c, 60c, 3fr); Engraved (others)

1963-67

96 A9 5c Prus bl, pur brn & cl ('66) 1.75 .50
a. 5c prus blue & claret ('72) 45.00 37.50
97 A9 10c brt grn, org brn & dk brn ('65) .25 .25
98 A9 15c dk pur, yel & brn .25 .25
99 A9 20c brt blue, gray & cit ('65) .55 .25
100 A9 25c vio, rose lil & org brn ('66) .75 .50
101 A9 30c lilac, brn & cit 1.00 .75
102 A9 40c dk bl & ver ('65) 1.25 1.50
103 A9 50c Prus bl, yel & green 1.10 .80
103A A9 60c dk bl & ver ('67) 1.00 .50
104 A9 1fr blue grn, blk & red ('66) 3.00 3.50
105 A9 2fr ol, blk & brn 4.00 2.00
106 A9 3fr org grn, brt grn & blk ('65) 10.00 7.00
107 A9 5fr indigo, dp bl & gray ('67) 15.00 *20.00*
Nos. 96-107 (13) 39.90 37.80

For surcharge see No. 141.

ITU Emblem CD317

Perf. 11x11½

1965, May 17 **Litho.** **Wmk. 314**

108 CD317 15c ver & ol bister .25 .25
109 CD317 60c ultra & ver .40 .25

Intl. Cooperation Year Issue

Common Design Type with Royal Cipher and "RF" Replacing Queen's Portrait

1965, Sept. 24 ***Perf. 14½***

110 CD318 5c blue grn & claret .25 .25
111 CD318 55c lt violet & green .25 .25

Churchill Memorial Issue

Common Design Type with Royal Cipher and "RF" Replacing Queen's Portrait

1966, Jan. 24 **Photo.** ***Perf. 14***

112 CD319 5c multicolored .30 .25
113 CD319 15c multicolored .50 .25
114 CD319 25c multicolored .75 .25
115 CD319 30c multicolored .75 .25
Nos. 112-115 (4) 2.30 1.00

World Cup Soccer Issue

Common Design Type with Royal Cipher and "RF" Replacing Queen's Portrait

1966, July 1 **Litho.** ***Perf. 14***

116 CD321 20c multicolored .30 .30
117 CD321 40c multicolored .70 .70

WHO Headquarters Issue

Common Design Type with Royal Cipher and "RF" Replacing Queen's Portrait

1966, Sept. 20 **Litho.** ***Perf. 14***

118 CD322 25c multicolored .25 .25
119 CD322 60c multicolored .50 .25

UNESCO Anniversary Issue

Common Design Type with Royal Cipher and "RF" Replacing Queen's Portrait

1966, Dec. 1 **Litho.** ***Perf. 14***

120 CD323 15c "Education" .35 .35
121 CD323 30c "Science" .60 .60
122 CD323 45c "Culture" .95 .95
Nos. 120-122 (3) 1.90 1.90

Coast Watchers — A11

25c, Map of South Pacific war zone, US Marine and Australian soldier. 60c, Australian cruiser Canberra. 1fr, Flying fortress taking off from Bauer Field, & view of Vila.

Perf. 14x13

1967, Sept. 26 **Photo.** **Wmk. 314**

123 A11 15c lt blue & multi .25 .25
124 A11 25c yellow & multi .30 .30
125 A11 60c multicolored .75 .75
126 A11 1fr pale salmon & multi 1.00 1.00
Nos. 123-126 (4) 2.30 2.30

25th anniv. of the Allied Forces' campaign in the South Pacific War Zone.

Globe and World Map A12

Designs: 25c, Ships La Boudeuse and L'Etoile and map of Bougainville Strait. 60c, Louis Antoine de Bougainville, ship's figure-head and bougainvillaea.

1968, May 23 **Engr.** ***Perf. 13***

127 A12 15c ver, emer & dull vio .25 .25
128 A12 25c ultra, olive & brn .25 .25
129 A12 60c magenta, grn & brn .30 .25
Nos. 127-129 (3) .80 .75

200th anniv. of Louis Antoine de Bougainville's (1729-1811) voyage around the world.

Concorde Airliner A13

Design: 60c, Concorde, sideview.

1968, Oct. 9 **Litho.** ***Perf. 14x13½***

130 A13 25c vio bl, red & lt bl .30 .25
131 A13 60c red, ultra & black .60 .50

Development of the Concorde supersonic airliner, a joint Anglo-French project to produce a high speed plane.

Kauri Pine — A14

Perf. 14x14½

1969, June 30 **Wmk. 314**

132 A14 20c brown & multi .30 .30

New Hebrides timber industry. Issued in sheets of 9 (3x3) on simulated wood grain background.

Relay Race, French and British Flags — A15

Design: 1fr, Runner at right.

Perf. 12½x13

1969, Aug. 13 **Photo.** **Unwmk.**

133 A15 25c ultra, car, brn & gold .25 .25
134 A15 1fr brn, car, ultra & gold .25 .25

3rd South Pacific Games, Port Moresby, Papua and New Guinea, Aug. 13-23.

Land Diver, Pentecost Island — A16

Designs: 15c, Diver in starting position on tower. 1fr, Diver nearing ground.

Wmk. 314

1969, Oct. 15 Litho. *Perf. 12½*

135 A16 15c yellow & multi .25 .25
136 A16 25c pink & multi .25 .25
137 A16 1fr gray & multi .25 .25
Nos. 135-137 (3) .75 .75

UPU Headquarters and Monument, Bern — A17

Unwmk.

1970, May 20 Engr. *Perf. 13*

138 A17 1.05fr org, lilac & slate .30 .30

Opening of the new UPU Headquarters, Bern.

Charles de Gaulle — A18

1970, July 20 Photo. *Perf. 13*

139 A18 65c brown & multi .25 .25
140 A18 1.10fr dp blue & multi .75 .75

30th anniv. of the rallying to the Free French.
For overprints see Nos. 144-145.

No. 99 Surcharged

1970, Oct. 15 Wmk. 314 *Perf. 12½*

141 A9 35c on 20c multi .30 .30

Virgin and Child, by Giovanni Bellini — A19

Christmas: 50c, Virgin and Child, by Giovanni Cima.

Perf. 14½x14

1970, Nov. 30 Litho. Wmk. 314

142 A19 15c tan & multi .25 .25
143 A19 50c lt green & multi .25 .25

Nos. 139-140 Overprinted with 2 Black Vertical Bars and Gold Inscription: "1890-1970 / IN MEMORIAM / 9-11-70"

Unwmk.

1971, Jan. 19 Photo. *Perf. 13*

144 A18 65c brown & multi .25 .25
145 A18 1.10fr dp blue & multi .35 .35

In memory of Gen. Charles de Gaulle (1890-1970), President of France.

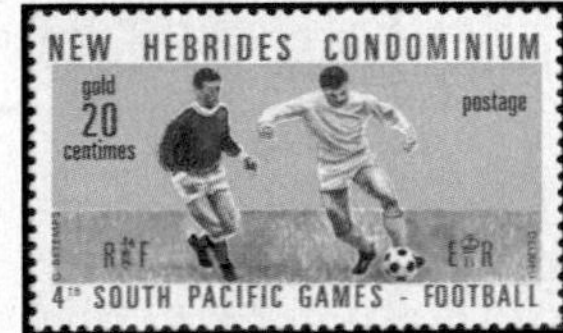

Soccer — A20

Design: 65c, Basketball, vert.

1971, July 13 Photo. *Perf. 12½*

146 A20 20c multicolored .25 .25
147 A20 65c multicolored .25 .25

4th South Pacific Games, Papeete, French Polynesia, Sept. 8-19.

Kauri Pine, Cone and Arms of Royal Society — A21

Perf. 14½x14

1971, Sept. 7 Litho. Wmk. 314

148 A21 65c multicolored .30 .30

Royal Society of London for the Advancement of Science expedition to study vegetation and fauna, July 1-October.

Adoration of the Shepherds, by Louis Le Nain — A22

Design: 50c, Adoration of the Shepherds, by Jacopo Tintoretto.

1971, Nov. 23 *Perf. 14x13½*

149 A22 25c lt green & multi .25 .25
150 A22 50c lt blue & multi .25 .25

Christmas. See Nos. 167-168.

Drover Mk III — A23

Airplanes: 25c, Sandringham seaplane. 30c, Dragon Rapide. 65c, Caravelle.

Perf. 13½x13

1972, Feb. 29 Photo. Unwmk.

151 A23 20c lt green & multi .25 .25
152 A23 25c ultra & multi .25 .25
153 A23 30c orange & multi .45 .45
154 A23 65c dk blue & multi .90 .90
Nos. 151-154 (4) 1.85 1.85

Headdress, South Malekula — A24

Baker's Pigeon — A25

Artifacts: 15c, Slit gong and carved figure, North Ambrym. 1fr, Carved figures, North Ambrym. 3fr, Ceremonial headdress, South Malekula.

Birds: 20c, Red-headed parrot-finch. 35c, Chestnut-bellied kingfisher. 2fr, Green palm lorikeet.

Sea shells: 25c, Cribraria fischeri. 30c, Oliva rubrolabiata. 65c, Strombus plicatus. 5fr, Turbo marmoratus.

1972, July 24 Photo. *Perf. 12½x13*

155 A24 5c plum & multi .25 .25
156 A25 10c blue & multi .25 .25
157 A24 15c red & multi .30 .40
158 A25 20c org brown & multi .35 .50
159 A24 25c dp blue & multi .50 .80
160 A24 30c dk green & multi .65 .85
161 A25 35c gray bl & multi .70 1.10
162 A24 65c dk green & multi 1.25 3.75
163 A24 1fr orange & multi 2.00 3.00
164 A25 2fr multicolored 4.50 4.50
165 A24 3fr yellow & multi 5.75 6.75
166 A24 5fr pink & multi 9.00 13.50
Nos. 155-166 (12) 25.50 35.65

For overprints and surcharges see #181-182, 217-228.

Christmas Type of 1971

Designs: 25c, Adoration of the Magi (detail), by Bartholomaeus Spranger. 70c, Virgin and Child, by Jan Provoost.

Perf. 14x13½

1972, Sept. 25 Litho. Wmk. 314

167 A22 25c lt green & multi .25 .25
168 A22 70c lt blue & multi .25 .25

Silver Wedding Issue, 1972

Common Design Type

Design: Elizabeth II and Prince Philip.

1972, Nov. 20 Photo. *Perf. 14x14½*

169 CD324 35c vio black & multi .25 .25
170 CD324 65c olive & multi .25 .25

Dendrobium Teretifolium — A26

Orchids: 30c, Ephemerantha comata. 35c, Spathoglottis petri. 65c, Dendrobium mohlianum.

1973, Feb. 26 Litho. *Perf. 14*

171 A26 25c blue vio & multi .40 .25
172 A26 30c multicolored .60 .35
173 A26 35c violet & multi .75 .45
174 A26 65c dk green & multi 1.25 .60
Nos. 171-174 (4) 3.00 1.65

New Wharf, Vila — A27

Design: 70c, New wharf, horiz.

1973, May 14 Wmk. 314

175 A27 25c multicolored .25 .25
176 A27 70c multicolored .30 .30

New wharf at Vila, finished Nov. 1972.

Wild Horses, Tanna Island A28

70c, Yasur Volcano, Tanna.

Perf. 13x12½

1973, Aug. 13 Photo. Unwmk.

177 A28 35c shown .45 .45
178 A28 70c multicolored 1.25 .90

Mother and Child, by Marcel Moutouh — A29

Christmas: 70c, Star over Lagoon, by Tatin d'Avesnieres.

Perf. 14x13½

1973, Nov. 19 Litho. Wmk. 314

179 A29 35c tan & multi .25 .25
180 A29 70c lilac rose & multi .25 .25

Nos. 161 and 164 Overprinted in Red or Black: "ROYAL VISIT / 1974"

Perf. 12½x13

1974, Feb. 11 Photo. Unwmk.

181 A25 35c multicolored (R) .35 .25
182 A25 2fr multicolored (B) .75 .60

Visit of British Royal Family, Feb. 11-12.

Pacific Dove A30

Designs: 35c, Night swallowtail. 70c, Green sea turtle. 1.15fr, Flying fox.

1974, Feb. 11 *Perf. 13x12½*

183 A30 25c gray & multi .75 .25
184 A30 35c gray & multi 1.10 .30
185 A30 70c gray & multi 1.90 1.00
186 A30 1.15fr gray & multi 3.25 1.75
Nos. 183-186 (4) 7.00 3.30

Nature conservation.

Old Post Office, Vila — A31

Design: 70c, New Post Office.

1974, May 6 Unwmk. *Perf. 12*
187 A31 35c blue & multi .25 .25
188 A31 70c red & multi .25 .25
a. Pair, #187-188 .50 .50

Opening of New Post Office, May, 1974.

Capt. Cook and Tanna Island A32

#190, William Wales, & boat landing on island. #191, William Hodges painting islanders & landscape. 1.15fr, Capt. Cook, "Resolution" & map of New Hebrides.

Wmk. 314
1974, Aug. 1 Litho. *Perf. 13*
Size: 40x25mm
189 A32 35c multicolored 1.50 1.00
190 A32 35c multicolored 1.50 1.00
191 A32 35c multicolored 1.50 1.00
a. Strip of 3, #189-191 4.75 *5.50*

Perf. 11
Size: 58x34mm
192 A32 1.15fr lilac & multi 3.00 3.00
Nos. 189-192 (4) 7.50 6.00

Bicentenary of the discovery of the New Hebrides by Capt. Cook. No. 191a has continuous design.

Exchange of Letters, UPU Emblem A33

Perf. 13x12½
1974, Oct. 9 Photo. Unwmk.
193 A33 70c multicolored .30 .30

Centenary of Universal Postal Union.

Nativity, by Gerard van Honthorst — A34

Christmas: 35c, Adoration of the Kings, by Velazquez, vert.

Wmk. 314
1974, Nov. 14 Litho. *Perf. 13½*
194 A34 35c multicolored .25 .25
195 A34 70c multicolored .25 .25

Charolais Bull — A35

1975, Apr. 29 Engr. *Perf. 13*
196 A35 10fr multicolored 10.00 *20.00*

For surcharge see No. 229.

A36

1975, Aug. 5 Litho. *Perf. 14x13½*
197 A36 25c Kayak race .25 .25
198 A36 35c Camp cooks .25 .25
199 A36 1fr Map makers .65 .65
200 A36 5fr Fishermen 4.50 4.50
Nos. 197-200 (4) 5.65 5.65

Nordjamb 75, 14th Boy Scout Jamboree, Lillehammer, Norway, July 29-Aug. 7.

A37

Christmas (After Michelangelo): 35c, Pitti Madonna. 70c, Bruges Madonna. 2.50fr, Taddei Madonna.

Perf. 14½x14
1975, Nov. 11 Litho. Wmk. 373
201 A37 35c ol green & multi .25 .25
202 A37 70c brown & multi .45 .45
203 A37 2.50fr blue & multi 1.40 1.40
Nos. 201-203 (3) 2.10 2.10

Concorde, British Airways Colors and Emblem — A38

Unwmk.
1976, Jan. 30 Typo. *Perf. 13*
204 A38 5fr blue & multi 7.50 7.50

First commercial flight of supersonic jet Concorde from London to Bahrain, Jan. 21.

Telephones, 1876 and 1976 — A39

Designs: 70c, Alexander Graham Bell. 1.15fr, Nouméa earth station and satellite.

1976, Mar. 31 Photo. *Perf. 13*
205 A39 25c black, car & blue .30 .30
206 A39 70c black & multi .40 .40
207 A39 1.15fr black, org & vio bl 1.00 1.00
Nos. 205-207 (3) 1.70 1.70

Centenary of first telephone call by Alexander Graham Bell, Mar. 10, 1876.

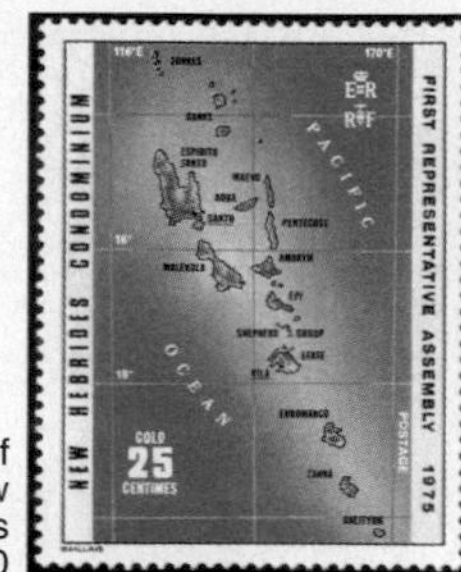

Map of New Hebrides A40

View of Santo A41

Design: 2fr, View of Vila.

1976, June 29 Photo. *Perf. 13*
208 A40 25c blue & multi .30 .30
209 A41 1fr multicolored .70 .70
210 A41 2fr multicolored 1.50 1.50
Nos. 208-210 (3) 2.50 2.50

Opening of First Representative Assembly, June 29 (25c); first Santo Municipal Council (1fr); first Vila Municipal Council (2fr).

See Nos. 263-264 for types of design A40 surcharged.

Flight into Egypt, by Francisco Vieira Lusitano — A42

Christmas (Portuguese 16th Cent. Paintings): 70c, Adoration of the Shepherds. 2.50fr, Adoration of the Kings.

Wmk. 373
1976, Nov. 8 Litho. *Perf. 14*
211 A42 35c purple & multi .25 .25
212 A42 70c blue & multi .25 .25
213 A42 2.50fr lt green & multi .60 .60
Nos. 211-213 (3) 1.10 1.10

Queen's Visit, 1974 — A43

70c, Imperial state crown. 2fr, The blessing.

1977, Feb. 7 *Perf. 14x13½*
214 A43 35c lt green & multi .25 .25
215 A43 70c blue & multi .25 .25
216 A43 2fr pink & multi .25 .25
Nos. 214-216 (3) .75 .75

25th anniv. of the reign of Elizabeth II.

Nos. 155-166, 196 Surcharged

Paris Overprints

Perf. 12½x13
1977, July 1 Photo. Unwmk.
217 A24 5fr on 5c multi .50 *.60*
218 A25 10fr on 10c multi .80 .40
219 A24 15fr on 15c multi .65 *1.75*
220 A25 20fr on 20c multi 1.30 .60
221 A24 25fr on 25c multi 1.75 2.00
222 A24 30fr on 30c multi 1.75 1.25
223 A25 35fr on 35c multi 1.75 1.50
224 A24 40fr on 65c multi 1.50 1.50
225 A24 50fr on 1fr multi 1.10 2.00
226 A25 70fr on 2fr multi 6.75 1.00
227 A24 100fr on 3fr multi 1.20 *4.00*
228 A24 200fr on 5fr multi 5.50 *14.00*

Wmk. 314
Engr. *Perf. 13*
229 A35 500fr on 10fr multi 15.00 17.50
Nos. 217-229 (13) 39.55 48.10

Nos. 155//166, 196 Surcharged with New Value, "FNH" and Bars

FNH FNH FNH 25 FNH
a b c d

Port Vila Overprints

Two settings of 35fr and 200fr surcharges: type 1, 1.4mm between new value and "FNH"; type 2, 2.1mm between value and "FNH."

Perf. 12½x13
1977-78 Photo. Unwmk.
217a A24 5fr on 5c (a) .60 .25
218a A25 10fr on 10c (b) .85 .25
219a A24 15fr on 15c (c) 2.00 1.00
221a A24 25fr on 25c (d) 60.00 24.00
222a A24 30fr on 30c (d) 275.00 75.00

223a A25 35fr on 35c (d), type 1 3.50 .90
b. Type 2 6.00 1.20
224a A24 40fr on 65c (d) 1.75 .65
225a A24 50fr on 1fr (d) 50.00 30.00
227a A24 100fr on (d) 50.00 *30.00*
228a A24 200fr on 5fr (d), type 1 20.00 15.00
b. Type 2 — —
229a A35 500fr on 10fr (d) 22.50 16.00
Nos. 217a-229a (11) 486.20 193.05

The 50fr and 100fr values were sold only through the philatelic bureau.

Issued: 10fr, 7/10; 15fr, 7/18; 5fr, 8/10; #228a, 8/22; 25fr, 30fr, #223a, 9/10; 40fr, 9/12; 500fr, 9/14; #223b, 1/6/78; #228b, 1/13/78.

Erromango and Kaori Tree — A44

Designs: 10fr, Archipelago and man making copra. 15fr, Espiritu Santo Island and cattle. 20fr, Efate Island and Post Office, Vila. 25fr, Malakula Island and headdresses. 30fr, Aoba and Maewo Islands and pig tusks. 35fr, Pentecost Island and land diving. 40fr, Tanna Island and Prophet John Frum's Red Cross. 50fr, Shepherd Island and canoe with sail. 70fr, Banks Island and dancers. 100fr, Ambrym Island and carvings. 200fr, Aneityum Island and decorated baskets. 500fr, Torres Islands and fishing with bow and arrow.

1977-78 Wmk. 373 Litho. *Perf. 14*

238 A44 5fr multicolored .25 .25
239 A44 10fr multicolored .25 .25
240 A44 15fr multicolored .25 .25
241 A44 20fr multicolored .30 .30
242 A44 25fr multicolored .40 .40
243 A44 30fr multicolored .50 .50
244 A44 35fr multicolored .55 .55
245 A44 40fr multicolored .60 .60
246 A44 50fr multicolored 1.25 .75
247 A44 70fr multicolored 1.50 *2.00*
248 A44 100fr multicolored 1.75 1.25
249 A44 200fr multicolored 2.50 2.50
250 A44 500fr multicolored 5.50 7.50
Nos. 238-250 (13) 15.60 17.10

Issue dates: 5fr, 20fr, 50fr, 100fr, 200fr, Sept. 7; 15fr, 25fr, 30fr, 40fr, Nov. 23, 1977; 10fr, 35fr, 70fr, 500fr, May 9, 1978.

Tempi Madonna, by Raphael — A45

Christmas: 15fr, Virgin and Child, by Gerard David. 30fr, Virgin and Child, by Pompeo Batoni.

1977, Dec. 8 Litho. *Perf. 12*

251 A45 10fr multicolored .25 .25
252 A45 15fr multicolored .25 .25
253 A45 30fr multicolored .30 .30
Nos. 251-253 (3) .80 .80

British Airways Concorde over New York City — A46

20fr, British Airways Concorde over London. 30fr, Air France Concorde over Washington. 40fr, Air France Concorde over Paris.

1978, May 9 Wmk. 373 *Perf. 14*

254 A46 10fr multicolored .85 .50
255 A46 20fr multicolored 1.10 1.10
256 A46 30fr multicolored 1.50 1.50
257 A46 40fr multicolored 1.75 1.75
Nos. 254-257 (4) 5.20 4.85

Concorde, 1st commercial flight, Paris to NYC.

Elizabeth II Coronation Anniversary Issue

Common Design Types
Souvenir Sheet

1978, June 2 Unwmk. *Perf. 15*

258 Sheet of 6 1.75 1.75
a. CD326 40fr White horse of Hanover .25 .25
b. CD327 40fr Elizabeth II .25 .25
c. CD328 40fr Gallic cock .25 .25

No. 258 contains 2 se-tenant strips of Nos. 258a-258c, separated by horizontal gutter with commemorative and descriptive inscriptions and showing central part of coronation procession with coach.

Virgin and Child, by Dürer — A47

Dürer Paintings: 15fr, Virgin and Child with St. Anne. 30fr, Virgin and Child with Goldfinch. 40fr, Virgin and Child with Pear.

Perf. 14x13½

1978, Dec. 1 Litho. Wmk. 373

259 A47 10fr multicolored .25 .25
260 A47 15fr multicolored .25 .25
261 A47 30fr multicolored .25 .25
262 A47 40fr multicolored .25 .25
Nos. 259-262 (4) 1.00 1.00

Christmas and 450th death anniv. of Albrecht Dürer (1471-1528), German painter.

Type of 1976 Surcharged with New Value, Bars over Denomination and Inscription at Right. Longitude changed to "166E."

1979, Jan. 11 Photo. *Perf. 13*

263 A40 10fr on 25c bl & multi .25 .25
264 A40 40fr on 25c lt grn & multi .25 .25

1st anniv. of Internal Self-Government.

New Hebrides No. 50 — A48

Rowland Hill and New Hebrides Stamps: 20fr, No. 136. 40fr, No. 43.

1979, Sept. 10 Litho. *Perf. 14*

265 A48 10fr multicolored .25 .25
266 A48 20fr multicolored .25 .25
a. Souvenir sheet of 2 .90 .90
267 A48 40fr multicolored .40 .40
Nos. 265-267 (3) .90 .90

Sir Rowland Hill (1795-1879), originator of penny postage. No. 266a contains New Hebrides, British, No. 266, and French, No. 286; margin shows Mulready envelope.

Arts Festival — A49

Designs: 10fr, Clubs and spears. 20fr, Ritual puppet. 40fr, Headdress.

1979, Nov. 16 Wmk. 373 *Perf. 14*

268 A49 5fr multicolored .25 .25
269 A49 10fr multicolored .25 .25
270 A49 20fr multicolored .25 .25
271 A49 40fr multicolored .40 .40
Nos. 268-271 (4) 1.15 1.15

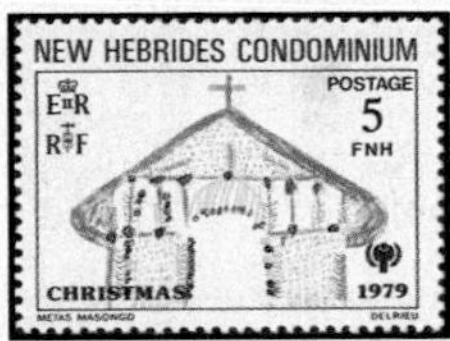

Church, IYC Emblem A50

IYC Emblem, Children's Drawings: 10fr, Father Christmas. 20fr, Cross and Bible, vert. 40fr, Stars, candle and Santa Claus, vert.

1979, Dec. 4 *Perf. 13x13½*

272 A50 5fr multicolored .25 .25
273 A50 10fr multicolored .25 .25
274 A50 20fr multicolored .25 .25
275 A50 40fr multicolored .35 .35
Nos. 272-275 (4) 1.10 1.10

Christmas; Intl. Year of the Child.

White-bellied Honeyeater — A51

1980, Feb. 27 Litho. *Perf. 14*

276 A51 10fr shown .85 .25
277 A51 20fr Scarlet robins 1.10 .45
278 A51 30fr Yellow white-eyes 1.50 .65
279 A51 40fr Fan-tailed brush cuckoo 1.75 .85
Nos. 276-279 (4) 5.20 2.20

New Hebrides stamps were replaced in 1980 by those of Vanuatu.

POSTAGE DUE STAMPS

British Issues

Type of 1925 Overprinted

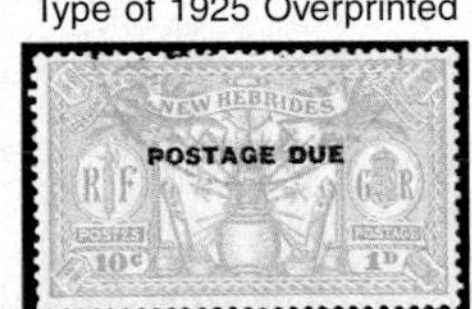

1925, June Engr. Wmk. 4 *Perf. 14*

J1 A3 1p (10c) green 37.50 1.25
J2 A3 2p (20c) gray 40.00 1.25
J3 A3 3p (30c) carmine 40.00 3.25
J4 A3 5p (50c) ultra 45.00 5.50
J5 A3 10p (1fr) car, *blue* 52.50 6.50
Nos. J1-J5 (5) 215.00 17.75

Values for Nos. J1-J5 are for toned stamps.

Regular Stamps of 1938 Overprinted in Black

1938, June 1 *Perf. 12*

J6 A5 5c green 20.00 *32.50*
J7 A5 10c dark orange 20.00 *32.50*
J8 A5 20c rose red 22.50 *50.00*
J9 A5 40c olive green 27.50 *57.50*
J10 A5 1fr car, *emerald* 35.00 *67.50*
Nos. J6-J10 (5) 125.00 *240.00*

Catalogue values for unused stamps in this section, from this point to the end of the section, are for Never Hinged items.

Regular Stamps of 1953 Overprinted in Black

1953, Apr. 30 *Perf. 12½*

J11 A6 5c green 4.75 *13.50*
J12 A6 10c red 2.25 *11.00*
J13 A6 20c ultramarine 6.00 *20.00*
J14 A6 40c black brown 8.50 *37.50*
J15 A6 1fr deep orange 5.50 *45.00*
Nos. J11-J15 (5) 27.00 *127.00*

Same on Nos. 82-83, 85, 88 and 90

1957, Sept. 3 *Perf. 13½x13*

J16 A8 5c green .25 *1.00*
J17 A8 10c red .35 *1.25*
J18 A8 20c ultramarine .75 *1.50*
J19 A8 40c sepia 1.00 *2.50*
J20 A8 1fr orange 2.00 *3.50*
Nos. J16-J20 (5) 4.35 *9.75*

NEW HEBRIDES, FRENCH

'nü 'he-brə-ˌdēz

LOCATION — A group of islands in the South Pacific Ocean lying north of New Caledonia

GOVT. — Condominium under the joint administration of Great Britain and France

AREA — 5,790 sq. mi.

POP. — 100,000 (est. 1976)

CAPITAL — Port-Vila (Vila)

Postage stamps are issued by both Great Britain and France. In 1911 a joint issue was made bearing the coats of arms of both countries. The British stamps bore the coat of arms of Great Britain and the value in British currency on the right and the French coat of arms and values at the left. On the French stamps the positions were reversed. This resulted in some confusion when the value of the French franc decreased following World War I but the situation was corrected by arranging that both series of stamps be sold for their value as expressed in French currency.

12 Pence = 1 Shilling

100 Centimes = 1 Franc

New Hebrides Franc (FNH) — 1977

Catalogue values for unused stamps in this country are for Never Hinged items, beginning with Scott 79 in the regular postage section, Scott J16 in the postage due section.

French Issues

Stamps of New Caledonia, 1905, Overprinted in Black or Red

Nos. 1-4

No. 5

1908 Unwmk. *Perf. 14x13½*

No.	Type	Description	Unused	Used
1	A16	5c green	11.00	*5.50*
2	A16	10c rose	11.00	*6.75*
3	A17	25c blue, *grnsh* (R)	9.50	*11.00*
4	A17	50c carmine, *org*	8.50	*12.00*
5	A18	1fr bl, *yel grn* (R)	26.00	*24.00*
		Nos. 1-5 (5)	66.00	*59.25*

For overprints and surcharges see #6-10, 33-35.

Stamps of 1908 with Additional Overprint

1910

No.	Type	Description	Unused	Used
6	A16	5c green	8.00	*3.00*
7	A16	10c rose	8.00	*3.00*
8	A17	25c blue, *grnsh* (R)	3.50	*6.00*
9	A17	50c car, *orange*	11.00	*25.00*
10	A18	1fr bl, *yel grn* (R)	28.00	*22.50*
		Nos. 6-10 (5)	58.50	*59.50*

A2

Perf. 14

1911, July 12 Engr. Wmk. 3

No.	Type	Description	Unused	Used
11	A2	5c pale green	1.00	*3.00*
12	A2	10c red	.55	*1.10*
13	A2	20c gray	2.00	*4.00*
14	A2	25c ultramarine	2.75	*7.00*
15	A2	30c vio, *yellow*	6.50	*8.00*
16	A2	40c red, *yellow*	4.00	*8.00*
17	A2	50c olive green	4.00	*8.00*
18	A2	75c brn orange	7.00	*30.00*
19	A2	1fr brn red, *bl*	6.00	*7.00*
20	A2	2fr violet	12.00	*22.50*
21	A2	5fr brn red, *grn*	14.00	*47.50*
		Nos. 11-21 (11)	59.80	*146.10*

For surcharges see Nos. 36-37, 43 and British issue No. 30.

1912 Wmk. R F in Sheet

No.	Type	Description	Unused	Used
22	A2	5c pale green	1.75	*5.50*
23	A2	10c red	1.75	*6.00*
24	A2	20c gray	2.10	*2.40*
25	A2	25c ultramarine	2.50	*7.00*
26	A2	30c vio, *yellow*	2.50	*17.00*
27	A2	40c red, *yellow*	24.00	*80.00*
28	A2	50c olive green	18.00	*30.00*
29	A2	75c brn orange	9.00	*42.50*
30	A2	1fr brn red, *bl*	9.00	*10.00*
31	A2	2fr violet	9.25	*50.00*
32	A2	5fr brn red, *grn*	32.50	*60.00*
		Nos. 22-32 (11)	112.35	310.40

In the watermark, "R F" (République Française initials) are large double-lined Roman capitals, about 120mm high. About one-fourth of the stamps in each sheet show parts of the watermark. The other stamps are without watermark.

For surcharges see Nos. 38-42 and British issue No. 31.

Nos. 9 and 8 Surcharged

1920 Unwmk. *Perf. 14x13½*

No.	Type	Description	Unused	Used
33	A17	5c on 50c red, *org*	2.50	*22.00*
34	A17	10c on 25c bl, *grnsh*	1.00	*1.50*

Same Surcharge on No. 4

No.	Type	Description	Unused	Used
35	A17	5c on 50c red, *org*	900.00	*1,100.*

British Issue No. 21 and French Issue No. 15 Surcharged

1921 Wmk. 3 *Perf. 14*

No.	Type	Description	Unused	Used
36	A1	10c on 5p ol grn	16.00	*60.00*
37	A2	20c on 30c vio, *yel*	15.00	*70.00*

Nos. 27 and 26 Surcharged

1921 Wmk. R F in Sheet

No.	Type	Description	Unused	Used
38	A2	5c on 40c red, *yel*	27.50	*100.00*
39	A2	20c on 30c vio, *yel*	11.50	*80.00*

Stamps of 1910-12 Surcharged with New Values as in 1920-21

1924

No.	Type	Description	Unused	Used
40	A2	10c on 5c pale grn	2.75	11.00
41	A2	30c on 10c red	2.75	3.00
42	A2	50c on 25c ultra	4.50	20.00

Wmk. 3

No.	Type	Description	Unused	Used
43	A2	50c on 25c ultra	40.00	*110.00*
		Nos. 40-43 (4)	50.00	144.00

A4

The values at the lower right denote the currency and amount for which the stamps were to be sold. The stamps could be purchased at the French post office and used to pay postage at the English rates.

1925 Engr. Wmk. R F in Sheet

No.	Type	Description	Unused	Used
44	A4	5c (½p) black	.90	*13.00*
45	A4	10c (1p) green	1.00	*9.00*
46	A4	20c (2p) grnsh gray	3.75	*3.75*
47	A4	25c (2½p) brown	1.50	*9.00*
48	A4	30c (3p) carmine	1.75	*18.00*
49	A4	40c (4p) car, *org*	2.50	*16.00*
50	A4	50c (5p) ultra	2.00	*11.00*
51	A4	75c (7½p) bis brn	1.75	*22.00*
52	A4	1fr (10p) car, *blue*	3.00	*14.50*
53	A4	2fr (1sh 8p) gray vio	3.50	37.50
54	A4	5fr (4sh) car, *grnsh*	7.00	*37.50*
		Nos. 44-54 (11)	28.65	*191.25*

For overprints see Nos. J1-J5.

Beach Scene A6

1938 *Perf. 12*

No.	Type	Description	Unused	Used
55	A6	5c green	2.50	*9.00*
56	A6	10c dark orange	2.50	*3.25*
57	A6	15c violet	2.50	*8.00*
58	A6	20c rose red	2.50	*5.50*
59	A6	25c brown	5.50	*7.50*
60	A6	30c dark blue	5.50	*8.00*
61	A6	40c olive grn	2.75	*15.00*
62	A6	50c brown violet	2.75	*5.00*
63	A6	1fr dk car, *grn*	3.75	*8.00*
64	A6	2fr blue, *grn*	25.00	*40.00*
65	A6	5fr red, *yellow*	37.50	*65.00*
66	A6	10fr vio, *blue*	80.00	*150.00*
		Nos. 55-66 (12)	172.75	*324.25*
		Set, never hinged	360.00	

For overprints see Nos. 67-78, J6-J15.

Stamps of 1938 Ovptd. in Black

1941

No.	Type	Description	Unused	Used
67	A6	5c green	3.00	*25.00*
68	A6	10c dark orange	4.00	*24.00*
69	A6	15c violet	5.50	*40.00*
70	A6	20c rose red	15.00	*30.00*
71	A6	25c brown	16.00	*40.00*
72	A6	30c dark blue	16.00	*35.00*
73	A6	40c olive green	16.00	*40.00*
74	A6	50c brn violet	14.00	*35.00*
75	A6	1fr dk car, *grn*	14.00	*37.50*
76	A6	2fr blue, *grn*	14.00	*37.50*
77	A6	5fr red, *yellow*	15.00	*42.50*
78	A6	10fr vio, *blue*	22.50	*45.00*
		Nos. 67-78 (12)	155.00	431.50
		Set, never hinged	225.00	

Catalogue values for unused stamps in this section, from this point to the end of the section, are for Never Hinged items.

UPU Issue

Common Design Type

Wmk. RF in Sheet

1949 Engr. *Perf. 13½x14*

No.	Type	Description	Unused	Used
79	CD309	10c red orange	3.50	3.50
80	CD309	15c violet	4.75	4.75
81	CD309	30c violet blue	7.50	7.50
82	CD309	50c rose violet	8.50	8.50
		Nos. 79-82 (4)	24.25	24.25

Some stamps in each sheet show part of the watermark; others show none.

Common Design Types pictured following the introduction.

A8

5c, 10c, 15c, 20c, Canoes with sails. 25c, 30c, 40c, 50c, Native carving. 1fr, 2fr, 5fr, Natives.

1953 *Perf. 12½*

No.	Type	Description	Unused	Used
83	A8	5c green	.65	*1.75*
84	A8	10c red	.65	*1.75*
85	A8	15c yellow	.65	*1.75*
86	A8	20c ultramarine	1.25	*2.75*
87	A8	25c olive	1.00	*2.50*
88	A8	30c light brown	1.50	*3.50*
89	A8	40c black brown	1.60	*4.50*
90	A8	50c violet	1.75	*5.00*
91	A8	1fr deep orange	10.00	*18.00*
92	A8	2fr red violet	19.00	*47.50*
93	A8	5fr scarlet	29.00	*82.50*
		Nos. 83-93 (11)	67.05	*171.50*

For overprints see Nos. J16-J20.

Discovery of New Hebrides, 1606 — A9

20c, 50c, Britannia, Marianne, Flags and Mask.

Perf. 14½x14

1956, Oct. 20 Unwmk. Photo.

No.	Type	Description	Unused	Used
94	A9	5c emerald	.75	.75
95	A9	10c crimson	.75	.75
96	A9	20c ultramarine	.90	.90
97	A9	50c purple	2.75	2.75
		Nos. 94-97 (4)	5.15	5.15

50th anniv. of the establishment of the Anglo-French Condominium.

Port Vila and Iririki Islet — A10

Designs: 25c, 30c, 40c, 50c, Tropical river and spear fisherman. 1fr, 2fr, 5fr, Woman drinking from coconut (inscribed: "Alliance Franco-Britannique 4 Mars 1947").

Wmk. RF in Sheet

1957 Engr. *Perf. 13½x13*

No.	Type	Description	Unused	Used
98	A10	5c green	.60	*1.25*
99	A10	10c red	.90	*.85*
100	A10	15c orange yel	1.00	*1.50*
101	A10	20c ultramarine	1.25	*1.50*
102	A10	25c olive	1.25	*1.25*
103	A10	30c light brown	1.75	*1.75*
104	A10	40c sepia	2.00	*2.25*
105	A10	50c violet	2.50	*3.50*
106	A10	1fr orange	6.75	*9.00*
107	A10	2fr rose lilac	14.50	*20.00*
108	A10	5fr black	28.00	*40.00*
		Nos. 98-108 (11)	60.50	*82.85*

For overprints see Nos. J21-J25.

Wheat Emblem and Globe A10a

1963, Sept. 2 Unwmk. *Perf. 13*

No.	Type	Description	Unused	Used
109	A10a	60c org brn & slate grn	19.00	19.00

FAO "Freedom from Hunger" campaign.

Centenary Emblem — A11

1963, Sept. 2 Unwmk.

No.	Type	Description	Unused	Used
110	A11	15c org, gray & car	12.50	12.50
111	A11	45c bis, gray & car	18.50	18.50

Centenary of International Red Cross.

Copra Industry
A12

Designs: 5c, Manganese loading, Forari Wharf. 10c, Cacao. 20c, Map of New Hebrides, tuna, marlin and ships. 25c, Striped triggerfish. 30c, Nautilus. 40c, 60c, Turkeyfish (pterois volitans). 50c, Lined tang (fish). 1fr, Cardinal honeyeater and hibiscus. 2fr, Buff-bellied flycatcher. 3fr, Thicket warbler. 5fr, White-collared kingfisher.

Perf. 12½ (10c, 20c, 40c, 60c); 14 (3fr); 13 (others)

Photo. (10c, 20c, 40c, 60c, 3fr); Engr. (others)

1963-67 Unwmk.

112 A12 5c Prus bl, pur brn & cl ('66) .65 .65
a. 5c prus blue & claret ('72) 57.50 *60.00*
113 A12 10c brt grn, org brn & dk brn ("RF" at left) ('65) 2.10 1.60
114 A12 15c dk pur, yel & brn .80 .80
115 A12 20c brt bl, gray & cit ("RF" at left) ('65) 3.00 2.75
116 A12 25c vio, rose lil & org brn ('66) .80 .80
117 A12 30c lil, brn & citron 6.00 1.60
118 A12 40c dk bl & ver ('65) 5.50 5.50
119 A12 50c Prus bl, yel & grn 5.00 2.40
119A A12 60c dk bl & ver ('67) 1.90 1.50
120 A12 1fr bl grn, blk & red ('66) 3.75 3.75
121 A12 2fr ol, blk & brn 17.50 9.00
122 A12 3fr org brn, brt grn & blk ("RF" at left) ('65) 16.00 *22.50*
123 A12 5fr ind, dp bl & gray ('67) 30.00 30.00
Nos. 112-123 (13) 93.00 82.85

See #146-148. For surcharge see #160.

Telegraph, Syncom Satellite and ITU Emblem — A13

1965, May 17 Unwmk. *Perf. 13*

124 A13 15c dk red brn, brt bl & emer 11.50 9.00
125 A13 60c Prus grn, mag & sl 29.00 25.00

ITU, centenary.

Intl. Cooperation Year Issue

Common Design Type with Royal Cipher and "RF" Replacing Queen's Portrait

1965, Oct. 24 Litho. *Perf. 14½*

126 CD318 5c blue grn & claret 4.00 4.00
127 CD318 55c lt violet & grn 8.00 8.00

International Cooperation Year.

Churchill Memorial Issue

Common Design Type with Royal Cipher and "RF" Replacing Queen's Portrait

1966, Jan. 24 Photo. *Perf. 14*

Design in Black, Gold and Carmine Rose

128 CD319 5c brt blue 1.00 1.00
129 CD319 15c green 1.50 1.50
130 CD319 25c brown 3.25 3.25
131 CD319 30c violet 4.50 4.50
Nos. 128-131 (4) 10.25 10.25

World Cup Soccer Issue

Common Design Type with Royal Cipher and "RF" Replacing Queen's Portrait

1966, July 1 Litho. *Perf. 14*

132 CD321 20c multicolored 2.75 2.75
133 CD321 40c multicolored 4.25 4.25

WHO Headquarters Issue

Common Design Type with Royal Cipher and "RF" Replacing Queen's Portrait

1966, Sept. 20 Litho. *Perf. 14*

134 CD322 25c multicolored 3.75 3.75
135 CD322 60c multicolored 5.00 5.00

UNESCO Anniversary Issue

Common Design Type with Royal Cipher and "RF" Replacing Queen's Portrait

1966, Dec. 1 Litho. *Perf. 14*

136 CD323 15c "Education" 1.50 1.50
137 CD323 30c "Science" 3.00 3.00
138 CD323 45c "Culture" 3.25 3.25
Nos. 136-138 (3) 7.75 7.75

US Marine, Australian Soldier and Map of South Pacific War Zone — A19

Designs: 15c, The coast watchers. 60c, Australian cruiser Canberra. 1fr, Flying fortress taking off from Bauer Field, and view of Vila.

Perf. 14x13

1967, Sept. 26 Photo. Unwmk.

139 A19 15c lt blue & multi 1.10 1.10
140 A19 25c yellow & multi 1.25 1.25
141 A19 60c multicolored 2.00 2.00
142 A19 1fr pale salmon & multi 2.50 2.50
Nos. 139-142 (4) 6.85 6.85

25th anniv. of the Allied Forces' campaign in the South Pacific War Zone.

L. A. de Bougainville, Ship's Figurehead and Bougainvillea — A20

15c, Globe & world map. 25c, Ships La Boudeuse & L'Etoile & map of Bougainville Strait.

1968, May 23 Engr. *Perf. 13*

143 A20 15c ver, emer & dl vio .45 .45
144 A20 25c ultra, ol & brn .65 .65
145 A20 60c mag, grn & brn 1.15 1.15
Nos. 143-145 (3) 2.25 2.25

200th anniv. of Louis Antoine de Bougainville's (1729-1811) voyage around the world.

Type of 1963-67 Redrawn, "E II R" at left, "RF" at Right

Designs as before.

1968, Aug. 5 Photo. *Perf. 12½*

146 A12 10c brt grn, org brn & dk brn 1.00 1.00
147 A12 20c brt bl, gray & citron 1.40 1.40

Perf. 14

148 A12 3fr org brn, brt grn & blk 9.50 9.50
Nos. 146-148 (3) 11.90 11.90

On Nos. 113, 115 and 122 "RF" is at left and "E II R" is at right.
For surcharge see No. 160.

Concorde Supersonic Airliner — A21

Design: 25c, Concorde seen from above.

1968, Oct. 9 Litho. *Perf. 14x13½*

149 A21 25c vio bl, red & lt bl 3.00 2.50
150 A21 60c red, ultra & blk 6.50 5.00

Development of the Concorde supersonic airliner, a joint Anglo-French project.

Kauri Pine — A22

1969, June 30 *Perf. 14½x14*

151 A22 20c brown & multi .60 .60

New Hebrides timber industry. Issued in sheets of 9 (3x3) on simulated wood grain background.

Relay Race, British and French Flags — A23

1969, Aug. 13 Photo. *Perf. 12½x13*

152 A23 25c shown .85 .85
153 A23 1fr Runner at right 1.60 1.60

3rd South Pacific Games, Port Moresby, Papua and New Guinea, Aug. 13-23.

Land Diver at Start, Pentecost Island — A24

1969, Oct. 15 Litho. *Perf. 12½*

154 A24 15c shown .50 .50
155 A24 25c Diver in mid-air .60 .60
156 A24 1fr Diver near ground 2.00 2.00
Nos. 154-156 (3) 3.10 3.10

Land divers of Pentecost Island.

UPU Headquarters and Monument, Bern — A25

1970, May 20 Engr. *Perf. 13*

157 A25 1.05fr org, lilac & slate 1.00 1.00

New UPU Headquarters, Bern.

Charles de Gaulle — A26

1970, July 20 Photo. *Perf. 13*

158 A26 65c brown & multi 2.00 2.00
159 A26 1.10fr dp blue & multi 2.75 2.75

Rallying of the Free French, 30th anniv.
For overprints see Nos. 163-164.

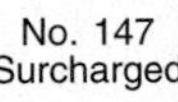
No. 147 Surcharged

1970, Oct. 15 Photo. *Perf. 12½*

160 A12 35c on 20c multi .50 *.60*

Virgin and Child, by Giovanni Bellini — A27

50c, Virgin and Child, by Giovanni Cima.

1970, Nov. 30 Litho. *Perf. 14½x14*

161 A27 15c tan & multi .25 .25
162 A27 50c lt grn & multi .50 .35

Christmas. See Nos. 186-187.

Nos. 158-159 Overprinted "1890-1970 / IN MEMORIAM / 9-11-70" in Gold, 2 Vertical Bars in Black

1971, Jan. 19 Photo. *Perf. 13*

163 A26 65c brown & multi .85 .85
164 A26 1.10fr dp blue & multi 2.00 2.00

In memory of Gen. Charles de Gaulle (1890-1970), President of France.

Soccer — A28

Design: 65c, Basketball, vert.

1971, July 13 Photo. *Perf. 12½*

165 A28 20c multicolored .75 .75
166 A28 65c multicolored 1.25 1.25

4th South Pacific Games, Papeete, French Polynesia, Sept. 8-19.

Breadfruit Tree and Fruit, Society Arms — A29

Perf. 14½x14

1971, Sept. 7 Litho. Unwmk.
167 A29 65c multicolored 1.75 1.75

Expedition of the Royal Society of London for the Advancement of Science to study vegetation and fauna, July 1-October.

Adoration of the Shepherds, by Louis Le Nain — A30

Christmas: 50c, Adoration of the Shepherds, by Jacopo Tintoretto.

1971, Nov. 23 ***Perf. 14x13½***
168 A30 25c lt green & multi .60 .60
169 A30 50c lt blue & multi .90 .90

Drover Mk III — A31

Airplanes: 25c, Sandringham seaplane. 30c, Dragon Rapide. 65c, Caravelle.

1972, Feb. 29 Photo. ***Perf. 13½x13***
170 A31 20c lt green & multi .90 .90
171 A31 25c ultra & multi 1.00 1.00
172 A31 30c orange & multi 1.10 1.10
173 A31 65c dk blue & multi 3.00 3.00
Nos. 170-173 (4) 6.00 6.00

Headdress, South Malekula — A32

Baker's Pigeon — A33

Artifacts: 15c, Slit gong and carved figure, North Ambrym. 1fr, Carved figures, North Ambrym. 3fr, Ceremonial headdress, South Malekula.

Birds: 20c, Red-headed parrot-finch. 35c, Chestnut-bellied kingfisher. 2fr, Green palm lorikeet.

Sea Shells: 25c, Cribraria fischeri. 30c, Oliva rubrolabiata. 65c, Strombus plicatus. 5fr, Turbo marmoratus.

1972, July 24 Photo. ***Perf. 12½x13***
174 A32 5c plum & multi .30 *1.00*
175 A33 10c blue & multi 2.25 *1.75*
176 A32 15c red & multi .35 1.00
177 A33 20c org brn & multi 2.50 1.50
178 A32 25c dp blue & multi 1.75 1.60
179 A32 30c dk green & multi 1.75 *1.75*
180 A33 35c gray bl & multi 3.00 2.50
181 A33 65c dk green & multi 3.75 3.00
182 A32 1fr orange & multi 2.75 *4.25*
183 A33 2fr multicolored 25.00 15.00
184 A32 3fr yellow & multi 9.75 *17.50*
185 A32 5fr pink & multi 21.00 *30.00*
Nos. 174-185 (12) 74.15 *80.85*

For overprints see Nos. 200-201. For surcharges see Nos. 236-247.

Christmas Type of 1970

Christmas: 25c, Adoration of the Magi (detail), by Bartholomaeus Spranger. 70c, Virgin and Child, by Jan Provoost.

1972, Sept. 25 Litho. ***Perf. 14x13½***
186 A27 25c lt green & multi .50 .50
187 A27 70c lt blue & multi .75 .75

Queen Elizabeth II and Prince Philip — A34

Perf. 14x14½

1972, Nov. 20 Photo. Wmk. 314
188 A34 35c violet blk & multi .45 .45
189 A34 65c olive & multi .60 .60

25th anniversary of the marriage of Queen Elizabeth II and Prince Philip.

Dendrobium Teretifolium — A35

Orchids: 30c, Ephemerantha comata. 35c, Spathoglottis petri. 65c, Dendrobium mohlianum.

Unwmk.

1973, Feb. 26 Litho. ***Perf. 14***
190 A35 25c blue vio & multi 2.00 2.00
191 A35 30c multicolored 2.00 2.00
192 A35 35c violet & multi 3.00 3.00
193 A35 65c dk green & multi 5.75 5.75
Nos. 190-193 (4) 12.75 12.75

New Wharf, Vila — A36

1973, May 14 Litho. ***Perf. 14***
194 A36 25c shown .85 .85
195 A36 70c New Wharf, horiz. 1.50 1.50

New wharf at Vila, completed Nov. 1972.

Wild Horses, Tanna A37

Design: 70c, Yasur Volcano, Tanna.

1973, Aug. 13 Photo. ***Perf. 13x13½***
196 A37 35c multicolored 2.75 2.75
197 A37 70c multicolored 3.50 3.50

Christmas A38

35c, Mother and Child, by Marcel Moutouh. 70c, Star over Lagoon, by Tatin D'Avesnieres.

1973, Nov. 19 Litho. ***Perf. 14x13½***
198 A38 35c tan & multi .60 .60
199 A38 70c lil rose & multi .90 .90

Nos. 180, 183 Overprinted in Red or Black: "VISITE ROYALE / 1974"

1974, Feb. 11 Photo. ***Perf. 12½x13***
200 A33 35c multi (R) 3.00 1.10
201 A33 2fr multi (B) 8.50 7.50

Visit of British Royal Family, Feb. 15-16.

Pacific Dove A39

Designs: 35c, Night swallowtail. 70c, Green sea turtle. 1.15fr, Flying fox.

1974, Feb. 11 ***Perf. 13x12½***
202 A39 25c gray & multi 4.50 3.00
203 A39 35c gray & multi 5.50 2.50
204 A39 70c gray & multi 6.75 4.75
205 A39 1.15fr gray & multi 7.75 9.50
Nos. 202-205 (4) 24.50 19.75

Nature conservation.

Old Post Office, Vila — A40

Design: 70c, New Post Office.

Unwmk.

1974, May 6 Photo. ***Perf. 12***
206 A40 35c blue & multi .60 .50
207 A40 70c red & multi 1.10 .90
a. Pair, #206-207 2.25 2.25

Opening of New Post Office, May, 1974.

Capt. Cook and Tanna Island A41

Designs: No. 209, William Wales and boat landing on island. No. 210, William Hodges painting islanders and landscape. 1.15fr, Capt. Cook, "Resolution" and map of New Hebrides.

1974, Aug. 1 Litho. ***Perf. 13***

Size: 40x25mm

208 A41 35c multicolored 4.50 2.75
209 A41 35c multicolored 4.50 2.75
210 A41 35c multicolored 4.50 2.75
a. Strip of 3, #208-210 18.00 18.00

Size: 58x34mm

Perf. 11

211 A41 1.15fr lilac & multi 7.50 7.50

Bicentenary of the discovery of the New Hebrides by Capt. James Cook.

No. 210a has a continuous design.

Exchange of Letters, UPU Emblem A42

1974, Oct. 9 Photo. ***Perf. 13x12½***
212 A42 70c multicolored 1.50 1.50

Centenary of Universal Postal Union.

Nativity, by Gerard Van Honthorst — A43

Christmas: 35c, Adoration of the Kings, by Velazquez, vert.

1974, Nov. 14 Litho. ***Perf. 13½***
213 A43 35c multicolored .25 .25
214 A43 70c multicolored .50 .50

Charolais Bull — A44

1975, Apr. 29 Engr. ***Perf. 13***
215 A44 10fr multicolored 27.50 *30.00*

For surcharge see No. 248.

Nordjamb Emblem, Kayaks — A45

1975, Aug. 5 Litho. ***Perf. 14x13½***
216 A45 25c shown .60 .50
217 A45 35c Camp cooks .80 .70
218 A45 1fr Map makers 1.75 1.75
219 A45 5fr Fishermen 8.50 8.50
Nos. 216-219 (4) 11.65 11.45

Nordjamb 75, 14th Boy Scout Jamboree, Lillehammer, Norway, July 29-Aug. 7.

Pitti Madonna, by Michelangelo A46

Christmas (After Michelangelo): 70c, Bruges Madonna. 2.50fr, Taddei Madonna.

1975, Nov. 11 Litho. *Perf. 14½x14*

220	A46	35c multicolored	.55	.55
221	A46	70c brown & multi	.70	.70
222	A46	2.50fr blue & multi	2.75	2.75
		Nos. 220-222 (3)	4.00	4.00

Concorde, Air France Colors and Emblem — A47

1976, Jan. 30 Typo. *Perf. 13*

223	A47	5fr blue & multi	13.50	13.50

1st commercial flight of supersonic jet Concorde from Paris to Rio, Jan. 21.

Telephones, 1876 and 1976 — A48

Designs: 70c, Alexander Graham Bell. 1.15fr, Nouméa Earth Station and satellite.

1976, Mar. 31 Photo. *Perf. 13*

224	A48	25c black, car & bl	.50	.50
225	A48	70c black & multi	1.50	1.50
226	A48	1.15fr blk, org & vio bl	2.00	2.00
		Nos. 224-226 (3)	4.00	4.00

Centenary of first telephone call by Alexander Graham Bell, Mar. 10, 1876.

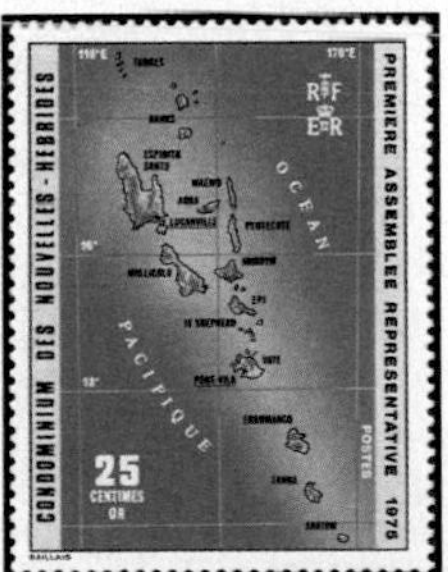

Map of New Hebrides A49

View of Luganville (Santo) A50

Design: 2fr, View of Vila.

1976, June 29 Unwmk. *Perf. 13*

227	A49	25c blue & multi	.55	.45
228	A50	1fr multicolored	1.25	1.00
229	A50	2fr multicolored	3.00	3.00
		Nos. 227-229 (3)	4.80	4.45

Opening of first Representative Assembly, June 29, 1976 (25c); first Luganville (Santo) Municipal Council (1fr); first Vila Municipal Council (2fr).

Nos. 228-229 exist with lower inscription reading "Premiere Assemblée Representative 1975" instead of "Premiere Municipalite de Luganville" on 1fr and "Premiere Municipalite de Port-Vila" on 2fr.

For surcharges, see No. 283-284.

Flight into Egypt, by Francisco Vieira Lusitano — A51

Portuguese 16th Cent. Paintings: 70c, Adoration of the Shepherds. 2.50fr, Adoration of the Kings.

1976, Nov. 8 Litho. *Perf. 14*

230	A51	35c purple & multi	.45	.35
231	A51	70c blue & multi	.65	.55
232	A51	2.50fr multicolored	2.00	2.00
		Nos. 230-232 (3)	3.10	2.90

Christmas 1976.

Queen's Visit, 1974 — A52

70c, Imperial State crown. 2fr, The blessing.

1977, Feb. 7 Litho. *Perf. 14x13½*

233	A52	35c lt green & multi	.35	.25
234	A52	70c blue & multi	.55	.50
235	A52	2fr pink & multi	1.00	1.00
		Nos. 233-235 (3)	1.90	1.75

Reign of Queen Elizabeth II, 25th anniv.

Nos. 174-185, 215 Surcharged

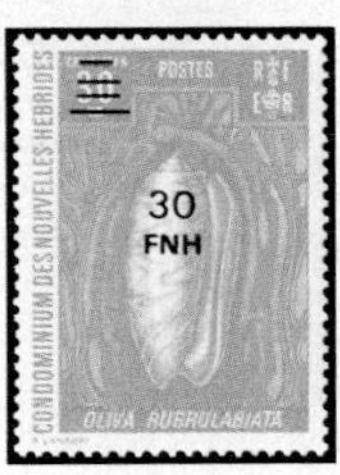

Paris Overprints

1977, July 1 Photo. *Perf. 12½x13*

236	A32	5fr on 5c multi	1.75	1.75
237	A33	10fr on 10c multi	2.75	1.50
238	A32	15fr on 15c multi	1.50	1.50
239	A33	20fr on 20c multi	3.00	1.75
240	A32	25fr on 25c multi	2.75	2.00
241	A32	30fr on 30c multi	2.75	2.50
242	A33	35fr on 35c multi	4.50	4.00
243	A32	40fr on 65c multi	3.50	3.00
244	A32	50fr on 1fr multi	2.25	*3.00*
245	A33	70fr on 2fr multi	7.50	4.00
246	A32	100fr on 3fr multi	3.00	*6.00*
247	A32	200fr on 5fr multi	10.00	*25.00*

Engr.

Perf. 13

248	A44	500fr on 10fr multi	20.00	*42.50*
		Nos. 236-248 (13)	65.25	*98.50*

Nos. 174/185, 215 Surcharged with New Value, "FNH" and Bars

FNH a — FNH b — FNH c — 25 FNH d

Port Vila Overprints

Two settings of 35fr and 200fr surcharges: type 1, 1.4mm between new value and "FNH"; type 2, 2.1mm between value and "FNH."

Perf. 12½x13

1977-78 Photo. Unwmk.

236a	A32	5fr on 5c (a)	3.00	3.00
237a	A33	10fr on 10c (b)	3.50	2.50
238a	A32	15fr on 15c (c)	5.00	3.25
240a	A32	25fr on 25c (d)	120.00	80.00
241a	A32	30fr on 30c (d)	250.00	80.00
242a	A33	35fr on 35c (d), type 1	8.00	6.50
b.		Type 2	37.50	22.50
243a	A32	40fr on 65c (d)	7.00	7.00
244a	A32	50fr on 1fr multi	80.00	
245a	A33	70fr on 2fr multi	80.00	
246a	A32	100fr on 3fr multi	80.00	
247a	A32	200fr on 5fr (d), type 1	55.00	*65.00*
b.		Type 2	65.00	65.00
248a	A44	500fr on 10fr (d)	65.00	*75.00*
		Nos. 236a-248a (12)	756.50	322.25

The 50fr, 70fr and 100fr values were sold only through the philatelic bureau.

Issued: 15fr, 7/18; 10fr, 7/20; 5fr, 8/10#247a, 8/22; 25fr, 30fr, #242a, 9/10; 40fr, 9/12; 500fr, 9/14; #242b, 1/6/78; #247b, 1/13/78.

Espiritu Santo and Cattle — A53

Designs: 5fr, Erromango Island and Kaori tree. 10fr, Archipelago and man making copra. 20fr, Efate Island and Post Office, Vila. 25fr, Malakula Island and headdresses. 30fr, Aoba and Maewo Islands and pig tusks. 35fr, Pentecost Island and land diving. 40fr, Tanna Island and Prophet John Frum's Red Cross. 50fr, Shepherd Island and canoe with sail. 70fr, Banks Island and dancers. 100fr, Ambrym Island and carvings. 200fr, Aneityum Island and decorated baskets. 500fr, Torres Islands and fishing with bow and arrow.

1977-78 Litho. *Perf. 14*

258	A53	5fr multicolored	.25	.25
259	A53	10fr multicolored	.40	.70
260	A53	15fr multicolored	.50	.70
261	A53	20fr multicolored	.60	.90
262	A53	25fr multicolored	.75	1.00
263	A53	30fr multicolored	1.00	1.10
264	A53	35fr multicolored	1.10	1.10
265	A53	40fr multicolored	1.25	1.25
266	A53	50fr multicolored	1.50	2.00
267	A53	70fr multicolored	2.50	3.25
268	A53	100fr multicolored	3.50	5.00
269	A53	200fr multicolored	6.75	10.00
270	A53	500fr multicolored	14.00	24.00
		Nos. 258-270 (13)	34.10	51.25

Issued: 5fr, 20fr, 50fr, 100fr, 200fr, 9/7/77; 15fr, 25fr, 30fr, 40fr, 11/23/77; 10fr, 35fr, 70fr, 500fr, 5/9/78.

Tempi Madonna, by Raphael — A54

Christmas: 15fr, Virgin and Child, by Gerard David. 30fr, Virgin and Child, by Pompeo Batoni.

1977, Dec. 8 Litho. *Perf. 12*

271	A54	10fr multicolored	.35	.35
272	A54	15fr multicolored	.50	.35
273	A54	30fr multicolored	.90	.90
		Nos. 271-273 (3)	1.75	1.60

British Airways Concorde over New York — A55

Designs: 20fr, British Airways Concorde over London. 30fr, Air France Concorde over Washington. 40fr, Air France Concorde over Paris.

1978, May 9 Litho. *Perf. 14*

274	A55	10fr multicolored	2.00	1.50
275	A55	20fr multicolored	2.75	1.75
276	A55	30fr multicolored	3.25	2.25
277	A55	40fr multicolored	4.50	3.50
		Nos. 274-277 (4)	12.50	9.00

Souvenir Sheet

White Horse of Hanover — A56

Elizabeth II — A57

Design: No. 278c, Gallic cock.

1978, June 2 Litho. *Perf. 15*

278		Sheet of 6	3.50	3.50
a.	A56	40fr greenish blue & multi	.25	.25
b.	A57	40fr greenish blue & multi	.25	.25
c.	A56	40fr greenish blue & multi	.25	.25

25th anniversary of coronation of Queen Elizabeth II.

No. 278 contains 2 se-tenant strips of Nos. 278a-278c, separated by horizontal gutter with commemorative and descriptive inscriptions and showing central part of coronation procession with coach.

Virgin and Child, by Dürer — A58

Christmas, Paintings by Albrecht Durer (1471-1528): 15fr, Virgin and Child with St. Anne. 30fr, Virgin and Child with Goldfinch. 40fr, Virgin and Child with Pear.

1978, Dec. 1 Litho. *Perf. 14x13½*
279 A58 10fr multicolored .25 .25
280 A58 15fr multicolored .25 .25
281 A58 30fr multicolored .25 .25
282 A58 40fr multicolored .35 .35
Nos. 279-282 (4) 1.10 1.10

Type of 1976 Surcharged with New Value, Bars over Old Denomination and Inscription at Right. Longitude changed to "166E."

1979, Jan. 11 Photo. *Perf. 13*
283 A49 10fr on 25c bl & multi 1.00 1.00
284 A49 40fr on 25c lt grn & multi 2.00 2.00

First anniv. of Internal Self-Government.

New Hebrides No. 155 and Hill Statue A59

Rowland Hill and New Hebrides Stamps: 10fr, No. 55. 40fr, No. 46.

1979, Sept. 10 Litho. *Perf. 14*
285 A59 10fr multicolored .25 .25
286 A59 20fr multicolored .25 .25
287 A59 40fr multicolored .40 .40
Nos. 285-287 (3) .90 .90

Sir Rowland Hill (1795-1879), originator of penny postage. A souvenir sheet containing No. 286 and British issue No. 266 is listed as No. 266a under New Hebrides, British issues.

Arts Festival — A60

Designs: 10fr, Clubs and spears. 20fr, Ritual puppet. 40fr, Headdress.

1979, Nov. 16 Litho. *Perf. 14*
288 A60 5fr multicolored .25 .25
289 A60 10fr multicolored .25 .25
290 A60 20fr multicolored .40 .40
291 A60 40fr multicolored .65 .65
Nos. 288-291 (4) 1.55 1.55

Church, IYC Emblem A61

IYC Emblem, Children's Drawings: 10fr, Father Christmas. 20fr, Cross and Bible, vert. 40fr, Stars, candle and Santa Claus, vert.

1979, Dec. 4 *Perf. 13x13½*
292 A61 5fr multicolored .70 .60
293 A61 10fr multicolored 1.00 .60
294 A61 20fr multicolored 1.40 .90
295 A61 40fr multicolored 1.75 1.75
Nos. 292-295 (4) 4.85 3.85

Christmas; Intl. Year of the Child.

White-bellied Honeyeater — A62

1980, Feb. 27 Litho. *Perf. 14*
296 A62 10fr shown .85 .85
297 A62 20fr Scarlet robins 1.40 1.60
298 A62 30fr Yellow white-eyes 2.75 2.75
299 A62 40fr Fan-tailed brush cuckoo 3.25 3.25
Nos. 296-299 (4) 8.25 8.45

Stamps of Vanuatu replaced those of New Hebrides in 1980.

POSTAGE DUE STAMPS

French Issues

Nos. 45-46, 48, 50, 52 Overprinted

1925 Wmk. R F in Sheet *Perf. 14*
J1 A4 10c green 50.00 4.75
J2 A4 20c greenish gray 50.00 4.75
J3 A4 30c carmine 50.00 4.75
J4 A4 50c ultramarine 50.00 4.75
J5 A4 1fr carmine, *blue* 50.00 4.75
Nos. J1-J5 (5) 250.00 23.75

Nos. 55-56, 58, 61, 63 Overprinted

1938 *Perf. 12*
J6 A6 5c green 11.00 *65.00*
J7 A6 10c dark orange 12.50 *65.00*
J8 A6 20c rose red 14.50 *70.00*
J9 A6 40c olive green 30.00 *140.00*
J10 A6 1fr dark car, *green* 35.00 *160.00*
Nos. J6-J10 (5) 103.00 *500.00*

Nos. J6-J10 Overprinted like Nos. 67-78

1941
J11 A6 5c green 11.00 *42.50*
J12 A6 10c dark orange 11.00 *42.50*
J13 A6 20c rose red 11.00 *42.50*
J14 A6 40c olive green 13.00 *42.50*
J15 A6 1fr dk car, *green* 12.00 *42.50*
Nos. J11-J15 (5) 58.00 *212.50*

Catalogue values for unused stamps in this section, from this point to the end of the section, are for Never Hinged items.

Nos. 83-84, 86, 89, 91 Overprinted

1953 Unwmk. *Perf. 12½*
J16 A8 5c green 6.00 *13.50*
J17 A8 10c red 8.00 *18.00*
J18 A8 20c ultramarine 14.00 *30.00*
J19 A8 40c black brown 19.00 *55.00*
J20 A8 1fr deep orange 27.50 *60.00*
Nos. J16-J20 (5) 74.50 *176.50*

Nos. 98-99, 101, 104, 106 Overprinted "TIMBRE-TAXE"

Wmk. R F in Sheet

1957 Engr. *Perf. 13½x13*
J21 A10 5c green 1.25 *3.50*
J22 A10 10c red 1.50 *4.25*
J23 A10 20c ultramarine 1.75 *5.25*
J24 A10 40c sepia 6.75 *19.00*
J25 A10 1fr orange 16.00 *45.00*
Nos. J21-J25 (5) 27.25 *77.00*

NEW REPUBLIC

'nü ri-'pə-blik

LOCATION — In South Africa, located in the northern part of the present province of Natal
GOVT. — A former Republic
CAPITAL — Vryheid

New Republic was created in 1884 by Boer adventurers from Transvaal who proclaimed Dinizulu king of Zululand and claimed as their reward a large tract of country as their own, which they called New Republic. This area was excepted when Great Britain annexed Zululand in 1887, but New Republic became a part of Transvaal in 1888 and was included in the Union of South Africa.

12 Pence = 1 Shilling
20 Shillings = 1 Pound

New Republic stamps were individually handstamped on gummed and perforated sheets of paper. Naturally many of the impressions are misaligned and touch or intersect the perforations. Values are for stamps with good color and, for Nos. 37-64, sharp embossing. The alignment does not materially alter the value of the stamp.

A1

Handstamped

1886 Unwmk. *Perf. 11½*
1 A1 1p violet, *yel* 20.00 22.50
a. "d" omitted, in pair with normal 2,750.
1A A1 1p black, *yel* *3,250.*
2 A1 2p violet, *yel* 22.50 *27.50*
a. "d" omitterd 4,750.
b. As "a", without date
c. tete-beche pair —
3 A1 3p violet, *yel* 50.00 *60.00*
a. Double impression
b. "d" omitted (Oct. 13 '86) *4,750.*
c. Tete-beche pair —
4 A1 4p violet, *yel* 85.00
a. Without date
b. "4d" omitted, in pair with normal *3,000.*
5 A1 6p violet, *yel* 65.00 *70.00*
a. Double impression
b. "6d" omitted in pair with normal —
6 A1 9p violet, *yel* 125.00
7 A1 1sh violet, *yel* 125.00
a. "1/S" 800.00
b. "1s" omitted in pair with normal —
8 A1 1/6 violet, *yel* 120.00
a. Without date
b. "1s6d" 600.00
c. as "b", tete-beche pair —
d. as "b", "d" omitted 150.00
9 A1 2sh violet, *yel* 75.00
a. tete-beche pair 875.00
10 A1 2sh6p violet, *yel* 190.00
a. Without date
b. "2/6" 190.00
11 A1 4sh violet, *yel*
a. "4/s" 825.00
12 A1 5sh violet, *yel* 55.00 *65.00*
a. Without date —
b. "s" omitted, in pair with normal 3,500.
13 A1 5/6 violet, *yel* 300.00
a. "5s6d" 550.00
14 A1 7sh6p violet, *yel* 175.00
a. "7/6" 250.00
15 A1 10sh violet, *yel* 225.00 *275.00*
a. Tete-beche pair —
16 A1 10sh6p violet, *yel* 250.00
b. "d" omitted 225.00
16A A1 13sh violet, *yel* 600.00
17 A1 £1 violet, *yel* 150.00
a. Tete-beche pair 650.00
18 A1 30sh violet, *yel* 150.00
a. tete-beche pair 750.00

Granite Paper

19 A1 1p violet, *gray* 30.00 *35.00*
a. "d" omitted 750.00
b. "1" omitted in pair with normal —
20 A1 2p violet, *gray* 22.50 *25.00*
a. "ZUID AFRIKA" omitted
b. "d" omitted *1,350.*
c. "2d." omitted in pair with normal —
21 A1 3p violet, *gray* 40.00 37.50
a. tete-beche pair 375.00
22 A1 4p violet, *gray* 55.00 *60.00*
23 A1 6p violet, *gray* 95.00 *95.00*
a. "6" omitted in pair with normal *2,750.*
24 A1 9p violet, *gray* 150.00
25 A1 1sh violet, *gray* 45.00 50.00
a. tete-beche pair 425.00
b. "1s." omitted in pair with normal 2,750.
26 A1 1sh6p violet, *gray* 125.00
a. tete-beche pair 750.00
b. "1/6" 190.00
c. "d" omitted —
27 A1 2sh violet, *gray* 150.00
a. "2s." omitted in pair with normal *3,250.*
28 A1 2sh6p violet, *gray* 3,500.
a. "2/6" 250.00
29 A1 4sh violet, *gray* 525.00
30 A1 5sh6p violet, *gray* 425.00
a. "5/6" 325.00
b. As "a," "/" omitted —
c. As "a," "6" omitted *4,500.*
31 A1 7/6 violet, *gray* 325.00
a. 7s. 6d violet gray 450.00
32 A1 10sh violet, *gray* 225.00 225.00
a. tete-beche pair 525.00
f. "s" omitted —
32B A1 10sh 6p vio, *gray* 275.00
c. Without date —
d. tete-beche pair —
e. "d" omitted 600.00
33 A1 12sh violet, *gray* 450.00
34 A1 13sh violet, *gray* 550.00
35 A1 £1 violet, *gray* 375.00
36 A1 30sh violet, *gray* 325.00

Same with Embossed Arms

37 A1 1p violet, *yel* 22.50 *25.00*
a. Arms inverted 30.00 35.00
b. Arms tete-beche, pair 125.00 *135.00*
c. tete-beche pair *950.00*
38 A1 2p violet, *yel* 27.50 *30.00*
a. Arms inverted 30.00 35.00
39 A1 4p violet, *yel* 80.00 85.00
a. Arms inverted 125.00 87.50
b. Arms tete-beche, pair 350.00
40 A1 6p violet, *yel* 375.00

Granite Paper

41 A1 1p violet, *gray* 30.00 30.00
a. Imperf. vert., pair
b. Arms inverted 40.00 45.00
c. Arms tete-beche, pair 550.00
42 A1 2p violet, *gray* 30.00 30.00
a. Imperf. horiz., pair
b. Arms inverted 55.00 *65.00*
c. Arms tete-beche, pair 550.00

There were several printings of the above stamps and the date upon them varies from "JAN 86" and "7 JAN 86" to "20 JAN 87."

Nos. 7, 8, 10, 13, 14, 26, 28 and 30 have the denomination expressed in two ways. Example: "1s 6d" or "1/6."

A2

1887 Arms Embossed
43 A2 3p violet, *yel* 27.50 *27.50*
a. Arms inverted 30.00 32.50
b. tete-beche pair 375.00 450.00
c. Imperf. vert., pair
d. Arms omitted
e. Arms tete-beche, pair 225.00
f. Arms sideways 375.00
44 A2 4p violet, *yel* 20.00 20.00
a. Arms inverted 25.00 25.00
45 A2 6p violet, *yel* 17.50 *17.50*
a. Arms inverted 50.00 50.00
b. Arms omitted 95.00
c. Arms tete-beche, pair 375.00
46 A2 9p violet, *yel* 17.50 *20.00*
a. Arms inverted 250.00
b. Arms tete-beche, pair 425.00
47 A2 1sh violet, *yel* 20.00 *20.00*
a. Arms inverted 75.00
b. Arms omitted
48 A2 1sh6p violet, *yel* 50.00 42.50
49 A2 2sh violet, *yel* 42.50 *45.00*
a. Arms inverted 65.00 60.00
b. Arms omitted 150.00
50 A2 2sh6p violet, *yel* 40.00 *40.00*
a. Arms inverted 45.00 *45.00*

50B A2 3sh violet, *yel* 65.00 65.00
c. Arms inverted 80.00 *80.00*
d. Arms tete-beche, pair 600.00
51 A2 4sh violet, *yel* 650.00
a. Arms omitted —
b. "4/s" 65.00 65.00
c. As "b," arms omitted 275.00
51B A2 4/s violet, *yel*
a. Arms omitted
52 A2 5sh violet, *yel* 60.00 60.00
a. Imperf. vert., pair
b. Arms inverted — 175.00
53 A2 5sh6p violet, *yel* 30.00 *35.00*
54 A2 7sh6p violet, *yel* 35.00 *35.00*
a. Arms inverted 125.00
b. Arms tete-beche, pair —
55 A2 10sh violet, *yel* 30.00 *35.00*
a. Arms inverted 40.00
b. Arms omitted 135.00 90.00
c. Imperf. vert., pair
d. Arms tete-beche, pair 150.00
56 A2 10sh6p violet, *yel* 27.50 *32.50*
a. Imperf. vert., pair
b. Arms inverted 55.00
c. Arms omitted
57 A2 £1 violet, *yel* 75.00 85.00
a. Arms inverted 80.00
b. tete-beche pair 650.00 750.00
58 A2 30sh violet, *yel* 225.00

Granite Paper

59 A2 1p violet, *gray* 32.50 20.00
a. Arms omitted 150.00 150.00
b. Arms inverted 30.00 30.00
c. Imperf. vert., pair
d. tete-beche pair 650.00
e. Arms tete-beche, pair —
f. Arms sideways —
60 A2 2p violet, *gray* 20.00 20.00
a. Arms omitted 135.00 125.00
b. Arms inverted 55.00 55.00
c. tete-beche pair 425.00
d. Arms tete-beche, pair —
61 A2 3p violet, *gray* 35.00 35.00
a. Arms inverted 65.00 65.00
b. tete-beche pair 450.00
c. Arms tete-beche, pair —
62 A2 4p violet, *gray* 30.00 27.50
a. Arms inverted 110.00
b. Tete-beche, pair 375.00
c. Arms tete-beche, pair 300.00
63 A2 6p violet, *gray* 35.00 35.00
a. Arms inverted 110.00
64 A2 1sh6p violet, *gray* 50.00 42.50
a. Arms inverted 175.00
b. Arms tete-beche, pair 475.00
65 A2 2/6 violet, *gray* — *1,150.*
Nos. 59-64 (6) 202.50 180.00

These stamps were valid only in New Republic.

All these stamps may have been valid for postage but bona-fide canceled examples of any but the 1p and 2p stamps are quite rare.

NEW ZEALAND

'nü 'zē-lənd

LOCATION — Group of islands in the south Pacific Ocean, southeast of Australia
GOVT. — Self-governing dominion of the British Commonwealth
AREA — 107,241 sq. mi.
POP. — 3,662,265 (1999 est.)
CAPITAL — Wellington

12 Pence = 1 Shilling
20 Shillings = 1 Pound
100 Cents = 1 Dollar (1967)

Catalogue values for unused stamps in this country are for Never Hinged items, beginning with Scott 246 in the regular postage section, Scott AR99 in the postal-fiscal section, Scott B9 in the semi-postal section, Scott J21 in the postage due section, Scott O92 in the officials section, Scott OY29 in the Life Insurance Department section, and Scott L1 in Ross Dependency.

Watermarks

Wmk. 6 — Large Star

Wmk. 59 — N Z

Wmk. 60 — Lozenges

This watermark includes the vertical word "INVICTA" once in each quarter of the sheet.

Wmk. 61 — N Z and Star Close Together

Wmk. 62 — N Z and Star Wide Apart

On watermark 61 the margins of the sheets are watermarked "NEW ZEALAND POSTAGE" and parts of the double-lined letters of these words are frequently found on the stamps. It occasionally happens that a stamp shows no watermark whatever.

Wmk. 63 — Double-lined N Z and Star

Wmk. 64 — Small Star Only

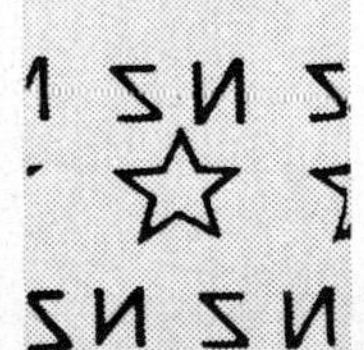
Wmk. 253 — Multiple N Z and Star

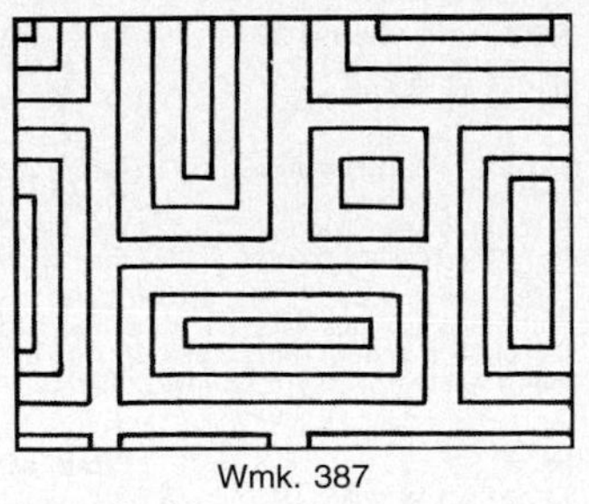
Wmk. 387

Values for unused stamps are for examples with original gum as defined in the catalogue introduction.

Very fine examples of the perforated issues between Nos. 7a-69, AR1-AR30, J1-J11, OY1-OY9 and P1-P4 will have perforations touching the framelines or design on one or more sides due to the narrow spacing of the stamps on the plates and imperfect perforating methods.

The rouletted and serrate rouletted stamps of the same period rarely have complete roulettes and are valued as sound and showing partial roulettes. Stamps with complete roulettes range from very scarce to very rare, are seldom traded, and command great premiums.

Victoria — A1

London Print
Wmk. 6

1855, July 20 **Engr.** ***Imperf.***
White Paper

1 A1 1p dull carmine *85,000.* *21,500.*
2 A1 2p deep blue *40,000.* 750.
3 A1 1sh yellow green *55,000.* *6,000.*
a. Half used as 6p on cover *45,000.*

The blueing of Nos. 2 and 3 was caused by chemical action in the printing process.

Auckland Print

1855-58 **Blue Paper** **Unwmk.**

4 A1 1p orange red 13,000. 2,150.
5 Al 2p blue ('56) 4,000. 325.
6 Al 1sh green ('58) *50,000.* 4,750.
a. Half used as 6p on cover *29,000.*

Nos. 4-6 may be found with parts of the papermaker's name in double-lined letters.

1857-61 **Unwmk.**
Thin Hard or Thick Soft White Paper

7 A1 1p orange ('58) 3,500. 825.
e. 1p org vermilion, Wmk. 6 ('56) *35,000.*
8 A1 2p blue ('58) 1,300. 200.
9 A1 6p brown ('59) 3,000. 325.
e. 6p bister brown ('59) 4,100. 550.
f. 6p chestnut ('59) 5,000. 650.
10 A1 1sh blue green ('61) 18,500. 2,000.
e. 1sh emerald ('58) 22,000. 2,000.

No. 7e is identical to a shade of No. 7. The only currently known example is a pair on a cover front. To qualify as No. 7e, a stamp must be on piece or on cover with a cancellation dated prior to 1862.

1859 ***Pin Rouletted 9-10***

7a A1 1p dull orange 6,000.
8a A1 2p blue 3,800.
9a A1 6p brown 4,600.
10a A1 1sh greenish blue 8,250.

1859 ***Serrate Rouletted 16, 18***

7b A1 1p dull orange 5,500.
8b A1 2p blue 4,100.
9b A1 6p brown 3,800.
g. 6p chestnut 7,750.
10b A1 1sh greenish blue 7,000.

Value for No. 10b is for a damaged stamp.

1859 ***Rouletted 7***

7c A1 1p dull orange *9,750.* 5,500.
f. Pair, imperf between —
8c A1 2p blue *8,250.* 3,500.
9c A1 6p brown *7,750.* 3,000.
l. Pair, imperf. between 27,500. 13,000.
10c A1 1sh greensh blue — 5,250.
10d A1 1sh emerald green — 5,250.

Roulettes are seldom complete or intact. Values for Nos. 7c to 10d are for stamps with partial roulettes.

1862 ***Perf. 13***

7d A1 1p orange vermilion 8,000.
8d A1 2p blue 8,250. 3,800.
9d A1 6p brown *7,000.*

See No. 26.

1862-63 **Wmk. 6** ***Imperf.***

11 A1 1p orange ver 1,100. 300.00
d. 1p carmine vermilion ('63) 500.00 325.00
e. 1p vermilion 775.00 300.00
12 A1 2p deep blue 1,000. 105.00
d. 2p slate blue 2,100. 215.00
e. Double impression 4,500.
g. 2p blue, worn plate 775.00 100.00
13 A1 3p brown lilac ('63) 950.00 175.00
14 A1 6p red brown ('63) 1,750. 125.00
d. 6p black brown 2,100. 140.00
e. 6p brown ('63) 2,200. 130.00
15 A1 1sh yellow green 2,750. 390.00
d. 1sh deep green 2,900. 410.00

See No. 7e.

1862 ***Pin Rouletted 9-10***

12a A1 2p deep blue — 3,250.
14a A1 6p black brown — 4,500.

1862 ***Serrate Rouletted 16, 18***

11b A1 1p orange vermilion 11,000. 2,500.
12b A1 2p blue — 1,300.
13b A1 3p brown lilac 6,250. 1,950.
14b A1 6p black brown — 2,000.
15b A1 1sh yellow green 4,750.

1862 ***Rouletted 7***

11c A1 1p vermilion 5,000. 875.
12c A1 2p blue 3,800. 525.
13c A1 3p brown lilac 3,800. 875.
14c A1 6p red brown 3,500. 550.
15c A1 1sh green 4,000. 1,000.

The 1p, 2p, 6p and 1sh come in two or more shades.

1863 ***Perf. 13***

16 A1 1p carmine ver 3,000. 440.00
17 A1 2p blue, no plate wear 3,000. 500.00
18 A1 3p brown lilac 2,750. 550.00
19 A1 6p red brown 1,500. 130.00
c. As "b," horiz. pair, imperf. btwn. —
20 A1 1sh green 3,000. 400.00

The 1p, 2p, 6p and 1sh come in two or more shades. See the *Scott Classic Specialized Catalogue.*

BUYING, SELLING, EXPERTIZATIONS, NEW ZEALAND & DEPENDENCIES
HELPING COLLECTORS AVOID THE MINEFIELDS!
Send Your Stamps & Covers with Confidence.
PHOTOGRAPHIC CERTIFICATES OF AUTHENTICITY
Reliable and Fast • Recognized • Competitively Priced • Contact Us for Terms and Prices
LIANE & SERGIO SISMONDO • PO Box 10035 • Syracuse, NY 13290-3301
T. 315-422-2331 • F. 315-422-2956 • EMAIL: sismondo@dreamscape.com

VISIT US ONLINE AT WWW.SISMONDOSTAMPS.COM

ASDA • PTS • CNEP • CSDA • FCFI

1862 Unwmk. *Imperf.*
Pelure Paper

21 A1 1p vermilion 12,000. 2,750.
b. Rouletted 7 6,500.
c. Serrate rouletted 13 10,500.
22 A1 2p pale dull ultra 5,500. 1,100.
c. 2p gray blue 6,000. 1,100.
23 A1 3p brown lilac *55,000.*
24 A1 6p black brown 3,500. 450.
b. Rouletted 7 4,000. 550.
c. Serrate rouletted 15 — *6,250.*
d. Serrate rouletted 13 *6,500.*
25 A1 1sh deep yel green 15,000. 1,250.
b. 1sh deep green 15,000. *1,250.*
c. Rouletted 7 16,000. *2,000.*
d. Serrate rouletted 15 *5,250.*
e. "Y" rouletted 18 *5,250.*

No. 23 was never placed in use.

1863 *Perf. 13*
21a A1 1p vermilion 16,000. 3,750.
22a A1 2p gray blue 9,250. 1,175.
b. 2p pale dull ultramarine 8,250. 1,175.
24a A1 6p black brown 8,250. 450.
25a A1 1sh deep green 15,000. 2,250.

1863 Unwmk. *Perf. 13*
Thick White Paper

26 A1 2p dull dark blue 3,750. 1,100.
a. Imperf 2,150. 1,100.
b. Pin roulette 9-10 2,250.

Nos. 26 and 26a differ from 8 and 8d by a white patch of wear at right of head.

1864 Wmk. 59 *Imperf.*
27 A1 1p carmine ver 1,000. 400.
28 A1 2p blue 1,750. 300.
29 A1 6p red brown 5,500. 800.
30 A1 1sh green 1,750. 340.

1864 *Rouletted 7*
27a A1 1p carmine vermilion 6,500. 3,250.
28a A1 2p blue 2,750. 825.
29a A1 6p deep red brown 7,500. 3,250.
30a A1 1sh green 5,000. 1,200.

1864 *Perf. 12½*
27B A1 1p carmine ver 12,500. 5,250.
28B A1 2p blue 475.00 85.00
29B A1 6p red brown 650.00 75.00
30B A1 1sh dp yel green 8,250. 3,250.

1864 *Perf. 13*
27C A1 1p carmine ver 12,500. 4,250.
d. "Y" roulette 18 *7,500.*
28C A1 2p blue 1,100. 250.
30C A1 1sh yellow green 2,500. 900.
d. Horiz. pair, imperf. btwn. *45,000.*
e. Perf. 6½x13 *5,000.*

1864-71 Wmk. 6 *Perf. 12½*
31 A1 1p vermilion 250.00 45.00
a. 1p orange ('71) 650.00 100.00
32 A1 2p blue 250.00 24.00
a. 2p blue, worn plate 350.00 32.50
b. Horiz. pair, imperf. btwn. (#32) *5,500.*
c. Perf. 10x12½ 20,000.
d. Imperf., pair (#32) 2,750. 2,000.
33 A1 3p lilac 225.00 37.50
a. 3p mauve 875.00 100.00
b. Imperf., pair (#33) 4,750. 2,100.
c. As "a", imperf., pair 5,250. 2,100.
d. 3p brown lilac *2,750.* *900.00*
34 A1 4p deep rose ('65) 4,000. 300.00
35 A1 4p yellow ('65) 275.00 145.00
a. 4p orange yellow *3,000.* 1,100.
36 A1 6p red brown 350.00 30.00
a. 6p brown 400.00 45.00
b. Horiz. pair, imperf. btwn. 3,000. 3,000.
37 A1 1sh pale yel green 400.00 135.00
a. 1sh yellow green 700.00 150.00
b. 1sh green 1,350. 400.00

The 1p, 2p and 6p come in two or more shades.

Imperforate examples of the 1p pale orange, worn plate; 2p dull blue and 6p dull chocolate brown are reprints. Value, each $100.

1871 Wmk. 6 *Perf. 10*
38 A1 1p deep brown 1,000. 140.00

1871 *Perf. 12½*
39 A1 1p brown 275.00 55.00
a. Imperf. 3,750. 2,250.
40 A1 2p orange 200.00 32.50
a. 2p vermilion 225.00 35.00
b. Imperf., pair 2,750. —
41 A1 6p blue 400.00 80.00
Nos. 39-41 (3) 875.00 167.50

Shades exist.

1871 *Perf. 10x12½*
42 A1 1p brown 450.00 60.00
43 A1 2p orange 325.00 45.00
44 A1 6p blue 2,500. 600.00
Nos. 42-44 (3) 3,275. 705.00

The 6p usually has only one side perf. 10, the 1p and 2p more rarely so.

Shades exist.

1873 Wmk. 59 *Perf. 12½*
45 A1 1p brown 8,750.
46 A1 2p vermilion 1,300. 375.00

1873 Unwmk. *Perf. 12½*
47 A1 1p brown 1,200. 275.00
48 A1 2p vermilion 175.00 60.00
49 A1 4p yellow orange 225.00 *925.00*

The watermark "T.H. SAUNDERS" in double-line capitals falls on 32 of the 240 stamps in a sheet. The 1p and 2p also are known with script "WT & CO" watermark.

1873 Wmk. 60
50 A1 2p vermilion *3,500.* 750.

A2 A3

A4

A5

A6

A7

Perf. 10x12½, 11½, 12, 12½
1874 Typo. Wmk. 62

51 A2 1p violet 125.00 15.50
a. Bluish paper 250.00 45.00
b. Imperf. 750.00 1,650.
52 A3 2p rose 130.00 9.00
a. Bluish paper 250.00 45.00
53 A4 3p brown 225.00 90.00
a. Bluish paper 425.00 120.00
54 A5 4p claret 325.00 75.00
a. Bluish paper 650.00 130.00
55 A6 6p blue 350.00 13.50
a. Bluish paper 500.00 60.00
56 A7 1sh green 650.00 40.00
a. Bluish paper 1,200. 210.00
Nos. 51-56 (6) 1,805. 243.00

1875 Wmk. 6 *Perf. 12½*
57 A2 1p violet 2,250. 400.00
58 A3 2p rose 825.00 45.00

A8

1878 Wmk. 62 *Perf. 12x11½*
59 A8 2sh deep rose 750.00 450.00
60 A8 5sh gray 800.00 500.00

No. 60 has numeral "5" in each of the four spandrels.

Beware of cleaned fiscally used examples of Nos. 59-60.

A9 A10

A11

A12

A13

A14

A15

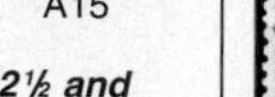

Perf. 10, 11, 11½, 12, 12½ and Compound
1882

61 A9 1p rose 12.00 .70
a. Vert. pair, imperf. horiz. *950.00*
b. Perf. 12x11½ 50.00 7.00
c. Perf. 12½ 300.00 175.00
d. Imperf., pair 900.00
62 A10 2p violet 13.50 .35
a. Vert. pair, imperf. btwn. *950.00*
b. Perf. 12½ 200.00 110.00
c. Imperf., pair 1,000.
63 A11 3p orange 60.00 9.50
a. 3p yellow 62.50 14.00
64 A12 4p blue green 62.50 4.50
a. Perf. 10x11 95.00 13.00
65 A13 6p brown 80.00 8.00
66 A14 8p blue 80.00 60.00
67 A15 1sh red brown 125.00 15.00
Nos. 61-67 (7) 433.00 98.05

See #87. For overprints see #O1-O2, O5, O7-O8.

A15a

A16

A17

1891-95
67A A15a ½p black ('95) 4.25 .25
b. Perf. 12x11½ 37.50 *90.00*
68 A16 2½p ultramarine 57.50 5.00
a. Perf. 12½ 375.00 200.00
69 A17 5p olive gray 70.00 25.00
Nos. 67A-69 (3) 131.75 30.25

In 1893 advertisements were printed on the backs of Nos. 61-67, 68-69.

See #86C. For overprints see #O3-O4, O9.

Mt. Cook — A18

Lake Taupo — A19

Pembroke Peak — A20

Mt. Earnslaw, Lake Wakitipu — A21

Mt. Earnslaw, Lake Wakltipu — A22

Huia, Sacred Birds — A23

White Terrace, Rotomahana
A24

Otira Gorge and Mt. Ruapehu
A25

Kiwi
A26

Maori Canoe
A27

Pink Terrace, Rotomahana
A28

Kea & Kaka (Hawk-billed Parrots)
A29

Milford Sound — A30

Mt. Cook — A31

Perf. 12 to 16
1898, Apr. 5 Engr. Unwmk.

70 A18 ½p lilac gray 9.25 1.75
a. Horiz. or vert. pair, imperf. btwn. 1,750. 1,450.
71 A19 1p yel brn & bl 6.50 .75
a. Horiz. or vert. pair, imperf. btwn. 1,300.
b. Imperf. pair 950.00 1,000.
72 A20 2p rose brown 57.50 .30
a. Horiz. pair, imperf. vert. 650.00
b. Vert. pair, imperf. btwn. 1,300.
73 A21 2½p bl *(Wakitipu)* 18.00 *50.00*
74 A22 2½p bl *(Wakatipu)* 50.00 10.00
75 A23 3p orange brn 37.50 10.00
76 A24 4p rose 18.00 *22.00*
77 A25 5p red brown 100.00 225.00
a. 5p violet brown 70.00 *25.00*
78 A26 6p green 120.00 55.00
79 A27 8p dull blue 75.00 50.00
80 A28 9p lilac 70.00 45.00
81 A29 1sh dull red 110.00 29.00
a. Pair, imperf. between 5,500.
82 A30 2sh blue green 300.00 160.00
a. Vert. pair, imperf. btwn. 5,000. 5,000.
83 A31 5sh vermilion 400.00 *550.00*
Nos. 70-83 (14) 1,371. *1,208.*

The 5sh stamps are often found with revenue cancellations that are embossed or show a crown on the top of a circle. These are worth much less.

See Nos. 84, 88-89, 91-98, 99B, 102, 104, 106-107, 111-112, 114-121, 126-128, 1508-1521. For overprint see No. O10.

A32 A33

1900 Wmk. 63 *Perf. 11*

Thick Soft Wove Paper

84 A18 ½p green 8.75 1.75
85 A32 1p carmine rose 15.00 .25
a. 1p lake 42.50 4.50
b. 1p crimson 15.00 .25
c. As "b," pair, imperf. btwn. 1,650. 1,550.
d. As "c," horiz. pair, imperf. vert. 650.00
86 A33 2p red violet 14.00 .90
a. Pair, imperf. btwn. 1,450.
Nos. 84-86 (3) 37.75 2.90

Nos. 84 and 86 are re-engravings of Nos. 70 and 72 and are slightly smaller.
See No. 110. For Handstamp see No. O18.

A34

1899-1900 Wmk. 63

86C A15a ½p black ('00) 9.50 *17.50*
87 A10 2p violet ('00) 30.00 17.50

Unwmk.

88 A22 2½p blue 30.00 3.75
a. Horiz. pair, imperf. vert. 1,450.
b. Vert. pair, imperf. btwn. 650.00 —
89 A23 3p org brown 35.00 2.50
a. Horiz. pair, imperf. vert. 650.00
b. Horiz. pair, imperf. btwn. 1,525.
90 A34 4p yel brn & bl ('00) 15.00 4.00
91 A25 5p red brown 50.00 10.00
a. 5p violet brown 42.50 5.00
92 A26 6p green 150.00 *82.50*
93 A26 6p rose ('00) 50.00 7.00
a. 6p carmine 50.00 7.00
d. As #93, horiz. pair, imperf. vert. 600.00
g. As #93, horiz. pair, imperf. btwn. 1,300.
94 A27 8p dark blue 45.00 16.50
95 A28 9p red lilac 52.50 30.00
96 A29 1sh red 100.00 10.00
97 A30 2sh blue green 250.00 60.00
98 A31 5sh vermilion 400.00 410.00
Revenue cancel 25.00
Nos. 86C-98 (13) 1,217. 671.25

See #113. For overprints see #O11-O15.
The 5sh stamps are often found with revenue cancellations that are embossed or show a crown on the top of a circle. These are worth much less.

"Commerce" — A35

1901, Jan. 1 Unwmk. *Perf. 12 to 16*

99 A35 1p carmine 8.00 *4.50*

Universal Penny Postage.
See Nos. 100, 103, 105, 108, 129. For overprint see Nos. 121a, O16, O18, O24, O32. Compare design A35 with A42.

Boer War Contingent A36

Perf. 14, 11x14, 14x11

1901 Thick Soft Paper Wmk. 63

99B A18 ½p green 15.00 5.50

Perf. 11, 14 and Compound

100 A35 1p carmine 18.00 .25
a. Horiz. pair, imperf. vert. 325.00 325.00
101 A36 1½p brown org 35.00 20.00
a. Vert. pair, imperf. horiz. 1,100.
b. Imperf., pair 1,200.
Nos. 99B-101 (3) 68.00 25.75

No. 101 was issued to honor the New Zealand forces in the South African War.
See No. 109.

Thin Hard Paper

102 A18 ½p green 29.00 27.50
103 A35 1p carmine 16.00 4.75
a. Horiz. pair, imperf. vert. 300.00

1902 Unwmk.

104 A18 ½p green 14.00 5.75
105 A35 1p carmine 14.00 3.25

1902 *Perf. 11*

Thin White Wove Paper

106 A26 6p rose red 45.00 7.00
a. Watermarked letters 100.00 100.00

The sheets of No. 106 are watermarked with the words "LISBON SUPERFINE" in two lines, covering ten stamps.

Perf. 11, 14, 11x14, 14x11

1902-07 Wmk. 61

107 A18 ½p green 8.00 1.35
a. Horiz. pair, imperf. vert. 300.00
108 A35 1p carmine 4.50 .25
a. 1p rose carmine 4.50 .25
b. Imperf., pair
c. Imperf. x serrate perf. 200.00
d. Imperf. horiz. or vert. pair 200.00
f. Booklet pane of 6 300.00
109 A36 1½p brown org ('07) 27.50 *60.00*
110 A33 2p dull vio ('03) 13.50 2.75
a. Horiz. pair, imperf. vert. 550.00 *875.00*
b. Vert. pair, imperf. horiz. 775.00
111 A22 2½p blue 32.00 7.00
112 A23 3p org brown 35.00 2.50
113 A34 4p yel brn & bl 11.00 4.00
a. Horiz. pair, imperf. vert. 650.00
114 A25 5p red brown 50.00 15.00
a. 5p violet brown 65.00 32.50
115 A26 6p rose red 45.00 8.50
a. 6p rose 45.00 8.50
b. 6p pink 65.00 8.75
c. 6p brick red 80.00 20.00
d. Horiz. pair, imperf. vert. 850.00
116 A27 8p deep blue 45.00 13.00
117 A28 9p red violet 50.00 9.25
118 A29 1sh scarlet 80.00 16.50
a. 1sh orange red 85.00 8.00
b. 1sh brown red 90.00 15.50
119 A30 2sh blue green 225.00 45.00
120 A31 5sh vermilion 500.00 *360.00*
Nos. 107-120 (14) 1,126. 545.10

Wmk. 61 is normally sideways on 3p, 5p, 6p, 8p and 1sh. The 6p exists with wmk. upright. The 1sh exists with wmk. upright and inverted.
The unique example of No. 113 with inverted center is used and is in the New Zealand National Philatelic Collection.
See No. 129. For overprints see Nos. O17-O22.
The 5sh stamps are often found with revenue cancellations that are embossed or show a crown on the top of a circle. These are worth much less.
In 1908 a quantity of the 1p carmine was overprinted "King Edward VII Land" and taken on a Shackleton expedition to the Antarctic. Because of the weather Shackleton landed at Victoria Land instead. The stamp was never sold to the public at face value. See No. 121a.
Similar conditions prevailed for the 1909-12 ½p green and 1p carmine overprinted "VICTORIA LAND." See Nos. 130d-131d.

1903 Unwmk. *Perf. 11*

Laid Paper

121 A30 2sh blue green 325.00 *250.00*

No. 108a Overprinted in Green: "King Edward VII Land" in Two Lines Reading Up

1908, Jan. 15 *Perf. 14*

121a A35 1p rose carmine 800.00 65.00

See note after No. 120.

Christchurch Exhibition Issue

Arrival of the Maoris A37

Maori Art — A38

Landing of Capt. Cook — A39

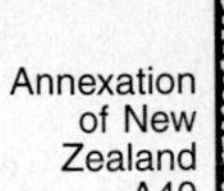

Annexation of New Zealand A40

Wmk. 61

1906, Nov. Typo. *Perf. 14*

122 A37 ½p emerald 37.50 *37.50*
123 A38 1p vermilion 18.00 27.50
a. 1p claret *15,000.* *25,000.*
124 A39 3p blue & brown 60.00 *115.00*
125 A40 6p gray grn & rose 220.00 *425.00*
Nos. 122-125 (4) 335.50 *605.00*

Value for No. 123a is for a fine example.

Designs of 1902-07 Issue, but smaller

Perf. 14, 14x13, 14x15

1907-08 Engr.

126 A23 3p orange brown *55.00* 17.50
127 A26 6p carmine rose *62.50* 11.50
128 A29 1sh orange red *225.00* 35.00
Nos. 126-128 (3) *342.50* 64.00

The small stamps are about 21mm high, those of 1898-1902 about 23mm.

Type of 1902 Redrawn

1908 Typo. *Perf. 14x14½*

129 A35 1p carmine 40.00 3.00

REDRAWN, 1p: The lines of shading in the globe are diagonal and the other lines of the design are generally thicker than on No. 108.

Edward VII A41

"Commerce" A42

1909-12 *Perf. 14x14½*

130 A41 ½p yellow green 7.25 .55
a. Booklet pane of 6 *225.00*
b. Booklet pane 5 + label *775.00*
c. Imperf., pair 250.00
131 A42 1p carmine 2.00 .25
a. Imperf., pair 410.00
b. Booklet pane of 6 225.00

Perf. 14x14½, 14x13½, 14

Engr.

Various Frames

132 A41 2p mauve 25.00 7.25
133 A41 3p orange brown 27.50 1.40
134 A41 4p red orange 32.50 *27.50*
135 A41 4p yellow ('12) 22.50 *13.50*
136 A41 5p red brown 22.00 5.00
137 A41 6p carmine rose 50.00 1.75
138 A41 8p deep blue 20.00 3.25
139 A41 1sh vermilion 75.00 6.75
Nos. 130-139 (10) 283.75 67.20

Nos. 133, 136-138 exist in vert. pairs with perf. 14x13½ on top and perf. 14x14½ on the bottom. These sell for a premium.
See #177. For overprints see Nos. 130d-131d, 130e-137e, O33-O37, O49, O54 and Cook Islands #49.

Nos. 130-131 Overprinted in Black: "VICTORIA LAND" in Two Lines

1911-13

130d A41 ½p yellow green *1,100.* *950.00*
131d A42 1p carmine 70.00 *150.00*

See note after No. 120.
Issue dates: 1p, Feb. 9; ½p, Jan. 18, 1913.

Stamps of 1909 Overprinted in Black

1913

130e A41 ½p yellow green 25.00 *55.00*
131e A42 1p carmine 35.00 *45.00*
133e A41 3p orange brown 250.00 *400.00*
137e A41 6p carmine rose 300.00 *500.00*
Nos. 130e-137e (4) 610.00 *1,000.*

This issue was valid only within New Zealand and to Australia from Dec. 1, 1913, to Feb. 28, 1914. The Auckland Stamp Collectors Club inspired this issue.

King George V — A43

1915 Typo. *Perf. 14x15*

144 A43 ½p yellow green 2.00 .25
b. Booklet pane of 6 *150.00*

See Nos. 163-164, 176, 178. For overprints see Nos. O41, O45-O46, MR1 and Cook Islands No. 48.

A44 A45

Perf. 14x14½, 14x13½

1915-22 Engr.

145 A44 1½p gray 4.25 2.00
146 A45 2p purple 14.50 *45.00*
147 A45 2p org yel ('16) 9.50 *35.00*
148 A44 2½p dull blue 9.00 *5.75*
149 A45 3p violet brown 16.50 1.40
150 A45 4p orange yellow 9.50 *57.50*
151 A45 4p purple ('16) 22.50 .55
c. 4p blackish violet 10.00 .55
d. Vert. pair, top stamp imperf, bottom stamp perf 3 sides *1,200.*
152 A44 4½p dark green 25.00 26.00
153 A45 5p light blue ('21) 19.00 1.10
a. Imperf., pair 250.00 200.00
154 A45 6p carmine rose 13.00 .55
a. Horiz. pair, imperf. vert.
155 A44 7½p red brown 22.50 *26.00*
156 A45 8p blue ('21) 25.00 *50.00*
157 A45 8p red brown ('22) 35.00 4.00
158 A45 9p olive green 30.00 5.00
a. Imperf., pair *1,500.*
159 A45 1sh vermilion 30.00 .60
a. Imperf., pair 450.00
Nos. 145-159 (15) 285.25 260.45

Nos. 145-156, 158-159 exist in vert. pairs with perf 14x13½ on top and perf 14x14½ on the bottom. These sell for a premium. The 5p and No. 151c exist with the perf varieties reversed. These are rare. No. 157 only comes perf 14x13½.
The former Nos. 151a and 151b probably were listed from sheets with No. 151d. They probably do not exist.
For overprints see Nos. O47-O48, O50-O53 and Cook Islands Nos. 53-60.

A46

A47

No. 160 No. 161

The engr. stamps have a background of geometric lathe-work; the typo. stamps have a background of crossed dotted lines.
Type A43 has three diamonds at each side of the crown, type A46 has two, and type A47 has one.

1916-19 Typo. *Perf. 14x15, 14*

160 A46 1½p gray black 9.00 1.40
161 A47 1½p gray black 11.00 .60
162 A47 1½p brown orange ('18) 3.50 .60
163 A43 2p yellow 2.60 .25
164 A43 3p chocolate ('19) 12.00 1.50
Nos. 160-164 (5) 38.10 4.35

In 1916 the 1½, 2, 3 and 6p of the 1915-16 issue and the 8p of the 1909 issue were printed on paper intended for the long rectangular stamps of the 1902-07 issue. In this paper the watermarks are set wide apart, so that the smaller stamps often show only a small part of the watermark or miss it altogether.
For overprints see Nos. O42-O44 and Cook Islands Nos. 50-52.

Victory Issue

"Peace" and British Lion — A48

Peace and Lion — A49

Maori Chief — A50

British Lion — A51

"Victory" — A52

King George V, Lion and Maori Fern at Sides — A53

1920, Jan. 27 ***Perf. 14***

165	A48	½p yellow green	3.25	2.75
166	A49	1p carmine	4.50	.65
167	A50	1½p brown orange	3.50	.55
168	A51	3p black brown	15.00	*16.00*
169	A52	6p purple	17.00	*19.00*
170	A53	1sh vermilion	25.00	*55.00*
		Nos. 165-170 (6)	68.25	*93.95*

No. 165 Surcharged in Red

1922, Mar.

174	A48	2p on ½p yellow green	6.00	1.50

Map of New Zealand — A54

1923 **Typo.** ***Perf. 14x15***

175	A54	1p carmine rose	3.50	.70

Restoration of Penny Postage. The paper varies from thin to thick.

Types of 1909-15
N Z and Star 'watermark' printed on back, usually in blue

1925 **Unwmk.** ***Perf. 14x14½***

176	A43	½p yellow green	3.50	*3.50*
177	A42	1p carmine	3.50	.90
178	A43	2p yellow	20.00	*62.50*
		Nos. 176-178 (3)	27.00	*66.90*

Exhibition Buildings A55

1925, Nov. 17 **Wmk. 61**
Surface Tinted Paper

179	A55	½p yel green, *grnsh*	3.50	*14.00*
180	A55	1p car rose, *pink*	4.25	*6.25*
181	A55	4p red violet, *lilac*	37.50	*80.00*
		Nos. 179-181 (3)	45.25	*100.25*

Dunedin Exhibition.

George V in Admiral's Uniform A56

In Field Marshal's Uniform A57

1926 ***Perf. 14, 14½x14***

182	A56	2sh blue	70.00	35.00
a.		2sh dark blue	65.00	*67.50*
183	A56	3sh violet	130.00	*175.00*
a.		3sh deep violet	110.00	*190.00*

Perf. 14, 14x14½

184	A57	1p rose red	1.25	.25
a.		Booklet pane of 6	150.00	
b.		Imperf., pair	250.00	
		Nos. 182-184 (3)	201.25	210.25

For overprints see Nos. O55-O56 and Cook Islands Nos. 74-75.

Pied Fantail and Clematis A58

Kiwi and Cabbage Palm A59

Maori Woman Cooking in Boiling Spring A60

Maori Council House (Whare) A61

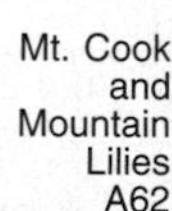

Mt. Cook and Mountain Lilies A62

Maori Girl Wearing Tiki — A63

Mitre Peak — A64

Striped Marlin A65

Harvesting — A66

Tuatara Lizard — A67

Maori Panel from Door — A68

Tui or Parson Bird — A69

Capt. Cook Landing at Poverty Bay — A70

Mt. Egmont, North Island A71

Perf. 14x14½, 14x13½, 13½x14, 13½

1935, May 1 **Engr.** **Wmk. 61**

185	A58	½p bright green	3.00	1.50
186	A59	1p copper red	2.50	1.00
186A	A59	1p copper red, re-engraved	9.00	4.00
b.		Booklet pane of 6 + ad labels	*80.00*	
187	A60	1½p red brown	6.50	*10.00*
188	A61	2p red orange	4.00	2.50
189	A62	2½p dull blue & dk brown	8.00	*22.50*
190	A63	3p chocolate	13.50	3.25
191	A64	4p blk brn & blk	4.25	3.25
192	A65	5p violet blue	26.00	*35.00*
193	A66	6p red	9.00	*12.00*
194	A67	8p dark brown	12.00	*15.00*

Litho.
Size: 18x21½mm

195	A68	9p blk & scar	16.00	6.00

Engr.

196	A69	1sh dk sl green	22.50	15.00
197	A70	2sh olive green	50.00	50.00
198	A71	3sh yel brn & brn black	25.00	*50.00*
		Nos. 185-198 (15)	211.25	231.00
		Set, never hinged	500.00	

On No. 186A, the horizontal lines in the sky are much darker.

The 2½p, 5p, 2sh and 3sh are perf. 13½ vertically; perf. 13-14 horizontally on each stamp.

See Nos. 203-216, 244-245. For overprints see Nos. O58-O71, O90.

Silver Jubilee Issue

Queen Mary and King George V A72

1935, May 7 ***Perf. 11x11½***

199	A72	½p blue green	.75	1.00
200	A72	1p dark car rose	1.00	.75
201	A72	6p vermilion	20.00	*30.00*
		Nos. 199-201 (3)	21.75	*31.75*
		Set, never hinged	29.00	

25th anniv. of the reign of King George V.

Types of 1935

Perf. 12½ to 15 and Compound

1936-42 **Wmk. 253**

203	A58	½p bright green	2.00	.25
204	A59	1p copper red	2.00	.25
205	A60	1½p red brown	9.50	6.00
206	A61	2p red orange	.25	.25
a.		Perf. 14	16.50	.90
b.		Perf. 14x15	21.00	*25.00*
c.		Perf. 12½	4.00	.25
207	A62	2½p dull blue & dk brn	1.50	*6.00*
208	A63	3p chocolate	20.00	1.50
209	A64	4p blk brn & blk	1.50	.25
a.		Perf. 12½	22.50	17.50
210	A65	5p violet blue	2.50	1.25
a.		Perf. 12½	11.00	3.50
211	A66	6p red	1.25	.25
a.		Perf. 12½	1.75	5.00
212	A67	8p dark brown	2.00	1.50
a.		Perf. 12½	2.25	1.60

Litho.
Size: 18x21½mm

213	A68	9p gray & scar	30.00	4.00
a.		9p black & scarlet	32.50	4.25

Engr.

214	A69	1sh dk sl grn	3.50	1.25
a.		Perf. 12½	35.00	25.00
215	A70	2sh olive green	6.50	1.50
a.		Perf. 13½x14	175.00	4.00
b.		Perf. 12½	12.50	9.50
216	A71	3sh yel brn & blk brn	5.50	3.25
a.		Perf. 12½ ('41)	45.00	50.00
		Nos. 203-216 (14)	88.00	27.50
		Set, never hinged	180.00	

Wool Industry A73

Butter Industry A74

Sheep Farming A75

Apple Industry A76

Shipping A77

1936, Oct. 1 **Wmk. 61** ***Perf. 11***

218	A73	½p deep green	.25	.30
219	A74	1p red	.25	.25
220	A75	2½p deep blue	1.25	*4.00*
221	A76	4p dark purple	1.00	*3.00*
222	A77	6p red brown	2.00	*3.50*
		Nos. 218-222 (5)	4.75	*11.05*
		Set, never hinged	6.50	

Congress of the Chambers of Commerce of the British Empire held in New Zealand.

Queen Elizabeth and King George VI A78

Perf. 13½x13

1937, May 13 **Wmk. 253**

223	A78	1p rose carmine	.25	.25
224	A78	2½p dark blue	.50	*1.25*
225	A78	6p vermilion	.65	*1.25*
		Nos. 223-225 (3)	1.40	*2.75*
		Set, never hinged	2.25	

Coronation of George VI and Elizabeth.

A79

A80

1938-44 **Engr.** ***Perf. 13½***

226	A79	½p emerald	4.75	.25
226B	A79	½p brown org ('41)	.25	.30
227	A79	1p rose red	3.75	.25
227A	A79	1p lt blue grn ('41)	.25	.25
228	A80	1½p violet brown	19.00	3.25

No.	Type	Denom.	Color	Unused	Used
228B	A80	1½p	red ('44)	.25	.35
228C	A80	3p	blue ('41)	.25	.25
			Nos. 226-228C (7)	28.50	4.90
			Set, never hinged	40.00	

See Nos. 258-264. For surcharges and overprints see Nos. 242-243, 279, 285, O72-O74, O88-O89, O92-O97.

Landing of the Maoris in 1350 A81

Captain Cook, His Map of New Zealand, 1769, H.M.S. Endeavour A82

Victoria, Edward VII, George V, Edward VIII and George VI — A83

Abel Tasman, Ship, and Chart of West Coast of New Zealand A84

Treaty of Waitangi, 1840 — A85

Pioneer Settlers Landing on Petone Beach, 1840 A86

The Progress of Transport A87

H.M.S. "Britomart" at Akaroa — A88

Route of Ship Carrying First Shipment of Frozen Mutton to England — A89

Maori Council A90

Gold Mining in 1861 and Modern Gold Dredge A91

Giant Kauri — A92

Perf. 13½x13, 13x13½, 14x13½

1940, Jan. 2 Engr. Wmk. 253

No.	Type	Denom.	Color	Unused	Used
229	A81	½p	dk blue green	.30	.25
230	A82	1p	scarlet & sepia	2.25	.25
231	A83	1½p	brt vio & ultra	.25	.60
232	A84	2p	blk brn & Prus grn	1.10	.25
233	A85	2½p	dk bl & myr grn	1.50	1.00
234	A86	3p	dp plum & dk vio	2.75	1.00
235	A87	4p	dk red vio & vio brn	10.00	1.60
236	A88	5p	brown & lt bl	6.00	4.00
237	A89	6p	vio & brt grn	8.00	1.50
238	A90	7p	org red & black	1.25	*4.50*
239	A90	8p	org red & black	8.00	5.00
240	A91	9p	dp org & olive	5.50	2.25
241	A92	1sh	dk sl grn & ol	10.00	4.00
			Nos. 229-241 (13)	56.90	26.20
			Set, never hinged	95.00	

Centenary of British sovereignty established by the treaty of Waitangi.

Imperfs of #229-241 exist. These probably are plate proofs.

For surcharge and overprints see Nos. 246, O76-O86.

Stamps of 1938 Surcharged with New Values in Black

1941 Wmk. 253 *Perf. 13½*

No.	Type	Surcharge		Unused	Used
242	A79	1p on ½p	emerald	1.00	.25
243	A80	2p on 1½p	violet brn	1.00	.25
			Set, never hinged	3.50	

Type of 1935 Redrawn

1941 Typo. Wmk. 61 *Perf. 14x15*

Size: 17½x20½mm

No.	Type	Denom.	Color	Unused	Used
244	A68	9p	int black & scarlet	70.00	30.00

Wmk. 253

No.	Type	Denom.	Color	Unused	Used
245	A68	9p	int black & scarlet	4.00	3.50
			Set, never hinged	160.00	

Catalogue values for unused stamps in this section, from this point to the end of the section, are for Never Hinged items.

No 231 Srchd. in Black

1944 *Perf. 13½x13*

No.	Type	Surcharge		Unused	Used
246	A83	10p on 1½p	brt vio & ultra	.45	.45

Peace Issue

Lake Matheson A93

Parliament House, Wellington — A94

St. Paul's Cathedral, London — A95

The Royal Family — A96

Badge of Royal New Zealand Air Force A97

New Zealand Army Overseas Badge A98

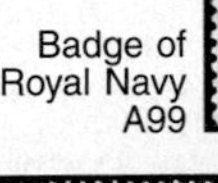

Badge of Royal Navy A99

New Zealand Coat of Arms A100

Knight, Window of Wellington Boys' College A101

Natl. Memorial Campanile, Wellington A103

Southern Alps and Chapel Altar A102

Engr.; Photo. (1½p, 1sh)

Perf. 13x13½, 13½x13

1946, Apr. 1 Wmk. 253

No.	Type	Denom.	Color	Unused	Used
247	A93	½p	choc & dk bl grn	.25	*.60*
248	A94	1p	emerald	.25	.25
249	A95	1½p	scarlet	.25	.25
250	A96	2p	rose violet	.25	.25
251	A97	3p	dk grn & ultra	.25	.25
252	A98	4p	brn org & ol grn	.25	.25
253	A99	5p	ultra & blue grn	.80	.80
254	A100	6p	org red & red brn	.25	.25
255	A101	8p	brown lake & blk	.30	.30
256	A102	9p	black & brt bl	.30	.30
257	A103	1sh	gray black	.80	.40
			Nos. 247-257 (11)	3.95	3.90

Return to peace at the close of WWII.

Imperfs exist from the printer's archives.

George VI Type of 1938 and

King George VI — A104

1947 Engr. *Perf. 13½*

No.	Type	Denom.	Color	Unused	Used
258	A80	2p	orange	.30	.25
260	A80	4p	rose lilac	.75	.50
261	A80	5p	gray	1.00	.50
262	A80	6p	rose carmine	1.00	.25
263	A80	8p	deep violet	1.00	1.00
264	A80	9p	chocolate	2.00	.40

Perf. 14

No.	Type	Denom.	Color	Unused	Used
265	A104	1sh	dk car rose & chnt	.75	.50
266	A104	1sh3p	ultra & chnt	2.50	1.00
267	A104	2sh	dk grn & brn org	6.25	2.00
268	A104	3sh	gray blk & chnt	5.00	3.00
			Nos. 258-268 (10)	20.55	9.40

Nos. 265-267 have watermark either upright or sideways. On No. 268 watermark is always sideways.

For overprints see Nos. O98-O99.

"John Wickliffe" and "Philip Laing" A105

Cromwell, Otago A106

First Church, Dunedin — A107

University of Otago A108

1948, Feb. 23 *Perf. 13½*

No.	Type	Denom.	Color	Unused	Used
269	A105	1p	green & blue	.25	.25
270	A106	2p	brown & green	.25	.25
271	A107	3p	violet	.35	.35
272	A108	6p	lilac rose & gray blk	.35	.35
			Nos. 269-272 (4)	1.20	1.20

Otago Province settlement, cent.

A Royal Visit set of four was prepared but not issued. Examples of the 3p have appeared in the stamp market.

A109

Black Surcharge

Wmk. 253

1950, July 28 Typo. *Perf. 14*

No.	Type	Denom.	Color	Unused	Used
273	A109	1½p	rose red	.40	.40

See No. 367.

Cathedral at Christchurch — A110

"They Passed this Way" A111

3p, John Robert Godley. 6p, Canterbury University College. 1sh, View of Timaru.

1950, Nov. 20 Engr. *Perf. 13x13½*

274 A110 1p blue grn & blue .50 .50
275 A111 2p car & red org .50 .50
276 A110 3p indigo & blue .50 .50
277 A111 6p brown & blue .70 .70
278 A111 1sh claret & blue .70 .70
Nos. 274-278 (5) 2.90 2.90

Centenary of the founding of Canterbury Provincial District.

Imperfs of #274-278 exist.

No. 227A Surcharged in Black

1952, Dec. *Perf. 13½*

279 A79 3p on 1p lt blue green .30 .25

Coronation Issue

Buckingham Palace and Elizabeth II — A112

Queen Elizabeth II — A113

Westminster Abbey — A114

Designs: 4p, Queen Elizabeth and state coach. 1sh6p, Crown and royal scepter.

Perf. 13x12½, 14x14½ (3p, 8p)

Engr., Photo. (3p, 8p)

1953, May 25

280 A112 2p ultramarine .40 .35
281 A113 3p brown .35 .25
282 A112 4p carmine 1.40 *2.00*
283 A114 8p slate black 1.00 *1.50*
284 A112 1sh6p vio blue & pur 2.50 *2.75*
Nos. 280-284 (5) 5.65 6.85

See Nos. 1869-1873.

No. 226B Surcharged in Black

1953, Sept. *Perf. 13½*

285 A79 1p on ½p brown orange .40 .25

Queen Elizabeth II — A115

Queen Elizabeth II and Duke of Edinburgh A116

Perf. 12½x13½, 13½x13

1953, Dec. 9 Engr.

286 A115 3p lilac .25 .25
287 A116 4p deep blue .25 .25

Visit of Queen Elizabeth II and the Duke of Edinburgh.

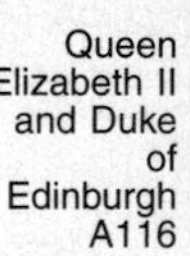

A117

A118

A119

1953-57 *Perf. 13½*

288 A117 ½p gray .25 *.30*
289 A117 1p orange .25 .25
290 A117 1½p rose brown .25 .25
291 A117 2p blue green .25 .25
292 A117 3p red .25 .25
293 A117 4p blue .40 .40
294 A117 6p rose violet .70 *1.50*
295 A117 8p rose car .60 .60
296 A118 9p emerald & org brn .60 .60
297 A118 1sh car & blk .70 .25
298 A118 1sh6p blue & blk 1.50 .50
298A A118 1sh9p org & blk 5.00 1.25
298B A119 2sh6p redsh brn 15.00 8.00
299 A119 3sh blue green 13.00 .50
300 A119 5sh rose car 27.50 4.50
301 A119 10sh vio blue 50.00 19.00
Nos. 288-301 (16) 116.25 38.40

The 1½p was issued in 1953; 1sh9p and 2sh6p in 1957; all others in 1954.

No. 298A exists on both ordinary and chalky paper.

Two dies of the 1sh differ in shading on the sleeve.

Imperfs of Nos. 298B-301 and tete-beche pairs of No. 301 and 312 exist from the printer's archives.

See Nos. 306-312. For surcharge see No. 320.

Maori Mailman A120

Queen Elizabeth II A121

Douglas DC-3 A122

Perf. 13½ (2p), 14 (3p), 13 (4p)

1955, July 18 Wmk. 253

302 A120 2p deep grn & brn .25 .25
303 A121 3p claret .25 .25
304 A122 4p ultra & black .50 .50
Nos. 302-304 (3) 1.00 1.00

Cent. of New Zealand's 1st postage stamps.

Type of 1953-54 Redrawn

1955-59 Wmk. 253 *Perf. 13½*

306 A117 1p orange ('56) .50 .25
307 A117 1½p rose brown .60 .25
308 A117 2p bl grn ('56) .40 .25
309 A117 3p vermilion ('56) .40 .25
310 A117 4p blue ('58) 1.00 .75
311 A117 6p violet 8.00 .25
312 A117 8p brown red ('59) 5.00 5.00
Nos. 306-312 (7) 15.90 7.00

The numeral has been enlarged and the ornament in the lower right corner omitted.

Nos. 306, 308-310 exist on both ordinary and chalky paper.

Imperfs exist.

For surcharges see Nos. 319, 354.

Whalers of Foveaux Strait A123

"Agriculture" with Cow and Sheep — A124

Notornis (Takahe) — A125

1956, Jan. *Perf. 13x12½, 13 (8p)*

313 A123 2p deep green .30 .25
314 A124 3p sepia .25 .25
315 A125 8p car & blue vio 1.25 1.25
Nos. 313-315 (3) 1.80 1.75

Southland centennial.

Lamb and Map of New Zealand — A126

Lamb, S. S. "Dunedin" and Refrigeration Ship — A127

Perf. 14x14½, 14½x14

1957, Feb. 15 Photo.

316 A126 4p bright blue .50 *1.00*
317 A127 8p brick red .75 *1.25*

New Zealand Meat Export Trade, 75th anniv.

Sir Truby King — A128

1957, May 14 Engr. *Perf. 13*

318 A128 3p rose red .25 .25

Plunket Society, 50th anniversary.

Imperfs exist. These probably are plate proofs.

Nos. 307, 290 Surcharged

1958, Jan. 15 *Perf. 13½*

319 A117 2p on 1½p (#307) .50 .25
a. Small surcharge .25 .25
320 A117 2p on 1½p (#290) 175.00 *200.00*
a. Small surcharge —

Surcharge measures 9½mm vert. on Nos. 319-320; 9mm on No. 319a-320a. Diameter of dot 4½mm on Nos. 319-320; 3¾mm on No. 319a-320a.

Counterfeits exist.

Sir Charles Kingsford-Smith and "Southern Cross" — A129

Perf. 14x14½

1958, Aug. 27 Engr. Wmk. 253

321 A129 6p brt violet blue .50 *.60*

1st air crossing of the Tasman Sea, 30th anniv.

See Australia No. 310.

Nelson Diocese Seal — A129a

1958, Sept. 29 *Perf. 13*

322 A129a 3p carmine rose .25 .25

Centenary of Nelson City.

Imperfs exist. These probably are plate proofs.

Statue of "Pania," Napier — A130

Gannet Sanctuary, Cape Kidnappers A131

Design: 8p, Maori shearing sheep.

Perf. 13½x14½, 14½x14

1958, Nov. 3 Photo. Wmk. 253

323 A130 2p yellow green .25 .25
324 A131 3p ultramarine .25 .25
325 A130 8p red brown 1.00 *1.50*
Nos. 323-325 (3) 1.50 2.00

Centenary of Hawkes Bay province.

Jamboree Kiwi Badge — A132

1959, Jan. 5 Engr. *Perf. 13*

326 A132 3p car rose & brown .30 .25

Pan-Pacific Scout Jamboree, Auckland, Jan. 3-10.

"Endeavour" at Ship Cove — A133

Designs: 3p, Shipping wool at Wairau bar, 1857. 8p, Salt Industry, Grassmere.

1959, Mar. 2 Photo. *Perf. 14½x14*

327 A133 2p green .30 .25
328 A133 3p dark blue .30 .25
329 A133 8p brown 1.10 *2.00*
Nos. 327-329 (3) 1.70 2.50

Centenary of Marlborough Province.

The Explorer — A134

Westland Centennial: 3p, The Gold Digger. 8p, The Pioneer Woman.

1960, May 16 *Perf. 14x14½*

330 A134 2p green .25 .25
331 A134 3p orange .30 .25
332 A134 8p gray 1.25 2.00
Nos. 330-332 (3) 1.80 2.50

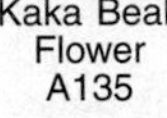

Kaka Beak Flower A135

Timber Industry A136

Tiki A137

Maori Rock Drawing A138

Butter Making A139

Designs: ½p, Manuka flower. 1p, Karaka flower. 2½p, Titoki flower. 3p, Kowhai flower. 4p, Hibiscus. 5p, Mountain daisy. 6p, Clematis. 7p, Koromiko flower. 8p, Rata flower. 9p, Flag. 1sh3p, Rainbow trout. 1sh9p, Plane spraying farmland. 3sh, Ngauruhoe Volcano, Tongariro National Park. 5sh, Sutherland Falls. 10sh, Tasman Glacier, Mount Cook. £1, Pohutu Geyser.

Perf. 14½x14, 14x14½

1960-66 **Photo.** **Wmk. 253**

333 A135 ½p dp car, grn & pale bl .25 .25
b. Green omitted 400.00
c. Pale blue omitted 300.00
334 A135 1p brn, org & grn .25 .25
b. Orange omitted 600.00 375.00
c. Perf. 14½x13, wmkd. sideways 1.50 *2.75*
335 A135 2p grn, rose car, blk & yel .25 .25
b. Black omitted 500.00
c. Yellow omitted 600.00
336 A135 2½p blk, grn, red & brn .90 .25
a. Brown omitted 300.00
b. Green & red omitted 950.00
c. Green omitted 350.00
d. Red omitted 800.00 600.00
337 A135 3p Prus bl, yel, brn & grn .30 .25
b. Yellow omitted 200.00
c. Brown omitted 200.00
d. Green omitted 250.00
e. Perf. 14½x13, wmkd. sideways 1.50 *2.75*
338 A135 4p bl, grn, yel & lil .40 .25
a. Yellow omitted 750.00
b. Lilac omitted 600.00 500.00
339 A135 5p pur, blk, yel & grn .90 .25
a. Yellow omitted 425.00 175.00
340 A135 6p dp grn, lt grn & lil .50 .25
a. Light green omitted 425.00
b. Lilac omitted 375.00
340C A135 7p pink, red, grn & yel .90 *1.25*
341 A135 8p gray, grn, pink & yel .40 .25
342 A136 9p ultra & car .45 .25
a. Carmine omitted 400.00
343 A136 1sh grn & brn .50 .25
344 A137 1sh3p bl, brn & carmine 2.00 .25
a. Carmine omitted 750.00
345 A137 1sh6p org brn & ol grn 1.00 .25
346 A136 1sh9p pale brn 13.00 .50
347 A138 2sh buff & blk 1.00 .25
348 A139 2sh6p red brn & yel 1.50 1.00
a. Yellow omitted 1,100. 800.00
349 A139 3sh gray brn 20.00 1.00
350 A138 5sh dk grn 2.50 .80
351 A139 10sh blue 3.50 3.50
352 A138 £1 magenta 11.00 8.50
Nos. 333-352 (21) 61.50 20.05

Nos. 334c and 337e were issued in coils.

Only on chalky paper: 2½p, 5p, 7p. On ordinary and chalky paper: 1p, 3p, 4p, 6p, 1sh9p, 2sh, 3sh, 5sh, 10sh. Others on ordinary paper only.

Issued: 2p, 4p, 1sh, 1sh3p, 1sh6p, 1sh9p, 2sh, 2sh6p, 3sh, 5sh, 10sh, £1, 7/11/60; ½p, 1p, 3p, 6p, 8p, 9p, 9/1/60; 2½p, 11/1/61; 5p, 5/14/62; 7p, 3/16/66; #334c, 11/63; #337e, 10/3/63.

See Nos. 360-361, 382-404.

Adoration of the Shepherds, by Rembrandt A140

Perf. 11½x12

1960, Nov. 1 **Wmk. 253**

353 A140 2p dp brn & red, *cream* .30 .25
a. Red omitted *400.00* *400.00*

Christmas. See No. 355.

No. 309 Surcharged with New Value and Bars

Two types of surcharge:
Type I — "2½d" is 5½mm wide.
Type II — "2½d" is 5mm wide.

1961, Sept. 1 **Engr.** *Perf. 13½*

354 A117 2½p on 3p vermilion, I .40 .25
a. Type II .40 .25

Christmas Type of 1960

2½p, Adoration of the Magi, by Dürer.

1961, Oct. 16 **Photo.** *Perf. 14½x14*
Size: 30x34mm

355 A140 2½p multicolored .25 .25

Morse Key and Port Hills, Lyttelton, 1862 A141

Design: 8p, Teleprinter and tape, 1962.

1962, June 1 **Wmk. 253**

356 A141 3p dk brn & grn .25 .25
a. Green omitted 2,750.
357 A141 8p dk red & gray .90 .75
a. Imperf., pair 2,500.
b. Gray omitted 2,250.

Centenary of the New Zealand telegraph.

Madonna in Prayer by Sassoferrato A142

1962, Oct. 15 *Perf. 14½x14*

358 A142 2½p multicolored .25 .25

Christmas.

Holy Family by Titian A143

1963, Oct. 14 **Photo.** *Perf. 12½*

359 A143 2½p multicolored .25 .25
a. Imperf., pair *250.00*
b. Yellow omitted *300.00*

Christmas.

Types of 1960-62

1sh9p, Plane spraying farmland. 3sh, Ngauruhoe volcano, Tongariro National Park.

1963-64 *Perf. 14½x14*

360 A136 1sh9p brt blue, grn & yel 2.50 1.00
361 A139 3sh bl, grn & bis 2.00 1.75

Issued: 1sh9p, 11/4/63; 3sh, 4/1/64.

Old and New Engines A144

1sh9p, Express train and Mt. Ruapehu.

1963, Nov. 25 *Perf. 14*

362 A144 3p multicolored .40 .25
a. Blue (sky) omitted *550.00*
363 A144 1sh9p bl, blk, yel & carmine 2.25 1.50
a. Carmine (value) omitted *2,500.*

Centenary of New Zealand Railways.

Cable Around World and Under Sea A144a

1963, Dec. 3 **Unwmk.** *Perf. 13½*

364 A144a 8p yel, car, blk & bl .90 *1.25*

Opening of the Commonwealth Pacific (telephone) cable service (COMPAC).

See Australia No. 381.

Map of New Zealand and Steering Wheel A145

Perf. 14½x14

1964, May 1 **Wmk. 253**

365 A145 3p multicolored .30 .25

National Road Safety Campaign.

Rev. Samuel Marsden Conducting First Christian Service, Rangihoua Bay, Christmas 1814 — A146

1964, Oct. 12 *Perf. 14x13½*

366 A146 2½p multicolored .25 .25

Christmas.

Postal-Fiscal Type of 1950

1964, Dec. 14 **Typo.** *Perf. 14*
Black Surcharge

367 A109 7p rose red .50 *1.10*

ANZAC Issue

Anzac Cove, Gallipoli A147

Design: 5p, Anzac Cove and poppy.

Perf. 12½

1965, Apr. 14 **Unwmk.** **Photo.**

368 A147 4p light brown .25 .25
369 A147 5p green & red .25 *.40*

50th anniv. of the landing of the Australian and New Zealand Army Corps, ANZAC, at Gallipoli, Turkey, Apr. 25, 1915.

ITU Emblem, Old and New Communication Equipment — A148

Perf. 14½x14

1965, May 17 **Photo.** **Wmk. 253**

370 A148 9p lt brown & dk blue .55 .35

Centenary of the ITU.

Sir Winston Spencer Churchill (1874-1965) A148a

1965, May 24 **Unwmk.** *Perf. 13½*

371 A148a 7p lt blue, gray & blk .30 *.40*

See Australia No. 389.

Provincial Council Building, Wellington A149

Perf. 14½x14

1965, July 26 **Photo.** **Wmk. 253**

372 A149 4p multicolored .25 .25

Centenary of the establishment of Wellington as seat of government. The design is from a water color by L. B. Temple, 1867.

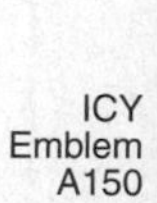

ICY Emblem A150

1965, Sept. 28 Litho. ***Perf. 14***

373 A150 4p ol bister & dk red .25 .25

International Cooperation Year.

"The Two Trinities" by Murillo — A151

1965, Oct. 11 Photo. ***Perf. 13½x14***

374 A151 3p multicolored .25 .25
a. Gold omitted 1,500.

Christmas.

Parliament House, Wellington and Commonwealth Parliamentary Association Emblem — A152

Designs: 4p, Arms of New Zealand and Queen Elizabeth II. 2sh, Wellington from Mt. Victoria.

1965, Nov. 30 Unwmk. ***Perf. 14***

375	A152	4p multicolored	.30	.25
a.		Blue omitted	*1,000.*	
376	A152	9p multicolored	.60	.60
377	A152	2sh multicolored	4.75	4.75
a.		Red omitted	*950.00*	
		Nos. 375-377 (3)	5.65	5.60

11th Commonwealth Parliamentary Assoc. Conf.

Scout Emblem, Maori Pattern — A153

Perf. 14x14½

1966, Jan. 5 Photo. Wmk. 253

378 A153 4p green & gold .25 .25
a. Gold omitted *1,100.*

4th National Scout Jamboree, Trentham.

Virgin with Child, by Carlo Maratta — A154

1966, Oct. 3 Wmk. 253 ***Perf. 14***

379 A154 3p multicolored .25 .25
a. Red omitted *350.00*

Christmas.

Queens Victoria and Elizabeth II — A155

New Zealand PO Savings Bank cent.: 9p, Reverse of half sovereign, 1867, and 1967 dollar.

Perf. 14x14½

1967, Feb. 3 Photo. Wmk. 253

380 A155 4p plum, gold & black .25 .25
381 A155 9p dk grn, bl, blk, sil & gold .25 .25

Decimal Currency

Types of 1960-62

Designs: ½c, Manuka flower. 1c, Karaka flower. 2c, Kaka beak flower. 2½c, Kowhai flower. 3c, Hibiscus. 4c, Mountain daisy. 5c, Clematis. 6c, Koromiko flower. 7c, Rata flower. 7½c, Brown trout. 8c, Flag. 10c, Timber industry. 15c, Tiki. 20c, Maori rock drawing. 25c, Butter making. 28c, Fox Glacier, Westland National Park. 30c, Ngauruhoe Volcano, Tongarino National Park. 50c, Sutherland Falls. $1, Tasman Glacier, Mount Cook. $2, Pohutu Geyser.

Wmk. 253, Unwmkd. (#400)

1967-70 Photo. ***Various Perfs.***

382	A135	½c multicolored	.25	.25
a.		Pale blue omitted		*325.00*
383	A135	1c multicolored	.25	.25
a.		Booklet pane of 5 + label	2.25	
384	A135	2c multicolored	.25	.25
385	A135	2½c multicolored	.25	.25
a.		Dark blue omitted	*3,750.*	
386	A135	3c multicolored	.25	.25
387	A135	4c multicolored	.30	.25
388	A135	5c multicolored	.50	.50
389	A135	6c multicolored	.50	*1.00*
390	A135	7c multicolored	.60	*1.00*
391	A137	7½c multicolored	.50	.50
392	A136	8c ultra & car	.60	.60
a.		Red omitted	*1,200.*	
393	A136	10c grn & brn	.60	.60
394	A137	15c org brn & slate grn	2.25	2.25
395	A137	15c grn, sl grn & red ('68)	1.00	1.00
396	A138	20c buff & black	1.00	.25
397	A139	25c brown & yel	1.25	*2.00*
398	A138	28c multi ('68)	.75	.25
399	A139	30c multicolored	1.75	.40
400	A139	30c multi ('70)	5.00	3.00
401	A138	50c dark green	2.00	.75
402	A139	$1 blue	11.00	1.50
403	A138	$2 magenta	7.50	5.00
404	A138	$2 multi ('68)	30.00	15.00
		Nos. 382-404 (23)	68.35	37.10

Perf. 13½x14: ½c to 3c, 5c, 7c. Perf. 14½x14: 4c, 6c, 8c, 10c, 25c, 30c, $1.

Perf. 13½: 7½c. Perf. 14x14½: 15c, 20c, 28c, 50c, $2.

Issued: 7½c, 8/29/67; No. 395, 3/19/68; 28c, 7/30/68; No. 404, 12/10/68; No. 400, 1970; others, 7/10/67.

The 7½c was issued to commemorate the centenary of the brown trout's introduction to New Zealand, and retained as part of the regular series.

No. 395 has been redrawn. The "c" on No. 395 lacks serif; No. 394 has serif.

No. 391 exists with watermarks either sideways or upright.

Like Postal-Fiscal Type PF5 of 1931

Coat of Arms — A155a

Decimal Currency

1967, July 10 Wmk. 253 ***Perf. 14***

404A	A155a	$4 purple	4.00	2.00
404B	A155a	$6 green	6.00	4.00
a.		Unwmk. ('87)	9.00	4.50
404C	A155a	$8 light blue	8.00	4.75
a.		Unwmk. ('87)	9.50	*12.00*
404D	A155a	$10 dark blue	10.00	*4.00*
a.		Unwmk. ('87)	11.00	9.00
		Nos. 404A-404D (4)	28.00	14.75

Adoration of the Shepherds, by Poussin — A156

Perf. 13½x14

1967, Oct. 3 Photo. Wmk. 253

405 A156 2½c multicolored .25 .25

Christmas.

Sir James Hector — A157

Design: 4c, Mt. Aspiring, aurora australis and Southern Cross.

1967, Oct. 10 Litho. ***Perf. 14***

406 A157 4c multicolored .25 .25
407 A157 8c multicolored .35 *.55*

Centenary of the Royal Society of New Zealand to Promote Science.

Maori Bible — A158

1968, Apr. 23 Litho. ***Perf. 13½***

408 A158 3c multicolored .25 .25
a. Gold omitted *160.00*

Publication of the Bible in Maori, cent.

Soldiers of Two Eras and Tank A159

10c, Airmen of two eras, insigne & plane. 28c, Sailors of two eras, insigne & battleships.

1968, May 7 ***Perf. 14x13½***

409	A159	4c multicolored	.25	.25
410	A159	10c multicolored	.50	.50
411	A159	28c multicolored	1.50	1.50
		Nos. 409-411 (3)	2.25	2.25

Issued to honor the Armed Services.

"Universal Suffrage" A160

Human Rights Flame A161

Perf. 13½

1968, Sept. 19 Photo. Unwmk.

412 A160 3c ol grn, lt bl & grn .25 .25
413 A161 10c dp grn, yel & red .30 .30

75th anniv. of universal suffrage in New Zealand; Intl. Human Rights Year.

Adoration of the Holy Child, by Gerard van Honthorst A162

Perf. 14x14½

1968, Oct. 1 Wmk. 253

414 A162 2½c multicolored .25 .25

Christmas.

Romney Marsh Sheep and Woolmark on Carpet A163

Designs: 7c, Trawler and catch. 8c, Apples and orchard. 10c, Radiata pines and stacked lumber. 20c, Cargo hoist and grazing cattle. 25c, Dairy farm in Taranaki, Mt. Egmont and crated dairy products.

Wmk. 253 (10c, 18c, 25c); others Unwmkd.

Perf. 13½; 14½x14 (10c, 25c)

1968-69 Litho.; Photo. (10c, 25c)

415	A163	7c multi ('69)	.90	.90
416	A163	8c multi ('69)	.75	.75
417	A163	10c multi	.50	.25
a.		Green omitted	*950.00*	
418	A163	18c multi ('69)	1.25	.55
419	A163	20c multi ('69)	1.00	.25
420	A163	25c multi	2.25	1.75
		Nos. 415-420 (6)	6.65	4.45

ILO Emblem A164

Perf. 14½x14

1969, Feb. 11 Photo. Wmk. 253

421 A164 7c scarlet & black .35 .35

50th anniv. of the ILO.

Law Society Coat of Arms — A165

Designs: 3c, Supreme Court Building, Auckland, horiz. 18c, "Justice" from memorial window of the University of Canterbury Hall, Christchurch.

1969, Apr. 8 Litho. ***Perf. 13½***

422	A165	3c multicolored	.25	.25
423	A165	10c multicolored	.40	.40
424	A165	18c multicolored	.65	.65
		Nos. 422-424 (3)	1.30	1.30

Centenary of New Zealand Law Society.

Otago University — A166

Design: 10c, Conferring degree and arms of the University, horiz.

1969, June 3

425 A166 3c multicolored .25 .25
426 A166 10c multicolored .35 .35

Centenary of the University of Otago.

Oldest House in New Zealand, Kerikeri A167

Design: 6c, Bay of Islands.

1969, Aug. 18 Litho. Wmk. 253

427 A167 4c multicolored .30 .30
428 A167 6c multicolored .75 .75

Early European settlements in New Zealand on the 150th anniv. of the founding of Kerikeri, the oldest existing European settlement.

Nativity, by Federico Fiori — A168

Perf. 13½x14

1969, Oct. 1 Photo. Wmk. 253

429 A168 2½c multicolored .25 .25

Unwmk.

430 A168 2½c multicolored .25 .25

Christmas.

Capt. Cook, Transit of Venus and Octant A169

Designs: 6c, Joseph Banks and bark Endeavour. 18c, Dr. Daniel Solander and matata branch (rhabdothamnus solandri). 28c, Queen Elizabeth II and map showing Cook's chart of 1769.

1969, Oct. 9 *Perf. 14½x14*

431 A169 4c dk bl, blk & brt rose .50 .50
a. Imperf., pair 425.00
432 A169 6c sl grn & choc 1.25 *1.25*
433 A169 18c choc, sl grn & black 2.00 2.00
434 A169 28c dk ultra, blk & brt rose 3.50 *3.50*
a. Souv. sheet of 4, #431-434 18.50 18.50
Nos. 431-434 (4) 7.25 7.25

Cook's landing in New Zealand, bicent.

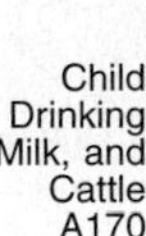

Child Drinking Milk, and Cattle A170

7c, Wheat and child with empty bowl.

1969, Nov. 18 Photo. *Perf. 13*

435 A170 7c multicolored 1.25 1.25
436 A170 8c multicolored 1.25 1.25

25th anniv. of CORSO (Council of Organizations for Relief Services Overseas).

Cardigan Bay A171

1970, Jan. 28 Unwmk. *Perf. 11½*

Granite Paper

437 A171 10c multicolored .40 .40

Return to New Zealand from the US of Cardigan Bay, 1st standard bred light-harness race horse to win a million dollars in stake money.

Glade Copper Butterfly A172

Scarlet Parrotfish A173

New Zealand Coat of Arms and Queen Elizabeth II — A174

Maori Fishhook A175

Egmont National Park A176

Hauraki Gulf Maritime Park — A177

Designs: 1c, Red admiral butterfly. 2c, Tussock butterfly. 2½c, Magpie moth. 3c, Lichen moth. 4c, Puriri moth. 6c, Sea horses. 7c, Leatherjackets (fish). 7½c, Garfish. 8c, John dory (fish). 18c, Maori club. 20c, Maori tattoo pattern. 30c, Mt. Cook National Park (chamois). 50c, Abel Tasman National Park. $1, Geothermal power plant. $2, Helicopter over field, molecule (agricultural technology).

1970-71 Wmk. 253 *Perf. 13½x13*

438 A172 ½c ultra & multi .25 .25
439 A172 1c dp bis & multi .25 .25
a. Bklt. pane of 3 + 3 labels ('71) 2.50
b. Red omitted 275.00
440 A172 2c ol grn & multi .25 .25
a. Black omitted 400.00
441 A172 2½c yel & multi .30 .25
442 A172 3c brown & multi .25 .25
443 A172 4c dk brown & multi .25 .25
a. Bright green omitted 250.00 110.00
444 A173 5c dk green & multi .35 *.80*
445 A173 6c dp car & multi .45 .80
446 A173 7c brn red & multi .50 1.50
447 A173 7½c dk vio & multi .75 .75
448 A173 8c blue grn & multi .50 .25

Perf. 14½x14

449 A174 10c dk bl, sil, red & ultra .45 .25

Perf. 14x13, 13x14

450 A175 15c brick red, sal & blk .75 .50
a. Brick red omitted 700.00
451 A177 18c yel grn, blk & red brn .75 .50
452 A175 20c yel brn & blk .75 .25

Nos. 439, 442 and 443 exist with watermark either sideways or upright.

Perf. 13½x12½

Unwmk.

453 A176 23c bl, grn & blk .60 .30

Litho.

Perf. 13½

454 A177 25c gray & multi 1.25 .50
a. Perf. 14 ('76) .60 .50
455 A177 30c tan & multi .60 .25
a. Perf. 14 ('76) 1.25 1.75

Photo.

Perf. 13½x12½

456 A176 50c sl grn & multi .75 .25
a. Apple grn omitted 27.50
b. Buff omitted 55.00
c. Slate grn omitted 350.00

Perf. 11½

Granite Paper

457 A175 $1 lt ultra & multi 1.50 1.00
458 A175 $2 ol & multi 3.25 1.50
Nos. 438-458 (21) 14.75 10.90

The 10c for the visit of Queen Elizabeth II, Prince Philip and Princess Anne.

Issued: 10c, 3/12/70; ½c-4c, 9/2/70; 5c-8c, 11/4/70; 15c-20c, 1/20/71; 25c-50c, 9/1/71; $1-$2, 4/14/71; 23c, 12/1/71.

See Nos. 533-546. For surcharge see No. 480.

EXPO '70 Emblem, Geyser Restaurant — A178

Designs: 8c, EXPO '70 emblem and New Zealand Pavilion. 18c, EXPO '70 emblem and bush walk (part of N.Z. exhibit).

Perf. 13x13½

1970, Apr. 8 Photo. Unwmk.

459 A178 7c multicolored .75 .75
460 A178 8c multicolored .75 .75
461 A178 18c multicolored 1.50 1.50
Nos. 459-461 (3) 3.00 3.00

EXPO '70 Intl. Expo., Osaka, Japan.

UN Headquarters, New York — A179

UN, 25th anniv.: 10c, Plowing toward the sun and "25" with laurel.

1970, June 24 Litho. *Perf. 13½*

462 A179 3c multicolored .25 .25
463 A179 10c yellow & red .35 .35

Adoration, by Correggio — A180

Tower, Catholic Church, Sockburn A181

Christmas: 3c, Holy Family, stained glass window, First Presbyterian Church, Invercargill.

1970, Oct. 1 Unwmk. *Perf. 12½*

464 A180 2½c multicolored .25 .25
465 A180 3c multicolored .25 .25
a. Green omitted 275.00
466 A181 10c silver, org & blk .45 .45
Nos. 464-466 (3) .95 .95

Chatham Islands Mollymawk — A182

1970, Dec. 2 Photo. *Perf. 13x13½*

467 A182 1c Chatham Islands lily .25 .25
468 A182 2c shown .25 .25

G Clef, Emblem and Spinning Wheel A183

Rotary Emblem and Map of New Zealand A184

1971, Feb. 10 Photo. *Perf. 13x13½*

469 A183 4c multicolored .25 .25
470 A184 10c lemon, dk blue & gold .35 .35

50th anniv. of Country Women's Inst. (4c) and Rotary Intl. in New Zealand (10c).

Ocean Racer A185

8c, One Ton Cup and blueprint of racing yacht.

1971, Mar. 3 Litho. *Perf. 13½x13*

471 A185 5c blue, blk & red .25 .25
472 A185 8c ultra & black .65 .65

First challenge in New Zealand waters for the One Ton Cup ocean race.

Coats of Arms A186

1971, May 12 Photo. *Perf. 13x13½*

473 A186 3c Palmerston North .25 .25
474 A186 4c Auckland .25 .25
475 A186 5c Invercargill .30 .30
Nos. 473-475 (3) .80 .80

Centenary of New Zealand cities.

Map of Antarctica — A187

1971, June 9 Photo. *Perf. 13x13½*

476 A187 6c dk blue, pur & grn 1.40 *1.40*

10th anniv. of the Antarctic Treaty pledging peaceful uses of and scientific cooperation in Antarctica.

Child on Swing — A188

1971, June 9 *Perf. 13½x13*

477 A188 7c yellow & multi 1.00 1.00

25th anniv. of UNICEF.

Opening of New Zealand's 1st Satellite Earth Station near Warkworth A189

1971, July 14 *Perf. 11½*

478 A189 8c Radar Station .75 .75
479 A189 10c Satellite .75 .75

No. 441 Surcharged

1971 **Wmk. 253** *Perf. 13½x13*

480 A172 4c on 2½c multi .45 .25
a. Narrow bars .25 .25

Surcharge typographed on No. 480, photogravure or typographed on No. 480a.

Holy Night, by Carlo Maratta — A190

The Three Kings — A191

Christmas: 4c, Annunciation, stained glass window, St. Luke's Anglican Church, Havelock North.

Perf. 13x13½

1971, Oct. 6 **Photo.** **Unwmk.**

481 A190 3c orange & multi .25 .25
482 A191 4c multicolored .25 .25
483 A191 10c dk blue & multi .50 .50
Nos. 481-483 (3) 1.00 1.00

World Rose Convention — A192

1971, Nov. 3 *Perf. 11½*

484 A192 2c Tiffany rose .25 .25
485 A192 5c Peace rose .35 .35
486 A192 8c Chrysler Imperial rose .85 .85
Nos. 484-486 (3) 1.45 1.45

Rutherford and Alpha Particles Passing Atomic Nucleus A193

7c, Lord Rutherford, by Sir Oswald Birley, and formula of disintegration of nitrogen atom.

1971, Dec. 1 **Litho.** *Perf. 13½x13*

487 A193 1c gray & multi .25 .25
488 A193 7c multicolored .75 .75

Centenary of the birth of Ernest Lord Rutherford (1871-1937), physicist.

Benz, 1895 — A194

Vintage Cars: 4c, Oldsmobile, 1904. 5c, Model T Ford, 1914. 6c, Cadillac service car, 1915. 8c, Chrysler, 1924. 10c, Austin 7, 1923.

1972, Feb. 2 *Perf. 14x14½*

489 A194 3c brn, car & multi .25 .25
490 A194 4c brt lilac & multi .25 .25
491 A194 5c lilac rose & multi .30 .30
492 A194 6c gray grn & multi .40 .40
493 A194 8c vio blue & multi .60 .60
494 A194 10c sepia & multi .75 .75
Nos. 489-494 (6) 2.55 2.55

13th International Vintage Car Rally, New Zealand, Feb. 1972.

Asian-Oceanic Postal Union — A195

Designs: 3c, Wanganui City arms and Drurie Hill tower, vert. 5c, De Havilland DH89 and Boeing 737 planes, vert. 8c, French frigate and Maori palisade at Moturoa, vert. 10c, Stone cairn at Kaeo (site of first Methodist mission).

1972, Apr. 5 *Perf. 13x14, 14x13*

495 A195 3c violet & multi .30 .30
496 A195 4c brn org, blk & brn .30 .30
497 A195 5c blue & multi .45 .45
498 A195 8c green & multi 1.25 1.25
499 A195 10c olive, yel & blk 1.50 1.50
Nos. 495-499 (5) 3.80 3.80

Cent. of Council government at Wanganui (3c); 10th anniv. of Asian-Oceanic Postal Union (4c); 25th anniv. of Nat. Airways Corp. (5c); bicent. of the landing by Marion du Fresne at the Bay of Islands (8c); 150th anniv. of the Methodist Church in New Zealand (10c).

Black Scree Cotula — A196

Alpine Plants: 6c, North Is. edelweiss. 8c, Haast's buttercup. 10c, Brown mountain daisy.

1972, June 7 **Litho.** *Perf. 13x14*

500 A196 4c orange & multi .55 .55
501 A196 6c dp blue & multi .70 .70
502 A196 8c rose lilac & multi 1.10 1.10
503 A196 10c yel green & multi 1.50 1.50
Nos. 500-503 (4) 3.85 3.85

Madonna and Child, by Murillo — A197

Christmas: 5c, Resurrection, stained-glass window, St. John's Methodist Church, Levin. 10c, Pohutukawa (New Zealand's Christmas flower).

1972, Oct. 4 **Photo.** *Perf. 11½*

504 A197 3c gray & multi .25 .25
505 A197 5c gray & multi .25 .25
506 A197 10c gray & multi .65 .65
Nos. 504-506 (3) 1.15 1.15

New Zealand Lakes — A198

1972, Dec. 6 **Photo.** **Unwmk.**

507 A198 6c Waikaremoana 1.25 1.25
508 A198 8c Hayes 1.50 1.50
509 A198 18c Wakatipu 2.25 *2.25*
510 A198 23c Rotomahana 3.00 *3.00*
Nos. 507-510 (4) 8.00 8.00

Old Pollen Street A199

Coal Mining and Landscape A200

Cloister, University of Canterbury A201

Forest, Birds and Lake A202

Rowing and Olympic Emblems A203

Progress Chart A204

1973, Feb. 7 **Litho.** *Perf. 13½x13*

511 A199 3c ocher & multi .25 .25
512 A200 4c blue & multi .25 .25
513 A201 5c multicolored .25 .25
514 A202 6c blue & multi .50 .50
515 A203 8c multicolored .60 .60
516 A204 10c blue & multi .60 .60
Nos. 511-516 (6) 2.45 2.45

Centenaries of Thames and Westport Boroughs (3c, 4c); centenary of the Univ. of Canterbury, Christchurch (5c); 50th anniv. of Royal Forest and Bird Protection Soc. (6c); success of New Zealand rowing team at 20th Olympic Games (8c); 25th anniv. of the Economic Commission for Asia and the Far East (ECAFE, 10c).

Class W Locomotive, 1889 — A205

New Zealand Steam Locomotives: 4c, Class X, 1908. 5c, "Passchendaele" Ab Class. 10c, Ja Class, last steam locomotive.

1973, Apr. 4 **Litho.** *Perf. 14½*

517 A205 3c lt green & multi .35 .25
518 A205 4c lil rose & multi .35 .25
519 A205 5c lt blue & multi .45 .45
520 A205 10c cream & multi 1.75 1.75
Nos. 517-520 (4) 2.90 2.70

Maori Woman and Child, by Hodgkins — A206

Paintings by Frances Hodgkins: 8c, The Hill Top. 10c, Barn in Picardy. 18c, Self-portrait, Still Life.

1973, June 6 **Photo.** *Perf. 12x11½*

521 A206 5c multicolored .50 .50
522 A206 8c multicolored .90 .90
523 A206 10c multicolored .90 .90
524 A206 18c multicolored 1.50 1.50
Nos. 521-524 (4) 3.80 3.80

Christmas in New Zealand — A207

Christmas: 3c, Tempi Madonna, by Raphael. 5c, Three Kings, stained-glass window, St. Theresa's R.C. Church, Auckland.

1973, Oct. 3 **Photo.** *Perf. 12½x13½*

525 A207 3c gold & multi .25 .25
526 A207 5c gold & multi .25 .25
527 A207 10c gold & multi .50 .50
Nos. 525-527 (3) 1.00 1.00

Mt. Ngauruhoe A208

Perf. 13x13½, 13½x13

1973, Dec. 5 **Photo.**

528 A208 6c Mitre Peak .65 .65
529 A208 8c shown .85 .85
530 A208 18c Mt. Sefton, horiz. 1.60 1.60
531 A208 23c Burnett Range, horiz. 1.90 1.90
Nos. 528-531 (4) 5.00 5.00

Types of 1970-71

Designs as before.

Perf. 13½x13

1973-76 **Photo.** **Unwmk.**

533 A172 1c multicolored .60 *1.00*
a. Bklt. pane of 3 + 3 labels ('74) 2.50
534 A172 2c multicolored .30 .25
536 A172 3c multicolored .50 .50
537 A172 4c multicolored .45 .25

538	A173	5c multicolored	.60	.60
539	A173	6c multicolored	1.50	1.50
540	A173	7c multicolored	4.00	2.75
542	A173	8c multicolored	4.75	3.50

Perf. 14x13½

543	A174	10c multicolored	1.25	.25

Perf. 13x14, 14x13

544	A175	15c multicolored	.50	.50
545	A177	18c multicolored	2.00	.60
546	A175	20c yel brn & blk	.80	.80
		Nos. 533-546 (12)	17.25	12.50

Issued: 2c, 10c, 6/73; 1c, 4c, 6c, 9/7/73; 5c, 1973; 3c, 7c, 8c, 18c, 20c, 1974; 15c, 8/2/76.
For surcharges see Nos. 630-631.

Hurdles and Games' Emblem — A209

Designs: 5c, Paraplegic ballplayer. 10c, Bicycling. 18c, Rifle shooting. 23c, Lawn bowling. 4c, 10c, 18c and 23c stamps also show Commonwealth Games' emblem.

1974, Jan. 9 Litho. *Perf. 13x13½*

547	A209	4c yellow & multi	.30	.30
548	A209	5c violet & black	.30	.30
549	A209	10c brt red & multi	.70	.70
550	A209	18c brown & multi	.45	.45
551	A209	23c yel green & multi	.55	.55
		Nos. 547-551 (5)	2.30	2.30

10th British Commonwealth Games, Christchurch, 1/24-2/2. #548 for the 4th Paraplegic Games, Dunedin, 1/10-20.

Souvenir Sheet

New Zealand Day — A210

1974, Feb. 6 Litho. *Perf. 13*

552	A210	Sheet of 5	1.60	1.60
a.		4c Treaty House, Waitangi	.25	.25
b.		4c Parliament extension buildings	.25	.25
c.		4c Signing Treaty of Waitangi	.25	.25
d.		4c Queen Elizabeth II	.25	.25
e.		4c Integrated school	.25	.25

New Zealand Day (Waitangi Day). No. 552 has marginal inscription and imprint.

"Spirit of Napier" Fountain — A211

Clock Tower, Bern — A212

Design: 8c, UPU emblem.

1974, Apr. 3 Photo. *Perf. 11½*

553	A211	4c blue green & multi	.25	.25
554	A212	5c brown & multi	.25	.25
555	A212	8c lemon & multi	.60	.60
		Nos. 553-555 (3)	1.10	1.10

Centenaries of Napier (4c); UPU (5c, 8c).

Boeing Seaplane, 1919 A213

Designs: 4c, Lockheed Electra, 1937. 5c, Bristol freighter, 1958. 23c, Empire S30 flying boat, 1940.

1974, June 5 Litho. *Perf. 14x13*

556	A213	3c multicolored	.35	.35
557	A213	4c multicolored	.40	.40
558	A213	5c multicolored	.40	.40
559	A213	23c multicolored	1.60	1.60
		Nos. 556-559 (4)	2.75	2.75

Development of New Zealand's air transport.

Adoration of the Kings, by Conrad Witz — A214

Christmas: 5c, Angels, stained glass window, St. Paul's Church, Wellington. 10c, Christmas lily (lilium candidum).

1974, Oct. 2 Photo. *Perf. 11½*
Granite Paper

560	A214	3c olive & multi	.25	.25
561	A214	5c lilac & multi	.25	.25
562	A214	10c orange & multi	.50	.50
		Nos. 560-562 (3)	1.00	1.00

Offshore Islands A215

1974, Dec. 4 Photo. *Perf. 13½x13*

563	A215	6c Great Barrier	.40	.40
564	A215	8c Stewart	.60	.60
565	A215	18c White	.85	.85
566	A215	23c The Brothers	1.00	1.00
		Nos. 563-566 (4)	2.85	2.85

Child Using Walker A216

Farm Woman and Children A217

IWY Symbol A218

Otago Medical School A219

1975, Feb. 5 Litho. *Perf. 13½x13*

567	A216	3c orange & multi	.25	.25
568	A217	5c green & multi	.25	.25
569	A218	10c blue & multi	.25	*.25*
570	A219	18c multicolored	.50	*.50*
		Nos. 567-570 (4)	1.25	1.25

New Zealand Crippled Children's Soc., 40th anniv. (3c); Women's Division Federated Farmers of N. Z., 50th anniv. (5c); IWY (10c); Otago Medical School cent. (18c).

Scow "Lake Erie," 1873 A220

Historic Sailing Ships: 5c, Schooner "Herald," 1826. 8c, Brigantine "New Zealander," 1828. 10c, Topsail schooner "Jessie Kelly," 1866. 18c, Barque "Tory," 1834. 23c, Clipper "Rangitiki," 1863.

1975, Apr. 2 Litho. *Perf. 13½x13*

571	A220	4c vermilion & blk	.30	.30
572	A220	5c grnsh blue & blk	.30	.30
573	A220	8c yellow & black	.45	.45
574	A220	10c yellow grn & blk	.55	.55
575	A220	18c brown & black	.80	.80
576	A220	23c dull lilac & blk	.85	.85
		Nos. 571-576 (6)	3.25	3.25

State Forest Parks A221

1975, June 4 Photo. *Perf. 13½x13*

577	A221	6c Lake Sumner	.50	.50
578	A221	8c North West Nelson	.80	.80
579	A221	18c Kaweka	1.00	1.00
580	A221	23c Coromandel	1.25	1.25
		Nos. 577-580 (4)	3.55	3.55

Virgin and Child, by Zanobi Machiavelli (1418-1479) — A222

Stained Glass Window, Greendale Methodist/Presbyterian Church — A223

Christmas: 10c, Medieval ships and doves.

Perf. 13½x14, 14x13½

1975, Oct. 1 Photo.

581	A222	3c multicolored	.25	.25
582	A223	5c multicolored	.25	.25
583	A223	10c multicolored	.45	.45
		Nos. 581-583 (3)	.95	.95

Sterling Silver — A224

Roses: 2c, Lilli Marlene. 3c, Queen Elizabeth. 4c, Super star. 5c, Diamond jubilee. 6c, Cresset. 7c, Michele Meilland. 8c, Josephine Bruce. 9c, Iceberg.

1975, Nov. 26 Photo. *Perf. 14½x14*

584	A224	1c multicolored	.25	.25
585	A224	2c orange & multi	.25	.25
586	A224	3c ultra & multi	.25	.25
a.		Perf. 14½ ('79)	.25	.25
587	A224	4c purple & multi	.25	.25
588	A224	5c brown & multi	.25	.25
589	A224	6c multicolored ('76)	.25	.25
a.		Perf. 14½	.50	.50
590	A224	7c multicolored ('76)	.25	.25
a.		Perf. 14½	.70	.60
591	A224	8c yellow & multi ('76)	.25	.25
a.		Perf. 14½	.70	.60
592	A224	9c blue & multi	.25	.25
		Nos. 584-592 (9)	2.25	2.25

For surcharges see Nos. 693, 695, 718.

Family and Mothers' League Emblem A225

Designs: 7c, "Weight, measure, temperature and capacity." 8c, 1st emigrant ship "William Bryan" and Mt. Egmont. 10c, Maori and Caucasian women and YWCA emblem. 25c, Telecommunications network on Goode's equal area projection.

1976, Feb. 4 Litho. *Perf. 14*

593	A225	6c olive & multi	.25	.25
594	A225	7c lilac & multi	.25	.25
595	A225	8c red & multi	.25	.25
596	A225	10c yellow & multi	.25	.25
597	A225	25c tan & multi	.35	.35
		Nos. 593-597 (5)	1.35	1.35

League of Mothers of New Zealand, 50th anniv. (6c); Metric conversion, 1976 (7c); cent. of New Plymouth (8c); YWCA in New Zealand, 50th anniv. (10c); cent. of link into Intl. telecommunications network (25c).

Gig A226

Farm Vehicles: 7c, Thornycroft truck. 8c, Scandi wagon. 9c, Traction engine. 10c, Wool wagon. 25c, One-horse cart.

1976, Apr. 7 Litho. *Perf. 14x13½*

598	A226	6c dk olive & multi	.25	.25
599	A226	7c gray & multi	.25	.25
600	A226	8c dk blue & multi	.40	.40
601	A226	9c maroon & multi	.30	.30
602	A226	10c brown & multi	.30	.30
603	A226	25c multicolored	.90	.90
		Nos. 598-603 (6)	2.40	2.40

Purakaunui Falls — A227

Waterfalls: 14c, Marakopa Falls. 15c, Bridal Veil Falls. 16c, Papakorito Falls.

1976, June 2 Photo. *Perf. 11½*

604	A227	10c blue & multi	.35	.35
605	A227	14c lilac & multi	.50	.50
606	A227	15c ocher & multi	.60	.60
607	A227	16c multicolored	.75	.75
		Nos. 604-607 (4)	2.20	2.20

Nativity, Carved Ivory, Spain, 16th Century — A228

Christmas: 11c, Risen Christ, St. Joseph's Church, Grey Lynn, Auckland, horiz. 18c, "Hark the Herald Angels Sing," horiz.

Perf. 14x14½, 14½x14

1976, Oct. 6 Photo.

608	A228	7c ocher & multi	.25	.25
609	A228	11c ocher & multi	.35	.35
610	A228	18c ocher & multi	.45	.45
		Nos. 608-610 (3)	1.05	1.05

Maripi (Carved Wooden Knife) — A229

Maori Artifacts: 12c, Putorino, carved flute. 13c, Wahaika, hardwood club. 14c, Kotiate, violin-shaped weapon.

1976, Nov. 24 Photo. *Perf. 11½*
Granite Paper

611	A229 11c multicolored	.25	.25
612	A229 12c multicolored	.25	.25
613	A229 13c multicolored	.25	.25
614	A229 14c multicolored	.25	.25
	Nos. 611-614 (4)	1.00	1.00

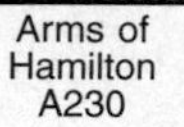

Arms of Hamilton
A230

Automobile Assoc. Emblem
A231

Designs: No. 616, Arms of Gisborne. No. 617, Arms of Masterton. No. 619, Emblem of Royal Australasian College of Surgeons.

1977, Jan. 19 Litho. *Perf. 13x13½*

615	A230 8c multicolored	.25	.25
616	A230 8c multicolored	.25	.25
617	A230 8c multicolored	.25	.25
a.	Strip of 3, #615-617	.75	*.75*
618	A231 10c multicolored	.30	.35
619	A230 10c multicolored	.30	.35
a.	Pair, #618-619	.60	*.75*
	Nos. 615-619 (5)	1.35	1.45

Centenaries of Hamilton, Gisborne and Masterton (cities); 75th anniv. of the New Zealand Automobile Assoc. and 50th anniv. of the Royal Australasian College of Surgeons.

Souvenir Sheet

Queen Elizabeth II, 1976 — A232

Designs: Various portraits.

1977, Feb. Photo. *Perf. 14x14½*

620	A232 Sheet of 5	1.25	*1.25*
a.-e.	8c single stamp	.25	.25
f.	Sheet imperf.	*1,350.*	

25th anniv. of the reign of Elizabeth II.

Physical Education, Maori Culture
A233

Education Dept., Geography, Science
A234

#623, Special school for the deaf; kindergarten. #624, Language class. #625, Home economics, correspondence school, teacher training.

1977, Apr. 6 Litho. *Perf. 13x13½*

621	A233 8c shown	.40	.40
622	A234 8c shown	.40	.40
623	A233 8c multicolored	.40	.40
624	A234 8c multicolored	.40	.40
625	A233 8c multicolored	.40	.40
a.	Strip of 5, #621-625	2.50	2.50
	Nos. 621-625 (5)	2.00	2.00

Cent. of Education Act, establishing Dept. of Education.

Karitane Beach — A235

Seascapes and beach scenes: 16c, Ocean Beach, Mount Maunganui. 18c, Piha Beach. 30c, Kaikoura Coast.

1977, June 1 Photo. *Perf. 14½*

626	A235 10c multicolored	.25	.25
627	A235 16c multicolored	.30	.30
628	A235 18c multicolored	.30	.30
629	A235 30c multicolored	.35	.35
	Nos. 626-629 (4)	1.20	1.20

Nos. 536-537 Surcharged with New Value and Heavy Bar

1977 Unwmk. *Perf. 13½x13*

630	A172 7c on 3c multicolored	.35	.35
631	A172 8c on 4c multicolored	.35	.35

Holy Family, by Correggio
A236

Window, St. Michael's and All Angels Church — A237

Partridge in a Pear Tree — A238

1977, Oct. 5 Photo. *Perf. 11½*

632	A236 7c multicolored	.25	.25
633	A237 16c multicolored	.30	.30
634	A238 23c multicolored	.50	.50
	Nos. 632-634 (3)	1.05	1.05

Christmas.

Merryweather Manual Pump, 1860 — A239

Fire Fighting Equipment: 11c, 2-wheel hose reel and ladder, 1880. 12c, Shand Mason Steam Fire Engine, 1873. 23c, Chemical fire engine, 1888.

1977, Dec. 7 Litho. *Perf. 14x13½*

635	A239 10c multicolored	.25	.25
636	A239 11c multicolored	.25	.25
637	A239 12c multicolored	.25	.25
638	A239 23c multicolored	.30	.30
	Nos. 635-638 (4)	1.05	1.05

A240

A240a

Parliament Building, Wellington — A241

1977-82 Photo. *Perf. 14½*

648	A240 10c ultra & multi	.25	.25
a.	Perf. 14½x14	.80	.50

Perf. 14½x14

649	A240a 24c blue & lt green	.30	.25
a.	Perf. 13x12½	.45	.25

Perf. 13

650	A241 $5 multicolored	4.00	2.00
	Nos. 648-650 (3)	4.55	2.50

Issued: No. 648, 2/79; No. 648a, 12/7/77; $5, 12/2/81; No. 649, 4/1/82; No. 649a, 12/13/82.

For surcharge see No. 694.

A242

Coil Stamps

1978 Photo. *Perf. 13½x13*

651	A242 1c red lilac	.25	.25
652	A242 2c orange	.25	.25
653	A242 5c brown	.25	.25

Perf. 14½x14

654	A242 10c ultramarine	.25	.25
	Nos. 651-654 (4)	1.00	1.00

Issue dates: 10c, May 3; others, June 9.

Ashburton
A244

Stratford
A245

Old Telephone — A246

Bay of Islands
A247

1978, Feb. 1 Litho. *Perf. 14*

656	A244 10c multicolored	.25	.25
657	A245 10c multicolored	.25	.25
a.	Pair, #656-657	.50	.50
658	A246 12c multicolored	.25	.25
659	A247 20c multicolored	.30	.30
	Nos. 656-659 (4)	1.05	1.05

Cent. of the cities of Ashburton, Stratford, the NZ Telephone Co. and Bay of Islands County.

Lincoln Univ. College of Agriculture, Cent. — A248

Designs: 10c, Students and Ivey Hall. 12c, Grazing sheep. 15c, Mechanical fertilization. 16c, Furrow, plow and tractor. 20c, Combine harvester. 30c, Grazing cattle.

1978, Apr. 26 *Perf. 14½*

660	A248 10c multicolored	.25	.25
661	A248 12c multicolored	.25	.25
662	A248 15c multicolored	.25	.25
663	A248 16c multicolored	.25	.25
664	A248 20c multicolored	.25	.25
665	A248 30c multicolored	.30	.30
	Nos. 660-665 (6)	1.55	1.55

Maui Gas Drilling Platform — A249

The sea and its resources: 15c, Fishing boat. 20c, Map of New Zealand and 200-mile limit. 23c, Whale and bottle-nosed dolphins. 35c, Kingfish, snapper, grouper and squid.

1978, June 7 Litho. *Perf. 13½x14*

666	A249 12c multicolored	.25	.25
667	A249 15c multicolored	.25	.25
668	A249 20c multicolored	.25	.25
669	A249 23c multicolored	.30	.30
670	A249 35c multicolored	.45	.45
	Nos. 666-670 (5)	1.50	1.50

All Saints Church, Howick
A250

Christmas: 7c, Holy Family, by El Greco, vert. 23c, Beach scene.

1978, Oct. 4 Photo. *Perf. 11½*

671	A250 7c gold & multi	.25	.25
672	A250 16c gold & multi	.30	.30
673	A250 23c gold & multi	.35	.35
	Nos. 671-673 (3)	.90	.90

Sea Shells — A251

20c, Paua (Haliotis Iris). 30c, Toheroa (paphies ventricosa). 40c, Coarse dosinia (dosinia anus). 50c, Spiny murex (poirieria zelandica).

1978, Nov. 29 Photo. *Perf. 13x12½*

674	A251 20c multicolored	.25	.25
675	A251 30c multicolored	.30	.25
676	A251 40c multicolored	.45	.30
677	A251 50c multicolored	.55	.40
	Nos. 674-677 (4)	1.55	1.20

See Nos. 696-697.

Julius Vogel — A252

19th cent. NZ statesmen: No. 679, George Grey. No. 680, Richard John Seddon.

1979, Feb. 7 Litho. *Perf. 13x13½*

678	A252 10c light & dark brown	.25	.25
679	A252 10c light & dark brown	.25	.25
680	A252 10c light & dark brown	.25	.25
a.	Strip of 3, #678-680	1.10	1.10

Riverlands Cottage, Blenheim — A253

Early NZ Architecture: 12c, Mission House, Waimate North, 1831-32. 15c, The Elms, Anglican Church Mission, Tauranga, 1847. 20c, Provincial Council Buildings, Christchurch, 1859.

1979, Apr. 4 ***Perf. 13½x13***
681 A253 10c multicolored .25 .25
682 A253 12c multicolored .25 .25
683 A253 15c black & gray .25 .25
684 A253 20c multicolored .25 .25
Nos. 681-684 (4) 1.00 1.00

Whangaroa Harbor — A254

Small Harbors: 20c, Kawau Island. 23c, Akaroa Harbor, vert. 35c, Picton Harbor, vert.

Perf. 13x13½, 13½x13
1979, June 6 **Photo.**
685 A254 15c multicolored .25 .25
686 A254 20c multicolored .25 .25
687 A254 23c multicolored .30 .30
688 A254 35c multicolored .40 .40
Nos. 685-688 (4) 1.20 1.20

IYC A255

1979, June 6 **Litho.** ***Perf. 14***
689 A255 10c Children playing .25 .25

Virgin and Child, by Lorenzo Ghiberti — A256

Christmas: 25c, Christ Church, Russell, 1835. 35c, Pohutukawa ("Christmas") tree.

1979, Oct. 3 **Photo.** ***Perf. 11½***
690 A256 10c multicolored .25 .25
691 A256 25c multicolored .35 .35
692 A256 35c multicolored .45 .45
Nos. 690-692 (3) 1.05 1.05

Nos. 591a, 648 and 589a Surcharged

1979, Sept. ***Perf. 14½, 14½x14 (14c)***
693 A224 4c on 8c multi .25 .25
694 A240 14c on 10c multi .25 .25
695 A224 17c on 6c multi .25 .25
Nos. 693-695 (3) .75 .75

Shell Type of 1978

$1, Scallop (pecten novaezelandiae). $2, Circular saw (astraea heliotropium).

1979, Nov. 26 **Photo.** ***Perf. 13x12½***
696 A251 $1 multicolored 1.25 .75
697 A251 $2 multicolored 2.50 1.00

Debating Chamber, House of Parliament A257

1979, Nov. 26 **Litho.** ***Perf. 14x13½***
698 A257 14c shown .25 .25
699 A257 20c Mace, black rod .25 .25
700 A257 30c Wall hanging .40 .40
Nos. 698-700 (3) .90 .90

25th Commonwealth Parliamentary Conference, Wellington, Nov. 26-Dec. 2.

NZ No. 1 A258

1980, Feb. 7 **Litho.** ***Perf. 14x13½***
701 A258 14c shown .25 .25
702 A258 14c No. 2 .25 .25
703 A258 14c No. 3 .25 .25
a. Souvenir sheet of 3, #701-703 2.00 2.00
b. Strip of 3, #701-703 .75 .75

NZ postage stamps, 125th anniv. No. 703a publicizes Zeapex '80 Intl. Stamp Exhib., Auckland, Aug. 23-31; it sold for 52c, of which 10c went to exhib. fund.

Maori Wood Carving, Tudor Towers A259

Earina Autumnalis and Thelymitra Venosa — A260

Tractor Plowing, Golden Plow Trophy A261

1980, Feb. 7 ***Perf. 14½***
704 A259 17c multicolored .25 .25
705 A260 25c multicolored .35 .35
706 A261 30c multicolored .45 .45
Nos. 704-706 (3) 1.05 1.05

Rotorua cent.; Intl. Orchid Conf., Auckland, Oct.; World Plowing Championship, Christchurch, May.

Ewelme Cottage, Parnell, 1864 A262

Early NZ Architecture: 17c, Broadgreen, Nelson, 1855. 25c, Courthouse, Oamaru, 1822, 30c, Government Buildings, Wellington, 1877.

1980, Apr. 2 **Litho.** ***Perf. 13½x13***
707 A262 14c multicolored .25 .25
708 A262 17c multicolored .25 .25
709 A262 25c green & black .30 .30
710 A262 30c multicolored .35 .35
Nos. 707-710 (4) 1.15 1.15

Harbors A263

1980, June 4 **Photo.** ***Perf. 13x13½***
711 A263 25c Auckland .30 .20
712 A263 30c Wellington .35 .35
713 A263 35c Lyttelton .40 .40
714 A263 50c Port Chalmers .65 .65
Nos. 711-714 (4) 1.70 1.60

Madonna and Child with Cherubim, by Andrea della Robbia — A264

1980, Oct. 1 **Photo.** ***Perf. 12***
715 A264 10c shown .25 .25
716 A264 25c St. Mary's Church, New Plymouth .30 .30
717 A264 35c Picnic .40 .40
Nos. 715-717 (3) .95 .95

Christmas.

No. 590 Surcharged

1980, Sept. 29 **Photo.** ***Perf. 14½x14***
718 A224 20c on 7c multicolored .25 .25

Te Heu Heu Tukino IV, Ngati Tuwharetoa Tribal Chief — A265

Maori Leaders: 25c, Te Hau-Takiri Wharepapa. 35c, Princess Te Puea Herangi. 45, Apirana Ngata. 60c, Hakopa Te Ata-o-tu.

1980, Nov. 26 ***Perf. 13***
719 A265 15c multicolored .25 .25
720 A265 25c multicolored .25 .25
721 A265 35c multicolored .35 .35
722 A265 45c multicolored .55 .55
723 A265 60c multicolored .60 .60
Nos. 719-723 (5) 2.00 2.00

Henry A. Feilding, Borough Emblem A266

1981, Feb. 4 **Litho.** ***Perf. 14½***
724 A266 20c multicolored .30 .25

Borough of Feilding centenary.

IYD A267

1981, Feb. 4
725 A267 25c orange & black .35 .35

Family and Dog — A268

1981, Apr. 1 **Litho.** ***Perf. 13***
726 A268 20c shown .25 .25
727 A268 25c Grandparents .30 .30
728 A268 30c Parents reading to children .35 .35
729 A268 35c Family outing .40 .40
Nos. 726-729 (4) 1.30 1.30

Shotover River — A269

1981, June 3 **Photo.** ***Perf. 13½***
730 A269 30c Kaiauai River, vert. .35 .35
731 A269 35c Mangahao River, vert. .40 .40
732 A269 40c shown .50 .50
733 A269 60c Cleddau River .65 .65
Nos. 730-733 (4) 1.90 1.90

Prince Charles and Lady Diana A270

1981, July 29 **Litho.** ***Perf. 14½***
734 A270 20c shown .30 .25
735 A270 20c St. Paul's Cathedral .30 .25
a. Pair, #734-735 .60 .60

Royal Wedding.

Golden Tainui — A271

Christmas: 14c, Madonna and Child, by Marco d'Oggiono, 15th cent. 30c, St. John's Church, Wakefield.

1981, Oct. **Photo.** ***Perf. 11½***
Granite Paper
736 A271 14c multicolored .25 .25
737 A271 30c multicolored .30 .30
738 A271 40c multicolored .45 .45
Nos. 736-738 (3) 1.00 1.00

SPCA Centenary A272

Intl. Science Year A273

Centenaries: No. 739, Tauranga. No. 740, Hawera. 30c, Frozen meat exports.

1982, Feb. 3 **Litho.** ***Perf. 14½***
739 A272 20c multicolored .25 .25
740 A272 20c multicolored .25 .25
a. Pair, #739-740 .60 .60
741 A272 25c multicolored .30 .30
742 A272 30c multicolored .40 .40
743 A273 35c multicolored .45 .45
Nos. 739-743 (5) 1.65 1.65

Alberton Farmhouse, Auckland, 1867 — A274

25c, Caccia Birch, Palmerston North, 1893. 30c, Dunedin Railway Station, 1904. 35c, PO, Ophir, 1886.

1982, Apr. 7 **Litho.**

744 A274 20c shown .25 .25
745 A274 25c multicolored .30 .30
746 A274 30c multicolored .45 .45
747 A274 35c multicolored .45 .45
Nos. 744-747 (4) 1.45 1.45

Summer, Kaiteriteri A275

40c, Autumn, Queenstown. 45c, Winter, Mt. Ngauruhoe. 70c, Spring, Wairarapa.

1982, June 2 **Photo.** ***Perf. 13½***

748 A275 35c shown .40 .40
749 A275 40c multicolored .45 .45
750 A275 45c multicolored .50 .50
751 A275 70c multicolored .85 .85
Nos. 748-751 (4) 2.20 2.20

Madonna with Child and Two Angels, by Piero di Cosimo — A276

Christmas: 35c, Rangiatea Maori Church, Otaki. 45c, Surf life-saving patrol.

1982, Oct. 6 **Photo.** ***Perf. 14***

752 A276 18c multicolored .25 .25
753 A276 35c multicolored .35 .35
754 A276 45c multicolored .60 .60
Nos. 752-754 (3) 1.20 1.20

Nephrite A277

Fruit Export A278

1982-83 **Litho.**

755 A277 1c shown .25 .25
a. Perf 13x12½ .40 .40
756 A277 2c Agate .25 .25
a. Perf 13x12½ 1.10 1.10
757 A277 3c Iron pyrites .25 .25
758 A277 4c Amethyst .25 .25
759 A277 5c Carnelian .25 .25
760 A277 9c Native sulphur .25 .25
761 A278 10c Grapes .25 .25
762 A278 20c Citrus fruit .30 .25
763 A278 30c Nectarines .35 .25
764 A278 40c Apples .40 .25
765 A278 50c Kiwifruit .45 .25
Nos. 755-765 (11) 3.25 2.75

Issued: A277, Dec. 1; A278, Dec. 7, 1983.

Native Birds — A279

1985-89 ***Perf. 14½***

766 A279 30c Kakapo .75 .25
767 A279 45c Falcon 1.25 .50
768 A279 $1 Kokako 1.25 .45
769 A279 $2 Black Robin 2.50 .70
a. Souvenir sheet of one 11.00 11.00
770 A279 $3 Stitchbird 4.00 2.75
770A A279 $4 Saddleback 4.75 3.25
Nos. 766-770A (6) 14.50 7.90

No. 769a for PHILEXFRANCE '89 and has margin picturing progressive proofs of No. 769. No. 769a sold for $3.50.

Issued: $1, $2, 4/24; $3, $4, 4/23/86; 30c, 45c, 5/1/86; No. 769a, 7/7/89.

See Nos. 830-835, 919-933.

Salvation Army in NZ Cent. — A280

Univ. of Auckland Cent. — A281

NZ-Australia Closer Economic Relationship Agreement — A282

Introduction of Rainbow Trout Cent. — A283

WCY — A284

Perf. 14, 14x13½ (35c)

1983, Feb. 2 **Litho.**

771 A280 24c multicolored .25 .25
772 A281 30c multicolored .30 .30
773 A282 35c multicolored .35 .35
774 A283 40c multicolored .60 .60
775 A284 45c multicolored .70 .70
Nos. 771-775 (5) 2.20 2.20

A285

1983, Mar. 14 **Litho.** ***Perf. 14***

776 A285 24c Queen Elizabeth II .30 .30
777 A285 35c Maori rock painting .35 .35
778 A285 40c Wool industry logos .45 .45
779 A285 45c Arms .65 .65
Nos. 776-779 (4) 1.75 1.75

Commonwealth Day.

Island Bay, by Rita Angus (1908-1970) A286

Landscapes.

1983, Apr. 6 **Litho.** ***Perf. 14½***

780 A286 24c shown .35 .35
781 A286 30c Central Otago .45 .45
782 A286 35c Wanaka .50 .50
783 A286 45c Tree, Greymouth .60 .60
Nos. 780-783 (4) 1.90 1.90

Lake Matheson A287

Perf. 13½x13, 13x13½

1983, June 1 **Photo.**

784 A287 35c Mt. Egmont, vert. .40 .40
785 A287 40c Cooks Bay, vert. .50 .50
786 A287 45c shown .60 .60
787 A287 70c Lake Alexandrina .95 .95
Nos. 784-787 (4) 2.45 2.45

Christmas 1983 — A288

18c, Holy Family of the Oak Tree, by Raphael. 35c, St. Patrick's Church, Greymouth. 45c, Star, poinsettias.

1983, Oct. 5 **Photo.** ***Perf. 12***

788 A288 18c multicolored .25 .25
789 A288 35c multicolored .45 .45
790 A288 45c multicolored .70 .70
Nos. 788-790 (3) 1.40 1.40

Antarctic Research A289

1984, Feb. 1 **Litho.** ***Perf. 13½x13***

791 A289 24c Geology .35 .35
792 A289 40c Biology .55 .55
793 A289 58c Glaciology .90 .90
794 A289 70c Meteorology .95 .95
a. Souvenir sheet of 4, #791-794 3.00 3.00
Nos. 791-794 (4) 2.75 2.75

Ferry Mountaineer, Lake Wakatipu, 1879 — A290

40c, Waikana, Otago Harbor, 1909. 58c, Britannia, Waitemata Harbor, 1885. 70c, Wakatere, Firth of Thames, 1896.

1984, Apr. 4 **Litho.** ***Perf. 13½***

795 A290 24c shown .40 .40
796 A290 40c multicolored .50 .50
797 A290 58c multicolored .65 .65
798 A290 70c multicolored .90 .90
Nos. 795-798 (4) 2.45 2.45

Skier, Mount Hutt — A291

1984, June 6 **Litho.** ***Perf. 13½x13***

799 A291 35c shown .40 .40
800 A291 40c Coronet Peak .50 .50
801 A291 45c Turoa .60 .60
802 A291 70c Whakapapa .85 .85
Nos. 799-802 (4) 2.35 2.35

Hamilton's Frog A292

1984, July 11 ***Perf. 13½***

803 A292 24c shown .25 .25
804 A292 24c Great barrier skink .25 .25
a. Pair, #803-804 .80 .80
805 A292 30c Harlequin gecko .30 .30
806 A292 58c Otago skink .60 .60
807 A292 70c Gold-striped gecko .80 .80
Nos. 803-807 (5) 2.20 2.20

No. 804a has continuous design.

Christmas A293

Designs: 18c, Adoration of the Shepherds, by Lorenzo Di Credi. 35c, Old St. Paul's Church, Wellington, vert. 45c, Bell, vert.

Perf. 13½x14, 14x13½

1984, Sept. 26 **Photo.**

808 A293 18c multicolored .25 .25
809 A293 35c multicolored .35 .35
810 A293 45c multicolored .50 .50
Nos. 808-810 (3) 1.10 1.10

Military History A294

1984, Nov. 7 **Litho.** ***Perf. 15x14***

811 A294 24c South Africa, 1901 .40 .40
812 A294 40c France, 1917 .60 .60
813 A294 58c North Africa, 1942 .80 .80
814 A294 70c Korea & Southeast Asia, 1950-72 .90 .90
a. Souvenir sheet of 4, #811-814 2.75 2.75
Nos. 811-814 (4) 2.70 2.70

St. John Ambulance Assoc. Cent. in NZ A295

1985, Jan. 16 **Litho.** ***Perf. 14***

815 A295 24c multicolored .25 .25
816 A295 30c multicolored .30 .30
817 A295 40c multicolored .45 .45
Nos. 815-817 (3) 1.00 1.00

Early Transportation — A296

24c, Nelson Horse Tram, 1862. 30c, Graham's Town-Steam, 1871. 35c, Dunedin Cable Car, 1881. 40c, Auckland Electric, 1902. 45c, Wellington Electric, 1904. 58c, Christchurch Electric, 1905.

1985, Mar. 6 **Litho.** ***Perf. 13½***

818 A296 24c multicolored .40 .25
819 A296 30c multicolored .40 .40
820 A296 35c multicolored .45 .45
821 A296 40c multicolored .50 .50
822 A296 45c multicolored .55 .55
823 A296 58c multicolored .60 .60
Nos. 818-823 (6) 2.90 2.75

Bridges A297

1985, June 12 **Photo.** ***Perf. 11½***

824 A297 35c Shotover .45 .45
825 A297 40c Alexandra .50 .50
826 A297 45c So. Rangitikei .65 .65
827 A297 70c Twin Bridges .90 .90
Nos. 824-827 (4) 2.50 2.50

Bird Type of 1985 and

Elizabeth II — A298

1985-89 Litho. *Perf. 14½x14*

828 A298 25c multicolored .40 .40
829 A298 35c multicolored .60 .60

Perf. 14½

830 A279 40c Blue duck .65 .25
831 A279 60c Brown teal 1.00 .65
832 A279 70c Paradise shelduck 1.05 .75
a. Souvenir sheet of 1 *10.00 10.00*
835 A279 $5 Takahe 7.00 6.00
Nos. 828-835 (6) 10.70 8.65

Size of 70c, 22x27mm.

No. 832a for World Stamp Expo '89. Sold for $1.50.

Issued: 25c, 35c, 7/1/85; 40c, 60c, 2/2/87; 70c, 6/7/88; $5, 4/20/88; #832a, 11/17/89.

Christmas A301

Carol "Silent Night, Holy Night," by Joseph Mohr (1792-1848), Austrian clergyman.

Perf. 13½x12½

1985, Sept. 18 Litho.

836 A301 18c Stable .25 .25
837 A301 40c Shepherds .55 .55
838 A301 50c Angels .60 .60
Nos. 836-838 (3) 1.40 1.40

Navy Ships A302

25c, Philomel, 1914-1947. 45c, Achilles, 1936-1946. 60c, Rotoiti, 1949-1965. 75c, Canterbury, 1971-.

1985, Nov. 6 Litho. *Perf. 13½*

839 A302 25c multicolored .40 .25
840 A302 45c multicolored .75 .75
841 A302 60c multicolored 1.00 1.00
842 A302 75c multicolored 1.25 1.25
a. Souvenir sheet of 4, #839-842 4.00 *4.00*
Nos. 839-842 (4) 3.40 3.25

Police Force Act, Cent. — A303

Designs: a, Radio operators, 1940-1985. b, Mounted policeman, 1890, forensic specialist in mobile lab, 1985. c, Police station, 1895, policewoman and badge, 1985. d, 1920 motorcycle, 1940s car, modern patrol cars and graphologist. e, Original Mt. Cook Training Center and modern Police College, Poriria.

1986, Jan. 15 *Perf. 14½x14*

843 Strip of 5 2.00 2.00
a.-e. A303 25c any single .35 .25

Intl. Peace Year — A304

1986, Mar. 5 *Perf. 13½x13*

844 25c Tree .35 .25
845 25c Dove .35 .25
a. A304 Pair, #844-845 .80 .70

Motorcycles — A305

1986, Mar. 5

846 A305 35c 1920 Indian Power Plus .50 .50
847 A305 45c 1927 Norton CS1 .60 .60
848 A305 60c 1930 BSA Sloper .75 .75
849 A305 75c 1915 Triumph Model H .95 .95
Nos. 846-849 (4) 2.80 2.80

Knight's Point — A306

1986, June 11 Litho. *Perf. 14*

850 A306 55c shown .65 .65
851 A306 60c Beck's Bay .70 .70
852 A306 65c Doubtless Bay .75 .75
853 A306 80c Wainui Bay .80 .80
a. Miniature sheet of one 1.90 1.90
Nos. 850-853 (4) 2.90 2.90

No. 853a sold for $1.20. Surtax benefited the "NZ 1990" executive committee.

No. 853a exists with Stockholmia '86 emblem. This sheet was sold only at the exhibition.

The Twelve Days of Christmas — A307

1986, Sept. 17 Photo. *Perf. 14½*

854 A307 25c First day .35 .25
855 A307 55c Second .55 .55
856 A307 65c Third .90 .90
Nos. 854-856 (3) 1.80 1.70

Music — A308

1986, Nov. 5 Litho. *Perf. 14½x14*

857 A308 30c Conductor .45 .30
858 A308 60c Brass band .60 .60
859 A308 80c Highland pipe band .95 .95
860 A308 $1 Country music 1.10 1.10
Nos. 857-860 (4) 3.10 2.95

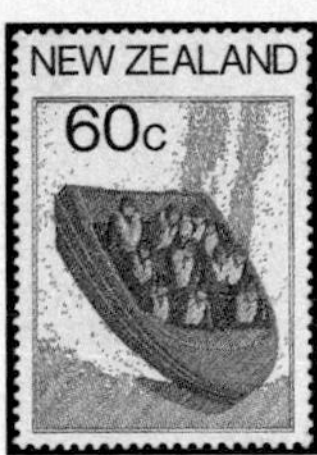

Tourism — A309

1987, Jan. 14 *Perf. 14½x14*

861 A309 60c Boating .75 .75
862 A309 70c Aviation .90 .90
863 A309 80c Camping 1.00 1.00
864 A309 85c Windsurfing 1.10 1.10
865 A309 $1.05 Mountain climbing 1.25 1.25
866 A309 $1.30 White water rafting 1.50 1.50
Nos. 861-866 (6) 6.50 6.50

Blue Water Classics A310

1987, Feb. 2 *Perf. 14x14½*

867 A310 40c Southern Cross Cup .60 .35
868 A310 80c Admiral's Cup 1.00 1.00
869 A310 $1.05 Kenwood Cup 1.25 1.25
870 A310 $1.30 America's Cup 1.50 1.50
Nos. 867-870 (4) 4.35 4.10

Vesting Day — A311

a, Motor vehicles, plane. b, Train, bicycle.

1987, Apr. 1 Litho. *Perf. 13½*

871 A311 Pair 1.75 1.75
a.-b. 40c any single .60 .40

Establishment of NZ Post Ltd., Apr. 1, replacing the NZ PO.

Royal NZ Air Force, 50th Anniv. A312

Designs: 40c, Avro 626, Wigram Airfield, c. 1937. 70c, P-40 Kittyhawks. 80c, Sunderland seaplane. 85c, A4 Skyhawks.

1987, Apr. 15 *Perf. 14x14½*

872 A312 40c multicolored .60 .60
873 A312 70c multicolored 1.00 1.00
874 A312 80c multicolored 1.10 1.10
875 A312 85c multicolored 1.25 1.25
a. Souvenir sheet of 4, #872-875 5.50 5.50
b. As "a," ovptd. with CAPEX '87 emblem in margin 10.00 10.00
Nos. 872-875 (4) 3.95 3.95

Natl. Parks System, Cent. — A313

1987, June 17 Litho. *Perf. 14½*

876 A313 70c Urewera .85 1.00
877 A313 80c Mt. Cook .90 1.10
878 A313 85c Fiordland 1.00 1.10
879 A313 $1.30 Tongariro 1.75 2.10
a. Souvenir sheet of one 3.50 3.50
b. As "a," ovptd. with CAPEX '87 emblem in margin 11.00 11.00
Nos. 876-879 (4) 4.50 5.30

No. 879a sold for $1.70 to benefit the NZ 1990 World Phil. Exhib., Auckland.

Christmas Carols — A314

1987, Sept. 16 Litho. *Perf. 14x14½*

880 A314 35c Hark! The Herald Angels Sing .50 .40
881 A314 70c Away in a Manger .90 .90
882 A314 85c We Three Kings of Orient Are 1.25 1.25
Nos. 880-882 (3) 2.65 2.55

Maori Fiber Art — A315

1987, Nov. 4 Litho. *Perf. 12*

883 A315 40c Knot .55 .45
884 A315 60c Binding .75 .75
885 A315 80c Plait .95 .95
886 A315 85c Flax fiber 1.00 1.00
Nos. 883-886 (4) 3.25 3.15

Royal Phil. Soc. of NZ, Cent. A316

Portrait of Queen Victoria by Chalon — A317

Queen Elizabeth II and: No. 887, No. 61 (blue background). No. 888, No. 62 (red background).

1988, Jan. 13 *Perf. 14x14½*

887 A316 40c multicolored .55 .45
888 A316 40c multicolored .55 .45
a. Pair, #887-888 1.25 1.25

Souvenir Sheet

889 A317 $1 multicolored 2.75 2.75
a. Overprinted with SYDPEX '88 emblem in margin 30.00 30.00

NZ Electrification, Cent. — A318

1988, Jan. 13 *Perf. 14x14½*

890 A318 40c Geothermal .45 .45
891 A318 60c Thermal .55 .55
892 A318 70c Gas .75 .75
893 A318 80c Hydroelectric 1.00 1.00
Nos. 890-893 (4) 2.75 2.75

Maori Rafter Paintings — A319

1988, Mar. 2 Litho. *Perf. 14½*
894 A319 40c Mangopare .65 .65
895 A319 40c Koru .65 .65
896 A319 40c Raupunga .65 .65
897 A319 60c Koiri .95 .95
Nos. 894-897 (4) 2.90 2.90

Greetings Messages A320

1988, May 18 Litho. *Perf. 13½x13*
Booklet Stamps
898 A320 40c Good luck .75 .75
899 A320 40c Keeping in touch .75 .75
900 A320 40c Happy birthday .75 .75

Size: 41x27mm
901 A320 40c Congratulations .75 .75
902 A320 40c Get well soon .75 .75
a. Bklt. pane of 5, #898-902 4.25

Landscapes A321

1988, June 8 *Perf. 14½*
903 A321 70c Milford Track .80 .80
904 A321 80c Heaphy Track .85 .85
905 A321 85c Copland Track .95 .95
906 A321 $1.30 Routeburn Track *1.50* 1.50
a. Miniature sheet of one 2.75 2.75
Nos. 903-906 (4) 4.10 4.10

No. 906a sold for $1.70 to benefit the exhibition.

NEW ZEALAND 1990
Souvenir Sheets
Four souvenir sheets were sold by the New Zealand post to benefit NEW ZEALAND 1990 World Stamp Exhibition. They each contain three $1 and one $2 "stamps" picturing antarctic scenes. They are not valid for postage.

Australia Bicentennial A322

Caricature: Kiwi and koala around campfire.

1988, June 21
907 A322 40c multicolored .55 .55

See Australia No. 1086.

Christmas Carols — A323

Illuminated manuscripts: 35c, O, Come All Ye Faithful, by John Francis Wade, 1742. 70c, Hark! the Herald Angels Sing. 80c, Ding Dong! Merrily on High. 85c, The First Noel, first published in Davies & Gilbert's Some Ancient Christmas Carols, 1832.

1988, Sept. 14 Litho. *Perf. 14½*
908 A323 35c multicolored .55 .40
909 A323 70c multicolored .95 .95
910 A323 80c multicolored 1.00 1.00
911 A323 85c multicolored 1.10 1.10
Nos. 908-911 (4) 3.60 3.45

New Zealand Heritage A324

The Land. Paintings by 19th cent. artists: 40c, Lake Pukaki, 1862, by John Gully. 60c, On the Grass Plain Below Lake Arthur, 1846, by William Fox. 70c, View of Auckland, 1873, by John Hoyte. 80c, Mt. Egmont from the Southward, 1840, by Charles Heaphy. $1.05, Anakiwa, Queen Charlotte Sound, 1871, by John Kinder. $1.30, White Terraces, Lake Rotomahana, 1880, by Charles Barraud.

1988, Oct. 5 Litho. *Perf. 14x14½*
912 A324 40c multicolored .50 .25
913 A324 60c multicolored .70 .70
914 A324 70c multicolored .90 .90
915 A324 80c multicolored 1.00 1.00
916 A324 $1.05 multicolored 1.20 1.20
917 A324 $1.30 multicolored 1.40 1.40
Nos. 912-917 (6) 5.70 5.45

Kiwi A325

1988, Oct. 19 Engr. *Perf. 14½*
918 A325 $1 green 2.50 2.50
a. Booklet pane of 6 12.50
b. Litho. 2.50 2.50

Value is for stamp with surrounding selvage. No. 918 issued in booklets only.
No. 918b is from No. 1161a.
See Nos. 1027, 1161, 1445, 1635, 1787, 2368-2370.

Bird Type of 1985
1988-95 Litho. *Perf. 14½x14*
Sizes: $10, 26x31½mm, Others, 22x27mm
919 A279 5c Spotless crake .25 .25
920 A279 10c Banded dotterel .25 .25
921 A279 20c Yellowhead .30 .25
a. Perf. 13½ .75 .75
922 A279 30c Silvereye .45 .25
923 A279 40c Brown kiwi .65 .30
c. Perf. 13½x13 3.00 3.00
924 A279 45c Rock wren .70 .25
b. Booklet pane of 10 6.50
925 A279 50c Kingfisher .80 .35
926 A279 60c Spotted shag .95 .80
a. Sheet of 8, #919-926 5.00 5.00
b. Perf. 13½ 7.00 7.00
927 A279 80c Fiordland crested penguin 1.25 1.00
928 A279 80c New Zealand falcon 1.25 1.00
Complete booklet, 10 #928 12.50
c. Perf. 12 on 3 sides 4.00 4.00
d. As "c," booklet pane of 10 40.00
Complete booklet, #928d 40.00
929 A279 90c South Is. robin 1.40 1.25
930 A279 $10 Little spotted kiwi 9.50 6.75
d. Souv. sheet of 1 20.00 20.00

Self-Adhesive
Die Cut Perf 11½
931 A279 40c like #923 .65 .50
932 A279 45c like #924 .70 .55

Die Cut Perf 10½x11
933 A279 45c like #924 .70 .55
Nos. 919-933 (15) 19.80 14.30

No. 933 has a darker blue background than No. 932 and has perf "teeth" at the corners while No. 932 does not. Perf "teeth" on the top and left side are staggered to line up with perf "holes" on the bottom and right on No. 933. "Teeth" line up with "teeth" on No. 932.
PHILAKOREA '94 (#926a). POST'X '95 Postal Exhibition (#930d).
Issued: $10, 4/19/89; #931, 4/17/91; 5c, #924, 932, 7/1/91; #933, 1991; #928, 3/31/93; #926a, 8/16/94; #930d, 2/3/95; #921a, 926b, 9/22/95; #923c, 11/8/89; others, 11/2/88.

Whales of the Southern Oceans A326

1988, Nov. 2 Litho. *Perf. 13½*
936 A326 60c Humpback .95 .95
937 A326 70c Killer 1.00 1.00
938 A326 80c Southern right 1.10 1.10
939 A326 85c Blue 1.25 1.25
940 A326 $1.05 Southern bottle-nose 1.50 1.50
941 A326 $1.30 Sperm 1.75 1.75
Nos. 936-941 (6) 7.55 7.55

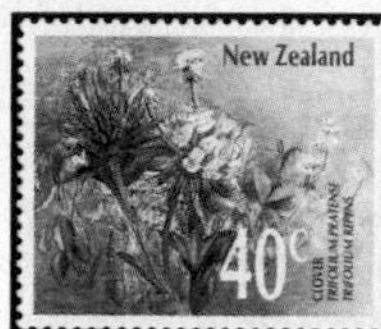

Wildflowers A327

1989, Jan. 18 Litho. *Perf. 14½*
942 A327 40c Clover .55 .55
943 A327 60c Lotus .75 .75
944 A327 70c Montbretia .80 .80
945 A327 80c Wild ginger .95 .95
Nos. 942-945 (4) 3.05 3.05

Authors — A328

Portraits: 40c, Katherine Mansfield (1888-1923). 60c, James K. Baxter (1926-1972). 70c, Bruce Mason (1921-1982). 80c, Ngaio Marsh (1899-1982).

1989, Mar. 1 Litho. *Perf. 12½*
946 A328 40c multicolored .45 .45
947 A328 60c multicolored .65 .65
948 A328 70c multicolored .70 .70
949 A328 80c multicolored .80 .80
Nos. 946-949 (4) 2.60 2.60

New Zealand Heritage A329

The people.

1989, May 17 *Perf. 14x14½*
950 A329 40c Moriori .60 .35
951 A329 60c Prospectors .85 .85
952 A329 70c Land settlers .70 .70
953 A329 80c Whalers .85 .85
954 A329 $1.05 Missionaries .95 .95
955 A329 $1.30 Maori 1.25 1.25
Nos. 950-955 (6) 5.20 4.95

Trees — A330

1989, June 7
956 A330 80c Kahikatea .90 .90
957 A330 85c Rimu .95 .95
958 A330 $1.05 Totara 1.25 1.25
959 A330 $1.30 Kauri 1.40 1.40
a. Miniature sheet of one 3.00 3.00
Nos. 956-959 (4) 4.50 4.50

No. 959a sold for $1.80. Surtax benefited the "NZ 1990" executive committee.

Christmas — A331

Star of Bethlehem illuminating settings: 35c, View of One Tree Hill from a bedroom window. 65c, A shepherd overlooking snow-capped mountains. 80c, Boats in harbor. $1, Earth.

1989, Sept. 13 Litho. *Perf. 14½*
960 A331 35c multicolored .40 .25
a. Booklet pane of 10 5.50
961 A331 65c multicolored .75 .75
962 A331 80c multicolored .95 .95
963 A331 $1 multicolored 1.10 1.10
Nos. 960-963 (4) 3.20 3.05

New Zealand Heritage A332

The sea.

1989, Oct. 11 Litho. *Perf. 14x14½*
964 A332 40c Windsurfing .50 .25
965 A332 60c Fishing .65 .65
966 A332 65c Swordfish .90 .90
967 A332 80c Harbor 1.00 1.00
968 A332 $1 Gulls over coast 1.25 1.25
969 A332 $1.50 Container ship 1.90 1.90
Nos. 964-969 (6) 6.20 5.95

14th Commonwealth Games, Auckland, Jan. 24-Feb. 3, 1990 — A333

1989, Nov. 8 *Perf. 14½*
970 A333 40c Emblem .45 .45
971 A333 40c Goldie character trademark .45 .45
a. Souvenir sheet of 2, #970-971, sailboats ('90) 2.75 2.75
b. As "a," stadium ('90) 2.75 2.75
972 A333 40c Gymnastics .45 .45
973 A333 50c Weight lifting .55 .55
974 A333 65c Swimming .75 .75
975 A333 80c Cycling .95 .95
976 A333 $1 Lawn bowling 1.00 1.00
977 A333 $1.80 Hurdles 1.50 1.50
Nos. 970-977 (8) 6.10 6.10

Air New Zealand, 50th Anniv. A334

1990, Jan. 17 *Perf. 13½x14½*
978 A334 80c multicolored 1.50 1.25

Souvenir Sheet

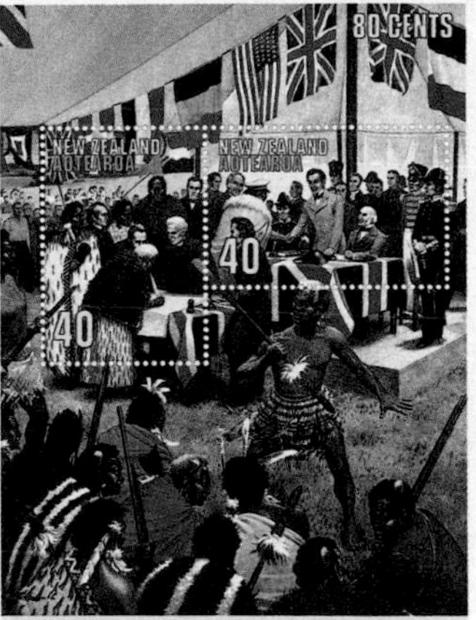

Treaty of Waitangi, 150th Anniv. — A335

Painting by Leonard Mitchell: a, Maori chief signing the treaty. b, Chief Hone Heke shaking hand of Lt.-Gov. William Hobson.

1990, Jan. 17 *Perf. 13½*

979	A335	Sheet of 2	3.50	3.50
a.-b.		40c any single	1.40	1.40

New Zealand Heritage A336

The Ships: No. 980, Polynesian double-hulled canoe, c. 1000. No. 981, Endeavour. No. 982, Tory. No. 983, Crusader. No. 984, Edwin Fox. No. 985, Arawa.

1990, Mar. 7 Litho. *Perf. 14x14½*

980	A336	40c multi	.60	.25
981	A336	50c multi	.75	.75
a.		Souvenir sheet of 1	*20.00*	*20.00*
982	A336	60c multi	.90	.90
983	A336	80c multi	1.40	1.40
984	A336	$1 multi	1.50	1.50
985	A336	$1.50 multi	2.00	2.00
		Nos. 980-985 (6)	7.15	6.80

No. 981a for Stamp World London '90. Sold for $1.30. Issued May 3.

Miniature Sheet

Orchids — A337

Designs: a, Sun. b, Spider. c, Winika. d, Greenhood. e, Odd-leaved orchid.

1990, Apr. 18 Litho. *Perf. 14½*

986		Sheet of 5	7.00	7.00
a.-d.		A337 40c any single	1.00	1.00
e.		A337 80c multicolored	2.00	2.00

No. 986 sold for $4.90. Surcharge for the intl. stamp exhibition, Auckland, Aug. 24-Sept 2. Imperf. sheets were available only in season tickets which were sold for $25. Value, $35

New Zealand Heritage A338

The Achievers: 40c, Grace Neill (1846-1926), nurse, journalist. 50c, Jean Batten (1909-1982), aviator. 60c, Katherine Sheppard (1848-1934), social worker. 80c, Richard Pearse (1877-1953), inventor. $1, Gov.-Gen. Bernard Freyberg (1889-1963). $1.50, Peter Buck (1877-1951), cabinet minister.

1990, May 16 Litho. *Perf. 14x14½*

987	A338	40c multicolored	.65	.30
988	A338	50c multicolored	.80	.80
989	A338	60c multicolored	.95	.95
990	A338	80c multicolored	1.25	1.25
991	A338	$1 multicolored	1.50	1.50
992	A338	$1.50 multicolored	1.75	1.75
		Nos. 987-992 (6)	6.90	6.55

Akaroa Harbor — A339

Early Settlements: $1, Durie Hill, Wanganui River. $1.50, Mt. Victoria, Wellington. $1.80, Rangitoto Island, Takapuna Beach, Auckland.

1990, June 13 Litho. *Perf. 14½*

993	A339	80c multicolored	1.00	1.00
994	A339	$1 multicolored	1.40	1.40
995	A339	$1.50 multicolored	2.25	2.25
996	A339	$1.80 multicolored	2.50	2.50
a.		Souvenir sheet of 1	4.25	4.25
		Nos. 993-996 (4)	7.15	7.15

No. 996a sold for $2.30. Surtax for world philatelic expo, New Zealand '90.

New Zealand Heritage A340

The Maori: 40c, Legend of Rangi and Papa. 50c, Maori feather cloak. 60c, Song. 80c, Maori tattoo. $1, War canoe prow. $1.50, Maori war dance.

1990, Aug. 24 Litho. *Perf. 14*

997	A340	40c multicolored	.55	.30
998	A340	50c multicolored	.65	.65
999	A340	60c multicolored	.75	.75
1000	A340	80c multicolored	.85	.85
1001	A340	$1 multicolored	1.25	1.25
1002	A340	$1.50 multicolored	1.75	1.75
		Nos. 997-1002 (6)	5.80	5.55

Souvenir Sheet

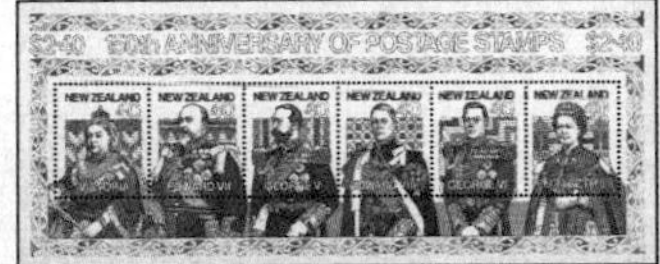

First Postage Stamps, 150th Anniv. — A341

Designs: a, Victoria. b, Edward VII. c, George V. d, Edward VIII. e, George VI. f, Elizabeth II.

1990, Aug. 29 Engr. *Perf. 14½x14*

1003	A341	40c Sheet of 6	5.25	5.25
a.-f.		any single	.75	.75

Christmas — A342

Various angels.

1990, Sept. 12 Litho. *Perf. 14*

1004	A342	40c multicolored	.55	.40
1005	A342	$1 multicolored	1.25	.25
1006	A342	$1.50 multicolored	2.00	1.25
1007	A342	$1.80 multicolored	2.25	2.00
		Nos. 1004-1007 (4)	6.05	3.90

Antarctic Petrel — A343

50c, Wilson's storm petrel. 60c, Snow petrel. 80c, Antarctic fulmar. $1, Chinstrap penguin. $1.50, Emperor penguin.

1990, Nov. 7 *Perf. 13½x13*

1008	A343	40c shown	.65	.35
1009	A343	50c multicolored	.80	.70
1010	A343	60c multicolored	.95	.85
1011	A343	80c multicolored	1.25	1.10
1012	A343	$1 multicolored	1.60	1.60
1013	A343	$1.50 multicolored	2.40	2.25
		Nos. 1008-1013 (6)	7.65	6.85

Sheep — A344

1991, Jan. 23 Litho. *Perf. 14½*

1014	A344	40c Coopworth	.55	.25
1015	A344	60c Perendale	.80	.80
1016	A344	80c Corriedale	1.00	1.00
1017	A344	$1 Drysdale	1.25	1.25
1018	A344	$1.50 South Suffolk	1.75	1.75
1019	A344	$1.80 Romney	2.00	2.00
		Nos. 1014-1019 (6)	7.35	7.05

Map, Royal Albatross, Designs from Moriori House, Moriori Man, Nikau Palm, Tree Carving — A345

Design: 80c, Map, sailing ship, carving, petroglyph, Moriori house, Tommy Solomon, last full-blooded Moriori.

1991, Mar. 6 Litho. *Perf. 13½*

1020	A345	40c shown	.65	.55
1021	A345	80c multicolored	1.25	1.10

Discovery of the Chatham Islands, Bicent.

New Zealand Football (Soccer) Assoc., Cent. A346

Designs: a, Goal. b, 5 players, referee.

1991, Mar. 6

1022		Pair	2.50	2.50
a.-b.		A346 80c any single	1.25	1.25

Tuatara A347

Designs: No. 1023, Juvenile. No. 1024, In burrow. No. 1025, Female. No. 1026, Male.

1991, Apr. 17 Litho. *Perf. 14½*

Denomination Color

1023	A347	40c gray blue	1.00	1.00
1024	A347	40c dark brown	1.00	1.00
1025	A347	40c olive green	1.00	1.00
1026	A347	40c orange brown	1.00	1.00
		Nos. 1023-1026 (4)	4.00	4.00

Kiwi Type of 1988

1991, Apr. 17 Engr. *Perf. 14½*

1027	A325	$1 red	1.60	1.25
a.		Litho.	1.75	1.50

Value is for stamp with surrounding selvage. No. 1027a is from Nos.1161a, 1635a.

Happy Birthday — A348

Thinking of You — A349

1991, May 15 Litho. *Perf. 14x13½*

Size of Nos. 1031-1032, 1036-1037: 41x27mm

1028	A348	40c Clown face	.90	.90
1029	A348	40c Balloons	.90	.90
1030	A348	40c Birthday hat	.90	.90
1031	A348	40c Present	.90	.90
1032	A348	40c Cake & candles	.90	.90
a.		Bklt. pane of 5, #1028-1032	6.00	
1033	A349	40c shown	.90	.90
1034	A349	40c Cat, slippers	.90	.90
1035	A349	40c Cat, alarm clock	.90	.90
1036	A349	40c Cat looking out window	.90	.90
1037	A349	40c Cat walking by door	.90	.90
a.		Bklt. pane of 5, #1033-1037	6.00	
		Nos. 1028-1037 (10)	9.00	9.00

See Nos. 1044-1053.

Rock Formations A350

40c, Punakaiki Rocks. 50c, Moeraki Boulders. 80c, Organ Pipes. $1, Castle Hill. $1.50, Te Kaukau Point. $1.80, Ahuriri River Clay Cliffs.

1991, June 12 Litho. *Perf. 14½*

1038	A350	40c multicolored	.60	.35
1039	A350	50c multicolored	.75	.75
1040	A350	80c multicolored	1.10	1.10
1041	A350	$1 multicolored	1.25	1.25
1042	A350	$1.50 multicolored	2.00	2.00
1043	A350	$1.80 multicolored	2.25	2.25
		Nos. 1038-1043 (6)	7.95	7.70

Greetings Types

1991, July 1 Litho. *Perf. 14x13½*

Size of Nos. 1047-1048, 1052-1053: 41x27mm

1044	A348	45c like #1028	.90	.90
1045	A348	45c like #1029	.90	.90
1046	A348	45c like #1030	.90	.90
1047	A348	45c like #1031	.90	.90
1048	A348	45c like #1032	.90	.90
a.		Bklt. pane of 5, #1044-1048	5.50	
1049	A349	45c like #1033	.90	.90
1050	A349	45c like #1034	.90	.90
1051	A349	45c like #1035	.90	.90
1052	A349	45c like #1036	.90	.90
1053	A349	45c like #1037	.90	.90
a.		Bklt. pane of 5, #1049-1053	5.50	
		Nos. 1044-1053 (10)	9.00	9.00

1991 Rugby World Cup — A351

1991, Aug. 21 Litho. *Perf. 14½x14*

1054 A351 80c Children's 1.00 1.00
1055 A351 $1 Women's 1.10 1.10
1056 A351 $1.50 Senior 2.00 2.00
1057 A351 $1.80 All Blacks 2.25 2.25
a. Souvenir sheet of 1 4.00 4.00
b. As "a," with Phila Nippon '91 emblem in margin *12.50 12.50*
Nos. 1054-1057 (4) 6.35 6.35

No. 1057a sold for $2.40 to benefit philatelic trust for hobby support.

Christmas A352

1991, Sept. 18 Litho. *Perf. 13½x14*

1058 A352 45c Shepherds .55 .55
1059 A352 45c Wise men, camels .55 .55
1060 A352 45c Mary, Baby Jesus .55 .55
1061 A352 45c Wise man, gift .55 .55
a. Block of 4, #1058-1061 3.00 3.00
1062 A352 65c Star .90 .90
1063 A352 $1 Crown 1.50 1.50
1064 A352 $1.50 Angel 2.00 2.00
Nos. 1058-1064 (7) 6.60 6.60

Butterflies A354

1991-2008 Litho. *Perf. 14¼*

1075 A354 $1 Forest ringlet 1.40 1.10
a. Perf. 14x14½ on 3 sides 5.00 5.00
b. Booklet pane of 5 + 5 labels Perf. 14x14½ on 3 sides 25.00
Complete booklet, #1075b 25.00
c. Perf. 13¾x14¼ 2.00 2.00
1076 A354 $2 Southern blue 3.00 2.25
a. Perf. 13¾x14¼ 15.00 15.00
1077 A354 $3 Yellow admiral 4.00 3.50
a. Souvenir sheet of 1 10.00 10.00
b. Perf. 13¾x14¼ 15.00 15.00
1078 A354 $4 Common copper 5.00 3.00
a. Perf. 13¾x14¼ 7.00 5.25
b. Perf. 14 ('08) 6.25 4.50
1079 A354 $5 Red admiral 6.50 5.00
a. Perf. 13¾x14¼ 8.50 6.00
Nos. 1075-1079 (5) 19.90 14.85

No. 1077a issued later for Phila Nippon '91.

Issued: #1075, 1075a, 1076, 1077, 11/6/91; $4-$5, 1/25/95; #1075b, 9/1/95; #1078a, 10/97; #1079a, 10/9/96; #1075c, 1076a, 11/6/96; #1077b, Aug. 1996..

Mount Cook — A356

Die Stamped & Engr.
Perf. 14½x15

1994, Feb. 18 Wmk. 387

1084 A356 $20 gold & blue 22.50 15.00

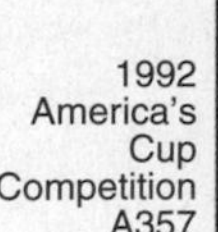

1992 America's Cup Competition A357

45c, KZ7 Kiwi Magic, 1987. 80c, KZ1 New Zealand, 1988. $1, America, 1851. $1.50, New Zealand, 1992.

1992, Jan. 22 Litho. *Perf. 14x14½*

1085 A357 45c multicolored .60 .25
1086 A357 80c multicolored .95 .95
1087 A357 $1 multicolored 1.25 1.25
1088 A357 $1.50 multicolored 1.50 1.50
Nos. 1085-1088 (4) 4.30 3.95

Sighting of New Zealand by Abel Tasman, 350th Anniv. A358

1992, Mar. 12 *Perf. 13½x14½*

1089 A358 45c Heemskerck .60 .30
1090 A358 80c Zeehaen 1.00 1.00
1091 A358 $1 Santa Maria 1.40 1.40
1092 A358 $1.50 Pinta and Nina 1.75 1.75
a. Souvenir sheet of 2, #1091-1092, Perf. 14x14½ 7.50 7.50
Nos. 1089-1092 (4) 4.75 4.45

Discovery of America, 500th anniv. (#1091-1092).

Issue date: No. 1092a, May 22. World Columbian Stamp Expo (#1092a).

1992 Summer Olympics, Barcelona A359

1992, Apr. 3 Litho. *Perf. 13½*

1093 A359 45c Runners .70 .60

Antarctic Seals — A360

1992, Apr. 8 *Perf. 14x13½*

1094 A360 45c Weddell seal .70 .60
1095 A360 50c Crabeater seal .80 .70
1096 A360 65c Leopard seal 1.00 .85
1097 A360 80c Ross seal 1.25 1.00
1098 A360 $1 Southern elephant seal 1.60 1.40
1099 A360 $1.80 Hooker's sea lion 2.75 2.50
Nos. 1094-1099 (6) 8.10 7.05

1992 Summer Olympics, Barcelona A361

1992, May 13 Litho. *Perf. 13½*

1100 A361 45c Cycling .65 .40
1101 A361 80c Archery 1.00 1.00
1102 A361 $1 Equestrian 1.25 1.25
1103 A361 $1.50 Board sailing 1.75 1.75
a. Souvenir sheet of 4, #1100-1103, perf 14x14½ 5.75 5.75
b. No. 1103a overprinted 11.00 11.00
Nos. 1100-1103 (4) 4.65 4.40

No. 1103b overprint consists of World Columbian Stamp Expo emblem in sheet margin. Issue date: No. 1103b, May 22.

Glaciers A362

45c, Glacier ice. 50c, Tasman glacier. 80c, Snowball glacier. $1, Brewster glacier. $1.50, Fox glacier. $1.80, Franz Josef glacier.

1992, June 12

1104 A362 45c multicolored .60 .30
1105 A362 50c multicolored .70 .70
1106 A362 80c multicolored .85 .85
1107 A362 $1 multicolored 1.25 1.25
1108 A362 $1.50 multicolored 1.60 1.60
1109 A362 $1.80 multicolored 1.75 1.75
Nos. 1104-1109 (6) 6.75 6.45

Camellias — A363

45c, Grand finale. 50c, Showa-no-sakae. 80c, Sugar dream. $1, Night rider. $1.50, E.G. Waterhouse. $1.80, Dr. Clifford Parks.

1992, July 8 *Perf. 14½*

1110 A363 45c multicolored .60 .30
1111 A363 50c multicolored .70 .70
1112 A363 80c multicolored .90 .90
1113 A363 $1 multicolored 1.10 1.10
1114 A363 $1.50 multicolored 1.50 1.50
1115 A363 $1.80 multicolored 1.75 1.75
Nos. 1110-1115 (6) 6.55 6.25

Scenic Views of New Zealand — A364

No. 1116, Tree, hills. No. 1117, Hills, stream. No. 1118, Hills, mountain tops. No. 1119, Glacier. No. 1120, Trees, green hills. No. 1121, Tree branch, rapids. No. 1122, Rocky shoreline. No. 1123, Fjord. No. 1124, Glacial runoff. No. 1125, Vegetation, stream.

1992, Sept. 1 Litho. *Perf. 14x14½*
Booklet Stamps

1116 A364 45c multicolored .65 .65
1117 A364 45c multicolored .65 .65
1118 A364 45c multicolored .65 .65
1119 A364 45c multicolored .65 .65
1120 A364 45c multicolored .65 .65
1121 A364 45c multicolored .65 .65
1122 A364 45c multicolored .65 .65
1123 A364 45c multicolored .65 .65
1124 A364 45c multicolored .65 .65
1125 A364 45c multicolored .65 .65
a. Bklt. pane of 10, #1116-1125 8.75
Nos. 1116-1125 (10) 6.50 6.50

No. 1125a has continous design.

Christmas — A365

No. 1126, Two reindeer over village. No. 1127, Two reindeer pulling Santa's sleigh. No. 1128, Christmas tree in window. No. 1129, Two children looking out window. 65c, Fireplace, stockings. $1, Church. $1.50, People beneath pohutukawa tree at beach.

1992, Sept. 16 *Perf. 14½*

1126 A365 45c multicolored .50 .50
1127 A365 45c multicolored .50 .50
1128 A365 45c multicolored .50 .50
1129 A365 45c multicolored .50 .50
a. Block of 4, #1126-1129 2.50 2.50
1130 A365 65c multicolored .75 .75
1131 A365 $1 multicolored 1.00 1.00
1132 A365 $1.50 multicolored 1.75 1.75
Nos. 1126-1132 (7) 5.50 5.50

No. 1129a has continous design.

A366

The Emerging Years: The 1920s: 45c, Flaming youth. 50c, Birth of broadcasting. 80c, All Blacks rugby player. $1, The swaggie. $1.50, Motorcar brings freedom. $1.80, Arrival of the air age.

1992, Nov. 4 Litho. *Perf. 13½*

1133 A366 45c multicolored .50 .25
1134 A366 50c multicolored .55 .35
1135 A366 80c multicolored .85 .85
1136 A366 $1 multicolored .95 .95
1137 A366 $1.50 multicolored 1.75 1.75
1138 A366 $1.80 multicolored 2.00 2.00
Nos. 1133-1138 (6) 6.60 6.15

Royal Doulton Ceramics A367

45c, Character jug, "Old Charley." 50c, Plate from "Bunnykins" series. 80c, Maori art tea ware. $1, Hand painted "Ophelia" plate. $1.50, Burslem figurine of St. George. $1.80, Salt glazed vase.

1993, Jan. 20 Litho. *Perf. 13*

1139 A367 45c multicolored .50 .25
1140 A367 50c multicolored .55 .55
1141 A367 80c multicolored .85 .85
1142 A367 $1 multicolored 1.00 1.00
1143 A367 $1.50 multicolored 1.50 1.50
1144 A367 $1.80 multicolored 1.75 1.75
a. Souvenir sheet of 1 2.50 2.50
Nos. 1139-1144 (6) 6.15 5.90

A368

The Emerging Years: The 1930's: 45c, Buttons and bows, the new femininity. 50c, The Great Depression. 80c, Race horse, Phar Lap. $1, State housing. $1.50, Free milk for schools. $1.80, The talkies.

1993, Feb. 17 Litho. *Perf. 14½x14*

1145 A368 45c multicolored .55 .25
1146 A368 50c multicolored .60 .60
1147 A368 80c multicolored .95 .95
1148 A368 $1 multicolored 1.00 1.00
1149 A368 $1.50 multicolored 1.50 1.50
1150 A368 $1.80 multicolored 1.75 1.75
Nos. 1145-1150 (6) 6.35 6.05

Woman Suffrage, Cent. — A369

1993, Mar. 31 Litho. *Perf. 13½*

1151 A369 45c First vote .55 .25
1152 A369 80c War work .85 .85
1153 A369 $1 Child care .95 .95
1154 A369 $1.50 Contemporary women 2.40 2.40
Nos. 1151-1154 (4) 4.75 4.45

Thermal Wonders A370

45c, Champagne Pool. 50c, Boiling mud, Rotorua. 80c, Emerald Pool. $1, Hakereteke Falls. $1.50, Warbrick Terrace. $1.80, Pohutu Geyser.

1993, May 5 Litho. *Perf. 12*

1155 A370 45c multicolored .55 .25
1156 A370 50c multicolored .65 .65
1157 A370 80c multicolored 1.00 1.00
1158 A370 $1 multicolored 1.10 1.10
1159 A370 $1.50 multicolored 1.50 1.50
1160 A370 $1.80 multicolored 2.00 2.00
a. Souvenir sheet of 1 3.50 3.50
Nos. 1155-1160 (6) 6.80 6.50

No. 1160a inscribed with Bangkok '93 emblem in sheet margin. Issue date: No. 1160a, Oct. 1.

Kiwi Type of 1988

1993, June 9 Engr. *Perf. 14½*

1161 A325 $1 blue 1.50 1.50
a. Souv. sheet of 3, #918b, 1027a, 1161 8.50 8.50
b. Litho. 2.25 1.75
c. Souv. sheet of 3, #918b, 1027a, 1161b 6.00 6.00

Taipei '93, Asian Intl. Stamp Exhibition (#1161a), Hong Kong '94 (#1161c).
Value is for stamp with surrounding selvage.
Issued: #1161a, 8/14/93; #1161c, 2/18/94.
See No. 1635a.

Species Unique to New Zealand A371

Designs: No. 1162, Yellow-eyed penguin, Hector's dolphin, New Zealand fur seal. 1162A, Taiko, Mt. Cook lily, blue duck. 1162B, Giant snail, rock wren, Hamilton's frog. 1162C, Kaka, Chatham Island pigeon, giant weta.
No. 1163, Tusked weta.

1993, June 9 Litho. *Perf. 14x14½*

1162 A371 45c multi .85 .85
1162A A371 45c multi .85 .85
1162B A371 45c multi .85 .85
1162C A371 45c multi .85 .85
d. As #1162-1162C, block of 4 4.25 4.25
1163 A371 45c multicolored 1.00 1.00
a. Booklet pane of 10 10.00 —
Complete booklet 10.50
Nos. 1162-1163 (5) 4.40 4.40

World Wildlife Fund.
Nos. 1162-1162C were issued both in sheets containing individual designs and in sheets containing the four values setenant (#1162d).

Christmas — A372

Christmas designs: No. 1164, Flowers from pohutukawa tree, denomination at UL. No. 1165, Like #1164, denomination at UR. No. 1166, Present with yellow ribbon, denomination at LL. No. 1167, Present with red ribbon, denomination at LR. $1.00, Ornaments, cracker, sailboats. $1.50, Wreath, sailboats, present.

1993, Sept. 1 Litho. *Perf. 14½x14*

1164 A372 45c multicolored .60 .60
1165 A372 45c multicolored .60 .60
1166 A372 45c multicolored .60 .60
1167 A372 45c multicolored .60 .60
a. Block of 4, #1164-1167 2.75 2.75
1168 A372 $1 multicolored 1.25 1.10
1169 A372 $1.50 multicolored 2.00 1.75
Nos. 1164-1169 (6) 5.65 5.25

Booklet Stamps
Perf. 12

1164a A372 45c multicolored 1.00 1.00
1165a A372 45c multicolored 1.00 1.00
1166a A372 45c multicolored 1.00 1.00
1167b A372 45c multicolored 1.00 1.00
c. Bklt. pane, 2 ea #1166a, 1167b, 3 ea #1164a-1165a 17.50

At least one edge of No. 1167c is guillotined.

Fish — A373

Designs: No. 1170, Paua (#1175). No. 1171, Greenshell mussels. No. 1172, Terakihi (#1171). No. 1173, Salmon (#1172). No. 1174, Southern bluefin tuna, albacore tuna, kahawai (#1173). No. 1175, Rock lobster (#1171). No. 1176, Snapper (#1177). No. 1177, Grouper ("Groper," #1178). No. 1178, Orange roughy (#1179). No. 1179, Squid, hoki, oreo dory (#1173, #1174, #1178).

1993, Sept. 1 *Perf. 13½*
Booklet Stamps

1170 A373 45c multicolored .80 .80
1171 A373 45c multicolored .80 .80
1172 A373 45c multicolored .80 .80
1173 A373 45c multicolored .80 .80
1174 A373 45c multicolored .80 .80
1175 A373 45c multicolored .80 .80
1176 A373 45c multicolored .80 .80
1177 A373 45c multicolored .80 .80
1178 A373 45c multicolored .80 .80
1179 A373 45c multicolored .80 .80
a. Booklet pane of 10, #1170-1179 + 2 labels 10.00
Nos. 1170-1179 (10) 8.00 8.00

Nos. 1179a has continuous design.

Dinosaurs — A374

1993, Oct. 1

1180 A374 45c Sauropod .60 .50
1181 A374 80c Pterosaur 1.10 1.10
1182 A374 $1 Ankylosaur 1.25 1.25
1183 A374 $1.20 Mauisaurus 1.50 1.50
1184 A374 $1.50 Carnosaur 1.60 1.60
a. Souvenir sheet of 1, perf. 14½x14 2.25 2.00
b. As "a," inscribed with Bangkok '93 emblem 3.00 2.75
Nos. 1180-1184 (5) 6.05 5.95

Booklet Stamp
Size: 25½x23½mm
Perf. 12

1185 A374 45c Carnosaur, sauropod .70 .55
a. Booklet pane of 10 + 2 labels 7.00 7.00

The 1940s — A375

Designs: 45c, New Zealand at war. 50c, Crop dusting. 80c, State produces hydroelectricity. $1, New Zealand Marching Assoc. $1.50, The American invasion. $1.80, Victory.

1993, Nov. 3 Litho. *Perf. 14*

1186 A375 45c multicolored .65 .30
1187 A375 50c multicolored .75 .75
1188 A375 80c multicolored 1.10 1.10
1189 A375 $1 multicolored 1.40 1.40
1190 A375 $1.50 multicolored 2.00 2.00
1191 A375 $1.80 multicolored 2.25 2.25
Nos. 1186-1191 (6) 8.15 7.80

Outdoor Adventure Sports — A376

1994, Jan. 19 Litho. *Perf. 12*

1192 A376 45c Bungy jumping .60 .30
1193 A376 80c Trout fishing .95 .95
1194 A376 $1 Jet boating, horiz. 1.25 1.25
1195 A376 $1.50 Tramping 1.75 1.75
1196 A376 $1.80 Heli-skiing 2.00 2.00
a. Souvenir sheet of 1 3.75 3.75
Nos. 1192-1196 (5) 6.55 6.25

No. 1196a inscribed in sheet margin with Hong Kong '94 emblem and text in English and Chinese. Issue date: No. 1196a, Feb. 18.

White Water Rafting — A377

1994, Jan. 19 Litho. *Perf. 12*
Booklet Stamp

1197 A377 45c multicolored .55 .55
a. Booklet pane of 10 + 4 labels 6.00

Whitbread Trans-Global Yacht Race — A378

1994, Jan. 19 *Perf. 15*

1198 A378 $1 Endeavour 1.40 1.40

Used value is for stamp with complete selvage.

The 1950's — A379

Designs: 45c, Rock and roll. 80c, Conquest of Mt. Everest. $1, Aunt Daisy, "Good Morning Everybody." $1.20, Royal visit, 1953. $1.50, Opo, the Friendly Dolphin. $1.80, The Coat Hanger (Auckland Harbor Bridge.)

1994, Mar. 24 Litho. *Perf. 14*

1199 A379 45c multicolored .60 .30
1200 A379 80c multicolored .95 .95
1201 A379 $1 multicolored 1.25 1.25
1202 A379 $1.20 multicolored 1.50 1.50
1203 A379 $1.50 multicolored 1.75 1.75
1204 A379 $1.80 multicolored 2.25 2.25
Nos. 1199-1204 (6) 8.30 8.00

Scenic Views of the Four Seasons A380

Designs: 45c, Winter, Mt. Cook, Mt. Cook lily. 70c, Spring, Lake Hawea, kowhai flower. $1.50, Summer, Opononi, pohutukawa flower. $1.80, Autumn, Mt. Cook, Lake Pukaki, puriri flower.

1994, Apr. 27 *Perf. 12*

1205 A380 45c multicolored .50 .30
1206 A380 70c multicolored .85 .85
1207 A380 $1.50 multicolored 1.25 1.25
1208 A380 $1.80 multicolored 1.75 1.75
a. Strip of 4, #1205-1208 5.00 5.00
Nos. 1205-1208 (4) 4.35 4.15

Paua Shell — A381

Pavlova Dessert A382

Jandals — A383

Bush Shirt — A384

Buzzy Bee Toy — A385

Kiwi Fruit — A386

Kiwiana: #1211, Hokey pokey ice cream. #1212, Fish and chips. #1216, Black singlet, gumboots. #1217, Rugby shoes, ball.

1994, Apr. 27 Litho. *Perf. 12*
Booklet Stamps

1209 A381 45c shown .55 .55
1210 A382 45c shown .55 .55
1211 A381 45c multicolored .55 .55
1212 A382 45c multicolored .55 .55
1213 A383 45c shown .55 .55
1214 A384 45c shown .55 .55
1215 A385 45c shown .55 .55
1216 A384 45c multicolored .55 .55
1217 A385 45c multicolored .55 .55
1218 A386 45c shown .55 .55
a. Booklet pane of 10, #1209-1218 7.50
Nos. 1209-1218 (10) 5.50 5.50

Maori Myths — A387

Designs: 45c, Maui pulls up Te Ika (the fish). 80c, Rona is snatched up by Marama (moon). $1, Maui attacks Tuna (eel). $1.20, Tane separates Rangi (sky) and Papa (earth). $1.50, Matakauri slays Giant of Wakatipu. $1.80, Panenehu shows Koura (crayfish) to Tangaroa.

1994, June 8 *Perf. 13*

1219 A387 45c multicolored .65 .35
1220 A387 80c multicolored .95 .95
1221 A387 $1 multicolored 1.25 1.25
1222 A387 $1.20 multicolored 1.50 1.50

1223 A387 $1.50 multicolored 1.90 1.90
1224 A387 $1.80 multicolored 2.25 2.25
Nos. 1219-1224 (6) 8.50 8.20

First Manned Moon Landing, 25th Anniv. — A388

1994, July 20 Litho. *Perf. 12*
1225 A388 $1.50 multicolored 2.25 2.25

No. 1225 has a holographic image. Soaking in water may affect the hologram.

People Reaching People — A389

Serpentine Die Cut 11
1994, July 20 Photo.
Self-Adhesive
1226 A389 45c multicolored .60 .50
a. Arrow partially covering hole in "B," serpentine die cut 11¼ 2.00 .75

No. 1226a issued Aug. 1995.
See No. 1311.

Wild Animals A390

1994, Aug. 16 Litho. *Perf. 14*
1227 A390 45c Hippopotamus .75 .75
1228 A390 45c Spider monkey .75 .75
1229 A390 45c Giant panda .75 .75
1230 A390 45c Polar bear .75 .75
1231 A390 45c African elephant .75 .75
1232 A390 45c White rhinoceros .75 .75
1233 A390 45c African lion .75 .75
1234 A390 45c Plains zebra .75 .75
1235 A390 45c Giraffe .75 .75
1236 A390 45c Siberian tiger .75 .75
a. Block of 10, #1227-1236 9.00 9.00
b. Souvenir sheet of 6, #1229-1231, 1233, 1235-1236 4.50 4.50
Nos. 1227-1236 (10) 7.50 7.50

PHILAKOREA '94 (#1236b). Nos. 1227-1236 printed in sheets of 100. Because of the design of these sheets, blocks or strips of Nos. 1227-1236 exist in 10 different arrangements. Value assigned to No. 1236a applies to all arrangements.

Christmas A391

Designs: No. 1237, Children, Nativity scene. 70c, Magi, father, child. 80c, Carolers, stained glass window. $1, Carolers, Christmas tree. $1.50, Children, candles. $1.80, Father, mother, infant.
No. 1243, Children, Christmas tree, Santa.

1994, Sept. 21 Litho. *Perf. 14*
1237 A391 45c multicolored .60 .50
1238 A391 70c multicolored .90 .90
1239 A391 80c multicolored 1.10 1.10
1240 A391 $1 multicolored 1.25 1.25
a. Souv. sheet, 1 ea #1237-1240 4.00 4.00
1241 A391 $1.50 multicolored 1.50 1.50
1242 A391 $1.80 multicolored 1.75 1.75
Nos. 1237-1242 (6) 7.10 7.00

Booklet Stamp
Size: 30x25mm
1243 A391 45c multicolored .55 .55
a. Booklet pane of 10 7.00

Cricket in New Zealand, Cent. — A392

Beach Cricket — A393

No. 1248: a, Woman with striped bathing suit in ocean. b, Person on bodyboard in ocean. c, Child holding float toy at water's edge. d, Boy with beach ball. e, Man holding ice cream cone. f, Beach umbrella at LL. g, Man in blue and red shorts holding cricket bat. h, Woman with cap holding cricket bat. i, Child with pail and shovel. j, Sunbather reading newspaper.

1994, Nov. 2 *Perf. 13½*
1244 A392 45c Batting .60 .40
1245 A392 80c Bowling 1.10 .80
1246 A392 $1 Wicketkeeping 1.25 1.25
1247 A392 $1.80 Fielding 2.00 2.00
Nos. 1244-1247 (4) 4.95 4.45
Perf. 12
1248 45c Bklt. pane of 10 8.00 8.00
a.-j. A393 Any single .70 .55

New Zealand at Night A394

1995, Feb. 22 Litho. *Perf. 12*
1249 A394 45c Auckland .65 .30
1250 A394 80c Wellington 1.00 .60
1251 A394 $1 Christchurch 1.40 1.00
1252 A394 $1.20 Dunedin 1.60 1.60
1253 A394 $1.50 Rotorua 1.75 1.75
1254 A394 $1.80 Queenstown 2.00 2.00
a. Souv. sheet of 6, #1249-1254 25.00 25.00
Nos. 1249-1254 (6) 8.40 7.25

Singapore '95, Jakarta '95 (#1254a).
Issued: No. 1254a, 9/1/95.

Golf Courses — A395

1995, Mar. 22 Litho. *Perf. 14*
1255 A395 45c Waitangi .65 .35
1256 A395 80c New Plymouth 1.00 1.00
1257 A395 $1.20 Rotorua 1.50 1.50
1258 A395 $1.80 Queenstown 2.50 2.50
Nos. 1255-1258 (4) 5.65 5.35

Environmental Protection A396

No. 1259, Native fauna, flora. No. 1260, Plant native trees, shrubs. No. 1261, Protect marine mammals. No. 1262, Conserve power, water. No. 1263, Enjoy natural environment. No. 1264, Control animal pests. No. 1265, Eliminate noxious plants. No. 1266, Return undersized catches. No. 1267, Control air, water quality. No. 1268, Dispose of trash properly.

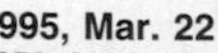

1995, Mar. 22
1259 A396 45c multicolored .65 .65
1260 A396 45c multicolored .65 .65
1261 A396 45c multicolored .65 .65
1262 A396 45c multicolored .65 .65
1263 A396 45c multicolored .65 .65
1264 A396 45c multicolored .65 .65
1265 A396 45c multicolored .65 .65
1266 A396 45c multicolored .65 .65
1267 A396 45c multicolored .65 .65
1268 A396 45c multicolored .65 .65
a. Booklet pane, #1259-1268 7.50
Complete booklet, #1268a 8.00
Nos. 1259-1268 (10) 6.50 6.50

Maori Language — A397

Designs: 45c, Treasured Language Nest. 70c, Sing to awaken the spirit. 80c, Acquire knowledge through stories. $1, The welcoming call. $1.50, Recite the genealogies that link people. $1.80, Tell the lore of the people.

1995, May 3 Litho. *Perf. 13½*
1269 A397 45c multicolored .60 .25
1270 A397 70c multicolored .90 .90
1271 A397 80c multicolored 1.10 1.10
1272 A397 $1 multicolored 1.25 1.25
1273 A397 $1.50 multicolored 2.00 2.00
1274 A397 $1.80 multicolored 2.25 2.25
Nos. 1269-1274 (6) 8.10 7.75

Asian Development Bank, 28th Meeting of the Board of Governors, Auckland — A398

Design: $1.50, Pacific Basin Economic Council, 28th Intl. Meeting, Auckland.

1995, May 3
1275 A398 $1 Map shown 1.25 1.25
1276 A398 $1.50 Map of Pacific 2.00 2.00

Team New Zealand, 1995 America's Cup Winner — A399

1995, May 16 *Perf. 12*
1277 A399 45c Black Magic yacht .70 .60

Rugby League, Cent. A400

Designs: No. 1278, Club Rugby League, Lion Red Cup. No. 1282, Trans Tasman. $1, Mini League. $1.50, George Smith, Albert Baskerville, Early Rugby League. $1.80, Intl. Rugby League, Courtney Intl. Goodwill Trophy.

1995, July 26 Litho. *Perf. 14*
1278 A400 45c multicolored .65 .25
1279 A400 $1 multicolored 1.40 1.40
1280 A400 $1.50 multicolored 2.10 2.10
1281 A400 $1.80 multicolored 2.50 2.50
a. Souvenir sheet of 1 3.00 3.00
Nos. 1278-1281 (4) 6.65 6.25

Booklet Stamp
Perf. 12 on 3 Sides
1282 A400 45c multicolored .60 .60
a. Booklet pane of 10 7.00
Complete booklet, #1282a 7.00

#1281a exists imperf from a "Limited Edition" album.

From 1995 onward, New Zealand Post has released a series of "Limited Edition" albums in editions of 2,000. Some contain souvenir sheets unique to these albums.

Farm Animals — A401

1995 Litho. *Perf. 14x14½*
Booklet Stamps
1283 A401 40c Sheep .50 .50
1284 A401 40c Deer .50 .50
1285 A401 40c Horses .50 .50
1286 A401 40c Cattle .50 .50
1287 A401 40c Goats .50 .50
1288 A401 40c Turkey .50 .50
1289 A401 40c Ducks .50 .50
1290 A401 40c Chickens .50 .50
1291 A401 40c Pigs .50 .50
1292 A401 40c Border collie .50 .50
a. Bklt. pane of 10, #1283-1292 6.25
Complete booklet 6.75
1293 A401 45c Sheep .75 .75
1294 A401 45c Deer .75 .75
1295 A401 45c Horses .75 .75
1296 A401 45c Cattle .75 .75
1297 A401 45c Goats .75 .75
1298 A401 45c Turkey .75 .75
1299 A401 45c Ducks .75 .75
1300 A401 45c Chickens .75 .75
1301 A401 45c Pigs .75 .75
1302 A401 45c Border collie .75 .75
a. Bklt. pane of 10, #1293-1302 8.25
Complete booklet, #1302a 8.75
b. Souvenir sheet of 5, #1298-1302, perf. 12 4.25 4.25
Nos. 1283-1302 (20) 12.50 12.50

Singapore '95 (#1302b).
#1302b exists imperf.
Issued: #1302a, 9/1/95; #1292a, 10/2/95.

Christmas A402

Stained glass windows: 40c, 45c, Archangel Gabriel. No. 1309A, Angel with trumpet. 70c, Mary. 80c, Shepherds. $1, Madonna and Child. $1.50, Two wise men. $1.80, One wise man.

1995 *Perf. 12*
1303 A402 40c multi .60 .25
1304 A402 45c multi .65 .35
1305 A402 70c multi .95 .95
1306 A402 80c multi 1.00 1.00
1307 A402 $1 multi 1.25 1.25
1308 A402 $1.50 multi 2.25 2.25
1309 A402 $1.80 multi 2.50 2.50
Nos. 1303-1309 (7) 9.20 8.55

Booklet Stamp
Size: 25x30mm
Perf. 14½x14
1309A A402 40c multi .55 .55
b. Booklet pane of 10 6.50
Complete booklet, #1309b 6.50

Issued: 45c-$1.80, 9/1; #1303, 10/2; #1309A, 11/9.
Nos. 1303-1309 exist in a souvenir sheet from a "Limited Edition" pack.

Nuclear Disarmament A403

1995, Sept. 1 Litho. *Perf. 13½*

1310 A403 $1 multicolored	1.40	1.40

People Reaching People Type of 1994

Serpentine Die Cut 11

1995, Oct. 2 Photo.

Self-Adhesive

1311 A389 40c multicolored	1.50	.50
a. Arrow partially covering hole in "B," serpentine die cut 11¼	1.00	1.00

No. 1311a, Nov. 1995.

Scenic Views

Mitre Peak — A404

1995, Oct. 2 Litho. *Perf. 13½*

1312 A404 40c multicolored	.65	.55
a. Perf 12	.65	.00
b. As "a," miniature sheet of 10	6.50	

Southpex '96 Stamp Show (No. 1312a).

See Nos. 1345-1360, 1405, 1412, 1636-1640, 1679-1680, 1909, 1929.

UN, 50th Anniv. — A405

1995, Oct. 4 *Perf. 14½*

1313 A405 $1.80 multicolored	2.50	2.50

Famous Living New Zealanders — A406

Person, career field: 40c, Dame Kiri Te Kanawa, performing arts. 80c, Charles Upham, service, business, development. $1, Barry Crump, fine arts, literature. $1.20, Sir Brian Barratt-Boyes, science, medicine, education. $1.50, Dame Whina Cooper, community leader, social campaigner. $1.80, Sir Richard Hadlee, sports.

1995, Oct. 4 *Perf. 12*

1314 A406 40c multicolored	.90	.45
1315 A406 80c multicolored	1.10	.85
1316 A406 $1 multicolored	1.25	1.25
1317 A406 $1.20 multicolored	1.50	1.50
1318 A406 $1.50 multicolored	2.00	2.00
1319 A406 $1.80 multicolored	2.50	2.50
Nos. 1314-1319 (6)	9.25	8.55

Nos. 1314-1319 issued with se-tenant tab inscribed "STAMP / MONTH / OCTOBER / 1995."

Commonwealth Heads of Government Meeting, Auckland — A407

Designs: 40c, Fern, sky, globe, $1.80, Fern, sea, national flag.

1995, Nov. 9 Litho. *Perf. 14*

1320 A407 40c multicolored	.65	.50
1321 A407 $1.80 multicolored	2.75	2.50

Racehorses A408

1996, Jan. 24 Litho. *Perf. 13½x14*

1322 A408 40c Kiwi	.75	.25
1323 A408 80c Rough Habit	1.00	1.00
1324 A408 $1 Blossom Lady	1.25	1.25
1325 A408 $1.20 Il Vicolo	1.75	1.75
1326 A408 $1.50 Horlicks	2.00	2.00
1327 A408 $1.80 Bonecrusher	2.50	2.50
Nos. 1322-1327 (6)	9.25	8.75

Booklet

1328 A408 Souvenir bklt.	*19.00*	

No. 1328 contains one booklet pane of Nos. 1322-1327, perf. 14, and individual panes of 1 each Nos. 1322-1327.

Maori Crafts — A409

1996, Feb. 21 Litho. *Perf. 14x13½*

1329 A409 40c Basket	.45	.25
1330 A409 80c Weapon	.85	.85
1331 A409 $1 Embroidery	1.10	1.10
1332 A409 $1.20 Greenstone	1.50	1.50
1333 A409 $1.50 Gourd	1.75	1.75
a. Souvenir sheet of 3, #1329, 1330, 1333, perf. 13	5.50	5.50
1334 A409 $1.80 Cloak	2.00	2.00
Nos. 1329-1334 (6)	7.65	7.45

No. 1333a for Hong Kong '97. Issued 2/12/97.

Seashore — A410

Designs: No. 1335, Black-backed gull. No. 1336, Sea cucumber, spiny starfish. No. 1337, Common shrimp. No. 1338, Gaudy nudibranch. No. 1339, Large rock crab, clingfish. No. 1340, Snake skin chiton, red rock crab. No. 1341, Estuarine triplefin, cat's eye shell. No. 1342, Cushion star, sea horse. No. 1343, Blue-eyed triplefin, yaldwyn's triplefin. No. 1344, Common octopus.

1996, Feb. 21 *Perf. 14x14½*

Booklet Stamps

1335 A410 40c multicolored	.55	.55
1336 A410 40c multicolored	.55	.55
1337 A410 40c multicolored	.55	.55
1338 A410 40c multicolored	.55	.55
1339 A410 40c multicolored	.55	.55
1340 A410 40c multicolored	.55	.55
1341 A410 40c multicolored	.55	.55
1342 A410 40c multicolored	.55	.55
1343 A410 40c multicolored	.55	.55
1344 A410 40c multicolored	.55	.55
a. Booklet pane, Nos. 1335-1344	6.50	
Complete booklet, No. 1344a	6.75	
Nos. 1335-1344 (10)	5.50	5.50

No. 1344a has a continuous design.

Serpentine Die Cut 11½

1996, Aug. 7 Litho.

Booklet Stamps

Self-Adhesive

1344B A410 40c like #1335	1.25	1.25
1344C A410 40c like #1336	1.25	1.25
1344D A410 40c like #1337	1.25	1.25
1344E A410 40c like #1338	1.25	1.25
1344F A410 40c like #1339	1.25	1.25
1344G A410 40c like #1340	1.25	1.25
1344H A410 40c like #1341	1.25	1.25
1344I A410 40c like #1342	1.25	1.25
1344J A410 40c like #1343	1.25	1.25
1344K A410 40c like #1344	1.25	1.25
l. Bklt pane, #1344B-1344K	14.00	
Nos. 1344B-1344K (10)	12.50	12.50

No. 1344Kl is a complete booklet. The peelable paper backing serves as a booklet cover.

Scenic Views Type of 1995

5c, Mt. Cook, horiz. 10c, Champagne Pool, horiz. 20c, Cape Reinga, horiz. 30c, Mackenzie Country, horiz. 50c, Mt. Ngauruhoe, horiz. 60c, Lake Wanaka. 70c, Giant Kauri-Tane Mahuta. 80c, Doubtful Sound. 90c, Waitomo Limestone Cave.

No. 1354, Tory Channel, Marlborough Sounds. No. 1355, Lake Wakatipu. No. 1356, Lake Matheson. No. 1357, Fox Glacier. No. 1358, Mt. Egmont, Taranaki. No. 1359, Piercy Island, Bay of Islands. No. 1354-1359 horiz.

1996, Mar. 27 Litho. *Perf. 13½*

1345 A404 5c multicolored	.25	.25
1346 A404 10c multicolored	.25	.25
1347 A404 20c multicolored	.25	.25
1348 A404 30c multicolored	.35	.35
1349 A404 50c multicolored	.50	.50
a. Souv. sheet of 4, #1346-1349	3.00	3.00
1350 A404 60c multicolored	.70	.70
1351 A404 70c multicolored	.80	.80
1352 A404 80c multicolored	1.00	1.00
1353 A404 90c multicolored	1.25	1.25
a. Souv. sheet of 4, #1350-1353	6.50	6.50
Nos. 1345-1353 (9)	5.35	5.35

CHINA '96 (#1349a). CAPEX '96 (#1353a.)

See No. 1405.

Serpentine Die Cut 11¼

1996, May 1 Photo.

Size: 26x21mm

Self-Adhesive

1354 A404 40c multicolored	.55	.55
1355 A404 40c multicolored	.55	.55
1356 A404 40c multicolored	.55	.55
1357 A404 40c multicolored	.55	.55
1358 A404 40c multicolored	.55	.55
1359 A404 40c multicolored	.55	.55
a. Strip of 6, Nos. 1354-1359	3.50	3.50
k. Sheet of 10, #1356, 1359, 2 each #1354-1355, 1357-1358	*35.00*	
l. Sheet of 10, #1355, 1358, 2 each #1354, 1356-1357, 1359	*35.00*	
m. Sheet of 10, #1354, 1357, 2 each #1355-1356, 1358-1359	*35.00*	
Nos. 1354-1359 (6)	3.30	3.30

Serpentine Die Cut 10x9¾

1998, Jan. 14 Litho.

Booklet Stamps

Size: 26x21mm

Self-Adhesive

1359B A404 40c like #1358	.55	.55
1359C A404 40c like #1357	.55	.55
1359D A404 40c like #1359	.55	.55
1359E A404 40c like #1356	.55	.55
1359F A404 40c like #1354	.55	.55
h. "Marlborough Sounds" omitted	*17.50*	
1359G A404 40c like #1355	.55	.55
i. Booklet pane, #1359D, 1359F, 1359Fh, 1359G, 2 #1359B-1359C, 1359E	*19.00*	
j. Booklet pane #1359D, 1359G, 2 each #1359B, 1359C, 1359E, 1359F	5.50	
n. Coil strip of 6, #1359B-1359G	3.60	
Nos. 1359B-1359G (6)	3.30	3.30

No. 1359Gi is a complete booklet.

Serpentine Die Cut 11½

1996, Aug. 7 Litho.

Size: 33x22mm

Self-Adhesive

Design: $1, Pohutukawa tree, horiz.

1360 A404 $1 multicolored	1.40	1.40
a. Booklet pane of 5	7.00	

By its nature No. 1360a is a complete booklet. The peelable paper backing serves as a booklet cover. The outside of the cover contains 5 peelable international airpost labels.

Rescue Services — A411

40c, Fire service, ambulance. 80c, Civil defense. $1, Air sea rescue. $1.50, Air ambulance, rescue helicopter. $1.80, Mountain rescue, Red Cross.

1996, Mar. 27 *Perf. 14½x15*

1361 A411 40c multicolored	.60	.45
1362 A411 80c multicolored	1.00	1.00
1363 A411 $1 multicolored	1.25	1.25
1364 A411 $1.50 multicolored	2.00	2.00
1365 A411 $1.80 multicolored	2.50	2.50
Nos. 1361-1365 (5)	7.35	7.20

Wildlife A412

Designs: 40c, Yellow-eyed penguin, vert. 80c, Royal albatross. $1, White heron. $1.20, Sperm whale. $1.50, Fur seal, vert. $1.80, Bottlenose dolphin, vert.

1996, May 1 Litho. *Perf. 14*

1366 A412 40c multicolored	.70	.50
1367 A412 80c multicolored	1.25	.90
1368 A412 $1 multicolored	1.40	1.40
1369 A412 $1.20 multicolored	1.50	1.50
1370 A412 $1.50 multicolored	1.75	1.75
a. Sheet of 2, #1368, 1370	6.50	6.50
1371 A412 $1.80 multicolored	2.00	2.00
a. Sheet of 2, #1367, 1371	5.00	5.00
b. Block, #1366-1371, + 2 labels	9.50	9.50
Nos. 1366-1371 (6)	8.60	8.05

No. 1370a for CHINA '96. Issued May 18.

No. 1371a for Taipei '96. Issued Oct. 2.

New Zealand Symphony Orchestra, 50th Anniv. — A413

1996, July 10 Litho. *Perf. 15x14½*

1372 A413 40c Violin	.60	.50
1373 A413 80c French horn	1.10	1.10

1996 Summer Olympics, Atlanta A414

1996, July 10 *Perf. 14½*

1374 A414 40c Swimming	.75	.30
1375 A414 80c Cycling	1.40	1.40
1376 A414 $1 Athletics	1.50	1.50
1377 A414 $1.50 Rowing	1.75	1.75
1378 A414 $1.80 Yachting	2.00	2.00
a. Sheet of 5, #1374-1378	8.00	8.00
Nos. 1374-1378 (5)	7.40	6.95

Used value is for stamp with complete selvage.

A miniature sheet containing #1374-1378, both perf and imperf within the sheet, exists. This comes from a "Limited Edition" collectors' pack.

See No. 1383.

A415

Motion pictures, cent.: 40c, Hinemoa. 80c, Broken Barrier. $1.50, Goodbye Pork Pie. $1.80, Once Were Warriors.

1996, Aug. 7 Litho. *Perf. 14½x15*

1379 A415 40c multicolored .60 .35
1380 A415 80c multicolored 1.10 1.10
1381 A415 $1.50 multicolored 1.75 1.75
1382 A415 $1.80 multicolored 2.00 2.00
Nos. 1379-1382 (4) 5.45 5.20

Nos. 1379-1382 are printed se-tenant with scratch and win labels for a contest available to New Zealand residents. Values 25% more with unscratched labels attached.

1996 Summer Olympics Type

Design: Danyon Loader, swimmer, Blyth Tait, horseman, 1996 gold medalists from New Zealand.

1996, Aug. 28 Litho. *Perf. 14½*

1383 A414 40c multicolored .65 .65

Used value is for stamp with complete selvage.
Leaves in selvage printed in six different patterns.

A416

1996, Sept. 4 *Perf. 12*

1384 A416 40c Beehive ballot box .65 .50

Mixed member proportional election, 1966. No. 1384 was issued in sheets of 10.

Christmas A417

Scenes from the Christmas story: No. 1385, Following the star. 70c, Shepherd finding baby in manger. 80c, Angel's announcement to shepherd. $1, The Nativity. $1.50, Journey to Bethlehem. $1.80, The annunciation.
No. 1391, Adoration of the Magi. No. 1392, Heavenly host praising God.

1996, Sept. 4 *Perf. 14*

1385 A417 40c multicolored .60 .30
1386 A417 70c multicolored 1.00 1.00
1387 A417 80c multicolored 1.10 1.10
1388 A417 $1 multicolored 1.25 1.25
1389 A417 $1.50 multicolored 1.75 1.75
1390 A417 $1.80 multicolored 2.00 2.00
Nos. 1385-1390 (6) 7.70 7.40

Size: 29x24mm
Self-Adhesive
Serpentine Die Cut 11½

1391 A417 40c multicolored .65 .55
a. Booklet pane 10 6.50
1392 A417 40c multicolored .65 .55

By its nature No. 1391a is a complete booklet. The peelable paper backing serves as a booklet cover.

Extinct Birds A418

1996, Oct. 2 Litho. *Perf. 13½*

1393 A418 40c Adzebill .60 .45
1394 A418 80c Laughing owl 1.10 1.10
1395 A418 $1 Piopio 1.50 1.50
1396 A418 $1.20 Huia 1.60 1.60
1397 A418 $1.50 Giant eagle 2.00 2.00
1398 A418 $1.80 Giant moa 2.25 2.25
a. Souvenir sheet 3.00 3.00
b. As "a," with added inscription 4.50 4.50
Nos. 1393-1398 (6) 9.05 8.90

Size: 29x24mm
Self-Adhesive
Serpentine Die Cut 11½

1399 A418 40c Stout-legged wren .65 .55
a. Booklet pane of 10 6.50

Inscriptions on backs of Nos. 1393-1398 describe each species. By its nature No. 1399a is a complete booklet. The peelable backing serves as a booklet cover.
No. 1398b contains Taipei '96 exhibition emblem in sheet margin.

Scenic Gardens — A419

Designs: 40c, Seymour Square Gardens, Blenheim. 80c, Pukekura Park Gardens, New Plymouth. $1, Wintergarden, Auckland. $1.50, Botanic Gardens, Christchurch. $1.80, Marine Parade Gardens, Napier.

1996, Nov. 13 Litho. *Perf. 13½*

1400 A419 40c multicolored .55 .45
1401 A419 80c multicolored 1.00 1.00
1402 A419 $1 multicolored 1.25 1.25
1403 A419 $1.50 multicolored 1.75 1.75
1404 A419 $1.80 multicolored 2.25 2.25
Nos. 1400-1404 (5) 6.80 6.70

New Zealand Post produced and distributed three souvenir sheets as rewards for purchases made from the post office during 1996. The sheets were not available through normal philatelic channels. The sheets are inscribed "NEW ZEALAND POST / Best of 1996" and the Stamp Points emblem. Each sheet contains 3 stamps; #1327, 1365, 1334; #1378, 1382, 1371; #1390, 1404, 1398.

Scenic Views Type of 1995

Serpentine Die Cut 11½

1996, Nov. 1 Litho.

Size: 21x26mm
Self-Adhesive

1405 A404 80c like No. 1352 1.10 1.10
a. Booklet pane of 10 12.50

By its nature No. 1405a is a complete booklet. The peelable paper backing serves as a booklet cover. The outside of the cover contains 10 peelable international airpost labels.

Cattle — A420

1997, Jan. 15 *Perf. 14x14½*

1406 A420 40c Holstein-Friesian .65 .30
1407 A420 80c Jersey 1.25 1.10
1408 A420 $1 Simmental 1.60 1.40
1409 A420 $1.20 Ayrshire 1.75 1.75
1410 A420 $1.50 Angus 2.00 2.00
a. Souvenir sheet of 3, #1407, 1408, 1410 9.00 9.00
1411 A420 $1.80 Hereford 2.25 2.25
Nos. 1406-1411 (6) 9.50 8.80

No. 1410a for Hong Kong '97. Issued 2/12/97.

Souvenir Sheets

The 1997 sheets contain: Nos. 1411, 1418, 1434; Nos. 1440, 1444, 1451; Nos. 1445, 1457, 1475.
See note following No. 1404.

Scenic Views Type of 1995

1997, Feb. 12 Litho. *Perf. 13½*

Size: 37x32mm

1412 A404 $10 Mt. Ruapehu 15.00 11.50

Discoverers — A421

40c, James Cook. 80c, Kupe. $1, Maui, vert. $1.20, Jean de Surville, vert. $1.50, Dumont d'Urville. $1.80, Abel Tasman.

1997, Feb. 12 *Perf. 14*

1413 A421 40c multicolored .75 .50
1414 A421 80c multicolored 1.10 1.10
1415 A421 $1 multicolored 1.40 1.40
1416 A421 $1.20 multicolored 1.75 1.75
1417 A421 $1.50 multicolored 2.25 2.25
1418 A421 $1.80 multicolored 2.50 2.50
Nos. 1413-1418 (6) 9.75 9.50

#1413-1418 exist in sheet of 6 created for a hard-bound millennium book that sold for $129.

"Wackiest Letterboxes" — A422

Serpentine Die Cut 11¼

1997, Mar. 19 Litho.

Self-Adhesive
Booklet Stamps

1419 A422 40c Log house .55 .55
1420 A422 40c Owl .55 .55
1421 A422 40c Whale .55 .55
1422 A422 40c "Kilroy is Back" .55 .55
1423 A422 40c House of twigs .55 .55
1424 A422 40c Scottish piper .55 .55
1425 A422 40c Diving helmet .55 .55
1426 A422 40c Airplane .55 .55
1427 A422 40c Water faucet .55 .55
1428 A422 40c Painted buildings .55 .55
a. Bklt. pane of 10, #1419-1428 7.00
b. Sheet of 10, #1419-1428 18.00
Nos. 1419-1428 (10) 5.50 5.50

By its nature No. 1428a is a complete booklet. The peelable paper backing serves as a booklet cover.

Vineyards — A423

40c, Central Otago. 80c, Hawke's Bay. $1, Marlborough. $1.20, Canterbury, Waipara. $1.50, Gisborne. $1.80, Auckland, Waiheke.

1997, Mar. 19 *Perf. 14*

1429 A423 40c multicolored .50 .30
a. Booklet pane of 1 .65
1430 A423 80c multicolored 1.10 1.10
a. Booklet pane of 1 1.10
1431 A423 $1 multicolored 1.50 1.50
a. Booklet pane of 1 1.50
1432 A423 $1.20 multicolored 1.75 1.75
a. Booklet pane of 1 1.75
1433 A423 $1.50 multicolored 2.50 2.50
a. Booklet pane of 1 2.50
b. Souvenir sheet of 3, #1429, 1431, 1433 8.50 8.50
1434 A423 $1.80 multicolored 2.50 2.50
a. Booklet pane of 1 2.50
b. Bklt. pane of 6, #1429-1434 10.00
Complete booklet, #1429a, 1430a, 1431a, 1432a, 1433a, 1434a, 1434b 21.00
Nos. 1429-1434 (6) 9.85 9.65

No. 1433b for PACIFIC 97. Issued: 5/29.

Pigeon Mail Service, Cent. A424

Design: 1899 local stamp.

1997, May 7 Litho. *Perf. 14*

1435 A424 40c red .65 .65
1436 A424 80c blue 1.25 1.25
a. Souv. sheet, 2 ea #1435-1436 9.50 9.50
b. As "a," diff. inscription 6.00 6.00

No. 1436a for PACIFIC 97. Issued: 5/29.
No. 1436b was inscribed in sheet margin for AUPEX '97 National Stamp Exhibition, Auckland. Issued 11/13.

Paintings by Colin McCahon (1919-87) — A425

Designs: 40c, The Promised Land, 1948. $1, Six Days in Nelson and Canterbury, 1950. $1.50, Northland Panels, 1958. $1.80, Moby Dick is sighted off Muriwai Beach, 1972.

1997, May 7

1437 A425 40c multicolored .65 .30
1438 A425 $1 multicolored 1.25 1.25
1439 A425 $1.50 multicolored 2.00 2.00
1440 A425 $1.80 multicolored 2.25 2.25
Nos. 1437-1440 (4) 6.15 5.80

See Nos. 1597-1600.

Fly Fishing — A426

Designs: 40c, Red setter fly, rainbow trout. $1, Grey ghost fly, sea-run brown trout. $1.50, Twilight beauty fly, brook trout. $1.80, Hare & copper fly, brown trout.

1997, June 18 Litho. *Perf. 13*

1441 A426 40c multicolored .60 .40
1442 A426 $1 multicolored 1.50 1.50
1443 A426 $1.50 multicolored 2.00 2.00
1444 A426 $1.80 multicolored 2.25 2.25
a. Souv. sheet of 2, #1441, 1444 6.00 6.00
Nos. 1441-1444 (4) 6.35 6.15

No.1444a issued 5/13/98 for Israel '98 World Stamp Exhibition, Tel Aviv.

Kiwi Type of 1988

1997, Aug. 6 Litho. *Perf. 14½*

1445 A325 $1 violet 1.25 1.25

Value is for stamp with surrounding selvage. Selvage comes with and without gold sunbursts.
See No. 1635a.

Scenic Trains A426a

Name of train, area scene, map of train route: 40c, Overlander, Paremata, Wellington, Wellington-Auckland. 80c, Trans-Alpine, Southern Alps, Christchurch-Greymouth. $1, Southerner, Canterbury, Invercargill-Christchurch. $1.20, Coastal Pacific, Kaikoura Coast, Christchurch-Picton. $1.50, Bay Express, Central Hawke's Bay, Wellington-Napier. $1.80, Kaimai Express, Tauranga Harbor, Tauranga-Auckland.

1997, Aug. 6 ***Perf. 14x14½***

1446 A426a 40c multicolored .60 .40
1447 A426a 80c multicolored 1.10 1.00
1448 A426a $1 multicolored 1.25 1.25
1449 A426a $1.20 multicolored 1.50 1.50
1450 A426a $1.50 multicolored 2.00 2.00
a. Sheet of 3, #1447-1448, 1450 7.50 7.50
1451 A426a $1.80 multicolored 2.25 2.25
Nos. 1446-1451 (6) 8.70 8.40

No. 1450a issued 5/13/98 for Israel '98 World Stamp Exhibition, Tel Aviv.

Nos. 1446-1451 exist in a sheet of 6 from a "Limited Edition" album.

Christmas A427

Scenes from first Christian service, Rangihoua Bay, and words from Christmas carol, "Te Harinui:" No. 1452, Samuel Marsden's ship, Active. 70c, Marsden preaching from pulpit. 80c, Marsden extending hand to local chiefs. $1, Mother, children from Rangihoua. $1.50, Maori and Pakeha hands, Marsden's memorial cross. $1.80, Pohutukawa flowers, Rangihoua Bay. No. 1458, Cross marking spot of service, flowers, bay.

1997, Sept. 3 **Litho.** ***Perf. 14***

1452 A427 40c multicolored .60 .25
1453 A427 70c multicolored .90 .90
1454 A427 80c multicolored 1.00 1.00
1455 A427 $1 multicolored 1.25 1.25
1456 A427 $1.50 multicolored 1.75 1.75
1457 A427 $1.80 multicolored 2.00 2.00
a. Block of 6, #1452-1457 10.00 10.00
Nos. 1452-1457 (6) 7.50 7.15

Self-Adhesive

Size: 30x24mm

Serpentine Die Cut 10

1458 A427 40c multicolored .50 .50
a. Booklet pane of 10 6.50

By its nature No. 1458a is a complete booklet. The peelable paper backing serves as a booklet cover.

"Creepy Crawlies" — A428

Serpentine Die Cut 11¼

1997, Oct. 1 **Litho.**

Booklet Stamps

1459 A428 40c Huhu beetle .55 .55
1460 A428 40c Giant land snail .55 .55
1461 A428 40c Giant weta .55 .55
1462 A428 40c Giant dragonfly .55 .55
1463 A428 40c Peripatus .55 .55
1464 A428 40c Cicada .55 .55
1465 A428 40c Puriri moth .55 .55
1466 A428 40c Veined slug .55 .55
1467 A428 40c Katipo .55 .55
1468 A428 40c Flaxweevil .55 .55
a. Booklet pane, #1459-1468 6.25
b. Sheet of 10, #1459-1468 10.00
Nos. 1459-1468 (10) 5.50 5.50

By its nature No. 1468a is a complete booklet. The peelable paper backing serves as a booklet cover.

China-New Zealand Stamp Expo — A429

1997, Oct. 9 ***Perf. 14***

1469 40c Rosa rugosa .65 .50
1470 40c Aotearoa-New Zealand .65 .50
a. A429 Pair, #1469-1470 1.40 1.10
b. Souvenir sheet, #1470a 2.00 2.00
c. As "b," diff. inscription 2.00 2.00

No. 1470c inscribed in gold and black in sheet margin for Shanghai 1997 Intl. Stamp & Coin Expo. Issued: 11/19/97.

See People's Republic of China Nos. 2797-2798.

Queen Elizabeth II and Prince Philip, 50th Wedding Anniv. — A430

1997, Nov. 12 **Litho.** ***Perf. 12***

1471 A430 40c multicolored .65 .45

Issued in sheets of 10.

Cartoonists A431

"Kiwis Taking on the World:" 40c, Kiwi flying on bee, by Garrick Tremain. $1, Kiwi using world as egg and having it for breakfast, by Jim Hubbard. $1.50, Kiwi in yacht race against the world, by Eric Heath. $1.80, Man with chain saw, trees on mountainside cut as peace symbol, by Burton Silver.

1997, Nov. 12 ***Perf. 14***

1472 A431 40c multicolored .65 .30
1473 A431 $1 multicolored 1.25 1.25
1474 A431 $1.50 multicolored 1.75 1.75
1475 A431 $1.80 multicolored 2.50 2.50
Nos. 1472-1475 (4) 6.15 5.80

Performing Arts — A432

1998, Jan. 14 **Litho.** ***Perf. 13½***

1476 A432 40c Modern dance .60 .35
a. Booklet pane of 1 .60
1477 A432 80c Music 1.00 .95
a. Booklet pane of 1 1.00
b. Perf 14 2.50 2.50
1478 A432 $1 Opera 1.25 1.25
a. Booklet pane of 1 1.25
1479 A432 $1.20 Theater 1.50 1.50
a. Booklet pane of 1 1.50
1480 A432 $1.50 Song 2.00 2.00
a. Booklet pane of 1 2.00
1481 A432 $1.80 Ballet 2.25 2.25
a. Booklet pane of 1 2.25
b. Bklt. pane of 6, #1476-1481 11.00
Complete booklet, 1 each #1476a-1481a, 1481b 22.50
c. Perf 14 5.50 5.50
Nos. 1476-1481 (6) 8.60 8.30

Museum of New Zealand Te Papa Tongarewa — A433

40c, People at entrance. $1.80, Waterfront location.

1998, Feb. 11 **Litho.** ***Perf. 14***

1482 A433 40c multicolored .50 .45
1483 A433 $1.80 multicolored 2.00 2.00

Souvenir Sheets

The 1998 sheets contain: Nos. 1489, 1483, 1481; Nos. 1491, 1521, 1525; Nos. 1531, 1537, 1562.

See note following No. 1404.

Domestic Cat — A434

1998, Feb. 11 ***Perf. 13½***

1484 A434 40c Moggy .55 .30
1485 A434 80c Burmese 1.00 1.00
1486 A434 $1 Birman 1.10 1.10
1487 A434 $1.20 British blue 1.25 1.25
1488 A434 $1.50 Persian 1.75 1.75
1489 A434 $1.80 Siamese 2.25 2.25
a. Souvenir sheet of 3, #1484, #1486, #1489 6.00 6.00
Nos. 1484-1489 (6) 7.90 7.65

Memorial Statues — A435

40c, "With Great Respect to the Mehmetcik, Gallipoli" (Turkish soldier carrying wounded ANZAC). $1.80, "Mother with Children," Natl. War Memorial, Wellington.

1998, Mar. 18 **Litho.** ***Perf. 13½***

1490 A435 40c multicolored .50 .40
1491 A435 $1.80 multicolored 2.00 2.00

See Turkey Nos. 2695-2696.

New Zealand's Multi-cultural Society — A436

Designs: 40c, The Maori. 80c, British/European settlers, 1840-1914. $1, Fortune seekers, 1800-1920. $1.20, Post-war British/European migrants, 1945-70. $1.50, Pacific Islanders, from 1960. $1.80, Asian arrivals, 1980s-90s.

1998, Mar. 18 ***Perf. 14***

1492 A436 40c multicolored .55 .25
1493 A436 80c multicolored 1.10 .90
1494 A436 $1 multicolored 1.40 1.10
1495 A436 $1.20 multicolored 1.50 1.50
1496 A436 $1.50 multicolored 1.75 1.75
1497 A436 $1.80 multicolored 2.00 2.00
Nos. 1492-1497 (6) 8.30 7.50

Nos. 1492-1497 exist in sheet of 6 created for a hard-bound millennium book that sold for $129.

"Stay in Touch" Greetings Stamps A437

Designs: No. 1498, Young and older person hugging, vert. No. 1499, Middle-aged couple wading in water at beach, vert. No. 1500, Characters giving "high five," vert. No. 1501, Stylized boy pointing way to old woman, vert. No. 1502, Cartoon of woman with tears embracing man. No. 1503, Couple kissing. No. 1504, Older couple with faces together. No. 1505, Two boys arm in arm in swimming pool. No. 1506, Stylized couple, clouds. No. 1507, Stylized couple seated on sofa.

Die Cut Perf. 10x10¼, 10¼x10

1998, Apr. 15 **Litho.**

Booklet Stamps

Self-Adhesive

1498 A437 40c multicolored .50 .50
1499 A437 40c multicolored .50 .50
1500 A437 40c multicolored .50 .50
1501 A437 40c multicolored .50 .50
a. Sheet of 4, #1498-1501 5.00
1502 A437 40c multicolored .50 .50
1503 A437 40c multicolored .50 .50
1504 A437 40c multicolored .50 .50
1505 A437 40c multicolored .50 .50
1506 A437 40c multicolored .50 .50
1507 A437 40c multicolored .50 .50
a. Booklet pane, #1498-1507 6.50
b. Sheet of 6, #1502-1507 10.00
Nos. 1498-1507 (10) 5.00 5.00

The peelable paper backing of No. 1507a serves as a booklet cover.

Types of 1898

1998, May 20 **Litho.** ***Perf. 14x14½***

1508 A18 40c Mt. Cook .55 .55
1509 A19 40c Lake Taupo .55 .55
1510 A20 40c Pembroke Peak .55 .55
1511 A23 40c Huia .55 .55
1512 A24 40c White Terrace .55 .55
1513 A26 40c Kiwi .55 .55
1514 A27 40c Maori canoe .55 .55
1515 A29 40c Hawk-billed parrots .55 .55

Perf. 14½

1516 A21 80c Wakitipu 1.00 1.00
1517 A22 80c Wakatipu 1.00 1.00
a. Souvenir sheet of 2, 1516-1517 4.75 4.75
1518 A25 $1 Otira Gorge 1.25 1.25
1519 A28 $1.20 Pink Terrace 1.50 1.50
1520 A30 $1.50 Milford Sound 1.75 1.75
a. Sheet of 2, #1517, 1520 4.00 4.00
1521 A31 $1.80 Mt. Cook 2.00 2.00
Nos. 1508-1521 (14) 12.90 12.90

No. 1517a issued 8/7/98 for Tarapex '98, Natl. Stamp Exhibition.

No. 1520a issued 10/23/98 for Italia '98.

Paintings by Peter McIntyre A438

Designs: 40c, Wounded at Cassino, 1944. $1, The Cliffs of Rangitikei, c. 1958. $1.50, Maori Children, King Country, 1963. $1.80, The Anglican Church, Kakahi, 1972.

1998, June 24 **Litho.** ***Perf. 13½***

1522 A438 40c multicolored .45 .30
1523 A438 $1 multicolored 1.10 1.10
1524 A438 $1.50 multicolored 1.50 1.50
1525 A438 $1.80 multicolored 1.75 1.75
a. Souvenir sheet, #1524-1525, perf 14 6.00 6.00
Nos. 1522-1525 (4) 4.80 4.65

No. 1525a issued 10/23/98 for Italia '98.

Nos. 1524-1525 exist in an imperf souvenir sheet from a "Limited Edition" album.

Scenic Skies — A439

1998, July 29 Litho. *Perf. 14½*

1526	A439	40c Cambridge	.60	.25
1527	A439	80c Lake Wanaka	1.10	.90
1528	A439	$1 Mt. Maunganui	1.25	1.10
1529	A439	$1.20 Kaikoura	1.40	1.40
1530	A439	$1.50 Whakatane	2.00	2.00
1531	A439	$1.80 Lindis Pass	2.25	2.25
a.		Souv. sheet of 2, #1526, 1531	3.75	3.75
		Nos. 1526-1531 (6)	8.60	7.90

No. 1531a issued 3/19/99 for Australia '99 World Stamp Expo.

Christmas A440

Designs: 40c, Madonna and Child. 70c, Shepherds approaching nativity scene. 80c, Joseph, Mary, Christ Child. $1, Magus. $1.50, Magi with gifts. $1.80, Angel telling shepherds about Messiah.

1998, Sept. 2 Litho. *Perf. 13x14*

1532	A440	40c multicolored	.55	.25
1533	A440	70c multicolored	.90	.80
1534	A440	80c multicolored	1.10	.90
1535	A440	$1 multicolored	1.25	1.25
1536	A440	$1.50 multicolored	1.75	1.75
1537	A440	$1.80 multicolored	2.00	2.00
		Nos. 1532-1537 (6)	7.55	6.95

Self-adhesive

Size: 24x30mm

Serpentine Die Cut 11½

1538	A440	40c multicolored	.50	.40
a.		Booklet pane of 10	6.50	

No. 1538a is a complete booklet. The peelable paper backing serves as a booklet cover.

Marine Life — A441

1998, Oct. 7 Litho. *Perf. 14*

1539	A441	40c Moonfish	.45	.45
1540	A441	40c Mako shark	.45	.45
1541	A441	40c Yellowfin tuna	.45	.45
1542	A441	40c Giant squid	.45	.45
a.		Block of 4, #1539-1542	2.50	2.50
1543	A441	80c Striped marlin	.90	.90
1544	A441	80c Porcupine fish	.90	.90
a.		Souvenir sheet of 4, #1539-1540, #1543-1544	5.25	5.25
1545	A441	80c Eagle ray	.90	.90
1546	A441	80c Sandager's wrasse	.90	.90
a.		Block of 4, #1543-1546	4.75	4.75
b.		Souvenir sheet of 4, #1541-1542, 1545-1546	8.00	8.00
		Nos. 1539-1546 (8)	5.40	5.40

No. 1544a issued 3/19/99 for Australia '99, World Stamp Expo. No. 1546b was issued 7/2/99 for PhilexFrance '99, World Philatelic Exhibition.

#1539-1546 exist in sheets of 8 from a "Limited Edition" album.

Famous Town Icons
A442 A443

Designs: No. 1547, L&P bottle, Paeroa. No. 1548, Carrot, Ohakune. No. 1549, Brown trout, Gore. No. 1550, Crayfish, Kaikoura. No. 1551, Sheep shearer, Te Kuiti. No. 1552, Pania of the Reef, Napier. No. 1553, Paua shell, Riverton. No. 1554, Kiwifruit, Te Puke. No. 1555, Border collie, Tekapo. No. 1556, Cow, Hawera.

Serpentine Die Cut 11½

1998, Oct. 7 Litho.

Self-Adhesive

1547	A442	40c multicolored	.45	.45
1548	A442	40c multicolored	.45	.45
1549	A443	40c multicolored	.45	.45
1550	A443	40c multicolored	.45	.45
1551	A443	40c multicolored	.45	.45
1552	A443	40c multicolored	.45	.45

Size: 25x30mm

1553	A443	40c multicolored	.45	.45
1554	A443	40c multicolored	.45	.45
1555	A443	40c multicolored	.45	.45
1556	A443	40c multicolored	.45	.45
a.		Sheet of 10, #1547-1556	10.00	
b.		Booklet pane, #1547-1556	5.75	
		Nos. 1547-1556 (10)	4.50	4.50

No. 1556b is a complete booklet. The peelable paper backing serves as a booklet cover.

Urban Transformation — A444

1998, Nov. 11 Litho. *Perf. 14x14½*

1557	A444	40c Wellington	.60	.35
1558	A444	80c Auckland	1.00	.65
1559	A444	$1 Christchurch	1.10	1.10
1560	A444	$1.20 Westport	1.40	1.40
1561	A444	$1.50 Tauranga	1.75	1.75
1562	A444	$1.80 Dunedin	2.25	2.25
		Nos. 1557-1562 (6)	8.10	7.50

#1557-1562 exist in sheet of 6 created for a hard-bound Millennium book that sold for $129.

Native Tree Flowers — A445

1999, Jan. 13 Litho. *Perf. 14½x14*

1563	A445	40c Kotukutuku	.50	.25
1564	A445	80c Poroporo	.85	.85
a.		Souv. sheet of 2, #1563-1564	3.50	3.50
1565	A445	$1 Kowhai	.95	.95
1566	A445	$1.20 Weeping broom	1.10	1.10
1567	A445	$1.50 Teteaweka	1.50	1.50
1568	A445	$1.80 Southern rata	2.00	2.00
		Nos. 1563-1568 (6)	6.90	6.65

No. 1564a was issued 8/21/99 for China 1999 World Philatelic Exhibition.

Nos. 1567-1568 exist in a souvenir sheet from a "Limited Edition" album.

Souvenir Sheets

The 1999 sheets contain: Nos. 1568, 1572, 1578; Nos. 1584, 1600, 1607; Nos. 1613, 1620, 1627.

See note following No. 1404.

Art Deco Buildings — A446

40c, Civic Theatre, Auckland. $1, Masonic Hotel, Napier. $1.50, Medical and Dental Offices, Hastings. $1.80, Buller County Offices, Westport.

1999, Feb. 10 Litho. *Perf. 14*

1569	A446	40c multicolored	.70	.25
1570	A446	$1 multicolored	1.75	1.00
1571	A446	$1.50 multicolored	1.75	1.75
1572	A446	$1.80 multicolored	2.00	2.00
		Nos. 1569-1572 (4)	6.20	5.00

Popular Pets — A447

Designs: 40c, Labrador puppy. 80c, Netherland dwarf rabbit. $1, Rabbit, tabby kitten. $1.20, Lamb. $1.50, Welsh pony. $1.80, Budgies.

1999, Feb. 10

1573	A447	40c multicolored	.50	.35
1574	A447	80c multicolored	1.00	.60
1575	A447	$1 multicolored	1.25	1.25
a.		Souvenir sheet, #1573-1575	4.25	4.25
b.		Souvenir sheet, #1573, 1575	5.50	5.50
1576	A447	$1.20 multicolored	1.50	1.50
1577	A447	$1.50 multicolored	1.75	1.75
1578	A447	$1.80 multicolored	2.25	2.25
		Nos. 1573-1578 (6)	8.25	7.70

New Year 1999, Year of the Rabbit (#1575a).

No. 1575b was issued 8/21/99 for China 1999 World Philatelic Exhibition.

Nostalgia A448

1999, Mar. 10 Litho. *Perf. 14*

1579	A448	40c Toys	.70	.25
1580	A448	80c Food	1.00	1.00
1581	A448	$1 Transport	1.25	1.25
1582	A448	$1.20 Household	1.50	1.50
1583	A448	$1.50 Collectibles	1.75	1.75
1584	A448	$1.80 Garden	2.00	2.00
		Nos. 1579-1584 (6)	8.20	7.75

#1579-1584 exist in sheet of 6 created for a hard-bound Millennium book that sold for $129.

Victoria University of Wellington, Cent. A449

1999, Apr. 7 Litho. *Perf. 14*

1585	A449	40c multicolored	.55	.45

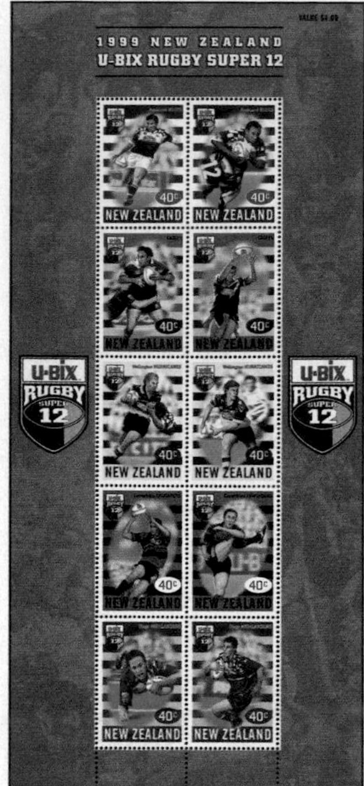

1999 New Zealand U-Bix Rugby Super 12 — A450

Auckland Blues: a, Kicking ball. b, Running with ball.

Chiefs: c, Being tackled. d, Catching ball.

Wellington Hurricanes: e, Being tackled. f, Passing.

Canterbury Crusaders: g, Catching ball. h, Kicking ball.

Otago Highlanders: i, Falling down with ball. j, Running with ball.

1999, Apr. 7 *Perf. 14½*

1586	A450	40c Sheet of 10, #a.-j.	12.50	12.50

Booklet Stamps

Self-Adhesive

Die Cut Perf. 12

1587	A450	40c like #1586a	.60	.45
1588	A450	40c like #1586b	.60	.45
a.		Bklt. pane, 5 ea #1587-1588	6.50	
1589	A450	40c like #1586c	.60	.45
1590	A450	40c like #1586d	.60	.45
a.		Bklt. pane, 5 ea #1589-1590	6.50	
1591	A450	40c like #1586e	.60	.45
1592	A450	40c like #1586f	.60	.45
a.		Bklt. pane, 5 ea #1591-1592	6.50	
1593	A450	40c like #1586g	.60	.45
1594	A450	40c like #1586h	.60	.45
a.		Bklt. pane, 5 ea #1593-1594	6.50	
1595	A450	40c like #1586i	.60	.45
1596	A450	40c like #1586j	.60	.45
a.		Bklt. pane, 5 ea #1595-1596	6.50	

Nos. 1587-1588, 1589-1590, 1591-1592, 1593-1594, 1595-1596 were also issued as pairs without surrounding selvage.

Nos. 1588a, 1590a, 1592a, 1594a and 1596a are all complete booklets.

Paintings Type of 1997

Paintings by Doris Lusk: 40c, The Lake, Tuai, 1948. $1, The Pumping Station, 1958. $1.50, Arcade Awning, St. Mark's Square, Venice (2), 1976. $1.80, Tuan St. II, 1982.

1999, June 16 Litho. *Perf. 14*

1597	A425	40c multicolored	.60	.25
1598	A425	$1 multicolored	1.25	1.25
1599	A425	$1.50 multicolored	1.50	1.50
1600	A425	$1.80 multicolored	2.25	2.25
a.		Souv. sheet of 2, #1597, 1600	5.00	5.00
		Nos. 1597-1600 (4)	5.60	5.25

No. 1600a was issued 7/2/99 for PhilexFrance '99, World Philatelic Exhibition.

Asia-Pacific Economic Cooperation (APEC) — A451

1999, July 21 Litho. *Perf. 14*

1601 A451 40c multicolored .50 .45

Scenic Walks A452

Designs: 40c, West Ruggedy Beach, Stewart Island. 80c, Ice Lake, Butler Valley, Westland. $1, Tonga Bay, Abel Tasman Natl. Park. $1.20, East Matakitaki Valley, Nelson Lakes Natl. Park. $1.50, Great Barrier Island. $1.80, Mt. Taranaki/Egmont.

1999, July 28

1602 A452 40c multicolored .50 .25
a. Booklet pane of 1 .55
1603 A452 80c multicolored .85 .85
a. Booklet pane of 1 .95
1604 A452 $1 multicolored 1.00 1.00
a. Booklet pane of 1 1.10
1605 A452 $1.20 multicolored 1.40 1.40
a. Booklet pane of 1 1.50
1606 A452 $1.50 multicolored 2.00 2.00
a. Booklet pane of 1 2.25
1607 A452 $1.80 multicolored 2.25 2.25
a. Booklet pane of 1 2.50
b. Bklt. pane of 6, #1602-1607 11.00
Complete booklet, 1 each #1602a-1607a, 1607b 22.50
c. Souvenir sheet of 1 3.50 3.50
Nos. 1602-1607 (6) 8.00 7.75

Issued: No. 1607c, 10/1.

Christmas A453

40c, Baby in manger. 80c, Virgin Mary. $1.10, Joseph and Mary. $1.20, Angel with harp. $1.50, Shepherds. $1.80, Three Magi.
No. 1614, Baby in manger.

1999, Sept. 8 Litho. *Perf. 13*

1608 A453 40c multicolored .50 .25
1609 A453 80c multicolored 1.00 1.00
1610 A453 $1.10 multicolored 1.40 1.40
1611 A453 $1.20 multicolored 1.50 1.50
1612 A453 $1.50 multicolored 1.75 1.75
1613 A453 $1.80 multicolored 2.00 2.00
Nos. 1608-1613 (6) 8.15 7.90

Self-Adhesive
Size: 23x27mm
Die Cut Perf. 9½x10

1614 A453 40c multicolored .50 .25
a. Booklet pane of 10 6.00

No. 1614a is a complete booklet.

Yachting — A454

1999, Oct. 20 Litho. *Perf. 14*

1615 A454 40c P Class .60 .25
1616 A454 80c Laser 1.00 .85
1617 A454 $1.10 18-foot skiff 1.25 1.25
1618 A454 $1.20 Hobie Cat 1.40 1.40
1619 A454 $1.50 Racing yacht 1.50 1.50
1620 A454 $1.80 Cruising yacht 1.75 1.75
a. Souvenir sheet of 6, #1615-1620 8.50 8.50
Nos. 1615-1620 (6) 7.50 7.00

Nos. 1615-1620 exist in an imperf souvenir sheet from a "Limited Edition" album.

Self-Adhesive
Size: 25x30mm
Die Cut Perf. 9½x10

1621 A454 40c Optimist .45 .40
a. Booklet pane of 10 6.00

No. 1621a is a complete booklet.

Millennium — A455

New Zealanders Leading the Way: 40c, Women, ballot box. 80c, Airplane of Richard Pearse, pioneer aviator. $1.10, Lord Ernest Rutherford, physicist. $1.20, Jet boat. $1.50, Sir Edmund Hillary, Mt. Everest. $1.80, Anti-nuclear protesters.

1999, Nov. 17 Litho. *Perf. 14x14¼*

1622 A455 40c multicolored .60 .25
1623 A455 80c multicolored 1.10 .60
1624 A455 $1.10 multicolored 1.50 1.50
1625 A455 $1.20 multicolored 1.60 1.60
1626 A455 $1.50 multicolored 1.75 1.75
1627 A455 $1.80 multicolored 2.00 2.00
Nos. 1622-1627 (6) 8.55 7.70

#1622-1627 exist in sheet of 6 created for a hard-bound millennium book that sold for $129.

Year 2000 A456

2000, Jan. 1 Litho. *Perf. 14¼*

1628 A456 40c multi .65 .45
a. Miniature sheet of 10 6.50 4.50

No. 1628 exists in a sheet of 6 created for a hard-bound Millennium book that sold for $129.

The third stamp in the left column on No. 1628a is missing the map and sun emblem between the time and country name.

New Year 2000 (Year of the Dragon) — A457

Spirits and guardians: 40c, Araiteuru. 80c, Kurangaituku. $1.10, Te Hoata and Te Pupu. $1.20, Patupaiarehe. $1.50, Te Ngarara-huarau. $1.80, Tuhirangi.

2000, Feb. 9 Litho. *Perf. 14*

1629 A457 40c multi .60 .25
1630 A457 80c multi .90 .45
1631 A457 $1.10 multi 1.25 1.25
1632 A457 $1.20 multi 1.50 1.50
1633 A457 $1.50 multi 1.75 1.75
1634 A457 $1.80 multi 2.25 2.25
a. Souv. sheet of 2, #1633-1634 5.25 5.25
Nos. 1629-1634 (6) 8.25 7.45

Nos. 1631-1632 exist in a souvenir sheet from a "Limited Edition" album.

Kiwi Type of 1988

2000, Mar. 6 Litho. *Perf. 14½*

1635 A325 $1.10 gold 1.50 1.50
a. Souv. sheet, #918b, 1027a, 1161b, 1445, 1635 8.25 8.25

Used value is for stamp with complete selvage.

#1635a issued 7/7 for World Stamp Expo 2000, Anaheim.

The 2000 sheets contain: #1694, 1635, 1671; #1662, 1634, 1638; #1677, 1665, 1656. See note following #1404.

Scenic Views Type of 1995

$1, Taiaroa Head. $1.10, Kaikoura Coast. $2, Great Barrier Is. $3, Cape Kidnappers.

2000 Litho. *Perf. 13¼x13½*
Size: 27x22mm

1636 A404 $1 multi 1.50 1.00
1637 A404 $1.10 multi 1.60 1.10
1638 A404 $2 multi 2.25 1.75
1639 A404 $3 multi 2.75 2.50
a. Souv. sheet, #1636, 1638-1639 9.00 9.00
Nos. 1636-1639 (4) 8.10 6.35

Self-Adhesive
Booklet Stamp
Die Cut Perf 10x9¾

1640 A404 $1.10 Like #1637 1.50 1.10
a. Booklet, 5 #1640 + 5 etiquettes 8.75

The Stamp Show 2000, London (No. 1639a).
Issued: #1639a, 5/22; #1640, 4/3; others, 3/6.

New Zealand Popular Culture — A458

Kiwi with: #1641, Insulated cooler. #1642, Pipis. #1643, Inflatable beach cushion. #1644, Chocolate fish. #1645, Beach house and surf board. #1646, Barbecue. #1647, Ug boots. #1648, Anzac biscuit. #1649, Hot dog. #1650, Meat pie.

Die Cut Perf. 9¾x10
2000, Apr. 3 Litho.
Booklet Stamps
Self-Adhesive

1641 A458 40c multi .55 .45
1642 A458 40c multi .55 .45
1643 A458 40c multi .55 .45
1644 A458 40c multi .55 .45
1645 A458 40c multi .55 .45
1646 A458 40c multi .55 .45
1647 A458 40c multi .55 .45
1648 A458 40c multi .55 .45
1649 A458 40c multi .55 .45
1650 A458 40c multi .55 .45
a. Booklet, #1641-1650 6.00
b. Sheet, #1641-1650 6.00
Nos. 1641-1650 (10) 5.50 4.50

No. 1650b has plain backing paper.

Automobiles A459

40c, Volkswagen Beetle. 80c, Ford Zephyr MK I. $1.10, Morris Mini MK II. $1.20, Holden HQ Kingswood. $1.50, Honda Civic EB2. $1.80, Toyota Corolla.

2000, June 1 *Perf. 14*

1651 A459 40c claret .55 .35
a. Booklet pane of 1 .55
1652 A459 80c blue .90 .65
a. Booklet pane of 1 .90
1653 A459 $1.10 brown 1.25 1.25
a. Booklet pane of 1 1.25
1654 A459 $1.20 green 1.50 1.50
a. Booklet pane of 1 1.50
1655 A459 $1.50 olive grn 2.00 2.00
a. Booklet pane of 1 2.00
1656 A459 $1.80 violet 2.25 2.25
a. Booklet pane of 1 2.25
b. Booklet pane, #1651-1656 9.00
Booklet, #1651a-1656a, 1656b 18.00
Nos. 1651-1656 (6) 8.45 8.00

A miniature sheet containing #1651-1656, both perf and imperf within the sheet, exists. This comes from a "Limited Edition" album.

Scenic Reflections A460

Designs: 40c, Lake Lyndon. 80c, Lake Wakatipu. $1.10, Mt. Ruapehu. $1.20, Rainbow Mountain Scenic Reserve. $1.50, Tairua Harbor. $1.80, Lake Alexandrina.

2000, July 7 Litho. *Perf. 14*

1657 A460 40c multi .60 .35
1658 A460 80c multi 1.10 .55
1659 A460 $1.10 multi 1.25 1.00
1660 A460 $1.20 multi 1.50 1.50
1661 A460 $1.50 multi 1.75 1.75
1662 A460 $1.80 multi 2.00 2.00
a. Souvenir Sheet, #1657, 1662 4.00 4.00
Nos. 1657-1662 (6) 8.20 7.15

No. 1662a issued 10/5/00 for Canpex 2000 Stamp Exhibition, Christchurch.

Queen Mother's 100th Birthday A461

Queen Mother in: 40c, 1907. $1.10, 1966. $1.80, 1997.

2000, Aug. 4

1663 A461 40c multi .60 .35
1664 A461 $1.10 multi 1.25 1.00
1665 A461 $1.80 multi 2.50 2.00
a. Souvenir sheet, #1663-1665 4.25 4.25
Nos. 1663-1665 (3) 4.35 3.35

Sports A462

2000, Aug. 4 *Perf. 14x14¼*

1666 A462 40c Rowing .60 .35
1667 A462 80c Equestrian 1.00 .55
1668 A462 $1.10 Cycling 1.50 1.00
1669 A462 $1.20 Triathlon 1.50 1.50
1670 A462 $1.50 Lawn bowling 1.75 1.75
1671 A462 $1.80 Netball 2.00 2.25
Nos. 1666-1671 (6) 8.35 7.40

2000 Summer Olympics, Sydney (Nos. 1666-1669).

Christmas A463

Designs: 40c, Madonna and child. 80c, Mary, Joseph and donkey. $1.10, Baby Jesus, cow, lamb. $1.20, Archangel. $1.50, Shepherd and lamb. $1.80, Magi.

2000, Sept. 6 *Perf. 14*

1672 A463 40c multi .60 .25
1673 A463 80c multi 1.00 .60
1674 A463 $1.10 multi 1.40 1.40
1675 A463 $1.20 multi 1.60 1.60
1676 A463 $1.50 multi 1.75 1.75
1677 A463 $1.80 multi 2.00 2.00
Nos. 1672-1677 (6) 8.35 7.60

Self-Adhesive
Size: 30x25mm
Serpentine Die Cut 11¼x11

1678 A463 40c multi .60 .25
a. Booklet of 10 6.50

Issued: No. 1678a, 11/1/00.

Scenic Views Type of 1995

Designs: 90c, Rangitoto Island. $1.30, Lake Camp, South Canterbury.

2000 Litho. *Perf. 13¼x13½*

Size: 27x22mm

No.	Type	Description	Unused	Used
1679	A404	90c multi	1.25	.75
1680	A404	$1.30 multi	1.75	1.10
a.		Souvenir sheet, #1636-1637, 1679-1680	6.00	6.00

Issued: Nos. 1679-1680, 10/2/00; No. 1680a, 3/16/01. 2001: A Stamp Odyssey Philatelic Exhibition, Invercargill (#1680a).

Teddy Bears and Dolls — A464

Designs: 40c+5c, Teddy bear "Geronimo," by Rose Hill. 80c+5c, Antique French and wooden Schoenhut dolls. $1.10, Chad Valley bear. $1.20, Doll "Poppy," by Debbie Pointon. $1.50, Teddy bears "Swanni," by Robin Rive, and "Dear John," by Rose Hill. $1.80, Doll "Lia," by Gloria Young, and teddy bear.

2000, Oct. 5 *Perf. 14½x14¾*

No.	Type	Description	Unused	Used
1681	A464	40c +5c multi	.65	.40
1682	A464	80c +5c multi	1.25	.70
a.		Souvenir sheet, #1681-1682	2.75	2.75
1683	A464	$1.10 multi	1.40	1.40
1684	A464	$1.20 multi	1.60	1.60
1685	A464	$1.50 multi	1.75	1.75
1686	A464	$1.80 multi	2.00	2.00
a.		Block of 6, #1681-1686	9.50	9.50

Coil Stamp

Size: 30x25mm

Self-Adhesive

Serpentine Die Cut 11¼

No.	Type	Description	Unused	Used
1687	A464	40c +5c multi	.55	.40

Endangered Birds — A465

Designs: No. 1688, Lesser kestrel. No. 1689, Orange fronted parakeet. 80c, Black stilt. $1.10, Stewart Island fernbird. $1.20, Kakapo. $1.50, North Island weka. $1.80, Okarito brown kiwi.

2000, Nov. 4 *Perf. 14*

No.	Type	Description	Unused	Used
1688	A465	40c multi	.60	.35
1689	A465	40c multi	.60	.35
a.		Pair, #1688-1689	1.75	1.75
1690	A465	80c multi	1.25	.90
1691	A465	$1.10 multi	1.40	1.40
1692	A465	$1.20 multi	1.50	1.50
1693	A465	$1.50 multi	1.75	1.75
1694	A465	$1.80 multi	2.00	2.00
a.		Souvenir sheet, #1693-1694	5.75	5.75
		Nos. 1688-1694 (7)	9.10	8.25

Nos. 1689-1690 exist in a souvenir sheet from a "Limited Edition" album.

Issued: No. 1694a, 2/1/01. Hong Kong 2001 Stamp Exhibition (#1694a). See France Nos. 2790-2791.

Penny Universal Postage, Cent. — A466

Methods of mail delivery: a, Steamship. b, Horse-drawn coach. c, Early mail truck. d, Paddle steamer. e, Railway traveling post office. f, Airplane with front cargo hatch. g, Bicycle. h, Tractor trailer. i, Airplane with side cargo hatch. j, Computer mouse.

2001, Jan. 1

No.	Type	Description	Unused	Used
1695		Sheet of 10	5.75	5.75
a.-j.		A466 40c Any single	.55	.55
k.		As No. 1695, with Belgica 2001 sheet margin	6.00	6.00

No. 1695k has no perforations running through sheet margin.

Marine Reptiles — A467

Designs: 40c, Green turtle. 80c, Leathery turtle. 90c, Loggerhead turtle. $1.30, Hawksbill turtle. $1.50, Banded sea snake. $2, Yellow-bellied sea snake.

2001, Feb. 1

No.	Type	Description	Unused	Used
1696	A467	40c multi	.75	.25
1697	A467	80c multi	1.10	.65
1698	A467	90c multi	1.25	1.25
1699	A467	$1.30 multi	1.75	1.75
1700	A467	$1.50 multi	2.00	2.00
1701	A467	$2 multi	2.25	2.25
a.		Souvenir sheet, #1700-1701	5.00	5.00
		Nos. 1696-1701 (6)	9.10	8.15

New Year 2001 (Year of the snake) (#1701a).

Flowers A468

2001, Mar. 7

No.	Type	Description	Unused	Used
1702	A468	40c Camellia	.55	.35
1703	A468	80c Siberian iris	.90	.55
1704	A468	90c Daffodil	1.10	1.10
1705	A468	$1.30 Chrysanthemum	1.50	1.50
1706	A468	$1.50 Sweet pea	1.75	1.75
1707	A468	$2 Petunia	2.50	2.50
a.		Souvenir sheet, #1702-1707	8.25	8.25
		Nos. 1702-1707 (6)	8.30	7.75

No. 1707a exists imperf from a "Limited Edition" album.

Art From Nature A469

2001, Apr. 4 Litho. *Perf. 14¼*

No.	Type	Description	Unused	Used
1708	A469	40c Greenstone	.55	.35
1709	A469	80c Oamaru stone	.90	.55
1710	A469	90c Paua	1.10	1.10
1711	A469	$1.30 Kauri gum	1.50	1.50
1712	A469	$1.50 Flax	1.75	1.75
1713	A469	$2 Fern	2.50	2.50
		Nos. 1708-1713 (6)	8.30	7.75

Within sheets of 25 printed for each stamp are four blocks of four showing a circular design, made by rotating each stamp design 90 degrees.

Aircraft A470

Designs: 40c, Douglas DC-3. 80c, Fletcher FU24 Topdresser. 90c, De Havilland DH82A Tiger Moth. $1.30, Fokker FVIIb/3m. $1.50, De Havilland DH100 Vampire. $2, Boeing & Westervelt Seaplane.

2001, May 2 *Perf. 14x14¼*

No.	Type	Description	Unused	Used
1714	A470	40c multi	.60	.35
a.		Booklet pane of 1	.60	
1715	A470	80c multi	.90	.65
a.		Booklet pane of 1	.90	
1716	A470	90c multi	1.25	1.25
a.		Booklet pane of 1	1.25	
1717	A470	$1.30 multi	1.50	1.50
a.		Booklet pane of 1	1.50	
1718	A470	$1.50 multi	1.75	1.75
a.		Booklet pane of 1	1.75	
1719	A470	$2 multi	2.50	2.50
a.		Booklet pane of 1	2.50	
b.		Booklet pane, #1714-1719	10.00	
		Booklet, #1714a-1719a, 1719b	20.00	
		Nos. 1714-1719 (6)	8.50	8.00

Greetings — A471

No. 1720: a, Heart. b, Balloons. c, Flower. d, Gift. e, Trumpet.

No. 1721: a, Candles. b, Stars. c, Roses and candle. d, Picture frame. e, Letter and fountain pen.

2001, June 6 *Perf. 14½x14*

No.	Type	Description	Unused	Used
1720		Vert. strip of 5 + 5 labels	2.75	2.75
a.-e.		A471 40c Any single + label	.50	.50
1721		Vert. strip of 5 + 5 labels	5.75	5.75
a.-e.		A471 90c Any single + label	.90	.90

Labels could be personalized on sheets that sold for $15.95 and $27.95 respectively.

Government Tourist Office, Cent. — A472

Designs: 40c, Bungee jumper, Queenstown. 80c, Canoeing on Lake Rotoiti. 90c, Sightseers on Mt. Alfred. $1.30, Fishing in Glenorchy River. $1.50, Kayakers in Abel Tasman Natl. Park. $2, Hiker in Fiordland Natl. Park.

2001 Litho. *Perf. 14¼*

No.	Type	Description	Unused	Used
1722	A472	40c multi	.50	.25
1723	A472	80c multi	.90	.90
1724	A472	90c multi	1.10	1.10
1725	A472	$1.30 multi	1.50	1.50
1726	A472	$1.50 multi	1.75	1.75
1727	A472	$2 multi	2.25	2.25
a.		Souvenir sheet, #1726-1727	4.75	4.75

Size: 26x21mm

Serpentine Die Cut 11¼x11

Self-Adhesive

No.	Type	Description	Unused	Used
1728	A472	40c multi	.60	.50
a.		Booklet of 10 + 10 etiquettes	6.50	
1729	A472	90c multi	1.25	1.25
a.		Booklet of 10 + 10 etiquettes	14.00	
1730	A472	$1.50 multi	2.25	2.25
a.		Horiz. strip, #1728-1730	4.50	
b.		Booklet of 5 + 5 etiquettes	12.00	

Coil Stamp

Size: 26x21mm

Self-Adhesive

Serpentine Die Cut 10x9¾

No.	Type	Description	Unused	Used
1730C	A472	40c Like #1722	.55	.35
		Nos. 1722-1730C (10)	12.65	12.10

Phila Nippon '01, Japan (No. 1727a). Issued: No. 1727a, 8/1; others, 7/4.

A sheet containing 3 each of Nos. 1722-1727 was included in a book that sold for $69.95.

Christmas — A473

Designs: 40c, In Excelsis Gloria. 80c, Away in the Manger. 90c, Joy to the World. $1.30, Angels We Have Heard on High. $1.50, O Holy Night. $2, While Shepherds Watched Their Flocks.

2001, Sept. 5 *Perf. 13¼x13¾*

No.	Type	Description	Unused	Used
1731	A473	40c multi	.60	.25
1732	A473	80c multi	1.10	.50
1733	A473	90c multi	1.25	1.25
1734	A473	$1.30 multi	1.50	1.50
1735	A473	$1.50 multi	1.75	1.75
1736	A473	$2 multi	2.00	2.00

Size: 21x26mm

Serpentine Die Cut 9¾x10

Self-Adhesive

No.	Type	Description	Unused	Used
1737	A473	40c multi	.65	.25
a.		Booklet of 10	6.50	
		Nos. 1731-1737 (7)	8.85	7.50

Issued: No. 1737a, 11/7/01.

Visit of Queen Elizabeth II, Oct. 2001 — A474

Queen in past visits: 40c, Arriving for opening of Parliament, 1953. 80c, With crowd, 1970. 90c, With crowd, 1977. $1.30, With crowd, 1986. $1.50, At Commonwealth Games, 1990. $2, 2001 portrait.

2001, Oct. 3 Litho. *Perf. 14*

No.	Type	Description	Unused	Used
1738	A474	40c multi	.65	.35
1739	A474	80c multi	1.10	.60
1740	A474	90c multi	1.25	1.25
1741	A474	$1.30 multi	1.50	1.50
1742	A474	$1.50 multi	1.75	1.75
1743	A474	$2 multi	2.25	2.25
a.		Horiz. strip, #1738-1743	8.50	8.50
		Nos. 1738-1743 (6)	8.50	7.70

Nos. 1738-1743 exist in a souvenir sheet from a "Limited Edition" album. Nos. 1738-1743 also exist imperf.

Penguins A475

Designs: 40c, Rockhopper. 80c, Little blue. 90c, Snares crested. $1.30, Erect-crested. $1.50, Fiordland crested. $2, Yellow-eyed.

2001, Nov. 7 *Perf. 14¼*

No.	Type	Description	Unused	Used
1744	A475	40c multi	.75	.40
1745	A475	80c multi	1.10	.60
1746	A475	90c multi	1.25	1.25
1747	A475	$1.30 multi	1.75	1.75
1748	A475	$1.50 multi	2.00	2.00
1749	A475	$2 multi	2.25	2.25
		Nos. 1744-1749 (6)	9.10	8.25

Filming in New Zealand of The Lord of the Rings Trilogy — A476

Scenes from "The Lord of the Rings: The Fellowship of the Ring:" 40c, Gandalf the Gray and Saruman the White, vert. 80c, Lady Galadriel, vert. 90c, Sam Gamgee and Frodo Baggins. $1.30, Guardian of Rivendell, vert. $1.50, Strider, vert. $2, Boromir, son of Denethor.

Perf. 14½x14, 14x14½

2001, Dec. 4 Litho.

No.	Type	Description	Unused	Used
1750	A476	40c multi	.75	.50
a.		Souvenir sheet of 1	2.25	1.75
b.		Sheet of 10 #1750	7.50	—
1751	A476	80c multi	1.75	1.75
a.		Souvenir sheet of 1	4.00	3.50
1752	A476	90c multi	2.00	2.00
a.		Souvenir sheet of 1	4.75	4.00
1753	A476	$1.30 multi	2.75	2.75
a.		Souvenir sheet of 1	6.50	5.75
1754	A476	$1.50 multi	3.00	3.00
a.		Souvenir sheet of 1	7.50	6.50
1755	A476	$2 multi	4.00	4.00
a.		Souvenir sheet of 1	11.00	8.75
b.		Souvenir sheet, #1754-1755	8.00	8.00
c.		Souvenir sheet, #1750, 1753, 1755	9.50	9.50

Self-Adhesive

Serpentine Die Cut 10x10¼, 10¼x10

Size: 22x33mm, 33x22mm

1756	A476	40c multi	.85	.85
1757	A476	80c multi	2.00	2.00
1758	A476	90c multi	2.25	2.25
1759	A476	$1.30 multi	3.00	3.00
1760	A476	$1.50 multi	3.25	3.25
1761	A476	$2 multi	4.25	4.25
a.		Pane, #1756-1761	*16.00*	
b.		Booklet pane, #1757, 1759-1761, 4 #1756, 2 #1758	*35.00*	
		Nos. 1750-1761 (12)	29.85	29.60

Issued: No. 1755b, 8/30/02; No. 1755c, 4/5/02. Other values, 12/4/01.

No. 1755b issued for Amphilex 2002 World Stamp Exhibition, Amsterdam; No. 1755c issued for Northpex 2002.

See Nos. 1835-1846, 1897-1908.

New Year 2002 (Year of the Horse) A477

Champion race horses: 40c, Christian Cullen. 80c, Lyell Creek. 90c, Yulestar. $1.30, Sunline. $1.50, Ethereal. $2, Zabeel.

2002, Feb. 7			***Perf. 14***	
1762	A477	40c multi	.55	.35
1763	A477	80c multi	.90	.90
1764	A477	90c multi	1.10	1.10
1765	A477	$1.30 multi	1.50	1.50
1766	A477	$1.50 multi	1.75	1.75
a.		Souvenir sheet, #1765-1766	4.50	4.50
1767	A477	$2 multi	2.50	2.50
		Nos. 1762-1767 (6)	8.30	8.10

Fungi — A478

Designs: 40c, Hygrocybe rubrocarnosa. 80c, Entoloma hochstetteri. 90c, Aseroe rubra. $1.30, Hericium coralloides. $1.50, Thaxterogaster porphyreus. $2, Ramaria aureorhiza.

2002, Mar. 6		**Litho.**	***Perf. 14***	
1768	A478	40c multi	.60	.40
1769	A478	80c multi	1.10	.60
1770	A478	90c multi	1.25	1.25
1771	A478	$1.30 multi	1.75	1.75
1772	A478	$1.50 multi	2.00	2.00
1773	A478	$2 multi	2.25	2.25
a.		Souvenir sheet, #1768-1773	9.00	9.00
		Nos. 1768-1773 (6)	8.95	8.25

No. 1773a exists as an imperforate souvenir sheet from a "Limited Edition" album.

A479

A480

Architectural Heritage — A481

Designs: 40c, War Memorial Museum, Auckland. 80c, Stone Store, Kerikeri. 90c, Arts Center, Christchurch. $1.30, Government buildings, Wellington. $1.50, Railway Station, Dunedin. $2, Sky Tower, Auckland.

2002, Apr. 3		**Litho.**	***Perf. 14½x14***	
1774	A479	40c multi	.65	.30
a.		Booklet pane of 1	.65	—
1775	A480	80c multi	1.10	.75
a.		Booklet pane of 1	1.10	—
1776	A481	90c multi	1.25	1.00
a.		Booklet pane of 1	1.25	—
1777	A481	$1.30 multi	1.50	1.50
a.		Booklet pane of 1	1.50	—
1778	A480	$1.50 multi	1.75	1.75
a.		Booklet pane of 1	1.75	—
1779	A479	$2 multi	2.00	2.00
a.		Booklet pane of 1	2.00	—
b.		Block of 6, #1774-1779	10.00	10.00
c.		Booklet pane, #1779b	11.00	—
		Booklet, #1774a-1779a, 1779c	20.00	
		Nos. 1774-1779 (6)	8.25	7.30

Booklet containing Nos. 1774a-1779a, 1779c sold for $16.95.

Art from Sweden and New Zealand A482

Designs: No. 1780, Maori basket, by Willa Rogers, New Zealand. No. 1781, Starfish Vessel, by Graeme Priddle, New Zealand. 80c, Catch II, by Raewyn Atkinson, New Zealand. 90c, Silver brooch, by Gavin Hithings, New Zealand. $1.30, Glass towers, by Emma Camden, New Zealand. $1.50, Pacific Rim, by Merilyn Wiseman. $2, Rain Forest, glass vase by Ola Höglund, Sweden.

Litho. & Engr. (#1780, 1786), Litho.

Perf. 12½x12¾ (#1780, 1786), 14

2002, May 2				
1780	A482	40c multi	.60	.35
1781	A482	40c multi	.60	.35
1782	A482	80c multi	1.10	.65
1783	A482	90c multi	1.25	1.25
1784	A482	$1.30 multi	1.50	1.50
1785	A482	$1.50 multi	1.75	1.75
1786	A482	$2 multi	2.00	2.00
		Nos. 1780-1786 (7)	8.80	7.85

See Sweden No. 2440.

Nos. 1780-1786 exist in a souvenir sheet from a "Limited Edition" album.

Kiwi Type of 1988

2002, June 5		**Litho.**	***Perf. 14½***	
1787	A325	$1.50 brown	2.00	1.50
a.		Souvenir sheet of 3	7.00	7.00

Used value is for stamp with complete selvage.

Issued: No. 1787a, 11/12/10. Palmpex 2010 Stamp Show, Palmerston North (No. 1787a).

Queen Mother Elizabeth (1900-2002) A483

2002, June 5			***Perf. 14¼***	
1788	A483	$2 multi	2.25	2.00

Children's Book Festival Stamp Design Contest Winners A484

Art by: No. 1789, Anna Poland, Cardinal McKeefry School, Wellington. No. 1790, Hee Su Kim, Glendowie Primary School, Auckland. No. 1791, Jayne Bruce, Rangiora Borough School, Rangiora. No. 1792, Teigan Stafford-Bush (bird), Ararimu School, Auckland. No. 1793, Hazel Gilbert, Gonville School, Wanganui. No. 1794, Gerard Mackle, Temuka High School, Temuka. No. 1795, Maria Rodgers, Salford School, Invercargill. No. 1796, Paul Read (hand and ball), Ararimu School, Auckland. No. 1797, Four students, Glendene Primary School, Auckland. No. 1798, Olivia Duncan, Taupo Normal Intermediate School, Auckland.

2002, June 5			***Perf. 14***	
1789	A484	40c multi	.75	.75
1790	A484	40c multi	.75	.75
1791	A484	40c multi	.75	.75
1792	A484	40c multi	.75	.75
1793	A484	40c multi	.75	.75
1794	A484	40c multi	.75	.75
1795	A484	40c multi	.75	.75
1796	A484	40c multi	.75	.75
1797	A484	40c multi	.75	.75
1798	A484	40c multi	.75	.75
a.		Block of 10, #1789-1798	7.75	7.75
b.		Sheet of 10, #1789-1798	8.00	8.00
		Nos. 1789-1798 (10)	7.50	7.50

Scenic Coastlines A485

Designs: 40c, Tongaporutu Cliffs, Taranaki. 80c, Lottin Point, East Cape. 90c, Curio Bay, Catlins. $1.30, Kaikoura Coast. $1.50, Meybille Bay, West Coast. $2, Papanui Point, Raglan.

2002, July 3			***Perf. 14***	
1799	A485	40c multi	.50	.30
1800	A485	80c multi	1.00	.60
1801	A485	90c multi	1.25	1.25
1802	A485	$1.30 multi	1.50	1.50
1803	A485	$1.50 multi	1.75	1.75
1804	A485	$2 multi	2.00	2.00

Size: 28x22mm

Self-Adhesive

Serpentine Die Cut 10x9¾

1805	A485	40c multi	.55	.55
a.		Booklet pane of 10	6.50	
b.		Serpentine die cut 11	.70	.70
c.		Booklet pane of 10 #1805b	7.50	
1806	A485	90c multi	1.25	1.25
a.		Booklet pane of 10	14.00	
1807	A485	$1.50 multi	2.40	1.50
a.		Booklet pane of 5	12.00	
b.		Coil strip of 3, #1805-1807	4.50	

Coil Stamp

Size: 28x22mm

Self-Adhesive

Die Cut Perf. 12¾

1808	A485	40c multi	.55	.40
		Nos. 1799-1808 (10)	12.75	11.10

Christmas A487

Church interiors: 40c, Saint Werenfried Catholic Church, Waihi Village, Tokaannu. 80c, St. David's Anglican Church, Christchurch. 90c, Orthodox Church of the Transfiguration of Our Lord, Masterton. $1.30, Cathedral of the Holy Spirit, Palmerston North. $1.50, Cathedral of St. Paul, Wellington. $2, Cathedral of the Blessed Sacrament, Christchurch.

2002, Sept. 4			***Perf. 14¼***	
1812	A487	40c multi	.50	.25
1813	A487	80c multi	1.00	.45
1814	A487	90c multi	1.25	1.00
1815	A487	$1.30 multi	1.75	1.75
1816	A487	$1.50 multi	2.00	2.00
1817	A487	$2 multi	2.25	2.25

Coil Stamp

Size: 21x26mm

Self-Adhesive

Die Cut Perf. 13x12¾

1818	A487	40c multi	.55	.25

Booklet Stamp

Size: 21x26mm

Self-Adhesive

Die Cut Perf 9¾x10

1818A	A487	40c Like No. 1818	.55	.25
b.		Booklet pane of 10	6.50	
		Nos. 1812-1818A (8)	9.85	8.20

Issued: No. 1818A, 11/6/02.

Boats A488

Designs: 40c, KZ1. 80c, High 5. 90c, Gentle Spirit. $1.30, NorthStar. $1.50, OceanRunner. $2, Salperton.

2002, Oct. 2		**Litho.**	***Perf. 14***	
1819	A488	40c multi	.60	.35
1820	A488	80c multi	1.00	.65
1821	A488	90c multi	1.10	1.10
1822	A488	$1.30 multi	1.50	1.50
1823	A488	$1.50 multi	2.00	2.00
1824	A488	$2 multi	2.25	2.25
a.		Souvenir sheet, #1819-1824	9.00	9.00
		Nos. 1819-1824 (6)	8.45	7.85

No. 1824a exists an an imperforate souvenir sheet from a "Limited Edition" album.

2003 America's Cup Yacht Races A489

Scenes from 2000 America's Cup finals: $1.30, Black Magic next to Luna Rossa. $1.50, Aerial view. $2, Black Magic passing Luna Rossa.

2002				
1825	A489	$1.30 multi	1.75	1.50
1826	A489	$1.50 multi	2.00	2.00
1827	A489	$2 multi	2.25	2.25
a.		Souvenir sheet, #1825-1827	7.50	7.50
b.		As "a," with Stampshow Melbourne 02 ovpt. in margin	7.00	7.00
		Nos. 1825-1827 (3)	6.00	5.75

Issued: No. 1827b, 10/4; others 10/2.

Vacation Homes A490

Various vacation homes with denominations over: No. 1828, Paua shell. No. 1829, Sunflower. No. 1830, Life preserver. No. 1831, Fish hook. No. 1832, Fish. No. 1833, Flower bouquet.

2002, Nov. 6		**Litho.**	***Perf. 14***	
1828	A490	40c multi	.70	.55
1829	A490	40c multi	.70	.55
1830	A490	40c multi	.70	.55
1831	A490	40c multi	.70	.55
1832	A490	40c multi	.70	.55
1833	A490	40c multi	.70	.55
		Nos. 1828-1833 (6)	4.20	3.30

Nativity, by Pseudo Ambrogio di Baldese — A491

2002, Nov. 21			***Perf. 14¼x14***	
1834	A491	$1.50 multi	2.10	1.75

See Vatican City No. 1232.

The Lord of the Rings Type of 2001

Scenes from *The Lord of the Rings: The Two Towers:* 40c, Aragorn and Eowyn. 80c, Orc raider. 90c, Gandalf the White, vert. $1.30, The Easterlings. $1.50, Frodo captured, vert. $2, Shield Maiden of Rohan.

2002, Dec. 4		***Perf. 14x14½, 14½x14***		
1835	A476	40c multi	.65	.40
a.		Souvenir sheet of 1	1.00	.65
1836	A476	80c multi	1.40	1.40
a.		Souvenir sheet of 1	2.00	2.00
1837	A476	90c multi	1.50	1.50
a.		Souvenir sheet of 1	2.25	2.25

1838 A476 $1.30 multi 2.25 2.25
a. Souvenir sheet of 1 3.25 3.25
1839 A476 $1.50 multi 2.50 2.50
a. Souvenir sheet of 1 3.75 3.75
1840 A476 $2 multi 3.25 3.25
a. Souvenir sheet of 1 4.25 4.25
Set of 6 souvenir sheets of 1 each, #1835a//1840a 16.50

Self-Adhesive

Size: 34x23mm, 23x34mm

Serpentine Die Cut 10¼x10, 10x10¼

1841 A476 40c multi .65 .40
1842 A476 80c multi 1.25 1.25
1843 A476 90c multi 1.40 1.40
1844 A476 $1.30 multi 2.10 2.10
1845 A476 $1.50 multi 2.40 2.40
1846 A476 $2 multi 3.25 3.25
a. Pane, #1841-1846 11.00
b. Booklet pane, #1842, 1844-1846, 2 #1843, 4 #1841 14.50
Nos. 1835-1846 (12) 22.60 22.10

The 2002 sheets contain: #1767, 1773, 1779, 1785, 1787, 1804, 1817, 1830, B170. See note following #1404.

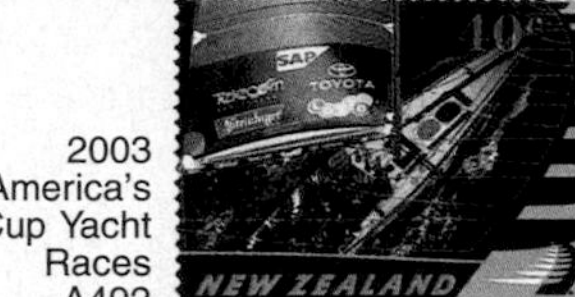

2003 America's Cup Yacht Races A492

Designs: 40c, Yacht and sail with sponsor's advertisements. 80c, Yachts circling. 90c, Yachts racing.

2003, Jan. 8 Litho. *Perf. 14*

1847 A492 40c multi .50 .35
1848 A492 80c multi 1.10 1.10
1849 A492 90c multi 1.25 1.25
a. Souvenir sheet of 3, #1847-1849 3.25 3.25
Nos. 1847-1849 (3) 2.85 2.70

New Year 2003 (Year of the Ram) A493

Designs: 40c, Sheep in high country. 90c, Sheep leaving pen. $1.30, Sheepdog and sheep. $1.50, Shearer. $2, Shearing gang.

2003, Feb. 5 Litho. *Perf. 14*

1850 A493 40c multi .55 .35
1851 A493 90c multi 1.00 .65
1852 A493 $1.30 multi 1.50 1.50
1853 A493 $1.50 multi 2.00 2.00
1854 A493 $2 multi 2.50 2.50
a. Souvenir sheet of 2, #1852, 1854 4.00 4.00
Nos. 1850-1854 (5) 7.55 7.00

Royal New Zealand Ballet, 50th Anniv. A494

Scenes from productions of: 40c, Carmina Burana, 1971, vert. 90c, Papillon, 1989. $1.30, Cinderella, 2000, vert. $1.50, FrENZy, 2001, vert. $2, Swan lake, 2002.

2003, Mar. 5 Litho. *Perf. 14*

1855 A494 40c multi .55 .40
1856 A494 90c multi 1.10 .75
1857 A494 $1.30 multi 1.50 1.50
1858 A494 $1.50 multi 2.00 2.00
1859 A494 $2 multi 2.50 2.50
a. Souvenir sheet, #1855, 1856, 1859 6.50 6.50
Nos. 1855-1859 (5) 7.65 7.15

No. 1859a issued for Bangkok 2003 World Philatelic Exhibition.

Nos. 1855-1859 exist in a souvenir sheet from a "Limited Edition" album.

Military Uniforms, Medals and Insignia — A495

No. 1860: a, Forest ranger, 1860s. b, Napier naval artillery volunteer officer, 1890s. c, Amuri mounted rifles officer, 1900-10. d, Mounted Rifles, South Africa, 1898-1902. e, Staff officer, France, 1918. f, Petty officer, 1914-18. g, Infantry, France, 1916-18. h, Engineer, 1939-45. i, Matron, RNZN Hospital, 1940s. j, WAAC, Egypt, 1942. k, Bomber pilot, Europe, 1943. l, Fighter pilot, Pacific, 1943. m, WAAF driver, 1943. n, Gunner, Korea, 1950-53. o, Petty officer, 1950s. p, SAS, Malaya, 1955-57. q, Canberra Pilot, 1960. r, Infantry, Viet Nam, 1960s. s, UN Peacekeeper, East Timor, 2000. t, Peace Monitor, Bougainville, 2001.

2003, Apr. 2 Litho. *Perf. 14*

1860 Sheet of 20 18.00 18.00
a.-t. A495 40c Any single .65 .45
u. Booklet pane, 2 each #a-d 6.00 —
v. Booklet pane, 2 each #e-h 6.00 —
w. Booklet pane, 2 each #i-l 6.00 —
x. Booklet pane, 2 each #m-p 6.00 —
y. Booklet pane, 2 each #q-t 6.00 —
Complete booklet, #u-y 30.00

Tourist Attractions A496

Designs: 50c, Ailsa Mountains. $1, Coromandel Peninsula. $1.50, Arrowtown. $2, Tongariro National Park. $5, Castlepoint.

2003, May 7 Litho. *Perf. 13¼x13½*

1861 A496 50c multi .65 .40
1862 A496 $1 multi 1.30 .90
1863 A496 $1.50 multi 1.75 1.40
1863A A496 $1.50 multi 1.75 1.40
1864 A496 $2 multi 2.75 2.00
1865 A496 $5 multi 5.75 4.75

Self-Adhesive

Serpentine Die Cut 10x9½

1866 A496 $1.50 multi 2.00 1.50
a. Booklet pane of 5 11.00
1866B A496 $1.50 As #1866, vignette 26mm wide 2.10 2.00
c. Booklet pane of 5 #1866b + 10 etiquettes 12.00
Nos. 1861-1866 (7) 15.95 12.35

Nos. 1861-1865 exist with silver fern leaf overprints from a limited printing.

Nos. 1866b, 1866c issued 3/27/07. Vignette of No. 1866 is 27mm wide. No. 1863A issued 2007.

Nos. 1863A and 1866B show a person on the sidewalk in front of the door of the house in the foreground (above the zero in the denomination). The person is not found on Nos. 1863 and 1866.

See Nos. 1926-1928B, 1972-1977, 2062-2067, 2129-2137, 2222, 2238, 2257-2263, 2316-2322, 2392, 2405-2409.

Ascent of Mt. Everest, 50th Anniv. A497

Designs: No. 1867, Sir Edmund Hillary, Mt. Everest. No. 1868, Tenzing Norgay, climbers on mountain.

2003, May 29 *Perf. 14*

1867 A497 40c multi .95 .95
1868 A497 40c multi .95 .95
a. Pair, #1867-1868 2.00 2.00

Coronation Type of 1953

Perf. 14x14½, 14½x14

2003, June 4 Litho.

1869 A112 40c Like #280 .60 .30
1870 A113 90c Like #281 1.10 .75
1871 A112 $1.30 Like #282 1.75 1.75
1872 A114 $1.50 Like #283 2.00 2.00
1873 A112 $2 Like #284 2.25 2.25
Nos. 1869-1873 (5) 7.70 7.05

Nos. 1869-1873 exist in a souvenir sheet from a "Limited Edition" album.

Test Rugby, Cent. A498

Designs: 40c, New Zealand vs. South Africa, 1937. 90c, New Zealand vs. Wales, 1963. $1.30, New Zealand vs. Australia, 1985. No.1877, New Zealand vs. France, 1986. No. 1878, All Blacks jersey. $2, New Zealand vs. England, 1997.

2003, July 2 *Perf. 14*

1874 A498 40c multi .65 .35
1875 A498 90c multi 1.25 .80
1876 A498 $1.30 multi 1.75 1.75
1877 A498 $1.50 multi 2.00 2.00
1878 A498 $1.50 multi 2.00 2.00
1879 A498 $2 multi 2.25 2.25
a. Souvenir sheet, #1874-1879 10.00 10.00
b. Sheet, #1877-1879 7.00 7.00
c. Souvenir sheet, #1878-1879 6.00 6.00
Nos. 1874-1879 (6) 9.90 9.15

No. 1879b issued 11/7 for Welpex 2003 Stampshow, Wellington. No. 1879b sold for $6.

No. 1879c issued 1/30/04 for 2004 Hong Kong Stamp Expo (#1879c).

Waterways A499

Designs: 40c, Papaaroha, Coromandel Peninsula. 90c, Waimahana Creek, Chatham Islands. $1.30, Blue Lake, Central Otago. $1.50, Waikato River, Waikato. $2, Hooker River, Canterbury.

2003, Aug. 6 Litho. *Perf. 14¼*

1880 A499 40c multi .55 .35
1881 A499 90c multi 1.00 .90
1882 A499 $1.30 multi 1.75 1.75
1883 A499 $1.50 multi 2.00 2.00
1884 A499 $2 multi 2.25 2.25
Nos. 1880-1884 (5) 7.55 7.25

Antique Automobiles A500

Designs: 40c, 1895 Benz Velo. 90c, 1903 Oldsmobile. $1.30, 1911 Wolseley. $1.50, 1915 Talbot. $2, 1915 Ford Model T.

2003, Sept. 3 Litho. *Perf. 13x13¼*

1885 A500 40c multi .60 .40
1886 A500 90c multi 1.10 .95
1887 A500 $1.30 multi 1.75 1.75
1888 A500 $1.50 multi 2.00 2.00
1889 A500 $2 multi 2.25 2.25
Nos. 1885-1889 (5) 7.70 7.35

Christmas A501

Tree decorations: 40c, Christ child. 90c, Dove. $1.30, Geometric (candles). $1.50, Bells. $2, Angel.

$1, Geometric (fleur-de-lis).

2003, Oct. 1 *Perf. 13½*

1890 A501 40c multi .60 .25
1891 A501 90c multi 1.10 .75
1892 A501 $1.30 multi 1.75 1.75
1893 A501 $1.50 multi 2.00 2.00
1894 A501 $2 multi 2.25 2.25

Self-Adhesive

Serpentine Die Cut 9½x10

Size: 21x26mm

1895 A501 40c multi .60 .40
a. Booklet pane of 10 6.50
1896 A501 $1 multi 1.25 1.25
a. Booklet pane of 8 + 8 etiquettes 13.00
Nos. 1890-1896 (7) 9.55 8.65

The Lord of the Rings Type of 2001

Scenes from *The Lord of the Rings: The Return of the King:* 40c, Legolas, vert. 80c, Frodo, vert. 90c, Merry and Pippin. $1.30, Aragorn, vert. $1.50, Gandalf the White, vert. $2, Gollum.

2003, Nov. 5 *Perf. 14½x14, 14x14½*

1897 A476 40c multi .65 .40
a. Souvenir sheet of 1 .90 .90
1898 A476 80c multi 1.10 1.10
a. Souvenir sheet of 1 1.50 1.50
1899 A476 90c multi 1.25 1.25
a. Souvenir sheet of 1 2.00 2.00
1900 A476 $1.30 multi 2.00 2.00
a. Souvenir sheet of 1 2.25 2.25
1901 A476 $1.50 multi 2.25 2.25
a. Souvenir sheet of 1 2.75 2.75
1902 A476 $2 multi 2.50 2.50
a. Souvenir sheet of 1 3.75 3.75
Set of 6 souvenir sheets of 1 each, #1897a-1902a 13.25

Self-Adhesive

Size: 23x34mm, 34x23mm

Serpentine Die Cut 10x10¼, 10¼x10

1903 A476 40c multi .65 .45
1904 A476 80c multi 1.10 1.00
1905 A476 90c multi 1.40 1.10
1906 A476 $1.30 multi 2.00 2.00
1907 A476 $1.50 multi 2.25 2.25
1908 A476 $2 multi 2.50 2.50
a. Pane, #1903-1908 10.00
b. Booklet pane, #1904, 1906-1908, 2 #1905, 4 #1903 14.00
Nos. 1897-1908 (12) 19.65 18.80

The 2003 sheets contain: #1854, 1859, 1864, 1873, 1879, 1884, 1889, 1894, 1902. See note following #1404.

Scenic Views Type of 1995

Serpentine Die Cut 10x9¾

2004, Jan. 28 Litho.

Booklet Stamp

Size: 26x21mm

Self-Adhesive

1909 A404 10c Like #1346 .40 .40
a. Booklet pane, 10 #1359F, 4 #1909 8.00

Zoo Animals — A502

Designs: 40c, Hamadryas baboon. 90c, Malayan sun bear. $1.30, Red panda. $1.50, Ring-tailed lemur. $2, Spider monkey.

2004, Jan. 28 Litho. *Perf. 13¼x13*

1910 A502 40c multi .60 .50
1911 A502 90c multi 1.25 1.25
1912 A502 $1.30 multi 2.00 2.00
1913 A502 $1.50 multi 2.25 2.25
1914 A502 $2 multi 2.50 2.50
a. Souvenir sheet, #1913-1914 5.00 5.00

Nos. 1910-1914 exist in a souvenir sheet from a "Limited Edition" album.

Self-Adhesive

Size: 21x26mm

Coil Stamp

Die Cut Perf. 12¾x12½

1915 A502 40c multi .60 .55

Booklet Stamp

Serpentine Die Cut 11¼

1916 A502 40c multi .60 .55
a. Booklet pane of 10 6.50
Nos. 1910-1916 (7) 9.80 9.60

New Year 2004 (Year of the Monkey) (#1914a).

Rugby Sevens A503

Designs: 40c, New Zealand Sevens. 90c, Hong Kong Sevens. $1.50, Hong Kong Stadium. $2, Westpac Stadium, Wellington.

2004, Feb. 25 Litho. *Perf. 14x14¼*

1917 A503 40c multi .60 .45
1918 A503 90c multi 1.25 1.25
1919 A503 $1.50 multi 1.75 1.75
1920 A503 $2 multi 2.75 2.75
a. Souvenir sheet, #1917-1920 7.00 7.00
b. Souvenir sheet, #1877, 1878, 1920 7.00 7.00
Nos. 1917-1920 (4) 6.35 6.20

No. 1920b issued 6/26 for Le Salon du Timbre 2004, Paris.

See Hong Kong Nos. 1084-1087.

Parliament, 150th Anniv. — A504

Designs: 40c, Parliament Building, Auckland, 1854. 90c, Parliament Buildings, Wellington (Provincial Chambers), 1865. $1.30, Parliament Buildings, Wellington, 1899. $1.50, Parliament House, Wellington, 1918. $2, Beehive, Wellington, 1977.

2004, Mar. 3 *Perf. 14½x14¼*

1921 A504 40c blk & purple .60 .45
1922 A504 90c blk & violet 1.25 1.10
1923 A504 $1.30 blk & gray 1.75 1.75
1924 A504 $1.50 blk & blue 2.00 2.00
1925 A504 $2 blk & green 2.50 2.50
a. Souvenir sheet, #1921-1925 9.75 9.75
Nos. 1921-1925 (5) 8.10 7.80

See No. 1935.

Tourist Attractions Type of 2003

Designs: 45c, Kaikoura. $1.35, Church of the Good Shepherd, Lake Tekapo.

Perf. 13¼x13½

2004, Mar. 22 Litho.

1926 A496 45c multi .60 .60

Perf. 14x14½

1927 A496 $1.35 multi 2.00 2.00
a. Perf. 13½ ('06) 2.10 2.10

Self-Adhesive

Serpentine Die Cut 11¼x11

1928 A496 45c multi .70 .70
a. Booklet pane of 10 7.00

Coil Stamp

1928B A496 45c multi .70 .70
Nos. 1926-1928B (4) 4.00 4.00

Country name on No. 1928B has an unserifed font, with horizontal bars in "e," and a symmetrical "w."

No. 1927a issued 8/2006.

Scenic Views Type of 1995

2004, Apr. 5 *Die Cut Perf. 10x9½*

Size: 27x22mm

Self-Adhesive

1929 A404 90c Like #1679 1.10 1.10
a. Booklet pane of 10 11.00

Historic Farm Equipment A505

Designs: 45c, Kinnard Haines tractor. 90c, Fordson F tractor with plow. $1.35, Burrell traction engine. $1.50, Threshing mill. $2, Duncan's seed drill.

2004, Apr. 5 *Perf. 14*

1930 A505 45c multi .65 .40
a. Booklet pane of 1, perf. 14x13¼ .90 —
1931 A505 90c multi 1.25 .75
a. Booklet pane of 1, perf. 14x13¼ 1.75 —
1932 A505 $1.35 multi 2.00 2.00
a. Booklet pane of 1, perf. 14x13¼ 2.75 —
1933 A505 $1.50 multi 2.25 2.25
a. Booklet pane of 1, perf. 14x13¼ 3.00 —
1934 A505 $2 multi 2.50 2.50
a. Booklet pane of 1, perf. 14x13¼ 4.00 —
b. Booklet pane of 5, #1930-1934, perf. 14x13¼ 10.00 —
Complete booklet, #1930a, 1931a, 1932a, 1933a, 1934a, 1934b 25.00
Nos. 1930-1934 (5) 8.65 7.90

The complete booklet sold for $19.95.

Parliament Type of 2004

2004, May 5 *Perf. 14½x14¼*

1935 A504 45c Like #1921 .65 .65

World of Wearable Art Awards Show — A506

Designs: 45c, Dragon Fish. 90c, Persephone's Descent. $1.35, Meridian. $1.50, Taunga Ika. $2, Cailleach Na Mara (Sea Witch).

2004, May 5 *Perf. 14*

1936 A506 45c multi .65 .35
1937 A506 90c multi 1.10 .85
1938 A506 $1.35 multi 1.75 1.75
1939 A506 $1.50 multi 2.00 2.00
1940 A506 $2 multi 2.50 2.50
Nos. 1936-1940 (5) 8.00 7.45

Nos. 1936-1940 exist imperf.

New Zealanders — A507

Designs: No. 1941, Man outside of Pungarehu Post Office. No. 1942, Children on horse. No. 1943, Elderly man and woman in front of house.

2004, Feb. Litho. *Die Cut Perf. 13½*

Booklet Stamps

Self-Adhesive

1941 A507 $1.50 multi 5.00 5.00
1942 A507 $1.50 multi 5.00 5.00
1943 A507 $1.50 multi 5.00 5.00
a. Booklet pane, 2 each # 1941-1943, 6 etiquettes and 10 stickers 30.00
Complete booklet, #1943a 30.00
Nos. 1941-1943 (3) 15.00 15.00

Wild Food — A508

Designs: No. 1944, Mountain oysters. No. 1945, Huhu grubs. No. 1946, Possum paté.

2004, Feb. Booklet Stamps

Self-Adhesive

1944 A508 $1.50 multi 5.00 5.00
1945 A508 $1.50 multi 5.00 5.00
1946 A508 $1.50 multi 5.00 5.00
a. Booklet pane, 2 each # 1944-1946, 6 etiquettes and 6 stickers 30.00
Complete booklet, #1946a 30.00
Nos. 1944-1946 (3) 15.00 15.00

New Zealand Post Emblem — A509

2004, Feb. Booklet Stamps

Self-Adhesive

1947 A509 $1.50 blue & red 6.00 6.00
1948 A509 $1.50 red 6.00 6.00
1949 A509 $1.50 green & red 6.00 6.00
a. Booklet pane, 2 each # 1947-1949, 6 etiquettes 35.00
Complete booklet, #1949a 35.00
Nos. 1947-1949 (3) 18.00 18.00

Country name is at bottom on No. 1948. A pane of eight stamps containing two each of Nos. 1947-1949 and two $1.50 purple and red stamps similar to No. 1948 came unattached in a folder together with a set of four markers, a sheet of decorative magnets and two sheets of self-adhesive plastic stickers. The pane of eight was not available without purchasing the other non-stamp items, which sold as a package for $19.95.

Flowers — A510

Designs: 45c, Magnolia "Vulcan." 90c, Helleborus "Unnamed Hybrid." $1.35, Nerine "Anzac." $1.50, Rhododendron "Charisma." $2, Delphinium "Sarita."

2004, June 2 *Perf. 13¼x13¾*

1950 A510 45c multi .65 .35
1951 A510 90c multi 1.25 .75
1952 A510 $1.35 multi 1.75 1.75
1953 A510 $1.50 multi 2.00 2.00
1954 A510 $2 multi 2.25 2.25
a. Souvenir sheet, #1950-1954 8.75 8.75
Nos. 1950-1954 (5) 7.90 7.10

The 45c stamp in the souvenir sheet was impregnated with a floral scent.

Numeral — A511

Serpentine Die Cut 5¾

2004, June 28 Litho.

Booklet Stamp

Self-Adhesive

1955 A511 5c multi 1.40 1.40
a. Booklet pane of 10 14.00

Postage Advertising Labels

In 2004, New Zealand Post began issuing "Postage Advertising Labels," which have the New Zealand Post emblem and curved side panel found on type A511. These stamps have various vignettes and denominations and were designed in conjunction with various private parties who contracted for and purchased the entire print run of these stamps. Though valid for domestic postage only as most of these stamps lack a country name, none of these stamps were made available to the general public by New Zealand Post.

In 2006, a limited number of Postal Advertising Labels began to be sold at face value by New Zealand Post when new contracts with the private parties were written. These agreements allowed New Zealand Post to print more items than the private party desired and to sell the overage to collectors.

Scene Locations from *The Lord of the Rings* Movie Trilogy A512

Designs: Nos. 1956, 1965, Skippers Canyon. Nos. 1957, 1964, Skippers Canyon (Ford of Bruinden) with actors. Nos. 1958, 1967, Mount Olympus. No. 1959, 1966, Mount Olympus (South of Rivendell) with actors. No. 1960, Erewhon. No. 1961, Erewhon (Edoras) with actors. No. 1962, Tongariro National Park. No. 1963, Tongariro National Park (Emyn Muil) with actors.

2004, July 7 *Perf. 14*

1956 A512 45c multi .65 .65
1957 A512 45c multi .65 .65
a. Vert. pair, #1956-1957 1.40 1.40
1958 A512 90c multi 1.25 1.25
1959 A512 90c multi 1.25 1.25
a. Vert. pair, #1958-1959 2.75 2.75
1960 A512 $1.50 multi 2.25 2.25
1961 A512 $1.50 multi 2.25 2.25
a. Vert. pair, #1960-1961 4.75 4.75
b. Souvenir sheet, #1958-1961 7.25 7.25
1962 A512 $2 multi 3.00 3.00
1963 A512 $2 multi 3.00 3.00
a. Vert. pair, #1962-1963 6.50 6.50
b. Horiz. block of 8, #1956-1963 15.50 15.50
c. Souvenir sheet, #1956-1963 15.50 15.50

No. 1963c exists imperf from a "Limited Edition" album.

Self-Adhesive

Serpentine Die Cut 11¼

Size: 30x25mm

1964 A512 45c multi .60 .60
1965 A512 45c multi .60 .60
1966 A512 90c multi 1.25 1.25
1967 A512 90c multi 1.25 1.25
a. Block of 4, #1964-1967 4.00
b. Booklet pane, 3 each #1964-1965, 2 each #1966-1967 9.25
Nos. 1956-1967 (12) 18.00 18.00

No. 1961b issued 8/28. World Stamp Championship (No. 1961b).

2004 Summer Olympics, Athens — A513

Gold medalists: 45c, John Walker, 1500 meters, Montreal, 1976. 90c, Yvette Williams, long jump, Helsinki, 1952. $1.50, Ian Ferguson and Paul MacDonald, 500 meters kayak doubles, Seoul, 1988. $2, Peter Snell, 800 meters, Rome, 1960.

Litho. with 3-Dimensional Plastic Affixed

Serpentine Die Cut 10¾

2004, Aug. 2 Self-Adhesive

1968 A513 45c multi .65 .50
1969 A513 90c multi 1.00 .80
1970 A513 $1.50 multi 1.75 1.75
1971 A513 $2 multi 2.25 2.25
a. Horiz. strip of 4, #1968-1971 7.00
Nos. 1968-1971 (4) 5.65 5.30

Tourist Attractions Type of 2003

Designs: No. 1972, Lake Wakatipu, Queenstown. No. 1973, Kaikoura. No. 1974, Bath House, Rotorua. No. 1975, Pohutu Geyser, Rotorua. No. 1976, Mitre Peak, Milford Sound. No. 1977, Hawke's Bay.

2004-05 Litho. *Perf. 13¼x13½*

1972 A496 $1.50 multi 1.90 1.90
a. Perf. 14x14¼ 1.90 1.90
1973 A496 $1.50 multi 1.90 1.90
1974 A496 $1.50 multi 1.90 1.90
1975 A496 $1.50 multi 1.90 1.90
a. Souvenir sheet, #1973, 1975 5.00 5.00
1976 A496 $1.50 multi 1.90 1.90
a. Perf. 14x14¼ 1.90 1.90
b. Souvenir sheet, #1972a, 1976a 4.50 4.50
1977 A496 $1.50 multi 1.90 1.90
a. Souvenir sheet, #1639, 1977 7.25 7.25
Nos. 1972-1977 (6) 11.40 11.40

Issued: Nos. 1972-1977, 8/28; No. 1977a, 10/29 for Baypex 2004; No. 1975a, 8/18/05 for Taipei 2005 Stamp Exhibition; Nos. 1972a,

1976a, 1976b, 8/3/07. Bangkok 2007 Asian International Stamp Exhibition (#1976b).

A514

Christmas — A515

Designs: 45c, Candle, wine bottle, turkey, ham. 90c, Hangi. $1, Christmas cards, fruit cake. $1.35, Barbecued shrimp. $1.50, Wine bottle, pie and salad. $2, Candelabra, pavlova and plum pudding.

2004, Oct. 4 ***Perf. 14¼***

1978 A514 45c multi .60 .25
1979 A514 90c multi 1.25 .50
1980 A514 $1.35 multi 1.50 1.50
1981 A514 $1.50 multi 1.75 1.75
1982 A514 $2 multi 2.50 2.50
Nos. 1978-1982 (5) 7.60 6.50

Self-Adhesive

Serpentine Die Cut 9½x10

1983 A515 45c multi .60 .40
a. Booklet pane of 10 7.00
1984 A515 90c multi 1.10 1.00
1985 A515 $1 multi 1.40 1.40
a. Booklet pane of 8 + 8 etiquettes 13.00
b. Horiz. strip, #1983-1985 3.75 3.75
Nos. 1983-1985 (3) 3.10 2.80

Extreme Sports A516

Designs: 45c, Whitewater rafting. 90c, Snow sports. $1.35, Skydiving. $1.50, Jet boating. $2, Bungy jumping.

2004, Dec. 1 ***Perf. 14***

1986 A516 45c multi .55 .25
a. Booklet pane of 1 .75 —
1987 A516 90c multi 1.00 .65
a. Booklet pane of 1 1.50 —
1988 A516 $1.35 multi 1.50 1.50
a. Booklet pane of 1 2.00 —
1989 A516 $1.50 multi 1.75 1.75
a. Booklet pane of 1 2.50 —
1990 A516 $2 multi 2.75 2.75
a. Booklet pane of 1 3.25 —
b. Booklet pane, #1986-1990 12.00 —
Complete booklet, #1986a, 1987a, 1988a, 1989a, 1990a, 1990b 24.00
Nos. 1986-1990 (5) 7.55 6.90

Complete booklet sold for $14.95.

The 2004 sheets contain: #1914, 1920, 1925, 1934, 1940, 1954, 1962, 1982, 1990. See note following #1404.

Farm Animals — A517

Designs: 45c, Ewe (with horns) and lambs. 90c, Scottish border collies. $1.35, Pigs. $1.50, Rooster and chicken. $2, Rooster and chicken, diff.

2005, Jan. 12 ***Perf. 14***

1991 A517 45c multi .60 .45
1992 A517 90c multi 1.25 .75
1993 A517 $1.35 multi 1.50 1.50
1994 A517 $1.50 multi 1.75 1.75
1995 A517 $2 multi 2.75 2.75
a. Horiz. strip, #1991-1995 10.00 10.00
b. Souvenir sheet, #1994-1995 5.25 5.25
Nos. 1991-1995 (5) 7.85 7.20

Nos. 1991-1995 exist in a souvenir sheet from a "Limited Edition" album.

Self-Adhesive

Size: 22x27mm

Serpentine Die Cut 11x11¼

1996 A517 45c multi .50 .60
a. Booklet pane of 10 6.50

New Year 2005 (Year of the Cock) (No. 1995b).

Community Groups A518

Designs: No. 1997, Canoeists, YMCA emblem. No. 1998, Three people holding cement, Rotary International emblem. No. 1999, People building track bed, Lions International emblem. No. 2000, Four people jumping, YMCA emblem. No. 2001, People building wall, Rotary International emblem. No. 2002, Miniature train, Lions International emblem.

2005, Feb. 2 **Litho.** ***Perf. 14***

1997 A518 45c multi .50 .40
1998 A518 45c multi .50 .40
1999 A518 45c multi .50 .40
2000 A518 $1.50 multi 2.00 2.00
a. Horiz. pair, #1997, 2000, + central label 3.00 3.00
b. Miniature sheet, 3 #2000a 8.00 8.00
2001 A518 $1.50 multi 2.00 2.00
a. Horiz. pair, #1998, 2001, + central label 3.00 3.00
b. Miniature sheet, 3 #2001a 8.00 8.00
2002 A518 $1.50 multi 2.00 2.00
a. Horiz. pair, #1999, 2002, + central label 3.00 3.00
b. Miniature sheet, #2000a, 2001a, 2002a 8.00 8.00
c. Miniature sheet, 3 #2002a 8.25 8.25
Nos. 1997-2002 (6) 7.50 7.20

New Zealand Postage Stamps, 150th Anniv. — A519

2005, Mar. 2 **Litho.** ***Perf. 14***

2003 A519 45c No. 1 .60 .35
2004 A519 90c No. P1 1.10 .75
2005 A519 $1.35 No. OY5 1.50 1.50
2006 A519 $1.50 No. 83 1.75 1.75
2007 A519 $2 No. 99 2.75 2.75
a. Souvenir sheet, #2003-2007 8.75 8.75
Nos. 2003-2007 (5) 7.70 7.10

2005, Apr. 6 **Litho.** ***Perf. 14***

2008 A519 45c No. 123a .60 .60
2009 A519 90c No. B3 1.10 .75
2010 A519 $1.35 No. C7 1.50 1.50
2011 A519 $1.50 No. 256 1.75 1.75
2012 A519 $2 No. 301 2.75 2.75
a. Souvenir sheet, #2008-2012 8.75 8.75
b. Souvenir sheet, #2007, 2012 6.50 6.50
Nos. 2008-2012 (5) 7.70 7.35

No. 2012b issued 4/21 for Pacific Explorer 2005 World Stamp Expo, Sydney.

Size: 25x30mm

Self-Adhesive

Coil Stamps

Serpentine Die Cut 12¾

2013 A519 45c No. 123a .55 .55
2014 A519 90c No. B3 1.00 1.00
a. Horiz. pair, #2013-2014 2.25

Booklet Stamps

Serpentine Die Cut 11x11¼

2015 A519 45c No. 123a .60 .50
a. Booklet pane of 10 7.00
2016 A519 90c No. B3 1.10 1.10
a. Booklet pane of 10 12.00
Nos. 2013-2016 (4) 3.25 3.15

2005, June 1 **Litho.** ***Perf. 14***

2017 A519 45c No. 369 .60 .25
2018 A519 90c No. 918 1.10 .75
2019 A519 $1.35 No. 989 1.50 1.50
2020 A519 $1.50 No. 1219 1.75 1.75
a. Souvenir sheet, #2006, 2011, 2020 7.25 7.25
2021 A519 $2 No. 1878 2.75 2.75
a. Souvenir sheet, #2017-2021 10.00 10.00
Nos. 2017-2021 (5) 7.70 7.00

No. 2020a issued 11/17 for New Zealand 2005 National Stamp Show, Auckland.

A miniature sheet containing Nos. 2003-2012 and 2017-2021 was sold only with a commemorative book.

Cafés — A520

2005, May 4 **Litho.** ***Die Cut***

Self-Adhesive

2022 A520 45c 1910s .60 .35
2023 A520 90c 1940s 1.25 .75
2024 A520 $1.35 1970s 1.50 1.50
2025 A520 $1.50 1990s 2.00 2.00
2026 A520 $2 2005 2.75 2.75
a. Horiz. strip, #2022-2026 10.00
Nos. 2022-2026 (5) 8.10 7.35

Rugby Team Shirts A521

Shirts of: Nos. 2027, 2029, All Blacks. Nos. 2028, 2030, British & Irish Lions.

2005, June 1 ***Die Cut***

Self-Adhesive

2027 A521 45c multi .55 .55
2028 A521 45c multi .55 .55
a. Horiz. pair, #2027-2028 1.30
2029 A521 $1.50 multi 2.00 2.00
2030 A521 $1.50 multi 2.00 2.00
a. Horiz. pair, #2029-2030 4.50
Nos. 2027-2030 (4) 5.10 5.10

Miniature Sheet

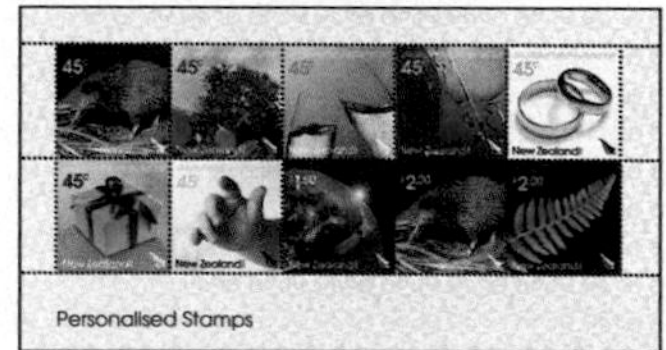

Greetings Stamps — A522

No. 2031: a, Kiwi. b, Pohutukawa flower. c, Champagne flutes. d, Balloons. e, Wedding rings. f, Gift. g, Baby's hand. h, New Zealand on globe. i, Kiwi. j, Fern.

2005, July 6 ***Perf. 14***

2031 A522 Sheet of 10 12.50 12.50
a.-g. 45c Any single .60 .50
h. $1.50 multi 2.10 1.75
i.-j. $2 Either single 3.00 3.00
k. Sheet of 20 #2031a + 20 labels 25.00 —
l. Sheet of 20 #2031b + 20 labels 25.00 —
m. Sheet of 20 #2031c + 20 labels 25.00 —
n. Sheet of 20 #2031d + 20 labels 25.00 —
o. Sheet of 20 #2031e + 20 labels 25.00 —
p. Sheet of 20 #2031f + 20 labels 25.00 —
q. Sheet of 20 #2031g + 20 labels 25.00 —
r. Sheet of 20 #2031h + 20 labels 50.00 —
s. Sheet of 20 #2031i + 20 labels 70.00 —
t. Sheet of 20 #2031j + 20 labels 70.00 —

Nos. 2031k-2031q each sold for $19.95; No. 2031r sold for $44.95; Nos. 2031s-2031t each sold for $54.95.

Examples of Nos. 2031a and 2031h without the "2005" year date were produced in sheets of 20 stamps + 20 labels for the Washington 2006 World Philatelic Exhibition and sold only at that show.

See Nos. 2070, 2120.

Worldwide Fund for Nature (WWF) A523

Kakapo and text: No. 2032, "Nocturnal bird living on the forest floor." No. 2033, "Endangered — only 86 known surviving." No. 2034, "Relies heavily on camouflage for defence." No. 2035, "Night Parrot unique to New Zealand."

2005, Aug. 3

2032 A523 45c multi .70 .70
2033 A523 45c multi .70 .70
2034 A523 45c multi .70 .70
2035 A523 45c multi .70 .70
a. Strip of 4, #2032-2035 2.75 2.75
Nos. 2032-2035 (4) 2.80 2.80

A524

Christmas — A525

Designs: 45c, Baby Jesus. 90c, Mary and Joseph. $1.35, Shepherd and sheep. $1.50, Magi. $2, Star of Bethlehem.

2005 **Litho.** ***Perf. 14¼***

2036 A524 45c multi .60 .30
2037 A524 90c multi 1.10 .70
2038 A524 $1.35 multi 1.50 1.50
2039 A524 $1.50 multi 1.75 1.75
2040 A524 $2 multi 2.75 2.75
a. Horiz. strip, #2036-2040 9.50 9.50
Nos. 2036-2040 (5) 7.70 7.00

Booklet Stamps

Size: 22x27mm

Self-Adhesive

Serpentine Die Cut 11x11¼

2041 A524 45c multi .65 .55
a. Booklet pane of 10 7.00
2042 A525 $1 multi 1.40 1.40
a. Booklet pane of 10 14.00

Issued: $1, 10/5; Nos. 2036-2041, 11/2.

Premiere of Movie, *King Kong* — A526

Characters: 45c, King Kong. 90c, Carl Denham. $1.35, Ann Darrow. $1.50, Jack Driscoll. $2, Darrow and Driscoll.

2005, Oct. 19 ***Perf. 14¾***

2043 A526 45c multi .70 .70
2044 A526 90c multi 1.40 1.40
2045 A526 $1.35 multi 2.10 2.10
2046 A526 $1.50 multi 2.40 2.40
2047 A526 $2 multi 3.25 3.25
a. Horiz. strip, #2043-2047 10.00 10.00
b. Souvenir sheet, #2047a 10.00 10.00
Nos. 2043-2047 (5) 9.85 9.85

Premiere of Film *Narnia: The Lion, The Witch and the Wardrobe* A527

Designs: 45c, Lucy and the Wardrobe. 90c, Lucy, Edmund, Peter and Susan, horiz. $1.35, White Witch and Edmund, horiz. $1.50, Frozen Army. $2, Aslan and Lucy, horiz.

Perf. 14x14¼, 14¼x14

2005, Dec. 1 **Litho.**

2048 A527 45c multi .70 .70
a. Souvenir sheet of 1 1.00 1.00
2049 A527 90c multi 1.40 1.40
a. Souvenir sheet of 1 1.90 1.90
2050 A527 $1.35 multi 2.10 2.10
a. Souvenir sheet of 1 3.00 3.00
2051 A527 $1.50 multi 2.40 2.40
a. Souvenir sheet of 1 3.25 3.25
2052 A527 $2 multi 3.25 3.25
a. Souvenir sheet of 1 4.25 4.25
Nos. 2048-2052 (5) 9.85 9.85
Set of 5 souvenir sheets of 1 each, #2048a//2052a 13.40 13.40

Self-Adhesive

Serpentine Die Cut 12½x12, 12x12½

2053 Sheet of 5 10.00
a. A527 45c multi, 26x37mm .70 .70
b. A527 90c multi, 37x26mm 1.40 1.40
c. A527 $1.35 multi, 37x26mm 2.10 2.10
d. A527 $1.50 multi, 26x37mm 2.40 2.40
e. A527 $2 multi, 37x26mm 3.25 3.25

Nos. 2048a-2052a sold as a set for $8.70.

The 2005 sheets contain: #2003, 2006, 2007, 2008, 2011, 2012, 2017, 2020, 2021. See note following #1404.

New Year 2006 (Year of the Dog) — A528

Designs: 45c, Labrador retriever. 90c, German shepherd. $1.35, Jack Russell terrier. $1.50, Golden retriever. $2, Huntaway.

Litho. & Embossed

2006, Jan. 4 ***Perf. 14***

2054 A528 45c multi .60 .30

Litho.

2055 A528 90c multi 1.10 1.10
2056 A528 $1.35 multi 1.50 1.50
2057 A528 $1.50 multi 2.00 2.00
2058 A528 $2 multi 2.75 2.75
a. Souvenir sheet, #2057-2058 5.75 5.75
Nos. 2054-2058 (5) 7.95 7.65

No. 2058a exists imperf in a limited edition album.

Self-Adhesive

Size: 25x30mm Coil Stamp

Coil Stamp

Die Cut Perf. 12¾

2059 A528 45c multi .65 .55

Booklet Stamp

Serpentine Die Cut 11x11¼

2060 A528 45c multi .65 .55
a. Booklet pane of 10 7.00

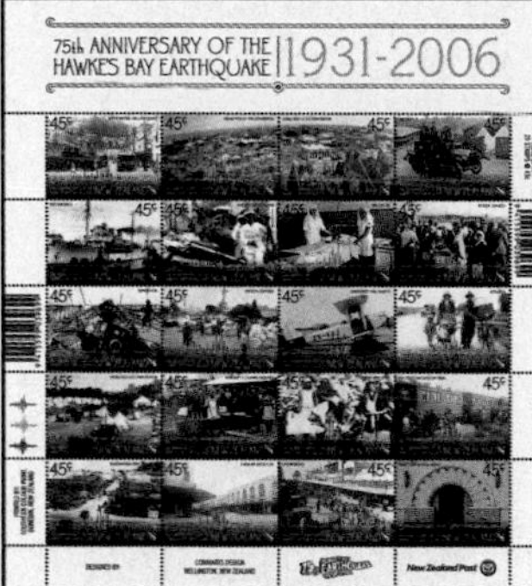

Hawke's Bay Earthquake, 75th Anniv. — A529

No. 2061: a, Napier before the earthquake. b, Aerial view of the devastation (denomination at left). c, Aerial view of the devastation (denomination at right). d, Fire service. e, HMS Veronica. f, HMS Veronica sailors. g, Red Cross. h, Rescue services. i, Devastation. j, Medical services. k, Emergency mail flights. l, Refugees. m, Emergency accommodation. n, Makeshift cooking facilities. o, Community spirit. p, Refugees evacuated by train. q, Building industry. r, A new Art Deco city. s, Celebrations. t, Hawke's Bay region today.

2006, Feb. 3 **Litho.** ***Perf. 14***

2061 A529 Sheet of 20 14.00 14.00
a.-t. 45c Any single .70 .70
u. Booklet pane, 2 each #2061a-2061c 4.75 —
v. Booklet pane, 2 each #2061r-2061t 4.75 —
w. Booklet pane, 2 each #2061d-2061f 4.75 —
x. Booklet pane, 2 each #2061g-2061h + 2 labels 3.25 —
y. Booklet pane, 2 each #2061i, 2061k, 2061p 4.75 —
z. Booklet pane, 2 each #2061j, 2061l, 2061m 4.75 —
aa. Booklet pane, 2 each #2061n, 2061o, 2061q 4.75 —
Complete booklet, #2061u-2061aa 32.50

Complete booklet sold for $19.95.

Tourist Attractions Type of 2003

Designs: No. 2062, Franz Josef Glacier, West Coast. No. 2063, Halfmoon Bay, Stewart Island. No. 2064, Cathedral Cove, Coromandel. No. 2065, Mount Taranaki. No. 2066, Huka Falls, Taupo. No. 2067, Lake Wanaka.

2006, Mar. 1 ***Perf. 13¼x13½***

2062 A496 $1.50 multi 2.00 2.00
2063 A496 $1.50 multi 2.00 2.00
2064 A496 $1.50 multi 2.00 2.00
2065 A496 $1.50 multi 2.00 2.00
2066 A496 $1.50 multi 2.00 2.00
2067 A496 $1.50 multi 2.00 2.00
Nos. 2062-2067 (6) 12.00 12.00

Queen Elizabeth II, 80th Birthday A530

Litho. & Embossed with Foil Application

2006, Apr. 21 ***Perf. 13½***

2068 A530 $5 dk bl & multi 8.00 8.00
a. $5 Prussian blue & multi 8.00 8.00
b. Souvenir sheet, #2068a, Jersey #1215a 27.50 27.50

Printed in sheets of 4.

No. 2068b sold for $17.50. See Jersey No. 1215.

Miniature Sheet

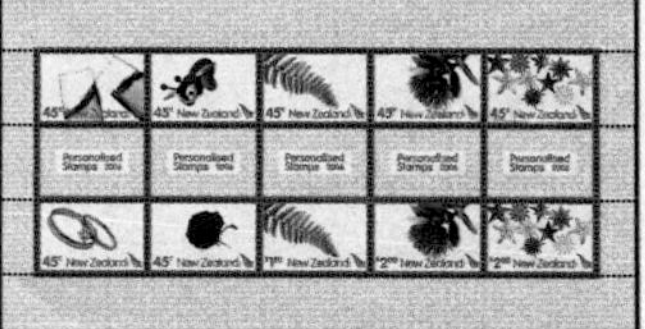

Greetings Stamps — A531

No. 2069: a, Champagne flutes. b, Child's toy. c, Fern. d, Pohutukawa flower. e, Stars. f, Wedding and engagement rings. g, Rose. h, Fern. i, Pohutukawa flower. j, Stars.

2006, May 3 **Litho.** ***Perf. 14***

2069 A531 Sheet of 10 + 5 labels 14.00 14.00
a.-g. 45c Any single .70 .70
h. $1.50 multi 2.40 2.40
i.-j. $2 Either single 3.25 3.25
k. Souvenir sheet, #2069i, 2 #2069h 8.00 8.00
l. Sheet of 20 #2069h + 20 labels 67.50 —
m. Sheet of 20 #2069i + 20 labels 82.50 —
n. Sheet of 20 #2069j + 20 labels 82.50 —

No. 2069k issued 11/16. Belgica'06 World Philatelic Exhibition, Brussels (#2069k).

Nos. 2069l-2069n issued 2007. No. 2069l sold for $44.90; Nos. 2069m and 2069n, each sold for $54.90. Labels could be personalized

A sheet of 20 #2069c + 20 labels depicting New Zealand's America's Cup Emirates Team yacht sold for $19.90. Labels on this sheet could not be personalized.

See Nos. 2138, 2292, 2326-2327, 2412.

Greetings Type of 2005 Redrawn

Souvenir Sheet

No. 2070: a, Like #2031i, without "2005" year date. b, Like #2031j, without "2005" year date.

2006, May 27 **Litho.** ***Perf. 14***

2070 Sheet of 2 + central label 6.50 6.50
a.-b. A522 $2 Either single 3.25 3.25
c. Souvenir sheet, #2070a-2070b 6.75 6.75

Washington 2006 World Philatelic Exhibition.

No. 2070c issued 11/2. Kiwipex 2006 National Stamp Exhibition, Christchurch (#2070c). No. 2070c lacks label, and sold for $5, with the extra $1 going to the NZ Philatelic Foundation.

A set of five gummed stamps, a self-adhesive coil stamp and a self-adhesive booklet stamp depicting Traditional Maori Performing Arts was prepared for release on June 7, 2006 but was withdrawn on June 2. Some mail orders for these stamps were fulfilled and shipped out inadvertantly prior to June 7, but apparently no examples were sold over post office counters. The editors request any evidence of sale of any of these stamps over post office counters.

Renewable Energy A532

Designs: 45c, Wind farm, Tararua. 90c, Roxburgh Hydroelectric Dam. $1.35, Biogas facility, Waikato. $1.50, Geothermal Power Station, Wairakei. $2, Solar panels on Cape Reinga Lighthouse, vert.

2006, July 5

2071 A532 45c multi .70 .70
2072 A532 90c multi 1.40 1.40
2073 A532 $1.35 multi 2.10 2.10
2074 A532 $1.50 multi 2.40 2.40
2075 A532 $2 multi 3.25 3.25
Nos. 2071-2075 (5) 9.85 9.85

Fruits and Vegetables A533

Slogan "5 + a day," and: 45c+5c, Tomatoes and "5." 90c+10c, Oranges and "+." $1.35, Onions and "a" (30x30mm). $1.50, Kiwi fruit and "Day," horiz. $2, Radicchio and hand.

2006, Aug. 2 **Litho.** ***Perf. 14***

2076 A533 45c +5c multi .70 .70
2077 A533 90c +10c multi 1.40 1.40
2078 A533 $1.35 multi 2.10 2.10
2079 A533 $1.50 multi 2.40 2.40
2080 A533 $2 multi 3.25 3.25
a. Souvenir sheet, #2076-2080 10.00 10.00
Nos. 2076-2080 (5) 9.85 9.85

Self-Adhesive

Size: 24x29mm

Serpentine Die Cut 9¾x10

2081 A533 45c +5c multi .70 .70

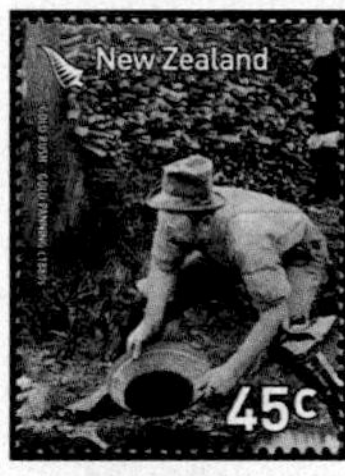

New Zealand Gold Rush — A534

Designs: 45c, Gold panner, c. 1880. 90c, Miners, Kuranui Creek, c. 1868, horiz. $1.35, Chinese miners, Tuapeka, c. 1900, horiz. $1.50, Gold escort coach, Roxburgh, 1901, horiz. $2, Dunedin harbor, c. 1900, horiz.

2006, Sept. 9 ***Perf. 14***

2082 A534 45c multi .70 .70
2083 A534 90c multi 1.40 1.40
2084 A534 $1.35 multi 2.10 2.10
2085 A534 $1.50 multi 2.40 2.40
2086 A534 $2 multi 3.25 3.25
Nos. 2082-2086 (5) 9.85 9.85

Souvenir Sheet

Litho. With Foil Application

2087 Sheet of 5 10.00 10.00
a. A534 45c gold & multi .70 .70
b. A534 90c gold & multi 1.40 1.40
c. A534 $1.35 gold & multi 2.10 2.10
d. A534 $1.50 gold & multi 2.40 2.40
e. A534 $2 gold & multi 3.25 3.25

Portions of the design of Nos. 2082 and 2087a are printed with a thermochromic ink that changes color when warmed that is applied by a thermographic process producing a shiny, raised effect.

No. 2087 exists Imperf in a limited edition album.

Christmas A535

Children's art by: Nos. 2088, 2098, Hanna McLachlan. No. 2089, Isla Hewitt. No. 2090, Caitlin Davidson. No. 2091, Maria Petersen. No. 2092, Deborah Yoon. No. 2093, Hannah Webster. 90c, Pierce Higginson. $1.35, Rosa Tucker. $1.50, Sylvie Webby. $2, Gemma Baldock.

2006, Oct. 4 **Litho.** ***Perf. 14¼***

2088 A535 45c multi .70 .70
2089 A535 45c multi .70 .70
2090 A535 45c multi .70 .70
2091 A535 45c multi .70 .70
2092 A535 45c multi .70 .70
2093 A535 45c multi .70 .70
a. Miniature sheet, #2088-2093 4.25 4.25
b. Horiz. strip of 5, #2089-2093 3.50 3.50
2094 A535 90c multi 1.40 1.40
2095 A535 $1.35 multi 2.10 2.10

2096 A535 $1.50 multi 2.40 2.40
2097 A535 $2 multi 3.25 3.25
Nos. 2088-2097 (10) 13.35 13.35

Self-Adhesive

Size: 21x26mm

Serpentine Die Cut 9¾x10

2098 A535 45c multi .70 .70
a. Booklet pane of 10 7.00
2099 A535 $1.50 multi 2.40 2.40
a. Horiz. pair, #2098-2099 3.00
b. Booklet pane of 10 24.00

No. 2099b sold for $13.50.

Summer Festivals A536

Designs: 45c, Dragon boat racing. 90c, Race day. $1.35, Teddy Bears' Picnic. $1.50, Outdoor concerts. $2, Jazz festivals.

2006, Nov. 1 ***Perf. 14¼***

2100 A536 45c multi .70 .70
2101 A536 90c multi 1.40 1.40
2102 A536 $1.35 multi 2.10 2.10
2103 A536 $1.50 multi 2.40 2.40
2104 A536 $2 multi 3.25 3.25
a. Horiz. strip of 5, #2100-2104 10.00 10.00
b. Miniature sheet, #2104a 10.00 10.00
Nos. 2100-2104 (5) 9.85 9.85

The 2006 sheets contain: #2058, 2061e, 2066, 2069i, 2075, 2080, 2086, 2097, 2104. See note following #1404.

Scott Base, Antarctica, 50th Anniv. — A537

Designs: 45c, Opening ceremony, 1957. 90c, Scott Base, 1990. $1.35, Aerial view, 2000. $1.50, Sign, 2003-04. $2, Aerial view, 2005.

2007, Jan. 20 ***Perf. 14¼x14***

2105 A537 45c multi .70 .70
a. Souvenir sheet of 1 1.00 1.00
2106 A537 90c multi 1.40 1.40
a. Souvenir sheet of 1 1.90 1.90
2107 A537 $1.35 multi 2.10 2.10
a. Souvenir sheet of 1 2.75 2.75
2108 A537 $1.50 multi 2.40 2.40
a. Souvenir sheet of 1 3.50 3.50
2109 A537 $2 multi 3.25 3.25
a. Souvenir sheet of 1 4.50 4.50
Nos. 2105-2109 (5) 9.85 9.85

Nos. 2105a-2109a sold as a set for $8.70. The souvenir sheets exist overprinted in a limited edition album.

New Year 2007 (Year of the Pig) A538

Pig breeds: 45c, Kunekune. 90c, Kunekune, diff. $1.35, Arapawa. $1.50, Auckland Island. $2, Kunekune, diff.

2007, Feb. 7 ***Perf. 14½x14***

2110 A538 45c multi .70 .70
2111 A538 90c multi 1.40 1.40
2112 A538 $1.35 multi 2.10 2.10
2113 A538 $1.50 multi 2.40 2.40
2114 A538 $2 multi 3.25 3.25
a. Souvenir sheet, #2113-2114 5.75 5.75

Nos. 2111-2112 exist in a souvenir sheet in a limited edition album.

Indigenous Animals — A539

Designs: 45c, Tuatara. 90c, Kiwi. $1.35, Hamilton's frog. $1.50, Yellow-eyed penguin. $2, Hector's dolphin.

Serpentine Die Cut

2007, Mar. 7 **Litho.**

Self-Adhesive

2115 A539 45c multi .65 .65
2116 A539 90c multi 1.25 1.25
2117 A539 $1.35 multi 1.90 1.90
2118 A539 $1.50 multi 2.10 2.10
2119 A539 $2 multi 2.75 2.75
a. Horiz. strip of 5, #2115-2119 8.65

Greetings Type of 2005 Redrawn

Souvenir Sheet

2007, Mar. 30 **Litho.** ***Perf. 14***

2120 Sheet , #2075, 2120a 6.00 6.00
a. A531 $2 Like #2069i, without "2006" year date 3.00 3.00

Northland 2007 National Stamp Exhibition, Whangarei.

Centenaries — A540

Designs: No. 2121, Scouts and Lieutenant Colonel David Cossgrove, founder of scouting movement in New Zealand. No. 2122, Infant, nurse, Dr. Frederic Truby King, founder of Plunket Society. No. 2123, Rugby players, Hercules "Bumper" Wright, first team captain. No. 2124, Sister of Compassion teaching children, Suzanne Aubert, founder of Sisters of Compassion. $1, Plunket Society emblem, family. $1.50, Sisters of Compassion emblem, women reading book. No. 2127, New Zealand Rugby League emblem, rugby players. No. 2128, Scouting emblem, scouts.

2007, Apr. 24 ***Perf. 14***

2121 A540 50c multi .75 .75
2122 A540 50c multi .75 .75
2123 A540 50c multi .75 .75
2124 A540 50c multi .75 .75
a. Horiz. strip of 4, #2121-2124 4.00 4.00
2125 A540 $1 multi 1.50 1.50
2126 A540 $1.50 multi 2.25 2.25
2127 A540 $2 multi 3.00 3.00
2128 A540 $2 multi 3.00 3.00
a. Block of 8, #2121-2128 12.75 12.75
b. Horiz. pair, #2127-2128 9.00 9.00

Tourist Attractions Type of 2003

Designs: 5c, Whakarewarewa geothermal area. 10c, Central Otago. 20c, Rainbow Falls, Northland. 50c, Lake Coleridge. $1, Rangitoto Island. $2.50, Abel Tasman National Park. $3, Tongaporutu, Taranaki.

2007, May 9 ***Perf. 13¼x13½***

2129 A496 5c multi .25 .25
2130 A496 10c multi .25 .25
2131 A496 20c multi .30 .30
2132 A496 50c multi .75 .75
2133 A496 $1 multi 1.50 1.50
2134 A496 $2.50 multi 3.75 3.75
2135 A496 $3 multi 4.50 4.50
Nos. 2129-2135 (7) 11.30 11.30

Self-Adhesive

Serpentine Die Cut 10x9½

2136 A496 50c multi .75 .75
a. Booklet pane of 10 7.50
2137 A496 $1 multi 1.50 1.50
a. Horiz. pair, #2136-2137 2.25 2.25
b. Booklet pane of 10 15.00

Greetings Type of 2006 Redrawn

No. 2138: a, Child's toy. b, Pohutukawa flower. c, Wedding and engagement rings. d, Fern. e, Champagne flutes. f, Rose. g, Stars.

2007, May 9 ***Perf. 14***

2138 A531 Sheet of 7 + 8 labels 5.25 5.25
a.-g. 50c Any single .75 .75
h. Sheet of 20 #2138a + 20 labels 32.50 —
i. Sheet of 20 #2138b + 20 labels 32.50 —
j. Sheet of 20 #2138c + 20 labels 32.50 —
k. Sheet of 20 #2138d + 20 labels 32.50 —
l. Sheet of 20 #2138e + 20 labels 32.50 —
m. Sheet of 20 #2138f + 20 labels 32.50 —
n. Sheet of 20 #2138g + 20 labels 32.50 —

Nos. 2138h-2138n each sold for $20.90.

Southern Skies and Observatories — A541

Designs: 50c, Southern Cross, Stardome Observatory. $1, Pleiades, McLellan Mt. John Observatory. $1.50, Trifid Nebula, Ward Observatory. $2, Southern Pinwheel, MOA telescope, Mt. John Observatory. $2.50, Large Magellanic Cloud, Southern African Large Telescope.

2007, June 6 ***Perf. 13x13¼***

2139 A541 50c multi .80 .80
a. Perf. 14 1.00 1.00
b. Booklet pane of 1 #2139a 1.00 —
2140 A541 $1 multi 1.60 1.60
a. Perf. 14 2.00 2.00
b. Booklet pane of 1 #2140a 2.00 —
2141 A541 $1.50 multi 2.40 2.40
a. Perf. 14 3.00 3.00
b. Booklet pane of 1 #2141a 3.00 —
2142 A541 $2 multi 3.00 3.00
a. Perf. 14 4.25 4.25
b. Booklet pane of 1 #2142a 4.25 —
2143 A541 $2.50 multi 3.75 3.75
a. Perf. 14 5.25 5.25
b. Booklet pane of 1 #2143a 5.25 —
c. Booklet pane of 5, #2139a-2143a 15.50 —
Complete booklet, #2139b, 2140b, 2141b, 2142b, 2143b, 2143c 31.00
d. Souvenir sheet, #2142a, 2143a 6.75 6.75
Nos. 2139-2143 (5) 11.55 11.55

No. 2143d issued 8/31. Huttpex 2007 Stampshow (#2143d).

Miniature Sheet

New Zealand Slang — A542

No. 2144 — Designs: a, "Good as gold," gold nugget. b, "Sweet as," kiwi fruit. c, "She'll be right," hand with thumb up. d, "Hissy fit," insect. e, "Sparrow fart," sun in sky. f, "Cuz," kiwi bird. g, "Away laughing," sandals. h, "Tiki tour," road sign. i, "Away with the fairies," cookies. j, "Wop-wops," house. k, "Hard yakka," shirt. l, "Cods wollop," fish. m, "Boots and all," rugby ball and athletic shoes. n, "Shark and taties," fish and chips. o, "Knackered," boots. p, "Laughing gear," mug. q, "Everyman and his dog," dog. r, "Bit of a dag," sheep. s, "Dreaded lurgy," box of tissues. t, "Rark up," hand pointing.

2007, July 4 ***Perf. 14***

2144 A542 Sheet of 20 16.00 16.00
a.-t. 50c Any single .80 .80

Portions of the design were covered with a thermographic ink that allowed printing below (definitinons of the slang phrases) to appear when the ink was warmed.

Technical Innovations by New Zealanders A543

Designs: 50c, Gallagher electric fence. $1, Spreadable butter. $1.50, Mountain buggy. $2, Hamilton jet boat. $2.50, Tranquilizer gun.

2007, Aug. 1

2145 A543 50c multi .75 .75
2146 A543 $1 multi 1.50 1.50
2147 A543 $1.50 multi 2.25 2.25
2148 A543 $2 multi 3.00 3.00
2149 A543 $2.50 multi 3.75 3.75
Nos. 2145-2149 (5) 11.25 11.25

Nos. 2145-2149 exist in a souvenir sheet in a limited edition album.

Wedding of Queen Elizabeth II and Prince Philip, 60th Anniv. — A544

Queen and Prince: 50c, In 2007. $2, On wedding day, 1947.

2007, Sept. 5 **Litho.** ***Perf. 14***

2150 A544 50c multi .70 .70
2151 A544 $2 multi 2.75 2.75
a. Souvenir sheet, #2150-2151 3.50 3.50

Christmas A545

Children's art by: 50c, Sione Vao. $1, Reece Cateley. $1.50, Emily Wang. $2, Alexandra Eathorne. $2.50, Jake Hooper.

2007, Oct. 3 ***Perf. 14¼***

2152 A545 50c multi .80 .80
2153 A545 $1 multi 1.50 1.50
2154 A545 $1.50 multi 2.40 2.40
2155 A545 $2 multi 3.00 3.00
2156 A545 $2.50 multi 4.00 4.00
Nos. 2152-2156 (5) 11.70 11.70

Size: 25x30mm

Self-Adhesive

Coil Stamps

Die Cut Perf. 13x12¾

2157 A545 50c multi .80 .80
2158 A545 $1.50 multi 2.40 2.40
a. Horiz. pair, #2157-2158 3.25

Booklet Stamps

Serpentine Die Cut 11x11¼

2159 A545 50c multi .80 .80
a. Booket pane of 10 8.00
2160 A545 $1.50 multi 2.10 2.10
a. Booklet pane of 10 21.00

No. 2160a sold for $13.50.

Miniature Sheet

Greetings Stamps — A546

No. 2161: a, "Go You Good Thing." b, "Look Who It Is." c, "Love Always." d, "Thanks a Million." e, "We've Got News." f, "Wish You Were Here." g, "Time to Celebrate." h, "Kia Ora." i, "You Gotta Love Christmas." j, Chinese characters.

2007, Nov. 7 ***Perf. 14***

2161 A546 Sheet of 10 + 5 labels 13.00 13.00
a.-f. 50c Any single .75 .75
g.-h. $1 Either single 1.50 1.50
i. $1.50 multi 2.40 2.40
j. $2 multi 3.00 3.00
k. Sheet of 20 #2161c + 20 labels 32.50 —
l. Sheet of 20 #2161d + 20 labels 32.50 —
m. Sheet of 20 #2161e + 20 labels 32.50 —
n. Sheet of 20 #2161f + 20 labels 32.50 —
o. Sheet of 20 #2161g + 20 labels 47.50 —
p. Sheet of 20 #2161h + 20 labels 47.50 —
q. Sheet of 20 #2161i + 20 labels 70.00 —
r. Sheet of 20 #2161j + 20 labels 85.00 —
s. As #2161h, perf 13¼x13½ (2224b) 1.25 1.25
t. As #2161j, perf 13¼x13½ (2224b) 2.40 2.40

Nos. 2161k-2161n each sold for $20.90; Nos. 2161o-2161p, for $30.90; No. 2161q, for $44.90; No. 2161r, for $54.90. Labels were personalizable on Nos. 2161k-2161r. Issued: Nos. 2161s, 2161t, 4/1/09.

The 2007 sheets contain: #2114, 2109, 2142; #2127, 2128, 2148; #2155, 2151, 2161j. See note following #1404.

Reefs A547

Marine life from: 50c, Dusky Sound, Fiordland. $1, Mayor Island, Bay of Plenty. $1.50, Fiordland. $2, Volkner Rocks, White Island, Bay of Plenty.

2008, Jan. 9 **Litho.** ***Perf. 13x13¼***

2162 A547 50c multi .80 .80
2163 A547 $1 multi 1.60 1.60
2164 A547 $1.50 multi 2.40 2.40
2165 A547 $2 multi 3.25 3.25
a. Souvenir sheet, #2162-2165 8.25 8.25
Nos. 2162-2165 (4) 8.05 8.05

Self-Adhesive

Size: 26x21mm

Serpentine Die Cut 11¼

2166 A547 50c multi .80 .80
a. Booklet pane of 10 8.00
2167 A547 $1 multi 1.60 1.60
a. Horiz. pair, #2166-2167 2.40
b. Booklet pane of 10 #2167 16.00

Pocket Pets A548

2008, Feb. 7 ***Perf. 14***

2168 A548 50c Rabbits .80 .80
2169 A548 $1 Guinea pigs 1.60 1.60
2170 A548 $1.50 Rats 2.40 2.40
2171 A548 $2 Mice 3.25 3.25
a. Souvenir sheet, #2170-2171 5.75 5.75
b. As #2171, perf. 13½x13¼ 3.25 3.25
c. Souvenir sheet, #2161j, 2171b 6.50 6.50

New Year 2008 (Year of the Rat), No. 2171a.
Nos. 2171b, 2171c issued 3/7. Taipei 2008 International Stamp Exhibition (#2171c).

Weather Extremes A549

Designs: No. 2172, Drought, Gisborne, 1998. No. 2173, Wind, Auckland, 2007. $1, Storm, Wellington, 2001. $1.50, Flooding, Hikurangi, 2007. $2, Snow storm, Southland, 2001. $2.50, Heat, Matarangi, 2005.

2008, Mar. 5 **Litho.** ***Perf. 14***

2172 A549 50c multi .80 .80
2173 A549 50c multi .80 .80
2174 A549 $1 multi 1.60 1.60
2175 A549 $1.50 multi 2.40 2.40
2176 A549 $2 multi 3.25 3.25
2177 A549 $2.50 multi 4.00 4.00
Nos. 2172-2177 (6) 12.85 12.85

Nos. 2172-2177 exist in a souvenir sheet in a limited edition album.

Australian and New Zealand Army Corps (ANZAC) A550

Designs: No. 2178, Dawn Parade. No. 2179, Soldiers at Gallipoli, 1915. $1, Soldiers at Western Front, 1916-18. $1.50, Chalk kiwi made by soldiers, England, 1919. $2, Soldier's Haka dance, Egypt, 1941. $2.50, Soldiers in Viet Nam, 1965-71.

2008, Apr. 2

2178 A550 50c multi .80 .80
a. Booklet pane of 1 1.00 —
2179 A550 50c multi .80 .80
a. Booklet pane of 1 1.00 —
2180 A550 $1 multi 1.60 1.60
a. Booklet pane of 1 2.00 —
2181 A550 $1.50 multi 2.40 2.40
a. Booklet pane of 1 3.00 —
b. Souvenir sheet, #2179-2181 3.50 3.50
2182 A550 $2 multi 3.25 3.25
a. Booklet pane of 1 4.00 —
2183 A550 $2.50 multi 4.00 4.00
a. Booklet pane of 1 5.00 —
b. Booklet pane of 6, #2178-2183 16.00 —
Complete booklet, #2178a, 2179a, 2180a, 2181a, 2182a, 2183a, 2183b 32.00
Nos. 2178-2183 (6) 12.85 12.85

No. 2181b issued 10/20. End of World War I, 90th anniv. (#2181b).

Maori King Movement, 150th Anniv. — A551

Various unnamed artworks by Fred Graham and English text: 50c, "There is but one eye of the needle. . ." $1.50, "Taupiri is the mountain. . ." $2.50, "After I am gone. . .," horiz.

2008, May 2 **Litho.** ***Perf. 14***

2184 A551 50c multi .80 .80
2185 A551 $1.50 multi 2.40 2.40
2186 A551 $2.50 multi 4.00 4.00
Nos. 2184-2186 (3) 7.20 7.20

Premiere of Film, *The Chronicles of Narnia: Prince Caspian* — A552

Designs: 50c, The Pevensie children. $1, Queen Susan. $1.50, High King Peter. $2, Prince Caspian.

2008, May 7 ***Perf. 14½x14***

2187 A552 50c multi .80 .80
a. Souvenir sheet of 1 1.10 1.10
2188 A552 $1 multi 1.60 1.60
a. Souvenir sheet of 1 2.25 2.25
2189 A552 $1.50 multi 2.40 2.40
a. Souvenir sheet of 1 3.25 3.25
2190 A552 $2 multi 3.25 3.25
a. Souvenir sheet of 1 4.50 4.50
Nos. 2187-2190 (4) 8.05 8.05

Nos. 2187a-2190a were sold as a set for $7.

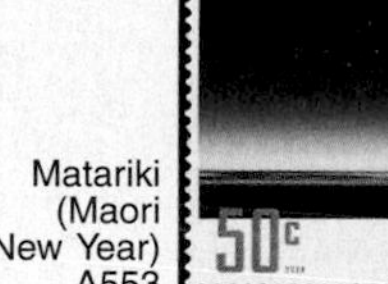

Matariki (Maori New Year) A553

Inscriptions: No. 2191, Ranginui. No. 2192, Te Moana nui a Kiwa. $1, Papatuanuku. $1.50, Whakapapa. $2, Takoha. $2.50, Te Tau Hou.

2008, June 5 **Litho.** ***Perf. 14***

2191 A553 50c multi .80 .80
2192 A553 50c multi .80 .80
2193 A553 $1 multi 1.60 1.60
2194 A553 $1.50 multi 2.40 2.40
2195 A553 $2 multi 3.25 3.25
a. Souvenir sheet, #2192, 2194, 2195 6.50 6.50
2196 A553 $2.50 multi 4.00 4.00
a. Miniature sheet, #2191-2196, perf. 13½x13¼ 13.00 13.00
Nos. 2191-2196 (6) 12.85 12.85

No. 2195a issued 9/18. Vienna Intl. Postage Stamp Exhibition (#2195a).
No. 2196a exists as an imperf miniature sheet from a limited edition album.

2008 Summer Olympics, Beijing — A554

2008, July 2 ***Perf. 14¼***

2197 A554 50c Rowing .80 .80
2198 A554 50c Cycling .80 .80
2199 A554 $1 Kayaking 1.60 1.60
2200 A554 $2 Running 3.00 3.00
Nos. 2197-2200 (4) 6.20 6.20

Compare with Type SP82.

Miniature Sheet

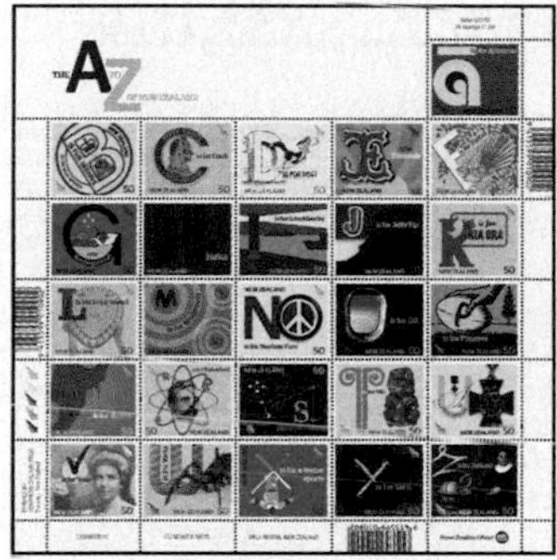

Alphabet — A555

No. 2201 — Inscriptions: a, A is for Aotearoa (Maori name for New Zealand). b, B is for Beehive (Parliament Building). c, C is for Cook (Capt. James Cook). d, D is for Dog (comic strip character). e, E is for Edmonds (Thomas J. Edmonds, cookbook producer). f, F is for Fantail (bird). g, G is for Goodnight Kiwi (cartoon). h, H is for Haka (Maori dance). i, I is for Interislander (ferry). j, J is for Jelly tip (ice cream bar). k, K is for Kia ora. l, L is for Log O'Wood (rugby trophy). m, M is for Mudpools. n, N is for Nuclear free. o, O is for O.E. (overseas experience). p, P is for Pinetree (Colin "Pinetree" Meads, rugby player). q, Q is for Quake. r, R is for Rutherford (Sir Ernest Rutherford, chemist and physicist). s, S is for Southern Cross (constellation). t, T is for Tiki (rock carving). u, U is for Upham (Capt. Charles Upham, war hero). v, V is for Vote. w, W is for Weta (insect). x, X is for X-treme sports. y, Y is for Yarn. z, Z is for Zeeland (Dutch province for which New Zealand was named).

2008, Aug. 6 ***Perf. 14¼***

2201 A555 Sheet of 26 18.50 18.50
a.-z. 50c Any single .70 .70

North Island Main Trunk Line, Cent. A556

Designs: 50c, Last spike ceremony, Manganui-o-te-Ao, 1908. $1, Locomotive at Taumarunui Station, 1958. $1.50, Train on Makatote Viaduct, 1963. $2, Train on Raurimi Spiral, 1964. $2.50, Train on Hapuawhenua Viaduct, 2003.

2008, Sept. 3 **Litho.** ***Perf. 14***

2202 A556 50c multi .70 .70
2203 A556 $1 multi 1.40 1.40
2204 A556 $1.50 multi 2.00 2.00
2205 A556 $2 multi 2.75 2.75
2206 A556 $2.50 multi 3.50 3.50
Nos. 2202-2206 (5) 10.35 10.35

Christmas A557

Winning art in children's stamp design competition: 50c, Sheep With Stocking Cap, by Kirsten Fisher-Marsters. $2, Pohutukawa and Koru, by Tamara Jenkin. $2.50, Kiwi and Pohutukawa, by Molly Bruhns.

2008, Oct. 1 ***Perf. 14¼***

2207 A557 50c multi .70 .70
2208 A557 $2 multi 2.75 2.75
2209 A557 $2.50 multi 3.25 3.25
Nos. 2207-2209 (3) 6.70 6.70

Christmas A558

Designs: 50c, Nativity. $1, Holy Family. $1.50, Madonna and Child.

2008, Oct. 1 ***Perf. 14¼***

2210 A558 50c multi .70 .70
2211 A558 $1 multi 1.40 1.40
2212 A558 $1.50 multi 2.00 2.00
Nos. 2210-2212 (3) 4.10 4.10

Size: 21x26mm

Self-Adhesive

Coil Stamps

Die Cut Perf. 12¾

2213 A558 50c multi .70 .70
2214 A558 $1.50 multi 2.00 2.00
a. Horiz. pair, #2213-2214 2.75

Booklet Stamps

Serpentine Die Cut 11¼

2215 A558 50c multi .70 .70
a. Booklet pane of 10 7.00
2216 A558 $1.50 multi 2.00 2.00
a. Booklet pane of 10 20.00
Nos. 2213-2216 (4) 5.40 5.40

Sir Edmund Hillary (1919-2008), Mountaineer A559

New Zealand flag and: 50c, Hillary. $1, Hillary and Tenzing Norgay on Mt. Everest, 1953. $1.50, Hillary on Trans-Antarctic Expedition, 1958. $2, Hillary with Nepalese people, 1964.

$2.50, Hillary at Order of the Garter ceremony, 1995.

2008, Nov. 5 Litho. *Perf. 14¾*

2217 A559 50c multi .60 .60
a. Perf. 14 .75 .75
2218 A559 $1 multi 1.25 1.25
a. Perf. 14 1.50 1.50
2219 A559 $1.50 multi 1.75 1.75
2220 A559 $2 multi 2.40 2.40
2221 A559 $2.50 multi 3.00 3.00
a. Perf. 14 3.75 3.75
b. Souvenir sheet, #2217a, 2218a, 2221a, + specimen of #1084 6.00 6.00
Nos. 2217-2221 (5) 9.00 9.00

Timpex 2009 National Stamp Exhibition, Timaru (Nos. 2217a, 2218a, 2221a-b); Issued 10/16/09.

Tourist Attractions Type of 2003
Souvenir Sheet

No. 2222: a, Like #2065, without year date. b, Like #2135, without year date.

2008, Nov. 7 *Perf. 13¼x13½*

2222 Sheet of 2 5.50 5.50
a. A496 $1.50 multi 1.75 1.75
b. A496 $3 multi 3.75 3.75

Tarapex 2008 Philatelic Exhibition, New Plymouth.

The 2008 sheets contain: #2165, 2171, 2177; #2183, 2186, 2196; #2206, 2212, 2221. See note following #1404.

New Year 2009 (Year of the Ox) — A560

Designs: 50c, Chinese character for "ox." $1, Ox. $2, Chinese lanterns and Auckland Harbor Bridge.

2009, Jan. 7 *Perf. 13¼x13*

2223 A560 50c multi .60 .60
2224 A560 $1 multi 1.25 1.25
a. Perf. 13¼x13½ 1.25 1.25
b. Souvenir sheet, #2161s, 2161t, 2224a 5.00 5.00
2225 A560 $2 multi 2.40 2.40
a. Souvenir sheet, #2223-2225 4.25 4.25
Nos. 2223-2225 (3) 4.25 4.25

China 2009 World Stamp Exhibition, Luoyand (#2224b). Issued: Nos. 2224a, 2224b, 4/1.

Lighthouses — A561

Designs: 50c, Pencarrow Lighthouse. $1, Dog Island Lighthouse. $1.50, Cape Brett Lighthouse. $2, Cape Egmont Lighthouse. $2.50, Cape Reinga Lighthouse.

2009, Jan. 7 *Perf. 13x13¼*

2226 A561 50c multi .60 .60
2227 A561 $1 multi 1.25 1.25
2228 A561 $1.50 multi 1.75 1.75
2229 A561 $2 multi 2.40 2.40
2230 A561 $2.50 multi 3.00 3.00
Nos. 2226-2230 (5) 9.00 9.00

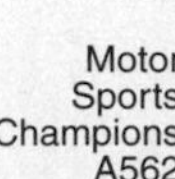

Motor Sports Champions A562

Designs: 50c, Scott Dixon. $1, Bruce McLaren. $1.50, Ivan Mauger. $2, Denny Hulme. $2.50, Hugh Anderson.

2009, Feb. 4 Litho. *Perf. 14*

2231 A562 50c multi .50 .50
2232 A562 $1 multi 1.00 1.00
2233 A562 $1.50 multi 1.50 1.50
2234 A562 $2 multi 2.10 2.10
2235 A562 $2.50 multi 2.60 2.60
a. Sheet, #2231-2235 7.75 7.75
Nos. 2231-2235 (5) 7.70 7.70

Self-Adhesive
Size: 26x21mm
Serpentine Die Cut 10x9¾

2236 A562 50c multi .50 .50
a. Booklet pane of 10 5.00
2237 A562 $1 multi 1.00 1.00
a. Booklet pane of 10 10.00
b. Horiz. pair, #2236-2237 1.50

Tourist Attractions Type of 2003

2009, Mar. 4 Litho. *Perf. 13¼x13½*

2238 Sheet of 2 #2238a 3.00 3.00
a. A496 $1.50 Like #2062, without year date 1.50 1.50

Intl. Polar Year.

Giants of New Zealand — A563

Designs: 50c, Giant moa. $1, Colossal squid. $1.50 Southern right whale. $2, Giant eagle. $2.50, Giant weta.

2009, Mar. 4 *Perf. 14½*

2239 A563 50c multi .75 .75
2240 A563 $1 multi 1.50 1.50
2241 A563 $1.50 multi 2.00 2.00
2242 A563 $2 multi 2.50 2.50
2243 A563 $2.50 multi 3.00 3.00
a. Miniature sheet, #2239-2243 8.00 8.00
Nos. 2239-2243 (5) 9.75 9.75

Australian and New Zealand Army Corps (ANZAC) A564

Poppy and: No. 2244, Funeral procession of the Unknown Warrior. No. 2245, New Zealand Maori Pioneer Battalion, World War I. $1, New Zealand No. 75 Squadron of the Royal Air Force, World War II. $1.50, HMS Achilles, World War II. $2, Kayforce soldiers, Korean War. $2.50, ANZAC Battalion, Vietnam War.

2009, Apr. 1 Litho. *Perf. 13½x13¼*

2244 A564 50c multi .60 .60
a. Perf. 14 .70 .70
b. Booklet pane of 1 #2244a .70 —
2245 A564 50c multi .60 .60
a. Perf. 14 .70 .70
b. Booklet pane of 1 #2245a .70 —
2246 A564 $1 multi 1.25 1.25
a. Perf. 14 1.50 1.50
b. Booklet pane of 1 #2246a 1.50 —
2247 A564 $1.50 multi 1.75 1.75
a. Perf. 14 2.25 2.25
b. Booklet pane of 1 #2247a 2.25 —
2248 A564 $2 multi 2.40 2.40
a. Perf. 14 3.00 3.00
b. Booklet pane of 1 #2248a 3.00 —
2249 A564 $2.50 multi 3.00 3.00
a. Perf. 14 3.75 3.75
b. Booklet pane of 1 #2249a 3.75 —
c. Booklet pane of 6, #2244a, 2245a, 2246a, 2247a, 2248a, 2249a 12.00 —
Complete booklet, #2244b, 2245b, 2246b, 2247b, 2248b, 2249b, 2249c 24.00
Nos. 2244-2249 (6) 9.60 9.60

Complete booklet sold for $19.90.

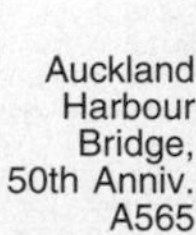

Auckland Harbour Bridge, 50th Anniv. A565

Various views of bridge with inscription: 50c, Opening Day 1959. $1, Our Bridge 2009. $1.50, Our Icon 1961. $2, Our Link 2009.

2009, May 1 *Perf. 13½x13¼*

2250 A565 50c multi .60 .60
2251 A565 $1 multi 1.25 1.25
2252 A565 $1.50 multi 1.75 1.75
2253 A565 $2 multi 2.25 2.25
Nos. 2250-2253 (4) 5.85 5.85

Self-Adhesive
Serpentine Die Cut 9½x10

2254 A565 50c multi .60 .60

Miniature Sheets

Matariki (Maori New Year) — A566

Nos. 2255 and 2256 — Various heitikis: a, Heitiki in Te Maori Exhibition. b, Heitiki carved by Raponi. c, Corian heitiki carved by Rangi Kipa. d, Female greenstone heitiki. e, Heitiki in Museum of New Zealand. f, Whalebone heitiki carved by Rangi Hetet.

Perf. 13¼x13½
2009, June 24 Litho.

2255 A566 Sheet of 6 11.50 11.50
a. 50c multi .60 .60
b. $1 multi 1.25 1.25
c. $1.50 multi 1.90 1.90
d. $1.80 multi 2.25 2.25
e. $2 multi 2.50 2.50
f. $2.30 multi 3.00 3.00

Self-Adhesive
Serpentine Die Cut 10x9½

2256 A566 Sheet of 6 11.50 11.50
a. 50c multi .60 .60
b. $1 multi 1.25 1.25
c. $1.50 multi 1.90 1.90
d. $1.80 multi 2.25 2.25
e. $2 multi 2.50 2.50
f. $2.30 multi 3.00 3.00

Tourist Attractions Type of 2003

Designs: 30c, Tolaga Bay. $1.80, Russell. $2.30, Lake Wanaka. $2.80, Auckland. $3.30, Rakaia River. $4, Wellington.

2009, July 1 *Perf. 13¼x13½*

2257 A496 30c multi .40 .40
2258 A496 $1.80 multi 2.25 2.25
2259 A496 $2.30 multi 3.00 3.00
2260 A496 $2.80 multi 3.50 3.50
2261 A496 $3.30 multi 4.25 4.25
2262 A496 $4 multi 5.00 5.00
Nos. 2257-2262 (6) 18.40 18.40

Self-Adhesive
Serpentine Die Cut 10x9½

2263 A496 $1.80 multi 2.25 2.25
a. Booklet pane of 5 11.50

Miniature Sheet

Tiki Tour of New Zealand — A567

No. 2264 — Parts of map of New Zealand and: a, Signpost and lighthouse, Cape Reinga, fisherman and red snapper, Tane Mahuta, quill pen, Stone Store, Kerikeri. b, Bird, boat on Hole in the Rock tour, dolphin. c, White heron, Maori snaring the Sun. d, Bird, airplane, yachts. e, Rangitoto Island volcano, Sky tower, Auckland, L&P Bottle, Paeroa, bird, surf boat, hibiscus, car and trailer. f, Fishing boat and marlin. g, Balloons, Maori canoe, bull playing rugby. h, Balloon, rower, statue of sheep shearer, Te Kuiti, trout, kiwifruit, Maori carving, Rotorua Mud Pools. i, Pohutukawa tree blossom, meeting house, surfer, horse and rider. j, Maui gas rig, Mt. Taranaki, hang glider, Wind Wand sculpture. k, Rubber boot, apple, pear, windmills, Waimarie River cruise boat, highway sign, Viking helmet, giant kiwi. l, Tractor and wagon, gannet, Pania of the Reef, Napier. m, Westport Municipal Building, statue, Greymouth, Pancake Rocks, Punakaiki. n, Mussel, fisherman, grapes, glass blowers and bottle. o, Birds, statue of Richard Seddon, daffodil, windsurfer, Cook Strait ferry, Golden Shears, Masterton, Westpac Stadium, Wellington. p, Mount Cook lily, bulldozer lifting coal, statue of Mackenzie sheep dog, Lake Tekapo. q, Red deer, punt on Avon River, trailer for selling crayfish, French flags, Chalice, sculpture by Neil Dawson, Christchurch. r, Birds, boat, whale, fish. s, Crayfish, black robin, fishing boat. t, Kayakers, skier, mountains, jetboat on Shotover River. u, Kea, biplane, clams, Museum, Oamaru, clock, Alexandra. v, Kakapo, Museum, Invercargill, Burt Munro motorcycle, musician at Country and Western Festival, Gore. w, Moeraki Boulders, Larnach Castle, Dunedin, curler, seal. x, Stewart Island shag, blue cod, Chain sculpture, Oban.

2009, Aug. 5 *Perf. 14¼*

2264 A567 Sheet of 24 + label 16.00 16.00
a.-x. 50c Any single .65 .65

Kiwistamps — A568

Designs: No. 2265, Cricket ball, bails and wickets. No. 2266, Kiwi fruit. No. 2267, Highway route sign. No. 2268, Wind turbine and man with broken umbrella. No. 2269, Rotary lawn mower. No. 2270, Trailer. No. 2271, Wall decorations (three birds). No. 2272, Fish and chips. No. 2273, Jacket on barbed-wire fence. No. 2274, Hot dog and barbecue.

Serpentine Die Cut 9¾x10
2009, Sept. 7 Litho.
Self-Adhesive

2265 A568 (50c) multi .75 .75
a. Serpentine die cut 11x11¼ .75 .75
b. As "a," with silver text .75 .75
c. Serpentine die cut 10x9¾ .75 .75
d. As "c," with silver text .75 .75
2266 A568 (50c) multi .75 .75
a. Serpentine die cut 11x11¼ .75 .75
b. As "a," with silver text .75 .75
c. Serpentine die cut 10x9¾ .75 .75
d. As "c," with silver text .75 .75
2267 A568 (50c) multi .75 .75
a. Serpentine die cut 11x11¼ .75 .75
b. As "a," with silver text .75 .75
c. Serpentine die cut 10x9¾ .75 .75
d. As "c," with silver text .75 .75
2268 A568 (50c) multi .75 .75
a. Serpentine die cut 11x11¼ .75 .75
b. As "a," with silver text .75 .75
c. Serpentine die cut 10x9¾ .75 .75
d. As "c," with silver text .75 .75
2269 A568 (50c) multi .75 .75
a. Serpentine die cut 11x11¼ .75 .75
b. As "a," with silver text .75 .75
c. Serpentine die cut 10x9¾ .75 .75
d. As "c," with silver text .75 .75
2270 A568 (50c) multi .75 .75
a. Serpentine die cut 11x11¼ .75 .75
b. As "a," with silver text .75 .75
c. Serpentine die cut 10x9¾ .75 .75
d. As "c," with silver text .75 .75
2271 A568 (50c) multi .75 .75
a. Serpentine die cut 11x11¼ .75 .75
b. As "a," with silver text .75 .75
c. Serpentine die cut 10x9¾ .75 .75
d. As "c," with silver text .75 .75
2272 A568 (50c) multi .75 .75
a. Serpentine die cut 11x11¼ .75 .75
b. As "a," with silver text .75 .75
c. Serpentine die cut 10x9¾ .75 .75
d. As "c," with silver text .75 .75
2273 A568 (50c) multi .75 .75
a. Serpentine die cut 11x11¼ .75 .75
b. As "a," with silver text .75 .75
c. Serpentine die cut 10x9¾ .75 .75
d. As "c," with silver text .75 .75
2274 A568 (50c) multi .75 .75
a. Serpentine die cut 11x11¼ .75 .75
b. As "a," with silver text .75 .75
c. Serpentine die cut 10x9¾ .75 .75
d. As "c," with silver text .75 .75
e. Block of 10, #2265-2274 7.50
f. Booklet pane of 10, #2265a-2274a 7.50
g. Booklet pane of 10, #2265b-2274b 7.50
h. Vert. coil strip of 10, #2265-2274 7.50
Nos. 2265-2274 (10) 7.50 7.50

A569

A570

Christmas
A571

Designs: Nos. 2275, 2281, Adoration of the Shepherds. No. 2276, Chair and Pohutukawa Tree, by Felix Wang. $1, Holy Family. $1.80, Adoration of the Magi. $2.30, New Zealand Pigeon, by Dannielle Aldworth. $2.80, Child, Gifts and Christmas Tree, by Apurv Bakshi.

2009, Oct. 7 Litho. *Perf. 14¼*
2275 A569 50c multi .75 .75
2276 A570 50c multi .75 .75
2277 A569 $1 multi 1.50 1.50
2278 A569 $1.80 multi 2.60 2.60
2279 A570 $2.30 multi 3.50 3.50
2280 A570 $2.80 multi 4.00 4.00
Nos. 2275-2280 (6) 13.10 13.10

Self-Adhesive

Serpentine Die Cut 10x9½
2281 A571 50c multi .75 .75
a. Booklet pane of 10 7.50
2282 A571 $1.80 multi 2.60 2.60
a. Booklet pane of 10 26.00
b. Horiz. pair, #2281-2282 3.50

No. 2282a sold for $15.

Sir Peter Blake (1948-2001), Yachtsman
A572

Photograph of Blake and New Zealand flag with inscription at lower right: 50c, Inspirational leader. $1, Yachtsman. $1.80, Record breaker. $2.30, Passionate Kiwi. $2.80, Environmentalist.

2009, Nov. 25 *Perf. 13¼x13½*
2283 A572 50c multi .75 .75
2284 A572 $1 multi 1.50 1.50
2285 A572 $1.80 multi 2.60 2.60
2286 A572 $2.30 multi 3.25 3.25
2287 A572 $2.80 multi 4.00 4.00
a. Souvenir sheet, #2283-2287 12.50 12.50
Nos. 2283-2287 (5) 12.10 12.10

The 2009 sheets contain: #2230, 2225, 2235; #2249, 2243, 2253; #2256f, 2278, 2287. See note following #1404.

New Year 2010 (Year of the Tiger) — A573

Designs: 50c, Chinese character for "tiger." $1, Tiger. $1.80 Tiger's head. $2.30, Bird and Wellington Beehive.

2010, Jan. 6 *Perf. 14*
2288 A573 50c multi .70 .70
a. Perf. 13½ .70 .70
2289 A573 $1 multi 1.40 1.40
a. Perf. 13½ 1.40 1.40
2290 A573 $1.80 multi 2.60 2.60
a. Perf. 13½ 2.60 2.60
2291 A573 $2.30 multi 3.25 3.25
a. Perf. 13½ 3.25 3.25
b. Souvenir sheet, #2288a-2291a 8.00 8.00
Nos. 2288-2291 (4) 7.95 7.95

Greetings Type of 2006 Redrawn Without Silver Frames

No. 2292: a, Heitiki. b, Champagne flutes. c, Wedding and engagement rings. d, Pohutukawa flower.

2010, Feb. 10 Litho. *Perf. 15x14½*
2292 Sheet of 4 + 2 labels 12.50 12.50
a. A531 $1.80 multi 2.60 2.60
b.-d. A531 $2.30 Any single 3.25 3.25
e. Sheet of 20 #2292a + 20 labels 72.50 72.50
f. Sheet of 20 #2292b + 20 labels 85.00 85.00
g. Sheet of 20 #2292c + 20 labels 85.00 85.00
h. Sheet of 20 #2292d + 20 labels 85.00 85.00

Labels are not personalizable on No. 2292.
No. 2292e sold for $50.90. Nos. 2292f-2292h each sold for $60.90. Labels could ber personalized on Nos. 2292e-2292h.

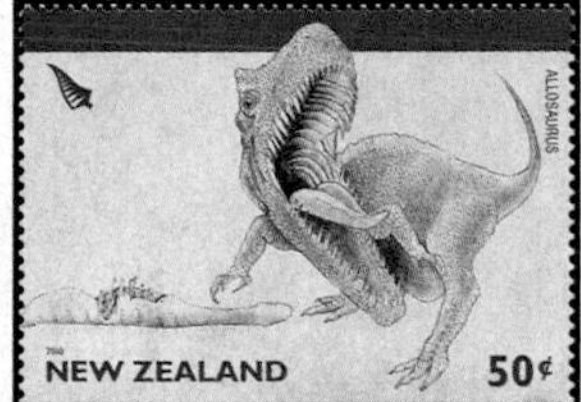

Prehistoric Animals — A574

Designs: 50c, Allosaurus. $1, Anhanguera. $1.80, Titanosaurus. $2.30, Moanasaurus. $2.80, Mauisaurus.

2010, Mar. 3 Litho. *Perf. 14¾*
2293 A574 50c multi .70 .70
2294 A574 $1 multi 1.40 1.40
2295 A574 $1.80 multi 2.50 2.50
2296 A574 $2.30 multi 3.25 3.25
2297 A574 $2.80 multi 4.00 4.00
Nos. 2293-2297 (5) 11.85 11.85

Self-Adhesive

Serpentine Die Cut 10x9¾
2298 Sheet of 5 12.00
a. A574 50c multi .70 .70
b. A574 $1 multi 1.40 1.40
c. A574 $1.80 multi 2.50 2.50
d. A574 $2.30 multi 3.25 3.25
e. A574 $2.80 multi 4.00 4.00

ANZAC Remembrance — A575

Designs: No. 2299, Silhouette of soldier. No. 2300, Gallipoli veterans marching on ANZAC Day, 1958. $1, Posthumous Victoria Cross ceremony for Te Moana-nui-a-Kiwa, 1943. $1.80, Nurses placing wreath in Cairo cemetery on ANZAC Day, 1940. $2.30, Unveiling of ANZAC War Memorial, Port Said, Egypt, 1932. $2.80, Veteran visiting Sangro War Cemetery, Italy, 2004.

2010, Apr. 7 Litho. *Perf. 13½x13¼*
2299 A575 50c multi .75 .75
a. Perf. 14 .80 .80
b. Booklet pane of 1, perf. 14 .80 —
2300 A575 50c multi .75 .75
a. Perf. 14 .80 .80
b. Booklet pane of 1, perf. 14 .80 —
2301 A575 $1 multi 1.50 1.50
a. Perf. 14 1.60 1.60
b. Booklet pane of 1, perf. 14 1.60 —
2302 A575 $1.80 multi 2.60 2.60
a. Perf. 14 3.00 3.00
b. Booklet pane of 1, perf. 14 3.00 —
2303 A575 $2.30 multi 3.25 3.25
a. Perf. 14 3.75 3.75
b. Booklet pane of 1, perf. 14 3.75 —
2304 A575 $2.80 multi 4.00 4.00
a. Perf. 14 4.50 4.50
b. Booklet pane of 1, perf. 14 4.50 —
c. Booklet pane of 6, #2299a-2304a 14.50 —
Complete booklet, #2299b-2304b, 2304c 29.00
d. Souvenir sheet of 3, #2299a, 2303a, 2304a 9.25 9.25
Nos. 2299-2304 (6) 12.85 12.85

Complete booklet sold for $19.90.
Issued: No. 2304d, 4/30. London 2010 Festival of Stamps (No. 2304d).

Expo 2010, Shanghai — A576

Designs: 50c, Pohutukawas and peonies. $1, Kaitiaki and Fu Dog. $1.80, Tane and Pan Gu. $2.30, Auckland and Shanghai. $2.80, Heitiki and Cong.

2010, Apr. 30 Litho. *Perf. 14*
2305 A576 50c multi .75 .75
2306 A576 $1 multi 1.50 1.50
2307 A576 $1.80 multi 2.60 2.60
2308 A576 $2.30 multi 3.50 3.50
2309 A576 $2.80 multi 4.25 4.25
a. Horiz. strip of 5, #2305-2309 13.00 13.00
b. Sheet of 5, #2305-2309, without back printing 13.00 13.00
Nos. 2305-2309 (5) 12.60 12.60

Maori Rugby, Cent. — A577

Designs: 50c, Centenary jersey. $1.80, Centenary emblem.

2010, June 9
2310 A577 50c multi .70 .70
2311 A577 $1.80 multi 2.50 2.50
a. Souvenir sheet of 2, #2310-2311 3.25 3.25

Traditional Maori Kites
A578

Designs: 50c, Manu Aute. $1, Manu Patiki, vert. $1.80, Manu Taratahi, vert. $2.30, Upoko Tangata.

2010, June 9
2312 A578 50c multi .70 .70
2313 A578 $1 multi 1.40 1.40
2314 A578 $1.80 multi 2.50 2.50
2315 A578 $2.30 multi 3.25 3.25
a. Souvenir sheet of 4, #2312-2315 8.00 8.00
Nos. 2312-2315 (4) 7.85 7.85

Tourist Attractions Type of 2003

Designs: $1.20, Mitre Peak, Milford Sound. $1.90, Queenstown. $2.40, Lake Rotorua. $2.90, Kaikoura. $3.40, Christchurch.

2010, Aug. 4 *Perf. 13¼x13½*
2316 A496 $1.20 multi 1.75 1.75
2317 A496 $1.90 multi 2.75 2.75
2318 A496 $2.40 multi 3.50 3.50
a. Souvenir sheet of 3, #2316-2318 8.50 8.50
2319 A496 $2.90 multi 4.25 4.25
2320 A496 $3.40 multi 5.00 5.00
Nos. 2316-2320 (5) 17.25 17.25

Self-Adhesive

Serpentine Die Cut 10x9½
2321 A496 $1.20 multi 1.75 1.75
a. Booklet pane of 10 17.50
2322 A496 $1.90 multi 2.75 2.75
a. Booklet pane of 5 14.00

Issued: No. 2318a, 2/12/11. Indipex 2011 (#2318a).

Emblem of All Blacks Rugby Team
A579

2010, Aug. 4 *Perf. 13½x13¼*
2323 A579 60c black .90 .90
2324 A579 $1.90 black 2.75 2.75
a. Miniature sheet of 6 60.00 60.00

Souvenir Sheet
2325 Sheet of 4, #2323, 2324, 2325a, 2325b 7.50 7.50
a. A579 60c black, 32x17mm, perf. 15x14½ .90 .90
b. A579 $1.90 black, 32x17mm, perf. 15x14½ .90 .90
c. Sheet of 20 #2325a + 20 labels 34.00 34.00
d. Sheet of 20 #2325b + 20 labels 77.50 77.50

2011 Rugby World Cup victory of New Zealand rugby team (No. 2324a). Issued: No. 2324a, 10/28/11. No. 2324a sold for $19.90.
No. 2325c sold for $22.90. No. 2325d sold for $52.90. Labels could be personalized on Nos. 2325c-2325d. In 2011, No. 2325c was made available for the same price with labels that could not be personalized.
See Nos. 2410-2411, 2519-2521.

Greetings Stamps Type of 2006 Without Silver Frames

No. 2326: a, Champagne flutes. b, Child's toy. c, Fern. d, Pohutukawa flower. e, Wedding and engagement rings. f, Rose. g, Heitiki. h, Teddy bear.
No. 2327: a, Heitiki. b, Champagne flutes. c, Wedding and engagement rings. d, Pohutukawa flower.

2010, Sept. 9 *Perf. 15x14½*
2326 A531 Sheet of 8 + 4 labels 7.25 7.25
a.-h. 60c Any single .90 .90
i. Sheet of 20 #2326a + 20 labels 34.00 34.00
j. Sheet of 20 #2326b + 20 labels 34.00 34.00
k. Sheet of 20 #2326c + 20 labels 34.00 34.00
l. Sheet of 20 #2326d + 20 labels 34.00 34.00
m. Sheet of 20 #2326e + 20 labels 34.00 34.00
n. Sheet of 20 #2326f + 20 labels 34.00 34.00
o. Sheet of 20 #2326g + 20 labels 34.00 34.00
p. Sheet of 20 #2326h + 20 labels 34.00 34.00
2327 A531 Sheet of 4 + 2 labels 13.50 13.50
a. $1.90 multi 2.75 2.75
b.-d. $2.40 Any single 3.50 3.50
e. Sheet of 20 #2327a + 20 labels 77.50 77.50
f. Sheet of 20 #2327b + 20 labels 92.50 92.50
g. Sheet of 20 #2327c + 20 labels 92.50 92.50
h. Sheet of 20 #2327d + 20 labels 92.50 92.50

Nos. 2326i-2326p each sold for $22.90. No. 2327e sold for $52.90. Nos. 2327f-2327h each sold for $62.90. Labels could be personalized on Nos. 2326i-2326p, 2327e-2327h.

Emblem of 2011 Rugby World Cup
A580

2010, Sept. 9 *Perf. 13½x13¼*
2328 A580 60c multi .90 .90
2329 A580 $1.90 multi 2.75 2.75

Souvenir Sheet
2330 Sheet of 4, #2328, 2329, 2330a, 2330b 7.50 7.50
a. A580 60c multi, 32x17mm, perf. 15x14½ .90 .90

b. A580 $1.90 multi, 32x17mm, perf. 15x14½ .90 .90
c. Sheet of 20 #2330a + 20 labels 34.00 34.00
d. Sheet of 20 #2330b + 20 labels 77.50 77.50

No. 2330c sold for $22.90. No. 2330d sold for $52.90. Labels could be personalized on Nos. 2330c-2330d. In 2011, No. 2330c was made available for the same price with labels that could not be personalized.

Miniature Sheet

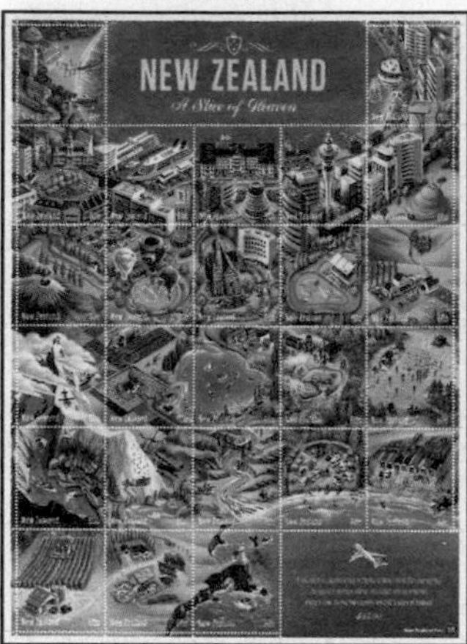

"A Slice of Heaven" — A581

No. 2331: a, Tane Mahuta kauri tree, Stone Store, Kerikeri, Waitangi Treaty Grounds, boat at dock. b, Carter Fountain, Oriental Bay, buildings. c, The Octagon, St. Paul's Cathedral, Dunedin. d, Cruise ship, Princes Wharf, Auckland. e, The Beehive, Wellington. f, Sky Tower, Auckland Ferry Terminal. g, Obelisk on grave of Sir John Logan Campbell on One Tree Hill, cable car, buildings. h, Mount Ruapehu (volcano), punts on Avon River, Christchurch. i, Fairfield Bridge, hot-air balloons over Basin Reserve Cricket Grounds, Wellington. j, Christchurch Cathedral, Bridge of Remembrance. k, Horse racing track. l, Road, small town, war memorial, sheep in field. m, Mountain climbers with flag on Mt. Cook, ski plane, helicopter. n, Farm house, storage shed, plowed field, cows in pasture, shore of Lake Taupo. o, Lake Taupo, Huka Falls. p, Champagne Pool, geyser, mud pool. q, Rugby field. r, TSS Earnslaw on Lake Wakatipu, parasailers, Queenstown. s, Biplane and glider over ski and golf resort. t, Suspension bridge over river, river mouth. u, Trailer park near beach, Moeraki Boulders. v, Line of boatsheds, Tihati Bay. w, Farmhouse, barn, tractor, silos. x, House, sheep pens, truck. y, Nugget Point Lighthouse, whale.

2010, Oct. 6 *Perf. 14¼*
2331 A581 Sheet of 25 22.50 22.50
a.-y. 60c Any single .90 .90

Christmas A582

New Zealand Christmas stamps of the past: 60c, #353. $1.20, #465. $1.90, #692. $2.40, #790. $2.90, #1672.

2010, Oct. 20 *Perf. 13¼x13½*

Stamps Without White Frames

2332 A582 60c multi .95 .95
2333 A582 $1.20 multi 1.90 1.90
2334 A582 $1.90 multi 3.00 3.00
2335 A582 $2.40 multi 4.00 4.00
2336 A582 $2.90 multi 4.75 4.75
Nos. 2332-2336 (5) 14.60 14.60

Stamps With White Frames

Coil Stamps

Self-Adhesive

Size: 21x26mm

Die Cut Perf. 12¾

2337 A582 60c multi .95 .95
2338 A582 $1.90 multi 3.00 3.00
a. Horiz. pair, #2337-2338 4.00

Booklet Stamps

Serpentine Die Cut 11¼

2339 A582 60c multi .95 .95
a. Booklet pane of 10 9.50
2340 A582 $1.90 multi 3.00 3.00
a. Booklet pane of 10 30.00
Nos. 2337-2340 (4) 7.90 7.90

New Zealand Christmas stamps, 50th anniv. No. 2339a sold for $5.40 and No. 2340a sold for $16.

Volunteer Lifeguard Clubs, Cent. A583

Designs: 60c, Surf lifeguard and beach flag. $1.20, Lifeguards on inflatable rescue boat. $1.90, Lifeguards on ski paddlers. $2.40, Lifeguards on surf boat. $2.90, Lifeguards marching on beach.

2010, Nov. 3 *Perf. 13x13¼*
2341 A583 60c multi .95 .95
2342 A583 $1.20 multi 1.90 1.90
2343 A583 $1.90 multi 3.00 3.00
2344 A583 $2.40 multi 4.00 4.00
2345 A583 $2.90 multi 4.75 4.75
Nos. 2341-2345 (5) 14.60 14.60

The 2010 sheets contain: #2291, 2297, 2304; #2309, 2315, B198; #2319, 2336, 2345. See note following #1404.

New Year 2011 (Year of the Rabbit) — A584

Designs: 60c, Chinese character for "rabbit." $1.20, Paper-cut rabbit. $1.90, Rabbit. $2.40, Kite, Christchurch Cathedral.

2011, Jan. 12 Litho. *Perf. 13½x13*
2346 A584 60c multi .95 .95
2347 A584 $1.20 multi 1.90 1.90
2348 A584 $1.90 multi 3.00 3.00
2349 A584 $2.40 multi 3.75 3.75
a. Souvenir sheet, #2346-2349 9.75 9.75
Nos. 2346-2349 (4) 9.60 9.60

Miniature Sheets

Kapa Haka — A585

Nos. 2350 and 2351: a, Whakaeke. b, Poi. c, Waiata-a-ringa. d, Haka. e, Whakawatea. f, Moteatea.

2011, Feb. 17 *Perf. 13¼x13½*
2350 A585 Sheet of 6 15.00 15.00
a.-b. 60c Either single .90 .90
c. $1.20 multi 1.90 1.90
d. $1.90 multi 3.00 3.00
e. $2.40 multi 3.75 3.75
f. $2.90 multi 4.50 4.50

Self-Adhesive

Serpentine Die Cut 10x9½

2351 A585 Sheet of 6 15.00 15.00
a.-b. 60c Either single .90 .90
c. $1.20 multi 1.90 1.90
d. $1.90 multi 3.00 3.00
e. $2.40 multi 3.75 3.75
f. $2.90 multi 4.50 4.50

Kiwistamps A586

Designs: Nos. 2352, 2357, Hokey pokey ice cream cone. Nos. 2353, 2358, Kiwi crossing road sign. Nos. 2354, 2359, People on beach. Nos. 2355, 2360, Trout fisherman. Nos. 2356, 2361, Mountain biking.

Serpentine Die Cut 10x9¾

2011, Mar. 23 Litho.

Self-Adhesive

Coil Stamps

2352 A586 (60c) multi .95 .95
2353 A586 (60c) multi .95 .95
2354 A586 (60c) multi .95 .95
2355 A586 (60c) multi .95 .95
2356 A586 (60c) multi .95 .95
a. Horiz. strip of 5, #2352-2356 4.75
Nos. 2352-2356 (5) 4.75 4.75

Booklet Stamps

Serpentine Die Cut 11

2357 A586 (60c) multi .95 .95
2358 A586 (60c) multi .95 .95
2359 A586 (60c) multi .95 .95
2360 A586 (60c) multi .95 .95
2361 A586 (60c) multi .95 .95
a. Booklet pane of 10, 2 each #2357-2361 9.50
Nos. 2357-2361 (5) 4.75 4.75

Wedding of Prince William and Catherine Middleton A587

Prince William and Catherine Middleton with Prince William wearing: No. 2362, Suit and tie. No. 2363, Sweater.

2011, Mar. 23 *Perf. 14½x14¾*
2362 A587 $2.40 multi 3.75 3.75
2363 A587 $2.40 multi 3.75 3.75
a. Horiz. pair, #2362-2363 7.50 7.50
b. Souvenir sheet of 2, #2362-2363 7.50 7.50

New Zealand's Victoria Cross Recipients A588

No. 2364: a, Charles Heaphy. b, William James Hardham. c, Cyril Royston Guyton Bassett. d, Donald Forrester Brown. e, Samuel Frickleton. f, Leslie Wilton Andrew. g, Henry James Nicholas. h, Richard Charles Travis. i, Samuel Forsyth. j, Reginald Stanley Judson. k, Harry John Laurent. l, James Crichton. m, John Gildroy Grant. n, James Edward Allen Ward. o, Charles Hazlitt Upham. p, Alfred Clive Hulme. q, John Daniel Hinton. r, Keith Elliott.s, Moana-nui-a-Kiwa Ngarimu. t, Lloyd Allen Trigg. u, Leonard Henry Trent. v, Bill Henry Apiata (medal only).

2011, Apr. 14 *Perf. 13¼x13½*
2364 Miniature sheet of 22 22.00 22.00
a.-v. A588 60c Any single 1.00 1.00

Miniature Sheet

Life Beyond the Coast — A589

No. 2365: a, Humpback whale. b, White-faced storm petrel, horiz. c, John Dory, horiz. d, Yellowfin tuna, horiz. e, Kingfish, horiz. f, Hammerhead shark, horiz. g, Snapper, horiz. h, Arrow squid, horiz. i, Lord Howe coralfish. j, Orange roughy, horiz. k, Yellow moray eel, horiz. l, King crab.

Serpentine Die Cut 10x9½, 9½x10

2011, May 4 Self-Adhesive
2365 A589 Sheet of 12 15.50
a.-j. 60c Any single .95 .95
k.-l. $1.90 Either single 3.00 3.00

Miniature Sheet

Matariki (Maori New Year) — A590

Nos. 2366 and 2367 — Various hei mataus (decorative fish hooks): a, Green pounamu fish hook by Lewis Gardiner. b, White whalebone fish hook, c. 1500-1800, in Museum of New Zealand. c, Inanga fish hook, c. 1800, in Museum of New Zealand. d, Pounamu, whalebone, feathers and flax fiber fish hook by Gardiner. e, Wooden fish hook, c. 1800, in Auckland War Memorial Museum. f, Whalebone fish hook, c. 1750-1850, in Museum of New Zealand.

2011, June 1 Litho. *Perf. 13¼x13½*
2366 A590 Sheet of 6 16.00 16.00
a.-b. 60c Either single 1.00 1.00
c. $1.20 multi 2.00 2.00
d. $1.90 multi 3.25 3.25
e. $2.40 multi 4.00 4.00
f. $2.90 multi 4.75 4.75

Self-Adhesive

Serpentine Die Cut 10x9½

2367 A590 Sheet of 6 16.00 16.00
a.-b. 60c Either single 1.00 1.00
c. $1.20 multi 2.00 2.00
d. $1.90 multi 3.25 3.25
e. $2.40 multi 4.00 4.00
f. $2.90 multi 4.75 4.75

Kiwi Type of 1988

2011 Litho. *Perf. 14½*
2368 A325 $1.20 black 2.00 2.00
2369 A325 $1.90 silver 3.25 3.25
a. Souvenir sheet, #2369, 2 #2324 9.75 9.75
2370 A325 $2.40 blue 4.00 4.00
a. Horiz. strip of 3, #2368-2370 9.25 9.25
b. Souvenir sheet of 3, #2368-2370 8.75 8.75
Nos. 2368-2370 (3) 9.25 9.25

Issued: Nos. 2368-2370, 7/6; No. 2369a, 7/28. No. 2370b, 11/11. Philanippon 2011 World Stamp Exhibition, Yokohama (#2369a). China 2011 Intl. Stamp Exhibition, Wuxi, China (#2370b).

Values for Nos. 2368-2370 are for stamps with surrounding selvage.

Miniature Sheet

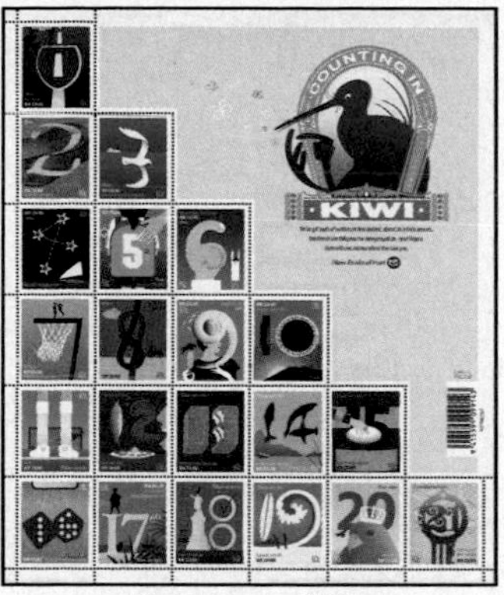

Numbers — A591

No. 2371 — Maori words for numbers and stylized numbers: a, 1 (State Highway 1 sign). b, 2 (2 beach sandals). c, 3 (sea gull, Cook Strait ferry). d, 4 (stars in Southern Cross, sailboat) e, 5 (child with backpack). f, 6 (hand, cricket umpire). g, 7 (netball goal and players). h, 8 (barbed wire, tractor). i, 9 (woman in fancy clothes, race horse). j, 10 (guitar). k, 11 (legs of soccer player). l, 12 (oyster shell, tongue, plate of oysters). m, 13 (Lamington cakes). n, 14 (dolphins, outrigger canoes in national parks). o, 15 (hand on rugby ball). p, 16 (dice hanging from rear-view mirror). q, 17 (Capt. James Cook and year of his arrival in New Zealand). r, 18 (bird on statue, ballot circles, Parliament building). s, 19 (surf board and wave). t, 20 (parrot with crown). u, 21 (key and streamers).

2011, Aug. 10 ***Perf. 14***
2371 A591 Sheet of 21 21.00 21.00
a.-u. 60c Any single 1.00 1.00

Webb Ellis Cup, Trophy of Rugby World Cup A592

Litho. With 3-Dimensional Plastic Affixed
Serpentine Die Cut 10¼
2011, Sept. 7 **Self-Adhesive**
2372 A592 $15 multi 25.00 25.00

The New Zealand Experience A593

Designs: No. 2373, Backpacker, paraglider, camp, hikers, mountains. No. 2374, Sailboaters, motor boat, sailboarder. $1.20, Fisherman and fish. $1.90, Maoris. $2.40, Skier, helicopter. $2.90, Bungee jumper, whitewater raft, hot air balloon.

2011, Sept. 7 **Litho.** ***Perf. 14***
2373 A593 60c multi .95 .95
2374 A593 60c multi .95 .95
2375 A593 $1.20 multi 1.90 1.90
2376 A593 $1.90 multi 3.00 3.00
2377 A593 $2.40 multi 3.75 3.75
2378 A593 $2.90 multi 4.50 4.50
a. Souvenir sheet of 6, #2373-2378 15.50 15.50
Nos. 2373-2378 (6) 15.05 15.05

A594

Christmas — A595

Star of Bethlehem and: 60c, Baby Jesus and livestock. $1.20, Angel appearing to shepherds. $1.90, Holy Family. $2.40, Adoration of the Shepherds. $2.90, Adoration of the Magi.

2011, Nov. 2 **Litho.** ***Perf. 14¼***
2379 A594 60c multi .95 .95
2380 A594 $1.20 multi 1.90 1.90
2381 A594 $1.90 multi 3.00 3.00
2382 A594 $2.40 multi 4.00 4.00
2383 A594 $2.90 multi 4.75 4.75
Nos. 2379-2383 (5) 14.60 14.60

Self-Adhesive
Serpentine Die Cut 9¾x10
2384 A595 60c multi .95 .95
2385 A595 $1.90 multi 3.00 3.00
a. Booklet pane of 10 30.00
2386 A595 $2.40 multi 4.00 4.00
a. Horiz. sheet of 3, #2384-2386 8.00
b. Booklet pane of 10 40.00

Booklet Stamp
Serpentine Die Cut 11¼
2387 A595 60c multi .95 .95
a. Booklet pane of 10 9.50
Nos. 2384-2387 (4) 8.90 8.90

Nos. 2385a and 2386b sold for $17.10 and $21.60, respectively. A se-tenant strip of Nos. 2379-2383 was not put on sale but was a reward for standing order customers.

The 2011 sheets contain: #2349, 2362, 2350f; #2364v, B202, 2366f; #2378, 2370, 2383. See note following #1404.

New Year 2012 (Year of the Dragon) — A596

Designs: 60c, Chinese character for "dragon." $1.20, Dragon. $1.90, Dragon lantern. $2.40, Dunedin Railroad Station, swallows.

2012, Jan. 5 **Litho.** ***Perf. 13¼x13½***
2388 A596 60c multi 1.00 1.00
2389 A596 $1.20 multi 2.00 2.00
2390 A596 $1.90 multi 3.25 3.25
2391 A596 $2.40 multi 4.00 4.00
a. Souvenir sheet of 4, #2388-2391 10.50 10.50
b. Souvenir sheet of 3, #2388, 2390, 2391 8.25 8.25
Nos. 2388-2391 (4) 10.25 10.25

Issued: No. 2391b, 11/2. 2012 Beijing Intl. Stamp and Coin Expo (#2391b).

Tourist Attractions Type of 2003
Serpentine Die Cut 10x9½
2012, Feb. 1 **Litho.**
Self-Adhesive
2392 A496 $2.40 Lake Rotorua 4.00 4.00
a. Booklet pane of 5 + 2 etiquettes 20.00

Native Trees — A597

Designs: 60c, Pohutukawa. $1.20, Cabbage tree. $1.90, Kowhai. $2.40, Nikau. $2.90, Manuka.

2012, Feb. 1 ***Perf. 13¼x13½***
2393 A597 60c multi 1.00 1.00
2394 A597 $1.20 multi 2.00 2.00
2395 A597 $1.90 multi 3.25 3.25
2396 A597 $2.40 multi 4.00 4.00
a. Souvenir sheet of 3, #2393, 2395, 2396 8.25 8.25
2397 A597 $2.90 multi 5.00 5.00
a. Souvenir sheet of 5, #2393-2397 15.50 15.50
Nos. 2393-2397 (5) 15.25 15.25

Issued: No. 2396a, 6/18. Indonesia 2012 World Stamp Championship and Exhibition, Jakarta (#2396a).

Miniature Sheet

Royal New Zealand Air Force, 75th Anniv. — A598

No. 2398 — Inscriptions: a, The Beginning. b, Air Training corps. c, WWII Europe. d, Women's Auxiliary Air Force. e, WWII Pacific. f, Aerial Topdressing. g, Territorial Air Force. h, Sout East Asia. i, ANZAC. j, Naval Support. k, Transport. l, Peacekeeping. m, Search and Rescue. n, Remembrance. o, The Future.

2012, Mar. 15 ***Perf. 14½***
2398 A598 Sheet of 15 15.00 15.00
a.-o. 60c Any single 1.00 1.00
p. Booklet pane of 4, 2 each #2398a-2398b 4.50 —
q. Booklet pane of 4, 2 each #2398c-2398d 4.50 —
r. Booklet pane of 4, 2 each #2398e-2398f 4.50 —
s. Booklet pane of 4, 2 each #2398g-2398h 4.50 —
t. Booklet pane of 4, 2 each #2398i-2398j 4.50 —
u. Booklet pane of 4, 2 each #2398k-2398l 4.50 —
v. Booklet pane of 4, 2 each #2398m, 2398o 4.50 —
w. Booklet pane of 2 #2398n 2.25 —
Complete booklet, #2398p-2398w 34.00

Complete booklet sold for $19.90.

Reign of Queen Elizabeth II, 60th Anniv. — A599

Photographs of: No. 2399, Queen, 2012. No. 2400, Queen and Prince Philip, 2012. $1.40, Queen and Prince Philip, 1986. $1.90, Queen and Prince Philip, 1981. $2.40, Queen and Prince Philip, 1977. $2.90, Queen, 1953.

Litho. With Foil Application
2012, May 9 ***Perf. 13¼x13½***
2399 A599 70c multi 1.10 1.10
2400 A599 70c multi 1.10 1.10
2401 A599 $1.40 multi 2.25 2.25
2402 A599 $1.90 multi 3.00 3.00
2403 A599 $2.40 multi 3.75 3.75
2404 A599 $2.90 multi 4.50 4.50
a. Souvenir sheet of 6, #2399-2404 16.00 16.00
b. Souvenir sheet of 3, #2399, 2402, 2404 9.25 9.25
Nos. 2399-2404 (6) 15.70 15.70

Issued: No. 2404b, 10/12. 2012 New Zealand National Stamp Exhibition, Blenheim (#2404b).

Tourist Attractions Type of 2003

Designs: $1.40, Cape Reinga Lighthouse. $2.10, Stewart Island. $3.50, Lake Matheson.

2012, May 23 **Litho.** ***Perf. 13¼x13½***
2405 A496 $1.40 multi 2.25 2.25
2406 A496 $2.10 multi 3.25 3.25
2407 A496 $3.50 multi 5.50 5.50
Nos. 2405-2407 (3) 11.00 11.00

Self-Adhesive
Serpentine Die Cut 10x9½
2408 A496 $1.40 multi 2.25 2.25
a. Booklet pane of 10 22.50
2409 A496 $2.10 multi 3.25 3.25
a. Booklet pane of 5 16.50
b. Horiz. pair, #2408-2409 5.50

All Blacks Type of 2010
2012, May 23 ***Perf. 13½x13¼***
2410 A579 70c black 1.10 1.10

Souvenir Sheet
2411 Sheet of 2, #2410, 2411a 2.25 2.25
a. A579 70c black, 32x17mm, perf. 15x14½ 1.10 1.10

Greetings Stamps Type of 2006 Without Silver Frames

No. 2412: a, Champagne flutes. b, Child's toy. c, Fern. d, Pohutukawa flower. e, Wedding and engagement rings. f, Rose. g, Heitiki. h, Tedddy bear.

2012, June 6 ***Perf. 15x14½***
2412 A531 Sheet of 8 + 4 labels 9.00 9.00
a.-h. 70c Any single 1.10 1.10

Miniature Sheets

Maori Rock Art — A600

Nos. 2413 and 2414: a, Pouakai, Pareora. b, Tiki, Maerewhenua. c, Mohiki, Opihi. d, Te Puawaitanga, Waitaki. e, Tiki, Te Ana a Wai. f, Taniwha, Opihi.

2012, June 6 ***Perf. 13½x13¼***
2413 A600 Sheet of 6 16.00 16.00
a.-b. 70c Either single 1.10 1.10
c. $1.40 multi 2.25 2.25
d. $1.90 multi 3.00 3.00
e. $2.40 multi 3.75 3.75
f. $2.90 multi 4.50 4.50

Self-Adhesive
Serpentine Die Cut 9½x10
2414 A600 Sheet of 6 16.00 16.00
a.-b. 70c Either single 1.10 1.10
c. $1.40 multi 2.25 2.25
d. $1.90 multi 3.00 3.00
e. $2.40 multi 3.75 3.75
f. $2.90 multi 4.50 4.50

Miniature Sheet

Tiki Tour of New Zealand — A601

No. 2415 — Places named on map of New Zealand: a, Cape Reinga, Ninety Mile Beach, Kaitaia. b, Whangarei, Bay of Islands. c, Cape Brett. d, Lion Rock. e, Auckland, Hamilton, Tauranga. f, White Island, East Cape. g, Mt. Taranaki, New Plymouth, Hawera. h, Rotorua, Taupo, Palmerston North. i, Gisborne, Napier. j, No place names (fish, boat, waves). k, Westport, Greymouth. l, Golden Bay, Nelson, Cook Strait, Kaikoura. m, Wellington, Castlepoint. n, Chatham Islands. o, Mitre Peak, Milford Sound. p, Queenstown, Aoraki (Mount Cook), Timaru. q, Christchurch, Ashburton. r, Gore, Invercargill, Foveaux Strait, Stewart Island. s, Dunedin. t, Taiaroa Head.

2012, July 4 *Perf. 14¼*

2415 A601 Sheet of 20 22.00 22.00
a.-t. 70c Any single 1.10 1.10

Samoan Head Combs — A602

Designs: 70c, Fu'a. $1.40, Niu. $1.90, Maota. $2.40, Tatau. $2.90, Malumalu.

2012, Aug. 1 *Perf. 14*

2416 A602 70c multi 1.25 1.25
2417 A602 $1.40 multi 2.40 2.40
2418 A602 $1.90 multi 3.25 3.25
2419 A602 $2.40 multi 4.00 4.00
2420 A602 $2.90 multi 4.75 4.75
a. Souvenir sheet of 5, #2416-2420 16.00 16.00
Nos. 2416-2420 (5) 15.65 15.65

Ships A603

Designs: 70c, Aramoana. $1.40, Waka. $1.90, Earnslaw. $2.40, Dunedin. $2.90, Rotomahana.

2012, Sept. 5

2421 A603 70c multi 1.25 1.25
2422 A603 $1.40 multi 2.25 2.25
2423 A603 $1.90 multi 3.25 3.25
2424 A603 $2.40 multi 4.00 4.00
2425 A603 $2.90 multi 4.75 4.75
a. Souvenir sheet of 5, #2421-2425 15.50 15.50
Nos. 2421-2425 (5) 15.50 15.50

A604

Christmas — A605

Designs: 70c, Holy Family. $1.40, Adoration of the Shepherds. $1.90, Angel. $2.40 Adoration of the Magi. $2.90, Magi and camels.

2012, Oct. 3 *Perf. 14*

2426 A604 70c multi 1.25 1.25
2427 A604 $1.40 multi 2.25 2.25
2428 A604 $1.90 multi 3.25 3.25
2429 A604 $2.40 multi 4.00 4.00
2430 A604 $2.90 multi 4.75 4.75
Nos. 2426-2430 (5) 15.50 15.50

Self-Adhesive

Serpentine Die Cut 11x11¼

2431 A605 70c multi 1.25 1.25
a. Booklet pane of 10 12.50
2432 A605 $1.90 multi 3.25 3.25
a. Booklet pane of 10 + 10 etiquettes 32.50
2433 A605 $2.40 multi 4.00 4.00
a. Booklet pane of 10 + 10 etiquettes 40.00
b. Horiz. sheet of 3, #2431-2433 8.50
Nos. 2431-2433 (3) 8.50 8.50

Nos. 2432 and 2433 are air mail. No. 2432a sold for $17.10. No. 2433a sold for $21.60.

Premiere of Movie *The Hobbit: An Unexpected Journey*
A606 A607

Characters: 70c, Bilbo Baggins. $1.40, Gollum. $1.90, Gandalf, horiz. $2.10, Thorin Oakenshield, horiz. $2.40, Radagast. $2.90, Elrond.

2012, Nov. 1 *Perf. 14½x14, 14x14½*

2434 A606 70c multi 1.25 1.25
a. Souvenir sheet of 1 1.50 1.50
2435 A606 $1.40 multi 2.40 2.40
a. Souvenir sheet of 1 3.00 3.00
2436 A606 $1.90 multi 3.25 3.25
a. Souvenir sheet of 1 4.00 4.00
2437 A606 $2.10 multi 3.50 3.50
a. Souvenir sheet of 1 4.50 4.50
2438 A606 $2.40 multi 4.00 4.00
a. Souvenir sheet of 1 5.00 5.00
2439 A606 $2.90 multi 4.75 4.75
a. Souvenir sheet of 1 6.25 6.25
Nos. 2434-2439 (6) 19.15 19.15

Self-Adhesive

Serpentine Die Cut 11¼

2440 Sheet of 6 19.50
a. A607 70c multi 1.25 1.25
b. A607 $1.40 multi 2.40 2.40
c. A607 $1.90 multi 3.25 3.25
d. A607 $2.10 multi 3.50 3.50
e. A607 $2.40 multi 4.00 4.00
f. A607 $2.90 multi 4.75 4.75
g. Booklet pane of 10, #2440c-2440f, 4 #2440a, 2 #2440b 25.50

Nos. 2434a-2439a sold as a set of 6 sheets for $14.40.

New Year 2013 (Year of the Snake) — A608

Designs: 70c, Chinese character for "snake." $1.40, Snake. $1.90, Snake on lantern. $2.40, Lanterns and Skyline Gondola, Queenstown.

2013, Jan. 9 *Perf. 13¼x13*

2441 A608 70c multi 1.25 1.25
2442 A608 $1.40 multi 2.40 2.40
2443 A608 $1.90 multi 3.25 3.25
2444 A608 $2.40 multi 4.00 4.00
a. Souvenir sheet of 4, #2441-2444 11.00 11.00
Nos. 2441-2444 (4) 10.90 10.90

Ferns A609

Designs: 70c, Hen and chickens fern. $1.40, Kidney fern. $1.90, Colenso's hard fern. $2.40, Umbrella fern. $2.90, Silver fern.

2013, Feb. 7 *Perf. 13x13¼*

2445 A609 70c multi 1.25 1.25
2446 A609 $1.40 multi 2.40 2.40
2447 A609 $1.90 multi 3.25 3.25
2448 A609 $2.40 multi 4.00 4.00
2449 A609 $2.90 multi 5.00 5.00
a. Souvenir sheet of 5, #2445-2449 16.00 16.00
b. Souvenir sheet of 2, #2448-2449, perf. 13½ 13.00 13.00
Nos. 2445-2449 (5) 15.90 15.90

Issued: No. 2449b, 9/13. Upper Hutt 2013 National Stamp Show (#2449b). No. 2449b sold for $7.80, with $2.50 of that amount going to the Philatelic Trust.

Children's Books by Margaret Mahy (1936-2012) — A610

Designs: 70c, A Lion in the Meadow. $1.40, A Summery Saturday Morning. $1.90, The Word Witch. $2.40, The Great White Man-Eating Shark. $2.90, The Changeover.

2013, Mar. 13 *Perf. 14*

2450 A610 70c multi 1.25 1.25
2451 A610 $1.40 multi 2.40 2.40
2452 A610 $1.90 multi 3.25 3.25
2453 A610 $2.40 multi 4.00 4.00
2454 A610 $2.90 multi 4.75 4.75
a. Souvenir sheet of 5, #2450-2454 16.00 16.00
Nos. 2450-2454 (5) 15.65 15.65

New Zealand Defense Force Missions Abroad A611

Mission in: No. 2455, Afghanistan. No. 2456, Timor. 140c, Solomon Islands. 190c, Bosnia and Herzegovina. 240c, Antarctica. 290c, Korea.

2013, Apr. 10

2455 A611 70c multi 1.25 1.25
a. Booklet pane of 1 1.25 1.25
2456 A611 70c multi 1.25 1.25
a. Booklet pane of 1 1.25 1.25
2457 A611 140c multi 2.40 2.40
a. Booklet pane of 1 2.40 2.40
2458 A611 190c multi 3.25 3.25
a. Booklet pane of 1 3.25 3.25
2459 A611 240c multi 4.00 4.00
a. Booklet pane of 1 4.00 4.00
2460 A611 290c multi 5.00 5.00
a. Booklet pane of 1 5.00 5.00
b. Booklet pane of 6, #2455-2460 17.50 —
Complete booklet, #2455a, 2456a, 2457a, 2458a, 2459a, 2460a, 2460b 35.00
Nos. 2455-2460 (6) 17.15 17.15

Complete booklet sold for $19.90.

Coronation of Queen Elizabeth II, 60th Anniv. — A612

Depictions of Queen Elizabeth II used on New Zealand currency by: No. 2461, Mary Gillick, 1953. No. 2462, Gillick, re-engraved in 1956. $1.40, Arnold Machin, 1967. $1.90, James Berry, 1979. $2.40, Raphael Maklouf, 1986. $2.90, Ian Rank-Broadley, 1999.

Litho. & Embossed With Foil Application

2013

2461 A612 70c multi 1.25 1.25
2462 A612 70c multi 1.25 1.25
2463 A612 $1.40 multi 2.25 2.25
2464 A612 $1.90 multi 3.00 3.00
2465 A612 $2.40 multi 4.00 4.00
2466 A612 $2.90 multi 4.75 4.75
a. Souvenir sheet of 6, #2461-2466 16.50 16.50
b. Souvenir sheet of 3, #2461, 2463, 2466 8.25 8.25
Nos. 2461-2466 (6) 16.50 16.50

Australia 2013 World Stamp Exhibition, Melbourne (#24266b). Issued: Nos. 2461-2466, 2466a, 5/8; No. 2466b, 5/10.

Miniature Sheets

Matariki (Maori New Year) — A613

Nos. 2467 and 2468 — Koru patterns: a, Piko. b, Manu Tukutuku. c, Nguru. d, Pataka. e, Kotiate. f, Patiki.

2013, June 5 Litho. *Perf. 13¾x13½*

2467 A613 Sheet of 6 16.50 16.50
a.-b. 70c Either single 1.25 1.25
c. $1.40 multi 2.25 2.25
d. $1.90 multi 3.00 3.00
e. $2.40 multi 4.00 4.00
f. $2.90 multi 4.75 4.75

Self-Adhesive

Serpentine Die Cut 9½x10

2468 A613 Sheet of 6 16.50 16.50
a.-b. 70c Either single 1.25 1.25
c. $1.40 multi 2.25 2.25
d. $1.90 multi 3.00 3.00
e. $2.40 multi 4.00 4.00
f. $2.90 multi 4.75 4.75

Honey Bees A614

Designs: 70c, Bee collecting nectar. 140c, Bees at hive entrance. 190c, Bees on honeycomb. 240c, Apiarist collecting honey. 290c, Harvested honeycomb.

2013, July 3 *Perf. 14*

2469 A614 70c multi 1.25 1.25
2470 A614 140c multi 2.25 2.25
2471 A614 190c multi 3.00 3.00
2472 A614 240c multi 4.00 4.00
2473 A614 290c multi 4.75 4.75
a. Souvenir sheet of 5, #2469-2473 15.50 15.50
Nos. 2469-2473 (5) 15.25 15.25

Classic Travel Posters — A615

No. 2474 — Travel poster depicting: a, Woman in bathing suit, Napier Carnival. b, Fishing boat and fish. c, Tree fern. d, Rata blossom, Franz Josef Glacier. e, Fisherman in river. f, Wellington. g, Contrail of TEAL Airlines emblem going through mouth of Maori carving, mountains. h, Queenstown. i, Timaru by the Sea. j, Lake and mountains. k, Man reaching for hand, Tauranga. l, Kea. m, Bus touring the Southern Alps. n, Marlborough Sounds. o, Sheep drover on horse, sheep herd, dog. p, Basket weaver. q, Skier at Mt. Cook. r, Mt. Egmont. s, Maori statues, mountains, geyser. t, Swimmers at Blue Baths, Rotorua.

2013, Aug. 7 ***Perf. 14x14½***

2474 A615 Sheet of 20 22.00 22.00
a.-t. 70c Any single 1.10 1.10

Coastlines and Lighthouses — A616

Designs: 70c, Castlepoint. $1.40, Nugget Point. $1.90, East Cape. $2.40, Pencarrow Head. $2.90, Cape Campbell.

2013, Sept. 4 ***Perf. 13¼x13½***

2475 A616 70c multi 1.10 1.10
2476 A616 $1.40 multi 2.25 2.25
2477 A616 $1.90 multi 3.00 3.00
2478 A616 $2.40 multi 4.00 4.00
2479 A616 $2.90 multi 4.75 4.75
a. Souvenir sheet of 5, #2475-2479 15.50 15.50
Nos. 2475-2479 (5) 15.10 15.10

Birth of Prince George of Cambridge A617

Designs: 70c, Duke, Duchess of Cambridge, Prince George. $1.90, Duke of Cambridge holding Prince George. $2.40, Duke, Duchess of Cambridge, Prince George, diff. $2.90, Duchess of Cambridge holding Prince George.

2013, Sept. 11 ***Perf. 14¾***

2480 A617 70c multi 1.25 1.25
2481 A617 $1.90 multi 3.25 3.25
2482 A617 $2.40 multi 4.00 4.00
2483 A617 $2.90 multi 4.75 4.75
a. Horiz. strip of 4, #2480-2483 13.50 13.50
Nos. 2480-2483 (4) 13.25 13.25

A618

Christmas — A619

Designs: 70c, Child receiving gift. $1.40, Christmas lunch. $1.90, Children decorating Christmas tree. $2.40, Children playing cricket on beach. $2.90, People singing Christmas carols.

2013, Oct. 2 ***Perf. 14¼***

2484 A618 70c multi 1.25 1.25
2485 A618 $1.40 multi 2.40 2.40
2486 A618 $1.90 multi 3.25 3.25
2487 A618 $2.40 multi 4.00 4.00
2488 A618 $2.90 multi 5.00 5.00
Nos. 2484-2488 (5) 15.90 15.90

Self-Adhesive

Serpentine Die Cut 9½x10¼

2489 Sheet of 3 8.50
a. A619 70c multi 1.25 1.25
b. A619 $1.90 multi 3.25 3.25
c. A619 $2.40 multi 4.00 4.00
d. Booklet pane of 10 #2489a 12.50
e. Booklet pane of 10 #2489b 32.50
f. Booklet pane of 10 #2489c 40.00

No. 2489a doesn not have a blue airmail panel at the bottom of the stamp. No. 2489e sold for $17.10. No. 2489f sold for $21.60.

Premiere of Movie *The Hobbit: The Desolation of Smaug*
A620 A621

Designs: 70c, Thorin Oakenshield. $1.40, Gandalf. $1.90, Tauriel, horiz. $2.10, Bilbo Baggins, horiz. $2.40, Legolas Greenleaf. $2.90, Bard the Bowman.

2013, Nov. 1 ***Perf. 14½x14, 14x14½***

2490 A620 70c multi 1.25 1.25
a. Souvenir sheet of 1 1.50 1.50
2491 A620 $1.40 multi 2.40 2.40
a. Souvenir sheet of 1 3.00 3.00
2492 A620 $1.90 multi 3.25 3.25
a. Souvenir sheet of 1 4.00 4.00
2493 A620 $2.10 multi 3.50 3.50
a. Souvenir sheet of 1 4.50 4.50
2494 A620 $2.40 multi 4.00 4.00
a. Souvenir sheet of 1 5.00 5.00
2495 A620 $2.90 multi 5.00 5.00
a. Souvenir sheet of 1 6.25 6.25
Nos. 2490-2495 (6) 19.40 19.40

Self-Adhesive

Serpentine Die Cut 10¼x10, 10x10¼

2496 Sheet of 6 19.50
a. A621 70c multi 1.25 1.25
b. A621 $1.40 multi 2.40 2.40
c. A621 $1.90 multi 3.25 3.25
d. A621 $2.10 multi 3.50 3.50
e. A621 $2.40 multi 4.00 4.00
f. A621 $2.90 multi 5.00 5.00
g. Booklet pane of 10, #2496c-2496f, 4 #2496a, 2 #2496b 26.00

Nos. 2490a-2495a were sold as a set for $14.40.

New Year 2014 (Year of the Horse) — A622

Designs: 70c, Chinese character for "horse." $1.40, Horse. $1.90, Horse jumping over hurdle. $2.40, Rotorua Museum, Chinese lantern.

2014, Jan. 8 **Litho.** ***Perf. 13½x13***

2497 A622 70c multi 1.25 1.25
2498 A622 $1.40 multi 2.40 2.40
2499 A622 $1.90 multi 3.25 3.25
2500 A000 $2.40 multi 4.00 4.00
a. Souvenir sheet of 4, #2497-2500 11.00 11.00
Nos. 2497-2500 (4) 10.90 10.90

Seaweeds A623

Map of New Zealand and: 70c, Hormosira banksii. $1.40, Landsburgia quercifolia. $1.90, Caulerpa brownii. $2.40, Marginariella boryana. $2.90, Pterocladia lucida.

2014, Feb. 5 **Litho.** ***Perf. 14***

2501 A623 70c multi 1.25 1.25
a. Perf. 13¼x13½ 1.25 1.25
2502 A623 $1.40 multi 2.40 2.40
a. Perf. 13¼x13½ 2.40 2.40
2503 A623 $1.90 multi 3.25 3.25
a. Perf. 13¼x13½ 3.25 3.25
2504 A623 $2.40 multi 4.00 4.00
a. Perf. 13¼x13½ 4.00 4.00
2505 A623 $2.90 multi 5.00 5.00
a. Perf. 13¼x13½ 5.00 5.00
b. Souvenir sheet of 5, #2501a-2505a 16.00 16.00
Nos. 2501-2505 (5) 15.90 15.90

Houses A624

Designs: 70c, Colonial cottage. $1.40, Villa. $1.90, Californian bungalow. $2.40, Art Deco. $2.90, State house.

2014, Mar. 5 **Litho.** ***Perf. 14***

2506 A624 70c multi 1.25 1.25
2507 A624 $1.40 multi 2.40 2.40
2508 A624 $1.90 multi 3.25 3.25
2509 A624 $2.40 multi 4.00 4.00
2510 A624 $2.90 multi 5.00 5.00
a. Souvenir sheet of 5, #2506-2510 5.00 5.00
Nos. 2506-2510 (5) 15.90 15.90

World War II Poster Art — A625

Posters inscribed: No. 2511, Duty Calls the Youth of New Zealand. No. 2512, Help Farm for Victory. $1.40, The Air Force Needs Men! $1.90, Navy Week. $2.40, Army Week. $2.90, Taringa Whakarongo!

2014, Apr. 2 **Litho.** ***Perf. 14¾***

2511 A625 70c multi 1.25 1.25
a. Perf. 13 1.25 1.25
b. Booklet pane of 1, #2511a 1.25 —
2512 A625 70c multi 1.25 1.25
a. Perf. 13 1.25 1.25
b. Booklet pane of 1, #2512a 1.25 —
2513 A625 $1.40 multi 2.40 2.40
a. Perf. 13 2.40 2.40
b. Booklet pane of 1, #2513a 2.40 —
2514 A625 $1.90 multi 3.25 3.25
a. Perf. 13 3.25 3.25
b. Booklet pane of 1, #2514a 3.25 —
2515 A625 $2.40 multi 4.00 4.00
a. Perf. 13 4.00 4.00
b. Booklet pane of 1, #2515a 4.00 —
2516 A625 $2.90 multi 5.00 5.00
a. Perf. 13 5.00 5.00
b. Booklet pane of 1, #2516a 5.00 —
c. Booklet pane of 6, #2511a-2516a 17.50 —
Complete booklet, #2511b, 2512b, 2513b, 2514b, 2515b, 2516b, 2516c 35.00
Nos. 2511-2516 (6) 17.15 17.15

Complete booklet sold for $19.90.

Visit to New Zealand of Duke and Duchess of Cambridge and Prince George A626

Various photos of Duke, Duchess and Prince.

2014, Apr. 7 **Litho.** ***Perf. 14½***

2517 A626 70c multi 1.25 1.25
2518 A626 $2.40 multi 4.25 4.25

All Blacks Type of 2010

2014, May 7 **Litho.** ***Perf. 13½x13¼***

2519 A579 80c black 1.40 1.40
2520 A579 $2.50 black 4.25 4.25

Souvenir Sheet

2521 Sheet of 4, #2519, 2520, 2521a, 2521b 11.50 11.50
a. A579 80c black, 32x17mm, perf. 15x14½ 1.40 1.40
b. A579 $2.50 black, 32x17mm, perf. 15x14½ 4.25 4.25

Tourist Attractions A627

Designs: 60c, Franz Josef Glacier. $1.60, Moeraki Boulders. $2, Mount Taranaki. $2.50, Pancake Rocks. $3.60, Waikato River.

2014, May 7 **Litho.** ***Perf. 13¼***

2522 A627 60c multi 1.00 1.00
2523 A627 $1.60 multi 2.75 2.75
2524 A627 $2.50 multi 4.25 4.25
2525 A627 $3.60 multi 6.25 6.25
Nos. 2522-2525 (4) 14.25 14.25

Self-Adhesive

Serpentine Die Cut 10x9½

2526 A627 $2 multi 3.50 3.50
a. Booklet pane of 5 17.50
2527 A627 $2.50 multi 4.25 4.25
a. Pair, #2526-2527 7.75
b. Booklet pane of 5 21.50

Miniature Sheets

Personalized Stamps — A628

No. 2528: a, Wedding rings. b, Fern fiddlehead. c, "Love." d, Champagne flutes. e, Teddy bear. f, Pohutukawa flowers. g, Cupcake with birthday candles. h, Bunch of balloons.

No. 2529: a, Wedding rings. b, Fern fiddlehead. c, Champagne flutes. d, Pohutukawa flowers.

2014, May 7 **Litho.** ***Perf. 15x14½***

2528 A628 Sheet of 8 + 4 labels 11.50 11.50
a.-h. 80c Any single 1.40 1.40

2529 A628 Sheet of 4 + 2 labels 15.50 15.50
a.-b. $2 Either single 3.50 3.50
c.-d. $2.50 Either single 4.25 4.25

Miniature Sheets

Matariki — A629

Nos. 2530 and 2531 — Maori art depicting the story of Papatuanuku and Ranginui: a, Te Wehenga o Rangi Raua ko Papa, by Cliff Whiting, b, Rangi and Papa, by Phil Mokaraka Berry. c, Te Whakamamae o te Wehenga, by Kura Te Waru Rewiri. d, The Separtation of Rangi and Papa, by Fred Graham, horiz. e, The Children of Rangi and Papa, by Pauline Kahurangi Yearbury, horiz. f, The Ranginui Doorway, by Robert Jahnke, horiz.

2014, June 4 Litho. *Perf. 13½*

2530 A629 Sheet of 6 18.50 18.50
a.-b. 80c Either single 1.40 1.40
c. $1.40 multi 2.40 2.40
d. $2 multi 3.50 3.50
e. $2.50 multi 4.25 4.25
f. $3 multi 5.25 5.25

Self-Adhesive

Serpentine Die Cut 10x9½ (vert. stamps), 9½x10 (horiz. stamps)

2531 A629 Sheet of 6 18.50
a.-b. 80c Either single 1.40 1.40
c. $1.40 multi 2.40 2.40
d. $2 multi 3.50 3.50
e. $2.50 multi 4.25 4.25
f. $3 multi 5.25 5.25

Miniature Sheet

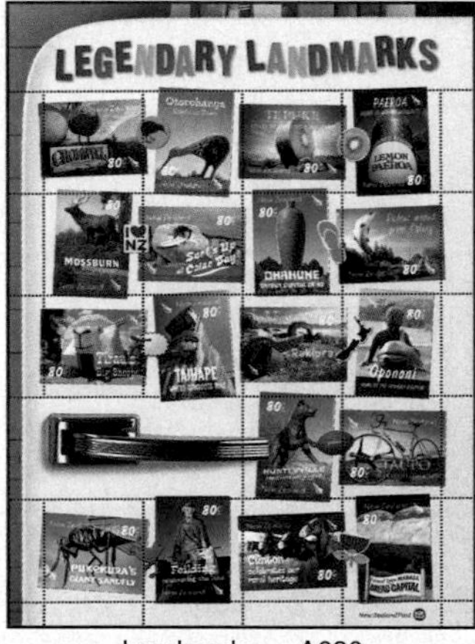

Landmarks — A630

No. 2532: a, Sculptures of peaches, Cromwell. b, Kiwi statue, Otorohanga. c, Kiwi fruit slice statue, Te Puke. d, Lemon and Paeroa bottle statue, Paeroa. e, Deer statue, Mossburn. f, Surfer statue, Colac Bay. g, Carrot statue, Ohakune. h, Fish statue, Rakaia. i, Sheep building, Tirau. j, Gumboot sculpture, Taihape. k, Chain sculpture, Raikura. l, Statue of boy and bottlenose dolphin, Opononi. m, Dog statue, Hunterville. n, Bicycle sculpture, Taupo. o, Sandfly sculpture, Pukekura. p, Sculpture of man and dog, Feilding. q, Clydesdale horses sculptures, Clinton. r, Sculpture of bread loaves, Manaia.

2014, July 2 Litho. *Perf. 14½*

2532 A630 Sheet of 18 + label 25.50 25.50
a.-r. 80c Any single 1.40 1.40

World War I, Cent. — A631

Designs: No. 2533, Lord Kitchener. No. 2534, Poster for military training. No. 2535, Announcement of war. No. 2536, Melville Mirfin in military uniform. No. 2537, Photograph of Mirfin family. No. 2538, Departure of troop ships. No. 2539, Training camp. No. 2540, Street scene, Karaka Bay. No. 2541, Letter from Mirfin from Samoa. No. 2542, New Zealand soldiers in Egypt.

2014, July 29 Litho. *Perf. 14½*

2533 A631 80c multi 1.40 1.40
a. Booklet pane of 1 2.00 —
2534 A631 80c multi 1.40 1.40
a. Booklet pane of 1 2.00 —
2535 A631 80c multi 1.40 1.40
a. Booklet pane of 1 2.00 —
2536 A631 80c multi 1.40 1.40
a. Booklet pane of 1 2.00 —
2537 A631 80c multi 1.40 1.40
a. Booklet pane of 1 2.00 —
2538 A631 80c multi 1.40 1.40
a. Booklet pane of 1 2.00 —
b. Booklet pane of 6, #2533-2538 12.00 —
c. Block of 6, #2533-2538 8.50 8.50
d. Souvenir sheet, #2533-2538 8.50 8.50
2539 A631 $2 multi 3.50 3.50
a. Booklet pane of 1 5.00 —
2540 A631 $2 multi 3.50 3.50
a. Booklet pane of 1 5.00 —
b. Horiz. pair, #2539-2540 7.00 7.00
2541 A631 $2.50 multi 4.25 4.25
a. Booklet pane of 1 6.25 —
2542 A631 $2.50 multi 4.25 4.25
a. Booklet pane of 1 6.25 —
b. Booklet pane of 4, #2539-2542 22.50 —
Complete booklet, #2533a, 2534a, 2535a, 2536a, 2537a. 2538a, 2538b, 2539a, 2540a, 2541a, 2542a, 2542b 69.00
c. Horiz. pair, #2541-2542 8.50 8.50
d. Souvenir sheet of 4, #2539-2542 15.50 15.50
e. Souvenir sheet of 10, #2533-2542 24.00 24.00
f. Souvenir sheet of 3, #2538, 2539, 2542 12.50 12.50
Nos. 2533-2542 (10) 23.90 23.90

Issued: No. 2542f, 11/14. Baypex 2014 National Stamp Exhibition, Hawke's Bay (No. 2542f). No. 2542f sold for $7.80 with surtax going to the Philatelic Trust. Complete booklet sold for $39.90. See Nos. 2574-2683, 2633-2642.

Endangered Seabirds — A632

Designs: 80c, Antipodean albatross. $1.40, New Zealand fairy tern. $2, Chatham Island shag. $2.50, Black-billed gull. $3, Chatham Island taiko.

2014, Sept. 3 Litho. *Perf. 14*

2543 A632 80c multi 1.25 1.25
a. Perf. 13½x13¼ 1.25 1.25
2544 A632 $1.40 multi 2.25 2.25
a. Perf. 13½x13¼ 2.25 2.25
2545 A632 $2 multi 3.25 3.25
a. Perf. 13½x13¼ 3.25 3.25
2546 A632 $2.50 multi 4.00 4.00
a. Perf. 13½x13¼ 4.00 4.00
2547 A632 $3 multi 4.75 4.75
a. Perf. 13½x13¼ 4.75 4.75
b. Souvenir sheet of 5, #2543a, 2544a, 2545a, 2546a, 2547a 15.50 15.50
Nos. 2543-2547 (5) 15.50 15.50

The silhouettes of birds were printed with thermochromic ink, which disappeared when warmed.

A633

Christmas — A634

Children in Nativity play depicting: 80c, Mary and Jesus. $1.40, Joseph. $2, Wise Man. $2.50, Angel. $3, Shepherd.

2014, Oct. 1 Litho. *Perf. 14*

2548 A633 80c multi 1.25 1.25
2549 A633 $1.40 multi 2.25 2.25
2550 A633 $2 multi 3.25 3.25
2551 A633 $2.50 multi 4.00 4.00
2552 A633 $3 multi 4.75 4.75
Nos. 2548-2552 (5) 15.50 15.50

Self-Adhesive

Serpentine Die Cut 10x9½

2553 Sheet of 3 8.50
a. A634 80c multi 1.25 1.25
b. A634 $2 multi 3.25 3.25
c. A634 $2.50 multi 4.00 4.00
d. Booklet pane of 10 #2553a 12.50
e. Booklet pane of 10 #2553b 32.50
f. Booklet pane of 10 #2553c 40.00

Nos. 2553b and 2553c are airmail. No. 2553e sold for $18. No. 2553f sold for $22.50.

Souvenir Sheet

Premiere of Movie *The Hobbit: The Battle of the Five Armies* — A635

Design: Characters from movie in costume.

2014, Oct. 15 Litho. *Perf. 14¾x14½*

2554 A635 Sheet of 2 5.25 5.25
a. 80c multi 1.25 1.25
b. $2.50 multi 4.00 4.00

Nos. 2554a and 2554b were each available in sheets of 20 + 20 personalizable labels.

Premiere of Movie *The Hobbit: The Battle of the Five Armies*
A636 A637

Designs: 80c, Smaug. $1.40, Bilbo Baggins. $2, Gandalf, horiz. $2.10, Thranduil, horiz. Nos. 2559, 2562e, Bard the Bowman. $3, Tauriel. No. 2561, Door to Bag End.

Perf. 14½x14, 14x14½

2014, Nov. 12 Litho.

2555 A636 80c multi 1.25 1.25
a. Souvenir sheet of 1 1.60 1.60
2556 A636 $1.40 multi 2.25 2.25
a. Souvenir sheet of 1 2.75 2.75
2557 A636 $2 multi 3.00 3.00
a. Souvenir sheet of 1 4.00 4.00
2558 A636 $2.10 multi 3.25 3.25
a. Souvenir sheet of 1 4.25 4.25
2559 A636 $2.50 multi 4.00 4.00
a. Souvenir sheet of 1 5.00 5.00
2560 A636 $3 multi 4.75 4.75
a. Souvenir sheet of 1 5.75 5.75

Litho. & Thermography

2561 A636 $2.50 multi 4.00 4.00
a. Souvenir sheet of 1 5.00 5.00
Nos. 2555-2561 (7) 22.50 22.50

Self-Adhesive

Litho.

Serpentine Die Cut 10¼x10, 10x10¼

2562 Sheet of 6 18.50
a. A637 80c multi 1.25 1.25
b. A637 $1.40 multi 2.25 2.25
c. A637 $2 multi 3.00 3.00
d. A637 $2.10 multi 3.25 3.25
e. A637 $2.50 multi 4.00 4.00
f. A637 $3 multi 4.75 4.75
g. Booklet pane of 10, #2562c-2562f, 4 #2562a, 2 #2562b 24.50

Particles of wood from the movie set are embedded in the thermographic ink on No. 2561. Nos. 2555a-2561a sold as a set for $17.80.

New Year 2015 (Year of the Sheep) — A638

Designs: 80c, Chinese character for "sheep." $1.40, Sheep in paper-cut design. $2, Sheep and fence, New Zealand. $2.50, Church of the Good Shepherd, Tekapo, and Chinese kite.

2015, Jan. 14 Litho. *Perf. 14*

2563 A638 80c multi 1.25 1.25
a. Perf. 13¼x13½ 1.25 1.25
2564 A638 $1.40 multi 2.10 2.10
a. Perf. 13¼x13½ 2.10 2.10
2565 A638 $2 multi 3.00 3.00
a. Perf. 13¼x13½ 3.00 3.00
2566 A638 $2.50 multi 3.75 3.75
a. Perf. 13¼x13½ 3.75 3.75
b. Souvenir sheet of 4, #2563a-2566a 10.50 10.50
Nos. 2563-2566 (4) 10.10 10.10

Air New Zealand, 75th Anniv. — A639

Designs: 80c, Short S-30 Flying Boat on first Auckland-Sydney flight, 1940. $1.40, Airplanes, Stewardess Margaret Gould, child, pilot, 1948. $2, Tasman Empire Airways Ltd. 1951-60 Coral Route baggage label. $2.50, Children and flight attendant, 1977. $3, Air New Zealand Boeing 787-9 taking off.

2015, Jan. 14 Litho. *Perf. 14¾*

2567 A639 80c multi 1.25 1.25
2568 A639 $1.40 multi 2.10 2.10
2569 A639 $2 multi 3.00 3.00
2570 A639 $2.50 multi 3.75 3.75
2571 A639 $3 multi 4.50 4.50
a. Souvenir sheet of 5, #2567-2571 15.00 15.00
Nos. 2567-2571 (5) 14.60 14.60

Souvenir Sheet

Treaty of Waitangi, 175th Anniv. — A640

Perf. 14x14½

2015, Feb. 4 Litho. Wmk. 387

2572 A640 $2.50 multi 3.75 3.75

Miniature Sheet

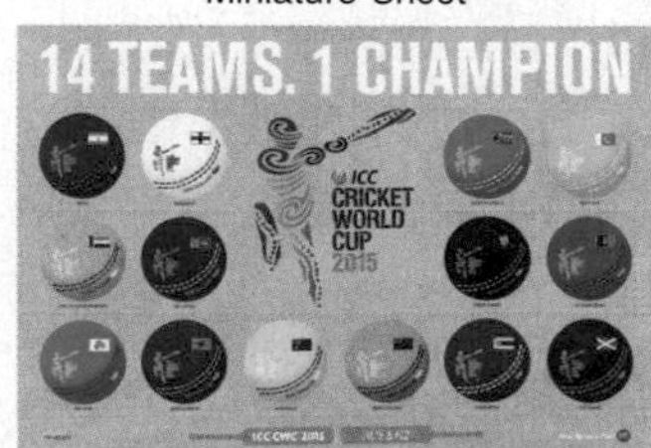

2015 ICC Cricket World Cup Tournament, Australia and New Zealand — A641

No. 2573 — Tournament emblem on cricket ball with flag of competing team: a, India (dark blue ball, red stitching). b, England (white ball, red stitching). c, South Africa (green ball, orange stitching). d, Pakistan (yellow green ball, yellow stitching). e, United Arab Emirates (gray ball, red stitching). f, Sri Lanka (dark blue ball, yellow stitching). g, West Indies (red violet ball, orange stitching). h, Afghanistan (blue ball, red stitching). i, Ireland (green ball, blue stitching). j, Bangladesh (red ball, green stitching). k, Australia (yellow ball, black stitching). l,

New Zealand (gray ball, black stitching). m, Zimbabwe (red ball, white stitching). n, Scotland (deep blue ball, blue stitching).

Unwmk.

2015, Feb. 4 Litho. ***Die Cut***

Self-Adhesive

2573 A641 Sheet of 14 17.50
a.-n. 80c Any single 1.25 1.25

World War I, Cent. Type of 2014

Designs: No. 2574, Evelyn Brooke, nurse. No. 2575, Postcard from Egypt. No. 2576, Landing at Anzac Cove. No. 2577, Chunuk Bair. No. 2578, Casualties return. No. 2579, Marquette Memorial. No. 2580, The Sapper and His Donkey, painting by Horace Moore-Jones. No. 2581, War census poster. No. 2582, Hospital ship Maheno. No. 2583, An Enduting Bond, poster by Otho Hewett.

2015, Mar. 23 Litho. ***Perf. 14½***

2574 A631 80c multi 1.25 1.25
a. Booklet pane of 1 1.75 —
2575 A631 80c multi 1.25 1.25
a. Booklet pane of 1 1.75 —
2576 A631 80c multi 1.25 1.25
a. Booklet pane of 1 1.75 —
2577 A631 80c multi 1.25 1.25
a. Booklet pane of 1 1.75 —
2578 A631 80c multi 1.25 1.25
a. Booklet pane of 1 1.75 —
2579 A631 80c multi 1.25 1.25
a. Booklet pane of 1 1.75 —
b. Booklet pane of 6, #2574-2579 10.50 —
c. Block of 6, #2574-2579 7.50 7.50
d. Souvenir sheet of 6, #2574-2579 7.50 7.50
2580 A631 $2 multi 3.00 3.00
a. Booklet pane of 1 4.50 —
2581 A631 $2 multi 3.00 3.00
a. Booklet pane of 1 4.50 —
b. Horiz. pair, #2580-2581 6.00 6.00
2582 A631 $2.50 multi 3.75 3.75
a. Booklet pane of 1 5.50 —
b. Souvenir sheet of 3, #2576, 2580, 2582 7.25 7.25
2583 A631 $2.50 multi 3.75 3.75
a. Booklet pane of 1 5.50 —
b. Booklet pane of 4, #2580-2583 20.00 —
Complete booklet, #2574a, 2575a, 2576a, 2577a, 2578a, 2579a, 2579b, 2580a, 2581a, 2582a, 2583a, 2583b 61.00
c. Horiz. pair, #2582-2583 7.50 7.50
d. Souvenir sheet of 4, #2580-2583 13.50 13.50
e. Souvenir sheet of 10, #2574-2583 21.00 21.00
Nos. 2574-2583 (10) 21.00 21.00

Complete booklet sold for $39.90.
Issued: No. 2582b, 10/23/15. 2015, Capital Stamp Show, Wellington, (No. 2582b).

Australian and New Zealand Army Corps, Cent. — A642

Soldier and bugler with bugler facing: 80c, Right. $2, Left.

2015, Apr. 7 Litho. ***Perf. 14½x14***

2584 A642 80c multi 1.25 1.25
2585 A642 $2 multi 3.00 3.00
a. Souvenir sheet of 2, #2584-2585 4.25 4.25

See Australia Nos. 4271-4274.

Shells — A643

Designs: 80c, Silver paua. $1.40, Scott's murex. $2, Golden volute. $2.50, Fan shell. $3, Opal top shell.

2015, May 6 Litho. ***Perf. 14***

2586 A643 80c multi 1.25 1.25
a. Perf. 13¼x13½ 1.25 1.25
2587 A643 $1.40 multi 2.10 2.10
a. Perf. 13¼x13½ 2.10 2.10
2588 A643 $2 multi 3.00 3.00
a. Perf. 13¼x13½ 3.00 3.00
2589 A643 $2.50 multi 3.75 3.75
a. Perf. 13¼x13½ 3.75 3.75
2590 A643 $3 multi 4.50 4.50
a. Perf. 13¼x13½ 4.50 4.50
b. Souvenir sheet of 5, #2586a-2590a 15.00 15.00
Nos. 2586-2590 (5) 14.60 14.60

Miniature Sheets

Matariki — A644

Nos. 2591 and 2592 — Kowhaiwhai: a, Digiwhaiwhai, by Johnson Witehira. b, Tenei Au Tenei Au, by Kura Te Waru Rewiri. c, Haki, by Kylie Tiuka. d, Banner Moon, by Buck Nin, horiz. e, Part of Te Hatete o Te Reo Series, by Ngatai Taepa, horiz. f, Taona Marama, by Sandy Adsett, horiz.

2015, June 3 Litho. ***Perf. 14***

2591 A644 Sheet of 6 14.50 14.50
a.-b. 80c Either single 1.10 1.10
c. $1.40 multi 1.90 1.90
d. $2 multi 2.75 2.75
e. $2.50 multi 3.50 3.50
f. $3 multi 4.00 4.00

Self-Adhesive

Serpentine Die Cut 10x9½ (vert. stamps), 9½x10 (horiz. stamps)

2592 A644 Sheet of 6 14.50 14.50
a.-b. 80c Either single 1.10 1.10
c. $1.40 multi 1.90 1.90
d. $2 multi 2.75 2.75
e. $2.50 multi 3.50 3.50
f. $3 multi 4.00 4.00

Miniature Sheet

Popular New Zealand Foods — A645

No. 2593: a, Aspargaus rolls. b, Kiwi onion dip. c, Puha and pork. d, Bluff oyster. e, Meat loaf. f, Hokey pokey ice cream. g, Shrimp cocktail. h, Cheese rolls. i, Pikelets. j, Lamington cake. k, Mince on toast. l, Whitebait fritters. m, Curried egg. n, Saveloy sausage and sauce. o, Bacon and egg pie. p, Pavlova. q, Fairy bread. r, Mouse trap.

2015, July 1 Litho. ***Perf. 14¼x14¾***

2593 A645 Sheet of 18 20.00 20.00
a.-r. 80c Any single 1.10 1.10

UNESCO World Heritage Sites — A646

Designs: 80c, Emerald Lakes, Tongariro National Park. $1.40, Franz Josef Glacier, Te Wahipounamu-South West New Zealand. $2, Enderby Island, New Zealand Sub-Antarctic Islands. $2.20, Mount Ngauruhoe, Tongariro National Park. $2.50, Lake Mackenzie, Te Wahipounamu-South West New Zealand. $3, Campbell Island, New Zealand Sub-Antarctic Islands.

2015, Aug. 5 Litho. ***Perf. 14***

2594 A646 80c multi 1.00 1.00
2595 A646 $1.40 multi 1.75 1.75
2596 A646 $2 multi 2.50 2.50
2597 A646 $2.20 multi 2.75 2.75
2598 A646 $2.50 multi 3.25 3.25
2599 A646 $3 multi 3.75 3.75
a. Souvenir sheet of 6, #2594-2599 15.00 15.00
Nos. 2594-2599 (6) 15.00 15.00

Parliament House, Wellington A647

2015, Aug. 14 Litho. ***Perf. 14½***

2600 A647 $2.50 multi 3.25 3.25

See Australia Nos. 4331-4333, Singapore Nos.

All Blacks Rugby Team Uniform Shirt — A648

Litho. With Fabric Affixed

2015, Sept. 2 ***Perf. 13¼x13½***

2601 A648 $15 multi 19.00 19.00

No. 2601 was sold individually in a folder.

Queen Elizabeth II, Longest-Reigning British Monarch — A649

Photograph of Queen Elizabeth II from: No. 2602, 1950s. No. 2603, 1960s. $1.40, 1970s. $2, 1980s. $2.20, 1990s. $2.50, 2000s. $3, 2010s.

2015, Oct. 7 Litho. ***Perf. 14¾x14¼***

2602 A649 80c multi 1.10 1.10
2603 A649 80c multi 1.10 1.10
2604 A649 $1.40 multi 1.90 1.90
2605 A649 $2 multi 2.75 2.75
2606 A649 $2.20 multi 3.00 3.00
2607 A649 $2.50 multi 3.50 3.50
2608 A649 $3 multi 4.00 4.00
a. Souvenir sheet of 7, #2602-2608 17.50 17.50
Nos. 2602-2608 (7) 17.35 17.35

Christmas
A650 A651

Stained-glass windows: 80c, Angel, St. Mark's Church, Carterton. $1.40, Dove, St. Aidan's Anglican Church, Remuera. $2, Madonna and Child, St. Mary's-in-Holy Trinity Cathedral, Parnell. $2.50, Pohutukawa flower, Christchurch Hospital Nurses Memorial Chapel. $3, Wise Men, St. Benedict's Church, Auckland.

2015, Nov. 4 Litho. ***Perf. 14***

2609 A650 80c multi 1.10 1.10
2610 A650 $1.40 multi 1.90 1.90
2611 A650 $2 multi 2.75 2.75
2612 A650 $2.50 multi 3.50 3.50
2613 A650 $3 multi 4.00 4.00
Nos. 2609-2613 (5) 13.25 13.25

Miniature Sheet

Translucent Paper

2614 Sheet of 5 13.50 13.50
a. A650 80c multi 1.10 1.10
b. A650 $1.40 multi 1.90 1.90
c. A650 $2 multi 2.75 2.75
d. A650 $2.50 multi 3.50 3.50
e. A650 $3 multi 4.00 4.00

Self-Adhesive

Serpentine Die Cut 9½x10

2615 A651 80c multi 1.10 1.10
a. Booklet pane of 10 9.00
2616 A651 $2 multi 2.75 2.75
a. Booklet pane of 10 + 10 etiquettes 27.50
2617 A651 $2.50 multi 3.50 3.50
a. Booklet pane of 10 + 10 etiquettes 35.00
b. Horiz. strip of 3, #2615-2617 7.50
Nos. 2615-2617 (3) 7.35 7.35

No. 2616a sold for $18. No. 2617a sold for $22.50.

New Year 2016 (Year of the Monkey) — A652

Designs: 80c, Chinese character for "monkey." $1.40, Monkey in paper-cut design. $2, Monkey hanging from branch. $2.50, Bar-tailed godwit and Monkey Island.

2016, Jan. 13 Litho. ***Perf. 14***

2618 A652 80c multi 1.10 1.10
a. Perf. 13¼x13½ 1.10 1.10
2619 A652 $1.40 multi 1.90 1.90
a. Perf. 13¼x13½ 1.90 1.90
2620 A652 $2 multi 2.60 2.60
a. Perf. 13¼x13½ 2.60 2.60
2621 A652 $2.50 multi 3.25 3.25
a. Perf. 13¼x13½ 3.25 3.25
b. Souvenir sheet of 4, #2618a-2621a 9.00 9.00
Nos. 2618-2621 (4) 8.85 8.85

Returned and Services' Association, Cent. A653

Inscription: 80c, The returned. $1.40, The poppy. $2, Supporting those who served. $2.20, At the RSA. $2.50, The badge. $3, We will remember them.

2016, Feb. 3 Litho. ***Perf. 14¼x14¾***

2622 A653 80c multi 1.10 1.10
2623 A653 $1.40 multi 1.90 1.90
2624 A653 $2 multi 2.75 2.75
2625 A653 $2.20 multi 3.00 3.00
2626 A653 $2.50 multi 3.50 3.50
2627 A653 $3 multi 4.00 4.00
a. Souvenir sheet of 6, #2622-2627 16.50 16.50
Nos. 2622-2627 (6) 16.25 16.25

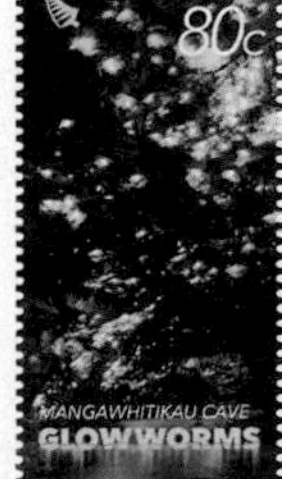

Glowworms
A654 A655

Glowworms from: 80c, Mangawhitikau Cave. $1.40, Nikau Cave. $2, Ruakuri Cave. $2.50, Waipu Cave.

2016, Mar. 2 Litho. *Perf. 14½x14*

2628	A654 80c multi		1.10	1.10
2629	A654 $1.40 multi		1.90	1.90
2630	A654 $2 multi		2.75	2.75
2631	A654 $2.50 multi		3.50	3.50
a.	Souvenir sheet of 4, #2628-2631		9.25	9.25
	Nos. 2628-2631 (4)		9.25	9.25

Self-Adhesive

Serpentine Die Cut 10x9½

2632	A655 $2 multi	2.75	2.75
a.	Booklet pane of 10	27.50	

No. 2632 was issued with backing paper with and without printing on the reverse.

World War I, Cent. Type of 2014

Designs: No. 2633, Solomon Isaacs, member of New Zealand Expeditionary Force. No. 2634, Pioneer Battalion. No. 2635, Inscriptions in Arras Tunnels. No. 2636, Newspaper story announcing introduction of conscription. No. 2637, New Zealand troops in the Middle East. No. 2638, Troops in trenches during the Somme Offensive. No. 2639, First ANZAC Day. No. 2640, Soldiers away from the front at Bloomsbury Square headquarters of New Zealand Expeditionary Force. No. 2641, Battle of Jutland. No. 2642, The home front (Kaikoura, New Zealand Post Office).

2016, Apr. 6 Litho. *Perf. 14½*

2633	A631 80c multi	1.10	1.10
a.	Booklet pane of 1	1.60	—
2634	A631 80c multi	1.10	1.10
a.	Booklet pane of 1	1.60	—
2635	A631 80c multi	1.10	1.10
a.	Booklet pane of 1	1.60	—
2636	A631 80c multi	1.10	1.10
a.	Booklet pane of 1	1.60	—
2637	A631 80c multi	1.10	1.10
a.	Booklet pane of 1	1.60	—
2638	A631 80c multi	1.10	1.10
a.	Booklet pane of 1	1.60	—
b.	Booklet pane of 6, #2633-2638	9.50	—
c.	Block of 6, #2633-2638	6.60	6.60
d.	Souvenir sheet, #2633-2638	6.60	6.60
2639	A631 $2 multi	2.75	2.75
a.	Booklet pane of 1	4.00	—
2640	A631 $2 multi	2.75	2.75
a.	Booklet pane of 1	4.00	—
b.	Horiz. pair, #2639-2640	5.50	5.50
2641	A631 $2.50 multi	3.50	3.50
a.	Booklet pane of 1	5.00	—
2642	A631 $2.50 multi	3.50	3.50
a.	Booklet pane of 1	5.00	—
b.	Booklet pane of 4, #2639-2642	17.50	—
	Complete booklet, #2633a, 2634a, 2635a, 2636a, 2637a. 2638a, 2638b, 2639a, 2640a, 2641a, 2642a, 2642b	55.00	
c.	Horiz. pair, #2641-2642	7.00	7.00
d.	Souvenir sheet of 4, #2639-2642	12.50	12.50
e.	Souvenir sheet of 10, #2633-2642	19.50	19.50
	Nos. 2633-2642 (10)	19.10	19.10

POSTAL-FISCAL STAMPS

In 1881 fiscal stamps of New Zealand of denominations over one shilling were made acceptable for postal duty. Values for canceled stamps are for postal cancellations. Denominations above £5 appear to have been used primarily for fiscal purposes.

Queen Victoria
PF1 PF2

Perf. 11, 12, 12½

1882 Typo. Wmk. 62

AR1	PF1	2sh blue	125.00	20.00
AR2	PF1	2sh6p dk brown	125.00	20.00
AR3	PF1	3sh violet	225.00	25.00
AR4	PF1	4sh brown vio	325.00	40.00
AR5	PF1	4sh red brn	275.00	40.00
AR6	PF1	5sh green	325.00	40.00
AR7	PF1	6sh rose	500.00	65.00
AR8	PF1	7sh ultra	550.00	150.00
AR9	PF1	7sh6p ol gray	1,500.	500.00
AR10	PF1	8sh dull blue	525.00	125.00
AR11	PF1	9sh org red	900.00	300.00
AR12	PF1	10sh red brn	350.00	75.00

1882-90

AR13	PF2	15sh dk grn	1,500.	400.00
AR15	PF2	£1 rose	700.00	150.00
AR16	PF2	25sh blue		—
AR17	PF2	30sh brown		—
AR18	PF2	£1 15sh yellow		—
AR19	PF2	£2 purple		—

PF3 PF4

AR20	PF3	£2 10sh red brn		—
AR21	PF3	£3 yel green		—
AR22	PF3	£3 10sh rose		—
AR23	PF3	£4 ultra		—
AR24	PF3	£4 10sh ol brn		—
AR25	PF3	£5 dark blue		—
AR26	PF4	£6 org red		—
AR27	PF4	£7 brn red		—
AR28	PF4	£8 green		—
AR29	PF4	£9 rose		—
AR30	PF4	£10 blue		—
AR30A	PF4	£20 yellow	—	—

No. AR31

With "COUNTERPART" at Bottom

1901

AR31	PF1 2sh6p brown	300.00	*400.00*

Perf. 11, 14, 14½x14

1903-15 Wmk. 61

AR32	PF1	2sh blue ('07)	80.00	12.00
AR33	PF1	2sh6p brown	80.00	12.00
AR34	PF1	3sh violet	175.00	14.00
AR35	PF1	4sh brn red	200.00	30.00
AR36	PF1	5sh grn ('06)	225.00	30.00
AR37	PF1	6sh rose	375.00	50.00
AR38	PF1	7sh dull blue	400.00	80.00
AR39	PF1	7sh6p ol gray ('06)	1,500.	400.00
AR40	PF1	8sh dk blue	450.00	75.00
AR41	PF1	9sh dl org ('06)	600.00	200.00
AR42	PF1	10sh dp clar	250.00	50.00
AR43	PF2	15sh blue grn	1,350.	350.00
AR44	PF2	£1 rose	500.00	150.00

Perf. 14½

AR45	PF2	£2 dp vio ('25)	600.00	150.00
a.		Perf. 14	700.00	150.00
		Nos. AR32-AR45 (14)	6,785.	1,603.

For overprints see Cook Islands Nos. 67-71.

Coat of Arms — PF5

1931-39 Wmk. 61 *Perf. 14*

Type PF5 (Various Frames)

AR46	1sh3p lemon	30.00	40.00
AR47	1sh3p org ('32)	8.00	9.00
AR48	2sh6p brown	16.00	5.25
AR49	4sh dull red ('32)	17.00	7.50
AR50	5sh green	21.00	12.50
AR51	6sh brt rose ('32)	37.50	15.00
AR52	7sh gray blue	32.50	25.00
AR53	7sh6p olive gray ('32)	75.00	92.50
AR54	8sh dark blue	50.00	37.50
AR55	9sh brn org	52.50	32.50
AR56	10sh dark car	27.50	10.50
AR57	12sh6p brn vio ('35)	250.00	250.00
AR58	15sh ol grn ('32)	70.00	42.50
AR59	£1 pink ('32)	75.00	22.50
AR60	25sh turq bl ('38)	550.00	600.00
AR61	30sh dk brn ('36)	300.00	200.00
AR62	35sh yel ('37)	6,000.	*7,500.*
AR63	£2 vio ('33)	400.00	70.00
AR64	£2 10sh dk red ('36)	400.00	*550.00*
AR65	£3 lt grn ('32)	400.00	210.00
AR66	£3 10sh rose ('39)	2,250.	2,250.
AR67	£4 light blue	400.00	175.00
AR68	£4 10sh dk ol gray ('39)	2,500.	2,500.
AR69	£5 dk blue ('32)	400.00	100.00

For overprints see Cook Islands Nos. 80-83.

No. AR62 Surcharged in Black

1939 *Perf. 14*

AR70	PF5 35sh on 35sh yel	500.00	350.00

Type PF5 Surcharged in Black

1940

AR71	3sh6p on 3sh6p dl green	28.50	21.00
AR72	5sh6p on 5sh6p rose lilac	60.00	57.50
AR73	11sh on 11sh pale yellow	125.00	150.00
AR74	22sh on 22sh scar	275.00	350.00
	Nos. AR71-AR74 (4)	488.50	578.50

Type of 1931

1940-58 Wmk. 253 *Perf. 14*

Type PF5 (Various Frames)

AR75	1sh3p orange	5.75	.60
AR76	2sh6p brown	5.75	.60
AR77	4sh dull red	6.75	.60
AR78	5sh green	11.50	.90
AR79	6sh brt rose	20.00	4.00
AR80	7sh gray bl	20.00	6.75
AR81	7sh6p ol gray ('50)	70.00	*70.00*
AR82	8sh dk blue	45.00	25.00
AR83	9sh orange ('46)	50.00	30.00
AR84	10sh dk carmine	25.00	3.25
AR85	15sh olive ('45)	55.00	20.00
AR86	£1 pink('45)	29.00	8.50
a.	Perf. 14x13½ ('58)	32.50	15.00
AR87	25sh blue ('46)	500.00	*550.00*
AR88	30sh choc ('46)	250.00	200.00
AR89	£2 violet ('46)	100.00	60.00
AR90	£2 10sh dk red ('51)	400.00	*525.00*
AR91	£3 lt grn ('46)	150.00	125.00
AR92	£3 10sh rose ('48)	2,250.	*2,500.*
AR93	£4 lt blue ('52)	150.00	160.00
AR94	£5 dk blue ('40)	175.00	150.00

Type PF5 Surcharged in Black

1942-45 Wmk. 253

AR95	3sh6p on 3sh6p grn	12.50	8.00
AR96	5sh6p on 5sh6p rose lil ('44)	26.00	8.50
AR97	11sh on 11sh yel	67.50	52.50
AR98	22sh on 22sh car ('45)	325.00	*275.00*
	Nos. AR95-AR98 (4)	431.00	344.00

Catalogue values for unused stamps in this section, from this point to the end of the section, are for Never Hinged items.

Type of 1931 Redrawn Surcharged in Black

1953 Typo.

AR99	PF5 3sh6p on 3sh6p green	32.50	35.00

Denomination of basic stamp is in small, sans-serif capitals without period after "sixpence."

Type of 1931

1955 Wmk. 253 *Perf. 14*

Denomination in Black

AR100	PF5 1sh3p orange	2.75	.90

1956 Denomination in Blue

AR101	PF5 1sh3p orange yel	17.50	14.50

For decimal-currency postage stamps of design No. PF5, see Nos. 404A-404D, 404Ba, 404Ca, 404Da.

SEMI-POSTAL STAMPS

Nurse — SP1

Inscribed: "Help Stamp out Tuberculosis, 1929"

Wmk. 61

1929, Dec. 11 Typo. *Perf. 14*

B1	SP1 1p + 1p scarlet	12.50	*20.00*

Nurse — SP2

Inscribed: "Help Promote Health, 1930"

1930, Oct. 29

B2	SP2 1p + 1p scarlet	30.00	*45.00*

Boy — SP3

1931, Oct. 31 *Perf. 14½x14*

B3	SP3 1p + 1p scarlet	100.00	90.00
B4	SP3 2p + 1p dark blue	100.00	75.00

Hygeia, Goddess of Health — SP4

1932, Nov. 18 Engr. *Perf. 14*

B5	SP4 1p + 1p carmine	22.50	*30.00*
	Never hinged	55.00	

Road to Health — SP5

1933, Nov. 8

B6	SP5 1p + 1p carmine	15.00	*20.00*
	Never hinged	35.00	

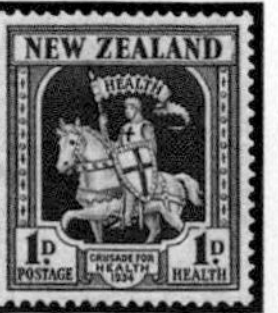

Crusader — SP6

1934, Oct. 25 *Perf. 14x13½*

B7	SP6 1p + 1p dark carmine	12.50	*20.00*
	Never hinged	25.00	

Child at Bathing Beach — SP7

1935, Sept. 30 ***Perf. 11***

B8 SP7 1p + 1p scarlet 3.00 3.25
Never hinged 5.00

Catalogue values for unused stamps in this section, from this point to the end of the section, are for Never Hinged items.

Anzac — SP8

1936, Apr. 27

B9 SP8 ½p + ½p green .70 *2.00*
B10 SP8 1p + 1p red .70 *1.60*

21st anniv. of Anzac landing at Gallipoli.

"Health" SP9

1936, Nov. 2

B11 SP9 1p + 1p red 2.00 *4.25*

Boy Hiker — SP10

1937, Oct. 1

B12 SP10 1p + 1p red 3.00 *4.00*

Children at Play — SP11

Perf. 14x13½

1938, Oct. 1 **Wmk. 253**

B13 SP11 1p + 1p red 6.25 3.25

Children at Play — SP12

Black Surcharge

1939, Oct. 16 **Wmk. 61** ***Perf. 11½***

B14 SP12 1p on ½p + ½p grn 5.00 5.00
B15 SP12 2p on 1p + 1p scar 5.00 5.00

1940, Oct. 1

B16 SP12 1p + ½p green 16.00 17.50
B17 SP12 2p + 1p org brown 16.00 17.50

The surtax was used to help maintain children's health camps.

Semi-Postal Stamps of 1940, Overprinted in Black "1941"

1941, Oct. 4 ***Perf. 11½***

B18 SP12 1p + ½p green 3.00 *3.50*
B19 SP12 2p + 1p org brown 3.00 *3.50*

Children in Swing — SP13

1942, Oct. 1 **Engr.**

B20 SP13 1p + ½p green .35 *1.10*
B21 SP13 2p + 1p dp org brown .35 *1.10*

Imperf plate proofs on card exist for #B22-B27, B32-B33, B38-B39, B46-B48, B59-B60. Imperfs exist for B44-B45, B49-B51. These are from the printer's archives.

Princess Elizabeth — SP14

Design: 1p+1/2p, Princess Margaret Rose.

1943, Oct. 1 **Wmk. 253** ***Perf. 12***

B22 SP14 1p + ½p dark green .25 .40
a. Vert. pair, imperf. between
B23 SP14 2p + 1p red brown .25 .40
a. Vert. pair, imperf. between

Princesses Margaret Rose and Elizabeth SP16

1944, Oct. 9 ***Perf. 13½***

B24 SP16 1p + ½p blue green .35 .45
B25 SP16 2p + 1p chalky blue .35 .35

Peter Pan Statue, London — SP17

1945, Oct. 1

B26 SP17 1p + ½p gray grn & bis brn .25 .35
B27 SP17 2p + 1p car & ol bis .25 .35

Soldier Helping Child over Stile SP18

1946, Oct. 24 ***Perf. 13½x13***

B28 SP18 1p + ½p dk grn & org brn .25 .35
B29 SP18 2p + 1p dk brn & org brn .25 .35

Statue of Eros, London — SP19

1947, Oct. 1 **Engr.** ***Perf. 13x13½***

B30 SP19 1p + ½p deep green .25 .35
B31 SP19 2p + 1p deep carmine .25 .35

Children's Health Camp SP20

1948, Oct. 1 ***Perf. 13½x13***

B32 SP20 1p + ½p blue grn & ultra .25 .35
B33 SP20 2p + 1p red & dk brn .25 .35

Nurse and Child — SP21

1949, Oct. 3 **Photo.** ***Perf. 14x14½***

B34 SP21 1p + ½p deep green .30 .35
B35 SP21 2p + 1p ultramarine .30 .35

Princess Elizabeth and Prince Charles — SP22

1950, Oct. 2

B36 SP22 1p + ½p green .25 .35
B37 SP22 2p + 1p violet brown .25 .35

Racing Yachts SP23

Perf. 13½x13

1951, Nov. 1 **Engr.** **Wmk. 253**

B38 SP23 1½p + ½p red & yel .25 *.35*
B39 SP23 2p + 1p dp grn & yel .25 .35

Princess Anne SP24

Prince Charles SP25

Perf. 14x14½

1952, Oct. 1 **Wmk. 253** **Photo.**

B40 SP24 1½p + ½p crimson .25 .35
B41 SP25 2p + 1p brown .25 .35

Girl Guides Marching SP26

Boy Scouts at Camp SP27

1953, Oct. 7

B42 SP26 1½p + ½p bright blue .25 .35
B43 SP27 2p + 1p deep green .25 .35

The border of No. B43 consists of Morse code reading "Health" at top and bottom and "New Zealand" on each side. On No. B42 the top border line is replaced by "Health" in Morse code.

Young Mountain Climber Studying Map — SP28

1954, Oct. 4 **Engr.** ***Perf. 13½***

B44 SP28 1½p + ½p pur & brn .25 *.35*
B45 SP28 2p + 1p vio gray & brn .25 *.35*

Child's Head — SP29

1955, Oct. 3 **Wmk. 253** ***Perf. 13***

B46 SP29 1½p + ½p brn org & sep .25 *.35*
B47 SP29 2p + 1p grn & org brn .25 *.35*
B48 SP29 3p + 1p car & sepia .25 .35
Nos. B46-B48 (3) .75 1.05

Children Picking Apples — SP30

1956, Sept. 24

B49 SP30 1½p + ½p chocolate .25 *.35*
B50 SP30 2p + 1p blue green .25 *.35*
B51 SP30 3p + 1p dk car .25 .35
Nos. B49-B51 (3) .75 1.05

Life-Saving Team SP31

3p+1p, Children playing and boy in canoe.

1957, Sept. 25 ***Perf. 13½***

B52 SP31 2p + 1p emer & blk .25 .35
a. Miniature sheet of 6 7.25 *25.00*
B53 SP31 3p + 1p car & ultra .25 .35
a. Miniature sheet of 6 7.25 *25.00*

The watermark is sideways on Nos. B52a and B53a. In a second printing, the watermark is upright; values double.

Girls' Life Brigade Cadet — SP32

Design: 3p+1p, Bugler, Boys' Brigade.

1958, Aug. 20 Photo. ***Perf. 14x14½***

B54 SP32 2p + 1p green .25 .45
a. Miniature sheet of 6 5.00 *25.00*
B55 SP32 3p + 1p ultramarine .25 .45
a. Miniature sheet of 6 5.00 *25.00*

75th anniv. of the founding of the Boys' Brigade.

The surtax on this and other preceding semi-postals was for the maintenance of children's health camps.

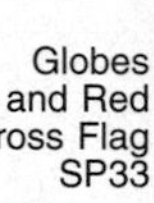

Globes and Red Cross Flag SP33

1959, June 3 ***Perf. 14½x14***

B56 SP33 3p + 1p ultra & car .25 .25
a. Red Cross omitted *2,000.*

The surtax was for the Red Cross.

Gray Teal (Tete) — SP34

Design: 3p+1p, Pied stilt (Poaka).

1959, Sept. 16 ***Perf. 14x14½***

B57 SP34 2p + 1p pink, blk, yel & gray .60 .75
a. Miniature sheet of 6 6.00 *20.00*
B58 SP34 3p + 1p blue, black & pink .60 .75
a. Miniature sheet of 6 6.00 *20.00*
b. Pink omitted *160.00*

Sacred Kingfisher (Kotare) — SP35

Design: 3p+1p, NZ pigeon (Kereru).

1960, Aug. 10 Engr. ***Perf. 13x13½***

B59 SP35 2p + 1p grnsh blue & sepia .60 .85
a. Min. sheet of 6, perf. 11½x11 13.00 *22.50*
B60 SP35 3p + 1p org & sepia .60 .85
a. Min. sheet of 6, perf. 11½x11 13.00 *22.50*

Type of 1959

Birds: 2p+1p, Great white egret (Kotuku). 3p+1p, New Zealand falcon (Karearea).

1961, Aug. 2 **Wmk. 253**

B61 SP34 2p + 1p pale lil & blk .60 .80
a. Miniature sheet of 6 13.00 *22.50*
B62 SP34 3p + 1p yel grn & blk brn .60 .80
a. Miniature sheet of 6 13.00 *22.50*

Type of 1959

Birds: 2½p+1p, Red-fronted parakeet (Kakariki). 3p+1p, Saddleback (Tieke).

1962, Oct. 3 Photo. ***Perf. 15x14***

B63 SP34 2½p + 1p lt bl, blk, grn & org .60 .80
a. Miniature sheet of 6 20.00 *27.50*
B64 SP34 3p + 1p salmon, blk, grn & org .60 .80
a. Miniature sheet of 6 20.00 *27.50*
b. Orange omitted *2,750.*

Prince Andrew — SP36

Design: 3p+1p, Prince without book.

1963, Aug. 7 Engr. ***Perf. 14***

B65 SP36 2½p + 1p ultra .35 .80
a. Miniature sheet of 6 13.00 *22.50*
B66 SP36 3p + 1p rose car .35 .25
a. Miniature sheet of 6 13.00 *22.50*

Red-billed Gull (Tarapunga) SP37

Design: 3p+1p, Blue penguin (Korora).

1964, Aug. 5 Photo. ***Perf. 14***

B67 SP37 2½p + 1p lt bl, pale yel, red & blk .45 .75
a. Miniature sheet of 8 22.50 *35.00*
b. Red omitted 325.00 225.00
c. Yellow omitted
B68 SP37 3p + 1p blue, yel & blk .45 .75
a. Miniature sheet of 8 22.50 *35.00*

Kaka — SP38

Design: 4p+1p, Fantail (Piwakawaka).

1965, Aug. 4 ***Perf. 14x14½***

B69 SP38 3p + 1p gray, red, brn & yellow .60 .85
a. Miniature sheet of 6 11.00 *27.50*
B70 SP38 4p + 1p yel, blk, emer & brn .60 .85
a. Miniature sheet of 6 11.00 *27.50*
b. As No. B70, green omitted *2,000. 2,000.*

Bellbird & Bough of Kowhai Tree — SP39

4p+1p, Flightless rail (Weka) and fern.

1966, Aug. 3 Photo. **Wmk. 253**

B71 SP39 3p + 1p lt bl & multi .60 .85
a. Miniature sheet of 6 9.00 *25.00*
B72 SP39 4p + 1p lt grn & multi .60 .85
a. Miniature sheet of 6 9.00 *25.00*
b. Brown omitted *2,250.*

National Team Rugby Player and Boy — SP40

Design: 3c+1c, Man and boy placing ball for place kick, horiz.

1967, Aug. 2 ***Perf. 14½x14, 14x14½***

B73 SP40 2½c + 1c multi .25 .25
a. Miniature sheet of 6 10.00 *20.00*
B74 SP40 3c + 1c multi .25 .25
a. Miniature sheet of 6 10.00 *20.00*

Boy Running and Olympic Rings — SP41

3c+1c, Girl swimming and Olympic rings.

1968, Aug. 7 ***Perf. 14½x14***

B75 SP41 2½c + 1c multi .25 .25
a. Miniature sheet of 6 9.50 *22.50*
b. As No. B75, blue omitted *400.00*
B76 SP41 3c + 1c multi .25 .25
a. Miniature sheet of 6 9.50 *22.50*
b. Red omitted, from No. B76a *3,350. 2,000.*
c. Dark blue omitted, from No. B76a *2,250.*

Boys Playing Cricket SP42

Dr. Elizabeth Gunn — SP43

Design: 3c+1c, playing cricket.

Perf. 13½x13, 13x13½

1969, Aug. 6 Litho. Unwmk.

B77 SP42 2½c + 1c multi .45 .75
a. Miniature sheet of 6 10.00 *25.00*
B78 SP42 3c + 1c multi .45 .75
a. Miniature sheet of 6 10.00 *25.00*
B79 SP43 4c + 1c multi .45 *2.50*
Nos. B77-B79 (3) 1.35 4.00

50th anniv. of Children's Health Camps, founded by Dr. Elizabeth Gunn.

Boys Playing Soccer SP44

2½c+1c, Girls playing basketball, vert.

1970, Aug. 5 Unwmk. ***Perf. 13½***

B80 SP44 2½c + 1c multi .30 .80
a. Miniature sheet of 6 10.00 *26.00*
B81 SP44 3c + 1c multi .30 .80
a. Miniature sheet of 6 10.00 *26.00*

Hygienist and Child SP45

Designs: 3c+1c, Girls playing hockey. 4c+1c, Boys playing hockey.

1971, Aug. 4 Litho. ***Perf. 13½***

B82 SP45 3c + 1c multicolored .50 .75
a. Miniature sheet of 6 10.00 *22.50*
B83 SP45 4c + 1c multicolored .50 .75
a. Miniature sheet of 6 10.00 *22.50*
B84 SP45 5c + 1c multicolored 1.00 *2.25*
Nos. B82-B84 (3) 2.00 3.75

50th anniv. of School Dental Service (No. B84).

Boy Playing Tennis — SP46

Design: 4c+1c, Girl playing tennis.

1972, Aug. 2 Litho. ***Perf. 13x13½***

B85 SP46 3c + 1c gray & lt brn .35 .60
a. Miniature sheet of 6 9.50 *20.00*
B86 SP46 4c + 1c brown, yel & gray .35 .60
a. Miniature sheet of 6 9.50 *20.00*

Prince Edward — SP47

1973, Aug. 1 **Photo.**

B87 SP47 3c + 1c grn & brn .35 .60
a. Miniature sheet of 6 9.00 *20.00*
B88 SP47 4c + 1c dk red & blk .35 .60
a. Miniature sheet of 6 9.00 *20.00*

Children with Cat and Dog — SP48

Designs: 4c+1c, Girl with dogs and cat. 5c+1c, Children and dogs.

1974, Aug. 7 Litho. ***Perf. 13½x14***

B89 SP48 3c + 1c multicolored .25 .60
B90 SP48 4c + 1c multicolored .30 .60
a. Miniature sheet of 10 20.00 *40.00*
B91 SP48 5c + 1c multicolored 1.10 1.75
Nos. B89-B91 (3) 1.65 2.95

Girl Feeding Lamb SP49

Designs: 4c+1c, Boy with hen and chicks. 5c+1c, Boy with duck and duckling.

1975, Aug. 6 Litho. ***Perf. 14x13½***

B92 SP49 3c + 1c multicolored .25 .35
B93 SP49 4c + 1c multicolored .25 .35
a. Miniature sheet of 10 15.00 *40.00*
B94 SP49 5c + 1c multicolored .75 *1.75*
Nos. B92-B94 (3) 1.25 2.45

Boy and Piebald Pony — SP50

Designs: 8c+1c, Farm girl and calf. 10c+1c, 2 girls watching nest-bound thrush.

1976, Aug. 4 Litho. ***Perf. 13½x14***

B95 SP50 7c + 1c multicolored .25 .35
B96 SP50 8c + 1c multicolored .25 .35
B97 SP50 10c + 1c multicolored .45 *.90*
a. Min. sheet, 2 each #B95-B97 4.25 *6.00*
Nos. B95-B97 (3) .95 1.60

Girl and Bluebird — SP51

8c+2c, Boy & frog. 10c+2c, Girl & butterfly.

1977, Aug. 3 Litho. *Perf. 13½x14*

B98 SP51 7c + 2c multi .25 .60
B99 SP51 8c + 2c multi .25 .65
B100 SP51 10c + 2c multi .50 *1.10*
 a. Miniature sheet of 6 2.50 *6.50*
 Nos. B98-B100 (3) 1.00 2.35

No. B100a contains 2 each of Nos. B98-B100 in 2 strips of continuous design.

NZ No. B1
SP52

Heart Surgery
SP53

1978, Aug. 2 Litho. *Perf. 13½x14*

B101 SP52 10c + 2c multi .35 .40
B102 SP53 12c + 2c multi .35 .45
 a. Min. sheet, 3 ea #B101-B102 1.40 *4.00*

50th Health Stamp issue (No. B101) and National Heart Foundation (No. B102).

No. B102a exists in two printings: with "HARRISON & SONS LTD., LONDON" imprint at bottom left margin (valued) and with imprint more centered across three bottom stamps (apparently very scarce). Both varieties are known on first day covers.

Demoiselle Fish
SP54

Designs: No. B104, Sea urchin. 12c+2c, Underwater photographer and red mullet, vert.

1979, July 25 *Perf. 13½x13, 13x13½*

B103 SP54 10c + 2c multi .35 .70
B104 SP54 10c + 2c multi .35 .70
 a. Pair, #B103-B104 .70 1.25
B105 SP54 12c + 2c multi .35 .70
 a. Min. sheet, 2 ea #B103-B105 1.50 *2.75*
 Nos. B103-B105 (3) 1.05 2.10

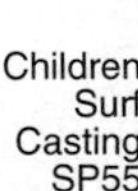

Children Surf Casting
SP55

No. B107, Wharf Fishing. B108, Underwater fishing.

1980, Aug. 6 Litho. *Perf. 13½x13*

B106 SP55 14c + 2c shown .35 .95
B107 SP55 14c + 2c multi .35 .95
 a. Pair, #B106-B107 .70 1.75
B108 SP55 17c + 2c multi .35 .65
 a. Min. sheet, 2 ea #B106-B108 1.90 *3.25*
 Nos. B106-B108 (3) 1.05 2.55

Boy and Girl at Rock Pool — SP56

1981, Aug. 5 Litho. *Perf. 14½*

B109 SP56 20c + 2c Girl, starfish .30 .75
B110 SP56 20c + 2c Boy fishing .30 .75
 a. Pair, #B109-B110 .60 1.50
B111 SP56 25c + 2c shown .30 .40
 a. Min. sheet, 2 ea #B109-B111 1.50 3.50
 Nos. B109-B111 (3) .90 1.90

Cocker Spaniel — SP57

1982, Aug. 4 Litho. *Perf. 13x13½*

B112 SP57 24c + 2c Labrador .90 1.10
B113 SP57 24c + 2c Border collie .90 1.10
 a. Pair, #B112-B113 1.90 2.25
B114 SP57 30c + 2c shown .90 1.10
 a. Min. sheet, 2 each #B112-B114, perf. 14x13½ 5.00 7.50
 Nos. B112-B114 (3) 2.70 3.30

Persian Cat — SP58

1983, Aug. 3 Litho. *Perf. 14½*

B115 SP58 24 + 2c Tabby .70 .85
B116 SP58 24 + 2c Siamese .70 .85
 a. Pair, #B115-B116 1.40 1.75
B117 SP58 30 + 2c shown .95 1.10
 a. Min. sheet, 2 ea #B115-B117 3.00 3.50
 Nos. B115-B117 (3) 2.35 2.80

Thoroughbreds — SP59

1984, Aug. 1 Litho. *Perf. 13½x13*

B118 SP59 24c + 2c Clydesdales .60 .85
B119 SP59 24c + 2c Shetlands .60 .85
 a. Pair, #B118-B119 1.25 1.75
B120 SP59 30c + 2c shown .60 .85
 a. Min. sheet, 2 ea #B118-B120 2.50 3.75
 Nos. B118-B120 (3) 1.80 2.55

Health — SP60

Princess Diana and: No. B121, Prince William. No. B122, Prince Henry. No. B123, Princes Charles, William and Henry.

1985, July 31 Litho. *Perf. 13½*

B121 SP60 25c + 2c multi 1.00 1.50
B122 SP60 25c + 2c multi 1.00 1.50
 a. Pair, #B121-B122 2.10 3.00
B123 SP60 35c + 2c multi 1.00 1.50
 a. Min. sheet, 2 ea #B121-B123 4.75 7.00
 Nos. B121-B123 (3) 3.00 4.50

Surtax for children's health camps.

Children's Drawings — SP61

No. B125, Children playing. No. B126, Skipping rope, horiz.

1986, July 30 Litho. *Perf. 14½x14*

B124 SP61 30c + 3c shown .50 .75
B125 SP61 30c + 3c multi .50 .75
 a. Pair, #B124-B125 1.00 1.50
B126 SP61 45c + 3c multi .75 .90
 a. Min. sheet, 2 ea #B124-B126 3.50 4.00
 Nos. B124-B126 (3) 1.75 2.40

Surtax for children's health camps.

No. B126a exists with Stockholmia '86 emblem. This sheet was sold only at the exhibition.

Children's Drawings
SP62

1987, July 29 Litho. *Perf. 14½*

B127 SP62 40c + 3c shown .90 1.75
B128 SP62 40c + 3c Swimming .90 1.75
 a. Pair, #B127-B128 1.90 3.50
B129 SP62 60c + 3c Riding horse, vert. 1.50 7.75
 a. Min. sheet, 2 ea #B127-B129 6.50 11.00
 Nos. B127-B129 (3) 3.30 11.25

Surtax benefited children's health camps.

1988 Summer Olympics, Seoul — SP63

1988, July 27 Litho. *Perf. 14½*

B130 SP63 40c + 3c Swimming .70 .80
B131 SP63 60c + 3c Running .95 1.25
B132 SP63 70c + 3c Rowing 1.10 1.25
B133 SP63 80c + 3c Equestrian 1.25 1.60
 a. Souv. sheet of 4, #B130-B133 4.00 5.00
 Nos. B130-B133 (4) 4.00 4.90

Children's Health — SP64

Designs: No. B134, Duke and Duchess of York, Princess Beatrice. No. B135, Duchess, princess. No. B136, Princess.

1989, July 23

B134 SP64 40c + 3c multi .90 1.75
B135 SP64 40c + 3c multi .90 1.75
 a. Pair, #B134-B135 1.90 3.50
B136 SP64 80c + 3c multi 1.60 2.00
 a. Min. sheet, 2 ea #B134-B136 6.75 8.75
 b. As "a," overprinted with World Stamp Expo '89 emblem in margin 17.50 17.50
 Nos. B134-B136 (3) 3.40 5.50

Athletes
SP65

40c+5c, Jack Lovelock (1910-1949), runner. 80c+5c, George Nepia (1905-1986), rugby player.

1990, July 25 Litho. *Perf. 14½x14*

B137 SP65 40c +5c multi .60 .95
B138 SP65 80c +5c multi 1.25 1.60
 a. Min. sheet, 2 ea #B137-B138 3.75 4.25

Hector's Dolphin
SP66

1991, July 24 Litho. *Perf. 14½*

B139 SP66 45c +5c 3 Swimming 1.00 1.40
B140 SP66 80c +5c 2 Jumping 1.40 2.25
 a. Souv. sheet, 2 ea #B139-B140 5.75 7.50

Surtax benefited children's health camps.

Anthony F. Wilding (1883-1915), Tennis Player — SP67

Design: No. B142, C.S. "Stewie" Dempster (1903-1974), cricket player.

1992, Aug. 12 Litho. *Perf. 14x13½*

B141 SP67 45c +5c multi 1.10 1.40
B142 SP67 80c +5c multi 1.40 1.75
 a. Souv. sheet, 2 each #B141-B142, perf. 14½ 4.50 6.25

Surtax for children's health camps.

SP68

1993, July 21 Litho. *Perf. 13½x14*

B143 SP68 45c +5c Boy, puppy .80 1.00
B144 SP68 80c +5c Girl, kitten 1.40 1.75
 a. Souvenir sheet, 2 each #B143-B144, perf. 14½ 4.50 5.00
 b. As "a," inscribed in sheet margin 7.00 7.00

Surtax for children's health camps.

No. B144b inscribed with "TAIPEI '93" emblem.

Issue date: No. B144b, Aug. 14.

SP69

Children's Health Camps, 75th Anniv.: No. B145, #B15, Children playing with ball. No. B146, #B34, Nurse holding child. No. B147, #B79, Children reading. 80c+5c, #B4, Boy.

1994, July 20 Litho. *Perf. 14*

B145 SP69 45c +5c multi .80 .90
B146 SP69 45c +5c multi .80 .90
B147 SP69 45c +5c multi .80 .90
B148 SP69 80c +5c multi 1.40 1.40
 a. Souv. sheet of 4, #B145-B148 4.50 5.00
 Nos. B145-B148 (4) 3.80 4.10

Surtax for children's health camps.

Children's Health Camps — SP70

Designs: 45c+5c, Boy on skateboard. 80c+5c, Child on bicycle.

1995, June 21 Litho. *Perf. 14½*

B149 SP70 45c +5c multi .85 1.25
B150 SP70 80c +5c multi 2.10 2.10
a. Souv. sheet, 2 ea #B149-B150 4.75 5.75
b. As "a," with added inscription 8.00 8.00

No. B150b inscribed with Stampex '95 emblem in sheet margin.

Surtax for children's health camps.

SP71

Children's Health: Nos. B151, B153, Infant buckled into child safety seat. 80c, Child holding adult's hand on pedestrian crossing.

1996, June 5 Litho. *Perf. 14x13½*

B151 SP71 40c +5c multi .80 .95
B152 SP71 80c +5c multi 1.40 1.50
a. Souvenir sheet, 2 each Nos. B151-B152, perf. 14x14½ 4.00 4.00
b. As "a" with added inscription 5.50 5.50

Self-Adhesive

Serpentine Die Cut 11½

B153 SP71 40c +5c multi .60 .85

No. B152b inscribed with CAPEX '96 emblem in sheet margin.

SP72

Original Design

1996, June 5 Litho. *Perf. 14x13½*

B154 SP72 40c +5c multi *1,000.* 1,200.

Self-Adhesive

Serpentine Die Cut 11½

B155 SP72 40c +5c multi 1,750. 1,750.

Nos. B154 and B155 were withdrawn before issue by New Zealand Post. Slightly over 1,000 examples of No. B154 and 500 examples of No. B155 were sold in error by two post offices within three days of June 5. A total of 402 examples of the souvenir sheet containing No. B154 were made available by the printer, but none were sold at post offices.

The stamps were withdrawn because the inclusion of the stuffed animal indicated that the infant was improperly belted into the vehicle.

Children's Health SP73

Children's designs of "Healthy Living:" No. B156, Child on beach. 80c+5c, Child riding horse on waterfront. No. B158, Mosaic of person collecting fruit from tree, vert.

1997, June 18 Litho. *Perf. 14*

B156 SP73 40c +5c multi .80 .85
B157 SP73 80c +5c multi 1.40 1.40

Souvenir Sheet

B157A Sheet of 3, #B156-B157, B157Ab 3.50 3.50
b. SP73 40c +5c like #B158 2.00 2.00

Size: 25x36mm

Self-Adhesive

Serpentine Die Cut 10½

B158 SP73 40c +5c multi .75 .70

Children's Water Safety — SP74

Designs: 40c+5c, Child in life jacket. 80c+5c Child learning to swim.

1998, June 24 Litho. *Perf. 13½*

B159 SP74 40c +5c multicolored .75 .60
B160 SP74 80c +5c multicolored 1.40 1.40
a. Sheet, 2 each #B159-B160 4.25 4.25

Size: 25x38mm

Self-Adhesive

Serpentine Die Cut 11½

B161 SP74 40c +5c multicolored .75 .45

Children's Health SP75

Scenes from children's books: #B162, Hairy Maclary's Bone, by Lynley Dodd. #B163, Lion in the Meadow, by Margaret Mahy. 80c+5c, Greedy Cat, by Joy Cowley.

Serpentine Die Cut 10¼

1999, June 16 Litho.

Self-Adhesive (#B162)

B162 SP75 40c +5c multi .75 .60

Perf. 14¼

B163 SP75 40c +5c multi .75 .60
B164 SP75 80c +5c multi 1.40 1.40

Souvenir Sheet

B165 Sheet of 3, #B163-B164, B165a 3.50 3.50
a. SP75 40c +5c like #B162 2.00 2.00

Nos. B162, B165a are 37x26mm.

For 2000 semi-postals, see Nos. 1681, 1682, 1682a and 1687.

Children's Health SP76

Designs: No. B166, Four cyclists. 90c+5c, Cyclist in air. No. B168, Cyclist riding through puddle.

2001, Aug. 1 Litho. *Perf. 14*

B166 SP76 40c +5c multi .75 .60
a. Sheet of 10 7.50 7.50
B167 SP76 90c +5c multi 1.50 1.40
a. Souvenir sheet, #B166-B167 2.10 2.10

Size: 30x25mm

Serpentine Die Cut 10x9¾

Self-Adhesive

B168 SP76 40c +5c multi .60 .60
Nos. B166-B168 (3) 2.85 2.60

Healthy Living SP77

Designs: B169, 40c+5c, Fruits. 90c+5c, Vegetables.

No. B171a, Fruits, diff. B172, Fruits diff. (like B171a).

2002, Aug. 7 *Perf. 14¼x14*

B169 SP77 40c +5c multi .75 .60
B170 SP77 90c +5c multi 1.50 1.50

Souvenir Sheet

B171 Sheet, #B169-B170, B171a 3.50 3.50
a. SP77 40c +5c multi (21x26mm) 2.00 2.00

Coil Stamp

Size: 21x26mm

Self-Adhesive

Serpentine Die Cut 9¾x10

B172 SP77 40c +5c multi .75 .50

Children's Health SP78

Designs: No. B173, 40c+5c, Children on swings. 90c+5c, Child with ball, girl playing hopscotch.

Nos. B175a, B176, 40c+ 5c, Girl on monkey bars.

2003, Aug. 6 Litho. *Perf. 14*

B173 SP78 40c +5c multi .75 .55
B174 SP78 90c +5c multi 1.50 1.50

Souvenir Sheet

B175 Sheet, #B173-B174, B175a 3.50 3.50
a. SP78 40c +5c multi (21x26mm), perf. 14½x14 2.00 2.00

Coil Stamp

Size: 21x26mm

Self-Adhesive

Serpentine Die Cut 9¾x10

B176 SP78 40c +5c multi .75 .55

Children's Health — SP79

Designs: No. B177, Children playing with beach ball in water. No. B178, People in boat. Nos. B179a, B180, People fishing.

2004, Sept. 1 Litho. *Perf. 14*

B177 SP79 45c +5c multi .75 .65
B178 SP79 90c +5c multi 1.50 1.50

Souvenir Sheet

B179 Sheet, #B177-B178, B179a 3.50 3.50
a. SP79 45c +5c multi (22x27mm), perf. 14¼x14 2.00 2.00

Self-Adhesive

Size: 22x27mm

Serpentine Die Cut 9½x10

B180 SP79 45c +5c multi .75 .65

Children's Health — SP80

Designs: No. B181, Girl and horse. 90c+5c, Boy and rabbit. Nos. B183a, B184, Children and dog.

2005, Aug. 3 Litho. *Perf. 14*

B181 SP80 45c +5c multi .75 .65
B182 SP80 90c +5c multi 1.50 1.50
B183 Souvenir sheet, #B181-B182, B183a 3.50 3.50
a. SP80 45c +5c multi, 20x25mm, perf. 14½x14 2.00 2.00

Self-Adhesive

Size: 20x25mm

Serpentine Die Cut 9½x10

B184 SP80 45c +5c multi .75 .65

Children's Health — SP81

Designs: No. B185, Girl releasing dove. $1+10c, Boy with origami bird. Nos. B187a, B188, Two children, peace lily (25x30mm).

2007, Sept. 5 Litho. *Perf. 14*

B185 SP81 50c +10c multi .85 .85
a. Perf. 13½ .85 .85
B186 SP81 $1 +10c multi 1.50 1.50
a. Perf. 13½ 1.50 1.50

Souvenir Sheet

B187 Sheet, #B185-B186, B187a 3.75 3.75
a. SP81 50c +10c multi, perf. 14½x14 2.50 2.50
b. As "a," perf. 14½x13½x14½x14 2.00 2.00
c. Souvenir sheet, #B185a, B186a, B187b 3.25 3.25

Self-Adhesive

Serpentine Die Cut 9½x10

B188 SP81 50c +10c multi .85 .85

Surtax for Children's Health Camps.

Children's Health — SP82

Child: No. B189, Cycling. $1+10c, Kayaking. Nos. B191a, B192, Running.

2008, July 2 Litho. *Perf. 14¼*

B189 SP82 50c +10c multi .75 .75
B190 SP82 $1 +10c multi 1.50 1.50

Souvenir Sheet

B191 Sheet, #B189-B190, B191a 4.00 4.00
a. SP82 50c +10c multi (36x36mm), perf. 14x14½ 1.75 1.75

Self-Adhesive

Serpentine Die Cut 9¾

Size: 34x34mm

B192 SP82 50c +10c multi .95 .95

Surtax for Children's Health Camps.

Children's Health Stamps, 80th Anniv. — SP83

Stamps in color: No. B193, #B151. $1+10c, #B5. Nos. B195a, B196, #B23.

2009, Sept. 7 Litho. *Perf. 13¼x13½*

B193 SP83 50c +10c multi .90 .90
a. Perf. 14 1.00 1.00
B194 SP83 $1 +10c multi 1.60 1.60
a. Perf. 14 1.75 1.75

Souvenir Sheet

B195 Sheet, #B193a, B194a, B195a 3.75 3.50
a. SP83 50c+10c multi, perf. 14½x14, 22x27mm 2.00 2.00

Self-Adhesive

Serpentine Die Cut 9½x10

Size: 21x26mm

B196 SP83 50c +10c multi .90 .90

Surtax for Children's Health Camps.

Butterflies SP84

Designs: No. B197, Monarch butterfly. $1+10c, Tussock butterfly. Nos. B199a, B200, Boulder copper butterfly, vert. (25x30mm).

2010, July 7 Litho. *Perf. 14*

B197 SP84 50c + 10c multi .75 .75
B198 SP84 $1 +10c multi 1.50 1.50

Souvenir Sheet

B199 Sheet of 3, #B197-B198, B199a 3.75 3.75
a. SP84 50c +10c multi 1.50 1.50

Self-Adhesive

Serpentine Die Cut 9½x10

B200 SP84 50c +10c multi 1.00 1.00

Surtax for Children's Health Camps.

Flightless Birds SP85

Designs: No. B201, Kiwi. $1.20+10c, Kakapo. Nos. B203a, B204, Takahe, vert. (25x30mm).

2011, July 6 Litho. *Perf. 14*

B201 SP85 60c + 10c multi 1.10 1.10
B202 SP85 $1.20 +10c multi 2.25 2.25

Souvenir Sheet

B203 Sheet of 3, #B201-B202, B203a 5.00 5.00
a. SP85 60c +10c multi 1.60 1.60

Self-Adhesive

Serpentine Die Cut 9½x10

B204 SP85 60c +10c multi 1.25 1.25

Surtax for Children's Health Camps.

New Zealand Sea Lions SP86

Designs: No. B205, Sea lion pup. $1.40+10c, Adolescent male sea lion. Nos. B207a, B208, Head of sea lion pup, vert. (23x27mm).

2012, Aug. 1 *Perf. 14*

B205 SP86 70c + 10c multi 1.25 1.25
B206 SP86 $1.40 +10c multi 2.50 2.50

Souvenir Sheet

B207 Sheet of 3, #B205-B206, B207a 5.75 5.75
a. SP86 70c +10c multi 2.00 2.00

Self-Adhesive

Serpentine Die Cut 9½x10

B208 SP86 70c +10c multi 1.40 1.40

Surtax for New Zealand Foundation for Child and Family Health and Development.

Children and Farm Pets — SP87

Designs: No. B209, Boy and lamb. $1.40 + 10c, Girl and piglets. Nos. B211a, B212, Boy and goat (22x27mm).

2013, Sept. 4 *Perf. 14*

B209 SP87 70c +10c multi 1.25 1.25
a. Perf. 13½ 1.25 1.25
B210 SP87 $1.40 +10c multi 2.40 2.40
a. Perf. 13½ 2.40 2.40

Souvenir Sheet

Perf. 13½

B211 Sheet of 3, #B209a, B210a, B211a 5.00 5.00
a. SP87 70c +10c multi 1.25 1.25

Self-Adhesive

Serpentine Die Cut 9½x10

B212 SP87 70c +10c multi 1.25 1.25

Surtax for Stand Children's Services.

Children and Vegetables SP88

Designs: No. B213, Girl and carrots. $1.40 + 10c, Boy and apples. Nos. B215a, B216, Boy and pumpkin.

2014, Sept. 3 Litho. *Perf. 14*

B213 SP88 80c +10c multi 1.40 1.40
a. Perf. 13½ 1.40 1.40
B214 SP88 $1.40 +10c multi 2.40 2.40
a. Perf. 13½ 2.40 2.40

Souvenir Sheet

B215 Sheet of 3, #B213a, B214a, B215a 5.25 5.25
a. SP88 80c +10c multi (22x27mm) 1.40 1.40

Self-Adhesive

Size: 21x26mm

B216 SP88 80c +10c multi 1.40 1.40

Surtax for Stand Children's Services Tu Maia Whanau.

Children and Sun Protection SP89

Designs: No. B217, Girl under beach umbrella. $1.40+10c, Girl wearing hat with ear flaps putting sun screen on hands. $2+10c, Girl with large hat over head. Nos. B220a, B221, Boy, large pair of sunglasses.

2015, Sept. 2 Litho. *Perf. 14*

B217 SP89 80c +10c multi 1.25 1.25
a. Perf. 13¼x13½ 1.25 1.25
B218 SP89 $1.40 +10c multi 1.90 1.90
a. Perf. 13¼x13½ 1.90 1.90
B219 SP89 $2 +10c multi 2.75 2.75
a. Perf. 13¼x13½ 2.75 2.75
Nos. B217-B219 (3) 5.90 5.90

Miniature Sheet

B220 Sheet of 4, #B217a, B218a, B219a, B220a 7.25 7.25
a. SP89 80c+10c multi, perf. 13¾x13½, 25x30mm 1.25 1.25

Self-Adhesive

Size: 25x30mm

Serpentine Die Cut 9½x10

B221 SP89 80c +10c multi 1.25 1.25

Surtax for Stand Children's Services Tu Maia Whanau.

AIR POST STAMPS

Plane over Lake Manapouri AP1

Perf. 14x14½

1931, Nov. 10 Typo. Wmk. 61

C1 AP1 3p chocolate 27.50 22.50
a. Perf. 14x15 150.00 *500.00*
C2 AP1 4p dark violet 27.50 27.50
C3 AP1 7p orange 30.00 27.50
Nos. C1-C3 (3) 85.00 77.50

Most examples of No. C1a are poorly centered.

Type of 1931 Surcharged in Red

1931, Dec. 18 *Perf. 14x14½*

C4 AP1 5p on 3p yel green 20.00 25.00

Type of 1931 Overprinted in Dark Blue

1934, Jan. 17

C5 AP1 7p bright blue 50.00 55.00

1st official air mail flight between NZ and Australia.

Airplane over Landing Field AP2

1935, May 4 Engr. *Perf. 14*

C6 AP2 1p rose carmine 1.10 .80
C7 AP2 3p dark violet 5.75 3.75
C8 AP2 6p gray blue 11.50 5.75
Nos. C6-C8 (3) 18.35 10.30
Set, never hinged 40.00

SPECIAL DELIVERY STAMPS

SD1

Perf. 14x14½,14x15

1903-26 Typo. Wmk. 61

E1 SD1 6p purple & red ('26) 60.00 40.00
a. 6p violet & red, perf. 11 70.00 50.00

Mail Car — SD2

1939, Aug. 16 Engr. *Perf. 14*

E2 SD2 6p violet 1.75 6.00

POSTAGE DUE STAMPS

D1

Wmk. 62

1899, Dec. 1 Typo. *Perf. 11*

J1 D1 ½p green & red 8.00 *19.00*
a. No period after "D" 75.00 60.00
J2 D1 1p green & red 12.50 2.10
J3 D1 2p green & red 40.00 6.25
J4 D1 3p green & red 20.00 6.00
J5 D1 4p green & red 42.50 25.00
J6 D1 5p green & red 45.00 *60.00*
J7 D1 6p green & red 45.00 *60.00*
J8 D1 8p green & red 110.00 *150.00*
J9 D1 10p green & red 175.00 *225.00*
J10 D1 1sh green & red 140.00 100.00
J11 D1 2sh green & red 225.00 *300.00*
Nos. J1-J11 (11) 863.00 953.35

Nos. J1-J11 may be found with N. Z. and D. varying in size.

D2

1902, Feb. 28 Unwmk.

J12 D2 ½p gray grn & red 3.00 7.50

Wmk. 61

J13 D2 ½p gray grn & red 3.00 2.10
J14 D2 1p gray grn & red 12.00 4.00
J15 D2 2p gray grn & red 150.00 150.00

1904-28 *Perf. 14, 14x14½*

J16 D2 ½p green & car 3.75 4.25
J17 D2 1p green & car 7.00 1.00
J18 D2 2p green & car 9.00 3.50
J19 D2 3p grn & rose ('28) 50.00 25.00
Nos. J16-J19 (4) 69.75 33.75

N Z and Star printed on the back in Blue

1925 Unwmk. *Perf. 14x14½, 14x15*

J20 D2 ½p green & rose 4.00 *26.00*
J21 D2 2p green & rose 9.00 *35.00*

Catalogue values for unused stamps in this section, from this point to the end of the section, are for Never Hinged items.

D3

1939 Wmk. 61 Typo. *Perf. 15x14*

J22 D3 ½p turquoise green 13.00 *9.00*
J23 D3 1p rose pink 5.00 .60
J24 D3 2p ultramarine 9.00 1.75
J25 D3 3p brown orange 26.00 29.00
Nos. J22-J25 (4) 53.00 40.35

1945-49 Wmk. 253

J27 D3 1p rose pink ('49) 5.00 25.00
J28 D3 2p ultramarine ('47) 7.00 9.00
J29 D3 3p brown orange 15.00 5.75
Nos. J27-J29 (3) 27.00 39.75

The use of postage due stamps was discontinued in Sept., 1951.

WAR TAX STAMP

No. 144 Overprinted in Black

Perf. 14x14½

1915, Sept. 24 **Wmk. 61**

MR1 A43 ½p green 2.10 .60

OFFICIAL STAMPS

Regular Issues of 1882-92 Overprinted & Handstamped

1892 **Wmk. 62** ***Perf as Before***

Rose or Magenta Handstamp

O1 A9 1p rose *600.*
O2 A10 2p violet *800.*
O3 A16 2½p ultramarine *700.*
O4 A17 5p olive gray *1,000.*
O5 A13 6p brown *1,200.*

Violet Handstamp

O6 N1 ½p rose *1,000.*
O7 A9 1p rose *600.*
O8 A10 2p violet

Handstamped on No. 67A in Rose

1899 ***Perf. 10, 10x11***

O9 A15a ½p black *600.*

Handstamped on No. 79 in Violet

Unwmk. ***Perf. 14, 15***

O10 A27 8p dull blue *1,200.*

Hstmpd. on Stamps of 1899-1900 in Violet

1902 ***Perf. 11***

O11 A22 2½p blue *650.*
O12 A23 3p org brown *1,000.*
O13 A25 5p red brown *900.*
O14 A27 8p dark blue *1,000.*

Green Handstamp

O15 A25 5p red brown *900.*

Handstamped on Stamp of 1901 in Violet

Wmk. 63 ***Perf. 11***

O16 A35 1p carmine *600.*

Handstamped on Stamps of 1902-07 in Violet or Magenta

1905-07 **Wmk. 61** ***Perf. 11, 14***

O17 A18 ½p green *600.*
O18 A35 1p carmine *600.*
O19 A22 2½p blue *700.*
O20 A25 5p red brown
O21 A27 8p deep blue
O22 A30 2sh blue green *5,000.*

The "O. P. S. O." handstamp is usually struck diagonally, reading up, but on No. O19 it also occurs horizontally. The letters stand for "On Public Service Only."

Overprinted in Black

On Stamps of 1902-07

1907 ***Perf. 14, 14x13, 14x14½***

O23 A18 ½p green 12.00 2.00
O24 A35 1p carmine 12.00 1.00
a. Booklet pane of 6 110.00
O25 A33 2p violet 20.00 2.00
O26 A23 3p orange brn 60.00 6.00
O27 A26 6p carmine rose 250.00 40.00
a. Horiz. pair, imperf. vert. *925.00*
O28 A29 1sh brown red 125.00 25.00
O29 A30 2sh blue green 175.00 150.00
a. Horiz. pair, imperf. vert. *1,400.*
O30 A31 5sh vermilion 350.00 350.00
Nos. O23-O30 (8) 1,004. 576.00

On No. 127

Perf. 14x13, 14x14½

O31 A26 6p carmine rose 325.00 65.00

On No. 129

1909 ***Perf. 14x14½***

O32 A35 1p car (redrawn) 90.00 3.00

On Nos. 130-131, 133, 137, 139

1910 ***Perf. 14, 14x13½, 14x14½***

O33 A41 ½p yel grn 10.00 1.00
a. Inverted overprint 1,600.
O34 A42 1p carmine 3.75 .25
O35 A41 3p org brn 20.00 2.00
O36 A41 6p car rose 30.00 10.00
O37 A41 1sh vermilion 70.00 40.00
Nos. O33-O37 (5) 133.75 53.25

For 3p see note on perf varieties following No. 139.

On Postal-Fiscal Stamps Nos. AR32, AR36, AR44

1911-14

O38 PF1 2sh blue ('14) 75.00 52.50
O39 PF1 5sh green ('13) 125.00 *200.00*
O40 PF2 £1 rose 1,000. 625.00
Nos. O38-O40 (3) 1,200. 877.50

On Stamps of 1909-19

Perf. 14x13½, 14x14½

1915-19 **Typo.**

O41 A43 ½p green 1.60 .25
O42 A46 1½p gray black ('16) 8.00 3.00
O43 A47 1½p gray black ('16) 5.75 1.00
O44 A47 1½p brown org ('19) 5.75 .60
O45 A43 2p yellow ('17) 5.75 .50
O46 A43 3p chocolate ('19) 16.00 1.50

Engr.

O47 A45 3p vio brn ('16) 8.00 1.50
O48 A45 6p car rose ('16) 12.00 1.00
O49 A41 8p dp bl (R) ('16) 20.00 *30.00*
O50 A45 1sh vermilion ('16) 7.50 2.25
a. 1sh orange 15.00 *20.00*
Nos. O41-O50 (10) 90.35 *41.60*

For 8p see note on perf varieties following No. 139.

1922 **On No. 157**

O51 A45 8p red brown 125.00 *200.00*

1925 **On Nos. 151, 158**

O52 A45 4p purple 20.00 4.25
O53 A45 9p olive green 45.00 42.50

On No. 177

1925 ***Perf. 14x14½***

O54 A42 1p carmine 5.00 5.00

On Nos. 184, 182

1927-28 **Wmk. 61** ***Perf. 14, 14½x14***

O55 A57 1p rose red 2.50 .25
O56 A56 2sh blue 125.00 140.00

On No. AR50

1933 ***Perf. 14***

O57 PF5 5sh green 450.00 450.00

Nos. 186, 187, 196 Overprinted in Black

1936 ***Perf. 14x13½, 13½x14, 14***

O58 A59 1p copper red 2.00 1.40
O59 A60 1½p red brown 14.00 *30.00*
O60 A69 1sh dark slate grn 30.00 *52.50*
Nos. O58-O60 (3) 46.00 83.90
Set, never hinged 120.00

Same Overprint Horizontally in Black or Green on Stamps of 1936

Perf. 12½, 13½, 13x13½, 14x13½, 13½x14, 14

1936-42 **Wmk. 253**

O61 A58 ½p brt grn ('37) 1.50 5.25
O62 A59 1p copper red 3.00 .60
O63 A60 1½p red brown 4.00 5.25
O64 A61 2p red org ('38) 1.00 .25
a. Perf. 12½ ('42) 110.00 62.50
O65 A62 2½p dk gray & dk brown 8.00 24.00
O66 A63 3p choc ('38) 27.50 4.00
O67 A64 4p blk brn & blk 5.00 1.10
O68 A66 6p red ('37) 5.75 .35
O68B A67 8p dp brn ('42) 8.50 20.00
O69 A68 9p blk & scar (G) ('38) 80.00 45.00
O70 A69 1sh dk slate grn 14.00 1.60
a. Perf. 12½ ('42) 27.50 1.75

Overprint Vertical

O71 A70 2sh ol grn ('37) 24.00 8.50
a. Perf. 12½ ('42) 90.00 25.00
Nos. O61-O71 (12) 182.25 115.90
Set, never hinged 550.00

Same Overprint Horizontally in Black on Nos. 226, 227, 228

1938

O72 A79 ½p emerald 5.75 1.75
O73 A79 1p rose red 7.25 .30
O74 A80 1½p violet brn 37.50 10.50
Nos. O72-O74 (3) 50.50 12.55
Set, never hinged 95.00

Same Overprint on No. AR50

1938 **Wmk. 61** ***Perf. 14***

O75 PF5 5sh green 75.00 47.50

Nos. 229-235, 237, 239-241 Overprinted in Red or Black

Perf. 13½x13, 13x13½, 14x13½

1940 **Wmk. 253**

O76 A81 ½p dk bl grn (R) .60 .75
a. "ff" joined 29.00 70.00
O77 A82 1p scar & sepia 2.25 .30
a. "ff" joined 29.00 70.00
O78 A83 1½p brt vio & ultra 1.10 *4.25*
O79 A84 2p blk brn & Prus grn 2.25 .30
a. "ff" joined 35.00 70.00
O80 A85 2½p dk bl & myr grn 1.40 4.50
a. "ff" joined 29.00 77.50
O81 A86 3p dp plum & dk vio (R) 5.75 .95
a. "ff" joined 24.00 55.00
O82 A87 4p dk red vio & vio brn 14.50 1.60
a. "ff" joined 70.00 92.50
O83 A89 6p vio & brt grn 14.50 1.60
a. "ff" joined 40.00 80.00
O84 A90 8p org red & blk 14.50 13.00
a. "ff" joined 40.00 110.00
O85 A91 9p dp org & olive 5.75 5.75
O86 A92 1sh dk sl grn & ol 35.00 5.25
Nos. O76-O86 (11) 97.60 38.25
Set, never hinged 190.00

Nos. 227A, 228C Overprinted in Black

1941 **Wmk. 253** ***Perf. 13½***

O88 A79 1p light blue green .30 .30
O89 A80 3p blue .75 .30
Set, never hinged 2.25

Same Overprint on No. 245

1944 ***Perf. 14x15***

Size: 17¼x20¼mm

O90 A68 9p int black & scar 20.00 17.00
Never Hinged 60.00

Same Overprint on No. AR78

Perf. 14

O91 PF5 5sh green 12.00 7.00
Never Hinged 20.00

Catalogue values for unused stamps in this section, from this point to the end of the section, are for Never Hinged items.

Same Ovpt. on Stamps of 1941-47

1946-51 ***Perf. 13½, 14***

O92 A79 ½p brn org ('46) 1.75 1.25
O92B A80 1½p red 5.75 1.25
O93 A80 2p orange .90 .30
O94 A80 4p rose lilac 4.00 1.25
O95 A80 6p rose carmine 5.75 1.25
O96 A80 8p deep violet 10.00 4.50
O97 A80 9p chocolate 11.50 5.75
O98 A104 1sh dk car rose & chestnut 11.50 1.75
O99 A104 2sh dk grn & brn org 26.00 8.50
Nos. O92-O99 (9) 77.15 25.80

Queen Elizabeth II — O1

Perf. 13½x13

1954, Mar. 1 **Engr.** **Wmk. 253**

O100 O1 1p orange 1.10 .50
O101 O1 1½p rose brown 4.25 5.75
O102 O1 2p green .45 .25
O103 O1 3p red .45 .25
O104 O1 4p blue 1.10 .60
O105 O1 9p rose carmine 10.50 2.50
O106 O1 1sh rose violet 1.10 .25
Nos. O100-O106 (7) 18.95 10.10

Exist imperf.

Nos. O102, O101 Surcharged with New Value and Dots

1959-61

O107 O1 2½p on 2p green ('61) 1.10 1.75
O108 O1 6p on 1½p rose brn .60 1.25

Exist imperf.

1963, Mar. 1

O109 O1 2½p dark olive 4.00 1.75
O111 O1 3sh slate 47.50 57.50

Exist imperf.

LIFE INSURANCE

Lighthouses — LI1

Perf. 10, 11, 10x11, 12x11½

1891, Jan. 2 **Typo.** **Wmk. 62**

OY1 LI1 ½p purple 110.00 7.00
OY2 LI1 1p blue 80.00 2.00
OY3 LI1 2p red brown 150.00 4.25
OY4 LI1 3p chocolate 425.00 22.50
OY5 LI1 6p green 550.00 70.00
OY6 LI1 1sh rose pink 800.00 140.00
Nos. OY1-OY6 (6) 2,115. 245.75

Stamps from outside rows of the sheets sometimes lack watermark.

1903-04 **Wmk. 61** ***Perf. 11, 14x11***

OY7 LI1 ½p purple 120.00 7.00
OY8 LI1 1p blue 75.00 1.10
OY9 LI1 2p red brown 200.00 10.00
Nos. OY7-OY9 (3) 395.00 18.10

Lighthouses — LI2

1905-32 ***Perf. 11, 14, 14x14½***

OY10 LI2 ½p yel grn ('13) 1.40 .90
OY11 LI2 ½p green ('32) 5.75 2.75
OY12 LI2 1p blue ('06) 375.00 29.00
OY13 LI2 1p dp rose ('13) 9.75 1.10
OY14 LI2 1p scarlet ('31) 4.25 2.00
OY15 LI2 1½p gray ('17) 14.00 4.25
OY16 LI2 1½p brn org ('19) 1.75 1.40
OY17 LI2 2p red brown 2,750. 200.00
OY18 LI2 2p violet ('13) 20.00 17.00
OY19 LI2 2p yellow ('21) 6.00 6.00
OY20 LI2 3p ocher ('13) 29.00 20.00
OY21 LI2 3p choc ('31) 11.00 26.00
OY22 LI2 6p car rose ('13) 20.00 26.00
OY23 LI2 6p pink ('31) 20.00 45.00
Nos. OY10-OY23 (14) 3,267. 381.40

#OY15, OY16 have "POSTAGE" at each side.

Stamps from outside rows of the sheets sometimes lack watermark.

1946-47 Wmk. 253 Perf. 14x15

No.	Type	Description	Unused	Used
OY24	LI2	½p yel grn ('47)	1.90	1.90
OY25	LI2	1p scarlet	1.40	1.25
OY26	LI2	2p yellow	2.25	*15.00*
OY27	LI2	3p chocolate	10.50	*30.00*
OY28	LI2	6p pink ('47)	8.50	*25.00*
		Nos. OY24-OY28 (5)	24.55	73.15
		Set, never hinged	42.50	

Catalogue values for unused stamps in this section, from this point to the end of the section, are for Never Hinged items.

New Zealand Lighthouses

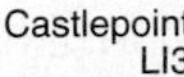
Castlepoint LI3

Taiaroa — LI4

Cape Palliser LI5

Cape Campbell LI6

Eddystone (England) LI7

Stephens Island LI8

The Brothers LI9

Cape Brett — LI10

Perf. 13½x13, 13x13½

1947-65 Engr. Wmk. 253

No.	Type	Description	Unused	Used
OY29	LI3	½p dk grn & red orange	1.75	1.70
OY30	LI4	1p dk ol grn & blue	1.75	1.10
OY31	LI5	2p int bl & gray	.90	.90
OY32	LI6	2½p ultra & blk ('63)	11.00	15.00
OY33	LI7	3p red vio & bl	3.50	.75
OY34	LI8	4p dk brn & org	4.50	1.75
a.		Wmkd. sideways ('65)	4.50	16.00
OY35	LI9	6p dk brn & bl	4.25	2.50
OY36	LI10	1sh red brn & bl	4.25	3.50
		Nos. OY29-OY36 (8)	31.90	27.20

Set first issued Aug. 1, 1947.
Exist imperf.

Nos. OY30, OY32-OY33, OY34a, OY35-OY36 and Types Surcharged

No. OY37

No. OY38

Perf. 13½x13, 13x13½

1967-68 Engr. Wmk. 253

No.	Type	Description	Unused	Used
OY37	LI4	1c on 1p	2.50	4.75
a.		Wmkd. upright ('68)	1.10	4.75
OY38	LI6	2c on 2½p	11.00	16.00
OY39	LI7	2½c on 3p, wmkd. upright	1.75	5.50
a.		Watermarked sideways ('68)	2.75	5.50
OY40	LI8	3c on 4p	5.25	6.25
OY41	LI9	5c on 6p	.85	7.00
OY42	LI10	10c on 1sh, wmkd. sideways	.85	4.75
a.		Watermarked upright	2.40	11.50
		Nos. OY37-OY42 (6)	22.20	44.25

The surcharge is different on each stamp and is adjusted to obliterate old denomination. One dot only on 2½c.
Set first issued July 10, 1967.

Moeraki Point Lighthouse — LI11

Lighthouses: 2½c, Puysegur Point, horiz. 3c, Baring Head. 4c, Cape Egmont, horiz. 8c, East Cape. 10c, Farewell Spit. 15c, Dog Island.

Perf. 13x13½, 13½x13, 14 (8c, 10c)

1969-76 Litho. Unwmk.

No.	Type	Description	Unused	Used
OY43	LI11	½c pur, bl & yel	.75	2.00
OY44	LI11	2½c yel, ultra & grn	.60	1.40
OY45	LI11	3c yellow & brown	.60	.85
OY46	LI11	4c lt ultra & ocher	.60	1.10
OY47	LI11	8c multicolored	.60	3.25
OY48	LI11	10c multicolored	.40	3.25
OY49	LI11	15c multicolored	.40	2.40
a.		Perf. 14 ('78)	1.00	2.50
		Nos. OY43-OY49 (7)	3.95	14.25

Cent. of Government Life Insurance Office.
Issued: #OY47-OY48, 11/17/76; others 3/27/69.

No. OY44 Surcharged with New Value and 4 Diagonal Bars

Perf. 13½x13

1978, Mar. 8 Litho. Wmk. 253

No.	Type	Description	Unused	Used
OY50	LI11	25c on 2½c multi	.85	2.00

Lighthouse — LI12

1981, June 3 Litho. Perf. 14½

No.	Type	Description	Unused	Used
OY51	LI12	5c multicolored	.25	.25
OY52	LI12	10c multicolored	.25	.25
OY53	LI12	20c multicolored	.25	.25
OY54	LI12	30c multicolored	.30	.30
OY55	LI12	40c multicolored	.35	.35
OY56	LI12	50c multicolored	.35	.50
		Nos. OY51-OY56 (6)	1.75	1.90

Government Life Insurance Stamps have been discontinued.

NEWSPAPER STAMPS

Queen Victoria — N1

Wmk. 59

1873, Jan. 1 Typo. Perf. 10

No.	Type	Description	Unused	Used
P1	N1	½p rose	140.00	47.50
a.		Perf. 12½x10	160.00	75.00
b.		Perf. 12½	210.00	75.00

The "N Z" watermark is widely spaced and intended for larger stamps. About a third of the stamps in each sheet are unwatermarked. They are worth a slight premium.
For overprint, see No. O6.

1875, Jan. Wmk. 64 Perf. 12½

No.	Type	Description	Unused	Used
P3	N1	½p rose	25.00	5.00
a.		Pair, imperf. between	800.00	500.00
b.		Perf. 12	70.00	12.50

1892 Wmk. 62 Perf. 12½

No.	Type	Description	Unused	Used
P4	N1	½p bright rose	11.00	1.50
a.		Unwatermarked	20.00	10.00

ROSS DEPENDENCY

Catalogue values for unused stamps in this section are for Never Hinged items.

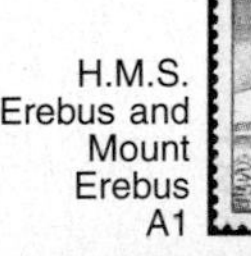
H.M.S. Erebus and Mount Erebus A1

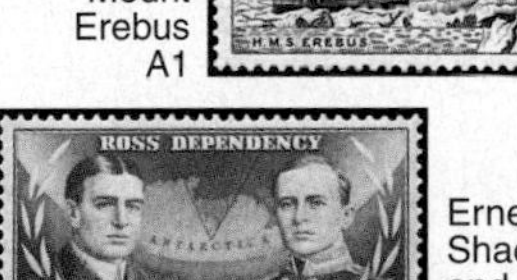
Ernest H. Shackleton and Robert F. Scott — A2

Map Showing Location of Ross Dependency A3

Queen Elizabeth II A4

Perf. 14, 13 (A4)

1957, Jan. 11 Engr. Wmk. 253

No.	Type	Description	Unused	Used
L1	A1	3p dark blue	3.00	1.25
L2	A2	4p dark carmine	3.00	1.25
L3	A3	8p ultra & car rose	3.00	1.25
L4	A4	1sh6p dull violet	3.00	1.25
		Nos. L1-L4 (4)	12.00	5.00

1967, July 10

No.	Type	Description	Unused	Used
L5	A1	2c dark blue	21.00	15.00
L6	A2	3c dark carmine	12.00	10.00
L7	A3	7c ultra & car rose	12.00	10.00
L8	A4	15c dull violet	12.00	10.00
		Nos. L5-L8 (4)	57.00	45.00

Skua — A5

Scott Base — A6

Designs: 4c, Hercules plane unloading at Williams Field. 5c, Shackleton's hut, Cape Royds. 8c, Naval supply ship Endeavour unloading. 18c, Tabular ice floe.

Perf. 13x13½

1972, Jan. 18 Litho. Unwmk.

No.	Type	Description	Unused	Used
L9	A5	3c lt bl, blk & gray	1.00	1.75
L10	A5	4c black & violet	.25	1.75
L11	A5	5c rose lil, blk & gray	.25	1.75
L12	A5	8c blk, dk gray & brn	.25	1.75
		Perf. 14½x14		
L13	A6	10c slate grn, brt grn & blk	.25	1.90
a.		Perf. 14½x13½ ('79)	.70	1.75
L14	A6	18c pur & black	.25	1.90
a.		Perf. 14½x13½ ('79)	1.60	3.00
		Nos. L9-L14 (6)	2.25	10.80

25th Anniv. of Scott Base — A7

5c, Adelie penguins. 10c, Tracked vehicles. 30c, Field party, Upper Taylor Valley. 40c, Vanda Station. 50c, Scott's hut, Cape Evans, 1911.

1982, Jan. 20 Litho. Perf. 15½

No.	Type	Description	Unused	Used
L15	A7	5c multicolored	1.40	1.60
L16	A7	10c multicolored	.25	.75
L17	A7	20c shown	.25	.75
L18	A7	30c multicolored	.25	.45
L19	A7	40c multicolored	.25	.45
L20	A7	50c multicolored	.25	.45
		Nos. L15-L20 (6)	2.65	4.45

Wildlife — A8

5c, South polar skua. 10c, Snow petrel chick. 20c, Black-browed albatross. 45c, Emperor penguins. 50c, Chinstrap penguins. 70c, Adelie penguins. 80c, Elephant seals. $1, Leopard seal. $2, Weddell seal. $3, Crabeater seal pup.

1994-95 Litho. Perf. 13½

No.	Type	Description	Unused	Used
L21	A8	5c multicolored	.25	.25
L22	A8	10c multicolored	.25	.25
L23	A8	20c multicolored	.30	.30
L23A	A8	40c like No. 24	.65	.65
L24	A8	45c multicolored	.70	.70
L25	A8	50c multicolored	.80	.80
L26	A8	70c multicolored	1.10	1.10
L27	A8	80c multicolored	1.25	1.25
L28	A8	$1 multicolored	1.60	1.60
L29	A8	$2 multicolored	3.25	3.25
L30	A8	$3 multicolored	4.75	4.75
		Nos. L21-L30 (11)	14.90	14.90

Issued: 40c, 10/2/95; others, 11/2/94.

Antarctic Explorers A9

Explorer, ships: 40c, James Cook, Resolution & Adventure. 80c, James Clark Ross, Erebus & Terror. $1, Roald Amundsen, Fram. $1.20, Robert Falcon Scott, Terra Nova. $1.50, Ernest Henry Shackleton, Endurance. $1.80, Richard Evelyn Byrd, Floyd Bennett (airplane).

1995, Nov. 9 Litho. Perf. 14½

No.	Type	Description	Unused	Used
L31	A9	40c multicolored	.65	.65
L32	A9	80c multicolored	1.25	1.25
L33	A9	$1 multicolored	1.60	1.60
L34	A9	$1.20 multicolored	1.90	1.90
L35	A9	$1.50 multicolored	2.40	2.40
L36	A9	$1.80 multicolored	2.75	2.75
		Nos. L31-L36 (6)	10.55	10.55

Antarctic Landscapes — A10

Designs: 40c, Inside ice cave, vert. 80c, Base of glacier, vert. $1, Glacier ice fall, vert. $1.20, Climbers on crater rim. $1.50, Pressure ridges. $1.80, Fumarole ice tower.

1996, Nov. 13 Litho. *Perf. 14*

L37	A10	40c	multicolored	.65	.65
L38	A10	80c	multicolored	1.25	1.25
L39	A10	$1	multicolored	1.60	1.60
L40	A10	$1.20	multicolored	1.90	1.90
L41	A10	$1.50	multicolored	2.40	2.40
L42	A10	$1.80	multicolored	2.75	2.75
			Nos. L37-L42 (6)	10.55	10.55

Antarctic Sea Birds — A11

40c, Snow petrel. 80c, Cape petrel. $1, Antarctic prion. $1.20, Antarctic fulmar. $1.50, Antarctic petrel. $1.80, Antarctic tern.

1997, Nov. 12 Litho. *Perf. 14*

L43	A11	40c	multi	.65	.65
L44	A11	80c	multi	1.25	1.25
L45	A11	$1	multi	1.75	1.50
L46	A11	$1.20	multi	2.25	2.00
L47	A11	$1.50	multi	2.50	2.25
L48	A11	$1.80	multi	3.00	15.00
			Nos. L43-L48 (6)	11.40	22.65
L48A			Block of 6, #L45, L48, L48b-L48e	20.00	20.00
b.			A11 40c As #L43, without WWF emblem	.90	.90
c.			A11 80c As #L44, without WWF emblem	1.75	1.75
d.			A11 $1.20 As #L46, without WWF emblem	2.75	2.75
e.			A11 $1.50 As #L47, without WWF emblem	3.50	3.50

World Wildlife Fund. Nos. L43-L44, L46-L47 have WWF emblem. Nos. L45 and L48 do not have emblem.

Ice Formations A12

Designs: 40c, Sculptured sea ice. 80c, Glacial tongue. $1, Stranded tabular iceberg. $1.20, Autumn at Cape Evans. $1.50, Sea ice in summer thaw. $1.80, Sunset on tabular icebergs.

1998, Nov. 11 Litho. *Perf. 14*

L49	A12	40c	multicolored	.65	.65
L50	A12	80c	multicolored	1.25	1.25
L51	A12	$1	multicolored	1.60	1.60
L52	A12	$1.20	multicolored	1.90	1.90
L53	A12	$1.50	multicolored	2.40	2.40
L54	A12	$1.80	multicolored	2.75	2.75
a.			Block of 6, #L49-L54	15.00	15.00
			Nos. L49-L54 (6)	10.55	10.55

Night Skies A13

Designs: 40c, Sea smoke, McMurdo Sound. 80c, Alpenglow, Mt. Erebus. $1.10, Sunset, Black Island. $1.20, Pressure ridges, Ross Sea. $1.50, Evening light, Ross Island. $1.80, Mother of pearl clouds, Ross Island.

1999, Nov. 17 Litho. *Perf. 14*

L55	A13	40c	multicolored	.65	.65
L56	A13	80c	multicolored	1.25	1.25
L57	A13	$1.10	multicolored	1.75	1.75
L58	A13	$1.20	multicolored	1.90	1.90
L59	A13	$1.50	multicolored	2.40	2.40
L60	A13	$1.80	multicolored	2.75	2.75
			Nos. L55-L60 (6)	10.70	10.70

Antarctic Transportation — A14

Designs: 40c, RNZAF C130 Hercules. 80c, Hagglunds BV206 All-terrain carrier. $1.10, Tracked 4x4 motorbike. $1.20, ASV Track truck. $1.50, Squirrel helicopter. $1.80, Elan Skidoo.

2000, Nov. 4 Litho. *Perf. 14*

L61	A14	40c	multi	.65	.65
L62	A14	80c	multi	1.25	1.25
L63	A14	$1.10	multi	1.75	1.75
L64	A14	$1.20	multi	1.90	1.90
L65	A14	$1.50	multi	2.40	2.40
L66	A14	$1.80	multi	2.75	2.75
			Nos. L61-L66 (6)	10.70	10.70

Penguins Type of 2001 of New Zealand

Designs: 40c, Emperor. 80c, Adelie. 90c, Emperor, diff. $1.30, Adelie, diff. $1.50, Emperor, diff. $2, Adelie, diff.

2001, Nov. 7 *Perf. 14¼*

L67	A475	40c	multi	.65	.65
L68	A475	80c	multi	1.25	1.25
L69	A475	90c	multi	1.40	1.40
L70	A475	$1.30	multi	2.10	2.10
L71	A475	$1.50	multi	2.40	2.40
L72	A475	$2	multi	3.25	3.25
			Nos. L67-L72 (6)	11.05	11.05

Discovery Expedition of Capt. Robert Falcon Scott, 1901-04 A15

Designs: 40c, Three men with sleds. 80c, HMS Discovery. 90c, HMS Discovery trapped in ice. $1.30, Edward Wilson, Ernest Shackleton and sleds. $1.50, Explorers with flags and dog. $2, Base hut.

2002, Nov. 6 Litho. *Perf. 14*

L73	A15	40c	multi	.65	.65
L74	A15	80c	multi	1.25	1.25
L75	A15	90c	multi	1.40	1.40
L76	A15	$1.30	multi	2.10	2.10
L77	A15	$1.50	multi	2.40	2.40
L78	A15	$2	multi	3.25	3.25
			Nos. L73-L78 (6)	11.05	11.05

Marine Life — A16

Designs: 40c, Odontaster validus. 90c, Beroe cucumis. $1.30, Macroptychaster accrescens. $1.50, Sterechinus neumayeri. $2, Perkinsiana littoralis.

2003, Oct. 1 Litho. *Perf. 13x13¼*

L79	A16	40c	multi	.65	.65
L80	A16	90c	multi	1.40	1.40
L81	A16	$1.30	multi	2.10	2.10
L82	A16	$1.50	multi	2.40	2.40
L83	A16	$2	multi	3.25	3.25
			Nos. L79-L83 (5)	9.80	9.80

Emperor Penguins and Map of Antarctica — A17

Various pictures of penguins.

2004, Nov. 3 Litho. *Perf. 13¼x14*
Color of Denomination

L84	A17	45c	yellow orange	.70	.70
L85	A17	90c	dark brown	1.40	1.40
L86	A17	$1.35	lilac	2.10	2.10
L87	A17	$1.50	red brown	2.40	2.40
L88	A17	$2	gray blue	3.25	3.25
			Nos. L84-L88 (5)	9.85	9.85

Photographs — A18

Designs: 45c, Dry Valleys, by Craig Potton. 90c, Emperor Penguins, by Andris Apse. $1.35, Fur Seal, by Mark Mitchell. $1.50, Captain Scott's Hut, by Colin Monteath. $2. Minke Whale, by Kim Westerskov.

2005, Nov. 2 Litho. *Perf. 13¼*

L89	A18	45c	multi	.70	.70
L90	A18	90c	multi	1.40	1.40
L91	A18	$1.35	multi	2.10	2.10
L92	A18	$1.50	multi	2.40	2.40
L93	A18	$2	multi	3.25	3.25
			Nos. L89-L93 (5)	9.85	9.85

A sheet containing Nos. L89-L93 was in a limited edition album.

New Zealand Antarctic Program, 50th Anniv. A19

Designs: 45c, Biologist. 90c, Hydrologist. $1.35, Geologist. $1.50, Meteorologist. $2, Marine biologist.

2006, Nov. 1 Litho. *Perf. 14*

L94	A19	45c	multi	.70	.70
L95	A19	90c	multi	1.40	1.40
L96	A19	$1.35	multi	2.10	2.10
L97	A19	$1.50	multi	2.40	2.40
L98	A19	$2	multi	3.25	3.25
			Nos. L94-L98 (5)	9.85	9.85

Commonwealth Trans-Antarctic Expedition, 50th Anniv. — A20

Designs: 50c, Man and Beaver airplane. $1, Man and sled. $1.50, Sled dogs. $2, TE20 Ferguson tractor. $2.50, HMNZS Endeavour.

2007, Nov. 7 Litho. *Perf. 14*

L99	A20	50c	multi	.80	.80
L100	A20	$1	multi	1.50	1.50
L101	A20	$1.50	multi	2.40	2.40
L102	A20	$2	multi	3.25	3.25
L103	A20	$2.50	multi	4.00	4.00
a.			Souvenir sheet, #L102-L103	7.25	7.25
			Nos. L99-L103 (5)	11.95	11.95

1907-09 British Antarctic Expedition A21

Designs: 50c, Departure of Nimrod from Lyttleton. $1, Expedition Hut, Cape Royds. $1.50, First vehicle on Antarctica. $2, First men to reach South Magnetic Pole. $2.50, First ascent of Mt. Erebus.

2008, Nov. 5 Litho. *Perf. 13½x13¼*

L104	A21	50c	multi	.80	.80
L105	A21	$1	multi	1.50	1.50
L106	A21	$1.50	multi	2.40	2.40
L107	A21	$2	multi	3.25	3.25
L108	A21	$2.50	multi	4.00	4.00
			Nos. L104-L108 (5)	11.95	11.95

Signing of Antarctic Treaty, 50th Anniv. — A22

Mountains and: 50c, Map of Antarctica. $1, Penguins. $1.80, Scientist and equipment. $2.30, Flags. $2.80, Seal.

Perf. 13¼x13½
2009, Nov. 25 Litho.

L109	A22	50c	multi	.75	.75
L110	A22	$1	multi	1.50	1.50
L111	A22	$1.80	multi	2.60	2.60
L112	A22	$2.30	multi	3.25	3.25
L113	A22	$2.80	multi	4.00	4.00
			Nos. L109-L113 (5)	12.10	12.10

Whales — A23

Designs: 60c, Sperm whale. $1.20, Minke whale. $1.90, Sei whale. $2.40, Killer whale. $2.90, Humpback whale.

2010, Nov. 17 Litho. *Perf. 15x14¾*

L114	A23	60c	multi	.95	.95
L115	A23	$1.20	multi	1.90	1.90
L116	A23	$1.90	multi	3.00	3.00
L117	A23	$2.40	multi	3.75	3.75
L118	A23	$2.90	multi	4.50	4.50
a.			Souvenir sheet of 5, #L114-L118	14.50	14.50
			Nos. L114-L118 (5)	14.10	14.10

Race to the South Pole A24

Map of Antarctica and: 60c, Roald Amundsen and ship, Fram. $1.20, Men of Amundsen's expedition. $1.90, Robert Falcon Scott and ship Terra Nova. $2.40, Men of Scott expedition, cross on cairn. $2.90, Flags of United Kingdom and Norway.

2011, Nov. 2 *Perf. 13½x13¼*

L119	A24	60c	multi	.95	.95
L120	A24	$1.20	multi	1.90	1.90
L121	A24	$1.90	multi	3.00	3.00
L122	A24	$2.40	multi	4.00	4.00
a.			Souvenir sheet of 2, #L121-L122	10.00	10.00
L123	A24	$2.90	multi	4.75	4.75
a.			Souvenir sheet of 5, #L119-L123	15.00	15.00
			Nos. L119-L123 (5)	14.60	14.60

Issued: No. L122a, 1/14/12. Christchurch Philatelic Society Centennial Stamp and Postcard Exhibition (#L122a).

Antarctic Landscapes — A25

Designs: 70c, Mount Erebus. $1.40, Beardmore Glacier. $1.90, Lake Vanda. $2.40, Cape Adare. $2.90, Ross Ice Shelf.

2012, Nov. 21

L124	A25	70c multi	1.25	1.25
L125	A25	$1.40 multi	2.40	2.40
L126	A25	$1.90 multi	3.25	3.25
L127	A25	$2.40 multi	4.00	4.00
L128	A25	$2.90 multi	4.75	4.75
a.		Souvenir sheet of 5, #L124-L128	16.00	16.00
		Nos. L124-L128 (5)	15.65	15.65

Antarctic Food Web — A26

Designs: 70c, Antarctic krill. $1.40, Lesser snow petrel. $1.90, Adélie penguin. $2.40, Crabeater seal. $2.90, Blue whale.

2013, Nov. 20 Litho. *Perf. 14*

L129	A26	70c multi	1.25	1.25
L130	A26	$1.40 multi	2.40	2.40
L131	A26	$1.90 multi	3.25	3.25
L132	A26	$2.40 multi	4.00	4.00
L133	A26	$2.90 multi	4.75	4.75
a.		Souvenir sheet of 5, #L129-L133	16.00	16.00
		Nos. L129-L133 (5)	15.65	15.65

Penguins

Designs: 80c, Emperor penguins. $1.40, Adélie penguin. $2, Macaroni penguins. $2.50, Gentoo penguin and eggs. $3, Chinstrap penguin.

2014, Nov. 19 Litho. *Perf. 14½*

L134	A27	80c multi	1.25	1.25
L135	A27	$1.40 multi	2.25	2.25
L136	A27	$2 multi	3.25	3.25
L137	A27	$2.50 multi	4.00	4.00
L138	A27	$3 multi	4.75	4.75
a.		Souvenir sheet of 1 + label	4.75	4.75
b.		Souvenir sheet of 5, #L134-L138	15.50	15.50
		Nos. L134-L138 (5)	15.50	15.50

Values for Nos. L134-L138 are for stamps with surrounding selvage. See Greenland No. 679a.

Imperial Trans-Antarctic Expedition, Cent. — A28

Designs: No. L139, S.Y. Endurance. No. L140, Ocean Camp. $1.40, Expedition members in boat going from Elephant Island to South Georgia. $2, S.Y. Aurora. $2.50, Expedition members laying depots. $3, Rescue of the Ross Sea Party.

2015, Nov. 4 Litho. *Perf. 14x14½*

L139	A28	80c multi	1.10	1.10
L140	A28	80c multi	1.10	1.10
L141	A28	$1.40 multi	1.90	1.90
a.		Souvenir sheet of 3, #L139-L141	4.25	4.25
L142	A28	$2 multi	2.75	2.75
L143	A28	$2.50 multi	3.50	3.50
L144	A28	$3 multi	4.00	4.00
a.		Souvenir sheet of 3, #L142-L144	10.50	10.50
		Nos. L139-L144 (6)	14.35	14.35

Advantage Stocksheets

Advantage Stocksheets fit directly in your 2-post or 3-ring National or Specialty album. Choose your favorite style, available with up to 8 pockets. **Stocksheets are sold in packages of 10.**

- Stocksheets match album pages in every respect, including size, border and color. Pages are punched to fit perfectly in your binder.
- These sheets are ideal for storing minor varieties and collateral material – a great place to keep new issues until the next supplement is available!
- Clear acetate pockets on heavyweight pages provide protection for your valuable stamps.

Retail Price $21.99 **AA* Price $19.99**

NUMBER OF POCKETS	POCKET SIZE	NATIONAL BORDER ITEM #	SPECIALTY BORDER ITEM #
1 Pocket	242mm	AD11	AD21
2 Pockets	119mm	AD12	AD22
3 Pockets	79mm	AD13	AD23
4 Pockets	58mm	AD14	AD24
5 Pockets	45mm	AD15	AD25
6 Pockets	37mm	AD16	AD26
7 Pockets	34mm	AD17	AD27
8 Pockets	31mm	AD18	AD28

Visit AmosAdvantage.com

Call 1-800-572-6885

Outside U.S. & Canada 937-498-0800

Mail to: P.O. Box 4129, Sidney OH 45365

ORDERING INFORMATION

1. *AA prices apply to paid subscribers of Amos Media titles, or for orders placed online.
2. Prices, terms and product availability subject to change. Taxes will apply in CA, OH, & IL.
3. Shipping & Handling: United States: Orders under $10 are only $3.99; Orders over $10 are 10% of order total. Minimum charge $7.99, Maximum charge $45. Canada: 20% of order total. Minimum charge $19.99, Maximum charge $200. Foreign orders are shipped via FedEx Intl and billed actual freight.

NICARAGUA

ˌni-kə-ˈrä-gwə

LOCATION — Central America, between Honduras and Costa Rica
GOVT. — Republic
AREA — 50,439 sq. mi.
POP. — 4,384,400 (1997 est.)
CAPITAL — Managua

100 Centavos = 1 Peso
100 Centavos = 1 Córdoba (1913)

Catalogue values for unused stamps in this country are for Never Hinged items, beginning with Scott 689 in the regular postage section, Scott C261 in the airpost section, Scott CO37 in the airpost official section, and Scott RA60 in the postal tax section.

ISSUES OF THE REPUBLIC

Watermarks

Wmk. 117 — Liberty Cap

Wmk. 209 — Multiple Ovals

Liberty Cap on Mountain Peak; From Seal of Country — A1

Unwmk.

1862, Dec. 2 Engr. *Perf. 12*

Yellowish Paper

1	A1	2c dark blue	75.00	20.00
2	A1	5c black	150.00	60.00

Designs of Nos. 1-2 measure 22½x18½mm. Perforations are invariably rough.

Values are for stamps without gum. Examples with gum sell for more. Nos. 1-2 were canceled only by pen.

There is one reported cover of No. 1, two of No. 2.

See No. C509.

A2 A3

1869-71 White Paper

3	A1	1c bister ('71)	3.00	1.25
4	A1	2c blue	3.00	1.25
5	A1	5c black	100.00	1.00
6	A2	10c vermilion	4.00	1.75
7	A3	25c green	7.50	4.00
		Nos. 3-7 (5)	117.50	9.25

Designs of Nos. 3-7 measure 22½x19mm. Perforations are clean cut.

There are two reported covers of No. 5, five of No. 7.

1878-80 *Rouletted 8½*

8	A1	1c brown	2.00	1.25
9	A1	2c blue	2.00	1.25
10	A1	5c black	50.00	1.00
11	A2	10c ver ('80)	2.50	1.50
12	A3	25c green ('79)	2.50	4.00
		Nos. 8-12 (5)	59.00	9.00

Most values exist on thicker soft paper.

Stamps with letter/numeral cancellations other than "3 G," "6 M," "9 C" sell for more.

Nos. 3-12 were reprinted in 1892. The corresponding values of the two series are printed in the same shades which is not usually true of the originals. They are, however, similar to some of the original shades and the only certain test is comparison. Originals have thin white gum; reprints have rather thick yellowish gum. Value 50c each. Unused examples of Nos. 3-12 without gum should be presumed to be reprints. Nos. 5 and 10 unused are extremely scarce and should be purchased with original gum and should be expertized.

Seal of Nicaragua — A4

1882 Engr. *Perf. 12*

13	A4	1c green	.25	.25
14	A4	2c carmine	.25	.25
15	A4	5c blue	.30	.25
16	A4	10c dull violet	.40	.75
17	A4	15c yellow	.80	25.00
18	A4	20c slate gray	1.60	5.00
19	A4	50c dull violet	2.25	25.00
		Nos. 13-19 (7)	5.85	56.50

Used Values

of Nos. 13-120 are for stamps with genuine cancellations applied while the stamps were valid. Various counterfeit cancellations exist.

Locomotive and Telegraph Key — A5

1890 Engr.

20	A5	1c yellow brown	.25	.25
21	A5	2c vermilion	.25	.25
22	A5	5c deep blue	.25	.25
23	A5	10c lilac gray	.25	.25
24	A5	20c red	.25	1.75
25	A5	50c purple	.25	5.00
26	A5	1p brown	.25	8.50
27	A5	2p dark green	.25	9.00
28	A5	5p lake	.25	
29	A5	10p orange	.25	
		Nos. 20-29 (10)	2.50	

The issues of 1890-1899 were printed by the Hamilton Bank Note Co., New York, to the order of N. F. Seebeck who held a contract for stamps with the government of Nicaragua. Reprints were made, for sale to collectors, of the 1896, 1897 and 1898, postage, postage due and official stamps. See notes following those issues.

For overprints see Nos. O1-O10.

Perforation Varieties

Imperfs and part perfs of all the Seebeck issues, Nos. 20-120, exist for all except originals of the 1898 issue, Nos. 99-109M.

Goddess of Plenty — A6

1891 Engr.

30	A6	1c yellow brn	.25	.35
31	A6	2c red	.25	.35
32	A6	5c dk blue	.25	.25
33	A6	10c slate	.25	.50
34	A6	20c plum	.25	2.00
35	A6	50c purple	.25	5.00
36	A6	1p black brn	.25	5.00
37	A6	2p green	.25	8.50
38	A6	5p brown red	.25	
39	A6	10p orange	.25	
		Nos. 30-39 (10)	2.50	

For overprints see Nos. O11-O20.

Columbus Sighting Land — A7

1892 Engr.

40	A7	1c yellow brn	.25	.25
41	A7	2c vermilion	.25	.25
42	A7	5c dk blue	.25	.25
43	A7	10c slate	.25	.25
44	A7	20c plum	.25	2.00
45	A7	50c purple	.25	7.00
46	A7	1p brown	.25	7.00
47	A7	2p blue grn	.25	8.50
48	A7	5p rose lake	.25	
49	A7	10p orange	.25	
		Nos. 40-49 (10)	2.50	

Commemorative of the 400th anniversary of the discovery of America by Columbus.

Stamps of the 1892 design were printed in other colors than those listed and overprinted "Telegrafos". The 1c blue, 10c orange, 20c slate, 50c plum and 2p vermilion are telegraph stamps which did not receive the overprint.

For overprints see Nos. O21-O30.

Arms — A8

1893 Engr.

51	A8	1c yellow brn	.25	.25
52	A8	2c vermilion	.25	.25
53	A8	5c dk blue	.25	.25
54	A8	10c slate	.25	.25
55	A8	20c dull red	.25	1.50
56	A8	50c violet	.25	4.00
57	A8	1p dk brown	.25	7.00
58	A8	2p blue green	.25	8.50
59	A8	5p rose lake	.25	
60	A8	10p orange	.25	
		Nos. 51-60 (10)	2.50	

The 1c blue and 2c dark brown are telegraph stamps which did not receive the "Telegrafos" overprint.

For overprints see Nos. O31-O41.

"Victory" — A9

1894 Engr.

61	A9	1c yellow brn	.25	.30
62	A9	2c vermilion	.25	.40
63	A9	5c dp blue	.25	.30
64	A9	10c slate	.25	.40
65	A9	20c lake	.25	2.00
66	A9	50c purple	.25	5.00
67	A9	1p brown	.25	9.50
68	A9	2p green	.25	17.50
69	A9	5p brown red	.25	45.00
70	A9	10p orange	.25	45.00
		Nos. 61-70 (10)	2.50	125.40

There were three printings of this issue. Only the first is known postally used. Unused values are for the third printing.

Used values are for stamps with "DIRECCION" cancels in black that were removed from post office new year cards.

Specialists believe the 25c yellow green, type A9, is a telegraph denomination never issued for postal purposes. Stamps in other colors are telegraph stamps without the usual "Telegrafos" overprint.

For overprints see Nos. O42-O51.

Coat of Arms — A10

1895 Engr.

71	A10	1c yellow brn	.25	.30
72	A10	2c vermilion	.25	.30
73	A10	5c deep blue	.25	.25
74	A10	10c slate	.25	.25
75	A10	20c claret	.25	.75
76	A10	50c light violet	50.00	5.00
77	A10	1p dark brown	.25	5.00
78	A10	2p deep green	.25	8.00
79	A10	5p brown red	.25	11.00
80	A10	10p orange	.25	
		Nos. 71-80 (10)	52.25	

Frames of Nos. 71-80 differ for each denomination.

A 50c violet blue exists. Its status is questioned. Value 25c.

There was little proper use of No. 80. Canceled examples are almost always c-t-o or have faked cancels.

For overprints see Nos. O52-O71.

Map of Nicaragua — A11

1896 Engr.

81	A11	1c violet	.30	1.00
82	A11	2c blue grn	.30	.50
83	A11	5c brt rose	.30	.30
84	A11	10c blue	.50	.50
85	A11	20c bister brn	3.00	4.00
86	A11	50c blue gray	.60	8.00
87	A11	1p black	.75	11.00
88	A11	2p claret	.75	15.00
89	A11	5p deep blue	.75	15.00
		Nos. 81-89 (9)	7.25	55.30

There were two printings of this issue. Only the first is known postally used. Unused values are for the second printing.

See italic note after No. 109M.

For overprints see Nos. O82-O117.

Wmk. 117

89A	A11	1c violet	3.75	.90
89B	A11	2c bl grn	3.75	1.25
89C	A11	5c brt rose	15.00	.30
89D	A11	10c blue	25.00	.90
89E	A11	20c bis brn	22.50	4.25
89F	A11	50c bl gray	42.50	9.00
89G	A11	1p black	37.50	12.50
89H	A11	2p claret		18.00
89I	A11	5p dp bl		40.00

Same, dated 1897

1897 Engr. Unwmk.

90	A11	1c violet	.50	.50
91	A11	2c bl grn	.50	.60
92	A11	5c brt rose	.50	.30
93	A11	10c blue	6.25	.75
94	A11	20c bis brn	2.50	3.75
95	A11	50c bl gray	9.00	9.50
96	A11	1p black	9.00	15.00
97	A11	2p claret	20.00	19.00
98	A11	5p dp bl	20.00	42.50
		Nos. 90-98 (9)	68.25	91.90

See italic note after No. 109M.

Wmk. 117

98A	A11	1c violet	14.00	.50
98B	A11	2c bl grn	14.00	.50
98C	A11	5c brt rose	20.00	.40
98D	A11	10c blue	22.50	.90
98E	A11	20c bis brn	22.50	4.25
98F	A11	50c bl gray	22.50	8.00
98G	A11	1p black	25.00	16.00
98H	A11	2p claret	25.00	25.00
98I	A11	5p dp bl	125.00	50.00
		Nos. 98A-98I (9)	290.50	105.55

Coat of Arms of "Republic of Central America" — A12

1898 Engr. Wmk. 117

99	A12	1c brown	.25	.40
100	A12	2c slate	.25	.40
101	A12	4c red brown	.25	.50
102	A12	5c olive green	40.00	22.50
103	A12	10c violet	15.00	.60
104	A12	15c ultra	.40	1.50
105	A12	20c blue	10.00	2.00
106	A12	50c yellow	10.00	9.50
107	A12	1p violet blue	.40	16.00
108	A12	2p brown	19.00	22.50
109	A12	5p orange	25.00	32.50
		Nos. 99-109 (11)	120.55	108.40

Unwmk.

109A	A12	1c brown	1.25	.30
109B	A12	2c slate	1.25	
109D	A12	4c red brown	2.25	.60
109E	A12	5c olive green	25.00	.25
109G	A12	10c violet	25.00	.60
109H	A12	15c ultra	25.00	

109I A12 20c blue 25.00
109J A12 50c yellow 25.00
109K A12 1p deep ultra 25.00
109L A12 2p olive brown 25.00
109M A12 5p orange 25.00
Nos. 109A-109M (11) 204.75

The paper of Nos. 109A to 109M is slightly thicker and more opaque than that of Nos. 81 to 89 and 90 to 98. The 5c and 10c also exist on very thin, semi-transparent paper.

Many reprints of Nos. 81-98, 98F-98H, 99-109M are on thick, porous paper, with and without watermark. The watermark is sideways. Paper of the originals is thinner for Nos. 81-109 but thicker for Nos. 109A-109M. Value 25c each.

In addition, reprints of Nos. 81-89 and 90-98 exist on thin paper, but with shades differing slightly from those of originals.

For overprints see Nos. O118-O128.

"Justice" — A13

1899 **Litho.**

110 A13 1c gray grn .25 *.35*
111 A13 2c brown .25 *.25*
112 A13 4c dp rose .35 *.40*
113 A13 5c dp bl .25 *.25*
114 A13 10c buff .25 *.30*
115 A13 15c chocolate .25 *.65*
116 A13 20c dk grn .35 *.75*
117 A13 50c brt rose .25 *3.00*
118 A13 1p red .25 *8.50*
119 A13 2p violet .25 *20.00*
120 A13 5p lt bl .25 *25.00*
Nos. 110-120 (11) 2.95 *59.45*

Nos. 110-120 exist imperf. and in horizontal pairs imperf. between.

Nos. 110-111, 113 exist perf 6x12 due to defective perforating equipment.

For overprints see Nos. O129-O139.

Mt. Momotombo A14

Imprint: "American Bank Note Co. NY"

1900, Jan. 1 **Engr.**

121 A14 1c plum .50 .25
122 A14 2c vermilion .50 .25
123 A14 3c green .75 .25
124 A14 4c ol grn 1.00 .25
125 A14 5c dk bl 4.00 .25
126 A14 6c car rose 14.00 5.00
127 A14 10c violet 7.00 .25
128 A14 15c ultra 8.00 .65
129 A14 20c brown 8.00 .65
130 A14 50c lake 7.00 1.10
131 A14 1p yellow 12.00 4.00
132 A14 2p salmon 10.00 2.25
133 A14 5p black 10.00 3.00
Nos. 121-133 (13) 82.75 18.15

Used values for #123, 126, 130-133 are for canceled to order examples.

See Nos. 159-161. For overprints and surcharges see Nos. 134-136, 144-151, 162-163, 175-178, O150-O154, 1L1-1L13, 1L16-1L19, 1L20, 2L1-2L10, 2L16-2L24, 2L36-2L39.

Mt. Momotombo — A14a

1902 **White Wove Paper** ***Imperf.***
Size: 55x52mm

133A A14a 5c blue
133B A14a 10c red violet
133C A14a 20c brown
133D A14a 30c black green
133E A14a 50c red

51x51mm

133F A14a 2c dk red, *buff*
133G A14a 4c red brown, *buff*

Nos. 133A-133G are documented on covers postmarked from 1902-04. Specimen pairs and blocks are from sheets of 35 (Nos. 133A-133E) or 28 (Nos. 133F-133G) sold in the 1990 American Bank Note Company archives sale. Nos. 133A-133G are not cutouts from similar postal envelopes issued in 1900.

Nos. 131-133 Surcharged in Black or Red

1901, Mar. 5

134 A14 2c on 1p yel 5.00 4.50
a. Bar below date 16.00 *9.00*
b. Inverted surcharge *35.00*
c. Double surcharge *50.00*
135 A14 10c on 5p blk (R) 12.00 4.50
a. Bar below date 17.50 8.00
136 A14 20c on 2p salmon 7.50 7.50
a. Bar below date 14.00 10.00
Nos. 134-136 (3) 24.50 16.50

A 2c surcharge on No. 121, the 1c plum, was not put on sale, though some are known used from a few sheets distributed by the post office to "government friends." Value, *$250.00.*

The 2c on 1p yellow without ornaments is a reprint.

Postage Due Stamps of 1900 Overprinted in Black or Gold

1901, Mar.

137 D3 1c plum 4.50 3.50
138 D3 2c vermilion 4.50 3.50
139 D3 5c dk bl 6.00 3.50
140 D3 10c pur (G) 8.50 8.50
a. Double overprint 14.00 14.00
141 D3 20c org brn 10.00 10.00
142 D3 30c dk grn 10.00 6.50
143 D3 50c lake 8.50 4.00
a. "1091" for "1901" 35.00 35.00
b. "Correo" 37.50
Nos. 137-143 (7) 52.00 39.50

In 1904 an imitation of this overprint was made to fill a dealer's order. The date is at top and "Correos" at bottom. The overprint is printed in black, sideways on the 1c and 2c and upright on the 5c and 10c. Some examples of the 2c were further surcharged "1 Centavo." None of these stamps was ever regularly used.

Nos. 126, 131-133 Surcharged

1901, Oct. 20 **Black Surcharge**

144 A14 3c on 6c rose 12.00 5.00
a. Bar below value 13.00 5.50
b. Inverted surcharge 14.00 8.00
c. Double surcharge 14.00 8.00
d. Double surch., one inverted 25.00 25.00
145 A14 4c on 6c rose 8.00 4.00
a. Bar below value 8.00 4.50
b. "1 cent" instead of "4 cent" 11.00 8.00
c. Double surcharge 20.00 20.00
146 A14 5c on 1p yellow 6.00 4.00
a. Three bars below value 7.00 4.50
b. Ornaments at each side of "1901" 30.00 4.50
c. Double surcharge, one in red 17.50 15.00
147 A14 10c on 2p salmon 6.50 4.00
a. Inverted surcharge 30.00 27.50
b. Double surcharge

Blue Surcharge

148 A14 3c on 6c rose 9.00 4.50
a. Bar below value 10.00 5.50
b. Double surcharge 11.00 8.00
149 A14 4c on 6c rose 12.00 5.00
a. Bar below value 13.00 7.50
b. "1 cent" instead of "4 cent" 20.00 10.00
c. Inverted surcharge 25.00 20.00

Red Surcharge

150 A14 5c on 1p yellow 8.00 6.50
a. Three bars below value 10.00 7.00
b. Ornaments at each side of "1901" 10.00 7.00
c. Inverted surcharge 20.00 12.00
d. Double surcharge, inverted 22.50 17.50
151 A14 20c on 5p black 5.50 3.50
a. Inverted surcharge 20.00 16.00
b. Double surcharge 22.50 22.50
c. Triple surcharge
Nos. 144-151 (8) 67.00 36.50

In 1904 a series was surcharged as above, but with "Centavos" spelled out. About the same time No. 122 was surcharged "1 cent." and "1901," "1902" or "1904." All of these surcharges were made to fill a dealer's order and none of the stamps was regularly issued or used.

Postage Due Stamps of 1900 Overprinted in Black

1901, Oct.

152 D3 1c red violet 1.00 .40
a. Ornaments at each side of the stamp 10.00 .65
b. Ornaments at each side of "1901" 1.10 .65
c. "Correos" in italics 1.50 1.50
d. Double overprint 14.00 14.00
153 D3 2c vermilion .75 .40
a. Double overprint 8.50 5.50
154 D3 5c dark blue 1.00 .60
a. Double overprint, one inverted
b. Double overprint 7.00 7.00
155 D3 10c purple 1.00 .60
b. Double overprint 10.00 10.00
c. Double overprint, one inverted 12.00 12.00
156 D3 20c org brn 1.25 1.25
b. Double overprint 7.00 7.00
157 D3 30c dk grn 1.00 1.10
a. Double overprint 9.00 9.00
b. Inverted overprint 19.00 19.00
158 D3 50c lake 1.00 1.10
a. Triple overprint 25.00 25.00
b. Double overprint 16.00 16.00
Nos. 152-158 (7) 7.00 5.45

One stamp in each group of 25 has the 2nd "o" of "Correos" italic. Value twice normal.

Momotombo Type of 1900
Without Imprint

1902 **Litho.** ***Perf. 14***

159 A14 5c blue .50 .25
a. Imperf., pair 3.75
160 A14 5c carmine .50 .25
a. Imperf., pair 3.75
161 A14 10c violet 1.50 .25
a. Imperf., pair 3.75
Nos. 159-161 (3) 2.50 .75

No. 161 was privately surcharged 6c, 1p and 5p in black in 1903. Not fully authorized but known postally used. Value of c-t-o peso denominations, $5 each.

Nos. 121 and 122 Surcharged in Black

1902, Oct. ***Perf. 12***

162 A14 15c on 2c ver 4.00 .75
a. Double surcharge 32.50
b. Blue surcharge 90.00
163 A14 30c on 1c plum 3.00 2.25
a. Double surcharge 12.00
b. Inverted surcharge 27.50

Counterfeits of No. 163 exist in slightly smaller type.

President José Santos Zelaya — A15

1903, Jan. **Engr.**

167 A15 1c emer & blk .45 .50
168 A15 2c rose & blk 1.00 .50
169 A15 5c ultra & blk .50 .50
170 A15 10c yel & blk .50 *.85*
171 A15 15c lake & blk .95 *2.00*
172 A15 20c vio & blk .95 *2.00*
173 A15 50c ol & blk .95 *5.00*
174 A15 1p red brn & blk .95 *6.00*
Nos. 167-174 (8) 6.25 *17.35*

10th anniv. of 1st election of Pres. Zelaya.

The so-called color errors-1c orange yellow and black, 2c ultramarine and black, 5c lake and black and 10c emerald and black-were also delivered to postal authorities. They were intended for official use though not issued as such. Value, $4 each.

No. 161 Surcharged in Blue

Nos. 175-176

No. 177

1904-05

175 A14 5c on 10c vio ('05) 1.75 .25
a. Inverted surcharge 5.50 3.00
b. Without ornaments 2.00 .70
c. Character for "cents" inverted 1.75 .40
d. As "b," inverted
e. As "c," inverted 2.75 2.75
f. Double surcharge 25.00 8.00
g. "5" omitted 2.75 2.75
176 A14 15c on 10c vio ('05) .90 .30
a. Inverted surcharge 3.00 1.40
b. Without ornaments 2.00 1.40
c. Character for "cents" inverted 2.00 1.10
d. As "b," inverted
e. As "c," inverted 5.00 1.75
f. Imperf. 7.00
h. As "a," imperf. 10.00 9.00
i. Double surcharge 16.00 14.00
177 A14 15c on 10c vio 4.50 2.75
a. Inverted surcharge 7.00 6.00
b. "Centcvos" 7.00 4.50
c. "5" of "15" omitted 12.50
d. As "b," inverted 8.50 8.50
e. Double surcharge 11.00 11.00
f. Double surcharge, inverted 13.00 13.00
g. Imperf., pair 9.00 9.00
Nos. 175-177 (3) 7.15 3.30

There are two settings of the surcharge on No. 175. In the 1st the character for "cents" and the figure "5" are 2mm apart and in the 2nd 4mm.

The 2c vermilion, No. 122, with surcharge "1 cent. / 1904" was not issued.

No. 161 Surcharged in Black

1905, June

178 A14 5c on 10c violet .60 .35
a. Inverted surcharge 13.50 10.00
b. Double surcharge 4.50 4.50
c. Surcharge in blue *75.00*

Coat of Arms — A18

Imprint: "American Bank Note Co. NY"

1905, July 25 **Engr.** ***Perf. 12***

179 A18 1c green .30 .25
180 A18 2c car rose .30 .25
181 A18 3c violet .45 .25
182 A18 4c org red .45 .25
183 A18 5c blue .45 .25
184 A18 6c slate .60 .40
185 A18 10c yel brn .85 .25
186 A18 15c brn olive .75 .35
187 A18 20c lake .60 .40
188 A18 50c orange 3.00 1.50
189 A18 1p black 1.50 1.50
190 A18 2p dk grn 1.50 2.00
191 A18 5p violet 1.75 2.50
Nos. 179-191 (13) 12.50 10.15

See Nos. 202-208, 237-248. For overprints and surcharges see Nos. 193-201, 212-216, 235-236, 249-265, O187-O198, O210-O222, 1L21-1L62, 1L73-1L95, 1LO1-1LO3, 2L26-2L35, 2L42-2L46, 2L48-2L72, 2LO1-2LO4.

Nos. 179-184 and 191 Surcharged in Black or Red Reading Up or Down

1906-08

193 A18 10c on 2c car rose (up) 7.00 4.50
a. Surcharge reading down 13.00 13.00
194 A18 10c on 3c vio (up) .60 .25
a. "¢" normal 2.75 1.35
b. Double surcharge 4.50 4.50
c. Double surch., up and down 7.00 5.00
d. Pair, one without surcharge 9.50
e. Surcharge reading down .30 .25
195 A18 10c on 4c org red (up) ('08) *35.00 20.00*
a. Surcharge reading down *32.50 26.00*
196 A18 15c on 1c grn (up) .60 .30
a. Double surcharge 7.50 7.50
b. Dbl. surch., one reading down 11.00 11.00
c. Surcharge reading down .40 .25
197 A18 20c on 2c car rose (down) ('07) .50 .30
a. Double surcharge 13.00 13.00
b. Surcharge reading up 37.50 32.50
c. "V" omitted 10.00 10.00
198 A18 20c on 5c bl (down) .75 .50
a. Surcharge reading up 35.00
199 A18 50c on 6c sl (R) (down) .60 .50
a. Double surcharge
b. Surcharge reading up 30.00 30.00
c. Yellow brown surcharge .60 .40
200 A18 1p on 5p vio (down) ('07) 42.50 25.00
Nos. 193-200 (8) *87.55 51.35*

There are several settings of these surcharges and many varieties in the shapes of the figures, the spacing, etc.

Surcharged in Red Vertically Reading Up

1908, May

201 A18 35c on 6c slate 3.50 2.25
a. Double surcharge (R) 25.00
b. Double surcharge (R + Bk) 65.00
c. Carmine surcharge 3.50 2.25

Arms Type of 1905

Imprint: "Waterlow & Sons, Ltd."

1907, Feb. ***Perf. 14 to 15***

202 A18 1c green .70 .40
203 A18 2c rose .80 .25
204 A18 4c brn org 2.00 .30
205 A18 10c yel brn 3.00 .25
206 A18 15c brn olive 4.50 .90
207 A18 20c lake 8.00 1.25
208 A18 50c orange 20.00 4.25
Nos. 202-208 (7) 39.00 7.60

Nos. 202-204, 207-208 Surcharged in Black or Blue (Bl) Reading Down

1907-08

212 A18 10c on 2c rose 1.50 .50
a. Double surcharge 10.00
b. "Vale" only 22.50
c. Surcharge reading up 14.00 6.50
213 A18 10c on 4c brn org (up) ('08) 2.25 .85
a. Double surcharge 10.00
b. Surcharge reading down 10.00
214 A18 10c on 20c lake ('08) 3.25 1.40
b. Surcharge reading up 80.00
215 A18 10c on 50c org (Bl) ('08) 2.00 .60
216 A18 15c on 1c grn ('08) 32.50 4.00
Nos. 212-216 (5) 41.50 7.35

Several settings of this surcharge provide varieties of numeral font, spacing, etc.

Revenue Stamps Overprinted "CORREO-1908" — A19

1908, June

217 A19 5c yel & blk .60 .40
a. "CORROE" 2.75 2.75
b. Overprint reading down 7.00
c. Double overprint 13.00
218 A19 10c lt bl & blk .50 .25
a. Double overprint 4.50 4.50
b. Overprint reading down .50 .25
c. Double overprint, up and down 13.00 13.00
219 A19 1p yel brn & blk .50 *2.00*
a. "CORROE" 10.00 *12.00*
220 A19 2p pearl gray & blk .50 *2.50*
a. "CORROE" 10.00 10.00
Nos. 217-220 (4) 2.10 *5.15*

The overprint exists on a 5p in green (value $200) and on a 50p in black (value $300).

Revenue Stamps Surcharged Vertically Reading Up in Red (1c, 15c), Blue(2c), Green (4c) or Orange (35c)

221 A19 1c on 5c yel & blk .40 .25
a. "1008" 2.00 *3.00*
b. "8908" 2.00 *3.00*
c. Surcharge reading down 4.00 4.00
d. Double surcharge 4.00 4.00
222 A19 2c on 5c yel & blk .50 .30
b. "ORREO" 1.75 1.75
c. "1008" 1.75 1.75
d. "8908" 2.50 *5.50*
f. Double surcharge 7.00 7.00
g. Double surcharge, one inverted 7.00 7.00
h. Surcharge reading down 9.00 9.00
223 A19 4c on 5c yel & blk .65 .35
a. "ORREO" 3.50 *7.50*
b. "1008" 2.00 2.00
c. "8908" 2.00 2.00
224 A19 15c on 50c ol & blk .60 .40
a. "1008" 7.50 *11.50*
b. "8908" 4.00 4.00
c. Surcharge reading down 10.00 10.00
225 A19 35c on 50c ol & blk 4.00 1.00
a. Double surcharge, one inverted 12.00 12.00
b. Surcharge reading down 12.00 12.00
c. Double surcharge, one in black
Nos. 221-225 (5) 6.15 2.30

For surcharges and overprints see Nos. 225D-225H, 230-234, 266-278, 1L63-1L72A, 1L96-1L106, 2L47.

Revenue Stamps Surcharged Vertically Reading Up in Blue, Black or Orange

1908, Nov.

225D A19 2c on 5c yel org & blk (Bl) 20.00 12.50
e. "9c" instead of "2c" 75.00 75.00
225F A19 10c on 50c ol & blk (Bk) *850.00 325.00*
g. Double surcharge *425.00*
225H A19 35c on 50c ol & blk (O) 17.50 10.00

In this setting there are three types of the character for "cents."

Revenue Stamps Overprinted or Surcharged in Various Colors

No. 226

No. 227

1908, Dec.

226 2c org (Bk) 3.50 2.00
a. Double overprint 6.00 6.00
b. Overprint reading up 5.00 5.00
227 4c on 2c org (Bk) 1.75 .90
a. Surcharge reading up 5.00 5.00
b. Blue surcharge 80.00 80.00
228 5c on 2c org (Bl) 1.50 .60
a. Surcharge reading up 6.00 6.00
229 10c on 2c org (G) 1.50 .30
a. "1988" for "1908" 4.00 3.00
b. Surcharge reading up 5.00 5.00
c. "¢" inverted 4.00 4.00
d. Double surcharge 7.50
Nos. 226-229 (4) 8.25 3.80

Two printings of No. 229 exist. In the first, the initial of "VALE" is a small capital, and in the second a large capital.

The overprint "Correos-1908." 35mm long, handstamped on 1c blue revenue stamp of type A20, is private and fraudulent.

Revenue Stamps Surcharged in Various Colors

1909, Feb. **Color: Olive & Black**

230 A19 1c on 50c (V) 4.00 1.60
231 A19 2c on 50c (Br) 7.00 3.00
232 A19 4c on 50c (G) 7.00 3.00
233 A19 5c on 50c (C) 4.00 1.75
a. Double surcharge 12.50 12.50
234 A19 10c on 50c (Bk) 1.10 .75
Nos. 230-234 (5) 23.10 10.10

Nos. 230 to 234 are found with three types of the character for "cents."

Nos. 190 and 191 Surcharged in Black

1909, Mar. ***Perf. 12***

235 A18 10c on 2p dk grn 20.00 12.00
236 A18 10c on 5p vio *100.00 70.00*

There are three types of the character for "cents."

Arms Type of 1905

Imprint: "American Bank Note Co. NY"

1909, Mar.

237 A18 1c yel grn .35 .25
238 A18 2c vermilion .35 .25
239 A18 3c red org .35 .25
240 A18 4c violet .35 .25
241 A18 5c dp bl .35 .25
242 A18 6c gray brn 3.00 1.50
243 A18 10c lake .85 .25
244 A18 15c black .85 .25
245 A18 20c brn olive .85 .25
246 A18 50c dp grn 1.25 .40
247 A18 1p yellow 1.25 .40
248 A18 2p car rose 1.00 .40
Nos. 237-248 (12) 10.80 4.70

Nos. 239 and 244, Surcharged in Black or Red

1910, July

249 A18 2c on 3c red org 2.75 1.10
250 A18 10c on 15c blk (R) 1.25 .30
a. "VLEA" 3.50 2.00
b. Double surcharge 17.50 17.50

There are two types of the character for "cents."

Nos. 239, 244, 245 Surcharged in Black or Red

1910

252 A18 2c on 3c (Bk) 1.50 1.25
a. Double surcharge 6.00 6.00
b. Pair, one without surcharge
c. "Vale" omitted 10.00 10.00
254 A18 5c on 20c (R) .40 .30
a. Double surcharge (R) 6.00 5.00
b. Inverted surcharge (R) 10.00 *32.50*
c. Black surcharge 100.00
d. Double surcharge (Bk) 140.00
e. Inverted surcharge (Bk) 110.00
255 A18 10c on 15c (Bk) .90 .30
a. "c" omitted 2.00 1.10
b. "10c" omitted 2.50 1.50
c. Inverted surcharge 4.00 4.00
d. Double surcharge 6.00 6.00
e. Double surch., one inverted 14.00 *18.50*
Nos. 252-255 (3) 2.80 1.85

There are several minor varieties in this setting, such as italic "L" and "E" and fancy "V" in "VALE," small italic "C," and italic "I" for "1" in "10."

Nos. 239, 244, 246 and 247, Surcharged in Black

1910, Dec. 10

256 A18 2c on 3c red org .85 .45
a. Without period 1.00 .75
b. Inverted surcharge 6.00 6.00
c. Double surcharge 6.00 6.00
257 A18 10c on 15c blk 2.00 .75
a. Without period 3.50 1.25
b. Double surcharge 6.00 3.00
c. Inverted surcharge 10.00 *18.00*
258 A18 10c on 50c dp grn 1.25 .40
a. Without period 1.50 .75
b. Double surcharge 10.00 *26.00*
c. Inverted surcharge 3.00 3.00
259 A18 10c on 1p yel .90 .40
a. Without period 1.25 .75
b. Double surcharge 3.00 3.00
Nos. 256-259 (4) 5.00 2.00

The 15c on 50c deep green is a telegraph stamp from which the "Telegrafos" overprint was omitted. It appears to have been pressed into postal service, as all examples are used with postal cancels. Value $450.

Nos. 240, 244-248 Surcharged in Black

Surcharge as on Nos. 256-259 but lines wider apart.

1911, Mar.

260 A18 2c on 4c vio .30 .25
a. Without period .35 .30
b. Double surcharge 3.50 3.00
c. Double surcharge, inverted 4.00 4.00
d. Double surcharge, one invtd. 9.00 *17.50*
e. Inverted surcharge 10.00 *18.50*
261 A18 5c on 20c brn ol .30 .25
a. Without period .60 .50
b. Double surcharge 2.50 2.50
c. Inverted surcharge 2.50 2.00
d. Double surcharge, one invtd. 6.00 6.00
262 A18 10c on 15c blk .40 .25
a. Without period 1.00 .50
b. "Yale" 12.00 12.00
c. Double surcharge 3.00 3.00
d. Inverted surcharge 3.00 3.00
e. Double surch., one inverted 5.00 4.00
f. Double surch., both inverted 12.00 12.00
263 A18 10c on 50c dp grn .25 .25
a. Without period 1.00 .50
b. Double surcharge 3.00 2.50
c. Double surcharge, one invtd. 5.00 4.00
d. Inverted surcharge 5.00 5.00
264 A18 10c on 1p yel 1.50 .40
a. Without period 2.00 1.50
b. Double surcharge 4.00 4.00
c. Double surcharge, one invtd. 7.50

265 A18 10c on 2p car rose .60 .50
a. Without period 2.00 1.50
b. Double surcharge 2.50 2.50
c. Double surcharge, one invtd. 6.00 6.00
d. Inverted surcharge 6.00 6.00
Nos. 260-265 (6) 3.35 1.90

Revenue Stamps Surcharged in Black

1911, Apr. 10 *Perf. 14 to 15*
266 A19 2c on 5p dl bl 1.00 *1.25*
a. Without period 1.25 *1.50*
b. Double surcharge 2.50 2.00
267 A19 2c on 5p ultra .35 *.40*
a. Without period .75 *1.25*
b. Double surcharge *3.50*
268 A19 5c on 10p pink .75 .40
a. Without period 1.50 1.00
b. "cte" for "cts" 1.50 1.00
c. Double surcharge 4.00 4.00
d. Inverted surcharge 2.50 2.50
269 A19 10c on 25c lilac .40 .25
a. Without period 1.00 .75
b. "cte" for "cts" 1.25 1.00
c. Inverted surcharge 4.00 4.00
d. Double surcharge 2.50 2.50
e. Double surcharge, one inverted 4.00 4.00
270 A19 10c on 2p gray .40 .25
a. Without period 1.00 .75
b. "cte" for "cts" 1.25 1.00
c. Double surcharge 5.00 5.00
d. Double surcharge, one inverted 4.00 3.00
271 A19 35c on 1p brown .40 .30
a. Without period 1.00 .75
b. "cte" for "cts" 1.25 1.00
c. "Corre" 1.50 1.50
d. Double surcharge 2.50 2.50
e. Double surcharge, one inverted 2.50 2.50
f. Double surcharge inverted 3.00 3.00
g. Inverted surcharge *5.00*
Nos. 266-271 (6) 3.30 2.85

These surcharges are in settings of twenty-five. One stamp in each setting has a large square period after "cts" and two have no period. One of the 2c has no space between "02" and "cts" and one 5c has a small thin "s" in "Correos."

Surcharged in Black

1911, June
272 A19 5c on 2p gray 1.50 1.00
a. Inverted surcharge 6.00 5.00

In this setting one stamp has a large square period and another has a thick up-right "c" in "cts."

Surcharged in Black

1911, June 12
273 A19 5c on 25c lilac 1.50 1.25
274 A19 5c on 50c ol grn 5.00 5.00
275 A19 5c on 5p blue 7.00 7.00
276 A19 5c on 5p ultra 7.50 6.00
a. Inverted surcharge 45.00
277 A19 5c on 50p ver 6.25 5.00
278 A19 10c on 50c ol grn 1.50 .50
Nos. 273-278 (6) 28.75 24.75

This setting has the large square period and the thick "c" in "cts." Many of the stamps have no period after "cts." Owing to broken type and defective impressions letters sometimes appear to be omitted.

A21

Revenue Stamps Surcharged on the Back in Black

a

b

Railroad coupon tax stamps (1st class red and 2nd class blue) are the basic stamps of Nos. 279-294. They were first surcharged for revenue use in 1903 in two types: I — "Timbre Fiscal" and "ctvs." II — "TIMBRE FISCAL" and "cents" (originally intended for use in Bluefields).

1911, July
279 A21 (a) 2c on 5c on 2 bl .25 .30
a. New value in yellow on face 6.00 6.00
b. New value in black on face 10.00 5.00
c. New value in red on face *100.00*
d. Inverted surcharge .75
e. Double surch., one inverted 7.50 7.50
f. "TIMBRE FISCAL" in black .75 .75
280 A21 (b) 2c on 5c on 2 bl .25 .30
a. New value in yellow on face 3.00 3.00
b. New value in black on face 9.00 4.00
c. New value in red on face *100.00*
d. Inverted surcharge .90 1.00
e. Double surch., one inverted 7.50 7.50
f. "TIMBRE FISCAL" in black 1.00 1.00
281 A21 (a) 5c on 5c on 2 bl .25 .25
a. Inverted surcharge .50 .35
b. "TIMBRE FISCAL" in black 1.00 1.00
c. New value in yellow on face
282 A21 (b) 5c on 5c on 2 bl .25 .25
a. Inverted surcharge .40 .35
b. "TIMBRE FISCAL" in black 1.00 1.00
c. New value in yellow on face
283 A21 (a) 10c on 5c on 2 bl .25 .25
a. Inverted surcharge .75 .50
b. "TIMBRE FISCAL" in black 1.00 1.00
c. New value in yellow on face *100.00*
d. Double surcharge 6.00 6.00
284 A21 (b) 10c on 5c on 2 bl .25 .25
a. Inverted surcharge .75 .50
b. "TIMBRE FISCAL" in black 1.00 1.00
c. Double surcharge 6.00 6.00
d. New value in yellow on face *110.00*
285 A21 (a) 15c on 10c on 1 red .25 .25
a. Inverted surcharge 1.00 1.25
b. "Timbre Fiscal" double 5.00
286 A21 (b) 15c on 10c on 1 red .40 .35
a. Inverted surcharge 1.00 1.00
b. "Timbre Fiscal" double 5.00
Nos. 279-286 (8) 2.15 2.20

These surcharges are in settings of 20. For listing, they are separated into small and large figures, but there are many other varieties due to type and arrangement.

The colored surcharges on the face of the stamps were trial printings. These were then surcharged in black on the reverse. The olive yellow surcharge on the face of the 2c was later applied to prevent use as a 5c revenue stamps. Other colors known on the face are orange and green. Forgeries exist.

For overprints and surcharges see Nos. 287-294, O223-O244, 1L107-1L108.

Surcharged on the Face in Black

1911, Oct.
287 A21 2c on 10c on 1 red 6.50 6.50
a. Inverted surcharge 1.40 1.40
b. Double surcharge 10.00 10.00
288 A21 20c on 10c on 1 red 4.50 4.50
a. Inverted surcharge 5.25 5.00
289 A21 50c on 10c on 1 red 5.25 4.50
a. Inverted surcharge 10.00 10.00
Nos. 287-289 (3) 16.25 15.50

There are two varieties of the figures "2" and "5" in this setting.

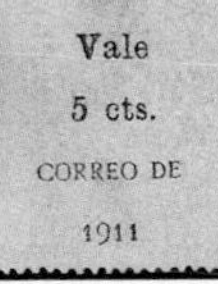

Surcharged on the Back in Black

1911, Nov.
289B A21 5c on 10c on 1 red 37.50
c. Inverted surcharge 20.00
289D A21 10c on 10c on 1 red 12.50
e. Inverted surcharge 24.00

Surcharged on the Face

1911, Dec.

Dark Blue Postal Surcharge

290 A21 2c on 10c on 1 red .25 .25
a. Inverted surcharge 2.50 2.50
b. Double surcharge 5.00 5.00
291 A21 5c on 10c on 1 red .30 .25
a. Double surcharge 2.50 2.50
b. Inverted surcharge 2.50 2.50
292 A21 10c on 10c on 1 red .35 .25
a. Inverted surcharge 2.50 2.50
b. Double surcharge 2.50 2.50
c. "TIMBRE FISCAL" on back 3.50 3.50

Black Postal Surcharge

293 A21 10c on 10c on 1 red 1.50 1.00
a. Inverted surcharge 7.00 7.00
b. New value surch. on back 12.00 12.00

Red Postal Surcharge

293C A21 5c on 5c on 2 blue 1.40 1.25
d. "TIMBRE FISCAL" in black 2.50 1.75
e. "5" omitted 3.75 3.75
f. Inverted surcharge 4.75 4.75
Nos. 290-293C (5) 3.80 3.00

Bar Overprinted on No. O234 in Dark Blue

294 A21 10c on 10c on 1 red 1.25 1.00
a. Inverted surcharge 2.50 2.50
b. Bar at foot of stamp 5.00 5.00

Nos. 290-294 each have three varieties of the numerals in the surcharge.

"Liberty" — A22

Coat of Arms — A23

1912, Jan. **Engr.** *Perf. 14, 15*
295 A22 1c yel grn .30 .25
296 A22 2c carmine .40 .25
297 A22 3c yel brn .30 .25
298 A22 4c brn vio .30 .25
299 A22 5c blue & blk .25 .25
300 A22 6c olive bister .30 .80
301 A22 10c red brn .25 .25
302 A22 15c vio .25 .25
303 A22 20c red .25 .25
304 A22 25c blue grn & blk .30 .25
305 A23 35c grn & chnt 2.00 1.50
306 A22 50c lt blue 1.00 .40
307 A22 1p org 1.40 2.00
308 A22 2p dark blue grn 1.50 2.25
309 A22 5p blk 3.50 3.50
Nos. 295-309 (15) 12.30 12.70

For overprints and surcharges see Nos. 310-324, 337A-348, 395-396, O245-O259.

No. 305 Surcharged in Violet

1913, Mar.
310 A23 15c on 35c .40 .25
a. "ats" for "cts" 7.50 6.00

Stamps of 1912 Surcharged in Red or Black

1913-14
311 A22 ½c on 3c yel brn (R) .40 .35
a. "Corooba" 2.50 2.50
b. "do" for "de" 2.50 2.50
c. Inverted surcharge 22.50
312 A22 ½c on 15c vio (R) .25 .25
a. "Corooba" 1.00 1.00
b. "do" for "de" 1.25 1.25
313 A22 ½c on 1p org .75 .25
a. "VALB" 3.00 *5.00*
b. "ALE" 4.00 3.50
c. "LE" 6.00 5.00
d. "VALE" omitted 3.50 3.50
314 A22 1c on 3c yel brn .95 .60
315 A22 1c on 4c brn vio .75 .25
316 A22 1c on 50c lt blue .25 .25
317 A22 1c on 5p blk .25 .25
318 A22 2c on 4c brn vio .35 .25
a. "do" for "de" 3.00 *12.00*
319 A22 2c on 20c red 3.50 *4.50*
a. "do" for "de" 17.50 12.50
320 A22 2c on 25c blue grn & blk .35 .25
a. "do" for "de" 3.50 2.50
321 A23 2c on 35c grn & chnt .25 .40
a. "9131" 4.00 *7.50*
b. "do" for "de" 2.50 2.00
322 A22 2c on 50c lt blue .25 .25
a. "do" for "de" 2.00 *4.00*
323 A22 2c on 2p dark blue grn .25 .25
a. "VALR" 1.25 1.25
b. "ALE" 2.50 1.25
c. "VALE" omitted 6.00
d. "VALE" and "dos" omitted 6.00
324 A22 3c on 6c olive bis .25 .25
a. "VALB" *35.00*
Nos. 311-324 (14) 8.80 8.35

Nos. 311, 312 surcharged in black were not regularly issued.

Surcharged on Zelaya Issue of 1912

325 Z2 ½c on 2c ver .60 *1.25*
a. "Corooba" 1.25 1.25
b. "do" for "de" 1.25 1.25
326 Z2 1c on 3c org brn .50 .25
327 Z2 1c on 4c car .50 .25
328 Z2 1c on 6c red brn .40 .25
329 Z2 1c on 20c dark vio .50 .25
330 Z2 1c on 25c grn & blk .50 .25
331 Z2 2c on 1c yel grn ('14) 6.75 1.25
a. "Centavos" 7.50 1.50
332 Z2 2c on 25c grn & blk 2.25 *3.00*
333 Z2 5c on 35c brn & blk .40 .25
334 Z2 5c on 50c ol grn .40 .25
a. Double surcharge 22.50
335 Z2 6c on 1p org .50 .25
336 Z2 10c on 2p org brn .90 .25
337 Z2 1p on 5p dk bl grn 1.00 .40
Nos. 325-337 (13) 15.20 8.15

On No. 331 the surcharge has a space of 2½mm between "Vale" and "dos."

Space between "Vale" and "dos" 2½mm instead of 1mm, "de Cordoba" in different type.

1914, Feb.
337A A22 2c on 4c brn vio 27.50 4.00
b. "Ccntavos" 12.00
337C A22 2c on 20c red 13.00 3.75
d. "Ccntavos" 4.00
337E A22 2c on 25c bl grn & blk 6.00
f. "Ccntavos" 12.00
337G A23 2c on 35c grn & chnt 8.50
h. "Ccntavos" 15.00
337I A22 2c on 50c lt bl 22.50 4.00
j. "Ccntavos" 10.00

No. 310 with Additional Surcharge

1913, Dec.
337K A23 ½c on 15c on 35c *300.00*

The word "Medio" is usually in heavy-faced, shaded letters. It is also in thinner, unshaded letters and in letters from both fonts mixed.

No. 310 Surcharged in Black and Violet

338 A23 ½c on 15c on 35c .50 .25
a. Double surcharge 3.50
b. Inverted surcharge 3.50
c. Surcharged on No. 305 12.00
339 A23 1c on 15c on 35c .25 .25
a. Double surcharge 4.00

Official Stamps of 1912 Surcharged

1914, Feb.
340 A22 1c on 25c lt bl .40 .25
a. Double surcharge 9.00
341 A23 1c on 35c lt bl .40 .25
a. "0.10" for "0.01" 10.00 10.00
341B A22 1c on 50c lt bl *200.00*
342 A22 1c on 1p lt bl .25 .25
342A A22 2c on 20c lt bl *200.00 150.00*
b. "0.12" for "0.02"
343 A22 2c on 50c lt bl .40 .25
a. "0.12" for "0.02" 150.00
344 A22 2c on 2p lt bl .40 .25
345 A22 2c on 5p lt bl *250.00*
346 A22 5c on 5p lt bl .25 .25

Red Surcharge

347 A22 5c on 1p lt bl *140.00*
348 A22 5c on 5p lt bl *500.00*

National Palace, Managua — A24

León Cathedral — A25

Various Frames

1914, May 13 **Engr.** ***Perf. 12***
349 A24 ½c lt blue .85 .25
350 A24 1c dk green .85 .25
351 A25 2c red orange .85 .25
352 A24 3c red brown 1.25 .30
353 A25 4c scarlet 1.25 .40
354 A24 5c gray black .45 .25
355 A25 6c black brn 9.00 5.50
356 A25 10c orange yel .85 .25
357 A24 15c dp violet 5.75 2.00
358 A25 20c slate 11.00 5.50
359 A24 25c orange 1.50 .45
360 A25 50c pale blue 1.40 .40
Nos. 349-360 (12) 35.00 15.80

In 1924 the 5c, 10c, 25c, 50c were issued in slightly larger size, 27x22¾mm. The original set was 26x22½mm.

No. 356 with overprint "Union Panamericana 1890-1940" in green is of private origin.

See Nos. 408-415, 483-495, 513-523, 652-664. For overprints and surcharges see Nos. 361-394, 397-400, 416-419, 427-479, 500, 540-548, 580-586, 600-648, 671-673, 684-685, C1-C3, C9-C13, C49-C66, C92-C105, C121-C134, C147-C149, C155-C163, C174-C185, CO1-CO24, O260-O294, O296-O319, O332-O376, RA1-RA5, RA10-RA11, RA26-RA35, RA39-RA40, RA44, RA47, RA52.

No. 355 Surcharged in Black

1915, Sept.
361 A25 5c on 6c blk brn 1.50 .40
a. Double surcharge 7.00 7.00

Stamps of 1914 Surcharged in Black or Red

1918-19 **New Value in Figures**
362 A24 1c on 3c red brn 6.50 2.25
a. Double surch., one invtd. 12.50
363 A25 2c on 4c scarlet 32.50 22.50
364 A24 5c on 15c dp vio (R) 7.50 1.50
a. Double surcharge 12.00
364C A24 5c on 15c dp vio 350.00

Surcharged in Black

365 A25 2c on 20c slate 110.00 60.00
a. "ppr" for "por" *500.00 300.00*
b. Double surcharge *300.00*
c. "Cordobo" *500.00 300.00*
365D A25 5c on 20c slate — *200.00*
e. Double surcharge (Bk + R) *300.00*
f. "Cordobo" *300.00*

The surcharge on No. 365 is in blue black, and that on No. 365D usually has an admixture of red.

Used only at Bluefields and Rama.

Surcharged in Black, Red or Violet

New Value in Words

366 A25 ½c on 6c blk brn 4.00 1.50
a. "Meio" 15.00
b. Double surcharge 12.00
367 A25 ½c on 10c yellow 2.50 .30
a. "Val" for "Vale" 3.00
b. "Codoba" 3.00
c. Inverted surcharge 5.00
d. Double surch., one inverted 10.00
368 A24 ½c on 15c dp vio 2.50 .60
a. Double surcharge 7.50
b. "Codoba" 4.00
c. "Meio" 6.00
369 A24 ½c on 25c orange 5.00 2.00
a. Double surcharge 8.00
b. Double surch., one inverted 6.00
370 A25 ½c on 50c pale bl 2.50 .30
a. "Meio" 6.00
b. Double surcharge 5.00
c. Double surch., one inverted 7.00
371 A25 ½c on 50c pale bl (R) 4.50 1.50
a. Double surcharge 10.00
372 A24 1c on 3c red brn 3.00 .30
a. Double surcharge 3.50
373 A25 1c on 6c blk brn 12.50 3.50
a. Double surcharge 9.00
374 A25 1c on 10c yellow 24.00 8.00
a. "nu" for "un" 22.50
375 A24 1c on 15c dp vio 4.50 .75
a. Double surcharge 10.00
b. "Codoba" 6.00
376 A25 1c on 20c slate *200.00 100.00*
a. Black surch. normal and red surch. invtd. *150.00*
b. Double surch., red & black *150.00*
c. Blue surcharge *200.00*
377 A25 1c on 20c sl (V) 110.00 70.00
a. Double surcharge (V + Bk) *150.00*
378 A25 1c on 20c sl (R) 2.50 .30
a. Double surch., one inverted
b. "Val" for "Vale" 3.50 3.00
379 A24 1c on 25c orange 4.50 1.00
a. Double surcharge 11.00
380 A25 1c on 50c pale bl 14.00 4.50
a. Double surcharge 17.50
381 A25 2c on 4c scarlet 3.50 .30
a. Double surcharge 10.00
b. "centavo" 5.00
c. "Val" for "Vale"
382 A25 2c on 6c blk brn 24.00 8.00
a. "Centavoss"
b. "Cordobas"
383 A25 2c on 10c yellow 24.00 4.50
a. "centavo"
384 A25 2c on 20c sl (R) 13.00 3.25
a. "pe" for "de" 15.00
b. Double surch., red & blk 27.50
c. "centavo" 12.00
d. Double surcharge (R) 17.50
385 A24 2c on 25c orange 5.50 .40
a. "Vle" for "Vale" 7.50
b. "Codoba" 7.50
c. Inverted surcharge 10.00
386 A25 5c on 6c blk brn 10.00 4.25
a. Double surcharge 13.50
387 A24 5c on 15c dp vio 3.50 .60
a. "cincoun" for "cinco" 15.00
b. "Vle" for "Vale" 12.50
c. "Codoba" 12.50
Nos. 366-387 (22) 479.50 215.85

No. 378 is surcharged in light red and brown red: the latter color is frequently offered as the violet surcharge (No. 377).

Official Stamps of 1915 Surcharged in Black or Blue

1919-21
388 A24 1c on 25c lt blue 1.50 .25
a. Double surcharge 10.00
b. Inverted surcharge 12.00
389 A25 2c on 50c lt blue 1.50 .25
a. "centavo" 4.00 4.00
b. Double surcharge 12.00
390 A25 10c on 20c lt blue 1.40 .40
a. "centovos" 5.00 5.00
b. Double surcharge 8.00
390F A25 10c on 20c lt bl (Bl) 65.00
Nos. 388-390 (3) 4.40 .90

There are numerous varieties of omitted, inverted and italic letters in the foregoing surcharges.

No. 358 Surcharged in Black

Types of the numerals

I II III IV

V VI VII VIII

I II III IV

V VI VII VIII

1919, May
391 A25 2c on 20c (I) *200.00 150.00*
a. Type II
b. Type III
c. Type IV
d. Type VI
e. Type VIII
392 A25 5c on 20c (I) 110.00 50.00
a. Type II 110.00 45.00
b. Type III 125.00 55.00
c. Type IV 125.00 50.00
d. Type V 140.00 60.00
e. Type VI 140.00 60.00
f. Type VII 400.00 250.00
h. Double surch., one inverted

No. 358 Surcharged in Black

393 A25 2 Cents on 20c (I) *200.00 150.00*
a. Type II
b. Type III
c. Type IV
d. Type V
e. Type VI
f. Type VII
393G A25 5 Cents on 20c sl, (VIII) 140.00 55.00

Nos. 391-393G used only at Bluefields and Rama.

No. 351 Surcharged in Black

1920, Jan.
394 A25 1c on 2c red org 1.50 .25
a. Inverted surcharge
b. Double surcharge

Official Stamps of 1912 Overprinted in Carmine

1921, Mar.
395 A22 1c lt blue 1.50 .60
a. "Parricular" 5.00 5.00
b. Inverted overprint 10.00
396 A22 5c lt blue 1.50 .40
a. "Parricular" 5.00 5.00

Official Stamps of 1915 Surcharged in Carmine

1921, May
397 A25 ½c on 2c light blue .50 .25
a. "Mddio" 2.50 2.50
398 A25 ½c on 4c light blue 1.25 .25
a. "Mddio" 2.50 2.50
399 A24 1c on 3c light blue 1.25 .30
Nos. 397-399 (3) 3.00 .80

No. 354 Surcharged in Red

1921, Aug.
400 A24 ½c on 5c gray blk .75 .75

Trial printings of this stamp were surcharged in yellow, black and red, and yellow and red. Some of these were used for postage.

Gen. Manuel José Arce — A26

José Cecilio del Valle — A27

Miguel Larreinaga A28

Gen. Fernando Chamorro A29

Gen. Máximo Jérez — A30

Gen. Pedro Joaquín Chamorro — A31

Rubén Darío — A32

1921, Sept. **Engr.**

401 A26 ½c lt bl & blk 1.60 1.60
402 A27 1c grn & blk 1.60 1.60
403 A28 2c rose red & blk 1.60 1.60
404 A29 5c ultra & blk 1.60 1.60
405 A30 10c org & blk 1.60 1.60
406 A31 25c yel & blk 1.60 1.60
407 A32 50c vio & blk 1.60 1.60
Nos. 401-407 (7) 11.20 11.20

Centenary of independence.

For overprints and surcharges see Nos. 420-421, RA12-RA16, RA19-RA23.

Types of 1914 Issue

1922 **Various Frames**

408 A24 ½c green .25 .25
409 A24 1c violet .25 .25
410 A25 2c car rose .25 .25
411 A24 3c ol gray .30 .25
411A A25 4c vermilion .35 .25
412 A25 6c red brn .25 .25
413 A24 15c brown .35 .25
414 A25 20c bis brn .50 .25
415 A25 1cor blk brn .90 .50
Nos. 408-415 (9) 3.40 2.50

In 1924 Nos. 408-415 were issued in slightly larger size, 27x22¾mm. The original set was 26x22½mm.

Nos. 408, 410 exist with signature controls. See note before No. 600. Same values.

No. 356 Surcharged in Black

1922, Nov.

416 A25 1c on 10c org yel 1.00 .35
417 A25 2c on 10c org yel 1.00 .25

Nos. 354 and 356 Surcharged in Red

1923, Jan.

418 A24 1c on 5c gray blk 1.25 .25
419 A25 2c on 10c org yel 1.25 .25
a. Inverted surcharge

Nos. 401 and 402 Overprinted in Red

1923

420 A26 ½c lt blue & blk 7.50 7.50
421 A27 1c green & blk 2.50 .85
a. Double overprint 7.50

Francisco Hernández de Córdoba — A33

1924 **Engr.**

422 A33 1c deep green 2.50 .30
423 A33 2c carmine rose 2.50 .30
424 A33 5c deep blue 2.00 .30
425 A33 10c bister brn 2.00 .60
Nos. 422-425 (4) 9.00 1.50

Founding of León & Granada, 400th anniv.

For overprint & surcharges see #499, 536, O295.

Stamps of 1914-22 Overprinted

Black, Red or Blue Overprint

1927, May 3

427 A24 ½c green (Bk) .25 .25
428 A24 1c violet (R) .25 .25
a. Double overprint 3.00
428B A24 1c violet (Bk) 85.00 55.00
429 A25 2c car rose (Bk) .25 .25
a. Inverted overprint 5.00
b. Double overprint 5.00
430 A24 3c ol gray (Bk) 1.25 1.25
a. Inverted overprint 5.00
b. Double overprint 6.00
c. Double ovpt., one inverted 9.00 7.00
430D A24 3c ol gray (Bl) 8.00 3.25
431 A25 4c ver (Bk) 16.00 13.00
a. Inverted overprint 30.00
432 A24 5c gray blk (R) 1.25 .25
a. Inverted overprint 7.50
432B A24 5c gray blk (Bk) .75 .25
c. Double ovpt., one inverted 8.00
d. Double overprint 8.00
433 A25 6c red brn (Bk) 13.00 11.00
a. Inverted overprint 17.50
b. Double overprint
c. "1297" for "1927" 250.00
434 A25 10c yellow (Bl) .65 .40
a. Double overprint 12.50
b. Double ovpt., one inverted 10.00
435 A24 15c brown (Bk) 6.00 2.50
436 A25 20c bis brn (Bk) 6.00 2.50
a. Double overprint 17.50
437 A24 25c orange (Bk) 27.50 5.00
438 A25 50c pale bl (Bk) 7.50 3.00
439 A25 1cor blk brn (Bk) 15.00 9.00
Nos. 427-439 (16) 188.65 107.15

Most stamps of this group exist with tall "1" in "1927." Counterfeits exist of normal stamps and errors of Nos. 427-478.

1927, May 19 **Violet Overprint**

440 A24 ½c green .25 .25
a. Inverted overprint 2.00 2.00
b. Double overprint 2.00 2.00
441 A24 1c violet .25 .25
a. Double overprint 2.00 2.00
442 A25 2c car rose .25 .25
a. Double overprint 2.00 2.00
b. "1927" double 5.00
d. Double ovpt., one inverted 2.00 2.00
443 A24 3c ol gray .25 .25
a. Inverted overprint 6.00
b. Overprinted "1927" only 12.00
c. Double ovpt., one inverted 9.00
444 A25 4c vermilion 37.50 27.50
a. Inverted overprint 75.00
445 A24 5c gray blk 1.00 .25
a. Double overprint, one inverted 6.00
446 A25 6c red brn 37.50 27.50
a. Inverted overprint 75.00
447 A25 10c yellow .35 .25
a. Double overprint 2.00 2.00
448 A24 15c brown .75 .30
a. Double overprint 5.00
b. Double overprint, one inverted 8.00
449 A25 20c bis brn .35 .25
a. Double overprint
450 A24 25c orange .40 .25
451 A25 50c pale bl .40 .25
a. Double ovpt., one inverted 4.00 4.00
452 A25 1cor blk brn .75 .25
a. Double overprint 3.00
b. "1927" double 5.00
c. Double ovpt., one inverted 6.00
Nos. 440-452 (13) 80.00 57.80

Stamps of 1914-22 Overprinted in Violet

1928, Jan. 3

453 A24 ½c green .25 .25
a. Double overprint 3.00
b. Double overprint, one inverted 4.00
454 A24 1c violet .25 .25
a. Inverted overprint 2.00
b. Double overprint 2.00
c. Double overprint, one inverted 2.00
d. "928" for "1928" 2.50
455 A25 2c car rose .25 .25
a. Inverted overprint 2.00
b. Double overprint 2.00
c. "1928" omitted 5.00
d. "928" for "1928" 2.50
e. As "d," inverted
f. "19" for "1928"
456 A24 3c ol gray .40 .25
457 A25 4c vermilion .25 .25
458 A24 5c gray blk .25 .25
a. Double overprint 5.00
b. Double overprint, one inverted 5.00
459 A25 6c red brn .25 .25
460 A25 10c yellow .25 .25
a. Double overprint 2.50
c. Inverted overprint
461 A24 15c brown .35 .25
462 A25 20c bis brn .50 .25
a. Double overprint
463 A24 25c orange .75 .25
a. Double overprint, one inverted 4.00
464 A25 50c pale bl 1.25 .25
465 A25 1cor blk brn 1.25 .35
Nos. 453-465 (13) 6.25 3.35

Stamps of 1914-22 Overprinted in Violet

1928, June 11

466 A24 ½c green .25 .25
467 A24 1c violet .25 .25
a. "928" omitted
469 A24 3c ol gray .75 .25
a. Double overprint 6.00
470 A25 4c vermilion .35 .25
471 A24 5c gray blk .25 .25
a. Double overprint 4.00
472 A25 6c red brn .40 .25
a. Double overprint 5.00
473 A25 10c yellow .50 .25
474 A24 15c brown 1.75 .25
a. Double overprint
475 A25 20c bis brn 2.00 .25
476 A24 25c orange 2.00 .25
a. Double overprint, one inverted 6.00
477 A25 50c pale bl 2.00 .25
478 A25 1cor blk brn 5.00 2.50
a. Double overprint 10.00
Nos. 466-478 (12) 15.50 5.25

No. 410 with above overprint in black was not regularly issued.

No. 470 with Additional Surcharge in Violet

1928

479 A25 2c on 4c ver 1.25 .35
a. Double surcharge 9.00

A34

Inscribed: "Timbre Telegrafico"

1928 **Red Surcharge**

480 A34 1c on 5c bl & blk .30 .25
a. Double surcharge 5.00
b. Double surcharge, one inverted
481 A34 2c on 5c bl & blk .30 .25
a. Double surcharge 5.00
482 A34 3c on 5c bl & blk .30 .25
Nos. 480-482 (3) .90 .75

Stamps similar to Nos. 481-482, but with surcharge in black and with basic stamp inscribed "Timbre Fiscal," are of private origin.

See designs A36, A37, A44, PT1, PT4, PT6, PT7.

Types of 1914 Issue

1928 **Various Frames**

483 A24 ½c org red .40 .25
484 A24 1c orange .40 .25
485 A25 2c green .40 .25
486 A24 3c dp vio .40 .25
487 A25 4c brown .40 .25
488 A24 5c yellow .40 .25
489 A25 6c lt bl .40 .25
490 A25 10c dk bl .90 .25
491 A24 15c car rose 1.40 .50
492 A25 20c dk grn 1.40 .50
493 A24 25c blk brn 27.50 6.00
494 A25 50c bis brn 3.25 1.00
495 A25 1cor dl vio 6.25 3.00
Nos. 483-495 (13) 43.50 13.00

No. 425 Overprinted in Violet

1929

499 A33 10c bis brn .75 .60

No. 408 Overprinted in Red

1929

500 A24 ½c green (R) .25 .25
a. Inverted overprint 5.50
b. Double overprint 5.00
c. Double overprint, one inverted 5.00

A36

Ovptd. Horiz. in Black "R. de T." Surcharged Vert. in Red

1929

504 A36 1c on 5c bl & blk (R) .25 .25
a. Inverted surcharge 3.00
b. Surcharged "0.10" for "0.01" 3.00
c. "0.0" instead of "0.01" 5.00
509 A36 2c on 5c bl & blk (R) .25 .25
a. Double surcharge 2.50
b. Double surcharge, one inverted 3.50
c. Inverted surcharge 5.00

Overprinted Horizontally in Black "R. de C." Surcharged Vertically in Red

510 A36 2c on 5c bl & blk (R) 22.50 1.25
a. Dbl. surcharge, one inverted 25.00

A37

Surcharged in Red

511 A37 1c on 10c dk grn & blk (R) .25 .25
a. Double surcharge
512 A37 2c on 5c bl & blk (R) .25 .25
Nos. 504-512 (5) 23.50 2.25

The varieties tall "1" in "0.01" and "O$" for "C$" are found in this surcharge.

Nos. 500, 504, 509-512 and RA38 were surcharged in red and sold in large quantities to the public. Surcharges in various other colors were distributed only to a favored few and not regularly sold at the post offices.

Types of 1914 Issue

1929-31 **Various Frames**

513 A24 1c ol grn .25 .25
514 A24 3c lt bl .30 .25
515 A25 4c dk bl ('31) .30 .25
516 A24 5c ol brn .40 .25
517 A25 6c bis brn ('31) .50 .30
518 A25 10c lt brn ('31) .60 .25
519 A24 15c org red ('31) .90 .25
520 A25 20c org ('31) 1.25 .35
521 A24 25c dk vio .25 .25

522 A25 50c grn ('31) .50 .25
523 A25 1cor yel ('31) 4.50 1.25
Nos. 513-523 (11) 9.75 3.90

Nos. 513-523 exist with signature controls. See note before No. 600. Same values.

New Post Office at Managua — A38

1930, Sept. 15 **Engr.**

525 A38 ½c olive gray 1.25 1.25
526 A38 1c carmine 1.25 1.25
527 A38 2c red org .90 .90
528 A38 3c orange 1.75 1.75
529 A38 4c yellow 1.75 1.75
530 A38 5c ol grn 2.25 2.25
531 A38 6c bl grn 2.25 2.25
532 A38 10c black 2.75 2.75
533 A38 25c dp bl 5.50 5.50
534 A38 50c ultra 9.00 9.00
535 A38 1cor dp vio 25.00 25.00
Nos. 525-535 (11) 53.65 53.65

Opening of the new general post office at Managua. The stamps were on sale on day of issuance and for an emergency in April, 1931.

No. 499 Surcharged in Black and Red

1931, May 29

536 A33 2c on 10c bis brn .50 1.60
a. Red surcharge omitted 2.50
b. Red surcharge double 5.00
c. Red surcharge inverted 6.00
d. Red surcharge double, one invtd.

Surcharge exists in brown.

Types of 1914-31 Issue Overprinted

1931, June 11

540 A24 ½c green .35 .25
a. Double overprint .80
b. Double ovpt., one inverted 1.40
c. Inverted overprint .80
541 A24 1c ol grn .35 .25
a. Double overprint .80
b. Double ovpt., one inverted 1.40
c. Inverted overprint
542 A25 2c car rose .35 .25
a. Double overprint .80
b. Double ovpt., both inverted 2.50
c. Inverted overprint 1.40
543 A24 3c lt bl .35 .25
a. Double overprint .80
b. Double ovpt., one inverted 1.40
c. Inverted overprint 1.40
544 A24 5c yellow 4.00 2.25
545 A24 5c ol brn 1.25 .25
a. Double overprint 4.50
b. Inverted overprint 4.50
546 A24 15c org red 1.50 .40
a. Double overprint 3.50
547 A24 25c blk brn 12.00 6.50
a. Double overprint 13.00 7.00
b. Inverted overprint 13.00 7.00
548 A24 25c dk vio 4.50 2.50
a. Double overprint 10.00
Nos. 540-548 (9) 24.65 12.90

Counterfeits exist of the scarcer values. The 4c brown and 6c light blue with this overprint are bogus.

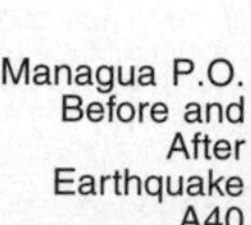

Managua P.O. Before and After Earthquake A40

1932, Jan. 1 **Litho.** ***Perf. 11½***

Soft porous paper, Without gum

556 A40 ½c emerald 1.50
557 A40 1c yel brn 1.90
558 A40 2c dp car 1.50
559 A40 3c ultra 1.50
560 A40 4c dp ultra 1.50
561 A40 5c yel brn 1.60
562 A40 6c gray brn 1.60
563 A40 10c yel brn 2.50
564 A40 15c dl rose 3.75
565 A40 20c orange 3.50
566 A40 25c dk vio 2.50
567 A40 50c emerald 2.50
568 A40 1cor yellow 6.25
Nos. 556-568 (13) 32.10

Issued in commemoration of the earthquake at Managua, Mar. 31, 1931. The stamps were on sale on Jan. 1, 1932, only. The money received from this sale was for the reconstruction of the Post Office building and for the improvement of the postal service. Many shades exist.

Sheets of 10.

Reprints are on thin hard paper and do not have the faint horiz. ribbing that is on the front or back of the originals. Fake cancels abound. Value 75 cents each.

See Nos. C20-C24. For overprints and surcharges see Nos. C32-C43, C47-C48.

Rivas Railroad Issue

"Fill" at El Nacascolo — A41

1c, Wharf at San Jorge. 5c, Rivas Station. 10c, San Juan del Sur. 15c, Train at Rivas Station.

1932, Dec. 17 **Litho.** ***Perf. 12***

Soft porous paper

570 A41 1c yellow 16.00
a. 1c ocher 18.00
571 A41 2c carmine 16.00
572 A41 5c blk brn 16.00
573 A41 10c chocolate 16.00
574 A41 15c yellow 16.00
a. 15c deep orange 18.00
Nos. 570-574 (5) 80.00

Inauguration of the railroad from San Jorge to San Juan del Sur. On sale only on Dec. 17, 1932.

Sheets of 4, without gum. See #C67-C71.

Reprints exist on five different papers ranging from thick soft light cream to thin very hard paper and do not have the faint horiz. ribbing that is normally on the front or back of the originals. Originals are on very white paper. Value of reprints, $5 each.

Leon-Sauce Railroad Issue

Bridge No. 2 at Santa Lucia — A42

Designs: 1c, Environs of El Sauce. 5c, Santa Lucia. 10c, Works at Km. 64. 15c, Rock cut at Santa Lucia.

1932, Dec. 30 ***Perf. 12***

Soft porous paper

575 A42 1c orange 16.00
576 A42 2c carmine 16.00
577 A42 5c blk brn 16.00
578 A42 10c brown 16.00
579 A42 15c orange 16.00
Nos. 575-579 (5) 80.00

Inauguration of the railroad from Leon to El Sauce. On sale only on Dec. 30, 1932.

Sheets of 4, without gum. See #C72-C76.

Reprints exist on thin hard paper and do not have the faint horiz. ribbing that is on the front or back of the originals. Value $5 each.

Nos. 514-515, 543 Surcharged in Red

1932, Dec. 10

580 A24 1c on 3c lt bl (514) .35 .25
a. Double surcharge 3.50
581 A24 1c on 3c lt bl (543) 4.00 3.50
582 A25 2c on 4c dk bl (515) .25 .25
a. Double surcharge 2.50
Nos. 580-582 (3) 4.60 4.00

Nos. 514, 516, 545 and 518 Surcharged in Black or Red

1933

583 A24 1c on 3c lt bl (Bk) (514) .25 .25
a. "Censavo" 4.00 2.25
b. Double surcharge, one inverted 4.00
584 A24 1c on 5c ol brn (R) (516) .25 .25
a. Inverted surcharge
b. Double surcharge
585 A24 1c on 5c ol brn (R) (545) 6.50 5.00
a. Red surcharge double 12.00
586 A25 2c on 10c lt brn (Bk) (518) .25 .25
a. Double surcharge 7.00 2.50
b. Inverted surcharge 6.00 3.50
c. Double surcharge, one inverted 7.00 2.50
Nos. 583-586 (4) 7.25 5.75

On No. 586 "Vale Dos" measures 13mm and 14mm.

No. 583 with green surcharge and No. 586 with red surcharge are bogus.

Flag of the Race Issue

Flag with Three Crosses for Three Ships of Columbus A43

1933, Aug. 3 **Litho.** ***Rouletted 9***

Without gum

587 A43 ½c emerald 1.75 1.75
588 A43 1c green 1.50 1.50
589 A43 2c red 1.50 1.50
590 A43 3c dp rose 1.50 1.50
591 A43 4c orange 1.50 1.50
592 A43 5c yellow 1.75 1.75
593 A43 10c dp brn 1.75 1.75
594 A43 15c dk brn 1.75 1.75
595 A43 20c vio bl 1.75 1.75
596 A43 25c dl bl 1.75 1.75
597 A43 30c violet 4.50 4.50
598 A43 50c red vio 4.50 4.50
599 A43 1cor ol brn 4.50 4.50
Nos. 587-599 (13) 30.00 30.00

Commemorating the raising of the symbolical "Flag of the Race"; also the 441st anniversary of the sailing of Columbus for the New World, Aug. 3, 1492. Printed in sheets of 10.

See Nos. C77-C87, O320-O331.

In October, 1933, various postage, airmail and official stamps of current issues were overprinted with facsimile signatures of the Minister of Public Works and the Postmaster-General. These overprints are control marks.

Nos. 410 and 513 Overprinted in Black

1935 ***Perf. 12***

600 A24 1c ol grn .25 .25
a. Inverted overprint 1.40 1.60
b. Double overprint 1.40 1.60
c. Double overprint, one inverted 1.60 1.60
601 A25 2c car rose .25 .25
a. Inverted overprint 1.60
b. Double overprint 1.60
c. Double overprint, one inverted 1.60
d. Double overprint, both inverted 2.50 2.25

No. 517 Surcharged in Red as in 1932

1936, June

602 A25 ½c on 6c bis brn .35 .25
a. "Ccentavo" .80 .80
b. Double surcharge 3.50 3.50

Regular Issues of 1929-35 Overprinted in Blue

1935, Dec.

603 A25 ½c on 6c bis brn .65 .25
604 A24 1c ol grn (#600) .80 .25
605 A25 2c car rose (#601) .80 .25
a. Black overprint inverted 6.00
606 A24 3c lt bl .80 .25
607 A24 5c ol brn 1.00 .25
608 A25 10c lt brn 1.60 .80
Nos. 603-608 (6) 5.65 2.05

Nos. 606-608 have signature control overprint. See note before No. 600.

Same Overprint in Red

1936, Jan.

609 A24 ½c dk grn .25 .25
610 A25 ½c on 6c bis brn (602) .25 .25
a. Double surch., one inverted 6.00 6.00
611 A24 1c ol grn (513) .25 .25
612 A24 1c ol grn (600) .25 .25
613 A25 2c car rose (410) .50 .25
614 A25 2c car rose (601) .25 .25
a. Black overprint inverted 12.00 2.50
b. Black ovpt. double, one invtd. 12.00 3.50
615 A24 3c lt bl .25 .25
616 A25 4c dk bl .25 .25
617 A24 5c ol brn .25 .25
618 A25 6c bis brn .25 .25
619 A25 10c lt brn .50 .25
620 A24 15c org red .25 .25
621 A25 20c orange .80 .25
622 A24 25c dk vio .25 .25
623 A25 50c green .35 .25
624 A25 1cor yellow .40 .25
Nos. 609-624 (16) 5.30 4.00

Red or blue "Resello 1935" overprint may be found inverted or double. Red and blue overprints on same stamp are bogus.

Nos. 615-624 have signature control overprint. See note before No. 600.

Regular Issues of 1922-29 Overprinted in Carmine

1936, May

625 A24 ½c green .25 .25
626 A24 1c olive green .25 .25
627 A25 2c carmine rose .50 .25
628 A24 3c light blue .25 .25
Nos. 625-628 (4) 1.25 1.00

No. 628 has signature control overprint. See note before No. 600.

Nos. 514, 516 Surcharged in Black

1936, June

629 A24 1c on 3c lt bl .25 .25
a. "1396" for "1936" 1.00 1.00
b. "Un" omitted 4.50 1.40
c. Inverted surcharge 1.60 1.60
d. Double surcharge 1.60 1.60
630 A24 2c on 5c ol brn .25 .25
a. "1396" for "1936" 1.40 1.40
b. Double surcharge 3.50 3.50

Regular Issues of 1929-31 Surcharged in Black or Red

1936

631 A24 ½c on 15c org red (R) .25 .25
a. Double surcharge 5.00
632 A25 1c on 4c dk bl (Bk) .25 .25
633 A24 1c on 5c ol brn (Bk) .25 .25
634 A25 1c on 6c bis brn (Bk) .40 .25
a. "1939" instead of "1936" 2.50 1.60
635 A24 1c on 15c org red (Bk) .25 .25
a. "1939" instead of "1936" 2.50 1.60
636 A25 1c on 20c org (Bk) .25 .25
a. "1939" intead of "1936" 2.50 1.60
b. Double surcharge 4.00

637 A25 1c on 20c org (R) .25 .25
638 A25 2c on 10c lt brn (Bk) .25 .25
639 A24 2c on 15c org red (Bk) 1.00 .80
640 A25 2c on 20c org (Bk) .50 .25
641 A24 2c on 25c dk vio (R) .35 .25
642 A24 2c on 25c dk vio (Bk) .35 .25
a. "1939" instead of "1936" 2.50 1.60
643 A25 2c on 50c grn (Bk) .35 .25
a. "1939" instead of "1936" 2.50 1.60
644 A25 2c on 1 cor yel (Bk) .35 .25
a. "1939" instead of "1936" 2.50 1.60
645 A25 3c on 4c dk bl (Bk) .65 .50
a. "1939" instead of "1936" 2.50 1.60
b. "s" of "Centavos" omitted and "r" of "Tres" inverted 2.50
Nos. 631-645 (15) 5.70 4.55

Nos. 634, 639, 643-644 exist with and without signature controls. Same values, except for No. 639, which is rare without the signature control. Nos. 635-636, 642, 645 do not have signature controls. Others have signature controls only. See note before No. 600.

Regular Issues of 1929-31 Overprinted in Black

1936, Aug.
646 A24 3c lt bl .35 .25
647 A24 5c ol brn .25 .25
648 A25 10c lt brn .50 .35
Nos. 646-648 (3) 1.10 .85

No. 648 bears script control mark.

A44

1936, Oct. 19 **Red Surcharge**
649 A44 1c on 5c grn & blk .25 .25
650 A44 2c on 5c grn & blk .25 .25

Types of 1914

1937, Jan. 1 **Engr.**
652 A24 ½c black .25 .25
653 A24 1c car rose .25 .25
654 A25 2c dp bl .25 .25
655 A24 3c chocolate .25 .25
656 A25 4c yellow .25 .25
657 A24 5c org red .25 .25
658 A25 6c dl vio .25 .25
659 A25 10c ol grn .25 .25
660 A24 15c green .25 .25
661 A25 20c red brn .25 .25
663 A25 50c brown .35 .25
664 A25 1cor ultra .60 .25
Nos. 652-664 (12) 3.45 3.00

See note after No. 360.

Mail Carrier — A45

Designs: 1c, Mule carrying mail. 2c, Mail coach. 3c, Sailboat. 5c, Steamship. 7½c, Train.

1937, Dec. **Litho.** ***Perf. 11***
665 A45 ½c green .25 .25
666 A45 1c magenta .25 .25
667 A45 2c brown .25 .25
668 A45 3c purple .25 .25
669 A45 5c blue .25 .25
670 A45 7½c red org .55 .35
Nos. 665-670 (6) 1.80 1.60

75th anniv. of the postal service in Nicaragua.

Nos. 665-670 were also issued in sheets of 4. Value, set of sheets $20.

The miniature sheets are ungummed, and also exist imperf. and part-perf.

Nos. 662, 663 and 664 Surcharged in Red

1938 ***Perf. 12***
671 A24 3c on 25c org .25 .25
672 A25 5c on 50c brn .25 .25
a. "e" of "Vale" omitted 1.60 1.00
673 A25 6c on 1cor ultra .25 .25
Nos. 671-673 (3) .75 .75

No. 672 has a script signature control and the surcharge is in three lines.

Dario Park A46

1939, Jan. **Engr.** ***Perf. 12½***
674 A46 1½c yel grn .25 .25
675 A46 2c dp rose .25 .25
676 A46 3c brt bl .25 .25
677 A46 6c brn org .25 .25
678 A46 7½c dp grn .25 .25
679 A46 10c blk brn .25 .25
680 A46 15c orange .25 .25
681 A46 25c lt vio .25 .25
682 A46 50c brt yel grn .25 .25
683 A46 1cor yellow .65 .40
Nos. 674-683 (10) 2.90 2.65

Nos. 660 and 661 Surcharged in Red

1939 ***Perf. 12***
684 A24 1c on 15c grn .25 .25
a. Inverted surcharge 2.00 2.00
685 A25 1c on 20c red brn .25 .25

No. C236 Surcharged in Carmine

1941 **Unwmk.** ***Perf. 12***
686 AP14 10c on 1c brt grn 1.00 .25
a. Double surcharge 10.00 2.50
b. Inverted surcharge 10.00 2.50

Rubén Darío A47

1941, Dec. **Engr.** ***Perf. 12½***
687 A47 10c red .40 .25
Nos. 687,C257-C260 (5) 2.00 1.30

25th anniversary of the death of Rubén Darío, poet and writer.

No. C236 Surcharged in Carmine

1943 ***Perf. 12***
688 AP14 10c on 1c brt grn 4.00 .25
a. Inverted surcharge 10.00
b. Double surcharge 10.00

Catalogue values for unused stamps in this section, from this point to the end of the section, are for Never Hinged items.

"Victory" — A48

1943, Dec. 8 **Engr.**
689 A48 10c vio & cerise .25 .25
690 A48 30c org brn & cerise .25 .25

2nd anniv. of Nicaragua's declaration of war against the Axis. See Nos. C261-C262.

Columbus and Lighthouse — A49

1945, Sept. 1 **Unwmk.** ***Perf. 12½***
691 A49 4c dk grn & blk .25 .25
692 A49 6c org & blk .25 .25
693 A49 8c dp rose & blk .35 .35
694 A49 10c bl & blk .40 .40
Nos. 691-694,C266-C271 (10) 6.30 5.50

Issued in honor of the discovery of America by Columbus and the Columbus Lighthouse near Ciudad Trujillo, Dominican Republic.

Franklin D. Roosevelt, Philatelist A50

Roosevelt Signing Declaration of War Against Japan — A51

8c, F. D. Roosevelt, Winston Churchill. 16c, Gen. Henri Giraud, Roosevelt, de Gaulle & Churchill. 32c, Stalin, Roosevelt, Churchill. 50c, Sculptured head of Roosevelt.

Engraved, Center Photogravure
1946, June 15 **Unwmk.** ***Perf. 12½***
Frame in Black
695 A50 4c sl grn .25 .25
696 A50 8c violet .30 .30
697 A51 10c ultra .30 .30
698 A50 16c rose red .40 .40
699 A50 32c org brn .30 .30
700 A51 50c gray .30 .30
Nos. 695-700,C272-C276 (11) 11.50 11.50

Issued to honor US Pres. Franklin D. Roosevelt (1882-1945). See Nos. C272-C276.

Projected Provincial Seminary — A56

Designs: 4c, Metropolitan Cathedral, Managua. 5c, Sanitation Building. 6c, Municipal Building. 75c, Communications Building.

1947, Jan. 10 **Frame in Black**
701 A56 4c carmine .25 .25
702 A56 5c blue .25 .25
703 A56 6c green .25 .25
704 A56 10c olive .25 .25
705 A56 75c golden brn .30 .30
Nos. 701-705,C277-C282 (11) 4.80 4.30

Centenary of the founding of the city of Managua. See Nos. C277-C282.

San Cristóbal Volcano A61

Designs: 3c, Tomb of Rubén Dario. 4c, Grandstand. 5c, Soldiers' monument. 6c, Sugar cane. 8c, Tropical fruit. 10c, Cotton industry. 20c, Horse race. 30c, Nicaraguan coffee. 50c, Steer. 1cor, Agriculture.

Engraved, Center Photogravure
1947, Aug. 29 **Frame in Black**
706 A61 2c orange .25 .25
707 A61 3c violet .25 .25
708 A61 4c gray .25 .25
709 A61 5c rose car .55 .25
710 A61 6c green .30 .25
711 A61 8c org brn .40 .25
712 A61 10c red .55 .25
713 A61 20c brt ultra 1.90 .50
714 A61 30c rose lilac 1.50 .50
715 A61 50c dp claret 3.25 .95
716 A61 1cor brn org 1.10 .50
Nos. 706-716,C283-C295 (24) 35.30 29.20

The frames differ for each denomination. For surcharge see No. 769.

Softball A62

Boy Scout, Badge and Flag — A63

Designs: 3c, Pole vault. 4c, Diving. 5c, Bicycling. 10c, Proposed stadium. 15c, Baseball. 25c, Boxing. 35c, Basketball. 40c, Regatta. 60c, Table tennis. 1 cor, Soccer. 2 cor, Tennis.

1949, July 15 **Photo.** ***Perf. 12***
717 A62 1c henna brn .45 .25
718 A63 2c ultra .80 .25
719 A63 3c bl grn .45 .25
720 A62 4c dp claret .30 .25
721 A63 5c orange .65 .25
722 A62 10c emerald .65 .25
723 A62 15c cerise .90 .25
724 A63 25c brt bl .90 .25
725 A63 35c olive grn 1.75 .25
726 A62 40c violet 2.50 .30
727 A62 60c olive gray 3.00 .40

728 A62 1cor scarlet 4.00 1.25
729 A62 2cor red vio 7.00 2.50
Nos. 717-729 (13) 23.35 6.70
Nos. 717-729,C296-C308 (26) 57.45 17.25

10th World Series of Amateur Baseball, 1948.

Each denomination was also issued in a souvenir sheet containing four stamps and marginal inscriptions. Value, set of 13 sheets, $375.

Rowland Hill — A64

Designs: 25c, Heinrich von Stephan. 75c, UPU Monument. 80c, Congress medal, obverse. 4cor, as 80c, reverse.

1950, Nov. 23 Engr. *Perf. 13*
Frame in Black

730 A64 20c car lake .25 .25
731 A64 25c yel grn .25 .25
732 A64 75c ultra .50 .25
733 A64 80c green .25 .25
734 A64 4cor blue 1.00 .80
Nos. 730-734 (5) 2.25 1.80
Nos. 730-734,C309-C315,CO45-CO50 (18) 11.45 9.45

75th anniv. (in 1949) of the UPU.

Each denomination was also issued in a souvenir sheet containing 4 stamps. Size: 115x123mm. Value, set of 5 sheets, $30.

For surcharge see #771.

Queen Isabella I — A65

Ships of Columbus A66

Designs: 98c, Santa Maria. 1.20cor, Map. 1.76cor, Portrait facing left.

1952, June 25 *Perf. 11½*

735 A65 10c lilac rose .25 .25
736 A66 96c deep ultra .75 .75
737 A65 98c carmine .75 .75
738 A65 1.20cor brown .90 .90
739 A65 1.76cor red violet 1.25 1.25
a. Souvenir sheet of 5, #735-739 10.00 3.75
Nos. 735-739 (5) 3.90 3.90
Nos. 735-739,C316-C320 (10) 16.40 13.90

Queen Isabella I of Spain, 500th birth anniv.

ODECA Flag — A67

Designs: 5c, Map of Central America. 6c, Arms of ODECA. 15c, Presidents of Five Central American Republics. 50c, ODECA Charter and Flags.

1953, Apr. 15 *Perf. 13½x14*

740 A67 4c dk bl .25 .25
741 A67 5c emerald .25 .25
742 A67 6c lt brn .25 .25
743 A67 15c lt ol grn .25 .25
744 A67 50c blk brn .25 .25
Nos. 740-744,C321-C325 (10) 3.00 2.90

Founding of the Organization of the Central American States (ODECA).

For surcharge see #767.

Pres. Carlos Solorzano — A68

Presidents: 6c, Diego Manuel Chamorro. 8c, Adolfo Diaz. 15c, Gen. Anastasio Somoza. 50c, Gen. Emiliano Chamorro.

Heads in Gray Black
Engr. (frames); Photo. (heads)
1953, June 25 *Perf. 12½*

745 A68 4c dk car rose .25 .25
746 A68 6c dp ultra .25 .25
747 A68 8c brown .25 .25
748 A68 15c car rose .25 .25
749 A68 50c bl grn .25 .25
Nos. 745-749,C326-C338 (18) 5.15 5.00

For surcharges see Nos. 768, 853.

Sculptor and UN Emblem — A69

4c, Arms of Nicaragua. 5c, Globe. 15c, Candle & Charter. 1cor, Flags of Nicaragua & UN.

Perf. 13½
1954, Apr. 30 Engr. Unwmk.

750 A69 3c olive .25 .25
751 A69 4c olive green .25 .25
752 A69 5c emerald .25 .25
753 A69 15c deep green .90 .25
754 A69 1cor blue green .75 .30
Nos. 750-754,C339-C345 (12) 11.05 7.30

UN Organization.

Capt. Dean L. Ray, USAF — A70

Designs: 2c, Sabre jet plane. 3c, Plane, type A-20. 4c, B-24 bomber. 5c, Plane, type AT-6. 15c, Gen. Anastasio Somoza. 1cor, Air Force emblem.

Frame in Black
Engraved; Center Photogravure
1954, Nov. 5 *Perf. 13*

755 A70 1c gray .25 .25
756 A70 2c gray .25 .25
757 A70 3c dk gray grn .25 .25
758 A70 4c orange .25 .25
759 A70 5c emerald .25 .25
760 A70 15c aqua .25 .25
761 A70 1cor purple .25 .25
Nos. 755-761,C346-C352 (14) 3.80 3.70

National Air Force.

Rotary Slogans and Wreath — A71

Map of the World and Rotary Emblem A72

20c, Handclasp, Rotary emblem & globe. 35c, Flags of Nicaragua & Rotary. 90c, Paul P. Harris.

1955, Aug. 30 Photo. *Perf. 11½*
Granite Paper.

762 A71 15c dp orange .25 .25
763 A71 20c dk olive grn .25 .25
764 A71 35c red violet .25 .25
765 A72 40c carmine .25 .25
766 A71 90c black & gray .35 .35
a. Souvenir sheet of 5, #762-766 5.75 4.25
Nos. 762-766,C353-C362 (15) 4.05 4.00

50th anniversary of Rotary International.

For surcharges see Nos. 770, 772, 876.

Issues of 1947-55 Surcharged in Various Colors

Perf. 13½x14, 12½, 11½, 13
Engraved, Photogravure
1956, Feb. 4 Unwmk.

767 A67 5c on 6c lt brn .25 .25
768 A68 5c on 6c ultra & gray blk (Ult) .25 .25
769 A61 5c on 8c blk & org brn .25 .25
770 A71 15c on 35c red vio (G) .25 .25
771 A64 15c on 80c blk & grn .25 .25
772 A71 15c on 90c blk & gray (Bl) .25 .25
Nos. 767-772,C363-C366 (10) 3.05 3.00

Spacing of surcharge varies to fit shape of stamps.

National Exhibition, Feb. 4-16, 1956.

Gen. Máximo Jerez — A73

Battle of San Jacinto A74

10c, Gen. Fernando Chamorro. 25c, Burning of Granada. 50c, Gen. José Dolores Estrada.

Perf. 12½x12, 12, 12½
1956, Sept. 14 Engr.

773 A73 5c brown .25 .25
774 A73 10c dk car rose .25 .25
775 A74 15c blue gray .25 .25
776 A74 25c brt red .25 .25
777 A73 50c brt red vio .40 .25
Nos. 773-777,C367-C371 (10) 4.80 4.40

National War, cent.

Boy Scout — A75

Designs: 15c, Cub Scout. 20c, Boy Scout. 25c, Lord Baden-Powell. 50c, Joseph A. Harrison.

Perf. 13½x14
1957, Apr. 9 Photo. Unwmk.

778 A75 10c violet & ol .25 .25
779 A75 15c dp plum & gray blk .25 .25
780 A75 20c ultra & brn .25 .25
781 A75 25c dl red brn & dp bluish grn .25 .25
782 A75 50c red & olive .25 .25
a. Souvenir sheet of 5, #778-782, imperf. 3.25 2.50
Nos. 778-782,C377-C386 (15) 3.80 3.80

Centenary of the birth of Lord Baden-Powell, founder of the Boy Scouts.

For surcharge see #C754.

Pres. Luis A. Somoza — A76

Portrait in Dark Brown
1957, July 2 *Perf. 14x13½*

783 A76 10c brt red .25 .25
784 A76 15c deep blue .25 .25
785 A76 35c rose violet .25 .25
786 A76 50c brown .30 .25
787 A76 75c gray green .65 .55
Nos. 783-787,C387-C391 (10) 3.95 3.80

President Luis A. Somoza.

Leon Cathedral A77

Bishop Pereira y Castellon — A78

Designs: 5c, Managua Cathedral. 15c, Archbishop Lezcano y Ortega. 50c, De la Merced Church, Granada. 1cor, Father Mariano Dubon.

Centers in Olive Gray
1957, July 12 *Perf. 13½x14, 14x13½*

788 A77 5c dull green .25 .25
789 A78 10c dk purple .25 .25
790 A78 15c dk blue .25 .25
791 A77 20c dk brown .30 .25
792 A77 50c dk slate grn .35 .25
793 A78 1cor dk violet .65 .30
Nos. 788-793,C392-C397 (12) 6.65 3.60

Honoring the Catholic Church in Nicaragua.

M. S. Honduras A79

5c, Gen. Anastasio Somoza & freighter. 6c, M. S. Guatemala. 10c, M. S. Salvador. 15c, Ship between globes. 50c, Globes & ship.

1957, Oct. 15 Litho. *Perf. 14*

794 A79 4c green, bl & blk .25 .25
795 A79 5c multi .25 .25
796 A79 6c red, bl & blk .25 .25
797 A79 10c brn, bl grn & blk .25 .25
798 A79 15c dk car, ultra & ol brn .25 .25
799 A79 50c violet, bl & mar .40 .25
Nos. 794-799,C398-C403 (12) 4.75 4.60

Issued to honor Nicaragua's Merchant Marine. For surcharge see No. C691.

Melvin Jones and Lions Emblem A80

Designs: 5c, Arms of Central American Republics. 20c, Dr. Teodoro A. Arias. 50c, Edward G. Barry. 75c, Motto and emblem. 1.50 cor, Map of Central America.

Emblem in Yellow, Red and Blue

1958, May 8 Unwmk. *Perf. 14*

800 A80 5c blue & multi .25 .25
801 A80 10c blue & org .25 .25
802 A80 20c blue & olive .25 .25
803 A80 50c blue & lilac .25 .25
804 A80 75c blue & pink .35 .25
805 A80 1.50cor blue, gray ol & sal .60 .45
a. Souvenir sheet of 6, #800-805 3.25 2.50
Nos. 800-805,C410-C415 (12) 5.30 4.70

17th convention of Lions Intl. of Central America, May, 1958.

For surcharge see #C686.

St. Jean Baptiste De La Salle — A81

Christian Brothers: 5c, Arms of La Salle. 10c, School, Managua, horiz. 20c, Bro. Carlos. 50c, Bro. Antonio. 75c, Bro. Julio. 1cor, Bro. Argeo.

1958, July 13 Photo. *Perf. 14*

806 A81 5c car, bl & yel .25 .25
807 A81 10c emer, blk & ultra .25 .25
808 A81 15c red brn, bis & blk .25 .25
809 A81 20c car, bis & blk .25 .25
810 A81 50c org, bis & brn blk .25 .25
811 A81 75c bl, lt grn & dk brn .25 .25
812 A81 1cor vio, bis & grnsh blk .30 .30
Nos. 806-812,C416-C423 (15) 6.85 5.65

For surcharges see Nos. C539A, C755-C756.

UN Emblem and Globe — A82

15c, UNESCO building. 25c, 45c, "UNESCO." 40c, UNESCO building and Eiffel tower.

1958, Dec. 15 Litho. *Perf. 11½*

813 A82 10c brt pink & bl .25 .25
814 A82 15c blue & brt pink .25 .25
815 A82 25c green & brn .25 .25
816 A82 40c red org & blk .25 .25
817 A82 45c dk bl & rose lil .25 .25
818 A82 50c brown & grn .25 .25
a. Miniature sheet of 6, #813-818 1.25 .75
Nos. 813-818,C424-C429 (12) 5.30 4.10

UNESCO Headquarters in Paris opening, Nov. 3.

Pope John XXIII and Cardinal Spellman — A83

Designs: 10c, Spellman coat of arms. 15c, Cardinal Spellman. 20c, Human rosary and Cardinal, horiz. 25c, Cardinal with Ruben Dario order.

1959, Nov. 26 Unwmk. *Perf. 12½*

819 A83 5c grnsh bl & brn .25 .25
820 A83 10c yel, bl & car .25 .25
821 A83 15c dk grn, blk & dk car .25 .25
822 A83 20c yel, dk bl & grn .25 .25
823 A83 25c ultra, vio & mag .25 .25
a. Min. sheet of 5, #819-823, perf. or imperf. 1.50 1.00
Nos. 819-823,C430-C436 (12) 4.90 3.90

Cardinal Spellman's visit to Managua, Feb. 1958.

For surcharges see #C638, C747, C752.

Abraham Lincoln — A84

Center in Black

1960, Jan. Engr. *Perf. 13x13½*

824 A84 5c dp carmine .25 .25
825 A84 10c green .25 .25
826 A84 15c dp orange .25 .25
827 A84 1cor plum .25 .25
828 A84 2cor ultra .35 .30
a. Souv. sheet of 5, #824-828, imperf. .90 .90
Nos. 824-828,C437-C442 (11) 4.00 3.50

150th anniv. of the birth of Abraham Lincoln.

For surcharges see #C500, C539, C637, C680, C753.

Nos. 824-828 Overprinted in Red

1960, Sept. 19 Center in Black

829 A84 5c deep carmine .25 .25
830 A84 10c green .25 .25
831 A84 15c deep orange .25 .25
832 A84 1cor plum .25 .25
833 A84 2cor ultra .50 .40
Nos. 829-833,C446-C451 (11) 4.45 3.85

Issued for the Red Cross to aid earthquake victims in Chile.

Gen. Tomas Martinez and Pres. Luis A. Somoza — A85

5c, Official decrees. 10c, Two envelopes.

Perf. 13½

1961, Aug. 29 Unwmk. Litho.

834 A85 5c grnsh bl & lt brn .25 .25
835 A85 10c green & lt brn .25 .25
836 A85 15c pink & brn .25 .25
Nos. 834-836 (3) .75 .75

Cent. (in 1960) of the postal rates regulation.

Arms of Nueva Segovia — A86

Coats of Arms: 3c, León. 4c, Managua. 5c, Granada. 6c, Rivas.

Arms in Original Colors; Black Inscriptions

1962, Nov. 22 *Perf. 12½x13*

837 A86 2c pink .25 .25
838 A86 3c lt blue .25 .25
839 A86 4c pale lilac .25 .25
840 A86 5c yellow .25 .25
841 A86 6c buff .25 .25
Nos. 837-841,C510-C514 (10) 3.15 3.05

For surcharge see #854.

No. RA73 Overprinted in Red: "CORREOS"

1964 Photo. *Perf. 11½*

842 PT13 5c gray, red & org .25 .25
a. Inverted overprint

Nos. RA66-RA75 Overprinted

1965 Photo. *Perf. 11½*

Orchids in Natural Colors

843 PT13 5c pale lilac & grn .60 .30
844 PT13 5c yellow & grn .60 .30
845 PT13 5c pink & grn .60 .30
846 PT13 5c pale vio & grn .60 .30
847 PT13 5c lt grnsh bl & red .60 .30
848 PT13 5c buff & lil .60 .30
849 PT13 5c yel grn & brn .60 .30
850 PT13 5c gray & red .60 .30
851 PT13 5c lt blue & dk bl .60 .30
852 PT13 5c lt green & brn .60 .30
Nos. 843-852 (10) 6.00 3.00

7th Central American Scout Camporee at El Coyotete. This overprint was also applied to each stamp on souvenir sheet No. C386a.

Use of Nos. 843-852 for postage was authorized by official decree.

Nos. 746 and 841 Surcharged with New Value and "RESELLO"

1968, May Engr. *Perf. 12½*

853 A68 5c on 6c dp ultra & gray blk .50 .50

Litho. *Perf. 12½x13*

854 A86 5c on 6c multi .50 .50

Nos. RA66-RA67, RA69 and RA71 Overprinted

1969 Photo. *Perf. 11½*

Orchids in Natural Colors

855 PT13 5c pale lil & grn .60 .60
856 PT13 5c yellow & grn .60 .60
857 PT13 5c pale vio & grn .60 .60
858 PT13 5c buff & lilac .60 .60
Nos. 855-858 (4) 2.40 2.40

Nos. RA66-RA75 Overprinted

1969 Photo. *Perf. 11½*

Orchids in Natural Colors

859 PT13 5c pale lil & grn .50 .30
860 PT13 5c yellow & grn .50 .30
861 PT13 5c pink & grn .50 .30
862 PT13 5c pale vio & grn .50 .30
863 PT13 5c lt grnsh bl & red .50 .30
864 PT13 5c buff & lil .50 .30
865 PT13 5c yel grn & brn .50 .30
866 PT13 5c gray & red .50 .30
867 PT13 5c lt & dk blue .50 .30
868 PT13 5c lt grn & brn .50 .30
Nos. 859-868 (10) 5.00 3.00

International Labor Organization, 50th anniv.

Pelé, Brazil — A87

Soccer Players: 10c, Ferenc Puskás, Hungary. 15c, Sir Stanley Matthews, England. 40c, Alfredo di Stefano, Argentina. 2cor, Giacinto Facchetti, Italy. 3cor, Lev Yashin, USSR. 5cor, Franz Beckenbauer, West Germany.

1970, May 11 Litho. *Perf. 13½*

869 A87 5c multicolored .25 .25
870 A87 10c multicolored .25 .25
871 A87 15c multicolored .25 .25
872 A87 40c multicolored .30 .25
873 A87 2cor multicolored 1.00 .75
874 A87 3cor multicolored 1.30 .90
875 A87 5cor multicolored 1.50 1.25
Nos. 869-875,C712-C716 (12) 8.70 6.80

Issued to honor the winners of the 1970 poll for the International Soccer Hall of Fame. Names of players and their achievements printed in black on back of stamps.

For surcharges and overprint see Nos. 899-900, C786-C788.

No. 766 Surcharged & Overprinted in Black

1971, Mar. Photo. *Perf. 11*

876 A71 30c on 90c blk & gray *200.00 100.00*

Egyptian Using Fingers to Count — A88

Symbolic Designs of Scientific Formulas: 15c, Newton's law (gravity). 20c, Einstein's theory (relativity). 1cor, Tsiolkovski's law (speed of rockets). 2cor, Maxwell's law (electromagnetism).

1971, May 15 Litho. *Perf. 13½*

877 A88 10c lt bl & multi .25 .25
878 A88 15c lt bl & multi .25 .25
879 A88 20c lt bl & multi .30 .25
880 A88 1cor lt bl & multi 1.00 .60
881 A88 2cor lt bl & multi 2.10 1.25
Nos. 877-881,C761-C765 (10) 7.90 4.45

Mathematical equations which changed the world. On the back of each stamp is a descriptive paragraph.

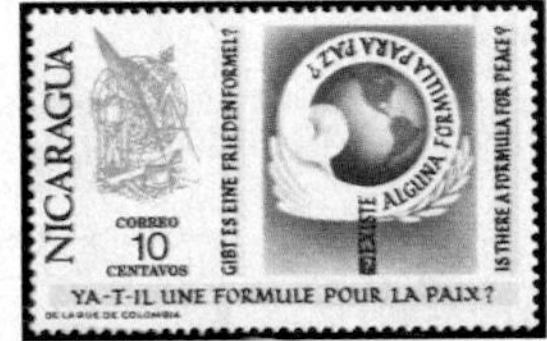

Symbols of Civilization, Peace Emblem with Globe — A89

1971, Sept. 6 Litho. *Perf. 14*

882 A89 10c blk & bl .25 .25
883 A89 15c vio bl, bl & blk .25 .25
884 A89 20c brn bl & blk .25 .25
885 A89 40c emer, bl & blk .30 .30
886 A89 50c mag, bl & blk .40 .40
887 A89 80c org, bl & blk .60 .60
888 A89 1cor ol, bl & blk .75 .75
889 A89 2cor vio, bl & blk 1.50 1.50
Nos. 882-889 (8) 4.30 4.30

"Is there a formula for peace?" issue.

Moses with Tablets of the Law, by Rembrandt
A90

The Ten Commandments (Paintings): 15c, Moses and the Burning Bush, by Botticelli (I). 20c, Jephthah's Daughter, by Degas, (II), horiz. 30c, St. Vincent Ferrer Preaching in Verona, by Domenico Morone (III). 35c, The Nakedness of Noah, by Michelangelo (IV), horiz. 40c, Cain and Abel, by Francesco Trevisani (V), horiz. 50c, Potiphar's wife, by Rembrandt (VI). 60c, Isaac Blessing Jacob, by Gerbrand van den Eeckhout (VII), horiz. 75c, Susanna and the Elders, by Rubens (VIII), horiz.

1971, Nov. 1 ***Perf. 11***

890 A90 10c ocher & multi .25 .25
891 A90 15c ocher & multi .25 .25
892 A90 20c ocher & multi .25 .25
893 A90 30c ocher & multi .25 .25
894 A90 35c ocher & multi .25 .25
895 A90 40c ocher & multi .25 .25
896 A90 50c ocher & multi .35 .35
897 A90 60c ocher & multi .55 .50
898 A90 75c ocher & multi .80 .75
Nos. 890-898,C776-C777 (11) 5.80 4.35

Descriptive inscriptions printed in gray on back of stamps.

Nos. 873-874 Surcharged

1972, Mar. 20 **Litho.** ***Perf. 13½***

899 A87 40c on 2cor multi .25 .25
900 A87 50c on 3cor multi .30 .25
Nos. 899-900,C786-C788 (5) 2.40 2.00

20th Olympic Games, Munich, 8/26-9/10.

Nos. RA66-RA69, RA71-RA74 Overprinted in Blue

1972, July 29 **Photo.** ***Perf. 11½***
Granite Paper

901 PT13 5c (#RA66) .30 .25
902 PT13 5c (#RA67) .30 .25
903 PT13 5c (#RA68) .30 .25
904 PT13 5c (#RA69) .30 .25
905 PT13 5c (#RA71) .30 .25
906 PT13 5c (#RA72) .30 .25
907 PT13 5c (#RA73) .30 .25
908 PT13 5c (#RA74) .30 .25
Nos. 901-908 (8) 2.40 2.00

Gown by Givenchy, Paris — A91

1973, July 26 **Litho.** ***Perf. 13½***

909 A91 1cor shown .30 .25
910 A91 2cor Hartnell, London .55 .50
911 A91 5cor Balmain, Paris 1.40 1.20
Nos. 909-911,C839-C844 (9) 3.75 3.45

Gowns by famous designers, modeled by Nicaraguan women. Inscriptions on back printed on top of gum give description of gown in Spanish and English.

Nos. 909-911 in perf. 11, see No. C844a.

Christmas A92

2c, 5c, Virginia O'Hanlon writing letter, father. 3c, 15c, letter. 4c, 20c, Virginia, father reading letter.

1973, Nov. 15 **Litho.** ***Perf. 15***

912 A92 2c multicolored .25 .25
913 A92 3c multicolored .25 .25
914 A92 4c multicolored .25 .25
915 A92 5c multicolored .25 .25
916 A92 15c multicolored .25 .25
917 A92 20c multicolored .25 .25
Nos. 912-917,C846-C848 (9) 3.50 3.50

Sir Winston Churchill (1874-1965) A93

Designs: 2c, Churchill speaking. 3c, Military planning. 4c, Cigar, lamp. 5c, Churchill with Roosevert and Stalin. 10c, Churchill walking ashore from landing craft.

1974, Apr. 30 ***Perf. 14½***

918 A93 2c multicolored .25 .25
919 A93 3c multicolored .25 .25
920 A93 4c multicolored .25 .25
921 A93 5c multicolored .25 .25
922 A93 10c multicolored .25 .25
Nos. 918-922,C849-C850 (7) 4.40 4.40

World Cup Soccer Championships, Munich — A94

Scenes from previous World Cup Championships with flags and scores of finalists.

1974, May 8 ***Perf. 14½***

923 A94 1c 1930 .25 .25
924 A94 2c 1934 .25 .25
925 A94 3c 1938 .25 .25
926 A94 4c 1950 .25 .25
927 A94 5c 1954 .25 .25
928 A94 10c 1958 .25 .25
929 A94 15c 1962 .25 .25
930 A94 20c 1966 .25 .25
931 A94 25c 1970 .25 .25
Nos. 923-931,C853 (10) 5.00 5.00

For overprint see No. C856.

A95

Wild Flowers and Cacti: 2c, Hollyhocks. 3c, Paguira insignis. 4c, Morning glory. 5c, Pereschia autumnalis. 10c, Cultivated morning glory. 15c, Hibiscus. 20c, Pagoda tree blossoms.

1974, June 11 **Litho.** ***Perf. 14***

932 A95 2c grn & multi .25 .25
933 A95 3c grn & multi .25 .25
934 A95 4c grn & multi .25 .25
935 A95 5c grn & multi .25 .25
936 A95 10c grn & multi .25 .25
937 A95 15c grn & multi .25 .25
938 A95 20c grn & multi .25 .25
Nos. 932-938,C854-C855 (9) 2.80 2.55

A96

Nicaraguan stamps,

1974, July 10 ***Perf. 14½***

939 A96 2c No. 670 .25 .25
940 A96 3c No. 669 .25 .25
941 A96 4c No. C110, horiz. .25 .25
942 A96 5c No. 667 .25 .25
943 A96 10c No. 666 .25 .25
944 A96 20c No. 665 .25 .25
Nos. 939-944,C855A-C855C (9) 4.05 4.05

UPU, Cent.

Four-toed Anteater A97

Designs: 2c, Puma. 3c, Raccoon. 4c, Ocelot. 5c, Kinkajou. 10c, Coypu. 15c, Peccary. 20c, Tapir.

1974, Sept. 10 **Litho.** ***Perf. 14½***

946 A97 1c multi .25 .25
947 A97 2c multi .25 .25
948 A97 3c multi .25 .25
949 A97 4c multi .25 .25
950 A97 5c multi .25 .25
951 A97 10c multi .25 .25
952 A97 15c multi .25 .25
953 A97 20c multi .25 .25
Nos. 946-953,C857-C858 (10) 3.65 3.45

Wild animals from San Diego and London Zoos.

Prophet Zacharias, by Michelangelo A98

Works of Michelangelo: 2c, The Last Judgment. 3c, The Creation of Adam, horiz. 4c, Sistine Chapel. 5c, Moses. 10c, Mouscron Madonna. 15c, David. 20c, Doni Madonna.

1974, Dec. 15

954 A98 1c dp rose & multi .25 .25
955 A98 2c yellow & multi .25 .25
956 A98 3c sal & multi .25 .25
957 A98 4c blue & multi .25 .25
958 A98 5c tan & multi .25 .25
959 A98 10c multicolored .25 .25
960 A98 15c multicolored .25 .25
961 A98 20c blue & multi .25 .25
Nos. 954-961,C859-C862 (12) 3.50 3.40

Christmas 1974 and 500th birth anniversary of Michelangelo Buonarroti (1475-1564), Italian painter, sculptor and architect.

Giovanni Martinelli, Othello A99

Opera Singers and Scores: 2c, Tito Gobbi, Simone Boccanegra. 3c, Lotte Lehmann, Der Rosenkavalier. 4c, Lauritz Melchior, Parsifal. 5c, Nellie Melba, La Traviata. 15c, Jussi Bjoerling, La Bohème. 20c, Birgit Nilsson, Turandot.

1975, Jan. 22 ***Perf. 14x13½***

962 A99 1c rose lil & multi .25 .25
963 A99 2c brt bl & multi .25 .25
964 A99 3c yel & multi .25 .25
965 A99 4c dl bl & multi .25 .25
966 A99 5c org & multi .25 .25
967 A99 15c lake & multi .25 .25
968 A99 20c gray & multi .25 .25
Nos. 962-968,C863-C870 (15) 6.45 4.15

Famous opera singers.

Jesus Condemned A100

Stations of the Cross: 2c, Jesus Carries the Cross. 3c, Jesus falls the first time. 4c, Jesus meets his mother. 5c, Simon of Cyrene carries the Cross. 15c, St. Veronica wipes Jesus' face. 20c, Jesus falls the second time. 25c, Jesus meets the women of Jerusalem. 35c, Jesus falls the third time. Designs from Leon Cathedral.

1975, Mar. 20 ***Perf. 14½***

969 A100 1c ultra & multi .25 .25
970 A100 2c ultra & multi .25 .25
971 A100 3c ultra & multi .25 .25
972 A100 4c ultra & multi .25 .25
973 A100 5c ultra & multi .25 .25
974 A100 15c ultra & multi .25 .25
975 A100 20c ultra & multi .25 .25
976 A100 25c ultra & multi .25 .25
977 A100 35c ultra & multi .25 .25
Nos. 969-977,C871-C875 (14) 4.15 4.05

Easter 1975.

The Spirit of 76, by Archibald M. Willard — A101

Designs: 2c, Pitt Addressing Parliament, by K. A. Hickel. 3c, The Midnight Ride of Paul Revere, horiz. 4c, Statue of George III Demolished, by W. Walcutt, horiz. 5c, Boston Massacre. 10c, Colonial coin and seal, horiz. 15c, Boston Tea Party, horiz. 20c, Thomas Jefferson, by Rembrandt Peale. 25c, Benjamin Franklin, by Charles Willson Peale. 30c, Signing Declaration of Independence, by John Trumbull, horiz. 35c, Surrender of Cornwallis, by Trumbull, horiz.

1975, Apr. 16 ***Perf. 14***

978 A101 1c tan & multi .25 .25
979 A101 2c tan & multi .25 .25
980 A101 3c tan & multi .25 .25
981 A101 4c tan & multi .25 .25

982 A101 5c tan & multi .25 .25
983 A101 10c tan & multi .25 .25
984 A101 15c tan & multi .25 .25
985 A101 20c tan & multi .25 .25
986 A101 25c tan & multi .25 .25
987 A101 30c tan & multi .25 .25
988 A101 35c tan & multi .25 .25
Nos. 978-988,C876-C879 (15) 6.20 5.85

American Bicentennial.

Scouts Saluting Flag, Scout Emblems A102

2c, Two-men canoe. 3c, Scouts of various races shaking hands. 4c, Scout cooking. 5c, Entrance to Camp Nicaragua. 20c, Group discussion.

1975, Aug. 15 ***Perf. 14½***

989 A102 1c multi .25 .25
990 A102 2c multi .25 .25
991 A102 3c multi .25 .25
992 A102 4c multi .25 .25
993 A102 5c multi .25 .25
994 A102 20c multi .25 .25
Nos. 989-994,C880-C883 (10) 4.05 3.50

Nordjamb 75, 14th World Boy Scout Jamboree, Lillehammer, Norway, July 29-Aug. 7.

Pres. Somoza, Map and Arms of Nicaragua — A103

1975, Sept. 10 ***Perf. 14***

995 A103 20c multi .25 .25
996 A103 40c org & multi .25 .25
Nos. 995-996,C884-C886 (5) 6.75 5.50

Reelection of Pres. Anastasio Somoza D.

King's College Choir, Cambridge — A104

Famous Choirs: 2c, Einsiedeln Abbey. 3c, Regensburg. 4c, Vienna Choir Boys. 5c, Sistine Chapel. 15c, Westminster Cathedral. 20c, Mormon Tabernacle.

1975, Nov. 15 ***Perf. 14½***

997 A104 1c silver & multi .25 .25
998 A104 2c silver & multi .25 .25
999 A104 3c silver & multi .25 .25
1000 A104 4c silver & multi .25 .25
1001 A104 5c silver & multi .25 .25
1002 A104 15c silver & multi .25 .25
1003 A104 20c silver & multi .25 .25
Nos. 997-1003,C887-C890 (11) 4.00 3.40

Christmas 1975.

The Chess Players, by Ludovico Carracci A105

History of Chess: 2c, Arabs Playing Chess, by Delacroix. 3c, Cardinals Playing Chess, by Victor Marais-Milton. 4c, Albrecht V of Bavaria and Anne of Austria Playing Chess, by Hans Muelich, vert. 5c, Chess Players, Persian manuscript, 14th century. 10c, Origin of Chess, Indian miniature, 17th century. 15c, Napoleon Playing Chess at Schönbrunn, by Antoni Uniechowski, vert. 20c, The Chess Game, by J. E. Hummel.

1976, Jan. 8 ***Perf. 14½***

1004 A105 1c brn & multi .25 .25
1005 A105 2c lt vio & multi .25 .25
1006 A105 3c ocher & multi .25 .25
1007 A105 4c multi .25 .25
1008 A105 5c multi .25 .25
1009 A105 10c multi .25 .25
1010 A105 15c blue & multi .25 .25
1011 A105 20c ocher & multi .25 .25
Nos. 1004-1011,C891-C893 (11) 4.50 4.05

Olympic Rings, Danish Crew — A107

Winners, Rowing and Sculling Events: 2c, East Germany, 1972. 3c, Italy, 1968. 4c, Great Britain, 1936. 5c, France, 1952. 35c, US, 1920, vert.

1976, Sept. 7 **Litho.** ***Perf. 14***

1022 A107 1c blue & multi .25 .25
1023 A107 2c blue & multi .25 .25
1024 A107 3c blue & multi .25 .25
1025 A107 4c blue & multi .25 .25
1026 A107 5c blue & multi .25 .25
1027 A107 35c blue & multi .25 .25
Nos. 1022-1027,C902-C905 (10) 6.75 6.00

Candlelight — A108

#1028, The Smoke Signal, by Frederic Remington. #1029, Space Signal Monitoring Center. #1031, Edison's laboratory & light bulb. #1032, Agriculture, 1776. #1033, Agriculture, 1976. #1034, Harvard College, 1726. #1035, Harvard University, 1976. #1036, Horse-drawn carriage. #1037, Boeing 747.

1976, May 25 **Litho.** ***Perf. 13½***

1028 A108 1c gray & multi .25 .25
1029 A108 1c gray & multi .25 .25
  a. Pair, #1028-1029 .25 .25
1030 A108 2c gray & multi .25 .25
1031 A108 2c gray & multi .25 .25
  a. Pair, #1030-1031 .25 .25
1032 A108 3c gray & multi .25 .25
1033 A108 3c gray & multi .25 .25
  a. Pair, #1032-1033 .25 .25
1034 A108 4c gray & multi .25 .25
1035 A108 4c gray & multi .25 .25
  a. Pair, #1034-1035 .25 .25
1036 A108 5c gray & multi .25 .25
1037 A108 5c gray & multi .25 .25
  a. Pair, #1036-1037 .25 .25
Nos. 1028-1037,C907-C912 (16) 5.60 4.80

American Bicentennial, 200 years of progress.

Zeppelin in Flight — A110

1c, Zeppelin in hangar. 3c, Giffard's dirigible airship, 1852. 4c, Zeppelin on raising stilts coming out of hangar. 5c, Zeppelin ready for take-off.

1977, Oct. 31 **Litho.** ***Perf. 14½***

1045 A110 1c multi .25 .25
1046 A110 2c multi .25 .25
1047 A110 3c multi .25 .25
1048 A110 4c multi .25 .25
1049 A110 5c multi .25 .25
Nos. 1045-1049,C921-C924 (9) 4.90 4.00

75th anniversary of Zeppelin.

Lindbergh, Map of Nicaragua — A111

2c, Spirit of St. Louis, map of Nicaragua. 3c, Lindbergh, vert. 4c, Spirit of St. Louis & NYC-Paris route. 5c, Lindbergh & Spirit of St. Louis. 20c, Lindbergh, NYC-Paris route & plane.

1977, Nov. 30

1050 A111 1c multi .25 .25
1051 A111 2c multi .25 .25
1052 A111 3c multi .25 .25
1053 A111 4c multi .25 .25
1054 A111 5c multi .25 .25
1055 A111 20c multi .25 .25
Nos. 1050-1055,C926-C929 (10) 4.40 3.90

Charles A. Lindbergh's solo transatlantic flight from NYC to Paris, 50th anniv.

Nutcracker Suite — A112

1c, Christmas party. 2c, Dancing dolls. 3c, Clara and Snowflakes. 4c, Snowflake and prince. 5c, Snowflake dance. 15c, Sugarplum fairy and prince. 40c, Waltz of the flowers. 90c, Chinese tea dance. 1cor, Bonbonnière. 10cor, Arabian coffee dance.

1977, Dec. 12

1056 A112 1c multi .25 .25
1057 A112 2c multi .25 .25
1058 A112 3c multi .25 .25
1059 A112 4c multi .25 .25
1060 A112 5c multi .25 .25
1061 A112 15c multi .25 .25
1062 A112 40c multi .25 .25
1063 A112 90c multi .25 .25
1064 A112 1cor multi .30 .25
1065 A112 10cor multi 2.25 2.00
Nos. 1056-1065 (10) 4.55 4.25

Christmas 1977. See No. C931.

Mr. and Mrs. Andrews, by Gainsborough — A113

Paintings: 2c, Giovanna Bacelli, by Gainsborough. 3c, Blue Boy by Gainsborough. 4c, Francis I, by Titian. 5c, Charles V in Battle of Muhlberg, by Titian. 25c, Sacred Love, by Titian.

1978, Jan. 11 **Litho.** ***Perf. 14½***

1066 A113 1c multi .25 .25
1067 A113 2c multi .25 .25
1068 A113 3c multi .25 .25
1069 A113 4c multi .25 .25
1070 A113 5c multi .25 .25
1071 A113 25c multi .25 .25
Nos. 1066-1071,C932-C933 (8) 4.70 3.95

Thomas Gainsborough (1727-1788), 250th birth anniv.; Titian (1477-1576), 500th birth anniv.

Gothic Portal, Lower Church, Assisi — A114

Designs: 2c, St. Francis preaching to the birds. 3c, St. Francis, painting. 4c, St. Francis and Franciscan saints, 15th century tapestry. 5c, Portiuncola, cell of St. Francis, now in church of St. Mary of the Angels, Assisi. 15c, Blessing of St. Francis for Brother Leo (parchment). 25c, Stained-glass window, Upper Church of St. Francis, Assisi.

1978, Feb. 23 **Litho.** ***Perf. 14½***

1072 A114 1c red & multi .25 .25
1073 A114 2c brt grn & multi .25 .25
1074 A114 3c bl grn & multi .25 .25
1075 A114 4c ultra & multi .25 .25
1076 A114 5c rose & multi .25 .25
1077 A114 15c yel & multi .25 .25
1078 A114 25c ocher & multi .25 .25
Nos. 1072-1078,C935-C936 (9) 3.90 3.75

St. Francis of Assisi (1182-1266), 750th anniversary of his canonization, and in honor of Our Lady of the Immaculate Conception, patron saint of Nicaragua.

Passenger and Freight Locomotives — A115

Locomotives: 2c, Lightweight freight. 3c, American. 4c, Heavy freight Baldwin. 5c, Light freight and passenger Baldwin. 15c, Presidential coach.

1978, Apr. 7 **Litho.** ***Perf. 14½***

1079 A115 1c lil & multi .25 .25
1080 A115 2c rose lil & multi .25 .25
1081 A115 3c bl & multi .25 .25
1082 A115 4c ol & multi .30 .25
1083 A115 5c yel & multi .30 .25
1084 A115 15c dp org & multi .40 .25
Nos. 1079-1084,C938-C940 (9) 4.90 4.40

Centenary of Nicaraguan railroads.

Michael Strogoff, by Jules Verne — A116

Jules Verne Books: 2c, The Mysterious Island. 3c, Journey to the Center of the Earth (battle of the sea monsters). 4c, Five Weeks in a Balloon.

1978, Aug. **Litho.** ***Perf. 14½***

1085 A116 1c multi .25 .25
1086 A116 2c multi .25 .25
1087 A116 3c multi .25 .25
1088 A116 4c multi .25 .25
Nos. 1085-1088,C942-C943 (6) 3.00 2.75

Jules Verne (1828-1905), science fiction writer.

Back inscriptions printed on top of gum describe illustrated stamp.

Rare Stamps: 2c, Western Australia #3a. 3c, Mauritius #1. 4c, Jamaica #83a. 5c, US #C3a. 10c, Basel #3L1. 25c, Canada #387a.

1976, Dec. ***Perf. 14***

1038 A109 1c multi .25 .25
1039 A109 2c multi .25 .25
1040 A109 3c multi .25 .25
1041 A109 4c multi .25 .25
1042 A109 5c multi .25 .25
1043 A109 10c multi .25 .25
1044 A109 25c multi .25 .25
Nos. 1038-1044,C913-C917 (12) 4.65 4.40

Montgolfier Balloon — A117

1c, Icarus. 3c, Wright Brothers' Flyer A. 4c, Orville Wright at control of Flyer, 1908.

Perf. 14½, horiz.

1978, Sept. 29 **Litho.**

1089 A117 1c multi, horiz. .25 .25
1090 A117 2c multi .25 .25
1091 A117 3c multi, horiz. .25 .25
1092 A117 4c multi .25 .25
Nos. 1089-1092,C945-C946 (6) 2.65 2.25

History of aviation & 75th anniv. of 1st powered flight.

Ernst Ocwirk and Alfredo Di Stefano — A118

Soccer Players: 25c, Ralf Edstroem and Oswaldo Piazza.

1978, Oct. 25 Litho. ***Perf. 13½x14***

1093 A118 20c multicolored .25 .25
1094 A118 25c multicolored .25 .25
Nos. 1093-1094,C948-C949 (4) 1.75 1.60

11th World Soccer Cup Championship, Argentina, June 1-25. See No. C950.

St. Peter, by Goya — A119

Paintings: 15c, St. Gregory, by Goya.

1978, Dec. 12 Litho. ***Perf. 13½x14***

1095 A119 10c multi .25 .25
1096 A119 15c multi .25 .25
Nos. 1095-1096,C951-C952 (4) 2.30 1.85

Christmas 1978. See No. C953.

San Cristobal Volcano and Map — A120

Designs: No. 1098, Lake Cosiguina. No. 1099, Telica Volcano. No. 1100, Lake Jiloa.

1978, Dec. 29 ***Perf. 14x13½***

1097 A120 5c multi .25 .25
1098 A120 5c multi .25 .25
a. Pair, #1097-1098 .25 .25
1099 A120 20c multi .25 .25
1100 A120 20c multi .25 .25
a. Pair, #1099-1100 .25 .25
Nos. 1097-1100,C954-C961 (12) 6.30 5.30

Volcanos, lakes and their locations.

Overprinted in Silver or Red — A120a

Overprint reads: 1979 / ANO DE LA LIBERACION / OLYMPIC RINGS / PARTICIPACION NICARAGUA / OLIMPIADAS 1980 / Litografia Nacional, Portugal symbol

International Year of the Child: 20c, Carousel. 90c, Playing soccer. 2cor, Collecting stamps. 2.20cor, Playing with model train, plane. 10cor, Playing baseball.

1980, Apr. 7 Litho. ***Perf. 13¾x14¼***

Overprinted in Silver

1101 A120a 20c multi
e. Red ovpt.
1101A A120a 90c multi
f. Red ovpt.
1101B A120a 2cor multi
g. Red ovpt.
1101C A120a 2.20cor multi
h. Red ovpt.
1101D A120a 10cor multi
i. Red ovpt.
Nos. 1101-1101D (5) 5.00 5.00

Overprinted for Year of Liberation and 1980 Olympic Games.

Nos. 1101-1101D, 1101e-1101i were not issued without overprint.

Nos. 1101A-1101D are airmail.

Numbers have been reserved for a set of 6 Rowland Hill stamps overprinted in silver or red like Nos. 1101-1101D. The editors would like to examine a set.

Overprinted in Silver — A120c

Overprint reads: 1979 / ANO DE LA LIBERACION / OLYMPIC RINGS / PARTICIPACION NICARAGUA / OLIMPIADAS 1980 / Litografia Nacional, Portugal symbol

Albert Einstein and: 5c, Albert Schweitzer. 10c, Theory of Relativity; 15c, Trylon & Perisphere, NY World's Fair, 1939. 20c, J. Robert Oppenheimer. 25c, Wailing Wall, Jerusalem. 1cor, Nobel Prize Medal. 2.75cor, Spaceship, radio telescope antenna.

Overprinted in Silver

1980, Apr. 7 Litho. ***Perf. 14¾***

1103 A120c 5c multi
1103A A120c 10c multi
1103B A120c 15c multi
1103C A120c 20c multi
1103D A120c 25c multi
1103E A120c 1cor multi
1103F A120c 2.75cor multi
Nos. 1103-1103F (7) 5.50 5.50

Overprinted for Intl. Year of the Child, Year of Liberation and 1980 Olympic Games.

Nos. 1103-1103F were not issued without overprint. Nos. 1103E-1103F are airmail.

The editors would like to examine the set overprinted in red.

1st Anniv. of the Revolution — A120d

Sandino portrait and: 40c, Rigoberto Lopez Perez. 75c, Street fighters. 1cor, Literacy Logo, Intl. Solidarity with Nicaragua, vert. 1.25cor, German Pomares Ordonez, jungle fighters. 1.85cor, Crowd celebrating, vert. 2.50cor, Carlos Fonseca, campfire, FSLN. 5cor, Map of Central America, Flag of Nicarauga, vert. 10cor, Literacy statement, rural scene.

1980, July 19 Litho. ***Perf. 14***

1104 A120d 40c multi
1104A A120d 75c multi
1104B A120d 1cor multi
1104C A120d 1.25cor multi
1104D A120d 1.85cor multi
1104E A120d 2.50cor multi
1104F A120d 5cor multi

Souvenir Sheet

Perf. 14½x14¼

1104G A120d 10cor multi

Numbers have been reserved for two sheets of 6 and a souvenir sheet overprinted for the 1980 Literacy Year, the Intl. Year of the Child, 1980 Olympic Games, and other subjects. The editors would like to examine all three items.

Intl. Year of the Child Type of 1980 Overprinted in Black — A120f

Overprint reads: 1980 ANO DE LA ALFABETIZACION and Litografia Nacional, Portugal symbol

Perf. 13¾x14¼

1980, Dec. 20 **Litho.**

1106 A120f 20c like #1101
1106A A120f 90c like #1101A
1106B A120f 2cor like #1101B
1106C A120f 2.20cor like #1101C
1106D A120f 10cor like #1101D

Nos. 1106-1106D were not issued without overprint. Nos. 1106A-1106D are airmail.

A number has been reserved for a souvenir sheet issued with this set. The editors would like to examine the sheet.

Einstein Type of 1980

Overprinted in Gold and Black: 1980 ANO DE LA ALFABETIZACION, Litografia Nacional, Portugal symbol

A120g

Additional overprints read: No. 1107, YURI GAGARIN / 12/IV/1961 / LER HOMBRE EN EL ESPACIO. No. 1107A, Space Shuttle and LUNABA 1981. No. 1107B, Space Shuttle. Nos. 1107C, 1107E, 1107F, 1980 ANO DE LA ALFABETIZACION and Litografia Nacional, Portugal symbol. No. 1107D, Apollo XI / 16/VII/1969 / LER HONBRE A LA LUNA. No. 1107G, Einstin and Gandhi, with LUNOJOD 1 Overprint. No. 1107H, Einstin holding clipboard, with Space Shuttle, LUNABA 1981, PLANETA SATURNO 1980 and VOYAGER overprints.

1981, May 15 Litho. ***Perf. 14½***

1107 A120g 5c like #1103
1107A A120g 10c like #1103A
1107B A120g 15c like #1103B
1107C A120g 20c like #1103C
1107D A120g 25c like #1103D
1107E A120g 1cor like #1103E
1107F A120g 2.75cor like #1103F
1107G A120g 10cor multi

Souvenir Sheet

Perf. 14¾

1107H A120g 10cor on 20cor multi

Nos. 1107-1107H were not issued without overprint. Nos. 1107E-1107H are airmail.

Souvenir Sheet

Quetzal — A121

1981, May 18 Litho. ***Perf. 13***

1108 A121 10cor multi 2.50 1.25

WIPA 1981 Phil. Exhib., Vienna, May 22-31.

1982 World Cup A122

Various soccer players and stadiums.

1981, June 25 ***Perf. 12x12½***

1109 A122 5c multi .25 .25
1109A A122 20c multi .25 .25
1109B A122 25c multi .25 .25
1109C A122 30c multi .25 .25
1109D A122 50c multi .25 .25
1109E A122 4cor multi .45 .25
1109F A122 5cor multi .55 .30
1109G A122 10cor multi 1.10 .65
Nos. 1109-1109G (8) 3.35 2.45

Souvenir Sheet

Perf. 13

1109H A122 10cor multi 2.00 1.00

2nd Anniv. of Revolution — A123

1981, July 19 ***Perf. 12½x12***

1110 A123 50c Adult education .25 .25
Nos. 1110,C975E-C975G (4) 8.50 1.20

20th Anniv. of the FSLN A124

1981, July 23

1111 A124 50c Armed citizen .25 .25

See No. C976.

Postal Union of Spain and the Americas, 12th Congress, Managua — A125

1981, Aug. 10
1112 A125 50c Mailman .25 .25
Nos. 1112,C977-C979 (4) 1.40 1.10

Natl. Literacy Campaign, 1st Anniv. — A125a

Designs: 5c, "S"ahino, man counting on fingers. 20c, "A"rmadillo, children marching. 30c, "N"utria, teacher with 2 women. 40c, "D"anto, teacher with 5 people.60c, "I"guana, teacher with 3 adults, hut. 6cor, "N"icaragua, map of Nicaragua with graph. 9cor, "O"so hormiguera, UNESCO Krupskaya medal.

1981, August **Litho.** ***Perf. 14***
1113 A125a 5c multi
1113A A125a 10c multi
1113B A125a 30c multi
1113C A125a 40c multi
1113D A125a 60c multi
1113E A125a 6cor multi
1113F A125a 9cor multi
Nos. 1113-1103F (7) 4.00 4.00

Aquatic Flowers (Nymphaea...) A126

1981, Sept. 15 ***Perf. 12½***
1114 A126 50c Capensis .25 .25
1115 A126 1cor Daubenyana .25 .25
1116 A126 1.20cor Marliacea .25 .25
1117 A126 1.80cor GT Moore .35 .25
1118 A126 2cor Lotus .40 .25
1119 A126 2.50cor BG Berry .55 .30
Nos. 1114-1119,C981 (7) 3.45 2.45

Tropical Fish A127

50c, Cheirodon axelrodi. 1cor, Poecilia reticulata. 1.85cor, Anostomus anostomus. 2.10cor, Corydoras arcuatus. 2.50cor, Cynolebias nigripinnis.

1981, Oct. 19
1120 A127 50c multicolored .25 .25
1121 A127 1cor multicolored .25 .25
1122 A127 1.85cor multicolored .35 .25
1123 A127 2.10cor multicolored .45 .25
1124 A127 2.50cor multicolored .55 .30
Nos. 1120-1124,C983-C984 (7) 3.35 1.90

Dryocopus Lineatus — A128

1.20cor, Ramphastos sulfuratus, horiz. 1.80cor, Aratinga finschi, horiz. 2cor, Ara macao.

1981, Nov. 30 ***Perf. 12½***
1125 A128 50c multi .30 .25
1126 A128 1.20cor multi .45 .25
1127 A128 1.80cor multi .50 .25
1128 A128 2cor multi .60 .25
Nos. 1125-1128,C986-C988 (7) 4.80 2.20

Space Communications — A129

Various communications satellites.

1981, Dec. 15 ***Perf. 13x12½***
1129 A129 50c multi .25 .25
1130 A129 1cor multi .25 .25
1131 A129 1.50cor multi .25 .25
1132 A129 2cor multi .30 .25
Nos. 1129-1132,C989-C991 (7) 4.05 1.90

Vaporcito 93 A130

1cor, Vulcan Iron Works, 1946. 1.20cor, 1911. 1.80cor, Hoist & Derriel, 1909. 2cor, U-10B, 1956. 2.50cor, Ferrobus, 1945.

1981, Dec. 30 ***Perf. 12½***
1133 A130 50c multi .25 .25
1134 A130 1cor multi .25 .25
1135 A130 1.20cor multi .25 .25
1136 A130 1.80cor multi .40 .25
1137 A130 2cor multi .40 .25
1138 A130 2.50cor multi .40 .30
Nos. 1133-1138,C992 (7) 3.70 2.10

1982 World Cup — A131

Designs: Various soccer players. 3.50cor horiz.

1982, Jan. 25
1139 A131 5c multi .25 .25
1140 A131 20c multi .25 .25
1141 A131 25c multi .25 .25
1142 A131 2.50cor multi .40 .35
1143 A131 3.50cor multi .55 .35
Nos. 1139-1143,C993-C994 (7) 3.70 2.55

Cocker Spaniels A132

20c, German shepherds. 25c, English setters. 2.50cor, Brittany spaniels.

1982, Feb. 18
1144 A132 5c multi .25 .25
1145 A132 20c multi .25 .25
1146 A132 25c multi .25 .25
1147 A132 2.50cor multi .45 .30
Nos. 1144-1147,C996-C998 (7) 3.45 2.15

Dynamine Myrrhina A133

1.20cor, Eunica alcmena. 1.50cor, Callizona acesta. 2cor, Adelpha leuceria.

1982, Mar. 26
1148 A133 50c multi .25 .25
1149 A133 1.20cor multi .25 .25
1150 A133 1.50cor multi .30 .25
1151 A133 2cor multi .35 .25
Nos. 1148-1151,C1000-C1002 (7) 3.65 2.00

Satellite A134

Designs: Various satellites. 5c, 50c, 1.50cor, 2.50cor horiz.

1982, Apr. 12
1152 A134 5c multi .25 .25
1153 A134 15c multi .25 .25
1154 A134 50c multi .25 .25
1155 A134 1.50cor multi .25 .25
1156 A134 2.50cor multi .45 .25
Nos. 1152-1156,C1003-C1004 (7) 3.20 2.15

UPU Membership Centenary — A135

1982, May 1 **Litho.** ***Perf. 13***
1157 A135 50c Mail coach .25 .25
1158 A135 1.20cor Ship .25 .25
Nos. 1157-1158,C1005-C1006 (4) 2.00 1.45

14th Central American and Caribbean Games (Cuba '82) — A136

1982, May 13
1159 A136 10c Bicycling .25 .25
1160 A136 15c Swimming, horiz. .25 .25
1161 A136 25c Basketball .25 .25
1162 A136 50c Weight lifting .25 .25
Nos. 1159-1162,C1007-C1009 (7) 4.00 2.35

3rd Anniv. of Revolution — A137

1982, July 19
1163 A137 50c multi .25 .25
Nos. 1163,C1012-C1014 (4) 2.50 1.50

George Washington (1732-1799) A138

19th Century Paintings. 50c, Mount Vernon. 1cor, Signing the Constitution, horiz. 2cor, Riding through Trenton.
Size of 50c: 45x35mm.

Perf. 13x12½, 12½x13
1982, June 20 **Litho.**
1164 A138 50c multicolored .25 .25
1165 A138 1cor multicolored .25 .25
1166 A138 2cor multicolored .40 .25
Nos. 1164-1166,C1015-C1018 (7) 3.90 2.35

Flower Arrangement, by R. Penalba A139

Paintings: 50c, Masked Dancers, by M. Garcia, horiz. 1cor, The Couple, by R. Perez. 1.20cor, Canales Valley, by A. Mejias, horiz. 1.85cor, Portrait of Mrs. Castellon, by T. Jerez. 2cor, Street Vendors, by L. Cerrato. 10cor, Cock Fight, by Gallos P. Ortiz.

1982, Aug. 17 ***Perf. 13***
1167 A139 25c multi .25 .25
1168 A139 50c multi .25 .25
1169 A139 1cor multi .25 .25
1170 A139 1.20cor multi .25 .25
1171 A139 1.85cor multi .30 .25
1172 A139 2cor multi .30 .25
Nos. 1167-1172,C1019 (7) 3.60 2.30

Souvenir Sheet

1173 A139 10cor multi 2.00 1.00

No. 1173 contains one 36x28mm stamp.

George Dimitrov, First Pres. of Bulgaria — A140

1982, Sept. 9
1174 A140 50c Lenin, Dimitrov, 1921 .25 .25
Nos. 1174,C1020-C1021 (3) 1.50 .90

26th Anniv. of End of Dictatorship — A141

1982, Sept. 21 ***Perf. 13x12½***
1175 A141 50c Ausberto Narvaez .25 .25
1176 A141 2.50cor Cornelio Silva .50 .30
Nos. 1175-1176,C1022-C1023 (4) 2.35 1.55

Ruins, Leon Viejo A142

1cor, Ruben Dario Theater and Park. 1.20cor, Independence Plaza, Granada. 1.80cor, Corn Island. 2cor, Santiago Volcano crater, Masaya.

1982, Sept. 25 *Perf. 13*

1177 A142 50c multi .25 .25
1178 A142 1cor multi .25 .25
1179 A142 1.20cor multi .25 .25
1180 A142 1.80cor multi .30 .25
1181 A142 2cor multi .30 .25
Nos. 1177-1181,C1024-C1025 (7) 2.20 1.75

Karl Marx (1818-1883) — A143

1982, Oct. 4 *Perf. 12½*

1182 A143 1cor Marx, birthplace .25 .25

Se-tenant with label showing Communist Manifesto titlepage. See No. C1026.

World Food Day (Oct. 16) A144

50c, Picking fruit. 1cor, Farm workers, vert. 2cor, Cutting sugar cane. 10cor, Emblems.

1982, Oct. 10 *Perf. 13*

1183 A144 50c multicolored .25 .25
1184 A144 1cor multicolored .25 .25
1185 A144 2cor multicolored .30 .25
1186 A144 10cor multicolored 1.50 1.25
Nos. 1183-1186 (4) 2.30 2.00

Discovery of America, 490th Anniv. — A145

1982, Oct. 12 *Perf. 12½x13*

1187 A145 50c Santa Maria .25 .25
1188 A145 1cor Nina .25 .25
1189 A145 1.50cor Pinta .30 .25
1190 A145 2cor Columbus, fleet .40 .30
Nos. 1187-1190,C1027-C1029 (7) 3.70 2.40

A146

50c, Lobelia laxiflora. 1.20cor, Bombacopsis quinata. 1.80cor, Mimosa albida. 2cor, Epidendrum alatum.

1982, Nov. 13 *Perf. 12½*

1191 A146 50c multi .25 .25
1192 A146 1.20cor multi .25 .25
1193 A146 1.80cor multi .40 .25
1194 A146 2cor multi .40 .25
Nos. 1191-1194,C1031-C1033 (7) 3.40 2.00

A147

1982, Dec. 10 *Perf. 13*

1195 A147 10c Coral snake .25 .25
1196 A147 50c Iguana, horiz. .25 .25
1197 A147 2cor Lachesis muta, horiz. .40 .25
Nos. 1195-1197,C1034-C1037 (7) 7.30 2.05

Telecommunications Day — A148

50c, Radio transmission station. 1cor, Telcor building, Managua.

1982, Dec. 12 **Litho.** *Perf. 12½*

1198 A148 50c multicolored .25 .25
1199 A148 1cor multicolored .25 .25

50c airmail.

Jose Marti, Cuban Independence Hero, 130th Birth Anniv. — A149

1983, Jan. 28 *Perf. 13*

1200 A149 1cor multi .25 .25

Boxing — A150

1983, Jan. 31 *Perf. 12½*

1201 A150 50c shown .25 .25
1202 A150 1cor Gymnast .25 .25
1203 A150 1.50cor Running .25 .25
1204 A150 2cor Weightlifting .35 .25
1205 A150 4cor Women's discus .70 .30
1206 A150 5cor Basketball .90 .40
1207 A150 6cor Bicycling 1.10 .50
Nos. 1201-1207 (7) 3.80 2.20

Souvenir Sheet

Perf. 13

1208 A150 15cor Sailing 2.25 1.25

23rd Olympic Games, Los Angeles, July 28-Aug. 12, 1984. Nos. 1205-1208 airmail. No. 1208 contains one 31x39mm stamp.

Local Flowers — A151

No. 1209, Bixa orellana. No. 1210, Brassavola nodosa. No. 1211, Cattleya lueddemanniana. No. 1212, Cochlospermum spec. No. 1213, Hibiscus rosa-sinensis. No. 1214, Laella spec. No. 1215, Malvaviscus arboreus. No. 1216, Neomarica coerulea. No. 1217, Plumeria rubra. No. 1218, Senecio spec. No. 1219, Sobralla macrantha. No. 1220, Stachytarpheta indica. No. 1221, Tabebula ochraceae. No. 1222, Tagetes erecta. No. 1223, Tecoma stans. No. 1224, Thumbergia alata.

1983, Feb. 5 *Perf. 12½*

1209 A151 1cor multicolored .25 .25
1210 A151 1cor multicolored .25 .25
1211 A151 1cor multicolored .25 .25
1212 A151 1cor multicolored .25 .25
1213 A151 1cor multicolored .25 .25
1214 A151 1cor multicolored .25 .25
1215 A151 1cor multicolored .25 .25
1216 A151 1cor multicolored .25 .25
1217 A151 1cor multicolored .25 .25
1218 A151 1cor multicolored .25 .25
1219 A151 1cor multicolored .25 .25
1220 A151 1cor multicolored .25 .25
1221 A151 1cor multicolored .25 .25
1222 A151 1cor multicolored .25 .25
1223 A151 1cor multicolored .25 .25
1224 A151 1cor multicolored .25 .25
Nos. 1209-1224 (16) 4.00 4.00

See #1515-1530, 1592-1607, 1828-1843.

Visit of Pope John Paul II A152

50c, Peace banner. 1cor, Map, girl picking coffee beans. 4cor, Pres. Rafael Rivas, Pope. 7cor, Pope, Managua Cathedral.
15cor, Pope, vert.

1983, Mar. 4 *Perf. 13*

1225 A152 50c multicolored .25 .25
1226 A152 1cor multicolored .25 .25
1227 A152 4cor multicolored .95 .60
1228 A152 7cor multicolored 1.60 1.00
Nos. 1225-1228 (4) 3.05 2.10

Souvenir Sheet

1229 A152 15cor multicolored 3.25 1.75

Nos. 1227-1229 airmail. No. 1229 contains one 31x39mm stamp.

Nocturnal Moths — A153

15c, Xilophanes chiron. 50c, Protoparce ochus. 65c, Pholus lasbruscae. 1cor, Amphypterus gannascus. 1.50cor, Pholus licaon. 2cor, Agrius cingulata. 10cor, Rothschildia jurulla, vert.

1983, Mar. 10

1230 A153 15c multi .25 .25
1231 A153 50c multi .25 .25
1232 A153 65c multi .25 .25
1233 A153 1cor multi .25 .25
1234 A153 1.50cor multi .25 .25
1235 A153 2cor multi .35 .25
1236 A153 10cor multi 1.50 .80
Nos. 1230-1236 (7) 3.10 2.30

No. 1236 airmail.

26th Anniv. of the Anti-Somoza Movement — A154

Various monuments and churches — 50c, Church of Subtiava, Leon. 1cor, La Immaculata Castle, Rio San Juan. 2cor, La Recoleccion Church, Leon, vert. 4cor, Ruben Dario monument, Managua, vert.

1983, Mar. 25 *Perf. 12½*

1237 A154 50c multi .25 .25
1238 A154 1cor multi .25 .25
1239 A154 2cor multi .35 .25
1240 A154 4cor multi .65 .40
Nos. 1237-1240 (4) 1.50 1.15

Nos. 1237-1239 has "correos" above date. No. 1240 has "aereo" above date.

Railroad Cars A155

1983, Apr. 15

1241 A155 15c Passenger .25 .25
1242 A155 65c Freight .25 .25
1243 A155 1cor Tank .25 .25
1244 A155 1.50cor Ore .25 .25
1245 A155 4cor Passenger, diff. .55 .30
1246 A155 5cor Flat .70 .40
1247 A155 7cor Rail bus .95 .50
Nos. 1241-1247 (7) 3.20 2.20

Nos. 1245-1247 airmail.

Red Cross Flood Rescue A156

1cor, Putting patient in ambulance. 4cor, 1972 earthquake & fire rescue. 5cor, Nurse examining soldier, 1979 Liberation War.

1983, May 8 *Perf. 13*

1248 A156 50c multi .25 .25
1249 A156 1cor multi .25 .25
1250 A156 4cor multi .65 .40
1251 A156 5cor multi .70 .40
Nos. 1248-1251 (4) 1.85 1.30

4cor, 5cor airmail. 4cor vert.

World Communications Year — A157

1983, May 17

1252 A157 1cor multi .40 .25

9th Pan-American Games, Aug. — A158

1983, May 30 **Litho.** *Perf. 13*

1253 A158 15c Baseball .25 .25
1254 A158 50c Water polo .25 .25
1255 A158 65c Running .25 .25
1256 A158 1cor Women's basketball, vert. .25 .25
1257 A158 2cor Weightlifting, vert. .35 .25
1258 A158 7cor Fencing 1.10 .55
1259 A158 8cor Gymnastics 1.25 .65
Nos. 1253-1259 (7) 3.70 2.45

Souvenir Sheet

1260 A158 15cor Boxing 2.50 1.25

Nos. 1258-1260 airmail. No. 1260 contains one 39x31mm stamp.

4th Anniv. of Revolution — A159

1cor, Port of Corinto. 2cor, Telecommunications Bldg., Leon.

1983, July 19 Litho. *Perf. 12½*
1261 A159 1cor multicolored .25 .25
1262 A159 2cor multicolored .40 .25

Founders of FSLN (Sandinista Party) — A160

1983, July 23 Litho. *Perf. 13*
1263 A160 50c multi .25 .25
1264 A160 1cor multi .25 .25
1265 A160 4cor multi, vert. .60 .35
Nos. 1263-1265 (3) 1.10 .85

No. 1265, airmail, 33x44mm.

Simon Bolivar, 200th Birth Anniv. A161

50c, Bolivar and Sandino. 1cor, Bolivar on horseback, vert.

1983, July 24 Litho. *Perf. 12½*
1266 A161 50c multicolored .25 .25
1267 A161 1cor multicolored .25 .25

14th Winter Olympic Games, Sarajevo, Yugoslavia, Feb. 8-19, 1984 — A162

1983, Aug. 5 Litho. *Perf. 13*
1268 A162 50c Speed skating .25 .25
1269 A162 1cor Slalom .25 .25
1270 A162 1.50cor Luge .25 .25
1271 A162 2cor Ski jumping .40 .25
1272 A162 4cor Ice dancing .65 .35
1273 A162 5cor Skiing .75 .40
1274 A162 6cor Biathlon 1.00 .50
Nos. 1268-1274 (7) 3.55 2.25

Souvenir Sheet

1983, Aug. 25 Litho. *Perf. 13*
1275 A162 15cor Hockey 2.50 1.40

No. 1275 contains one 39x32mm stamp. Nos. 1272-1275 airmail.

Chess Moves — A163

1983, Aug. 20 Litho. *Perf. 13*
1276 A163 15c Pawn .25 .25
1277 A163 65c Knight .25 .25
1278 A163 1cor Bishop .25 .25
1279 A163 2cor Castle .35 .25
1280 A163 4cor Queen .60 .35
1281 A163 5cor King .70 .40
1282 A163 7cor Player 1.00 .55
Nos. 1276-1282 (7) 3.40 2.30

Nos. 1280-1282 airmail.

Archaeological Finds — A164

1983, Aug. 20 *Perf. 13x12½*
1283 A164 50c Stone figurine .25 .25
1284 A164 1cor Covered dish .25 .25
1285 A164 2cor Vase .40 .25
1286 A164 4cor Platter .70 .35
Nos. 1283-1286 (4) 1.60 1.10

No. 1286 airmail.

Madonna of the Chair, by Raphael (1483-1517) A165

Paintings: 1cor, The Eszterhazy Madonna. 1.50cor, Sistine Madonna. 2cor, Madonna of the Linnet. 4cor, Madonna of the Meadow. 5cor, La Belle Jardiniere. 6cor, Adoration of the Kings. 15cor, Madonna de Foligno. 4, 5, 6, 15cor airmail.

1983, Sept. 15
1287 A165 50c multi .25 .25
1288 A165 1cor multi .25 .25
1289 A165 1.50cor multi .25 .25
1290 A165 2cor multi .35 .25
1291 A165 4cor multi .60 .35
1292 A165 5cor multi .70 .40
1293 A165 6cor multi .90 .45
Nos. 1287-1293 (7) 3.30 2.20

Souvenir Sheet

1984, Sept. 15 Litho. *Perf. 13*
1293A A165 15cor multi 2.75 1.25

Mining Industry Nationalization — A166

1cor, Pouring molten metal. 4cor, Mine headstock, workers.

1983, Oct. 2 *Perf. 13*
1294 A166 1cor multicolored .25 .25
1295 A166 4cor multicolored .60 .40

4cor airmail.

Ship-to-Shore Communications — A167

1983, Oct. 7 *Perf. 12½*
1296 A167 1cor shown .25 .25
1297 A167 4cor Radio tower, view .60 .40

FRACAP '83, Federation of Central American and Panamanian Radio Amateurs Cong., Oct. 7-9.

Agrarian Reform — A168

1983, Oct. 16
1298 A168 1cor Tobacco .25 .25
1299 A168 2cor Cotton .35 .25
1300 A168 4cor Corn .60 .25
1301 A168 5cor Sugar cane .70 .35
1302 A168 6cor Cattle .90 .40
1303 A168 7cor Rice paddy 1.00 .45
1304 A168 8cor Coffee beans 1.20 .55
1305 A168 10cor Bananas 1.50 .65
Nos. 1298-1305 (8) 6.50 3.15

See Nos. 1531-1538, 1608-1615.

Fire Engine A169

Various Fire Engines.

1983, Oct. 17 *Perf. 13*
1306 A169 50c multi .25 .25
1307 A169 1cor multi .25 .25
1308 A169 1.50cor multi .25 .25
1309 A169 2cor multi .35 .25
1310 A169 4cor multi .60 .35
1311 A169 5cor multi .70 .40
1312 A169 6cor multi .90 .45
Nos. 1306-1312 (7) 3.30 2.20

Nos. 1308-1311 airmail.

Nicaraguan-Cuban Solidarity — A170

1cor, José Marti, Gen. Sandino. 4cor, Education, health, industry.

1983, Oct. 24
1313 A170 1cor multicolored .25 .25
1314 A170 4cor multicolored .60 .40

4cor airmail.

A171

Christmas (Adoration of the Kings Paintings by): 50c, Hugo van der Goes. 1 cor, Ghirlandaio. 2cor, El Greco. 7cor, Konrad von Soest. 7cor airmail.

1983, Dec. 1
1315 A171 50c multi .25 .25
1316 A171 1cor multi .25 .25
1317 A171 2cor multi .30 .25
1318 A171 7cor multi 1.20 .40
Nos. 1315-1318 (4) 2.00 1.15

A172

1984, Jan. 10
1319 A172 50c Biathlon .25 .25
1320 A172 50c Bobsledding .25 .25
1321 A172 1cor Speed skating .25 .25
1322 A172 1cor Slalom .25 .25
1323 A172 4cor Downhill skiing .65 .35
1324 A172 5cor Ice dancing .80 .40
1325 A172 10cor Ski jumping 1.40 .75
Nos. 1319-1325 (7) 3.85 2.50

Souvenir Sheet

1326 A172 15cor Hockey 3.50 1.75

1984 Winter Olympics. No. 1326 contains one 31x39mm stamp. Nos. 1323-1326 airmail.

Domestic Cats — A173

No. 1327, Chinchilla. No. 1328, Long-haired Angel. No. 1329, Red tabby. No. 1330, Tortoiseshell. No. 1331, Siamese. No. 1332, Blue Burmese. No. 1333, Silver long-haired.

1984, Feb. 15 *Perf. 12½*
1327 A173 50c multicolored .25 .25
1328 A173 50c multicolored .25 .25
1329 A173 1cor multicolored .40 .25
1330 A173 2cor multicolored .60 .25
1331 A173 3cor multicolored .50 .30
1332 A173 4cor multicolored 1.00 .40
1333 A173 7cor multicolored 2.00 .60
Nos. 1327-1333 (7) 5.00 2.30

Nos. 1331, 1333 airmail.

Augusto Cesar Sandino (d. 1934) — A174

1984, Feb. 21
1334 A174 1cor Arms .25 .25
1335 A174 4cor Portrait .60 .40

4cor airmail.

Intl. Women's Day — A175

1984, Mar. 8
1336 A175 1cor Blanca Arauz .40 .25

Bee-pollinated Flowers A176

No. 1337, Poinsettia. No. 1338, Sunflower. No. 1339, Antigonan leptopus. No. 1340, Cassia alata. No. 1341, Bidens pilosa. No. 1342, Althea rosea. No. 1343, Rivea corymbosa.

1984, Mar. 20

1337	A176	50c multicolored	.25	.25
1338	A176	50c multicolored	.25	.25
1339	A176	1cor multicolored	.25	.25
1340	A176	1cor multicolored	.25	.25
1341	A176	3cor multicolored	.40	.25
1342	A176	4cor multicolored	.60	.35
1343	A176	5cor multicolored	.70	.40
		Nos. 1337-1343 (7)	2.70	2.00

Nos. 1341-1343 airmail.

Space Annivs. — A177

No. 1344, Soyuz 6,7,8, 1969. No. 1345, Soyuz 6,7,8, diff. No. 1346, Apollo 11, 1969. No. 1347, Luna 1, 1959. No. 1348, Luna 2, 1959. No. 1349, Luna 3, 1959. No. 1350, Painting by Koroliov, 1934.

1984, Apr. 20

1344	A177	50c multicolored	.25	.25
1345	A177	50c multicolored	.25	.25
1346	A177	1cor multicolored	.25	.25
1347	A177	2cor multicolored	.35	.25
1348	A177	3cor multicolored	.50	.25
1349	A177	4cor multicolored	.65	.35
1350	A177	9cor multicolored	1.40	.50
		Nos. 1344-1350 (7)	3.65	2.10

Nos. 1348-1350 airmail.

Noli Me Tangere, by Correggio A178

No. 1352, Madonna of San Girolamo. No. 1353, Allegory of the Virtues. No. 1354, Allegory of Placer. No. 1355, Ganimedes. No. 1356, Danae. No. 1357, Leda.
No. 1358, St. John the Evangelist.

1984, May 17 Litho. *Perf. 12½*

1351	A178	50c shown	.25	.25
1352	A178	50c multicolored	.25	.25
1353	A178	1cor multicolored	.25	.25
1354	A178	2cor multicolored	.35	.25
1355	A178	3cor multicolored	.50	.25
1356	A178	5cor multicolored	.80	.40
1357	A178	8cor multicolored	1.25	.65
		Nos. 1351-1357 (7)	3.65	2.30

Souvenir Sheet

1358	A178	15cor multicolored	3.25	1.25

No. 1358 contains one 31x39mm stamp. Nos. 1355-1358 airmail.

Vintage Cars A179

No. 1359, Abadal, 1914. No. 1360, Daimler, 1886, vert. No. 1361, Ford, 1903, vert. No. 1362, Renault, 1899, vert. No. 1363, Rolls Royce, 1910. No. 1364, Metallurgique, 1907. No. 1365, Bugatti Mode 40.

1984, May 18

1359	A179	1cor multicolored	.25	.25
1360	A179	1cor multicolored	.25	.25
1361	A179	2cor multicolored	.35	.25
1362	A179	2cor multicolored	.35	.25
1363	A179	3cor multicolored	.50	.25
1364	A179	4cor multicolored	.65	.35
1365	A179	7cor multicolored	1.10	.60
		Nos. 1359-1365 (7)	3.45	2.20

Birth sesquicentennial of Gottlieb Daimler. Nos. 1363-1365 airmail.

1984 Summer Olympics A180

1984, July 6

1366	A180	50c Volleyball	.25	.25
1367	A180	50c Basketball	.25	.25
1368	A180	1cor Field hockey	.25	.25
1369	A180	2cor Tennis	.35	.25
1370	A180	3cor Soccer	.50	.25
1371	A180	4cor Water polo	.65	.35
1372	A180	9cor Net ball	1.40	.70
		Nos. 1366-1372 (7)	3.65	2.30

Souvenir Sheet

Perf. 13

1373	A180	15cor Baseball	2.25	1.25

No. 1373 contains one 40x31mm stamp. Nos. 1370-1373 airmail and horiz.

5th Anniv. of Revolution — A181

1984, July 19

1374	A181	50c Construction	.25	.25
1375	A181	1cor Transportation	.25	.25
1376	A181	4cor Agriculture	.65	.35
1377	A181	7cor Govt. building	1.25	.55
		Nos. 1374-1377 (4)	2.40	1.40

Nos. 1376-1377 airmail.

UNESCO Nature Conservation Campaign — A182

50c, Children dependent on nature. 1cor, Forest. 2cor, River. 10cor, Seedlings, field, vert.

1984, Aug. 3 *Perf. 12½x13, 13x12½*

1378	A182	50c multicolored	.25	.25
1379	A182	1cor multicolored	.25	.25
1380	A182	2cor multicolored	.35	.25
1381	A182	10cor multicolored	1.50	.80
		Nos. 1378-1381 (4)	2.35	1.55

No. 1381 airmail.

Nicaraguan Red Cross, 50th Anniv. — A183

1984, Sept. 16 *Perf. 12½x12*

1382	A183	1cor Air ambulance	.25	.25
1383	A183	7cor Battle field	1.00	.55

No. 1383 airmail.

History of Baseball — A184

Portraits and national colors: #1384, Ventura Escalante, Dominican Republic. #1385, Daniel Herrera, Mexico. #1386, Adalberto Herrera, Venezuela. #1387, Roberto Clemente, Puerto Rico. #1388, Carlos Colas, Cuba. #1389, Stanley Cayasso, Nicaragua. #1390, Babe Ruth, US.

1984, Oct. 25 Litho. *Perf. 12½*

1384	A184	50c multi	.25	.25
1385	A184	50c multi	.25	.25
1386	A184	1cor multi	.35	.25
1387	A184	1cor multi	.35	.25
1388	A184	3cor multi	.90	.25
1389	A184	4cor multi	1.25	.25
1390	A184	5cor multi	1.50	.35
		Nos. 1384-1390 (7)	4.85	1.85

Nos. 1388-1390 are airmail.

Tapirus Bairdii A185

1984, Dec. 28 *Perf. 13*

1391	A185	25c In water	.30	.25
1392	A185	25c In field	.30	.25
1393	A185	3cor Baring teeth	.70	.25
1394	A185	4cor Female and young	.90	.25
		Nos. 1391-1394 (4)	2.20	1.00

Wildlife conservation. Nos. 1393-1394 are airmail. Compare with type A202.

1986 World Cup Soccer Championships, Mexico — A186

Evolution of soccer.

1985, Jan. 20

1395	A186	50c 1314	.25	.25
1396	A186	50c 1500	.25	.25
1397	A186	1cor 1846	.25	.25
1398	A186	1cor 1872	.25	.25
1399	A186	2cor 1883	.25	.25
1400	A186	4cor 1890	.40	.25
1401	A186	6cor 1953	.60	.30
		Nos. 1395-1401 (7)	2.25	1.80

Souvenir Sheet

Perf. 12½

1402	A186	10cor 1985	2.00	1.00

Nos. 1399-1402 are airmail. No. 1402 contains one 40x32mm stamp.

Mushrooms A187

No. 1403, Boletus calopus. No. 1404, Strobilomyces retisporus. No. 1405, Boletus luridus. No. 1406, Xerocomus illudens. No. 1407, Gyrodon merulioides. No. 1408, Tylopilus plumbeoviolaceus. No. 1409, Gyroporus castaneus.

1985, Feb. 20

1403	A187	50c multicolored	.25	.25
1404	A187	50c multicolored	.25	.25
1405	A187	1cor multicolored	.25	.25
1406	A187	1cor multicolored	.25	.25
1407	A187	4cor multicolored	.50	.25
1408	A187	5cor multicolored	.60	.25
1409	A187	8cor multicolored	1.00	.40
		Nos. 1403-1409 (7)	3.10	1.90

Nos. 1406-1409 are airmail.

Postal Union of the Americas and Spain, 13th Congress A188

UPAE emblem and: 1cor, Chasqui, mail runner and map of Realejo-Nicaragua route. 7cor, Monoplane and Nicaraguan air network.

1985, Mar. 11 *Perf. 12½x13*

1410	A188	1cor multi	.55	.25
1411	A188	7cor multi	2.10	.40

No. 1411 is airmail.

City Railway Engine A189

Various locomotives.

1985, Apr. 5 *Perf. 12½*

1412	A189	1cor Electric	.25	.25
1413	A189	1cor Steam	.25	.25
1414	A189	9cor shown	.80	.25
1415	A189	9cor Tram	.80	.25
1416	A189	15cor steam, diff.	1.40	.40
1417	A189	21cor steam, diff.	2.00	.35
		Nos. 1412-1417 (6)	5.50	1.75

Souvenir Sheet

Perf. 13

1418	A189	42cor steam, diff.	5.75	5.75

German Railroads, 150th Anniv. #1418 also for 100th anniv. of Nicaraguan railroads. #1418 contains one 40x32mm stamp. #1414-1418 are airmail.

Motorcycle Cent. — A190

1985, Apr. 30 Litho. *Perf. 12½*

1419	A190	50c F.N., 1928	.25	.25
1420	A190	50c Douglas, 1928	.25	.25
1421	A190	1cor Puch, 1938	.40	.25
1422	A190	2cor Wanderer, 1939	.50	.25
1423	A190	4cor Honda, 1949	1.00	.25

1424 A190 5cor BMW, 1984 1.40 .25
1425 A190 7cor Honda, 1984 1.75 .40
Nos. 1419-1425 (7) 5.55 1.90

Nos. 1419-1425 se-tenant with labels picturing manufacturers' trademarks. Nos. 1422-1425 are airmail.

Flowers — A194

No. 1454, Metelea quirosii. No. 1455, Ipomea nil. No. 1456, Lysichitum americanum. No. 1457, Clusia sp. No. 1458, Vanilla planifolia. No. 1459, Stemmadenia obovata.

1985, May 20 Litho. *Perf. 13*

1454 A194 50c multicolored .25 .25
1455 A194 50c multicolored .25 .25
1456 A194 1cor multicolored .40 .25
1457 A194 2cor multicolored .70 .25
1458 A194 4cor multicolored 1.40 .35
1459 A194 7cor multicolored 2.50 .60
a. Miniature sheet of 6, #1454-1459 5.75
Nos. 1454-1459 (6) 5.50 1.95

Nos. 1457-1459 are airmail.
Stamps in No. 1459a do not have white border.

End of World War II, 40th Anniv. — A195

9.50cor, German army surrenders. 28cor, Nuremberg trials, horiz.

1985, May *Perf. 12x12½, 12½x12*

1460 A195 9.50cor multi .80 .35
1461 A195 28cor multi 2.25 1.00

No. 1461 is airmail.

Lenin, 115th Birth Anniv. A196

Design: 21cor, Lenin speaking to workers.

1985, June Litho. *Perf. 12x12½*

1462 A196 4cor multicolored .50 .25
1463 A196 21cor multicolored 2.50 1.10

Souvenir Sheet

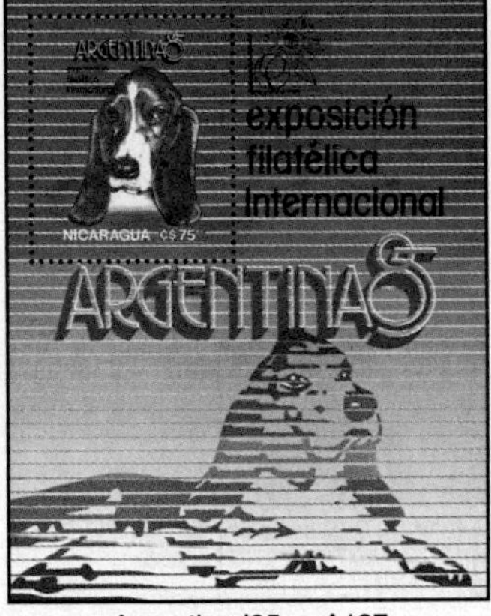

Argentina '85 — A197

1985, June 5 Litho. *Perf. 13*

1464 A197 75cor multicolored 4.25 2.00

World Stamp Exposition.

Birds — A198

1985, Aug. 25

1465 A198 50c Ring-neck pheasant .25 .25
1466 A198 50c Chicken .25 .25
1467 A198 1cor Guinea hen .30 .25
1468 A198 2cor Goose .60 .25
1469 A198 6cor Turkey 1.90 .60
1470 A198 8cor Duck 2.40 .80
Nos. 1465-1470 (6) 5.70 2.40

Intl. Music Year A199

No. 1471, Luis A. Delgadillo, vert. No. 1473, Parade. No. 1474, Managua Cathedral. No. 1475, Masked dancer. No. 1476, Parade, diff.

1985, Sept. 1

1471 A199 1cor multicolored .25 .25
1472 A199 1cor shown .25 .25
1473 A199 9cor multicolored .90 .35
1474 A199 9cor multicolored .90 .35
1475 A199 15cor multicolored 1.40 .55
1476 A199 21cor multicolored 1.90 .75
Nos. 1471-1476 (6) 5.60 2.50

Nos. 1473-1476 are airmail.

Natl. Fire Brigade, 6th Anniv. A200

1985, Oct. 18

1477 A200 1cor Fire station .25 .25
1478 A200 1cor Fire truck .25 .25
1479 A200 1cor shown .25 .25
1480 A200 3cor Ambulance .30 .25
1481 A200 9cor Airport fire truck .90 .30
1482 A200 15cor Waterfront fire 1.50 .50
1483 A200 21cor Hose team, fire 2.10 .75
a. Min. sheet of 7, #1474-1483 + 2 labels 5.50
Nos. 1477-1483 (7) 5.55 2.55

Stamps from No. 1483a have orange borders. Nos. 1480-1483 are airmail.

Halley's Comet — A201

No. 1484, Edmond Halley. No. 1485, Map of comet's track, 1910. No. 1486, Tycho Brahe's observatory. No. 1487, Astrolabe, map. No. 1488, Telescopes. No. 1489, Telescope designs.

1985, Nov. 26

1484 A201 1cor multicolored .25 .25
1485 A201 3cor multicolored .35 .25
1486 A201 3cor multicolored .35 .25
1487 A201 9cor multicolored .90 .25
1488 A201 15cor multicolored 1.50 .40
1489 A201 21cor multicolored 2.25 .60
Nos. 1484-1489 (6) 5.60 2.00

Nos. 1487-1489 are airmail.

Tapirus Bairdii A202

1985, Dec. 30

1490 A202 1cor Eating .40 .25
1491 A202 3cor Drinking .60 .25
1492 A202 5cor Grazing in field 1.00 .25
1493 A202 9cor With young 1.90 .45
Nos. 1490-1493 (4) 3.90 1.20

Nos. 1491-1493 are airmail.

Roses — A203

1986, Jan. 15 *Perf. 12½*

1494 A203 1cor Spinosissima .25 .25
1495 A203 1cor Canina .25 .25
1496 A203 3cor Eglanteria .40 .25
1497 A203 5cor Rubrifolia .40 .25
1498 A203 9cor Foetida .40 .25
1499 A203 100cor Rugosa 4.00 1.10
Nos. 1494-1499 (6) 5.70 2.35

Nos. 1497-1499 are airmail.

Birds — A204

1986, Feb. 10 *Perf. 13x12½*

1500 A204 1cor Colibri topacio .25 .25
1501 A204 3cor Paraulata picodorado .30 .25
1502 A204 3cor Troupial .30 .25
1503 A204 5cor Vereron pintado .30 .25
1504 A204 10cor Tordo ruisenor .45 .25
1505 A204 21cor Buho real .90 .25
1506 A204 75cor Gran kiskadee 3.00 1.10
Nos. 1500-1506 (7) 5.50 2.60

Nos. 1504-1506 are airmail.

A205

World Cup Soccer Championships, Mexico: Soccer players and pre-Columbian artifacts. No. 1514, Player's foot, ball.

1986, Mar. 20 *Perf. 12½*

Shirt Colors

1507 A205 1cor blue & yel .25 .25
1508 A205 1cor yel & green .25 .25
1509 A205 3cor blue & white .25 .25
1510 A205 3cor red & white .25 .25
1511 A205 5cor red .25 .25
1512 A205 9cor blk & yel .25 .25
1513 A205 100cor red & grn 2.25 1.10
Nos. 1507-1513 (7) 3.75 2.60

Souvenir Sheet

Perf. 13

1514 A205 100cor multicolored 2.50 1.25

Nos. 1509-1514 are airmail.

Flower Type of 1983

1986, Mar. Litho. *Perf. 12½*

1515 A151 5cor like #1209 .35 .25
1516 A151 5cor like #1210 .35 .25
1517 A151 5cor like #1211 .35 .25
1518 A151 5cor like #1212 .35 .25
1519 A151 5cor like #1213 .35 .25
1520 A151 5cor like #1214 .35 .25
1521 A151 5cor like #1215 .35 .25
1522 A151 5cor like #1216 .35 .25
1523 A151 5cor like #1217 .35 .25
1524 A151 5cor like #1218 .35 .25
1525 A151 5cor like #1219 .35 .25
1526 A151 5cor like #1220 .35 .25
1527 A151 5cor like #1221 .35 .25
1528 A151 5cor like #1222 .35 .25
1529 A151 5cor like #1223 .35 .25
1530 A151 5cor like #1224 .35 .25
Nos. 1515-1530 (16) 5.60 4.00

Agrarian Reform Type of 1983

1986, Apr. 15 *Perf. 12½*

1531 A168 1cor dk brown .25 .25
1532 A168 9cor purple .25 .25
1533 A168 15cor rose violet .30 .25
1534 A168 21cor dk car rose .45 .25
1535 A168 33cor orange .75 .35
1536 A168 42cor green .95 .45
1537 A168 50cor brown 1.10 .55
1538 A168 100cor blue 2.25 1.10
Nos. 1531-1538 (8) 6.30 3.45

Writers A207

No. 1539, Alfonso Cortes. No. 1540, Salomon de la Selva. No. 1541, Azarias H. Pallais. No. 1542, Ruben Dario. No. 1543, Pablo Neruda. No. 1544, Alfonso Reyes. No. 1545, Pedro Henriquez Urena.

1986, Apr. 23 *Perf. 12½x13*

1539 A207 1cor multicolored .25 .25
1540 A207 3cor multicolored .25 .25
1541 A207 3cor multicolored .25 .25
1542 A207 5cor multicolored .25 .25
1543 A207 9cor multicolored .30 .25

1544 A207 15cor multicolored .45 .25
1545 A207 100cor multicolored 3.50 1.10
Nos. 1539-1545 (7) 5.25 2.60

Nos. 1544-1545 are airmail.

Nuts & Fruits — A208

No. 1546, Maranon (cashew). No. 1547, Zapote. No. 1548, Pitahaya. No. 1549, Granadilla. No. 1550, Anona. No. 1551, Melocoton (starfruit). No. 1552, Mamey.

1986, June 20 *Perf. 12x12½*
1546 A208 1cor multicolored .25 .25
1547 A208 1cor multicolored .25 .25
1548 A208 3cor multicolored .30 .25
1549 A208 3cor multicolored .30 .25
1550 A208 5cor multicolored .30 .25
1551 A208 21cor multicolored .75 .25
1552 A208 100cor multicolored 3.25 1.10
Nos. 1546-1552 (7) 5.40 2.60

FAO, 40th Anniv. Nos. 1550-1552 are airmail.

Lockheed L-1011 Tristar — A209

Airplanes: No. 1554, YAK 40. No. 1555, BAC 1-11. No. 1556, Boeing 747. 9cor, A-300. 15cor, TU-154. No. 1559, Concorde, vert. No. 1560, Fairchild 340.

1986, Aug. 22 *Perf. 12½*
1553 A209 1cor multicolored .25 .25
1554 A209 1cor multicolored .25 .25
1555 A209 3cor multicolored .25 .25
1556 A209 3cor multicolored .30 .25
1557 A209 9cor multicolored .40 .25
1558 A209 15cor multicolored .50 .25
1559 A209 100cor multicolored 3.50 1.10
Nos. 1553-1559 (7) 5.45 2.60

Souvenir Sheet

Perf. 13

1560 A209 100cor multicolored 3.75 3.75

Stockholmia '86. No. 1560 contains one 40x32mm stamp.
Nos. 1557-1560 airmail.

A210

NICARAGUA CORREO AEREO
JUAN DE LA COSA
C$9.00

A210a

Discovery of America, 500th Anniv. (in 1992) — A210b

No. 1561, 1 of Columbus' ships. No. 1562, 2 of Columbus' ships. No. 1563, Juan de la Cosa. No. 1564, Columbus. No. 1565, Ferdinand, Isabella. No. 1566, Columbus before throne.

1986, Oct. 12 *Perf. 12½x12*
1561 A210 1cor multi .25 .25
1562 A210 1cor multi .25 .25
a. Pair, #1561-1562 .25 .25
b. Souv. sheet of 2, #1561-1562 .30 .25

Perf. 12x12½

1563 A210a 9cor multi .30 .25
1564 A210a 9cor multi .30 .25
a. Pair, #1563-1564 .65 .25
1565 A210b 21cor multi .80 .25
1566 A210b 100cor multi 3.50 1.10
a. Pair, #1565-1566 4.50 1.40
b. Souv. sheet of 4, #1563-1566 5.00 1.50
Nos. 1561-1566 (6) 5.40 2.35

Nos. 1563-1566 are airmail. Nos. 1564a, 1566a have continuous design.

Butterflies A211

No. 1567, Theritas coronata. No. 1568, Charayes nitebis. No. 1569, Salamis cacta. No. 1570, Papilio maacki. No. 1571, Euphaedro cyparissa. No. 1572, Palaeochrysophonus hippothoe. No. 1573, Ritra aurea.

1986, Dec. 12 *Perf. 12½*
1567 A211 10cor multi .45 .25
1568 A211 15cor multi .70 .25
1569 A211 15cor multi .70 .25
1570 A211 15cor multi .70 .25
1571 A211 25cor multi 1.10 .30
1572 A211 25cor multi 1.10 .30
1573 A211 30cor multi 1.50 .35
Nos. 1567-1573 (7) 6.25 1.95

Nos. 1568-1573 are airmail.

Ruben Dario Order of Cultural Independence A212

Dario Order Winning Writers: No. 1574, Ernesto Mejia Sanchez. No. 1575, Fernando Gordillo C. No. 1576, Francisco Perez Estrada. 30cor, Julio Cortazar. 60cor, Enrique Fernandez Morales.

1987, Jan. 18 **Litho.** *Perf. 13*
1574 A212 10cor multicolored .25 .25
1575 A212 10cor multicolored .25 .25
1576 A212 10cor multicolored .25 .25
1577 A212 15cor multicolored .30 .25
1578 A212 30cor multicolored .65 .30
1579 A212 60cor multicolored 1.25 .65
a. Strip of 6, #1574-1579 2.90 1.50
b. Min. sheet of 6, #1574-1579 2.90 2.90

1988 Winter Olympics, Calgary — A213

#1580, Speed skating. #1581, Ice hockey. #1582, Women's figure skating. #1583, Ski jumping. 20cor, Biathalon. 30cor, Slalom skiing. 40cor, Downhill skiing. 110cor, Ice hockey, diff., horiz.

1987, Feb. 3 *Perf. 13*
1580 A213 10cor multi .45 .25
1581 A213 10cor multi .45 .25
1582 A213 15cor multi .60 .25
1583 A213 15cor multi .60 .25
1584 A213 20cor multi .75 .25
1585 A213 30cor multi 1.10 .30
1586 A213 40cor multi 1.75 .40
Nos. 1580-1586 (7) 5.70 1.95

Souvenir Sheet

Perf. 12½

1587 A213 110cor multi 3.75 3.75

Nos. 1582-1587 are airmail. No. 1587 contains one 40x32mm stamp.

Children's Welfare Campaign A214

1987, Mar. 18 *Perf. 13*
1588 A214 10cor Growth & development .25 .25
1589 A214 25cor Vaccination .90 .30
1590 A214 30cor Rehydration 1.50 .35
1591 A214 50cor Breastfeeding 5.00 .60
Nos. 1588-1591 (4) 7.65 1.50

Nos. 1589-1591 are airmail. For surcharges, see Nos. 1674A-1674D.

Flower Type of 1983

No. 1592, Bixa orellana. No. 1593, Brassavola nodosa. No. 1594, Cattleya lueddemanniana. No. 1595, Cochlospermum spec. No. 1596, Hibiscus rosa-sinensis. No. 1597, Laella spec. No. 1598, Malvaviscus arboreus. No. 1599, Neomarica coerulea. No. 1600, Plumeria rubra. No. 1601, Senecio spec. No. 1602, Sobralla macrantha. No. 1603, Stachytarpheta indica. No. 1604, Tabebula ochraceae. No. 1605, Tagetes erecta. No. 1606, Tecoma stans. No. 1607, Thumbergia alata.

1987, Mar. 25 *Perf. 12½*
1592 A151 10cor multicolored .35 .25
1593 A151 10cor multicolored .35 .25
1594 A151 10cor multicolored .35 .25
1595 A151 10cor multicolored .35 .25
1596 A151 10cor multicolored .35 .25
1597 A151 10cor multicolored .35 .25
1598 A151 10cor multicolored .35 .25
1599 A151 10cor multicolored .35 .25
1600 A151 10cor multicolored .35 .25
1601 A151 10cor multicolored .35 .25
1602 A151 10cor multicolored .35 .25
1603 A151 10cor multicolored .35 .25
1604 A151 10cor multicolored .35 .25
1605 A151 10cor multicolored .35 .25
1606 A151 10cor multicolored .35 .25
1607 A151 10cor multicolored .35 .25
Nos. 1592-1607 (16) 5.60 4.00

Agrarian Reform Type of 1983 Inscribed "1987"

Designs: No. 1608, Tobacco. No. 1609, Cotton. 15cor, Corn. 25cor, Sugar. 30cor, Cattle. 50cor, Coffee Beans. 60cor, Rice. 100cor, Bananas.

1987, Mar. 25 *Perf. 12½*
1608 A168 10cor dk brown .30 .25
1609 A168 10cor purple .30 .25
1610 A168 15cor rose violet .45 .25
1611 A168 25cor dk car rose .70 .35
1612 A168 30cor orange .85 .45
1613 A168 50cor brown 1.40 .65
1614 A168 60cor green 1.75 .90
1615 A168 100cor blue 2.75 1.40
Nos. 1608-1615 (8) 8.50 4.50

77th Interparliamentary Conf., Managua — A215

1987, Apr. 27
1616 A215 10cor multicolored .25 .25

Prehistoric Creatures — A216

1987, May 25 *Perf. 13*
1617 A216 10cor Mammoth .35 .25
1618 A216 10cor Dimetrodon .35 .25
1619 A216 10cor Triceratops .35 .25
1620 A216 15cor Dinichthys .60 .25
1621 A216 15cor Uintaterium .60 .25
1622 A216 30cor Pteranodon 1.25 .25
1623 A216 40cor Tilosaurus 1.75 .30
Nos. 1617-1623 (7) 5.25 1.80

Nos. 1620-1623 are airmail.

CAPEX '87 — A217

Various tennis players in action.

1987, June 2 *Perf. 13*
1624 A217 10cor Male player .30 .25
1625 A217 10cor Female player .30 .25
1626 A217 15cor Player at net .60 .25
1627 A217 15cor Female player, diff. .60 .25
1628 A217 20cor multi .70 .25
1629 A217 30cor multi 1.25 .30
1630 A217 40cor multi 1.90 .40
Nos. 1624-1630 (7) 5.65 1.95

Souvenir Sheet

Perf. 12½

1631 A217 110cor Doubles partners, vert. 3.75 3.75

Nos. 1626-1631 are airmail. No. 1631 contains one 32x40mm stamp.

Dogs — A218

No. 1632, Doberman pinscher. No. 1633, Bull Mastiff. No. 1634, Japanese Spaniel. No. 1635, Keeshond. No. 1636, Chihuahua. No. 1637, St. Bernard. No. 1638, West Gotha spitz.

1987, June 25 *Perf. 13*

1632 A218 10cor multicolored .25 .25
1633 A218 10cor multicolored .25 .25
1634 A218 15cor multicolored .60 .25
1635 A218 15cor multicolored .60 .25
1636 A218 20cor multicolored .80 .25
1637 A218 30cor multicolored 1.25 .30
1638 A218 40cor multicolored 1.75 .40
Nos. 1632-1638 (7) 5.50 1.95

Nos. 1634-1638 are airmail.

Cacti
A219

No. 1639, Lophocereus schottii. No. 1640, Opuntia acanthocarpa. No. 1641, Echinocereus engelmanii. No. 1642, Lemaireocereus thurberi. No. 1643, Saguaros. No. 1644, Opuntia fulgida. No. 1645, Opuntia ficus.

1987, July 25 *Perf. 12½*

1639 A219 10cor multicolored .30 .25
1640 A219 10cor multicolored .30 .25
1641 A219 10cor multicolored .30 .25
1642 A219 20cor multicolored .80 .25
1643 A219 20cor multicolored .80 .25
1644 A219 30cor multicolored 1.25 .30
1645 A219 50cor multicolored 2.00 .50
Nos. 1639-1645 (7) 5.75 2.05

Nos. 1642-1645 are airmail.

10th Pan American Games, Indianapolis — A220

1987, Aug. 7 *Perf. 13*

1646 A220 10cor High jump .30 .25
1647 A220 10cor Volleyball .30 .25
1648 A220 15cor Sprinter .55 .25
1649 A220 15cor Gymnastics .55 .25
1650 A220 20cor Baseball .70 .30
1651 A220 30cor Synchronized swimming 1.10 .45
1652 A220 40cor Weightlifting 1.50 .60
Nos. 1646-1652 (7) 5.00 2.35

Souvenir Sheet

1653 A220 110cor Rhythmic gymnastics 3.50 3.50

Nos. 1648-1653 are airmail. No. 1653 contains one 32x40mm stamp. Nos. 1651-1653 are vert.

Satellites
A221

1987, Oct. 4

1654 A221 10cor Sputnik .30 .25
1655 A221 10cor Cosmos .30 .25
1656 A221 15cor Proton .50 .25
1657 A221 25cor Meteor .90 .25
1658 A221 25cor Luna .90 .25
1659 A221 30cor Electron 1.00 .30
1660 A221 50cor Mars 1 1.60 .50
Nos. 1654-1660 (7) 5.50 2.05

Cosmonauts' Day. Nos. 1656-1660 are airmail.

Fish
A222

Designs: No. 1661, Tarpon atlanticus. No. 1662, Cichlasoma managuense. No. 1663, Atractoteus tropicus. No. 1664, Astyana fasciatus. No. 1665, Cichlasoma citrimellum. 20cor, Cichlosoma dowi. 50cor, Caracharhinus nicaraguensis.

1987, Oct. 18 *Perf. 12½*

1661 A222 10cor multicolored .35 .25
1662 A222 10cor multicolored .35 .25
1663 A222 10cor multicolored .35 .25
1664 A222 15cor multicolored .60 .25
1665 A222 15cor multicolored .60 .25
1666 A222 20cor multicolored .80 .25
1667 A222 50cor multicolored 2.00 .50
Nos. 1661-1667 (7) 5.05 2.00

Nos. 1663-1667 are airmail.

October Revolution, 70th Anniv. — A223

Designs: 30cor, Cruiser Aurora, horiz. 50cor, USSR natl. arms.

1987, Nov. 7 *Perf. 13*

1668 A223 10cor multicolored .25 .25
1669 A223 30cor multicolored .60 .35
1670 A223 50cor multicolored 1.00 .60
Nos. 1668-1670 (3) 1.85 1.20

Nos. 1669-1670 are airmail.

Christmas Paintings by L. Saenz — A224

10cor, Nativity. 20cor, Adoration of the Magi. 25cor, Adoration of the Magi, diff. 50cor, Nativity, diff.

1987, Nov. 15 *Perf. 13*

1671 A224 10cor multicolored .25 .25
1672 A224 20cor multicolored .35 .25
1673 A224 25cor multicolored .40 .25
1674 A224 50cor multicolored .80 .40
Nos. 1671-1674 (4) 1.80 1.15

Nos. 1588-1591 Surcharged

Methods and Perfs As Before

1987, Dec. 26

1674A A214 400cor on 10cor #1588 — —
1674B A214 600cor on 50cor #1591 — —
1674C A214 1000cor on 25cor #1589 — —
1674D A214 5000cor on 30cor #1590 — —
Nos. 1674A-1674D (4) *30.00*

1988 Winter Olymmpics, Calgary — A225

No. 1675, Biathlon. No. 1676, Cross-country skiing, vert. No. 1677, Hockey, vert. No. 1678, Women's figure skating, vert. No. 1679, Slalom skiing, vert. No. 1680, Ski jumping. No. 1681, Men's downhill skiing, vert.

No. 1682, Pairs figure skating.

1988, Jan. 30 **Litho.** *Perf. 12½*

1675 A225 10cor multicolored .25 .25
1676 A225 10cor multicolored .25 .25
1677 A225 15cor multicolored .50 .25
1678 A225 20cor multicolored .75 .25
1679 A225 25cor multicolored 1.00 .30
1680 A225 30cor multicolored 1.10 .40
1681 A225 40cor multicolored 1.50 .50
Nos. 1675-1681 (7) 5.35 2.20

Souvenir Sheet

Perf. 13

1682 A225 100cor multicolored 3.75 3.75

Nos. 1675-1681 printed with se-tenant label showing Canadian flag and wildlife.

No. 1682 contains one 40x32mm stamp.

Nicaraguan Journalists Assoc., 10th Anniv. — A226

Design: 5cor, Churches of St. Francis Xavier and Fatima, and speaker addressing journalists, horiz.

1988, Feb. 10

1683 A226 1cor shown .25 .25
1684 A226 5cor multicolored .75 .40

No. 1684 is airmail.

1988 Summor Olympics, Seoul — A227

1988, Feb. 28

1685 A227 10cor Gymnastics .25 .25
1686 A227 10cor Basketball .25 .25
1687 A227 15cor Volleyball .50 .25
1688 A227 20cor Long jump .75 .25
1689 A227 25cor Soccer 1.00 .25
1690 A227 30cor Water polo 1.10 .40
1691 A227 40cor Boxing 1.75 .55
Nos. 1685-1691 (7) 5.60 2.20

Souvenir Sheet

1692 A227 100cor Baseball 3.75 3.75

No. 1692 contains one 40x32mm stamp.

European Soccer Championships, Essen — A228

Designs: Various soccer players in action.

1988, Apr. 14 *Perf. 13x12½, 12½x13*

1693 A228 50c multicolored .35 .25
1694 A228 1cor multicolored .35 .25
1695 A228 2cor multi, vert. .40 .25
1696 A228 3cor multi, vert. .70 .25
1697 A228 4cor multi, vert. .95 .25
1698 A228 5cor multi, vert. 1.25 .35
1699 A228 6cor multicolored 1.50 .40
Nos. 1693-1699 (7) 5.50 2.00

Souvenir Sheet

Perf. 13

1700 A228 15cor multi, vert. 3.75 3.75

Nos. 1695-1700 are airmail. No. 1700 contains one 32x40mm stamp.

Sandinista Revolution, 9th Anniv. — A229

1988, July 19 *Perf. 13*

1701 A229 1cor shown .25 .25
1702 A229 5cor Volcanoes, dove .60 .30

No. 1702 is airmail.

Animals — A230

1988, Mar. 3 *Perf. 13x12½*

1703 A230 10c Bear, cub .25 .25
1704 A230 15c Lion, cubs .25 .25
1705 A230 25c Spaniel, pups .25 .25
1706 A230 50c Wild boars .25 .25
1707 A230 4cor Cheetah, cubs 1.10 .35
1708 A230 7cor Hyenas 1.60 .70
1709 A230 8cor Fox, kit 2.00 .80
Nos. 1703-1709 (7) 5.70 2.85

Souvenir Sheet

Perf. 12½

1710 A230 15cor House cat, kittens, vert. 3.75 3.75

Nos. 1707-1710 are airmail. No. 1710 contains one 32x40mm stamp.

Helicopters — A231

1988, June 1 *Perf. 12½x12*

1711 A231 4cor B-206B-JRIII .25 .25
1712 A231 12cor BK-117A-3 .25 .25
1713 A231 16cor B-360 .50 .25
1714 A231 20cor 109-MRII .60 .25
1715 A231 24cor S-61 .80 .25
1716 A231 28cor SA-365N-D2 .90 .25
1717 A231 56cor S-76 1.75 .50
Nos. 1711-1717 (7) 5.05 2.00

Souvenir Sheet

Perf. 13

1718 A231 120cor NH-90 3.75 3.75

Nos. 1712-1718 are airmail. No. 1718 contains one 40x32mm stamp.

Shells — A232

4cor, Strombus pugilis. 12cor, Polymita picta. 16cor, Architectonica maximum. 20cor, Pectens laqueatus. 24cor, Guildfordia triumphans. 28cor, Ranella pustulosa. 50cor, Trochus maculatus.

1988, Sept. 20 *Perf. 13*

1719 A232 4cor multicolored .25 .25
1720 A232 12cor multicolored .30 .25
1721 A232 16cor multicolored .50 .25
1722 A232 20cor multicolored .70 .25
1723 A232 24cor multicolored .90 .25
1724 A232 28cor multicolored .95 .30
1725 A232 50cor multicolored 1.75 .50
Nos. 1719-1725 (7) 5.35 2.05

Nos. 1720-1725 are airmail.

Insects — A233

4cor, Chrysina macropus. 12cor, Plusiotis victoriana. 16cor, Ceratotrupes bolivari. 20cor, Gymnetosoma stellata. 24cor, Euphoria lineoligera. 28cor, Euphoria candezei. 50cor, Sulcophanaeus chryseicollis.

1988, Nov. 10

1726 A233 4cor multicolored .25 .25
1727 A233 12cor multicolored .40 .25
1728 A233 16cor multicolored .55 .25
1729 A233 20cor multicolored .80 .25
1730 A233 24cor multicolored .95 .25
1731 A233 28cor multicolored 1.05 .30
1732 A233 50cor multicolored 1.75 .50
Nos. 1726-1732 (7) 5.75 2.05

Nos. 1727-1732 are airmail.

Heroes of the Revolution — A234

Designs: 4cor, Casimiro Sotelo Montenegro. 12cor, Ricardo Morales Aviles. 16cor, Silvio Mayorga Delgado. 20cor, Pedro Arauz Palacios. 24cor, Oscar A. Turcios Chavarrias. 28cor, Julio C. Buitrago Urroz. 50cor, Jose B. Escobar Perez. 100cor, Eduardo E. Contreras Escobar.

1988, Aug. 27 *Perf. 12½x12*

1733 A234 4cor sky blue .25 .25
1734 A234 12cor red lilac .25 .25
1735 A234 16cor yel grn .30 .25
1736 A234 20cor org brown .40 .25
1737 A234 24cor brown .45 .25
1738 A234 28cor purple .55 .30
1739 A234 50cor henna brn .95 .50
1740 A234 100cor plum 1.90 .95
Nos. 1733-1740 (8) 5.05 3.00

Nos. 1734-1740 are airmail.

Flowers — A235

Designs: 4cor, Acacia baileyana. 12cor, Anigozanthos manglesii. 16cor, Telopia speciosissima. 20cor, Eucalyptus ficifolia. 24cor, Boronia heterophylla. 28cor, Callistemon speciosus. 30cor, Nymphaea caerulea, horiz. 50cor, Clianthus formosus.

1988, Aug. 30 *Perf. 13*

1741 A235 4cor multicolored .25 .25
1742 A235 12cor multicolored .35 .25
1743 A235 16cor multicolored .45 .25
1744 A235 20cor multicolored .60 .25
1745 A235 24cor multicolored .70 .25
1746 A235 28cor multicolored .80 .50
1747 A235 30cor multicolored .90 .30
1748 A235 50cor multicolored 1.50 .45
Nos. 1741-1748 (8) 5.55 2.50

Nos. 1742-1748 are airmail.

Pre-Columbian Art — A236

Designs: 4cor, Zapotec funeral urn. 12cor, Mochica ceramic kneeling man. 16cor, Mochica ceramic head. 20cor, Taina ceramic vase. 28cor, Nazca cup, horiz. 100cor, Inca pipe, horiz. 120cor, Aztec ceramic vessel, horiz.

1988, Oct. 12 *Perf. 12x12½, 12½x12*

1749 A236 4cor multi + label .25 .25
1750 A236 12cor multi + label .35 .25
1751 A236 16cor multi + label .45 .25
1752 A236 20cor multi + label .60 .25
1753 A236 28cor multi + label .80 .30
1754 A236 100cor multi + label 2.75 1.00
Nos. 1749-1754 (6) 5.20 2.30

Souvenir Sheet

Perf. 13x13½

1755 A236 120cor multicolored 3.75 3.75

Discovery of America, 500th anniv. (in 1992). Nos. 1750-1755 are airmail. No. 1755 contains one 40x32mm stamp.

Publication of Blue, by Ruben Dario, Cent. — A237

1988, Oct. 12 *Perf. 12x12½*

1756 A237 25cor multi + label .45 .25

No. 1756 is airmail.

Tourism — A238

4cor, Pochomil. 12cor, Granada. 20cor, Olof Palme Convention Center. 24cor, Masaya Volcano Natl. Park. 28cor, La Boquita. 30cor, Xiloa. 50cor, Hotels of Managua.
160cor, Montelimar.

1989, Feb. 5 *Perf. 12½x12*

1757 A238 4cor multicolored .25 .25
1758 A238 12cor multicolored .35 .25
1759 A238 20cor multicolored .65 .25
1760 A238 24cor multicolored .70 .25
1761 A238 28cor multicolored .90 .25
1762 A238 30cor multicolored .95 .25
1763 A238 50cor multicolored 1.75 .45
Nos. 1757-1763 (7) 5.55 1.95

Souvenir Sheet

Perf. 13

1764 A238 160cor multicolored 3.75 3.75

Nos. 1758-1764 are airmail. No. 1764 contains one 40x32mm stamp.

French Revolution, Bicentennial — A240

Designs: 50cor, Procession of the Estates General, Versailles. 300cor, Oath of the Tennis Court. 600cor, 14th of July, vert. 1000cor, Dancing Around the Liberty Tree. 2000cor, Liberty Guiding the People, vert. 3000cor, Storming the Bastille. 5000cor, Lafayette Swearing Allegiance to the Constitution, vert. 9000cor, La Marseillaise, vert.

Perf. 12½x13 (50cor), 13x12½ (600, 2000cor), 12½

1989, July 14

Sizes: 50cor, 40x25mm

600cor, 2000cor, 33x44mm

1773 A240 50cor multicolored .25 .25
1774 A240 300cor shown .25 .25
1775 A240 600cor multicolored .30 .25
1776 A240 1000cor multicolored .45 .25
1777 A240 2000cor multicolored .80 .30
1778 A240 3000cor multicolored 1.40 .40
1779 A240 5000cor multicolored 2.10 .65
Nos. 1773-1779 (7) 5.55 2.35

Souvenir Sheet

Perf. 12½

1780 A240 9000cor multicolored 4.50 4.50

Philexfrance '89. #1774-1780 are airmail. #1780 contains one 32x40mm stamp.

Currency Reform

Currency reform took place Mar. 4, 1990. Until stamps in the new currency were issued, mail was to be handstamped "Franqueo Pagado," (Postage Paid). Stamps were not used again until Apr. 25, 1991. The following four sets and one airmail set were sold by the post office but were not valid for postage.

Ships

Stamp World London '90: 500cor, Director. 1000cor, Independence. 3000cor, Orizaba. 5000cor, SS Lewis. 10,000cor, Golden Rule. 30,000cor, Santiago de Cuba. 75,000cor, Bahia de Corinto. 100,000cor, North Star.

1990, Apr. 3 *Perf. 12½x12*

Set of 7 5.50

Souvenir Sheet

Perf. 12½

75,000cor 4.25

World Cup Soccer Championships, Italy

Designs: Various soccer players in action.

1990, Apr. 30 *Perf. 13*

Set of 7 5.50

Souvenir Sheet

Perf. 12½

75,000cor 4.00

1992 Winter Olympics, Albertville

Designs: 500cor, Ski jumping. 1000cor, Downhill skiing. 3000cor, Figure skating, vert. 5000cor, Speed skating, vert. 10,000cor, Biathlon, vert. 30,000cor, Cross country skiing, vert. 75,000cor, Two-man bobsled, vert. 100,000cor, Ice hockey, vert.

1990, July 25 *Perf. 13*

Set of 7 5.50

Souvenir Sheet

Perf. 12½

75,000cor 4.00

1992 Summer Olympics, Barcelona

Designs: 500cor, Javelin. 1000cor, Steeplechase. 3000cor, Handball. 5000cor, Basketball. 10,000cor, Gymnastics. 30,000cor, Cycling. 75,000cor, Soccer. 100,000cor, Boxing, horiz.

1990, Aug. 10 *Perf. 13*

Set of 7 5.50

Souvenir Sheet

75,000cor 4.00

Birds A245

Designs: No. 1813, Apteryx owenii. No. 1814, Notornis mantelli. 10c, Cyanoramphus novaezelandiae. 20c, Gallirallus australis. 30c, Rhynochetos jubatus, vert. 60c, Nestor notabilis. 70c, Strigops habroptilus. 1.50cor, Cygnus atratus.

1990, Aug. 14 **Litho.** *Perf. 12½*

1813 A245 5c multicolored .25 .25
1814 A245 5c multicolored .25 .25
1815 A245 10c multicolored .25 .25
1816 A245 20c multicolored .50 .25
1817 A245 30c multicolored .85 .30
1818 A245 60c multicolored 1.75 .65
1819 A245 70c multicolored 2.00 .75
Nos. 1813-1819 (7) 5.85 2.70

Souvenir Sheet

1820 A245 1.50cor multicolored 4.00 3.75

New Zealand '90, Intl. Philatelic Exhibition.

Fauna A246

No. 1821, Panthera onca. No. 1822, Felis pardalis, vert. No. 1823, Atelles geoffrogi, vert. No. 1824, Tapirus bairdi. No. 1825, Dasypus novencintus. No. 1826, Canis latrans. No. 1827, Choloepus hoffmanni.

1990, Oct. 10

1821 A246 5c multicolored .25 .25
1822 A246 5c multicolored .25 .25
1823 A246 10c multicolored .25 .25
1824 A246 20c multicolored .50 .25
1825 A246 30c multicolored .85 .30

1826 A246 60c multicolored 1.60 .65
1827 A246 70c multicolored 2.00 .75
Nos. 1821-1827 (7) 5.70 2.70

FAO, 45th anniv.

Flower Type of 1983 Redrawn Without Date

1991, Apr. 24 Litho. ***Perf. 14x13½***

Size: 19x22mm

1828 A151 1cor like #1220 .40 .25
1829 A151 2cor like #1212 .80 .25
1830 A151 3cor like #1218 1.25 .25
1831 A151 4cor like #1219 1.60 .25
1832 A151 5cor like #1217 2.00 .25
1833 A151 6cor like #1210 2.40 .25
1834 A151 7cor like #1216 2.75 .25
1835 A151 8cor like #1215 3.25 .25
1836 A151 9cor like #1211 3.50 .25
1837 A151 10cor like #1221 4.00 .25
1838 A151 11cor like #1214 4.50 .25
1839 A151 12cor like #1222 4.75 .25
1840 A151 13cor like #1213 5.25 .25
1841 A151 14cor like #1224 5.50 .25
1842 A151 15cor like #1223 6.00 .25
1843 A151 16cor like #1209 6.50 .25
Nos. 1828-1843 (16) 54.45 4.00

Dr. Pedro Joaquin Chamorro — A247

1991, Apr. 25 ***Perf. 14½x14***

1844 A247 2.25cor multicolored .95 .45

1990 World Cup Soccer Championships, Italy — A248

Designs: No. 1845, Two players. No. 1846, Four players, vert. 50c, Two players, referee. 1cor, Germany, five players, vert. 1.50cor, One player, vert. 3cor, Argentina, five players, vert. 3.50cor, Italian players. 7.50cor, German team with trophy.

1991, July 16 ***Perf. 14x14½, 14½x14***

1845 A248 25c multicolored .25 .25
1846 A248 25c multicolored .25 .25
1847 A248 50c multicolored .25 .25
1848 A248 1cor multicolored .40 .25
1849 A248 1.50cor multicolored .60 .30
1850 A248 3cor multicolored 1.25 .60
1851 A248 3.50cor multicolored 1.40 .70
Nos. 1845-1851 (7) 4.40 2.60

Souvenir Sheet

1852 A248 7.50cor multicolored 3.00 1.50
a. Overprinted in sheet margin ('93) 3.25 1.60

No. 1852a overprint reads "COPA DE FOOTBALL / U.S.A. '94."

Butterflies — A249

Designs: No. 1853, Prepona praeneste. No. 1854, Anartia fatima. 50c, Eryphanis aesacus. 1cor, Heliconius melpomene. 1.50cor, Chlosyne janais. 3cor, Marpesia iole. 3.50cor, Metamorpha epaphus. 7.50cor, Morpho peleides.

1991, July 16 ***Perf. 14½x14***

1853 A249 25c multicolored .25 .25
1854 A249 25c multicolored .25 .25
1855 A249 50c multicolored .25 .25
1856 A249 1cor multicolored .40 .25
1857 A249 1.50cor multicolored .60 .30
1858 A249 3cor multicolored 1.25 .60
1859 A249 3.50cor multicolored 1.40 .70
Nos. 1853-1859 (7) 4.40 2.60

Souvenir Sheet

1860 A249 7.50cor multicolored 3.00 1.50

Fauna of Rainforest — A250

No. 1861 a, Yellow-headed amazon. b, Toucan. c, Scarlet macaw (lapa roja). d, Quetzal. e, Spider monkey (mono arana). f, Capuchin monkey. g, Sloth (cucala). h, Oropendola. i, Violet sabrewing (colibri violeta). j, Tamandua. k, Jaguarundi. l, Boa constrictor. m, Iguana. n, Jaguar. o, White-necked jacobin. p, Doxocopa clothilda. q, Dismorphia deione. r, Golden arrow-poison frog (rana venenosa). s, Callithomia hezia. t, Chameleon.

1991, Aug. 7 Litho. ***Perf. 14x14½***

1861 A250 2.25cor Sheet of 20, #a.-t. 24.00 12.00

America Issue — A251

1990, Oct. 12 ***Perf. 14½x14***

1862 A251 2.25cor Concepcion volcano 1.40 .55

Orchids A252

Designs: No. 1863, Isochilus major. No. 1864, Cycnoches ventricosum. 50c, Vanilla odorata. 1cor, Helleriella nicaraguensis. 1.50cor, Barkeria spectabilis. 3cor, Maxillaria hedwigae. 3.50cor, Cattleya aurantiaca. 7.50cor, Psygmorchis pusilla, vert.

1991 Litho. ***Perf. 14x14½***

1863 A252 25c multicolored .25 .25
1864 A252 25c multicolored .25 .25
1865 A252 50c multicolored .25 .25
1866 A252 1cor multicolored .35 .25
1867 A252 1.50cor multicolored .60 .25
1868 A252 3cor multicolored 1.10 .50
1869 A252 3.50cor multicolored 1.40 .55
Nos. 1863-1869 (7) 4.20 2.30

Souvenir Sheet

Perf. 14½x14

1870 A252 7.50cor multicolored 3.00 1.50

Locomotives of South America — A253

Various steam locomotives.

1991, Apr. 21 ***Perf. 14½x14***

1871 A253 25c Bolivia .25 .25
1872 A253 25c Peru .25 .25
1873 A253 50c Argentina .25 .25
1874 A253 1.50cor Chile .60 .25
1875 A253 2cor Colombia .80 .30
1876 A253 3cor Brazil 1.10 .50
1877 A253 3.50cor Paraguay 1.30 .55
Nos. 1871-1877 (7) 4.55 2.35

Souvenir Sheets

1878 A253 7.50cor Nicaragua 3.50 3.00
1879 A253 7.50cor Guatemala 3.50 3.00

Birds — A254

Designs: 50c, Eumomota supercilliosa. 75c, Trogon collaris. 1cor, Electron platyrhynchum. 1.50cor, Teleonema filicauda. 1.75cor, Tangara chilensis, horiz. No. 1885, Pharomachrus mocino. No. 1886, Phlegopsis nigromaculata. No. 1887, Hylophylax naevioides, horiz. No. 1888, Aulacorhynchus haematopygius, horiz.

1991 ***Perf. 14½x14, 14x14½***

1880 A254 50c multicolored .25 .25
1881 A254 75c multicolored .30 .25
1882 A254 1cor multicolored .40 .25
1883 A254 1.50cor multicolored .65 .25
1884 A254 1.75cor multicolored .70 .30
1885 A254 2.25cor multicolored 1.00 .35
1886 A254 2.25cor multicolored 1.00 .35
Nos. 1880-1886 (7) 4.30 2.00

Souvenir Sheets

1887 A254 7.50cor multicolored 3.00 3.00
1888 A254 7.50cor multicolored 3.00 3.00

Paintings by Vincent Van Gogh A255

Designs: No. 1889, Head of a Peasant Woman Wearing a Bonnet. No. 1890, One-Eyed Man. 50c, Self-Portrait. 1cor, Vase with Carnations and Other Flowers. 1.50cor, Vase with Zinnias and Geraniums. 3cor, Portrait of Pere Tanguy. 3.50cor, Portrait of a Man, horiz. 7.50cor, Path Lined with Poplars, horiz.

1991 ***Perf. 14x13½, 13½x14***

1889 A255 25c multicolored .25 .25
1890 A255 25c multicolored .25 .25
1891 A255 50c multicolored .30 .25
1892 A255 1cor multicolored .40 .25
1893 A255 1.50cor multicolored .65 .25
1894 A255 3cor multicolored 1.20 .50
1895 A255 3.50cor multicolored 1.60 .55
Nos. 1889-1895 (7) 4.65 2.30

Size: 128x102mm

Imperf

1896 A255 7.50cor multicolored 2.50 1.25

Phila Nippon '91 A256

Designs: 25c, Golden Hall. 50c, Phoenix Hall. 1cor, Bunraku puppet head. 1.50cor, Japanese cranes. 2.50cor, Himeji Castle. 3cor, Statue of the Guardian. 3.50cor, Kabuki warrior. 7.50cor, Vase.

1991 ***Perf. 14x14½***

1897 A256 25c multicolored .25 .25
1898 A256 50c multicolored .25 .25
1899 A256 1cor multicolored .45 .25
1900 A256 1.50cor multicolored .65 .25
1901 A256 2.50cor multicolored 1.00 .40
1902 A256 3cor multicolored 1.25 .50
1903 A256 3.50cor multicolored 1.40 .55
Nos. 1897-1903 (7) 5.25 2.45

Souvenir Sheet

1904 A256 7.50cor multicolored 3.00 3.00

Inscriptions are switched on 50c and 2.50cor.

Child's Drawing A257

1991

1905 A257 2.25cor multicolored 1.10 .45

Central American Bank of Economic Integration, 30th Anniv. — A258

1991, Aug. 1 Litho. ***Perf. 14***

1906 A258 1.50cor multicolored 1.05 .50

No. 1906 printed with se-tenant label.

Discovery of America, 500th Anniv. (in 1992) — A259

1991, Oct. 12 ***Perf. 14½x14***

1907 A259 2.25cor Columbus' fleet 1.05 .75

Swiss Confederation, 700th Anniv. (in 1991) — A260

1992, Aug. 1 Litho. ***Perf. 14x14½***

1908 A260 2.25cor black & red 1.20 .75

Contemporary Art — A261

Designs: No. 1909, Pitcher, by Jose Ortiz. No. 1910, Black jar, by Lorenza Pineda Cooperative, vert. 50c, Vase, by Elio Gutierrez, vert. 1cor, Christ on Cross, by Jose de Los Santos, vert. 1.50cor, Sculpture of family, by Erasmo Moya, vert. 3cor, Bird and fish, by Silvio Chavarria Cooperative. 3.50cor, Filigree jar, by Maria de Los Angeles Bermudez, vert. 7.50cor, Masks by Jose Flores.

Perf. 14x14½, 14½x14

1992, Sept. 17 Litho.

1909 A261 25c multicolored .25 .25
1910 A261 25c multicolored .25 .25
1911 A261 50c multicolored .25 .25
1912 A261 1cor multicolored .45 .25
1913 A261 1.50cor multicolored .65 .30
1914 A261 3cor multicolored 1.25 .65
1915 A261 3.50cor multicolored 1.50 .75
Nos. 1909-1915 (7) 4.60 2.70

Imperf

Size: 100x70mm

1916 A261 7.50cor multicolored 3.25 1.60

Miniature Sheet

Fauna and Flora of Rainforest — A262

No. 1917: a, Colibri magnifico (b). b, Aguila arpia (f). c, Orchids. d, Toucan, Mariposa morpho. e, Quetzal (i). f, Guardabarranco (g, k). g, Mono aullador (howler monkey). h, Perezoso (sloth). i, Mono ardilla (squirrel monkey). j, Guacamaya (macaw) (n). k, Boa esmeralda, Tanagra escarlata (emerald boa, scarlet tanager). l, Rana flecha venenosa (arrow frog). m, Jaguar. n, Oso hormiguero (anteater) (o). o, Ocelot. p, Coati.

1992, Nov. 12 ***Perf. 14½x14***

1917 A262 1.50cor Sheet of 16, #a.-p. 12.00 6.00

1992 Winter Olympics, Albertville A263

No. 1918, Ice hockey. No. 1919, 4-man bobsled. No. 1920, Combined slalom, vert. No. 1921, Speed skating. No. 1922, Cross-country skiing. No. 1923, Double luge. No. 1924, Ski jumping, vert. No. 1925, Slalom.

Perf. 14x14½, 14½x14

1992, Sept. 17

1918	A263	25c multi	.25	.25
1919	A263	25c multi	.25	.25
1920	A263	50c multi	.25	.25
1921	A263	1cor multi	.45	.25
1922	A263	1.50cor multi	.65	.30
1923	A263	3cor multi	1.40	.65
1924	A263	3.50cor multi	1.50	.75
		Nos. 1918-1924 (7)	4.75	2.70

Imperf

Size: 100x70mm

1925 A263 7.50cor multi 3.25 1.60

a. Overprinted ('93) 3.25 1.60

No. 1925a overprint reads "JUEGOS PRE OLIMPICOS DE INVIERNO / LILLEHAMMER, NORUEGA."

1992 Summer Olympics, Barcelona A264

No. 1926, Javelin. No. 1927, Fencing. No. 1928, Basketball. No. 1929, 1500-meter race. No. 1930, Long jump. No. 1931, Women's 10,000-meter race. No. 1932, Equestrian. No. 1933, Canoeing

Perf. 14x14½, 14½x14

1992, Sept. 17 **Litho.**

1926	A264	25c multi	.25	.25
1927	A264	25c multi	.25	.25
1928	A264	50c multi	.25	.25
1929	A264	1.50cor multi	.65	.30
1930	A264	2cor multi	.85	.40
1931	A264	3cor multi	1.25	.65
1932	A264	3.50cor multi	1.50	.75
		Nos. 1926-1932 (7)	5.00	2.85

Imperf

Size: 100x70mm

1933 A264 7.50cor multi 3.25 1.60

a. Overprinted ('93) 3.25 1.60

Nos. 1927-1932 are vert. Dated 1991.

No. 1933a overprint reads "JUEGOS PRE OLIMPICOS DE VERANO / ATLANTA, GA. / ESTADOS UNIDOS DE AMERICA."

Father R. M. Fabretto and Children A265

1992, Nov. 12 **Litho.** ***Perf. 14x14½***

1934 A265 2.25cor multicolored .95 .50

Nicaraguan Natives, by Claudia Gordillo — A266

1992, Nov. 12

1935 A266 2.25cor black & brn .95 .50

Nicaraguan Caciques, by Milton Jose Cruz — A267

1992, Nov. 12

1936 A267 2.25cor multicolored .95 .50

Contemporary Paintings — A268

Paintings by: No. 1937, Alberto Ycaza, vert. No. 1938, Alejandro Arostegui, vert. 50c, Bernard Dreyfus. 1.50cor, Orlando Sobalvarro. 2cor, Hugo Palma. 3cor, Omar D'Leon. 3.50cor, Carlos Montenegro, vert. 7.50cor, Federico Nordalm.

Perf. 14½x14, 14x14½

1992, Nov. 12

1937	A268	25c multicolored	.25	.25
1938	A268	25c multicolored	.25	.25
1939	A268	50c multicolored	.25	.25
1940	A268	1.50cor multicolored	.65	.30
1941	A268	2cor multicolored	.85	.40
1942	A268	3cor multicolored	1.25	.65
1943	A268	3.50cor multicolored	1.50	.75
		Nos. 1937-1943 (7)	5.00	2.85

Imperf

Size: 100x70mm

1944 A268 7.50cor multicolored 3.25 1.60

Monument to Columbus, Rivas — A269

1993, Mar. 22 ***Perf. 14½x14***

1945 A269 2.25cor multicolored .95 .50

UPAEP issue. Dated 1992.

Catholic Religion in Nicaragua, 460th Anniv. — A270

Designs: 25c, Eucharistic gonfalon. 50c, Statue of Virgin Mary. 1cor, Document, 1792-93. 1.50cor, Baptismal font. 2cor, Statue of Madonna and Child. 2.25cor, Monsignor Diego Alvarez Osario. 3cor, Christ on cross.

1993, Mar. 22

1946	A270	25c multicolored	.25	.25
1947	A270	50c multicolored	.25	.25
1948	A270	1cor multicolored	.40	.25
1949	A270	1.50cor multicolored	.65	.30
1950	A270	2cor multicolored	.85	.40
1951	A270	2.25cor multicolored	.95	.50
1952	A270	3cor multicolored	1.25	.65
		Nos. 1946-1952 (7)	4.60	2.60

Dated 1992.

A271

Archdiocese of Managua: a, 3cor, Cathedral of the Immaculate Conception. b, 4cor, Cross, map.

1993, Apr. 30

1953 A271 Pair, #a.-b. 3.00 1.75

Dated 1992.

A272

Player, country: 50c, Brolin, Sweden. No. 1955, Karas, Poland; Costa, Brazil. No. 1956, Bossis, Platini, France. 1.50cor, Schumacher, Germany. 2cor, Zubizarreta, Spain. 2.50cor, Matthaeus, Germany; Maradona, Argentina. 3.50cor, Robson, England; Santos, Portugal. 10cor, Biyik, Cameroun; Valderrama, Colombia.

1994, Jan. 28 **Litho.** ***Perf. 14***

1954	A272	50c multicolored	.25	.25
1955	A272	1cor multicolored	.40	.25
1956	A272	1cor multicolored	.40	.25
1957	A272	1.50cor multicolored	.65	.30
1958	A272	2cor multicolored	.85	.40
1959	A272	2.50cor multicolored	1.10	.55
1960	A272	3.50cor multicolored	1.50	.75
		Nos. 1954-1960 (7)	5.15	2.75

Souvenir Sheet

1961 A272 10cor multicolored 4.25 2.00

1994 World Cup Soccer Championships, US.

Sonatina, by Alma Iris Prez — A272a

1993, Oct. 29 **Litho.** ***Perf. 13½x14***

1961A A272a 3cor multicolored 1.00 1.00

Butterflyfish A273

No. 1962: a, Chaetodon lunula. b, Chaetodon rainfordi. c, Chaetodon reticulatus. d, Chaetodon auriga. e, Heniochus acuminatus. f, Coradion fulvocinctus. g, Chaetodon speculum. h, Chaetodon lineolatus. i, Chaetodon bennetti. j, Chaetodon melanotus. k, Chaetodon aureus. l. Chaetodon ephippium. m, Hemitaurichthys polylepis. n, Chaetodon semeion. o, Chaetodon kleinii. p, Chelmon rostratus.

1993, Nov. 18 **Litho.** ***Perf. 14***

1962 Sheet of 16 8.00 5.00

a.-p. A273 1.50cor Any single .40 .30

q. Inscribed with Bangkok '93 emblem in sheet margin 8.00 5.00

r. Inscribed with Indopex '93 emblem in sheet margin 8.00 5.00

s. Inscribed with Taipei '93 emblem in sheet margin 8.00 5.00

Issue date: No. 1962, Nov. 1, 1993.

No. 1962 is without any show emblem in sheet margin.

1994 Winter Olympics, Lillehammer, 1996 Summer Olympics, Atlanta — A274

No. 1963, Downhill skiing. No. 1964, Fourman bobsled. No. 1965, Swimming. No. 1966, Diving. No. 1967, Speed skating. No. 1968, Race walking. No. 1969, Hurdles. No. 1970, Ski jumping. No. 1971, Women's gymnastics. No. 1972, Women's figure skating. No. 1973, Pairs figure skating. No. 1974, Javelin. No. 1975, Biathlon. No. 1976, Running.

No. 1977, Torch, hands. No. 1978, Flags.

1993, Nov. 18

1963	A274	25c multicolored	.25	.25
1964	A274	25c multicolored	.25	.25
1965	A274	25c multicolored	.25	.25
1966	A274	25c multicolored	.25	.25
1967	A274	50c multicolored	.25	.25
1968	A274	50c multicolored	.25	.25
1969	A274	1cor multicolored	.40	.25
1970	A274	1.50cor multicolored	.65	.30
1971	A274	1.50cor multicolored	.65	.30
1972	A274	2cor multicolored	.85	.40
1973	A274	3cor multicolored	1.25	.65
1974	A274	3cor multicolored	1.25	.65
1975	A274	3.50cor multicolored	1.50	.75
1976	A274	3.50cor multicolored	1.50	.75
		Nos. 1963-1976 (14)	9.55	5.55

Souvenir Sheets

1977 A274 7.50cor multicolored 3.25 1.50

1978 A274 7.50cor multicolored 4.25 1.50

1994 Winter Olympics (#1963-1964, 1967, 1970, 1972-1973, 1975, 1978). Others, 1996 Summer Olympics.

Pan-American Health Organization, 90th Anniv. — A275

1993, June 16 ***Perf. 14½***
1979 A275 3cor multicolored 1.25 .65

Organization of American States, 23rd General Assembly — A276

1993, June 7 ***Perf. 13½x14***
1980 A276 3cor multicolored 1.25 .65

Christmas — A276a

Paintings: 1cor, Holy Family, by unknown painter. 4cor, Birth of Christ, by Lezamon.

1994, Feb. 23 **Litho.** ***Perf. 13½x14***
1980A A276a 1cor multicolored .35 .25
1980B A276a 4cor multicolored 1.40 .70

Fauna and Flora of Rainforest — A277

No. 1981: a, Bromeliacae. b, Tilmatura dupontii. c, Anolis biporcatus (b). d, Fulgara laternaria. e, Bradypus. f, Spizaetus ornatus. g, Cotinga amabilis. h, Bothrops schlegelii. i, Odontoglossum. j, Agalychnis callidryas. k, Heliconius spaho. l, Passiflora vitifolia.

No. 1982, Dasyprocta punctata. No. 1983, Melinaea lilis.

1994, Jan. 20 ***Perf. 14***
1981 A277 2cor Sheet of 12, #a.-l. 12.00 6.00

Souvenir Sheets

1982 A277 10cor multicolored 3.50 1.75
1983 A277 10cor multicolored 3.50 1.75

Hong Kong '94 A278

No. 1984 — Butterflies: a, Callicore patelina. b, Chlosyne narva. c, Anteos maerula. d, Marpesia petreus. e, Pierella helvetia. f, Eurytides epidaus. g, Heliconius doris. h, Smyrna blomfildia. i, Eueides lybia. j, Adelpha heraclea. k, Heliconius hecale. l, Parides montezuma. m, Morpho polyphemus. n, Eresia alsina. o, Prepona omphale. p, Morpho granadensis.

1994, Feb. 18 **Litho.** ***Perf. 14***
1984 A278 1.50cor Sheet of 16, #a.-p. 10.00 6.00

Astronomers — A279

No. 1985 — Copernicus and: a, Satellite. b, Tycho Brahe (1546-1601), making observations. c, Galileo probe, Galileo. d, Isaac Newton, Newton telescope. e, Giotto probe to Halley's comet, Edmund Halley. f, James Bradley (1693-1762), Greenwich Observatory. g, 1793 telescope, William Herschel (1738-1822). h, John Goodricke (1764-86), stellar eclipse. i, Gottingen observatory, Karl Fredrich Gauss (1777-1855). j, Friedrich Bessell (1784-1846), astronomical instrument. k, Harvard College Observatory, William Granch (1783-1859). l, George B. Airy (1801-92), stellar disc. m, Lowell Observatory, Flagstaff, Arizona, Percival Lowell (1855-1916). n, George A. Halle (1868-1938), solar spectrograph. o, Space telescope, Edwin Hubble (1889-1953). p, Gerard Kuiper (1905-73), Uranus' moon Miranda.

10cor, Nicolas Copernicus, interstellar probe.

1994, Apr. 4
1985 A279 1.50cor Sheet of 16, #a.-p. 9.00 4.50

Souvenir Sheet

1986 A279 10cor multicolored 3.50 2.00

Automotive Anniversaries — A280

No. 1987: a, 1886 Benz three-wheel car. b, 1909 Benz Blitzen. c, 1923 Mercedes Benz 24/100/140. d, 1928 Mercedes Benz SSK. e, 1934 Mercedes Benz Cabriolet 500k. f, 1949 Mercedes Benz 170S. g, 1954 Mercedes Benz W196. h, 1954 Mercedes Benz 300SL. i, 1896 Ford four-wheel car. j, 1920 Ford taxi. k, 1928 Ford Roadster. l, 1932 Ford V-8. m, 1937 Ford 78 (V-8). n, 1939 Ford 91 Deluxe Tudor Sedan. o, 1946 Ford V-8 Sedan Coupe. p, 1958 Ford Custom 300.

10cor, Henry Ford (1863-1947), 1903 Ford Model A; Karl Benz (1844-1929), 1897 Benz 5CH.

1994, Apr. 5
1987 A280 1.50cor Sheet of 16, #a.-p. 9.00 4.50

Souvenir Sheet

1988 A280 10cor multicolored 3.50 2.00

First Benz four-wheeled vehicle, cent. (Nos. 1987a-1987h). First Ford gasoline engine, cent. (Nos. 1987i-1987p).

Graf Zeppelin A281

No. 1989 — Graf Zeppelin and: a, Dr. Hugo Eckener, Count Zeppelin (inside cabin). b, New York City, 1928. c, Tokyo, 1929. d, San Simeon, California, 1929. e, Col. Charles Lindbergh, Dr. Hugo Eckener, 1929. f, Moscow, 1930. g, Paris, 1930. h, Cairo, 1931. i, Arctic waters. j, Rio de Janeiro, 1932. k, London, 1935. l, St. Peter's Basilica, Vatican City. m, Swiss Alps. n, Brandenburg Gate. o, Eckener in control room. p, Ernest A. Lehman, DO-X.

No. 1990, Graf Zeppelin, Count Zeppelin. No. 1991, Zeppelin, Eckener.

1994, Apr. 6
1989 A281 1.50cor Sheet of 16, #a.-p. 9.00 4.50

Souvenir Sheets

1990 A281 10cor multicolored 3.50 1.75
1991 A281 10cor multicolored 3.50 1.75

Dr. Hugo Eckener (1868-1954) (#1991).

Contemporary Crafts — A282

Designs: No. 1992, 50c, Basket weaving, by Rosalia Sevilla, horiz. No. 1993, 50c, Wood carving, by Julio Lopez. No. 1994, 1cor, Woman carrying sack, by Indiana Robleto. No. 1995, 1cor, Church, by Auxiliadora Bush. 2.50cor, Carving, by Jose de Los Santos. 3cor, Costumed doll with horse's head, by Ines Gutierrez de Chong. 4cor, Ceramic container, by Elio Gutierrez.

10cor, Metate, by Saul Carballo.

Perf. 13½x14, 14x13½

1994, Feb. 15 **Litho.**
1992-1998 A282 Set of 7 4.25 2.00

Imperf

Size: 96x66mm

1999 A282 10cor multicolored 3.25 1.60

Dated 1993.

Stone Carvings, Chontal Culture — A283

Color of inscription tablet: No. 2000, 50c, Yellow. No. 2001, 50c, Yellow brown. No. 2002, 1cor, Green. No. 2003, 1cor, Yellow green. 2.50cor, Greenish blue. 3cor, Blue. 4cor, Grey green.

10cor, Two stone totems seen against landscape painting.

1994, Feb. 23 ***Perf. 14***
2000-2006 A283 Set of 7 4.25 2.00

Imperf

Size: 96x66mm

2007 A283 10cor multicolored 3.25 1.60

Dated 1993.

Contemporary Art — A284

Designs: No. 2008, 50c, Lady Embroidering, by Guillermo Rivas Navas. No. 2009, 50c, Virgin of Nicaragua, by Cella Lacayo. No. 2010, 1cor, The Dance, by June Beer. No. 2011, 1cor, Song of Peace, by Alejandro Canales. 2.50cor, Fruits, by Genaro Lugo, horiz. 3cor, Figures and Fragments, by Leonel Vanegas. 4cor, Eruption of Volcano of Water, by Asilia Guillen, horiz.

10cor, Still life, by Alejandro Alonso Rochi.

1994, Mar. 15 ***Perf. 14x13½, 13½x14***
2008-2014 A284 Set of 7 4.25 2.00

Imperf

Size: 96x66mm

2015 A284 10cor multicolored 3.25 1.60

Dated 1993.

Prominent Nicaraguan Philatelists — A285

Designs: 1cor, Gabriel Horvilleur (1907-91). 3cor, Jose S. Cuadra A. (1932-92). 4cor, Alfredo Pertz (1864-1948).

1994, Apr. 18 **Litho.** ***Perf. 14***
2016-2018 A285 Set of 3 2.75 1.40

Dated 1993.

First Tree Conference of Nicaragua A286

1994, June 5 ***Perf. 14x13½***
2019 A286 4cor multicolored 1.40 .70

Souvenir Sheets

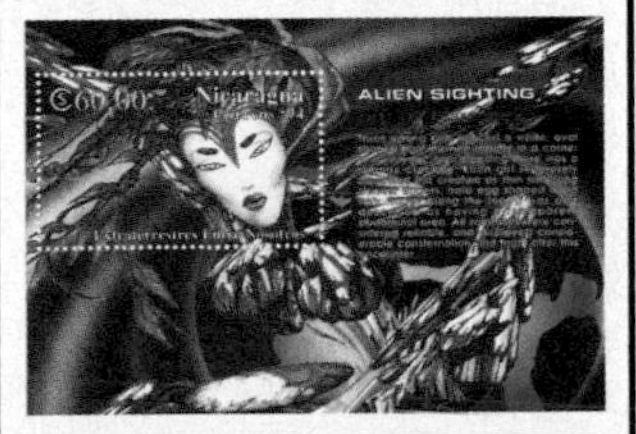

Reported Alien Sightings — A287

Date and location of sighting: No. 2020, 60cor, July 21, 1991, Missouri. No. 2021, 60cor, July 28, 1965, Argentina. No. 2022, 60cor, Aug. 21, 1955, Kentucky. No. 2023, 60cor, Oct. 25, 1973, Pennsylvania. No. 2024, 60cor, Sept. 19, 1961, New Hampshire. No. 2025, 60cor, Nov. 7, 1989, Kansas. No. 2026, 60cor, Sept. 26, 1976, Grand Canary Island. No. 2027, 60cor, May 8, 1973, Texas.

1994, May 25 **Litho.** ***Perf. 14***
2020-2027 A287 Set of 8 *30.00 30.00*

Sacred Art — A288

Designs: No. 2028, 50c, Pulpit, Cathedral of Leon. No. 2029, 50c, Statue of Saint Ann, Chinandega Parish. No. 2030, 1cor, Statue of St. Joseph, San Pedro Parish, Rivas. No. 2031, 1cor, Statue of St. James, Jinotepe Parish. 2.50cor, Chalice, Subtiava Temple, Leon. 3cor, Processional cross, Nequinohoma Parish, Masaya. 4cor, Crucifix, Temple of Miracles, Managua.

10cor, Silver frontal, San Pedro Parish, Rivas.

1994, July 11 Litho. *Perf. 14*
2028-2034 A288 Set of 7 4.25 2.25
Size: 96x66mm
Imperf
2036 A288 10cor multicolored 3.50 1.75
No. 2035 is unassigned.

A289

1994, July 4 Litho. *Perf. 14*
2037 A289 3cor multicolored 1.00 1.00
Intl. Conference of New or Restored Democracies.

A290

1994, Aug. 2
2038 A290 4cor multicolored 1.50 1.50
32nd World Amateur Baseball Championships.

PHILAKOREA '94 — A291

No. 2039: a, Soraksan. b, Statue of Kim Yu-Shin. c, Solitary Rock. d, Waterfall, Hallasan Valley. e, Mirukpong and Pisondae. f, Chonbuldong Valley. g, Bridge of the Seven Nymphs. h, Piryong Falls.
No. 2040, Boy on first birthday, gifts of fruit.

1994, Aug. 16
2039 A291 1.50cor Sheet of 8, #a.-h. 4.00 4.00
Souvenir Sheet
2040 A291 10cor multicolored 3.00 3.00

Dinosaurs A292

No. 2041: a, Tyrannosaurus rex. b, Plateosaurus (f-g). c, Pteranodon (b). d, Camarasaurus (c). e, Euplocephalus. f, Sacuanjoche. g, Deinonychus (h). h, Chasmosaurus (d). i, Dimorphodon. j, Ametriorhynchids (i). k, Ichthyosaurus (j). l, Pterapsis, Compsognathus. m, Cephalopod. n, Archelon (o). o, Griphognatus, Gyroptychius. p, Plesiosaur (o), Navtiloid.

1994, Sept. 1
2041 A292 1.50cor Sheet of 16, #a.-p. 9.50 8.50

1994 World Cup Soccer Championships, US — A293

Players: a, Rai. b, Freddy Rincon. c, Luis Garcia. d, Thomas Dooley. e, Franco Baresi. f, Tony Meola. g, Enzo Francescoli. h, Roy Wegerle.
No. 2043, 10cor, Faustino Asprilla. No. 2044, 10cor, Adolfo Valencia, horiz.

1994, Sept. 19
2042 A293 3cor Sheet of 8, #a.-h. 8.50 7.50
Souvenir Sheets
2043-2044 A293 Set of 2 6.00 6.00

D-Day, 50th Anniv. A294

No. 2045: a, British fighter plane. b, C-47 transports dropping paratroopers. c, HMS Mauritius bombards Houlgate. d, Mulberry artificial harbor. e, Churchill tank. f, Landing craft approaching beach.

1994, Sept. 26
2045 A294 3cor Sheet of 6, #a.-f. 7.25 6.00

Ruben Dario National Theater, 25th Anniv. — A295

1994, Sept. 30
2046 A295 3cor multicolored 1.10 1.00

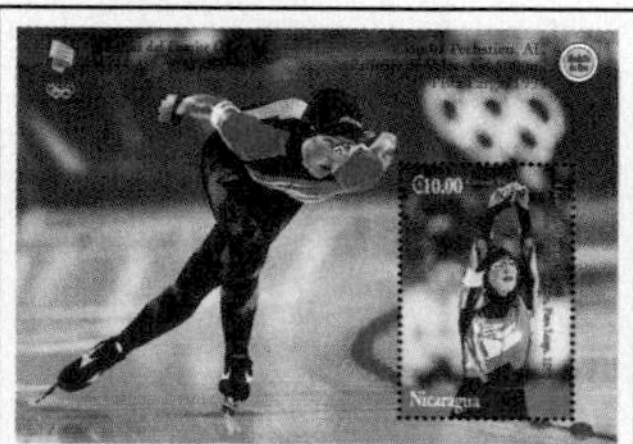

A296

Intl. Olympic Committee, Cent. — A297

Gold Medalists: No. 2047, Cassius Clay (Muhammad Ali), boxing, 1960. No. 2048, Renate Stecher, track, 1972, 1976. 10cor, Claudia Pechstein, speed skating, 1994.

1994, Oct. 3
2047 A296 3.50cor multicolored 1.25 1.25
2048 A296 3.50cor multicolored 1.25 1.25
Souvenir Sheet
2049 A297 10cor multicolored 3.25 3.25

La Carreta Nagua, by Erick Joanello Montoya A298

1994, Oct. 19
2050 A298 4cor multicolored 1.25 1.25

Motion Pictures, Cent. — A299

No. 2051 — Film and director: a, The Kid, Charlie Chaplin. b, Citizen Kane, Orson Welles. c, Lawrence of Arabia, David Lean. d, Ivan the Terrible, Sergei Eisenstein. e, Metropolis, Fritz Lang. f, The Ten Commandments, Cecil B. DeMille. g, Gandhi, Richard Attenborough. h, Casablanca, Michael Curtis. i, Platoon, Oliver Stone. j, The Godfather, Francis Ford Coppola. k, 2001: A Space Odyssey, Stanley Kubrick. l, The Ocean Depths, Jean Renoir.
No. 2052, Gone With the Wind, Victor Fleming.

1994, Nov. 14
2051 A299 2cor Sheet of 12, #a.-l. 8.00 8.00
Souvenir Sheet
2052 A299 15cor multicolored 5.00 5.00

Wildlife A300

No. 2053: a, Nyticorax nyticorax. b, Ara macao. c, Bulbulcus ibis. d, Coragyps atratus. e, Epicrates cenchria. f, Cyanerpes cyaneus. g, Ortalis vetula. h, Bradypus griseus. i, Felis onca. j, Anhinga anhinga. k, Tapirus bairdi. l, Myrmecophaga jubata. m, Iguana iguana. n, Chelydra serpentina. o, Dendrocygna autumnalis. p, Felis paradalis.

1994, Oct. 31
2053 A300 2cor Sheet of 16, #a.-p. 10.00 10.00

First Manned Moon Landing, 25th Anniv. — A301

No. 2054: a, Docking command, lunar modules. b, Lift-off. c, Entering lunar orbit. d, Footprint on moon. e, Separation of first stage. f, Trans-lunar insertion. g, Lander descending toward moon. h, Astronaut on moon.
No. 2055, 10cor, Astronaut saluting, flag. No. 2056, 10cor, Astronauts in quarantine, horiz.

1994, Oct. 17
2054 A301 3cor Sheet of 8, #a.-h. 9.50 8.00
Souvenir Sheets
2055-2056 A301 Set of 2 6.50 6.50
Nos. 2055-2056 each contain one 29x47mm stamp.

Contemporary Paintings by Rodrigo Penalba — A302

Designs: 50c, Discovery of America. 1cor, Portrait of Maurice. 1.50cor, Portrait of Franco. 2cor, Portrait of Mimi Hammer. 2.50cor, Seated Woman. 3cor, Still Life, horiz. 4cor, Portrait of Maria Augusta. 15cor, Entrance to Anticoli.

1994, Nov. 15
2057-2063 A302 Set of 7 4.75 4.75
Size: 66x96mm
Imperf
2064 A302 15cor multicolored 4.75 4.75

Domestic Cats — A303

No. 2065: a, Chocolate point Himalayan. b, Red Somalian. c, American long hair. d, Russian blue. e, Scottish folded ear. f, Persian chinchilla. g, Egyptian mau. h, Manx blue cream. i, Burmese blue Malaysian. j, Balinesian seal point. k, Oriental long-haired blue. l, Persian chinchilla cameo. m, Angora. n, Siamese. o, Burmese seal point. p, Mixed red.
15cor, Golden shoulder Persian.

1994, Dec. 20 Litho. *Perf. 14*
2065 A303 1.50cor Sheet of 16, #a.-p. 9.00 8.00
Souvenir Sheet
2066 A303 15cor multicolored 5.00 5.00
No. 2066 contains one 38x51mm stamp.

Wild Fowl A304

No. 2067 — Penelopina nigra: a, 50c, Male, female on tree branch. b, 1cor, Head of male, male on tree branch. c, 2.50cor, Head of female, female on tree branch. d, 3cor, Male spreading wings, female.
No. 2068, 15cor, Heads of male and female Penelopina nigra. No. 2069, 15cor, Anhinga anhinga.

1994, Dec. 20 Litho. *Perf. 14*
2067 A304 Vert. strip of 4, #a.-d. 2.75 2.25
Souvenir Sheets
2068-2069 A304 Set of 2 10.00 10.00
World Wildlife Fund (#2067).
No. 2067 was issued in minature sheets of 3 strips.

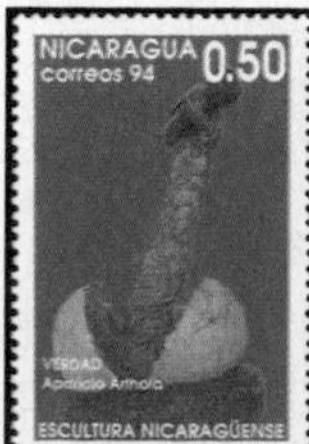

Sculpture — A305

Designs: 50c, Truth, by Aparicio Arthola. 1cor, Owl, by Orlando Sobalvarro. 1.50cor, Small Music Player, by Noel Flores Castro. 2cor, Exodus II, by Miguel Angel Abarca.

2.50cor, Raza, by Fernando Saravia. 3cor, Dolor Incognito, by Edith Gron. 4cor, Heron, by Ernesto Cardenal.

No. 2077, 15cor, Atlante, by Jorge Navas Cordonero. No. 2078, 15cor, Motherhood, by Rodrigo Penalba.

1995, Feb. 23 Litho. *Perf. 14½*

2070-2076 A305 Set of 7 4.50 4.50

Size: 66x96mm

Imperf

2077-2078 A305 Set of 2 9.00 9.00

Historic Landmarks — A306

Designs: 50c, Animas Chapel, Granada, vert. 1cor, San Francisco Convent, Granada. 1.50cor, Santiago Tower, Leon, vert. 2cor, Santa Ana Church, Nindiri. 2.50cor, Santa Ana Church, Nandaime, vert. 3cor, Lion Gate, Granada. 4cor, Castle of the Immaculate Conception, Rio San Juan.

15cor, Hacienda San Jacinto, Managua.

1995 Litho. *Perf. 14*

2079-2085 A306 Set of 7 4.50 4.50

Size: 96x66mm

2086 A306 15cor multicolored 4.50 4.50

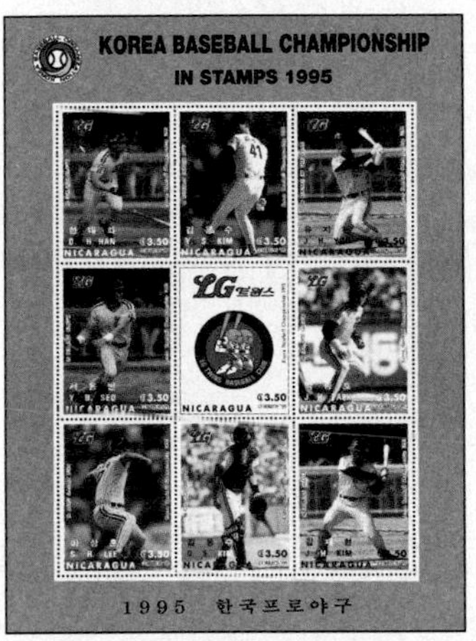

Korean Baseball Championships — A307

No. 2087, 3.50cor — LG Twins: No. 2087a, D.H. Han. b, Y.S. Kim. c, J.H. Yoo. d, Y.B. Seo. e, Team logo. f, J.H. Park. g, S.H. Lee. h, D.S. Kim. i, J.H. Kim.

No. 2088, 3.50cor — Samsung Lions: a, J.L. Ryu. b, S.Y. Kim. c, S.R. Kim. d, B.C. Dong. e, Team logo. f, K.W. Kang. g, C.S. Park. h, J.H. Yang. i, T.H. Kim.

No. 2089, 3.50cor — SBW Raiders: a, H.J. Park. b, K.J. Cho. c, K.T. Kim. d, W.H. Kim. e, Team logo. f, I.H. Baik. g, S.K. Park. h, K.L. Kim. i, J.S. Park.

No. 2090, 3.50cor — Doosan OB Bears: a, M.S. Lee. b, C.S. Park. c, H.S. Lim. d, K.W. Kim. e, Team logo. f, J.S. Kim. g, T.H. Kim. h, H.S. Kim. i, S.J. Kim.

No. 2091, 3.50cor — Pacific Dolphins: a, M.W. Jung. b, K.K. Kim. c, H.J. Kim. d, M.T. Chung. e, Team logo. f, B.W. An. g, D.G. Yoon. h, S.D. Choi. i, D.K. Kim.

No. 2092, 3.50cor — Hanwha Eagles: a, J.H. Jang. b, Y.D. Han. c, K.D. Lee. d, J.S. Park. e, Team logo. f, M.C. Jeong. g, J.W. Song. h, J.G. Kang. i, D.S. Koo.

No. 2093, 3.50cor — Lotte Giants: a, H.K. Yoon. b, D.H. Park. c, H.K. Joo. d, E.G. Kim. e, Team logo. f, J.T. Park. g, P.S. Kong. h, J.S. Yeom. i, M.H. Kim.

No. 2094, 3.50cor — Haitai Tigers: a, D.Y. Sun. b, J.B. Lee. c, J.S. Kim. d, S.H. Kim. e, Team logo. f, G.C. Lee. g, G.H. Cho. h, S.H. Kim. i, S.C. Lee.

1995, Mar. 25 Litho. *Perf. 14*

Sheets of 9, #a-i

2087-2094 A307 Set of 8 77.50 77.50

Nature Paintings — A308

Designs: 1cor, Advancing Forward, by Maria Jose Zamora. 2cor, Natural Death, by Rafael Castellon. 4cor, Captives of Water, by Alvaro Gutierrez.

1995, Apr. 4 Litho. *Perf. 14*

2095-2097 A308 Set of 3 2.25 2.25

British-Nicaragua Expedition, San Juan River — A309

1995, May 5

2098 A309 4cor multicolored 1.25 1.25

Boaco Festival — A310

1995, May 10

2099 A310 4cor multicolored 1.25 1.25

Printed with se-tenant label.

Contemporary Paintings, by Armando Morales — A311

Designs: 50c, Ferry Boat. 1cor, Oliverio Castañeda, vert. 1.50cor, Sitting Nude, vert. 2cor, Señoritas at the Port of Cabeza. 2.50cor, The Automobile and Company, vert. 3cor, Bullfight, vert. 4cor, Still life.

15cor, Woman Sleeping.

1995, Oct. 31 Litho. *Perf. 14*

2100-2106 A311 Set of 7 4.50 4.50

Size: 96x66mm

2107 A311 15cor multicolored 4.50 4.50

Louis Pasteur (1822-95) — A312

1995, Sept. 28 Litho. *Perf. 14*

2108 A312 4cor multicolored 1.25 1.25

First Place in Childrens' Painting Contest A313

Nature scene, by Brenda Jarquin Gutierrez.

1995, Oct. 9

2109 A313 3cor multicolored .90 .90

Animals A314

No. 2110: a, Crocodile. b, Opossum. c, Zahina. d, Guardatinale. e, Frog. f, Iguana. g, Macaw. h, Capybara. i, Vampire bat.

No. 2111, 15cor, Jaguar, vert. No. 2112, 15cor, Eagle, vert.

1995, Oct. 9

2110 A314 2.50cor Sheet of 9, #a.-i. 6.75 6.75

Souvenir Sheets

2111-2112 A314 Set of 2 9.00 9.00

Issued: #2112, 4/15; #2110-2111, 10/9.

FAO, 50th Anniv. — A315

1995, Oct. 16

2113 A315 4cor multicolored 1.25 1.25

UN, 50th Anniv. — A316

No. 2114: a, 3cor, UN flag, doves, rainbow. b, 4cor, Rainbow, lion, lamb. c, 5cor, Rainbow, dove on soldier's helmet.

No. 2115, Children holding hands under sun, dove.

1995, Oct. 31

2114 A316 Strip of 3, #a.-c. 3.75 3.75

Souvenir Sheet

2115 A316 10cor multicolored 3.00 3.00

No. 2114 is a continuous design.

Rotary Intl., 90th Anniv. — A317

1995, Nov. 17

2116 A317 15cor Paul Harris, logo 4.50 4.50

Souvenir Sheet

2117 A317 25cor Old, new logos 7.50 7.50

Butterflies, Moths — A318

No. 2118: a, Cyrestis camillus. b, Salamis cacta. c, Charaxes castor. d, Danaus formosa. e, Graphium ridleyanus. f, Hewitsonia boisduvali. g, Charaxes zoolina. h, Kallima cymodoce i, Precis westermanni. j, Papilo antimachus. k, Cymothoe sangaris. l, Papillo zalmoxis.

No. 2119, Danaus formosa, vert.

1995, Nov. 17

2118 A318 2.50cor Sheet of 12, #a.-l. 9.00 9.00

Souvenir Sheet

2119 A318 15cor multicolored 4.50 4.50

1996 Summer Olympics, Atlanta — A319

No. 2120: a, Michael Jordan. b, Heike Henkel. c, Linford Christie. d, Vitaly Chtcherbo. e, Heike Drechsler. f, Mark Tewksbury.

Pierre de Coubertin and: No. 2121, 20cor, Javelin thrower, horiz. No. 2122, 20cor, Runner.

1995, Dec. 1 Litho. *Perf. 14*

2120 A319 5cor Sheet of 6, #a.-f. 9.00 9.00

Souvenir Sheets

2121-2122 A319 Set of 2 12.00 12.00

John Lennon (1940-80) — A320

1995, Dec. 8

2123 A320 2cor multicolored 1.00 .60

Issued in sheets of 16.

Trains A321

Designs: No. 2124, 2cor, Mombasa mail train, Uganda. No. 2125, 2cor, Steam locomotive, East Africa. No. 2126, 2cor, Electric locomotive, South Africa. No. 2127, 2cor, Beyer-Garrat steam locomotive, South Africa. No. 2128, 2cor, Beyer-Garrat steam locomotive, Rhodesia. No. 2129, 2cor, Class 30 steam locomotive, East Africa.

No. 2130: a, New York Central & Hudson River RR 4-4-0, #999, US. b, Australian Class 638, 4-6-2, Pacific. c, Baldwin 2-10-2, Bolivia. d, Vulcan 4-8-4, China. e, Paris-Orleans 4-6-2 Pacific, France. f, Class 062, 4-6-4, Japan.

No. 2131, 15cor, Siberian cargo train. No. 2132, 15cor, Midland 4-4-0 train, Great Britain. No. 2133, 15cor, Soviet steam locomotive.

1995, Dec. 11

2124-2129 A321 Set of 6 4.00 3.75

Miniature Sheet

2130 A321 4cor Sheet of 6, #a.-f. 7.25 7.25

Souvenir Sheets

2131-2133 A321 Set of 3 13.50 13.50

#2131-2133 each contain one 85x28mm stamp.

Establishment of Nobel Prize Fund, Cent. — A322

No. 2134: a, Otto Meyerhof, medicine, 1922. b, Léon Bourgeois, peace, 1920. c, James Franck, physics, 1925. d, Leo Esaki, physics, 1973. e, Miguel Angel Asturias, literature, 1967. f, Henri Bergson, literature, 1927. g, Friedrich Bergius, chemistry, 1931. h, Klaus von Klitzing, physics, 1985. i, Eisaku Sato, Japan, peace, 1974.

No. 2135: a, Wilhelm C. Roentgen, physics, 1901. b, Theodor Mommsen, literature, 1902. c, Philipp E.A. von Lenard, physics, 1905. d, Walther H. Nernst, chemistry, 1920. e, Hans Spemann, medicine, 1935. f, Jean Paul Sartre, literature, 1964. g, T.S. Eliot, literature, 1948. h, Albert Camus, literature, 1957. i, Ludwig Quidde, peace, 1927. j, Werner Heisenberg, physics, 1932. k, Joseph Brodsky, literature, 1987. l, Carl von Ossietzky, peace, 1935.

No. 2136, 15cor, Sin-itiro Tomonaga, physics, 1965. No. 2137, 15cor, Johannes Stark, physics, 1919. No. 2138, 15cor, Oscar Arias Sánchez, peace, 1987.

1995, Dec. 11

2134 A322 2.50cor Sheet of 9, #a.-i. 6.75 6.75
2135 A322 2.50cor Sheet of 12, #a.-l. 9.00 9.00

Souvenir Sheets

2136-2138 A322 Set of 3 13.50 13.50

Orchids A323

No. 2139: a, Cattleya dowinana. b, Odontoglossum maculatum. c, Barkeria lindleyana. d, Rossioglossum grnde. e, Brassavpia digbyana. f, Miltonia schroederiana. g, Ondidium ornithorhynchum. h, Odontoglossum cervantesii. i, Chysis tricostata.

No. 2140. a, Lycaste auburn. b, Lemboglossum cordatum. c, Cyrtochilum macranthum. d, Miltassia Aztec "Nalo." e, Masdevaltia ignea. f, Oncidium sniffen "Jennifer Dauro." g, Brassolaeliocattleya Alma Kee. h, Ascocenda blue boy. i, Phalaenopsis.

15cor, Odontogiossum uro-skinneri.

1995, Dec. 15

2139 A323 2.50cor Sheet of 9, #a.-i. 6.75 6.75
2140 A323 3cor Sheet of 9, #a.-i. 8.25 8.25

Souvenir Sheet

2141 A323 15cor multicolored 4.50 4.50

World War II, 50th Anniv. A324

No. 2142: a, Patton's troops crossing the Rhine. b, Churchill, Roosevelt, and Stalin at Yalta. c, US flag being raised at Iwo Jima. d, Marine infantry taking possession of Okinawa. e, US troops greeting Russian troops at Torgau. f, Liberation of concentration camps. g, Signing UN Charter, June 1945. h, Ships arriving at Tokyo after war's end.

10cor, German Bf-109 fighter plane.

1996, Jan. 24 Litho. *Perf. 14*

2142 A324 3cor Sheet of 8, #a.-h. + label 7.25 7.25

Souvenir Sheet

2143 A324 10cor multicolored 3.00 3.00

Miniature Sheet

Exotic Birds — A325

No. 2144: a, Paradisiaea apoda. b, Dryocopus galeatus. c, Psarisomus dalhousiae (g). d, Psarocolius montezuma. e, Halcyon pileata. f, Calocitta formosa. g, Ara chloroptera. h, Platycercus eximius. i, Polyplectron emphanum. j, Cariama cristata. k, Opisthocomus hoatzin. l, Coracias cyanogaster.

10cor, Dryocopus galeatus.

1996, Feb. 1

2144 A325 2cor Sheet of 12, #a.-l. 7.25 7.25

Souvenir Sheet

2145 A325 10cor multicolored 3.00 3.00

Town of Rivas, 275th Anniv. — A326

1995, Sept. 23 Litho. *Perf. 14*

2146 A326 3cor multi +label .90 .90

Christmas A327

1995, Dec. 8

2147 A327 4cor multicolored 1.25 1.25

20th Century Writers — A328

No. 2148 — Writer, country flag: a, C. Drummond de Andrade (1902-87), Brazil. b, Cesar Vallejo (1892-1938), Peru. c, J. Luis Borges (1899-1986), Argentina. d, James Joyce (1882-1941), Italy. e, Marcel Proust (1871-1922), France. f, William Faulkner (1897-1962), US. g, Vladmir Maiakovski (1893-1930), Russia. h, Ezra Pound (1885-1972), US. i, Franz Kafka (1883-1924), Czechoslovakia. j, T.S. Eliot (188-1965), United Kingdom. k, Rainer Rilke (1875-1926), Austria. l, Federico G. Lorca (1898-1936), Spain.

1995, Oct. 15 *Perf. 14½x14*

2148 A328 3cor Sheet of 12, #a.-l. 12.50 12.50

Classic Sailing Ships A329

No. 2149, 2.50cor: a, Mayflower, England. b, Young America, US. c, Preussen, Germany. d, Lateen-rigged pirate ship, Caribbean Sea. e, Cutty Sark, England. f, Square-rigged pirate ship, Caribbean Sea. g, Galeón, Spain. h, The Sun King, France. i, Santa Maria, Spain.

No. 2150, 2.50cor: a, HMS Bounty, England. b, The President, US. c, Prince William, Holland. d, Flying Cloud, US. e, Markab, Nile River, Egypt. f, Europa, Holland. g, Vasa, Sweden. h, Foochow junk, China. i, San Gabriel, Portugal.

No. 2151, 15cor, Passat, Germany. No. 2152, 15cor, Japanese junk, vert.

1996, Jan. 10 Litho. *Perf. 14*

Sheets of 9, #a-i

2149-2150 A329 Set of 2 13.50 13.50

Souvenir Sheets

2151-2152 A329 Set of 2 9.00 9.00

Visit of Pope John Paul II — A330

1996, Feb. 7

2153 A330 5cor multicolored 1.50 1.50

Puppies — A331

Various breeds: No. 2154, 1cor, Holding red leash in mouth. No. 2155, 1cor, With red bandanna around neck. No. 2156, 2cor, Spaniel playing with ball. No. 2157, 2cor, With dog biscuit in mouth. No. 2158, 3cor, Akita. No. 2159, 3cor, Bull dog. No. 2160, 4cor, With newspaper in mouth. No. 2161, 4cor, Dalmatian with cat.

No. 2162, 16cor, Bending down on front paws. No. 2163, 16cor, Poodle.

1996, Mar. 6

2154-2161 A331 Set of 8 7.25 7.25

Souvenir Sheets

2162-2163 A331 Set of 2 9.50 9.50

Famous Women — A332

No. 2164: a, Indira Gandhi. b, Mme. Chiang Kai-shek. c, Mother Teresa. d, Marie Curie. e, Margaret Thatcher. f, Eleanor Roosevelt. g, Eva Perón. h, Golda Meir. i, Violeta Barrios de Chamorro.

No. 2165, 15cor, Jacqueline Kennedy Onassis, vert. No. 2166, 15cor, Aung San Suu Kyi, vert. No. 2167, 15cor, Valentina Tereshkova, vert.

1996, Mar. 8 *Perf. 14x13½*

2164 A332 2.50cor Sheet of 9, #a.-i. 7.25 7.25

Souvenir Sheets

Perf. 13½x14

2165-2167 A332 Set of 3 13.50 13.50

Members of Baseball's Hall of Fame A333

No. 2168 — Player, year inducted: a, Lou Gehrig, 1944. b, Rogers Hornsby, 1946. c, Mike Schmidt, 1995. d, Honus Wagner, 1936. e, Ty Cobb, 1936. f, Roberto Clemente, 1973. g, Babe Ruth, 1936. h, Johnny Bench, 1987. i, Tom Seaver, 1993.

10cor, Reggie Jackson, 1993.

1996, Mar. 15 Litho. *Perf. 13½x14*

2168 A333 4cor Sheet of 9, #a.-i. 11.00 11.00

Souvenir Sheet

2169 A333 10cor multicolored 9.25 9.25

1996 Summer Olympics, Atlanta A334

Designs: 1cor, Takehide Nakatani, Japan. 2cor, Olympic Stadium, Tokyo, 1964. 3cor, Al Oerter, US, vert. 10cor, Discus thrower from ancient games.

No. 2174, 2.50cor, vert. — Gold medal winners in boxing: a, Andrew Maynard, U.S. b, Rudi Fink, Germany. c, Peter Lessov, Bulgaria. d, Angel Herrera, Cuba. e, Patrizio Oliva, Italy. f, Armando Martinez, Cuba. g, Slobodan Kacar, Yugoslavia. h, Teofilo Stevenson, Cuba. i, George Foreman, U.S.

No. 2175, 2.50cor — Events: a, Basketball. b, Baseball. c, Boxing. d, Long jump. e, Judo. f, Team handball. g, Volleyball. h, Water polo. i, Tennis.

25cor, Cassius Clay (Muhammad Ali), US.

1996, Mar. 28 *Perf. 14*

2170-2173 A334 Set of 4 4.75 4.75

Sheets of 9, #a-i

2174-2175 A334 Set of 2 13.50 13.50

Souvenir Sheet

2176 A334 25cor multicolored 7.50 7.50

Race Horses A335

Carousel Horses — A336

Race horses: 1cor, "Wave." 2cor, "Charming Traveler." 2.50cor, "Noble Vagabond." No. 2180, 3cor, "Golden Dancer," vert. No. 2181,

3cor, "Wave Runner." No. 2182, 4cor, "Ebony Champion." No. 2183, 4cor, "Wave Tamer."

Antique carousel horses: No. 2184a, Persian light infantry horse, 18th cent. b, Italian parade horse, 15th cent. c, German armored horse, 15th cent. d, Turkish light infantry horse, 17th cent.

16cor, "Proud Heart." 25cor, German armored horse, 16th cent.

1996, Apr. 15

2177-2183 A335 Set of 7 6.00 6.00
2184 A336 2cor Sheet of 4, #a.-d. 2.50 2.50

Souvenir Sheets

2185 A335 16cor multi 6.50 6.50
2186 A336 25cor multi 7.50 7.50

Marine Life A337

No. 2187, 2.50cor: a, Butterflyfish (d). b, Barracuda (a). c, Manatee. d, Jellyfish. e, Octopus (b, d, f, g, h). f, Small yellow-striped fish. g, Lemon shark. h, Striped fish. i, Red fish.

No. 2188, 2.50cor: a, Reef shark. b, Diver, hammerhead shark (c, e). c, Moray eel (f). d, Macrela ojos de caballo (a, b, e). e, Hammerhead shark. f, Butterflyfish. g, Mediterranean grouper. h, Octopus, diff. i, Manta ray.

No. 2189, 20cor, Angelfish. No. 2190, 20cor, Saddleback butterflyfish.

1996, Apr. 29 Litho. *Perf. 14*

Sheets of 9, #a-i

2187-2188 A337 Set of 2 14.50 14.50

Souvenir Sheets

2189-2190 A337 Set of 2 13.00 13.00

Chinese Lunar Calendar A338

Year signs: a, Rat. b, Ox. c, Tiger. d, Hare. e, Dragon. f, Snake. g, Horse. h, Sheep. i, Monkey. j, Rooster. k, Dog. l, Boar.

1996, May 6

2191 A338 2cor Sheet of 12, #a.-l. 6.50 6.50

China'96.

Central American Integration System (SICA) A339

1996, May 8 *Perf. 14½*

2192 A339 5cor multicolored 1.60 1.60

20th Century Events A340

No. 2193: a, Russian revolution, 1917. b, Chinese revolution, 1945. c, Creation of the UN, 1945. d, Tearing down the Berlin Wall, 1989. e, World War I, vert. f, Creation of the State of Israel, 1948, vert. g, World War II, vert. h, 2nd Vatican Council, 1962-65, vert. i, Atom bombing of Hiroshima, 1945. j, Viet Nam War, 1962-73. k, Persian Gulf War, 1991. l, End of Apartheid, 1991.

1996 *Perf. 14*

2193 A340 3cor Sheet of 12, #a.-l. + label 11.50 11.50

Souvenir Sheet

New Year 1997 (Year of the Ox) — A341

1996 Litho. *Perf. 15x14*

2194 A341 10cor multicolored 3.00 3.00

Wuhan Huanghelou — A342

1996, May 20 Litho. *Perf. 14*

2195 A342 4cor multicolored 1.25 1.25

China '96. No. 2195 was not available until March 1997.

Red Parrot, by Ernesto Cardenal — A343

1996, June 5 Litho. *Perf. 14½x14*

2196 A343 4cor multicolored 1.25 1.25

Friendship Between Nicaragua and Republic of China A344

Designs: 10cor, Painting, "Landscape with Bags," by Fredrico Nordalm, vert. 20cor, Dr. Lee Teng-Hui, Pres. of Republic of China and Violeta Barrios de Chamorro, President of Nicaragua.

Perf. 14½x14, 14x14½

1996, June 26 Litho.

2197 A344 10cor multicolored 1.75 1.75
2198 A344 20cor multicolored 3.50 3.50

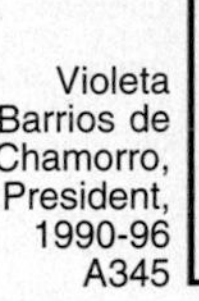

Violeta Barrios de Chamorro, President, 1990-96 A345

Serpentine Die Cut

1997, Jan. 27 Litho.

Self-Adhesive

2199 A345 3cor multicolored .90 .90
a. Booklet pane of 9 + 2 labels 8.25

The peelable paper backing serves as a booklet cover.

"Plan International," Intl. Children's Organization, 60th Anniv. — A346

1997, Feb. 24 *Serpentine Die Cut*

Self-Adhesive

2200 A346 7.50cor multicolored 2.25 2.25
a. Booklet pane of 12 27.00

The peelable paper backing serves as a booklet cover.

"Iberoamerica," Spanish-America Art Exhibition — A347

Painting, "Night with Two Figures," by Alejandro Aróstegui.

1998, May 8 *Perf. 13½*

2201 A347 7.50cor multicolored 2.00 2.00

Butterflies — A348

No. 2202: a, Metamorpha stelenes. b, Erateina staudingeri. c, Premolis semirufa. d, Heliconius eisini. e, Phoebis phlea. f, Dione juno. g, Helicopis cupido. h, Catonephele numili. i, Anteos clorinde.

No. 2203, 25cor, Thecla coronata. No. 2204, 25cor, Ufefheisa bela.

1999, Mar. 15 Litho. *Perf. 14*

2202 A348 2.50cor Sheet of 9, #a.-i. 4.25 4.25

Souvenir Sheets

2203-2204 A348 Set of 2 15.50 15.50

Dated 1996.

Fauna of Central America — A349

No. 2205, 2cor: a, Red banded parrot. b, Sloth. c, Porcupine. d, Toucan. e, Howler monkey. f, Anteater. g, Kinkajou. h, Owl monkey. i, Red-footed land turtle. j, Red deer. k, Armadillo. l, Paca.

No. 2206, 2cor: a, Vulture. b, Tarantula. c, Palm viper. d, Ocelot. e, Fighting spider. f, Large fruit bat. g, Jaguar. h, Venomous tree frog. i, Viper. j, Grison. k, Rattlesnake. l, Puma.

No. 2207, 25cor, Tapir. No. 2208, 25cor, Caiman.

1999, Mar. 15 Sheets of 12, #a-l

2205-2206 A349 Set of 2 9.00 9.00

Souvenir Sheets

2207-2208 A349 Set of 2 9.00 9.00

Dated 1996.

Endangered Species — A350

No. 2209, 2.50cor: a, Owls, gorilla. b, Cheetahs. c, Giraffes. d, Gazelle, elephants. e, Elephants. f, Lion, okapi. g, Rhinoceros. h, Hippopotamus. i, Lion.

No. 2210, 2.50cor, vert: a, Lemurs. b, Blue gliding parrot. c, Toucan. d, Boa. e, Jaguar. f, Margay. g, Loris. h, White egrot. i, Armadillo.

No. 2211, 2.50cor, vert: a, Prezwalski horse. b, Red deer. c, Zebra. d, Golden lion monkey. e, African elephant. f, Black bear. g, Tiger. h, Orangutan. i, Snow leopard.

25cor, Chimpanzee. 25.50cor, Panda, vert.

1999, Mar. 15 Sheets of 9, #a-i

2209-2211 A350 Set of 3 13.00 13.00

Souvenir Sheets

2212 A350 25cor multi 4.50 4.50
2213 A350 25.50cor multi 4.75 4.75

Dated 1996.

India's Independence, 50th Anniv. — A351

1998, Aug. 13 Litho. *Perf. 14½*

2214 A351 3cor blue & multi .50 .50
2215 A351 9cor brn yel & multi 1.50 1.50

Dated 1997.

Nature Reserves and Natl. Parks A352

Designs: 1.50cor, Mombacho Volcano Nature Reserve. 2.50cor, La Flor Wildlife Refuge. 3cor, Zapatera Archipelago Natl. Park. 3.50cor, Miraflor Nature Reserve. 5cor, Cosigüina Volcano Natl. Park. 6.50cor, Masaya Volcano Natl. Park. 7.50cor, Juan Venado Island Nature Reserve. 8cor, Escalante Chacoonte River Wildlife Refuge. 10cor, Protected Areas, Natl. Park System.

12cor, Trees, first Biosphere Reserve.

1998, Aug. 20 *Perf. 10½*

2216 A352 1.50cor multicolored .25 .25
2217 A352 2.50cor multicolored .45 .45
2218 A352 3cor multicolored .50 .50
2219 A352 3.50cor multicolored .60 .60
2220 A352 5cor multicolored .85 .85
2221 A352 6.50cor multicolored 1.10 1.10
2222 A352 7.50cor multicolored 1.25 1.25
2223 A352 8cor multicolored 1.40 1.40
2224 A352 10cor multicolored 1.75 1.75
Nos. 2216-2224 (9) 8.15 8.15

Size: 65x95mm

Imperf

2225 A352 12cor multicolored 2.60 2.00

National Museum, Cent A353

1998, Aug. 25
2226 A353 3.50cor Footprints .80 .60

Paintings by Rodrigo Peñalba (1908-1979) A354

Designs: 2.50cor, "Descendimiento." 3.50cor, "Victoria y Piere With Child." 5cor, "Motherhood."
10cor, "El Güegüense."

1998, Aug. 26 ***Perf. 10½***
2227 A354 2.50cor multicolored .45 .45
2228 A354 3.50cor multicolored .60 .60
2229 A354 5cor multicolored .85 .85
Nos. 2227-2229 (3) 1.90 1.90

Size: 95x65mm

Imperf

2230 A354 10cor multicolored 1.90 1.75

Child's Painting, "Children Love Peace" — A355

1998, Aug. 28 ***Perf. 14½***
2231 A355 50c multicolored .30 .25
Dated 1997.

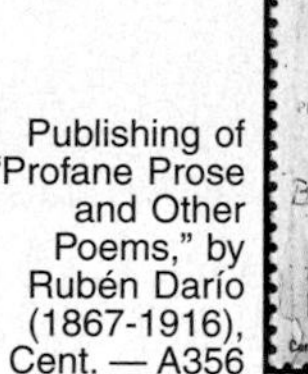

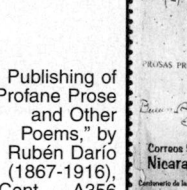

Publishing of "Profane Prose and Other Poems," by Rubén Darío (1867-1916), Cent. — A356

1998, Sept. 11 ***Perf. 10½***
2232 A356 3.50cor shown .60 .60
2233 A356 5cor Portrait .85 .85

Naturaleza '98 — A357

Painting by Bayron Gómez Chavarría.

1998, Sept. 25
2234 A357 3.50cor multicolored .80 .60

World Stamp Day — A358

1998, Oct. 9
2235 A358 6.50cor multicolored 1.10 1.10

Dialogue of Nicaragua A359

1998, Oct. 12
2236 A359 5cor multicolored .85 .85

Famous Nicaraguan Women — A360

America issue: 3.50cor, Lolita Soriano de Guerrero (b. 1922), writer. 7.50cor, Violeta Barrios de Chamorro (b. 1929), former president.

1998, Oct. 16
2237 A360 3.50cor multicolored .60 .60
2238 A360 7.50cor multicolored 1.40 1.25

Universal Declaration of Human Rights, 50th Anniv. A361

1998, Dec. 10 ***Perf. 13½***
2239 A361 12cor multicolored 2.10 2.10

Christmas — A362

Nativity scenes: 50c, Molded miniature, vert. 1cor, Drawing on pottery, vert. 2cor, Adoration of the Magi. 3cor, Painting.
7.50cor, Painting of angel over modern village.

1998, Dec. 14 ***Perf. 14***
2240 A362 50c multicolored .25 .25
2241 A362 1cor multicolored .25 .25
2242 A362 2cor multicolored .35 .35
2243 A362 3cor multicolored .50 .50
Nos. 2240-2243 (4) 1.35 1.35

Size: 95x64mm

Imperf

2244 A362 7.50cor multicolored 1.25 1.25
Dated 1997.

Managua Earthquake, 25th Anniv. (in 1997) — A363

Designs: 3cor, Managua in 1997, vert. 7.50cor, Devastation after earthquake in 1972. 10.50cor, Buildings toppling, clock, vert.

1998, Dec. 23
2245 A363 3cor multicolored .50 .50
2246 A363 7.50cor multicolored 1.25 1.25

Souvenir Sheet

2247 A363 10.50cor multicolored 1.75 1.75
Dated 1997.

Diana, Princess of Wales (1961-97) — A364

Designs: 5cor, Wearing hat. 7.50cor, Wearing tiara. 10cor, Wearing white dress.

1999, Apr. 29 Litho. ***Perf. 13½***
2248-2250 A364 Set of 3 3.75 3.75

Nos. 2248-2250 were each issued in sheets of 6.

Butterflies A365

Designs: 3.50cor, Papilionidae ornithoptera. 8cor, Nymphalidae cepheuptychia. 12.50cor, Pieridae phoebis.
No. 2254: a, Nymphalidae eryphanis. b, Nymphalidae callicore. c, Nymphalidae hypolimmas. d, Nymphalidae precis. e, Papilionidae troides. f, Nymphalidae cithaerias. g, Papilionidae parides. h, Nymphalidae heliconius. i, Nymphalidae morpho.
15cor, Papilionidae papilio.

1999, Apr. 30 ***Perf. 14***
2251-2253 A365 Set of 3 4.25 4.25
2254 A365 9cor Sheet of 9, #a.-i. 14.00 14.00

Souvenir Sheet

2255 A365 15cor multicolored 2.50 2.50

Sailing Ships — A366

Paintings: 2cor, Eagle, 1851, US. 4cor, Contest, 1800, US. 5cor, Architect, 1847, US. 10cor, Edward O'Brien, 1863, UK.
No. 2260, vert: a, HMS Rodney, 1830, UK. b, Boyne, 1700's, Great Britain. c, Castor, 1800's, UK. d, Mutin, 1800's, UK. e, Britainnia, 1820, UK. f, Gouden Leeuw, 1600, Holland. g, Hercules, 1600, Holland. h, Resolution, 1667, Great Britain. i, Royal George, 1756, Great Britain. j, Vanguard, 1700's, Great Britain. k, Prince Royal, 1600, Great Britain. l, Zeven Provincien, 1600, Holland.
No. 2261, 15cor, Pamir, 1905, US. No. 2262, 15cor, Great Expedition, 1700's, Great Britain.

1999, May 31 Litho. ***Perf. 14x13½***
2256-2259 A366 Set of 4 3.75 3.75

Perf. 14½x14¼

2260 A366 3cor Sheet of 12, #a.-l. 6.50 6.50

Souvenir Sheets

Perf. 13½x14

2261-2262 A366 Set of 2 5.50 5.50

No. 2260 contains twelve 28x36mm stamps.

Flora and Fauna A367

Designs: 5cor, Anteos clorinde. 6cor, Coereba flaveola. No. 2265, 7.50cor, Rynchops niger. No. 2266, 7.50cor, Chaetodon striatus.
No. 2267, vert: a, Palm tree. b, Phaethon lepturus. c, Cinclocerthia ruficauda. d, Myadestes genibarbis. e, Rosa sinesis. f, Cyanophala bicolor. g, Delphinus delphis. h, Anolis carolinensis (l). i, Dynastes tityus. j, Heliconia psittacorum. k, Iguana iguana (j). l, Propona meander.
No. 2268, 10cor, Ceryle torquata, vert. No. 2269, 10cor, Anisotremus virginicus.

1999, June 14 ***Perf. 14x14¼***
2263-2266 A367 Set of 4 4.75 4.75

Perf. 14¼x14

2267 A367 5cor Sheet of 12, #a.-l. 11.00 11.00

Souvenir Sheet

2268-2269 A367 Set of 2 3.50 3.50

No. 2267 l is inscribed 3cor, but the editors believe the sheet was sold as sheet of 5cor stamps.

Birds — A368

Designs: 5cor, Eudyptes chrysocome. 5.50cor, Spheniscus magellanious. 6cor, Pygoscelis antarctica. 7.50cor, Magadyptes antipodes.
No. 2274, horiz.: a, Phalacrocorax punctatus featherstoni. b, Phalacrocorax bougainvillii. c, Anhinga anhinga. d, Phalacrocorax punctatus punctatus. e, Phalacrocorax sulcirostris. f, Pelecanus occidentalis.
No. 2275, 12cor, Aptenodytes forsteri, horiz. No. 2276, 12cor, Pygoscelis papua.

1999, May 25 Litho. ***Perf. 14***
2270-2273 A368 Set of 4 4.00 4.00
2274 A368 6cor Sheet of 6, #a.-f. 6.00 6.00

Souvenir Sheets

2275-2276 A368 Set of 2 4.00 4.00
Dated 1998.

Dinosaurs A369

No. 2277: a, Sordes. b, Dimorphodon. c, Anurognathus. d, Rhamphorhynchus. e, Pterodaustro. f, Pteranodon.
No. 2278: a, Macroplata. b, Coelurus. c, "Stegosaurus." d, "Corythosaurus." e, Thadeosaurus. f, "Brachisaurus."
No. 2279, 12cor, Platecarpus. No. 2280, 12cor, Pterodactylus.

1999, June 1 Litho. *Perf. 14*

2277 A369 5cor Sheet of 6, #a.-f. 5.00 5.00
2278 A369 6cor Sheet of 6, #a.-f. 6.00 6.00

Souvenir Sheets

2279-2280 A369 Set of 2 4.00 4.00

Dated 1998. Stamp inscriptions on Nos. 2278c, 2278d and 2278f, and perhaps others, are incorrect or misspelled.

Trains A370

Designs: 1cor, U25B, Rock Island Line. 5cor, C-630 Santa Fe Railroad. 6.50cor, Class D. D. 40 AX, Union Pacific Railroad. 7.50cor, F Series B. B. EMD, Maryland Department of Transportation.

No. 2285: a, CR Alco RS11. b, Metra EMD F40. c, British Columbia Railways GF6C. d, Amtrak AEM7. e, C-40-9, Norfolk Southern. f, C-630, Reading Railroad.

No. 2286: a, British Columbia Railways GF6C, diff. b, Indian Railways WDM C-C. c, Class 421, Australia. d, Class M821, Australia. e, LRC B.B., Via Canada. f, GM Class X, Victorian Railways, Australia.

No. 2287, 15cor, Queen Victoria. No. 2288, 15cor, Donald Smith driving last spike of Trans-Canada Railway, vert.

1999, June 28 Litho. *Perf. 14*

2281-2284 A370 Set of 4 3.25 3.25
2285 A370 5cor Sheet of 6, #a.-f. 5.00 5.00
2286 A370 6cor Sheet of 6, #a.-f. 6.00 6.00

Souvenir Sheets

2287-2288 A370 Set of 2 5.00 5.00

Dated 1998. Stamp inscription on No. 2284, and perhaps others, is misspelled.

Mushrooms and Insects — A371

No. 2289: a, Tricholoma ustaloides, leaf beetle. b, Tricholoma pardinum, grasshopper. c, Amanita echinocephala, crickets. d, Tricholoma saponaceum, red-tipped clearwing moth. e, Amanita inaurata, hanging scorpionfly. f, Amanita rubescens, assassin bug.

No. 2290: a, Amanita citrina, banded agrion. b, Cryoptotrama asprata, clouded yellow butterfly. c, Amanita gemmata, mayfly. d, Catathelasma imperiale, variable reed beetle. e, Collybia fusipes, black swallowtail caterpillar. f, Collybia butyracea, South African savannah grasshopper.

No. 2291, 12.50cor, Tricholomopsis rutilans, lesser cloverleaf weevil. No. 2292, 12.50cor, Tricholoma virgatum, rose weevil.

1999, Oct. 27 Litho. *Perf. 13¼x13½*

2289 A371 5.50cor Sheet of 6, #a.-f. 5.50 5.50
2290 A371 7.50cor Sheet of 6, #a.-f. 7.25 7.25

Souvenir Sheets

2291-2292 A371 Set of 2 4.00 4.00

Dated 1998.

Ballooning — A372

No. 2293, 12cor: a, Solo Spirit 3. b, Emblem of Breitling Orbiter 3, first balloon to make non-stop circumnavigation, 1999. c, ICO Global.

No. 2294, 12cor: a, Breitling Orbiter 3 over mountains. b, Leonardo da Vinci. c, Brian Jones and Bertrand Piccard, pilots of Breitling Orbiter 3.

No. 2295, 12cor: a, Tiberius Cavallo. b, Breitling Orbiter 3 on ground. c, Piccard and Jones, diff.

No. 2296, 12cor: a, Jones. b, Breitling Orbiter 3 in flight. c, Piccard.

No. 2297, 25cor, Jean-Francois Pilatre de Rozier. No. 2298, 25cor, Jean-Pierre Blanchard. No. 2299, 25cor, Madame Thible. No. 2300, 25cor, J. A. C. Charles.

1999, Nov. 12 *Perf. 13½x13¼*

Sheets of 3, #a-c

2293-2296 A372 Set of 4 24.00 24.00

Souvenir Sheets

2297-2300 A372 Set of 4 16.00 16.00

Dated 1998.

Orchids — A373

Designs: 2cor, Cattleya, skinneri. 4cor, Lycaste aromatica. 5cor, Odontoglossum cervantesii. 10cor, Brassia verrucosa.

No. 2305, 3cor: a, Odontoglossum rossii. b, Cattleya aurantiaca. c, Encyclia cordigera. d, Phragmipedium bessae. e, Brassavola nodosa. f, Cattleya forbesii.

No. 2306, 3cor: a, Barkeria spectabilis. b, Dracula erythrochaete. c, Cochleanthes discolor. d, Encyclia cochleata. e, Lycaste aromatica. f, Brassia maculata.

No. 2307, 25cor, Odontoglossum rossii, diff. No. 2308, 25cor, Phragmipedium longifolium.

1999, Nov. 10

2301-2304 A373 Set of 4 4.00 3.50

Sheets of 6, #a.-f.

2305-2306 A373 Set of 2 7.25 6.00

Souvenir Sheets

2307-2308 A373 Set of 2 8.00 8.00

Rubén Darío Natl. Theater, 30th Anniv. A374

1999, Dec. 6 *Perf. 13¼x13½*

2309 A374 7.50cor multi 1.25 1.25

Inter-American Development Bank, 40th Anniv. — A375

1999, Nov. 18 *Perf. 13¼*

2310 A375 7.50cor multi 1.25 1.25

America Issue, A New Millennium Without Arms — A376

1999, Nov. 25 *Perf. 13½*

2311 A376 7.50cor multi 1.25 1.25

Japanese-Nicaraguan Friendship — A377

Designs: a, 3.50cor, Fishing boats, Puertos Cabezas. b, 9cor, Hospital. c, 5cor, Combine in field. d, 6cor, Japanese school. e, 7.50cor, Bridge on Pan-American Highway. f, 8cor, Aqueduct.

1999, Nov. 12 *Perf. 13x13¼*

2312 A377 Sheet of 6, #a.-f. 7.50 7.50

UPU, 125th Anniv. — A378

1999, Dec. 20 Litho. *Perf. 13½*

2313 A378 7.50cor multi 1.40 1.40

Cities of Granada and León, 475th Anniv. A379

No. 2314 — Granada: a, City Hall. b, Guadalupe Church. c, Buildings on central square. d, Houses with porches. e, House of the Leones. f, El Consulado Street.

No. 2315 — León: a, Cathedral. b, Municipal theater. c, La Recolección Church. d, Rubén Dario Museum. e, Post and Telegraph office. f, Cural de Subtiava house.

1999, Dec. 13 *Perf. 13x13½*

2314 A379 3.50cor Sheet of 6, #a.-f. 3.50 3.50
2315 A379 7.50cor Sheet of 6, #a.-f. 7.25 7.25

Dogs and Cats — A380

Designs: 1cor, Azawakh. 2cor, Chihuahua. 2.50cor, Chocolate colorpoint Birman, horiz. 3cor, Norwegian Forest cat, horiz.

No. 2320: a, Clumber spaniel. b, Australian shepherd. c, German wire-haired pointer. d, Unnamed. e, Ibizan hound. f, Norwegian elkhound.

No. 2321, horiz.: a, Blue European Shorthair. b, Turkish Angora. c, Red Tiffany. d, Persian. e, Calico Shorthair. f, Russian Blue.

No. 2322, 12cor, Braque du Bourbonnais. No. 2323, 12cor, Burmese, horiz.

Perf. 13¾x13½, 13½x13¾

2000, July 20 Litho.

2316-2319 A380 Set of 4 1.50 1.50
2320 A380 6cor Sheet of 6, #a-f 6.25 6.25
2321 A380 6.50cor Sheet of 6, #a-f 6.75 6.75

Souvenir Sheets

2322-2323 A380 Set of 2 4.25 4.25

No. 2322 contains one 42x56mm stamp; No. 2323 contains one 56x42mm stamp.

Trains A381

Designs: 3cor, Class 470 APT-P, Great Britain. 4cor, X-2000, Sweden. 5cor, XPT, Australia. 10cor, High speed train, Great Britain.

No. 2328: a, Metro North B-25-7. b, Long Island Railroad EMD DE30. c, EMD F40 PHM-2C. d, Pennsylvania Railroad GG1. e, New Jersey Transit MK GP40 FH-2. f, Amtrak EMD F59 PHI.

No. 2329: a, DM-3, Sweden. b, EW 165, New Zealand. c, Class 87, Great Britain. d, Class 40, Great Britain. e, GE 6/6, Switzerland. f, Class 277, Spain.

No. 2330, Metra EMD P69PN-AC. No. 2331, Class 44, Great Britain.

2000, Aug. 21 Litho. *Perf. 14*

2324-2327 A381 Set of 4 3.75 3.75

Sheets of 6, #a-f

2328-2329 A381 3cor Set of 2 6.25 6.25

Souvenir Sheets

2330-2331 A381 25cor Set of 2 8.50 8.50

Marine Life A382

Designs: 3.50cor, Great white shark. 5cor, Humpback whale. 6cor, Sea turtle. 9cor, Sperm whale.

No. 2336, 7.50cor: a, Puffer fish. b, Manta ray. c, Black grouper. d, Tiger grouper. e, Golden-tailed eel. f, Atlantic squid.

No. 2337, 7.50cor: a, Hawksbill turtle. b, Moon jellyfish. c, Caribbean reef shark. d, Turtle. e, Spotted dolphin. f, Southern sting ray.

No. 2338, Tiger shark. No. 2339, Spotted dolphins.

2000, Aug. 22 *Perf. 14*

2332-2335 A382 Set of 4 4.00 4.00

Sheets of 6, #a-f

2336-2337 A382 Set of 2 17.50 17.50

Souvenir Sheets

2338-2339 A382 25cor Set of 2 9.50 9.50

Queen Mother, 100th Birthday — A383

No. 2340: a, As young woman. b, In 1970. c, With King George VI. d, As old woman.

Litho. (Margin Embossed)

2000, July 25 *Perf. 14*

2340 A383 10cor Sheet of 4, #a-d + label 7.00 7.00

Souvenir Sheet

Perf. 13¾

2341 A383 25cor In 1948 4.25 4.25

No. 2341 contains one 38x51mm stamp.

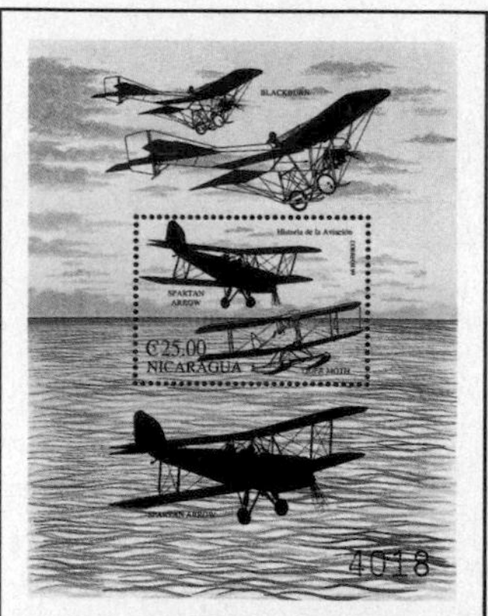

History of Aviation — A384

No. 2342, 7.50cor: a, Montgolfier balloon (blue background), vert. b, Hawker Hart. c, Lysander. d, Bleriot and Fox Moth, vert. e, Harrier. f, VC10.

No. 2343, 7.50cor: a, Montgolfier balloon (tan background), vert. b, Bristol F2B. c, Jet Provost. d, Avro 504K and Redwing II trainer, vert. e, Hunter. f, Wessex.

No. 2344, 25cor, Spartan Arrow (top) and Tiger Moth. No. 2345, 25cor, Tiger Moth (top) and Spartan Arrow.

2000, July 27 Litho. *Perf. 14½x14*

Sheets of 6, #a-d

2342-2343 A384 Set of 2 15.00 15.00

Souvenir Sheets

2344-2345 A384 Set of 2 8.50 8.50

Size of Nos. 2342a, 2342d, 2343a, 2343d: 41x60mm.

Birds — A385

Designs: 5cor, Cotinga amabilis. 7.50cor, Galbula ruficauda. 10cor, Guiraca caerulea. 12.50cor, Momotus momota.

No. 2350: a, Ara macao. b, Amazona ochrocephala. c, Chloroceryle americana. d, Archilocus colubris. e, Pharamachrus mocinno. f, Ramphastos sulfuratus. g, Coereba flaveola. h, Piculus rubiginosus. i, Passerina ciris. j, Busarellus nigricollis.

No. 2351, 25cor, Aulacorhynchus prasinus. No. 2352, 25cor, Ceryle alcyon.

2000, Aug. 23 *Perf. 14*

2346-2349 A385 Set of 4 7.00 7.00

2350 A385 3cor Sheet of 10, #a-j 6.00 6.00

Souvenir Sheets

2351-2352 A385 Set of 2 8.50 8.50

Space Exploration — A386

No. 2353, 5cor: a, Donald K. Slayton. b, M. Scott Carpenter. c, Walter M. Schirra. d, John H. Glenn, Jr. e, L. Gordon Cooper. f, Virgil I. Grissom. g, Mercury Redsone 3 rocket. h, Alan B. Shepard.

No. 2354, 5cor, horiz.: a, Recovery of Mercury 8. b, View of Earth from space. c, Carpenter in life raft. d, Shepard in water. e, USS Intrepid. f, Friendship 7. g, Mercury 9 splashdown. h, Recovery of Mercury 6.

No. 2355, 25cor, Glenn, diff. No. 2356, 25cor, Shepard, horiz.

2000, Aug. 25 Litho.

Sheets of 8, #a-h

2353-2354 A386 Set of 2 14.00 14.00

Souvenir Sheets

2355-2356 A386 Set of 2 8.50 8.50

Millennium — A387

No. 2357: a, Pope Leo XIII. b, Rerum Novarum. c, Pope Pius X. d, Revision of ecclesiatic music. e, Pope Benedict XV. f, Canonization of Joan of Arc. g, Pope Pius XI. h, Establishment of Radio Vatican. i, Pope John XXIII. j, Peace symbol. k, Pope Paul VI. l, Arms of Paul VI. m, Pope John Paul I. n, Lamb and cross. o, Pope John Paul II. p, Globe, hands holding dove.

No. 2358, 25cor, John XXIII. No. 2359, 25cor, John Paul II.

2000, Sept. 7 *Perf. 13¼*

2357 A387 3cor Sheet of 16, #a-p + label 9.50 9.50

Souvenir Sheets

2358-2359 A387 Set of 2 10.00 10.00

No. 2357 contains sixteen 30x40mm stamps.

Butterflies — A388

No. 2360, 8cor: a, Catonephele numilla esite. b, Marpesia marcella. c, Heliconius hecalesia. d, Actinote thalia anteas. e, Doxocopa larentia cherubina. f, Napeogenes tolosa mombachoensis.

No. 2361, 9cor: a, Heliconius cydno galanthus. b, Nessaea agiaura. c, Godyris zavaleta sosunga. d, Caligo atreus dionysos. e, Morpho amatonte. f, Eryphanis polyxena lycomedon.

No. 2362, 25cor, Papilio garamas. No. 2363, 25cor, Cithaerias menander.

2000, Sept. 27 *Perf. 14*

Sheets of 6, #a-f

2360-2361 A388 Set of 2 22.50 22.50

Souvenir Sheets

2362-2363 A388 Set of 2 10.00 10.00

20th Century National Leaders — A389

No. 2364, 5cor: a, Kemal Ataturk, dam. b, Ataturk, Turkish flag, horiz. c, John F. Kennedy, wife Jacqueline, Soviet missiles, horiz. d, John F. Kennedy, rocket. e, Winston Churchill, bomb explosion. f, Churchill, airplane, horiz. g, Jomo Kenyatta, tribesman, animals, horiz. h, Kenyatta, Mt. Kenya.

No. 2365, 5cor: a, Indira Gandhi. b, Indira Gandhi, soldier, elephant, horiz. c, Ronald Reagan, airplanes, horiz. d, Reagan, American flags. e, Lenin. f, Lenin, hammer and sickle, horiz. g, Charles de Gaulle, Eiffel Tower, horiz. h, De Gaulle, monument.

No. 2366, 25cor, Chiang Kai-shek. No. 2367, 25cor, Theodore Roosevelt.

2000, Oct. 5 *Perf. 14*

Sheets of 8, #a-h

2364-2365 A389 Set of 2 14.00 14.00

Souvenir Sheets

2366-2367 A389 Set of 2 8.50 8.50

Horizontal stamps are 56x42mm.

Lions Intl. — A390

No. 2368, horiz.: a, Melvin Jones and other founding members, Chicago, 1917. b, Old headquarters building, Chicago. c, Helen Keller and dog. d, UN Secretary General Kofi Annan greeting Lions Intl. Pres. Kajit Habananda. e, Jones and globe. f, André de Villiers, winner of 1998-99 Peace Poster contest.

2000, Oct. 26 Litho.

2368 A390 5cor Sheet of 6, #a-f 6.00 6.00

Souvenir Sheet

2369 A390 25cor Melvin Jones 5.50 5.50

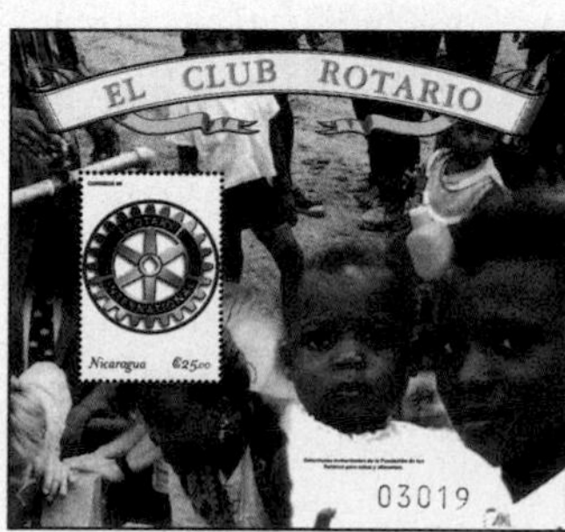

Rotary Intl. — A391

No. 2370: a, Clowns and child in Great Britain. b, Polio vaccination in Egypt. c, Burkina Faso natives at well. d, School for girls in Nepal. e, Assisting the disabled in Australia. f, Discussing problem of urban violence.

2000, Oct. 26 *Perf. 14*

2370 A391 7cor Sheet of 6, #a-f 7.25 7.25

Souvenir Sheet

2371 A391 25cor Rotary emblem 4.25 4.25

Campaign Against AIDS A392

2000, Dec. 1 Litho. *Perf. 13¼*

2372 A392 7.50cor multi 1.60 1.60

Third Conference of States Signing Ottawa Convention — A393

Designs: 7.50cor, People, world map. 10cor, People opposing land mines on globe.

2001, Sept. 18 *Perf. 13x13½*

2373-2374 A393 Set of 2 3.25 3.25

Miniature Sheet

Bridges Built With Japanese Assistance — A394

No. 2375: a, 6.50cor, Tamarindo Bridge. b, 7.50cor, Ochomogo Bridge. c, 9cor, Gil González Bridge. d, 10cor, Las Lajas Bridge. e, 12cor, Río Negro Bridge.

2001, Oct. 23 *Perf. 13x13¼*

2375 A394 Sheet of 5, #a-e, + label 8.00 8.00

World Post Day — A395

2001, Nov. 21 *Perf. 13½*

2376 A395 6.50cor multi 1.40 1.40

Dated 2000.

America Issue — Old Léon Ruins, UNESCO World Heritage Site A396

2001, Nov. 23 *Perf. 13½*

2377 A396 10cor multi 1.90 1.90

Order of Piarists in Nicaragua, 50th Anniv. — A397

Perf. 13¼x13½

2001, Nov. 27 **Litho.**

2378 A397 7cor multi 1.25 1.25

Dated 2000.

Miniature Sheet

Endangered Wildlife — A398

No. 2379: a, 5cor, Rhamphastos swaisonii. b, 6.50cor, Amazona auropalliata. c, 8cor, Buteo magnirostris. d, 9cor, Atteles geoffroyi. 10cor, Leopardus wiedii. 12cor, Puma concolor.

2001, Nov. 27 *Perf. 13¼x13*

2379 A398 Sheet of 6, #a-f 7.50 7.50

Dated 2000.

SOS Children's Villages, 50th Anniv. — A399

2001, Dec. 6 *Perf. 13¼x13½*

2380 A399 5.50cor multi 1.00 1.00

Dated 2000.

Miguel Cardinal Obando Bravo A400

2002, Jan. 3 **Litho.** *Perf. 13½*

2381 A400 6.50cor multi 1.25 1.25

Souvenir Sheet

Friendship Between Nicaragua and People's Republic of China — A401

No. 2382: a, 3cor, Presidential House, Managua. b, 7.50cor, Ministry of Foreign Affairs Building, Managua.

2002, Jan. 4 **Litho.** *Perf. 13x13¼*

2382 A401 Sheet of 2, #a-b — —

Visit of UN Secretary General Kofi Annan to Nicaragua A402

2002, Mar. 15 **Litho.** *Perf. 13¼*

2383 A402 14cor multi 2.25 2.25

Sister Maria Romero A403

2002, Apr. 9 *Perf. 13x13¼*

2384 A403 7.50cor multi 1.50 1.50

Discovery of Nicaragua, 500th Anniv. A404

Design: 12cor, Natives watching ships on horizon, vert.

2002, Sept. 12 **Litho.** *Perf. 13x13¼*

2385 A404 7.50cor shown 1.50 1.50

Souvenir Sheet

Perf. 13¼x13

2386 A404 12cor multi 2.75 2.00

America Issue - Youth, Education and Literacy — A405

2002, Nov. 29 **Litho.** *Perf. 13¼x13*

2387 A405 7.50cor multi 1.50 1.50

Canonization of St. Josemaría Escrivá de Balaguer — A406

2002, Nov. 29 *Perf. 13x13¼*

2388 A406 2.50cor multi .50 .50

Port of Corinto A407

2002, Dec. 10

2389 A407 5cor multi 1.00 1.00

Managua Earthquake, 30th Anniv. — A408

Pictures of earthquake damage: 3.50cor, Avenida del Mercado Central. 7.50cor, Managua Cathedral, vert.

Perf. 13¼x13½, 13½x13¼

2002, Dec. 13

2390-2391 A408 Set of 2 2.25 2.25

Visit of Grand Duke Henri and Princess Maria Teresa of Luxembourg A409

2003, Feb. 5 *Perf. 13¼x13*

2392 A409 12cor multi 2.50 2.50

Paintings — A410

Designs: 3cor, En Diriamba de Nicaragua, Capturaronme Amigo, by Roger Pérez de la Rocha. 5cor, San Gabriel Arcangel, by Orlando Sobalvarro. 6.50cor, Ava Fénix, by Alejandro Aróstegui. 7.50cor, Abstracción de Frutas, by Leonel Vanegas. 8cor, Suite en Turquesa y Azules, by Bernard Dreyfus, horiz. 9cor, Ana III, by Armando Morales, horiz. 10cor, Coloso IV, by Arnoldo Guillén, horiz.

Perf. 14x13½, 13½x14

2003, Oct. 23 **Litho.**

2393-2399 A410 Set of 7 8.50 8.50

Souvenir Sheet

Pontificate of Pope John Paul II, 25th Anniv. — A411

No. 2400: a, 3cor, Pope wearing zucchetto. b, 10cor, Pope wearing miter.

2003, Oct. 28 **Litho.** *Perf. 13¼x13*

2400 A411 Sheet of 2, #a-b 2.50 2.50

Christian Brothers (La Salle Order) in Nicaragua, Cent. — A412

Designs: 3cor, San Juan de Dios Hospice, horiz. 5cor, Brother Octavio de Jesús. 6.50cor, Brother Bodrán Marie. 7.50cor, Brother Agustin Hervé. 9cor, Brother Vauthier de Jesús. 10cor, Father Mariano Dubón.

12cor, St. Jean-Baptiste de la Salle.

Perf. 13½x14, 14x13½

2003, Nov. 14 **Litho.**

2401-2406 A412 Set of 6 6.50 6.50

Souvenir Sheet

2407 A412 12cor multi 2.25 1.60

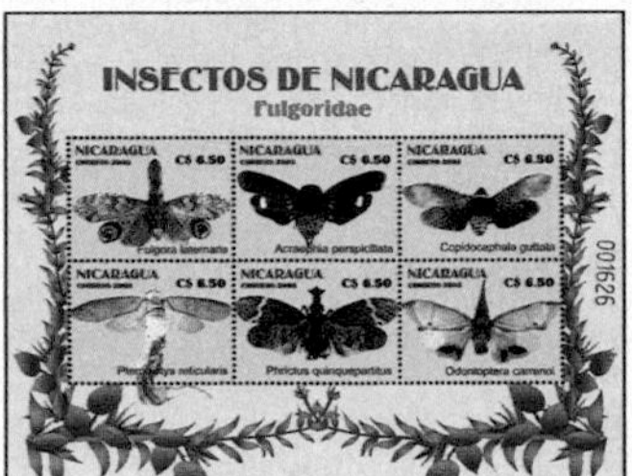

Insects — A413

No. 2408, 6.50cor: a, Fulgora laternaria. b, Acraephia perspicillata. c, Copidocephala guttata. d, Pterodictya reticularis. e, Phrictus quinquepartitus. f, Odontoptera carrenoi.

No. 2409, 8cor: a, Golofa pizarro. b, Phaneus pyrois. c, Plusiotis aurigans. d, Polyphylla concurrens. e, Dynastes hercules septentrionalis. f, Phaneus demon excelsus.

2003, Nov. 19 *Perf. 13x13½*

Sheets of 6, #a-f

2408-2409 A413 Set of 2 14.00 14.00

Contemporary Crafts — A414

Designs: 3cor, Marble sculpture, vert. 5cor, Dolls. 6.50cor, Balsa wood fish and birds. 7.50cor, Cord and jipijapa hats. 8cor, Ceramics. 9cor, Saddle. 10cor, Clay rendition of Léon Cathedral.

Perf. 14x13½, 13½x14

2003, Nov. 20

2410-2416 A414 Set of 7 8.00 8.00

Lake and River Mail Steamships A415

Designs: 3cor, Victoria. 5cor, Irma. 6.50cor, Hollenbeck. 7.50cor, Managua.

2003, Nov. 28 *Perf. 13½x14*

2417-2420 A415 Set of 4 3.50 3.50

America Issue - Flora and Fauna A416

Designs: 10cor, Corytophanes cristatus. 12.50cor, Guaiacum sanctum.

2003, Dec. 4 ***Perf. 13x13¼***
2421-2422 A416 Set of 2 3.75 3.75

San Juan del Sur, 150th Anniv. A417

2003, Dec. 9 **Litho.**
2423 A417 10cor multi 1.75 1.75

Miniature Sheet

Toyota Motor Vehicles — A418

No. 2424: a, 1936 Model AA. b, 1936 Model AB Phaeton. c, 1947 Model SA. d, 1951 Model BJ. e, 1955 Model Crown RSD. f, 1958 Model FJ28VA.

2003, Dec. 11
2424 A418 7.50cor Sheet of 6, #a-f 6.00 6.00

Publication of Tierras Solares, by Rubén Darío, Cent. A419

2004, June 22 ***Perf. 13x13¼***
2425 A419 10cor multi 1.75 1.75

Flora A420

Designs: 3cor, Tabebuia rosea. 5cor, Cassia fistula. 6.50cor, Delonix regia.

2004, June 24
2426-2428 A420 Set of 3 2.60 2.60

America Issue - Environmental Protection — A421

Designs: No. 2429, 7.50cor, Bosawas Río Bocay Biosphere Reserve. No. 2430, 7.50cor, Cerro Kilambé Nature Reserve.

2004, June 30
2429-2430 A421 Set of 2 2.75 2.75

2004 Summer Olympics, Athens — A422

Designs: 7.50cor, Track athletes. 10cor, Swimmers. 12cor, Rifleman.

2004, Aug. 13 ***Perf. 13¼x13***
2431-2433 A422 Set of 3 4.75 4.75

Central American Student's Games, Managua A423

Designs: 3cor, Judo. 5cor, Soccer, baseball. 6.50cor, High jump, swimming.

2004, Sept. 17
2434-2436 A423 Set of 3 2.75 2.75

Birds — A424

Designs: 5cor, Selenidera spectabilis. 6.50cor, Nycticorax nycticorax. 7.50cor, Caracara plancus. 10cor, Myiozetetes similis.

2004, Sept. 28 **Litho.**
2437-2440 A424 Set of 4 5.00 5.00

Granada Railroad Station A425

2004, Oct. 8 ***Perf. 13x13¼***
2441 A425 3cor multi .50 .40

Tourist Attractions A426

Designs: No. 2442, 7.50cor, Río Tapou, Río San Juan Forest Refuge. No. 2443, 7.50cor, Mombacho Volcano Natural Reserve.

2004, Oct. 12
2442-2443 A426 Set of 2 2.50 2.50

Contemporary Paintings — A427

Designs: 3cor, Frutas Ocultas, by Federico Nordalm. 7.50cor, Nicaraguapa, by Efrén Medina, vert. 10cor, Bambues, by Genaro Lugo.

2004, Nov. 4 ***Perf. 13x13¼, 13¼x13***
2444-2446 A427 Set of 3 3.50 3.50

Dogma of the Immaculate Conception, 150th Anniv. — A428

2004, Dec. 6 ***Perf. 13¼x13***
2447 A428 3cor multi .50 .40

Pablo Neruda (1904-73), Poet — A429

2004, Dec. 16
2448 A429 7.50cor multi 1.25 1.25

Publication of *Songs of Life and Hope,* by Rubén Darío, Cent. — A430

2005, Feb. 7 **Litho.** ***Perf. 13¼x13½***
2449 A430 7.50col multi + label 1.40 1.40

Souvenir Sheet

Nicaragua — Japan Diplomatic Relations, 70th Anniv. — A431

No. 2450: a, 3col, Adult volunteer teaching student. b, 7.50col, Momotombo Volcano. c, 10col, Vado Bridge, Bocana de Paiwas. d, 12col, Flowers.

2005, Feb. 21 ***Perf. 13x13¼***
2450 A431 Sheet of 4, #a-d 5.00 5.00

Orchids — A432

Designs: 3.50cor, Eleanthus hymeniformis. 5cor, Laelia superbens. 6.50cor, Cattleya aurentiaca. 7.50cor, Bletia roezlii. 10cor, Dimerandra emarginata. 12cor, Epidendrum wercklei. 25cor, Cyhysis tricostata.

2005 **Litho.** ***Perf. 13¼x13***
2451-2456 A432 Set of 6 6.25 6.25

Souvenir Sheet

2457 A432 25cor multi 3.75 3.75

Endangered Reptiles and Amphibians — A433

Designs: 3cor, Dendrobates pumilio. 6.50cor, Drymodius melanotropis. 7.50cor, Cochranella granulosa. 10cor, Bolitoglossa mombachoensis. 12cor, Caiman crocodilus. 15cor, Polychrus gutturosus.
25cor, Lepidochelys olivacea.

2005 **Litho.** ***Perf. 13x13¼***
2458-2463 A433 Set of 6 7.75 7.75

Souvenir Sheet

2464 A433 25cor multi 3.75 3.75

Intl. Year of Microcredit A434

2005 **Litho.** ***Perf. 13¼x13***
2465 A434 3.50cor multi .60 .45

Europa Stamps, 50th Anniv. A435

Designs: Nos. 2466, 2470a, 14cor, Morpho peleides. Nos. 2467, 2470b, 14cor, Amazona autumnalis. Nos. 2468, 2470c, 15cor, Rubén Dario Monument. Nos. 2469, 2470d, 25cor, Antigua Cathedral, Managua.

2006 ***Perf. 13¾x13½***
2466-2469 A435 Set of 4 10.00 10.00

Souvenir Sheet

Imperf

2470 A435 Sheet of 4, #a-d 12.50 12.50

No. 2470 contains four 40x30mm stamps.

Souvenir Sheet

Second Intl. Poetry Festival, Granada — A436

No. 2471: a, 4.50cor, Jose Coronel Urtecho (1906-94), poet. b, 7cor, Guadalupe Church,

1856. c, 10cor, Church of St. Francis. d, 12cor, Joaquin Pasos (1914-47), poet.

2006 **Litho.** ***Perf. 14***
2471 A436 Sheet of 4, #a-d 4.75 4.75

Environmental Protection — A437

Designs: 4.50cor, Casmerodius albus. 11.50cor, Amazilia tzacatl. 13.50cor, Jacana spinosa. 14.50cor, Mico River.

2007 **Litho.** ***Perf. 13x13¼***
2472-2475 A437 Set of 4 6.50 6.50

Gen. Augusto C. Sandino (1893-1934) A438

Various photographs of Sandino: 8.50cor, 10.50cor, 12.50cor.

2007 ***Perf. 13¼x13***
2476-2478 A438 Set of 3 5.00 5.00

Land Mine Clearance Program, 15th Anniv. A439

2007 **Litho.** ***Perf. 13x13¼***
2479 A439 19cor multi 3.25 3.25

Literacy Campaign, 27th Anniv. — A440

Various literacy campaign workers and students: 1cor, 2cor, 2.50cor, 4.50cor.

2007 ***Perf. 13¼x13***
2480-2483 A440 Set of 4 1.75 1.75

Second Edition of "Cantos de Vida y Esperanza," by Rubén Darío — A441

Designs: 4cor, Baptismal font, León Cathedral. 10cor, Photograph of Darío at age 5. 13.50cor, Birthplace of Darío, monument. 16cor, Portrait of Darío as diplomat in Spain.

2007, May 4 **Litho.** ***Perf. 13¼x13***
2484-2487 A441 Set of 4 6.50 6.50

Port Facilities A442

Designs: 1cor, Port of Corinto. 2cor, Port of Rama. 5cor, Port of Granada. 10cor, Port of San Juan del Sur. 15cor, Port of Sandino. 25cor, Salvador Allende Port.

2009, Apr. 28 **Litho.** ***Perf. 10½***
2488-2493 A442 Set of 6 7.50 7.50

Gen. Augusto C. Sandino (1895-1934) A443

Designs: No. 2494, 10cor, Sandino and wife, Blanca Aráuz. No. 2495, 10cor, Statue of Sandino.

2009, May 18 **Litho.** ***Perf. 10½***
2494-2495 A443 Set of 2 3.00 3.00

Víctor Raúl Haya de la Torre (1895-1979), President of Peruvian Constitutional Assembly — A444

2009, May 27 **Litho.** ***Perf. 10½***
2496 A444 12cor multi 1.90 1.90

Nicaraguan Social Security Institute, 50th Anniv. A445

50th anniversary emblem and: 4cor, Nurse examining child. 14cor, Hands, map of Nicaragua. 16cor, Elderly women. 25cor, Workman wearing air filter.

2009, July 30 **Litho.** ***Perf. 10½***
2497-2500 A445 Set of 4 8.00 8.00

A446

Sandinista Revolution, 30th Anniv. A447

Designs: 4cor, General Augusto C. Sandino. 5cor, Victory celebration, July 19, 1979. 60cor, Soldier.

2009, July 30
2501 A446 4cor multi .60 .60
2502 A446 5cor multi .80 .80
2503 A447 60cor multi 8.00 8.00
Nos. 2501-2503 (3) 9.40 9.40

Caribbean Coast Autonomy Law, 22nd Anniv. A448

Designs: 6.50cor, Creole children. 10cor, Map and Mayagna people. 14cor, Garifuna people, vert. 60cor, Dancers wrapping ribbons around pole.

2009, Oct. 9 **Litho.** ***Perf. 10½***
2504-2507 A448 Set of 4 8.75 8.75

Central American Court of Justice, 17th Anniv. — A449

2009
2508 A449 25cor multi 2.40 2.40

Central Bank of Nicaragua, 50th Anniv. A450

Designs: No. 2509, 15cor, 50th anniversary emblem. No. 2510, 15cor, Nicaraguan banknotes.

2010, Jan. 6
2509-2510 A450 Set of 2 3.00 3.00

National Assembly, 25th Anniv. A451

2010, Jan. 9
2511 A451 60cor multi 5.75 5.75

Venezuelan Independence, Bicent. — A452

2010
2512 A452 60cor multi 5.50 5.50

Mexican Revolution, Cent. — A453

Mexican Independence, Bicent. — A454

2010 ***Imperf.***
2513 A453 10cor multi .95 .95
2514 A454 13.50cor multi 1.40 1.40

Miniature Sheet

Ecuadoran Independence, Bicent. — A455

No. 2515: a, 50c, Manuel Rodríguez de Quiroga. b, 4cor, Eugenio de Santa Cruz y Espejo. c, 5cor, Juan Salinas. d, 6.50cor, José Joaquín Olmedo. e, 10cor, Juan Pio Montufar.

2010 ***Perf. 10½***
2515 A455 Sheet of 5, #a-e, + label 2.40 2.40

Postal Union of the Americas, Spain and Portugal (UPAEP), Cent. — A456

2011, Sept. 1
2516 A456 12cor multi 1.10 1.10

Bernardo O'Higgins (1778-1842), Chilean General — A457

2011
2517 A457 15cor multi 1.40 1.40

José de San Martín (1778-1850), Argentine General — A458

2011
2518 A458 25cor multi 2.25 2.25

Argentine independence, bicent.

Souvenir Sheet

Preservation of Polar Regions and Glaciers — A459

2011 **Litho.**

2519 A459 50.50cor multi 4.50 4.50

Miniature Sheet

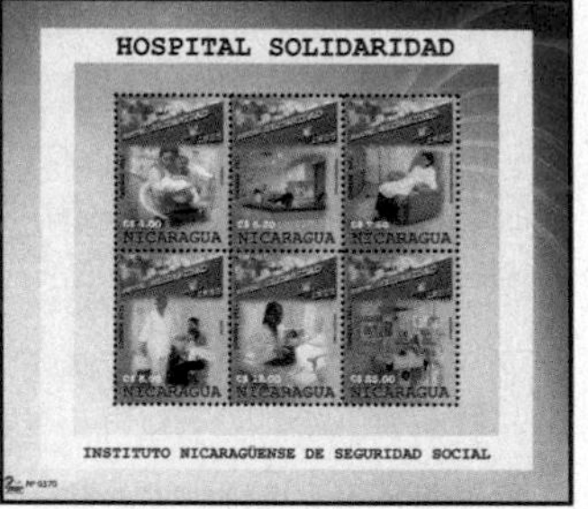

Solidarity Hospital, Managua — A460

No. 2520: a, 4cor, Woman in chair holding infant in neo-natal unit. b, 6.50cor, Nurse's station. c, 7.50cor, Woman in chair receiving chemotherapy. d, 8cor, Pediatrician, mother and child. e, 12cor, Woman sitting on hospital bed holding infant. f, 25cor, Pediatrics unit equipment.

2011 ***Perf. 10½***

2520 A460 Sheet of 6, #a-f 5.50 5.50

Central American Parliament, 20th Anniv. — A461

2011, Aug. 9 **Litho.** ***Perf. 10½***

2521 A461 16cor multi — —

Colombian Independence, Bicent. (in 2010) — A462

2012, Feb. 29 **Litho.** ***Perf. 10½***

2522 A462 50.50cor multi 4.50 4.50

Dated 2011.

Paintings — A463

Designs: No. 2523, 50c, La Embarcacíon, by Leonel Vanegas. No. 2524, 50c, La Princesa Está Triste, by Vanegas. No. 2525, 1cor, La Montaña Mágica, by Leoncio Sáenz. No. 2426, 1cor, La Gigantona I, by Sáenz. No. 2527, 2cor, No Olvides Monimbó, by Roger Pérez de la Rocha. No. 2528, 2cor, Campesinas, by Pérez de la Rocha. 10cor, Amanecer, by Arnoldo Guillén. 13.50cor, Esta Tierra ni se Vende, ni se Rinde, Guillén. 15cor, Metamorfosis de las Mujeres del Cua, by Orlando Sobalvarro. 16cor, Verano, by Sobalvarro.

2012, Sept. 6

2523-2532 A463 Set of 10 5.25 5.25

Miniature Sheet

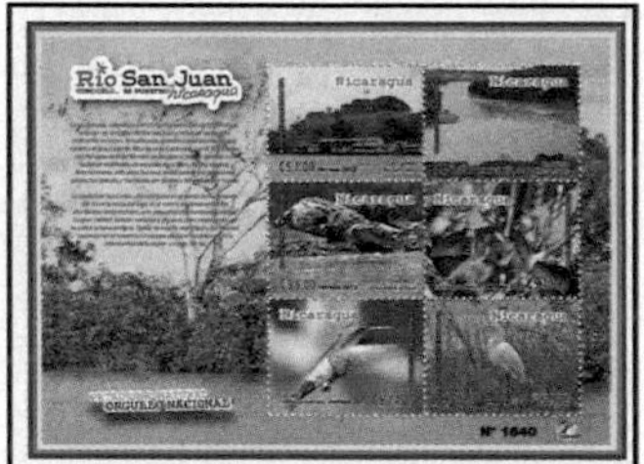

San Juan River — A464

No. 2533: a, 1cor, El Castillo. b, 4cor, River and its shores. c, 5cor, Crocodylus acutus. d, 10cor, Ctenosaura similis. e, 14cor, Mellisuga helenae. f, 50cor, Egretta alba.

2012, Sept. 6

2533 A464 Sheet of 6, #a-f 7.25 7.25

Miniature Sheet

Diplomatic Relations Between Nicaragua and South Korea, 50th Anniv. — A465

No. 2534: a, 4cor, Solar panels. b, 5cor, Water pump, Juigalpa. c, 13.50cor, Machinery in factory. d, 25cor, Building in free trade zone.

2012, Sept. 30

2534 A465 Sheet of 4, #a-d 4.00 4.00

Souvenir Sheet

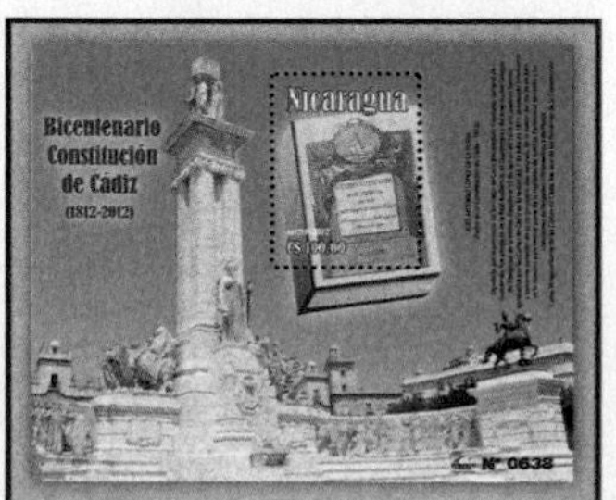

Cádiz Constitution (First Spanish Constitution), Bicent. — A466

2012, Oct. 16

2535 A466 100cor multi 8.50 8.50

Souvenir Sheet

Spanish Agency for Intl. Development Cooperation, 25th Anniv. — A467

2013, Nov. 21 **Litho.** ***Perf. 10½***

2536 A467 25cor multi 2.00 2.00

America Issue — A468

Flags and Hugo Chávez (1954-2013), President of Venezuela: 5cor, Waving. 10cor, Holding map of South America.

2014, Mar. 5 **Litho.** ***Perf. 10½***

2537-2538 A468 Set of 2 1.25 1.25

AIR POST STAMPS

Counterfeits exist of almost all scarce surcharges among Nos. C1-C66.

Regular Issues of 1914-28 Overprinted in Red

1929, May 15 **Unwmk.** ***Perf. 12***

C1 A24 25c orange 1.75 1.75
- *a.* Double overprint, one inverted 50.00
- *b.* Inverted overprint 50.00
- *c.* Double overprint 50.00

C2 A24 25c blk brn 2.25 2.25
- *a.* Double overprint, one inverted 50.00
- *b.* Double overprint 50.00
- *c.* Inverted overprint 30.00

There are numerous varieties in the setting of the overprint. The most important are: Large "1" in "1929" and large "A" in "Aereo" and "P. A. A."

Similar Overprint on Regular Issue of 1929 in Red

1929, June

C3 A24 25c dk vio 1.25 .75
- *a.* Double overprint 50.00
- *b.* Inverted overprint 50.00
- *c.* Double overprint, one inverted 50.00

Nos. C1-C3 (3) 5.25 4.75

The stamps in the bottom row of the sheet have the letters "P. A. A." larger than usual.

Similar overprints, some including an airplane, have been applied to postage issues of 1914-20, officials of 1926 and Nos. 401-407. These are, at best, essays.

Airplanes over Mt. Momotombo — AP1

1929, Dec. 15 **Engr.**

C4 AP1 25c olive blk .50 .40
C5 AP1 50c blk brn .75 .75
C6 AP1 1cor org red 1.00 1.00
Nos. C4-C6 (3) 2.25 2.15

See Nos. C18-C19, C164-C168. For surcharges and overprints see Nos. C7-C8, C14-C17, C25-C31, C106-C120, C135-C146, C150-C154, C169-C173, CO25-CO29.

No. C4 Surcharged in Red or Black

1930, May 15

C7 AP1 15c on 25c ol blk (R) .50 .40
- *a.* "$" inverted 3.50
- *b.* Double surcharge (R + Bk) 7.00
- *c.* As "b," red normal, blk invtd. 7.00
- *d.* Double red surch., one inverted 7.00

C8 AP1 20c on 25c ol blk (Bk) .75 .60
- *a.* "$" inverted 7.00
- *b.* Inverted surcharge 15.00

Nos. C1, C2 and C3 Surcharged in Green

1931, June 7

C9 A24 15c on 25c org 70.00 50.00
C10 A24 15c on 25c blk brn 100.00 100.00
C11 A24 15c on 25c dk vio 15.00 15.00
- *c.* Inverted surcharge 47.50

C12 A24 20c on 25c dk vio 10.00 10.00
- *c.* Inverted surcharge 100.00
- *d.* Double surcharge 100.00

C13 A24 20c on 25c blk brn *375.00*

No. C13 was not regularly issued.

"1391"

C9a	A24	15c on 25c	
C10a	A24	15c on 25c	
C11a	A24	15c on 25c	60.00
d.	As "a," inverted		400.00
C12a	A24	20c on 25c	*75.00*
e.	As "a," inverted		400.00
g.	As "a," double		400.00
C13a	A24	20c on 25c	

"1921"

C9b	A24	15c on 25c	
C10b	A24	15c on 25c	400.00
C11b	A24	15c on 25c	60.00
e.	As "b," inverted		400.00
C12b	A24	20c on 25c	*100.00*
f.	As "b," inverted		400.00
h.	As "b," double		400.00
C13b	A24	20c on 25c	

Nos. C8, C4-C6 Surcharged in Blue

1931, June

C14 AP1 15c on 20c on 25c 26.00 9.00
- *b.* Blue surcharge inverted 37.50
- *c.* "$" in blk, surch. invtd. 50.00
- *d.* Blue surch. dbl., one invtd. 30.00

C15 AP1 15c on 25c 5.50 5.50
- *b.* Blue surcharge inverted 100.00
- *c.* Double surch., one invtd. 25.00

C16 AP1 15c on 50c 40.00 40.00
C17 AP1 15c on 1cor 100.00 100.00
Nos. C14-C17 (4) 171.50 154.50

"1391"

C14a	AP1	15c on 20c on 25c	50.00
C15a	AP1	15c on 25c	30.00
C16a	AP1	15c on 50c	80.00
C17a	AP1	15c on 1cor	225.00
	Nos. C14a-C17a (4)		385.00

Momotombo Type of 1929

1931, July 8

C18 AP1 15c deep violet .25 .25
C19 AP1 20c deep green .40 .40

Managua Post Office Before and After Earthquake AP2

Without gum, Soft porous paper

1932, Jan. 1 Litho. *Perf. 11*

C20 AP2 15c lilac 1.50 *1.25*
a. 15c violet 22.50
b. Vert. pair, imperf. btwn. 35.00
C21 AP2 20c emerald 2.00
b. Horizontal pair, imperf. between 35.00
C22 AP2 25c yel brn 6.50
b. Vertical pair, imperf. between 60.00
C23 AP2 50c yel brn 8.00
C24 AP2 1cor dp car 12.00
a. Vert. or horiz. pair, imperf. btwn. 80.00
Nos. C20-C24 (5) 30.00

Sheets of 10. See note after No. 568.

For overprint and surcharges see #C44-C46.

Reprints: see note following No. 568. Value $1 each.

Nos. C5 and C6 Surcharged in Red or Black

1932, July 12 *Perf. 12*

C25 AP1 30c on 50c (Bk) 1.50 1.50
a. "Valc" 25.00
b. Double surcharge 15.00
c. Double surch., one inverted 15.00
d. Period omitted after "O" 25.00
e. As "a," double 300.00
C26 AP1 35c on 50c (R) 1.50 1.50
a. "Valc" 30.00
b. Double surcharge 12.00
c. Double surch., one inverted 12.00
d. As "a," double 300.00
C27 AP1 35c on 50c (Bk) 35.00 35.00
a. "Valc" 250.00
C28 AP1 40c on 1cor (Bk) 1.75 1.75
a. "Valc" 25.00
b. Double surcharge 15.00
c. Double surch., one inverted 15.00
d. Inverted surcharge 15.00
e. As "a," inverted 300.00
f. As "a," double 300.00
C29 AP1 55c on 1cor (R) 1.75 1.75
a. "Valc" 25.00
b. Double surcharge 12.00
c. Double surch., one inverted 12.00
d. Inverted surcharge 12.00
e. As "a," inverted 300.00
f. As "a," double 300.00
Nos. C25-C29 (5) 41.50 41.50

No. C18 Overprinted in Red

1932, Sept. 11

C30 AP1 15c dp vio 70.00 70.00
a. "Aerreo" 150.00 150.00
b. Invtd. "m" in "Septiembre" 150.00

International Air Mail Week.

No. C6 Surcharged

1932, Oct. 12

C31 AP1 8c on 1 cor org red 20.00 20.00
a. "1232" 30.00 30.00
b. 2nd "u" of "Inauguration" invtd. 30.00 30.00

Inauguration of airmail service to the interior.

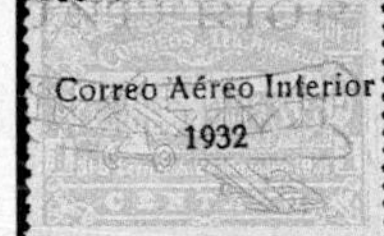

Regular Issue of 1932 Overprinted in Red

1932, Oct. 24 *Perf. 11½*

Without Gum

C32 A40 1c yel brn 20.00 20.00
a. Inverted overprint 125.00 125.00
C33 A40 2c carmine 20.00 20.00
a. Inverted overprint 125.00 125.00
b. Double overprint 100.00 100.00
C34 A40 3c ultra 9.50 9.50
a. Inverted overprint 150.00 150.00
b. As "a," vert. pair, imperf. btwn. 500.00
C35 A40 4c dp ultra 9.50 9.50
a. Inverted overprint 125.00 125.00
b. Double overprint 100.00 100.00
c. Vert. or horiz. pair, imperf. btwn. 300.00
C36 A40 5c yel brn 9.50 9.50
a. Inverted overprint 125.00 125.00
b. Vert. pair, imperf. btwn. 75.00
C37 A40 6c gray brn 9.50 9.50
a. Inverted overprint 100.00 100.00
C38 A40 50c green 9.00 9.00
a. Inverted overprint 125.00 125.00
C39 A40 1cor yellow 9.50 9.50
a. Inverted overprint 125.00 125.00
b. Horiz. pair, imperf. btwn. 200.00
Nos. C32-C39 (8) 96.50 96.50

Nos. 564, C20-C21 exist overprinted as C32-C39. The editors believe they were not regularly issued.

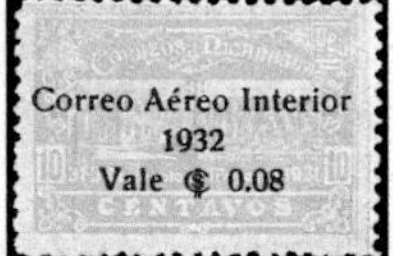

Surcharged in Red

1932, Oct. 24

C40 A40 8c on 10c yel brn 9.00 9.00
a. Inverted surcharge 125.00 125.00
C41 A40 16c on 20c org 9.00 9.00
a. Inverted surcharge 125.00 125.00
C42 A40 24c on 25c dp vio 9.00 9.00
a. Inverted surcharge 125.00 125.00
b. Horiz. pair, imperf. vert. 300.00

Surcharged in Red as No. C40 but without the word "Vale"

C43 A40 8c on 10c yel brn 45.00 45.00
a. Inverted surcharge 125.00 125.00
b. Horiz. pair, imperf. vert. 300.00

No. C22 Overprinted in Red

1932, Oct. 24

C44 AP2 25c yel brn 8.00 8.00
a. Inverted overprint 125.00 125.00

Nos. C23 and C24 Surcharged in Red

1932, Oct. 24

C45 AP2 32c on 50c yel brn 9.50 9.50
a. Inverted surcharge 125.00 125.00
b. "Interior-1932" inverted 150.00 150.00
c. "Vale $0.32" inverted 150.00 150.00
d. Horiz. pair, imperf. btwn. 200.00
C46 AP2 40c on 1cor car 7.00 7.00
a. Inverted surcharge 125.00 125.00
b. "Vale $0.40" inverted 200.00 200.00

Nos. 557-558 Overprinted in Black like Nos. C32 to C39

1932, Nov. 16

C47 A40 1c yel brn 25.00 22.50
a. "1232" 45.00 45.00
b. Inverted overprint 125.00 125.00
c. Double ovpt., one invtd. 125.00 125.00
d. As "a," inverted 500.00
C48 A40 2c dp car 20.00 17.50
a. "1232" 45.00 45.00
b. Inverted overprint 125.00 125.00
c. As "a," inverted 500.00

Excellent counterfeits exist of Nos. C27, C30-C48. Forged overprints and surcharges as on Nos. C32-C48 exist on reprints of Nos. C20-C24.

Regular Issue of 1914-32 Surcharged in Black

1932 *Perf. 12*

C49 A25 1c on 2c brt rose .65 .30
C50 A24 2c on 3c lt bl .65 .30
C51 A25 3c on 4c dk bl .65 .30
C52 A24 4c on 5c gray brn .65 .30
C53 A25 5c on 6c ol brn .65 .30
C54 A25 6c on 10c lt brn .65 .30
a. Double surcharge 25.00
C55 A24 8c on 15c org red .65 .30
C56 A25 16c on 20c org .65 .35
C57 A24 24c on 25c dk vio 2.50 1.00
C58 A24 25c on 25c dk vio 2.50 1.00
a. Double surcharge 25.00
C59 A25 32c on 50c grn 2.50 1.25
C60 A25 40c on 50c grn 3.00 1.40
C61 A25 50c on 1cor yel 4.25 2.25
C62 A25 1cor on 1cor yel 6.50 3.00
Nos. C49-C62 (14) 26.45 12.35

Nos. C49-C62 exist with inverted surcharge.

In addition to C49 to C62, four other stamps, Type A25, exist with this surcharge:
40c on 50c bister brown, black surcharge.
1cor on 2c bright rose, black surcharge.
1cor on 1cor yellow, red surcharge.
1cor on 1cor dull violet, black surcharge.

The editors believe they were not regularly issued.

Surcharged on Nos. 548, 547

1932

C65 A24 24c on 25c dk vio 45.00 45.00
C66 A24 25c on 25c blk brn 50.00 50.00

Counterfeits of Nos. C65 and C66 are plentiful.

Rivas Railroad Issue

La Chocolata Cut — AP3

El Nacascola — AP4

Designs: 25c, Cuesta cut. 50c, Mole of San Juan del Sur. 1cor, View of El Estero.

1932, Dec. Litho.

Soft porous paper

C67 AP3 15c dk vio 20.00
C68 AP4 20c bl grn 20.00
C69 AP4 25c dk brn 20.00
C70 AP4 50c blk brn 20.00
C71 AP4 1cor rose red 20.00
Nos. C67-C71 (5) 100.00

Inauguration of the railroad from San Jorge to San Juan del Sur, Dec. 18, 1932. Printed in sheets of 4, without gum.

Reprints: see note following No. 574. Value, $6 each.

Leon-Sauce Railroad Issue

"Fill" at Santa Lucia River — AP5

Designs: 15c, Bridge at Santa Lucia. 25c, Malpaicillo Station. 50c, Panoramic view. 1cor, San Andres.

1932, Dec. 30 Soft porous paper

C72 AP5 15c purple 20.00
C73 AP5 20c bl grn 20.00
C74 AP5 25c dk brn 20.00
C75 AP5 50c blk brn 20.00
C76 AP5 1cor rose red 20.00
Nos. C72-C76 (5) 100.00

Inauguration of the railroad from Leon to El Sauce, 12/30/32. Sheets of 4, without gum.

Reprints: see note following No. 579. Value, $6 each.

Flag of the Race Issue

1933, Aug. 3 Litho. *Rouletted 9*

Without gum

C77 A43 1c dk brn 1.50 1.50
C78 A43 2c red vio 1.50 1.50
C79 A43 4c violet 2.50 2.25
C80 A43 5c dl bl 2.25 2.25
C81 A43 6c vio bl 2.25 2.25
C82 A43 8c dp brn .70 .70
C83 A43 15c ol brn .70 .70
C84 A43 20c yellow 2.25 2.25
a. Horiz. pair, imperf. btwn. 15.00
b. Horiz. pair, imperf. vert. 15.00
C85 A43 25c orange 2.25 2.25
C86 A43 50c rose 2.25 2.25
C87 A43 1cor green 11.00 11.00
Nos. C77-C87 (11) 29.15 28.90

See note after No. 599. Printed in sheets of 10.

Reprints exist, shades differ from postage and official stamps.

Imperf., Pairs

C78a A43 2c 14.00
C79a A43 4c 10.00
C81a A43 6c 10.00
C82a A43 8c 10.00
C83a A43 15c 10.00
C87a A43 1cor 30.00

AP7

1933, Nov. *Perf. 12*

C88 AP7 10c bis brn 1.60 1.60
a. Vert. pair, imperf. between 35.00
C89 AP7 15c violet 1.25 1.25
a. Vert. pair, imperf. between 37.50
C90 AP7 25c red 1.50 1.50
a. Horiz. pair, imperf. between 22.50
C91 AP7 50c dp bl 1.60 1.60
Nos. C88-C91 (4) 5.95 5.95

Intl. Air Post Week, Nov. 6-11, 1933. Printed in sheets of 4. Counterfeits exist.

Stamps and Types of 1928-31 Surcharged in Black

1933, Nov. 3

C92 A25 1c on 2c grn .25 .25
C93 A24 2c on 3c ol gray .25 .25
C94 A25 3c on 4c car rose .25 .25
C95 A24 4c on 5c lt bl .25 .25
C96 A25 5c on 6c dk bl .25 .25
C97 A25 6c on 10c ol brn .25 .25
C98 A24 8c on 15c bis brn .25 .25
C99 A25 16c on 20c brn .25 .25
C100 A24 24c on 25c ver .25 .25
C101 A24 25c on 25c org .25 .25
C102 A25 32c on 50c vio .25 .25
C103 A25 40c on 50c grn .25 .25

C104 A25 50c on 1cor yel .25 .25
C105 A25 1cor on 1cor org red .35 .25
Nos. C92-C105 (14) 3.60 3.50

Nos. C100, C102-C105 exist without script control overprint. Value, each $1.50.

Type of Air Post Stamps of 1929 Surcharged in Black

1933, Oct. 28

C106 AP1 30c on 50c org red *2.00* .25
C107 AP1 35c on 50c lt bl *2.00* .25
C108 AP1 40c on 1cor yel *5.00* .25
C109 AP1 55c on 1cor grn *4.00* .25
Nos. C106-C109 (4) *13.00* 1.00

No. C19 Surcharged in Red

1934, Mar. 31

C110 AP1 10c on 20c grn .30 .25
a. Inverted surcharge 15.00
b. Double surcharge, one inverted 15.00
c. "Ceutroamericano" 10.00

No. C110 with black surcharge is believed to be of private origin.

No. C4 Surcharged in Red

1935, Aug.

C111 AP1 10c on 25c ol blk .25 .25
a. Small "v" in "vale" (R) 5.00
b. "centrvos" (R) 5.00
c. Double surcharge (R) 25.00
d. Inverted surcharge (R) 25.00
g. As "a," inverted 400.00
h. As "a," double 400.00

No. C111 with blue surcharge is believed to be private origin.

The editors do not recognize the Nicaraguan air post stamps overprinted in red "VALIDO 1935" in two lines and with or without script control marks as having been issued primarily for postal purposes.

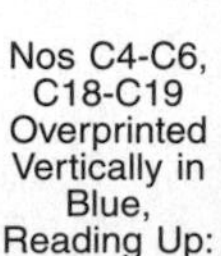

Nos C4-C6, C18-C19 Overprinted Vertically in Blue, Reading Up:

1935-36

C112 AP1 15c dp vio 1.00 1.00
C113 AP1 20c dp grn 1.75 1.75
C114 AP1 25c ol blk 2.25 2.25
C115 AP1 50c blk brn 5.00 5.00
C116 AP1 1cor org red 40.00 40.00
Nos. C112-C116 (5) 50.00 50.00

Same Overprint on Nos. C106-C109 Reading Up or Down

C117 AP1 30c on 50c org red 1.50 1.40
C118 AP1 35c on 50c lt bl 6.50 6.50
C119 AP1 40c on 1cor yel 6.50 6.50
C120 AP1 55c on 1cor grn 6.50 6.50
Nos. C117-C120 (4) 21.00 20.90
Nos. C112-C120 (9) 71.00 70.90

Same Overprint in Red on Nos. C92-C105

1936

C121 A25 1c on 2c grn .25 .25
C122 A24 2c on 3c ol gray .25 .25
C123 A25 3c on 4c car rose .25 .25
C124 A24 4c on 5c lt bl .25 .25
C125 A25 5c on 6c dk bl .25 .25
C126 A25 6c on 10c ol brn .25 .25
C127 A24 8c on 15c bis brn .25 .25
C128 A25 16c on 20c brn .30 .25
C129 A24 24c on 25c ver .50 .30
C130 A24 25c on 25c org .35 .25
C131 A25 32c on 50c vio .35 .25
C132 A25 40c on 50c grn 1.00 .50
C133 A25 50c on 1cor yel .85 .25
C134 A25 1cor on 1cor org red 3.50 .65
Nos. C121-C134 (14) 8.60 4.20

Nos. C121 to C134 are handstamped with script control mark.

Overprint Reading Down on No. C110

C135 AP1 10c on 20c grn *350.00*

This stamp has been extensively counterfeited.

Overprinted in Red on Nos. C4 to C6, C18 and C19

C136 AP1 15c dp vio 1.00 .25
C137 AP1 20c dp grn 1.25 .60
C138 AP1 25c ol blk 1.25 .55
C139 AP1 50c blk brn 1.00 .55
C140 AP1 1cor org red 3.25 .55

On Nos. C106 to C109

C141 AP1 30c on 50c org red 2.25 .60
C142 AP1 35c on 50c lt bl 2.25 .40
C143 AP1 40c on 1cor yel 2.25 .55
C144 AP1 55c on 1cor grn 2.25 .50

Same Overprint in Red or Blue on No. C111 Reading Up or Down

C145 AP1 10c on 25c, down 3.00 .45
a. "Centrvos" 25.00
C146 AP1 10c on 25c (Bl), up 6.00 1.00
a. "Centrvos" 25.00
Nos. C136-C146 (11) 25.75 6.00

Overprint on No. C145 is at right, on No. C146 in center.

Nos. C92, C93 and C98 Overprinted in Black

1936

C147 A25 1c on 2c grn 2.00 .25
C148 A24 2c on 3c ol gray 2.00 .25
a. "Resello 1936" dbl., one invtd. 7.50
C149 A24 8c on 15c bis brn 2.00 .25
Nos. C147-C149 (3) 6.00 .75

With script control handstamp.

Nos. C5 and C6 Surcharged in Red

1936, Nov. 26

C150 AP1 15c on 50c blk brn .40 .25
C151 AP1 15c on 1cor org red .40 .25

Nos. C18 and C19 Overprinted in Carmine

1936, July 2

C152 AP1 15c dp vio .60 .25
C153 AP1 20c dp grn .60 .25

Overprint reading up or down.

No. C4 Surcharged and Overprinted in Red

C154 AP1 10c on 25c olive blk .50 .30
a. Surch. and ovpt. inverted 3.50

Same Overprint in Carmine on Nos. C92 to C99

C155 A25 1c on 2c green .75 .25
C156 A24 2c on 3c olive gray 4.00 2.00
C157 A25 3c on 4c car rose .75 .25
C158 A24 4c on 5c light blue .75 .25
C159 A25 5c on 6c dark blue .75 .25
C160 A25 6c on 10c olive brn .75 .25
C161 A24 8c on 15c bister brn .75 .25
C162 A25 16c on 20c brown .75 .25
Nos. C154-C162 (9) 9.75 4.05

No. 518 Overprinted in Black

C163 A25 10c lt brn .75 .25
a. Overprint inverted 3.50
b. Double overprint 3.50

Two fonts are found in the sheet of #C163.

Momotombo Type of 1929

1937

C164 AP1 15c yel org 1.00 .25
C165 AP1 20c org red 1.00 .25
C166 AP1 25c black 1.00 .25
C167 AP1 50c violet 1.00 .25
C168 AP1 1cor orange 4.50 .25
Nos. C164-C168 (5) 8.50 1.25

Surcharged in Black

1937

C169 AP1 30c on 50c car rose 1.25 .25
C170 AP1 35c on 50c olive grn 1.25 .25
C171 AP1 40c on 1cor green 1.25 .25
C172 AP1 55c on 1cor blue 1.25 .25
Nos. C169-C172 (4) 5.00 1.00

No. C168 Surcharged in Violet

1937 Unwmk. *Perf. 12*

C173 AP1 10c on 1cor org .45 .25
a. "Centauos" 10.00

No. C98 with Additional Overprint "1937"

C174 A24 8c on 15c bis brn .65 .25
a. "1937" double 6.50

Nos. C92-C102 with Additional Overprint in Blue reading "HABILITADO 1937"

C175 A25 1c on 2c grn .90 .25
a. Blue overprint double *3.50*
C176 A24 2c on 3c ol gray .90 .25
a. Double surch., one inverted *3.50*
C177 A25 3c on 4c car rose .90 .25
C178 A24 4c on 5c lt bl .90 .25
C179 A25 5c on 6c dk bl .90 .25
C180 A25 6c on 10c ol brn .90 .25
C181 A24 8c on 15c bis brn .90 .25
a. "Habilitado 1937" double 4.50
C182 A25 16c on 20c brn .90 .25
a. Double surcharge 3.50
C183 A24 24c on 25c ver .90 .25
C184 A24 25c on 25c org .90 .25
C185 A25 32c on 50c vio .90 .25
Nos. C175-C185 (11) 9.90 2.75

Map of Nicaragua AP8

For Foreign Postage

1937, July 30 Engr.

C186 AP8 10c green .40 .25
C187 AP8 15c dp bl .40 .25
C188 AP8 20c yellow .40 .25
C189 AP8 25c bl vio .40 .25
C190 AP8 30c rose car .40 .25
C191 AP8 50c org yel .50 .25
C192 AP8 1cor ol grn 1.00 .55
Nos. C186-C192 (7) 3.50 2.05

Presidential Palace AP9

For Domestic Postage

C193 AP9 1c rose car .40 .25
C194 AP9 2c dp bl .40 .25
C195 AP9 3c ol grn .40 .25
C196 AP9 4c black .40 .25
C197 AP9 5c dk vio .40 .25
C198 AP9 6c chocolate .40 .25
C199 AP9 8c bl vio .40 .25
C200 AP9 16c org yel .40 .25
C201 AP9 24c yellow .40 .25
C202 AP9 25c yel grn .40 .25
Nos. C193-C202 (10) 4.00 2.50

No. C201 with green overprint "Union Panamericana 1890-1940" is of private origin.

Managua AP10

Designs: 15c, Presidential Palace. 20c, Map of South America. 25c, Map of Central America. 30c, Map of North America. 35c, Lagoon of Tiscapa, Managua. 40c, Road Scene. 45c, Park. 50c, Another park. 55c, Scene in San Juan del Sur. 75c, Tipitapa River. 1cor, Landscape.

Wmk. 209

1937, Sept. 17 Typo. *Perf. 11*

Center in Dark Blue

C203 AP10 10c yel grn 2.25 1.20
C204 AP10 15c orange 2.25 1.40
C205 AP10 20c red 1.75 1.00
C206 AP10 25c vio brn 1.75 1.00
a. Center, double impression —
C207 AP10 30c bl grn 1.75 1.00
a. Great Lakes omitted 40.00 40.00
C208 AP10 35c lemon .75 .45
C209 AP10 40c green .75 .40
C210 AP10 45c brt vio .75 .35
C211 AP10 50c rose lil .75 .35
a. Vert. pair, imperf. btwn. 140.00
C212 AP10 55c lt bl .75 .35
C213 AP10 75c gray grn .75 .35

Center in Brown Red

C214 AP10 1cor dk bl 1.75 .50
Nos. C203-C214 (12) 16.00 8.35

150th anniv. of the Constitution of the US.

Diriangen — AP11

Designs: 4c, 10c, Nicarao. 5c, 15c, Bartolomé de Las Casas. 8c, 20c, Columbus.

For Domestic Postage
Without gum

1937, Oct. 12 Unwmk. *Perf. 11*

C215 AP11 1c green .25 .25
C216 AP11 4c brn car .25 .25
C217 AP11 5c dk vio .25 .25
a. Without imprint .40
C218 AP11 8c dp bl .25 .25
a. Without imprint .50

For Foreign Postage
Wmk. 209
With Gum

C219 AP11 10c lt brn .25 .25
C220 AP11 15c pale bl .25 .25
a. Without imprint 1.00
C221 AP11 20c pale rose .25 .25
Nos. C215-C221 (7) 1.75 1.75

Nos. C215-C221 printed in sheets of 4.

Imperf., Pairs

C215a AP11 1c .25 .25
C216a AP11 4c .25 .25
C217b AP11 5c .25 .25
C217c AP11 5c Without imprint
C218b AP11 8c .25
C218c AP11 8c Without imprint
C219a AP11 10c .25 .25
C220b AP11 15c .25 .25
C220c AP11 15c Without imprint
C221a AP11 20c .35 .35

Gen. Tomas Martinez — AP11a

Design: 10c-50c, Gen. Anastasio Somoza.

For Domestic Postage
Without Gum

Perf. 11½, Imperf.

1938, Jan. 18 Typo. Unwmk.

Center in Black

C221B AP11a 1c orange .25 .25
C221C AP11a 5c red vio .25 .25
C221D AP11a 8c dk bl .25 .25
C221E AP11a 16c brown .25 .25
f. Sheet of 4, 1c, 5c, 8c, 16c 2.25 2.25

For Foreign Postage

C221G AP11a 10c green .25 .25
C221H AP11a 15c dk bl .25 .25
C221J AP11a 25c violet .40 .40
C221K AP11a 50c carmine .50 .45
m. Sheet of 4, 10c, 15c, 25c, 50c 3.25 3.25
Nos. C221B-C221K (8) 2.40 2.35

75th anniv. of postal service in Nicaragua. Printed in sheets of four.

Stamps of type AP11a exist in changed colors and with inverted centers, double centers and frames printed on the back. These varieties were private fabrications.

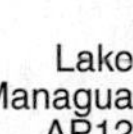

Lake Managua AP12

President Anastasio Somoza — AP13

For Domestic Postage

1939 Unwmk. Engr. *Perf. 12½*

C222 AP12 2c dp bl .25 .25
C223 AP12 3c green .25 .25
C224 AP12 8c pale lil .25 .25
C225 AP12 16c orange .25 .25
C226 AP12 24c yellow .25 .25
C227 AP12 32c dk grn .25 .25
C228 AP12 50c dp rose .25 .25

For Foreign Postage

C229 AP13 10c dk brn .25 .25
C230 AP13 15c dk bl .25 .25
C231 AP13 20c org yel .25 .25
C232 AP13 25c dk pur .25 .25
C233 AP13 30c lake .25 .25
C234 AP13 50c dp org .25 .25
C235 AP13 1cor dk ol grn .35 .40
Nos. C222-C235 (14) 3.60 3.65

For Domestic Postage

Will Rogers and View of Managua AP14

Designs: 2c, Rogers standing beside plane. 3c, Leaving airport office. 4c, Rogers and US Marines. 5c, Managua after earthquake.

1939, Mar. 31 Engr. *Perf. 12*

C236 AP14 1c brt grn .25 .25
C237 AP14 2c org red .25 .25
C238 AP14 3c lt ultra .25 .25
C239 AP14 4c dk bl .25 .25
C240 AP14 5c rose car .25 .25
Nos. C236-C240 (5) 1.25 1.25

Will Rogers' flight to Managua after the earthquake, Mar. 31, 1931.

For surcharges see Nos. 686, 688.

Pres. Anastasio Somoza in US House of Representatives — AP19

President Somoza and US Capitol AP20

President Somoza, Tower of the Sun and Trylon and Perisphere AP21

For Domestic Postage

1940, Feb. 1

C241 AP19 4c red brn .25 .25
C242 AP20 8c blk brn .25 .25
C243 AP19 16c grnsh bl .25 .25
C244 AP20 20c brt plum .50 .30
C245 AP21 32c scarlet .25 .25

For Foreign Postage

C246 AP19 25c dp bl .25 .25
C247 AP19 30c black .25 .25
C248 AP20 50c rose pink .45 .40
C249 AP21 60c green .50 .30
C250 AP19 65c dk vio brn .50 .25
C251 AP19 90c ol grn .65 .30
C252 AP21 1cor violet 1.00 .55
Nos. C241-C252 (12) 5.10 3.60

Visit of Pres. Somoza to US in 1939.

For surcharge see No. C636.

L. S. Rowe, Statue of Liberty, Nicaraguan Coastline, Flags of 21 American Republics, US Shield and Arms of Nicaragua — AP22

1940, Aug. 2 Engr. *Perf. 12½*

C253 AP22 1.25cor multi 2.00 1.00

50th anniversary of Pan American Union.

For overprint see No. C493.

First Nicaraguan Postage Stamp and Sir Rowland Hill — AP23

1941, Apr. 4

C254 AP23 2cor brown 2.50 .80
C255 AP23 3cor dk bl 8.25 1.40
C256 AP23 5cor carmine 22.50 3.50
Nos. C254-C256 (3) 33.25 5.70

Centenary of the first postage stamp.

Nos. C254-C256 imperf. are proofs.

Rubén Darío AP24

1941, Dec. 23

C257 AP24 20c pale lil .25 .25
C258 AP24 35c yel grn .30 .25
C259 AP24 40c org yel .40 .25
C260 AP24 60c lt bl .65 .30
Nos. C257-C260 (4) 1.60 1.05

25th anniversary of the death of Rubén Darío, poet and writer.

Catalogue values for unused stamps in this section, from this point to the end of the section, are for Never Hinged items.

Victory Type

1943, Dec. 8 *Perf. 12*

C261 A48 40c dk bl grn & cer .25 .25
C262 A48 60c lt bl & cer .30 .25

Red Cross — AP26

Cross and Globes — AP27

Red Cross Workers AP28

1944, Oct. 12 Engr.

C263 AP26 25c red lil & car .65 .30
C264 AP27 50c ol brn & car 1.00 .55
C265 AP28 1cor dk bl grn & car 2.00 2.00
Nos. C263-C265 (3) 3.65 2.85

International Red Cross Society, 80th anniv.

Caravels of Columbus and Columbus Lighthouse AP29

Landing of Columbus AP30

1945, Sept. 1 *Perf. 12½*

C266 AP29 20c dp grn & gray .25 .25
C267 AP29 35c dk car & blk .35 .30
C268 AP29 75c ol grn & rose pink .50 .40
C269 AP29 90c brick red & aqua .80 .75
C270 AP29 1cor blk & pale bl .90 .30
C271 AP30 2.50cor dk bl & car rose 2.25 2.25
Nos. C266-C271 (6) 5.05 4.25

Issued in honor of the discovery of America by Columbus and the Columbus Lighthouse near Ciudad Trujillo, Dominican Republic.

Roosevelt Types

Designs: 25c, Franklin D. Roosevelt and Winston Churchill. 75c, Roosevelt signing declaration of war against Japan. 1cor, Gen. Henri Giraud, Roosevelt, Gen. Charles de Gaulle and Churchill. 3cor, Stalin, Roosevelt and Churchill. 5cor, Sculptured head of Roosevelt.

Engraved, Center Photogravure

1946, June 15 *Perf. 12½*

Frame in Black

C272 A50 25c orange .25 .25
a. Horiz. pair, imperf. btwn. 225.00
b. Imperf., pair 175.00
C273 A51 75c carmine .25 .25
a. Imperf., pair 175.00
C274 A50 1cor dark green .40 .40
C275 A50 3cor violet 3.75 3.75
C276 A51 5cor greenish blue 5.00 5.00
Nos. C272-C276 (5) 9.65 9.65

Issued to honor Franklin D. Roosevelt.

Projected Provincial Seminary — AP36

Designs: 20c, Communications Building. 35c, Sanitation Building. 90c, National Bank. 1cor, Municipal Building. 2.50cor, National Palace.

1947, Jan. 10 Frame in Black

C277 AP36 5c violet .25 .25
a. Imperf., pair 125.00
C278 AP36 20c gray grn .25 .25
C279 AP36 35c orange .25 .25
C280 AP36 90c red lil .40 .30
C281 AP36 1cor brown .60 .45
C282 AP36 2.50cor rose lil 1.75 1.50
Nos. C277-C282 (6) 3.50 3.00

City of Managua centenary.

Rubén Darío Monument — AP42

Designs: 6c, Tapir. 8c, Stone Highway. 10c, Genizaro Dam. 20c, Detail of Dario Monument. 25c, Sulphurous Lake of Nejapa. 35c, Mercedes Airport. 50c, Prinzapolka River delta. 1cor, Tipitapa Spa. 1.50cor, Tipitapa River. 5cor, United States Embassy. 10cor, Indian fruit vendor. 25cor, Franklin D. Roosevelt Monument.

Engraved, Center Photogravure

1947, Aug. 29 Unwmk. *Perf. 12½*

C283 AP42 5c dk bl grn & rose car .25 .25
C284 AP42 6c blk & yel .25 .25
C285 AP42 8c car & ol .25 .25
C286 AP42 10c brn & bl .25 .25
C287 AP42 20c bl vio & org .30 .30
C288 AP42 25c brn red & emer .35 .35
C289 AP42 35c gray & bis .30 .30
C290 AP42 50c pur & sep .25 .25
C291 AP42 1cor blk & lil rose .75 .75
C292 AP42 1.50cor red brn & aqua .80 .80
C293 AP42 5cor choc & car rose 6.25 6.25
C294 AP42 10cor vio & dk brn 5.00 5.00
C295 AP42 25cor dk bl grn & yel 10.00 10.00
Nos. C283-C295 (13) 25.00 25.00

The frames differ for each denomination.

For surcharge see No. C750.

Tennis — AP43

Designs: 2c, Soccer. 3c, Table tennis. 4c, Proposed stadium. 5c, Regatta. 15c, Basketball. 25c, Boxing. 30c, Baseball. 40c, Bicycling. 75c, Diving. 1cor, Pole vault. 2cor, Boy Scouts. 5cor, Softball.

1949, July Photo. *Perf. 12*

C296 AP43 1c cerise .35 .25
C297 AP43 2c ol gray .35 .25
C298 AP43 3c scarlet .35 .25
C299 AP43 4c dk bl gray .35 .25
C300 AP43 5c aqua .35 .25
C301 AP43 15c bl grn .35 .25
C302 AP43 25c red vio 3.00 .30
C303 AP43 30c red brn 2.75 .30
C304 AP43 40c violet .75 .30
C305 AP43 75c magenta 7.50 2.75
C306 AP43 1cor lt bl 9.00 1.40
C307 AP43 2cor brn ol 4.00 1.75
C308 AP43 5cor lt grn 5.00 2.25
a. Set of 13 souv. sheets of 4 *450.00 450.00*
Nos. C296-C308 (13) 34.10 10.55

10th World Series of Amateur Baseball, 1948.

Rowland Hill — AP44

Designs: 20c, Heinrich von Stephan. 25c, First UPU Bldg. 30c, UPU Bldg., Bern. 85c, UPU Monument. 1.10cor, Congress medal, obverse. 2.14cor, as 1.10cor, reverse.

1950, Nov. 23 Engr. *Perf. 13*
Frames in Black

C309 AP44 16c cerise .25 .25
C310 AP44 20c orange .25 .25
C311 AP44 25c gray .25 .25
C312 AP44 30c cerise .40 .25
C313 AP44 85c dk bl grn .75 .65
C314 AP44 1.10cor chnt brn 1.50 .45
C315 AP44 2.14cor ol grn 2.25 2.25
Nos. C309-C315 (7) 5.65 4.35

75th anniv. (in 1949) of the UPU.
Each denomination was also issued in a souvenir sheet containing four stamps and marginal inscriptions. Size: 126x114mm. Value, set of 7 sheets, $35.
For surcharges see Nos. C501, C758.

Queen Isabela I Type

Designs: 2.30cor, Portrait facing left. 2.80cor, Map. 3cor, Santa Maria. 3.30cor, Columbus' ships. 3.60cor, Portrait facing right.

1952, June 25 Unwmk. *Perf. 11½*

C316 A65 2.30cor rose car 2.50 2.00
C317 A65 2.80cor red org 2.25 1.75
C318 A65 3cor green 2.50 2.00
C319 A66 3.30cor lt bl 2.50 2.00
C320 A65 3.60cor yel grn 2.75 2.25
a. Souv. sheet of 5, #C316-C320 12.50 12.50
Nos. C316-C320 (5) 12.50 10.00

For overprint see No. C445.

Arms of ODECA AP47

Designs: 25c, ODECA Flag. 30c, Presidents of five Central American countries. 60c, ODECA Charter and Flags. 1cor, Map of Central America.

1953, Apr. 15 *Perf. 13½x14*

C321 AP47 20c red lil .25 .25
C322 AP47 25c lt bl .25 .25
C323 AP47 30c sepia .25 .25
C324 AP47 60c dk bl grn .30 .25
C325 AP47 1cor dk vio .70 .65
Nos. C321-C325 (5) 1.75 1.65

Founding of the Organization of Central American States (ODECA).

Leonardo Arguello — AP48

Presidents: 5c, Gen. Jose Maria Moncada. 20c, Juan Bautista Sacasa. 25c, Gen. Jose Santos Zelaya. 30c, Gen. Anastasio Somoza. 35c, Gen. Tomas Martinez. 40c, Fernando Guzman. 45c, Vicente Cuadra. 50c, Pedro Joaquin Chamorro. 60c, Gen. Joaquin Zavala. 85c, Adan Cardenas. 1.10cor, Evaristo Carazo. 1.20cor, Roberto Sacasa.

Engraved (frames); Photogravure (heads)

1953, June 25 *Perf. 12½*
Heads in Gray Black

C326 AP48 4c dp car .25 .25
C327 AP48 5c dp org .25 .25
C328 AP48 20c dk Prus bl .25 .25
C329 AP48 25c blue .25 .25
C330 AP48 30c red brn .25 .25
C331 AP48 35c dp grn .25 .25
C332 AP48 40c dk vio brn .25 .25
C333 AP48 45c olive .25 .25
C334 AP48 50c carmine .30 .25
C335 AP48 60c ultra .30 .25
C336 AP48 85c brown .40 .35
C337 AP48 1.10cor purple .45 .45
C338 AP48 1.20cor ol bis .45 .45
Nos. C326-C338 (13) 3.90 3.75

For surcharges see Nos. C363-C364, C757.

Torch and UN Emblem — AP49

Designs: 4c, Raised hands. 5c, Candle and charter. 30c, Flags of Nicaragua and UN. 2cor, Globe. 3cor, Arms of Nicaragua. 5cor, Type A69 inscribed "Aereo."

1954, Apr. 30 Engr. *Perf. 13½*

C339 AP49 3c rose pink .25 .25
C340 AP49 4c dp org .25 .25
C341 AP49 5c red .25 .25
C342 AP49 30c cerise 1.00 .25
C343 AP49 2cor magenta 1.40 1.00
C344 AP49 3cor org brn 2.50 1.75
C345 AP49 5cor brn vio 3.00 2.25
Nos. C339-C345 (7) 8.65 6.00

Honoring the United Nations.
For overprint & surcharge see #C366, C443.

Capt. Dean L. Ray, USAF — AP50

Designs: 15c, Sabre jet plane. 20c, Air Force emblem. 25c, National Air Force hangars. 30c, Gen. A. Somoza. 50c, AT-6's in formation. 1cor, Plane, type P-38.

Frame in Black
Engraved; Center Photogravure

1954, Nov. 5 *Perf. 13*

C346 AP50 10c gray .25 .25
C347 AP50 15c gray .25 .25
C348 AP50 20c claret .25 .25
C349 AP50 25c red .25 .25
C350 AP50 30c ultra .25 .25
C351 AP50 50c blue .45 .45
C352 AP50 1cor green .35 .25
Nos. C346-C352 (7) 2.05 1.95

Issued to honor the National Air Force.

Rotary Intl. Type

Designs: 1c, 1cor, Paul P. Harris. 2c, 50c, Handclasp, Rotary emblem and globe. 3c, 45c, Map of world and Rotary emblem. 4c, 30c, Rotary slogans and wreath. 5c, 25c, Flags of Nicaragua and Rotary.

Perf. 11½

1955, Aug. 30 Unwmk. Photo.
Granite Paper

C353 A71 1c vermilion .25 .25
C354 A71 2c ultra .25 .25
C355 A72 3c pck grn .25 .25
C356 A71 4c violet .25 .25
C357 A71 5c org brn .25 .25
C358 A71 25c brt grnsh bl .25 .25
C359 A71 30c dl pur .25 .25
C360 A72 45c lil rose .35 .30
C361 A71 50c lt bl grn .25 .25
C362 A71 1cor ultra .35 .35
a. Souv. sheet of 5, #C358-C362 9.50 9.50
Nos. C353-C362 (10) 2.70 2.65

For surcharge see No. C365.

Nos. C331, C333, C360, C345 Surcharged in Green or Black

Engraved, Photogravure

1956, Feb. 4 *Perf. 13½x13, 11½*

C363 AP48 30c on 35c (G) .25 .25
C364 AP48 30c on 45c (G) .25 .25
C365 A72 30c on 45c .25 .25
C366 AP49 2cor on 5cor .80 .75
Nos. C363-C366 (4) 1.55 1.50

National Exhibition, Feb. 4-16, 1956.
See note after No. 772.

Gen. Jose D. Estrada — AP53

The Stoning of Andres Castro AP54

1.50 cor, Emanuel Mongalo. 2.50 cor, Battle of Rivas. 10 cor, Com. Hiram Paulding.

1956, Sept. 14 Engr. *Perf. 12½*

C367 AP53 30c dk car rose .25 .25
C368 AP54 60c chocolate .25 .25
C369 AP53 1.50cor green .25 .25
C370 AP54 2.50cor dk ultra .40 .40
C371 AP53 10cor red org 2.25 2.00
Nos. C367-C371 (5) 3.40 3.15

Centenary of the National War.
For overprint and surcharge see #C444, C751.

President Somoza — AP55

1957, Feb. 1 Photo. *Perf. 14x13½*
Various Frames: Centers in Black

C372 AP55 15c gray blk .25 .25
C373 AP55 30c indigo .25 .25
C374 AP55 2cor purple 1.00 1.00
C375 AP55 3cor dk grn 2.00 2.00
C376 AP55 5cor dk brn 3.25 3.25
Nos. C372-C376 (5) 6.75 6.75

President Anastasio Somoza, 1896-1956.

Type of Regular Issue and

Handshake and Globe — AP56

Designs: 4c, Scout emblem, globe and Lord Baden-Powell. 5c, Cub Scout. 6c, Crossed flags and Scout emblem. 8c, Scout symbols. 30c, Joseph A. Harrison. 40c, Pres. Somoza receiving decoration at first Central American Camporee. 75c, Explorer Scout. 85c, Boy Scout. 1cor, Lord Baden-Powell.

1957, Apr. 9 Unwmk. *Perf. 13½x14*

C377 AP56 3c red org & ol .25 .25
C378 A75 4c dk brn & dk Prus grn .25 .25
C379 A75 5c grn & brn .25 .25
C380 A75 6c pur & ol .25 .25
C381 A75 8c grnsh blk & red .25 .25
C382 A75 30c Prus grn & gray .25 .25
C383 AP56 40c dk bl & grysh blk .25 .25
C384 A75 75c mar & brn .25 .25
C385 A75 85c red & gray .25 .25
C386 A75 1cor dl red brn & sl grn .30 .30
a. Souv. sheet of 5, #C382-C386, imperf. 2.50 2.50
Nos. C377-C386 (10) 2.55 2.55

Centenary of the birth of Lord Baden-Powell, founder of the Boy Scouts.
No. C386a with each stamp overprinted "CAMPOREE SCOUT 1965" was issued in 1965 along with Nos. 843-852.
For surcharge see No. C754.

Pres. Luis A. Somoza — AP57

1957, July 2 *Perf. 14x13½*
Portrait in Dark Brown

C387 AP57 20c dp bl .25 .25
C388 AP57 25c lil rose .25 .25
C389 AP57 30c blk brn .25 .25
C390 AP57 40c grnsh bl .25 .25
C391 AP57 2cor brt vio 1.25 1.25
Nos. C387-C391 (5) 2.25 2.25

Issued to honor President Luis A. Somoza.

Church Types of Regular Issue

Designs: 30c, Archbishop Lezcano y Ortega. 60c, Managua Cathedral. 75c, Bishop Pereira y Castellon. 90c, Leon Cathedral. 1.50cor, De la Merced Church, Granada. 2cor, Father Mariano Dubon.

1957, July 16 Unwmk.
Centers in Olive Gray

C392 A78 30c dk grn .35 .25
C393 A77 60c chocolate .35 .25
C394 A78 75c dk bl .35 .25
C395 A77 90c brt red .55 .30
C396 A77 1.50cor Prus grn 1.25 .40
C397 A78 2cor brt pur 1.75 .60
Nos. C392-C397 (6) 4.60 2.05

Merchant Marine Type of 1957

Designs: 25c, M. S. Managua. 30c, Ship's wheel and map. 50c, Pennants. 60c, M. S. Costa Rica. 1 cor, M. S. Nicarao. 2.50 cor, Flag, globe & ship.

1957, Oct. 24 Litho. *Perf. 14*

C398 A79 25c ultra grysh bl & gray .25 .25
C399 A79 30c red brn, gray & yel .25 .25
C400 A79 50c vio, ol gray & bl .30 .30
C401 A79 60c lake, grnsh bl & blk .35 .35
C402 A79 1cor crim, brt bl & blk .45 .45
C403 A79 2.50cor blk, bl & red brn 1.50 1.50
Nos. C398-C403 (6) 3.10 3.10

For surcharge see No. C691.

Fair Emblem — AP58

Designs: 30c, 2cor, Arms of Nicaragua. 45c, 10cor, Pavilion of Nicaragua, Brussels.

1958, Apr. 17 Unwmk. *Perf. 14*

C404 AP58 25c bluish grn, blk & yel .25 .25
C405 AP58 30c multi .25 .25

C406 AP58 45c bis, bl & blk .25 .25
C407 AP58 1cor pale brn, lt bl & blk .25 .25
C408 AP58 2cor multi .40 .30
C409 AP58 10cor pale bl, lil & brn 2.10 1.60
a. Souv. sheet of 6, #C404-C409 12.00 12.00
Nos. C404-C409 (6) 3.50 2.90

World's Fair, Brussels, Apr. 17-Oct. 19.

Lions Type of Regular Issue

Designs: 30c, Dr. Teodoro A. Arias. 60c, Arms of Central American Republics. 90c, Edward G. Barry. 1.25cor, Melvin Jones. 2cor, Motto and emblem. 3cor, Map of Central America.

1958, May 8 Litho.
Emblem in Yellow, Red and Blue

C410 A80 30c bl & org .25 .25
C411 A80 60c multi .25 .25
C412 A80 90c blue .35 .30
C413 A80 1.25cor bl & ol .45 .40
C414 A80 2cor bl & grn .80 .70
C415 A80 3cor bl, lil & pink 1.25 1.10
a. Souv. sheet of 6, #C410-C415 4.25 4.25
Nos. C410-C415 (6) 3.35 3.00

For surcharge see No. C686.

Christian Brothers Type of 1958

Designs: 30c, Arms of La Salle. 60c, School, Managua, horiz 85c, St. Jean Baptiste De La Salle. 90c, Bro. Carlos. 1.25cor, Bro. Julio. 1.50cor, Bro. Antonio. 1.75cor, Bro. Argeo. 2cor, Bro. Eugenio.

1958, July 13 Photo. *Perf. 14*

C416 A81 30c bl, car & yel .25 .25
C417 A81 60c gray, brn & lil .35 .25
C418 A81 85c red, bl & grnsh blk .35 .30
C419 A81 90c ol grn, ocher & blk .50 .35
C420 A81 1.25cor car, ocher & blk .70 .50
C421 A81 1.50cor lt grn, gray & vio blk .80 .55
C422 A81 1.75cor brn, bl & grnsh blk .85 .65
C423 A81 2cor ol grn, gray & vio blk 1.25 1.00
Nos. C416-C423 (8) 5.05 3.85

For surcharges see Nos. C539A, C755-C756.

UNESCO Building, Paris — AP59

75c, 5cor, "UNESCO." 90c, 3cor, UNESCO building, Eiffel tower. 1cor, Emblem, globe.

Perf. 11½
1958, Dec. 15 Unwmk. Litho.

C424 AP59 60c brt pink & bl .30 .25
C425 AP59 75c grn & red brn .30 .25
C426 AP59 90c lt brn & grn .30 .25
C427 AP59 1cor ultra & brt pink .30 .25
C428 AP59 3cor gray & org 1.00 .65
C429 AP59 5cor rose lil & dk bl 1.60 .95
a. Min. sheet of 6, #C424-C429 4.00 4.00
Nos. C424-C429 (6) 3.80 2.60

UNESCO Headquarters Opening in Paris, Nov. 3.
For overprints see Nos. C494-C499.

Type of Regular Issue, 1959 and

Nicaraguan, Papal and US Flags — AP60

Designs: 35c, Pope John XXIII and Cardinal Spellman. 1cor, Spellman coat of arms. 1.05cor, Cardinal Spellman. 1.50cor, Human rosary and Cardinal, horiz. 2cor, Cardinal with Ruben Dario order.

1959, Nov. 26 *Perf. 12½*

C430 AP60 30c vio bl, yel & red .25 .25
C431 A83 35c dp org & grnsh blk .25 .25
C432 A83 1cor yel, bl & car .25 .25
C433 A83 1.05cor red, blk & dk car .40 .30
C434 A83 1.50cor dk bl & yel .40 .30
C435 A83 2cor multi .50 .40
C436 AP60 5cor multi 1.60 .90
a. Min. sheet of 7, #C430-C436, perf. or imperf. 4.00 4.00
Nos. C430-C436 (7) 3.65 2.65

Visit of Cardinal Spellman to Managua, Feb. 1958.
For surcharges see #C538, C638, C747, C752.

Type of Lincoln Regular Issue and

AP61

Perf. 13x13½, 13½x13
1960, Jan. 21 Engr. Unwmk.
Portrait in Black

C437 A84 30c indigo .25 .25
C438 A84 35c brt car .25 .25
C439 A84 70c plum .25 .25
C440 A84 1.05cor emerald .25 .25
C441 A84 1.50cor violet .40 .30
C442 AP61 5cor int blk & bis 1.25 .90
a. Souv. sheet of 6, #C437-C442, imperf. 4.00 4.00
Nos. C437-C442 (6) 2.65 2.20

150th anniv. of the birth of Abraham Lincoln.
For overprints and surcharges see Nos. C446-C451, C500, C539, C637, C680, C753.

Nos. C343, C370 and C318 Overprinted

1960, July 4 Engr.

C443 AP49 2cor magenta .90 .70
C444 AP54 2.50cor dk ultra .90 .75
C445 A65 3cor green 1.25 1.10
Nos. C443-C445 (3) 3.05 2.55

10th anniversary of the Philatelic Club of San Jose, Costa Rica.

Nos. C437-C442 Overprinted in Red

Perf. 13x13½, 13½x13
1960, Sept. 19 Unwmk.
Center in Black

C446 A84 30c indigo .25 .25
C447 A84 35c brt car .25 .25
C448 A84 70c plum .25 .25
C449 A84 1.05cor emerald .30 .25
C450 A84 1.50cor violet .50 .35
C451 AP61 5cor int blk & bis 1.40 1.10
Nos. C446-C451 (6) 2.95 2.45

Issued for the Red Cross to aid earthquake victims in Chile. The overprint on No. C451 is horizontal and always inverted.

People and World Refugee Year Emblem AP62

5cor, Crosses, globe and WRY emblem.

1961, Dec. 30 Litho. *Perf. 11x11½*

C452 AP62 2cor multi .50 .30
C453 AP62 5cor multi 1.00 .65
a. Souv. sheet of 2, #C452-C453 2.50 2.50

World Refugee Year, July 1, 1959-June 30, 1960.

Consular Service Stamps Surcharged in Red, Black or Blue — AP63

Unwmk.
1961, Feb. 21 Engr. *Perf. 12*
Red Marginal Number

C454 AP63 20c on 50c dp bl (R) .25 .25
C455 AP63 20c on 1cor grnsh blk (R) .25 .25
C456 AP63 20c on 2cor grn (R) .25 .25
C457 AP63 20c on 3cor dk car .25 .25
C458 AP63 20c on 5cor org (Bl) .25 .25
C459 AP63 20c on 10cor vio (R) .25 .25
C460 AP63 20c on 20cor red brn (R) .25 .25
C461 AP63 20c on 50cor brn (R) .25 .25
C462 AP63 20c on 100cor mag .25 .25
Nos. C454-C462 (9) 2.25 2.25

See Nos. CO51-CO59, RA63-RA64.

Charles L. Mullins, Anastasio Somoza and Franklin D. Roosevelt AP64

Standard Bearers with Flags of Nicaragua and Academy — AP65

Designs: 25c, 70c, Flags of Nicaragua and Academy. 30c, 1.05cor, Directors of Academy: Fred T. Cruse, LeRoy Bartlett, Jr., John F. Greco, Anastasio Somoza Debayle, Francisco Boza, Elias Monge. 40c, 2cor, Academy Emblem. 45c, 5cor, Anastasio Somoza Debayle and Luis Somoza Debayle.

Perf. 11x11½, 11½x11
1961, Feb. 24 Litho. Unwmk.

C463 AP64 20c rose, gray & buff .25 .25
C464 AP65 25c bl, red & blk .25 .25
C465 AP64 30c bl, gray & yel .25 .25
C466 AP65 35c multi .25 .25
C467 AP65 40c multi .25 .25
C468 AP64 45c pink, gray & buff .25 .25
a. Min. sheet of 6, #C463-C468, imperf. .90 .70
C469 AP64 60c brn, gray & buff .25 .25
C470 AP65 70c multi .25 .25
C471 AP64 1.05cor clar, gray & yel .25 .25
C472 AP65 1.50cor multi .25 .25
C473 AP65 2cor multi .30 .25
C474 AP64 5cor gray & buff .70 .55
a. Min. sheet of 6, #C469-C474, imperf. 3.50 3.50
Nos. C463-C474 (12) 3.50 3.30

20th anniversary (in 1959) of the founding of the Military Academy of Nicaragua.
In 1977, Nos. C468a and C474a were overprinted in black: "1927-1977 50 ANIVERSARIO / Guardia Nacional de Nicaragua." Value, $7 for both.
For surcharges see #C692, C748, C759.

Emblem of Junior Chamber of Commerce — AP66

Designs: 2c, 15c, Globe showing map of Americas, horiz. 4c, 35c, Globe and initials, horiz. 5c, 70c, Chamber credo. 6c, 1.05cor, Handclasp. 10c, 5cor, Regional map.

Perf. 11x11½, 11½x11
1961, May 16 Unwmk.

C475 AP66 2c multi .25 .25
C476 AP66 3c yel & blk .25 .25
C477 AP66 4c multi .25 .25
C478 AP66 5c crim & blk .25 .25
C479 AP66 6c brn, yel & blk .25 .25
C480 AP66 10c red org, blk & bl .25 .25
C481 AP66 15c bl, blk & grn .25 .25
C482 AP66 30c bl & blk .25 .25
C483 AP66 35c multi .25 .25
C484 AP66 70c yel, blk & crim .25 .25
C485 AP66 1.05cor multi .25 .25
C486 AP66 5cor multi .55 .55
Nos. C475-C486 (12) 3.30 3.30

13th Regional Congress of the Junior Chamber of Commerce of Nicaragua and the Intl. Junior Chamber of Commerce.
The imperforates of Nos. C475-C486 were not authorized.
For overprints and surcharges see Nos. C504-C508, C537, C634, C687, C749.

Rigoberto Cabezas — AP67

Map of Costa Rica and View of Cartago AP68

Designs: 45c, Newspaper. 70c, Building. 2cor, Cabezas quotation. 10cor, Map of lower Nicaragua with Masaya area.

1961, Aug. 29 Litho. *Perf. 13½*

C487 AP67 20c org & dk bl .25 .25
C488 AP68 40c lt bl & claret .25 .25
C489 AP68 45c citron & brn .25 .25
C490 AP68 70c beige & grn .25 .25
C491 AP68 2cor pink & dk bl .30 .25
C492 AP68 10cor grnsh bl & cl 1.40 1.10
Nos. C487-C492 (6) 2.70 2.35

Centenary of the birth of Rigoberto Cabezas, who acquired the Mosquito Territory (Atlantic Littoral) for Nicaragua.

No. C253 Overprinted in Red: "Convención Filatélica-Centro-América-Panama-San Salvador-27 Julio 1961"

1961, Aug. 23 Engr. *Perf. 12½*

C493 AP22 1.25cor multi .90 .90
a. Inverted overprint 75.00

Central American Philatelic Convention, San Salvador, July 27.

Nos. C424-C429 Overprinted in Red: "Homenaje a Hammarskjold Sept. 18-1961"

1961 Litho. *Perf. 11½*

C494 AP59 60c brt pink & bl .25 .25
C495 AP59 75c grn & red brn .30 .30
C496 AP59 90c lt brn & grn .30 .30
C497 AP59 1cor ultra & brt pink .30 .30
C498 AP59 3cor gray & org .65 .65
C499 AP59 5cor rose lil & dk bl 1.75 1.75
Nos. C494-C499 (6) 3.55 3.55

Issued in memory of Dag Hammarskjold, Secretary General of the United Nations, 1953-61.

Nos. C314 and C440 Surcharged in Red

Perf. 13x13½, 13

1962, Jan. 20 — Engr.

C500 A84 1cor on 1.05cor .25 .25
C501 AP44 1cor on 1.10cor .25 .25

UNESCO Emblem and Crowd — AP69

Design: 5cor, UNESCO and UN Emblems.

Unwmk.

1962, Feb. 26 — Photo. — *Perf. 12*

C502 AP69 2cor multi .40 .25
C503 AP69 5cor multi .85 .70
a. Souv. sheet of 2, #C502-C503, imperf. 1.25 1.25

15th anniv. (in 1961) of UNESCO.

Nos. C480 and C483-C486 Overprinted

Perf. 11x11½, 11½x11

1962, July — Litho.

C504 AP66 10c multi .30 .25
C505 AP66 35c multi .40 .25
C506 AP66 70c multi .50 .30
C507 AP66 1.05cor multi .65 .45
C508 AP66 5cor multi 1.10 1.40
Nos. C504-C508 (5) 2.95 2.65

WHO drive to eradicate malaria.

Souvenir Sheet

Stamps and Postmarks of 1862 — AP69a

1962, Sept. 9 — Litho. — *Imperf.*

C509 AP69a 7cor multi 3.50 2.75

Cent. of Nicaraguan postage stamps.

Arms Type of Regular Issue, 1962

30c, Nueva Segovia. 50c, León. 1cor, Managua. 2cor, Granada. 5cor, Rivas.

1962, Nov. 22 — *Perf. 12½x13*

Arms in Original Colors; Black Inscriptions

C510 A86 30c rose .25 .25
C511 A86 50c salmon .25 .25
C512 A86 1cor lt grn .25 .25
C513 A86 2cor gray .30 .30
C514 A86 5cor lt bl .85 .75
Nos. C510-C514 (5) 1.90 1.80

Liberty Bell AP70

1963, May 15 — Litho. — *Perf. 13x12*

C515 AP70 30c lt bl, blk & ol bis .25 .25

Sesquicentennial of the 1st Nicaraguan declaration of Independence (in 1961).

Paulist Brother Comforting Boy — AP71

60c, Nun comforting girl. 2cor, St. Vincent de Paul and St. Louisa de Marillac, horiz.

1963, May 15 — Photo. — *Perf. 13½*

C516 AP71 60c gray & ocher .25 .25
C517 AP71 1cor salmon & blk .30 .25
C518 AP71 2cor crimson & blk .50 .50
Nos. C516-C518 (3) 1.05 1.00

300th anniv. of the deaths of St. Vincent de Paul and St. Louisa de Marillac (in 1960).

Map of Central America — AP72

Lithographed and Engraved

1963, Aug. 2 — Unwmk. — *Perf. 12*

C519 AP72 1cor bl & yel .25 .25

Issued to honor the Federation of Central American Philatelic Societies.

Cross over World — AP73

1963, Aug. 6

C520 AP73 20c yel & red .25 .25

Vatican II, the 21st Ecumenical Council of the Roman Catholic Church.

Wheat and Map of Nicaragua AP74

Design: 25c, Dead tree on parched earth.

1963, Aug. 6

C521 AP74 10c lt grn & grn .25 .25
C522 AP74 25c yel & dk brn .25 .25

FAO "Freedom from Hunger" campaign.

Boxing — AP75

Lithographed and Engraved

1963, Dec. 12 — Unwmk. — *Perf. 12*

C523 AP75 2c shown .25 .25
C524 AP75 3c Running .25 .25
C525 AP75 4c Underwater .25 .25
C526 AP75 5c Soccer .25 .25
C527 AP75 6c Baseball .25 .25
C528 AP75 10c Tennis .25 .25
C529 AP75 15c Bicycling .25 .25
C530 AP75 20c Motorcycling .25 .25
C531 AP75 35c Chess .25 .25
C532 AP75 60c Deep-sea fishing .30 .30
C533 AP75 1cor Table tennis .40 .40
C534 AP75 2cor Basketball .80 .80
C535 AP75 5cor Golf 2.00 2.00
Nos. C523-C535 (13) 5.75 5.75

Publicizing the 1964 Olympic Games.

For overprints and surcharge see Nos. C553-C558, C635.

Central American Independence Issue

Flags of Central American States — AP75a

1964, Sept. 15 — Litho. — *Perf. 13x13½*

Size: 27x43mm

C536 AP75a 40c multi .25 .25

Nos. C479, C430, C437 and C416 Surcharged in Black or Red

a

b

1964 — Litho. — *Perf. 11½x11*

C537 AP66 (a) 5c on 6c .25 .25

Perf. 12½

C538 AP60 (a) 10c on 30c .50 .25

Engr.

Perf. 13x13½

C539 A84 (a) 15c on 30c (R) .65 .25

Photo.

Perf. 14

C539A A81 (b) 20c on 30c .25 .25
Nos. C537-C539A (4) 1.65 1.00

Floating Red Cross Station AP76

Designs: 5c, Alliance for Progress emblem, vert. 15c, Highway. 20c, Plowing with tractors, and sun. 25c, Housing development. 30c, Presidents Somoza and Kennedy and World Bank Chairman Eugene Black. 35c, Adult education. 40c, Smokestacks.

1964, Oct. 15 — Litho. — *Perf. 12*

C540 AP76 5c yel, brt bl, grn & gray .25 .25
C541 AP76 10c multi .25 .25
C542 AP76 15c multi .25 .25
C543 AP76 20c org brn, yel & blk .25 .25
C544 AP76 25c multi .25 .25
C545 AP76 30c dk bl, blk & brn .25 .25
C546 AP76 35c lil rose, dk red & blk .25 .25
C547 AP76 40c dp car, blk & yel 3.00 .25
Nos. C540-C547 (8) 4.75 2.00

Alliance for Progress.

For surcharges see Nos. C677, C693.

Map of Central America and Central American States AP77

Designs (Map of Central America and): 25c, Grain. 40c, Cogwheels. 50c, Heads of cattle.

1964, Nov. 30 — Litho. — *Perf. 12*

C548 AP77 15c ultra & multi .25 .25
C549 AP77 25c multi .25 .25
C550 AP77 40c multi .25 .25
C551 AP77 50c multi .25 .25
Nos. C548-C551 (4) 1.00 1.00

Central American Common Market.

For surcharge see No. C678.

Nos. C523-C525, C527 and C533-C534 Overprinted: "OLIMPIADAS / TOKYO-1964"

Lithographed and Engraved

1964, Dec. 19 — Unwmk. — *Perf. 12*

C553 AP75 2c multi .25 .25
C554 AP75 3c multi .25 .25
C555 AP75 4c multi .25 .25
C556 AP75 6c multi .25 .25
C557 AP75 1cor multi 2.25 2.00
C558 AP75 2cor multi 2.75 2.50
Nos. C553-C558 (6) 6.00 5.50

18th Olympic Games, Tokyo, Oct. 10-25.

Blood Transfusion AP78

Designs: 20c, Volunteers and priest rescuing wounded man. 40c, Landscape during storm. 10cor, Red Cross over map of Nicaragua.

1965, Jan. 28 — Litho. — *Perf. 12*

C559 AP78 20c yel, blk & red .25 .25
C560 AP78 25c red, blk & ol bis .25 .25
C561 AP78 40c grn, blk & red .25 .25
C562 AP78 10cor multi 1.75 1.10
Nos. C559-C562 (4) 2.50 1.85

Centenary (in 1963) of the Intl. Red Cross.

Stele — AP79

Antique Indian artifacts: 5c, Three jadeite statuettes, horiz. 15c, Dog, horiz. 20c, Talamanca pendant. 25c, Decorated pottery bowl and vase, horiz. 30c, Stone pestle and mortar on animal base. 35c, Three statuettes, horiz. 40c, Idol on animal pedestal. 50c, Decorated pottery bowl and vase. 60c, Vase and metate (tripod bowl), horiz. 1cor, Metate.

Perf. 13½x13, 13x13½

1965, Mar. 24 Litho. Unwmk.

Black Margin and Inscription

No.	Type	Description	Unused	Used
C563	AP79	5c yel & multi	.30	.25
C564	AP79	10c multi	.30	.25
C565	AP79	15c multi	.30	.25
C566	AP79	20c sal & dk brn	.30	.25
C567	AP79	25c lil & multi	.30	.25
C568	AP79	30c lt grn & multi	.30	.25
C569	AP79	35c multi	.30	.25
C570	AP79	40c cit & multi	.30	.25
C571	AP79	50c ocher & multi	.30	.25
C572	AP79	60c multi	.30	.25
C573	AP79	1cor car & multi	.40	.25
		Nos. C563-C573 (11)	3.40	2.75

For surcharges see Nos. C596-597, C679, C688-C690.

Pres. John F. Kennedy (1917-63) — AP80

Photogravure & Lithographed

1965, Apr. 28 *Perf. 12½x13½*

No.	Type	Description	Unused	Used
C574	AP80	35c blk & brt grn	.25	.25
C575	AP80	75c blk & brt pink	.35	.25
C576	AP80	1.10cor blk & dk bl	.50	.40
C577	AP80	2cor blk & yel brn	1.25	1.00
		Nos. C574-C577 (4)	2.35	1.90
		Set of 4 souvenir sheets	5.50	5.50

Nos. C574-C577 each exist in souvenir sheets containing one imperf. block of 4.

For surcharge see No. C760.

Andrés Bello AP81

1965, Oct. 15 Litho. *Perf. 14*

No.	Type	Description	Unused	Used
C578	AP81	10c dk brn & red brn	.25	.25
C579	AP81	15c ind & lt bl	.25	.25
C580	AP81	45c blk & dl lil	.25	.25
C581	AP81	80c blk & yel grn	.25	.25
C582	AP81	1cor dk brn & yel	.25	.25
C583	AP81	2cor blk & gray	.30	.30
		Nos. C578-C583 (6)	1.55	1.55

Centenary of the death of Andrés Bello (1780?-1864), Venezuelan writer and educator.

Winston Churchill — AP82

Winston Churchill: 35c, 1cor, Broadcasting, horiz. 60c, 3cor, On military inspection. 75c, As young officer.

1966, Feb. 7 Unwmk. *Perf. 14*

No.	Type	Description	Unused	Used
C584	AP82	20c cer & blk	.25	.25
C585	AP82	35c dk ol grn & blk	.25	.25
C586	AP82	60c brn & blk	.25	.25
C587	AP82	75c rose red	.30	.25
C588	AP82	1cor vio blk	.45	.25
C589	AP82	2cor lil & blk	.80	.50
a.		Souv. sheet of 4	3.25	3.25
C590	AP82	3cor ind & blk	1.25	.70
		Nos. C584-C590 (7)	3.55	2.45

Sir Winston Spencer Churchill (1874-1965), statesman and World War II leader.

No. C589a contains four imperf. stamps similar to Nos. C586-C589 with simulated perforations.

Pope John XXIII — AP83

35c, Pope Paul VI. 1cor, Archbishop Gonzalez y Robleto. 2cor, St. Peter's, Rome. 3cor, Arms of Pope John XXIII & St. Peter's.

1966, Dec. 15 Litho. *Perf. 13*

No.	Type	Description	Unused	Used
C591	AP83	20c multi	.25	.25
C592	AP83	35c multi	.25	.25
C593	AP83	1cor multi	.25	.25
C594	AP83	2cor multi	.40	.35
C595	AP83	3cor multi	.65	.50
		Nos. C591-C595 (5)	1.80	1.60

Closing of the Ecumenical Council, Vatican II.

Nos. C571-C572 Surcharged in Red

1967 *Perf. 13x13½, 13½x13*

No.	Type	Description	Unused	Used
C596	AP79	10c on 50c multi	.25	.25
C597	AP79	15c on 60c multi	.25	.25

Rubén Dario and Birthplace — AP84

Portrait and: 10c, Monument, Managua. 20c, Leon Cathedral, site of Dario's tomb. 40c, Centaurs. 75c, Swans. 1cor, Roman triumphal march. 2cor, St. Francis and the Wolf. 5cor, "Faith" defeating "Death."

1967, Jan. 18 Litho. *Perf. 13*

No.	Type	Description	Unused	Used
C598	AP84	5c lt brn, tan & blk	.25	.25
C599	AP84	10c org, pale org & blk	.25	.25
C600	AP84	20c vio, lt bl & blk	.25	.25
C601	AP84	40c grn, dk grn & blk	.25	.25
a.		Souv. sheet of 4, #C598-C601	1.00	1.00
C602	AP84	75c ultra, pale bl & blk	.25	.25
C603	AP84	1cor red, pale red & blk	.25	.25
C604	AP84	2cor rose pink, car & blk	.30	.30
C605	AP84	5cor dp ultra, vio bl, & blk	.75	.65
a.		Souv. sheet of 4, #C602-C605	3.50	3.50
		Nos. C598-C605 (8)	2.55	2.45

Rubén Dario (pen name of Felix Rubén Garcia Sarmiento, 1867-1916), poet, newspaper correspondent and diplomat.

Sheets were issued perf. and imperf.

Megalura Peleus AP85

Designs: Various butterflies. 5c, 10c, 30c, 35c, 50c and 1cor are vertical.

1967, Apr. 20 Litho. *Perf. 14*

No.	Type	Description	Unused	Used
C606	AP85	5c multi	.30	.25
C607	AP85	10c multi	.35	.25
C608	AP85	15c multi	.35	.25
C609	AP85	20c multi	.35	.25
C610	AP85	25c multi	.35	.25
C611	AP85	30c multi	.45	.25
C612	AP85	35c multi	.45	.25
C613	AP85	40c multi	.45	.25
C614	AP85	50c multi	.55	.25
C615	AP85	60c multi	.55	.25
C616	AP85	1cor multi	.70	.40
C617	AP85	2cor multi	1.10	.75
		Nos. C606-C617 (12)	5.95	3.65

Com. James McDivitt and Maj. Edward H. White AP86

Gemini 4 Space Flight: 10c, 40c, Rocket launching and astronauts. 15c, 75c, Edward H. White walking in space. 20c, 1cor, Recovery of capsule.

1967, Sept. 20 Litho. *Perf. 13*

No.	Type	Description	Unused	Used
C618	AP86	5c red & multi	.25	.25
C619	AP86	10c org & multi	.25	.25
C620	AP86	15c multi	.25	.25
C621	AP86	20c multi	.25	.25
C622	AP86	35c ol & multi	.25	.25
C623	AP86	40c ultra & multi	.25	.25
C624	AP86	75c brn & multi	.25	.25
C625	AP86	1cor multi	.25	.25
		Nos. C618-C625 (8)	2.00	2.00

Saquanjoche, National Flower of Nicaragua — AP87

National Flowers: No. C626, White nun orchid, Guatemala. No. C627, Rose, Honduras. No. C629, Maquilishuat, Salvador. No. C630, Purple guaria orchid, Costa Rica.

1967, Nov. 22 Litho. *Perf. 13½*

No.	Type	Description	Unused	Used
C626	AP87	40c multi	.25	.25
C627	AP87	40c multi	.25	.25
C628	AP87	40c multi	.25	.25
C629	AP87	40c multi	.25	.25
C630	AP87	40c multi	.25	.25
a.		Strip of 5, #C626-C630	.75	.50

5th anniversary of the General Treaty for Central American Economic Integration.

Presidents of Nicaragua and Mexico — AP88

Designs: 40c Pres. Gustavo Diáz Ordaz of Mexico and Pres. René Schick of Nicaragua signing statement, horiz. 1cor, President Diáz.

1968, Feb. 28 Litho. *Perf. 12½*

No.	Type	Description	Unused	Used
C631	AP88	20c black	.25	.25
C632	AP88	40c slate grn	.25	.25
C633	AP88	1cor dp brn	.25	.25
		Nos. C631-C633 (3)	.75	.75

Issued to commemorate the visit of the President of Mexico, Gustavo Diáz Ordaz.

Nos. C479, C527, C242, C440 and C434 Surcharged "Resello" and New Value in Black, Red (#C637) or Yellow (#C638)

1968, May Litho.; Engr.

No.	Type	Description	Unused	Used
C634	AP66	5c on 6c multi	.25	.25
C635	AP75	5c on 6c multi	.25	.25
C636	AP20	5c on 8c blk brn	.25	.25
C637	A84	1cor on 1.05cor emer & blk	.25	.25
C638	A83	1cor on 1.50cor dk bl & yel	.25	.25
		Nos. C634-C638 (5)	1.25	1.25

Mangos — AP89

1968, May 15 Litho. *Perf. 14*

No.	Type	Description	Unused	Used
C639	AP89	5c shown	.25	.25
C640	AP89	10c Pineapples	.25	.25
C641	AP89	15c Orange	.25	.25
C642	AP89	20c Papaya	.25	.25
C643	AP89	30c Bananas	.25	.25
C644	AP89	35c Avocado	.25	.25
C645	AP89	50c Watermelon	.25	.25
C646	AP89	75c Cashews	.25	.25
C647	AP89	1cor Sapodilla	.40	.25
C648	AP89	2cor Cacao	.75	.45
		Nos. C639-C648 (10)	3.15	2.70

The Last Judgment, by Michelangelo — AP90

Paintings: 10c, The Crucifixion, by Fra Angelo, horiz. 35c, Madonna with Child and St. John, by Raphael. 2cor, The Disrobing of Christ, by El Greco. 3cor, The Immaculate Conception, by Murillo. 5cor, Christ of St. John of the Cross, by Salvador Dali.

1968, July 22 Litho. *Perf. 12½*

No.	Type	Description	Unused	Used
C649	AP90	10c gold & multi	.25	.25
C650	AP90	15c gold & multi	.25	.25
C651	AP90	35c gold & multi	.25	.25
C652	AP90	2cor gold & multi	.45	.40
C653	AP90	3cor gold & multi	.65	.55
		Nos. C649-C653 (5)	1.85	1.70

Miniature Sheet

No.	Type	Description	Unused	Used
C654	AP90	5cor gold & multi	2.75	2.75

Nos. C649-C652 Overprinted: "Visita de S.S. Paulo VI C.E. de Bogota 1968"

1968, Oct. 25 Litho. *Perf. 12½*

No.	Type	Description	Unused	Used
C655	AP90	10c gold & multi	.25	.25
C656	AP90	15c gold & multi	.25	.25
C657	AP90	35c gold & multi	.25	.25
C658	AP90	2cor gold & multi	.50	.40
		Nos. C655-C658 (4)	1.25	1.15

Visit of Pope Paul VI to Bogota, Colombia, Aug. 22-24. The overprint has 3 lines on the 10c stamp and 5 lines on others.

Basketball AP91

Sports: 15c, Fencing, horiz. 20c, Diving. 35c, Running. 50c, Hurdling, horiz. 75c, Weight lifting. 1cor, Boxing, horiz. 2cor, Soccer.

1968, Nov. 28 Litho. *Perf. 14*

No.	Type	Description	Unused	Used
C659	AP91	10c multi	.25	.25
C660	AP91	15c org red, blk & gray	.25	.25
C661	AP91	20c multi	.25	.25
C662	AP91	35c multi	.25	.25
C663	AP91	50c multi	.25	.25
C664	AP91	75c multi	.25	.25
C665	AP91	1cor yel & multi	.30	.30
C666	AP91	2cor gray & multi	.80	.80
a.		Souv. sheet of 4, #C663-C666	1.75	1.75
		Nos. C659-C666 (8)	2.60	2.60

19th Olympic Games, Mexico City, 10/12-27.

Cichlasoma Citrinellum — AP92

Fish: 15c, Cichlasoma nicaraguensis. 20c, Carp. 30c, Gar (lepisosteus tropicus). 35c, Swordfish. 50c, Phylipnus dormitor, vert. 75c, Tarpon atlanticus, vert. 1cor, Eulamia nicaraguensis, vert. 2cor, Sailfish, vert. 3cor, Sawfish, vert.

Perf. 13½x13, 13x13½

1969, Mar. 12 **Litho.**

C667	AP92	10c vio bl & multi	.35	.25
C668	AP92	15c org & multi	.35	.25
C669	AP92	20c grn & multi	.35	.25
C670	AP92	30c pur & multi	.35	.25
C671	AP92	35c yel & multi	.35	.25
C672	AP92	50c brn & multi	.35	.25
C673	AP92	75c ultra & multi	.35	.25
C674	AP92	1cor org & multi	.35	.25
C675	AP92	2cor dk bl & multi	.60	.25
C676	AP92	3cor multi	.90	.40
a.		Min. sheet of 4, #C673-C676	4.25	4.25
		Nos. C667-C676 (10)	4.30	2.65

Nos. C544, C549, C567 and C439 Srchd. in Black or Red

1969, Mar. **Litho.** ***Perf. 12, 13½x13***

C677	AP76	10c on 25c multi	.25	.25
C678	AP77	10c on 25c multi	.25	.25
C679	AP79	15c on 25c multi	.25	.25

Engr.

C680	A84	50c on 70c (R)	.25	.25
		Nos. C677-C680 (4)	1.00	1.00

Size of 50c surcharge: 11½x9mm.

View, Exhibition Tower and Emblem — AP93

1969, May 30 **Litho.** ***Perf. 13½x13***

C681	AP93	30c dk vio bl & red	.25	.25
C682	AP93	35c blk & red	.25	.25
C683	AP93	75c car rose & vio bl	.25	.25
C684	AP93	1cor dp plum & blk	.25	.25
C685	AP93	2cor dk brn & blk	.45	.35
a.		Souv. sheet of 4, #C681-C682, C684-C685	1.25	1.25
		Nos. C681-C685 (5)	1.45	1.35

HEMISFAIR 1968 Exhibition.

Nos. C410, C482, C567-C569, C399, C465, C546 Srchd. in Black or Red

1969 **Litho.** ***Perfs. as before***

C686	A80	10c on 30c multi	.55	.25
C687	AP66	10c on 30c bl & blk (R)	.55	.25
C688	AP79	10c on 25c multi	.55	.25
C689	AP79	10c on 30c multi	.55	.25
C690	AP79	15c on 35c multi (R)	.55	.25
C691	A79	20c on 30c multi	.55	.25
C692	AP64	20c on 30c multi	.55	.25
C693	AP76	20c on 35c multi	.55	.25
		Nos. C686-C693 (8)	4.40	2.00

Products of Nicaragua AP94

5c, Minerals (miner). 10c, Fishing. 15c, Bananas. 20c, Timber (truck). 35c, Coffee. 40c, Sugar cane. 60c, Cotton. 75c, Rice and corn. 1cor, Tobacco. 2cor, Meat.

1969, Sept. 22 **Litho.** ***Perf. 13x13½***

C694	AP94	5c gold & multi	.25	.25
C695	AP94	10c gold & multi	.25	.25
C696	AP94	15c gold & multi	.25	.25
C697	AP94	20c gold & multi	.25	.25
C698	AP94	35c gold & multi	.25	.25
C699	AP94	40c gold & multi	.25	.25
C700	AP94	60c gold & multi	.25	.25
C701	AP94	75c gold & multi	.25	.25
C702	AP94	1cor gold & multi	.25	.25
C703	AP94	2cor gold & multi	.40	.25
		Nos. C694-C703 (10)	2.65	2.50

Woman Carrying Jar, Conference Emblem — AP95

1970, Feb. 26 **Litho.** ***Perf. 13½x14***

C704	AP95	10c multi	.25	.25
C705	AP95	15c grn & multi	.25	.25
C706	AP95	20c ultra & multi	.25	.25
C707	AP95	35c multi	.25	.25
C708	AP95	50c multi	.25	.25
C709	AP95	75c multi	.25	.25
C710	AP95	1cor lil & multi	.45	.30
C711	AP95	2cor multi	.85	.50
		Nos. C704-C711 (8)	2.80	2.30

8th Inter-American Conf. on Savings & Loans.

Soccer Type of Regular Issue and

Flags of Participating Nations, World Cup, 1970 — AP96

Soccer Players: 20c, Djalma Santos, Brazil. 80c, Billy Wright, England. 4cor, Jozef Bozsik, Hungary. 5cor, Bobby Charlton, England.

1970, May 11 **Litho.** ***Perf. 13½***

C712	A87	20c multi	.25	.25
C713	A87	80c multi	.30	.25
C714	AP96	1cor multi	.40	.25
C715	A87	4cor multi	1.40	.90
C716	A87	5cor multi	1.50	1.25
		Nos. C712-C716 (5)	3.85	2.90

Issued to honor the winners of the 1970 poll for the International Soccer Hall of Fame. No. C714 also publicizes the 9th World Soccer Championships for the Jules Rimet Cup, Mexico City, May 30-June 21, 1970.

Names of players and their achievements printed in black on back of stamps.

For overprint and surcharges see Nos. C786-788.

EXPO Emblem, Mt. Fuji and Torii — AP97

1970, July 5 **Litho.** ***Perf. 13½x14***

C717	AP97	25c multi	.25	.25
C718	AP97	30c multi	.25	.25
C719	AP97	35c multi	.25	.25
C720	AP97	75c multi	.25	.25
C721	AP97	1.50cor multi	.40	.30
C722	AP97	3cor multi	.75	.75
a.		Souv. sheet of 3, #C720-C722, imperf.	1.00	1.00
		Nos. C717-C722 (6)	2.15	2.05

EXPO '70 International Exhibition, Osaka, Japan, Mar. 15-Sept. 13, 1970.

Moon Landing, Apollo 11 Emblem and Nicaragua Flag AP98

Apollo 11 Emblem, Nicaragua Flag and: 40c, 75c, Moon surface and landing capsule. 60c, 1cor, Astronaut planting US flag.

1970, Aug. 12 **Litho.** ***Perf. 14***

C723	AP98	35c multi	.25	.25
C724	AP98	40c multi	.25	.25
C725	AP98	60c pink & multi	.25	.25
C726	AP98	75c yel & multi	.25	.25
C727	AP98	1cor vio & multi	.40	.25
C728	AP98	2cor org & multi	.65	.40
		Nos. C723-C728 (6)	2.05	1.65

Man's 1st landing on the moon, July 20, 1969. See note after US No. C76.

Franklin D. Roosevelt — AP99

Roosevelt Portraits: 15c, 1cor, as stamp collector. 20c, 50c, 2cor, Full face.

1970, Oct. 12

C729	AP99	10c blk & bluish blk	.25	.25
C730	AP99	15c blk & brn vio	.25	.25
C731	AP99	20c blk & ol grn	.25	.25
C732	AP99	35c blk & brn vio	.25	.25
C733	AP99	50c brown	.25	.25
C734	AP99	75c blue	.25	.25
C735	AP99	1cor rose red	.25	.25
C736	AP99	2cor black	.40	.25
		Nos. C729-C736 (8)	2.15	2.00

Franklin Delano Roosevelt (1882-1945).

Christmas 1970 — AP100

Paintings: Nos. C737, C742, Annunciation, by Matthias Grunewald. Nos. C738, C743, Nativity, by El Greco. Nos. C739, C744, Adoration of the Magi, by Albrecht Dürer. Nos. C740, C745, Virgin and Child, by J. van Hemessen. Nos. C741, C746, Holy Shepherd, Portuguese School, 16th century.

1970, Dec. 1 **Litho.** ***Perf. 14***

C737	AP100	10c multi	.25	.25
C738	AP100	10c multi	.25	.25
C739	AP100	10c multi	.25	.25
C740	AP100	10c multi	.25	.25
C741	AP100	10c multi	.25	.25
C742	AP100	15c multi	.25	.25
C743	AP100	20c multi	.25	.25
C744	AP100	35c multi	.25	.25
C745	AP100	75c multi	.25	.25
C746	AP100	1cor multi	.25	.25
		Nos. C737-C746 (10)	2.50	2.50

Nos. C737-C741 printed se-tenant.

Issues of 1947-67 Surcharged

1971, Mar.

C747	A83	10c on 1.05cor, #C433	.30	.30
C748	AP64	10c on 1.05cor, #C471	.30	.30
C749	AP66	10c on 1.05cor, #C485	.30	.30
C750	AP42	15c on 1.50cor, #C292	.40	.40
C751	AP53	15c on 1.50cor, #C369	.40	.40
C752	A83	15c on 1.50cor, #C434	.40	.40
C753	A84	15c on 1.50cor, #C441	.40	.40
C754	A75	20c on 85c, #C385	.50	.50
C755	A81	20c on 85c, #C418	.50	.50
C756	A81	25c on 90c, #C419	.70	.70
C757	AP48	30c on 1.10cor, #C337	.85	.85
C758	AP44	40c on 1.10cor, #C314	1.10	1.10
C759	AP65	40c on 1.50cor, #C472	1.10	1.10
C760	AP80	1cor on 1.10cor, #C576	2.75	2.75
		Nos. C747-C760 (14)	10.00	10.00

The arrangement of the surcharge differs on each stamp.

Mathematics Type of Regular Issue

Symbolic Designs of Scientific Formulae: 25c, Napier's law (logarithms). 30c, Pythagorean theorem (length of sides of right-angled triangle). 40c, Boltzman's equation (movement of gases). 1cor, Broglie's law (motion of particles of matter). 2cor, Archimedes' principle (displacement of mass).

1971, May 15 **Litho.** ***Perf. 13½***

C761	A88	25c lt bl & multi	.25	.25
C762	A88	30c lt bl & multi	.30	.25
C763	A88	40c lt bl & multi	.45	.25
C764	A88	1cor lt bl & multi	1.10	.35
C765	A88	2cor lt bl & multi	1.90	.75
		Nos. C761-C765 (5)	4.00	1.85

On the back of each stamp is a descriptive paragraph.

Montezuma Oropendola AP101

Birds: 15c, Turquoise-browed motmot. 20c, Magpie-jay. 25c, Scissor-tailed flycatchers. 30c, Spot-breasted oriole, horiz. 35c, Rufous-naped wren. 40c, Great kiskadee. 75c, Red-legged honeycreeper, horiz. 1cor, Great-tailed grackle, horiz. 2cor, Belted kingfisher.

1971, Oct. 15 **Litho.** ***Perf. 14***

C766	AP101	10c multi	.40	.25
C767	AP101	15c multi	.40	.25
C768	AP101	20c gray & multi	.40	.25
C769	AP101	25c multi	.40	.25
C770	AP101	30c multi	.40	.25
C771	AP101	35c multi	.45	.25
C772	AP101	40c multi	.45	.25
C773	AP101	75c yel & multi	.55	.25
C774	AP101	1cor org & multi	.70	.25
C775	AP101	2cor org & multi	1.20	.30
		Nos. C766-C775 (10)	5.35	2.55

Ten Commandments Type of Regular Issue

Designs: 1cor, Bathsheba at her Bath, by Rembrandt (IX). 2cor, Naboth's Vineyard, by James Smetham (X).

1971, Nov. 1 ***Perf. 11***

C776	A90	1cor ocher & multi	1.00	.45
C777	A90	2cor ocher & multi	1.60	.80

Descriptive inscriptions printed in gray on back of stamps.

U Thant, Anastasio Somoza, UN Emblem AP102

1972, Feb. 15 ***Perf. 14x13½***

C778 AP102 10c pink & mar .25 .25
C779 AP102 15c green .25 .25
C780 AP102 20c blue .25 .25
C781 AP102 25c rose claret .25 .25
C782 AP102 30c org & brn .25 .25
C783 AP102 40c gray & sl grn .25 .25
C784 AP102 1cor ol grn .25 .25
C785 AP102 2cor brown .45 .25
Nos. C778-C785 (8) 2.20 2.00

25th anniv. of the United Nations (in 1970).

Nos. C713, C715, C716 Surcharged or Overprinted Like Nos. 899-900

1972, Mar. 20 **Litho.** ***Perf. 13½***

C786 A87 20c on 80c multi .30 .25
C787 A87 60c on 4cor multi .30 .25
C788 A87 5cor multi 1.25 1.00
Nos. C786-C788 (3) 1.85 1.50

20th Olympic Games, Munich, 8/26-9/11.

Ceramic Figure, Map of Nicaragua — AP103

Pre-Columbian ceramics (700-1200 A.D.) found at sites indicated on map of Nicaragua.

1972, Sept. 16 **Litho.** ***Perf. 14x13½***

C789 AP103 10c blue & multi .25 .25
C790 AP103 15c blue & multi .25 .25
C791 AP103 20c blue & multi .25 .25
C792 AP103 25c blue & multi .25 .25
C793 AP103 30c blue & multi .25 .25
C794 AP103 35c blue & multi .25 .25
C795 AP103 40c blue & multi .25 .25
C796 AP103 50c blue & multi .25 .25
C797 AP103 60c blue & multi .25 .25
C798 AP103 80c blue & multi .25 .25
C799 AP103 1cor blue & multi .25 .25
C800 AP103 2cor blue & multi .40 .25
Nos. C789-C800 (12) 3.15 3.00

Lord Peter Wimsey, by Dorothy L. Sayers AP104

Designs (Book and): 10c, Philip Marlowe, by Raymond Chandler. 15c, Sam Spade, by Dashiell Hammett. 20c, Perry Mason, by Erle S. Gardner. 25c, Nero Wolfe, by Rex Stout. 35c, Auguste Dupin, by Edgar Allan Poe. 40c, Ellery Queen, by Frederick Dannay and Manfred B. Lee. 50c, Father Brown, by G. K. Chesterton. 60c, Charlie Chan, by Earl Derr Biggers. 80c, Inspector Maigret, by Georges Simenon. 1cor, Hercule Poirot, by Agatha Christie. 2cor, Sherlock Holmes, by A. Conan Doyle.

1972, Nov. 13 **Litho.** ***Perf. 14x13½***

C801 AP104 5c blue & multi .30 .25
C802 AP104 10c blue & multi .30 .25
C803 AP104 15c blue & multi .30 .25
C804 AP104 20c blue & multi .30 .25
C805 AP104 25c blue & multi .30 .25
C806 AP104 35c blue & multi .40 .25
C807 AP104 40c blue & multi .40 .25
C808 AP104 50c blue & multi .50 .30
C809 AP104 60c blue & multi .70 .40
C810 AP104 80c blue & multi .85 .50
C811 AP104 1cor blue & multi 1.10 .65
C812 AP104 2cor blue & multi 2.25 1.25
Nos. C801-C812 (12) 7.70 4.85

50th anniv. of INTERPOL, intl. police organization. Designs show famous fictional detectives. Inscriptions on back, printed on top of gum, give thumbnail sketch of character and author.

Shepherds Following Star AP105

Legend of the Christmas Rose: 15c, Adoration of the kings and shepherds. 20c, Shepherd girl alone crying. 35c, Angel appears to girl. 40c, Christmas rose (Helleborus niger). 60c, Girl thanks angel. 80c, Girl and Holy Family. 1cor, Girl presents rose to Christ Child. 2cor, Adoration.

1972, Dec. 20

C813 AP105 10c multi .25 .25
C814 AP105 15c multi .25 .25
C815 AP105 20c multi .25 .25
C816 AP105 35c multi .25 .25
C817 AP105 40c multi .25 .25
C818 AP105 60c multi .25 .25
C819 AP105 80c multi .25 .25
C820 AP105 1cor multi .25 .25
C821 AP105 2cor multi .40 .30
a. Souv. sheet of 9, #C813-C821 1.25 1.25
Nos. C813-C821 (9) 2.40 2.30

Christmas 1972.

No. C821a exists with red marginal overprint, "TERREMOTO DESASTRE," for the Managua earthquake of Dec. 22-23, 1972. It was sold abroad, starting in Jan. 1973.

Sir Walter Raleigh, Patent to Settle New World — AP106

Events and Quotations from Contemporary Illustrations: 15c, Mayflower Compact, 1620. 20c, Acquittal of Peter Zenger, 1735, vert. 25c, William Pitt, 1766, vert. 30c, British revenue stamp for use in America No. RM31, vert. 35c, "Join or Die" serpent, 1768. 40c, Boston Massacre and State House, 1770, vert. 50c, Boston Tea Party and 3p coin, 1774. 60c, Patrick Henry, 1775, vert. 75c, Battle scene ("Our cause is just, our union is perfect," 1775). 80c, Declaration of Independence, 1776. 1cor, Liberty Bell, Philadelphia. 2cor, Seal of US, 1782, vert.

1973, Feb. 22 **Photo.** ***Perf. 13½***

C822 AP106 10c olive & multi .25 .25
C823 AP106 15c olive & multi .25 .25
C824 AP106 20c olive & multi .25 .25
C825 AP106 25c olive & multi .25 .25
C826 AP106 30c olive & multi .25 .25
C827 AP106 35c ol, gold & blk .35 .25
C828 AP106 40c olive & multi .35 .25
C829 AP106 50c olive & multi .35 .35
C830 AP106 60c olive & multi .40 .35
C831 AP106 75c olive & multi .50 .40
C832 AP106 80c olive & multi .50 .40
C833 AP106 1cor olive & multi .80 .50
C834 AP106 2cor olive & multi 1.50 1.00
Nos. C822-C834 (13) 6.00 4.75

Inscriptions on back, printed on top of gum, give brief description of subject and event.

Baseball, Player and Map of Nicaragua AP107

1973, May 25 **Litho.** ***Perf. 13½x14***

C835 AP107 15c lil & multi .25 .25
C836 AP107 20c multi .25 .25
C837 AP107 40c multi .25 .25
C838 AP107 10cor multi 1.75 1.50
a. Souvenir sheet of 4 10.00 10.00
Nos. C835-C838 (4) 2.50 2.25

20th International Baseball Championships, Managua, Nov. 15-Dec. 5, 1972. No. C838a contains 4 stamps similar to Nos. C835-C838 with changed background colors (15c, olive; 20c, gray; 40c, lt. green; 10cor, lilac), and 5 labels.

Fashion Type of 1973

10c, Lourdes Nicaragua. 15c, Halston, New York. 20c, Pino Lancetti, Rome. 35c, Madame Ges, Paris. 40c, Irene Galitzine, Rome. 80c, Pedro Rodriguez, Barcelona.

1973, July 26 **Litho.** ***Perf. 13½***

C839 A91 10c multicolored .25 .25
C840 A91 15c multicolored .25 .25
C841 A91 20c multicolored .25 .25
C842 A91 35c multicolored .25 .25
C843 A91 40c multicolored .25 .25
C844 A91 80c multicolored .25 .25
a. Souv. sheet of 9, #909-911, C839-C844, perf. 11 + 3 labels *12.00* *12.00*
Nos. C839-C844 (6) 1.50 1.50

Inscriptions on back printed on top of gum give description of gown in Spanish and English.

Type of Air Post Semi-Postal Issue

Design: 2cor, Pediatric surgery.

1973, Sept. 25

C845 SPAP1 2cor multi .40 .35
Nos. C845,CB1-CB11 (12) 3.20 3.10

Planned Children's Hospital. Inscription on back, printed on top of gum gives brief description of subject shown.

Christmas Type

1cor, Virginia O'Hanlon writing letter, father. 2cor, Letter. 4cor, Virginia, father reading letter.

1973, Nov. 15 **Litho.** ***Perf. 15***

C846 A92 1cor multicolored .30 .30
C847 A92 2cor multicolored .60 .60
C848 A92 4cor multicolored 1.10 1.10
a. Souvenir sheet of 3, #C846-C848, perf. 14½ 4.00 4.00
Nos. C846-C848 (3) 2.00 2.00

Churchill Type

#C851, Silhouette, Parliament. #C852, Silhouette, #10 Downing St. 5cor, Showing "V" sign. 6cor, "Bulldog" Churchill protecting England.

1974, Apr. 30 ***Perf. 14½***

C849 A93 5cor multicolored 1.40 1.40
C850 A93 6cor multicolored 1.75 1.75

Souvenir Sheets

Perf. 15

C851 A93 4cor blk, org & bl 1.40 1.40
C852 A93 4cor blk, org, & grn 1.40 1.40

Nos. C851-C852 contain one 28x42mm stamp.

World Cup Type

Scenes from previous World Cup Championships with flags and scores of finalists.

1974, May 8 ***Perf. 14½***

C853 A94 10cor Flags of participants 2.75 2.75

Souvenir Sheets

C853A A94 4cor like No. 928 1.10 1.10
C853B A94 5cor like No. 930 1.40 1.40

For overprint see No. C856.

Flower Type of 1974

Wild Flowers and Cacti: 1 cor, Centrosema. 3 cor, Night-blooming cereus.

1974, June 11 **Litho.** ***Perf. 14***

C854 A95 1cor green & multi .30 .25
C855 A95 3cor green & multi .75 .55

Nicaraguan Stamps Type

1974, July 10 ***Perf. 14½***

C855A A96 40c #835 .25 .25
C855B A96 3cor #C313, horiz. .90 .90
C855C A96 5cor #734 1.40 1.40
Nos. C855A-C855C (3) 2.55 2.55

Souvenir Sheet

Imperf

C855D Sheet of 3 2.25
e. A96 1cor #665 .30
f. A96 2cor #C110, horiz. .55
g. A96 4cor Globe, stars 1.40

UPU, Cent.

No. C853 Ovptd.

1974, July 12

C856 A94 10cor Flags 2.75 2.25

Animal Type of 1974

3cor, Colorado deer. 5cor, Jaguar.

1974, Sept. 10 **Litho.** ***Perf. 14½***

C857 A97 3cor multi .65 .55
C858 A97 5cor multi 1.00 .90

Christmas Type of 1974

Works of Michelangelo: 40c, Madonna of the Stairs. 80c, Pitti Madonna. 2cor, Pietà. 5cor, Self-portrait.

1974, Dec. 15

C859 A98 40c multi .25 .25
C860 A98 80c multi .25 .25
C861 A98 2cor multi .30 .25
C862 A98 5cor multi .70 .65
Nos. C859-C862 (4) 1.50 1.40

An imperf. souvenir sheet exists containing 2cor and 5cor stamps. Value, $3.50.

Opera Type of 1975

Opera Singers and Scores: 25c, Rosa Ponselle, Norma. 35c, Giuseppe de Luca, Rigoletto. 40c, Joan Sutherland, La Figlia del Reggimento. 50c, Ezio Pinza, Don Giovanni. 60c, Kirsten Flagstad, Tristan and Isolde. 80c, Maria Callas, Tosca. 2cor, Fyodor Chaliapin, Boris Godunov. 5cor, Enrico Caruso, La Juive.

1975, Jan. 22 ***Perf. 14x13½***

C863 A99 25c grn & multi .30 .25
C864 A99 35c multi .30 .25
C865 A99 40c multi .30 .25
C866 A99 50c org & multi .30 .25
C867 A99 60c rose & multi .30 .25
C868 A99 80c lake & multi .40 .25
C869 A99 2cor sep & multi .80 .25
C870 A99 5cor multi 2.00 .65
a. Souvenir sheet of 3 4.00 4.00
Nos. C863-C870 (8) 4.70 2.40

No. C870a contains one each of Nos. C869-C870 and a 1cor with design and colors of No. C868. Exists imperf.

Easter Type of 1975

Stations of the Cross: 40c, Jesus stripped of his clothes. 50c, Jesus nailed to the Cross. 80c, Jesus dies on the Cross. 1cor, Descent from the Cross. 5cor, Jesus laid in the tomb.

1975, Mar. 20 ***Perf. 14½***

C871 A100 40c ultra & multi .25 .25
C872 A100 50c ultra & multi .25 .25
C873 A100 80c ultra & multi .25 .25
C874 A100 1cor ultra & multi .25 .25
C875 A100 5cor ultra & multi .90 .80
Nos. C871-C875 (5) 1.90 1.80

American Bicentennial Type of 1975

Designs: 40c, Washington's Farewell, 1783. 50c, Washington Addressing Continental Congress by J. B. Stearns. 2cor, Washington Arriving for Inauguration. 5cor, Statue of Liberty and flags of 1776 and 1976. 40c, 50c, 2cor, horiz.

1975, Apr. 16 ***Perf. 14***

C876 A101 40c tan & multi .25 .25
C877 A101 50c tan & multi .30 .25
C878 A101 2cor tan & multi .90 .70
C879 A101 5cor tan & multi 2.00 1.90
Nos. C876-C879 (4) 3.45 3.10

Perf. and imperf. 7cor souv. sheets exist. Value, $3.50.

Nordjamb 75 Type of 1975

Designs (Scout and Nordjamb Emblems and): 35c, Camp. 40c, Scout musicians. 1cor, Campfire. 10cor, Lord Baden-Powell.

1975, Aug. 15 ***Perf. 14½***

C880 A102 35c multi .25 .25
C881 A102 40c multi .25 .25
C882 A102 1cor multi .30 .25
C883 A102 10cor multi 1.75 1.25
Nos. C880-C883 (4) 2.55 2.00

Two airmail souvenir sheets of 2 exist. One, perf., contains 2cor and 3cor with designs of Nos. 992 and 990. The other, imperf., contains 2cor and 3cor with designs of Nos. 993 and C882. Size: 125x101mm. Value, pair $18.

Pres. Somoza Type of 1975

1975, Sept. 10 *Perf. 14*
C884 A103 1cor vio & multi .25 .25
C885 A103 10cor bl & multi 2.00 1.75
C886 A103 20cor multi 4.00 3.00
Nos. C884-C886 (3) 6.25 5.00

Choir Type of 1975

Famous Choirs: 50c, Montserrat Abbey. 1cor, St. Florian Choir Boys. 2cor, Choir Boys of the Wooden Cross, vert. 5cor, Boys and Pope Paul VI (Pueri Cantores International Federation).

1975, Nov. 15 *Perf. 14½*
C887 A104 50c sil & multi .25 .25
C888 A104 1cor sil & multi .25 .25
C889 A104 2cor sil & multi .35 .30
C890 A104 5cor sil & multi 1.40 .85
Nos. C887-C890 (4) 2.25 1.65

A 10cor imperf. souvenir sheet exists (Oberndorf Memorial Chapel Choir and score of "Holy Night-Silent Night"). Value, $12.50.

Chess Type of 1976

Designs: 40c, The Chess Players, by Thomas Eakins. 2cor, Bobby Fischer and Boris Spasski in Reykjavik, 1972. 5cor, Shakespeare and Ben Johnson Playing Chess, by Karel van Mander.

1976, Jan. 8 *Perf. 14½*
C891 A105 40c multi .25 .25
C892 A105 2cor vio & multi .75 .55
C893 A105 5cor multi 1.50 1.25
Nos. C891-C893 (3) 2.50 2.05

A souvenir sheet contains one each of Nos. C892-C893, perf. and imperf. Size: 143x67mm. Value, pair $10.

Olympic Winner Type 1976

Winners, Rowing and Sculling Events: 55c, USSR, 1956, 1960, 1964, vert. 70c, New Zealand, 1972, vert. 90c, New Zealand, 1968. 10cor, Women's rowing crew, US, 1976, vert. 20cor, US, 1956.

1976, Sept. 7 Litho. *Perf. 14*
C902 A107 55c bl & multi .25 .25
C903 A107 70c bl & multi .25 .25
C904 A107 90c bl & multi .25 .25
C905 A107 20cor bl & multi 4.50 3.75
Nos. C902-C905 (4) 5.25 4.50

Souvenir Sheet

C906 A107 10cor multi 3.00 2.00

No. C906 for the 1st participation of women in Olympic rowing events, size of stamp: 37x50mm.

The overprint "Republica Democratica Alemana Vencedor en 1976" was applied in 1976 to No. C905 in black in 3 lines and to the margin of No. C906 in gold in 2 lines.

Bicentennial Type of 1976

American Bicentennial Emblem and: #C907, Philadelphia, 1776. #C908, Washington, 1976. #C909, John Paul Jones' ships. #C910, Atomic submarine. #C911, Wagon train. #C912, Diesel train.

1976, May 25 Litho. *Perf. 13½*
C907 A108 80c multi .25 .25
C908 A108 80c multi .25 .25
a. Pair, #C907-C908 .35 .30
C909 A108 2.75cor multi .50 .40
C910 A108 2.75cor multi .50 .40
a. Pair, #C909-C910 1.00 .80
C911 A108 4cor multi .80 .50
C912 A108 4cor multi .80 .50
a. Pair, #C911-C912 1.75 1.00
Nos. C907-C912 (6) 3.10 2.30

A souvenir sheet contains two 10cor stamps showing George Washington and Gerald R. Ford with their families. Size: 140x111mm. Value, $5.

Rare Stamps Type of 1976

Rare Stamps: 40c, Hawaii #1. 1cor, Great Britain #1. 2cor, British Guiana #13. 5cor, Honduras #C12. 10cor, Newfoundland #C1.

1976, Dec. *Perf. 14*
C913 A109 40c multi .25 .25
C914 A109 1cor multi .25 .25
C915 A109 2cor multi .30 .25
C916 A109 5cor multi .70 .65
C917 A109 10cor multi 1.40 1.25
Nos. C913-C917 (5) 2.90 2.65

Inscriptions on back printed on top of gum give description of illustrated stamp. A 4cor imperf. souvenir sheet shows 1881 Great Britain-Nicaragua combination cover. Size: 140x101mm. Value, $2.

Olga Nuñez de Saballos — AP108

Designs: 1cor, Josefa Toledo de Aguerri. 10cor, Hope Portocarrero de Somoza.

1977, Feb. Litho. *Perf. 13½*
C918 AP108 35c multi .25 .25
C919 AP108 1cor red & multi .25 .25
C920 AP108 10cor multi 2.00 1.75
Nos. C918-C920 (3) 2.50 2.25

Famous Nicaraguan women and for International Women's Year (in 1975).

Zeppelin Type of 1977

Designs: 35c, Ville de Paris airship. 70c, Zeppelin "Schwaben." 3cor, Zeppelin in flight. 10cor, Vickers "Mayfly" before take-off. 20cor, Zeppelin with leadlines extended.

1977, Oct. 31 Litho. *Perf. 14½*
C921 A110 35c multi .25 .25
C922 A110 70c multi .25 .25
C923 A110 3cor multi .65 .50
C924 A110 10cor multi 2.50 1.75
Nos. C921-C924 (4) 3.65 2.75

Souvenir Sheet

C925 A110 20cor multi 5.00 2.75

Lindbergh Type of 1977

Designs: 55c, Lindbergh's plane approaching Nicaraguan airfield, 1928. 80c, Spirit of St. Louis and map of New York-Paris route. 2cor, Plane flying off Nicaragua's Pacific Coast. 10cor, Lindbergh flying past Momotombo Volcano on way to Managua. 20cor, Spirit of St. Louis.

1977, Nov. 30
C926 A111 55c multi .25 .25
C927 A111 80c multi .25 .25
C928 A111 2cor multi .40 .30
C929 A111 10cor multi 2.00 1.60
Nos. C926-C929 (4) 2.90 2.40

Souvenir Sheet

C930 A111 20cor multi 5.00 3.50

Christmas Type of 1977
Souvenir Sheet

Design: 20cor, Finale of Nutcracker Suite.

1977, Dec. 12
C931 A112 20cor multi 4.50 4.50

Painting Type of 1978

Rubens Paintings: 5cor, Hippopotamus and Crocodile Hunt. 100cor, Duke de Lerma on Horseback. 20cor, Self-portrait.

1978, Jan. 11 Litho. *Perf. 14½*
C932 A113 5cor multi 1.10 .85
C933 A113 10cor multi 2.10 1.60

Souvenir Sheet

C934 A113 20cor multi 5.75 4.00

Peter Paul Rubens (1577-1640), 400th birth anniversary.

St. Francis Type of 1978

Designs: 80c, St. Francis and the wolf. 10cor, St. Francis, painting. 20cor, Our Lady of Conception, statue in Church of El Viejo.

1978, Feb. 23 Litho. *Perf. 14½*
C935 A114 80c lt brn & multi .25 .25
C936 A114 10cor bl & multi 1.90 1.75

Souvenir Sheet

C937 A114 20cor multi 3.50 2.50

Railroad Type of 1978

Locomotives: 35c, Light-weight American. 4cor, Heavy Baldwin. 10cor, Juniata, 13-ton. 20cor, Map of route system.

1978, Apr. 7 Litho. *Perf. 14½*
C938 A115 35c lt grn & multi .25 .25
C939 A115 4cor dp org & multi .90 .75
C940 A115 10cor cit & multi 2.00 1.90
Nos. C938-C940 (3) 3.15 2.90

Souvenir Sheet

C941 A115 20cor multi 7.50 4.00

Jules Verne Type of 1978

Designs: 90c, 20,000 Leagues under the Sea. 10cor, Around the World in 80 Days. 20cor, From the Earth to the Moon.

1978, Aug. Litho. *Perf. 14½*
C942 A116 90c multi .25 .25
C943 A116 10cor multi 1.75 1.50

Souvenir Sheet

C944 A116 20cor multi 7.50 5.00

Aviation History Type of 1978

Designs: 55c, Igor Sikorsky in his helicopter, 1913, horiz. 10cor, Space shuttle, horiz. 20cor, Flyer III, horiz.

1978, Sept. 29 Litho. *Perf. 14½*
C945 A117 55c multi .25 .25
C946 A117 10cor multi 1.40 1.00

Souvenir Sheet

C947 A117 20cor multi 5.00 4.00

Soccer Type of 1978

Soccer Players: 50c, Denis Law and Franz Beckenbauer. 5cor, Dino Zoff and Pelé. 20cor, Dominique Rocheteau and Johan Neeskens.

1978, Oct. 25 Litho. *Perf. 13½x14*
C948 A118 50c multi .25 .25
C949 A118 5cor multi 1.00 .85

Souvenir Sheet

C950 A118 20cor multi 5.00 4.00

Christmas Type of 1978

Paintings: 3cor, Apostles John and Peter, by Dürer. 10cor, Apostles Paul and Mark, by Dürer. 20cor, Virgin and Child with Garlands, by Dürer.

1978, Dec. 12 Litho. *Perf. 13½x14*
C951 A119 3cor multi .40 .35
C952 A119 10cor multi 1.40 1.00

Souvenir Sheet

C953 A119 20cor multi 5.00 2.50

Volcano Type of 1978

Designs: No. C954, Cerro Negro Volcano. No. C955, Lake Masaya. No. C956, Momotombo Volcano. No. C957, Lake Asososca. No. C958, Mombacho Volcano. No. C959, Lake Apoyo. No. C960, Concepcion Volcano. No. C961, Lake Tiscapa.

1978, Dec. 29 *Perf. 14x13½*
C954 A120 35c multi .25 .25
C955 A120 35c multi .25 .25
a. Pair, #C549-C955 .30 .30
C956 A120 90c multi .25 .25
C957 A120 90c multi .25 .25
a. Pair, #C956-C957 .35 .30
C958 A120 1cor multi .25 .25
C959 A120 1cor multi .25 .25
a. Pair, #C958-C959 .40 .30
C960 A120 10cor multi 1.90 1.40
C961 A120 10cor multi 1.90 1.40
a. Pair, #C960-C961 4.00 3.00
Nos. C954-C961 (8) 5.30 4.30

Bernardo O'Higgins AP109

1979, Mar. 7 Litho. *Perf. 14*
C962 AP109 20cor multi 4.25 3.25

Bernardo O'Higgins (1778-1842), Chilean soldier and statesman.

Red Ginger and Rubythroated Hummingbird — AP110

Designs: 55c, Orchid. 70c, Poinsettia. 80c, Flower and bees. 2cor, Lignum vitae and blue morpho butterfly. 4cor, Cattleya.

1979, Apr. 6 Litho. *Perf. 14x13½*
C963 AP110 50c multi .25 .25
C964 AP110 55c multi .25 .25
C965 AP110 70c multi .25 .25
C966 AP110 80c multi .25 .25
C967 AP110 2cor multi .60 .30
C968 AP110 4cor multi 1.25 .50
Nos. C963-C968 (6) 2.85 1.80

Endangered Turtles Overprinted in Red — AP110a

Overprint reads: 1979 / ANO DE LA LIBERACION / OLYMPIC RINGS / PARTICIPACION NICARAGUA / OLIMPIADAS 1980 / Litografia Nacional, Portugal symbol

Turtles: 90c, Loggerhead. 2cor, Correoso. 2.20cor, Ridley. 10cor, Pico Halcón.

1980, Apr. 7 Litho. *Perf. 14¼x13¾*
C969 AP110a 90c multi
C969A AP110a 2cor multi
C969B AP110a 2.20cor multi
C969C AP110a 10cor multi
Nos. C969-C969C (4) 7.00 7.00

Overprinted for Year of Liberation and 1980 Olympic Games.

Nos. C969-C969C were not issued without overprints.

Souvenir Sheet

Intl. Year of the Child — AP110b

Designs: a, 5cor, like #1101C. b, 15cor, Dr. Hermann Gmeiner.

1980, May 3 Litho. *Perf. 14½*
C970 AP110b Sheet of 2, #a-b. 21.00

No. C970 exists imperf.

Numbers have been reserved for 4 souvenir sheets celebrating the Year of Liberation and featuring Rowland Hill, Albert Einstein and Endangered Turtles. The editors would like to examine these sheets.

Numbers have been reserved for miniature sheets celebrating Natl. Literacy Campaign overprinted on Nos. C436a, C503a, C937, C415a, C509, C722a and C925. The editors would like to examine these sheets.

No. C930 Overprinted in Gold, Purple and Green

1980, Sept. 30 *Perf. 14½*
C973 A111 20cor multi

Souvenir Sheet

Overprinted & Surcharged in Black & Silver — AP110h

Overprint reads: 1980 ANO DE LA ALFABETIZACION / 1980 MOSCU and Litografia Nacional, Portugal symbol

1980, Dec. 20 Litho. ***Perf. 14½***

C974F AP110h 10cor on 20cor multi

Overprinted & surcharged for Literacy Year.
No. 974F was not issued without surcharge. Numbers have been reserved for 6 additional stamps in this set. The editors would like to examine these stamps.

Endangered Turtles Type of 1980 Overprinted in Red — AP110j

Overprint reads: 1980 ANO DE LA ALFABETIZACION and Litografia Nacional, Portugal symbol

No. C975D, Green (Verde) turtle.

1981, May 15 Litho. ***Perf. 14¼x13¾***

C975 AP110j 90c like #C969
C975A AP110j 2cor like #C969A
C975B AP110j 2.20cor like #C969B
C975C AP110j 10cor like #C969C

Souvenir Sheet

C975D AP110j 5cor on 20cor multi *15.00*

Overprinted for Literacy Year.
Nos. C975-C975D were not issues without overprints and surcharge.

Revolution Type of 1981

1981, July 19 Litho. ***Perf. 12½x12***

C975E A123 2.10cor March 1.25 .25
C975F A123 3cor Construction 2.00 .25
C975G A123 6cor Health programs 5.00 .45
Nos. C975E-C975G (3) 8.25 .95

FSLN Type of 1981

1981, July 23

C976 A124 4cor Founder .55 .35

Postal Union Type of 1981

1981, Aug. 10

C977 A125 2.10cor Pony express .25 .25
C978 A125 3cor Headquarters .30 .25
C979 A125 6cor Members' flags .60 .35
Nos. C977-C979 (3) 1.15 .85

1300th Anniv. of Bulgaria — AP112

1981, Sept. 2 ***Imperf.***

C980 AP112 10cor multi 2.50 1.00

Size: 96x70mm.

Aquatic Flower Type of 1981

10cor, Nymphaea gladstoniana.

1981, Sept. 15 ***Perf. 12½***

C981 A126 10cor multi 1.40 .90

Souvenir Sheet

Panda Bear — AP113

1981, Oct. 9 ***Perf. 13***

C982 AP113 10cor multi 1.75 1.00

Philatokyo Stamp Exhibition, Tokyo.

Tropical Fish Type of 1981

3.50cor, Pterolebias longipinnis. 4cor, Xiphophorus helleri.

1981, Oct. 19 ***Perf. 12½***

C983 A127 3.50cor multi .70 .30
C984 A127 4cor multi .80 .30

Souvenir Sheet

Frigate — AP114

1981, Nov. 2 ***Perf. 13***

C985 AP114 10cor multi 1.75 1.00

Espamer '81 Stamp Exhibition, Buenos Aires, Nov. 13-22.

Bird Type of 1981

3cor, Trogon massena. 4cor, Campylopterus hemileucurus, horiz. 6cor, Momotus momota.

1981, Nov. 30 ***Perf. 12½***

C986 A128 3cor multicolored .70 .25
C987 A128 4cor multicolored 1.00 .40
C988 A128 6cor multicolored 1.25 .55
Nos. C986-C988 (3) 2.95 1.20

Satellite Type of 1981

1981, Dec. 15 ***Perf. 13x12½***

C989 A129 3cor multi .75 .25
C990 A129 4cor multi 1.00 .30
C991 A129 5cor multi 1.25 .35
Nos. C989-C991 (3) 3.00 .90

Railroad Type of 1981

1981, Dec. 30 ***Perf. 12½***

C992 A130 6cor Ferrobus, 1967 1.75 .55

World Cup Type of 1982

1982, Jan. 25

C993 A131 4cor multi .60 .30
C994 A131 10cor multi, horiz. 1.40 .80

Souvenir Sheet

Perf. 13

C995 A131 10cor multi 2.75 1.10

No. C995 contains one 39x31mm stamp.

Dog Type of 1982

1982, Feb. 18

C996 A132 3cor Boxers .60 .30
C997 A132 3.50cor Pointers .65 .30
C998 A132 6cor Collies 1.00 .50
Nos. C996-C998 (3) 2.25 1.10

Intl. ITU Congress — AP115

1982, Mar. 12

C999 AP115 25cor multi 3.50 2.25

Butterfly Type of 1982

3cor, Parides iphidamas. 3.50cor, Consul hippona. 4cor, Morpho peleides.

1982, Mar. 26

C1000 A133 3cor multi .75 .30
C1001 A133 3.50cor multi .85 .30
C1002 A133 4cor multi .90 .40
Nos. C1000-C1002 (3) 2.50 1.00

Satellite Type of 1982

1982, Apr. 12

C1003 A134 5cor multi, horiz. .75 .40
C1004 A134 6cor multi 1.00 .50

UPU Type of 1982

1982, May 1 Litho. ***Perf. 13***

C1005 A135 3.50cor Train .40 .25
C1006 A135 10cor Jet 1.10 .70

Sports Type of 1982

2.50cor, Women's volleyball, vert. 3cor, Boxing. 9cor, Soccer.
10cor, Baseball, vert.

1982, May 13

C1007 A136 2.50cor multi .50 .25
C1008 A136 3cor multi .60 .30
C1009 A136 9cor multi 1.90 .80
Nos. C1007-C1009 (3) 3.00 1.35

Souvenir Sheet

C1010 A136 10cor multi 2.00 .80

No. C1010 contains one 29x36mm stamp.

Souvenir Sheet

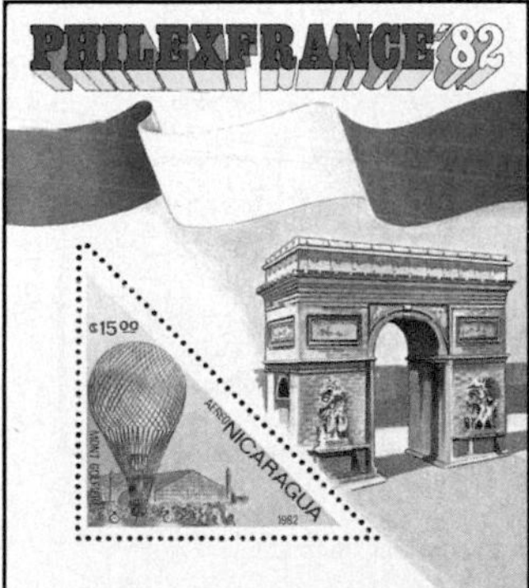

PHILEXFRANCE '82 Intl. Stamp Exhibition, Paris, June 11-21 — AP116

1982, June 9 ***Perf. 13x12½***

C1011 AP116 15cor multi 2.75 1.25

Revolution Type of 1982

Symbolic doves. 2.50cor, 4cor vert.

1982, July 19 ***Perf. 13***

C1012 A137 2.50cor multi .45 .25
C1013 A137 4cor multi .70 .40
C1014 A137 6cor multi 1.10 .60
Nos. C1012-C1014 (3) 2.25 1.25

Washington Type of 1982

2.50cor, Crossing the Delaware. 3.50cor, At Valley Forge. 4cor, Battle of Trenton. 6cor, Washington in Princeton.

Perf. 12½x13, 13x12½

1982, June 20 Litho.

C1015 A138 2.50cor multi, horiz. .50 .25
C1016 A138 3.50cor multi, horiz. .65 .35
C1017 A138 4cor multi .75 .40
C1018 A138 6cor multi 1.10 .60
Nos. C1015-C1018 (4) 3.00 1.60

Painting Type of 1982

9cor, Seated Woman, by A. Morales.

1982, Aug. 17 ***Perf. 13***

C1019 A139 9cor multi 2.00 .80

Dimitrov Type of 1982

2.50cor, Dimitrov, Yikov, Sofia, 1946. 4cor, Portrait, flag.

1982, Sept. 9

C1020 A140 2.50cor multi .45 .25
C1021 A140 4cor multi .80 .40

Dictatorship Type of 1982

4cor, Rigoberto Lopez Perez. 6cor, Edwin Castro.

1982, Sept. 21 ***Perf. 13x12½***

C1022 A141 4cor multi .60 .40
C1023 A141 6cor multi 1.00 .60

Tourism Type of 1982

2.50cor, Coyotepe Fortress, Masaya. 3.50cor, Velazquez Park, Managua.

1982, Sept. 25 ***Perf. 13***

C1024 A142 2.50cor multi .40 .25
C1025 A142 3.50cor multi .45 .25

Marx Type of 1982

4cor, Marx, Highgate Monument.

1982, Oct. 4 ***Perf. 12½***

C1026 A143 4cor multi .55 .35

Discovery of America Type of 1982

2.50cor, Trans-atlantic voyage. 4cor, Landing of Columbus. 7cor, Death of Columbus.
10cor, Columbus' fleet.

1982, Oct. 12 ***Perf. 12½x13***

C1027 A145 2.50cor multi .50 .25
C1028 A145 4cor multi .75 .40
C1029 A145 7cor multi 1.25 .70
a. Sheet, 2 each #1187-1190, C1027-C1029, + 2 labels — —
Nos. C1027-C1029 (3) 2.50 1.35

Souvenir Sheet

Perf. 13

C1030 A145 10cor multi 2.25 1.10

No. C1030 contains one 31x39mm stamp.

Flower Type of 1982

2.50cor, Pasiflora foetida. 3.50cor, Clitoria sp. 5cor, Russelia sarmentosa.

1982, Nov. 13 ***Perf. 12½***

C1031 A146 2.50cor multi .60 .25
C1032 A146 3.50cor multi .70 .30
C1033 A146 5cor multi .80 .45
Nos. C1031-C1033 (3) 2.10 1.00

Reptile Type of 1982

2.50cor, Turtle, horiz. 3cor, Boa constrictor. 3.50cor, Crocodile, horiz. 5cor, Sistrurus catenatus, horiz.

1982, Dec. 10 ***Perf. 13***

C1034 A147 2.50cor multi 1.25 .25
C1035 A147 3cor multi 1.40 .30
C1036 A147 3.50cor multi 1.50 .30
C1037 A147 5cor multi 2.25 .45
Nos. C1034-C1037 (4) 6.40 1.30

Non-aligned States Conference, Jan. 12-14 — AP117

1983, Jan. 10 Litho. ***Perf. 12½x13***

C1038 AP117 4cor multi .90 .40

Geothermal Electricity Generating Plant, Momotombo Volcano — AP118

1983, Feb. 25 *Perf. 13*
C1039 AP118 2.50cor multi .40 .25

Souvenir Sheet

TEMBAL '83 Philatelic Exhibition, Basel, Switzerland — AP119

1983, May 21 Litho. *Perf. 13*
C1040 AP119 15cor Chamoix 2.40 1.40

Souvenir Sheet

1st Nicaraguan Philatelic Exhibition — AP120

1983, July 17 Litho. *Perf. 13*
C1041 AP120 10cor Nicaragua Airlines jet 2.40 1.40

Armed Forces AP121

1983, Sept. 2 Litho. *Perf. 13*
C1042 AP121 4cor Frontier guards, watch dog .40 .25

Souvenir Sheet

BRASILIANA '83 Intl. Stamp Show, Rio de Janeiro, July 29-Aug. 7 — AP122

1983
C1043 AP122 15cor Jaguar 5.00 1.75

Cuban Revolution, 25th Anniv. AP122a

6cor, Castro, Guevara, flag.

1984, Jan. 1 Litho. *Perf. 13*
C1043A AP122a 4cor shown .80 .40
C1043B AP122a 6cor multi 1.20 .60

Souvenir Sheet

Cardinal Infante Don Fernando, by Diego Velazquez — AP123

1984, May 2 Litho. *Perf. 13*
C1044 AP123 15cor multi 3.75 1.25

ESPANA '84.

Souvenir Sheet

Hamburg '84 — AP124

1984, June 19 Litho. *Perf. 13*
C1045 AP124 15cor Dirigible 3.75 1.25

1984 UPU Congress — AP125

15cor, Mail transport.

1984, June 24 *Perf. 12½*
C1046 AP125 15cor multi 2.00 1.00

Souvenir Sheet

Expofilnic '84 (2nd Natl. Stamp Exhibition) — AP126

15cor, Communications Museum.

1984, July 15
C1047 AP126 15cor multi 2.00 1.00

Souvenir Sheet

Ausipex '84 — AP127

1984, Sept. 21
C1048 AP127 15cor Explorer ship 2.00 1.00

Souvenir Sheet

OLYMPHILEX '85 — AP128

1985, Mar. 18 Litho. *Perf. 12½*
C1049 AP128 15cor Bicycle race 1.50 .75

Souvenir Sheet

ESPAMER '85, Havana, Mar. 19-24 — AP129

1985, Mar. 19
C1050 AP129 10cor Crocodylus rhombifer 1.50 .75

Victory of Sandanista Revolution, 6th Anniv. AP134

1985, July 19 Litho. *Perf. 12½*
C1125 AP134 9cor Soldier, flag .90 .60
C1126 AP134 9cor Sugar mill .90 .60

Benjamin Zeledon, Birth Cent. — AP135

1985, Oct. 4 Litho. *Perf. 12½*
C1127 AP135 15cor multicolored .90 .40

Henri Dunant (1828-1910), Founder of Red Cross — AP136

1985, Oct. 10 *Perf. 12½x12*
C1128 AP136 3cor shown .30 .25
C1129 AP136 15cor Dunant, air ambulance 1.10 .45
a. Pair, #C1128-C1129 + label 1.45 .55

Nicaraguan Stamps, 125th Anniv. AP137

1986, May 22 *Perf. 12½x13*
C1130 AP137 30cor No. C1 .80 .30
C1131 AP137 40cor No. 174 1.00 .40
C1132 AP137 50cor No. 48 1.25 .50
C1133 AP137 100cor No. 1 2.40 1.10
Nos. C1130-C1133 (4) 5.45 2.30

Intl. Peace Year — AP138

1986, July 19 *Perf. 12½*
C1134 AP138 5cor shown .25 .25
C1135 AP138 10cor Globe, dove .25 .25

Carlos Fonseca, 10th Death Anniv. — AP139

1986, Aug. 11 Litho. *Perf. 12½*
C1136 AP139 15cor multicolored .30 .25

Formation of the Sandinista Front, 25th anniv.

AP140

1986, Nov. 20 *Perf. 13*
C1137 AP140 15cor Rhinoceros .40 .25
C1138 AP140 15cor Zebra .40 .25
C1139 AP140 25cor Elephant .55 .30
C1140 AP140 25cor Giraffe .55 .30
C1141 AP140 50cor Mandrill 1.20 .55
C1142 AP140 50cor Tiger 1.20 .55
Nos. C1137-C1142 (6) 4.30 2.20

AP141

World Cup Soccer Championships, Mexico: Various soccer players and natl. flags.

1986, Dec. 20 *Perf. 13*

Shirt Colors

C1143 AP141 10cor blue .30 .25
C1144 AP141 10cor blk & white .30 .25
C1145 AP141 10cor blue & white .30 .25
C1146 AP141 15cor pink & white .45 .25
C1147 AP141 15cor grn & blk .45 .25
C1148 AP141 25cor blk & white, red .70 .30
C1149 AP141 50cor grn & yel, red, horiz. 1.40 .55
Nos. C1143-C1149 (7) 3.90 2.10

Souvenir Sheet

Perf. 12½

C1150 AP141 100cor blk & white, bl & white 2.75 1.10

Vassil Levski, 150th Birth Anniv. — AP142

1987, Apr. 18 *Perf. 13*
C1151 AP142 30cor multicolored .70 .30

Intl. Year of Shelter for the Homeless — AP143

1987, Aug. 2
C1152 AP143 20cor multicolored .55 .25
C1153 AP143 30cor Housing, diff. .85 .35

For surcharges, see Nos. C1160B-C1160C.

Souvenir Sheet

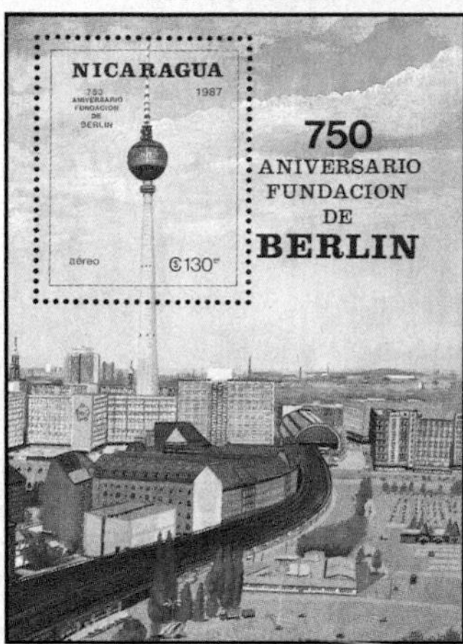

Berlin, 750th Anniv. — AP144

1987, Sept. 25 Litho. *Perf. 13*
C1154 AP144 130cor multi 3.50 1.00

Discovery of America, 500th Anniv. (in 1992) — AP145

No. C1155, Indian village. No. C1156, Sailing ships. No. C1157, Battle in village. No. C1158, Battle, prisoners. No. C1159, Spanish town. No. C1160, Cathedral.

1987, Oct. 12 *Perf. 13*
C1155 AP145 15cor multicolored .50 .25
C1156 AP145 15cor multicolored .50 .25
C1157 AP145 20cor multicolored .65 .25
C1158 AP145 30cor multicolored 1.00 .30
C1159 AP145 40cor multicolored 1.40 .40
C1160 AP145 50cor multicolored 1.60 .50
a. Min. sheet of 6, #C1155-C1160 5.75 5.75
Nos. C1155-C1160 (6) 5.65 1.95

Nos. C1152-C1153 Surcharged

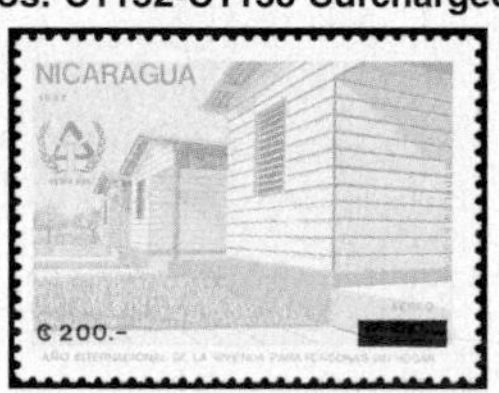

Methods and Perfs As Before

1987, Dec. 26
C1160B AP143 200cor on 20cor #C1152 — —
C1160C AP143 3000cor on 30cor #C1153 — —

Cuban Revolution, 30th Anniv. — AP146

1989, Jan. 1 *Perf. 13*
C1161 AP146 20cor multicolored .75 .25

AP147

Designs: Various soccer players in action.

1989, Feb. 20 *Perf. 13x12½*
C1162 AP147 100cor multi .30 .25
C1163 AP147 200cor multi .30 .25
C1164 AP147 600cor multi .30 .25
C1165 AP147 1000cor multi .45 .25
C1166 AP147 2000cor multi .90 .45
C1167 AP147 3000cor multi 1.40 .40
C1168 AP147 5000cor multi 2.10 .65
Nos. C1162-C1168 (7) 5.75 2.50

Souvenir Sheet

Perf. 13

C1169 AP147 9000cor multi 4.00 2.25

World Cup Soccer Championships, Italy. No. C1169 contains one 32x40mm stamp.

AP148

Design: 9000cor, Concepcion Volcano.

1989, July 19 *Perf. 13*
C1170 AP148 300cor multi .25 .25

Souvenir Sheet

C1171 AP148 9000cor multi 3.00 2.25

Sandinista Revolution, 10th Anniv. No. C1171 contains one 40x32mm stamp.

AP149

Birds: 100cor, Anhinga anhinga. 200cor, Elanoides forficatus. 600cor, Eumomota superciliosa. 1000cor, Setophaga picta. 2000cor, Taraba major, horiz. 3000cor, Onychorhynchus mexicanus. 5000cor, Myrmotherula axillaris, horiz. 9000cor, Amazona ochrocephala.

1989, July 18 *Perf. 13x12½, 12½x13*
C1172 AP149 100cor multi .25 .25
C1173 AP149 200cor multi .25 .25
C1174 AP149 600cor multi .25 .25
C1175 AP149 1000cor multi .40 .25
C1176 AP149 2000cor multi .90 .30
C1177 AP149 3000cor multi 1.40 .45
C1178 AP149 5000cor multi 2.40 .75
Nos. C1172-C1178 (7) 5.85 2.50

Souvenir Sheet

Perf. 13

C1179 AP149 9000cor multi 4.00 2.00

Brasiliana '89. No. C1179 contains one 32x40mm stamp.

AP150

Designs: 50cor, Downhill skiing. 300cor, Ice hockey. 600cor, Ski jumping. 1000cor, Pairs figure skating. 2000cor, Biathalon. 3000cor, Slalom skiing. 5000cor, Cross country skiing. 9000cor, Two-man luge.

1989, Mar. 25 *Perf. 13*
C1180 AP150 50cor multi .60 .25
C1181 AP150 300cor multi .60 .25
C1182 AP150 600cor multi .60 .25
C1183 AP150 1000cor multi .60 .25
C1184 AP150 2000cor multi 1.00 .25
C1185 AP150 3000cor multi 1.10 .25
C1186 AP150 5000cor multi 1.25 .25
Nos. C1180-C1186 (7) 5.75 1.75

Souvenir Sheet

C1187 AP150 9000cor multi 4.00 2.00

1992 Winter Olympics, Albertville. No. C1187 contains one 32x40mm stamp.

AP151

Designs: 100cor, Water polo. 200cor, Running. 600cor, Diving. 1000cor, Gymnastics. 2000cor, Weight lifting. 3000cor, Volleyball. 5000cor, Wrestling. 9000cor, Field hockey.

1989, Apr. 23
C1188 AP151 100cor multi .60 .25
C1189 AP151 200cor multi .60 .25
C1190 AP151 600cor multi .60 .25
C1191 AP151 1000cor multi .60 .25
C1192 AP151 2000cor multi 1.00 .25
C1193 AP151 3000cor multi 1.10 .25
C1194 AP151 5000cor multi 1.25 .25
Nos. C1188-C1194 (7) 5.75 1.75

Souvenir Sheet

C1195 AP151 9000cor multi 3.75 .45

1992 Summer Olympics, Barcelona. No. C1195 contains one 32x40mm stamp.

AP152

1989, Oct. 12
C1196 AP152 2000cor Vase .70 .30

Discovery of America, 500th Anniv. (in 1992).

Currency Reform

Currency reform took place Mar. 4, 1990. Until stamps in the new currency were issued, mail was to be hand-stamped "Franqueo Pagado," (Postage Paid). Stamps were not used again until Apr. 25, 1991. The following set was sold by the post office but was not valid for postage. Value $5.65

Mushrooms

Designs: 500cor, Morchella esculenta. 1000cor, Boletus edulis. 5000cor, Lactarius deliciosus. 10,000cor, Panellus stipticus. 20,000cor, Craterellus cornucopioides. 40,000cor, Cantharellus cibarius. 50,000cor, Armillariella mellea.

1990, July 15 *Perf. 13*

500cor-50,000cor

AIR POST SEMI-POSTAL STAMPS

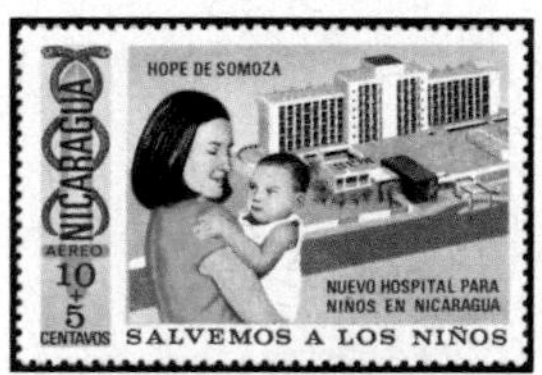

Mrs. Somoza and Children's Hospital — SPAP1

Designs: 5c+5c, Children and weight chart. 15c+5c, Incubator and Da Vinci's "Child in Womb." 20c+5c, Smallpox vaccination. 30c+5c, Water purification. 35c+5c, 1cor+50c, like 10c+5c. 50c+10c, Antibiotics. 60c+15c, Malaria control. 70c+10c, Laboratory. 80c+20c, Gastroenteritis (sick and well babies).

1973, Sept. 25 Litho. *Perf. 13½x14*

CB1 SPAP1 5c + 5c multi .25 .25
CB2 SPAP1 10c + 5c multi .25 .25
CB3 SPAP1 15c + 5c multi .25 .25
CB4 SPAP1 20c + 5c multi .25 .25
CB5 SPAP1 30c + 5c multi .25 .25
CB6 SPAP1 35c + 5c multi .25 .25
CB7 SPAP1 50c + 10c multi .25 .25
CB8 SPAP1 60c + 15c multi .25 .25
CB9 SPAP1 70c + 10c multi .25 .25
CB10 SPAP1 80c + 20c multi .25 .25
CB11 SPAP1 1cor + 50c multi .30 .25
Nos. CB1-CB11 (11) 2.30 2.25

The surtax was for hospital building fund. See No. C845. Inscriptions on back, printed on top of gum give brief description of subjects shown.

AIR POST OFFICIAL STAMPS

OA1

"Typewritten" Overprint on #O293

1929, Aug. Unwmk. *Perf. 12*

CO1 OA1 25c orange 50.00 45.00

Excellent counterfeits of No. CO1 are plentiful.

Official Stamps of 1926 Ovptd. in Dark Blue

1929, Sept. 15

CO2 A24 25c orange .50 .50
a. Inverted overprint 25.00
b. Double overprint 25.00
CO3 A25 50c pale bl .75 .75
a. Inverted overprint 25.00
b. Double overprint 25.00
c. Double overprint, one inverted 25.00

Nos. 519-523 Overprinted in Black

1932, Feb.

CO4 A24 15c org red .40 .40
a. Inverted overprint 25.00
b. Double overprint 25.00
c. Double overprint, one invtd. 25.00
CO5 A25 20c orange .45 .45
a. Double overprint 25.00
CO6 A24 25c dk vio .45 .45
CO7 A25 50c green .55 .55
CO8 A25 1cor yellow 1.00 1.00
Nos. CO4-CO8 (5) 2.85 2.85

Nos. CO4-CO5, CO7-CO8 exist with signature control overprint. Value, each, $2.50.

Overprinted on Stamp No. 547

CO9 A24 25c blk brn 42.50 42.50

The varieties "OFICAL", "OFIAIAL" and "CORROE" occur in the setting and are found on each stamp of the series.

Counterfeits of No. CO9 are plentiful.

Stamp No. CO4 with overprint "1931" in addition is believed to be of private origin.

Type of Regular Issue of 1914 Overprinted Like Nos. CO4-CO8

1933

CO10 A24 25c olive .25 .25
CO11 A25 50c ol grn .25 .25
CO12 A25 1cor org red .40 .40

On Stamps of 1914-28

CO13 A24 15c dp vio .25 .25
CO14 A25 20c dp grn .25 .25
Nos. CO10-CO14 (5) 1.40 1.40

Nos. CO10-CO14 exist without signature control mark. Value, each $2.50.

Air Post Official Stamps of 1932-33 Ovptd. in Blue

1935

CO15 A24 15c dp vio 1.00 .80
CO16 A25 20c dp grn 2.00 1.60
CO17 A24 25c olive 3.00 2.50
CO18 A25 50c ol grn 35.00 30.00
CO19 A25 1cor org red 40.00 37.50
Nos. CO15-CO19 (5) 81.00 72.40

Overprinted in Red

CO20 A24 15c dp vio .25 .25
CO21 A25 20c dp grn .25 .25
CO22 A24 25c olive .25 .25
CO23 A25 50c ol grn .80 .80
CO24 A25 1cor org red .80 .80
Nos. CO20-CO24 (5) 2.35 2.35

Nos. CO15 to CO24 are handstamped with script control mark. Counterfeits of blue overprint are plentiful.

The editors do not recognize the Nicaraguan air post Official stamps overprinted in red "VALIDO 1935" in two lines and with or without script control marks as having been issued primarily for postal purposes.

Nos. C164-C168 Overprinted in Black

1937

CO25 AP1 15c yel org .80 .55
CO26 AP1 20c org red .80 .60
CO27 AP1 25c black .80 .70
CO28 AP1 50c violet .80 .70
CO29 AP1 1cor orange .80 .70
Nos. CO25-CO29 (5) 4.00 3.25

Pres. Anastasio Somoza — OA2

1939, Feb. 7 Engr. *Perf. 12½*

CO30 OA2 10c brown .25 .25
CO31 OA2 15c dk bl .25 .25
CO32 OA2 20c yellow .25 .25
CO33 OA2 25c dk pur .25 .25
CO34 OA2 30c lake .25 .25
CO35 OA2 50c dp org .65 .65
CO36 OA2 1cor dk ol grn 1.25 1.25
Nos. CO30-CO36 (7) 3.15 3.15

Catalogue values for unused stamps in this section, from this point to the end of the section, are for Never Hinged items.

Mercedes Airport — OA3

Designs: 10c, Sulphurous Lake of Nejapa. 15c, Ruben Dario Monument. 20c, Tapir. 25c, Genizaro Dam. 50c, Tipitapa Spa. 1cor, Stone Highway. 2.50cor, Franklin D. Roosevelt Monument.

Engraved, Center Photogravure

1947, Aug. 29

Various Frames in Black

CO37 OA3 5c org brn .50 .25
CO38 OA3 10c blue .50 .25
CO39 OA3 15c violet .50 .25
CO40 OA3 20c red org .50 .25
CO41 OA3 25c blue .50 .25
CO42 OA3 50c car rose .50 .25
CO43 OA3 1cor slate .70 .45
CO44 OA3 2.50cor red brn 2.00 1.25
Nos. CO37-CO44 (8) 5.70 3.20

Rowland Hill — OA4

Designs: 10c, Heinrich von Stephan. 25c, 1st UPU Bldg. 50c, UPU Bldg., Bern. 1cor, UPU Monument. 2.60cor, Congress medal, reverse.

1950, Nov. 23 Engr. *Perf. 13*

Frames in Black

CO45 OA4 5c rose vio .25 .25
CO46 OA4 10c dp grn .25 .25
CO47 OA4 25c rose vio .25 .25
CO48 OA4 50c dp org .25 .25
CO49 OA4 1cor ultra .30 .30
CO50 OA4 2.60cor gray blk 2.25 2.00
Nos. CO45-CO50 (6) 3.35 3.10

75th anniv. (in 1949) of the UPU.

Each denomination was also issued in a souvenir sheet containing four stamps and marginal inscriptions. Size: 121x96mm. Value, set of 6 sheets, $35.

Consular Service Stamps Surcharged "Oficial Aéreo" and New Denomination in Red, Black or Blue

1961, Nov. Unwmk. Engr. *Perf. 12*

Red Marginal Number

CO51 AP63 10c on 1cor grnsh blk (R) .25 .25
CO52 AP63 15c on 20cor red brn (R) .25 .25
CO53 AP63 20c on 100cor mag .25 .25
CO54 AP63 25c on 50c dp bl (R) .25 .25
CO55 AP63 35c on 50cor brn (R) .25 .25
CO56 AP63 50c on 3cor dk car .25 .25
CO57 AP63 1cor on 2cor grn (R) .25 .25
CO58 AP63 2cor on 5cor org (Bl) .40 .40
CO59 AP63 5cor on 10cor vio (R) 1.00 1.00
Nos. CO51-CO59 (9) 3.15 3.15

POSTAGE DUE STAMPS

D1

1896 Unwmk. Engr. *Perf. 12*

J1 D1 1c orange .50 *1.25*
J2 D1 2c orange .50 *1.25*
J3 D1 5c orange .50 *1.25*
J4 D1 10c orange .50 *1.25*
J5 D1 20c orange .50 *1.25*
J6 D1 30c orange .50 *1.25*
J7 D1 50c orange .50 *1.50*
Nos. J1-J7 (7) 3.50 *9.00*

Wmk. 117

J8 D1 1c orange 1.00 *1.50*
J9 D1 2c orange 1.00 *1.50*
J10 D1 5c orange 1.00 *1.50*
J11 D1 10c orange 1.00 *1.50*
J12 D1 20c orange 1.25 *1.50*
J13 D1 30c orange 1.00 *1.50*
J14 D1 50c orange 1.00 *1.50*
Nos. J8-J14 (7) 7.25 *10.50*

1897 Unwmk.

J15 D1 1c violet .50 *1.50*
J16 D1 2c violet .50 *1.50*
J17 D1 5c violet .50 *1.50*
J18 D1 10c violet .50 *1.50*
J19 D1 20c violet 1.25 *2.00*
J20 D1 30c violet .50 *1.50*
J21 D1 50c violet .50 *1.50*
Nos. J15-J21 (7) 4.25 *11.00*

Wmk. 117

J22 D1 1c violet .50 *1.50*
J23 D1 2c violet .50 *1.50*
J24 D1 5c violet .50 *1.50*
J25 D1 10c violet .50 *1.50*
J26 D1 20c violet 1.00 *2.00*
J27 D1 30c violet .50 *1.50*
J28 D1 50c violet .50 *1.50*
Nos. J22-J28 (7) 4.00 *11.00*

Reprints of Nos. J8-J28 are on thick, porous paper. Color of 1896 reprints, reddish orange; or 1897 reprints, reddish violet. On watermarked reprints, liberty cap is sideways. Value 25c each.

D2

1898 Litho. Unwmk.

J29 D2 1c blue green .25 *2.00*
J30 D2 2c blue green .25 *2.00*
J31 D2 5c blue green .25 *2.00*
J32 D2 10c blue green .25 *2.00*
J33 D2 20c blue green .25 *2.00*
J34 D2 30c blue green .25 *2.00*
J35 D2 50c blue green .25 *2.00*
Nos. J29-J35 (7) 1.75 *14.00*

1899

J36 D2 1c carmine .25 *2.00*
J37 D2 2c carmine .25 *2.00*
J38 D2 5c carmine .25 *2.00*
J39 D2 10c carmine .25 *2.00*

J40 D2 20c carmine .25 *2.00*
J41 D2 50c carmine .25 *2.00*
Nos. J36-J41 (6) 1.50 *12.00*

Some denominations are found in se-tenant pairs.

Various counterfeit cancellations exist on #J1-J41.

D3

1900 **Engr.**
J42 D3 1c plum .75
J43 D3 2c vermilion .75
J44 D3 5c dk bl .75
J45 D3 10c purple .75
J46 D3 20c org brn .75
J47 D3 30c dk grn 1.50
J48 D3 50c lake 1.50
Nos. J42-J48 (7) 6.75

Nos. J42-J48 were not placed in use as postage due stamps. They were only issued with "Postage" overprints. See Nos. 137-143, 152-158, O72-O81, 2L11-2L15, 2L25, 2L40-2L41.

OFFICIAL STAMPS

Types of Postage Stamps Overprinted in Red Diagonally Reading up

1890 **Unwmk.** **Engr.** ***Perf. 12***
O1 A5 1c ultra .25 *.30*
O2 A5 2c ultra .25 *.30*
O3 A5 5c ultra .25 *.30*
O4 A5 10c ultra .25 *.40*
O5 A5 20c ultra .25 *.45*
O6 A5 50c ultra .25 *.75*
O7 A5 1p ultra .25 *1.25*
O8 A5 2p ultra .25 *1.60*
O9 A5 5p ultra .25 *2.40*
O10 A5 10p ultra .25 *4.00*
Nos. O1-O10 (10) 2.50 *11.75*

All values of the 1890 issue are known without overprint and most of them with inverted or double overprint, or without overprint and imperforate. There is no evidence that they were issued in these forms.

Official stamps of 1890-1899 are scarce with genuine cancellations. Forged cancellations are plentiful.

Overprinted Vertically Reading Up

1891 **Litho.**
O11 A6 1c green .25 *.30*
O12 A6 2c green .25 *.30*
O13 A6 5c green .25 *.30*
O14 A6 10c green .25 *.30*
O15 A6 20c green .25 *.50*
O16 A6 50c green .25 *1.10*
O17 A6 1p green .25 *1.25*
O18 A6 2p green .25 *1.30*
O19 A6 5p green .35 *2.40*
O20 A6 10p green .50 *4.00*
Nos. O11-O20 (10) 2.85 *11.75*

All values of this issue except the 2c and 5p exist without overprint and several with double overprint. They are not known to have been issued in this form.

Many of the denominations may be found in se-tenant pairs.

Overprinted in Dark Blue

1892 **Engr.**
O21 A7 1c yellow brown .25 *.30*
O22 A7 2c yellow brown .25 *.30*
O23 A7 5c yellow brown .25 *.30*
O24 A7 10c yellow brown .25 *.30*
O25 A7 20c yellow brown .25 *.50*
O26 A7 50c yellow brown .25 *1.00*
O27 A7 1p yellow brown .25 *1.25*
O28 A7 2p yellow brown .25 *1.60*
O29 A7 5p yellow brown .25 *2.40*
O30 A7 10p yellow brown .25 *4.00*
Nos. O21-O30 (10) 2.50 *11.95*

The 2c and 1p are known without overprint and several values exist with double or inverted overprint. These probably were not regularly issued.

Commemorative of the 400th anniversary of the discovery of America by Christopher Columbus.

Overprinted in Red

1893 **Engr.**
O31 A8 1c slate .25 *.30*
O32 A8 2c slate .25 *.30*
O33 A8 5c slate .25 *.30*
O34 A8 10c slate .25 *.30*
O35 A8 20c slate .25 *.50*
O36 A8 25c slate .25 *.75*
O37 A8 50c slate .25 *.85*
O38 A8 1p slate .25 *1.00*
O39 A8 2p slate .25 *2.00*
O40 A8 5p slate .25 *2.50*
O41 A8 10p slate .25 *5.50*
Nos. O31-O41 (11) 2.75 *14.30*

The 2, 5, 10, 20, 25, 50c and 5p are known without overprint but probably were not regularly issued. Some values exist with double or inverted overprints.

Overprinted in Black

1894
O42 A9 1c orange .30 .35
O43 A9 2c orange .30 .35
O44 A9 5c orange .30 .35
O45 A9 10c orange .30 .35
O46 A9 20c orange .30 *.50*
O47 A9 50c orange .30 *.75*
O48 A9 1p orange .30 *1.50*
O49 A9 2p orange .30 *2.00*
O50 A9 5p orange 2.00 *3.00*
O51 A9 10p orange 2.00 *4.00*
Nos. O42-O51 (10) 6.40 *13.15*

Reprints are yellow.

Overprinted in Dark Blue

1895
O52 A10 1c green .25 *.35*
O53 A10 2c green .25 *.35*
O54 A10 5c green .25 *.35*
O55 A10 10c green .25 *.35*
O56 A10 20c green .25 *.50*
O57 A10 50c green .25 *1.00*
O58 A10 1p green .25 *1.50*
O59 A10 2p green .25 *2.00*
O60 A10 5p green .25 *3.00*
O61 A10 10p green .25 *4.00*
Nos. O52-O61 (10) 2.50 *13.40*

Wmk. 117
O62 A10 1c green
O63 A10 2c green
O64 A10 5c green
O65 A10 10c green
O66 A10 20c green
O67 A10 50c green
O68 A10 1p green
O69 A10 2p green
O70 A10 5p green
O71 A10 10p green

Nos. O62-O71 probably exist only as reprints. Value, each 15 cents.

Postage Due Stamps of Same Date Handstamped in Violet

1896 **Unwmk.**
O72 D1 1c orange 7.00
O73 D1 2c orange 7.00
O74 D1 5c orange 5.00
O75 D1 10c orange 5.00
O76 D1 20c orange 10.00
Nos. O72-O76 (5) 34.00

Wmk. 117
O77 D1 1c orange 7.00
O78 D1 2c orange 7.00
O79 D1 5c orange 4.00
O80 D1 10c orange 4.00
O81 D1 20c orange 4.00
Nos. O77-O81 (5) 26.00

Nos. O72-O81 were handstamped in rows of five. Several handstamps were used, one of which had the variety "Oftcial." Most varieties are known inverted and double.

Forgeries exist.

Types of Postage Stamps Overprinted in Red

1896 **Unwmk.**
O82 A11 1c red 2.50 3.00
O83 A11 2c red 2.50 3.00
O84 A11 5c red 2.50 3.00
O85 A11 10c red 2.50 3.00
O86 A11 20c red 3.00 3.00
O87 A11 50c red 5.00 *5.00*
O88 A11 1p red 12.00 *12.00*
O89 A11 2p red 12.00 *12.00*
O90 A11 5p red 16.00 *16.00*
Nos. O82-O90 (9) 58.00 *60.00*

Wmk. 117
O91 A11 1c red 3.00 3.50
O92 A11 2c red 3.00 3.50
O93 A11 5c red 3.00 3.50
O94 A11 10c red 3.00 3.50
O95 A11 20c red 5.00 5.00
O96 A11 50c red 3.00 *5.00*
O97 A11 1p red 14.00 *14.00*
O98 A11 2p red 16.00 *16.00*
O99 A11 5p red 25.00 *25.00*
Nos. O91-O99 (9) 75.00 *79.00*

Used values for Nos. O88-O90, O97-O99 are for CTO examples. Postally used examples are not known.

Same, Dated 1897

1897 **Unwmk.**
O100 A11 1c red 3.00 3.00
O101 A11 2c red 3.00 3.00
O102 A11 5c red 3.00 2.50
O103 A11 10c red 3.00 3.00
O104 A11 20c red 3.00 4.00
O105 A11 50c red 5.00 *5.00*
O106 A11 1p red 12.00 *12.00*
O107 A11 2p red 12.00 *12.00*
O108 A11 5p red 16.00 *16.00*
Nos. O100-O108 (9) 60.00 *60.50*

Wmk. 117
O109 A11 1c red 5.00 5.00
O110 A11 2c red 5.00 5.00
O111 A11 5c red 5.00 5.00
O112 A11 10c red 10.00 10.00
O113 A11 20c red 10.00 10.00
O114 A11 50c red 12.00 *12.00*
O115 A11 1p red 20.00 *20.00*
O116 A11 2p red 20.00 *20.00*
O117 A11 5p red 20.00 *20.00*
Nos. O109-O117 (9) 107.00 *107.00*

Reprints of Nos. O82-O117 are described in notes after No. 109M. Value 15c each.

Used values for Nos. O106-O108, O115-O117 are for CTO examples. Postally used examples are not known.

Overprinted in Blue

1898 **Unwmk.**
O118 A12 1c carmine 3.25 3.25
O119 A12 2c carmine 3.25 3.25
O120 A12 4c carmine 3.25 3.25
O121 A12 5c carmine 2.50 2.50
O122 A12 10c carmine 4.00 4.00
O123 A12 15c carmine 6.00 6.00
O124 A12 20c carmine 6.00 6.00
O125 A12 50c carmine 8.50 *8.50*
O126 A12 1p carmine 11.00 *11.00*
O127 A12 2p carmine 11.00 *11.00*
O128 A12 5p carmine 11.00 *11.00*
Nos. O118-O128 (11) 69.75 *69.75*

Stamps of this set with sideways watermark 117 or with black overprint are reprints. Value 25c each.

Used values for Nos. O126-O128 are for CTO examples. Postally used examples are not known.

Overprinted in Dark Blue

1899
O129 A13 1c gray grn .35 *1.00*
O130 A13 2c bis brn .35 *1.00*
O131 A13 4c lake .35 *1.00*
O132 A13 5c dk bl .35 *.50*
O133 A13 10c buff .35 *1.00*
O134 A13 15c chocolate .35 *2.00*
O135 A13 20c dk grn .35 *3.00*
O136 A13 50c car rose .35 *3.00*
O137 A13 1p red .35 *10.00*
O138 A13 2p violet .35 *10.00*
O139 A13 5p lt bl .35 *15.00*
Nos. O129-O139 (11) 3.85 *47.50*

Counterfeit cancellations on Nos. O129-O139 are plentiful.

"Justice" — O5

1900 **Engr.**
O140 O5 1c plum .60 .60
O141 O5 2c vermilion .50 .50
O142 O5 4c ol grn .60 .60
O143 O5 5c dk bl 1.25 .45
O144 O5 10c purple 1.25 .35
O145 O5 20c brown .90 .35
O146 O5 50c lake 1.25 .50
O147 O5 1p ultra 3.50 2.50
O148 O5 2p brn org 4.00 4.00
O149 O5 5p grnsh blk 5.00 5.00
Nos. O140-O149 (10) 18.85 14.85

For surcharges see Nos. O155-O157.

Nos. 123, 161 Surcharged in Black

1903 ***Perf. 12, 14***
O150 A14 1c on 10c violet .25 .30
a. "Centovo" 1.00
b. "Contavo" 1.00
c. With ornaments .30
d. Inverted surcharge 1.00
e. "1" omitted at upper left 2.00
O151 A14 2c on 3c green .30 .40
a. "Centovos" 1.00
b. "Contavos" 1.00
c. With ornaments .35
d. Inverted surcharge 1.00
O152 A14 4c on 3c green 1.25 1.25
a. "Centovos" 2.50
b. "Contavos" 2.50
c. With ornaments 2.50
d. Inverted surcharge
O153 A14 4c on 10c violet 1.25 1.25
a. "Centovos" 2.50
b. "Contavos" 2.50
c. With ornaments 2.00
d. Inverted surcharge

O154 A14 5c on 3c green .25 .25
- *a.* "Centovos" 1.00
- *b.* "Contavos" 1.00
- *c.* With ornaments .30
- *d.* Double surcharge 2.00
- *e.* Inverted surcharge

Nos. O150-O154 (5) 3.30 3.45

These surcharges are set up to cover 25 stamps. Some of the settings have bars or pieces of fancy border type below "OFICIAL." There are 5 varieties on #O150, 3 on #O151, 1 each on #O152, O153, O154.

In 1904 #O151 was reprinted to fill a dealer's order. This printing lacks the small figure at the upper right. It includes the variety "OFICILA." At the same time the same setting was printed in carmine on official stamps of 1900, 1c on 10c violet and 2c on 1p ultramarine. Also the 1, 2 and 5p official stamps of 1900 were surcharged with new values and the dates 1901 or 1902 in various colors, inverted, etc. It is doubtful if any of these varieties were ever in Nicaragua and certain that none of them ever did legitimate postal duty.

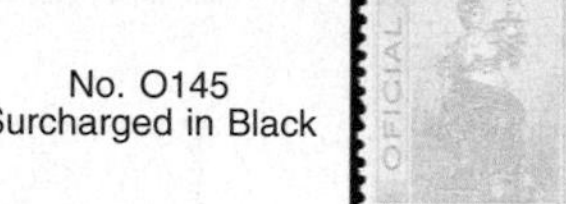

No. O145 Surcharged in Black

1904 *Perf. 12*

O155 O5 10c on 20c brn .25 .25
- *a.* No period after "Ctvs" 1.00 .75

O156 O5 30c on 20c brn .25 .25
O157 O5 50c on 20c brn .50 .35
- *a.* Lower "50" omitted 2.50 2.50
- *b.* Upper figures omitted 2.50 2.50
- *c.* Top left and lower figures omitted 3.50 3.50

Nos. O155-O157 (3) 1.00 .85

Coat of Arms — O6

1905, July 25 **Engr.**

O158 O6 1c green .25 .25
O159 O6 2c rose .25 .25
O160 O6 5c blue .25 .25
O161 O6 10c yel brn .25 .25
O162 O6 20c orange .25 .25
O163 O6 50c brn ol .25 .25
O164 O6 1p lake .25 .25
O165 O6 2p violet .25 .25
O166 O6 5p gray blk .25 .25
Nos. O158-O166 (9) 2.25 2.25

Surcharged Vertically Up or Down

1907

O167 O6 10c on 1c grn .75 .75
O168 O6 10c on 2c rose 25.00 22.50
O169 O6 20c on 2c rose 22.50 *26.00*
O170 O6 50c on 1c grn 1.50 1.50
O171 O6 50c on 2c rose 22.50 *23.00*

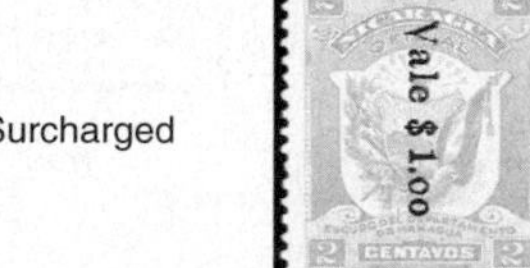

Surcharged

O172 O6 1p on 2c rose 1.50 1.50
O173 O6 2p on 2c rose 1.50 1.50
O174 O6 3p on 2c rose 1.50 1.50
O175 O6 4p on 2c rose
O176 O6 4p on 5c blue 2.25 2.25

The setting for this surcharge includes various letters from wrong fonts, the figure "1" for "I" in "Vale" and an "I" for "1" in "$1.00."

Surcharged

O177 O6 20c on 1c green 1.00 1.00
- *a.* Double surcharge 5.00 5.00

Nos. O167-O174,O176-O177 (10) 80.00 81.50

The preceding surcharges are vertical, reading both up and down.

Revenue Stamps Surcharged

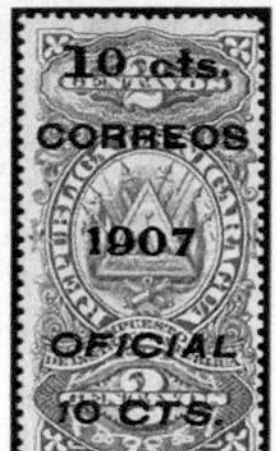

O7

1907 *Perf. 14 to 15*

O178 O7 10c on 2c org (Bk) .25 .25
O179 O7 35c on 1c bl (R) .25 .25
- *a.* Inverted surcharge 3.00 3.00

O180 O7 70c on 1c bl (V) .25 .25
- *a.* Inverted surcharge 3.00 3.00

O181 O7 70c on 1c bl (O) .25 .25
- *a.* Inverted surcharge 3.00 3.00

O182 O7 1p on 2c org (G) .25 .25
- *a.* Inverted surcharge 14.00 14.00

O183 O7 2p on 2c org (Br) .25 .25
O184 O7 3p on 5c brn (Bl) .25 .25
O185 O7 4p on 5c brn (G) .25 .25
- *a.* Double surcharge 3.00 3.00

O186 O7 5p on 5c brn (G) .25 .25
- *a.* Inverted surcharge 3.50 3.50

Nos. O178-O186 (9) 2.25 2.25

Letters and figures from several fonts were mixed in these surcharges.

See Nos. O199-O209.

No. 202 Surcharged

1907, Nov.

Black or Blue Black Surcharge

O187 A18 10c on 1c grn 15.00 15.00
O188 A18 15c on 1c grn 15.00 20.00
O189 A18 20c on 1c grn 15.00 15.00
O190 A18 50c on 1c grn 15.00 20.00

Red Surcharge

O191 A18 1(un)p on 1c grn 14.00 15.00
O192 A18 2(dos)p on 1c grn 14.00 15.00
Nos. O187-O192 (6) 88.00 100.00

No. 181 Surcharged

1908 **Yellow Surcharge** *Perf. 12*

O193 A18 10c on 3c vio 15.00 15.00
O194 A18 15c on 3c vio 15.00 15.00
O195 A18 20c on 3c vio 15.00 15.00
O196 A18 35c on 3c vio 15.00 15.00
O197 A18 50c on 3c vio 15.00 15.00
Nos. O193-O197 (5) 75.00 75.00

Black Surcharge

O198 A18 35c on 3c vio *100.00 100.00*

Revenue Stamps Surcharged like 1907 Issue Dated "1908"

1908 *Perf. 14 to 15*

O199 O7 10c on 1c bl (V) .75 .50
- *a.* Inverted surcharge 3.50 3.50

O200 O7 35c on 1c bl (Bk) .75 .50
- *a.* Inverted surcharge 3.50 3.50
- *b.* Double surcharge 4.00 4.00

O201 O7 50c on 1c bl (R) .75 .50
O202 O7 1p on 1c bl (Br) 37.50 37.50
- *a.* Inverted surcharge 65.00 65.00

O203 O7 2p on 1c bl (G) .90 .75
O204 O7 10c on 2c org (Bk) 1.10 .65
O205 O7 35c on 2c org (R) 1.10 .65
- *a.* Double surcharge 3.50

O206 O7 50c on 2c org (Bk) 1.10 .65
O207 O7 70c on 2c org (Bl) 1.10 .65
O208 O7 1p on 2c org (G) 1.10 .65
O209 O7 2p on 2c org (Br) 1.10 .65
Nos. O199-O209 (11) 47.25 43.65

There are several minor varieties in the figures, etc., in these surcharges.

Nos. 243-248 Overprinted in Black

1909 *Perf. 12*

O210 A18 10c lake .25 .25
- *a.* Double overprint 2.50 2.50

O211 A18 15c black .60 .50
O212 A18 20c brn ol 1.00 .75
O213 A18 50c dp grn 1.50 1.00
O214 A18 1p yellow 1.75 1.25
O215 A18 2p car rose 6.50 2.00
Nos. O210-O215 (6) 11.60 5.75

Overprinted in Black

1910

O216 A18 15c black 1.50 1.25
- *a.* Double overprint 4.00 4.00

O217 A18 20c brn ol 2.50 2.00
O218 A18 50c dp grn 2.50 2.00
O219 A18 1p yellow 2.75 2.50
- *a.* Inverted overprint 16.00 7.50

O220 A18 2p car rose 4.00 3.00
Nos. O216-O220 (5) 13.25 10.75

Nos. 239-240 Surcharged in Black

No. O221

No. O222

1911

O221 A18 5c on 3c red org 10.00 6.00
O222 A18 10c on 4c vio 12.00 5.00
- *a.* Double surcharge 24.00 24.00
- *b.* Pair, one without new value 35.00

Revenue Stamps Surcharged in Black

1911, Nov. *Perf. 14 to 15*

O223 A21 10c on 10c on 1 red 3.00 3.00
- *a.* Inverted surcharge 4.50
- *b.* Double surcharge 4.50

O224 A21 15c on 10c on 1 red 3.00 3.00
- *a.* Inverted surcharge 5.00
- *b.* Double surcharge 4.50

O225 A21 20c on 10c on 1 red 3.00 3.00
- *a.* Inverted surcharge 5.00

O226 A21 50c on 10c on 1 red 3.75 3.75
- *a.* Inverted surcharge 4.50

O227 A21 1p on 10c on 1 red 5.00 *7.00*
- *a.* Inverted surcharge 6.00

O228 A21 2p on 10c on 1 red 5.50 *10.00*
- *a.* Inverted surcharge 7.50
- *b.* Double surcharge 7.50

Nos. O223-O228 (6) 23.25 29.75

Surcharged in Black

1911, Nov.

O229 A21 10c on 10c on 1 red 22.50
O230 A21 15c on 10c on 1 red 22.50
O231 A21 20c on 10c on 1 red 22.50
O232 A21 50c on 10c on 1 red 16.00
Nos. O229-O232 (4) 83.50

Surcharged in Black

1911, Dec.

O233 A21 5c on 10c on 1 red 4.50 *6.00*
- *a.* Double surcharge 7.50
- *b.* Inverted surcharge 7.50
- *c.* "5" omitted 6.00

O234 A21 10c on 10c on 1 red 5.50 *7.00*
O235 A21 15c on 10c on 1 red 6.00 *7.50*
O236 A21 20c on 10c on 1 red 6.50 *8.50*
O237 A21 50c on 10c on 1 red 7.50 *10.00*
Nos. O233-O237 (5) 30.00 39.00

Nos. O233 to O237 have a surcharge on the back like Nos. 285 and 286 with "15 cts" obliterated by a heavy horizontal bar.

Surcharged Vertically in Black

1912

O238 A21 5c on 10c on 1 red 8.00 8.00
O239 A21 10c on 10c on 1 red 8.00 8.00
O240 A21 15c on 10c on 1 red 8.00 8.00
O241 A21 20c on 10c on 1 red 8.00 8.00
O242 A21 35c on 10c on 1 red 8.00 8.00
O243 A21 50c on 10c on 1 red 8.00 8.00
O244 A21 1p on 10c on 1 red 8.00 8.00
Nos. O238-O244 (7) 56.00 56.00

Nos. O238 to O244 are printed on Nos. 285 and 286 but the surcharge on the back is obliterated by a vertical bar.

Types of Regular Issue of 1912 Overprinted in Black

1912 *Perf. 12*

O245 A22 1c light blue .25 .25
O246 A22 2c light blue .25 .25
O247 A22 3c light blue .25 .25
O248 A22 4c light blue .25 .25
O249 A22 5c light blue .25 .25
O250 A22 6c light blue .35 .25
O251 A22 10c light blue .35 .25
O252 A22 15c light blue .35 .25
O253 A22 20c light blue .35 .25
O254 A22 25c light blue .35 .25
O255 A23 35c light blue .40 .25
O256 A22 50c light blue 3.75 2.00
O257 A22 1p light blue .65 .45
O258 A22 2p light blue .75 .55
O259 A22 5p light blue 1.00 .75
Nos. O245-O259 (15) 9.55 6.50

On the 35c the overprint is 15½mm wide, on the other values it is 13mm.

Types of Regular Issue of 1914 Overprinted in Black

1915, May

O260 A24 1c light blue .25 .25
O261 A25 2c light blue .25 .25
O262 A24 3c light blue .25 .25
O263 A25 4c light blue .25 .25
O264 A24 5c light blue .25 .25
O265 A25 6c light blue .25 .25
O266 A25 10c light blue .25 .25
O267 A24 15c light blue .25 .25
O268 A25 20c light blue .25 .25
O269 A24 25c light blue .30 .30
O270 A25 50c light blue .60 .60
Nos. O260-O270 (11) 3.15 3.15

Regular Issues of 1914-22 Overprinted in Red

1925
O271 A24 ½c dp grn .25 .25
a. Double overprint 2.50 2.50
O272 A24 1c violet .25 .25
O273 A25 2c car rose .25 .25
O274 A24 3c ol grn .25 .25
O275 A25 4c vermilion .25 .25
a. Double overprint *4.00 4.00*
O276 A24 5c black .25 .25
a. Double overprint *4.00 4.00*
O277 A25 6c red brn .25 .25
O278 A25 10c yellow .30 .30
a. Double overprint *4.25 4.25*
O279 A24 15c red brn .40 .40
O280 A25 20c bis brn .50 .50
O281 A24 25c orange .60 .60
a. Inverted overprint *60.00 40.00*
O282 A25 50c pale bl .75 .75
a. Double overprint *20.00 20.00*
Nos. O271-O282 (12) 4.30 4.30

Type II overprint has "f" and "i" separated. Comes on Nos. O272-O274 and O276.

Regular Issues of 1914-22 Overprinted in Black

1926
O283 A24 ½c dk grn .25 .25
O284 A24 1c dp vio .25 .25
O285 A25 2c car rose .25 .25
O286 A24 3c ol gray .25 .26
O287 A25 4c vermilion .25 .25
O288 A24 5c gray blk .25 .25
O289 A25 6c red brn .25 .25
O290 A25 10c yellow .25 .25
O291 A24 15c dp brn .25 .25
O292 A25 20c bis brn .25 .25
O293 A24 25c orange .25 .25
O294 A25 50c pale bl .25 .25
Nos. O283-O294 (12) 3.00 3.00

No. 499 Surcharged in Black

1931
O295 A33 5c on 10c bis brn .25 .25

Nos. 517-518 Overprinted in Red

1931
O296 A25 6c bis brn .25 .25
O297 A25 10c lt brn .25 .25

Nos. 541, 543, 545 With Additional Overprint in Red

O298 A24 1c ol grn .25 .25
O299 A24 3c lt bl .25 .25
a. "OFICIAL" inverted .80 .80
O300 A24 5c gray brn .25 .25
a. "1931" double .80 .80
Nos. O298-O300 (3) .75 .75

Regular Issues of 1914-31 Overprinted in Black

1932, Feb. 6
O301 A24 1c ol grn .25 .25
a. Double overprint 1.40 1.40
O302 A25 2c brt rose .25 .25
a. Double overprint 1.40 1.40
O303 A24 3c lt bl .25 .25
a. Double overprint .50 .50
O304 A25 4c dk bl .25 .25
O305 A24 5c ol brn .25 .25
O306 A25 6c bis brn .25 .25
a. Double overprint 2.00 2.00
O307 A25 10c lt brn .30 .25
O308 A24 15c org red .40 .25
a. Double overprint 2.25 2.25
O309 A25 20c orange .70 .35
O310 A24 25c dk vio 2.00 .50
O311 A25 50c green .25 .25
O312 A25 1cor yellow .25 .25
Nos. O301-O312 (12) 5.40 3.35

With Additional Overprint in Black

1932, Feb. 6
O313 A24 1c ol grn 5.50 5.50
O314 A25 2c brt rose 6.50 6.50
a. Double overprint 8.25 8.25
O315 A24 3c lt bl 5.00 5.00
O316 A24 5c ol brn 5.00 5.00
O317 A24 15c org red .65 .65
O318 A24 25c blk brn .65 .65
O319 A24 25c dk vio 1.50 1.50
Nos. O313-O319 (7) 24.80 24.80

The variety "OFIAIAL" occurs once in each sheet of Nos. O301 to O319 inclusive.

Despite the 1932 release date, the "1931" overprint on Nos. O313-O319 is correct.

Flag of the Race Issue

1933, Aug. 9 Litho. *Rouletted 9*
Without gum
O320 A43 1c orange 1.25 1.25
O321 A43 2c yellow 1.25 1.25
O322 A43 3c dk brn 1.25 1.25
O323 A43 4c dp brn 1.25 1.25
O324 A43 5c gray brn 1.25 1.25
O325 A43 6c dp ultra 1.50 1.50
O326 A43 10c dp vio 1.50 1.50
O327 A43 15c red vio 1.50 1.50
O328 A43 20c dp grn 1.50 1.50
O329 A43 25c green 2.50 2.50
O330 A43 50c carmine 3.00 3.00
O331 A43 1cor red 5.00 5.00
Nos. O320-O331 (12) 22.75 22.75

See note after No. 599.

Reprints of Nos. O320-O331 exist.

A 25c dull blue exists. Its status is questioned.

Regular Issue of 1914-31 Overprinted in Red

1933, Nov. *Perf. 12*
O332 A24 1c ol grn .25 .25
O333 A25 2c brt rose .25 .25
O334 A24 3c lt bl .25 .25
O335 A25 4c dk bl .25 .25
O336 A24 5c ol brn .25 .25
O337 A25 6c bis brn .25 .25
O338 A25 10c lt brn .25 .25
O339 A24 15c red org .25 .25
O340 A25 20c orange .25 .25
O341 A24 25c dk vio .25 .25
O342 A25 50c green .25 .25
O343 A25 1cor yellow .35 .25
Nos. O332-O343 (12) 3.10 3.00

Nos. O332-O343 exist with or without signature control overprint. Values are the same.

Official Stamps of 1933 Overprinted as Nos. CO15-CO19 in Blue

1935, Dec.
O344 A24 1c ol grn .65 .40
O345 A25 2c brt rose .65 .50
O346 A24 3c lt bl 1.60 .50
O347 A25 4c dk bl 1.60 1.60
O348 A24 5c ol brn 1.60 1.60
O349 A25 6c bis brn 2.00 2.00
O350 A25 10c lt brn 2.00 2.00
O351 A24 15c org red 27.50 27.50
O352 A25 20c orange 27.50 27.50
O353 A24 25c dk vio 27.50 27.50
O354 A25 50c green 27.50 27.50
O355 A25 1cor yellow 27.50 27.50
Nos. O344-O355 (12) 147.60 146.10

Nos. O344-O355 have signature control overprints. Counterfeits of overprint abound.

Same Overprinted in Red

1936, Jan.
O356 A24 1c ol grn .25 .25
O357 A25 2c brt rose .25 .25
O358 A24 3c lt bl .25 .25
a. Double overprint
O359 A25 4c dk bl .25 .25
O360 A24 5c ol brn .25 .25
O361 A25 6c bis brn .25 .25
O362 A25 10c lt brn .25 .25
O363 A24 15c org red .25 .25
O364 A25 20c orange .25 .25
O365 A24 25c dk vio .25 .25
O366 A25 50c green .25 .25
O367 A25 1cor yellow .35 .35
Nos. O356-O367 (12) 3.10 3.10

Nos. O356-O367 have signature control overprints.

Nos. 653 to 655, 657, 659 660, 662 to 664 Overprinted in Black

1937
O368 A24 1c car rose .25 .25
O369 A25 2c dp bl .25 .25
O370 A24 3c chocolate .25 .25
O371 A24 5c org red .35 .25
O372 A25 10c ol grn .65 .40
O373 A24 15c green .80 .50
O374 A24 25c orange 1.00 .65
O375 A25 50c brown 1.40 .80
O376 A25 1cor ultra 2.50 1.25
Nos. O368-O376 (9) 7.45 4.60

Islands of the Great Lake
O9

1939, Jan. Engr. *Perf. 12½*
O377 O9 2c rose red 1.00 .25
O378 O9 3c lt bl 1.00 .25
O379 O9 6c brn org 1.00 .25
O380 O9 7½c dp grn 1.00 .25
O381 O9 10c blk brn 1.00 .25
O382 O9 15c orange 1.00 .25
O383 O9 25c dk vio 1.50 .25
O384 O9 50c brt yel grn 4.00 .75
Nos. O377-O384 (8) 11.50 2.50

POSTAL TAX STAMPS

Official Stamps of 1915 Surcharged in Black

1921, July Unwmk. *Perf. 12*
RA1 A24 1c on 5c lt bl 1.50 .60
RA2 A25 1c on 6c lt bl .65 .25
a. Double surcharge, one inverted
RA3 A25 1c on 10c lt bl 1.00 .25
a. Double surcharge 3.50 3.50
RA4 A24 1c on 15c lt bl 1.50 .25
a. Double surcharge, one inverted 5.00 5.00
Nos. RA1-RA4 (4) 4.65 1.35

"R de C" signifies "Reconstruccion de Comunicaciones." The stamps were intended to provide a fund for rebuilding the General Post Office which was burned in April, 1921. One stamp was required on each letter or parcel, in addition to the regular postage. In the setting of one hundred there are five stamps with antique "C" and twenty-one with "R" and "C" smaller than in the illustration. One or more stamps in the setting have a dotted bar, as illustrated over No. 388, instead of the double bar.

The use of the "R de C" stamps for the payment of regular postage was not permitted.

Official Stamp of 1915 Overprinted in Black

1921, July
RA5 A24 1c light blue 6.00 1.75

This stamp is known with the dotted bar as illustrated over No. 388, instead of the double bar.

Coat of Arms — PT1

1921, Sept. Red Surcharge
RA6 PT1 1c on 1c ver & blk .25 .25
RA7 PT1 1c on 2c grn & blk .25 .25
a. Double surcharge 3.00 3.00
b. Double surcharge, one inverted 4.00 4.00
RA8 PT1 1c on 4c org & blk .25 .25
a. Double surcharge 4.00 4.00
RA9 PT1 1c on 15c dk bl & blk .25 .25
a. Double surcharge 3.00 3.00
Nos. RA6-RA9 (4) 1.00 1.00

PT2

1922, Feb. Black Surcharge
RA10 PT2 1c on 10c yellow .25 .25
a. Period after "de" .50 .40
b. Double surcharge 2.00 2.00
c. Double inverted surcharge 3.75 3.75
d. Inverted surcharge 3.00 3.00
e. Without period after "C" 1.00 1.00

No. 409 Overprinted in Black

1922
RA11 A24 1c violet .25 .25
a. Double overprint 2.00 2.00

This stamp with the overprint in red is a trial printing.

Nos. 402, 404-407 Surcharged in Black

1922, June
RA12 A27 1c on 1c grn & blk .75 .75
RA13 A29 1c on 5c ultra & blk .75 .75
RA14 A30 1c on 10c org & blk .75 .40
RA15 A31 1c on 25c yel & blk .75 .30
a. Inverted surcharge 5.00 5.00
RA16 A32 1c on 50c vio & blk .30 .25
a. Double surcharge 4.00 4.00
Nos. RA12-RA16 (5) 3.30 2.45

PT3

Surcharge in Red or Dark Blue

1922, Oct. ***Perf. 11½***

RA17 PT3 1c yellow (R) .25 .25
a. No period after "C" 1.00 1.00
RA18 PT3 1c violet (DBl) .25 .25
a. No period after "C" 1.00 1.00

Surcharge is inverted on 22 out of 50 of No. RA17, 23 out of 50 of No. RA18.
See No. RA24.

Nos. 403-407 Surcharged in Black

1923 ***Perf. 12***

RA19 A28 1c on 2c rose red & black .50 .45
RA20 A29 1c on 5c ultra & blk .55 .25
RA21 A30 1c on 10c org & blk .25 .25
RA22 A31 1c on 25c yel & blk .35 .30
RA23 A32 1c on 50c vio & blk .25 .25
Nos. RA19-RA23 (5) 1.90 1.50

The variety no period after "R" occurs twice on each sheet.

Red Surcharge
Wmk. Coat of Arms in Sheet
Perf. 11½

RA24 PT3 1c pale blue .25 .25

Type of 1921 Issue

Without Surcharge of New Value

Unwmk.

RA25 PT1 1c ver & blk .25 .25
a. Double overprint, one inverted 3.00 3.00

No. 409 Overprinted in Blue

1924

RA26 A24 1c violet .25 .25
a. Double overprint 8.00 8.00

There are two settings of the overprint on No. RA26, with "1924" 5½mm or 6½mm wide.

No. 409 Overprinted in Blue

1925

RA27 A24 1c violet .25 .25

No. 409 Overprinted in Blue

1926

RA28 A24 1c violet .25 .25

No. RA28 Overprinted in Various Colors

1927

RA29 A24 1c vio (R) .25 .25
a. Double overprint (R) 2.00 2.00
b. Inverted overprint (R) 3.00 3.00
RA30 A24 1c vio (V) .25 .25
a. Double overprint 2.50 2.50
b. Inverted overprint 2.50 2.50
RA31 A24 1c vio (Bl) .25 .25
a. Double overprint 5.00 5.00
RA32 A24 1c vio (Bk) .25 .25
a. Double ovpt., one invtd. 4.25 4.25
b. Double overprint 4.25 4.25

Same Overprint on No. RA27

RA33 A24 1c vio (Bk) 15.00 10.00
Nos. RA29-RA33 (5) 16.00 11.00

No. RA28 Overprinted in Violet

1928

RA34 A24 1c violet .25 .25
a. Double overprint 2.00 2.00
b. "928" 1.00 1.00

Similar to No. RA34 but 8mm space between "Resello" and "1928"

Black Overprint

RA35 A24 1c violet .40 .25
a. "1828" 2.00 2.00

PT4

Inscribed "Timbre Telegrafico"
Horiz. Srch. in Black,
Vert. Srch. in Red

RA36 PT4 1c on 5c bl & blk .60 .25
a. Comma after "R" 1.25 1.25
b. No period after "R" 1.25 1.25
c. No periods after "R" and "C" 1.25 1.25

("CORREOS" at right) — PT5

1928 **Engr.** ***Perf. 12***

RA37 PT5 1c plum .25 .25

See Nos. RA41-RA43. For overprints see Nos. RA45-RA46, RA48-RA51.

PT6

1929 **Red Surcharge**

RA38 PT6 1c on 5c bl & blk .25 .25
a. Inverted surcharge 3.00 3.00
b. Double surcharge 2.00 2.00
c. Double surcharge, one inverted 2.00 2.00
d. Period after "de" 1.25 1.25
e. Comma after "R" 1.25 1.25

See note after No. 512.

Regular Issue of 1928 Overprinted in Blue

RA39 A24 1c red orange .25 .25

No. RA39 exists both with and without signature control overprint.

An additional overprint, "1929" in black or blue on No. RA39, is fraudulent.

No. 513 Overprinted in Red

1929

RA40 A24 1c ol grn .25 .25
a. Double overprint .75 .75

No. RA40 is known with overprint in black, and with overprint inverted. These varieties were not regularly issued, but copies have been canceled by favor.

Type of 1928 Issue Inscribed at right "COMUNICACIONES"

1930-37

RA41 PT5 1c carmine .25 .25
RA42 PT5 1c orange ('33) .25 .25
RA43 PT5 1c green ('37) .25 .25
Nos. RA41-RA43 (3) .75 .75

No. RA42 has signature control. See note before No. 600.

No. RA39 Overprinted in Black

1931

RA44 A24 1c red orange .25 .25
a. "1931" double overprint .35 .35
b. "1931" double ovpt., one invtd. .40 .40

No. RA44 exists with signature control overprint. See note before No. 600. Value is the same.

No. RA42 Overprinted Vertically, up or down, in Black

1935

RA45 PT5 1c orange .25 .25
a. Double overprint 1.00 1.00
b. Double ovpt., one inverted

No. RA45 and RA45a Overprinted Vertically, Reading Down, in Blue

RA46 PT5 1c orange .50 .25
a. Black overprint double 2.00 2.00

Same Overprint in Red on Nos. RA39, RA42 and RA45

RA47 A24 1c red org (#RA39) *50.00 50.00*
RA48 PT5 1c org (#RA42) .25 .25
RA49 PT5 1c org (#RA45) .25 .25
a. Black overprint double .80 .80

Overprint is horizontal on No. RA47 and vertical, reading down, on Nos. RA48-RA49.
No. RA48 exists with signature control overprint. See note before No. 600. Same values.

No. RA42 Overprinted Vertically, Reading Down, in Carmine

1935 **Unwmk.** ***Perf. 12***

RA50 PT5 1c orange .25 .25

No. RA45 with Additional Overprint "1936", Vertically, Reading Down, in Red

1936

RA51 PT5 1c orange .50 .25

No. RA39 with Additional Overprint "1936" in Red

RA52 A24 1c red orange .50 .25

No. RA52 exists only with script control mark.

PT7

1936 **Vertical Surcharge in Red**

RA53 PT7 1c on 5c grn & blk .25 .25
a. "Cenavo" 1.40 1.40
b. "Centavos" 1.40 1.40

Horizontal Surcharge in Red

RA54 PT7 1c on 5c grn & blk .25 .25
a. Double surcharge 1.40 1.40

Baseball Player PT8

1937 **Typo.** ***Perf. 11***

RA55 PT8 1c carmine .60 .25
RA56 PT8 1c yellow .60 .25
RA57 PT8 1c blue .60 .25
RA58 PT8 1c green .60 .25
b. Sheet of 4, #RA55-RA58 6.00 3.00
Nos. RA55-RA58 (4) 2.40 1.00

Issued for the benefit of the Central American Caribbean Games of 1937.
Control mark in red is variously placed. See dark oval below "OLIMPICO" in illustration.

Tête bêche Pairs

RA55a PT8 1c .75 .75
RA56a PT8 1c .75 .75
RA57a PT8 1c .75 .75
RA58a PT8 1c .75 .75
Nos. RA55a-RA58a (4) 3.00 3.00

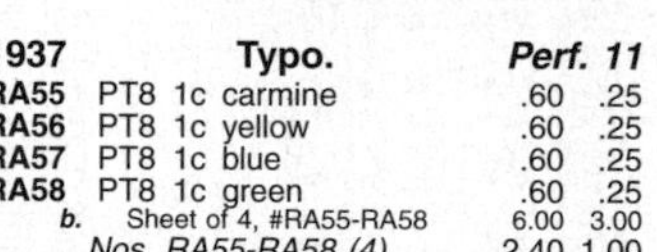

Catalogue values for unused stamps in this section, from this point to the end of the section, are for Never Hinged items.

Proposed Natl. Stadium, Managua — PT9

1949 **Photo.** ***Perf. 12***

RA60 PT9 5c greenish blue .25 .25
a. Souvenir sheet of 4 3.75 3.75

10th World Series of Amateur Baseball, 1948. The tax was used toward the erection of a national stadium at Managua.

Type Similar to 1949, with "Correos" omitted

1952

RA61 PT9 5c magenta .25 .25

The tax was used toward the erection of a national stadium at Managua.

PT10

1956 **Engr.** ***Perf. 12½x12***

RA62 PT10 5c deep ultra .25 .25

The tax was used for social welfare.

PT11

Surcharged in Red or Black

1959 Unwmk. *Perf. 12*

Red Marginal Number

RA63 PT11 5c on 50c vio bl (R) .25 .25
RA64 PT11 5c on 50c vio bl (B) .25 .25

Nos. RA63-RA64 are surcharged on consular revenue stamps. Surcharge reads "Sobre Tasa Postal CO.O5." Vertical surcharge on No. RA63, horizontal on No. RA64.

Jesus and Children — PT12

1959 Photo. *Perf. 16*

RA65 PT12 5c ultra .25 .25

Hexisia Bidentata — PT13

Orchids: No. RA67, Schomburgkia tibicinus. No. RA68, Stanhopea ecornuta. No. RA69, Lycaste macrophylla. No. RA70, Maxillaria tenuifolia. No. RA71, Cattleya skinneri. No. RA72, Cycnoches egertonianum. No. RA73, Bletia roezlii. No. RA74, Sobralia pleiantha. No. RA75, Oncidium oobolleta and ascendens.

1962, Feb. Photo. *Perf. 11½*

Granite Paper

Orchids in Natural Colors

RA66 PT13 5c pale lil & grn .25 .25
RA67 PT13 5c yel & grn .25 .25
RA68 PT13 5c pink & grn .25 .25
RA69 PT13 5c pale vio & grn .25 .25
RA70 PT13 5c lt grnsh bl & red .25 .25
RA71 PT13 5c buff & lil .25 .25
RA72 PT13 5c yel grn & brn .25 .25
RA73 PT13 5c gray & red .25 .25
RA74 PT13 5c lt bl & dk bl .25 .25
RA75 PT13 5c lt grn & brn .25 .25
Nos. RA66-RA75 (10) 2.50 2.50

For overprints see #842-852, 855-868, 901-908.

Exist imperf. Value, each pair $100.

PROVINCE OF ZELAYA

(Bluefields)

A province of Nicaragua lying along the eastern coast. Special postage stamps for this section were made necessary because for a period two currencies, which differed materially in value, were in use in Nicaragua. Silver money was used in Zelaya and Cabo Gracias a Dios while the rest of Nicaragua used paper money. Later the money of the entire country was placed on a gold basis.

Dangerous counterfeits exist of most of the Bluefields overprints.

Regular Issues of 1900-05 Handstamped in Black (4 or more types)

1904-05 Unwmk. *Perf. 12, 14*

On Engraved Stamps of 1900

1L1 A14 1c plum 1.50 .75
1L2 A14 2c vermilion 1.50 .75
1L3 A14 3c green 1.90 1.50
1L4 A14 4c ol grn 11.00 9.00
1L5 A14 15c ultra 3.00 1.90
1L6 A14 20c brown 3.00 1.90
1L7 A14 50c lake 10.50 9.00
1L8 A14 1p yellow 21.00
1L9 A14 2p salmon 30.00
1L10 A14 5p black 37.50
Nos. 1L1-1L10 (10) 120.90
Nos. 1L1-1L7 (7) 24.80

On Lithographed Stamps of 1902

1L11 A14 5c blue 3.00 .75
1L12 A14 5c carmine 1.90 .90
1L13 A14 10c violet 1.50 .75
Nos. 1L11-1L13 (3) 6.40 2.40

On Postage Due Stamps Overprinted "1901 Correos"

1L14 D3 20c brn (No. 156) 4.50 1.90
1L15 D3 50c lake (No. 158) — —

On Surcharged Stamps of 1904-05

1L16 A14 5c on 10c (#175) 1.50 1.10
1L17 A14 5c on 10c (#178) 3.00 1.50
1L18 A14 15c on 10c vio (#176) 1.50 1.50
1L19 A14 15c on 10c vio (#177) 14.00 4.50
Nos. 1L16-1L19 (4) 20.00 8.60

On Surcharged Stamp of 1901

1L20 A14 20c on 5p blk 18.00 3.00

On Regular Issue of 1905

1906-07 *Perf. 12*

1L21 A18 1c green .30 .30
1L22 A18 2c car rose .30 .30
1L23 A18 3c violet .30 .30
1L24 A18 4c org red .45 .45
1L25 A18 5c blue .25 .25
1L26 A18 10c yel brn 3.00 1.50
1L27 A18 15c brn ol 4.50 1.75
1L28 A18 20c lake 9.00 7.50
1L29 A18 50c orange 35.00 30.00
1L30 A18 1p black 30.00 27.50
1L31 A18 2p dk grn 37.50
1L32 A18 5p violet 45.00
Nos. 1L21-1L32 (12) 165.60
Nos. 1L21-1L30 (10) 69.85

On Surcharged Stamps of 1906-08

1L33 A18 10c on 3c vio .40 .40
1L34 A18 15c on 1c grn .50 .50
1L35 A18 20c on 2c rose 3.50 3.50
1L36 A18 20c on 5c bl 1.50 1.50
1L37 A18 50c on 6c sl (R) 1.50 3.00
Nos. 1L33-1L37 (5) 7.40 8.90

Handstamped

Stamps with the above overprints were made to fill dealers' orders but were never regularly issued or used. Stamps with similar overprints handstamped are bogus.

Surcharged Stamps of 1906 Overprinted in Red, Black or Blue

1L38 A18 15c on 1c grn (R) 2.75 2.75
a. Red overprint inverted

1L39 A18 20c on 2c rose (Bk) 1.90 1.90
1L40 A18 20c on 5c bl (R) 3.00 3.00
1L41 A18 50c on 6c sl (Bl) 14.00 14.00
Nos. 1L38-1L41 (4) 21.65 21.65

Stamps of the 1905 issue overprinted as above No. 1L38 or similarly overprinted but with only 2¼mm space between "B" and "Dpto. Zelaya" were made to fill dealers' orders but not placed in use.

No. 205 Handstamped in Black

Perf. 14 to 15

1L42 A18 10c yel brn 24.00 24.00

Stamps of 1907 Overprinted in Red or Black

1L43 A18 15c brn ol (R) 3.00 3.00
1L44 A18 20c lake .90 .90
a. Inverted overprint 11.00 11.00

With Additional Surcharge

1L45 A18 5c brn org .50 .45
a. Inverted surcharge 7.50 7.50

With Additional Surcharge

1L46 A18 5c on 4c brn org 12.00 12.00

On Provisional Postage Stamps of 1907-08 in Black or Blue

1L47 A18 10c on 2c rose (Bl) 4.50 4.50
1L48 A18 10c on 2c rose 300.00
1L48A A18 10c on 4c brn org 300.00
1L49 A18 10c on 20c lake 3.00 3.00
1L50 A18 10c on 50c org (Bl) 3.00 2.25

Arms Type of 1907 Overprinted in Black or Violet

1907

1L51 A18 1c green .30 .25
1L52 A18 2c rose .30 .25
1L53 A18 3c violet .40 .40
1L54 A18 4c brn org .45 .45
1L55 A18 5c blue 4.50 2.25
1L56 A18 10c yel brn .40 .30
1L57 A18 15c brn ol .75 .40
1L58 A18 20c lake .75 .45
1L59 A18 50c orange 2.25 1.50
1L60 A18 1p blk (V) 2.25 1.50
1L61 A18 2p dk grn 2.25 1.90
1L62 A18 5p violet 3.75 2.25
Nos. 1L51-1L62 (12) 18.35 11.90

Nos. 217-225 Overprinted in Green

1908

1L63 A19 1c on 5c yel & blk (R) .45 .40
1L64 A19 2c on 5c yel & blk (Bl) .45 .40
1L65 A19 4c on 5c yel & blk (G) .45 .40
a. Overprint reading down 11.00 11.00
b. Double overprint, reading up and down 18.00 18.00
1L66 A19 5c yel & blk .45 .45
a. "CORROE" 4.50
b. Double overprint 11.00 11.00
c. Double overprint, reading up and down 19.00 19.00
d. "CORREO 1908" double 15.00 15.00
1L67 A19 10c lt bl & blk .45 .45
a. Ovpt. reading down .50 .50
b. "CORREO 1908" triple 37.50
1L68 A19 15c on 50c ol & blk (R) .90 .90
a. "1008" 4.50
b. "8908" 4.50
1L69 A19 35c on 50c ol & blk 1.40 1.40
1L70 A19 1p yel brn & blk 1.90 1.90
a. "CORROE" 12.00 12.00
1L71 A19 2p pearl gray & blk 2.25 2.25
a. "CORROE" 15.00 15.00
Nos. 1L63-1L71 (9) 8.70 8.55

Overprinted Horizontally in Black or Green

1L72 A19 5c yel & blk 9.00 7.50
1L72A A19 2p pearl gray & blk (G) *300.00*

On Nos. 1L72-1L72A, space between "B" and "Dpto. Zelaya" is 13mm.

Nos. 237-248 Overprinted in Black

Imprint: "American Bank Note Co. NY"

1909 *Perf. 12*

1L73 A18 1c yel grn .25 .25
1L74 A18 2c vermilion .25 .25
a. Inverted overprint
1L75 A18 3c red org .25 .25
1L76 A18 4c violet .25 .25
1L77 A18 5c dp bl .30 .25
a. Inverted overprint 9.00 9.00
b. "B" inverted 7.50 7.50
c. Double overprint 12.00 12.00
1L78 A18 6c gray brn 4.50 3.00
1L79 A18 10c lake .30 .30
a. "B" inverted 9.00 9.00
1L80 A18 15c black .45 .40
a. "B" inverted 11.00 11.00
b. Inverted overprint 12.00 12.00
c. Double overprint 14.00 14.00
1L81 A18 20c brn ol .50 .50
a. "B" inverted 19.00 19.00
1L82 A18 50c dp grn 1.50 1.50
1L83 A18 1p yellow 5.00 2.25
1L84 A18 2p car rose 6.00 3.00
a. Double overprint 27.50 27.50
Nos. 1L73-1L84 (12) 19.55 12.20

One stamp in each sheet has the "o" of "Dpto." sideways.

Overprinted in Black

1910

1L85 A18 3c red org .40 .40
1L86 A18 4c violet .40 .40
a. Inverted overprint 14.00 14.00
1L87 A18 15c black 4.50 2.25
1L88 A18 20c brn ol .25 .30
1L89 A18 50c dp grn .30 .40

1L90 A18 1p yellow .30 .45
a. Inverted overprint 7.50
1L91 A18 2p car rose .40 .75
Nos. 1L85-1L91 (7) 6.55 4.95

Black Ovpt., Green Srch., Carmine Block-outs

Z1

1910
1L92 Z1 5c on 10c lake 3.75 3.00

There are three types of the letter "B." It is stated that this stamp was used exclusively for postal purposes and not for telegrams.

No. 247 Surcharged in Black

1911
1L93 A18 5c on 1p yellow .75 .75
a. Double surcharge 14.00
1L94 A18 10c on 1p yellow 1.50 1.50
1L95 A18 15c on 1p yellow .75 .75
a. Inverted surcharge 9.00
b. Double surcharge 9.00
c. Double surcharge, one invtd. 9.00
Nos. 1L93-1L95 (3) 3.00 3.00

Revenue Stamps Surcharged in Black

Perf. 14 to 15
1L96 A19 5c on 25c lilac .75 1.10
a. Without period 1.50 1.50
b. Inverted surcharge 9.00 9.00
1L97 A19 10c on 1p yel brn 1.10 .75
a. Without period 1.90 1.90
b. "01" for "10" 9.00 7.50
c. Inverted surcharge 13.00 13.00

Surcharged in Black

1L98 A19 5c on 1p yel brn 1.50 1.50
a. Without period 2.25
b. "50" for "05" 14.00 14.00
c. Inverted surcharge 15.00 15.00
1L99 A19 5c on 10p pink 1.50 1.50
a. Without period 2.25 2.25
b. "50" for "05" 11.00 11.00
1L100 A19 10c on 1p yel brn 82.50 82.50
a. Without period 95.00 95.00
1L101 A19 10c on 25p grn .75 .75
a. Without period 2.25 2.25
b. "1" for "10" 7.50
1L102 A19 10c on 50p ver 11.00 11.00
a. Without period 16.00
b. "1" for "10" 22.50
Nos. 1L98-1L102 (5) 97.25 97.25

With Additional Overprint "1904"
1L103 A19 5c on 10p pink 14.00 14.00
a. Without period 24.00 24.00
b. "50" for "05" 110.00 110.00
1L104 A19 10c on 2p gray .75 .75
a. Without period 1.90
b. "1" for "10" 7.50
1L105 A19 10c on 25p grn 92.50
a. Without period 100.00
1L106 A19 10c on 50p ver 7.50 7.50
a. Without period 14.00
b. "1" for "10" 18.00
c. Inverted surcharge

The surcharges on Nos. 1L96 to 1L106 are in settings of twenty-five. One stamp in each setting has a large square period after "cts" and another has a thick upright "c" in that word. There are two types of "1904".

No. 293C Overprinted

1911
1L107 A21 5c on 5c on 2c bl (R) 32.50
a. "5" omitted 37.50
b. Red overprint inverted 40.00
c. As "a" and "b" 47.50

Same Overprint On Nos. 290, 291, 292 and 289D with Lines of Surcharge spaced 2½mm apart Reading Down
1L107D A21 2c on 10c on 1c red *250.00*
e. Overprint reading up *250.00*
1L107F A21 5c on 10c on 1c red *150.00*
1L107G A21 10c on 10c on 1c red (#292) *200.00*
1L108 A21 10c on 10c on 1c red (#289D) *200.00*

Locomotive — Z2

1912 **Engr.** ***Perf. 14***
1L109 Z2 1c yel grn 1.50 .50
1L110 Z2 2c vermilion 1.25 .25
1L111 Z2 3c org brn 1.50 .45
1L112 Z2 4c carmine 1.50 .30
1L113 Z2 5c dp bl 1.50 .45
1L114 Z2 6c red brn 9.00 3.50
1L115 Z2 10c slate 1.50 .30
1L116 Z2 15c dl lil 1.50 .60
1L117 Z2 20c bl vio 1.50 .60
1L118 Z2 25c grn & blk 2.25 .80
1L119 Z2 35c brn & blk 3.00 1.25
1L120 Z2 50c ol grn 3.00 1.25
1L121 Z2 1p orange 4.00 1.75
1L122 Z2 2p org brn 7.50 3.25
1L123 Z2 5p dk bl grn 18.00 7.50
Nos. 1L109-1L123 (15) 58.50 22.75

The stamps of this issue were for use in all places on the Atlantic Coast of Nicaragua where the currency was on a silver basis.

For surcharges see Nos. 325-337.

OFFICIAL STAMPS

Regular Issue of 1909 Overprinted in Black

1909 **Unwmk.** ***Perf. 12***
1LO1 A18 20c brn ol 15.00 12.00
a. Double overprint 30.00

No. O216 Overprinted in Black

1LO2 A18 15c black 15.00 10.00

Same Overprint on Official Stamp of 1911

1911
1LO3 A18 5c on 3c red org 22.50 17.50

CABO GRACIAS A DIOS

A cape and seaport town in the extreme northeast of Nicaragua. The name was coined by Spanish explorers who had great difficulty finding a landing place along the Nicaraguan coast and when eventually locating this harbor expressed their relief by designating the point "Cape Thanks to God." Special postage stamps came into use for the same reasons as the Zelaya issues. See Zelaya.

Dangerous counterfeits exist of most of the Cabo Gracias a Dios overprints. Special caution should be taken with double and inverted handstamps of Nos. 2L1-2L25, as most are counterfeits. Expert opinion is required.

Regular Issues of 1900-04 Handstamped in Violet

On Engraved Stamps of 1900

1904-05 **Unwmk.** ***Perf. 12, 14***
2L1 A14 1c plum 2.25 1.10
2L2 A14 2c vermilion 4.50 1.25
2L3 A14 3c green 6.00 4.50
2L4 A14 4c ol grn 9.75 9.75
2L5 A14 15c ultra 35.00 22.50
2L6 A14 20c brown 3.00 2.25
Nos. 2L1-2L6 (6) 60.50 41.35

On Lithographed Stamps of 1902
2L7 A14 5c blue 24.00 24.00
2L8 A14 10c violet 24.00 24.00

On Surcharged Stamps of 1904
2L9 A16 5c on 10c vio 22.50 22.50
2L10 A16 15c on 10c vio

On Postage Due Stamps
Violet Handstamp
2L11 D3 20c org brn (#141) 5.00 1.25
2L12 D3 20c org brn (#156) 3.50 1.25
2L13 D3 30c dk grn (#157) 14.00 14.00
2L14 D3 50c lake (#158) 3.75 .75
Nos. 2L11-2L14 (4) 26.25 17.25

Black Handstamp
2L15 D3 30c dk grn (#157) 24.00 24.00

Stamps of 1900-05 Handstamped in Violet

On Engraved Stamps of 1900
2L16 A14 1c plum 2.75 2.25
2L17 A14 2c vermilion 27.50 24.00
2L18 A14 3c green 37.50 27.50
2L19 A14 4c ol grn 40.00 37.50
2L20 A14 15c ultra 45.00 45.00
Nos. 2L16-2L20 (5) 152.75 136.25

On Lithographed Stamps of 1902
2L22 A14 5c dk bl 95.00 50.00
2L23 A14 10c violet 27.50 24.00

On Surcharged Stamp of 1904
2L24 A14 5c on 10c vio

On Postage Due Stamp
2L25 D3 20c org brn (#141)

The editors have no evidence that stamps with this handstamp were issued. Examples were sent to the UPU and covers are known.

Stamps of 1900-08 Handstamped in Violet

1905 **On Stamps of 1905**
2L26 A18 1c green 1.10 1.10
2L27 A18 2c car rose 1.50 1.50
2L28 A18 3c violet 1.50 1.50
2L29 A18 4c org red 3.75 3.75
2L30 A18 5c blue 1.50 1.10
2L31 A18 6c slate 3.75 3.75
2L32 A18 10c yel brn 3.00 1.90
2L33 A18 15c brn ol 4.50 4.50
2L34 A18 1p black 20.00 20.00
2L35 A18 2p dk grn 35.00 35.00
Nos. 2L26-2L35 (10) 75.60 74.10

Magenta Handstamp
2L26a A18 1c 3.75 3.00
2L27a A18 2c 3.00 2.75
2L28a A18 3c 3.75 3.00
2L30a A18 5c 7.50 6.00
2L33a A18 15c 13.50 11.00
Nos. 2L26a-2L33a (5) 31.50 25.75

On Stamps of 1900-04
2L36 A14 5c on 10c vio 14.00 14.00
2L37 A14 10c violet
2L38 A14 20c brown 12.00 12.00
2L39 A14 20c on 5p blk 95.00

On Postage Due Stamps Overprinted "Correos"
2L40 D3 20c org brn (#141) 9.00 9.00
2L41 D3 20c org brn (#156) 5.00 4.50

On Surcharged Stamps of 1906-08
2L42 A18 10c on 3c vio *250.00*
2L43 A18 20c on 5c blue 9.00 9.00
2L44 A18 50c on 6c slate 24.00 24.00

On Stamps of 1907
Perf. 14 to 15
2L44A A18 2c rose *250.00*
2L45 A18 10c yel brn *100.00 75.00*
2L46 A18 15c brn ol *90.00 75.00*

On Provisional Stamp of 1908 in Magenta
2L47 A19 5c yel & blk 7.50 7.50

Stamps with the above large handstamp in black instead of violet, are bogus. There are also excellent counterfeits in violet.

The foregoing overprints being handstamped are found in various positions, especially the last type.

Stamps of 1907 Type A18, Overprinted in Black or Violet

1907
2L48 A18 1c green .35 .30
a. Vert. pair, imperf. btwn. —
2L49 A18 2c rose .35 .30
2L50 A18 3c violet .35 .30
a. Vert. pair, imperf. btwn. *350.00*
2L51 A18 4c brn org .50 .40
2L52 A18 5c blue .60 .50
2L53 A18 10c yel brn .50 .40
2L54 A18 15c brn ol .85 .75
2L55 A18 20c lake .85 .75
2L56 A18 50c orange 2.25 1.50
2L57 A18 1p blk (V) 2.50 1.90
2L58 A18 2p dk grn 3.50 2.25
2L59 A18 5p violet 5.00 3.75
Nos. 2L48-2L59 (12) 17.60 13.10

Nos. 237-248 Overprinted in Black

Imprint: American Bank Note Co.

1909 ***Perf. 12***
2L60 A18 1c yel grn .35 .40
2L61 A18 2c vermilion .35 .40
2L62 A18 3c red org .35 .40
2L63 A18 4c violet .35 .40

2L64 A18 5c dp bl .35 .60
2L65 A18 6c gray brn 6.00 6.00
2L66 A18 10c lake .60 .75
2L67 A18 15c black .90 .90
2L68 A18 20c brn ol 1.00 *4.00*
2L69 A18 50c dp grn 2.50 2.50
2L70 A18 1p yellow 4.00 4.00
2L71 A18 2p car rose 5.75 5.75
Nos. 2L60-2L71 (12) 22.50 26.10

No. 199 Overprinted Vertically

2L72 A18 50c on 6c slate (R) 7.50 7.50

CABO GRACIAS A DIOS OFFICIAL STAMPS

Official Stamps of 1907 Overprinted in Red or Violet

1907
2LO1 A18 10c on 1c green *60.00*
2LO2 A18 15c on 1c green *75.00*
2LO3 A18 20c on 1c green *100.00*
2LO4 A18 50c on 1c green *125.00*

NIGER

'nī-jər

LOCATION — Northern Africa, directly north of Nigeria
GOVT. — Republic
AREA — 458,075 sq. mi.
POP. — 9,962,242 (1999 est.)
CAPITAL — Niamey

The colony, formed in 1922, was originally a military territory. The Republic of the Niger was proclaimed December 18, 1958. In the period between issues of the colony and the republic, stamps of French West Africa were used. Full Independence from France was proclaimed August 3, 1960.

100 Centimes = 1 Franc

Catalogue values for unused stamps in this country are for Never Hinged items, beginning with Scott 91 in the regular postage section, Scott B14 in the semi-postal section, Scott C14 in the airpost section, Scott J22 in the postage due section, and Scott O1 in the official section.

Watermark

Wmk. 385

Stamps of Upper Senegal and Niger Type of 1914, Overprinted

Camel and Rider — A1

In the overprint, normal spacing between the words "DU" and "NIGER" is 2½mm. In one position (72) of all sheets in the first printing, the space between the two words is 3mm.

1921-26 Unwmk. *Perf. 13½x14*
1 A1 1c brn vio & vio .25 *.40*
2 A1 2c dk gray & dl vio .25 *.40*
3 A1 4c black & blue .35 *.50*
4 A1 5c ol brn & dk brn .30 *.50*
5 A1 10c yel grn & bl grn 1.60 *2.00*
6 A1 10c mag, *bluish* ('26) .95 *1.20*
7 A1 15c red brn & org .40 *.55*
8 A1 20c brn vio & blk .35 *.50*
9 A1 25c blk & bl grn .80 *.80*
10 A1 30c red org & rose 2.75 *3.50*
11 A1 30c bl grn & red org ('26) .80 *.80*
12 A1 35c rose & violet .95 *1.20*
13 A1 40c gray & rose .95 *1.20*
14 A1 45c blue & ol brn 1.40 *1.40*
15 A1 50c ultra & bl .80 *1.20*
16 A1 50c dk gray & bl vio ('25) 1.60 *1.60*
17 A1 60c org red ('26) 1.40 *2.00*
18 A1 75c yel & ol brn 1.40 *1.60*
19 A1 1fr dk brn & dl vio 1.60 *2.00*
20 A1 2fr green & blue 1.60 *2.00*
21 A1 5fr violet & blk 2.75 *4.00*
Nos. 1-21 (21) 23.25 *29.35*

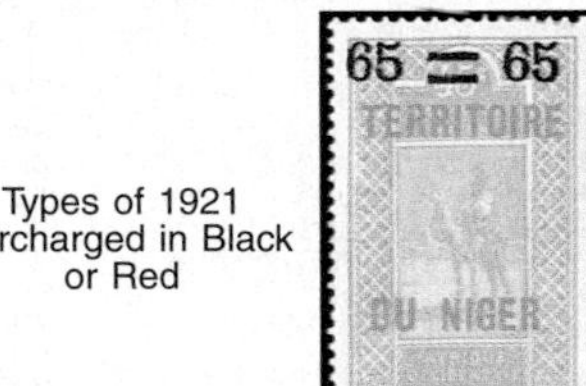
Types of 1921 Surcharged in Black or Red

1922-26
22 A1 25c on 15c red brn & org ('25) .95 .80
a. Multiple surcharge 260.00
b. "25c" inverted 140.00
23 A1 25c on 2fr grn & bl (R) ('24) .90 .80
24 A1 25c on 5fr vio & blk (R) ('24) .95 .80
a. Double surcharge 225.00
25 A1 60c on 75c vio,*pnksh* .90 *1.20*
26 A1 65c on 45c bl & ol brn ('25) 2.75 *3.50*
27 A1 85c on 75c yel & ol brn ('25) 2.75 *3.50*
28 A1 1.25fr on 1fr dp bl & lt bl (R) ('26) 1.10 *1.20*
a. Surcharge omitted 260.00
b. As "a," in pair with unsurcharged stamp 1,700.
Nos. 22-28 (7) 10.30 11.80

Nos. 22-24 are surcharged "25c," No. 28, "1f25." Nos. 25-27 are surcharged like illustration.

Drawing Water from Well — A2

Zinder Fortress — A4

Boat on Niger River — A3

Perf. 13x14, 13½x14, 14x13, 14x13½
1926-40 Typo.
29 A2 1c lil rose & ol .25 *.40*
30 A2 2c dk gray & dl red .25 *.40*
31 A2 3c red vio & ol gray ('40) .25 *.40*
32 A2 4c amber & gray .25 *.40*
33 A2 5c ver & yel grn .25 *.40*
34 A2 10c dp bl & Prus bl .25 *.40*
35 A2 15c gray grn & yel grn .55 *.80*
36 A2 15c gray lil & lt red ('28) .40 .40
37 A3 20c Prus grn & ol brn .40 *.55*
38 A3 25c black & dl red .40 .50
39 A3 30c bl grn & yel grn .80 *1.20*
40 A3 30c yel & red vio ('40) .30 *.50*
41 A3 35c brn org & turq bl, *bluish* .80 *1.20*
42 A3 35c bl grn & dl grn ('38) 1.20 *1.60*
43 A3 40c red brn & slate .40 *.50*
44 A3 45c yel & red vio 1.60 *1.90*
45 A3 45c bl grn & dl grn ('40) .30 *.50*
46 A3 50c scar & grn, *grnsh* .40 .40
47 A3 55c dk car & brn ('38) 2.00 2.00
48 A3 60c dk car & brn ('40) .55 *.70*
49 A3 65c ol grn & rose .40 *.55*
50 A3 70c ol grn & rose ('40) 2.00 *2.50*
51 A3 75c grn & vio, *pink* 2.00 *2.25*
a. Center and value double 225.00
52 A3 80c cl & ol grn ('38) 1.60 *2.00*
53 A3 90c brn red & ver 1.60 *1.90*
54 A3 90c brt rose & yel grn ('39) 2.00 *2.40*
55 A4 1fr rose & yel grn 8.00 8.75
56 A4 1fr dk red & red org ('38) 2.00 *2.40*
57 A4 1fr grn & red ('40) .80 .80
58 A4 1.10fr ol brn & grn 4.00 *6.50*
59 A4 1.25fr grn & red ('33) 2.40 2.40
60 A4 1.25fr dk red & red org ('39) .80 *1.20*
61 A4 1.40fr red vio & dk brn ('40) .80 *1.50*
62 A4 1.50fr dp bl & pale bl .55 *.70*
63 A4 1.60fr ol brn & grn ('40) 1.75 *2.00*
64 A4 1.75fr red vio & dk brn ('33) 1.60 2.40
65 A4 1.75fr dk bl & vio bl ('38) 1.25 *1.60*
66 A4 2fr red org & ol brn .30 *.50*
67 A4 2.25fr dk bl & vio bl ('39) 1.20 *1.60*
68 A4 2.50fr blk brn ('40) 1.20 *1.60*
69 A4 3fr dl vio & blk ('27) .55 *.80*
70 A4 5fr vio brn & blk, *pink* .80 *1.20*
71 A4 10fr chlky bl & mag 1.60 *2.00*
72 A4 20fr yel grn & red org 1.60 *2.00*
Nos. 29-72 (44) 52.40 *66.70*

For surcharges see Nos. B7-B10.

Common Design Types pictured following the introduction.

Colonial Exposition Issue
Common Design Types

1931 Typo. *Perf. 12½*
Name of Country in Black
73 CD70 40c deep green 5.00 5.00
74 CD71 50c violet 5.00 5.00
75 CD72 90c red orange 5.75 5.75
76 CD73 1.50fr dull blue 5.75 5.75
Nos. 73-76 (4) 21.50 21.50

Paris International Exposition Issue
Common Design Types

1937 *Perf. 13*
77 CD74 20c deep violet 2.00 2.00
78 CD75 30c dark green 2.00 2.00
79 CD76 40c carmine rose 2.00 2.00
80 CD77 50c dark brown 1.60 1.60
81 CD78 90c red 1.60 1.60
82 CD79 1.50fr ultra 2.00 2.00
Nos. 77-82 (6) 11.20 11.20

Colonial Arts Exhibition Issue
Souvenir Sheet
Common Design Type

1937 *Imperf.*
83 CD74 3fr magenta 10.00 *14.00*

Caillie Issue
Common Design Type

1939 *Perf. 12½x12*
84 CD81 90c org brn & org .35 .35
85 CD81 2fr brt violet .35 1.00
86 CD81 2.25fr ultra & dk bl .35 1.00
Nos. 84-86 (3) 1.05 2.35

New York World's Fair Issue
Common Design Type

1939, May 10
87 CD82 1.25fr car lake .70 1.40
88 CD82 2.25fr ultra .70 1.40

Zinder Fortress and Marshal Pétain — A5

1941 Unwmk. Engr. *Perf. 12x12½*
89 A5 1fr green .35
90 A5 2.50fr dark blue .35
Set, never hinged 1.40

Nos. 89-90 were issued by the Vichy government in France, but were not placed on sale in Niger.

For surcharges, see Nos. B13A-B13B.

See French West Africa No. 68 for additional stamp inscribed "Niger" and "Afrique Occidentale Francaise."

Catalogue values for unused stamps in this section, from this point to the end of the section, are for Never Hinged items.

Republic of the Niger

Giraffes — A6

1fr, 2fr, Crested cranes. 5fr, 7fr, Saddle-billed storks. 15fr, 20fr, Barbary sheep. 25fr, 30fr, Giraffes. 50fr, 60fr, Ostriches. 85fr, 100fr, Lion.

1959-60 Unwmk. Engr. *Perf. 13*
91 A6 1fr multi .35 .25
92 A6 2fr multi .35 .25
93 A6 5fr blk, car & ol .50 .25
94 A6 7fr grn, blk & red .60 .25
95 A6 15fr grnsh bl & dk brn .25 .25
96 A6 20fr vio, blk & ind .25 .25
97 A6 25fr multi .35 .25
98 A6 30fr multi .45 .30
99 A6 50fr ind & org brn 4.75 .70
100 A6 60fr dk brn & emer 6.50 1.00
101 A6 85fr org brn & bis 2.25 .80
102 A6 100fr bis & yel grn 3.00 1.25
Nos. 91-102 (12) 19.60 5.80

Issue years: #97, 1959; others, 1960.
For surcharge see No. 103.

Imperforates
Most stamps of the republic exist imperforate in issued and trial colors, and also in small presentation sheets in issued color.

No. 102 Surcharged with New Value and: "Indépendance 3-8-60"

1960
103 A6 200fr on 100fr 14.00 14.00

Niger's independence.

C.C.T.A. Issue
Common Design Type

1960 Engr. *Perf. 13*
104 CD106 25fr buff & red brn .85 .45

Emblem of the Entente — A6a

1960, May 29 Photo. *Perf. 13x13½*
105 A6a 25fr multi .85 .45

1st anniversary of the Entente (Dahomey, Ivory Coast, Niger and Upper Volta).

Pres. Diori Hamani — A7

1960, Dec. 18 Engr. *Perf. 13*
106 A7 25fr ol bis & blk .60 .30

2nd anniversary of the proclamation of the Republic of the Niger.

Dugong A8

1962, Jan. 29 Unwmk. *Perf. 13*
107 A8 50c grn & dk sl grn .40 .25
108 A8 10fr red brn & dk grn .65 .25

Abidjan Games Issue
Common Design Type

25fr, Basketball & Soccer. 85fr, Track, horiz.

1962, May 26 Photo. *Perf. 12x12½*
109 CD109 15fr multi .40 .25
110 CD109 25fr multi .60 .25
111 CD109 85fr multi 1.60 .60
Nos. 109-111 (3) 2.60 1.10

African-Malgache Union Issue
Common Design Type

1962, Sept. 8 *Perf. 12½x12*
112 CD110 30fr multi .80 .40

Pres. Diori Hamani and Map of Niger in Africa A10

1962, Dec. 18 Photo. *Perf. 12½x12*
113 A10 25fr multi .60 .25

Woman Runner — A11

15fr, Swimming, horiz. 45fr, Volleyball.

Unwmk.
1963, Apr. 11 Engr. *Perf. 13*
114 A11 15fr brt bl & dk brn .25 .25
115 A11 25fr dk brn & red .60 .25
116 A11 45fr grn & blk 1.10 .40
Nos. 114-116 (3) 1.95 .90

Friendship Games, Dakar, Apr. 11-21.

Woodworker — A12

10fr, Tanners, horiz. 25fr, Goldsmith. 30fr, Mat makers, horiz. 85fr, Decoy maker.

Perf. 12x12½, 12½x12
1963, Aug. 30 Photo.
117 A12 5fr brn & multi .25 .25
118 A12 10fr dk grn & multi .35 .25
119 A12 25fr blk & multi .60 .25
120 A12 30fr vio & multi .90 .30
121 A12 85fr dk bl & multi 2.00 .80
Nos. 117-121,C26 (6) 6.85 3.35

Berberi (Nuba) Woman's Costume — A13

Costume Museum, Niamey — A14

Costumes: 20fr, Hausa woman. 25fr, Tuareg woman. 30fr, Tuareg man. 60fr, Djerma woman.

Perf. 12x12½, 12½x12
1963, Oct. 15 Photo.
122 A13 15fr multi .35 .25
123 A13 20fr blk & bl .50 .25
124 A13 25fr multi .70 .25
125 A13 30fr multi .75 .25
126 A13 60fr multi 1.75 .60
127 A14 85fr multi 2.00 .70
Nos. 122-127 (6) 6.05 2.30

Man, Globe and Scales — A15

Unwmk.
1963, Dec. 10 Engr. *Perf. 13*
128 A15 25fr lt ol grn, ultra & brn org .65 .30

15th anniversary of the Universal Declaration of Human Rights.

Parkinsonia Aculeata — A16

Flowers: 10fr, Russelia equisetiformis. 15fr, Red sage (lantana). 20fr, Argyreia nervosa. 25fr, Luffa cylindrica. 30fr, Hibiscus rosa sinensis. 45fr, Red jasmine (frangipani). 50fr,
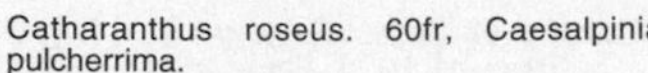
Catharanthus roseus. 60fr, Caesalpinia pulcherrima.

1964-65 Photo. *Perf. 13½x13*
129 A16 5fr dk red, grn & yel .75 .30
130 A16 10fr multi .60 .30
131 A16 15fr multi 1.00 .40
132 A16 20fr multi 1.00 .40
133 A16 25fr multi 1.00 .40
134 A16 30fr multi 1.25 .55
135 A16 45fr multi ('65) 2.25 .85
136 A16 50fr dk red, brt pink & grn ('65) 2.25 .85
137 A16 60fr multi ('65) 4.00 1.10
Nos. 129-137 (9) 14.10 5.15

Solar Flares and IQSY Emblem — A17

1964, May 12 Engr. *Perf. 13*
138 A17 30fr dp org, vio & blk .60 .45

International Quiet Sun Year, 1964-65.

Mobile Medical Unit — A18

30fr, Mobile children's clinic. 50fr, Mobile women's clinic. 60fr, Outdoor medical laboratory.

1964, May 26
139 A18 25fr bl, org & ol .40 .25
140 A18 30fr multi .50 .25
141 A18 50fr vio, org & bl .80 .30
142 A18 60fr grnsh bl, org & dk brn .90 .40
Nos. 139-142 (4) 2.60 1.20

Nigerian mobile health education organization, OMNES (Organisation Médicale Mobile Nigérienne d'Education Sanitaire).

Cooperation Issue
Common Design Type

1964, Nov. 7 Unwmk. *Perf. 13*
143 CD119 50fr vio, dk brn & org .80 .40

Tuareg Tent of Azawak A19

Designs: 20fr, Songhai house. 25fr, Wogo and Kourtey tents. 30fr, Djerma house. 60fr, Huts of Sorkawa fishermen. 85fr, Hausa town house.

1964-65 Engr.
144 A19 15fr ultra, dl grn & red brn .25 .25
145 A19 20fr multi .30 .25
146 A19 25fr Prus bl, dk brn & org brn .40 .25
147 A19 30fr multi ('65) .50 .30
148 A19 60fr red, grn & bis ('65) 1.00 .30
149 A19 85fr multi ('65) 1.40 .50
Nos. 144-149 (6) 3.85 1.85

Leprosy Examination — A20

1964, Dec. 15 Photo. *Perf. 13x12½*
150 A20 50fr multi .70 .45

Issued to publicize the fight against leprosy.

Abraham Lincoln — A21

1965, Apr. 3 *Perf. 13x12½*
151 A21 50fr vio bl, blk, & ocher .70 .45

Centenary of death of Abraham Lincoln.

Teaching with Radio and Pictures — A22

Designs: 25fr, Woman studying arithmetic: "A better life through knowledge." 30fr, Adult education class. 50fr, Map of Niger and 5 tribesmen, "Literacy for adults."

1965, Apr. 16 Engr. *Perf. 13*
152 A22 20fr dk bl, dk brn & ocher .40 .25
153 A22 25fr sl grn, brn & ol brn .50 .25
154 A22 30fr red, sl grn & vio brn .60 .25
155 A22 50fr dp bl, brn & vio brn .85 .35
Nos. 152-155 (4) 2.35 1.10

Issued to promote adult education and "a better life through knowledge."

Ader Portable Telephone — A23

Designs: 30fr, Wheatstone telegraph interrupter. 50fr, Early telewriter.

1965, May 17 Unwmk. *Perf. 13*
156 A23 25fr red brn, dk grn & ind .60 .25
157 A23 30fr lil, slate grn & red .70 .30
158 A23 50fr red, slate grn & pur 1.00 .40
Nos. 156-158 (3) 2.30 .95

International Telecommunication Union, cent.

Runner — A24

Designs: 10fr, Hurdler, horiz. 20fr, Pole vaulter, horiz. 30fr, Long jumper.

1965, July 1 Engr. *Perf. 13*
159 A24 10fr brn, ocher & blk .25 .25
160 A24 15fr gray, brn & red .45 .25
161 A24 20fr dk grn, brn & vio bl .60 .25
162 A24 30fr maroon, brn & grn .70 .25
Nos. 159-162 (4) 2.00 1.00

African Games, Brazzaville, July 18-25.

Radio Interview and Club Emblem A25

45fr, Recording folk music, vert. 50fr, Group listening to broadcast, vert. 60fr, Public debate.

1965, Oct. 1 Engr. *Perf. 13*

163 A25 30fr brt vio, emer & red brn .40 .25
164 A25 45fr blk, car & buff .55 .25
165 A25 50fr dk car, bl & lt brn .60 .30
166 A25 60fr bis, ultra & brn .75 .35
Nos. 163-166 (4) 2.30 1.15

Issued to promote radio clubs.

Water Cycle — A26

1966, Feb. 28 Engr. *Perf. 13*

167 A26 50fr vio, ocher & bl .80 .35

Hydrological Decade, 1965-74.

Carvings, Mask and Headdresses — A27

50fr, Carvings and wall decorations. 60fr, Carvings and arch. 100fr, Architecture and handicraft.

1966, Apr. 12

168 A27 30fr red brn, blk & brt grn .55 .35
169 A27 50fr brt bl, ocher & pur .80 .35
170 A27 60fr car lake, dl pur & yel brn .90 .50
171 A27 100fr brt red, bl & blk 1.75 .90
Nos. 168-171 (4) 4.00 2.10

Intl. Negro Arts Festival, Dakar, Senegal, Apr. 1-24.

Soccer Player — A28

50fr, Goalkeeper, horiz. 60fr, Player kicking ball.

1966, June 17 Engr. *Perf. 13*

172 A28 30fr dk brn, brt bl & rose red .60 .30
173 A28 50fr bl, choc & emer .75 .35
174 A28 60fr bl, lil & brn .90 .45
Nos. 172-174 (3) 2.25 1.10

8th World Soccer Cup Championship, Wembley, England, July 11-30.

Color Guard — A29

20fr, Parachutist, horiz. 45fr, Tanks, horiz.

Perf. 12½x13, 13x12½

1966, Aug. 23 Photo.

175 A29 20fr multi .40 .25
176 A29 30fr multi .50 .25
177 A29 45fr multi .65 .30
Nos. 175-177 (3) 1.55 .80

5th anniv. of the National Armed Forces.

Cow Receiving Injection A30

1966, Sept. 26 Litho. *Perf. 12½x13*

178 A30 45fr org brn, bl & blk 1.25 .50

Campaign against cattle plague.

UNESCO Emblem — A31

1966, Nov. 4 Litho. *Perf. 13x12½*

179 A31 50fr multi .70 .40

20th anniversary of UNESCO.

Cement Works Malbaza A32

Designs: 10fr, Furnace, vert. 20fr, Electric center. 50fr, Handling of raw material.

1966, Dec. 17 Engr. *Perf. 13*

180 A32 10fr ind, brn & org .30 .25
181 A32 20fr dk ol grn & dl bl .45 .25
182 A32 30fr bl, gray & red brn .45 .25
183 A32 50fr ind, bl & brn .70 .30
Nos. 180-183 (4) 1.90 1.05

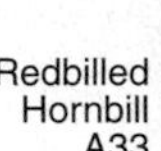

Redbilled Hornbill A33

Birds: 2fr, Pied kingfisher. 30fr, Barbary shrike. 45fr, 65fr, Little weaver and nest. 70fr, Chestnut-bellied sand grouse.

1967-81 Engr. *Perf. 13*

184 A33 1fr red, sl grn & dk brn .70 .35
185 A33 2fr brn, brt grn & blk .70 .35
186 A33 30fr multi 3.50 .65
187 A33 45fr multi 1.75 .40
188 A33 65fr multi ('81) 3.25 .75
189 A33 70fr multi 3.25 .65
Nos. 184-189 (6) 13.15 3.15

Issued: 1fr, 2fr, 30fr, 2/8; 45fr, 70fr, 11/18; 65fr, 9/81. See #237.

Villard-de-Lans and Olympic Emblem — A34

Olympic Emblem and Mountains: 45fr, Autrans and ski jump. 60fr, Saint Nizier du Moucherotte and ski jump. 90fr, Chamrousse and course for downhill and slalom races.

1967, Feb. 24

190 A34 30fr grn, ultra & brn .50 .25
191 A34 45fr grn, ultra & brn .70 .40
192 A34 60fr grn, ultra & brn .95 .50
193 A34 90fr grn, ultra & brn 1.40 .75
Nos. 190-193 (4) 3.55 1.90

10th Winter Olympic Games, Grenoble, 1968.

Lions Emblem and Family — A35

1967, Mar. 4

194 A35 50fr dk grn, brn red & ultra 1.00 .40

Lions International, 50th anniversary.

ITY Emblem, Views, Globe and Plane A36

1967, Apr. 28 Engr. *Perf. 13*

195 A36 45fr vio, brt grn & red lil .70 .35

International Tourist Year, 1967.

1967 Jamboree Emblem and Scouts — A37

Designs (Jamboree Emblem and): 45fr, Scouts gathering from all directions, horiz. 80fr, Campfire.

1967, May 25 Engr. *Perf. 13*

196 A37 30fr mar, Prus bl & ol .50 .25
197 A37 45fr org, vio bl & brn ol .70 .30
198 A37 80fr multi 1.40 .75
Nos. 196-198 (3) 2.60 1.30

12th Boy Scout World Jamboree, Farragut State Park, Idaho, Aug. 1-9.

Red Cross Aides Carrying Sick Man — A38

Designs: 50fr, Nurse, mother and infant. 60fr, Physician examining woman.

1967, July 13 Engr. *Perf. 13*

199 A38 45fr blk, grn & car .65 .30
200 A38 50fr grn, blk & car .90 .50
201 A38 60fr blk, grn & car 1.25 .55
Nos. 199-201 (3) 2.80 1.35

Issued for the Red Cross.

Europafrica Issue

Map of Europe and Africa — A39

1967, July 20 Photo. *Perf. 12½x12*

202 A39 50fr multi .75 .30

Women and UN Emblem — A40

1967, Oct. 21 Engr. *Perf. 13*

203 A40 50fr brn, brt bl & yel .70 .40

UN Commission on Status of Women.

Monetary Union Issue

Common Design Type

1967, Nov. 4 Engr. *Perf. 13*

204 CD125 30fr grn & dk gray .45 .25

Human Rights Flame, Globe, People and Statue of Liberty A41

1968, Feb. 19 Engr. *Perf. 13*

205 A41 50fr brn, indigo & brt bl .70 .40

International Human Rights Year.

Woman Dancing and WHO Emblem — A42

1968, Apr. 8 Engr. *Perf. 13*

206 A42 50fr brt bl, blk & red brn .75 .40

20th anniv. of WHO.

Gray Hornbill A43

Birds: 10fr, Woodland kingfisher. 15fr, Senegalese coucal. 20fr, Rose-ringed parakeets. 25fr, Abyssinian roller. 50fr, Cattle egret.

Dated "1968"

1968, Nov. 15 Photo. *Perf. 12½x13*

207 A43 5fr dk grn & multi .60 .40
208 A43 10fr grn & multi .70 .40
209 A43 15fr bl vio & multi 1.25 .40
210 A43 20fr pink & multi 1.25 .50
211 A43 25fr ol & multi 2.00 .60
212 A43 50fr pur & multi 2.75 1.50
Nos. 207-212 (6) 8.55 3.80

See Nos. 233-236, 316.

ILO Emblem and "Labor Supporting the World" A44

1969, Apr. 22 Engr. *Perf. 13*

213 A44 30fr yel grn & dk car .50 .25
214 A44 50fr dk car & yel grn .65 .40

50th anniv. of the World Labor Organization.

Red Crosses, Mother and Child — A45

Designs: 50fr, People, globe, red crosses, horiz. 70fr, Man with gift parcel and red crosses.

1969, May 5 Engr. *Perf. 13*

215 A45 45fr bl, red & brn ol .80 .25
216 A45 50fr dk grn, red & gray .80 .35
217 A45 70fr ocher, red & dk brn 1.25 .60
Nos. 215-217 (3) 2.85 1.20

50th anniv. of the League of Red Cross Societies.

Mouth and Ear — A46

1969, May 20 Photo. *Perf. 12½x12*

218 A46 100fr multi 1.25 .55

First (cultural) Conference of French-speaking Community at Niamey.

National Administration College — A47

1969, July 8 Photo. *Perf. 12½x12*

219 A47 30fr emer & dp org .60 .30

Development Bank Issue
Common Design Type

1969, Sept. 10 Engr. *Perf. 13*

220 CD130 30fr pur, grn & ocher .60 .30

ASECNA Issue
Common Design Type

1969, Dec. 12 Engr. *Perf. 12*

221 CD132 100fr car rose 1.25 .70

Classical Pavilion, National Museum A48

Pavilions, National Museum: 45fr, Temporary exhibitions. 50fr, Audio-visual. 70fr, Nigerian musical instruments. 100fr, Craftsmanship.

1970, Feb. 23 Engr. *Perf. 13*

222 A48 30fr brt bl, sl grn & brn .40 .25
223 A48 45fr emer, Prus bl & brn .55 .25
224 A48 50fr sl grn, vio bl & brn .60 .25
225 A48 70fr brn, sl grn & lt bl .90 .45
226 A48 100fr sl grn, vio bl & brn 1.40 .60
Nos. 222-226 (5) 3.85 1.80

Map of Africa and Vaccination Gun — A49

1970, Mar. 31 Engr. *Perf. 13*

227 A49 50fr ultra, dp yel grn & mag .75 .40

Issued to commemorate the 100 millionth smallpox vaccination in West Africa.

Mexican Figurine and Soccer Player A50

Designs: 70fr, Figurine, globe and soccer ball. 90fr, Figurine and 2 soccer players.

1970, Apr. 25

228 A50 40fr dk brn, red lil & emer .75 .35
229 A50 70fr red brn, bl & plum 1.05 .50
230 A50 90fr blk & red 1.40 .70
Nos. 228-230 (3) 3.20 1.55

9th World Soccer Championship for the Jules Rimet Cup, Mexico City, 5/29-6/21.

UPU Headquarters Issue
Common Design Type

1970, May 20 Engr. *Perf. 13*

231 CD133 30fr brn, dk gray & dk red .40 .25
232 CD133 60fr vio bl, dk car & vio .80 .35

Bird Types of 1967-68

Birds: 5fr, Gray hornbill. 10fr, Woodland kingfisher. 15fr, Senegalese coucal. 20fr, Rose-ringed parakeets. 40fr, Red bishop.

Dated "1970"

1970-71 Photo. *Perf. 13*

233 A43 5fr multi ('71) .40 .25
234 A43 10fr multi ('71) .40 .25
235 A43 15fr multi ('71) .65 .25
236 A43 20fr multi ('71) .90 .30

Engr.

237 A33 40fr multi 3.00 1.00
Nos. 233-237 (5) 5.35 2.05

Issue dates: 40fr, Dec. 9; others Jan. 4.

World Map with Niamey in Center A51

1971, Mar. 3 Photo. *Perf. 12½x12*

238 A51 40fr brn & multi .75 .40

First anniversary of founding of the cooperative agency of French-speaking countries.
For overprint see No. 289.

Scout Emblem, Merit Badges, Mt. Fuji, Japanese Flag — A52

Designs: 40fr, Boy Scouts and flags, vert. 45fr, Map of Japan, Boy Scouts and compass rose, vert. 50fr, Tent and "Jamboree."

1971, July 5 Engr. *Perf. 13*

239 A52 35fr rose lil, dp car & org .50 .25
240 A52 40fr dk pur, grn & mar .55 .25
241 A52 45fr ultra, cop red & grn .70 .30
242 A52 50fr multi .80 .30
Nos. 239-242 (4) 2.55 1.10

13th Boy Scout World Jamboree, Asagiri Plain, Japan, Aug. 2-10.

Maps of Europe and Africa — A53

1971, July 29 Photo. *Perf. 13x12*

243 A53 50fr lt bl & multi .80 .35

Renewal of the agreement on economic association between Europe and Africa, 2nd anniv.

Broad-tailed Whydah A54

1971, Aug. 17 *Perf. 12½x12*

244 A54 35fr yel grn & multi 3.25 1.25

See No. 443.

Garaya, Haoussa — A55

Stringed Instruments of Niger: 25fr, Gouroumi, Haoussa. 30fr, Molo, Djerma. 40fr, Godjie, Djerma-Sonrai. 45fr, Inzad, Tuareg. 50fr, Kountigui, Sonrai.

1971-72 Engr. *Perf. 13*

245 A55 25fr red, emer & brn .45 .25
246 A55 30fr emer, pur & brn .50 .25
247 A55 35fr brn red, emer & ind .55 .40
248 A55 40fr emer, org & dk brn .65 .45
249 A55 45fr Prus bl, grn & bis .85 .50
250 A55 50fr blk, red & brn 1.10 .60
Nos. 245-250 (6) 4.10 2.45

Issued: 35, 40, 45fr, 10/13/71; others, 6/16/72.

UNICEF Emblem, Children of 4 Races — A56

1971, Dec. 11 Photo. *Perf. 11*

251 A56 50fr multi .65 .40

25th anniversary of UNICEF.

Star with Globe, Book, UNESCO Emblem A57

Design: 40fr, Boy reading, UNESCO emblem, sailing ship, plane, mosque.

1972, Mar. 27 Engr. *Perf. 13*

252 A57 35fr mag & emer .30 .25
253 A57 40fr dk car & Prus bl .65 .25

International Book Year 1972.

Cattle Egret A58

1972, July 31 Photo. *Perf. 12½x12*

254 A58 50fr tan & multi 5.25 2.75

See No. 425.

Cattle at Salt Pond of In-Gall A59

1972, Aug. 25 *Perf. 13*

255 A59 35fr shown .85 .40
256 A59 40fr Cattle wading in pond 1.25 .45

Salt cure for cattle.
For surcharge see No. 282.

Lottery Drum — A60

1972, Sept. 18

257 A60 35fr multi .65 .40

6th anniversary of the national lottery.

West African Monetary Union Issue
Common Design Type

Design: 40fr, African couple, city, village and commemorative coin.

1972, Nov. 2 Engr. *Perf. 13*

258 CD136 40fr brn, lil & gray .55 .30

Dromedary Race — A61

Design: 40fr, Horse race.

1972, Dec. 15 Engr. *Perf. 13*

259 A61 35fr brt bl, dk red & brn .90 .45
260 A61 40fr sl grn, mar & brn 1.25 .65

Pole Vault, Map of Africa — A62

Map of Africa and: 40fr, Basketball. 45fr, Boxing. 75fr, Soccer.

1973, Jan. 15 Engr. *Perf. 13*

261 A62 35fr claret & multi .35 .25
262 A62 40fr grn & multi .45 .25
263 A62 45fr red & multi .55 .30
264 A62 75fr dk bl & multi .75 .40
Nos. 261-264 (4) 2.10 1.20

2nd African Games, Lagos, Nigeria, 1/7-18.

Knight, Pawn, Chessboard A63

1973, Feb. 16 Engr. *Perf. 13*

265 A63 100fr dl red, sl grn & bl 3.00 1.25

World Chess Championship, Reykjavik, Iceland, July-Sept. 1972.

Abutilon Pannosum — A64

Rare African Flowers: 45fr, Crotalaria barkae. 60fr, Dichrostachys cinerea. 80fr, Caralluma decaisneana.

1973, Feb. 26 Photo. *Perf. 12x12½*
266 A64 30fr dk vio & multi .75 .40
267 A64 45fr red & multi .90 .40
268 A64 60fr ultra & multi 1.25 .50
269 A64 80fr ocher & multi 1.75 .60
Nos. 266-269 (4) 4.65 1.90

Interpol Emblem — A65

1973, Mar. 13 Typo. *Perf. 13x12½*
270 A65 50fr brt grn & multi .60 .40

50th anniversary of International Criminal Police Organization (INTERPOL).

Dr. Hansen, Microscope and Petri Dish — A66

1973, Mar. 29 Engr. *Perf. 13*
271 A66 50fr vio bl, sl grn & dk brn 1.25 .50

Centenary of the discovery by Dr. Armauer G. Hansen of the Hansen bacillus, the cause of leprosy.

Nurse Treating Infant, UN and Red Cross Emblems — A67

1973, Apr. 3 Engr. *Perf. 13*
272 A67 50fr red, bl & brn .60 .25

25th anniversary of WHO.

Crocodile A68

Animals from W National Park: 35fr, Elephant. 40fr, Hippopotamus. 80fr, Wart hog.

1973, June 5 Typo. *Perf. 12½x13*
273 A68 25fr gray & blk .90 .25
274 A68 35fr blk, gold & gray 1.25 .30
275 A68 40fr red, lt bl & blk 1.25 .35
276 A68 80fr multi 2.50 .50
Nos. 273-276 (4) 5.90 1.40

Eclipse over Mountains A69

1973, June 21 Engr. *Perf. 13*
277 A69 40fr dk vio bl .60 .40

Solar eclipse, June 30, 1973.

Palominos — A70

Horses: 75fr, French trotters. 80fr, English thoroughbreds. 100fr, Arabian thoroughbreds.

1973, Aug. 1 Photo. *Perf. 13x12½*
278 A70 50fr ultra & multi 1.00 .45
279 A70 75fr gray & multi 1.40 .50
280 A70 80fr emer & multi 1.75 .65
281 A70 100fr ocher & multi 2.25 .85
Nos. 278-281 (4) 6.40 2.45

No. 255 Srchd. with New Value, 2 Bars, and Ovptd. in Ultramarine: "SECHERESSE/SOLIDARITE AFRICAINE"

1973, Aug. 16 *Perf. 13*
282 A59 100fr on 35fr multi 1.60 1.00

African solidarity in drought emergency.

Diesel Engine and Rudolf Diesel A71

Designs: Various Diesel locomotives.

1973, Sept. 7 *Perf. 13x12½*
283 A71 25fr gray, choc & Prus bl .70 .25
284 A71 50fr sl bl, gray & dk grn 1.25 .40
285 A71 75fr red lil, sl bl & gray 1.60 .65
286 A71 125fr brt grn, vio bl & car 2.75 1.10
Nos. 283-286 (4) 6.30 2.40

Rudolf Diesel (1858-1913), inventor of an internal combustion engine, later called Diesel engine.

African Postal Union Issue
Common Design Type

1973, Sept. 12 Engr. *Perf. 13*
287 CD137 100fr ol, dk car & sl grn .90 .60

TV Set, Map of Niger, Children A72

1973, Oct. 1 Engr. *Perf. 13*
288 A72 50fr car, ultra & brn .75 .35

Educational television.

Type of 1971 Overprinted

1973, Oct. 12 Photo. *Perf. 13*
289 A51 40fr red & multi .75 .30

3rd Conference of French-speaking countries, Liège, Sept. 15-Oct. 14.

Apollo of Belvedère — A73

Classic Sculpture: No. 291, Venus of Milo. No. 292, Hercules. No. 293, Atlas.

1973, Oct. 15 Engr.
290 A73 50fr brn & sl grn 1.00 .45
291 A73 50fr rose car & pur 1.00 .45
292 A73 50fr red brn & dk brn 1.00 .45
293 A73 50fr red brn & blk 1.00 .45
Nos. 290-293 (4) 4.00 1.80

Beehive, Bees and Globes A74

1973, Oct. 31 Engr. *Perf. 13*
294 A74 40fr dl red, ocher & dl bl .75 .30

World Savings Day.

Tcherka Songhai Blanket — A75

Design: 35fr, Kounta Songhai blanket, vert.

Perf. 12½x13, 13x12½
1973, Dec. 17 Photo.
295 A75 35fr brn & multi .75 .40
296 A75 40fr brn & multi .75 .45

Textiles of Niger.

WPY Emblem, Infant and Globe A76

1974, Mar. 4 Engr. *Perf. 13*
297 A76 50fr multi .70 .35

World Population Year 1974.

Locomotives, 1938 and 1948 — A77

75fr, Locomotive, 1893. 100fr, Locomotives, 1866 and 1939. 150fr, Locomotives, 1829.

1974, May 24 Engr. *Perf. 13*
298 A77 50fr shown .95 .40
299 A77 75fr multicolored 1.50 .55
300 A77 100fr multicolored 2.10 .85
301 A77 150fr multicolored 3.25 1.40
Nos. 298-301 (4) 7.80 3.20

Map and Flags of Members A78

1974, May 29 Photo. *Perf. 13x12½*
302 A78 40fr bl & multi .70 .35

15th anniversary of the Council of Accord.

Marconi Sending Radio Signals to Australia — A79

1974, July 1 Engr. *Perf. 13*
303 A79 50fr pur, bl & dk brn .75 .35

Centenary of the birth of Guglielmo Marconi (1874-1937), Italian inventor and physicist.

Hand Holding Sapling — A80

1974, Aug. 2 Engr. *Perf. 13*
304 A80 35fr multi .75 .35

National Tree Week.

Camel Saddle — A81

Design: 50fr, 3 sculptured horses, horiz.

1974, Aug. 20 Engr. *Perf. 13*
305 A81 40fr ol brn, bl & red .60 .30
306 A81 50fr ol brn, bl & red .75 .35

Chopin and Polish Eagle A82

Design: No. 308, Ludwig van Beethoven and allegory of Ninth Symphony.

1974
307 A82 100fr multi 2.00 .80
308 A82 100fr multi 2.00 .80

125th anniversary of the death of Frederic Chopin (1810-1849), composer and 150th anniversary of Beethoven's Ninth Symphony, composed 1823.

Issue dates: #307, Sept. 4; #308, Sept. 19.

Don-Don Drum — A83

1974, Nov. 12 Engr. *Perf. 13*
309 A83 60fr multi 1.10 .55

Tenere Tree, Compass Rose and Caravan — A84

1974, Nov. 24 Engr. *Perf. 13*
310 A84 50fr multi 2.50 1.10

Tenere tree, a landmark in Sahara Desert, first death anniversary.

Satellite over World Weather Map — A85

1975, Mar. 23 Litho. *Perf. 13*
311 A85 40fr bl, blk & red .60 .30

World Meteorological Day, Mar. 23, 1975.

"City of Truro," English, 1903 — A86

Locomotives and Flags: 75fr, "5.003," Germany, 1937. 100fr, "The General," United States, 1863. 125fr, "Electric BB 15.000," France, 1971.

1975, Apr. 24 Typo. *Perf. 13*
312 A86 50fr org & multi 1.50 .35
313 A86 75fr yel grn & multi 2.00 .65
314 A86 100fr lt bl & multi 2.40 .80
315 A86 125fr multi 3.00 1.00
Nos. 312-315 (4) 8.90 2.80

Bird Type of 1968 Dated "1975"

1975, Apr. Photo. *Perf. 13*
316 A43 25fr ol & multi 2.00 .60

Zabira Leather Bag — A87

Handicrafts: 40fr, Damier tapestry. 45fr, Vase. 60fr, Gourd flask.

1975, May 28 Litho. *Perf. 12½*
317 A87 35fr dp bl & multi .35 .25
318 A87 40fr dp grn & multi .50 .30
319 A87 45fr brn & multi .70 .40
320 A87 60fr dp org & multi 1.10 .40
Nos. 317-320 (4) 2.65 1.35

Mother and Child, IWY Emblem — A88

1975, June 9 Engr. *Perf. 13*
321 A88 50fr claret, brn & bl .80 .35

International Women's Year 1975.

Dr. Schweitzer and Lambarene Hospital — A89

1975, June 23 Engr. *Perf. 13*
322 A89 100fr brn, grn & blk 1.40 .75

Dr. Albert Schweitzer (1875-1965), medical missionary.

Peugeot, 1892 — A90

Early Autos: 75fr, Daimler, 1895. 100fr, Fiat, 1899. 125fr, Cadillac, 1903.

1975, July 16 Engr. *Perf. 13*
323 A90 50fr rose & vio bl 1.05 .40
324 A90 75fr bl & vio brn 1.60 .45
325 A90 100fr brt grn & mag 2.50 .70
326 A90 125fr brick red & brt grn 2.75 .80
Nos. 323-326 (4) 7.90 2.35

Sun, Tree and Earth — A91

1975, Aug. 2 Engr. *Perf. 13*
327 A91 40fr multi .80 .35

National Tree Week.

Boxing — A92

Designs: 35fr, Boxing, horiz. 45fr, Wrestling, horiz. 50fr, Wrestling.

1975, Aug. 25 Engr. *Perf. 13*
328 A92 35fr blk, org & brn .45 .25
329 A92 40fr bl grn, brn & blk .50 .30
330 A92 45fr blk, brt bl & brn .80 .35
331 A92 50fr red, brn & blk .85 .40
Nos. 328-331 (4) 2.60 1.30

Lion's Head Tetradrachm, Leontini, 460 B.C. — A93

Greek Coins: 75fr, Owl tetradrachm, Athens, 500 B.C. 100fr, Crab didrachm, Himera, 480 B.C. 125fr, Minotaur tetradrachm, Gela, 460 B.C.

1975, Sept. 12 Engr. *Perf. 13*
332 A93 50fr red, dl bl & blk .90 .30
333 A93 75fr lil, brt bl & blk 1.25 .35
334 A93 100fr bl, org & blk 1.60 .60
335 A93 125fr grn, pur & blk 2.25 .70
Nos. 332-335 (4) 6.00 1.95

Starving Family A94

45fr, Animal skeletons. 60fr, Truck bringing food.

1975, Oct. 21 Engr. *Perf. 13x12½*
336 A94 40fr multi .80 .40
337 A94 45fr ultra & brn 1.50 .60
338 A94 60fr grn, org & dk bl 1.35 .50
Nos. 336-338 (3) 3.65 1.50

Fight against drought.

Niger River Crossing — A95

Designs: 45fr, Entrance to Boubon camp. 50fr, Camp building.

1975, Nov. 10 Litho. *Perf. 12½*
339 A95 40fr multi .70 .30
340 A95 45fr multi .75 .30
341 A95 50fr multi .80 .40
Nos. 339-341 (3) 2.25 1.00

Tourist publicity.

Teacher and Pupils A96

Each stamp has different inscription in center.

1976, Jan. 12 Photo. *Perf. 13*
342 A96 25fr ol & multi .25 .25
343 A96 30fr vio bl & multi .25 .25
344 A96 40fr multi .25 .25
345 A96 50fr multi .40 .25
346 A96 60fr multi .50 .25
Nos. 342-346 (5) 1.65 1.25

Literacy campaign 1976.
For overprints see Nos. 371-375.

12th Winter Olympic Games, Innsbruck — A97

1976, Feb. 20 Litho. *Perf. 14x13½*
347 A97 40fr Ice hockey .35 .25
348 A97 50fr Luge .55 .30
349 A97 150fr Ski jump 1.10 .60
Nos. 347-349,C266-C267 (5) 5.75 3.15

Satellite, Telephone, ITU Emblem — A98

1976, Mar. 10 Litho. *Perf. 13*
350 A98 100fr org, bl & vio bl 1.25 .60

Centenary of first telephone call by Alexander Graham Bell, Mar. 10, 1876.

WHO Emblem, Red Cross Truck, Infant — A99

1976, Apr. 7 Engr. *Perf. 13*
351 A99 50fr multi .75 .25

World Health Day 1976.

Statue of Liberty and Washington Crossing the Delaware — A100

50fr, Statue of Liberty and call to arms.

1976, Apr. 8 Litho. *Perf. 14x13½*

352 A100 40fr multi .30 .25
353 A100 50fr multi .40 .25
Nos. 352-353,C269-C271 (5) 6.05 2.45

American Bicentennial.

The Army Helping in Development — A101

Design: 50fr, Food distribution, vert.

Perf. 12½x13, 13x12½
1976, Apr. 15 Litho.

354 A101 50fr multi .45 .25
355 A101 100fr multi .90 .40

National Armed Forces, 2nd anniv. of take-over.

Europafrica Issue

Maps, Concorde, Ship and Grain — A102

1976, June 9 Litho. *Perf. 13*

356 A102 100fr multi 1.25 .50

Road Building A103

Design: 30fr, Rice cultivation.

1976, June 26 *Perf. 12½*

357 A103 25fr multi .25 .25
358 A103 30fr multi .40 .25

Community labor.

Motobecane 125, France — A104

Motorcycles: 75fr, Norton Challenge, England. 100fr, BMW 90 S, Germany. 125fr, Kawasaki 1000, Japan.

1976, July 16 Engr. *Perf. 13*

359 A104 50fr vio bl & multi .70 .30
360 A104 75fr dp grn & multi 1.00 .35
361 A104 100fr dk brn & multi 1.50 .70
362 A104 125fr slate & multi 1.75 .80
Nos. 359-362 (4) 4.95 2.15

Boxing A105

Designs: 50fr, Basketball. 60fr, Soccer. 80fr, Cycling, horiz. 100fr, Judo, horiz.

1976, July 17 Litho. *Perf. 14*

363 A105 40fr multi .50 .30
364 A105 50fr multi .60 .30
365 A105 60fr multi .70 .30
366 A105 80fr multi .80 .30
367 A105 100fr multi 1.10 .35
Nos. 363-367 (5) 3.70 1.55

21st Summer Olympic games, Montreal. See No. C279.

Map of Niger, Planting Seedlings A106

Designs: 50fr, Woman watering seedling, vert. 60fr, Women planting seedlings, vert.

1976, Aug. 1 Litho. *Perf. 12½x13*

368 A106 40fr org & multi .45 .25
369 A106 50fr yel & multi .55 .30
370 A106 60fr grn & multi .70 .35
Nos. 368-370 (3) 1.70 .90

Reclamation of Sahel Region.

Nos. 342-346 Overprinted: "JOURNEE / INTERNATIONALE / DE L'ALPHABETISATION"

1976, Sept. 8 Photo. *Perf. 13*

371 A96 25fr ol & multi .25 .25
372 A96 30fr vio bl & multi .25 .25
373 A96 40fr multi .30 .25
374 A96 50fr multi .40 .25
375 A96 60fr multi .45 .30
Nos. 371-375 (5) 1.65 1.30

Literacy campaign.

Hairdresser — A107

Designs: 40fr, Woman weaving straw, vert. 50fr, Women potters, vert.

1976, Oct. 6 *Perf. 13*

376 A107 40fr buff & multi .45 .25
377 A107 45fr bl & multi .50 .25
378 A107 50fr red & multi .70 .30
Nos. 376-378 (3) 1.65 .80

Niger Women's Association.

Rock Carvings A108

Archaeology: 50fr, Neolithic sculptures. 60fr, Dinosaur skeleton.

1976, Nov. 15 Photo. *Perf. 13x12½*

379 A108 40fr blk, sl & yel 2.25 .55
380 A108 50fr blk, red & bis 2.50 .55
381 A108 60fr bis, blk & brn 5.00 .75
Nos. 379-381 (3) 9.75 1.85

Benin Head — A109

Weaver, Dancers and Musicians — A110

1977, Jan. 15 Engr. *Perf. 13*

382 A109 40fr dk brn .45 .25
383 A110 50fr gray bl 1.00 .30

2nd World Black and African Festival, Lagos, Nigeria, Jan. 15-Feb. 12.

First Aid, Student, Blackboard and Plow — A111

Designs: Inscriptions on blackboard differ on each denomination.

1977, Jan. 23 Photo. *Perf. 12½x13*

384 A111 40fr multi .40 .25
385 A111 50fr multi .50 .30
386 A111 60fr multi .70 .40
Nos. 384-386 (3) 1.60 .95

Literacy campaign.

Midwife — A112

Design: 50fr, Midwife examining newborn.

1977, Feb. 23 Litho. *Perf. 13*

387 A112 40fr multi .45 .25
388 A112 50fr multi .75 .30

Village health service.

Titan Rocket Launch A113

80fr, Viking orbiter near Mars, horiz.

1977, Mar. 15 Litho. *Perf. 14*

389 A113 50fr multi .45 .25
390 A113 80fr multi .75 .25
Nos. 389-390,C283-C285 (5) 4.70 1.80

Viking Mars project.
For overprints see #497-498, C295-C297.

Marabous A114

Design: 90fr, Harnessed antelopes.

1977, Mar. 18 Engr. *Perf. 13*

391 A114 80fr multi 2.00 1.00
392 A114 90fr multi 2.25 1.00

Nature protection.

Weather Map, Satellite, WMO Emblem A115

1977, Mar. 23

393 A115 100fr multi 1.25 .60

World Meteorological Day.

Group Gymnastics — A116

50fr, High jump. 80fr, Folk singers.

1977, Apr. 7 Litho. *Perf. 13x12½*

394 A116 40fr dl yel & multi .45 .25
395 A116 50fr bl & multi .60 .30
396 A116 80fr org & multi .75 .35
Nos. 394-396 (3) 1.80 .90

2nd Tahoua Youth Festival, Apr. 7-14.

Red Cross, WHO Emblems and Children — A117

1977, Apr. 25 Engr. *Perf. 13*

397 A117 80fr lil, org & red .85 .40

World Health Day: "Immunization means protection of your children."

Eye with WHO Emblem, and Sword Killing Fly — A118

1977, May 7
398 A118 100fr multi 1.25 .60

Fight against onchocerciasis, a roundworm infection, transmitted by flies, causing blindness.

Guirka Tahoua Dance A119

50fr, Mailfilafili Gaya. 80fr, Naguihinayan Loga.

1977, June 7 Photo. *Perf. 13x12½*
399 A119 40fr multi .55 .30
400 A119 50fr multi .75 .40
401 A119 80fr multi 1.10 .55
Nos. 399-401 (3) 2.40 1.25

Popular arts and traditions.

Cavalry — A120

Traditional chief's cavalry, different groups.

1977, July 7 Litho. *Perf. 13x12½*
402 A120 40fr multi .70 .40
403 A120 50fr multi .80 .45
404 A120 60fr multi 1.20 .60
Nos. 402-404 (3) 2.70 1.45

Planting and Cultivating — A121

1977, Aug. 10
405 A121 40fr multi .60 .30

Reclamation of Sahel Region.

Albert John Luthuli Peace — A122

Designs: 80fr, Maurice Maeterlinck, literature. 100fr, Allan L. Hodgkin, medicine. 150fr, Albert Camus, literature. 200fr, Paul Ehrlich, medicine.

1977, Aug. 20 Litho. *Perf. 14*
406 A122 50fr multi .35 .25
407 A122 80fr multi .45 .25
408 A122 100fr multi .70 .25
409 A122 150fr multi 1.10 .40
410 A122 200fr multi 1.50 .50
Nos. 406-410 (5) 4.10 1.65

Nobel prize winners. See No. C287.

Mao Tse-tung — A123

1977, Sept. 9 Engr. *Perf. 13*
411 A123 100fr blk & red 3.75 1.50

Argentina '78 Emblem, Soccer Players and Coach, Vittorio Pozzo, Italy — A124

Designs (Argentina '78 emblem, soccer players and coach): 50fr, Vincente Feola, Spain. 80fr, Aymore Moreira, Portugal. 100fr, Sir Alf Ramsey, England. 200fr, Helmut Schoen, Germany. 500fr, Sepp Herberger, Germany.

1977, Oct. 12 Litho. *Perf. 13½*
412 A124 40fr multi .40 .25
413 A124 50fr multi .50 .25
414 A124 80fr multi .65 .25
415 A124 100fr multi 1.10 .35
416 A124 200fr multi 1.75 .65
Nos. 412-416 (5) 4.40 1.75

Souvenir Sheet

417 A124 500fr multi 4.25 1.75

World Cup Soccer championship, Argentina '78.
For overprints see Nos. 453-458.

Horse's Head, Parthenon and UNESCO Emblem — A125

1977, Nov. 12 Engr. *Perf. 13*
418 A125 100fr multi 1.75 .75

Woman Carrying Water Pots — A126

Design: 50fr, Women pounding corn.

1977, Nov. 23 Photo. *Perf. 12½x13*
419 A126 40fr multi .45 .25
420 A126 50fr red & multi .55 .30

Niger Women's Association.

Crocodile's Skull, 100 Million Years Old — A127

Design: 80fr, Neolithic flint tools.

1977, Dec. 14 *Perf. 13*
421 A127 50fr multi 1.10 .55
422 A127 80fr multi 1.50 .80

Raoul Follereau and Lepers A128

40fr, Raoul Follereau and woman leper, vert.

1978, Jan. 28 Engr. *Perf. 13*
423 A128 40fr multi .45 .25
424 A128 50fr multi .50 .30

25th anniversary of Leprosy Day. Follereau (1903-1977) was "Apostle to the Lepers" and educator of the blind.

Bird Type of 1972 Redrawn

1978, Feb. Photo. *Perf. 13*
425 A58 50fr tan & multi 2.50 1.00

No. 425 is dated "1978" and has only designer's name in imprint. No. 254 has printer's name also.

Assumption, by Rubens A129

Rubens Paintings: 70fr, Rubens and Friends, horiz. 100fr, History of Marie de Medici. 150fr, Alathea Talbot and Family. 200fr, Marquise de Spinola. 500fr, Virgin and St. Ildefonso.

1978, Feb. 25 Litho. *Perf. 14*
426 A129 50fr multi .40 .25
427 A129 70fr multi .45 .25
428 A129 100fr multi .85 .30
429 A129 150fr multi 1.25 .40
430 A129 200fr multi 1.80 .50
Nos. 426-430 (5) 4.75 1.70

Souvenir Sheet
Perf. 13½

431 A129 500fr gold & multi 5.00 1.50

Peter Paul Rubens (1577-1640), 400th birth anniversary.

Shot Put A130

1978, Mar. 22 Photo. *Perf. 13*
432 A130 40fr shown .30 .25
433 A130 50fr Volleyball .40 .25
434 A130 60fr Long jump .45 .25
435 A130 100fr Javelin .80 .35
Nos. 432-435 (4) 1.95 1.10

Natl. University Games' Championships.

First Aid and Red Crosses A131

1978, May 13 Litho.
436 A131 40fr red & multi .35 .25

Niger Red Cross.

Goudel Earth Station A132

1978, May 23
437 A132 100fr multi .75 .40

Soccer Ball, Flags of Participants A133

Argentina '78 Emblem and: 50fr, Ball in net. 100fr, Globe with South America, Soccer field. 200fr, Two players, horiz. 300fr, Player and globe.

1978, June 18 Litho. *Perf. 13½*
438 A133 40fr multi .30 .25
439 A133 50fr multi .50 .25
440 A133 100fr multi .75 .35
441 A133 200fr multi 1.50 .60
Nos. 438-441 (4) 3.05 1.45

Souvenir Sheet

442 A133 300fr multi 2.50 1.25

11th World Cup Soccer Championship, Argentina, June 1-25.

Bird Type of 1971 Redrawn

1978, June Photo. *Perf. 13*
443 A54 35fr bl & multi 3.25 .80

No. 443 has no year date, nor Delrieu imprint.

Post Office, Niamey — A134

Design: 60fr, Post Office, different view.

1978, Aug. 12 Litho.
444 A134 40fr multi .30 .25
445 A134 60fr multi .45 .25

Goudel Water Works
A135

1978, Sept. 25 Photo. *Perf. 13*

446 A135 100fr multi .85 .55

Giraffe — A136

Animals and Wildlife Fund Emblem: 50fr, Ostrich. 70fr, Cheetah. 150fr, Oryx, horiz. 200fr, Addax, horiz. 300fr, Hartebeest, horiz.

1978, Nov. 20 Litho. *Perf. 15*

447 A136 40fr multi *1.00* .50
448 A136 50fr multi *1.75* .60
449 A136 70fr multi *2.40* .80
450 A136 150fr multi *5.00* 1.40
451 A136 200fr multi *8.00* 2.00
452 A136 300fr multi *10.00* 2.75
Nos. 447-452 (6) *28.15* 8.05

Endangered species.

Nos. 412-417 Overprinted in Silver

a. "EQUIPE QUATRIEME: ITALIE"
b. "EQUIPE TROISIEME: BRESIL"
c. "EQUIPE / SECONDE: / PAYS BAS"
d. "EQUIPE VAINQUEUR: ARGENTINE"
e. "ARGENTINE-PAYS BAS 3-1"

1978, Dec. 1 *Perf. 13½*

453 A124(a) 40fr multi .35 .25
454 A124(b) 50fr multi .45 .25
455 A124(c) 80fr multi .70 .30
456 A124(d) 100fr multi 1.00 .40
457 A124(e) 200fr multi 1.75 .75
Nos. 453-457 (5) 4.25 1.95

Souvenir Sheet

458 A124(e) 500fr multi 4.25 1.75

Winners, World Soccer Cup Championship, Argentina, June 1-25.

Tinguizi — A137

Musicians: No. 460, Dan Gourmou. No. 461, Chetima Ganga, horiz.

1978, Dec. 11 Litho. *Perf. 13*

459 A137 100fr multi 1.00 .50
460 A137 100fr multi 1.00 .50
461 A137 100fr multi 1.00 .50
Nos. 459-461 (3) 3.00 1.50

Virgin Mary, by Dürer
A138

50fr, The Homecoming, by Honoré Daumier (1808-79). 150fr, 200fr, 500fr, Virgin and Child, by Albrecht Dürer (1471-1528), diff.

1979, Jan. 31 Litho. *Perf. 13½*

462 A138 50fr multi .70 .25
463 A138 100fr multi .75 .30
464 A138 150fr multi 1.25 .40
465 A138 200fr multi 1.75 .60
Nos. 462-465 (4) 4.45 1.55

Souvenir Sheet

466 A138 500fr multi 4.50 1.50

Solar Panels and Tank — A139

Design: 40fr, Tank and panels on roof, vert.

1979, Feb. 28 *Perf. 12½x12, 12x12½*

467 A139 40fr multi .35 .25
468 A139 50fr multi .45 .25

Hot water from solar heat.

Children with Building Blocks — A140

Children and IYC Emblem: 100fr, Reading books. 150fr, With model plane.

1979, Apr. 10 Litho. *Perf. 13½*

469 A140 40fr multi .40 .25
470 A140 100fr multi .80 .30
471 A140 150fr multi 1.60 .40
Nos. 469-471 (3) 2.80 .95

International Year of the Child.

The Langa, Traditional Sport
A141

Design: 50fr, The langa, diff.

1979, Apr. 10 Litho. *Perf. 12½x12*

472 A141 40fr multi .35 .25
473 A141 50fr multi .45 .25

Rowland Hill, Mail Truck and France No. 8 — A142

Designs (Hill and): 100fr, Canoes and Austria #P4. 150fr, Air Niger plane and US #122. 200fr, Streamlined mail train and Canada type A6. 400fr, Electric train and Niger #51.

1979, June 6 Litho. *Perf. 14*

474 A142 40fr multi .50 .25
475 A142 100fr multi 1.00 .30
476 A142 150fr multi 1.50 .40
477 A142 200fr multi 1.80 .55
Nos. 474-477 (4) 4.80 1.50

Souvenir Sheet

478 A142 400fr multi 4.00 1.50

Sir Rowland Hill (1795-1879), originator of penny postage.

Zabira Handbag and Niger No. 135 — A143

Design: 150fr, Heads with communications waves, world map, UPU emblem and satellite.

1979, June 8 Litho. *Perf. 12x12½*

479 A143 50fr multi 1.25 .60

Engr. *Perf. 13*

480 A143 150fr brt red & ultra 3.25 1.60

Philexafrique II, Libreville, Gabon, June 8-17. Nos. 479, 480 each printed in sheets of 10 and 5 labels showing exhibition emblem.

Djermakoye Palace — A144

1979, Sept. 26 Litho. *Perf. 13x12½*

481 A144 100fr multi .75 .40

Bororo Festive Headdress — A145

60fr, Bororo women's traditional costumes.

Perf. 13x12½, 12½x13

1979, Sept. 26

482 A145 45fr multi .35 .25
483 A145 60fr multi, vert. .50 .30

Annual Bororo Festival.

Olympic Emblem, Flame and Boxers — A146

Designs: 100fr, 150fr, 250fr, 500fr, Olympic emblem, flame and boxers, diff.

1979, Oct. 6 *Perf. 13½*

484 A146 45fr multi .40 .25
485 A146 100fr multi .85 .30
486 A146 150fr multi 1.30 .40
487 A146 250fr multi 2.25 .65
Nos. 484-487 (4) 4.80 1.60

Souvenir Sheet

488 A146 500fr multi 4.00 1.75

Pre-Olympic Year.

John Alcock, Arthur Whitten Brown, Vickers-Vimy Biplane — A147

1979, Sept. 3 *Perf. 13½*

489 A147 100fr multi 1.25 .50

First Transatlantic flight, 60th anniversary.

Road and Traffic Safety — A148

1979, Nov. 20 Litho. *Perf. 12½*

490 A148 45fr multi .45 .30

Four-Man Bobsledding, Lake Placid '80 Emblem — A149

Lake Placid '80 Emblem and: 60fr, Downhill skiing. 100fr, Speed skating. 150fr, Two-man bobsledding. 200fr, Figure skating. 300fr, Cross-country skiing.

1979, Dec. 10 *Perf. 14½*

491 A149 40fr multi .30 .25
492 A149 60fr multi .45 .25
493 A149 100fr multi .75 .30
494 A149 150fr multi 1.10 .40
495 A149 200fr multi 1.50 .75
Nos. 491-495 (5) 4.10 1.95

Souvenir Sheet

496 A149 300fr multi 2.50 1.00

13th Winter Olympic Games, Lake Placid, NY, Feb. 12-24, 1980.

For overprints see Nos. 501-506.

Nos. 389, 390 Overprinted in Silver or Black "alunissage/apollo XI/juillet 1969" and Emblem

1979, Dec. 20 Litho. *Perf. 14*

497 A113 50fr multi (S) .35 .25
498 A113 80fr multi .60 .30
Nos. 497-498,C295-C296 (4) 3.80 2.10

Apollo 11 moon landing, 10th anniv. See #C297.

Court of Sultan of Zinder — A150

1980, Mar. 25 Litho. *Perf. 13x12½*
499 A150 45fr shown .35 .25
500 A150 60fr Sultan's court, diff. .45 .25

Nos. 491-496 Overprinted

(a)

(b)

(c)

(d)

(e)

(f)

1980, Mar. 31 Litho. *Perf. 14½*
501 A149 (a) 40fr multi .30 .25
502 A149 (b) 60fr multi .45 .25
503 A149 (c) 100fr multi .75 .40
504 A149 (d) 150fr multi 1.10 .50
505 A149 (e) 200fr multi 1.50 .70
Nos. 501-505 (5) 4.10 2.10

Souvenir Sheet

506 A149 (f) 300fr multi 2.40 1.50

Javelin, Olympic Rings — A151

1980, Apr. 17
507 A151 60fr shown .45 .25
508 A151 90fr Walking .75 .25
509 A151 100fr High jump, horiz. .90 .30
510 A151 300fr Marathon runners, horiz. 2.00 .80
Nos. 507-510 (4) 4.10 1.60

Souvenir Sheet

511 A151 500fr High jump, horiz. 3.50 1.50

22nd Summer Olympic Games, Moscow, July 19-Aug. 3.
For overprints see Nos. 527-531.

Man Smoking Cigarette, Runner — A152

1980, Apr. 7 *Perf. 13*
512 A152 100fr multi .70 .40

World Health Day; fight against cigarette smoking.

Health Year A153

1980, May 15 Photo. *Perf. 13x12½*
513 A153 150fr multi 1.10 .65

Shimbashi-Yokohama Locomotive — A154

60fr, American type. 90fr, German Reichsbahn series 61. 100fr, Prussian Staatsbahn P2. 130fr, L'Aigle.
425fr, Stephenson's Rocket.

1980, June Litho. *Perf. 12½*
514 A154 45fr shown .55 .30
515 A154 60fr multicolored .80 .35
516 A154 90fr multicolored 1.05 .50
517 A154 100fr multicolored 1.40 .65
518 A154 130fr multicolored 1.75 .85
Nos. 514-518 (5) 5.55 2.65

Souvenir Sheet

519 A154 425fr multicolored 7.50 2.25

For overprint see No. 674.

Steve Biko, 4th Anniversary of Death — A155

1980, Sept. 12 Litho. *Perf. 13*
520 A155 150fr org & blk 1.00 .60

Soccer Players — A156

Designs: Various soccer scenes.

1980, Oct. 15 *Perf. 12½*
521 A156 45fr multi .30 .25
522 A156 60fr multi .40 .25
523 A156 90fr multi .70 .25
524 A156 100fr multi .80 .30
525 A156 130fr multi .90 .35
Nos. 521-525 (5) 3.10 1.40

Souvenir Sheet

526 A156 425fr multi 4.00 1.25

World Soccer Cup 1982.

Nos. 507-511 Overprinted in Gold with Winner's Name and Country

1980, Sept. 27 Litho. *Perf. 14½*
527 A151 60fr multi .45 .25
528 A151 90fr multi .70 .30
529 A151 100fr multi .80 .35
530 A151 300fr multi 2.40 1.00
Nos. 527-530 (4) 4.35 1.90

Souvenir Sheet

531 A151 500fr multi, horiz. 4.00 2.50

African Postal Union, 5th Anniversary A157

1980, Dec. 24 Photo. *Perf. 13½*
532 A157 100fr multi .75 .40

Terra Cotta Kareygorou Head — A158

Designs: Terra Cotta Kareygorou Statues, 5th-12th cent. 45fr, 150fr, horiz.

1981, Jan. 23 Litho. *Perf. 13*
533 A158 45fr multi .30 .25
534 A158 60fr multi .45 .25
535 A158 90fr multi .60 .30
536 A158 150fr multi 1.10 .50
Nos. 533-536 (4) 2.45 1.30

Ostrich — A159

1981, Mar. 17 Litho. *Perf. 12½*
537 A159 10fr shown 1.10 .30
538 A159 20fr Oryx .40 .30
539 A159 25fr Gazelle .40 .30
540 A159 30fr Great bustard 1.80 .60
541 A159 60fr Giraffe .75 .40
542 A159 150fr Addax 1.80 .80
Nos. 537-542 (6) 6.25 2.70

7th Anniv. of the F.A.N. A160

1981, Apr. 14 Litho. *Perf. 13*
543 A160 100fr multi .75 .40

One-armed Archer — A161

1981, Apr. 24 Engr.
544 A161 50fr shown .70 .30
545 A161 100fr Draftsman 1.10 .60

Intl. Year of the Disabled.

Scene from Mahalba Ballet, 1980 Youth Festival, Dosso A162

1981, May 17 Litho.
546 A162 100fr shown .75 .40
547 A162 100fr Ballet, diff. .75 .40

Prince Charles and Lady Diana, Coach — A163

Designs: Couple and coaches.

1981, July 15 Litho. *Perf. 14½*
548 A163 150fr multi 1.10 .45
549 A163 200fr multi 1.40 .65
550 A163 300fr multi 2.00 .90
Nos. 548-550 (3) 4.50 2.00

Souvenir Sheet

551 A163 400fr multi 3.00 1.50

Royal wedding.
For overprints see Nos. 595-598.

Hegira 1500th Anniv. — A164

1981, July 15 *Perf. 13½x13*
552 A164 100fr multi .80 .40

Alexander Fleming (1881-1955) A165

1981, Aug. 6 **Engr.** ***Perf. 13***

553 A165 150fr multi 2.00 .95

25th Intl. Letter Writing Week, Oct. 6-12 — A167

1981, Oct. 9 **Surcharged in Black**

554 A167 65fr on 40fr multi .55 .30
555 A167 85fr on 60fr multi .75 .50

Nos. 554-555 not issued without surcharge.

World Food Day — A168

1981, Oct. 16 **Litho.**

556 A168 100fr multi .75 .40

Espana '82 World Cup Soccer — A169

Designs: Various soccer players.

1981, Nov. 18 **Litho.** ***Perf. 14x13½***

557 A169 40fr multi .30 .25
558 A169 65fr multi .50 .25
559 A169 85fr multi .60 .25
560 A169 150fr multi 1.10 .45
561 A169 300fr multi 2.00 .90
Nos. 557-561 (5) 4.50 2.10

Souvenir Sheet

562 A169 500fr multi 4.00 1.75

For overprints see Nos. 603-608.

75th Anniv. of Grand Prix — A170

Designs: Winners and their cars — 20fr, Peugeot, 1912. 40fr, Bugatti, 1924. 65fr, Lotus-Climax, 1962. 85fr, Georges Boillot, 1912. 150fr, Phil Hill, 1960.
450fr, Race.

1981, Nov. 30 ***Perf. 14***

563 A170 20fr multicolored .40 .25
564 A170 40fr multicolored .55 .25
565 A170 65fr multicolored .80 .25
566 A170 85fr multicolored 1.00 .50
567 A170 150fr multicolored 1.50 .80
Nos. 563-567 (5) 4.25 2.05

Souvenir Sheet

568 A170 450fr multicolored 5.00 1.75

For overprint see No. 675.

Christmas 1981 — A171

Designs: Virgin and Child paintings.

1981, Dec. 24

569 A171 100fr Botticelli .80 .35
570 A171 200fr Botticini 1.40 .75
571 A171 300fr Botticelli, diff. 2.40 1.00
Nos. 569-571 (3) 4.60 2.10

School Gardens A172

1982, Feb. 19 **Litho.** ***Perf. 13x13½***

572 A172 65fr shown .55 .30
573 A172 85fr Garden, diff. .70 .45

L'Estaque, by Georges Braque (1882-1963) — A173

Anniversaries: 120fr, Arturo Toscanini (1867-1957), vert. 140fr, Fruit on a Table, by Edouard Manet (1832-1883). 300fr, George Washington (1732-99), vert. 400fr, Goethe (1749-1832), vert. Nos. 579-580, 21st birthday of Diana, Princess of Wales (portraits), vert.

1982, Mar. 8 **Litho.** ***Perf. 13***

574 A173 120fr multi 1.15 .45
575 A173 140fr multi 1.60 .50
576 A173 200fr multi 2.75 .75
577 A173 300fr multi 3.25 1.15
578 A173 400fr multi 4.00 1.50
579 A173 500fr multi 5.00 2.00
Nos. 574-579 (6) 17.75 6.35

Souvenir Sheet

580 A173 500fr multi 4.00 1.75

Palace of Congress — A174

1982, Mar. 17

581 A174 150fr multi 1.25 .70

7th Youth Festival, Agadez — A175

1982, Apr. 7 ***Perf. 12½***

582 A175 65fr Martial arts, horiz. .50 .30
583 A175 100fr Wrestling .90 .50

Reafforestation Campaign — A176

1982, Apr. 16 ***Perf. 13***

584 A176 150fr Tree planting 1.20 .50
585 A176 200fr Trees, Desert 1.40 .75

For overprints see Nos. 668-669.

Scouting Year A177

1982, May 13

586 A177 65fr Canoeing .60 .25
587 A177 85fr Scouts in rubber boat .85 .30
588 A177 130fr Canoeing, diff. 1.25 .45
589 A177 200fr Rafting 1.75 .75
Nos. 586-589 (4) 4.45 1.75

Souvenir Sheet

590 A177 400fr Beach scene 3.25 1.75

For overprint see No. 673.

13th Meeting of Islamic Countries Foreign Affairs Ministers, Niamey, Aug. 20-27 A178

1982, June 6

591 A178 100fr multi .90 .40

West African Economic Community — A179

1982, June 28

592 A179 200fr Map 1.25 .85

Fishermen in Canoe A180

1982, July 18 ***Perf. 13x12½***

593 A180 65fr shown .60 .35
594 A180 85fr Bringing in nets .75 .40

Nos. 548-551 Overprinted in Blue: "NAISSANCE ROYALE 1982"

1982, Aug. 4 ***Perf. 14½***

595 A163 150fr multi 1.10 .50
596 A163 200fr multi 1.40 .70
597 A163 300fr multi 2.40 1.00
Nos. 595-597 (3) 4.90 2.20

Souvenir Sheet

598 A163 400fr multi 2.75 1.50

Flautist, by Norman Rockwell A181

1982, Sept. 10 **Litho.** ***Perf. 14***

599 A181 65fr shown .50 .25
600 A181 85fr Clerk .70 .30
601 A181 110fr Teacher and Pupil .90 .35
602 A181 150fr Girl Shopper 1.25 .50
Nos. 599-602 (4) 3.35 1.40

Nos. 557-562 Overprinted with Past and Present Winners in Black on Silver

1982, Sept. 28 ***Perf. 14x13½***

603 A169 40fr multi .30 .25
604 A169 65fr multi .45 .25
605 A169 85fr multi .55 .30
606 A169 150fr multi 1.20 .45
607 A169 300fr multi 2.25 1.10
Nos. 603-607 (5) 4.75 2.35

Souvenir Sheet

608 A169 500fr multi 4.00 2.75

Italy's victory in 1982 World Cup.

ITU Plenipotentiaries Conference, Nairobi, Sept. — A182

1982, Sept. 28 ***Perf. 13***

609 A182 130fr black & blue .90 .50

Laboratory Workers A183

Various laboratory workers.

1982, Nov. 9 **Litho.** ***Perf. 13***

610 A183 65fr multi .60 .35
611 A183 115fr multi .90 .55

Self-sufficiency in Food Production — A184

1983, Feb. 16 Litho. ***Perf. 13½x13***

612 A184 65fr Rice harvest .60 .30
613 A184 85fr Planting rice, vert. .90 .40

Grand Ducal Madonna, by Raphael A185

Raphael Paintings: 65fr, Miraculous Catch of Fishes. 100fr, Deliverance of St. Peter. 150fr, Sistine Madonna. 200fr, Christ on the Way to Calvary. 300fr, Deposition. 400fr, Transfiguration. 500fr, St. Michael Slaying the Dragon.

1983, Mar. 30 Litho. ***Perf. 14***

614 A185 65fr multi, vert. .50 .25
615 A185 85fr multi .60 .25
616 A185 100fr multi, vert. .80 .25
617 A185 150fr multi 1.10 .40
618 A185 200fr multi 1.40 .55
619 A185 300fr multi, vert. 2.00 .80
620 A185 400fr multi 3.00 1.10
621 A185 500fr multi 4.00 1.25
Nos. 614-621 (8) 13.40 4.85

African Economic Commission, 25th Anniv. — A186

1983, Mar. 18 ***Perf. 12½x13***

622 A186 120fr multi .90 .45
623 A186 200fr multi 1.40 .85

Army Surveyors A187

1983, Apr. 14 ***Perf. 13x12½***

624 A187 85fr shown .60 .40
625 A187 150fr Road building 1.10 .75

Agadez Court A188

1983, Apr. 26 Litho. ***Perf. 13x12½***

626 A188 65fr multi .45 .25

Mail Van — A189

1983, June 25 Litho.

627 A189 65fr Van .45 .40
628 A189 100fr Van, map .75 .45

Palestine Solidarity — A190

1983, Aug. 21 Litho. ***Perf. 12½***

629 A190 65fr multi .60 .25

Intl. Literacy Year — A191

Various adult education classes. 65fr, 150fr vert.

Perf. 13½x14½, 14½x13½

1983, Sept. 8 Litho.

630 A191 40fr multi .35 .25
631 A191 65fr multi .45 .25
632 A191 85fr multi .60 .30
633 A191 100fr multi .75 .40
634 A191 150fr multi 1.25 .90
Nos. 630-634 (5) 3.40 2.10

7th Ballet Festival of Dosso Dept. A192

Various dancers.

1983, Oct. 7 ***Perf. 14½x13½***

635 A192 65fr multi .50 .35
636 A192 85fr multi .70 .45
637 A192 120fr multi 1.10 .60
Nos. 635-637 (3) 2.30 1.40

World Communications Year — A193

1983, Oct. 18 ***Perf. 13x12½, 12½x13***

638 A193 80fr Post Office, mail van .60 .45
639 A193 120fr Sorting mail .85 .50
640 A193 150fr Emblem, vert. 1.25 .60
Nos. 638-640 (3) 2.70 1.55

Solar Energy For Television — A194

1983, Nov. 26 ***Perf. 13***

641 A194 85fr Antenna .60 .40
642 A194 130fr Car 1.00 .40

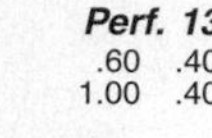

Local Butterflies — A195

75fr, Hypolimnas misippus. 120fr, Papilio demodocus. 250fr, Vanessa antiopa. 350fr, Charesex jasius. 500fr, Danaus chrisippus.

1983, Dec. 9 ***Perf. 12½***

643 A195 75fr multicolored .90 .40
644 A195 120fr multicolored 1.25 .50
645 A195 250fr multicolored 2.25 .90
646 A195 350fr multicolored 3.50 1.25
647 A195 500fr multicolored 5.50 1.60
Nos. 643-647 (5) 13.40 4.65

SAMARIYA Natl. Development Movement — A196

1984, Jan. 18 Litho. ***Perf. 13x13½***

648 A196 80fr multi .60 .40

Alestes Bouboni A197

1984, Mar. 28 Litho. ***Perf. 13***

649 A197 120fr multi 3.00 .80

Military Pentathlon A198

1984, Apr. 10

650 A198 120fr Hurdles .85 .40
651 A198 140fr Shooting 1.00 .60

Radio Broadcasting Building Opening A199

1984, May 14 Litho. ***Perf. 13***

652 A199 120fr multi .90 .40

25th Anniv. of Council of Unity — A200

1984, May 29 ***Perf. 12½***

653 A200 65fr multi .45 .35
654 A200 85fr multi .75 .45

Renault, 1902 — A201

80fr, Paris. 100fr, Gottlieb Daimler. 120fr, Three-master Jacques Coeur. 150fr, Barque Bosphorus. 250fr, Delage D8. 300fr, Three-master Comet. 400fr, Maybach Zeppelin.
Vintage cars (#656, 658, 660, 662) & ships.

1984, June 12 ***Perf. 12½***

655 A201 80fr multicolored .60 .30
656 A201 100fr multicolored .75 .40
657 A201 120fr multicolored .75 .40
658 A201 140fr shown 1.00 .50
659 A201 150fr multicolored 1.10 .60
660 A201 250fr multicolored 1.90 .75
661 A201 300fr multicolored 2.00 .75
662 A201 400fr multicolored 3.00 1.00
Nos. 655-662 (8) 11.10 4.70

1984 UPU Congress A202

1984, June 20 Engr. ***Perf. 13x12½***

663 A202 300fr Ship, emblems 3.00 1.75

Ayerou Market Place A203

1984, July 18 Litho. ***Perf. 12½***

664 A203 80fr shown .75 .50
665 A203 120fr River scene 1.10 .60

Vipere Echis Leucogaster — A204

1984, Aug. 16 ***Perf. 13x12½***

666 A204 80fr multi 1.05 .55

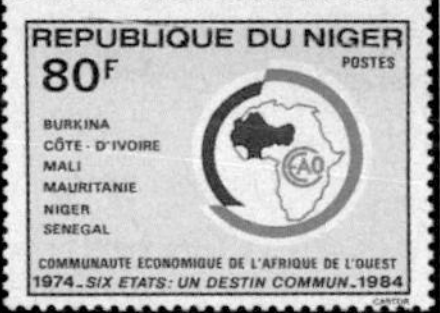

West African Union, CEAO, 10th Anniv. A205

1984, Oct. 26 **Litho.** ***Perf. 13½***

667 A205 80fr multi .60 .40

UN Disarmament Campaign, 20th Anniv. — A205a

1984, Oct. 31 ***Perf. 13***

667A A205a 400fr brt grn & blk 2.75 1.50

667B A205a 500fr brt bl & blk 3.25 2.00

Nos. 584-585 Overprinted "Aide au Sahel 84"

1984 **Litho.** ***Perf. 13***

668 A176 150fr multi 1.40 .75

669 A176 200fr multi 1.60 1.10

World Tourism Organization, 10th Anniv. — A206

1984, Jan. 2 **Litho.** ***Perf. 12½***

670 A206 110fr WTO emblem .90 .45

Infant Survival Campaign A207

1985, Jan. 28 **Litho.** ***Perf. 12½***

671 A207 85fr Breastfeeding .65 .35

672 A207 110fr Weighing child, giving liquids .90 .50

Nos. 590, 519 and 568 Overprinted with Exhibitions in Red

Souvenir Sheets

Perf. 13, 12½, 14

1985, Mar. 11 **Litho.**

673 A177 400fr MOPHILA '85 / HAMBOURG 4.50 4.50

674 A154 425fr TSUKUBA EXPO '85 4.50 4.50

675 A170 450fr ROME, ITALIA '85 emblem 4.50 4.50

See Nos. C356-C357.

Technical & Cultural Cooperation Agency, 15th Anniv. — A208

1985, Mar. 20 ***Perf. 13***

676 A208 110fr vio, brn & car rose .75 .40

8th Niamey Festival A209

Gaya Ballet Troupe. No. 678 vert.

1985, Apr. 8 ***Perf. 12½x13, 13x12½***

677 A209 85fr multi .60 .40

678 A209 110fr multi .75 .55

679 A209 150fr multi 1.10 .70

Nos. 677-679 (3) 2.45 1.65

Intl. Youth Year — A210

Authors and scenes from novels: 85fr, Jack London (1876-1916). 105fr, Joseph Kessel (1898-1979). 250fr, Herman Melville. 450fr, Rudyard Kipling.

1985, Apr. 29 ***Perf. 13***

680 A210 85fr multi .75 .35

681 A210 105fr multi .80 .40

682 A210 250fr multi 2.00 .90

683 A210 450fr multi 3.50 1.75

Nos. 680-683 (4) 7.05 3.40

PHILEXAFRICA '85, Lome, Togo — A211

1985, May 6 ***Perf. 13x12½***

684 A211 200fr Tree planting 1.50 1.10

685 A211 200fr Industry 1.50 1.10

a. Pair, Nos. 684-685 + label 4.50 4.50

Victor Hugo and His Son Francois, by A. de Chatillon — A212

1985, May 22 ***Perf. 12½***

686 A212 500fr multi 4.00 1.80

Europafrica A213

1985, June 3 ***Perf. 13***

687 A213 110fr multi .95 .50

World Wildlife Fund — A214

50fr, 60fr, Addax. 85fr, 110fr, Oryx.

1985, June 15

688 A214 50fr Head, vert. *2.75 .65*

689 A214 60fr Grazing *3.50 .85*

690 A214 85fr Two adults *4.25 1.05*

691 A214 110fr Head, vert. *5.50 1.25*

Nos. 688-691 (4) 16.00 3.80

Environ-destroying Species — A215

85fr, Oedaleus sp. 110fr, Dysdercus volkeri. 150fr, Tolyposporium ehrenbergii, Sclerospora graminicola, horiz. 210fr, Passer luteus. 390fr, Quelea quelea.

1985, July 1 ***Perf. 13x12½, 12½x13***

692 A215 85fr multi .90 .35

693 A215 110fr multi 1.00 .40

694 A215 150fr multi 1.60 .60

695 A215 210fr multi 2.25 .90

696 A215 390fr multi 4.25 1.75

Nos. 692-696 (5) 10.00 4.00

Official Type of 1988 and

Cross of Agadez — A216

1985-94 **Engr.** ***Perf. 13***

697 A216 85fr green .75 .40

698 O2 110fr brown 1.00 .50

699 A216 125fr blue green —

700 A216 175fr emerald —

701 A216 210fr orange — —

Issued: 85fr, 110fr, 7/85; 125fr, 175fr, 210fr, 5/15/94.

Natl. Independence, 25th Anniv. — A217

1985, Aug. 3 **Litho.** ***Perf. 13x12½***

707 A217 110fr multi .90 .40

Protected Trees A218

Designs: 30fr, No. 711, Adansonia digitata and pod, vert. 85fr, 210fr, Acacia albida. No. 710, 390fr, Adansonia digitata, diff. Nos. 708-710 inscribed "DES ARBRES POUR LE NIGER."

1985 ***Perf. 13x12½, 12½x13***

708 A218 30fr grn & multi .55 .40

709 A218 85fr brn & multi .85 .50

710 A218 110fr mag & multi 1.20 .60

711 A218 110fr blk & multi 1.05 .55

712 A218 210fr blk & multi 1.75 1.10

713 A218 390fr blk & multi 3.50 1.60

Nos. 708-713 (6) 8.90 4.75

Issued: #708-710, 10/1; #711-713, 8/19.

Niamey-Bamako Motorboat Race — A219

110fr, Boats on Niger River. 150fr, Helicopter, competitor. 250fr, Motorboat, map.

1985, Sept. 16 ***Perf. 13½***

714 A219 110fr multicolored .75 .40

715 A219 150fr multicolored 1.00 .60

716 A219 250fr multicolored 1.90 1.00

Nos. 714-716 (3) 3.65 2.00

Mushrooms — A220

85fr, Boletus. 110fr, Hypholoma fasciculare. 200fr, Coprinus comatus. 300fr, Agaricus arvensis. 400fr, Geastrum fimbriatum.

1985, Oct. 3

717 A220 85fr multicolored .80 .35

718 A220 110fr multicolored 1.10 .40

719 A220 200fr multicolored 1.90 .75

720 A220 300fr multicolored 3.25 1.10

721 A220 400fr multicolored 4.25 1.60

Nos. 717-721 (5) 11.30 4.20

Nos. 717-719 vert.

PHILEXAFRICA '85, Lome, Togo — A221

No. 722, Village water pump. No. 723, Children playing dili.

1985, Oct. 21 ***Perf. 13x12½***

722 A221 250fr multicolored 2.00 1.25

723 A221 250fr multicolored 2.00 1.25

a. Pair, Nos. 722-723 4.50 4.50

61st World Savings Day A222

1985, Oct. 31 *Perf. 12½x13*
724 A222 210fr multi 1.60 .90

European Music Year A223

Traditional instruments.

1985, Nov. 4 *Perf. 13½*
725 A223 150fr Gouroumi, vert. 1.25 .80
726 A223 210fr Gassou 1.75 1.25
727 A223 390fr Algaita, vert. 3.00 1.75
Nos. 725-727 (3) 6.00 3.80

Souvenir Sheet

Perf. 12½

728 A223 500fr Biti 4.00 4.00

Civil Statutes Reform — A224

1986, Jan. 2 Litho. *Perf. 13x12½*
729 A224 85fr Natl. identity card .60 .40
730 A224 110fr Family services .85 .50

Traffic Safety — A225

1986, Mar. 26 Litho. *Perf. 12½x13*
731 A225 85fr Obey signs .60 .35
732 A225 110fr Speed restriction .85 .50

Artists — A226

60fr, Oumarou Ganda, filmmaker. 85fr, Ida Na Dadaou, entertainer. 100fr, Dan Gourmou, entertainer. 130fr, Koungoui, comedian.

1986, Apr. 11 *Perf. 12½*
733 A226 60fr multi .45 .30
734 A226 85fr multi .60 .40
735 A226 100fr multi .75 .50
736 A226 130fr multi 1.00 .55
Nos. 733-736 (4) 2.80 1.75

Hunger Relief Campaign, Trucks of Hope — A227

85fr, Relief supply truck. 110fr, Mother, child, vert.

1986, Aug. 27 Litho. *Perf. 12½*
737 A227 85fr multicolored .75 .40
738 A227 110fr multicolored 1.00 .50

Intl. Solidarity Day — A228

200fr, Nelson Mandela and Walter Sisulu, Robben Island prison camp. 300fr, Mandela.

1986, Oct. 8 *Perf. 13½*
739 A228 200fr multi 1.80 .90
740 A228 300fr multi 2.75 1.40

FAO, 40th Anniv. A229

50fr, Cooperative peanut farm. 60fr, Fight desert encroachment. 85fr, Irrigation management. 100fr, Breeding livestock. 110fr, Afforestation.

1986, Oct. 16 *Perf. 13*
741 A229 50fr multicolored .40 .30
742 A229 60fr multicolored .45 .30
743 A229 85fr multicolored .60 .40
744 A229 100fr multicolored .75 .40
745 A229 110fr multicolored 1.00 .40
Nos. 741-745 (5) 3.20 1.80

Improved Housing for a Healthier Niger — A230

1987, Feb. 26 Litho. *Perf. 13½*
746 A230 85fr Albarka .75 .30
747 A230 110fr Mai Sauki .95 .50

Insects Protecting Growing Crops — A231

1987, Mar. 26 *Perf. 13x12½*
748 A231 85fr Sphodromantis 1.00 .50
749 A231 110fr Delta 1.50 .60
750 A231 120fr Cicindela 1.75 .85
Nos. 748-750 (3) 4.25 1.95

Liptako-Gourma Telecommunications Link Inauguration — A232

1987, Apr. 10 *Perf. 13½*
751 A232 110fr multi .75 .50

Samuel Morse — A233

120fr, Telegraph key, operator, horiz. 350fr, Receiver, horiz.

1987, May 21 Litho. *Perf. 12x12½*
752 A233 120fr multicolored .75 .40
753 A233 200fr shown 1.50 .75
754 A233 350fr multicolored 3.00 1.50
Nos. 752-754 (3) 5.25 2.65

Invention of the telegraph, 150th anniv.

1988 Seoul Summer Olympics — A234

1987, July 15
755 A234 85fr Tennis .55 .40
756 A234 110fr Pole vault .85 .40
757 A234 250fr Soccer 2.00 .85
Nos. 755-757 (3) 3.40 1.65

Souvenir Sheet

758 A234 500fr Running 4.00 2.75

1988 Winter Olympics, Calgary — A235

1987, July 28 Litho. *Perf. 12½*
759 A235 85fr Ice hockey .60 .35
760 A235 110fr Speed skating .85 .40
761 A235 250fr Pairs figure skating 2.00 .85
Nos. 759-761 (3) 3.45 1.60

Souvenir Sheet

762 A235 500fr Downhill skiing 4.00 2.75

For overprints see Nos. 783-785.

African Games, Nairobi — A236

1987, Aug. 5 *Perf. 13*
763 A236 85fr Runners .60 .35
764 A236 110fr High jump .75 .40
765 A236 200fr Hurdles 1.50 .75
766 A236 400fr Javelin 3.00 1.50
Nos. 763-766 (4) 5.85 3.00

Natl. Tourism Office, 10th Anniv. A237

85fr, Chief's stool, scepter, vert. 110fr, Nomad, caravan, scepter. 120fr, Moslem village. 200fr, Bridge over Niger River.

1987, Sept. 10 *Perf. 13½*
767 A237 85fr multicolored .50 .35
768 A237 110fr multicolored 1.00 .40
769 A237 120fr multicolored 1.00 .40
770 A237 200fr multicolored 1.75 .75
Nos. 767-770 (4) 4.25 1.90

Aga Khan Architecture Prize, 1986 — A238

1987, Oct. 7 *Perf. 13*
771 A238 85fr Yaama Mosque, dawn .60 .30
772 A238 110fr At night .80 .40
773 A238 250fr In daylight 1.75 .90
Nos. 771-773 (3) 3.15 1.60

Niamey Court of Appeal A239

1987, Nov. 17 *Perf. 13x12½*
774 A239 85fr multi .60 .30
775 A239 110fr multi .75 .40
776 A239 140fr multi 1.00 .50
Nos. 774-776 (3) 2.35 1.20

Christmas 1987 — A240

Paintings: 110fr, The Holy Family with Lamb, by Raphael. 500fr, The Adoration of the Magi, by Hans Memling (c. 1430-1494).

Wmk. 385

1987, Dec. 24 Litho. *Perf. 12½*
777 A240 110fr multi 1.00 .50

Souvenir Sheet

778 A240 500fr multi 4.00 2.50

No. 778 is airmail.

Modern Services for a Healthy Community — A241

1988, Jan. 21 *Perf. 13*

779 A241 85fr Water drainage .95 .55
780 A241 110fr Sewage 1.10 .70
781 A241 165fr Garbage removal 1.90 .95
Nos. 779-781 (3) 3.95 2.20

Dan-Gourmou Prize — A242

1988, Feb. 16 **Litho.** *Perf. 13½*

782 A242 85fr multi 1.10 .70

Natl. modern music competition.

Nos. 759-761 Ovptd. "Medaille d'or" and Name of Winner in Gold

1988, Mar. 29 *Perf. 12½*

783 A235 85fr USSR .60 .40
784 A235 110fr Gusafson, Sweden .80 .50
785 A235 250fr Gordeeva and Grinkov, USSR 2.00 1.20
Nos. 783-785 (3) 3.40 2.10

New Market Building, Niamey A243

1988, Apr. 9 **Litho.** *Perf. 13x12½*

786 A243 85fr multi .75 .40

WHO 40th Anniv., Universal Immunization Campaign — A244

1988, May 26 **Litho.** *Perf. 12½x13*

787 A244 85fr Mother and child .65 .40
788 A244 110fr Visiting doctor .90 .45

Organization for African Unity (OAU), 25th Anniv. — A245

1988, June 28 *Perf. 12½*

789 A245 85fr multi .65 .35

Construction of a Sand Break to Arrest Desert Encroachment — A246

1988, Sept. 27 **Litho.** *Perf. 12½x13*

790 A246 85fr multi 1.10 .50

Intl. Red Cross and Red Crescent Organizations, 125th Annivs. — A247

1988, Oct. 26 *Perf. 13x12½*

791 A247 85fr multi .60 .35
792 A247 110fr multi .80 .40

Niger Press Agency A248

1989, Jan. 31 **Litho.** *Perf. 12½*

793 A248 85fr blk, org & grn .65 .35

Fight Against AIDS — A249

1989, Feb. 28 *Perf. 13½*

794 A249 85fr multi .65 .35
795 A249 110fr multi .80 .40

Intl. Maritime Organization, 30th Anniv. — A250

1989, Mar. 29 **Litho.** *Perf. 12½x13*

796 A250 100fr multi .90 .40
797 A250 120fr multi 1.20 .50

FAN Seizure of Government, 15th Anniv. — A251

1989, Apr. 14

798 A251 85fr Gen. Ali Saibou .60 .30
799 A251 110fr Raising of the flag .80 .35

PHILEXFRANCE '89 — A252

1989, July 1 **Litho.** *Perf. 13*

800 A252 100fr Eiffel Tower .75 .40
801 A252 200fr Simulated stamps 1.50 .70

French Revolution, Bicent. — A253

250fr, Planting a tree for liberty.

1989, July 1

802 A253 250fr multicolored 2.25 1.10

Zinder Regional Museum — A253a

Perf. 14¾x14¼

1989, Aug. 23 **Litho.**

802A A253a 85fr multicolored *20.00*

African Development Bank, 25th Anniv. — A254

1989, Aug. 30 **Litho.** *Perf. 13½*

803 A254 100fr multicolored .75 .35

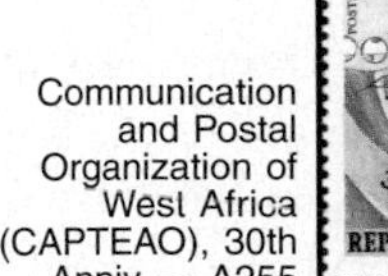

Communication and Postal Organization of West Africa (CAPTEAO), 30th Anniv. — A255

1989, July 3 **Litho.** *Perf. 13½*

804 A255 85fr multicolored .65 .35

Verdant Field, Field After Locust Plague — A256

1989, Oct. 1 **Litho.** *Perf. 13*

805 A256 85fr multicolored 1.25 .35

Lumiere Brothers, Film Pioneers A256a

Designs: 150fr, Auguste Lumiere (1862-1954). 250fr, Louis Lumiere (1864-1948).

1989, Nov. 21 **Litho.** *Perf. 13½*

805A A256a 150fr multicolored 1.50 .75
805B A256a 250fr multicolored 2.25 1.00
805C A256a 400fr multicolored 3.50 1.75
Nos. 805A-805C (3) 7.25 3.50

Rural Development Council, 30th Anniv. — A256b

1989 **Litho.** *Perf. 15x14*

805D A256b 75fr multicolored *20.00*

Flora — A257

10fr, Russelia equisetiformis. 20fr, Argyreia nervosa. 30fr, Hibiscus rosa-sinensis. 50fr, Catharanthus roseus. 100fr, Cymothoe sangaris, horiz.

1989, Dec. 12 **Litho.** *Perf. 13*

806 A257 10fr multicolored .25 .25
807 A257 20fr multicolored .25 .25
808 A257 30fr multicolored .25 .25
809 A257 50fr multicolored .45 .25
810 A257 100fr multicolored 1.00 .40
Nos. 806-810 (5) 2.20 1.40

Dunes of Temet A257a

1989 **Litho.** *Perf. 15x14*

810A A257a 145fr Caravan *55.00 45.00*
810B A257a 165fr shown *55.00 45.00*

Pan-African Postal Union, 10th Anniv. — A258

1990, Jan. 18 *Perf. 12½*

811 A258 120fr multicolored 1.00 .50

Intl. Literacy Year — A259

1990, Feb. 27 *Perf. 13½x13*

812 A259 85fr shown .65 .30
813 A259 110fr Class, diff. .95 .40

Islamic Conference Organization, 20th anniv. — A260

1990, Mar. 15 *Perf. 13x12½*

814 A260 85fr OCI emblem .70 .35

U.S. Congressman Mickey Leland — A261

1990, Mar. 29 **Litho.** ***Perf. 13½***

No.	Type	Description	Unused	Used
815	A261	300fr multicolored	2.40	1.25
816	A261	500fr multicolored	4.00	2.00

Leland died Aug. 7, 1989 in a plane crash on a humanitarian mission.

Natl. Development Society, 1st Anniv. — A262

1990, May 15 **Litho.** ***Perf. 13½***

No.	Type	Description	Unused	Used
817	A262	85fr multicolored	.70	.35

Multinational Postal School, 20th Anniv. — A263

1990, May 31 ***Perf. 13x12½***

No.	Type	Description	Unused	Used
818	A263	85fr multicolored	.75	.35

1992 Summer Olympics, Barcelona — A263a

1990, June 4 **Litho.** ***Perf. 13½***

No.	Type	Description	Unused	Used
818A	A263a	85fr Gymnastics	.65	.30
818B	A263a	110fr Hurdles	.85	.40
818C	A263a	250fr Running	2.00	1.00
818D	A263a	400fr Equestrian	3.00	1.50
818E	A263a	500fr Long jump	4.00	2.00
		Nos. 818A-818E (5)	10.50	5.20

Souvenir Sheet

No.	Type	Description	Unused	Used
818F	A263a	600fr Cycling	4.75	2.75

Nos. 818D-818F are airmail.

Independence, 30th Anniv. — A264

1990, Aug. 3 ***Perf. 12½***

No.	Type	Description	Unused	Used
819	A264	85fr gray grn & multi	.60	.35
820	A264	110fr buff & multi	.90	.45

UN Development Program, 40th Anniv. — A265

1990, Oct. 24 **Litho.** ***Perf. 13½***

No.	Type	Description	Unused	Used
821	A265	100fr multicolored	.80	.40

A266

Butterflies and Mushrooms — A266a

Designs: 85fr, Amanita rubescens. 110fr, Graphum pylades. 200fr, Pseudacraea hostilia. 250fr, Russula virescens. 400fr, Boletus impolitus. 500fr, Precis octavia. 600fr, Cantharellus cibarius & pseudacraea boisduvali.

1991, Jan. 15 **Litho.** ***Perf. 13½***

No.	Type	Description	Unused	Used
822	A266	85fr multicolored	.65	.30
823	A266	110fr multicolored	.75	.40
824	A266	200fr multicolored	1.20	.80
825	A266	250fr multicolored	2.25	1.00
826	A266	400fr multicolored	3.25	1.50
827	A266	500fr multicolored	3.50	1.60
		Nos. 822-827 (6)	11.60	5.60

Souvenir Sheet

No.	Type	Description	Unused	Used
828	A266a	600fr multicolored	5.00	5.00

Nos. 826-828 are airmail. No. 828 contains one 30x38mm stamp.

Palestinian Uprising — A267

1991, Mar. 30 **Litho.** ***Perf. 12½***

No.	Type	Description	Unused	Used
829	A267	110fr multicolored	1.00	.45

Christopher Columbus (1451-1506) A268

Hypothetical portraits and: 85fr, Santa Maria. 110fr, Frigata, Portuguese caravel, 15th cent. 200fr, Four-masted caravel, 16th cent. 250fr, Estremadura, Spanish caravel, 1511. 400fr, Vija, Portuguese caravel, 1600. 500fr, Pinta. 600fr, Nina.

1991, Mar. 19 **Litho.** ***Perf. 13½***

No.	Type	Description	Unused	Used
830	A268	85fr multicolored	.75	.35
831	A268	110fr multicolored	.90	.40
832	A268	200fr multicolored	1.60	.80
833	A268	250fr multicolored	2.00	1.00
834	A268	400fr multicolored	3.25	1.40
835	A268	500fr multicolored	3.75	1.90
		Nos. 830-835 (6)	12.25	5.85

Souvenir Sheet

No.	Type	Description	Unused	Used
835A	A268	600fr multicolored	5.00	4.00

Nos. 834-835A are airmail.

Timia Falls — A269

African Tourism Year — A270

Designs: 85fr, Boubon Market, horiz. 130fr, Ruins of Assode, horiz.

1991, July 10

No.	Type	Description	Unused	Used
836	A269	85fr multicolored	.70	.30
837	A269	110fr multicolored	.95	.45
838	A269	130fr multicolored	1.10	.50
839	A270	200fr multicolored	1.75	.85
		Nos. 836-839 (4)	4.50	2.10

Anniversaries and Events — A270a

85fr, Chess players Anatoly Karpov and Garry Kasparov. 110fr, Race car drivers Ayrton Senna and Alain Prost. 200fr, An official swears allegiance to the constitution, Honoré-Gabriel Riqueti (Comte de Mirabeau). 250fr, Gen. Dwight D. Eisenhower, Winston Churchill, Field Marshal Bernard Montgomery and Republic P-4D Thunderbolt. 400fr, Charles de Gaulle and Konrad Adenauer. 500fr, German Chancellor Helmut Kohl, Brandenburg Gate. 600fr, Pope John Paul II's visit to Africa.

1991, July 15 **Litho.** ***Perf. 13½***

No.	Type	Description	Unused	Used
839A	A270a	85fr multicolored	.45	.25
839B	A270a	110fr multicolored	.60	.25
839C	A270a	200fr multicolored	1.10	.35
839D	A270a	250fr multicolored	6.00	1.25
839E	A270a	400fr multicolored	2.25	.75
839F	A270a	500fr multicolored	2.75	.85
839G	A270a	600fr multicolored	5.00	5.00
		Nos. 839A-839G (7)	18.15	8.70

French Revolution, bicent. (#839C). Franco-German Cooperation Agreement, 28th anniv. (#839E). #839E is airmail & exists in a souvenir sheet of 1. German reunification (#839F). Nos. 839F and 839G are airmail and exist in souvenir sheets of 1.

For surcharge see No. 865.

Women's Hairstyles A271

1991

No.	Type	Description	Unused	Used
840	A271	85fr multicolored	.95	.30
841	A271	110fr multicolored	1.25	.40
842	A271	165fr multicolored	1.90	.65
843	A271	200fr multicolored	2.10	.75
		Nos. 840-843 (4)	6.20	2.10

Transportation — A271a

Design: 85fr, Earth Resources Satellite, ERS-1, Japan; 110fr, EXOS-D satellite for observation of the Aurora Borealis, Japan; 200fr, Louis Favre (1826-1879), Congo-Ocean locomotive BB 415; 250fr, Congo-Ocean locomotive BB.BB.301; 400fr, Locomotive BB BB 302; 500fr, Anglo-French Concorde, F117 stealth fighter, US. 600fr, George Nagelmacker (1845-1905), Orient Express.

1991, Oct. 15 **Litho.** ***Perf. 13½x13¼***

No.	Type	Description	Unused	Used
843A	A271a	85fr multi	.45	.25
843B	A271a	110fr multi	.60	.25
843C	A271a	200fr multi	2.10	.35
843D	A271a	250fr multi	2.50	.40
843E	A271a	400fr multi	3.75	.55
843F	A271a	500fr multi	2.75	.50
		Nos. 843A-843F (6)	12.15	2.30

Souvenir Sheet

No.	Type	Description	Unused	Used
843G	A271a	600fr multi	2.75	.50

Nos. 843E-843G are airmail. Nos. 843A-843F exist in souvenir sheets of one. A souvenir sheet of 3 containing Nos. 843A-843B, 843F exists.

Natl. Conference of Niger — A272

1991, Dec. 17 **Litho.** ***Perf. 12½***

No.	Type	Description	Unused	Used
844	A272	85fr multicolored	.70	.35

House Built Without Wood A273

1992, May 25 **Litho.** ***Perf. 12½***

No.	Type	Description	Unused	Used
845	A273	85fr multicolored	.75	.40

World Population Day — A274

Designs: 85fr, Assembling world puzzle. 110fr, Globe on a kite string.

1992, July 11 **Litho.** ***Perf. 12½***

No.	Type	Description	Unused	Used
846	A274	85fr multicolored	.75	.40
847	A274	110fr multicolored	.95	.50

Discovery of America, 500th Anniv. — A275

1992, Sept. 16 *Perf. 13*
848 A275 250fr multicolored 2.25 1.10

Hadjia Haoua Issa (1927-1990), Singer — A276

1992, Sept. 23 *Perf. 12½x13*
849 A276 150fr multicolored 1.25 .65

Intl. Conference on Nutrition, Rome — A277

1992 **Litho.** *Perf. 12½*
850 A277 145fr tan & multi 1.40 .60
851 A277 350fr blue & multi 3.00 1.50

African School of Meteorology and Civil Aviation, 30th Anniv. — A278

1993, Feb. 7 *Perf. 13½*
852 A278 110fr bl, grn & blk .90 .45

Environmental Protection A279

1993, June 26 **Litho.** *Perf. 12½*
853 A279 85fr salmon & multi .75 .40
854 A279 165fr green & multi 1.50 .75

World Population Day A280

110fr, Buildings, person with globe as head, tree.

1993, July 11 **Litho.** *Perf. 13½*
855 A280 85fr multicolored .65 .30
856 A280 110fr multicolored .85 .40

Holy City of Jerusalem — A281

1993, Nov. 8 **Litho.** *Perf. 13x12½*
857 A281 110fr multicolored .95 .45

Artisans at Work — A282b

1994 **Litho.** *Perf. 13x13¼*
857D A282b 125fr Tailor —
857E A282b 175fr Weaver, vert. — —

Nelson Mandela, F.W. De Klerk, Winners of 1993 Nobel Peace Prize — A282

1994, Feb. 11 **Litho.** *Perf. 13*
858 A282 270fr multicolored 1.10 .55

A282a

1994 **Litho.** *Perf. 12½x13*
858B A282a 110fr Hills —
858C A282a 165fr Mountain —

An 85fr stamp was released with this set. The editors would like to examine that stamp.

Cultural Cooperation & Technique Agency, 25th Anniv. — A283

1995 **Litho.** *Perf. 13½x13*
859 A283 100fr multicolored .50 .25

Animals Used for Transportation — A284

1995 *Perf. 13x13½*
860 A284 500fr Donkey cart 1.75 1.10
861 A284 1000fr Man, saddled horse 4.00 2.25

Economic Community of West African States (ECOWAS), 20th Anniv. — A285

1995 **Litho.** *Perf. 13½*
862 A285 125fr multicolored .70 .35

Cattle Ranching A286

Design: 300fr, Irrigating fields.

1995 *Perf. 13½x13*
863 A286 125fr shown .60 .35
864 A286 300fr multicolored 1.20 .75

Souvenir Sheet of No. 839E Ovptd.

1995, Nov. 8 **Litho.** *Perf. 13½*
865 A270a 400fr multicolored *6.50 4.00*

African Development Bank, 30th Anniv. — A287

1995 **Litho.** *Perf. 14*
866 A287 300fr green & red 1.25 .80

Boy Scouts A288

350fr, Robert Baden-Powell. 500fr, Scout saluting.

1996 *Perf. 13½*
867 A288 350fr multicolored 1.25 .75
868 A288 500fr multicolored 2.00 1.20

Nos. 867-868 exist imperf. and in souvenir sheets of 1 both perf. and imperf.

UN, UNICEF, 50th Anniv. — A289

Designs: 150fr, Child with head bandaged, UNICEF emblem. 225fr, Boy carrying bowl of food on head, dove, globes. 475fr, Woman, boy playing on artillery piece, space station Mir. 550fr, Boy, race car driver Michael Schumacher, UNICEF emblem.

1996
869 A289 150fr multicolored .70 .35
870 A289 225fr multicolored 1.00 .50
871 A289 475fr multicolored 2.25 1.10
a. Sheet of 2, #870-871 + label *11.00 5.50*
872 A289 550fr multicolored 2.50 1.25
a. Sheet of 2, #869, 872 + label *11.00 5.50*
Nos. 869-872 (4) 6.45 3.20

Entertainers — A290

No. 873, Bob Marley. No. 874, Janis Joplin. No. 874A, Madonna. No. 875, Jerry Garcia. No. 876, Elvis Presley. No. 877, Marilyn Monroe. No. 878, John Lennon. No. 879, Monroe, diff. No. 880, Presley, diff.
No. 881, Presley, diff. No. 882, Monroe, diff.

1996
873 A290 175fr multicolored .70 .45
874 A290 300fr multicolored 1.10 .90
874A A290 400fr multicolored 1.60 1.20
875 A290 600fr multicolored 2.50 1.75
876 A290 700fr multicolored 2.75 2.10
877 A290 700fr multicolored 2.75 2.10
878 A290 750fr multicolored 3.25 2.25
879 A290 800fr multicolored 3.25 2.40
880 A290 800fr multicolored 3.25 2.40
Nos. 873-880 (9) 21.15 15.55

Souvenir Sheets

881 A290 2000fr multicolored 7.00 6.00
882 A290 2000fr multicolored 7.00 6.00

Nos. 873-882 exist imperf. and in souvenir sheets of 1 both perf. and imperf.
No. 874A exists in a souvenir sheet of 1.

Butterflies A291

Boy Scout Jamboree emblem and: 150fr, Chrysiridia ripheария. 200fr, Palla ussheri. 750fr, Mylothris chloris. 800fr, Papilo dardanus.

1996 **Litho.** *Perf. 13½*
883 A291 150fr multicolored .60 .35
884 A291 200fr multicolored .80 .50
885 A291 750fr multicolored 2.75 2.25
886 A291 800fr multicolored 2.90 2.40
Nos. 883-886 (4) 7.05 5.50

Nos. 883-886 exist imperf. and in souvenir sheets of 1 both perf. and imperf.

Wild Animals — A292

Boy Scout Jamboree emblem, Rotary emblem and: 150fr, Erythrocebus patas. 200fr, Panthera pardus. 900fr, Balearica regulorum. 1000fr, Alcelaphus buselaphus.
2000fr, Panthera leo.

1996

887	A292	150fr multicolored	.55	.35
888	A292	200fr multicolored	.70	.55
889	A292	900fr multicolored	3.00	2.50
890	A292	1000fr multicolored	3.50	2.75
		Nos. 887-890 (4)	7.75	6.15

Souvenir Sheet

891 A292 2000fr multicolored 7.00 6.00

Nos. 887-890 exist in souvenir sheets of 1.

Rotary International A292a

Designs: 200fr, Boy holding fruits and vegetables. 700fr, Girl holding sheaves of grain.

1996 Litho. ***Perf. 13½***

891A	A292a	200fr multicolored	.90	.55
891B	A292a	700fr multicolored	3.00	1.90

Intl. Red Cross and Lions Intl. — A293

Designs: 250fr, Jean-Henri Dunant as young man. 300fr, Lions Intl. emblems, boy with books. 400fr, Dunant as old man. 600fr, Older boy carrying younger boy, Lions Intl. emblems.

1996 Litho. ***Perf. 13½***

892	A293	250fr multicolored	.90	.60
893	A293	300fr multicolored	1.05	.55
894	A293	400fr multicolored	1.50	1.25
895	A293	600fr multicolored	2.25	1.75
		Nos. 892-895 (4)	5.70	4.15

Traditional Musical Instruments A294

1996 Litho. ***Perf. 13½***

896	A294	125fr violet & multi	.55	.30
897	A294	175fr pink & multi	.80	.40

Sports A295

1996

898	A295	300fr Golf	1.05	.70
899	A295	500fr Tennis	1.75	1.40
900	A295	700fr Table tennis	2.60	1.80
		Nos. 898-900 (3)	5.40	3.90

Nos. 898-900 exist in souvenir sheets of one.

1996 Summer Olympic Games, Atlanta A296

Designs: 250fr, Track & field. 350fr, Women's gymnastics, table tennis. 400fr, Tennis, swimming. 600fr, Hurdles, pole vault. 1500fr, Men's track and field.

1996 Litho. ***Perf. 13½***

901	A296	250fr multicolored	.90	.60
902	A296	350fr multicolored	1.25	1.05
903	A296	400fr multicolored	1.50	1.25
904	A296	600fr multicolored	2.10	1.80
		Nos. 901-904 (4)	5.75	4.70

Souvenir Sheet

904A A296 1500fr multicolored 6.00 6.00

Souvenir Sheet

CHINA '96 — A297

Statues from Yunguang Grottoes, Datong, China: a, Head of Buddha. b, Side view.

1996

905 A297 140fr Sheet of 2, #a.-b. 2.00 1.00

1998 Winter Olympic Games, Nagano A298

1996

906	A298	85fr Hockey	.40	.25
907	A298	200fr Downhill skiing	.90	.45
908	A298	400fr Slalom skiing	1.75	.90
909	A298	500fr Pairs figure skating	2.25	1.10
		Nos. 906-909 (4)	5.30	2.70

Nos. 906-909 were not issued without metallic blue overprint on stamps dated 1991. Nos. 908-909 are airmail.

Nos. 906-909 exist with red metallic overprint. A 600fr souvenir sheet with red metallic overprint exists in limited quantities.

Formula I Race Car Drivers A299

Designs: 450fr, Jacques Villeneuve. 2000fr, Ayrton Senna (1960-94).

1996

910 A299 450fr multicolored 1.60 .80

Souvenir Sheet

911 A299 2000fr multicolored 7.00 6.00

No. 910 exists in souvenir sheet of 1. No. 911 contains one 39x57mm stamp.

Tockus Nasutus A300

Coracias Abyssinica A301

Designs: 15fr, Psittacula krameri. 25fr, Coracias abyssinica. 35fr, Bulbucus ibis.

1996 Litho. ***Perf. 13½x13***

912	A300	5fr multi	—
912A	A300	15fr multi	
912B	A300	25fr multi	—
912C	A300	35fr multi	

Perf. 13

913	A301	25fr multi	
914	A301	35fr multi	

Compare type A300 to types A301 and A309. The editors would like to examine two stamps of type A301 with 5fr and 15fr denominations.

1998 Winter Olympic Games, Nagano, Japan A302

1996 Litho. ***Perf. 13x13½***

915	A302	125fr Ice hockey	.55	.30
916	A302	175fr Slalom skiing	.75	.35
917	A302	700fr Pairs figure skating	3.00	1.50
918	A302	800fr Speed skating	3.50	1.75
		Nos. 915-918 (4)	7.80	3.90

Souvenir Sheet

919 A302 1500fr Downhill skiing 6.50 3.25

No. 919 contains one 57x51mm stamp. Nos. 915-918 exist in souvenir sheets of 1.

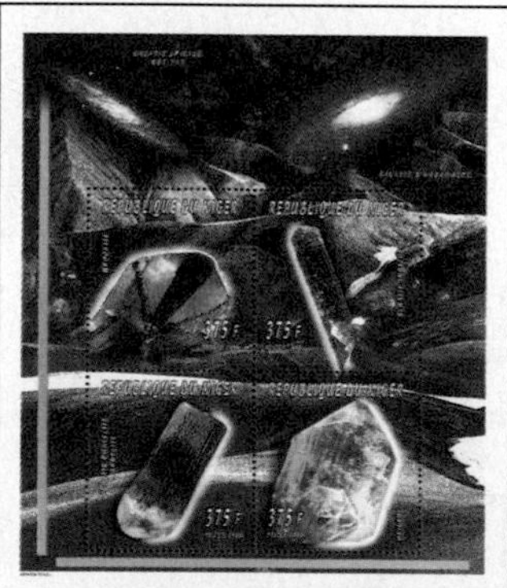

Minerals — A303

No. 920: a, Brookite. b, Elbaite indicolite. c. Elbaite rubellite verdelite. d, Olivine.

No. 921: a, Topaz. b, Autunite. c, Leucite. d, Struvite.

1996 Litho. ***Perf. 13½***

920	A303	375fr Sheet of 4, #a.-d.	5.50	3.25
921	A303	500fr Sheet of 4, #a.-d.	7.00	4.50

Souvenir Sheet

922 A303 2000fr Pyrargyrite 6.50 3.25

No. 922 contains one 42x39mm stamp.

World Driving Champion Michael Schumacher — A304

Schumacher: a, Grand Prix of Spain. b, In race car in pit. c, Ahead of another car. d, Behind another car.

1996 Litho. ***Perf. 13½***

923 A304 375fr Sheet of 4, #a.-d. 5.50 4.00

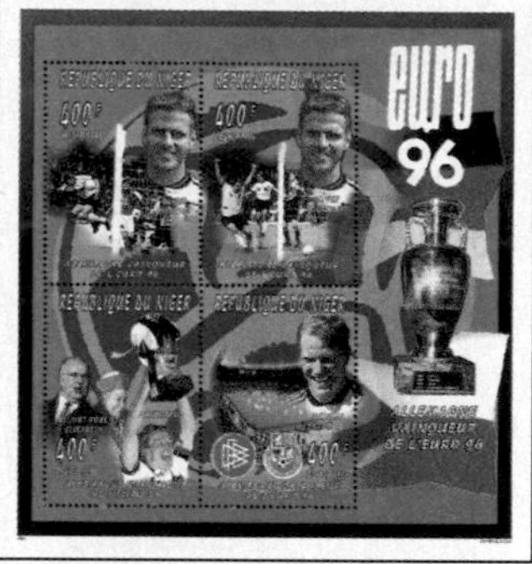

German Soccer Team, Euro '96 Champions — A305

No. 924: a, Oliver Bierhoff, player jumping up. b, Bierhoff, player holding up arms. c, ChancellorHelmut Kohl, Queen Elizabeth II, Klinsmann. d, Stadium, Mathias Sammer. logos.

1996 Litho. ***Perf. 13½***

924 A305 400fr Sheet of 4, #a.-d. 6.00 4.50

Dinosaurs — A306

No. 925: a, Ouranosaurus. b, Spinosaurus. c, Polacanthus. d, Deinonychus.

No. 926: a, Camptosaurus. b, Allosaurus. c, Nodosaurus. d, Kritosaurus.

2000fr, Protoceratops, oviraptor, horiz.

1996

925	A306	300fr Sheet of 4, #a.-d.	7.00	7.00
926	A306	450fr Sheet of 4, #a.-d.	11.00	11.00

Souvenir Sheet

927 A306 2000fr multicolored 6.75 6.00

France '98, World Soccer Cup Championships — A307

World Cup Trophy and: 125fr, American player. 175fr, Brazilian player. 750fr, Italian player. 1000fr, German player.
1500fr, Player in action scene.

1996

928	A307	125fr multicolored	.55	.30
929	A307	175fr multicolored	.75	.45
930	A307	750fr multicolored	3.25	1.90
931	A307	1000fr multicolored	4.25	2.40
		Nos. 928-931 (4)	8.80	5.05

Souvenir Sheet

932 A307 1500fr multicolored 6.00 4.00

No. 932 contains one 57x51mm stamp.

New Year 1997 (Year of the Ox) — A308

1997 **Litho.** ***Perf. 13½***

933	A308	500fr shown	2.00	1.00
934	A308	500fr Riding three oxen	2.00	1.00

Nos. 933-934 exist in souvenir sheets of 1, design extending to perfs on No. 933.

Birds A309

5fr, Tockus nasutus. 15fr, Psittacula kramer. 25fr, Coracias abyssinica. 35fr, Bulbucus ibis.

1997 **Litho.** ***Perf. 13½***

935	A309	5fr multicolored	.30	.25
936	A309	15fr multicolored	.30	.25
937	A309	25fr multicolored	.30	.25
938	A309	35fr multicolored	.30	.25
		Nos. 935-938 (4)	1.20	1.00

See No. 1050.

19th Dakar-Agades-Dakar Rally — A310

Designs: 125fr, Truck, child in traditional dress. 175fr, Ostrich, three-wheel vehicle. 300fr, Camel, heavy-duty support truck. 500fr, Motorcycles.

1997

939	A310	125fr multicolored	.50	.30
940	A310	175fr multicolored	.70	.40
941	A310	300fr multicolored	1.20	.75
942	A310	500fr multicolored	1.90	1.25
a.		Souvenir sheet, #939-942	4.50	4.50
b.		Strip of 4, #939-942	4.50	4.50

Deng Xiaoping (1904-97), Chinese Leader — A311

Designs: a, Deng, flag, eating at table, Deng as young man. b, Farming with oxen, Deng holding girl, flag. c, Flag, Deng with soldiers, camp. d, Deng bathing, ships in port, combining grain, launching space vehicle. e, Huts, heavy equipment vehicle, men working. f, Airplane, man holding up flask, operating room, Deng.

1997

943 A311 150fr Sheet of 6, #a.-f. 3.50 2.00

Diana, Princess of Wales (1961-97) A312

No. 944: Various portraits performing humanitarin deeds, on world tours, with various figures.
No. 945: Various portraits in designer dresses.
No. 946: With Mother Teresa (in margin).

1997, Sept. 30 **Litho.** ***Perf. 13½***

944	A312	180fr Sheet of 9, #a.-i.	6.50	4.00
945	A312	180fr Sheet of 9, #a.-i.	6.50	4.00

Souvenir Sheets

946	A312	2000fr multicolored	7.25	5.00
947	A312	4000fr multicolored	14.00	14.00

No. 947 contains one 40x46mm stamp depicting Princess Diana in red coat, holding bouquet.
A number of other stamps and souvenir sheets having similar type fonts depicting Princess Diana exist. These were declared to be not authorized by Niger postal authorites.

Famous Americans — A313

No. 948 — Various portraits: a-b, John F. Kennedy. c-d, Pres. Bill Clinton.
No. 949 — Various pprtraits: a, Kennedy. b, Dr. Martin Luther King (1929-68). c-d, Clinton.
2000fr, John F. Kennedy.

1997 **Litho.** ***Perf. 13½***

948	A313	350fr Sheet of 4, #a.-d.	4.75	3.00
949	A313	400fr Sheet of 4, #a.-d.	5.75	5.75

Souvenir Sheet

950 A313 2000fr multicolored 6.75 4.00

No. 950 contains one 42x60mm stamp.

Stars of American Cinema — A314

No. 951: a, Eddie Murphy. b, Elizabeth Taylor. c, Bruce Willis. d, James Dean. e, Clint Eastwood. f, Elvis Presley. g, Michelle Pfeiffer. h, Marilyn Monroe. i, Robert Redford.

1997 **Litho.** ***Perf. 13½***

951 A314 300fr Sheet of 9, #a.-i. 10.50 6.00

Communications — A315

No. 952: a, 80fr, Satellite transmission, radios. b, 100fr, Computers. c, 60fr, Cellular phone transmission around world. d, 120fr, Hand holding car phone. e, 180fr, Satellite, earth. f, 50fr, Transmission tower, cellular phone.

1997

952 A315 Sheet of 6, #a.-f. 2.25 1.10

Prof. Abdou Moumouni Dioffo — A316

1997 **Litho.** ***Perf. 13½x13***

953 A316 125fr multicolored *125.00*

Methods of Transportation — A317

Bicycles, motorcycles: No. 954: a, Jan Ullrich, 1997 Tour de France winner, Eiffel Tower. b, Diana 250, Harley Davidson. c, MK VIII motorcycle, bicycles of 1819, 1875. d, Brands Match Motorcycle Race, Great Britain.
Modern locomotives, country flags: No. 955: a, Pendolino ETR 470, Italy. b, Rame TGV 112, France. c, Eurostar, France, Belgium, UK. d, Intercity Express ICE train, Germany.
Early locomotives, country flags: No. 956: a, Trevithick, UK. b, Pacific North Chapelon, France. c, Buddicom, UK, France. d, PLM "C", France.
Trains of Switzerland: No. 957: a, Crocodile, St. Gothard. b, RE 460. c, Red Streak, RAE 2/4 1001. d, Limmat.
Classic cars, modern sports cars: No. 958: a, Mercedes 300 SL Gullwing, Mercedes E320 Cabriolet. b, Aston Martin V8, Aston Martin DBR2. c. Ferrari F50, Ferrari 250 GT Berlinette. d, Ford Thunderbird, Ford GT40.
Air flight: No. 959: a, Clement Ader's Avion 111, dirigible R101. b, Concorde jet, X36 NASA/MCDD prototype. c, Aile volante FW900, Airbus A340. d, Gaudron GIII, Montgolfier's balloon.
Space travel: No. 960: a, HII rocket, Japan, Copernicus. b, Galileo, Ariane rocket. c, Space shuttle, Neil Armstrong. d, Yuri Gagarin, orbital space station, Soyuz.
1500fr, Swiss train, RE 4/4 II 11349, vert. No. 962, Hubble Space Telescope, Concorde jet. No. 963, TGV mail train, 1958 Chevrolet Corvette.

1997 **Litho.** ***Perf. 13½***

954	A317	300fr Sheet of 4, #a.-d.	4.00	4.00
955	A317	350fr Sheet of 4, #a.-d.	5.00	5.00
956	A317	375fr Sheet of 4, #a.-d.	5.00	5.00
957	A317	400fr Sheet of 4, #a.-d.	6.00	6.00
958	A317	450fr Sheet of 4, #a.-d.	6.00	6.00
959	A317	500fr Sheet of 4, #a.-d.	6.75	6.75
960	A317	600fr Sheet of 4, #a.-d.	7.50	7.50

Souvenir Sheets

961	A317	1500fr multicolored	5.75	5.75
962	A317	2000fr multicolored	6.75	6.75
963	A317	2000fr multicolored	6.75	6.75

Swiss Railroad, 150th anniv. (#957, #961). Nos. 961-963 each contain one 50x60mm stamp.

Diana, Princess of Wales (1961-97) — A318

Various portraits.
1500fr, Wearing red dress. No. 966, Wearing blue dress.

1997 **Litho.** ***Perf. 13½***

964	A318	250fr Sheet of 9, #a.-i.	8.75	4.50
964J	A318	300fr Sheet of 9, #k.-s.	10.50	5.25

Souvenir Sheets

965	A318	1500fr multicolored	5.25	3.50
966	A318	2000fr multicolored	7.00	4.50

Nos. 965-966 contain one 42x60mm stamp.

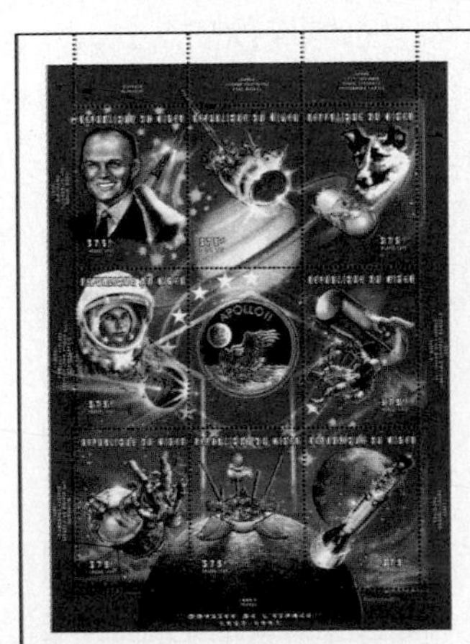

Man in Space — A319

No. 967: a, John Glenn, Mercury capsule. b, Cassini/Huygens satellite. c, Laika, first dog in space, Sputnik 2. d, Valentina Tereshkova, first woman in space, Vostok 6. e. Edward White, first American to walk in space, Gemini 4. f, Alexi Leonov, first Soviet to walk in space. g, Luna 9. h, Gemini capsule docked to Agena.

No. 968: a, Skylab space station. b, Pioneer 13, Venus 2. c, Giotto probe, Halley's Comet. d, Apollo-Soyuz mission. e, Mariner 10. f, Viking 1. g, Venera 11. h, Surveyor 1.

No. 969, 2000fr, Yuri Gagarin, first man in space, Sergei Korolev, RD107 rocket. No. 970, 2000fr, John F. Kennedy, Apollo 11, Neil Armstrong, first man to set foot on the moon.

1997 Litho. *Perf. 13½*

967 A319 375fr Sheet of 8 + label 10.00 8.00
968 A319 450fr Sheet of 8 + label 13.00 9.00

Souvenir Sheets

969-970 A319 Set of 2 14.00 10.00

Nos. 969-970 each contain one 42x60mm stamp.

Pres. Ibrahim Mainassara-Bare — A320

1997 Litho. & Embossed *Perf. 13½*

971 A320 500fr gold & multi 1.75 1.10

Scouting, Intl., 90th Anniv. (in 1997) — A321

No. 972 — Scout and: a, Lion. b, Rhinoceros. c, Giraffe. d, Elephant.

No. 972E — Girl Scout: f, Building bird house. g, Examining flower with magnifying glass. h, Identifying flower from book. i, Playing with bird.

No. 973: a, Butterfly. b, Bird with berries in mouth. c, Bird. d, Brown & white butterfly.

No. 974: a, Holding up rock to light. b, Using magnifying glass. c, Looking at rock. d, On hands and knees.

No. 975 — Scout, mushroom, with background color of: a, Yellow. b, White. c, Pink. d, Green.

2000fr, Robert Baden-Powell, Scouts chasing butterflies, mushroom.

1998 Litho.

972 A321 350fr Sheet of 4, #a.-d. 5.00 2.75
972E A321 400fr Sheet of 4, #f.-i. 5.75 3.50
973 A321 450fr Sheet of 4, #a.-d. 6.50 3.75
974 A321 500fr Sheet of 4, #a.-d. 7.00 4.00
975 A321 600fr Sheet of 4, #a.-d. 8.50 4.75

Souvenir Sheet

975E A321 2000fr multicolored 7.00 4.00

Greenpeace — A322

No. 976 — Turtles: a, Being caught in net. b, One swimming right. c, Mating. d, One swimming left.

1998

976 A322 400fr Block of 4, #a.-d 9.00 4.50
e. Souvenir sheet, #976 16.00 16.00

Sheets overprinted "CHINA 99 World Philatelic Exhibition" are not authorized.

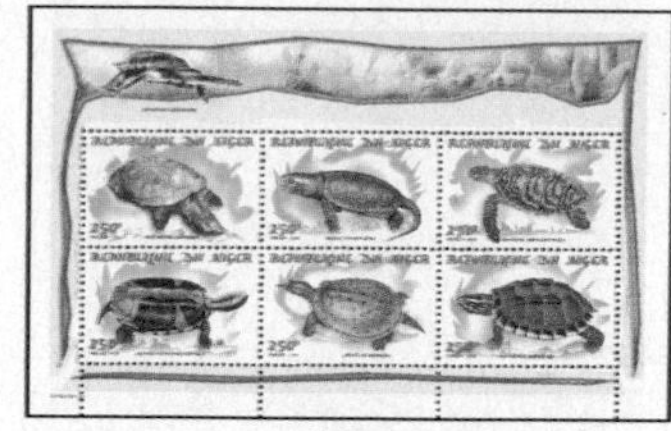

A323

No. 977 — Turtles: a, Pelomedusa subruta. b, Megacephalum shiui. c, Eretmochelus imbricata. d, Platycephala platycephala. e, Spinifera spinifera. f, Malayemys subtrijuga.

No. 978 — Raptors: a, Aquila uerreauxii. b, Asia otus. c, Bubo bubo. d, Surnia ulula. e, Asio flammeus. f, Falco biarnicus.

No. 979 — Orchids: a, Oeceoclades saundersiana. b, Paphiopedilum venustum. c, Maxillaria picta. d, Masdevallia triangularis. e, Zugopetalum. f, Encyllia nemoralis.

No. 980 — Butterflies: a, Danaus plexippus. b, Leto venus. c, Callioratis millari. d, Hippotion celerio. e, Euchloron megaera. f, Teracotona euprepia.

No. 981 — Mushrooms: a, Phaeolepotia aurea. b, Disciotis venosa. c, Gomphidius glutinosus. d, Amanita vaginata. e, Tremellodon gelatinosum. f, Voluariella voluacea.

1998, Sept. 29 Litho. *Perf. 13½*

977 A323 250fr Sheet of 6, #a.-f. 5.50 2.50
978 A323 300fr Sheet of 6, #a.-f. 6.50 3.75
979 A323 350fr Sheet of 6, #a.-f. 7.50 4.00
980 A323 400fr Sheet of 6, #a.-f. 8.50 4.75
981 A323 450fr Sheet of 6, #a.-f. 9.75 5.25

Marine Life — A324

No. 982: a, Tursiops truncatus. b, Phocoenoides dalli. c, Sousa teuszii. d, Stegostoma fasciatum. e, Delphinus delphis, balaenoptera musculus. f, Carcharodon carcharias. g, Argonauta argo, heterodontus portusjacksoni. h, Mitsukurina owstoni. i, Sphyrna mokarran. j, Homarus gammarus, prostheceraeus vittatus. k, Glossodoris valenciennesi, cephalopodes decapodes. l, Nemertien anople, elysia viridis.

1998, Sept. 29 Litho. *Perf. 13½*

982 A324 175fr Sheet of 12, #a-l 8.00 4.00

World Wildlife Fund A325

Gazella dorcas: No. 983, Doe, fawn. No. 984, Adult lying down. No. 985, Two adults standing still. No. 986 Adult walking.

1998

983 A325 250fr multicolored 1.25 .85
984 A325 250fr multicolored 1.25 .85
985 A325 250fr multicolored 1.25 .85
986 A325 250fr multicolored 1.25 .85
a. Souvenir sheet, #983-986 *40.00 35.00*
Nos. 983-986 (4) 5.00 3.40

Similar items without WWF emblem are not authorized.

Pope John Paul II — A326

Various portraits of pontiff thoughout his life.

1998, Sept. 29 Litho. *Perf. 13½*

987 A326 250fr Sheet of 9, #a.-i. 8.75 4.50

Souvenir Sheet

988 A326 2000fr multicolored 7.75 4.00

No. 988 contains one 57x51mm stamp.

Frank Sinatra (1915-98) — A327

Various portraits.

1998

989 A327 300fr Sheet of 9, #a.-i. 10.50 6.00

Explorers — A328

No. 990: a, Juan Sebastian del Cano (1476-1526), commander of vessel that completed circumnavigation of globe. b, Globe, sailing ships. c, Ferdinand Magellan (1480-1521).

No. 991 — Vasco da Gama (1469-1524): a. Portrait. b, Angels, explorers, soldiers, flag. c, Sailing ship, da Gama's tomb, Lisbon.

No. 992 — Aviator Roland Garros (1888-1918): a, Arriving at Utrecht. b, Flying across Mediterranean, 1913. c, Portrait.

1998, Sept. 29

990 A328 350fr Sheet of 3, #a.-c. 4.00 2.00
991 A328 400fr Sheet of 3, #a.-c. 4.75 2.25
992 A328 450fr Sheet of 3, #a.-c. 5.25 2.50

Nos. 990b, 991b, 992b are 60x51mm.

Jacques-Yves Cousteau (1910-97), Environmentalist — A329

No. 993: a, Whales. b, Fish, diver, whales, sled dog team. c, Portrait of Cousteau surrounded by ship, explorers in polar region, whale, fish.

No. 994: a, Cousteau, children, bird. b, Ship, marine life. c, Cousteau in diving gear, fish.

1998, Sept. 29

993 A329 500fr Sheet of 3, #a.-c. 5.75 3.00
994 A329 600fr Sheet of 3, #a.-c. 7.00 3.50

Nos. 993b and 994b are 60x51mm.

1998 World Cup Soccer Championships, France — A330

No. 995: a, Emmanuel Petit. b, Zinedine Zidane. c, Fabien Barthez. d, Lilian Thuram. e, Didier Deschamps. f, Youri Djorkaeff. g, Marcel Desailly, Christian Karembeu. h, Bixente Lizarazu. i, Frank Leboeuf, Stephane Guivarc'h.

1998

995 A330 250fr Sheet of 9, #a.-i. 8.75 4.50

A331

FIMA Niger '98 African Fashion Festival — A332

1998 Litho. *Perf. 13½x13*

996 A331 175fr multi 1.20 .75
997 A332 225fr multi 1.50 .75

Flowers — A333

Designs: 10fr, Roses and anemone. 20fr, Asystasia vogeliana, horiz. 30fr, Agrumes, horiz. 40fr, Angraecum sesquipedale. 45fr, Dissotis rotundifolia. 50fr, Hibiscus rosa-sinensis. 100fr, Datura.

1998 Litho. *Perf. 13¼x13½*

997A	A333	10fr multi	—	—
997B	A333	20fr multi	—	—
997C	A333	30fr multi	—	—
997D	A333	40fr multi	—	—
997E	A333	45fr multi	—	—
998	A333	50fr multi	—	—
999	A333	100fr multi	—	—

A number of items inscribed "Republique du Niger" were not authorized by Niger postal authorities. These include:

Dated 1996: Overprinted 500fr souvenir sheet for 20th anniv. first commercial flight of the Concorde.

Dated 1998: Martin Luther King, Jr., 2000fr souvenir sheet;

Ferrari automobile, 2000fr stamp and souvenir sheet;

Trains, 650fr sheet of 4, 2500fr souvenir sheet, two 3000fr souvenir sheets;

Titanic, 650fr sheet of 4, four 650fr souvenir sheets, 2500fr souvenir sheet;

Paintings by Toulouse-Lautrec, Gauguin, Renoir, Matisse, Delacroix, Van Gogh, sheets of nine 250fr, 300fr, 375fr 400fr, 425fr, 500fr stamps, sheet of three 725fr Matisse stamps, 200fr, Delacroix souvenir sheet;

French and Italian performers, sheet of nine 675fr stamps;

Sailing vessels, sheets of four 525fr, 875fr stamps;

Events of the 20th Century, 3 sheets of nine 225fr stamps, 2 sheets of nine 375fr stamps, 3 sheets of nine 500fr stamps, fourteen 225fr souvenir sheets, three 2000fr souvenir sheets;

Space events of the 20th Century, two 2000fr souvenir sheets;

Papal visits, sheet of nine 500fr stamps, sheet of two 1500fr stamps;

Cats, sheetlet of 5 stamps, various denominations, 500fr souvenir sheet;

African Music, sheet of nine 225fr stamps;

Pinocchio, sheet of nine 200fr stamps;

Dated 1999: History of the Cinema (Marilyn Monroe), sheet of nine 275fr stamps, 2000fr souvenir sheet;

History of American Cinema (various actors), sheet of nine 400fr stamps;

John F. Kennedy, Jr., sheet of nine 500fr stamps;

Sheets of nine stamps of various denominations depicting Cats, Panda, Dinosaurs, Kennedy Space Center, Mushrooms, Butterflies, Eagles, Tiger Woods, Chess Pieces (2 different sheets);

Sheets of six stamps of various denominations depicting Butterflies, Cartoon Network Cartoon Characters.

Additional issues may be added to this list.

Wildlife — A334

Designs: No. 1000, 180fr, Tiger, Rotary emblem, vert. No. 1001, 250fr, Tigers, Lions emblem. No. 1002, 375fr, Tiger, Scouting, scouting jamboree emblems. 500fr, Owl, vert.

No. 1003, vert. — Rotary emblem and: a, Lions. b, Leopard. c, Red-headed cranes. d, Owl. e, Buzzards. f, Gazelles (long horns). g, Elands (twisted horns). h, Antelope (short horns).

No. 1004 — Lions emblem and: a, Lion, looking left. b, Lion, lioness. c, Lion reclining. d, Leopards. e, Leopard on rock. f, Lion, looking right. g, Lion in grass. h, Lion cub.

No. 1005 — Scouting and scouting jamboree emblems and: a, Leopard, mouth open. b, Leopard overlooking plains. c, Leopard looking right. d, Cat. e, Pair of leopards. f, Leopard and trees. g, Leopard reclining. h, Leopard standing on rock.

1000fr, Tiger in water, horiz. 2500fr, Leopards.

1998 Litho. *Perf. 13½*

1000-1002	A334	Set of 3	
1003	A334	180fr Sheet of 9, #a-h, 1000	
1004	A334	250fr Sheet of 9, #a-h, 1001	
1005	A334	375fr Sheet of 9, #a-h, 1002	

Souvenir Sheets

1005I	A334	500fr multi	—	—
1006	A334	1000fr mutli		
1007	A334	2500fr multi		

New Year 1998, Year of the Tiger, Nos. 1000-1002, 1006. Nos. 1006-1007 each contain one 46x40mm stamp.

No. 1005I contains one 40x46mm stamp. Italia '98 Intl. Philatelic Exhibition (No. 1005I).

Jerry Garcia — A335

No. 1008: a, In brown shirt. b, In blue shirt, with flower. c, In yellow shirt. d, in green shirt. e, With fists clenched. f, In blue shirt. g, In black jacket. h, Holding glasses. i, In black shirt, with black guitar strap.

1998

1008	A335	350fr Sheet of 9, #a-i	10.00 10.00

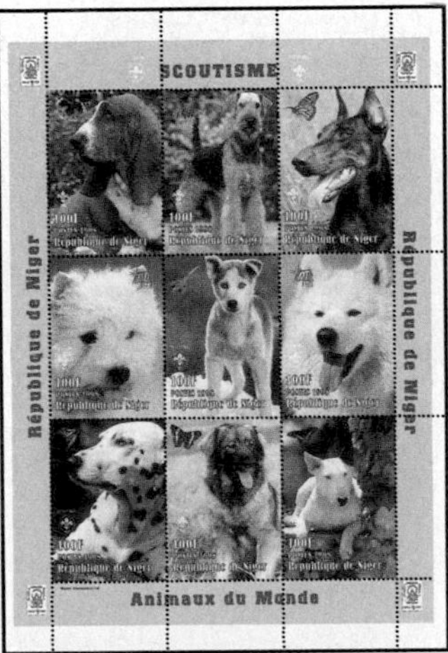

Dogs and Birds — A336

No. 1009, 100fr — Scouting emblem and: a, Beagle, butterfly. b, Airedale terrier, Italia 98 emblem. c, Doberman pinscher, butterfly. d, Small white dog, Italia emblem. e, Husky pup, Concorde. f, White Eskimo dog, Italia emblem. g, Dalmatian, butterfly. h, Retriever, butterfly. i, Pit bull, butterfly.

No. 1010, 300fr — a-i, Scouting jamboree emblem and various penguins.

No. 1011, 500fr — a-i, Various parrots.

1999 Sheets of 9, #a-i

1009-1011	A336	Set of 3	*15.00 15.00*

Intl. Year of the Ocean (No. 1010). Dated 1998.

Sailing — A337

No. 1012: a, Sailboat, lighthouse. b, Man, woman in sailboat. c, Sailor, large waves. d, Yachts racing.

1999

1012	A337	750fr Sheet of 4, #a-d

Dated 1998. Sheets of four 525fr and 875fr stamps were not authorized by Niger Post.

Trains — A338

Various trains. Sheets of 4, each stamp denominated: 225fr, 325fr, 375fr, 500fr.

1999 Sheets of 4, #a-d

1013-1017	A338	Set of 5

Dated 1998. PhilexFrance 99 (#1017). A sheet of four similar stamps with 650fr denominations, 750fr souvenir sheet, 2500fr souvenir sheet, and two 3000fr souvenir sheets were not authorized by Niger Post.

Astronauts — A339

No. 1018, 450fr: a, James Lovell. b, Alan Shepard. c, David Scott. d, John Young.

No. 1019, 500fr: a, Neil Armstrong. b, Michael Collins. c, Edwin Aldrin. d, Alan Bean.

No. 1020, 600fr: a, Walter Schirra. b, Robert Crippen. c, Thomas Stafford. d, Owen Garriott.

No. 1021, 750fr: a, John Glenn. b, Gordon Cooper. c, Scott Carpenter. d, Virgil Grissom.

2000fr, Collins, Armstrong and Aldrin.

1999 Sheets of 4, #a-d

1018-1021	A339	Set of 4	*40.00 40.00*

Souvenir Sheet

1022	A339	2000fr multi	*9.00 9.00*

No. 1022 contains one 56x51mm stamp.

Chess — A340

No. 1023, 350fr: a, Tigran Petrosian. b, Robert Fischer. c, Boris Spassky. d, Viktor Korchnoi. e, Garry Kasparov. f, Anatoly Karpov.

No. 1024, 400fr: a, Richard Reti. b, Alexander Alekhine. c, Max Euwe. d, Paul Keres. e, Mikhail Botvinnik. f, Mikhail Tal.

No. 1025, 500fr: a, Philidor. b, Adolf Anderssen. c, Joseph Henry Blackburne. d, Emanuel Lasker. e, Frank Marshall. f, José Raul Capablanca.

2000fr, head of Kasparov, Leo Tolstoy playing chess.

1999 Sheets of 6, #a-f

1023-1025	A340	Set of 3	*35.00 35.00*

Souvenir Sheet

1026	A340	2000fr multi	*10.00 10.00*

Nos. 1023-1025 each contain six 51x36mm stamps. Dated 1998.

Baseball Players — A341

No. 1027, 200fr, Various views of Lou Gehrig.

No. 1028, 250fr, Various views of Ty Cobb.

Nos. 1029, 1031, Gehrig, diff. Nos. 1030, 1032, Cobb, diff.

1999 Sheets of 9, #a-i

1027-1028	A341	Set of 2	*19.00 19.00*

Souvenir Sheets

1029-1030	A341	1500fr Set of 2	*15.00 15.00*
1031-1032	A341	2000fr Set of 2	*15.00 15.00*

Animals and Mushrooms — A342

No. 1033, 300fr: a, Snake. b, Tortoise. c, Scorpion. d, Lizard.

No. 1034, 400fr: a, Vulture. b, Gray cuckoo. c, Jackdaw. d, Turtle dove.

No. 1035, 600fr: a, Ham the chimpanzee. b, Laika the dog. c, Cat. d, Spider.

No. 1036, 750fr: a, Nymphalidae palla. b, Nymphalidae perle. c, Nymphalidae diademebleu. d, Nymphalidae pirate.

No. 1037, 1000fr: a, Clitocybe rouge brique. b, Lactaire a odeur de camphre. c, Strophaire vert-de-gris. d, Lepiote a ecailles aigues.

Illustration reduced.

1999, Nov. 23 Sheets of 4, #a-d

1033-1037	A342	Set of 5	*50.00 50.00*

Council of the Entente, 40th Anniv. A343

1999, May 29 Litho. *Perf. 13x13¼*

1039 A343 175fr multi 2.00 2.00

An additional stamp was issued in this set. The editors would like to examine any examples.

First French Stamps, 150th Anniv. A344

Litho. With Hologram Applied

1999, Oct. 7 *Perf. 13*

1040 A344 200fr France Type A1 1.50 1.50

Fire Fighting Equipment — A345

No. 1041 — Automobiles: a, Bugatti Type 37. b, Chevrolet Corvette. c, Lotus Elise. d, Ferrari 550 Maranello.

No. 1042: a, Canadair airplane. b, Hook and ladder truck. c, Water pumper of middle ages. d, 1914 pumper.

No. 1043 — Trains: a, Union Pacific, 1869. b, Prussian State Railway P8, 1905. c, Pennsylvania Railroad T1, 1942. d, German Railways Series 015, 1962.

No. 1044 — Airplanes: a, De Havilland Comet. b, Airbus A340. c, Boeing 747. d, Concorde.

No. 1045 — Trains: a, Diesel-electric locomotive. b, Bullet train, Japan. c, Thalys. d, X2000, China.

No. 1046 — Spacecraft: a, Atlas rocket, Mercury capsule. b, RD-107 Soyuz. c, Saturn V rocket, Apollo capsule. d, Space shuttle.

1999, Nov. 23 Litho. *Perf. 13½*

1041 A345 450fr Sheet of 4, #a-d *10.00 10.00*
1042 A345 500fr Sheet of 4, #a-d *11.50 11.50*
1043 A345 600fr Sheet of 4, #a-d *13.00 13.00*
1044 A345 650fr Sheet of 4, #a-d *14.50 14.50*
1045 A345 750fr Sheet of 4, #a-d *16.00 16.00*
1046 A345 800fr Sheet of 4, #a-d *12.50 12.50*

Intl. Anti-Desertification Day — A346

Designs: 150fr, Trenches. 200fr, Men in field. 225fr, Trees in desert.

2000, June 17 Litho. *Perf. 13½*

1047-1049 A346 Set of 3 1.75 1.75

Bird Type of 1997

2000, June 20 *Perf. 13¼*

1050 A309 150fr Psittacula krameri 1.00 1.00

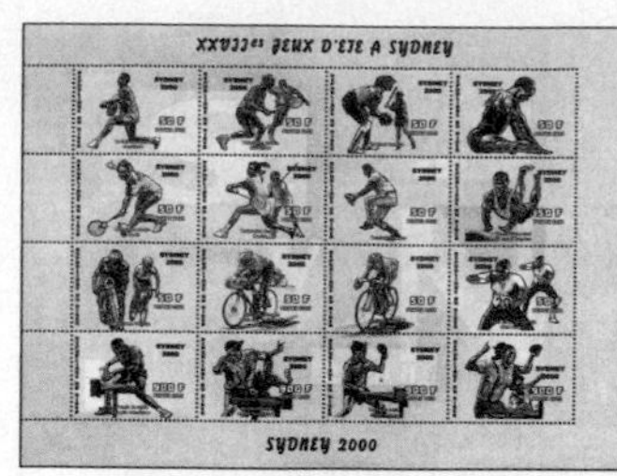

2000 Summer Olympics, Sydney — A347

No. 1051: a, 50fr, Men's singles, badminton. b, 50fr, Men's doubles, badminton. c, 50fr, Softball. d, 50fr, Men's floor exercises. e, 50fr, Women's singles, badminton. f, 50fr, Women's doubles, badminton. g, 50fr, Baseball. h, 50fr, Men's long horse vault. i, 50fr, Women's cycling. j, 50fr, Women's pursuit cycling. k, 50fr, Women's road race cycling. l, 50fr, Women's shot put. m, 900fr, Men's singles, table tennis. n, 900fr, Men's doubles, table tennis. o, 900fr, Women's singles, table tennis. p, 900fr, Women's doubles, table tennis.

No. 1052: a, 100fr, Women's freestyle swimming. b, 100fr, Women's butterfly. c, 100fr, Men's prone rifle. d, 100fr, Women's sport pistol. e, 100fr, Women's 3-meter diving. f, 100fr, Women's 10-meter diving. g, 100fr, Women's three-position rifle. h, 100fr, Women's double trap. i, 100fr, Women's beach volleyball. j, 100fr, Women's volleyball. k, 100fr, Women's handball. l, 100fr, Men's sailboarding. m, 700fr, Women's kayak singles. n, 700fr, Women's kayak pairs. o, 700fr, Women's kayak fours. p, 700fr, Women's eight-oared shell with coxswain.

2000, July 27 Litho.

Sheets of 16, #a-p

1051-1052 A347 Set of 2 *70.00 70.00*

Modern and Prehistoric Fauna — A348

No. 1053, 200fr — Butterflies: a, Epiphora bauhiniae. b, Cymothoe sangaris. c, Cyrestris camillus. d, Precis clelia. e, Precis octavia amestris. f, Nudaurelia zambesina.

No. 1054, 200fr — Insects: a, Stenocara eburnea. b, Chalcocoris anchorago. c, Scarabaeus aeratus. d, Pseudocreobotra wahlbergi. e, Schistocera gregaria. f, Anopheles gambiae.

No. 1055, 225fr — Prehistoric winged animals: a, Sordes pilosus. b, Quetzalcoatlus. c, Dimorphodon. d, Podopteryx. e, Archaeopteryx. f, Pteranodon.

No. 1056, 225fr — Birds: a, Bec-en-sabot. b, Euplecte ingnicolore. c, Spreo royal. d, Calao trompette. e, Pseudocanari parasite. f, Gonolek rouge et noir.

No. 1057, 400fr — Cats: a, Egyptian mau. b, Domestic. c, African wildcat. d, Chat dore. e, Chat a pieds noirs. f, Chat des sables.

No. 1058, 400fr — Dogs: a, Chien du pharaon. b, Saluki. c, Rhodesian ridgeback. d, Beagle. e, Spitz. f, Basenji.

No. 1059, 450fr — Modern and prehistoric African animals: a, Proconsul africanus. b, Chimpanzee. c, Metamynodon planifrons. d, Black rhinoceros. e, Hyrachius eximus. f, White rhinoceros.

No. 1060, 450fr — Modern and prehistoric African animals: a, Canis familiaris. b, Black and white basenji. c, Hipparion mediterraneum. d, Burchell zebra. e, Moeritherium. f, African elephant.

No. 1061, 475fr — Modern and prehistoric reptiles: a, Palaeobatrachus. b, African frog. c, Metoposaurus. d, Salamander. e, Tylosaurus. f, Varan du Nil.

No. 1062, 475fr — Modern and prehistoric African animals: a, Basilosaurus. b, Solalie du Cameroun. c, Mesosaurus. d, Cordylus giganteus. e, Sarcosuchus. f, Nile crocodile

2000, Oct. 27 *Perf. 13¼*

Sheets of 6, #a-f

1053-1062 A348 Set of 10 *120.00 120.00*

2002 World Cup Soccer Championships, Japan and Korea — A349

No. 1063, 400fr: a, Castro. b, Orsi. c, Piola. d, Ghiggia.

No. 1064, 400fr: a, Morlock. b, Pele. c, Amarildo. d, Hurst.

No. 1065, 400fr: a, Jairzinho. b, Müller. c, Kempes. d, Rossi.

No. 1066, 400fr: a, Burruchaga. b, Brehme. c, Dunga. d, Petit.

2001, Jan. 16 Sheets of 4, #a-d

1063-1066 A349 Set of 4 22.50 22.50

Dated 2000.

Universal Postal Union, 125th Anniv. (in 1999) — A350

No. 1067, 150fr — Ships: a, Transat, Citta di Catania. b, Great Eastern, Julius Caesar. c, Caledonia, Mercury. d, Braganza, Westland.

No. 1068, 225fr — Vehicles: a, Horse-drawn omnibus, postal bus. b, 1899 automobile, rural omnibus. c, 1904 van, postal automobile and bicycle. d, 1906 automobile, Swiss postal bus.

No. 1069, 450fr — Trains: a, 25NC Modder Kimberley locomotive, CDJR diesel. b, Pacific Karoo, Budd diesel. c, 141 Maghreb locomotive, EAR Diesel-electric locomotive. d, 230 Series 6 C.G.A., Postal TGV train.

No. 1070, 500fr — Airplanes: a, Late-28, Super Constellation. b, Douglas DC-4, Nord Atlas. c, Boeing 707, Concorde. d, Boeing 747, Airbus A3XX.

No. 1071, 550fr — Spacecraft: a, 1934 postal rocket, Asian telecommunications satellite. b, Space capsules. c, Apollo 15, Astra 1 H telecommunications satellite. d, Voyager, Space Station and shuttle.

No. 1072, 700fr — Trains: a, 230 locomotive, Senegal, 141 locomotive, Tanganyika. b, 141 locomotive, Niger. 242 locomotive, South Africa. c, 130+031 locomotive, Ivory Coast, Garrat 242+242. d, 040 locomotive, Cameroun, 14R locomotive.

2001, Jan. 16 *Perf. 13¼*

Sheets of 4, #a-d

1067-1072 A350 Set of 6 50.00 50.00

Dated 2000.

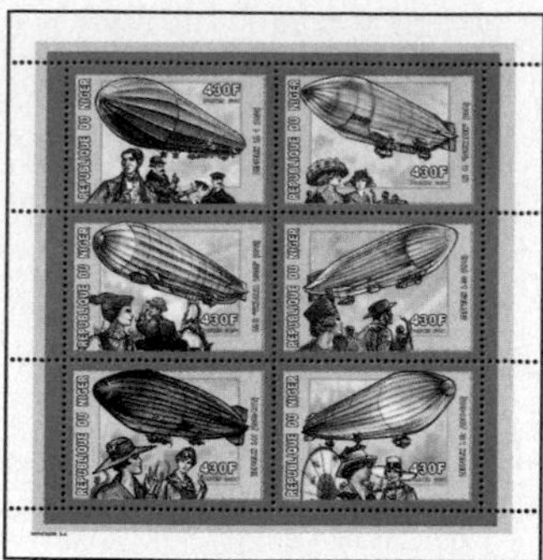

Zeppelins and Satellites — A351

No. 1073, 430fr — Zeppelins: a, LZ-1. b, LZ-10 Schwaben. c, LZ II Viktoria Luise. d, L-30. e, L-11. f, L-59.

No. 1074, 460fr — Zeppelins: a, LZ-120 Bodensee. b, L-72 Dixmude. c, LZ-127 Graf Zeppelin. d, LZ-129 Hindenburg. e, LZ-130. f, D-LZFN.

No. 1075, 750fr, vert. — Satellites: a, Meteosat. b, GOMS. c, GMS. d, Insat 1A. e, GOES. f, FY-2.

2001, June 20 Litho.

Sheets of 6, #a-f

1073-1075 A351 Set of 3 40.00 40.00

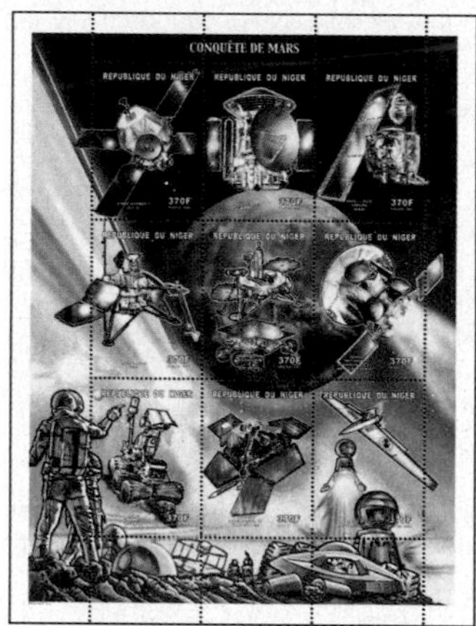

Space Exploration — A352

No. 1076, 370fr — Conquest of Mars: a, Mariner 9. b, Mars 3. c, Mars Climate Orbiter. d, Mars Lander. e, Mars Rover. f, Netlander. g, Robot on Mars. h, Beagle 2. i, Ames Research plane for Mars.

No. 1077, 390fr — Orbital and Lunar Exploration: a, Yuri Gagarin, Vostok capsule. b, John Glenn, Mercury capsule. c, Space shuttle. d, Alan Shepard, Apollo 14. e, Neil Armstrong, Apollo 11. f, Charles Conrad, Apollo 12. g, Edward White, Gemini 4. h, James Irwin, Apollo 15. i, Lunar base and shuttle.

No. 1078, 490fr — Planetary and Interstellar Exploration: a, Pioneer 10. b, Mariner 10. c, Venera 13. d, Pioneer 13, Venus 2. e, Probe for detecting "Big Bang." f, Interstellar spacecraft. g, Inhabited space station. h, Giotto probe, Astronaut on comet. i, Galileo probe.

2001, June 20 Litho.

Sheets of 9, #a-i

1076-1078 A352 Set of 3 50.00 50.00

African History — A353

No. 1079, 390fr: a, Gahna Empire, 10th cent. b, Kankou Moussa, Emperor of Mali, 1324. c, Sankore, University of Tombouctou,

15th cent. d, Sonni Ali Ber, Songhai Emperor. e, Bantu migrations, 15th and 16th cents. f, Slave trade, 1513.

No. 1080, 490fr: a, Ramses II, 1301-1235 B.C., Battle of Qadesh. b, Mummification. c, Religion. d, Instruction. e, Justice. f, Artisans.

No. 1081, 530fr: a, Djoser, Third Dynasty, 2650 B.C. b, Rahotep and wife, Fourth Dynasty, 2570 B.C. c, Cheops and Pyramid, Fourth Dynasty, 2600 B.C. d, Chephren, Fourth Dynasty, 2500 B.C. e, Akhenaton and Nefertiti, 18th Dynasty, 1372-1354 B.C. f, Tutankhamen, 18th Dynasty, 1354-1346 B.C.

2001, July 24 **Litho.**

Sheets of 6, #a-f

1079-1081 A353 Set of 3 35.00 35.00

Air Chiriet — A354

2001 ***Perf. 13x13¼***

1082 A354 150fr multi 1.00 1.00

Intl. Volunteers Year — A355

2001

1083 A355 150fr multi 1.00 1.00

Birds, Butterflies, Meteorites, and Mushrooms — A356

No. 1084, 530fr — Birds: a, Falco peregrinus. b, Falco biarmicus. c, Vultur gryphus.

No. 1085, 575fr — Butterflies: a, Junonia orithya. b, Salamis parhassus. c, Amauris echeria.

No. 1086, 750fr — Meteorites: a, P. Pallas, 1772. b, Iron meteorite. c, Bouvante rock.

No. 1087, 825fr — Mushrooms: a, Otidea onotica. b, Lentinus sajor-caju. c, Pleurotus luteoalbus.

2002, Apr. 24 ***Perf. 13¼***

Sheets of 3, #a-c

1084-1087 A356 Set of 4 27.50 27.50

Souvenir sheets of 1 of each of the individual stamps exist.

Cow's Head A357

2002, Sept. 17 **Litho.** ***Perf. 13¼***

1088 A357 50fr multi .50 .50

Toubou Spears — A358

2002, Sept. 17 **Litho.** ***Perf. 13x12½***

1089 A358 100fr multi .90 .90

Birds — A359

2002, Sept. 17 **Litho.** ***Perf. 13***

1090 A359 225fr multi 1.10 1.10

Hippopotamus in Captivity — A360

Boudouma Cow A361

Boudouma Calf — A362

2003, Dec. 3 **Litho.** ***Perf. 13x13¼***

1091 A360 100fr multi .60 .60

Perf. 13

1092 A361 150fr multi .80 .80

Perf. 13¼

1093 A362 225fr multi 1.10 1.10

Nos. 1091-1093 (3) *2.50 2.50*

Values for No. 1092 are for stamps with surrounding selvage.

Pottery — A363

Camel and Rider A364

2004 ***Perf. 13x13¼***

1094 A363 150fr multi 1.00 1.00

Perf. 13

1095 A364 1000fr multi *5.00 5.00*

Values for No. 1095 are for stamps with surrounding selvage.

In Universal Postal Union Circular 388, issued Nov. 28, 2005, Niger postal officials declared illegal additional items bearing the inscription "Republique du Niger." As this circular contains a somewhat unintelligible list of items which lacks specifics as to denominations found on the illegal items or the sizes of sheets, some of the items may be duplicative of items mentioned in the note on illegal stamps following No. 999. Also, because of the lack of clarity of the list, some catalogued items may now be items cited as "illegal" in Circular 388. The text of this circular can be seen on the UPU's WNS website, www.wnsstamps.ch.

Emblem of 2005 Francophone Games — A365

2005, May 12 **Litho.** ***Perf. 13x13¼***

1096 A365 150fr multi .65 .65

World Summit on the Information Society, Tunis — A366

2005, May 26 ***Perf. 13¼***

1097 A366 225fr multi 1.25 1.25

Mascot of 2005 Francophone Games — A367

2005, Aug. 22 ***Perf. 13***

1098 A367 225fr multi 1.00 1.00

Léopold Sédar Senghor (1906-2001), First President of Senegal — A368

2006, Apr. 6 **Litho.** ***Perf. 12¾***

1099 A368 175fr multi .85 .85

Pres. Tandja Mamadou — A369

2006, July 14

1100 A369 750fr multi 3.50 3.50

Boubou Hama (1906-82), Writer — A370

Background colors: 150fr, Green. 175fr, Orange brown. 325fr, Light blue.

2006, Sept. 23 **Litho.** ***Perf. 13x12¾***

1101-1103 A370 Set of 3 3.50 3.50

Messenger From Madaoua — A371

2006, Nov. 6 **Litho.** ***Perf. 13x12¾***

1104 A371 25fr multi —

Dated 2004.

24th UPU Congress, Geneva, Switzerland — A373

2007, Nov. 9 **Litho.** ***Perf. 13***

1106 A373 500fr multi 2.25 2.25

Values are for stamps with surrounding selvage. UPU Congress was moved to Geneva after political violence in Nairobi, Kenya.

Wildlife
A374

Designs: 200fr, Giraffes. 400fr, Addax. 600fr, Ostriches.

2007, Nov. 9 *Perf. 12¾*
1107-1109 A374 Set of 3 5.50 5.50

Grain Grinding
A375

Bororo Dance
A376

Chief's Guard
A377

2008, Aug. 8 *Perf. 12¾*
1110 A375 100fr multi .45 .45
1111 A376 350fr multi 1.60 1.60
1112 A377 1000fr multi 4.75 4.75
Nos. 1110-1112 (3) 6.80 6.80

Women At Well — A378

Hunters — A379

2009, Nov. 20 *Perf. 13*
1113 A378 300fr multi 1.40 1.40
1114 A379 450fr multi 2.10 2.10

Baobab Tree
A380

Téra-téra Blanket
A381

Women's Hairstyles
A382

2010, June 4 *Perf. 12¾*
1115 A380 500fr multi 1.90 1.90

Perf. 13

1116 A381 700fr multi 2.60 2.60

Perf. 13¼

1117 A382 1500fr multi 5.50 5.50
Nos. 1115-1117 (3) 10.00 10.00

Values for No. 1116 are for stamps with surrounding selvage.

Independence, 50th Anniv. — A383

2010, June 30 *Perf. 13*
1118 A383 1000fr multi 4.00 4.00

Hut of Sultan Usman Dan Fodio (1754-1817) — A384

Lété Island
A385

2011, May 30 *Perf. 12¾*
1119 A384 175fr multi .80 .80
1120 A385 320fr multi 1.40 1.40

Violet de Galmi Onions
A386

Djado Ruins
A387

Gen. Salou Djibo, Head of State of Niger — A388

2011, Oct. 19
1121 A386 500fr multi 2.10 2.10
1122 A387 735fr multi 3.25 3.25
1123 A388 1000fr multi 4.25 4.25
Nos. 1121-1123 (3) 9.60 9.60

Worldwide Fund for Nature (WWF) — A389

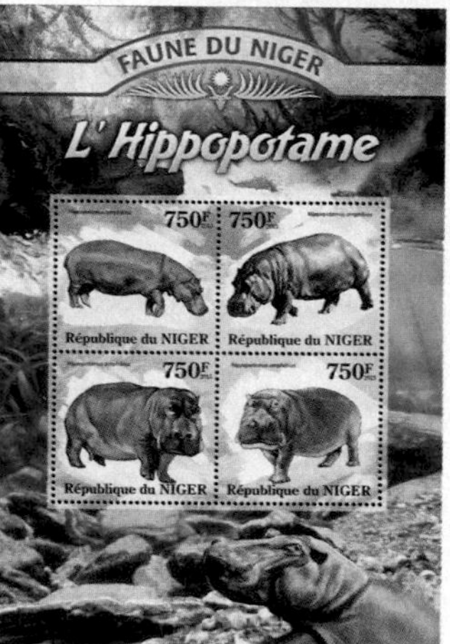
Wildlife — A390

No. 1124 — Giraffa camelopardalis peralta with: a, WWF emblem at LR, animal name at UR. b, WWF emblem at UL, animal name at bottom. c, WWF emblem at LR, animal name at UL. d, WWF emblem at UR, animal name at bottom.

No. 1125, 750fr — Hippopotamus amphibius: a, Denomination at UR, head down, facing right. b, Denomination at UL. c, Denomination at UR, head up at right. d, Denomination at UR, head up at left.

No. 1126, 750fr — Syncerus caffer: a, Denomination at UR, animal name at UL. b, Denomination at UL, animal name at top, animal facing right. c, Denomination at UL, animal name at top, animal facing left. d, Denomination at UR, animal name at LL.

No. 1127, 750fr — Foxes: a, Vulpes rueppellii, animal name at UL. b, Vulpes zerda, animal name at UL, end of name even with top of denomination. c, Vulpes zerda, animal name at left, end of name lower than denomination. d, Vulpes rueppellii, animal name at LR.

No. 1128, 750fr — Hyenas: a, Crocuta crocuta, animal name at LL. b, Hyaena hyaena, animal name at UR. c, Hyaena hyaena, animal name at UL. d, Crocuta crocuta, animal name at top.

No. 1129, 750fr — Antelopes: a, Oryx dammah. b, Ammotragus lervia. c, Nanger dama. d, Tragelaphus eurycerus.

No. 1130, 750fr — Primates: a, Galago senegalensis. b, Chlorocebus tantalus. c, Erythrocebus patas. d, Papio anubis.

No. 1131, 750fr — Bats: a, Eidolon helvum. b, Micropteropus pusillus. c, Lavia frons. d, Nycteris thebaica.

No. 1132, 750fr — Lions and leopards: a, Male Panthera leo. b, One Panthera pardus. c, Two Panthera pardus. d, Two female Panthera leo.

No. 1133, 750fr — Wildcats: a, Felis silvestris lybica. b, Felis margarita. c, Leptailurus serval. d, Felis margarita airensis.

No. 1134, 750fr — Lycaon pictus: a, Denomination at UR, animal name at UL. b, Denomination at UL, animal name at UR. c, Denomination at UL, animal name at top center. d, Denomination at UR, animal name at top center.

No. 1135, 750fr — Loxodonta africana: a, Denomination at right center, animal name at UL. b, Denomination at UR, animal name at UL. c, Denomination at UL, animal name at left. d, Denomination at UR, animal name at right center.

No. 1136, 750fr — Trichechus senegalensis: a, Animal name at UL, left flipper above "b" in "République." b, Animal name at UL, right flipper above "d" in "du." c, Animal name at UL, right fin above space between "République" and "du." d, Animal name at LL.

No. 1137, 750fr — Owls: a, Scotopelia peli. b, Glaucidium perlatum. c, Otus senegalensis. d, Ptilopsis leucotis.

No. 1138, 750fr — Doves: a, Colombar waalia. b, Oena capensis. c, Columba guinea. d, Columba arquatrix.

No. 1139, 750fr — Parrots: a, Poicephalus robustus. b, Psittacula krameri, animal name below denomination. c, Psittacula krameri, animal name to left of denomination. d, Psittacus erithacus, Psittacula krameri.

No. 1140, 750fr — Birds: a, Chalcomitra senegalensis. b, Hedydipna platurus. c, Cinnyris pulchella. d, Cinnyris cupreus.

No. 1141, 750fr — Water birds: a, Ardea cinerea in flight. b, Ardeola rufiventris. c, Ardea cinerea with fish. d, Ardea goliath.

No. 1142, 750fr — Birds of prey: a, Circaetus cinereus. b, Hieraaetus pennatus. c, Aquila rapax. d, Aquila pomarina.

No. 1143, 750fr — Butterflies: a, Pinacopteryx eriphia. b, Colotis antevippe with orange wing tips. c, Colotis antevippe with yellow and black coloratiion. d, Zizeeria knysna.

No. 1144, 750fr — Butterflies: a, Catopsilia florella. b, Coeliades forestan. c, Acraea neobule. d, Hypolimnas misippus.

No. 1145, 750fr — Fish: a, Hemichromis fasciatus. b, Fundulosoma thierryi. c, Aphyosemion bitaeniatum. d, Arnoldichthys spilopterus.

No. 1146, 750fr — Turtles: a, Psammobates geometricus. b, Pelomedusa subrufa. c, Pelusios niger. d, Astrochelys yniphora.

No. 1147, 750fr — Crocodiles: a, Crocodylus niloticus, animal name at UL. b, Crocodylus cataphractus, denomination at UL. c, Crocodylus cataphractus, denomination at UR. d, Crocodylus niloticus, animal name at LL.

No. 1148, 750fr — Snakes: a, Dasypeltis sahelensis. b, Dromophis praeornatus. c, Dromophis lineatus. d, Dasypeltis gansi.

No. 1149, 2500fr, Giraffa camelopardalis peralta, diff. No. 1150, 2500fr, Hippopotamus amphibius, diff. No. 1151, 2500fr, Syncerus caffer, diff. No. 1152, 2500fr, Vulpes rueppellii, diff. No. 1153, 2500fr, Crocuta crocuta, diff. No. 1154, 2500fr, Ammotragus lervia, diff. No. 1155, 2500fr, Papio anubis, diff. No. 1156, 2500fr, Micropterопus pusillus, diff. No. 1157, 2500fr, Panthera pardus, diff. No. 1158, 2500fr, Caracal caracal. No. 1159, 2500fr, Lycaon pictus, diff. No. 1160, 2500fr, Loxodonta africana, diff. No. 1161, 2500fr, Trichechus senegalensis, diff. No. 1162, 2500fr, Bubo ascalaphus. No. 1163, 2500fr, Colombar waalia, diff. No. 1164, 2500fr, Psittacus erithacus, diff. No. 1165, 2500fr, Cinnyris coccinigastrus. No. 1166, 2500fr, Ardea cinerea, diff. No. 1167, 2500fr, Falco naumanii. No. 1168, 2500fr, Spialia spio. No. 1169, 2500fr, Danaus chysippus. No. 1170, 2500fr, Oreochromis aureus. No. 1171, 2500fr, Pelusios sinuatus. No. 1172, 2500fr, Crocodylus niloticus, diff. No. 1173, 2500fr, Atracaspis microlepidota.

2013, Mar. 1 *Perf. 13¼x13*
1124 Strip of 4 12.00 12.00
a.-d. A389 750fr Any single 3.00 3.00
e. Souvenir sheet of 8, 2 each #1124a-1124d, + 2 labels 24.00 24.00

Sheets of 4, #a-d

Perf. 13¼

1125-1148 A390 Set of 24 285.00 285.00

Souvenir Sheets

1149-1173 A390 Set of 25 250.00 250.00

Pres. Issoufou Mahamadou
A391

2013, Mar. 8 *Perf. 13¼x13*
1174 A391 500fr multi 2.00 2.00

A392

No. 1175, 500fr — Mahatma Gandhi (1869-1948), Indian independence leader: a, On Russia #3639, denomination at LR. b, On cover of *Time* magazine, denomination at LL. c, Denomination at UR. d, With hands together, denomination at UL.

No. 1176, 500fr — Yang Liwei, Chinese astronaut, and Shenzhou 5 with: a, Denomination at LR. b, Denomination at LL. c, Denomination at UR. d, Denomination at UL.

No. 1177, 675fr — Pope Benedict XVI with: a, Denomination at LR. b, Denomination at LL. c, Denomination at UR. d, Denomination at UL.

No. 1178, 675fr — Garry Kasparov, chess champion, and chess pieces with: a, Denomination at LR. b, Denomination at LL. c, Denomination at UR. d, Denomination at UL.

No. 1179, 675fr — Cat breeds: a, Cymric. b, Maine coon cat. c, Persian. d, Oriental.

No. 1180, 675fr — Small dog breeds: a, Chihuahua. b, Spitz. c, Russian toy terrier. d, Yorkshire terrier.

No. 1181, 750fr — Paintings by Albrecht Dürer (1471-1528): a, Portrait of Barbara Dürer, denomination at LR. b, Nativity, denomination at LL. c, Young Hare, denomination at UR. d, Feast of the Rosary, denomination at UL.

No. 1182, 750fr — Paintings by Paul Signac (1863-1935): a, Calvados, denomination at LR. b, Road to Gennevilliers, denomination at LL. c, The Gas Tanks at Clichy, denomination at UR. d, The Railroad at Bois Colombes, denomination at UL.

No. 1183, 750fr — Paintings by Joan Miró (1893-1983): a, Carneval d'Arlequin, denomination at LR. b, Catalan Landscape (The Hunter), denomination at LL. c, Circus, denomination at UR. d, The Poetess, denomination at UL.

No. 1184, 750fr — Bobby Fischer (1943-2008), chess champion: a, On Iceland #1203, denomination at LR. b, On cover of *Life* magazine, denomination at LL. c, With chess pieces, denomination at UR. d, With chess pieces, denomination at UL.

No. 1185, 750fr — Audrey Hepburn (1929-93), actress: a, Wearing red dress. b, With Peter O'Toole. c, With Cary Grant. d, With Gregory Peck.

No. 1186, 750fr — Ancient Egyptian monuments: a, Sculpted head of Amenhotep III. Temple of Horus. b, Bust of Nefertiti. c, Sphinx and Pyramids. d, Pyramids.

No. 1187, 750fr — Lighthouses: a, Biloxi Lighthouse, U.S. b, Rotesand Lighthouse, Germany. c, Execution Rocks Lighthouse, U.S. d, Coney Island Lighthouse, U.S.

No. 1188, 750fr — Cessation of Concorde flights, 10th anniv.: a, Concorde, Buckingham Palace, Queen Elizabeth II, Prince Philip. b, Concorde, Heathrow Airport, Brian Trubshaw, pilot. c, Concorde, Tower Bridge, British flag. d, Concorde, Arc de Triomphe, French flag.

No. 1189, 750fr — Space Shuttle Columbia disaster, 10th anniv.: a, Explosion. b, Columbia, map of U.S.. c, Memorial to Columbia astronauts. d, Columbia on launch pad.

No. 1190, 750fr — Tour de France bicycle race, cent.: a, Lucien Petit-Breton. b, Philippe Thys. c, Greg LeMond. d, Cadel Evans.

No. 1191, 750fr — 2013 African Cup of Nations soccer tournament: a, Two players, denomination at LR. b, One player, denomination at LL. c, One player, denomination at UR. d, Two players, denomination at UL.

No. 1192, 750fr — 2014 Winter Olympics, Sochi: a, Luge. b, Figure skating. c, Ice hockey. d, Speed skating.

No. 1193, 750fr — Dinosaurs: a, Jobaria tiguidensis. b, Afrovenator abakensis. c, Spinophorosaurus nigerensis. d, Suchomimus tenerensis.

No. 1194, 825fr — Paintings by Vincent van Gogh (1853-90): a, Portrait of Postman Joseph Roulin, denomination at LR. b, Self-portrait, Agostina Segatori Sitting in the Cafe du Tambourin, denomination at LL. c, Self-portrait, Olive Trees, denomination at UR. d, The Drinkers, denomination at UL.

No. 1195, 825fr — Hamadou Djibo Issaka, Nigerien rower at 2012 Summer Olympics: a, Denomination at LR. b, Denomination at LL. c, Denomination at UR. d, Denomination at UL.

No. 1196, 825fr — Scouting: a, Scouts building bridge, denomination at LR. b, Scout at campfire, denomination at LL. c, Map, Scout with pocket watch. d, Scouts erecting tents, denomination at UL.

No. 1197, 825fr — Rotary International Flood Aid to Niger: a, Denomination at LR. b, Denomination at LL. c, Denomination at UR. d, Denomination at UL.

No. 1198, 825fr — Scenes from the Djado Plateau: a, Denomination at LR. b, Denomination at LL. c, Denomination at UR. d, Denomination at UL.

No. 1199, 825fr — Minerals of Niger: a, Diamond, denomination at LR. b, Gold, denomination at LL. c, Tin, denomination at UR. d, Silver, denomination at UL.

No. 1200, 2000fr, Gandhi, diff. No. 1201, 2000fr, Yang Liwei and Shenzhou 5, diff. No. 1202, 2000fr, Pope Benedict XVI, diff. No. 1203, 2000fr, Kasparov, diff. No. 1204, 2000fr, Cymric cat, diff. No. 1205, 2000fr, Papillon. No. 1206, 2500fr, Adoration of the Magi, by Dürer. No. 1207, 2500fr, Evening Calm, Concarneau, by Signac. No. 1208, 2500fr, Women and Birds at Sunrise, by Miró. No. 1209, 2500fr, Fischer, diff. No. 1210, 2500fr, Hepburn and husband, Mel Ferrer. No. 1211, 2500fr, Bust of Nefertiti, diff. No. 1212, 2500fr, Mohegan Lighthouse, U.S. No. 1213, 2500fr, Concorde and London. No. 1214, 2500fr, Crew of Space Shuttle Columbia flight STS-107. No. 1215, 2500fr, Bradley Wiggins, cyclist. No. 1216, 2500fr, Two soccer players, diff. No. 1217, 2500fr, Freestyle skiing. No. 1218, 2500fr, Kryptops palaios. No. 1219, 3000fr, Pietà, by van Gogh. No. 1220, 3000fr, Issaka, diff. No. 1221, 3000fr, Scouts and tent. No. 1222, 3000fr, Map of Niger, Rotary International emblem, child and Gaston Kaba, Niamey Rotary president. No. 1223, 3000fr, Djado Plateau rock painting. No. 1224, 3000fr, Salt, map of Niger.

2013, Apr. 15 *Perf. 13¼*

Sheets of 4, #a-d

1175-1199 A392 Set of 25 290.00 290.00

Souvenir Sheets

1200-1224 A392 Set of 25 250.00 250.00

A393

No. 1225, 750fr — Yuri Gagarin (1934-68), first man in space: a, Blue panel, Gagarin without cap at left. b, Red panel, Gagarin wearing space helmet at left. c, Red panel, Gagarin wearing military cap at left. d, Blue panel, Gagarin wearing military cap.

No. 1226, 750fr — Space tourism: a, International Space Station, XCOR Lynx Mark II. b, WhiteKnightTwo, SpaceShipOne. c, SpaceShipTwo. d, International Space Station, Astrium Suborbital Space Plane.

No. 1227, 750fr — Steam trains: a, South African Class 26. b, LNER Peppercorn Class A1 60163 Tornado. c, LB&SCR Class B4. d, Reading Blue Mountain & Northern Railway 425.

No. 1228, 750fr — High-speed trains: a, Acela Express, New York City skyline. b, Chinese CRH380A UEM, Yongdinghe Bridge, Beijing. c, Maglev train, Shanghai. d, Alfa train, Lisbon, Portugal skyline.

No. 1229, 750fr — Ships and lighthouses: a, Barque Europa, 2007. b, Mahatao Lighthouse, Philippines. c, Amerigo Vespucci, 1976. d, Isle of May Lighthouse, Scotland.

No. 1230, 750fr — French airplanes: a, Concorde. b, Dassault Rafale. c, Breguet 14. d, Dassault Mirage F1.

No. 1231, 750fr — Fire trucks: a, SACFS Isuzu 800. b, Atego Mercedes-Benz LF 10/6 Ziegler. c, Valdosta, Georgia Airport E-7 fire truck. d, Kronenburg MAC 11.

No. 1232, 750fr — Motorcycles and actors: a, 1953 Triumph Thunderbird, Marlon Brando. b, 1955 Triumph TR5, James Dean, Marilyn Monroe. c, 1934 Harley-Davidson RL, Clark Gable. d, 1940 Indian Four Cylinder, Steve McQueen.

No. 1233, 750fr — Elvis Presley (1935-77), with panel color of: a, Blue. b, Purple. c, Olive green. d, Red.

No. 1234, 750fr — Marilyn Monroe (1926-62), with panel color of: a, Prussian blue. b, Red. c, Violet. d, Brown orange.

No. 1235, 750fr — 60th anniv. of coronation of Queen Elizabeth II, with panel color of: a, Blue. b, Red. c, Green. d, Brown orange.

No. 1236, 750fr — Pope Francis, with panel color of: a, Blue. b, Brown orange. c, Green. d, Red.

No. 1237, 750fr — Dr. Albert Schweitzer (1875-1965), 1952 Nobel Peace laureate, with panel color of: a, Dark brown. b, Prussian blue. c, Dark blue. d, Brown orange.

No. 1238, 750fr — Louis Pasteur (1822-95), microbiologist, with panel colors of: a, Brown. b, Prussian blue. c, Dark blue. d, Brown orange.

No. 1239, 750fr — Mao Zedong (1893-1976), Chinese Communist leader: a, Holding book at right, gray panel. b, Clapping at right, brown orange panel. c, Holding book at right, brown orange panel. d, With raised arm at right, gray panel.

No. 1240, 750fr — Table tennis players: a, Zhang Jike. b, Ding Ning. c, Ma Long. d, Xu Xin.

No. 1241, 750fr — Paul Cézanne (1839-1906), painter, and: a, Compotier, Pitcher and Fruit, 1894. b, Mont Saint-Victoire and Chateau Noir, 1904-06. c, Lac d'Annecy, 1896. d, Apples and Oranges, 1899.

No. 1242, 750fr — Pierre-Auguste Renoir (1841-1919), painter, and: a, Luncheon of the Boating Party, 1881. b, La Grenouillère, 1869. c, Chestnut Tree in Bloom, 1881. d, Madame Georges Charpontier and Her Children, 1878.

No. 1243, 750fr — Volcanoes and minerals: a, Chaíten Volcano, Chile, Vanadinite. b, Popocatépetl, Mexico, Calcite. c, Tungurahua, Ecuador, Hemimorphite. d, Redoubt Volcano, Alaska, Calcite and hematite.

No. 1244, 750fr — Dolphins and shells: a, Lagenorhynchus obscurus. b, Turbinella pyrum. c, Cymbiola vespertilio. d, Tursiops truncatus.

No. 1245, 750fr — Owls and mushrooms: a, Tyto alba, unnamed mushrooms. b, Gomphidus glutinosus, unnamed owl. c, Bubo virginianus, unnamed mushrooms. d, Sarcodon imbricatus, unnamed owl.

No. 1246, 750fr — Orchids and butterflies: a, Encyclia vitellina, unnamed butterflies. b, Papilio maackii, unnamed orchid. c, Vanda sanderiana, unnamed butterflies. d, Bhutanitis lidderdalii, unnamed orchid.

No. 1247, 750fr — Year of the Horse: a, Horse, brown orange panel. b, Two horses, blue panel. c, Two horses, purple panel. d, Horse, black panel.

No. 1248, 2500fr, Gagarin, diff. No. 1249, 2500fr, Richard Branson, SpaceShip Two. No. 1250, 2500fr, Southern Railway Class Ps-4. No. 1251, 2500fr, Shinkansen Series 800, Japan. No. 1252, 2500fr, Fastnet Lighthouse, Ireland, and ship. No. 1253, 2500fr, Blériot XI. No. 1254, 2500fr, Oshkosh Striker T-3000. No. 1255, 2500fr, 1964 Triumph Tiger 100, Bob Dylan. No. 1256, 2500fr, Presley, diff. No. 1257, 2500fr, Monroe, diff. No. 1258, 2500fr, Queen Elizabeth II, diff. No. 1259, 2500fr, Pope Francis, diff. No. 1260, 2500fr, Schweitzer, diff. No. 1261, 2500fr, Pasteur, diff. No. 1262, 2500fr, Mao Zedong, diff. No. 1263, 2500fr, Timo Boll, table tennis player. No. 1264, 2500fr, Cézanne, Mont Sainte-Victoire, 1885-87. No. 1265, 2500fr, Renoir, Ball at the Moulin de la Galette, 1876. No. 1266, 2500fr, Mount Etna, Italy, Pyrite. No. 1267, 2500fr, Stenella coeruleoalba. No. 1268, 2500fr, Strix aluco, unnamed mushrooms. No. 1269, 2500fr, Atrophaneura hector, unnamed orchid. No. 1270, 2500fr, Horse, diff.

2013, July 1 **Litho.** *Perf. 13¼*

Sheets of 4, #a-d

1225-1247 A393 Set of 23 275.00 275.00

Souvenir Sheets

1248-1270 A393 Set of 23 230.00 230.00

2013 China International Collection Expo (Nos. 1239, 1262).

Photography by Sergey Tkachenko and Russian Philatelic Items — A394

No. 1271 — Photograph and: a, Post card depicting Graf Zeppelin. b, Russia #C24. c, Russia #C21. d, Russia #C20.

2500fr, Photograph and Russia #6016.

2013, July 1 **Litho.** *Perf. 12¾x13¼*

1271 A394 750fr Sheet of 4, #a-d 12.00 12.00

Souvenir Sheet

1272 A394 2500fr multi 10.00 10.00

Souvenir Sheet

Mao Zedong (1893-1976), Chinese Communist Leader — A395

2013, July 1 **Litho.** *Perf. 12¾x13¼*

On Wood Veneer

Self-Adhesive

1273 A395 6500fr multi 26.00 26.00

Souvenir Sheet

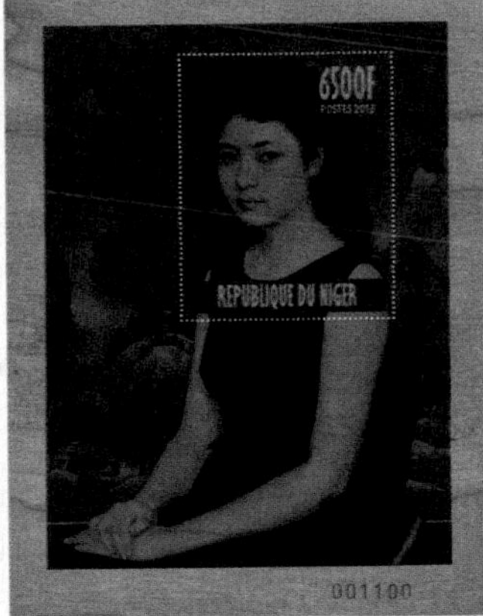

Peng Liyuan, Singer and Wife of Xi Jinping, President of People's Republic of China — A396

2013, July 1 **Litho.** *Perf. 12¾x13¼*

On Wood Veneer

Self-Adhesive

1274 A396 6500fr multi 26.00 26.00

Cooperation Between Niger and Algeria — A397

Perf. 12¾x13¼

2013, Sept. 10 **Litho.**

1275 A397 1060fr multi 4.50 4.50

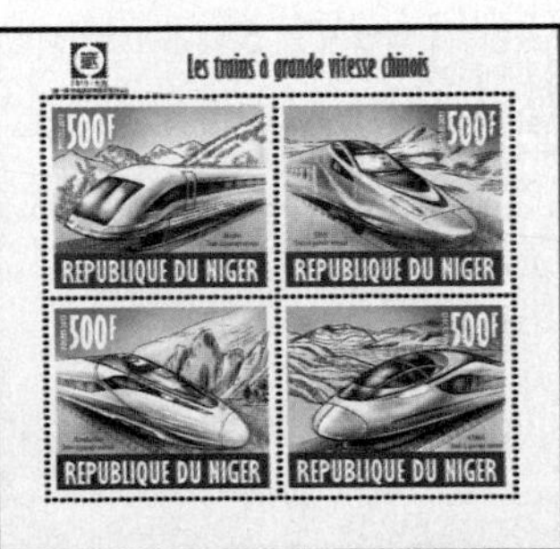

A398

No. 1276, 500fr — Chinese high-speed trains: a, Maglev. b, CRH5. c, Bombardier. d, CRH6A.

No. 1277, 500fr — Shenzhou 10: a, Astronaut Wang Yaping, Shenzhou 10. b, Astronaut Nie Haisheng, Shenzhou 10. c, Astronaut Zhang Xiaoguang, rocket on launch pad. d, Shenzhou 10 and emblem.

No. 1278, 675fr — Nanger Dama: a, Head of gazelle facing left, gazelle in background. b, Gazelle leaping. c, Gazelle resting. d, Adult and juvenile gazelles.

No. 1279, 675fr — African mammals: a, Equus burchelli. b, Phacochoerus africanus. c, Hippopotamus amphibius. d, Alcelaphus buselaphus caama.

No. 1280, 675fr — Wildcats: a, Caracal caracal. b, Leptailurus serval. c, Acinonyx jubatus. d, Panthera pardus.

No. 1281, 750fr — Whales: a, Megaptera novaeangliae. b, Balaenoptera borealis. c, Balaenoptera musculus. d, Eschrichtius robustus.

No. 1282, 750fr — Apis mellifera and flowers: a, Chaenomeles japonica. b, Tanacetum parthenium. c, Paeonia cambessedesii. d, Odontoglossum rossii.

No. 1283, 750fr — Birds: a, Halcyon malimbica. b, Caprimulgus eximius. c, Scopus umbretta. d, Musophaga violacea.

No. 1284, 750fr — Reptiles: a, Python regius. b, Crocodylus niloticus. c, Varanus griseus. d, Trionyx triunguis.

No. 1285, 750fr — Campaign against malaria: a, Red Cross worker feeling head of sick child. b, Children under mosquito netting, mosquito at right. c, Children under mosquito netting, mosquito at left. d, Red Cross worker wearing gloves treating sick child.

No. 1286, 750fr — Prehistoric man: a, Homo georgicus. b, Homo neanderthalensis. c, Homo tyrolensis. d, Homo erectus.

No. 1287, 750fr — Military aircraft: a, Argentine Air Force Douglas A-4 Skyhawk. b, Iranian Air Force F14 Tomcat. c, U.S. Air Force Northrop Grumman RQ-4 Global Hawk. d, U.S. Air Force Lockheed Martin F35B Stealth fighter.

No. 1288, 750fr — Special transportation: a, BMW R1200RT police motorcycle. b, Agusta A-109 K2 helicopter ambulance. c, Pierce Arrow 105-foot X-ladder fire truck. d, Chevrolet C4500 ambulance.

No. 1289, 750fr — Famous cricket players: a, Inzamam-ul-Haq. b, Malcolm Marshall. c, Sanath Jayasuriya. d, Sachin Tendulkar.

No. 1290, 750fr — Pierre de Coubertin (1863-1937), founder of International Olympic Committee, and: a, Runner. b, High jumper. c, Wrestlers. d, Gymnast.

No. 1291, 750fr — Giuseppe Verdi (1813-1901), composer, and performers from opera: a, Rigoletto. b, Hermani. c, Macbeth. d, La Pucelle d'Orléans (Giovanna d'Arco).

No. 1292, 750fr — Richard Wagner (1813-83), composer, and performers from opera: a, Lohengrin. b, Tristan and Isolde. c, The Mastersingers of Nuremberg (Les Maîtres Chanteurs de Nuremberg). d, The Flying Dutchman (Le Vaisseau Fantôme).

No. 1293, 750fr — Nelson Mandela (1918-2013), President of South Africa, and: a, Princess Diana. b, Dove. c, Michael Jackson. d, Bill Gates.

No. 1294, 750fr — Pope John Paul II (1920-2005): a, Waving. b, Seated. c, Seated holding crucifix. d, Standing and praying.

No. 1295, 750fr — Grace Kelly (1929-82), actress and Princess of Monaco: a, Wearing red dress in background. b, In scene from *To Catch a Thief*, 1955. c, In scene from *Dial M for Murder*, 1954. d, Wearing blue dress in background.

No. 1296, 750fr — Paintings by Francisco Goya (1746-1828): a, Witches' Sabbath, 1798. b, The Grape Harvest, 1787. c, The Parasol, 1777. d, Gaspar Melchor de Jovellanos, 1798.

No. 1297, 750fr — Paintings by American Impressionists: a, The Hammock, by Joseph DeCamp. b, Five O'Clock, by Guy Rose. c, Madonna of the Apples, by Joseph Kleitsch. d, Marjorie and Little Edmund, by Edmund C. Tarbell.

No. 1298, 750fr — Paintings by Pablo Picasso (1881-1973): a, Woman at Fountain, 1901. b, Still Life with a Bull's Skull, 1939. c, Science and Charity, 1897. d, The Red Armchair, 1931 (incorrect inscription).

No. 1299, 750fr — Birth of Prince George of Cambridge: a, Prince Charles, Princess Diana and Prince William. b, Duke and Duchess of Cambridge with Prince George outside hospital. c, Duke and Duchess of Cambridge with Prince George in nursery. d, Princess Diana, Princes William and Harry.

No. 1300, 875fr — Rotary International emblem and: a, Paul P. Harris (1868-1947), founder of Rotary International, Acraea neobule. b, Polio virus. c, Rotarians giving baby polio vaccine, Hypolimnas misippus. d, Hands touching, Colotis danae.

No. 1301, 2000fr, CRH3 train. No. 1302, 2000fr, Nanger dama, diff. No. 1303, 2000fr, Ceratotherium simum. No. 1304, 2000fr, Panthera leo. No. 1305, 2500fr, Wang Yaping, Shenzhou 10, diff. No. 1306, 2500fr, Orcinus orca. No. 1307, 2500fr, Apis mellifera, Raphanus sativus. No. 1308, 2500fr, Halcyon chelicuti. No. 1309, 2500fr, Geochelone sulcata. No. 1310, 2500fr, Red Cross emblem, medical worker giving child an injection. No. 1311, 2500fr, Homo neanderthalensis, cave drawing. No. 1312, 2500fr, Russian Air Force Sukhoi PAK FA. No. 1313, 2500fr, Ford F150 fire truck. No. 1314, 2500fr, Cricket player Andrew Flintoff. No. 1315, 2500fr, Coubertin, meeting of International Olympic Committee. No. 1316, 2500fr, Verdi. No. 1317, 2500fr, Wagner. No. 1318, 2500fr, Mandela and Queen Elizabeth II. No. 1319, 2500fr, Popes John Paul II and Benedict XVI. No. 1320, 2500fr, Kelly. No. 1321, 2500fr, Two Boys with a Giant Mastiff, by Goya. No. 1322, 2500fr, Spring on the Riviera, by Rose. No. 1323, 2500fr, Bullfight, by Picasso. No. 1324, 2500fr, Duke and Duchess of Cambridge, Prince George, vert. No. 1325, 3000fr, Harris, Rotary International emblem, Charaxes jasius.

2013, Sept. 30 Litho. *Perf. 13¼*

Sheets of 4, #a-d

1276-1300	A398	Set of 25	300.00	300.00

Souvenir Sheets

1301-1325	A398	Set of 25	255.00	255.00

A399

A400

A401

Chinese Chang'e 3 Mission to the Moon — A402

Perf. 12¾x13¼

2013, Dec. 20 Litho.

1326	Horiz. strip of 4	13.00	13.00
a.	A399 750fr multi	3.25	3.25
b.	A400 750fr multi	3.25	3.25
c.	A401 750fr multi	3.25	3.25
d.	A402 750fr multi	3.25	3.25

Polo — A403

No. 1327 — Polo players on horses: a, Adolfo Cambiaso. b, Mariano Aguerre. c, Bartolomé Castagnola. d, Facundo Pieres.

2500fr, Polo player on horse.

2013, Dec. 20 Litho. *Perf.*

1327	A403	750fr Sheet of 4, #a-d	13.00	13.00

Souvenir Sheet

1328	A403	2500fr multi	10.50	10.50

A404

No. 1329, 750fr — Pan troglodytes: a, Sitting on rock. b, Sitting next to tree, looking forward. c, Adult and juvenile. d, Sitting on branch looking left.

No. 1330, 750fr — Dugong dugon with Latin name: a, At LL, animal facing left. b, At UR, animal facing forward. c, At UR, with animal's head touching sea floor. d, At LL, with animal looking forward.

No. 1331, 750fr — Dolphins: a, Tursiops truncatus, Latin name at LR. b, Two Tursiops truncatus, Latin name at LL. c, Two Tursiops truncatus, Latin name at UR. d, Two Delphinus delphi.

No. 1332, 750fr — Tropical fish: a, Chelmon rostratus. b, Pygoplites diacanthus. c, Chaetodon auriga. d, Amphiprion ocellaris.

No. 1333, 750fr — Turtles: a, Geochelone sulcata. b, Chelonoidis denticulata. c, Geochelone nigra. d, Trachemys scripta elegans.

No. 1334, 750fr — Dinosaurs: a, Diceratops. b, Dicraeosaurus. c, Diplodocus. d, Tyrannosaurus.

No. 1335, 750fr — Endangered animals: a, Eretmochelys imbricata. b, Ailuropoda melanoleuca. c, Loxodonta cyclotis. d, Panthera pardus orientalis.

No. 1336, 750fr — Climate change: a, Arctocephalus gazella on shore. b, Ursus maritimus in water. c, Giraffa camelopardalis in water. d, Odobenus rosmarus on ice.

No. 1337, 750fr — Orchids: a, Paphiopedilum callosum. b, Cattleya auera. c, Cattleya labiata. d, Miltonia spectabilis.

No. 1338, 750fr — Mushrooms: a, Macrolepiota procera. b, Sarcodon imbricatus. c, Cantharellus cibarius. d, Leccinum aurantiacum.

No. 1339, 750fr — Minerals: a, Jasper. b, Amethyst. c, Malachite. d, Smoky quartz.

No. 1340, 750fr — Lighthouses: a, Rubjerg Knude Lighthouse, Denmark. b, Green Cape Lighthouse, Australia (incorrect inscription on stamp). c, Fingal Head Lighthouse, Australia (incorrect inscription on stamp). d, Hov Fyr Lighthouse, Denmark.

No. 1341, 750fr — Windmills in: a, Campo de Criptana, Spain. b, Kuzelov, Czech Republic. c, Kinderdijk, Netherlands. d, Volendam, Netherlands.

No. 1342, 750fr — Japanese high-speed trains: a, E3 Series Shinkansen. b, 700 Series Shinkansen. c, E2 Series Shinkansen. d, E3 R1 Akita Shinkansen.

No. 1343, 750fr — Fire trucks: a, Ural. b, 1938 Quad. c, Magirus-Deutz LF 16-TS. d, Steam-driven wagon.

No. 1344, 750fr — Ferrari automobiles: a, F40. b, 458. c, FF. d, "Enzo Ferrari".

No. 1345, 750fr — Chess: a, White piece tilting wooden king on white square. b, White and black queens. c, Timer. d, Player holding white piece tilting wooden king on black square.

No. 1346, 750fr — Campaign against AIDS: a, Women wearing head covering, child. b, Mother and infant meeting with doctor. c, Woman. d, Doctor examining infant held in woman's arms.

No. 1347, 750fr — Niger culture: a, Aerial view of desert village. b, Buildings in Agadez. c, Mural. d, Mountains in desert.

No. 1348, 750fr — Composers: a, Joseph Haydn (1732-1809). b, Johann Sebastian Bach (1685-1750). c, Robert Schumann (1810-56). d, Wolfgang Amadeus Mozart (1756-91).

No. 1349, 750fr — Paintings by Eugène Delacroix (1798-1863): a, Combat of Horsemen in the Countryside, 1824. b, The Dying Turk, 1825-30. c, Horse Frightened by a Storm, 1824. d, A Mortally Wounded Brigand Quenches His Thirst, 1825.

No. 1350, 750fr — Pope Benedix XVI with top inscription: a, In white on one line. b, In black on two lines. c, In white on two lines. d, In black on three lines.

No. 1351, 750fr — Nelson Mandela (1918-2013), President of South Africa: a, With hand clenched at LL. b, Waving. c, Saluting. d, With flag of South Africa.

No. 1352, 2500fr, Adult and juvenile Pan troglodytes, diff. No. 1353, 2500fr, Dugong dugon, diff. No. 1354, 2500fr, Tursiops truncatus, diff. No. 1355, 2500fr, Heniochus acuminatus. No. 1356, 2500fr, Chelonia mydas. No. 1357, 2500fr, Spinosaurus. No. 1358, 2500fr, Diceros bicornis. No. 1359, 2500fr, Pygoscelis papua. No. 1360, 2500fr, Oncidium altissimum. No. 1361, 2500fr, Boletus edulis. No. 1362, 2500fr, Chalcedony. No. 1363, 2500fr, Michigan City East Lighthouse, Michigan City, Indiana. No. 1364, 2500fr, Windmill at Lithuanian Ethnographic Museum. No. 1365, 2500fr, E3-2000 Series Shinkansen. No. 1366, 2500fr, Mercedes-Benz Zetros fire truck. No. 1367, 2500fr, Enzo Ferrari (1898-1988), automobile manufacturer. No. 1368, 2500fr, Chess board and timer. No. 1369, 2500fr, Two women, infant, red cross. No. 1370, 2500fr, Sahara Desert rock paintings. No. 1371, 2500fr, Ludwig van Beethoven (1770-1827), composer. No. 1372, 2500fr, The Combat of the Giaour and Hassan, by Delacroix. No. 1373, 2500fr, Pope Benedict XVI, diff. No. 1374, 2500fr, Mandela with fist raised. No. 1375, 2500fr, Mandela and flag of South Africa, diff.

2013, Dec. 20 Litho. *Perf. 13¼*

Sheets of 4, #a-d

1329-1351	A404	Set of 23	290.00	290.00

Souvenir Sheets

1352-1375	A404	Set of 24	250.00	250.00

SEMI-POSTAL STAMPS

Curie Issue

Common Design Type

1938 Unwmk. Engr. *Perf. 13*

B1	CD80	1.75fr + 50c brt ultra	15.00	15.00

French Revolution Issue

Common Design Type

1939 Photo. *Perf. 13*

Name and Value Typo. in Black

B2	CD83	45c + 25c grn	12.00	12.00
B3	CD83	70c + 30c brn	12.00	12.00
B4	CD83	90c + 35c red org	12.00	12.00
B5	CD83	1.25fr + 1fr rose pink	12.00	12.00
B6	CD83	2.25fr + 2fr blue	12.00	12.00
		Nos. B2-B6 (5)	60.00	60.00

Stamps of 1926-38, Surcharged in Black

1941 *Perf. 14x13½, 13½x14*

B7	A3	50c + 1fr scar & grn, *grnsh*	3.25	3.25
B8	A3	80c + 2fr cl & ol grn	7.25	7.25
B9	A4	1.50fr + 2fr dp bl & pale bl	7.25	7.25
B10	A4	2fr + 3fr red org & ol brn	7.25	7.25
		Nos. B7-B10 (4)	25.00	25.00

Common Design Type and

Colonial Cavalry — SP1

Soldiers and Tank SP2

1941 Unwmk. Photo. *Perf. 13½*

B11 SP2	1fr + 1fr red	1.10	
B12 CD86	1.50fr + 3fr claret	1.10	
B13 SP1	2.50fr + 1fr blue	1.10	
	Nos. B11-B13 (3)	3.30	
	Set, never hinged	5.25	

Nos. B11-B13 were issued by the Vichy government in France, but were not placed on sale in Niger.

Nos. 89-90 Surcharged in Black or Red

1944 Engr. *Perf. 12x12½*

B13A	50c + 1.50fr on 2.50fr deep blue (R)	.35
B13B	+ 2.50fr on 1fr green	.35
	Set, never hinged	1.40

Colonial Development Fund.

Nos. B13A-B13B were issued by the Vichy government in France, but were not placed on sale in Niger.

Catalogue values for unused stamps in this section, from this point to the end of the section, are for Never Hinged items.

Republic of the Niger Anti-Malaria Issue

Common Design Type

Perf. 12½x12

1962, Apr. 7 Engr. Unwmk.

B14 CD108 25fr + 5fr brn .60 .60

Freedom from Hunger Issue

Common Design Type

1963, Mar. 21 *Perf. 13*

B15 CD112 25fr + 5fr gray ol, red lil & brn .60 .60

Dome of the Rock — SP3

1978, Dec. 11 Litho. *Perf. 12½*

B16 SP3 40fr + 5fr multi .45 .30

Surtax was for Palestinian fighters and their families.

AIR POST STAMPS

Common Design Type

1940 Unwmk. Engr. *Perf. 12½x12*

C1	CD85 1.90fr ultra	.35	.35
C2	CD85 2.90fr dk red	.35	.35
C3	CD85 4.50fr dk gray grn	.70	.70
C4	CD85 4.90fr yel bis	.70	.70
C5	CD85 6.90fr dp org	1.40	1.40
	Nos. C1-C5 (5)	3.50	3.50

Common Design Types

1942

C6	CD88 50c car & bl	.30
C7	CD88 1fr brn & blk	.35
C8	CD88 2fr multi	.70
C9	CD88 3fr multi	.70
C10	CD88 5fr vio & brn red	.70

Frame Engraved, Center Typographed

C11	CD89 10fr multi	1.00
C12	CD89 20fr multi	1.40
C13	CD89 50fr multi	1.75
	Nos. C6-C13 (8)	6.90
	Set, never hinged	10.00

There is doubt whether Nos. C6-C13 were officially placed in use. They were issued by the Vichy government.

Catalogue values for unused stamps in this section, from this point to the end of the section, are for Never Hinged items.

Republic of the Niger

Wild Animals, W National Park — AP1

1960, Apr. 11 Engr. *Perf. 13*

C14 AP1 500fr multi 17.50 8.00

For overprint see No. C112.

Nubian Carmine Bee-eater — AP2

1961, Dec. 18 Unwmk. *Perf. 13*

C15 AP2 200fr multi 8.00 3.00

UN Headquarters and Emblem, Niger Flag and Map — AP3

1961, Dec. 16

C20	AP3 25fr multi	.60	.35
C21	AP3 100fr multi	2.00	1.25

Niger's admission to the United Nations.
For overprints see Nos. C28-C29.

Air Afrique Issue

Common Design Type

1962, Feb. 17 Unwmk. *Perf. 13*

C22 CD107 100fr multi 1.75 .90

Mosque at Agadez and UPU Emblem — AP4

Designs: 85fr, Gaya Bridge. 100fr, Presidential Palace, Niamey.

1963, June 12 Photo. *Perf. 12½*

C23	AP4 50fr multi	.90	.50
C24	AP4 85fr multi	1.60	.70
C25	AP4 100fr multi	1.60	.80
	Nos. C23-C25 (3)	4.10	2.00

2nd anniv. of Niger's admission to the UPU.

Type of Regular Issue, 1963

Design: 100fr, Building boats (kadei), horiz.

1963, Aug. 30 *Perf. 12½x12*

Size: 47x27mm

C26 A12 100fr multi 2.75 1.50

African Postal Union Issue

Common Design Type

1963, Sept. 8 *Perf. 12½*

C27 CD114 85fr multi 1.25 .60

Nos. C20-C21 Overprinted "Centenaire de la Croix-Rouge" and Cross in Red

1963, Sept. 30 Engr. *Perf. 13*

C28	AP3 25fr multi	.75	.50
C29	AP3 100fr multi	1.75	.90

Centenary of International Red Cross.

White and Black before Rising Sun — AP5

1963, Oct. 25 Photo. *Perf. 12x13*

C30 AP5 50fr multi 3.00 2.25

See note after Mauritania No. C28.

Peanut Cultivation — AP6

Designs: 45fr, Camels transporting peanuts to market. 85fr, Men closing bags. 100fr, Loading bags on truck.

1963, Nov. 5 Engr. *Perf. 13*

C31	AP6 20fr grn, bl & red brn	.60	.25
C32	AP6 45fr red brn, bl & grn	1.00	.40
C33	AP6 85fr multi	2.00	.70
C34	AP6 100fr red brn, ol bis & bl	2.25	1.00
a.	Souv. sheet of 4, #C31-C34	6.00	6.00
	Nos. C31-C34 (4)	5.85	2.35

To publicize Niger's peanut industry.

1963 Air Afrique Issue

Common Design Type

1963, Nov. 19 Photo. *Perf. 13x12*

C35 CD115 50fr multi .90 .50

Telstar and Capricornus and Sagittarius Constellations — AP7

100fr, Relay satellite, Leo & Virgo constellations.

1964, Feb. 11 Engr. *Perf. 13*

C36	AP7 25fr olive gray & vio	.50	.30
C37	AP7 100fr grn & rose claret	1.40	.85

Ramses II Holding Crook and Flail, Abu Simbel — AP8

1964, Mar. 9

C38	AP8 25fr bis brn & dl bl grn	.80	.50
C39	AP8 30fr dk bl & org brn	1.25	.65
C40	AP8 50fr dp claret & dk bl	2.25	1.25
	Nos. C38-C40 (3)	4.30	2.40

Issued to publicize the UNESCO world campaign to save historic monuments in Nubia.

Tiros I Weather Satellite over Globe and WMO Emblem — AP9

1964, Mar. 23 Unwmk. *Perf. 13*

C41 AP9 50fr emer, dk bl & choc 1.25 .65

4th World Meteorological Day, Mar. 23.

Rocket, Stars and "Stamp" — AP10

1964, June 5 Engr.

C42 AP10 50fr dk bl & magenta 1.10 .65

"PHILATEC," International Philatelic and Postal Techniques Exhibition, Paris, June 5-21, 1964.

Europafrica Issue, 1963

Common Design Type

50fr, European & African shaking hands, emblems of industry & agriculture.

1964, July 20 Photo. *Perf. 12x13*

C43 CD116 50fr multi .85 .50

John F. Kennedy — AP11

Perf. 12½

1964, Sept. 25 Unwmk. Photo.

C44	AP11 100fr multi	1.90	1.25
a.	Souvenir sheet of 4	8.50	8.50

President John F. Kennedy (1917-1963).

Discobolus and Discus Thrower — AP12

60fr, Water polo, horiz. 85fr, Relay race, horiz. 250fr, Torch bearer & Pierre de Coubertin.

1964, Oct. 10 Engr. *Perf. 13*

C45	AP12	60fr red brn & sl grn	1.00	.50
C46	AP12	85fr ultra & red brn	1.50	.60
C47	AP12	100fr brt grn, dk red & sl	1.50	.70
C48	AP12	250fr yel brn, brt grn & sl	3.50	1.75
a.		Min. sheet of 4, #C45-C48	11.00	11.00
		Nos. C45-C48 (4)	7.50	3.55

18th Olympic Games, Tokyo, Oct. 10-25.

Pope John XXIII (1881-1963) AP13

1965, June 3 Photo. *Perf. 12½x13*

C49 AP13 100fr multi 1.50 .75

Hand Crushing Crab — AP14

1965, July 15 Engr. *Perf. 13*

C50 AP14 100fr yel grn, blk & brn 1.40 .85

Issued to publicize the fight against cancer.

Sir Winston Churchill — AP15

Perf. 12½x13

1965, Sept. 3 Photo. Unwmk.

C51 AP15 100fr multi 1.40 .85

Symbols of Agriculture, Industry, Education AP16

1965, Oct. 24 Engr. *Perf. 13*

C52 AP16 50fr henna brn, blk & ol .90 .50

International Cooperation Year, 1965.

Flags and Niamey Fair — AP17

1965, Dec. 10 Photo. *Perf. 13x12½*

C53 AP17 100fr multi 1.40 .80

International Fair at Niamey.

Dr. Schweitzer, Crippled Hands and Symbols of Medicine, Religion and Music — AP18

1966, Jan. 4 Photo. *Perf. 12½x13*

C54 AP18 50fr multi 1.00 .50

Weather Survey Frigate and WMO Emblem — AP19

1966, Mar. 23 Engr. *Perf. 13*

C55 AP19 50fr brt rose lil, dl grn & dk vio bl 1.50 .60

6th World Meteorological Day, Mar. 23.

Edward H. White Floating in Space and Gemini IV — AP20

#C57, Alexei A. Leonov & Voskhod II.

1966, Mar. 30

C56	AP20	50fr dk red brn, blk & brt grn	1.00	.50
C57	AP20	50fr pur, slate & org	1.00	.50

Issued to honor astronauts Edward H. White and Alexei A. Leonov.

A-1 Satellite and Earth — AP21

45fr, Diamant rocket and launching pad. 90fr, FR-1 satellite. 100fr, D-1 satellite.

1966, May 12 Photo. *Perf. 13*

C58	AP21	45fr multi, vert.	.75	.45
C59	AP21	60fr multi	.90	.50
C60	AP21	90fr multi	1.10	.70
C61	AP21	100fr multi	1.75	.90
		Nos. C58-C61 (4)	4.50	2.55

French achievements in space.

Maps of Europe and Africa and Symbols of Industry — AP22

1966, July 20 Photo. *Perf. 12x13*

C62 AP22 50fr multi .80 .40

Third anniversary of economic agreement between the European Economic Community and the African and Malgache Union.

Air Afrique Issue, 1966

Common Design Type

1966, Aug. 31 Photo. *Perf. 13*

C63 CD123 30fr gray, yel grn & blk .65 .35

Gemini 6 and 7 — AP23

1966, Oct. 14 Engr. *Perf. 13*

C64	AP23	50fr Voskhod 1, vert.	.80	.40
C65	AP23	100fr shown	1.60	.75

Russian & American achievements in space.

Torii and Atom Destroying Crab — AP24

1966, Dec. 2 Photo. *Perf. 13*

C66 AP24 100fr dp claret, brn, vio & bl grn 1.50 .70

9th Intl. Anticancer Cong., Tokyo, Oct. 23-29.

New Mosque, Niamey — AP25

1967, Jan. 11 Engr. *Perf. 13*

C67 AP25 100fr grn & brt bl 1.75 .80

Albrecht Dürer, Self-portrait AP26

Self-portraits: 100fr, Jacques Louis David. 250fr, Ferdinand Delacroix.

1967, Jan. 27 Photo. *Perf. 12½*

C68	AP26	50fr multi	1.10	.70
C69	AP26	100fr multi	2.00	1.00
C70	AP26	250fr multi	4.50	2.25
		Nos. C68-C70 (3)	7.60	3.95

See No. C98.

Maritime Weather Station — AP27

1967, Mar. 23 Engr. *Perf. 13*

C71 AP27 50fr brt bl, dk car rose & blk 1.50 .70

7th World Meteorological Day.

View of EXPO '67, Montreal — AP28

1967, Apr. 28 Engr. *Perf. 13*

C72 AP28 100fr lil, brt bl & blk 1.25 .70

Issued for EXPO '67, International Exhibition, Montreal, Apr. 28-Oct. 27, 1967.

Audio-visual Center, Stylized Eye and People — AP29

1967, June 22 Engr. *Perf. 13*

C73 AP29 100fr brt bl, pur & grn 1.25 .60

National Audio-Visual Center.

Apollo 11, 1969 — AP119

Space Conquest: Views of Columbia space shuttle, 1981.

1981, Mar. 30 Litho. *Perf. 12½*

C305 AP119 100fr multi .80 .30
C306 AP119 150fr multi 1.25 .35
C307 AP119 200fr multi 1.40 .45
C308 AP119 300fr multi 2.25 .75
Nos. C305-C308 (4) 5.70 1.85

Souvenir Sheet

C309 AP119 500fr multi 4.00 1.25

For overprint see No. C356.

Girl in a Room, by Picasso — AP120

Picasso Birth Centenary: 60fr, Olga in an Armchair. 90fr, Family of Acrobats. 120fr, Three Musicians. 200fr, Paul on a Donkey. All vert.

1981, June 25 Litho. *Perf. 12½*

C310 AP120 60fr multi .50 .25
C311 AP120 90fr multi .80 .30
C312 AP120 120fr multi 1.00 .40
C313 AP120 200fr multi 1.75 .60
C314 AP120 400fr multi 3.50 1.10
Nos. C310-C314 (5) 7.55 2.65

Christmas 1982 AP121

Rubens Paintings — 200fr, Adoration of the Kings. 300fr, Mystical Marriage of St. Catherine. 400fr, Virgin and Child.

1982, Dec. 24 Litho. *Perf. 14*

C315 AP121 200fr multi 1.40 .30
C316 AP121 300fr multi 2.10 .65
C317 AP121 400fr multi 2.75 .80
Nos. C315-C317 (3) 6.25 1.75

Manned Flight Bicentenary AP122

65fr, Montgolfiere balloon, 1783, vert. 85fr, Hydrogen balloon, 1783, vert. 200fr, Zeppelin. 250fr, Farman plane. 300fr, Concorde. 500fr, Apollo 11, vert.

1983, Jan. 24

C318 AP122 65fr multi .50 .25
C319 AP122 85fr multi .75 .25
C320 AP122 200fr multi 1.50 .40
C321 AP122 250fr multi 2.00 .55
C322 AP122 300fr multi 2.25 .65
C323 AP122 500fr multi 4.00 1.00
Nos. C318-C323 (6) 11.00 3.10

Pre-Olympic Year — AP123

1983, May 25 Litho. *Perf. 13*

C324 AP123 85fr Javelin .60 .25
C325 AP123 200fr Shot put 1.60 .55
C326 AP123 250fr Hammer, vert. 1.90 .70
C327 AP123 300fr Discus 2.40 .80
Nos. C324-C327 (4) 6.50 2.30

Souvenir Sheet

C328 AP123 500fr Shot put, diff. 4.00 1.25

For overprint see No. C357.

Christmas 1983 — AP124

Botticelli Paintings — 120fr, Virgin and Child with Angels, vert. 350fr, Adoration of the Kings. 500fr, Virgin of the Pomegranate, vert.

Wmk. 385 Cartor

1983 Litho. *Perf. 13*

C329 AP124 120fr multi .90 .35
C330 AP124 350fr multi 2.75 .75
C331 AP124 500fr multi 3.75 1.10
Nos. C329-C331 (3) 7.40 2.20

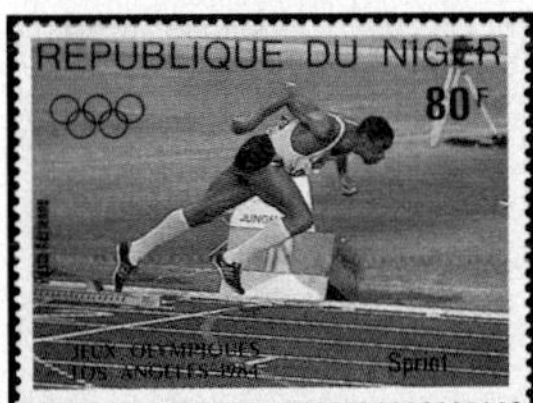

1984 Summer Olympics — AP125

Unwmk.

1984, Feb. 22 Litho. *Perf. 13*

C332 AP125 80fr Sprint .55 .25
C333 AP125 120fr Pole vault .80 .25
C334 AP125 140fr High jump 1.25 .40
C335 AP125 200fr Triple jump, vert. 1.75 .40
C336 AP125 350fr Long jump, vert. 2.75 .90
Nos. C332-C336 (5) 7.10 2.20

Souvenir Sheet

C337 AP125 500fr 110-meter hurdles 3.50 1.25

1984, Oct. 8 Litho.

Designs: Winners of various track events. Nos. C338-C341 vert.

C338 AP125 80fr Carl Lewis .55 .35
C339 AP125 120fr J. Cruz .90 .45
C340 AP125 140fr A. Cova 1.00 .50
C341 AP125 300fr Al Joyner 2.10 1.10
Nos. C338-C341 (4) 4.55 2.40

Souvenir Sheet

C342 AP125 500fr D. Mogenburg, high jump 3.50 2.00

World Soccer Cup — AP126

1984, Nov. 19 Litho. *Perf. 13*

C345 AP126 150fr multi 1.00 .60
C346 AP126 250fr multi 1.75 1.05
C347 AP126 450fr multi 3.25 1.60
C348 AP126 500fr multi 3.50 1.90
Nos. C345-C348 (4) 9.50 5.15

Christmas 1984 AP127

Paintings: 100fr, The Visitation, by Ghirlandajo. 200fr, Virgin and Child, by the Master of Santa Verdiana. 400fr, Virgin and Child, by J. Koning.

1984, Dec. 24 Litho. *Perf. 13*

C349 AP127 100fr multi .80 .45
C350 AP127 200fr multi 1.60 .95
C351 AP127 400fr multi 3.25 1.40
Nos. C349-C351 (3) 5.65 2.80

Audubon Birth Bicentennial — AP128

110fr, Himantopus mexicanus. 140fr, Phoenicopterus ruber, vert. 200fr, Fratercula arctica. 350fr, Sterna paradisaea, vert.

1985, Feb. 6 Litho. *Perf. 13*

C352 AP128 110fr multi .90 .50
C353 AP128 140fr multi 1.40 .55
C354 AP128 200fr multi 1.75 .85
C355 AP128 350fr multi 3.25 1.40
Nos. C352-C355 (4) 7.30 3.30

Nos. C309, C328 Ovptd. in Silver with Exhibition Emblems

1985, Mar. 11 Litho. *Perf. 12½, 13*

C356 AP119 500fr ARGENTINA '85 BUENOS AIRES 4.75 3.00
C357 AP123 500fr OLYMPHILEX '85 LAUSANNE 4.75 3.00

Religious Paintings by Bartolome Murillo (1617-1682) AP129

110fr, Virgin of the Rosary. 250fr, The Immaculate Conception. 390fr, Virgin of Seville.

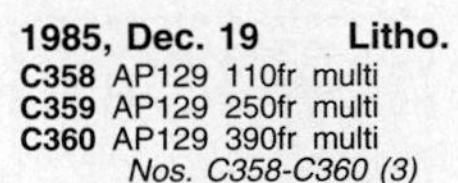

1985, Dec. 19 Litho. *Perf. 13*

C358 AP129 110fr multi .80 .45
C359 AP129 250fr multi 1.90 .85
C360 AP129 390fr multi 3.25 1.40
Nos. C358-C360 (3) 5.95 2.70

Christmas 1985.

Halley's Comet — AP130

110fr, Over Paris, 1910. 130fr, Over New York. 200fr, Giotto space probe. 300fr, Vega probe. 390fr, Planet A probe.

1985, Dec. 26

C361 AP130 110fr multi .80 .40
C362 AP130 130fr multi 1.00 .55
C363 AP130 200fr multi 1.75 .80
C364 AP130 300fr multi 2.50 1.20
C365 AP130 390fr multi 3.25 1.60
Nos. C361-C365 (5) 9.30 4.55

Martin Luther King, Jr. (1929-1968), Civil Rights Activist — AP131

1986, Apr. 28 Litho. *Perf. 13½*

C366 AP131 500fr multi 4.00 2.00

1986 World Cup Soccer Championships, Mexico — AP132

Various soccer plays, stamps and labels.

1986, May 21 *Perf. 13*

C367 AP132 130fr No. 228 .90 .40
C368 AP132 210fr No. 229 1.40 .70
C369 AP132 390fr No. 230 2.75 1.25
C370 AP132 400fr Aztec drawing 2.75 1.25
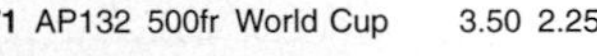
Nos. C367-C370 (4) 7.80 3.60

Souvenir Sheet

C371 AP132 500fr World Cup 3.50 2.25

Statue of Liberty, Cent. AP133

1986, June 19

C372 AP133 300fr Bartholdi, statue 2.40 1.25

1988 Summer Olympics, Seoul AP134

Olympic Rings, Pierre de Coubertin and: 85fr, One-man kayak, vert. 165fr, Crew racing. 200fr, Two-man kayak. 600fr, One-man kayak, diff., vert. 750fr, One-man kayak, diff., vert.

1988, June 22 **Litho.** ***Perf. 13***

C373	AP134	85fr multi	.65	.30
C374	AP134	165fr multi	1.25	.60
C375	AP134	200fr multi	1.60	.80
C376	AP134	600fr multi	4.50	2.25
		Nos. C373-C376 (4)	8.00	3.95

Souvenir Sheet

C377	AP134	750fr multi	6.00	4.50

First Moon Landing, 20th Anniv. AP135

1989, July 27 **Litho.** ***Perf. 13***

C378	AP135	200fr Launch	1.60	.75
C379	AP135	300fr Crew	2.40	1.25
C380	AP135	350fr Lunar experiments	2.75	1.40
C381	AP135	400fr Raising flag	3.25	1.50
		Nos. C378-C381 (4)	10.00	4.90

1990 World Cup Soccer Championships, Italy — AP136

Athletes & views or symbols of Italian cities.

1990, Mar. 6 **Litho.** ***Perf. 13***

C382	AP136	130fr Florence	.90	.40
C383	AP136	210fr Verona	1.50	.75
C384	AP136	500fr Bari	3.50	1.75
C385	AP136	600fr Rome	4.25	2.10
		Nos. C382-C385 (4)	10.15	5.00

1992 Winter Olympics, Albertville — AP138

110fr, Speed skating. 300fr, Ice hockey. 500fr, Downhill skiing. 600fr, Luge.

1991, Mar. 28 **Litho.** ***Perf. 13***

C392	AP138	110fr multicolored	.80	.35
C393	AP138	300fr multicolored	2.40	1.25
C394	AP138	500fr multicolored	4.00	2.00
C395	AP138	600fr multicolored	4.75	2.40
		Nos. C392-C395 (4)	11.95	6.00

AIR POST SEMI-POSTAL STAMPS

Dahomey types SPAP1-SPAP3 inscribed Niger

Perf. 13½x12½, 13 (#CB3)

Photo, Engr. (#CB3)

1942, June 22

CB1	SPAP1	1.50fr + 3.50fr green	.35	*5.00*
CB2	SPAP2	2fr + 6fr brown	.35	*5.00*
CB3	SPAP3	3fr + 9fr car red	.35	*5.00*
		Nos. CB1-CB3 (3)	1.05	15.00
		Set, never hinged	2.00	

Native children's welfare fund.

Colonial Education Fund

Common Design Type

Perf. 12½x13½

1942, June 22 **Engr.**

CB4	CD86a	1.20fr + 1.80fr blue & red	.35	*5.00*
		Never hinged	.70	

POSTAGE DUE STAMPS

1914 Upper Senegal and Niger Postage Due Stamps Ovptd.

1921 **Unwmk.** ***Perf. 14x13½***

J1	D1	5c green	.70	*.95*
J2	D1	10c rose	.70	*.95*
J3	D1	15c gray	.70	*1.05*
J4	D1	20c brown	.70	*1.05*
J5	D1	30c blue	.70	*1.20*
J6	D1	50c black	.70	*1.20*
J7	D1	60c orange	1.40	*2.00*
J8	D1	1fr violet	1.40	*2.00*
		Nos. J1-J8 (8)	7.00	*10.40*

Caravansary Near Timbuktu D2

1927 **Typo.**

J9	D2	2c dk bl & red	.35	*.35*
J10	D2	4c ver & blk	.35	*.35*
J11	D2	5c org & vio	.35	*.35*
J12	D2	10c red brn & blk vio	.35	*.35*
J13	D2	15c grn & org	.35	.35
J14	D2	20c cer & ol brn	.35	.70
J15	D2	25c blk & ol brn	.35	*.70*
J16	D2	30c dl vio & blk	1.40	*1.40*
J17	D2	50c dp red, *grnsh*	.70	*1.10*
J18	D2	60c gray vio & org, *bluish*	.70	.70
J19	D2	1fr ind & ultra, *bluish*	1.00	*1.20*
J20	D2	2fr rose red & vio	1.10	*1.40*
J21	D2	3fr org brn & ultra	1.75	2.00
		Nos. J9-J21 (13)	9.10	*10.95*

Catalogue values for unused stamps in this section, from this point to the end of the section, are for Never Hinged items.

Republic of the Niger

Cross of Agadez D3

Native Metalcraft: 3fr, 5fr, 10fr, Cross of Iferouane. 15fr, 20fr, 50fr, Cross of Tahoua.

Perf. 12½

1962, July 1 **Unwmk.** **Photo.**

J22	D3	50c emerald	.25	.25
J23	D3	1fr violet	.25	.25
J24	D3	2fr slate green	.25	.25
J25	D3	3fr lilac rose	.25	.25
J26	D3	5fr green	.25	.25
J27	D3	10fr orange	.25	.25
J28	D3	15fr deep blue	.25	.25
J29	D3	20fr carmine	.25	.25
J30	D3	50fr chocolate	.35	.35
		Nos. J22-J30 (9)	2.35	2.35

1993 **Litho.** ***Perf. 12½***

Designs as Before

Size: 50x50mm

J31	D3	5fr green	.25	.25
J32	D3	10fr orange	.25	.25
J33	D3	15fr blue	.25	.25
J34	D3	20fr red	.25	.25
J35	D3	50fr chocolate	.40	.40
		Nos. J31-J35 (5)	1.40	1.40

Imprint on Nos. J31-J35 is in black.

OFFICIAL STAMPS

Catalogue values for unused stamps in this section are for Never Hinged items.

Djerma Girl Carrying Jug — O1

Denomination in Black

Perf. 14x13½

1962-71 **Typo.** **Unwmk.**

O1	O1	1fr dark purple	.25	.25
O2	O1	2fr yel grn	.25	.25
O3	O1	5fr brt blue	.25	.25
O4	O1	10fr deep red	.25	.25
O5	O1	20fr vio blue	.25	.25
O6	O1	25fr orange	.25	.25
O7	O1	30fr light blue ('65)	.30	.25
O8	O1	35fr pale grn ('71)	.40	.30
O9	O1	40fr brown ('71)	.40	.30
O10	O1	50fr black	.40	.30
O11	O1	60fr rose red	.60	.35
O12	O1	85fr blue green	.90	.35
O13	O1	100fr red lilac	.95	.35
O14	O1	200fr dark blue	2.00	.75
		Nos. O1-O14 (14)	7.45	4.45

Djerma Girl Carrying Jug — O2

Denomination Same Color As Design

1988, Nov. **Typo.** ***Perf. 13***

O15	O2	5fr brt blue	.25	.25
O16	O2	10fr henna brn	.25	.25
O17	O2	20fr vio blue	.25	.25
O18	O2	50fr greenish blk	.50	.25

1989-96(?)

O19	O2	15fr bright yellow	.25	.25
O20	O2	45fr orange	.30	.25
O21	O2	85fr blue green		
O22	O2	100fr red lilac		

Issued: 15, 45fr, 3/89; 85, 100fr, 1996(?).
See No. 698.

NIGER COAST PROTECTORATE

'nī-jər 'kōst prə-'tek-t̩ə-ˌrət

(Oil Rivers Protectorate)

LOCATION — West coast of Africa on Gulf of Guinea
GOVT. — British Protectorate

This territory was originally known as the Oil Rivers Protectorate, and its affairs were conducted by the British Royal Niger Company. The Company surrendered its charter to the Crown in 1899. In 1900 all of the territories formerly controlled by the Royal Niger Company were incorporated into the two protectorates of Northern and Southern Nigeria, the latter absorbing the area formerly known as Niger Coast Protectorate. In 1914 Northern and Southern Nigeria joined to form the Crown Colony of Nigeria. (See Nigeria, Northern Nigeria, Southern Nigeria and Lagos.)

12 Pence = 1 Shilling

Stamps of Great Britain, 1881-87, Overprinted in Black

1892 **Wmk. 30** ***Perf. 14***

1	A54	½p vermilion	22.50	13.00
2	A40	1p lilac	13.00	11.00
a.		"OIL RIVERS" at top	*10,000.*	
b.		Half used as ½p on cover		*2,750.*
3	A56	2p green & car	40.00	9.50
a.		Half used as 1p on cover		*2,500.*
4	A57	2½p violet, *bl*	10.00	2.75
5	A61	5p lilac & blue	20.00	7.25
6	A65	1sh green	77.50	*100.00*
		Nos. 1-6 (6)	183.00	143.50

For surcharges see Nos. 7-36, 50.

Dangerous forgeries exist of all surcharges.

No. 2 Surcharged in Red or Violet

1893

7	A40	½p on half of 1p (R)	175.	160.
c.		Unsevered pair	550.	500.
d.		As "c," surcharge inverted and dividing line reversed		*27,500.*
e.		"½" omitted		
f.		Straight top to "1" in "½"	390.	*400.*
g.		Double surcharge in pair with normal		*2,100.*
7A	A40	½p on half of 1p (V)	*7,750.*	*5,500.*
b.		Surcharge double	*27,500.*	
c.		Unsevered pair	*20,000.*	*17,500.*

Nos. 3-6 Handstamp Srchd. in Violet, Red, Carmine, Bluish Black, Deep Blue, Green or Black

1893 **Wmk. 30** ***Perf. 14***

8	A56	½p on 2p (V)	*525.*	325.
a.		Surcharge inverted	*19,000.*	
b.		Surcharge diagonal, inverted	*18,500.*	
9	A57	½p on 2½p (V)	14,000.	
10	A57	½p on 2½p (R)	425.	275.
a.		Surcharge inverted	*12,500.*	
b.		Surcharge diagonal, inverted	*14,500.*	
11	A57	½p on 2½p (C)	*25,000.*	*24,500.*
12	A57	½p on 2½p (B)	*40,000.*	—
13	A57	½p on 2½p (G)	550.	

14	A56	½p on 2p (V)	500.	375.
15	A56	½p on 2p (Bl)	2,200.	825.
16	A57	½p on 2½p (V)	*7,750.*	
17	A57	½p on 2½p (R)	650.	*775.*
18	A57	½p on 2½p (Bl)	475.	450.
19	A57	½p on 2½p (G)	500.	*550.*

20	A56	½p on 2p (V)	550.	775.
a.		Surcharge inverted	17,500.	
21	A57	½p on 2½p (R)	600.	475.
a.		Surcharge inverted	20,000.	
b.		Surcharge diagonal, inverted	8,250.	
22	A57	½p on 2½p (C)	475.	500.
23	A57	½p on 2½p (Bl Bk)	5,500.	
24	A57	½p on 2½p (Bl)	475.	525.
25	A57	½p on 2½p (G)	325.	275.
a.		Surcharge diagonal, inverted		
26	A57	½p on 2½p (Bk)	4,750.	
a.		Surcharge inverted	15,500.	
b.		Surcharge diagonal, inverted	13,500.	

27	A57	½p on 2½p (R)	10,000.	
28	A57	½p on 2½p (G)	550.	500.

29	A56	1sh on 2p (V)	500.	425.
a.		Surcharge inverted	13,500.	
b.		Surcharge diagonal, inverted	12,500.	
30	A56	1sh on 2p (R)	825.	4,500.
a.		Surcharge inverted	18,000.	
31	A56	1sh on 2p (Bk)	6,500.	
a.		Surcharge inverted	21,000.	

32	A56	5sh on 2d (V)	10,000.	11,500.
a.		Surcharge inverted	55,000.	
33	A61	10sh on 5p (R)	7,250.	11,000.
a.		Surcharge inverted	55,000.	
34	A65	20sh on 1sh (V)	165,000.	
a.		Surcharge inverted	190,000.	
35	A65	20sh on 1sh (R)	145,000.	
36	A65	20sh on 1sh (Bk)	145,000.	

The handstamped 1893 surcharges are known inverted, vertical, etc.

Queen Victoria
A8 A9

A10

A11

A12

A13

1893 Unwmk. *Perf. 12 to 15*

37	A8	½p vermilion	10.00	*11.00*
38	A9	1p light blue	6.75	5.25
a.		Half used as ½p on cover		825.00
39	A10	2p green	47.50	47.50
a.		Half used as 1p on cover		*1,000.*
b.		Horiz. pair, imperf. between		*17,500.*
40	A11	2½p car lake	17.50	4.50
41	A12	5p gray lilac	22.50	17.50
a.		5p lilac	16.50	24.00
42	A13	1sh black	15.50	16.00
		Nos. 37-42 (6)	119.75	101.75

For surcharge see No. 49.

A15

A16

A17

A18

A19 A20

1894 Engr.

43	A15	½p yel green	5.25	5.50
44	A16	1p vermilion	15.00	9.50
a.		1p orange vermilion	25.00	17.50
b.		Diagonal half, used as ½p on cover		875.00
45	A17	2p car lake	35.00	7.25
a.		Half used as 1p on cover		—
46	A18	2½p blue	20.00	4.50
47	A19	5p dp violet	14.00	6.00
48	A20	1sh black	90.00	26.00
		Nos. 43-48 (6)	179.25	58.75

See #55-59, 61. For surcharges see #51-54.

Halves of Nos. 38, 3 & 44 Srchd. in Red, Blue, Violet or Black

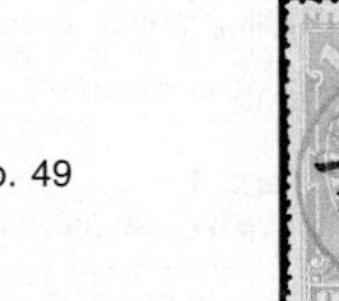

No. 49

No. 50

Nos. 51-53

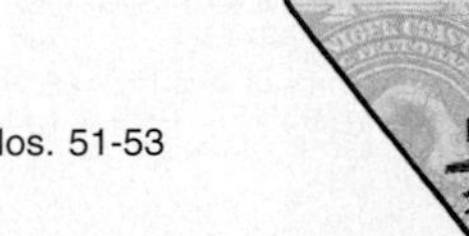

1894

49	A9	½p on half of 1p (R)	1,300.	425.
a.		Inverted surcharge	*15,500.*	

Perf. 14

Wmk. 30

50	A56	1p on half of 2p (R)	1,950.	425.
a.		Double surcharge	7,250.	1,350.
b.		Inverted surcharge		2,250.

Perf. 12 to 15

Unwmk.

51	A16	½p on half of 1p (Bl)	3,850.	550.
a.		Double surcharge		
52	A16	½p on half of 1p (V)	4,400.	775.
53	A16	½p on half of 1p (Bk)	*6,000.*	*1,100.*

This surcharge is found on both vertical and diagonal halves of the 1p.

No. 46 Surcharged in Black

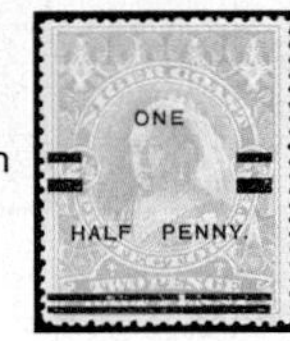

1894

54	A18	½p on 2½p blue	475.	275.
a.		Double surcharge	8,750.	2,500.

The surcharge is found in eight types. The "OIE" variety is broken type.

A27

A28

A29

1897-98 Wmk. 2

55	A15	½p yel green	8.00	1.75
56	A16	1p vermilion	8.00	1.60
57	A17	2p car lake	4.50	2.50
58	A18	2½p blue	16.00	3.25
a.		2½p slate blue	8.50	3.00
59	A19	5p dp violet	18.00	*90.00*
60	A27	6p yel brn ('98)	8.00	8.25
61	A20	1sh black	17.50	*32.50*
62	A28	2sh6p olive bister	24.00	*90.00*
63	A29	10sh dp pur ('98)	140.00	*250.00*
a.		10sh bright purple	135.00	*225.00*
		Nos. 55-63 (9)	244.00	*479.85*

The stamps of Niger Coast Protectorate were superseded in Jan. 1900, by those of Northern and Southern Nigeria.

NIGERIA

nī-ˈjir-ē-ə

LOCATION — West coast of Africa, bordering on the Gulf of Guinea
GOVT. — Republic
AREA — 356,669 sq. mi.
POP. — 113,828,587 (1999 est.)
CAPITAL — Abuja

The colony and protectorate were formed in 1914 by the union of Northern and Southern Nigeria. The mandated territory of Cameroons (British) was also attached for administrative purposes. The Federation of Nigeria was formed in 1960. It became a republic in 1963. See Niger Coast Protectorate, Lagos, Northern Nigeria and Southern Nigeria.

12 Pence = 1 Shilling
20 Shillings = 1 Pound
100 Kobo = 1 Naira (1973)

Catalogue values for unused stamps in this country are for Never Hinged items, beginning with Scott 71 in the regular postage section, Scott B1 in the semi-postal section and Scott J1 in the postage due section.

Watermarks

Wmk. 335 — FN Multiple

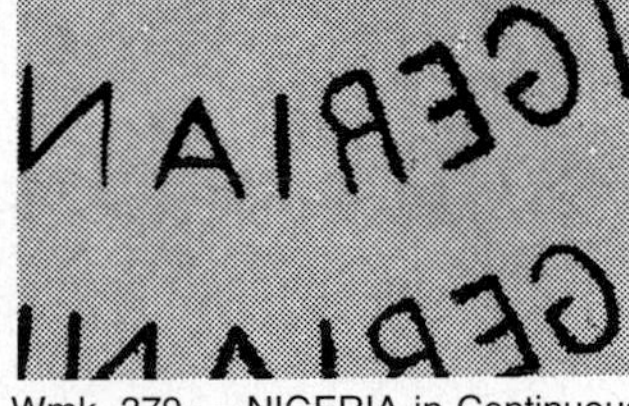
Wmk. 379 — NIGERIA in Continuous Wavy Lines

King George V — A1

Numerals of 3p, 4p, 6p, 5sh and £1 of type A1 are in color on plain tablet.

Dies I and II are described at front of this volume.

Die I

Ordinary Paper

Wmk. Multiple Crown and CA (3)

1914-27 Typo. *Perf. 14*

1	A1	½p green	5.50	.70
a.		Booklet pane of 6		
2	A1	1p carmine	5.25	.25
a.		Booklet pane of 6		
b.		1p scarlet ('16)	13.00	.25
3	A1	2p gray	9.00	2.00
a.		2p slate gray ('18)	10.00	.85
4	A1	2½p ultramarine	10.00	5.50
a.		2½p dull blue ('15)	26.00	9.00

Chalky Paper

5	A1	3p violet, *yel*	1.60	3.00
6	A1	4p blk & red, *yel*	1.10	*4.75*
7	A1	6p dull vio & red vio	10.00	11.00
8	A1	1sh black, *green*	1.10	*10.00*
a.		1sh black, *emerald*	1.40	*15.00*
b.		1sh black, *bl grn*, ol back	60.00	*60.00*
c.		As "a," olive back ('20)	9.00	*47.50*
9	A1	2sh6p blk & red, *bl*	17.50	7.25
10	A1	5sh grn & red, *yel*, white back	22.50	*62.50*
11	A1	10sh grn & red, *grn*	60.00	*95.00*
a.		10sh grn & red, *emer*	40.00	*110.00*
b.		10sh green & red, *blue grn*, olive back	1,000.	*1,700.*
c.		As "a," olive back	160.00	250.00
12	A1	£1 vio & blk, *red*	190.00	*250.00*
a.		Die II ('27)	275.00	*350.00*
		Nos. 1-12 (12)	333.55	*451.95*

Surface-colored Paper

13	A1	3p violet, *yel*	3.50	*12.00*
14	A1	4p black & red, *yel*	1.60	*11.50*
15	A1	1sh black, *green*	1.60	*25.00*
a.		1sh black, *emerald*	*225.00*	
16	A1	5sh grn & red, *yel*	21.00	*55.00*
17	A1	10sh grn & red, *grn*	50.00	*180.00*
		Nos. 13-17 (5)	77.70	*283.50*

Die II

1921-33 Ordinary Paper Wmk. 4

18	A1	½p green	6.50	.90
a.		Die I	1.25	.40

19 A1 1p carmine 1.75 .55
a. Booklet pane of 6 27.50
b. Die I 3.25 .35
c. Booklet pane of 6, Die I 37.50
20 A1 1½p orange ('31) 8.00 .35
21 A1 2p gray 10.00 .50
a. Die I 1.60 *8.00*
b. Booklet pane of 6, Die I 55.00
22 A1 2p red brown ('27) 5.00 1.00
a. Booklet pane of 6 60.00
23 A1 2p dk brown ('28) 3.00 .25
a. Booklet pane of 6 50.00
b. Die I ('32) 6.00 .75
24 A1 2½p ultra (die I) 1.25 *12.00*
25 A1 3p dp violet 11.00 1.10
a. Die I ('24) 6.00 3.50
26 A1 3p ultra ('31) 10.00 1.10

Chalky Paper

27 A1 4p blk & red, *yel* .70 .60
a. Die I ('32) 6.25 7.75
28 A1 6p dull vio & red vio 8.00 *9.00*
a. Die I 14.00 *40.00*
29 A1 1sh black, *emerald* 5.50 2.25
30 A1 2sh6p blk & red, *bl* 7.25 *47.50*
a. Die I ('32) 50.00 *85.00*
31 A1 5sh green & red, *yel* ('26) 16.00 *80.00*
a. Die I ('32) 75.00 *250.00*
32 A1 10sh green & red, *emer* 67.50 *225.00*
a. Die I ('32) 130.00 *500.00*
Nos. 18-32 (15) 161.45 382.10

Silver Jubilee Issue
Common Design Type

1935, May 6 Engr. *Perf. 11x12*
34 CD301 1½p black & ultra 1.00 *1.50*
35 CD301 2p indigo & green 2.00 *1.75*
36 CD301 3p ultra & brown 3.50 *19.00*
37 CD301 1sh brown vio & ind 6.75 *37.50*
Nos. 34-37 (4) 13.25 *59.75*
Set, never hinged 24.00

Wharf at Apapa — A2

Picking Cacao Pods — A3

Dredging for Tin — A4

Timber — A5

Fishing Village — A6

Ginning Cotton — A7

Minaret at Habe — A8

Fulani Cattle — A9

Victoria-Buea Road — A10

Oil Palms A11

View of Niger at Jebba A12

Nigerian Canoe A13

1936, Feb. 1 *Perf. 11½x13*
38 A2 ½p green 1.50 1.40
39 A3 1p rose car .50 .40
40 A4 1½p brown 2.00 .40
a. Perf. 12½x13½ 85.00 4.50
41 A5 2p black .50 *.80*
42 A6 3p dark blue 2.00 1.50
a. Perf. 12½x13½ 150.00 25.00
43 A7 4p red brown 2.50 2.00
44 A8 6p dull violet .70 .60
45 A9 1sh olive green 2.25 *5.00*

Perf. 14

46 A10 2sh6p ultra & blk 8.00 *40.00*
47 A11 5sh ol grn & blk 20.00 *60.00*
48 A12 10sh slate & blk 90.00 *140.00*
49 A13 £1 orange & blk 130.00 *200.00*
Nos. 38-49 (12) 259.95 *452.10*
Set, never hinged 400.00

Common Design Types pictured following the introduction.

Coronation Issue
Common Design Type

1937, May 12 *Perf. 11x11½*
50 CD302 1p dark carmine .50 *2.00*
51 CD302 1½p dark brown 1.25 *2.50*
52 CD302 3p deep ultra 1.50 *4.00*
Nos. 50-52 (3) 3.25 8.50
Set, never hinged 6.50

George VI — A14

Victoria-Buea Road — A15

Niger at Jebba A16

1938-51 Wmk. 4 *Perf. 12*
53 A14 ½p deep green .25 .25
a. Perf. 11½ ('50) 1.40 *1.75*
54 A14 1p dk carmine .40 .30
55 A14 1½p red brown .25 .25
a. Perf. 11½ ('50) .25 .25
56 A14 2p black .25 *3.00*
57 A14 2½p orange ('41) .25 *3.00*
58 A14 3p deep blue .25 .25
59 A14 4p orange 32.50 4.00
60 A14 6p brown violet .30 .25
a. Perf. 11½ ('51) 1.40 .60
61 A14 1sh olive green .40 .25
a. Perf. 11½ ('50) .90 .25
62 A14 1sh3p turq blue ('40) .60 .70
a. Perf. 11½ ('50) 2.10 .70
63 A15 2sh6p ultra & blk ('51) 1.50 4.50
a. Perf. 13½ ('42) 2.25 *7.00*
b. Perf. 14 ('42) 2.00 *3.50*
c. Perf. 13x11½ 37.50 24.00
64 A16 5sh org & blk, perf. 13½ ('42) 4.50 *4.50*
a. Perf. 12 ('49) 5.50 4.00
b. Perf. 14 ('48) 6.75 3.00
c. Perf. 13x11½ 67.50 21.00

1944, Dec. 1 *Perf. 12*
65 A14 1p red violet .25 .30
a. Perf. 11½ ('50) .60 .60
66 A14 2p deep red .25 *3.00*
a. Perf. 11½ ('50) .35 *.70*
67 A14 3p black .25 *3.50*
68 A14 4p dark blue .25 *4.00*
Nos. 53-68 (16) 42.45 *32.05*
Set, never hinged 75.00

Issue date: Nos. 65a, 66a, Feb. 15.

Catalogue values for unused stamps in this section, from this point to the end of the section, are for Never Hinged items.

Peace Issue
Common Design Type

1946, Oct. 21 Engr. *Perf. 13½x14*
71 CD303 1½p brown .35 .25
72 CD303 4p deep blue .35 *2.50*

Silver Wedding Issue
Common Design Types

1948, Dec. 20 Photo. *Perf. 14x14½*
73 CD304 1p brt red violet .35 .30

Perf. 11½x11
Engraved; Name Typographed

74 CD305 5sh brown orange 17.50 *22.50*

UPU Issue
Common Design Types
Engr.; Name Typo. on 3p, 6p
Perf. 13½, 11x11½

1949, Oct. 10 Wmk. 4
75 CD306 1p red violet .25 .25
76 CD307 3p indigo .35 *3.50*
77 CD308 6p rose violet .80 *3.50*
78 CD309 1sh olive 1.40 *2.00*
Nos. 75-78 (4) 2.80 *9.25*

Coronation Issue
Common Design Type

1953, June 2 Engr. *Perf. 13½x13*
79 CD312 1½p brt grn & blk .45 .25

Manilla (Bracelet) Currency A17

Olokun Head, Ife — A18

Designs: 1p, Bornu horsemen. 1½p, Peanuts, Kano City. 2p, Mining tin. 3p, Jebba Bridge over Niger River. 4p, Cocoa industry. 1sh, Logging. 2sh6p, Victoria harbor. 5sh, Loading palm oil. 10sh, Goats and Fulani cattle. £1, Lagos waterfront, 19th and 20th centuries.

1953, Sept. 1 *Perf. 14*
Size: 35½x22½mm

80 A17 ½p red org & blk .25 .25
81 A17 1p ol gray & blk .25 .25
82 A17 1½p blue green .50 .25
83 A17 2p bister & blk 4.00 .30
84 A17 3p purple & blk .50 .30
85 A17 4p ultra & black 2.50 .25
86 A18 6p blk & org brn .30 .25
87 A17 1sh brn vio & blk .50 .25

Size: 40½x24½mm

88 A17 2sh6p green & black 16.00 1.25
89 A17 5sh ver & black 5.50 1.40
90 A17 10sh red brn & blk 24.00 3.25

Size: 42x31½mm

91 A17 £1 violet & black 32.50 16.00
Nos. 80-91 (12) 86.80 24.00

Booklet panes of 4 of Nos. 80, 81, 84, 87 were issued in 1957. They are identical to margin blocks of 4 from sheets.
See No. 93.

No. 83 Overprinted in Black

1956, Jan. 28 Wmk. 4 *Perf. 13½*
92 A17 2p bister & black .40 .30

Visit of Queen Elizabeth II to Nigeria, Jan.-Feb., 1956.

Mining Tin Type of 1953

Two types:
I — Broken row of dots between "G" and miner's head.
II — Complete row of dots.

1956-57
93 A17 2p bluish gray (shades) (I) 3.00 2.00
b. 2p gray (shades) (II) 4.75 .40

Booklet pane of 4 of No. 93 was issued in 1957. See note after No. 91.

Ambas Bay, Victoria Harbor A19

Wmk. 314

1958, Dec. 1 Engr. *Perf. 13½*
94 A19 3p purple & black .40 .30

Cent. of the founding of Victoria, Southern Cameroons.

1959, Mar. 14

3p, Lugard Hall, Kaduna. 1sh, Kano Mosque.

95 A19 3p purple & black .30 .25
96 A19 1sh green & black .75 .50

Attainment of self-government by the Northern Region, Mar. 15, 1959.

Federation of Nigeria

Federal Legislature A20

3p, Man Paddling Canoe. 6p, Federal Supreme Court. 1sh3p, Map of Africa, dove and torch.

Wmk. 335

1960, Oct. 1 Photo. *Perf. 13½*
Size: 35x22mm

97 A20 1p carmine & black .25 .25
98 A20 3p blue & black .25 .25
99 A20 6p dk red brn & emer .25 .25

Size: 39½x23½mm

100 A20 1sh3p ultra & yellow .25 .25
Nos. 97-100 (4) 1.00 1.00

Nigeria's independence, Oct. 1, 1960.

Peanuts — A21

Central Bank, Lagos A22

Designs: 1p, Coal miner. 1½p, Adult education. 2p, Potter. 3p, Oyo carver. 4p, Weaver. 6p, Benin mask. 1sh, Yellow-casqued hornbill. 1sh3p, Camel train and map. 5sh, Nigeria museum and sculpture. 10sh, Kano airport. £1, Lagos terminal.

Perf. 14½x14

1961, Jan. 1 **Wmk. 335**

101 A21 ½p emerald .30 *.60*
102 A21 1p purple .80 .30
a. Booklet pane of 6 5.00
103 A21 1½p rose red .80 *2.25*
104 A21 2p ultra .30 .30
105 A21 3p dk grn .40 .30
a. Booklet pane of 6 2.50
106 A21 4p blue .30 *2.00*
107 A21 6p blk & yol .80 .30
a. Booklet pane of 6 5.00
b. Yellow omitted *2,750.* *1,300.*
108 A21 1sh yel grn 4.00 .30
109 A21 1sh3p orange 1.50 .30
a. Booklet pane of 6 9.00
110 A22 2sh6p yellow & blk 2.75 .30
111 A22 5sh emer & blk 1.25 1.25
112 A22 10sh dp ultra & blk 3.75 3.75
113 A22 £1 dp car & blk 13.00 *14.00*
Nos. 101-113 (13) 29.95 25.95

For overprint see No. 198.

Globe and Train A23

1961, July 25 **Wmk. 335**

114 A23 1p shown .25 .25
115 A23 3p Truck .25 .25
116 A23 1sh3p Plane .35 .35
117 A23 2sh6p Ship .80 .80
Nos. 114-117 (4) 1.65 1.65

Nigeria's admission to the UPU.

Coat of Arms — A24

Map and Natural Resources — A25

Designs: 6p, Eagle carrying banner. 1sh3p, Flying eagles forming flag. 2sh6p, Young couple looking at flag and government building.

Perf. 14½x14, 14x14½

1961, Oct. 1 **Photo.** **Wmk. 335**

118 A24 3p multicolored .25 .25
119 A25 4p org, yel grn & dk red .25 .25
120 A25 6p emerald .25 .25
121 A25 1sh3p ultra, emer & gray .25 .25
122 A25 2sh6p blue, emer & sep .50 .50
Nos. 118-122 (5) 1.50 1.50

First anniversary of independence.

Map of Africa and Staff of Aesculapius — A26

Map of Africa and: 3p, Lyre, book and scroll. 6p, Cogwheel. 1sh, Radio beacon. 1sh3p, Hands holding globe.

1962, Jan. 25 ***Perf. 14x14½***

123 A26 1p bister .25 .25
124 A26 3p deep magenta .25 .25
125 A26 6p blue green .25 .25
126 A26 1sh chestnut .25 .25
127 A26 1sh3p bright blue .25 .25
Nos. 123-127 (5) 1.25 1.25

Issued to honor the conference of heads of state of African and Malagasy Governments.

Malaria Eradication Emblem and Larvae — A27

Emblem and: 6p, Man with spray gun. 1sh3p, Plane spraying insecticide. 2sh6p, Microscope, retort and patient.

1962, Apr. 7 ***Perf. 14½***

128 A27 3p emer, brn & ver .25 .25
129 A27 6p lil rose & dk blue .25 .25
130 A27 1sh3p dk blue & lil rose .25 .25
131 A27 2sh6p yel brown & blue .30 .80
Nos. 128-131 (4) 1.05 1.55

WHO drive to eradicate malaria.

National Monument, Lagos A28

Ife Bronze Head and Flag — A29

Perf. 14½x14, 14x14½

1962, Oct. 1 **Wmk. 335** **Photo.**

132 A28 3p lt ultra & emer .25 .25
a. Emerald omitted 800.00 475.00
133 A29 5sh vio, emer & org red 1.25 1.25

Second anniversary of independence.

Fair Emblem — A30

Designs (horizontal): 6p, "Wheels of Industry." 1sh, Cornucopia, goods and trucks. 2sh6p, Oil derricks and tanker.

1962, Oct. 27 **Wmk. 335**

134 A30 1p brown olive & org .25 .25
135 A30 6p crimson & blk .25 .25
136 A30 1sh dp orange & blk .25 .25
137 A30 2sh6p dk ultra, yel & blk .30 .25
Nos. 134-137 (4) 1.05 1.00

Lagos Intl. Trade Fair, Oct. 27-Nov. 8.

Globe and Arrows — A31

4p, Natl. Hall & Commonwealth emblem, horiz. 1sh3p, Palm tree, emblem & doves.

1962, Nov. 5

138 A31 2½p sky blue .25 *1.00*
139 A31 4p dp rose & slate bl .25 .25
140 A31 1sh3p gray & yellow .25 .25
Nos. 138-140 (3) .75 1.50

8th Commonwealth Parliamentary Conf., Lagos.

Herdsman with Cattle — A32

Design: 6p, Tractor and corn, horiz.

1963, Mar. 21 **Photo.** ***Perf. 14½***

141 A32 3p olive green 1.10 .25
142 A32 6p brt lilac rose 1.40 .25

FAO "Freedom from Hunger" campaign.

US Mercury Capsule over Kano Tracking Station — A33

Design: 1sh3p, Syncom II satellite and US tracking ship "Kingsport," Lagos harbor.

1963, June 21 ***Perf. 14½***

143 A33 6p dk blue & yel grn .25 .25
144 A33 1sh3p black & dp green .30 .30

Peaceful uses of outer space.

Printed in sheets of 12 (4x3) with ornamental borders and inscriptions.

Nigerian and Greek Scouts Shaking Hands and Jamboree Emblem — A34

1sh, Scouts dancing around campfire.

1963, Aug. 1 **Photo.** ***Perf. 14***

145 A34 3p gray olive & red .30 .25
146 A34 1sh red & black .60 .60
a. Souvenir sheet of 2, #145-146 1.60 1.60

11th Boy Scout Jamboree, Marathon, Greece, Aug. 1963.

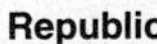

Republic

First Aid — A35

Designs: 6p, Blood donors and ambulances. 1sh3p, Helping the needy.

1963, Sept. 1 **Wmk. 335** ***Perf. 14½***

147 A35 3p dk blue & red .35 .25
148 A35 6p dk green & red .55 .30
149 A35 1sh3p black & red 1.50 1.00
a. Souvenir sheet of 4, #149 12.00 12.00
Nos. 147-149 (3) 2.40 1.55

Cent. of the Intl. Red Cross.

Pres. Nnamdi Azikiwe and State House — A36

Designs: 1sh3p, President and Federal Supreme Court. 2sh6p, President and Parliament Building.

1963, Oct. 1 **Unwmk.** ***Perf. 14x13***

150 A36 3p dull grn & yel grn .25 .25
151 A36 1sh3p brown & bister .25 .25
a. Bister (head) omitted
152 A36 2sh6p vio bl & brt grnsh bl .25 .25
Nos. 150-152 (3) .75 .75

Independence Day, Oct. 1, 1963.

"Freedom of Worship" — A37

3p, Charter & broken whip, horiz. 1sh3p, "Freedom from Want." 2sh6p, "Freedom of Speech."

1963, Dec. 10 **Wmk. 335** ***Perf. 13***

153 A37 3p vermilion .25 .25
154 A37 6p green .25 .25
155 A37 1sh3p deep ultra .25 .25
156 A37 2sh6p red lilac .30 .30
Nos. 153-156 (4) 1.05 1.05

15th anniv. of the Universal Declaration of Human Rights.

Queen Nefertari — A38

1964, Mar. 8 **Photo.** ***Perf. 14***

157 A38 6p shown 1.00 .35
158 A38 2sh6p Ramses II 2.00 2.25

UNESCO world campaign to save historic monuments in Nubia.

John F. Kennedy, US and Nigerian Flags A39

1sh3p, Kennedy bust & laurel. 5sh, Kennedy coin (US), flags of US & Nigeria at half-mast.

1964, Aug. 20 **Unwmk.** ***Perf. 13x14***

159 A39 1sh3p black & lt vio .25 .25
160 A39 2sh6p multicolored .65 .75
161 A39 5sh multicolored 1.40 1.75
a. Souvenir sheet of 4 7.50 7.50
Nos. 159-161 (3) 2.30 2.75

Pres. John F. Kennedy (1917-63). No. 161a contains 4 imperf. stamps similar to No. 161 with simulated perforations.

Pres. Nnamdi Azikiwe — A40

Herbert Macaulay — A41

Design: 2sh6p, King Jaja of Opobo.

Perf. 14x13, 14

1964, Oct. 1 Photo. Unwmk.

162 A40 3p red brown .25 .25
163 A41 1sh3p green .25 .25
164 A41 2sh6p slate green .60 .60
Nos. 162-164 (3) 1.10 1.10

First anniversary of the Republic.

Boxing Gloves and Torch A42

Hurdling — A43

6p, High jump. 1sh3p, Woman runner, vert.

1964, Oct. ***Perf. 14½***

165 A42 3p olive grn & sepia .25 .25
166 A42 6p dk blue & emer .35 .35
167 A42 1sh3p olive & brown .55 .55

Perf. 14

168 A43 2sh6p orange red & brn 1.50 1.50
a. Souvenir sheet of 4 4.25 4.25
Nos. 165-168 (4) 2.65 2.65

18th Olympic Games, Tokyo, Oct. 10-25.
No. 168a contains 4 imperf. stamps similar to No. 168 with simulated perforations.

Mountain Climbing Scouts — A44

3p, Golden Jubilee emblem. 6p, Nigeria's Scout emblem & merit badges. 1sh3p, Lord Baden-Powell & Nigerian Boy Scout.

1965, Jan. Photo. ***Perf. 14½***

169 A44 1p brown .25 .25
170 A44 3p emer, blk & red .25 .25
171 A44 6p yel grn, red & blk .25 .25
172 A44 1sh3p sep, yel & dk grn .35 .75
a. Souvenir sheet of 4 7.25 7.25
Nos. 169-172 (4) 1.10 1.50

Founding of the Nigerian Boy Scouts, 50th anniv.
No. 172a contains four imperf. stamps similar to No. 172 with simulated perforation.

IQSY Emblem and Telstar, Map of Africa — A45

1sh3p, Explorer XII over map of Africa.

1965, Apr. 1 Unwmk. ***Perf. 14x13***

173 A45 6p grnsh bl & vio .25 .25
174 A45 1sh3p lilac & green .30 .30

Intl. Quiet Sun Year, 1964-65. Printed in sheets of 12 (4x3) with ornamental borders and inscriptions.

ITU Emblem, Drummer, Man at Desk and Telephone A46

Cent. of the ITU: 1sh3p, ITU emblem and telecommunication tower, vert. 5sh, ITU emblem, Syncom satellite and map of Africa showing Nigeria.

Perf. 11x11½, 11½x11

1965, Aug. 2 Photo. Unwmk.

175 A46 3p ocher, red & blk .30 .25
176 A46 1sh3p ultra, grn & blk 1.50 1.50
177 A46 5sh multicolored 6.00 6.00
Nos. 175-177 (3) 7.80 7.75

ICY Emblem, Diesel Locomotive and Camel Caravan A47

ICY Emblem and: 1sh, Students and hospital, Lagos. 2sh6p, Kainji Dam, Niger River.

Perf. 14x15

1965, Sept. 1 Wmk. 335

178 A47 3p orange, grn & car 3.50 .35
179 A47 1sh ultra, blk & yel 3.00 .50
180 A47 2sh6p ultra, yel & grn 10.00 7.50
Nos. 178-180 (3) 16.50 8.35

Intl. Cooperation Year and 20th anniv. of the UN.

Stone Images, Ikom — A48

Designs: 3p, Carved frieze, horiz. 5sh, Seated man, Taba bronze.

Perf. 14x15, 15x14

1965, Oct. 1 Photo. Unwmk.

181 A48 3p ocher, blk & red .25 .25
182 A48 1sh3p lt ultra, grn & reddish brn .25 .25
183 A48 5sh emer, dk brn & reddish brn .60 1.25
Nos. 181-183 (3) 1.10 1.75

Second anniversary of the Republic.

Elephants A49

Designs: ½p, Lioness and cubs, vert. 1½p, Splendid sunbird. 2p, Weaverbirds. 3p, Cheetah. 4p, Leopard and cubs. 6p, Saddle-billed storks, vert. 9p, Gray parrots. 1sh, Kingfishers. 1sh3p, Crowned cranes. 2sh6p, Buffon's kobs (antelopes). 5sh, Giraffes. 10sh, Hippopotami, vert. £1, Buffalos.

"MAURICE FIEVET" below Design

Perf. 12x12½, 12½x12, 14x13½ (1p, 2p, 3p, 4p, 9p)

1965-66 Photo.

Size: 23x38mm, 38x23mm

184 A49 ½p multicolored 1.00 *2.50*
185 A49 1p red & multi .50 .25
186 A49 1½p lt blue & multi 8.00 *9.50*
187 A49 2p brt red & multi 3.75 .25
a. White "2d" ('70) 4.50 2.50
188 A49 3p brt grn, yel & dl brn 1.25 .30
189 A49 4p lilac & multi .30 .25
a. Perf 12½x12 .60 *3.00*
b. "4" 5mm wide ('71) 60.00 8.00
190 A49 6p violet & multi 2.10 .40
191 A49 9p blue & orange 3.00 .60

Perf. 12½

Size: 45x26mm, 26x45mm

192 A49 1sh gray & multi 5.00 .60
a. Red omitted
193 A49 1sh3p brt bl & multi 9.00 2.00
194 A49 2sh6p dk brn, yel & ocher 1.00 *2.00*
195 A49 5sh brn, yel & red brown 2.25 3.50
196 A49 10sh grnsh bl & multi 7.00 3.25
197 A49 £1 brt grn & multi 18.50 9.00
Nos. 184-197 (14) 62.65 34.40

The designer's name, Maurice Fievet, appears at right or left, in small or large capitals. Nos. 187a and 189b have "MAURICE FIEVET" at right, 5mm wide. No. 187a has "2d" in white instead of yellow. No. 189b has "REPUBLIC" and "4d" larger, bolder.

Issued: ½p, 1p, 11/1/65; 2p, 4/1/66; 1½p, #189a, 6p, 1sh, 1sh3p, 2sh6p, 5sh, 10sh, 1£, 5/2/66; 3p, 9p, 10/17/66; 4p, 1966.

Nine values were overprinted "F. G. N./ F. G. N." (Federal Government of Nigeria) in 1968. They were not issued, but some were sold by accident in 1968. Later the Nigerian Philatelic Service sold examples, stating they were not postally valid. However, some were used by government agencies in 1969.

See Nos. 258-267.

No. 110 Overprinted in Red: "COMMONWEALTH / P.M. MEETING / 11. Jan. 1966"

Perf. 14½x14

1966, Jan. 11 Photo. Wmk. 335

198 A22 2sh6p yellow & black .35 .35

Conf. of British Commonwealth Prime Ministers, Lagos.

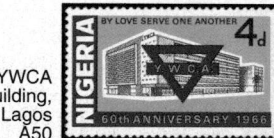

YWCA Building, Lagos A50

Unwmk.

1966, Sept. 1 Litho. ***Perf. 14***

199 A50 4p yel, green & multi .25 .25
200 A50 9p brt green & multi .25 .50

60th anniv. of the Nigerian YWCA.

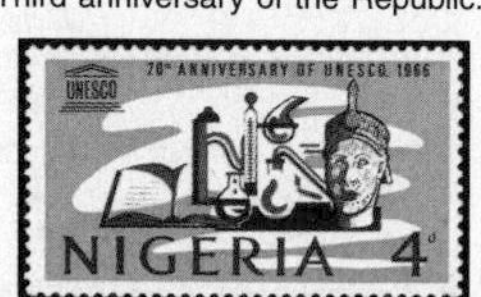

Lineman and Telephone A51

Designs: 4p, Flag and letter carrying pigeon, vert. 2sh6p, Niger Bridge.

Perf. 14½x14, 14x14½

1966, Oct. 1 Photo. Wmk. 335

201 A51 4p green .25 .25
202 A51 1sh6p lilac, blk & sep .30 .50
203 A51 2sh6p multicolored .70 1.75
Nos. 201-203 (3) 1.25 2.50

Third anniversary of the Republic.

Surveyors and Hydrological Decade Emblem — A53

Book, Chemical Apparatus, Carved Head and UNESCO Emblem A52

1966, Nov. 4 ***Perf. 14½x14***

204 A52 4p dl org, mar & blk .50 .25
205 A52 1sh6p bl grn, plum & blk 1.75 2.50
206 A52 2sh6p pink, plum & blk 3.50 6.00
Nos. 204-206 (3) 5.75 8.75

20th anniv. of UNESCO.

Design: 2sh6p, Water depth gauge on dam and Hydrological Decade emblem, vert.

Perf. 14½x14, 14x14½

1967, Feb. 1 Photo. Wmk. 335

207 A53 4p multicolored .25 .25
208 A53 2sh6p multicolored .50 1.25

Hydrological Decade (UNESCO), 1965-74.

Weather Satellite Orbiting Earth A54

1sh6p, Storm over land & sea & World Meteorological Organization emblem.

1967, Mar. 23 Photo. ***Perf. 14½x14***

209 A54 4p dp ultra & brt rose .25 .25
210 A54 1sh6p ultra & yellow .65 .90

World Meteorological Day, March 23.

Eyo Masqueraders — A55

1sh6p, Acrobat. 2sh6p, Stilt dancer, vert.

Perf. 11x11½, 11½x11

1967, Oct. 1 Photo. Unwmk.

211 A55 4p multicolored .25 .25
212 A55 1sh6p turq bl & multi .50 1.25
213 A55 2sh6p pale grn & multi .75 2.50
Nos. 211-213 (3) 1.50 4.00

4th anniversary of the Federal Republic.

Rinderpest Eradication Campaign

Vaccination of Cattle A56

1967, Dec. 1 ***Perf. 14½x14***

214 A56 4p maroon & multi .25 .25
215 A56 1sh6p ultra & multi .70 *1.25*

Campaign to eradicate cattle plague.

1/6d NIGERIA

WORLD HEALTH ORGANIZATION

Anopheles Mosquito and Sick Man — A57

20th anniv. of the WHO: 4p, WHO emblem and vaccination.

1968, Apr. 7 Litho. ***Perf. 14***

216 A57 4p dp lil rose & blk .25 .25
217 A57 1sh6p org yel & blk .55 .80

Shackled Hands, Map of Nigeria and Human Rights Flame A58

Design: 1sh6p, Flag of Nigeria and human rights flame, vert.

1968, July 1 Photo. *Perf. 14*

218 A58 4p dp blue, yel & blk .25 .25
219 A58 1sh6p green, blk & red .45 .80

International Human Rights Year.

Hand and Doves — A59

1968, Oct. 1 Unwmk. *Perf. 14*

220 A59 4p brt blue & multi .25 .25
221 A59 1sh6p black & multi .25 .25

5th anniversary of the Federal Republic.

Olympic Rings, Nigerian Flag and Athletes A60

4p, Map of Nigeria and Olympic rings.

1968, Oct. 14 Photo. *Perf. 14*

222 A60 4p red, blk & emer .25 .25
223 A60 1sh6p multicolored .50 .35

19th Olympic Games, Mexico City, 10/12-27.

G.P.O., Lagos A61

1969, Apr. 11 Unwmk. *Perf. 14*

224 A61 4p emerald & black .25 .25
225 A61 1sh6p dk blue & black .25 .40

Opening of the Nigerian Philatelic Service of the GPO, Lagos.

Gen. Yakubu Gowon and Victoria Zakari A62

Perf. 13x13½

1969, Sept. 20 Litho. Unwmk.

226 A62 4p emerald & choc .30 .25
227 A62 1sh6p emerald & black .70 .45

Wedding of Yakubu Gowon, head of state of Nigeria, and Miss Victoria Zakari, Apr. 19, 1969.

Development Bank Emblem and "5" — A63

Design: 1sh6p, Emblem and rays.

1969, Oct. 18 Litho. *Perf. 14*

228 A63 4p dk bl, blk & org .25 .25
229 A63 1sh6p dk pur, yel & blk .35 *1.00*

African Development Bank, 5th anniv.

ILO Emblem A64

50th anniv. of the ILO: 1sh6p, ILO emblem and world map.

1969, Nov. 15 Photo.

230 A64 4p purple & black .25 .25
231 A64 1sh6p green & black .65 *1.25*

Tourist Year Emblem and Musicians — A65

Designs: 4p, Olumo Rock and Tourist Year emblem, horiz. 1sh6p, Assob Falls.

1969, Dec. 30 Photo. *Perf. 14*

232 A65 4p blue & multi .25 .25
233 A65 1sh emerald & black .30 .30
234 A65 1sh6p multicolored 1.25 .85
Nos. 232-234 (3) 1.80 1.40

International Year of African Tourism.

12-Spoke Wheel and Arms of Nigeria — A66

Designs: 4p, Map of Nigeria and tree with 12 fruits representing 12 tribes. 1sh6p, People bound by common destiny and map of Nigeria. 2sh, Torch with 12 flames and map of Africa, horiz.

Perf. 11½x11, 11x11½

1970, May 28 Photo. Unwmk.

235 A66 4p gold, blue & blk .25 .25
236 A66 1sh gold & multi .25 .25
237 A66 1sh6p green & black .25 .25
238 A66 2sh bl, org, gold & black .25 .25
Nos. 235-238 (4) 1.00 1.00

Establishment of a 12-state administrative structure in Nigeria.

Opening of New UPU Headquarters, Bern — A67

1970, June 29 Unwmk. *Perf. 14*

239 A67 4p purple & yellow .30 .25
240 A67 1sh6p blue & vio blue .45 .35

UN Emblem and Charter — A68

25th anniv. of the UN: 1sh6p, UN emblem and headquarters, New York.

1970, Sept. 1 Photo. *Perf. 14*

241 A68 4p brn org, buff & blk .25 .25
242 A68 1sh6p dk bl, gold & bis brn .25 .25

Student — A69

Designs: 2p, Oil drilling platform. 6p, Durbar horsemen. 9p, Soldier and sailors raising flag. 1sh, Soccer player. 1sh6p, Parliament Building. 2sh, Kainji Dam. 2sh6p, Export products: Timber, rubber, peanuts, cocoa and palm produce.

1970, Sept. 30 Litho. *Perf. 14x13½*

243 A69 2p blue & multi .25 .25
244 A69 4p blue & multi .25 .25
245 A69 6p blue & multi .30 .25
246 A69 9p blue & multi .45 .25
247 A69 1sh blue & multi .45 .25
248 A69 1sh6p blue & multi .45 .40
249 A69 2sh blue & multi .80 .90
250 A69 2sh6p blue & multi .80 1.00
Nos. 243-250 (8) 3.75 3.55

Ten years of independence.

Black and White Men Uprooting Racism — A70

Designs: 4p, Black and white school children and globe, horiz. 1sh6p, World map with black and white stripes. 2sh, Black and white men, shoulder to shoulder, horiz.

Perf. 13½x14, 14x13½

1971, Mar. 22 Photo. Unwmk.

251 A70 4p multicolored .25 .25
252 A70 1sh yellow & multi .25 .25
253 A70 1sh6p blue, yel & blk .25 .65
254 A70 2sh multicolored .25 1.25
Nos. 251-254 (4) 1.00 2.40

Intl. year against racial discrimination.

Ibibio Mask, c. 1900 — A71

Nigerian Antiquities: 1sh3p, Bronze mask of a King of Benin, c. 1700. 1sh9p, Bronze figure of a King of Ife.

1971, Sept. 30 *Perf. 13½x14*

255 A71 4p lt blue & black .25 .25
256 A71 1sh3p yellow bis & blk .25 .35
257 A71 1sh9p apple grn, dp grn & blk .25 1.00
Nos. 255-257 (3) .75 1.60

Type of 1965-66 Redrawn

Imprint: "N.S.P. & M. Co. Ltd." Added to "MAURICE FIEVET"

Perf. 13x13½; 14x13½ (6p)

1969-72 Photo.

Size: 38x23mm

258 A49 1p red & multi 3.00 2.25
259 A49 2p brt red & multi 4.00 1.50
260 A49 3p multi ('71) .75 *2.00*
261 A49 4p lilac & multi 8.50 .25
262 A49 6p brt vio & multi ('71) 2.25 .25
263 A49 9p dl bl & dp org ('70) 7.00 .50

Size: 45x26mm

264 A49 1sh multi ('71) 3.00 .25
265 A49 1sh3p multi ('71) 11.00 3.50
266 A49 2sh6p multi ('72) 15.00 7.00
267 A49 5sh multi ('72) 3.50 *17.50*
Nos. 258-267 (10) 58.00 35.00

"Maurice Fievet" imprint on No. 259 exists in two lengths, 5mm and 5½mm.

"Maurice Fievet" imprint on No. 260 exists in two lengths, 5½mm and 8½mm.

UNICEF Emblem and Children — A72

UNICEF 25th anniv.: 1sh3p, Mother and child. 1sh9p, African mother carrying child on back.

1971, Dec. 11 *Perf. 14*

270 A72 4p purple & yellow .25 .25
271 A72 1sh3p org, pur & plum .25 *.45*
272 A72 1sh9p blue & dk blue .25 *.90*
Nos. 270-272 (3) .75 1.60

Satellite Earth Station — A73

Various views of satellite communications earth station, Lanlate, Nigeria. All horiz.

1971, Dec. 30 Photo. *Perf. 14*

273 A73 4p multicolored .25 .25
274 A73 1sh3p blue, blk & grn .25 .65
275 A73 1sh9p orange & blk .30 .95
276 A73 3sh brt pink & blk .55 1.75
Nos. 273-276 (4) 1.35 3.60

Satellite communications earth station, Lanlate, Nigeria.

Fair Emblem — A74

Fair Emblem and: 1sh3p, Map of Africa, horiz. 1sh9p, Globe with map of Africa.

Perf. 13½x13, 13x13½

1972, Feb. 23 Litho.

277 A74 4p multicolored .25 .25
278 A74 1sh3p dull pur, yel & gold .25 *.40*
279 A74 1sh9p orange, yel & blk .25 *1.25*
Nos. 277-279 (3) .75 1.90

First All-Africa Trade Fair, Nairobi, Kenya, Feb. 23-Mar. 5.

Traffic A75

Designs: 1sh3p, Traffic flow at circle. 1sh9p, Car and truck on road. 3sh, Intersection with lights and pedestrians.

1972, June 23 Photo. *Perf. 13x13½*

280 A75 4p orange & blk .50 .25
281 A75 1sh3p lt blue & multi 1.50 1.00
282 A75 1sh9p emerald & multi 1.75 1.25
283 A75 3sh yellow & multi 3.00 *3.50*
Nos. 280-283 (4) 6.75 6.00

Introduction of right-hand driving in Nigeria, Apr. 2, 1972.

Nok Style Terra-cotta Head, Katsina Ala — A76

1sh3p, Roped bronze vessel, Igbo Ukwu. 1sh9p, Bone harpoon, Daima, horiz.

Perf. 13½x13, 13x13½

1972, Sept. 1 Litho.

284 A76 4p dk blue & multi .25 .25
285 A76 1sh3p gold & multi .45 *.60*
286 A76 1sh9p dp blue & multi .55 *1.60*
Nos. 284-286 (3) 1.25 2.45

All-Nigeria Festival of the Arts, Kaduna, Dec. 9.

Games Emblem and Soccer A77

Designs: 5k, Running. 18k, Table tennis. 25k, Stadium, vert.

1973, Jan. 8 Litho. *Perf. 13x13½*

287 A77 5k lilac, blue & blk .25 .25
288 A77 12k multicolored .35 .55
289 A77 18k yellow & multi .60 *1.10*
290 A77 25k brown & multi 1.00 *1.50*
Nos. 287-290 (4) 2.20 3.40

2nd All-Africa Games, Lagos, Jan. 7-18.

Hides and Skins A78

Designs: 2k, Natural gas tanks. 3k, Cement works. 5k, Cattle ranching. 7k, Lumbermill. 8k, Oil refinery. 10k, Leopards, Yankari Game Reserve. 12k, New civic building. 15k, Sugar cane harvesting. 18k, Palm oil production, vert. 20k, Vaccine production. 25k, Modern docks. 30k, Argungu Fishing Festival, vert. 35k, Textile industry. 50k, Pottery, vert. 1n, Eko Bridge. 2n, Teaching Hospital, Lagos.

Imprint at left: "N S P & M Co Ltd"
6mm on Litho. Stamps, 5¼ mm on Photo. Stamps
Litho.; Photo. (50k)

1973-74 Unwmk. *Perf. 14*

291 A78 1k multi, buff imprint *.25* *.25*
292 A78 2k multi ('74) *3.00* *.90*
293 A78 3k multi ('74) *.25* *.25*
294 A78 5k grn & multi ('74) *3.75* *.90*
295 A78 7k multicolored *.35* *1.25*
296 A78 8k multicolored *.40* *.25*
297 A78 10k multicolored *5.00* *.25*
298 A78 12k multicolored *.50* *2.00*
299 A78 15k multicolored *.35* *.60*
300 A78 18k multicolored *.55* *.30*
301 A78 20k multicolored *.65* *.30*
302 A78 25k multicolored *.85* *.45*
303 A78 30k multicolored *.50* *1.50*
304 A78 35k multicolored *6.00* *4.00*
305 A78 50k black background *2.00* *2.50*
306 A78 1n multicolored *1.00* *.90*
307 A78 2n multicolored *1.00* *2.25*
Nos. 291-307 (17) *26.40* *18.85*

Imprint on 35k has periods.

Imprint at left: "N S P & M Co Ltd"

1973 Photo., Imprint 5¼mm

291a A78 1k multi, dk grn foliage *1.00* *.75*
291b A78 1k multi, brt grn foliage *.25* *.25*
292a A78 2k multicolored *.35* *.25*
294a A78 5k multi, emer fields *.60* *.75*
294b A78 5k multi, yel grn fields *.50* *.25*
297a A78 10k multicolored *.75* *.80*
298a A78 12k multicolored *12.00* *10.00*
300a A78 18k multicolored *12.00* *2.00*
301a A78 20k multicolored *13.00* *3.00*
303a A78 30k multicolored *12.00* *7.50*
305a A78 50k dk brn background *.75* *.90*
306a A78 1n multicolored *2.00* *4.00*
Nos. 291a-306a (12) *55.20* *30.45*

Nos. 300a, 305a and 306a have periods in the imprint. The liquid in the flasks is gray on No. 301, black on No. 301a, and blue on No. 301b.

1975-80 Wmk. 379

291c A78 1k multi, dk grn foliage *1.50* *2.00*
292b A78 2k multi ('75) *1.75* *.25*
293a A78 3k multi ('75) *.25* *.25*
294c A78 5k emerald fields ('76) *2.25* *.25*
295a A78 7k multi ('80) *3.50* *3.50*
296a A78 8k multi ('76) *1.75* *2.00*
297b A78 10k multi ('76) *2.00* *.25*
299a A78 15k multicolored *3.00*
300b A78 18k multi ('78) *4.25* *4.00*
301b A78 20k multi, pale pink table, door, windows ('79) *3.25* *3.50*
302a A78 25k multi, pur barges *3.25* *.25*
302b A78 25k multi, brn barges *3.25* *.25*
305b A78 50k dk brn background, grn imprint *3.50* *3.75*
307a A78 2n multicolored *5.50* *6.50*

OAU Headquarters — A79

Designs: 18k, OAU flag, vert. 30k, Stairs leading to OAU emblem, vert.

1973, May 25 Litho. *Perf. 14*

308 A79 5k blue & multi .25 .25
309 A79 18k olive grn & multi .35 *.50*
310 A79 30k lilac & multi .55 *.80*
Nos. 308-310 (3) 1.15 1.55

Org. for African Unity, 10th anniv.

WMO Emblem, Weather Vane A80

1973, Sept. 4 Litho. *Perf. 13*

311 A80 5k multicolored .30 .25
312 A80 30k multicolored 1.50 *2.25*

Cent. of intl. meteorological cooperation.

View of Ibadan University A81

Designs: 12k, Campus, crest and graph showing growth, vert. 18k, Campus, students and crest. 30k, Teaching hospital.

1973, Nov. 17 *Perf. 14*

313 A81 5k lt blue & multi .25 .25
314 A81 12k lilac & multi .25 .30
315 A81 18k orange & multi .45 .40
316 A81 30k blue, org & blk .65 *.80*
Nos. 313-316 (4) 1.60 1.75

University of Ibadan, 25th anniversary.

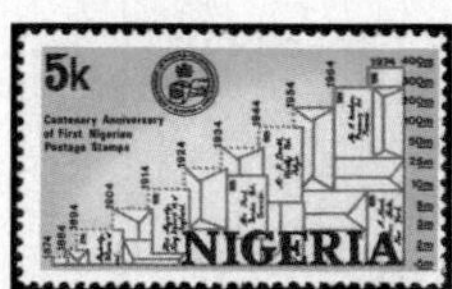

Growth of Mail, 1874-1974 A82

12k, Nigerian Post emblem & Northern Nigeria #18A. 18k, Postal emblem & Lagos #1. 30k, Map of Nigeria &means of transportation.

1974, June 10 Litho. *Perf. 14*

317 A82 5k green, black & org .25 .25
318 A82 12k green & multi .60 .60
319 A82 18k green, lilac & blk 1.00 1.00
320 A82 30k black & multi 1.75 1.75
Nos. 317-320 (4) 3.60 3.60

Centenary of first Nigerian postage stamps.

Globe and UPU Emblem A83

UPU cent.: 18k, World map and means of transportation. 30k, Letters.

1974, Oct. 9

321 A83 5k blue & multi .25 .25
322 A83 18k orange & multi 2.50 .60
323 A83 30k brown & multi 2.00 1.75
Nos. 321-323 (3) 4.75 2.60

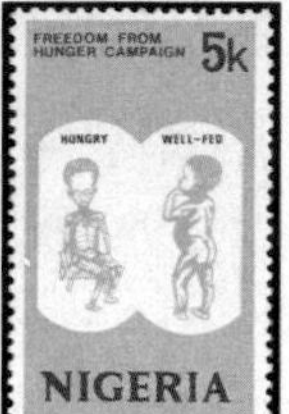

Hungry and Well-fed Children — A84

Designs: 12k, Chicken farm, horiz. 30k, Irrigation project.

1974, Nov. 25 Litho. *Perf. 14*

324 A84 5k orange, blk & grn .25 .25
325 A84 12k multicolored .35 .50
326 A84 30k multicolored .80 *1.50*
Nos. 324-326 (3) 1.40 2.25

Freedom from Hunger.

A85

Map of Nigeria with Telex Network, Teleprinter — A86

1975, July 3 Litho. *Perf. 14*

327 A85 5k multicolored .25 .25
328 A85 12k multicolored .25 .25
329 A86 18k multicolored .30 .30
330 A86 30k multicolored .55 .55
Nos. 327-330 (4) 1.35 1.35

Inauguration of Nigeria Telex Network.

Queen Amina of Zaria (1536-1566) — A87

1975, Aug. 18 Litho. *Perf. 14*

331 A87 5k multicolored .25 .25
332 A87 18k multicolored 1.10 .90
333 A87 30k multicolored 1.40 *1.75*
Nos. 331-333 (3) 2.75 2.90

International Women's Year.

Alexander Graham Bell — A88

Designs: 18k, Hands beating gong, modern telephone operator, horiz. 25k, Telephones, 1876, 1976.

1976, Mar. 10 Wmk. 379

334 A88 5k pink, black & ocher .25 .25
335 A88 18k deep lilac & multi .45 .55
336 A88 25k lt bl, vio bl & blk .90 1.10
Nos. 334-336 (3) 1.60 1.90

Centenary of first telephone call by Alexander Graham Bell, Mar. 10, 1876.

Children Going to School — A89

Designs: 5k, Child learning to write, horiz. 25k, Classroom.

1976, Sept. 20 Litho. *Perf. 14*

337 A89 5k multicolored .25 .25
338 A89 18k multicolored .55 .75
339 A89 25k multicolored .70 1.00
Nos. 337-339 (3) 1.50 2.00

Launching of universal primary education in 1976.

Traditional Musical Instruments A90

5k, Carved mask (festival emblem). 10k, Natl. Arts Theater, Lagos. 12k, Nigerian & African women's hair styles. 30k, Nigerian carvings.

1976-77 Wmk. 379

340 A90 5k black, gold & grn .25 .25
341 A90 10k multicolored .40 .40
342 A90 12k multicolored .75 .75
343 A90 18k brown, ocher & blk .90 .90
344 A90 30k multicolored 1.10 1.25
Nos. 340-344 (5) 3.40 3.55

2nd World Black and African Festival of Arts and Culture, Lagos, Jan. 15-Feb. 12, 1977.

Issued: 5k, 18k, 11/1; others 1/15/77.

Gen. Muhammed Broadcasting and Map of Nigeria — A91

Designs: 18k, Gen. Muhammed as Commander in Chief, vert. 30k, in battle dress, vert.

1977, Feb. 13 Litho. *Perf. 14*

345 A91 5k multicolored .25 .25
346 A91 18k multicolored .45 .45
347 A91 30k multicolored .80 .80
Nos. 345-347 (3) 1.50 1.50

Gen. Murtala Ramat Muhammed, Head of State and Commander in Chief, 1st death anniversary.

Scouts Clearing Street A92

5k, Senior and Junior Boy Scouts saluting, vert. 25k, Scouts working on farm. 30k, African Scout Jamboree emblem, map of Africa.

1977, Apr. 1 **Wmk. 379**

348 A92 5k multicolored .30 .30
349 A92 18k multicolored .70 .70
350 A92 25k multicolored .90 1.10
351 A92 30k multicolored 1.25 1.75
Nos. 348-351 (4) 3.15 3.85

First All-Africa Boy Scout Jamboree, Sherehills, Jos, Nigeria, Apr. 2-8, 1977.

Trade Fair Emblem A93

Emblem and: 5k, View of Fair grounds. 30k, Weaver and potter.

1977, Nov. 27 **Litho.** ***Perf. 13***

352 A93 5k multicolored .25 .25
353 A93 18k multicolored .35 .35
354 A93 30k multicolored .65 .65
Nos. 352-354 (3) 1.25 1.25

1st Lagos Intl. Trade Fair, Nov. 27-Dec. 11.

Nigeria's 13 Universities A94

12k, Map of West African highways and telecommunications network. 18k, Training of technicians, and cogwheel. 30k, World map and map of Argentina with Buenos Aires.

1978, Apr. 28 **Wmk. 379**

355 A94 5k multicolored .25 .25
356 A94 12k multicolored .25 .25
357 A94 18k multicolored .30 .30
358 A94 30k multicolored .65 .65
Nos. 355-358 (4) 1.45 1.45

Global Conf. on Technical Cooperation among Developing Countries, Buenos Aires.

Antenna and ITU Emblem A95

1978, May 17 **Litho.** ***Perf. 14***

359 A95 30k multicolored .75 .75

10th World Telecommunications Day.

Students on Cassava Plantation A96

"Operation Feed the Nation": 18k, Woman working in backyard vegetable garden. 30k, Plantain harvest, vert.

1978, July 7 **Litho.** ***Perf. 14***

360 A96 5k multicolored .25 .25
361 A96 18k multicolored .30 .30
362 A96 30k multicolored .50 .50
Nos. 360-362 (3) 1.05 1.05

Mother Holding Sick Child A97

Designs: 12k, Sick boy at health station. 18k, Vaccination of children. 30k, Syringe and WHO emblem, vert.

1978, Aug. 31 **Wmk. 379**

363 A97 5k multicolored .25 .25
364 A97 12k multicolored .30 .30
365 A97 18k multicolored .45 .45
366 A97 30k multicolored .75 .75
Nos. 363-366 (4) 1.75 1.75

Global eradication of smallpox.

Bronze Horseman from Benin — A98

Nigerian antiquities: 5k, Nok terracotta figure from Bwari. 12k, Bronze snail and animal from Igbo-Ukwu. 18k, Bronze statue of a king of Ife.

1978, Oct. 27 **Litho.** ***Perf. 14***

367 A98 5k multicolored .25 .25
368 A98 12k multicolored, horiz. .25 .25
369 A98 18k multicolored .30 .30
370 A98 30k multicolored .50 .50
Nos. 367-370 (4) 1.30 1.30

Anti-Apartheid Emblem — A99

1978, Dec. 10 ***Perf. 14***

371 A99 18k red, yellow & black .35 .35

Anti-Apartheid Year.

Wright Brothers, Flyer A A100

18k, Nigerian Air Force fighters in formation.

1978, Dec. 28

372 A100 5k multicolored .30 .30
373 A100 18k multicolored .60 .60

75th anniversary of powered flight.

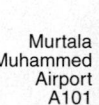

Murtala Muhammed Airport A101

1979, Mar. 15 **Litho.** ***Perf. 14***

374 A101 5k bright blue & black .50 .30

Inauguration of Murtala Muhammed Airport.

Young Stamp Collector A102

1979, Apr. 11

375 A102 5k multicolored .35 .25

Philatelic Week; Natl. Philatelic Service, 10th anniv.

Mother Nursing Child, IYC Emblem A103

18k, Children at study. 25k, Children at play, vert.

1979, June 28 **Wmk. 379** ***Perf. 14***

376 A103 5k multicolored .25 .25
377 A103 18k multicolored .30 .30
378 A103 25k multicolored .35 .35
Nos. 376-378 (3) .90 .90

International Year of the Child.

A104

Design: 10k, Preparation of audio-visual material. 30k, Adult education class.

1979, July 25 **Photo. & Engr.**

379 A104 10k multicolored .25 .25
380 A104 30k multicolored .40 .40

Intl. Bureau of Education, Geneva, 50th anniv.

A105

1979, Sept. 20 **Litho.** ***Perf. 13½x14***

381 A105 10k Necom house, Lagos .30 .30

Intl. Radio Consultative Committee (CCIR) of the ITU, 50th anniv.

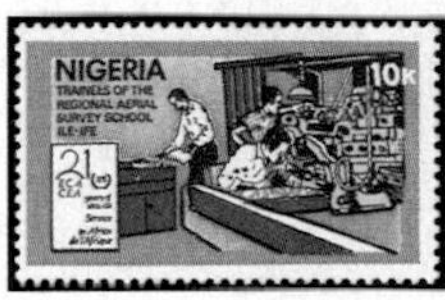

Trainees and Survey Equipment A106

1979, Dec. 12 **Photo.** ***Perf. 14***

382 A106 10k multicolored .30 .30

Economic Commission for Africa, 21st anniv.

Soccer Cup and Ball on Map of Nigeria A107

1980, Mar. 8

383 A107 10k shown .25 .25
384 A107 30k Player, vert. .60 .60

12th African Cup of Nations Soccer Championship, Lagos and Ibadan, Mar.

Swimming, Moscow '80 Emblem A108

Litho. & Engr.

1980, July 19 ***Perf. 14***

385 A108 10k Wrestling, vert. .25 .25
386 A108 20k Long jump, vert. .25 .25
387 A108 30k shown .30 .30
388 A108 45k Women's basketball, vert. .35 .35
Nos. 385-388 (4) 1.15 1.15

22nd Summer Olympic Games, Moscow, July 19-Aug. 3.

Men Holding OPEC Emblem A109

1980, Sept. 15 **Litho. & Engr.**

389 A109 10k shown .25 .25
390 A109 45k Anniversary emblem, vert. .75 .75

OPEC, 20th anniversary.

First Steam Locomotive in Nigeria A110

1980, Oct. 2 **Wmk. 379** ***Perf. 14***

391 A110 10k shown .50 .50
392 A110 20k Unloading freight car 1.40 1.40
393 A110 30k Freight train 2.10 2.10
Nos. 391-393 (3) 4.00 4.00

Nigerian Railway Corp., 75th anniv.

Technician Performing Quality Control Test A111

1980, Oct. 14

394 A111 10k Scale, ruler, vert. .25 .25
395 A111 30k shown .45 .45

World Standards Day.

Map of West Africa showing ECOWAS Members, Modes of Communication — A112

1980, Nov. 5 **Litho. & Engr.**

396 A112 10k shown .25 .25
396A A112 25k Transportation .30 .30
397 A112 30k Map, cow, cocoa .40 .40
398 A112 45k Map, industrial symbols .55 .55
Nos. 396-398 (4) 1.50 1.50

Woman with Cane Sweeping — A113

Wmk. 379

1981, June 25 **Litho.** ***Perf. 14***

399 A113 10k shown .25 .25
400 A113 30k Amputee photographer .50 .50

Intl. Year of the Disabled.

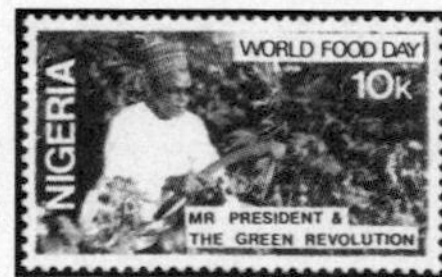

World Food Day
A114

1981, Oct. 16 **Litho. & Engr.**

401 A114 10k Pres. Shenu Shagari .25 .25
402 A114 25k Produce, vert. .30 .30
403 A114 30k Tomato crop, vert. .40 .40
404 A114 45k Pig farm .55 .55
Nos. 401-404 (4) 1.50 1.50

Anti-apartheid Year — A115

1981, Dec. 10 **Litho.**

405 A115 30k Soweto riot .40 .55
406 A115 45k Police hitting man, vert. .60 1.00

Scouting Year
A116

1982, Feb. 22 **Litho.** ***Perf. 14***

407 A116 30k Animal first aid .60 .65
408 A116 45k Baden-Powell, scouts 1.10 1.25

TB Bacillus Centenary
A117

1982, Mar. 24 **Litho.** ***Perf. 14***

409 A117 10k Inoculation .30 .30
410 A117 30k Research .50 .60
411 A117 45k Patient being x-rayed, vert. .80 1.40
Nos. 409-411 (3) 1.60 2.30

10th Anniv. of UN Conference on Human Environment — A118

10k, Keep your environment clean. 20k, Check air pollution. 30k, Preserve natural environment. 45k, Reafforestation concerns all.

1982, June 10 **Litho.**

412 A118 10k multicolored .25 .25
413 A118 20k multicolored .25 .35
414 A118 30k multicolored .35 .50
415 A118 45k multicolored .60 .80
Nos. 412-415 (4) 1.45 1.90

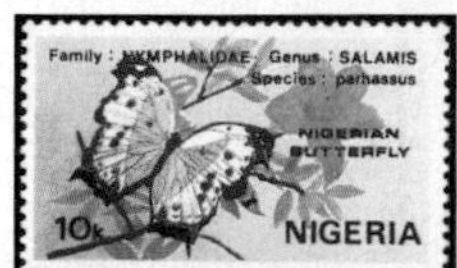

Salamis Parnassus
A119

1982, Sept. 15 **Litho.**

416 A119 10k shown .35 .25
417 A119 20k Papilio zalmoxis .65 .55
418 A119 30k Pachylophus beckeri 1.00 1.00
419 A119 45k Papilio hesperus 1.50 1.40
Nos. 416-419 (4) 3.50 3.20

25th Anniv. of Natl. Museum
A120

1982, Nov. 18 **Wmk. 379**

420 A120 10k Statuettes, vert. .25 .25
421 A120 20k Bronze leopard .35 .35
422 A120 30k Soapstone seated figure, vert. .40 .40
423 A120 45k Wooden helmet mask .60 .60
Nos. 420-423 (4) 1.60 1.60

Family Day — A121

1983, Mar. 8 **Litho.** ***Perf. 14***

424 A121 10k Extended family, house, horiz. .25 .25
425 A121 30k Family .50 .50

Commonwealth Day — A122

10k, Satellite view, horiz. 25k, Natl. Assembly buildings, horiz. 30k, Oil exploration. 45k, Runners.

1983, Mar. 14

426 A122 10k multicolored .25 .25
427 A122 25k multicolored .35 .35
428 A122 30k multicolored .45 .45
429 A122 45k multicolored .55 .55
Nos. 426-429 (4) 1.60 1.60

10th Anniv. of Natl. Youth Service Corps
A123

1983, May 25 **Litho.** ***Perf. 14***

430 A123 10k Construction .25 .25
431 A123 25k Climbing wall, vert. .45 .45
432 A123 30k Marching, vert. .65 .65
Nos. 430-432 (3) 1.35 1.35

World Communications Year — A124

10k, Mailman, vert. 25k, Newspaper stand. 30k, Traditional horn messenger. 45k, TV news broadcast.

Wmk. 379

1983, July 22 **Litho.** ***Perf. 14***

433 A124 10k multicolored .25 .25
434 A124 25k multicolored .35 .35
435 A124 30k multicolored .55 .55
436 A124 45k multicolored .45 .45
Nos. 433-436 (4) 1.60 1.60

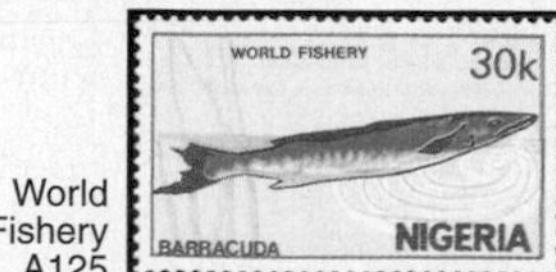

World Fishery
A125

1983, Sept. 22 **Litho.** **Wmk. 379**

437 A125 10k Pink shrimp .30 .30
438 A125 25k Long neck croaker .45 .45
439 A125 30k Barracuda .55 .55
440 A125 45k Fishing technique .65 .65
Nos. 437-440 (4) 1.95 1.95

Boys' Brigade, 75th Anniv.
A126

1983, Oct. 14 ***Perf. 14***

441 A126 10k Boys, emblem, vert. .30 .30
442 A126 30k Food production 1.50 1.50
443 A126 45k Skill training 2.25 2.25
Nos. 441-443 (3) 4.05 4.05

Fight Against Polio Campaign
A127

1984, Feb. 29 **Litho.** ***Perf. 14***

444 A127 10k Crippled boy, vert. .25 .25
445 A127 25k Vaccination .60 .60
446 A127 30k Healthy child, vert. .80 .80
Nos. 444-446 (3) 1.65 1.65

Hartebeests — A128

1984, May 25 **Wmk. 379** ***Perf. 14***

447 A128 10k Waterbuck, vert. .50 .30
448 A128 25k shown .45 .45
449 A128 30k Buffalo .65 .65
450 A128 45k African golden monkey, vert. 1.00 1.00
Nos. 447-450 (4) 2.60 2.40

Central Bank of Nigeria, 25th Anniv.
A129

1984, July 2 **Wmk. 379**

451 A129 10k £1 note, 1968 .25 .25
452 A129 25k Bank .55 .55
453 A129 30k £5 note, 1959 .70 .70
Nos. 451-453 (3) 1.50 1.50

1984 Summer Olympics, Los Angeles — A130

Wmk. 379

1984, Aug. 9 **Litho.** ***Perf. 14***

454 A130 10k Boxing .25 .25
455 A130 25k Discus .40 .40
456 A130 30k Weight lifting .50 .50
457 A130 45k Bicycling .75 .75
Nos. 454-457 (4) 1.90 1.90

African Development Bank, 20th Anniv. — A131

10k, Irrigation project, Lesotho. 25k, Bomi Hills roadway, Liberia. 30k, Education development, Seychelles. 45k, Coal mining & transportation, Niger. #459-461 horiz.

1984, Sept. 10

458 A131 10k multicolored .30 .30
459 A131 25k multicolored .55 .55
460 A131 30k multicolored .75 .75
461 A131 45k multicolored 1.20 1.20
Nos. 458-461 (4) 2.80 2.80

A132

A132a

A132b

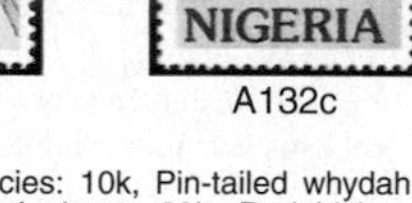

A132c

Rare bird species: 10k, Pin-tailed whydah. 25k, Spur-winged plover. 30k, Red bishop. 45k, Francolin.

1984, Oct. 24

462 A132 10k multicolored .75 .75
463 A132a 25k multicolored 1.25 1.25
464 A132b 30k multicolored 1.75 1.75
465 A132c 45k multicolored 2.75 2.75
Nos. 462-465 (4) 6.50 6.50

Intl. Civil Aviation Organization, 40th Anniv. — A132d

1984, Dec. 7 **Litho.** ***Perf. 14***

465A A132d 10k shown .50 .50
465B A132d 45k Jet circling Earth 2.00 2.00

Fight Against Indiscipline
A133

20k, Encourage punctuality. 50k, Discourage bribery.

1985, Feb. 27

466 A133 20k multicolored .30 .30
467 A133 50k multicolored .90 .90

Intl. Youth Year — A134

1985, June 5

468 A134 20k Sports, horiz. .25 .25
469 A134 50k Nationalism .60 .60
470 A134 55k Service organizations .70 .70
Nos. 468-470 (3) 1.55 1.55

OPEC, 25th Anniv. — A135

1985, Sept. 15

471 A135 20k shown .90 .90
472 A135 50k World map, horiz. 1.75 1.75

Natl. Independence, 25th Anniv. — A136

1985, Sept. 25

473 A136 20k Oil refinery .25 .25
474 A136 50k Map of states .60 .60
475 A136 55k Monument .65 .65
476 A136 60k Eleme Oil Refinery .75 .75
a. Souvenir sheet of 4, #473-476 5.50 *5.50*
Nos. 473-476 (4) 2.25 2.25

World Tourism Day — A137

1985, Sept. 27

477 A137 20k Waterfalls .25 .25
478 A137 50k Crafts, horiz. .55 .55
479 A137 55k Carved calabashes, flag .60 .60
480 A137 60k Leather goods, rug .65 .65
Nos. 477-480 (4) 2.05 2.05

UN, 40th Anniv. — A138

1985, Oct. 7

481 A138 20k Emblem, map, flag .30 .30
482 A138 50k UN building, horiz. .80 .80
483 A138 55k Emblem, horiz. .90 .90
Nos. 481-483 (3) 2.00 2.00

Admission of Nigeria to UN, 25th anniv.

African Reptiles A139

1986, Apr. 15 Wmk. 379 *Perf. 14*

484 A139 10k Python .30 .30
485 A139 20k Crocodile .50 .50
486 A139 25k Gopher tortoise .60 .60
487 A139 30k Chameleon .70 .70
Nos. 484-487 (4) 2.10 2.10

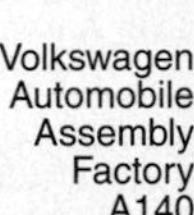
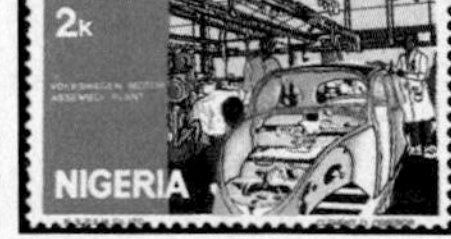

Volkswagen Automobile Assembly Factory A140

Designs: 1k, Social worker with children, vert. 5k, Modern housing development. 10k, Modern method of harvesting coconuts, vert. 15k, Port activities. 20k, Tecoma stans, flower, vert. 25k, Medical care. 30k, Birom folk dancers. 35k, Telephone operators. 40k, Nkpokiti dancers, vert. 45k, Hibiscus. 50k, Modern p.o. 1n, Stone quarry. 2n, Technical education.

1986, June 16 Wmk. 379 *Perf. 14*

488 A140 1k multicolored .40 .40
489 A140 2k multicolored .40 .40
490 A140 5k multicolored .25 .25
491 A140 10k multicolored .25 .25
492 A140 15k multicolored .90 .25
493 A140 20k multicolored .25 .25
494 A140 25k multicolored .30 .45
494A A140 30k multicolored .50 .50
495 A140 35k multicolored .30 .25
496 A140 40k multicolored .30 .25
497 A140 45k multicolored .30 .25
498 A140 50k multicolored .90 .60
499 A140 1n multicolored .40 .40
500 A140 2n multicolored .40 .40
Nos. 488-500 (14) 5.85 4.90

Use of some denominations began as early as 1984. Date of issue of the 30k is not definite.

See Nos. 560A-560D, 615C.

Intl. Peace Year A141

1986, June 20 Litho. *Perf. 14*

501 A141 10k Emblem .30 .30
502 A141 20k Hands touching globe .50 .50

Insects A142

1986, July 14

503 A142 10k Goliath beetle .35 .35
504 A142 20k Wasp .80 .80
505 A142 25k Cricket 1.00 1.00
506 A142 30k Carpet beetle 1.25 1.25
a. Souvenir sheet of 4, #503-506 5.75 5.75

Nos. 503-506 and 506a exist imperf. Values: 503-506, set $6; 506a, $12.

Nos. 503-506 (4) 3.40 3.40

UNICEF, 40th Anniv. — A143

1986, Nov. 11

507 A143 10k Oral rehydration .25 .25
508 A143 20k Immunization .35 .35
509 A143 25k Breast-feeding .70 .70
510 A143 30k Mother playing with child .80 .80
Nos. 507-510 (4) 2.10 2.10

UN Child Survival Campaign.

Institute of Intl. Affairs, 25th Anniv. — A144

1986, Dec. 13

511 A144 20k Intl. understanding, horiz. .70 .70
512 A144 30k shown .90 .90

Nos. 511-512 exist imperf. Value, set $2.50.

Seashells A145

1987, Mar. 31

513 A145 10k Freshwater clam 1.25 1.25
514 A145 20k Periwinkle 1.50 1.50
515 A145 25k Bloddy cockle 1.75 1.75
516 A145 30k Mangrove oyster 2.00 2.00
Nos. 513-516 (4) 6.50 6.50

A146

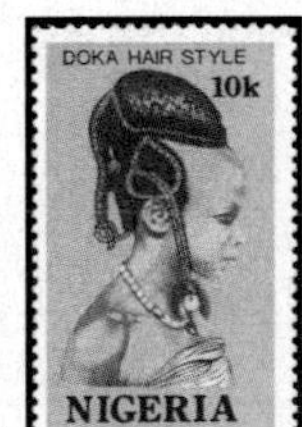

A147

10k, Blue pea but. 20k, Hibiscus. 25k, Acanthus montanus. 30k, Combretum racemosum.

1987, May 28

517 A146 10k multicolored .25 .25
518 A146 20k multicolored .25 .25
519 A147 25k multicolored .25 .25
520 A147 30k multicolored .25 .25
Nos. 517-520 (4) 1.00 1.00

Hair Styles — A148

1987, Sept. 15 Wmk. 379 *Perf. 14*

521 A148 10k Doka .30 .30
522 A148 20k Eting .30 .30
523 A148 25k Agogo .30 .30
524 A148 30k Goto .30 .30
Nos. 521-524 (4) 1.20 1.20

Intl. Year of Shelter for the Homeless — A149

1987, Dec. 10 Litho.

525 A149 20k Homeless family .25 .25
526 A149 30k Moving to new home .25 .25

A150

1988, Feb. 17 Litho. *Perf. 14*

527 A150 20k Help the Needy .70 .50
528 A150 30k Care for the sick 1.10 .90

Intl. Red Cross and Red Crescent Organizations, 125th annivs.

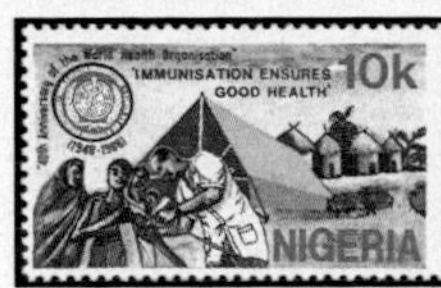

A151

1988, Apr. 7 Wmk. 379 *Perf. 14*

529 A151 10k Immunization .30 .25
530 A151 20k Map, globe, emblem .60 .60
531 A151 30k Mobile hospital .70 .70
Nos. 529-531 (3) 1.60 1.55

WHO, 40th anniv.

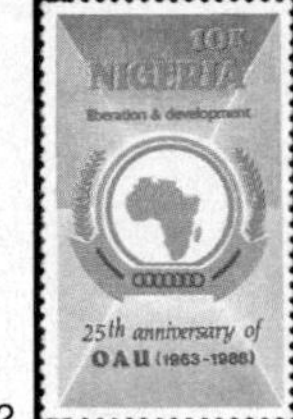

A152

1988, May 25

532 A152 10k shown .25 .25
533 A152 20k Emblem, map, 4 men .25 .25

Organization of African Unity, 25th anniv.

Shrimp A153

1988, June 2

534 A153 10k Pink shrimp .30 .30
535 A153 20k Tiger shrimp .50 .50
536 A153 25k Deepwater roseshrimp .60 .60
537 A153 30k Estuarine prawn .70 .70
a. Miniature sheet of 4, #534-537 2.50 2.50
Nos. 534-537 (4) 2.10 2.10

1988 Summer Olympics, Seoul A154

1988, Sept. 6 Wmk. 379 *Perf. 14*

538 A154 10k Weight lifting .30 .30
539 A154 20k Boxing .30 .30
540 A154 30k Running, vert. .30 .30
Nos. 538-540 (3) .90 .90

A155

A156

Nigerian Security Printing and Minting Co., Ltd., 25th Anniv. A157

1988, Oct. 28

541 A155 10k Bank note production .35 .35
542 A155 20k Coin production .35 .35
543 A156 25k Products .35 .35
544 A157 30k Anniv. emblem .35 .35
Nos. 541-544 (4) 1.40 1.40

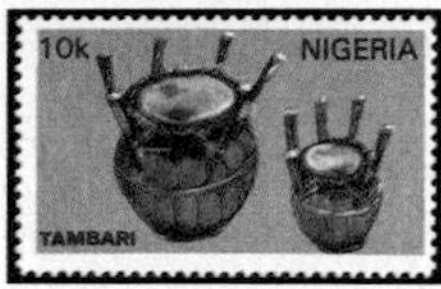

Traditional Musical Instruments A158

Wmk. 379

1989, June 29 Litho. *Perf. 14*

545 A158 10k Tambari .40 .40
546 A158 20k Kundung .40 .40
547 A158 25k Ibid .40 .40
548 A158 30k Dundun .40 .40
Nos. 545-548 (4) 1.60 1.60

African Development Bank, 25th Anniv. — A159

10k, Reservoir, Mali. 20k, Irrigation project, Gambia. 25k, Bank headquarters.

1989, Sept. 10

549 A159 10k multicolored .25 .25
550 A159 20k multicolored .25 .25
551 A159 25k multicolored .25 .25
552 A159 30k shown .25 .25
Nos. 549-552 (4) 1.00 1.00

Nos. 549-551 horiz.

Nigerian Girl Guides Assoc., 70th Anniv. — A160

1989, Sept. 16

553 A160 10k Campfire, horiz. .50 .50
554 A160 20k shown .50 .50

A161

Traditional costumes.

1989, Oct. 26

555 A161 10k Etubom .40 .40
556 A161 20k Fulfulde .40 .40
557 A161 25k Aso-ofi .40 .40
558 A161 30k Fuska Kura .40 .40
Nos. 555-558 (4) 1.60 1.60

A162

1990, Jan. 18

559 A162 10k shown .35 .35
560 A162 20k Map, delivery .40 .40

Pan-African Postal Union, 10th anniv.

National Theater — A162a

20n, Ancient wall, Kano. 50n, Rock bridge. 100n, Ekpe masquerade, vert.

1990, May 23 Litho. *Perf. 14*

560A A162a 20n multicolored *13.00* 2.00
560B A162a 50n multicolored *9.00* 4.00
560C A162a 100n multicolored *7.00* 7.00
560D A162a 500n multicolored *37.50* 25.00
e. Perf. 13, unwatermarked (NSPMPLC inscription at LL) — —
Nos. 560A-560D (4) *66.50* 38.00

Postal counterfeits are known of No. 560B. Issued: No. 560De, 2010.

Pottery A163

1990, May 24

561 A163 10k Oil lamp .25 .25
562 A163 20k Water pot .25 .25
563 A163 25k Musical pots .25 .25
564 A163 30k Water jug .25 .25
a. Sheet of 4, #561-564 with yellow frames, + 4 labels 1.75 1.75
Nos. 561-564 (4) 1.00 1.00

Inscriptions, including country name, denomination and descriptions vary widely in size and style.

Intl. Literacy Year A164

1990, Aug. 8

565 A164 20k multicolored .25 .25
566 A164 30k multicolored .25 .25

A165

A166

1990, Sept. 14

567 A165 10k shown .25 .25
568 A166 20k Flags .25 .25
569 A165 25k Globe .25 .25
570 A166 30k shown .25 .25
Nos. 567-570 (4) 1.00 1.00

Organization of Petroleum Exporting Countries (OPEC), 30th anniv.

A167

1990, Nov. 8

571 A167 20k Grey parrot .30 .30
572 A167 30k Roan antelope .40 .40
573 A167 1.50n Grey-necked rock fowl 1.25 1.25
574 A167 2.50n Mountain gorilla 1.75 1.75
a. Souvenir sheet of 4, #571-574 4.25 4.25
Nos. 571-574 (4) 3.70 3.70

Inscriptions vary widely in size and style.

A168

A169

1991, Mar. 20

575 A168 10k Eradication .25 .25
576 A169 20k shown .25 .25
577 A168 30k Prevention .25 .25
Nos. 575-577 (3) .75 .75

Natl. Guineaworm Eradication Day.

A170

1991, May 26

578 A170 20k Progress .25 .25
579 A170 30k Unity .25 .25
580 A170 50k Freedom .25 .25
Nos. 578-580 (3) .75 .75

OAU Heads of State Meeting, Abiya.

ECOWAS Summit, Abuja A171

1991, July 4

581 A171 20k Flags .40 .40
582 A171 50k Map of West Africa .40 .40

Economic Community of West African States.

Fish A172

1991, July 10

583 A172 10k Electric catfish .30 .30
584 A172 20k Niger perch .45 .45
585 A172 30k Talapia .50 .50
586 A172 50k African catfish .60 .60
a. Souvenir sheet of 4, #583-586 2.75 2.75
Nos. 583-586 (4) 1.85 1.85

Telecom '91 — A173

1991, Oct. 7

587 A173 20k shown .25 .25
588 A173 50k multi, vert. .40 .40

Sixth World Forum and Exposition on Telecommunications, Geneva, Switzerland.

1992 Summer Olympics, Barcelona A174

1992, Jan. 24 Unwmk.

589 A174 50k Boxing .30 .30
590 A174 1n Running .30 .30
591 A174 1.50n Table tennis .40 .40
592 A174 2n Taekwondo .50 .50
a. Souvenir sheet of 4, #589-592, wmk. 379 3.50 3.50
Nos. 589-592 (4) 1.50 1.50

1992 Summer Olympics, Barcelona — A175

Wmk. 379

1992, Apr. 3 Litho. *Perf. 14*

593 A175 1.50n multicolored .55 .55

World Health Day — A176

Designs: 50k, Heart and blood pressure gauge. 1n, Globe and blood pressure guage. 1.50n, Heart in rib cage. 2n, Cross-section of heart.

1992, Apr. 7 Unwmk.

594 A176 50k multicolored .25 .25
595 A176 1n multicolored .25 .25
596 A176 1.50n multicolored .30 .30
597 A176 2n multicolored .40 .40
a. Souvenir sheet of 4, #594-597 1.50 1.50
Nos. 594-597 (4) 1.20 1.20

Intl. Institute of Tropical Agriculture, 25th Anniv. A177

Designs: 50k, Plantain, vert. 1n, Food products. 1.50n, Harvesting cassava tubers, vert. 2n, Yam barn, vert.

1992, July 17

598	A177	50k	multicolored	.25	.25
599	A177	1n	multicolored	.25	.25
600	A177	1.50n	grn, blk & brown	.25	.25
601	A177	2n	multicolored	.30	.30
a.			Souvenir sheet of 4, #598-601	2.40	2.40
			Nos. 598-601 (4)	1.05	1.05

Olymphilex '92 — A178

1.50n, Stamp under magnifying glass.

Wmk. 379

1992, July 3 Litho. *Perf. 14*

602	A178	50k	multicolored	.25	.25
603	A178	1.50n	multicolored	.45	.45
a.			Souvenir sheet of 2, #602-603 + 4 labels, unwmkd.	2.25	2.25

Maryam Babangida, Natl. Center for Women's Development
A179 A180

A180a

Designs: 50k, Emblem of Better Life Program. 1n, Women harvesting corn. 1.50n, Natl. Center, horiz. 2n, Woman using loom.

1992, Oct. 16

604	A179	50k	multicolored	.25	.25
605	A180	1n	multicolored	.25	.25
606	A180	1.50n	multicolored	.30	.30
607	A180a	2n	multicolored	.35	.35
			Nos. 604-607 (4)	1.15	1.15

Traditional Dances — A181

Unwmk.

1992, Dec. 15 Litho. *Perf. 14*

608	A181	50k	Sabada	.25	.25
609	A181	1n	Sato	.25	.25
610	A181	1.50n	Asian Ubo Ikpa	.30	.30
611	A181	2n	Dundun	.35	.35
a.			Souvenir sheet of 4, #608-611	2.25	2.25
			Nos. 608-611 (4)	1.15	1.15

Intl. Conference on Nutrition, Rome A182

1992, Dec. 1 Litho. *Perf. 14*

612	A182	50k	Vegetables	.25	.25
613	A182	1n	Child eating	.25	.25
614	A182	1.50n	Fruits, vert.	.30	.30
615	A182	2n	Vegetables, diff.	.35	.35
a.			Souvenir sheet of 4, #611-615	2.75	2.75
			Nos. 612-615 (4)	1.15	1.15

African Elephant — A182a

Stanley Crane — A182b

Lekki Beach — A182c

Roan Antelopes — A182d

Lion — A182e

1992-93 Litho. *Perf. 14*

615A	A182a	1.50n	multi	4.25	1.50
615B	A182b	5n	multi	5.00	1.00
615C	A182c	10n	multi	2.50	1.00
615D	A182d	20n	multi	9.00	4.00
615E	A182e	30n	multi	12.00	6.00
			Nos. 615A-615E (5)	32.75	13.50

World Environment Day — A183

Designs: 1n, Clean environment ensures good health. 1.50n, Check water polution. 5n, Preserve your environment. 10n, Environment and nature.

1993, June 4 Litho. *Perf. 14*

616	A183	1n	multicolored	.25	.25
617	A183	1.50n	multicolored	.30	.30
618	A183	5n	multicolored	.80	.80
619	A183	10n	multicolored	1.00	1.00
			Nos. 616-619 (4)	2.35	2.35

Natl. Commission for Museums and Monuments, 50th Anniv. — A184

1993, July 28 Litho. *Perf. 14*

620	A184	1n	Oni figure, vert.	.25	.25
621	A184	1.50n	Queen Mother head, vert.	.30	.30
622	A184	5n	Pendant	.45	.45
623	A184	10n	Nok head, vert.	.75	.75
			Nos. 620-623 (4)	1.75	1.75

Orchids — A185

1993, Oct. 28 Litho. *Perf. 14*

624	A185	1n	Bulbophyllum distans	.30	.30
625	A185	1.50n	Eulophia cristata	.35	.35
626	A185	5n	Eulophia horsfalli	.60	.60
627	A185	10n	Eulophia quartiniana	1.25	1.25
a.			Souv. sheet of 4, #624-627	*3.50*	*3.50*
			Nos. 624-627 (4)	2.50	2.50

No. 627a exists with perforations through either the bottom or top margins.

Intl. Year of the Family A186

1.50n, Child abuse, classroom scene. 10n, Fending for the family, market scene.

1994, Mar. 30 Litho. *Perf. 14*

628	A186	1.50n	multicolored	.50	.50
629	A186	10n	multicolored	1.10	1.10

Nigerian Philatelic Service, 25th Anniv. A187

1n, #224. 1.50n, Bureau building. 5n, Map made of stamps. 10n, Counter staff, customers.

1994, Apr. 11

630	A187	1n	multicolored	.25	.25
631	A187	1.50n	multicolored	.30	.30
632	A187	5n	multicolored	.50	.50
633	A187	10n	multicolored	1.20	1.20
			Nos. 630-633 (4)	2.25	2.25

First Nigerian Postage Stamps, 120th Anniv. A188

Designs: 1n, "I love stamps." 1.50n, "I collect stamps." 5n, Methods of transporting mail. 10n, Lagos type A1 on airmail envelope.

1994, June 10 Litho. *Perf. 14*

634	A188	1n	multicolored	.25	.25
635	A188	1.50n	multicolored	.30	.30
636	A188	5n	multicolored	.50	.50
637	A188	10n	multicolored	1.20	1.20
			Nos. 634-637 (4)	2.25	2.25

PHILAKOREA '94 — A189

1994, Aug. 16 Litho. *Perf. 14*

638	A189	30n	multicolored	3.00	3.00
a.			Souvenir sheet of 1, #638	5.50	5.50

Crabs A190

1994, Aug. 12 Litho. *Perf. 14*

639	A190	1n	Geryon quinquedens	.25	.25
640	A190	1.50n	Spider crab	.35	.35
641	A190	5n	Red spider	.75	.75
642	A190	10n	Geryon maritae	1.50	1.50
			Nos. 639-642 (4)	2.85	2.85

African Development Bank, 30th Anniv. — A191

1994, Sept. 16

643	A191	1.50n	Water treatment plant	.25	.25
644	A191	30n	Emblem, field	2.75	2.75

NIPOST/NITEL, 10th Anniv. — A192

Designs: 1n, Putting letter into mailbox, vert. 1.50n, Airmail letter. 5n, NIPOST, NITEL logos. 10n, Telephones, vert.

1995, Jan. 1 Litho. *Perf. 14*

645	A192	1n	multicolored	.25	.25
646	A192	1.50n	multicolored	.25	.25
647	A192	5n	multicolored	.40	.40
648	A192	10n	multicolored	.80	.80
			Nos. 645-648 (4)	1.70	1.70

Family Support Program A194

Designs: 1n, Feed the family. 1.50n, Monitoring child education. 5n, Caring for the family. 10n, Support agriculture.

1995, July 20 Litho. *Perf. 14*

653	A194	1n	multicolored	.25	.25
654	A194	1.50n	multicolored	.25	.25
655	A194	5n	multicolored	.40	.40
656	A194	10n	multicolored	.80	.80
			Nos. 653-656 (4)	1.70	1.70

First Telephone in Nigeria, Cent. — A195

Designs: 1.50n, Dial telephone, c. 1919. 10n, Crank telephone, c. 1885.

1995, Oct. 9 Litho. *Perf. 14*

657	A195	1.50n	multicolored	.30	.30
658	A195	10n	multicolored	1.10	1.10

FAO, 50th Anniv. A196

1995, Oct. 16

659	A196	1.50n	shown	.25	.25
660	A196	30n	Fishing boats	3.00	3.00

UN, 50th Anniv. A197

Designs: 1n, Emblem of justice, vert. 1.50n, Against illegal dumping of toxic chemicals. 5n, Tourism. 10n, Peace-keeping soldiers.

1995, Oct. 24

661	A197	1n multicolored	.25	.25
662	A197	1.50n multicolored	.25	.25
663	A197	5n multicolored	.40	.40
664	A197	10n multicolored	.80	.80
		Nos. 661-664 (4)	1.70	1.70

Niger Dock, 10th Anniv. A198

5n, Overall view of dock. 10n, Boat being lifted. 20n, Boats in dock area. 30n, Boat on water.

1996, Apr. 29 **Litho.** ***Perf. 14***

665	A198	5n multicolored	.40	.40
666	A198	10n multicolored	1.00	1.00
667	A198	20n multicolored	1.75	1.75
668	A198	30n multicolored	2.50	2.50
		Nos. 665-668 (4)	5.65	5.65

Economic Community of West African States (ECOWAS), 21st Anniv. A199

5n, Developing agriculture and scientific research. 30n, Free movement of people.

1996, May 5 **Litho.** ***Perf. 14***

669	A199	5n multicolored	.50	.50
670	A199	30n multicolored	2.50	2.50

A200

1996, June 28

671	A200	5n Judo	.40	.40
672	A200	10n Tennis	1.00	1.00
673	A200	20n Relay race	1.75	1.75
674	A200	30n Soccer	2.50	2.50
		Nos. 671-674 (4)	5.65	5.65

1996 Summer Olympic Games, Atlanta.

Natl. Flag, Logo — A201

1996, Oct. 10 **Litho.** ***Perf. 14***

675	A201	30n multicolored	3.00	3.00

Istanbul '96.

Mushrooms A202

Designs: 5n, Volvariella esculenta. 10n, Lentinus subnudus. 20n, Tricholoma lobayensis. 30n, Pleurotus tuber-regium.

1996, Nov. 19

676	A202	5n multicolored	.50	.50
677	A202	10n multicolored	.90	.90
678	A202	20n multicolored	2.10	2.10
679	A202	30n multicolored	3.00	3.00
		Nos. 676-679 (4)	6.50	6.50

UNICEF, 50th Anniv. A203

Designs: 5n, "Child's right to play," vert. 30n, "Educate the girl child."

1996, Dec. 10

680	A203	5n multicolored	.50	.50
681	A203	30n multicolored	2.50	2.50

Mass Literacy Commission, 5th Anniv. — A204

Designs: 5n, "Teach one to teach one." 30n, "Education through co-operation."

1996, Dec. 30

682	A204	5n grn, blk & dk grn	.45	.45
683	A204	30n grn, blk & dk grn	2.40	2.40

1998 World Cup Soccer Championships, France — A205

1998, June 10 **Litho.** ***Perf. 13***

684	A205	5n shown	.45	.45
685	A205	10n Player, vert.	.90	.90
686	A205	20n Player, diff., vert.	1.60	1.60
687	A205	30n Two players	2.50	2.50
		Nos. 684-687 (4)	5.45	5.45

ECOMOG (Military Co-operation Organization), 8th Anniv. — A206

Designs: 5n, Silhouette of ship. 30n, Flag colors of Gambia, Ghana, Guinea, Mali, Nigeria, Senegal, Sierra Leone. 50n, Flag colors of Gambia, Ghana, Nigeria, Guinea, Mali, Senegal, Sierra Leone, Niger, Ivory Coast, Benin, Burkina Faso.

1998, Nov. 30 **Litho.** ***Perf. 14***

688	A206	5n multicolored	.40	.40
689	A206	30n multicolored	2.40	2.40
690	A206	50n multicolored	4.00	4.00
		Nos. 688-690 (3)	6.80	6.80

Nigerian Railroad, Cent. A207

5n, Caged locomotive. 10n, Iddo Terminal. 20n, Locomotive. 30n, Passenger tram.

1999, Jan. 20 ***Perf. 13***

691	A207	5n multicolored	.40	.40
692	A207	10n multicolored	.85	.85
693	A207	20n multicolored	1.75	1.75
694	A207	30n multicolored	2.50	2.50
		Nos. 691-694 (4)	5.50	5.50

Rain Forest — A207a

1999, May 10 **Litho.** ***Perf. 13***

694A	A207a	10n multi	—	—

University of Ibadan, 50th Anniv. A208

1998, Nov. 17 **Litho.** ***Perf. 14***

695	A208	5n University building	.50	.50
696	A208	30n "50," Crest	2.25	2.25

Federal Environmental Protection Agency, 10th Anniv. — A209

5n, Water resources. 10n, Natural resources. 20n, Endangered species. 30n, One earth, one family.

1999, June 8 **Litho.** ***Perf. 13***

697	A209	5n multicolored	.50	.50
698	A209	10n multicolored	.75	.75
699	A209	20n multicolored	1.75	1.75
700	A209	30n multicolored	2.50	2.50
		Nos. 697-700 (4)	5.50	5.50

NICON Insurance Corp., 30th Anniv. A210

Emblem and: 5n, Airplane, ship, oil refinery, vert. 30n, Building.

Perf. 12¾x13, 13x12¾

1999, Aug. 31 **Litho.**

701	A210	5n multi	.40	.40
702	A210	30n multi	2.00	2.00

Millennium A211

Designs: 10n, Map of Northern and Southern Protectorates, 1900-14. 20n, Map of Nigeria, 1914. 30n, Coat of arms. 40n, Map of 36 states, 1996.

2000 **Litho.** ***Perf. 13***

703-706	A211	Set of 4	2.10	2.10

World Meteorological Organization, 50th Anniv. — A212

Designs: 10n, Sunshine hour recorder, vert. 30n, Meteorological station.

2000 ***Perf. 12¾x13, 13x12¾***

707-708	A212	Set of 2	1.00	1.00

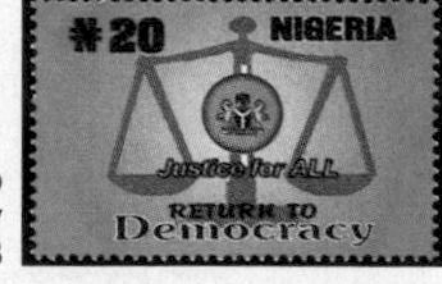

Return to Democracy A213

Designs: 10n, Flag, "Freedom of the press," vert. 20n, Scales of justice. 30n, Legislative mace, vert. 40n, Pres. Olusegun Obasanjo, flag, vert.

2000 ***Perf. 14¾***

709-712	A213	Set of 4	3.25	3.25
712a		Souvenir sheet, #709-712	5.00	5.00

2000 Summer Olympics, Sydney A214

Designs: 10n, Boxing. 20n, Weight lifting. 30n, Soccer. 40n, Soccer, diff.

2000, Sept. 7 **Litho.** ***Perf. 13x12¾***

713-716	A214	Set of 4	3.25	3.25
716a		Souvenir sheet, #713-716 + 4 labels	5.00	5.00

A215

Independence, 40th anniv.: 10n, Obafemi Awolowo (1909-87), promoter of federal constitution. 20n, Prime Minister Abubakar Tafawa Balewa (1912-66). 30n, Pres. Nnamdi Azikiwe (1904-96). 40n, Liquified gas refinery, horiz. 50n, Ship carrying exports, horiz.

Perf. 12¾x13, 13x12¾

2000, Sept. 27 **Litho.**

717-721	A215	Set of 5	3.75	3.75

A216

Fruit: 20n, Hug plum. 30n, White star apple. 40n, African breadfruit. 50n, Akee apple.

2001, Jan. 16 ***Perf. 14***

722-725	A216	Set of 4	3.00	3.00

Nigeria Daily Times Newspaper, 75th Anniv. A217

Designs: 20n, Corporate headquarters, Lagos. 30n, First issue. 40n, Daily Times complex, Lagos. 50n, Masthead.

2001, June 1 **Litho.** ***Perf. 13x12¾***

726-729	A217	Set of 4	3.25	3.25

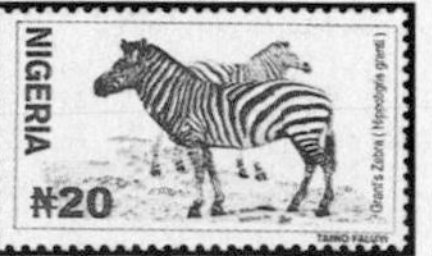

Fauna A218

Designs: 10n, Broad-tailed paradise whydahs, vert. 15n, Fire-bellied woodpeckers, vert. 20n, Grant's zebras. 25n, Aardvark. 30n,

Preuss's guenon, vert. 40n, Giant ground pangolin. 50n, Bonobo. 100n, Red-eared guenon, vert.

2001, June 15 ***Perf. 14***

730 A218 10n multi .40 .25
731 A218 15n multi .50 .25
732 A218 20n multi .60 .35
a. Thinner inscriptions, perf. 13x13¼ ('05) .30 .30
733 A218 25n multi .70 .45
734 A218 30n multi .80 .60
735 A218 40n multi .90 .80
736 A218 50n multi 1.00 .90
a. Thinner inscriptions, perf. 13x13¼ ('05) .80 .80
737 A218 100n multi 2.50 2.00
a. Perf. 13¼x13 — —
Nos. 730-737 (8) 7.40 5.60

Inscriptions vary widely in size and style. Issued: Nos. 732a, 736a, 737a, 2005.

Year of Dialogue Among Civilizations — A219

2001, Oct. 9 **Litho.** ***Perf. 13***

738 A219 20n multi .90 .90

New Millennium A220

Designs: 20n, Peace. 30n, Age of globalization. 40n, Reconciliation. 50n, Love.

2002, Feb. 13 **Litho.** ***Perf. 13x12¾***

739-742 A220 Set of 4 3.00 3.00

Crops A221

Designs: 20n, Kola nuts. 30n, Oil palm. 40n, Cassava. 50n, Corn, vert.

2002, May 10 ***Perf. 13x12¾, 12¾x13***

743-746 A221 Set of 4 2.60 2.60

2002 World Cup Soccer Championships, Japan and Korea — A222

Emblem and: 20n, Nigerian player and opponent, vert. 30n, Globe and soccer balls, vert. 40n, Player's legs and ball. 50n, World Cup trophy, vert.

Perf. 12¾x13, 13x12¾

2002, June 14

747-750 A222 Set of 4 2.75 2.75

World AIDS Day — A223

Designs: 20n, Nurse, patient, flowers. 50n, AIDS counseling.

2003, May 3 **Litho.** ***Perf. 13x12¾***

751-752 A223 Set of 2 1.70 1.70
752a Souvenir sheet, #751-752 3.50 3.50

A224

Universal basic education: 20n, Students. 50n, Student writing, horiz.

Perf. 12¾x13, 13x12¾

2003, Sept. 22 **Litho.**

753-754 A224 Set of 2 2.00 2.00

A225

Eighth All Africa Games: 20n, Runner. 30n, High jump, horiz. 40n, Taekwondo, horiz. 50n, Long jump

2003, Oct. 4

755-758 A225 Set of 4 2.50 2.50
758a Souvenir sheet, #755-758 + 4 labels 3.00 3.00

Worldwide Fund for Nature (WWF) A226

Side-striped jackal: 20n, Adult and pups. 40n, Adult in grass. 80n, Two adults. 100n, Adult in grass, diff.

2003, Dec. 12 ***Perf. 13x12¾***

759-762 A226 Set of 4 4.25 3.75
762a Block of 4, #759-762 4.75 4.75

Commonwealth Heads of Government Meeting, Abuja — A227

Emblem and: 20n, Map of Nigeria. 50n, Flag of Nigeria, vert.

Perf. 13x12¾, 12¾x13

2003, Dec. 7 **Litho.**

763-764 A227 Set of 2 2.00 2.00

2004 Summer Olympics, Athens — A228

Designs: 50n, Runners. 120n, Basketball.

2004, Aug. 18 **Litho.** ***Perf. 12¾x13***

765-766 A228 Set of 2 3.00 3.00
766a Souvenir sheet of 2, #765-766, + 4 labels — —

No. 766a sold for 150n.

A229 A232

A230

Winning Children's Stamp Art Contest Designs — A231

Perf. 12¾x13, 13x12¾

2004, Oct. 29 **Litho.**

767 A229 50n multi .75 .75
768 A230 90n multi 1.40 1.40
769 A231 120n multi 1.90 1.90
770 A232 150n multi 2.25 2.25
a. Souvenir sheet, #767-770, + 12 labels 6.50 6.50
Nos. 767-770 (4) 6.30 6.30

Rotary International, Cent. — A233

Designs: 50n, "100" with Rotary emblems for zeroes. 120n, Rotary emblem and world map.

2005, Aug. 9 **Litho.** ***Perf. 13x12¾***

771-772 Set of 2 3.50 3.50
772a A233 Horiz. pair, #771-772 3.50 3.50

Nigerian Postage Stamps, 131st Anniv. A234

Designs: 50n, Text in simulated stamp. 90n, Map of Nigeria, simulated stamp. 120n, Map of Nigeria, years "1874" and "2005." 150n, Nigeria #118, 746, vert.

2005, Oct. 9 ***Perf. 13x12¾, 12¾x13***

773-776 A234 Set of 4 6.50 6.50

World Summit on the Information Society, Tunis A235

Summit emblems, globe and: 20n, Nigeria Post emblem. 50n, Postman on motorcycle, vert. 120n, Like 20n.

Perf. 13x12¾, 12¾x13

2005, Nov. 4 **Litho.**

777-779 A235 Set of 3 3.50 3.50

Writers A236

Designs: 20n, Prof. Chinua Achebe. 40n, Dr. Abubakar Imam (1911-81). 50n, Prof. Wole Soyinka.

2006, Jan. 18 ***Perf. 13x12¾***

780-782 A236 Set of 3 1.75 1.75

Scholars — A237

Designs: No. 783, 50n, No. 786, 100n, Prof. Ayodele Awojobi (1937-84), engineer. No. 784, 50n, No. 787, 120n, Prof. Gabriel Oyibo, mathematician. No. 785, 50n, No. 788, 150n, Philip Emeagwali, computer scientist.

2006, Jan. 18 ***Perf. 12¾x13***

783-788 A237 Set of 6 8.25 8.25

Dated 2005.

52nd Commonwealth Parliamentary Conference, Abuja — A238

Designs: No. 789, International Conference Center. No. 790, National Assembly Building. No. 791: a, 20n, Like No. 789 with smaller-sized denomination in green and white. b, 50n, Like No. 790 with denomination in green.

2006, Sept. 4 **Litho.** ***Perf. 13x12¾***

789 A238 20n multi — —
790 A238 50n multi — —

Souvenir Sheet

Imperf

791 A238 Sheet of 2, #a-b — —

Queen Elizabeth II, 80th Birthday A239

Designs: 20n, Queen at public ceremony, in pink hat. 50n, Queen in pink hat, vert.

2006, Oct. 9 **Litho.** ***Perf. 13***

792-793 A239 Set of 2 1.40 1.40

Agbani Darego, 2001 Miss World — A240

Darego and: 20n, Map of Nigeria. 50n, Map of world, horiz.

2006, Nov. 9

794-795 A240 Set of 2 1.10 1.10

Abuja, 30th Anniv. A241

Designs: 20n, Gate, fireworks, palm trees, map of Nigeria. 50n, Emblem, hands beating drum, vert.

2006, Dec. 13

796-797 A241 Set of 2 1.10 1.10

143rd Extraordinary Conference of OPEC, Abuja — A242

2006, Dec. 14
798 A242 50n multi .80 .80

The editors have been shown numerous examples of this stamp on cover, but Nigerian postal authorities state that it was issued "strictly for the validation of documents, and not for postage," and that use of the stamp on mail was probably done out of ignorance.

Mungo Park (1771-1806), Explorer — A243

Park and: 20n, Monument. 50n, River, horiz.

2007, Mar. 29 Litho. *Perf. 13*
799-800 A243 Set of 2 1.10 1.10

Second World Black and African Festival of Arts and Culture, 30th Anniv.
A244

2007, Mar. 29 Litho. *Perf. 13*
801 A244 50n multi .80 .80
h. Sheet of 2 #801, imperf. — —

24th UPU Congress — A244a

Ceremonial costumes: No. 801A, Fulani man. No. 801B, Igbo man and woman. No. 801C, South Zone man and woman. No. 801D, Tiv man and woman, horiz. No. 801E, 50n, Yoruba man and woman. No. 801F, North East Zone women.

Perf. 13x12¾, 12¾x13
2007, Oct. 9 Litho.
801A A244a 20n multi — —
801B A244a 20n multi — —
801C A244a 30n multi — —
801D A244a 30n multi — —
801E A244a 50n multi — —
801F A244a 50n multi — —
g. Souvenir sheet of 6, #801A-801F, imperf. — —

The 24th UPU Congress, scheduled to be held in Nairobi, was moved to Geneva, Switzerland, because of political unrest in Kenya.

A245

Cross river gorilla: 20n, Adult. 50n, Two adults, horiz. 100n, Adult and juvenile, horiz. 150n, Head.

2008, Mar. 26 Litho. *Perf. 13*
802-805 A245 Set of 4 5.00 5.00

Worldwide Fund for Nature (WWF).

A246

Designs: 20n, Hands, money. 50n, Campaign to end violation of 419 law. 100n, Clasped hands.

2008, Apr. 10
806-808 A246 Set of 3 3.00 3.00
808a Souvenir sheet of 3, #806-808, imperf. — —

Economic & Financial Crimes Commission anti-corruption campaign.

2008 Summer Olympics, Beijing A247

Designs: 20n, Runners at finish line. 50n, Soccer. 100n, Wrestling, vert.

2008, Aug. 8
809-811 A247 Set of 3 3.00 3.00

Federal Road Safety Commission, 20th Anniv. — A247a — 811A

2008, Nov. 13 Litho. *Perf. 13*
811A A247a 50n multi 1.25 1.00

Nigerian Institute of Advanced Legal Studies A248

2009, Sept. 4 Litho. *Perf. 13*
812 A248 50n multi .65 .65

Pan-African Postal Union, 30th Anniv. — A248a

2010, Jan. 8 Litho. *Perf. 13x12¾*
812A A248a 50n multi 1.00 1.00

Dated 2009.

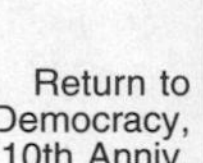

Return to Democracy, 10th Anniv. A249

Designs: No. 813, 50n, Nigerian flag, Pres. Umaru Musa Yar'Adua. No. 814, 50n, Mace, scales of justice, barrister's wig, vert.

Perf. 13x12¾, 12¾x13
2010, Apr. 6 Litho.
813-814 A249 Set of 2 1.75 1.75

Dated 2009.

GT Bank, 20th Anniv. A250

Woman, globe, 20th anniversary emblem, bank emblem and background color of: 20n, Red. 50n, Gray. 100n, Pale yellow. 120n, Gray green.

2010, July 14 Litho. *Perf. 13x12¾*
815-818 A250 Set of 4 5.50 5.50

Organization of Petroleum Exporting Countries, 50th Anniv. — A251

Designs: 50n, Oil droplet, 50th anniversary emblem. 120n, 50th anniversary emblem.

2010, Aug. 12 Litho. *Perf. 12¾x13*
819-820 A251 Set of 2 3.00 3.00

2010 World Cup Soccer Championships, South Africa — A252

Design: 20n, Two soccer players and ball. 30n, Soccer ball, globe, World Cup, vert. 50n, Soccer players and stadium.

2010 *Perf. 13x12¾, 12¾x13*
821 A252 20n multi *.50* —
821A A252 30n multi *1.00* —
821B A252 50n multi *1.75* —

Terracotta Head — A253

Terracotta Head — A253a

Bronze Bowl — A254

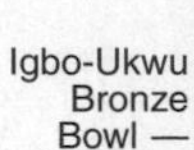

Igbo-Ukwu Bronze Bowl — A254a

Slave Chain A255

Lander Brothers Anchorage A256

Lander Brothers Anchorage — A256a

Nok Terracotta Head — A257

Monkey Colony, Lagwa-Mbaise A258

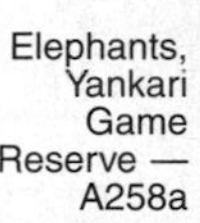

Elephants, Yankari Game Reserve — A258a

Argungu Fishing Festival, Kebbi State A259

Seated Human Figurine — A260

Lander Brothers Anchorage — A260a

Perf. 12¼x12½, 13 (Nos. 822A, 823A, 825A, 826, 827, 828), 12½x12¼ (No. 827A)

Litho. With Hologram Applied

2010-11

822	A253	20n multi	*.75*	—
822A	A253a	20n multi	—	—
823	A254	30n multi	—	—
823A	A254a	30n multi	—	—
824	A255	50n multi	—	—
825	A256	50n multi	—	—
825A	A256a	50n multi	—	—
826	A257	50n multi	—	—
827	A258	50n multi	—	—
827A	A258a	90n multi	—	—
828	A259	100n multi		*4.00*
829	A260	120n multi	*3.50*	—

Litho.

Perf. 12¾x13

829A	A260a	50n multi	*20.00*	*20.00*

Issued: No. 822A, 823A, 825A, 2011; No. 829A, 2010; others, 10/9/2010. No. 822A is dated 2010. No. 829A is dated 2009.

Independence, 50th Anniv. — A261

Nigerian arms and: 20n, Nigerian flag on pole, man holding pole with British flag, 50th anniv. emblem. 30n, Map and symbols of Nigeria. No. 832, 50n, Four men and Nigerian flag, 50th anniv. emblem, horiz. (77x22mm). No. 833, 50n, Photographs of Nigerian crops and industries, 50th anniv. emblem, horiz. (53x37mm).

Perf. 13, 13¼ (#832), 13¼x13 (#833)

2010 **Litho.**

830-833	A261	Set of 4	3.50	3.50

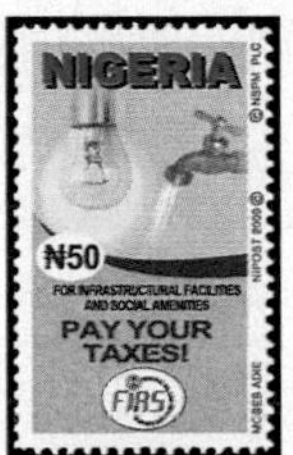

Federal Inland Revenue Service — A262

Emblem of Federal Inland Revenue Service and: 20n, Heart, map of Nigeria. 50n, Light bulb, water faucet. 100n, Taxcard.

2011 **Litho.** ***Perf. 13***

834	A262	20n multi	*.75*	—
835	A262	50n multi	*1.25*	—
836	A262	100n multi	*2.50*	—

Dated 2009.

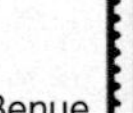

Benue State A263

Map of Benue State and: 20n, Gugur Waterfall. 30n, Food basket. 50n, Senator Joseph Sawuan Tarka (1932-80). 100n, Benue Bridge.

2011 **Litho.** ***Perf. 13***

837-840	A263	Set of 4	4.50	4.50
840a		Souvenir sheet of 4, #837-840, imperf.	*14.00*	*14.00*

Nigerian Institute of Management, 50th Anniv. — A264

2011, Sept. 27

841	A264	50n multi	1.00	1.00
a.		Souvenir sheet of 1, imperf.	—	—

Phila Africa 2012 Stamp Exhibition — A265

2012, Jan. 31

842	A265	50n multi	1.00	1.00

An imperforate souvenir sheet of 1 sold for 400n.

Enugu, Cent. (in 2009) — A266

2012, Sept. 27 **Litho.** ***Perf. 12¾x13***

843	A266	50n multi	—	—

Ahmadu Bello University, Zaria, 50th Anniv. — A267

50th Anniv. emblem and: Nos. 844, 848, Sir Ahmadu Bello (1910-66), Premier of Northern Nigeria. Nos. 845, 849, Ahmadu Bello University Senate Building, horiz. 90n, University crest. 120n, Shika brown chickens, horiz.

Litho. With Hologram Applied

2012, Nov. 24 ***Perf. 13***

844	A267	50n multi	—	—
845	A267	50n multi	—	—
846	A267	90n multi	—	—
847	A267	120n multi	—	—

Litho.

Perf. 13¼x14

Booklet Stamps

848	A267	50n multi	—	—
849	A267	50n multi	—	—
850	A267	90n multi	—	—
851	A267	120n multi	—	—
a.		Booklet pane of 4, #848-851	—	—
		Complete booklet, 3 #851a	—	

Diplomatic Relations Between Nigeria and Philippines, 50th Anniv. A268

Flags of Philippines and Nigeria and: 50n, Coat of arms of Nigeria, daisy. 120n, Coat of arms of Philippines, sampaguita.

Litho. With Hologram Applied

2013, Dec. 24 ***Perf. 12¾x13¼***

853	A268	50n multi	—	—
854	A268	120n multi	—	—

See Philippines No. 3511.

SEMI-POSTAL STAMPS

Catalogue values for unused stamps in this section are for Never Hinged items.

Children Drinking Milk at Orphanage SP1

Designs: 1sh6p+3p, Civilian first aid, vert. 2sh6p+3p, Military first aid.

1966, Dec. 1 **Photo.** ***Perf. 14½x14***

B1	SP1	4p + 1p pur, blk & red	.35	.35
B2	SP1	1sh6p + 3p multi	.80	.80
B3	SP1	2sh6p + 3p multi	1.25	1.25
		Nos. B1-B3 (3)	2.40	2.40

The surtax was for the Nigerian Red Cross.

Dr. Armauer G. Hansen — SP2

1973, July 30 **Litho.** ***Perf. 14***

B4	SP2	5k + 2k blk, brn & buff	.50	*1.00*

Centenary of the discovery of the Hansen bacillus, the cause of leprosy. The surtax was for the Nigerian Anti-Leprosy Association.

Nigeria '99, FIFA World Youth Championships — SP3

5n+5n, Soccer ball, FIFA emblem. 10n+5n, Throwing ball. 20n+5n, Kicking ball into goal. 30n+5n, Map of Nigeria. 40n+5n, FIFA emblem, eagle, soccer ball. 50n+5n, Tackling.

1999, Mar. 31 **Litho.** ***Perf. 13x14***

B5	SP3	5n +5n multi	.25	.25
B6	SP3	10n +5n multi	.30	.30
B7	SP3	20n +5n multi	.55	.55
B8	SP3	30n +5n multi	.65	.65
B9	SP3	40n +5n multi	.90	.90
B10	SP3	50n +5n multi	1.20	1.20
a.		Souvenir sheet of 6, #B5-B10	3.75	3.75
		Nos. B5-B10 (6)	3.85	3.85

POSTAGE DUE STAMPS

Catalogue values for unused stamps in this section are for Never Hinged items.

D1

Perf. 14½x14

1959, Jan. 4 **Wmk. 4** **Litho.**

J1	D1	1p orange	.25	*1.00*
J2	D1	2p orange	.25	*1.25*
J3	D1	3p orange	.25	*1.75*
J4	D1	6p orange	.80	*6.25*
J5	D1	1sh black	1.25	*11.00*
		Nos. J1-J5 (5)	2.80	*21.25*

1961, Aug. 1 **Wmk. 335**

J6	D1	1p red	.25	*.40*
J7	D1	2p blue	.25	*.50*
J8	D1	3p emerald	.25	*.75*
J9	D1	6p yellow	.25	*2.00*
J10	D1	1sh dark blue	.40	*4.00*
		Nos. J6-J10 (5)	1.40	*7.65*

D2

Perf. 12½x13½

1973, May 3 **Litho.** **Unwmk.**

J11	D2	2k red	.25	.25
J12	D2	3k blue	.25	.25
J13	D2	5k orange	.25	.25
J14	D2	10k yellow green	.25	.25
		Nos. J11-J14 (4)	1.00	1.00

1987-94 ***Rouletted 9***

J15	D2	2k red	1.75	*2.50*
J16	D2	5k yellow	4.50	*5.00*
J17	D2	10k green	9.00	*10.00*
		Nos. J15-J17 (3)	15.25	*17.50*

D3

2004 **Litho.** ***Perf. 12¾***

J18	D3	20n yel green	*.75*	—
J19	D3	40n red	*.95*	—

NIUE

nē-'ü-‚ā

LOCATION — Island in the south Pacific Ocean, northeast of New Zealand
GOVT. — Self-government, in free association with New Zealand
AREA — 100 sq. mi.
POP. — 1,708 (1997 est.)
CAPITAL — Alofi

Niue, also known as Savage Island, was annexed to New Zealand in 1901 with the Cook Islands. Niue achieved internal self-government in 1974.

12 Pence = 1 Shilling
20 Shillings = 1 Pound
100 Cents = 1 Dollar (1967)

Catalogue values for unused stamps in this country are for Never Hinged items, beginning with Scott 90 in the regular postage section, Scott B1 in the semi-postal section, Scott C1 in the air post section, and Scott O1 in the officials section.

Watermarks

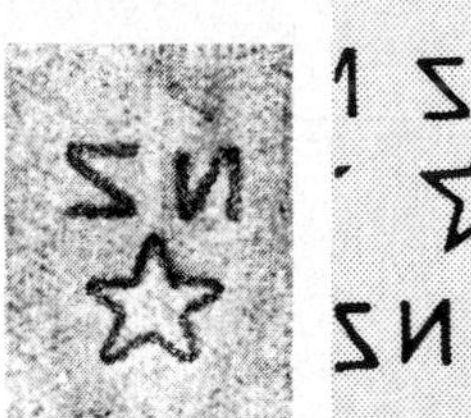

Wmk. 61 — Single-lined NZ and Star Close Together

Wmk. 253 — NZ and Star

New Zealand No. 100 Handstamped in Green

1902 Wmk. 63 *Perf. 11*
Thick Soft Paper

1 A35 1p carmine 375.00 375.00

Stamps of New Zealand Surcharged in Carmine, Vermilion or Blue

1/2p

1p

2 1/2p

Perf. 14
Thin Hard Paper

3 A18 ½p green (C) 5.50 *7.00*
a. Inverted surcharge 325.00 *600.00*
b. Double surcharge 1,200.
4 A35 1p carmine (Bl), perf. 11x14 2.00 *3.50*
a. No period after "PENI" 50.00 *70.00*
b. Perf. 14 50.00 *55.00*
c. As "a," perf. 14 500.00 600.00

Perf. 14
Wmk. 61

6 A18 ½p green (V) 1.25 1.25
7 A35 1p carmine (Bl) .85 1.10
a. No period after "PENI" 9.00 *17.00*
b. Double surcharge *1,800. 2,000.*

Perf. 11
Unwmk.

8 A22 2½p blue (C) 2.50 *4.50*
a. No period after "PENI" 35.00 *55.00*
9 A22 2½p blue (V) 1.75 2.00
a. No period after "PENI" 20.00 25.00
b. Double surcharge 2,500.

The surcharge on the ½ & 1p stamps is printed in blocks of 60. Two stamps in each block have a space between the "U" and "E" of "NIUE" and one of the 1p stamps has a broken "E" like an "F."

Blue Surcharge on Stamps of New Zealand, Types of 1898

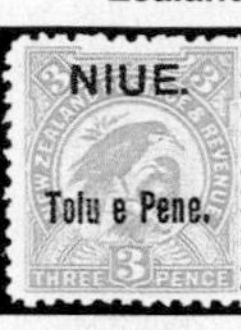

e

f

g

h

1903 Wmk. 61 *Perf. 11*

10 A23(e) 3p yellow brown 11.00 5.50
11 A26(f) 6p rose 15.00 12.50
13 A29(g) 1sh brown red 40.00 *47.50*
a. 1sh scarlet 40.00 *47.50*
b. 1sh orange red 50.00 *52.50*
c. As "b," surcharge "h" (error) 750.00
Nos. 10-13 (3) 66.00 *65.50*

Surcharged in Carmine or Blue on Stamps of New Zealand — j

1911-12 *Perf. 14, 14x14½*

14 A41(j) ½p yellow grn (C) .60 .70
15 A41(f) 6p car rose (Bl) 2.50 *7.50*
16 A41(g) 1sh vermilion (Bl) 8.00 *50.00*
Nos. 14-16 (3) 11.10 *58.20*

1915 *Perf. 14*

18 A22(d) 2½p dark blue (C) 26.00 *55.00*

Surcharged in Brown or Dark Blue on Stamps of New Zealand

1917 *Perf. 14x13½, 14x14½*

19 A42 1p carmine (Br) 24.00 6.25
a. No period after "PENI" 850.00
20 A45(e) 3p violet brn (Bl) 50.00 95.00
a. No period after "Pene" 850.00

New Zealand Stamps of 1909-19 Overprinted in Dark Blue or Red — k

1917-20 Typo.

21 A43 ½p yellow grn (R) .80 *2.75*
22 A42 1p carmine (Bl) 11.00 *14.00*
23 A47 1½p gray black (R) 1.10 *2.50*
24 A47 1½p brown org (R) 1.00 *8.50*
25 A43 3p chocolate (Bl) 1.60 *37.50*

Engr.

26 A44 2½p dull blue (R) 1.50 *14.00*
27 A45 3p violet brown (Bl) 1.75 *2.25*
28 A45 6p car rose (Bl) 6.00 *26.00*
29 A45 1sh vermilion (Bl) 7.50 *30.00*
Nos. 21-29 (9) 32.25 *137.50*

Same Overprint On Postal-Fiscal Stamps of New Zealand, 1906-15

Perf. 14, 14½ and Compound

1918-23

30 PF1 2sh blue (R) 18.00 *35.00*
31 PF1 2sh6p bn (Bl) ('23) 24.00 *55.00*
32 PF1 5sh green (R) 29.00 *57.50*
33 PF1 10sh red brn (Bl) ('23) 130.00 *170.00*
34 PF2 £1 rose (Bl) ('23) 170.00 *275.00*
Nos. 30-34 (5) 371.00 *592.50*

Landing of Captain Cook A16

Avarua Waterfront A17

Capt. James Cook — A18

Coconut Palm — A19

Arorangi Village — A20

Avarua Harbor — A21

Unwmk.

1920, Aug. 23 Engr. *Perf. 14*

35 A16 ½p yel grn & blk 4.25 4.25
36 A17 1p car & black 2.25 1.40
37 A18 1½p red & black 2.75 *18.00*
38 A19 3p pale blue & blk 1.25 *16.00*
39 A20 6p dp grn & red brn 4.75 *21.00*
a. Center inverted *1,000.*
40 A21 1sh blk brn & blk 3.00 *21.00*
Nos. 35-40 (6) 18.25 *81.65*

See Nos. 41-42. For surcharge see No. 48.

Types of 1920 Issue and

Rarotongan Chief (Te Po) — A22

Avarua Harbor — A23

1925-27 Wmk. 61

41 A16 ½p yel grn & blk ('26) 2.00 *11.00*
42 A17 1p car & black 2.00 1.00
43 A22 2½p dk blue & blk ('27) 4.50 *13.00*
44 A23 4p dull vio & blk ('27) 8.00 *22.50*
Nos. 41-44 (4) 16.50 *47.50*

New Zealand No. 182 Overprinted Type "k" in Red

1927

47 A56 2sh blue 18.00 *35.00*
a. 2sh dark blue 17.00 *47.50*

No. 37 Surcharged

1931 Unwmk. *Perf. 14*

48 A18 2p on 1½p red & blk 4.25 1.10

New Zealand Postal-Fiscal Stamps of 1931-32 Overprinted Type "k" in Blue or Red

1931, Nov. 12 Wmk. 61

49 PF5 2sh6p deep brown 5.00 13.00
50 PF5 5sh green (R) 40.00 *75.00*
51 PF5 10sh dark car 40.00 *110.00*
52 PF5 £1 pink ('32) 75.00 *160.00*
Nos. 49-52 (4) 160.00 *358.00*

See Nos. 86-89D, 116-119.

Landing of Captain Cook — A24

Capt. James Cook — A25

Polynesian Migratory Canoe — A26

Islanders Unloading Ship — A27

View of Avarua Harbor — A28

R.M.S. Monowai — A29

King George V — A30

Perf. 13, 14 (4p, 1sh)

1932, Mar. 16 Engr. Unwmk.

53 A24 ½p yel grn & blk 14.00 *25.00*
a. Perf. 14x13 275.00
54 A25 1p dp red & blk 1.10 .55
55 A26 2p org brn & blk 6.50 *4.50*
a. Perf. 14x13x13x13 150.00 *190.00*
56 A27 2½p indigo & blk 8.50 *80.00*
a. Center inverted 350.00
57 A28 4p Prus blue & blk 16.00 *60.00*
a. Perf. 13 15.00 *65.00*
58 A29 6p dp org & blk 2.75 2.25
59 A30 1sh dull vio & blk 2.50 *5.50*
Nos. 53-59 (7) 51.35 *177.80*

For types overprinted see Nos. 67-69.

1933-36 Wmk. 61 *Perf. 14*

60 A24 ½p yel grn & blk .50 *3.50*
61 A25 1p deep red & blk .50 *2.25*
62 A26 2p brown & blk ('36) .50 *1.75*
63 A27 2½p indigo & blk .50 *4.75*
64 A28 4p Prus blue & blk 2.00 *4.25*
65 A29 6p org & blk ('36) .80 *.90*
66 A30 1sh dk vio & blk ('36) 9.00 *25.00*
Nos. 60-66 (7) 13.80 *42.40*

See Nos. 77-82.

Silver Jubilee Issue

Types of 1932 Overprinted in Black or Red

1935, May 7 *Perf. 14*

67 A25 1p car & brown red .80 *3.50*
68 A27 2½p indigo & bl (R) 4.25 *13.00*
a. Vert. pair, imperf. horiz. 275.00
69 A29 6p dull org & grn 5.50 *10.00*
Nos. 67-69 (3) 10.55 *26.50*
Set, never hinged 16.00

The vertical spacing of the overprint is wider on No. 69.

No. 68a is from proof sheets.

Coronation Issue

New Zealand Stamps of 1937 Overprinted in Black

Perf. 13½x13

1937, May 13 **Wmk. 253**

70 A78 1p rose carmine .25 .25
71 A78 2½p dark blue .25 *1.50*
72 A78 6p vermilion .30 .30
Nos. 70-72 (3) .80 *2.05*
Set, never hinged 1.25

George VI — A31

Village Scene — A32

Coastal Scene with Canoe — A33

1938, May 2 **Wmk. 61** *Perf. 14*

73 A31 1sh dp violet & blk 5.00 8.00
74 A32 2sh dk red brown & blk 6.50 *17.00*
75 A33 3sh yel green & blue 18.50 17.00
Nos. 73-75 (3) 30.00 42.00
Set, never hinged 55.00

See Nos. 83-85.

Mt. Ikurangi behind Avarua — A34

Perf. 13½x14

1940, Sept. 2 **Engr.** **Wmk. 253**

76 A34 3p on 1½p rose vio & blk .45 .25
Never hinged .75

Examples without surcharge are from printer's archives. Value, $250 unused.

Types of 1932-38

1944-46 **Wmk. 253** *Perf. 14*

77 A24 ½p yel grn & blk .40 *2.25*
78 A25 1p dp red & blk ('45) .40 *1.25*
79 A26 2p org brn & blk ('46) 3.75 *6.00*
80 A27 2½p dk bl & blk ('45) .50 *1.00*
81 A28 4p Prus blue & blk 2.75 .90
82 A29 6p dp orange & blk 1.40 1.40
83 A31 1sh dp vio & blk .85 1.00
84 A32 2sh brn car & blk ('45) 8.50 3.75
85 A33 3sh yel grn & bl ('45) 11.00 8.50
Nos. 77-85 (9) 29.55 26.05
Set, never hinged 35.00

New Zealand Postal-Fiscal Stamps Overprinted Type "k" (narrow "E") in Blue or Red

1941-45 **Wmk. 61** *Perf. 14*

86 PF5 2sh6p brown 55.00 *60.00*
87 PF5 5sh green (R) 225.00 150.00
88 PF5 10sh rose 95.00 *150.00*
89 PF5 £1 pink 150.00 *225.00*
Nos. 86-89 (4) 525.00 *585.00*
Set, never hinged 775.00

Wmk. 253

89A PF5 2sh6p brown 2.50 *11.00*
89B PF5 5sh green (R) 5.25 *12.50*
e. 5sh light yellow green, wmkd. sideways ('67) 35.00 *95.00*
89C PF5 10sh rose 37.50 *110.00*
89D PF5 £1 pink 30.00 *67.50*
Nos. 89A-89D (4) 75.25 *201.00*
Set, never hinged 120.00

No. 89Be exists in both line and comb perf.

Catalogue values for unused stamps in this section, from this point to the end of the section, are for Never Hinged items.

Peace Issue

New Zealand Nos. 248, 250, 254 and 255 Overprinted in Black or Blue

p

q

1946, June 4 *Perf. 13x13½, 13½x13*

90 A94 (p) 1p emerald .40 .35
91 A96 (q) 2p rose violet (Bl) .40 .35
92 A100 (p) 6p org red & red brn .40 *.75*
93 A101 (p) 8p brn lake & blk (Bl) .50 *.75*
Nos. 90-93 (4) 1.70 *2.20*

Map of Niue — A35

H.M.S. Resolution — A36

Designs: 2p, Alofi landing. 3p, Thatched Dwelling. 4p, Arch at Hikutavake. 6p, Alofi bay. 9p, Fisherman. 1sh, Cave at Makefu. 2sh, Gathering bananas. 3sh, Matapa Chasm.

Perf. 14x13½, 13½x14

1950, July 3 **Engr.** **Wmk. 253**

94 A35 ½p red orange & bl .25 *1.25*
95 A36 1p green & brown 2.50 2.50
96 A36 2p rose car & blk 1.10 *2.00*
97 A36 3p blue vio & blue .25 .25
98 A36 4p brn vio & ol grn .40 .40
99 A36 6p brn org & bl grn .70 *1.40*
100 A35 9p dk brn & brn org .85 *1.40*
101 A36 1sh black & purple 1.00 .60
102 A35 2sh dp grn & brn org 1.35 *5.00*
103 A35 3sh black & dp blue 4.00 *5.00*
Nos. 94-103 (10) 12.40 *19.80*

For surcharges see Nos. 106-115.

Coronation Issue

Queen Elizabeth II — A36a

Westminster Abbey — A36b

1953, May 24 **Photo.** *Perf. 14x14½*

104 A36a 3p brown .50 .50
105 A36b 6p slate black 1.25 1.25

Nos. 94-103 Surcharged

Perf. 14x13½, 13½x14

1967, July 10 **Engr.** **Wmk. 253**

106 A35 ½c on ½p red org & blue .25 .25
107 A36 1c on 1p green & brn .40 .25
108 A36 2c on 2p rose car & blk .25 .25
109 A36 2½c on 3p bl vio & bl .25 .25
110 A36 3c on 4p brn vio & ol grn .25 .25
111 A36 5c on 6p brn org & grn .25 .25
112 A35 8c on 9p dk brn & brn org .25 .25
113 A36 10c on 1sh blk & pur .25 .25
114 A35 20c on 2sh dp grn & brn org .30 *1.25*
115 A35 30c on 3sh blk & dp bl .50 *1.25*
Nos. 106-115 (10) 2.95 4.50

The position of the numeral varies on each denomination. The surcharge on the ½c, 2½c, 8c, 10c and 20c contains one dot only.

New Zealand Arms — A37

Wmk. 253

1967, July 10 **Typo.** *Perf. 14*

Black Surcharge

116 A37 25c yellow brown .50 .45
117 A37 50c green .85 .90
118 A37 $1 cerise .55 1.75
119 A37 $2 pale pink .85 3.00
Nos. 116-119 (4) 2.75 6.10

1967 *Perf. 11*

116a A37 25c 8.25 13.00
117a A37 50c 9.50 15.00
118a A37 $1 12.00 15.00
119a A37 $2 15.00 20.00
Nos. 116a-119a (4) 44.75 63.00

The perf. 11 stamps were produced when a normal perforating machine broke down and 2,500 of each denomination were perforated on a treadle machine first used by the N.Z. Post Office in 1899.

Christmas Issues

Adoration of the Shepherds, by Poussin — A37a

Perf. 13½x14

1967, Oct. 3 **Photo.** **Wmk. 253**

120 A37a 2½c multicolored .30 .25

Nativity, by Federico Fiori — A37b

1969, Oct. 1 **Photo.** **Wmk. 253**

121 A37b 2½c multicolored .30 .25

Pua — A38

Flowers (except 20c): 1c, Golden shower. 2c, Flamboyant. 2½c, Frangipani. 3c, Niue crocus. 5c, Hibiscus. 8c, Passion fruit. 10c, Kamapui. 20c, Queen Elizabeth II. 30c, Tapeu orchid.

Perf. 12½x13

1969, Nov. 27 **Litho.** **Unwmk.**

122 A38 ½c green & multi .25 .25
123 A38 1c orange & multi .25 .25
124 A38 2c gray & multi .25 .25
125 A38 2½c bister & multi .25 .25
126 A38 3c blue & multi .25 .25
127 A38 5c ver & multi .25 .25
128 A38 8c violet & multi .25 .25
129 A38 10c yellow & multi .25 .25
130 A38 20c dk blue & multi .75 *1.50*
131 A38 30c olive grn & multi 1.00 *2.00*
Nos. 122-131 (10) 3.75 5.50

See Nos. 678.

Edible Crab A39

Perf. 13½x12½

1969, Aug. 19 **Litho.**

132 A39 3c Kalahimu .25 .25
133 A39 5c Kalavi .25 .25
134 A39 30c Unga .40 .40
Nos. 132-134 (3) .90 .90

Christmas Issue

Adoration, by Correggio — A39a

1970, Oct. 1 **Litho.** *Perf. 12½*

135 A39a 2½c multicolored .30 .25

Plane over Outrigger Canoe A40

Designs: 5c, Plane over ships in harbor. 8c, Civair plane over island.

1970, Dec. 9 **Litho.** *Perf. 13½*

136 A40 3c multicolored .25 .25
137 A40 5c multicolored .25 .25
138 A40 8c multicolored .25 .25
Nos. 136-138 (3) .75 .75

Opening of Niue Airport.

Polynesian Triller (Heahea) A41

Birds: 10c, Crimson-crowned fruit pigeon (kulukulu). 20c, Blue-crowned lory (henga).

1971, June 23 **Litho.** *Perf. 13½x13*

139 A41 5c multicolored .25 .25
140 A41 10c multicolored .50 .25
141 A41 20c multicolored .85 .25
Nos. 139-141 (3) 1.60 .75

Christmas Issue

Holy Night, by Carlo Maratta — A41a

1971, Oct. 6 Photo. ***Perf. 13x13½***
142 A41a 3c orange & multi .35 .25

People of Niue — A42

1971, Nov. 17
143 A42 4c Boy .25 .25
144 A42 6c Girl .25 .25
145 A42 9c Man .25 .35
146 A42 14c Woman .25 .70
Nos. 143-146 (4) 1.00 1.55

Octopus Lure and Octopus — A43

5c, Warrior and weapons. 10c, Sika (spear) throwing, horiz. 25c, Vivi dance, horiz.

1972, May 3 Litho. ***Perf. 13x13½***
147 A43 3c blue & multi .25 .25
148 A43 5c rose & multi .25 .25
149 A43 10c blue & multi .25 .25
150 A43 25c yellow & multi .25 .25
Nos. 147-150 (4) 1.00 1.00

So. Pacific Festival of Arts, Fiji, May 6-20.

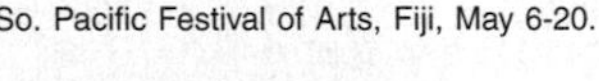

Alofi Wharf A44

South Pacific Commission Emblem and: 5c, Health service. 6c, School children. 18c, Cattle and dwarf palms.

1972, Sept. 6 Litho. ***Perf. 13½x14***
151 A44 4c blue & multi .25 .25
152 A44 5c blue & multi .25 .25
153 A44 6c blue & multi .25 .25
154 A44 18c blue & multi .25 .25
Nos. 151-154 (4) 1.00 1.00

So. Pacific Commission, 25th anniv.

Christmas Issue

Madonna and Child, by Murillo — A44a

1972, Oct. 4 Photo. ***Perf. 11½***
155 A44a 3c gray & multi .30 .25

Pempheris Oualensis A45

Designs: Various fish.

Perf. 13½x13
1973, June 27 Litho. Unwmk.
156 A45 8c shown .35 .35
157 A45 10c Cephalopholis .35 .35
158 A45 15c Variola louti .40 .40
159 A45 20c Etelis carbunculus .45 .45
Nos. 156-159 (4) 1.55 1.55

Flowers, by Jan Breughel — A46

Paintings of Flowers: 5c, by Hans Bollongier. 10c, by Rachel Ruysch.

1973, Nov. 21 Litho. ***Perf. 13½x13***
160 A46 4c bister & multi .25 .25
161 A46 5c orange brn & multi .25 .25
162 A46 10c emerald & multi .25 .25
Nos. 160-162 (3) .75 .75

Christmas.

Capt. Cook and "Resolution" — A47

Capt. Cook and: 3c, Cook's landing place and ship. 8c, Map of Niue. 20c, Administration Building and flag of 1774.

1974, June 20 Litho. ***Perf. 13½x14***
163 A47 2c multicolored .25 .25
164 A47 3c multicolored .25 .25
165 A47 8c multicolored .25 .30
166 A47 20c multicolored .35 .55
Nos. 163-166 (4) 1.10 1.35

Bicentenary of Cook's landing on Niue.

King Fataaiki — A48

Annexation Day, Oct. 19, 1900 — A49

Village Meeting A50

Design: 10c, Legislative Assembly Building.

Perf. 14x13½, 13½x14
1974, Oct. 19 Litho.
167 A48 4c multicolored .25 .25
168 A49 8c multicolored .25 .25
169 A50 10c multicolored .25 .25
170 A50 20c multicolored .25 .25
Nos. 167-170 (4) 1.00 1.00

Referendum for Self-government, 9/3/74.

Decorated Bicycle — A51

Christmas: 10c, Decorated motorcycle. 20c, Going to church by truck.

1974, Nov. 13 Litho. ***Perf. 12½***
171 A51 3c green & multi .25 .25
172 A51 10c dull blue & multi .25 .25
173 A51 20c brown & multi .25 .25
Nos. 171-173 (3) .75 .75

Children Going to Church A52

Children's Drawings: 5c, Child on bicycle trailing balloons. 10c, Balloons and gifts hanging from tree.

1975, Oct. 29 Litho. ***Perf. 14½***
174 A52 4c multicolored .25 .25
175 A52 5c multicolored .25 .25
176 A52 10c multicolored .25 .25
Nos. 174-176 (3) .75 .75

Christmas.

Opening of Tourist Hotel A53

Design: 20c, Hotel, building and floor plan.

1975, Nov. 19 Litho. ***Perf. 14x13½***
177 A53 8c multicolored .25 .25
178 A53 20c multicolored .25 .25

Preparing Ground for Taro A54

2c, Planting taro (root vegetable). 3c, Banana harvest. 4c, Bush plantation. 5c, Shellfish gathering. 10c, Reef fishing. 20c, Luku (fern) harvest. 50c, Canoe fishing. $1, Husking coconuts. $2, Hunting uga (land crab).

1976, Mar. 3 Litho. ***Perf. 13½x14***
179 A54 1c multicolored .25 .25
180 A54 2c multicolored .25 .25
181 A54 3c multicolored .25 .25
182 A54 4c multicolored .25 .25
183 A54 5c multicolored .25 .25
184 A54 10c multicolored .25 .25
185 A54 20c multicolored .25 .25
186 A54 50c multicolored .25 .50
187 A54 $1 multicolored .25 .75
188 A54 $2 multicolored .75 1.00
Nos. 179-188 (10) 3.00 4.00

See #222-231. For surcharges see #203-210.

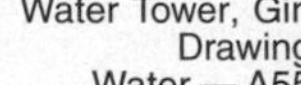

Water Tower, Girl Drawing Water — A55

15c, Teleprinter & Niue radio station. 20c, Instrument panel, generator & power station.

1976, July 7 Litho. ***Perf. 14x14½***
189 A55 10c multicolored .25 .25
190 A55 15c multicolored .25 .25
191 A55 20c multicolored .25 .25
Nos. 189-191 (3) .75 .75

Technical achievements.

Christmas Tree (Flamboyant) and Administration Building — A56

Christmas: 15c, Avatele Church, interior.

1976, Sept. 15 Litho. ***Perf. 14½***
192 A56 9c orange & multi .25 .25
193 A56 15c orange & multi .25 .25

Elizabeth II, Coronation Portrait, and Westminster Abbey — A57

Design: $2, Coronation regalia.

1977, June 7 Photo. ***Perf. 13½***
194 A57 $1 multicolored .50 .50
195 A57 $2 multicolored 1.25 .75
a. Souvenir sheet of 2, #194-195 2.00 2.00

25th anniv. of reign of Elizabeth II. Nos. 194-195 each printed in sheets of 5 stamps and label showing Niue flag and Union Jack.

For surcharge see No. 213.

Mothers and Infants A58

Designs: 15c, Mobile school dental clinic. 20c, Elderly couple and home.

1977, June 29 Litho. ***Perf. 14½***
196 A58 10c multicolored .25 .25
197 A58 15c multicolored .25 .25
198 A58 20c multicolored .25 .25
Nos. 196-198 (3) .75 .75

Personal (social) services.

For surcharges see Nos. 211-212.

Annunciation, by Rubens — A59

Rubens Paintings (details, Virgin and Child): 12c, Adoration of the Kings. 20c, Virgin with Garland. 35c, Holy Family.

1977, Nov. 15 Photo. ***Perf. 13x13½***
199 A59 10c multicolored .25 .25
200 A59 12c multicolored .25 .25
201 A59 20c multicolored .35 .50
202 A59 35c multicolored .40 .80
a. Souvenir sheet of 4, #199-202 1.75 1.75
Nos. 199-202 (4) 1.25 1.80

Christmas and 400th birth anniversary of Peter Paul Rubens (1577-1640). Nos. 199-202 each printed in sheets of 6 stamps.

Stamps of 1976-77 Surcharged with New Value and 4 Bars in Black or Gold
Printing and Perforations as Before

1977, Nov. 15

No.	Type	Description	Unused	Used
203	A54	12c on 1c (#179)	.45	.25
204	A54	16c on 2c (#180)	.50	.30
205	A54	30c on 3c (#181)	.50	.40
206	A54	35c on 4c (#182)	.50	.45
207	A54	40c on 5c (#183)	.50	.50
208	A54	60c on 20c (#185)	.50	.50
209	A54	70c on $1 (#187)	.50	.50
210	A54	85c on $2 (#188)	.50	.60
211	A58	$1.10 on 10c (#196)	.50	.60
212	A58	$2.60 on 20c (#198)	.85	.65
213	A57	$3.20 on $2 (#195, G)	1.05	.75
		Nos. 203-213 (11)	6.35	5.50

"An Inland View in Atooi," by John Webber — A60

Scenes in Hawaii, by John Webber: 16c, A View of Karakooa in Owyhee. 20c, An Offering Before Capt. Cook in the Sandwich Islands. 30c, Tereoboo, King of Owyhee, bringing presents (boats). 35c, Masked rowers in boat.

1978, Jan. 18 Photo. *Perf. 13½*

No.	Type	Description	Unused	Used
214	A60	12c gold & multi	.70	.35
215	A60	16c gold & multi	.75	.40
216	A60	20c gold & multi	.75	.50
217	A60	30c gold & multi	.85	.60
218	A60	35c gold & multi	.90	.65
a.		Souv. sheet, #214-218 + label	4.50	2.75
		Nos. 214-218 (5)	3.95	2.50

Bicentenary of Capt. Cook's arrival in Hawaii. Nos. 214-218 printed in sheets of 5 stamps and one label showing flags of Hawaii and Niue.

Descent from the Cross, by Caravaggio A61

Easter: 20c, Burial of Christ, by Bellini.

1978, Mar. 15 Photo. *Perf. 13x13½*

No.	Type	Description	Unused	Used
219	A61	10c multicolored	.25	.25
220	A61	20c multicolored	.35	.25
a.		Souv. sheet, #219-220, perf. 13½	1.00	1.00

Nos. 219-220 issued in sheets of 8.
See Nos. B1-B2.

Souvenir Sheet

Elizabeth II — A62

1978, June 26 Photo. *Perf. 13*

No.	Type	Description	Unused	Used
221	A62	Sheet of 6	3.00	3.00
a.		$1.10 Niue and UK flags	.50	.75
b.		$1.10 shown	.50	.75
c.		$1.10 Queen's New Zealand flag	.50	.75
d.		Souvenir sheet of 3	2.25	2.25

25th anniv. of coronation of Elizabeth II. No. 221 contains 2 horizontal se-tenant strips of Nos. 221a-221c, separated by horizontal gutter showing coronation coach. No. 221d contains a vertical se-tenant strip of Nos. 221a-221c.

Type of 1977

12c, Preparing ground for taro. 16c, Planting taro. 30c, Banana harvest. 35c, Bush plantation. 40c, Shellfish gathering. 60c, Reef fishing. 75c, Luku (fern) harvest. $1.10, Canoe fishing. $3.20, Husking coconuts. $4.20, Hunting uga (land crab).

1978, Oct. 27 Litho. *Perf. 14*

No.	Type	Description	Unused	Used
222	A54	12c multicolored	.25	.25
223	A54	16c multicolored	.25	.25
224	A54	30c multicolored	.25	.25
225	A54	35c multicolored	.25	.25
226	A54	40c multicolored	.25	.25
227	A54	60c multicolored	.30	.35
228	A54	75c multicolored	.35	.40
229	A54	$1.10 multicolored	.45	.50
230	A54	$3.20 multicolored	1.25	1.50
231	A54	$4.20 multicolored	1.90	2.25
		Nos. 222-231 (10)	5.50	6.25

Celebration of the Rosary, by Dürer — A63

Designs: 30c, Nativity, by Dürer. 35c, Adoration of the Kings, by Dürer.

1978, Nov. 30 Photo. *Perf. 13*

No.	Type	Description	Unused	Used
232	A63	20c multicolored	.30	.30
233	A63	30c multicolored	.45	.45
234	A63	35c multicolored	.50	.50
a.		Souv. sheet, #232-234 + label	1.60	1.60
		Nos. 232-234 (3)	1.25	1.25

Christmas and 450th death anniversary of Albrecht Dürer (1471-1528). Nos. 232-234 each printed in sheets of 5 stamps and descriptive label.
See Nos. B3-B5.

Pietà, by Gregorio Fernandez — A64

Easter: 35c, Burial of Christ, by Pedro Roldan.

1979, Apr. 2

No.	Type	Description	Unused	Used
235	A64	30c multicolored	.35	.35
236	A64	35c multicolored	.40	.40
a.		Souvenir sheet of 2, #235-236	1.50	1.50

See Nos. B6-B7.

Child, by Franz Hals — A65

IYC (Emblem and Details from Paintings): 16c, Nurse and Child. 20c, Child of the Duke of Osuna, by Goya. 30c, Daughter of Robert Strozzi, by Titian. 35c, Children Eating Fruit, by Murillo.

1979, May 31 Photo. *Perf. 14*

No.	Type	Description	Unused	Used
237	A65	16c multicolored	.25	.25
238	A65	20c multicolored	.35	.35
239	A65	30c multicolored	.40	.40
240	A65	35c multicolored	.50	.50
a.		Souvenir sheet of 4, #237-240	2.10	2.10
		Nos. 237-240 (4)	1.50	1.50

See Nos. B8-B11.

Penny Black, Bath Mail Coach, Rowland Hill — A66

30c, Basel #3L1 & Alpine village coach. 35c, US #1 & 1st US transatlantic mail ship. 50c, France #3 & French railroad mail car, 1849. 60c, Bavaria #1 & Bavarian mail coach.

1979, July 3 Photo. *Perf. 14*

No.	Type	Description	Unused	Used
241	A66	20c Pair, #a.-b.	.40	.40
242	A66	30c Pair, #a.-b.	.55	.55
243	A66	35c Pair, #a.-b.	.65	.65
244	A66	50c Pair, #a.-b.	1.00	1.00
245	A66	60c Pair, #a.-b.	1.10	1.10
c.		Souv. sheet of 10, #241-245 + 2 labels	4.25	4.25
		Nos. 241-245 (5)	3.70	3.70

Sir Rowland Hill (1795-1879), originator of penny postage.
For overprints and surcharges see Nos. 281-285, B16, B21, B26, B30, B33, B41.

Cook's Landing at Botany Bay A68

18th Century Paintings: 30c, Cook's Men during a Landing on Erromanga. 35c, Resolution and Discovery in Queen Charlotte's Sound. 75c, Death of Capt. Cook on Hawaii, by Johann Zoffany.

1979, July 30 Photo. *Perf. 14*

No.	Type	Description	Unused	Used
251	A68	20c multicolored	.65	.30
252	A68	30c multicolored	.85	.40
253	A68	35c multicolored	1.10	.50
254	A68	75c multicolored	1.10	.90
a.		Souv. sheet, #251-254, perf. 13½	3.75	3.75
		Nos. 251-254 (4)	3.70	2.10

200th death anniv. of Capt. James Cook.
For surcharges see Nos. B18, B23, B28, B36.

Apollo 11 Lift-off — A69

1979, Sept. 27 Photo. *Perf. 13½*

No.	Type	Description	Unused	Used
255	A69	30c shown	.35	.35
256	A69	35c Lunar module	.40	.40
257	A69	60c Splashdown	.70	.70
a.		Souvenir sheet of 3	1.90	1.90
		Nos. 255-257 (3)	1.45	1.45

Apollo 11 moon landing, 10th anniversary. No. 257a contains Nos. 255-257 in changed colors.
For surcharges see Nos. B24, B29, B35.

Virgin and Child, by P. Serra — A70

Virgin and Child by: 25c, R. di Mur. 30c, S. diG. Sasseta. 50c, J. Huguet.

1979, Nov. 29 Photo. *Perf. 13*

No.	Type	Description	Unused	Used
258	A70	20c multicolored	.25	.25
259	A70	25c multicolored	.25	.25
260	A70	30c multicolored	.25	.25
261	A70	50c multicolored	.25	.25
a.		Souvenir sheet of 4, #258-261	1.40	1.40
		Nos. 258-261 (4)	1.00	1.00

Christmas. See Nos. B12-B15. For surcharges see Nos. B19-B20, B25, B32.

Pietà, by Giovanni Bellini — A71

Easter (Pietà, Paintings by): 30c, Botticelli. 35c, Anthony Van Dyck.

1980, Apr. 2 Photo. *Perf. 13*

No.	Type	Description	Unused	Used
262	A71	25c multicolored	.30	.30
263	A71	30c multicolored	.35	.35
264	A71	35c multicolored	.40	.40
		Nos. 262-264 (3)	1.05	1.05

See Nos. B37-B40.

A72

#265a, Ceremonial Stool, New Guinea (shown). #265b, Ku-Tagwa plaque. #265c, Suspension hook. #266a, Platform post. #266b, Canoe ornament. #266c, Carved figure. #266d, Woman and child. #267a, God A'a, statue. #267b, Tangaroa, statue. #267c, Ivory pendant. #267d, Tapa cloth. #268a, Maori feather box. #268b, Hei-tiki. #268c, House post. #268d, God Ku, feather image.

1980, July 30 Photo. *Perf. 13*

No.	Type	Description	Unused	Used
265	A72	20c Strip of 4, #a.-d.	.65	.65
266	A72	25c Strip of 4, #a.-d.	.80	.80
267	A72	30c Strip of 4, #a.-d.	.95	.95
268	A72	35c Strip of 4, #a.-d.	1.10	1.10

Souvenir Sheets of 4

No.	Description	Unused	Used
e.	#265a, 266a, 267a, 268a	1.10	1.10
f.	#265b, 266b, 267b, 268b	1.10	1.10
g.	#265c, 266c, 267c, 268c	1.10	1.10
h.	#265d, 266d, 267d, 268d	1.10	1.10
	Nos. 265-268 (4)	3.50	3.50

3rd South Pacific Festival of Arts, Port Moresby, Papua New Guinea, June 30-July 12. Stamps in souvenir sheets have 2c surtax.
For surcharges see Nos. 626-629.

Nos. 241-250, Overprinted in Black on Silver

1980, Aug. 22 *Perf. 14*

No.	Type	Description	Unused	Used
281	A66	20c Pair, #a.-b.	.50	.50
282	A66	30c Pair, #a.-b.	.70	.70
283	A66	35c Pair, #a.-b.	.80	.80
284	A66	50c Pair, #a.-b.	1.10	1.10
285	A66	60c Pair, #a.-b.	1.40	1.40
		Nos. 281-285 (5)	4.50	4.50

ZEAPEX '80, New Zealand International Stamp Exhibition, Auckland, Aug. 23-31.

Queen Mother Elizabeth, 80th Birthday — A73

1980, Sept. 15 Photo. ***Perf. 13x13½***

291	A73	$1.10 multicolored	.90	1.40

Souvenir Sheet

292	A73	$3 multicolored	2.00	2.00

No. 291 issued in sheets of 5 and label showing coad of arms.

A74

#293a, 100-meter dash. #293b, Allen Wells, England. #294a, 400-Meter freestyle. #294b, Ines Diers, DDR. #295a, Soling class yachting. #295b, Denmark. #296a, Soccer. #296b, Czechoslovakia.

1980, Oct. 30 Photo. ***Perf. 14***

293	A74	20c Pair, #a.-b.	.45	.45
294	A74	25c Pair, #a.-b.	.50	.50
295	A74	30c Pair, #a.-b.	.60	.60
296	A74	35c Pair, #a.-b.	.70	.70
		Nos. 293-296 (4)	2.25	2.25

22nd Summer Olympic Games, Moscow, July 19-Aug. 3.

See No. B42.

Virgin and Child, by del Sarto — A76

Paintings of Virgin & Child, by Andrea del Sarto.

1980, Nov. 28 Photo. ***Perf. 13x13½***

301	A76	20c multicolored	.25	.25
302	A76	25c multicolored	.25	.25
303	A76	30c multicolored	.25	.25
304	A76	35c multicolored	.25	.25
a.		Souvenir sheet of 4, #301-304	1.00	1.25
		Nos. 301-304 (4)	1.00	1.00

Christmas and 450th death anniversary of Andrea del Sarto.

See Nos. B43-B46.

A77

Golden Shower Tree — A77a

#317a, Phalaenopsis sp. #317b, Moth Orchid. #318a, Euphorbia pulcherrima. #318b, Poinsettia. #319a, Thunbergia alata. #319b, Black-eyed Susan. #320a, Cochlospermum hibiscoides. #320b, Buttercup tree. #321a, Begonia sp. #321b, Begonia. #322a, Plumeria sp. #322b, Frangipani. #323a, Sterlitzia reginae. #323b, Bird of paradise. #324a, Hibiscus syriacus. #324b, Rose of Sharon. #325a, Nymphaea sp. #325b, Water lily. #326a, Tibouchina sp. #326b, Princess flower. #327a, Nelumbo sp. #327b, Lotus. #328a, Hybrid hibiscus. #328b, Yellow hibiscus.

1981-82 Photo. ***Perf. 13x13½***

317	A77	2c Pair, #a.-b.	.25	.25
318	A77	5c Pair, #a.-b.	.25	.25
319	A77	10c Pair, #a.-b.	.25	.25
320	A77	15c Pair, #a.-b.	.30	.30
321	A77	20c Pair, #a.-b.	.40	.40
322	A77	25c Pair, #a.-b.	.50	.50
323	A77	30c Pair, #a.-b.	.55	.55
324	A77	35c Pair, #a.-b.	.65	.65
325	A77	40c Pair, #a.-b.	.70	.70
326	A77	50c Pair, #a.-b.	1.00	1.00
327	A77	60c Pair, #a.-b.	1.10	1.10
328	A77	80c Pair, #a.-b.	1.60	1.60

Perf. 13½

329	A77a	$1 shown	1.00	1.00
330	A77a	$2 Orchid var.	2.00	2.00
331	A77a	$3 Orchid sp.	2.75	2.75
332	A77a	$4 Poinsettia	4.00	4.00
333	A77a	$6 Hybrid hibiscus	5.75	5.75
334	A77a	$10 Hibiscus rosa-sinensis	10.00	10.00
		Nos. 317-334 (18)	33.05	33.05

Issued: 2c, 5c, 10c, 15c, 20c, 25c, Apr. 2; 30c, 35c, 40c, 50c, 60c, 80c, May 26; $1, $2, $3, Dec. 9, 1981; $4, $6, $10, Jan. 15, 1982.

For surcharges and overprints see Nos. 406-409, 413E, 594-595, O14, O16, O19.

Jesus Defiled, by El Greco A78

Easter (Paintings): 50c, Pieta, by Fernando Gallego. 60c, The Supper of Emaus, by Jacopo da Pontormo.

1981, Apr. 10 ***Perf. 14***

337	A78	35c multicolored	.40	.40
338	A78	50c multicolored	.65	.65
339	A78	60c multicolored	.75	.75
		Nos. 337-339 (3)	1.80	1.80

See Nos. B47-B50.

Prince Charles and Lady Diana — A79

1981, June 26 Photo. ***Perf. 14***

340	A79	75c Charles	.50	.50
341	A79	95c Lady Diana	.65	.65
342	A79	$1.20 shown	.90	.90
a.		Souvenir sheet of 3, #340-342	2.50	2.50
		Nos. 340-342 (3)	2.05	2.05

Royal Wedding. Nos. 340-342 each printed in sheets of 5 plus label showing St. Paul's Cathedral.

For overprints and surcharges see Nos. 357-359, 410, 412, 455, 596-598, B52-B55.

1982 World Cup Soccer A80

1981, Oct. 16 Photo. ***Perf. 13***

343		Strip of 3	.80	.80
a.		A80 30c any single	.25	.25
344		Strip of 3	1.05	1.05
a.		A80 35c any single	.35	.35
345		Strip of 3	1.20	1.20
a.		A80 40c any single	.40	.40
		Nos. 343-345 (3)	3.05	3.05

See No. B51.

Christmas 1981 — A81

Rembrandt Paintings: 20c, Holy Family with Angels, 1645. 35c, Presentation in the Temple, 1631. 50c, Virgin and Child in Temple, 1629. 60c, Holy Family, 1640.

1981-82 Photo. ***Perf. 14x13***

346	A81	20c multicolored	.35	.35
347	A81	35c multicolored	.80	.80
348	A81	50c multicolored	1.10	1.10
349	A81	60c multicolored	1.25	1.25
a.		Souvenir sheet of 4, #346-349	3.50	3.50
		Nos. 346-349 (4)	3.50	3.50

Souvenir Sheets

350	A81	80c + 5c like #346	.80	.80
351	A81	80c + 5c like #347	.80	.80
352	A81	80c + 5c like #348	.80	.80
353	A81	80c + 5c like #349	.80	.80

Surtax was for school children.

Issued: #346-349, 12/11; others, 1/22/82.

21st Birthday of Princess Diana — A82

1982, July 1 ***Perf. 14***

354	A82	50c Charles	.50	.50
355	A82	$1.25 Wedding	1.25	1.25
356	A82	$2.50 Diana	2.25	2.25
a.		Souvenir sheet of 3, #354-356	6.00	6.00
		Nos. 354-356 (3)	4.00	4.00

Nos. 354-356 each printed in sheets of 5 plus label showing wedding day picture.

For overprints and surcharges see Nos. 359B-359D, 411, 413, 456.

Nos. 340-342a Overprinted

Type I

Type II

Type III

1982, July 23 ***Perf. 14***

357	A79	75c multi (I)	1.40	1.40
357A	A79	75c multi (II)	1.40	1.40
358	A79	95c multi (I)	1.75	1.75
358A	A79	95c multi (II)	1.75	1.75
359	A79	$1.20 multi (I)	2.25	2.25
359A	A79	$1.20 multi (II)	2.25	2.25
		Nos. 357-359A (6)	10.80	10.80

Souvenir Sheet

359B	A79	Sheet of 3, #a.-c.	7.50	7.50
a.		75c multi (III)	2.00	2.00
b.		95c multi (III)	2.00	2.00
c.		$1.20 multi (III)	2.00	2.00

Nos. 357/357A, 358/358A and 359/359A were printed in small sheets containing three stamps overprinted Type I, two overprinted type II and one label.

Birthday Type of 1982 Inscribed in Silver

1982 Photo. ***Perf. 14***

359C	A82	50c like #354	.70	.70
359D	A82	$1.25 like #355	1.75	1.75
359E	A82	$2.50 like #356	3.25	3.25
a.		Souvenir sheet of 3	7.00	7.00
		Nos. 359C-359E (3)	5.70	5.70

Christmas — A83

Princess Diana Holding Prince William and Paintings of Infants by: 40c, Bronzino (1502-1572). 52c, Murillo (1617-1682). 83c, Murillo, diff. $1.05, Boucher (1703-1770). Singles in No. 363a: 34x30mm, showing paintings only.

1982, Dec. 3 Photo. ***Perf. 13½x14½***

360	A83	40c multicolored	1.20	1.20
361	A83	52c multicolored	1.40	1.40
362	A83	83c multicolored	2.40	2.40
363	A83	$1.05 multicolored	3.50	3.50
a.		Souvenir sheet of 4, #364-367	6.75	6.75
		Nos. 360-363 (4)	8.50	8.50

Souvenir Sheets

364	A83	80c + 5c like #360	2.40	2.40
365	A83	80c + 5c like #361	2.40	2.40
366	A83	80c + 5c like #362	2.40	2.40
367	A83	80c + 5c like #363	2.40	2.40

Nos. 364-367 each contain one 30x42mm stamp showing Royal family. Surtax was for children's funds.

Commonwealth Day — A84

1983, Mar. 14 Photo. ***Perf. 13***

368	A84	70c Flag, Premier Robert R. Rex	.75	.75
369	A84	70c Resolution, Adventurer	.75	.75
370	A84	70c Passion flower	.75	.75
371	A84	70c Lime branch	.75	.75
a.		Block of 4, #368-371	3.00	3.00

For overprints see Nos. 484-487.

Scouting Year — A85

1983, Apr. 28 Photo. ***Perf. 13***

372	A85	40c Flag signals	.70	.70
373	A85	50c Tree planting	.80	.80
374	A85	83c Map reading	1.50	1.50
		Nos. 372-374 (3)	3.00	3.00

Souvenir Sheet

375		Sheet of 3	3.00	3.00
a.		A85 40c + 3c like 40c	.75	.75
b.		A85 50c + 3c like 50c	.80	.80
c.		A85 83c + 3c like 83c	1.30	1.30

Nos. 372-375 Overprinted in Black on Silver: "XV WORLD JAMBOREE CANADA"

1983, July 14 — Photo.

376 A85 40c multicolored .60 .60
377 A85 50c multicolored .75 .75
378 A85 83c multicolored 1.15 1.15
Nos. 376-378 (3) 2.50 2.50

Souvenir Sheet

379 Sheet of 3 2.75 2.75
a. A85 40c + 3c multicolored .60 .60
b. A85 50c + 3c multicolored .70 .70
c. A85 83c + 3c multicolored 1.40 1.40

Save the Whales Campaign — A86

1983, Aug. 15 — *Perf. 13x14*

380 A86 12c Right whale .90 .50
381 A86 25c Fin whale 1.30 .60
382 A86 35c Sei whale 1.75 .95
383 A86 40c Blue whale 2.00 1.10
384 A86 58c Bowhead whale 2.25 1.25
385 A86 70c Sperm whale 2.75 1.25
386 A86 83c Humpback whale 3.00 1.75
387 A86 $1.05 Lesser rorqual 3.75 1.90
388 A86 $2.50 Gray whale 5.00 3.25
Nos. 380-388 (9) 22.70 12.55

Manned Flight Bicentenary — A87

25c, Montgolfier, 1783. 40c, Wright Bros. Flyer, 1903. 58c, Graf Zeppelin, 1928. 70c, Boeing 247, 1933. 83c, Apollo VIII, 1968. $1.05, Columbia space shuttle.

1983, Oct. 14 — Photo. — *Perf. 14*

389 A87 25c multicolored .50 .50
390 A87 40c multicolored .75 .75
391 A87 58c multicolored 1.25 1.25
392 A87 70c multicolored 1.75 1.75
393 A87 83c multicolored 2.10 2.10
394 A87 $1.05 multicolored 2.40 2.40
a. Souvenir sheet of 6 5.50 5.50
Nos. 389-394 (6) 8.75 8.75

No. 394a contains Nos. 389-394 inscribed "AIRMAIL."

Christmas A87a

Paintings by Raphael (1483-1520): 30c, Garvagh Madonna, National Gallery, London. 40c, Granduca Madonna, Pitti Gallery, Florence. 58c, Goldfinch Madonna, Uffizi Gallery, Florence. 70c, Holy Family of Francis I, Louvre, Paris. 83c, Holy Family with Saints, Alte Pinakothek, Munich

1983 — Photo. — *Perf. 14*

395 A87a 30c multicolored .60 .60
396 A87a 40c multicolored .80 .80
397 A87a 58c multicolored 1.20 1.20
398 A87a 70c multicolored 1.30 1.30
399 A87a 83c multicolored 1.60 1.60
Nos. 395-399 (5) 5.50 5.50

Souvenir Sheets

Perf. 13½

400 Sheet of 5 4.00 4.00
a. A87a 30c + 3c like #395 .40 .40
b. A87a 40c + 3c like #396 .55 .55
c. A87a 58c + 3c like #397 .80 .80
d. A87a 70c + 3c like #398 .90 .90
e. A87a 83c + 3c like #399 1.10 1.10
401 A87a 85c + 5c like #395 1.20 1.20
402 A87a 85c + 5c like #396 1.20 1.20
403 A87a 85c + 5c like #397 1.20 1.20
404 A87a 85c + 5c like #398 1.20 1.20
405 A87a 85c + 5c like #399 1.20 1.20

500th birth anniv. of Raphael.
Issued: #395-400, 11/25; #401-405, 12/29.

Nos. 323, 326-328, 341, 355, 342, 356 and 331 Surcharged in Black or Gold with One or Two Bars

1983, Nov. 30 — Photo.

Pairs, #a.-b. (#406-409)

406 A77 52c on 30c 1.60 1.60
407 A77 58c on 50c 1.75 1.75
408 A77 70c on 60c 2.25 2.25
409 A77 83c on 80c 2.75 2.75
410 A79 $1.10 on 95c #341 1.60 1.60
411 A82 $1.10 on $1.25 #355 (G) 1.60 1.60
412 A79 $2.60 on $1.20 #342 4.00 4.00
413 A82 $2.60 on $2.50 #356 (G) 4.00 4.00
413A A77a $3.70 on $3 #331 5.50 5.50
Nos. 406-413A (9) 25.05 25.05

World Communications Year — A88

1984, Jan. 23 — Photo. — *Perf. 13x13½*

414 A88 40c Telegraph sender .45 .45
415 A88 52c Early telephone .65 .65
416 A88 83c Satellite 1.10 1.10
a. Souvenir sheet of 3, #414-416 2.00 2.00
Nos. 414-416 (3) 2.20 2.20

Moth Orchid — A89

Golden Shower Tree A90

25c, Poinsettia. 30c, Buttercup tree. 35c, Begonia. 40c, Frangipani. 52c, Bird of paradise. 58c, Rose of Sharon. 70c, Princess flower. 83c, Lotus. $1.05, Yellow hibiscus. $2.30, Orchid var. $3.90, Orchid sp. $5, Poinsettia, diff. $6.60, Hybrid hibiscus. $8.30, Hibiscus rosasinensis.

1984 — *Perf. 13x13½*

417 A89 12c shown .25 .25
418 A89 25c multicolored .35 .35
419 A89 30c multicolored .50 .50
420 A89 35c multicolored .50 .50
421 A89 40c multicolored .55 .55
422 A89 52c multicolored .70 .70
423 A89 58c multicolored .80 .80
424 A89 70c multicolored 1.00 1.00
425 A89 83c multicolored 1.10 1.10
426 A89 $1.05 multicolored 1.60 1.60
427 A90 $1.75 shown 1.60 1.60
428 A90 $2.30 multicolored 2.25 2.25
429 A90 $3.90 multicolored 3.50 3.50
430 A90 $5 multicolored 4.50 4.50
431 A90 $6.60 multicolored 6.00 6.00
431A A90 $8.30 multicolored 8.00 8.00
Nos. 417-431A (16) 33.20 33.20

Issued: #417-426, 2/20; #427-429, 5/10; others 6/18.

For overprints see #O1-O13, O15, O17-O18.

1984 Summer Olympics A91

Designs: Greek pottery designs, 3rd cent. BC. 30c, 70c vert.

1984, Mar. 15 — Photo. — *Perf. 14*

432 A91 30c Discus .45 .45
433 A91 35c Running .50 .50
434 A91 40c Equestrian .55 .55
435 A91 58c Boxing .80 .80
436 A91 70c Javelin .95 .95
Nos. 432-436 (5) 3.25 3.25

For overprints and surcharges see #446-450, 480-483.

AUSIPEX '84, Australian Animals — A92

1984 — Photo. — *Perf. 14*

437 A92 25c Koala .30 .30
438 A92 35c Koala, diff. .40 .40
439 A92 40c Koala, diff. .65 .65
440 A92 58c Koala, diff. 1.00 1.00
441 A92 70c Koala, diff. 1.30 1.30
442 A92 83c Kangaroo with joey 1.50 1.50
443 A92 $1.05 Kangaroo with joey, diff. 1.75 1.75
444 A92 $2.50 Kangaroo, diff. 4.00 4.00
Nos. 437-444 (8) 10.90 10.90

Souvenir Sheets

445 Sheet of 2 + label 5.00 5.00
a. A92 $1.75 Wallaby 2.50 2.50
b. A92 $1.75 Koala, diff. 2.50 2.50
c. Sheet, #437-441, 445b, perf 13½ 4.50 4.50
d. Sheet, #442-444, 445a, perf 13½ 6.50 6.50

Nos. 442-444 airmail.
Issued: #437-444, Aug. 24; $445, Sept. 20.

Nos. 432-436 Ovptd. with Event, Names of Gold Medalists, Country in Gold or Red

1984, Sept. 7 — *Perf. 14*

446 A91 30c Danneberg .40 .40
447 A91 35c Coe (R) .50 .50
448 A91 40c Todd .55 .55
449 A91 58c Biggs .80 .80
450 A91 70c Haerkoenen 1.00 1.00
Nos. 446-450 (5) 3.25 3.25

10th Anniv. of Self Government — A93

1984, Oct. 19 — Photo. — *Perf. 13*

451 A93 40c Niue flag .55 .55
452 A93 58c Niue map 1.00 1.00
453 A93 70c Ceremony 1.15 1.15
a. Souvenir sheet of 3, #451-453 2.50 2.50
Nos. 451-453 (3) 2.70 2.70

Souvenir Sheet

454 A93 $2.50 like 70c 2.50 2.50

For overprints and surcharges see Nos. 655-660.

Nos. 340, 354 Surcharged "Prince Henry / 15.9.84" and Bars and New Values in Red or Silver

1984, Oct. 22 — Photo. — *Perf. 14*

455 A79 $2 on 75c multi (R) 2.25 2.25
456 A82 $2 on 50c multi (S) 2.25 2.25

Nos. 455-456 issued in sheets of 5 + label.

Christmas A94

Paintings: 40c, The Nativity, by A. Vaccaro. 58c, Virgin with Fly, anonymous. 70c, Adoration of the Shepherds, by B. Murillo. 83c, Flight into Egypt, by B. Murillo.

1984, Oct. 19 — Photo. — *Perf. 13x13½*

457 A94 40c multicolored .55 .55
458 A94 58c multicolored .80 .80
459 A94 70c multicolored 1.00 1.00
460 A94 83c multicolored 1.10 1.10
Nos. 457-460 (4) 3.45 3.45

Souvenir Sheets

461 Sheet of 4 3.25 3.25
a. A94 40c + 5c Like 40c .55 .55
b. A94 58c + 5c Like 58c .70 .70
c. A94 70c + 5c Like 70c .90 .90
d. A94 83c + 5c Like 83c 1.00 1.00

Perf. 13½

462 A94 95c + 10c Like 40c 1.25 1.25
463 A94 95c + 10c Like 58c 1.25 1.25
464 A94 95c + 10c Like 70c 1.25 1.25
465 A94 95c + 10c Like 83c 1.25 1.25

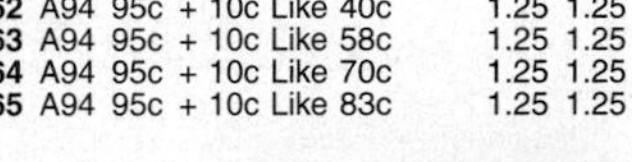

Audubon Birth Bicentenary A95

Illustrations of North American bird species by artist/naturalist John J. Audubon: 40c, House wren. 70c, Veery. 83c, Grasshopper sparrow. $1.05, Henslow's sparrow. $2.50, Vesper sparrow.

1985, Apr. 15 — Photo. — *Perf. 14½*

466 A95 40c multicolored 1.50 1.50
467 A95 70c multicolored 2.00 2.00
468 A95 83c multicolored 2.75 2.75
469 A95 $1.05 multicolored 3.25 3.25
470 A95 $2.50 multicolored 7.50 7.50
Nos. 466-470 (5) 17.00 17.00

Souvenir Sheets

Perf. 14

471 A95 $1.75 like #466 2.50 2.50
472 A95 $1.75 like #467 2.50 2.50
473 A95 $1.75 like #468 2.50 2.50
474 A95 $1.75 like #469 2.50 2.50
475 A95 $1.75 like #470 2.50 2.50
Nos. 471-475 (5) 12.50 12.50

Queen Mother, 85th Birthday A96

Designs: 70c, Wearing mantle of the Order of the Garter. $1.15, With Queen Elizabeth II. $1.50, With Prince Charles. $3, Writing letter.

1985, June 14 — *Perf. 13½x13*

476 A96 70c multicolored 1.00 1.00
477 A96 $1.15 multicolored 1.25 1.25
478 A96 $1.50 multicolored 1.75 1.75
a. Souvenir sheet of 3 + label, #476-478 8.00 8.00
Nos. 476-478 (3) 4.00 4.00

Souvenir Sheet

Perf. 13½

479 A96 $3 multicolored 4.25 4.25

Nos. 476-478 issued in sheets of 5 plus label. No. 479 contains one 39x36mm stamp. No. 478a issued 8/4/86, for 86th birthday.

Nos. 432-433, 435-436 Overprinted "Mini South Pacific Games, Rarotonga" and Surcharged with Gold Bar and New Value in Black

1985, July 26 *Perf. 14*

480 A91 52c on 95c multi .55 .55
481 A91 83c on 58c multi 1.15 1.15
482 A91 95c on 35c multi 1.30 1.30
483 A91 $2 on 30c multi 2.50 2.50
Nos. 480-483 (4) 5.50 5.50

Nos. 368-371 Overprinted with Conference Emblem and: "Pacific Islands Conference, Rarotonga"

1985, July 26 *Perf. 13½x13*

484 A84 70c on #368 .75 .75
485 A84 70c on #369 .75 .75
486 A84 70c on #370 .75 .75
487 A84 70c on #371 .75 .75
a. Block of 4, #484-487 3.00 3.00

A97

Paintings of children: 58c, Portrait of R. Strozzi's Daughter, by Titian. 70c, The Fifer, by Manet. $1.15, Portrait of a Young Girl, by Renoir. $1.50, Portrait of M. Berard, by Renoir.

1985, Oct. 11 *Perf. 13*

488 A97 58c multicolored 1.75 1.75
489 A97 70c multicolored 2.00 2.00
490 A97 $1.15 multicolored 3.50 3.50
491 A97 $1.50 multicolored 4.50 4.50
Nos. 488-491 (4) 11.75 11.75

Souvenir Sheets

Perf. 13x13½

492 A97 $1.75 + 10c like #488 5.00 5.00
493 A97 $1.75 + 10c like #489 5.00 5.00
494 A97 $1.75 + 10c like #490 5.00 5.00
495 A97 $1.75 + 10c like #491 5.00 5.00

Intl. Youth Year.

A98

Christmas, Paintings (details) by Correggio: 58c, No. 500a, Virgin and Child. 85c, No. 500b, Adoration of the Magi. $1.05, No. 500c, Virgin and Child, diff. $1.45, No. 500d, Virgin and Child with St. Catherine.

1985, Nov. 29 Photo. *Perf. 13x13½*

496 A98 58c multicolored 1.25 1.25
497 A98 85c multicolored 2.25 2.25
498 A98 $1.05 multicolored 2.75 2.75
499 A98 $1.45 multicolored 3.75 3.75
Nos. 496-499 (4) 10.00 10.00

Souvenir Sheets

500 Sheet of 4 5.50 5.50
a.-d. A98 60c + 10c, any single 1.30 1.30

Imperf

501 A98 65c like #496 1.25 1.25
502 A98 95c like #497 1.75 1.75
503 A98 $1.20 like #498 2.50 2.50
504 A98 $1.75 like #499 3.50 3.50
Nos. 500-504 (5) 14.50 14.50

Nos. 501-504 each contain one 61x71mm stamp.

Halley's Comet — A99

The Constellations, fresco by Giovanni De Vecchi, Farnesio Palace, Caprarola, Italy.

1986, Jan. 24 *Perf. 13½*

505 A99 60c multicolored .90 .90
506 A99 75c multicolored 1.10 1.00
507 A99 $1.10 multicolored 1.50 1.50
508 A99 $1.50 multicolored 2.40 2.40
Nos. 505-508 (4) 5.90 5.80

Souvenir Sheet

509 Sheet of 4 8.00 8.00
a. A99 95c like #505 2.00 2.00
b. A99 95c 95c like #506 2.00 2.00
c. A99 95c like #507 2.00 2.00
d. A99 95c like #508 2.00 2.00

A100

Elizabeth II, 60th Birthday: $1.10, No. 513a, Elizabeth and Prince Philip at Windsor Castle. $1.50, No. 513b, At Balmoral. $2, No. 513c, Elizabeth at Buckingham Palace. $3, Elizabeth seated and Prince Philip.

1986, Apr. 28 *Perf. 14½x13½*

510 A100 $1.10 multicolored 1.00 1.00
511 A100 $1.50 multicolored 1.50 1.50
512 A100 $2 multicolored 2.00 2.00
Nos. 510-512 (3) 4.50 4.50

Souvenir Sheets

513 Sheet of 3 2.75 2.75
a.-c. A100 75c any single .90 .90
514 A100 $3 multicolored 3.50 3.50

For surcharges see Nos. 546-547.

A101

AMERIPEX '86: #515a, Washington, US #1. #515b, Jefferson, Roosevelt, Lincoln.

1986, May 22 Photo. *Perf. 14*

515 A101 $1 Pair, #a.-b. 7.75 7.75

A102

Paintings: $1, Statue under construction, 1883, by Victor Dargaud. $2.50, Unveiling the Statue of Liberty, 1886, by Edmund Morand (1829-1901).

1986, July 4 *Perf. 13x13½*

517 A102 $1 multicolored 2.25 2.25
518 A102 $2.50 multicolored 5.50 5.50

Souvenir Sheet

519 Sheet of 2 4.00 4.00
a. A102 $1.25 like #517 2.00 2.00
b. A102 $1.25 like #518 2.00 2.00

Statue of Liberty, cent.

Wedding of Prince Andrew and Sarah Ferguson — A103

Designs: $2.50, Portraits, Westminster Abbey. $5, Portraits.

1986, July 23 *Perf. 13½x13*

520 A103 $2.50 multicolored 4.00 4.00

Souvenir Sheet

521 A103 $5 Portraits 8.25 8.25

No. 520 printed in sheets of 4. No. 521 contains one 45x32mm stamp.

STAMPEX '86, Adelaide, Aug. 4-10 — A104

Birds — 40c, Egretta alba, vert. 60c, Emblema picta. 75c, Aprosmictus scapularis, vert. 80c, Malurus lamberti. $1, Falco peregrinus, vert. $1.65, Halcyon azurea. $2.20, Melopsittacus undulatus, vert. $4.25,

Perf. 13x13½, 13½x13

1986, Aug. 4 **Photo.**

522 A104 40c multi 1.10 1.10
523 A104 60c multi 1.60 1.60
524 A104 75c multi 2.25 2.25
525 A104 80c multi 2.50 2.50
526 A104 $1 multi 3.00 3.00
527 A104 $1.65 multi 4.75 4.75
528 A104 $2.20 multi 7.00 7.00
529 A104 $4.25 multi 13.00 13.00
Nos. 522-529 (8) 35.20 35.20

Christmas A105

Paintings in the Vatican Museum: 80c, No. 534a, Virgin and Child, by Perugino (1446-1523). $1.15, No. 534b, Virgin of St. N. dei Frari, by Titian. $1.80, No. 534c, Virgin with Milk, by Lorenzo di Credi (1459-1537). $2.60, $7.50, No. 534d, Foligno Madonna, by Raphael.

1986, Nov. 14 Litho. *Perf. 14*

530 A105 80c multi 1.60 1.60
531 A105 $1.15 multi 2.25 2.25
532 A105 $1.80 multi 4.00 4.00
533 A105 $2.60 multi 6.00 6.00
Nos. 530-533 (4) 13.85 13.85

Souvenir Sheets

Perf. 13½

534 Sheet of 4 11.00 11.00
a.-d. A105 $1.50 any single 2.75 2.75

Perf. 14½x13½

535 A105 $7.50 multi 12.00 12.00

For surcharges see Nos. B56-B61.

Souvenir Sheets

Statue of Liberty, Cent. — A106

Photographs: No. 536a, Tall ship, bridge. No. 536b, Workmen, flame from torch. No. 536c, Workman, flame, diff. No. 536d, Ships, New York City. No. 536e, Tall ship, sailboat, bridge. No. 537a, Statue, front. No. 537b, Statue, left side. No. 537c, Torch dismantled. No. 537d, Statue, right side. No. 537e, Welder.

1987, May 20

536 A106 Sheet of 5 + label 3.75 3.75
a.-e. 75c any single .75 .75
537 A106 Sheet of 5 + label 3.75 3.75
a.-e. 75c any single, vert. .75 .75

Tennis Champions — A107

Olympic emblem, coin and: 80c, $1.15, $1.40, $1.80, Boris Becker. 85c, $1.05, $1.30, $1.75, Steffi Graf. Various action scenes.

1987

538 A107 80c multi 2.50 2.50
539 A107 85c multi 2.10 2.10
540 A107 $1.05 multi 2.50 2.50
541 A107 $1.15 multi 2.60 2.60
542 A107 $1.30 multi 2.50 2.50
543 A107 $1.40 multi 3.00 3.00
544 A107 $1.75 multi 3.00 3.00
545 A107 $1.80 multi 3.75 3.75
Nos. 538-545 (8) 21.95 21.95

Issued: 80c, $1.15, $1.40, $1.80, 9/25; others, 10/20.

For overprints see Nos. 560-563.

Nos. 511-512 Surcharged "40th /WEDDING / ANNIV." with Denomination in Black on Gold

Perf. 14½x13½

1987, Nov. 20 **Photo.**

546 A100 $4.85 on $1.50 #511 6.00 6.00
547 A100 $4.85 on $2 #512 6.00 6.00

40th Wedding anniv. of Queen Elizabeth II and Prince Philip, Duke of Edinburgh.

Christmas — A108

Paintings (details) by Albrecht Durer (Angel with Lute on 80c, $1.05, $2.80): 80c, No. 551a, The Nativity. $1.05, No. 551b, Adoration of the Magi. $2.80, No. 551c, $7.50, Celebration of the Rosary.

1987, Dec. 4 Photo. *Perf. 13½*

548 A108 80c multi 1.75 1.75
549 A108 $1.05 multi 2.25 2.25
550 A108 $2.80 multi 5.00 5.00
Nos. 548-550 (3) 9.00 9.00

Souvenir Sheets

551 Sheet of 3 9.00 9.00
a.-c. A108 $1.30 any single 3.00 3.00
552 A108 $7.50 multi 11.00 11.00

Size of Nos. 551a-551c: 49½x38½mm. No. 552 contains one 51x33mm stamp.

European Soccer Championships — A109

Highlights from Franz Beckenbauer's career: 20c, Match scene. 40c, German all-star team. 60c, Brussels, 1974. 80c, England, 1966. $1.05, Mexico, 1970. $1.30, Munich, 1974. $1.80, FC Bayern Munchen vs. Athletico Madrid.

1988, June 20 Litho. *Perf. 14*

553 A109 20c multi .40 .40
554 A109 40c multi .80 .80
555 A109 60c multi 1.25 1.25
556 A109 80c multi 1.60 1.60
557 A109 $1.05 multi 2.25 2.25
558 A109 $1.30 multi 3.00 3.00
559 A109 $1.80 multi 3.75 3.75
Nos. 553-559 (7) 13.05 13.05

Nos. 539-540, 542 and 543 Ovptd.

a. "AUSTRALIA 24 JAN 88 / FRENCH OPEN 4 JUNE 88"
b. "WIMBLEDON 2 JULY 88 / U S OPEN 10 SEPT. 88"
c. "WOMEN'S TENNIS GRAND / SLAM: 10 SEPTEMBER 88"
d. "SEOUL OLYMPIC GAMES / GOLD MEDAL WINNER"

1988, Oct. 14 Litho. *Perf. 13½x14*

560 A107(a) 85c on No. 539 1.75 1.75
561 A107(b) $1.05 on No. 540 2.25 2.25
562 A107(c) $1.30 on No. 542 2.75 2.75
563 A107(d) $1.75 on No. 543 3.75 3.75
Nos. 560-563 (4) 10.50 10.50

Steffi Graf, 1988 Olympic gold medalist; opportunities for youth in sports.

Christmas A110

Adoration of the Shepherds, by Rubens: 60c, Angels. 80c, Joseph and witness. $1.05, Madonna. $1.30, Christ child. $7.20, Entire painting.

1988, Oct. 28 Photo. *Perf. 13½*

564 A110 60c multi 1.40 1.40
565 A110 80c multi 2.40 2.40
566 A110 $1.05 multi 3.50 3.50
567 A110 $1.30 multi 4.00 4.00
Nos. 564-567 (4) 11.30 11.30

Souvenir Sheet

568 A110 $7.20 multi 10.00 10.00

No. 568 contains one 40x50mm stamp.

First Moon Landing, 20th Anniv. A111

Apollo 11: #a, Mission emblem and astronaut. #b, Earth, Moon and simplified flight plan. #c, Olive branch, Apollo 1 mission emblem and astronaut on Moon. Printed in continuous design.

1989, July 20 Photo. *Perf. 14*

571 A111 $1.50 Strip of 3, #a.-c. 14.50 14.50

Souvenir Sheet of 3

Perf. 13½x13

572 A111 $1.15 #a.-c. 8.00 8.00

Christmas — A112

Details of Presentation in the Temple, 1631, by Rembrandt, Royal Cabinet of Paintings, The Hague: 70c, Priests. 80c, Madonna. $1.05, Joseph. $1.30, Christ child. $7.20, Entire painting.

1989, Nov. 22 Photo. *Perf. 13x13½*

573 A112 70c multicolored 2.60 2.60
574 A112 80c multicolored 2.75 2.75
575 A112 $1.05 multicolored 3.50 3.50
576 A112 $1.30 multicolored 4.50 4.50
Nos. 573-576 (4) 13.35 13.35

Souvenir Sheet

Perf. 13½

577 A112 $7.20 multicolored 13.50 13.50

No. 577 contains one 39x50mm stamp.

Emblem of the German Natl. Soccer Team and Signatures — A113

Former team captains: 80c, Fritz Walter. $1.15, Franz Beckenbauer. $1.40, Uwe Seeler.

1990, Feb. 5 Photo. *Perf. 13½*

578 A113 80c multicolored 2.25 2.25
579 A113 $1.15 multicolored 2.60 2.60
580 A113 $1.40 multicolored 4.50 4.50
581 A113 $1.80 shown 5.25 5.25
Nos. 578-581 (4) 14.60 14.60

1990 World Cup Soccer Championships, Italy.

First Postage Stamp, 150th Anniv. — A114

Paintings by Rembrandt showing letters: 80c, No. 586d, Merchant Maarten Looten (1632). $1.05, No. 586c, Rembrandt's son Titus holding pen (1655). $1.30, No. 586b, The Shipbuilder and his Wife (1633). $1.80, No. 586a, Bathsheba with King David's letter (1654).

1990, May 2 Photo. *Perf. 13½*

582 A114 80c multicolored 2.25 2.25
583 A114 $1.05 multicolored 3.00 3.00
584 A114 $1.30 multicolored 4.50 4.50
585 A114 $1.80 multicolored 6.00 6.00
Nos. 582-585 (4) 15.75 15.75

Souvenir Sheet

586 Sheet of 4 11.00 11.00
a.-d. A114 $1.50 any single 2.75 2.75

A115

1990, July 23 *Perf. 13x13½*

587 A115 $1.25 multicolored 5.00 5.00

Souvenir Sheet

588 A115 $7 multicolored 16.00 16.00

Queen Mother, 90th birthday.

A116

Christmas (Paintings): 70c, Adoration of the Magi by Bouts. 80c, Holy Family by Fra Bartolomeo. $1.05, The Nativity by Memling. $1.30, Adoration of the King by Pieter Bruegel, the Elder. $7.20, Virgin and Child Enthroned by Cosimo Tura.

1990, Nov. 27 Litho. *Perf. 14*

589 A116 70c multicolored 2.25 2.25
590 A116 80c multicolored 3.00 3.00
591 A116 $1.05 multicolored 3.50 3.50
592 A116 $1.30 multicolored 4.25 4.25
Nos. 589-592 (4) 13.00 13.00

Souvenir Sheet

593 A116 $7.20 multicolored 13.00 13.00

No. 334 Overprinted in Silver

1990, Dec. 5 *Perf. 13x13½*

594 A77a $10 multicolored 16.00 16.00

Birdpex '90, 20th Intl. Ornithological Congress, New Zealand.

No. 333 Overprinted "SIXTY FIFTH BIRTHDAY QUEEN ELIZABETH II"

1991, Apr. 22 Litho. *Perf. 13x13½*

595 A77a $6 multicolored 8.00 8.00

Nos. 340-342 Overprinted in Black or Silver

T E N T H ANNIVERSARY — Typo.
T E N T H ANNIVERSARY — Litho.

1991, June 26 Photo. *Perf. 14*

596 A79 75c on #340 (S) 1.50 1.50
a. Litho. overprint 1.50 1.50
597 A79 95c on #341 2.25 2.25
a. Litho. overprint 2.25 2.25
598 A79 $1.20 on #342 3.25 3.25
a. Litho. overprint 3.25 3.25
Nos. 596-598 (3) 7.00 7.00
Nos. 596a-598a (3) 7.00 7.00

Nos. 596-598 issued in miniature sheets of 5 with typo. overprint. Nos. 596a-598a issued in uncut panes of 4 miniature sheets of 5. Letters of typo. overprint are taller and thinner than litho. overprint.

Christmas — A117

Paintings: 20c, The Virgin and Child with Saints Jerome and Dominic, by Filippino Lippi. 50c, The Isenheim Altarpiece, The Virgin and Child, by Grunewald. $1, The Nativity, by Pittoni. $2, Adoration of the Kings, by Jan Brueghel, the Elder. $7, The Adoration of the Shepherds, by Reni.

1991, Nov. 11 Litho. *Perf. 14*

599 A117 20c multicolored .50 .50
600 A117 50c multicolored 1.40 1.40
601 A117 $1 multicolored 3.00 3.00
602 A117 $2 multicolored 5.50 5.50
Nos. 599-602 (4) 10.40 10.40

Souvenir Sheet

603 A117 $7 multicolored 11.00 11.00

Birds — A118

20c, Banded rail. 50c, Red-tailed tropicbird. 70c, Purple swamphen. $1, Pacific pigeon. $1.50, White-collared kingfisher. $2, Blue-crowned lory. $3, Crimson-crowned fruit dove. $5, Barn owl. $7, Longtailed cockoo. $10, Reef heron. $15, Polynesian triller.

1992-93 Litho. *Perf. 14x13½*

604 A118 20c multicolored .30 .30
605 A118 50c multicolored .70 .70
606 A118 70c multicolored 1.00 1.00
607 A118 $1 multicolored 1.50 1.50
608 A118 $1.50 multicolored 2.00 2.00
609 A118 $2 multicolored 2.75 2.75
610 A118 $3 multicolored 4.25 4.25
611 A118 $5 multicolored 6.50 6.50

Perf. 13

Size: 51x38mm

612 A118 $7 multicolored 8.50 8.50

Size: 49x35mm

613 A118 $10 multicolored 11.50 11.50
614 A118 $15 multicolored 18.00 18.00
Nos. 604-614 (11) 57.00 57.00

Issued $1.50, $2, 3/20; $3, 4/16; $5, 5/15; $7, 3/26/93; $10, 4/16/93; $15, 8/10/93; others, 2/92.

For overprints & surcharges see Nos. O20-O25, 676-677.

This is an expanding set. Numbers may change.

Discovery of America, 500th Anniv. — A119

$2, Queen Isabella supports Columbus. $3, Columbus' fleet. $5, Columbus landing in America.

1992 Litho. *Perf. 13*

621 A119 $2 multicolored 2.55 2.55
622 A119 $3 multicolored 4.50 4.50
623 A119 $5 multicolored 7.50 7.50
Nos. 621-623 (3) 14.55 14.55

1992 Summer Olympics, Barcelona — A120

#624: a, $10 coin, tennis player. b, Flags, torch. c, Gymnast, $10 coin. $5, Water polo player.

1992, July 22 Litho. *Perf. 13½x13*

624 A120 $2.50 Strip of 3, #a.-c. 17.00 17.00

Souvenir Sheet

625 A120 $5 multicolored 10.50 10.50

Nos. 265-268 Surcharged

1992, Sept. 30 Photo. *Perf. 13*

Strips of 4, #a.-d.

626 A72 $1 on 20c 4.75 4.75
627 A72 $1 on 25c 4.75 4.75
628 A72 $1 on 30c 4.75 4.75
629 A72 $1 on 35c 4.75 4.75
Nos. 626-629 (4) 19.00 19.00

6th South Pacific Festival of the Arts.

Christmas A121

Design: Different details from St. Catherine's Mystic Marriage, by Hans Memling.

1992, Nov. 18 Litho. *Perf. 13½*

642 A121 20c multicolored .35 .35
643 A121 50c multicolored 1.00 1.00
644 A121 $1 multicolored 2.40 2.40
645 A121 $2 multicolored 4.00 4.00
Nos. 642-645 (4) 7.75 7.75

Souvenir Sheet

646 A121 $7 like #643 11.50 11.50

No. 646 contains one 39x48mm stamp.

Queen Elizabeth II's Accession to the Throne, 40th Anniv. — A122

Various portraits of Queen Elizabeth II.

1992, Dec. 7 *Perf. 14*

647 A122 70c multicolored .60 .60
648 A122 $1 multicolored 1.75 1.75
649 A122 $1.50 multicolored 3.50 3.50
650 A122 $2 multicolored 4.25 4.25
Nos. 647-650 (4) 10.10 10.10

Dolphins A123

Designs: 20c, Rough-toothed dolphin. 50c, Fraser's dolphin. 75c, Pantropical spotted dolphin. $1, Risso's dolphin.

1993, Jan. 13 Litho. *Perf. 14*

651 A123 20c multicolored 1.25 .75
652 A123 50c multicolored 3.50 1.50
653 A123 75c multicolored 4.75 2.50
654 A123 $1 multicolored 6.00 4.50
Nos. 651-654 (4) 15.50 9.25

World Wildlife Fund.

Nos. 451-453 Ovptd.

1993, Mar. 15 Photo. *Perf. 13*

655 A93 40c on #451 multi .65 .65
656 A93 58c on #452 multi 1.25 1.25
657 A93 70c on #453 multi 1.75 1.75

Nos. 655-657 Surcharged

1993, Mar. 15

658 A93 $1 on 40c #655 3.25 3.25
659 A93 $1 on 58c #656 3.25 3.25
660 A93 $1 on 70c #657 3.25 3.25
Nos. 655-660 (6) 13.40 13.40

Queen Elizabeth II, 40th Anniv. of Coronation — A124

1993, June 2 Litho. *Perf. 14*

661 A124 $5 multicolored 10.50 10.50

Christmas A125

Details from Virgin of the Rosary, by Guido Reni: 20c, Infant Jesus. 70c, Cherubs. $1, Two men, one pointing upward. $1.50, Two men looking upward. $3, Madonna and child.

1993, Oct. 29 Litho. *Perf. 14*

662 A125 20c multicolored .30 .30
663 A125 70c multicolored 1.20 1.20
664 A125 $1 multicolored 1.75 1.75
665 A125 $1.50 multicolored 3.25 3.25

Size: 32x47mm

Perf. 13½

666 A125 $3 multicolored 6.00 6.00
Nos. 662-666 (5) 12.50 12.50

1994 World Cup Soccer Championships, U.S. — A126

1994, June 17 Litho. *Perf. 14*

667 A126 $4 multicolored 8.00 8.00

First Manned Moon Landing, 25th Anniv. — A127

Designs: a, Flight to Moon, astronaut opening solar wind experiment lunar surface. b, Astronaut holding flag. c, Astronaut standing by lunar experiment package.

1994, July 20 Litho. *Perf. 14*

668 A127 $2.50 Tryptic, #a.-c. 20.00 20.00

Christmas A128

Entire paintings or details: No. 669a, The Adoration of the Kings, by Jan Gossaert. b, Madonna & Child with Saints John & Catherine, by Titian. c, The Holy Family and Shepherd, by Titian. d, Virgin & Child with Saints, by Gerard David.

No. 670: a-b, Adoration of the Shepherds, by N. Poussin. c, Madonna & Child with Saints Joseph & John, by Sebastiano. d, Adoration of the Kings, by Veronese.

1994, Nov. 28 Litho. *Perf. 14*

669 A128 70c Block of 4, #a.-d. 4.50 4.50
670 A128 $1 Block of 4, #a.-d. 7.00 7.00

Robert Louis Stevenson (1850-94), Writer — A129

a, Treasure Island. b, Dr. Jekyll and Mr. Hyde. c, Kidnapped. d, Stevenson, tomb, inscription.

1994, Dec. 14 *Perf. 15x14*

671 A129 $1.75 Block of 4, #a.-d. 15.00 15.00

Flowers — A130

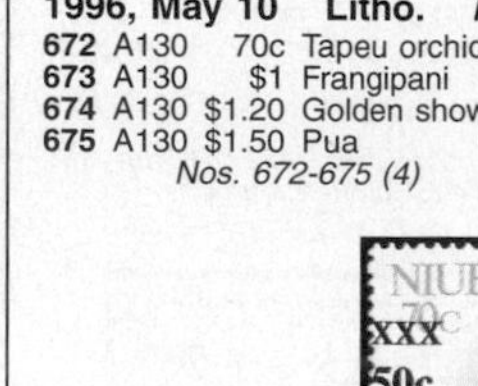

1996, May 10 Litho. *Perf. 14½x14*

672 A130 70c Tapeu orchid .90 .90
673 A130 $1 Frangipani 1.40 1.40
674 A130 $1.20 Golden shower 1.60 1.60
675 A130 $1.50 Pua 2.10 2.10
Nos. 672-675 (4) 6.00 6.00

Nos. 606, 608 Surcharged

1996, Feb. 19 Litho. *Perf. 14x13½*

676 A118 50c on 70c #606 11.50 8.50
677 A118 $1 on $1.50 #608 13.50 10.50

Flower Type of 1969 Redrawn

Design: 20c, Hibiscus.

1996, Aug. 22 Litho. *Rouletted 7*

678 A38 20c red & green .45 .45

Yachting A131

1996 Litho. *Perf. 14½*

679 A131 70c Jackfish 1.00 1.00
680 A131 $1 S/V Jennifer 1.40 1.40
681 A131 $1.20 Mikeva 2.00 2.00
682 A131 $2 Eye of the Wind 3.50 3.50
Nos. 679-682 (4) 7.90 7.90

Souvenir Sheet

Perf. 14

683 A131 $1.50 Desert Star 2.50 2.50

Issued: Nos. 679-682, 9/30/96. No. 683, 10/96 (Taipei '96). No. 683 contains one 30x30mm stamp.

Coral A132

20c, Acropora gemmifera. 50c, Acropora nobilis. 70c, Goniopora lobata. $1, Stylaster. $1.20, Alveopora catalai. $1.50, Fungia scutaria. $2, Porites solida. $3, Millepora. $4, Pocillopora eydouxi. $5, Platygyra pini.

1996, Dec. 20 Litho. *Perf. 14*

684-693 A132 Set of 10 26.00 26.00

Souvenir Sheet

New Year 1997 (Year of the Ox) — A133

1997, Feb. 10 Litho. *Perf. 13*

694 A133 $1.50 multicolored 2.50 2.50

Hong Kong '97.

Humpback Whale — A134

20c, Whale in water. 50c, Killer whale. 70c, Minke whale. $1, Adult, young whale swimming upward. $1.20, Sperm whale. $1.50, Whale breaching.

1997 Litho. *Perf. 14*

695	A134	20c multi	.40	.40
696	A134	50c multi, vert.	1.05	1.05
697	A134	70c multi, vert.	1.40	1.40
698	A134	$1 multi, vert.	2.25	2.25
699	A134	$1.20 multi, vert.	2.60	2.60
700	A134	$1.50 multi, vert.	3.50	3.50
a.		Souvenir sheet, #695, 698, 700	4.25	4.25
		Nos. 695-700 (6)	11.20	11.20

Pacific '97 (#700a).
Issued: 20c, $1, $1.50, 5/29; others, 9/3.

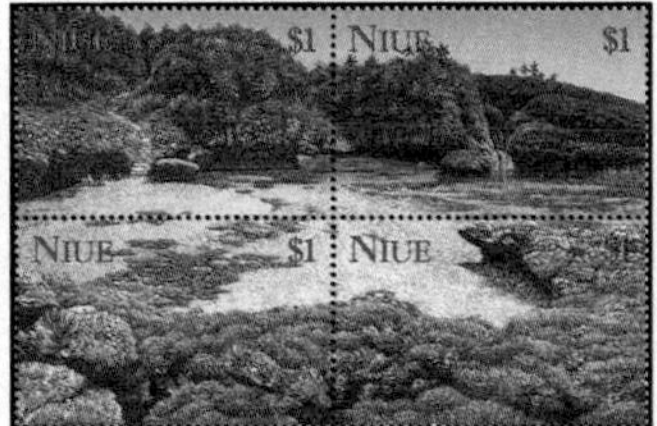

Island Scenes — A135

Designs: a, Steps leading over island along inlet. b, Island, vegetagion, sky. c, Coral reef, undersea vegetation. d, Reef, vegetation, diff.

1997, Apr. 18 Litho. *Perf. 13½x14*

701	A135	$1 Block of 4, #a.-d.	5.50	5.50

Christmas A136

Bouquets of various flowers.

1997, Nov. 26 Litho. *Perf. 14*

702	A136	20c deep plum & multi	.30	.30
703	A136	50c green & multi	.70	.70
704	A136	70c blue & multi	1.00	1.00
705	A136	$1 red & multi	1.50	1.50
		Nos. 702-705 (4)	3.50	3.50

Diana, Princess of Wales (1961-97)
Common Design Type

Various portraits: a, 20c. b, 50c. c, $1. d, $2.

1998, Apr. 29 Litho. *Perf. 14½x14*

706	CD355	Sheet of 4, #a.-d.	5.50	5.50

No. 706 sold for $3.70 + 50c, with surtax from international sales being donated to the Princess of Wales Memorial fund and surtax from national sales being donated to designated local charity.

Diving A137

Designs: 20c, Two snorkeling beneath water's surface. 70c, One diver, coral. $1, Diving into underwater canyon, vert. $1.20, Two divers, coral. $1.50, Divers exploring underwater cavern.

Wmk. Triangles

1998, May 20 Litho. *Perf. 14½*

707	A137	20c multicolored	.40	.40
708	A137	70c multicolored	1.00	1.00
709	A137	$1 multicolored	1.40	1.40
710	A137	$1.20 multicolored	1.75	1.75
711	A137	$1.50 multicolored	2.40	2.40
		Nos. 707-711 (5)	6.95	6.95

Sea Birds A138

Designs: 20c, Pacific black duck. 70c, Fairy tern. $1, Great frigatebird, vert. $1.20, Lesser golden plover. $2, Brown noddy.

Perf. 14½x14, 14x14½
Wmk. Triangles

1998, July 23 Litho.

712	A138	20c multicolored	.55	.55
713	A138	70c multicolored	1.20	1.20
714	A138	$1 multicolored	2.10	2.10
715	A138	$1.20 multicolored	2.40	2.40
716	A138	$2 multicolored	3.50	3.50
		Nos. 712-716 (5)	9.75	9.75

Shells A139

Two views of various shells from the Pacific Ocean.

Perf. 14½

1998, Sept. 23 Litho. Unwmk.

717	A139	20c multicolored	.50	.50
718	A139	70c multicolored	1.15	1.15
719	A139	$1 multicolored	2.40	2.40
720	A139	$5 multicolored	7.50	7.50
		Nos. 717-720 (4)	11.55	11.55

Ancient Weapons — A140

Perf. 14x14½

1998, Nov. 18 Litho. Unwmk.

721	A140	20c Clubs	.50	.50
722	A140	$1.20 Spears	1.50	1.50
723	A140	$1.50 Spears, diff.	1.90	1.90
724	A140	$2 Throwing stones	2.60	2.60
		Nos. 721-724 (4)	6.50	6.50

Nos. 722-723 are each 60x23mm.

Maritime Heritage — A141

Designs: 70c, First migration of Niue Fekai. $1, Crew of Resolution discover Niue. $1.20, LMS John Williams. $1.50, Captain James Cook (1728-79).

1999, Feb. 24 Litho. *Perf. 14½x14*

725	A141	70c bright violet blue	.90	.90
726	A141	$1 bright violet blue	1.40	1.40
727	A141	$1.20 bright violet blue	1.75	1.75
728	A141	$1.50 bright violet blue	2.10	2.10
		Nos. 725-728 (4)	6.15	6.15

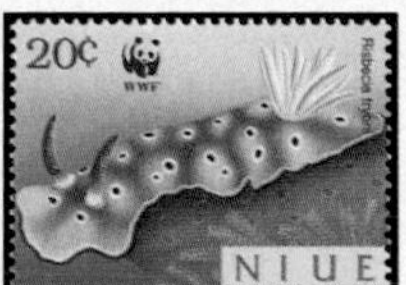

Nudibranchs A142

World Wide Fund for Nature: 20c, Risbecia tryoni. $1, Chromodoris lochi. $1.20, Chromodoris elizabethina. $1.50, Chromodoris bullocki.

1999, Mar. 17 Litho. *Perf. 14½*

729	A142	20c multicolored	.40	.40
730	A142	$1 multicolored	1.40	1.40
731	A142	$1.20 multicolored	1.50	1.50
732	A142	$1.50 multicolored	2.25	2.25
a.		Souv. sheet, 2 ea #729-732	11.50	11.50
		Nos. 729-732 (4)	5.55	5.55

Scenic Views A143

$1, Togo Chasm, vert. $1.20, Matapa Chasm, vert. $1.50, Tufukia. $2, Talava Arches.

1999, June 16 Litho. *Perf. 14*

734	A143	$1 multicolored	1.40	1.40
735	A143	$1.20 multicolored	1.50	1.50
736	A143	$1.50 multicolored	1.90	1.90
737	A143	$2 multicolored	2.75	2.75
		Nos. 734-737 (4)	7.55	7.55

Woven Baskets A144

Various styles and patterns: #738a, 20c. #738b, $1. #739a, 70c. #739b, $3.

1999, Sept. 18 Litho. *Perf. 12*

738	A144	Pair, a.-b.	2.00	2.00
739	A144	Pair, a.-b.	4.00	4.00

Nos. 738b, 739b are each 45x35mm.

Souvenir Sheet

Self-Government, 25th Anniv. — A145

Designs: a, 20c, Natives, boats. b, $5, Fish, tree, diver, child.

Litho. with Foil application

1999, Dec. 1 *Perf. 15x14¾*

740	A145	Sheet of 2, #a.-b	6.00	6.00

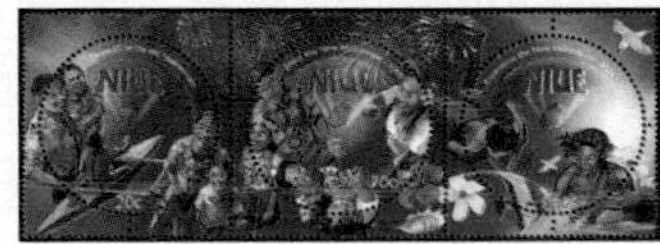

Millennium — A146

a, 20c, Man in outrigger canoe. b, 70c, Women pointing up. c, $4, Swimmers, bird, fish.

1999, Dec. 31 Litho. *Perf. 14¼x15*

741	A146	Strip of 3, #a.-c.	6.50	6.50

Birds and Flora — A147

20c, Purple-capped fruit dove, mamane. $1, Purple swamphen, fig. $1.20, Barn owl, koa. $2, Blue-crowned lory, ohia lehua.

2000, Apr. 5 Litho. *Perf. 13x13¼*

742-745	A147	Set of 4	6.50	6.50

Royal Birthdays A148

Designs: $1.50, Queen Mother, 100th birthday, vert. $3, Prince William, 18th birthday, and Queen Mother.

2000, May 22 *Perf. 13¼x13, 13x13¼*

746-747	A148	Set of 2	4.50	4.50

2000 Summer Olympics, Sydney A149

Designs: 50c, Pole vault. 70c, Diving. $1, Hurdles. $3, Gymnastics.

Perf. 13½x13¼

2000, Sept. 16 Litho.

748-751	A149	Set of 4	5.00	5.00

Dancers — A150

No. 752: a, Couple. b, Woman with red garments. c, Woman with white garments. d, Child with garments made of leaves.

2000, Nov. 22 Litho. *Perf. 13¼x13*

752		Horiz. strip of 4	5.00	5.00
a.		A150 20c multi	.30	.30
b.		A150 70c multi	.65	.65
c.		A150 $1.50 multi	1.30	1.30
d.		A150 $3 multi	2.75	2.75

Niue Postage Stamps, Cent. (in 2002) — A151

Designs: 70c, #1. $3, #34.

2001, Jan. 31

753-754	A151	Set of 2	3.25	3.25

Butterflies A152

No. 755: a, Large green-banded blue. b, Leafwing. c, Cairns birdwing. d, Meadow argus.

2001, Mar. 22 *Perf. 13½x13¼*

755	Horiz. strip of 4	4.00	4.00
a.	A152 20c multi	.25	.25
b.	A152 70c multi	.60	.60
c.	A152 $1.50 multi	1.40	1.40
d.	A152 $2 multi	1.75	1.75

Turtles A153

Designs: 50c, Green turtle hatching. $1, Hawksbill turtle. $3, Green turtle on beach.

2001, May 10

756-758 A153	Set of 3	4.00	4.00

Coconut Crabs — A154

Crab: 20c, In water. 70c, On beach. $1.50, Climbing tree. $3, With coconut.

2001, July 7 *Perf. 14*

759-762 A154	Set of 4	5.00	5.00

Annexation by New Zealand, Cent. A155

Designs: $1.50, Building. $2, Man and woman.

2001, Oct. 19 Litho. *Perf. 13½x13¼*

763-764 A155	Set of 2	3.25	3.25

Christmas — A156

Designs: 20c, Magi. 70c, Dove. $1, Angel. $2, Star.

2001, Dec. 13 *Perf. 13x13¼*

765-768 A156	Set of 4	3.50	3.50
768a	Horiz. strip, #765-768	3.50	3.50

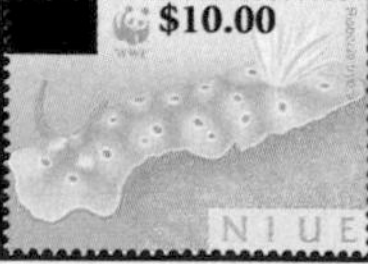

No. 729 Surcharged

2002, July 7 Litho. *Perf. 14½*

769 A142	$10 on 20c multi	*75.00*	*65.00*

Worldwide Fund for Nature (WWF) — A156a

Various depictions of small giant clam.

2002, Nov. 7 Litho. *Perf. 13¼x13*

769A	Horiz. strip of 4	4.50	4.50
b.	A156a 50c multi	.60	.60
c.	A156a 70c multi	.75	.70
d.	A156a $1 multi	1.10	1.10
e.	A156a $1.50 multi	1.60	1.60
f.	As #769Ab, without emblem	—	—
g.	As #760Ac, without emblem	—	—
h.	As #769Ad, without emblem	—	—
i.	As #769Ae, without emblem	—	—
j.	Souvenir sheet of 4, #769Af-769Ai	—	—

General Motors Automobiles — A157

No. 770, $1.50 — Cadillacs: a, 1953 Eldorado. b, 2002 Eldorado. c, 1967 Eldorado. d, 1961 Sedan de Ville.

No. 771, $1.50 — Corvettes: a, 1954 convertible. b, 1979. c, 1956 convertible. d, 1964 Stingray.

No. 772, $4, 1978 Cadillac Seville. No. 773, $4, 1979 Corvette.

2003 Litho. *Perf. 14*

Sheets of 4, #a-d

770-771 A157	Set of 2	24.00	24.00

Souvenir Sheets

772-773 A157	Set of 2	22.00	22.00

Issued: Nos. 770, 772, 8/25; Nos. 771, 773, 9/2.

Coronation of Queen Elizabeth II, 50th Anniv. — A158

No. 774: a, Wearing crown as younger woman. b, Wearing tiara. c, Wearing crown as older woman.

$4, Wearing hat.

2003, Sept. 2

774 A158	$1.50 Sheet of 3, #a-c	9.00	9.00

Souvenir Sheet

775 A158	$4 multi	9.00	9.00

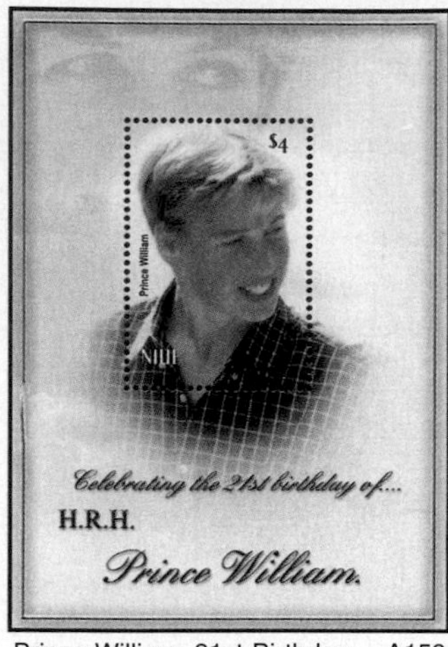

Prince William, 21st Birthday — A159

No. 776: a, Wearing blue checked tie. b, Wearing shirt and jacket. c, Wearing striped shirt and tie.

$4, Wearing shirt.

2003, Sept. 2

776 A159	$1.50 Sheet of 3, #a-c	9.00	9.00

Souvenir Sheet

777 A159	$4 multi	8.50	8.50

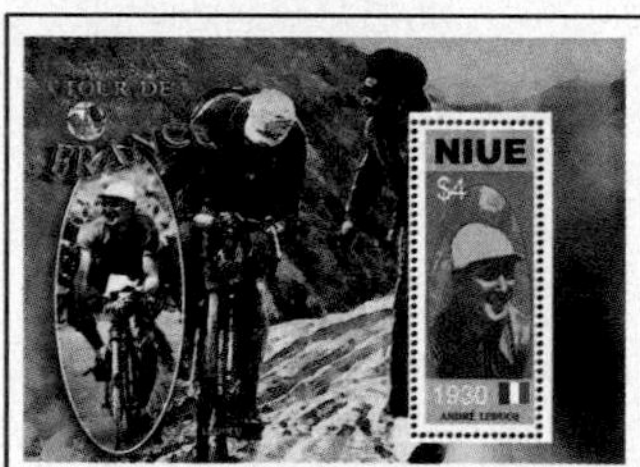

Tour de France Bicycle Race, Cent. — A160

No. 778: a, Nicholas Frantz, 1927. b, Frantz, 1928. c, Maurice de Waele, 1929. d, André Leducq, 1930.

$4, Leducq, 1930, diff.

2003, Sept. 2 *Perf. 13½x13¼*

778 A160	$1.50 Sheet of 4, #a-d	10.50	10.50

Souvenir Sheet

779 A160	$4 multi	8.75	8.75

Powered Flight, Cent. — A161

No. 780: a, Boeing 737-200. b, Boeing Stratocruiser. c, Boeing Model SA-307B. d, Douglas DC-2. e, Wright Flyer I. f, De Havilland D.H.4A.

$4, Boeing 767.

2003, Sept. 2 *Perf. 14*

780 A161	80c Sheet of 6, #a-f	9.00	9.00

Souvenir Sheet

781 A161	$4 multi	9.00	9.00

Birds, Butterflies and Fish — A162

No. 782, $1.50, vert. — Birds: a, Wrinkled hornbill. b, Toco toucan. c, Roseate spoonbill. d, Blue and gold macaw.

No. 783, $1.50 — Butterflies: a, Agrias beata. b, Papilio blumei. c, Cethosia bibbis. d, Cressida cressida.

No. 784, $1.50 — Fish: a, Garibaldi fish. b, Golden damselfish. c, Squarespot anthias. d, Orange-fin anemonefish.

No. 785, $3, Green-wing macaw. No. 786, $3, Blue morpho butterfly. No. 787, $3, Maculosus angelfish.

Perf. 13½x13¼, 13¼x13½

2004, Aug. 16 **Litho.**

Sheets of 4, #a-d

782-784 A162	Set of 3	24.00	24.00

Souvenir Sheets

785-787 A162	Set of 3	12.00	12.00

Miniature Sheet

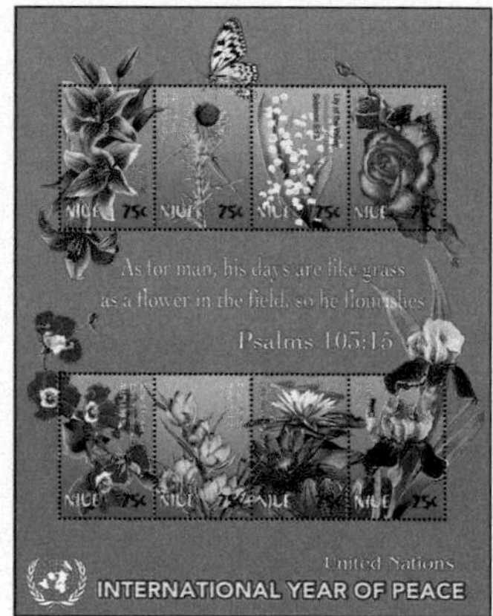

Intl. Year of Peace — A163

No. 788: a, Lily. b, Thistle. c, Lily of the valley. d, Rose. e, Garland flower. f, Crocus. g, Lotus. h, Iris.

2004, Oct. 13 *Perf. 13½x13¼*

788 A163	75c Sheet of 8, #a-h	8.50	8.50

Miniature Sheet

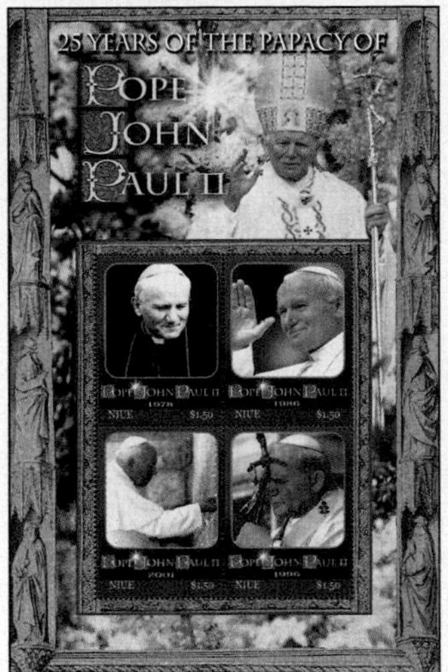

Election of Pope John Paul II, 25th Anniv. (in 2003) — A164

No. 789 — Pope in: a, 1978. b, 1986. c, 2001. d, 1996.

2004, Oct. 13 ***Perf. 13¼***
789 A164 $1.50 Sheet of 4, #a-d 8.50 8.50

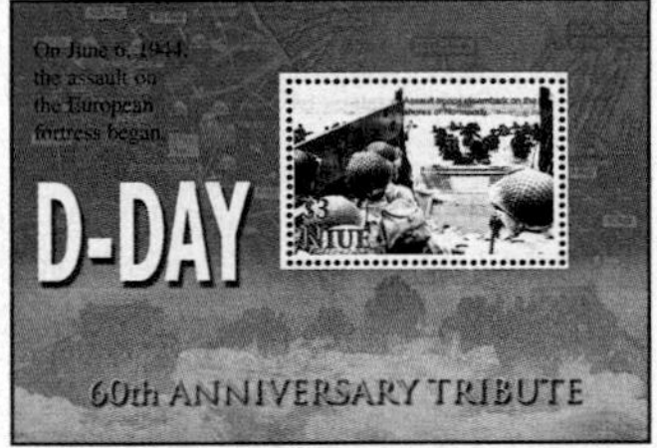

D-Day, 60th Anniv. — A165

No. 790: a, Allied Air Forces begin bombing German coastal batteries. b, Allied naval guns pound Atlantic Wall. c, Paratroopers drop over Normandy. d, Allies advance and the Germans begin to surrender.
$3, Assault troops disembark on the shores of Normandy.

2004, Oct. 13 ***Perf. 13¼x13½***
790 A165 $1.50 Sheet of 4, #a-d 8.50 8.50

Souvenir Sheet

791 A165 $3 multi 4.50 4.50

Locomotives, 200th Anniv. — A166

No. 792: a, 520 Class 4-8-4, Australia. b, FEF-2 Class 4-8-4, US. c, Royal Scot Class 4-6-0, Great Britain. d, A4 Class 4-6-2, Great Britain.
$3, Class GS-4 4-8-4, US.

2004, Oct. 13
792 A166 $1.50 Sheet of 4, #a-d 8.50 8.50

Souvenir Sheet

793 A166 $3 multi 4.50 4.50

Pope John Paul II (1920-2005) — A167

2005, Dec. 13 **Litho.** ***Perf. 13¼***
794 A167 $2 multi 3.00 3.00

Printed in sheets of 4.

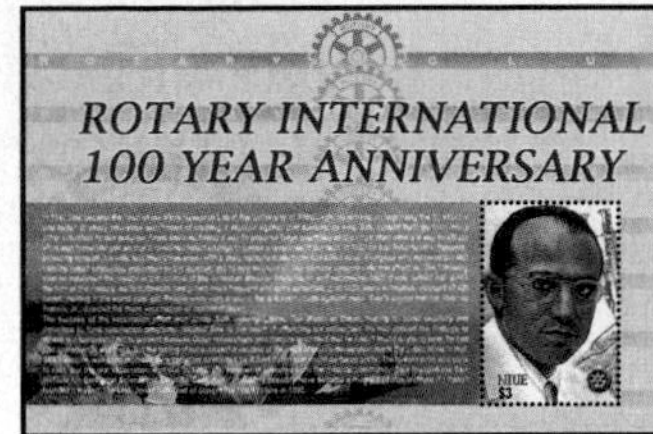

Rotary International, Cent. — A168

No. 795: a, Children. b, Paul P. Harris, Rotary founder. c, Carlo Ravizza, 1999-2000 Rotary International President.
$3, Dr. Jonas Salk, polio vaccine pioneer.

2005, Dec. 22
795 A168 $1.50 Sheet of 3, #a-c 6.50 6.50

Souvenir Sheet

796 A168 $3 multi 4.50 4.50

Pope Benedict XVI — A169

2005, Dec. 27
797 A169 $1.50 multi 2.25 2.25

Printed in sheets of 4.

Hans Christian Andersen (1805-75), Author — A170

No. 798 — Andersen and country name and denomination in: a, Lilac. b, Ocher. c, Red.
$3, Andersen facing left.

2005, Dec. 27
798 A170 $1.50 Sheet of 3, #a-c 6.50 6.50

Souvenir Sheet

799 A170 $3 multi 4.50 4.50

World Cup Soccer Championships, 75th Anniv. — A171

No. 800: a, Frank Bauman. b, Marcus Babbel. c, Dietmar Hamann.
$3, Christian Worns.

2005, Dec. 27
800 A171 $1.50 Sheet of 3, #a-c 6.50 6.50

Souvenir Sheet

801 A171 $3 multi 4.50 4.50

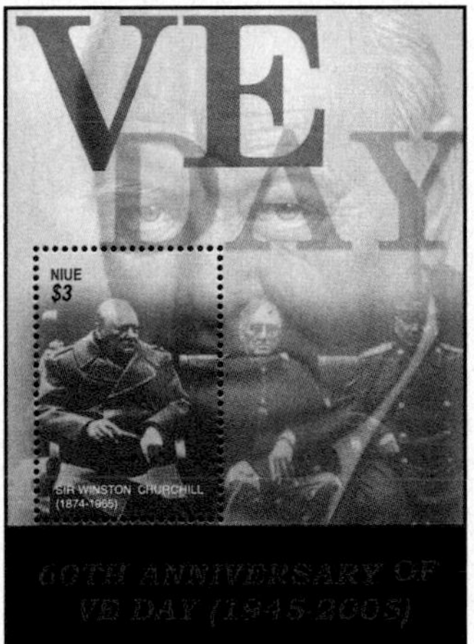

End of World War II, 60th Anniv. — A172

No. 802, horiz.: a, Entertaining the troops in the Pacific. b, USS Argonaut sailors reading letters from home. c, Japan surrenders on USS Missouri. d, A toast to peace. e, Entertainment at sea. f, Welcoming peace.

No. 803: a, D-Day invasion, Normandy, France. b, Lt. Meyrick Clifton-James, double for Field Marshal Bernard Montgomery. c, RAF Hawker Typhoon over French coast. d, Allied war cemetery, St. Laurent-sur-Mer, France.

No. 804, $3, Sir Winston Churchill. No. 805, $3, Pres. Franklin D. Roosevelt.

2005, Dec. 27
802 A172 75c Sheet of 6, #a-f 6.75 6.75
803 A172 $1.25 Sheet of 4, #a-d 7.50 7.50

Souvenir Sheets

804-805 A172 Set of 2 9.00 9.00

Souvenir Sheets

National Basketball Association Players and Team Emblems — A173

No. 806, $4.50: a, LeBron James. b, Cleveland Cavaliers emblem.

No. 807, $4.50: a, Tim Duncan. b, San Antonio Spurs emblem.

No. 808, $4.50: a, Allen Iverson. b, Denver Nuggets emblem.

No. 809, $4.50: a, Kobe Bryant. b, Los Angeles Lakers emblem.

No. 810, $4.50: a, Tracy McGrady. b, Houston Rockets emblem.

No. 811, $4.50: a, Jermaine O'Neal. b, Indiana Pacers emblem.

Litho. & Embossed

2007, Feb. 4 ***Imperf.***

Without Gum

Sheets of 2, #a-b

806-811 A173 Set of 6 77.50 77.50

Miniature Sheet

Elvis Presley (1935-77) — A174

No. 812 — Presley: a, With hands resting on guitar. b, In green shirt, playing guitar. c, In brown red shirt, playing guitar. d, Holding guitar by neck.

2007, Feb. 15 **Litho.** ***Perf. 12¾***
812 A174 $1.50 Sheet of 4, #a-d 8.50 8.50

Miniature Sheets

Space Achievements — A175

No. 813: a, Stardust probe at Kennedy Space Center. b, Stardust dust collector with aerogel. c, Stardust navigational camera. d, Stardust Whipple shield. e, Cometary and interstellar dust analyzer. f, Stardust and Comet Wild 2.

No. 814, horiz. — Artist's rendition of future projects: a, Astrobiology field laboratory. b, Deep-drill lander. c, Mars science laboratory. d, Phoenix lander.

2007, Feb. 15
813 A175 $1 Sheet of 6, #a-f 8.50 8.50
814 A175 $1.50 Sheet of 4, #a-d 8.50 8.50

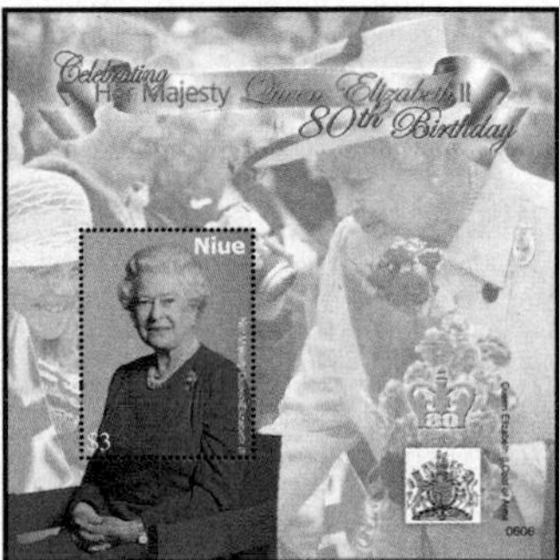

Queen Elizabeth II, 80th Birthday (in 2006) — A176

No. 815 — Dress color: a, Brown. b, Pink. c, Red. d, White.
$3, Purple.

2007, Feb. 15 ***Perf. 12¼x12***
815 A176 $1.50 Sheet of 4, #a-d 8.50 8.50

Souvenir Sheet

Perf. 13¼

816 A176 $3 multi 4.50 4.50

Rembrandt (1606-69), Painter A177

Designs: 75c, Life Study of a Young Man Pulling a Rope. $1.25, Self-portrait. $1.50, Joseph Telling His Dreams. $2, The Blindness of Tobit.

$3, Christ in the Storm on the Lake of Galilee.

2007, Feb. 15 *Perf. 12¼x12*

817-820 A177 Set of 4 8.25 8.25

Imperf

Size: 70x100mm

821 A177 $3 multi 4.75 4.75

Princess Diana (1961-97) — A178

No. 822 — Diana wearing: a, Purple dress. b, Tiara and black dress. c, Green dress, close-up. d, Purple dress, close-up. e, Tiara, close-up. f, Green dress.

$3, Diana with head on hand.

2007, May 3 *Perf. 13½x13¼*

822 A178 $1 Sheet of 6, #a-f 9.50 9.50

Souvenir Sheet

823 A178 $3 multi 4.75 4.75

Local Attractions, Flora and Fauna — A179

Designs: 20c, Palaha Cave. 70c, White pua flower. $1, Talava Natural Arch. $1.20, Avaiki Pool. $1.50, Coral rock spears. $2, Humpback whale. $3, Spinner dolphins.

2007, July 9 **Litho.** *Perf. 14x14¾*

824	A179	20c multi	.35	.35
825	A179	70c multi	1.20	1.20
826	A179	$1 multi	1.60	1.60
827	A179	$1.20 multi	2.00	2.00
828	A179	$1.50 multi	2.40	2.40
829	A179	$2 multi	3.25	3.25
830	A179	$3 multi	4.75	4.75
		Nos. 824-830 (7)	15.55	15.55

Miniature Sheets

Concorde — A180

No. 831, $1: a, Concorde and hangar, blue tint. b, Concorde in air, normal tint. c, Concorde and hangar, red tint. d, Concorde in air, pink tint. e, Concorde and hangar, normal tint. f, Concorde in air, blue tint.

No. 832, $1: a, Concorde landing, yellow green frame. b, Concorde being towed, gray frame. c, Concorde landing, green gray frame. d, Concorde being towed, brown frame. e, Concorde landing, gray frame. f, Concorde being towed, blue frame.

2007, July 21 *Perf. 13¼*

Sheets of 6, #a-f

831-832 A180 Set of 2 19.00 19.00

Wedding of Queen Elizabeth II and Prince Philip, 60th Anniv. — A181

No. 833, vert.: a, Queen and Prince, "N" of "Niue" and denomination over white area, parts of flag in faded area between country name and denomination. b, Queen, "N" of "Niue" and denomination over white and blue areas. c, Queen, flower buds in faded area between country name and denomination. d, Queen and Prince, "N" of "Niue" and denomination over gray area, parts of flag in faded area between country name and denomination. e, Queen and Prince, country name and denomination over solid gray area. f, Queen, country name and denomination over solid gray area.

$3, Queen and Prince.

2007, July 21 *Perf. 13¼*

833 A181 $1 Sheet of 6, #a-f 9.25 9.25

Souvenir Sheet

834 A181 $3 multi 4.25 4.25

Miniature Sheets

A182

Marilyn Monroe (1926-62), Actress — A183

Various portraits.

2007, Aug. 21

835 A182 $1.50 Sheet of 4, #a-d 8.50 8.50

836 A183 $1.50 Sheet of 4, #a-d 8.50 8.50

Jamestown, Virginia, 400th Anniv. — A184

No. 837: a, Marriage of John Rolfe to Pocahontas. b, First settlers reach Jamestown. c, Tobacco plant. d, Capt. John Smith. e, Jamestown Tercentenary Monument. f, Map of Jamestown.

$3, Queen Elizabeth II and Prince Philip at Jamestown.

2007, Aug. 21

837 A184 $1 Sheet of 6, #a-f 9.00 9.00

Souvenir Sheet

838 A184 $3 multi 4.50 4.50

Pope Benedict XVI — A185

2007, Dec. 3 **Litho.** *Perf. 13¼*

839 A185 70c multi 1.25 1.25

Printed in sheets of 8.

Miniature Sheet

Ferrari Automobiles, 60th Anniv. — A186

No. 840: a, 1949 166 FL. b, 1991 512 TR. c, 2003 Challenge Stradale. d, 1988 F1 87/88C. e, 2007 F2007. f, Building with Ferrari sign.

2007, Dec. 10

840 A186 $1 Sheet of 6, #a-f 10.50 10.50

Tourism A187

Designs: 10c, Coconut palm. 20c, Tropical sunset. 30c, Humpback whale. 50c, Rainbow over rainforest. $1, Hio Beach. $1.20, Talava Arches. $1.40, Limu Pools. $1.70, Limestone caves. $2, Snorkeling in Limu Pools. $3, Panoramic coastline. $5, Liku Caves.

Perf. 13½x13¼

2009, Sept. 14 **Litho.**

841	A187	10c multi	.25	.25
842	A187	20c multi	.30	.30
843	A187	30c multi	.45	.45
844	A187	50c multi	.75	.75
845	A187	$1 multi	1.50	1.50
846	A187	$1.20 multi	1.75	1.75
a.		Miniature sheet of 6, #841-846, perf. 14	5.00	5.00
847	A187	$1.40 multi	2.00	2.00
848	A187	$1.70 multi	2.50	2.50
849	A187	$2 multi	3.00	3.00
850	A187	$3 multi	4.50	4.50
851	A187	$5 multi	7.25	7.25
a.		Miniature sheet of 5, #847-851, perf. 14	19.50	19.50
		Nos. 841-851 (11)	24.25	24.25

Christmas A188

Stained-glass window depicting: 30c, Man facing right, Ekalesia Millennium Hall. 80c, Dove, Lakepa Ekalesia Church. $1.20, Chalice and bread, Lakepa Ekalesia Church. $1.40, Man facing left, Ekalesia Millennium Hall.

Perf. 13¼x13½

2009, Nov. 25 **Litho.**

852-855 A188 Set of 4 5.50 5.50

855a Souvenir sheet, #852-855 5.50 5.50

Butterflies A189

Designs: $1.40, Hypolimnas bolina. $1.70, Junonia villida, vert. (22x26mm). $2.40, Hypolimnas antilope.

2010, July 7 **Litho.** *Perf. 14*

856-858 A189 Set of 3 8.00 8.00

858a Souvenir sheet of 3, #856-858 8.00 8.00

Christmas A190

2010, Oct. 20 *Perf. 13¼x13½*

859	Horiz. strip of 4	12.00	12.00
a.	A190 30c Annunciation	.45	.45
b.	A190 $1.40 Journey to Bethlehem	2.10	2.10
c.	A190 $2 Nativity	3.00	3.00
d.	A190 $4 Adoration of the Shepherds	6.00	6.00

Whales A191

Designs: 80c, Whale's flukes. $1.20, Two whales raising heads out of water. $1.40, Calf breaching surface. $2, Mother and calf playing.

2010, Nov. 17 **Litho.** *Perf. 14*

860-863 A191 Set of 4 8.50 8.50

863a Souvenir sheet, #860-863 8.50 8.50

Wedding of Prince William and Catherine Middleton — A192

No. 864: a, $2.40, Catherine Middleton. b, $3.40, Prince William.

2011, Mar. 23

864 A192 Horiz. pair, #a-b 9.25 9.25

c. Souvenir sheet, #864a-864b 9.25 9.25

Birds — A193

Designs: $1.70, Aplonis tabuensis. $2, Lalage maculosa, vert. (25x30mm). $2.40, Ptilinopus porphyraceus.

2011, July 6
865-867 A193 Set of 3 10.50 10.50
867a Souvenir sheet of 3, #865-867 10.50 10.50

Christmas A194

Designs: 30c, Pacific sunset. $1.40, Matapa Chasm. $2, Coconut palms. $4, Centennial Church, Alofi.

2011, Nov. 16 ***Perf. 13¼x13½***
868-871 A194 Set of 4 12.00 12.00
871a Souvenir sheet of 4, #868-871 12.00 12.00

Shells A195

Designs: $1.20, Map cowrie. $1.40, Geography cone. $1.70, Partridge tun. $2, Tiger cowrie.

2012, Apr. 11 ***Perf. 13½x13¼***
872-875 A195 Set of 4 10.50 10.50
875a Souvenir sheet of 4, #872-875 10.50 10.50

Reign of Queen Elizabeth II, 60th Anniv. — A196

Hibiscus flowers and photograph of Queen Elizabeth II from: $2.40, 1953. $3.40, 2012.

2012, May 23 ***Perf. 13¼x13½***
876-877 A196 Set of 2 9.00 9.00
877a Souvenir sheet of 2, #876-877 9.00 9.00
877b Horiz. pair, #876-877 9.00 9.00

Worldwide Fund For Nature (WWF) A197

Various depictions of Giant sea fan: $1.20, $1.40, $1.70, $2.

2012, Sept. 5 ***Perf. 13½x13¼***
878-881 A197 Set of 4 10.50 10.50
881a Souvenir sheet of 4, #878-881 10.50 10.50

Christmas A198

Designs: 30c, Angel and infant Jesus. $1.40, Holy Family. $2, Magi. $4, Shepherds.

2012, Nov. 21
882-885 A198 Set of 4 13.00 13.00

Niue Blue Butterfly A199

Designs: $1.20, Male underside. $1.40, Male upperside. $1.70, Female underside. $2, Female upperside.

2013, Apr. 10 ***Perf. 13½***
886-889 A199 Set of 4 10.50 10.50
889a Souvenir sheet of 4, #886-889 10.50 10.50

Coronation of Queen Elizabeth II, 60th Anniv. — A200

Designs: $2.40, Queen Elizabeth II. $3.40, Queen Elizabeth II, Prince Philip, Princess Margaret, Queen Mother.

2013, May 8 ***Perf. 13¼x13½***
890-891 A200 Set of 2 9.25 9.25
891a Souvenir sheet of 2, #890-891 9.25 9.25

Christmas A201

Designs: 30c, Dove. $1.40, Angel. $2, Star of Bethlehem. $4, Bells.

Perf. 13¼x13¾
2013, Nov. 20 **Litho.**
892-895 A201 Set of 4 13.00 13.00
895a Souvenir sheet of 4, #892-895 13.00 13.00

Traditional Dress A202

Designs: 30c, Pulou (hat). $1.40, Pipi (belt). $2, Tiputa (poncho). $4, Patutiti (skirt).

2014, Apr. 23 **Litho.** ***Perf. 13½x13¼***
896-899 A202 Set of 4 13.50 13.50
899a Souvenir sheet of 4 #896-899 13.50 13.50

Fish A203

Designs: 30c, Whitemouth moray. $1.40, Orangefin anemonefish. $2, Fire dartfish. $4, Longnose butterflyfish.

Perf. 13½x13¼
2014, June 18 **Litho.**
900-903 A203 Set of 4 13.50 13.50
903a Souvenir sheet of 4 #900-903 13.50 13.50

Island Views — A204

Designs: 20c, Talava Arches. 30c, Mutalau. $1, Avaiki Caves. $1.20, Lakepa Village Church. $1.40, Golf course. $1.70, Huvalu Forest. $2, Tepa Point. $4, Togo Chasm.

2014, Oct. 18 **Litho.** ***Perf. 14x14¼***

904	A204	20c	multi	.35	.35
905	A204	30c	multi	.50	.50
906	A204	$1	multi	1.60	1.60
907	A204	$1.20	multi	1.90	1.90
908	A204	$1.40	multi	2.25	2.25
909	A204	$1.70	multi	2.75	2.75
910	A204	$2	multi	3.25	3.25
911	A204	$4	multi	6.25	6.25
	Nos. 904-911 (8)			18.85	18.85

Christmas A205

Various Christmas ornaments in: 30c Blue. $1.40, Red. $2, Green. $4, Purple.

Perf. 13¼x13½
2014, Dec. 10 **Litho.**
912-915 A205 Set of 4 12.00 12.00
915a Souvenir sheet of 4, #912-915 12.00 12.00

Haipo (Tapa Cloths) A206

Various haipo designs: 30c, $1.40, $2, $4.

2015, Apr. 7 **Litho.** ***Perf. 13½***
916-919 A206 Set of 4 12.00 12.00
919a Souvenir sheet of 4, #916-919 12.00 12.00

Flora — A207

Designs: 30c, Hibiscus tiliaceus. $1.40, Fagraea Berteroana. $2, Alphitonia zizyphoides. $4, Cordyline fruticosa.

2015, June 3 **Litho.** ***Perf. 13½***
920-923 A207 Set of 4 10.50 10.50
923a Souvenir sheet of 4, #920-923 10.50 10.50

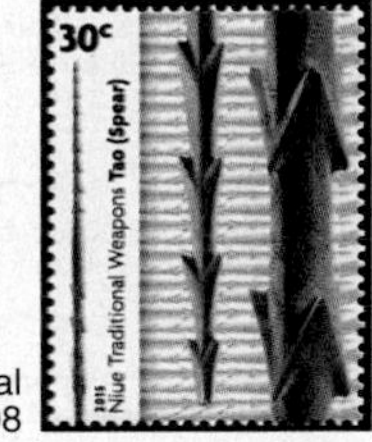
Traditional Weapons — A208

Designs: 30c, Spear. $1.40, Club. $3, Spear, diff. $4, Club, diff.

2015, Aug. 5 **Litho.** ***Perf. 13½***
924-927 A208 Set of 4 11.00 11.00
927a Souvenir sheet of 4, #924-927 11.00 11.00

Miniature Sheet

World War I, Cent. — A209

No. 928: a, 20c, Life in Niue, pre-war. b, 30c, Soldiers at Narrow Neck Camp, Auckland. c, $1, Troops departing for war from Auckland. d, $1.20, Badge of New Zealand Pioneer Battalion, map of Egypt. e, $1.40, Trench in Armentières, France. f, $1.70, New Zealand Convalescent Hospital, Hornchurch, England. g, $2, Soldiers and nurses recovering in Auckland. h, $4, War Memorial, Niue.

2015, Oct. 13 **Litho.** ***Perf. 14x14½***
928 A209 Sheet of 8, #a-h 16.00 16.00

Christmas A210

Carols: 30c, Silent Night. $1.40, Joy to the World. $2, Away in the Manger. $4, Deck the Halls.

2015, Nov. 25 **Litho.** ***Perf. 14½***
929-932 A210 Set of 4 10.50 10.50
932a Souvenir sheet of 4, #929-932 10.50 10.50

SEMI-POSTAL STAMPS

Catalogue values for unused stamps in this section are for Never Hinged items.

Easter Type of 1978
Souvenir Sheets

Designs: No. B1, Descent from the Cross, by Caravaggio. No. B2, Burial of Christ, by Bellini. Sheets show paintings from which stamp designs were taken.

1978, Mar. 15 **Photo.** ***Perf. 13½***
B1 A61 70c + 5c multi 1.00 1.00
B2 A61 70c + 5c multi 1.00 1.00

Surtax was for school children in Niue.

Christmas Type of 1978
Souvenir Sheets

1978, Nov. 30 **Photo.** ***Perf. 13***

B3	A63	60c + 5c like #232	.90	.90
B4	A63	60c + 5c like #233	.90	.90
B5	A63	60c + 5c like #234	.90	.90
	Nos. B3-B5 (3)		2.70	2.70

Surtax was for school children of Niue. The sheets show paintings from which designs of stamps were taken.

Easter Type of 1979

Souvenir Sheets

1979, Apr. 2

B6 A64 70c + 5c like #235 1.10 1.10
B7 A64 70c + 5c like #236 1.10 1.10

Surtax was for school children of Niue. The sheets show altarpiece from which designs of stamps were taken.

IYC Type of 1979

Souvenir Sheets

1979, May 31 Photo. *Perf. 13*

B8 A65 70c + 5c like #237 .85 .85
B9 A65 70c + 5c like #238 .85 .85
B10 A65 70c + 5c like #239 .85 .85
B11 A65 70c + 5c like #240 .85 .85
Nos. B8-B11 (4) 3.40 3.40

Sheets show paintings from which designs of stamps were taken.

Christmas Type of 1979

Souvenir Sheets

1979, Nov. 29 Photo. *Perf. 13*

B12 A70 85c + 5c like #258 .80 .80
B13 A70 85c + 5c like #259 .80 .80
B14 A70 85c + 5c like #260 .80 .80
B15 A70 85c + 5c like #261 .80 .80
Nos. B12-B15 (4) 3.20 3.20

Multicolored margins show entire paintings.

Nos. 241-245, 251-254, 255-257, 258-261 Srchd. in Black (2 lines) or Silver (3 lines)

1980, Jan. 25 Photo. *Perf. 14, 13½*

B16 A66 20c + 2c pair .55 .55
B18 A68 20c + 2c multi (S) .30 .30
B19 A70 20c + 2c multi (S) .30 .30
B20 A70 25c + 2c multi (S) .40 .40
B21 A66 30c + 2c pair .80 .80
B23 A68 30c + 2c multi (S) .45 .45
B24 A69 30c + 2c multi (S) .45 .45
B25 A70 30c + 2c multi (S) .45 .45
B26 A66 35c + 2c pair 1.00 1.00
B28 A68 35c + 2c multi (S) .55 .55
B29 A69 35c + 2c multi (S) .55 .55
B30 A66 50c + 2c pair 1.20 1.20
B32 A70 50c + 2c multi (S) .65 .65
B33 A66 60c + 2c pair 1.40 1.40
B35 A69 60c + 2c multi (S) .80 .80
B36 A68 75c + 2c multi (S) 1.00 1.00
Nos. B16-B36 (16) 10.85 10.85

Easter Type of 1980

Souvenir Sheets

1980, Apr. 2 Photo. *Perf. 13*

B37 Sheet of 3 1.05 1.05
a. A71 25c + 2c like #262 .30 .30
b. A71 30c + 2c like #263 .35 .35
c. A71 35c + 2c like #264 .40 .40

1980, Apr. 2

B38 A71 85c + 5c like #262 .75 .75
B39 A71 85c + 5c like #263 .75 .75
B40 A71 85c + 5c like #264 .75 .75
Nos. B38-B40 (3) 2.25 2.25

Surtax was for hurricane relief.

No. 245a Overprinted Like Nos. 281-285 and Surcharged

Souvenir Sheet

1980, Aug. 22 Photo. *Perf. 14*

B41 Sheet of 10 5.00 5.00
a. A66 20c + 2c pair .50 .50
b. A66 30c + 2c pair .65 .65
c. A66 35c + 2c pair .80 .80
d. A66 50c + 2c pair 1.25 1.25
e. A66 60c + 2c pair 1.60 1.60

ZEAPEX '80, New Zealand Intl. Stamp Exhib., Auckland, Aug. 23-31.

Nos. 293a-296a Surcharged in Black

Souvenir Sheet

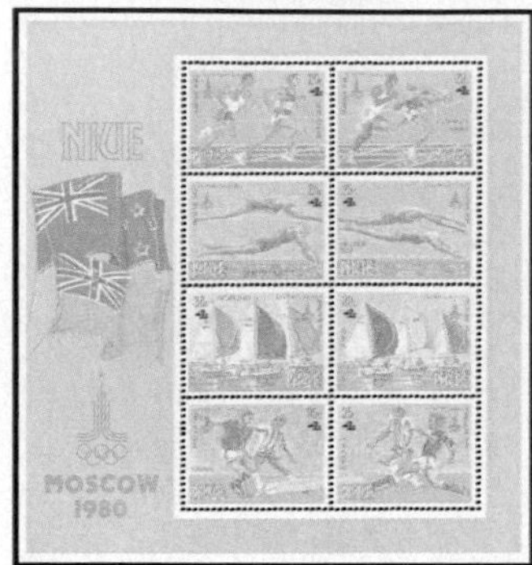

1980, Oct. 30 Photo. *Perf. 14*

B42 Sheet of 8, #a.-h. 2.50 2.50

22nd Summer Olympic Games, Moscow, July 19-Aug. 3.

Christmas Type of 1980

Souvenir Sheets

1980, Nov. 28 Photo. *Perf. 13½x13*

B43 A76 80c + 5c like #301 .75 .75
B44 A76 80c + 5c like #302 .75 .75
B45 A76 80c + 5c like #303 .75 .75
B46 A76 80c + 5c like #304 .75 .75
Nos. B43-B46 (4) 3.00 3.00

Nos. B43-B46 each contain one 31x39mm stamp.

Easter Type of 1981

Souvenir Sheets

1981, Apr. 10 Photo. *Perf. 13½*

B47 Sheet of 3 1.75 1.75
a. A78 35c + 2c like #337 .40 .40
b. A78 50c + 2c like #338 .50 .50
c. A78 60c + 2c like #339 .60 .60
B48 A78 80c + 5c like #337 .75 .75
B49 A78 80c + 5c like #338 .75 .75
B50 A78 80c + 5c like #339 .75 .75
Nos. B47-B50 (4) 4.00 4.00

Soccer Type of 1981

1981, Oct. 16 Photo. *Perf. 13*

B51 A80 Sheet of 9 3.25 3.25

#B51 contains #343-345 each with 3c surtax.

Nos. 340-342a Surcharged

1981, Nov. 3 Photo. *Perf. 14*

B52 A79 75c + 5c like #340 1.00 1.00
B53 A79 95c + 5c like #341 1.25 1.25
B54 A79 $1.20 + 5c like #342 1.50 1.50
Nos. B52-B54 (3) 3.75 3.75

Souvenir Sheet

B55 Sheet of 3 4.50 4.50
a. A79 75c + 10c like #340 1.20 1.20
b. A79 95c + 10c like #341 1.40 1.40
c. A79 $1.20 + 10c like #342 1.75 1.75

Intl. Year of the Disabled. Surtax was for disabled.

Nos. 530-535 Surcharged in Black on Silver

1986, Nov. 21 Litho. *Perf. 14*

B56 A105 80c + 10c multi 2.75 2.75
B57 A105 $1.15 + 10c multi 3.75 3.75
B58 A105 $1.80 + 10c multi 5.50 5.50
B59 A105 $2.60 + 10c multi 8.00 8.00
Nos. B56-B59 (4) 20.00 20.00

Souvenir Sheets

Perf. 13½

B60 Sheet of 4 18.00 18.00
a.-d. A105 $1.50 + 10c on #534a-534d 4.50 4.50

Perf. 14½x13½

B61 A105 $7.50 + 50c multi 18.00 18.00

No. B60 ovptd. "FIRST VISIT OF A POPE TO SOUTH PACIFIC" and "HIS HOLINESS POPE JOHN PAUL II" on margin. No. B61 ovptd. on margin only "Visit of Pope John Paul II, Nov 21-24 1986 / First Papal Visit to the South Pacific."

Souvenir Sheets

Aupex '97 Stamp Exhibition — SP1

1997, June 9 Litho. *Perf. 14x15*

B62 SP1 $2 +20c like #1 3.75 3.75

Perf. 14½x15

B63 SP1 $2 +20c like #34 3.25 3.25

No. B63 contains one 31x60mm stamp.

AIR POST STAMPS

Catalogue values for unused stamps in this section are for Never Hinged items.

Type of 1977

Designs: 15c, Preparing ground for taro. 20c, Banana harvest. 23c, Bush plantation. 50c, Canoe fishing. 90c, Reef fishing. $1.35, Preparing ground for taro. $2.10, Shellfish gathering. $2.60, Luku harvest.

1979 Litho. *Perf. 14*

C1 A54 15c gold & multi .25 .25
C2 A54 20c gold & multi .25 .25
C3 A54 23c gold & multi .30 .30
C4 A54 50c gold & multi .45 .45
C5 A54 90c gold & multi .70 .70
C6 A54 $1.35 gold & multi 1.10 1.10
C7 A54 $2.10 gold & multi 1.75 1.75
C8 A54 $2.60 gold & multi 2.25 2.25
C9 A54 $5.10 like #187 4.25 4.25
C10 A54 $6.35 like #188 5.50 5.50
Nos. C1-C10 (10) 16.80 16.80

Issue dates: Nos. C1-C5, Feb. 26. Nos. C6-C8, Mar. 30. C9-C10, May 28.

OFFICIAL STAMPS

Catalogue values for unused stamps in this section are for Never Hinged items.

Nos. 417-430, 332-334, 431-431A Ovptd. in Metallic Blue or Gold

Perf. 13½, 13½x13, 13x13½, 13

1985-87 Photo.

O1 A89 12c multi .25 .25
O2 A89 25c multi .25 .25
O3 A89 30c multi .25 .25
O4 A89 35c multi .25 .25
O5 A89 40c multi .30 .30
O6 A89 52c multi .40 .40
O7 A89 58c multi .50 .50
O8 A89 70c multi .55 .55
O9 A89 83c multi .65 .65
O10 A89 $1.05 multi .75 .75
O11 A90 $1.75 multi 1.50 1.50
O12 A90 $2.30 multi 2.50 2.50
O13 A90 $3.90 multi 4.75 4.75
O14 A77a $4 multi (G) 4.50 4.50
O15 A90 $5 multi 5.50 5.50
O16 A77a $6 multi ('87) (G) 10.00 10.00
O17 A90 $6.60 multi ('86) 7.00 7.00
O18 A90 $8.30 multi ('86) 9.00 9.00
O19 A77a $10 multi ('87) (G) 16.00 16.00
Nos. O1-O19 (19) 64.90 64.90

Nos. 604-613 Ovptd. in Gold

1993-94 Litho. *Perf. 14x13½*

O20 A118 20c multicolored .30 .30
O21 A118 50c multicolored .55 .55
O22 A118 70c multicolored .80 .80
O23 A118 $1 multicolored 1.25 1.25
O24 A118 $1.50 multicolored 2.00 2.00
O25 A118 $2 multicolored 3.50 3.50
O26 A118 $3 multicolored 4.25 4.25
O27 A118 $5 multicolored 6.50 6.50
O28 A118 $7 multicolored 9.00 9.00
O29 A118 $10 multicolored 13.00 13.00
O30 A118 $15 multicolored 20.00 20.00
Nos. O20-O30 (11) 61.15 61.15

Nos. O20-O30 were not sold unused to local customers.

Issued: 20c-$2, 12/10/93; $3, $5, 4/27/94; $7, $10, 9/1/94; $15, 9/30/94.

NORFOLK ISLAND

'nor-fək 'ī-lənd

LOCATION — Island in the south Pacific Ocean, 900 miles east of Australia
GOVT. — Territory of Australia
AREA — 13½ sq. mi.
POP. — 1,905 (1999 est.)

12 Pence = 1 Shilling
100 Cents = 1 Dollar (1966)

Catalogue values for all unused stamps in this country are for Never Hinged items.

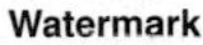

Watermark

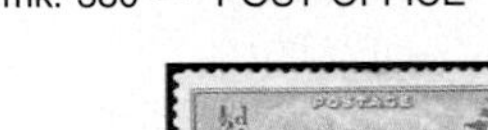

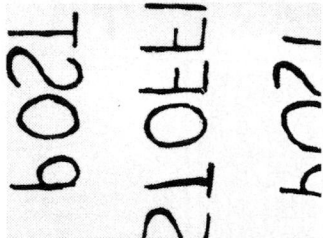

Wmk. 380 — "POST OFFICE"

View of Ball Bay — A1

Unwmk.

1947, June 10 Engr. *Perf. 14*

On Toned Paper

1	A1	½p deep orange	.60	.50
2	A1	1p violet	.40	.50
3	A1	1½p bright green	.45	.50
4	A1	2p red violet	.50	.25
5	A1	2½p red	.65	.40
6	A1	3p brown orange	.60	.60
7	A1	4p rose lake	1.50	.30
8	A1	5½p slate	.95	.40
9	A1	6p sepia	1.15	.40
10	A1	9p lilac rose	1.75	.60
11	A1	1sh gray green	1.75	.60
12	A1	2sh olive bister	3.50	1.25
		Nos. 1-12 (12)	13.80	6.30

Nos. 1-4 were reprinted in 1956-59 on white paper. Values, set: never hinged $140; used $220.

See Nos. 23-24.

Warder's Tower — A2

Airfield — A3

Designs: 7½p, First Governor's Residence. 8½p, Barracks entrance. 10p, Salt House. 5sh, Bloody Bridge.

1953, June 10 *Perf. 14½*

13	A2	3½p rose brown	1.25	1.00
14	A3	6½p dark green	2.50	3.00
15	A3	7½p deep ultra	2.00	3.00
16	A2	8½p chocolate	2.25	4.75
17	A2	10p rose lilac	1.40	.75
18	A3	5sh dark brown	32.50	8.50
		Nos. 13-18 (6)	41.90	21.00

See Nos. 35, 40. For surcharges see Nos. 21-22, 27. For types surcharged see Nos. 26, 28.

Original Norfolk Seal and First Settlers — A4

1956, June 8

19	A4	3p bluish green	.75	.50
20	A4	2sh violet	3.25	*3.50*

Cent. of the landing of the Pitcairn Islanders on Norfolk Island.

Nos. 15 and 16 Surcharged with New Value and Bars

1958, July 1

21	A3	7p on 7½p dp ultra	1.50	*1.40*
22	A2	8p on 8½p choc	1.50	*1.75*

Ball Bay Type of 1947

1959, July 6 Engr. *Perf. 14*

23	A1	3p green	15.00	8.00
24	A1	2sh dark blue	16.00	10.00

A5

Australia #332 Surcharged in Red

1959, Dec. 7

25	A5	5p on 4p dk gray blue	1.25	1.25

No. 14 and Types of 1953 Surcharged with New Values and Bars

1960, Sept. 26 *Perf. 14½*

26	A2	1sh1p on 3½p dk bl	4.00	2.75
27	A3	2sh5p on 6½p dk grn	5.50	4.25
28	A3	2sh8p on 7½p dk brn	7.25	5.75
		Nos. 26-28 (3)	16.75	12.75

Types of 1953 and

Island Hibiscus — A6

Fairy Tern — A7

Red-Tailed Tropic Bird — A8

Designs: 2p, Lagunaria patersonii (flowers). 5p, Lantana. 8p, Red hibiscus. 9p, Cereus and Queen Elizabeth II. 10p, Salt House. 1sh1p, Fringed hibiscus. 2sh, Providence petrel, vert. 2sh5p, Passion flower. 2sh8p, Rose apple. 5sh, Bloody Bridge.

1960-62 Unwmk. Engr. *Perf. 14½*

29	A6	1p blue green	.25	.25
30	A6	2p gray grn & brt pink	.25	.25
31	A7	3p brt green ('61)	.40	.25
32	A6	5p lilac	.85	.55
33	A6	8p vermilion	1.50	1.10
34	A6	9p ultramarine	1.50	1.10
35	A2	10p pale pur & brn ('61)	2.60	1.25
36	A6	1sh1p dark red ('61)	2.00	1.10
37	A6	2sh sepia ('61)	2.00	1.25
38	A6	2sh5p dk purple ('62)	2.00	1.25
39	A6	2sh8p green & sal ('62)	3.25	1.50
40	A3	5sh green & gray ('61)	4.75	2.10

Perf. 14½x14

41	A8	10sh green ('61)	32.50	30.00
		Nos. 29-41 (13)	53.85	41.95

See #585-586. For surcharges see #71-82.

Map of Norfolk Island — A9

1960, Oct. 24 Engr. *Perf. 14*

42	A9	2sh8p rose violet	14.00	12.00

Introduction of local government for Norfolk Island.

Open Bible and Candle — A9a

1960, Nov. 21 *Perf. 14½*

43	A9a	5p bright lilac rose	2.00	2.00

Christmas.

Page from Book of Hours, 15th Century A9b

1961, Nov. 20 *Perf. 14½x14*

44	A9b	5p slate blue	1.00	1.00

Nos. 43-44 were issued to mark the beginning and the end of the 350th anniversary year of the publication of the King James translation of the Bible.

Madonna and Child — A9c

1962, Nov. 19 *Perf. 14½*

45	A9c	5p blue	1.00	1.00

Christmas.

Overlooking Kingston — A10

Dreamfish — A11

Designs: 6p, Tweed trousers (fish). 8p, Kingston scene. 9p, "The Arches." 10p, Slaughter Bay. 11p, Trumpeter fish. 1sh, Po'ov (wrasse). 1sh6p, Queensland grouper. 2sh3p, Ophie (carangidae).

Perf. 14½x14

1962-64 Unwmk. Photo.

49	A10	5p multi ('64)	.45	.40
50	A11	6p multi	.55	.55
51	A10	8p multi ('64)	.70	.60
52	A10	9p multi ('64)	1.00	.90
53	A10	10p multi ('64)	1.15	1.15
54	A11	11p multi ('63)	1.75	1.15
55	A11	1sh olive, bl & pink	2.00	1.60
57	A11	1sh3p bl, mar & grn ('63)	2.25	2.00
58	A11	1sh6p bl, brn & lil ('63)	2.50	2.50
60	A11	2sh3p dl bl, yel & red ('63)	3.00	2.75
		Nos. 49-60 (10)	15.35	13.60

Star of Bethlehem — A11a

1963, Nov. 11 Engr. *Perf. 14½*

65	A11a	5p vermilion	.90	.90

Christmas.

Symbolic Pine Tree — A12

1964, July 1 Photo. *Perf. 13½x13*

66	A12	5p orange, blk & red	.75	.75
67	A12	8p gray green, blk & red	1.00	1.00

50th anniv. of Norfolk Island as an Australian Territory.

Child Looking at Nativity Scene — A12a

1964, Nov. 9 *Perf. 13½*

68	A12a	5p multicolored	.75	.75

Christmas.

"Simpson and His Donkey" by Wallace Anderson — A12b

1965, Apr. 14 Photo. *Perf. 13½x13*

69	A12b	5p brt grn, sepia & blk	.55	.45

ANZAC issue. See note after Australia No. 387.

Nativity — A12c

1965, Oct. 25 Unwmk. *Perf. 13½*

70	A12c	5p gold, blk, ultra & redsh brn	.40	.40

Christmas. No. 70 is luminescent. See note after Australia No. 331.

Nos. 29-33 and 35-41 Surcharged in Black on Overprinted Metallic Rectangles

Two types of 1c on 1p:
I. Silver rectangle 4x5½mm.
II. Silver rectangle 5½x5¼mm.
Two types of $1 on 10sh:
I. Silver rectangle 7x6½mm.
II. Silver rectangle 6x4mm.

Perf. 14½, 14½x14

1966, Feb. 14 Engr.

71	A6	1c on 1p bl grn (I)	.25	.25
a.		Type II	.30	.30
72	A6	2c on 2p gray grn & brt pink	.25	.25
73	A7	3c on 3p brt green	.35	*.60*
74	A6	4c on 5p lilac	.25	.25
75	A6	5c on 8p vermilion	.25	.25
76	A2	10c on 10p pale pur & brn	.70	.25
77	A6	15c on 1sh1p dark red	.30	.40
78	A6	20c on 2sh sepia	2.75	2.25
79	A6	25c on 2sh5p dk pur	1.10	.30
80	A6	30c on 2sh8p grn & sal	.75	.40
81	A3	50c on 5sh grn & gray	2.75	.55
82	A8	$1 on 10sh green (I)	2.50	2.00
a.		Type II	5.00	5.00
		Nos. 71-82 (12)	12.20	7.75

Headstone Bridge — A13

1966, June 27 Photo. *Perf. 14½*

88	A13 7c shown		.25	.25
89	A13 9c Cemetery road		.40	.40

St. Barnabas Chapel — A14

Design: 4c, Interior of St. Barnabas Chapel.

Perf. 14x14½

1966, Aug. 23 Photo. Unwmk.

97	A14 4c multicolored	.25	.25
98	A14 25c multicolored	.45	.45

Centenary of the Melanesian Mission.

Star over Philip Island — A15

1966, Oct. 24 Photo. *Perf. 14½*

99	A15 4c violet, grn, blue & sil	.35	.35

Christmas.

H.M.S. Resolution, 1774 — A16

Ships: 2c, La Boussole and Astrolabe, 1788. 3c, Brig Supply, 1788. 4c, Sirius, 1790. 5c, The Norfolk, 1798. 7c, Survey cutter Mermaid, 1825. 9c, The Lady Franklin, 1853. 10c The Morayshire, 1856. 15c, Southern Cross, 1866. 20c, The Pitcairn, 1891. 25c, Norfolk Island whaleboat, 1895. 30c, Cable ship Iris, 1907. 50c, The Resolution, 1926. $1, S.S. Morinda, 1931.

1967-68 Photo. *Perf. 14x14½*

100	A16 1c multicolored	.25	.25
101	A16 2c multicolored	.25	.25
102	A16 3c multicolored	.25	.25
103	A16 4c multicolored	.40	.25
104	A16 5c multicolored	.25	.25
105	A16 7c multicolored	.25	.25
106	A16 9c multicolored	.30	.25
107	A16 10c multicolored	.40	.35
108	A16 15c multicolored	.60	.55
109	A16 20c multicolored	.90	.80
110	A16 25c multicolored	1.40	1.25
111	A16 30c multicolored	1.75	1.50
112	A16 50c multicolored	2.25	2.00
113	A16 $1 multicolored	3.50	3.25
	Nos. 100-113 (14)	12.75	11.45

Issued: #100-103, 4/17; #104-107, 8/19; #108-110, 3/18/68; #111-113, 6/18/68.

Lions Intl., 50th Anniv. — A16a

1967, June 7 Photo. *Perf. 13½*

114	A16a 4c citron, blk & bl grn	.40	.40

Printed on luminescent paper; see note after Australia No. 331.

John Adams' Prayer A17

1967, Oct. 16 Photo. *Perf. 14x14½*

115	A17 5c brick red, blk & buff	.40	.40

Christmas.

Queen Elizabeth II Type of Australia, 1966-67

Coil Stamps

Perf. 15 Horizontally

1968-71 Photo. Unwmk.

116	A157 3c brn org, blk & buff	.25	.25
117	A157 4c blue grn, blk & buff	.25	.25
118	A157 5c brt purple, blk & buff	.25	.25
118A	A157 6c dk red, brn, blk & buff	.30	.40
	Nos. 116-118A (4)	1.05	1.15

Issued: 6c, 8/2/71; others, 8/5/68.

DC-4 Skymaster and Lancastrian Plane — A18

1968, Sept. 25 *Perf. 14½x14*

119	A18 5c dk car, sky bl & ind	.25	.25
120	A18 7c dk car, bl grn & sep	.25	.25

21st anniv. of the Sydney to Norfolk Island air service by Qantas Airways.

Star and Hibiscus Wreath — A19

Photo.; Silver Impressed (Star)

1968, Oct. 24 *Perf. 14½x14*

121	A19 5c sky blue & multi	.35	.35

Christmas.

Map of Pacific, Transit of Venus before Sun, Capt. Cook and Quadrant A20

1969, June 3 Photo. *Perf. 14x14½*

122	A20 10c brn, ol, pale brn & yel	.35	.35

Bicent. of the observation at Tahiti by Capt. James Cook of the transit of the planet Venus across the sun.

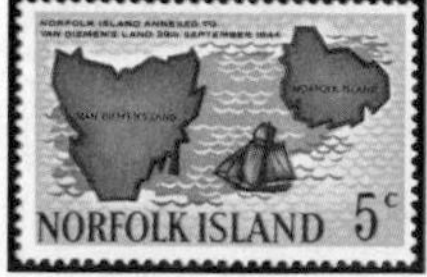

Map of Van Diemen's Land and Norfolk Island A21

1969, Sept. 29 *Perf. 14x14½*

123	A21 5c multicolored	.25	.25
124	A21 30c multicolored	.50	.50

125th anniv. of the annexation of Norfolk Island by Van Diemen's Land (Tasmania).

Nativity (Mother-of-Pearl carving) — A22

1969, Oct. 27 Photo. *Perf. 14½x14*

125	A22 5c brown & multi	.35	.35

Christmas.

Norfolk Island Flyeater A23

Birds of Norfolk Island from Book by Gregory Mathews: 1c, Robins, vert. 2c, Norfolk Island whistlers (thickheads), vert. 4c, Long-tailed cuckoos. 5c, Red-fronted parakeet, vert. 7c, Long-tailed trillers, vert. 9c, Island thrush. 10c, Owl, vert. 15c, Norfolk Island pigeon (extinct; vert.). 20c, White-breasted white-eye. 25c, Norfolk Island parrots, vert. 30c, Gray fantail. 45c, Norfolk Island starlings. 50c, Crimson rosella, vert. $1, Sacred kingfisher.

Perf. 14x14½, 14½x14

1970-71 Photo. Unwmk.

126	A23 1c multicolored	.25	.25
127	A23 2c multicolored	.25	.30
128	A23 3c multicolored	.25	.25
129	A23 4c multicolored	.45	.30
130	A23 5c multicolored	1.25	.80
131	A23 7c multicolored	.35	.25
132	A23 9c multicolored	.55	.30
133	A23 10c multicolored	1.40	1.60
134	A23 15c multicolored	1.25	.75
135	A23 20c multicolored	5.75	3.50
136	A23 25c multicolored	2.00	1.25
137	A23 30c multicolored	5.75	3.00
138	A23 45c multicolored	2.50	1.40
139	A23 50c multicolored	3.00	2.25
140	A23 $1 multicolored	8.25	7.00
	Nos. 126-140 (15)	33.25	23.20

Issued: 3c, 4c, 9c, 45c, 2/25; 1c, 7c, 10c, 25c, 7/22; 2c, 2c, 5c, 15c, 50c, 2/24/71; 20c, 30c, $1, 6/16/71.

Map of Australia, James Cook and Southern Cross A24

Design: 10c, "Endeavour" entering Botany Bay, Apr. 29, 1770, and aborigine with spear. The 1776 portrait of James Cook on the 5c is by John Webber.

1970, Apr. 29 Photo. *Perf. 14x14½*

141	A24 5c multicolored	.25	.25
142	A24 10c multicolored	.25	.25

200th anniv. of Cook's discovery and exploration of the eastern coast of Australia.

First Christmas, Sydney Bay, 1788 — A25

1970, Oct. 15 Photo. *Perf. 14x14½*

143	A25 5c multicolored	.25	.25

Christmas.

Bishop Patteson, Open Bible — A26

#145, Bible opened to Acts Chap. 7, martyrdom of St. Stephen, & knotted palm fronds. #146, Bishop Patteson, rose window of Melanesian Mission Chapel on Norfolk Island. #147, Cross erected at Nukapu where Patteson died & his arms.

1971, Sept. 20

144	A26 6c brown & multi	.25	.25
145	A26 6c brown & multi	.25	.25
a.	Pair, #144-145	.45	.45
146	A26 10c purple & multi	.25	.25
147	A26 10c purple & multi	.25	.25
a.	Pair, #146-147	.55	.55
	Nos. 144-147 (4)	1.00	1.00

Centenary of the death of Bishop John Coleridge Patteson (1827-1871), head of the Melanesian mission.

Rose Window, St. Barnabas Chapel, Norfolk Island — A27

1971, Oct. 25 *Perf. 14x13½*

148	A27 6c dk vio blue & multi	.30	.30

Christmas.

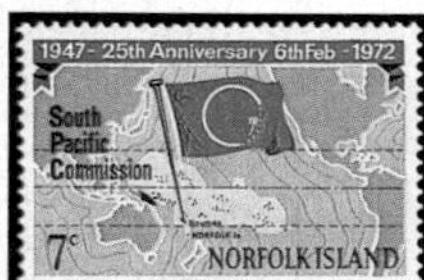

Map of South Pacific and Commission Flag — A28

1972, Feb. 7 *Perf. 14x14½*

149	A28 7c multicolored	.35	.35

So. Pacific Commission, 25th anniv.

Stained-glass Window — A29

1972, Oct. 16 Photo. *Perf. 14x14½*

150	A29 7c dark olive & multi	.30	.30

Christmas. The stained-glass window by Edward Coley Burne-Jones is in All Saints Church, Norfolk Island.

Cross, Church, Pines — A30

1972, Nov. 20

151	A30 12c multicolored	.30	.30
a.	Purple omitted	*1,600.*	

Centenary of All Saints Church, first built by Pitcairners on Norfolk Island.

"Resolution" in Antarctica — A31

1973, Jan. 17 Photo. *Perf. 14½x14*

152	A31	35c multicolored	3.25	3.25

200th anniv. of the 1st crossing of the Antarctic Circle by Cook, Jan. 17, 1773.

Sleeping Child, and Christmas Tree — A32

Christmas: 35c, Star over lagoon.

1973, Oct. 22 Photo. *Perf. 14x14½*

153	A32	7c black & multi	.25	.25
154	A32	12c black & multi	.30	.30
155	A32	35c black & multi	1.05	1.05
		Nos. 153-155 (3)	1.60	1.60

Protestant Clergyman's House — A33

Designs: 2c, Royal Engineer Office. 3c, Double quarters for free overseers. 4c, Guard House. 5c, Pentagonal Gaol entrance. 7c, Pentagonal Gaol, aerial view. 8c, Convict barracks. 10c, Officers' quarters, New Military Barracks. 12c, New Military Barracks. 14c, Beach stores. 15c, Magazine. 20c, Old Military Barracks, entrance. 25c, Old Military Barracks. 30c, Old stores, Crankmill. 50c, Commissariat stores. $1, Government House.

1973-75 Photo. *Perf. 14x14½*

156	A33	1c multicolored	.25	.25
157	A33	2c multicolored	.25	.25
158	A33	3c multicolored	.35	*.70*
159	A33	4c multicolored	.25	.25
160	A33	5c multicolored	.25	.25
161	A33	7c multicolored	.35	.35
162	A33	8c multicolored	1.40	1.40
163	A33	10c multicolored	.50	.50
164	A33	12c multicolored	.50	.40
165	A33	14c multicolored	.50	*.65*
166	A33	15c multicolored	1.25	.90
167	A33	20c multicolored	.50	.50
168	A33	25c multicolored	1.25	1.25
169	A33	30c multicolored	.50	.50
170	A33	50c multicolored	.55	*1.10*
171	A33	$1 multicolored	1.10	*1.75*
		Nos. 156-171 (16)	9.75	11.00

Issued: 1c, 5c, 10c, 50c, 11/19/73; 2c, 7c, 12c, 30c, 5/1/74; 4c, 14c, 20c, $1, 7/12/74; 3c, 8c, 15c, 25c, 2/19/75.

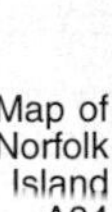

Map of Norfolk Island A34

1974, Feb. 8 Photo. *Perf. 14x14½*

172	A34	7c red lilac & multi	.35	.35
173	A34	25c dull blue & multi	1.00	1.00

Visit of Queen Elizabeth II and the Duke of Edinburgh, Feb. 11-12.

Gipsy Moth over Norfolk Island A35

1974, Mar. 28 Litho. *Perf. 14x14½*

174	A35	14c multicolored	1.25	1.25

1st aircraft to visit Norfolk, Sir Francis Chichester's "Mme. Elijah," Mar. 28, 1931.

Capt. Cook — A36

Designs: 10c, "Resolution," by Henry Roberts. 14c, Norfolk Island pine, cone and seedling. 25c, Norfolk Island flax, by George Raper, 1790. Portrait of Cook on 7c by William Hodges, 1770.

1974, Oct. 8 Litho. *Perf. 14*

175	A36	7c multicolored	.65	.65
176	A36	10c multicolored	1.60	1.60
177	A36	14c multicolored	1.30	1.30
178	A36	25c multicolored	1.30	1.30
		Nos. 175-178 (4)	4.85	4.85

Bicentenary of the discovery of Norfolk Island by Capt. James Cook.

Nativity — A37

1974, Oct. 18 Photo. *Perf. 14*

179	A37	7c rose & multi	.25	.25
180	A37	30c violet & multi	1.00	1.00

Christmas.

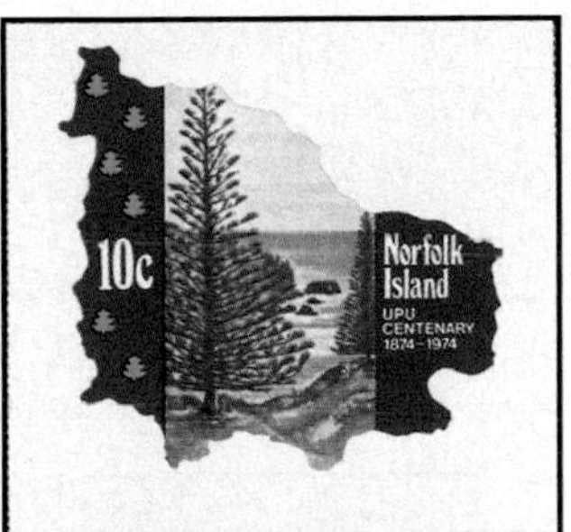

Norfolk Island Pine — A38

15c, Off-shore islands. 35c, Crimson rosella and sacred kingfisher. 40c, Map showing Norfolk's location. Stamps in shape of Norfolk Island.

1974, Dec. 16 Litho. *Imperf.*
Self-adhesive

181	A38	10c brown & multi	.30	.30
182	A38	15c dk blue & multi	.40	.40
183	A38	35c dk purple & multi	1.05	1.05
184	A38	40c dk blue grn & multi	1.25	2.10
a.		Souvenir sheet of 4	22.50	24.00
		Nos. 181-184 (4)	3.00	3.85

Cent. of UPU. Stamps printed on peelable paper backing. No. 184a contains 4 imperf. stamps similar to Nos. 181-184 in reduced size on a background of map of Norfolk Island. Peelable paper backing shows beach scene on Norfolk Island.

Survey Cutter "Mermaid," 1825 — A39

Design: 35c, Kingston, 1835, after painting by Thomas Seller. Stamps outlined in shape of Norfolk Island map.

1975, Aug. 18 Litho. *Imperf.*
Self-adhesive

185	A39	10c multicolored	.35	.35
186	A39	35c multicolored	.65	.65

Sesquicentennial of 2nd settlement of Norfolk Island. Printed on peelable paper backing with green and black design and inscription.

Star over Norfolk Island Pine and Map — A40

1975, Oct. 6 Photo. *Perf. 14½x14*

187	A40	10c lt blue & multi	.25	.25
188	A40	15c lt brown & multi	.40	.40
189	A40	35c lilac & multi	.55	.55
		Nos. 187-189 (3)	1.20	1.20

Christmas.

Brass Memorial Cross — A41

Design: 60c, Laying foundation stone, 1875, and chapel, 1975, horiz.

Perf. 14½x14, 14x14½
1975, Nov. 24 Photo.

190	A41	30c multicolored	.35	.35
191	A41	60c multicolored	.90	.90

St. Barnabas Chapel, centenary.

Launching "Resolution" A42

Design: 45c, "Resolution" under sail.

1975, Dec. 1 *Perf. 14x14½*

192	A42	25c multicolored	.40	.40
193	A42	45c multicolored	.85	.85

50th anniversary of launching of schooner "Resolution."

Bedford Flag, Charles W. Morgan Whaler A43

Designs: 25c, Grand Union Flag, church interior. 40c, 15-stari flag, 1795, and plane over island, WWII. 45c, 13-star flag and California quail.

1976, July 5 Photo. *Perf. 14*

194	A43	18c multicolored	.30	.35
195	A43	25c multicolored	.30	.30
196	A43	40c multicolored	.65	.75
197	A43	45c multicolored	.75	.85
		Nos. 194-197 (4)	2.00	2.25

American Bicentennial.

Bird in Flight, Brilliant Sun — A44

1976, Oct. 4 Photo. *Perf. 14*

198	A44	18c blue grn & multi	.30	.30
199	A44	25c dp blue & multi	.50	.50
200	A44	45c violet & multi	.80	.80
		Nos. 198-200 (3)	1.60	1.60

Christmas.

Bassaris Itea — A45

Butterflies and Moths: 2c, Utetheisa pulchelloides vaga. 3c, Agathia asterias jowettorum. 4c, Cynthia kershawi. 5c, Leucania loreyimima. 10c, Hypolimnas bolina nerina. 15c, Pyrrhorachis pyrrhogona. 16c, Austrocarea iocephala millsi. 17c, Pseudocoremia christiani. 18c, Cleora idiocrossa. 19c, Simplicia caeneusalis buffetti. 20c, Austrocidaria ralstonae. 30c, Hippotion scrofa. 40c, Papilio ilioneus. 50c, Tiracola plagiata. $1, Precis villida. $2, Cepora perimale.

1976-77 Photo. *Perf. 14*

201	A45	1c multicolored	.25	*.40*
202	A45	2c multicolored	.25	*.40*
203	A45	3c multicolored	.25	.30
204	A45	4c multicolored	.25	.30
205	A45	5c multicolored	.25	*.70*
206	A45	10c multicolored	.25	*.70*
207	A45	15c multicolored	.25	.30
208	A45	16c multicolored	.25	.30
209	A45	17c multicolored	.30	.30
210	A45	18c multicolored	.30	.30
211	A45	19c multicolored	.30	.30
212	A45	20c multicolored	.35	.30
213	A45	30c multicolored	.45	*.60*
214	A45	40c multicolored	.50	.35
215	A45	50c multicolored	.65	*.75*
216	A45	$1 multicolored	.70	*.75*
217	A45	$2 multicolored	1.10	*1.30*
		Nos. 201-217 (17)	6.65	*8.35*

Issued: 1c, 5c, 10c, 16c, 18c, $1, 11/17; others, 1977.

View of Kingston A46

1977, June 10

218	A46	25c multicolored	.50	.50

25th anniv. of reign of Elizabeth II.

Hibiscus and 19th Century Whaler's Lamp — A47

1977, Oct. 4 Photo. *Perf. 14½*

219	A47	18c multicolored	.25	.25
220	A47	25c multicolored	.25	.25
221	A47	45c multicolored	.40	.40
		Nos. 219-221 (3)	.90	.90

Christmas.

Capt. Cook, by Nathaniel Dance — A48

Designs: 25c, Discovery of Northern Hawaiian Islands (Cook aboard ship), horiz. 80c, British flag and Island, horiz.

1978, Jan. 18	**Photo.**	***Perf. 14½***	
222 A48 18c multicolored		.35	.35
223 A48 25c multicolored		.35	.35
224 A48 80c multicolored		.70	.70
Nos. 222-224 (3)		1.40	1.40

Bicentenary of Capt. Cook's arrival in Hawaiian Islands.

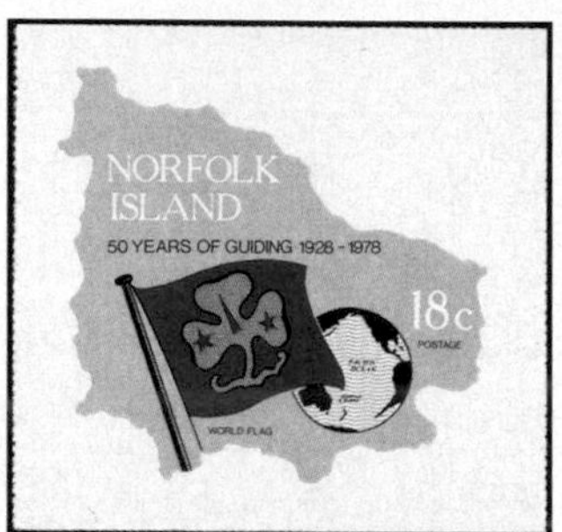

World Guides Flag and Globe — A49

Designs: 25c, Norfolk Guides' scarf badge and trefoil. 35c, Elizabeth II and trefoil. 45c, FAO Ceres medal with portrait of Lady Olive Baden-Powell, and trefoil. Stamps outlined in shape of Norfolk Island map.

1978, Feb. 22	**Litho.**	***Imperf.***	
Self-adhesive			
225 A49 18c lt ultra & multi		.30	.30
226 A49 25c yellow & multi		.30	.30
227 A49 35c lt green & multi		.40	.40
228 A49 45c yellow grn & multi		.50	.50
Nos. 225-228 (4)		1.50	1.50

50th anniversary of Norfolk Island Girl Guides. Printed on peelable paper backing with green multiple pines and tourist publicity inscription.

St. Edward's Crown A50

Design: 70c, Coronation regalia.

1978, June 29	**Photo.**	***Perf. 14½***	
229 A50 25c multicolored		.30	.30
230 A50 70c multicolored		.70	.70

25th anniv. of coronation of Elizabeth II.

Norfolk Island Boy Scouts, 50th Anniv. — A51

Designs: 20c, Cliffs, Duncombe Bay, Scout Making Fire. 25c, Emily Bay, Philip and Nepean Islands from Kingston. 35c, Anson Bay, Cub and Boy Scouts. 45c, Sunset and Lord Baden-Powell. Stamps outlined in shape of Norfolk Island map.

1978, Aug. 22	**Litho.**	***Imperf.***	
Self-adhesive			
231 A51 20c multicolored		.40	.40
232 A51 25c multicolored		.45	.45
233 A51 35c multicolored		.65	.65
234 A51 45c multicolored		.70	.70
Nos. 231-234 (4)		2.20	2.20

Printed on peelable paper backing with green multiple pines and tourist publicity inscription and picture.

Map of Bering Sea and Pacific Ocean, Routes of Discovery and Resolution — A52

Design: 90c, Discovery and Resolution trapped in ice, by John Webber.

1978, Aug. 29	**Photo.**	***Perf. 14½***	
235 A52 25c multicolored		.40	.40
236 A52 90c multicolored		1.00	1.00

Northernmost point of Cook's voyages.

Poinsettia and Bible — A53

Christmas: 30c, Native oak (flowers) and Bible. 55c, Hibiscus and Bible.

1978, Oct. 3	**Photo.**	***Perf. 14½***	
237 A53 20c multicolored		.25	.25
238 A53 30c multicolored		.30	.30
239 A53 55c multicolored		.60	.60
Nos. 237-239 (3)		1.15	1.15

Capt. Cook, View of Staithes A54

80c, Capt. Cook and view of Whitby harbor.

1978, Oct. 27			
240 A54 20c multicolored		.40	*.50*
241 A54 80c multicolored		1.10	*1.25*

Resolution, Map of Asia and Australia — A55

Designs: No. 243, Map of Hawaii and Americas, Cook's route and statue. No. 244, Capt. Cook's death. No. 245, Ships off Hawaii.

1979, Feb. 14	**Photo.**	***Perf. 14½***	
242 20c multicolored		.30	.30
243 20c multicolored		.30	.30
a. A55 Pair, #242-243		.60	.60
244 40c multicolored		.65	.65
245 40c multicolored		.65	.65
a. A55 Pair, #244-245		1.30	1.30
Nos. 242-245 (4)		1.90	1.90

Bicentenary of Capt. Cook's death.

Rowland Hill and Tasmania No. 1 A56

Rowland Hill and: 30c, Great Britain No. 8. 55c, Norfolk Island No. 2.

1979, Aug. 27		***Perf. 14x14½***	
246 A56 20c multicolored		.30	.30
247 A56 30c multicolored		.30	.30
248 A56 55c multicolored		.40	.40
a. Souvenir sheet of 1		1.00	1.00
Nos. 246-248 (3)		1.00	1.00

Sir Rowland Hill (1795-1879), originator of penny postage.

Legislative Assembly — A57

1979, Aug.	**Photo.**	***Perf. 14½x14***	
249 A57 $1 multicolored		.90	.90

First session of Legislative Assembly.

Map of Pacific Ocean, IYC Emblem A58

1979, Sept. 25	**Litho.**	***Perf. 15***	
250 A58 80c multicolored		.75	.75

International Year of the Child.

Emily Bay Beach — A59

1979, Oct. 2	**Photo.**	***Perf. 12½x13***	
251 15c Beach		.25	.25
252 20c Emily Bay		.25	.25
253 30c Salt House		.30	.30
a. Souv. sheet of 3, #251-253, perf. 14x14½		1.25	1.25
b. A59 Strip of 3, #251-253		.80	.80

Christmas. #253b has continuous design.

Lions District Convention 1980 — A60

1980, Jan. 25	**Litho.**	***Perf. 15***	
254 A60 50c multicolored		.50	.50

Rotary International, 75th Anniversary — A61

1980, Feb. 21			
255 A61 50c multicolored		.55	.55
a. Black omitted		*11,000.*	

No. 255a is unique.

DH-60 "Gypsy Moth" A62

1c, Hawker Siddeley HS-748. 3c, Curtiss P-40 Kittyhawk. 4c, Chance Vought Corsair. 5c, Grumman Avenger. 15c, Douglas Dauntless. 20c, Cessna 172. 25c, Lockheed Hudson. 30c, Lockheed PV-1 Ventura. 40c, Avro York. 50c, DC-3. 60c, Avro 691 Lancastrian. 80c, DC-4. $1, Beechcraft Super King Air. $2, Fokker Friendship. $5, Lockheed C-130 Hercules.

1980-81	**Litho.**	***Perf. 14½***	
256 A62 1c multicolored		.25	.25
257 A62 2c multicolored		.25	.25
258 A62 3c multicolored		.25	.25
259 A62 4c multicolored		.25	.25
260 A62 5c multicolored		.25	.25
261 A62 15c multicolored		.25	.25
262 A62 20c multicolored		.30	.30
262A A62 25c multicolored		.40	.40
263 A62 30c multicolored		.50	.50
264 A62 40c multicolored		.60	.60
265 A62 50c multicolored		.75	.75
266 A62 60c multicolored		.85	.85
267 A62 80c multicolored		1.30	1.30
268 A62 $1 multicolored		1.50	1.50
269 A62 $2 multicolored		1.90	1.90
270 A62 $5 multicolored		5.00	5.00
Nos. 256-270 (16)		14.60	14.60

Issued: 2, 3, 20c, $5, 3/25; 4, 5, 15c, $2, 8/19; 30, 50, 60, 80c, 1/13/81; 1, 25, 40c, $1, 3/3/81.

Queen Mother Elizabeth, 80th Birthday A63

1980, Aug. 4	**Litho.**	***Perf. 14½***	
271 A63 22c multicolored		.25	.25
272 A63 60c multicolored		.65	.65

Red-tailed Tropic Birds — A64

1980, Oct. 28	**Litho.**	***Perf. 14x14½***	
273 A64 15c shown		.25	.25
274 A64 22c Fairy terns		.25	.25
275 A64 35c White-capped noddys		.40	.40
a. Strip of 3, #273-275		1.00	1.00
276 A64 60c Fairy terns, diff.		.75	.75
Nos. 273-276 (4)		1.65	1.65

Christmas. No. 275a has continuous design.

Citizens Arriving at Norfolk Island A65

1981, June 5	**Litho.**	***Perf. 14½***	
277 A65 5c Departure		.25	.25
278 A65 35c shown		.40	.40
279 A65 60c Settlement		.70	.70
a. Souvenir sheet of 3, #277-279		1.50	1.50
Nos. 277-279 (3)		1.35	1.35

Pitcairn migration to Norfolk Island, 125th anniv.

Common Design Types pictured following the introduction.

Royal Wedding Issue
Common Design Type

1981, July 22	**Litho.**	***Perf. 14***	
280 CD331 35c Bouquet		.30	.30
281 CD331 55c Charles		.50	.50
282 CD331 60c Couple		.55	.55
Nos. 280-282 (3)		1.35	1.35

Nos. 280-282 each se-tenant with decorative label.

Uniting Church of Australia
A66

24c, Seventh Day Adventist Church. 30c, Church of the Sacred Heart. $1, St. Barnabas Church.

1981, Sept. 15 Litho. *Perf. 14½*

283 A66 18c shown .25 .25
284 A66 24c multicolored .25 .25
285 A66 30c multicolored .25 .25
286 A66 $1 multicolored .90 .90
Nos. 283-286 (4) 1.65 1.65

Christmas.

White-breasted Silvereye — A67

1981, Nov. 10 Litho. *Perf. 14½*

287 Strip of 5 2.75 2.75
a.-e. A67 35c any single .50 .50

Philip Island
A68

Views, Flora and Fauna: No. 288, Philip Isld. No. 289, Nepean Island.

1982, Jan. 12 Litho. *Perf. 14*

288 Strip of 5 1.25 1.25
a.-e. A68 24c any single .25 .25
289 Strip of 5 2.00 2.00
a.-e. A68 35c any single .40 .40

Sperm Whale
A69

1982, Feb. 23 Litho. *Perf. 14½*

290 A69 24c shown .50 .50
291 A69 55c Southern right whale 1.00 1.00
292 A69 80c Humpback whale 1.75 1.75
Nos. 290-292 (3) 3.25 3.25

Shipwrecks — A70

1982 Litho. *Perf. 14½*

293 A70 24c Sirius, 1790 .55 .55
294 A70 27c Diocet, 1873 .60 .60
295 A70 35c Friendship, 1835 .95 .95
296 A70 40c Mary Hamilton, 1873 1.05 1.05
297 A70 55c Fairlie, 1840 1.25 1.25
298 A70 65c Warrigal, 1918 1.60 1.60
Nos. 293-298 (6) 6.00 6.00

Christmas and 40th Anniv. of Aircraft Landing
A71

1982, Sept. 7 *Perf. 14*

299 A71 27c Supplies drop .35 .35
300 A71 40c Landing .60 .60
301 A71 75c Sharing supplies 1.25 1.25
Nos. 299-301 (3) 2.20 2.20

A72

British Army Uniforms, Second Settlement, 1839-1848: 27c, Battalion Company Officer, 50th Regiment, 1835-1842. 40c, Light Company Officer, 58th Reg., 1845. 55c, Private, 80th Bat., 1838. 65c, Bat. Company Officer, 11th Reg., 1847.

1982, Nov. 9 *Perf. 14½*

302 A72 27c multicolored .30 .30
303 A72 40c multicolored .50 .50
304 A72 55c multicolored .55 .55
305 A72 65c multicolored .70 .70
Nos. 302-305 (4) 2.05 2.05

A73

Local mushrooms — 27c, Panaeolus papilonaceus. 40c, Coprinus domesticus. 55c, Marasmius niveus. 65c, Cymatoderma elegans.

1983, Mar. 29 Litho. *Perf. 14x13½*

306 A73 27c multicolored .35 .35
307 A73 40c multicolored .55 .55
308 A73 55c multicolored .70 .70
309 A73 65c multicolored .90 .90
Nos. 306-309 (4) 2.50 2.50

Manned Flight Bicentenary
A74

1983, July 12 Litho. *Perf. 14½x14*

310 A74 10c Beech 18, aerial mapping .25 .25
311 A74 27c Fokker F-28 .30 .30
312 A74 45c DC4 .65 .65
313 A74 75c Sikorsky helicopter .95 .95
a. Souvenir sheet of 4, #310-313 2.50 2.50
Nos. 310-313 (4) 2.15 2.15

Christmas — A75

Stained-glass Windows by Edward Burne-Jones (1833-1898), St. Barnabas Chapel.

1983, Oct. 4 Litho. *Perf. 14*

314 A75 5c multicolored .25 .25
315 A75 24c multicolored .30 .30
316 A75 30c multicolored .35 .35
317 A75 45c multicolored .45 .45
318 A75 85c multicolored .90 .90
Nos. 314-318 (5) 2.25 2.25

World Communications Year — A76

ANZCAN Cable Station: 30c, Chantik, Cable laying Ship. 45c, Shore end. 75c, Cable Ship Mercury. 85c, Map of cable route.

1983, Nov. 15 Litho. *Perf. 14½x14*

319 A76 30c multicolored .30 .30
320 A76 45c multicolored .50 .50
321 A76 75c multicolored .90 .90
322 A76 85c multicolored 1.00 1.00
Nos. 319-322 (4) 2.70 2.70

Local Flowers — A77

1c, Myoporum obsurum. 2c, Ipomoea pes-caprae. 3c, Phreatia crassiuscula. 4c, Streblorrhiza speciosa. 5c, Rhopalostylis baueri. 10c, Alyxia gynopogon. 15c, Ungeria floribunda. 20c, Capparis nobilis. 25c, Lagunaria patersonia. 30c, Cordyline obtecta. 35c, Hibiscus insularis. 40c, Millettia australis. 50c, Jasminum volubile. $1, Passiflora aurantia. $3, Oberonia titania. $5, Araucaria heterophylla.

1984 Litho. *Perf. 14*

323 A77 1c multicolored .25 .25
324 A77 2c multicolored .25 .25
325 A77 3c multicolored .25 .25
326 A77 4c multicolored .25 .25
327 A77 5c multicolored .25 .25
328 A77 10c multicolored .25 .25
329 A77 15c multicolored .25 .25
330 A77 20c multicolored .25 .25
331 A77 25c multicolored .25 .25
332 A77 30c multicolored .35 .35
333 A77 35c multicolored .40 .40
334 A77 40c multicolored .45 .45
335 A77 50c multicolored .55 .55
336 A77 $1 multicolored 1.10 1.10
337 A77 $3 multicolored 3.50 3.50
338 A77 $5 multicolored 5.50 5.50
Nos. 323-338 (16) 14.10 14.10

Issued: 2-3, 10, 20-25, 40-50c, $5, 1/10; others 3/27.

Reef Fish — A78

30c, Painted morwong. 45c, Black-spot goatfish. 75c, Ring-tailed surgeon fish. 85c, Three-striped butterfly fish.

Perf. 13½x14

1984, Apr. 17 Litho. Wmk. 373

339 A78 30c multicolored .40 .40
340 A78 45c multicolored .55 .55
341 A78 75c multicolored 1.00 1.00
342 A78 85c multicolored 1.10 1.10
Nos. 339-342 (4) 3.05 3.05

Boobook Owl — A79

Designs: a, Laying eggs. b, Standing at treehole. c, Sitting on branch looking sideways. d, Looking head on. e, Flying.

Wmk. 373

1984, July 17 Litho. *Perf. 14*

343 Strip of 5 6.00 6.00
a.-e. A79 30c any single 1.20 1.20

AUSIPEX '84 — A80

1984, Sept. 18 Litho. *Perf. 14½*

344 A80 30c Nos. 15 and 176 .45 .45
345 A80 45c First day cover .70 .70
346 A80 75c Presentation pack 1.30 1.30
a. Souvenir sheet of 3, #344-346 6.00 6.00
Nos. 344-346 (3) 2.45 2.45

Christmas — A81

5c, The Font. 24c, Church at Kingston, interior. 30c, Pastor and Mrs. Phelps. 45c, Phelps, Church of Chester. 85c, Phelps, Methodist Church, modern interior.

1984, Oct. 9 Litho. *Perf. 13½*

347 A81 5c multicolored .25 .25
348 A81 24c multicolored .30 .30
349 A81 30c multicolored .35 .35
350 A81 45c multicolored .55 .55
351 A81 85c multicolored 1.05 1.05
Nos. 347-351 (5) 2.50 2.50

A82

1984, Nov. 6 Litho. *Perf. 14x15*

352 A82 30c As teacher .35 .35
353 A82 45c As minister .45 .45
354 A82 75c As chaplain .80 .80
355 A82 85c As community leader 1.00 1.00
Nos. 352-355 (4) 2.60 2.60

Rev. George Hunn Nobbs, death centenary.

Whaling Ships — A83

1985 Litho. *Perf. 13½x14*

356 A83 5c Fanny Fisher .25 .25
357 A83 15c Waterwitch .30 .30
358 A83 20c Canton .40 .40
359 A83 33c Costa Rica Packet .60 .60
360 A83 50c Splendid .90 .90
361 A83 60c Aladin 1.50 1.50
362 A83 80c California 1.75 1.75
363 A83 90c Onward 2.25 2.25
Nos. 356-363 (8) 7.95 7.95

Issued: 5c, 33c, 50c, 90c, 2/19; others 4/30.

Queen Mother 85th Birthday

Common Design Type

5c, Portrait, 1926. 33c, With Princess Anne. 50c, Photograph by N. Parkinson. 90c, Holding Prince Henry.

$1, With Princess Anne, Ascot Races.

Perf. 14½x14

1985, June 6 Litho. Wmk. 384

364 CD336 5c multicolored .25 .25
365 CD336 33c multicolored .45 .45
366 CD336 50c multicolored .60 .60
367 CD336 90c multicolored 1.25 1.25
Nos. 364-367 (4) 2.55 2.55

Souvenir Sheet

368 CD336 $1 multicolored 2.50 2.50

Intl. Youth Year — A84

Children's drawings.

1985, July 9 Litho. *Perf. 13½x14*

369 A84 33c Swimming .60 .60
370 A84 50c Nature walk 1.00 1.00

Girl, Prize-winning Cow — A85

Designs: 90c, Embroidery, jam-making, baking, animal husbandry.

1985, Sept. 10 Litho. *Perf. 13½x14*

371 A85 80c multicolored 1.00 1.00
372 A85 90c multicolored 1.10 1.10
a. Souvenir sheet of 2, #371-372 3.00 3.00

Royal Norfolk Island Agricultural & Horticultural Show, 125th anniv.

Christmas — A86

1985, Oct. 3 *Perf. 13½*

373 A86 27c Three Shepherds .35 .35
374 A86 33c Journey to Bethlehem .50 .50
375 A86 50c Three Wise Men .65 .65
376 A86 90c Nativity 1.30 1.30
Nos. 373-376 (4) 2.80 2.80

Marine Life — A87

1986, Jan. 14 *Perf. 13½x14*

377 A87 5c Long-spined sea urchin .25 .25
378 A87 33c Blue starfish .50 .50
379 A87 55c Eagle ray .85 .85
380 A87 75c Moray eel 1.20 1.20
a. Souvenir sheet of 4, #377-380 4.00 4.00
Nos. 377-380 (4) 2.80 2.80

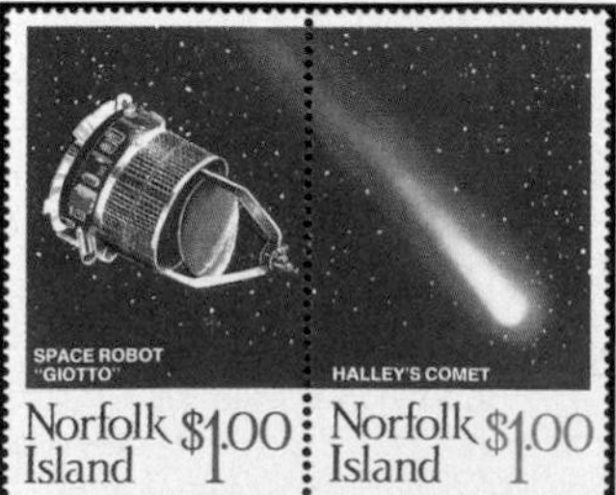

Halley's Comet — A88

Designs: a, Giotto space probe. b, Comet.

1986, Mar. 11 *Perf. 15*

381 A88 Pair 3.25 3.25
a.-b. $1 any single 1.60 1.60

Se-tenant in continuous design.

AMERIPEX '86 — A89

Designs: 33c, Isaac Robinson, US consul in Norfolk, 1887-1908, vert. 50c, Ford Model-T. 80c, Statue of Liberty.

1986, May 22 Litho. *Perf. 13½*

382 A89 33c multicolored .45 .45
383 A89 50c multicolored .70 .70
384 A89 80c multicolored 1.10 1.10
a. Souvenir sheet of #382-384 2.75 2.75
Nos. 382-384 (3) 2.25 2.25

Queen Elizabeth II, 60th Birthday — A90

Various portraits — 5c, As Princess. 33c, Contemporary photograph. 80c, Opening N.I. Golf Club. 90c,

1986, June 12

385 A90 5c multicolored .25 .25
386 A90 33c multicolored .65 .65
387 A90 80c multicolored 1.40 1.40
388 A90 90c multicolored 1.75 1.75
Nos. 385-388 (4) 4.05 4.05

Christmas A91

1986, Sept. 23 Litho. *Perf. 13½x14*

389 A91 30c multicolored .40 .40
390 A91 40c multicolored .50 .50
391 A91 $1 multicolored 1.30 1.30
Nos. 389-391 (3) 2.20 2.20

Commission of Gov. Phillip, Bicent. — A92

36c, British prison, 1787. 55c, Transportation, Court of Assize. No. 394, Gov. meeting Home Society. No. 395, Gov. meeting Home Secretary. $1, Gov. Phillip, 1738-1814.

1986 Litho. *Perf. 14x13½*

392 A92 36c multicolored 1.00 .75
393 A92 55c multicolored 1.75 1.15
394 A92 90c multicolored 3.00 3.00
395 A92 90c multicolored 3.00 3.00
396 A92 $1 multicolored 4.00 4.00
Nos. 392-396 (5) 12.75 11.90

No. 395 was issued because No. 394 is incorrectly inscribed.

Issued: #395, Dec. 16; others, Oct. 14.

See #417-420, 426-436.

Commission of Gov. Phillip, Bicent. — A93

1986, Dec. 16 *Perf. 13½*

397 A93 36c Maori chief 1.25 1.25
398 A93 36c Bananas, taro 1.25 1.25
399 A93 36c Stone tools 1.25 1.25
400 A93 36c Polynesian outrigger 1.25 1.25
Nos. 397-400 (4) 5.00 5.00

Pre-European occupation of the Island.

Island Scenery — A94

1c, Cockpit Creek Bridge. 2c, Cemetery Bay Beach. 3c, Guesthouse. 5c, Philip Island from Point Ross. 15c, Cattle grazing. 30c, Rock fishing. 37c, Old home. 40c, Shopping center. 50c, Emily Bay. 60c, Bloody Bridge. 80c, Pitcairner-style shop. 90c, Government House. $1, Melanesian Memorial Chapel. $2, Kingston convict settlement. $3, Ball Bay. $5, Northerly cliffs.

1987-88 Litho. *Perf. 13½*

401 A94 1c multicolored .25 *.35*
402 A94 2c multicolored .25 *.35*
403 A94 3c multicolored .25 *.35*
404 A94 5c multicolored .25 *.35*
405 A94 15c multicolored .25 *.35*
406 A94 30c multicolored .45 *.65*
407 A94 37c multicolored .55 *.75*
408 A94 40c multicolored .60 *.85*
409 A94 50c multicolored .75 *1.05*
410 A94 60c multicolored .85 *1.20*
411 A94 80c multicolored 1.10 *1.60*
412 A94 90c multicolored 1.25 *1.75*
413 A94 $1 multicolored 1.50 *2.25*
414 A94 $2 multicolored 3.00 *4.25*
415 A94 $3 multicolored 4.50 *6.50*
416 A94 $5 multicolored 10.00 *14.50*
Nos. 401-416 (16) 25.80 *37.10*

Issued: 5c, 50c, 90c, $1, 2/17; 30c, 40c, 80c, $2, 4/17; 15c, 37c, 60c, $3, 7/27; 1c, 2c, 3c, $5, 5/17/88.

Bicentennial Type of 1986

Designs: 5c, Loading supplies at Deptford, England, 1787. No. 418, First Fleet sailing from Spithead (buoy in water). No. 419, Sailing from Spithead (ship flying British merchant flag). $1, Convicts below deck.

1987, May 13 Litho. *Perf. 14x13½*

417 A92 5c multicolored .55 .55
418 A92 55c multicolored 1.75 1.75
419 A92 55c multicolored 1.75 1.75
a. Pair, #418-419 4.25 4.25
420 A92 $1 multicolored 2.75 2.75
Nos. 417-420 (4) 6.80 6.80

No. 419a has a continuous design.

A96

World Wildlife Fund: Green parrot.

1987, Sept. 16 Unwmk.

421 Strip of 4 *17.50 17.50*
a. A96 5c Parrot facing right *3.00 2.25*
b. A96 15c Parrot, chick, egg *3.50 1.75*
c. A96 36c Parrots *4.75 3.50*
d. A96 55c Parrot facing left *6.50 4.50*

Christmas A97

Children's party: 30c, Norfolk Island pine tree, restored convicts' settlement. 42c, Santa Claus, children opening packages. 58c, Santa, children, gifts in fire engine. 63c, Meal.

Perf. 13½x14

1987, Oct. 13 Litho. Wmk. 384

422 A97 30c multicolored .45 .45
423 A97 42c multicolored .65 .65
424 A97 58c multicolored .85 .85
425 A97 63c multicolored .95 .95
Nos. 422-425 (4) 2.90 2.90

Bicentennial Type of 1986

Designs: 5c, Lt. Philip Gidley King. No. 427, La Perouse and Louis XVI of France. No. 428, Gov. Phillip sailing in ship's cutter from Botany Bay to Port Jackson. No. 429, Flag raising on Norfolk Is. 55c, Lt. King and search party exploring the island. 70c, Landfall, Sydney Bay. No. 432, L'Astrolabe and La Boussole off coast of Norfolk. No. 433, HMS Supply. No. 434, Wrecking of L'Astrolabe off the Solomon Isls. No. 435, First Fleet landing at Sydney Cove. No. 436, First settlement, Sydney Bay, 1788.

1987-88 Litho. *Perf. 14x13½*

426 A92 5c multicolored .25 .25
427 A92 37c multicolored .85 .85
428 A92 37c multicolored .85 .85
429 A92 37c multicolored .85 .85
430 A92 55c multicolored 1.75 1.75
431 A92 70c multicolored 1.50 1.50
432 A92 90c multicolored 2.75 2.75
433 A92 90c multicolored 2.25 2.25
434 A92 $1 multicolored 2.75 2.75
435 A92 $1 multicolored 2.50 2.50
436 A92 $1 multicolored 2.50 2.50
Nos. 426-436 (11) 18.80 18.80

Visit of Jean La Perouse (1741-88), French navigator, to Norfolk Is. (Nos. 427, 432, 434); arrival of the First Fleet at Sydney Cove (Nos. 428, 435); founding of Norfolk Is. (Nos. 426, 429-431, 433, 436).

Issued: #427, 432, 434, Dec. 8, 1987; #428, 435, Jan. 25, 1988; others, Mar. 4, 1988.

SYDPEX '88, July 30-Aug. 7 A98

Sydney-Norfolk transportation and communication links — No. 437, Air and sea transports, vert. No. 439, Telecommunications, vert.

Perf. 14x13½, 13½x14

1988, July 30 Litho.

437 A98 37c multicolored .90 .90
438 A98 37c shown .90 .90
439 A98 37c multicolored .90 .90
a. Souvenir sheet of 3, #437-439 8.50 8.50
Nos. 437-439 (3) 2.70 2.70

No. 438 exists perf. 13½ within No. 439a.

Christmas — A99

1988, Sept. 27 Litho. *Perf. 14x13½*

440 A99 30c shown .45 .45
441 A99 42c Flowers, diff. .65 .65
442 A99 58c Trees, fish .95 .95
443 A99 63c Trees, sailboats .95 .95
Nos. 440-443 (4) 3.00 3.00

Convict Era Georgian Architecture, c. 1825-1850
A100

Designs: 39c, Waterfront shop and boat shed. 55c, Royal Engineers' Building. 90c, Old military barracks. $1, Commissary and new barracks.

1988, Dec. 6 Litho. *Perf. 13½x14*

444 A100 39c multicolored .55 .55
445 A100 55c multicolored .80 .80
446 A100 90c multicolored 1.30 1.30
447 A100 $1 multicolored 1.50 1.50
Nos. 444-447 (4) 4.15 4.15

Indigenous Insects
A101

39c, Lamprima aenea. 55c, Insulascirtus nythos. 90c, Caedicia araucariae. $1, Thrincophora aridela.

Perf. 13½x14

1989, Feb. 14 Litho. Unwmk.

448 A101 39c multicolored .85 .85
449 A101 55c multicolored 1.15 1.15
450 A101 90c multicolored 1.75 1.75
451 A101 $1 multicolored 2.25 2.25
Nos. 448-451 (4) 6.00 6.00

Mutiny on the Bounty
A102

Designs: 5c, *Bounty's* landfall, Adventure Bay, Tasmania. 39c, Mutineers and Polynesian maidens, c. 1790. 55c, Cumbria, Christian's home county. $1.10, Capt. Bligh and crewmen cast adrift.

Perf. 13½

1989, Apr. 28 Litho. Unwmk.

452 A102 5c multicolored .70 .70
453 A102 39c multicolored 2.40 2.40
454 A102 55c multicolored 3.00 3.00
455 A102 $1.10 multicolored 4.50 4.50
Nos. 452-455 (4) 10.60 10.60

Souvenir Sheet

456 Sheet of 3 + label (#453, 456a-456b) 8.25 8.25
a. A102 90c Isle of Man No. 393 3.25 3.25
b. A102 $1 Pitcairn Isls. No. 321d 3.50 3.50

See Isle of Man Nos. 389-394 and Pitcairn Isls. Nos. 320-322.

A103

Perf. 14x13½

1989, Aug. 10 Litho. Unwmk.

457 A103 41c Flag .95 .95
458 A103 55c Ballot box 1.05 1.05
459 A103 $1 Norfolk Is. Act of 1979 2.25 2.25
460 A103 $1.10 Norfolk Is. crest 2.40 2.40
Nos. 457-460 (4) 6.65 6.65

Self-Government, 10th anniv.

A104

Perf. 13½x13

1989, Sept. 25 Litho. Unwmk.

461 A104 $1 dark ultra & dark red 4.00 4.00

Natl. Red Cross, 75th anniv.

Bounty Hymns
A105

Designs: 36c, "While nature was sinking in stillness to rest, The last beams of daylight show dim in the west." 60c, "There's a land that is fairer than day, And by faith we can see it afar." 75c, "Let the lower lights be burning, Send a gleam across the wave." 80c, "Oh, have you not heard of that beautiful stream That flows through our father's lands."

1989, Oct. 9 *Perf. 13½x14*

462 A105 36c multicolored .90 .90
463 A105 60c multicolored 1.75 1.75
464 A105 75c multicolored 2.60 2.60
465 A105 80c multicolored 2.60 2.60
Nos. 462-465 (4) 7.85 7.85

A106

41c, Announcer John Royle. 65c, Sound waves on map. $1.10, Jacko, the laughing kookaburra.

1989, Nov. 21 *Perf. 14x13½*

466 A106 41c multicolored 1.50 1.50
467 A106 65c multicolored 2.10 2.10
468 A106 $1.10 multicolored 3.25 3.25
Nos. 466-468 (3) 6.85 6.85

Radio Australia, 50th anniv.

A107

Settlement of Pitcairn (The Norfolk Islanders): 70c, The *Bounty* on fire. $1.10, Armorial ensign of Norfolk.

Perf. 15x14½

1990, Jan. 23 Litho. Unwmk.

469 A107 70c multicolored 3.50 3.50
470 A107 $1.10 multicolored 3.75 3.75

Salvage Team at Work
A108

Designs: No. 471, HMS *Sirius* striking reef. No. 472, HMS *Supply* clearing reef. $1, Map of salvage sites, artifacts.

1990, Mar. 19 *Perf. 14x13½*

Size of Nos. 471-472: 40x27

471 A108 41c multicolored 2.00 2.00
472 A108 41c multicolored 2.00 2.00
a. Pair, #471-472 4.50 4.50
473 A108 65c shown 3.00 3.00
474 A108 $1 multicolored 3.25 3.25
Nos. 471-474 (4) 10.25 10.25

Wreck of HMS *Sirius*, 200th anniv. No. 472a has continuous design.

Lightering Cargo Ashore, Kingston
A109

MV Ile de Lumiere
A110

45c, La Dunkerquoise. 50c, Dmitri Mendeleev. 65c, Pacific Rover. 75c, Norfolk Trader. 80c, Roseville. 90c, Kalia. $1, HMS Bounty. $2, HMAS Success. $5, HMAS Whyalia.

1990-91 Litho. *Perf. 14x14½*

479 A109 5c shown .30 .30
480 A109 10c like #479 .30 .30

Perf. 14½

481 A110 45c multicolored .70 .70
482 A110 50c multicolored .80 .80
483 A110 65c multicolored 1.05 1.05
484 A110 70c shown 1.10 1.10
485 A110 75c multicolored 1.20 1.20
486 A110 80c multicolored 1.20 1.20
487 A110 90c multicolored 1.40 1.40
488 A110 $1 multicolored 1.60 1.60
489 A110 $2 multicolored 3.25 3.25
490 A110 $5 multicolored 8.25 8.25
Nos. 479-490 (12) 21.15 21.15

Issued: 5c, 10c, 70c, $2, 7/17/90; 45c, 50c, 65c, $5, 2/19/91; 75c, 80c, 90c, $1, 8/13/91.

Christmas — A111

38c, Island home. 43c, New post office. 65c, Sydney Bay, Kingston, horiz. 85c, Officers' Quarters, 1836, horiz.

1990, Sept. 25 Litho. *Perf. 14½*

491 A111 38c multicolored .90 .90
492 A111 43c multicolored .95 .95
493 A111 65c multicolored 2.10 2.10
494 A111 85c multicolored 2.40 2.40
Nos. 491-494 (4) 6.35 6.35

A112

Designs: 70c, William Charles Wentworth (1790-1872), Australian politician. $1.20, Thursday October Christian (1790-1831).

1990, Oct. 11 Litho. *Perf. 15x14½*

495 A112 70c brown 1.50 1.50
496 A112 $1.20 brown 2.25 2.25

Norfolk Island Robin
A113 A114

1990, Dec. 3 Litho. *Perf. 14½*

497 A113 65c multicolored 1.50 1.50
498 A113 $1 shown 2.50 2.50
499 A113 $1.20 multi, diff. 3.00 3.00
Nos. 497-499 (3) 7.00 7.00

Souvenir Sheet

500 Sheet of 2 7.00 7.00
a. A114 $1 shown 3.00 3.00
b. A114 $1 Two robins 3.00 3.00

Birdpex '90, 20th Intl. Ornithological Congress, New Zealand.

Ham Radio — A115

1991, Apr. 9 Litho. *Perf. 14½*

501 A115 43c Island map 1.60 1.60
502 A115 $1 World map 3.50 3.50
503 A115 $1.20 Regional location 3.50 3.50
Nos. 501-503 (3) 8.60 8.60

Museum Displays
A116

43c, Ship's bow, Sirius Museum, vert. 70c, House Museum. $1, Carronade, Sirius Museum. $1.20, Pottery, Archaeology Museum, vert.

1991, May 16 Litho. *Perf. 14½*

504 A116 43c multicolored 1.20 1.20
505 A116 70c multicolored 2.10 2.10
506 A116 $1 multicolored 2.40 2.40
507 A116 $1.20 multicolored 2.75 2.75
Nos. 504-507 (4) 8.45 8.45

Wreck of HMS Pandora, Aug. 28, 1791
A117

Design: $1.20, HMS Pandora searching for Bounty mutineers.

1991, July 2 Litho. *Perf. 13½x14*

508 A117 $1 shown 4.00 4.00
509 A117 $1.20 multicolored 4.50 4.50

Christmas
A118

1991, Sept. 23 Litho. *Perf. 14½*

510 A118 38c multicolored .80 .80
511 A118 43c multicolored 1.10 1.10
512 A118 65c multicolored 1.75 1.75
513 A118 85c multicolored 2.10 2.10
Nos. 510-513 (4) 5.75 5.75

Start of World War II in the Pacific, 50th Anniv. A119

1991, Dec. 9 Litho. *Perf. 14½*

514	A119	43c Tank and soldier	1.60	1.60
515	A119	70c B-17	2.75	2.75
516	A119	$1 War ships	3.75	3.75
		Nos. 514-516 (3)	8.10	8.10

A120

1992, Feb. 11 Litho. *Perf. 14½*

517	A120	45c Columbus' Coat of Arms	.90	.90
518	A120	$1.05 Santa Maria	2.25	2.25
519	A120	$1.20 Columbus at globe	2.75	2.75
		Nos. 517-519 (3)	5.90	5.90

Discovery of America, 500th anniv.

A121

Designs: No. 520, Map of Coral Sea Battle area. No. 521, Battle area, Midway. No. 522, HMAS Australia. No. 523, Catalina PBY5. No. 524, USS Yorktown. No. 525, Dauntless dive bomber.

1992, May 4 Litho. *Perf. 14½*

520	A121	45c multicolored	1.00	1.00
521	A121	45c multicolored	1.00	1.00
522	A121	70c multicolored	1.75	1.75
523	A121	70c multicolored	1.75	1.75
524	A121	$1.05 multicolored	2.75	2.75
525	A121	$1.05 multicolored	2.75	2.75
		Nos. 520-525 (6)	11.00	11.00

Battles of the Coral Sea and Midway, 50th anniv.

US Invasion of Guadalcanal, 50th Anniv. A122

Designs: 45c, Troops landing on beach. 70c, Troops in battle. $1.05, Map, flags.

1992, Aug. 6 Litho. *Perf. 14½*

526	A122	45c multicolored	1.40	1.40
527	A122	70c multicolored	2.25	2.25
528	A122	$1.05 multicolored	4.00	4.00
		Nos. 526-528 (3)	7.65	7.65

Christmas — A123

Scenes of Norfolk Island: 40c, Ball Bay, looking over Point Blackbourne. 45c, Headstone Creek. 75c, Ball Bay. $1.20, Rocky Point Reserve.

1992, Oct. 29 Litho. *Perf. 15x14½*

529	A123	40c multicolored	.75	.75
530	A123	45c multicolored	.85	.85
531	A123	75c multicolored	1.75	1.75
532	A123	$1.20 multicolored	2.50	2.50
		Nos. 529-532 (4)	5.85	5.85

Tourism A124

Tourist sites at Kingston: a, Boat shed, flaghouses. b, Old military barracks. c, All Saints Church. d, Officers quarters. e, Quality row.

1993, Feb. 23 Litho. *Perf. 14½*

533	A124	45c Strip of 5, #a.-e.	5.50	5.50

Emergency Services A125

45c, Volunteer fire service. 70c, Rescue squad. 75c, St. John ambulance. $1.20, Police service.

1993, May 18 Litho. *Perf. 14½*

534	A125	45c multicolored	1.25	1.25
535	A125	70c multicolored	1.50	1.50
536	A125	75c multicolored	1.90	1.90
537	A125	$1.20 multicolored	3.50	3.50
		Nos. 534-537 (4)	8.15	8.15

Nudibranchs A126

No. 538, Phyllidia ocellata. No. 539, Glaucus atlanticus. 75c, Bornella sp. 85c, Glossodoris rubroannolata. 95c, Halgerda willeyi. $1.05, Chromodoris amoena.

1993, July 7 Litho. *Perf. 14½*

538	A126	45c multicolored	1.25	1.25
539	A126	45c multicolored	1.50	1.50
540	A126	75c multicolored	1.75	1.75
541	A126	85c multicolored	2.00	2.00
542	A126	95c multicolored	2.25	2.25
543	A126	$1.05 multicolored	2.50	2.50
		Nos. 538-543 (6)	11.25	11.25

No. 539 identified as "glauc."

A127

Designs: 70c, Maori patus. $1.20, First Maori map of New Zealand on paper, 1793.

1993, Oct. 28 Litho. *Perf. 14½*

544	A127	70c tan, buff & black	1.75	1.75
545	A127	$1.20 tan, buff & black	3.25	3.25

Cultural contact with New Zealand, bicent.

A128

1993, Oct. 28

546	A128	40c blue & multi	.95	.95
547	A128	45c red & multi	1.05	1.05
548	A128	75c green & multi	1.75	1.75
549	A128	$1.20 black & multi	2.75	2.75
		Nos. 546-549 (4)	6.50	6.50

Early Pacific Explorers A129

Explorer, ship: 5c, Vasco Nunez de Balboa, Barbara. 10c, Ferdinand Magellan, Victoria. 20c, Juan Sebastian de Elcano, Victoria. 50c, Alvaro de Saavedra, Florida. 70c, Ruy Lopez de Villalobos, San Juan. 75c, Miguel Lopez de Legaspi, San Lesmes. 80c, Sir Frances Drake, Golden Hinde. 85c, Alvaro de Mendana, Santiago. 90c, Pedro Fernandes de Quiros, San Pedro Paulo. $1, Luis Baez de Torres, San Perico. $2, Abel Tasman, Heemskerk. $5, William Dampier, Cygnet. No. 562, Golden Hinde (Francis Drake).

1994 Litho. *Perf. 14½*

550	A129	5c multicolored	.35	.35
551	A129	10c multicolored	.40	.40
552	A129	20c multicolored	.75	.75
554	A129	50c multicolored	1.10	1.10
556	A129	70c multicolored	1.40	1.40
557	A129	75c multicolored	1.60	1.60
558	A129	80c multicolored	1.60	1.60
559	A129	85c multicolored	1.75	1.75
560	A129	90c multicolored	2.00	2.00
560A	A129	$1 multicolored	2.25	2.25
561	A129	$2 multicolored	4.50	4.50
561A	A129	$5 multicolored	10.00	10.00
		Nos. 550-561A (12)	27.70	27.70

Souvenir Sheet

Perf. 13

562	A129	$1.20 multicolored	4.75	4.75

No. 562 contains one 32x52mm stamp.

Issued: 50c, 70c, 75c, $2, No. 562, 2/8/94; 5c, 10c, 20c, $5, 5/3/94. 80c, 85c, 90c, $1, 7/26/94.

A130

Seabirds: a, Sooty tern. b, Red-tailed tropic bird. c, Australasian gannet. d, Wedge-tail shearwater. e, Masked booby.

1994, Aug. 17 Litho. *Perf. 14½x14*

565	A130	45c Strip of 5, #a.-e.	7.00	7.00
		Booklet, 2 #565	14.00	

A131

Christmas: 45c, Church, flowers, words from Pitcairn anthem. 75c, Stained glass windows, "To God be the glory." $1.20, Rainbow, ship, "Ship of Fame."

1994, Oct. 27 Litho. *Die Cut*

Self-Adhesive

566	A131	45c multicolored	1.50	1.50
567	A131	75c multicolored	1.75	1.75
568	A131	$1.20 multicolored	3.00	3.00
		Nos. 566-568 (3)	6.25	6.25

Vintage Cars — A132

45c, 1926 Chevrolet. 75c, 1928 Model A Ford. $1.05, 1929 Model A A/C Ford truck. $1.20, 1930 Model A Ford.

1995, Feb. 7 Litho. *Perf. 14x14½*

569	A132	45c multicolored	.80	.80
570	A132	75c multicolored	1.60	1.60
571	A132	$1.05 multicolored	2.25	2.25
572	A132	$1.20 multicolored	3.00	3.00
		Nos. 569-572 (4)	7.65	7.65

Humpback Whales A133

Perf. 14x14½, 14½x14

1995, May 9 Litho.

573	A133	45c Tail fluke	1.30	1.30
574	A133	75c Mother & calf	2.00	2.00
575	A133	$1.05 Breaching, vert.	2.75	2.75
		Nos. 573-575 (3)	6.05	6.05

Souvenir Sheet

Perf. 14x14½

576	A133	$1.20 Bubble netting, vert.	4.25	4.25
a.		Overprinted in gold & black	4.00	4.00

No. 576 contains one 30x50mm stamp and is a continuous design.

Overprint in margin of No. 576a has "Selamat Hari Merdeka" and JAKARTA '95 exhibition emblem.

Butterfly Fish — A134

Chaetodon: 5c, pelewensis. 45c, plebeius. $1.20, tricinctus. $1.50, auriga.

1995, June 15 Litho. *Perf. 14*

577	A134	5c multicolored	1.10	1.10
578	A134	45c multicolored	1.75	1.75
579	A134	$1.20 multicolored	3.50	3.50
580	A134	$1.50 multicolored	4.00	4.00
		Nos. 577-580 (4)	10.35	10.35

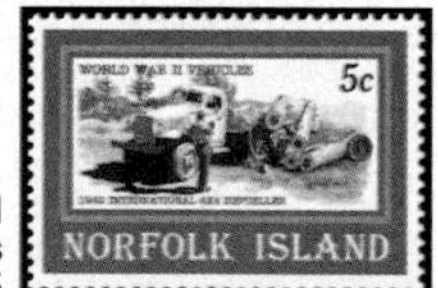

World War II Vehicles A135

Designs: 5c, 1942 Intl. 4x4 refueler. 45c, 1942 Ford 5 passenger sedan. $1.20, 1942 Ford 3-ton tipper. $2, D8 Caterpillar with scraper.

1995, Aug. 8 Litho. *Perf. 14x15*

Black Vignettes

581	A135	5c brown & tan	.60	.60
582	A135	45c blue & red lil	1.50	1.50
583	A135	$1.20 grn & org	3.25	3.25
584	A135	$2 red & gray	5.25	5.25
		Nos. 581-584 (4)	10.60	10.60

Island Flower Type of 1960

1995, Sept. 1 Litho. *Rouletted 7*

Booklet Stamps

585	A6	5c like No. 30	.30	.30
a.		Booklet pane of 18 + 3 labels	5.50	
586	A6	5c like No. 33	.30	.30
a.		Booklet pane of 18 + 3 labels	5.50	
		Complete booklet, 1 each #585a-586a	11.00	

A136

Victory in the Pacific Day, 50th Anniv. A136a

Designs: 5c, Fighter plane en route. 45c, Sgt. T.C. Derrick, VC, vert. 75c, Gen. MacArthur, vert. $1.05, Girls at victory party.

1995, Sept. 1 Litho. *Perf. 12*

587 A136 5c multicolored .40 .40
588 A136 45c multicolored .95 .95
589 A136 75c multicolored 1.60 1.60
590 A136 $1.05 multicolored 2.50 2.50
Nos. 587-590 (4) 5.45 5.45

Litho. & Embossed

591 A136a $10 Medals 24.00 24.00

Singapore '95.

UN, 50th Anniv. — A137

45c, Dove. 75c, Christmas star. $1.05, Christmas candles. $1.20, Olive branch.

1995, Nov. 7 Litho. *Perf. 14½x14*

592 A137 45c multicolored .90 .90
593 A137 75c multicolored 1.30 1.30
594 A137 $1.05 multicolored 1.75 1.75
595 A137 $1.20 multicolored 2.40 2.40
Nos. 592-595 (4) 6.35 6.35

Christmas (#593-594).

Skinks and Geckos A138

World Wildlife Fund: a, 5c, Skink crawling left. b, 45c, Skink crawling right. c, 5c, Gecko crawling right. d, 45c, Gecko crawling left, flower.

1996, Feb. 7 Litho. *Perf. 14½x15*

596 A138 Strip of 4, #a.-d. 4.00 4.00

No. 596 was issued in sheets of 4 strips with stamps in each strip in different order.

Royal Australian Air Force, 75th Anniv. — A139

1996, Apr. 22 Litho. *Perf. 14*

597 A139 45c Sopwith pup .85 .85
598 A139 45c Wirraway .85 .85
599 A139 75c F-111C 1.40 1.40
600 A139 85c F/A-18 Hornet 1.60 1.60
Nos. 597-600 (4) 4.70 4.70

Souvenir Sheet

New Year 1996 (Year of the Rat) — A140

1996, May 17 Litho. *Perf. 12*

601 A140 $1 multicolored 3.00 3.00
a. With addl. inscription in sheet margin 3.00 3.00

No. 601a is inscribed in sheet margin with China '96 exhibition emblem.

Shells — A141

Designs: No. 602, Argonauta nodosa. No. 603, Janthina janthina. No. 604, Naticarius oncus. No. 605, Cypraea caputserpentis.

1996, July 2 Litho. *Perf. 14*

602 A141 45c multicolored 1.00 1.00
603 A141 45c multicolored 1.00 1.00
604 A141 45c multicolored 1.00 1.00
605 A141 45c multicolored 1.00 1.00
Nos. 602-605 (4) 4.00 4.00

Tourism A142

1996, Sept. 17 Litho. *Perf. 13½x14*

606 A142 45c Shopping .85 .85
607 A142 75c Bounty day 1.40 1.40
608 A142 $2.50 Horse riding 4.50 4.50
609 A142 $3.70 Working the ship 6.75 6.75
Nos. 606-609 (4) 13.50 13.50

A143

Christmas: Cow, star, Bible verse, and: No. 610, Nativity scene. No. 611, Boats, boathouses. 75c, House, trees. 85c, Flowers, fruits.

1996, Nov. 5 Litho. *Perf. 15*

610 A143 45c multicolored .75 .75
611 A143 45c multicolored .75 .75
612 A143 75c multicolored 1.25 1.25
613 A143 85c multicolored 1.40 1.40
Nos. 610-613 (4) 4.15 4.15

A144

No. 614, Natl. Arms. No. 615, Natl. Seal.

1997, Jan. 22 Litho. *Roulette 7*

614 A144 5c yellow & green .40 .40
a. Booklet pane of 10 4.00
615 A144 5c tan & brown .40 .40
a. Booklet pane of 10 4.00
Complete booklet, 2 each #614a-615a 8.00

Souvenir Sheet

Beef Cattle — A145

1997, Feb. 11 *Perf. 13½x13*

616 A145 $1.20 multicolored 3.00 3.00
a. Inscribed in sheet margin 30.00 25.00

No. 616a is inscribed with Hong Kong '97 exhibition emblem.

Butterflies A146

Designs: 75c, Cepora perimale perimale. 90c, Danaus chrysippus petilia. $1, Danaus bamata bamata. $1.20, Danaus plexippus.

1997, Mar. 28 *Perf. 14½*

617 A146 75c multicolored 1.50 1.50
618 A146 90c multicolored 1.75 1.75
619 A146 $1 multicolored 2.00 2.00
620 A146 $1.20 multicolored 2.50 2.50
Nos. 617-620 (4) 7.75 7.75

Dolphins — A147

1997, May 29 Litho. *Perf. 14*

621 A147 45c Dusky dolphin 1.25 1.25
622 A147 75c Common dolphin 2.50 2.50

Souvenir Sheet

623 A147 $1.05 Dolphin, diff. 3.50 3.50
a. Inscribed in sheet margin 4.50 4.50

No. 623a is inscribed in sheet margin with PACIFIC 97 exhibition emblem.

First Norfolk Island Stamp, 50th Anniv. A148

Designs: $1, View of Ball Bay. $1.50, #4. $8, #12, view of Ball Bay.

1997, June 10 *Perf. 12*

624 A148 $1.00 multicolored 1.75 1.75
625 A148 $1.50 multicolored 2.75 2.75
a. Pair, #624-625 4.50 4.50

Size: 90x45mm

626 A148 $8 multicolored 13.00 13.00

Queen Elizabeth II & Prince Philip, 50th Wedding Anniv. — A149

Designs: 20c, Queen. No. 628, Prince guiding 4-in-hand team. No. 629, Prince in formal suit, hat. 50c, Queen riding in royal coach. $1.50, Younger picture of Queen, Prince riding in carriage.

1997, Aug. 12 Litho. *Perf. 14½*

627 A149 20c multicolored .50 .50
628 A149 25c multicolored .60 .60
a. Pair, #627-628 1.10 1.10
629 A149 25c multicolored .60 .60
630 A149 50c multicolored 1.30 1.30
a. Pair, #629-630 1.90 1.90

Souvenir Sheet

631 A149 $1.50 multicolored 3.25 3.25

Souvenir Sheet

Return of Hong Kong to China — A150

1997, Sept. 16 Litho. *Perf. 14*

632 A150 45c Royal Yacht Britannia 2.00 2.00

Greetings Stamps — A151

1997, Nov. 4 Litho. *Perf. 13x13½*

633 A151 45c Christmas .75 .75
634 A151 75c New Year's Eve 1.25 1.25
635 A151 $1.20 Valentine's Day 2.00 2.00
Nos. 633-635 (3) 4.00 4.00

Souvenir Sheet

Oriental Pearl TV Tower, Shanghai — A152

1997, Nov. 18 *Perf. 14½*

636 A152 45c multicolored 1.50 1.50

Shanghai '97, Intl. Stamp & Coin Expo.

Souvenir Sheet

New Year 1998 (Year of the Tiger) — A153

1998, Feb. 12 Litho. *Perf. 12*
637 A153 45c multicolored 2.00 2.00

Paintings of Cats — A154

1998, Feb. 26 *Perf. 14½*
638 A154 45c "Pepper" .75 .75
639 A154 45c "Tabitha" .75 .75
640 A154 75c "Midnight" 1.25 1.25
641 A154 $1.20 "Rainbow" 2.00 2.00
Nos. 638-641 (4) 4.75 4.75

Island Scenes, by Brent Hilder — A155

Designs: No. 642, Penal Settlement, 1825-56. No. 643, First settlement, 1788-1814.

1998, Feb. 27 *Rouletted 7*
642 A155 5c blue & black .30 .30
a. Booklet pane of 10 3.00
643 A155 5c blue green & black .30 .30
a. Booklet pane of 10 3.00
Complete booklet, 2 each 1642a-1643a 6.00

Diana, Princess of Wales (1961-97)
Common Design Type

#645: a, Wearing blue & white dress. b, Wearing pearl pendant earrings. c, In striped dress.

1998, Apr. 28 Litho. *Perf. 14½x14*
644 CD355 45c multicolored .75 .75

Sheet of 4
645 CD355 45c #a.-c., #644 4.50 4.50

No. 644 sold for $1.80 + 45c, with surtax from international sales being donated to the Princess Diana Memorial fund and surtax from national sales being dontated to designated local charity.

Reef Fish — A156

Designs: 10c, Tweed trousers. 20c, Conspicuous angelfish. 30c, Moon wrasse. 45c, Wide-stiped clownfish. 50c, Raccoon butterfly fish. 70c, Artooti. 75c, Splendid hawkfish. 85c, Scorpion fish. 90c, Orange fairy basslet. $1, Sweetlip. $3, Moorish idol. $4, Gold ribbon soapfish.
$1.20, Shark.

1998 Litho. *Perf. 14½*
646 A156 10c multicolored .25 .25
647 A156 20c multicolored .30 .30
648 A156 30c multicolored .45 .45
649 A156 45c multicolored .65 .65
650 A156 50c multicolored .75 .75
651 A156 70c multicolored 1.00 1.00
652 A156 75c multicolored 1.10 1.10
653 A156 85c multicolored 1.25 1.25
654 A156 90c multicolored 1.25 1.25
655 A156 $1 multicolored 1.50 1.50
656 A156 $3 multicolored 4.50 4.50
657 A156 $4 multicolored 6.00 6.00
Nos. 646-657 (12) 19.00 19.00

Souvenir Sheet
Perf. 14x14½
658 A156 $1.20 multicolored 2.50 2.50

No. 658 contains 30x40mm stamp.
Issued: 10c, 30c, 50c, 75c, 90c, $1.20, $4, 5/5; others, 6/29.

16th Commonwealth Games, Kuala Lumpur — A157

Designs: 75c, Hammer throw, vert. 95c, Trap shooting. $1.05, Lawn bowling, vert.
85c, Flag bearer, vert.

1998, July 23 Litho. *Perf. 14½*
659 A157 75c black & red 1.00 1.00
660 A157 95c black & violet blue 1.20 1.20
661 A157 $1.05 black & red lilac 1.25 1.25
Nos. 659-661 (3) 3.45 3.45

Souvenir Sheet
662 A157 85c black & greenish blue 1.60 1.60

The Norfolk, Bicent. A158

1998, Sept. 24 Litho. *Perf. 13*
663 A158 45c multicolored 2.25 2.25

Souvenir Sheet
664 A158 $1.20 multicolored 4.50 4.50

Souvenir Sheet

Whales — A159

1998, Oct. 23 Litho. *Perf. 13½x14*
665 A159 $1.50 multicolored 4.25 4.25

See Namibia No. 919, South Africa No. 1095.

Christmas A160

Designs: 45c, "Peace on earth." 75c, "Joy to the World." $1.05, Doves, "A season of love." $1.20, Candle, "Light of the World."

1998, Nov. 10 *Perf. 13x13½*
666 A160 45c multicolored .65 .65
667 A160 75c multicolored 1.10 1.10
668 A160 $1.05 multicolored 1.50 1.50
669 A160 $1.20 multicolored 1.75 1.75
Nos. 666-669 (4) 5.00 5.00

Airplanes A161

1999, Jan. 28 Litho. *Roulette 7*
Booklet Stamps
670 A161 5c S23 Sandringham .60 .60
a. Booklet pane of 10 5.00
671 A161 5c DC4 "Norfolk Trader" .60 .60
a. Booklet pane of 10 6.00
Complete booklet, 2 ea #670a-671a 12.00

Souvenir Sheet

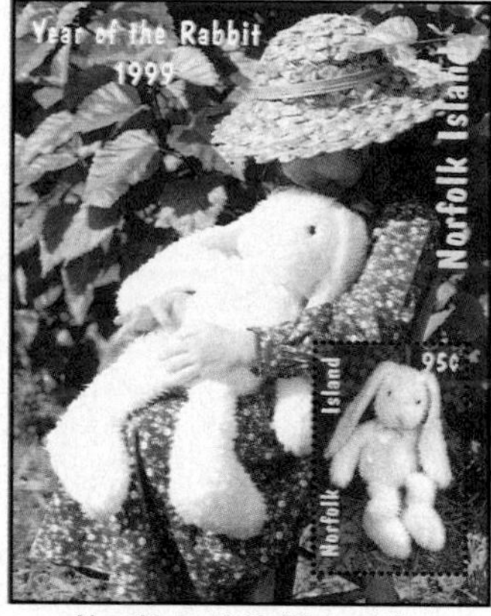

New Year 1999 (Year of the Rabbit) — A162

1999, Feb. 9 Litho. *Perf. 14*
672 A162 95c multicolored 2.25 2.25
a. With additional sheet margin inscription 4.50 4.50

No. 672a is inscribed in sheet margin with China '99 exhibition emblem. Issued: 8/23/99.

Trading Ship Resolution A163

Designs: No. 673, Under construction. No. 674, Launch day. No. 675, Emily Bay. No. 676, Cascade. No. 677, Docked at Auckland.

1999, Mar. 19 *Perf. 13x13½*
Booklet Stamps
673 A163 45c multicolored 1.40 1.40
674 A163 45c multicolored 1.40 1.40
675 A163 45c multicolored 1.40 1.40
676 A163 45c multicolored 1.40 1.40
677 A163 45c multicolored 1.40 1.40
a. Booklet pane, #673-677 + label 7.00
Complete booklet, #677a 7.00

Australia '99, World Stamp Expo.

Souvenir Sheet

Pacific Black Duck — A164

1999, Apr. 27 Litho. *Perf. 14*
678 A164 $2.50 multicolored 6.00 6.00

IBRA '99, Intl. Philatelic Exhibition, Nuremberg, Germany.

Providence Petrel A165

1999, May 27 Litho. *Perf. 14½*
679 A165 75c In flight, vert. 2.40 2.40
680 A165 $1.05 Up close 3.50 3.50
681 A165 $1.20 Adult, young 3.75 3.75
Nos. 679-681 (3) 9.65 9.65

Souvenir Sheet
Perf. 13
682 A165 $4.50 In flight 8.50 8.50

No. 682 contains one 35x51mm stamp.
See No. 710.

Roses — A166

1999, July 30 Litho. *Perf. 14½x14*
683 A166 45c Cecile Brunner .85 .85
684 A166 75c Green 1.25 1.25
685 A166 $1.05 David Buffett 1.90 1.90
Nos. 683-685 (3) 4.00 4.00

Souvenir Sheet
686 A166 $1.20 A Country Woman 2.25 2.25

Handicrafts — A167

Designs: a, 45c, Pottery. b, 45c, Woodcarving. c, 75c, Quilting. d, $1.05, Weaving.

1999, Sept. 16 *Perf. 14¼x14¾*
687 A167 Strip of 4, #a.-d. 4.75 4.75

Queen Mother's Century
Common Design Type

Queen Mother: No. 688, Inspecting bomb damage at Buckingham Palace, 1940. No. 689, With royal family at Abergeldy Castle, 1955. 75c, With Queen Elizabeth, Prince William, 94th birthday. $1.20, As colonel-in-chief of King's Regiment.
$3, With Amy Johnson, pilot of 1930 flight to Australia.

Wmk. 384

1999, Oct. 12 Litho. *Perf. 13½*

688 CD358	45c multicolored	.75	.75
689 CD358	45c multicolored	.75	.75
690 CD358	75c multicolored	1.30	1.30
691 CD358	$1.20 multicolored	2.00	2.00
	Nos. 688-691 (4)	4.80	4.80

Souvenir Sheet

692 CD358	$3 multicolored	5.50	5.50

Melanesian Mission, 150th Anniv. — A168

Christmas: a, 45c, Bishop George Augustus Selwyndd. b, 45c, Bishop John Coleridge Patteson. c, 75c, Text. d, $1.05, Stained glass. e, $1.20, Southern Cross.

1999, Nov. 10 Litho. *Perf. 14*

693 A168	Strip of 5, #a.-e.	9.00	9.00

See Solomon Islands No. 890.

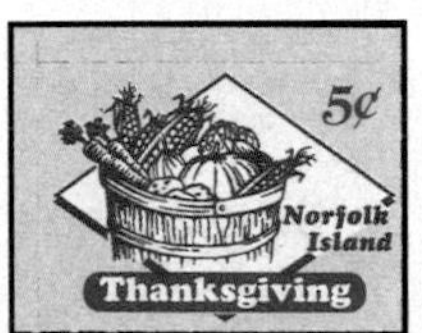

Festivals A169

No. 694, Thanksgiving. No. 695, Country music festival.

2000, Jan. 31 Litho. *Roulette 5¾*

Booklet Stamps

694 A169	5c lav & blk	.25	.25
695 A169	5c blue & blk	.25	.25
a.	Booklet pane, 5 each #694-695	1.75	
	Complete booklet, 4 #695a	7.00	

Souvenir Sheet

New Year 2000 (Year of the Dragon) — A170

2000, Feb. 7 Litho. *Perf. 13¼*

696 A170	$2 multi	3.25	3.25

Fowl — A171

Designs: 45c, Domestic goose. 75c, Pacific black duck. $1.05, Mallard drake. $1.20, Aylesbury duck.

2000, Feb. 18 Litho. *Perf. 14¼*

697 A171	45c multi	1.00	1.00
698 A171	75c multi	1.50	1.50
699 A171	$1.05 multi	2.00	2.00
700 A171	$1.20 multi	2.50	2.50
	Nos. 697-700 (4)	7.00	7.00

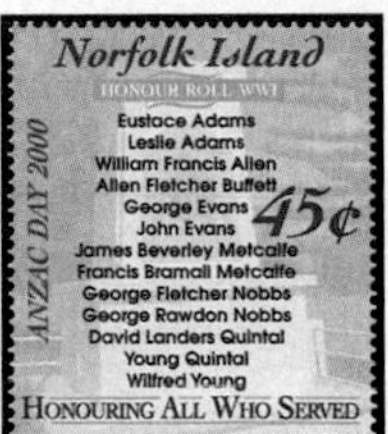

Anzac Day — A172

Monument and lists of war dead from: 45c, WWI. 75c, WWII and Korean War.

2000, Apr. 25 Litho. *Perf. 14x14¾*

701-702 A172	Set of 2	3.00	3.00

Souvenir Sheets

Whaler Project — A173

Designs: No. 703, shown. No. 704, As #703, with gold overprints for The Stamp Show 2000, London, and Crown Agents.

Perf. 14¼, Imperf. (#704)

2000, May 1

703-704 A173	$4 Set of 2	17.50	17.50

Bounty Day — A174

Designs: 45c, Capt. William Bligh. 75c, Fletcher Christian.

2000, June 8 *Perf. 14¼*

705-706 A174	Set of 2	4.00	4.00

Eighth Festival of Pacific Arts, New Caledonia — A175

Designs: 45c, Pot and broom.

No. 708: a, 75c, Turtle and shells. $1.05, Paintings. $1.20, Spear, mask. $2, Decorated gourds.

2000, June 19 *Die cut 9x9½*

Self-Adhesive

707 A175	45c multi	1.75	1.75

Souvenir Sheet

Perf. 13¾

Water-Activated Gum

708 A175	Sheet of 4, #a-d	8.75	8.75

No. 708 contains four 30x38mm stamps.

Souvenir Sheet

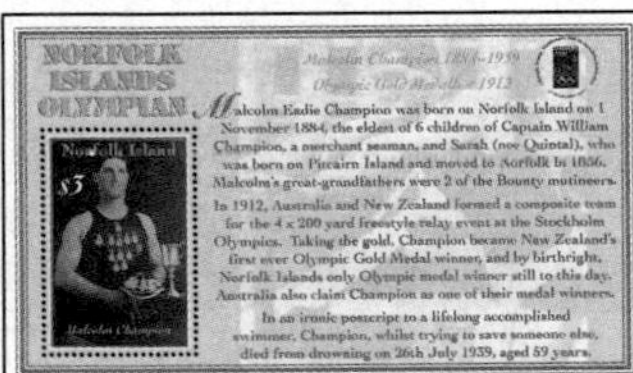

Malcolm Eadie Champion, 1912 Olympic Gold Medalist — A176

2000, Sept. 15 Litho. *Perf. 14x14¼*

709 A176	$3 multi	6.75	6.75

Olymphilex 2000 Stamp Exhibition, Sydney.

Providence Petrel Type of 1999

Souvenir Sheet

2000, Oct. 5 *Perf. 14½x14¾*

710	Sheet of 2 #710a	7.50	7.50
a.	A165 $1.20 Like #681, 32x22mm, with white frame	3.75	3.75

Canpex 2000 Stamp Exhibition, Christchurch, New Zealand.

Christmas A177

Words from "Silent Night" and: 45c, Sun. 75c, Candle. $1.05, Moon. $1.20, Stars.

2000, Oct. 20 *Perf. 13¼x13*

711-714 A177	Set of 4	9.00	9.00

Millennium A178

Children's art by: No. 715, 45c, Jessica Wong and Mardi Pye. No. 716, 45c, Roxanne Spreag. No. 717, 75c, Tara Grube. No. 718, 75c, Tom Greenwood.

2000, Nov. 26 *Perf. 14¾x14½*

715-718 A178	Set of 4	9.50	9.50

Green Parrot — A179

2001, Jan. 26 *Rouletted 5½*

Booklet Stamp

719 A179	5c green & red	.25	.25
a.	Booklet pane of 10	2.25	
	Booklet, 4 #719a	9.00	

Tarler Bird — A180

Designs: $2.30, Norfolk island eel and tarler bird.

2001, Feb. 1 *Perf. 13¼*

720 A180	45c multi	1.75	1.75

Imperf

Size: 110x70mm

721 A180	$2.30 multi	6.25	6.25

No. 720 issued in sheet of 5 + label. New Year 2001 (Year of the snake), Hong Kong 2001 Stamp Exhibition (#721).

Australian Federation, Cent. — A181

Pre-federation political cartoons from The Bulletin Magazine: No. 722, 45c, Promises, Promises! No. 723, 45c, The Gout of Federation. No. 724, 45c, The Political Garotters. No. 725, 45c, Tower of Babel. No. 726, 45c, Old Clothes. No. 727, 45c, The Federal Spirit. 75c, Australia Faces the Dawn. $1.05, The Federal Capital Question. $1.20, The Imperial Fowl Yard.

2001, Mar. 12 Litho. *Perf. 14x14¾*

722-730 A181	Set of 9	8.50	8.50

Souvenir Sheet

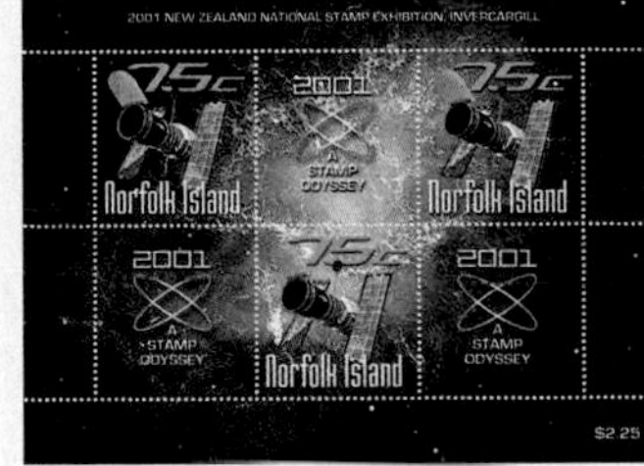

2001 A Stamp Odyssey Stamp Show, Invercargill, New Zealand — A182

Blue portion of background at: a, Right. b, Left. c, Top.

2001, Mar. 16 *Perf. 13*

731 A182	75c Sheet of 3, #a-c, + 3 labels	4.50	4.50

Bounty Day — A183

2001, June 8 *Rouletted 6*

732 A183	5c green & black	.25	.25
a.	Booklet pane of 10	1.50	
	Booklet, 4 #732a	6.00	

Tourism A184

Perfume bottle and: 45c, Jasminium simplicifolium. 75c, Woman's face in perfume bottle. $1.05, Woman with roses. $1.20, Taylors Road. $1.50, Couple shopping for perfume. $3, Woman and Norfolk pine trees.

2001, June 9 *Perf. 13¼*

733 A184	45c multi	1.00	1.00
734 A184	75c multi	2.00	2.00
a.	Booklet pane, #733-734	3.00	—
735 A184	$1.05 multi	2.00	2.00
736 A184	$1.20 multi	2.25	2.25
a.	Booklet pane, #735-736	4.25	—
737 A184	$1.50 multi	3.25	2.75
a.	Booklet pane of 1	3.25	—

Souvenir Sheet

738 A184	$3 multi	6.00	6.00

Booklet Stamp

Size: 154x97mm

Microrouletted at Left

739 A184	$3 Like #738	6.00	6.00
a.	Booklet pane of 1	6.00	—
	Booklet, #734a, 736a, 737a, 739a	16.50	

Nos. 733-739 are impregnated with jasmine perfume. No. 738 contains one 60x72mm stamp.

No. 739 has perfume bottle at LR, country name moved on one line at UL, and is impregnated with jasmine perfume. No. 739a has binding stub at left. Booklet sold for $10 and includes postal card.

For overprint see No. 824.

Boats A185

Designs: 45c, Whaler, vert. No. 741, $1, Rowers in boat. No. 742, $1, Motorboat, vert. $1.50, Men in cutter.

Perf. 14½x14¼, 14¼x14½

2001, Aug. 1 **Litho.**

740-743 A185 Set of 4 6.75 6.75

Coil Stamp

Self-Adhesive

Die Cut Perf. 14¼x14¾

744 A185 45c multi 1.00 1.00

Peace Keepers in Japan — A186

No. 745: a, Australian soldiers playing cards. b, Soldiers with birthday cake.

No. 746: a, Soldiers on Christmas float. b, Soldiers controlling traffic.

2001, Sept. 9 ***Perf. 14½x14¾***

745 Pair with central label 3.00 3.00
a. A186 45c multi .90 .90
b. A186 $1 multi 2.10 2.10

746 Pair with central label 3.00 3.00
a. A186 45c multi .90 .90
b. A186 $1 multi 2.10 2.10

6th South Pacific Mini Games — A187

2001, Oct. 1 ***Rouletted 6***

747 A187 10c green & brown .30 .30
a. Booklet pane of 10 3.00 —
Booklet, 2 #747a 6.00

Two souvenir sheets publicizing the 6th South Pacific Mini-Games, featuring four 45c and four $1 values, respectively, were scheduled for release but were withdrawn from sale upon arrival in Norfolk, when serious design errors were discovered. A small quantity had previously been sold by Crown Agents. Value for pair of sheets, $150.

Christmas A188

Christmas carols and flora: No. 748, 45c, Hark, the Herald Angels Sing, strawberry guava. No. 749, 45c, Deck the Halls, poinsettia. No., 750, $1, The First Noel, hibiscus. No. 751, $1, Joy to the World, Christmas croton. $1.50, We Wish You a Merry Christmas, Indian shot.

2001, Oct. 26 ***Perf. 12½***

748-752 A188 Set of 5 9.00 9.00

Sacred Kingfisher — A189

2002, Jan. 15 **Litho.** ***Rouletted 5¾***

Booklet Stamp

753 A189 10c aqua & dk bl .25 .25
a. Booklet pane of 10 2.50 —
Booklet, 2 #753a 5.00

Cliff Ecology A190

Designs: 45c, Red-tailed tropicbird. No. 755, $1, White oak tree. No. 756, $1, White oak flower. $1.50, Eagle ray.

2002, Jan. 21 **Unwmk.** ***Perf. 13***

754-757 A190 Set of 4 9.00 9.00

Reign Of Queen Elizabeth II, 50th Anniv. Issue

Common Design Type

Designs: Nos. 758, 762a, 45c, Queen Mother with Princesses Elizabeth and Margaret, 1930. Nos. 759, 762b, 75c, Wearing scarf, 1977. Nos. 760, 762c, $1, Wearing crown, 1953. Nos. 761, 762d, $1.50, Wearing yellow hat, 2000. No. 762e, $3, 1955 portrait by Annigoni (38x50mm).

Perf. 14¼x14½, 13¾ (#762e)

2002, Feb. 6 **Litho.** **Wmk. 373**

With Gold Frames

758 CD360 45c multicolored .90 .90
759 CD360 75c multicolored 1.50 1.50
760 CD360 $1 multicolored 2.10 2.10
761 CD360 $1.50 multicolored 3.00 3.00
Nos. 758-761 (4) 7.50 7.50

Souvenir Sheet

Without Gold Frames

762 CD360 Sheet of 5, #a-e 12.00 12.00

The Age of Steam — A191

Perf. 14½x14¾

2002, Mar. 21 **Litho.** **Unwmk.**

763 A191 $4.50 multi 9.00 9.00

South Pacific Mini Games — A192

Designs: 50c, Track and field. $1.50, Tennis.

2002, Mar. 21 ***Perf. 13¾x14¼***

764-765 A192 Set of 2 4.25 4.25

2002 Bounty Bowls Tournament A193

2002, May 6 ***Rouletted 6***

Booklet Stamp

766 A193 10c multi .25 .25
a. Booklet pane of 10 2.00 —
Booklet, 2 #766a 4.00

Phillip Island Flowers — A194

Designs: 10c, Streblorrhiza speciocа. 20c, Plumbago zeylanica. 30c, Canavalia rosea. 40c, Ipomoea pes-caprae. 45c, Hibiscus insularis. 50c, Solanum laciniatum. 95c, Phormium tenax. $1, Lobelia anceps. $1.50, Carpobrotus glaucescens. $2, Abutilon julianae. $3, Wollastonia biflora. $5, Oxalis corniculata.

2002 ***Perf. 14½***

767 A194 10c multi .25 .25
768 A194 20c multi .35 .35
769 A194 30c multi .50 .50
770 A194 40c multi .65 .65
771 A194 45c multi .70 .70
772 A194 50c multi .80 .80
773 A194 95c multi 1.75 1.75
774 A194 $1 multi 2.00 2.00
775 A194 $1.50 multi 2.75 2.75
776 A194 $2 multi 3.75 3.75
777 A194 $3 multi 5.50 5.50
778 A194 $5 multi 9.00 9.00
Nos. 767-778 (12) 28.00 28.00

Issued: 20c, 40c, 45c, 95c, $2, $5, 5/21; others 9/18.

2002 Commonwealth Games, Manchester, England — A195

Designs: 10c, Track and field, vert. 45c, Cycling. $1, Lawn bowling, vert. $1.50, Shooting.

2002, July 25

779-782 A195 Set of 4 7.25 7.25

Operation Cetacean — A196

No. 783: a, Sperm whale and calf. b, Sperm whale and squid.

2002, Sept. 18 ***Perf. 14***

783 A196 Horiz. pair with central label 8.00 8.00
a.-b. $1 Either single 4.00 4.00

See New Caledonia No. 906.

Christmas A197

White tern: No. 784, 45c, Hatchling. No. 785, 45c, Bird on egg in nest. $1, Pair in flight. $1.50, One in flight.

2002, Nov. 12 **Litho.** ***Perf. 14***

784-787 A197 Set of 4 8.00 8.00

Horses on Norfolk Island A198

No. 788: a, Horses with riders near stable. b, Horses grazing. c, Show jumping. d, Horse racing. e, Horses pulling carriage.

2003, Jan. 14

788 Horiz. strip of 5 8.00 8.00
a.-c. A198 45c Any single 1.00 1.00
d.-e. A198 75c Either single 2.25 2.25

Year of the horse (in 2002).

Island Scenes — A199

Photographs by Mary Butterfield: 50c, Buildings. 95c, Boat on beach. $1.10 Cattle grazing. $1.65 Tree near water.

2003, Mar. 18 ***Perf. 14x14¼***

789-792 A199 Set of 4 9.50 9.50

See Nos. 805-808.

Day Lilies — A200

No. 793: a, Southern Prize. b, Becky Stone. c, Cameroons. d, Chinese Autumn. e, Scarlet Orbit. f, Ocean Rain. g, Gingerbread man. h, Pink Corduroy. i, Elizabeth Hinrichsen. j, Simply Pretty.

2003, June 10 **Litho.** ***Perf. 14¼***

793 Block of 10 9.50 9.50
a.-j. A200 50c Any single .95 .95
Complete booklet, #793 9.50

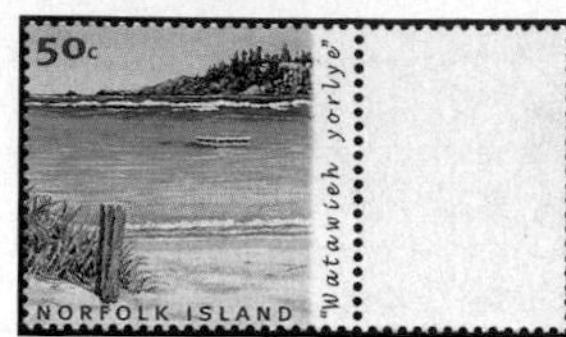

Island Views — A201

No. 794: a, Large trees at left, ocean. b, Beach. c, Rocks at shoreline. d, Cattle grazing.

2003, July 21 ***Perf. 14***

794 Horiz. strip of 4 + 4 labels 7.75 7.75
a.-d. A201 50c Any single + label 1.20 1.20

No. 794 was issued in sheets of five strips that had labels that could be personalized for an additional fee.

First Norfolk Island Writer's Festival — A202

No. 795: a, Maeve and Gil Hitch. b, Alice Buffett. c, Nan Smith. d, Archie Bigg. e, Colleen McCullough. f, Peter Clarke. g, Bob Tofts. h, Merval Hoare.

2003, July 21 ***Perf. 14½***

795 Block of 8 + 2 labels 6.75 6.75
a.-d. A202 10c Any single .30 .30
e.-h. A202 50c Any single .95 .95

Souvenir Sheet

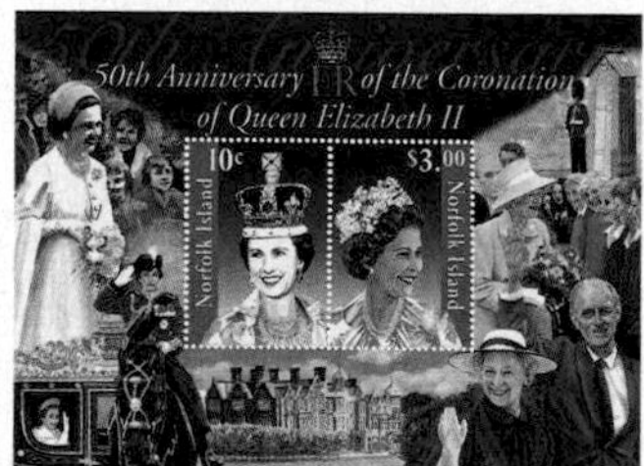

Coronation of Queen Elizabeth II, 50th Anniv. — A203

No. 796: a, 10c, Queen wearing crown. b, $3, Queen wearing hat.

2003, July 29 ***Perf. 14½***

796 A203 Sheet of 2, #a-b 7.00 7.00

Christmas — A204

Designs: No. 797, 50c, Dove, rainbow, "Joy to the World." No. 798, 50c, Earth, "Peace on

Earth." $1.10, Heart, "Give the gift of Love." $1.65, Candle, "Trust in Faith."

2003, Oct. 21 *Perf. 14¼x14*
797-800 A204 Set of 4 9.00 9.00

Powered Flight, Cent. A205

Designs: 50c, Seaplane. $1.10, QANTAS airliner in flight. No. 803, $1.65, QANTAS airliner on ground.
No. 804, $1.65, Wright Flyer.

2003, Dec. 2 *Perf. 14x14¼*
801-803 A205 Set of 3 10.00 10.00

Souvenir Sheet

Perf. 14½x14

804 A205 $1.65 multi 6.50 6.50

No. 804 contains one 48x30mm stamp.
Limited quantities of No. 804 exist with an 85c surcharge and a 2004 Hong Kong Stamp Expo emblem in the margin. These were sold only at the exhibition. Value, mint never hinged or cto, $60.

Island Scenes Type of 2003

Designs: 50c, Houses, boat prow with foliage, vert. 95c, Waterfall, vert. $1.10, Cattle, vert. $1.65, Sea shore, vert.

2004, Feb. 10 Litho. *Perf. 14¼x14*
805-808 A199 Set of 4 10.00 10.00

Sharks — A206

Designs: 10c, Whale shark. 50c, Hammerhead shark. $1.10, Tiger shark. $1.65, Bronze whaler shark.

2004, Apr. 6 *Perf. 14¾*
809-812 A206 Set of 4 11.00 11.00

Spiders A207

Designs: No. 813, 50c, Golden orb spider. No. 814, 50c, Community spider. $1, St. Andrew's cross spider. $1.65, Red-horned spider.
$1.50, Red-horned spider, diff.

2004, June 1 *Perf. 14½*
813-816 A207 Set of 4 8.50 8.50

Souvenir Sheet

Perf. 14½x14

817 A207 $1.50 multi 4.25 4.25

No. 817 contains one 47x40mm stamp.

Unloading of Ship Cargo — A208

Designs: 50c, Men climbing on cargo nets. $1.10, Small boat with men and cargo. No. 820, $1.65, Two small boats.
No. 821, $1.65, Two small boats at dock.

2004, July 13 Litho. *Perf. 14¾*
818-820 A208 Set of 3 7.25 7.25

Souvenir Sheet

821 A208 $1.65 multi 4.25 4.25

Souvenir Sheet

Quota International, 25th Anniv. on Norfolk Island — A209

No. 822: a, 50c, Three children. b, $1.10, "We Care" on feet. c, $1.65, Child drawing "Quota" in sand.

2004, Aug. 16 *Perf. 14¼*
822 A209 Sheet of 3, #a-c 7.25 7.25

Day Lilies A210

No. 823 — Hippeastrum varieties: a, Apple Blossom. b, Carnival. c, Cherry Blossom. d, Lilac Wonder. e, Millenium Star. f, Cocktail. g, Milady. h, Pacific Sunset. i, Geisha Girl. j, Lady Jane.

2004, Aug. 16 *Perf. 14½*
823 Block of 10 12.00 12.00
a.-j. A210 50c Any single 1.20 1.20
Complete booklet, #823 12.50

No. 738 Overprinted in Silver

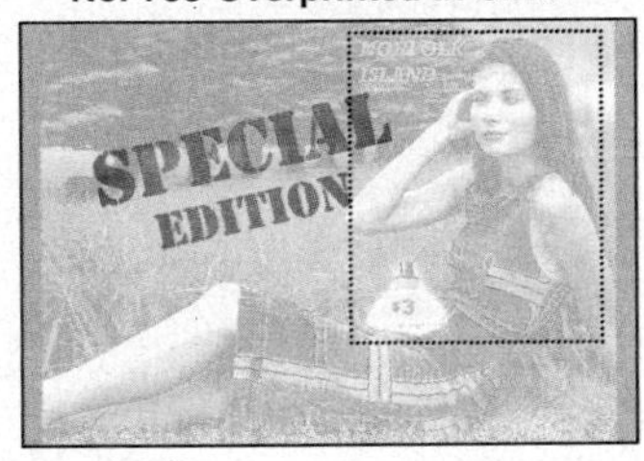

Souvenir Sheet

2004, Aug. Litho. *Perf. 13¼*
824 A184 $3 multi 7.50 7.50

No. 824 is impregnated with jasmine perfume.

Flora — A211

Designs: No. 825, Norfolk Island tree fern. No. 826, Norfolk Island palm.

2004, Sept. 28 *Rouletted 6*

Booklet Stamps

825 A211 10c bl grn & blk .40 .30
a. Booklet pane of 10 4.00 —
826 A211 10c yel & blk .40 .25
a. Booklet pane of 10 4.00 —
Complete booklet, #825a, 826a 8.00

Christmas — A212

Norfolk pine and words from: No. 827, 50c, Silent Night. No. 828, 50c, 'Twas the Night Before Christmas. $1.10, On the First Day of Christmas. $1.65, Oh, Holy Night.

2004, Oct. 26 *Perf. 14¼*
827-830 A212 Set of 4 7.50 7.50

Legislative Assembly, 25th Anniv. — A213

2004, Dec. 14 *Perf. 14*
831 A213 $5 multi 10.50 10.50

Worldwide Fund for Nature (WWF) — A214

Sacred kingfisher: No. 832, 50c, Two birds on tree branch. No. 833, 50c, Bird in flight with insect in beak. $1, Bird on branch. $2, Bird on branch, diff.

2004, Dec. 14
832-835 A214 Set of 4 9.00 9.00
835a Miniature sheet, 2 each #832-835 17.50 17.50

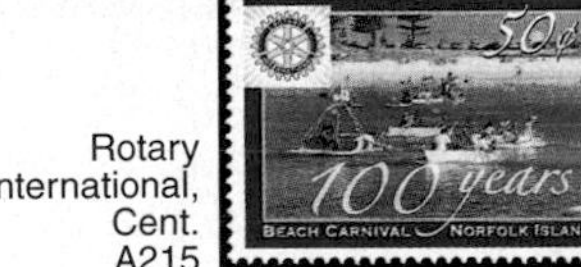

Rotary International, Cent. A215

Emblem and: No. 836, 50c, Beach Carnival. No. 837, 50c, Tree planting, vert. $1.20, Paul Harris. $1.80, Rotary Youth Leadership Awards, vert.
$2, District 9910 ceremony.

2005, Feb. 23 Litho. *Perf. 14½*
836-839 A215 Set of 4 8.00 8.00

Souvenir Sheet

840 A215 $2 multi 5.00 5.00

No. 840 contains one 40x30mm stamp.

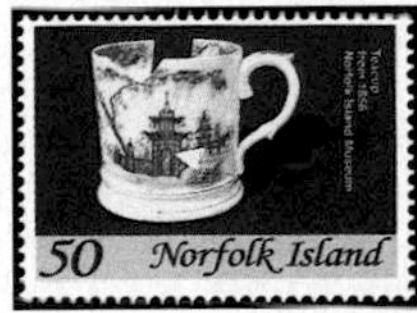

Items From Norfolk Island Museum A216

Designs: No. 841, 50c, Teacup, 1856. No. 842, 50c, Salt cellar from HMAV Bounty, 1856. $1.10, Medicine cups, 1825-55. $1.65, Stoneware jar, 1825-55.

2005, Apr. 5
841-844 A216 Set of 4 9.00 9.00

Pacific Explorers A217

Designs: 50c, Polynesian explorer, boat and fish. $1.20, Magellan's ship and bird. $1.80, Captain James Cook, ship and flower.
$2, Old map of world, horiz.

2005, Apr. 21 *Perf. 14*
845-847 A217 Set of 3 7.50 7.50

Souvenir Sheet

Perf. 14¾

848 A217 $2 multi 5.00 5.00

Pacific Explorer 2005 World Stamp Expo, Sydney. No. 848 contains one 46x32mm stamp.

Old Houses A218

Designs: No. 849, 50c, Greenacres. No. 850, 50c, Branka House. $1.20, Ma Annas. $1.80, Naumai.

2005, June 16 Litho. *Perf. 14½*
849-852 A218 Set of 4 7.75 7.75

Sea Birds — A219

Designs: 10c, Red-tailed tropicbird. 50c, Australasian gannet. $1.50 Gray ternlet. $2, Masked booby. $5, White-necked petrel.
$4, Red-tailed tropicbird, horiz.

2005, Aug. 9
853-857 A219 Set of 5 21.00 21.00

Souvenir Sheet

858 A219 $4 multi 9.00 9.00

See Nos. 883-888. For surcharge, see No. 1044.

Hibiscus Varieties A220

No. 859: a, Marjory Brown. b, Aloha. c, Pulau Tree. d, Ann Miller. e, Surfrider. f, Philip Island. g, Rose of Sharon. h, D. J. O'Brien. i, Elaine's Pride. j, Castle White. k, Skeleton Hibiscus. l, Pink Sunset.

2005, Aug. 30 *Perf. 14¼x14*
859 Block of 12 12.00 12.00
a.-l. A220 50c Any single 1.00 1.00
Complete booklet, #859 12.00

Christmas — A221

Designs: 50c, Anson Bay. $1.20, Cascade Bay. $1.80, Ball Bay.

2005, Oct. 25 Litho. *Perf. 14¼x14*
860-862 A221 Set of 3 6.75 6.75

Jazz Festival — A222

Designs: 50c, Drummer. $1.20, Saxophonist. $1.80, Guitarist.

2005, Dec. 6 ***Perf. 14x14¼***
863-865 A222 Set of 3 7.25 7.25

Queen's Baton Relay for 2006 Commonwealth Games — A223

No. 866: a, 50c, Baton relay runner, boat's prow. b, $1.50, Baton.

2006, Jan. 16 Litho. ***Perf. 14½x14¾***
866 A223 Horiz. pair, #a-b 4.25 4.25

2006 Commonwealth Games, Melbourne — A224

Norfolk Island flag and: 50c, Shooting. $1.50, Lawn bowling. $2, Squash.

2006, Mar. 14 Litho. ***Perf. 14½***
867-869 A224 Set of 3 7.25 7.25

Pitcairn Migration, 150th Anniv. — A225

Pitcairn Island history: No. 870, 50c, The Bounty at Portsmouth. No. 871, 50c, Collecting breadfruit at Tahiti. $1.20, The mutiny. $1.50, Burning of the Bounty at Pitcairn Island. $1.80, Pitcairners arrive at Norfolk Island, 1856.

2006, May 4 ***Perf. 14x14½***
870-874 A225 Set of 5 11.00 11.00

Bounty Anniversary Day — A226

Designs: 10c, Re-enactment procession. 30c, Remembering old soldiers. No. 877, 50c, Honoring ancestors. No. 878, 50c, Community picnic. $4, Bounty Ball.

2006, June 7
875-879 A226 Set of 5 10.50 10.50

See Pitcairn Islands No. 643.

Traditional Hat Making — A227

No. 880, 50c — Purple panel: a, Hat with flowers on brim. b, Hat with no flowers.
No. 881, 50c — Blue green panel: a, Hat with flowers on brim. b, Hat with feather at right.
No. 882, 50c — Green panel: a, Hat with flowers on brim. b, Hat with no flowers.

2006, June 7 ***Perf. 15¼x14¾***
Horiz. Pairs, #a-b
880-882 A227 Set of 3 5.75 5.75

Sea Birds Type of 2005

Designs: 25c, White tern. 40c, Sooty tern. 70c, Black-winged petrel. $1, Black noddy. $3, Wedge-tailed shearwater.
$2.50, Sooty tern, diff.

2006, Aug. 9 ***Perf. 14½***
883-887 A219 Set of 5 10.00 10.00

Souvenir Sheet
888 A219 $2.50 multi 5.50 5.50

Dogs — A228

Dogs named: 10c, Wal. 50c, Axel. $1, Wag. $2.65, Gemma.

2006, Sept. 12 ***Perf. 14½***
889-892 A228 Set of 4 9.00 9.00

Norfolk Island Central School, Middlegate, Cent. — A229

Designs: No. 893, $2, Sepia-toned photograph. No. 894, $2, Color photograph.

2006, Oct. 3
893-894 A229 Set of 2 8.50 8.50

Christmas — A230

Ornaments showing: No. 895, 50c, Birds. No. 896, 50c, House. $1.20, Building. $1.80, Flower.

2006, Nov. 21 **Litho.**
Stamp + Label
895-898 A230 Set of 4 *15.00 15.00*

Weeds A231

Designs: No. 899, 50c, Ageratina riparia. No. 900, 50c, Lantana camara. $1.20, Ipomoea cairica. $1.80, Solanum mauritianum.

2007, Feb. 6 ***Perf. 14¼***
899-902 A231 Set of 4 7.50 7.50

Adventure Sports A232

Designs: No. 903, 50c, Wind surfing. No. 904, 50c, Sea kayaking. $1.20, Mountain biking. $1.80, Surfing.

2007, Apr. 3 Litho. ***Perf. 14½***
903-906 A232 Set of 4 8.00 8.00

Souvenir Sheet

Kentia Palm Seed Harvest — A233

No. 907: a, Ladder and trees, vert. b, Dog and buckets of seeds. c, Man pouring seeds into box. d, Seeds on tree, vert.

Perf. 14 (14½ on Short Side Not Adjacent to Another Stamp)
2007, May 29
907 A233 50c Sheet of 4, #a-d, + central label 5.00 5.00

Ghosts — A234

Designs: 10c, Violinist, musical notes, building. 50c, Graveyard. $1, Female ghost on dock steps. $1.80, Ghosts on building steps.

2007, June 26 ***Perf. 14½***
908-911 A234 Set of 4 7.50 7.50

Queen Victoria — A235

2007, July 31 ***Die Cut***
Self-Adhesive
Booklet Stamp (10c)
912 A235 10c multi .40 .40
a. Booklet pane of 10 4.00

Size: 21x28mm
913 A235 $5 multi 11.00 11.00

Queen Victoria Scholarship, 120th anniv.

13th South Pacific Games, Samoa — A236

Designs: 50c, Squash. $1, Golf. $1.20, Netball. $1.80, Running.
$2, Games emblem.

2007, Aug. 28 ***Perf. 14¼***
914-917 A236 Set of 4 9.00 9.00

Souvenir Sheet
918 A236 $2 multi 4.00 4.00

Closure of First Convict Settlement, Bicent. A237

Designs: 10c, HMS Sirius and Supply off Kingston. 50c, Shipping signal, Kingston. $1.20, First settlement, Kingston. $1.80, Ship Lady Nelson leaving for Tasmania.

2007, Nov. 13
919-922 A237 Set of 4 7.75 7.75

Banyan Park Play Center A238

Children and slogans: 50c, "Friendship." $1, "Community." $1.20, "Play, learn, grow together." $1.80, "Read books."

2007, Nov. 27 Litho. ***Perf. 14x14¼***
923-926 A238 Set of 4 8.75 8.75

Christmas A239

Items with Christmas lights: 50c, Christmas tree. $1.20, Building. $1.80, Rowboat.

2007, Nov. 27
927-929 A239 Set of 3 6.75 6.75

Automobiles A240

Designs: 50c, 1965 Ford Falcon XP. $1, 1952 Chevrolet Styleline. $1.20, 1953 Pontiac Silver Arrow. $1.80, 1971 Rolls Royce Silver Shadow.

2008, Feb. 5
930-933 A240 Set of 4 8.25 8.25

Norfolk Islanders With Pitcairn Islands Heritage — A241

Designs: 50c, Andre Nobbs. $1, Darlene Buffett. $1.20, Colin "Boonie" Lindsay Buffett. $1.80, Tania Grube.

2008, Apr. 4 Litho. ***Perf. 14½***
934-937 A241 Set of 4 8.50 8.50

Jewish Gravestones A242

Gravestone of: 50c, Carl Hans Nathan Strauss. $1.20, Meta Kienhuize. $1.80, Johan Jacobus Kienhuize.
$2, Sally Kadesh.

2008, May 14 ***Perf. 14½***
938-940 A242 Set of 3 6.75 6.75

Souvenir Sheet
Perf. 13½

941 A242 $2 multi 4.00 4.00

2008 World Stamp Championship, Israel (#941). No. 941 contains one 30x40mm stamp.

Calves A243

Designs: 50c, Limousin Cross. $1, Murray Grey. $1.20, Poll Hereford. $1.80, Brahman Cross.

2008, May 30 ***Perf. 14¼***
942-945 A243 Set of 4 8.75 8.75

St. John Ambulance, 25th Anniv. on Norfolk Island — A244

Designs: 30c, Past and present members. 40c, Re-enactment of treatment of accident victim at scene. 95c, Accident victim being placed in ambulance. $4, Accident victim entering hospital.

2008, June 27 ***Perf. 14½***
946-949 A244 Set of 4 11.00 11.00

Ferns — A245

No. 950, 20c: a, Netted brakefern. b, Pteris zahlbruckneriana.
No. 951, 50c: a, Robinsonia. b, Asplenium australasicum.
No. 952, 80c: a, Hanging fork fern. b, Tmesipteris norfolkensis.
No. 953, $2: a, King fern. b, Marattia salicina.

2008, Aug. 1 **Litho.** ***Perf. 14¼***
Horiz. Pairs, #a-b
950-953 A245 Set of 4 13.00 13.00

Ships Built On Norfolk Island — A246

Designs: 50c, Sloop Norfolk, 1798. $1.20, Schooner Resolution, 1925. $1.80, Schooner Endeavour, 1808.

2008, Sept. 2
954-956 A246 Set of 3 5.75 5.75

A247

Designs: 25c, Prison buildings. 55c, Gate and prison buildings. $1.75, Graveyard. $2.50, Building and walls.

2008, Oct. 27 **Litho.** ***Perf. 14½***
957-960 A247 Set of 4 7.00 7.00

Isles of Exile Conference, Norfolk Island.

A248

Christmas: 55c, Adoration of the Shepherds. $1.40, Madonna and Child. $2.05, Adoration of the Magi.

2008, Nov. 7 ***Perf. 14¼***
961-963 A248 Set of 3 5.50 5.50

Mosaics A249

Designs: 5c, Fish. No. 965, 15c, Flower. 55c, Bird. $1.40, Tree.
No. 968, 15c, Turtle. No. 969, 15c, Starfish.

2009, Feb. 16 ***Perf. 14x14¼***
964-967 A249 Set of 4 3.00 3.00

Booklet Stamps
Self-Adhesive
Serpentine Die Cut 9½x10

968-969 A249 Set of 2 .75 .75
969a Booklet pane of 12, 6 each #968-969 4.50 4.50

Cattle Breeds A250

Designs: 15c, Shorthorn. 55c, South Devon. $1.40, Norfolk Blue. $2.05, Lincoln Red.
$5.00, Three calves.

2009, Apr. 24 **Litho.** ***Perf. 14x14¼***
970-973 A250 Set of 4 6.00 6.00

Souvenir Sheet
Perf. 14¼

974 A250 $5 multi 7.25 7.25

Mushrooms — A251

Designs: 15c, Gyrodon sp. 55c, Stereum ostrea. $1.40, Cymatoderma elegans. $2.05, Chlorophyllum molybdites.

2009, May 29 **Litho.** ***Perf. 14½x14***
975-978 A251 Set of 4 6.75 6.75
978a Souvenir sheet, #975-978 6.75 6.75
978b As "a," overprinted with Intl. Stamp & Coin Expo emblem and text in sheet margin in gold 8.25 8.25

Issued: No. 978b, 11/7/10.

Endangered Wildlife — A252

Designs: No. 979, Bridled nailtail wallaby. No. 980, Norfolk Island green parrot. No. 981, Subarctic fur seal. No. 982, Christmas Island blue-tailed skink. No. 983, Green turtle.

2009, Aug. 4 **Litho.** ***Perf. 14¾x14***
"Norfolk Island" Above Denomination

979 A252 55c multi .95 .95
980 A252 55c multi .95 .95
981 A252 55c multi .95 .95
982 A252 55c multi .95 .95
983 A252 55c multi .95 .95
a. Horiz. strip of 5, #979-983 4.75 4.75
Nos. 979-983 (5) 4.75 4.75

Miniature Sheet

984 A252 55c Sheet of 5, #980, Australia #3126, 3128-3130 5.25 5.25

See Australia Nos. 3126-3136. No. 984 is identical to Australia No. 3131. Australia No. 3127 is similar to No. 980, but has "Australia" above denomination.

Birds — A253

Designs: 15c, Gray fantail. 55c, Pacific robin, vert. $1.40, Golden whistler, vert. $2.05, Sacred kingfisher.

2009, Aug. 19 ***Perf. 14½***
985 A253 15c multi .25 .25
986 A253 55c multi .95 .95
Complete booklet, 10 #986 9.50
987 A253 $1.40 multi 2.40 2.40
988 A253 $2.05 multi 3.50 3.50
Nos. 985-988 (4) 7.10 7.10

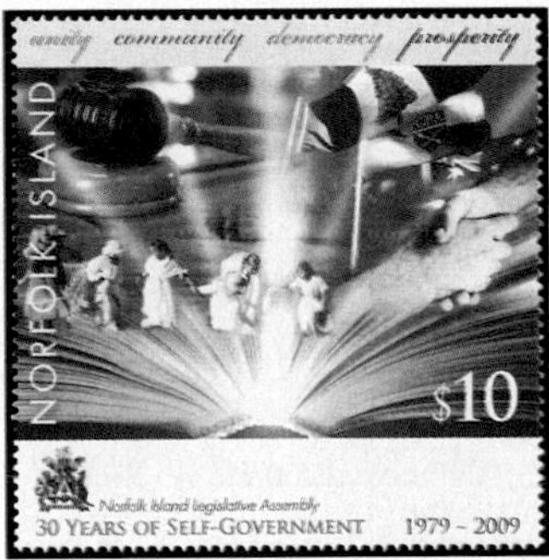
Self-government, 30th Anniv. — A254

2009, Aug. 19 ***Perf. 14***
989 A254 $10 multi 17.00 17.00

Christmas A255

Stained-glass windows depicting: 15c, St. Matthew. 50c, Roses. $1.45, Christ in Glory. $2.10, Saint with Chalice.

2009, Nov. 2 **Litho.** ***Perf. 14¼***
990-993 A255 Set of 4 7.75 7.75

Historical Artifacts A256

Designs: 5c, China from second convict settlement, drawing of man and woman. 55c, Polynesian ivory fish hook, drawing of fishing boat. $1.10, Regimental badge, painting of soldiers. $1.45, Brass wall fitting from HMS Sirius shipwreck, drawing of shipwreck. $1.65, Bottles from convict settlement's Civil Hospital, drawing of treatment of an ill woman. $2.10, Bounty wedding ring, painting of the Bounty.

2010, Feb. 22 **Litho.** ***Perf. 14½***
994 A256 5c multi .25 .25
995 A256 55c multi 1.00 1.00
996 A256 $1.10 multi 1.10 1.10
997 A256 $1.45 multi 2.60 2.60
998 A256 $1.65 multi 3.00 3.00
999 A256 $2.10 multi 3.75 3.75
Nos. 994-999 (6) 11.70 11.70

See Nos. 1021-1026.

Cruise Ships A257

Designs: 55c, Pacific Jewel. $1.45, Pacific Sun. $1.65, Pacific Pearl. $1.75, Pacific Dawn. $2.10, RMS Strathaird.

2010, Mar. 26 **Litho.** ***Perf. 14x14½***
1000-1004 A257 Set of 5 14.00 14.00

1856 Emigration of Pitcairn Islanders to Norfolk Island A258

Ship Morayshire and: 55c, Pitcairn Island girls on Norfolk Island, 1857. $1.10, Passengers aboard ship, 1856. $1.45, Pitcairn Island men on Norfolk Island, 1861. $2.75, Naomi and Jane Nobbs.

2010, June 15 ***Perf. 13½x13¼***
1005-1008 A258 Set of 4 10.00 10.00

History of Whaling A259

Designs: No. 1009, 60c, Blessing of the fleet. No. 1010, 60c, Launching of boats. $1.20, Cliff top navigational fires. $3, Products made from whales.

2010, Aug. 16 **Litho.** ***Perf. 14x14¼***
1009-1012 A259 Set of 4 10.00 10.00

Christmas A260

Parrots and: 15c, Bells. 55c, Conifer sprig. 60c, Gift. $1.30, Christmas ornament.

2010, Oct. 18 **Litho.** ***Perf. 13¼x13½***
1013-1016 A260 Set of 4 5.25 5.25

2010 World Bowls Champion of Champions Lawn Bowling Tournament, Norfolk Island — A261

Designs: 60c, Woman holding trophy. $1.50, Man bowling. $2.20, Bowling balls.

2010, Nov. 23 Litho. *Perf. 14*

1017-1019 A261 Set of 3 8.75 8.75

Souvenir Sheet

St. Barnabas Chapel, 130th Anniv. — A262

No. 1020: a, Chapel under construction. b, Congregation in front of chapel. c, Two men in front of chapel.

2010, Dec. 7 *Perf. 14½x14*

1020 A262 60c Sheet of 3, #a-c 3.75 3.75

Historical Artifacts Type of 2010

Designs: 15c, Women, iron. 60c, Thursday October Christian and his mug. $1.20, Soldiers, bone dominoes. $1.50, Soldier in front of Civil Hospital, clay pipe and ceramic shards. $1.80, Woman and child, doll and doll's head. $3, People at Melanesian Mission, wooden and shell hair items.

2011, Feb. 22 *Perf. 14½*

1021	A256	15c multi	.30	.30
1022	A256	60c multi	1.25	1.25
1023	A256	$1.20 multi	2.50	2.50
1024	A256	$1.50 multi	3.00	3.00
1025	A256	$1.80 multi	3.75	3.75
1026	A256	$3 multi	6.25	6.25
		Nos. 1021-1026 (6)	17.05	17.05

Shells — A263

Designs: 15c, Cirostrema zelebori, Canarium labiatum. 60c, Janthina janthina, Spirula spirula. $1.50, Conus capitaneus, Conus ebraeus. $1.80, Cypraea vitellus, Cypraea caputserpentis. $3, Nerita atramentosa, Neritina turrita.

2011, Apr. 21 Litho. *Perf. 14½*

1027-1031 A263 Set of 5 15.00 15.00

Norfolk Island National Park, 25th Anniv. A264

Park emblem and: 25c, Abutilon julianae. 60c, Hibiscus insularis. $1.55, Myoporum obscurum. $2.25, Meryta latifolia.

2011, June 24 *Perf. 13½x13¼*

1032-1035 A264 Set of 4 10.00 10.00

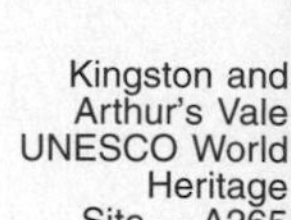

Kingston and Arthur's Vale UNESCO World Heritage Site — A265

No. 1036: a, Guard House, 1796-1826. b, Graveyard, 1790s-1825. c, Government House, 1804-28. d, Pier Store, 1825. e, Crank Mill, 1827. f, Bloody Bridge, 1835. g, Commissariat Store, 1835. h, Kingston Pier, 1839. i, No. 9 Quality Row, 1839. j, Flaghouses, 1840s. k, New Jail, 1847. l, Royal Engineers Office, 1851.

2011, Aug. 1 *Die Cut Perf. 9¾x10*

Self-Adhesive

1036 Booklet pane of 12 15.00

a.-l. A265 60c Any single 1.25 1.25

Norfolk Island Police Force, 80th Anniv. A266

Designs: 60c, Mounted policeman on Bounty Day, c. 1933. $1.55, 1970s police car. $2.25, Policeman observing ship.

2011, Oct. 14 Litho. *Perf. 13x13¼*

1037-1039 A266 Set of 3 9.25 9.25

Christmas A267

Various flowers: 15c, 55c, 60c, $1.35.

2011, Oct. 14 *Perf. 14½*

1040-1043 A267 Set of 4 5.50 5.50

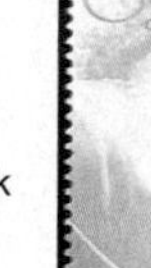

No. 853 Surcharged in Brown and Black

Methods and Perfs As Before

2012, Feb. 13

1044 A219 $4 on 10c #853 8.75 8.75

Iconic Activities A268

Designs: 60c, Collecting hi hi shells. 75c, Collecting whale bird eggs. $1.55, Fishing off the rocks. $2.75, Clifftop barbecue.

2012, Apr. 10 Litho. *Die Cut*

Self-Adhesive

1045-1048 A268 Set of 4 11.50 11.50

Souvenir Sheet

Reign of Queen Elizabeth II, 60th Anniv. — A269

No. 1049: a, Commemorative plaque on Queen Elizabeth Avenue. b, Beacon at Queen Elizabeth Lookout. c, Decorated pine tree at Government House.

Litho. With Foil Application

2012, Aug. 20 *Perf. 14½*

1049 A269 $1.60 Sheet of 3, #a-c 10.00 10.00

Sunshine Club, 51st Anniv. A270

Designs: 60c, Baked goods. $1.60, Basket with bananas, flour and sugar. $1.65, Cook book and pie ingredients. $2.35, Hands.

2012, Oct. 19 Litho. *Perf. 14*

1050-1053 A270 Set of 4 13.00 13.00

Christmas A271

Various pearl inlays from pews in St. Barnabas Chapel and lyrics from Christmas carols: 15c, 55c, $1.55, $2.35.

2012, Nov. 1

1054-1057 A271 Set of 4 9.75 9.75

Airplanes Landing on Norfolk Island, 70th Anniv. — A272

No. 1058: a, Royal New Zealand Air Force Hudson Bomber. b, DC-3. c, Lancastrian. d, DC-4 Skymaster. e, Fokker F27 Friendship. f, Beechcraft Super King Air 200. g, Fokker F28 Fellowship. h, C-130 Hercules. i, BAe 146. j, Boeing 737-300. k, F/A-18 Hornet. l, Airbus A320.

Serpentine Die Cut 9¾x10

2012, Dec. 24

1058 Booklet pane of 12 15.00

a.-l. A272 60c Any single 1.25 1.25

Bell, All Saints Church, Kingston — A273

2013, Apr. 9 *Perf. 14*

1059 A273 $5 multi 10.50 10.50

Norfolk Island Country Music Festival, 20th Anniv. A274

Designs: 15c, Boots, Emily Bay Beach. 60c, Adam Harvey with guitar. $1.60, Guitar. $1.65, Dennis Marsh with guitar. $2.35, Street perfomer with guitar.

2013, May 20

1060-1064 A274 Set of 5 12.00 12.00

Shorelines — A275

Designs: 15c, Ball Bay. 60c, Second Sands. 95c, Anson Bay. $1.20, Slaughter Bay. $1.70, Bumboras. $1.85, Emily Bay.

2013, Sept. 30 Litho. *Perf. 13½*

1065	A275	15c multi	.30	.30
1066	A275	60c multi	1.10	1.10
1067	A275	95c multi	1.90	1.90
1068	A275	$1.20 multi	2.25	2.25
1069	A275	$1.70 multi	3.25	3.25
1070	A275	$1.85 multi	3.50	3.50
		Nos. 1065-1070 (6)	12.30	12.30

See Nos. 1079-1084.

Christmas A276

Locally-made Christmas ornamentation: 15c, Wreath. 55c, Christmas tree made of driftwood. $1.10, Bird made of driftwood. $1.65, Three stars.

2013, Nov. 1 Litho. *Perf. 14½*

1071-1074 A276 Set of 4 6.50 6.50

Trans-Tasman Freestyle Motocross Challenge — A277

Flag of Norfolk Island and New Zealand motorcyclists performing stunts on motorcycle: 50c, Joe McNaughton. $1, McNaughton, diff. $1.50, McNaughton, diff. $1.60, Callum Shaw.

2013, Dec. 18 Litho. *Perf. 13½*

1075-1078 A277 Set of 4 8.25 8.25

Shorelines Type of 2013

Designs: 5c, Cemetery Beach. 10c, Beefsteak. 25c, Crystal Pool. 70c, Cascade Bay. $1.75, Garnet Point. $2.60, Duncombe Bay.

2014, May 7 Litho. *Perf. 13½*

1079	A275	5c multi	.25	.25
1080	A275	10c multi	.25	.25
1081	A275	25c multi	.50	.50
1082	A275	70c multi	1.40	1.40
1083	A275	$1.75 multi	3.25	3.25
1084	A275	$2.60 multi	4.75	4.75
		Nos. 1079-1084 (6)	10.40	10.40

Wearable Art — A278

Designs: 15c, Fishing for the Groom, by Wayne Boniface. 70c, Pasta Bella, by Boniface. $1.40, Flora Abunda Metallica, by Tony Gazzard., $1.50, Romeo and Julieta, by Julie Paris. $3.50, Bamboo Princess Warrior, by Robyn Butterfield.

2014, May 26 Litho. *Perf. 14*
1085-1089 A278 Set of 5 13.50 13.50

Norfolk Island Pine — A279

Norfolk Island Pine and: 20c, Cottesloe Beach, Western Australia. 70c, Old Military Barracks, Kingston, Norfolk Island.

2014, July 22 Litho. *Perf. 14x14¾*
1090-1091 A279 Set of 2 1.75 1.75

See Australia Nos. 4145-4146.

Norfolk Island Quota International Club, 35th Anniv. — A280

Designs: 15c, Picnic table near Emily Bay. 70c, Telescope on Queen Elizabeth Lookout. $3.20, Family on bench overlooking ocean.

2014, Aug. 15 Litho. *Perf. 14*
1092-1094 A280 Set of 3 7.50 7.50

Souvenir Sheet

Red Cross on Norfolk Island, Cent. — A281

2014, Sept. 29 Litho. *Perf. 14*
1095 A281 $3.50 multi 6.25 6.25

Tip of Norfolk Island Pine — A282

Developing Norfolk Island Pine Cone — A283

Norfolk Island Pine Seedling A284

Norfolk Island Pine Forest A285

Norfolk Island Pine Seeds A286

Norfolk Island Pine Branches A287

Shed Norfolk Island Pine Needles — A288

Hollowed-out Norfolk Island Pine — A289

Norfolk Island Pines — A290

Norfolk Island Pine — A291

Serpentine Die Cut 10¾x10

2014, Sept. 29 Litho.

Self-Adhesive

1096	Booklet pane of 10	12.50	
a.	A282 70c multi	1.25	1.25
b.	A283 70c multi	1.25	1.25
c.	A284 70c multi	1.25	1.25
d.	A285 70c multi	1.25	1.25
e.	A286 70c multi	1.25	1.25
f.	A287 70c multi	1.25	1.25
g.	A288 70c multi	1.25	1.25
h.	A289 70c multi	1.25	1.25
i.	A290 70c multi	1.25	1.25
j.	A291 70c multi	1.25	1.25

See No. 1109.

Quilts — A292

Designs: 15c, Memory Quilt, by Julie South. 70c, Sampler Quilt, by Kay Greenbury, Raewyn Maxwell, Rowena Massicks and Barbara Solomon. $1.40, Sunset at Puppy's Point, by Greenbury. $1.50, Southern Cross Shared, by Greenbury. $3.50, Storm at Sea, by Massicks.

2014, Oct. 17 Litho. *Perf. 14½*
1097-1101 A292 Set of 5 12.50 12.50

Christmas — A293

Fabric designs by Sue Pearson depicting: 15c, Breadfruit leaves. 65c, Passion fruit flowers. $1.70, Turtles. $1.80, Taro leaves. $2.55, Hibiscus flowers.

2014, Nov. 3 Litho. *Perf. 14¼x14*
1102-1106 A293 Set of 5 12.00 12.00

Sinking of HMS Sirius, 225th Anniv. A294

No. 1107: a, Diver at underwater memorial. b, HMS Sirius, painting by John Allcott. c, The Melancholy Loss of HMS Sirius, painting by George Rapet. d, Cross belt plate from HMS Sirius. e, Capt. John Hunter of the HMS Sirius. f, Anchor of HMS Sirius. g, HMS Sirius, painting by Francis J. Bayldon. h, Carronades of HMS Sirius. i, Bronze shackle from HMS Sirius. j, Pantograph from HMS Sirius.

Serpentine Die Cut 10x10¾

2015, Mar. 19 Litho.

Self-Adhesive

1107	Booklet pane of 10	11.00	
a.-j.	A294 70c Any single	1.10	1.10

Souvenir Sheet

Battle of Gallipoli, Cent. — A295

Litho. With Foil Application

2015, Apr. 24 *Perf. 13½*
1108 A295 $5 multi 8.00 8.00

Norfolk Island Pine Types of 2014

Designs as before.

Serpentine Die Cut 10¾x10

2015, June 1 Litho.

Self-Adhesive

1109	Booklet pane of 10	2.50	
a.	A282 15c multi	.25	.25
b.	A283 15c multi	.25	.25
c.	A284 15c multi	.25	.25
d.	A285 15c multi	.25	.25
e.	A286 15c multi	.25	.25
f.	A287 15c multi	.25	.25
g.	A288 15c multi	.25	.25
h.	A289 15c multi	.25	.25
i.	A290 15c multi	.25	.25
j.	A291 15c multi	.25	.25

Celebrities at Christmas in July Festival A296

Designs: 25c, John Rowles, singer. 35c, Suzanne Prentice, singer. 45c, Normie Rowe, singer. $1.40, Glenn A. Baker, journalist and 2015 festival master of ceremonies. $1.95, Colleen McCullough (1937-2015), writer.

2015, July 13 Litho. *Perf. 14¼x14*
1110-1114 A296 Set of 5 6.50 6.50

Christmas A297

Ornaments made from plant fibers: 15c, Bird. 65c, Star. $1.30, Fish. $1.70, Rings around glass balls, candle. $2.55, Netting around glass ball.

2015, Oct. 1 Litho. *Perf. 14½x14¾*
1115-1119 A297 Set of 5 9.00 9.00

Norfolk's Ocean Challenge Canoe Races — A298

Various participants with panel color of: No. 1120, $1, Cerise. No. 1121, $1, Cobalt. $1.85, Green. $2.75, Gray blue.

2016, Jan. 14 Litho. *Perf. 14x14½*
1120-1123 A298 Set of 4 9.50 9.50

NORTH BORNEO

'north 'bor-nē-ˌō

LOCATION — Northeast part of island of Borneo, Malay archipelago
GOVT. — British colony
AREA — 29,388 sq. mi.
POP. — 470,000 (est. 1962)
CAPITAL — Jesselton

The British North Borneo Company administered North Borneo, under a royal charter granted in 1881, until 1946 when it became a British colony. Labuan (q.v.) became part of the new colony. As "Sabah," North Borneo joined with Singapore, Sarawak and Malaya to form the Federation of Malaysia on Sept. 16, 1963.

100 Cents = 1 Dollar

Quantities of most North Borneo stamps through 1912 have been canceled to order with an oval of bars. Values given for used stamps beginning with No. 6 are for those with this form of cancellation. Stamps from No. 6 through Nos. 159 and J31 that do not exist CTO have used values in italics. Stamps with dated town cancellations sell for much higher prices.

Catalogue values for unused stamps in this country are for Never Hinged items, beginning with Scott 238.

North Borneo

Coat of Arms — A1

1883-84 Unwmk. Litho. *Perf. 12*

No.			Unused	Used
1	A1	2c brown	47.50	*75.00*
a.		Horiz. pair, imperf. btwn.	20,000.	
2	A1	4c rose ('84)	65.00	*70.00*
3	A1	8c green ('84)	90.00	*60.00*
		Nos. 1-3 (3)	202.50	*205.00*

For surcharges see Nos. 4, 19-21.

No. 1 Surcharged in Black

No.			Unused	Used
4	A1	8c on 2c brown	500.00	*210.00*
a.		Double surcharge		*6,000.*

Coat of Arms with Supporters
A4 A5

Perf. 14

No.			Unused	Used
6	A4	50c violet	225.00	40.00
7	A5	$1 red	160.00	17.50

1886 *Perf. 14*

No.			Unused	Used
8	A1	½c magenta	120.00	*200.00*
9	A1	1c orange	*210.00*	*350.00*
a.		Imperf., pair	300.00	
b.		Vert. pair, imperf horiz.	1,500.	
10	A1	2c brown	47.50	42.50
a.		Horiz. pair, imperf. between	700.00	
11	A1	4c rose	20.00	*55.00*
a.		Horiz. pair, imperf. between	—	1,700.
12	A1	8c green	22.50	*50.00*
a.		Horiz. pair, imperf. between	*900.00*	
13	A1	10c blue	55.00	*65.00*
a.		Imperf., pair	375.00	
		Nos. 8-13 (6)	475.00	*762.50*

Nos. 8, 11, 12 and 13 Surcharged or Overprinted in Black

b

c

d

1886

No.			Unused	Used
14	A1 (b)	½c magenta	225.00	*325.00*
15	A1 (c)	3c on 4c rose	130.00	*150.00*
16	A1 (d)	3c on 4c rose	1,800.	
17	A1 (c)	5c on 8c green	140.00	*150.00*
a.		Inverted surcharge	2,750.	
18	A1 (b)	10c blue	300.00	*375.00*

On Nos. 2 and 3

Perf. 12

No.			Unused	Used
19	A1 (c)	3c on 4c rose	325.00	*375.00*
20	A1 (d)	3c on 4c rose	—	*16,000.*
a.		Double surcharge, both types of "3"		—
21	A1 (c)	5c on 8c green	325.00	*375.00*

British North Borneo

A9

1886 Unwmk. Litho. *Perf. 12*

No.			Unused	Used
22	A9	½c lilac rose	400.00	*700.00*
23	A9	1c orange	250.00	*400.00*

Perf. 14

No.			Unused	Used
25	A9	½c rose	4.25	*19.00*
a.		½c lilac rose	*21.00*	50.00
b.		Imperf., pair	70.00	
26	A9	1c orange	2.25	*16.00*
a.		Imperf., pair	80.00	
b.		Vert. pair, imperf. btwn.	425.00	
27	A9	2c brown	2.25	*16.00*
a.		Imperf., pair	50.00	
28	A9	4c rose	5.50	*19.00*
a.		Cliché of 1c in plate of 4c	350.00	*1,300.*
b.		Imperf., pair	50.00	
c.		As "a," imperf. in pair with #28	7,500.	
d.		Horiz. pair, imperf vert.	425.00	
29	A9	8c green	30.00	*28.00*
a.		Imperf., pair	55.00	*55.00*
30	A9	10c blue	15.00	*45.00*
a.		Imperf., pair	55.00	
b.		Vert. pair, imperf btwn.	425.00	
		Nos. 25-30 (6)	59.25	*143.00*

For surcharges see Nos. 54-55.

A10

A11

A12

A13

No.			Unused	Used
31	A10	25c slate blue	475.00	25.00
a.		Imperf., pair	475.00	50.00
32	A11	50c violet	475.00	25.00
a.		Imperf., pair	550.00	50.00
33	A12	$1 red	400.00	24.00
a.		Imperf., pair	600.00	50.00
34	A13	$2 sage green	700.00	30.00
a.		Imperf., pair	600.00	55.00
		Nos. 31-34 (4)	2,050.	104.00
		Nos. 22-34 (12)	2,759.	*1,347.*

See Nos. 44-47.

A14

1887-92 *Perf. 14*

No.			Unused	Used
35	A14	½c rose	1.50	.60
a.		½c magenta	4.00	*3.00*
36	A14	1c orange	6.50	.50
37	A14	2c red brown	7.50	.50
b.		As "a," horiz. pair imperf. between		*425.00*
38	A14	3c violet	2.75	.50
39	A14	4c rose	13.00	.50
a.		Horiz. pair, imperf. vert.		*250.00*
40	A14	5c slate	3.00	.50
41	A14	6c lake ('92)	18.00	.50
42	A14	8c green	29.00	1.00
a.		Horiz. pair, imperf. between		
43	A14	10c blue	7.25	.50
		Nos. 35-43 (9)	88.50	5.10

Exist imperf. Value $20 each, unused, $4.50 used. Forgeries exist, perf. 11½.
For surcharges see Nos. 52-53, 56-57.

Redrawn

25c. The letters of "BRITISH NORTH BORNEO" are 2mm high instead of 1½mm.

50c. The club of the native at left does not touch the frame. The 0's of "50" are flat at top and bottom instead of being oval.

$1.00. The spear of the native at right does not touch the frame. There are 14 pearls at each side of the frame instead of 13.

$2.00. "BRITISH" is 11mm long instead of 12mm. There are only six oars at the side of the dhow.

1888

No.			Unused	Used
44	A10	25c slate blue	100.00	.75
b.		Horiz. pair, imperf. between		*300.00*
c.		Imperf., pair	500.00	22.50
45	A11	50c violet	120.00	.75
a.		Imperf., pair	600.00	21.00
46	A12	$1 red	60.00	.75
a.		Imperf., pair	450.00	22.50
47	A13	$2 sage green	225.00	1.50
a.		Imperf., pair	750.00	25.00
		Nos. 44-47 (4)	505.00	3.75

For surcharges see Nos. 50-51, 58.

A15

A16

1889

No.			Unused	Used
48	A15	$5 red violet	350.00	9.00
a.		Imperf., pair	750.00	55.00
49	A16	$10 brown	350.00	12.50
b.		Imperf., pair	950.00	65.00

No. 44 Surcharged in Red — e

1890

No.			Unused	Used
50	A10	2c on 25c slate blue	75.00	*100.00*
a.		Inverted surcharge	450.00	*450.00*
b.		With additional surcharge "2 cents" in black		
51	A10	8c on 25c slate blue	105.00	*125.00*

Surcharged in Black On #42-43 — f

1891-92

No.			Unused	Used
52	A14	6c on 8c green	25.00	*11.00*
a.		"c" of "cents" inverted	550.00	*650.00*
b.		"cetns"	550.00	*650.00*
c.		Inverted surcharge	450.00	*500.00*
53	A14	6c on 10c blue	160.00	*27.50*

On Nos. 29 and 30

No.			Unused	Used
54	A9	6c on 8c green	9,000.	*4,750.*
55	A9	6c on 10c blue	67.50	*22.50*
a.		Inverted surcharge	300.00	*300.00*
b.		Double surcharge	1,000.	
c.		Triple surcharge	550.00	

BUYING, SELLING, EXPERTIZATIONS, NORTH BORNEO & LABUAN

HELPING COLLECTORS AVOID THE MINEFIELDS! Send Your Stamps & Covers with Confidence.

PHOTOGRAPHIC CERTIFICATES OF AUTHENTICITY

Reliable and Fast • Recognized • Competitively Priced • Contact Us for Terms and Prices

LIANE & SERGIO SISMONDO • PO Box 10035 • Syracuse, NY 13290-3301

T. 315-422-2331 • F. 315-422-2956 • EMAIL: sismondo@dreamscape.com

VISIT US ONLINE AT WWW.SISMONDOSTAMPS.COM

ASDA • PTS • CNEP • CSDA • FCFI

Nos. 39, 40 and 44 Surcharged in Red

1892

No.	Type	Description	Unused	Used
56	A14	1c on 4c rose	25.00	15.00
a.		Double surcharge	1,500.	
b.		Surcharged on face & back		*675.00*
57	A14	1c on 5c slate	8.00	6.50
58	A10	8c on 25c blue	150.00	*175.00*
		Nos. 56-58 (3)	183.00	*196.50*

North Borneo

Dyak Chief — A21

Malayan Sambar — A22

Malay Dhow — A26

Sago Palm — A23

Saltwater Crocodile — A27

Argus Pheasant A24

Mt. Kinabalu A28

Coat of Arms — A25

Coat of Arms with Supporters — A29

A30

A31

A32

A33

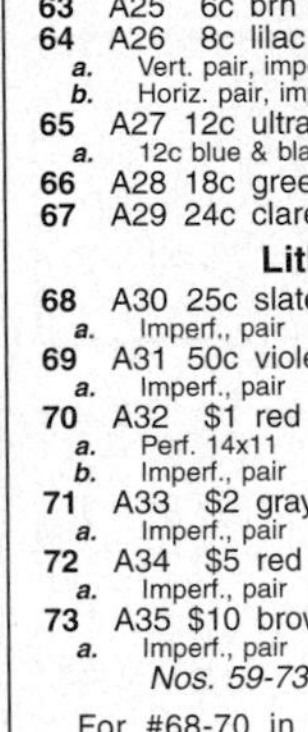

A34

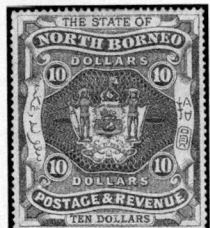

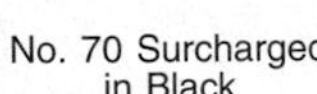

A35

Perf. 12 to 15 and Compound

1894 Engr. Unwmk.

No.	Type	Description	Unused	Used
59	A21	1c bis brn & blk	1.40	.50
a.		Vert. pair, imperf. btwn.	*950.00*	
60	A22	2c rose & black	5.50	.75
a.		Horiz. pair, imperf. btwn.	*950.00*	*950.00*
b.		Vert. pair, imperf. btwn.	*950.00*	*950.00*
61	A23	3c vio & ol green	4.00	.55
a.		Horiz. pair, imperf. btwn.	—	*850.00*
b.		Vert. pair, imperf. btwn.	1,350.	
62	A24	5c org red & blk	14.00	.75
a.		Horiz. pair, imperf. btwn.	850.00	
63	A25	6c brn ol & blk	4.50	.60
64	A26	8c lilac & black	6.50	.75
a.		Vert. pair, imperf. btwn.	550.00	*350.00*
b.		Horiz. pair, imperf. btwn.	*750.00*	
65	A27	12c ultra & black	47.50	3.00
a.		12c blue & black	30.00	2.75
66	A28	18c green & black	30.00	2.00
67	A29	24c claret & blue	25.00	2.00

Litho. ***Perf. 14***

No.	Type	Description	Unused	Used
68	A30	25c slate blue	10.00	1.00
a.		Imperf., pair	60.00	12.00
69	A31	50c violet	42.50	2.00
a.		Imperf., pair		12.00
70	A32	$1 red	12.50	1.25
a.		Perf. 14x11	300.00	
b.		Imperf., pair	47.50	12.00
71	A33	$2 gray green	22.50	2.75
a.		Imperf., pair		18.00
72	A34	$5 red violet	275.00	16.00
a.		Imperf., pair	650.00	60.00
73	A35	$10 brown	300.00	16.00
a.		Imperf., pair	650.00	60.00
		Nos. 59-73 (15)	800.90	49.90

For #68-70 in other colors see Labuan #63a-65a.

For surcharges & overprints see #74-78, 91-94, 97-102, 115-119, 130-135, 115-119, 150-151, 158-159, J1-J8.

No. 70 Surcharged in Black

1895, June

No.	Type	Description	Unused	Used
74	A32	4c on $1 red	7.00	1.25
a.		Double surcharge	1,000.	
75	A32	10c on $1 red	26.00	.60
76	A32	20c on $1 red	47.50	.60
77	A32	30c on $1 red	40.00	1.25
78	A32	40c on $1 red	47.50	1.25
		Nos. 74-78 (5)	168.00	4.95

See No. 99.

A37

A38

A39

A40

A41

A42

A43

"Postal Revenue" — A44

No "Postal Revenue" — A45

Perf. 13 to 16 and Compound

1897-1900 Engr.

No.	Type	Description	Unused	Used
79	A37	1c bis brn & blk	12.00	.55
a.		Horiz. pair, imperf. btwn.		600.00
80	A38	2c dp rose & blk	25.00	.55
81	A38	2c grn & blk ('00)	60.00	.60
82	A39	3c lilac & ol green	24.00	.55
83	A40	5c orange & black	110.00	.75
84	A41	6c ol brown & blk	45.00	.50
85	A42	8c brn lilac & blk	13.00	.75
86	A43	12c blue & black	140.00	1.50
87	A44	18c green & black	27.50	3.00
a.		Vert. pair, imperf. btwn.		*350.00*
b.		Horiz. pair, imperf. vert.		*95.00*
c.		Imperf, pair		*200.00*
88	A45	24c claret & blue	26.00	3.00
		Nos. 79-88 (10)	482.50	11.75

For overprints and surcharges see Nos. 105-107, 109-112, 124-127, J9-J17, J20-J22, J24-J26, J28.

"Postage & Revenue"
A46 A47

1897

No.	Type	Description	Unused	Used
89	A46	18c green & black	100.00	1.75
90	A47	24c claret & blue	50.00	2.10

For surcharges & overprints see #95-96, 128-129, 113-114, J18-J19, J30-J31.

Stamps of 1894-97 Surcharged in Black

1899

No.	Type	Description	Unused	Used
91	A40	4c on 5c org & blk	40.00	*12.50*
92	A41	4c on 6c ol brn & blk	20.00	*25.00*
93	A42	4c on 8c brn lil & blk	16.00	*13.00*
94	A43	4c on 12c bl & blk	29.00	*15.00*
a.		Horiz. pair, imperf. btwn.	850.00	
b.		Vert. pair, imperf. btwn.		950.00
95	A46	4c on 18c grn & blk	16.00	*18.00*
96	A47	4c on 24c cl & blue	25.00	*20.00*
a.		Perf. 16	55.00	*55.00*
97	A30	4c on 25c sl blue	6.00	*10.00*
98	A31	4c on 50c violet	18.00	*18.00*
99	A32	4c on $1 red	6.25	*14.00*
100	A33	4c on $2 gray grn	6.25	*19.00*

"CENTS" 8½mm below "4"

No.	Type	Description	Unused	Used
101	A34	4c on $5 red vio	7.25	*18.00*
a.		Normal spacing	170.00	*250.00*
102	A35	4c on $10 brown	7.25	*18.00*
a.		Normal spacing	130.00	*250.00*
		Nos. 91-102 (12)	197.00	*200.50*

No. 99 differs from No. 74 in the distance between "4" and "cents" which is 4¾mm on No. 99 and 3¾mm on No. 74.

Orangutan — A48

1899-1900 Engr.

No.	Type	Description	Unused	Used
103	A48	4c green & black	10.00	1.75
104	A48	4c dp rose & blk ('00)	40.00	.75

For overprints see Nos. 108, J13, J23.

Stamps of 1894-1900 Overprinted in Red, Black, Green or Blue — m

1901-05

No.	Type	Description	Unused	Used
105	A37	1c bis brn & blk (R)	4.00	.35
106	A38	2c grn & blk (R)	3.50	.35
107	A39	3c lil & ol grn (Bk)	2.00	.35
108	A48	4c dp rose & blk (G)	10.00	.35
109	A40	5c org & blk (G)	16.00	.35
110	A41	6c ol brn & blk (R)	4.50	.75
111	A42	8c brn & blk (Bl)	4.25	.55
a.		Vert. pair, imperf. btwn.		425.00
112	A43	12c blue & blk (R)	60.00	1.50
113	A46	18c grn & blk (R)	15.00	1.40
114	A47	24c red & blue (Bk)	18.00	1.75
115	A30	25c slate blue (R)	3.00	.60
a.		Inverted overprint	700.00	
116	A31	50c violet (R)	3.00	.70
117	A32	$1 red (R)	20.00	3.75
118	A32	$1 red (Bk)	10.00	2.75
a.		Double overprint		425.00
119	A33	$2 gray grn (R)	37.50	4.00
a.		Double overprint	1,600.	
		Nos. 105-119 (15)	210.75	19.50

Nos. 110, 111 and 122 are known without period after "PROTECTORATE."

See Nos. 122-123, 150-151.

Bruang (Sun Bear) — A49

Railroad Train — A50

1902 Engr.

No.	Type	Description	Unused	Used
120	A49	10c slate & dk brn	130.00	3.25
a.		Vertical pair, imperf. between		575.00
121	A50	16c yel brn & grn	150.00	3.75

Overprinted type "m" in Red or Black

No.	Type	Description	Unused	Used
122	A49	10c sl & dk brn (R)	75.00	1.10
a.		Double overprint	900.00	350.00
123	A50	16c yel brn & grn (Bk)	150.00	2.50
		Nos. 120-123 (4)	505.00	10.60

For overprints see Nos. J27, J29.

Stamps of 1894-97 Surcharged in Black

1904

No.	Type	Description	Unused	Used
124	A40	4c on 5c org & blk	50.00	14.00
125	A41	4c on 6c ol brn & blk	8.00	14.00
a.		Inverted surcharge	350.00	
126	A42	4c on 8c brn lil & blk	15.00	14.00
a.		Inverted surcharge	350.00	
127	A43	4c on 12c blue & blk	40.00	14.00
128	A46	4c on 18c grn & blk	16.00	14.00
129	A47	4c on 24c cl & bl	20.00	14.00
130	A30	4c on 25c sl blue	5.00	14.00
131	A31	4c on 50c violet	5.50	14.00
132	A32	4c on $1 red	7.00	14.00
133	A33	4c on $2 gray grn	10.50	14.00
134	A34	4c on $5 red vio	14.00	14.00
135	A35	4c on $10 brown	14.00	14.00
a.		Inverted surcharge	2,750.	
		Nos. 124-135 (12)	205.00	168.00

Malayan Tapir — A51

Traveler's Palm — A52

Railroad Station — A53

Meeting of the Assembly — A54

Elephant and Mahout A55

Sumatran Rhinoceros A56

Natives Plowing — A57

Wild Boar — A58

Palm Cockatoo A59

Rhinoceros Hornbill A60

Banteng (Wild Ox) A61 A62

Cassowary A63

1909-22 Unwmk. Engr. *Perf. 14*

Center in Black

No.	Type	Description	Unused	Used
136	A51	1c chocolate	7.00	.30
b.		Perf. 13½		
c.		Perf. 15	47.50	.40
137	A52	2c green	1.00	.30
b.		Perf. 15	3.25	.30
138	A53	3c deep rose	3.25	.30
b.		Perf. 15	42.50	.55
139	A53	3c green ('22)	42.50	*.40*
140	A54	4c dull red	2.75	.30
b.		Perf. 13½	*11.00*	*10.50*
c.		Perf. 15	21.00	.40
141	A55	5c yellow brn	16.00	.40
b.		Perf. 15		
142	A56	6c olive green	13.00	.30
b.		Perf. 15	80.00	1.00
143	A57	8c rose	4.00	.60
b.		Perf 15		*12.00*
144	A58	10c blue	45.00	2.00
b.		Perf. 13½		—
c.		Perf. 15	70.00	*6.50*
145	A59	12c deep blue	42.50	1.00
c.		Perf. 15		*12.00*
146	A60	16c red brown	26.00	1.25
b.		Perf. 13½	30.00	6.50
147	A61	18c blue green	120.00	1.25
148	A62	20c on 18c bl grn (R)	7.00	.55
b.		Perf. 15	250.00	*75.00*
149	A63	24c violet	28.00	1.75
		Nos. 136-149 (14)	358.00	10.70

Issued: #139, 1922; others, July 1, 1909.

See #167-178. #136a-149a follow #162.

For surcharges and overprints see #160-162, 166, B1-B12, B14-B24, B31-B41, J32-J49.

Nos. 72-73 Overprinted type "m" in Red

1910

No.	Type	Description	Unused	Used
150	A34	$5 red violet	325.00	9.00
151	A35	$10 brown	550.00	11.00
a.		Double overprint		
b.		Inverted overprint	2,700.	450.00

A64 A65

1911 Engr. *Perf. 14*

Center in Black

No.	Type	Description	Unused	Used
152	A64	25c yellow green	18.00	2.00
a.		Perf. 15	19.00	
b.		Imperf., pair	55.00	
153	A64	50c slate blue	18.00	2.25
a.		Perf. 15	24.00	*22.50*
b.		Imperf., pair	90.00	
154	A64	$1 brown	18.00	4.00
a.		Perf. 15	60.00	*8.00*
c.		Imperf., pair	180.00	
155	A64	$2 dk violet	75.00	5.00
156	A65	$5 claret	150.00	32.50
a.		Perf. 13½	*150.00*	
b.		Imperf., pair	200.00	
157	A65	$10 vermilion	500.00	90.00
a.		Imperf., pair	475.00	
		Nos. 152-157 (6)	779.00	*135.75*

See #179-184. #152c-153c follow #162.

For overprint and surcharges see Nos. B13, B25-B30, B42-B47.

Nos. 72-73 Overprinted in Red

1912

No.	Type	Description	Unused	Used
158	A34	$5 red violet	1,500.	9.25
159	A35	$10 brown	1,800.	9.25

Nos. 158 and 159 were prepared for use but not regularly issued.

Nos. 138, 142 and 145 Surcharged in Black or Red

1916 Center in Black *Perf. 14*

No.	Type	Description	Unused	Used
160	A53	2c on 3c dp rose	30.00	15.00
a.		Inverted "S"	110.00	95.00
161	A56	4c on 6c ol grn (R)	30.00	20.00
a.		Inverted "S"	110.00	100.00
162	A59	10c on 12c bl (R)	60.00	*70.00*
a.		Inverted "S"	180.00	*190.00*
		Nos. 160-162 (3)	120.00	105.00

Stamps and Types of 1909-11 Overprinted in Red or Blue

1922 Center in Black

No.	Type	Description	Unused	Used
136a	A51	1c brown	20.00	*70.00*
137a	A52	2c green	2.50	*25.00*
138a	A53	3c deep rose (B)	16.00	*65.00*
140a	A54	4c dull red (B)	3.75	*45.00*
141a	A55	5c yel brown (B)	9.50	*65.00*
142a	A56	6c olive green	9.50	*70.00*
143a	A57	8c rose (B)	8.50	*42.50*
144a	A58	10c gray blue	20.00	*65.00*
145a	A59	12c deep blue	12.00	*45.00*
146a	A60	16c red brown (B)	26.00	*75.00*
148a	A62	20c on 18c bl grn	27.50	*90.00*
149a	A63	24c violet	50.00	*75.00*
152c	A64	25c yel green	12.00	*65.00*
153c	A64	50c slate blue	17.50	*70.00*
		Nos. 136a-153c (14)	234.75	*867.50*

Industrial fair, Singapore, 3/31-4/15/22.

No. 140 Surcharged in Black

1923

No.	Type	Description	Unused	Used
166	A54	3c on 4c dull red & blk	2.75	*6.00*
a.		Double surcharge	*1,300.*	

Types of 1909-22 Issues

1926-28 Engr. *Perf. 12½*

Center in Black

No.	Type	Description	Unused	Used
167	A51	1c chocolate	1.00	.70
168	A52	2c lake	.85	.60
169	A53	3c green	3.00	.75
170	A54	4c dull red	.50	.25
171	A55	5c yellow brown	6.00	3.50
172	A56	6c yellow green	10.00	.90
173	A57	8c rose	4.75	.50
174	A58	10c bright blue	4.25	.90
175	A59	12c deep blue	24.00	.80
176	A60	16c orange brn	37.50	*225.00*
177	A62	20c on 18c bl grn (R)	16.00	4.00
178	A63	24c dull violet	60.00	*170.00*
179	A64	25c yellow grn	16.00	5.50
180	A64	50c slate blue	25.00	*14.00*
181	A64	$1 brown	25.00	*500.00*
182	A64	$2 dark violet	85.00	*650.00*
183	A65	$5 deep rose	200.00	*1,300.*
184	A65	$10 dull vermilion	550.00	*1,500.*
		Nos. 167-184 (18)	1,068.	*4,377.*

Murut — A66

Orangutan — A67

Dyak — A68

Mt. Kinabalu A69

Clouded Leopard A70

Coat of Arms — A71

Arms with Supporters and Motto A72

Arms with Supporters — A73

1931, Jan. 1 Engr. *Perf. 12½*

Center in Black

No.	Type	Description	Unused	Used
185	A66	3c blue green	1.50	*1.50*
186	A67	6c orange red	17.50	4.75
187	A68	10c carmine	4.50	*13.00*
188	A69	12c ultra	4.75	*8.00*
189	A70	25c deep violet	40.00	35.00
190	A71	$1 yellow green	27.50	*110.00*
191	A72	$2 red brown	47.50	*110.00*
192	A73	$5 red violet	160.00	*500.00*
		Nos. 185-192 (8)	303.25	*782.25*

50th anniv. of the North Borneo Co.

Buffalo Transport A74

Palm Cockatoo — A75

Murut — A76

Proboscis Monkey — A77

Bajaus — A78

Map of North Borneo and Surrounding Lands — A79

Orangutan — A80

Murut with Blowgun — A81

Dyak — A82

River Scene — A83

Proa — A84

Mt. Kinabalu — A85

Coat of Arms — A86

Arms with Supporters A87

1939, Jan. 1 *Perf. 12½*

No.	Type	Denom.	Description	Unused	Used
193	A74	1c	red brn & dk grn	2.75	2.25
194	A75	2c	Prus bl & red vio	3.25	2.25
195	A76	3c	dk grn & sl blue	3.50	2.50
196	A77	4c	rose vio & ol grn	8.50	.50
197	A78	6c	dp cl & dk blue	7.75	14.00
198	A79	8c	red	11.00	2.00
199	A80	10c	olive grn & vio	26.00	7.00
200	A81	12c	ultra & grn	27.50	8.00
201	A82	15c	bis brn & brt bl grn	21.00	13.00
202	A83	20c	ind & rose vio	14.50	7.00
203	A84	25c	dk brn & bl grn	21.00	15.00
204	A85	50c	purple & brn	22.50	14.00
205	A86	$1	car & brown	72.50	22.50
206	A86	$2	ol grn & pur	120.00	*150.00*
207	A87	$5	blue & indigo	350.00	*375.00*
			Nos. 193-207 (15)	711.75	635.00
			Set, never hinged	1,200.	

For overprints see #208-237, MR1-MR2, N1-N15, N16-N31.

Nos. 193 to 207 Overprinted in Black

1945, Dec. 17 **Unwmk.** *Perf. 12½*

No.	Type	Denom.	Description	Unused	Used
208	A74	1c	red brn & dk grn	9.50	2.25
209	A75	2c	Prus bl & red vio	10.00	2.00
210	A76	3c	dk grn & sl bl	.90	1.25
211	A77	4c	rose vio & ol grn	12.00	*16.00*
212	A78	6c	dp cl & dk bl	.90	1.25
213	A79	8c	red	2.10	.75
214	A80	10c	ol green & vio	2.10	.40
215	A81	12c	ultra & green	4.25	3.50
216	A82	15c	bis brn & brt bl grn	1.20	1.10
217	A83	20c	ind & rose vio	4.25	2.50
218	A84	25c	dk brn & bl grn	4.75	1.50
219	A85	50c	purple & brn	3.00	2.50
220	A86	$1	carmine & brn	35.00	*40.00*
221	A86	$2	ol green & pur	35.00	*42.50*
a.			Double overprint	4,000.	
222	A87	$5	blue & indigo	18.00	18.00
			Nos. 208-222 (15)	142.95	135.50
			Set, never hinged	235.00	

"BMA" stands for British Military Administration.

Nos. 193 to 207 Ovptd. in Black or Carmine

1947

No.	Type	Denom.	Description	Unused	Used
223	A74	1c	red brn & dk grn	.25	1.00
224	A75	2c	Prus bl & red vio	1.25	.80
225	A76	3c	dk grn & sl bl (C)	.25	.80
226	A77	4c	rose vio & ol grn	.50	.80
227	A78	6c	dp cl & dk bl (C)	.25	.25
228	A79	8c	red	.25	.25
229	A80	10c	olive grn & vio	1.10	.35
230	A81	12c	ultra & grn	2.40	2.75
231	A82	15c	bis brn & brt bl grn	1.75	.30
232	A83	20c	ind & rose vio	2.40	.85
233	A84	25c	dk brn & bl grn	2.40	.50
234	A85	50c	purple & brn	2.00	.85
235	A86	$1	carmine & brn	8.50	1.75
236	A86	$2	ol green & pur	11.50	*18.00*
237	A87	$5	blue & ind (C)	19.00	*25.00*
			Nos. 223-237 (15)	53.80	54.25
			Set, never hinged	80.00	

The bars obliterate "The State of" and "British Protectorate."

Catalogue values for unused stamps in this section, from this point to the end of the section, are for Never Hinged items.

Silver Wedding Issue

Common Design Types

Perf. 14x14½

1948, Nov. 1 **Wmk. 4** **Photo.**

No.	Type	Denom.	Description	Unused	Used
238	CD304	8c	scarlet	.30	*.75*

Perf. 11½x11

Engraved; Name Typographed

No.	Type	Denom.	Description	Unused	Used
239	CD305	$10	purple	35.00	*45.00*

Common Design Types pictured following the introduction.

UPU Issue

Common Design Types

Engr.; Name Typo. on 10c and 30c

1949, Oct. 10 *Perf. 13½, 11x11½*

No.	Type	Denom.	Description	Unused	Used
240	CD306	8c	rose carmine	.65	.25
241	CD307	10c	chocolate	3.25	1.75
242	CD308	30c	deep orange	1.50	1.75
243	CD309	55c	blue	1.75	*2.75*
			Nos. 240-243 (4)	7.15	6.50

Mount Kinabalu — A88

Coconut Grove — A89

Designs: 2c, Musician. 4c, Hemp drying. 5c, Cattle at Kota Belud. 8c, Map. 10c, Logging. 15c, Proa at Sandakan. 20c, Bajau Chief. 30c, Suluk Craft. 50c, Clock tower. $1, Bajau horsemen. $2, Murut with blowgun. $5, Net fishing. $10, Arms.

Perf. 13½x14½, 14½x13½

1950, July 1 **Photo.**

No.	Type	Denom.	Description	Unused	Used
244	A88	1c	red brown	.25	*1.25*
245	A88	2c	blue	.25	*.50*
246	A89	3c	green	.25	.25
247	A89	4c	red violet	.25	.25
248	A89	5c	purple	.25	.25
249	A88	8c	red	1.25	.85
250	A88	10c	violet brn	1.75	.25
251	A88	15c	brt ultra	2.00	.65
252	A88	20c	dk brown	2.25	.25
253	A89	30c	brown	5.50	.25
254	A89	50c	cer *(Jessleton)*	1.75	4.75
255	A89	$1	red orange	6.00	1.75
256	A88	$2	dark green	15.00	*20.00*
257	A88	$5	emerald	25.00	*30.00*
258	A88	$10	gray blue	65.00	*90.00*
			Nos. 244-258 (15)	126.75	151.25

Redrawn

1952, May 1 *Perf. 14½x13½*

No.	Type	Denom.	Description	Unused	Used
259	A89	50c	cerise *(Jesselton)*	16.00	3.25

Coronation Issue

Common Design Type

1953, June 3 **Engr.** *Perf. 13½x13*

No.	Type	Denom.	Description	Unused	Used
260	CD312	10c	carmine & black	2.00	1.00

Types of 1950 with Portrait of Queen Elizabeth II

Perf. 13½x14½, 14½x13½

1954-57 **Photo.**

No.	Type	Denom.	Description	Unused	Used
261	A88	1c	red brown	.25	.30
262	A88	2c	brt blue ('56)	1.25	.25
263	A89	3c	green ('57)	4.00	2.00
264	A89	4c	red violet ('55)	1.75	.25
265	A89	5c	purple	1.00	.25
266	A88	8c	red	1.25	.30
267	A88	10c	violet brown	.40	.25
268	A88	15c	brt ultra ('55)	1.00	.25
269	A88	20c	dk brown	.50	.25
270	A89	30c	brown	3.25	.25
271	A89	50c	cerise ('56)	6.25	.25
272	A89	$1	red orange ('55)	7.50	.25
273	A88	$2	dk green ('55)	15.00	1.25
274	A88	$5	emerald ('57)	12.50	*32.50*
275	A88	$10	gray blue ('57)	27.50	*35.00*
			Nos. 261-275 (15)	83.40	73.60

Issued: 10c, 3/1; 5c, 7/1; 20c, 30c, 8/3; 1c, 8c, 10/1; $1, 4/1/55; 4c, 15c, 5/16/55; $2, 10/1/55; 50c, 2/10/56; 2c, 6/1/56; 3c, $5, $10, 2/1/57.

In 1960, the 30c plate was remade, using a finer, smaller-dot (250) screen instead of the 200 screen. The background appears smoother. Value, $2.75 unused.

Borneo Railway, 1902 — A90

Comp. Arms — A91

15c, Proa (sailboat). 35c, Mount Kinabalu.

Perf. 13x13½, 13½x13

1956, Nov. 1 **Engr.** **Wmk. 4**

No.	Type	Denom.	Description	Unused	Used
276	A90	10c	rose car & blk	1.25	.40
277	A90	15c	red brown & blk	.65	.30
278	A90	35c	green & blk	.65	1.50
279	A91	$1	slate & blk	1.50	2.50
			Nos. 276-279 (4)	4.05	4.70

75th anniv. of the founding of the Chartered Company of North Borneo.

Malayan Sambar — A92

Orangutan — A93

Designs: 4c, Honey bear. 5c, Clouded leopard. 6c, Dusun woman with gong. 10c, Map of Borneo. 12c, Banteng (wild ox). 20c, Butterfly orchid. 25c, Rhinoceros. 30c, Murut with blowgun. 35c, Mount Kinabalu. 50c, Dusun with buffalo transport. 75c, Bajau horsemen. $2, Rhinoceros hornbill. $5, Crested wood partridge. $10, Coat of arms.

Perf. 13x12½, 12½x13

1961, Feb. 1 **Wmk. 314** **Engr.**

No.	Type	Denom.	Description	Unused	Used
280	A92	1c	lt red brn & grn	.25	.25
281	A92	4c	orange & olive	.90	.90
282	A92	5c	violet & sepia	.30	.25
283	A92	6c	bluish grn & sl	.75	.40
284	A92	10c	rose red & lt grn	1.25	.25
285	A92	12c	dull grn & brn	.50	.25
286	A92	20c	ultra & bl grn	4.00	.25
287	A92	25c	rose red & gray	1.25	*1.50*
288	A92	30c	gray ol & sep	1.25	.25
289	A92	35c	redsh brn & stl bl	2.50	2.25
290	A92	50c	brn org & bl grn	2.25	.25
291	A92	75c	red vio & sl bl	16.00	.90
292	A93	$1	yel grn & brn	14.00	.80
293	A93	$2	slate & brown	35.00	3.75
294	A93	$5	brn vio & grn	37.50	22.50
295	A93	$10	blue & car	50.00	50.00
			Nos. 280-295 (16)	167.70	84.75

Freedom from Hunger Issue

Common Design Type

1963, June 4 **Photo.** *Perf. 14x14½*

No.	Type	Denom.	Description	Unused	Used
296	CD314	12c	ultramarine	1.90	.75

SEMI-POSTAL STAMPS

Nos. 136-138, 140-146, 148-149, 152 Ovptd. in Carmine or Vermilion

1916 **Unwmk.** ***Perf. 14***

Center in Black

B1 A51 1c chocolate 7.50 *35.00*
B2 A52 2c green 30.00 *80.00*
a. Perf. 15 35.00 *80.00*
B3 A53 3c deep rose 27.50 *50.00*
B4 A54 4c dull red 7.25 *32.50*
a. Perf. 15 275.00 *180.00*
B5 A55 5c yellow brown 50.00 *55.00*
B6 A56 6c olive green 70.00 *75.00*
a. Perf. 15 225.00 225.00
B7 A57 8c rose 24.00 *60.00*
B8 A58 10c brt blue 55.00 *70.00*
B9 A59 12c deep blue 100.00 *100.00*
B10 A60 16c red brown 110.00 *110.00*
B11 A62 20c on 18c bl grn 55.00 *100.00*
B12 A63 24c violet 130.00 *130.00*

Perf. 15

B13 A64 25c yellow green 375.00 *425.00*
Nos. B1-B13 (13) 1,041. *1,322.*

All values exist with the vermilion overprint and all but the 4c with the carmine.

Of the total overprinting, a third was given to the National Philatelic War Fund Committee in London to be auctioned for the benefit of the wounded and veterans' survivors. The balance was lost en route from London to Sandakan when a submarine sank the ship. Very few were postally used.

Nos. 136-138, 140-146, 149, 152-157 Surcharged

1918 **Center in Black** ***Perf. 14***

B14 A51 1c + 2c choc 3.50 *14.00*
B15 A52 2c + 2c green 1.00 *8.50*
B16 A53 3c + 2c dp rose 14.00 *19.00*
a. Perf. 15 30.00 *65.00*
B17 A54 4c + 2c dull red .70 *5.00*
a. Inverted surcharge 450.00
B18 A55 5c + 2c yel brn 8.00 *29.00*
B19 A56 6c + 2c olive grn 5.00 *29.00*
a. Perf. 15 225.00 *250.00*
B20 A57 8c + 2c rose 5.50 *11.00*
B21 A58 10c + 2c brt blue 8.00 *27.50*
B22 A59 12c + 2c deep bl 21.00 *55.00*
a. Inverted surcharge 700.00
B23 A60 16c + 2c red brn 22.50 *45.00*
B24 A63 24c + 2c violet 22.50 *45.00*
B25 A64 25c + 2c yel grn 12.00 *42.50*
B26 A64 50c + 2c sl blue 14.00 *42.50*
B27 A64 $1 + 2c brown 50.00 *55.00*
B28 A64 $2 + 2c dk vio 75.00 *95.00*
B29 A65 $5 + 2c claret 425.00 *650.00*
B30 A65 $10 + 2c ver 475.00 *700.00*
Nos. B14-B30 (17) 1,162. *1,873.*

On Nos. B14-B24 the surcharge is 15mm high, on Nos. B25-B30 it is 19mm high.

Nos. 136-138, 140-146, 149, 152-157 Surcharged in Red

1918 **Center in Black**

B31 A51 1c + 4c choc .60 *5.00*
B32 A52 2c + 4c green .65 *8.00*
B33 A53 3c + 4c dp rose 1.00 *3.75*
B34 A54 4c + 4c dull red .40 *4.75*
B35 A55 5c + 4c yel brn 2.00 *22.50*
B36 A56 6c + 4c olive grn 2.00 *12.00*
a. Vert. pair, imperf. btwn. 2,500.
B37 A57 8c + 4c rose 1.25 *9.50*
B38 A58 10c + 4c brt blue 3.75 *12.00*
B39 A59 12c + 4c dp blue 14.00 *14.00*
B40 A60 16c + 4c red brn 8.00 *16.00*
B41 A63 24c + 4c violet 11.00 *20.00*
B42 A64 25c + 4c yel grn 9.00 *50.00*
B43 A64 50c + 4c sl blue 15.00 *45.00*
a. Perf. 15 60.00
B44 A64 $1 + 4c brown 22.50 *60.00*
a. Perf. 15 *180.00*
B45 A64 $2 + 4c dk vio 55.00 *80.00*
B46 A65 $5 + 4c claret 300.00 *400.00*
B47 A65 $10 + 4c ver 375.00 *450.00*
Nos. B31-B47 (17) 821.15 *1,212.*

POSTAGE DUE STAMPS

Regular Issues Overprinted

On Nos. 60 to 67

Reading Up Vert. (V), or Horiz. (H)

1895, Aug. 1 **Unwmk.** ***Perf. 14, 15***

J1 A22 2c rose & blk (V) 30.00 2.50
J2 A23 3c vio & ol grn (V) 6.00 1.25
J3 A24 5c org red & blk (V) 60.00 3.25
a. Period after "DUE" (V) 275.00
J4 A25 6c ol brn & blk (V) 20.00 2.75
J5 A26 8c lilac & blk (H) 50.00 3.00
a. Double ovpt. (H) *400.00*
J6 A27 12c blue & blk (H) 70.00 3.00
a. Double overprint (H) *325.00*
J7 A28 18c green & blk (V) 70.00 4.25
a. Ovpt. reading down 600.00 *350.00*
b. Overprinted horizontally 70.00 4.25
c. Same as "b" inverted 375.00 *400.00*
J8 A29 24c claret & bl (H) 40.00 4.00
Nos. J1-J8 (8) 346.00 24.00

1897 **On Nos. 80 and 85**

J9 A38 2c dp rose & blk (V) 8.50 1.50
a. Overprinted horizontally 23.00 *15.00*
J10 A42 8c brn lil & blk (H) 65.00 *80.00*
a. Period after "DUE" 30.00 *75.00*

On Nos. 81-88 and 104 Vertically reading up

1901

J11 A38 2c green & blk 75.00 .70
a. Overprinted horizontally 225.00
J12 A39 3c lilac & ol grn 32.00 .50
a. Period after "DUE" 70.00 *70.00*
J13 A48 4c dp rose & blk 70.00 .50
J14 A40 5c orange & blk 28.00 .90
a. Period after "DUE" 90.00
J15 A41 6c olive brn & blk 7.00 .50
J16 A42 8c brown & blk 9.00 .50
a. Overprinted horizontally 30.00
b. Period after "DUE" (H) 23.00 75.00
J17 A43 12c blue & blk 150.00 4.00
J18 A46 18c green & blk 80.00 4.00
J19 A47 24c red & blue 50.00 2.50
Nos. J11-J19 (9) 501.00 14.10

On Nos. 105-114, 122-123 Horizontally

1903-11 ***Perf. 14***

J20 A37 1c bis brn & blk, period after "DUE" 4.50 55.00
a. Period omitted
J21 A38 2c green & blk 27.50 .30
a. Ovpt. vert., perf. 16 550.00 *275.00*
b. Perf 15 (ovpt. horiz.) 55.00 *55.00*
J22 A39 3c lilac & ol grn 7.00 .35
a. Ovpt. vert. 140.00 *140.00*
b. Perf. 15 (ovpt. horiz.) 50.00 *45.00*
J23 A48 4c dp rose & blk, perf. 15 11.00 2.00
a. "Postage Due" double 550.00 170.00
b. Perf. 14 21.00 1.00
J24 A40 5c orange & blk 45.00 .45
a. Ovpt. vert., perf. 15 250.00 *160.00*
b. Perf. 13½ (ovpt. horiz.)
c. Perf. 15 (ovpt. horiz.) 85.00 *35.00*
J25 A41 6c olive brn & blk 24.00 .40
a. "Postage Due" double *750.00*
b. "Postage Due" inverted 500.00 *125.00*
c. Perf. 16 90.00 *37.50*
J26 A42 8c brown & blk 27.50 .50
a. Overprint vertical 200.00 *125.00*
J27 A49 10c slate & brn 130.00 1.60
J28 A43 12c blue & blk 42.50 3.75
J29 A50 16c yel brn & grn 85.00 3.75
J30 A46 18c green & blk 17.50 1.50
a. "Postage Due" double *500.00* *100.00*
J31 A47 24c claret & blue 17.50 3.75
a. "Postage Due" double *350.00* *125.00*
b. Overprint vertical 325.00 *140.00*
Nos. J20-J31 (12) 439.00 73.35

On Nos. 137 and 139-146

1921-31 ***Perf. 14, 15***

J32 A52 2c green & blk 27.50 *80.00*
a. Perf. 13½ 11.00 *75.00*
J33 A53 3c green & blk 5.25 *50.00*
J34 A54 4c dull red & blk 1.25 1.25
J35 A55 5c yel brn & blk 9.50 *30.00*
J36 A56 6c olive grn & blk 17.00 17.00
J37 A57 8c rose & blk 2.00 2.00
J38 A58 10c blue & blk 16.00 *19.00*
a. Perf. 15 120.00 *200.00*
J39 A59 12c dp vio & blk 70.00 55.00
J40 A60 16c red brn & blk 26.00 65.00
Nos. J32-J40 (9) 174.50 319.25

On Nos. 168 to 176

1926-28 ***Perf. 12½***

J41 A52 2c lake & blk .75 *2.00*
J42 A53 3c green & blk 10.00 *32.50*
J43 A54 4c dull red & blk 3.25 *2.00*
J44 A55 5c yel brown & blk 8.50 *90.00*
J45 A56 6c yel green & blk 14.00 3.00
J46 A57 8c rose & black 11.00 *22.50*
J47 A58 10c brt blue & blk 12.00 *90.00*
J48 A59 12c dp blue & blk 32.50 *160.00*
J49 A60 16c org brn & blk 75.00 *225.00*
Nos. J41-J49 (9) 167.00 *627.00*

Crest of British North Borneo Company — D1

1939, Jan. 1 **Engr.** ***Perf. 12½***

J50 D1 2c brown 4.25 *80.00*
J51 D1 4c carmine 4.75 *110.00*
J52 D1 6c dp rose violet 17.50 *150.00*
J53 D1 8c dk blue green 22.50 *300.00*
J54 D1 10c deep ultra 50.00 *450.00*
Nos. J50-J54 (5) 99.00 *1,090.*
Set, never hinged 160.00

WAR TAX STAMPS

Nos. 193-194 Overprinted

No. MR1

No. MR2

1941, Feb. 24 **Unwmk.** ***Perf. 12½***

MR1 A74 1c red brn & dk grn 2.75 4.50
MR2 A75 2c Prus blue & red violet 11.00 4.75

For overprints see Nos. N15A-N15B.

OCCUPATION STAMPS

Issued under Japanese Occupation

Nos. 193-207 Handstamped in Violet or Black

On Nos. N1-N15B, the violet overprint is attributed to Jesselton, the black to Sandakan. Nos. N1-N15 are generally found with violet overprint, Nos. N15A-N15B with black.

1942 **Unwmk.** ***Perf. 12½***

N1 A74 1c 200.00 250.00
N2 A75 2c 220.00 275.00
N3 A76 3c 175.00 300.00
N4 A77 4c 325.00 390.00
N5 A78 6c 200.00 355.00
N6 A79 8c 275.00 210.00
N7 A80 10c 250.00 360.00
N8 A81 12c 275.00 525.00
N9 A82 15c 220.00 525.00
N10 A83 20c 300.00 *650.00*
N11 A84 25c 300.00 *700.00*
N12 A85 50c 400.00 *775.00*
N13 A86 $1 440.00 *925.00*
N14 A86 $2 650.00 *1,250.*
N15 A87 $5 775.00 *1,350.*
Nos. N1-N15 (15) 5,005. *8,840.*

For overprints see Nos. N22a, N31a.

Same Overprint on Nos. MR1-MR2 in Black or Violet

1942

N15A A74 1c *775.00* *325.00*
N15B A75 2c *2,100.* *650.00*

Nos. 193 to 207 Overprinted in Black

1944, Sept. 30 **Unwmk.** ***Perf. 12½***

N16 A74 1c 8.25 13.00
N17 A75 2c 8.25 10.00
N18 A76 3c 8.25 11.00
N19 A77 4c 16.50 25.00
N20 A78 6c 12.00 7.00
N21 A79 8c 11.00 *18.50*
N22 A80 10c 9.25 *14.50*
a. On No. N7 500.00
N23 A81 12c 17.50 *14.50*
N24 A82 15c 17.50 *17.50*
N25 A83 20c 35.00 *55.00*
N26 A84 25c 35.00 *55.00*
N27 A85 50c 87.50 *130.00*
N28 A86 $1 105.00 *165.00*
Nos. N16-N28 (13) 371.00 *536.00*

Nos. N1 and 205 Surcharged in Black

No. N30

No. N31

1944, May

N30 A74 $2 on 1c *5,500.* *4,750.*
N31 A86 $5 on $1 5,000. 3,750.
a. On No. N13 10,000. 6,000.

Mt. Kinabalu OS1

Boat and Traveler's Palm OS2

1943, Apr. 29 **Litho.**

N32 OS1 4c dull rose red 30.00 60.00
N33 OS2 8c dark blue 25.00 55.00

Stamps of Japan, 1938-43, Overprinted in Black

1s, War factory girl. 2s, Gen. Maresuke Nogi. 3s, Power plant. 4s, Hyuga Monument and Mt. Fuji. 5s, Adm. Heihachiro Togo. 6s, Garambi Lighthouse, Formosa. 8s, Meiji Shrine, Tokyo. 10s, Palms and map of "Greater East Asia." 15s, Aviator saluting and Japanese flag. 20s, Mt. Fuji and cherry blossoms. 25s, Horyu Temple, Nara. 30s, Miyajima Torii, Itsukushima shrine. 50s, Golden Pavilion, Kyoto. 1y, Great Buddha, Kamakura. See Burma, Vol. 1, for illustrations of 2s, 3s, 5s, 8s, 20s and watermark. For others, see Japan.

Wmk. Curved Wavy Lines (257)

1944, Sept. 30 ***Perf. 13***

N34 A144 1s orange brown 10.00 *35.00*
N35 A84 2s vermilion 8.25 *30.00*
N36 A85 3s green 10.00 *35.00*
N37 A146 4s emerald 18.50 *27.50*
N38 A86 5s brown lake 15.50 *30.00*
N39 A88 6s orange 24.00 *32.50*
N40 A90 8s dk purple & pale vio 7.00 *32.50*
N41 A148 10s crim & dull rose 15.00 *35.00*
N42 A150 15s dull blue 14.00 *32.50*
N43 A94 20s ultra 95.00 *100.00*

N44	A95	25s brown		65.00	*95.00*
N45	A96	30s peacock blue		195.00	*105.00*
N46	A97	50s olive		87.50	*87.50*
N47	A98	1y lt brown		95.00	*120.00*
		Nos. N34-N47 (14)		659.75	*797.50*

The overprint translates "North Borneo."

OCCUPATION POSTAGE DUE STAMPS

Nos. J50-J51, J53 Handstamped in Black

1942, Sept. 30

NJ1	D1	2c brown	—	*5,000.*
NJ2	D1	4c carmine	—	*5,000.*
NJ3	D1	8c dk blue green	—	*5,000.*

NORTHERN NIGERIA

'nor-thə͏r͏n nī-'jir-ē-ə

LOCATION — Western Africa
GOVT. — British Protectorate
AREA — 281,703 sq. mi.
POP. — 11,866,250
CAPITAL — Zungeru

In 1914 Northern Nigeria united with Southern Nigeria to form the Colony and Protectorate of Nigeria.

12 Pence = 1 Shilling
20 Shillings = 1 Pound

Victoria — A1

Numerals of 5p and 6p, types A1 and A2, are in color on plain tablet.

Wmk. Crown and C A (2)

1900, Mar. Typo. *Perf. 14*

1	A1	½p	lilac & grn	8.00	*22.00*
2	A1	1p	lilac & rose	5.00	5.50
3	A1	2p	lilac & yel	16.00	*60.00*
4	A1	2½p	lilac & blue	13.00	*45.00*
5	A1	5p	lilac & brn	30.00	*70.00*
6	A1	6p	lilac & vio	30.00	*50.00*
7	A1	1sh	green & blk	32.50	*85.00*
8	A1	2sh6p	green & blue	180.00	*550.00*
9	A1	10sh	green & brn	325.00	*900.00*
			Nos. 1-9 (9)	639.50	*1,787.*

Edward VII — A2

1902, July 1

10	A2	½p	violet & green	2.00	1.25
11	A2	1p	vio & car rose	5.00	1.00
12	A2	2p	violet & org	2.50	*3.00*
13	A2	2½p	violet & ultra	2.00	*11.00*
14	A2	5p	vio & org brn	7.00	*7.50*
15	A2	6p	violet & pur	18.50	*7.00*
16	A2	1sh	green & black	7.50	*7.50*
17	A2	2sh6p	green & ultra	17.00	*75.00*
18	A2	10sh	green & brown	55.00	*60.00*
			Nos. 10-18 (9)	116.50	*173.25*

1904, Apr. Wmk. 3

18A	A2	£25	green & car	*60,000.*

No. 18A was available for postage but probably was used only for fiscal purposes.

1905

19a	A2	½p	violet & grn	6.00	5.50
20a	A2	1p	violet & car rose	6.00	1.25
21	A2	2p	violet & org	19.00	*32.50*
22	A2	2½p	violet & ultra	7.25	*10.00*
23	A2	5p	violet & org brn	32.50	*85.00*
24	A2	6p	violet & pur	29.00	*65.00*
25a	A2	1sh	green & black	24.00	*55.00*
26a	A2	2sh6p	green & ultra	42.50	*60.00*
			Nos. 19a-26a (8)	166.25	314.25

All values except the 2½p exist on ordinary and chalky papers. The less expensive values are given above. For detailed listings, see the *Scott Classic Specialized Catalogue of Stamps and Covers 1840-1940.*

1910-11 Ordinary Paper

28	A2	½p	green	2.25	1.25
29	A2	1p	carmine	5.25	1.25
30	A2	2p	gray	9.50	*4.50*
31	A2	2½p	ultra	3.50	*9.50*

Chalky Paper

32	A2	3p	violet, *yel*	4.50	1.00
33	A2	5p	vio & ol grn	6.00	*16.00*
34	A2	6p	vio & red vio ('11)	6.00	*6.00*
a.			6p violet & deep violet	7.50	*26.00*
35	A2	1sh	black, *green*	4.25	.75
36	A2	2sh6p	blk & red, *bl*	17.50	*45.00*
37	A2	5sh	grn & red, *yel*	27.50	*75.00*
38	A2	10sh	grn & red, *grn*	55.00	*50.00*
			Nos. 28-38 (11)	141.25	210.25

George V — A3

For description of dies I and II, see A pages in front section of catalogue.

Die I

1912 Ordinary Paper

40	A3	½p	green	4.50	1.00
41	A3	1p	carmine	4.50	.60
42	A3	2p	gray	6.75	*15.00*

Chalky Paper

43	A3	3p	violet, *yel*	2.25	1.25
44	A3	4p	blk & red, *yel*	1.25	*2.25*
45	A3	5p	vio & ol grn	4.50	*18.00*
46	A3	6p	vio & red vio	4.25	*4.50*
47	A3	9p	violet & scar	2.25	*12.00*
48	A3	1sh	blk, *green*	5.00	2.25
49	A3	2sh6p	blk & red, *bl*	9.25	*55.00*
50	A3	5sh	grn & red, *yel*	25.00	*90.00*
51	A3	10sh	grn & red, *grn*	45.00	*50.00*
52	A3	£1	vio & blk, *red*	200.00	120.00
			Nos. 40-52 (13)	314.50	*371.85*

Numerals of 3p, 4p, 5p and 6p, type A3, are in color on plain tablet.

Stamps of Northern Nigeria were replaced in 1914 by those of Nigeria.

NORTHERN RHODESIA

'nor-thə͏r͏n rō-'dē-zhē-ə

LOCATION — In southern Africa, east of Angola and separated from Southern Rhodesia by the Zambezi River.
GOVT. — British Protectorate
AREA — 287,640 sq. mi.
POP. — 2,550,000 (est. 1962)
CAPITAL — Lusaka

Prior to April 1, 1924, Northern Rhodesia was administered by the British South Africa Company. It joined the Federation of Rhodesia and Nyasaland in 1953 and used its stamps in 1954-63. It resumed issuing its own stamps in December, 1963, after the Federation was dissolved. On Oct. 24, 1964, Northern Rhodesia became the independent republic of Zambia. See Rhodesia, Southern Rhodesia, Rhodesia and Nyasaland, Zambia.

12 Pence = 1 Shilling
20 Shillings = 1 Pound

Catalogue values for unused stamps in this country are for Never Hinged items, beginning with Scott 46 in the regular postage section and Scott J5 in the postage due section.

A1

King George V — A2

1925-29 Engr. Wmk. 4 *Perf. 12½*

1	A1	½p	dk green	1.75	.80
2	A1	1p	dk brown	1.75	.25
3	A1	1½p	carmine	4.25	.30
4	A1	2p	brown org	4.50	.25
5	A1	3p	ultra	4.50	1.30
6	A1	4p	dk violet	7.50	.50
7	A1	6p	gray	8.00	.40
8	A1	8p	rose lilac	8.00	*60.00*
9	A1	10p	olive grn	8.00	*50.00*
10	A2	1sh	black & org	4.25	2.25
11	A2	2sh	ultra & brn	27.50	*40.00*
12	A2	2sh6p	green & blk	24.00	*15.00*
13	A2	3sh	indigo & vio	40.00	25.00
14	A2	5sh	dk vio & gray	50.00	22.50
15	A2	7sh6p	blk & lil rose	160.00	*275.00*
16	A2	10sh	black & green	100.00	*100.00*
17	A2	20sh	rose lil & red	275.00	*325.00*
			Nos. 1-17 (17)	729.00	*918.55*

High values with revenue cancellations are inexpensive.

Issue dates: 3sh, 1929; others, Apr. 1.

Common Design Types pictured following the introduction.

Silver Jubilee Issue

Common Design Type

1935, May 6 *Perf. 13½x14*

18	CD301	1p	olive grn & ultra	1.50	1.50
19	CD301	2p	indigo & grn	2.50	2.25
20	CD301	3p	blue & brown	4.00	*10.00*
21	CD301	6p	brt vio & indigo	8.75	2.50
			Nos. 18-21 (4)	16.75	16.25
			Set, never hinged	25.00	

Coronation Issue

Common Design Type

1937, May 12 *Perf. 11x11½*

22	CD302	1½p	dark carmine	.25	.25
23	CD302	2p	yellow brown	.30	*.75*
24	CD302	3p	deep ultra	.40	*1.25*
			Nos. 22-24 (3)	.95	2.25
			Set, never hinged	1.50	

King George VI — A3

1938-52 Wmk. 4 *Perf. 12½*

Size: 19x24mm

25	A3	½p	green	.25	.25
26	A3	½p	dk brn ('51)	1.40	*1.50*
a.			Perf. 12½x14	1.00	*6.00*
27	A3	1p	dk brown	.25	.25
28	A3	1p	green ('51)	.90	*2.25*
29	A3	1½p	carmine	30.00	.75
a.			Horiz. pair, imperf. between	*27,000.*	
30	A3	1½p	brn org ('41)	.30	.25
31	A3	2p	brown org	30.00	1.75
32	A3	2p	carmine ('41)	1.00	.50
33	A3	2p	rose lilac ('51)	.40	*1.50*
34	A3	3p	ultra	.45	.30
35	A3	3p	red ('51)	.30	*3.00*
36	A3	4p	dk violet	.30	.40
37	A3	4½p	dp blue ('52)	1.75	*12.00*
38	A3	6p	dark gray	.30	.25
39	A3	9p	violet ('52)	1.75	*12.00*

Size: 21½x26¾mm

40	A3	1sh	blk & brn org	2.50	.60
41	A3	2sh6p	green & blk	7.50	7.00
42	A3	3sh	ind & dk vio	14.00	*17.50*
43	A3	5sh	violet & gray	15.00	*17.50*
44	A3	10sh	black & green	18.00	*35.00*
45	A3	20sh	rose lil & red	42.50	*80.00*
			Nos. 25-45 (21)	168.85	*194.55*
			Set, never hinged	275.00	

Catalogue values for unused stamps in this section, from this point to the end of the section, are for Never Hinged items.

Peace Issue

Common Design Type

1946, Nov. 26 Engr. *Perf. 13½x14*

46	CD303	1½p	deep orange	1.00	*1.50*
a.			Perf. 13½	14.00	*13.00*
47	CD303	2p	carmine	.25	*.50*

Silver Wedding Issue

Common Design Types

1948, Dec. 1 Photo. *Perf. 14x14½*

48	CD304	1½p	orange	.30	.25

Perf. 11½x11

Engr.

49	CD305	20sh	rose brown	92.50	90.00

UPU Issue

Common Design Types

Engr.; Name Typo. on 3p, 6p

Perf. 13½, 11x11½

1949, Oct. 10 Wmk. 4

50	CD306	2p	rose carmine	.50	.50
51	CD307	3p	indigo	2.00	*3.00*
52	CD308	6p	gray	1.50	1.50
53	CD309	1sh	red orange	1.00	*1.50*
			Nos. 50-53 (4)	5.00	*6.50*

Victoria Falls and Railway Bridge, Cecil Rhodes and Elizabeth II — A4

1953, May 30 Engr. *Perf. 12x11*

54	A4	½p	brown	.55	*1.25*
55	A4	1p	green	.45	*1.25*
56	A4	2p	deep claret	.80	.40
57	A4	4½p	deep blue	.55	*4.00*
58	A4	1sh	gray & orange	1.25	*4.25*
			Nos. 54-58 (5)	3.60	11.15

Cecil Rhodes (1853-1902).

Exhibition Seal — A5

1953, May 30 *Perf. 14x13½*

59	A5	6p	purple	.70	*1.25*

Central African Rhodes Centenary Exhib.

Coronation Issue

Common Design Type

1953, June 2 *Perf. 13½x13*

60	CD312	1½p	orange & black	.70	.25

Elizabeth II — A6

Perf. 12½x13½

1953, Sept. 15 Engr.

Size: 19x23mm

61	A6	½p	dark brown	.65	.25
62	A6	1p	green	.75	.25
63	A6	1½p	brown orange	1.25	.25
64	A6	2p	rose lilac	1.40	.25
65	A6	3p	red	.80	.25
66	A6	4p	dark violet	1.25	*2.00*
67	A6	4½p	deep blue	1.50	*4.25*
68	A6	6p	dark gray	1.25	.40
69	A6	9p	violet	1.25	*4.25*

Size: 21x27mm

70	A6	1sh	black & brn org	1.00	.25
71	A6	2sh6p	green & blk	15.00	8.00
72	A6	5sh	violet & gray	16.00	*15.00*
73	A6	10sh	black & green	12.00	*32.50*
74	A6	20sh	rose lilac & red	30.00	*37.50*
			Nos. 61-74 (14)	84.10	105.40

Coat of Arms — A7

Size: 23x19mm

Perf. 14½

1963, Dec. 1 Unwmk. Photo.

Arms in Black, Blue and Orange

No.	Design	Description	Unused	Used
75	A7	½p violet & blk	.70	*1.00*
a.		Value omitted	1,100.	
b.		Orange (eagle) omitted	1,400.	
76	A7	1p blue & blk	1.50	.25
a.		Value omitted	12.50	
77	A7	2p brown & blk	.70	.25
78	A7	3p orange & blk	.25	.25
a.		Bklt. pane of 4	1.00	
b.		Value omitted	120.00	
c.		Orange (eagle) omitted	*1,200.*	—
d.		Value and orange (eagle) omitted	325.00	
79	A7	4p green & blk	.70	.30
a.		Value omitted	130.00	
80	A7	6p yel grn & blk	1.00	.25
a.		Value omitted	800.00	
81	A7	9p ocher & blk	.70	*1.60*
a.		Value omitted	600.00	
b.		Value and orange (eagle) omitted	600.00	
82	A7	1sh dk gray & blk	.50	.25
83	A7	1sh3p brt red lil & blk	2.25	.25

Perf. 13

Size: 27x23mm

No.	Design	Description	Unused	Used
84	A7	2sh dp org & blk	2.50	*5.25*
85	A7	2sh6p maroon & blk	2.50	2.25
86	A7	5sh dk car rose & blk	10.00	8.00
a.		Value omitted	*2,750.*	
87	A7	10sh brt pink & blk	17.00	*22.50*
88	A7	20sh dk blue & blk	22.00	*40.00*
a.		Value omitted	1,100.	
		Nos. 75-88 (14)	62.30	*82.40*

Stamps of Northern Rhodesia were replaced by those of Zambia, starting Oct. 24, 1964.

POSTAGE DUE STAMPS

D1

1929 Typo. Wmk. 4 *Perf. 14*

No.	Design	Description	Unused	Used
J1	D1	1p black	3.00	*2.75*
a.		Wmk. 4a (error)	6,000.	
J2	D1	2p black	6.00	*3.50*
a.		Bisected, used as 1d, on cover		*850.00*
J3	D1	3p black	3.50	*27.50*
a.		Crown in watermark missing	600.00	
b.		Wmk. 4a (error)	375.00	
J4	D1	4p black	12.00	*42.50*
		Nos. J1-J4 (4)	24.50	*76.25*

Catalogue values for unused stamps in this section, from this point to the end of the section, are for Never Hinged items.

D2

1964 Unwmk. Litho. *Perf. 12½*

No.	Design	Description	Unused	Used
J5	D2	1p orange	3.00	*5.50*
J6	D2	2p dark blue	3.00	*4.50*
J7	D2	3p rose claret	3.00	*7.50*
J8	D2	4p violet blue	3.00	*13.00*
J9	D2	6p purple	9.50	*10.00*
J10	D2	1sh emerald	11.00	*30.00*
		Nos. J5-J10 (6)	32.50	*70.50*

NORTH INGERMANLAND

'north 'iŋ-gər-mən-ˌland

LOCATION — In Northern Russia lying between the River Neva and Finland

CAPITAL — Kirjasalo

In 1920 the residents of this territory revolted from Russian rule and set up a provisional government. The new State existed only a short period as the revolution was quickly quelled by Soviet troops.

100 Pennia = 1 Markka

Arms — A1

Perf. 11½

1920, Mar. 21 Unwmk. Litho.

No.	Design	Description	Unused	Used
1	A1	5p green	2.75	*3.50*
2	A1	10p rose red	2.75	*3.50*
3	A1	25p bister	2.75	*3.50*
b.		Horiz. pair, imperf. btwn.	50.00	
4	A1	50p dark blue	2.50	*3.50*
5	A1	1m car & black	30.00	*42.50*
6	A1	5m lilac & black	175.00	*175.00*
7	A1	10m brown & blk	225.00	*250.00*
		Nos. 1-7 (7)	440.75	*481.50*

Well centered examples sell for twice the values shown.

Imperf., Pairs

No.	Design	Denomination	Unused
1a	A1	5p	45.00
2a	A1	10p	45.00
3a	A1	25p	50.00
4a	A1	50p	50.00
5a	A1	1m	65.00
6a	A1	5m	200.00
7a	A1	10m	350.00

Arms — A2

Peasant — A3

Plowing — A4

Milking — A5

Planting — A6

Ruins of Church — A7

Peasants Playing Zithers — A8

1920, Aug. 2

No.	Design	Description	Unused	Used
8	A2	10p gray grn & ultra	3.50	*7.00*
9	A3	30p buff & gray grn	3.50	*7.00*
a.		Horiz. pair, imperf. btwn.	100.00	
10	A4	50p ultra & red brn	3.50	*7.00*
11	A5	80p claret & slate	3.50	*7.00*
12	A6	1m red & slate	22.50	*45.00*
13	A7	5m dk vio & dl rose	9.00	*18.00*
14	A8	10m brn & violet	9.00	*18.00*
a.		Center inverted	1,000.	
		Nos. 8-14 (7)	54.50	*109.00*

Counterfeits abound.

Nos. 8-14 exist imperf. Value for set in pairs, $200.

NORTH WEST PACIFIC ISLANDS

'north 'west pə-'si-fik 'ī-ləndz

LOCATION — Group of islands in the West Pacific Ocean including a part of New Guinea and adjacent islands of the Bismarck Archipelago

GOVT. — Australian military government

AREA — 96,160 sq. mi.

POP. — 636,563

Stamps of Australia were overprinted for use in the former German possessions of Nauru and German New Guinea which Australian troops had captured. Following the League of Nations' decision which placed these territories under mandate to Australia, these provisional issues were discontinued. See German New Guinea, New Britain, Nauru and New Guinea.

12 Pence = 1 Shilling

20 Shillings = 1 Pound

Stamps of Australia Overprinted — a

Type a: "P" of "PACIFIC" above "S" of "ISLANDS."

There are two varieties of the letter "S" in the Type "a" overprint. These occur in three combinations: a, both normal "S"; b, 1st "S" with small head and long bottom stroke, 2nd "S" normal; c, both "S" with small head and long bottom stroke.

DESIGN A1

Die I — The inside frameline has a break at left, even with the top of the letters of the denomination.

Die II — The frameline does not show a break.

Die IV — As Die III, with a break in the top outside frameline above the "ST" of "AUSTRALIA." The upper right inside frameline has an incomplete corner.

Dies are only indicated when there are more than one for any denomination.

1915-16 Wmk. 8 *Perf. 12*

No.	Design	Description	Unused	Used
1	A1	2p gray	25.00	*75.00*
2	A1	2½p dark blue	5.00	*22.50*
3	A1	3p ol bis, die I	25.00	*65.00*
a.		Die II	385.00	*600.00*
b.		Pair, #3, 3a	825.00	*1,200.*
c.		Pair, die I and die II	2,500.	
4	A1	6p ultra	120.00	*130.00*
5	A1	9p violet	60.00	*72.50*
6	A1	1sh blue green	75.00	*77.50*
8	A1	5sh yel & gray ('16)	2,750.	*3,850.*
9	A1	10sh pink & gray	170.00	*200.00*
		Revenue cancel		
10	A1	£1 ultra & brown	*600.00*	*775.00*
		Nos. 1-6,8-10 (9)	*3,830.*	*5,267.*

For surcharge see No. 27.

Wmk. Wide Crown and Narrow A (9)

Perf. 12, 14

ONE PENNY

Die I — Normal die, having outside the oval band with "AUSTRALIA" a white line and a heavy colored line.

Die Ia — As die I with a small white spur below the right serif at foot of the "1" in left tablet.

Dies are only indicated when there are more than one for any denomination.

No.	Design	Description	Unused	Used
11	A4	½p emerald	3.25	*10.00*
a.		Double overprint		
12	A4	1p car (Die I)	7.75	7.25
a.		1p carmine rose (Die I)	120.00	*150.00*
b.		1p carmine (Die Ia)	110.00	*120.00*
13	A1	2p gray	20.00	*45.00*
14	A1	2½p dk bl ('16)	*30,000.*	*30,000.*
16	A4	4p orange	4.50	*17.50*
17	A4	5p org brown	2.75	*19.00*
18	A1	6p ultra	11.00	*13.00*
19	A1	9p violet	17.50	*24.00*
20	A1	1sh blue green	12.50	*27.50*
21	A1	2sh brown	110.00	*130.00*
22	A1	5sh yel & gray	82.50	*120.00*
		Nos. 11-13,16-22 (10)	271.75	*413.25*

For surcharge see No. 28.

1915-16 Wmk. 10 *Perf. 12*

No.	Design	Description	Unused	Used
23	A1	2p gray, die I	9.00	*28.00*
24	A1	3p ol bis, die I	7.00	*15.00*
a.		Die II	125.00	*190.00*
b.		Pair, #24, 24a	250.00	
25	A1	2sh brown ('16)	45.00	*65.00*
26	A1	£1 ultra & brn ('16)	400.00	*525.00*
		Nos. 23-26 (4)	461.00	*633.00*

Nos. 6 and 17 Surcharged

1918, May 23 Wmk. 8 *Perf. 12*

No.	Design	Description	Unused	Used
27	A1	1p on 1sh bl grn	125.00	100.00

Wmk. 9 *Perf. 14*

No.	Design	Description	Unused	Used
28	A4	1p on 5p org brn	110.00	100.00

Stamps of Australia Overprinted — b

Type "b": "P" of "PACIFIC" above space between "I" and "S" of "ISLANDS."

1918-23 Wmk. 10 *Perf. 12*

No.	Design	Description	Unused	Used
29	A1	2p gray	8.50	*30.00*
a.		Die II	13.50	*57.50*
30	A1	2½p dk bl ('19)	6.50	*19.00*
a.		"1" of fraction omitted	*13,000.*	*16,500.*
31	A1	3p ol bis, die I	27.50	*30.00*
a.		Die II	80.00	*100.00*
b.		Pair, #31, 31a	500.00	*650.00*
32	A1	6p ultra ('19)	7.50	*16.50*
a.		6p chalky blue	50.00	*75.00*
33	A1	9p violet ('19)	11.50	*60.00*
34	A1	1sh bl grn ('18)	16.50	*37.50*
a.		1sh emerald green	7.00	*32.50*
35	A1	2sh brown	25.00	*42.50*
36	A1	5sh yel & gray ('19)	75.00	*80.00*
37	A1	10sh pink & gray ('19)	200.00	*275.00*
38	A1	£1 ultra & brn	4,250.	*5,500.*
		Nos. 29-37 (9)	378.00	*590.50*

1919 Wmk. 11 *Perf. 14*

No.	Design	Description	Unused	Used
39	A4	½p emerald	5.00	*6.00*

1918-23 **Wmk. 9**

No.	Design	Description	Unused	Used
40	A4	½p emerald	2.00	*4.00*
41	A4	1p car red, die 1	4.25	1.75
a.		1p carmine red, die Ia	125.00	90.00
42	A4	1p scar, die I, rough paper	1,000.	675.00
a.		1p rose red, die Ia, rough paper	1,000.	675.00
43	A4	1p violet ('22)	2.75	*7.25*
44	A4	2p orange	8.75	2.75
45	A4	2p red ('22)	10.50	2.25
46	A4	4p yel org	4.00	*17.50*
47	A4	4p violet ('22)	22.50	*45.00*
a.		"Four Penc" in thinner letters	900.00	*1,550.*
48	A4	4p light ultra ('22)	12.50	*65.00*
a.		"Four Penc" in thinner letters	1,000.	*2,000.*
49	A4	5p brown	4.25	*13.50*
		Nos. 40-41,43-49 (9)	71.50	*159.00*

North West Pacific Islands stamps were largely used in New Britain. Some were used in Nauru. They were intended to serve the Bismarck Archipelago and other places.

NORWAY

'nor-,wā

LOCATION — Western half of the Scandinavian Peninsula in northern Europe
GOVT. — Kingdom
AREA — 125,051 sq. mi.
POP. — 4,644,457 (2008 est.)
CAPITAL — Oslo

120 Skilling = 1 Specie Daler
100 Ore = 1 Krone (1877)

Catalogue values for unused stamps in this country are for Never Hinged items, beginning with Scott 275 in the regular postage section, Scott B27 in the semi-postal section, and Scott O65 in the official section.

Watermarks

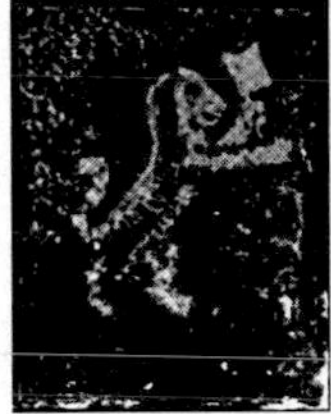

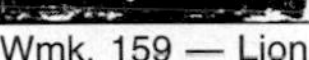

Wmk. 159 — Lion

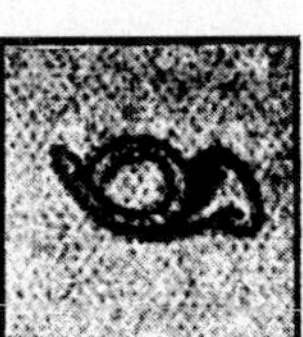

Wmk. 160 — Post Horn

Coat of Arms — A1

Wmk. 159

1855, Jan. 1 **Typo.** ***Imperf.***

No.	Design	Description	Unused	Used
1	A1	4s blue	*4,250.*	175.
a.		Double foot on right hind leg of lion		3,000.

Only a few genuine unused examples of No. 1 exist. Stamps often offered have had pen-markings removed. The unused catalogue value is for a stamp without gum. Stamps with original gum sell for much more.

No. 1 was reprinted in 1914 and 1924 unwatermarked. Lowest value reprint, $75.

ROULETTED REPRINTS

1963: No. 1, value $25; Nos. 2-5, 15, value each $15.

1966: Nos. 57, 70a, 100, 152, J1, O1. Value each $12.

1969: Nos. 69, 92, 107, 114, 128, J12. Value each $12.

King Oscar I — A2

1856-57 **Unwmk.** ***Perf. 13***

No.	Design	Description	Unused	Used
2	A2	2s yellow ('57)	800.00	160.00
3	A2	3s lilac ('57)	550.00	120.00
4	A2	4s blue	450.00	20.00
a.		Imperf.		*10,000.*
b.		Half used as 2s on cover		—
5	A2	8s dull lake	1,450.	65.00

Nos. 2-5 were reprinted in 1914 and 1924, perf. 13½. Lowest valued reprint, $50 each.

A3

1863 **Litho.** ***Perf. 14½x13½***

No.	Design	Description	Unused	Used
6	A3	2s yellow	1,250.	300.00
7	A3	3s gray lilac	850.00	600.00
8	A3	4s blue	275.00	18.00
9	A3	8s rose	1,200.	80.00
10	A3	24s brown	55.00	65.00
		Nos. 6-10 (5)	3,630.	1,063.

There are four types of the 2, 3, 8 and 24 skilling and eight types of the 4 skilling. See note on used value of No. 10 following No. 21.

No. 8 exists imperf. Value, unused $900.

A4

1867-68 **Typo.**

No.	Design	Description	Unused	Used
11	A4	1s black, coarse impression ('68)	100.00	70.00
12	A4	2s orange	35.00	30.00
b.		Vert. pair, imperf between	*1,750.*	
13	A4	3s dl lil, coarse impression ('68)	600.00	160.00
14	A4	4s blue, thin paper	175.00	15.00
15	A4	8s car rose	750.00	70.00
a.		8s rose, clear impression	1,900.	550.00
		Nos. 11-15 (5)	1,660.	345.00

See note on used value of #12 following #21.

For surcharges see Nos. 59-61, 149.

No. 15 was reprinted in 1914 and 1924, perf. 13½. Lowest valued reprint, $50.

Post Horn and Crown — A5

1872-75 **Wmk. 160**

No.	Design	Description	Unused	Used
16	A5	1s yel grn ('75)	13.50	*25.00*
a.		1s deep green ('73)	375.00	100.00
b.		"E.EN"	25.00	*75.00*
d.		Vert. pair, imperf between	—	
17	A5	2s ultra ('74)	20.00	*40.00*
a.		2s Prussian blue ('74)	*17,000.*	*5,000.*
b.		2s gray blue	15.00	*30.00*
18	A5	3s rose	85.00	35.00
a.		3s carmine	95.00	16.00
b.		3s carmine, *bluish* thin paper	450.00	50.00
19	A5	4s lilac, thin paper ('75)	19.00	*30.00*
a.		4s dark violet, *bluish,* thin paper	700.00	200.00
b.		4s brown violet, *bluish,* thin paper ('73)	700.00	250.00
c.		4s violet, *white,* thick paper ('73)	120.00	80.00
20	A5	6s org brn ('75)	675.00	90.00
21	A5	7s red brn ('73)	75.00	65.00
		Nos. 16-21 (6)	887.50	285.00

In this issue there are 12 types each of Nos. 16, 17, 18 and 19; 12 types of No. 20 and 20 types of No. 21. The differences are in the words of value.

Nos. 10, 12, 16, 17, 19 and 21 were re-released in 1888 and used until March 31, 1908. Used values of these stamps are for examples canceled in this later period, usually with a two-ring cancellation. Examples bearing clear dated cancellations before 1888 are worth considerably more, as follows: No. 10 $165, No. 12 $70, No. 16 $60, No. 17 $100, No. 17b $450, No. 19 $90, No. 21 $100.

No. 21 exists imperf. Value, unused without gum $800.

No. 19 comes on thin and thick paper.

For surcharges see Nos. 62-63.

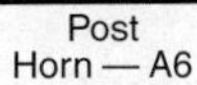

Post Horn — A6

King Oscar II — A7

"NORGE" in Sans-serif Capitals, Ring of Post Horn Shaded

1877-78

No.	Design	Description	Unused	Used
22	A6	1o drab	12.00	*14.00*
23	A6	3o orange	125.00	45.00
24	A6	5o ultra	40.00	18.00
a.		5o dull blue	800.00	125.00
b.		5o bright blue	300.00	70.00
c.		No period after "Postfrim"	57.50	20.00
d.		Retouched plate	200.00	25.00
e.		As "c," retouched plate	225.00	27.50
25	A6	10o rose	120.00	4.50
b.		Retouched plate	120.00	5.50
26	A6	12o lt green	150.00	30.00
27	A6	20o orange brn	450.00	20.00
28	A6	25o lilac	600.00	150.00
29	A6	35o bl grn ('78)	30.00	20.00
a.		Retouched plate	250.00	110.00
30	A6	50o maroon	65.00	12.50
31	A6	60o dk bl ('78)	70.00	12.50
32	A7	1k gray grn & grn ('78)	45.00	12.50
33	A7	1.50k ultra & bl ('78)	100.00	50.00
34	A7	2k rose & mar ('78)	55.00	25.00
		Nos. 22-34 (13)	1,862.	414.00

There are 6 types each of Nos. 22, 26 and 28 to 34; 12 types each of Nos. 23, 24, 25 and 27. The differences are in the numerals.

A 2nd plate of the 5o ultramarine has 100 types, the 10o, 200 types.

The retouch on 5o, 10o and 35o shows as a thin white line between crown and post horn.

Post Horn — A8

"NORGE" in Sans-serif Capitals, Ring of Horn Unshaded

1882-93 **Wmk. 160** ***Perf. 14½x13½***

No.	Design	Description	Unused	Used
35	A8	1o blk brn ('86)	25.00	*30.00*
a.		No period after "Postfrim"	60.00	60.00
b.		Small "N" in "NORGE"	60.00	60.00
36	A8	1o gray ('93)	15.00	15.00
37	A8	2o brown ('90)	8.00	*10.00*
38	A8	3o yellow ('89)	100.00	12.50
a.		3o orange ('83)	300.00	25.00
b.		Perf. 13½x12½ ('93)	12,000.	4,000.
39	A8	5o bl grn ('89)	95.00	4.00
a.		5o gray green ('86)	120.00	6.00
b.		5o emerald ('88)	300.00	12.50
c.		5o yellow green ('91)	100.00	4.50
d.		Perf. 13½x12½ ('93)	*5,000.*	*1,200.*
40	A8	10o rose	80.00	2.00
a.		10o rose red ('86)	80.00	2.00
b.		10o carmine ('91)	80.00	2.00
c.		As "b," imperf. ('91)	*3,000.*	*2,750.*
41	A8	12o green ('84)	1,800.	500.00
42	A8	12o org brn ('84)	50.00	35.00
a.		12o bister brown ('83)	100.00	70.00
43	A8	20o brown	200.00	25.00
44	A8	20o blue ('86)	125.00	3.50
a.		20o ultramarine ('83)	500.00	25.00
b.		No period after "Postfrim" ('85)	700.00	30.00
c.		As "a," imperf. ('90)	*2,500.*	*3,000.*
d.		20o Prussian blue	350.00	30.00
45	A8	25o dull vio ('84)	25.00	30.00

Dies vary from 20 to 21mm high. Numerous types exist due to different production methods, including separate handmade dies for value figures. Many shades exist.

No. 42 and 42a Surcharged in Black

1888 ***Perf. 14½x13½***

No.	Design	Description	Unused	Used
46	A8	2o on 12o org brn	3.50	*4.50*
a.		2o on 12o bister brown	7.00	5.50

Post Horn — A10

"NORGE" in Roman instead of Sans-serif capitals

Perf. 14½x13½

1893-1908 **Wmk. 160**

Size: 16x20mm

No.	Design	Description	Unused	Used
47	A10	1o gray ('99)	4.50	*5.00*
48	A10	2o pale brn ('99)	3.25	*3.00*
49	A10	3o orange yel	2.75	.40
50	A10	5o dp green ('98)	7.00	.30
b.		Booklet pane of 6	*800.00*	
51	A10	10o carmine ('98)	16.00	.30
b.		Booklet pane of 6	*1,100.*	
d.		10o rose ('94)	350.00	4.00
e.		Imperf		*4,000.*
52	A10	15o brown ('08)	65.00	16.00
53	A10	20o dp ultra	30.00	.40
b.		Booklet pane of 6		
54	A10	25o red vio ('01)	85.00	5.00
55	A10	30o sl gray ('07)	65.00	5.50
56	A10	35o dk bl grn ('98)	18.00	12.50
57	A10	50o maroon ('94)	75.00	3.00
58	A10	60o dk blue ('00)	85.00	16.00
		Nos. 47-58 (12)	456.50	67.40

Two dies exist of 3, 10 and 20o.

See Nos. 74-95, 162-166, 187-191, 193, 307-309, 325-326, 416-419, 606, 709-714, 960-968, 1141-1145.

For overprints and surcharge see Nos. 99, 207-211, 220-224, 226, 329.

Norway
and Scandinavia
• Free Catalog • Stamps
• Postal History • Literature
• Want Lists Filled • Albums
• New Issue Service
www.JaySmith.com

CALL TOLL FREE
1-800-447-8267
(U.S. and CANADA)
or 336-376-9991
FAX 336-376-6750

Jay Smith
P.O. Box 650-X952
Snow Camp, NC 27349
email:info-X952@JaySmith.com

The Scandinavia Specialist Since 1973

1893-98 Wmk. 160 *Perf. 13½x12½*

47a A10 1o gray ('95) 25.00 *45.00*
49a A10 3o orange ('95) 50.00 12.00
50a A10 5o green 35.00 1.75
51a A10 10o carmine ('96) 35.00 1.50
c. 10o rose ('95) 100.00 3.25
53a A10 20o dull ultra ('95) 110.00 7.50
54a A10 25o red violet ('98) 140.00 55.00
56a A10 35o dark blue green ('95) 100.00 30.00
57a A10 50o maroon ('97) 350.00 25.00
Nos. 47a-57a (8) 845.00 177.75

Two dies exist of each except 25 and 35o.

No. 12 Surcharged in Green, Blue or Carmine

1905 Unwmk. *Perf. 14½x13½*

59 A4 1k on 2s org (G) 57.50 50.00
60 A4 1.50k on 2s org (Bl) 100.00 85.00
61 A4 2k on 2s org (C) 110.00 100.00
Nos. 59-61 (3) 267.50 235.00

Used values are for stamps canceled after 1910. Stamps used before that sell for twice as much.

Nos. 19 and 21 Surcharged in Black

1906-08 Wmk. 160 *Perf. 14½x13½*

62 A5 15o on 4s lilac ('08) 8.50 8.50
a. 15o on 4s violet ('08) 20.00 17.50
63 A5 30o on 7s red brn 16.00 12.00
a. Inverted overprint *10,000.*

Used values are for stamps canceled after 1914. Stamps used before that sell for twice as much.

King Haakon VII — A11

Die A

Die B

Die C

Die A — Background of ruled lines. The coils at the sides are ornamented with fine cross-lines and small dots. Stamps 20¼mm high.

Die B — Background of ruled lines. The coils are ornamented with large white dots and dashes. Stamps 21¼mm high.

Die C — Solid background. The coils are without ornamental marks. Stamps 20¾mm high.

Die A

1907 Typo. *Perf. 14½x13½*

64 A11 1k yellow grn 70.00 40.00
65 A11 1.50k ultra 120.00 90.00
66 A11 2k rose 185.00 125.00
Nos. 64-66 (3) 375.00 255.00

Used values are for stamps postmarked after 1910. Stamps postmarked before that sell for twice as much. Stamps postmarked after 1914 sell for one-half the values listed. See note after No. 180.

1909-10 Die B

67 A11 1k green 225.00 130.00
68 A11 1.50k ultra 260.00 *375.00*
69 A11 2k rose 200.00 8.00
Nos. 67-69 (3) 685.00 *513.00*

Used values are for stamps canceled after 1914. Stamps used before that sell for twice as much.

1911-18 Die C

70 A11 1k light green .90 .25
a. 1k dark green 90.00 3.50
71 A11 1.50k ultra 3.50 1.00
72 A11 2k rose ('15) 4.50 1.50
73 A11 5k dk violet ('18) 6.00 6.00
Nos. 70-73 (4) 14.90 8.75
Set, never hinged 40.00

See note following No. 180.

Post Horn Type Redrawn

Original

Redrawn

In the redrawn stamps the white ring of the post horn is continuous instead of being broken by a spot of color below the crown. On the 3 and 30 ore the top of the figure "3" in the oval band is rounded instead of flattened.

1910-29 *Perf. 14½x13½*

74 A10 1o pale olive .40 *.75*
75 A10 2o pale brown .40 *.50*
76 A10 3o orange .40 *.50*
77 A10 5o green 4.50 .25
a. Booklet pane of 6 175.00
Complete booklet, 4 #77a 3,200.
78 A10 5o magenta ('22) .80 .25
79 A10 7o green ('29) .80 .25
80 A10 10o car rose 6.50 .25
a. Booklet pane of 6 100.00
Complete booklet, 2 #80a 500.00
81 A10 10o green ('22) 8.00 .50
82 A10 12o purple ('17) 1.00 1.50
83 A10 15o brown 8.00 .50
a. Booklet pane of 6 25.00
Complete booklet, 2 #83a 90.00
84 A10 15o indigo ('20) 9.00 .25
85 A10 20o deep ultra 9.00 .25
a. Booklet pane of 6 400.00
Complete booklet, 2 #85a *4,000.*
86 A10 20o ol grn ('21) 11.00 .30
87 A10 25o red lilac 55.00 .50
88 A10 25o car rose ('22) 9.00 .80
89 A10 30o slate gray 12.00 .50
90 A10 30o lt blue ('27) 10.00 8.00
91 A10 35o dk olive ('20) 15.00 .50
92 A10 40o ol grn ('17) 6.00 .50
93 A10 40o dp ultra ('22) 30.00 .30
94 A10 50o claret 25.00 .50
95 A10 60o deep blue 30.00 .50
Nos. 74-95 (22) 251.80 18.15
Set, never hinged 1,500.

Constitutional Assembly of 1814 — A12

1914, May 10 Engr. *Perf. 13½*

96 A12 5o green 1.25 .75
97 A12 10o car rose 3.00 .75
98 A12 20o deep blue 10.00 12.00
Nos. 96-98 (3) 14.25 13.50
Set, never hinged 80.00

Norway's Constitution of May 17, 1814.

No. 87 Surcharged

1922, Mar. 1 *Perf. 14½x13½*

99 A10 5o on 25o red lilac 1.00 *1.50*
Never hinged 2.00

Lion Rampant — A13

"NORGE" in Roman capitals, Line below "Ore"

1922-24 Typo. *Perf. 14½x13½*

100 A13 10o dp grn ('24) 10.00 .60
101 A13 20o dp vio 16.00 .25
102 A13 25o scarlet ('24) 27.50 .75
103 A13 45o blue ('24) 2.00 1.50
Nos. 100-103 (4) 55.50 3.10
Set, never hinged 250.00

For surcharge see No. 129.

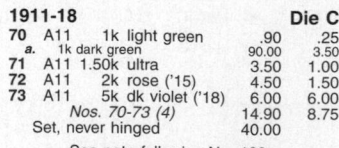

Polar Bear and Airplane — A14

1925, Apr. 1

104 A14 2o yellow brn 2.25 *3.50*
105 A14 3o orange 4.50 *6.00*
106 A14 5o magenta 12.00 *22.50*
107 A14 10o yellow grn 16.00 *35.00*
108 A14 15o dark blue 15.00 *32.50*
109 A14 20o plum 25.00 *40.00*
110 A14 25o scarlet 6.00 *8.00*
Nos. 104-110 (7) 80.75 147.50
Set, never hinged 180.00

Issued to help finance Roald Amundsen's attempted flight to the North Pole.

A15

1925, Aug. 19

111 A15 10o yellow green 7.00 *15.00*
112 A15 15o indigo 5.00 *9.00*
113 A15 20o plum 7.00 *2.50*
114 A15 45o dark blue 6.00 *9.00*
Nos. 111-114 (4) 25.00 35.50
Set, never hinged 100.00

Annexation of Spitsbergen (Svalbard). For surcharge see No. 130.

A16

"NORGE" in Sans-serif Capitals, No Line below "Ore"

1926-34 Wmk. 160

Size: 16x19½mm

115 A16 10o yel grn .70 .25
116 A16 14o dp org ('29) 2.25 3.00
117 A16 15o olive gray .85 .25
118 A16 20o plum 30.00 .40
119 A16 20o scar ('27) 1.00 .25
a. Booklet pane of 6 80.00
Complete booklet, 2 #119a 375.00
120 A16 25o red 12.00 3.00
121 A16 25o org brn ('27) 1.25 .25
122 A16 30o dull bl ('28) 1.25 .25
123 A16 35o ol brn ('27) 75.00 .25
124 A16 35o red vio ('34) 2.00 .25
125 A16 40o dull blue 5.00 1.50
126 A16 40o slate ('27) 2.00 .25
127 A16 50o claret ('27) 2.00 .25
128 A16 60o Prus bl ('27) 2.00 .25
Nos. 115-128 (14) 137.30 10.40
Set, never hinged 675.00

See Nos. 167-176, 192, 194-202A. For overprints and surcharges see Nos. 131, 212-219, 225, 227-234, 302-303.

Nos. 103 and 114 Surcharged

1927, June 13

129 A13 30o on 45o blue 13.00 3.00
130 A15 30o on 45o dk blue 7.00 10.00
Set, never hinged 60.00

20
NORGE

No. 120 Surcharged

1928

131 A16 20o on 25o red 2.50 2.50
Never hinged 15.00

See Nos. 302-303.

Henrik Ibsen — A17

1928, Mar. 20 Litho.

132 A17 10o yellow grn 10.00 5.00
133 A17 15o chnt brown 4.00 4.50
134 A17 20o carmine 3.50 .90
135 A17 30o dp ultra 7.00 5.00
Nos. 132-135 (4) 24.50 15.40
Set, never hinged 85.00

Ibsen (1828-1906), dramatist.

Postage Due Stamps of 1889-1923 Overprinted

a

b

1929, Jan.

136 D1 (a) 1o gray .90 *1.75*
137 D1 (a) 4o lilac rose .60 .60
138 D1 (a) 10o green 2.50 *5.00*
139 D1 (b) 15o brown 3.50 *8.00*
140 D1 (b) 20o dull vio 1.25 1.00
141 D1 (b) 40o deep ultra 2.00 1.00
142 D1 (b) 50o maroon 10.00 10.00
143 D1 (a) 100o orange yel 4.25 *4.25*
144 D1 (b) 200o dk violet 5.50 5.00
Nos. 136-144 (9) 30.50 36.60
Set, never hinged 75.00

Niels Henrik Abel — A18

1929, Apr. 6 Litho. *Perf. 14½x13½*

145 A18 10o green 3.50 1.00
146 A18 15o red brown 3.50 2.50
147 A18 20o rose red 1.25 .50
148 A18 30o deep ultra 3.25 3.00
Nos. 145-148 (4) 11.50 7.00
Set, never hinged 50.00

Abel (1802-1829), mathematician.

14 ØRE 14

No. 12 Surcharged

Perf. 14½x13½

1929, July 1 Unwmk.

149 A4 14o on 2s orange 3.50 *8.00*
Never hinged 7.00

Saint Olaf A19

Trondheim Cathedral A20

Death of Olaf in Battle of Stiklestad A21

Typo.; Litho. (15o)
Perf. 14½x13½

1930, Apr. 1 **Wmk. 160**

150 A19 10o yellow grn 14.00 .70
151 A20 15o brn & blk 1.75 1.00
152 A19 20o scarlet 1.25 .50

Engr.
Perf. 13½

153 A21 30o deep blue 4.50 5.00
Nos. 150-153 (4) 21.50 7.20
Set, never hinged 90.00

King Olaf Haraldsson (995-1030), patron saint of Norway.

Björnson — A22

1932, Dec. 8 ***Perf. 14½x13½***

154 A22 10o yellow grn 10.00 .75
155 A22 15o black brn 1.50 1.50
156 A22 20o rose red 1.00 .50
157 A22 30o ultra 3.50 *4.50*
Nos. 154-157 (4) 16.00 7.25
Set, never hinged 60.00

Björnstjerne Björnson (1832-1910), novelist, poet and dramatist.

Holberg — A23

1934, Nov. 23

158 A23 10o yellow grn 4.50 .90
159 A23 15o brown 1.00 1.25
160 A23 20o rose red 18.00 .50
161 A23 30o ultra 4.00 4.50
Nos. 158-161 (4) 27.50 7.15
Set, never hinged 90.00

Ludvig Holberg (1684-1754), Danish man of letters.

Types of 1893-1900, 1926-34
Second Redrawing
Perf. 13x13½

1937 **Wmk. 160** **Photo.**
Size: 17x21mm

162 A10 1o olive .70 2.00
163 A10 2o yellow brn .70 1.75
164 A10 3o deep orange 1.75 *4.00*
165 A10 5o rose lilac .55 .40
166 A10 7o brt green .70 .40
167 A16 10o brt green .45 .30
Complete booklet, 2 panes of 6 #167 675.00
168 A16 14o dp orange 3.00 6.00
169 A16 15o olive bis 1.75 .25
170 A16 20o scarlet 1.25 .25
Complete booklet, 2 panes of 6 #170 1,250.
Complete booklet, panes of 6 ea of #165, 167, 170 500.00
171 A16 25o dk org brn 6.00 .50
172 A16 30o ultra 3.50 .50
173 A16 35o brt vio 2.50 .25
174 A16 40o dk slate grn 3.50 .25
175 A16 50o deep claret 3.50 .75
176 A16 60o Prussian bl 2.50 .25
Nos. 162-176 (15) 32.35 17.85
Set, never hinged 125.00

Nos. 162 to 166 have a solid background inside oval. Nos. 74, 75, 76, 78, 79 have background of vertical lines.

King Haakon VII — A24

1937-38

177 A24 1k dark green .25 .25
178 A24 1.50k sapphire ('38) 1.00 2.00
179 A24 2k rose red ('38) 1.00 1.25
180 A24 5k dl vio ('38) 9.00 *10.00*
Nos. 177-180 (4) 11.25 13.50
Set, never hinged 25.00

Nos. 64-66, 67-69, 70-73, 177-180 and B11-B14 were demonitized and banned on Sept. 30, 1940. Nos. 267, B19, B32-B34 and B38-B41 were demonetized on May 15, 1945. All of these stamps became valid again Sept. 1, 1981. Nos. 64-66, 67-69 and 70-73 rarely were used after 1981, and values represent stamps used in the earlier period. Values for Nos. B11-B14 used are for stamps used in the earlier period, and used examples in the later period are worth the same as mint stamps. Values for the other stamps used are for examples used in the later period, and stamps with dated cancellations prior to May 15, 1945 sell for more. False cancellations exist.

Reindeer — A25 Borgund Church — A26

Jolster in Sunnfiord A27

Perf. 13x13½, 13½x13

1938, Apr. 20 **Wmk. 160**

181 A25 15o olive brn 1.25 1.25
182 A26 20o copper red 4.00 .55
183 A27 30o brt ultra 4.00 2.50
Nos. 181-183 (3) 9.25 4.30
Set, never hinged 40.00

1939, Jan. 16 **Unwmk.**

184 A25 15o olive brn .50 .75
185 A26 20o copper red .50 .25
186 A27 30o brt ultra .50 .50
Nos. 184-186 (3) 1.50 1.50
Set, never hinged 3.00

Types of 1937
Perf. 13x13½

1940-49 **Unwmk.** **Photo.**
Size: 17x21mm

187 A10 1o olive grn ('41) .25 .25
188 A10 2o yel brn ('41) .25 .25
189 A10 3o dp org ('41) .25 .25
190 A10 5o rose lilac ('41) .35 .25
191 A10 7o brt green ('41) .40 .25
192 A16 10o brt green .35 .25
Complete booklet, 2 panes of 6 #192 50.00
193 A10 12o brt vio .80 2.00
194 A16 14o dp org ('41) 1.50 4.00
195 A16 15o olive bister .50 .25
196 A16 20o red .45 .25
Complete booklet, 2 panes of 6 #196 60.00
Complete booklet, pane of 6 ea of #190, 192, 196 200.00
Complete booklet, pane of 10 ea of #190, 192, 196 125.00
197 A16 25o dk org brn 1.25 .25
197A A16 25o scarlet ('46) .50 .25
Complete booklet, pane of 10 ea of #190, 192, 197A 110.00
Complete booklet, pane of 10 ea of #192, 195, 197A 100.00
198 A16 30o brt ultra ('41) 1.75 .40
198A A16 30o gray ('49) 6.00 .25
199 A16 35o brt vio ('41) 1.75 .25
200 A16 40o dk sl grn ('41) 1.00 .25
200A A16 40o dp ultra ('46) 3.75 .40
201 A16 50o dp claret ('41) 1.00 .25
201A A16 55o dp org ('46) 15.00 .40
202 A16 60o Prus bl ('41) 1.25 .25
202A A16 80o dk org brn ('46) 14.00 .40
Nos. 187-202A (21) 52.35 11.35
Set, never hinged 150.00

Lion Rampant — A28

1940 **Unwmk.** **Photo.** ***Perf. 13x13½***

203 A28 1k brt green 1.00 .25
204 A28 1½k deep blue 1.75 .30
205 A28 2k bright red 2.50 1.25
206 A28 5k dull purple 7.00 *7.00*
Nos. 203-206 (4) 12.25 8.80
Set, never hinged 40.00

For overprints see Nos. 235-238.

Stamps of 1937-41, Types A10, A16, A28, Overprinted in Black

1941 **Wmk. 160** ***Perf. 13x13½***

207 A10 1o olive .50 *9.00*
208 A10 2o yellow brn .50 *12.00*
209 A10 3o orange 2.50 *25.00*
210 A10 5o rose lilac .50 *2.50*
211 A10 7o brt green .50 *6.00*
212 A16 10o brt green 7.50 *40.00*
213 A16 14o dp orange 1.00 *22.50*
214 A16 15o olive bis .30 *1.25*
215 A16 30o ultra 3.00 *5.00*
216 A16 35o brt violet 1.00 *1.00*
217 A16 40o dk slate grn 7.50 *12.50*
218 A16 50o dp claret 275.00 *750.00*
Never hinged 600.00
219 A16 60o Prus blue 1.00 *2.50*
Nos. 207-217,219 (12) 25.80 *139.25*
Set, never hinged 55.00

The "V" overprint exists on Nos. 170-171, but these were not regularly issued.

Unwmk.

220 A10 1o olive .35 *6.00*
221 A10 2o yellow brn .35 *10.00*
222 A10 3o deep orange .35 *7.50*
223 A10 5o rose lilac .35 .50
224 A10 7o brt green 1.25 *10.00*
225 A16 10o brt green .35 .25
226 A10 12o brt violet 1.10 *20.00*
227 A16 15o olive bis 1.90 *25.00*
228 A16 20o red .35 .25
a. Inverted overprint 1,250. 1,750.
229 A16 25o dk orange brn .50 .40
230 A16 30o brt ultra 1.50 *5.00*
231 A16 35o brt violet 1.25 .70
232 A16 40o dk slate grn .70 .90
233 A16 50o dp claret 1.00 *3.50*
234 A16 60o Prus blue 3.00 2.00
235 A28 1k brt green 1.25 .75
236 A28 1½k dp blue 3.75 *18.00*
237 A28 2k bright red 12.00 *70.00*
238 A28 5k dull purple 22.50 *150.00*

Lion Rampant with "V" — A29

Coil Stamp

239 A29 10o brt green 1.25 *15.00*
Nos. 220-239 (20) 55.05 *345.75*
Set, never hinged 100.00

No. 239 has a white "V" incorporated into design, rather than an overprint. Nos. 207-239 were demonitized March 29, 1944. Used values are for stamps with postmarks dated prior to March 29, 1944. Forged cancellations exist.

Dream of Queen Ragnhild A30

Snorri Sturluson A32

Einar Tambarskjelve in Fight at Svolder — A31

Designs: 30o, King Olaf sailing in wedding procession to Landmerket. 50o, Syipdag's sons and followers going to Hall of Seven Kings. 60o, Before Battle of Stiklestad.

1941 ***Perf. 13½x13, 13x13½***

240 A30 10o bright green .35 .50
241 A31 15o olive brown .40 .75
242 A32 20o dark red .35 .25
243 A31 30o blue 1.75 *2.50*
244 A31 50o dull violet 1.10 *2.00*
245 A31 60o Prus blue 2.00 2.25
Nos. 240-245 (6) 5.95 8.25
Set, never hinged 20.00

700th anniversary of the death of Snorri Sturluson, writer and historian

University of Oslo — A36

1941, Sept. 2 ***Perf. 13x13½***

246 A36 1k dk olive grn 50.00 80.00
Never hinged 80.00

Centenary of cornerstone laying of University of Oslo building.

Richard (Rikard) Nordraak (1842-66), Composer — A37

"Broad Sails Go over the North Sea" A38

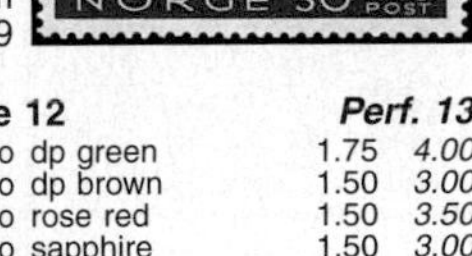

View of Coast and Lines of National Anthem A39

1942, June 12 ***Perf. 13***

247 A37 10o dp green 1.75 *4.00*
248 A38 15o dp brown 1.50 *3.00*
249 A37 20o rose red 1.50 *3.50*
250 A39 30o sapphire 1.50 *3.00*
Nos. 247-250 (4) 6.25 13.50
Set, never hinged 18.00

Johan Herman Wessel (1742-1785), Author — A40

1942, Oct. 6

251 A40 15o dull brown .30 .50
252 A40 20o henna .30 .50
Set, never hinged 1.00

Designs of 1942 and 1855 Stamps of Norway A41

1942, Oct. 12

253 A41 20o henna .25 1.75
254 A41 30o sapphire .35 2.75
Set, never hinged 1.25

European Postal Congress at Vienna, October, 1942.

Nos. 253-254, B24-B27, B31 and B35-B37 were demonitized May 15, 1945. Used values are for stamps with postmarks dated prior to May 15, 1945. Forged cancellations exist.

Edvard Grieg (1843-1907), Composer — A42

1943, June 15

No.	Type	Description	Unused	Used
255	A42	10o deep green	.25	*.50*
256	A42	20o henna	.25	*.50*
257	A42	40o grnsh black	.25	*.50*
258	A42	60o dk grnsh blue	.25	*.50*
		Nos. 255-258 (4)	1.00	2.00
		Set, never hinged	2.50	

Destroyer Sleipner — A43

5o, 10o, "Sleipner." 7o, 30o, Convoy under midnight sun. 15o, Plane and pilot. 20o, "We will win." 40o, Ski troops. 60o, King Haakon VII.

1943-45 Unwmk. Engr. *Perf. 12½*

No.	Type	Description	Unused	Used
259	A43	5o rose vio ('45)	.25	.25
260	A43	7o grnsh blk ('45)	.25	.75
261	A43	10o dk blue grn	.25	.25
262	A43	15o dk olive grn	.60	*2.00*
263	A43	20o rose red	.25	.25
264	A43	30o dp ultra	.65	*2.00*
265	A43	40o olive black	1.00	*1.75*
266	A43	60o dark blue	1.00	*1.75*
		Nos. 259-266 (8)	4.25	*9.00*
		Set, never hinged	10.00	

Nos. 261-266 were used for correspondence carried on Norwegian ships until after the liberation of Norway, when they became regular postage stamps.

Nos. 261-266 exist with overprint "London 17-5-43" and serial number. Value for set, unused, $850; canceled $1,500.

Gran's Plane and Map of His North Sea Flight Route A49

1944, July 30 *Perf. 13*

No.	Type	Description	Unused	Used
267	A49	40o dk grnsh blue	.40	.40
		Never hinged	.60	

20th anniv. of the 1st flight over the North Sea, made by Tryggve Gran on July 30, 1914.

Value for used stamp postmarked before May 15, 1945, $6. See note following No. 180.

New National Arms of 1943 — A50

1945, Feb. 15 Typo. *Perf. 13*

No.	Type	Description	Unused	Used
268	A50	1½k dark blue	1.25	.60
		Never hinged	4.00	

Henrik Wergeland — A51

1945, July 12 Photo.

No.	Type	Description	Unused	Used
269	A51	10o dk olive green	.30	*.50*
270	A51	15o dark brown	.85	1.25
271	A51	20o dark red	.25	.30
		Nos. 269-271 (3)	1.40	2.05
		Set, never hinged	2.00	

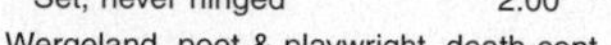

Wergeland, poet & playwright, death cent.

Lion Rampant — A52

1945, Dec. 19

No.	Type	Description	Unused	Used
272	A52	10o dk olive green	.50	.50
273	A52	20o red	.50	.50
		Set, never hinged	3.50	

Norwegian Folklore Museum, 50th anniv.

Pilot and Mechanic — A53

1946, Mar. 22 Engr. *Perf. 12*

No.	Type	Description	Unused	Used
274	A53	15o brown rose	.40	*2.00*
		Never hinged	1.00	

Issued in honor of Little Norway, training center in Canada for Norwegian pilots.

Catalogue values for unused stamps in this section, from this point to the end of the section, are for Never Hinged items.

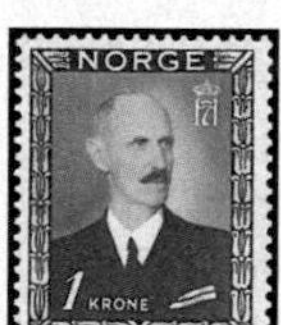

King Haakon VII — A54

1946, June 7 Photo. *Perf. 13*

No.	Type	Description	Unused	Used
275	A54	1k bright green	3.00	.25
276	A54	1½k Prus blue	7.50	.25
277	A54	2k henna brown	60.00	.25
278	A54	5k violet	50.00	.50
		Nos. 275-278 (4)	120.50	1.25

Hannibal Sehested — A55

Designs: 10o, Letter carrier, 1700. 15o, Adm. Peter W. Tordenskjold. 25o, Christian Magnus Falsen. 30o, Cleng Peerson and "Restaurationen." 40o, Post ship "Constitution." 45o, First Norwegian locomotive. 50o, Sven Foyn and whaler. 55o, Fridtjof Nansen and Roald Amundsen. 60o, Coronation of King Haakon VII and Queen Maud, 1906. 80o, Return of King Haakon, June 7, 1945.

1947, Apr. 15 Photo. *Perf. 13*

No.	Type	Description	Unused	Used
279	A55	5o red lilac	.50	.25
280	A55	10o green	.80	.25
281	A55	15o brown	1.50	.25
282	A55	25o orange red	1.25	.25
283	A55	30o gray	2.50	.25
284	A55	40o blue	8.00	.25
285	A55	45o violet	3.00	.75
286	A55	50o orange brn	5.50	.35
287	A55	55o orange	8.00	.35
288	A55	60o slate gray	8.00	2.00
289	A55	80o dk brown	8.00	.35
		Nos. 279-289 (11)	47.05	5.30

Establishment of the Norwegian Post Office, 300th anniv.

Petter Dass — A66

1947, July 1 Unwmk.

No.	Type	Description	Unused	Used
290	A66	25o bright red	2.00	1.75

300th birth anniv. of Petter Dass, poet.

King Haakon VII — A67

1947, Aug. 2

No.	Type	Description	Unused	Used
291	A67	25o orange red	1.00	1.00

75th birthday of King Haakon.

Axel Heiberg — A68

1948, June 15

No.	Type	Description	Unused	Used
292	A68	25o deep carmine	1.25	.60
293	A68	80o dp red brown	3.50	.30

50th anniv. of the Norwegian Society of Forestry; birth cent. of Axel Heiberg, its founder.

Alexander L. Kielland — A69

1949, May 9

No.	Type	Description	Unused	Used
295	A69	25o rose brown	2.00	.50
296	A69	40o greenish blue	2.50	.75
297	A69	80o orange brown	3.00	1.00
		Nos. 295-297 (3)	7.50	2.25

Birth cent. of Alexander L. Kielland, author.

Symbols of UPU Members A70

Stylized Pigeons and Globe A71

Symbolical of the UPU A72

1949, Oct. 8 *Perf. 13*

No.	Type	Description	Unused	Used
299	A70	10o dk green & blk	.75	.60
300	A71	25o scarlet	.75	.50
301	A72	40o dull blue	.90	.75
		Nos. 299-301 (3)	2.40	1.85

75th anniv. of the formation of the UPU.

Nos. 196 and 200A Surcharged with New Value and Bar in Black

1949 *Perf. 13x13½*

No.	Type	Description	Unused	Used
302	A16	25o on 20o red	.75	.25
303	A16	45o on 40o dp ultra	3.75	.65

King Harald Haardraade and Oslo City Hall — A73

1950, May 15 Photo. *Perf. 13*

No.	Type	Description	Unused	Used
304	A73	15o green	.90	1.00
305	A73	25o red	1.00	.50
306	A73	45o ultramarine	1.00	1.00
		Nos. 304-306 (3)	2.90	2.50

900th anniversary of Oslo.

Redrawn Post Horn Type of 1937

1950-51 Photo. *Perf. 13x13½*

Size: 17x21mm

No.	Type	Description	Unused	Used
307	A10	10o grnsh gray	1.00	.25
		Complete booklet, pane of 10 #307	250.00	
308	A10	15o dark green	2.50	.50
309	A10	20o chnt brn ('51)	5.00	3.00
		Nos. 307-309 (3)	8.50	3.75

King Haakon VII — A74

1950-51 Photo. *Perf. 13x13½*

No.	Type	Description	Unused	Used
310	A74	25o dk red ('50)	1.00	.25
		Complete booklet, pane of 10 ea of #307, 308, 310	85.00	
311	A74	30o gray	10.00	.75
312	A74	35o red brn	20.00	.35
313	A74	45o brt blue	2.00	3.00
314	A74	50o olive brn	6.00	.25
315	A74	55o orange	2.50	1.50
316	A74	60o gray blue	18.00	.25
317	A74	80o chnt brn	4.00	.40
		Nos. 310-317 (8)	63.50	6.75

See Nos. 322-324, 345-352. For surcharge see No. 321.

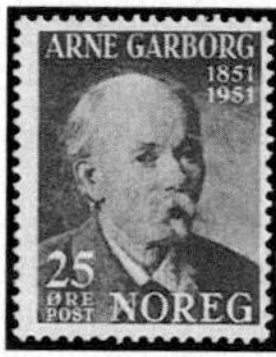

Arne Garborg — A75

1951, Jan. 25 *Perf. 13*

No.	Type	Description	Unused	Used
318	A75	25o red	1.00	.50
319	A75	45o dull blue	3.75	4.00
320	A75	80o brown	3.75	2.00
		Nos. 318-320 (3)	8.50	6.50

Birth cent. of Arne Garborg, poet.

No. 310 Surcharged with New Value in Black

1951 *Perf. 13x13½*

No.	Type	Description	Unused	Used
321	A74	30o on 25o dk red	1.00	.30

Haakon Type of 1950-51

1951-52 Photo.

No.	Type	Description	Unused	Used
322	A74	25o gray	25.00	.25
323	A74	30o dk red ('52)	.90	.25
		Complete booklet, pane of 10 ea of #307, 308, 323	225.00	
		Complete booklet, pane of 10 ea of #307, 325, 323	110.00	
324	A74	55o blue ('52)	2.50	.50
		Nos. 322-324 (3)	28.40	1.00

Redrawn Post Horn Type of 1937

1952, June 3 *Perf. 13x13½*

No.	Type	Description	Unused	Used
325	A10	15o org brn	.70	.25
326	A10	20o green	.70	.25

King Haakon VII — A76

1952, Aug. 3 Unwmk. *Perf. 13*
327 A76 30o red .50 .50
328 A76 55o deep blue 1.50 1.50

80th birthday of King Haakon VII.

No. 308 Surcharged with New Value

1952, Nov. 18 *Perf. 13x13½*
329 A10 20o on 15o dk grn .60 .25

Medieval Sculpture, Nidaros Cathedral — A77

1953, July 15 *Perf. 13*
330 A77 30o henna brn 1.75 .75

800th anniv. of the creation of the Norwegian Archbishopric of Nidaros.

Train of 1854 and Horse-drawn Sled — A78

Designs: 30o, Diesel train. 55o, Engineer.

1954, Apr. 30 Photo.
331 A78 20o green 1.25 .60
332 A78 30o red 1.50 .40
333 A78 55o ultra 2.00 1.50
Nos. 331-333 (3) 4.75 2.50

Inauguration of the first Norwegian railway, cent.

Carsten T. Nielsen — A79

Designs: 30o, Government radio towers. 55o, Lineman and telegraph poles in snow.

1954, Dec. 10
334 A79 20o ol grn & blk .60 .60
335 A79 30o brt red .60 .40
336 A79 55o blue 1.50 1.25
Nos. 334-336 (3) 2.70 2.25

Centenary (in 1955) of the inauguration of the first Norwegian public telegraph line.

Norway No. 1 — A80

Stamp Reproductions: 30o, Post horn type A5. 55o, Lion type A13.

1955, Jan. 3 *Perf. 13*
337 A80 20o dp grn & gray bl .45 .45
338 A80 30o red & carmine .40 .40
339 A80 55o gray bl & dp bl .95 .50
Nos. 337-339 (3) 1.80 1.35

Centenary of Norway's first postage stamp.

Nos. 337-339 Overprinted in Black

1955, June 4
340 A80 20o dp grn & gray bl 20.00 20.00
341 A80 30o red & carmine 20.00 20.00
342 A80 55o gray bl & dp bl 20.00 20.00
Nos. 340-342 (3) 60.00 60.00

Norway Philatelic Exhibition, Oslo, 1955. Sold at exhibition post office for face value plus 1kr admission fee.

King Haakon VII and Queen Maud in Coronation Robes — A81

1955, Nov. 25 Photo. *Perf. 13*
343 A81 30o rose red .40 .40
344 A81 55o ultra .75 .75

Haakon's 50th anniv. as King of Norway.

Haakon Type of 1950-51

1955-57 Unwmk. *Perf. 13x13½*
345 A74 25o dk grn ('56) 1.50 .25
346 A74 35o brn red ('56) 6.00 .25
Complete booklet, pane of 10 ea of #307, 325, 346 100.00
347 A74 40o pale pur 2.25 .25
Complete booklet, pane of 10 ea of #307, 325, 347 80.00
348 A74 50o bister ('57) 6.00 .25
349 A74 65o ultra ('56) 1.50 .40
350 A74 70o brn ol ('56) 25.00 .25
351 A74 75o mar ('57) 3.00 .25
352 A74 90o dp org 2.00 .25
Nos. 345-352 (8) 47.25 2.15

Northern Countries Issue

Whooper Swans — A81a

1956, Oct. 30 Engr. *Perf. 12½*
353 A81a 35o rose red .95 .60
354 A81a 65o ultra .95 .85

Close bonds connecting the northern countries: Denmark, Finland, Iceland, Norway and Sweden.

Jan Mayen Island A82

Map of Spitsbergen — A83

Design: 65o, Map of South Pole with Queen Maud Land.

Perf. 12½x13, 13x12½

1957, July 1 Photo. Unwmk.
355 A82 25o slate green .75 .60
356 A83 35o dk red & gray 1.00 .50
357 A83 65o dk grn & bl 1.00 .70
Nos. 355-357 (3) 2.75 1.80

Intl. Geophysical Year, 1957-58.

King Haakon VII — A84

1957, Aug. 3 *Perf. 13*
358 A84 35o dark red .80 .50
359 A84 65o ultra 1.40 1.25

85th birthday of King Haakon VII.

King Olav V — A85

1958-60 Photo. *Perf. 13x13½*
360 A85 25o emerald 1.50 .25
Complete booklet, pane of 4 of #360 150.00
361 A85 30o purple ('59) 2.50 .25
361A A85 35o brown car ('60) 1.25 .25
362 A85 40o dark red 1.25 .25
Complete booklet, pane of 10 of ea of #307, 325, 362 115.00
363 A85 45o scarlet 1.90 .25
Complete booklet, pane of 10 of #363 75.00
Complete booklet, pane of 10 ea of #307, 325, 363 100.00
364 A85 50o bister ('59) 8.50 .25
365 A85 55o dk gray ('59) 2.25 1.00
366 A85 65o blue 3.50 .50
367 A85 80o org brn ('60) 14.00 1.00
368 A85 85o olive brn ('59) 2.50 .25
369 A85 90o orange ('59) 2.00 .25
Nos. 360-369 (11) 41.15 4.50

See Nos. 408-412.

King Olav V — A86

1959, Jan. 12
370 A86 1k green 1.50 .25
371 A86 1.50k dark blue 4.50 .25
372 A86 2k crimson 4.50 .25
373 A86 5k lilac 70.00 .25
374 A86 10k dp orange 10.00 .25
Nos. 370-374 (5) 90.50 1.25

See Phosphorescence note following No. 430.

Asbjörn Kloster — A87

1959, Feb. 2
375 A87 45o violet brown .70 .40

Centenary of the founding of the Norwegian Temperance Movement; Asbjörn Kloster, its founder.

Agricultural Society Medal — A88

1959, May 26
376 A88 45o red & ocher .80 .75
377 A88 90o blue & gray 2.50 2.50

150th anniversary of the Royal Agricultural Society of Norway.

Sower — A89

Design: 90o, Grain, vert.

1959, Oct. 1 Photo. *Perf. 13*
378 A89 45o ocher & blk 1.00 .75
379 A89 90o blue & blk 2.00 1.50

Agricultural College of Norway, cent.

Society Seal — A90

1960, Feb. 26 Unwmk.
380 A90 45o carmine .75 .50
381 A90 90o dark blue 2.50 2.00

Bicentenary of the Royal Norwegian Society of Sciences, Trondheim.

Viking Ship A91

25o, Caravel & fish. 45o, Sailing ship & nautical knot. 55o, Freighter & oil derricks. 90o, Passenger ship & Statue of Liberty.

1960, Aug. 27 *Perf. 12½x13*
382 A91 20o gray & blk 2.50 1.75
383 A91 25o yel grn & blk 1.50 1.50
384 A91 45o ver & blk 1.50 .40
385 A91 55o ocher & blk 4.00 3.50
386 A91 90o Prus bl & blk 5.00 2.50
Nos. 382-386 (5) 14.50 9.65

Norwegian shipping industry.

Common Design Types pictured following the introduction.

Europa Issue
Common Design Type

1960, Sept. 19 *Perf. 13*
Size: 27x21mm
387 CD3 90o blue 1.25 1.25

DC-8 Airliner — A91a

1961, Feb. 24 Photo. *Perf. 13*
388 A91a 90o dark blue 1.00 1.00

Scandinavian Airlines System, SAS, 10th anniv.

Javelin Thrower — A92

1961, Mar. 15
389 A92 20o shown 1.25 1.00
390 A92 25o Skater 1.25 1.00
391 A92 45o Ski jumper 1.00 .50
392 A92 90o Sailboat 1.75 1.75
Nos. 389-392 (4) 5.25 4.25

Norwegian Sports Federation centenary.

Haakonshallen — A93

1961, May 25 *Perf. 12½x13*
393 A93 45o maroon & gray 1.00 .50
394 A93 1k gray green & gray 1.50 .50

700th anniv. of Haakonshallen, castle in Bergen.

Domus Media, Oslo University A94

1961, Sept. 2 Photo. *Perf. 12½x13*

395 A94 45o dark red 1.00 .50
396 A94 1.50k Prus blue 1.50 .50

150th anniversary of Oslo University.

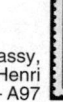

Fridtjof Nansen — A95

1961, Oct. 10 *Perf. 13*

397 A95 45o orange red & gray 1.25 .40
398 A95 90o chlky blue & gray 2.00 1.75

Birth centenary of Fridtjof Nansen, explorer.

Roald Amundsen A96

Design: 90o, Explorers and tent at Pole.

1961, Nov. 10 Unwmk. *Perf. 13*

399 A96 45o dl red brn & gray 1.50 .75
400 A96 90o dk & lt blue 2.50 2.00

50th anniversary of Roald Amundsen's arrival at the South Pole.

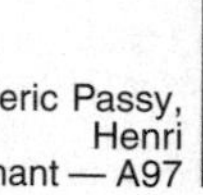

Frederic Passy, Henri Dunant — A97

1961, Dec. 9 Photo.

401 A97 45o henna brown .50 .50
402 A97 1k yellow green 1.75 .50

Winners of the first Nobel Peace prize. Frederic Passy, a founder of the Interparliamentary Union, and Henri Dunant, founder of the International Red Cross.

Vilhelm Bjerknes — A98

1962, Mar. 14 *Perf. 13*

403 A98 45o dk red & gray .50 .40
404 A98 1.50k dk blue & gray 1.25 .50

Vilhelm Bjerknes (1862-1951), physicist, mathematician, meteorologist, etc.

German Rumpler Taube over Oslo Fjord A99

1962, June 1 Photo.

405 A99 1.50k dl bl & blk 4.50 .85

50th anniversary of Norwegian aviation.

Fir Branch and Cone — A100

1962, June 15

406 A100 45o salmon & blk .75 .75
407 A100 1k pale grn & blk 8.00 .50

Olav Type of 1958-60

1962 Unwmk. *Perf. 13x13½*

408 A85 25o slate grn 1.75 .25
Complete booklet, pane of 4 of #408 150.00
Complete booklet, pane of 10 ea of #190, 307, 408 40.00
409 A85 35o emerald 7.50 .25
410 A85 40o gray 5.00 2.50
411 A85 50o scarlet 11.50 .25
Complete booklet, pane of 10 of #411 200.00
412 A85 60o violet 8.00 .75
Nos. 408-412 (5) 33.75 4.00

Europa Issue
Common Design Type

1962, Sept. 17 Photo. *Perf. 13*
Size: 37x21mm

414 CD5 50o dp rose & maroon .75 .50
415 CD5 90o blue & dk blue 1.50 1.75

Post Horn Type of 1893-1908 Redrawn and

Rock Carvings A101

Boatswain's Knot A102

Designs: 30o, 55o, 85o, Rye and fish. 65o, 80o, Stave church and northern lights.

1962-63 Engr. *Perf. 13x13½*

416 A10 5o rose cl .25 .25
417 A10 10o slate .25 .25
Complete booklet, pane of 10 of #417 40.00
418 A10 15o orange brn .30 .25
419 A10 20o green .25 .25
Complete booklet, pane of 4 ea of #416, 419 20.00
420 A101 25o gray grn ('63) 1.50 .25
Complete booklet, pane of 4 of #420 25.00
Complete booklet, pane of 10 ea of #416, 417, 420 45.00
421 A101 30o olive brn ('63) 5.00 5.00
422 A102 35o brt green ('63) .30 .25
423 A101 40o lake ('63) 3.50 .25
424 A102 50o vermilion 4.75 .25
Complete booklet, pane of 10 of #424 100.00
425 A101 55o orange brn ('63) .50 .55
426 A102 60o dk grnsh gray ('63) 15.00 .25
427 A102 65o dk blue ('63) 3.50 .35
Complete booklet, pane of 10 of #427 110.00
428 A102 80o rose lake ('63) 2.50 2.50
429 A101 85o sepia ('63) .50 .25
430 A101 90o blue ('63) .30 .25
Nos. 416-430 (15) 38.40 11.15

Nos. 416-419 have been redrawn and are similar to 1910-29 issue, with vertical lines inside oval and horizontal lines in oval frame. See Nos. 462-470, 608-615.

Phosphorescence
Nos. 370-372, 416-419, 423, 425, 428, 430, 462, 466, O65-O68, O75, O78-O82, O83-O84 and O88 have been issued on both ordinary and phosphorescent paper.

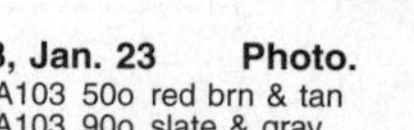

Camilla Collett (1813-1895), Author — A103

1963, Jan. 23 Photo. *Perf. 13*

431 A103 50o red brn & tan 1.00 .50
432 A103 90o slate & gray 1.75 1.25

Girl in Boat Loaded with Grain — A104

Still Life A105

1963, Mar. 21 Unwmk. *Perf. 13*

433 A104 25o yellow brown .75 .75
434 A104 35o dark green .75 .75
435 A105 50o dark red .75 .50
436 A105 90o dark blue 1.50 1.10
Nos. 433-436 (4) 3.75 3.10

FAO "Freedom from Hunger" campaign.

River Boat A106

Design: 90o, Northern sailboat.

1963, May 20 Unwmk. *Perf. 13*

437 A106 50o brown red 1.50 1.00
438 A106 90o blue 4.00 4.00

Tercentenary of regular postal service between Northern and Southern Norway.

Ivar Aasen — A107

1963, Aug. 5 Photo.

439 A107 50o dk red & gray .75 .50
440 A107 90o dk blue & gray 2.50 1.75

150th birth anniv. of Ivar Aasen, poet and philologist.

Europa Issue
Common Design Type

1963, Sept. 14 Unwmk. *Perf. 13*
Size: 27x21½mm

441 CD6 50o dull rose & org 1.00 .50
442 CD6 90o blue & yel grn 3.75 2.50

Patterned Fabric A108

1963, Sept. 24

443 A108 25o olive & ol grn 1.00 1.00
444 A108 35o Prus bl & dk bl 1.50 1.50
445 A108 50o dk car rose & plum .85 .50
Nos. 443-445 (3) 3.35 3.00

Norwegian textile industry, 150th anniv.

"Loneliness" A109

Paintings by Edvard Munch (1863-1944): 25o, Self-portrait, vert. 35o, "Fertility." 90o, "Girls on Bridge," vert.

1963, Dec. 12 Litho. *Perf. 13*

446 A109 25o black .50 .50
447 A109 35o dark green .50 .50
448 A109 50o deep claret .85 .50
449 A109 90o gray bl & dk bl 1.25 1.25
Nos. 446-449 (4) 3.10 2.75

Eilert Sundt — A110

50o, Beehive, Workers' Society emblem.

1964, Feb. 17 Photo.

450 A110 25o dark green .75 .75
451 A110 50o dk red brown .75 .25

Centenary of the Oslo Workers' Society.

Cato M. Guldberg and Peter Waage by Stinius Fredriksen A111

1964, Mar. 11 Unwmk. *Perf. 13*

452 A111 35o olive green .90 .90
453 A111 55o bister 2.00 1.75

Centenary of the presentation of the Law of Mass Action (chemistry) by Professors Cato M. Guldberg and Peter Waage in the Oslo Scientific Society.

Eidsvoll Building A112

Design: 90o, Storting (Parliament House).

1964, May 11 Photo.

454 A112 50o hn brn & blk 1.40 .50
455 A112 90o Prus bl & dk bl 2.75 2.50

150th anniv. of Norway's constitution.

Church and Ships in Harbor A113

1964, Aug. 17 *Perf. 13*

456 A113 25o dk sl grn & buff .75 .75
457 A113 90o dk bl & gray 2.50 2.50

Centenary of the Norwegian Seamen's Mission, which operates 32 stations around the world.

Europa Issue
Common Design Type

1964, Sept. 14 Photo. *Perf. 13*

458 CD7 90o dark blue 4.50 4.50

Herman Anker and Olaus Arvesen A114

1964, Oct. 31 Litho. Unwmk.

459 A114 50o rose 1.00 .50
460 A114 90o blue 3.25 3.25

Centenary of the founding of Norwegian schools of higher education (Folk High Schools).

Types of Regular Issue, 1962-63

Type I

Type II

Two types of 60o:
I — Four twists across bottom of knot.
II — Five twists.

Designs: 30o, 45o, Rye and fish. 40o, 100o, Rock carvings. 50o, 60o, 65o, 70o, Boatswain's knot.

1964-70 Engr. *Perf. 13x13½*

462 A101	30o dull green	.40	.25
463 A101	40o lt bl grn ('68)	.30	.25
464 A101	45o lt yel grn ('68)	.75	.75
465 A102	50o indigo ('68)	.50	.25
466 A102	60o brick red, II ('75)	2.50	.50
a.	Type I	1.50	.30
	Complete booklet, pane of 10 of #466a	90.00	
467 A102	65o lake ('68)	.65	.25
	Complete booklet, pane of 10 of #467	55.00	
468 A102	70o brown ('70)	.50	.25
	Complete booklet, pane of 10 of #468	50.00	
469 A101	100o violet bl ('70)	.70	.25
	Complete booklet, pane of 4 ea of #416, 419, 469	9.00	
	Nos. 462-469 (8)	6.30	2.75

See Phosphorescence note following #430.

Coil Stamp

1965 *Perf. 13½ Horiz.*

470 A101 30o dull green 5.00 3.50

Telephone Dial and Waves — A115

Design: 90o, Television mast and antenna.

1965, Apr. 1 Engr. *Perf. 13*

471 A115 60o redsh brown .75 .50
472 A115 90o slate 1.75 1.75

ITU, centenary.

Mountain Scene A116

Design: 90o, Coastal view.

1965, June 4 Unwmk. *Perf. 13*

473 A116 60o brn blk & car 1.00 .60
474 A116 90o slate bl & car 4.50 4.50

Centenary of the Norwegian Red Cross.

Europa Issue
Common Design Type

1965, Sept. 25 Photo. *Perf. 13*
Size: 27x21mm

475 CD8 60o brick red 1.25 .60
476 CD8 90o blue 2.75 2.50

St. Sunniva and Buildings of Bergen — A117

90o, St. Sunniva and stylized view of Bergen.

1965, Oct. 25 *Perf. 13*

477 A117 30o dk green & blk .55 .50
478 A117 90o blue & blk, horiz. 2.00 1.75

Bicentenary of Bergen's philharmonic society "Harmonien."

Rondane Mountains by Harold Sohlberg — A118

1965, Nov. 29 Photo. *Perf. 13*

484 A118 1.50k dark blue 3.00 .25

Rock Carving of Skier, Rodoy Island, c. 2000 B.C. — A120

Designs: 55o, Ski jumper. 60o, Cross country skier. 90o, Holmenkollen ski jump, vert.

1966, Feb. 8 Engr. *Perf. 13*

486 A120 40o sepia 1.50 1.50
487 A120 55o dull green 2.00 2.00
488 A120 60o dull red 1.00 .50
489 A120 90o blue 2.00 2.00
Nos. 486-489 (4) 6.50 6.00

World Ski Championships, Oslo, Feb. 17-27.

Open Bible and Chrismon A121

1966, May 20 Photo. *Perf. 13*

490 A121 60o dull red .75 .50
491 A121 90o slate blue 1.50 1.50

150th anniv. of the Norwegian Bible Society.

Engine-turned Bank Note Design — A122

Bank of Norway — A123

1966, June 14 Engr.

492 A122 30o green .85 .85
493 A123 60o dk carmine rose .55 .25

150th anniversary of Bank of Norway.

Johan Sverdrup — A124

1966, July 30 Photo. *Perf. 13*

494 A124 30o green .50 .50
495 A124 60o rose lake .50 .50

Johan Sverdrup (1816-92), Prime Minister of Norway (1884-89).

> **Canceled to Order**
> The Norwegian philatelic agency began in 1966 to sell commemorative and definitive issues canceled to order at face value.

Europa Issue
Common Design Type

1966, Sept. 26 Engr. *Perf. 13*
Size: 21x27mm

496 CD9 60o dark carmine 1.75 .50
497 CD9 90o blue gray 3.25 2.50

Nitrogen Molecule in Test Tube — A125

Design: 55o, Wheat and laboratory bottle.

1966, Oct. 29 Photo. *Perf. 13x12½*

498 A125 40o bl & dp bl 1.75 1.75
499 A125 55o red, org & lil rose 2.25 2.25

Centenary of the birth of Kristian Birkeland (1867-1917), and of Sam Eyde (1866-1940), who together developed the production of nitrates.

EFTA Emblem — A126

1967, Jan. 16 Engr. *Perf. 13*

500 A126 60o rose red .50 .35
501 A126 90o dark blue 2.25 2.25

European Free Trade Association. Tariffs were abolished Dec. 31, 1966, among EFTA members: Austria, Denmark, Finland, Great Britain, Norway, Portugal, Sweden, Switzerland.

Sabers, Owl and Oak Leaves A127

1967, Feb. 16 Engr. *Perf. 13*

502 A127 60o chocolate 1.00 1.00
503 A127 90o black 4.00 4.00

Higher military training in Norway, 150th anniv.

Europa Issue
Common Design Type

1967, May 2 Photo. *Perf. 13*
Size: 21x27mm

504 CD10 60o magenta & plum 1.00 .50
505 CD10 90o bl & dk vio bl 2.25 2.25

Johanne Dybwad, by Per Ung — A128

1967, Aug. 2 Photo. *Perf. 13*

506 A128 40o slate blue .55 .45
507 A128 60o dk carmine rose .55 .45

Johanne Dybwad (1867-1950), actress.

Missionary L.O. Skrefsrud A129

Ebenezer Church, Benagaria, Santal A130

1967, Sept. 26 Engr. *Perf. 13*

508 A129 60o red brown .55 .45
509 A130 90o blue gray 1.50 1.50

Norwegian Santal (India) mission, cent.

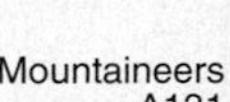

Mountaineers A131

Designs: 60o, Mountain view. 90o, Glitretind mountain peak.

1968, Jan. 22 Engr. *Perf. 13*

510 A131 40o sepia 1.50 1.50
511 A131 60o brown red 1.00 .30
512 A131 90o slate blue 1.75 1.75
Nos. 510-512 (3) 4.25 3.55

Centenary of the Norwegian Mountain Touring Association.

Two Smiths A132

1968, Mar. 30 Photo. *Perf. 12½x13*

513 A132 65o dk car rose & brn .45 .25
514 A132 90o blue & brown 1.50 1.50

Issued to honor Norwegian craftsmen.

A. O. Vinje — A133

1968, May 21 Engr. *Perf. 13*

515 A133 50o sepia .75 .50
516 A133 65o maroon .50 .25

Aasmund Olafsson Vinje (1818-1870), poet, journalist and language reformer.

Cross and Heart — A134

1968, Sept. 16 Photo.

517 A134 40o brt grn & brn red 3.25 3.25
518 A134 65o brn red & vio bl .65 .25

Centenary of the Norwegian Lutheran Home Mission Society.

Cathinka Guldberg — A135

1968, Oct. 31 Engr. *Perf. 13*

519 A135 50o bright blue .65 .45
520 A135 65o dull red .65 .25

Nursing profession; centenary of Deaconess House in Oslo. Cathinka Guldberg was a pioneer of Norwegian nursing and the first deaconess.

Klas P. Arnoldson and Fredrik Bajer — A136

1968, Dec. 10 Engr. *Perf. 13*

521 A136 65o red brown .65 .30
522 A136 90o dark blue 2.00 2.00

60th anniv. of the awarding of the Nobel Peace prize to Klas P. Arnoldson (1844-1916), Swedish writer and statesman, and to Fredrik Bajer (1837-1922), Danish writer and statesman.

Nordic Cooperation Issue

Five Ancient Ships — A136a

1969, Feb. 28 Engr. *Perf. 13*
523 A136a 65o red .35 .30
524 A136a 90o blue 1.50 1.50

50th anniv. of the Nordic Society and centenary of postal cooperation among the northern countries. The design is taken from a coin found on the site of Birka, an ancient Swedish town.

See Demark Nos. 454-455, Finland No. 481, Iceland Nos. 404-405 and Sweden Nos. 808-810.

Ornament from Urnes Stave Church — A137

Traena Island A138

1969 Engr. *Perf. 13*
526 A137 1.15k sepia 1.25 .50
529 A138 3.50k bluish blk 2.00 .25

Issue dates: 1.15k, Jan. 23, 3.50k, June 18.

Plane, Train, Ship and Bus A139

Child Crossing Street A140

1969, Mar. 24 Photo. *Perf. 13*
531 A139 50o green 1.25 1.25
532 A140 65o slate grn & dk red .75 .25

No. 531 for the centenary of the publication of "Rutebok of Norway" (Communications of Norway); No. 532 publicizes traffic safety.

Europa Issue
Common Design Type

1969, Apr. 28 Size: 37x21mm
533 CD12 65o dk red & gray 1.00 .35
534 CD12 90o chalky bl & gray 2.75 2.00

Johan Hjort — A141

Design: 90o, different emblem.

1969, May 30 Engr. *Perf. 13*
535 A141 40o brn & bl 1.50 1.25
536 A141 90o bl & grn 2.50 2.25

Zoologist and oceanographer (1869-1948).

King Olav V — A142

1969-83 Engr. *Perf. 13*
537 A142 1k lt ol grn ('70) .65 .25
538 A142 1.50k dk blue ('70) .85 .25
539 A142 2k dk red ('70) .85 .25
540 A142 5k vio bl ('70) 2.50 .25
541 A142 10k org brn ('70) 5.00 .25
542 A142 20k brown 12.00 .25
543 A142 50k dk ol grn ('83) 22.00 1.00
Nos. 537-543 (7) 43.85 2.50

Man, Woman and Child, by Vigeland A143

65o, Mother and Child, by Gustav Vigeland.

1969, Sept. 8 Photo. *Perf. 13*
545 A143 65o car rose & blk .50 .35
546 A143 90o blue & black 1.50 1.50

Gustav Vigeland (1869-1943), sculptor.

People A144

1969, Oct. 10
547 A144 65o Punched card .75 .35
548 A144 90o shown 1.50 1.50

1st Norwegian census, 200th anniv.

Queen Maud — A145

1969, Nov. 26 Engr. *Perf. 13*
549 A145 65o dk carmine .80 .40
550 A145 90o violet blue 1.50 1.50

Queen Maud (1869-1938), wife of King Haakon VII.

Pulsatilla Vernalis — A146

European Nature Conservation Year: 40o, Wolf. 70o, Voringsfossen (waterfall). 100o, White-tailed sea eagle, horiz.

1970, Apr. 10 Photo. *Perf. 13*
551 A146 40o sep & pale bl 1.50 1.50
552 A146 60o lt brn & gray 3.00 3.00
553 A146 70o pale bl & brn 1.50 .60
554 A146 100o pale bl & brn 2.50 2.50
Nos. 551-554 (4) 8.50 7.60

"V" for Victory — A147

Design: 100o, Convoy, horiz.

Perf. 13x12½, 12½x13
1970, May 8 Photo.
555 A147 70o red & lilac 2.50 .65
556 A147 100o vio bl & brt grn 2.50 2.25

Norway's liberation from the Germans, 25th anniv.

"Citizens" — A148

Designs: 70o, "The City and the Mountains." 100o, "Ships."

1970, June 23 Engr. *Perf. 13*
557 A148 40o green 2.50 2.00
558 A148 70o rose claret 3.00 .50
559 A148 100o violet blue 2.50 2.50
Nos. 557-559 (3) 8.00 5.00

City of Bergen, 900th anniversary.

Olive Wreath and Hands Upholding Globe — A149

1970, Sept. 15 Engr. *Perf. 13*
560 A149 70o dk car rose 3.00 .50
561 A149 100o steel blue 2.00 1.75

25th anniversary of the United Nations.

Georg Ossian Sars (1837-1927) — A150

Portraits: 50o, Hans Strom (1726-1797). 70o, Johan Ernst Gunnerus (1718-1773). 100o, Michael Sars (1805-1869).

1970, Oct. 15 Engr. *Perf. 13*
562 A150 40o brown 1.75 1.75
563 A150 50o dull purple 1.50 1.25
564 A150 70o brown red 1.50 .50
565 A150 100o bright blue 1.75 1.50
Nos. 562-565 (4) 6.50 5.00

Issued to honor Norwegian zoologists.

Central School of Gymnastics, Oslo, Cent. — A151

50o, Ball game, vert. 70o, Leapfrog.

1970, Nov. 17 Photo. *Perf. 13*
566 A151 50o dk blue, brn 1.00 .40
567 A151 70o red, brn, blk 1.50 .25

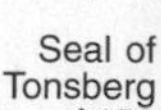

Seal of Tonsberg A152

1971, Jan. 20 Photo. *Perf. 13*
568 A152 70o dark red .85 .30
569 A152 100o blue black 1.75 1.50

City of Tonsberg, 1,100th anniversary.

Parliament A153

1971, Feb. 23
570 A153 70o red brn & lil .75 .30
571 A153 100o dk bl & sl grn 1.75 1.50

Centenary of annual sessions of Norwegian Parliament.

Hand, Heart and Eye A154

1971, Mar. 26 Photo. *Perf. 13*
572 A154 50o emerald & blk .75 .75
573 A154 70o scarlet & blk .75 .30

Joint northern campaign for the benefit of refugees.

"Haugianerne" by Adolph Tiedemand — A155

1971, Apr. 27 Photo. *Perf. 13*
574 A155 60o dark gray .75 .75
575 A155 70o brown .75 .35

Hans Nielsen Hauge (1771-1824), church reformer.

Worshippers Coming to Church — A156

Design: 70o, Building first church, vert.

1971, May 21
576 A156 70o black & dk red .50 .35
577 A156 1k black & blue 2.25 2.00

900th anniversary of the Bishopric of Oslo.

Roald Amundsen, Antarctic Treaty Emblem A157

1971, June 23 Engr. *Perf. 13*
578 A157 100o blue & org red 4.00 3.00

Antarctic Treaty pledging peaceful uses of and scientific cooperation in Antarctica, 10th anniv.

The Farmer and the Woman — A158

Designs: 50o, The Preacher and the King, horiz. 70o, The Troll and the Girl. Illustrations for legends and folk tales by Erik Werenskiold.

1971, Nov. 17 Photo. *Perf. 13*

579 A158 40o olive & blk 1.00 .50
580 A158 50o blue & blk 1.00 .50
581 A158 70o magenta & blk .85 .25
Nos. 579-581 (3) 2.85 1.25

Engine Turning A159

1972, Apr. 10 Photo. *Perf. 13*

582 A159 80o red & gold .80 .30
583 A159 1.20k ultra & gold 1.50 1.25

Norwegian Savings Bank sesquicentennial.

Norway #18 — A160

Engr. & Photo.

1972, May 6 *Perf. 12*

584 A160 80o shown .75 .50
585 A160 1k Norway #17 .75 .50
a. Souvenir sheet of 2, #584-585 6.00 10.00

Centenary of the post horn stamps. No. 585a sold for 2.50k.

Dragon's Head, Oseberg Viking Ship — A161

Ancient Artifacts: 50o, Horseman from Stone of Alstad. 60o, Horseman, wood carving, stave church, Hemsedal. 1.20k, Sword hilt, found at Lodingen.

1972, June 7 Engr. *Perf. 13*

586 A161 50o yellow grn .75 .75
587 A161 60o brown 1.75 1.75
588 A161 80o dull red 2.00 .45
589 A161 1.20k ultra 1.75 1.75
Nos. 586-589 (4) 6.25 4.70

1,100th anniversary of unification.

King Haakon VII (1872-1957) — A162

1972, Aug. 3 Engr. *Perf. 13*

590 A162 80o brown orange 3.50 .35
591 A162 1.20k Prussian bl 2.00 2.00

"Joy" — A163

Design: 1.20k, "Solidarity."

1972, Aug. 15 Photo. *Perf. 13x13½*

592 A163 80o brt magenta .75 .30
593 A163 1.20k Prussian blue 1.75 1.50

2nd Intl. Youth Stamp Exhib., INTERJUNEX 72, Kristiansand, Aug. 25-Sept. 3.

Nos. 592-593 Overprinted "INTERJUNEX 72"

1972, Aug. 25

594 A163 80o brt magenta 3.25 3.75
595 A163 1.20k Prussian blue 3.25 3.75

Opening of INTERJUNEX 72. Sold at exhibition only together with 3k entrance ticket.

"Fram." — A164

Polar Exploration Ships: 60o, "Maud." 1.20k, "Gjoa."

1972, Sept. 20 *Perf. 13½x13*

596 A164 60o olive & green 1.75 1.25
597 A164 80o red & black 3.50 .35
598 A164 1.20k blue & red brn 2.50 2.00
Nos. 596-598 (3) 7.75 3.60

"Little Man" — A165

Illustrations for folk tales by Theodor Kittelsen (1857-1914): 60o, The Troll who wondered how old he was. 80o, The princess riding the polar bear.

1972, Nov. 15 Litho. *Perf. 13½x13*

599 A165 50o green & blk 1.00 .25
600 A165 60o blue & blk 1.25 1.25
601 A165 80o pink & blk 1.00 .25
Nos. 599-601 (3) 3.25 1.75

Dr. Armauer G. Hansen and Leprosy Bacillus Drawing — A166

Design: 1.40k, Dr. Hansen and leprosy bacillus, microscopic view.

1973, Feb. 28 Engr. *Perf. 13x13½*

602 A166 1k henna brn & bl .75 .25
603 A166 1.40k dk bl & dp org 1.50 1.50

Centenary of the discovery of the Hansen bacillus, the cause of leprosy.

Europa Issue

Common Design Type

1973, Apr. 30 Photo. *Perf. 12½x13*

Size: 37x20mm

604 CD16 1k red, org & lil *4.00* .40
605 CD16 1.40k dk grn, grn & bl *2.25* 2.00

Types of 1893 and 1962-63

Designs: 75o, 85o, Rye and fish. 80o, 140o, Stave church. 100o, 110o, 120o, 125o, Rock carvings.

1972-75 Engr. *Perf. 13x13½*

606 A10 25o ultra ('74) .25 .25
Complete booklet, pane of 4 of #606 2.50
608 A101 75o green ('73) .25 .25
609 A102 80o red brown .50 .35
Complete booklet, pane of 10 of #609 65.00
610 A101 85o bister ('74) .25 .25
611 A101 100o red ('73) .75 .25
Complete booklet, pane of 10 of #611 50.00
612 A101 110o rose car ('74) .50 .25
613 A101 120o gray blue .75 .50
614 A101 125o red ('75) .85 .25
Complete booklet, pane of 10 of #614 20.00
615 A102 140o dk blue ('73) .75 .35
Nos. 606-615 (9) 4.85 2.70

Nordic Cooperation Issue

Nordic House, Reykjavik A167

1973, June 26 Engr. *Perf. 12½*

617 A167 1k multi 1.25 .40
618 A167 1.40k multi 1.50 1.75

A century of postal cooperation among Denmark, Finland, Iceland, Norway and Sweden; Nordic Postal Conference, Reykjavik, Iceland.

King Olav V — A168

1973, July 2 Engr. *Perf. 13*

619 A168 1k car & org brn 1.50 .25
620 A168 1.40k blue & org brn 1.75 1.75

70th birthday of King Olav V.

Jacob Aall — A169

1973, Aug. 22 Engr. *Perf. 13*

621 A169 1k deep claret .75 .25
622 A169 1.40k dk blue gray 1.50 1.50

Jacob Aall (1773-1844), mill owner and industrial pioneer.

Blade Decoration — A170

Handicraft from Lapland: 1k, Textile pattern. 1.40k, Decoration made of tin.

1973, Oct. 9 Photo. *Perf. 13x12½*

623 A170 75o blk brn & buff .60 .60
624 A170 1k dp car & buff 1.25 .30
625 A170 1.40k blk & dl bl 1.50 1.50
Nos. 623-625 (3) 3.35 2.40

Viola Biflora — A171

1973, Nov. 15 Litho. *Perf. 13*

626 A171 65o shown .60 .50
627 A171 70o Veronica Fruticans .75 .75
628 A171 1k Phyllodoce corrulea .75 .25
Nos. 626-628 (3) 2.10 1.50

See Nos. 754-756, 770-771.

Surveyor in Northern Norway, 1907 — A172

1.40k, South Norway Mountains map, 1851.

1973, Dec. 14 Engr. *Perf. 13*

629 A172 1k red orange .50 .25
630 A172 1.40k slate blue 1.50 1.50

Geographical Survey of Norway, bicent.

Lindesnes A173

Design: 1.40k, North Cape.

1974, Apr. 25 Photo. *Perf. 13*

631 A173 1k olive 1.50 .50
632 A173 1.40k dark blue 3.00 3.00

Ferry in Hardanger Fjord, by A. Tidemand and H. Gude A174

Classical Norwegian paintings: 1.40k, Stugunoset from Filefjell, by Johan Christian Dahl.

1974, May 21 Litho. *Perf. 13*

633 A174 1k multi .75 .25
634 A174 1.40k multi 1.50 1.50

Gulating Law Manuscript, 1325 A175

King Magnus VI Lagaböter A176

1974, June 21 Engr.

635 A175 1k red & brn .75 .25
636 A176 1.40k ultra & brn 1.75 1.75

700th anniv. of the National Code given by King Magnus VI Lagaböter (1238-80).

Saw Blade and Pines — A177

Design: 1k, Cog wheel and guard.

1974, Aug. 12 Photo. *Perf. 13*

637 A177 85o grn, ol & dk grn 2.50 2.50
638 A177 1k org, plum & dk red 1.75 .40

Safe working conditions.

J.H.L. Vogt — A178

Geologists: 85o, V. M. Goldschmidt. 1k, Theodor Kjerulf. 1.40k, Waldemar C. Brogger.

1974, Sept. 4 Engr. *Perf. 13*

639 A178 65o olive & red brn .50 .25
640 A178 85o mag & red brn 2.00 2.00
641 A178 1k org & red brn .75 .25
642 A178 1.40k blue & red brn 1.50 1.50
Nos. 639-642 (4) 4.75 4.00

"Man's Work," Famous Buildings A179

Design: 1.40k, "Men, our brethren," people of various races.

1974, Oct. 9 Photo. *Perf. 13*
643 A179 1k green & brn 1.00 .25
644 A179 1.40k brn & grnsh bl 1.50 1.50

Centenary of Universal Postal Union.

Horseback Rider A180

Flowers A181

1974, Nov. 15 Litho. *Perf. 13*
645 A180 85o multicolored .50 .50
646 A181 1k multicolored .50 .25

Norwegian folk art, rose paintings from furniture decorations.

Woman Skier, c. 1900 A182

1975, Jan. 15 Litho. *Perf. 13*
647 A182 1k shown 1.00 .25
648 A182 1.40k Telemark turn 1.25 1.25

"Norway, homeland of skiing."

Women — A183

Design: Detail from wrought iron gates of Vigeland Park, Oslo.

1975, Mar. 7 Litho. *Perf. 13*
649 A183 1.25k brt rose lil & dk bl .65 .25
650 A183 1.40k bl & dk bl 1.25 1.25

International Women's Year.

Nusfjord Fishing Harbor — A184

1.25k, Street in Stavanger. 1.40k, View of Roros.

1975, Apr. 17 Litho. *Perf. 13*
651 A184 1k yellow green 1.00 .65
652 A184 1.25k dull red .75 .25
653 A184 1.40k blue 1.50 1.50
Nos. 651-653 (3) 3.25 2.40

European Architectural Heritage Year.

Norwegian Krone, 1875 — A185

Ole Jacob Broch — A186

1975, May 20 Engr. *Perf. 13*
654 A185 1.25k dark carmine 1.00 .25
655 A186 1.40k blue 1.25 1.25

Centenary of Monetary Convention of Norway, Sweden and Denmark (1.25k); and of Intl. Meter Convention, Paris, 1875. Ole Jacob Broch (1818-1889) was first director of Intl. Bureau of Weights and Measures.

Scouting in Summer A187

Design: 1.40k, Scouting in winter (skiers).

1975, June 19 Litho. *Perf. 13*
656 A187 1.25k multicolored 1.25 .35
657 A187 1.40k multicolored 1.50 1.50

Nordjamb 75, 14th Boy Scout Jamboree, Lillehammer, July 29-Aug. 7.

Sod Hut and Settlers A188

Cleng Peerson and Letter from America, 1874 A189

1975, July 4 Engr.
658 A188 1.25k red brown 1.00 .25
659 A189 1.40k bluish blk 1.50 1.50

Sesquicentennial of Norwegian emigration to America.

Templet, Tempelfjord, Spitsbergen A190

Miners Leaving Coal Pit — A191

Design: 1.40k, Polar bear.

1975, Aug. 14 Engr. *Perf. 13*
660 A190 1k olive black 1.25 1.00
661 A191 1.25k maroon 1.25 .25
662 A191 1.40k Prus blue 2.50 2.25
Nos. 660-662 (3) 5.00 3.50

50th anniversary of union of Spitsbergen (Svalbard) with Norway.

Microphone with Ear Phones — A192

Radio Tower and Houses — A193

Designs after children's drawings.

1975, Oct. 9 Litho. *Perf. 13*
663 A192 1.25k multi .60 .25
664 A193 1.40k multi 1.10 1.10

50 years of broadcasting in Norway.

Annunciation A194

Nativity — A195

Painted vault of stave church of Al, 13th cent: 1k, Visitation. 1.40k, Adoration of the Kings.

1975, Nov. 14
665 A194 80o red & multi .60 .25
666 A194 1k red & multi .75 .50
667 A195 1.25k red & multi .60 .25
668 A195 1.40k red & multi 1.00 1.25
Nos. 665-668 (4) 2.95 2.25

Sigurd and Regin — A196

1976, Jan. 20 Engr. *Perf. 13*
669 A196 7.50k brown 4.00 .25

Norwegian folk tale, Sigurd the Dragon-killer. Design from portal of Hylestad stave church, 13th century.

Halling, Hallingdal Dance — A197

Folk Dances: 1k, Springar, Hordaland region. 1.25k, Gangar, Setesdal.

1976, Feb. 25 Litho. *Perf. 13*
670 A197 80o black & multi 1.00 .75
671 A197 1k black & multi 1.00 .75
672 A197 1.25k black & multi .75 .25
Nos. 670-672 (3) 2.75 1.75

Silver Sugar Shaker, Stavanger, c. 1770 — A198

1.40k, Goblet, Nostetangen glass, c. 1770.

1976, Mar. 25 Engr. *Perf. 13*
673 A198 1.25k multicolored .85 .40
674 A198 1.40k multicolored 1.00 1.25

Oslo Museum of Applied Art, centenary.

Ceramic Bowl Shaped Like Bishop's Mitre A199

Europa: 1.40k, Plate and CEPT emblem. Both designs after faience works from Herrebo Potteries, c. 1760.

1976, May 3 Litho. *Perf. 13*
675 A199 1.25k rose mag & brn *.75 .40*
676 A199 1.40k brt bl & vio bl *1.25 1.25*

The Pulpit, Lyse Fjord — A200

Gulleplet (Peak), Sogne Fjord — A201

Perf. 13 on 3 Sides
1976, May 20 Litho.
677 A200 1k multi .60 .25
a. Booklet pane of 10 6.50
Complete booklet, #677a 7.50
678 A201 1.25k multi 1.00 .25
a. Booklet pane of 10 10.00
Complete booklet, #678a 12.00

Nos. 677-678 issued only in booklets.

Graph Paper, Old and New Subjects — A202

Design: 2k, Graph of national product.

1976, July 1 Engr. *Perf. 13*
679 A202 1.25k red brown .70 .25
680 A202 2k dark blue 1.00 .50

Central Bureau of Statistics, centenary.

Olav Duun on Dun Mountain A203

1976, Sept. 10 Engr. *Perf. 13*
681 A203 1.25k multi .70 .25
682 A203 1.40k multi 1.00 1.00

Olav Duun (1876-1939), novelist.

"Birches" by Th. Fearnley (1802-1842) A204

Design: 1.40k, "Gamle Furutraer" (trees), by L. Hertervig (1830-1902).

1976, Oct. 8 Litho. *Perf. 13*
683 A204 1.25k multi .80 .25
684 A204 1.40k multi 1.25 1.25

"April" — A205

"May" — A206

Baldishol Tapestry — A207

80o, 1k, Details from 13th cent. Baldishol tapestry, found in Baldishol stave church.

1976, Nov. 5 Litho. *Perf. 13*

685	A205	80o	multi	.50	.25
686	A206	1k	multi	.65	.50
687	A207	1.25k	multi	.60	.25
			Nos. 685-687 (3)	1.75	1.00

Five Water Lilies — A208

Photo. & Engr.

1977, Feb. 2 *Perf. 12½*

688	A208	1.25k	multi	.75	.30
689	A208	1.40k	multi	.75	1.00

Nordic countries cooperation for protection of the environment and 25th Session of Nordic Council, Helsinki, Feb. 19.

Akershus Castle, Oslo — A209

Steinviksholm Fort, Asen Fjord — A210

Torungen Lighthouses, Arendal — A211

1977, Feb. 24 Engr. *Perf. 13*

690	A209	1.25k	red	.70	.25
			Complete booklet pane of 10 #690	12.00	
			Complete booklet pane of 8 #690	8.50	
691	A210	1.30k	olive brown	.75	.25
692	A211	1.80k	blue	.85	.25
			Nos. 690-692 (3)	2.30	.75

See Nos. 715-724, 772-774.

Europa Issue

Hamnoy, Lofoten, Fishing Village — A212

Huldre Falls, Loen — A213

Perf. 13 on 3 Sides

1977, May 2 Litho.

693	A212	1.25k	multi	1.00	.25
a.			Booklet pane of 10	10.00	
			Complete booklet, #693a	12.00	
694	A213	1.80k	multi	1.00	1.00
a.			Booklet pane of 10	10.00	
			Complete booklet, #694a	12.00	

Nos. 693-694 issued only in booklets.

Norwegian Trees — A214

1977, June 1 Engr. *Perf. 13*

695	A214	1k	Spruce	.75	.50
696	A214	1.25k	Fir	.75	.25
697	A214	1.80k	Birch	1.25	1.25
			Nos. 695-697 (3)	2.75	2.00

"Constitutionen," Norway's 1st Steamship, at Arendal — A215

Designs: 1.25k, "Vesteraalen" off Bodo, 1893. 1.30k, "Kong Haakon," 1904 and "Dronningen," 1893, off Stavanger. 1.80k, "Nordstjernen" and "Harald Jari" at pier, 1970.

1977, June 22

698	A215	1k	brown	.60	.25
699	A215	1.25k	red	1.00	.25
700	A215	1.30k	green	2.00	1.75
701	A215	1.80k	blue	1.50	1.25
			Nos. 698-701 (4)	5.10	3.50

Norwegian ships serving coastal routes.

Fishermen and Boats — A216

Fish and Fishhooks A217

1977, Sept. 22 Engr. *Perf. 13*

702	A216	1.25k	buff, lt brn & dk brn	1.00	.25
703	A217	1.80k	lt bl, bl & dk bl	1.25	1.25

Men, by Halfdan Egedius A218

Landscape, by August Cappelen A219

1977, Oct. 7 Litho. *Perf. 13*

704	A218	1.25k	multi	.60	.25
705	A219	1.80k	multi	1.25	1.25

Norwegian classical painting.

David with the Bells — A220

Christmas: 1k, Singing Friars. 1.25k, Virgin and Child, horiz. Designs from Bible of Bishop Aslak Bolt, 13th century.

1977, Nov. 10 Litho. *Perf. 13*

Size: 21x27mm

706	A220	80o	multi	.50	.25
707	A220	1k	multi	.50	.35

Size: 34x27mm

708	A220	1.25k	multi	.75	.25
			Nos. 706-708 (3)	1.75	.85

Post Horn Type of 1893 and Scenic Types of 1977

Designs: 1k, Austrat Manor, 1650. 1.10k, Trondenes Chruch, early 13th Cent. 1.40k, Ruins of Hamar Cathedral, 12th Cent. 1.75k, Seamen's Hall, Stavern, 1926, vert. 2k, Tofte Estate, Dovre, 16-17th cent., vert. 2.25k, Oscarhall, Oslofijord, 1847, vert. 2.50k, Log house, Breiland, 1785. 2.75k, Damsgard Building, Lakesvag, 1770. 3k, Selje Monastery, 11th cent. 3.50k, Lighthouse, Lindesnes, 1655.

Perf. 13x13½, 13½x13

1978-83 Engr.

709	A10	40o	olive	.30	.25
710	A10	50o	dull purple	.30	.25
711	A10	60o	vermilion	.30	.25
712	A10	70o	orange	.50	.30
713	A10	80o	red brown	.50	.35
714	A10	90o	brown	.60	.60
715	A209	1k	green	.50	.25
			Complete booklet, pane of 4 ea #416, 419, 715	15.00	
716	A209	1.10k	rose mag	.75	.25
717	A209	1.40k	dark purple	.90	.30
718	A211	1.75k	green ('82)	.75	.25
719	A211	2k	brown red ('82)	.75	.25
720	A211	2.25k	dp vio ('82)	1.00	.50
721	A209	2.50k	brn red ('83)	1.00	.25
722	A209	2.75k	dp mag ('82)	1.50	1.25
723	A209	3k	dk bl ('82)	1.25	.25
724	A209	3.50k	dp vio ('83)	1.25	.30
			Nos. 709-724 (16)	12.15	5.85

See Nos. 772-774.

Peer Gynt, and Reindeer by Per Krogh — A222

Henrik Ibsen, by Erik Werenskiold, 1895 — A223

1978, Mar. 10 Litho. *Perf. 13*

725	A222	1.25k	buff & blk	.80	.25
726	A223	1.80k	multicolored	1.25	1.00

Ibsen (1828-1906), poet and dramatist.

Heddal Stave Church, c. 1250 — A224

Europa: 1.80k, Borgund stave church.

1978, May 2 Engr. *Perf. 13*

727	A224	1.25k	dk brn & red	1.25	.45
728	A224	1.80k	sl grn & bl	1.75	1.50

Lenangstindene and Jaegervasstindene — A225

1.25k, Gaustatoppen, mountain, Telemark.

Perf. 13 on 3 Sides

1978, June 1 Litho.

729	A225	1k	multi	.55	.40
a.			Booklet pane of 10	6.50	
			Complete booklet, #729a	8.00	
730	A225	1.25k	multi	.70	.25
a.			Booklet pane of 10	9.00	
			Complete booklet, #730a	10.00	

Nos. 729-730 issued only in booklets.

Olav V Sailing A226

Design: 1.80k, King Olav delivering royal address in Parliament, vert.

1978, June 30 Engr. *Perf. 13*

731	A226	1.25k	red brown	1.25	.25
732	A226	1.80k	violet blue	1.25	1.25

75th birthday of King Olav V.

Norway No. 107 — A227

Stamps: b, #108. c, #109. d, #110. e, #111. f, #112. g, #113. h, #114.

Perf. 13 on 3 Sides

1978, Sept. 19 Litho.

733			Booklet pane of 8	8.00	8.00
a.-h.	A227	1.25k,	any single	1.00	1.00
			Complete booklet, #733	8.00	

NORWEX '80 Philatelic Exhibition, Oslo, June 13-22, 1980. Booklet sold for 15k; the additional 5k went for financing the exhibition.

Willow Pipe Player A228

Musical Instruments: 1.25k, Norwegian violin. 1.80k, Norwegian zither. 7.50k, Ram's horn.

1978, Oct. 6 Engr. *Perf. 13*

734	A228	1k	deep green	.35	.25
735	A228	1.25k	dk rose car	.55	.25
736	A228	1.80k	dk violet blue	1.00	1.00
737	A228	7.50k	gray	4.50	.25
			Nos. 734-737 (4)	6.40	1.75

Wooden Doll, 1830 — A229

Christmas: 1k, Toy town 1896-97. 1.25k, Wooden horse from Torpo in Hallingdal.

1978, Nov. 10 Litho.

738	A229	80o	multi	.50	.25
739	A229	1k	multi	.50	.25
740	A229	1.25k	multi	.70	.25
			Nos. 738-740 (3)	1.70	.75

Ski Jump, Huseby Hill, c. 1900 — A230

1.25k, Crown Prince Olav, Holmenkollen ski jump competition, 1922. 1.80k, Cross-country race, Holmenkollen, 1976.

1979, Mar. 2 Engr. *Perf. 13*

741	A230	1k	green	.75	.50
742	A230	1.25k	red	1.00	.25
743	A230	1.80k	blue	1.50	1.25
			Nos. 741-743 (3)	3.25	2.00

Huseby Hills and Holmenkollen ski competitions, centenary.

Girl, by Mathias Stoltenberg A231

1.80k, Boy, by H. C. F. Hosenfelder.

1979, Apr. 26 Litho. *Perf. 13*

744	A231	1.25k	multi	.75	.25
745	A231	1.80k	multi	1.00	1.00

International Year of the Child.

Road to Briksdal Glacier — A232

1.25k, Boat on Skjernoysund, near Mandal.

1979, June 13 *Perf. 13 on 3 Sides*

746 A232 1k multi .60 .25
a. Booklet pane of 10 6.00
Complete booklet, #746a 7.00
747 A232 1.25k multi .75 .25
a. Booklet pane of 10 7.50
Complete booklet, #747a 9.00

Nos. 746-747 issued only in booklets.

Johan Falkberget, by Harald Dal — A233

1.80k, "Ann-Magritt and the Hovi Bullock" (by Falkberget), monument by Kristofer Leirdal.

1979, Sept. 4 **Engr.** *Perf. 13*

748 A233 1.25k deep claret .75 .25
749 A233 1.80k Prus blue 1.10 1.00

Johan Falkberget (1879-1967), novelist.

Kylling Bridge, Verma, 1923 — A234

Norwegian Engineering: 2k, Vessingsjo Dam, Nea, 1960. 10k, Stratfjord A, oil drilling platform in North Sea.

1979, Oct. 5

750 A234 1.25k black & brown .60 .25
751 A234 2k dk blue & blue 1.00 .40
752 A234 10k brown & bister 5.00 .45
Nos. 750-752 (3) 6.60 1.10

Souvenir Sheet

Dornier Wal over Polar Map — A235

Arctic Aviation and Polar Maps: 2k, Dirigible Norge. 2.80k, Loening air yacht amphibian. 4k, Reidar Viking DC-7C.

1979, Oct. 5 **Litho.** *Perf. 13*

753 Sheet of 4 7.00 7.00
a. A235 1.25k multi 1.50 1.50
b. A235 2k multi 1.50 1.50
c. A235 2.80k multi 1.50 1.50
d. A235 4k multi 1.50 1.50

Norwex '80 Intl. Phil. Exhib., Oslo, June 13-22, 1980. No. 753 sold for 15k.

Mountain Flower Type of 1973

80o, Ranunculus glacialis. 1k, Potentilla crantzii. 1.25k, Saxiflora oppositifolia.

1979, Nov. 22 **Litho.** *Perf. 13½*

754 A171 80o multicolored .50 .25
755 A171 1k multicolored .50 .25
756 A171 1.25k multicolored .70 .25
Nos. 754-756 (3) 1.70 .75

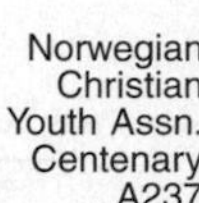

Norwegian Christian Youth Assn. Centenary A237

1980, Feb. 26 **Litho.** *Perf. 13*

757 A237 100o shown .70 .25
758 A237 180o Emblems and doves 1.00 1.00

Oyster Catcher — A238

Perf. 13 on 3 Sides

1980, Apr. 18 **Litho.**

759 A238 100o shown .35 .25
760 A238 100o Mallard .35 .25
a. Bklt. pane, 5 #759, 5 #760 4.00
Complete booklet, #760a 5.00
761 A238 125o Dipper .55 .25
762 A238 125o Great tit .55 .25
a. Bklt. pane, 5 #761, 5 #762 5.50
Complete booklet, #762a 6.00
Nos. 759-762 (4) 1.80 1.00

Nos. 759-762 issued in booklets only. See Nos. 775-778, 800-801, 821-822.

Dish Antenna, Old Phone A239

National Telephone Service Centenary: 1.80k, Erecting telephone pole.

1980, May 9 **Litho.** *Perf. 13½*

763 A239 1.25k multi .60 .25
764 A239 1.80k multi 1.00 1.00

Souvenir Sheet

NORWEX '80 Stamp Exhibition — A240

1980, June 13

765 A240 Sheet of 4 6.50 6.50
a. 1.25k Paddle Steamer "Bergen" 1.50 1.50
b. 2k Train, 1900 1.50 1.50
c. 2.80k Bus, 1940 1.50 1.50
d. 4k Boeing 737 1.50 1.50

NORWEX '80 Stamp Exhibition, Oslo, June 13-22. Sold for 15k.

Nordic Cooperation Issue

Vulcan as an Armourer, by Henrich Bech, 1761 — A241

Henrich Bech Cast Iron Stove Ornament: 1.80k, Hercules at a Burning Altar, 1769.

1980, Sept. 9 **Engr.** *Perf. 13*

766 A241 1.25k dk vio brn .60 .25
767 A241 1.80k dark blue 1.00 1.00

Self-Portrait, by Christian Skredsvig (1854-1924) A242

Paintings: 1.25k, Fire, by Nikolai Astrup.

1980, Nov. 14 **Litho.** *Perf. 13½x13*

768 A242 1.25k multi .80 .25
769 A242 1.80k multi 1.25 1.00

Mountain Flower Type of 1973

1980, Nov. 14 *Perf. 13*

770 A171 80o Sorbus aucuparia .50 .25
771 A171 1k Rosa canina .50 .25

Scenic Type of 1977

1.50k, Stavanger Cathedral, 13th cent. 1.70k, Rosenkrantz Tower, Bergen, 13th-16th cent. 2.20k, Church of Tromsdalen (Arctic Cathedral), 1965.

Perf. 13x13½, 13½x13

1981, Feb. 26 **Engr.**

772 A211 1.50k brown red .75 .25
773 A211 1.70k olive green 1.00 .75
774 A209 2.20k dark blue 1.25 .45
Nos. 772-774 (3) 3.00 1.45

Bird Type of 1980

Perf. 13 on 3 Sides

1981, Feb. 26 **Litho.**

775 A238 1.30k Anser erythropus .50 .50
776 A238 1.30k Peregrine falcon .50 .50
a. Booklet pane of 10 (5 each) 5.50
Complete booklet, #776a 6.50
777 A238 1.50k Black guillemot .65 .25
778 A238 1.50k Puffin .65 .25
a. Booklet pane of 10 (5 each) 6.50
Complete booklet, #778a 7.50
Nos. 775-778 (4) 2.30 1.50

Nos. 775-778 issued in booklets. See Nos. 800-801, 821-822.

Nat'l Milk Producers Assn. Centenary A244

1981, Mar. 24 **Litho.** *Perf. 13x13½*

779 A244 1.10k Cow .75 .25
780 A244 1.50k Goat .75 .25

A245

Europa: 1.50k, The Mermaid, painted dish, Hol. 2.20k, The Proposal, painted box, Nes.

1981, May 4 **Litho.** *Perf. 13*

781 A245 1.50k multi 1.00 .25
782 A245 2.20k multi 1.25 .75

A246

Designs: 1.30k, Weighing anchor. 1.50k, Climbing rigging, vert. 2.20k, Training Ship Christian Radich.

1981, May 4 **Engr.**

783 A246 1.30k dk olive grn .75 .50
784 A246 1.50k orange red .75 .25
785 A246 2.20k dark blue 1.25 .75
Nos. 783-785 (3) 2.75 1.50

Paddle Steamer Skibladner, 1856, Mjosa Lake — A247

Lake Transportation: 1.30k, Victoria, 1882, Bandak Channel. 1.50k, Faemund II, 1905, Fermund Lake. 2.30k, Storegut, 1956, Tinnsjo Lake.

1981, June 11 **Engr.** *Perf. 13*

786 A247 1.10k dark brown .75 .35
787 A247 1.30k green 1.00 .50
788 A247 1.50k red .75 .25
789 A247 2.30k dark blue 1.25 .50
Nos. 786-789 (4) 3.75 1.60

Group Walking Arm in Arm — A248

1981, Aug. 25 **Engr.**

790 A248 1.50k shown .75 .25
791 A248 2.20k Group, diff. 1.00 1.00

Intl. Year of the Disabled.

A249

Paintings: 1.50k, Interior in Blue, by Harriet Backer (1845-1932). 1.70k, Peat Moor on Jaeren, by Kitty Lange Kielland (1843-1914).

1981, Oct. 9 **Litho.** *Perf. 13*

792 A249 1.50k multi .75 .25
793 A249 1.70k multi 1.00 .75

A250

Tapestries: 1.10k, One of the Three Kings, Skjak, 1625. 1.30k, Adoration of the Infant Christ, tapestry, Skjak, 1625. 1.50k, The Marriage of Cana, Storen, 18th cent.

1981, Nov. 25 **Litho.** *Perf. 13½*

794 A250 1.10k multi .40 .25
795 A250 1.30k multi .50 .50

Size: 29x37mm

796 A250 1.50k multi .55 .25
Nos. 794-796 (3) 1.45 1.00

1921 Nobel Prize Winners Christian L. Lange (1869-1938) and Hjalmar Branting (1860-1925) A251

1981, Nov. 25 **Engr.** *Perf. 13*

797 A251 5k black 3.00 .40

World Skiing Championship, Oslo — A252

1982, Feb. 16 *Perf. 13½*

798 A252 2k Poles .75 .25
799 A252 3k Skis 1.10 .60

City of Christiansand, 350th Anniv. — A343

Litho. & Engr.

1991, Apr. 16 ***Perf. 13***

991 A343 3.20k Early view 1.50 .25
992 A343 5.50k Modern view 2.75 .50

Lifeboat Service, Cent. — A344

Designs: 3.20k, Rescue boat, Skomvaer III, horiz. 27k, Sailboat Colin Archer.

Litho & Engr.

1991, June 7 ***Perf. 13***

993 A344 3.20k multicolored 1.75 .25
994 A344 27k multicolored 14.00 2.00

Tourism — A345

Designs: 3.20k, Fountain, Vigeland Park. 4k, Globe, North Cape.

1991, June 7 Litho. ***Perf. 13½x13***

995 A345 3.20k multicolored 1.75 .25
996 A345 4k multicolored 3.50 2.00

Winter Olympic Type of 1989

Souvenir Sheet

Gold medal winners: a, Birger Ruud, ski jumping. b, Johan Grottumsbraten, cross country skiing. c, Knut Johannesen, speed skating. d, Magnar Solberg, biathlon.

1991, Oct. 11 LItho. ***Perf. 13½x13***

997 Sheet of 4 10.00 10.00
a.-d. A323 4k any single 2.50 2.50

Sold for 20k to benefit Olympic sports promotion.

A346

Natl. Stamp Day: a, Hands engraving. b, Magnifying glass above hands. c, View of hands through magnifying glass. d, Printed label being removed from plate.

1991, Oct. 11 ***Perf. 13x13½***

Souvenir Sheet

998 Sheet of 4 12.00 12.00
a. A346 2.70k multicolored 2.50 2.50
b. A346 3.20k multicolored 2.50 2.50
c. A346 4k multicolored 2.50 2.50
d. A346 5k multicolored 2.50 2.50

Sold for 20k.

A347

Christmas: No. 1000, People with lantern.

Perf. 13½x13 on 3 Sides

1991, Nov. 22 **Litho.**

Booklet Stamps

999 A347 3.20k multicolored 1.25 .25
1000 A347 3.20k multicolored 1.25 .25
a. Bklt. pane, 5 each #999-1000 12.50
Complete booklet, #1000a 14.00

Queen Sonja A348

King Harald A349

A349a

Perf. 13x13½, 12½x13½ (6.50k)

1992-2002 **Litho. & Engr.**

1004	A348	2.80k	multi	1.75	.25
1005	A348	3k	multi	1.50	.25
1007	A349	3.30k	multi	2.00	.25
1008	A349	3.50k	multi	1.75	.25
1009	A349	4.50k	carmine	2.25	.50
1011	A349	5.50k	multi	2.25	.25
1012	A349	5.60k	multi	2.50	.40
1014	A349	6.50k	green	3.00	.40
1015	A349	6.60k	multi	3.25	.50
1016	A349	7.50k	violet	3.75	2.00
1016A	A349	8.50k	brown	4.00	2.25

Perf. 13½x13

1017	A349a	10k	dark grn	5.00	.25
a.		Perf. 13½x13¾		4.00	.75
1019	A349a	20k	deep vio	10.00	.50
b.		Perf. 13½x13¾		8.50	.75
1019A	A349a	30k	dark blue	12.00	.50
1020	A349a	50k	olive black	17.00	1.00
a.		Perf. 13½x13¾		18.00	2.00
	Nos. 1004-1020 (15)			72.00	9.55

Issued: 2.80k, 3.30k, 5.60k, 6.60k, 2/21/92; 50k, 6/12/92; 3k, 3.50k, 5.50k, 2/23/93; 10k, 20k, 6/17/93; 6.50k, 2/12/94; 30k, 11/18/94; 4.50k, 7.50k, 8.50k, 11/24/95; Nos. 1019b, 1020a, Dec. 2001. No. 1017a, 2002.

Winter Olympic Type of 1989

Souvenir Sheet

Gold Medal winners: a, Hallgeir Brenden, cross-country skiing. b, Arnfinn Bergmann, ski jumping. c, Stein Eriksen, giant slalom. d, Simon Slattvik, Nordic combined.

1992, Feb. 21 Litho. ***Perf. 13½x13***

1021 Sheet of 4 9.00 9.00
a.-d. A323 4k any single 2.00 2.00

Sold for 20k to benefit Olympic sports promotion.

Expo '92, Seville A350

Designs: 3.30k, Norwegian pavilion, ship. 5.20k, Mountains, boat and fish.

1992, Apr. 20 Litho. ***Perf. 13x13½***

1022 A350 3.30k multicolored 1.50 .25
1023 A350 5.20k multicolored 2.25 .75

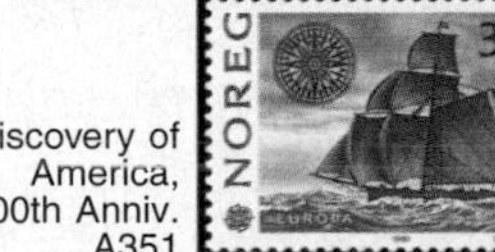

Discovery of America, 500th Anniv. A351

Europa: 3.30k, Sailing ship Restauration at sea, 1825. 4,20k, Stavangerfjord in New York Harbor, 1918.

Litho. & Engr.

1992, Apr. 21 ***Perf. 13x13½***

1024 A351 3.30k multicolored 2.25 .30
1025 A351 4.20k multicolored 2.75 1.00

Kristiansund, 250th Anniv. — A352

Litho. & Engr.

1992, June 12 ***Perf. 13***

1026 A352 3.30k brn, bl & blk 1.50 .25
1027 A352 3.30k View of Molde 1.50 .25

Molde, 250th anniv. (#1027).

Souvenir Sheet

Glass — A353

Stamp Day: a, Decorated vase. b, Carafe with gold design. c, Cut glass salad bowl. d, Decorated cup.

1992, Oct. 9 Litho. ***Perf. 13x13½***

1028 A353 Sheet of 4 12.00 12.00
a. 2.80k multicolored 2.50 2.50
b. 3.30k multicolored 2.50 2.50
c. 4.20k multicolored 2.50 2.50
d. 5.20k multicolored 2.50 2.50

No. 1028 sold for 20k.

A354

Designs: 3.30k, Flags, buildings in Lillehammer. 4.20k, Flag.

1992, Oct. 9 Litho. ***Perf. 13x13½***

1029 A354 3.30k multicolored 1.50 .25
1030 A354 4.20k multicolored 2.50 .75

1994 Winter Olympics, Lillehammer. See Nos. 1047-1048, 1053-1058.

A355

Christmas: No. 1031, Elves in front of mailbox. No. 1032, One elf holding other on shoulders to mail letters.

Perf. 13 on 3 Sides

1992, Nov. 23 **Litho.**

Booklet Stamps

1031 A355 3.30k multicolored 1.00 .25
1032 A355 3.30k multicolored 1.00 .25
b. Booklet pane, 5 each #1031-1032 12.00
Complete booklet, #1032b 15.00

Butterflies — A356

Designs: No. 1033, Anthocharis cardamines. No. 1034, Aglais urticae.

Perf. 13½x13 on 3 Sides

1993, Feb. 23 **Litho.**

Booklet Stamps

1033 A356 3.50k multicolored 1.25 .25
1034 A356 3.50k multicolored 1.25 .25
b. Booklet pane, 5 each #1033-1034 12.50
Complete booklet, #1034b 15.00

See Nos. 1051-1052.

Winter Olympic Type of 1989

Souvenir Sheet

1992 Gold Medal winners: a, Finn Christian Jagge, slalom. b, Bjorn Daehlie, cross-country skiing. c, Geir Karlstad, speed skating. d, Vegard Ulvang, cross-country skiing.

1993, Feb. 23 ***Perf. 13½x13***

1035 Sheet of 4 9.00 9.00
a.-d. A323 4.50k any single 2.00 2.00

No. 1035 sold for 22k to benefit Olympic sports promotion.

Norden — A357

1993, Apr. 23 Litho. ***Perf. 13½x13***

1036 A357 4k Canoe on lake 2.25 2.25
1037 A357 4.50k River rafting 2.25 .50

Edvard Grieg A358

Litho. & Engr.

1993, Apr. 23 ***Perf. 13x13½***

1038 A358 3.50k Portrait 1.75 .25
1039 A358 5.50k Landscape 2.50 .50

1993 World Championships in Norway — A359

1993, June 17 Litho. ***Perf. 13½x13***

1040 A359 3.50k Team handball 1.50 .25
1041 A359 5.50k Cycling 2.50 .50

Hurtigruten Shipping Line, Cent. A360

Litho. & Engr.

1993, June 17 ***Perf. 12½x13***

1042 A360 3.50k Richard With, ship 2.00 .25
1043 A360 4.50k Ship, officers 2.25 .75

Worker's Organization, Cent. A361

1993, Sept. 24 Engr. ***Perf. 13x13½***

1044 A361 3.50k Johan Castberg 2.00 .40
1045 A361 12k Betzy Kjelsberg 6.00 .75

Souvenir Sheet

Carvings — A362

Stamp Day: a, Spiral leaf scroll. b, Interlocking scroll. c, "1754" surrounded by scroll. d, Face with scroll above.

1993, Sept. 24 Litho. *Perf. 13½x13*

1046 A362 Sheet of 4, #a.-d. 12.00 12.00
a. 3k multicolored 2.50 2.50
b. 3.50k multicolored 2.50 2.50
c. 4.50k multicolored 2.50 2.50
d. 5.50k multicolored 2.50 2.50

No. 1046 sold for 21k.
See No. 1069.

1994 Winter Olympic Type of 1992

#1047, Flags, cross country skier. #1048, Flags, buildings in Lillehammer.

1993, Nov. 27 Litho. *Perf. 13x13½*

1047 A354 3.50k multicolored 1.50 .25
1048 A354 3.50k multicolored 1.50 .25
a. Pair, #1047-1048 3.25 2.00

No. 1048a has a continuous design.

Christmas — A363

Designs: No. 1049, Store Mangen Chapel. No. 1050, Church of Stamnes, Sandnes.

Perf. 13½x13 on 3 Sides

1993, Nov. 27 Booklet Stamps

1049 A363 3.50k shown 1.25 .25
1050 A363 3.50k multicolored 1.25 .25
b. Booklet pane, 5 each #1049-1050 12.50
Complete booklet, #1050b 15.00

Butterfly Type of 1993

Perf. 13½x13 on 3 Sides

1994, Feb. 12 Litho.

Booklet Stamps

1051 A356 3.50k Colias hecla 1.25 .25
1052 A356 3.50k Clossiana freija 1.25 .25
b. Booklet pane, 5 each #1051-1052 12.50
Complete booklet, #1052b 15.00

1994 Winter Olympic Type of 1992

Designs: No. 1053, Stylized Norwegian flag, Olympic rings UR. No. 1054, Stylized Norwegian flag, Olympic rings, UL. No. 1055, Olympic rings, buildings in Lillehammer. No. 1056, Olympic rings, ski jump. 4.50k, Flags of Norway, Belgium, Greece, Switzerland, Sweden, Germany, United Kingdom. 5.50k, Flags of Australia, New Zealand, Brazil, Canada, US, Japan, Mexico, South Korea.

1994, Feb. 12 *Perf. 13x13½*

1053 A354 3.50k multicolored 1.50 .30
1054 A354 3.50k multicolored 1.50 .30
1055 A354 3.50k multicolored 1.50 .30
1056 A354 3.50k multicolored 1.50 .30
a. Block of 4, #1053-1056 7.00 8.00
1057 A354 4.50k multicolored 2.00 .60
1058 A354 5.50k multicolored 2.25 .50
Nos. 1053-1058 (6) 10.25 2.30

1994 Paralympics A365

1994, Mar. 10 Litho. *Perf. 13*

1059 A365 4.50k Skier 1.75 .60
1060 A365 5.50k Skier, diff. 2.00 .50

Tromso Charter, Bicent. A366

Litho. & Engr.

1994, Apr. 19 *Perf. 13*

1061 A366 3.50k Royal seal 1.75 .25
1062 A366 4.50k Cathedral 2.25 .75

Norwegian Folk Museum, Cent. A367

Designs: 3k, Log buildings, Osterdal Valley. 3.50k, Sled, 1750.

Litho. & Engr.

1994, June 14 *Perf. 12½x13*

1063 A367 3k multicolored 1.50 .50
1064 A367 3.50k multicolored 1.75 .25

Research in Norway A368

Abstract designs with various formulas, microchips, glass flasks.

1994, June 14 Litho.

1065 A368 4k multicolored 1.75 .60
1066 A368 4.50k multicolored 2.25 .60

Electric Tram Lines, Cent. A369

Litho. & Engr.

1994, Sept. 23 *Perf. 13x13½*

1067 A369 3.50k Early tram, map 1.75 .25
1068 A369 12k Modern tram, map 6.00 .60

Stamp Day Type of 1993

Ornamental broaches: a, Gold, embossed designs. b, Silver, embossed designs. c, Silver, circular designs. d, Gold, jeweled center.

1994, Sept. 23 Litho. *Perf. 13½x13*

1069 Sheet of 4, #a.-d. 12.50 12.50
a. A362 3k multicolored 2.50 2.50
b. A362 3.50k multicolored 2.50 2.50
c. A362 4.50k multicolored 2.50 2.50
d. A362 5.50k multicolored 2.50 2.50

No. 1069 sold for 21k.

Christmas — A370

Perf. 13½x13 on 3 Sides

1994, Nov. 18 Litho.

Booklet Stamps

1070 A370 3.50k Sled 1.50 .25
1071 A370 3.50k Kick sled 1.50 .25
a. Booklet pane, 5 each 15.00
Complete booklet, #1071a 16.00

Berries — A371

No. 1086, Vaccinium vitis. No. 1087, Vaccinium myrtillus. No. 1088, Fragaria vesca. No. 1089, Rubus chamaemorus.

Booklet Stamps

1995-96 Litho. *Perf. 13½x13*

1086 A371 3.50k multi 1.25 .25
1087 A371 3.50k multi 1.25 .25
a. Bklt. pane, 4 ea #1086-1087 10.00
Complete booklet, #1087a 12.00
1088 A371 3.50k multi 1.25 .25
1089 A371 3.50k multi 1.25 .25
a. Bklt. pane, 4 ea #1088-1089 10.00
Complete booklet, #1089a 12.00
Nos. 1086-1089 (4) 5.00 1.00

Issued: #1086-1087, 2/23/95; #1088-1089, 2/22/96.

A372

Apothecary Shops, 400th Anniv.: 3.50k, Swan Pharmacy, Bergen. 25k, Apothecary's tools.

Litho. & Engr.

1995, Feb. 23 *Perf. 13½x13*

1090 A372 3.50k multicolored 1.75 .25
1091 A372 25k multicolored 12.00 1.25

A373

Tourism: 4k, Skudeneshavn Harbor. 4.50k, Torghatten mountain, Helgeland coastline.

1995, May 8 Litho. *Perf. 13½x13*

Booklet Stamps

1092 A373 4k multicolored 1.50 .75
a. Booklet pane of 8 12.00
Complete booklet, #1092a 14.00
1093 A373 4.50k multicolored 1.75 .75
a. Booklet pane of 8 14.00
Complete booklet, #1093a 16.00

Christianity in Norway A374

3.50k, Old Moster Church, c. 1100. 15k, Slettebakken Church, Bergen, 1970.

Litho. & Engr.

1995, May 8 *Perf. 13x13½*

1094 A374 3.50k multicolored 1.75 .25
1095 A374 15k multicolored 7.00 1.00

End of World War II, 50th Anniv. A375

Designs: 3.50k, German commander saluting Terje Rollem in 1945, German forces marching down Karl Johans Gate from Royal Palace, 1940. 4.50k, King Haakon VII, Crown Prince leaving Norway in 1940, King saluting upon return in 1945. 5.50k, Children waving Norwegian flags, 1945.

1995, May 8 Litho. *Perf. 13½x13*

1096 A375 3.50k multicolored 1.75 .25
1097 A375 4.50k multicolored 2.25 .60
1098 A375 5.50k multicolored 2.75 .50
Nos. 1096-1098 (3) 6.75 1.35

Kirsten Flagstad (1895-1962), Opera Singer — A376

Design: 5.50k, In Lohengrin.

1995, June 26 Litho. *Perf. 13*

1099 A376 3.50k multicolored 2.00 .25
1100 A376 5.50k multicolored 2.75 .60

Conciliation Boards, Bicent. A377

Designs: 7k, Three-man board between two people facing away from each other. 12k, Seated board member, two people talking to each other.

1995, June 26 *Perf. 13½*

1101 A377 7k multicolored 3.25 .60
1102 A377 12k multicolored 5.00 .60

UN, 50th Anniv. A378

UN emblem and: 3.50k, Trygve Lie, Secretary General 1946-53. 5.50k, Woman drinking from clean water supply.

Litho. & Engr.

1995, Sept. 22 *Perf. 13*

1103 A378 3.50k multicolored 2.00 .25
1104 A378 5.50k multicolored 2.75 .50

Norway Post, 350th Anniv. A379

#1105, Signature, portrait of Hannibal Sehested, letter post, 1647. #1106, Wax seal, registered letters, 1745. #1107, Christiania, etc. postmarks. #1108, Funds transfer, coins, canceled envelopes, 1883. #1109, "Norske Intelligenz-Seddeler," first newspaper, newspapers, magazines, 1660. #1110, Postmarks, label, parcel post, 1827. #1111, No. 1, Type A5, stamps, 1855. #1112, Savings book stamps, bank services, 1950.

Booklet Stamps

1995, Sept. 22 Litho.

1105 A379 3.50k multicolored 1.25 .50
1106 A379 3.50k multicolored 1.25 .50
1107 A379 3.50k multicolored 1.25 .50
1108 A379 3.50k multicolored 1.25 .50
1109 A379 3.50k multicolored 1.25 .50
1110 A379 3.50k multicolored 1.25 .50
1111 A379 3.50k multicolored 1.25 .50
a. Missing gray stamp at LR *12.50* 5.00
1112 A379 3.50k multicolored 1.25 .50
a. Booklet pane, #1105-1112 12.50 18.00
Complete booklet, #1112a 15.00
b. Booklet pane, #1105-1110, #1111a, 1112 25.00 25.00
Complete booklet, #1112b 27.50

Christmas — A380

Booklet Stamps

Perf. 13 on 3 Sides

1995, Nov. 24 **Litho.**

1113	A380 3.50k Knitted cap	1.25	.25
1114	A380 3.50k Knitted mitten	1.25	.25
a.	Bklt. pane, 4 ea #1113-1114	10.00	
	Complete booklet, #1114a	12.00	

Svalbard Islands A381

1996, Feb. 22 **Litho.** ***Perf. 13***

1115	A381 10k Advent Bay	5.00	.75
1116	A381 20k Polar bear	10.00	1.25

Olympic Games, Cent. — A382

Children's drawings: 3.50k, Cross country skier. 5.50k, Runner.

1996, Apr. 18 **Litho.** ***Perf. 13½***

1117	A382 3.50k multicolored	1.75	.25
1118	A382 5.50k multicolored	2.50	.50

Tourism — A383

1996, Apr. 18 ***Perf. 13 on 3 Sides***

1119	A383 4k Besseggen	1.25	.75
a.	Booklet pane of 8	10.00	
	Complete booklet, #1119a	12.00	
1120	A383 4.50k Urnes Stave Church	1.50	.75
a.	Booklet pane of 8	12.00	
	Complete booklet, #1120a	14.00	
1121	A383 5.50k Alta Rock Carvings	1.75	.75
a.	Booklet pane of 8	14.00	
	Complete booklet, #1121a	16.00	
	Nos. 1119-1121 (3)	4.50	2.25

See Nos. 1155-1157.

Railway Centennials — A384

Litho. & Engr.

1996, June 19 ***Perf. 13***

1122	A384 3k Urskog-Holand	1.50	.50
1123	A384 4.50k Setesdal	2.00	1.25

The Troll Offshore Gasfield A385

3.50k, Size of Troll platform compared to Eiffel Tower. 25k, Troll platform, map of gas pipelines.

1996, June 19 **Litho.**

1124	A385 3.50k multicolored	1.75	.25
1125	A385 25k multicolored	11.00	1.25

Norway Post, 350th Anniv. A386

#1126, Postal courier on skis. #1127, Fjord boat, SS "Framnaes," 1920's. #1128, Mail truck, Oslo, 1920's. #1129, Early airmail service. #1130, Unloading mail, East Railroad Station, Oslo, 1950's. #1131, Using bicycle for rural mail delivery, 1970's. #1132, Customer, mail clerk, Elverum post office. #1133, Computer, globe, E-mail service.

Booklet Stamps

1996, Sept. 20 **Litho.** ***Perf. 13***

1126	A386 3.50k multicolored	1.25	.85
1127	A386 3.50k multicolored	1.25	.85
1128	A386 3.50k multicolored	1.25	.85
1129	A386 3.50k multicolored	1.25	.85
1130	A386 3.50k multicolored	1.25	.85
1131	A386 3.50k multicolored	1.25	.85
1132	A386 3.50k multicolored	1.25	.85
1133	A386 3.50k multicolored	1.25	.85
a.	Booklet pane, #1126-1133	12.00	14.00
	Complete booklet, #1133a	13.00	

Motion Pictures, Cent. A387

Film strips showing: 3.50k, Leif Juster, Sean Connery, Liv Ullmann, The Olsen Gang Films, Il Temp Gigante. 5.50k, Wenche Foss, Jack Fjeldstad, Marilyn Monroe, murder, blood, shooting. 7k, Charlie Chaplin, Ottar Gladvedt, Laurel & Hardy, Marlene Dietrich.

1996, Sept. 20

1134	A387 3.50k multicolored	1.50	.25
1135	A387 5.50k multicolored	2.25	.50
1136	A387 7k multicolored	2.75	.60
	Nos. 1134-1136 (3)	6.50	1.35

A388

Christmas (Embroidered motif from Norwegian folk costume): Denomination at UL (#1137), UR (#1138).

Perf. 13 on 3 Sides

1996, Nov. 21 **Litho.**

1137	A388 3.50k multicolored	1.25	.25
1138	A388 3.50k multicolored	1.25	.25
a.	Bklt. pane, 4 ea #1137-1138	10.00	
	Complete booklet, #1138a	12.00	

A389

Amalie Skram (1846-1905), Novelist: 3.50k, Portrait. 15k, Scene from performance of Skram's "People of Hellemyr."

1996, Nov. 21 **Engr.**

1139	A389 3.50k claret	1.75	.35
1140	A389 15k claret & dk blue	6.50	1.50

Posthorn Type of 1893 Redrawn

1997, Jan. 2 **Litho.** ***Perf. 13x13½***

Color of Oval

1141	A10 10o red	.25	.25
1142	A10 20o blue	.25	.25
a.	Perf. 13¾x13¼	.50	.50
1143	A10 30o orange	.25	.25
1144	A10 40o gray	.25	.25
1145	A10 50o green, green numeral	.25	.25
	Nos. 1141-1145 (5)	1.25	1.25

Numerous design differences exist in the vertical shading lines, the size and shading of the posthorn, and in the corner wings.

See No. 1282A for stamp similar to No. 1145 but with blue numeral.

Issued: No. 1142a, Dec. 2000.

Insects — A390

1997, Jan. 2 ***Perf. 13 on 3 Sides***

1146	A390 3.70k Bumblebee	1.25	.25
1147	A390 3.70k Ladybug	1.25	.25
a.	Bklt. pane, 4 ea #1146-1147	10.00	
	Complete booklet	12.00	

See Nos. 1180-1181.

Flowers — A391

1997, Jan. 2 ***Perf. 13***

1148	A391 3.20k Red clover	1.25	.40
1149	A391 3.70k Coltsfoot	1.50	.35
1150	A391 4.30k Lily of the Valley	2.00	.40
1151	A391 5k Harebell	2.25	.45
1152	A391 6k Oxeye daisy	2.50	.55
	Nos. 1148-1152 (5)	9.50	2.15

See #1182-1187, 1210-1212, 1244-1247.

World Nordic Skiing Championships, Trondheim A392

1997, Feb. 20

1153	A392 3.70k Ski jumping	1.75	.40
1154	A392 5k Cross-country skiing	2.50	.60

Tourism Type of 1996

Perf. 13 on 3 Sides

1997, Apr. 16 **Litho.**

Booklet Stamps

1155	A383 4.30k Roros	1.75	1.00
a.	Booklet pane of 8	14.00	
	Complete booklet, #1155a	16.00	
1156	A383 5k Faerder Lighthouse	2.00	.75
a.	Booklet pane of 8	16.00	
	Complete booklet, #1156a	18.00	
1157	A383 6k Nusfjord	2.25	.60
a.	Booklet pane of 8	18.00	
	Complete booklet #1157a	20.00	

King Harald, Queen Sonja, 60th Birthdays A393

1997, Apr. 16 **Litho.** ***Perf. 13***

1158	A393 3.70k shown	1.75	.40
1159	A393 3.70k King Harald, vert.	1.75	.40

Norway Post, 350th Anniv. A394

Post-World War II development: No. 1160, Tools for construction, 1945. No. 1161, Kon-Tiki Expedition, 1947. No. 1162, Environmental protection, establishing national parks, 1962. No. 1163, Welfare, help for the elderly, 1967. No. 1164, Off-shore oil drilling, 1969. No. 1165, Grete Waitz, marathon winner, 1983. No. 1166, Askoy Bridge, 1992. No. 1167, Winter Olympic Games, Lillehammer, 1994.

1997, Apr. 16 **Booklet Stamps**

1160	A394 3.70k multicolored	1.25	.85
1161	A394 3.70k multicolored	1.25	.85
1162	A394 3.70k multicolored	1.25	.85
1163	A394 3.70k multicolored	1.25	.85
1164	A394 3.70k multicolored	1.25	.85
1165	A394 3.70k multicolored	1.25	.85
1166	A394 3.70k multicolored	1.25	.85
1167	A394 3.70k multicolored	1.25	.85
a.	Booklet pane, #1160-1167	12.00	14.00
	Complete booklet, #1167a	14.00	12.00

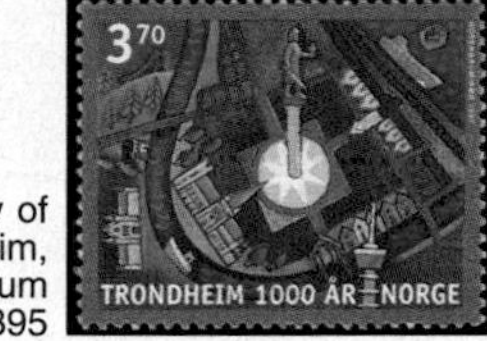

City of Trondheim, Millenium A395

Stylized designs: 3.70k, New Trondheim. 12k, Ships entering harbor, King, early settlements in Old Nidaros.

1997, June 6 **Litho.** ***Perf. 13½x13***

1168	A395 3.70k multicolored	2.00	.40
1169	A395 12k multicolored	6.00	1.00

Einar Gerhardsen (1897-1987), Prime Minister — A396

Caricatures: 3.70k, In front on government buildings. 25k, Scenes of Norway.

1997, June 6 ***Perf. 13½***

1170	A396 3.70k multicolored	2.00	.40
1171	A396 25k multicolored	12.00	1.50

Junior Stamp Club — A397

Topics found on stamps: No. 1172, Insect, butterfly (silhouette of person's face), cartoon character, fish, flag, hand holding pen, heart, tiger, horn, boy with dog, globe. No. 1173, Flag, hand holding pen, tree, butterfly (silhouette of person's face), ladybug, cartoon character, antique postal vehicle, soccer ball, stylized bird, man on bicycle, lighthouse.

1997, Sept. 29 **Litho.** ***Perf. 13***

1172	A397 3.70k multicolored	1.75	.40
1173	A397 3.70k multicolored	1.75	.40

Harald Saeverud (1897-1992), Composer — A398

15k, Tarjei Vesaas (1897-1970), writer.

Litho. & Engr.

1997, Sept. 19 ***Perf. 13½x13***

1174	A398 10k blue	5.50	1.00
1175	A398 15k green	7.50	1.50

Petter Dass (1647-1706), Poet, Priest — A399

Designs: 3.20k, Dass standing in rowboat, verse. 3.70k, Dass, church on island of Alsten.

Litho. & Engr.

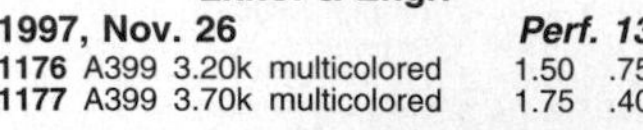

1997, Nov. 26 *Perf. 13*
1176 A399 3.20k multicolored 1.50 .75
1177 A399 3.70k multicolored 1.75 .40

Christmas A400

Various designs from Norwgian calendar stick, medieval forerunner of modern day calendar.

Serpentine Die Cut 13½ on 3 Sides
1997, Nov. 26 **Litho.**
Self-Adhesive
Booklet Stamps
1178 A400 3.70k yellow & multi 1.25 .30
1179 A400 3.70k blue & multi 1.25 .30
a. Bklt. pane, 2 ea #1178-1179 6.00
Complete booklet, 2 #1179a 12.00

Insect Type of 1997
1998, Jan. 2 ***Perf. 13½ on 3 Sides***
Booklet Stamps
1180 A390 3.80k Dragonfly 1.50 .25
1181 A390 3.80k Grasshopper 1.50 .25
a. Bklt. pane, 4 ea #1180-1181 12.00
Complete booklet, #1181a 14.00

Flower Type of 1997

3.40k, Marsh marigold. 3.80k, Wild pansy. 4.50k, White clover. 5.50k, Hepatica. 7.50k, Pale pasqueflower. 13k, Purple saxifrage.

1998, Jan. 2 **Litho.** *Perf. 13*
1182 A391 3.40k multi 1.25 .25
1183 A391 3.80k multi 1.50 .25
1184 A391 4.50k multi 2.00 .40
1185 A391 5.50k multi 2.25 .40
1186 A391 7.50k multi 3.00 .50
1187 A391 13k multi 5.00 .50
Nos. 1182-1187 (6) 15.00 2.30

Valentine's Day — A401

1998, Feb. 9 ***Die Cut Perf. 14x13***
Self-Adhesive
1188 A401 3.80k multicolored 1.50 .50

No. 1188 was issued in sheets of 3 + 4 labels.

A402

Coastal Shipping: 3.80k, Mail boat, SS Hornelen. 4.50k, Catamaran, Kommandoren.

Litho. & Engr.
1998, Apr. 20 ***Perf. 13x13½***
1189 A402 3.80k dark bl & grn 1.50 .30
1190 A402 4.50k bl & dark grn 2.00 1.00

A403

Tourism: 3.80k, Holmenkollen ski jump, Oslo. 4.50k, Fisherman, city of Alesund. 5.50k, Summit of Hamaroyskaftet Mountain.

Perf. 13 on 3 Sides
1998, Apr. 20 **Litho.**
1191 A403 3.80k multicolored 1.50 .25
a. Booklet pane of 8 12.00
Complete booklet, #1191a 12.00
1192 A403 4.50k multicolored 1.75 1.00
a. Booklet pane of 8 14.00
Complete booklet, #1192a 14.00
1193 A403 5.50k multicolored 2.00 .75
a. Booklet pane of 8 16.00
Complete booklet, #1193a 16.00
Nos. 1191-1193 (3) 5.25 2.00

Town of Egersund, Bicent. A404

Designs: 3.80k, Port, herring boats. 6k, Pottery, white stoneware.

Litho. & Engr.
1998, Apr. 20 *Perf. 13*
1194 A404 3.80k dk blue & pink 1.50 .30
1195 A404 6k mag & dp bl 2.50 .60

Minerals — A405

1998, June 18 **Litho.** *Perf. 13*
1196 A405 3.40k Silver 1.50 .70
1197 A405 5.20k Cobaltite 2.25 .75

Contemporary Art — A406

Designs: 6k, "Water Rider," painting by Frans Widerberg. 7.50k, "Red Moon," tapestry by Synnove Anker Aurdal. 13k, "King Haakon VII," sculpture by Nils Aas.

1998, June 18
1198 A406 6k multicolored 2.40 .50
1199 A406 7.50k multicolored 3.00 1.25
1200 A406 13k multicolored 5.00 1.25
Nos. 1198-1200 (3) 10.40 3.00

Children's Games A407

1998, Sept. 18 **Litho.** *Perf. 13*
1201 A407 3.80k Hopscotch 1.50 .50
1202 A407 5.50k Pitching coins 2.25 1.00

New Airport, Gardermoen — A408

1998, Sept. 18 *Perf. 13½*
1203 A408 3.80k DC-3 2.00 .50
1204 A408 6k Boeing 737 3.00 .75
1205 A408 24k New airport 10.00 1.50
Nos. 1203-1205 (3) 15.00 2.75

The Royal Palace A409

1998, Nov. 20 **Engr.** ***Perf. 13x13½***
1206 A409 3.40k Royal Guard 1.50 1.00
1207 A409 3.80k Facade 1.50 .50

Christmas A410

Serpentine Die Cut 14x13 on 3 Sides
1998, Nov. 20 **Photo.**
Self-Adhesive
Booklet Stamps
1208 A410 3.80k red & multi 1.50 .30
1209 A410 3.80k blue & multi 1.50 .30
a. Bklt. pane, 2 ea #1208-1209 6.00
Complete booklet, 2 #1209a 12.00

Flower Type of 1997
1999, Jan. 2 **Litho.** ***Perf. 13***
1210 A391 3.60k Red campion 1.50 .30
1211 A391 4k Wood anemone 1.75 .25
1212 A391 7k Yellow wood violet 2.75 .50
Nos. 1210-1212 (3) 6.00 1.05

Norwegian Inventions — A411

Designs: 3.60k, Cheese slicer, by Thor Bjorklund. 4k, Paper clip, by Johan Vaaler.

Die Cut Perf. 13
1999, Jan. 2 **Photo.**
Self-Adhesive
1213 A411 3.60k blue & black 1.25 .25
1214 A411 4k red & gray 1.50 .25

See No. 1260.

Salmon — A412

Cod — A413

Die Cut Perf. 14x13
1999, Jan. 2 **Litho. & Photo.**
Self-Adhesive
Booklet Stamps
1215 A412 4k multicolored 1.25 .25
1216 A413 4k multicolored 1.25 .25
a. Bklt. pane, 2 ea #1215-1216 5.00
Complete booklet, 2 #1216a 10.00

St. Valentine's Day — A414

1999, Feb. 14 **Litho.** ***Perf. 13x13½***
1217 A414 4k multicolored 1.75 .50

A415

Litho. & Engr.
1999, Apr. 12 ***Perf. 13***
1218 A415 4k multicolored 1.50 .50

Norwegian Confederation of Trade Unions, Cent.

A416

Tourism: 4k, Swans on lake. 5k, Hamar Cathedral. 6k, Man in traditional attire.

1999, Apr. 12 **Litho.** ***Perf. 13***
Booklet Stamps
1219 A416 4k multicolored 1.25 .40
a. Booklet pane of 8 10.00
Complete booklet, #1219a 10.00
1220 A416 5k multicolored 1.75 .50
a. Booklet pane of 8 14.00
Complete booklet, #1220a 14.00
1221 A416 6k multicolored 2.00 .75
a. Booklet pane of 8 16.00
Complete booklet, #1221a 16.00

Ice Hockey World Championships — A417

Designs: 4k, Poland vs Norway, 1998 Class B Championships. 7k, Sweden vs Switzerland, 1998 Class A Championships.

1999, Apr. 12 ***Perf. 13½***
1222 A417 4k multicolored 1.50 .50
1223 A417 7k multicolored 3.00 .75

Millennium Stamps A418

Events from 1000-1899: 4k, Family leaving Sejestad Station, emigration period, 1800's. 6k, Statue of St. Olav (995-1030), Christian III Bible, 1550, Christianization period. 14k, King Christian IV speciedaler, miners, union period, 1380-1814. 26k, Textile factory, paper mill on Aker River, Oslo, 1850's, industrialization period.

Litho. & Engr.
1999, June 11 ***Perf. 12¾x13***
1224 A418 4k multicolored 1.75 .50
1225 A418 6k multicolored 2.75 .75
1226 A418 14k multicolored 6.50 1.25
1227 A418 26k multicolored 10.00 1.75
Nos. 1224-1227 (4) 21.00 4.25

Pictures of Everyday Life — A419

No. 1228, Carriage on ferry. No. 1229, Men with hammers. No. 1230, Pumping gasoline. No. 1231, Milking cow. No. 1232, Rakers. No. 1233, Skier. No. 1234, Boat captain. No. 1235, Soccer player.

1999, Sept. 9 **Litho.** ***Perf. 13***
1228 A419 4k multicolored 1.75 .50
1229 A419 4k multicolored 1.75 .50
1230 A419 4k multicolored 1.75 .50
1231 A419 4k multicolored 1.75 .50
1232 A419 4k multicolored 1.75 .50
1233 A419 4k multicolored 1.75 .50
1234 A419 4k multicolored 1.75 .50
1235 A419 4k multicolored 1.75 .50
a. Souv. sheet of 8, #1228-1235 14.00 12.50

Children's Games — A420

1999, Sept. 9 Litho. *Perf. 13¼*

1236 A420 4k Skateboarder 1.50 .50
1237 A420 6k Roller skater 2.50 .75

National Theater, Cent. A421

Designs: 3.60k, Scene from "An Ideal Husband." 4k, Scene from "Peer Gynt."

1999, Nov. 19 Engr. *Perf. 12¾x13¼*

1238 A421 3.60k claret & org yel 1.50 1.50
1239 A421 4k dk bl & royal bl 1.25 .50

Christmas — A422

Designs: No. 1240, Mother, children at door. No. 1241, Mother, children at window.

Die Cut Perf. 14x13 on 3 sides

1999, Nov. 19 Litho.

Self-Adhesive

1240 A422 4k multi 1.50 .30
1241 A422 4k multi 1.50 .30
a. Bklt. pane, 2 ea #1240-1241 5.00
Complete booklet, 2 #1241a 12.00

Millennium A423

Winners of photo competition: No. 1242, "Winter Night." No. 1243, "Sunset."

Die Cut Perf. 13¼x13

1999, Dec. 31 Litho. & Photo.

Self-Adhesive

1242 A423 4k multi 1.75 .50
1243 A423 4k multi 1.75 .50
a. Bklt. pane of 2, #1242-1243 5.00
Complete booklet, #1240a 18.00
b. Bklt. pane, 2 ea #1242-1243 8.00
Complete booklet, 2 #1243b 16.00

One complete booklet containing No. 1243a was given free to each Norwegian household in January 2000.

Flower Type of 1997

Designs: 5.40k, Oeder's lousewort. 8k, White water lily. 14k, Globe flower. 25k, Melancholy thistle.

2000, Feb. 9 Litho. *Perf. 12¾x13¼*

1244 A391 5.40k multi 2.00 .60
1245 A391 8k multi 3.25 .75
1246 A391 14k multi 5.00 1.00
1247 A391 25k multi 10.00 1.25
Nos. 1244-1247 (4) 20.25 3.60

Love — A424

2000, Feb. 9 *Perf. 13x13¼*

1248 A424 4k multi 1.50 .50

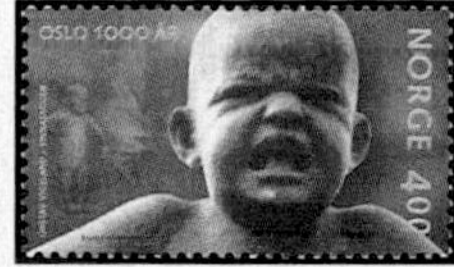

Oslo, 1000th Anniv. A425

4k, Angry Child sculpture, Frogner Park. 6k, Statue of King Christian IV, by C. L. Jacobsen. 8k, Oslo City Hall. 27k, Oslo Stock Exchange.

2000, Apr. 7 Litho. *Perf. 13¼*

1249 A425 4k multi 1.75 .50
1250 A425 6k multi 2.50 .75
1251 A425 8k multi 3.50 1.00
1252 A426 27k multi 11.00 1.50
Nos. 1249-1252 (4) 18.75 3.75

Fauna — A426

2000, Apr. 7 *Perf. 13¼ on 3 sides*

Booklet Stamps

1253 A426 5k Golden eagle 1.75 .75
a. Booklet pane of 8 14.00
Booklet, #1253a 15.00
1254 A426 6k Elk 2.00 .75
a. Booklet pane of 8 16.00
Booklet, #1254a 18.00
1255 A426 7k Whale 2.25 .75
a. Booklet pane of 8 18.00
Complete booklet, #1255a 20.00
Nos. 1253-1255 (3) 6.00 2.25

Expo 2000, Hanover A427

Artwork of Marianne Heske: 4.20k, The Quiet Room. 6.30k, Power and Energy.

2000, June 1 *Perf. 13¼*

1256 A427 4.20k multi 1.75 1.00
1257 A427 6.30k multi 2.75 .50

Royal Norwegian Military Academy, 250th Anniv. — A428

Litho. & Engr.

2000, June 2 *Perf. 13x13¼*

1258 A428 3.60k 1750 Cadets 1.75 2.00
1259 A428 8k 2000 Cadets 3.25 1.00

Inventions Type of 1999

4.20k, Aerosol container, by Erik Rotheim.

Die Cut Perf. 12¾

2000, June 2 Photo.

Self-Adhesive

1260 A411 4.20k green & black 1.50 .25

Mackerel — A429

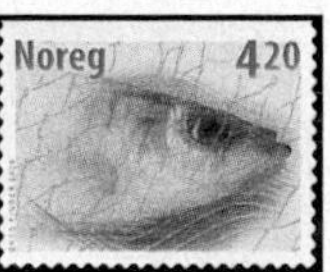

Herring — A430

Die Cut Perf. 14x13 on 3 sides

2000, June 2 Photo. & Litho.

Self-Adhesive

Booklet Stamps

1261 A429 4.20k multi 1.50 .25
1262 A430 4.20k multi 1.50 .25
a. Booklet pane, 2 each #1261-1262 6.00
Complete booklet, 2#1262a 12.00

A431

Litho. & Engr.

2000, Sept. 15 *Perf. 13¼x13*

1263 A431 5k multi 2.25 1.00

Lars Levi Laestadius (1800-61), botanist.

A432

Intl. Museum of Children's Art, Oslo: 4.20k, Astronaut, by May-Therese Vorland. 6.30k, Rocket, by Jann Fredrik Ronning.

Perf. 13¼x13¾

2000, Sept. 15 Litho.

1264 A432 4.20k multi 1.75 .50
1265 A432 6.30k multi 2.50 .60

Skien, 1000th Anniv. — A433

Designs: 4.20k, Monument to loggers. 15k, Skien Church.

2000, Sept. 15 *Perf. 13¼x13*

1266 A433 4.20k multi 1.75 .75
1267 A433 15k multi 6.25 1.50

Church Altar Pieces A434

2000, Nov. 17 Litho. *Perf. 13x13¼*

1268 A434 3.60k Hamaroy Church 1.50 1.25
1269 A434 4.20k Ski Church 1.75 .75

Comic Strips — A435

Designs: No. 1270, Nils og Blamman, by Sigurd Winsnes and Ivar Mauritz-Hansen. No. 1271, Nr. 91 Stomperud, by Ernst Garvin and Torbjorn Wen.

Die Cut Perf. 14x13 on 3 sides

2000, Nov. 17 Photo. & Litho.

Booklet Stamps

Self-Adhesive

1270 A435 4.20k multi 1.50 .25
1271 A435 4.20k multi 1.50 .25
a. Booklet pane, 2 each #1270-1271 6.00
Complete booklet, 2 #1271a 12.00

Rose Varieties A436

Designs: No. 1272, Sekel (green denomination). No. 1273, Namdal (brown denomination).

Die Cut Perf.13¼ on 3 sides

2001, Jan. 2 Photo.

Booklet Stamps

Self-Adhesive

1272 A436 4.50k multi 1.50 .25
1273 A436 4.50k multi 1.50 .25
a. Booklet pane, 2 each #1272-1273 7.00
Complete booklet, 2 #1273a 14.00

See Nos. 1303-1304.

Crafts — A437

Designs: 4k, Mat of bound birch roots. 4.50k, Birch bark basket. 7k, Embroidered bunad.

2001, Jan. 2 *Die Cut Perf. 12¾*

Coil Stamps

Self-Adhesive

1274 A437 4k multi 1.50 .30
1275 A437 4.50k multi 1.75 .25
1276 A437 7k multi 2.50 .50
Nos. 1274-1276 (3) 5.75 1.05

See Nos. 1305-1307, 1354.

Actors and Actresses A438

Designs: 4k, Aase Bye (1904-91). 4.50k, Per Aabel (1902-99). 5.50k, Alfred Maurstad (1896-1967). 7k, Lillebil Ibsen (1899-1989). 8k, Tore Segelcke (1901-79).

2001, Jan. 2 Litho. *Perf. 14x12¾*

1277 A438 4k brn & blk 1.50 .75
1278 A438 4.50k bl & blk 2.00 .50
1279 A438 5.50k gold & blk 2.25 .75
1280 A438 7k pur & blk 2.75 1.00
1281 A438 8k bl gray & blk 3.00 1.00
Nos. 1277-1281 (5) 11.50 4.00

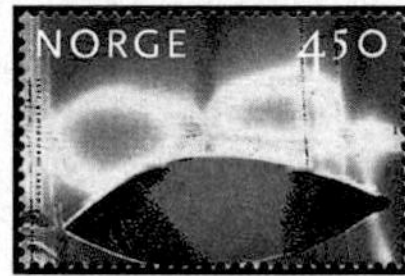

Ties That Bind, by Magne Furuholmen A439

2001, Feb. 7 Litho. *Perf. 14¾x14*

1282 A439 4.50k multi 1.75 .50

Redrawn Posthorn — A439a

2001-06 Litho. *Perf. 13¾x13¼*

Color of Oval

1282A A439a 50o green, blue denomination .25 .25
1283 A439a 1k green .50 .40
a. Horiz. rows of dots between vert. lines 1.00 .75
1284 A439a 2k Prus blue 1.00 .75
a. Horiz. rows of dots between vert. lines 1.00 .75
1285 A439a 3k blue 1.00 .50
1287 A439a 5k purple 3.00 .75
a. Horiz. rows of dots between vert. lines 3.00 .25
1288 A439a 6k purple 2.00 .45
1289 A439a 7k brown 2.50 .90
1291 A439a 9k orange brn 4.50 .75
a. Horiz. rows of dots between vert. lines 4.00 .75
Nos. 1282A-1291 (8) 14.75 4.75

Numerous design differences exist between types A10 and A439a in the vertical shading lines, the size and shading of the posthorn and in the corner wings.

No. 1282A has no dots between vertical lines. Dots between vertical lines on Nos.

1283-1284, 1287-1288 and 1291 are arranged diagonally. Nos. 1285 and 1289 have horizontal rows of dots between vertical lines.

Issued: Nos.1283, 1284, 6k, 2/7/01; 50o, 3/01; 5k, 9k, 2/11/02; Nos. 1283a, 1284a, 1291a, 2003; 3k, 7k, 4/15/05; No. 1287a, 2006.

See No. 1145 for green 50o stamp with green denomination. See Nos. 1628-1630, 1661, 1690, 1723-1724, 1749-1752, 1783.

School Bands, Cent. A440

Designs: 4.50k, Tuba player. 9k, Drum majorette.

2001, Apr. 20 Litho. ***Perf. 14¾x14***
1292 A440 4.50k multi 1.75 .50
1293 A440 9k multi 3.50 1.50

Adventure Sports — A441

Designs: 4.50k, Kayaking. 7k, Rock climbing.

Serpentine Die Cut 14x13 on 3 Sides

2001, Apr. 20 Photo. & Litho.

Booklet Stamps

Self-Adhesive

1294 A441 4.50k multi 1.75 .50
a. Booklet of 8 15.00
1295 A441 7k multi 2.50 .75
a. Booklet of 8 20.00

Norwegian Architecture A442

Designs: 5.50k, Bank of Norway, Oslo, by Christian Heinrich Grosch. 8.50k, Ivar Aasen Center, Orsta, by Sverre Fehn.

2001, June 22 Litho. ***Perf. 14¾x14***
1296 A442 5.50k multi 2.00 .75
1297 A442 8.50k multi 3.00 1.00

Actors and Actresses — A443

Designs: 5k, Lalla Carlsen (1889-1967). 5.50k, Leif Juster (1910-95). 7k, Kari Diesen (1914-87). 9k, Arvid Nilssen (1913-76). 10k, Einar Rose (1898-1979).

2001, June 22 ***Perf. 13x14***
1298 A443 5k multi 1.75 1.00
1299 A443 5.50k multi 2.00 .50
1300 A443 7k multi 2.25 1.25
1301 A443 9k multi 3.25 1.25
1302 A443 10k multi 3.75 1.00
Nos. 1298-1302 (5) 13.00 5.00

Rose Type of 2001

Die Cut Perf. 13¼x13 on 3 Sides

2001, June 22 Photo. & Litho.

Booklet Stamps

Self-Adhesive

1303 A436 5.50k Red roses 1.75 .30
1304 A436 5.50k Pink roses 1.75 .30
a. Booklet pane, 2 each #1303-1304 7.00
Booklet, 2 #1304a 16.00

Nos. 1303-1304 are impregnated with a rose scent.

Roses on No. 1303 have white centers. Compare with Illustration A460.

Crafts Type of 2001

Designs: 5k, Carved bird-shaped drinking vessel. 5.50k, Doll with crocheted clothing. 8.50k, Knitted cap.

Die Cut Perf. 14½

2001, June 22 Photo.

Coil Stamps

Self-Adhesive

1305 A437 5k multi 3.50 3.50
1306 A437 5.50k multi 3.50 3.50
1307 A437 8.50k multi 5.00 5.00
Nos. 1305-1307 (3) 12.00 12.00

2001, June 22 Photo.

Coil Stamps

Self-Adhesive

1305a Die cut perf. 12¾ 1.75 .30
1306a Die cut perf. 12¾ 1.75 .25
1307a Die cut perf. 12¾ 3.00 .50

Nobel Peace Prize, Cent. A444

Designs: No. 1308, 1991 winner Aung San Suu Kyi. No. 1309, 1993 winner Nelson Mandela. No. 1310, Alfred Nobel. No. 1311, 1901 winner Henri Dunant. No. 1312, 1922 winner Fridjof Nansen. No. 1313, 1990 winner, Mikhail S. Gorbachev. No. 1314, 1964 winner, Dr. Martin Luther King, Jr. No. 1315, 1992 winner Dr. Rigoberta Menchú Tum.

Perf. 13¼x13¾

2001, Sept. 14 Litho. & Engr.
1308 A444 5.50k multi 2.00 .75
1309 A444 5.50k multi 2.00 .75
a. Vert. pair, #1308-1309 4.00 3.50
1310 A444 7k multi 2.50 1.25
a. Souvenir sheet of 1 3.50 2.75
1311 A444 7k multi 2.50 1.25
a. Vert. pair, #1310-1311 5.00 4.50
1312 A444 9k multi 3.25 1.50
1313 A444 9k multi 3.25 1.50
a. Vert. pair, #1312-1313 6.50 5.00
1314 A444 10k multi 3.75 1.25
1315 A444 10k multi 3.75 1.25
a. Vert. pair, #1314-1315 7.50 4.50
Nos. 1308-1315 (8) 23.00 9.50

Pets — A445

2001, Sept. 14 Litho. ***Perf. 14x13¼***
1316 A445 5.50k Kittens 2.00 .50
1317 A445 7.50k Goat 3.00 1.25

Aurora Borealis A446

2001, Nov. 15
1318 A446 5k Trees 2.00 1.25
1319 A446 5.50k Reindeer 2.25 1.00

Christmas A447

Gingerbread: No. 1320, Man. No. 1321, House.

Serp. Die Cut 14x13 on 3 Sides

2001, Nov. 15 Photo. & Litho.

Booklet Stamps

Self-Adhesive

1320 A447 5.50k multi 1.75 .30
1321 A447 5.50k multi 1.75 .30
a. Booklet pane, 2 each #1320-1321 7.00
Complete booklet, 2 #1321a 14.00

Actors and Actresses — A448

Designs: 5k, Tordis Maurstad (1901-97). 5.50k, Rolf Just Nilsen (1931-81). 7k, Lars Tvinde (1886-1973). 9k, Henry Gleditsch (1902-42). 10k, Norma Balean (1907-89).

2002, Feb. 11 Litho. ***Perf. 13x14***

Background Color

1322 A448 5k rose lilac 1.75 1.25
1323 A448 5.50k lilac 2.00 .50
1324 A448 7k beige 2.50 1.25
1325 A448 9k light green 3.25 1.50
1326 A448 10k dull rose 3.50 1.50
Nos. 1322-1326 (5) 13.00 6.00

Contemporary Sculpture — A449

Designs: 7.50k, Monument to Whaling, by Sivert Donali. 8.50k, Throw, by Kare Groven.

2002, Apr. 12 Litho. ***Perf. 13¼x13¾***
1327 A449 7.50k multi 2.50 1.50
1328 A449 8.50k multi 2.75 1.25

Fairy Tales

A450 A451

Designs: No. 1329, Askeladden and the Good Helpers, by Ivo Caprino. No. 1330, Giant Troll on Karl Johan, by Theodor Kittelsen.

Serpentine Die Cut 13x14 on 3 Sides

2002, Apr. 12 Photo. & Litho.

Booklet Stamps

Self-Adhesive

1329 A450 5.50k multi 1.75 .25
a. Booklet pane of 4 7.00
Booklet, 2 #1329a 14.00
1330 A451 9k multi 3.00 1.25
a. Booklet pane of 4 12.00
Booklet, 2 #1330a 24.00

Norwegian Soccer Association, Cent. — A452

No. 1331: a, Boys playing soccer. b, Referee pointing, player. c, Girls playing soccer. d, Boy kicking ball.

2002, Apr. 12 ***Die Cut Perf.***

Self-Adhesive

1331 Booklet pane of 4 7.50
a.-d. A452 5.50k Any single 1.75 .30
Booklet, 2 #1331 15.00

The margins of the two panes in the booklet differ.

Niels Henrik Abel (1802-29), Mathematician — A453

Designs: 5.50k, Abel, formula and curves. 22k, Formula, front page of book by Abel, curve.

Perf. 13¼x13¾

2002, June 5 Litho. & Engr.
1332 A453 5.50k multi 2.00 .75
1333 A453 22k multi 8.00 2.25

For overprints, see No. 1346-1347.

City Charter Anniversaries — A454

Designs: No. 1334, Holmestrand, 250th anniv. No. 1335, Kongsberg, 200th anniv.

2002, June 5 Litho.
1334 A454 5.50k multi 2.00 .75
1335 A454 5.50k multi 2.00 .75

Authors — A455

Designs: 11k, Johan Collett Muller Borgen (1902-79). 20k, Nordahl Grieg (1902-43).

2002, June 5 ***Perf. 14¼x14***
1336 A455 11k multi 4.00 1.50
1337 A455 20k multi 7.50 2.25

Europa — A456

Designs: 5.50k, Clown juggling balls. 8.50k, Elephant, monkey on rocking horse.

2002, Sept. 20 ***Perf. 14x14¾***
1338 A456 5.50k multi 2.00 .75
1339 A456 8.50k multi 3.00 1.25

Great Moments in Norwegian Soccer A457

Players involved in: 5k, Victory against Germany in 1936 Olympics. No. 1341, Victory against Brazil in 1998 World Cup tournament. No. 1342, Victory of women's team against US in 2000 Olympics. 7k, Victory against Sweden, 1960. 9k, Victory against England, 1981. 10k, Rosenborg's victory against Milan, in Champions League tournament, 1996.

2002, Sept. 20 ***Perf. 13¼x13¾***
1340 A457 5k multi 1.75 .75
1341 A457 5.50k multi 2.00 .50
1342 A457 5.50k multi 2.00 .50
1343 A457 7k multi 2.50 1.25
1344 A457 9k multi 3.25 1.25
1345 A457 10k multi 3.50 1.25
a. Souvenir sheet, #1340-1345 + 6 labels 15.00 15.00
Nos. 1340-1345 (6) 15.00 5.50

Norwegian Soccer Association, cent.

Nos. 1332-1333 Overprinted

Perf. 13¼x13¾

2002, Oct. 10 **Litho. & Engr.**

1346 A453 5.50k multi 6.00 6.00
1347 A453 22k multi 13.00 13.00

Pastor Magnus B. Landstad (1802-80), Hymn Writer and Folk Song Collector A458

Designs: 5k, Landstad on horse, front page of 1853 book of folk songs. 5.50k, Church's hymn board, front page of 1870 hymn book, portrait of Landstad.

2002, Nov. 20

1348 A458 5k multi 1.75 1.00
1349 A458 5.50k multi 2.00 .75

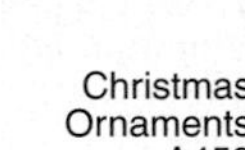

Christmas Ornaments A459

Die Cut Perf. 13½x13 on 3 Sides

2002, Nov. 20 **Photo.**

Booklet Stamps

Self-Adhesive

1350 A459 5.50k Hearts 1.90 .30
1351 A459 5.50k Star 1.90 .30
a. Booklet pane, 2 each #1350-1351 7.75
Booklet, 2 #1351a 15.50

Rose Type of 2001 and

Grand Prix Rose — A460

Design: No. 1353, Champagne roses (light yellow).

Die Cut Perf. 13¼x13 on 3 Sides

2003, Feb. 10 **Photo. & Litho.**

Booklet Stamps

Self-Adhseive

1352 A460 5.50k multi 2.25 .25
1353 A436 5.50k multi 2.25 .25
a. Booklet pane, 2 each #1352-1353 9.00
Booklet, 2 #1353a 18.00

Roses on No. 1303 have white centers, while those on No. 1352 do not.

Crafts Type of 2001

2003, Feb. 10 *Die Cut Perf. 12¾*

Self-Adhesive

1354 A437 5.50k Duodji knife handle 1.75 .25

Graphic Arts — A461

Designs: 5k, Nordmandens Krone, by Kaare Espolin Johnson. 8.50k, Bla Hester, by Else Hagen. 9k, Dirigent og Solist, by Niclas Gulbrandsen. 11k, Olympia, by Svein Strand. 22k, Still Life XVII, by Rigmor Hansen.

Perf. 13¼x12¾

2003, Feb. 10 **Litho.**

1355 A461 5k multi 1.75 1.00
1356 A461 8.50k multi 3.00 1.50
1357 A461 9k multi 3.25 1.75
1358 A461 11k multi 4.00 1.50
1359 A461 22k multi 8.00 2.00
a. Perf. 14x12¾ 8.00 2.25
Nos. 1355-1359 (5) 20.00 7.75

St. Valentine's Day — A462

Inscriptions beneath scratch-off heart: b, Elsker deg! c, Jusen kyss! d, Glad i dag! e, Klem fra meg! f, Du er sot! g, Min beste venn! h, Yndlings-bror. i, Yndlings-soster. j, Verdens beste far. k, Verdens beste mor.

2003, Feb. 10 *Perf. 14¾x14*

1360 Sheet of 10 20.00 18.00
a. A462 5.50k Any single, unscrached 2.00 1.00
b.-k. A462 5.50k Any single, scratched .65

Unused value for No. 1360a is for stamp with attached selvage. Inscriptions are shown in selvage next to each stamp.

Fairy Tale Illustrations by Theodor Kittelsen (1857-1914)
A463 A464

Serpentine Die Cut 13x14 on 3 Sides

2003, May 22 **Photo. & Litho.**

Booklet Stamps

Self-Adhesive

1361 A463 5.50k Forest troll 1.90 .30
a. Booklet pane of 4 7.75
Complete booklet, 2 #1361a 15.50

Serpentine Die Cut 14x13 on 3 Sides

1362 A464 9k Water sprite 3.00 1.25
a. Booklet pane of 4 12.00
Complete booklet, 2 #1362a 24.00

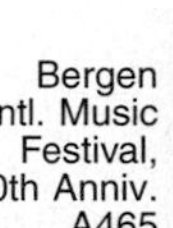

Bergen Intl. Music Festival, 50th Anniv. A465

Musical score and: 5.50k, Violinist. 10k, Children.

2003, May 22 **Litho.** *Perf. 13¼x14*

1363 A465 5.50k multi 2.00 1.00
1364 A465 10k multi 3.75 2.00

Public Health Service, 400th Anniv. A466

Designs: 5.50k, Heart transplant operation. 7k, Infant welfare clinic.

2003, May 22

1365 A466 5.50k multi 2.00 1.00
1366 A466 7k multi 2.50 1.75

Norwegian Refugee Council, 50th Anniv. A467

Designs: 5.50k, Child with bread. 10k, Line of refugees.

2003, June 20

1367 A467 5.50k multi 2.00 1.00
1368 A467 10k multi 4.00 1.10

King Olav V (1903-91) — A468

Designs: 5.50k, As child, with parents. 8.50k, With Crown Princess Märtha. 11k, In uniform.

Litho. & Engr.

2003, June 20 *Perf. 14x13¼*

1369 A468 5.50k multi 2.00 1.00
1370 A468 8.50k multi 3.00 1.50
1371 A468 11k multi 4.00 2.00
a. Souvenir sheet, #1369-1371 13.50 13.50
Nos. 1369-1371 (3) 9.00 4.50

Norwegian Nobel Laureates A469

Designs: 11k, Bjornsterne Bjornson, Literature, 1903. 22k, Lars Onsager, Chemistry, 1968.

Perf. 13¼x13¾

2003, Sept. 19 **Litho. & Engr.**

1372 A469 11k multi 4.00 1.75
1373 A469 22k multi 8.00 2.50

See nos. 1414-1415.

Europa — A470

Poster art: 8.50k, Dagbladet newspaper poster, by Per Krohg. 9k, Travel poster, by Knut Yran. 10k, 1985 North of Norway Music Festival poster, by Willibald Storn.

2003, Sept. 19 **Litho.** *Perf. 13¾*

1374 A470 8.50k multi 3.00 1.75
1375 A470 9k multi 3.25 1.75
1376 A470 10k multi 3.75 1.75
Nos. 1374-1376 (3) 10.00 5.25

Special Occasions A471

Designs: No. 1377, Baby, children's names. No. 1378, Children, birthday cake, toys. No. 1379, Man and woman at party, musical notes. No. 1380, Hands, Cupid. No. 1381, Lily.

Die Cut Perf. 13x13½

2003, Sept. 19 **Photo.**

Self-Adhesive

1377 A471 5.50k multi 2.00 1.00
1378 A471 5.50k multi 2.00 1.00
1379 A471 5.50k multi 2.00 1.00
1380 A471 5.50k multi 2.00 1.00
1381 A471 5.50k multi 2.00 1.00
Nos. 1377-1381 (5) 10.00 5.00

Graphic Arts — A472

Designs: 5k, Winter Landscape, woodcut by Terje Grostad. 5.50k, Goatherd and Goats, by Rolf Nesch.

Perf. 13¾x12¾

2003, Nov. 21 **Litho.**

1382 A472 5k multi 1.75 1.25
1383 A472 5.50k multi 1.75 1.25

Christmas A473

Serpentine Die Cut 13¼x13 on 3 Sides

2003, Nov. 21 **Photo.**

Booklet Stamps

Self-Adhesive

1384 A473 5.50k Santa Claus 1.75 .30
1385 A473 5.50k Gift 1.75 .30
a. Booklet pane, 2 each #1384-1385 9.50
Complete booklet, 2 #1385a 20.00

Paintings — A474

Designs: 6k, Idyll, by Christian Skredsvig. 9.50k, Stetind in Fog, by Peder Balke. 10.50k, Worker's Protest, by Reidar Aulie.

2004, Jan. 2 **Litho.** *Perf. 13x14*

1386 A474 6k multi 2.25 .85
1387 A474 9.50k multi 3.25 1.75
1388 A474 10.50k multi 3.75 2.00
Nos. 1386-1388 (3) 9.25 4.60

Marine Life — A475

Designs: 5.50k, Periphylla periphylla. 6k, Anarhichas lupus. 9k, Sepiola atlantica.

Die Cut Perf. 15½x14¼

2004, Jan. 2 **Photo.**

Self-Adhesive

1389 A475 5.50k multi 2.00 .30
1390 A475 6k multi 2.25 .25
1391 A475 9k multi 3.25 .50
Nos. 1389-1391 (3) 7.50 1.05

See Nos. 1440-1441.

"Person to Person" A476

Stylized: No. 1392, Man and woman. No. 1393, Globe.

Serpentine Die Cut 13¼x13 on 3 Sides

2004, Jan. 2 **Photo. & Litho.**

Self-Adhesive

Booklet Stamps

1392 A476 6k multi 2.00 .25
1393 A476 6k multi 2.00 .25
a. Booklet pane, 2 each #1392-1393 8.00
Complete booklet, 2 #1393a 18.00

Sunflower Heart — A477

2004, Feb. 6 Litho. ***Perf. 14x13¼***

1394 A477 6k multi 2.25 .75

Printed in sheets of 6 stamps and 3 labels.

Europa A478

Designs: 6k, Bicyclist in Moskenes. 7.50k, Kayaker on Oslo Fjord. 9.50k, Hikers crossing Stygge Glacier.

Die Cut Perf. 13½x13 on 3 Sides
2004, Mar. 26 Photo. & Litho.
Self-Adhesive
Booklet Stamps

1395 A478 6k multi 2.00 .50
a. Booklet pane of 4 8.00
Complete booklet, 2 #1395a 16.00
1396 A478 7.50k multi 2.50 1.00
a. Booklet pane of 4 10.00
Complete booklet, 2 #1396a 20.00
1397 A478 9.50k multi 3.25 1.25
a. Booklet pane of 4 13.00
Complete booklet, 2 #1397a 26.00
Nos. 1395-1397 (3) 7.75 2.75

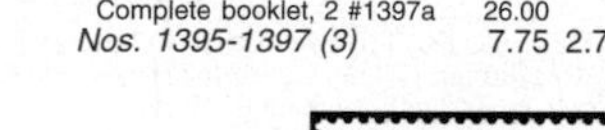

Otto Sverdrup (1854-1930), Arctic Explorer — A479

Litho. & Engr.
2004, Mar. 26 ***Perf. 13¼***

1398 A479 6k shown 2.25 1.25
1399 A479 9.50k Ship "Fram" 3.50 2.10
a. Souvenir sheet, #1398-1399 + label 7.50 7.50

See Canada Nos. 2026-2027, Greenland No. 426.

Norse Mythology A480

Designs: 7.50k, Njord, god of wind, sea and fire and ship. 10.50k, Nanna, wife of Balder, Balder's horse, ship.

Perf. 14¼x13¾
2004, Mar. 26 Litho.

1400 A480 7.50k multi 2.75 1.75
1401 A480 10.50k multi 4.00 2.25
a. Souvenir sheet, #1400-1401 9.00 9.00

Souvenir Sheet

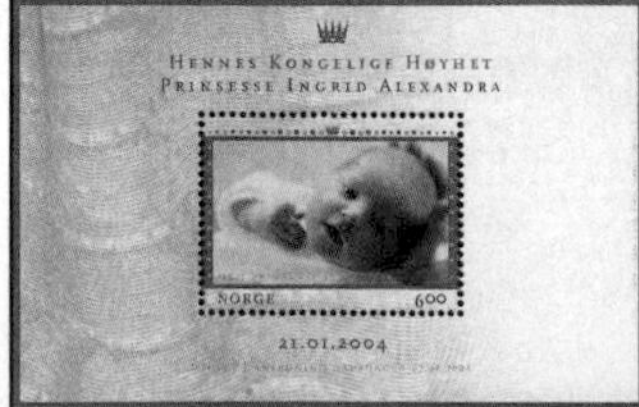

Birth of Princess Ingrid Alexandra — A481

2004, Apr. 17 ***Perf. 13¾***

1402 A481 6k multi 3.25 3.25

King Haakon IV Haakonson (1204-63) A482

Designs: 12k, Silhouette of King Haakon IV Haakonson, bows of Viking ships. 22k, Sword and Haakon's Hall, Bergen.

2004, June 18 ***Perf. 14¼x14¾***

1403 A482 12k multi 4.00 2.50
1404 A482 22k multi 7.50 2.50

Railways in Norway, 150th Anniv. A483

Designs: 6k, Koppang Station. 7.50k, Dovre Station. 9.50k, Locomotive, Kylling Bridge. 10.50k, Airport Express train.

2004, June 18 ***Perf. 13¼***

1405 A483 6k multi 2.00 .65
1406 A483 7.50k multi 2.50 1.50
1407 A483 9.50k multi 3.25 1.75
1408 A483 10.50k multi 3.50 2.25
Nos. 1405-1408 (4) 11.25 6.15

A484

Children's Stamps — A485

2004, Sept. 17 ***Perf. 13¼x14***

1409 A484 6k multi 2.00 .75
1410 A485 9k multi 3.00 1.50

Oseberg Excavations, Cent. — A486

Designs: 7.50k, Archaeologists uncovering ship's stern, excavated containers. 9.50k, Textile fragment, ceremonial sleigh. 12k, Bed and rattle.

Litho. & Engr.
2004, Sept. 17 ***Perf. 13x13¼***

1411 A486 7.50k multi 2.50 1.75
1412 A486 9.50k multi 3.25 1.75
1413 A486 12k multi 4.00 1.75
Nos. 1411-1413 (3) 9.75 5.25

Norwegian Nobel Laureates Type of 2003

Designs: 5.50k, Odd Hassel, Chemistry, 1969. 6k, Christian Lous Lange, Peace, 1921.

Perf. 13¼x13¾
2004, Nov. 19 Litho. & Engr.

1414 A469 5.50k multi 1.90 1.40
1415 A469 6k multi 2.00 1.00

Christmas — A487

Winning art in UNICEF children's stamp design contest: No. 1416, Children and sun, by Hanne Soteland. No. 1417, Child on woman's lap, by Synne Amalie Lund Kallak.

Serpentine Die Cut 13x13¼ on 3 Sides
2004, Nov. 19 Photo. & Litho.
Self-Adhesive
Booklet Stamps

1416 A487 6k multi 2.00 .30
1417 A487 6k multi 2.00 .30
a. Booklet pane, 2 each #1416-1417 8.00
Complete booklet, 2 #1417a 16.00

Illustrations From "The Three Princesses in the Blue Hill," by Erik Werenskiold (1855-1936) A488

Designs: 7.50k, Princesses and guard. 9.50k, Baby in cradle.

2005, Jan. 7 Litho. ***Perf. 14¼x14***

1418 A488 7.50k multi 2.50 1.75
1419 A488 9.50k multi 3.25 2.25

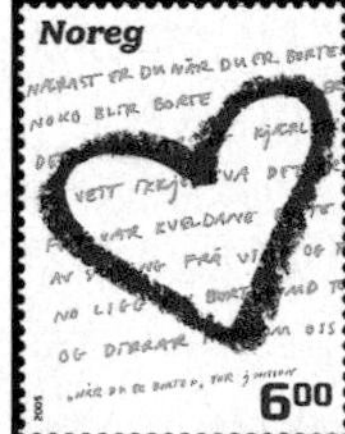

St. Valentine's Day — A489

2005, Feb. 4 ***Perf. 13¼x13¾***

1420 A489 6k red & silver 2.00 1.00

Church City Missions, 150th Anniv. A490

Designs: 5.50k, Soup kitchen. 6k, Ministers administering communion.

2005, Feb. 4 ***Perf. 13¾x14¼***

1421 A490 5.50k multi 1.75 1.25
1422 A490 6k multi 2.00 1.00

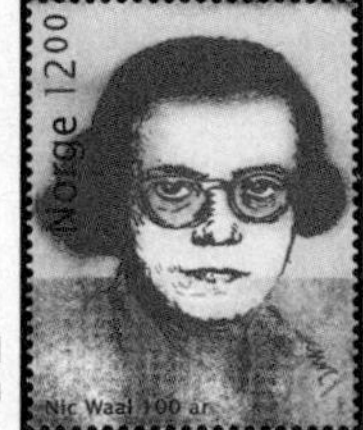

Children's Mental Health Pioneers — A491

Designs: 12k, Nic Waal (1905-60), first Norwegian child psychiatrist. 22k, Aase Gruda Skard (1905-85), first Norwegian child psychologist.

2005, Feb. 4 ***Perf. 14¼x14¾***

1423 A491 12k multi 4.00 2.00
1424 A491 22k multi 7.50 2.00

A492

Children's Drawings of Norway in 2105 — A493

2005, Apr. 15 Litho. ***Perf. 14x12¾***

1425 A492 6k multi 2.00 1.00
1426 A493 7.50k multi 2.50 1.50

Tourism — A494

Designs: 6k, Geiranger Fjord. 9.50k, Kjofossen Waterfall, Flam. 10.50k, Polar bear, Svalbard.

Die Cut Perf. 13x13¼ on 3 Sides
2005, Apr. 15 Photo. & Litho.
Booklet Stamps
Self-Adhesive

1427 A494 6k multi 2.00 .30
a. Booklet pane of 4 8.00
Complete booklet, 2 #1427a 17.00
1428 A494 9.50k multi 3.25 1.50
a. Booklet pane of 4 13.00
Complete booklet, 2 #1428a 26.00
1429 A494 10.50k multi 3.50 1.75
a. Booklet pane of 4 14.00
Complete booklet, 2 #1429a 28.00
Nos. 1427-1429 (3) 8.75 3.55

Dissolution of Union with Sweden, Cent. — A495

Designs: 6k, Norwegian Prime Minister Christian Michelsen, Norwegian negotiators and signatures. 7.50k, King Haakon VII, ships.

Perf. 12½x12¾
2005, May 27 Litho. & Engr.

1430 A495 6k multi 2.00 1.00
1431 A495 7.50k multi 2.50 1.25
a. Souvenir sheet, #1430-1431 5.00 6.00

See Sweden No. 2514.

Historic Events Since Dissolution of Union with Sweden A496

Designs: No. 1432, King Haakon VII taking oath of allegiance, 1905. No. 1433, Crown Prince Olav celebrating end of World War II, 1945. No. 1434, King Olav V at inauguration of Norwegian television broadcasting, 1960. No. 1435, Prime Minister Trygve Bratteli opening Ekofisk oil field, 1971. No. 1436, Victory of Norwegian World Cup soccer team over Brazil, 1998.

2005, June 7 Litho. ***Perf. 13¾***

1432 A496 6k multi 2.00 1.00
1433 A496 6k multi 2.00 1.00
1434 A496 6k multi 2.00 1.00
1435 A496 6k multi 2.00 1.00
1436 A496 9k multi 3.00 1.50
Nos. 1432-1436 (5) 11.00 5.50

Tall Ships — A497

Designs: 6k, Christian Radich. 9.50k, Sorlandet. 10.50k, Statsraad Lehmkuhl.

2005, June 7 ***Perf. 13¾x13½***

1437 A497 6k multi 2.00 1.00
1438 A497 9.50k multi 3.25 1.75
1439 A497 10.50k multi 3.50 2.40
Nos. 1437-1439 (3) 8.75 5.15

Marine Life Type of 2004

Designs: B, Orcinus orca. A, Urticina eques.

Die Cut Perf. 15½x14¼

2005, Sept. 1 **Photo.**

Self-Adhesive

1440 A475 B multi 1.75 .30
1441 A475 A multi 2.00 .30

No. 1440 sold for 5.50k and No. 1441 sold for 6k on day of issue.

Lighthouses A498

Designs: No. 1442, Jomfruland (white lighthouse). No. 1443, Tranoy (red and white lighthouse).

Die Cut Perf. 13¼x13 on 3 Sides

2005, Sept. 1 **Photo. & Litho.**

Self-Adhesive

Booklet Stamps

1442 A498 A multi 2.00 .30
1443 A498 A multi 2.00 .30
a. Booklet pane, 2 each #1442-1443 8.00
Complete booklet, 2 #1443a 17.00

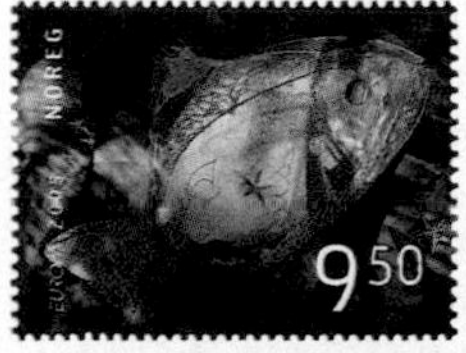

Europa A499

2005, Sept. 16 **Litho.** ***Perf. 14¾x14***

1444 A499 9.50k Fish 3.25 2.25
1445 A499 10.50k Table 3.50 2.00

Norwegian Telegraph Service, 150th Anniv. A500

Designs: 6k, Telegraph key and poles. 10.50k, Woman and symbols of modern communication.

Perf. 13½x13¾

2005, Sept. 16 **Litho. & Engr.**

1446 A500 6k multi 2.00 1.40
1447 A500 10.50k multi 3.50 2.00

Geological Society of Norway, Cent. — A501

Designs: 5.50k, Thortveitite and feldspar. 6k, Oil rig, ship, map of Norway, microfossil and stylized rock layers.

2005, Sept. 16 **Litho.** ***Perf. 13¾***

1448 A501 5.50k multi 1.75 1.40
1449 A501 6k multi 2.00 1.25

Norwegian Postage Stamps, 150th Anniv. — A502

Designs: A, Eye, vignette and spandrels of Norway #1. 12k, Norway #1, woman writing letter.

Litho., Engr. & Silk Screened

2005, Nov. 17 ***Perf. 14x14¼***

1450 A502 A multi 2.00 1.00

Souvenir Sheet

1451 Sheet, #1450, 1451a 6.50 6.50
a. A502 12k multi 4.50 4.00

No. 1450 sold for 6k on day of issue.

Royal House, Cent. — A503

Designs: No. 1452, Norwegian Prime Minister greeting King Haakon VII and Crown Prince Olav, 1905. No. 1453, Royal coat of arms, King Haakon VII, Queen Maud and Crown Prince Olav, 1945, King Harald V, Crown Prince Haakon, and Princess Ingrid Alexandra, 2004.

2005, Nov. 18 **Litho.** ***Perf. 14x13½***

1452 A503 6k multi 2.00 1.00
1453 A503 6k multi 2.50 1.00

Christmas — A504

Designs: No. 1454, Gingerbread Christmas tree. No. 1455, Oranges studded with cloves on bed of nuts.

Serpentine Die Cut 13x13¼ on 3 Sides

2005, Nov. 19 **Photo. & Litho.**

Booklet Stamps

Self-Adhesive

1454 A504 A multi 2.00 .30
1455 A504 A multi 2.00 .30
a. Booklet pane, 2 each #1454-1455 8.00
Complete booklet, 2, #1455a 16.00

Nos. 1454-1455 each sold for 6k on day of issue and are impregnated with a cinnamon scent.

Norwegian Language Society, Cent. — A505

2006, Feb. 3 **Litho.** ***Perf. 13¼x13¾***

1456 A505 6k multi 2.00 1.40

St. Valentine's Day — A506

2006, Feb. 3 ***Perf. 13¾x14¼***

1457 A506 A multi 2.00 1.00

Sold for 6k on day of issue.

2006 Winter Olympics, Turin — A507

Designs: 6k, Kari Traa, freestyle skier. 22k, Ole Einar Bjorndalen, biathlon.

2006, Feb. 3 ***Perf. 14¼x14¾***

1458 A507 6k multi 2.00 1.00
1459 A507 22k multi 7.50 2.00

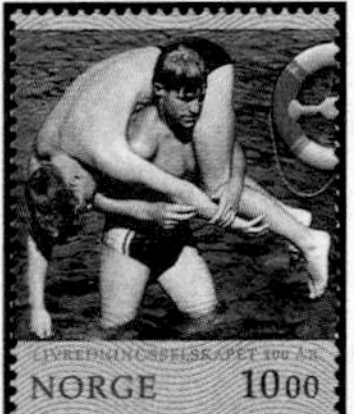

Norwegian Lifesaving Society, Cent. — A508

Designs: 10k, Lifeguard carrying man. 10.50k, Child swimming.

2006, Feb. 24 ***Perf. 13¾***

1460 A508 10k multi 3.50 2.50
1461 A508 10.50k multi 3.50 2.75

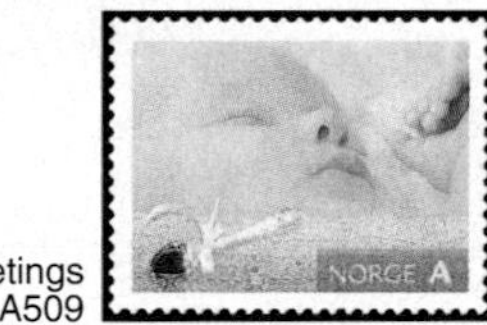

Greetings A509

Designs: No. 1462, Baby and spoon. No. 1463, Birthday cake. No. 1464, Heart and wedding rings. No. 1465, Flower.

2006, Feb. 24 ***Die Cut Perf. 13¼***

Self-Adhesive

1462 A509 A multi 2.00 1.00
1463 A509 A multi 2.00 1.00
1464 A509 A multi 2.00 1.00
1465 A509 A multi 2.00 1.00
Nos. 1462-1465 (4) 8.00 4.00

Each stamp sold for 6k on day of issue. Each stamp was issued on a white paper backing with surrounding selvage and in coils on a translucent paper backing without surrounding selvage.

Polycera Quadrilineata A510

Die Cut Perf. 15½x14½

2006, Mar. 29 **Photo.**

Coil Stamp

1466 A510 10k multi 3.50 .50

Wildlife A511

2006, Mar. 29 **Litho.** ***Perf. 13¼x14***

1467 A511 6.50k Lynx 2.25 .50
1468 A511 8.50k Capercaillie 2.75 2.00
1469 A511 10k Golden eagle 3.25 2.00
1470 A511 10.50k Arctic fox 3.50 2.50
1471 A511 13k Arctic hare 4.25 2.50
Nos. 1467-1471 (5) 16.00 9.50

See Nos. 1498-1499, 1531-1533, 1565-1567, 1600-1602, 1636-1637, 1726C-1728, 1756, 1763.

Souvenir Sheet

Norse Mythology — A512

No. 1472: a, Design on Sami shaman's drum. b, Carved door post from Hylestad Stave Church depicting dragon and dragon slayer.

2006, Mar. 29 ***Perf. 14x14¼***

1472 A512 Sheet of 2 7.50 8.00
a. A multi 2.75 2.75
b. 10.50k multi 3.25 3.25

No. 1472a sold for 6k on day of issue.

Norwegian Arctic Expeditions, Cent. — A513

Designs: 6.50k, Gunnar Isachsen and assistant surveying terrain. 8.50k, Coal cable car terminal, Store Norske Spitzbergen mines. 22k, Longyearbyen.

Litho. & Engr.

2006, June 9 ***Perf. 13½x14***

1473 A513 6.50k multi 2.25 .75
1474 A513 8.50k multi 2.75 2.00

Litho.

1475 A513 22k multi 7.00 4.25
a. Souvenir sheet, #1473-1475 12.50 12.50
Nos. 1473-1475 (3) 12.00 7.00

Tourism A514

Designs: No. 1476, Paddle steamer Skibladner. No. 1477, Maihaugen Museum, Lillehammer. No. 1478, Kirkeporten natural arch. No. 1479, North Cape. No. 1480, Bryggen UNESCO World Heritage Site. No. 1481, Storeseisundet Bridge on Atlantic Road.

Die Cut Perf. 13¼x13½

2006, June 9 **Photo.**

Self-Adhesive

Booklet Stamps

1476 A514 6.50k multi 2.25 .50
1477 A514 6.50k multi 2.25 .50
a. Booklet pane, 5 each #1476-1477 22.50
1478 A514 8.50k multi 2.75 2.00
1479 A514 8.50k multi 2.75 2.00
a. Booklet pane, 5 each #1478-1479 27.50

1480 A514 10.50k multi 3.50 2.50
1481 A514 10.50k multi 3.50 2.50
a. Booklet pane, 5 each #1480-1481 35.00
Nos. 1476-1481 (6) 17.00 10.00

Consumer Cooperatives, Cent. — A515

2006, June 9 Litho. ***Perf. 13½x14***
1482 A515 6.50k multi 2.25 1.00

Personalized Stamp — A516

Serpentine Die Cut 11¾ Syncopated
2006, Aug. 22 Self-Adhesive
1483 A516 A multi 2.50 2.00

No. 1483 sold for 6.50k on the day of issue. The image shown is the generic image sold at face value. Stamps could be personalized, presumably for an extra fee.

Marine Life — A517

Designs: B, Strongylocentrotus droebachiensis. A, Labrus bimaculatus.

Die Cut Perf. 15½x14½
2006, Sept. 15 Photo.
Self-Adhesive
Coil Stamps
1484 A517 B multi 2.00 .50
1485 A517 A multi 2.25 .30

On day of issue, No. 1484 sold for 6k; No. 1485 for 6.50k.

King's Guard, 150th Anniv. A518

Designs: 6.50k, King's Guard in dress uniforms. 13k, In field uniforms, with helicopter.

2006, Sept. 15 Litho. ***Perf. 14x13¼***
1486 A518 6.50k multi 2.25 1.25
1487 A518 13k multi 4.50 3.00
a. Souvenir sheet, #1486-1487 7.00 7.00

Europa A519

Designs: 8.50k, Five children. 13k, Three children playing soccer.

2006, Nov. 17 ***Perf. 13¾***
1488 A519 8.50k multi 2.75 2.00
1489 A519 13k multi 4.50 3.00

Christmas A520

Designs: No. 1490, Children and Christmas tree. No. 1491, Child and snowman.

Die Cut Perf. 13¼x13½
2006, Nov. 17 Photo. & Litho.
Self-Adhesive
Booklet Stamps
1490 A520 A multi 2.25 .50
1491 A520 A multi 2.25 .50
a. Booklet pane, 5 each #1490-1491 22.50

On day of issue each stamp sold for 6.50k.

Personalized Stamp — A521

Serpentine Die Cut 11¾ Syncopated
2006, Nov. 17 Litho.
Self-Adhesive
1492 A521 A multi 2.50 2.10

No. 1492 sold for 6.50k on the day of issue. The image shown is the generic image sold at face value. Stamps could be personalized, presumably for an extra fee.

St. Valentine's Day — A522

2007, Feb. 6 Litho. ***Perf. 13¼***
1493 A522 A multi 2.25 1.50

Sold for 6.50k on day of issue. Values are for stamps with surrounding selvage.

Winter Rally Race Cars A523

Designs: No. 1494, Petter Solberg's Subaru Impreza. No. 1495, Henning Solberg's Peugeot 307. No. 1496, Thomas Schie's Ford Focus.

Litho. With Foil Application
2007, Feb. 6 ***Perf. 13¼x13¾***
1494 A523 A Innland multi 2.25 1.50
1495 A523 A Europa multi 2.75 2.25
1496 A523 A Verden multi 3.50 3.00
a. Souvenir sheet, #1494-1496 8.50 8.50
Nos. 1494-1496 (3) 8.50 6.75

On day of issue, No. 1494 sold for 6.50k; No. 1495, for 8.50k; No. 1496, for 10.50k.

King Harald V, 70th Birthday — A524

Perf. 13¾x13¼
2007, Feb. 21 Litho.
1497 A524 6.50k multi 2.25 1.50

Wildlife Type of 2006
2007, Feb. 21 ***Perf. 13¼x13¾***
1498 A511 12k Hedgehog 4.00 1.75
1499 A511 22k Red squirrel 7.50 2.50

Souvenir Sheet

Intl. Polar Year — A526

No. 1500: a, Ice core, oceanographic equipment. b, K/V Svalbard, dish antenna.

2007, Feb. 21
1500 A526 Sheet of 2 8.50 8.50
a. 10.50k multi 3.75 3.75
b. 13k multi 4.75 4.75

Porsgrunn, Bicent. — A527

2007, Apr. 27
1501 A527 A Innland multi 2.40 1.50

Sold for 7k on day of issue.

Illustrations by Theodor Kittelsen (1857-1914) A528

Designs: No. 1502, An Attack (grasshoppers, mosquito, flower). No. 1503, Premature Delivery (frogs, hatched bird).

2007, Apr. 27 ***Perf. 14x13½***
1502 A528 A Europa multi 3.00 2.00
1503 A528 A Verden multi 3.75 2.75

On day of issue, No. 1502 sold for 9k; No. 1503, for 11k.

Skydivers A529

Cyclists A530

Buildings, Roros A531

Bridge, Fredrikstad A532

Pilot House, Portor A533

Reine Harbor A534

Die Cut Perf. 13¼x13¾
2007, Apr. 27
Self-Adhesive
Booklet Stamps
1504 A529 A Innland multi 2.40 .50
1505 A530 A Innland multi 2.40 .50
a. Booklet pane, 5 each #1504-1505 24.00
1506 A531 A Europa multi 3.00 1.00
1507 A532 A Europa multi 3.00 1.00
a. Booklet pane, 5 each #1506-1507 30.00
1508 A533 A Verden multi 3.75 1.00
1509 A534 A Verden multi 3.75 1.00
a. Booklet pane, 5 each #1508-1509 37.50
Nos. 1504-1509 (6) 18.30 5.00

On day of issue, Nos. 1504-1505 each sold for 7k; Nos. 1506-1507 each sold for 9k; Nos. 1508-1509 each sold for 11k.

Marine Life — A535

Designs: No. 1510, Pandalus montagui. No. 1511, Homarus gammarus. No. 1512, Cancer pagurus. No. 1513, Galathea strigosa. 11k, Scomber scombrus.

2007 ***Die Cut Perf. 15½x14½***
Self-Adhesive
Coil Stamps
1510 A535 A Innland multi 2.60 .50
1511 A535 A Innland multi 2.60 .50
1512 A535 A Innland multi 2.60 .50
1513 A535 A Innland multi 2.60 .50
a. Horiz. strip of 4, #1510-1513 10.50
1514 A535 11k multi 3.75 .90
Nos. 1510-1514 (5) 14.15 2.90

Issued; Nos. 1510-1513, 9/21; No. 1514, 5/2. On day of issue, Nos. 1510-1513 each sold for 7k.

Europa A536

Designs: 9k, Scouts, knots. 11k, Hitch diagrams, camp gateway.

Perf. 13¼x13¾
2007, May 11 Litho. & Engr.
1515 A536 9k multi 3.00 2.00
1516 A536 11k multi 3.75 2.50

Scouting, cent.

Building Anniversaries — A537

Designs: 14k, Church of Our Lady, Trondheim, 800th anniv. 23k, Vardohus Fortress, 700th anniv.

2007, May 11
1517 A537 14k multi 4.75 3.00
1518 A537 23k multi 7.75 5.00

Riksmaal Society, Cent. A538

2007, June 15 **Litho.**
1519 A538 7k multi 2.40 1.25

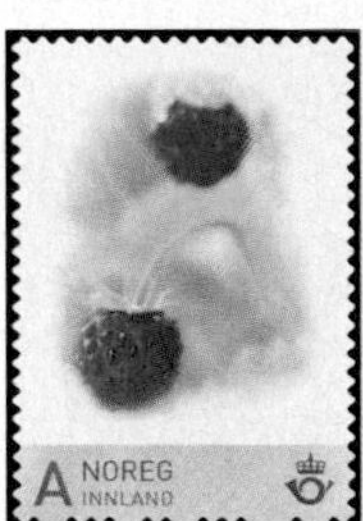
Personalized Stamp — A539

Serpentine Die Cut 11½ Syncopated
2007, June 15
1520 A539 A Innland multi 2.75 2.75

No. 1520 sold for 7k on day of issue. The image shown is the generic image sold at face value. Stamps could be personalized, presumably for an extra fee.

Ona Lighthouse, Romsdal A540

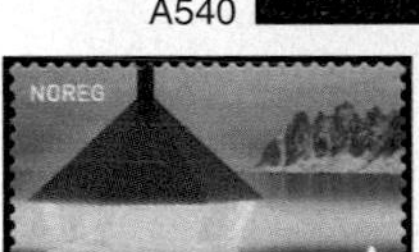
Tungeneset Lighthouse, Ersfjorden A541

Die Cut Perf. 13¼x13¾
2007, June 15
1521 A540 A Innland multi 2.40 .50
1522 A541 A Innland multi 2.40 .50
a. Booklet pane, 5 each #1521-1522 24.00

Nos. 1521-1522 each sold for 7k on day of issue.

Haldis Moren Vesaas (1907-95), Poet — A542

Litho. With Foil Application
2007, Sept. 21 ***Perf. 14x13½***
1523 A542 23k multi 8.00 5.00

Mining Academy, Kongsberg, 250th Anniv. — A543

Norwegian Academy of Science and Letters, 150th Anniv. — A544

Perf. 13¼x13¾
2007, Nov. 23 **Litho. & Engr.**
1524 A543 14k multi 4.50 3.50
1525 A544 14k multi 4.50 3.50

Personalized Stamp — A545

Booklet Stamp
Serpentine Die Cut 10¼ Syncopated
2007, Nov. 23 **Self-Adhesive**
1526 A545 A Innland multi 2.60 2.25
a. Booklet pane of 8 21.00

No. 1526 sold for 7k on day of issue. The image shown is the generic image sold at face value. Stamps could be personalized, presumably for an extra fee.

Christmas Star — A546

Adoration of the Magi — A547

Die Cut Perf. 13¼x13¾
2007, Nov. 23 **Photo.**
Self-Adhesive
Booklet Stamps
1527 A546 A Innland multi 2.25 .50
1528 A547 A Innland multi 2.25 .50
a. Booklet pane, 5 each #1527-1528 22.50

On day of issue, Nos. 1527-1528 each sold for 7k.

A548

St. Valentine's Day — A549

2008, Feb. 8 **Litho.** ***Perf. 13¼x13¾***
1529 A548 A Innland multi 2.25 1.50
1530 A549 A Europa multi 3.00 2.00

On day of issue, Nos. 1529-1530 sold for 7k and 9k, respectively.

Wildlife Type of 2006
2008, Feb. 21
1531 A511 11k Elk 3.75 2.50
1532 A511 14k Bear 4.50 3.50
1533 A511 23k Wolf 8.00 5.00
Nos. 1531-1533 (3) 16.25 11.00

Thorleif Haug, 1924 Olympic Cross-country Skiing Gold Medalist — A551

Espen Bredesen, 1994 Olympic Ski Jumping Gold Medalist A552

Children Skiing A553

Kjetil André Aamodt, 1992, 2002, and 2006 Olympic Alpine Skiing Gold Medalist A554

Die Cut Perf. 15½x14½
2008, Mar. 14 **Photo.**
Coil Stamps
Self-Adhesive
1534 A551 A Innland multi 2.50 .70
1535 A552 A Innland multi 2.50 .70
1536 A553 A Innland multi 2.50 .70
1537 A554 A Innland multi 2.50 .70
a. Horiz. strip of 4, #1534-1537 10.00

On day of issue, Nos. 1534-1537 each sold for 7k. Norwegian Ski Federation, cent.

Souvenir Sheet

Norse Mythology — A555

No. 1538: a, Harald Fairhair meeting Snofrid. b, Snohetta Mountain.

2008, Mar. 27 **Litho.** ***Perf. 14x14¼***
1538 A555 Sheet of 2 6.00 6.00
a. A Innland multi 2.50 2.50
b. A Europa multi 3.50 3.50

On day of issue, No. 1538a sold for 7k, and No. 1538b sold for 9k.

Opera House, Oslo — A556

Litho. With Foil Application
2008, Apr. 12 ***Perf. 14x13½***
1539 A556 A Innland multi 2.50 1.50

Sold for 7k on day of issue.

Famous Men — A557

Designs: No. 1540, Frederik Stang (1808-84), Interior Minister. No. 1541, Henrik Wergeland (1808-45), lyricist.

Perf. 13¼x13¾
2008, Apr. 12 **Litho. & Engr.**
1540 A557 A Innland multi 2.50 1.50
1541 A557 A Innland multi 2.50 1.50

On day of issue, Nos. 1540-1541 each sold for 7k.

Oslo Harbor A558

Divers, Sculpture, by Ola Enstad, Oslo — A559

The Blade, Sunnmore Alps — A560

Kjerag Boulder A561

Sailboat and Lyngor Lighthouse A562

Lyngor A563

Die Cut Perf. 13¼x13¾
2008, Apr. 12 **Photo.**
Booklet Stamps
Self-Adhesive
1542 A558 A Innland multi 2.50 .70
1543 A559 A Innland multi 2.50 .70
a. Booklet pane of 10, 5 each #1542-1543 25.00
1544 A560 A Europa multi 3.00 2.50
1545 A561 A Europa multi 3.00 2.50
a. Booklet pane of 10, 5 each #1544-1545 30.00
1546 A562 A Varden multi 3.75 2.75
1547 A563 A Varden multi 3.75 2.75
a. Booklet pane of 10, 5 each #1546-1547 37.50
Nos. 1542-1547 (6) 18.50 11.90

On day of issue, Nos. 1542-1543 each sold for 7k; Nos. 1544-1545, for 9k; Nos. 1546-1547, for 11k.

Stavanger, 2008 European Cultural Capital — A564

Designs: 7k, Dancer in a Cultural Landscape, photograph by Marcel Lelienhof. 14k, Swords in Rock, sculpture by Fritz Roed. 23k,

Scene from musical, The Thousandth Heart, vert.

Perf. 14x13½, 13½x14

2008, June 6 **Litho.**

1548	A564	7k multi	2.50	1.50
1549	A564	14k multi	5.00	3.50
1550	A564	23k multi	8.00	5.00
a.		Souvenir sheet, #1548-1550	17.00	17.00
		Nos. 1548-1550 (3)	15.50	10.00

No. 1550a issue 10/23. Nordia 2008 Philatelic Exhibition, Stavenger (#1550a).

Transportation Centenaries — A565

Designs: 7k, SS Boroysund. 9k, SS Oster. 25k, Automobile used on first bus route. 30k, Train on Thamshavn electric railroad line.

Perf. 13¼x13¾

2008, June 6 **Litho. & Engr.**

1551	A565	7k ocher & green	2.50	1.50
1552	A565	9k rose pink & blue	3.00	2.50
1553	A565	25k lt bl & brown	8.50	5.50
1554	A565	30k pur & green	10.00	6.50
		Nos. 1551-1554 (4)	24.00	16.00

2008 Summer Olympics, Beijing A566

Designs: 9k, Andreas Thorkildsen, javelin thrower. 23k, Women's handball player, Gro Hammerseng.

2008, Aug. 8 **Litho.** ***Perf. 14¾x14¼***

1555	A566	9k multi	3.00	2.25
1556	A566	23k multi	8.00	5.00

Personalized Stamp — A567

No. 1558: a, Like No. 1557, but with line of post horns running through middle of top line of "E" in "Norge." b, "Bring."

Serpentine Die Cut 11¾ Syncopated

2008, Sept. 5 **Litho.**

Self-Adhesive

1557	A567	A Innland multi	2.50	2.50

Souvenir Sheet

1558		Sheet of 2	*32.50*	
a.		A567 A Innland red & gray	*16.00*	*16.00*
b.		A567 A Innland green & gray	*16.00*	*16.00*

No. 1557 sold for 7k on day of issue. The image shown is the generic image sold at face value. Stamps could be personalized for an extra fee.

No. 1557 has line of post horn running through the right side of the top line of the "E" in "Norge."

About 375,000 examples of No. 1558 were distributed free of charge by Norway Post to the general public at post offices throught Norway and through their agents abroad in a campaign to promote the sale of personalized stamps. The sheet was never offered for sale by Norway Post or their agents. Nos. 1558a and 1558b each had a franking value of 7k, and could not be personalized.

Art — A568

Designs: No. 1559, In the Forecourt of the Revolution, by Arne Ekeland. No. 1560, Svalbard Motif, by Kare Tveter. No. 1561, Composition in Red, by Inger Sitter. No. 1562, From Sagorsk, c. 1985, by Terje Bergstad.

Die Cut Perf. 15½x14½

2008, Oct. 24 **Photo.**

Coil Stamps

Self-Adhesive

1559	A568	A Innland multi	2.50	.70
1560	A568	A Innland multi	2.50	.70
1561	A568	A Innland multi	2.50	.70
1562	A568	A Innland multi	2.50	.70
a.		Horiz. strip of 4, #1559-1562	11.50	11.50
		Nos. 1559-1562 (4)	10.00	2.80

On day of issue, Nos. 1559-1562 each sold for 7k.

Gnomes, Amperhaugen Farm, Stor-Elvdal A569

Gnome, Nordre Lien Farm, Stor-Elvdal A570

Booklet Stamps

Die Cut Perf. 13¼x13¾

2008, Nov. 17 **Self-Adhesive**

1563	A569	A Innland multi	2.25	.50
1564	A570	A Innland multi	2.25	.50
a.		Booklet pane of 10, 5 each #1563-1564	22.50	

Christmas. On day of issue, Nos. 1563-1564 each sold for 7k.

Wildlife Type of 2006

2009, Jan. 2 **Litho.** ***Perf. 13¼x13¾***

1565	A511	11.50k Roe deer	4.00	2.50
1566	A511	15.50k Reindeer	5.50	2.50
1567	A511	25k Willow grouse	9.00	4.50
		Nos. 1565-1567 (3)	18.50	9.50

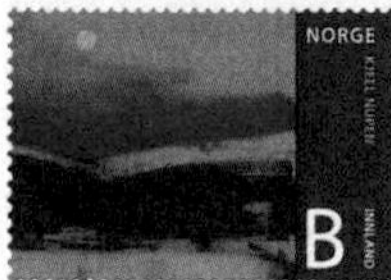

Art — A572

Designs: B, Summer Night, a Tribute to E. M., by Kjell Nupen. 12k, Light at Whitsuntide, by Irma Salo Jaeger.

Die Cut Perf. 15½x14½

2009, Jan. 2 **Photo.**

Coil Stamps

Self-Adhesive

1568	A572	B Innland multi	2.50	.75
1569	A572	12k multi	4.00	1.00

No. 1568 sold for 7.50k on day of issue.

Souvenir Sheet

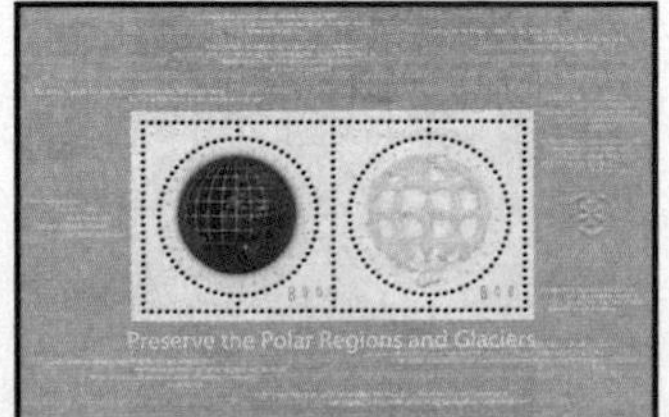

Global Warming — A573

No. 1570: a, Warm globe. b, Globe with melting ice at meridians.

Litho. (#1570a), Litho and Embossed (#1570b)

2009, Feb. 20 ***Perf. 13½***

1570	A573	Sheet of 2	6.00	6.00
a.-b.		8k Either single	2.75	2.75

Personalized Stamp — A574

Serpentine Die Cut 10x10¼ Syncopated

2009, Mar. 2 **Litho.**

Booklet Stamp

Self-Adhesive

1571	A574	A Innland gray	2.75	2.25
a.		Booklet pane of 8	22.00	

No. 1571 sold for 8k on day of issue. The image shown is the generic image sold at face value. Stamps could be personalized for an extra fee.

National Anthem by Bjornestjerne Bjornson, 150th Anniv. — A575

Litho. & Engr.

2009, Apr. 17 ***Perf. 13½x14***

1572	A575	12k multi	4.00	3.25

Bergen Line Train in Mountains A576

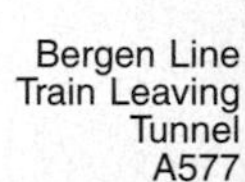

Bergen Line Train Leaving Tunnel A577

Stotta Fjord — A578

Rocky Shore, Revtangen A579

Aurora Borealis A580

Pot Rock, Vagsoy A581

Die Cut Perf. 13¼x13½

2009, Apr. 17 **Photo.**

Booklet Stamps

Self-Adhesive

1573	A576	A Innland multi	3.00	1.25
1574	A577	A Innland multi	3.00	1.25
a.		Booklet pane of 10, 5 each #1573-1574	30.00	
1575	A578	A Europa multi	3.50	2.00
1576	A579	A Europa multi	3.50	2.00
a.		Booklet pane of 10, 5 each #1575-1576	35.00	
1577	A580	A Verden multi	4.00	2.50
1578	A581	A Verden multi	4.00	2.50
a.		Booklet pane of 10, 5 each #1577-1578	40.00	
		Nos. 1573-1578 (6)	21.00	11.50

On day of issue, Nos. 1573-1574 each sold for 8k, Nos. 1575-1576 each sold for 10k, and Nos. 1577-1578 each sold for 12k.

Royal Norwegian Society for Development, Bicent. — A582

Perf. 13¼x13¾

2009, June 12 **Litho.**

1579	A582	12k multi	4.00	3.25

Submarine Branch of Norwegian Navy, Cent. — A583

Designs: 14.50k, The Kobben. 15.50k, Ula Class submarine.

Litho. & Engr.

2009, June 12 ***Perf. 13¼x14***

1580	A583	14.50k multi	5.00	4.00
1581	A583	15.50k multi	5.50	4.00

Norwegian Year of Cultural Heritage A584

Designs: No. 1582, Kurér radio, 1950. No. 1583, Telephone booth, 1932.

Die Cut Perf. 15½x14½

2009, June 12 **Litho.**

Coil Stamps

Self-Adhesive

1582	A584	A Innland multi	2.75	1.25
1583	A584	A Innland multi	2.75	1.25
a.		Horiz. pair, #1582-1583	5.50	5.50

On day of issue, Nos. 1582-1583 each sold for 8k.

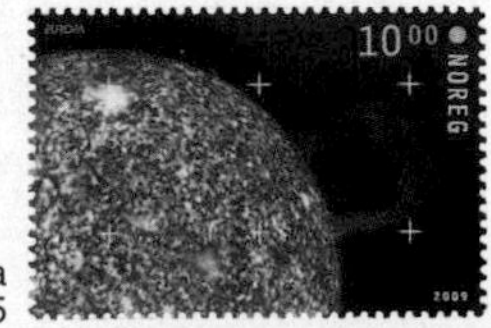

Europa A585

Designs: 10k, Solar explosion. 12k, Moon.

2009, June 12 ***Perf. 14¼x13¾***

1584	A585	10k multi	3.50	2.50
1585	A585	12k multi	4.00	3.00
a.		Souvenir sheet of 2, #1584-1585	9.00	9.00

Intl. Year of Astronomy.

Knut Hamsun (1859-1952), 1920 Nobel Literature Laureate A586

Litho. & Engr.

2009, Aug. 4 *Perf. 14¼*

1586	A586	25k multi	9.00	5.00

Rock 'n' Roll Pioneers A587

Designs: No. 1587, Per "Elvis" Granberg (1941-80). No. 1588, Roald Stensby. No. 1589, Rocke-Pelle (Per Hartvig) (1938-80). No. 1590, Jan Rohde (1942-2005).

Die Cut Perf. 15½x14½

2009. Aug. 21 **Photo.**

Coil Stamps

Self-Adhesive

1587	A587	A Innland multi	2.75	1.25
1588	A587	A Innland multi	2.75	1.25
1589	A587	A Innland multi	2.75	1.25
1590	A587	A Innland multi	2.75	1.25
a.		Horiz. strip of 4, #1587-1590	11.00	11.00

On day of issue, Nos. 1587-1590 each sold for 8k.

Norwegian Shipowners' Association, Cent. — A588

Perf. 13¾x13¼

2009, Sept. 15 **Litho.**

1591	A588	15.50k multi	5.50	4.00

Norwegian Association of the Blind, Cent. — A589

Litho. & Embossed

2009, Oct. 8 *Perf. 13¼x14*

1592	A589	8k red	3.00	2.50

Sculptures A590

Designs: No. 1593, Woman on a Man's Lap, by Gustav Vigeland. No. 1594, Crow, by Nils Aas. No. 1595, Birds in Flight, by Arnold Haukeland. No. 1596, Granite Head Lying on its Side, by Kristian Blystad.

Die Cut Perf. 15½x14½

2009, Nov. 16 **Photo.**

Coil Stamps

Self-Adhesive

1593	A590	A Innland multi	3.00	1.25
1594	A590	A Innland multi	3.00	1.25
1595	A590	A Innland multi	3.00	1.25
1596	A590	A Innland multi	3.00	1.25
a.		Horiz. strip of 4, #1593-1596	12.00	
		Nos. 1593-1596 (4)	12.00	5.00

Nos. 1593-1596 each sold for 8k on day of issue.

Christmas A591

Text and: No. 1597, Apple and snowflakes. No. 1598, Stars.

Die Cut Perf. 13¼x13¾

2009, Nov. 16 **Photo.**

Booklet Stamps

Self-Adhesive

1597	A591	A Innland multi	3.00	1.25
1598	A591	A Innland multi	3.00	1.25
a.		Booklet pane of 10, 5 each #1597-1598	30.00	

Nos. 1597-1598 each sold for 8k on day of issue.

Man Drinking, Sculpture bu Per Palle Storm A592

Die Cut Perf. 15½x14½

2010, Jan. 2 **Litho.**

Coil Stamp

Self-Adhesive

1599	A592	13k multi	4.50	2.50

Wildlife Type of 2006

2010, Jan. 2 *Perf. 13¼x13¾*

1600	A511	15k European otter	5.25	3.00
1601	A511	16k Lemming	5.50	3.00
1602	A511	26k Wolverine	9.00	4.50
		Nos. 1600-1602 (3)	19.75	10.50

Famous Men — A595

Designs: No. 1603, Peter Andreas Munch (1810-63), historian, and illuminated text. No. 1604, Ole Bull (1810-80), violinist.

2010, Feb. 5 *Die Cut Perf. 15½x14½*

Coil Stamps

Self-Adhesive

1603	A595	A Innland multi	3.00	1.25
1604	A595	A Innland multi	3.00	1.25
a.		Horiz. pair, #1603 1604	6.00	

On day of issue, Nos. 1603-1604 each sold for 8.50k.

Souvenir Sheet

Dried Cod — A596

Perf. 13¼x13¾

2010, Mar. 24 **Litho.**

1605	A596	A Europa multi	4.50	4.50

No. 1605 sold for 11k on day of issue.

Personalized Stamp — A597

Serpentine Die Cut 10x10¼
Syncopated

2010, Apr. 16 **Self-Adhesive**

1606	A597	A Europa gray	3.75	3.75

No. 1606 sold for 11k on day of issue. The image shown is the generic image sold at face value. Stamps could be personalized for an additional fee.

Valdresflya Road A598

Gamle Strynefjellsvegen Road — A599

Sognefjellet Road A600

Trollstigen Road A601

Helgelandskysten Nord Road — A602

Lofoten National Tourist Road A603

Booklet Stamps

Die Cut Perf. 13¼x13½

2010, Apr. 16 **Self-Adhesive**

1607	A598	A Innland multi	3.00	3.00
1608	A599	A Innland multi	3.00	3.00
a.		Booklet pane of 10, 5 each #1607-1608	30.00	
1609	A600	A Europa multi	4.00	3.00
1610	A601	A Europa multi	4.00	3.00
a.		Booklet pane of 10, 5 each #1609-1610	40.00	
1611	A602	A Verda multi	4.50	4.50
1612	A603	A Verda multi	4.50	4.50
a.		Booklet pane of 10, 5 each #1611-1612	45.00	
		Nos. 1607-1612 (6)	23.00	21.00

On day of issue, Nos. 1607-1608 each sold for 8.50k, Nos. 1609-1610 each sold for 11k, and Nos. 1611-1612 each sold for 13k.

Norwegian Eurovision Song Contest Contestants A604

Designs: No. 1613, Bobbysocks, 1985 winner. No. 1614, Secret Garden, 1995 winner. No. 1615, Alexander Rybak, 2009 winner. No. 1616, Jahn Teigen, 1978 finalist.

Coil Stamps

Die Cut Perf. 15½x14½

2010, May 18 **Self-Adhesive**

1613	A604	A Innland multi	3.00	1.25
1614	A604	A Innland multi	3.00	1.25
1615	A604	A Innland multi	3.00	1.25
1616	A604	A Innland multi	3.00	1.25
a.		Horiz. strip of 4, #1613-1616	12.00	
		Nos. 1613-1616 (4)	12.00	5.00

On day of issue, Nos. 1613-1616 each sold for 8.50k.

Molde Jazz Festival, 50th Anniv. — A605

2010, June 18 *Perf. 13¼x13¾*

1617	A605	13k gray & blue	4.50	3.50

Norwegian National Health Association, Cent. — A606

2010, June 18 **Litho. & Engr.**

1618	A606	26k multi	9.00	6.75

A607

A608

A609

Television in Norway, 50th Anniv. A610

Designs: Nos. 1619a, 1620, Children's television characters Bjornen Teodor, Kometkameratene, Pompel & Pilt, Titten Tei. No. 1621, Comedy stars Trond Kirkvag, Robert Stoltenberg, Rolv Wesenlund and Trond-Viggo Torgersen. Nos. 1619b, 1622, Erik Diesen, Dan Borge Akero, Ivar Dyrhaug and Anne Grosvold. No. 1623, Arne Scheie, Ingrid Espelid Hovig, Erik Bye and Ragnhild Saelthun Fjortoft.

2010, Aug. 20 **Litho.** *Perf. 13¼x13*

1619		Sheet of 2	7.00	7.00
a.		A607 A Innland multi	3.00	3.00
b.		A609 A Innland multi	3.00	3.00

Coil Stamps

Self-Adhesive

Die Cut Perf. 15½x14½

1620	A607	A Innland multi	3.00	1.25
1621	A608	A Innland multi	3.00	1.25
1622	A609	A Innland multi	3.00	1.25

1623 A610 A Innland multi 3.00 1.25
a. Horiz. strip of 4, #1620-1623 12.00
Nos. 1620-1623 (4) 12.00 5.00

On day of issue, Nos. 1619a-1619b, 1620-1623 each sold for 8.50k.

Norwegian Press Association, Norwegian Media Businesses Association, Cent. — A611

2010, Sept. 15 *Perf. 13¼x13¾*
1624 A611 11k multi 4.00 3.00

Norwegian Seafarers' Union, Cent. — A612

2010, Sept. 15 *Perf. 13¾x13¼*
1625 A612 16k multi 5.50 4.25

Norwegian University of Technology and Science, Cent. — A613

Royal Norwegian Society of Science and Letters, 250th Anniv. — A614

Perf. 13¼x13¾
2010, Sept. 15 **Litho. & Engr.**
1626 A613 8.50k multi 3.00 2.25
1627 A614 13k multi 4.50 3.50

Redrawn Posthorn Type of 2001-06
Perf. 13¾x13¼
2010, Nov. 15 **Litho.**
Color of Oval
1628 A439a 4k blue 1.40 1.00
1629 A439a 8k brown 2.75 2.00
1630 A439a 30k dull violet 10.00 6.00
Nos. 1628-1630 (3) 14.15 9.00

No. 1630 has a silver frame.

A615

Europa — A616

Illustrations from children's books by Anne-Cath. Vestly (1920-2008): A Innland, Marte and Grandma and Grandma and Morten. A Europa, The House in the Woods — A New Home.

Litho. With Foil Application
2010, Nov. 15 *Perf. 13¼*
1631 A615 A Innland multi 3.00 2.25
1632 A616 A Europa multi 4.00 3.00

On day of issue, No. 1631 sold for 8.50k and No. 1632 sold for 11k.

Christmas A617

Designs from embroidered Christmas tablecloth: No. 1633, Straw billy goat. No. 1634, Candlesticks and mistletoe.

Die Cut Perf. 13¼x13¾
2010, Nov. 15 **Litho.**
Booklet Stamps
Self-Adhesive
1633 A617 A Innland multi 3.00 1.25
1634 A617 A Innland multi 3.00 1.25
a. Booklet pane of 10, 5 each #1633-1634 30.00

On day of issue, Nos. 1633-1634 each sold for 8.50k.

Norwegian Sports Confederation, 150th Anniv. — A618

Die Cut Perf. 15½x15
2011, Jan. 3 **Litho.**
Coil Stamp
Self-Adhesive
1635 A618 14k multi 5.00 3.00

Wildlife Type of 2006
2011, Jan. 3 **Litho.** *Perf. 13¼x13¾*
1636 A511 17k Polar bear 6.00 3.00
a. Perf. 14¼x13¾ 6.25 3.50
1637 A511 27k Musk ox 9.50 4.00

2011 World Nordic Skiing Championships, Oslo — A619

Designs: 9k, Holmenkollen ski jump. 12k, Skiers, Holmenkollen Ski Stadium.

2011, Feb. 23 *Perf. 13½x13¼*
1638 A619 9k multi 3.25 2.50
1639 A619 12k multi 4.50 2.50
a. Souvenir sheet of 2, #1638-1639 9.00 9.00

Fridtjof Nansen (1861-1930), Explorer and Statesman — A620

2011, Apr. 15 **Litho.** *Perf. 14x13¼*
1640 A620 12k multi 4.50 3.25

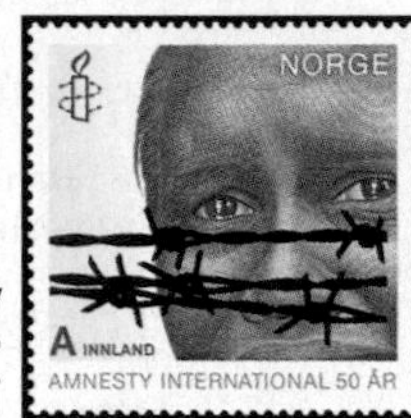

Amnesty International, 50th Anniv. A621

Perf. 14¼x14½
2011, Apr. 15 **Litho. & Engr.**
1641 A621 A Innland multi 3.50 2.50

No. 1641 sold for 9k on day of issue.

Roald Amundsen Expedition to South Pole, Cent. — A622

Designs: 14k, Amundsen (1872-1928), men on expedition, Norwegian flag. 17k, Polar ship Fram and sled dogs.

2011, Apr. 15 **Litho.** *Perf. 14x13¼*
1642 A622 14k multi 5.25 3.75
1643 A622 17k multi 6.50 4.50

Buildings A623

Designs: No. 1644, Global Seed Vault, Svalbard. No. 1645, Visitor's Center, Borgund. No. 1646, Preikestolen Mountain Lodge, Lysefjorden.

Booklet Stamps
Die Cut Perf. 13¼x13½
2011, Apr. 15 **Self-Adhesive**
1644 A623 A Innland multi 3.50 1.25
a. Booklet pane of 10 35.00
1645 A623 A Europa multi 4.50 2.50
a. Booklet pane of 10 45.00
1646 A623 A Verden multi 5.25 2.25
a. Booklet pane of 10 52.50
Nos. 1644-1646 (3) 13.25 6.00

On day of issue, Nos. 1644-1646 sold for 9k, 12k and 14k, respectively.

Drammen, Bicent. — A624

2011, May 20 *Perf. 14x13¼*
1647 A624 9k multi 3.50 2.50

Fire and Rescue Services, 150th Anniv. A625

Designs: 9k, Firemen and fire truck from Sagene Fire Station, Oslo. 27k, Firemen training.

2011, June 3 *Perf. 13¼x13¾*
1648 A625 9k multi 3.50 2.50
1649 A625 27k multi 10.00 6.50

Europa — A626

Designs: 12k, Logging, Bjornsasen. 14k, Forest, Farrisvannet.

2011, June 10 **Litho.**
1650 A626 12k multi 4.50 3.25
1651 A626 14k multi 5.25 3.75

Intl. Year of Forests.

University of Oslo, Bicent. — A627

2011, Sept. 2 **Litho. & Engr.**
1652 A627 9k ver & brn 3.25 2.50

Comic Strip Art — A628

Designs: 9k, Bird in nest, by John Arne Saeteroy. 14k, Hold Brillan (man opening envelope), by Cristopher Nielsen. 17k, Nemi (women with index finger and pinkie raised), by Lise Myhre. 20k, Pondus (soccer player), by Frode Overli.

2011, Sept. 16 **Litho.**
1653 A628 9k multi 3.25 2.50
1654 A628 14k multi 5.00 3.75
1655 A628 17k multi 6.00 4.50
1656 A628 20k multi 7.00 5.50
Nos. 1653-1656 (4) 21.25 16.25

Female Singers A629

Designs: No. 1657, Wenche Myhre. No. 1658, Inger Lise Rypdal. No. 1659, Mari Boine. No. 1660, Sissel Kyrkjebo.

Coil Stamps
Die Cut Perf. 15½x14½
2011, Sept. 16 **Self-Adhesive**
1657 A629 A Innland multi 3.25 1.25
1658 A629 A Innland multi 3.25 1.25
1659 A629 A Innland multi 3.25 1.25
1660 A629 A Innland multi 3.25 1.25
a. Horiz. coil strip of 4, #1657-1660 13.00
Nos. 1657-1660 (4) 13.00 5.00

On day of issue, Nos. 1657-1660 each sold for 9k.

Redrawn Posthorn Type of 2001-06
Perf. 13¾x13¼
2011, Nov. 11 **Litho.**
Color of Oval
1661 A439a 50k blue gray 18.00 9.00

No. 1661 has a silver frame.

Christmas — A630

Designs: No. 1662, Boy holding letter. No. 1663, Girl holding gifts.

Die Cut Perf. 13½x13¼

2011, Nov. 11 Litho.

Self-Adhesive

1662	A630 A Innland multi	3.25	1.25
1663	A630 A Innland multi	3.25	1.25
a.	Horiz. pair, #1662-1663, on tan backing paper	6.50	
b.	Booklet pane of 10, 5 each #1662-1663	32.50	

On day of issue, Nos. 1662-1663 each sold for 9k. On No. 1663b, Nos. 1662 and 1663 are arranged in vertical pairs.

Personalized Stamp — A631

Serpentine Die Cut 10x10¼ Syncopated

2012, Feb. 21 Self-Adhesive

1664	A631 A Innland multi	3.50	3.50

No. 1664 sold for 9.50k on day of issue. The image shown is the generic image sold at face value. Stamps could be personalized for an additional fee.

75th Birthdays of King and Queen A632

Designs: 9.50k, Queen Sonja. 13k, King Harald V.

Perf. 14¼x14½

2012, Feb. 21 Litho. & Engr.

1665	A632 9.50k multi	3.50	2.75
1666	A632 13k multi	4.75	3.50

A booklet containing booklet panes of 2 No. 1665, 2 No. 1666 and 1 each of Nos. 1665-1666 sold for 99k. Value $35.

Griffin From Roof Of National Gallery Oslo, Sculpture by Lars Utne — A633

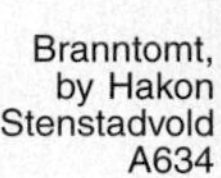

Branntomt, by Hakon Stenstadvold A634

Die Cut Perf. 15½x14½

2012, Feb. 21 Litho.

Coil Stamps

Self-Adhesive

1667	A633 B Innland multi	3.25	1.25
1668	A634 14k multi	5.00	3.00

No. 1667 sold for 9k on day of issue. An etiquette alternates with No. 1667 on rolls produced for sale to the public. On later printings, the etiquette is not present on the rolls.

Souvenir Sheet

Rescue Helicopter — A635

2012, Mar. 21 ***Perf. 14x13½***

1669	A635 A Europa multi	5.00	5.00

No. 1669 sold for 13k on day of issue.

Famous People A636

Designs: No. 1670, Sonja Henie (1912-69), figure skater. No. 1671, Close-up of Henie. No. 1672, Thorbjorn Egner (1912-90), writer of children's books. No. 1673, Egner's illustration of Kardemomme Town.

Coil Stamps

Die Cut Perf. 15½x14½

2012, Apr. 13 Self-Adhesive

1670	A636 A Innland multi	3.50	1.25
1671	A636 A Innland multi	3.50	1.25
1672	A636 A Innland multi	3.50	1.25
1673	A636 A Innland multi	3.50	1.25
a.	Horiz. strip of 4, #1670-1673	14.00	
	Nos. 1670-1673 (4)	14.00	5.00

On day of issue, Nos. 1670-1673 each sold for 9.50k. No. 1673a was made available with stamps on the strip in a different order and having a different distance between stamps.

Nidaros Cathedral, Trondheim A637

Abbey Ruins, Selja Island — A638

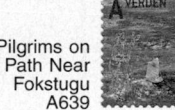

Pilgrims on Path Near Fokstugu A639

Die Cut Perf. 13¼x13½

2012, Apr. 13 Self-Adhesive

1674	A637 A Innland multi	3.50	1.25
a.	Booklet pane of 10 on white backing paper	35.00	
1675	A638 A Europa multi	4.50	2.50
a.	Booklet pane of 10 on white backing paper	45.00	
1676	A639 A Verden multi	5.25	3.00
a.	Booklet pane of 10 on white backing paper	52.50	
	Nos. 1674-1676 (3)	13.25	6.75

Europa. On day of issue Nos. 1674-1676 each sold for 9.50k, 13k and 15k, respectively. Values for unused examples of Nos. 1674-1676 are for copies either on white backing paper (from booklet panes) or tan backing paper (single stamps).

Norwegian Aviation, Cent. — A640

Designs: 14k, Start (Rumpler Taube), first airplane of Navy Air Service. 15k, Douglas DC-3 Dakota. 27k, Glider.

2012, May 18 Litho. ***Perf. 13¼***

1677	A640 14k multi	4.75	4.75
1678	A640 15k multi	5.00	5.00
1679	A640 27k multi	9.00	9.00
a.	Souvenir sheet of 3, #1677-1679	19.00	19.00
	Nos. 1677-1679 (3)	18.75	18.75

Hadeland Glassworks, 250th Anniv. — A641

Perf. 13¼x13¾

2012, June 15 Litho. & Engr.

1680	A641 13k multi	4.25	4.25

Kavringen Lighthouse A642

Medfjordbaen Lighthouse A643

Die Cut Perf. 13½x13¼

2012, June 15 Litho.

Self-Adhesive

1681	A642 A Innland multi	3.25	3.25
1682	A643 A Innland multi	3.25	3.25
a.	Horiz. pair, #1681-1682, on tan backing paper	6.50	
b.	Booklet pane of 10, 5 each # 1681-1682	32.50	

On day of issue, Nos. 1681-1682 each sold for 9.50k. On No. 1682b, Nos. 1681 and 1682 are arranged in vertical pairs.

Norwegian Nurses Organization, Cent. — A644

2012, Sept. 14 ***Perf. 13¼x13¾***

1683	A644 13k multi	4.50	4.50

Famous Men — A645

Designs: 14k, Knud Knudsen (1812-95), linguist. 15k, Peter Christen Asbjornsen (1812-85) and Jorgen Moe (1813-82), collectors of Norwegian folklore.

2012, Sept. 14 ***Perf. 14x13¼***

1684	A645 14k multi	5.00	5.00
1685	A645 15k multi	5.25	5.25

Popular Musicians A646

Designs: No. 1686, Sondre Lerche. No. 1687, Ole Paus. No. 1688, Age Aleksandersen. No. 1689, Morten Abel.

Coil Stamps

Die Cut Perf. 15½x14½

2012, Sept. 14 Self-Adhesive

1686	A646 A Innland multi	3.50	3.50
1687	A646 A Innland multi	3.50	3.50
1688	A646 A Innland multi	3.50	3.50
1689	A646 A Innland multi	3.50	3.50
a.	Horiz. strip of 4, #1686-1689	14.00	
	Nos. 1686-1689 (4)	14.00	14.00

Redrawn Posthorn Type of 2001-06

Perf. 13¾x13¼

2012, Nov. 12 Litho.

Color of Oval

1690	A439a 40k gray	14.00	14.00

No. 1690 has a silver frame.

Ruins of Hamar Cathedral A647

2012, Nov. 12 Litho.

1691	A647 15k multi	5.25	5.25

Directorate for Cultural Heritage, cent.

Santa Claus and Carpenter Andersen A648

Mrs. Claus and Children A649

Die Cut Perf. 13¼x13¾

2012, Nov. 12 Self-Adhesive

1692	A648 A Innland multi	3.50	3.50
1693	A649 A Innland multi	3.50	3.50
a.	Booklet pane of 10, 5 each #1692-1693, on white backing paper	35.00	

Nos. 1692-1693 each sold for 9.50k on day of issue. Horizontal pairs of Nos. 1692-1693 are on white backing paper, which are from No. 1693a, and a tan backing paper, which were prepared for philatelic sale. The stamps on the tan backing paper were only made available as pairs, and were not available in coil rolls.

Fashion A650

Fashion designs by: No. 1694, Nina Skarras. No. 1695, Camilla Bruerberg.

2013, Jan. 2 ***Die Cut Perf. 15½x14½***

Coil Stamps

Self-Adhesive

1694	A650 15k multi	5.50	5.50
1695	A650 15k multi	5.50	5.50
a.	Horiz. pair, #1694-1695	11.00	

Paintings by Edvard Munch (1863-1944) — A651

Details from: 13k, Self-Portrait in Front of the House Wall, 1926. 15k, The Sick Child, 1898. 17k, Madonna, 1895. No. 1699, The Scream, 1893.
No. 1700, The Sun, 1911.

2013, Feb. 15 ***Perf. 14x13¼***

1696	A651 13k multi	4.50	4.50
a.	Booklet pane of 1	7.50	—
1697	A651 15k multi	5.25	5.25
a.	Booklet pane of 1	8.50	—
1698	A651 17k multi	6.00	6.00
a.	Booklet pane of 1	9.75	—
1699	A651 20k multi	7.00	7.00
a.	Booklet pane of 1	11.50	—
	Nos. 1696-1699 (4)	22.75	22.75

Souvenir Sheet

1700	A651 20k multi	7.00	7.00
a.	Booklet pane of 1	11.50	—
	Complete booklet, #1696a, 1697a, 1698a, 1699a, 1700a	49.00	

Complete booklet sold for 139k.

Statue of King Karl Johan, by Brynjulv Bergslien A652

Perf. 14¼x14½

2013, Apr. 19 **Litho. & Engr.**

1701	A652 30k multi	10.50	10.50

King Karl Johan (1763-1844).

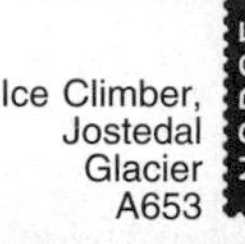
Ice Climber, Jostedal Glacier A653

Boya Glacier A654

Hikers at Gaustatoppen A655

Hikers at Gaustatoppen A656

Rafters, Sjoa River — A657

Riverboarder, Sjoa River — A658

Die Cut Perf. 13¼x13½

2013, Apr. 19 **Litho.**

Booklet Stamps
Self-Adhesive

1702	A653 A Innland multi	3.25	3.25
1703	A654 A Innland multi	3.25	3.25
a.	Booklet pane of 10, 5 each #1702-1703	32.50	
1704	A655 A Europa multi	4.50	4.50
1705	A656 A Europa multi	4.50	4.50
a.	Booklet pane of 10, 5 each #1704-1705	45.00	
1706	A657 A Verden multi	5.25	5.25
1707	A658 A Verden multi	5.25	5.25
a.	Booklet pane of 10, 5 each #1706-1707	52.50	
	Nos. 1702-1707 (6)	26.00	26.00

On day of issue, Nos. 1702-1703 each sold for 9.50k, Nos. 1704-1705 each sold for 13k, and Nos. 1706-1707 each sold for 15k.

Norwegian Student Society, 200th Anniv. — A659

2013, June 10 **Litho.** ***Perf. 13¼***

1708	A659 17k multi	6.00	6.00

Europa — A660

Postal vehicles: 13k, 1932 Harley-Davidson motorcycles and sidecars. 15k, Ford electric vans.

2013, June 10 **Litho.** ***Perf. 14x13½***

1709	A660 13k multi	4.50	4.50
1710	A660 15k multi	5.25	5.25

Crown Prince Haakon A661

Crown Princess Mette-Marit A662

Crown Prince Haakon, Crown Princess Mette-Marit and Their Children A663

King Harald V, Crown Prince Haakon, Princess Ingrid Alexandra A664

Die Cut Perf. 15½x14½

2013, June 10 **Litho.**

Coil Stamps
Self-Adhesive

1711	A661 A Innland multi	3.50	3.50
1712	A662 A Innland multi	3.50	3.50
1713	A663 A Innland multi	3.50	3.50
1714	A664 A Innland multi	3.50	3.50
a.	Horiz. strip of 4, #1711-1714	14.00	
	Nos. 1711-1714 (4)	14.00	14.00

Fortieth birthdays of Crown Prince Haakon and Crown Princess Mette-Marit. On day of issue, Nos. 1711-1714 each sold for 9.50k.

Woman Suffrage, Cent. — A665

Designs: 17k, Camilla Collett (1813-95), feminist writer, front page of *Amtmandens Døttre*. 30k, Anna Rogstad (1854-1938), first female in Parliament, Parliament Building.

Perf. 13¼x13¾

2013, Sept. 9 **Litho. & Engr.**

1715	A665 17k multi	5.75	5.75
1716	A665 30k multi	10.00	10.00

National Language Year — A666

Designs: No. 1717, Lasse Kolstad (1922-2012), actor. No. 1718, Ivar Aasen (1813-96), writer and lexicographer.

Die Cut Perf. 15½x14½

2013, Sept. 9 **Litho.**

Coil Stamps
Self-Adhesive

1717	A666 A Innland multi	3.25	3.25
1718	A666 A Innland multi	3.25	3.25
a.	Horiz. pair, #1717-1718	6.50	

Nos. 1717-1718 each sold for 9.50k on day of issue.

Rock Bands — A667

Designs: No. 1719, The Pussycats. No. 1720, DumDum Boys. No. 1721, Turbonegro. No. 1722, DeLillos.

Die Cut Perf. 15½x14½

2013, Oct. 4 **Litho.**

Coil Stamps
Self-Adhesive

1719	A667 A Innland multi	3.25	3.25
1720	A667 A Innland multi	3.25	3.25
1721	A667 A Innland multi	3.25	3.25
1722	A667 A Innland multi	3.25	3.25
a.	Horiz. strip of 4, #1719-1722	13.00	
	Nos. 1719-1722 (4)	13.00	13.00

Nos. 1719-1722 each sold for 9.50k on day of issue.

Redrawn Posthorn Type of 2001-06

Perf. 13¾x13¼

2013, Nov. 11 **Litho.**

Color of Oval

1723	A439a 10k brown	3.25	3.25
1724	A439a 20k brown	6.50	6.50

Solan Gundersen A668

Nabonissen House A669

Die Cut Perf. 13½x13¼

2013, Nov. 11 **Litho.**

Self-Adhesive

1725	A668 A Innland multi	3.25	3.25
1726	A669 A Innland multi	3.25	3.25
a.	Horiz. pair, #1725-1726, on tan backing paper	6.50	
b.	Booklet pane of 10, 5 each #1725-1726, on white backing paper	32.50	

Christmas. Nos. 1725-1726 each sold for 9.50k on day of issue.

Wildlife Type of 2006

2014 **Litho.** ***Perf. 14¼x13¾***

Self-Adhesive

1726C	A511 16k Lemming	5.25	5.25
1727	A511 19k Red deer	6.25	6.25
1728	A511 35k Badger	11.50	11.50
	Nos. 1726C-1728 (3)	23.00	23.00

Issued: Nos 1727-1728, 1/2; 1726C, 1/22.

Norwegian Church Abroad, 150th Anniv. — A670

Die Cut Perf. 14½x15½

2014, Jan. 2 **Litho.**

Coil Stamp
Self-Adhesive

1729	A670 15k multi	5.00	5.00

Marit Bjorgen A671

Tora Berger A672

Petter Northug A673

Aksel Lund Svindal A674

Die Cut Perf. 13¼x13½

2014, Feb. 7 **Litho.**

Coil Stamps
Self-Adhesive

1730	A671 A Innland multi	3.50	3.50
1731	A672 A Innland multi	3.50	3.50
1732	A673 A Innland multi	3.50	3.50
1733	A674 A Innland multi	3.50	3.50
a.	Horiz. strip of 4, #1730-1733	14.00	
	Nos. 1730-1733 (4)	14.00	14.00

2014 Winter Olympics, Sochi, Russia. Nos. 1730-1733 each sold for 10k on day of issue.

Souvenir Sheet

Supply Ship MS Normand Arctic — A675

2014, Mar. 17 **Litho.** ***Perf. 14x13¼***

1734	A675 A Europe multi	4.50	4.50

No. 1734 sold for 13k on day of issue.

Viking Buckle, Longhouse and Woman in Viking Costume Sewing
A676

Viking Helmet, Actors Recreating Viking Fight — A677

Draken Harald Harfagre, Dragon Figurehead
A678

Die Cut Perf. 13¼x13½

2014, Apr. 28 **Litho.**

Self-Adhesive

1735 A676 A Innland multi 3.50 3.50
a. Booklet pane of 10 35.00
1736 A677 A Europa multi 4.50 4.50
a. Booklet pane of 10 45.00
1737 A678 A Verda multi 5.50 5.50
a. Booklet pane of 10 55.00
Nos. 1735-1737 (3) 13.50 13.50

On day of issue, No. 1735 sold for 10k; No. 1736, for 13k; No. 1737, for 16k. Nos. 1735-1737 are on brownish translucent paper (single stamps for sale to collectors) and white translucent paper (stamps in booklet panes).

Thor Heyerdahl (1914-2002), Ethnographer
A679

Kon-Tiki
A680

Easter Island Moai — A681

Ra II — A682

2014, Apr. 28 **Litho.** ***Perf. 13¾x14***

Booklet Stamps

1737B A679 A Innland multi 6.00 6.00
f. Booklet pane of 1 6.00 —
1737C A680 A Innland multi 6.00 6.00
g. Booklet pane of 1 6.00 —
1737D A681 A Innland multi 6.00 6.00
h. Booklet pane of 1 6.00 —
1737E A682 A Innland multi 6.00 6.00
i. Booklet pane of 1 6.00 —
j. Booklet pane of 4, #1737B-1737E 24.00 —
Complete booklet, #1737Bf, 1737Cg, 1737Dh, 1737Ei, 1737Ej 48.00
Nos. 1737B-1737E (4) 24.00 24.00

Coil Stamps

Self-Adhesive

Die Cut Perf. 13x13½

1738 A679 A Innland multi 3.50 3.50
1739 A680 A Innland multi 3.50 3.50
1740 A681 A Innland multi 3.50 3.50
1741 A682 A Innland multi 3.50 3.50
a. Horiz. strip of 4, #1738-1741 14.00
Nos. 1738-1741 (4) 14.00 14.00

Nos. 1737B-1737E each had a franking value of 10k on day of issue. Complete booklet sold for 139k. Nos. 1738-1741 each sold for 10k on day of issue.

Norwegian Constitution, 200th Anniv. — A683

Designs: 13k, Constituent Assembly meeting at Eidsvoll, 1814. 16k, Prince Christian Frederik and 1814 Constitution. 19k, Lion statue at Parliament, May 17 parade. 30k, Hands forming heart, 1814 Constitution.

Litho. & Engr.

2014, May 16 ***Perf. 14x13¼***

1742 A683 13k multi 4.50 4.50
1743 A683 16k multi 5.50 5.50
1744 A683 19k multi 6.50 6.50
1745 A683 30k multi 10.00 10.00
Nos. 1742-1745 (4) 26.50 26.50

Personalized Stamp — A684

Serpentine Die Cut 10¼x10 Syncopated

2014, May 16 **Litho.**

Self-Adhesive

1746 A684 A Verden multi 5.50 5.50

No. 1746 sold for 16k on day of issue. The image shown, depicting the Aurora Borealis, is the generic image sold at face value. Stamps could be personalized for an additional fee.

Alf Proysen (1914-70), Writer, and Radio — A685

Mrs. Pepperpot and Mouse
A686

Die Cut Perf. 15½x14½

2014, June 13 **Litho.**

Coil Stamps

Self-Adhesive

1747 A685 A Innland multi 3.25 3.25
1748 A686 A Innland multi 3.25 3.25
a. Horiz. pair, #1747-1748 6.50

Nos. 1747-1748 each sold for 10k on day of issue.

Redrawn Posthorn Type of 2001-06

2014-15 **Litho.** ***Perf. 13¾x13¼***

Self-Adhesive

Color of Oval

1749 A439a 1k green .25 .25
1750 A439a 5k purple 1.60 1.60
1751 A439a 50k blue gray 16.00 16.00
1752 A439a 70k gray grn 22.00 22.00
Nos. 1749-1752 (4) 39.85 39.85

Issued: No. 1749, 1/7/15. No. 1750, 9/9; No. 1752, 9/12.

Norwegian Chess Federation, Cent. — A687

Litho. & Engr.

2014, Aug. 1 ***Perf. 13¼***

1753 A687 15k multi 4.75 4.75

Solvguttene Boys' Choir — A688

Characters From Production of *Putti Plutti Pott* — A689

Die Cut Perf. 13¼x13½

2014, Nov. 10 **Litho.**

Self-Adhesive

1754 A688 A Innland multi 3.00 3.00
1755 A689 A Innland multi 3.00 3.00
a. Horiz. pair, #1754-1755, on tan backing paper 6.00
b. Booklet pane of 10, 5 each #1754-1755 30.00

Christmas. Nos. 1754-1755 both sold for 10k on day of issue.

Wildlife Type of 2006

2015, Jan. 2 **Litho.** ***Perf. 14¼x13¾***

Self-Adhesive

1756 A511 31k Eurasian eagle owl 8.25 8.25

Birds — A690

Designs: No. 1757, Cyanistes caeruleus. No. 1758, Lophophanes cristatus.

Die Cut Perf. 15½x14½

2015, Jan. 2 **Litho.** **Coil Stamps**

Self-Adhesive

1757 A690 16k multi 4.25 4.25
1758 A690 16k multi 4.25 4.25
a. Horiz. pair, #1757-1758 8.50

Norwegian Red Cross, 150th Anniv.
A691

Designs: No. 1759, Rescue team members in snow. No. 1760, Visitor service representative meeting with elderly woman. No. 1761, Emergency aid worker with Philippine children. No. 1762, Attempt to create world's largest human cross, 2010.

Die Cut Perf. 15½x14½

2015, Feb. 20 **Litho.**

Coil Stamps

Self-Adhesive

1759 A691 A Innland multi 2.75 2.75
1760 A691 A Innland multi 2.75 2.75
1761 A691 A Innland multi 2.75 2.75
1762 A691 A Innland multi 2.75 2.75
a. Horiz. strip of 4, #1759-1762 11.00
Nos. 1759-1762 (4) 11.00 11.00

On day of issue, Nos. 1759-1762 each sold for 10.50k.

Wildlife Type of 2006

2015, Mar. 4 **Litho.** ***Perf. 14¼x13¾***

Self-Adhesive

1763 A511 14k Bear 3.75 3.75

Halden, 350th Anniv. — A692

Litho. & Engr.

2015, Apr. 10 ***Perf. 14½***

1764 A692 20k multi 5.50 5.50

Photographs by Anders Beer Wilse (1865-1949) — A693

Design: A Innland, Street View of Oslo, 1924. 14k, Kyrkja Mountain, 1933. 16k, Three Large Cod, 1910.
20k, Setesdal on the Way to Church, 1934.

2015, Apr. 16 **Litho.** ***Perf. 14x13½***

1765 A693 A Innland multi 3.00 3.00
1766 A693 14k multi 3.75 3.75
1767 A693 16k multi 4.25 4.25
Nos. 1765-1767 (3) 11.00 11.00

Souvenir Sheet

1768 A693 20k multi 5.50 5.50

No. 1765 sold for 10.50k on day of issue. No. 1768 contains one 70x30mm stamp.

Europa
A694

Old toys: 14k, Anne dolls. 17k Tomte Ford F-100 truck and firetruck.

2015, June 5 **Litho.** ***Perf. 14¼x14½***

1769 A694 14k multi 3.50 3.50
1770 A694 17k multi 4.25 4.25

Halfdan Kjerulf (1815-68), Composer
A695

Agnar Mykle (1915-94), Writer — A696

Die Cut Perf. 15½x14½

2015, June 5 **Litho.**

Coil Stamps

Self-Adhesive

1771 A695 A Innland multi 2.60 2.60
1772 A696 A Innland multi 2.60 2.60
a. Horiz. pair, #1771-1772 5.20

Nos. 1771-1772 each sold for 10.50k on day of issue.

Lighthouses — A697

Designs: No. 1773, Kvitsoy Lighthouse. No. 1774, Slatteroy Lighthouse. No. 1775, Lindesnes Lighthouse. No. 1776, Kjeungskjaeret Lighthouse.

Die Cut Perf. 13¾x13¼

2015, June 5 **Litho.**

Self-Adhesive

1773 A697 A Europa multi 3.50 3.50
1774 A697 A Europa multi 3.50 3.50
a. Booklet pane of 10, 5 each #1773-1774 35.00

1775 A697 A Verda multi 4.25 4.25
1776 A697 A Verda multi 4.25 4.25
a. Horiz. strip of 4, #1773-1776, on tan backing paper 15.50
b. Booklet pane of 10, 5 each #1773-1774 42.50
Nos. 1773-1776 (4) 15.50 15.50

On day of issue, Nos. 1773-1774 each sold for 14k and Nos. 1775-1776 each sold for 17k.

Bergen Philharmonic Orchestra, 250th Anniv. — A698

2015, Aug. 20 Litho. *Perf. 14x13½*
1777 A698 31k multi 7.50 7.50

Supreme Court of Norway, 200th Anniv. — A699

Litho. & Engr.
2015, Oct. 3 *Perf. 13½x14*
1778 A699 20k multi 4.75 4.75

Birds — A700

Designs: No. 1779, Somateria spectabilis. No. 1780, Somateria mollissima. No. 1781, Motacilla alba. No. 1782, Oenanthe oenanthe.

Die Cut Perf. 15½x14½
2015, Oct. 3 Litho.
Coil Stamps
Self-Adhesive
1779 A700 B Innland 2.25 2.25
1780 A700 B Innland 2.25 2.25
1781 A700 A Innland 2.50 2.50
1782 A700 A Innland 2.50 2.50
a. Horiz. strip of 4, #1779-1782 9.50
Nos. 1779-1782 (4) 9.50 9.50

On day of issue, Nos. 1779-1780 each sold for 9.50k and Nos. 1781-1782 each sold for 10.50k.

Redrawn Posthorn Type of 2001-06
Perf. 13¾x13¼
2015, Nov. 13 Litho.
Self-Adhesive
Color of Oval
1783 A439a 60k dull bl grn 14.00 14.00

A701

Christmas — A702

Serpentine Die Cut 11
2015, Nov. 13 Litho.
Booklet Stamps
Self-Adhesive
1784 A701 A Innland 2.50 2.50
1785 A702 A Innland 2.50 2.50
a. Booklet pane of 8, 4 each #1784-1785 20.00

Reign of King Harald V, 25th Anniv. — A703

Die Cut Perf. 14½x15½
2016, Jan. 11 Litho.
Coil Stamp
Self-Adhesive
1786 A703 17k multi 4.00 4.00

Youth Winter Olympic Games, Lillehammer — A704

Designs: No. 1787, Skier. No. 1788, Person on mountain top.

Die Cut Perf. 13½x13¼
2016, Jan. 11 Litho.
Self-Adhesive
1787 A704 A Innland multi 2.50 2.50
1788 A704 A Innland multi 2.50 2.50
a. Horiz. pair on tan backing paper 5.00
b. Booklet pane of 10, 5 each #1787-1788 25.00

World Biathlon Championships, Oslo — A705

Two competitors: 21k, Skiing. 33k, Shooting.

Litho. With Foil Application
2016, Feb. 19 *Perf. 14x13½*
1789 A705 21k multi 5.00 5.00
1790 A705 33k multi 7.75 7.75

Cities A706

Designs: 11k, Harbor of Grimstad, statue of fisherman by Terje Vigen. 17k, Cannons of Nyholmd Skandse, Bodo, Bishop Mathias Bonsach Krogh, city founder. 18k, Cannons near Kragero, *Winter, Kragero,* by Edvard Munch. 21k, Waterfall, Sarpsborg, statue of St. Olav by Finn Eirik Modahl.

2016, Apr. 15 Litho. *Perf. 13½x13¾*
1791 A706 11k multi 2.75 2.75
1792 A706 17k multi 4.25 4.25
1793 A706 18k multi 4.50 4.50
1794 A706 21k multi 5.00 5.00
Nos. 1791-1794 (4) 16.50 16.50

Grimstad, 200th anniv.; Bodo, 200th anniv.; Kragero, 350th anniv.; Sarpsborg, 1000th anniv.

Nordic Food Culture — A707

Designs: No. 1795, Glazed langoustines, by Chef Espen Holmboe Bang. No. 1796, Beetroot barley risotto with Atlantic cod and kale, by Chef Freddy Storaker Bruu.

2016, Apr. 15 Litho. *Perf. 14x13½*
1795 A707 14k multi 3.50 3.50
1796 A707 14k multi 3.50 3.50
a. Souvenir sheet of 2, #1795-1796 7.00 7.00

SEMI-POSTAL STAMPS

North Cape Issue

North Cape — SP1

Perf. 13½x14
1930, June 28 Wmk. 160 Photo.
Size: 33¼x21½mm
B1 SP1 15o + 25o blk brn 2.00 *6.00*
B2 SP1 20o + 25o car 35.00 *80.00*
B3 SP1 30o + 25o ultra 90.00 *110.00*
Nos. B1-B3 (3) 127.00 *196.00*
Set, never hinged 275.00

The surtax was given to the Tourist Association. See Nos. B9-B10, B28-B30, B54-B56, B59-B61.

Radium Hospital SP2

1931, Apr. 1 *Perf. 14½x13½*
B4 SP2 20o + 10o carmine 16.00 10.00
Never hinged 65.00

The surtax aided the Norwegian Radium Hospital.

Fridtjof Nansen — SP3

1935, Dec. 13 *Perf. 13½*
B5 SP3 10o + 10o green 3.50 *7.00*
B6 SP3 15o + 10o red brn 10.00 *15.00*
B7 SP3 20o + 10o crimson 5.00 4.50
B8 SP3 30o + 10o brt ultra 12.00 *16.00*
Nos. B5-B8 (4) 30.50 42.50
Set, never hinged 55.00

The surtax aided the International Nansen Office for Refugees.

North Cape Type of 1930
1938, June 20 *Perf. 13x13½*
Size: 27x21mm
B9 SP1 20o + 25o brn car 3.50 *9.00*
B10 SP1 30o + 25o dp ultra 13.50 32.50
Set, never hinged 27.50

Surtax given to the Tourist Assoc.

Queen Maud — SP4

Perf. 13x13½
1939, July 24 Photo. Unwmk.
B11 SP4 10o + 5o brt grn .40 10.00
B12 SP4 15o + 5o red brn .40 10.00
B13 SP4 20o + 5o scarlet .50 7.50
B14 SP4 30o + 5o brt ultra .40 12.00
Nos. B11-B14 (4) 1.70 39.50
Set, never hinged 4.00

The surtax was used for charities.

Fridtjof Nansen — SP5

1940, Oct. 21
B15 SP5 10o + 10o dk grn 3.50 4.50
B16 SP5 15o + 10o henna brn 4.00 6.00
B17 SP5 20o + 10o dark red .75 1.50
B18 SP5 30o + 10o ultra 2.50 4.50
Nos. B15-B18 (4) 10.75 16.50
Set, never hinged 16.00

The surtax was used for war relief work.

SP6

Ancient Sailing Craft off Lofoten Islands.

1941, May 16
B19 SP6 15o + 10o deep blue 1.75 .80
Never hinged 4.50

Haalogaland Exposition. Surtax for relief fund for families of lost fishermen.

Value for used stamp postmarked before May 15, 1945, $9.50. See note following No. 180.

Nos. 70-73, 177-180, 267, B19, B32-B34 and B38-B41 were demonetized from May 15, 1945 until Sept. 1, 1981. Used values are for stamps canceled after this period. Stamps with dated cancellations prior to May 15, 1945 sell for more. False cancellations exist.

Colin Archer and Lifeboat — SP7 Lifeboat — SP8

1941, July 9 *Perf. 13x13½, 13½x13*
B20 SP7 10o + 10o yel grn 1.25 2.50
B21 SP7 15o + 10o dk ol brn 1.75 3.50
B22 SP8 20o + 10o brt red .50 .75
B23 SP8 30o + 10o ultra 5.00 9.00
Nos. B20-B23 (4) 8.50 15.75
Set, never hinged 15.00

Norwegian Lifeboat Society, 50th anniv.

Legionary, Norwegian and Finnish Flags — SP9

1941, Aug. 1 *Perf. 13½x13*
B24 SP9 20o + 80o scar ver 60.00 120.00
Never hinged 120.00

The surtax was for the Norwegian Legion.

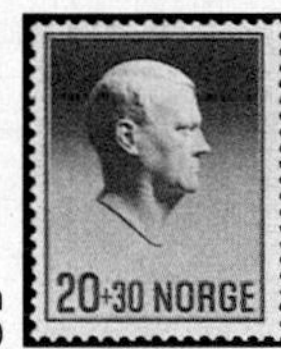

Vidkun Quisling — SP10

1942, Feb. 1
B25 SP10 20o + 30o henna 6.50 *25.00*
Never hinged 11.00

Overprinted in Red

B26 SP10 20o + 30o henna 7.00 *30.00*
Never hinged 12.00

Inauguration of Quisling as prime minister.

Catalogue values for unused stamps in this section, from this point to the end of the section, are for Never Hinged items.

Vidkun Quisling — SP11

1942, Sept. 26 *Perf. 13*
B27 SP11 20o + 30o henna .90 *9.00*

8th annual meeting of Nasjonal Samling, Quisling's party. The surtax aided relatives of soldiers killed in action.

North Cape Type of 1930

1943, Apr. 1 **Size: 27x21mm**
B28 SP1 15o + 25o olive brn 2.00 2.00
B29 SP1 20o + 25o dark car 3.50 3.50
B30 SP1 30o + 25o chalky blue 3.50 3.50
Nos. B28-B30 (3) 9.00 9.00

The surtax aided the Tourist Association.

Frontier Guardsmen Emblem — SP12

1943, Aug. 2 **Unwmk.**
B31 SP12 20o + 30o henna .90 *9.00*

The surtax aided the Frontier Guardsmen (Norwegian Nazi Volunteers).

Fishing Village — SP13

Drying Grain — SP14

Barn in Winter — SP15

1943, Nov. 10
B32 SP13 10o + 10o gray green 2.00 .60
B33 SP14 20o + 10o henna 2.00 .60
B34 SP15 40o + 10o grnsh blk 2.50 .60
Nos. B32-B34 (3) 6.50 1.80

The surtax was for winter relief.

Value, set postmarked before May 15, 1945, $15. See note following No. B19.

The Baroy Sinking — SP16

Sanct Svithun Aflame — SP17

Design: 20o+10o, "Irma" sinking.

1944, May 20
B35 SP16 10o + 10o gray grn 2.50 *7.00*
B36 SP17 15o + 10o dk olive 1.75 *7.00*
B37 SP16 20o + 10o henna 1.75 *7.00*
Nos. B35-B37 (3) 6.00 *21.00*

The surtax aided victims of wartime ship sinkings, and their families.

Spinning SP19

Plowing SP20

Tree Felling — SP21

Child Care — SP22

1944, Dec. 1
B38 SP19 5o + 10o deep mag 1.50 .40
B39 SP20 10o + 10o dark yel grn 1.50 .40
B40 SP21 15o + 10o chocolate 1.50 .40
B41 SP22 20o + 10o henna 1.50 .40
Nos. B38-B41 (4) 6.00 1.60

The surtax was for National Welfare.

Value, set postmarked before May 15, 1945, $20. See note following No. B19.

Red Cross Nurse — SP23

1945, Sept. 22
B42 SP23 20o + 10o red 1.00 *1.75*

80th anniv. of the founding of the Norwegian Red Cross. The surtax was for that institution.

For surcharge see No. B47.

Crown Prince Olav — SP24

1946, Mar. 4 **Unwmk.**
B43 SP24 10o + 10o ol grn .75 .60
B44 SP24 15o + 10o ol brn .75 .60
B45 SP24 20o + 10o dk red 1.00 .60
B46 SP24 30o + 10o brt bl 2.50 2.50
Nos. B43-B46 (4) 5.00 4.30

The surtax was for war victims.

No. B42 Surcharged in Black

1948, Dec. 1
B47 SP23 25o + 5o on 20o+10o 1.00 *1.75*

The surtax was for Red Cross relief work.

Child Picking Flowers — SP25

1950, Aug. 15 **Photo.** *Perf. 13*
B48 SP25 25o + 5o brt red 2.50 1.75
B49 SP25 45o + 5o dp bl 9.00 10.00

The surtax was for poliomyelitis victims.

Skater — SP26

Winter Scene SP27

Design: 30o+10o, Ski jumper.

1951, Oct. 1
B50 SP26 15o + 5o olive grn 2.75 3.50
B51 SP26 30o + 10o red 4.00 4.50
B52 SP27 55o + 20o blue 15.00 *16.00*
Nos. B50-B52 (3) 21.75 24.00

Olympic Winter Games, Oslo, 2/14-29/52.

Kneeling Woman — SP28

1953, June 1 **Photo. & Litho.**
B53 SP28 30o + 10o red & cr 2.50 2.50

The surtax was for cancer research.

North Cape Type of 1930

1953, June 15 **Photo.**
Size: 27x21mm
B54 SP1 20o + 10o green 15.00 15.00
B55 SP1 30o + 15o red 17.00 17.00
B56 SP1 55o + 25o gray blue 20.00 20.00
Nos. B54-B56 (3) 52.00 52.00

The surtax aided the Tourist Association.

Crown Princess Martha — SP29

1956, Mar. 28 *Perf. 13*
B57 SP29 35o + 10o dark red 2.00 2.00
B58 SP29 65o + 10o dark blue 5.00 5.00

The surtax was for the Crown Princess Martha Memorial Fund.

North Cape Type of 1930

1957, May 6 **Size: 27x21mm**
B59 SP1 25o + 10o green 8.50 8.50
B60 SP1 35o + 15o red 10.00 12.00
B61 SP1 65o + 25o gray blue 4.50 3.50
Nos. B59-B61 (3) 23.00 24.00

The surtax aided the Tourist Association.

White Anemone — SP30

Design: 90o+10o, Hepatica.

1960, Jan. 12 **Litho.** *Perf. 13*
B62 SP30 45o + 10o brt red & grn 4.00 4.00
B63 SP30 90o + 10o bl, org & grn 12.00 *15.00*

The surtax was for anti-tuberculosis work.

Mother, Child, WRY Emblem — SP31

1960, Apr. 7 **Photo.** **Unwmk.**
B64 SP31 45o + 25o rose & blk 8.00 9.00
B65 SP31 90o + 25o bl & blk 16.00 20.00

World Refugee Year, July 1, 1959-June 30, 1960. The surtax was for aid to refugees.

Severed Chain and Dove SP32

Design: 60o+10o, Norwegian flags.

1965, May 8 **Photo.** *Perf. 13*
B66 SP32 30o + 10o grn, blk & tan .50 .50
B67 SP32 60o + 10o red & dk bl .90 .75

20th anniversary of liberation from the Germans. The surtax was for war cripples.

Souvenir Sheet

Offshore Oil Drilling — SP33

Designs: a, Ekofisk Center. b, Treasure Scout drilling rig and Odin Viking supply vessel at Tromsoflaket, 1982. c, Statfjord C oil platform, 1984. d, Men working on deck of Neptune Nordraug.

1985, Oct. 4 **Litho.** *Perf. 13½x13*
B68 SP33 Sheet of 4 10.00 12.00
a.-d. 2k + 1k, any single 2.50 2.50

Stamp Day 1985. Surtax for philatelic promotion.

Souvenir Sheet

Paper Industry — SP34

Paper mill: a, Wood aging containers. b, Boiling plant. c, Paper-making machine. d, Paper dryer.

1986, Oct. 17 Litho. *Perf. 13½*
B69 SP34 Sheet of 4 14.00 16.00
a.-d. 2.50k + 1k, any single 3.50 3.50

Surtax for philatelic promotion. Nos. B69a-B69b and B69c-B69d printed in continuous designs.

Souvenir Sheet

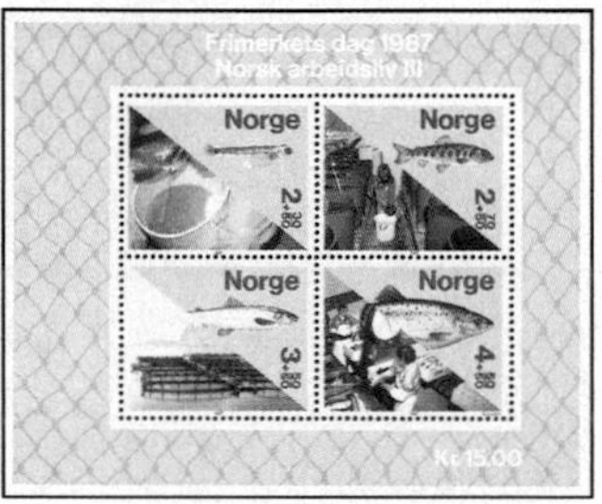

Salmon Industry — SP35

Designs: a, Eggs and milt pressed out of fish by hand. b, Cultivation of eggs in tanks. c, Outdoor hatchery. d, Market.

1987, Oct. 9 Litho. *Perf. 13½x13*
B70 SP35 Sheet of 4 14.00 16.00
a. 2.30k +50o multi 3.50 3.50
b. 2.70k +50o multi 3.50 3.50
c. 3.50k +50o multi 3.50 3.50
d. 4.50k +50o multi 3.50 3.50

Souvenir Sheet

Norwegian Constituent Assembly, 200th Anniv. — SP36

No. B71: a, Prince Christian Frederik, Constitution of 1814. b, Parliament Lion sculpture, parade.

2014, Nov. 21 Litho. *Perf. 14x13¼*
B71 SP36 Sheet of 2 12.00 12.00
a. 16k multi 5.50 5.50
b. 19k multi 6.50 6.50

Nordia 2014 Stamp Exhibition, Oslo. No. B71 sold for 41k, with 6k defraying the costs of the exhibition.

AIR POST STAMPS

Airplane over Akershus Castle — AP1

Perf. 13½x14½
1927-34 Typo. Wmk. 160
C1 AP1 45o lt bl, strong frame line ('34) 4.50 *5.00*
Never hinged 20.00
a. Faint or broken frame line 25.00 9.00
Never hinged 150.00

Airplane over Akershus Castle — AP2

1937, Aug. 18 Photo. *Perf. 13*
C2 AP2 45o Prussian blue .90 .70
Never hinged 4.50

1941, Nov. 10 Unwmk.
C3 AP2 45o indigo .50 .25
Never hinged 2.50

POSTAGE DUE STAMPS

Numeral of Value — D1

Inscribed "at betale"

Perf. 14½x13½
1889-1914 Typo. Wmk. 160
J1 D1 1o olive green ('15) 1.25 *2.50*
Never hinged 2.40
J2 D1 4o magenta ('11) 2.00 2.00
Never hinged 12.00
J3 D1 10o carmine rose ('99) 5.00 .90
Never hinged 15.00
a. 10o rose red ('89) 90.00 25.00
J4 D1 15o brown ('14) 4.50 1.75
J5 D1 20o ultra ('99) 3.50 .65
Never hinged 15.00
a. Perf. 13½x12½ ('95) 250.00 115.00
J6 D1 50o maroon ('89) 6.50 4.00
Never hinged 30.00
Nos. J1-J6 (6) 22.75 11.80

See #J7-J12. For overprint see #136-144.

1922-23 Inscribed "a betale"
J7 D1 4o lilac rose 11.00 18.00
Never hinged 35.00
J8 D1 10o green 5.00 3.50
Never hinged 22.50
J9 D1 20o dull violet 8.00 8.00
Never hinged 30.00
J10 D1 40o deep ultra 12.00 1.50
Never hinged 40.00
J11 D1 100o orange yel 35.00 17.00
Never hinged 150.00
J12 D1 200o dark violet 75.00 30.00
Never hinged 160.00
Nos. J7-J12 (6) 146.00 78.00

OFFICIAL STAMPS

Coat of Arms — O1

Perf. 14½x13½
1926 Typo. Wmk. 160
O1 O1 5o rose lilac .75 *1.50*
O2 O1 10o yellow green .50 .50
O3 O1 15o indigo 2.00 *4.50*
O4 O1 20o plum .50 .25
O5 O1 30o slate 4.50 *10.00*
O6 O1 40o deep blue 2.50 *2.00*
O7 O1 60o Prussian blue 5.00 *10.00*
Nos. O1-O7 (7) 15.75 *28.75*
Set, never hinged 40.00

Official Stamp of 1926 Surcharged

1929, July 1
O8 O1 2o on 5o magenta .60 *1.75*
Never hinged 2.00

Coat of Arms — O2

Perf. 14½x13½
1933-34 Litho. Wmk. 160
Size: 35x19¼mm
O9 O2 2o ocher .60 *1.75*
O10 O2 5o rose lilac 4.50 *7.00*
O11 O2 7o orange 4.50 *10.00*
O12 O2 10o green 30.00 1.25
O13 O2 15o olive .60 *1.25*
O14 O2 20o vermilion 30.00 .60
O15 O2 25o yellow brn .60 *1.00*
O16 O2 30o ultra .90 *1.25*
O18 O2 40o slate 30.00 1.25
O19 O2 60o blue 18.00 2.00
O20 O2 70o olive brn 1.50 *4.00*
O21 O2 100o violet 2.00 3.50
Nos. O9-O16,O18-O21 (12) 123.20 34.85
Same, never hinged 600.00

On the lithographed stamps, the lion's left leg is shaded.

Typo.
Size: 34x18¾mm
O10a O2 5o rose lilac 1.50 4.00
O11a O2 7o orange 8.00 *22.50*
O12a O2 10o green .70 .60
O13a O2 15o olive 6.00 *20.00*
O14a O2 20o vermilion .70 .50
O17 O2 35o red violet ('34) .90 .90
O18a O2 40o slate 1.00 .90
O19a O2 60o blue 1.25 1.25
Nos. O10a-O14a,O17,O18a-O19a (8) 20.05 *50.65*
Same, never hinged 60.00

Coat of Arms — O3

1937-38 Photo. *Perf. 13½x13*
O22 O3 5o rose lilac ('38) .75 1.50
O23 O3 7o dp orange .75 4.00
O24 O3 10o brt green .40 .50
O25 O3 15o olive bister .55 1.00
O26 O3 20o carmine ('38) 2.50 5.00
O27 O3 25o red brown ('38) 1.00 1.00
O28 O3 30o ultra 1.00 1.00
O29 O3 35o red vio ('38) 1.75 .60
O30 O3 40o Prus grn ('38) 1.00 .60
O31 O3 60o Prus bl ('38) 1.25 .60
O32 O3 100o dk vio ('38) 2.00 1.50
Nos. O22-O32 (11) 12.95 *17.30*
Set, never hinged 35.00

See Nos. O33-O43, O55-O56. For surcharge see No. O57.

1939-47 Unwmk.
O33 O3 5o dp red lil ('41) .25 .25
O34 O3 7o dp orange ('41) .30 *1.50*
O35 O3 10o brt green ('41) .25 .25
O36 O3 15o olive ('45) .25 .25
O37 O3 20o carmine .25 .25
O38 O3 25o red brown 3.00 *20.00*
O38A O3 25o scarlet ('46) .25 .25
O39 O3 30o ultra 2.75 2.75
O39A O3 30o dk gray ('47) .65 .55
O40 O3 35o brt lilac ('41) .60 .50
O41 O3 40o grnsh blk ('41) .55 .25
O41A O3 40o dp ultra ('46) 3.00 .25
O42 O3 60o Prus blue ('41) .65 .50
O43 O3 100o dk violet ('41) 1.00 .25
Nos. O33-O43 (14) 13.75 *27.80*
Set, never hinged 40.00

Norwegian Nazi Party Emblem — O4

1942-44
O44 O4 5o magenta .25 *2.00*
O45 O4 7o yellow org .25 *2.00*
O46 O4 10o emerald .25 .25
O47 O4 15o olive ('44) 1.50 *30.00*
O48 O4 20o bright red .25 .25
O49 O4 25o red brn ('43) 4.00 *40.00*
O50 O4 30o brt ultra ('44) 3.00 *40.00*
O51 O4 35o brt pur ('43) 3.00 *18.00*
O52 O4 40o grnsh blk ('43) .25 .50
O53 O4 60o indigo ('43) 2.25 *20.00*
O54 O4 1k blue vio ('43) 2.25 *25.00*
Nos. O44-O54 (11) 17.25 *178.00*
Set, never hinged 30.00

Type of 1937
1947, Nov. 1
O55 O3 50o deep magenta .70 .25
O56 O3 200o orange 2.25 .65
Set, never hinged 5.00

No. O37 Surcharged in Black

1949, Mar. 15
O57 O3 25o on 20o carmine .25 .50
Never hinged .75

Norway Coat of Arms — O5

1951-52 Unwmk. Photo. *Perf. 13*
O58 O5 5o rose lilac .75 .50
O59 O5 10o dk gray .75 .25
O60 O5 15o dp org brn ('52) 1.00 .90
O61 O5 30o scarlet .35 .25
O62 O5 35o red brn ('52) 1.25 .70
O63 O5 60o blue gray .90 .25
O64 O5 100o vio bl ('52) 1.25 .30
Nos. O58-O64 (7) 6.25 3.15
Set, never hinged 15.00

Catalogue values for unused stamps in this section, from this point to the end of the section, are for Never Hinged items.

Norway Coat of Arms — O6

1955-61
O65 O6 5o rose lilac .25 .25
O66 O6 10o slate .25 .25
O67 O6 15o orange brn .65 2.75
O68 O6 20o bl grn ('57) .65 .25
O69 O6 25o emer ('59) .90 .25
O70 O6 30o scarlet 4.00 .90
O71 O6 35o brown red .70 .25
O72 O6 40o blue lilac 1.50 .25
O73 O6 45o scar ('58) 1.50 .25
O74 O6 50o gldn brn ('57) 4.00 .25
O75 O6 60o blue 16.00 .70
O76 O6 70o brn olive ('56) 7.00 1.25
O77 O6 75o maroon ('57) 25.00 18.00
O78 O6 80o org brn ('58) 9.00 1.25
O79 O6 90o org ('58) 1.25 .25
O80 O6 1k vio ('57) 2.25 .25
O81 O6 2k gray grn ('60) 4.00 .25
O82 O6 5k red lil ('61) 9.00 .85
Nos. O65-O82 (18) 87.90 28.45

See Phosphorescence note after No. 430.

1962-74 Photo.
O83 O6 30o green ('64) 2.00 .25
O84 O6 40o ol grn ('68) 2.00 .50
O85 O6 50o scarlet 2.50 .25
O86 O6 50o slate ('69) .70 .25
O87 O6 60o dk red ('64) 1.10 .25
O87A O6 60o grnsh bl ('72) 5.00 10.00
O88 O6 65o dk red ('68) 1.75 .25
O89 O6 70o dk red ('70) .50 .25
O90 O6 75o lt grn ('73) 1.25 .75
O90A O6 80o red brn ('72) 1.25 .25
O91 O6 85o ocher ('74) .95 2.00
O92 O6 1k dp org ('73) .50 .25
O93 O6 1.10k car lake ('74) 1.25 1.25
Nos. O83-O93 (13) 20.75 16.50

Shades exist of several values of type O6. Nos O87A, O90A are on phosphored paper.

1975-82 Litho.
O94 O6 5o rose lil ('80) .30 1.75
O95 O6 10o bluish gray ('82) .30 3.00
O96 O6 15o henna brn .90 4.00
O97 O6 20o green ('82) 1.50 5.50
O98 O6 25o yellow grn .40 .25
O99 O6 40o ol grn ('79) 2.25 10.00
O100 O6 50o grnsh gray ('76) 1.00 .25
O101 O6 60o dk grnsh bl 2.25 10.00
O102 O6 70o dk red ('82) 5.50 15.00

O103 O6 80o red brn ('76) .60 .25
O104 O6 1k vio ('80) 1.40 .50
O105 O6 1.10k red ('80) 2.50 3.50
O106 O6 1.25k dull red .60 .25
O107 O6 1.30k lilac ('81) 2.00 2.25
O108 O6 1.50k red ('81) .70 .25
O109 O6 1.75k dl bl grn ('82) 2.25 2.00
O110 O6 2k dk gray grn 1.00 .25
O111 O6 2k cerise ('82) 1.40 .30
O112 O6 3k purple ('82) 1.50 .50
O113 O6 5k lt vio 40.00 3.50
O114 O6 5k blue ('77) 2.50 .25
Nos. O94-O114 (21) 70.85 63.55

In lithographed set, shield's background is dotted; on photogravure stamps it is solid color.

Official stamps invalid as of Apr. 1, 1985.

NOSSI-BE

ˌno-sē-ˈbā

LOCATION — Island in the Indian Ocean, off the northwest coast of Madagascar
GOVT. — French Protectorate
AREA — 130 sq. mi.
POP. — 9,000 (approx. 1900)
CAPITAL — Hellville

In 1896 the island was placed under the authority of the Governor-General of Madagascar and postage stamps of Madagascar were placed in use.

100 Centimes = 1 Franc

Stamps of French Colonies Surcharged in Blue

a

b

c

On the following issues the colors of the French Colonies stamps, type A9, are: 5c, green, *greenish*; 10c, black, *lavender*; 15c, blue; 20c, red, *green*; 30c, brown, *bister*; 40c, vermilion, *straw*; 75c, carmine, *rose*; 1fr, bronze green, *straw*.

1889 Unwmk. *Imperf.*

1 A8(a) 25 on 40c red, *straw* 2,600. 1,100.
a. Double surcharge 3,400.
b. Inverted surcharge 3,750. 1,600.
2 A8(b) 25c on 40c red, *straw* 3,100. 2,000.
a. Double surcharge 5,500. 2,800.
b. Inverted surcharge 5,500. 2,800.
c. Pair, "a" and "c"

Perf. 14x13½

3 A9(b) 5c on 10c 3,750. 1,450.
a. Double surcharge 3,500.
b. Inverted surcharge 5,000. 3,100.
4 A9(b) 5c on 20c 4,000. 1,600.
a. Inverted surcharge 5,000. 3,100.
5 A9(c) 5c on 10c 3,100. 1,100.
a. Inverted surcharge 5,600.
6 A9(c) 5c on 20c 3,600. 2,400.
7 A9(a) 15 on 20c 2,800. 1,100.
a. Double surcharge 2,400.
b. Inverted surcharge 4,250. 1,750.
c. 15 on 30c (error) *32,000. 28,000.*
8 A9(a) 25 on 30c 2,800. 950.
a. Double surcharge 2,200.
b. Inverted surcharge 3,600. 1,600.
9 A9(a) 25 on 40c 2,400. 1,100.
a. Double surcharge 2,000.
b. Inverted surcharge 3,600. 1,600.

d

e

f

1890 Black Surcharge

10 A9(d) 25c on 20c 425.00 300.00
11 A9(e) 0.25 on 20c 425.00 300.00
12 A9(f) 25 on 20c 1,000. 675.00
13 A9(d) 25c on 75c 425.00 300.00
14 A9(e) 0.25 on 75c 425.00 300.00
15 A9(f) 25 on 75c 1,000. 675.00
16 A9(d) 25c on 1fr 425.00 300.00
17 A9(e) 0.25 on 1fr 425.00 300.00
18 A9(f) 25 on 1fr 1,000. 675.00

The 25c on 20c with surcharge composed of "25 c." as in "d," "N S B" as in "e," and frame as in "f" is an essay.

Surcharged or Overprinted in Black, Carmine, Vermilion or Blue

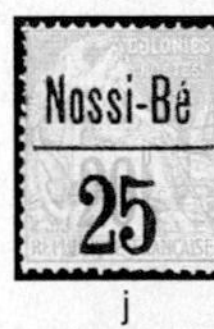
j

k

m

1893

23 A9(j) 25 on 20c (Bk) 52.50 45.00
24 A9(j) 50 on 10c (Bk) 67.50 47.50
a. Inverted surcharge 400.00 260.00
25 A9(j) 75 on 15c (Bk) 300.00 240.00
26 A9(j) 1fr on 5c (Bk) 150.00 110.00
a. Inverted surcharge 400.00 275.00
27 A9(k) 10c (C) 28.00 24.00
a. Inverted overprint 130.00 120.00
28 A9(k) 10c (V) 27.50 24.00
29 A9(k) 15c (Bk) 32.50 32.50
a. Inverted overprint 140.00 130.00
30 A9(k) 20c (Bk) 500.00 75.00
31 A9(m) 20c (Bl) 130.00 67.50
a. Inverted overprint 190.00 180.00

Counterfeits exist of surcharges and overprints of Nos. 1-31.

Navigation and Commerce — A14

1894 Typo. *Perf. 14x13½*
Name of Colony in Blue or Carmine

32 A14 1c blk, *lil bl* 1.60 1.60
33 A14 2c brn, *buff* 2.00 2.00
34 A14 4c claret, *lav* 2.75 2.00
35 A14 5c grn, *greenish* 4.00 3.25
36 A14 10c blk, *lav* 9.50 6.50
37 A14 15c blue, quadrille paper 13.50 6.50
38 A14 20c red, *grn* 9.50 6.50
39 A14 25c blk, *rose* 16.00 9.50
40 A14 30c brn, *bister* 16.00 14.50
41 A14 40c red, *straw* 22.50 16.00
42 A14 50c carmine, *rose* 22.50 16.00
43 A14 75c dp vio, *orange* 37.50 37.50
44 A14 1fr brnz grn, *straw* 27.50 27.50
Nos. 32-44 (13) 184.85 149.35

Perf. 13½x14 stamps are counterfeits.

POSTAGE DUE STAMPS

Stamps of French Colonies Surcharged in Black

n

o

1891 Unwmk. *Perf. 14x13½*

J1 A9(n) 20 on 1c blk, *lil bl* 425.00 300.00
a. Inverted surcharge 925.00 675.00
b. Surcharged vertically 1,200. *1,400.*
c. Surcharge on back 1,050. 1,050.
J2 A9(n) 30 on 2c brn, *buff* 400.00 300.00
a. Inverted surcharge 875.00 675.00
b. Surcharge on back 1,000. *1,200.*
J3 A9(n) 50 on 30c brn, *bister* 120.00 105.00
a. Inverted surcharge 925.00 675.00
b. Surcharge on back 1,050. *1,300.*
J4 A9(o) 35 on 4c cl, *lav* 450.00 325.00
a. Inverted surcharge 925.00 675.00
b. Surcharge on back 1,100. *1,300.*
c. Pair, one without surcharge
J5 A9(o) 35 on 20c red, *green* 450.00 325.00
a. Inverted surcharge 925.00 675.00
J6 A9(o) 1fr on 35c vio, *orange* 325.00 240.00
a. Inverted surcharge 925.00 625.00

p

q

r

1891

J7 A9(p) 5c on 20c 225.00 225.00
J8 A9(q) 5c on 20c 275.00 275.00
b. In se-tenant pair with #J7 725.00
J9 A9(r) 0.10c on 5c 27.50 24.00
J10 A9(p) 10c on 15c 225.00 225.00
J11 A9(q) 10c on 15c 275.00 275.00
b. In se-tenant pair with #J10 725.00
J12 A9(p) 15c on 10c 200.00 200.00
J13 A9(q) 15c on 10c 210.00 210.00
b. In se-tenant pair with #J12 725.00
J14 A9(r) 0.15c on 20c 32.50 32.50
a. 25c on 20c (error) *40,000. 35,000.*
J15 A9(p) 25c on 5c 180.00 180.00
J16 A9(q) 25c on 5c 200.00 200.00
b. In se-tenant pair with #J15 700.00
J17 A9(r) 0.25c on 75c 650.00 575.00

Inverted Surcharge

J7a A9(p) 5c on 20c 425.00 425.00
J8a A9(q) 5c on 20c 425.00 425.00
J10a A9(p) 10c on 15c 425.00 425.00
J11a A9(q) 10c on 15c 425.00 425.00
J12a A9(p) 15c on 10c 425.00 425.00
J13a A9(q) 15c on 10c 425.00 425.00
J15a A9(p) 25c on 5c 425.00 425.00
J16a A9(q) 25c on 5c 425.00 425.00
J17a A9(r) 0.25c on 75c 1,800. 1,500.

Stamps of Nossi-Be were superseded by those of Madagascar.

Counterfeits exist of surcharges on #J1-J17.

NYASALAND PROTECTORATE

nī-ˈa-sə-ˌland prə-ˈtek-t̩ə-ˌrət

LOCATION — In southern Africa, bordering on Lake Nyasa
GOVT. — British Protectorate
AREA — 49,000 sq. mi.
POP. — 2,950,000 (est. 1962)
CAPITAL — Zomba

For previous issues, see British Central Africa.

Nyasaland joined the Federation of Rhodesia and Nyasaland in 1953, using its stamps until 1963. As the Federation began to dissolve in 1963, Nyasaland withdrew its postal services and issued provisional stamps. On July 6, 1964, Nyasaland became the independent state of Malawi.

12 Pence = 1 Shilling
20 Shillings = 1 Pound

Catalogue values for unused stamps in this country are for Never Hinged items, beginning with Scott 68 in the regular postage section and Scott J1 in the postage due section.

A1

King Edward VII — A2

Wmk. Crown and C A (2)
1908, July 22 Typo. *Perf. 14*
Chalky Paper

1 A1 1sh black, *green* 6.00 *17.00*

Wmk. Multiple Crown and C A (3)
Ordinary Paper

2 A1 ½p green 2.00 2.25
3 A1 1p carmine 8.50 1.10

Chalky Paper

4 A1 3p violet, *yel* 1.75 *4.75*
5 A1 4p scar & blk, *yel* 1.75 *1.75*
6 A1 6p red vio & vio 5.75 *12.50*
7 A2 2sh6p car & blk, *bl* 75.00 *110.00*
8 A2 4sh black & car 110.00 *180.00*
9 A2 10sh red & grn, *grn* 200.00 *325.00*
10 A2 £1 blk & vio, *red* 650.00 *750.00*
11 A2 £10 ultra & lilac 12,000. *8,000.*
Nos. 1-10 (10) 1,060. 1,404.

A3

King George V — A4

1913-19 Ordinary Paper

12 A3 ½p green 1.75 *2.25*
13 A3 1p scarlet 6.00 1.00
a. 1p carmine 3.00 2.00
14 A3 2p gray 9.00 1.00
15 A3 2½p ultra 2.50 *7.50*

Chalky Paper

16 A3 3p violet, *yel* 6.00 4.50
17 A3 4p scar & blk, *yel* 2.00 *2.50*
18 A3 6p red vio & dull vio 5.00 *10.00*
19 A3 1sh black, *green* 2.00 *9.00*
a. 1sh black, *emerald* 4.50 *7.00*
b. 1sh blk, *bl grn*, olive back 6.00 1.60
20 A4 2sh6p red & blk, *bl* ('18) 12.50 *26.00*
21 A4 4sh blk & red ('18) 50.00 *90.00*
22 A4 10sh red & grn, *grn* 130.00 *160.00*
23 A4 £1 blk & vio, *red* ('18) 200.00 170.00
24 A4 £10 brt ultra & slate vio ('19) *4,000. 2,000.*
Revenue cancel 275.00
a. £10 pale ultra & dull vio ('14) 8,000.
Revenue cancel 300.00
Nos. 12-23 (12) 426.75 *483.75*

Stamps of Nyasaland Protectorate overprinted "N. F." are listed under German East Africa.

1921-30 Wmk. 4 Ordinary Paper

25 A3 ½p green 3.25 .50
26 A3 1p rose red 3.25 .50
27 A3 1½p orange 4.00 *17.50*
28 A3 2p gray 3.50 .50

Chalky Paper

29 A3 3p violet, *yel* 20.00 3.25
30 A3 4p scar & blk, *yel* 5.50 *11.00*
31 A3 6p red vio & dl vio 5.75 3.25
32 A3 1sh blk, *grn* ('30) 14.50 4.50
33 A4 2sh ultra & dl vio, *bl* 20.00 15.00
34 A4 2sh6p red & blk, *bl* ('24) 25.00 19.00
35 A4 4sh black & car 26.00 *45.00*
36 A4 5sh red & grn, *yel* ('29) 55.00 85.00
37 A4 10sh red & grn, *emer* 120.00 *120.00*
Nos. 25-37 (13) 305.75 *325.00*

George V and Leopard A5

1934-35 Engr. *Perf. 12½*

38 A5 ½p green .75 *1.25*
39 A5 1p dark brown .75 .75
40 A5 1½p rose .75 *3.50*
41 A5 2p gray 1.00 *1.25*
42 A5 3p dark blue 3.00 1.50
43 A5 4p rose lilac ('35) 6.50 4.00
44 A5 6p dk violet 3.50 2.00
45 A5 9p olive bis ('35) 8.50 *13.00*
46 A5 1sh orange & blk 22.50 *15.00*
Nos. 38-46 (9) 47.25 *42.25*

Common Design Types pictured following the introduction.

Silver Jubilee Issue
Common Design Type

1935, May 6 *Perf. 11x12*

47 CD301 1p gray blk & ultra 1.00 *2.50*
48 CD301 2p indigo & grn 2.75 2.75
49 CD301 3p ultra & brn 8.50 *20.00*
50 CD301 1sh brown vio & ind 27.50 *55.00*
Nos. 47-50 (4) 39.75 *80.25*
Set, never hinged 60.00

Coronation Issue
Common Design Type

1937, May 12 *Perf. 11x11½*

51 CD302 ½p deep green .25 .30
52 CD302 1p dark brown .40 .40
53 CD302 2p gray black .40 .60
Nos. 51-53 (3) 1.05 1.30
Set, never hinged 1.75

A6

King George VI — A7

1938-44 Engr. *Perf. 12½*

54 A6 ½p green .25 *2.00*
54A A6 ½p dk brown ('42) .25 *2.25*
55 A6 1p dark brown 2.50 *.35*
55A A6 1p green ('42) .25 *1.75*
56 A6 1½p dark carmine 4.00 *6.00*
56A A6 1½p gray ('42) .25 *5.75*
57 A6 2p gray 5.00 1.25
57A A6 2p dark car ('42) .25 *2.00*
58 A6 3p blue .60 1.00
59 A6 4p rose lilac 1.60 2.00
60 A6 6p dark violet 2.00 2.00
61 A6 9p olive bister 2.00 *4.75*
62 A6 1sh orange & blk 2.10 *3.25*

Typo.
Perf. 14
Chalky Paper

63 A7 2sh ultra & dl vio, *bl* 7.00 *17.50*
64 A7 2sh6p red & blk, *bl* 8.00 *19.50*
65 A7 5sh red & grn, *yel* 35.00 30.00
a. 5sh dk red & dp grn, *yel* ('44) 55.00 *140.00*
66 A7 10sh red & grn, *grn* 35.00 *70.00*

Wmk. 3

67 A7 £1 blk & vio, *red* 30.00 *45.00*
Nos. 54-67 (18) 136.05 *216.35*
Set, never hinged 220.00

Catalogue values for unused stamps in this section, from this point to the end of the section, are for Never Hinged items.

Canoe on Lake Nyasa — A8

Soldier of King's African Rifles — A9

Tea Estate, Mlanje Mountain A10

Map and Coat of Arms — A11

Fishing Village, Lake Nyasa — A12

Tobacco Estate — A13

Arms of Nyasaland and George VI A14

1945, Sept. 1 Engr. *Perf. 12*

68 A8 ½p brn vio & blk .50 .25
69 A9 1p dp green & blk .25 .75
70 A10 1½p gray grn & blk .35 .45
71 A11 2p scarlet & blk 1.50 .80
72 A12 3p blue & blk .45 .30
73 A13 4p rose vio & blk 2.00 .80
74 A10 6p violet & blk 3.00 .90
75 A8 9p ol grn & blk 3.50 *3.00*
76 A11 1sh myr grn & ind 3.75 .55
77 A12 2sh dl red brn & grn 9.50 5.50
78 A13 2sh6p ultra & green 9.50 7.00
79 A14 5sh ultra & lt vio 7.00 *6.50*
80 A11 10sh green & lake 22.50 18.00
81 A14 20sh black & scar 29.00 *35.00*
Nos. 68-81 (14) 92.80 79.80

Peace Issue
Common Design Type
Perf. 13½x14

1946, Dec. 16 Wmk. 4

82 CD303 1p bright green .25 .25
83 CD303 2p red orange .25 .25

A15

1947, Oct. 20 *Perf. 12*

84 A15 1p emerald & org brn .65 .50

Silver Wedding Issue
Common Design Types

1948, Dec. 15 Photo. *Perf. 14x14½*

85 CD304 1p dark green .25 .25

Engr.; Name Typo.
Perf. 11½x11

86 CD305 10sh purple 19.00 *32.50*

UPU Issue
Common Design Types
Engr.; Name Typo. on 3p, 6p
Perf. 13½, 11x11½

1949, Nov. 21 Wmk. 4

87 CD306 1p blue green .35 .35
88 CD307 3p Prus blue 2.50 2.50
89 CD308 6p rose violet .85 .85
90 CD309 1sh violet blue .35 .35
Nos. 87-90 (4) 4.05 4.05

Arms of British Central Africa and Nyasaland Protectorate — A16

1951, May 15 Engr. *Perf. 11x12*
Arms in Black

91 A16 2p rose 1.50 1.50
92 A16 3p blue 1.50 1.50
93 A16 6p purple 1.50 *2.25*
94 A16 5sh deep blue 5.00 *8.00*
Nos. 91-94 (4) 9.50 *13.25*

60th anniv. of the Protectorate, originally British Central Africa.

Exhibition Seal — A17

1953, May 30 *Perf. 14x13½*

95 A17 6p purple .65 .50

Central African Rhodes Cent. Exhib.

Coronation Issue
Common Design Type

1953, June 2 *Perf. 13½x13*

96 CD312 2p orange & black .75 .75

Types of 1945-47 with Portrait of Queen Elizabeth II and

Grading Cotton A18

1953, Sept. 1 *Perf. 12*

97 A8 ½p red brn & blk .25 *1.25*
a. Booklet pane of 4 3.75
b. Perf. 12x12½ ('54) .25 *1.25*
98 A15 1p emer & org brn .65 .25
a. Booklet pane of 4 3.75
99 A10 1½p gray grn & blk .25 *1.90*
100 A11 2p orange & blk .85 .30
a. Booklet pane of 4 4.25
b. Perf. 12x12½ ('54) .40 .30
101 A18 2½p blk & brt grn .30 *.50*
102 A13 3p scarlet & blk .30 .30
103 A12 4½p blue & blk .90 .45
104 A10 6p violet & blk 1.25 1.25
a. Booklet pane of 4 11.50
b. Perf. 12x12½ ('54) 2.00 .90
105 A8 9p olive & blk 1.25 *2.75*
106 A11 1sh myr grn & ind 3.75 .50
107 A12 2sh rose brn & grn 3.50 *3.75*
108 A13 2sh6p ultra & grn 4.25 *7.50*
109 A14 5sh Prus bl & rose lil 11.00 7.50
110 A11 10sh green & lake 12.00 *20.00*
111 A14 20sh black & scar 26.00 *35.00*
Nos. 97-111 (15) 66.50 *83.20*

Issue date: Nos. 97b, 100b, 104b, Mar. 8.

Revenue Stamps Overprinted in Black

Arms of Nyasaland A19

Perf. 11½x12

1963, Nov. 1 Engr. Unwmk.

112 A19 ½p on 1p blue .30 .30
113 A19 1p green .30 .25
114 A19 2p rose red .30 .30
115 A19 3p dark blue .30 .25
116 A19 6p rose lake .30 .25
117 A19 9p on 1sh car rose .40 .40
118 A19 1sh purple .45 2.75
119 A19 2sh6p black 1.25 *2.00*
120 A19 5sh brown 3.50 6.50
121 A19 10sh gray olive 6.00 *8.50*
122 A19 £1 violet 6.00 *8.50*
Nos. 112-122 (11) 19.10 *30.00*

Nos. 112, 117 have 3 bars over old value.

Mother and Child — A20

Designs: 1p, Chambo fish. 2p, Zebu bull. 3p, Peanuts. 4p, Fishermen in boat. 6p, Harvesting tea. 1sh, Lumber and tropical pine branch. 1sh3p, Tobacco industry. 2sh6p, Cotton industry. 5sh, Monkey Bay, Lake Nyasa. 10sh, Afzelia tree (pod mahogany). £1, Nyala antelope, vert.

Perf. 14½

1964, Jan. 1 Unwmk. Photo.
Size: 23x19mm

123 A20 ½p lilac .25 *.35*
124 A20 1p green & blk .25 *.30*
125 A20 2p red brown .25 *.30*
126 A20 3p pale brn, brn red & grn .25 *.30*
127 A20 4p org yel & indigo .30 *.35*

Size: 41½x25mm, 25x41½mm

128 A20 6p bl pur & brt yel grn .70 *.70*
129 A20 1sh yel brn & dk grn .75 .30
130 A20 1sh3p red brn & olive 3.75 .30
131 A20 2sh6p blue & brn 3.25 .65
132 A20 5sh grn, bl, sep & yel 2.00 1.75
133 A20 10sh org brn grn & gray 3.25 *4.00*
134 A20 £1 yel & dk brn 8.00 *14.00*
Nos. 123-134 (12) 23.00 23.30

POSTAGE DUE STAMPS

Catalogue values for unused stamps in this section are for Never Hinged items.

D1

Perf. 14

1950, July 1 Wmk. 4 Typo.

J1 D1 1p rose red 4.50 *32.50*
J2 D1 2p ultramarine 19.00 *32.50*
J3 D1 3p green 16.00 *8.00*
J4 D1 4p claret 30.00 *60.00*
J5 D1 6p ocher 42.50 *160.00*
Nos. J1-J5 (5) 112.00 *293.00*

NYASSA

nī-ˈa-sə

LOCATION — In the northern part of Mozambique in southeast Africa
AREA — 73,292 sq. mi.
POP. — 3,000,000 (estimated)
CAPITAL — Porto Amelia

The district formerly administered by the Nyassa Company is now a part of Mozambique.

1000 Reis = 1 Milreis
100 Centavos = 1 Escudo (1919)

Mozambique Nos. 24-35 Overprinted in Black

1898 Unwmk. *Perf. 11½, 12½*

No.	Type	Description	Unused	Used
1	A3	5r yellow	3.00	1.50
2	A3	10r redsh violet	3.00	1.50
3	A3	15r chocolate	3.00	1.50
4	A3	20r gray violet	3.00	1.50
5	A3	25r blue green	3.00	1.50
6	A3	50r light blue	3.00	1.50
a.		Inverted overprint		
b.		Perf. 12½	6.00	3.50
7	A3	75r rose	4.00	2.00
8	A3	80r yellow grn	4.00	2.00
9	A3	100r brown, *buff*	4.00	2.00
10	A3	150r car, *rose*	6.50	4.00
11	A3	200r dk blue, *blue*	5.00	3.00
12	A3	300r dk blue, *salmon*	5.00	3.00
		Nos. 1-12 (12)	46.50	25.00

Reprints of Nos. 1, 5, 8, 9, 10 and 12 have white gum and clean-cut perforation 13½. Value of No. 9, $15; others $3 each.

Same Overprint on Mozambique Issue of 1898

1898 *Perf. 11½*

No.	Type	Description	Unused	Used
13	A4	2½r gray	2.50	.80
14	A4	5r orange	2.50	.80
15	A4	10r light green	2.50	.80
16	A4	15r brown	3.00	1.00
17	A4	20r gray violet	3.00	1.00
18	A4	25r sea green	3.00	1.00
19	A4	50r blue	3.00	1.00
20	A4	75r rose	2.75	1.00
21	A4	80r violet	3.50	.80
22	A4	100r dk bl, *bl*	3.50	.80
23	A4	150r brown, *straw*	3.50	.80
24	A4	200r red lilac, *pnksh*	3.75	1.00
25	A4	300r dk blue, *rose*	4.00	1.00
		Nos. 13-25 (13)	40.50	11.80

Giraffe — A5

Camels — A6

1901 Engr. *Perf. 14*

No.	Type	Description	Unused	Used
26	A5	2½r blk & red brn	1.60	.55
27	A5	5r blk & violet	1.60	.55
28	A5	10r blk & dp grn	1.60	.55
29	A5	15r blk & org brn	1.60	.55
30	A5	20r blk & org red	1.60	.70
31	A5	25r blk & orange	1.60	.70
32	A5	50r blk & dl bl	1.60	.70
33	A6	75r blk & car lake	1.75	.70
34	A6	80r blk & lilac	1.75	.90
35	A6	100r blk & brn bis	1.75	.90
36	A6	150r blk & dp org	1.90	1.00
37	A6	200r blk & grnsh bl	2.00	1.00
38	A6	300r blk & yel grn	2.00	1.00
		Nos. 26-38 (13)	22.35	9.80

Nos. 26 to 38 are known with inverted centers but are believed to be purely speculative and never regularly issued. Value $80 each.

Perf 13½, 14½, 15½ & compound also exist.

For overprints and surcharges see Nos. 39-50, 63-80.

Nos. 34, 36, 38 Surcharged

1903

No.	Type	Description	Unused	Used
39	A6	65r on 80r	1.00	.75
40	A6	115r on 150r	1.00	.75
41	A6	130r on 300r	1.00	.75
		Nos. 39-41 (3)	3.00	2.25

Nos. 29, 31 Overprinted

1903

No.	Type	Description	Unused	Used
42	A5	15r black & org brn	1.00	.75
43	A5	25r black & orange	1.00	.75

Nos. 34, 36, 38 Surcharged

1903

No.	Type	Description	Unused	Used
44	A6	65r on 80r	32.50	15.00
45	A6	115r on 150r	32.50	15.00
46	A6	130r on 300r	32.50	15.00
		Nos. 44-46 (3)	97.50	45.00

Nos. 29, 31 Overprinted

1903

No.	Type	Description	Unused	Used
47	A5	15r black & org brn	500.00	100.00
48	A5	25r black & orange	150.00	100.00

Forgeries exist of Nos. 44-48.

Nos. 26, 35 Surcharged

1910

No.	Type	Description	Unused	Used
49	A5	5r on 2½r	1.00	.75
50	A6	50r on 100r	1.00	.75
a.		"50 REIS" omitted	300.00	

Reprints of Nos. 49-50, made in 1921, have 2mm space between surcharge lines, instead of 1½mm. Value, each 25 cents.

Zebra — A7

Vasco da Gama's Flagship "San Gabriel" — A8

Designs: Nos. 51-53, Camels. Nos. 57-59, Giraffe and palms.

1911 Red Overprint

No.	Type	Description	Unused	Used
51	A7	2½r blk & dl vio	1.00	.55
52	A7	5r black	1.00	.55
53	A7	10r blk & gray grn	1.00	.55
54	A7	20r blk & car lake	1.00	.55
55	A7	25r blk & vio brn	1.00	.55
56	A7	50r blk & dp bl	1.00	.55
57	A8	75r blk & brn	1.00	.55
58	A8	100r blk & brn, *grn*	1.00	.55
59	A8	200r blk & dp grn, *sal*	1.10	1.00
60	A8	300r blk, *blue*	2.40	1.60
61	A8	400r blk & dk brn	3.00	2.00
a.		Pair, one without overprint		
62	A8	500r ol & vio brn	4.00	3.00
		Nos. 51-62 (12)	18.50	12.00

Nos. 51-62 exist without overprint but were not issued in that condition. Value $7.50 each.

For surcharges see Nos. 81-105.

Stamps of 1901-03 Surcharged

1918 On Nos. 26-38

No.	Type	Description	Unused	Used
63	A5	¼c on 2½r	140.00	95.00
64	A5	½c on 5r	140.00	95.00
65	A5	1c on 10r	140.00	95.00
66	A5	1½c on 15r	2.10	1.10
67	A5	2c on 20r	1.25	1.00
68	A5	3½c on 25r	1.50	1.00
69	A5	5c on 50r	1.25	1.00
70	A6	7½c on 75r	1.25	1.00
71	A6	8c on 80r	1.25	1.00
72	A6	10c on 100r	1.25	1.00
73	A6	15c on 150r	2.10	2.00
74	A6	20c on 200r	2.00	2.00
75	A6	30c on 300r	3.25	2.40
		On Nos. 39-41		
76	A6	40c on 65r on 80r	18.00	16.50
77	A6	50c on 115r on 150r	3.00	2.00
78	A6	1e on 130r on 300r	5.00	2.00
		On Nos. 42-43		
79	A5	1½c on 15r	7.00	3.00
80	A5	3½c on 25r	2.00	1.00
		Nos. 63-80 (18)	472.20	323.00

On Nos. 70-78 there is less space between "REPUBLICA" and the new value than on the other stamps of this issue.

On Nos. 76-78 the 1903 surcharge is canceled by a bar.

The surcharge exists inverted on #64, 66-70, 72, 76, 78-80, and double on #64, 67, 69.

Nos. 51-62 Surcharged in Black or Red

Numerals: The "1" (large or small) is thin, sharp-pointed, and has thin serifs. The "2" is italic, with the tail thin and only slightly wavy. The "3" has a flat top. The "4" is open at the top. The "7" has thin strokes.

Centavos: The letters are shaded, i.e., they are thicker in some parts than in others. The "t" has a thin cross bar ending in a downward stroke at the right. The "s" is flat at the bottom and wider than in the next group.

1921 Lisbon Surcharges

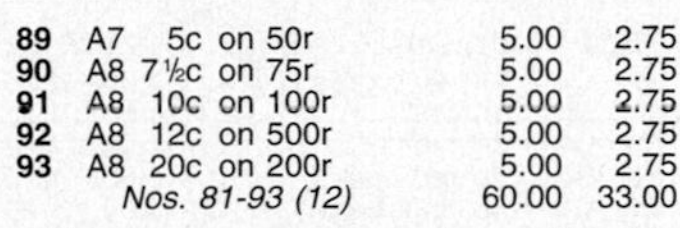

No.	Type	Description	Unused	Used
81	A7	¼c on 2½r	5.00	2.75
83	A7	½c on 5r (R)	5.00	2.75
a.		½c on 2½r (R) (error)	275.00	250.00
84	A7	1c on 10r	5.00	2.75
a.		Pair, one without surcharge		
85	A8	1½c on 300r (R)	5.00	2.75
86	A7	2c on 20r	5.00	2.75
87	A7	2½c on 25r	5.00	2.75
88	A8	3c on 400r	5.00	2.75
a.		"Republica" omitted		
89	A7	5c on 50r	5.00	2.75
90	A8	7½c on 75r	5.00	2.75
91	A8	10c on 100r	5.00	2.75
92	A8	12c on 500r	5.00	2.75
93	A8	20c on 200r	5.00	2.75
		Nos. 81-93 (12)	60.00	33.00

The surcharge exists inverted on Nos. 83-85, 87-88 and 92, and double on Nos. 81, 83 and 86.

Forgeries exist of Nos. 81-93.

London Surcharges

Numerals — The "1" has the vertical stroke and serifs thicker than in the Lisbon printing. The "2" is upright and has a strong wave in the tail. The small "2" is heavily shaded. The "3" has a rounded top. The "4" is closed at the top. The "7" has thick strokes.

Centavos — The letters are heavier than in the Lisbon printing and are of even thickness throughout. The "t" has a thick cross bar with scarcely any down stroke at the end. The "s" is rounded at the bottom and narrower than in the Lisbon printing.

No.	Type	Description	Unused	Used
94	A7	¼c on 2½r	1.50	1.25
95	A7	½c on 5r (R)	1.50	1.25
96	A7	1c on 10r	1.50	1.25
97	A8	1½c on 300r (R)	1.50	1.25
98	A7	2c on 20r	1.50	1.25
99	A7	2½c on 25r	1.50	1.25
100	A8	3c on 400r	1.50	1.25
101	A7	5c on 50r	1.50	1.25
102	A8	7½c on 75r	1.50	1.25
a.		Inverted surcharge		
103	A8	10c on 100r	1.50	1.25
104	A8	12c on 500r	1.50	1.25
105	A8	20c on 200r	1.50	1.25
		Nos. 94-105 (12)	18.00	15.00

A9

Zebra and Warrior — A10

Designs: 2c-6c, Vasco da Gama. 7½c-20c, "San Gabriel." 2e-5e, Dhow and warrior.

Perf. 12½, 13½-15 & Compound

1921-23 Engr.

No.	Type	Description	Unused	Used
106	A9	¼c claret	1.00	.70
107	A9	½c steel blue	1.00	.70
108	A9	1c grn & blk	1.00	.70
109	A9	1½c blk & ocher	1.00	.70
110	A9	2c red & blk	1.00	.70
111	A9	2½c blk & ol grn	1.00	.70
112	A9	4c blk & org	1.00	.70
113	A9	5c ultra & blk	1.00	.70
114	A9	6c blk & vio	1.00	.70
115	A9	7½c blk & blk brn	1.00	.70
116	A9	8c blk & ol grn	1.00	.70
117	A9	10c blk & red brn	1.00	.70
118	A9	15c blk & carmine	1.00	.70
119	A9	20c blk & pale bl	1.00	.70
120	A10	30c blk & bister	1.00	.70
121	A10	40c blk & gray bl	1.00	.70
122	A10	50c blk & green	1.00	.70
123	A10	1e blk & red brn	1.00	.70
124	A10	2e red brn & blk ('23)	3.25	2.50
125	A10	5e ultra & red brn ('23)	3.00	2.25
		Nos. 106-125 (20)	24.25	17.35

POSTAGE DUE STAMPS

Giraffe — D1

½c, 1c, Giraffe. 2c, 3c, Zebra. 5c, 6c, 10c, "San Gabriel." 20c, 50c, Vasco da Gama.

1924	Unwmk.	Engr.	Perf. 14	
J1	D1	½c deep green	1.00	*1.75*
J2	D1	1c gray	1.00	*1.75*
J3	D1	2c red	1.00	*1.75*
J4	D1	3c red orange	1.00	*1.75*
J5	D1	5c dark brown	1.00	*1.75*
J6	D1	6c orange brown	1.00	*1.75*
J7	D1	10c brown violet	1.00	*1.75*
J8	D1	20c carmine	1.00	*1.75*
J9	D1	50c lilac gray	1.00	*1.75*
		Nos. J1-J9 (9)	9.00	*15.75*

Used values are for c-t-o copies.

NEWSPAPER STAMP

Mozambique No. P6 Ovptd. Like Nos. 1-25 in Black

1898	Unwmk.	Perf. 13½	
P1	N3 2½r brown	2.00	1.00

Reprints have white gum and clean-cut perf. 13½. Value $1.

POSTAL TAX STAMPS

Pombal Issue

Mozambique Nos. RA1-RA3 Overprinted "NYASSA" in Red

1925	Unwmk.	Perf. 12½	
RA1	CD28 15c brown & blk	5.00	5.00
RA2	CD29 15c brown & blk	5.00	5.00
RA3	CD30 15c brown & blk	5.00	5.00
	Nos. RA1-RA3 (3)	15.00	15.00

POSTAL TAX DUE STAMPS

Pombal Issue

Mozambique Nos. RAJ1-RAJ3 Overprinted "NYASSA" in Red

1925	Unwmk.	Perf. 12½	
RAJ1	CD28 30c brown & blk	12.50	7.75
RAJ2	CD29 30c brown & blk	12.50	7.75
RAJ3	CD30 30c brown & blk	12.50	7.75
	Nos. RAJ1-RAJ3 (3)	37.50	23.25

See the World with Scott Album Kits

All-inclusive Scott Album Kits let you explore the world through the beauty of stamps. Each kit contains a complete set of Specialty Series album pages, as well as a large Scott 3-ring binder with matching slipcase and binder label. What a convenient way to save money!

Item	Description	Pages	Retail	AA*
713S014	Namibia 2014 #19	5	$5.99	$4.99
621S015	Nepal 2015 #16	7	$7.99	$6.99
335S014	Netherlands 2014 #65	36	$26.99	$21.99
220S014	New Zealand 2014 #30	18	$16.99	$13.99
220S014	New Zealand Dependencies 2014 #66	20	$16.99	$13.99
345NR14	Norway 2014 #19	4	$5.99	$4.99
345NR15	Norway 2015 #20	4	$5.99	$4.99
550S014	Oman 2014 #14	5	$5.99	$4.99
673S015	Pakistan 2015 #17	6	$6.99	$5.99
632S014	Pitcairn Islands 2014 #21	4	$5.99	$4.99
338S014	Poland 2014 #63	14	$14.99	$11.99
340S014	Portugal 2014 #65	19	$16.99	$13.99
340S015	Portugal 2015 #66	22	$16.99	$13.99
341S015	Portuguese Colonies 2015 #63	7	$14.99	$11.99
360S014	Russia 2014 #64	14	$14.99	$11.99
633S014	Samoa 2014 #14	9	$9.99	$7.99
328S014	San Marino 2014 #64	6	$6.99	$5.99
328S015	San Marino 2015 #65	6	$6.99	$5.99

Album kits are available in a globe-spanning selection of countries. To see the entire collection, visit AmosAdvantage.com

AMOS ADVANTAGE

Call: 1-800-572-6885

Outside U.S. & Canada Call: (937) 498-0800

Visit: www.AmosAdvantage.com

ORDERING INFORMATION: *AA prices apply to paid subscribers of Amos Media titles, or for orders placed online. Prices, terms and product availability subject to change.

OBOCK

'ō-,bäk

LOCATION — A seaport in eastern Africa on the Gulf of Aden, directly opposite Aden.

Obock was the point of entrance from which French Somaliland was formed. The port was acquired by the French in 1862 but was not actively occupied until 1884 when Sagallo and Tadjoura were ceded to France. In 1888 Djibouti was made into a port and the seat of government moved from Obock to the latter city. In 1902 the name Somali Coast was adopted on the postage stamps of Djibouti, these stamps superseding the individual issues of Obock.

100 Centimes = 1 Franc

Counterfeits exist of Nos. 1-31.

Stamps of French Colonies Handstamped in Black

#1-11, J1-J4

#12-20, J5-J18

1892 Unwmk. Perf. 14x13½

No.	Type	Description	Unused	Used
1	A9	1c blk, *lil bl*	45.00	45.00
2	A9	2c brn, *buff*	45.00	45.00
3	A9	4c claret, *lav*	450.00	475.00
4	A9	5c grn, *grnsh*	40.00	32.50
5	A9	10c blk, *lavender*	80.00	47.50
6	A9	15c blue	72.50	50.00
7	A9	25c blk, *rose*	110.00	80.00
8	A9	35c vio, *org*	450.00	450.00
9	A9	40c red, *straw*	400.00	425.00
10	A9	75c car, *rose*	450.00	475.00
11	A9	1fr brnz grn, *straw*	500.00	550.00
		Nos. 1-11 (11)	2,642.	2,675.

No. 3 has been reprinted. On the reprints the second "O" of "OBOCK" is 4mm high instead of 3½mm. Value $32.50.

1892

No.	Type	Description	Unused	Used
12	A9	4c claret, *lav*	27.50	27.50
13	A9	5c grn, *grnsh*	27.50	27.50
14	A9	10c blk, *lavender*	27.50	27.50
15	A9	15c blue	27.50	27.50
16	A9	20c red, *grn*	47.50	45.00
17	A9	25c blk, *rose*	35.00	27.50
18	A9	40c red, *straw*	60.00	52.50
19	A9	75c car, *rose*	325.00	275.00
20	A9	1fr brnz grn, *straw*	87.50	80.00
		Nos. 12-20 (9)	665.00	590.00

Exists inverted or double on all denominations.

Nos. 14, 15, 17, 20 with Additional Surcharge Handstamped in Red, Blue or Black

Nos, 21-30

No. 31

1892

No.	Type	Description	Unused	Used
21	A9	1c on 25c blk, *rose*	20.00	20.00
22	A9	2c on 10c blk, *lav*	72.50	60.00
23	A9	2c on 15c blue	22.50	20.00
24	A9	4c on 15c bl (Bk)	20.00	20.00
25	A9	4c on 25c blk, *rose* (Bk)	20.00	20.00
26	A9	5c on 25c blk, *rose*	27.50	27.50
27	A9	20c on 10c blk, *lav*	95.00	95.00
28	A9	30c on 10c blk, *lav*	120.00	110.00
29	A9	35c on 25c blk, *rose*	100.00	92.50
a.		"3" instead of "35"	950.00	950.00
30	A9	75c on 1fr brnz grn, *straw*	110.00	110.00
b.		"57" instead of "75"	8,750.	9,250.
c.		"55" instead of "75"	8,750.	9,250.
31	A9	5fr on 1fr brnz grn, *straw* (Bl)	775.00	700.00
		Nos. 21-31 (11)	1,382.	1,275.

Exists inverted on most denominations.

Navigation and Commerce — A4

Obock in Red (1c, 5c, 15c, 25c, 75c, 1fr) or Blue

1892 Typo. Perf. 14x13½

No.	Type	Description	Unused	Used
32	A4	1c blk, *lil bl*	2.75	2.75
33	A4	2c brn, *buff*	2.00	2.00
34	A4	4c claret, *lav*	2.75	2.75
35	A4	5c grn, *grnsh*	6.25	4.00
36	A4	10c blk, *lavender*	8.00	5.25
37	A4	15c bl, quadrille paper	19.50	11.50
38	A4	20c red, *grn*	27.50	27.50
39	A4	25c blk, *rose*	27.50	24.00
40	A4	30c brn, *bis*	24.00	20.00
41	A4	40c red, *straw*	24.00	20.00
42	A4	50c car, *rose*	28.00	24.00
43	A4	75c vio, *org*	32.50	24.00
a.		Name double	350.00	350.00
b.		Name inverted	5,500.	5,500.
44	A4	1fr brnz grn, *straw*	47.50	40.00
		Nos. 32-44 (13)	252.25	207.75

Perf. 13½x14 stamps are counterfeits.

Camel and Rider — A5

Quadrille Lines Printed on Paper

1893 Size: 32mm at base Imperf.

No.	Type	Description	Unused	Used
44A	A5	2fr brnz grn	65.00	55.00

Size: 45mm at base

No.	Type	Description	Unused	Used
45	A5	5fr red	140.00	125.00

Somali Warriors A7

A8

1894 Imperf.

Quadrille Lines Printed on Paper

No.	Type	Description	Unused	Used
46	A7	1c blk & rose	2.75	2.75
47	A7	2c vio brn & grn	2.75	2.75
48	A7	4c brn vio & org	2.75	2.75
49	A7	5c bl grn & brn	3.50	3.50
50	A7	10c blk & grn	9.50	8.00
a.		Half used as 5c on cover ('01)		350.00
51	A7	15c bl & rose	9.50	7.25
52	A7	20c brn org & mar	9.50	8.00
a.		Half used as 10c on cover ('01)		325.00
53	A7	25c blk & bl	10.50	6.50
a.		Right half used as 5c on cover ('01)		300.00
b.		Left half used as 2c on cover ('03)		300.00
54	A7	30c bis & yel grn	20.00	14.50
a.		Half used as 15c on cover ('01)		2,200.
55	A7	40c red & bl grn	17.00	13.00
56	A7	50c rose & bl	15.00	12.00
a.		Half used as 25c on cover		3,400.
57	A7	75c gray lil & org	20.00	13.00
58	A7	1fr ol grn & mar	17.00	10.50

Size: 37mm at base

No.	Type	Description	Unused	Used
60	A8	2fr vio & org	120.00	120.00

Size: 42mm at base

No.	Type	Description	Unused	Used
61	A8	5fr rose & bl	95.00	95.00

Size: 46mm at base

No.	Type	Description	Unused	Used
62	A8	10fr org & red vio	160.00	160.00
63	A8	25fr brn & bl	875.00	875.00
64	A8	50fr red vio & grn	1,000.	1,000.

Counterfeits exist of Nos. 63-64.

Stamps of Obock were replaced in 1901 by those of Somali Coast. The 5c on 75c, 5c on 25fr and 10c on 50fr of 1902 are listed under Somali Coast.

POSTAGE DUE STAMPS

Postage Due Stamps of French Colonies Handstamped Like #1-20

1892 Unwmk. Imperf.

No.	Type	Description	Unused	Used
J1	D1	5c black	11,000.	
J2	D1	10c black	240.00	275.00
J3	D1	30c black	375.00	450.00
J4	D1	60c black	475.00	550.00
J5	D1	1c black	55.00	55.00
J6	D1	2c black	45.00	45.00
J7	D1	3c black	52.50	52.50
J8	D1	4c black	45.00	45.00
J9	D1	5c black	16.00	16.00
J10	D1	10c black	35.00	35.00
J11	D1	15c black	24.00	24.00
J12	D1	20c black	32.50	32.50
J13	D1	30c black	32.50	32.50
J14	D1	40c black	60.00	60.00
J15	D1	60c black	80.00	80.00
J16	D1	1fr brown	225.00	225.00
J17	D1	2fr brown	240.00	240.00
J18	D1	5fr brown	525.00	525.00
		Nos. J2-J18 (17)	2,557.	2,742.

Overprint Inverted

No.	Type	Description	Unused	Used
J5a	D1	1c black	200.00	200.00
J6a	D1	2c black	200.00	200.00
J7a	D1	3c black	200.00	200.00
J8a	D1	4c black	200.00	200.00
J9a	D1	5c black	200.00	200.00
J10a	D1	10c black	250.00	250.00
J11a	D1	15c black	200.00	200.00
J15a	D1	60c black	275.00	275.00
J16a	D1	1fr brown	550.00	550.00
J17a	D1	2fr brown	550.00	550.00

Double Overprint

No.	Type	Description	Unused	Used
J5b	D1	1c black	200.00	200.00
J6b	D1	2c black	200.00	200.00
J9b	D1	5c black	250.00	250.00
J10b	D1	10c black	300.00	300.00
J11b	D1	15c black	250.00	250.00
J12b	D1	20c black	250.00	250.00
J13b	D1	30c black	300.00	300.00

These handstamped overprints may be found double on some values. Counterfeits exist of Nos. J1-J18.

No. J1 has been reprinted. The overprint on the original measures 12½x3¾mm and on the reprint 12x3¼mm. Value, $325.

OLTRE GIUBA

,ol-tra-'jü-bə

(Italian Jubaland)

LOCATION — A strip of land, 50 to 100 miles in width, west of and parallel to the Juba River in East Africa

GOVT. — Former Italian Protectorate

AREA — 33,000 sq. mi.

POP. — 12,000

CAPITAL — Kismayu

Oltre Giuba was ceded to Italy by Great Britain in 1924 and in 1926 was incorporated with Italian Somaliland. In 1936 it became part of Italian East Africa.

100 Centesimi = 1 Lira

Watermark

Wmk. 140 — Crown

Italian Stamps of 1901-26 Overprinted

On #1-15

On #16-20

1925, July 29 Wmk. 140 Perf. 14

No.	Type	Description	Unused	Used
1	A42	1c brown	5.50	30.00
a.		Inverted overprint	475.00	
2	A43	2c yel brown	4.25	30.00
3	A48	5c green	4.25	12.50
4	A48	10c claret	4.25	12.50
5	A48	15c slate	4.25	17.50
6	A50	20c brn orange	4.25	17.50
7	A49	25c blue	4.25	17.50
8	A49	30c org brown	5.50	22.50
9	A49	40c brown	11.00	17.50
10	A49	50c violet	11.00	17.50
11	A49	60c carmine	11.00	22.50
12	A46	1 l brn & green	16.00	30.00
13	A46	2 l dk grn & org	85.00	60.00
14	A46	5 l blue & rose	110.00	87.50
15	A51	10 l gray grn & red	21.00	95.00
		Nos. 1-15 (15)	301.50	490.00

1925-26

No.	Type	Description	Unused	Used
16	A49	20c green	7.00	17.50
17	A49	30c gray	10.00	22.50
18	A46	75c dk red & rose	42.50	95.00
19	A46	1.25 l bl & ultra	87.50	160.00
20	A46	2.50 l dk grn & org	120.00	275.00
		Nos. 16-20 (5)	267.00	570.00

Issue years: #18-20, 1926; others 1925.

Victor Emmanuel Issue

Italian Stamps of 1925 Overprinted

1925-26 Unwmk. Perf. 11

No.	Type	Description	Unused	Used
21	A78	60c brown car	1.60	16.00
a.		Perf. 13½	12,000.	
22	A78	1 l dark blue	1.60	25.00
a.		Perf. 13½	650.00	2,400.
23	A78	1.25 l dk bl ('26)	6.50	40.00
a.		Perf. 13½	0.50	40.00
		Nos. 21-23 (3)	9.70	81.00

Saint Francis of Assisi Issue

Italian Stamps and Type of 1926 Overprinted

1926, Apr. 12 Wmk. 140 Perf. 14

No.	Type	Description	Unused	Used
24	A79	20c gray green	2.50	45.00
25	A80	40c dark violet	2.50	45.00
26	A81	60c red brown	2.50	65.00

Overprinted in Red

Unwmk.

27 A82 1.25 l dk bl, perf. 11 2.50 *87.50*
28 A83 5 l + 2.50 l ol grn, perf. 13½ 8.00 *135.00*
Nos. 24-28 (5) 18.00 *377.50*

Map of Oltre Giuba — A1

1926, Apr. 21 Typo. Wmk. 140

29 A1 5c yellow brown 1.60 *35.00*
30 A1 20c blue green 1.60 *35.00*
31 A1 25c olive brown 1.60 *35.00*
32 A1 40c dull red 1.60 *35.00*
33 A1 60c brown violet 1.60 *35.00*
34 A1 1 l blue 1.60 *35.00*
35 A1 2 l dark green 1.60 *35.00*
Nos. 29-35 (7) 11.20 *245.00*

Oltre Giuba was incorporated with Italian Somaliland on July 1, 1926, and stamps inscribed "Oltre Giuba" were discontinued.

SEMI-POSTAL STAMPS

Note preceding Italy semi-postals applies to No. 28.

Colonial Institute Issue

"Peace" Substituting Spade for Sword — SP1

Wmk. 140

1926, June 1 Typo. *Perf. 14*

B1 SP1 5c + 5c brown 1.20 *9.50*
B2 SP1 10c + 5c ol grn 1.20 *9.50*
B3 SP1 20c + 5c blue grn 1.20 *9.50*
B4 SP1 40c + 5c brn red 1.20 *9.50*
B5 SP1 60c + 5c orange 1.20 *9.50*
B6 SP1 1 l + 5c blue 1.20 *20.00*
Nos. B1-B6 (6) 7.20 *67.50*

Surtax for Italian Colonial Institute.

SPECIAL DELIVERY STAMPS

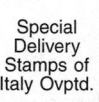

Special Delivery Stamps of Italy Ovptd.

1926 Wmk. 140 *Perf. 14*

E1 SD1 70c dull red 32.50 *65.00*
E2 SD2 2.50 l blue & red 67.50 *180.00*

POSTAGE DUE STAMPS

Italian Postage Due Stamps of 1870-1903 Ovptd. Like Nos. E1-E2

1925, July 29 Wmk. 140 *Perf. 14*

J1 D3 5c buff & magenta 24.00 24.00
J2 D3 10c buff & magenta 24.00 24.00
J3 D3 20c buff & magenta 24.00 *40.00*
J4 D3 30c buff & magenta 24.00 *40.00*
J5 D3 40c buff & magenta 24.00 *45.00*
J6 D3 50c buff & magenta 32.50 *55.00*
J7 D3 60c buff & brown 32.50 *65.00*
J8 D3 1 l blue & magenta 35.00 *80.00*
J9 D3 2 l blue & magenta 175.00 *275.00*
J10 D3 5 l blue & magenta 225.00 275.00
Nos. J1-J10 (10) 620.00 *923.00*

PARCEL POST STAMPS

These stamps were used by affixing them to the waybill so that one half remained on it following the parcel, the other half staying on the receipt given the sender. Most used halves are right halves. Complete stamps were obtainable canceled, probably to order. Both unused and used values are for complete stamps.

Italian Parcel Post Stamps of 1914-22 Overprinted

1925, July 29 Wmk. 140 *Perf. 13½*

Q1 PP2 5c brown 21.00 *45.00*
Q2 PP2 10c blue 17.50 *45.00*
Q3 PP2 20c black 17.50 *45.00*
Q4 PP2 25c red 17.50 *45.00*
Q5 PP2 50c orange 21.00 *45.00*
Q6 PP2 1 l violet 17.50 *100.00*
a. Double overprint 550.00
Q7 PP2 2 l green 28.00 *100.00*
Q8 PP2 3 l bister 65.00 *130.00*
Q9 PP2 4 l slate 29.00 *130.00*
Q10 PP2 10 l rose lilac 95.00 *225.00*
Q11 PP2 12 l red brown 175.00 *350.00*
Q12 PP2 15 l olive green 160.00 *350.00*
Q13 PP2 20 l brown violet 160.00 *350.00*
Nos. Q1-Q13 (13) 824.00 1,960.

Halves Used

Q1-Q4 1.75
Q5-Q7 3.00
Q8-Q9 4.75
Q10 9.25
Q11 15.00
Q12-Q13 10.00

OMAN

'ō-ˌmän

Muscat and Oman

LOCATION — Southeastern corner of the Arabian Peninsula
GOVT. — Sultanate
AREA — 105,000 sq. mi.
POP. — 2,446,645 (1999 est.)
CAPITAL — Muscat

Nos. 16-93, the stamps with "value only" surcharges, were used not only in Muscat, but also in Dubai (Apr. 1, 1948 - Jan. 6, 1961), Qatar (Aug. 1950 - Mar. 31, 1957), and Abu Dhabi (Mar. 30, 1963 - Mar. 29, 1964). Occasionally they were also used in Bahrain and Kuwait.

The Sultanate of Muscat and Oman changed its name to Oman in 1970.

12 Pies = 1 Anna
16 Annas = 1 Rupee
100 Naye Paise = 1 Rupee (1957)
64 Baizas = 1 Rupee (1966)
1000 Baizas = 1 Rial Saidi (1970)

Catalogue values for all unused stamps in this country are for Never Hinged items, beginning with No. 25 and including Nos. O1-O10.

Muscat

Stamps of India 1937-43 Overprinted in Black

On #1-13 the overprint is smaller — 13x6mm.

Wmk. Multiple Stars (196)

1944, Nov. 20 *Perf. 13½x14*

1 A83 3p slate .40 *8.00*
2 A83 ½a rose violet .40 *8.00*
3 A83 9p lt green .40 *8.00*
4 A83 1a carmine rose .40 *8.00*
5 A84 1½a dark purple .40 *8.00*
a. Double overprint 300.00
6 A84 2a scarlet .50 *8.00*
7 A84 3a violet 1.00 *8.00*
8 A84 3½a ultra 1.00 *8.00*
9 A85 4a chocolate 1.10 *8.00*
10 A85 6a pck blue 1.25 *8.00*
11 A85 8a blue violet 1.40 *8.50*
12 A85 12a car lake 1.50 *8.50*
13 A81 14a rose violet 2.75 *13.50*
14 A82 1r brown & slate 1.75 *12.50*
15 A82 2r dk brn & dk vio 5.00 *20.00*
Nos. 1-15 (15) 19.25 *143.00*

200th anniv. of Al Busaid Dynasty.

Used values for Nos. 1-15 are for stamps canceled with contemporaneous postmarks of the Indian postal administration. Examples with later British post office cancellations are worth much less.

Great Britain, Nos. 258 to 263, 243, 248, 249A Surcharged

Perf. 14½x14

1948, Apr. 1 Wmk. 251

16 A101 ½a on ½p green 3.00 *8.00*
17 A101 1a on 1p vermilion 3.25 *.30*
18 A101 1½a on 1½p lt red brn 15.00 *4.25*
19 A101 2a on 2p lt org 2.25 *3.50*
20 A101 2½a on 2½p ultra 4.25 *8.50*
21 A101 3a on 3p violet 4.00 *.25*
22 A102 6a on 6p rose lilac 4.50 *.25*
23 A103 1r on 1sh brown 5.00 *.75*

Wmk. 259 *Perf. 14*

24 A104 2r on 2sh6p yel grn 14.00 *52.50*
Nos. 16-24 (9) 55.25 *78.30*

Catalogue values for unused stamps in this section from this point to the end of the section are for Never Hinged items.

Silver Wedding Issue

Great Britain, Nos. 267 and 268, Surcharged with New Value in Black

Perf. 14½x14, 14x14½

1948, Apr. 26 Wmk. 251

25 A109 2½a on 2½p brt ultra 3.50 *5.00*
26 A110 15r on £1 dp chlky bl 42.50 *42.50*

Three bars obliterate the original denomination on No. 26.

Olympic Games Issue

Great Britain, Nos. 271 to 274, Surcharged with New Value in Black

1948, July 29 *Perf. 14½x14*

27 A113 2½a on 2½p brt ultra .75 *2.75*
28 A114 3a on 3p dp violet .85 *2.75*
29 A115 6a on 6p red violet .95 *3.00*
30 A116 1r on 1sh dk brn 2.25 *4.25*
a. Double surcharge 1,500.
Nos. 27-30 (4) 4.80 12.75

A square of dots obliterates the original denomination on Nos. 28-30.

UPU Issue

Great Britain Nos. 276 to 279 Surcharged with New Value and Square of Dots in Black

1949, Oct. 10 Photo.

31 A117 2½a on 2½p brt ultra .75 *2.75*
32 A118 3a on 3p brt violet .95 *3.75*
33 A119 6a on 6p red violet 1.10 *2.50*
34 A120 1r on 1sh brown 2.75 *6.75*
Nos. 31-34 (4) 5.55 15.75

Great Britain Nos. 280-286 Surcharged with New Value in Black

1951

35 A101 ½a on ½p lt org 1.00 *9.00*
36 A101 1a on 1p ultra .60 *7.50*
37 A101 1½a on 1½p green 17.00 *35.00*
38 A101 2a on 2p lt red brn .85 *8.00*
39 A101 2½a on 2½p vermilion 1.50 *16.00*
40 A102 4a on 4p ultra 1.25 *3.25*

Perf. 11x12

Wmk. 259

41 A121 2r on 2sh6p green 45.00 7.00
Nos. 35-41 (7) 67.20 *85.75*

Two types of surcharge on No. 41.

Stamps of Great Britain, 1952-54, Srchd. with New Value in Black and Dark Blue

1952-54 Wmk. 298 *Perf. 14½x14*

42 A126 ½a on ½p red org ('53) .35 *2.00*
43 A126 1a on 1p ultra ('53) .35 *2.00*
44 A126 1½a on 1½p grn ('52) .40 *2.00*
45 A126 2a on 2p red brn ('53) .50 .25
46 A127 2½a on 2½p scar ('52) .35 .25
47 A127 3a on 3p dk pur (dk bl) .50 *1.00*
48 A128 4a on 4p ultra ('53) 2.25 *3.75*
49 A129 6a on 6p lilac rose .60 .45
50 A132 12a on 1sh3p dk grn ('53) 8.00 .90
51 A131 1r on 1sh6p dk bl ('53) 3.00 .75
Nos. 42-51 (10) 16.30 13.35

Coronation Issue

Great Britain Nos. 313-316 Surcharged

1953, June 10

52 A134 2½a on 2½p scarlet 2.50 3.00
53 A135 4a on 4p brt ultra 2.50 1.25
54 A136 12a on 1sh3p dk grn 4.50 1.25
55 A137 1r on 1sh6p dk blue 5.75 1.00
Nos. 52-55 (4) 15.25 6.50

Squares of dots obliterate the original denominations on Nos. 54-55.

Great Britain Stamps of 1955-56 Surcharged

Perf. 14½x14

1955-57 Wmk. 308 Photo.

56 A126 1a on 1p ultra .50 *.60*
56A A126 1½a on 1½p grn 6,000. *950.00*
57 A126 2a on 2p red brn .85 *2.00*
58 A127 2½a on 2½p scar 1.00 *3.00*
59 A127 3a on 3p dk pur 1.10 *7.50*
60 A128 4a on 4p ultra 6.50 *19.00*
61 A129 6a on 6p lilac rose 1.40 *6.50*
62 A131 1r on 1sh6p dk bl 8.00 *.50*

Engr. *Perf. 11x12*

63 A133 2r on 2sh6p dk brown 8.00 1.50
64 A133 5r on 5sh crimson 14.00 3.50
Nos. 56,57-64 (9) 41.35 *44.10*

Surcharge on No. 63 exists in three types, on No. 64 in two types.

Issued: 2r, 9/23/55; 2a, 2½a, 6/8/56; 1r, 8/2/56; 4a, 12/9/56; 1½a, 1956; 3a, 2/3/57; 6a, 2/10/57; 5r, 3/1/57; 1a, 3/4/57.

Great Britain Nos. 317-325, 328, 332 Surcharged

1957, Apr. 1 *Perf. 14½x14*

65 A129 1np on 5p lt brown .25 *.90*
66 A126 3np on ½p red org .35 *2.00*
67 A126 6np on 1p ultra .40 *2.25*
68 A126 9np on 1½p green .50 *1.50*
69 A126 12np on 2p red brown .55 *1.75*
70 A127 15np on 2½p scar, I .65 .50
a. Type II .55 *3.00*
71 A127 20np on 3p dk pur .40 .30
72 A128 25np on 4p ultra 1.00 *6.00*
73 A129 40np on 6p lilac rose .75 .60
74 A130 50np on 9p dp ol grn 1.50 2.50
75 A132 75np on 1sh3p dk grn 3.00 .75
Nos. 65-75 (11) 9.35 *19.05*

The arrangement of the surcharge varies on different values; there are three bars through value on No. 74.

Jubilee Jamboree Issue

Great Britain Nos. 334-336 Surcharged with New Value and Square of Dots

Perf. 14½x14

1957, Aug. 1 Wmk. 308

76 A138 15np on 2½p scar 1.40 1.50
77 A138 25np on 4p ultra 1.40 1.50
78 A138 75np on 1sh3p dk grn 1.75 1.50
Nos. 76-78 (3) 4.55 4.50

50th anniv. of the Boy Scout movement and the World Scout Jubilee Jamboree, Aug. 1-12.

Great Britain Stamps of 1958-60 Surcharged

Perf. 14½x14

1960-61 Wmk. 322 Photo.

79 A129 1np on 5p lt brn .25 *.30*
80 A126 3np on ½p red org 1.00 *1.25*
81 A126 5np on 1p ultra 1.75 *3.00*

82 A126 6np on 1p ultra 1.25 1.00
83 A126 10np on 1½p green 1.00 *2.50*
84 A126 12np on 2p red brn 3.00 3.00
85 A127 15np on 2½p scar .50 .25
86 A127 20np on 3p dk pur .50 .25
87 A128 30np on 4½p hn brn .75 *1.10*
88 A129 40np on 6p lil rose .85 .30
89 A130 50np on 9p dp ol grn 1.50 *2.25*
90 A132 75np on 1sh3p dk grn 4.00 1.75
91 A131 1r on 1sh6p dk blue 30.00 6.50
92 A133 2r on 2sh6p dk brn 15.00 *37.50*
93 A133 5r on 5sh crim 35.00 *55.00*
Nos. 79-93 (15) 96.35 *115.95*

Issued: 15np, 4/26; 3np, 6np, 12np, 6/21; 1np, 8/8; 20np, 40np, 9/28; 5np, 10np, 30np, 50np-5r, 4/8/61.

Muscat and Oman

Crest — A1

View of Harbor — A2

Nakhal Fort — A3

BAIZAS

RUPEES

Crest and: 50b, Samail Fort. 1r, Sohar Fort. 2r, Nizwa Fort. 5r, Matrah Fort. 10r, Mirani Fort.

Perf. 14½x14 (A1), 14x14½ (A2), 14x13½ (A3)

1966, Apr. 29 Photo. Unwmk.

94 A1 3b plum .25 .25
95 A1 5b brown .25 .25
96 A1 10b red brown .25 .25
97 A2 15b black & violet 1.00 .25
98 A2 20b black & ultra 1.50 .25
99 A2 25b black & orange 2.25 .60
100 A3 30b dk blue & lil rose 2.75 .65
101 A3 50b red brn & brt grn 3.75 1.50
a. Value in "baizas" in Arabic 225.00 110.00
102 A3 1r org & dk bl 7.50 1.75
103 A3 2r grn & brn org 14.00 5.00
104 A3 5r dp car & vio 30.00 17.00
105 A3 10r dk vio & car rose 60.00 35.00
Nos. 94-105 (12) 123.50 62.75

No. 101 has value in rupees in Arabic.

See Nos. 110-121. For overprints & surcharges see Nos. 122-133C.

Mina al Fahal Harbor A4

Designs: 25b, Oil tanks. 40b, Oil installation in the desert. 1r, View of Arabian Peninsula from Gemini IV.

Perf. 13½x13

1969, Jan. 1 Litho. Unwmk.

106 A4 20b multicolored 5.00 1.00
107 A4 25b multicolored 7.00 1.50
108 A4 40b multicolored 10.00 2.25
109 A4 1r multicolored 26.00 6.75
Nos. 106-109 (4) 48.00 11.50

1st oil shipment from Muscat & Oman, July, 1967.

Types of 1966

Designs: 50b, Nakhal Fort. 75b, Samail Fort. 100b, Sohar Fort. ¼r, Nizwa Fort. ½r, Matrah Fort. 1r, Mirani Fort.

Perf. 14½x14 (A1), 14x14½ (A2), 14x13½ (A3)

1970, June 27 Photo. Unwmk.

110 A1 5b plum 1.00 .25
111 A1 10b brown 2.00 .40
112 A1 20b red brown 2.25 .45
113 A2 25b black & vio 4.00 .60
114 A2 30b black & ultra 5.00 1.00
115 A2 40b black & org 6.00 1.25
116 A3 50b dk blue & lil rose 8.00 1.50
117 A3 75b red brn & brt grn 9.50 2.00
118 A3 100b orange & dk bl 11.00 2.25
119 A3 ¼r grn & brn org 27.50 6.75
120 A3 ½r brn car & vio 50.00 19.00
121 A3 1r dk vio & car rose 90.00 32.50
Nos. 110-121 (12) 216.25 67.95

Sultanate of Oman

Nos. 110-121 Overprinted

a

b

c

5b, 10b 20b:

Type 1 — Lower bars 15¼mm long; letter "A" has low, thick crossbar.

Type 2 — Lower bars 14¾mm; "A" crossbar high, thin.

Perf. 14½x14, 14x14½, 14x13½

1971, Jan. 16 Photo. Unwmk.

122 A1 (a) 5b plum 12.50 .60
a. Type 2 *50.00 25.00*
123 A1 (a) 10b brown 35.00 17.50
a. Type 2 *55.00 30.00*
124 A1 (a) 20b red brown 16.00 .80
a. Type 2 *55.00 30.00*
125 A2 (b) 25b black & vio 2.25 .50
126 A2 (b) 30b black & ultra 3.25 .80
127 A2 (b) 40b black & org 4.00 1.00
128 A3 (c) 50b dk bl & lil rose 5.50 1.25
129 A3 (c) 75b red brn & brt grn 8.25 2.00
130 A3 (c) 100b org & dk bl 11.00 3.50
131 A3 (c) ¼r grn & brn org 27.50 8.50
132 A3 (c) ½r brn car & vio 55.00 15.00
133 A3 (c) 1r dk vio & car rose 120.00 30.00
Nos. 122-133 (12) 300.25 81.45

For surcharge see No. 133B.

No. 94 Surcharged Type "a," Nos. 127, 102 Surcharged

Perf. 14½x14, 14x14½, 14½x13½

1971-72

133A A1 5b on 3b *160.00 22.50*
133B A2 25b on 40b *160.00 160.00*
133C A3 25b on 1r *160.00 160.00*
Nos. 133A-133C (3) 480.00 342.50

No. 133C surcharge resembles type "c" with "Sultanate of Oman" omitted and bars of criss-cross lines.

No. 133A exists with inverted surchagre and in pair, one with surcharge omitted. No. 133C exists with Arabic "2" or "5" omitted.

Issued: 5b, Nov; #133C, 6/6/7; #133B, 7/1/72.

Sultan Qaboos bin Said and New Buildings — A5

National Day: 40b, Sultan Qaboos and free-dom symbols. 50b, Crest of Oman and health clinic. 100b, Crest of Oman, classrooms and school.

1971, July 23 Litho. *Perf. 13½x14*

134 A5 10b multicolored 3.25 .45
135 A5 40b multicolored 12.00 .90
136 A5 50b multicolored 15.00 1.50
137 A5 100b multicolored 30.00 5.00
Nos. 134-137 (4) 60.25 7.85

Open Book A6

1972, Jan. 3 *Perf. 14x14½*

138 A6 25b ap grn, dk bl & dk red 30.00 5.00

International Book Year, 1972.

View of Muscat, 1809 A7

Designs: 5, 10, 20, 25b, View of Matrah, 1809. 30, 40, 50, 75b, View of Shinas, 1809.

Wmk. 314 Sideways

1972, July 23 Litho. *Perf. 14x14½*

Size: 21x17mm

139 A7 5b tan & multi 1.00 .30
140 A7 10b blue & multi 1.75 .30
141 A7 20b gray grn & multi 2.00 .30
142 A7 25b violet & multi 2.75 .30

Perf. 14½x14

Size: 25x21mm

143 A7 30b tan & multi 3.50 .35
144 A7 40b gray blue & multi 3.50 .40
145 A7 50b rose brn & multi 4.50 .50
146 A7 75b olive & multi 10.00 .90

Perf. 14

Size: 41x25mm

147 A7 100b lilac & multi 13.50 1.50
148 A7 ¼r green & multi 30.00 3.00
149 A7 ½r bister & multi 57.50 9.50
150 A7 1r dull bl grn & multi 87.50 19.00
Nos. 139-150 (12) 217.50 36.35

Perf. 14x14½, 14½x14

1972-75 Wmk. 314 Upright

139a A7 5b tan & multi ('75) .45 .25
140a A7 10b blue & multi ('75) 1.25 .35
141a A7 20b gray grn & multi ('75) 2.50 .65
142a A7 25b violet & multi ('75) 3.50 .90
143a A7 30b tan & multi 4.75 1.20
144a A7 40b blue & multi 7.50 1.50
145a A7 50b rose brn & multi 8.00 1.75
146a A7 75b olive & multi 13.50 5.00
Nos. 139a-146a (8) 41.45 11.60

Issue dates: Nov. 17, 1972, Sept. 11, 1975.

Perf. 14x14½, 14½x14, 14

1976-82 Wmk. 373

139b A7 5b tan & multi ('78) .80 .60
140b A7 10b blue & multi ('78) 1.25 .50
141b A7 20b gray grn & multi ('82) 2.00 .55
142b A7 25b vio & multi ('78) 2.50 .60
143b A7 30b tan & multi 3.00 .85
144b A7 40b blue & multi 4.00 1.25
145b A7 50b rose brn & multi 5.00 1.40
146b A7 75b olive & multi 8.75 1.60
147b A7 100b lilac & multi 9.00 2.25
148a A7 ¼r grn & multi ('78) 26.00 6.50
149a A7 ½r bister & multi 37.50 11.00
150a A7 1r dull bl grn & multi 82.50 22.50
Nos. 139b-150a (12) 182.30 49.60

Issued: 4/12/76; 1/27/78; 3/15/82.

Ministerial Complex — A8

Litho.; Date Typo.

1973, Sept. 20 Unwmk. *Perf. 13*

151 A8 25b emerald & multi 3.75 1.25
152 A8 100b brown org & multi 13.00 3.00

Opening of ministerial complex.

Nos. 151-152 exist with date omitted and hyphen omitted.

Dhows — A9

Perf. 12½x12

1973, Nov. 18 Litho. Wmk. 314

153 A9 15b shown 2.25 .55
154 A9 50b Seeb Airport 10.00 2.25
155 A9 65b Dhow and tanker 11.00 2.50
156 A9 100b Camel rider 16.50 4.00
Nos. 153-156 (4) 39.75 9.30

National Day.

Port Qaboos — A10

1974, July 30 Litho. *Perf. 13*

157 A10 100b multicolored 16.50 5.00

Opening of Port Qaboos.

Open Book, Map of Arab World A11

100b, Hands reaching for book, vert.

1974, Sept. 8 Wmk. 314 *Perf. 14½*

158 A11 25b multicolored 3.75 .55
159 A11 100b multicolored 12.00 3.25

International Literacy Day, Sept. 8.

Sultan Qaboos, UPU and Arab Postal Union Emblems — A12

1974, Oct. 29 Litho. *Perf. 13½*

160 A12 100b multicolored 4.50 2.00

Centenary of Universal Postal Union.

Arab Scribe A13

1975, May 8 Photo. *Perf. 13x14*

161 A13 25b multicolored 12.00 3.00

Eradication of illiteracy.

New Harbor at Mina Raysoot — A14

Designs: 50b, Stadium and map of Oman. 75b, Water desalination plant. 100b, Oman color television station. 150b, Satellite earth station and map. 250b, Telephone, radar, cable and map.

Perf. 14x13½

1975, Nov. 18 Litho. Wmk. 373

162 A14 30b multicolored 1.50 .65
163 A14 50b multicolored 3.00 .75
164 A14 75b multicolored 4.00 1.25
165 A14 100b multicolored 5.50 2.25
166 A14 150b multicolored 7.50 3.25
167 A14 250b multicolored 14.00 7.00
Nos. 162-167 (6) 35.50 15.15

National Day 1975.
For surcharges see Nos. 190A, 190C.

Mother with Child, Nurse, Globe, Red Crescent, IWY Emblem — A15

Design: 150b, Hand shielding mother and children, Omani flag, IWY emblem, vert.

Perf. 13½x14, 14x13½

1975, Dec. 27 Litho.

168 A15 75b citron & multi 4.00 1.25
169 A15 150b ultra & multi 6.50 2.25

International Women's Year 1975.
For surcharge see No. 190B.

Sultan Presenting Colors and Opening Seeb-Nizwa Road — A16

National Day: 40b, Paratroopers bailing out from plane and mechanized harvester. 75b, Helicopter squadron and Victory Day procession. 150b, Army building road and Salalah television station.

1976, Nov. 15 Litho. *Perf. 14½*

173 A16 25b multicolored 1.25 .25
174 A16 40b multicolored 3.50 .50
175 A16 75b multicolored 7.00 1.50
176 A16 150b multicolored 8.75 2.50
Nos. 173-176 (4) 20.50 4.75

Great Bath at Mohenjo-Daro — A17

1977, Jan. 6 Wmk. 373 *Perf. 13½*

177 A17 125b multicolored 8.25 3.00

UNESCO campaign to save Mohenjo-Daro excavations in Pakistan.

APU Emblem, Members' Flags — A18

1977, Apr. 4 Litho. *Perf. 12*

178 A18 30b emerald & multi 3.50 1.00
179 A18 75b blue & multi 8.00 2.75

Arab Postal Union, 25th anniversary.

Coffeepots — A19

Designs: 75b, Earthenware. 100b, Stone tablet, Khor Rori, 100 B.C. 150b, Jewelry.

1977, Nov. 18 Litho. *Perf. 13½*

180 A19 40b multicolored 2.00 .50
181 A19 75b multicolored 4.00 1.00
182 A19 100b multicolored 6.00 1.50
183 A19 150b multicolored 9.00 2.00
Nos. 180-183 (4) 21.00 5.00

National Day 1977.

Forts A20

Wmk. 373

1978, Nov. 18 Litho. *Perf. 14*

184 A20 20b Jalali 1.25 .30
185 A20 25b Nizwa 1.50 .40
186 A20 40b Rostaq 3.50 .80
187 A20 50b Sohar 4.00 .90
188 A20 75b Bahla 4.50 1.50
189 A20 100b Jibrin 7.50 2.00
Nos. 184-189 (6) 22.25 5.90

National Day 1978.

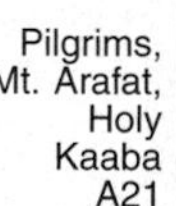

Pilgrims, Mt. Arafat, Holy Kaaba A21

1978, Nov. 1 Litho. *Perf. 13½*

190 A21 40b multicolored 7.25 2.50

Pilgrimage to Mecca.

Nos. 166, 169 and 167 Surcharged

Perf. 14x13½

1978, July 30 Litho. Wmk. 373

190A A14 40b on 150b *450.00 450.00*
190B A15 50b on 150b *475.00 475.00*
190C A14 75b on 250b *2,250. 2,250.*
Nos. 190A-190C (3) 3,175. 3,175.

World Map, Book, Symbols of Learning A22

1979, Mar. 22 Litho. *Perf. 14x13½*

191 A22 40b multicolored 2.75 .60
192 A22 100b multicolored 5.50 1.50

Cultural achievements of the Arabs.

Girl on Swing, IYC Emblem A23

1979, Oct. 28 Litho. *Perf. 14*

193 A23 40b multicolored 4.75 2.50

International Year of the Child.

Gas Plant — A24

National Day: 75b, Fisheries.

1979, Nov. 18 Photo. *Perf. 11½*

194 A24 25b multicolored 3.50 .85
195 A24 75b multicolored 9.00 2.75

Sultan on Horseback, Military Symbols — A25

Design: 100b, Soldier, parachutes, tank.

1979, Dec. 11

196 A25 40b multicolored 8.50 1.75
197 A25 100b multicolored 14.00 4.00

Armed Forces Day.

Hegira (Pilgrimage Year) — A26

1980, Nov. 9 Photo. *Perf. 11½*

198 A26 50b shown 7.00 1.10
199 A26 150b Hegira emblem 11.00 3.75

Omani Women — A27

1980, Nov. 18 Granite Paper

200 A27 75b Bab Alkabir 2.75 1.10
201 A27 100b Corniche Highway 4.00 2.00
202 A27 250b Polo match 7.00 4.75
203 A27 500b shown 14.00 8.75
Nos. 200-203 (4) 27.75 16.60

10th National Day.
For surcharges see Nos. 212-213.

Sultan and Patrol Boat — A28

1980, Dec. 11 Granite Paper

204 A28 150b shown 6.00 3.00
205 A28 750b Sultan, mounted troops 32.50 15.00

Armed Forces Day.
For surcharges see Nos. 210-211.

Policewoman and Children Crossing Street — A29

1981, Feb. 7 Litho. *Perf. 13½x14*

206 A29 50b shown 4.00 1.00
207 A29 100b Marching band 5.00 2.00
208 A29 150b Mounted police on beach 6.00 3.00
209 A29 ½r Headquarters 15.00 9.50
Nos. 206-209 (4) 30.00 15.50

First National Police Day.

Nos. 204-205, 200, 203 Surcharged in Black on Silver

1981, Apr. 8 Photo. *Perf. 11½*

210 A28 20b on 150b multi 5.50 1.00
211 A28 30b on 750b multi 7.00 1.25
212 A27 20b on 75b multi 8.00 2.25
213 A27 100b on 500b multi 13.00 3.75
Nos. 210-213 (4) 33.50 8.25

Welfare of the Blind — A30

1981, Oct. 14 Photo. *Perf. 11½*

214 A30 10b multicolored 27.50 2.75

World Food Day — A31

1981, Oct. 16 Photo. *Perf. 12*

215 A31 50b multicolored 7.50 2.50

Hegira (Pilgrimage Year) — A32

1981, Oct. 25 Litho. *Perf. 14½*

216 A32 50b multicolored 8.25 3.25

11th Natl. Day — A32a

160b, Al-Razha match (sword vs. stick). 300b, Sultan, map, vert.

1981, Nov. 18 Photo. *Perf. 12*
216A A32a 160b multicolored 6.00 3.25
216B A32a 300b multicolored 10.00 5.00

Voyage of Sinbad A33

50b, Muscat Port, 1981. 100b, Dhow Shohar. 130b, Map. 200b, Muscat Harbor, 1650.

1981, Nov. 23 Litho. *Perf. 14½x14*
217 A33 50b multicolored 2.50 1.10
218 A33 100b multicolored 5.25 3.00
219 A33 130b multicolored 6.25 4.00
220 A33 200b multicolored 8.75 5.50
a. Souvenir sheet of 4, #217-220 57.50 57.50
Nos. 217-220 (4) 22.75 13.60

Armed Forces Day — A34

1981, Dec. 11 Photo. *Perf. 11½*
221 A34 100b Sultan, planes 7.00 3.25
222 A34 400b Patrol boats 18.00 8.75

Natl. Police Day A35

1982, Jan. 5 Litho. *Perf. 14½*
223 A35 50b Patrol launch 3.75 1.50
224 A35 100b Band, vert. 6.50 3.00

Nerium Mascatense A36

Red-legged Partridge A37

10b, Dionysia mira. 20b, Teucrium mascatense. 25b, Geranium mascatense. 30b, Cymatium boschi, horiz. 40b, Acteon eloiseae, horiz. 50b, Cypraea teulerei, horiz. 75b, Cypraea pulchra, horiz. "1/4}r, Hoopoe. "1/2}r, Tahr. 1r, Arabian oryx.

1982, July 7 Photo. *Perf. 12½*
Granite Paper
225 A36 5b multicolored .35 .25
226 A36 10b multicolored .35 .25
227 A36 20b multicolored .65 .25
228 A36 25b multicolored .65 .30
229 A36 30b multicolored 1.00 .45
230 A36 40b multicolored 1.00 .55
231 A36 50b multicolored 1.25 .65
232 A36 75b multicolored 1.50 .95
233 A37 100b multicolored 5.00 1.25
234 A37 ¼r multicolored 11.50 5.75

Size: 25x38mm
235 A37 ½r multicolored 14.00 8.25
236 A37 1r multicolored 22.50 15.50
Nos. 225-236 (12) 59.75 34.40

2nd Municipalities Week (1981) — A38

1982, Oct. 28 Litho. *Perf. 13½x14½*
237 A38 40b multicolored 8.50 3.00

ITU Plenipotentiaries Conference, Nairobi, Sept. — A39

1982, Nov. 6 *Perf. 14½x13½*
238 A39 100b multicolored 12.00 4.00

12th Natl. Day A40

40b, State Consultative Council inaugural session. 100b, Oil refinery.

1982, Nov. 18 *Perf. 12*
239 A40 40b multicolored 5.00 2.00
240 A40 100b multicolored 9.50 3.50

Armed Forces Day — A41

1982, Dec. 11 *Perf. 13½x14*
241 A41 50b Soldiers 5.00 2.00
242 A41 100b Mounted band 9.50 4.00

Arab Palm Tree Day — A42

Perf. 13½x14½
1982, Sept. 19 Litho.
243 A42 40b Picking coconuts 5.50 2.25
244 A42 100b Dates 11.00 3.50

Natl. Police Day — A43

1983, Jan. 5 Litho. *Perf. 14x13½*
245 A43 50b multicolored 8.50 2.50

World Communications Year — A44

1983, May 17 *Perf. 13½x14*
246 A44 50b multicolored 6.75 2.50

Bees — A45

Designs: a, Beehive. b, Bee, flower.

1983, Aug. 15 Litho. *Perf. 13½*
247 A45 Pair 22.50 22.50
a.-b. 50b any single 5.00 3.25

Hegira (Pilgrimage Year) — A46

1983, Sept. 14 Photo. *Perf. 13½*
248 A46 40b multicolored 11.50 3.25

Youth Year — A47

Perf. 12½x13½
1983, Nov. 15 Litho.
249 A47 50b multicolored 7.00 2.75

National Day 1983 — A48

50b, Sohar Copper Factory. 100b, Sultan Qaboos University.

1983, Nov. 18 Litho. *Perf. 13½x14*
250 A48 50b multicolored 5.25 2.25
251 A48 100b multicolored 9.25 4.50

Armed Forces Day A49

1983, Dec. 11 Litho. *Perf. 13½x14*
252 A49 100b multicolored 8.50 3.00

Police Day A50

1984, Jan. 5 Litho. *Perf. 13½x14*
253 A50 100b multicolored 11.00 3.50

7th Arabian Gulf Soccer Tournament, Muscat, Mar. 9-26 — A51

1984, Mar. 9 Litho. *Perf. 13½*
254 A51 40b Players, cup, vert. 3.50 1.60
255 A51 50b Emblem 5.75 2.50

Pilgrims at Stone-Throwing Ceremony — A52

1984, Sept. 5 Litho. *Perf. 13½x14*
256 A52 50b multicolored 7.50 2.75

Pilgrimage to Mecca.

National Day 1984 — A53

130b, Mail sorting, new p.o. 160b, Map, vert.

Perf. 13½x14, 14x13½
1984, Nov. 18 Litho.
257 A53 130b multicolored 7.50 3.25
258 A53 160b multicolored 9.50 4.00

Inauguration of the new Central P.O., development of telecommunications.

16th Arab Scout Conference, Muscat — A54

No. 259, Setting-up camp. No. 260, Map reading. No. 261, Saluting natl. flag. No. 262, Scouts and girl guides.

1984, Dec. 5 Litho. *Perf. 14½*

259 A54 50b multicolored 2.25 .75
260 A54 50b multicolored 2.25 .75
a. Pair, #259-260 9.50 9.50
261 A54 130b multicolored 7.00 2.25
262 A54 130b multicolored 7.00 2.25
a. Pair, #261-262 22.50 22.50
Nos. 259-262 (4) 18.50 6.00

Armed Forces Day A55

1984, Dec. 11 *Perf. 13½x14*

263 A55 100b multicolored 11.50 4.50

Police Day — A56

1985, Jan. 5 *Perf. 14x13½*

264 A56 100b multicolored 11.50 4.00

Hegira (Pilgrimage Year) — A57

50b, Al-Khaif Mosque, Mina.

1985, Aug. 20 Litho. *Perf. 13½x14*

265 A57 50b multicolored 6.75 2.00

Intl. Youth Year A58

50b, Emblems. 100b, Emblem, youth activities.

1985, Sept. 22 Litho. *Perf. 13½x14*

266 A58 50b multicolored 3.75 1.00
267 A58 100b multicolored 6.75 2.25

Jabrin Palace Restoration — A59

1985, Sept. 22 Litho. *Perf. 13½x14*

268 A59 100b Interior 3.50 2.00
269 A59 250b Restored ceiling 8.75 5.75

Intl. Symposium on Traditional Music — A60

1985, Oct. 6 Litho. *Perf. 13½x14*

270 A60 50b multicolored 6.50 2.00

UN Child Survival Campaign — A61

1985, Oct. 25 Litho. *Perf. 13½x14*

271 A61 50b multicolored 5.25 1.50

Flags, Map and Sultan Qaboos — A62

1985, Nov. 3 Litho. *Perf. 12½*

272 A62 40b shown 3.25 1.25
273 A62 50b Supreme Council, vert. 4.25 1.50

6th Session of Arab Gulf States Supreme Council, Muscat.

Natl. Day 1985 — A63

Progress and development. 20b, Sultan Qaboos University. 50b, Date picking, plowing field. 100b, Port Qaboos Cement Factory. 200b, Post, transportation and communications. 250b, Sultan Qaboos, vert.

1985, Nov. 18

274 A63 20b multicolored 1.10 1.00
275 A63 50b multicolored 2.75 2.00
276 A63 100b multicolored 5.00 3.00
277 A63 200b multicolored 8.25 5.25
278 A63 250b multicolored 9.75 6.00
Nos. 274-278 (5) 26.85 17.25

Armed Forces Day A64

1985, Dec. 11 *Perf. 13½x14*

279 A64 100b multicolored 10.50 2.25

Fish and Crustaceans A65

20b, Chaetodon collaris. 50b, Chaetodon melapterus. 100b, Chaetodon gardineri. 150b, Scomberomorus commerson. 200b, Panulirus homarus.

Perf. 11½x12, 12x11½

1985, Dec. 15 Photo.

280 A65 20b multicolored .65 .25
281 A65 50b multicolored 1.25 .45
282 A65 100b multicolored 2.00 1.00
283 A65 150b multicolored 3.00 2.10
284 A65 200b multicolored 4.25 2.75
Nos. 280-284 (5) 11.15 6.55

Nos. 280-282, vert.

Frankincense Trees in Oman — A66

1985, Dec. 15 Litho. *Perf. 13½x14*

285 A66 100b multicolored 1.75 1.25
286 A66 3r multicolored 47.50 32.50

Police Day A67

1986, Jan. 5 Litho. *Perf. 13½x14*

287 A67 50b Camel Corps, Muscat 5.75 1.75

Statue of Liberty, Cent. A68

Maps and: 50b, Sultanah, voyage from Muscat to US 1840. 100b, Statue, Shabab Oman voyage from Oman to US, 1986, and fortress.

1986, July 4 *Perf. 14½*

288 A68 50b multicolored 4.75 1.75
289 A68 100b multicolored 8.00 3.00
a. Souvenir sheet of 2, #288-289 32.50 22.50

No. 289a sold for 250b.

Pilgrimage to Mecca — A69

1986, Aug. 9

290 A69 50b Holy Kaaba 4.75 1.50

17th Arab Scout Camp — A70

1986, Aug. 20

291 A70 50b Erecting tent 3.50 1.25
292 A70 100b Surveying 5.50 2.50

Sultan Qaboos Sports Complex Inauguration — A71

1986, Oct. 18 Litho. *Perf. 14½*

293 A71 100b multicolored 4.50 2.00

Intl. Peace Year A72

1986, Oct. 24 *Perf. 13½x13*

294 A72 130b multicolored 4.50 1.75

A73

A74

Natl. Day 1986 — A75

1986, Nov. 18 *Perf. 14½*

295 A73 50b mutlicolored 1.75 1.00
296 A74 100b multicolored 4.25 2.10

Perf. 13½x13

297 A75 130b multicolored 5.00 2.50
Nos. 295-297 (3) 11.00 5.60

Police Day A76

1987, Jan. 5 *Perf. 13½x14*

298 A76 50b multicolored 4.25 1.75

Second Arab Gulf Week for Social Work, Bahrain A77

1987, Mar. 21 *Perf. 13½x13*

299 A77 50b multicolored 3.50 1.25

Intl. Environment Day — A78

Perf. 13½x13, 13x13½

1987, June 5 Litho.

300 A78 50b Flamingos in flight 3.00 1.00
301 A78 130b Irrigation canal, vert. 5.00 1.50

Pilgrimage to Mecca A79

Stages of Pilgrimage (not in consecutive order): a, Pilgrims walking the tawaf, circling the Holy Kaaba 7 times. b, Tent City, Mina. c, Symbolic stoning of Satan. d, Pilgrims in Muzdalifah at dusk, picking up stones. e, Veneration of the prophet (pilgrims praying), Medina. f, Pilgrims wearing ihram, Pilgrim's Village, Jeddah.

1987, July 29 Litho. *Perf. 13½*

302 Strip of 6 25.00 25.00
a.-f. A79 50b any single 1.75 1.25

Third Municipalities Month — A80

1987, Oct. 1 *Perf. 13x13½*

303 A80 50b multicolored 2.75 1.10

Natl. Day A81

Designs: 50b, Marine Biology and Fisheries Center. 130b, Royal Hospital.

1987, Nov. 18 Litho. *Perf. 13½x13*

304 A81 50b multicolored 1.25 .75
305 A81 130b multicolored 3.00 2.00

Royal Omani Amateur Radio Soc., 15th Anniv. — A82

1987, Dec. 23 Litho. *Perf. 13½x13*

306 A82 130b multicolored 4.20 1.75

Traditional Handicrafts — A83

1988, June 1 Photo. *Perf. 12x11½*
Granite Paper

307 A83 50b Weaver 1.25 .75
308 A83 100b Potter 2.00 1.00
309 A83 150b Halwa maker 2.75 1.75
310 A83 200b Silversmith 3.25 2.25
a. Souvenir sheet of 4, #307-310 20.00 17.50
Nos. 307-310 (4) 9.25 5.75

No. 310a sold for 600b.

A84

1988, Sept. 17 Litho. *Perf. 14½*

311 A84 100b Equestrian 1.75 1.10
312 A84 100b Field hockey 1.75 1.10
313 A84 100b Soccer 1.75 1.10
314 A84 100b Running 1.75 1.10
315 A84 100b Swimming 1.75 1.10
316 A84 100b Shooting 1.75 1.10
a. Block of 6, #311-316 22.50 22.50
b. Souvenir sheet of 6, #311-316 30.00 30.00

1988 Summer Olympics, Seoul.

A85

1988, Nov. 1 Litho. *Perf. 13½*

317 A85 100b multicolored 2.50 1.50

WHO, 40th anniv.

Natl. Day, Agriculture Year A86

1988, Nov. 18 *Perf. 14½x13½*

318 A86 100b Tending crops 1.75 1.25
319 A86 100b Animal husbandry 1.75 1.25
a. Pair, #318-319 5.25 5.25

No. 319a has a continuous design.

Women Wearing Regional Folk Costume — A87

Designs: 200b-1r, Men wearing regional folk costumes.

1989 Photo. *Perf. 11½x12*
Granite Paper

320 A87 30b Dhahira .75 .25
321 A87 40b Eastern 1.00 .40
322 A87 50b Batinah 1.25 .55
323 A87 100b Interior 2.00 1.00
324 A87 130b Southern 2.50 2.25
325 A87 150b Muscat 3.50 2.75
a. Souvenir sheet of 6, #320-325 22.50 22.50
326 A87 200b Dhahira 2.00 1.40
327 A87 ¼r Eastern 2.50 1.60
328 A87 ½r Southern 4.00 4.00
329 A87 1r Muscat 8.50 6.75
a. Souvenir sheet of 4, #326-329 35.00 32.50
Nos. 320-329 (10) 28.00 20.95

No. 325a sold for 700b, No. 329a for 2r. Issued: 30b-150b, 8/26; 200b-1r, 11/11.

National Day, Agriculture Year — A88

1989, Nov. 18 *Perf. 12½x13*

330 A88 100b Fishing 2.00 1.00
331 A88 100b Farming 2.00 1.00
a. Pair, #330-331 5.00 4.50

Printed se-tenant in a continuous design.

10th Session of Supreme Council of the Cooperation Council for Arab Gulf States — A89

1989, Dec. 18 Litho. *Perf. 13x12*

332 A89 50b Flags, Omani crest 2.25 .75
333 A89 50b Sultan Qaboos, council emblem 2.25 .75
a. Pair, #332-333 5.00 4.00

No. 333a has a continuous design.

Gulf Investment Corp., 5th Anniv. (in 1989) — A90

1990, Jan. 1 Litho. *Perf. 13x12*

334 A90 50b multicolored 2.50 1.00
335 A90 130b multicolored 3.25 1.75

Gulf Air, 40th Anniv. A91

1990, Mar. 24 *Perf. 13x13½*

336 A91 80b multicolored 6.00 2.00

Symposium on the Oman Ophiolite — A92

1990, Apr. 22 Photo. *Perf. 11½*
Granite Paper

337 A92 80b shown 1.75 1.00
338 A92 150b multicolored 3.50 2.00

First Omani Envoy to the U.S., 150th Anniv. A93

1990, Apr. 30 Litho. *Perf. 13*

339 A93 200b multicolored 3.50 2.00

Sultan Qaboos Rose — A94

1990, May 5 Photo. *Perf. 11½*
Granite Paper

340 A94 200b multicolored 3.25 2.00

20th National Day A95

100b, Natl. Day emblem. 200b, Sultan Qaboos.

Litho. & Embossed

1990, Nov. 18 *Perf. 12x11½*
Granite Paper

341 A95 100b gold, red & green 1.50 1.00
342 A95 200b gold, green & red 3.75 2.10
a. Souvenir sheet of 2, #341-342 8.50 8.50

No. 342a sold for 500b.

Blood Donors — A96

1991, Apr. 22 Litho. *Perf. 13½x13*

343 A96 50b multicolored .80 .60
344 A96 200b multicolored 4.25 2.00
a. Pair, #343-344 25.00 25.00

National Day — A97

1991, Nov. 18 Photo. *Perf. 13½*

345 A97 100b shown 3.50 1.10
346 A97 200b Sultan Qaboos 5.75 2.25
a. Souvenir sheet of 2, #345-346 10.00 8.00

No. 346a sold for 400b.

Armed Forces Day A98

1991, Dec. 11 Litho. *Perf. 14½*
347 A98 100b multicolored 3.50 1.25

A99

1992, Jan. 29 Litho. *Perf. 13½x14*
348 A99 100b multicolored 3.25 1.25
a. Sheet of 1, perf. 13x13½ 13.00 9.00

Inauguration of Omani-French Museum, Muscat. No. 348a sold for 300b.

A100

1992, Mar. 23 Litho. *Perf. 14½*
349 A100 200b multicolored 4.25 1.75

World Meteorological Day.

A101

1992, June 5 Litho. *Perf. 13x13½*
350 A101 100b multicolored 2.50 1.25

World Environment Day.

A102

1992, Sept. 26 Litho. *Perf. 13½x14*
351 A102 70b multicolored 2.50 .75

Welfare of Handicapped Children.

Sultan Qaboos Encyclopedia of Arab Names — A103

1992, Oct. 10 *Perf. 14½*
352 A103 100b gold & multi 2.50 1.25

National Day — A104

Sultan Qaboos and emblems of: 100b, Year of Industry. 200b, Majlis As'shura.

1992, Nov. 18 Litho. *Perf. 14x13½*
353 A104 100b multicolored 3.00 1.75
354 A104 200b multicolored 4.25 2.50

Royal Oman Police Day A105

1993, Jan. 5 Litho. *Perf. 13½x14*
355 A105 80b multicolored 3.25 1.10

1993 Census A106

1993, Sept. 4 Litho. *Perf. 14x13½*
356 A106 100b multicolored 2.50 1.25

Royal Navy Day — A107

1993, Nov. 3 Litho. *Perf. 13*
357 A107 100b multicolored 3.25 1.50

23rd National Day A108

1993, Nov. 18 Photo. *Perf. 12*
Granite Paper
358 A108 100b Year of Youth emblem 2.25 1.50
359 A108 200b Sultan Qaboos 3.50 2.00

Scouting — A109

#360, Emblem of Scouts & Guides, Scout Headquarters. #361, Scout camp, Sultan Qaboos.

1993, Nov. 20 Litho. *Perf. 13x13½*
360 A109 100b multicolored 1.75 1.25
361 A109 100b multicolored 1.75 1.25
a. Pair, #360-361 5.00 5.00

Scouting movement in Oman, 61st anniv. (#360). Installation of Sultan Qaboos as chief scout, 10th anniv. (#361).

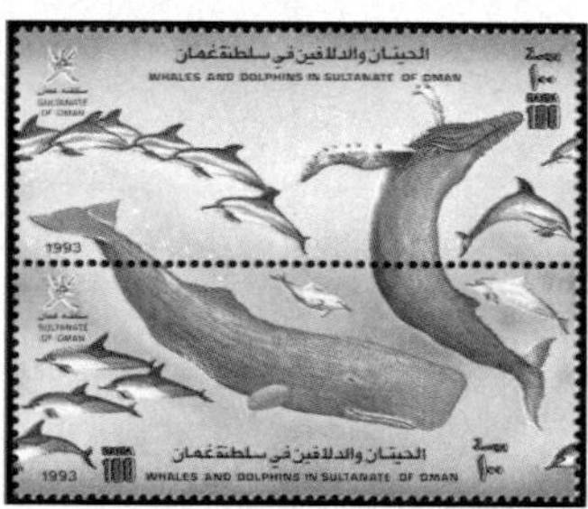

Whales and Dolphins — A110

#362, Dolphins, humpback whale. #363, Dolphins, sperm whale.

1993, Dec. 8 *Perf. 14½*
362 100b multicolored 3.75 1.75
363 100b multicolored 3.75 1.75
a. A110 Pair, #362-363 12.00 12.00
b. Souvenir sheet of 2, #362-363 45.00 45.00

No. 363a has a continuous design. No. 363b sold for 400b and has a white border surrounding the stamps.

World Day for Water — A111

1994, Mar. 22 Litho. *Perf. 13½*
364 A111 50b multicolored 2.25 .75

Muscat Municipality, 70th Anniv. — A112

1994, Apr. 16
365 A112 50b multicolored 2.50 1.00

Intl. Olympic Committee, Cent. — A113

1994, Aug. 29 Litho. *Perf. 13½*
366 A113 100b multicolored 16.00 8.25

Al Busaid Dynasty, 250th Anniv. — A114

Natl. arms or sultan, dates: a, 1744-75. b, 1775-79. c, 1779-92. d, 1792-1804. e, 1804-7. f, Sa'id ibn Sultan, 1807-56. g, 1856-65. h, 1866-68. i, 1868-71. j, Sultan, 1871-88. k, Sultan, 1888-1913. l, Sultan Taymur ibn Faysal, 1913-32. m, Sultan Qaboos, laurel tree. n, Sultan Sa'id ibn Taymur, 1932-70. o, Sultan Qaboos, 1970-.

200b, Sultan Qaboos atop family "tree," Arabic listing of former Sultans, years in power.

Litho. & Embossed

1994, Dec. 28 *Perf. 11½*
367 A114 50b Block of 15, #a.-o. *30.00 30.00*

Litho. & Typo.

Imperf

Size: 140x110mm

367P A114 200b gold & multi 7.00 5.50

Nos. 367f, 367j-367o contain portraits of sultans.

Open Parliament — A115

1995, Jan. 7 Litho. *Perf. 14*
Granite Paper
368 A115 50b silver & multi 2.25 1.00

24th National Day, Year of the Heritage — A116

1994, Nov. 18 Litho. *Perf. 13½*
369 A116 50b Emblem 1.00 .75
370 A116 50b Sultan Qaboos 1.00 .75
a. Pair, #369-370 6.25 6.25

ICAO, 50th Anniv. A117

1994, Dec. 7 *Perf. 13½x14*
371 A117 100b multicolored 7.25 3.00

Arab League, 50th Anniv. — A118

1995, Mar. 22 Litho. *Perf. 13*
372 A118 100b multicolored 2.50 1.00

UN, 50th Anniv. A119

1995, Sept. 2 *Perf. 13½*
373 A119 100b multicolored 4.50 1.50

16th Session of Supreme Council of the Co-operative Council for Arab Gulf States A120

Designs: 100b, Emblem. 200b, Flags of Arab Gulf States, map, Sultan Qaboos.

1995, Dec. 4 *Perf. 12*
Granite Paper
374 A120 100b multicolored 2.00 .70
375 A120 200b multicolored 4.00 1.25
a. Pair, #374-375 *30.00 20.00*

25th National Day A121

Portraits of Sultan Qaboos: 50b, In traditional attire. 100b, In military uniform.

Litho. & Embossed
1995, Nov. 18 *Perf. 11½*
Granite Paper
376 A121 50b multicolored 1.75 .80
377 A121 100b multicolored 3.25 1.00
a. Souvenir sheet of 2, #376-377 7.75 5.75

No. 377a sold for 300b.

1996 Summer Olympic Games, Atlanta — A122

a, Shooting. b, Swimming. c, Cycling. d, Running.

1996, July 19 Litho. *Perf. 14½*
378 A122 100b Strip of 4, #a.-d. 27.50 22.50

13th Arabian Gulf Cup Soccer Tournament — A123

1996, Oct. 15 *Perf. 13½*
379 A123 100b multicolored 2.00 1.00

UN Decade Against Drug Abuse — A124

1996, June 26 *Perf. 13½x14*
380 A124 100b multicolored 23.00 15.00

UNICEF, 50th Anniv. A125

1996, Dec. 11 Litho. *Perf. 14½*
381 A125 100b multicolored 2.25 1.10

26th National Day — A126

Designs: No. 382, Sultan Qaboos waving, boats in harbor. No. 383, Boats in harbor, Sultan Qaboos.

1996, Nov. 26 *Perf. 13½*
382 50b multicolored 1.50 .90
383 50b multicolored 1.50 .90
a. A126 Pair, #382-383 4.25 4.25

No. 383a is a continuous design.

Traditional Boats — A127

1996, Apr. 15 Photo. *Perf. 13½x14*
384 A127 50b Ash'Shashah .30 .25
385 A127 100b Al-Battil .65 .60
386 A127 200b Al-Boum 1.25 1.10
387 A127 250b Al-Badan 1.75 1.40
388 A127 350b As'Sanbuq 2.50 2.00
389 A127 450b Al-Galbout 3.25 2.50
390 A127 650b Al-Baghlah 4.25 3.50
391 A127 1r Al-Ghanjah 7.50 5.50
Nos. 384-391 (8) 21.45 16.85

Souvenir Sheet
Imperf
392 A127 600b Designs of #384-391 10.00 8.00

No. 392 has simulated perfs. and individual stamps are defaced and not valid for postage.

Tourism — A128

a, Oasis fort among palm trees. b, Small waterfalls, trees. c, Highway, coastline, castle on hilltop. d, Lake, mountains. e, Ruins of ancient fort on cliff. f, Waterfall, mountain stream.

1997 Litho. *Perf. 13½x14*
393 A128 100b Block of 6, #a.-f. 13.50 13.50

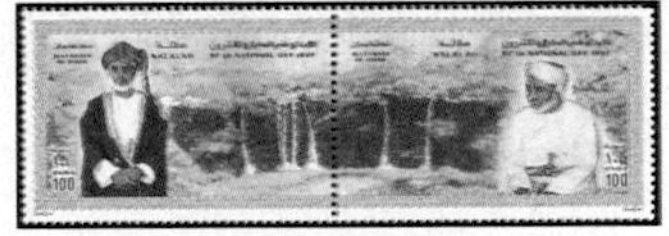

27th National Day — A129

Waterfall, Sultan Qaboos wearing: No. 394, Multicolored outfit. No. 395, Wearing white outfit.

1997, Nov. 18 Litho. *Perf. 13½*
394 100b multicolored 2.50 1.25
395 100b multicolored 2.50 1.25
a. A129 Pair, #394-395 8.00 8.00

Girl Guides in Oman, 25th Anniv. A130

1997, Nov. 30 *Perf. 14½*
396 A130 100b multicolored 2.75 1.50

Amateur Radio Society, 25th Anniv. — A131

1997, Dec. 23 *Perf. 13½*
397 A131 100b multicolored 3.75 2.00

Al-Khanjar Assaidi — A132

1997 Granite Paper *Perf. 11½*
398 A132 50b red & multi .85 .70
399 A132 50b green & multi .85 .70
400 A132 100b purple & multi 2.25 1.50
401 A132 200b brown & multi 3.25 2.25
Nos. 398-401 (4) 7.20 5.15

See No. 418.

Traffic Week A133

1998 *Perf. 13½*
402 A133 100b multicolored 8.00 4.00

Tourism — A134

Designs: a, Fort. b, Rocky mountainside, lake. c, City. d, Men raising swords, drummers. e, Stream running through countryside. f, Girls standing beside stream, trees.

1998 *Perf. 13½x13*
403 A134 100b Block of 6, #a.-f. 14.00 14.00

4th Arab Gulf Countries Philatelic Exhibition, Muscat — A135

1998 Litho. *Perf. 13½*
404 A135 50b multicolored 2.00 .80

Sultan Qaboos, Recipient of Intl. Peace Award A136

1998
405 A136 500b multicolored 21.00 14.00

28th National Day — A137

1998 *Perf. 12½*
406 A137 100b Sultan Qaboos 2.25 1.00
407 A137 100b Emblem, map 2.25 1.00
a. Pair, #406-407 6.50 6.50
b. Souvenir sheet, #406-407 *40.00 40.00*

Opening of Raysut Port-Salalah Container Terminal — A138

1998 *Perf. 13x13½*
408 A138 50b multicolored 5.50 2.25

World Stamp Day — A139

1998 *Perf. 13½*
409 A139 100b multicolored 2.00 1.50

Royal Air Force of Oman, 40th Anniv. — A140

1999 Litho. *Perf. 13½x13¾*
410 A140 100b multicolored 4.00 1.75

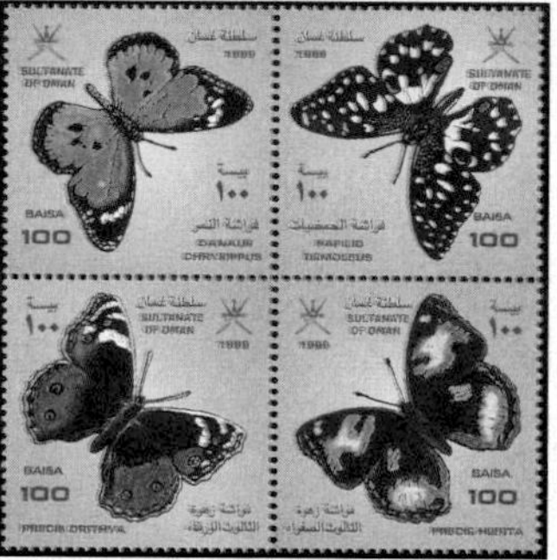

Butterflies — A141

Designs: a, Danaus chrysippus. b, Papilio demoleus. c, Precis orithya. d, Precis hierta.

1999 Litho. *Perf. 13¼*
411 A141 100b Block of 4, #a.-d. 13.00 13.00
e. Souvenir sheet of 4, #a.-d. 35.00 35.00

See No. 421.

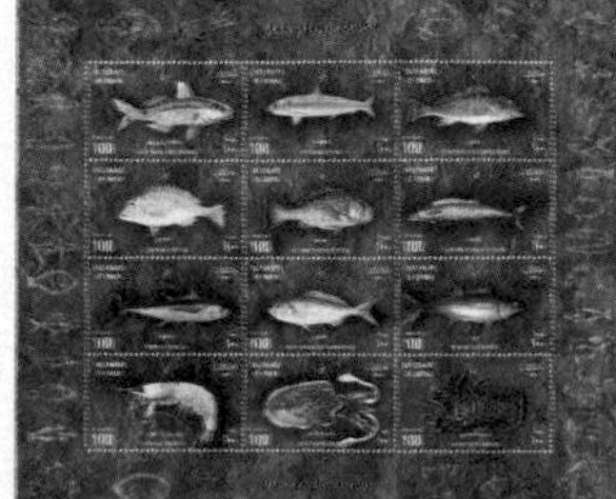

Marine Life — A142

Designs: a, Parupeneus macronema. b, Etrumeus teres. c, Epinephelus chlorostigma. d, Lethrinus lentjan. e, Lutjanus erythropterus. f, Acanthocybium solandri. g, Thunnus tongol. h, Pristipomoides filamentosus. i, Thunnus albacares. j, Penaeus indicus. k, Sepia pharaonis. l, Panulirus homarus.

1999 Litho. *Perf. 13½x13*
412 A142 100b Sheet of 12, #a.-l. 21.00 21.00

Wildlife — A143

Designs: a, Sand cat. b, Genet. c, Leopard. d, Sand fox. e, Caracal lynx. f, Hyena.

1999 Litho. *Perf. 13½x13*
413 100b Block of 6, #a.-f. 11.50 11.50
g. A143 Souvenir sheet, #a.-f. 40.00 40.00

UPU, 125th Anniv. A144

1999 *Perf. 11*
414 A144 200b multi 2.75 2.25

29th National Day — A145

1999 Litho. *Perf. 13½*
415 100b Sultan in black 2.25 1.25
416 100b Sultan in white 2.25 1.25
a. A145 Pair, #415-416 6.00 6.00

Souvenir Sheet

Millennium — A146

Litho. & Embossed with Foil Application

2000, Jan. 1 *Perf. 13¼*
417 A146 500b multi 15.00 15.00

Al-Khanjar Assaidi Type of 1997

2000, Feb. 12 Litho. *Perf. 11½*
Granite Paper
418 A132 80b orange & multi 1.75 1.25

GCC Water Week — A147

2000 Litho. *Perf. 13¼*
419 A147 100b multi 2.00 1.10

Gulf Air, 50th Anniv. — A148

2000 *Perf. 13½*
420 A148 100b multi 2.00 1.10

Butterfly Type of 1999

No. 421: a, Colotis danae. b, Anaphaeis aurota. c, Tarucus rosaceus. d, Lampides boeticus.

2000 Litho. *Perf. 13½*
421 Block of 4 12.00 12.00
a.-d. A141 100b Any single 2.50 1.25
e. Souvenir sheet, #421 30.00 30.00

Fish — A148a

No. 421F: g, Hippocampus kuda. h, Ostracion cubicus. i, Monocentris japonicus. j, Pterois antennata. k, Phinecanthus assasi. l, Taenura lymma.

Perf. 13½x13¾
2000, June 12 Litho.
421F A148a 100b Block of 6, #g-l 22.50 17.50
m. Souvenir sheet, #421F 24.00 17.50

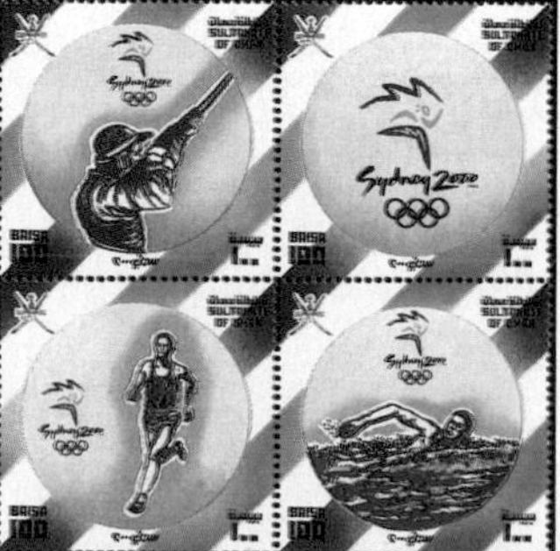

2000 Summer Olympics, Sydney — A149

Designs: a, Shooting. b, Emblem of Sydney Games. c, Running. d, Swimming.

2000, Sept. 15 *Perf. 13½x13¾*
422 A149 100b Block of 4, #a-d 10.00 10.00
e. Souvenir sheet, #422 32.50 32.50

Coup by Sultan Qaboos, 30th Anniv. — A150

No. 423: a, Emblem, Sultan in blue hat. b, Emblem, Sultan seated. c, Emblem, Sultan in red beret. d, Emblem, Sultan in white hat. e, Emblem. f, Emblem, Sultan in black hat.

Litho. & Embossed

2000, Nov. 18 *Perf. 13½*
423 Block of 6 17.50 14.00
a.-f. A150 100b Any single 2.25 1.25
g. Souvenir sheet, #423 16.00 16.00

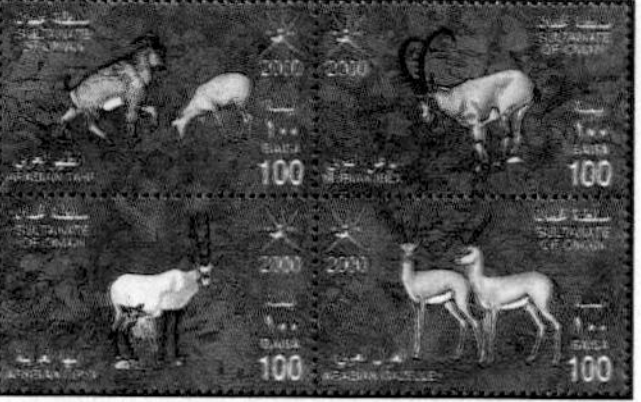

Wildlife — A151

No. 424: a, Arabian tahr. b, Nubian ibex. c, Arabian oryx. d, Arabian gazelle.

2000, July 23 Litho. *Perf. 13½x13*
424 A151 100b Block of 4, #a-d 15.00 11.00
e. Souvenir sheet, #424 22.50 13.00

Souvenir Sheet

Environment Day — A152

2001, Jan. 8 Litho. *Perf. 13¾x14¼*
425 A152 200b multi 16.00 12.00

Souvenir Sheet

Palestinian Uprising in Jerusalem — A153

Litho. & Embossed

2001, July 31 *Perf. 13½x13*
426 A153 100b multi 8.00 3.00

Al-Khanjar A'Suri — A154

Perf. 14½x13¾
2001, Mar. 19 Litho.
427 A154 50b red & multi .75 .50
428 A154 80b yel org & multi 1.25 1.00

Size: 26x34mm

Perf. 13¼x13

429 A154 100b blue & multi 1.50 1.25
430 A154 200b multi 3.00 2.50
a. Miniature sheet, #427-430 9.00 7.50

See Nos. 474-476.

Souvenir Sheets

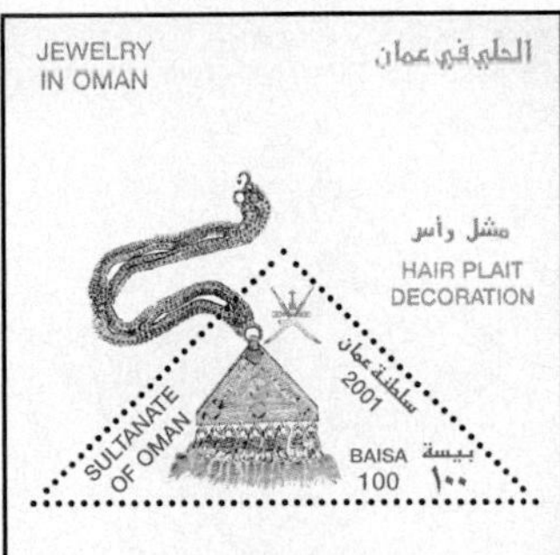

Jewelry — A155

Litho., Typo. & Embossed

2001 ***Perf. 12¾x12½***

431 A155 100b Hair plait decoration 5.25 3.00

Stamp Size: 62x27mm

Perf. 13¼x13¾

432 A155 100b Pendant 5.25 3.00

Stamp Size: 44x44mm

Perf. 12¾

433 A155 100b Necklace 5.25 3.00

Stamp Size: 38mm Diameter

Perf.

434 A155 100b Mazrad 5.25 3.00
Nos. 431-434 (4) 21.00 12.00

Supreme Council of Arab Gulf Cooperation Council States, 22nd Session A156

Designs: 50b, Map. 100b, Sultan Qaboos.

2001 Litho. & Typo. ***Perf. 14x14¼***

435-436 A156 Set of 2 2.50 1.50

Year of Dialogue Among Civilizations A157

2001 Litho. ***Perf. 13¾x13¼***

437 A157 200b multi 6.50 3.25

Shells — A157a

No. 437A: b, Nassarius coronatus. c, Epitoneum pallasii d, Cerithium caeruleum. e, Cerithidea cingulata.

2001 Litho. ***Perf. 13¼***

437A A157a 100b Block of 4, #b-e 7.00 5.75

31st National Day — A158

No. 438: a, Map of Oman, tree. b, Sultan Qaboos.

2001 ***Perf. 13¼***

438 A158 100b Horiz. pair, #a-b 4.75 4.75

Turtles — A159

No. 439: a, Olive Ridley. b, Green. c, Hawksbill. d, Loggerhead.

2002, Aug. 12 Litho. ***Perf. 13¼x13***

439 A159 100b Block of 4, #a-d 8.75 7.50
e. Souvenir sheet, #439a-439d 12.50 9.50

Sultan Qaboos Grand Mosque — A160

No. 440: a, Interior view of dome and chandelier. b, Exterior view of mosque and minaret. c, Exterior view of archway. d, Interior view of corner arches.

100b, Aerial view of mosque.

Litho. With Foil Application

2002, May 25 ***Perf. 13¼***

440 A160 50b Block of 4, #a-d 6.00 4.75

Size: 120x90mm

Imperf

441 A160 100b multi 7.50 4.75

Souvenir Sheet

32nd National Day — A160a

Design: 100b, Sultan Qaboos, flowers in corners.

Litho. With Foil Application

2002, Nov. 18 ***Perf. 13x13¼***

441A A160a 100b multi 5.25 3.00
441B A160a 200b shown 3.50 2.75

Birds — A161

No. 442: a, Streptopelia decaocto. b, Tchagra senegala. c, Ploceus galbula. d, Hieraaetus fasciatus. e, Pycnonotus xanthopygos. f, Bubo bubo. g, Eremalauda dunni. h, Burhinus capensis. i, Prinia gracilis. j, Francolinus pondicerianus. k, Onychognathus tristramii. l, Hoplopterus indicus. m, Corvus splendens. n, Chlamydotis undulata. o, Halcyon chloris. p, Pterocles coronatus.

2002, Dec. 15 ***Perf. 13x13¼***

442 A161 50b Sheet of 16, #a-p 22.50 17.50

Early Intervention for Children With Special Needs — A161a

2002, Oct. 30 Litho. ***Perf. 13x13¼***

442Q A161a 100b multi 3.50 1.75

Booklet Stamp

Self-Adhesive

442R A161a 100b multi 4.00 2.00
s. Booklet pane of 10 40.00 —

Oman - People's Republic of China Diplomatic Relations, 25th Anniv. — A163

2003, May 25 Litho. ***Perf. 12***

444 A163 70b multi 2.50 1.25

Souvenir Sheets

A164

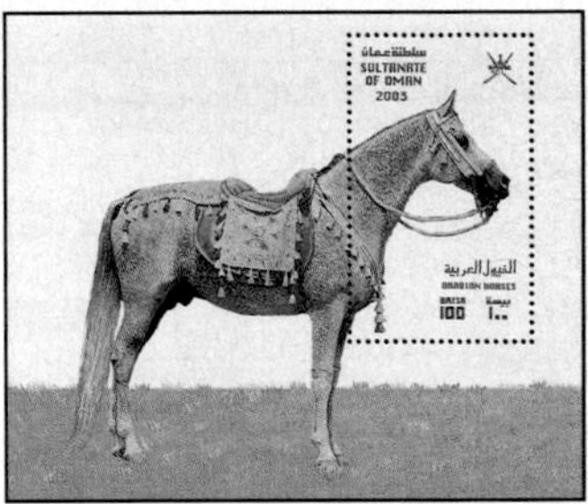

Arabian Horses — A165

2003, Apr. 8 ***Perf. 13¼x12¾***

445 A164 100b shown 2.75 1.50
446 A165 100b shown 2.75 1.50
447 A165 100b White horse facing left 2.75 1.50
448 A165 100b Brown horse 2.75 1.50
Nos. 445-448 (4) 11.00 6.00

Census — A166

No. 449: a, Emblem, buildings. b, Emblem, blue circle.

2003, Sept. 16 Litho. ***Perf. 13***

449 A166 50b Horiz. pair, #a-b 2.10 1.00

Intl. Day of Peace — A167

2003, Sept. 21 ***Perf. 13¼x12¾***

450 A167 200b multi 2.75 2.50

Muscat Festival 2003 A162

2003, Jan. 8 ***Perf. 14½***

443 A162 100b multi 2.00 1.00

Organization of the Islamic Conference — A168

Litho. & Embossed

2003, Sept. 25 *Perf. 13*
451 A168 100b multi 2.25 1.75

Self-Employment and National Autonomous Development Program — A169

2003, Oct. 6 Litho. *Perf. 13¼*

Souvenir Sheet

452 A169 100b multi 2.00 2.00

Booklet Stamp

Self-Adhesive

Serpentine Die Cut 12½

453 A169 100b multi 1.60 1.10
a. Booklet pane of 4 6.50
Complete booklet, 3 #453a 19.50

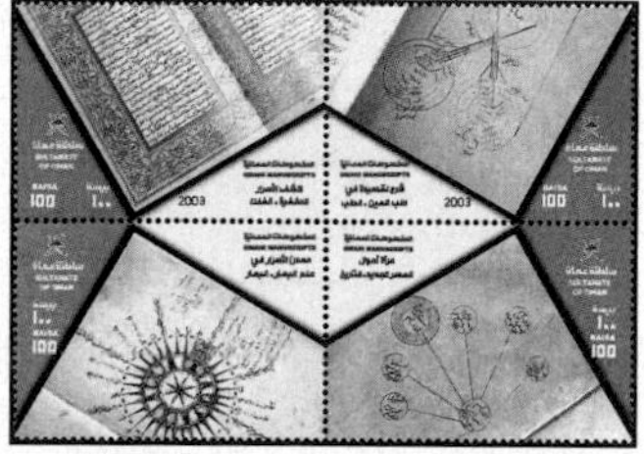

A170

Manuscripts — A171

No. 454: a, Denomination at lower left. b, Denomination at lower right. c, Denomination at left center. d, Denomination at right center.

No. 455: a, Illustrations of ships. b, Illustration of connected circles. c, Illustration of concentric circles. d, Text in large red circle.

2003, Oct. 14 Litho. *Perf. 13½x13¼*
454 A170 100b Block of 4, #a-d 5.00 5.00

Miniature Sheet

Litho. With Foil Application

Perf. 13¼

455 A171 50b Sheet of 4, #a-d 4.75 4.00

33rd National Day — A172

No. 456 — Sultan Qaboos and background color of: a, Light green. b, Light blue. c, Buff. d, Light red violet.

Litho. & Embossed

2003, Nov. 18 *Perf. 13x13¼*
456 A172 50b Block fo 4, #a-d 3.50 3.50

Flowers — A173

No. 457: a, Anogeissus dhofarica. b, Tecomella undulata. c, Euryops pinifolius. d, Aloe dhufarensis. e, Cleome glaucescens. f, Cassia italica. g, Cibirhiza dhofarensis. h, Ipomoea nil. i, Viola cinerea. j, Dyschoriste dalyi. k, Calotropis procera. l, Lavandula dhofarensis. m, Teucrium mascatense. n, Capparis mucronifolia. o, Geranium mascatense. p, Convolvulus arvensis.

2004, Jan. 24 Litho. *Perf. 14½*
457 Sheet of 16 11.50 11.50
a.-p. A173 50b Any single .60 .50

FIFA (Fédération Internationale de Football Association), Cent. — A174

Litho. & Embossed

2004, May 21 *Perf. 13¾*
458 A174 250b multi 4.25 3.75

Worldwide Fund for Nature (WWF) — A175

No. 459 — Arabian leopard: a, Front feet on mound. b, Pair of leopards. c, Rear feet on mound. d. Feet in depression.

2004, June 5 Litho. *Perf. 13¾x13½*
459 A175 Horiz. strip of 4 5.00 5.00
a.-d. 50b Any single .85 .75

Corals A176

No. 460: a, Montipora. b, Porites. c, Acropora. d, Cycloseris.

2004, Aug. 1 *Perf. 13¾*
460 Horiz. strip of 4 7.00 7.00
a.-d. A176 100b Any single .90 .75

Intl. Day of Peace — A177

Designs: 50b, Dove and green circle. 100b, Doves and Earth.

2004, Sept. 21 *Perf. 13½x13¾*
461-462 A177 Set of 2 1.50 1.50

Souvenir Sheet

Intl. White Cane Day — A178

2004 Litho. *Perf. 14x13¼*
463 A178 100b black 4.25 4.25

Braille text was applied by a thermographic process producing a shiny, raised effect.

34th National Day — A179

No. 464 — Sultan Qaboos with kaffiyah in: a, Red. b, Blue green. c, Gray and white. d, Black and white.

Litho. & Embossed With Foil Application

2004, Nov. 18 *Perf. 13¾x13½*
464 A179 100b Block of 4, #a-d 3.50 3.50

Water Supply Projects — A180

No. 465: a, Al Massarat. b, Ash'Sharqiyah.

2004, Dec. 1 Litho. *Perf. 14*
465 A180 50b Horiz. pair, #a-b 3.25 3.25

10th Gulf Cooperation Council Stamp Exhibition — A181

2004, Dec. 4 *Perf. 13½*
466 A181 50b multi 1.75 1.75

Self-Adhesive

Booklet Stamp

Serpentine Die Cut 12½

467 A181 50b multi 1.40 1.00
a. Booklet pane of 4 5.50
Complete booklet, 3 #467a 17.00

Civil Defense — A182

Designs: 50b, Civil defense workers, Omani people. 100b, Rescue workers in action.

2005, May 14 Litho. *Perf. 14*
468-469 A182 Set of 2 2.10 2.10

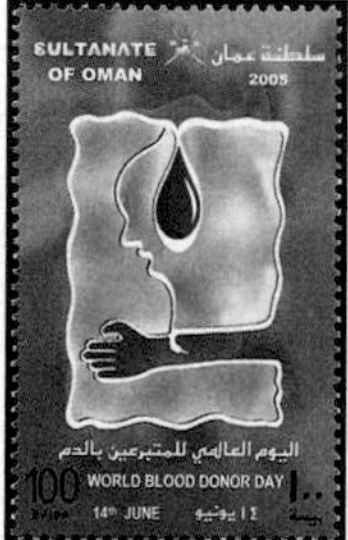

World Blood Donor Day — A183

2005, June 14 Litho. *Perf. 13¾x14*
470 A183 100b multi 1.50 1.50

Agricultural Census — A184

No. 471 — Census taker and: a, Herder and livestock. b, Farmer and crops.

2005, July 18 *Perf. 14x13¼*
471 A184 100b Horiz. pair, #a-b 3.25 3.25

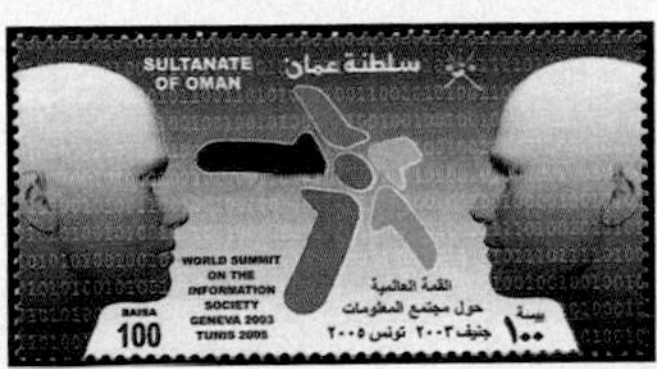

World Summit on the Information Society, Tunis — A185

2005, Nov. 16 ***Perf. 14***
472 A185 100b multi 1.75 1.75

Miniature Sheet

35th National Day — A186

No. 473: a, Airplane, dish antennas. b, Helicopter, mounted soldiers. c, Sultan Qaboos. d, People in costumes. e, Military aircraft, ship, vehicle. f, Tower, highway. g, Tower, people at computers. h, Emblem of 35th National Day. i, Man at oasis. j, Petroleum facility.

Litho., Litho. & Embossed With Foil Application (#473c)

2005, Nov. 18 ***Perf. 13¼x13½***
473 A186 100b Sheet of 10, #a-j 14.00 14.00

Al-Khanjar A'Suri Type of 2001

2005, Dec. 7 Litho. ***Perf. 13¼x13***

Size: 26x34mm

474 A154 250b bl grn & multi 1.40 1.40
475 A154 300b red vio & multi 1.60 1.60
476 A154 400b yel brn & multi 2.10 2.10
Nos. 474-476 (3) 5.10 5.10

A187

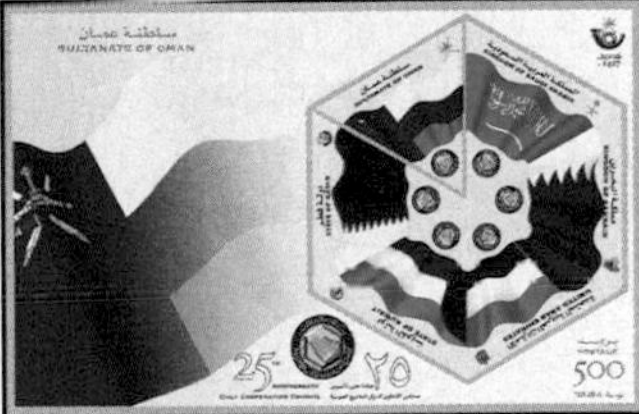

Gulf Cooperation Council, 25th Anniv. — A188

Litho. With Foil Application

2006, May 25 ***Perf. 14***
477 A187 100b multi 7.00 7.00

Imperf

Size: 165x100mm

478 A188 500b multi 26.00 26.00

See Bahrain Nos. 628-629, Kuwait Nos. 1646-1647, Qatar Nos. 1007-1008, Saudi Arabia No. 1378, and United Arab Emirates Nos. 831-832.

Souvenir Sheet

Muscat, 2006 Capital of Arab Culture — A189

2006, Aug. 26 Litho. ***Perf. 14***
479 A189 100b multi 3.00 3.00

Tourism — A190

No. 480: a, Man picking flowers, houses on mountain. b, Six men, building. c, Scuba diver, turtle on beach. d, Women with clothing on line, camels.

2006, Sept. 27 Litho. ***Perf. 14***
480 A190 100b Block of 4, #a-d 6.00 6.00

Oman Post Emblem A191

Text in: 100b, Blue. 250b, White.

Litho. With Foil Application

2006, Nov. 6 ***Perf. 13¾x13½***
481-482 A191 Set of 2 4.75 4.75

36th National Day — A192

2006, Nov. 18 ***Perf. 13x13½***
483 A192 100b multi 1.50 1.50

Sultan Qaboos Prize for Cultural Innovation — A193

2006, Dec. 24 Litho. ***Perf. 13¼x13***
484 A193 250b multi 4.00 4.00

Exportation of Crude Oil, 40th Anniv. — A194

No. 485: a, Oil tanker and oil storage facility. b, Oil storage facility and oil well.

2007, July 27 Litho. ***Perf. 13¾***
485 A194 100b Horiz. pair, #a-b 1.75 1.75

Symposium on Agricultrual Development A195

2007, Oct. 1 Litho. ***Perf. 13¾x14***
486 A195 100b multi 1.25 1.25

37th National Day — A196

2008, Nov. 18 ***Perf. 13***
487 A196 100b multi 2.00 2.00

Khasab Castle — A197

No. 488: a, Exterior of castle. b, Man behind table. c, People reading. d, Men and cannons near door.

2007, Dec. 1 ***Perf. 13¼x13***
488 A197 100b Block of 4, #a-d 2.75 2.75

Scouting, Cent., and Scouting in Oman, 75th Anniv. — A198

2007, Dec. 20 ***Perf. 13¾x13¼***
489 A198 250b multi 2.25 2.25

19th Arabian Gulf Cup Soccer Tournament — A199

2008, Jan. 4 Litho. ***Perf. 12¾x13¼***
490 A199 100b multi .70 .70

38th National Day A200

Litho. & Embossed With Foil Application

2008, Nov. 18 ***Perf. 13¾***
491 A200 200b multi 1.40 1.40

Souvenir Sheet

Arab Postal Day — A201

No. 492 — Emblem and: a, World map, pigeon. b, Camel caravan.

Perf. 14½x13¾

2008, Dec. 21 Litho.
492 A201 200b Sheet of 2, #a-b 4.00 4.00

Supreme Council of Gulf Cooperation Council, 29th Session — A202

Emblem and: 100b, Flags. 300b, Rulers of Council states.

Litho. With Foil Application

2008, Dec. 29 ***Perf. 13¼x13***
493 A202 100b multi 1.60 1.60

Size: 162x81mm

Imperf

494 A202 300b multi 4.00 4.00

Jerusalem, 2009 Capital of Arab Culture — A203

2009, Nov. 10 Litho. ***Perf. 13¾***
495 A203 250b multi 1.75 1.75

Souvenir Sheet

With White Frame Around Stamp

496 A203 250b multi *9.00 9.00*

15th Gulf Cooperation Council Stamps Exhibition, Oman — A204

No. 497: a, Part of Bahrain flag at right. b, Part of Bahrain flag at left, part of United Arab Emirates flag at right. c, Part of United Arab Emirates flag at left. d, Part of Oman flag at right. e, Part of Oman flag at left, part of Saudi Arabia flag at right. f, Part of Saudi Arabia flag at left. g, Part of Kuwait flag at right. h, Part of Kuwait flag at left, part of Qatar flag at right. i, Part of Qatar flag at left.

50b, No flag in background.

2009 Litho. *Perf. 13*

497 Sheet of 9 + 6 labels 13.00 13.00
a.-i. A204 200b Any single 1.40 1.40

Booklet Stamp
Self-Adhesive
Serpentine Die Cut 12¾

498 A204 50b multi .35 .35
a. Booklet pane of 12 4.25 4.25

39th National Day — A205

Litho. & Embossed

2009, Nov. 18 *Perf. 13¼*

499 A205 200b multi 1.40 1.40

Oman, Champions of 19th Arabian Gulf Cup Soccer Tournament A206

2009, Dec. 19 Litho. *Perf. 13¼*

500 A206 200b multi 1.40 1.40

Censuses A207

Emblem of: No. 502, 50b, Third census of Oman. No. 503, 50b, Joint Gulf Cooperation Council census.

2010, Feb. 2 Litho. *Perf. 13¼*

502-503 A207 Set of 2 .70 .70

Arab Water Day A209

2010, Mar. 3 Litho. *Perf. 14¼*

506 A209 100b multi .70 .70

A210

Expo 2010, Shanghai A211

2010, May 1 *Perf. 12¾x13¼*

Souvenir Sheet

507 A210 100b multi .70 .70

Self-Adhesive
Serpentine Die Cut

508 A211 50b multi .35 .35

Souvenir Sheet

Jewel of Muscat — A212

2010, July 3 *Perf. 13¾x13¼*

509 A212 100b multi .70 .70

Miniature Sheet

Renaissance Day — A213

No. 510 — Sultan Qaboos in: a, Blue uniform. b, Brown uniform, red brown background. c, White uniform. d, Beige uniform. e, Brown uniform, gray brown background.

Litho. & Embossed

2010, July 23 *Perf. 13¼*

510 A213 50b Sheet of 5, #a-e 1.75 1.75

Souvenir Sheet

40th National Day — A214

No. 511 — Doves and: a, 100b, Map of Oman. b, 150b, Sultan Qaboos.

2010, Oct. 18 *Perf.*

511 A214 Sheet of 2, #a-b 1.75 1.75

Traffic Safety Day — A215

2010, Oct. 18 Litho. *Perf. 13¼*

Souvenir Sheet

512 A215 100b multi .70 .70

Self-Adhesive
Serpentine Die Cut 13¼

513 A215 50b white & multi .35 .35

Miniature Sheet

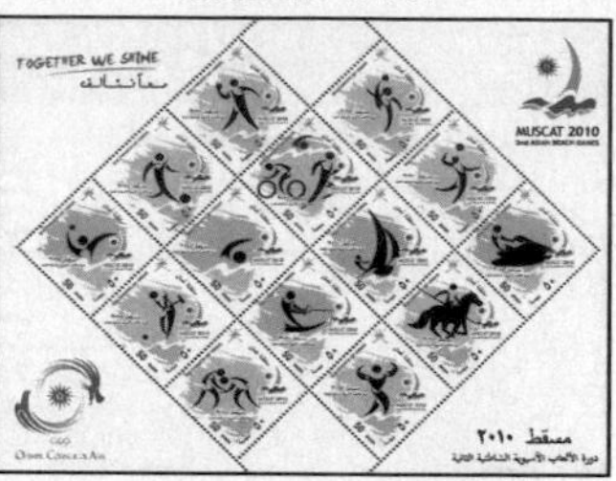

Second Asian Beach Games, Muscat — A216

No. 514: a, Handball. b, Sepak takraw (player kicking ball in air). c, Soccer player dribbling ball. d, Triathlon. e, Volleyball. f, Water polo. g, Swimming. h, Sailing. i, Jet skiing. j, Woodball (player with mallet and ball). k, Water skiing. l, Tent pegging (rider on horse). m, Kabbadi (two athletes wrestling). n, Body building.

2010, Dec. 8 Litho. *Perf. 13¼*

514 A216 50b Sheet of 14, #a-n 5.00 5.00

Miniature Sheet

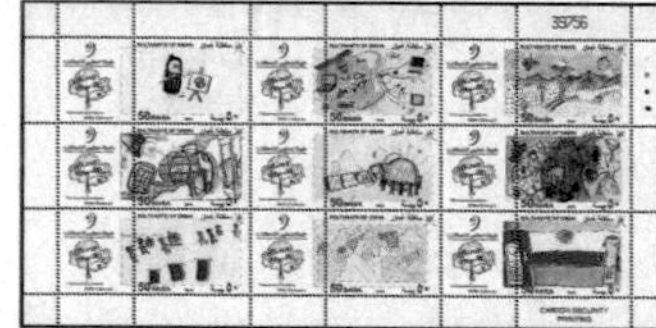

Children's Art — A217

No. 515: a, Cell phone with palette and brush painting Earth on easel. b, Satellite, satellite dish, electronic devices, scissors cutting cables. c, Car on road near buildings and mountains with satellite dishes. d, Cell phone, hand pointing at electronic options, telephone handset. e, Electronic devices, film strip, people circling Earth. f, Spider web, satellite dish, cell phones, antenna towers. g, Children and boxes with colored squares. h, Boy using cell phone. i, Flag of Oman, Sun, cell phones.

2010, Dec. 19 *Perf. 14¼x14*

515 A217 50b Sheet of 9, #a-i, + 9 labels 3.25 3.25

Sultan Qaboos University, 25th Anniv. — A218

Emblems, tower, and: 50b, Symbols of science and industry. 100b, Sultan Qaboos, horiz.

2011, Nov. 9 *Perf. 13¾x13¼*

516 A218 50b multi .25 .25

Size: 90x65mm
Imperf

517 A218 100b multi .55 .55

41st National Day — A219

Sultan Qaboos, Royal Opera House, Muscat, and scenes from various productions: 50b, 100b, 150b.

2011, Nov. 18

518-520 A219 Set of 3 1.60 1.60

Intl. Year of Chemistry A220

2011, Dec. 27 *Perf. 14¼x14*

521 A220 100b multi .55 .55

Friendship With Japan, 40th Anniv. — A221

2012, May 7 *Perf. 14x13¼*

522 A221 100b multi .70 .70

Frankincense and Incense Burner — A222

2012, June 21 Litho. *Perf. 13¼x14*

523 A222 250b multi 1.75 1.75

Salalah Tourism Festival. Portions of No. 523 have a scratch-and-sniff covering with a frankincese aroma.

Miniature Sheet

Muscat, 2012 Arab Tourism Capital — A223

No. 524: a, Old Muscat. b, Sultan Qaboos Grand Mosque. c, Matrah and port. d, Royal Opera House at night. e, Matrah Corniche with docked ships. f, Barr al Jissah Resort.

2012, July 23 Litho. *Perf. 14¼x14*

524 A223 50b Sheet of 6, #a-f, + 6 labels 2.10 2.10

Arab Postal Day A224

Litho. & Embossed

2012, Aug. 3 *Perf. 13½*

525 A224 100b multi .70 .70

Sultan Qaboos Sailing Trophy A225

Litho. & Embossed With Foil Application

2012, Nov. 3 *Perf. 14x13½*
526 A225 250b multi 1.75 1.75

42nd National Day — A226

Sultan Qaboos and various ships at Oman Drydock Company: 50b, 100b, 150b.

Perf. 13½x13¼

2012, Nov. 18 **Litho.**
527-529 A226 Set of 3 2.10 2.10

Miniature Sheets

Arabian Horses — A227

No. 530, 100b — Horse named Dorar: a, Facing right, black background. b, Facing left, outdoors. c, Head, facing right, and hindquarters, black background, vert. d, Facing left, black background. e, Standing, facing right, outdoors.
No. 531, 100b — Horse named: a, Ajlad, standing and facing right. b, Psymamon, vert. c, Ajlad, head only, vert. d, Modheeah. e, Sadeed, vert.

2012, Dec. 12 **Litho.** *Perf. 13¼*
Sheets of 5, #a-e
530-531 A227 Set of 2 7.00 7.00

Girl Guides 20th Arab Regional Conference — A231

2013, Aug. 24 **Litho.** *Perf. 14¼x14*
538 A231 100b multi .70 .70

Oman Boy Scouts 16th Intl. Youth Gathering for Cultural Exchange — A232

2013, Sept. 4 **Litho.** *Perf. 14¼x14*
539 A232 200b multi 1.40 1.40

A233

Omani Women's Day — A234

Litho. & Embossed

2013, Oct. 17 *Perf. 14*
540 A233 100b multi .70 .70
541 A234 100b multi .70 .70

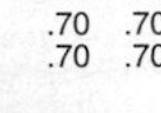

Traffic Safety Day — A235

2013, Oct. 18 **Litho.** *Perf. 14*
542 A235 50b multi .35 .35

A236

A237

Sultan Qaboos — A238

2013, Nov. 18 **Litho.** *Perf. 13½x13*
543 A236 200b multi 1.40 1.40
544 A237 200b multi 1.40 1.40
545 A238 200b multi 1.40 1.40
Nos. 543-545 (3) 4.20 4.20

43rd National Day. Nos. 543-545 each were printed in sheets of 4.

Sultan's Armed Forces Museum, 25th Anniv. A239

Designs: 50b, Museum exterior. 100b, Sultan Qaboos in museum.

2013, Dec. 11 **Litho.** *Perf. 13½*
546-547 A239 Set of 2 1.10 1.10

Salalah Festival A241

Emblem and: 100b, People, raised hands, flag.
150b, Building, vert.

2014, July 30 **Litho.** *Perf. 13¼*
551 A241 100b multi .70 .70

Souvenir Sheet
Perf. 13½x13
552 A241 150b multi 1.10 1.10

No. 552 contains one 30x40mm stamp.

Muscat Festival A242

2014, Aug. 14 **Litho.** *Perf. 13x13½*
553 A242 100b multi .70 .70

Souvenir Sheet

Tour of Oman Bicycle Race — A243

2014, Aug. 14 **Litho.** *Perf. 13x13½*
554 A243 250b multi 1.75 1.75

Architectural Details From Castles and Forts — A244

No. 555: a, Jabreen Castle. b, Nizwa Fort. c, Bahla Fort. d, Al Hazm Castle.
No. 556, 250b, Like #555a. No. 557, 250b, Like #555b. No. 558, 250b, Like #555c. No. 559, 250b, Like #555d.

2014, Sept. 29 **Litho.** *Perf. 13½x13*
555 A244 150b Sheet of 4, #a-d 4.25 4.25

Souvenir Sheets
556-559 A244 Set of 4 7.00 7.00

44th National Day — A245

No. 560 — Sultan Qaboos with background color of: a, Purple brown. b, Blue. c, Green. d, Purple.
200b, Sultan Qaboos, diff.

2014, Nov. 18 **Litho.** *Perf. 13½x13*
560 A245 100b Sheet of 4, #a-d 2.75 2.75

Souvenir Sheet
Litho. With Foil Application
Imperf
561 A245 200b gold & multi 1.40 1.40

SEMI-POSTAL STAMP

UNICEF Emblem, Girl with Book — SP1

Wmk. 314

1971, Dec. 25 **Litho.** *Perf. 14*
B1 SP1 50b + 25b multicolored 42.50 6.50

25th anniv. of UNICEF.

OFFICIAL STAMPS

Official Stamps of India 1938-43 Overprinted in Black

Perf. 13½x14

1944, Nov. 20 **Wmk. 196**

O1	O8	3p	slate	.80	*15.00*
O2	O8	½a	dk rose violet	.80	*15.00*
O3	O8	9p	green	.80	*15.00*
O4	O8	1a	carmine rose	.80	*15.00*
O5	O8	1½a	dull purple	.80	*15.00*
O6	O8	2a	scarlet	.80	*15.00*
O7	O8	2½a	purple	5.50	*15.00*
O8	O8	4a	dark brown	2.00	*15.00*
O9	O8	8a	blue violet	3.50	*17.50*
O10	A82	1r	brown & slate	6.00	*27.50*
			Nos. O1-O10 (10)	21.80	*165.00*

Al Busaid Dynasty, 200th anniv. On Nos. O1-O9 the overprint is smaller — 13x6mm.
Used values for Nos. O1-O10 are for stamps canceled with contemporaneous postmarks of the Indian postal administration. Examples

with the later British post office cancellations are worth much less.

ORANGE RIVER COLONY

'är-inj 'ri-vər 'kä-lə-nē

(Orange Free State)

LOCATION — South Africa, north of the Cape of Good Hope between the Orange and Vaal Rivers
GOVT. — A former British Crown Colony
AREA — 49,647 sq. mi.
POP. — 528,174 (1911)
CAPITAL — Bloemfontein

Orange Free State was an independent republic, 1854-1900. Orange River Colony existed from May, 1900, to June, 1910, when it united with Cape of Good Hope, Natal and the Transvaal to form the Union of South Africa.

12 Pence = 1 Shilling

Values for unused stamps are for examples with original gum as defined in the catalogue introduction. Very fine examples of Nos. 1-60c will have perforations touching the design on one or more sides due to the narrow spacing of the stamps on the plates. Stamps with perfs clear of the design on all four sides are scarce and will command higher prices.

Een = 1
Twee = 2
Drie = 3
Vier = 4

Issues of the Republic

Orange Tree — A1

1868-1900 Unwmk. Typo. *Perf. 14*

1 A1 ½p red brown ('83) 7.50 .75
2 A1 ½p orange ('97) 3.00 .60
a. ½p yellow ('97) 3.00 .40
3 A1 1p red brown 22.50 .50
a. 1p pale brown 32.50 2.50
b. 1p deep brown 32.50 .60
4 A1 1p violet ('94) 5.00 .35
5 A1 2p violet ('83) 20.00 1.50
a. 2p pale mauve ('83-'84) 23.00 .50
6 A1 3p ultra ('83) 8.25 2.25
7 A1 4p ultra ('78) 5.75 4.50
a. 4p pale blue ('78) 26.00 5.25
8 A1 6p car rose ('90) 30.00 13.00
a. 6p rose ('71) 37.50 8.00
b. 6p pale rose ('68) 72.50 8.75
c. 6p bright carmine ('94) 18.50 2.25
9 A1 6p ultramarine ('00) 80.00
10 A1 1sh orange 65.00 1.75
a. 1sh orange buff *110.00 7.25*
11 A1 1sh brown ('97) 32.50 1.75
12 A1 5sh green ('78) 14.00 *20.00*
Nos. 1-8,10-12 (11) 213.50 46.95

No. 8b was not placed in use without surcharge.

For surcharges see #13-53, 44j-53c, 57-60.

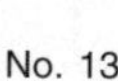
No. 13

No. 8a Surcharged in Four Different Types

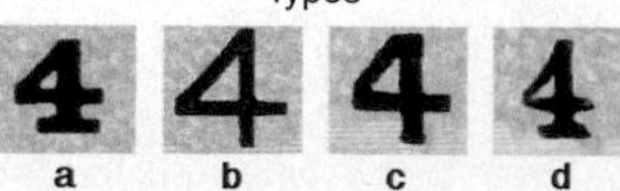

1877

13 (a) 4p on 6p rose 450.00 65.00
a. Inverted surcharge — 600.00
b. Double surcharge, one inverted ("a" + "c" inverted) *4,250.*
c. Double surcharge, one inverted ("a" inverted + "c" *6,000.*
14 (b) 4p on 6p rose 1,450. 225.00
a. Inverted surcharge — 1,250.
b. Double surcharge, one inverted ("b" and "d") —
15 (c) 4p on 6p rose 220.00 42.50
a. Inverted surcharge — 400.00
16 (d) 4p on 6p rose 325.00 50.00
a. Inverted surcharge *1,500.* 500.00
b. Double surcharge, one inverted ("d" and "c" inverted) — *4,250.*
c. Double surcharge, one inverted ("d" inverted and "c") — *6,500.*

No. 17

No. 12 Surcharged with Bar and

1d. f 1d. g 1d. h
1d. i 1d. k 1d. l

1881

First Printing

17 (f) 1p on 5sh green 120.00 32.50

Second Printing

18 (g) 1p on 5sh green 65.00 32.50
a. Inverted surcharge — *1,250.*
b. Double surcharge *1,450.*
19 (h) 1p on 5sh green 300.00 95.00
a. Inverted surcharge — *1,450.*
b. Double surcharge — *1,650.*
20 (i) 1p on 5sh green 100.00 32.50
a. Double surcharge — *1,325.*
b. Inverted surcharge *2,000. 1,000.*
21 (k) 1p on 5sh green 600.00 275.00
a. Inverted surcharge — *2,500.*
b. Double surcharge *2,500.*

Third Printing

21C (l) 1p on 5sh green 95.00 32.50
d. Inverted surcharge — *875.00*
e. Double surcharge *900.00*
Nos. 17-21C (6) 1,280. 500.00

No. 12 Surcharged

1882

22 A1 ½p on 5sh green 25.00 5.50
a. Double surcharge 550.00 400.00
b. Inverted surcharge *1,500. 1,000.*

No. 7 Surcharged with Thin Line and

m

n

o

p

 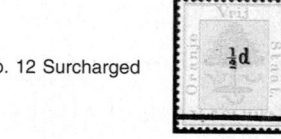
q

1882

23 (m) 3p on 4p ultra 100.00 35.00
a. Double surcharge 1,400.
24 (n) 3p on 4p ultra 100.00 20.00
a. Double surcharge 1,400.
25 (o) 3p on 4p ultra 55.00 25.00
a. Double surcharge 1,400.
26 (p) 3p on 4p ultra 275.00 80.00
a. Double surcharge 3,500.
27 (q) 3p on 4p ultra 100.00 24.00
a. Double surcharge 1,400.
Nos. 23-27 (5) 630.00 184.00

No. 6 Surcharged

1888

28 A1 2p on 3p ultra 60.00 2.25
a. Wide "2" at top 77.50 10.00
b. As No. 28, invtd. surch. 350.00
c. As No. 28a, invtd. surch. 825.00
d. Curved base on "2" *1,450. 650.00*

Nos. 6 and 7 Surcharged

r

s

t

1890-91

29 (r) 1p on 3p ultra ('91) 9.50 1.00
a. Double surcharge 100.00 77.50
b. "1" and "d" wide apart 170.00 135.00
30 (r) 1p on 4p ultra 45.00 12.50
a. Double surcharge 170.00 135.00
b. Triple surcharge *3,250.*
31 (s) 1p on 3p ultra ('91) 25.00 3.00
a. Double surcharge 325.00 300.00
32 (s) 1p on 4p ultra 95.00 60.00
a. Double surcharge 475.00 375.00
33 (t) 1p on 4p ultra *2,500. 675.00*

No. 6 Surcharged

1892

34 A1 2½p on 3p ultra 21.00 .80
a. Without period 92.50 55.00

No. 6 Surcharged

v

w

x

y

z

1896

35 (v) ½p on 3p ultra 8.50 12.00
a. Double surcharge "v" and "y" 15.50 15.50
36 (w) ½p on 3p ultra 14.50 3.00
a. Double surcharge "w" and "y" 15.00 11.00
37 (x) ½p on 3p ultra 14.50 2.50
38 (y) ½p on 3p ultra 9.00 5.50
a. Double surcharge 14.50 11.00
b. Triple surcharge 77.50 77.50
39 (z) ½p on 3p ultra 14.50 2.50

Surcharged as "v" but "1" with Straight Serif

40 A1 ½p on 3p ultra 15.50 *16.50*
a. Double surcharge, one type "y" 75.00 75.00

Surcharged as "z" but "1" with Straight Serif

41 A1 ½p on 3p ultra 15.50 15.50
a. Double surcharge, one type "y" 75.00 75.00
Nos. 35-41 (7) 92.00 57.50

No. 6 Surcharged

1896

42 A1 ½p on 3p ultra 1.10 .65
a. No period after "Penny" 22.50 *35.00*
b. "Peuny" 22.50 *35.00*
c. Inverted surcharge 65.00 *72.50*
d. Double surch., one inverted 200.00 *225.00*
e. Without bar 10.00
f. With additional surcharge as on Nos. 35-41 37.50
g. As "a", inverted surcharge 2,250.
h. As "b", inverted surcharge 1,750.

No. 6 Surcharged

1897

43 A1 2½p on 3p ultra 10.50 .90
a. Roman "I" instead of "1" in "½" 185.00 100.00

Issued under British Occupation

Nos. 2-8, 8a, 10-12 Surcharged or Overprinted

Periods in "V.R.I." Level with Bottoms of Letters

1900, Mar.-Apr. Unwmk. *Perf. 14*

44 A1 ½p on ½p org 5.00 *6.50*
a. No period after "V" 25.00 *35.00*
b. No period after "I" 175.00 175.00
c. "I" and period after "R" omitted 300.00 275.00
f. "½" omitted *210.00 210.00*
g. Small "½" 65.00 65.00
h. Double surcharge 200.00
i. As "g," double surcharge 575.00
45 A1 1p on 1p violet 3.00 1.60
a. No period after "V" 20.00 18.50
b. "I" and period after "R" omitted 300.00 300.00
d. "1" of "1d" omitted 225.00 225.00
e. "d" omitted 425.00 425.00
f. "1d" omitted, "V.R.I." at top 475.00
45O A1 1p on 1p brown *675.00 450.00*
y. No period after "V" *4,000.*
46 A1 2p on 2p violet 4.75 2.50
a. No period after "V" 20.00 24.00
b. No period after "R" 360.00 360.00
c. No period after "I" 360.00 360.00
47 A1 '2½' on 3p ultra 21.00 22.50
a. No period after "V" 105.00 105.00
b. Roman "I" in "½" 275.00 275.00
48 A1 3p on 3p ultra 3.25 4.75
a. No period after "V" 25.00 30.00
b. Dbl. surch. one diagonal 600.00
c. Pair, one with surcharge omitted 725.00
j. "3d" omitted 275.00 275.00
k. "V.R.I." omitted 275.00 275.00
49 A1 4p on 4p ultra 11.00 *18.50*
a. No period after "V" 72.50 *82.50*
50 A1 6p on 6p car rose 50.00 45.00
a. No period after "V" 275.00 300.00
b. "6" omitted 340.00 325.00
51 A1 6p on 6p ultra 14.50 6.50
a. No period after "V" 55.00 55.00
c. "6" omitted 95.00 *100.00*
h. "V.R.I." omitted 550.00 425.00
52 A1 1sh on 1sh brown 8.00 3.00
a. No period after "V" 55.00 35.00
c. "1" of "1s" omitted 165.00 155.00
j. "1s" omitted 225.00 220.00
k. "V.R.I." omitted 225.00 220.00

No.	Type	Description	Unused	Used
52G	A1	1sh on 1sh org	*4,100.*	*2,750.*
53	A1	5sh on 5sh green	32.50	60.00
a.		No period after "V"	300.00	*360.00*
b.		"5" omitted	1,100.	1,100.

#47, 47c overprinted "V.R.I." on #43.

No. 45f ("1d" omitted) with "V.R.I." at bottom is a shift which sells for a fifth of the value of the listed item. Varieties such as "V.R.I." omitted, denomination omitted and pair, one without surcharge are also the result of shifts.

For surcharges see Nos. 57, 60.

Nos. 2, 4-12 Surcharged or Overprinted

Periods in "V.R.I." Raised Above Bottoms of Letters

1900-01

No.	Type	Description	Unused	Used
44j	A1	½p on ½p orange	.35	.25
k.		Mixed periods	3.25	2.25
l.		Pair, one with level periods	15.50	*20.00*
m.		No period after "V"	4.00	*4.25*
n.		No period after "I"	42.50	42.50
o.		"V" omitted	675.00	
p.		Small "½"	20.00	*22.50*
q.		"1" for "I" in "V.R.I."	10.00	
r.		Thick "V"	6.00	4.00
45i	A1	1p on 1p violet	.35	.25
j.		Mixed periods	2.00	*2.50*
k.		Pair, one with level periods	25.00	*25.00*
l.		No period after "V"	6.00	*7.00*
m.		No period after "R"	19.00	19.00
n.		No period after "I"	19.00	19.00
p.		Double surcharge	120.00	120.00
q.		Inverted surcharge	425.00	
s.		Small "1" in "1d"	120.00	120.00
t.		"1" for "I" in "V.R.I."	13.00	
u.		Thick "V"	7.50	.40
v.		As "u," invtd. "1" for "I" in "V.R.I."	24.00	24.00
w.		As "u," double surcharge	375.00	360.00
z.		As "u," no period after "R"	50.00	*55.00*
za.		Pair, one without surchage	275.00	
zb.		Stamp double impression, one inverted	2,750.	
46e	A1	2p on 2p violet	2.25	.35
f.		Mixed periods	6.00	5.25
g.		Pair, one with level periods	10.00	*10.50*
h.		Inverted surcharge	360.00	360.00
i.		Thick "V"	16.50	15.50
j.		As "i," invtd. "1" for "I" in "V.R.I."	32.50	*35.00*
47c	A1	'2½' on 3p ultra	250.00	250.00
d.		Thick "V"	4,250.	
f.		As "d," Roman "I" on "½"	—	
48d	A1	3p on 3p ultra	1.60	.35
e.		Mixed periods	9.50	9.50
f.		Pair, one with level periods	25.00	*25.00*
g.		Double surcharge	440.00	
h.		Thick "V"	7.50	*17.50*
i.		As "h," invtd. "1" for "I" in "V.R.I."	72.50	*85.00*
l.		Double surcharge, one diagonal	450.00	
m.		As "l", thick "V"	*600.00*	
n.		As "l", mixed periods	*7,500.*	
o.		As "n", thick "V"	—	
49b	A1	4p on 4p ultra	3.25	*3.75*
c.		Mixed periods	11.00	*16.00*
d.		Pair, one with level periods	24.00	*35.00*
50c	A1	6p on 6p car rose	45.00	*55.00*
d.		Mixed periods	160.00	*175.00*
e.		Pair, one with level periods	300.00	*350.00*
f.		Thick "V"	*500.00*	*525.00*
51d	A1	6p on 6p ultra	1.10	.45
e.		Mixed periods	10.50	*11.00*
f.		Pair, one with level periods	25.00	*30.00*
g.		Thick "V"	25.00	35.00
i.		"6d" omitted	500.00	
52e	A1	1sh on 1sh brown	10.00	.50
f.		Mixed periods	27.50	25.00
h.		Pair, one with level periods	50.00	*55.00*
i.		Thick "V"	32.50	11.00
52j	A1	1sh on 1sh orange	*1,500.*	*1,500.*
53c	A1	5sh on 5sh green	10.50	*15.00*
d.		Mixed periods	400.00	400.00
e.		Pair, one with level periods	*1,600.*	
f.		"5" with short flag	65.00	*77.50*
g.		Thick "V"	72.50	*60.00*

Stamps with mixed periods have one or two periods level with the bottoms of letters. One stamp in each pane had all periods level. Later settings had several stamps with thick "V." Forgeries of the scarcer varieties exist.

"V.R.I." stands for Victoria Regina Imperatrix. On No. 59, "E.R.I." stands for Edward Rex Imperator.

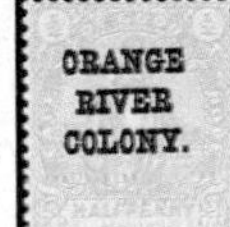

Cape of Good Hope Stamps of 1893-98 Overprinted

1900				**Wmk. 16**
54	A15	½p green	.65	.25
a.		No period after "COLONY"	12.00	*25.00*
b.		Double overprint	900.00	775.00
55	A13	2½p ultramarine	3.50	1.00
a.		No period after "COLONY"	82.50	82.50

Overprinted as in 1900

1902, May

No.	Type	Description	Unused	Used
56	A15	1p carmine rose	2.25	.25
a.		No period after "COLONY"	25.00	*30.00*

Nos. 51d, 53c, Surcharged and No. 8b Surcharged like No. 51 but Reading "E.R.I."

Carmine or Vermilion and Black Surcharges

1902				**Unwmk.**
57	A1	4p on 6p on 6p ultra	1.60	2.25
a.		Thick "V"	2.75	*8.25*
b.		As "a," invtd. "1" instead of "I"	7.25	*18.50*
c.		No period after "R"	42.50	*55.00*

Black Surcharge

No.	Type	Description	Unused	Used
59	A1	6p on 6p ultra	6.00	*19.00*
a.		Double surcharge, one invtd.	—	—

Orange Surcharge

No.	Type	Description	Unused	Used
60	A1	1sh on 5sh on 5sh grn	10.50	*25.00*
a.		Thick "V"	17.50	*55.00*
b.		"5" with short flag	80.00	*95.00*
c.		Double surcharge	1,100.	
		Nos. 57-60 (3)	18.10	*46.25*

"E.R.I." stands for Edward Rex Imperator.

King Edward VII — A8

1903-04		**Wmk. 2**		**Typo.**
61	A8	½p yellow green	10.00	2.50
62	A8	1p carmine	8.50	.25
63	A8	2p chocolate	10.00	1.00
64	A8	2½p ultra	6.00	1.25
65	A8	3p violet	10.50	1.25
66	A8	4p olive grn & car	42.50	5.50
67	A8	6p violet & car	9.25	1.25
68	A8	1sh bister & car	50.00	3.00
69	A8	5sh red brn & bl ('04)	160.00	30.00
		Nos. 61-69 (9)	306.75	46.00

Some of the above stamps are found with the overprint "C. S. A. R." for use by the Central South African Railway.

The "IOSTAGE" variety on the 4p is the result of filled in type.

Issue dates: 1p, Feb. 3. ½p, 2p, 2½p, 3p, 4p, 6p, 1sh, July 6. 5sh, Oct. 31.

1907-08				**Wmk. 3**
70	A8	½p yellow green	16.50	1.10
71	A8	1p carmine	10.50	.35
72	A8	4p olive grn & car	5.00	5.25
73	A8	1sh bister & car	85.00	25.00
		Nos. 70-73 (4)	117.00	31.70

The "IOSTAGE" variety on the 4p is the result of filled-in type.

Stamps of Orange River Colony were replaced by those of Union of South Africa.

MILITARY STAMP

M1

1899, Oct. 15		**Unwmk.**		***Perf. 12***
M1	M1	black, *bister yellow*	50.00	60.00

No. M1 was provided to members of the Orange Free State army on active service during the Second Boer War. Soldiers' mail carried free was required to bear either No. M1 or be signed by the sender's unit commander. The stamps were used extensively from Oct. 1899 until the fall of Kroonstad in May 1900.

No. M1 was typeset and printed by Curling & Co., Bloemfontein, in sheets of 20 (5x4), with each row of five containing slightly different types.

Forgeries exist. The most common counterfeits either have 17 pearls, rather than 16, in the top and bottom frames, or omit the periods after "BRIEF" and "FRANKO."

PAKISTAN

'pa-ki-,stan

LOCATION — In southern, central Asia
GOVT. — Republic
AREA — 307,293 sq. mi.
POP. — 130,579,571 (1998)
CAPITAL — Islamabad

Pakistan was formed August 14, 1947, when India was divided into the Dominions of the Union of India and Pakistan, with some princely states remaining independent. Pakistan became a republic on March 23, 1956.

Pakistan had two areas made up of all or part of several predominantly Moslem provinces in the northwest and northeast corners of pre-1947 India. West Pakistan consists of the entire provinces of Baluchistan, Sind (Scinde) and "Northwest Frontier," and 15 districts of the Punjab. East Pakistan, consisting of the Sylhet district in Assam and 14 districts in Bengal Province, became independent as Bangladesh in December 1971.

The state of Las Bela was incorporated into Pakistan.

12 Pies = 1 Anna
16 Annas = 1 Rupee
100 Paisa = 1 Rupee (1961)

Catalogue values for all unused stamps in this country are for Never Hinged items.

Watermarks

Wmk. 274

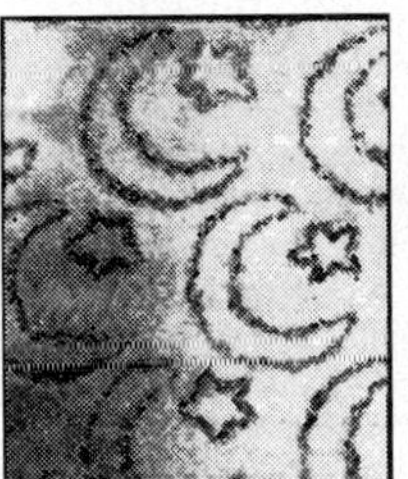

Wmk. 351 — Crescent and Star Multiple

Stamps of India, 1937-43, Overprinted in Black

Nos. 1-12

Nos. 13-19

Perf. 13½x14

1947, Oct. 1				**Wmk. 196**
1	A83	3p slate	.25	.25
2	A83	½a rose violet	.25	.25
3	A83	9p lt green	.25	.25
4	A83	1a car rose	.25	.25
4A	A84	1a3p bister ('49)	4.75	*5.75*
5	A84	1½a dk purple	.25	.25
6	A84	2a scarlet	.25	.40
7	A84	3a violet	.25	.40
8	A84	3½a ultra	1.25	*3.00*
9	A85	4a chocolate	.55	.30
10	A85	6a peacock blue	2.10	1.25
11	A85	8a blue violet	.65	*.85*
12	A85	12a carmine lake	2.10	.40
13	A81	14a rose violet	5.75	3.50
14	A82	1r brn & slate	3.50	1.50
a.		Inverted overprint	310.00	
b.		Pair, one without ovpt.	900.00	
15	A82	2r dk brn & dk vio	6.50	3.25
16	A82	5r dp ultra & dk grn	8.00	5.00
17	A82	10r rose car & dk vio	10.00	6.50
18	A82	15r dk grn & dk brn	90.00	*110.00*
19	A82	25r dk vio & bl vio	70.00	70.00
		Nos. 1-19 (20)	206.90	213.35
		Set, hinged	135.00	

Provisional use of stamps of India with handstamped or printed "PAKISTAN" was authorized in 1947-49. Nos. 4A, 14a 14b exist only as provisional issues.

Used values are for postal cancels. Telegraph cancels (concentric circles) sell for much less.

Constituent Assembly Building, Karachi A1

Crescent and Urdu Inscription — A2

Designs: 2½a, Karachi Airport entrance. 3a, Lahore Fort gateway.

Unwmk.

1948, July 9		**Engr.**		***Perf. 14***
20	A1	1½a bright ultra	1.25	*2.00*
21	A1	2½a green	1.25	.25
22	A1	3a chocolate	1.25	.30

Perf. 12

No.	Type	Description	Unused	Used
23	A2	1r red	1.25	.85
a.		Perf. 14	6.00	*10.00*
		Nos. 20-23 (4)	5.00	3.40

Pakistan's independence, Aug. 15, 1947.

Examples of No. 23a used on cover are unknown. Used examples of No. 23a are cto.

Scales, Star and Crescent A3

Star and Crescent A4

Karachi Airport Building A5

Karachi Port Authority Building — A6

Khyber Pass — A7

2½a, 3½a, 4a, Ghulan Muhammed Dam, Indus River, Sind. 1r, 2r, 5r, Salimullah Hostel.

Perf. 12½, 14 (3a, 10a), 14x13½ (2½a, 3½a, 6a, 12a)

1948-57 **Unwmk.**

24 A3 3p org red, perf. 12½ .25 .25
a. Perf. 13½ ('54) 2.00 1.00
25 A3 6p pur, perf. 12½ 1.25 .25
a. Perf. 13½ ('54) 4.00 3.50
26 A3 9p dk grn, perf. 12½ .55 .25
a. Perf. 13½ ('54) 3.50 1.75
27 A4 1a dark blue .25 .50
28 A4 1½a gray green .25 .25
29 A4 2a orange red 4.50 .70
30 A6 2½a green 6.50 *5.00*
31 A5 3a olive green 8.00 1.00
32 A6 3½a violet blue 6.50 *4.00*
33 A6 4a chocolate 1.25 .25
34 A6 6a deep blue 2.00 .55
35 A6 8a black 2.00 *1.25*
36 A5 10a red 8.00 *8.00*
37 A6 12a red 8.00 1.25

Perf. 14

38 A5 1r ultra 19.00 .25
a. Perf. 13½ ('54) 25.00 7.00
39 A5 2r dark brown 20.00 .80
a. Perf. 13½ ('54) 30.00 3.00

Perf. 13½

40 A5 5r car ('54) 13.00 .40
a. Perf. 13½x14 17.00 2.25

Perf. 13

41 A7 10r rose lilac ('51) 19.00 2.50
a. Perf. 14 14.00 *26.00*
b. Perf. 12 110.00 8.50
42 A7 15r blue green ('57) 20.00 16.00
a. Perf. 14 20.00 *65.00*
b. Perf. 12 32.50 20.00

Perf. 14

43 A7 25r purple 55.00 *67.50*
a. Perf. 13 ('54) 40.00 27.50
b. Perf. 12 32.50 *37.50*
Nos. 24-43 (20) 195.30 110.95
Set, hinged 100.00

Many compound perforations exist.

See No. 259, types A9-A11. For surcharges and overprints see Nos. 124, O14-O26, O35-O37, O41-O43A, O52, O63, O68.

Imperfs of Nos. 24-43 are from proof sheets improperly removed from the printer's archives.

"Quaid-i-Azam" (Great Leader), "Mohammed Ali Jinnah" — A8

1949, Sept. 11 **Engr.** ***Perf. 13½x14***

44 A8 1½a brown 2.25 1.75
45 A8 3a dark green 2.25 1.50
46 A8 10a blk *(English inscriptions)* 7.00 *8.00*
Nos. 44-46 (3) 11.50 11.25

1st anniv. of the death of Mohammed Ali Jinnah (1876-1948), Moslem lawyer, president of All-India Moslem League and first Governor General of Pakistan.

Re-engraved (Crescents Reversed)

A9

A10

A11

Perf. 12½, 13½x14 (3a, 10a), 14x13½ (6a, 12a)

1949-53

47 A10 1a dk blue ('50) 4.00 .85
a. Perf. 13 ('52) 7.00 .25
48 A10 1½a gray green 7.00 3.00
a. Perf. 13 ('53) 3.50 .25
49 A10 2a orange red 4.50 .25
a. Perf. 13 ('53) 4.50 .25
50 A9 3a olive green 15.00 1.00
51 A11 6a deep blue ('50) 20.00 2.50
52 A11 8a black ('50) 20.00 2.50
53 A9 10a red 25.00 3.75
54 A11 12a red ('50) 26.00 .60
Nos. 47-54 (8) 121.50 14.45

For overprints see #O27-O31, O38-O40.

Vase and Plate — A12

Star and Crescent, Plane and Hour Glass — A13

Moslem Leaf Pattern — A14

Arch and Lamp of Learning A15

1951, Aug. 14 **Engr.** ***Perf. 13***

55 A12 2½a dark red 1.90 1.25
56 A13 3a dk rose lake 1.00 .25
57 A12 3½a dp ultra (Urdu "⅓3") 1.25 *8.00*
57A A12 3½a dp ultra (Urdu "3½") ('56) 4.50 6.00
58 A14 4a deep green 1.50 .25
59 A14 6a red orange 1.50 .25
60 A15 8a brown 4.50 .25
61 A15 10a purple 2.25 1.25
62 A13 12a dk slate blue 2.00 .25
Nos. 55-62 (9) 20.40 17.75

Fourth anniversary of independence.

On No. 57, the characters of the Urdu denomination at right appears as "⅓3." On the reengraved No. 57A, they read "3½."

Issue date: Dec. 1956.

See Nos. 88, O32-O34.

For surcharges see Nos. 255, 257.

Scinde District Stamp and Camel Train A16

1952, Aug. 14

63 A16 3a olive green, *citron* 1.00 .85
64 A16 12a dark brown, *salmon* 1.75 .25

5th anniv. of Pakistan's Independence and the cent. of the 1st postage stamps in the Indo-Pakistan sub-continent.

Peak K-2, Karakoram Mountains A17

1954, Dec. 25

65 A17 2a violet .50 .30

Conquest of K-2, world's 2nd highest mountain peak, in July 1954.

Kaghan Valley — A18

Gilgit Mountains A19

Tea Garden, East Pakistan A20

Designs: 1a, Badshahi Mosque, Lahore. 1½a, Emperor Jahangir's Mausoleum, Lahore. 1r, Cotton field. 2r, River craft and jute field.

1954, Aug. 14 **Engr.**

66 A18 6p rose violet .25 .25
67 A19 9p blue *4.50* 1.50
68 A19 1a carmine rose .25 .25
69 A18 1½a red .25 .25
70 A20 14a dark green 5.00 .25
71 A20 1r yellow green 11.00 .25
72 A20 2r orange 3.00 .25
Nos. 66-72 (7) 24.25 3.00

Seventh anniversary of independence.

Nos. 66, 69 exist in booklet panes of 4 torn from sheets. Value of booklet, $9.

For overprints & surcharges see #77, 101, 123, 126, O44-O50, O53-O56, O60-O62, O67, O69-O71.

Karnaphuli Paper Mill, East Pakistan (Urdu "½2") — A21

6a, Textile mill. 8a, Jute mill. 12a, Sui gas plant.

1955, Aug. 14 **Unwmk.** ***Perf. 13***

73 A21 2½a dk car (Urdu "½2") .50 *1.50*
73A A21 2½a dk car (Urdu "2½") ('56) 1.00 *1.50*
74 A21 6a dark blue 1.50 .25
75 A21 8a violet 4.00 .25
76 A21 12a car lake & org 4.00 .25
Nos. 73-76 (5) 11.00 3.75

Eighth anniversary of independence.

On No. 73, the characters of the Urdu denomination at right appear as "½2." On the reengraved No. 73A, they read "2½."

Issue date: Dec. 1956.

See No. 87. For overprints and surcharges see Nos. 78, 102-103, 256, O51, O58-O59.

Map of West Pakistan — A22

1955, Dec. 7 **Unwmk.** ***Perf. 13½x13***

79 A22 1½a dark green .65 *.75*
80 A22 2a dark brown .60 .25
81 A22 12a deep carmine 1.00 .50
Nos. 79-81 (3) 2.25 1.50

West Pakistan unification, Nov. 14, 1955.

Nos. 79-81 from the bottom (eighth) row of the sheet are 1mm taller. Value, $4 each.

National Assembly A23

1956, Mar. 23 **Litho.** ***Perf. 13x12½***

82 A23 2a green .75 .25

Proclamation of the Republic of Pakistan, Mar. 23, 1956.

Crescent and Star — A24

1956, Aug. 14 **Engr.** ***Perf. 13***

83 A24 2a red .90 .25

Ninth anniversary of independence.

For surcharges and overprints see Nos. 127, O57, O72-O73.

Map of East Pakistan — A25

1956, Oct. 15 ***Perf. 13½x13***

84 A25 1½a dark green .40 *1.50*
85 A25 2a dark brown .50 .25
86 A25 12a deep red .40 *1.25*
Nos. 84-86 (3) 1.30 3.00

1st Session at Dacca (East Pakistan) of the National Assembly of Pakistan.

Nos. 84-86 from the bottom (eighth) row of the sheet are 1mm taller. Value, $4 each.

Redrawn Types of 1951, 1955 and

Orange Tree — A26

Perf. 13x13½, 13½x13

1957, Mar. 23 **Engr.**

87 A21 2½a dark carmine .25 .25
88 A12 3½a bright blue .35 .25
89 A26 10r dk green & orange .90 .40
Nos. 87-89 (3) 1.50 .90

Nos. 87-89 inscribed "Pakistan" in English, Urdu and Bengali. Denomination in English only.

Islamic Republic of Pakistan, 1st anniv.

See Nos. 95, 258, 475A. For surcharge and overprint see Nos. 159, O64.

Flag and Broken Chain — A27

1957, May 10 Litho. *Perf. 13*

90 A27 1½a green .50 .25
91 A27 12a blue 1.25 .50

Cent. of the struggle for Independence (Indian Mutiny).

Examples of Nos. 90-91 exist that are 1mm taller than other stamps from the sheet. Value, $4 each.

Industrial Plants and Roses as Symbols of Progress A28

1957, Aug. 14 Unwmk. *Perf. 13½*

92 A28 1½a light ultra .25 .25
93 A28 4a orange vermilion .50 *1.50*
94 A28 12a red lilac .50 .45
Nos. 92-94 (3) 1.25 2.20

Tenth anniversary of independence.

Type of 1957

Design: 15r, Coconut Tree.

1958, Mar. 23 Engr. *Perf. 13½x13*

95 A26 15r rose lilac & red 2.50 1.50

Issued to commemorate the second anniversary of the Islamic Republic of Pakistan.

Verse of Iqbal Poem A29

1958, Apr. 21 Photo. *Perf. 14½x14*
Black Inscriptions

96 A29 1½a citron .50 *.40*
97 A29 2a orange brown .50 .25
98 A29 14a aqua *2.50 3.00*
Nos. 96-98 (3) 3.50 *3.65*

20th anniv. of the death of Mohammad Iqbal (1877-1938), Moslem poet and philosopher.

Globe and Book — A30

1958, Dec. 10 Litho. *Perf. 13*

99 A30 1½a Prus blue .25 .25
100 A30 14a dark brown .50 *.25*

10th anniv. of the signing of the Universal Declaration of Human Rights.

Nos. 66 and 75 Overprinted: "Pakistan Boy Scout 2nd National Jamboree Chittagong Dec. 58-Jan. 59"

1958, Dec. 28 Engr. *Perf. 13*

101 A18 6p rose violet .25 .25
102 A21 8a violet .40 .25

2nd National Boy Scout Jamboree held at Chittagong, Dec. 28-Jan. 4.

No. 74 Overprinted in Red: "Revolution Day, Oct. 27, 1959."

1959, Oct. 27

103 A21 6a dark blue .80 .25

First anniversary of the 1958 Revolution.

Red Cross — A31

Engr.; Cross Typo.

1959, Nov. 19 Unwmk. *Perf. 13*

104 A31 2a green & red .30 .25
105 A31 10a dk blue & red .60 .25

Armed Forces Emblem — A32

1960, Jan. 10 Litho. *Perf. 13*

106 A32 2a blue grn, red & ultra .40 .25
107 A32 14a ultra & red .90 .25

Issued for Armed Forces Day.

Map Showing Disputed Areas A33

1960, Mar. 23 Engr. Unwmk.

108 A33 6p purple .35 .25
109 A33 2a copper red .55 .25
110 A33 8a green 1.10 .25
111 A33 1r blue 1.75 .25
Nos. 108-111 (4) 3.75 1.00

Publicizing the border dispute with India over Jammu and Kashmir, Junagarh and Manavadar.

For overprints and surcharges see Nos. 122, 125, 128, 178, O65-O66, O74-O75.

Uprooted Oak Emblem — A34

1960, Apr. 7

112 A34 2a carmine rose .25 .25
113 A34 10a green .25 *.25*

Issued to publicize World Refugee Year, July 1, 1959-June 30, 1960.

House, Field and Column (Allegory of Democratic Development) A35

1960, Oct. 27 Photo. *Perf. 13*

114 A35 2a brown, pink & grn .25 .25
a. Green & pink omitted 18.00
115 A35 14a multicolored .50 *.75*

Revolution Day, Oct. 27, 1960.

No. 114a is easily counterfeited.

Punjab Agricultural College, Lyallpur A36

Design: 8a, College shield.

1960, Oct. Engr. *Perf. 12½x14*

116 A36 2a rose red & gray blue .25 .25
117 A36 8a lilac & green .25 .30

50th anniv. of the Punjab Agricultural College, Lyallpur.

Caduceus, College Emblem — A37

1960, Nov. 16 Photo. *Perf. 13½x13*

118 A37 2a blue, yel & blk .50 .25
119 A37 14a car rose, blk & emerald 1.75 1.00

King Edward Medical College, Lahore, cent.

Map of South-East Asia and Commission Emblem — A38

1960, Dec. 5 Engr. *Perf. 13*

120 A38 14a red orange .50 *.25*

Conf. of the Commission on Asian and Far Eastern Affairs of the Intl. Chamber of Commerce, Karachi, Dec. 5-9.

"Kim's Gun" and Scout Badge A39

Perf. 12½x14

1960, Dec. 24 Unwmk.

121 A39 2a dk green, car & yel .75 .25

3rd Natl. Boy Scout Jamboree, Lahore, Dec. 24-31.

No. 110 Ovptd. in Red

1961, Feb. 12

122 A33 8a green .95 .95

10th Lahore Stamp Exhibition, Feb. 12.

New Currency

Nos. 24, 68-69, 83, 108-109 Surcharged with New Value in Paisa

1961 *Perf. 13*

123 A18 1p on 1½a red .40 .25
124 A3 2p on 3p orange red .25 .25
125 A33 3p on 6p purple .25 .25
126 A19 7p on 1a car rose .40 .25
127 A24 13p on 2a red .40 .25
128 A33 13p on 2a copper red .30 .25
Nos. 123-128 (6) 2.00 1.50

Various violet handstamped surcharges were applied to a variety of regular-issue stamps. Most of these repeat the denomination of the basic stamp and add the new value. Example: "8 Annas (50 Paisa)" on No. 75. Many errors exist from printer's waste.

For overprints see Nos. O74-O75.

Many errors exist from No. 123 onwards on stamps printed within Pakistan. These are generally printer's waste.

Khyber Pass — A40

Chota Sona Masjid Gate — A41

Design: 10p, 13p, 25p, 40p, 50p, 75p, 90p, Shalimar Gardens, Lahore.

Type I

Type II

Two types of 1p, 2p and 5p:

I — First Bengali character beside "N" lacks appendage at left side of loop.

II — This character has a downward-pointing appendage at left side of loop, correcting "sh" to read "p".

On Nos. 129, 130, 132 the corrections were made individually on the plates, and each stamp may differ slightly. On No. 131a, the corrected letter is more clearly corrected, and the added appendage comes close to, almost touching, the leg of the first Bengali character.

1961-63 Engr. *Perf. 13½x14*

129 A40 1p violet (II) 1.00 .25
a. Type I 1.50 .25
130 A40 2p rose red (II) 1.00 .25
a. Type I 1.50 .25
131 A40 3p magenta .75 .25
a. Retouched plate 5.00 5.00
132 A40 5p ultra (II) 4.50 1.00
a. Type I 3.00 .25
133 A40 7p emerald 2.00 .25
134 A40 10p brown .25 .25
135 A40 13p blue vio .25 .25
136 A40 25p dark blue ('62) 5.00 .25
137 A40 40p dull purple ('62) .25 .25
138 A40 50p dull green ('62) .25 .25
139 A40 75p dk carmine ('62) .45 .70
140 A40 90p lt olive grn ('62) .70 .70

Perf. 13½x13

141 A41 1r vermilion ('63) 1.00 .25
142 A41 1.25r purple .75 .75
143 A41 2r orange ('63) 2.00 .25
144 A41 5r green ('63) 6.00 2.25
Nos. 129-144 (16) 26.15 8.15

See #200-203. For surcharge and overprints see Nos. 184, O76-O82, O85-O93A.

Designs Redrawn

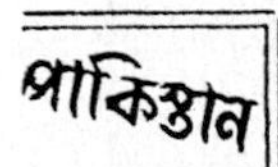

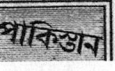

1961-62 Bengali Inscription

Redrawn Bengali Inscription

Bengali inscription redrawn with straight connecting line across top of characters. Shading of scenery differs, especially in Shalimar Gardens design where reflection is strengthened and trees at right are composed of horizontal lines instead of vertical lines and dots.

Designs as before; 15p, 20p, Shalimar Gardens.

1963-70 *Perf. 13½x14*

129b A40 1p violet .25 .25
130b A40 2p rose red ('64) 1.75 .25
131b A40 3p magenta ('70) 8.00 2.50
132b A40 5p ultra .25 .25
133a A40 7p emerald ('64) 7.00 1.50
134a A40 10p brown .25 .25
135a A40 13p blue violet .25 .25
135B A40 15p rose lilac ('64) .25 .25
135C A40 20p dull green ('70) .25 .25
136a A40 25p dark blue 7.00 .50
137a A40 40p dull purple ('64) .25 .25
138a A40 50p dull green ('64) .25 .25
139a A40 75p dark carmine ('64) 1.25 .70
140a A40 90p lt olive green ('64) 4.00 1.00
Nos. 129b-140a (14) 31.00 8.45

For overprints see #174, O76b, O77b, O78a, O79b, O80a, O81a, O82a, O83-O84A, O85a, O86a.

Warsak Dam, Kabul River
A42

1961, July 1 Engr. *Perf. 12½x13½*

150 A42 40p black & lt ultra .60 .25

Dedication of hydroelectric Warsak Project.

Symbolic Flower — A43

1961, Oct. 2 Unwmk. *Perf. 14*

151 A43 13p greenish blue .50 .25
152 A43 90p red lilac 1.00 .25

Issued for Children's Day.

Roses — A44

1961, Nov. 4 *Perf. 13½x13*

153 A44 13p deep green & ver .40 .25
154 A44 90p blue & vermilion .90 .90

Cooperative Day.

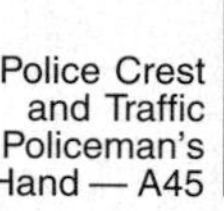
Police Crest and Traffic Policeman's Hand — A45

1961, Nov. 30 Photo. *Perf. 13x12½*

155 A45 13p dk blue, sil & blk .50 .25
156 A45 40p red, silver & blk 1.00 .25

Centenary of the police force.

"Eagle Locomotive, 1861" — A46

Design: 50pa, Diesel Engine, 1961.

1961, Dec. 31 *Perf. 13½x14*

157 A46 13p yellow, green & blk .75 .80
158 A46 50p green, blk & yellow 1.00 1.50

Centenary of Pakistan railroads.

No. 87 Surcharged in Red with New Value, Boeing 720-B Jetliner and: "FIRST JET FLIGHT KARACHI-DACCA"

1962, Feb. 6 Engr. *Perf. 13*

159 A21 13p on 2½a dk carmine 1.75 1.25

1st jet flight from Karachi to Dacca, Feb. 6, 1962.

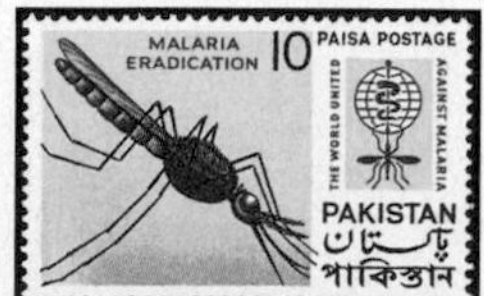

Mosquito and Malaria Eradication Emblem — A47

13p, Dagger pointing at mosquito, and emblem.

1962, Apr. 7 Photo. *Perf. 13½x14*

160 A47 10p multicolored .45 .25
161 A47 13p multicolored .45 .25

WHO drive to eradicate malaria.

Map of Pakistan and Jasmine — A48

1962, June 8 Unwmk. *Perf. 12*

162 A48 40p grn, yel grn & gray 1.00 .25

Introduction of new Pakistan Constitution.

Soccer
A49

13p, Hockey & Olympic gold medal. 25p, Squash rackets & British squash rackets championship cup. 40p, Cricket & Ayub challenge cup.

1962, Aug. 14 Engr. *Perf. 12½x13½*

163 A49 7p blue & black .25 .25
164 A49 13p green & black .60 1.50
165 A49 25p lilac & black .25 .25
166 A49 40p brown org & blk 2.00 2.25
Nos. 163-166 (4) 3.10 4.25

Marble Fruit Dish and Clay Flask — A50

13p, Sporting goods. 25p, Camel skin lamp, brass jug. 40p, Wooden powder bowl, cane basket. 50p, Inlaid box, brassware.

1962, Nov. 10 *Perf. 13½x13*

167 A50 7p dark red .25 .25
168 A50 13p dark green 1.50 1.00
169 A50 25p bright purple .25 .25
170 A50 40p yellow green .25 .25
171 A50 50p dull red .25 .25
Nos. 167-171 (5) 2.50 2.00

Pakistan Intl. Industries Fair, Oct. 12-Nov. 20, publicizing Pakistan's small industries.

Children's Needs
A51

1962, Dec. 11 Photo. *Perf. 13½x14*

172 A51 13p blue, plum & blk .35 .25
173 A51 40p multicolored .35 .25

16th anniv. of UNICEF.

No. 135a Overprinted in Red: "U.N. FORCE W. IRIAN"

1963, Feb. 15 Engr. Unwmk.

174 A40 13p blue violet .25 .60

Issued to commemorate the dispatch of Pakistani troops to West New Guinea.

Camel, Bull, Dancing Horse and Drummer
A52

1963, Mar. 13 Photo. *Perf. 12*

175 A52 13p multicolored .25 .25

National Horse and Cattle Show, 1963.

Wheat and Tractor
A53

Design: 50p, Hands and heap of rice.

1963, Mar. 21 Engr. *Perf. 12½x13½*

176 A53 13p brown orange 2.50 .25
177 A53 50p brown 4.00 .55

FAO "Freedom from Hunger" campaign.

No. 109 Surcharged with New Value and: "INTERNATIONAL/DACCA STAMP/EXHIBITION/1963"

1963, Mar. 23 *Perf. 13*

178 A33 13p on 2a copper red .50 .50

International Stamp Exhibition at Dacca.

Centenary Emblem — A54

Engr. and Typo.

1963, June 25 *Perf. 13½x12½*

179 A54 40p dark gray & red 1.50 .25

International Red Cross, cent.

Paharpur Stupa
A55

Designs: 13p, Cistern, Mohenjo-Daro, vert. 40p, Stupas, Taxila. 50pa, Stupas, Mainamati.

Perf. 12½x13½, 13½x12½

1963, Sept. 16 Engr. Unwmk.

180 A55 7p ultra .60 .25
181 A55 13p brown .60 .25
182 A55 40p carmine rose 1.10 .25
183 A55 50p dark violet 1.40 .65
Nos. 180-183 (4) 3.70 1.40

No. 131 Surcharged and Overprinted: "100 YEARS OF P.W.D. OCTOBER, 1963"

1963, Oct. 7 *Perf. 13½x14*

184 A40 13p on 3pa magenta .25 .25

Centenary of Public Works Department.

Atatürk Mausoleum, Ankara
A56

1963, Nov. 10 *Perf. 13x13½*

185 A56 50p red .65 .25

25th anniv. of the death of Kemal Atatürk, pres. of Turkey.

Globe and UNESCO Emblem
A57

1963, Dec. 10 Photo. *Perf. 13½x14*

186 A57 50p dk brn, vio blue & red .45 .25

15th anniv. of the Universal Declaration of Human Rights.

Multan Thermal Power Station
A58

1963, Dec. 25 Engr. *Perf. 12½x13½*

187 A58 13p ultra .25 .25

Issued to mark the opening of the Multan Thermal Power Station.

Type of 1961-63

Perf. 13½x13

1963-65 Engr. Wmk. 351

200 A41 1r vermilion .40 .25
201 A41 1.25r purple ('64) 2.75 .30
202 A41 2r orange 1.00 .25
203 A41 5r green ('65) 6.75 .60
Nos. 200-203 (4) 10.90 1.40

For overprints see Nos. O92-O93A.

A59

13p, Temple of Thot, Dakka, and Queen Nefertari with Goddesses Hathor and Isis. 50p, Ramses II, Abu Simbel, and View of Nile.

Perf. 13x13½

1964, Mar. 30 Unwmk.

204 A59 13p brick red & turq blue .60 .25
205 A59 50p black & rose lilac 1.20 .25

UNESCO world campaign to save historic monuments in Nubia.

Pakistan Pavilion and Unisphere
A60

1.25r, Pakistan pavilion, Unisphere, vert.

Perf. 12½x14, 14x12½

1964, Apr. 22 Engr. Unwmk.

206 A60 13p ultramarine .25 .25
207 A60 1.25r dp orange & ultra .40 .25

New York World's Fair, 1964-65.

Mausoleum of Shah Abdul Latif — A61

1964, June 25 *Perf. 13½x13*

208 A61 50p magenta & ultra 1.00 .25

Bicentenary (?) of the death of Shah Abdul Latif of Bhit (1689-1752).

Examples of No. 208 exist that are 1mm taller than other stamps from the sheet. Value, $4.

Mausoleum of Jinnah — A62

Design: 15p, Mausoleum, horiz.

1964, Sept. 11 Unwmk. *Perf. 13*
209 A62 15p green .75 .25
210 A62 50p greenish gray 1.50 .25

16th anniv. of the death of Mohammed Ali Jinnah (1876-1948), the Quaid-i-Azam (Great Leader), founder and president of Pakistan.

Bengali Alphabet on Slate and Slab with Urdu Alphabet A63

1964, Oct. 5 Engr.
211 A63 15p brown .25 .25

Issued for Universal Children's Day.

West Pakistan University of Engineering and Technology — A64

1964, Dec. 21 *Perf. 12½x14*
212 A64 15p henna brown .25 .25

1st convocation of the West Pakistan University of Engineering & Technology, Lahore, Dec. 1964.

Eyeglasses and Book — A65

Perf. 13x13½
1965, Feb. 28 Litho. Unwmk.
213 A65 15p yellow & ultra .25 .25

Issued to publicize aid for the blind.

ITU Emblem, Telegraph Pole and Transmission Tower — A66

1965, May 17 Engr. *Perf. 12½x14*
214 A66 15p deep claret 1.90 .30

Cent. of the ITU.

ICY Emblem A67

1965, June 26 Litho. *Perf. 13½*
215 A67 15p blue & black .50 .25
216 A67 50p yellow & green 1.50 .40

International Cooperation Year, 1965.

Hands Holding Book — A68

50p, Map & flags of Turkey, Iran & Pakistan.

Perf. 13½x13, 13x12½
1965, July 21 Litho. Unwmk.
Size: 46x35mm
217 A68 15p org brn, dk brn & buff .25 .25
Size: 54x30½mm
218 A68 50p multicolored 1.10 .25

1st anniv. of the signing of the Regional Cooperation for Development Pact by Turkey, Iran and Pakistan.
See Iran 1327-1328, Turkey 1648-1649.

Tanks, Army Emblem and Soldier — A69

Designs: 15p, Navy emblem, corvette No. O204 and officer. 50p, Air Force emblem, two F-104 Starfighters and pilot.

1965, Dec. 25 Litho. *Perf. 13½x13*
219 A69 7p multicolored 1.50 .25
220 A69 15p multicolored 1.50 .25
221 A69 50p multicolored 2.50 .30
Nos. 219-221 (3) 5.50 .80

Issued to honor the Pakistani armed forces.

Emblems of Pakistan Armed Forces — A70

1966, Feb. 13 Litho. *Perf. 13½x13*
222 A70 15p buff, grn & dk bl 1.00 .25

Issued for Armed Forces Day.

Atomic Reactor, Islamabad — A71

Unwmk.
1966, Apr. 30 Engr. *Perf. 13*
223 A71 15p black .25 .25

Pakistan's first atomic reactor.

Habib Bank Emblem A72

Perf. 12½x13½
1966, Aug. 25 Litho. Unwmk.
224 A72 15p brown, org & dk grn .25 .25

25th anniversary of the Habib Bank.

Boy and Girl — A73

1966, Oct. 3 Litho. *Perf. 13x13½*
225 A73 15p multicolored .25 .25

Issued for Children's Day.

UNESCO Emblem A74

1966, Nov. 24 Unwmk. *Perf. 14*
226 A74 15p multicolored 1.50 .30

20th anniv. of UNESCO.

Secretariat Buildings, Islamabad, Flag and Pres. Mohammed Ayub Khan — A75

1966, Nov. 29 Litho. *Perf. 13*
227 A75 15p multicolored .30 .25
228 A75 50p multicolored .60 .25

Publicizing the new capital, Islamabad.

Avicenna — A76

1966, Dec. 3 *Perf. 13½*
229 A76 15p sal pink & slate grn .30 .25

Issued to publicize the Health Institute.

Mohammed Ali Jinnah — A77

Design: 50p, Different frame.

Lithographed and Engraved
1966, Dec. 25 Unwmk. *Perf. 13*
230 A77 15p orange, blk & bl .25 .25
231 A77 50p lilac, blk & vio bl .35 .25

90th anniv. of the birth of Mohammed Ali Jinnah (1876-1948), 1st Governor General of Pakistan.

ITY Emblem — A78

1967, Jan. 1 Litho.
232 A78 15p bis brn, blue & blk .25 .25

International Tourist Year, 1967.

Red Crescent Emblem — A79

1967, Jan. 10 Litho. *Perf. 13½*
233 A79 15p brn, brn org & red .25 .25

Tuberculosis eradication campaign.

Scout Sign and Emblem A80

Perf. 12½x13½
1967, Jan. 29 Photo.
234 A80 15p dp plum & brn org .25 .25

4th National Pakistan Jamboree.
"Faisa" is a plate flaw, not an error. Value, unused or used, $5.

Justice Holding Scales — A81

Unwmk.
1967, Feb. 17 Litho. *Perf. 13*
235 A81 15p multicolored .25 .25

Centenary of High Court of West Pakistan.

Mohammad Iqbal — A82

1967, Apr. 21 Litho. *Perf. 13*
236 A82 15p red & brown .25 .25
237 A82 1r dk green & brn .60 .25

90th anniv. of the birth of Mohammad Iqbal (1877-1938), poet and philosopher.

Flag of Valor — A83

1967, May 15 Litho. *Perf. 13*
238 A83 15p multicolored .25 .25

Flag of Valor awarded to the cities of Lahore, Sialkot and Sargodha.

Star and "20" — A84

1967, Aug. 14 Photo. Unwmk.
239 A84 15p red & slate green .25 .25

20th anniversary of independence.

Rice Plant and Globe A85

Cotton Plant, Bale and Cloth — A86

Design: 50p, Raw jute, bale and cloth.

1967, Sept. 26 Photo. *Perf. 13x13½*
240 A85 10p dk blue & yellow .25 .25

Perf. 13

241 A86 15p orange, bl grn & yel .25 .25
242 A86 50p blue grn, brn & tan .25 .25
Nos. 240-242 (3) .75 .75

Issued to publicize major export products.

Toys — A87

1967, Oct. 2 Litho. *Perf. 13*
243 A87 15p multicolored .25 .25

Issued for International Children's Day.

Shah and Empress Farah of Iran — A88

Lithographed and Engraved

1967, Oct. 26 *Perf. 13*
244 A88 50p yellow, blue & lilac 1.50 .25

Coronation of Shah Mohammed Riza Pahlavi and Empress Farah of Iran.

"Each for all, . . ." — A89

1967, Nov. 4 Litho. *Perf. 13*
245 A89 15p multicolored .25 .25

Cooperative Day, 1967.

Mangla Dam — A90

1967, Nov. 23 Litho. *Perf. 13*
246 A90 15p multicolored .25 .25

Indus Basin Project, harnessing the Indus River for flood control and irrigation.

"Fight Against Cancer" — A91

1967, Dec. 26
247 A91 15p red & dk brown .70 .25

Issued to publicize the fight against cancer.

Human Rights Flame — A92

1968, Jan. 31 Photo. *Perf. 14x12½*
248 A92 15p Prus green & red .25 .25
249 A92 50p yellow, silver & red .25 .25

International Human Rights Year 1968.

Agricultural University and Produce A93

1968, Mar. 28 Litho. *Perf. 13½*
250 A93 15p multicolored .25 .25

Issued to publicize the first convocation of the East Pakistan Agricultural University.

WHO Emblem — A94

1968, Apr. 7 Photo. *Perf. 13½x12½*
251 A94 15p emerald & orange .25 .25
252 A94 50p orange & dk blue .25 .25

20th anniv. of WHO. "Pais" is a plate flaw, not an error. Value $2.

Kazi Nazrul Islam A95

Lithographed and Engraved

1968, June 25 Unwmk. *Perf. 13*
253 A95 15p dull yellow & brown .35 .25
254 A95 50p rose & brown .65 .25

Kazi Nazrul Islam, poet and composer.

Nos. 56, 61 and 74 Surcharged with New Value and Bars in Black or Red

1968, Sept. Engr. *Perf. 13*
255 A13 4p on 3a dk rose lake 1.00 *1.75*
256 A21 4p on 6a dk blue (R) 1.25 *1.75*
257 A15 60p on 10a purple (R) 1.00 .35
a. Black surcharge 1.50 2.00
Nos. 255-257 (3) 3.25 3.85

Types of 1948-57

1968 Wmk. 351 Engr. *Perf. 13*
258 A26 10r dk grn & org 5.00 4.00
259 A7 25r purple 6.00 6.00

Children with Hoops A96

Unwmk.

1968, Oct. 7 Litho. *Perf. 13*
260 A96 15p buff & multi .25 .25

Issued for International Children's Day.

Symbolic of Political Reforms — A97

Designs: 15p, Agricultural and industrial development. 50p, Defense. 60p, Scientific and cultural advancement.

1968, Oct. 27 Litho. *Perf. 13*
261 A97 10p multicolored .25 .25
262 A97 15p multicolored .25 .25
263 A97 50p multicolored 1.75 .35
264 A97 60p multicolored .50 .35
Nos. 261-264 (4) 2.75 1.20

Development Decade, 1958-1968.

Chittagong Steel Mill — A98

1969, Jan. 7 Unwmk. *Perf. 13*
265 A98 15p lt gray grn, lt blue & blk .25 .25

Opening of Pakistan's first steel mill.

Family of Four A99

1969, Jan. 14 Litho. *Perf. 13½*
266 A99 15p lt blue & plum .25 .25

Issued to publicize family planning.

Hockey Player and Medal — A100

1969, Jan. 30 Photo. *Perf. 13½*
267 A100 15p green, lt bl, blk & gold 1.00 .30
268 A100 1r grn, sal pink, blk & gold 2.25 .80

Pakistan's hockey victory at the 19th Olympic Games in Mexico.

Mirza Ghalib — A101

1969, Feb. 15 Litho. *Perf. 13*
269 A101 15p blue & multi .25 .25
270 A101 50p multicolored .60 .25

Mirza Ghalib (Asad Ullab Beg Khan, 1797-1869), poet who modernized the Urdu language.

Dacca Railroad Station A102

1969, Apr. 27 Litho. *Perf. 13*
271 A102 15p yel, grn, blk & dl bl .60 .25

Opening of the new railroad station in Kamalpur area of Dacca.

ILO Emblem and Ornamental Border — A103

1969, May 15 Litho. *Perf. 13½*
272 A103 15p brt grn & ocher .25 .25
273 A103 50p car rose & ocher .40 .25

50th anniv. of the ILO.

Lady on Balcony, Mogul Miniature, Pakistan A104

50p, Lady Serving Wine, Safavi miniature, Iran. 1r, Sultan Suleiman Receiving Sheik Abdul Latif, 16th cent. miniature, Turkey.

1969, July 21 Litho. *Perf. 13*

274 A104 20p multicolored .30 .25
275 A104 50p multicolored .30 .25
276 A104 1r multicolored .50 .25
Nos. 274-276 (3) 1.10 .75

5th anniv. of the signing of the Regional Cooperation for Development Pact by Turkey, Iran and Pakistan.

See Iran 1513-1515, Turkey 1813-1815.

Eastern Refinery, Chittagong A105

1969, Sept. 14 Photo. *Perf. 13½*

277 A105 20p yel, blk & vio bl .25 .25

Opening of the 1st oil refinery in East Pakistan.

Children Playing — A106

1969, Oct. 6 *Perf. 13*

278 A106 20p blue & multi .25 .25

Issued for Universal Children's Day.

Japanese Doll, Map of Dacca-Tokyo Pearl Route — A107

1969, Nov. 1 Litho. *Perf. 13½x13*

279 A107 20p multicolored .60 .25
280 A107 50p ultra & multi .90 .30

Inauguration of the Pakistan International Airways' Dacca-Tokyo "Pearl Route."

Reflection of Light Diagram — A108

1969, Nov. 4 *Perf. 13*

281 A108 20p multicolored .25 .25

Alhazen (abu-Ali al Hasan ibn-al-Haytham, 965-1039), astronomer and optician.

Vickers Vimy and London-Darwin Route over Karachi — A109

1969, Dec. 2 Photo. *Perf. 13½x13*

282 A109 50p multicolored 1.10 .30

50th anniv. of the 1st England to Australia flight.

View of EXPO '70, Sun Tower, Flags of Pakistan, Iran and Turkey A110

1970, Feb. 15 Litho. *Perf. 13*

283 A110 50p multicolored .25 .25

Issued to publicize EXPO '70 International Exhibition, Osaka, Japan, Mar. 15-Sept. 13.

UPU Headquarters, Bern — A111

1970, May 20 Litho. *Perf. 13½x13*

284 A111 20p multicolored .25 .25
285 A111 50p multicolored .25 .25

Opening of new UPU headquarters in Bern.

A souvenir sheet of 2 exists, inscribed "U.P.U. Day 9th Oct. 1971". It contains stamps similar to Nos. 284-285, imperf. Value, $25.

UN Headquarters, New York — A112

Design: 50p, UN emblem.

1970, June 26

286 A112 20p green & multi .25 .25
287 A112 50p violet & multi .25 .25

25th anniversary of the United Nations.

Education Year Emblem and Open Book — A113

1970, July 6 Litho. *Perf. 13*

288 A113 20p blue & multi .25 .25
289 A113 50p orange & multi .25 .25

International Education Year, 1970.

Saiful Malook Lake, Pakistan A114

Designs: 50p, Seeyo-Se-Pol Bridge, Esfahan, Iran. 1r, View, Fethiye, Turkey.

1970, July 21

290 A114 20p yellow & multi .25 .25
291 A114 50p yellow & multi .35 .25
292 A114 1r yellow & multi .35 .25
Nos. 290-292 (3) .95 .75

6th anniv. of the signing of the Regional Cooperation for Development Pact by Pakistan, Iran and Turkey.

See Iran 1558-1560, Turkey 1857-1859.

Asian Productivity Year Emblem — A115

1970, Aug. 18 Photo. *Perf. 12½x14*

293 A115 50p black, yel & grn .25 .25

Asian Productivity Year, 1970.

Dr. Maria Montessori A116

1970, Aug. 31 Litho. *Perf. 13*

294 A116 20p red & multi .25 .25
295 A116 50p multicolored .25 .25

Maria Montessori (1870-1952) Italian educator and physician.

Tractor and Fertilizer Factory — A117

1970, Sept. 12

296 A117 20p yel grn & brn org .25 .25

10th Regional Food and Agricultural Organization Conf. for the Near East in Islamabad.

Boy, Girl, Open Book — A118

1970, Oct. 5 Photo. *Perf. 13*

297 A118 20p multicolored .25 .25

Issued for Children's Day.

Flag and Inscription — A119

1970, Dec. 7 Litho. *Perf. 13½x13*

298 A119 20p violet & green .25 .25
299 A119 20p brt pink & green .25 .25

No. 298 inscribed "Elections for National Assembly 7th Dec. 1970," No. 299 inscribed "Elections for Provincial Assemblies 17th Dec. 1970."

Emblem and Burning of Al Aqsa Mosque — A120

1970, Dec. 26 *Perf. 13½x12½*

300 A120 20p multicolored .25 .25

Islamic Conference of Foreign Ministers, Karachi, Dec. 26-28.

Coastal Embankment — A121

1971, Feb. 25 Litho. *Perf. 13*

301 A121 20p multicolored .25 .25

Development of coastal embankments in East Pakistan.

Men of Different Races — A122

1971, Mar. 21 Litho. *Perf. 13*

302 A122 20p multicolored .25 .25
303 A122 50p lilac & multi .25 .25

Intl. Year against Racial Discrimination.

Cement Factory, Daudkhel — A123

1971, July 1 Litho. *Perf. 13*
304 A123 20p purple, blk & brn .25 .25

20th anniversary of Colombo Plan.

Badshahi Mosque, Lahore — A124

Designs: 10pa, Mosque of Selim, Edirne, Turkey. 50pa, Religious School, of Chaharbagh, Isfahan, Iran, vert.

1971, July 21 Litho. *Perf. 13*
305 A124 10p red & multi .25 .25
306 A124 20p green & multi .25 .25
307 A124 50p blue & multi .50 .30
Nos. 305-307 (3) 1.00 .80

7th anniversary of Regional Cooperation among Pakistan, Iran and Turkey.
See Iran 1599-1601, Turkey 1886-1888.

Electric Train and Boy with Toy Locomotive — A125

1971, Oct. 4 Litho. *Perf. 13*
308 A125 20p slate & multi 1.50 .50

Children's Day.

Messenger and Statue of Cyrus the Great — A126

1971, Oct. 15
309 A126 10p green & multi .30 .25
310 A126 20p blue & multi .50 .30
311 A126 50p red & multi .90 .50
Nos. 309-311 (3) 1.70 1.05

2500th anniversary of the founding of the Persian Empire by Cyrus the Great.
A souvenir sheet of 3 contains stamps similar to Nos. 309-311, imperf. Value, $52.50.

Hockey Player and Cup — A127

1971, Oct. 24
312 A127 20p red & multi 1.75 .50

First World Hockey Cup, Barcelona, Spain, Oct. 15-24.

Great Bath at Mohenjo-Daro — A128

1971, Nov. 4
313 A128 20p dp org, dk brn & blk .25 .25

25th anniv. of UNESCO.

UNICEF Emblem A129

1971, Dec. 11 Litho. *Perf. 13*
314 A129 50p dull bl, org & grn .25 .25

25th anniv. of UNICEF.

King Hussein and Jordan Flag A130

1971, Dec. 25
315 A130 20p blue & multi .25 .25

50th anniversary of the Hashemite Kingdom of Jordan.

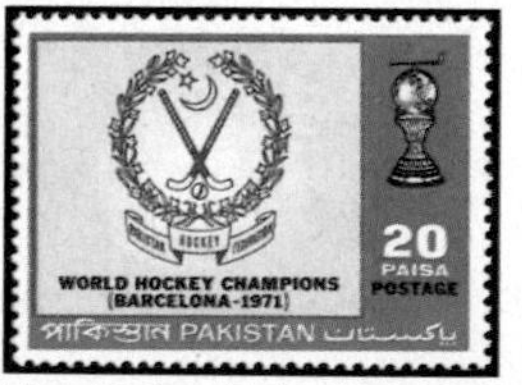

Pakistan Hockey Federation Emblem, and Cup — A131

1971, Dec. 31
316 A131 20p yellow & multi 2.50 .75

Pakistan, world hockey champions, Barcelona, Oct. 1971.

Arab Scholars A132

1972, Jan. 15 Litho. *Perf. 13½*
317 A132 20p brown, blk & blue .25 .30

International Book Year 1972.

Angels and Grand Canal, Venice — A133

1972, Feb. 5 *Perf. 13*
318 A133 20p blue & multi .35 .35

UNESCO campaign to save Venice.

ECAFE Emblem A134

1972, Mar. 28 Litho. *Perf. 13*
319 A134 20p blue & multi .25 .30

Economic Commission for Asia and the Far East (ECAFE), 25th anniversary.

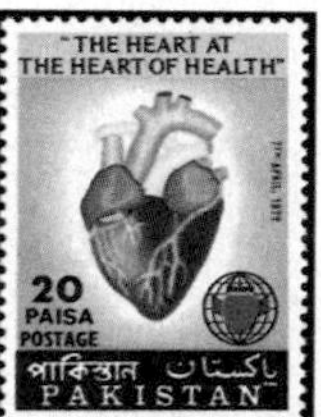

"Your Heart is your Health" — A135

1972, Apr. 7 *Perf. 13x13½*
320 A135 20p vio blue & multi .25 .30

World Health Day 1972.

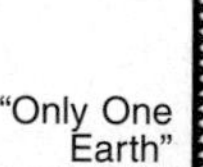

"Only One Earth" A136

1972, June 5 Litho. *Perf. 12½x14*
321 A136 20p ultra & multi .25 .30

UN Conference on Human Environment, Stockholm, June 5-16.

Young Man, by Abdur Rehman Chughtai A137

Paintings: 10p, Fisherman, by Cevat Dereli (Turkey). 20p, Persian Woman, by Behzad.

1972, July 21 Litho. *Perf. 13*
322 A137 10p multicolored .30 .25
323 A137 20p multicolored .50 .30
324 A137 50p multicolored 1.20 .60
Nos. 322-324 (3) 2.00 1.15

Regional Cooperation for Development Pact among Pakistan, Turkey and Iran, 8th anniversary.
See Iran 1647-1649, Turkey 1912-1914.

Jinnah and Independence Memorial A138

"Land Reforms" — A139

Designs: Nos. 326-329, Principal reforms. 60pa, State Bank, Islamabad, meeting-place of National Assembly, horiz.

Perf. 13 (A138), 13½x12½ (A139)
1972, Aug. 14
325 A138 10p shown .25 .25
326 A139 20p shown .25 .25
327 A139 20p Labor reforms .25 .25
328 A139 20p Education .25 .25
329 A139 20p Health care .25 .25
a. Vert. strip of 4, As #326-329 plus "labels" 1.00 1.00
330 A138 60p rose lilac & car .35 .30
Nos. 325-330 (6) 1.60 1.55

25th anniversary of independence. No. 329a contains designs of Nos. 326-329, each with a decorative label, separated by simulated perfs.

Blood Donor, Society Emblem — A140

1972, Sept. 6 Litho. *Perf. 14x12½*
331 A140 20p multicolored .25 .35

Pakistan National Blood Transfusion Service.

Census Chart A141

1972, Sept. 16 Litho. *Perf. 13½*
332 A141 20p multicolored .25 .25

Centenary of population census.

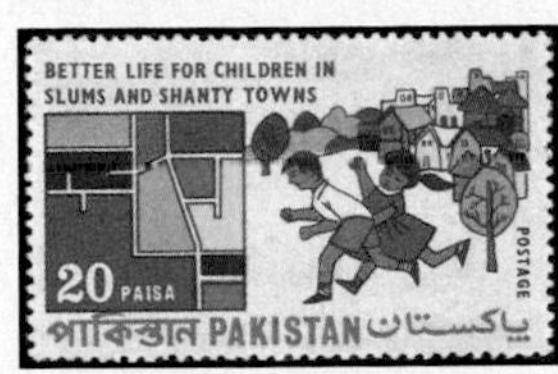

Children Leaving Slum for Modern City — A142

1972, Oct. 2 **Litho.** ***Perf. 13***
333 A142 20p multicolored .25 .30

Children's Day.

Giant Book and Children A143

1972, Oct. 23
334 A143 20p purple & multi .25 .30

Education Week.

Nuclear Power Plant, Karachi A144

1972, Nov. 28 **Litho.** ***Perf. 13***
335 A144 20p multicolored .25 .40

Pakistan's first nuclear power plant.

Copernicus in Observatory, by Jan Matejko — A145

1973, Feb. 19 **Litho.** ***Perf. 13***
336 A145 20p multicolored .60 .30

Dancing Girl, Public Baths, Mohenjo-Daro — A146

1973, Feb. 23 ***Perf. 13½x13***
337 A146 20p multicolored .35 .30

Mohenjo-Daro excavations, 50th anniv.

Radar, Lightning, WMO Emblem — A147

1973, Mar. 23 **Litho.** ***Perf. 13***
338 A147 20p multicolored .25 .40

Cent. of intl. meteorological cooperation.

Prisoners of War — A148

1973, Apr. 18
339 A148 1.25r black & multi 1.50 *2.50*

A plea for Pakistani prisoners of war in India.

National Assembly, Islamabad A149

1973, Apr. 21 ***Perf. 12½x13½***
340 A149 20p green & multi .55 .55

Constitution Week.

State Bank and Emblem — A150

1973, July 1 **Litho.** ***Perf. 13***
341 A150 20p multicolored .25 .25
342 A150 1r multicolored .30 .35

State Bank of Pakistan, 25th anniversary.

Street, Mohenjo-Daro, Pakistan A151

Designs: 20p, Statue of man, Shahdad, Kerman, Persia, 4000 B.C. 1.25r, Head from mausoleum of King Antiochus I (69-34 B.C.), Turkey.

1973, July 21 ***Perf. 13x13½***
343 A151 20p blue & multi .25 .25
344 A151 60p emerald & multi .65 .35
345 A151 1.25r red & multi 1.00 .75
Nos. 343-345 (3) 1.90 1.35

Regional Cooperation for Development Pact among Pakistan, Turkey and Iran, 9th anniversary.
See Iran 1714-1716, Turkey 1941-1943.

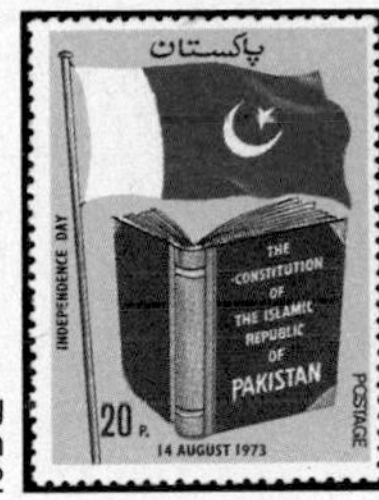

Pakistani Flag and Constitution A152

1973, Aug. 14 **Litho.** ***Perf. 13***
346 A152 20p blue & multi .25 .25

Independence Day.

Mohammed Ali Jinnah — A153

1973, Sept. 11 **Litho.** ***Perf. 13***
347 A153 20p emerald, yel & blk .25 .25

Mohammed Ali Jinnah (1876-1948), president of All-India Moslem League.

Wallago Attu — A154

Fish: 20p, Labeo rohita. 60p, Tilapia mossambica. 1r, Catla catla.

1973, Sept. 24 **Litho.** ***Perf. 13½***
348 A154 10p multicolored 1.10 1.10
349 A154 20p multicolored 1.25 1.25
350 A154 60p multicolored 1.40 1.40
351 A154 1r ultra & multi 1.40 1.40
a. Strip of 4, #348-351 5.75 5.75

Book, Torch, Child and School — A155

1973, Oct. 1
352 A155 20p multicolored .25 .25

Universal Children's Day.

Sindhi Farmer and FAO Emblem A156

1973, Oct. 15 **Litho.** ***Perf. 13***
353 A156 20p multicolored .75 .35

World Food Organization, 10th anniv.

Kemal Ataturk and Ankara — A157

1973, Oct. 29
354 A157 50p multicolored .75 .40

50th anniversary of Turkish Republic.

Scout Pointing to Planet and Stars — A158

Perf. 13½x12½
1973, Nov. 11 **Litho.**
355 A158 20p dull blue & multi 2.00 .50

25th anniversary of Pakistani Boy Scouts and Silver Jubilee Jamboree.

Human Rights Flame, Sheltered Home — A159

1973, Nov. 16
356 A159 20p multicolored .45 .40

25th anniversary of the Universal Declaration of Human Rights.

al-Biruni and Jhelum Observatory — A160

1973, Nov. 26 **Litho.** ***Perf. 13***
357 A160 20p multicolored .50 .25
358 A160 1.25r multicolored 1.25 .50

International Congress on Millenary of abu-al-Rayhan al-Biruni, Nov. 26-Dec. 12.

Dr. A. G. Hansen A161

1973, Dec. 29
359 A161 20p ultra & multi 1.20 .50

Centenary of the discovery by Dr. Armauer Gerhard Hansen of the Hansen bacillus, the cause of leprosy.

Family and WPY Emblem A162

1974, Jan. 1 Litho. *Perf. 13*
360 A162 20p yellow & multi .30 .25
361 A162 1.25r salmon & multi .30 .40

World Population Year 1974.

Summit Emblem and Ornament — A163

Emblem, Crescent and Rays A164

1974, Feb. 22 *Perf. 14x12½, 13*
362 A163 20p multicolored .25 .25
363 A164 65p multicolored .30 .40
a. Souvenir sheet of 2 2.00 3.25

Islamic Summit Meeting. No. 363a contains two stamps similar to Nos. 362-363 with simulated perforations.

Metric Measures A165

1974, July 1 Litho. *Perf. 13*
364 A165 20p multicolored .25 .30

Introduction of metric system.

Kashan Rug, Lahore A166

Designs: 60p, Persian rug, late 16th century. 1.25r, Anatolian rug, 15th century.

1974, July 21
365 A166 20p multicolored .25 .25
366 A166 60p multicolored .40 .50
367 A166 1.25r multicolored .75 1.00
Nos. 365-367 (3) 1.40 1.75

10th anniversary of the Regional Cooperation for Development Pact among Pakistan, Iran and Turkey.
See Iran 1806-1808, Turkey 1979-1981.

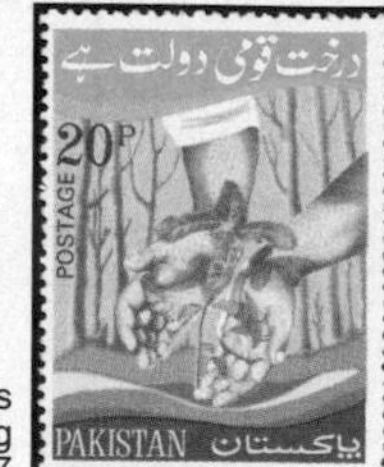

Hands Protecting Sapling — A167

1974, Aug. 9 Litho. *Perf. 13*
368 A167 20p multicolored .60 .60

Arbor Day.

Torch over Map of Africa with Namibia — A168

1974, Aug. 26
369 A168 60p green & multi .55 .60

Namibia (South-West Africa) Day. See note after United Nations No. 241.

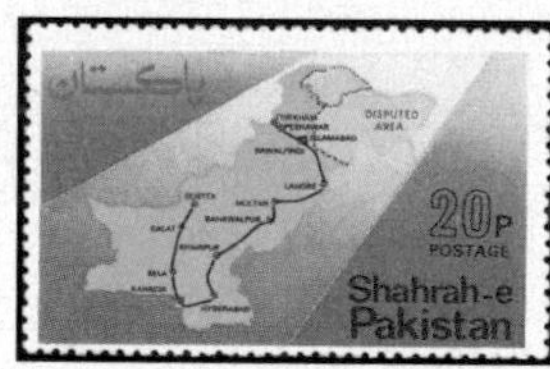

Map of Pakistan with Highways and Disputed Area — A169

1974, Sept. 23
370 A169 20p multicolored 1.25 1.00

Highway system under construction.

Child and Students A170

1974, Oct. 7 Litho. *Perf. 13*
371 A170 20p multicolored .40 .50

Universal Children's Day.

UPU Emblem — A171

2.25r, Jet, UPU emblem, mail coach.

1974, Oct. 9 Size: 24x36mm
372 A171 20p multicolored .25 .25

Size: 29x41mm
373 A171 2.25r multicolored .55 .70
a. Souv. sheet of 2, #372-373, imperf. 1.50 1.50

Centenary of Universal Postal Union.

Liaqat Ali Khan — A172

1974, Oct. 16 Litho. *Perf. 13x13½*
374 A172 20p black & red .45 .35

Liaqat Ali Khan, Prime Minister 1947-1951.

Mohammad Allama Iqbal — A173

1974, Nov. 9 Litho. *Perf. 13*
375 A173 20p multicolored .45 .35

Mohammad Allama Iqbal (1877-1938), poet and philosopher.

Dr. Schweitzer on Ogowe River, 1915 — A174

1975, Jan. 14 Litho. *Perf. 13*
376 A174 2.25r multicolored 4.50 *4.50*

Dr. Albert Schweitzer (1875-1965), medical missionary, birth centenary.

Tourism Year 75 Emblem A175

1975, Jan. 15
377 A175 2.25r multicolored .60 .80

South Asia Tourism Year, 1975.

Flags of Participants, Memorial and Prime Minister Bhutto — A176

1975, Feb. 22 Litho. *Perf. 13*
378 A176 20p lt blue & multi .25 .25
379 A176 1r brt pink & multi 1.25 1.00

2nd Lahore Islamic Summit, Feb. 22, 1st anniv.

IWY Emblem and Woman Scientist — A177

Design: 2.25r, Old woman and girl learning to read and write.

1975, June 15 Litho. *Perf. 13*
380 A177 20p multicolored .25 .25
381 A177 2.25r multicolored 1.40 1.75

International Women's Year 1975.

Globe with Dates, Arabic "X" — A178

1975, July 14 Litho. *Perf. 13*
382 A178 20p multicolored .75 .60

International Congress of Mathematical Sciences, Karachi, July 14-20.

Camel Leather Vase, Pakistan A179

60p, Ceramic plate and RCD emblem, Iran, horiz. 1.25r, Porcelain vase, Turkey.

1975, July 21
383 A179 20p lilac & multi .30 .25
384 A179 60p violet blk & multi .60 .75
385 A179 1.25r blue & multi 1.00 1.10
Nos. 383-385 (3) 1.90 2.10

Regional Cooperation for Development Pact among Turkey, Iran and Pakistan.
See Iran 1871-1873, Turkey 2006-2008.

Sapling, Trees and Ant — A180

1975, Aug. 9 Litho. *Perf. 13x13½*
386 A180 20p multicolored .45 .45

Tree Planting Day.

Black Partridge A181

1975, Sept. 30 Litho. *Perf. 13*

387 A181 20p blue & multi 1.50 .25
388 A181 2.25r yellow & multi 4.50 3.50

Wildlife Protection.

Girls — A182

1975, Oct. 6

389 A182 20p multicolored .45 .50

Universal Children's Day.

Hazrat Amir Khusrau, Sitar and Tabla — A183

1975, Oct. 24 Litho. *Perf. 14x12½*

390 A183 20p lt blue & multi .25 .50
391 A183 2.25r pink & multi 1.00 2.00

700th anniversary of Hazrat Amir Khusrau (1253-1325), musician who invented the sitar and tabla instruments.

Mohammad Iqbal — A184

1975, Nov. 9 *Perf. 13*

392 A184 20p multicolored .50 .50

Mohammad Allama Iqbal (1877-1938), poet and philosopher, birth centenary.

Wild Sheep of the Punjab — A185

1975, Dec. 31 Litho. *Perf. 13*

393 A185 20p multicolored .35 .25
394 A185 3r multicolored 2.00 1.75

Wildlife Protection. See Nos. 410-411.

Mohenjo-Daro and UNESCO Emblem A186

View of Mohenjo-Daro excavations.

1976, Feb. 29 Litho. *Perf. 13*

395 A186 10p multicolored .65 .80
396 A186 20p multicolored .75 .90
397 A186 65p multicolored .75 .90
398 A186 3r multicolored .75 .90
399 A186 4r multicolored .85 1.00
a. Strip of 5, #395-399 4.00 4.00

UNESCO campaign to save Mohenjo-Daro excavations.

Dome and Minaret of Rauza-e-Mubarak Mausoleum — A187

1976, Mar. 3 Photo. *Perf. 13½x14*

400 A187 20p blue & multi .25 .25
401 A187 3r gray & multi .75 .70

International Congress on Seerat, the teachings of Mohammed, Mar. 3-15.

Alexander Graham Bell, 1876 Telephone and Dial — A188

1976, Mar. 10 *Perf. 13*

402 A188 3r blue & multi 1.50 2.00

Centenary of first telephone call by Alexander Graham Bell, Mar. 10, 1876.

College Emblem — A189

1976, Mar. 15 Litho. *Perf. 13*

403 A189 20p multicolored .45 .45

Cent. of Natl. College of Arts, Lahore.

Peacock A190

1976, Mar. 31 Litho. *Perf. 13*

404 A190 20p lt blue & multi 1.00 .40
405 A190 3r pink & multi 4.00 3.75

Wildlife protection.

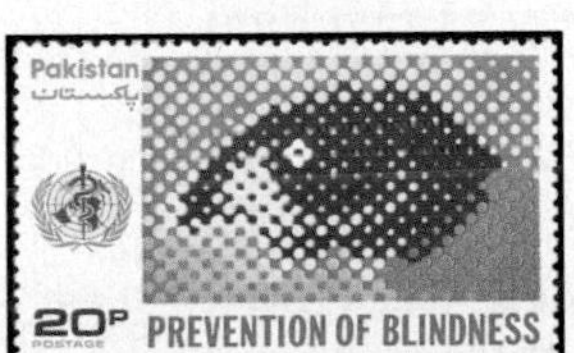

Eye and WHO Emblem — A191

1976, Apr. 7

406 A191 20p multicolored 1.10 .75

World Health Day: "Foresight prevents blindness."

Mohenjo-Daro, UNESCO Emblem, Bull (from Seal) — A192

1976, May 31 Litho. *Perf. 13*

407 A192 20p multicolored .45 .40

UNESCO campaign to save Mohenjo-Daro excavations.

Jefferson Memorial, US Bicentennial Emblem — A193

Declaration of Independence, by John Trumbull — A194

1976, July 4 *Perf. 13*

408 A193 90p multicolored .75 .50

Perf. 13½x13

409 A194 4r multicolored 3.00 *3.50*

American Bicentennial.

Wildlife Type of 1975

Wildlife protection: 20p, 3r, Ibex.

1976, July 12

410 A185 20p multicolored .35 .35
411 A185 3r multicolored 1.40 2.00

Mohammed Ali Jinnah — A195

65p, Riza Shah Pahlavi. 90p, Kemal Ataturk.

1976, July 21 Litho. *Perf. 14*

412 A195 20p multicolored .70 .50
413 A195 65p multicolored .70 .50
414 A195 90p multicolored .70 .50
a. Strip of 3, #412-414 2.50 3.25

Regional Cooperation for Development Pact among Pakistan, Turkey and Iran, 12th anniversary.

See Iran 1903-1905, Turkey 2041-2043.

Ornament A196

Jinnah and Wazir Mansion A197

Designs (Jinnah and): 40p, Sind Madressah (building). 50p, Minar Qarardad (minaret). 3r, Mausoleum.

1976, Aug. 14 Litho. *Perf. 13½*

415 A196 5p multicolored .25 .25
416 A196 10p multicolored .25 .25
417 A196 15p multicolored .25 .25
418 A197 20p multicolored .25 .25
419 A197 40p multicolored .25 .25
420 A197 50p multicolored .25 .25
421 A196 1r multicolored .35 .40
422 A197 3r multicolored .50 .50
a. Block of 8, #415-422 3.50 3.50

Mohammed Ali Jinnah (1876-1948), first Governor General of Pakistan, birth centenary. Horizontal rows of types A196 and A197 alternate in sheet.

Mohenjo-Daro and UNESCO Emblem — A198

1976, Aug. 31 *Perf. 14*

423 A198 65p multicolored .45 .50

UNESCO campaign to save Mohenjo-Daro excavations.

Racial Discrimination Emblem — A199

Perf. 12½x13½

1976, Sept. 15 Litho.

424 A199 65p multicolored .45 .45

Fight against racial discrimination.

Child's Head, Symbols of Health, Education and Food — A200

1976, Oct. 4 *Perf. 13*

425 A200 20p blue & multi .60 .45

Universal Children's Day.

Verse by Allama Iqbal A201

1976, Nov. 9 Litho. *Perf. 13*

426 A201 20p multicolored .25 .30

Mohammed Allama Iqbal (1877-1938), poet and philosopher, birth centenary.

Scout Emblem, Jinnah Giving Salute — A202

1976, Nov. 20

427 A202 20p multicolored 1.10 .45

Quaid-I-Azam Centenary Jamboree, Nov. 1976.

Children Reading A203

1976, Dec. 15 Litho. *Perf. 13*

428 A203 20p multicolored .60 .30

Books for children.

Mohammed Ali Jinnah — A204

Lithographed and Embossed

1976, Dec. 25 *Perf. 12½*

429 A204 10r gold & green 3.00 3.00

Mohammed Ali Jinnah (1876-1948), 1st Governor General of Pakistan.

An imperf presentation sheet of 1 exists. Value $100.

Farm Family and Village, Tractor, Ambulance A205

1977, Apr. 14 Litho. *Perf. 13*

430 A205 20p multicolored .45 .25

Social Welfare and Rural Development Year, 1976-77.

Terracotta Bullock Cart, Pakistan — A206

Designs: 20p, Terra-cotta jug, Turkey. 90p, Decorated jug, Iran.

1977, July 21 Litho. *Perf. 13*

431 A206 20p ultra & multi .45 .25
432 A206 65p blue green & multi .65 .35
433 A206 90p lilac & multi 1.00 1.40
Nos. 431-433 (3) 2.10 2.00

Regional Cooperation for Development Pact among Pakistan, Turkey and Iran, 13th anniversary.

See Iran 1946-1948, Turkey 2053-2055.

Trees — A207

1977, Aug. 9 Litho. *Perf. 13*

434 A207 20p multicolored .25 .30

Tree planting program.

Desert A208

1977, Sept. 5 Litho. *Perf. 13*

435 A208 65p multicolored .45 .30

UN Conference on Desertification, Nairobi, Kenya, Aug. 29-Sept. 9.

"Water for the Children" — A209

1977, Oct. 3 Litho. *Perf. 14x12½*

436 A209 50p multicolored .45 .40

Universal Children's Day.

Aga Khan III — A210

1977, Nov. 2 Litho. *Perf. 13*

437 A210 2r multicolored .75 .75

Aga Khan III (1877-1957), spiritual ruler of Ismaeli sect, statesman, birth centenary.

Mohammad Iqbal — A211

20p, Spirit appearing to Iqbal, painting by Behzad. 65p, Iqbal looking at Jamaluddin Afghani & Saeed Halim offering prayers, by Behzad. 1.25r, Verse in Urdu. 2.25r, Verse in Persian.

1977, Nov. 9

438 A211 20p multicolored .60 .60
439 A211 65p multicolored .60 .60
440 A211 1.25r multicolored .70 .70
441 A211 2.25r multicolored .75 .75
442 A211 3r multicolored .85 .85
a. Strip of 5, #438-442 4.50 4.50

Mohammad Allama Iqbal (1877-1938), poet and philosopher, birth centenary.

Holy Kaaba, Mecca A212

1977, Nov. 21 *Perf. 14*

443 A212 65p green & multi .45 .30

1977 pilgrimage to Mecca.

Healthy and Sick Bodies — A213

1977, Dec. 19 Litho. *Perf. 13*

444 A213 65p blue green & multi .45 .30

World Rheumatism Year.

Woman from Rawalpindi-Islamabad — A214

1978, Feb. 5 Litho. *Perf. 12½x13½*

445 A214 75p multicolored .45 .25

Indonesia-Pakistan Economic and Cultural Cooperation Organization.

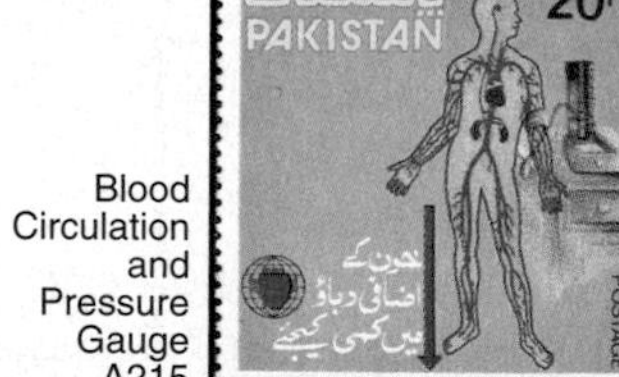

Blood Circulation and Pressure Gauge A215

1978, Apr. 20 Litho. *Perf. 13*

446 A215 20p blue & multi .25 .25
447 A215 2r yellow & multi .85 .75

Campaign against hypertension.

Henri Dunant, Red Cross, Red Crescent A216

1978, May 8 *Perf. 14*

448 A216 1r multicolored 1.00 .30

Henri Dunant (1828-1910), founder of Red Cross, 150th birth anniversary.

Red Roses, Pakistan — A217

90p, Pink roses, Iran. 2r, Yellow rose, Turkey.

1978, July 21 Litho. *Perf. 13½*

449 A217 20p multicolored .35 .25
450 A217 90p multicolored .50 .25
451 A217 2r multicolored .75 .35
a. Strip of 3, #449-451 2.00 2.00

Regional Cooperation for Development Pact among Turkey, Iran and Pakistan.

See Iran 1984-1986, Turkey 2094-2096.

Hockey Stick and Ball, Championship Cup — A218

Fair Building, Fountain, Piazza Tourismo A219

1978, Aug. 26 Litho. *Perf. 13*

452 A218 1r multicolored 1.25 .25
453 A219 2r multicolored .50 .30

Riccione '78, 30th International Stamp Fair, Riccione, Italy, Aug. 26-28. No. 452 also commemorates Pakistan as World Hockey Cup Champion.

Globe and Cogwheels A220

1978, Sept. 3

454 A220 75p multicolored .45 .25

UN Conference on Technical Cooperation among Developing Countries, Buenos Aires, Argentina, Sept. 1978.

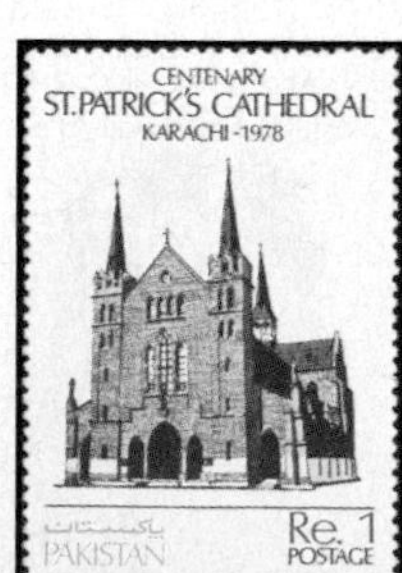

St. Patrick's Cathedral, Karachi A221

Design: 2r, Stained-glass window.

1978, Sept. 29 Litho. *Perf. 13*

455 A221 1r multicolored .25 .25
456 A221 2r multicolored .65 .25

St. Patrick's Cathedral, Karachi, centenary.

"Four Races" — A222

1978, Nov. 20 Litho. *Perf. 13*

457 A222 1r multicolored .45 .25

Anti-Apartheid Year.

Maulana Jauhar — A223

1978, Dec. 10 Litho. *Perf. 13*

458 A223 50p multicolored .55 .25

Maulana Muhammad Ali Jauhar, writer, journalist and patriot, birth centenary.

Type of 1957 and

Qarardad Monument — A224

Tractor — A225

Tomb of Ibrahim Khan Makli — A225a

Engr.; Litho. (10p, 25p, 40p, 50p, 90p)

1978-81 *Perf. 14*

459 A224 2p dark green .25 .25
460 A224 3p black .25 .25
461 A224 5p violet blue .25 .25
462 A225 10p lt blue & blue ('79) .25 .25
463 A225 20p yel green ('79) .40 .25
464 A225 25p rose car & grn ('79) .75 .25
465 A225 40p carmine & blue .25 .25
466 A225 50p bl grn & vio ('79) .25 .25
467 A225 60p black .25 .25
468 A225 75p dull red .50 .25
469 A225 90p blue & carmine .25 .25

Perf. 13½x13

Engr. Wmk. 351

470 A225a 1r olive ('80) .25 .25
471 A225a 1.50r dp org ('79) .25 .25
472 A225a 2r car rose ('79) .25 .25
473 A225a 3r indigo ('80) .25 .25
474 A225a 4r black ('81) .25 .25
475 A225a 5r dk brn ('81) .25 .25
475A A226 15r rose lil & red ('79) 1.50 1.50
Nos. 459-475A (18) 6.65 5.75

Lithographed stamps, type A225, have bottom panel in solid color with colorless lettering and numerals 2mm high instead of 3mm.

For overprints see Nos. O94-O110.

Tornado Jet Fighter, de Havilland Rapide and Flyer A — A226

Wright Flyer A and: 1r, Phantom F4F jet fighter & Tristar airliner. 2r, Bell X15 fighter & TU-104 airliner. 2.25r, MiG fighter & Concorde.

Unwmk.

1978, Dec. 24 Litho. *Perf. 13*

476 A226 65p multicolored 1.10 1.60
477 A226 1r multicolored 1.20 1.90
478 A226 2r multicolored 1.25 2.00
479 A226 2.25r multicolored 1.25 2.00
a. Block of 4, #476-479 6.00 6.00

75th anniv. of 1st powered flight.

Koran Lighting the World and Mohammed's Tomb — A227

1979, Feb. 10 Litho. *Perf. 13*

480 A227 20p multicolored .45 .25

Mohammed's birth anniversary.

Mother and Children A228

1979, Feb. 25

481 A228 50p multicolored .75 .25

APWA Services, 30th anniversary.

Lophophorus Impejanus — A229

Pheasants: 25p, Lophura leucomelana. 40p, Puccrasia macrolopha. 1r, Catreus walichii.

1979, June 17 Litho. *Perf. 13*

482 A229 20p multicolored 1.25 .60
483 A229 25p multicolored 1.25 .75
484 A229 40p multicolored 1.50 1.75
485 A229 1r multicolored 3.00 2.00
Nos. 482-485 (4) 7.00 5.10

For overprint see No. 525.

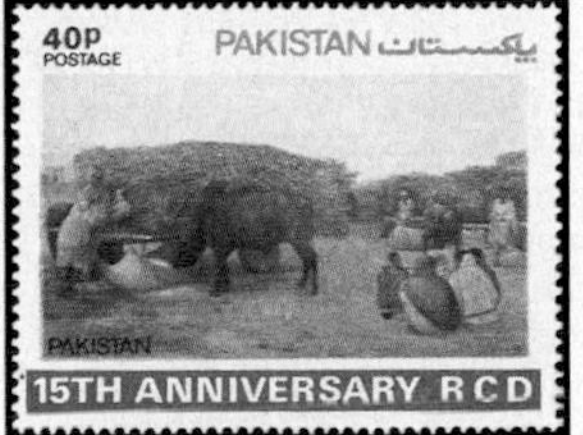

At the Well, by Allah Baksh — A230

Paintings: 75p, Potters, by Kamalel Molk, Iran. 1.60r, Plowing, by Namik Ismail, Turkey.

1979, July 21 Litho. *Perf. 14x13*

486 A230 40p multicolored .25 .25
487 A230 75p multicolored .25 .25
488 A230 1.60r multicolored .25 .25
a. Strip of 3, #486-488 .90 .90

Regional Cooperation for Development Pact among Pakistan, Iran and Turkey, 15th anniversary.

See Iran 2020-2022, Turkey 2112-2114.

Guj Embroidery — A231

Handicrafts: 1r, Enamel inlay brass plate. 1.50r, Baskets. 2r, Peacock, embroidered rug.

1979, Aug. 23 Litho. *Perf. 14x13*

489 A231 40p multicolored .25 .25
490 A231 1r multicolored .25 .25
491 A231 1.50r multicolored .30 .30
492 A231 2r multicolored .40 .35
a. Block of 4, #489-492 1.50 1.50

Children, IYC and SOS Emblems — A232

1979, Sept. 10 Litho. *Perf. 13*

493 A232 50p multicolored .50 .30

SOS Children's Village, Lahore, opening.

Playground, IYC Emblem — A233

IYC Emblem and: Children's drawings.

1979, Oct. 22 *Perf. 14x12½*

494 A233 40p multicolored .25 .25
495 A233 75p multicolored .25 .25
496 A233 1r multicolored .25 .30
497 A233 1.50r multicolored .30 .30
a. Block of 4, #494-497 1.25 1.25

Souvenir Sheet

Imperf

498 A233 2r multi, vert. 1.25 *2.10*

IYC. For overprints see #520-523.

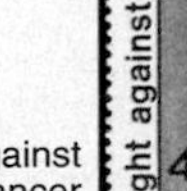

Fight Against Cancer A234

Unwmk.

1979, Nov. 12 Litho. *Perf. 14*

499 A234 40p multicolored .75 .70

Pakistan Customs Service Centenary — A235

1979, Dec. 10 *Perf. 13x13½*

500 A235 1r multicolored .35 .25

"1378" is a plate flaw, not an error.

Tippu Sultan Shaheed — A236

15r, Syed Ahmad Khan. 25r, Altaf Hussain Hali.

1979, Mar. 23 Wmk. 351 *Perf. 14*

501 A236 10r shown .75 1.00
502 A236 15r multicolored 1.00 1.50
503 A236 25r multicolored 1.50 2.25
a. Strip of 3, #501-503 4.00 4.00

See No. 699.

A237 A238

Ornament — A239

Perf. 12x11½, 11½x12

1980 Unwmk.

506 A237 10p dk grn & yel org .25 .25
507 A237 15p dk grn & apple grn .25 .25
508 A237 25p multicolored .25 .25
509 A237 35p multicolored .25 .25
510 A238 40p red & lt brown .25 .25
511 A239 50p olive & vio bl .25 .25
512 A239 80p black & yel grn .25 .30
Nos. 506-512 (7) 1.75 1.80

Issued: 25, 35, 50, 80p, 3/10; others, 1/15.

See Nos. O111-O117.

Pakistan International Airline, 25th Anniversary — A240

1980, Jan. 10 Litho. *Perf. 13*

516 A240 1r multicolored 2.00 1.00

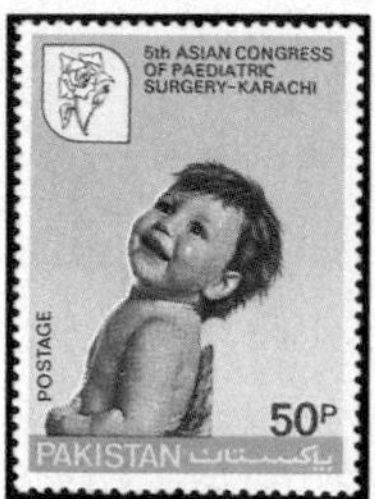

Infant, Rose — A241

1980, Feb. 16 *Perf. 13*

517 A241 50p multicolored 1.00 1.25

5th Asian Congress of Pediatric Surgery, Karachi, Feb. 16-19.

Conference Emblem A242

1980, May 17 Litho. *Perf. 13*

518 A242 1r multicolored .80 .50

11th Islamic Conference of Foreign Ministers, Islamabad, May 17-21.

Lighthouse, Oil Terminal, Map Showing Karachi Harbor — A243

1980, July 15 *Perf. 13½*

519 A243 1r multicolored 1.75 1.50

Karachi Port, cent. of independent management.

Nos. 494-497 Overprinted in Red: RICCIONE 80

1980, Aug. 30 Litho. *Perf. 14x12½*

520 A233 40p multicolored .30 *.50*
521 A233 75p multicolored .40 *.60*
522 A233 1r multicolored .45 *.65*
523 A233 1.50r multicolored .60 *.75*
a. Block of 4, #520-523 2.00 *3.00*

RICCIONE 80 International Stamp Exhibition, Riccione, Italy, Aug. 30-Sept. 2.

Quetta Command and Staff College, 75th Anniversary A244

1980, Sept. 18 Litho. *Perf. 13*

524 A244 1r multicolored .25 .40

No. 485 Overprinted: "World Tourism Conference/Manila 80"

1980, Sept. 27

525 A229 1r multicolored 1.00 .50

World Tourism Conf., Manila, Sept. 27.

Birth Centenary of Mohammed Shairani — A245

1980, Oct. 5 Litho. *Perf. 13*

526 A245 40p multicolored .45 .45

Aga Khan Architecture Award — A246

1980, Oct. 23 Litho. *Perf. 13½*

527 A246 2r multicolored .60 .55

Rising Sun A247

1981, Mar. 7 Litho. *Perf. 13*

Size: 30x41mm

528 A247 40p Hegira emblem .25 .40

1980, Nov. 6 Litho. *Perf. 13*

529 A247 40p shown .25 .25

Perf. 14

Size: 33x33mm

530 A247 2r Moslem symbols .25 .35

Perf. 13x13½

Size: 31x54mm

531 A247 3r Globe, hands holding Koran .25 .50
Nos. 528-531 (4) 1.00 1.50

Souvenir Sheet

Imperf

532 A247 4r Candles .75 .75

Hegira (Pilgrimage Year).

Airmail Service, 50th Anniversary — A248

Postal History: No. 533, Postal card cent. No. 534, Money order service cent.

1980-81 *Perf. 13*

533 A248 40p multi, vert. .25 .35
534 A248 40p multi, vert. .25 .35
535 A248 1r multi .75 .25
Nos. 533-535 (3) 1.25 .95

Issued: #533, 12/27; #534, 12/20; #535, 2/15/81.

Heinrich von Stephan, UPU Emblem A249

1981, Jan. 7 *Perf. 13½*

536 A249 1r multicolored .45 .25

Von Stephan (1831-97), founder of UPU.

Conference Emblem, Afghan Refugee A250

Conference Emblem, Flags of Participants, Men — A251

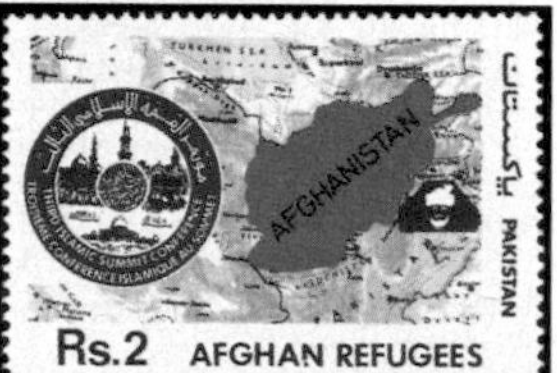

Conference Emblem, Map of Afghanistan — A252

Conference Emblem in Ornament A253

Conference Emblem, Flags of Participants A254

1981, Mar. 29 Litho. *Perf. 13*

537 A250 40p multicolored .25 .25
538 A251 40p multicolored .25 .25
539 A250 1r multicolored .50 .25
540 A251 1r multicolored .50 .25
541 A252 2r multicolored .65 .35
Nos. 537-541 (5) 2.15 1.35

1981, Mar. 29 *Perf. 13½*

542 A253 40p multicolored .25 .25
543 A254 40p multicolored .25 .25
544 A253 85p multicolored .25 .25
545 A254 85p multicolored .25 .25
Nos. 542-545 (4) 1.00 1.00

3rd Islamic Summit Conference, Makkah al-Mukarramah, Jan. 25-28.

Kemal Ataturk (1881-1938), First President of Turkey — A255

1981, May 19 Litho. *Perf. 13x13½*

546 A255 1r multicolored .60 .25

Green Turtle A256

1981, June 20 Litho. *Perf. 12x11½*

547 A256 40p multicolored 1.40 .75

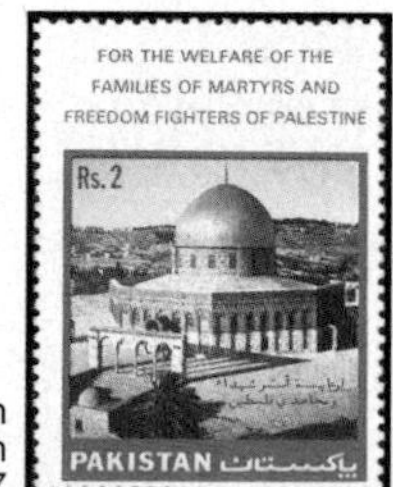

Palestinian Cooperation A257

1981, July 25 Litho. *Perf. 13*

548 A257 2r multicolored .55 .25

Mountain Ranges and Peaks — A258

1981, Aug. 20 *Perf. 14x13½*

549 40p Malubiting West, range .45 .30
550 40p Peak .45 .30
a. A258 Pair, #549-550 1.00 1.00
551 1r Mt. Maramosh, range .65 .50
552 1r Mt. Maramosh, peak .65 .50
a. A258 Pair, #551-552 1.50 1.50
553 1.50r K6, range .80 .60
554 1.50r Peak .80 .60
a. A258 Pair, #553-554 1.75 1.75
555 2r K2, range .80 .80
556 2r Peak .80 .80
a. A258 Pair, #555-556 1.75 1.75
Nos. 549-556 (8) 5.40 4.40

Inauguration of Pakistan Steel Furnace No. 1, Karachi A260

1981, Aug. 31 *Perf. 13*

557 A260 40p multicolored .25 .25
558 A260 2r multicolored .60 .75

Western Tragopan in Summer A261

1981, Sept. 15 Litho. *Perf. 14*

559 A261 40p shown 2.25 .75
560 A261 2r Winter 4.50 4.00

Intl. Year of the Disabled A262

1981, Dec. 12 Litho. *Perf. 13*

561 A262 40p multicolored .25 .30
562 A262 2r multicolored 1.25 1.00

World Cup Championship A263

1982, Jan. 31 Litho. *Perf. 13½x13*

563 A263 1r Cup, flags in arc 2.00 1.00
564 A263 1r shown 2.00 1.00
a. Pair, #563-564 4.50 4.50

Nos. 563-564 were printed with a vertical strip of labels, picturing different scenes, in the middle of each sheet, allowing for pairs with label between. Value, pair with label $4.

Camel Skin Lampshade A264

1982, Feb. 20 Litho. *Perf. 14*

565 A264 1r shown .70 .60
566 A264 1r Hala pottery .70 .60

See Nos. 582-583.

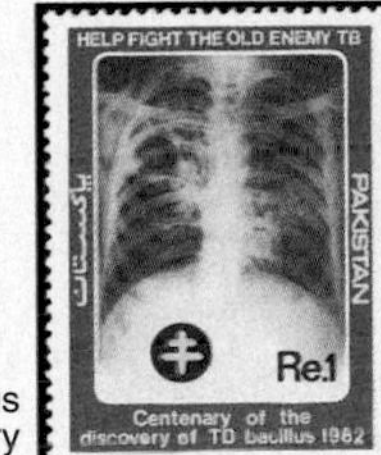

TB Bacillus Centenary A265

1982, Mar. 24

567 A265 1r multicolored 1.50 1.25

Blind Indus Dolphin A266

1982, Apr. 24 Litho. *Perf. 12x11½*

568 A266 40p Dolphin 1.50 .75
569 A266 1r Dolphin, diff. 3.50 1.50

Peaceful Uses of Outer Space — A267

1982, June 7 Litho. *Perf. 13*

570 A267 1r multicolored 2.00 1.10

No. 570 was printed with a vertical strip of labels, picturing different space satellites, in the middle of each sheet, allowing for pairs with label between. Value, pair with label $4.

50th Anniv. of Sukkur Barrage — A268

1982, July 17 Litho. *Perf. 13*

571 A268 1r multicolored .35 .25

For overprint see No. 574.

Independence Day — A269

1982, Aug. 14

572 A269 40p Flag .25 .25
573 A269 85p Map .50 .50

No. 571 Overprinted "RICCIONE-82/1932-1982"

1982, Aug. 28

574 A268 1r multicolored .25 .25

RICCIONE '82 Intl. Stamp Exhibition, Riccione, Italy, Aug. 28-30.

University of the Punjab Centenary — A270

1982, Oct. 14 Litho. *Perf. 13½*

575 A270 40p multicolored 1.20 .40

No. 575 was printed with a vertical strip of labels, picturing different university buildings, in the middle of each sheet, allowing for pairs with label between. Value, pair with label: $4.

Scouting Year — A271

1982, Dec. 23 Litho. *Perf. 13*

576 A271 2r Emblem .50 .35

Quetta Natural Gas Pipeline Project A272

1983, Jan. 6 Litho. *Perf. 13*

577 A272 1r multicolored .35 .25

Common Peacock A273

1983, Feb. 15 Litho. *Perf. 14*

578 A273 40p shown 1.25 .25
579 A273 50p Common rose 1.50 .25
580 A273 60p Plain tiger 1.75 .55
581 A273 1.50r Lemon butterfly 2.50 2.25
Nos. 578-581 (4) 7.00 3.30

Handicraft Type of 1982

1983, Mar. 9

582 A264 1r Straw mats .25 .25
583 A264 1r Five-flower cloth design .25 .25

Opening of Aga Khan University — A274

1983, Mar. 16 *Perf. 13½*

584 A274 2r multicolored 1.50 1.00

No. 584 was printed with a vertical strip of labels, picturing different university views, in the middle of each sheet, allowing for pairs with label between. Value, pair with label $4.

Yak Caravan, Zindiharam-Darkot Pass, Hindu Kush Mountains — A275

1983, Apr. 28 Litho. *Perf. 13*

585 A275 1r multicolored 1.60 .50

Marsh Crocodile A276

1983, May 19 *Perf. 13½x14*

586 A276 3r multicolored 3.75 1.60

1983, June 20 Litho. *Perf. 14*
Size: 50x40mm

587 A276 1r Gazelle 3.25 1.60

36th Anniv. of Independence A277

1983, Aug. 14 *Perf. 13*

588 A277 60p Star .25 .25
589 A277 4r Torch .40 .40

25th Anniv. of Indonesia-Pakistan Economic and Cultural Cooperation Org. — A278

Weavings — No. 590, Pakistani (geometric). No. 591, Indonesian (figures).

1983, Aug. 19 Litho. *Perf. 13*

590 A278 2r multicolored .30 .25
591 A278 2r multicolored .30 .25

Siberian Cranes — A279

1983, Sept. 8 *Perf. 13½*

592 A279 3r multicolored 4.00 3.00

World Communications Year — A280

1983, Oct. 9 Litho. *Perf. 13*
593 A280 2r multicolored .35 .25

Size: 33x33mm

594 A280 3r Symbol, diff. .30 .25

World Food Day A281

1983, Oct. 24 Litho. *Perf. 13*

595 A281 3r Livestock	1.50	1.50
596 A281 3r Fruit	1.50	1.50
597 A281 3r Grain	1.50	1.50
598 A281 3r Seafood	1.50	1.50
a. Strip of 4, #595-598	6.50	6.50

A282

1983, Oct. 24 Litho. *Perf. 13½*
599 A282 60p multicolored .25 .25

National Fertilizer Corp.

View of Lahore City, 1852 — A283

1983, Nov. 13 Litho. *Perf. 13*
600 Strip of 6 3.50 3.50
a.-f. A283 60p any single .50 .50

PAKPHILEX '83 Natl. Stamp Exhibition.

Yachting Victory in 9th Asian Games, 1982 — A284

1983, Dec. 31 Litho. *Perf. 13*
601 A284 60p OK Dinghy 1.75 1.75
602 A284 60p Enterprise 1.75 1.75

Snow Leopard — A285

1984, Jan. 21 *Perf. 14*
603 A285 40p lt green & multi 2.00 1.00
604 A285 1.60r blue & multi 5.00 5.00

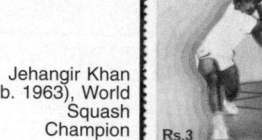

Jehangir Khan (b. 1963), World Squash Champion A286

1984, Mar. 17 Litho. *Perf. 13*
605 A286 3r multicolored 2.75 1.40

Pakistan Intl. Airway China Service, 20th Anniv. A287

1984, Apr. 29 Litho. *Perf. 13*
606 A287 3r Jet 5.75 4.50

Glass Work, Lahore Fort — A288

Various glass panels.

1984, May 31 Litho. *Perf. 13*

607 A288 1r green & multi	.25	.25
608 A288 1r purple & multi	.25	.25
609 A288 1r vermilion & multi	.25	.25
610 A288 1r brt blue & multi	.25	.25
Nos. 607-610 (4)	1.00	1.00

Forts — A289

1984-88 Litho. *Perf. 11*

613 A289 5p Kot Diji	*.40*	.25
614 A289 10p Rohtas	*.40*	.25
615 A289 15p Bala Hissar ('86)	*.75*	.25
616 A289 20p Attock	*1.50*	.25
617 A289 50p Hyderabad ('86)	*1.50*	.25
618 A289 60p Lahore	*1.25*	.25
619 A289 70p Sibi ('88)	*1.50*	.25
620 A289 80p Ranikot ('86)	*1.50*	.25
Nos. 613-620 (8)	*8.80*	2.00

Issued: 5p, 11/1; 10p, 9/25; 80p, 7/1.
For overprints see Nos. O118-O124.

Shah Rukn-i-Alam Tomb, Multan — A290

1984, June 26 Litho. *Perf. 13*
624 A290 60p multicolored 3.00 1.40

Aga Khan Award for Architecture.

Asia-Pacific Broadcasting Union, 20th Anniv. — A290a

1984, July 1 Litho. *Perf. 13*
625 A290a 3r multicolored .90 .50

1984 Summer Olympics, Los Angeles — A291

1984, July 31

626 A291 3r Athletics	1.25	1.00
627 A291 3r Boxing	1.25	1.00
628 A291 3r Hockey	1.25	1.00
629 A291 3r Yachting	1.25	1.00
630 A291 3r Wrestling	1.25	1.00
Nos. 626-630 (5)	6.25	5.00

Issued in sheets of 10.

A press sheet containing sheets of 10 each of Nos. 626-630 was produced for limited sales overseas. Value, $100.

Independence, 37th Anniv. — A292

1984, Aug. 14
631 A292 60p Jasmine .25 .25
632 A292 4r Lighted torch .50 .45

Intl. Trade Fair, Sept. 1-21, Karachi A293

1984, Sept. 1
633 A293 60p multicolored .60 .30

1984 Natl. Tourism Convention, Karachi, Nov. 5-8 — A293a

Shah Jahan Mosque: a, Main dome interior. b, Tile work. c, Entrance. d, Archways. e, Dome interior, diff.

1984, Nov. 5 Litho. *Perf. 13½*
634 Strip of 5 3.00 3.00
a.-e. A293a 1r any single .50 .40

United Bank Limited, 25th Anniv. A294

1984, Nov. 7
635 A294 60p multicolored .75 .60

UNCTAD, UN Conference on Trade and Development, 20th Anniv. — A294a

1984, Dec. 24 *Perf. 14½x14*
636 A294a 60p multicolored .85 .35

Postal Life Insurance, Cent. — A295

1984, Dec. 29 *Perf. 13½x14*
637 A295 60p multicolored .50 .25
638 A295 1r multicolored .75 .25

UNESCO World Heritage Campaign — A296

No. 639, Unicorn, rock painting. No. 640, Unicorn seal, round.

1984, Dec. 31
639 2r multicolored 1.50 .80
640 2r multicolored 1.50 .80
a. A296 Pair, #639-640 3.50 3.50

Restoration of Mohenjo-Daro.

IYY, Girl Guides 75th Anniv. A297

1985, Jan. 5 *Perf. 13½*
641 A297 60p Emblems 4.00 1.25

Smelting A298

Pouring Steel — A299

1985, Jan. 15 *Perf. 13*
642 A298 60p multicolored .75 .30
643 A299 1r multicolored 1.25 .40

Referendum Reinstating Pres. Zia — A300

1985, Mar. 20 Litho. *Perf. 13*
644 A300 60p Map, sunburst 1.25 .40

Minar-e-Qarardad-e-Pakistan Tower — A301

Ballot Box A302

1985 Elections.

1985, Mar. 23
645 A301 1r multicolored .70 .25
646 A302 1r multicolored .70 .25

Mountaineering — A303

40p, Mt. Rakaposhi, Karakoram. 2r, Mt. Nangaparbat, Western Himalayas.

1985, May 27 Litho. *Perf. 14*
647 A303 40p multicolored 2.00 .75
648 A303 2r multicolored 4.25 5.50

Championship Pakistani Men's Field Hockey Team — A304

Design: 1984 Olympic gold medal, 1985 Dhaka Asia Cup, 1982 Bombay World Cup.

1985, June 5 Litho. *Perf. 13*
649 A304 1r multicolored 2.50 1.25

King Edward Medical College, Lahore, 125th Anniv. — A305

1985, July 28 Litho. *Perf. 13*
650 A305 3r multicolored 2.25 .80

Natl. Independence Day — A306

Designs: No. 651a, 37th Independence Day written in English. No. 651b, In Urdu.

1985, Aug. 14
651 A306 Pair + 2 labels .75 .75
a.-b. 60p any single .35 .30

Printed in sheets of 4 stamps + 4 labels.

Sind Madressah-Tul-Islam, Karachi, Education Cent. — A307

1985, Sept. 1
652 A307 2r multicolored 2.10 .80

Mosque, Jinnah Avenue, Karachi — A308

1985, Sept. 14
653 A308 1r Mosque by day 1.00 .35
654 A308 1r At night 1.00 .35

35th anniv. of the Jamia Masjid Pakistan Security Printing Corporation's miniature replica of the Badshahi Mosque, Lahore.

Lawrence College, Murree, 125th Anniv. — A309

1985, Sept. 21
655 A309 3r multicolored 2.50 .75

UN, 40th Anniv. — A310

1985, Oct. 24 Litho. *Perf. 14x14½*
656 A310 1r UN building, sun .40 .25
657 A310 2r Building emblem .60 .30

10th Natl. Scouting Jamboree, Lahore, Nov. 8-15 — A311

1985, Nov. 8 *Perf. 13*
658 A311 60p multicolored 3.00 1.90

Islamabad and Capital Development Authority Emblem — A312

1985, Nov. 30 *Perf. 14½*
659 A312 3r multicolored 2.10 .50

Islamabad, capital of Pakistan, 25th anniv.

Flags and Map of SAARC Nations A313

Flags as Flower Petals A314

1985, Dec. 8 *Perf. 13½, 13*
660 A313 1r multicolored 2.50 3.50
661 A314 2r multicolored 1.00 1.75

SAARC, South Asian Assoc. for Regional Cooperation.

Dove and World Map A315

1985, Dec. 14 *Perf. 13*
662 A315 60p multicolored 1.00 .60

UN Declaration on the Granting of Independence to Colonial Countries and Peoples, 25th Anniv.

Shaheen Falcon — A316

1986, Jan. 20 *Perf. 13½x14*
663 A316 1.50r multicolored 5.00 4.00

Agricultural Development Bank, 25th Anniv. — A317

1986, Feb. 18 Litho. *Perf. 13*
664 A317 60p multicolored 1.00 .40

Sadiq Egerton College, Bahawalpur, Cent. — A318

1986, Apr. 25
665 A318 1r multicolored 3.50 1.00

A319

1986, May 11 *Perf. 13½*
666 A319 1r multicolored 3.25 .85

Asian Productivity Organization, 25th anniv.

A320

1986, Aug. 14 Litho. *Perf. 14½x14*

667 A320 80p "1947-1986" 1.50 .60
668 A320 1r Urdu text, fireworks 1.50 .60

Independence Day, 39th anniv.

A321

1986, Sept. 8 *Perf. 13*

669 A321 1r Teacher, students 1.75 .60

Intl. Literacy Day.

A322

1986, Oct. 28 Litho. *Perf. 13½x13*

670 A322 80p multicolored 2.50 .40

UN Child Survival Campaign.

Aitchison College, Lahore, Cent. — A323

1986, Nov. 3 *Perf. 13½*

671 A323 2.50r multicolored 1.75 .60

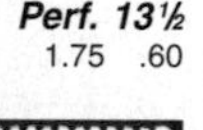

Intl. Peace Year — A324

1986, Nov. 20 *Perf. 13*

672 A324 4r multicolored .65 .55

4th Asian Cup Table Tennis Tournament, Karachi A325

1986, Nov. 25 *Perf. 14½*

673 A325 2r multicolored 2.50 .50

Marcopolo Sheep — A326

1986, Dec. 4 Litho. *Perf. 14*

674 A326 2r multicolored 3.25 2.50

See No. 698.

Eco Philex '86 — A327

Mosques: No. 675a, Selimiye, Turkey. No. 675b, Gawhar Shad, Iran. No. 675c, Grand Mosque, Pakistan.

1986, Dec. 20 *Perf. 13*

675 Strip of 3 4.00 4.00
a.-c. A327 3r any single 1.25 1.25

St. Patrick's School, Karachi, 125th Anniv. — A328

1987, Jan. 29 Litho. *Perf. 13*

676 A328 5r multicolored 3.00 1.10

Savings Bank Week — A329

Birds, berries and: a, National defense. b, Education. c, Agriculture. d, Industry.

1987, Feb. 21 Litho. *Perf. 13*

677 Block of 4 + 2 labels 5.00 5.00
a.-d. A329 5r any single 1.00 .75

Parliament House Opening, Islamabad — A330

1987, Mar. 23

678 A330 3r multicolored .60 .25

Fight Against Drug Abuse A331

1987, June 30 Litho. *Perf. 13*

679 A331 1r multicolored .60 .25

Natl. Independence, 40th Anniv. — A332

Natl. flag and: 80p, Natl. anthem, written in Urdu. 3r, Jinnah's first natl. address, the Minar-e-Qarardad-e-Pakistan and natl. coat of arms.

1987, Aug. 14 Litho. *Perf. 13*

680 A332 80p multicolored .75 .25
681 A332 3r multicolored 2.00 .75

Miniature Sheet

Air Force, 40th Anniv. — A333

Aircraft: a, Tempest II. b, Hawker Fury. c, Super Marine Attacker. d, F86 Sabre. e, F104 Star Fighter. f, C130 Hercules. g, F6. h, Mirage III. i, A5. j, F16 Fighting Falcon.

1987, Sept. 7 Litho. *Perf. 13½*

682 Sheet of 10 16.00 16.00
a.-j. A333 3r any single 1.25 1.00

Tourism Convention 1987 — A334

Views along Karakoram Highway: a, Pasu Glacier. b, Apricot trees. c, Highway winding through hills. d, Khunjerab peak.

1987, Oct. 1 *Perf. 13*

683 Block of 4 2.50 2.50
a.-d. A334 1.50r any single .50 .25

Shah Abdul Latif Bhitai Mausoleum — A335

1987, Oct. 8 *Perf. 13*

684 A335 80p multicolored .25 .25

D.J. Sind Government Science College, Karachi, Cent. — A336

1987, Nov. 7

685 A336 80p multicolored .25 .25

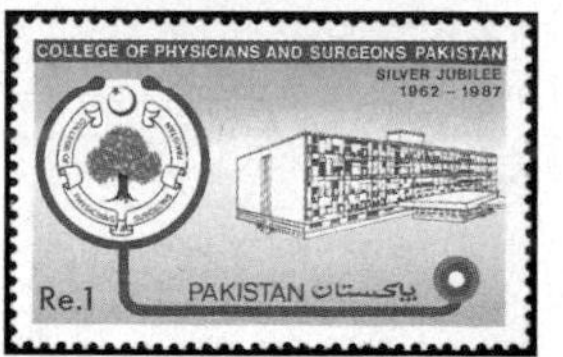

College of Physicians and Surgeons, 25th Anniv. — A337

1987, Dec. 9 Litho. *Perf. 13*

686 A337 1r multicolored 1.75 .60

Intl. Year of Shelter for the Homeless A338

1987, Dec. 15

687 A338 3r multicolored .50 .35

Cathedral Church of the Resurrection, Lahore, Cent. — A339

1987, Dec. 20

688 A339 3r multicolored .50 .25

Natl. Postal Service, 40th Anniv. A340

1987, Dec. 28
689 A340 3r multicolored .50 .25

Radio Pakistan A341

1987, Dec. 31
690 A341 80p multicolored .25 .25

Jamshed Nusserwanjee Mehta (1886-1952), Mayor of Karachi, Member of the Sind Legislative Assembly — A342

1988, Jan. 7
691 A342 3r multicolored .50 .35

World Leprosy Day — A343

1988, Jan. 31
692 A343 3r multicolored .75 .25

World Health Organization, 40th Anniv. — A344

1988, Apr. 7 Litho. ***Perf. 13***
693 A344 4r multicolored .75 .30

Intl. Red Cross and Red Crescent Organizations, 125th Annivs. — A345

1988, May 8
694 A345 3r multicolored .70 .45

Independence Day, 41st Anniv. — A346

1988, Aug. 14 Litho. ***Perf. 13½***
695 A346 80p multicolored .35 .25
696 A346 4r multicolored .35 .35

Miniature Sheet

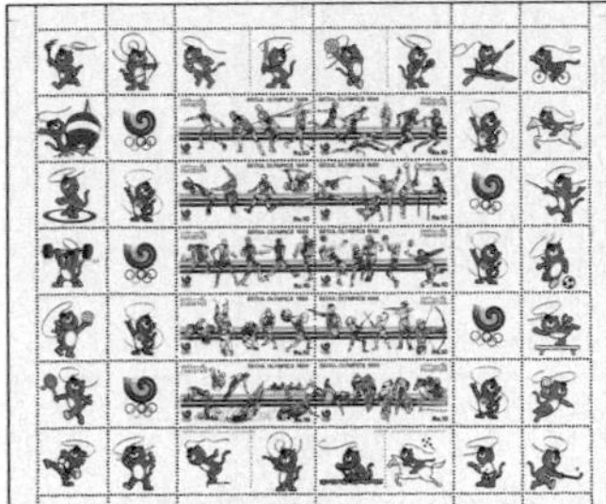

1988 Summer Olympics, Seoul — A347

Events: a, Discus, shot put, hammer throw, javelin. b, Relay, hurdles, running, walking. c, High jump, long jump, triple jump, pole vault. d, Gymnastic floor exercises, rings, parallel bars. e, Table tennis, tennis, field hockey, baseball. f, Volleyball, soccer, basketball, team handball. g, Wrestling, judo, boxing, weight lifting. h, Sport pistol, fencing, rifle shooting, archery. i, Swimming, diving, yachting, quadruple-sculling, kayaking. j, Equestrian jumping, cycling, steeplechase.

1988, Sept. 17 Litho. ***Perf. 13½x13***
697 A347 Sheet of 10+32 labels 13.00 13.00
a.-j. 10r any single 1.00 1.00

Labels contained in No. 697 picture the Seoul Games character trademark or emblem. Size of No. 697: 251x214mm.

Fauna Type of 1986

1988, Oct. 29 Litho. ***Perf. 14***
698 A326 2r Suleman markhor, vert. .85 .40

Pioneers of Freedom Type of 1979

1989, Jan. 23 Litho. Wmk. 351
699 A236 3r Maulana Hasrat Mohani .45 .25

Islamia College, Peshawar, 75th Anniv. — A348

1988, Dec. 22 Unwmk. ***Perf. 13½***
700 A348 3r multicolored .60 .25

SAARC Summit Conference, Islamabad — A349

Designs: 25r, Flags, symbols of commerce. 50r, Globe, communication and transportation. 75r, Bangladesh #69, Maldive Islands #1030, Bhutan #132, Pakistan #403, Ceylon #451, India #580, Nepal #437.

1988, Dec. 29 ***Perf. 13***
701 A349 25r shown 1.50 1.50

No. 701 exists with attached label. Values: *$10* mint, *$20* used.

Size: 33x33mm
Perf. 14
702 A349 50r multicolored 4.50 3.25

Size: 52x28mm
Perf. 13½x13
703 A349 75r multicolored 3.50 *3.50*
Nos. 701-703 (3) 9.50 8.25

No. 703 exists with attached label. Value, strip of three with label $20.

Adasia '89, 16th Asian Advertising Congress, Lahore, Feb. 18-22 — A350

1989, Feb. 18 Litho. ***Perf. 13***
704 Strip of 3 3.50 3.25
a. A350 1r deep rose lilac & multi .95 .65
b. A350 1r green & multi .95 .65
c. A350 1r bright vermilion & multi .95 .65

Printed in sheets of 9.

Pres. Zulfikar Ali Bhutto (1928-1979), Ousted by Military Coup and Executed A351

Portraits.

1989, Apr. 4 Litho. ***Perf. 13***
705 A351 1r shown .25 .25
706 A351 2r multi, diff. .40 .25

Submarine Operations, 25th Anniv. — A352

Submarines: a, *Agosta*. b, *Daphne*. c, *Fleet Snorkel*.

1989, June 1 Litho. ***Perf. 13½***
707 Strip of 3 4.25 4.25
a.-c. A352 1r any single 1.25 1.25

Oath of the Tennis Court, by David — A353

1989, June 24 Litho. ***Perf. 13½***
708 A353 7r multicolored 2.25 .80

French revolution, bicent.

Archaeological Heritage — A354

Terra cotta vessels excavated in Baluchistan: a, Pirak, c. 2200 B.C. b, Nindo Damb, c. 2300 B.C. c, Mehrgarh, c. 3600 B.C. d, Nausharo, c. 2600 B.C.

1989, June 28 ***Perf. 14½x14***
709 Block of 4 1.25 1.25
a.-d. A354 1r any single .25 .25

Asia-Pacific Telecommunity, 10th Anniv. — A355

1989, July 1 ***Perf. 13½x14***
710 A355 3r multicolored .50 .25

Laying the Foundation Stone for the 1st Integrated Container Terminal, Port Qasim A356

1989, Aug. 5 Litho. ***Perf. 14***
711 A356 6r Ship in berth 3.25 3.25

Mohammad Ali Jinnah — A357

Litho & Engr.
1989, Aug. 14 Wmk. 351 ***Perf. 13***
712 A357 1r multicolored .65 .25
713 A357 1.50r multicolored .80 .25
714 A357 2r multicolored .90 .25
715 A357 3r multicolored 1.00 .30
716 A357 4r multicolored 1.50 .35
717 A357 5r multicolored 1.75 .40
Nos. 712-717 (6) 6.60 1.80

Independence Day.

Nos. 712-717 exist overprinted "NATIONAL SEMINAR ON PHILATELY MULTAN 1992." These were available only at the seminar and were not sold in post offices. Value $125. Beware of forgeries.

Abdul Latif Bhitai Memorial A358

1989, Sept. 16 Litho. Unwmk.
718 A358 2r multicolored .60 .25

245th death and 300th birth annivs. of Shah Abdul Latif Bhitai.

World Wildlife Fund — A359

Himalayan black bears and WWF emblem: a, Bear on slope, emblem UR. b, Bear on slope, emblem UL. c, Bear on top of rock, emblem UR. d, Seated bear, emblem UL.

Perf. 14x13½
1989, Oct. 7 Litho. Unwmk.
719 A359 Block of 4 4.00 4.00
a.-d. 4r, any single .75 .75

World Food Day — A360

1989, Oct. 16 ***Perf. 14x12½***
720 A360 1r multicolored .45 .30

Quilt and Bahishiti Darwaza (Heavenly Gate) — A361

1989, Oct. 20 ***Perf. 13***
721 A361 3r multicolored .50 .25

800th Birth anniv. of Baba Farid.

4th SAF Games, Islamabad A362

1989, Oct. 20
722 A362 1r multicolored .45 .40

Pakistan Television, 25th Anniv. A363

1989, Nov. 26 Litho. ***Perf. 13½***
723 A363 3r multicolored .50 .25

SAARC Year Against Drug Abuse and Drug Trafficking A364

1989, Dec. 8 ***Perf. 13***
724 A364 7r multicolored 2.50 .85

Murray College, Sialkot, Cent. A365

1989, Dec. 18 ***Perf. 14***
725 A365 6r multicolored .60 .40

Government College, Lahore, 125th Anniv. — A366

1989, Dec. 21 ***Perf. 13***
726 A366 6r multicolored .60 .50

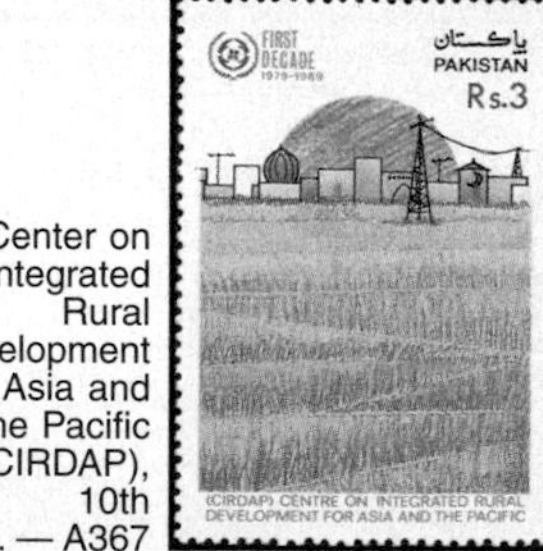

Center on Integrated Rural Development for Asia and the Pacific (CIRDAP), 10th Anniv. — A367

1989, Dec. 31
727 A367 3r multicolored .60 .40

Organization of the Islamic Conference (OIC), 20th Anniv. — A368

1990, Feb. 9 Litho. ***Perf. 13***
728 A368 1r multicolored 1.40 .50

7th World Field Hockey Cup, Lahore, Feb. 12-23 — A369

1990, Feb. 12 ***Perf. 14x13½***
729 A369 2r multicolored 5.25 4.00

A370

Pakistan Resolution, 50th Anniv. — A371

Designs: a, Allama Mohammad Iqbal addressing the Allahabad Session of the All-India Muslim League and swearing-in of Liat Ali Khan as league secretary-general. b, Freedom fighter Maulana Mohammad Ali Jauhar at Muslim rally and Mohammed Ali Jinnah at microphone. c, Muslim woman holding flag and swearing-in of Mohammed Ali Jinnah as governor-general of Pakistan, Aug. 14, 1947. 7r, English and Urdu translations of the resolution, natl. flag and Minar-e-Qarardade Pakistan.

1990, Mar. 23 Litho. ***Perf. 13***
730 Strip of 3 3.00 3.00
a.-c. A370 1r any single 1.00 .75

Size: 90x45mm
Perf. 13½
731 A371 7r multicolored 2.00 2.00

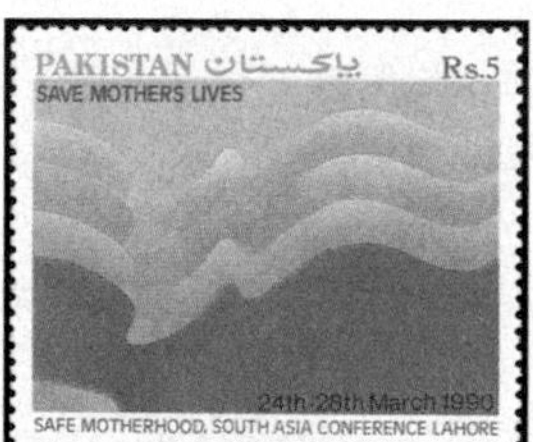

Safe Motherhood South Asia Conference, Lahore — A372

1990, Mar. 24 ***Perf. 13½***
732 A372 5r multicolored .75 .50

Calligraphic Painting of a Ghalib Verse, by Shakir Ali (1916-1975) — A373

1990, Apr. 19 Litho. ***Perf. 13½x13***
733 A373 1r multicolored 2.25 .65

See Nos. 757-758.

Badr-1 Satellite — A374

1990, July 26 Litho. ***Perf. 13***
734 A374 3r multicolored 3.75 2.50

Pioneers of Freedom A375

No. 735: a, Allama Mohammad Iqbal (1877-1938). b, Mohammad Ali Jinnah (1876-1948). c, Sir Syed Ahmad Khan (1817-98). d, Nawab Salimullah (1884-1915). e, Mohtarma Fatima Jinnah (1893-1967). f, Aga Khan III (1877-1957). g, Nawab Mohammad Ismail Khan (1884-1958). h, Hussain Shaheed Suhrawardy (1893-1963). i, Syed Ameer Ali (1849-1928).

No. 736: a, Nawab Bahadur Yar Jung (1905-44). b, Khawaja Nazimuddin (1894-1964). c, Maulana Obaidullah Sindhi (1872-1944). d, Sahibzada Abdul Qaiyum Khan (c. 1863-1937). e, Begum Jahanara Shah Nawaz (1896-1979). f, Sir Ghulam Hussain Hidayatullah (1879-1948). g, Qazi Mohammad Isa (1913-76). h, Sir M. Shahnawaz Khan Mamdot (1883-1942). i, Pir Shaib of Manki Sharif (1923-60).

No. 737: a, Liaquat Ali Khan (1895-1951). b, Maulvi A.K. Fazl-Ul-Haq (1873-1962). c, Allama Shabbir Ahmad Usmani (1885-1949). d, Sardar Abdur Rab Nishtar (1899-1958). e, Bi Amma (c. 1850-1924). f, Sir Abdullah Haroon (1872-1942). g, Chaudhry Rahmat Ali (1897-1951). h, Raja Sahib of Mahmudabad (1914-73). i, Hassanally Effendi (1830-1895).

No. 737J: k, Maulana Zafar Ali Khan (1873-1956). l, Maulana Mohamed Ali Jauhar (1878-1931). m, Chaudhry Khaliquzzaman (1889-1973). n, Hameed Nizami (1915-62). o, Begum Ra'ana Liaquat Ali Khan (1905-90). p, Mirza Abol Hassan Ispahani (1902-81). q, Raja Ghazanfar Ali Khan (1895-1963). r, Malik Barkat Ali (1886-1946). s, Mir Jaffer Khan Jamali (c. 1911-67).

1990-91 Litho. ***Perf. 13***
Miniature Sheets

735 Sheet of 9 3.50 3.50
a.-i. A375 1r any single .40 .25
736 Sheet of 9 3.50 3.50
a.-i. A375 1r any single .40 .25
737 Sheet of 9 3.50 3.50
a.-i. A375 1r any single .40 .25
737J Sheet of 9 ('91) 6.00 6.00
k.-s. A375 1r any single .40 .25
Nos. 735-737J (4) 16.50 16.50

Issued: #735-737, Aug. 19; #737J, 1991.

See Nos. 773, 792, 804, 859-860, 865, 875-876, 922-924.

Indonesia Pakistan Economic and Cultural Cooperation Organization, 1968-1990 — A376

1990, Aug. 19
738 A376 7r multicolored 3.50 1.10

Intl. Literacy Year — A377

1990, Sept. 8
739 A377 3r multicolored 1.25 .75

A378

1990, Sept. 22
740 A378 2r multicolored 1.10 .40

Joint meeting of Royal College of Physicians, Edinburgh and College of Physicians and Surgeons, Pakistan.

World Summit for Children A379

1990, Sept. 19
741 A379 7r multicolored .85 .50

Year of the Girl Child A380

1990, Nov. 21 Litho. *Perf. 13½*
742 A380 2r multicolored .75 .50

Security Papers Ltd., 25th Anniv. — A381

1990, Dec. 8 *Perf. 13*
743 A381 3r multicolored 4.50 1.50

Intl. Civil Defense Day — A382

1991, Mar. 1 Litho. *Perf. 13*
744 A382 7r multicolored 2.75 2.00

South & West Asia Postal Union — A383

1991, Mar. 21
745 A383 5r multicolored 2.10 1.50

World Population Day — A384

1991, July 11
746 A384 10r multicolored 2.50 1.50

Intl. Special Olympics A385

1991, July 19
747 A385 7r multicolored 2.10 1.50

Habib Bank Limited, 50th Anniv. — A386

1991, Aug. 25 Litho. *Perf. 13*
748 A386 1r brt red & multi 1.25 .45
749 A386 5r brt green & multi 4.50 3.25

St. Joseph's Convent School, Karachi — A387

1991, Sept. 8
750 A387 5r multicolored 4.25 3.00

Emperor Sher Shah Suri (c. 1472-1545) A388

1991, Oct. 5
751 A388 5r multicolored 1.75 1.75

Souvenir Sheet
Size: 90x81mm
Imperf

752 A388 7r multicolored 2.00 2.00

Pakistani Scientific Expedition to Antarctica — A389

1991, Oct. 28
753 A389 7r multicolored 3.50 2.50

Houbara Bustard — A390

1991, Nov. 4
754 A390 7r multicolored 3.00 2.00

Asian Development Bank, 25th Anniv. — A391

1991, Dec. 19 Litho. *Perf. 13*
755 A391 7r multicolored 3.50 1.50

Hazrat Sultan Bahoo, 300th Death Anniv. A392

1991, Dec. 22
756 A392 7r multicolored 2.10 1.10

Painting Type of 1990

Paintings and artists: No. 757, Village Life, by Allah Ustad Bux (1892-1978). No. 758, Miniature of Royal Procession, by Muhammad Haji Sharif (1889-1978).

1991, Dec. 24
757 A373 1r multicolored 2.25 1.25
758 A373 1r multicolored 2.25 1.25

American Express Travelers Cheques, 100th Anniv. — A393

1991, Dec. 26 *Perf. 13½*
759 A393 7r multicolored 2.50 1.50

Muslim Commercial Bank, First Year of Private Operation — A394

7r, City skyline, worker, cogwheels, computer operators.

1992, Apr. 8 Litho. *Perf. 13*
760 A394 1r multicolored .25 .25
761 A394 7r multicolored 1.00 .65

Pakistan, 1992 World Cricket Champions — A395

World Cricket Cup and: 2r, Pakistani player, vert. 7r, Pakistan flag, fireworks, vert.

1992, Apr. 27
762 A395 2r multicolored .75 .50
763 A395 5r multicolored 1.75 1.10
764 A395 7r multicolored 2.00 1.40
Nos. 762-764 (3) 4.50 3.00

Intl. Space Year — A396

Design: 2r, Globe, satellite.

1992, June 7 Litho. *Perf. 13*
771 A396 1r multicolored .35 .25
772 A396 2r multicolored .55 .35

30th anniv. of first Pakistani rocket (#771).

Pioneers of Freedom Type of 1990

Designs: a, Syed Suleman Nadvi (1884-1953). b, Nawab Iftikhar Hussain Khan Mamdot (1906-1969). c, Maulana Muhammad Shibli Naumani (1857-1914).

1992, Aug. 14 Litho. *Perf. 13*
773 A375 1r Strip of 3, #a.-c. 4.50 3.75

World Population Day — A397

1992, July 25
774 A397 6r multicolored 1.10 1.10

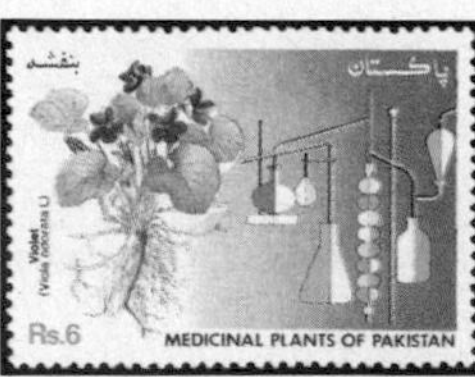

Medicinal Plants — A398

1992, Nov. 22 **Litho.** ***Perf. 13***
775 A398 6r multicolored 3.75 3.50

See No. 791.

Extraordinary Session of Economic Cooperation Organization Council of Ministers, Islamabad — A399

1992, Nov. 28
776 A399 7r multicolored 1.40 1.00

Intl. Conference on Nutrition, Rome A400

1992, Dec. 5 ***Perf. 14***
777 A400 7r multicolored .85 .85

A401

1992, Dec. 14 ***Perf. 13***
778 A401 7r Alhambra, Spain .60 .60

Islamic cultural heritage.

A402

1992, Aug. 23 ***Perf. 14x12½***
779 A402 6r 6th Jamboree .70 .60
780 A402 6r 4th Conference .70 .60

Islamic Scouts, Islamabad.

Government Islamia College, Lahore, Cent. — A403

1992, Nov. 1 ***Perf. 13***
781 A403 3r multicolored .60 .60

Industries A404

Designs: a, 10r, Surgical instruments. b, 15r, Leather goods. c, 25r, Sports equipment.

1992, July 5 **Litho.** ***Perf. 13½x13***
782 A404 Strip of 3, #a.-c. 5.50 5.50

World Telecommunications Day — A405

1993, May 17 **Litho.** ***Perf. 13***
783 A405 1r multicolored 1.50 .55

21st Islamic Foreign Ministers Conference A406

1993, Apr. 25
784 A406 1r buff & multi .50 .50
785 A406 6r green & multi 2.25 1.40

A407

Traditional costumes of provinces.

1993, Mar. 10
786 A407 6r Sindh 1.50 1.50
787 A407 6r North West Frontier 1.50 1.50
788 A407 6r Baluchistan 1.50 1.50
789 A407 6r Punjab 1.50 1.50
Nos. 786-789 (4) 6.00 6.00

A408

Birds: a, Gadwall. b, Common shelduck. c, Mallard. d, Greylag goose.

The order of the birds is different on each row. Therefore the arc of the rainbow is different on each of the 4 Gadwalls, etc.

1992, Dec. 31 ***Perf. 14x13***
790 A408 5r Sheet of 16 10.00 *15.00*
a.-d. Any single .60 .60
e. Horiz. strip of 4, #a-d 2.00 *3.00*

Medicinal Plants Type

1993, June 20 **Litho.** ***Perf. 13***
791 A398 6r Fennel, chemistry equipment 3.25 1.25

Pioneers of Freedom Type of 1990

Designs: a, Rais Ghulam Mohammad Bhurgri (1878-1924). b, Mir Ahmed Yar Khan, Khan of Kalat (1902-1977). c, Mohammad Abdul Latif Pir Sahib Zakori Sharif (1914-1978).

1993, Aug. 14 **Litho.** ***Perf. 13***
792 A375 1r Strip of 3, #a.-c. 3.50 2.50

Gordon College, Rawalpindi, Cent. — A410

1993, Sept. 1
793 A410 2r multicolored 1.75 1.75

Juniper Forests, Ziarat — A411

1993, Sept. 30
794 A411 7r multicolored 7.50 3.00

See No. 827.

World Food Day — A412

1993, Oct. 16 ***Perf. 14***
795 A412 6r multicolored 1.00 1.00

A413

Wmk. 351

1993, Dec. 25 **Litho.** ***Perf. 13½***
796 A413 1r multicolored 2.25 .55

Wazir Mansion, birthplace of Muhammad Ali Jinnah.

A414

Perf. 13x13½

1993, Oct. 28 **Unwmk.**
797 A414 7r multicolored 3.00 3.00

Burn Hall Institutions, 50th anniv.

South & West Asia Postal Union — A415

1993, Nov. 18 ***Perf. 13***
798 A415 7r multicolored 3.50 3.50

Pakistani College of Physicians & Surgeons, Intl. Medical Congress A416

1993, Dec. 10
799 A416 1r multicolored 2.75 .65

ILO, 75th Anniv. A417

1994, Apr. 11 **Litho.** ***Perf. 13***
800 A417 7r multicolored 2.00 2.00

Bio-diversity — A418

a, Ratan jot, medicinal plant. b, Wetlands. c, Mahseer fish. d, Himalayan brown bear.

1994, Apr. 20 **Litho.** ***Perf. 13½***
801 A418 6r Strip or block of 4, #a.-d. 2.00 2.00

Intl. Year of the Family — A419

1994, May 15 ***Perf. 13***
802 A419 7r multicolored .75 .75

World Population Day — A420

1994, July 11 **Litho.** ***Perf. 13***
803 A420 7r multicolored .75 .75

Pioneers of Freedom Type of 1990

Miniature Sheet of 8

Designs: a, Nawab Mohsin-Ul-Mulk (1837-1907). b, Sir Shahnawaz Bhutto (1888-1957). c, Nawab Viqar-Ul-Mulk (1841-1917). d, Pir Ilahi Bux (1890-1975). e, Sheikh Sir Abdul Qadir (1874-1950). f, Dr. Sir Ziauddin Ahmed (1878-1947). g, Jam Mir Ghulam Qadir Khan

(1920-88). h, Sardar Aurangzeb Khan (1899-1953).

1994, Aug. 14 Litho. *Perf. 13*
804 A375 1r #a.-h. + label 3.25 3.25

A421

1994, Oct. 2 *Perf. 13x13½*
805 A421 2r multicolored 1.50 .45

First Intl. Festival of Islamic Artisans.

A422

1994, Sept. 8
806 A422 7r multicolored .75 .75

Intl. Literacy Day.

Hyoscyamus Niger — A423

1994 *Perf. 13*
807 A423 6r multicolored 1.00 .75

Mohammad Ali Jinnah — A424

Litho. & Engr.
1994, Sept. 11 Wmk. 351 *Perf. 13*

808	A424	1r slate & multi	.35	.25
809	A424	2r claret & multi	.50	.25
810	A424	3r bright bl & multi	.65	.25
811	A424	4r emerald & multi	.70	.25
812	A424	5r lake & multi	.75	.25
813	A424	7r blue & multi	1.00	.25
814	A424	10r green & multi	.80	.30
815	A424	12r orange & multi	.90	.60
816	A424	15r violet & multi	1.00	.80
817	A424	20r rose & multi	1.10	1.00
818	A424	25r brown & multi	1.25	1.25
818A	A424	28r blk & multi		—
819	A424	30r olive brn & multi	1.75	1.25
		Nos. 808-819 (12)	10.75	6.70

Issued: 28r, 9/30/2011.

2nd SAARC & 12th Natl. Scout Jamboree, Quetta — A425

1994, Sept. 22 Litho.
820 A425 7r multicolored 1.00 .60

Publication of Ferdowsi's Book of Kings, 1000th Anniv. — A426

1994, Oct. 27
821 A426 1r multicolored .50 .50

Indonesia-Pakistan Economic & Cultural Cooperation Organization — A427

1994, Aug. 19
822 A427 10r Hala pottery 1.25 .60
823 A427 10r Lombok pottery 1.25 .60
a. Pair, #822-823 4.25 4.25

See Indonesia Nos. 1585-1586.

Lahore Museum, Cent. — A428

Wmk. 351
1994, Dec. 27 Litho. *Perf. 13*
824 A428 4r multicolored .60 .60

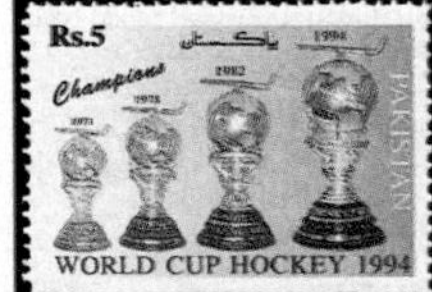
Pakistan, 1994 World Cup Field Hockey Champions A429

1994, Dec. 31
825 A429 5r multicolored 1.00 .40

World Tourism Organization, 20th Anniv. — A430

1995, Jan. 2
826 A430 4r multicolored 1.00 .30

Juniper Forests Type of 1993

1995, Feb. 14 Litho. *Perf. 13*
827 A411 1r like #794 .75 .25

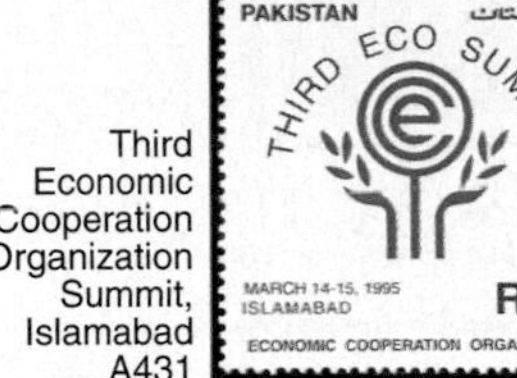
Third Economic Cooperation Organization Summit, Islamabad A431

1995, Mar. 14 Litho. *Perf. 14*
828 A431 6r multicolored 1.60 1.10

Khushall Khan Khatak (1613-89) A432

1995, Feb. 28 *Perf. 13*
829 A432 7r multicolored 2.50 2.25

Earth Day A433

Wmk. 351
1995, Apr. 20 Litho. *Perf. 13*
830 A433 6r multicolored .75 .75

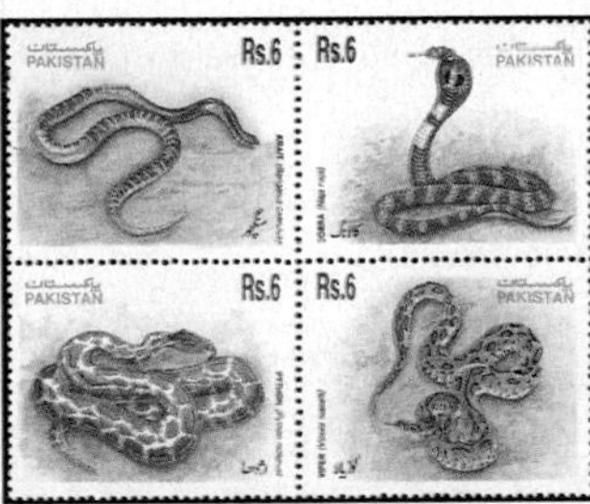
Snakes — A434

a, Krait. b, Cobra. c, Python. d, Viper.

1995, Apr. 15 Unwmk. *Perf. 13½*
831 A434 6r Block of 4, #a.-d. 4.00 4.00

Traditional Means of Transportation — A435

Wmk. 351
1995, May 22 Litho. *Perf. 13*
832 A435 5r Horse-drawn carriage 1.00 .85

Louis Pasteur (1822-95) A436

Wmk. 351
1995, Sept. 28 Litho. *Perf. 13*
833 A436 5r multicolored .85 .80

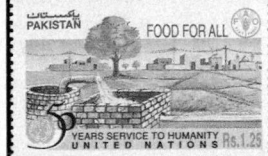

UN, FAO, 50th Anniv. A437

1995, Oct. 16
834 A437 1.25r multicolored 1.00 .25

Kinnaird College for Women, Lahore — A438

1995, Nov. 3 *Perf. 14x13*
835 A438 1.25r multicolored 1.00 .25

4th World Conference on Women, Beijing — A439

Women in various activities: a, Playing golf, in armed forces, repairing technical device. b, Graduates, student, chemist, computer operator, reading gauge. c, At sewing machine, working with textiles. d, Making rugs, police woman, laborers.

1995, Sept. 15 *Perf. 13*
836 A439 1.25r Strip of 4, #a.-d. 1.40 1.40

Presentation Convent School, Rawalpindi, Cent. A440

Wmk. 351
1995, Sept. 8 Litho. *Perf. 13½*
837 A440 1.25r multicolored .80 .45

A440a

Panel colors: 5p, Orange. 15p, Violet. 25p, Red. 75p, Red brown.

1995-96 Litho. Unwmk. *Perf. 13½*
837A-837D A440a Set of 4 2.50 .60

Issued: 5p, 15p, 10/10/95; 25p, 9/28/95; 75p, 5/15/96.

Liaquat Ali Khan (1895-1951) — A441

1995, Oct. 1 *Perf. 13*
838 A441 1.25r multicolored 1.00 .40

1st Conference of Women Parliamentarians from Muslim Countries — A442

Designs: No. 839, Dr. Tansu Ciller, Prime Minister of Turkey. No. 840, Mohtarma Benazir Bhutto, Prime Minister of Pakistan.

1995, Aug. 1 Unwmk.
839 A442 5r multicolored .90 .90
840 A442 5r multicolored .90 .90
a. Pair, #839-840 2.00 2.00

Intl. Conference of Writers and Intellectuals A443

Wmk. 351
1995, Nov. 30 Litho. *Perf. 14*
841 A443 1.25r multicolored 1.00 .40

Allama Iqbal Open University, 20th Anniv. — A444

1995, Dec. 16 *Perf. 13*
842 A444 1.25r multicolored .45 .30

Butterflies — A445

Designs: a, Érasmie. b, Catogramme. c, Ixias. d, Héliconie.

Wmk. 351
1995, Sept. 1 Litho. *Perf. 13½*
843 A445 6r Strip of 4, #a.-d. 2.50 2.50

Fish — A446

Designs: a, Sardinella long. b, Tilapia mossambica. c, Salmo fario. d, Labeo rohita.

1995, Sept. 1
844 A446 6r Strip of 4, #a.-d. 3.50 3.50

SAARC, 10th Anniv. — A447

1995, Dec. 8 *Perf. 13*
845 A447 1.25r multicolored .45 .40

UN, 50th Anniv. — A448

Wmk. 351
1995, Oct. 24 Litho. *Perf. 13½*
846 A448 7r multicolored 1.25 1.25

Karachi '95, Natl. Water Sports Gala — A449

Designs: a, Man on jet ski. b, Gondola race. c, Sailboard race. d, Man water skiing.

1995, Dec. 14 *Perf. 14x13*
847 A449 1.25r Block of 4, #a.-d. 1.50 1.50

University of Baluchistan, Quetta, 25th Anniv. — A452

Wmk. 351
1995, Dec. 31 Litho. *Perf. 13*
850 A452 1.25r multicolored .60 .55

Zulfikar Ali Bhutto (1928-79), Politician, President — A455

Designs: 1.25r, Bhutto, flag, crowd of people, vert. 8r, like No. 855

Wmk. 351
1996, Apr. 4 Litho. *Perf. 13*
855 A455 1.25r multicolored .75 .35
856 A455 4r shown 2.25 1.10

Size: 114x69mm
Imperf
857 A455 8r multicolored 2.50 2.50

Raja Aziz Bhatti Shaheed (1928-65) — A456

Wmk. 351
1995, Sept. 5 Litho. *Perf. 13*
858 A456 1.25r multicolored 1.75 .40

See Nos. 953, 983, 997, 1016.

Pioneers of Freedom Type of 1990

#859, Maulana Shaukat Ali (1873-1938). #860, Chaudhry Ghulam Abbas (1904-67).

1995, Aug. 14 Unwmk. *Perf. 13*
859 A375 1r green & brown .80 .50
860 A375 1r green & brown .80 .50
a. Pair, #859-860 1.75 1.75

1996 Summer Olympic Games, Atlanta — A457

Design: 25r, #861-864 without denominations, simulated perfs, Olympic rings, "100," Atlanta '96 emblem.

Wmk. 351
1996, Aug. 3 Litho. *Perf. 13*
861 A457 5r Wrestling .70 .70
862 A457 5r Boxing .70 .70
863 A457 5r Pierre de Coubertin .70 .70
864 A457 5r Field hockey .70 .70
Nos. 861-864 (4) 2.80 2.80

Imperf
Size: 111x101mm
864A A457 25r multicolored 3.00 3.00

Pioneers of Freedom Type of 1990

Allama Abdullah Yousuf Ali (1872-1953).

Unwmk.
1996, Aug. 14 Litho. *Perf. 13*
865 A375 1r green & brown .45 .40

Restoration of General Post Office, Lahore A458

1996, Aug. 21 Wmk. 351 *Perf. 14*
866 A458 5r multicolored .45 .45

Intl. Literacy Day A459

1996, Sept. 8 Wmk. 351 *Perf. 13*
867 A459 2r multicolored .45 .40

Yarrow — A459a

Wmk. 351
1996, Nov. 25 Litho. *Perf. 13*
867A A459a 3r multicolored 1.00 .65

Faiz Ahmed Faiz, Poet, 86th Birthday A460

Unwmk.
1997, Feb. 13 Litho. *Perf. 13*
868 A460 3r multicolored .80 .55

Tamerlane (1336-1405) A461

Unwmk.
1997, Apr. 8 Litho. *Perf. 13*
869 A461 3r multicolored .45 .40

Famous Men — A462

Designs: No. 870, Allama Mohammad Iqbal. No. 871, Jalal-Al-Din Moulana Rumi.

1997, Apr. 21 ***Perf. 13½***
870 A462 3r multicolored .25 .25
871 A462 3r multicolored .25 .25

Compare with Iran 2726-2727.

Pakistani Independence, 50th Anniv. — A463

1997, Mar. 23 ***Perf. 13***
872 A463 2r multicolored .45 .45

Special Summit of Organization of Islamic Countries, Islamabad.

World Population Day — A464

Unwmk.

1997, July 11 **Litho.** ***Perf. 13***
873 A464 2r multicolored .45 .40

Intl. Atomic Energy Agency-Pakistan Atomic Energy Commission Cooperation, 40th Anniv. — A465

1997, July 29 ***Perf. 14***
874 A465 2r multicolored .90 .40

Pioneers of Freedom Type of 1990

#875, Begum Salma Tassaduq Hussain (1908-95). #876, Mohammad Ayub Khuhro (1901-80).

1997, Aug. 14 **Litho.** ***Perf. 13***
875 A375 1r green & brown .55 .55
876 A375 1r green & brown .55 .55

Fruits of Pakistan A466

1997, May 8
877 A466 2r Apples .45 .45

Independence, 50th Anniv. — A467

Designs: a, Allama Mohammad Iqbal. b, Mohammad Ali Jinnah. c, Liaquat Ali Khan. d, Mohtarma Fatima Jinnah.

Block of 4 + 2 Labels

1997, Aug. 14
878 A467 3r #a.-d. 2.50 .75

No. 878 exists with No. 878d unretouched. Value, $5 mint or used.

Lophophorus Impejanus A468

Wmk. 351

1997, Oct. 29 **Litho.** ***Perf. 13***
879 A468 2r multicolored 2.50 .90

Lahore College for Women, 75th Anniv. — A469

1997, Sept. 23
880 A469 3r multicolored 1.50 1.00

Intl. Day of the Disabled A470

Unwmk.

1997, Dec. 3 **Litho.** ***Perf. 13***
881 A470 4r multicolored 1.40 .45

Protection of the Ozone Layer — A471

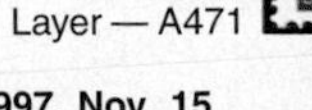

1997, Nov. 15
882 A471 3r multicolored 1.60 1.00

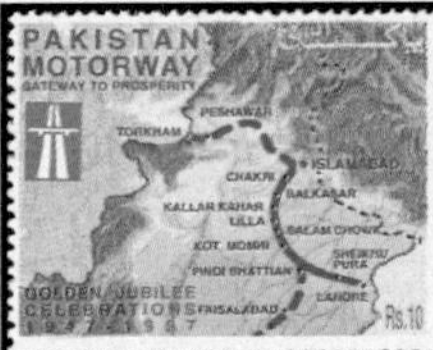

Pakistan Motorway, 50th Anniv. A472

1997, Nov. 26 ***Perf. 13½***
883 A472 10r multicolored 2.25 2.25
a. Souvenir sheet of 1 2.50 2.50

No. 883a sold for 15r.

Karachi Grammar School, 150th Anniv. A473

1997, Dec. 30 **Litho.** ***Perf. 13½***
884 A473 2r multicolored 1.10 1.10

Garlic A474

1997, Oct. 22 ***Perf. 13***
885 A474 2r multicolored 1.50 .25

Mirza Asad Ullah Khan Ghalib (1797-1869), Poet — A475

1998, Feb. 15
886 A475 2r multicolored .50 .50

Pakistan Armed Forces, 50th Anniv. A476

Wmk. 351

1997, Mar. 23 **Litho.** ***Perf. 13½***
887 A476 7r multicolored 1.00 1.00

Sir Syed Ahmad Khan (1817-98), Educator, Jurist, Author — A477

1998, Mar. 27 ***Perf. 14***
888 A477 7r multicolored 1.00 1.00

27th Natl. Games, Peshawar A478

Wmk. 351

1998, Apr. 22 **Litho.** ***Perf. 13***
889 A478 7r multicolored 1.00 1.00

Jimsonweed A479

1998, Apr. 27
890 A479 2r multicolored 1.40 1.40

Faisalabad Government College, Cent. (in 1997) — A480

1998, Aug. 14 **Litho.** ***Perf. 13***
891 A480 5r multicolored .70 .70

Pakistan Senate, 25th Anniv. A481

1998, Aug. 6 ***Perf. 13½***
892 A481 2r green & multi .25 .25
893 A481 5r blue & multi .80 .80

Mohammed Ali Jinnah — A482

Litho. & Engr.

1998-2001 Wmk. 351 *Perf. 14*

893A	A482	1r red & black	.25	.25
894	A482	2r dk bl & red	.25	.25
895	A482	3r slate grn & brn	.65	.25
896	A482	4r dp vio blk & org	.65	.25
897	A482	5r dp brn & grn	.90	.65
898	A482	6r dp grn & bl grn	1.10	.75
899	A482	7r dp brn red & dp vio	1.10	.90
		Nos. 894-899 (6)	4.65	3.05

Nos. 894 issued 8/14/98. No. 893A, 2001(?).

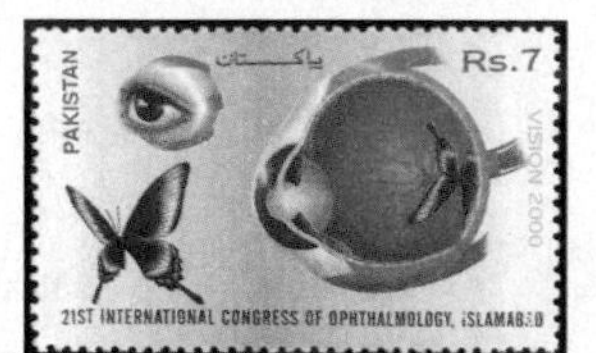

21st Intl. Congress of Ophthalmology, Islamabad — A483

Wmk. 351

1998, Sept. 11 Litho. *Perf. 13*

900 A483 7r multicolored 1.60 1.60

Syed Ahmed Shah Patrus Bukhari, Birth Cent. A484

1998, Oct. 1

901 A484 5r multicolored 1.25 1.00

Philately in Pakistan, 50th Anniv. — A485

Various portions of stamps inside "50," #20-23.

1998, Oct. 4

902 A485 6r multicolored .60 .60

World Food Day A486

Wmk. 351

1998, Oct. 16 Photo. *Perf. 13*

903 A486 6r multicolored .75 .75

Mohammad Ali Jinnah (1876-1948) A487

Wmk. 351

1998, Sept. 11 Photo. *Perf. 13½*

904 A487 15r multicolored 2.25 2.25
a. Souvenir sheet of 1, unwmk. 2.25 2.25

No. 904a sold for 20r.

Universal Declaration of Human Rights, 50th Anniv. A488

Perf. 13x14

1998, Dec. 10 Wmk. 351

905 A488 6r multicolored 1.40 1.00

Better Pakistan, 2010 A489

#906, Harvesting grain. #907, Health care. #908, Satellite dishes. #909, Airplane.

1998, Nov. 27 Unwmk.

906	A489	2r multicolored	.45	.35
907	A489	2r multicolored	.45	.35
908	A489	2r multicolored	.45	.35
909	A489	2r multicolored	.45	.35
		Nos. 906-909 (4)	1.80	1.40

Dr. Abdus Salam, Scientist A490

Unwmk.

1998, Nov. 21 Litho. *Perf. 13*

910 A490 2r multicolored .75 .50

See No. 916.

National Flag March A491

1998, Dec. 16 Wmk. 351

911 A491 2r multicolored .45 .30

Intl. Year of the Ocean A492

1998, Dec. 15 *Perf. 14*

912 A492 5r multicolored 1.50 1.00

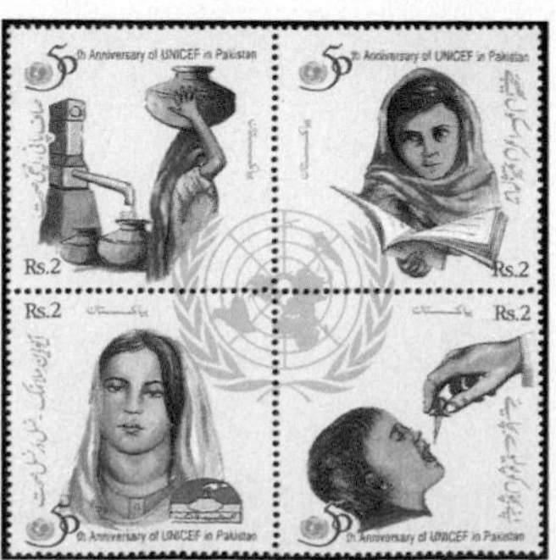

UNICEF in Pakistan, 50th Anniv. — A493

a, Distributing water. b, Child holding book. c, Girl. d, Child receiving oral vaccine.

1998, Dec. 15

913 A493 2r Block of 4, #a.-d. 1.50 1.50

Kingdom of Saudi Arabia, Cent. — A494

Perf. 13½

1999, Jan. 27 Litho. Unwmk.

914	A494	2r Emblem on sand	.50	.50
915	A494	15r Emblem on carpet	1.50	1.50
a.		Souvenir sheet of 1	2.75	2.75

No. 915a sold for 20r.

Scientists of Pakistan Type

Dr. Salimuz Zaman Siddiqui (1897-1994).

1999, Apr. 14 *Perf. 13*

916 A490 5r multicolored .60 .60

Pakistani Nuclear Test, 1st Anniv. — A495

1999, May 28 Litho. *Perf. 13*

917 A495 5r multicolored .60 .60

Completion of Data Darbar Mosque Complex — A496

1999, May 31 Litho. *Perf. 13*

918 A496 7r multicolored .80 .80

Fasting Buddha, c. 3-4 A.D. — A497

1999, July 21 Litho. *Perf. 13½x13¾*

919	A497	7r shown	1.00	1.00
920	A497	7r Facing forward	1.00	1.00
a.		Souv. sheet of 2, #919-920	3.00	3.00

No. 920a sold for 25r. China 1999 World Philatelic Exhibition (No. 920a).

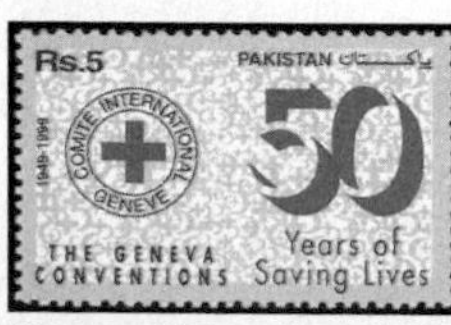

Geneva Conventions, 50th Anniv. — A498

Perf. 12¾x13¾

1999, Aug. 12 Litho.

921 A498 5r pink, black & red .60 .60

Pioneers of Freedom Type of 1990

Designs: No. 922, Chaudhry Muhammad Ali (1905-80), 1st Secretary General. No. 923, Sir Adamjee Haji Dawood (1880-1948), banker. No. 924, Maulana Abdul Hamid Badayuni (1898-1970), religious scholar.

1999, Aug. 14 Litho. *Perf. 13*

922	A375	2r green & brown	.45	.45
923	A375	2r green & brown	.45	.45
924	A375	2r green & brown	.45	.45
		Nos. 922-924 (3)	1.35	1.35

Ustad Nusrat Fateh Ali Khan (1948-97), Singer — A499

1999, Aug. 16

925 A499 2r multicolored .75 .75

Islamic Development Bank, 25th Anniv. (in 2000) — A500

1999, Sept. 18

926 A500 5r multicolored 1.00 1.00

People's Republic of China, 50th Anniv. — A501

2r, Gate of Heavenly Peace. 15r, Arms, Mao Zedong, horiz.

1999, Sept. 21

927	A501	2r multicolored	.25	.25
928	A501	15r multicolored	1.50	1.50

Ninth Asian Sailing Championship — A502

No. 929: a, Enterprise class. b, 470 class. c, Optimist class. d, Laser class. e, Mistral class.

1999, Sept. 28 *Perf. 13½x13¼*

929 A502 2r Strip of 5, #a.-e. 2.25 2.25

10th Asian Optimist Sailing Championships — A502a

1999, Oct. 7 Litho. *Perf. 13¾x13½*

929F A502a 2r multi + label .80 .80

A503

1999, Oct. 9 *Perf. 14¼*
930 A503 10r multicolored 1.00 1.00

UPU, 125th anniv.

Hakim Mohammed Said (1920-98), Physician A504

1999, Oct. 17 Litho. *Perf. 13*
931 A504 5r multicolored .65 .65

National Bank of Pakistan, 50th Anniv. — A505

Perf. 13¼x13¾

1999, Nov. 8 Litho. Wmk. 351
932 A505 5r multi .80 .80

Shell Oil in Pakistan, Cent. — A506

Perf. 13¼x13

1999, Nov. 15 Wmk. 351
933 A506 4r multi .60 .60

Rights of the Child, 10th Anniv. — A507

Perf. 13x13¼

1999, Nov. 20 Unwmk.
934 A507 2r multi .60 .60

Allam Iqbal Open University, Islamabad — A508

Designs: 2r, University crest, flasks, microphone, mortarboard, book, computer. 3r, Similar to 2r, crest in center. 5r, Crest, map, mortarboard, book.

Unwmk.

1999, Nov. 20 Litho. *Perf. 13*
935 A508 2r bl grn & multi .25 .25
936 A508 3r multi .30 .30
937 A508 5r multi 1.20 .75
Nos. 935-937 (3) 1.75 1.30

Shabbir Hassan Khan Josh Malihabadi (1898-1982), Poet — A509

1999, Dec. 5
938 A509 5r multi .60 .60

Dr. Afzal Qadri (1912-74), Entomologist — A510

1999, Dec. 6
939 A510 3r multi .60 .60

Ghulam Bari Aleeg (1907-49), Journalist A511

1999, Dec. 10 Litho. *Perf. 13*
940 A511 5r multi .60 .60

See No. 982.

Plantain — A512

1999, Dec. 20
941 A512 5r multi 1.60 1.60

Eid-Ul-Fitr — A513

Perf. 13¾x13½

1999, Dec. 24 Litho.
942 A513 2r green & multi .75 .75
943 A513 15r blue & multi 2.25 2.25

SOS Children's Villages of Pakistan, 25th Anniv. — A514

2000, Mar. 12 *Perf. 13*
944 A514 2r multi .50 .50

International Cycling Union, Cent. — A515

2000, Apr. 14 Litho. *Perf. 13¼*
945 A515 2r multi 1.50 1.50

Convention on Human Rights and Dignity — A516

Perf. 13¼

2000, Apr. 21 Litho. Unwmk.
946 A516 2r multi .50 .50

Edwardes College, Peshawar, Cent. — A517

2000, Apr. 24 *Perf. 13½*
947 A517 2r multi .50 .50

Mahomed Ali Habib (1904-59), Banker, Philantropist — A518

2000, May 15 Litho. *Perf. 13*
948 A518 2r multi .50 .50

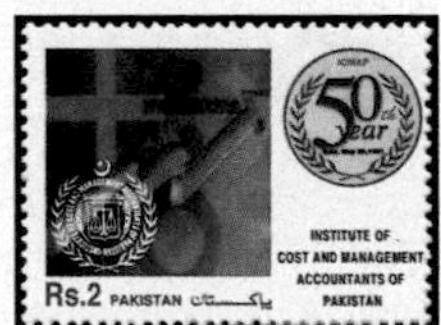

Institute of Cost and Management Accountants, 50th Anniv. — A519

Design: 2r, Arrow. 15r, Globe.

2000, June 23 Litho. *Perf. 13*
949 A519 2r multi .30 .30
950 A519 15r multi 2.00 2.00

Ahmed E. H. Jaffer (1909-90), Politician A520

2000, Aug. 9 Litho. *Perf. 13*
951 A520 10r multi 1.25 1.25

Creation of Pakistan, 53rd Anniv. — A521

a, No tree. b, Tree in foreground. c, Tree behind people, cart. d, Tree in distance.

2000, Aug. 14 Litho. *Perf. 13*
952 A521 5r Strip of 4, #a-d 2.00 2.00

Nishan-e-Haider Medal Type of 1995

Nishan-e-haider gallantry award winners: a, Capt. Muhammad Sarwar Shaheed (1910-48). b, Maj. Tufail Muhammad (1914-58).

2000, Sept. 6 Litho. *Perf. 13*
953 A456 5r Pair, #a-b 2.00 2.00

2000 Summer Olympics, Sydney — A523

No. 954: a, Runners. b, Field hockey. c, Weight lifting. d, Cycling.

2000, Sept. 20 *Perf. 14¼*
954 A523 4r Block of 4, #a-d 2.25 2.25

Natl. College of Arts, 125th Anniv. A524

2000, Oct. 28
955 A524 5r multi .45 .45

Creating the Future — A525

2000, Nov. 4 *Perf. 13½x13¼*
956 A525 5r multi 1.00 1.00

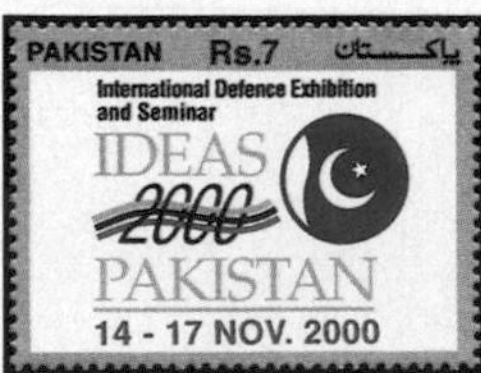

Intl. Defense Exhibition and Seminar — A526

2000, Nov. 14 **Litho.** ***Perf. 13***
957 A526 7r multi 1.10 1.10

Licorice — A527

2000, Nov. 28 **Litho.** ***Perf. 13***
958 A527 2r multi 2.00 2.00

Rotary Intl. Campaign Against Polio — A528

2000, Dec. 13
959 A528 2r multi .75 .75

UN High Commissioner for Refugees, 50th Anniv. — A529

2000, Dec. 14
960 A529 2r multi .45 .45

Poets — A530

Design: 2r, Hafeez Jalandhri (1900-82). 5r, Khawaja Ghulam Farid.

2001 **Litho.** ***Perf. 13***
961 A530 2r multi .50 .50
962 A530 5r multi 1.25 1.25

Issued: 2r, 1/14. 5r, 9/25.
See No. 986.

Habib Bank AG Zurich — A531

2001, Mar. 20 **Litho.** ***Perf. 13***
963 A531 5r multi 1.75 1.25

Chashma Nuclear Power Plant A532

2001, Mar. 29
964 A532 4r multi 1.40 1.25

9th SAF Games, Islamabad A533

Background colors: No. 965, 4r, Light blue. No. 966, 4r, Lilac.

2001, Apr. 9 ***Perf. 13½x13¼***
965-966 A533 Set of 2 1.40 1.40

Pakistan-People's Rep. of China Diplomatic Relations, 50th Anniv. — A534

Designs: No. 967, Yugur and Hunza women, flags.

No. 968 — Paintings by Yao Youdou: a, Ma Gu's Birthday Offering. b, Two Pakistani Women Drawing Water.

2001, May 12 ***Perf. 13***
967 A534 4r multi .25 .25
968 A534 4r Horiz. pair, #a-b 1.50 1.50

Mohammed Ali Jinnah (1876-1948) A535

2001, Aug. 14
969 A535 4r multi .90 .90

Sindh Festival A536

Unwmk.

2001, Sept. 22 **Litho.** ***Perf. 13***
970 A536 4r multi .75 .75

Year of Dialogue Among Civilizations A537

2001, Oct. 9 ***Perf. 13½***
971 A537 4r multi .75 .75

Turkmenistan, 10th Anniv. of Independence A538

2001, Oct. 27 ***Perf. 13***
972 A538 5r multi .90 .90

Convent of Jesus and Mary, Lahore, 125th Anniv. — A539

2001, Nov. 15 **Wmk. 351**
973 A539 4r multi 1.00 1.00

Men of Letters Type of 1999

Design: 4r, Dr. Ishtiaq Husain Qureshi (1903-81), historian.

2001, Nov. 20 **Unwmk.**
974 A511 4r multi .75 .75

Birds — A540

No. 975: a, Blue throat. b, Hoopoe. c, Pin-tailed sandgrouse. d, Magpie robin.

2001, Nov. 26 ***Perf. 13¼x13***
975 A540 4r Block of 4, #a-d 6.00 6.00

Pakistan — United Arab Emirates Friendship, 30th Anniv. — A541

Designs: 5r, Flags, handshake, vert. 30r, Sheik Zaid bin Sultan al Nahayan, Mohammed Ali Jinnah.

2001, Dec. 2 ***Perf. 13***
976-977 A541 Set of 2 3.75 3.75

Nishtar Medical College, Multan, 50th Anniv. — A542

2001, Dec. 20
978 A542 5r multi .75 .75

Quaid Year — A543

No. 979: a, Mohammed Ali Jinnah reviewing troops, 1948. b, Jinnah, soldiers, artillery gun, 1948.

No. 980, vert.: a, Jinnah taking oath as Governor General, 1947. b, Jinnah at opening ceremony of State Bank of Pakistan, 1948. c, Jinnah saluting at presentation of colors, 1948.

2001, Dec. 25 ***Perf. 13***
979 Horiz. pair .80 .80
a.-b. A543 4r Any single .25 .25

Size: 33x56mm

Perf. 13x13¼

980 Horiz. strip of 3 1.00 1.00
a.-c. A543 4r Any single .25 .25

Pakistan Ordnance Factories, 50th Anniv. — A544

2001, Dec. 28 ***Perf. 13¼x13½***
981 A544 4r multi 1.00 1.00

Men of Letters Type of 1999

Design: 5r, Syed Imtiaz Ali Taj (1900-70), playwright.

2001, Oct. 13 ***Perf. 13***
982 A511 5r multi .60 .60

Nishan-e-Haider Type of 1995

No. 983: a, Maj. Mohammad Akram Shaheed (1938-71). b, Maj. Shabbir Sharif Shaheeb (1943-71).

2001, Sept. 6 ***Perf. 13***
983 Horiz. pair 1.50 1.50
a.-b. A456 4r Any single .75 .75

Peppermint A545

Design: 5r, Hyssop.

2001-02 **Litho.** **Wmk. 351** ***Perf. 13***
984 A545 4r multi 1.00 1.00
985 A545 5r multi .80 .80

Issued: 4r, 11/12/01. 5r, 2/15/02.

Poets Type of 2001

Design: Samandar Khan Samandar (1901-90).

2002, Jan. 17 Litho. ***Perf. 13***
986 A530 5r multi .60 .60

Pakistan — Japan Diplomatic Relations, 50th Anniv. A546

2002, Apr. 28 Litho. ***Perf. 14***
987 A546 5r multi .60 .60

Pakistan - Kyrgyzstan Diplomatic Relations, 10th Anniv. — A547

2002, May 27 ***Perf. 13¾x12¾***
988 A547 5r multi .60 .60

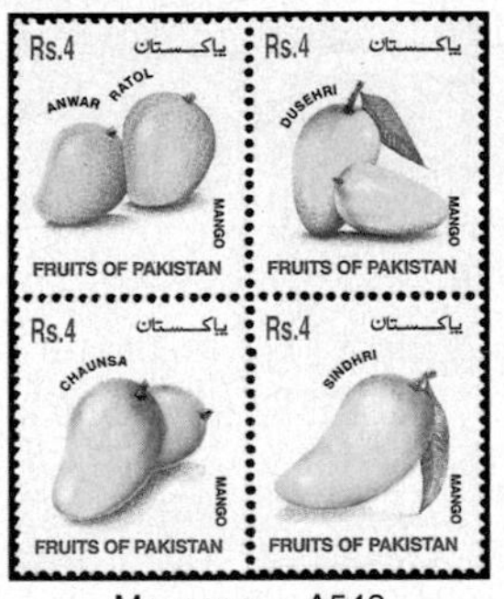

Mangoes — A548

No. 989: a, Anwar Ratol. b, Dusheri. c, Chaunsa. d, Sindhri.

2002, June 18
989 A548 4r Block of 4, #a-d 2.40 2.40

Independence, 55th Anniv. — A549

Famous people: No. 990, 4r, Noor-us-Sabah Begum (1908-78), Muslim leader and writer. No. 991, 4r, Prime Minister Ismail I. Chundrigar (1897-1960). No. 992, 4r, Habib Ibrahim Rahimtoola (1912-91), governmental minister. No. 993, 4r, Qazi Mureed Ahmed (1913-89), politician.

2002, Aug. 14 Litho. ***Perf. 13¼x13***
990-993 A549 Set of 4 2.40 2.40

World Summit on Sustainable Development, Johannesburg A550

Designs: No. 994, 4r, Children, Pakistani flag, dolphin, goat. No. 995, 4r, Water droplet, mountain (33x33mm).

2002, Aug. 26 ***Perf. 13¼, 14¼ (#995)***
994-995 A550 Set of 2 1.00 1.00

Mohammad Aly Rangoonwala (1924-98), Philanthropist A551

2002, Aug. 31 ***Perf. 13***
996 A551 4r multi .60 .60

Nishan-e-Haidar type of 1995

No. 997: a, Lance Naik Muhammad Mahfuz Shaheed (1944-71). b, Sawar Muhammad Hussain Shaheed (1949-71).

2002, Sept. 6 ***Perf. 13***
997 Horiz. pair 1.25 1.25
a.-b. A456 4r Either single .25 .25

Muhammad Iqbal Year — A552

No. 998: a, Iqbal wearing hat. b, Iqbal without hat.

Unwmk.
2002, Nov. 9 Litho. ***Perf. 13***
998 A552 4r Horiz. pair, #a-b 1.60 1.60

Eid ul-Fitr — A553

Perf. 13¾x14
2002, Nov. 14 Wmk. 351
999 A553 4r multi .60 .60

Shifa-ul-Mulk Hakim Muhammad Hassan Qarshi (1896-1974), Physician A554

2002, Dec. 20 Unwmk. ***Perf. 13½***
1000 A554 4r multi 1.00 1.00

Pakistan 2003 Natl. Philatelic Exhibition, Karachi — A555

Wmk. 351
2003, Jan. 31 Litho. ***Perf. 13***
1001 A555 4r multi + label 1.50 1.50

Pakistan Academy of Sciences, 50th Anniv. A556

2003, Feb. 15 Unwmk. ***Perf. 14¼***
1002 A556 4r multi .60 .60

North West Frontier Province, Cent. — A557

Perf. 13½x13¼
2003, Mar. 23 Litho. Wmk. 351
1003 A557 4r multi .60 .60

Pakistan Council of Scientific and Industrial Research, 50th Anniv. — A558

2003, Mar. 31 ***Perf. 14x13¾***
1004 A558 4r multi .60 .60

A. B. A. Haleem (1897-1975), Educator A559

2003, Apr. 20 ***Perf. 13½x13¼***
1005 A559 2r multi .60 .60

Campaign Against Illegal Drugs — A560

2003, Apr. 21 ***Perf. 13***
1006 A560 2r multi 1.00 1.00

Sir Syed Memorial, Islamabad A561

2003, Apr. 30 ***Perf. 13¼x13½***
1007 A561 2r multi .60 .60

Rosa Damascena A562

Perf. 13¼x12¾
2003, July 14 Unwmk.
1008 A562 2r multi 1.60 1.60

Mohtarma Fatima Jinnah (1893-1967), Presidential Candidate in 1964 — A563

2003, July 31 Litho.
1009 A563 4r multi .60 .60

Famous Men — A564

Designs: No. 1010, 2r, M. A. Rahim (1919-2003), labor leader. No. 1011, 2r, Abdul Rahman (1959-2002), slain postal worker.

2003, Aug. 3 ***Perf. 12¾x13¼***
1010-1011 A564 Set of 2 1.00 1.00

Famous Men — A565

Designs: No. 1012, 2r, Moulana Abdul Sattar Khan Niazi (1915-2001), politician. No. 1013, 2r, Muhammad Yousaf Khattak (1917-91), politician. No. 1014, 2r, Moulana Muhammad Ismail Zabeeh (1913-2001), political leader and journalist.

2003, Apr. 14 ***Perf. 13¼x12¾***
1012-1014 A565 Set of 3 1.75 1.75

UN Literacy Decade, 2003-12 — A566

2003, Sept. 6
1015 A566 1r multi .60 .60

Nishan-e-Haider Type of 1995

2003, Sept. 7 ***Perf. 14***
1016 A456 2r Pilot Officer Rashid Minhas Shaheed 1.25 1.25

Pakistan Academy of Letters, 25th Anniv. — A567

2003, Sept. 24 ***Perf. 13¼x12¾***
1017 A567 2r multi .60 .60

Karakoram Highway, 25th Anniv. — A568

Perf. 12¾x13
2003, Oct. 1 Litho. Unwmk.
1018 A568 2r multi .60 .60

Pakistan Air Force Public School, Sargodha, 50th Anniv. — A569

Perf. 13x13¼

2003, Oct. 10 Litho. Wmk. 351
1019 A569 4r multi 1.25 1.25

First Ascent of Nanga Parbat, 50th Anniv. — A570

Perf. 12¾x13

2003, Oct. 6 Litho. Unwmk.
1020 A570 2r multi 1.25 1.25

Exports — A571

No. 1021: a, Leather garments. b, Towels. c, Ready-made garments. d, Karachi Port Trust and Port Qasim. e, Fisheries. f, Yarn. g, Sporting goods. h, Fabrics. i, Furniture. j, Surgical instruments. k, Gems and jewelry. l, Leather goods. m, Information technology. n, Rice. o, Auto parts. p, Carpets. q, Marble and granite. r, Fruits. s, Cutlery. t, Engineering goods.

2003, Oct. 20 *Perf. 13x12¾*
1021 Sheet of 20 6.00 6.00
a.-t. A571 1r Any single .35 .35

Intl. Day of the Disabled A572

2003, Dec. 3 *Perf. 12¾x13*
1022 A572 2r multi 1.00 1.00

World Summit on the Information Society, Geneva, Switzerland A573

2003, Dec. 10 *Perf. 13x12¾*
1023 A573 2r multi .60 .60

Submarines A574

Khalid Class (Agosta 90B) submarine and flag of: 1r, Pakistan Navy, vert. 2r, Pakistan.

2003, Dec. 12 *Perf. 13x12¾, 12¾x13*
1024-1025 A574 Set of 2 3.00 3.00

Powered Flight, Cent. — A575

Designs: No. 1026, 2r, Pakistan Air Force's transition into jet age, 1956. No. 1027, 2r, Air Force in action at Siachen, 1988-90.

2003, Dec. 17 *Perf. 12¾x13*
1026-1027 A575 Set of 2 1.75 1.75

12th South Asian Association for Regional Cooperation Summit, Islamabad A576

2004, Jan. 4
1028 A576 4r multi .60 .60

Sadiq Public School, Bahawalpur, 50th Anniv. — A577

2004, Jan. 28 Litho. *Perf. 14*
1029 A577 4r multi .60 .60

Ninth SAF Games, Islamabad — A578

No. 1030: a, Gold medal. b, Running. c, Squash (yellow and blue uniform). d, Boxing. e, Wrestling. f, Judo. g, Javelin. h, Soccer. i, Rowing. j, Shooting. k, Shot put. l, Badminton (white uniform). m, Weight lifting. n, Volleyball. o, Table tennis. p, Swimming.

2004, Mar. 29 Litho. *Perf. 13x12¾*
1030 A578 2r Sheet of 16, #a-p 5.25 5.25

Pir Muhammad Karam Shah Al-Azhari (1918-98), Jurist — A579

2004, Apr. 7
1031 A579 2r multi .60 .60

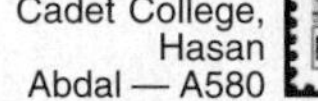
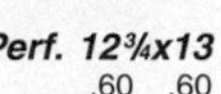

Cadet College, Hasan Abdal — A580

2004, Apr. 8 *Perf. 12¾x13*
1032 A580 4r multi .60 .60

Central Library, Bahawalpur A581

2004, Apr. 26 Litho. *Perf. 13x12¾*
1033 A581 2r multi .60 .60

Mosque, Bhong — A582

2004, May 12 *Perf. 12¾x13*
1034 A582 4r multi .60 .60

FIFA (Fédération Internationale de Football Association), Cent. — A583

No. 1035 — FIFA centenary emblem and: a, Player. b, Blue panel at bottom. c, Player, green panel at bottom.

2004, May 21 *Perf. 14*
1035 A583 Horiz. strip of 3 2.40 2.40
a.-c. 5r Any single .70 .70

Silk Road — A584

Designs: No. 1036, 4r, Indus River near Chilas. No. 1037, 4r, Haramosh Peak near Gilgit, vert.

2004, June 7 *Perf. 12¾x13, 13x12¾*
1036-1037 A584 Set of 2 1.00 1.00

Sui Southern Gas Company, 50th Anniv. — A585

2004, July 24 Litho. *Perf. 12¾x13*
1038 A585 4r multi .60 .60

First Ascent of K2, 50th Anniv. — A586

2004, July 31 *Perf. 13x12¾*
1039 A586 5r shown .60 .60

Imperf

Size: 95x64mm

1040 A586 30r Tent, K2 2.75 2.75

2004 Summer Olympics, Athens — A587

No. 1041: a, Track. b, Boxing. c, Field hockey. d, Wrestling.

2004, Aug. 13 *Perf. 13x12¾*
1041 A587 Horiz. strip of 4 2.40 2.40
a.-d. 5r Any single .60 .60

7 Lines of Text — A588

6½ Lines of Text — A589

6 Lines of Text — A590

6¾ Lines of Text — A591

2004, Aug. 14
1042 Horiz. strip of 4 1.50 1.50
a. A588 5r multi .30 .30
b. A589 5r multi .30 .30
c. A590 5r multi .30 .30
d. A591 5r multi .30 .30

Independence, 57th anniv.

Maulvi Abdul Haq (1870-1961), Lexicographer A592

2004, Aug. 16
1043 A592 4r multi .60 .60

Fourth Intl. Calligraphy and Calligraphic Art Exhibitiion and Competition, Lahore — A593

2004, Oct. 1
1044 A593 5r multi .40 .40

Tropical Fish — A594

No. 1045: a, Neon tetra. b, Striped gourami. c, Black widow. d, Yellow dwarf cichlid. e, Tiger barb.

2004, Oct. 9 ***Perf. 12½***
1045 Horiz. strip of 5 2.75 2.75
a.-e. A594 2r Any single .50 .50

Japanese Economic Assistance, 50th Anniv. A595

Designs: No. 1046, 5r, Training for handicapped. No. 1047, 5r, Polio eradication. No. 1048, 5r, Ghazi Barotha hydroelectric power project. No. 1049, 5r, Kohat Friendship Tunnel. 30r, Vignettes of Nos. 1046-1049, Friendship Tunnel.

2004, Nov. 8 Litho. ***Perf. 12¾x13***
1046-1049 A595 Set of 4 3.00 3.00

Imperf

1050 A595 multi 3.00 3.00

Year of Child Welfare and Rights — A596

2004, Nov. 20 ***Perf. 12½***
1051 A596 4r multi .45 .45

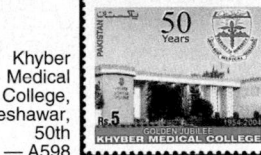

Allama Iqbal Open University, Islamabad, 30th Anniv. — A597

2004, Dec. 6 ***Perf. 12¾x13***
1052 A597 20r multi 1.50 1.50

Khyber Medical College, Peshawar, 50th Anniv. — A598

2004, Dec. 30
1053 A598 5r multi .60 .60

Prof. Ahmed Ali (1910-94), Writer — A599

2005, Jan. 14 Litho. ***Perf. 13x12¾***
1054 A599 5r multi .50 .50

Pakistan — Romania Friendship A600

Poets Mihai Eminescu and Allama Iqbal and: No. 1055, 5r, Flags of Romania and Pakistan. No. 1056, 5r, Flags, monument to Eminescu and Iqbal by Emil Ghitulescu, Islamabad.

2005, Jan. 14
1055-1056 A600 Set of 2 1.40 1.40

Saadat Hasan Manto (1912-55), Writer — A601

2005, Jan. 18 ***Perf. 13x12¾***
1057 A601 5r multi .50 .50

A602

A603

A604

Pakistan Air Force, 50th Anniv. — A605

2005, Mar. 23 Litho. ***Perf. 12¾x13***
1058 A602 5r multi 1.00 1.00
1059 A603 5r multi 1.00 1.00
1060 A604 5r multi 1.00 1.00

Perf. 13x12¾

1061 A605 5r multi 1.00 1.00
Nos. 1058-1061 (4) 4.00 4.00

Command and Staff College, Quetta, Cent. — A606

2005, Apr. 2 ***Perf. 12¾x13***
1062 A606 5r multi .50 .50

Turkish Grand National Assembly, 85th Anniv. — A607

No. 1063 — Assembly building and: a, Kemal Ataturk, Turkish flag. b, Ataturk, Mohammed Ali Jinnah, Turkish and Pakistani flags.

2005, Apr. 23 ***Perf. 14***
1063 A607 10r Horiz. pair, #a-b 2.00 2.00

Institute of Business Administration, Karachi, 50th Anniv. — A608

Various views of campus with country name at: No. 1064, 3r, Right. No. 1065, 3r, Bottom.

2005, Apr. 30 ***Perf. 12¾x13***
1064-1065 A608 Set of 2 1.00 1.00

Islamia High School, Quetta, 95th Anniv. — A609

2005, May 25 ***Perf. 13x12¾***
1066 A609 5r multi .50 .50

Akhtar Shairani (1905-48), Poet — A610

2005, June 30
1067 A610 5r multi .50 .50

World Summit on Information Technology, Tunis, Tunisia — A611

2005, July 15
1068 A611 5r multi .50 .50

Abdul Rehman Baba (1632-1707), Poet — A612

2005, Aug. 4
1069 A612 5r multi .50 .50

Lahore Marathon A613

2005, Sept. 10 ***Perf. 12¾x13***
1070 A613 5r multi .50 .50

Mushrooms — A614

No. 1071: a, Lepiota procera. b, Tricholoma gambosum. c, Amanita caesarea. d, Cantharellus cibarius. e, Boletus luridus. f, Morchella vulgaris. g, Amanita vaginata. h, Agaricus arvensis. i, Coprinus comatus. j, Clitocybe geotropa.

2005, Oct. 1 Litho. ***Perf. 13¼x12¾***
1071 A614 Block of 10 7.50 7.50
a.-j. 5r Any single .40 .40

Intl. Year of Sports and Physical Education A615

2005, Nov. 5 ***Perf. 14***
1072 A615 5r multi .50 .50

South Asian Association for Regional Cooperation, 20th Anniv. — A616

2005, Nov. 12 ***Perf. 13¼x12¾***
1073 A616 5r multi .50 .50

Khwaja Sarwar Hasan (1902-73), Diplomat — A617

2005, Nov. 18 ***Perf. 14***
1074 A617 5r multi .50 .50

SOS Children's Villages in Pakistan, 30th Anniv. A618

2005, Nov. 20 ***Perf. 12¾x13¼***
1075 A618 5r multi .50 .50

20th World Men's Team Squash Championships, Islamabad — A619

2005, Dec. 8 Litho. ***Perf. 14***
1076 A619 5r multi .50 .50

Supreme Court, 50th Anniv. A620

Supreme Court Building: 4r, In daylight. 15r, At night.

2006, Mar. 23
1077-1078 A620 Set of 2 2.75 2.75

Mohammed Ali Jinnah's 1948 Visit to Armored Corps Center — A621

Jinnah, soldiers and: No. 1079, 5r, Tanks. No. 1080, 5r, Flags, vert.

2006, Apr. 14
1079-1080 A621 Set of 2 1.00 1.00

Begum Ra'na Liaquat Ali Khan (1905-90), Diplomat A622

2006, June 13 ***Perf. 13½***
1081 A622 4r multi .60 .50

Sri Arjun Dev Jee (1563-1606), Sikh Guru — A623

2006, June 16
1082 A623 5r multi .50 .50

Polo at Shandur Pass A624

2006, July 1 ***Perf. 14***
1083 A624 5r multi 1.00 .75

Tourism — A625

No. 1084: a, Hanna Lake. b, Lake Payee. c, Lake Saiful Maluk. d, Lake Dudi Pat Sar.

2006, July 20
1084 A625 5r Block of 4, #a-d 2.75 2.75

Miniature Sheet

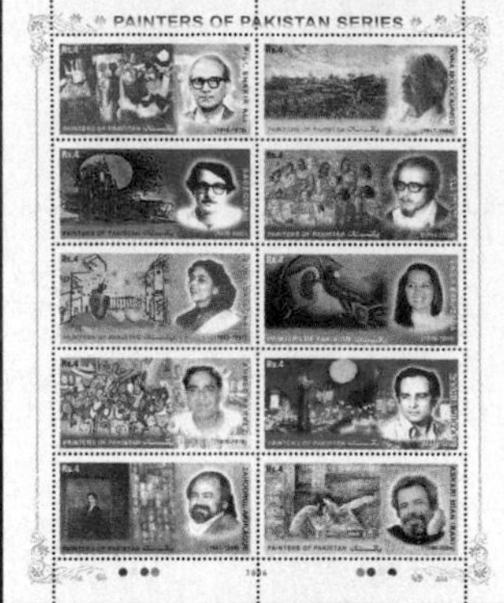

Painters — A626

No. 1085: a, Shakir Ali (1916-75). b, Anna Molka Ahmed (1917-94). c, Sadequain (1930-87). d, Ali Imam (1924-2002). e, Zubeida Agha (1922-97). f, Laila Shahzada (1926-94). g, Ahmed Parvez (1926-79). h, Bashir Mirza (1941-2000). i, Zahoorul Akhlaque (1941-99). j, Askari Mian Irani (1940-2004).

2006, Aug. 14 ***Perf. 13x12¾***
1085 A626 4r Sheet of 10, #a-j 2.50 2.50

Hamdard Services, Cent. — A627

2006, Aug. 25 ***Perf. 13¼x13***
1086 A627 5r multi .60 .50

Oct. 8, 2005 Earthquake, 1st Anniv. — A628

2006, Oct. 8 ***Perf. 13½x13¾***
1087 A628 5r multi .60 .50

Medicinal Plants A629

Designs: No. 1088, 5r, Aloe vera. No. 1089, 5r, Chamomile, vert.

Perf. 13½x13¼, 13¼x13½
2006, Oct. 28
1088-1089 A629 Set of 2 1.00 1.00

Intl. Anti-Corruption Day — A630

2006, Dec. 9 ***Perf. 13***
1090 A630 5r multi .60 .60

Baltit Fort Heritage Trust, 10th Anniv. A631

2006, Dec. 20 ***Perf. 13¼***
1091 A631 15r multi 1.50 1.50

Miniature Sheet

Muslim League, Cent. — A632

No. 1092: a, Mohammed Ali Jinnah's letter requesting membership in Muslim League. b, Jinnah in sherwani and cap. c, Jinnah addressing Lucknow session. d, Jinnah and wife with youth and women's wing. e, Jinnah hoisting Muslim League flag. f, Jinnah addressing Lahore session. g, Crowd, flags and ballot box. h, Jinnah addressing first Constituent Assembly.

Wmk. 351
2006, Dec. 28 **Litho.** ***Perf. 13***
1092 A632 4r Sheet of 8, #a-h 2.50 2.50

Karachi Municipal Corporation Building, 75th Anniv. A633

2007, Jan. 16 ***Perf. 14¼***
1093 A633 10r multi .60 .60

Cadet College Petaro, 50th Anniv. A634

Wmk. 351
2007, Feb. 28 **Litho.** ***Perf. 14¼***
1094 A634 10r multi .60 .60

Intl. Women's Day — A635

2007, Mar. 8 ***Perf. 13***
1095 A635 10r multi .60 .60

Hugh Catchpole (1907-97), Educator A636

2007, May 26
1096 A636 10r multi .60 .60

Pakistan Post Emblem A637

2007, June 7 ***Perf. 14¼***
1097 A637 4r multi .60 .60

First Public Appearance of JF-17 Thunder Airplane — A638

2007, Sept. 6 ***Perf. 13***
1098 A638 5r multi .60 .60

Completion of Term of National Assembly — A639

2007, Nov. 15
1099 A639 15r multi 1.50 1.50

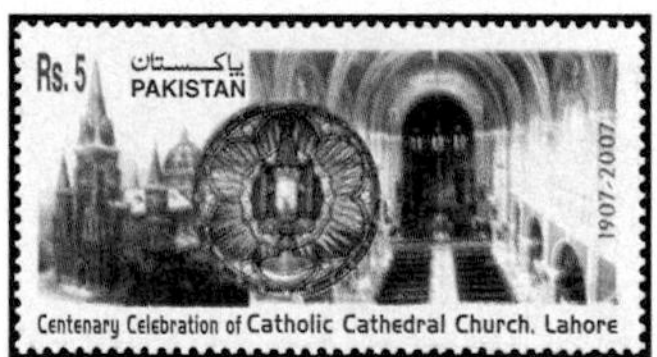

Catholic Cathedral, Lahore, Cent. — A640

2007, Nov. 19
1100 A640 5r multi .60 .60

Third Meeting of Economic Cooperation Organization Postal Authorities, Tehran (in 2006) — A641

Sir Muhammad Iqbal (1877-1938), Poet — A733

Wmk. 351

2013, Apr. 21 Litho. *Perf. 13½*
1190 A733 15r multi .90 .90

Reopening of Pakistan Army Museum, Rawalpindi — A734

2013, Apr. 30 *Perf. 13x13¼*
1191 A734 15r multi .90 .90

2013 General Elections — A735

2013, May 11
1192 A735 8r multi .60 .60

Recipients of Pakistan's Highest Military Medals — A736

No. 1193: a, Capt. Karnal Sher Khan Shaheed (1970-99), Nishan-e-Haider medal. b, Havildar Lalak Jan Shaheed (1967-99), Nishan-e-Haider medal. c, Naik Saif Ali Janjua Shaheed (1922-48), Hilal-i-Kashmir medal.

Perf. 13½x13¼
2013, Apr. 30 Litho. Wmk. 351
1193 A736 Horiz. strip of 3 1.50 1.50
a.-c. 8r Any single .50 .50

Sadiq Muhammad Khan Abbasi V (1904-66), Nawab of Bahawalpur A737

Wmk. 351
2013, May 24 Litho. *Perf. 13*
1194 A737 8r multi .60 .60

Islamia College, Peshawar, Cent. — A738

2013, May 30
1195 A738 8r multi .60 .60

Men of Letters Type of 2012

Design: Ibn-e-Insha (1927-78), poet.

2013, June 15
1196 A725 8r multi .50 .50

All-Pakistan Newspaper Society, 60th Anniv. — A739

2013, June 20
1197 A739 8r multi .60 .60

Red-vented Bulbul A740

Perf. 13½x13¼
2013, July 1 Litho. Wmk. 351
1198 A740 8r multi .60 .60

Frigate PNS Aslat — A742

Wmk. 351
2013, Sept. 3 Litho. *Perf. 13¼*
1200 A742 10r multi .60 .60

Noor Jahan (1926-2000), Singer — A743

Wmk. 351
2013, Sept. 21 Litho. *Perf. 13¼*
1201 A743 8r multi .60 .60

Men of Letters Type of 2012

Design: Jon Elia (1931-2002), writer.

Wmk. 351
2013, Nov. 8 Litho. *Perf. 13*
1202 A725 8r multi .50 .50

Two Decades of Extended Cooperation with Economic Cooperation Organization A744

Perf. 13¼x13
2013, Nov. 28 Litho. Wmk. 351
1203 A744 25r multi .60 .60

Perveen Shakir (1952-94), Poet — A745

Wmk. 351
2013, Dec. 26 Litho. *Perf. 13*
1204 A745 10r multi .60 .60

Pakistan Bible Society, 150th Anniv. — A746

Wmk. 351
2013, Dec. 28 Litho. *Perf. 13*
1205 A746 8r multi .60 .60

Men of Letters Type of 2012

Design: Habib Jalib (1928-93), poet.

Wmk. 351
2014, Mar. 12 Litho. *Perf. 13*
1206 A725 15r multi .50 .50

Air Commodore Muhammad Mahmood Alam (1935-2013) — A747

Perf. 13¾x13½
2014, Mar. 20 Litho. Wmk. 351
1207 A747 8r multi .60 .60

Hyder M. Habib (1931-2011), Banker — A748

Wmk. 351
2014, Apr. 6 Litho. *Perf. 13*
1208 A748 8r multi .60 .60

Forman Christian College, 150th Anniv. — A749

Wmk. 351
2014, May 14 Litho. *Perf. 13*
1209 A749 8r multi .25 .25

Pakistan Navy Submarine Force, 50th Anniv. — A750

Wmk. 351
2014, June 1 Litho. *Perf. 13*
1210 A750 10r multi .25 .25

Frontier Constabulary, Cent. — A751

Wmk. 351
2014, July 11 Litho. *Perf. 13½*
1211 A751 8r multi .25 .25

Sahiwal Cattle Conservation, Cent. — A752

Perf. 13x13¼
2014, Aug. 5 Litho. Wmk. 351
1212 A752 8r multi .25 .25

A753

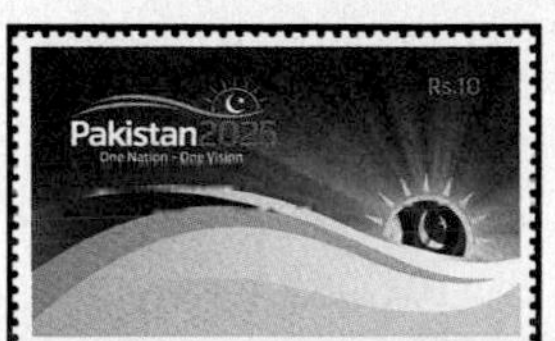
Pakistan 2025 Planning Program — A754

Perf. 13½x13¼
2014, Aug. 11 Litho. Wmk. 351
1213 A753 8r multi .25 .25

Perf. 13
1214 A754 10r multi .25 .25

Norman Borlaug (1914-2009), 1970 Nobel Peace Laureate — A755

Perf. 13x13¼

2014, Dec. 4 Litho. Wmk. 351

1215 A755 8r multi .25 .25

Intl. Anti-Corruption Day — A756

Perf. 13x13¼

2014, Dec. 9 Litho. Wmk. 351

1216 A756 8r multi .25 .25

Gems and Minerals A757

No. 1217: a, Apatite. b, Aquamarine. c, Black tourmaline. d, Garnet. e, Epidot. f, Vesuvianite. g, Topaz. h, Sphene.

Perf. 13x13¼

2014, Dec. 11 Litho. Wmk. 351

1217 Block of 8 1.60 1.60

a.-h. A757 10r Any single .25 .25

14th National Scout Jamboree, Khairpur — A758

Perf. 13x13¼

2014, Dec. 23 Litho. Wmk. 351

1218 A758 8r multi .25 .25

Artifacts of Ancient Civilizations — A759

No. 1219: a, Artifacts from Trypillia, Ukraine archaeological site, flag of Ukraine. b, Artifacts from Mohenjo-daro, Pakistan archaeological site, flag of Pakistan.

Perf. 13¼x13

2014, Dec. 25 Litho. Wmk. 351

1219 A759 20r Horiz. pair, #a-b .80 .80

c. Souvenir sheet of 2, #1219a-1219b, imperf. 1.00 1.00

No. 1219c has simulated perforations and sold for 50r.

See Ukraine No. 997.

Moulana Altaf Hussain Hali (1837-1914), Poet — A760

Perf. 13x13¼

2014, Dec. 31 Litho. Wmk. 351

1220 A760 8r multi .25 .25

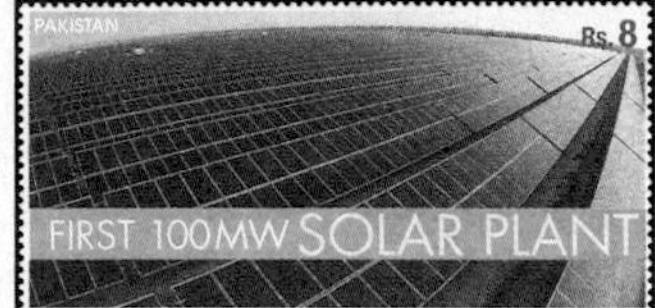

First 100 Megawatt Solar Plant in Pakistan — A762

Wmk. 351

2015, May 4 Litho. *Perf. 13½*

1222 A762 8r multi .25 .25

Year of Pakistan-China Friendly Exchanges — A763

No. 1223: a, Flag of People's Republic of China and Pres. Xi Jinping. b, Great Wall of China. c, Karakoram Highway. d, Shalimar Garden, Pakistan. e, Flag of Pakistan and Prime Minister Nawaz Sharif.

Wmk. 351

2015, Aug. 14 Litho. *Perf. 13*

1223 Horiz. strip of 5 1.25 1.25

a.-f. A763 10r Any single .25 .25

A764

A765

A766

A767

A768

India-Pakistan War, 50th Anniv. — A769

Perf. 13x13¼

2015, Sept. 7 Litho. Wmk. 351

1224 Block of 6 1.50 1.50

a. A764 10r multi .25 .25

b. A765 10r multi .25 .25

c. A766 10r multi .25 .25

d. A767 10r multi .25 .25

e. A768 10r multi .25 .25

f. A769 10r multi .25 .25

Cadet College, Kohat, 50th Anniv. — A770

Wmk. 351

2015, Oct. 10 Litho. *Perf.*

1225 A770 8r multi .25 .25

Urdu Language in Turkey, Cent. — A771

Wmk. 351

2015, Oct. 12 Litho. *Perf. 13*

1226 A771 10r multi .25 .25

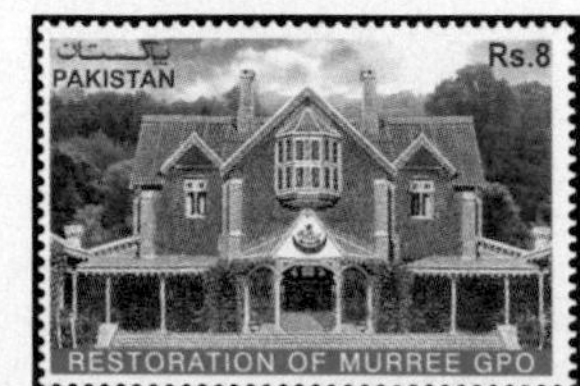

Restoration of Murree General Post Office — A772

Wmk. 351

2015, Nov. 4 Litho. *Perf. 13*

1227 A772 8r multi .25 .25

Army Public School Massacre, 1st Anniv. — A773

Wmk. 351

2015, Dec. 16 Litho. *Perf. 13*

1228 A773 16r multi .30 .30

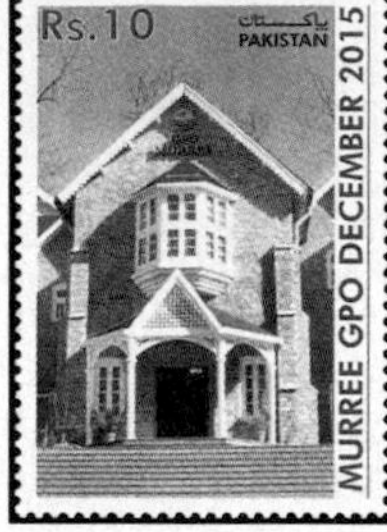

Reopening of Murree General Post Office — A774

Wmk. 351

2015, Dec. 29 Litho. *Perf. 13*

1229 A774 10r multi .25 .25

SEMI-POSTAL STAMPS

Earthquake Relief — SP1

2005, Oct. 27 Litho. *Perf. 13¾x14*

B1 SP1 4r +(8.50r) multi 1.50 1.50

Printed in sheets of 8 stamps +17 labels.

Child and Man at Refugee Camp — SP2

Perf. 13x13½

2009, Aug. 1 Litho. Unwmk.

B2 SP2 5r +(7.50r) multi 2.50 2.50

Printed in sheets of eight stamps + 17 labels. Surtax for Prime Minister's Relief Fund for Swat Refugees.

OFFICIAL STAMPS

Official Stamps of India, 1939-43, Overprinted in Black

1947-49 Wmk. 196 *Perf. 13½x14*

O1	O8	3p	slate	1.75	.90
O2	O8	½a	dk rose vio	.60	.25
O3	O8	9p	green	5.50	1.50
O4	O8	1a	carmine rose	.60	.25
O4A	O8	1a3p	bister ('49)	*9.00*	*25.00*
O5	O8	1½a	dull purple	.60	.25
O6	O8	2a	scarlet	.60	.40
O7	O8	2½a	purple	7.00	*11.00*
O8	O8	4a	dk brown	1.40	*.95*
O9	O8	8a	blue violet	2.00	*4.00*

India Nos. O100-O103 Overprinted in Black

O10 A82 1r brown & slate 1.00 *1.25*
O11 A82 2r dk brn & dk vio 7.50 1.50
O12 A82 5r dp ultra & dk grn 30.00 *55.00*
Telegraph cancel 7.50
O13 A82 10r rose car & dk vio 75.00 *130.00*
Telegraph cancel 5.00
Nos. O1-O13 (14) 142.55 232.25
Set, hinged 90.00

Regular Issue of 1948 Overprinted in Black or Carmine — a

"C" in "SERVICE" is nearly round.

Perf. 12½, 13, 13½x14, 14x13½

1948, Aug. 14 Unwmk.

O14 A3 3p orange red .25 .25
O15 A3 6p purple (C) .25 .25
O16 A3 9p dk green (C) .25 .25
O17 A4 1a dk blue (C) 4.25 .25
O18 A4 1½a gray grn (C) 4.00 .25
O19 A4 2a orange red 1.75 .25
O20 A5 3a olive green 29.00 14.00
O21 A6 4a chocolate 1.25 .25
O22 A6 8a black (C) 2.50 *10.00*
O23 A5 1r ultra 1.25 .30
O24 A5 2r dark brown 17.50 10.00
O25 A5 5r carmine 50.00 20.00
O26 A7 10r rose lil, perf. 14x13½ 22.50 *60.00*
a. Perf. 12 25.00 *65.00*
b. Perf. 13 22.50 *70.00*
Nos. O14-O26 (13) 134.75 116.05
Set, hinged 72.50

Issued: No. O26a, 10/10/51; No. O26b, 1954(?).

Nos. 47-50 and 52 Overprinted Type "a" in Black or Carmine

1949-50 *Perf. 12½, 13½x14*

O27 A10 1a dark blue (C) 2.10 .25
O28 A10 1½a gray green (C) .65 .25
a. Inverted ovpt. 275.00 45.00
O29 A10 2a orange red 2.10 .25
O30 A9 3a olive grn ('49) 37.50 7.50
O31 A11 8a black (C) 57.50 25.00
Nos. O27-O31 (5) 99.85 33.25

No. O32

No. O33

No. O34

Inscribed "SERVICE"

Unwmk.

1951, Aug. 14 Engr. *Perf. 13*

O32 A13 3a dark rose lake 9.25 *10.00*
O33 A14 4a deep green 2.40 .40
O34 A15 8a brown *10.00* 5.00
Nos. O32-O34 (3) 21.65 *15.40*

See Nos. 56, 58, 60.

Nos. 24-26, 47-49, 38-41 Overprinted in Black or Carmine — b

"C" in "SERVICE" is oval.

1954

O35 A3 3p orange red .25 .25
O36 A3 6p purple (C) .25 .25
O37 A3 9p dk green (C) .25 .25
O38 A10 1a dk blue (C) .25 .25
O39 A10 1½a gray grn (C) .25 .25
O40 A10 2a orange red .25 .25
O41 A5 1r ultra 12.00 5.00
O42 A5 2r dark brown 5.50 .25
O43 A5 5r carmine 42.50 26.00
O43A A7 10r rose lilac 37.50 *70.00*
Nos. O35-O43A (10) 99.00 *102.75*

Nos. 66-72 Overprinted Type "b" in Carmine or Black

1954, Aug. 14

O44 A18 6p rose violet (C) .25 *3.25*
O45 A19 9p blue (C) 1.75 *8.50*
O46 A19 1a carmine rose .25 *2.50*
O47 A18 1½a red .25 *2.50*
O48 A20 14a dk green (C) 1.25 *8.00*
O49 A20 1r yellow grn (C) 1.40 .25
O50 A20 2r orange 4.00 .25
Nos. O44-O50 (7) 9.15 *25.25*

No. 75 Overprinted in Carmine Type "b" Overprint: 13x2½mm

1955, Aug. 14 Unwmk. *Perf. 13*

O51 A21 8a violet .75 .25

Nos. 24, 40, 66-72, 74-75, 83, 89 Overprinted in Black or Carmine — c

1957-61

O52 A3 3p org red ('58) .25 .25
O53 A18 6p rose vio (C) .25 .25
O54 A19 9p blue (C) ('58) .25 *.25*
O55 A19 1a carmine rose .25 .25
O56 A18 1½a red .25 .25
O57 A24 2a red ('58) .25 .25
O58 A21 6a dk bl (C) ('60) .25 .25
O59 A21 8a vio (C) ('58) .25 .25
O60 A20 14a dk grn (C) ('58) .50 *4.25*
O61 A20 1r yel grn (C) ('58) .50 .25
O62 A20 2r orange ('58) 5.50 .25
O63 A5 5r carmine ('58) 7.50 .25
O64 A26 10r dk grn & org (C) ('61) 7.00 *9.00*
Nos. O52-O64 (13) 23.00 16.00

For surcharges see Nos. O67-O73.

Nos. 110-111 Overprinted Type "c"

1961, Apr.

O65 A33 8a green .25 .25
O66 A33 1r blue .25 .25
a. Inverted overprint 7.50

New Currency

Nos. O52, O55-O57 Surcharged with New Value in Paisa

1961

O67 A18 1p on 1½a red .25 .25
a. Overprinted type "b" 5.00 1.75
O68 A3 2p on 3p orange red .25 .25
a. Overprinted type "b" 8.50 5.00
O69 A19 6p on 1a car rose
O70 A19 7p on 1a car rose .25 .25
a. Overprinted type "b" 9.50 *11.00*
O71 A18 9p on 1½a red
O72 A24 13p on 2a red ("PAISA") .25 .25
O73 A24 13p on 2a red ("Paisa")

Nos. O69, O71, O73 were locally overprinted at Mastung. On these stamps "paisa" is in lower case.

Forgeries of No. O69, O71 and O73 abound.

Nos. 125, 128 Overprinted Type "c"

1961

O74 A33 3p on 6p purple .25 .25
O75 A33 13p on 2a copper red .25 .25

Various violet handstamped surcharges were applied to several official stamps. Most of these repeat the denomination of the basic stamp and add the new value. Example: "4 ANNAS (25 Paisa)" on No. O33.

Nos. 129-135, 135B, 135C, 136a, 137-140a Overprinted in Carmine — d

1961-78 *Perf. 13½x14*

O76 A40 1p violet (II) .25 .25
a. Type I .40 .40
O77 A40 2p rose red (II) .25 .25
a. Type I .40 .40
O78 A40 3p magenta .25 .25
O79 A40 5p ultra (II) .25 .25
a. Type I .40 .40
O80 A40 7p emerald 5.00 5.00
O81 A40 10p brown .25 .25
O82 A40 13p blue violet .25 .25
O85 A40 40p dull pur ('62) .25 .25
O86 A40 50p dull grn ('62) .25 .25
O87 A40 75p dk car ('62) .25 .25
Nos. O76-O87 (10) 7.25 7.25

1961-78 Designs Redrawn

O76b A40 1p violet (#129b) ('63) .25 .25
O77b A40 2p rose red (#130b) ('64) .25 .25
O78a A40 3p mag (#131a) ('66) 3.00 3.00
O78b A40 3p mag (#131b) 3.00 1.00
O79b A40 5p ultra (#132b) ('63) .25 .25
O80a A40 7p emerald (#133a) 25.00 14.00
O81a A40 10p brown (#134a) ('64) .25 .25
O82a A40 13p blue vio (#135a) ('63) .25 .25
O83 A40 15p rose lil (#135B; '64) .25 .25
O84 A40 20p dl grn (#135C; '70) .25 .25
O84A A40 25p dk blue (#136a; '77) 5.00 5.00
O85a A40 40p dull purple (#137a) 20.00 8.00
O86a A40 50p dull grn (#138a) ('64) .25 .25
O87a A40 75p dark carmine (#139a) 15.00 7.50
O88 A40 90p lt ol grn (#140a; '78) 5.00 5.00
Nos. O76b-O88 (14) 75.00 44.50

Nos. 141, 143-144 Overprinted Type "c" in Black or Carmine

1963, Jan. 7 Unwmk. *Perf. 13½x13*

O89 A41 1r vermilion .35 .25
O90 A41 2r orange 1.50 .25
O91 A41 5r green (C) 4.25 7.00
Nos. O89-O91 (3) 6.10 7.50

Nos. 200, 202-203 Overprinted Type "c"

1968-? Wmk. 351 *Perf. 13½x13*

O92 A41 1r vermilion 3.75 1.00
O93 A41 2r orange 16.00 2.00
O93A A41 5r green (C) 29.00 8.00
Nos. O92-O93A (3) 48.75 11.00

Nos. 459-468, 470-475 Overprinted Type "d" in Carmine or Black

1979-84

O94 A224 2p dark green .25 *.30*
O95 A224 3p black .25 *.30*
O96 A224 5p violet blue .25 *.30*
O97 A225 10p grnsh blue .25 *.30*
O98 A225 20p yel grn ('81) .25 .25
O99 A225 25p rose car & grn ('81) .25 .25
O100 A225 40p car & bl .45 .25
O101 A225 50p bl grn & vio .25 .25
O102 A225 60p black 1.75 .25
O103 A225 75p dp orange 1.75 .25
O105 A225a 1r olive ('81) 4.00 .25
O106 A225a 1.50r dp orange .25 *.30*
O107 A225a 2r car rose .25 .25
O108 A225a 3r indigo ('81) .30 .30
O109 A225a 4r black ('84) 3.50 .50
O110 A225a 5r dk brn ('84) 3.50 .50
Nos. O94-O110 (16) 17.50 4.80

Types A237-A239 Inscribed "SERVICE POSTAGE"

No. O111

No. O115

No. O117

1980 Litho. *Perf. 12x11½, 11½x12*

O111 A237 10p dk grn & yel org 1.40 .25
O112 A237 15p dk grn & ap grn 1.40 .25
O113 A237 25p dp vio & rose car .25 *1.00*
O114 A237 35p rose pink & brt yel grn .25 *7.50*
O115 A238 40p red & lt brn 1.40 .25
O116 A239 50p olive & vio bl .25 *.60*
O117 A239 80p blk & yel grn .40 *1.50*
Nos. O111-O117 (7) 5.35 *11.35*

Issued: 10p, 15p, 40p, 1/15; others, 3/10.

Nos. 613-614, 616-620 Ovptd. "SERVICE" in Red

1984-87 Litho. *Perf. 11*

O118 A289 5p Kot Diji .25 .60
O119 A289 10p Rohtas .25 .25
O120 A289 20p Attock Fort .30 .40
O121 A289 50p Hyderabad .40 .40
O122 A289 60p Lahore ('86) .45 *.50*
O123 A289 70p Sibi .50 *.70*
O124 A289 80p Ranikot .55 *.70*
Nos. O118-O124 (7) 2.70 3.55

Issued: 10p, 9/25; 80p, 8/3/87.

No. 712 Ovptd. "SERVICE"

Litho. & Engr.

1989, Dec. 24 *Perf. 13*

O124A A357 1r multicolored *5.00 5.00*

National Assembly, Islamabad — O1

Wmk. 351

1991-99 Litho. *Perf. 13½*

O125 O1 1r green & red .25 .25
O126 O1 2r rose car & red .25 .25
O127 O1 3r ultra & red .35 .25
O128 O1 4r red brown & red .45 .25
O129 O1 5r rose lilac & red .50 .25
O130 O1 10r brown & red 1.25 .40
Nos. O125-O130 (6) 3.05 1.65

Issued: 10r, 2/6/99; others, 4/12/91.

1999 Unwmk.

O131 O1 2r rose car & red .40 .25

National Assembly Type of 1991-99

Perf. 13¼x13½

2012 ? Litho. Wmk. 351

O132 O1 8r claret & red .25 .25

BAHAWALPUR

LOCATION — A State of Pakistan.
AREA — 17,494 sq. mi.
POP. — 1,341,209 (1941)
CAPITAL — Bahawalpur

Bahawalpur was an Indian princely state that was autonomous from Aug. 15-Oct. 3, 1947, when it united with Pakistan. These stamps had franking power solely within Bahawalpur.

Used values are for c-t-o or favor cancels.

India George VI stamps of 1937-40 and 1941-43 were overprinted for use in Bahawalpur during the brief period of that state's independence, following the creation of the separate dominions of India and Pakistan on Aug. 15, 1947. These stamps were withdrawn when Bahawalpur united with Pakistan on Oct. 3, 1947. Until 1953, Pakistan stamps were valid for use in Bahawalpur.

Stamps of India Used in Bahawalpur

Overprinted in Red or Black

1947, Aug. 15

A1 A83 3p slate (R) 30.00
A2 A83 ½a rose vio 30.00
A3 A83 9p light grn (R) 30.00
A4 A83 1a car rose 30.00
A5 A84 1½a dark pur (R) 30.00
A6 A84 2a scarlet 30.00
a. Double overprint 3,500.

A7 A84 3a violet (R) 30.00
A8 A84 3½a ultramarine (R) 30.00
A9 A85 4a chocolate 30.00
A10 A85 6a peacock bl (R) 30.00
a. Double overprint 3,500.
A11 A85 8a blue vio (R) 30.00
A12 A85 12a carm lake 30.00
A13 A81 14a rose vio 75.00
A14 A82 1r brn & slate 35.00
a. Double overprint, one albino 400.00
A15 A82 2r dk brn & dk vio (R) 2,250.
A16 A82 5r dp ultra & dk grn (R) 2,250.
A17 A82 10r rose car & dk vio 2,250.

Catalgoue values for unused stamps in this section, from this point to the end of the section are for Never Hinged items.

Amir Muhammad Bahawal Khan I Abbasi — A1

Perf. 12½x12

1947, Dec. 1 Wmk. 274 Engr.
1 A1 ½a brt car rose & blk 4.00 *8.00*

Bicentenary of the ruling family.

Nawab Sadiq Muhammad Khan V Abbasi Bahadur — A2

Tombs of the Amirs — A3

Mosque, Sadiq Garh — A4

Fort Dirawar A5

Nur-Mahal Palace — A6

Palace, Sadiq Garh — A7

Nawab Sadiq Muhammad Khan V Abbasi Bahadur — A8

A9

Perf. 12½ (A2), 12x12½ (A3, A5, A6, A7), 12½x12 (A4, A8), 13x13½ (A9)

1948, Apr. 1 Engr. Wmk. 274
2 A2 3p dp blue & blk 2.00 *14.00*
3 A2 ½a lake & blk 2.00 *14.00*
4 A2 9p dk green & blk 2.00 *14.00*
5 A2 1a dp car & blk 2.00 *14.00*
6 A2 1½a violet & blk 3.00 *14.00*
7 A3 2a car & dp grn 3.00 *14.00*
8 A4 4a brn & org red 3.00 *14.00*
9 A5 6a dp bl & vio brn 3.50 *14.00*
10 A6 8a brt pur & car 3.75 *14.00*
11 A7 12a dp car & dk bl grn 4.50 *16.00*
12 A8 1r chocolate & vio 25.00 *35.00*
13 A8 2r dp mag & dk grn 50.00 *60.00*
14 A8 5r purple & black 50.00 *70.00*
15 A9 10r black & car 45.00 *110.00*
Nos. 2-15 (14) 198.75 *417.00*

See #18-21. For overprints see #O17-O24.

Soldiers of 1848 and 1948 — A10

1948, Oct. 15 Engr. *Perf. 11½*
16 A10 1½a dp car & blk 1.75 *8.00*

Centenary of the Multan Campaign.

Amir Khan V and Mohammed Ali Jinnah — A11

1948, Oct. 3 *Perf. 13x12½*
17 A11 1½a grn & car rose 1.50 *5.25*

1st anniv. of the union of Bahawalpur with Pakistan.

Types of 1948

1948 *Perf. 12x11½*
18 A8 1r orange & dp grn 1.75 *17.00*
19 A8 2r carmine & blk 1.90 *21.00*
20 A8 5r ultra & red brn 2.25 *37.50*

Perf. 13½

21 A9 10r green & red brn 2.75 *50.00*
Nos. 18-21 (4) 8.65 *125.50*

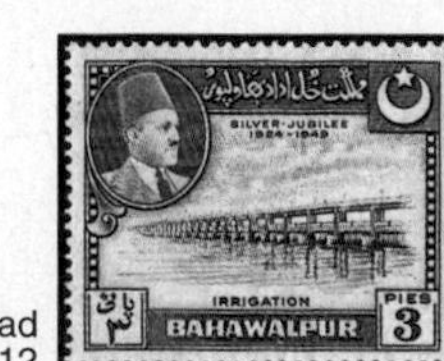
Panjnad Weir — A12

1949, Mar. 3 *Perf. 14*
22 A12 3p shown .25 *8.00*
23 A12 ½a Wheat .25 *8.00*
24 A12 9p Cotton .25 *8.00*
25 A12 1a Sahiwal Bull .25 *8.00*
Nos. 22-25 (4) 1.00 *32.00*

25th anniv. of the acquisition of full ruling powers by Amir Khan V.

UPU Monument, Bern — A13

1949, Oct. 10 *Perf. 13*

Center in Black

26 A13 9p green .25 *3.00*
27 A13 1a red violet .25 *3.00*
28 A13 1½a brown orange .25 *3.00*
29 A13 2½a blue .25 *3.00*
Nos. 26-29 (4) 1.00 *12.00*

UPU, 75th anniv. Exist perf 17½x17; value, each $2. Exist imperf.

For overprints see Nos. O25-O28.

OFFICIAL STAMPS

Two printings of Nos. O1-O10 exist. The first printing has brownish, streaky gum, and the second printing has clear, even gum.

Panjnad Weir — O1

Camel and Colt — O2

Antelopes O3

Pelicans O4

Juma Masjid Palace, Fort Derawar O5

Temple at Pattan Munara O6

Red Overprint

Wmk. 274

1945, Jan. 1 Engr. *Perf. 14*
O1 O1 ½a brt grn & blk 4.50 *12.50*
O2 O2 1a carmine & blk 5.75 *12.50*
O3 O3 2a violet & blk 5.00 *12.50*
O4 O4 4a olive & blk 12.50 *16.00*
O5 O5 8a brown & blk 22.00 20.00
O6 O6 1r orange & blk 22.00 20.00
Nos. O1-O6 (6) 71.75 *93.50*

For types overprinted see Nos. O7-O9, O11-O13.

Types of 1945, Without Red Overprint, Srchd. in Black

1945 Unwmk.
O7 O5 ½a on 8a lake & blk 6.00 6.00
O8 O6 1½a on 1r org & blk 40.00 10.00
O9 O1 1½a on 2r ultra & blk 200.00 20.00
Nos. O7-O9 (3) 246.00 36.00

Camels — O7

1945, Mar. 10 Red Overprint
O10 O7 1a brown & black 80.00 *75.00*

Types of 1945, Without Red Overprint, Ovptd. in Black

1945
O11 O1 ½a carmine & black 1.75 *7.00*
O12 O2 1a carmine & black 3.00 *7.00*
O13 O3 2a orange & black 5.25 *7.00*
Nos. O11-O13 (3) 10.00 *21.00*

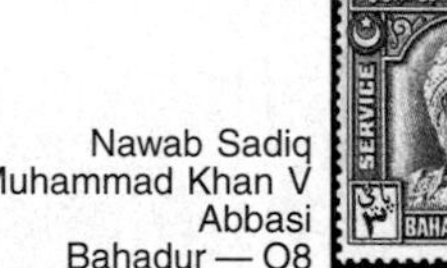
Nawab Sadiq Muhammad Khan V Abbasi Bahadur — O8

1945
O14 O8 3p dp blue & blk 4.50 *8.00*
O15 O8 1½a dp violet & blk 27.50 17.00

Flags of Allied Nations O9

1946, May 1
O16 O9 1½a emerald & gray 5.50 *7.00*

Victory of Allied Nations in World War II.

Stamps of 1948 Overprinted in Carmine or Black

Perf. 12½, 12½x12, 12x11½, 13½

1948 **Wmk. 274**

O17	A2	3p dp bl & blk (C)	1.00	*17.50*
O18	A2	1a dp carmine & blk	1.00	*17.50*
O19	A3	2a car & dp grn	1.00	*17.50*
O20	A4	4a brown & org red	1.00	*17.50*
O21	A8	1r org & dp grn (C)	1.00	*17.50*
O22	A8	2r car & blk (C)	1.00	*17.50*
O23	A8	5r ultra & red brn (C)	1.00	*17.50*
O24	A9	10r grn & red brn (C)	1.00	*17.50*
		Nos. O17-O24 (8)	8.00	*140.00*

Same Ovpt. in Carmine on #26-29

1949 **Center in Black** *Perf. 13, 18*

O25	A13	9p green	.25	*7.50*
O26	A13	1a red violet	.25	*7.50*
O27	A13	1½a brown orange	.25	*7.50*
O28	A13	2½a blue	.25	*7.50*
		Nos. O25-O28 (4)	1.00	*30.00*

75th anniv. of the UPU. Exist perf 17½x17; value, each *$10*. Exist imperf.

PALAU

pə-'lau

LOCATION — Group of 100 islands in the West Pacific Ocean about 1,000 miles southeast of Manila
AREA — 179 sq. mi.
POP. — 18,467 (1999 est.)
CAPITAL — Melekeok

Palau, the western section of the Caroline Islands (Micronesia), was part of the US Trust Territory of the Pacific, established in 1947. By agreement with the USPS, the republic began issuing its own stamps in 1984, with the USPS continuing to carry the mail to and from the islands.

On Jan. 10, 1986 Palau became a Federation as a Sovereign State in Compact of Free Association with the US.

100 Cents = 1 Dollar

Catalogue values for all unused stamps in this country are for Never Hinged items.

Inauguration of Postal Service — A1

1983, Mar. 10 **Litho.** *Perf. 14*

1	A1 20c	Constitution preamble	.55	.55
2	A1 20c	Hunters	.55	.55
3	A1 20c	Fish	.55	.55
4	A1 20c	Preamble, diff.	.55	.55
a.		Block of 4, #1-4	2.75	2.75

Palau Fruit Dove — A2

1983, May 16 *Perf. 15*

5	A2 20c	shown	.45	.45
6	A2 20c	Palau morningbird	.45	.45
7	A2 20c	Giant white-eye	.45	.45
8	A2 20c	Palau fantail	.45	.45
a.		Block of 4, #5-8	2.50	2.50

Sea Fan — A3

1983-84 **Litho.** *Perf. 13½x14*

9	A3 1c	shown	.25	.25
10	A3 3c	Map cowrie	.25	.25
11	A3 5c	Jellyfish	.25	.25
12	A3 10c	Hawksbill turtle	.25	.25
13	A3 13c	Giant Clam	.25	.25
a.		Booklet pane of 10	*10.00*	—
b.		Bklt. pane of 10 (5 #13, 5 #14)	*12.00*	—
14	A3 20c	Parrotfish	.35	.35
b.		Booklet pane of 10	*11.00*	—
15	A3 28c	Chambered Nautilus	.45	.45
16	A3 30c	Dappled sea cucumber	.50	.50
17	A3 37c	Sea Urchin	.55	.55
18	A3 50c	Starfish	.80	.80
19	A3 $1	Squid	1.60	1.60

Perf. 15x14

20	A3 $2	Dugong	4.25	4.25
21	A3 $5	Pink sponge	10.50	10.50
		Nos. 9-21 (13)	20.25	20.25

See Nos. 75-85.

Humpback Whale, World Wildlife Emblem — A4

1983, Sept. 21 *Perf. 14*

24	A4 20c	shown	1.25	1.25
25	A4 20c	Blue whale	1.25	1.25
26	A4 20c	Fin whale	1.25	1.25
27	A4 20c	Great sperm whale	1.25	1.25
a.		Block of 4, #24-27	6.50	6.50

Christmas 1983 — A5

Paintings by Charlie Gibbons, 1971 — No. 28, First Child ceremony. No. 29, Spearfishing from Red Canoe. No. 30, Traditional feast at the Bai. No. 31, Taro gardening. No. 32, Spearfishing at New Moon.

1983, Oct. **Litho.** *Perf. 14½*

28	A5 20c	multicolored	.50	.50
29	A5 20c	multicolored	.50	.50
30	A5 20c	multicolored	.50	.50
31	A5 20c	multicolored	.50	.50
32	A5 20c	multicolored	.50	.50
a.		Strip of 5, #28-32	2.75	2.75

A6

Capt. Wilson's Voyage, Bicentennial — A7

1983, Dec. 14 *Perf. 14x15*

33	A6 20c	Capt. Henry Wilson	.45	.45
34	A7 20c	Approaching Pelew	.45	.45
35	A7 20c	Englishman's Camp on Ulong	.45	.45
36	A6 20c	Prince Lee Boo	.45	.45
37	A6 20c	King Abba Thulle	.45	.45
38	A7 20c	Mooring in Koror	.45	.45
39	A7 20c	Village scene of Pelew Islands	.45	.45
40	A6 20c	Ludee	.45	.45
a.		Block or strip of 8, #33-40	5.00	5.00

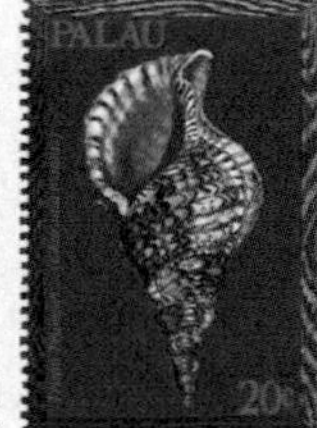

Local Seashells — A8

Shell paintings (dorsal and ventral) by Deborah Dudley Max.

1984, Mar. 15 **Litho.** *Perf. 14*

41	A8 20c	Triton trumpet, d.	.45	.45
42	A8 20c	Horned helmet, d.	.45	.45
43	A8 20c	Giant clam, d.	.45	.45
44	A8 20c	Laciniate conch, d.	.45	.45
45	A8 20c	Royal cloak scallop, d.	.45	.45
46	A8 20c	Triton trumpet, v.	.45	.45
47	A8 20c	Horned helmet, v.	.45	.45
48	A8 20c	Giant clam, v.	.45	.45
49	A8 20c	Laciniate conch, v.	.45	.45
50	A8 20c	Royal cloak scallop, v.	.45	.45
a.		Block of 10, #41-50	5.50	5.50

Explorer Ships A9

1984, June 19 **Litho.** *Perf. 14*

51	A9 40c	Oroolong, 1783	.85	.85
52	A9 40c	Duff, 1797	.85	.85
53	A9 40c	Peiho, 1908	.85	.85
54	A9 40c	Albatross, 1885	.85	.85
a.		Block of 4, #51-54	4.25	4.25

UPU Congress.

Ausipex '84 — A10

Fishing Methods.

1984, Sept. 6 **Litho.** *Perf. 14*

55	A10 20c	Throw spear fishing	.40	.40
56	A10 20c	Kite fishing	.40	.40
57	A10 20c	Underwater spear fishing	.40	.40
58	A10 20c	Net fishing	.40	.40
a.		Block of 4, #55-58	2.25	2.25

Christmas Flowers — A11

1984, Nov. 28 **Litho.** *Perf. 14*

59	A11 20c	Mountain Apple	.40	.40
60	A11 20c	Beach Morning Glory	.40	.40
61	A11 20c	Turmeric	.40	.40
62	A11 20c	Plumeria	.40	.40
a.		Block of 4, #59-62	2.00	2.00

Audubon Bicentenary — A12

1985, Feb. 6 **Litho.** *Perf. 14*

63	A12 22c	Shearwater chick	.85	.85
64	A12 22c	Shearwater's head	.85	.85
65	A12 22c	Shearwater in flight	.85	.85
66	A12 22c	Swimming	.85	.85
a.		Block of 4, #63-66	4.50	4.50
		Nos. 63-66,C5 (5)	4.50	4.50

Canoes and Rafts — A13

1985, Mar. 27 **Litho.**

67	22c Cargo canoe	.55	.55
68	22c War canoe	.55	.55
69	22c Bamboo raft	.55	.55
70	22c Racing/sailing canoe	.55	.55
a.	A13 Block of 4, #67-70	2.25	2.25

Marine Life Type of 1983

14c, Trumpet triton. 22c, Bumphead parrotfish. 25c, Soft coral, damsel fish. 33c, Sea anemone, clownfish. 39c, Green sea turtle. 44c, Pacific sailfish. $10, Spinner dolphins.

1985, June 11 **Litho.** *Perf. 14½x14*

75	A3 14c	multicolored	.30	.30
a.		Booklet pane of 10	*8.50*	—
76	A3 22c	multicolored	.55	.55
a.		Booklet pane of 10	*10.50*	—
b.		Booklet pane, 5 14c, 5 22c	*12.00*	—
77	A3 25c	multicolored	.60	.60
79	A3 33c	multicolored	.80	.80
80	A3 39c	multicolored	.95	.95
81	A3 44c	multicolored	1.10	1.10

Perf. 15x14

85	A3 $10	multicolored	19.00	19.00
		Nos. 75-85 (7)	23.30	23.30

A14

IYY emblem and children of all nationalities joined in a circle.

1985, July 15 **Litho.** *Perf. 14*

86	A14 44c	multicolored	.85	.85
87	A14 44c	multicolored	.85	.85
88	A14 44c	multicolored	.85	.85
89	A14 44c	multicolored	.85	.85
a.		Block of 4, #86-89	3.75	3.75

No. 89a has a continuous design.

A15

Christmas: Island mothers and children.

1985, Oct. 21 Litho. *Perf. 14*
90 A15 14c multicolored .35 .35
91 A15 22c multicolored .50 .50
92 A15 33c multicolored .80 .80
93 A15 44c multicolored 1.10 1.10
Nos. 90-93 (4) 2.75 2.75

Souvenir Sheet

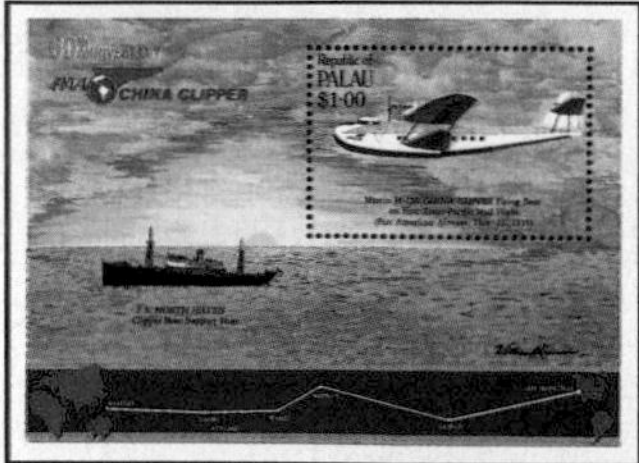

Pan American Airways Martin M-130 China Clipper — A16

1985, Nov. 21 Litho. *Perf. 14*
94 A16 $1 multicolored 2.50 2.50

1st Trans-Pacific Mail Flight, Nov. 22, 1935.
See Nos. C10-C13.

Return of Halley's Comet A17

Fictitious local sightings — No. 95, Kaeb canoe, 1758. No. 96, U.S.S. Vincennes, 1835. No. 97, S.M.S. Scharnhorst, 1910. No. 98, Yacht, 1986.

1985, Dec. 21 Litho. *Perf. 14*
95 A17 44c multicolored .80 .80
96 A17 44c multicolored .80 .80
97 A17 44c multicolored .80 .80
98 A17 44c multicolored .80 .80
a. Block of 4, #95-98 4.00 4.00

Songbirds — A18

No. 99, Mangrove flycatcher. No. 100, Cardinal honeyeater. No. 101, Blue-faced parrotfinch. No. 102, Dusky and bridled white-eyes.

1986, Feb. 24 Litho. *Perf. 14*
99 A18 44c multicolored .85 .85
100 A18 44c multicolored .85 .85
101 A18 44c multicolored .85 .85
102 A18 44c multicolored .85 .85
a. Block of 4, #99-102 4.00 4.00

World of Sea and Reef — A19

Designs: a, Spear fisherman. b, Native raft. c, Sailing canoes. d, Rock islands, sailfish. e, Inter-island boat, flying fish. f, Bonefish. g, Common jack. h, Mackerel. i, Sailfish. j, Barracuda. k, Triggerfish. l, Dolphinfish. m, Spear fisherman, grouper. n, Manta ray. o, Marlin. p, Parrotfish. q, Wrasse. r, Red snapper. s, Herring. t, Dugong. u, Surgeonfish. v, Leopard ray. w, Hawksbill turtle. x, Needlefish. y, Tuna. z, Octopus. aa, Clownfish. ab, Squid. ac, Grouper. ad, Moorish idol. ae, Queen conch, starfish. af, Squirrelfish. ag, Starfish, sting ray. ah, Lion fish. ai, Angel fish. aj, Butterfly fish. ak, Spiny lobster. al, Mangrove crab. am, Tridacna. an, Moray eel.

1986, May 22 Litho. *Perf. 15x14*
103 Sheet of 40 *37.50*
a.-an. A19 14c any single .75 .50

AMERIPEX '86, Chicago, May 22-June 1
See No. 854.

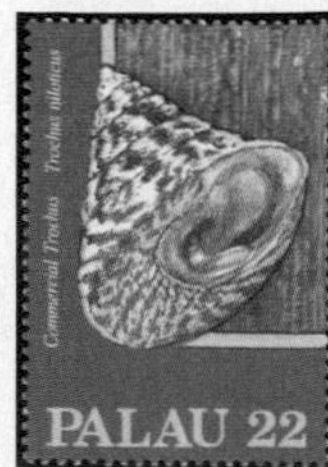

Seashells — A20

1986, Aug. 1 Litho. *Perf. 14*
104 A20 22c Commercial trochus .55 .55
105 A20 22c Marble cone .55 .55
106 A20 22c Fluted giant clam .55 .55
107 A20 22c Bullmouth helmet .55 .55
108 A20 22c Golden cowrie .55 .55
a. Strip of 5, #104-108 3.25 3.25

See Nos. 150-154, 191-195, 212-216.

Intl. Peace Year — A21

1986, Sept. 19 Litho.
109 22c Soldier's helmet .75 .75
110 22c Plane wreckage .75 .75
111 22c Woman playing guitar .75 .75
112 22c Airai vista .75 .75
a. A21 Block of 4, #109-112 3.50 3.50
Nos. 109-112,C17 (5) 4.00 4.00

Reptiles A22

1986, Oct. 28 Litho. *Perf. 14*
113 A22 22c Gecko .65 .65
114 A22 22c Emerald tree skink .65 .65
115 A22 22c Estuarine crocodile .65 .65
116 A22 22c Leatherback turtle .65 .65
a. Block of 4, #113-116 2.75 2.75

Christmas — A23

Joy to the World, carol by Isaac Watts and Handel: No. 117, Girl playing guitar, boys, goat. No. 118, Girl carrying bouquet, boys singing. No. 119, Palauan mother and child. No. 120, Children, baskets of fruit. No. 121, Girl, fairy tern. Nos. 117-121 printed in a continuous design.

1986, Nov. 26 Litho.
117 A23 22c multicolored .40 .40
118 A23 22c multicolored .40 .40
119 A23 22c multicolored .40 .40
120 A23 22c multicolored .40 .40
121 A23 22c multicolored .40 .40
a. Strip of 5, #117-121 2.50 2.50

Butterflies — A23a

No. 121B, Tangadik, soursop. No. 121C, Dira amartal, sweet orange. No. 121D, Ilhuochel, swamp cabbage. No. 121E, Bauosech, fig.

1987, Jan. 5 Litho. *Perf. 14*
121B A23a 44c multicolored 1.00 .90
121C A23a 44c multicolored 1.00 .90
121D A23a 44c multicolored 1.00 .90
121E A23a 44c multicolored 1.00 .90
f. Block of 4, #121B-121E 4.50 4.50

See Nos. 183-186.

Fruit Bats — A24

1987, Feb. 23 Litho.
122 44c In flight .85 .85
123 44c Hanging .85 .85
124 44c Eating .85 .85
125 44c Head .85 .85
a. A24 Block of 4, #122-125 4.00 4.00

Indigenous Flowers — A25

1c, Ixora casei. 3c, Lumnitzera littorea. 5c, Sonneratia alba. 10c, Tristellateria australasiae. 14c, Bikkia palauensis. 15c, Limnophila aromatica. 22c, Bruguiera gymnorhiza. 25c, Fagraea ksid. 36c, Ophiorrhiza palauensis. 39c, Cerbera manghas. 44c, Sandera indica. 45c, Maesa canfieldiae. 50c, Dolichandrone spathacea. $1, Barringtonia racemosa. $2, Nepenthes mirabilis. $5, Dendrobium palawense. $10, Bouquet.

1987-88 Litho. *Perf. 14*
126 A25 1c multicolored .25 .25
127 A25 3c multicolored .25 .25
128 A25 5c multicolored .25 .25
129 A25 10c multicolored .25 .25
130 A25 14c multicolored .25 .25
a. Booklet pane of 10 4.00 —
131 A25 15c multi ('88) .25 .25
a. Booklet pane of 10 ('88) 3.25 —
132 A25 22c multicolored .40 .40
a. Booklet pane of 10 6.50 —
b. Booklet pane, 5 each 14c, 22c 6.50 —
133 A25 25c multi ('88) .50 .50
a. Booklet pane of 10 ('88) 5.00 —
b. Booklet pane, 5 each 15c, 25c ('88) 5.00 —
134 A25 36c multi ('88) .65 .65
135 A25 39c multicolored .70 .70
136 A25 44c multicolored .85 .85
137 A25 45c multi ('88) .90 .90
138 A25 50c multicolored 1.00 1.00
139 A25 $1 multicolored 2.00 2.00
140 A25 $2 multicolored 4.25 4.00
141 A25 $5 multicolored 10.00 9.50

Size: 49x28mm
142 A25 $10 multi ('88) 17.00 16.00
Nos. 126-142 (17) 39.75 38.00

Issued: 3/12; $10, 3/17; 15c, 25c, 36c, 45c, 7/1; #131a, 133a-133b, 7/5.

CAPEX '87 — A26

1987, June 15 Litho. *Perf. 14*
146 22c Babeldaob Is. .50 .50
147 22c Floating Garden Isls. .50 .50
148 22c Rock Is. .50 .50
149 22c Koror .50 .50
a. A26 Block of 4, #146-149 2.25 2.25

Seashells Type of 1986

1987, Aug. 25 Litho. *Perf. 14*
150 A20 22c Black-striped triton .55 .55
151 A20 22c Tapestry turban .55 .55
152 A20 22c Adusta murex .55 .55
153 A20 22c Little fox miter .55 .55
154 A20 22c Cardinal miter .55 .55
a. Strip of 5, #150-154 3.00 3.00

US Constitution Bicentennial A27

Excerpts from Articles of the Palau and US Constitutions and Seals: No. 155, Art. VIII, Sec. 1, Palau. No. 156, Presidential seals. No. 157, Art. II, Sec. 1, US. No. 158, Art. IX, Sec. 1, Palau. No. 159, Legislative seals. No. 160, Art. I, Sec. 1, US. No. 161, Art X, Sec. 1, Palau. No. 162, Supreme Court seals. No. 163, Art. III, Sec. 1, US.

1987, Sept. 17 Litho. *Perf. 14*
155 A27 14c multicolored .25 .25
156 A27 14c multicolored .25 .25
157 A27 14c multicolored .25 .25
a. Triptych + label, #155-157 .80 .80
158 A27 22c multicolored .40 .40
159 A27 22c multicolored .40 .40
160 A27 22c multicolored .40 .40
a. Triptych + label, #158-160 1.50 1.50
161 A27 44c multicolored .75 .75
162 A27 44c multicolored .75 .75
163 A27 44c multicolored .75 .75
a. Triptych + label, #161-163 3.00 3.00
Nos. 155-163 (9) 4.20 4.20

Nos. 156, 159 and 162 are each 28x42mm. Labels picture national flags.

Japanese Links to Palau — A28

Japanese stamps, period cancellations and installations: 14c, No. 257 and 1937 Datsun sedan used as mobile post office, near Ngerchelechuus Mountain. 22c, No. 347 and phosphate mine at Angaur. 33c, No. B1 and Japan Airways DC-2 over stone monuments at Badrulchau. 44c, No. 201 and Japanese post office, Koror. $1, Aviator's Grave, Japanese Cemetary, Peleliu, vert.

1987, Oct. 16 Litho. *Perf. 14x13½*
164 A28 14c multicolored .30 .30
165 A28 22c multicolored .45 .45
166 A28 33c multicolored .65 .65
167 A28 44c multicolored .85 .85
Nos. 164-167 (4) 2.25 2.25

Souvenir Sheet
Perf. 13½x14
168 A28 $1 multicolored 2.25 2.25

Christmas — A30

Verses from carol "I Saw Three Ships," Biblical characters, landscape and Palauans in outrigger canoes.

1987, Nov. 24 Litho. *Perf. 14*
173 A30 22c I saw... .50 .50
174 A30 22c And what was... .50 .50
175 A30 22c 'Twas Joseph... .50 .50
176 A30 22c Saint Michael... .50 .50
177 A30 22c And all the bells... .50 .50
a. Strip of 5, #173-177 3.00 3.00

Symbiotic Marine Species — A31

#178, Snapping shrimp, goby. #179, Mauve vase sponge, sponge crab. #180, Pope's damselfish, cleaner wrasse. #181, Clown anemone fish, sea anemone. #182, Four-color nudibranch, banded coral shrimp.

1987, Dec. 15

178 A31 22c multicolored .55 .55
179 A31 22c multicolored .55 .55
180 A31 22c multicolored .55 .55
181 A31 22c multicolored .55 .55
182 A31 22c multicolored .55 .55
a. Strip of 5, #178-182 3.25 3.25

Butterflies and Flowers Type of 1987

Designs: No. 183, Dannaus plexippus, Tournefotia argentia. No. 184, Papilio machaon, Citrus reticulata. No. 185, Captopsilia, Crataeva speciosa. No. 186, Colias philodice, Crataeva speciosa.

1988, Jan. 25

183 A23a 44c multicolored .75 .75
184 A23a 44c multicolored .75 .75
185 A23a 44c multicolored .75 .75
186 A23a 44c multicolored .75 .75
a. Block of 4, #183-186 3.50 3.50

Ground-dwelling Birds — A32

1988, Feb. 29 Litho. *Perf. 14*

187 A32 44c Whimbrel .75 .75
188 A32 44c Yellow bittern .75 .75
189 A32 44c Rufous night-heron .75 .75
190 A32 44c Banded rail .75 .75
a. Block of 4, #187-190 3.50 3.50

Seashells Type of 1986

1988, May 11 Litho. *Perf. 14*

191 A20 25c Striped engina .55 .55
192 A20 25c Ivory cone .55 .55
193 A20 25c Plaited miter .55 .55
194 A20 25c Episcopal miter .55 .55
195 A20 25c Isabelle cowrie .55 .55
a. Strip of 5, #191-195 4.00 4.00

Souvenir Sheet

Postal Independence, 5th Anniv. — A33

FINLANDIA '88: a, Kaep (pre-European outrigger sailboat). b, Spanish colonial cruiser. c, German colonial cruiser SMS Cormoran, c. 1885. d, Japanese mailbox, WWII machine gun, Koror Museum. e, US Trust Territory ship, Malakal Harbor. f, Koror post office.

1988, June 8 Litho. *Perf. 14*

196 A33 Sheet of 6 3.00 3.00
a.-f. 25c multicolored .45 .45

Souvenir Sheet

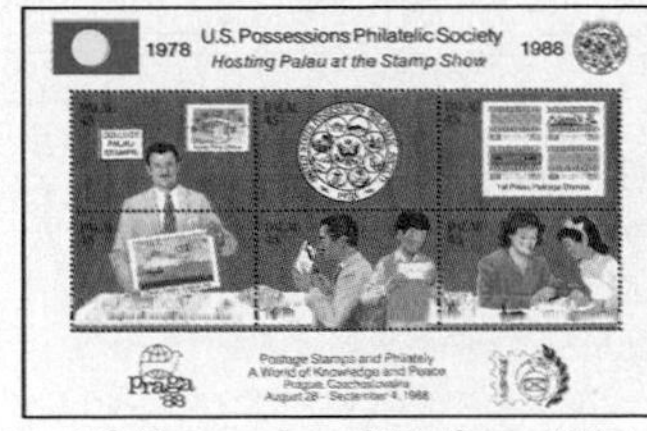

US Possessions Phil. Soc., 10th Anniv. — A34

PRAGA '88: a, "Collect Palau Stamps," original artwork for No. 196f and head of a man. b, Soc. emblem. c, Nos. 1-4. d, China Clipper original artwork and covers. e, Man and boy studying covers. f, Girl at show cancel booth.

1988, Aug. 26 Litho. *Perf. 14*

197 A34 Sheet of 6 5.00 5.00
a.-f. 45c any single .80 .80

Christmas — A35

Hark! The Herald Angels Sing: No. 198, Angels playing the violin, singing and sitting. No. 199, 3 angels and 3 children. No. 200, Nativity. No. 201, 2 angels, birds. No. 202, 3 children and 2 angels playing horns. Se-tenant in a continuous design.

1988, Nov. 7 Litho. *Perf. 14*

198 A35 25c multicolored .50 .50
199 A35 25c multicolored .50 .50
200 A35 25c multicolored .50 .50
201 A35 25c multicolored .50 .50
202 A35 25c multicolored .50 .50
a. Strip of 5, #199-202 2.75 2.75

Miniature Sheet

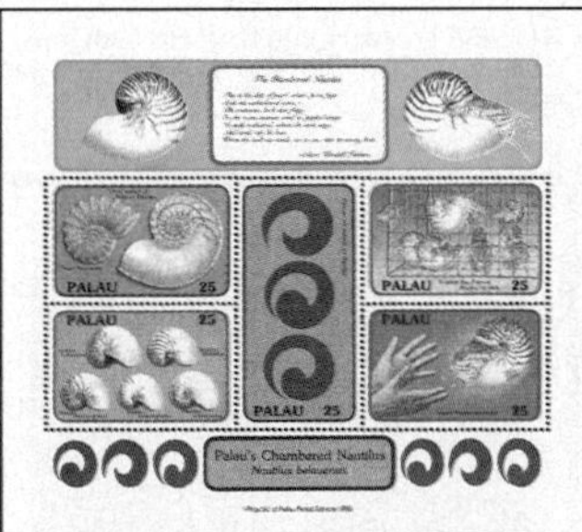

Chambered Nautilus — A36

Designs: a, Fossil and cross section. b, Palauan *bai* symbols for the nautilus. c, Specimens trapped for scientific study. d, *Nautilus belauensis, pompilius, macromphalus, stenomphalus* and *scrobiculatus.* e, Release of a tagged nautilus.

1988, Dec. 23 Litho. *Perf. 14*

203 A36 Sheet of 5 3.00 3.00
a.-e. 25c multicolored .60 .60

Endangered Birds of Palau — A37

1989, Feb. 9 Litho. *Perf. 14*

204 A37 45c Nicobar pigeon .85 .85
205 A37 45c Ground dove .85 .85
206 A37 45c Micronesian megapode .85 .85
207 A37 45c Owl .85 .85
a. Block of 4, #204-207 4.00 4.00

Exotic Mushrooms — A38

1989, Mar. 16 Litho. *Perf. 14*

208 A38 45c Gilled auricularia .90 .80
209 A38 45c Rock mushroom .90 .80
210 A38 45c Polyporous .90 .80
211 A38 45c Veiled stinkhorn .90 .80
a. Block of 4, #208-211 4.00 4.00

Seashells Type of 1986

1989, Apr. 12 Litho. *Perf. 14x14½*

212 A20 25c Robin redbreast triton .55 .55
213 A20 25c Hebrew cone .55 .55
214 A20 25c Tadpole triton .55 .55
215 A20 25c Lettered cone .55 .55
216 A20 25c Rugose miter .55 .55
a. Strip of 5, #212-216 3.25 3.25

Souvenir Sheet

A Little Bird, Amidst Chrysanthemums, 1830s, by Hiroshige (1797-1858) — A39

1989, May 17 Litho. *Perf. 14*

217 A39 $1 multicolored 2.25 2.25

Hirohito (1901-1989) and enthronement of Akihito as emperor of Japan.

Miniature Sheet

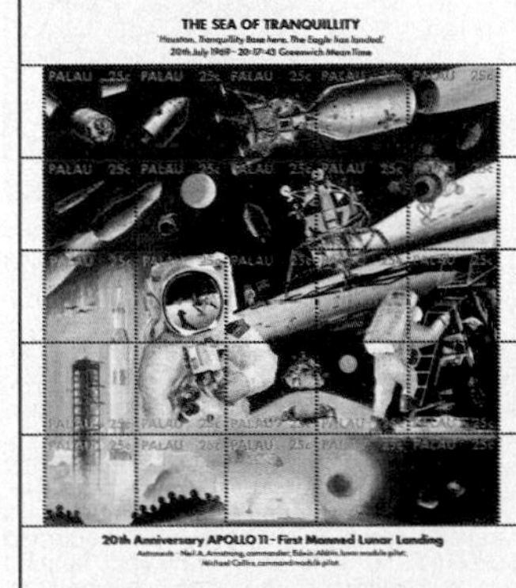

First Moon Landing, 20th Anniv. — A40

Apollo 11 mission: a, Third stage jettison. b, Lunar spacecraft. c, Module transposition *(Eagle).* d, *Columbia* module transposition (command module). e, *Columbia* module transposition (service module). f, Third stage burn. g, Vehicle entering orbit, Moon. h, *Columbia* and *Eagle.* i, *Eagle* on the Moon. j, *Eagle* in space. k, Three birds, Saturn V third stage, lunar spacecraft and escape tower. l, Astronaut's protective visor, pure oxygen system. m, Astronaut, American flag. n, Footsteps on lunar plain Sea of Tranquillity, pure oxygen system. o, Armstrong descending from *Eagle.* p, Mobile launch tower, Saturn V second stage. q, Space suit remote control unit and oxygen hoses. r, *Eagle* lift-off from Moon. s, Armstrong's first step on the Moon. t, Armstrong descending ladder, module transposition *(Eagle* and *Columbia).* u, Launch tower, spectators and Saturn V engines achieving thrust. v, Spectators, clouds of backwash. w, Parachute splashdown, U.S. Navy recovery ship and helicopter. x, Command module reentry. y, Jettison of service module prior to reentry.

1989, July 20 Litho. *Perf. 14*

218 A40 Sheet of 25 12.00 12.00
a.-y. 25c any single .45 .45

Buzz Aldrin Photographed on the Moon by Neil Armstrong — A41

1989, July 20 *Perf. 13½x14*

219 A41 $2.40 multicolored 4.75 4.75

First Moon landing 20th anniv.

Literacy — A42

Imaginary characters and children reading: a, Youth astronaut. b, Boy riding dolphin. c, Cheshire cat in palm tree. d, Mother Goose. e, New York Yankee at bat. f, Girl reading. g, Boy reading. h, Mother reading to child. i, Girl holding flower and listening to story. j, Boy dressed in baseball uniform. Printed se-tenant in a continuous design.

1989, Oct. 13 Litho. *Perf. 14*

220 A42 Block of 10 4.75 4.75
a.-j. 25c any single .40 .40

No. 220 printed in sheets containing two blocks of ten with strip of 5 labels between. Inscribed labels contain book, butterflies and "Give Them / Books / Give Them / Wings." Value, sheet $15.

Miniature Sheet

Stilt Mangrove Fauna — A43

World Stamp Expo '89: a, Bridled tern. b, Sulphur butterfly. c, Mangrove flycatcher. d, Collared kingfisher. e, Fruit bat. f, Estuarine crocodile. g, Rufous night-heron. h, Stilt mangrove. i, Bird's nest fern. j, Beach hibiscus tree. k, Common eggfly. l, Dog-faced watersnake. m, Jingle shell. n, Palau bark cricket. o, Periwinkle, mangrove oyster. p, Jellyfish. q, Striped mullet. r, Mussels, sea anemones, algae. s, Cardinalfish. t, Snapper.

1989, Nov. 20 Litho. *Perf. 14½*

221 A43 Block of 20 12.00 12.00
a.-t. 25c any single .55 .55

Christmas — A44

Whence Comes this Rush of Wings? a carol: No. 222, Dusky tern, Audubon's shearwater, angels, island. No. 223, Fruit pigeon, angel. No. 224, Madonna and Child, ground pigeons, fairy terns, rails, sandpipers. No. 225, Angel, blue-headed green finch, red flycatcher, honeyeater. No. 226, Angel, black-headed gulls. Printed se-tenant in a continuous design.

1989, Dec. 18 Litho. *Perf. 14*

222 A44 25c multicolored .55 .55
223 A44 25c multicolored .55 .55
224 A44 25c multicolored .55 .55
225 A44 25c multicolored .55 .55
226 A44 25c multicolored .55 .55
a. Strip of 5, #222-226 3.25 3.25

Soft Coral — A45

1990, Jan. 3

227 A45 25c Pink coral .50 .50
228 A45 25c Pink & violet coral .50 .50
229 A45 25c Yellow coral .50 .50
230 A45 25c Red coral .50 .50
a. Block of 4, #227-230 3.00 3.00

Birds of the Forest A46

1990, Mar. 16

231 A46 45c Siberian rubythroat .85 .85
232 A46 45c Palau bush-warbler .85 .85
233 A46 45c Micronesian starling .85 .85
234 A46 45c Cicadabird .85 .85
a. Block of 4, #231-234 4.00 4.00

Miniature Sheet

State Visit of Prince Lee Boo of Palau to England, 1784 — A47

Prince Lee Boo, Capt. Henry Wilson and: a, HMS *Victory* docked at Portsmouth. b, St. James's Palace, London. c, Rotherhithe Docks, London. d, Capt. Wilson's residence, Devon. e, Lunardi's Grand English Air Balloon. f, St. Paul's and the Thames. g, Lee Boo's tomb, St. Mary's Churchyard, Rotherhithe. h, St. Mary's Church. i, Memorial tablet, St. Mary's Church.

1990, May 6 Litho. *Perf. 14*

235 A47 Sheet of 9 4.50 4.50
a.-i. 25c any single .45 .45

Stamp World London '90.

Souvenir Sheet

Penny Black, 150th Anniv. — A48

1990, May 6

236 A48 $1 Great Britain #1 2.00 2.00

Orchids — A49

No. 237, Corymborkis veratrifolia. No. 238, Malaxis setipes. No. 239, Dipodium freycinetianum. No. 240, Bulbophyllum micronesiacum. No. 241, Vanda teres and hookeriana.

1990, June 7 *Perf. 14*

237 A49 45c multicolored .90 .90
238 A49 45c multicolored .90 .90
239 A49 45c multicolored .90 .90
240 A49 45c multicolored .90 .90
241 A49 45c multicolored .90 .90
a. Strip of 5, #237-241 5.00 5.00

Butterflies and Flowers A50

1990, July 6 Litho. *Perf. 14*

242 A50 45c Wedelia strigulosa .85 .85
243 A50 45c Erthrina variegata .85 .85
244 A50 45c Clerodendrum inerme .85 .85
245 A50 45c Vigna marina .85 .85
a. Block of 4, #242-245 3.75 3.75

Miniature Sheet

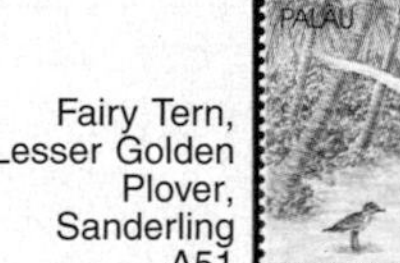

Fairy Tern, Lesser Golden Plover, Sanderling A51

Lagoon life: b, Bidekill fisherman. c, Sailing yacht, insular halfbeaks. d, Palauan kaeps. e, White-tailed tropicbird. f, Spotted eagle ray. g, Great barracuda. h, Reef needlefish. i, Reef blacktip shark. j, Hawksbill turtle. k, Octopus. l, Batfish. m, Lionfish. n, Snowflake moray. o, Porcupine fish, sixfeeler threadfins. p, Blue sea star, regal angelfish, cleaner wrasse. q, Clown triggerfish. r, Spotted garden eel and orange fish. s, Blue-lined sea bream, blue-green chromis, sapphire damselfish. t, Orangespine unicornfish, white-tipped soldierfish. u, Slatepencil sea urchin, leopard sea cucumber. v, Partridge tun shell. w, Mandarinfish. x, Tiger cowrie. y, Feather starfish, orange-fin anemonefish.

1990, Aug. 10 Litho. *Perf. 15x14½*

246 A51 25c Sheet of 25, #a.-y. 12.50 12.50

Nos. 246a-246y inscribed on reverse.

Pacifica — A52

1990, Aug. 24 Litho. *Perf. 14*

247 45c Mailship, 1890 1.50 1.50
248 45c US #803 on cover, fork-lift, plane 1.50 1.50
a. A52 Pair, #247-248 3.25 3.25

Christmas — A53

Here We Come A-Caroling: No. 250, Girl with music, poinsettias, doves. No. 251, Boys playing guitar, flute. No. 252, Family. No. 253, Three girls singing.

1990, Nov. 28

249 A53 25c multicolored .50 .40
250 A53 25c multicolored .50 .40
251 A53 25c multicolored .50 .40
252 A53 25c multicolored .50 .40
253 A53 25c multicolored .50 .40
a. Strip of 5, #249-253 3.00 3.00

US Forces in Palau, 1944 A54

Designs: No. 254, B-24s over Peleliu. No. 255, LCI launching rockets. No. 256, First Marine Division launching offensive. No. 257, Soldier, children. No. 258, USS *Peleliu.*

1990, Dec. 7

254 A54 45c multicolored 1.00 .85
255 A54 45c multicolored 1.00 .85
256 A54 45c multicolored 1.00 .85
257 A54 45c multicolored 1.00 .85
a. Block of 4, #254-257 4.25 4.25

Souvenir Sheet

Perf. 14x13½

258 A54 $1 multicolored 2.50 2.50

No. 258 contains one 51x38mm stamp.

See No. 339 for No. 258 with added inscription.

Coral — A55

1991, Mar. 4 Litho. *Perf. 14*

259 30c Staghorn .65 .65
260 30c Velvet Leather .65 .65
261 30c Van Gogh's Cypress .65 .65
262 30c Violet Lace .65 .65
a. A55 Block of 4, #259-262 3.25 3.25

Miniature Sheet

Angaur, The Phosphate Island — A56

Designs: a, Virgin Mary Statue, Nkulangelul Point. b, Angaur kaep, German colonial postmark. c, Swordfish, Caroline Islands No. 13. d, Phosphate mine locomotive. e, Copra ship off Lighthouse Hill. f, Dolphins. g, Estuarine crocodile. h, Workers cycling to phosphate plant. i, Ship loading phosphate. j, Hammerhead shark, German overseer. k, Marshall Islands No. 15. l, SMS Scharnhorst. m, SMS Emden. n, Crab-eating macaque monkey. o, Great sperm whale. p, HMAS Sydney.

1991, Mar. 14

263 A56 30c Sheet of 16, #a.-p. 10.00 10.00

Nos. 263b-263c, 263f-263g, 263j-263k, 263n-263o printed in continuous design showing map of island.

Birds — A57

1c, Palau bush-warbler. 4c, Common moorhen. 6c, Banded rail. 19c, Palau fantail. 20c, Mangrove flycatcher. 23c, Purple swamphen. 29c, Palau fruit dove. 35c, Great crested tern. 40c, Pacific reef heron. 45c, Micronesian pigeon. 50c, Great frigatebird. 52c, Little pied cormorant. 75c, Jungle night jar. 95c, Cattle egret. $1.34, Great sulphur-crested cockatoo. $2, Blue-faced parrotfinch. $5, Eclectus parrot. $10, Palau bush warbler.

Perf. 14½x15, 13x13½

1991-92 Litho.

266 A57 1c multicolored .25 .25
267 A57 4c multicolored .25 .25
268 A57 6c multicolored .25 .25
269 A57 19c multicolored .35 .30
b. Booklet pane, 10 #269 3.50 —
Complete booklet, #269b 3.75
270 A57 20c multicolored .40 .30
271 A57 23c multicolored .45 .35
272 A57 29c multicolored .55 .45
a. Booklet pane, 5 each #269, #272 5.00 —
Complete booklet, #272a 5.25
b. Booklet pane, 10 #272 4.50 —
Complete booklet, #272b 4.50
273 A57 35c multicolored .70 .55
274 A57 40c multicolored .80 .60
275 A57 45c multicolored .90 .70
276 A57 50c multicolored 1.00 .80
277 A57 52c multicolored 1.00 .90
278 A57 75c multicolored 1.50 1.25
279 A57 95c multicolored 2.00 1.50
280 A57 $1.34 multicolored 2.25 2.00
281 A57 $2 multicolored 3.25 3.00
282 A57 $5 multicolored 8.00 7.75

Size: 52x30mm

283 A57 $10 multicolored 16.00 15.00
Nos. 266-283 (18) 39.90 36.20

The 1, 6, 20, 52, 75c, $10 are perf. 14½x15.

Issued: 1, 6, 20, 52, 75c, $5, 4/6/92; $10, 9/10/92; #269b, 272a, 272b, 8/23/91; others, 4/18/91.

Miniature Sheet

Christianity in Palau, Cent. — A58

Designs: a, Pope Leo XIII, 1891. b, Ibedul Ilengelekei, High Chief of Koror, 1871-1911. c, Fr. Marino de la Hoz, Br. Emilio Villar, Fr. Elias Fernandez. d, Fr. Edwin G. McManus (1908-1969), compiler of Palauan-English dictionary. e, Sacred Heart Church, Koror. f, Pope John Paul II.

1991, Apr. 28 *Perf. 14½*

288 A58 29c Sheet of 6, #a.-f. 3.50 3.50

Miniature Sheet

Marine Life A59

Designs: a, Pacific white-sided dolphin. b, Common dolphin. c, Rough-toothed dolphin. d, Bottlenose dolphin. e, Harbor porpoise. f, Killer whale. g, Spinner dolphin, yellowfin tuna. h, Dall's porpoise. i, Finless porpoise. j, Map of Palau, dolphin. k, Dusky dolphin. l, Southern right-whale dolphin. m, Striped dolphin. n, Fraser's dolphin. o, Peale's dolphin. p, Spectacled porpoise. q, Spotted dolphin. r, Hourglass dolphin. s, Risso's dolphin. t, Hector's dolphin.

1991, May 24 Litho. *Perf. 14*
289 A59 29c Sheet of 20, #a.-t. 13.50 13.50

Miniature Sheet

Operations Desert Shield / Desert Storm — A60

Designs: a, F-4G Wild Weasel fighter. b, F-117A Stealth fighter. c, AH-64A Apache helicopter. d, TOW missle launcher on M998 HMMWV. e, Pres. Bush. f, M2 Bradley fighting vehicle. g, Aircraft carrier USS Ranger. h, Corvette fast patrol boat. i, Battleship Wisconsin.

1991, July 2 Litho. *Perf. 14*
290 A60 20c Sheet of 9, #a.-i. 3.75 3.75

Size: 38x51mm

291 A60 $2.90 Fairy tern, yellow ribbon 5.25 5.25

Souvenir Sheet

292 A60 $2.90 like #291 5.75 5.75

No. 291 has a white border around design. No. 292 printed in continuous design.

Republic of Palau, 10th Anniv. — A61

Designs: a, Palauan bai. b, Palauan bai interior, denomination UL. c, Same, denomination UR. d, Demi-god Chedechuul. e, Spider, denomination at UL. f, Money bird facing right. g, Money bird facing left. h, Spider, denomination at UR.

1991, July 9 *Perf. 14½*
293 A61 29c Sheet of 8, #a.-h. 5.00 5.00

See No. C21.

Miniature Sheet

Giant Clams — A62

Designs: a, Tridacna squamosa, Hippopus hippopus, Hippopus porcellanus, and Tridacna derasa. b, Tridacna gigas. c, Hatchery and tank culture. d, Diver, bottom-based clam nursery. e, Micronesian Mariculture Demonstration Center.

1991, Sept. 17 Litho. *Perf. 14*
294 A62 50c Sheet of 5, #a.-e. 5.00 5.00

No. 294e is 109x17mm and imperf on 3 sides, perf 14 at top.

Miniature Sheet

Japanese Heritage in Palau — A63

Designs: No. 295: a, Marine research. b, Traditional arts, carving story boards. c, Agricultural training. d, Archaeological research. e, Training in architecture and building. f, Air transportation. $1, Map, cancel from Japanese post office at Parao.

1991, Nov. 19
295 A63 29c Sheet of 6, #a.-f. 3.50 3.50

Souvenir Sheet

296 A63 $1 multicolored 3.00 3.00

Phila Nippon '91.

Miniature Sheet

Peace Corps in Palau, 25th Anniv. — A64

Children's drawings: No. 297a, Flag, doves, children, and islands. b, Airplane, people being greeted. c, Red Cross instruction. d, Fishing industry. e, Agricultural training. f, Classroom instruction.

1991, Dec. 6 Litho. *Perf. 13½*
297 A64 29c Sheet of 6, #a.-f. 3.75 3.75

Christmas — A65

Silent Night: No. 298: a, Silent night, holy night. b, All is calm, all is bright. c, Round yon virgin, mother and Child. d, Holy Infant, so tender and mild. e, Sleep in heavenly peace.

1991, Nov. 14 *Perf. 14*
298 A65 29c Strip of 5, #a.-e. 2.75 2.75

Miniature Sheet

World War II in the Pacific A66

Designs: No. 299a, Pearl Harbor attack begins. b, Battleship Nevada gets under way. c, USS Shaw explodes. d, Japanese aircraft carrier Akagi sunk. e, USS Wasp sunk off Guadalcanal. f, Battle of the Philippine Sea. g, US landing craft approach Saipan. h, US 1st Cavalry on Leyte. i, Battle of Bloody Nose Ridge, Peleliu. j, US troops land on Iwo Jima.

1991, Dec. 6 *Perf. 14½x15*
299 A66 29c Sheet of 10, #a.-j. 8.50 8.50

See No. C22.

A67

Butterflies: a, Troides criton. b, Alcides zodiaca. c, Papillio poboroi. d, Vindula arsinoe.

1992, Jan. 20 Litho. *Perf. 14*
300 A67 50c Block of 4, #a.-d. 4.00 4.00

A68

Shells: a, Common hairy triton. b, Eglantine cowrie. c, Sulcate swamp cerith. d, Black-spined murex. e, Black-mouth moon.

1992, Mar. 11
301 A68 29c Strip of 5, #a.-e. 3.00 3.00

Miniature Sheet

Age of Discovery A69

Designs: a, Columbus. b, Magellan. c, Drake. d, Wind as shown on old maps.
Maps and: e, Compass rose. f, Dolphin, Drake's ship Golden Hinde. g, Corn, Santa Maria. h, Fish. i, Betel palm, cloves and black pepper. j, Victoria, shearwater and great crested tern. k, White-tailed tropicbird, bicolor parrotfish, pineapple and potatoes. l, Compass. m, Sea monster. n, Paddles and astrolabe. o, Parallel ruler, dividers and Inca gold treasures. p, Back staff.
Portraits: q, Wind, diff. r, Vespucci. s, Pizarro. t, Balboa.

1992, May 25 Litho. *Perf. 14*
302 A69 29c Sheet of 20, #a.-t. 12.00 12.00

Miniature Sheet

Biblical Creation of the World — A70

Designs: a, "And darkness was..." b, Sun's rays. c, Water, sun's rays. d, "...and it was good." e, "Let there be a..." f, Land forming. g, Water and land. h, "...and it was so." i, "Let the waters..." j, Tree branches. k, Shoreline. l, Shoreline, flowers, tree. m, "Let there be lights..." n, Comet, moon. o, Mountains. p, Sun, hillside. q, "Let the waters..." r, Birds. s, Fish, killer whale. t, Fish. u, "Let the earth..." v, Woman, man. w, Animals. x, "...and it was very good."

1992, June 5 *Perf. 14½*
303 A70 29c Sheet of 24, #a.-x. 14.00 14.00

Nos. 303a-303d, 303e-303h, 303i-303l, 303m-303p, 303q-303t, 303u-303x are blocks of 4.

Souvenir Sheets

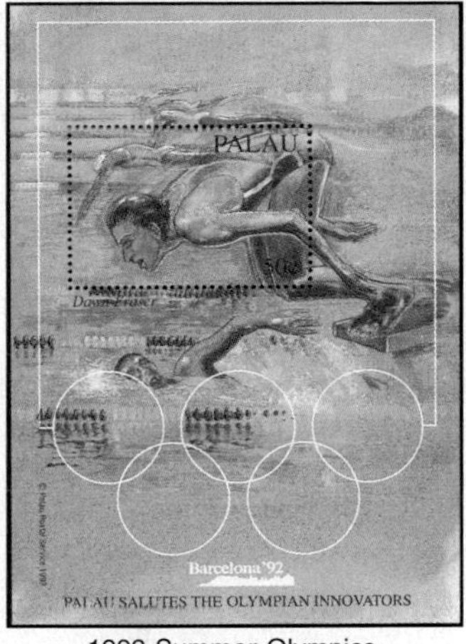

1992 Summer Olympics, Barcelona — A71

1992, July 10 *Perf. 14*

304 A71 50c Dawn Fraser	1.00	1.00
305 A71 50c Olga Korbut	1.00	1.00
306 A71 50c Bob Beamon	1.00	1.00
307 A71 50c Carl Lewis	1.00	1.00
308 A71 50c Dick Fosbury	1.00	1.00
309 A71 50c Greg Louganis	1.00	1.00
Nos. 304-309 (6)	6.00	6.00

Miniature Sheet

Elvis Presley A72

Various portraits.

1992, Aug. 17 *Perf. 13½x14*
310 A72 29c Sheet of 9, #a.-i. 7.00 7.00

See No. 350.

Christmas — A73

The Friendly Beasts carol depicting animals in Nativity Scene: No. 312a, "Thus Every Beast." b, "By Some Good Spell." c, "In The Stable Dark Was Glad to Tell." d, "Of The Gift He Gave Emanuel." e, "The Gift He Gave Emanuel."

1992, Oct. 1 Litho. *Perf. 14*
312 A73 29c Strip of 5, #a.-e. 3.00 3.00

Fauna A74

Designs: a, Dugong. b, Masked booby. c, Macaque. d, New Guinean crocodile.

1993, July 9 Litho. *Perf. 14*
313 A74 50c Block of 4, #a.-d. 4.00 4.00

Seafood A75

Designs: a, Giant crab. b, Scarlet shrimp. c, Smooth nylon shrimp. d, Armed nylon shrimp.

1993, July 22
314 A75 29c Block of 4, #a.-d. 2.25 2.25

Sharks A76

Designs: a, Oceanic whitetip. b, Great hammerhead. c, Leopard. d, Reef black-tip.

1993, Aug. 11 Litho. *Perf. 14½*
315 A76 50c Block of 4, #a.-d. 4.00 4.00

Miniature Sheet

World War II in the Pacific A77

Actions in 1943: a, US takes Guadalcanal, Feb. b, Hospital ship Tranquility supports action. c, New Guineans join Allies in battle. d, US landings in New Georgia, June. e, USS California participates in every naval landing. f, Dauntless dive bombers over Wake Island, Oct. 6. g, US flamethrowers on Tarawa, Nov. h, US landings on Makin, Nov. i, B-25s bomb Simpson Harbor, Rabaul, Oct. 23. j, B-24s over Kwajalein, Dec. 8.

1993, Sept. 23 Litho. *Perf. 14½x15*
316 A77 29c Sheet of 10, #a.-j. + label 8.00 8.00

See Nos. 325-326.

Christmas — A78

Christmas carol, "We Wish You a Merry Christmas," with Palauan customs: a, Girl, goat. b, Goats, children holding leis, prow of canoe. c, Santa Claus. d, Children singing. e, Family with fruit, fish.

1993, Oct. 22 Litho. *Perf. 14*
317 A78 29c Strip of 5, #a.-e. 3.00 3.00

Miniature Sheet

Prehistoric and Legendary Sea Creatures — A79

1993, Nov. 26 Litho. *Perf. 14*
318 A79 29c Sheet of 25, #a.-y. 14.00 14.00

Miniature Sheet

Intl. Year of Indigenous People — A80

Paintings, by Charlie Gibbons: No. 319: a, After Child-birth Ceremony. b, Village in Early Palau.

Storyboard carving, by Ngiraibuuch: $2.90, Quarrying of Stone Money, vert.

1993, Dec. 8 *Perf. 14x13½*
319 A80 29c Sheet, 2 ea #a.-b. 2.25 2.25

Souvenir Sheet
Perf. 13½x14
320 A80 $2.90 multicolored 6.00 6.00

Miniature Sheet

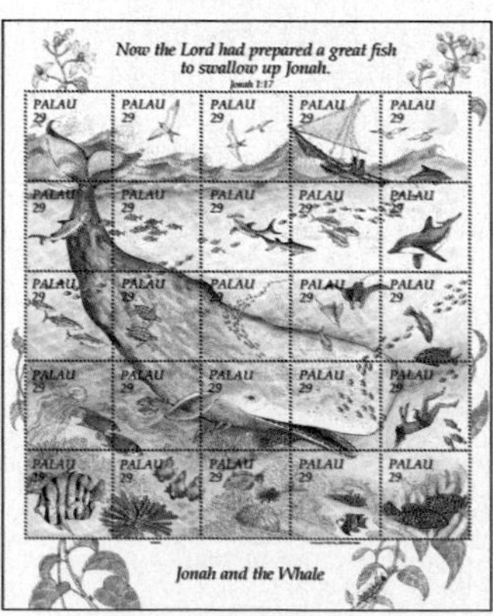

Jonah and the Whale — A81

1993, Dec. 28 Litho. *Perf. 14*
321 A81 29c Sheet of 25, #a.-y. 14.50 14.50

Hong Kong '94 A82

Rays: a, Manta (b). b, Spotted eagle (a). c, Coachwhip (d). d, Black spotted.

1994, Feb. 18 Litho. *Perf. 14*
322 A82 40c Block of 4, #a.-d. 3.00 3.00

Estuarine Crocodile A83

Designs: a, With mouth open. b, Hatchling. c, Crawling on river bottom. d, Swimming.

1994, Mar. 14
323 A83 20c Block of 4, #a.-d. 3.50 3.50

World Wildlife Fund.

Large Seabirds — A84

a, Red-footed booby. b, Great frigatebird. c, Brown booby. d, Little pied cormorant.

1994, Apr. 22 Litho. *Perf. 14*
324 A84 50c Block of 4, #a.-d. 4.00 4.00

World War II Type of 1993

Miniature Sheets

Action in the Pacific, 1944: No. 325: a, US Marines capture Kwajalien, Feb. 1-7. b, Japanese enemy base at Truk destroyed, Feb. 17-18. c, SS-284 Tullibee participates in Operation Desecrate, March. d, US troops take Saipan, June 15-July 9. e, Great Marianas Turkey Shoot, June 19-20. f, Guam liberated, July-Aug. g, US troops take Peleliu, Sept. 15-Oct. 14. h, Angaur secured in fighting, Sept. 17-22. i, Gen. Douglas MacArthur returns to Philippines, Oct. 20. j, US Army Memorial, Palau, Nov. 27.

D-Day, Allied Invasion of Normandy, June 6, 1944: No. 326: a, C-47 transport aircraft dropping Allied paratroopers. b, Allied warships attack beach fortifications. c, Commandos attack from landing craft. d, Tanks land. e, Sherman flail tank beats path through minefields. f, Allied aircraft attack enemy reinforcements. g, Gliders deliver troops behind enemy lines. h, Pegasus Bridge, first French house liberated. i, Allied forces move inland to form bridgehead. j, View of beach at end of D-Day.

1994, May Sheets of 10 *Perf. 14½*
325 A77 29c #a.-j. + label 8.50 8.50
326 A77 50c #a.-j. + label 12.00 12.00

Pierre de Coubertin (1863-1937) — A85

Winter Olympic medalists: No. 328, Anne-Marie Moser, vert. No. 329, James Craig. No. 330, Katarina Witt. No. 331, Eric Heiden, vert. No. 332, Nancy Kerrigan. $2, Dan Jansen.

1994, July 20 Litho. *Perf. 14*
327 A85 29c multicolored .70 .70

Souvenir Sheets
328 A85 50c multicolored 1.00 1.00
329 A85 50c multicolored 1.00 1.00
330 A85 $1 multicolored 2.00 2.00
331 A85 $1 multicolored 2.00 2.00
332 A85 $1 multicolored 2.00 2.00
333 A85 $2 multicolored 4.00 4.00

Intl. Olympic Committee, cent.

Miniature Sheets

PHILAKOREA '94 — A86

Wildlife carrying letters: No. 334: a, Sailfin goby. b, Sharpnose puffer. c, Lightning butterflyfish. d, Clown anemonefish. e, Parrotfish. f, Batfish. g, Clown triggerfish. h, twinspot wrasse.

No. 335a, Palau fruit bat. b, Crocodile. c, Dugong. d, Banded sea snake. e, Bottle-nosed dophin. f, Hawksbill turtle. g, Octopus. h, Manta ray.

No. 336: a, Palau fantail. b, Banded crake. c, Island swiftlet. d, Micronesian kingfisher. e. Red-footed booby. f, Great frigatebird. g, Palau owl. h, Palau fruit dove.

1994, Aug. 16 Litho. *Perf. 14*
334 A86 29c Sheet of 8, #a.-h. 6.00 6.00
335 A86 40c Sheet of 8, #a.-h. 8.00 8.00
336 A86 50c Sheet of 8, #a.-h. 10.00 10.00

No. 336 is airmail.

Miniature Sheet

First Manned Moon Landing, 25th Anniv. — A87

Various scenes from Apollo moon missions.

1994, July 20
337 A87 29c Sheet of 20, #a.-t. 12.00 12.00

Independence Day — A88

#338: b, Natl. seal. c, Pres. Kuniwo Nakamura, Palau, US Pres. Clinton. d, Palau, US flags. e, Musical notes of natl. anthem.

1994, Oct. 1 *Perf. 14*
338 A88 29c Strip of 5, #a.-e. 2.75 2.75

No. 338c is 57x42mm.

No. 258 with added text "50th ANNIVERSARY / INVASION OF PELELIU / SEPTEMBER 15, 1944"

1994 Litho. *Perf. 14X13½*
339 A54 $1 multicolored 2.50 2.50

Miniature Sheet

Disney Characters Visit Palau — A89

No. 340: a, Mickey, Minnie arriving. b, Goofy finding way to hotel. c, Donald enjoying beach. d, Minnie, Daisy learning the Ngloik. e, Minnie, Mickey sailing to Natural Bridge. f, Scrooge finding money in Babeldaob jungle. g, Goofy, Napoleon Wrasse. h, Minnie, Clam Garden. i, Grandma Duck weaving basket.

No. 341, Mickey exploring underwater shipwreck. No. 342, Donald visiting Airai Bai on Babeldaob. No. 343, Pluto, Mickey in boat, vert.

1994, Oct. 14 ***Perf. 13½x14***

340 A89 29c Sheet of 9, #a.-i. 6.00 6.00

Souvenir Sheets

341-342 A89 $1 each 3.00 3.00

Perf. 14x13½

343 A89 $2.90 multicolored 7.75 7.75

Miniature Sheet

Intl. Year of the Family — A90

Story of Tebruchel: a, With mother as infant. b, Father. c, As young man. d, Wife-to-be. e, Bringing home fish. f, Pregnant wife. g, Elderly mother. h, Elderly father. i, With first born. j, Wife seated. k, Caring for mother. l, Father, wife and baby.

1994, Nov. 1 **Litho.** ***Perf. 14***

344 A90 20c Sheet of 12, #a.-l. 4.75 4.75

Christmas — A91

O Little Town of Bethlehem: a, Magi, cherubs. b, Angel, shepherds, sheep. c, Angels, nativity. d, Angels hovering over town, shepherd, sheep. e, Cherubs, doves.

1994, Nov. 23 **Litho.** ***Perf. 14***

345 A91 29c Strip of 5, #a-e 3.00 3.00

No. 345 is a continuous design and is printed in sheets containing three strips. The bottom strip is printed with se-tenant labels.

Miniature Sheets

1994 World Cup Soccer Championships, US — A92

US coach, players: No. 346: a, Bora Milutinovic. b, Cle Kooiman. c, Ernie Stewart. d, Claudio Reyna. e, Thomas Dooley. f, Alexi Lalas. g, Dominic Kinnear. h, Frank Klopas. i, Paul Caligiuri. j, Marcelo Balboa. k, Cobi Jones. l, US flag, World Cup trohpy.

US players: No. 347a, Tony Meola. b, John Doyle. c, Eric Wynalda. d, Roy Wegerle. e, Fernando Clavijo. f, Hugo Perez. g, John Harkes. h, Mike Lapper. i, Mike Sorber. j, Brad Friedel. k, Tab Ramos. l, Joe-Max Moore.

No. 348: a, Babeto, Brazil. b, Romario, Brazil. c, Franco Baresi, Italy. d, Roberto Baggio, Italy. e, Andoni Zubizarreta, Spain. f, Oleg Salenko, Russia. g, Gheorghe Hagi, Romania. h, Dennis Bergkamp, Netherlands. i, Hristo Stoichkov, Bulgaria. j, Tomas Brolin, Sweden. k, Lothar Matthaus, Germany. l, Arrigo Sacchi, Italy, Carlos Alberto Parreira, Brazil, flags of Italy & Brazil, World Cup trophy.

1994, Dec. 23

346 A92 29c Sheet of 12, #a.-l. 6.25 6.25
347 A92 29c Sheet of 12, #a.-l. 6.25 6.25
348 A92 50c Sheet of 12, #a.-l. 10.50 10.50

Elvis Presley Type of 1992

Miniature Sheet

Various portraits.

1995, Feb. 28 **Litho.** ***Perf. 14***

350 A72 32c Sheet of 9, #a.-i. 6.25 6.25

Fish — A93

1c, Cube trunkfish. 2c, Lionfish. 3c, Longjawed squirrelfish. 4c, Longnose filefish. 5c, Ornate butterflyfish. 10c, Yellow seahorse. 20c, Magenta dottyback. 32c, Reef lizardfish. 50c, Multibarred goatfish. 55c, Barred blenny. $1, Fingerprint sharpnose puffer. $2, Longnose hawkfish. $3, Mandarinfish. $5, Blue surgeonfish. $10, Coral grouper.

1995, Apr. 3 **Litho.** ***Perf. 14½***

351	A93	1c multicolored	.25	.25
352	A93	2c multicolored	.25	.25
353	A93	3c multicolored	.25	.25
354	A93	4c multicolored	.25	.25
355	A93	5c multicolored	.25	.25
356	A93	10c multicolored	.25	.25
357	A93	20c multicolored	.35	.30
358	A93	32c multicolored	.50	.45
359	A93	50c multicolored	.85	.70
360	A93	55c multicolored	1.00	.75
361	A93	$1 multicolored	1.75	1.50
362	A93	$2 multicolored	3.50	3.00
363	A93	$3 multicolored	5.00	4.50
364	A93	$5 multicolored	8.50	7.75

Size: 48x30mm

365 A93 $10 multicolored 17.50 16.00
Nos. 351-365 (15) 40.45 36.45

Booklet Stamps

Size: 18x21mm

Perf. 14x14½ Syncopated

366 A93 20c multicolored .40 .40
a. Booklet pane of 10 3.75
Complete booklet, #366a 4.00
367 A93 32c multicolored .60 .60
a. Booklet pane of 10 6.00
Complete booklet, #367a 6.25
b. Booklet pane, 5 ea #366, 367 5.25
Complete booklet, #367b 5.50

Miniature Sheet

Lost Fleet of the Rock Islands A94

Underwater scenes, silhouettes of Japanese ships sunk during Operation Desecrate, 1944: a, Unyu Maru 2. b, Wakatake. c, Teshio Maru. d, Raizan Maru. e, Chuyo Maru. f, Shinsei Maru. g, Urakami Maru. h, Ose Maru. i, Iro. j, Shosei Maru. k, Patrol boat 31. l, Kibi Maru. m, Amatsu Maru. n, Gozan Maru. o, Matuei Maru. p, Nagisan Maru. q, Akashi. r, Kamikazi Maru.

1995, Mar. 30 **Litho.** ***Perf. 14***

368 A94 32c Sheet of 18, #a.-r. 12.00 12.00

Miniature Sheet

Flying Dinosaurs A95

Designs: a, Pteranodon sternbergi. b, Pteranodon ingens (a, c). c, Pterodoctyls (b). d, Dorygnathus (e). e, Dimorphodon (f). f, Nyctosaurus (e, c). g, Pterodactylus kochi. h, Ornithodesmus (g, i). i, Diatryma (l). j, Archaeopteryx. k, Campylognathoides (l). l, Gallodactylus. m, Batrachognathus (j). n, Scaphognathus (j, k, m, o). o, Peteinosaurus (l). p, Ichthyorinis. q, Ctenochasma (m, p, r). r, Rhamphorhynchus (n, o, q).

1995 **Litho.** ***Perf. 14***

369 A95 32c Sheet of 18, #a.-r. 12.00 12.00

Earth Day, 25th anniv.

Miniature Sheet

Research & Experimental Jet Aircraft — A96

Designs: a, Fairey Delta 2. b, B-70 "Valkyrie." c, Douglas X-3 "Stilletto." d, Northrop/NASA HL-10. e, Bell XS-1. f, Tupolev Tu-144. g, Bell X-1. h, Boulton Paul P.111. i, EWR VJ 101C. j, Handley Page HP-115. k, Rolls Royce TMR "Flying Bedstead." l, North American X-15.

$2, BAC/Aerospatiale Concorde SST.

1995 **Litho.** ***Perf. 14***

370 A96 50c Sheet of 12, #a.-l. 12.00 12.00

Souvenir Sheet

371 A96 $2 multicolored 3.75 3.75

No. 370 is airmail. No. 371 contains one 85x29mm stamp.

Miniature Sheet

Submersibles — A97

Designs: a, Scuba gear. b, Cousteau diving saucer. c, Jim suit. d, Beaver IV. e, Ben Franklin. f, USS Nautilus. g, Deep Rover. h, Beebe Bathysphere. i, Deep Star IV. j, DSRV. k, Aluminaut. l, Nautile. m, Cyana. n, FNRS Bathyscaphe. o, Alvin. p, Mir 1. q, Archimede. r, Trieste.

1995, July 21 **Litho.** ***Perf. 14***

372 A97 32c Sheet of 18, #a.-r. 12.00 12.00

Singapore '95 — A98

Designs: a, Dolphins, diver snorkeling, marine life. b, Turtle, diver, seabirds above. c, Fish, coral, crab. d, Coral, fish, diff.

1995, Aug. 15 **Litho.** ***Perf. 13½***

373 A98 32c Block of 4, #a.-d. 2.50 2.50

No. 373 is a continuous design and was issued in sheets of 24 stamps.

UN, FAO, 50th Anniv. A99

Designs: No. 374a, Outline of soldier's helmet, dove, peace. b, Outline of flame, Hedul Gibbons, human rights. c, Books, education. d, Outline of tractor, bananas, agriculture.

No. 375, Palau flag, bird, UN emblem. No. 376, Water being put on plants, UN emblem, vert.

1995, Sept. 15 **Litho.** ***Perf. 14***

374 A99 60c Block of 4, #a.-d. 4.75 4.75

Souvenir Sheets

375 A99 $2 multicolored 4.00 4.00
376 A99 $2 multicolored 4.00 4.00

Independence, 1st Anniv. — A100

Palau flag and: a, Fruit doves. b, Rock Islands. c, Map of islands. d, Orchid, hibiscus. 32c, Marine life.

1995, Sept. 15 ***Perf. 14½***

377 A100 20c Block of 4, #a.-d. 1.50 1.50
378 A100 32c multicolored .65 .65

No. 377 was issued in sheets of 16 stamps. See US No. 2999.

Miniature Sheets

A101

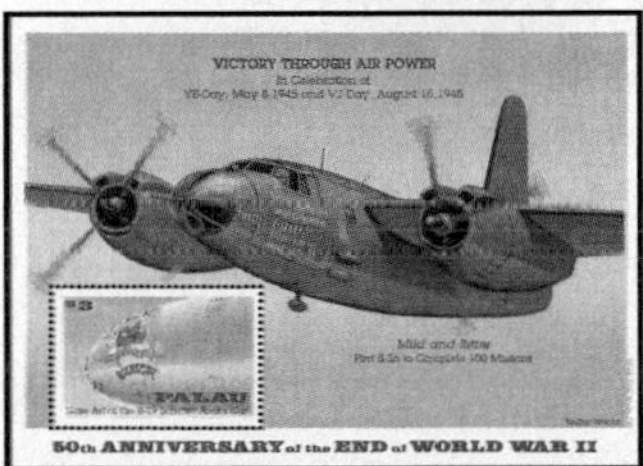

End of World War II, 50th Anniv. — A102

Paintings by Wm. F. Draper: No. 379a, Preparing Tin-Fish. b, Hellcats Take-off into Palau's Rising Sun. c, Dauntless Dive Bombers over Malakai Harbor. d, Planes Return from Palau. e, Communion Before Battle. f,

The Landing. g, First Task Ashore. h, Fire Fighters Save Flak-torn Pilot.

Paintings by Tom Lea: No. 379i, Young Marine Headed for Peleliu. j, Peleliu. k, Last Rites. l, The Thousand-Yard Stare.

Portraits by Albert Murray, vert.: No. 380a, Adm. Chester W. Nimitz. b, Adm. William F. Halsey. c, Adm. Raymond A. Spruance. d, Vice Adm. Marc A. Mitscher. e, Gen. Holland M. Smith, USMC.

$3, Nose art of B-29 Bock's Car.

1995, Oct. 18 ***Perf. 14x13½***

379 A101 32c Sheet of 12, #a.-l 7.75 7.75

Perf. 13½x14

380 A101 60c Sheet of 5, #a.-e. 7.50 7.50

Souvenir Sheet

Perf. 14

381 A102 $3 multicolored 6.00 6.00

Christmas — A103

Native version of "We Three Kings of Orient Are:" a, Angel, animals. b, Two wise men. c, Joseph, Mary, Jesus in manger. d, Wise man, shepherd, animals. e, Girl with fruit, goat, shepherd.

1995, Oct. 31 **Litho.** ***Perf. 14***

382 A103 32c Strip of 5, #a.-e. 3.00 3.00

No. 382 is a continuous design and was issued in sheets of 15 stamps + 5 labels se-tenant with bottom row of sheet.

Miniature Sheet

Life Cycle of the Sea Turtle — A104

Small turtles, arrows representing routes during life cycle and: a, Large turtle. b, Upper half of turtle shell platter, Palau map. c, Rooster in tree, island scene. d, Native woman. e, Lower half of turtle shell platter, Palau map, island couple. f, Fossil, palm trees, native house

1995, Nov. 15 **Litho.** ***Perf. 14***

383 A104 32c Sheet of 12, 2 each, #a.-f. 9.50 9.50

John Lennon (1940-80) — A105

1995, Dec. 8 **Litho.** ***Perf. 14***

384 A105 32c multicolored 1.10 1.10

No. 384 was issued in sheets of 16.

Miniature Sheet

New Year 1996 (Year of the Rat) — A106

Stylized rats in parade: No. 385: a, One carrying flag, one playing horn. b, Three playing musical instruments. c, Two playing instruments. d, Family in front of house.

Mirror images, diff. colors: No. 386: a, Like #385c-385d. b, Like #385a-385b.

1996, Feb. 2 **Litho.** ***Perf. 14***

385 A106 10c Strip of 4, #a.-d. 1.75 1.75

Miniature Sheet

386 A106 60c Sheet of 2, #a.-b. 2.25 2.25

No. 385 was issued in sheets of 2 + 4 labels like No. 386. Nos. 386a-386b are airmail and are each 56x43mm.

UNICEF, 50th Anniv. — A107

Three different children from Palau in traditional costumes, child in middle wearing: a, Red flowerd dress. b, Pink dress. c, Blue shorts. d, Red headpiece and shorts.

1996, Mar. 12 **Litho.** ***Perf. 14***

387 A107 32c Block of 4, #a.-d. 2.50 2.50

No. 387 was issued in sheets of 4.

Marine Life — A108

Letter spelling "Palau," and: a, "P," fairy basslet, vermiculate parrotfish. b, "A," yellow cardinalfish. c, "L," Marten's butterflyfish. d, "A," starry moray, slate pencil sea urchin. e, "U," cleaner wrasse, coral grouper.

1996, Mar. 29 **Litho.** ***Perf. 14***

388 A108 32c Strip of 5, #a.-e. 3.00 3.00

No. 388 was issued in miniature sheets of 3.

China '96, Intl. Stamp Exhibition, Beijing.

Capex '96 A109

Circumnavigators of the earth: No. 389: a, Ferdinand Magellan, ship Victoria. b, Charles Wilkes, ship Vincennes. c, Joshua Slocum, oyster boat Spray. d, Ben Carlin, amphibious vehicle Half-Safe. e, Edward L. Beach, submarine USS Triton. f, Naomi James, yacht Express Crusader. g, Sir Ranulf Fiennes, polar vehicle. h, Rick Hansen, wheel chair. i, Robin Knox-Johnson, catamaran Enza New Zealand.

No. 390: a, Lowell Smith, Douglas World Cruisers. b, Ernst Lehmann, Graf Zeppelin. c, Wiley Post, Lockheed Vega Winnie Mae. d, Yuri Gagarin, spacecraft Vostok I. e, Jerrie Mock, Cessna 180 Spirit of Columbus. f, Ross Perot, Jr., Bell Longranger III, Spirit of Texas. g, Brooke Knapp, Gulfstream III, The American Dream. h, Jeana Yeager, Dick Rutan, airplane Voyager. i, Fred Lasby, piper Commanche.

Each $3: No. 391, Bob Martin, Mark Sullivan, Troy Bradley, Odyssey Gondola. No. 392, Sir Francis Chichester, yacht Gipsy Moth IV.

1996, May 3 **Litho.** ***Perf. 14***

389 A109 32c Sheet of 9, #a.-i. 5.50 5.50

390 A109 60c Sheet of 9, #a.-i. 11.00 11.00

Souvenir Sheets

391-392 A109 Set of 2 12.00 12.00

No. 390 is airmail.

Miniature Sheet

Disney Sweethearts — A110

1c, like #393a. 2c, #393c. 3c, #393d. 4c, like #393e. 5c, #393f. 6c, #393h.

#393: a, Simba, Nala, Timon. b, Bernard, Bianca, Mr. Chairman. c, Georgette, Tito, Oliver. d, Duchess, O'Malley, Marie. e, Bianca, Jake, Polly. f, Tod, Vixey, Copper. g, Robin Hood, Maiden Marian, Alan-a-Dale. h, Thumper, Flower, their sweethearts. i, Pongo, Perdita, puppies.

Each $2: #394, Lady, vert. #395, Bambi, Faline.

1996, May 30 **Litho.** ***Perf. 14x13½***

392A-392F A110 Set of 6 1.00 1.00

Sheet of 9

393 A110 60c #a.-i. 13.50 13.50

Souvenir Sheets

Perf. 13½x14, 14x13½

394-395 A110 Set of 2 9.50 9.50

Jerusalem, 3000th Anniv. — A111

Biblical illustrations of the Old Testament appearing in "In Our Image," by Guy Rowe (1894-1969): a, Creation. b, Adam and Eve. c, Noah and his Wife. d, Abraham. e, Jacob's Blessing. f, Jacob Becomes Israel. g, Joseph and his Brethren. h, Moses and the Burning Bush. i, Moses and the Tablets. j, Balaam. k, Joshua. l, Gideon. m, Jephthah. n, Samson. o, Ruth and Naomi. p, Saul Anointed. q, Saul Denounced. r, David and Jonathan. s, David and Nathan. t, David Mourns. u, Solomon Praying. v, Solomon Judging. w, Elijah. x, Elisha. y, Job. z, Isaiah. aa, Jeremiah. ab, Ezekiel. ac, Nebuchadnezzar's Dream. ad, Amos.

1996, June 15 **Litho.** ***Perf. 14***

396 A111 20c Sheet of 30, #a.-ad. 12.00 12.00

For overprint see No. 461.

1996 Summer Olympics, Atlanta A112

No. 397, Fanny Blankers Koen, gold medalist, 1948, vert. No. 398, Bob Mathias, gold medalist, 1948, 1952, vert. No. 399, Torchbearer entering Wembley Stadium, 1948. No. 400, Olympic flag, flags of Palau and U.K. before entrance to Stadium, Olympia, Greece.

Athletes: No. 401: a, Hakeem Olajuwan, US. b, Pat McCormick, US. c, Jim Thorpe, US. d, Jesse Owens, US. e, Tatyana Gutsu, Unified Team. f, Michael Jordan, US. g, Fu Mingxia, China. h, Robert Zmelik, Czechoslovakia. i, Ivan Pedroso, Cuba. j, Nadia Comaneci, Romania. k, Jackie Joyner-Kersee, US. l, Michael Johnson, US. m, Kristin Otto, E. Germany. n, Vitali Scherbo, Unified Team. o, Johnny Weissmuller, US. p, Babe Didrikson, US. q, Eddie Tolan, US. r, Krisztina Egerszegi, Hungary. s, Sawao Kato, Japan. t, Alexander Popov, Unified Team.

1996, June 17 **Litho.** ***Perf. 14***

397 A112 40c multicolored .90 .90

398 A112 40c multicolored .90 .90

a. Pair, #397-398 2.00 2.00

399 A112 60c multicolored 1.40 1.40

400 A112 60c multicolored 1.40 1.40

a. Pair, #399-400 3.00 3.00

401 A112 32c Sheet of 20, #a.-t. 13.00 13.00

Nos. 398a, 400a were each issued in sheets of 20 stamps. No. 401 is a continuous design.

Birds Over Palau Lagoon A113

Designs: a, Lakkotsiang, female. b, Maladaob. c, Belochel (g). d, Lakkotsiang, male. e, Sechosech. f, Mechadelbedaoch (j). g, Laib. h, Cheloteachel. i, Deroech. j, Kerkirs. k, Dudek. l, Lakkotsiang. m, Bedaoch. n, Bedebedchaki. o, Sechou (gray Pacific reef-heron) (p). p, Kekereiderariik. q, Sechou (white Pacific reef-heron). r, Ochaieu. s, Oltirakladial. t, Omechederiibabad.

1996, July 10

402 A113 50c Sheet of 20, #a.-t. 20.00 20.00

Aircraft A114

Stealth, surveillance, and electronic warfare: No. 403: a, Lockheed U-2. b, General Dynamics EF-111A. c, Lockheed YF-12A. d, Lockheed SR-71. e, Teledyne-Ryan-Tiere II Plus. f, Lockheed XST. g, Lockhood ER-2. h, Lockheed F-117A Nighthawk. i, Lockheed EC-130E. j, Ryan Firebee. k, Lockheed Martin/Boeing "Darkstar." l, Boeing E-3A Sentry.

No. 404: a, Northrop XB-35. b, Leduc O.21. c, Convair Model 118. d, Blohm Und Voss BV 141. e, Vought V-173. f, McDonnell XF-85 Goblin. g, North American F-82B Twin Mustang. h, Lockheed XFV-1. i, Northrop XP-79B. j, Saunders Roe SR/A1. k, Caspian Sea Monster. l, Grumman X-29.

No. 405, Northrop B-2A Stealth Bomber. No. 406, Martin Marietta X-24B.

1996, Sept. 9 **Litho.** ***Perf. 14***

403 A114 40c Sheet of 12, #a.-l. 10.00 10.00

404 A114 60c Sheet of 12, #a.-l. 15.00 15.00

Souvenir Sheets

405 A114 $3 multicolored 6.50 6.50

406 A114 $3 multicolored 6.50 6.50

No. 404 is airmail. No. 406 contains one 85x28mm stamp.

Independence, 2nd Anniv. — A115

Paintings, by Koh Sekiguchi: No. 407, "In the Blue Shade of Trees-Palau (Kirie). No. 408 "The Birth of a New Nation (Kirie).

1996, Oct. 1 Litho. *Perf. 14½*

407	20c multicolored	.40	.40
408	20c multicolored	.40	.40
a.	A115 Pair, #407-408	.80	.80

#408a issued in sheets of 16 stamps.

Christmas — A116

Christmas trees: a, Pandanus. b, Mangrove. c, Norfolk Island pine. d, Papaya. e, Casuarina.

1996, Oct. 8 *Perf. 14*

409 A116 32c Strip of 5, #a.-e.	3.25	3.25

No. 409 was issued in sheets of 3.

Voyage to Mars — A117

No. 410: a, Viking 1 (US) in Mars orbit. b, Mars Lander fires de-orbit engines. c, Viking 1 symbol (top). d, Viking 1 symbol (bottom). e, Martian moon phobos. f, Mariner 9 in Mars orbit. g, Viking lander enters Martian atmosphere. h, Parachute deploys for Mars landing, heat shield jettisons. i, Proposed manned mission to Mars, 21st cent., US-Russian spacecraft (top). j, US-Russian spacecraft (botton). k, Lander descent engines fire for Mars landing. l, Viking 1 lands on Mars, July 20, 1976.

Each $3: No. 411, NASA Mars rover. No. 412, NASA water probe on Mars. Illustration reduced.

1996, Nov. 8 Litho. *Perf. 14x14½*

410 A117 32c Sheet of 12, #a.-l.	7.75	7.75

Souvenir Sheets

411-412 A117 Set of 2	12.00	12.00

No. 411 contains one 38x30mm stamp.

Souvenir Sheet

New Year 1997 (Year of the Ox) — A117a

1997, Jan. 2 Litho. *Perf. 14*

412A A117a $2 multicolored	4.25	4.25

Souvenir Sheet

South Pacific Commission, 50th Anniv. — A118

1997, Feb. 6 Litho. *Perf. 14*

413 A118 $1 multicolored	2.00	2.00

Hong Kong '97 — A119

Flowers: 1c, Pemphis acidula. 2c, Sea lettuce. 3c, Tropical almond. 4c, Guettarda. 5c, Pacific coral bean. $3, Sea hibiscus.

No. 420: a, Black mangrove. b, Cordia. c, Lantern tree. d, Palau rock-island flower.

No. 421: a, Fish-poison tree. b, Indian mulberry. c, Pacific poison-apple. d, Ailanthus.

1997, Feb. 12 *Perf. 14½, 13½ (#419)*

414-419 A119 Set of 6	7.00	7.00
420 A119 32c Block of 4, #a.-d.	2.50	2.50
421 A119 50c Block of 4, #a.-d.	4.00	4.00

Size of No. 419 is 73x48mm.

Nos. 420-421 were each issued in sheets of 16 stamps.

Bicent. of the Parachute A120

Uses of parachute: No. 422: a, Apollo 15 Command Module landing safely. b, "Caterpillar Club" flyer ejecting safely over land. c. Skydiving team formation. d, Parasailing. e, Military parachute demonstration teams. f, Parachute behind dragster. g, Dropping cargo from C-130 aircraft. h, "Goldfish Club" flyer ejecting safely at sea.

No. 423: a, Demonstrating parachute control. b, A.J. Gernerin, first succussful parachute descent, 1797. c, Slowing down world land-speed record breaking cars. d, Dropping spies behind enemy lines. e, C-130E demonstrating "LAPES." f, Parachutes used to slow down high performance aircraft. g, ARD parachutes. g, US Army parachutist flying Parafoil.

Each $2: No. 424 Training tower at Ft. Benning, Georgia. No. 425, "Funny Car" safety chute.

Perf. 14½x14, 14x14½

1997, Mar. 13 Litho.

422 A120 32c Sheet of 8, #a.-h.	5.25	5.25
423 A120 60c Sheet of 8, #a.-h.	9.75	9.75

Souvenir Sheets

Perf. 14

424-425 A120 Set of 2	10.00	10.00

Nos. 422a-423a, 422b-423b, 422g-423g, 422h-423h are 20x48mm. No. 424 contains one 28x85mm, No. 425 one 57x42mm stamps.

No. 423 is airmail.

Postage Stamp Mega-Event, NYC, Mar. 1997 (#422-423).

Native Birds A121

a, Gray duck, banana tree. b, Red junglefowl, calamondin. c, Nicobar pigeon, fruited parinari tree. d, Cardinal honeyeater, wax apple tree. e, Yellow bittern, purple swamphen, giant taro, taro. f, Eclectus parrot, pangi football fruit tree. g, Micronesian pigeon, Rambutan. h, Micronesian starling, mango tree. i, Fruit bat, breadfruit tree. j, Collared kingfisher, coconut palm. k, Palau fruit dove, sweet orange tree. l, Chestnut mannikin, soursop tree.

1997, Mar. 27 Litho. *Perf. 13½x14*

426 A121 20c Sheet of 12, #a.-l.	5.00	5.00

UNESCO, 50th Anniv. — A122

Sites in Japan, vert: Nos. 427: a, c-h, Himeji-jo. b, Kyoto.

Sites in Germany: Nos. 428: a-b, Augustusburg Castle. c, Falkenlust Castle. d, Roman ruins, Trier. e, Historic house, Trier.

Each $2: No. 429, Forest, Shirakami-Sanchi, Japan. No. 430, Yakushima, Japan.

Perf. 13½x14, 14x13½

1997, Apr. 7 Litho.

Sheets of 8 or 5 + Label

427 A122 32c #a.-h.	5.50	5.50
428 A122 60c #a.-e.	6.25	6.25

Souvenir Sheets

429-430 A122 Set of 2	8.75	8.75

A123

Paintings by Hiroshige (1797-1858): No. 431: a, Swallows and Peach Blossoms under a Full Moon. b, A Parrot on a Flowering Branch. c, Crane and Rising Sun. d, Cock, Umbrella, and Morning Glories. e, A Titmouse Hanging Head Downward on a Camellia Branch.

Each $2: No. 432, Falcon on a Pine Tree with the Rising Sun. No. 433, Kingfisher and Iris.

1997, June 2 Litho. *Perf. 14*

431 A123 32c Sheet of 5, #a.-e.	4.00	4.00

Souvenir Sheets

432-433 A123 Set of 2	8.25	8.25

A124

Volcano Goddesses of the Pacific: a, Darago, Philippines. b, Fuji, Japan. c, Pele, Hawaii. d, Pare, Maori. e, Dzalarhons, Haida. f, Chuginadak, Aleuts.

1997 Litho. *Perf. 14*

434 A124 32c Sheet of 6, #a.-f.	4.50	4.50

PACIFIC 97.

Independence, 3rd Anniv. — A125

1997, Oct. 1 Litho. *Perf. 14*

435 A125 32c multicolored	.65	.65

No. 435 was issued in sheets of 12.

Oceanographic Research — A126

Ships: No. 436: a, Albatross. b, Mabahiss. c, Atlantis II. d, Xarifa. e, Meteor. f, Egabras III. g, Discoverer. h, Kaiyo. i, Ocean Defender.

Each $2: No. 437, Jacques-Yves Cousteau (1910-97). No. 438, Cousteau, diff., vert. No. 439, Pete Seeger, vert.

1997, Oct. 1 *Perf. 14x14½, 14½x14*

436 A126 32c Sheet of 9, #a.-i.	6.00	6.00

Souvenir Sheets

437-439 A126 Set of 3	13.00	13.00

Diana, Princess of Wales (1961-97) A127

1997, Nov. 26 Litho. *Perf. 14*

440 A127 60c multicolored	1.25	1.25

No. 440 was issued in sheets of 6.

Disney's "Let's Read" — A128

Various Disney characters: 1c, like #447i. 2c, like #447d. 3c, like #447c. 4c, like #447f. 5c, #447b. 10c, like #447h.

No. 447: a, "Exercise your right to read." b, "Reading is the ultimate luxury." c, "Share your knowledge." d, "Start them Young." e, "Reading is fundamental." f, "The insatiable reader." g, "Reading time is anytime." h, "Real men read." i, "I can read by myself."

No. 448, Daisy, "The library is for everyone," vert. No. 449, Mickey, "Books are magical."

1997, Oct. 21 ***Perf. 14x13½, 13½x14***

441-446 A128 Set of 6 1.00 1.00

Sheet of 9

447 A128 32c #a.-i. 5.75 5.75

Souvenir Sheets

448 A128 $2 multicolored 4.50 4.50
449 A128 $3 multicolored 6.50 6.50

Christmas — A129

Children singing Christmas carol, "Some Children See Him:" No. 450: a, Girl, boy in striped shirt. b, Boy, girl in pigtails. c, Girl, boy, Madonna and Child. d, Girl, two children. e, Boy, girl with long black hair.

1997, Oct. 28 ***Perf. 14***

450 A129 32c Strip of 5, #a.-e. 3.25 3.25

No. 450 was issued in sheets of 3 strips, bottom strip printed se-tenant with 5 labels containing lyrics.

Souvenir Sheets

New Year 1998 (Year of the Tiger) — A130

Chinese toys in shape of tiger: No. 451, White background. No. 452, Green background.

1998, Jan. 2 **Litho.** ***Perf. 14***

451 A130 50c multicolored 1.25 1.25
452 A130 50c multicolored 1.25 1.25

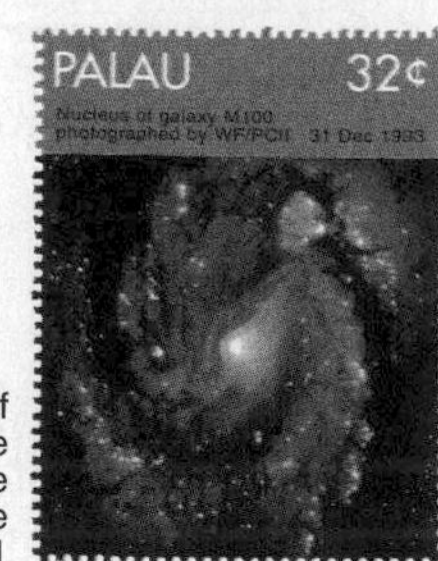
Repair of Hubble Space Telescope A131

No. 453: a, Photograph of nucleus of galaxy M100. b, Top of Hubble telescope with solar arrays folded. c, Astronaut riding robot arm. d, Astronaut anchored to robot arm. e, Astronaut in cargo space with Hubble mounted to shuttle Endeavor. f, Hubble released after repair.

Each $2: No. 454, Hubble cutaway, based on NASA schematic drawing. No. 455, Edwin Hubble (1889-1953), astronomer who proved existence of star systems beyond Milky Way. No. 456, Hubble Mission STS-82/Discovery.

1998, Mar. 9 **Litho.** ***Perf. 14***

453 A131 32c Sheet of 6, #a.-f. 4.00 4.00

Souvenir Sheets

454-456 A131 Set of 3 12.50 12.50

Mother Teresa (1910-97) — A132

Various portraits.

1998, Mar. 12 **Litho.** ***Perf. 14***

457 A132 60c Sheet of 4, #a.-d. 5.00 5.00

Deep Sea Robots A133

No. 458: a, Ladybird ROV. b, Slocum Glider. c, Hornet. d, Scorpio. e, Odyssey AUV. f, Jamstec Survey System Launcher. g, Scarab. h, USN Torpedo Finder/Salvager. i, Jamstec Survey System Vehicle. j, Cetus Tether. k, Deep Sea ROV. l, ABE. m, OBSS. n, RCV 225G Swimming Eyeball. o, Japanese UROV. p, Benthos RPV. q, CURV. r, Smartie.

Each $2: No. 459, Jason Jr. inspecting Titanic. No. 460, Dolphin 3K.

1998, Apr. 21

458 A133 32c Sheet of 18, #a.-r. 12.00 12.00

Souvenir Sheets

459-460 A133 Set of 2 8.50 8.50

UNESCO Intl. Year of the Ocean.

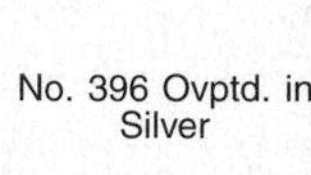
No. 396 Ovptd. in Silver

1998, May 13 **Litho.** ***Perf. 14***

461 A111 20c Sheet of 30, #a.-ad. 12.00 12.00

No. 461 is overprinted in sheet margin, "ISRAEL 98 — WORLD STAMP EXHIBITION / TEL AVIV 13-21 MAY 1998." Location of overprint varies.

Legend of Orachel — A134

#462: a, Bai (hut), people. b, Bai, lake. c, Bai, lake, person in canoe. d, Bird on branch over lake. e, Men rowing in canoe. f, Canoe, head of snake. g, Alligator under water. h, Fish, shark. i, Turtle, body of snake. j, Underwater bai, "gods". k, Snails, fish, Orachel swimming. l, Orachel's feet, coral, fish.

1998, May 29 **Litho.** ***Perf. 14***

462 A134 40c Sheet of 12, #a.-l. 9.50 9.50

1998 World Cup Soccer Championships, France — A135

Players, color of shirt — #463: a, Yellow, black & red. b, Blue, white & red. c, Green & white. d, White, red & blue. e, Green & white (black shorts). f, White, red & black. g, Blue & yellow. h, Red & white.

$3, Pele.

1998, June 5

463 A135 50c Sheet of 8, #a.-h. 8.00 8.00

Souvenir Sheet

464 A135 $3 multicolored 6.00 6.00

4th Micronesian Games, Palau — A136

Designs: a, Spear fishing. b, Spear throwing. c, Swimming. d, Pouring milk from coconut. e, Logo of games. f, Climbing coconut trees. g, Canoeing. h, Husking coconut. i, Deep sea diving.

1998, July 31 **Litho.** ***Perf. 14***

465 A136 32c Sheet of 9, #a.-i. 5.75 5.75

Rudolph The Red-Nosed Reindeer — A137

Christmas: a, Rudolph, two reindeer, girl. b, Two reindeer, girl holding flowers. c, Girl, two reindeer, boy. d, Two reindeer, girl smiling. e, Santa, children, Christmas gifts.

1998, Sept. 15 **Litho.** ***Perf. 14***

466 A137 32c Strip of 5, #a.-e. 3.25 3.25

No. 466 is a continuous design and was issued in sheets of 15 stamps.

Disney/Pixar's "A Bug's Life" — A138

No. 467: a, Dot. b, Heimlich, Francis, Slim. c, Hopper. d, Princess Atta.

No. 468: Various scenes with Flik, Princess Atta.

No. 469, horiz.: a, Circus bugs. b, Slim, Francis, Heimlich. c, Manny. d, Francis.

No. 470: a, Slim, Flik. b, Heimlich, Slim, Francis performing. c, Manny, Flik. d, Gypsy, Manny, Rosie.

Each $2: No. 471, Gypsy. No. 472, Princess Atta, Flik, horiz. No. 473, Slim, Francis, Heimlich, horiz. No. 474, Francis, Slim, Flik, Heimlich, horiz.

Perf. 13½x14, 14x13½

1998, Dec. 1 **Litho.** **Sheets of 4**

467 A138 20c #a.-d. 1.75 1.75
468 A138 32c #a.-d. 2.75 2.75
469 A138 50c #a.-d. 4.25 4.25
470 A138 60c #a.-d. 5.25 5.25

Souvenir Sheets

471-474 A138 Set of 4 18.00 18.00

Nos. 473-474 each contain one 76x51mm stamp.

John Glenn's Return to Space — A139

No. 475, Various photos of Project Mercury, Friendship 7 mission, 1962, each 60c.

No. 476, Various photos of Discovery Space Shuttle mission, 1998, each 60c.

Each $2: No. 477, Portrait, 1962. No. 478, Portrait, 1998.

1999, Jan. 7 **Litho.** ***Perf. 14***

Sheets of 8, #a-h

475-476 A139 Set of 2 19.00 19.00

Souvenir Sheets

477-478 A139 Set of 2 8.50 8.50

Nos. 477-478 each contain one 28x42mm stamp.

Environmentalists — A140

a, Rachel Carson. b, J.N. "Ding" Darling, US Duck stamp #RW1. c, David Brower. d, Jacques Cousteau. e, Roger Tory Peterson. f, Prince Philip. g, Joseph Wood Krutch. h, Aldo Leopold. i, Dian Fossey. j, US Vice-President Al Gore. k, David Attenborough. l, Paul McCready. m, Sting (Gordon Sumner). n, Paul Winter. o, Ian MacHarg. p, Denis Hayes.

1999, Feb. 1 **Litho.** ***Perf. 14½***

479 A140 33c Sheet of 16, #a.-p. 10.50 10.50

No. 479i shows Dian Fossey's name misspelled "Diane."

MIR Space Station A141

No. 480: a, Soyuz Spacecraft, Science Module. b, Specktr Science Module. c, Space Shuttle, Spacelab Module. d, Kvant 2, Scientific and Air Lock Module. e, Kristall Technological Module. f, Space Shutle, Docking Module.

Each $2: No. 481, Astronaut Charles Precout, Cosmonaut Talgat Musabayev. No. 482, Cosmonaut Valeri Poliakov. No. 483, US Mission Specialist Shannon W. Lucid, Cosmonaut Yuri Y. Usachov. No. 484, Cosmonaut Anatoly Solovyov.

1999, Feb. 18 Litho. *Perf. 14*

480 A141 33c Sheet of 6, #a.-f. 3.75 3.75

Souvenir Sheets

481-484 A141 Set of 4 16.00 16.00

Personalities — A142

1c, Haruo Remiliik. 2c, Lazarus Salil. 20c, Charlie W. Gibbons. 22c, Adm. Raymond A. Spruance. 33c, Kuniwo Nakamura. 50c, Adm. William F. Halsey. 55c, Col. Lewis "Chesty" Puller. 60c, Franklin D. Roosevelt. 77c, Harry S Truman. $3.20, Jimmy Carter.

1999, Mar. 4 *Perf. 14x15*

485	A142	1c	green	.25	.25
486	A142	2c	purple	.25	.25
487	A142	20c	violet	.40	.40
488	A142	22c	bister	.45	.45
489	A142	33c	red brown	.65	.65
490	A142	50c	brown	1.00	1.00
491	A142	55c	blue green	1.10	1.10
492	A142	60c	orange	1.25	1.25
493	A142	77c	yellow brown	1.50	1.50
494	A142	$3.20	red violet	6.50	6.50
	Nos. 485-494 (10)			13.35	13.35

Nos. 485, 492 exist dated 2001.

Australia '99 World Stamp Expo A143

Endangered species — #495: a, Leatherback turtle. b, Kemp's ridley turtle. c, Green turtle. d, Marine iguana. e, Table mountain ghost frog. f, Spiny turtle. g, Hewitt's ghost frog. h, Geometric tortoise. i, Limestone salamander. j, Desert rain frog. k, Cape plantanna. l, Long-toed tree frog.

Each $2: No. 496, Marine crocodile. No. 497, Hawksbill turtle.

1999, Mar. 19 Litho. *Perf. 13*

495 A143 33c Sheet of 12, #a.-l. 8.00 8.00

Souvenir Sheets

496-497 A143 Set of 2 8.00 8.00

IBRA '99, Nuremburg — A144

No. 498, Leipzig-Dresden Railway, Caroline Islands Type A4. No. 499, Gölsdorf 4-8-0, Caroline Islands #8, 10.

$2, Caroline Islands #1.

1999, Apr. 27 Litho. *Perf. 14*

498-499 A144 55c Set of 2 2.25 2.25

Souvenir Sheet

500 A144 $2 multicolored 4.00 4.00

Exploration of Mars A145

No. 501: a, Mars Global Surveyor. b, Mars Climate Orbiter. c, Mars Polar Lander. d, Deep Space 2. e, Mars Surveyor 2001 Orbiter. f, Mars Surveyor 2001 Lander.

Each $2: No. 502, Mars Global Surveyor. No. 503, Mars Climate Orbiter. No. 504, Mars Polar Lander. No. 505, Mars Surveyor 2001 Lander.

1999, May 10 Litho. *Perf. 14*

501 A145 33c Sheet of 6, #a.-f. 4.00 4.00

Souvenir Sheets

502-505 A145 Set of 4 16.00 16.00

Nos. 502-505 each contain one 38x50mm stamp.

See Nos. 507-511.

Earth Day — A146

Pacific insects: a, Banza Natida. b, Drosophila heteroneura. c, Nesomicromus vagus. d, Megalagrian leptodemus. e, Pseudopsectra cookearum. f, Ampheida neacaledonia. g, Pseudopsectra swezeyi. h, Deinacrida heteracantha. i, Beech forest butterfly. j, Hercules moth. k, Striped sphinx moth. l, Tussock butterfly. m. Elytrocheilus. n, Bush cricket. o, Longhorn beetle. p, Abathrus bicolor. q, Stylagymnusa subantartica. r, Moth butterfly. s, Paraconosoma naviculare. t, Ornithoptera priamus.

1999, May 24

506 A146 33c Sheet of 20, #a.-t. 13.50 13.50

Space Type

International Space Station — #507: a, Launch 1R. b, Launch 14A. c, Launch 8A. d, Launch 1J. e, Launch 1E. f, Launch 16A.

Each $2: No. 508, Intl. Space Station. No. 509, Cmdr. Bob Cabana, Cosmonaut Sergei Krikalev. No. 510, Crew of Flight 2R, horiz. No. 511, X-38 Crew Return Vehicle, horiz.

1999, June 12 Litho. *Perf. 14*

507 A145 33c Sheet of 6, #a.-f. 4.00 4.00

Souvenir Sheets

508-511 A145 Set of 4 16.00 16.00

20th Century Visionaries A147

Designs: a, William Gibson, "Cyberspace." b, Danny Hillis, Massively Parallel Processing. c, Steve Wozniak, Apple Computer. d, Steve Jobs, Apple Computer. e, Nolan Bushnell, Atari, Inc. f, John Warnock, Adobe, Inc. g, Ken Thompson, Unix. h, Al Shugart, Seagate Technologies. i, Rand & Robyn Miller, "MYST." j, Nicolas Negroponte, MIT Media Lab. k, Bill Gates, Microsoft, Inc. l, Arthur C. Clarke, Orbiting Communications Satellite. m, Marshall Mcluhan, "The Medium is the Message." n, Thomas Watson, Jr., IBM. o, Gordon Moore, Intel Corporation, "Moore's Law." p, James Gosling, Java. q, Sabeer Bhatia & Jack Smith, Hotmail.com. r, Esther Dyson, "Release 2.0." s, Jerry Yang, David Filo, Yahoo! t, Jeff Bezos, Amazon.com. u, Bob Kahn, TCP-IP. v, Jaron Lanter, "Virtual Reality." w, Andy Grove, Intel Corporation. x, Jim Clark, Silicon Graphics, Inc., Netscape Communications Corp. y, Bob Metcalfe, Ethernet, 3com.

1999, June 30 Litho. *Perf. 14*

512 A147 33c Sheet of 25, #a.-y. 17.00 17.00

Paintings by Hokusai (1760-1849) — A148

#513, each 33c: a, Women Divers. b, Bull and Parasol. c, Drawings of Women (partially nude). d, Drawings of Women (seated, facing forward). e, Japanese spaniel. f, Porters in Landscape.

#514, each 33c: a, Bacchanalian Revelry. b, Bacchanalian Revelry (two seated back to back). c, Drawings of Women (crawling). d, Drawings of Women (facing backward). e, Ox-Herd. f, Ox-Herd (man on bridge).

Each $2: No. 515, Mount Fuji in a Thunderstorm, vert. No. 516, At Swan Lake in Shinano.

1999, July 20 *Perf. 14x13¾*

Sheets of 6, #a-f

513-514 A148 Set of 2 8.00 8.00

Souvenir Sheets

515-516 A148 Set of 2 8.00 8.00

Apollo 11, 30th Anniv. A149

No. 517: a, Lift-off, jettison of stages. b, Earth, moon, capsule. c, Astronaut on lunar module ladder. d, Lift-off. e, Planting flag on moon. f, Astronauts Collins, Armstrong and Aldrin.

Each $2: No. 518, Rocket on launch pad. No. 519, Astronaut on ladder, earth. No. 520, Lunar module above moon. No. 521, Capsule in ocean.

1999, July 20 Litho. *Perf. 13½x14*

517 A149 33c Sheet of 6, #a.-f. 4.00 4.00

Souvenir Sheets

518-521 A149 Set of 4 16.00 16.00

Queen Mother (b. 1900) — A150

No. 522: a, In Australia, 1958. b, In 1960. c, In 1970. d, In 1987.

$2, Holding book, 1947.

Gold Frames

522 A150 60c Sheet of 4, #a.-d., + label 4.75 4.75

Souvenir Sheet

Perf. 13¾

523 A150 $2 black 4.00 4.00

No. 523 contains one 38x51mm stamp.

See Nos. 636-637.

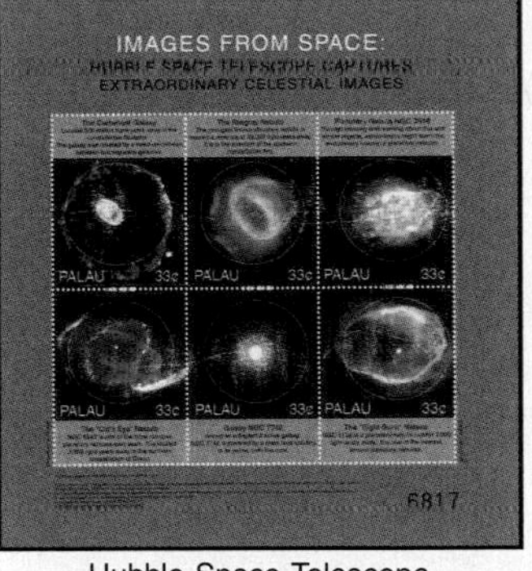

Hubble Space Telescope Images — A151

No. 524: a, Cartwheel Galaxy. b, Stingray Nebula. c, NGC 3918. d, Cat's Eye Nebula (NGC 6543). e, NGC 7742. f, Eight-burst Nebula (NGC 3132).

Each $2: No. 525, Eta Carinae. No. 526, Planetary nebula M2-9. No. 527, Supernova 1987-A. No. 528, Infrared aurora of Saturn.

1999, Oct. 15 Litho. *Perf. 13¾*

524 A151 33c Sheet of 6, #a.-f. 4.00 4.00

Souvenir Sheets

525-528 A151 Set of 4 16.00 16.00

Christmas — A152

Birds and: a, Cows, chickens. b, Donkey, geese, rabbit. c, Infant, cat, lambs. d, Goats, geese. e, Donkey, rooster.

1999, Nov. 15 *Perf. 14*

529 A152 20c Strip of 5, #a.-e. 2.00 2.00

Love for Dogs — A153

No. 530: a, Keep safe. b, Show affection. c, A place of one's own. d, Communicate. e, Good food. f, Annual checkup. g, Teach rules. h, Exercise & play. i, Let him help. j, Unconditional love.

Each $2: No. 531, Pleasure of your company. No. 532, Love is a gentle thing.

1999, Nov. 23 Litho. *Perf. 14*

530 A153 33c Sheet of 10, #a.-j. 6.75 6.75

Souvenir Sheets

531-532 A153 Set of 2 8.00 8.00

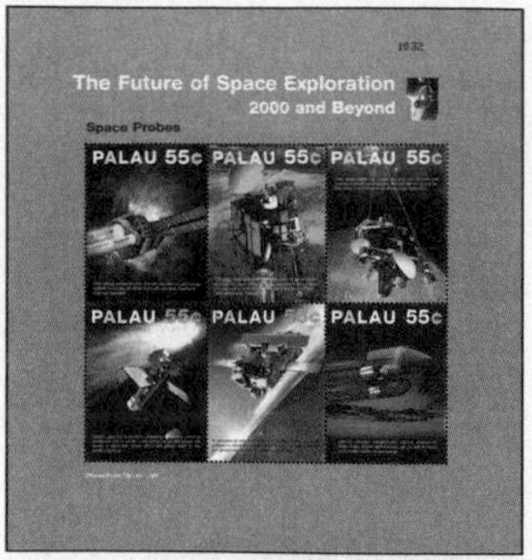

Futuristic Space Probes — A154

Text starting with — No. 533: a, Deep space probes like. . . b, This piggy-back. . . c, Deep space telescope. . . d, Mission planning. . . e, In accordance. . . f, Utilizing onboard. . .

Each $2: No. 534, This secondary. . . No. 535, Deep space probes are an integral. . . No. 536, Deep space probes are our. . . , horiz. No. 537, With the. . . , horiz.

2000, Jan. 18 Litho. *Perf. 13¾*

533 A154 55c Sheet of 6, #a.-f. 6.00 6.00

Souvenir Sheets

534-537 A154 Set of 4 16.00 16.00

Millennium — A155

Highlights of 1800-50 — No. 538, each 20c: a, Brazilian Indians. b, Haiti slave revolt. c, Napoleon becomes Emperor of France. d, Shaka Zulu. e, "Frankenstein" written. f, Simon Bolivar. g, Photography invented. h, First water purification works built. i, First all-steam railway. j, Michael Faraday discovers electromagnetism. k, First use of anesthesia. l, Samuel Morse completes first telegraph line. m, Women's rights convention in Seneca Falls, NY. n, Birth of Karl Marx. o, Revolution in German Confederation. p, Charles Darwin's voyages on the "Beagle" (60x40mm). q, Beijing, China.

Highlights of 1980-89 — No. 539, each 20c; a, Lech Walesa organizes Polish shipyard workers. b, Voyager I photographs Saturn. c, Ronald Reagan elected US president. d, Identification of AIDS virus. e, Wedding of Prince Charles and Lady Diana Spencer. f, Compact discs go into production. g, Bhopal, India gas disaster. h, I. M. Pei's Pyramid entrance to the Louvre opens. i, Mikhail Gorbachev becomes leader of Soviet Union. j, Chernobyl nuclear disaster. k, Explosion of Space Shuttle "Challenger." l, Klaus Barbie convicted of crimes against humanity. m, Life of author Salman Rushdie threatened by Moslems. n, Benazir Bhutto becomes first woman prime minister of a Moslem state. o, Tiananmen Square revolt. p, Berlin Wall falls (60x40mm). q, World Wide Web.

2000, Feb. 2 Litho. *Perf. 12¾x12½*

Sheets of 17, #a.-q.

538-539 A155 Set of 2 14.00 14.00

Misspellings and historical inaccuracies abound on Nos. 538-539.

See No. 584.

New Year 2000 (Year of the Dragon) — A156

2000, Feb. 5 *Perf. 13¾*

540 A156 $2 multi 4.00 4.00

US Presidents — A157

2000, Mar. 1 Litho. *Perf. 13½x13¼*

541	A157	$1 Bill Clinton	2.00	2.00
542	A157	$2 Ronald Reagan	4.00	4.00
543	A157	$3 Gerald Ford	6.00	6.00
544	A157	$5 George Bush	10.00	10.00

Size: 40x24mm

Perf. 14¾x14

545	A157	$11.75 Kennedy	22.50	22.50
		Nos. 541-545 (5)	44.50	44.50

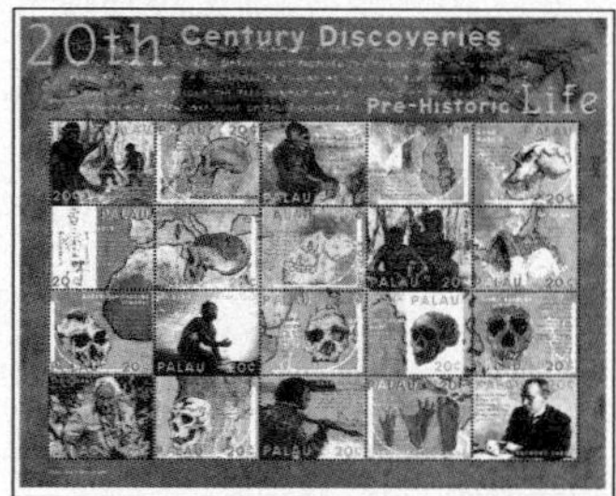

20th Century Discoveries About Prehistoric Life — A158

Designs: a, Australopithecines. b, Australopithecine skull. c, Homo habilis. d, Hand axe. e, Homo habilis skull. f, Lucy, Australopithecine skeleton. g, Archaic Homo sapiens skull. h, Diapithicine skull. i, Homo erectus. j, Wood hut. k, Australopithecine ethopsis skull. l, Dawn of mankind. m, Homo sapiens skull. n, Taung baby's skull. o, Homo erectus skull. p. Louis Leakey (1903-72), paleontologist. q, Neanderthal skull. r, Neandertahal. s, Evolution of the foot. t, Raymond Dart (1893-1988), paleontologist.

2000, Mar. 15 *Perf. 14¼*

546 A158 20c Sheet of 20, #a.-t. 8.00 8.00

Misspellings and historical inaccuracies are found on Nos. 546g, 546m, 546p, 546t and perhaps others.

2000 Summer Olympics, Sydney — A159

Designs: a, Charlotte Cooper, tennis player at 1924 Olympics. b, Women's shot put. c, Helsinki Stadium, site of 1952 Olympics. d, Ancient Greek athletes.

2000, Mar. 31 *Perf. 14*

547 A159 33c Sheet of 4, #a.-d. 2.75 2.75

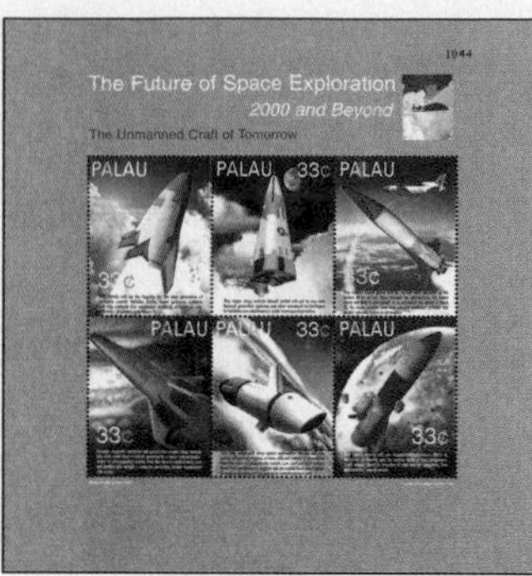

Future of Space Exploration — A160

Text starting with — No. 548: a, This vehicle will be. . . b, This single stage. . . c, This robotic rocket. . . d, Dynamic. . . e, This fully. . . f, This launch vehicle. . .

Each $2: No. 549, Increasingly, space travel. . . No. 550, Designed with projects. . ., horiz. No. 551, Design is currently. . ., horiz. No. 552, Inevitably, the future. . ., horiz.

2000, Apr. 10 *Perf. 13¾*

548 A160 33c Sheet of 6, #a.-f. 4.00 4.00

Souvneir Sheets

549-552 A160 Set of 4 16.00 16.00

Birds — A161

No. 553: a, Slatey-legged crake. b, Micronesian kingfisher. c, Little pied cormorant. d, Pacific reed egret. e, Nicobar pigeon. f, Rufous night heron.

No. 554: a, Palau ground dove. b, Palau scops owl. c, Mangrove flycatcher. d, Palau bush warbler. e, Palau fantail. f, Morningbird.

Each $2: No. 555, Palau fruit dove, horiz. No. 556, Palau white-eye, horiz.

2000, Apr. 14 Litho. *Perf. 14¼*

553	A161	20c Sheet of 6, #a.-f.	2.40	2.40
554	A161	33c Sheet of 6, #a.-f.	4.00	4.00

Souvenir Sheets

555-556 A161 Set of 2 8.00 8.00

Visionaries of the 20th Century — A162

a, Booker T. Washington. b, Buckminster Fuller. c, Marie Curie. d, Walt Disney. e, F. D. Roosevelt. f, Henry Ford. g, Betty Friedan. h, Sigmund Freud. i, Mohandas Gandhi. j, Mikhail Gorbachev. k, Stephen Hawking. l, Martin Luther King, Jr. m, Toni Morrison. n, Georgia O'Keeffe. o, Rosa Parks. p, Carl Sagan. q, Jonas Salk. r, Sally Ride. s, Nikola Tesla. t, Wilbur and Orville Wright.

2000, Apr. 28 Litho. *Perf. 14¼x14½*

557 A162 33c Sheet of 20, #a.-t. 13.50 13.50

20th Century Science and Medicine Advances — A163

No. 558, each 33c: a, James D. Watson, 1962 Nobel laureate. b, Har Gobind Khorana and Robert Holley, 1968 Nobel laureates. c, Hamilton O. Smith and Werner Arber, 1978 Nobel laureates. d, Extraction fo DNA from cells. e, Richard J. Roberts, 1993 Nobel laureate.

No. 559, each 33c: a, Francis Crick, 1962 Nobel laureate. b, Marshall W. Nirenberg, 1968 Nobel laureate. c, Daniel Nathans, 1978 Nobel laureate. d, Harold E. Varmus and J. Michael Bishop, 1989 Nobel laureates. e, Phillip A. Sharp, 1993 Nobel laureate.

No. 560, each 33c: a, Maurice H. F. Wilkins, 1962 Nobel laureate. b, DNA strand. c, Frederick Sanger and Walter Gilbert, 1980 Nobel laureates. d, Kary B. Mullis, 1993 Nobel laureate. e, Two DNA strands.

No. 561, each 33c: a, Four sheep, test tube. b, Two DNA strands, diagram of DNA fragments. c, Paul Berg, 1980 Nobel laureate. d, Michael Smith, 1993 Nobel laureate. e, Deer, DNA strands.

Each $2: #562, Deer. #563, Dolly, 1st cloned sheep.

Illustration reduced.

2000, May 10 *Perf. 13¾*

Sheets of 5, #a.-e.

558-561 A163 Set of 4 14.00 14.00

Souvenir Sheets

562-563 A163 Set of 2 8.00 8.00

Nos. 562-563 each contain one 38x50mm stamp.

Marine Life — A164

No. 564, each 33c: a, Prawn. b, Deep sea angler. c, Rooster fish. d, Grenadier. e, Platyberix opalescens. f, Lantern fish.

No. 565, each 33c: a, Emperor angelfish. b, Nautilus. c, Moorish idol. d, Sea horse. e, Clown triggerfish. f, Clown fish.

Each $2: No. 566, Giant squid. No. 567, Manta ray.

2000, May 10 Litho. *Perf. 14*

Sheets of 6, #a-f

564-565 A164 Set of 2 8.00 8.00

Souvenir Sheets

566-567 A164 Set of 2 8.00 8.00

Millennium — A165

No. 568, horiz. — "2000," hourglass, and map of: a, North Pacific area. b, U.S. and Canada. c, Europe. d, South Pacific. e, South America. f, Southern Africa.

No. 569 — Clock face and: a, Sky. b, Building. c, Cove and lighthouse. d, Barn. e, Forest. f, Desert.

2000, May 25 *Perf. 13¾*

568 A165 20c Sheet of 6, #a-f 2.40 2.40
569 A165 55c Sheet of 6, #a-f 6.75 6.75

The Stamp Show 2000, London.

New and Recovering Species — A166

No. 570, each 33c: a, Aleutian Canada goose. b, Western gray kangaroo. c, Palau scops owl. d, Jocotoco antpitta. e, Orchid. f, Red lechwe.

No. 571, each 33c: a, Bald eagle. b, Small-whorled pogonia. c, Arctic peregrine falcon. d, Golden lion tamarin. e, American alligator. f, Brown pelican.

Each $2: No. 572, Leopard. No. 573, Lahontan cutthroat trout, horiz.

2000, June 20 *Perf. 14*

Sheets of 6, #a-f

570-571 A166 Set of 2 8.00 8.00

Souvenir Sheets

572-573 A166 Set of 2 8.00 8.00

Dinosaurs — A167

No. 574: a, Rhamphorhynchus. b, Ceratosaurus. c, Apatosaurus. d, Stegosaurus. e, Archaeopteryx. f, Allosaurus.

No. 575: a, Parasaurolophus. b, Pteranodon. c, Tyrannosaurus. d, Triceratops. e, Ankylosaurus. f, Velociraptor.

Each $2: No. 576, Jurassic era view. No. 577, Cretaceous era view.

2000, June 20

574 A167 20c Sheet of 6, #a-f 2.40 2.40
575 A167 33c Sheet of 6, #a-f 4.00 4.00

Souvenir Sheets

576-577 A167 Set of 2 8.00 8.00

Queen Mother, 100th Birthday — A168

No. 578, 55c: a, With King George VI. b, Wearing brown hat.

No. 579, 55c: a, Wearing green hat. b, Wearing white hat.

2000, Sept. 1 Litho. *Perf. 14*

Sheets of 4, 2 each #a-b

578-579 A168 Set of 2 9.00 9.00

Souvenir Sheet

580 A168 $2 Wearing yellow hat 4.00 4.00

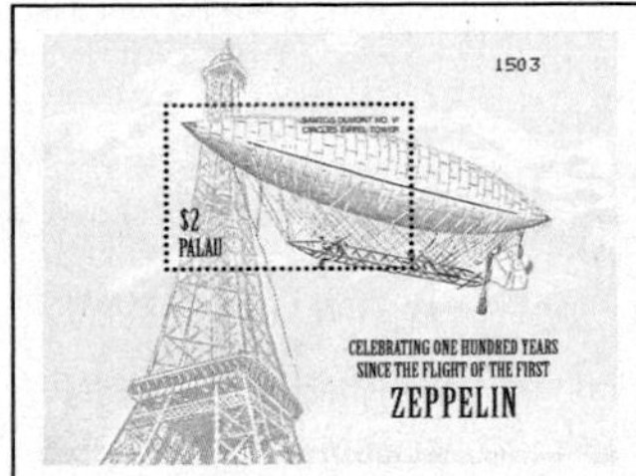

First Zeppelin Flight, Cent. — A169

No. 581: a, Le Jaune. b, Forlanini's Leonardo da Vinci. c, Baldwin's airship. d, Astra-Torres I. e, Parseval PL VII. f, Lebaudy's Liberte.

No. 582, $2, Santos-Dumont No. VI. No. 583, $2, Santos-Dumont Baladeuse No. 9.

2000, Sept. 1

581 A169 55c Sheet of 6, #a-f 6.75 6.75

Souvenir Sheets

582-583 A169 Set of 2 8.00 8.00

Millennium Type of 2000

Sheet of 17

Undersea History and Exploration: a, Viking diver. b, Arab diver Issa. c, Salvage diver. d, Diver. e, Diving bell. f, Turtle. g, Siebe helmet. h, C.S.S. Hunley. i, Argonaut. j, Photosphere. k, Helmet diver. l, Bathysphere. m, Coelacanth. n, WWII charioteers. o, Trieste. p, Alvin visits geothermal vents (60x40mm). q, Jim suit.

2000, Oct. 16 *Perf. 12¾x12½*

584 A155 33c #a-q + label 13.00 13.00

Photomosaic of Pope John Paul II — A170

Various photos with religious themes.

2000, Dec. 1 *Perf. 13¾*

585 A170 50c Sheet of 8, #a-h 8.00 8.00

Souvenir Sheets

New Year 2001 (Year of the Snake) — A171

Snake color: #586, Black. #587, Red.

2000, Dec. 1 *Perf. 14¼*

586-587 A171 60c Set of 2 2.40 2.40

Pacific Ocean Marine Life — A172

No. 588: a, Scalloped hammerhead shark. b, Whitetip reef shark. c, Moon jellyfish. d, Lionfish. e, Seahorse. f, Spotted eagle ray.

2000 *Perf. 14½x14¼*

588 A172 55c Sheet of 6, #a-f 6.75 6.75

Atlantic Ocean Fish — A173

No. 589, horiz.: a, Reef bass. b, White shark. c, Sharptail eel. d, Sailfish. e, Southern stingray. f, Ocean triggerfish.

#590, Short bigeye. #591, Gafftopsail catfish.

2000 *Perf. 13¾*

589 A173 20c Sheet of 6, #a-f 2.40 2.40

Souvenir Sheets

590-591 A173 $2 Set of 2 8.00 8.00

Pacific Arts Festival — A174

No. 592: a, Dancers, by S. Adelbai. b, Story Board Art, by D. Inabo. c, Traditional Money, by M. Takeshi. d, Clay Lamp and Bowl, by W. Watanabe. e, Meeting House, by Pasqual Tiakl. f, Outrigger Canoe, by S. Adelbai. g, Weaver, by M. Vitarelli. h, Rock Island Scene, by W. Marcil. i, Contemporary Music, by J. Imetuker.

2000, Nov. 1 Litho. *Perf. 14¼*

592 A174 33c Sheet of 9, #a-i 6.00 6.00

National Museum, 45th Anniv. — A175

No. 593: a, Klilt, turtle shell bracelet. b, Sculpture by H. Hijikata. c, Turtle shell women's money. d, Cherecheroi, by T. Suzuki. e, Money jar, by B. Sylvester. f, Prince Lebu by Ichikawa. g, Beach at Lild, by H. Hijikata. h, Traditional mask. i, Taro platter, by T. Rebluud. j, Meresebang, by Ichikawa. k, Wood sculpture, by B. Sylvester. l, Birth Ceremony, by I. Kishigawa.

2000, Nov. 1 *Perf. 14x14¾*

593 A175 33c Sheet of 12, #a-l 8.00 8.00

Butterflies A176

Designs: No. 594, 33c, Indian red admiral. No. 595, 33c, Fiery jewel. No. 596, 33c, Checkered swallowtail. No. 597, 33c, Yamfly.

No. 598, 33c: a, Large green-banded blue. b, Union Jack. c, Broad-bordered grass yellow. d, Striped blue crow. e, Red lacewing. f, Palmfly.

No. 599, 33c: a, Cairn's birdwing. b, Meadow argus. c, Orange albatross. d, Glass-wing. e, Beak. f, Great eggfly.

No. 600, $2, Clipper. No. 601, $2, Blue triangle.

2000, Dec. 15 *Perf. 14*

594-597 A176 Set of 4 2.75 2.75

Sheets of 6, #a-f

598-599 A176 Set of 2 8.00 8.00

Souvenir Sheets

600-601 A176 Set of 2 8.00 8.00

Flora and Fauna — A177

No. 602, 33c: a, Giant spiral ginger. b, Good luck plant. c, Ti tree, coconuts. d, Butterfly. e, Saltwater crocodile. f, Orchid.

No. 603, 33c: a, Little kingfisher. b, Mangrove snake. c, Bats, breadfruit. d, Giant tree frog. e, Giant centipede. f, Crab-eating macaque.

No. 604, $2, Soft coral, surgeonfish. No. 605, $2, Land crab, vert.

2000, Dec. 29 ***Perf. 14x14¼, 14¼x14***

Sheets of 6, #a-f

602-603	A177	Set of 2	8.00	8.00

Souvenir Sheets

604-605	A177	Set of 2	8.00	8.00

Personalities Type of 1999

Designs: 11c, Lazarus Salil. 70c, Gen. Douglas MacArthur. 80c, Adm. Chester W. Nimitz. $12.25, John F. Kennedy.

2001 **Litho.** ***Perf. 14x14¾***

606	A142	11c purple	.25	.25
607	A142	70c lilac	1.40	1.40
608	A142	80c green	1.60	1.60
609	A142	$12.25 red	25.00	25.00
		Nos. 606-609 (4)	28.25	28.25

Issued: Nos. 607-609, 6/10.

Phila Nippon '01, Japan — A178

No. 610, 60c: a, Ono no Komachi Washing the Copybook, by Kiyomitsu Torii. b, Woman Playing Samisen and Woman Reading al Letter, by School of Matabei Iwasa. c, The Actor Danjura Ichikawa V as a Samurai in a Wrestling Arena Striking a Pose on a Go Board, by Shunsho Katsukawa. d, Gentleman Entertained by Courtesans, by Kiyonaga Torii. e, Geisha at a Teahouse in Shinagawa, by Kiyonaga Torii.

No. 611, 60c: a, Preparing Sashimi, by Utamaro. b, Ichimatsu Sanogawa I as Sogo no Goro and Kikugoro Onoe as Kyo no Jiro in Umewakana Futaba Soga, by Toyonobu Ishikawa. c, Courtesan Adjusting Her Comb, by Dohan Kaigetsudo. d, The Actor Tomijuro Nakamura I in a Female Role Dancing, by Shunsho Katsukawa. e, Woman with Poem Card and Writing Brush, by Gakutei Yashima.

No. 612, Six panels of screen, Kitano Shrine in Kyoto, by unknown artist.

No. 613, $2, Raiko Attacks a Demon Kite, by Hokkei Totoya. No. 614, $2, Beauty Writing a Letter, by Doshin Kaigetsudo. No. 615, $2, Fireworks at Ikenohata, by Kiyochika Kobayashi.

2001, Aug. 13 **Litho.** ***Perf. 14***

Sheets of 5, #a-e

610-611	A178	Set of 2	12.00	12.00
612	A178	60c Sheet of 6, #a-f	7.25	7.25

Souvenir Sheets

613-615	A178	Set of 3	12.00	12.00

Moths — A179

Designs: 20c, Veined tiger moth. 21c, Basker moth. 80c, White-lined sphinx moth. $1, Isabella tiger moth.

No. 620, 34c: a, Cinnabar moth. b, Beautiful tiger moth. c, Great tiger moth. d, Provence burnet moth. e, Jersey tiger moth. f, Ornate moth.

No. 621, 70c: a, Hoop pine moth. b, King's bee hawk moth. c, Banded bagnest moth. d, Io moth. e, Tau emperor moth. f, Lime hawkmoth.

No. 622, $2, Spanish moon moth. No. 623, $2, Owl moth.

2001, Oct. 15 **Litho.** ***Perf. 14***

616-619	A179	Set of 4	4.50	4.50

Sheets of 6, #a-f

620-621	A179	Set of 2	12.50	12.50

Souvenir Sheets

622-623	A179	Set of 2	8.00	8.00

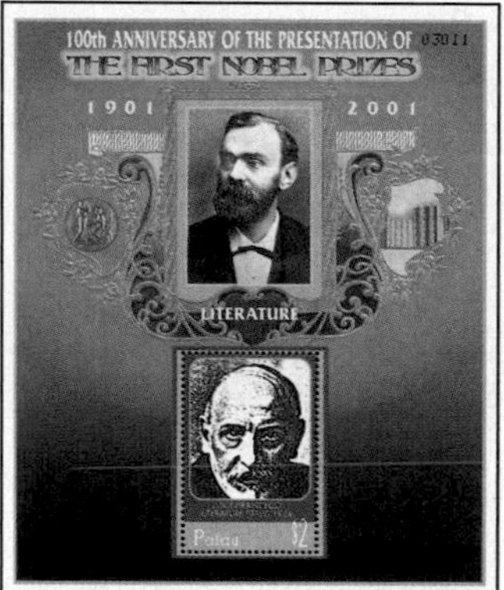

Nobel Prizes, Cent. — A180

Literature laureates — No. 624, 34c: a, Ivo Andric, 1961. b, Eyvind Johnson, 1974. c, Salvatore Quasimodo, 1959. d, Mikhail Sholokhov, 1965. e, Pablo Neruda, 1971. f, Saul Bellow, 1976.

No. 625, 70c: a, Boris Pasternak, 1958. b, Francois Mauriac, 1952. c, Frans Eemil Sillanpää, 1939. d, Roger Martin du Gard, 1937. e, Pearl Buck, 1938. f, André Gide, 1947.

No. 626, 80c: a, Karl Gjellerup, 1917. b, Anatole France, 1921. c, Sinclair Lewis, 1930. d, Jacinto Benavente, 1922. e, John Galsworthy, 1932. f, Erik. A. Karlfeldt, 1931.

No. 627, $2, Luigi Pirandello, 1934. No. 628, $2, Bertrand Russell, 1950. No. 629, Harry Martinson, 1974.

2001, Oct. 30 **Sheets of 6, #a-f**

624-626	A180	Set of 3	22.50	22.50

Souvenir Sheets

627-629	A180	Set of 3	12.00	12.00

2002 World Cup Soccer Championships, Japan and Korea — A181

No. 630, 34c — World Cup posters from: a, 1950. b, 1954. c, 1958. d, 1962. e, 1966. f, 1970.

No. 631, 80c — World Cup posters from: a, 1978. b, 1982. c, 1986. d, 1990. e, 1994. f, 1998.

No. 632, $2, World Cup poster, 1930. No. 633, $2, Head and globe from World Cup trophy.

2001, Nov. 29 ***Perf. 13¾x14¼***

Sheets of 6, #a-f

630-631	A181	Set of 2	14.00	14.00

Souvenir Sheets

Perf. 14½x14¼

632-633	A181	Set of 2	8.00	8.00

Christmas — A182

Denominations: 20c, 34c.

2001, Nov. 29 ***Perf. 14***

634-635	A182	Set of 2	1.10	1.10

Queen Mother Type of 1999 Redrawn

No. 636: a, In Australia, 1958. b, In 1960. c, In 1970. d, In 1987.

$2, Holding book, 1947.

2001, Dec. 13 ***Perf. 14***

Yellow Orange Frames

636	A150	60c Sheet of 4, #a-d, + label	4.75	4.75

Souvenir Sheet

Perf. 13¾

637	A150	$2 black	4.00	4.00

Queen Mother's 101st birthday. No. 637 contains one 38x51mm stamp that is slightly darker than that found on No. 523. Sheet margins of Nos. 636-637 lack embossing and gold arms and frames found on Nos. 522-523.

Pasturing Horses, by Han Kan — A183

2001, Dec. 17 ***Perf. 14x14¾***

638	A183	60c multi	1.25	1.25

New Year 2002 (Year of the Horse). Printed in sheets of 4.

Birds — A184

No. 639, 55c: a, Yellow-faced myna. b, Red-bellied pitta. c, Red-bearded bee-eater. d, Superb fruit dove. e, Coppersmith barbet. f, Diard's trogon.

No. 640, 60c: a, Spectacled monarch. b, Banded pitta. c, Rufous-backed kingfisher. d, Scarlet robin. e, Golden whistler. f, Jewel babbler.

No. 641, $2, Paradise flycatcher. No. 642, $2, Common kingfisher.

2001, Dec. 26 ***Perf. 14***

Sheets of 6, #a-f

639-640	A184	Set of 2	14.00	14.00

Souvenir Sheets

Perf. 14¾

641-642	A184	Set of 2	8.00	8.00

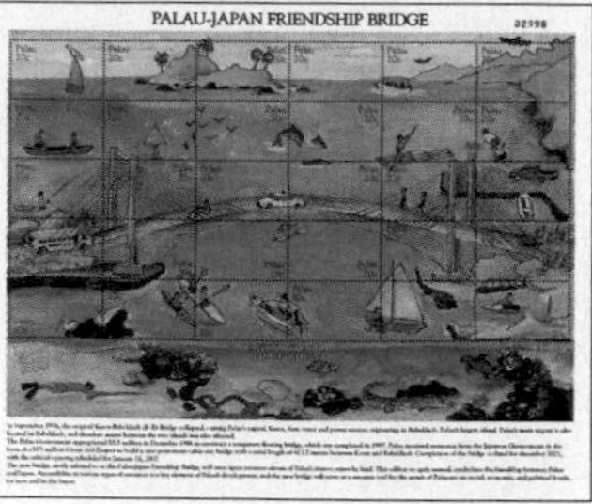

Opening of Palau-Japan Frendship Bridge — A185

No. 643, 20c; No. 644, 34c: a, Bird on orange rock. b, Island, one palm tree. c, Island, three palm trees. d, Rocks, boat prow. e, Boat, bat. f, Cove, foliage. g, Red boat with two people. h, Buoy, birds. i, Birds, dolphin's tail. j, Dolphins. k, Person on raft. l, Two people standing in water. m, Person with fishing pole in water. n, Bridge tower. o, Bicyclist, taxi. p, Front of taxi. q, People walking on bridge, bridge tower. r, Truck, boat. s, School bus. t, Base of bridge tower. u, Birds under bridge, oar. v, Birds under bridge. w, Base of bridge tower, tip of sail. x, Motorcyclist. y, Birds on black rock. z, Kayakers. aa, Kayak, boat. ab, Boat, sailboat. ac, Sailboat, jetty. ad, Jetski.

2002, Jan. 11 ***Perf. 13***

Sheets of 30, #a-ad

643-644	A185	Set of 2	32.50	32.50

United We Stand — A186

2002, Jan. 24 ***Perf. 14***

645	A186	$1 multi	2.00	2.00

Reign of Queen Elizabeth II, 50th Anniv. — A187

No. 646: a, In uniform. b, Wearing flowered hat. c, Prince Philip. d, Wearing tiara.

$2, Wearing white dress.

2002, Feb. 6 ***Perf. 14¼***

646	A187	80c Sheet of 4, #a-d	6.50	6.50

Souvenir Sheet

647	A187	$2 multi	4.00	4.00

Birds — A188

Designs: 1c, Gray-backed white-eye. 2c, Great frigatebird. 3c, Eclectus parrot. 4c, Red-footed booby. 5c Cattle egret. 10c, Cardinal honeyeater. 11c, Blue-faced parrot-finch. 15c, Rufous fantail. 20c, White-faced storm petrel. 21c, Willie wagtail. 23c, Black-headed gull. 50c, Sanderling. 57c, White-tailed tropicbird. 70c, Rainbow lorikeet. 80c, Moorhen. $1, Buff-banded rail. $2, Beach thick-knee. $3, Common tern. $3.50, Ruddy turnstone. $3.95, White-collared kingfisher. $5, Sulphur-crested cockatoo. $10, Barn swallow.

2002, Feb. 20 *Perf. 14¼*

648	A188	1c multi	.25	.25
649	A188	2c multi	.25	.25
650	A188	3c multi	.25	.25
651	A188	4c multi	.25	.25
652	A188	5c multi	.25	.25
653	A188	10c multi	.25	.25
654	A188	11c multi	.25	.25
655	A188	15c multi	.30	.30
656	A188	20c multi	.40	.40
657	A188	21c multi	.40	.40
658	A188	23c multi	.45	.45
659	A188	50c multi	1.00	1.00
660	A188	57c multi	1.10	1.10
661	A188	70c multi	1.40	1.40
662	A188	80c multi	1.60	1.60
663	A188	$1 multi	2.00	2.00
664	A188	$2 multi	4.00	4.00
665	A188	$3 multi	6.00	6.00
666	A188	$3.50 multi	7.00	7.00
667	A188	$3.95 multi	8.00	8.00
668	A188	$5 multi	10.00	10.00
669	A188	$10 multi	20.00	20.00
		Nos. 648-669 (22)	65.40	65.40

Flowers — A189

Designs: 20c, Euanthe sanderiana. 34c, Ophiorrhiza palauensis. No. 672, 60c, Cerbera manghas. 80c, Mendinilla pterocaula.

No. 674, 60c: a, Bruguiera gymnorhiza. b, Samadera indiccal. c, Maesa canfieldiae. d, Lumnitzera litorea. e, Dolichandrone palawense. f, Limnophila aromatica (red and white orchids).

No. 675, 60c: a, Sonneratia alba. b, Barringtonia racemosa. c, Ixora casei. d, Tristellateia australasiae. e, Nepenthes mirabilis. f, Limnophila aromatica (pink flowers).

No. 676, $2, Fagraea ksid. No. 677, $2, Cerbera manghas, horiz.

2002, Mar. 4 *Perf. 14*

670-673	A189	Set of 4	4.00	4.00

Sheets of 6, #a-f

674-675	A189	Set of 2	14.50	14.50

Souvenir Sheets

676-677	A189	Set of 2	8.00	8.00

2002 Winter Olympics, Salt Lake City A190

Skier with: No. 678, $1, Blue pants. No. 679, $1, Yellow pants.

2002, Mar. 18 *Perf. 14¼*

678-679	A190	Set of 2	4.00	4.00
679a		Souvenir sheet, #678-679	4.00	4.00

Cats and Dogs — A191

No. 680, 50c, horiz.: a, Himalayan. b, Norwegian forest cat. c, Havana. d, Exotic shorthair. e, Persian. f, Maine coon cat.

No. 681, 50c, horiz.: a, Great Dane. b, Whippet. c, Bedlington terrier. d, Golden retriever. e, Papillon. f, Doberman pinscher.

No. 682, $2, British shorthair. No. 683, $2, Shetland sheepdog.

2002, Mar. 18 **Litho.** *Perf. 14*

Sheets of 6, #a-f

680-681	A191	Set of 2	12.00	12.00

Souvenir Sheets

682-683	A191	Set of 2	8.00	8.00

Intl. Year of Mountains — A192

No. 684: a, Mt. Fuji, Japan. b, Mt. Everest, Nepal and China. c, Mt. Owen, US. d, Mt. Huascarán, Peru.

$2, Mt. Eiger, Switzerland.

2002, June 17 **Litho.** *Perf. 14*

684	A192	80c Sheet of 4, #a-d	6.50	6.50

Souvenir Sheet

685	A192	$2 multi	4.00	4.00

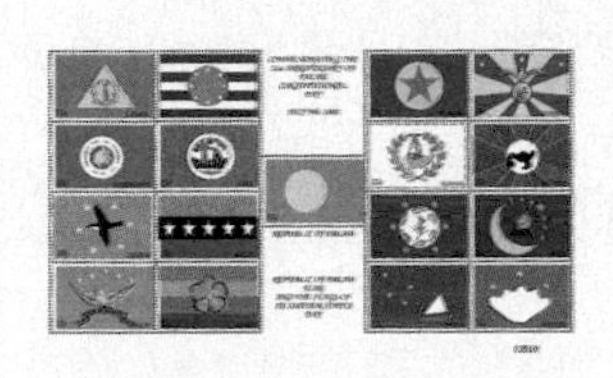

Flags of Palau and its States — A193

No. 686: a, Palau (no inscription). b, Kayangel. c, Ngarchelong. d, Ngaraard. e, Ngardmau. f, Ngaremlengui. g, Ngiwal. h, Ngatpang. i, Melekeor. j, Ngchesar. k, Aimeliik. l, Airai. m, Koror. n, Peleliu. o, Angaur. p, Sonsorol. q, Hatohobei.

2002, July 9

686	A193	37c Sheet of 17, #a-q	13.00	13.00

All stamps on No. 686 lack country name.

Winter Olympics Type of 2002 Redrawn with White Olympic Rings

Skier with: No. 687, $1, Blue pants. No. 688, $1, Yellow pants.

2002, July 29 *Perf. 13½*

687-688	A190	Set of 2	4.00	4.00
688a		Souvenir sheet, #687-688	4.00	4.00

Intl. Year of Ecotourism — A194

No. 689: a, Divers, angelfish facing right. b, Ray. c, Sea cucumber. d, Emperor angelfish facing left. e, Sea turtle. f, Nautilus.

$2, Person in canoe.

2002, Apr. 26 *Perf. 14½x14¼*

689	A194	60c Sheet of 6, #a-f	7.25	7.25

Souvenir Sheet

690	A194	$2 multi	4.00	4.00

Japanese Art — A195

No. 691, vert. (38x50mm): a, The Actor Shuka Bando as Courtesan Shiraito, by Kunisada Utagawa. b, The Actor Danjuro Ichikawa VII as Sugawara no Michizane, by Kunisada Utagawa. c, The Actor Sojuro Sawamura III as Yuranosuke Oboshi, by Toyokuni Utagawa. d, The Actor Nizaemon Kataoka VII as Shihei Fujiwara, by Toyokuni Utagawa. e, Bust Portrait of the Actor Noshio Nakamura II, by Kunimasa Utagawa. f, The Actor Gon-Nosuke Kawarazaki as Daroku, by Kunichika Toyohara.

No. 692, 80c, vert. (27x88mm): a, Bush Clover Branch and Sweetfish, by Kuniyoshi Utagawa. b, Catfish, by Kuniyoshi Utagawa. c, Scene at Takanawa, by Eisen Keisai. d, Ochanomizu, by Keisai.

No. 693, 80c (50x38mm): a, Gaslight Hall, by Kiyochika Kobayashi. b, Cherry Blossoms at Night at Shin Yoshiwara, by Yasuji Inoue. c, Night Rain at Oyama, by Toyokuni Utagawa II. d, Kintai Bridge, by Keisai.

No. 694, $2, Okane, a Strong Woman of Omi, by Kuniyoshi Utagawa. No. 695, $2, Scene on the Banks of the Oumaya River, by Kuniyoshi Utagawa.

Perf. 14¼, 13½ (#692)

2002, Sept. 23

691	A195	60c Sheet of 6, #a-f	7.25	7.25

Sheets of 4, #a-d

692-693	A195	Set of 2	13.00	13.00

Size: 105x85mm

Imperf

694-695	A195	Set of 2	8.00	8.00

Popeye — A196

No. 696, vert.: a, Wimpy. b, Swee'Pea. c, Popeye. d, Fish. e, Jeep. f, Brutus.

$2, Popeye golfing.

2002, Oct. 7 *Perf. 14*

696	A196	60c Sheet of 6, #a-f	7.25	7.25

Souvenir Sheet

697	A196	$2 multi	4.00	4.00

Elvis Presley (1935-77) — A197

No. 698: a, On horse. b, Holding guitar, wearing white jacket, no hat. c, Wearing black hat. d, With guitar with two necks. e, Holding guitar, wearing colored jacket, no hat. f, Wearing shirt.

2002, Oct. 23

698	A197	37c Sheet of 6, #a-f	4.75	4.75

Christmas A198

Designs: 23c, Presentation of Jesus in the Temple, by Perugino, vert. 37c, Madonna and Child Enthroned Between Angels and Saints, by Domenico Ghirlandaio, vert. 60c, Maesta, by Simone Martini, vert. 80c, Sacred Conversation, by Giovanni Bellini. $1, Nativity, by Ghirlandaio.

$2, Sacred Conversation (detail), by Bellini.

2002, Nov. 5

699-703	A198	Set of 5	6.00	6.00

Souvenir Sheet

704	A198	$2 multi	4.00	4.00

The painting shown on No. 704 does not appear to be a detail of the painting shown on No. 702.

Teddy Bears, Cent. — A199

No. 705: a, Accountant bear. b, Computer programmer bear. c, Businesswoman bear. d, Lawyer bear.

2002, Nov. 19

705	A199	60c Sheet of 4, #a-d	5.00	5.00

Queen Mother Elizabeth (1900-2002) — A200

No. 706: a, Holding bouquet. b, Wearing blue blouse and pearls. c, Wearing purple hat. d, Wearing tiara.
$2, Wearing flowered hat.

2002, Dec. 30

706 A200 80c Sheet of 4, #a-d 6.50 6.50

Souvenir Sheet

707 A200 $2 multi 4.00 4.00

20th World Scout Jamboree, Thailand (in 2002) — A201

No. 708, horiz.: a, Scout climbing rocks. b, Scout emblem, knife. c, Branches lashed together with rope. d, Cub scout (wearing cap). e, Knot. f, Boy scout (without cap).
$2 Lord Robert Baden-Powell.

2003, Jan. 13 ***Perf. 14***

708 A201 60c Sheet of 6, #a-f 7.25 7.25

Souvenir Sheet

709 A201 $2 multi 4.00 4.00

Shells — A202

No. 710: a, Leafy murex. b, Trumpet triton. c, Giant tun. d, Queen conch. e, Spotted tun. f, Emperor helmet.
$2, Angular triton.

2003, Jan. 13

710 A202 60c Sheet of 6, #a-f 7.25 7.25

Souvenir Sheet

711 A202 $2 multi 4.00 4.00

New Year 2003 (Year of the Ram) — A203

No. 712: a, Ram facing right. b, Ram facing forward. c, Ram facing left.

2003, Jan. 27 ***Perf. 14¼x13¾***

712 A203 37c Vert. strip of 3, #a-c 2.25 2.25
Sheet of 2 strips 4.50

No. 712 printed in sheets of 2 strips with slightly different backgrounds.

Pres. John F. Kennedy (1917-63) — A204

No. 713: a, Wearing cap. b, Facing left. c, Facing right. d, Holding ship's wheel.

2003, Feb. 10 ***Perf. 14***

713 A204 80c Sheet of 4, #a-d 6.50 6.50

Bird Type of 2002 With Unserifed Numerals

Designs: 26c, Golden whistler. 37c, Pale white-eye.

2003, Mar. 1 ***Perf. 14¼x13¾***

714 A188 26c multi .55 .55
715 A188 37c multi .75 .75

Astronauts Killed in Space Shuttle Columbia Accident — A205

No. 716: a, Mission Specialist 1 David M. Brown. b, Commander Rick D. Husband. c, Mission Specialist 4 Laurel Blair Salton Clark. d, Mission Specialist 4 Kalpana Chawla. e, Payload Commander Michael P. Anderson. f, Pilot William C. McCool. g, Payload Specialist 4 Ilan Ramon.

2003, Apr. 7 ***Perf. 13¼***

716 A205 37c Sheet of 7, #a-g 5.25 5.25

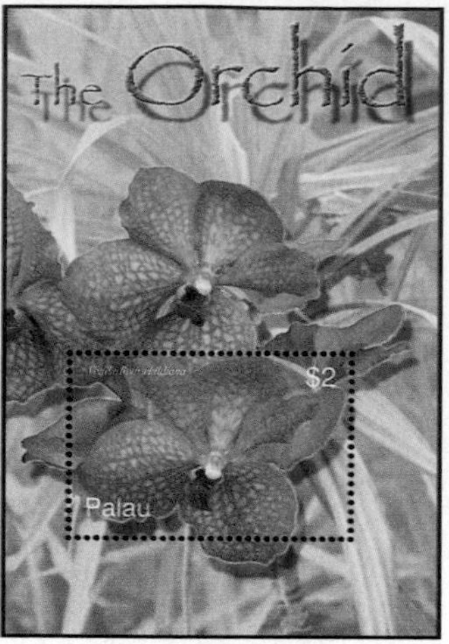

Orchids — A206

No. 717: a, Phalaenopsis grex. b, Cattleya loddigesii. c, Phalaenopsis joline. d, Dendrobium. e, Laelia anceps. f, Cymbidium Stanley Fouracre.
$2, Vanda rothschildiana.

2003, Jan. 13 **Litho.** ***Perf. 14***

717 A206 60c Sheet of 6, #a-f 7.25 7.25

Souvenir Sheet

718 A206 $2 multi 4.00 4.00

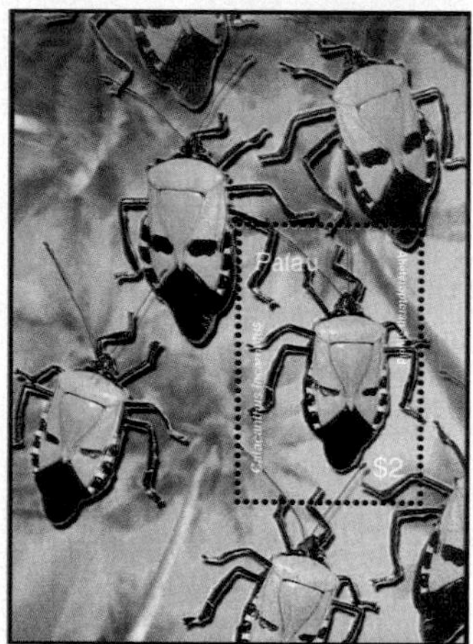

Insects — A207

No. 719: a, Giant water bug. b, Weevil. c, Blister beetle. d, Bess beetle. e, Metallic stag beetle. f, Violin beetle.
$2, Aheteropteran shield.

2003, Jan. 13

719 A207 60c Sheet of 6, #a-f 7.25 7.25

Souvenir Sheet

720 A207 $2 multi 4.00 4.00

First Non-stop Solo Transatlantic Flight, 75th Anniv. — A208

No. 721: a, Charles Lindbergh, Donald Hall and Spirit of St. Louis. b, Spirit of St. Louis, Apr. 28, 1927. c, Spirit of St. Louis towed from Curtiss Field, May 20, 1927. d, Spirit of St. Louis takes off, May 20, 1927. e, Arrival in Paris, May 21, 1927. f, New York ticker tape parade.

2003, Feb. 10

721 A208 60c Sheet of 6, #a-f 7.25 7.25

Pres. Ronald Reagan — A209

Reagan with: a, Orange bandana. b, Red shirt. c, Blue shirt, head at left. d, Blue shirt, head at right.

2003, Feb. 10

722 A209 80c Sheet of 4, #a-d 6.50 6.50

Princess Diana (1961-97) — A210

Diana and clothing worn in: a, India. b, Canada. c, Egypt. d, Italy.

2003, Feb. 10

723 A210 80c Sheet of 4, #a-d 6.50 6.50

Coronation of Queen Elizabeth II, 50th Anniv. — A211

No. 724 — Queen with: a, Tiara. b, Pink dress. c, Hat.
$2, Tiara, diff.

2003, May 13

724 A211 $1 Sheet of 3, #a-c 6.00 6.00

Souvenir Sheet

725 A211 $2 multi 4.00 4.00

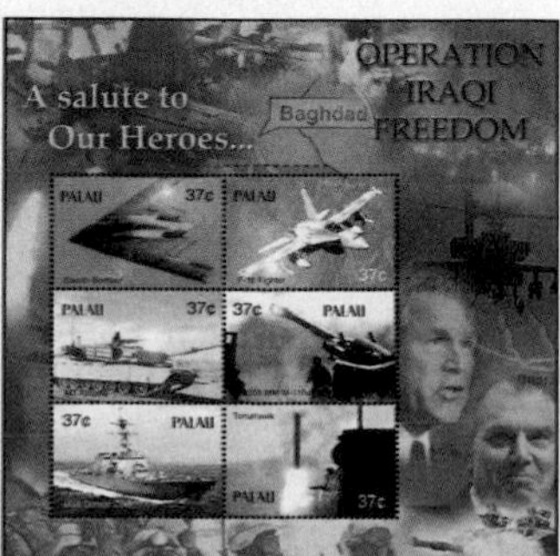

Operation Iraqi Freedom — A212

No. 726: a, Stealth bomber. b, F-18 fighter. c, MT Abrams tank. d, 203mm M-110s. e, USS Donald Cook. f, Tomahawk missile.

2003, May 14
726 A212 37c Sheet of 6, #a-f 4.50 4.50

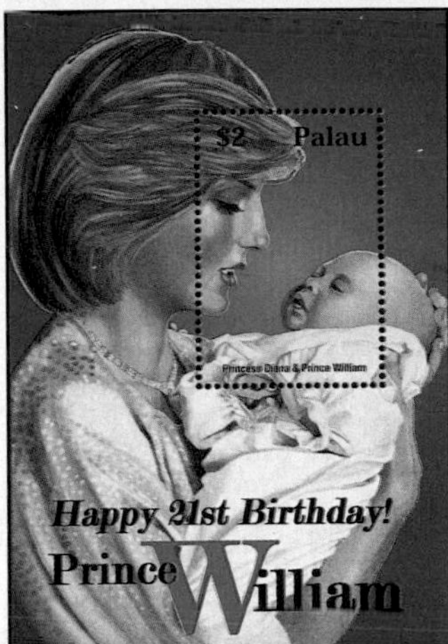

Prince William, 21st Birthday — A213

No. 727 — William: a, In yellow green shirt. b, As infant. c, In black sweater.
$2, As infant with Princess Diana.

2003, June 21
727 A213 $1 Sheet of 3, #a-c 6.00 6.00

Souvenir Sheet

728 A213 $2 multi 4.00 4.00

Tour de France Bicycle Race, Cent. — A214

No. 729: a, Henri Pelissier, 1923. b, Ottavio Bottecchia, 1924. c, Bottecchia, 1925. d, Lucien Buysse, 1926.
$2, Philippe Thys, 1920.

2003, Aug. 23 ***Perf. 13¼***
729 A214 60c Sheet of 4, #a-d 5.00 5.00

Souvenir Sheet

730 A214 $2 multi 4.00 4.00

Powered Flight, Cent. — A215

No. 731: a, Fokker 70. b, Boeing 747-217B. c, Curtiss T-32 Condor. d, Vickers Viscount Type 761. e, Wright Flyer III. f, Avro Ten Achilles.
$2, Wright Flyer III, diff.

2003, Aug. 25 ***Perf. 14***
731 A215 55c Sheet of 6, #a-f 6.75 6.75

Souvenir Sheet

732 A215 $2 multi 4.00 4.00

Paintings by James McNeill Whistler — A216

Designs: 37c, Blue and Silver: Trouville. 55c, The Last of Old Westminster. 60c, Wapping. $1, Cremorne Gardens, No. 2.
No. 737, vert.: a, Arrangement in Flesh Color and Black, Portrait of Theodore Duret. b, Arrangement in White and Black. c, Harmony in Pink and Gray, Portrait of Lady Meux. d, Arrangement in Black and Gold, Comte Robert de Montesquiou-Fezensac.
$2, Arrangement in Gray and Black No. 1, Portrait of Painter's Mother, vert.

Perf. 14¼, 13¼ (#737)

2003, Sept. 22
733-736 A216 Set of 4 5.25 5.25
737 A216 80c Sheet of 4, #a-d 6.50 6.50

Souvenir Sheet

738 A216 $2 multi 4.00 4.00

No. 737 contains four 35x71mm stamps.

Circus Performers — A217

No. 739, 80c — Clowns: a, Apes. b, Mo Life. c, Gigi. d, "Buttons" McBride.
No. 740, 80c: a, Dogs. b, Olena Yaknenko. c, Mountain High. d, Chinese Circus.

2003, Sept. 29 ***Perf. 14***

Sheets of 4, #a-d

739-740 A217 Set of 2 13.00 13.00

Christmas A218

Designs: 37c, Madonna della Melagrana, by Botticelli. 60c, Madonna del Magnificat, by Botticelli. 80c, Madonna and Child with the Saints and the Angels, by Andrea del Sarto. $1, La Madonna del Roseto, by Botticelli.
$2, Madonna and Child with the Angels and Saints, by Domenico Ghirlandaio.

2003, Dec. 1 ***Perf. 14¼***
741-744 A218 Set of 4 5.75 5.75

Souvenir Sheet

745 A218 $2 multi 4.00 4.00

Sea Turtles — A219

No. 746: a, Mating. b, Laying eggs at night. c, Hatching. d, Turtles going to sea. e, Growing up at sea. f, Returning to lay eggs.
$2, Head of sea turtle.

2004, Feb. 6 ***Perf. 14***
746 A219 60c Sheet of 6, #a-f 7.25 7.25

Souvenir Sheet

747 A219 $2 multi 4.00 4.00

Paintings by Norman Rockwell — A220

No. 748, vert.: a, The Connoisseur. b, Artist Facing a Blank Canvas (Deadline). c, Art Critic. d, Stained Glass Artistry.
$2, Painting Tavern Sign.

2004, Feb. 6 **Litho.** ***Perf. 14¼***
748 A220 80c Sheet of 4, #a-d 6.50 6.50

Souvenir Sheet

749 A220 $2 multi 4.00 4.00

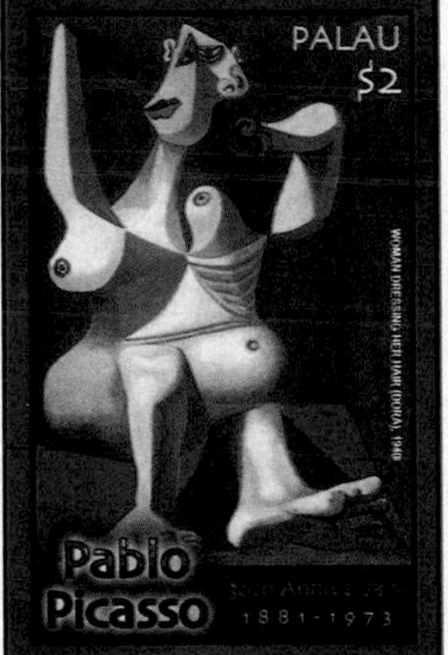

Paintings by Pablo Picasso — A221

No. 750: a, Dora Maar. b, The Yellow Sweater (Dora). c, Woman in Green (Dora). d, Woman in an Armchair (Dora).
$2, Woman Dressing Her Hair (Dora).

2004, Feb. 16 **Litho.** ***Perf. 14¼***
750 A221 80c Sheet of 4, #a-d 6.50 6.50

Imperf

751 A221 $2 multi 4.00 4.00

No. 750 contains four 37x50mm stamps.

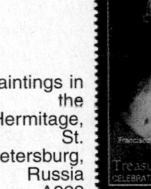

Paintings in the Hermitage, St. Petersburg, Russia A222

Designs: 37c, Antonia Zarate, by Francisco de Goya. 55c, Portrait of a Lady, by Antonio Correggio. 80c, Portrait of Count Olivarez, by Diego Velázquez. $1, Portrait of a Young Man With a Lace Collar, by Rembrandt.
$2, Family Portrait, by Anthony Van Dyck.

2004, Feb. 16 **Litho.** ***Perf. 14¼***
752-755 A222 Set of 4 5.50 5.50

Size: 62x81mm

Imperf

756 A222 $2 multi 4.00 4.00

Marine Life — A223

No. 757: a, Coral hind. b, Sea octopus. c, Manta ray. d, Dugong. e, Marine crab. f, Grouper.
$2, Gray reef shark.

2004, Feb. 16 ***Perf. 14¼***
757 A223 55c Sheet of 6, #a-f 6.75 6.75

Souvenir Sheet

758 A223 $2 multi 4.00 4.00

Minerals — A224

No. 759: a, Phosphate. b, Antimony. c, Limonite. d, Calcopyrite. e, Bauxite. f, Manganite.
$2, Gold.

2004, Feb. 16
759 A224 55c Sheet of 6, #a-f 6.75 6.75

Souvenir Sheet

760 A224 $2 multi 4.00 4.00

New Year 2004 (Year of the Monkey) A225

Green Bamboo and a White Ape, by Ren Yu: 50c, Detail. $1, Entire painting.

2004, Mar. 9 *Perf. 13¼*

761 A225 50c multi 1.00 1.00

Souvenir Sheet

Perf. 13½x13¼

762 A225 $1 multi 2.00 2.00

No. 761 printed in sheets of 4. No. 762 contains one 27x83mm stamp.

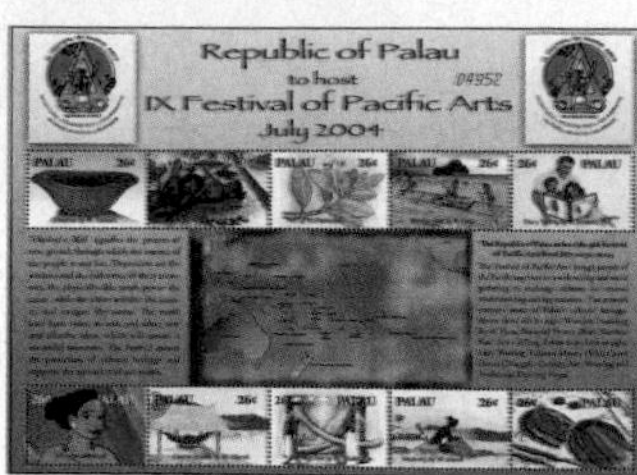

Ninth Festival of Pacific Arts — A226

No. 763, 26c: a, Oraschel, by M. Takeshi. b, Flute, by Sim Adelbai. c, Rur, by W. Watanabe. d, Bamboo Raft, by P. Tiakl. e, Story Telling, by K. Murret. f, Yek, by A. Imetuker. g, Canoe House, by W. Marsil. h, Carving Axe, by Watanabe. i, Weaving, by Marsil. j, Dancing Props, by Adelbai.

No. 764, 37c: a, Ongall, by Tiakl. b, Bai, by S. Weers. c, Taro Plant, by S. Smaserui. d, Toluk, by Watanabe. e, Medicinal Plants, by Smaserui. f, War Canoe, by Takeshi. g, Painting, by Adelbai. h, Pounding Taro, by Imetuker. h, Llengel, by Takeshi. i, Spear Technique, by Imetuker.

2004, Apr. 13 *Perf. 13*

Sheets of 10, #a-j

763-764 A226 Set of 2 13.00 13.00

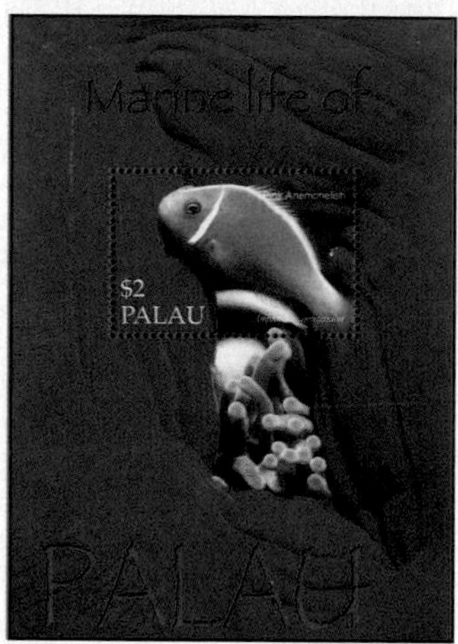

Marine Life — A227

No. 765, 26c: a, Cuttlefish. b, Long fin bannerfish. c, Red sponge, Medusa worm. d, Risbecia tryoni. e, Emperor angelfish. f, Chromodoris coi.

No. 766, 37c: a, Spotted eagle ray. b, Jellyfish. c, Nautilus. d, Gray reef shark. e, Tunicates. f, Manta ray.

No. 767, $2, Pink anemonefish. No. 768, $2, Dusky anemonefish.

2004, May 20 *Perf. 14*

Sheets of 6, #a-f

765-766 A227 Set of 2 7.75 7.75

Souvenir Sheets

767-768 A227 Set of 2 8.00 8.00

No. 765 contains six labels.

Intl. Year of Peace — A228

No. 769, vert.: a, Mahatma Gandhi. b, Nelson Mandela. c, Dr. Martin Luther King, Jr. $2, Dove.

2004, May 24 *Perf. 13½x13¼*

769 A228 $3 Sheet of 3, #a-c 18.00 18.00

Souvenir Sheet

Perf. 13¼x13½

770 A228 $2 multi 4.00 4.00

2004 Summer Olympics, Athens — A229

Designs: 37c, Athletes. 55c, Gold medals, Atlanta, 1996. 80c, Johannes Edström, Intl. Olympic Committee President, 1942-52, vert. $1, Women's soccer, Atlanta, 1996.

2004, June 18 *Perf. 14¼*

771-774 A229 Set of 4 5.50 5.50

Election of Pope John Paul, 25th Anniv. (in 2003) — A230

Pope John Paul II: a, With Mehmet Agca, 1983. b, Visiting Poland, 2002. c, At concert in Ischia, Italy, 2002. d, With Patriarch Zakka, 2003.

2004, June 18

775 A230 80c Sheet of 4, #a-d 6.50 6.50

Souvenir Sheet

Deng Xiaoping (1904-97) Chinese Leader — A231

2004, June 18

776 A231 $2 multi 4.00 4.00

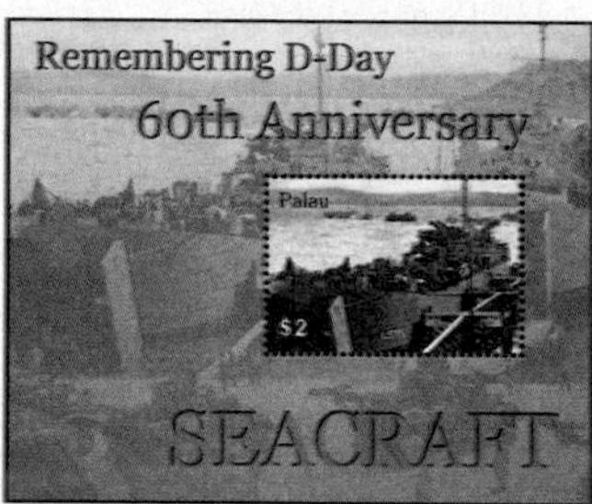

D-Day, 60th Anniv. — A232

No. 777: a, LCA 1377. b, Landing Craft, Infantry. c, LCVP. d, U-309. e, HMS Begonia. f, HMS Roberts.

$2, LSTs.

2004, June 18

777 A232 50c Sheet of 6, #a-f 6.00 6.00

Souvenir Sheet

778 A232 $2 multi 4.00 4.00

European Soccer Championships, Portugal — A233

No. 779, vert.: a, Rinus Michels. b, Rinat Dasaev. c, Marco Van Basten. d, Olympiastadion.

$2, 1988 Netherlands team.

2004, June 18

779 A233 80c Sheet of 4, #a-d 6.50 6.50

Souvenir Sheet

780 A233 $2 multi 4.00 4.00

No. 779 contains four 28x42mm stamps.

Babe Ruth (1895-1948), Baseball Player — A234

Ruth and: No. 781, 37c, Signed baseball. No. 782, 37c, World Series 100th anniversary emblem.

2004, Sept. 3 *Perf. 13½x13¼*

781-782 A234 Set of 2 1.50 1.50

Nos. 781-782 each printed in sheets of 8.

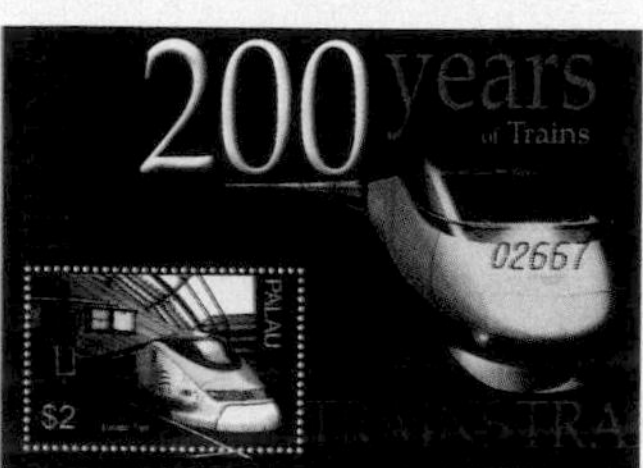

Trains, Bicent. — A235

No. 783: a, ATSF 315. b, Amtrak 464. c, Railway N52. d, SD 70 MAC Diesel-electric locomotive. No. 784, 50c: a, CS SO2002. b, P 36 N0032. c, SW-600. d, Gambier LNV 9703 4-4-0 NG.

No. 785, $2, CN5700 locomotive. No. 786, $2, Eurostar.

2004, Sept. 27 *Perf. 13¼x13½*

783 A235 26c Sheet of 4, #a-d 2.10 2.10

784 A235 50c Sheet of 4, #a-d 4.00 4.00

Souvenir Sheet

785 A235 $2 multi 4.00 4.00

786 A235 $2 multi 4.00 4.00

Butterflies, Reptiles, Amphibians and Birds — A236

No. 787, 80c — Butterflies: a, Cethosia hypsea. b, Cethosia myrina. c, Charaxes durnfordi. d, Charaxes nitebis.

No. 788, 80c — Reptiles: a, Bull snake. b, Garter snake. c, Yellow-lipped sea snake. d, Yellow-bellied sea snake.

No. 789, 80c, vert. — Birds: a, Blue-faced parrot finch. b, Mangrove flycatcher. c, Palau swiftlet. d, Bridled white-eye.

No. 790, $2, Charaxes nitebis, diff. No. 791, $2, Glass frog. No. 792, $2, Dusky white-eye, vert.

2004, Oct. 13 **Litho.** *Perf. 14*

Sheets of 4, #a-d

787-789 A236 Set of 3 19.50 19.50

Souvenir Sheets

790-792 A236 Set of 3 12.00 12.00

Dinosaurs — A237

No. 793, 26c, vert.: a, Kritosaurus. b, Triceratops. c, Hypselosaurus. d, Yingshanosaurus.

No. 794, 80c: a, Hadrosaurus. b, Pterodaustro. c, Agilisaurus. d, Amargasaurus.

No. 795, 80c, vert.: a, Corythosaurus. b, Dryosaurus. c, Euoplocephalus. d, Compsognathus.

No. 796, $2, Ornithomimus. No. 797, $2, Archaeopteryx. No. 798, $2, Deinonychus, vert.

2004, Oct. 13 **Sheets of 4, #a-d**

793-795 A237 Set of 3 15.00 15.00

Souvenir Sheets

796-798 A237 Set of 3 12.00 12.00

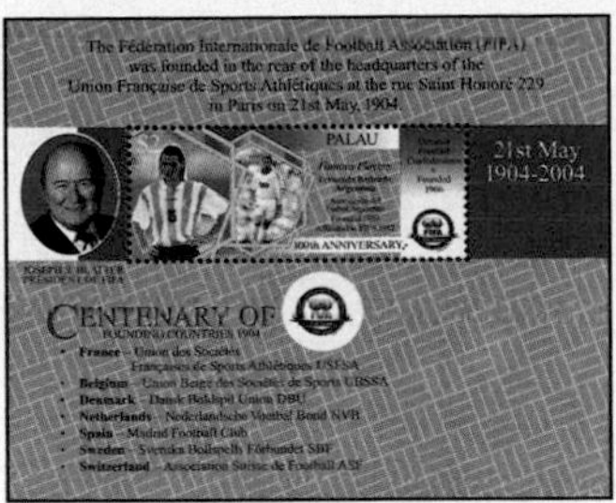

FIFA (Fédération Internationale de Football Association), Cent. — A238

No. 799: a, Diego Maradona. b, David Seaman. c, Andreas Brehme. d, Paul Ince. $2, Fernando Redondo.

2004, Oct. 27 ***Perf. 12¾x12½***
799 A238 80c Sheet of 4, #a-d 6.50 6.50

Souvenir Sheet

800 A238 $2 multi 4.00 4.00

National Basketball Association Players — A239

Designs: No. 801, 26c, Chris Bosh, Toronto Raptors. No. 802, 26c, Tim Duncan, San Antonio Spurs. No. 803, 26c, Kevin Garnett, Minnesota Timberwolves.

2004, Nov. 3 ***Perf. 14***
801-803 A239 Set of 3 1.60 1.60

Each stamp printed in sheets of 12.

Christmas — A240

Paintings of Madonna and Child by: 37c, Quentin Metsys. 60c, Adolphe William Bouguereau. 80c, William Dyce. $1, Carlo Crivelli. $2, Peter Paul Rubens, vert.

2004, Dec. 23 ***Perf. 14¼***
804-807 A240 Set of 4 5.75 5.75

Souvenir Sheet

808 A240 $2 multi 4.00 4.00

Miniature Sheet

Palau — Republic of China Diplomatic Relations, 5th Anniv. — A241

No. 809: a, Agricultural products. b, Republic of China Navy ship. c, Ngarachamayong Cultural Center. d, Palau National Museum.

2004, Dec. 29 ***Perf. 14***
809 A241 80c Sheet of 4, #a-d 6.50 6.50

Souvenir Sheet

New Year 2005 (Year of the Rooster) — A242

No. 810: a, Rooster facing right, tail feathers at LL. b, Rooster facing left, tail feathers at LR. c, Rooster facing right, no tail feathers at LL. d, Rooster facing left, no tail feathers at LR.

2005, Jan. 26 Litho. ***Perf. 12½***
810 A242 50c Sheet of 4, #a-d 4.00 4.00

Souvenir Sheet

Rotary International, Cent. — A243

No. 811: a, Rotary International emblem. b, Rotary Centennial bell. c, Flags of Rotary International, US, Great Britain, Canada, Germany, China and Italy. d, James Wheeler Davidson.

2005, Apr. 4 ***Perf. 14***
811 A243 80c Sheet of 4, #a-d 6.50 6.50

Friedrich von Schiller (1759-1805), Writer — A244

No. 812 — Schiller facing: a, Right (sepia tone). b, Right (color). c, Left (sepia tone). $2, Facing left, diff.

2005, Apr. 4
812 A244 $1 Sheet of 3, #a-c 6.00 6.00

Souvenir Sheet

813 A244 $2 multi 4.00 4.00

Hans Christian Andersen (1805-75), Author — A245

No. 814, vert. — Book covers: a, Hans Christian Andersen Fairy Tales. b, Hans Christian Andersen's The Ugly Duckling. c, Tales of Hans Christian Andersen. $2, The Little Match Girl.

2005, Apr. 4
814 A245 $1 Sheet of 3, #a-c 6.00 6.00

Souvenir Sheet

815 A245 $2 multi 4.00 4.00

Battle of Trafalgar, Bicent. — A246

Various ships in battle: 37c, 55c, 80c, $1. $2, Admiral Horatio Nelson Wounded During Battle of Trafalgar.

2005, Apr. 4 ***Perf. 14¼***
816-819 A246 Set of 4 5.50 5.50

Souvenir Sheet

820 A246 $2 multi 4.00 4.00

End of World War II, 60th Anniv. — A247

No. 821, 80c — Dambuster Raid: a, Pilots review routes prior to mission. b, Dambuster crew. c, Ground crews prepare Lancaster bomber. d, Bomber over Möhne Dam.

No. 822, 80c — Battle of Kursk: a, Russian tanks move forward. b, Tank commanders review maps. c, Russian and German armor clash. d, Destroyed German tank.

No. 823, $2, Squadron 617 leader Guy Gibson and "Highball Bouncing Bomb." No. 824, $2, Russian troops converge on destroyed German tank.

2005, May 9 ***Perf. 13½***

Sheets of 4, #a-d

821-822 A247 Set of 2 13.00 13.00

Souvenir Sheets

823-824 A247 Set of 2 8.00 8.00

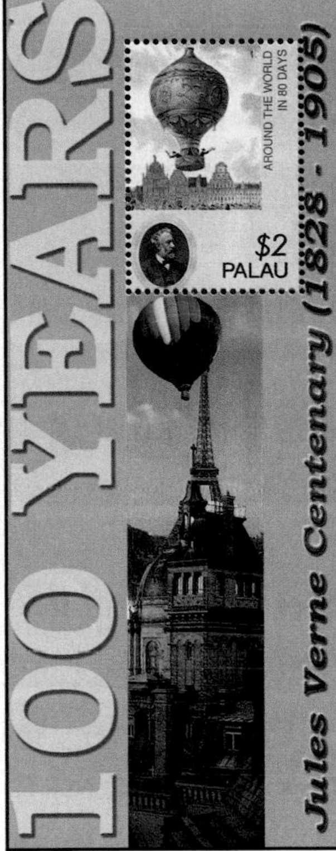

Jules Verne (1828-1905), Writer — A248

No. 825, horiz.: a, 20,000 Leagues Under the Sea. b, Mysterious Island. c, Journey to the Center of the Earth. $2, Around the World in 80 Days.

2005, June 7 ***Perf. 12¾***
825 A248 $1 Sheet of 3, #a-c 6.00 6.00

Souvenir Sheet

826 A248 $2 multi 4.00 4.00

Pope John Paul II (1920-2005) A249

2005, June 27 ***Perf. 13½x13¼***
827 A249 $1 multi 2.00 2.00

A250

Elvis Presley (1935-77) — A251

No. 829 — Color of Presley: a, Blue. b, Green. c, Yellow. d, Orange.

2005, July 2 *Perf. 14*
828 A250 80c multi 1.60 1.60
829 A251 80c Sheet of 4, #a-d 6.50 6.50

No. 828 printed in sheets of 4.

Trains Type of 2004

No. 830: a, Birney N62 Interurban. b, C62-2-103103. c, WR MO 2007. d, Atchison, Topeka & Santa Fe locomotive 314.
$2, Royal Hudson #2860, vert.

2005 *Perf. 13¼x13½*
830 A235 80c Sheet of 4, #a-d 6.50 6.50

Souvenir Sheet
Perf. 13½x13¼
831 A235 $2 multi 4.00 4.00

V-J Day, 60th Anniv. — A252

No. 832, vert.: a, Audie Murphy. b, John F. Kennedy. c, Fleet Admiral Chester W. Nimitz. d, Marines recapture Guam from the Japanese.
$2, Sailors going home.

2005, June 7 **Litho.** *Perf. 12¾*
832 A252 80c Sheet of 4, #a-d 6.50 6.50

Souvenir Sheet
833 A252 $2 multi 4.00 4.00

Miniature Sheet

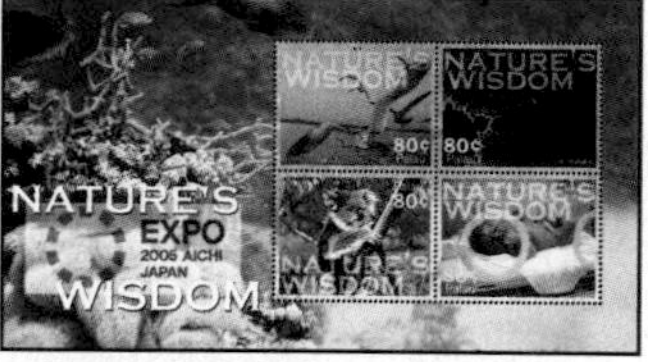

Expo 2005, Aichi, Japan — A253

No. 834: a, Seagulls. b, The cosmos. c, Koala. d, Childbirth.

2005, June 27 *Perf. 12*
834 A253 80c Sheet of 4, #a-d 6.50 6.50

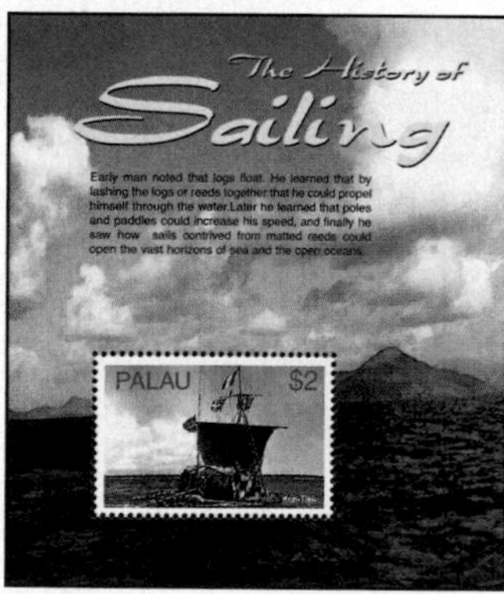

Sailing — A254

No. 835: a, Tepukei. b, Tainui. c, Palauan canoe. d, Yap outrigger.
$2, Kon-Tiki.

2005, June 27 *Perf. 12¾*
835 A254 80c Sheet of 4, #a-d 6.50 6.50

Souvenir Sheet
836 A254 $2 multi 4.00 4.00

World Cup Soccer Championships, 75th Anniv. — A255

No. 837, $1 — Scene from final match of: a, 1954. b, 1966. c, 1974.
No. 838, $1: a, Scene from 2002 final match. b, Lothar Matthias. c, Gerd Muller.
No. 839, $2, Sepp Herberger. No. 840, $2, Franz Beckenbauer.

2005, July 19 *Perf. 12*
Sheets of 3, #a-c
837-838 A255 Set of 2 12.00 12.00

Souvenir Sheets
839 A255 $2 multi 4.00 4.00
Perf. 12¾
840 A255 $2 multi 4.00 4.00

No. 840 contains one 42x28mm stamp.

Vatican City No. 61 — A256

2005, Aug. 9 *Perf. 13x13¼*
841 A256 37c multi .75 .75

Printed in sheets of 12.

Miniature Sheet

Taipei 2005 Intl. Stamp Exhibition — A257

No. 842: a, Wildeve rose. b, Graham Thomas rose. c, Crocus rose. d, Tes of the d'Urbervilles rose.

2005, Aug. 19 *Perf. 14*
842 A257 80c Sheet of 4, #a-d 6.50 6.50

Miniature Sheet

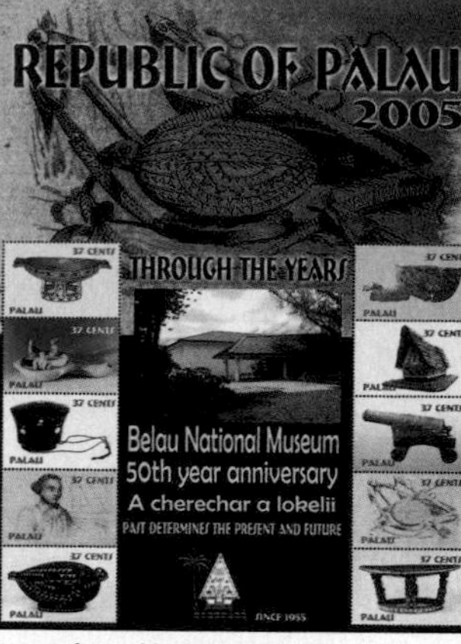

Items from National Museum — A258

No. 843: a, Decorated bowl, light yellow background. b, Potsherds, dull rose background. c, Sculpture with three people, blue background. d, Model of native house, light yellow background. e, Lidded container with strings. f, Cannon. g, Drawing of man on ship. h, Drawing of native craftwork. i, Bird-shaped figurine. j, Decorated bowl, pink background.

2005, Sept. 30
843 A258 37c Sheet of 10, #a-j 7.50 7.50

Pope Benedict XVI — A259

2005, Nov. 21 *Perf. 13¾x13½*
844 A259 80c multi 1.60 1.60

Printed in sheets of 4.

Christmas — A260

Paintings: 37c, Madonna and Child, by Daniel Seghers. 60c, Madonna and Child, by Raphael. 80c, The Rest on the Flight to Egypt, by Gerard David. $1, Granducci Madonna, by Raphael.
$2, Madonna and Child, by Bartolome Esteban Murillo.

2005, Dec. 21 *Perf. 14*
845-848 A260 Set of 4 5.75 5.75

Souvenir Sheet
849 A260 $2 multi 4.00 4.00

New Year 2006 (Year of the Dog) A261

2006, Jan. 3 *Perf. 13¼*
850 A261 50c multi 1.00 1.00

Printed in sheets of 4.

Birds A262

Designs: 24c, Black oystercatcher. 39c, Great blue heron, vert.

2006, Feb. 21 **Litho.** *Perf. 12*
851 A262 24c multi .50 .50
852 A262 39c multi .80 .80

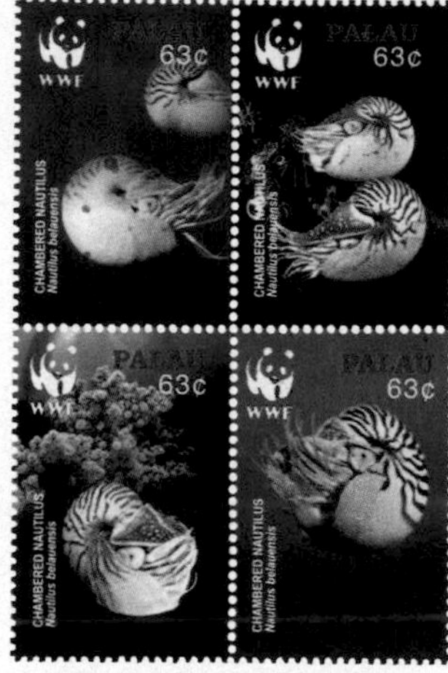

Worldwide Fund for Nature (WWF) — A263

No. 853 — Chambered nautilus: a, Two facing right. b, Two facing left. c, One, near coral. d, One, no coral.

2006, Feb. 21 *Perf. 12¾*
853 A263 63c Block of 4, #a-d 5.25 5.25
e. Sheet, 2 each #853a-853d 10.50 10.50

World of Sea and Reef Type of 1986 Redrawn
Miniature Sheet

No. 854: a, Spear fisherman. b, Native raft. c, Sailing canoes. d, Rock islands, sailfish. e, Inter-island boat, flying fish. f, Bonefish. g, Common jack. h, Mackerel. i, Sailfish. j, Barracuda. k, Triggerfish. l, Dolphinfish. m, Spear fisherman, grouper. n, Manta ray. o, Marlin. p, Parrotfish. q, Wrasse. r, Red snapper. s, Herring. t, Dugong. u, Surgeonfish. v, Leopard ray. w, Hawksbill turtle. x, Needlefish. y, Tuna. z, Octopus. aa, Clownfish, ab, Squid. ac, Grouper. ad, Moorish idol. ae, Queen conch. af, Squirrelfish. ag, Starfish, sting ray. ah, Lionfish. ai, Angelfish. aj, Butterflyfish. ak, Spiny lobster. al, Mangrove crab, am, Tridacna. an, Moray eel.

2006, May 29 **Litho.** *Perf. 13*
854 Sheet of 40 14.50 14.50
a.-an. A19 18c Any single .35 .35

Washington 2006 World Philatelic Exhibition.

Souvenir Sheet

Wolfgang Amadeus Mozart (1756-91), Composer — A264

2006, June 23 *Perf. 12¾*
855 A264 $2 multi 4.00 4.00

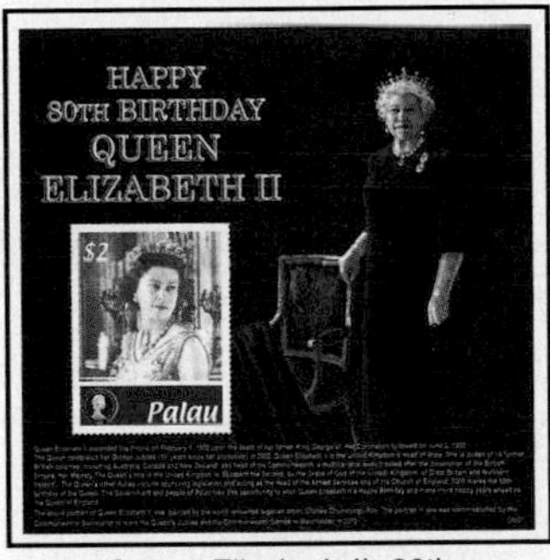

Queen Elizabeth II, 80th Birthday — A265

No. 856 — Queen wearing crown or tiara with background color of: a, Tan. b, Red. c, Blue. d, Lilac.
$2, Sepia photograph.

2006, June 23 ***Perf. 14¼***
856 A265 84c Sheet of 4, #a-d 6.75 6.75

Souvenir Sheet

857 A265 $2 multi 4.00 4.00

Rembrandt (1606-69), Painter — A266

No. 858: a, Old Man in a Fur Hat. b, Head of a Man. c, An Old Man in a Cap. d, Portrait of an Old Man.
$2, Saskia With a Veil.

2006, June 23 ***Perf. 13¼***
858 A266 $1 Sheet of 4, #a-d 8.00 8.00

Size: 70x100mm

Imperf

859 A266 $2 multi 4.00 4.00

No. 858 contains four 38x50mm stamps.

A267

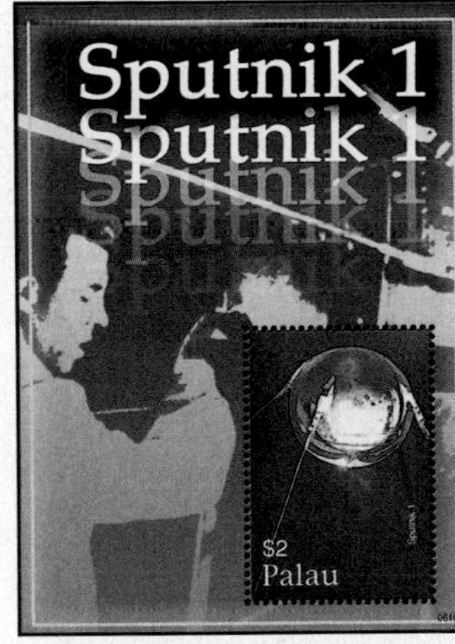

Space Achievements — A268

No. 860 — Inscription, "International Space Station": a, At left. b, At UR, in white. c, At LL. d, AT UR, in black.

No. 861, 75c — Viking 1: a, Viking orbiting Mars. b, Simulation of Viking on Mars. c, Viking probe. d, Solar panels. e, Picture from Viking on Mars, parts of spacecraft at right. f, Picture from Viking on Mars, large rock at right.

No. 862, 75c, vert. — First flight of Space Shuttle Columbia: a, Shuttle on launch pad. b, Half of shuttle, denomination at UL. c, Half of shuttle, denomination at UR. d, Mission emblem. e, Astronaut Robert Crippen. f, Commander John Young.

No. 863, $2, Sputnik 1. No. 864, $2, Apollo 11. No. 865, $2, Space Shuttle Columbia lifting off.

2006, July 10 ***Perf. 14¼***
860 A267 $1 Sheet of 4, #a-d 8.00 8.00

Sheets of 6, #a-f

861-862 A267 Set of 2 18.00 18.00

Souvenir Sheets

863-865 A268 Set of 3 12.00 12.00

Souvenir Sheet

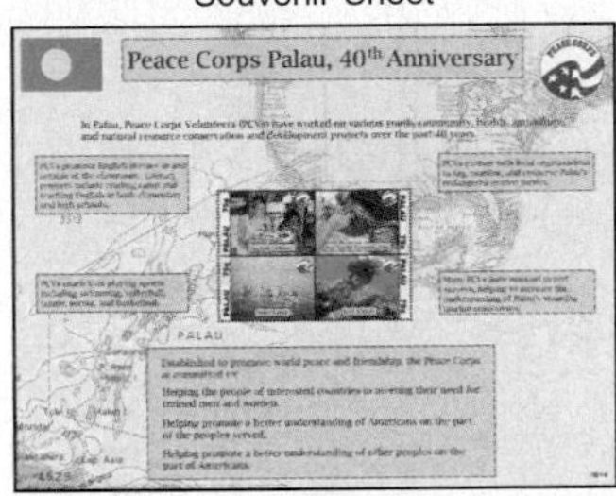

Peace Corps, 40th Anniv. — A269

No. 867: a, English literacy. b, Sea turtle conservation. c, Swim camp. d, Reef survey.

2006, Nov. 6 Litho. ***Perf. 14x14¾***
867 A269 75c Sheet of 4, #a-d 6.00 6.00

Concorde — A270

No. 868, 75c: a, Concorde over New York City. b, Concorde over London
No. 869, 75c: a, Wheel. b, Nose.

2006, Dec. 20 ***Perf. 13¼x13½***

Pairs, #a-b

868-869 A270 Set of 2 6.00 6.00

Souvenir Sheet

Christmas — A271

No. 870 — Tree ornaments: a, Soldier. b, Santa Claus. c, Elf holding gift. d, Mice in sleigh.

2006 ***Perf. 13¼***
870 A271 84c Sheet of 4, #a-d 6.75 6.75

New Year 2007 (Year of the Pig) — A272

2007, Jan. 3 Litho. ***Perf. 13¼***
871 A272 75c multi 1.50 1.50

Printed in sheets of 4.

Souvenir Sheet

Marilyn Monroe (1926-62), Actress — A273

Various drawings.

2007, Feb. 15
872 A273 84c Sheet of 4, #a-d 6.75 6.75

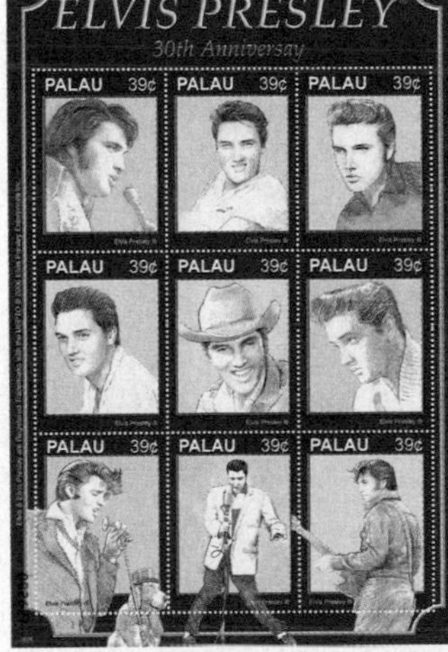

A274

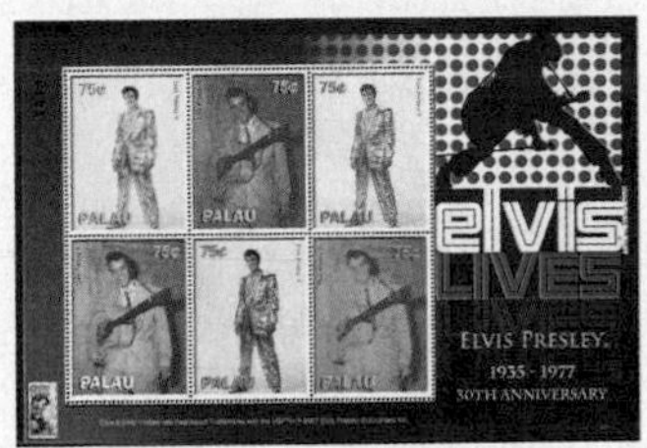

Elvis Presley (1935-77) — A275

No. 873 — Presley with: a, Microphone. b, Shirt with design on pocket. c, Dark shirt. d, White shirt. e, Hat. f, Sweater. g, Dog. h, Jacket and microphone. i, Guitar.

No. 874 — Presley with or without guitar and background color of: a, Yellow. b, Red violet. c, Pale green. d, Red. e, Pale blue. f, Orange.

2007, Feb. 15 ***Perf. 13¼***
873 A274 39c Sheet of 9, #a-i 7.25 7.25

Perf. 14¼

874 A275 75c Sheet of 6, #a-f 9.00 9.00

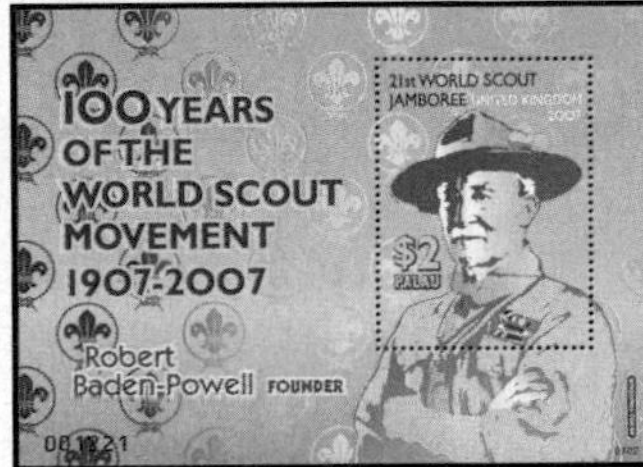

Scouting, Cent. — A276

No. 875, horiz. — Dove, Scouting flag, globe featuring Europe and frame color of: a, Purple. b, Bright pink. c, Green and blue.
$2, Lord Robert Baden-Powell.

2007, Feb. 15 ***Perf. 13¼***
875 A276 $1 Sheet of 3, #a-c 6.00 6.00

Souvenir Sheet

876 A276 $2 multi 4.00 4.00

Mushrooms — A277

No. 877, vert.: a, Entoloma hochstetteri. b, Aseroe rubra. c, Omphalotus nidiformis. d, Amanita sp.
$2, Aseroe rubra, diff.

2007, Feb. 15 ***Perf. 14¼x14***
877 A277 $1 Sheet of 4, #a-d 8.00 8.00

Souvenir Sheet

Perf. 14x14¼

878 A277 $2 multi 4.00 4.00

Helicopters, Cent. — A278

Designs: 10c, Bell 206B JetRanger III. 19c, McDonnell Douglas MD500D. 20c, McDonnell Douglas AH-64A Apache. 22c, Aérospatiale AS 332 Super Puma. 75c, Aérospatiale AS 355F-1 Twin Squirrel. 84c, MBB Eurocopter BO 105DBS/4. $1, Sikorsky MH-53J Pave Low III.
$2, Boeing Helicopters 234LR Chinook.

2007, Feb. 26 ***Perf. 14x14¼***
879-885 A278 Set of 7 6.75 6.75

Souvenir Sheet

886 A278 $2 multi 4.00 4.00

Souvenir Sheet

Triton Horn Shell — A279

2007, Mar. 1 ***Perf. 13¼***

887 A279 $2 multi 4.00 4.00

Miniature Sheets

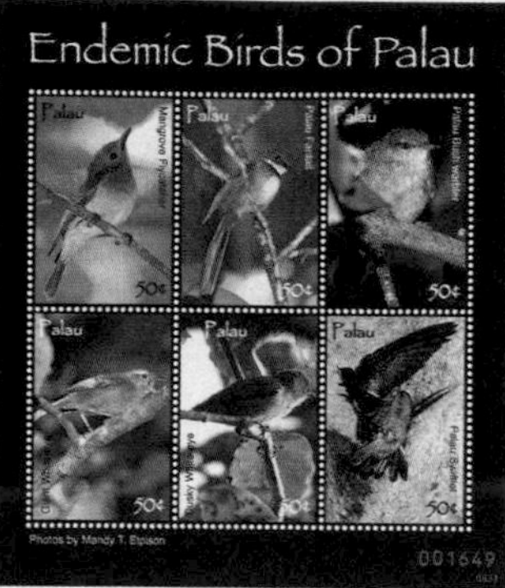

Birds — A280

No. 888, 50c: a, Mangrove flycatcher. b, Palau fantail. c, Palau bush warbler. d, Giant white-eye. e, Dusky white-eye. f, Palau swiftlet.

No. 889, 50c: a, Palau owl. b, Palau fruit dove. c, Palau ground dove. d, Morning bird. e, Palau megapode. f, Rusty-capped kingfisher.

2007, Mar. 1 **Litho.**

Sheets of 6, #a-f

888-889 A280 Set of 2 12.00 12.00

Wedding of Queen Elizabeth II and Prince Philip, 60th Anniv. A281

No. 890 — Photograph from: a, July 1947. b, November 1947.

2007, May 1

890 A281 60c Pair, #a-b 2.40 2.40

Printed in sheets containing three of each stamp.

Souvenir Sheet

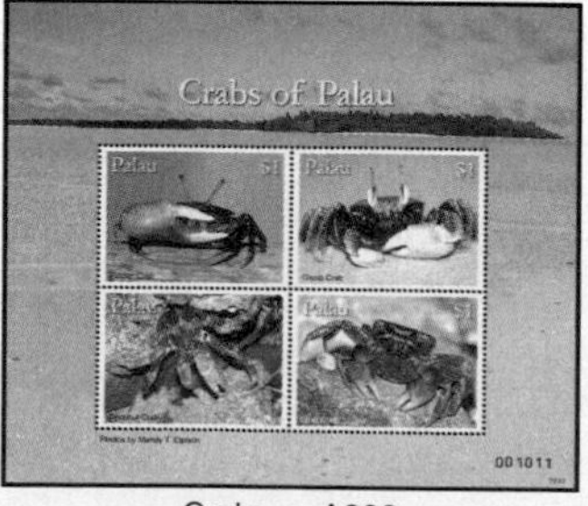

Crabs — A282

No. 891: a, Fiddler crab. b, Ghost crab. c, Coconut crab. d, Land crab.

2007, May 16

891 A282 $1 Sheet of 4, #a-d 8.00 8.00

Flowers — A283

No. 892: a, Plumeria. b, Streptosolen jamesonii. c, Heliconia pseudoaemygdiana. d, Mananita.
$2, Spider lily.

2007, May 16 ***Perf. 13¼***

892 A283 $1 Sheet of 4, #a-d 8.00 8.00

Souvenir Sheet

893 A283 $2 multi 4.00 4.00

Pope Benedict XVI — A284

2007, June 20

894 A284 41c multi .85 .85

Printed in sheets of 8.

Princess Diana (1961-97) — A285

No. 895 — Diana with: a, Earring at right, white dress. b, Choker. c, Earring at right. d, Earring at left, country name in white.
$2, Wearing veiled hat.

2007, June 20

895 A285 90c Sheet of 4, #a-d 7.25 7.25

Souvenir Sheet

896 A285 $2 multi 4.00 4.00

Butterflies — A286

Designs: 2c, Troides amphrysus. 3c, Paraeronia boebera. 4c, Delias catisa. 5c, Chilasa clytia. 11c, Ornithoptera goliath. 15c, Graphium delesserii. 20c, Euploea sp. 23c, Papilio euchenor. 26c, Ornithoptera tithonus. 41c, Hypolimnas misippus. 45c, Delias meeki. 50c, Papilio ulysses autolycus. 75c, Ornithoptera croesus. 90c, Trogonoptera brookiana. $1, Idea lynceus. $2, Parantica weiskei. $3, Graphium weiskei. $4, Ornithoptera goliath titan. $5, Attacus lorquini. $10, Delias henningia voconia.

2007, July 5 ***Perf. 12½x13½***

897	A286	2c multi	.25	.25
898	A286	3c multi	.25	.25
899	A286	4c multi	.25	.25
900	A286	5c multi	.25	.25
901	A286	11c multi	.25	.25
902	A286	15c multi	.30	.30
903	A286	20c multi	.40	.40
904	A286	23c multi	.50	.50
905	A286	26c multi	.55	.55
906	A286	41c multi	.85	.85
907	A286	45c multi	.90	.90
908	A286	50c multi	1.00	1.00
909	A286	75c multi	1.50	1.50
910	A286	90c multi	1.90	1.90
911	A286	$1 multi	2.00	2.00
912	A286	$2 multi	4.00	4.00
913	A286	$3 multi	6.00	6.00
914	A286	$4 multi	8.00	8.00
915	A286	$5 multi	10.00	10.00
916	A286	$10 multi	20.00	20.00
		Nos. 897-916 (20)	59.15	59.15

Miniature Sheet

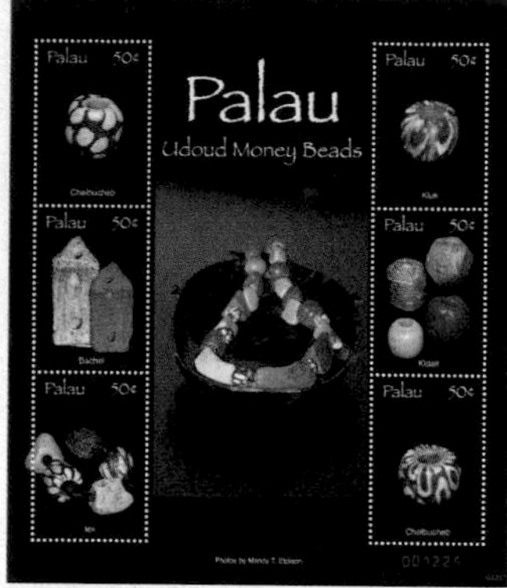

Udoud Money Beads — A287

No. 917: a, Black and white Chelbucheb. b, Kluk. c, Bachel. d, Kldait. e, lek. f, Green and white Chelbucheb.

2007, Mar. 1 **Litho.** ***Perf. 13¼***

917 A287 50c Sheet of 6, #a-f 6.00 6.00

Miniature Sheet

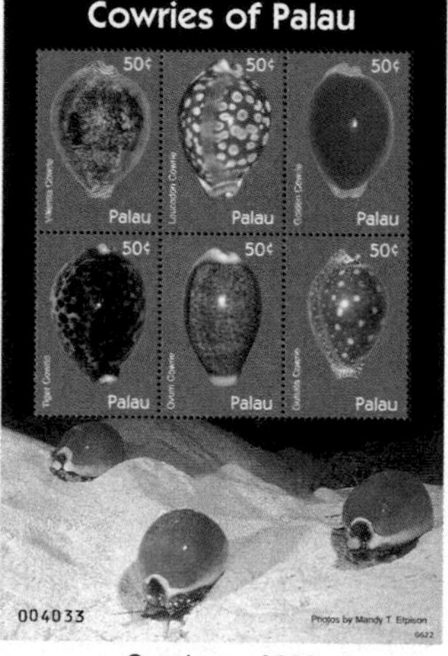

Cowries — A288

No. 918: a, Valentia cowrie. b, Leucodon cowrie. c, Golden cowrie. d, Tiger cowrie. e, Ovum cowrie. f, Guttata cowrie.

2007, Mar. 1

918 A288 50c Sheet of 6, #a-f 6.00 6.00

Miniature Sheet

Children and Wildlife — A289

No. 919: a, Praying mantis. b, Boy holding lobster. c, Boy holding bat. d, Dolphins.

2007, Mar. 1

919 A289 75c Sheet of 4, #a-d, + 4 labels 6.00 6.00

Birds of Southeast Asia — A290

No. 920: a, Red-billed leiothrix. b, Unidentified bird. c, Wahne's parotia. d, White-bellied yuhina.
$2, Wilson's bird-of-paradise.

2007, May 16

920 A290 80c Sheet of 4, #a-d 6.50 6.50

Souvenir Sheet

921 A290 $2 multi 4.00 4.00

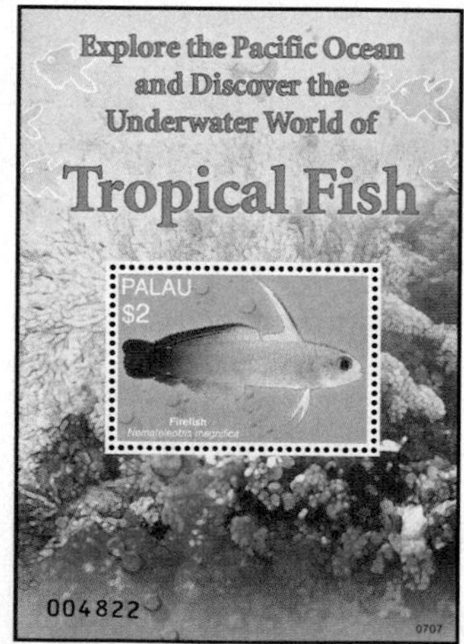

Tropical Fish — A291

No. 922: a, Boxfish. b, Copperband butterflyfish. c, Long-nosed hawkfish. d, Emperor angelfish.
$2, Firefish.

2007, May 16

922 A291 80c Sheet of 4, #a-d 6.50 6.50

Souvenir Sheet

923 A291 $2 multi 4.00 4.00

Miniature Sheet

Intl. Holocaust Remembrance Day — A292

No. 924 — United Nations diplomats and delegates: a, Eduardo J. Sevilla Somoza, Nicaragua. b, Aminu Bashir Wali, Nigeria. c, Stuart Beck, Palau. d, Ricardo Alberto Arias, Panama. e, Robert G. Aisi, Papua New Guinea. f, Eladio Loizaga, Paraguay. g, Jorge Voto-Bernales, Peru. h, Ban-Ki Moon, United Nations Secretary General.

2007, Nov. 20
924 A292 50c Sheet of 8, #a-h 8.00 8.00

Christmas A293

Color of ornament: 22c, Red. 26c, Green. 41c, Blue. 90c, Yellow brown.

2007, Nov. 20 Litho. *Perf. 12*
925-928 A293 Set of 4 3.75 3.75

32nd America's Cup Yacht Races A294

Various yachts.

2007, Dec. 13 *Perf. 13¼*

929	Strip of 4	8.50 8.50
a.	A294 26c multi	.50 .50
b.	A294 80c multi	1.60 1.60
c.	A294 $1.14 multi	2.40 2.40
d.	A294 $2 multi	4.00 4.00

New Year 2008 (Year of the Rat) — A295

2008, Jan. 2 *Perf. 12*
930 A295 50c multi 1.00 1.00

Printed in sheets of 4.

Miniature Sheet

Pres. John F. Kennedy (1917-63) — A296

No. 931: a, Crowd, Kennedy campaign poster. b, Kennedy shaking hands with crowd. c, Kennedy at lectern. d, Kennedy behind microphones, with hands showing.

2008, Jan. 2 *Perf. 14¼*
931 A296 90c Sheet of 4, #a-d 7.25 7.25

2008 Summer Olympics, Beijing — A297

No. 932 — Items and athletes from 1908 London Olympics: a, Fencing poster. b, Program cover. c, Wyndham Halswelle, track gold medalist. d, Dorando Pietri, marathon runner.

2008, Jan. 8
932 A297 50c Sheet of 4, #a-d 4.00 4.00

Taiwan Tourist Attractions — A298

No. 933: a, National Taiwan Democracy Memorial Hall. b, Chinese ornamental garden, Taipei. c, Taipei skyline. d, Eastern coast of Taiwan.
$2, Illuminated temple, Southern Taiwan.

2008, Apr. 11 *Perf. 11½*
933 A298 50c Sheet of 4, #a-d 4.00 4.00

Souvenir Sheet
Perf. 13¼

934 A298 $2 multi 4.00 4.00

2008 Taipei Intl. Stamp Exhibition. No. 933 contains four 40x30mm stamps.

2008 World Stamp Championships, Israel — A299

2008, May 14 *Imperf.*
935 A299 $3 multi 6.00 6.00

Miniature Sheet

Sir Edmund Hillary (1919-2008), Mountaineer — A300

No. 936: a, Hillary and Prince Charles. b, Hillary. c, Hillary and Nepal Prime Minister Lokendra Bahadur Chand. d, Hillary with bird on shoulder.

2008, May 28 *Perf. 13¼*
936 A300 90c Sheet of 4, #a-d 7.25 7.25

Miniature Sheet

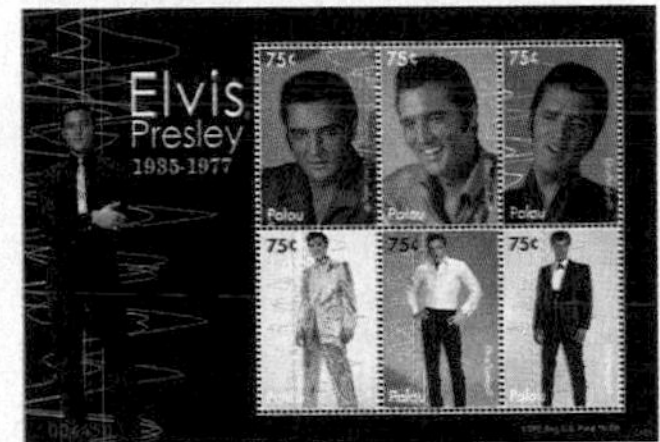

Elvis Presley (1935-77) — A301

No. 301 — Presley wearing: a, Gray shirt. b, Green shirt. c, Red shirt. d, Gold suit. e, White shirt, no jacket. f, White shirt, black suit.

2008, June 12
937 A301 75c Sheet of 6, #a-f 9.00 9.00

Miniature Sheet

Visit to United States of Pope Benedict XVI — A302

No. 938 — Pope Benedict XVI and US flag faintly in background: a, Part of flag star on Pope's head (no frame line above denomination). b, Red stripe under "au" of "Palau." c, Red stripe under "P" of Palau. d, Red stripe under entire country name.

2008, July 28
938 A302 90c Sheet of 4, #a-d 7.25 7.25

Miniature Sheets

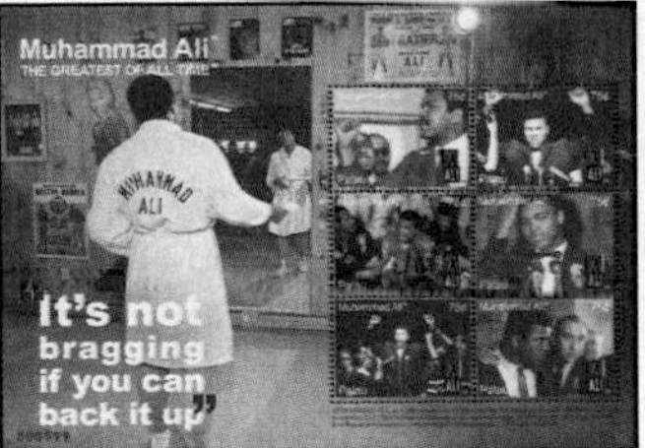

Muhammad Ali, Boxer — A303

No. 939 — Ali: a, In suit, clenching fist. b, Behind microphones, with both arms raised, with hands around his right forearm. c, Behind microphones, with towel around neck. d, Behind microphones, scratching head. e, Behind microphones, raising arms, with crowd. f, With hand of Howard Cosell on shoulder.

No. 940 — Ali: a, Pointing up, wearing short-sleeved shirt. b, Pointing to left, wearing suit. c, Making fist, in robe. d, Pointing to right, wearing suit.

2008, Sept. 22 *Perf. 11½x12*
939 A303 75c Sheet of 6, #a-f 9.00 9.00

Perf. 13¼

940 A303 94c Sheet of 4, #a-d 7.50 7.50

No. 940 contains four 50x37mm stamps.

Miniature Sheets

Space Exploration, 50th Anniv. (in 2007) — A304

No. 941, 75c — Mir Space Station: a, With black background. b, With Earth at bottom. c, Technical drawing. d, Above clouds. e, With Space Shuttle Atlantis. f, Against starry background.

No. 942, 75c: a, Pres. John F. Kennedy. b, Apollo 11 Command Module. c, Apollo 11 Lunar Module, Earth and Moon. d, Lunar Module and Moon. e, Kennedy, Astronaut John Glenn and Friendship 7 capsule. f, Edwin "Buzz" Aldrin on Moon.

No. 943, 94c: a, Technical drawing of R-7 launch vehicle. b, Sputnik 1, antennae at right. c, Technical drawing of Sputnik 1. d, Sputnik 1, antennae at left.

No. 944, 94c: a, Yuri Gagarin, first man in space, wearing medals. b, Technical drawing of Vostok rocket. c, Technical drawing of Vostok 1. d, Gagarin in space helmet.

2008, Sept. 22 *Perf. 13¼*

Sheets of 6, #a-f

941-942 A304 Set of 2 18.00 18.00

Sheets of 4, #a-d

943-944 A304 Set of 2 15.00 15.00

Miniature Sheets

Star Trek The Next Generation — A305

No. 945: a, Capt. Jean-Luc Picard. b, Lt. Commander Data. c, Commander William T. Riker. d, Counselor Deanna Troi. e, Lt. Commander Geordi La Forge. f, Lieutenant Worf.

No. 946: a, Wesley Crusher. b, Worf. c, Picard. d, Dr. Beverly Crusher.

2008, Dec. 4 ***Perf. 11½***

945 A305 75c Sheet of 6, #a-f 9.00 9.00

Perf. 13¼

946 A305 94c Sheet of 4, #a-d 7.50 7.50

No. 946 contains four 37x50mm stamps.

Christmas A306

Designs: 22c, Angel holding candle. 26c, Angel with violin. 42c, Angel and conifer wreath. 94c, Angel in light display.

2008, Dec. 11 Litho. ***Perf. 14x14¾***

947-950 A306 Set of 4 3.75 3.75

Inauguration of US Pres. Barack Obama — A307

No. 951, horiz. — Pres. Obama: a, Holding microphone. b, Smiling, denomination at LL. c, Smiling, denomination at UL. d, With index finger raised.

$2, Head of Pres. Obama.

2009, Jan. 20 ***Perf. 11½x11¼***

951 A307 94c Sheet of 4, #a-d 7.75 7.75

Souvenir Sheet

952 A307 $2 multi 4.00 4.00

No. 951 contains four 40x30mm stamps.

New Year 2009 (Year of the Ox) — A308

No. 953 — Ox and Chinese characters in diamond in: a, Black. b, White.

2009, Jan. 26 ***Perf. 12***

953 A308 94c Horiz. pair, #a-b 4.00 4.00

Printed in sheets containing two pairs.

Miniature Sheet

Teenage Mutant Ninja Turtles, 25th Anniv. — A309

No. 954: a, Donatello. b, Raphael. c, Michelangelo. d, Leonardo.

2009, Feb. 25 ***Perf. 13¼***

954 A309 94c Sheet of 4, #a-d 7.75 7.75

Miniature Sheets

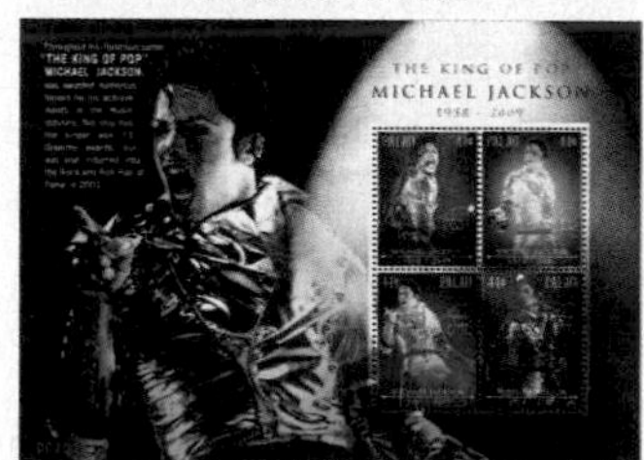

A310

Michael Jackson (1958-2009), Singer — A311

No. 955 — Background color: a, Red (Jackson with mouth open). b, Green. c, Blue. d, Red (Jackson with mouth closed).

No. 956 — Jackson dancing with denomination at: a, 28c, Right. b, 28c, Left. c, 75c, Right. d, 75c, Left.

2009, Sept. 3 ***Perf. 12x11½***

955 A310 44c Sheet of 4, #a-d 3.75 3.75

956 A311 Sheet of 4, #a-d 4.25 4.25

Miniature Sheet

Palau Pacific Resort, 25th Anniv. — A312

No. 957: a, Four beach umbrellas, shadow of palm trees. b, Palm trees near beach under cloudy skies. c, Resort at night. d, Lounge chairs on beach. e, Swimming pool. f, Palm tree, two beach umbrellas.

2009, Oct. 5 ***Perf. 11½***

957 A312 26c Sheet of 6, #a-f 3.25 3.25

Dolphins A313

Designs: 28c, Spinner dolphin. 44c, Hourglass dolphin. 98c, Costero. $1.05, Risso's dolphin.

No. 962: a, Heaviside's dolphin. b, Chilean dolphin. c, Dusky dolphin. d, Commerson's dolphin. e, Fraser's dolphin. f, Striped dolphin.

2009, Oct. 13 ***Perf. 14¾x14***

958-961 A313 Set of 4 5.50 5.50

962 A313 75c Sheet of 6, #a-f 9.00 9.00

Shells A314

Designs: 28c, Morula musiva. 44c, Littoraria articulata. 98c, Architectonica perdix. $1.05, Scalptia crossei.

No. 967: a, Pugilina cochlidium. b, Epitonium scalare. c, Ellobium tornatelliforme. d, Polinices sebae. e, Cyclophorus siamensis. f, Acrosterigma maculosum.

2009, Oct. 13

963-966 A314 Set of 4 5.50 5.50

967 A314 75c Sheet of 6, #a-f 9.00 9.00

A315

Cats — A316

No. 968: a, Devon Rex cream lynx point sirex. b, Ocicat chocolate. c, Asian chocolate smoke. d, Burmilla lilac shaded. e, Egyptian Mau bronze. f, Himalayan blue tortie point.

No. 969: a, Turkish Van and fireplace. b, Tiffany. c, Turkish Van, diff. d, Birman seal lynx point.

No. 970, $2, Golden Persian. No. 971, $2, Red silver tabby.

2009, Oct. 13 ***Perf. 14***

968 A315 75c Sheet of 6, #a-f 9.00 9.00

969 A315 94c Sheet of 4, #a-d 7.75 7.75

Souvenir Sheets

970-971 A316 Set of 2 8.00 8.00

Miniature Sheet

Fish — A317

No. 972: a, Two-spot snappers. b, Goggle-eye. c, Bluestreak cardinalfish. d, Bluefin trevally. e, Rainbow runners. f, Fire goby.

2009, Oct. 13 ***Perf. 11½x11¼***

972 A317 75c Sheet of 6, #a-f 9.00 9.00

Miniature Sheet

Pres. Abraham Lincoln (1809-65) — A318

No. 973 — Photographs of Lincoln: a, Hands showing, denomination in white. b, Hands not showing, denomination in white. c, Hands not showing, denomination in black. d, Hand showing, denomination in black.

2009, Oct. 13 ***Perf. 11¼x11½***

973 A318 44c Sheet of 4, #a-d 3.75 3.75

Souvenir Sheet

Visit of Pope Benedict XVI to Yad Vashem Holocaust Memorial, Israel — A319

No. 974 — Pope Benedict XVI: a, 98c, Looking at flame (30x40mm). b, $2, Praying in front of flowers (60x40mm).

2009, Oct. 13

974 A319 Sheet of 3, #974b, 2 #974a 8.00 8.00

Souvenir Sheets

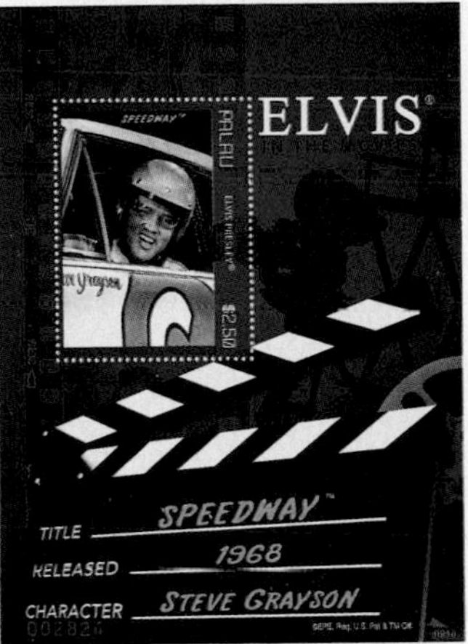

A320

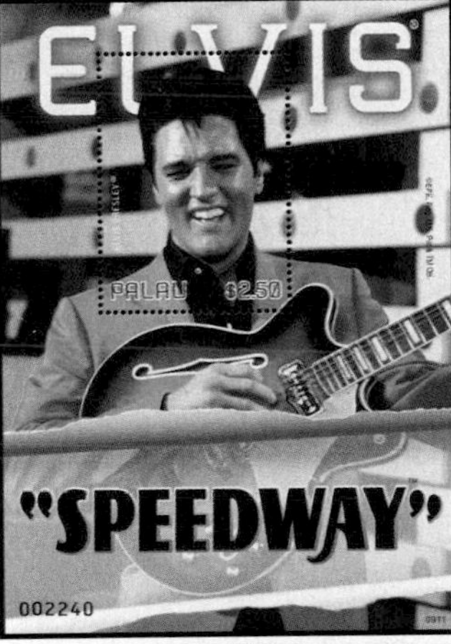

A321

A322

Elvis Presley (1935-77) — A323

2009, Oct. 13 *Perf. 13¼*

975 A320 $2.50 multi	5.00	5.00
976 A321 $2.50 multi	5.00	5.00
977 A322 $2.50 multi	5.00	5.00
978 A323 $2.50 multi	5.00	5.00
Nos. 975-978 (4)	20.00	20.00

A324

Fish — A325

Designs: 1c, Giant trevally. 2c, Pink anemonefish. 3c, Gray reef shark. 4c, Leaf fish. 5c, Scissor-tailed fusiliers. 26c, Helfrich's dartfish. 44c, Bigscale soldierfish. $1, Peach anthias. $2, Spotted eagle ray. $3, African pompano. $4, Harlequin grouper. $5, Pyramid butterflyfish. $10, Longnose hawkfish.

2009, Oct. 13 **Litho.** *Perf. 11¾x12¼*

979 A324 1c multi	.25	.25
980 A324 2c multi	.25	.25
981 A324 3c multi	.25	.25
982 A324 4c multi	.25	.25
983 A324 5c multi	.25	.25
984 A325 26c multi	.55	.55
985 A324 44c multi	.90	.90
986 A324 $1 multi	2.00	2.00
987 A324 $2 multi	4.00	4.00
988 A324 $3 multi	6.00	6.00
989 A324 $4 multi	8.00	8.00
990 A324 $5 multi	10.00	10.00
991 A324 $10 multi	20.00	20.00
Nos. 979-991 (13)	52.70	52.70

Worldwide Fund for Nature (WWF) — A326

No. 992 — Red lionfish: a, Two fish. b, One fish facing forward, brown background. c, One fish facing right. d, One fish facing forward, blue background.

2009, Nov. 9 **Litho.** *Perf. 13¼*

992 A326 53c Block of 4, #a-d	4.25	4.25
a. Sheet of 8, 2 each #992a-992d	8.50	8.50

Miniature Sheet

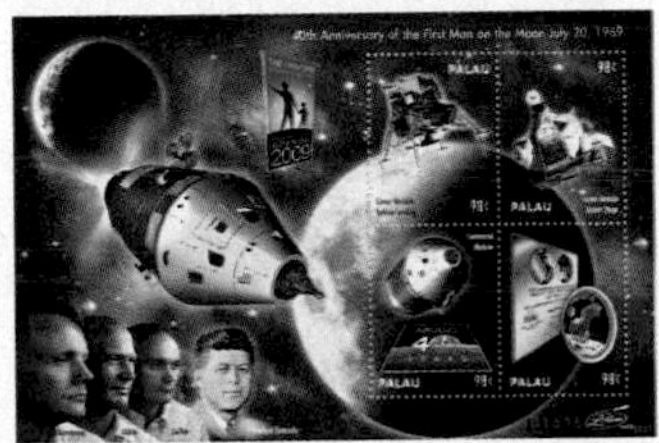

First Man on the Moon, 40th Anniv. — A327

No. 993: a, Lunar Module before landing. b, Lunar Module ascent stage. c, Command module. d, Mission patch and plaque left on Moon.

2009, Dec. 10 *Perf. 12x11½*

993 A327 98c Sheet of 4, #a-d 8.00 8.00

Intl. Year of Astronomy.

Christmas A328

Designs: 26c, Christmas ornaments and stocking on coral. 44c, Wreath and "Merry Christmas." 98c, Gingerbread house with flag of Palau. $2, Wreath and bell.

2009, Dec. 10 *Perf. 14¼x14¾*

994-997 A328 Set of 4 7.50 7.50

Miniature Sheet

Charles Darwin (1809-82), Naturalist — A329

No. 998: a, HMS Beagle. b, Captain Robert Fitzroy. c, Sextant of HMS Beagle. d, Diagram of HMS Beagle. e, Darwin. f, Darwin's report on the zoology of the voyage of the HMS Beagle.

2010, Mar. 2 *Perf. 13¼*

998 A329 75c Sheet of 6, #a-f 9.00 9.00

Reptiles and Amphibians — A330

Designs: 26c, Bufo marinus. 44c, Chelonia mydas. 98c, Lepidodactylus lugubris. $1.05, Varanus olivaceus.

No. 1003: a, Northern forest dragon. b, Common house gecko. c, Hawksbill turtle. d, Indopacific tree gecko. e, Amboina box turtle. f, Flying dragon.

2010, Mar. 2 *Perf. 12*

999-1002 A330 Set of 4	5.50	5.50
1003 A330 75c Sheet of 6, #a-f	9.00	9.00

Pope John Paul II (1920-2005) A331

2010, Apr. 22 *Perf. 12x11½*

1004 A331 75c multi 1.50 1.50

Printed in sheets of 4. Compare with type A451.

Miniature Sheet

Pres. Abraham Lincoln (1809-65) — A332

No. 1005 — Lincoln: a, Without beard. b, With beard, no cowlick on forehead. c, With beard, cowlick on forehead, point of shirt above "M." d, With beard, cowlick on forehead, point of shirt above "LIN."

2010, Apr. 22 *Perf. 11½*

1005 A332 75c Sheet of 4, #a-d 6.00 6.00

Miniature Sheet

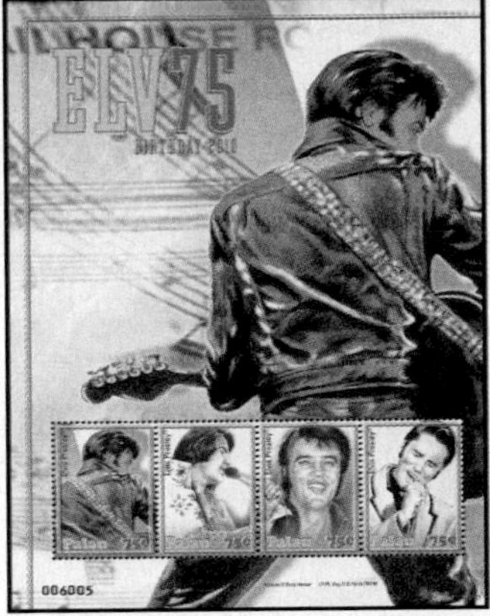

Elvis Presley (1935-77) — A333

No. 1005 — Presley: a, Facing backwards. b, Wearing sequined suit. c, With hand and microphone cord at left. d, Wearing suit with bordered lapels.

2010, Apr. 22 *Perf. 11½*

1006 A333 75c Sheet of 4, #a-d 6.00 6.00

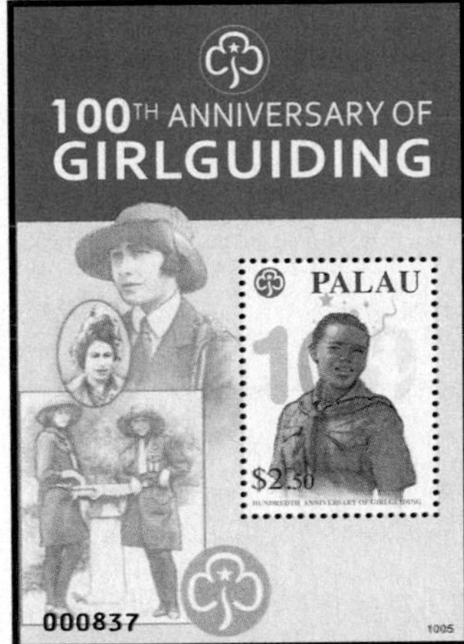

Girl Guides, Cent. — A334

No. 1007, horiz.: a, Two Girl Guides in blue uniforms. b, Two Girl Guides, one wearing cap. c, Girl Guide playing bongo drum. d, Four Girl Guides.

$2.50, Girl Guide in green uniform.

2010, June 9 *Perf. 11½x12*

1007 A334 94c Sheet of 4, #a-d 7.75 7.75

Souvenir Sheet

Perf. 11½

1008 A334 $2.50 multi 5.00 5.00

Souvenir Sheet

Governmental Buildings — A335

No. 1009: a, Executive Building. b, OEK Congress. c, Judiciary Building.

2010, July 1 *Perf. 13½*

1009 A335 $1 Sheet of 3, #a-c 6.00 6.00

Princess Diana (1961-97) — A336

No. 1010 — Princess Diana wearing: a, Tiara. b, Blue violet gown.

2010, Sept. 8 ***Perf. 12x11½***
1010 A336 75c Pair, #a-b 3.00 3.00

Printed in sheets containing two pairs.

Miniature Sheet

Mother Teresa (1910-97), Humanitarian — A337

No. 1011 — Mother Teresa and: a, Blue sky behind name and country name. b, Blue sky behind country name, cloud behind name. c, Cloud behind country name, blue sky partly behind name. d, Blue sky partly behind country name, cloud behind name.

2010, Sept. 8 ***Perf. 11½***
1011 A337 94c Sheet of 4, #a-d 7.75 7.75

Henri Dunant (1828-1910), Founder of Red Cross — A338

No. 1012 Dunant and: a, Frédèric Passy. b, Czar Nicholas II, c, Henri Dufour. d, Bertha von Suttner.
$2.50, Obverse and reverse of Nobel medal.

2010, Sept. 8 ***Perf. 11½x12***
1012 A338 94c Sheet of 4, #a-d 7.75 7.75

Souvenir Sheet
Perf. 11½

1013 A338 $2.50 multi 5.00 5.00

Paintings by Sandro Botticelli (1445-1510) — A339

No. 1014, vert.: a, Madonna and Child. b, Nastagio Degli Onesti. c, Calumny of Apelles. d, Primavera.
$2.50, Orazione Nell'Orto.

2010, Sept. 8 ***Perf. 12x11½***
1014 A339 94c Sheet of 4, #a-d 7.75 7.75

Souvenir Sheet
Perf. 11½

1015 A339 $2.50 multi 5.00 5.00

Souvenir Sheet

Issuance of the Penny Black, 170th Anniv. — A340

No. 1016: a, Penny Black (Great Britain #1). b, Palau #2.

2010, Sept. 8 ***Perf. 13¼***
1016 A340 $2 Sheet of 2, #a-b 8.00 8.00

Christmas A341

Paintings: 26c, Adoration of the Magi, by Leonardo da Vinci. 44c, Adoration of the Shepherds, by Carlo Crivelli. 98c, Adoration of the Magi, by Hieronymus Bosch. $2, Adoration of the Magi, by Albrecht Altdorfer.

2010, Sept. 8 ***Perf. 11½***
1017-1020 A341 Set of 4 7.50 7.50

Miniature Sheets

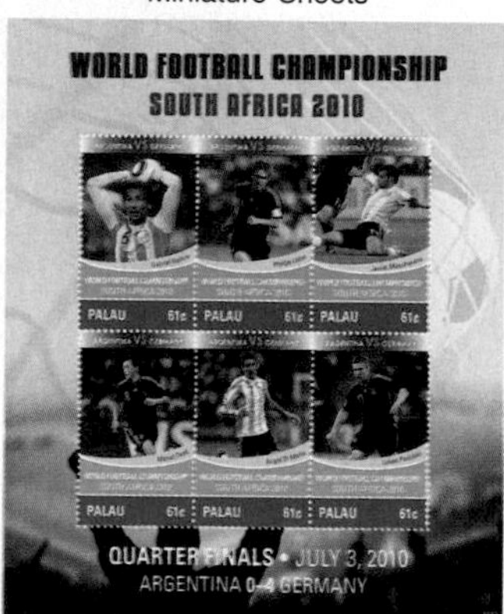

2010 World Cup Soccer Championships, South Africa — A342

No. 1021, 61c: a, Gabriel Heinze. b, Philipp Lahm. c, Javier Mascherano. d, Mesut Dezil. e, Angel Di Maria. f, Lukas Podolski.
No. 1022, 61c: a, Antolin Alcaraz. b, Cesc Fabregas. c, Dario Veron. d, Carlos Puyol. e, Victor Caceres. f, Xabi Alonso.

2010, Dec. 16 ***Perf. 12***
Sheets of 6, #a-f
1021-1022 A342 Set of 2 15.00 15.00

Paintings by Michelangelo Merisi da Caravaggio (1571-1610) — A343

No. 1023.: a, Supper at Emmaus. b, Ecce Homo. c, Omnia Vincit Amor. d, Flagellazione di Cristo.
$2.50, The Incredulity of Saint Thomas.

2010, Dec. 16 ***Perf. 12***
1023 A343 94c Sheet of 4, #a-d 7.75 7.75

Souvenir Sheet
Perf. 12½

1024 A343 $2.50 multi 5.00 5.00

No. 1023 contains four 40x30mm stamps.

Pope Benedict XVI A344

2010, Dec. 16 ***Perf. 12***
1025 A344 75c multi 1.50 1.50

Printed in sheets of 4 with slight color differences in the background.

Miniature Sheets

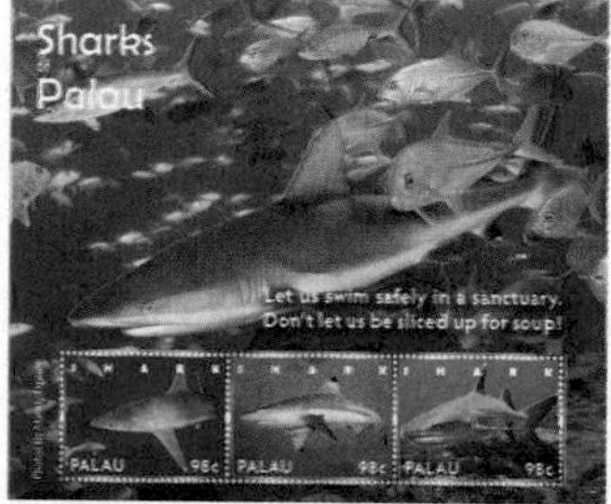

Sharks — A346

Sea Turtles — A347

Dugongs — A348

No. 1027 — Shark with dorsal fin: a, Touching "R" in "Shark." b, Between "A" and "R" in "Shark." c, Touching "A" in "Shark."
No. 1028 — Sea turtle: a, Swimming left. b, At ocean floor. c, Swimming right.
No. 1029: a, Dugong at water's surface. b, Two dugongs. c, Dugong and fish.

Perf. 13 Syncopated

2010, Dec. 21 **Litho.**

1027 A346 98c Sheet of 3, #a-c	6.00	6.00
1028 A347 98c Sheet of 3, #a-c	6.00	6.00
1029 A348 98c Sheet of 3, #a-c	6.00	6.00
Nos. 1027-1029 (3)	18.00	18.00

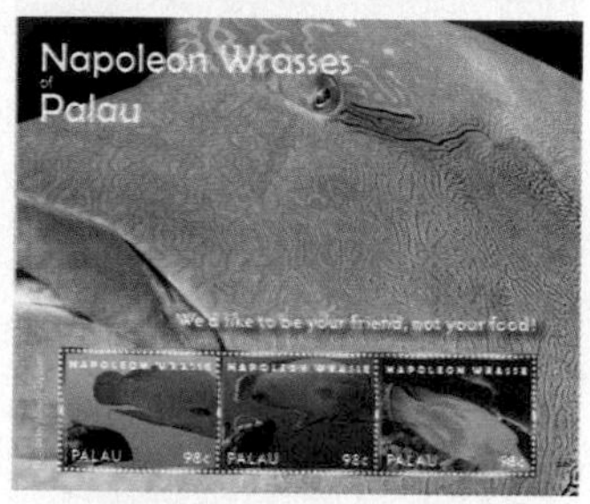

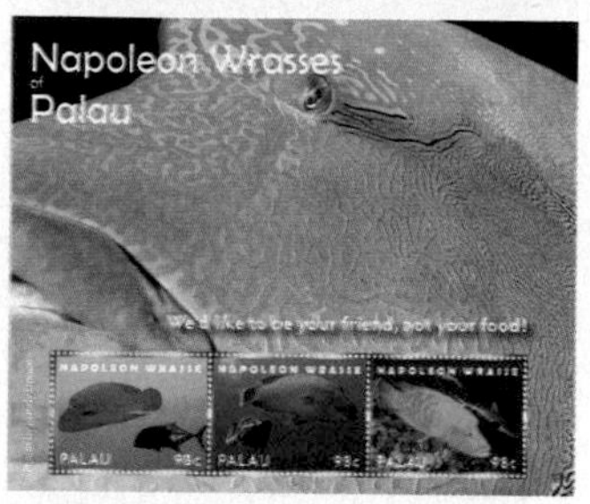

The top sheet, containing poorly cropped stamp images, was received by Palau postal officials but was never put on sale in Palau. The bottom sheet was sold by dealers, but was never received by Palau postal officials.

Miniature Sheet

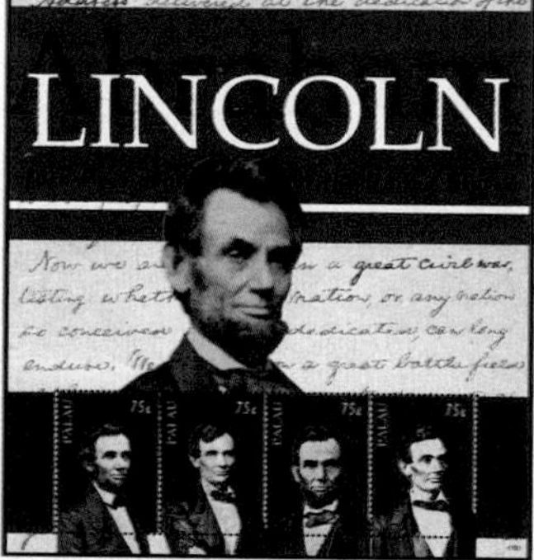

Pres. Abraham Lincoln (1809-65) — A349

Various photographs of Lincoln.

2011, Mar. 11 ***Perf. 12***
1030 A349 75c Sheet of 4, #a-d 6.00 6.00

Miniature Sheet

Inauguration of Pres. John F. Kennedy, 50th Anniv. — A350

No. 1031 — Kennedy: a, Behind microphone. b, At inauguration. c, In rocking chair. d, Shaking person's hand.

2011, Mar. 11
1031 A350 75c Sheet of 4, #a-d 6.00 6.00

Miniature Sheet

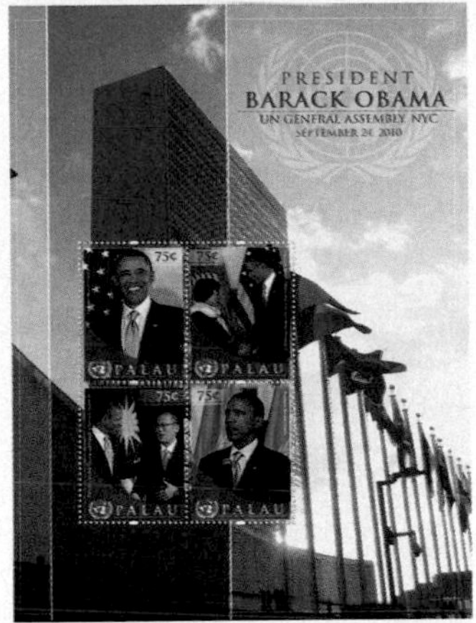

Pres. Barack Obama's Visit to the United Nations — A351

No. 1032 — Pres. Obama and: a, US flag. b, Kyrgyzstan Pres. Rosa Otunbaeva. c, Philippines Pres. Benigno Aquino III. d, United Nations flags.

2011, Mar. 11 ***Perf. 13 Syncopated***
1032 A351 75c Sheet of 4, #a-d 6.00 6.00

Indipex 2011 Intl. Philatelic Exhibition, New Delhi — A352

No. 1033: a, Bhagat Singh (1907-31), nationalist. b, Lal Bahadur Shastri (1904-66), Prime Minister. c, Subhas Chandra Bose (1897-1945), politician. d, Dr. Rajendra Prasad (1884-1963), politician. e, Jawaharlal Nehru (1889-1964), Prime Minister. f, Sardar Patel (1875-1950), Deputy Prime Minister.
$2.50, Mohandas K. Gandhi (1869-1948), independence leader.

2011, Mar. 11 ***Perf. 12***
1033 A352 50c Sheet of 6, #a-f 6.00 6.00

Souvenir Sheet
Perf. 13 Syncopated
1034 A352 $2.50 multi 5.00 5.00

Whales — A353

No. 1035: a, Blainville's beaked whale. b, Shepherd's beaked whale. c, Cuvier's beaked whale. d, Baird's beaked whale. e, Stejneger's beaked whale. f, Ginkgo-toothed beaked whale.
$2.50, Pygmy sperm whale.

2011, Mar. 11 ***Perf. 13 Syncopated***
1035 A353 75c Sheet of 6, #a-f 9.00 9.00

Souvenir Sheet
1036 A353 $2.50 multi 5.00 5.00

Visit to Spain of Pope Benedict XVI — A354

No. 1037: a, Pope Benedict XVI, Prince Felipe and Princess Letizia of Spain. b, Santiago de Compostela Cathedral. c, Pope Benedict XVI celebrating mass. d, King Juan Carlos and Queen Sofia of Spain.
$2.50, Pope Benedict XVI and Sagrada Familia Basilica, Barcelona, vert.

2011, Mar. 11 **Litho.**
1037 A354 94c Sheet of 4, #a-d 7.75 7.75

Souvenir Sheet
1038 A354 $2.50 multi 5.00 5.00

Miniature Sheet

Pres. Ronald Reagan (1911-2004) — A355

No. 1039: a, Pres. Reagan at podium. b, Pres. Reagan with wife, Nancy. c, Pres. Reagan. d, Pres. Reagan with Soviet Union General Secretary Mikhail Gorbachev.

2011, Apr. 5 ***Perf. 13 Syncopated***
1039 A355 98c Sheet of 4, #a-d 8.00 8.00

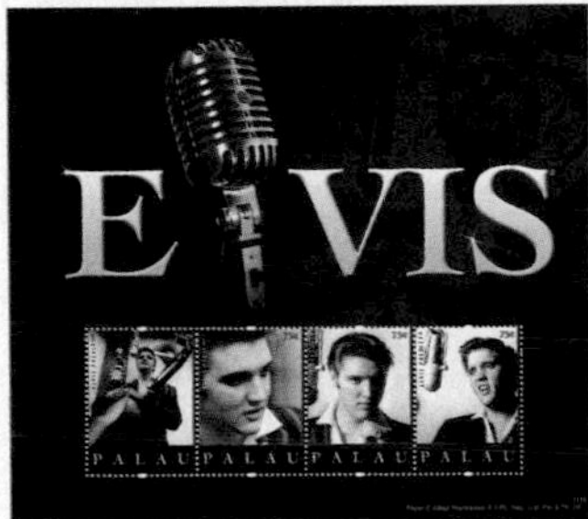

A356

A357

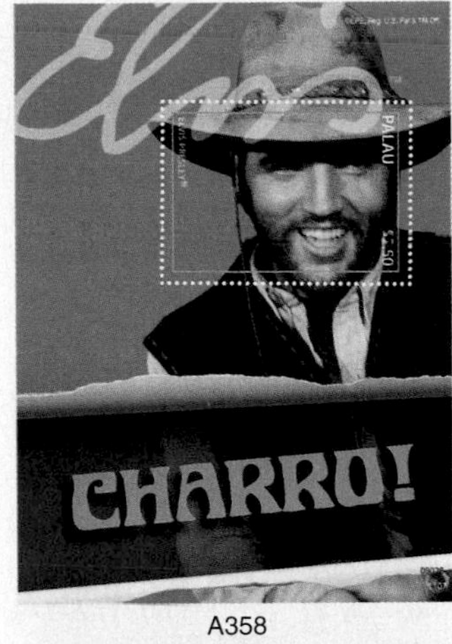

A358

A359

A360

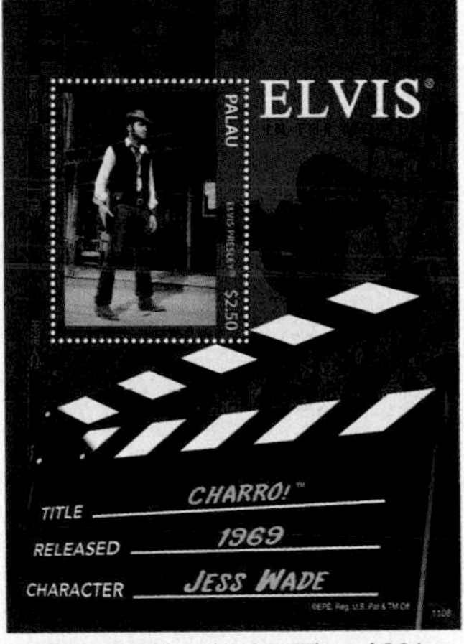

Elvis Presley (1935-77) — A361

No. 1040: a, Presley with guitar, two microphones. b, Presley facing right. c, Presley with closed mouth, microphone at left. d, Presley singing, microphone at left.
No. 1041 — Presley: a, With hand on ear. b, Microphone at left. c, Microphone at right, denomination in white. d, Microphone at right, denomination in black.

2011 ***Perf. 13 Syncopated***
1040 A356 75c Sheet of 4, #a-d 6.00 6.00
1041 A357 75c Sheet of 4, #a-d 6.00 6.00

Souvenir Sheets
Perf. 12¾
1042 A358 $2.50 multi 5.00 5.00
1043 A359 $2.50 multi 5.00 5.00
1044 A360 $2.50 multi 5.00 5.00
1045 A361 $2.50 multi 5.00 5.00
Nos. 1042-1045 (4) 20.00 20.00

Issued: Nos. 1040-1041, 7/14; Nos. 1042-1045, 4/5.

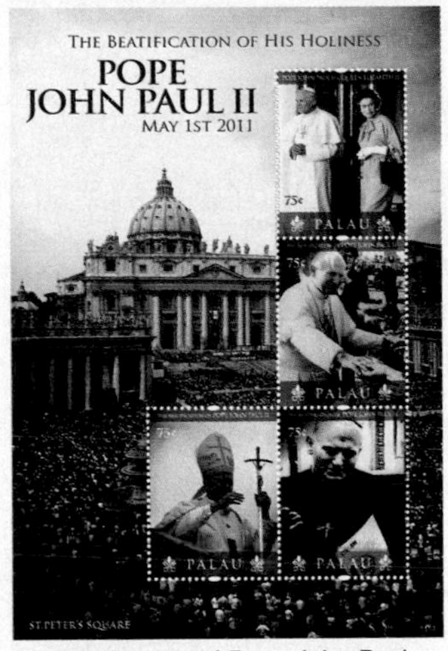

Beatification of Pope John Paul II — A362

No. 1046 — Pope John Paul II: a, With Queen Elizabeth II. b, Greeting crowd. c, Wearing miter. d, Holding paper.
$2.50, Wearing miter, priests in background.

2011, May 25 ***Perf. 13 Syncopated***
1046 A362 75c Sheet of 4, #a-d 6.00 6.00

Souvenir Sheet
Perf. 12¾
1047 A362 $2.50 multi 5.00 5.00

No. 1047 contains one 38x51mm stamp.

Wedding of Prince William and Catherine Middleton A363

Designs: 98c, Couple.
No. 1049, $2, Prince William. No. 1050, $2, Catherine Middleton.

2011, June 17 ***Perf. 12x12½***
1048 A363 98c multi 2.00 2.00

Souvenir Sheets
Perf. 13½
1049-1050 A363 Set of 2 8.00 8.00

Nos. 1049-1050 each contain one 51x32mm triangular stamp.

Miniature Sheets

A364

Princess Diana (1961-97) — A365

No. 1051 — Princess Diana wearing: a, Black lace dress and choker on black ribbon. b, White dress. c, Pink hat. d, Black dress, no choker.

No. 1052 — Princess Diana wearing: a, Earring. b, Plaid jacket. c, Red Cross uniform. d, Black hat with veil.

2011, July 6 ***Perf. 13 Syncopated***

1051 A364 75c Sheet of 4, #a-d 6.00 6.00
1052 A365 75c Sheet of 4, #a-d 6.00 6.00

Taro Festival — A366

No. 1053 — Taro plant and inscription: a, Dung er a terrekaki. b, Renged. c, Meuarch. d, Okelang. e, Metengal e ngas. f, Kirang. g, Rriu. h, Ngerbachel. i, Saikerei. j, Oiremech. k, Terebkul. l, Esuuch. m, Dungersuul. n, Ngesuas. o, Kerdeu. p, Terrekaki. q, Ngiroilang. r, Dilisior. s, Brak. t, Ulechem. u, Homusted. v, Besechel. w, Ungildil. x, Urungel. y, Ngatmadei. z, Dois. aa, Bsachel. ab, Ochab. ac, Kirang (redil). ad, Ngeruuch.

2011, July 8 ***Perf. 12¾x13***

1053 Sheet of 30 18.00 18.00
a.-ad. A366 29c Any single .60 .60

Souvenir Sheet

Haruo I. Remeliik (1933-85), First President of Palau — A367

2011, July 8 ***Perf. 13¼***

1054 A367 $2 multi 4.00 4.00

Birds — A368

No. 1055, 98c: a, Black-headed gull. b, Red-tailed tropicbird. c, Intermediate egret. d, Yellow bittern.

No., 1056, 98c, vert.: a, Cattle egret. b, Red-footed booby. c, Australian pelican. d, Little pied cormorant.

No. 1057, $2, Greater crested tern. No. 1058, $2, Brown noddy, vert.

2011, July 14 ***Perf. 13 Syncopated***

Sheets of 4, #a-d

1055-1056 A368 Set of 2 16.00 16.00

Souvenir Sheets

1057-1058 A368 Set of 2 8.00 8.00

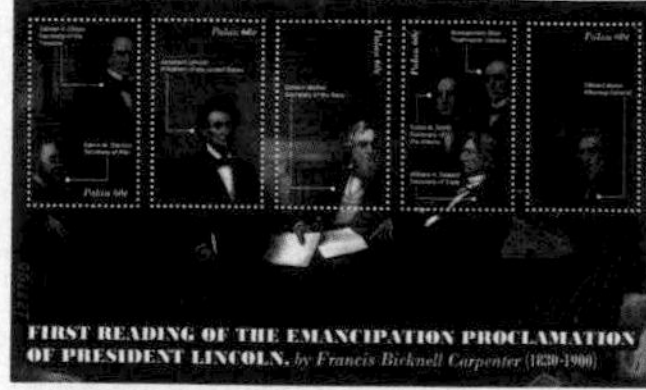

Pres. Abraham Lincoln (1809-65) — A369

No. 1059 — Details from First Reading of the Emancipation Proclamation of President Lincoln, by Francis Bicknell Carpenter: a, Treasury Secretary Salmon P. Chase, Secretary of War Edwin M. Stanton. b, Lincoln. c, Secretary of the Navy Gideon Welles. d, Postmaster General Montgomery Blair, Interior Secretary, Caleb B. Smith, Secretary of State William H. Seward. e, Attorney General Edward Bates.

$2.50, Photograph of Lincoln.

2011, July 27 ***Perf. 11½x11¾***

1059 A369 60c Sheet of 5, #a-d 6.00 6.00

Souvenir Sheet

Perf. 12x12½

1060 A369 $2.50 multi 5.00 5.00

No. 1060 contains one 30x80mm stamp.

Miniature Sheet

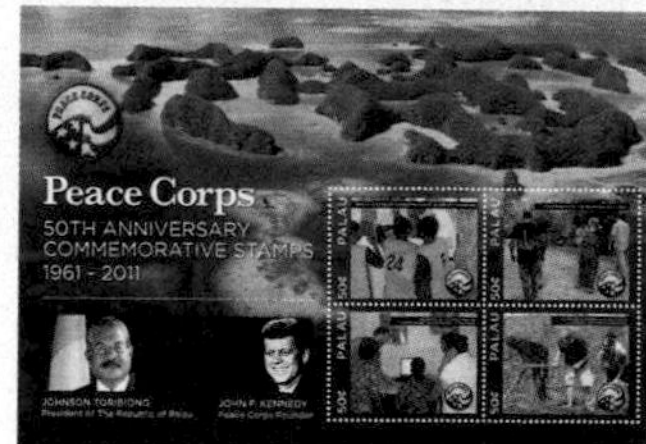

Peace Corps, 50th Anniv. — A370

No. 1061 — Peace Corps emblem and: a, Students and volunteer painting. b, Palauan host family and volunteers walking. c, Volunteer and teachers work on Internet project. d, Volunteers working in community garden.

2011, Aug. 2 ***Perf. 13x13¼***

1061 A370 50c Sheet of 4, #a-d 4.00 4.00

Sept. 11, 2001 Terrorist Attacks, 10th Anniv. — A371

No. 1062 — Firefighters, soldiers, U.S. flag and: a, Firefighter on rubble pile. b, Flags and flowers. c, Person looking at candlelight tribute. d, Tribute in light.

$2.50, World Trade Center and U.S flag.

2011, Sept. 11 ***Perf. 12***

1062 A371 75c Sheet of 4, #a-d 6.00 6.00

Souvenir Sheet

Perf. 12¾

1063 A371 $2.50 multi 5.00 5.00

No. 1063 contains one 38x51mm stamp.

Miniature Sheets

A372

Women's World Cup Soccer Championships, Germany — A373

No. 1064: a, Nahomi Kawasumi. b, Japanese team members lifting trophy, "Team Japan" in black. c, Members of Japanese team. d, Yuki Nagasato.

No. 1065: a, Japan coach Norio Sasaki. b, Japanese team members lifting trophy, "Team Japan" in white. c, U.S. team. d, U.S. coach Pia Sundhage.

2011, Sept. 21 ***Perf. 12x12½***

1064 A372 98c Sheet of 4, #a-d 8.00 8.00
1065 A373 98c Sheet of 4, #a-d 8.00 8.00

Pres. Barack Obama, 50th Birthday — A374

No. 1066 — Pres. Obama, White House, and one-quarter of Presidential Seal at: a, LR. b, LL. c, UR. d, UL.

$2.50, Pres. Obama.

2011, Oct. 26 ***Perf. 13 Syncopated***

1066 A374 98c Sheet of 4, #a-d 8.00 8.00

Souvenir Sheet

1067 A374 $2.50 multi 5.00 5.00

Crustaceans — A375

No. 1068, $1.25, vert.: a, Calcinus elegans. b, Dardanus pedunculatus. c, Odontodactylus scyllarus. d, Dardanus megistos.

No. 1069, $1.25, vert.: a, Birgus latro. b, Goneplax rhomboides. c, Bellia picta. d, Etisus dentatus.

No. 1070, $3, Grapsus grapsus. No. 1071, $3, Zebra mantis shrimp, vert.

2011, Oct. 26 ***Perf. 12***

Sheets of 4, #a-d

1068-1069 A375 Set of 2 20.00 20.00

Souvenir Sheets

1070-1071 A375 Set of 2 12.00 12.00

No. 1071 contains one 30x50mm stamp.

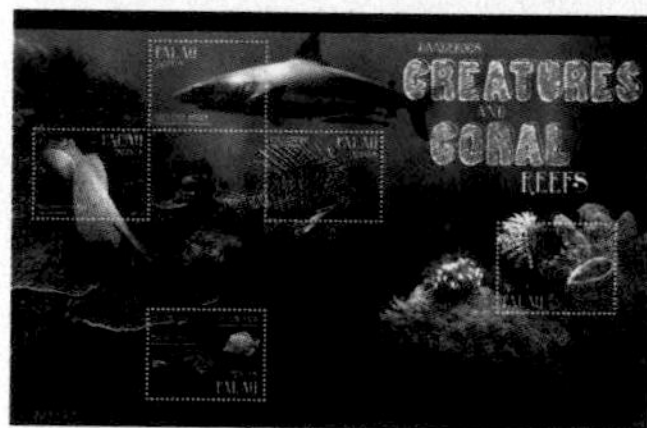

Marine Life — A376

No. 1072: a, Gray reef shark. b, Blue-spotted ray. c, Red lionfish. d, Feather duster worm. e, Regal tang, Yellow tang.

No. 1073: a, Pfeffer's flamboyant cuttlefish. b, Striped surgeonfish. c, Spiny sea urchin.

No. 1074, Box jellyfish, vert. No. 1075, Sawtooth barracuda.

2011, Nov. 29 ***Perf. 11½x12***

1072 A376 75c Sheet of 5, #a-e 7.50 7.50

Perf. 12½x12

1073 A376 $1 Sheet of 3, #a-c 6.00 6.00

Souvenir Sheets

Perf. 13½

1074 A376 $2.50 multi 5.00 5.00

Perf.

1075 A376 $2.50 multi 5.00 5.00

No. 1074 contains one 38x51mm stamp. No. 1075 contains one 35mm diameter stamp.

Christmas — A377

Paintings: 22c, Landscape with the Flight into Egypt, by Annibale Carracci. 44c, Madonna and Saints, by Giovanni Bellini. 98c, Merode Altarpiece, by Robert Campin. $4.25, The Annunciation, by Matthias Grünewald.

2012, Jan. 2 ***Perf. 14***

1076-1079 A377 Set of 4 12.00 12.00

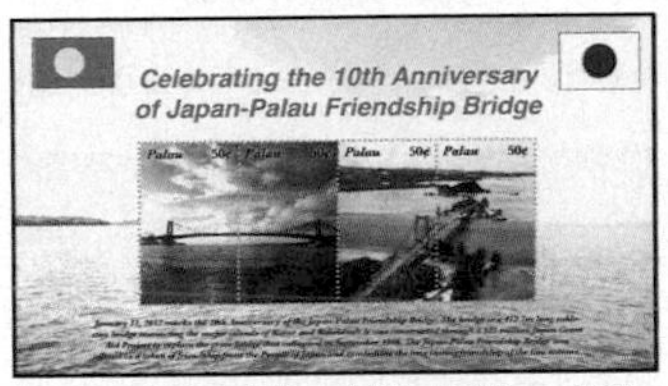

Lizards — A378

No. 1080, 98c: a, Snake-eyed skink. b, Solomon Islands skink. c, Vanuatu gecko. d, White-bellied skink.

No. 1081, 98c: a, Emerald tree skink. b, Common dwarf gecko. c, Mourning gecko. d, Moth skink.

No. 1082, $2.50, White-line gecko. No. 1083, $2.50, Mangrove monitor.

2012, Jan. 2 ***Perf. 13 Syncopated***

Sheets of 4, #a-d

1080-1081 A378 Set of 2 16.00 16.00

Souvenir Sheets

1082-1083 A378 Set of 2 10.00 10.00

Miniature Sheet

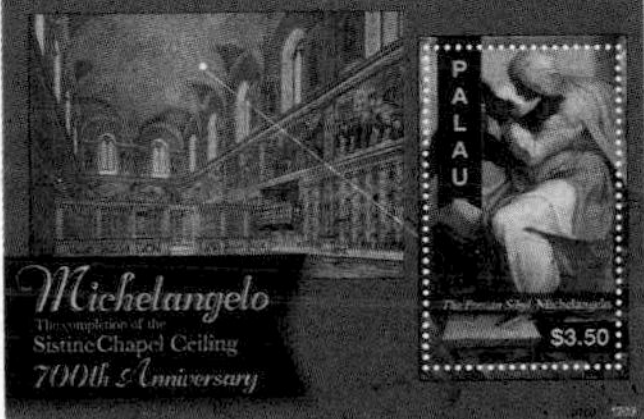

Japan-Palau Friendship Bridge, 10th Anniv. — A379

No. 1084: a, Side view of bridge, tower at left. b, Side view of bridge, tower at right. c, Aerial view of bridge, approach at bottom. d, Aerial view of bridge with road connecting other islands in distance.

2012, Jan. 11 ***Perf. 12***

1084 A379 50c Sheet of 4, #a-d 4.00 4.00

Painting of the Sistine Chapel Ceiling by Michelangelo, 500th Anniv. — A380

No. 1085, horiz.: a, Downfall of Adam and Eve. b, The Ignudi. c, The Prophet Jonah.

$3.50, The Persian Sibyl.

2012, Jan. 24 ***Perf. 12***

1085 A380 $1.25 Sheet of 3, #a-c 7.50 7.50

Souvenir Sheet

1086 A380 $3.50 multi 7.00 7.00

Nos. 1085 and 1086 are erroneously inscribed "700th Anniversary."

Sinking of the Titanic, Cent. — A381

No. 1087: a, Titanic at sea. b, Lifeboat. c, Man walking on deck. d, People reading newspapers reporting on the sinking.

$3, Titanic, diff.

2012, Jan. 25 ***Perf. 13 Syncopated***

1087 A381 $1 Sheet of 4, #a-d 8.00 8.00

Souvenir Sheet

1088 A381 $3 multi 6.00 6.00

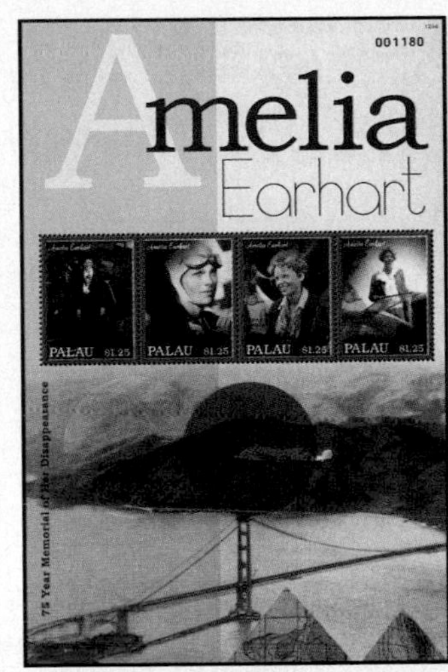

Disappearance of Amelia Earhart, 75th Anniv. — A382

No. 1089 — Earhart: a, Standing in front of airplane without helmet, hands visible. b, Wearing helmet and goggles. c, Standing in front of airplane without helmet, hands not visible. d, Standing in airplane cockpit without helmet.

No. 1090 — Earhart in helmet and goggles, airplane diagram, and text, "Amelia Earhart" in: a, White. b, Black.

2012, Feb. 6 ***Perf. 13½***

1089 A382 $1.25 Sheet of 4, #a-d 10.00 10.00

Souvenir Sheet

Perf. 12x12½

1090 A382 $1.25 Sheet of 2, #a-b 5.00 5.00

Miniature Sheet

2012 Summer Olympics, London — A383

No. 1091: a, Tennis. b, Swimming. c, Weight lifting. d, Basketball.

2012, Mar. 26 ***Perf. 13¼x13***

1091 A383 80c Sheet of 4, #a-d 6.50 6.50

Cherry Trees in Bloom and Washington Monument — A384

No. 1092, horiz. — Blossoms of flowering trees: a, Washington hawthorn. b, Flowering dogwood. c, Callery pear. d, Crabapple. e, Magnolia. f, Eastern redbud.

2012, Mar. 26 ***Perf. 12***

1092 A384 $1 Sheet of 6, #a-f 12.00 12.00

Souvenir Sheet

1093 A384 $3.50 shown 7.00 7.00

Miniature Sheets

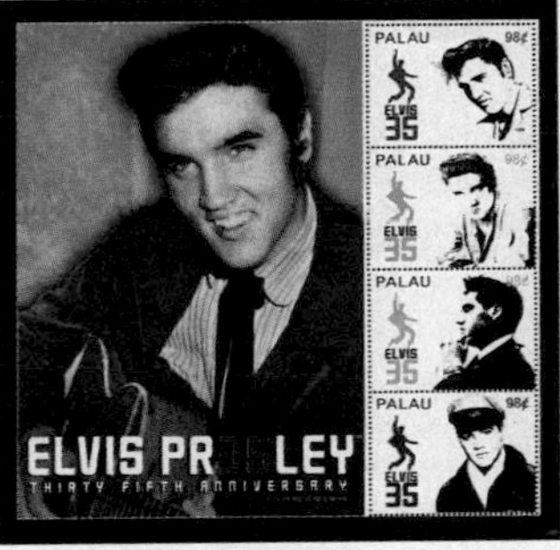

A385

Elvis Presley (1935-77) — A386

No. 1094 — Color of "35" and silhouette: a, Red violet. b, Green. c, Yellow. d, Violet.

No. 1095 — Presley wearing: a, Red jacket, white shirt. b, Tan shirt. c, Red jacket, black shirt. d, Gray jacket, white shirt.

2012, Apr. 11 ***Perf. 12½***

1094 A385 98c Sheet of 4, #a-d 8.00 8.00

1095 A386 98c Sheet of 4, #a-d 8.00 8.00

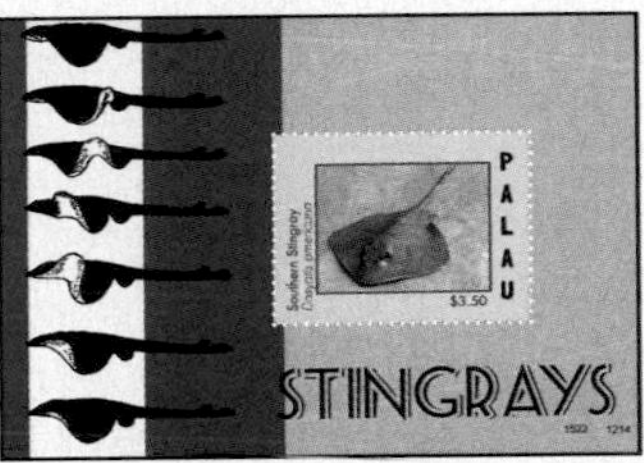

Stingrays — A387

No. 1096: a, Spotted eagle ray. b, Pacific electric ray. c, Blue-spotted stingray. d, Blotched fantail ray.

$3.50, Southern stingray.

2012, May 7 ***Perf. 12***

1096 A387 $1.25 Sheet of 4, #a-d 10.00 10.00

Souvenir Sheet

1097 A387 $3.50 multi 7.00 7.00

Souvenir Sheets

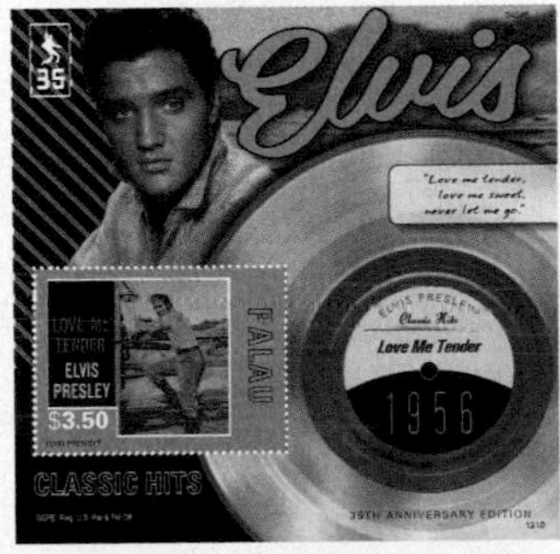

Elvis Presley (1935-77) — A388

Designs: No. 1098, $3.50, Presley on *Love Me Tender* record cover. No. 1099, $3.50, Presley on *Jailhouse Rock* album cover. No. 1100, $3.50, Presley on *Blue Hawaii* album cover. No. 1101, $3.50, Presley on *Just Tell Her Jim Said Hello/She's Not You* record cover. No. 1102, $3.50, Presley on *G.I. Blues* record cover.

2012, May 14 ***Perf. 12½***

1098-1102 A388 Set of 5 35.00 35.00

Miniature Sheet

Characters From *Peter Pan*, by Sir James M. Barrie (1860-1937) — A389

No. 1103: a, Peter Pan. b, Tiger Lily. c, Captain Hook. d, Wendy Darling.

2012, June 7 ***Perf. 12***

1103 A389 $1.25 Sheet of 4, #a-d 10.00 10.00

Miniature Sheet

Televised Tour of the White House, 50th Anniv. — A390

No. 1104: a, Jacqueline Kennedy, chandelier. b, Jacqueline Kennedy, table and chairs. c, Pres. John F. Kennedy, picture frame. d, Pres. Kennedy, White House.

2012, Aug. 28 **Litho.**

1104 A390 $1.25 Sheet of 4, #a-d 10.00 10.00

Pope Benedict XVI, 85th Birthday — A391

No. 1105 — Pope Benedict wearing: a, Miter. b, Zucchetto.

2012, Aug. 28 ***Perf. 14***

1105 A391 $1.25 Horiz. pair, #a-b 5.00 5.00

Printed in sheets containing two pairs.

Miniature Sheets

End of Apollo Moon Missions, 40th Anniv. — A392

No. 1106, $1.25: a, Apollo 9. b, Apollo 7. c, Apollo 15. d, Apollo 12.

No. 1107, $1.25: a, Apollo 14. b, Apollo 17. c, Apollo 8. d, Apollo 11.

2012, Aug. 28 ***Perf. 13 Syncopated***
Sheets of 4, #a-d

1106-1107 A392 Set of 2 20.00 20.00

Paintings by Raphael — A393

No. 1108: a, Giuliano de' Medici. b, Saint Sebastian. c, Portrait of Julius II. d, Bindo Altoviti.
$3, St. Catherine of Alexandria.

2012, Sept. 5 ***Perf. 12½***

1108 A393 $1 Sheet of 4, #a-d 8.00 8.00

Souvenir Sheet

1109 A393 $3 multi 6.00 6.00

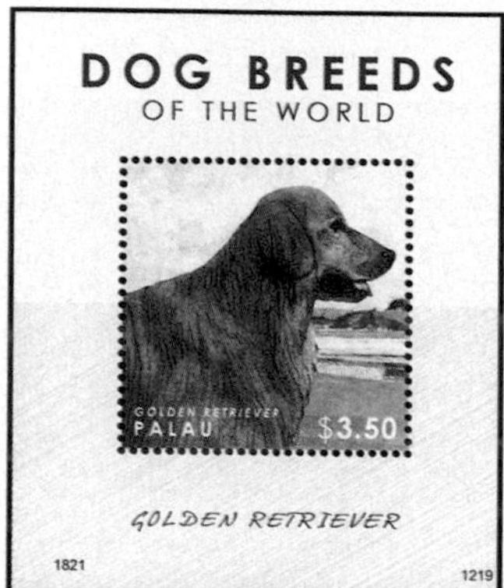

Dog Breeds — A394

No. 1110: a, Akita. b, Cane Corso. c, Collie. d, Rottweiler.
$3.50, Golden retriever.

2012, Sept. 5 ***Perf. 13¾***

1110 A394 $1.25 Sheet of 4, #a-d 10.00 10.00

Souvenir Sheet

1111 A394 $3.50 multi 7.00 7.00

Souvenir Sheets

Famous Speeches — A395

Orators of famous speeches: No. 1112, $3.50, Pres. Theodore Roosevelt. No. 1113, $3.50, Mahatma Gandhi. No. 1114, $3.50, Pres. John F. Kennedy. No. 1115, $3.50, Dr. Martin Luther King, Jr.

2012, Sept. 5 ***Perf. 12½***

1112-1115 A395 Set of 4 28.00 28.00

Carnivorous Plants — A396

No. 1116: a, Pale butterwort. b, Corkscrew plant. c, Alice sundew. d, Zigzag bladderwort.
$3.50, King sundew, vert.

2012, Nov. 28 ***Perf. 13¾***

1116 A396 $1.20 Sheet of 4, #a-d 9.75 9.75

Souvenir Sheet
Perf. 12½

1117 A396 $3.50 multi 7.00 7.00

No. 1117 contains one 38x51mm stamp.

Christmas A397

Paintings by Albrecht Dürer: No. 1118, 29c, Madonna and Child. No. 1119, 29c, The Flight to Egypt. No. 1120, 45c, The Virgin and Child with St. Anne. No. 1121, 45c, Virgin and Child Holding a Half-eaten Pear. No. 1122, $1.05, Mother of Sorrows. No. 1123, $1.05, The Virgin Mary in Prayer.
$3.50, Jesus Boy with a Globe.

2012, Dec. 24 ***Perf. 12½***

1118-1123 A397 Set of 6 7.25 7.25

Souvenir Sheet

1124 A397 $3.50 multi 7.00 7.00

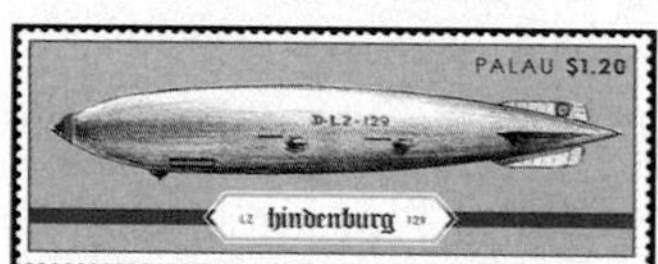

The Hindenburg — A398

Designs: $1.20, Hindenburg. $3.50, Hindenburg, Chrysler Building, Eiffel Tower, Empire State Building, 40 Wall Street Building, vert.

2012, Dec. 31 ***Perf. 12***

1125 A398 $1.20 multi 2.40 2.40

Souvenir Sheet
Perf. 12½

1126 A398 $3.50 multi 7.00 7.00

No. 1125 was printed in sheets of 4. No. 1126 contains one 38x51mm stamp.

World Radio Day — A399

No. 1127: a, Microphone. b, Antenna and waves. c, Table radio. d, Radio waves, diagram of ear canals.
$3.50, Solar system, radio wave, horiz.

2013, Jan. 2 **Litho.** ***Perf. 13¾***

1127 A399 $1.20 Sheet of 4, #a-d 9.75 9.75

Souvenir Sheet
Perf. 12½

1128 A399 $3.50 multi 7.00 7.00

No. 1128 contains one 51x38mm stamp.

Paintings by Paul Signac (1863-1935) — A400

No. 1129: a, L'Orage (The Storm). b, The Pine, Saint Tropez. c, Portrait of Félix Fénéon.
$3.50, Femmes au Puits (Women at the Well).

2013, Jan. 8 **Litho.** ***Perf. 12½***

1129 A400 $1.50 Sheet of 3, #a-c 9.00 9.00

Souvenir Sheet

1130 A400 $3.50 multi 7.00 7.00

Reign of Queen Elizabeth II, 60th Anniv. (in 2012) — A401

No. 1131 — Queen Elizabeth II: a, With Prince Philip. b, With dog. c, Waving. d, With Prince Charles.
$3.50, Queen Elizabeth II, vert.

2013, Jan. 8 **Litho.** ***Perf. 13¾***

1131 A401 $1.20 Sheet of 4, #a-d 9.75 9.75

Souvenir Sheet
Perf. 12½

1132 A401 $3.50 multi 7.00 7.00

No. 1132 contains one 38x51mm stamp.

Shells — A402

No. 1133: a, Conus gloriamaris. b, Hydatina albocincta. c, Marginella strigata. d, Conus betulinus.
$3.50, Tellina pharaonis, horiz.

2013, Mar. 20 **Litho.** ***Perf. 12***

1133 A402 $1.20 Sheet of 4, #a-d 9.75 9.75

Souvenir Sheet

1134 A402 $3.50 multi 7.00 7.00

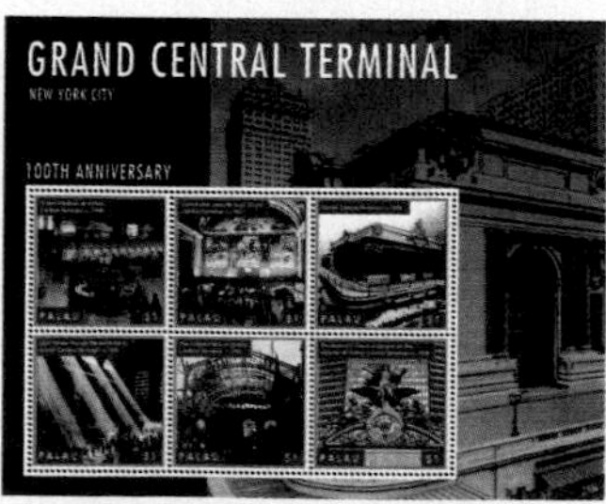

Cat Breeds — A403

Cat Depictions From Other Cultures — A404

No. 1135, $1.20: a, Russian Blue. b, Turkish Angora. c, Norwegian forest cat. d, Siamese.
No. 1136, $1.20: a, Siberian. b, Oriental shorthair. c, Japanese bobtail. d, Chartreux.
No. 1137, $3.50, Egyptian goddess Bastet. No. 1138, $3.50, Japanese Maneki-neko figurine.

2013, Mar. 20 **Litho.** ***Perf. 12***
Sheets of 4, #a-d

1135-1136 A403 Set of 2 19.50 19.50

Souvenir Sheets
Perf. 13¾

1137-1138 A404 Set of 2 14.00 14.00

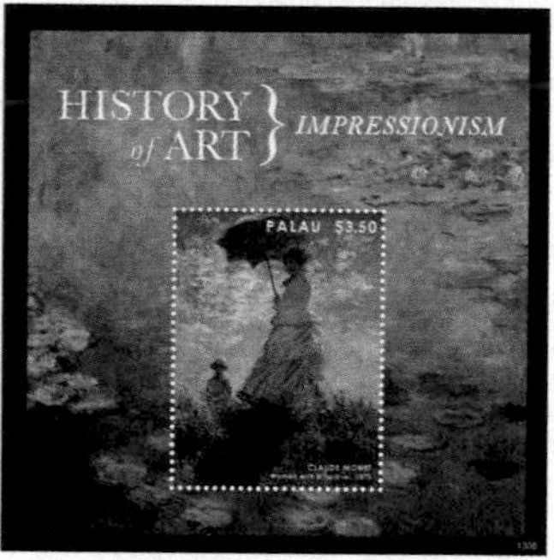

History of Art — A405

No. 1139, $1.50: a, Sunset at Ivry, by Armand Guillaumin. b, Landscape with Big Trees, by Camille Pissarro. c, A Box at the Theater, by Pierre-Auguste Renoir.
No. 1140, $1.50: a, Sunshine in the Blue Room, by Anna Ancher. b, Woman Washing Her Feet in a Brook, by Pissarro. c, Woman in the Bath, by Edgar Degas.
No. 1141, $3.50, Woman with a Parasol, by Claude Monet. No. 1142, $3.50, The Star, by Edgar Degas.

2013, Apr. 4 **Litho.** ***Perf. 12½***
Sheets of 3, #a-c

1139-1140 A405 Set of 2 18.00 18.00

Souvenir Sheets

1141-1142 A405 Set of 2 14.00 14.00

Grand Central Terminal, New York City, Cent. — A406

No. 1143: a, Ticket window, c. 1945. b, Commuters in station, c. 1941. c, Terminal exterior, c, 1920. d, Light shining through windows, c. 1930. e, Terminal under construction, c. 1907. f, Mercury Clock, c. 1988.
$3.50, Terminal exterior, horiz.

2013, Apr. 29 **Litho.** ***Perf. 13¾***

1143 A406 $1 Sheet of 6, #a-f 12.00 12.00

Souvenir Sheet

Perf. 12½

1144 A406 $3.50 multi 7.00 7.00

No. 1144 contains one 51x38mm stamp.

A407

Pres. John F. Kennedy (1917-63) — A408

No. 1145 — Black-and-white images of Pres. Kennedy: a, Facing right, flag in background. b, Facing left, flag in background. c, With people in background. d, With door in background.

No. 1146 — Color images of Pres. Kennedy: a, Facing right, with woman's head in background. b, With black background. c, With tie pattern visible. d, Facing right, with indistinguishable light reflections in background.

No. 1147, $3.50, Pres. Kennedy, country name at LL in blue panel. No. 1148, $3.50, Pres. Kennedy pointing, country name at UL in blue panel.

Perf. 13 Syncopated

2013, Apr. 29 **Litho.**

1145 A407 $1.20 Sheet of 4, #a-d 9.75 9.75

1146 A408 $1.20 Sheet of 4, #a-d 9.75 9.75

Souvenir Sheets

1147-1148 A408 Set of 2 14.00 14.00

Election of Pope Francis — A409

No. 1150 — Pope Francis: a, Waving to crowd below (orange background). b, Addressing crowd from balcony of St. Peter's Basilica (with cardinals). c, Behind microphone, addressing crowd, with assistant holding Bible. d, Waving to crowd (shadow and wall in background).

$3.50, Pope Francis, diff.

2013, June 3 **Litho.** ***Perf. 12***

1149 A409 $1.20 Sheet of 4, #a-d 9.75 9.75

Souvenir Sheet

Perf. 12½

1150 A409 $3.50 multi 7.00 7.00

No. 1150 contains one 38x51mm stamp.

Lady Margaret Thatcher (1925-2013), British Prime Minister — A410

No. 1151 — Thatcher: a, Wearing black dress. b, With Pres. George H. W. Bush. c, Wearing gray striped dress. d, Wearing black dresss with whtie dots.

$3.50, Thatcher in doorway of bus.

2013, June 3 **Litho.** ***Perf. 12***

1151 A410 $1.25 Sheet of 4, #a-d 10.00 10.00

Souvenir Sheet

Perf. 12½

1152 A410 $3.50 multi 7.00 7.00

No. 1152 conatins one 38x51mm stamp.

Henry Ford (1863-1947), Automobile Manufacturer — A411

No. 1153: a, Ford and first car. b, Assembly line. c, Parked Model T autombiles. d, Ford and Model T.

$3.50, Ford, vert.

2013, June 25 **Litho.** ***Perf. 12***

1153 A411 $1.20 Sheet of 4, #a-d 9.75 9.75

Souvenir Sheet

1154 A411 $3.50 multi 7.00 7.00

Tropical Fish — A412

No. 1155, $1.20: a, Australasian snapper. b, Tomato clownfish. c, Pennant coralfish. d, Yellow watchman goby.

No. 1156, $1.20: a, Pink-spotted shirmp goby. b, Ocellated dragonet. c, Common warehou. d, Gray moray.

No. 1157, $3.50, Blue-eyed triplefin. No. 1158, $3.50, Barred mudskipper.

2013, June 25 **Litho.** ***Perf. 12***

Sheets of 4, #a-d

1155-1156 A412 Set of 2 19.50 19.50

Souvenir Sheets

1157-1158 A412 Set of 2 14.00 14.00

Thailand 2013 World Stamp Exhibition, Bangkok — A413

No. 1159: a, Mondop Staircases. b, Floating market. c, Asian elephants. d, Buddhist temple.

$3.50, Sedge hats.

2013, July 7 **Litho.** ***Perf. 12***

1159 A413 $1.20 Sheet of 4, #a-d 9.75 9.75

Souvenir Sheet

1160 A413 $3.50 multi 7.00 7.00

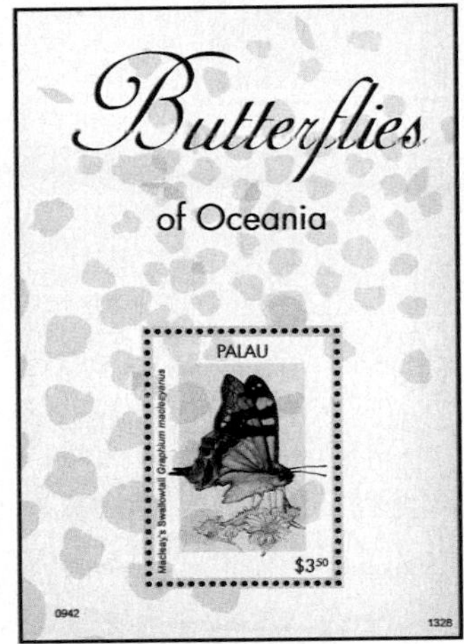

Butterflies — A414

No. 1161, horiz.: a, Tailed jay swallowtail. b, Old world swallowtail. c, Common albatross. d, Australian lurcher.

$3.50, Macleay's swallowtail.

2013, Sept. 17 **Litho.** ***Perf. 12***

1161 A414 $1.20 Sheet of 4, #a-d 9.75 9.75

Souvenir Sheet

1162 A414 $3.50 multl 7.00 7.00

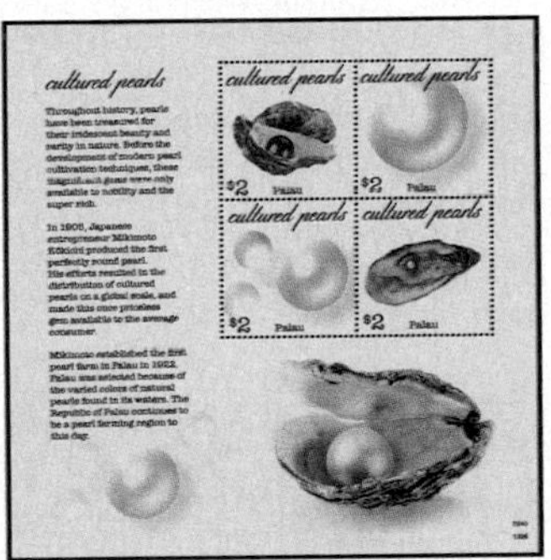

Cultured Pearls — A415

No. 1163: a, Large brown pearl in oyster shell, upper shell. b, Large white pearl. c, Three pearls. d, Small pearl in oyster shell.

$4, Pearl, tan background.

2013, Sept. 17 **Litho.** ***Perf. 13¾***

1163 A415 $2 Sheet of 4, #a-d 16.00 16.00

Souvenir Sheet

1164 A415 $4 multi 8.00 8.00

Birth of Prince George of Cambridge — A416

No. 1165: a, Duchess of Cambridge holding Prince George. b, Prince George, close-up. c, Prince Charles, Princess Diana, Prince William. d, Duke and Duchess of Cambridge with Prince George.

$3.50, Duke and Duchess of Cambridge with Prince George, diff.

2013, Sept. 17 **Litho.** ***Perf. 14***

1165 A416 $1.20 Sheet of 4, #a-d 9.75 9.75

Souvenir Sheet

Perf. 12

1166 A416 $3.50 multi 7.00 7.00

No. 1166 contains one 30x50mm stamp.

Miniature Sheets

Photographs by Kevin Davidson — A417

No. 1167: a, Oxypora coral, country name at UL, reading across. b, Coral dweller cobie, country name at UL, reading across. c, Bannerfish. d, Mushroom Rock Island, country name at UL, reading across. e, Medusa worm on red sponge. f, Eagle ray, decimal point of denomination to right of ray, wing of ray just touching vertical line of first "1" in denomination.

No. 1168: a, Baby green turtles. b, Mandarin fish, country name at UL, reading across. c, Eagle ray, decimal point of denomination on ray. d, Pink anemone fish, country name at UL, reading across. e, Head of fish (incorrectly inscribed "Medusa worm on red sponge"). f, Masked angelfish.

No. 1169: a, Harlequin sweetlips. b, Nautilus. c, Eagle Ray, decimal point of denomination to right of ray, wing of ran not touching vertical line of first "1" in denomination. d, Red sea fan. e, Soft coral crab.

No. 1170: a, Oxypora coral, country name at left, reading up. b, Coral dweller cobie, country name at left, reading up. c, Pink anemone fish, country name at left, reading up. d, Mushroom Rock Island, country name at left, reading up. e, Mandarin fish, country name at left, reading up. f, Longnose hawkfish.

No. 1171, vert.: a, Three jellyfish. b, Starfish on red coral fan, country name at UL, reading across. c, Jellyfish and diver. d, Oxypora coral, country name at UL, reading across. e, Seahorse. f, Lionfish.

No. 1172, vert.: a, Coconut climber. b, Pink anemone fish, country name at UL, reading across. c, Cup coral, country name at UL, reading across. d, Humphead wrasse, e, Shark.

No. 1173, vert.: a, Cup coral, country name at UL, reading up. b, Manta ray. c, Rock Island. d, Red seahorse. e, Pink anemone fish, country name at UL, reading up. f, Starfish on red coral fan, country name at UL, reading up.

2013, Oct. 1 **Litho.** ***Perf. 12***

1167 A417 $1.10 Sheet of 6, #a-f 13.50 13.50

1168 A417 $1.10 Sheet of 6, #a-f 13.50 13.50

1169 A417 $1.10 Sheet of 6, #a-e, 1168f 13.50 13.50

1170 A417 $1.10 Sheet of 6, #a-f 13.50 13.50

1171 A417 $1.10 Sheet of 6, #a-f 13.50 13.50

1172 A417 $1.10 Sheet of 6, #a-e, 1171d 13.50 13.50
1173 A417 $1.10 Sheet of 6, #a-f 13.50 13.50
Nos. 1167-1173 (7) 94.50 94.50

Souvenir Sheet

Elvis Presley (1935-77) — A418

Litho., Margin Embossed With Foil Application

2013, Oct. 1 ***Imperf.***
1174 A418 $10 multi 20.00 20.00

Coronation of Queen Elizabeth II, 60th Anniv. — A419

No. 1175 — Queen Elizabeth II: a, With Prince Philip. b, Wearing pink hat. c, Wearing white hat. d, Alone, wearing sash and tiara.
$3.50, Queen Elizabeth II in coach, vert.

2013, Oct. 7 **Litho.** ***Perf. 14***
1175 A419 $1.20 Sheet of 4, #a-d 9.75 9.75

Souvenir Sheet

1176 A419 $3.50 multi 7.00 7.00

World Water Day — A420

Designs: $1.20, Water droplets. $3.50, Water droplet, vert.

2013, Nov. 18 **Litho.** ***Perf. 13¾***
1177 A420 $1.20 multi 2.40 2.40

Souvenir Sheet

Perf. 12½

1178 A420 $3.50 multi 7.00 7.00

No. 1177 was printed in sheets of 4. No. 1178 contains one 38x51mm stamp.

Christmas A421

Paintings: 29c, Madonna Worshipping the Child and an Angel, by Biagio D'Antonio Tucci. 44c, Nativity, by unknown artist. $1.05, The Annunciation, by Simone Martini. $3.50, Virgin and Child, by Gentile da Fabriano.

2013, Dec. 2 **Litho.** ***Perf. 12½***
1179-1182 A421 Set of 4 11.00 11.00

A422

Nelson Mandela (1918-2013), President of South Africa — A423

No. 1183: a, Mandela and wife, Winnie, waving. b, Mandela as young man wearing traditional collar. c, Mandela in crowd, laughing.
No. 1184 — Mandela: a, wearing black and gray shirt. b, Wearing suit and tie, building in background. c, Holding microphone stand. d, Seated. e, Behind microphone, pointing. f, With raised fist.
No. 1185, $3.50, Mandela holding ballot, wearing shirt with pens in pocket, vert. No. 1186, $3.50, Mandela with arm raised, wearing patterned shirt, vert.

2013, Dec. 15 **Litho.** ***Perf. 13¾***
1183 A422 $1.20 Vert. strip of 3, #a-c 7.25 7.25
1184 A423 $1.20 Sheet of 6, #a-f 14.50 14.50

Souvenir Sheets

Perf. 12½

1185-1186 A423 Set of 2 14.00 14.00

No. 1183 was printed in sheet of 6 stamps containing two each of Nos. 1183a-1183c. Nos. 1185-1186 each contain on 38x51mm stamp.

Orchids — A424

No. 1187: Various Phalaenopsis orchids, as shown.
$3.50, Lady's slipper, horiz.

2013, Dec. 18 **Litho.** ***Perf. 13¾***
1187 A424 $1 Sheet of 6, #a-f 12.00 12.00

Souvenir Sheet

Perf. 12½

1188 A424 $3.50 multi 7.00 7.00

No. 1188 contains one 51x38mm stamp.

Chess in Art — A425

No. 1189: a, Etude of the Life of the Russian Tsars, by Vyacheslav Schwarz (players, table with green tablecloth). b, Scene from the Court of King Christian VII, by Kristian Zahrtmann (woman and man playing). c, The Chess Players, by Giulio Rosati (players on bench). d, The Chess Game, by Charles Bargue (woman and cardinal playing).
$3.50, Proposal, by Knut Ekwall, vert.

2013, Dec. 23 **Litho.** ***Perf. 12½***
1189 A425 $1.20 Sheet of 4, #a-d 9.75 9.75

Souvenir Sheet

1190 A425 $3.50 multi 7.00 7.00

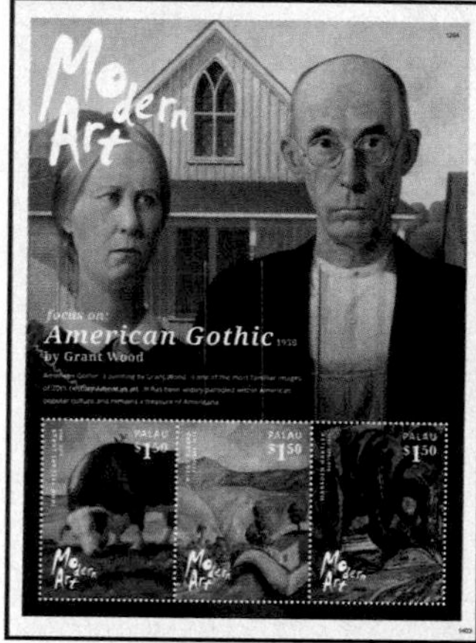

Modern Art — A426

No. 1191, $1.50 — Paintings: a, Ajax, by John Steuart Curry. b, Landscape, by Diego Rivera. c, Red Tree, by Marsden Hartley.
No. 1192, $1.50 — Photographs: a, Power Farming Displaces Tenants, by Dorothea Lange. b, Toward Los Angeles, California, by Lange. c, Power House Mechanic Working on Steam Pump, by Lewis Hine.
No. 1193, $3.50, Red Cavalry, by Kazimir Malevich. No. 1194, $3.50, The Alarm Clock, by Rivera.

2014, Jan. 2 **Litho.** ***Perf. 12½***

Sheets of 3, #a-c

1191-1192 A426 Set of 2 18.00 18.00

Souvenir Sheets

1193-1194 A426 Set of 2 14.00 14.00

Shells — A427

No. 1195, $1.75: a, Chicoreus palma-rosae. b, Phalium glaucum. c, Conus generalis (blue background at top). d, Conus episcopus.
No. 1196, $1.75: a, Conus generalis (purple background at top). b, Harpa articularis. c, Strombus minimus. d, Strombus gibberulus.
No. 1197, $3.50: a, Chicoreus ramosus. b, Murex troscheli.
No. 1198, $3.50: a, Charonia tritonis. b, Syrinx aruanus.

2014, Feb. 26 **Litho.** ***Perf. 12***

Sheets of 4, #a-d

1195-1196 A427 Set of 2 28.00 28.00

Souvenir Sheets of 2, #a-b

Perf. 12½

1197-1198 A427 Set of 2 28.00 28.00

Nos. 1197-1198 each contain two 38x51mm stamps.

Caroline Kennedy, United States Ambassador to Japan — A428

No. 1199 — Caroline Kennedy: a, Greeting Japanese students. b, With parents and brother. c, As young woman at graduation ceremony. d, As child, with father.
$4, Caroline Kennedy, vert.

2014, Mar. 5 **Litho.** ***Perf. 13¾***
1199 A428 $1.50 Sheet of 4, #a-d 12.00 12.00

Souvenir Sheet

Perf. 12½

1200 A428 $4 multi 8.00 8.00

No. 1200 contains one 38x51mm stamp.

Miniature Sheets

Winter Sports — A429

No. 1201: a, Ice hockey. b, Speed skating. c, Bobsled. d, Figure skating.

No. 1202, horiz.: a, Freestyle skiing. b, Nordic combined skiing. c, Curling. d, Luge. f, Skeleton. g, Bobsled, diff.

2014, Mar. 5 Litho. *Perf. 12½*

1201 A429 $1.20 Sheet of 4, #a-d 9.75 9.75

Perf. 14

1202 A429 $1.20 Sheet of 6, #a-f 14.50 14.50

No. 1202 contains six 40x30mm stamps.

Pope Francis — A430

No. 1203, $1.20: a, Pres. Horacio Cartes of Paraguay. b, Pope Francis (painting in backgound). c, Pres. Cartes and Pope Francis (painting in background). d, Pres. Cartes and Pope Francis (painting and table in background).

No. 1204, $1.20: a, Pres. Denis Sassou Nguesso of Congo Republic. b, Pope Francis (book shelves in background). c, Pres. Sassou Nguesso and Pope Francis (painting and chairs in background). d, Pres. Sassou Nguesso and Pope Francis (corner of room in background).

No. 1205, $2: a, Pope Francis hugging person. b, Pope Francis patting child's head.

No. 1206, $2: a, Pope Francis looking upwards. b, Pope Francis with hands together.

2014, Mar. 10 Litho. *Perf. 12½*

Sheets of 4, #a-d

1203-1204 A430 Set of 2 19.50 19.50

Souvenir Sheets of 2, #a-b

Perf. 12

1205-1206 A430 Set of 2 16.00 16.00

Nos. 1205-1206 each contain two 30x40mm stamps.

World War I, Cent. — A431

No. 1207, $2.50: a, London Scottish Regiment drill. b, British Army recruits in training. c, New recruits with officers, London. d, British Army volunteers, Aldershot.

No. 1208, $2.50: a, Bergmann MP18 machine gun, Germany. b, Carl Gustav Mauser M96, Sweden. c, Browning 1917 A1 machine gun, Belgium. d, Fedorov Avtomat rifle, Russia.

No. 1209, $2: a, Herbert Henry Asquith, British Prime Minister. b, Winston Churcill, First Lord of the Admiralty.

No. 1210, $2: a, Luger P08, Germany. b, Model 1892 revolver, France.

2014, Apr. 23 Litho. *Perf. 14*

Sheets of 4, #a-d

1207-1208 A431 Set of 2 40.00 40.00

Souvenir Sheets of 2, #a-b

Perf. 12½

1209-1210 A431 Set of 2 16.00 16.00

Nos. 1209-1210 each contain two 51x38mm stamps.

Miniature Sheet

South Korean Stamps — A432

No. 1211: a, South Korea #936 (1975 stamp). b, South Korea #1398 (1985 stamp). c, South Korea #1635 (1991 stamp). d, South Korea #704 (1970 stamp). e, South Korea #948 (1975 stamp). f, Never-used stamp of 1884. g, South Korea #861 (1973 stamp). h, South Korea #300 (1959 stamp).

2014, May 12 Litho. *Perf. 12*

1211 A432 $1 Sheet of 8, #a-h 16.00 16.00

Philakorea 2014 World Stamp Exhibition, Seoul.

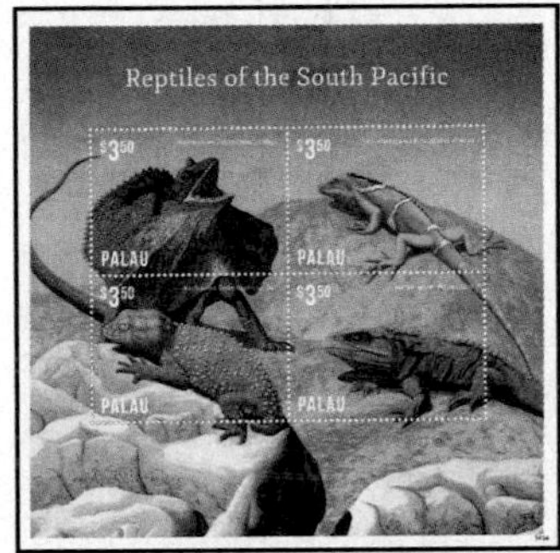

Reptiles — A433

No. 1212, $3.50: a, Frilled lizard. b, Fiji crested iguana. c, Knob-tailed gecko. d, Tuatara.

No. 1213, $3.50: a, Eastern brown snake (35x35mm). b, Children's python (35x35mm). c, Copperhead (35x70mm). d, Red-bellied black snake (35x35mm).

No. 1214, $3.50, Green sea turtle. No. 1215, $3.50, Saltwater crocodile.

Perf. 12½, 13¾ (#1213)

2014, July 1 Litho.

Sheets of 4, #a-d

1212-1213 A433 Set of 2 56.00 56.00

Souvenir Sheets

1214-1215 A433 Set of 2 14.00 14.00

Miniature Sheets

A434

Seagulls — A435

Various depictions of seagulls, as shown.

Perf. 13 Syncopated

2014, July 21 Litho.

1216 A434 $1 Sheet of 6, #a-f 12.00 12.00
1217 A435 $1 Sheet of 6, #a-f 12.00 12.00

Prince George of Cambridge — A436

No. 1218: a, Duke and Duchess of Cambridge, Prince George. b, Prince George. c, Duchess of Cambridge and Prince George.

No. 1219: a, Duke of Cambridge and Prince George. b, Prince George, diff.

No. 1220, $4, Prince George facing left, horiz. No. 1221, $4, Prince George facing right, horiz.

2014, July 21 Litho. *Perf. 14*

1218 A436 75c Horiz. strip of 3, #a-c 4.50 4.50
1219 A436 $1 Pair, #a-b 4.00 4.00

Souvenir Sheets

1220-1221 A436 Set of 2 16.00 16.00

No. 1218 was printed in sheets of 8 stamps containing 4 #1218b and 2 each #1218a and 1218c. No. 1219 was printed in sheets containing 3 pairs.

Miniature Sheet

Fish — A437

No. 1222: a, Brown surgeonfish. b, Striped surgeonfish. c, Convict surgeonfish. d, Eyestripe surgeonfish. e, Roundspot surgeonfish. f, Yellowfin surgeonfish.

2014, July 30 Litho. *Perf. 12½x13¼*

1222 A437 45c Sheet of 6, #a-f 5.50 5.50

45th Pacific Islands Forum, Palau.

Illustrations for *Alice's Adventures in Wonderland,* by Sir John Tenniel (1820-1914) — A438

No. 1223, $1.75: a, Alice, Flamingo and Duchess (club in panel). b, Playing Cards painting rose bush (diamond in panel). c, Fish delivers letter to frog (heart in panel). d, Alice and the Queen of Hearts (spade in panel).

No. 1224, $1.75: a, Alice at tea party (club in panel). b, Alice and flowers (diamond in panel). c, Alice holding bottle (heart in panel). d, Alice and playing cards (spade in panel).

No. 1225, $2.50: a, King of Hearts (club in panel). b, Queen of Hearts (heart in panel).

No. 1226, $2.50: a, Knave of Hearts (spade in panel) b, Birds in powdered wigs (diamond in panel).

2014, July 31 Litho. *Perf. 12½*

Sheets of 4, #a-d

1223-1224 A438 Set of 2 28.00 28.00

Souvenir Sheets of 2, #a-b

1225-1226 A438 Set of 2 20.00 20.00

Tourist Attractions in Russia — A439

No. 1227: a, Uzon Caldera. b, Mt. Elbrus. c, Trans-Siberian Railway.

No. 1228, vert.: a, Peter and Paul Cathedral, St. Petersburg. b, St. Sophia Cathedral, Vologda.

2014, Aug. 14 Litho. *Perf. 12*

1227 A439 $1.50 Sheet of 3, #a-c 9.00 9.00

Souvenir Sheet

1228 A439 $2 Sheet of 2, #a-b 8.00 8.00

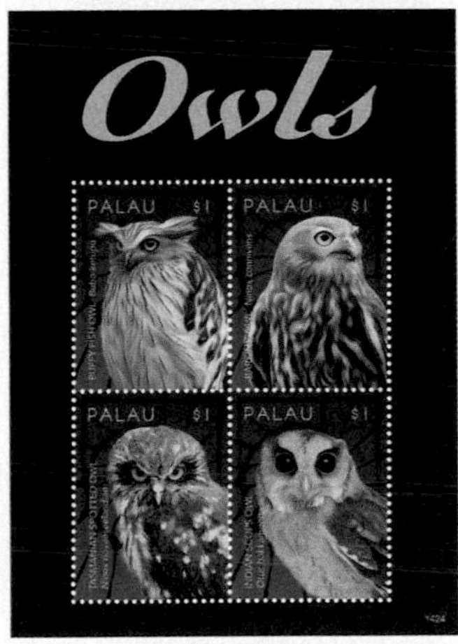

Owls — A440

No. 1229: a, Buffy fish owl. b, Barking owl. c, Tasmanian spotted owl. d, Indian scops owl. $3, Ural owl. $4, Short-eared owl.

2014, Aug. 14 Litho. *Perf. 12*

1229 A440 $1 Sheet of 4, #a-d 8.00 8.00

Souvenir Sheets

1230 A440 $3 multi 6.00 6.00
1231 A440 $4 multi 8.00 8.00

Marine Life — A441

Designs: 2c, Damselfish. 3c, Green sea turtle. 5c, Mailed butterflyfish. 10c, Ornate butterflyfish. 15c, Queen triggerfish. 20c, Reef manta ray. 75c, Yellow boxfish. $1, Palau nautilus.

2014, Aug. 27 Litho. *Perf. 13¾*

1232 A441 2c multi .25 .25
1233 A441 3c multi .25 .25
1234 A441 5c multi .25 .25
1235 A441 10c multi .25 .25

1236 A441 15c multi .30 .30
1237 A441 20c multi .40 .40
1238 A441 75c multi 1.50 1.50
1239 A441 $1 multi 2.00 2.00
Nos. 1232-1239 (8) 5.20 5.20

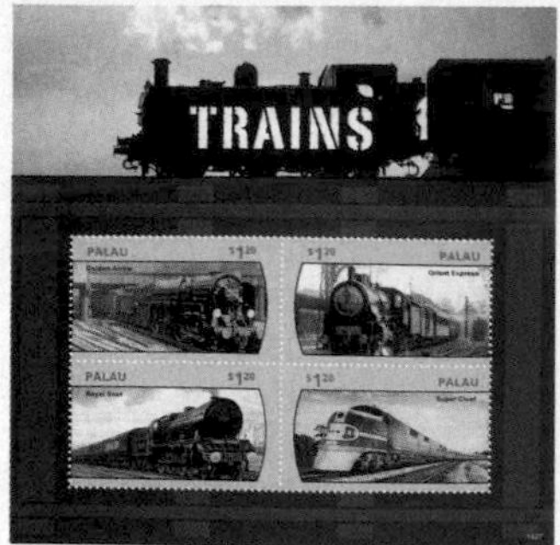

Trains — A442

No. 1240: a, Golden Arrow. b, Orient Express. c. Royal Scot. d, Super Chief.
$3.50, 20th Century Limited.

2014, Sept. 3 Litho. *Perf. 12*
1240 A442 $1.20 Sheet of 4, #a-d 9.75 9.75

Souvenir Sheet

1241 A442 $3.50 multi 7.00 7.00

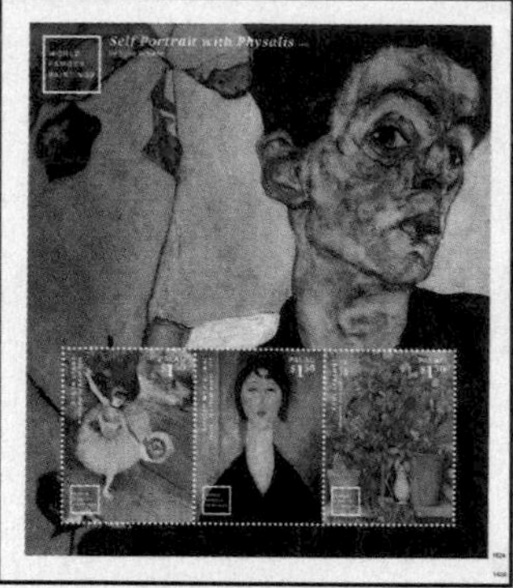

Paintings — A443

No. 1242, $1.50: a, Dancer Taking a Bow, by Edgar Degas. b, Portrait of a Young Woman, by Amedeo Modigliani. c, Terracotta Pots and Flowers, by Paul Cézanne.
No. 1243, $1.50: a, The Ballet Class, by Degas. b, Anxiety, by Edvard Munch. c, The Child's Bath, by Mary Cassatt.
No. 1244, $4, In the Kitchen, by Carl Larsson. No. 1245, $4, Farewell, by August Macke.

2014, Sept. 3 Litho. *Perf. 12½*
Sheets of 3, #a-c

1242-1243 A443 Set of 2 18.00 18.00

Size: 100x100mm
Imperf

1244-1245 A443 Set of 2 16.00 16.00

Frogs and Toads — A444

No. 1246, $1.20: a, Rough-backed forest frog. b, Common tree frog. c, Luzon frog. d, Wrinkled ground frog.
No. 1247, $1.20: a, Taylor's wrinkled ground frog. b, Woodworth's wart frog. c, Pygmy forest frog. d, Kalinga narrowmouth toad.
No. 1248, $4, Luzon fanged frog. No. 1249, $4, Harlequin tree frog.

Perf. 14, 12 (#1249)
2014, Sept. 15 Litho.
Sheets of 4, #a-d

1246-1247 A444 Set of 2 19.50 19.50

Souvenir Sheets

1248-1249 A444 Set of 2 16.00 16.00

Miniature Sheets

Characters From *Downton Abbey* Television Series — A445

No. 1250, $1.20: a, Dowager Countess of Grantham. b, Earl of Grantham. c, Countess of Grantham. d, Lady Mary Crawley. e, Lady Edith Crawley.
No. 1251, $1.20: a, Thomas Barrow. b, Mr. Carson. c, Mrs. Hughes. d, Mrs. Patmore. e, Daisy Mason.

2014, Nov. 11 Litho. *Perf. 14*
Sheets of 5, #a-e

1250-1251 A445 Set of 2 24.00 24.00

Christmas A446

Paintings and details of paintings by Raphael: 34c, The Adoration of the Magi. 49c, The Adoration of the Magi, diff. $1.50, Ansidei Madonna. $3.50, Colonna Madonna.

2014, Nov. 24 Litho. *Perf. 12½*
1252-1255 A446 Set of 4 12.00 12.00

Worldwide Fund for Nature (WWF) — A447

Nos. 1256 and 1257 — Lagoon jellyfish: a, Near water's surface. b, Two jellyfish. c, Above seafloor. d, In sea cave.

2014, Dec. 1 Litho. *Perf. 14*
1256 A447 40c Block or horiz. strip of 4, #a-d 3.25 3.25
1257 A447 90c Block or horiz. strip of 4, #a-d 7.25 7.25

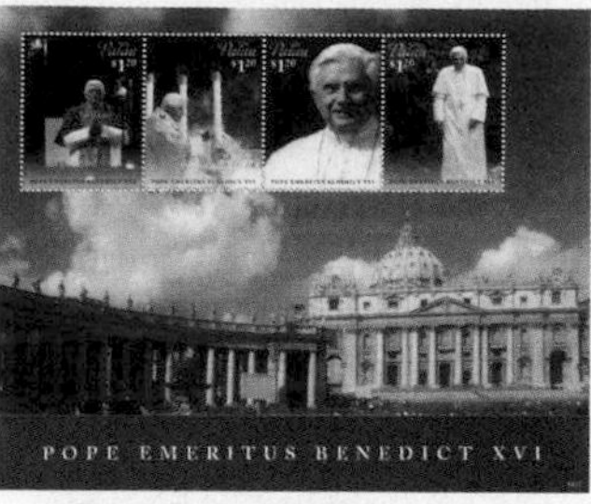

Pope Benedict XVI — A448

No. 1258 — Pope Benedict XVI: a, Wearing red vestments. b, Swinging censer. c, Close-up. d, Standing in front of bushes.
$4, Pope Benedict XVI in green vestments.

2014, Dec. 16 Litho. *Perf. 14*
1258 A448 $1.20 Sheet of 4, #a-d 9.75 9.75

Souvenir Sheet

1259 A448 $4 multi 8.00 8.00

Dinosaurs — A449

No. 1260, $1.20: a, Nigersaurus. b, Iguanodon. c, Agustinia. d, Doliosauriscus.
No. 1261, $1.20: a, Ankylosaurus. b, Giganotosaurus. c, Diplodocus. d, Tyrannosaurus.
No. 1262, $4, Stegosaurus. No. 1263, $4, Gigantspinosaurus.

2014, Dec. 22 Litho. *Perf. 12*
Sheets of 4, #a-d

1260-1261 A449 Set of 2 19.50 19.50

Souvenir Sheets

1262-1263 A449 Set of 2 16.00 16.00

No. 1261 contains four 50x30mm stamps.

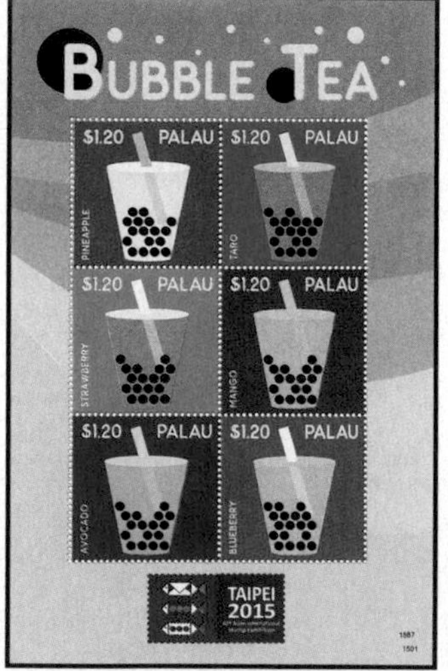

Bubble Tea — A450

No. 1264 — Cup of tea with straw and inscription of: a, Pineapple. b, Taro. c, Strawberry. d, Mango. e, Avocado. f, Blueberry.
$4, Cup of tea with lid and straw.

2015, Jan. 5 Litho. *Perf. 13¾*
1264 A450 $1.20 Sheet of 6, #a-f 14.50 14.50

Souvenir Sheet
Perf. 12

1265 A450 $4 multi 8.00 8.00

No. 1265 contains one 30x40mm stamp.
Asian International Stamp Exhibition, 30th Anniv.

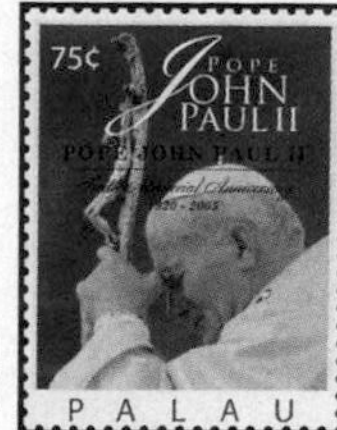

Pope John Paul II (1920-2005) A451

2015, Feb. 2 Litho. *Perf. 12*
1266 A451 75c multi 1.50 1.50

Printed in sheets of 4. Compare with type A331.

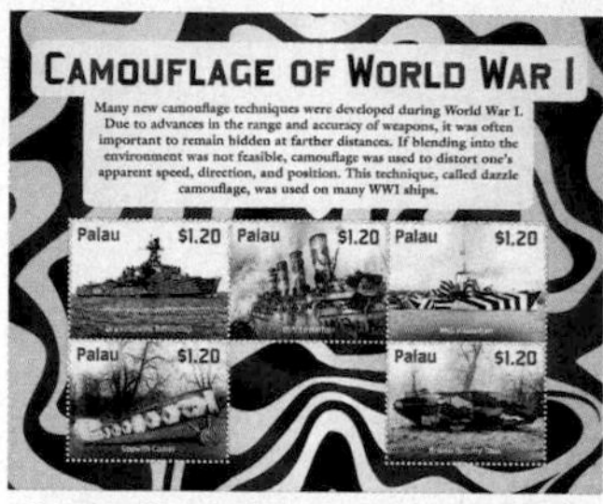

Camouflage of World War I — A452

No. 1267: a, Dreadnought Battleship. b, USS Leviathan. c, HMS Kildangan. d, Sopwith Camel airplane. e, British dummy tank.
$4, Soldier in tree-climbing camouflage.

2015, Feb. 2 Litho. *Perf. 14*
1267 A452 $1.20 Sheet of 5, #a-e 12.00 12.00

Souvenir Sheet
Perf. 13¾

1268 A452 $4 multi 8.00 8.00

No. 1268 contains one 35x35mm stamp.

UNESCO World Heritage Sites — A453

No. 1269: a, Great Barrier Reef, Australia. b, Prambanan Temple Compounds, Indonesia. c, Rice Terraces of the Philippine Cordilleras, Philippines. d, Kinabalu Park, Malaysia. e, Komodo National Park, Indonesia.
$4, Rock Islands Southern Lagoon, Palau.

2015, Mar. 9 Litho. *Perf. 14*
1269 A453 $1.20 Sheet of 5, #a-e 12.00 12.00

Souvenir Sheet
Perf. 13¾

1270 A453 $4 multi 8.00 8.00

No. 1270 contains one 70x35mm stamp.

Ships Involved in the 1940 Evacuation of Dunkirk — A454

No. 1271, 45c: a, Minnehaha, b, Cygnet. c, Rapid. d, Skylark. e, Wanda. f, Marchioness. g, Jovial. h, Fedalma II. i, Jane Hannah MacDonald. j, Massey Shaw. k, Mimosa. l, Aberdonia. m, Reda. n, Blue Bird. o, Dorian. p, White Heathe.

No. 1272, 45c: a, Cachalot. b, Fervant. c, Omega. d, Greater London. e, Jane Holland. f, Lucy Lavers. g, Tom Tit. h, Cyril and Lillian Bishop. i, Latona. j, Endeavour. k, Polly. l, Tigris. m, Eothen. n, Lazy Days. o, Wairakei II. p, Matoya.

2015, May 25 Litho. *Perf. 14*
Sheets of 16, #a-p, + Label
1271-1272 A454 Set of 2 29.00 29.00

Queen Elizabeth II, Longest-Reigning British Monarch — A455

No. 1273 — Queen Elizabeth II wearing: a, Dark green dress, light green hat and gloves. b, Pink dress and hat, black gloves. c, Green coat. b, Dark blue dress. c, White gown and tiara. d, Lilac dress.

$4, Queen Elizabeth II in white and blue dress with blue buttons and matching hat.

2015, May 25 Litho. *Perf. 14*
1273 A455 $1.20 Sheet of 6, #a-f 14.50 14.50

Souvenir Sheet
Perf. 12
1274 A455 $4 multi 8.00 8.00

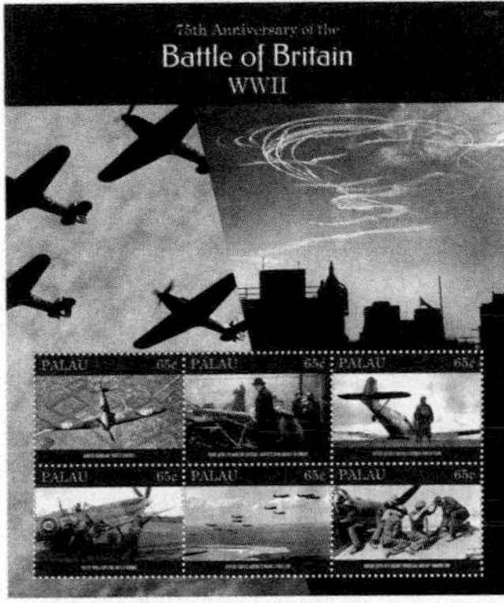

Battle of Britain, 75th Anniv. — A456

No. 1275: a, Hawker Hurricane. b, Prime Minister Winston Churchill inspects bomb damage in London. c, British soldier guards a German fighter plane. d, Pilots push a Spitfire onto a runway. e, Spitfires patrol a coastline. f, Ground crew replenishes Hurricane aircraft ammunition.

$4, Churchill and Queen Elizabeth inspect damage to Buckingham Palace.

2015, June 1 Litho. *Perf. 12*
1275 A456 65c Sheet of 6, #a-f 8.00 8.00

Souvenir Sheet
1276 A456 $4 multi 8.00 8.00

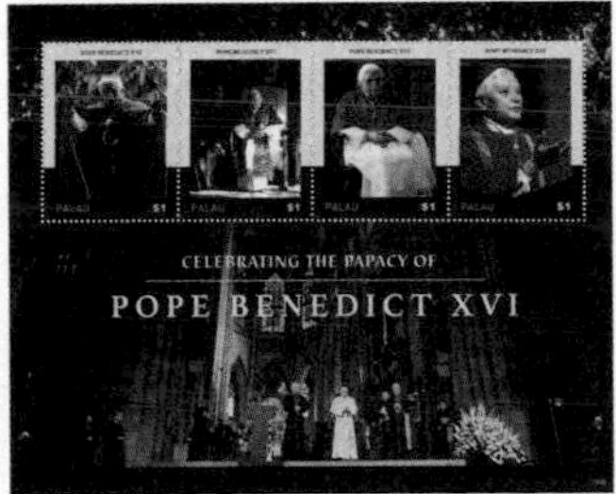

Pope Benedict XVI — A457

No. 1277 — Pope Benedict XVI: a, With arms raised. b, Seated next to bishop. c, Seated alone. d, With hand outstretched.

$3.50, Pope Benedict XVI wearing large crucifix.

2015, June 8 Litho. *Perf. 12½*
1277 A457 $1 Sheet of 4, #a-d 8.00 8.00

Souvenir Sheet
1278 A457 $3.50 multi 7.00 7.00

Birds — A458

No. 1279: a, Eclectus parrot (30x40mm). b, Brahminy kite (60x40mm). c, Whiskered tern (30x40mm). d, Black-winged stilt (30x40mm). e, Collared kingfisher (60x40mm). f, Black kite (30x40mm).

$4, Sulphur-crested cockatoo, horiz.

2015, June 15 Litho. *Perf. 12*
1279 A458 65c Sheet of 6, #a-f 8.00 8.00

Souvenir Sheet
1280 A458 $4 multi 8.00 8.00

No. 1280 contains one 40x30mm stamp.

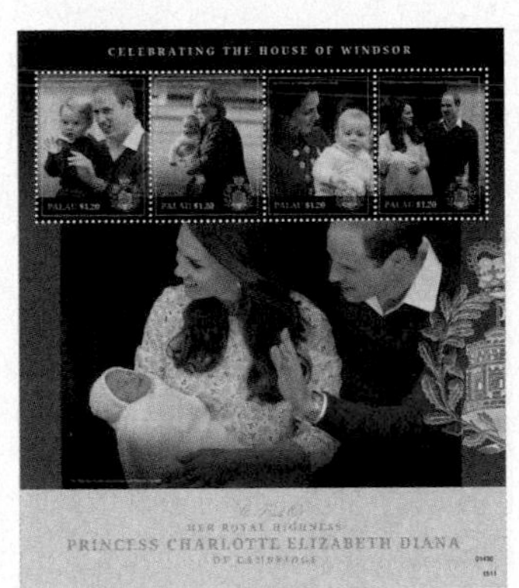

Birth of Princess Charlotte of Cambridge — A459

No. 1281: a, Duke of Cambridge and Prince George. b, Princess Diana and Prince William. c, Duchess of Cambridge and Prince George. d, Duke and Duchess of Cambridge, Princess Charlotte.

$4, Duchess of Cambridge holding Princess Charlotte.

2015, July 13 Litho. *Perf. 12*
1281 A459 $1.20 Sheet of 4, #a-d 9.75 9.75

Souvenir Sheet
1282 A459 $4 multi 8.00 8.00

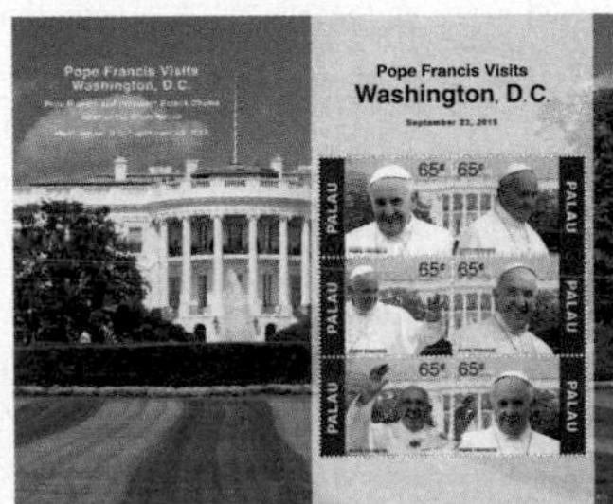

Visit of Pope Francis to Washington, D.C. — A460

No. 1283 — Pope Francis: a, Smiling, denomination at UR. b, Facing right, denomination at UL. c, Waving, hand at right, denomination at UR. d, Smiling, denomination at UL. e, Waving, hand at left, denomination at UR. f, Waving, hand at left, denomination at UL.

$4, Pope Francis with Pres. Barack Obama and wife, Michelle.

2015, Nov. 25 Litho. *Perf. 14*
1283 A460 65c Sheet of 6, #a-f 8.00 8.00

Souvenir Sheet
1284 A460 $4 multi 8.00 8.00

No. 1284 contains one 80x30mm stamp.

Pres. Dwight D. Eisenhower (1890-1969) — A461

No. 1285 — Pres. Eisenhower: a, Wearing golf cap. b, With three men on golf course. c, Giving "V" for victory sign. d, Holding baseball. e, Waving to crowd from train. f, Wearing military uniform, standing in car.

$4, Pres. Eisenhower with wife, Mamie, horiz.

2015, Dec. 7 Litho. *Perf. 14*
1285 A461 65c Sheet of 6, #a-f 8.00 8.00

Souvenir Sheet
Perf. 12½
1286 A461 $4 multi 8.00 8.00

No. 1286 contains one 51x38mm stamp.

Sir Winston Churchill (1874-1965), British Prime Minister — A462

No. 1287 — Churchill: a, Smoking cigar. b, Aiming submachine gun. c, With Pres. Franklin D. Roosevelt. d, Giving "V" for Victory sign.

$4, Churchill speaking in front of picture of Abraham Lincoln, horiz.

2015, Dec. 7 Litho. *Perf. 12½*
1287 A462 $1.20 Sheet of 4, #a-d 9.75 9.75

Souvenir Sheet
1288 A462 $4 multi 8.00 8.00

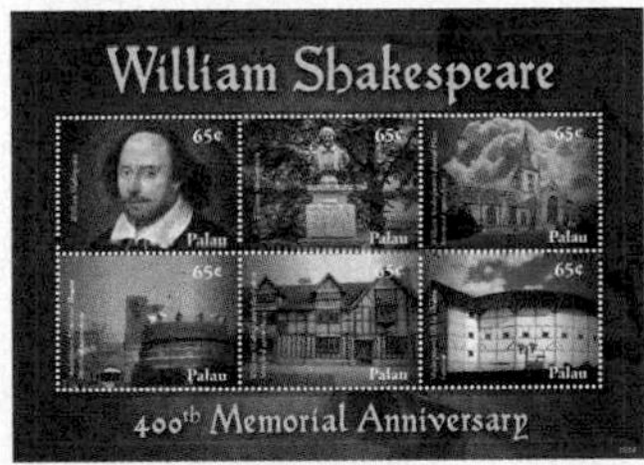

William Shakespeare (1564-1616), Writer — A463

No. 1289: a, Portrait of Shakespeare. b, Statue of Shakespeare. c, Shakespeare's burial place, Stratford-upon-Avon, Great Britain. d, Shakespeare Memorial Theater, Stratford-upon-Avon. e, Shakespeare's birthplace, Stratford-upon-Avon. f, Globe Theater, London.

$4, Shakespeare's first folio, 1623, vert.

2015, Dec. 7 Litho. *Perf. 14*
1289 A463 65c Sheet of 6, #a-f 8.00 8.00

Souvenir Sheet
Perf. 12
1290 A463 $4 multi 8.00 8.00

No. 1290 contains one 30x50mm stamp.

Christmas A464

Paintings by Bartolomé Esteban Murillo: 34c, The Annunciation. 49c, Virgin and Child in Glory. $1, Madonna and Child. $2, Virgin with Child.

2015, Dec. 7 Litho. *Perf. 12½*
1291-1294 A464 Set of 4 7.75 7.75

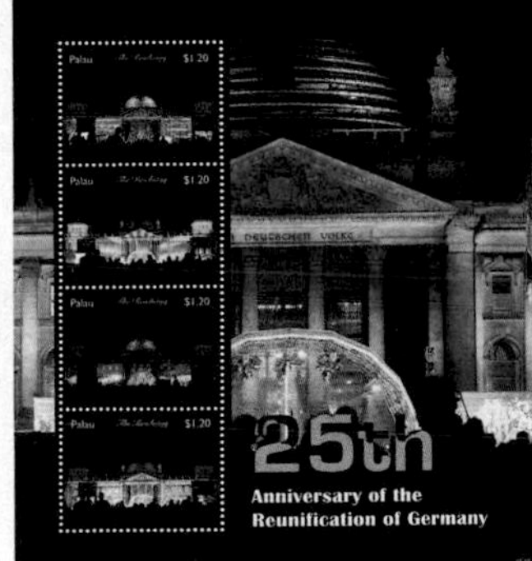

German Reunification, 25th Anniv. — A465

No. 1295 — Reichstag Building, Berlin: a, Side towers in red light. b, Side towers in yellow light. c, Side towers in purple light, statues near dome not visible. d, Side towers in purple light, statues near dome in blue light.

$4, Reichstag Building with columns in red and white light, vert.

2015, Dec. 17 Litho. *Perf. 12*
1295 A465 $1.20 Sheet of 4, #a-d 9.75 9.75

Souvenir Sheet
Perf. 12½
1296 A465 $4 multi 8.00 8.00

No. 1296 contains one 38x51mm stamp.

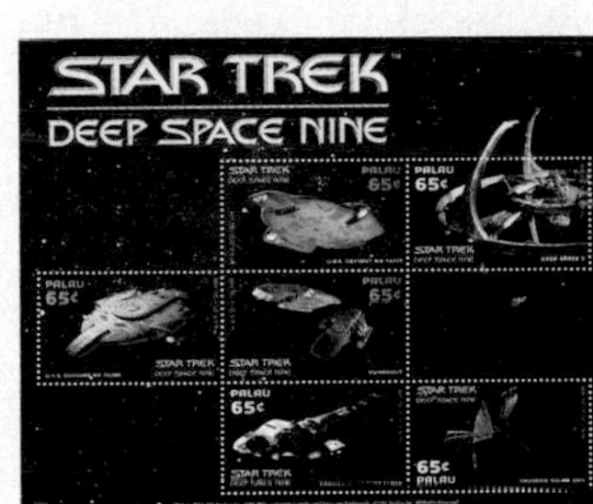

Spacecraft from *Star Trek Deep Space Nine* — A466

No. 1297: a, U.S.S. Defiant, denomination at UR. b, Deep Space 9. c, U.S.S. Defiant, denomination at UL. d, Runabout. e, Cardassian Galor Class. f, Bajoran Solar Sail.

$4, U.S.S. Defiant, diff.

2015, Dec. 31 Litho. *Perf. 12*
1297 A466 65c Sheet of 6, #a-f 8.00 8.00

Souvenir Sheet
Perf. 14
1298 A466 $4 multi 8.00 8.00

No. 1298 contains one 80x30mm stamp.

Mollusks — A467

No. 1299: a, Palau nautilus, tentacles at left. b, Chambered nautilus, tentacles at left. c, Palau nautilus, tentacles at right. d, Chambered nautilus, tentacles at right.
$4, Palau nautilus, vert.

2015, Dec. 31 Litho. *Perf. 14*

1299 A467 $1.20 Sheet of 4, #a-d 9.75 9.75

Souvenir Sheet

Perf. 12

1300 A467 $4 multi 8.00 8.00

Coral Reef Snakes — A468

No. 1301: a, Turtle-headed sea snake, name in white at top. b, Turtle-headed sea snake, name in black at bottom. c, Yellow-lipped sea krait, snake's body extending to right. d, Yellow-lipped sea krait, snake's body extending to left. e, Yellow-lipped sea krait and orange rock. f, Yellow-lipped sea krait, snake's body going through coral.
$4, Head of Yellow-lipped sea krait, horiz.

2015, Dec. 31 Litho. *Perf.*

1301 A468 65c Sheet of 6, #a-f 8.00 8.00

Souvenir Sheet

1302 A468 $4 multi 8.00 8.00

No. 1302 contains one 44x33mm oval stamp.

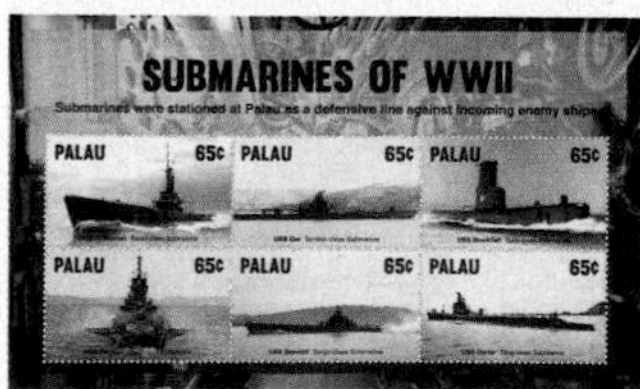

World War II Submarines — A469

No. 1303: a, USS Archerfish. b, USS Gar. c, USS Blackfish. d, USS Tullibee, e, USS Seawolf. f, USS Darter.
$4, USS Seal.

2015, Dec. 31 Litho. *Perf. 12*

1303 A469 65c Sheet of 6, #a-f 8.00 8.00

Souvenir Sheet

Perf. 14

1304 A469 $4 multi 8.00 8.00

No. 1304 contains one 80x30mm stamp.

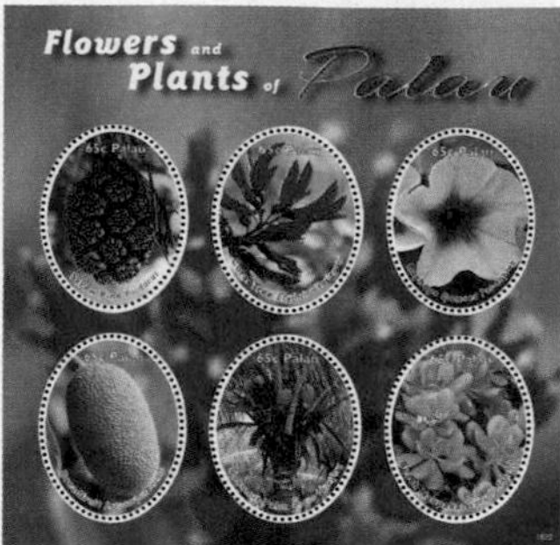

Flora — A470

No. 1305: a, Screw pine. b, Coral tree flowers. c, Bayhops. d, Breadfruit. e, Coconut palm. f, Beach naupaka.
$4, Mangrove flowers.

2016, Feb. 2 Litho. *Perf.*

1305 A470 65c Sheet of 6, #a-f 8.00 8.00

Souvenir Sheet

1306 A470 $4 multi 8.00 8.00

SEMI-POSTAL STAMPS

Olympic Sports SP1

No. B1, Baseball glove, player. No. B2, Running shoe, athlete. No. B3, Goggles, swimmer. No. B4, Gold medal, diver.

1988, Aug. 8 Litho. *Perf. 14*

B1 SP1 25c +5c multi .50 .50
B2 SP1 25c +5c multi .50 .50
a. Pair, #B1-B2 1.25 1.25
B3 SP1 45c +5c multi 1.25 1.25
B4 SP1 45c +5c multi 1.25 1.25
a. Pair, #B3-B4 2.75 2.75

AIR POST STAMPS

White-tailed Tropicbird — AP1

1984, June 12 Litho. *Perf. 14*

C1 AP1 40c shown .75 .75
C2 AP1 40c Fairy tern .75 .75
C3 AP1 40c Black noddy .75 .75
C4 AP1 40c Black-naped tern .75 .75
a. Block of 4, #C1-C4 3.50 3.50

Audubon Type of 1985

1985, Feb. 6 Litho. *Perf. 14*

C5 A12 44c Audubon's Shear-water 1.10 1.10

Palau-Germany Political, Economic & Cultural Exchange Cent. — AP2

Germany Nos. 40, 65, Caroline Islands Nos. 19, 13 and: No. C6, German flag-raising at Palau, 1885. No. C7, Early German trading post in Angaur. No. C8, Abai architecture recorded by Prof. & Frau Kramer, 1908-1910. No. C9, S.M.S. Cormoran.

1985, Sept. 19 Litho. *Perf. 14x13½*

C6 AP2 44c multicolored .95 .95
C7 AP2 44c multicolored .95 .95
C8 AP2 44c multicolored .95 .95
C9 AP2 44c multicolored .95 .95
a. Block of 4, #C6-C9 4.50 4.50

Trans-Pacific Airmail Anniv. Type of 1985

Aircraft: No. C10, 1951 Trans-Ocean Airways PBY-5A Catalina Amphibian. No. C11, 1968 Air Micronesia DC-6B Super Cloudmaster. No. C12, 1960 Trust Territory Airline SA-16 Albatross. No. C13, 1967 Pan American Douglas DC-4.

1985, Nov. 21 Litho. *Perf. 14*

C10 A16 44c multicolored .85 .85
C11 A16 44c multicolored .85 .85
C12 A16 44c multicolored .85 .85
C13 A16 44c multicolored .85 .85
a. Block of 4, #C10-C13 3.75 3.75

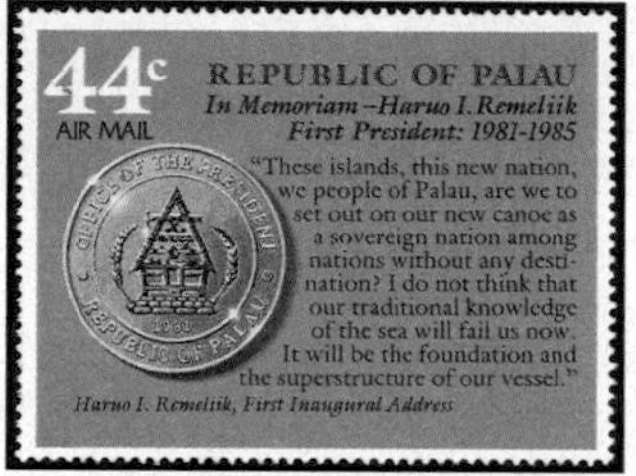

Haruo I. Remeliik (1933-1985), 1st President — AP3

Designs: No. C14, Presidential seal, excerpt from 1st inaugural address. No. C15, War canoe, address excerpt, diff. No. C16, Remeliik, US Pres. Reagan, excerpt from Reagan's speech, Pacific Basin Conference, Guam, 1984.

1986, June 30 Litho. *Perf. 14*

C14 AP3 44c multicolored 1.10 1.10
C15 AP3 44c multicolored 1.10 1.10
C16 AP3 44c multicolored 1.10 1.10
a. Strip of 3, #C14-C16 3.75 3.75

Intl. Peace Year, Statue of Liberty Cent. — AP4

1986, Sept. 19 Litho.

C17 AP4 44c multicolored 1.00 1.00

Aircraft — AP5

36c, Cessna 207 Skywagon. 39c, Embraer EMB-110 Bandeirante. 45c, Boeing 727.

1989, May 17 Litho. *Perf. 14x14½*

C18 AP5 36c multicolored .65 .65
a. Booklet pane of 10 7.00 —
C19 AP5 39c multicolored .85 .85
a. Booklet pane of 10 7.50 —
C20 AP5 45c multicolored 1.00 1.00
a. Booklet pane of 10 8.25 —
b. Booklet pane, 5 each 36c, 45c 8.50 —
Nos. C18-C20 (3) 2.50 2.50

Palauan Bai Type

1991, July 9 Litho. *Die Cut*

Self-Adhesive

C21 A61 50c like #293a 1.50 1.50

World War II in the Pacific Type

Miniature Sheet

Aircraft: No. C22: a, Grumman TBF Avenger, US Navy. b, Curtiss P-40C, Chinese Air Force "Flying Tigers." c, Mitsubishi A6M Zero-Sen, Japan. d, Hawker Hurricane, Royal Air Force. e, Consolidated PBY Catalina, Royal Netherlands Indies Air Force. f, Curtiss Hawk 75, Netherlands Indies. g, Boeing B-17E, US Army Air Force. h, Brewster Buffalo, Royal Australian Air Force. i, Supermarine Walrus, Royal Navy. j, Curtiss P-40E, Royal New Zealand Air Force.

1992, Sept. 10 Litho. *Perf. 14½x15*

C22 A66 50c Sheet of 10, #a.-j. 11.00 11.00

Birds — AP6

a, Palau swiftlet. b, Barn swallow. c, Jungle nightjar. d, White-breasted woodswallow.

1994, Mar. 24 Litho. *Perf. 14*

C23 AP6 50c Block of 4, #a.-d. 4.00 4.00

No. C23 is printed in sheets of 16 stamps.

PALESTINE

'pa-lə-ˌstin

LOCATION — Western Asia bordering on the Mediterranean Sea
GOVT. — Former British Mandate
AREA — 10,429 sq. mi.
POP. — 1,605,816 (estimated)
CAPITAL — Jerusalem

Formerly a part of Turkey, Palestine was occupied by the Egyptian Expeditionary Forces of the British Army in World War I and was mandated to Great Britain in 1923. Mandate ended May 14, 1948.

10 Milliemes = 1 Piaster
1000 Milliemes = 1 Egyptian Pound
1000 Mils = 1 Palestine Pound (1928)

Jordan stamps overprinted with "Palestine" in English and Arabic are listed under Jordan.

Watermark

Wmk. 33

Issued under British Military Occupation

For use in Palestine, Transjordan, Lebanon, Syria and in parts of Cilicia and northeastern Egypt

A1

Wmk. Crown and "GvR" (33)

1918, Feb. 10 Litho. ***Rouletted 20***

1	A1	1pi deep blue	190.00	105.00
2	A1	1pi ultra	2.50	2.50

Nos. 2 & 1 Surcharged in Black

1918, Feb. 16

3	A1	5m on 1pi ultra	8.50	4.25
a.		5m on 1pi gray blue	110.00	*600.00*

Nos. 1 and 3a were issued without gum. No. 3a is on paper with a surface sheen.

1918 Typo. ***Perf. 15x14***

4	A1	1m dark brown	.35	*.45*
5	A1	2m blue green	.35	*.50*
6	A1	3m light brown	.40	.40
7	A1	4m scarlet	.40	*.45*
8	A1	5m orange	.75	.35
9	A1	1pi indigo	.50	.30
10	A1	2pi olive green	3.50	1.00
11	A1	5pi plum	3.75	2.50
12	A1	9pi bister	11.50	7.50
13	A1	10pi ultramarine	12.00	4.50
14	A1	20pi gray	16.00	*20.00*
		Nos. 4-14 (11)	49.50	37.95

Many shades exist.

Nos. 4-11 exist with rough perforation.

Issued: 1m, 2m, 4m, 2pi, 5pi, 7/16; 5m, 9/25; 1pi, 11/9; 3m, 9pi, 10pi, 12/17; 20pi, 12/27.

Nos. 4-11 with overprint "O. P. D. A." (Ottoman Public Debt Administration) or "H.J.Z." (Hejaz-Jemen Railway) are revenue stamps; they exist postally used.

For overprints on stamps and types see #15-62 & Jordan #1-63, 73-90, 92-102, 130-144, J12-J23.

Issued under British Administration

Overprinted at Jerusalem

Stamps and Type of 1918 Overprinted in Black or Silver

1920, Sept. 1 Wmk. 33 ***Perf. 15x14***
Arabic Overprint 8mm long

15	A1	1m dark brown	9.00	2.25
16	A1	2m bl grn, perf 14	4.50	1.75
d.		Perf 15x14	14.00	6.00
17	A1	3m lt brown	17.50	8.50
d.		Perf 14	110.00	62.50
e.		Inverted overprint	550.00	*700.00*
18	A1	4m scarlet	5.25	1.75
19	A1	5m org, perf 14	8.00	.75
e.		Perf 15x14	27.50	10.00
20	A1	1pi indigo (S)	5.75	1.25
21	A1	2pi olive green	7.00	2.50
22	A1	5pi plum	27.50	*30.00*
23	A1	9pi bister	15.00	*23.00*
24	A1	10pi ultra	13.00	*19.50*
25	A1	20pi gray	35.00	*50.00*
		Nos. 15-25 (11)	147.50	141.25

Forgeries exist of No. 17e.

Similar Ovpt., with Arabic Line 10mm Long, Arabic "S" and "T" Joined, ".." at Left Extends Above Other Letters

1920-21 ***Perf. 15x14***

15a	A1	1m dark brown	2.25	1.20
e.		Perf. 14	700.00	850.00
g.		As "a," invtd. ovpt.	450.00	
16a	A1	2m blue green	10.00	4.50
e.		"PALESTINE" omitted	*2,500.*	*1,500.*
f.		Perf. 14	4.75	4.50
17a	A1	3m light brown	3.75	1.20
18a	A1	4m scarlet	5.50	1.40
b.		Perf. 14	70.00	87.50
19a	A1	5m orange	2.60	.90
f.		Perf. 14	9.50	1.25
20a	A1	1pi indigo, perf. 14 (S) ('21)	57.50	1.40
d.		Perf. 15x14	525.00	32.50
21a	A1	2pi olive green ('21)	75.00	30.00
22a	A1	5pi plum ('21)	52.50	11.00
d.		Perf. 14	225.00	*525.00*
		Nos. 15a-22a (8)	209.10	51.60

This overprint often looks grayish to grayish black. In the English line the letters are frequently uneven and damaged.

Similar Ovpt., with Arabic Line 10mm Long, Arabic "S" and "T" Separated and 6mm Between English and Hebrew Lines

1920, Dec. 6

15b	A1	1m dk brn, perf 14	57.50	37.50
17b	A1	3m lt brn, perf 15x14	60.00	37.50
19b	A1	5m orange, perf 14	400.00	37.50
d.		Perf. 15x14	*16,000.*	*13,750.*
		Nos. 15b-19b (3)	517.50	112.50

Overprinted as Before, 7½mm Between English and Hebrew Lines, ".." at Left Even With Other Letters

1921 ***Perf. 15x14***

15c	A1	1m dark brown	15.00	4.00
f.		1m dull brown, perf 14		*2,300.*
16c	A1	2m blue green	25.00	6.25
17c	A1	3m light brown	35.00	3.50
18c	A1	4m scarlet	35.00	4.00
19c	A1	5m orange	70.00	1.10
20c	A1	1pi indigo (S)	21.00	.90
21c	A1	2pi olive green	26.50	7.00
22c	A1	5pi plum	29.00	9.25
23c	A1	9pi bister	57.50	*100.00*
24c	A1	10pi ultra	70.00	16.00
25c	A1	20pi pale gray	100.00	57.50
d.		Perf. 14	*13,750.*	*2,900.*
		Nos. 15c-25c (11)	484.00	*209.50*

Overprinted at London

Stamps of 1918 Overprinted

1921 ***Perf. 15x14***

37	A1	1m dark brown	1.50	.35
38	A1	2m blue green	2.50	.35
39	A1	3m light brown	2.75	.35
40	A1	4m scarlet	3.25	.70
41	A1	5m orange	3.00	.35
42	A1	1pi bright blue	2.25	.40
43	A1	2pi olive green	3.75	.45
44	A1	5pi plum	10.00	5.75
45	A1	9pi bister	20.00	16.00
46	A1	10pi ultra	26.00	*600.00*
47	A1	20pi gray	65.00	*1,600.*
		Nos. 37-47 (11)	140.00	
		Nos. 37-45 (9)		24.70

The 2nd character from left on bottom line that looks like quotation marks consists of long thin lines.

Deformed or damaged letters exist in all three lines of the overprint.

Similar Overprint on Type of 1921

1922 Wmk. 4 ***Perf. 14***

48	A1	1m dark brown	1.75	.35
a.		Inverted overprint	—	*13,750.*
b.		Double overprint	260.00	500.00
49	A1	2m yellow	2.50	.35
50	A1	3m Prus blue	2.75	.25
51	A1	4m rose	2.75	.25
52	A1	5m orange	3.25	.35
53	A1	6m blue green	2.50	.35
54	A1	7m yellow brown	2.50	.35
55	A1	8m red	2.50	.35
56	A1	1pi gray	3.00	.35
57	A1	13m ultra	3.50	.25
58	A1	2pi olive green	3.50	.40
a.		Inverted overprint	350.00	*575.00*
b.		2pi yellow bister	*140.00*	*7.50*
59	A1	5pi plum	5.50	1.40
a.		Perf. 15x14	62.50	4.50

Perf. 15x14

60	A1	9pi bister	10.00	10.00
a.		Perf. 14	1,050.	225.00
61	A1	10pi light blue	8.50	3.00
a.		Perf. 14	75.00	15.00
62	A1	20pi violet	10.50	6.25
a.		Perf. 14	180.00	120.00
		Nos. 48-62 (15)	65.00	24.25

The 2nd character from left on bottom line that looks like quotation marks consists of short thick lines.

The "E. F. F." for "E. E. F." on No. 61 is caused by damaged type.

Rachel's Tomb — A3

Mosque of Omar (Dome of the Rock) — A4

Citadel at Jerusalem A5

Tiberias and Sea of Galilee A6

1927-42 Typo. ***Perf. 13½x14½***

63	A3	2m Prus blue	2.75	.25
64	A3	3m yellow green	1.75	.25
65	A4	4m rose red	9.00	1.40
66	A4	4m violet brn ('32)	2.50	.25
67	A5	5m brown org	4.25	.25
c.		Perf. 14½x14 (coil stamp) ('36)	16.00	*21.00*
68	A4	6m deep green	1.25	.25
69	A5	7m deep red	10.00	.70
70	A5	7m dk violet ('32)	1.00	.25
71	A4	8m yellow brown	17.50	7.00
72	A4	8m scarlet ('32)	1.50	.25
73	A3	10m deep gray	1.75	.25
a.		Perf. 14½x14 (coil stamp) ('38)	23.50	*27.50*
74	A4	13m ultra	17.50	.40
75	A4	13m olive bister ('32)	2.75	.25
76	A4	15m ultra ('32)	4.75	.50
77	A5	20m olive green	1.75	.25

Perf. 14

78	A6	50m brown purple	2.75	.40
79	A6	90m bister	70.00	*60.00*
80	A6	100m bright blue	2.60	.80
81	A6	200m dk violet	9.25	5.75
82	A6	250m dp brown ('42)	7.50	3.50
83	A6	500m red ('42)	7.50	3.50
84	A6	£1 gray black ('42)	10.00	4.00
		Nos. 63-84 (22)	189.60	90.45

Issued: 3m, #74, 6/1; 2m, 5m, 6m, 10m, #65, 69, 71, 77-81, 8/14; #70, 72, 6/1/32; #75, 15m, 8/1/32; #66, 11/1/32; #82-84, 1/15/42.

POSTAGE DUE STAMPS

D1

1923 Unwmk. Typo. ***Perf. 11***

J1	D1	1m bister brown	20.00	*29.00*
b.		Horiz. pair, imperf. btwn.	1,300.	*750.00*
J2	D1	2m green	16.00	11.50
J3	D1	4m red	12.00	*12.00*
J4	D1	8m violet	8.50	*8.50*
b.		Horiz. pair, imperf. btwn.		*2,300.*
J5	D1	13m dark blue	7.50	*7.50*
a.		Horiz. pair, imperf. btwn.	1,050.	
		Nos. J1-J5 (5)	64.00	*68.50*

Imperfs. of 1m, 2m, 8m, are from proof sheets.

Values for Nos. J1-J5 are for fine centered copies.

D2

1924, Dec. 1 **Wmk. 4**

J6	D2	1m brown	1.10	2.00
J7	D2	2m yellow	4.00	1.75
J8	D2	4m green	2.00	1.50
J9	D2	8m red	3.00	1.00
J10	D2	13m ultramarine	2.75	2.50
J11	D2	5pi violet	13.00	1.75
		Nos. J6-J11 (6)	25.85	10.50

D3

1928-45 ***Perf. 14***

J12	D3	1m lt brown	2.25	1.00
a.		Perf. 15x14 ('45)	42.50	80.00
J13	D3	2m yellow	3.00	.70
J14	D3	4m green	3.50	1.60
a.		4m bluish grn, perf. 15x14 ('45)	75.00	*97.50*
J15	D3	6m brown org ('33)	17.50	5.00
J16	D3	8m red	2.75	1.25
J17	D3	10m light gray	2.00	.70
J18	D3	13m ultra	4.50	2.25
J19	D3	20m olive green	4.50	1.25
J20	D3	50m violet	4.50	1.50
		Nos. J12-J20 (9)	44.50	15.25

The Hebrew word for "mil" appears below the numeral on all values but the 1m.

Issued: 6m, Oct. 1933; others, Feb. 1, 1928.

PALESTINIAN AUTHORITY

'pa-lə-,s-ti-nē-ən 'o-thōr-itē

LOCATION — Areas of the West Bank and the Gaza Strip.
AREA — 2,410 sq. mi.
POP. — 2,825,000 (2000 est.)

1000 Fils (Mils) = 5 Israeli Shekels
1000 Fils = 1 Jordanian Dinar (Jan. 1, 1998)

Catalogue values for all unused stamps in this country are for Never Hinged items.

Hisham Palace, Jericho — A1

5m, 10m, 20m, Hisham Palace. 30m, 40m, 50m, 75m, Mosque, Jerusalem. 125, 150m, 250m, 300m, 500m, Flag. 1000m, Dome of the Rock.

1994 Litho. *Perf. 14*

1 A1 5m multicolored .25 .25
2 A1 10m multicolored .25 .25
3 A1 20m multicolored .25 .25
4 A1 30m multicolored .25 .25
5 A1 40m multicolored .25 .25
6 A1 50m multicolored .35 .35
7 A1 75m multicolored .40 .40
8 A1 125m multicolored .65 .65
9 A1 150m multicolored .90 .90
10 A1 250m multicolored 1.25 1.25
11 A1 300m multicolored 1.75 1.75

Size: 51x29mm

12 A1 500m multicolored 3.00 3.00
13 A1 1000m multicolored 5.00 5.00
Nos. 1-13 (13) 14.55 14.55

Issued: 125m-500m, 8/15; others, 9/1.

Nos. 1-13 Surcharged "FILS" in English and Arabic in Black or Silver and with Black Bars Obliterating "Mils"

1995, Apr. 10 Litho. *Perf. 14*

14 A1 5f multicolored .25 .25
15 A1 10f multicolored .25 .25
16 A1 20f multicolored .25 .25
17 A1 30f multicolored (S) .25 .25
18 A1 40f multicolored (S) .30 .30
19 A1 50f multicolored (S) .35 .35
20 A1 75f multicolored (S) .40 .40
21 A1 125f multicolored .55 .55
22 A1 150f multicolored .65 .65
23 A1 250f multicolored 1.10 1.10
24 A1 300f multicolored 1.40 1.40

Size: 51x29mm

25 A1 500f multicolored 2.25 2.25
26 A1 1000f multicolored 5.00 5.00
Nos. 14-26 (13) 13.00 13.00

Palestine No. 63 — A2

350f, Palestine #67. 500f, Palestine #72.

1995, May 17 Litho. *Perf. 14*

27 A2 150f multicolored 1.00 1.00
28 A2 350f multicolored 1.75 1.75
29 A2 500f multicolored 2.25 2.25
Nos. 27-29 (3) 5.00 5.00

Traditional Costumes — A3

Women wearing various costumes.

1995, May 31

30 A3 250f multicolored 1.00 1.00
31 A3 300f multicolored 1.10 1.10
32 A3 550f multicolored 2.25 2.25
33 A3 900f multicolored 3.50 3.50
Nos. 30-33 (4) 7.85 7.85

Christmas — A4

Designs: 10f, Ancient view of Bethlehem. 20f, Modern view of Bethlehem. 50f, Entrance to grotto, Church of the Nativity. 100f, Yasser Arafat, Pope John Paul II. 1000f, Star of the Nativity, Church of the Nativity, Bethlehem.
10f, 20f, 100f, 1000f are horiz.

1995, Dec. 18

34 A4 10f multicolored .25 .25
35 A4 20f multicolored .25 .25
36 A4 50f multicolored .25 .25
37 A4 100f multicolored .60 .60
38 A4 1000f multicolored 5.00 5.00
Nos. 34-38 (5) 6.35 6.35

Pres. Yasser Arafat — A5

1996, Mar. 20

39 A5 10f red vio & bluish blk .25 .25
40 A5 20f yellow & bluish black .25 .25
41 A5 50f blue & bluish black .25 .25
42 A5 100f apple grn & bluish blk .50 .50
43 A5 1000f org & bluish blk 4.25 4.25
Nos. 39-43 (5) 5.50 5.50

1996 Intl. Philatelic Exhibitions — A6

Exhibition, site: 20f, CHINA '96, Summer Palace, Beijing. 50f, ISTANBUL '96, Hagia Sofia. 100f, ESSEN '96, Villa Hugel. 1000f, CAPEX '96, Toronto skyline.

1996, May 18

44 A6 20f multicolored .25 .25
45 A6 50f multicolored .30 .30
46 A6 100f multicolored .45 .45
47 A6 1000f multicolored 4.50 4.50
a. Sheet, 2 each #44-47 + 2 labels 13.00
Nos. 44-47 (4) 5.50 5.50

Souvenir Sheet

1st Palestinian Parliamentary & Presidential Elections — A7

1996, May 20

48 A7 1250f multicolored 5.50 5.50

1996 Summer Olympic Games, Atlanta — A8

Designs: 30f, Boxing. 40f, Medal, 1896. 50f, Runners. 150f, Olympic flame. 1000f, Palestinian Olympic Committee emblem.

1996, July 19 *Perf. 13½*

49 A8 30f multicolored .25 .25
50 A8 40f multicolored .25 .25
51 A8 50f multicolored .35 .35
52 A8 150f multicolored .70 .70
a. Sheet of 3, #49, 51-52 5.50 5.50
53 A8 1000f multicolored 4.25 4.25
Nos. 49-53 (5) 5.80 5.80

Flowers — A9

1996, Nov. 22

54 A9 10f Poppy .25 .25
55 A9 25f Hibiscus .25 .25
56 A9 100f Thyme .50 .50
57 A9 150f Lemon .70 .70
58 A9 750f Orange 3.00 3.00
Nos. 54-58 (5) 4.70 4.70

Souvenir Sheet

59 A9 1000f Olive 4.50 4.50

Souvenir Sheet

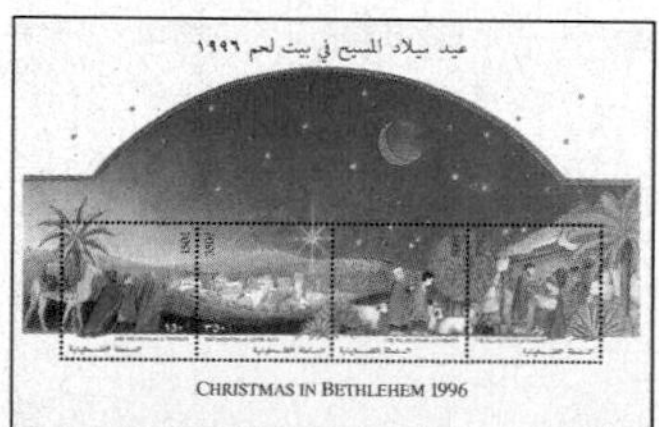

Christmas — A10

a, 150f, Magi. b, 350f, View of Bethlehem. c, 500f, Shepherds, sheep. d, 750f, Nativity scene.

1996, Dec. 14 *Perf. 14*

60 A10 Sheet of 4, #a.-d. 6.50 6.50

Birds — A11

1997, May 29

61 A11 25f Great tit .30 .30
62 A11 75f Blue rock thrush .40 .40
63 A11 150f Golden oriole .85 .85
64 A11 350f Hoopoe 2.00 2.00
65 A11 600f Peregrine falcon 2.75 2.75
Nos. 61-65 (5) 6.30 6.30

Historic Views — A12

1997, June 19

66 A12 350f Gaza, 1839 1.50 1.50
67 A12 600f Hebron, 1839 2.50 2.50

Souvenir Sheet

Return of Hong Kong to China — A13

1997, July 1

68 A13 225f multicolored 3.00 3.00

Friends of Palestine — A14

#69, Portraits of Yasser Arafat, Hans-Jürgen Wischnewski. #70, Wischnewski shaking hands with Arafat. #71, Mother Teresa. #72, Mother Teresa with Arafat.

1997 Litho. *Perf. 14*

69 A14 600f multicolored 1.75 1.75
70 A14 600f multicolored 1.75 1.75
a. Pair, #69-70 4.50 4.50
71 A14 600f multicolored 2.00 2.00
72 A14 600f multicolored 2.00 2.00
a. Pair, #71-72 4.75 4.75
Nos. 69-72 (1) 1.75 1.75

#70a, 72a were issued in sheets of 4 stamps.

Issued: #69-70, 7/24; #71-72, 12/17.

Christmas — A15

1997, Nov. 28

73 A15 350f multicolored 1.25 1.25
74 A15 700f multicolored 2.25 2.25
a. Pair, #73-74 3.75 3.75

Mosaics from Floor of Byzantine Church, Jabalia-Gaza
A16

50f, Rabbit, palm tree. 125f, Goat, rabbit, dog. 200f, Basket, fruit tree, jar. 400f, Lion.

1998, June 22 Litho. *Perf. 13½*

75	A16	50f multicolored	.30	.30
76	A16	125f multicolored	1.00	.60
77	A16	200f multicolored	1.75	1.00
78	A16	400f multicolored	3.50	1.75
		Nos. 75-78 (4)	6.55	3.65

Souvenir Sheet

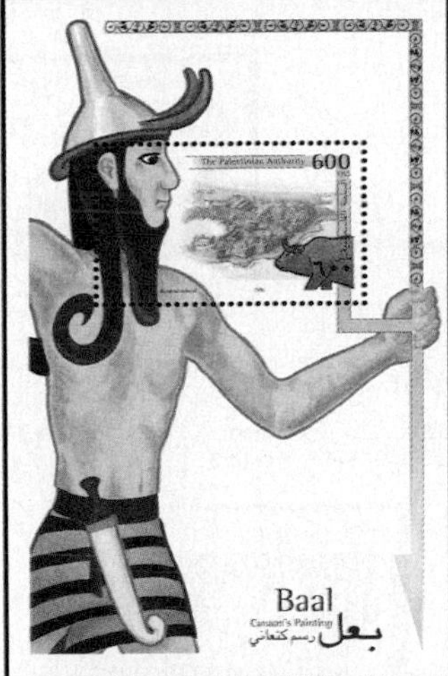

Baal — A17

1998, June 15 *Perf. 14*

79 A17 600f multicolored 2.75 2.75

A18

Medicinal plants.

1998, Sept. 30 Litho. *Perf. 14*

80	A18	40f Urginea maritima	.25	.25
81	A18	80f Silybum marianum	.30	.30
82	A18	500f Foeniculum vulgare	1.50	1.50
83	A18	800f Inula viscosa	3.00	3.00
		Nos. 80-83 (4)	5.05	5.05

Raptors
A19

1998, Nov. 12 Litho. *Perf. 14*

84	A19	20f Bonelli's eagle	.25	.25
85	A19	60f Hobby	.30	.30
86	A19	340f Verreaux's eagle	1.75	1.75
87	A19	600f Bateleur	2.75	2.75
88	A19	900f Buzzard	3.75	3.75
		Nos. 84-88 (5)	8.80	8.80

Souvenir Sheet

Granting of Additional Rights to Palestinian Authority's Observer to UN — A20

1998, Nov. 12

89 A20 700f multicolored 3.00 3.00

Butterflies — A21

Designs: a, 100f, Papilio alexanor. b, 200f, Danaus chrysippus. c, 300f, Gonepteryx cleopatra. d, 400f, Melanargia titea.

1998, Dec. 3

90 A21 Sheet of 4, #a.-d. 4.50 4.50

Souvenir Sheet

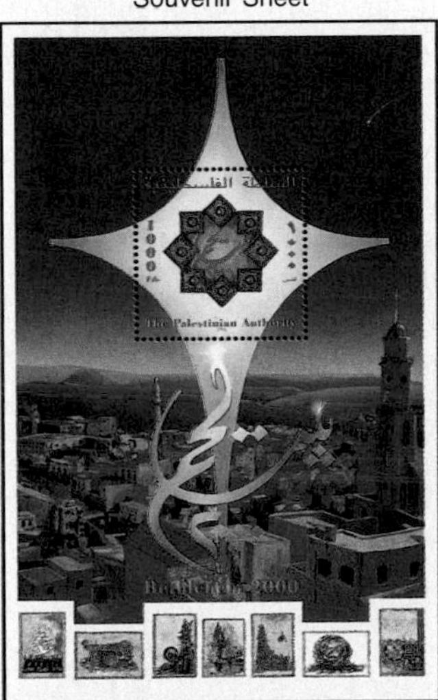

Christmas, Bethlehem 2000 — A22

1998, Dec. 3

91 A22 1000f multicolored 4.25 4.25

Souvenir Sheet

Signing of Middle East Peace Agreement, Wye River Conference, Oct. 23, 1998 — A23

Palestinian Pres. Yasser Arafat and US Pres. Bill Clinton.

1999 Litho. *Perf. 14*

92 A23 900f multicolored 3.75 3.75

New Airport, Gaza
A24

Designs: 80f, Control tower, vert. 300f, Airplane. 700f, Terminal building.

1999

93	A24	80f multicolored	.25	.25
94	A24	300f multicolored	.90	.90
95	A24	700f multicolored	2.50	2.50
		Nos. 93-95 (3)	3.65	3.65

Intl. Philatelic Exhibitions & UPU, 125th Anniv. — A25

a, 20f, Buildings, China 1999. b, 260f, Buildings, Germany, IBRA '99. c. 80f, High-rise buildings, Australia '99. d, 340f, Eiffel Tower, Philex France '99. e, 400f, Aerial view of countryside, denomination LR, UPU, 125th anniv. f, 400f, like #96e, denomination LL.

1999

96 A25 Block of 6, #a.-f. 6.75 6.75

Hebron — A26

a, 400f, Lettering in gold. b, 500f, Lettering in white.

1999, Aug. 20 Litho. *Perf. 14*

97 A26 Pair, #a.-b. 4.00 4.00

Arabian Horses — A27

a, 25f. b, 75f. c, 150f. d, 350f. e, 800f.

1999, Apr. 27

98 A27 Strip of 5, #a.-e. 5.50 5.50

Souvenir Sheet

Palestinian Sunbird — A28

1999 Litho. *Perf. 13¾*

99 A28 750f multi 3.50 3.50

A29

Christmas, Bethlehem 2000 — A30

Giotto Paintings (Type A30): 200f, 280f, 2000f, The Nativity. 380f, 460f, The Adoration of the Magi. 560f, The Flight into Egypt. Inscription colors: Nos. 108a, 110a, Black. Nos. 109a, 111a, White. No. 112a, Yellow. Nos. 108b-112b have silver inscriptions and frames. No. 113, country name at lower left. No. 113A, country name at upper right, denomination at lower left.

1999, Dec. 8 Litho. *Perf. 13¼x13*

Background Color

100	A29	60f black	.25	.25
101	A29	80f light blue	.25	.25
102	A29	100f dark gray	.35	.35
103	A29	280f lilac rose	.90	.90
104	A29	300f green	.95	.95
105	A29	400f red violet	1.40	1.40
106	A29	500f dark red	1.60	1.60
107	A29	560f light gray	1.90	1.90

Perf. 13¼

108	A30	200f Pair, #a.-b	*2.50*	*2.50*
109	A30	280f Pair, #a.-b.	*2.75*	*2.75*
110	A30	380f Pair, #a.-b.	*3.25*	*3.25*
111	A30	460f Pair, #a.-b.	*4.25*	*4.25*
112	A30	560f Pair, #a.-b.	*7.00*	*7.00*

Litho. & Embossed Foil Application

113	A30	2000f multi	8.50	8.50
113A	A30	2000f multi, booklet pane of 1	9.50	9.50
		Nos. 100-113 (14)	*35.85*	*35.85*

Nos. 108-112 each printed in sheets of 10 containing 9 "a" +1 "b." No. 113 printed in sheets of 4. Nos. 108a-112a also exist in sheets of 10.

Issued: No. 113A, 2000.

Easter — A31

Designs: 150f, Last Supper, by Giotto, white inscriptions. 200f, Last Supper, yellow inscriptions. 300f, Lamentation, by Giotto, white inscriptions. 350f, Lamentation, yellow inscriptions. 650f, Crucifix, by Giotto, orange frame.

No. 119, 2000f, Crucifix, gold frame, denomination and country name in orange. No. 119A, 2000f, denomination and country name in white.

2000 **Litho.** ***Perf. 13¼***
114-118 A31 Set of 5 5.50 5.50

Souvenir Sheet

Litho. & Embossed Foil Application

119 A31 2000f multi 8.50 8.50
119A A31 2000f multi, booklet pane of 1 9.50

See Nos. 140-144.

Christmas — A32

Madonna of the Star by Fra Angelico.

Litho. & Embossed Foil Application

2000 ***Perf. 13¼***
120 A32 2000f Miniature sheet of 1 8.50 8.50
a. Booklet pane of 1 9.50 9.50
Complete booklet, #113A, 119A, 120a 28.50

See Nos. 134-139.

Holy Land Visit of Pope John Paul II — A33

Designs: 500f, Pope, Yasser Arafat holding hands. 600f, Pope with miter. 750f, Pope touching Arafat's shoulder. 800f, Pope, creche. 1000f, Pope, back of Arafat's head.

2000 **Litho.** ***Perf. 13¾***
121-125 A33 Set of 5 12.00 12.00

Intl. Children's Year — A34

Designs: 50f, Landscape. 100f, Children. 350f, Domed buildings. 400f, Family.

2000
126-129 A34 Set of 4 3.50 3.50

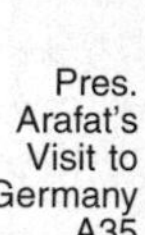

Pres. Arafat's Visit to Germany A35

Arafat and: 200f, German Chancellor Gerhard Schröder. 300f, German President Johannes Rau.

2000 ***Perf. 14x14¼***
130-131 A35 Set of 2 2.75 2.75

Marine Life — A36

No. 132: a, Parrotfish. b, Mauve stinger. c, Ornate wrasse. d, Rainbow wrasse. e, Red starfish. f, Common octopus. g, Purple sea urchin. h, Striated hermit crab.

2000 **Litho.** ***Perf. 13¾***
132 A36 700f Sheet of 8, #a-h 17.50 17.50

Souvenir Sheet

Blue Madonna — A37

2000 ***Perf. 14x13¾***
133 A37 950f multi 3.25 3.25

Christmas Type of 2000

Designs: No. 134, 100f, No. 138, 500f, Nativity, by Gentile da Fabriano, horiz. No. 135, 150f, Adoration of the Magi, by Fabriano, horiz. No. 136, 250f, Immaculate Conception, by Fabriano, horiz. No. 137, 350f, No. 139, 1000f, Like #120.

2000 **Litho.** ***Perf. 13¼***
134-139 A32 Set of 6 7.75 7.75

Easter Type of 2000

Designs: 150f, Christ Carrying Cross, by Fra Angelico, blue inscriptions. 200f, Christ Carrying Cross, white inscriptions. 300f, Removal of Christ from Cross, by Fra Angelico, yellow inscriptions. 350f, Removal of Christ from the Cross, white inscriptions.
2000f, Crucifix, by Giotto, vert.

2001 **Litho.** ***Perf. 13¼***
140-143 A31 Set of 4 3.25 3.25

Souvenir Sheet

Litho. & Embossed

144 A31 2000f gold & multi 7.50 7.50

A38

Palestinian Authority flag and flag of various organizations: 50f, 100f, 200f, 500f.

2001 **Litho.** ***Perf. 13¾***
145-148 A38 Set of 4 2.75 2.75

Souvenir Sheet

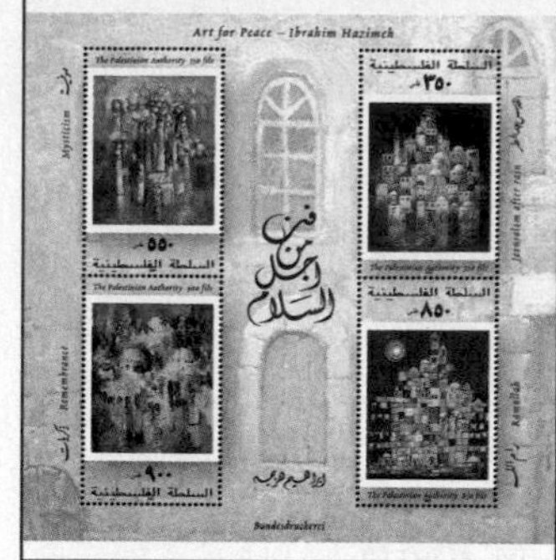

Art by Ibrahim Hazimeh — A39

No. 149: a, 350f, Jerusalem After Rain. b, 550f, Mysticism. c, 850f, Ramallah. d, 900f, Remembrance.

2001 ***Perf. 14x13¾***
149 A39 Sheet of 4, #a-d 9.00 9.00

Worldwide Fund for Nature (WWF) — A40

No. 150 — Houbara bustard, WWF emblem at: a, 350f, UR. b, 350f, LR. c, 750f, UL. d, 750f, LL.

2001 **Litho.** ***Perf. 13¾x14***
150 A40 Block of 4, #a-d 11.50 11.50

Graf Zeppelin Over Holy Land — A41

Zeppelin and: 200f, Map of voyage. 600f, Hills.

2001 ***Perf. 13¾***
151-152 A41 Set of 2 3.00 3.00

Legends A42

Designs: 300f, Man with magic lamp, buildings. 450f, Eagle, snake, gemstones, man. 650f, Man and woman on flying horse. 800f, Man hiding behind tree.

2001 ***Perf. 13¾x14***
153-156 A42 Set of 4 7.00 7.00

Souvenir Sheet

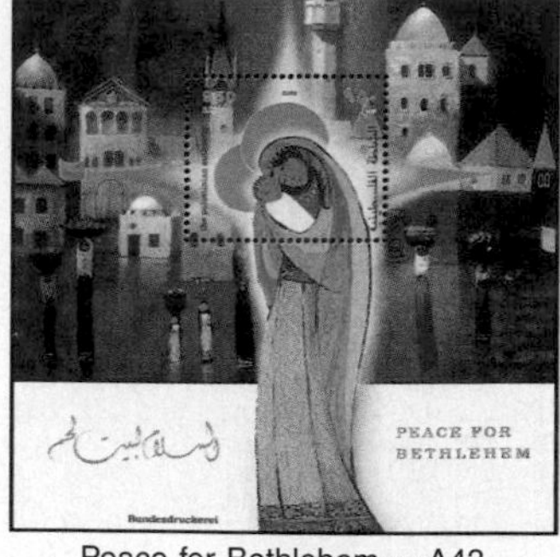

Peace for Bethlehem — A43

2001 ***Perf. 14x13¾***
157 A43 950f multi 3.75 3.75

City Views — A44

Designs: 450f, Jerusalem. 650f, El-Eizariya. 850f, Nablus.

2002 **Litho.** ***Perf. 13¾***
158-160 A44 Set of 3 7.25 7.25

Women's Traditional Clothing — A44a

Various costumes: 50f, 100f, 500f.

2002, June **Litho.** ***Perf. 14***
160A-160C A44a Set of 3 5.50 5.50

Souvenir Sheet

Christmas — A45

2002, Dec. 20 ***Perf. 14¼x14***
161 A45 1000f multi 3.75 3.75

Succulent Plants — A46

Designs: 550f, Prickly pear. 600f, Big-horned euphorbia. 750f, Century plant.

2003, May 10 **Litho.** ***Perf. 13¾x14***
162-164 A46 Set of 3 9.00 9.00
164a Souvenir sheet, #162-164 9.50 9.50

Trees — A47

Designs: 300f, Olive tree. 700f, Blessing tree.

2003, July 12
165-166 A47 Set of 2 6.00 6.00

Universities — A48

Designs: 250f, Al-Azhar University, Gaza. 650f, Hebron University, Hebron. 800f, Arab American University, Jenin.

2003, July 19
167-169 A48 Set of 3 9.50 9.50

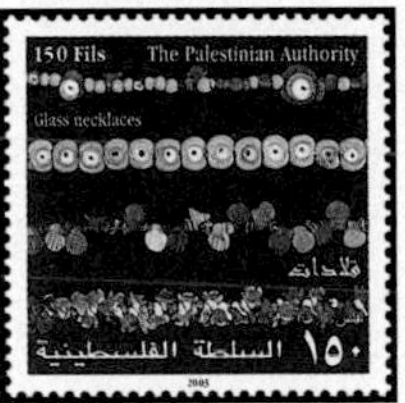

Handicrafts A49

Designs: 150f, Glass necklaces. 200f, Headdress. 450f, Embroidery. 500f, Costume embroidery. 950f, Head veil.

2003, Oct. 11 Litho. *Perf. 13¾*
170-174 A49 Set of 5 12.50 12.50

French President Jacques Chirac A50

No. 175 — Chirac and: a, 200f, Yasser Arafat, French flag. b, 450f, Palestinian flag.

2004 Litho. *Perf. 14*
175 A50 Pair, #a-b 5.25 5.25

Printed in sheets containing two each of Nos. 175a-175b

Souvenir Sheet

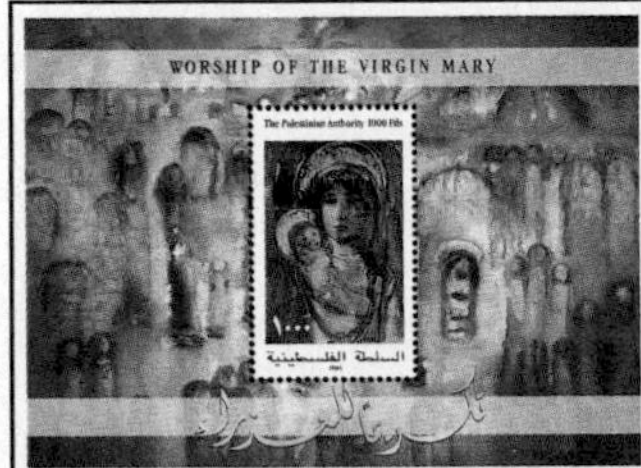

Worship of the Virgin Mary — A51

2004
176 A51 1000f multi 5.50 5.50

Souvenir Sheet

Arab League, 60th Anniv. — A52

2005 Litho. *Perf. 13¾*
177 A52 750f multi 3.50 3.50

Mahmoud Darwish (1941-2008), Poet — A53

Denominations: 150f, 250f, 350f, 400f.

2008, July 29 Litho. *Perf. 13*
178-181 A53 Set of 4 9.25 9.25

A54

Jericho, 10,000th Anniv. — A55

2010, Dec. 26 *Perf. 13¼x13*

Background Color

182	A54	50f white	.40	.40
183	A55	150f pink	1.25	1.25
184	A54	350f gray	2.75	2.75
185	A55	1000f light green	7.75	7.75
		Nos. 182-185 (4)	12.15	12.15

Christmas — A56

Color of panel above denomination: 100f, Red. 150f, Purple. 250f, Green. 500f, Blue.

2010, Dec. 26
186-189 A56 Set of 4 7.50 7.50

Souvenir Sheet

Arab Postal Day — A57

No. 190 — Emblem and: a, 350f, Camel caravan. b, 500f, Pigeon and map.

Litho. With Foil Application

2011, Mar. 17 *Perf. 13¾x13¼*
190 A57 Sheet of 2, #a-b 9.50 9.50

Ramadan A58

Designs: 50f, Dome of the Rock, crescent, arches, flag. 100f, Lantern, arabesque, flag. 250f, Lantern, crescent, arabesque, arch, flag. 500f, Dome of the Rock, crescent, flag.

No. 195, 1000f, Dome of the Rock, lantern, crescent. No. 196, 1000f, Flag, crescent, Arabic text.

2011, Aug. 1 Litho. *Perf. 13x13¼*
191-194 A58 Set of 4 8.50 8.50

Souvenir Sheets

Perf. 13¼x14¼
195-196 A58 Set of 2 18.50 18.50

Nos. 195 and 196 each contain one 45x35mm stamp.

Yasser Arafat (1929-2004), President of the Palestinian Authority A59

Various photographs of Arafat: 50f, 100f, 150f, 5000f.

2012, June 6 Litho. *Perf. 14¼*
197-200 A59 Set of 4 21.00 21.00

A booklet containing five 250f, three 500f, three 750f, and four 1000f stamps, each depicting Arafat, sold for 20,000f.

Souvenir Sheet

Soccer Ball and Flag of Palestinian Authority — A60

2012, June 6 Litho. *Perf. 13*
201 A60 1000f multi 4.25 4.25

Recognition by FIFA of first home soccer match of Palestinian Authority team, 4th anniv. Compare with type A68.

Miniature Sheet

Governmental Ministries — A61

No. 202 — Ministry of: a, Transport. b, Public Works and Housing. c, Telecommunication and Information Technology. d, Finance. e, Interior.

2012, June 6 Litho. *Perf. 13¼*
202 A61 300f Sheet of 5, #a-e 7.25 7.25

Miniature Sheet

Fruit — A62

No. 203: a, 150f, Grapes. b, 300f, Oranges. c, 350f, Bananas. d, 450f, Dates.

2012, June 6 Litho. *Perf. 14*
203 A62 Sheet of 8, 2 each #a-d 12.00 12.00

The two examples of Nos. 203a-203d on the sheet have different frames, being placed in different areas on the marginal illustration depicting trees.

Arab Postal Day A63

Denominations: 150f, 250f, 350f, 1000f, 5000f.

2012, Aug. 3 Litho. *Perf. 13¼*
204-208 A63 Set of 5 30.00 30.00

Christmas — A64

Various depictions of Christmas trees: 20f, 250f, 600f.

1000f, Man praying.

2012, Dec. 24 Litho. *Perf. 14*
209-211 A64 Set of 3 3.75 3.75

Souvenir Sheet
212 A64 1000f multi 4.25 4.25

Intl. Day of Civil Defense A65

Designs: 200f, Firemen in smoke. 250f, Firemen and fire truck. 500f, Firemen spraying water on building, ladder truck.

1000f, Firemen and fire truck, diff.

2013 **Litho.** ***Perf. 14***
213-215 A65 Set of 3 4.50 4.50

Souvenir Sheet

216 A65 1000f multi 5.00 5.00

Flora and Fauna — A66

Designs: 20f, White flower. 100f, Caracal. 200f, Bird. 480f, Poppies. 720f, Turtle. 1080f, Nubian ibex.
No. 223, 1000f, Daisies, horiz. No. 224, 1000f, Eagle, horiz.

2013, June 3 **Litho.** ***Perf. 14***
217-222 A66 Set of 6 13.50 13.50

Souvenir Sheets

223-224 A66 Set of 2 12.00 12.00

Police A67

Designs: 100f, Policeman directing traffic. 200f, Policemen inspecting plants. 250f, Policemen with pick and hoe.
500f, Policeman assisting elderly woman, vert.

2013 **Litho.** ***Perf. 14***
225-227 A67 Set of 3 3.25 3.25

Souvenir Sheet

228 A67 500f multi 3.00 3.00

Souvenir Sheet

Soccer Ball and Flag of Palestinian Authority — A68

2013 **Litho.** ***Perf. 13***
229 A68 1000f multi 9.00 9.00

Recognition by FIFA of first home soccer match of Palestinian Authority team, 5th anniv. Compare with type A60.

UNESCO Recognition of State of Palestine A69

Dove, text, UNESCO emblem and panel color of: 100f, Green. 200f, Red brown. 420f, Black.
1000f, Dove, text and UNESCO emblem on Palestinian Authority flag, vert.

2013, Oct. 31 **Litho.** ***Perf. 14***
230-232 A69 Set of 3 4.25 4.25

Souvenir Sheet

233 A69 1000f multi 5.75 5.75

SEMI-POSTAL STAMPS

Souvenir Sheet

Gaza-Jericho Peace Agreement — SP1

1994, Oct. 7 **Litho.** ***Perf. 14***
B1 SP1 750m +250m multi 6.75 6.75

For surcharge see No. B3.

Souvenir Sheet

Arab League, 50th Anniv. — SP2

Painting: View of Palestine, by Ibrahim Hazimeh.

1995, Mar. 22 ***Perf. 13½***
B2 SP2 750f +250f multi 3.75 3.75

No. B1 Surcharged "FILS" in English & Arabic and with Added Text at Left and Right

1995, Apr. 10 **Litho.** ***Perf. 14***
B3 SP1 750f +250f multi 7.00 7.00

Honoring 1994 Nobel Peace Prize winners Arafat, Rabin and Peres.

OFFICIAL STAMPS

Natl. Arms — O1

1994, Aug. 15 **Litho.** ***Perf. 14***

O1	O1	50m yellow	.25	.25
O2	O1	100m green blue	.35	.35
O3	O1	125m blue	.50	.50
O4	O1	200m orange	.75	.75
O5	O1	250m olive	1.00	1.00
O6	O1	400m maroon	1.40	1.40
		Nos. O1-O6 (6)	4.25	4.25

Nos. O1-O6 could also be used by the general public, and non-official-use covers are known.

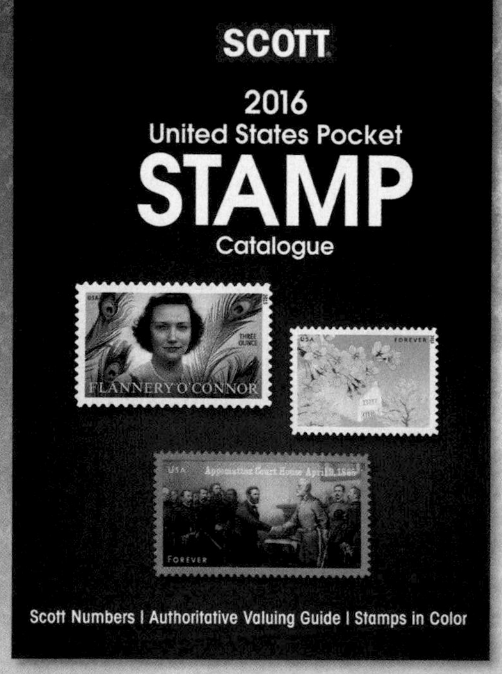

2016 SCOTT U.S. STAMP POCKET CATALOGUE

With pages designed to be a convenient inventory checklist, the Scott U.S. Stamp Pocket Catalogue is a perfect compact companion at shows, club meetings, and your desk. Full-color stamp illustrations accompany listings and values for more than 4,000 U.S. stamps, all identified by Scott Catalogue numbers.

Item	Retail	AA*
P112016	$32.50	$26.99

Visit AmosAdvantage.com
Call 1-800-572-6885
Outside U.S. & Canada 937-498-0800
P.O. Box 4129, Sidney OH 45365

TERMS & CONDITIONS
1. *AA prices apply to paid subscribers of Amos Media publications, or orders placed online.
2. Prices, terms and product availability subject to change. Taxes will apply in CA, OH & IL.
3. Shipping & Handling: United States: Orders under $10 are only $3.99. 10% of order over $10 total. Minimum Freight Charge $7.99; Maximum Freight Charge $45.00. Canada: 20% of order total. Minimum Freight Charge $19.99; Maximum Freight Charge $200.00. Foreign: Orders are shipped via FedEx Economy International or USPS and billed actual freight. Brokerage, Customs or duties are the responsibility of the customer.

AMOS ADVANTAGE

PANAMA

'pa-nə-ˌmä

LOCATION — Central America between Costa Rica and Colombia
GOVT. — Republic
AREA — 30,134 sq. mi.
POP. — 2,778,526 (1999 est.)
CAPITAL — Panama

Formerly a department of the Republic of Colombia, Panama gained its independence in 1903. Dividing the country at its center is the Panama Canal.

100 Centavos = 1 Peso
100 Centesimos = 1 Balboa (1904)

Catalogue values for unused stamps in this country are for Never Hinged items, beginning with Scott 350 in the regular postage section, Scott C82 in the airpost section, Scott CB1 in the airpost semi-postal section, and Scott RA21 in the postal tax section.

Watermarks

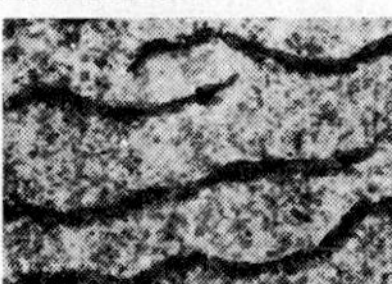

Wmk. 229 — Wavy Lines

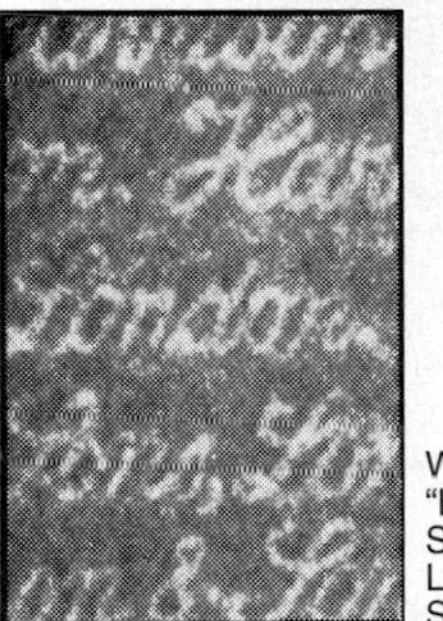

Wmk. 233 — "Harrison & Sons, London." in Script

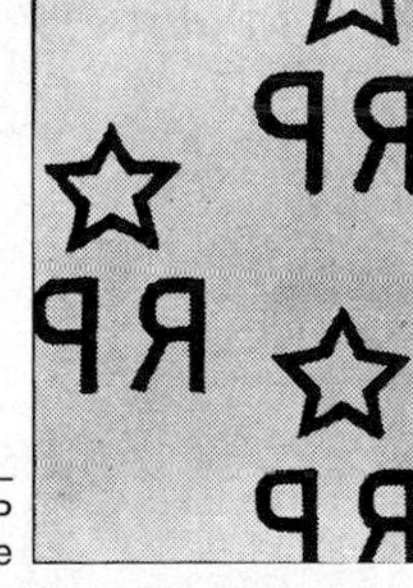

Wmk. 311 — Star and RP Multiple

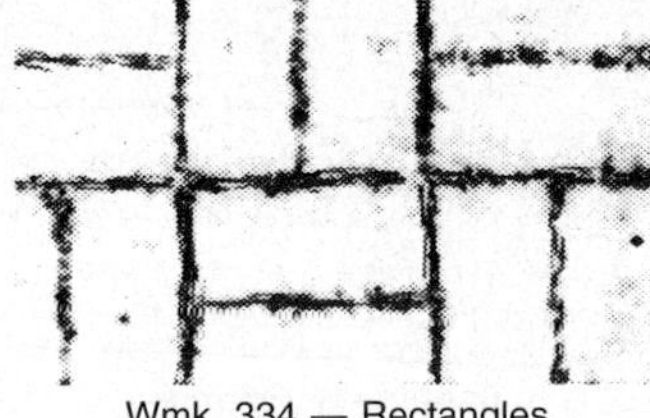

Wmk. 334 — Rectangles

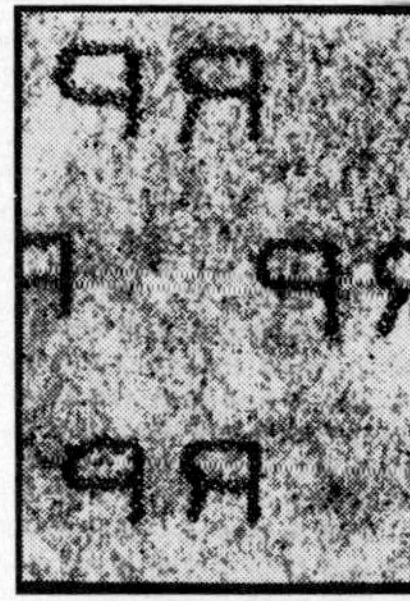

Wmk. 343 — RP Multiple

Wmk. 365 — Argentine Arms, Casa de Moneda de la Nacion & RA Multiple

Wmk. 377 — Interlocking Circles

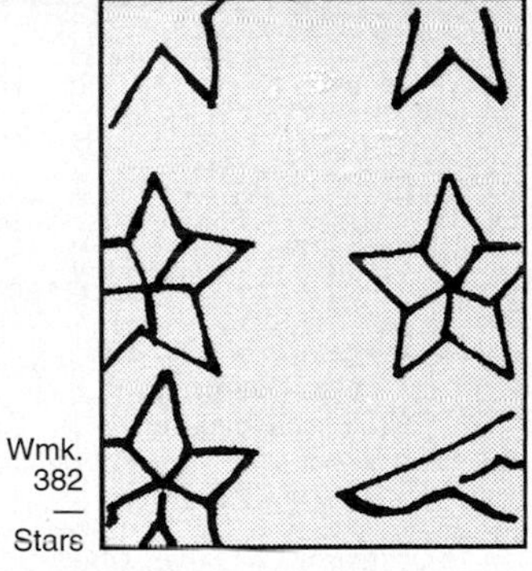

Wmk. 382 — Stars

Wmk. 382 may be a sheet watermark. It includes stars, wings with sun in middle and "Panama R de P."

Issues of the Sovereign State of Panama Under Colombian Dominion

Valid only for domestic mail.

Coat of Arms
A1 A2

1878 Unwmk. Litho. *Imperf.*

Thin Wove Paper

1	A1	5c gray green	25.00	30.00
a.		5c yellow green	25.00	30.00
2	A1	10c blue	60.00	60.00
3	A1	20c rose red	40.00	32.50
		Nos. 1-3 (3)	125.00	122.50

Very Thin Wove Paper

4	A2	50c buff	*1,500.*	

All values of this issue are known rouletted unofficially.

Medium Thick Paper

5	A1	5c blue green	25.00	30.00
6	A1	10c blue	65.00	70.00
7	A2	50c orange	13.00	
		Nos. 5-7 (3)	103.00	100.00

Nos. 5-7 were printed before Nos. 1-4, according to Panamanian archives.

Values for used Nos. 1-5 are for handstamped postal cancellations.

These stamps have been reprinted in a number of shades, on thin to moderately thick, white or yellowish paper. They are without gum or with white, crackly gum. All values have been reprinted from new stones made from retouched dies. The marks of retouching are plainly to be seen in the sea and clouds. On the original 10c the shield in the upper left corner has two blank sections; on the reprints the design of this shield is completed. The impression of these reprints is frequently blurred.

Reprints of the 50c are rare. Beware of remainders of the 50c offered as reprints.

Issues of Colombia for use in the Department of Panama

Issued because of the use of different currency.

Map of Panama — A3

1887-88 *Perf. 13½*

8	A3	1c black, *green*	.90	.80
9	A3	2c black, *pink* ('88)	1.60	1.25
a.		2c black, *salmon*	1.60	
10	A3	5c black, *blue*	.90	.35
11	A3	10c black, *yellow*	.90	.40
a.		Imperf., pair		
12	A3	20c black, *lilac*	1.00	.50
13	A3	50c brown ('88)	2.00	1.00
a.		Imperf.		
		Nos. 8-13 (6)	7.30	4.30

See No. 14. For surcharges and overprints see Nos. 24-30, 107-108, 115-116, 137-138.

1892 Pelure Paper

14	A3	50c brown	2.50	1.10

The stamps of this issue have been reprinted on papers of slightly different colors from those of the originals.

These are: 1c yellow green, 2c deep rose, 5c bright blue, 10c straw, 20c violet.

The 50c is printed from a very worn stone, in a lighter brown than the originals. The series includes a 10c on lilac paper.

All these stamps are to be found perforated, imperforate, imperforate horizontally or imperforate vertically. At the same time that they were made, impressions were struck upon a variety of glazed and surface-colored papers.

Map of Panama — A4

Wove Paper

1892-96 Engr. *Perf. 12*

15	A4	1c green	.25	.25
16	A4	2c rose	.40	.25
17	A4	5c blue	1.50	.50
18	A4	10c orange	.35	.25
19	A4	20c violet ('95)	.50	.35
20	A4	50c bister brn ('96)	.50	.40
21	A4	1p lake ('96)	6.50	4.00
		Nos. 15-21 (7)	10.00	6.00

In 1903 Nos. 15-21 were used in Cauca and three other southern Colombia towns. Stamps canceled in these towns are worth much more.

For surcharges and overprints see Nos. 22-23, 51-106, 109-114, 129-136, 139, 151-161, 181-184, F12-F15, H4-H5.

Nos. 16, 12-14 Surcharged

a b

c

d

e

f

g

1894 Black Surcharge

22	(a)	1c on 2c rose	.50	.40
a.		Inverted surcharge	2.50	2.50
b.		Double surcharge		
23	(b)	1c on 2c rose	.40	.50
a.		"CCNTAVO"	2.50	2.50
b.		Inverted surcharge	2.50	2.50
c.		Double surcharge		

Red Surcharge

24	(c)	5c on 20c black, *lil*	2.50	1.50
a.		Inverted surcharge	12.50	12.50
b.		Double surcharge		
c.		Without "HABILITADO"		
25	(d)	5c on 20c black, *lil*	3.50	3.00
a.		"CCNTAVOS"	7.50	7.50
b.		Inverted surcharge	12.50	12.50
c.		Double surcharge		
d.		Without "HABILITADO"		
26	(e)	5c on 20c black, *lil*	6.00	5.00
a.		Inverted surcharge	12.50	12.50
b.		Double surcharge		
27	(f)	10c on 50c brown	3.00	3.00
a.		"1894" omitted		
b.		Inverted surcharge		
c.		"CCNTAVOS"	15.00	
28	(g)	10c on 50c brown	12.50	12.50
a.		"CCNTAVOS"	32.50	
b.		Inverted surcharge		

Pelure Paper

29	(f)	10c on 50c brown	4.00	3.00
a.		"1894" omitted	7.50	
b.		Inverted surcharge	12.50	12.50
c.		Double surcharge		
30	(g)	10c on 50c brown	10.00	10.00
a.		"CCNTAVOS"		
b.		Without "HABILITADO"		
c.		Inverted surcharge	25.00	25.00
d.		Double surcharge		
		Nos. 22-30 (9)	42.40	38.90

There are several settings of these surcharges. Usually the surcharge is about 15½mm high, but in one setting, it is only 13mm. All the types are to be found with a comma after "CENTAVOS." Nos. 24, 25, 26, 29 and 30 exist with the surcharge printed sideways. Nos. 23, 24 and 29 may be found with an inverted "A" instead of "V" in "CENTAVOS." There are also varieties caused by dropped or broken letters.

Issues of the Republic Issued in the City of Panama

Stamps of 1892-96 Overprinted

1903, Nov. 16 Rose Handstamp

51	A4	1c green	2.00	1.50
52	A4	2c rose	5.00	3.00
53	A4	5c blue	2.00	1.25
54	A4	10c yellow	2.00	2.00
55	A4	20c violet	4.00	3.50
56	A4	50c bister brn	10.00	7.00
57	A4	1p lake	50.00	40.00
		Nos. 51-57 (7)	75.00	58.25

Blue Black Handstamp

58	A4	1c green	2.00	1.25
59	A4	2c rose	1.00	1.00
60	A4	5c blue	7.00	6.00

61 A4 10c yellow 5.00 3.50
62 A4 20c violet 10.00 7.50
63 A4 50c bister brn 10.00 7.50
64 A4 1p lake 50.00 42.50
Nos. 58-64 (7) 85.00 69.25

The stamps of this issue are to be found with the handstamp placed horizontally, vertically or diagonally; inverted; double; double, one inverted; double, both inverted; in pairs, one without handstamp; etc.

This handstamp is known in brown rose on the 1, 5, 20 and 50c, in purple on the 1, 2, 50c and 1p, and in magenta on the 5, 10, 20 and 50c.

Reprints were made in rose, black and other colors when the handstamp was nearly worn out, so that the "R" of "REPUBLICA" appears to be shorter than usual, and the bottom part of "LI" has been broken off. The "P" of "PANAMA" leans to the left and the tops of "NA" are broken. Many of these varieties are found inverted, double, etc.

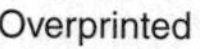
Overprinted

Bar in Similar Color to Stamp

1903, Dec. 3 **Black Overprint**

65 A4 2c rose 2.50 2.50
 a. "PANAMA" 15mm long 3.50
 b. Violet bar 5.00
66 A4 5c blue 100.00
 a. "PANAMA" 15mm long 100.00
67 A4 10c yellow 2.50 2.50
 a. "PANAMA" 15mm long 6.00
 b. Horizontal overprint 17.50

Gray Black Overprint

68 A4 2c rose 2.00 2.00
 a. "PANAMA" 15mm long 2.50

Carmine Overprint

69 A4 5c blue 2.50 2.50
 a. "PANAMA" 15mm long 3.50
 b. Bar only 75.00 75.00
 c. Double overprint
70 A4 20c violet 7.50 6.50
 a. "PANAMA" 15mm long 10.00
 b. Double overprint, one in black 150.00
Nos. 65,67-70 (5) 17.00 16.00

This overprint was set up to cover fifty stamps. "PANAMA" is normally 13mm long and 1¾mm high but, in two rows in each sheet, it measures 15 to 16mm.

This word may be found with one or more of the letters taller than usual; with one, two or three inverted "V's" instead of "A's"; with an inverted "Y" instead of "A"; an inverted "N"; an "A" with accent; and a fancy "P."

Owing to misplaced impressions, stamps exist with "PANAMA" once only, twice on one side, or three times.

Overprinted in Red

1903, Dec.

71 A4 1c green .75 .60
 a. "PANAMA" 15mm long 1.25
 b. "PANAMA" reading down 3.00 .75
 c. "PANAMA" reading up and down 3.00
 d. Double overprint 8.00
72 A4 2c rose .50 .40
 a. "PANAMA" 15mm long 1.00
 b. "PANAMA" reading down .75 .50
 c. "PANAMA" reading up and down 4.00
 d. Double overprint 8.00
73 A4 20c violet 1.50 1.00
 a. "PANAMA" 15mm long 2.25
 b. "PANAMA" reading down
 c. "PANAMA" reading up and down 8.00 8.00
 d. Double overprint 18.00 18.00
74 A4 50c bister brn 3.00 2.50
 a. "PANAMA" 15mm long 5.00
 b. "PANAMA" reading up and down 12.00 12.00
 c. Double overprint 6.00 6.00
75 A4 1p lake 6.00 4.50
 a. "PANAMA" 15mm long 6.25
 b. "PANAMA" reading up and down 15.00 15.00
 c. Double overprint 15.00
 d. Inverted overprint 25.00
Nos. 71-75 (5) 11.75 9.00

This setting appears to be a re-arrangement (or two very similar re-arrangements) of the previous overprint. The overprint covers fifty stamps. "PANAMA" usually reads upward but sheets of the 1, 2 and 20c exist with the word reading upward on one half the sheet and downward on the other half.

In one re-arrangement one stamp in fifty has the word reading in both directions. Nearly all the varieties of the previous overprint are repeated in this setting excepting the inverted "Y" and fancy "P." There are also additional varieties of large letters and "PANAMA" occasionally has an "A" missing or inverted. There are misplaced impressions, as the previous setting.

Overprinted in Red

1904-05

76 A4 1c green .25 .25
 a. Both words reading up 1.50
 b. Both words reading down 2.75
 c. Double overprint
 d. Pair, one without overprint 15.00
 e. "PANAAM" 20.00
 f. Inverted "M" in "PANAMA" 5.00
77 A4 2c rose .25 .25
 a. Both words reading up 2.50
 b. Both words reading down 2.50
 c. Double overprint 10.00
 d. Double overprint, one inverted 14.00
 e. Inverted "M" in "PANAMA" 5.00
78 A4 5c blue .30 .25
 a. Both words reading up 3.00
 b. Both words reading down 4.25
 c. Inverted overprint 12.50
 d. "PANAAM" 25.00
 e. "PANANA" 8.00
 f. "PAMANA" 5.00
 g. Inverted "M" in "PANAMA" 5.00
 h. Double overprint 20.00
79 A4 10c yellow .30 .25
 a. Both words reading up 5.00
 b. Both words reading down 5.00
 c. Double overprint 15.00
 d. Inverted overprint 6.75
 e. "PAMANA" 8.00
 f. Inverted "M" in "PANAMA" 15.00
 g. Red brown overprint 7.50 3.50
80 A4 20c violet 2.00 1.00
 a. Both words reading up 5.00
 b. Both words reading down 10.00
81 A4 50c bister brn 2.00 1.60
 a. Both words reading up 10.50
 b. Both words reading down 10.00
 c. Double overprint
82 A4 1p lake 5.00 5.00
 a. Both words reading up 12.50
 b. Both words reading down 12.50
 c. Double overprint
 d. Double overprint, one inverted 20.00
 e. Inverted "M" in "PANAMA" 45.00
Nos. 76-82 (7) 10.10 8.60

This overprint is also set up to cover fifty stamps. One stamp in each fifty has "PANAMA" reading upward at both sides. Another has the word reading downward at both sides, a third has an inverted "V" in place of the last "A" and a fourth has a small thick "N." In a resetting all these varieties are corrected except the inverted "V." There are misplaced overprints as before.

Later printings show other varieties and have the bar 2½mm instead of 2mm wide. The colors of the various printings of Nos. 76-82 range from carmine to almost pink.

Experts consider the black overprint on the 50c to be speculative.

The 20c violet and 50c bister brown exist with bar 2½mm wide, including the error "PAMANA," but are not known to have been issued. Some examples have been canceled "to oblige."

Issued in Colon

Handstamped in Magenta or Violet

1903-04 **On Stamps of 1892-96**

101 A4 1c green .75 .75
102 A4 2c rose .75 .75
103 A4 5c blue 1.00 1.00
104 A4 10c yellow 3.50 3.00
105 A4 20c violet 8.00 6.50
106 A4 1p lake 80.00 70.00

On Stamps of 1887-92

Ordinary Wove Paper

107 A3 50c brown 25.00 20.00
Nos. 101-107 (7) 119.00 102.00

Pelure Paper

108 A3 50c brown 70.00

Handstamped in Magenta, Violet or Red

On Stamps of 1892-96

109 A4 1c green 5.50 5.00
110 A4 2c rose 5.50 5.00
111 A4 5c blue 5.50 5.00
112 A4 10c yellow 8.25 7.00
113 A4 20c violet 12.00 9.00
114 A4 1p lake 70.00 60.00

On Stamps of 1887-92

Ordinary Wove Paper

115 A3 50c brown 35.00 25.00
Nos. 109-115 (7) 141.75 116.00

Pelure Paper

116 A3 50c brown 50.00 37.50

The first note after No. 64 applies also to Nos. 101-116.

The handstamps on Nos. 109-116 have been counterfeited.

Stamps with this overprint were a private speculation. They exist on cover. The overprint was to be used on postal cards.

Overprinted On Stamps Of 1892-96

On Stamps of 1892-96

Carmine Overprint

129 A4 1c green .40 .40
 a. Inverted overprint 6.00
 b. Double overprint 2.25
 c. Double overprint, one inverted 6.00
130 A4 5c blue .50 .50

Brown Overprint

131 A4 1c green 12.00
 a. Double overprint, one inverted

Black Overprint

132 A4 1c green 60.00 30.00
 a. Vertical overprint 42.50
 b. Inverted overprint 42.50
 c. Double overprint, one inverted 42.50
133 A4 2c rose .50 .50
 a. Inverted overprint
134 A4 10c yellow .50 .50
 a. Inverted overprint 4.00
 b. Double overprint 16.00
 c. Double overprint, one inverted 6.00
135 A4 20c violet .50 .50
 a. Inverted overprint 4.00
 b. Double overprint 5.50
136 A4 1p lake 16.00 14.00

On Stamps of 1887-88

Blue Overprint

Ordinary Wove Paper

137 A3 50c brown 3.00 3.00

Pelure Paper

138 A3 50c brown 3.00 3.00
 a. Double overprint 14.00

This overprint is set up to cover fifty stamps. In each fifty there are four stamps without accent on the last "a" of "Panama," one with accent on the "a" of "Republica" and one with a thick, upright "i."

Overprinted in Carmine

On Stamp of 1892-96

139 A4 20c violet *200.00*
 a. Double overprint

Unknown with genuine cancels.

Issued in Bocas del Toro

Stamps of 1892-96 Overprinted Handstamped in Violet

1903-04

151 A4 1c green 20.00 14.00
152 A4 2c rose 20.00 14.00
153 A4 5c blue 25.00 16.00
154 A4 10c yellow 15.00 8.25
155 A4 20c violet 50.00 30.00
156 A4 50c bister brn 100.00 55.00
157 A4 1p lake 140.00 110.00
Nos. 151-157 (7) 370.00 247.25

The handstamp is known double and inverted. Counterfeits exist.

Handstamped in Violet

158 A4 1c green *100.00*
159 A4 2c rose *70.00*
160 A4 5c blue *80.00*
161 A4 10c yellow *100.00*
Nos. 158-161 (4) *350.00*

This handstamp was applied to these 4 stamps only by favor, experts state. Counterfeits are numerous. The 1p exists only as a counterfeit.

General Issues

A5

1905, Feb. 4 **Engr.** ***Perf. 12***

179 A5 1c green .60 .40
180 A5 2c rose .80 .50

Panama's Declaration of Independence from the Colombian Republic, Nov. 3, 1903.

Surcharged in Vermilion on Stamps of 1892-96 Issue

1906

181 A4 1c on 20c violet .25 .25
 a. "Panrma" 2.25 2.25
 b. "Pnnama" 2.25 2.25
 c. "Pauama" 2.25 2.25
 d. Inverted surcharge 4.00 4.00
 e. Double surcharge 3.50 3.50
 f. Double surcharge, one inverted

Stamps of 1892-96 Surcharged in Vermilion

182 A4 2c on 50c bister brn .25 .25
 a. 3rd "A" of "PANAMA" inverted 2.25 2.25
 b. Both "PANAMA" reading down 4.00 4.00
 c. Double surcharge
 d. Inverted surcharge 2.50

The 2c on 20c violet was never issued to the public. All examples are inverted. Value, 75c.

Carmine Surcharge

183 A4 5c on 1p lake .60 .40
 a. Both "PANAMA" reading down 6.00 6.00
 b. "5" omitted
 c. Double surcharge
 d. Inverted surcharge
 e. 3rd "A" of "PANAMA" inverted 5.50 5.50

On Stamp of 1903-04, No. 75

184 A4 5c on 1p lake .60 .40
 a. "PANAMA" 15mm long
 b. "PANAMA" reading up and down
 c. Both "PANAMA" reading down
 d. Inverted surcharge
 e. Double surcharge
 f. 3rd "A" of "PANAMA" inverted
Nos. 181-184 (4) 1.70 1.30

National Flag — A6

Vasco Núñez de Balboa — A7

Fernández de Córdoba — A8

Coat of Arms — A9

Justo Arosemena A10

Manuel J. Hurtado A11

José de Obaldía — A12

Tomás Herrera — A13

José de Fábrega — A14

1906-07 Engr. *Perf. 11½*

185	A6	½c orange & multi	.70	.35
186	A7	1c dk green & blk ('07)	.70	.35
187	A8	2c scarlet & blk	1.00	.35
188	A9	2½c red orange	1.00	.35
189	A10	5c blue & black	1.75	.35
a.		5c ultramarine & black	2.00	.50
190	A11	8c purple & blk	1.50	.65
191	A12	10c violet & blk	1.50	.50
192	A13	25c brown & blk	3.50	1.10
193	A14	50c black	9.00	3.50
		Nos. 185-193 (9)	20.65	7.50

Inverted centers exist of Nos. 185-187, 189, 189a, 190-193, Value, each $25. Nos. 185-193 exist imperf.

For surcharge see No. F29.

Issued: Nos. 185, 188-193, 11/20; No. 187, 9/1.

Map — A17

Balboa — A18

Córdoba — A19

Arms — A20

Arosemena A21

Obaldía A23

1909-16 *Perf. 12*

195	A17	½c org ('11)	1.00	.30
196	A17	½c rose ('15)	.70	.60
197	A18	1c dk grn & blk	1.00	.50
a.		Inverted center	7,500.	7,500.
b.		Booklet pane of 6 ('16)	*160.00*	
		Complete booklet, 4 #197b	—	
198	A19	2c ver & blk	1.00	.30
a.		Booklet pane of 6	*160.00*	
199	A20	2½c red orange	1.50	.30
200	A21	5c blue & blk	2.00	.30
a.		Booklet pane of 6 ('16)	*175.00*	
201	A23	10c violet & blk	3.75	1.10
		Complete booklet, panes of 6 (3x2) of #195 (3), 197 (3), 199 (2), 200, 201 ('11)	—	
		Nos. 195-201 (7)	10.95	3.40

Value for No. 197a used is for an off-center example with faults.

The panes contained in the booklet listed following No. 201 are marginal blocks of 6 (3x2), without gum, stapled within the booklet cover, with advertising paper interleaving. The complete booklet was sold for B1.50.

Nos. 197b and 198a are gummed panes of 6 (2x3), imperf on outside edges.

For overprints and surcharges see #H23, I4-I7.

Balboa Sighting Pacific Ocean, His Dog "Leoncico" at His Feet — A24

1913, Sept. 1

202	A24	2½c dk grn & yel grn	1.75	.65

400th anniv. of Balboa's discovery of the Pacific Ocean.

Panama-Pacific Exposition Issue

Chorrera Falls — A25

Map of Panama Canal — A26

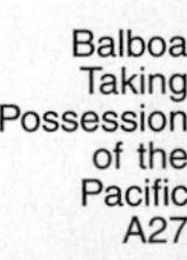

Balboa Taking Possession of the Pacific A27

Ruins of Cathedral of Old Panama A28

Palace of Arts — A29

Gatun Locks — A30

Culebra Cut — A31

Santo Domingo Monastery's Flat Arch — A32

1915, Mar. 1 *Perf. 12*

204	A25	½c ol grn & blk	.40	.30
205	A26	1c dk grn & blk	.95	.30
206	A27	2c car & blk	.75	.30
a.		2c ver & blk ('16)	.75	.30
208	A28	2½c scarlet & blk	.95	.35
209	A29	3c violet & blk	1.00	.55
210	A30	5c blue & blk	2.10	.35
a.		Center inverted	1,500.	650.00
211	A31	10c orange & blk	2.10	.70
212	A32	20c brown & blk	10.50	3.25
a.		Center inverted	300.00	—
		Nos. 204-212 (8)	19.35	6.10

For surcharges and overprints see Nos. 217, 233, E1-E2.

Manuel J. Hurtado — A33

1916

213	A33	8c violet & blk	9.00	4.25

For surcharge see No. F30.

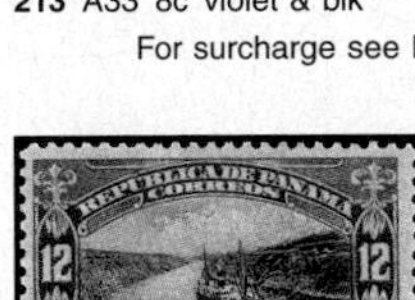
S. S. Panama in Culebra Cut Aug. 11, 1914 A34

S. S. Panama in Culebra Cut Aug. 11, 1914 A35

S. S. Cristobal in Gatun Lock — A36

1918, Aug. 23

214	A34	12c purple & blk	15.00	5.75
215	A35	15c brt blue & blk	10.00	3.50
216	A36	24c yellow brn & blk	15.00	3.50
		Nos. 214-216 (3)	40.00	12.75

No. 208 Surcharged in Dark Blue

1919, Aug. 15

217	A28	2c on 2½c scar & blk	.35	.35
a.		Inverted surcharge	11.00	5.00
b.		Double surcharge	15.00	6.00

City of Panama, 400th anniversary.

Dry Dock at Balboa A38

Ship in Pedro Miguel Lock — A39

1920, Sept. 1 Engr.

218	A38	50c orange & blk	30.00	22.50
219	A39	1b dk violet & blk	40.00	27.50

For overprint and surcharge see Nos. C6, C37.

Arms of Panama City — A40

José Vallarino — A41

"Land Gate" — A42

Simón Bolivar — A43

Statue of Cervantes — A44

Bolívar's Tribute — A45

Carlos de Ycaza — A46

Municipal Building in 1821 and 1921 — A47

Statue of Balboa — A48

Villa de Los Santos Church — A49

Herrera — A50

Fábrega — A51

1921, Nov.

No.	Type	Description	Unused	Used
220	A40	½c orange	.80	.25
221	A41	1c green	1.00	.25
222	A42	2c carmine	1.25	.25
223	A43	2½c red	2.75	1.10
224	A44	3c dull violet	2.75	1.10
225	A45	5c blue	2.75	.35
226	A46	8c olive green	10.00	3.50
227	A47	10c violet	6.75	1.50
228	A48	15c lt blue	8.00	2.00
229	A49	20c olive brown	14.50	3.50
230	A50	24c black brown	14.50	4.25
231	A51	50c black	25.00	8.00
		Nos. 220-231 (12)	90.05	26.05

Centenary of independence.

For overprints and surcharges see Nos. 264, 275-276, 299, 304, 308-310, C35.

Hurtado — A52

1921, Nov. 28

No.	Type	Description	Unused	Used
232	A52	2c dark green	.65	.65

Manuel José Hurtado (1821-1887), president and folklore writer.

For overprints see Nos. 258, 301.

No. 208 Surcharged in Black

1923

No.	Type	Description	Unused	Used
233	A28	2c on 2½c scar & blk	.45	.45
a.		"1923" omitted	4.00	
b.		Bar over "CENTESIMOS"	4.00	
c.		Inverted surcharge	4.00	
d.		Double surcharge	4.00	
e.		Pair, one without surcharge	4.00	

Two stamps in each sheet have a bar above "CENTESIMOS" (No. 233b).

Arms — A53

1924, May **Engr.**

No.	Type	Description	Unused	Used
234	A53	½c orange	.25	.25
235	A53	1c dark green	.25	.25
236	A53	2c carmine	.25	.25
237	A53	5c dark blue	.45	.25
238	A53	10c dark violet	.60	.25
239	A53	12c olive green	.75	.40
240	A53	15c ultra	.95	.40
241	A53	24c yellow brown	1.90	.60
242	A53	50c orange	4.50	1.10
243	A53	1b black	6.75	2.50
		Nos. 234-243 (10)	16.65	6.25

For overprints & surcharges see Nos. 277, 321A, 331-338, 352, C19-C20, C68, RA5, RA10-RA22.

Bolívar — A54

Statue of Bolívar — A55

Bolívar Hall — A56

1926, June 10 ***Perf. 12½***

No.	Type	Description	Unused	Used
244	A54	½c orange	.55	.25
245	A54	1c dark green	.55	.25
246	A54	2c scarlet	.70	.30
247	A54	4c gray	.90	.35
248	A54	5c dark blue	1.40	.50
249	A55	8c lilac	2.25	.80
250	A55	10c dull violet	1.60	.80
251	A55	12c olive green	2.50	1.00
252	A55	15c ultra	3.25	1.25
253	A55	20c brown	6.75	1.60
254	A56	24c black violet	8.00	2.00
255	A56	50c black	13.50	5.00
		Nos. 244-255 (12)	41.95	14.10

Bolivar Congress centennial.

For surcharges and overprints see Nos. 259-263, 266-267, 274, 298, 300, 302-303, 305-307, C33-C34, C36, C38-C39.

Lindbergh's Airplane, "The Spirit of St. Louis" — A57

Lindbergh's Airplane and Map of Panama — A58

1928, Jan. 9 **Typo.** ***Rouletted 7***

No.	Type	Description	Unused	Used
256	A57	2c dk red & blk, *salmon*	.40	.25
257	A58	5c dk blue, *grn*	.60	.40

Visit of Colonel Charles A. Lindbergh to Central America by airplane.

No. 256 has black overprint.

No. 232 Overprinted in Red

1928, Nov. 1 ***Perf. 12***

No.	Type	Description	Unused	Used
258	A52	2c dark green	.25	.25

25th anniversary of the Republic.

No. 247 Surcharged in Black

1930, Dec. 17 ***Perf. 12½, 13***

No.	Type	Description	Unused	Used
259	A54	1c on 4c gray	.25	.25

Centenary of the death of Simón Bolívar, the Liberator.

Nos. 244-246 Overprinted in Red or Blue

1932 ***Perf. 12½***

No.	Type	Description	Unused	Used
260	A54	½c orange (R)	.25	.25
261	A54	1c dark green (R)	.35	.25
a.		Double overprint	18.00	
262	A54	2c scarlet (Bl)	.35	.25

No. 252 Surcharged in Red

No.	Type	Description	Unused	Used
263	A55	10c on 15c ultra	1.00	.50
a.		Double surcharge	55.00	
		Nos. 260-263 (4)	1.95	1.25

No. 220 Overprinted as in 1932 in Black

1933, May 25 ***Perf. 12***

Overprint 19mm Long

No.	Type	Description	Unused	Used
264	A40	½c orange	.35	.25
a.		Overprint 17mm long		—

Dr. Manuel Amador Guerrero — A60

1933, June 30 **Engr.** ***Perf. 12½***

No.	Type	Description	Unused	Used
265	A60	2c dark red	.50	.25

Centenary of the birth of Dr. Manuel Amador Guerrero, founder of the Republic of Panama and its first President.

No. 251 Surcharged in Red

1933

No.	Type	Description	Unused	Used
266	A55	10c on 12c olive grn	1.25	.65

No. 253 Overprinted in Red

No.	Type	Description	Unused	Used
267	A55	20c brown	2.25	1.75

José Domingo de Obaldía — A61

Quotation from Emerson — A63

National Institute — A64

Designs: 2c, Eusebio A. Morales. 12c, Justo A. Facio. 15c, Pablo Arosemena.

1934, July 24 **Engr.** ***Perf. 14***

No.	Type	Description	Unused	Used
268	A61	1c dark green	1.00	.50
269	A61	2c scarlet	1.00	.45
270	A63	5c dark blue	1.25	.80
271	A64	10c brown	3.25	1.50
272	A61	12c yellow green	6.50	2.00
273	A61	15c Prus blue	8.50	2.50
		Nos. 268-273 (6)	21.50	7.75

25th anniv. of the Natl. Institute.

Nos. 248, 227 Overprinted in Black or Red

1935-36 ***Perf. 12½, 12***

No.	Type	Description	Unused	Used
274	A54	5c dark blue	.90	.30
275	A47	10c violet (R) ('36)	1.25	.60

No. 225 Surcharged in Red

1936. Sept. 19 ***Perf. 11½***

No.	Type	Description	Unused	Used
276	A45	1c on 5c blue	.40	.40
a.		Lines of surcharge 1½mm btwn.	6.50	

No. 241 Surcharged in Blue

1936, Sept. 24 ***Perf. 12***

No.	Type	Description	Unused	Used
277	A53	2c on 24c yellow brn	.60	.50
a.		Double surcharge	20.00	

Centenary of the birth of Pablo Arosemena, president of Panama in 1910-12. See Nos. C19-C20.

Panama Cathedral A67

Designs: ½c, Ruins of Custom House, Portobelo. 1c, Panama Tree. 2c, "La Pollera." 5c, Simon Bolivar. 10c, Cathedral Tower Ruins. Old Panama. 15c, Francisco Garcia y Santos, 20c, Madden Dam, Panama Canal. 25c, Columbus. 50c, Gaillard Cut. 1b, Panama Cathedral.

1936, Dec. 1 **Engr.** ***Perf. 11½***

No.	Type	Description	Unused	Used
278	A67	½c yellow org	.55	.25
279	A67	1c blue green	.55	.25
280	A67	2c carmine rose	.55	.25
281	A67	5c blue	.80	.50
282	A67	10c dk violet	1.75	.75
283	A67	15c turq blue	1.75	.75
284	A67	20c red	2.00	1.50
285	A67	25c black brn	3.50	2.00
286	A67	50c orange	7.75	5.00
287	A67	1b black	18.00	12.00
		Nos. 278-287,C21-C26 (16)	62.70	40.00

4th Postal Congress of the Americas and Spain.

Stamps of 1936 Overprinted in Red or Blue

1937, Mar. 9

No.	Type	Description	Unused	Used
288	A67	½c yellow org (R)	.35	.30
a.		Inverted overprint	25.00	
289	A67	1c blue green (R)	.45	.25
290	A67	2c car rose (Bl)	.45	.25
291	A67	5c blue (R)	.70	.25
292	A67	10c dk vio (R)	1.10	.35
293	A67	15c turq bl (R)	5.25	3.25
294	A67	20c red (Bl)	2.00	1.25
295	A67	25c black brn (R)	2.75	1.25
296	A67	50c orange (Bl)	9.00	6.00
297	A67	1b black (R)	14.50	10.00
		Nos. 288-297,C27-C32 (16)	84.60	54.15

Stamps of 1921-26 Overprinted in Red or Blue

1937, July ***Perf. 12, 12½***

298 A54	½c orange (R)	1.10	.80
a.	Inverted overprint	30.00	
299 A41	1c green (R)	.35	.25
a.	Inverted overprint	30.00	
300 A54	1c dk green (R)	.35	.25
301 A52	2c dk green (R)	.45	.35
302 A54	2c scarlet (Bl)	.55	.35

Stamps of 1921-26 Surcharged in Red

303 A54	2c on 4c gray	.70	.45
304 A46	2c on 8c ol grn	.70	.60
305 A55	2c on 8c lilac	.70	.45
306 A55	2c on 10c dl vio	.70	.50
307 A55	2c on 12c ol grn	.70	.45
308 A48	2c on 15c lt blue	.70	.60
309 A50	2c on 24c blk brn	.70	.75
310 A51	2c on 50c black	.70	.35
	Nos. 298-310 (13)	8.40	6.15

Ricardo Arango A77

Juan A. Guizado A78

La Concordia Fire — A79

Modern Fire Fighting Equipment A80

Firemen's Monument A81

David H. Brandon A82

Perf. 14x14½, 14½x14

1937, Nov. 25 **Photo.** **Wmk. 233**

311 A77	½c orange red	2.10	.35
312 A78	1c green	2.10	.35
313 A79	2c red	2.10	.25
314 A80	5c brt blue	4.00	.50
315 A81	10c purple	7.25	1.25
316 A82	12c yellow grn	11.50	2.00
	Nos. 311-316,C40-C42 (9)	44.80	7.05

50th anniversary of the Fire Department.

Old Panama Cathedral Tower and Statue of Liberty Enlightening the World, Flags of Panama and US — A83

Engr. & Litho.

1938, Dec. 7 **Unwmk.** ***Perf. 12½***

Center in Black; Flags in Red and Ultramarine

317 A83	1c deep green	.35	.25
318 A83	2c carmine	.55	.25
319 A83	5c blue	.80	.30
320 A83	12c olive	1.40	.75
321 A83	15c brt ultra	1.75	1.25
	Nos. 317-321,C49-C53 (10)	22.45	15.35

150th anniv. of the US Constitution.

No. 236 Overprinted in Black

1938, June 5 ***Perf. 12***

321A A53	2c carmine	.45	.25
b.	Inverted overprint	22.50	
	Nos. 321A,C53A-C53B (3)	1.25	1.05

Opening of the Normal School at Santiago, Veraguas Province, June 5, 1938.

Gatun Lake — A84

Designs: 1c, Pedro Miguel Locks. 2c, Allegory. 5c, Culebra Cut. 10c, Ferryboat. 12c, Aerial View of Canal. 15c, Gen. William C. Gorgas. 50c, Dr. Manuel A. Guerrero. 1b, Woodrow Wilson.

1939, Aug. 15 **Engr.** ***Perf. 12½***

322 A84	½c yellow	.35	.25
323 A84	1c dp blue grn	.55	.25
324 A84	2c dull rose	.65	.25
325 A84	5c dull blue	1.00	.25
326 A84	10c dk violet	1.10	.35
327 A84	12c olive green	1.10	.50
328 A84	15c ultra	1.10	.80
329 A84	50c orange	2.75	1.60
330 A84	1b dk brown	5.75	3.00
	Nos. 322-330,C54-C61 (17)	34.35	14.45

25th anniversary of the opening of the Panama Canal. For surcharges see Nos. C64, G2.

Stamps of 1924 Overprinted in Black or Red

1941, Jan. 2 ***Perf. 12***

331 A53	½c orange	.35	.25
332 A53	1c dk grn (R)	.35	.30
333 A53	2c carmine	.35	.25
334 A53	5c dk bl (R)	.55	.30
335 A53	10c dk vio (R)	.80	.50
336 A53	15c ultra (R)	1.75	.65
337 A53	50c dp org	6.25	3.50
338 A53	1b blk (R)	14.50	6.00
	Nos. 331-338,C67-C71 (13)	49.90	31.25

New Panama constitution, effective 1/241.

Black Overprint

1942, Feb. 19 **Engr.**

339 A93	10c purple	1.40	1.00

Surcharged with New Value

340 A93	2c on 5c dk bl	1.75	.50
	Nos. 339-340,C72 (3)	7.15	4.00

Flags of Panama and Costa Rica A94

Engraved and Lithographed

1942, April 25

341 A94	2c rose red, dk bl & dp rose	.30	.25

1st anniv. of the settlement of the Costa Rica-Panama border dispute. See No. C73.

National Emblems — A95

Farm Girl in Work Dress — A96

Cart Laden with Sugar Cane (Inscribed "ACARRERO DE CAÑA") — A97

Balboa Taking Possession of the Pacific A98

Golden Altar of San José — A99

San Blas Indian Woman and Child — A101

Santo Tomas Hospital A100

Modern Highway A102

Engr.; Flag on ½c Litho.

1942, May 11

342 A95	½c dl vio, bl & car	.25	.25
343 A96	1c dk green	.25	.25
344 A97	2c vermilion	.25	.25
345 A98	5c dp bl & blk	.25	.25
346 A99	10c car rose & org	.65	.25
347 A100	15c lt bl & blk	1.00	.50
348 A101	50c org red & ol blk	2.50	1.00
349 A102	1b black	3.50	1.00
	Nos. 342-349 (8)	8.65	3.75

See Nos. 357, 365, 376-377, 380, 395, 409.

For surcharges and overprints see Nos. 366-370, 373-375, 378 379, 381, 387-388, 396, C129-C130, RA23.

Catalogue values for unused stamps in this section, from this point to the end of the section, are for Never Hinged items.

Flag of Panama — A103

Arms of Panama — A104

Engraved; Flag on 2c Lithographed

1947, Apr. 7 **Unwmk.** ***Perf. 12½***

350 A103	2c car, bl & red	.25	.25
351 A104	5c deep blue	.25	.25

Natl. Constitutional Assembly of 1945, 2nd anniv.

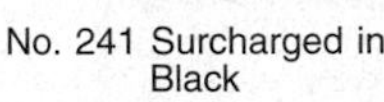

No. 241 Surcharged in Black

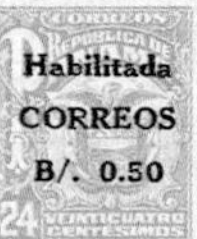

1947, Oct. 29 ***Perf. 12***

352 A53	50c on 24c yel brn	2.00	1.50
a.	"Habiiltada"	2.00	2.00

Nos. C6C, C75, C74 and C87 Surcharged in Black or Carmine

353 AP5	½c on 8c gray blk	.25	.25
a.	"B/.0.0½ CORREOS" (transposed)	2.50	2.50
354 AP34	½c on 8c dk ol brn & blk (C)	.25	.25
355 AP34	1c on 7c rose car	.25	.25
356 AP42	2c on 8c vio	.25	.25
	Nos. 352-356 (5)	3.00	2.50

Flag Type of 1942

1948 **Engr. and Litho.**

357 A95	½c car, org, bl & dp car	.25	.25

Monument to Firemen of Colon — A105

American-La France Fire Engine — A106

20c, Firemen & hose cart. 25c, New Central Fire Station, Colon. 50c, Maximino Walker. 1b, J. J. A. Ducruet.

1948, June 10 **Engr.**

Center in Black

358 A105	5c dp car	.65	.25
359 A106	10c orange	.90	.25
360 A106	20c gray bl	1.75	.40
361 A106	25c chocolate	1.75	.70

362 A105 50c purple 3.50 .70
363 A105 1b dp grn 5.00 1.50
Nos. 358-363 (6) 13.55 3.80

50th anniversary of the founding of the Colon Fire Department.
For overprint see No. C125.

Cervantes A107

1948, Nov. 15 Unwmk. *Perf. 12½*
364 A107 2c car & blk .80 .25
Nos. 364,C105-C106 (3) 2.25 .75

Miguel de Cervantes Saavedra, novelist, playwright and poet, 400th birth anniv.

Oxcart Type of 1942 Redrawn
Inscribed: "ACARREO DE CANA"

1948 *Perf. 12*
365 A97 2c vermilion .60 .25

No. 365 Surcharged or Overprinted in Black

1949, May 26
366 A97 1c on 2c ver .25 .25
367 A97 2c vermilion .25 .25
a. Inverted overprint 10.00 5.00
Nos. 366-367,C108-C111 (6) 3.90 3.90

Incorporation of Chiriqui Province, cent.

Stamps and Types of 1942-48 Issues Overprinted in Black or Red

1949, Sept. 9 Engr.
368 A96 1c dk green .25 .25
369 A97 2c ver (#365) .45 .25
370 A98 5c blue (R) .70 .25
Nos. 368-370,C114-C118 (8) 8.70 4.55

75th anniv. of the UPU.
Overprint on No. 368 is slightly different and smaller, 15½x12mm.

Francisco Javier de Luna — A108

1949, Dec. 7 *Perf. 12½*
371 A108 2c car & blk .25 .25

200th anniversary of the founding of the University of San Javier. See No. C119.

Dr. Carlos J. Finlay — A109

1950, Jan. 12 Unwmk. *Perf. 12*
372 A109 2c car & gray blk .45 .25

Issued to honor Dr. Carlos J. Finlay (1833-1915), Cuban physician and biologist who found that a mosquito transmitted yellow fever. See No. C120.

Nos. 343, 357 and 345, Overprinted or Surcharged in Carmine or Black

1950, Aug. 17
373 A96 1c dk green .25 .25
374 A95 2c on ½c car, org, bl & dp car (Bk) .25 .25
375 A98 5c dp bl & blk .30 .25
Nos. 373-375,C121-C125 (8) 5.65 3.75

Gen. José de San Martin, death cent.
The overprint is in four lines on No. 375.

Types of 1942

1950, Oct. 13 Engr.
376 A97 2c ver & blk .25 .25
377 A98 5c blue .25 .25

No. 376 is inscribed "ACARREO DE CANA."

Nos. 376 and 377 Overprinted in Green or Carmine

1951, Sept. 26
378 A97 2c ver & blk (G) .25 .25
a. Inverted overprint 20.00 20.00
b. First line omitted, second line repeated 20.00 20.00
379 A98 5c blue (C) .45 .25
a. Inverted overprint 20.00 20.00

St. Jean-Baptiste de la Salle, 500th birth anniv.

Altar Type of 1942

1952 Engr. *Perf. 12*
380 A99 10c pur & org .75 .25

No. 357 Surcharged in Black

1952, Oct. 29
381 A95 1c on ½c multi .25 .25

Queen Isabella I and Arms — A110

1952, Oct. 20 Engr. *Perf. 12½*
Center in Black
382 A110 1c green .45 .25
383 A110 2c carmine .45 .25
384 A110 5c dk bl .45 .25
385 A110 10c purple .70 .25
Nos. 382-385,C131-C136 (10) 15.35 5.70

Queen Isabella I of Spain. 500th birth anniv.

No. 380 and Type of 1942 Srchd. "B/ .0.01 1953" in Black or Carmine

1953 *Perf. 12*
387 A99 1c on 10c pur & org .25 .25
388 A100 1c on 15c black (C) .25 .25

Issued: No. 387, 4/22; No. 388, 9/4.
A similar surcharge on No. 346 was privately applied.

A111

A112

2c, Baptism of the Flag. 5c, Manuel Amador Guerrero & Senora de Amador. 12c, Santos Jorge A. & Jeronimo de la Ossa. 20c, Revolutionary Junta. 50c, Old city hall. 1b, Natl. coinage.

1953, Nov. 2 Engr. *Perf. 12*
389 A111 2c purple .45 .25
390 A112 5c red orange .55 .25
391 A112 12c dp red vio 1.25 .25
392 A112 20c slate gray 2.25 .25
393 A111 50c org yel 3.50 .60
394 A112 1b blue 5.75 1.25
Nos. 389-394 (6) 13.75 2.85

Founding of the Republic of Panama, 50th anniv.
See #C140-C145. For surcharge see #413.

Farm Girl Type of 1942

1954 Unwmk. *Perf. 12*
395 A96 1c dp car rose .25 .25

Surcharged in Black

396 A96 3c on 1c dp car rose .25 .25

Issued: No. 395, 4/21; No. 396, 6/21.

Monument to Gen. Tomas Herrera — A113

1954, Dec. 4 Litho. *Perf. 12½*
397 A113 3c purple .25 .25
Nos. 397,C148-C149 (3) 4.50 2.75

Gen. Tomas Herrera, death cent.

Tocumen International Airport A114

1955, Apr. 16
398 A114 ½c org brn .45 .25

For surcharges see Nos. 411-412.

General Remon Cantera, 1908-1955 — A115

1955, June 1
399 A115 3c lilac rose & blk .25 .25

See No. C153.

Victor de la Guardia y Ayala and Miguel Chiari A116

1955, Sept. 12
400 A116 5c violet .35 .25

Centenary of province of Coclé.

Ferdinand de Lesseps — A117

First Excavation of Panama Canal A118

Design: 50c, Theodore Roosevelt.

1955, Nov. 22
401 A117 3c rose brn, *rose* .55 .25
402 A118 25c vio bl, *lt bl* 2.25 1.40
403 A117 50c vio, *lt vio* 3.00 1.50
Nos. 401-403,C155-C156 (5) 11.15 5.90

Ferdinand de Lesseps, 150th birth anniv., French promoter connected with building of Panama Canal. 75th anniv. of the 1st French excavations.
Imperfs exist, but were not sold at any post office.

Popes

A set of twelve stamps picturing various Popes exists. Value, approximately $100.

Arms of Panama City — A119

Perf. 12½

1956, Aug. 17 Litho. Unwmk.

404 A119 3c green .25 .25

Sixth Inter-American Congress of Municipalities, Panama City, Aug. 14-19, 1956.
For souvenir sheet see C182a.

Carlos A. Mendoza — A120

1956, Oct. 31 Wmk. 311

405 A120 10c rose red & dp grn .35 .25

Pres. Carlos A. Mendoza, birth cent.

National Archives A121

1956, Nov. 27

406 A121 15c shown .70 .25
407 A121 25c Pres. Belisario Porras 1.00 .50
Nos. 406-407,C183-C184 (4) 2.40 1.25

Centenary of the birth of Pres. Belisario Porras. For surcharge see No. 446.

Pan-American Highway, Panama — A122

1957, Aug. 1

408 A122 3c gray green .25 .25
Nos. 408,C185-C187 (4) 3.90 3.30

7th Pan-American Highway Congress.

Hospital Type of 1942

Unwmk.

1957, Aug. 17 Engr. *Perf. 12*

409 A100 15c black .50 .30

Manuel Espinosa Batista — A123

Wmk. 311

1957, Sept. 12 Litho. *Perf. 12½*

410 A123 5c grn & ultra .25 .25

Centenary of the birth of Manuel Espinosa B., independence leader.

No. 398 Surcharged "1957" and New Value in Violet or Black

1957, Dec. 21 Unwmk.

411 A114 1c on ½c org brn (V) .25 .25
412 A114 3c on ½c org brn .25 .25

No. 391 Surcharged "1958," New Value and Dots

1958, June 6 Engr. *Perf. 12*

413 A112 3c on 12c dp red vio .25 .25

Flags of 21 American Nations — A124

Center yellow & black; flags in national colors

Perf. 12½

1958, Aug. 12 Litho. Unwmk.

414 A124 1c lt gray .25 .25
415 A124 2c brt yel grn .25 .25
416 A124 3c red org .25 .25
417 A124 7c vio bl .25 .25
Nos. 414-417,C203-C206 (8) 4.45 3.70

Organization of American States, 10th anniv.

Brazilian Pavilion, Brussels Fair — A125

3c, Argentina. 5c, Venezuela. 10c, Great Britain.

1958, Sept. 8 Wmk. 311

418 A125 1c org yel & emer .25 .25
419 A125 3c lt bl & olive .25 .25
420 A125 5c lt brn & slate .25 .25
421 A125 10c aqua & redsh brn .25 .25
Nos. 418-421,C207-C209 (7) 3.55 3.30

World's Fair, Brussels, Apr. 17-Oct. 19.

Pope Pius XII as Young Man — A126

Wmk. 311

1959, Jan. 21 Litho. *Perf. 12½*

422 A126 3c orange brown .25 .25
Nos. 422,C210-C212 (4) 2.05 1.55

Pope Pius XII, 1876-1958. See #C212a.

UN Headquarters Building — A127

Design: 15c, Humanity looking into sun.

1959, Apr. 14 Wmk. 311

423 A127 3c maroon & olive .25 .25
424 A127 15c orange & emer .35 .25
Nos. 423-424,C213-C217 (7) 3.90 3.30

10th anniv. (in 1958) of the signing of the Universal Declaration of Human Rights.
For overprints see Nos. 425-426, C219-C221.

Nos. 423-424 Overprinted in Dark Blue

1959, May 16

425 A127 3c maroon & olive .25 .25
426 A127 15c orange & emer .35 .25
Nos. 425-426,C218-C221 (6) 3.80 3.15

Issued to commemorate the 8th Reunion of the Economic Commission for Latin America.

Eusebio A. Morales — A128

National Institute A129

Wmk. 311

1959, Aug. 5 Litho. *Perf. 12½*

427 A128 3c shown .25 .25
428 A128 13c Abel Bravo .45 .25
429 A129 21c shown .70 .25
Nos. 427-429,C222-C223 (5) 1.90 1.25

50th anniversary, National Institute.

Soccer — A130

1959, Oct. 26

430 A130 1c shown .25 .25
431 A130 3c Swimming .35 .25
432 A130 20c Hurdling 1.75 .80
Nos. 430-432,C224-C226 (6) 6.15 3.05

3rd Pan American Games, Chicago, 8/27-9/7/59.
For overprint and surcharge see #C289, C349.

Fencing — A131

Wmk. 343

1960, Sept. 23 Litho. *Perf. 12½*

433 A131 3c shown .25 .25
434 A131 5c Soccer .45 .25
Nos. 433-434,C234-C237 (6) 4.85 2.55

17th Olympic Games, Rome, 8/25-9/11.
For surcharges & overprints see #C249-C250, C254, C266-C270, C290, C298, C350, RA40.

Agricultural Products and Cattle A132

1961, Mar. 3 Wmk. 311 *Perf. 12½*

435 A132 3c blue green .25 .25

Issued to publicize the second agricultural and livestock census, Apr. 16, 1961.

Children's Hospital A133

1961, May 2

436 A133 3c greenish blue .25 .25
Nos. 436,C245-C247 (4) 1.15 1.00

25th anniv. of the Lions Club of Panama. See #C245-C247.

Flags of Panama and Costa Rica A134

1961, Oct. 2 Wmk. 343 *Perf. 12½*

437 A134 3c car & bl .25 .25

Meeting of Presidents Mario Echandi of Costa Rica and Roberto F. Chiari of Panama at Paso Canoa, Apr. 21, 1961. See No. C251.

Arms of Colon — A135

1962, Feb. 28 Litho. Wmk. 311

438 A135 3c car, yel & vio bl .25 .25

3rd Central American Municipal Assembly, Colon, May 13-17. See No. C255.

Mercury and Cogwheel — A136

1962, Mar. 16 Wmk. 343

439 A136 3c red orange .25 .25

First industrial and commercial census.

Social Security Hospital A137

1962, June 1 *Perf. 12½*

440 A137 3c vermilion & gray .25 .25

Opening of the Social Security Hospital.
For surcharge see No. 445.

San Francisco de la Montana Church, Veraguas
A138

Ruins of Old Panama Cathedral (1519-1671)
A139

Designs: 3c, David Cathedral. 5c, Natá Church. 10c, Don Bosco Church. 15c, Church of the Virgin of Carmen. 20c, Colon Cathedral. 25c, Greek Orthodox Temple. 50c, Cathedral of Panama. 1b, Protestant Church of Colon.

1960-64 Litho. Wmk. 343

Buildings in Black

441 A138 1c red & bl .25 .25
441A A139 2c red & yel .25 .25
441B A138 3c vio & yel .25 .25
441C A139 5c rose & lt grn .25 .25
441D A139 10c grn & yel .25 .25
441E A139 10c red & bl ('64) .25 .25
441F A139 15c ultra & lt grn .35 .25
441G A139 20c red & pink .55 .25
441H A138 25c grn & pink .65 .45
441I A139 50c ultra & pink 1.10 .60
441J A138 1b lilac & yel 2.75 1.60
Nos. 441-441J (11) 6.90 4.65

Freedom of religion in Panama.
Issued: #441E, 6/4/64; others, 7/29/60.
See #C256-C265; souvenir sheet #C264a.
For surcharges and overprints see Nos. 445A, 451, 467, C288, C296-C297, C299.

Bridge of the Americas during Construction — A140

1962, Oct. 12 ***Perf. 12½***
442 A140 3c carmine & gray .25 .25

Opening of the Bridge of the Americas (Thatcher Ferry Bridge), Oct. 12, 1962. See No. C273. For surcharge see No. 445B.

Fire Brigade Exercises, Inauguration of Aqueduct, 1906 — A141

Portraits of Fire Brigade Officials: 3c, Lt. Col. Luis Carlos Endara P., Col. Raul Arango N. and Major Ernesto Arosemena A. 5c, Guillermo Patterson Jr., David F. de Castro, Pres. T. Gabriel Duque, Telmo Rugliancich and Tomas Leblanc.

1963, Jan. 22 Wmk. 311 ***Perf. 12½***
443 A141 1c emer & blk .25 .25
443A A141 3c vio bl & blk .30 .25
444 A141 5c mag & blk .50 .25
Nos. 443-444,C279-C281 (6) 2.75 1.75

75th anniversary (in 1962) of the Panamanian Fire Brigade.
For surcharge see No. 445C.

Nos. 440, 441A, 442, 443A and 407 Surcharged "VALE" and New Value in Black or Red

1963 Wmk. 343 ***Perf. 12½***
445 A137 4c on 3c ver & gray .25 .25
445A A138 4c on 3c vio & yel .25 .25
445B A140 4c on 3c car & gray .25 .25

Wmk. 311

445C A141 4c on 3c vio bl & blk .25 .25
446 A121 10c on 25c dk car rose & bluish blk (R) .35 .25
Nos. 445-446 (5) 1.35 1.25

Issued: Nos. 445-445C, 8/30; No. 446, 10/9.

1964 Winter Olympics, Innsbruck — 141a

Perf. 14x13½, 13½x14 (#447A, 447C)

1963, Dec. 20 Litho.
447 A141a ½c Mountains .25 .25
447A A141a 1c Speed skating .25 .25
447B A141a 3c like No. 447 .55 .25
447C A141a 4c like No. 447A .65 .25
447D A141a 5c Slalom skiing .80 .25
447E A141a 15c like No. 447D 1.50 .60
447F A141a 21c like No. 447D 2.75 1.00
447G A141a 31c like No. 447D 4.00 1.50
h. Souv. sheet of 2, #447F-447G, perf. 13½x14 18.00 10.00
Nos. 447-447G (8) 10.75 4.35

#447D-447G are airmail. #447Gh exists imperf., with background colors switched. Value, $17.50.

Pres. Francisco J. Orlich, Costa Rica — A142

Flags and Presidents: 2c, Luis A. Somoza, Nicaragua. 3c, Dr. Ramon Villeda M., Honduras. 4c, Roberto F. Chiari, Panama.

Perf. 12½x12

1963, Dec. 18 Litho. Unwmk.

Portrait in Slate Green

448 A142 1c lt grn, red & ultra .25 .25
448A A142 2c lt bl, red & ultra .25 .25
448B A142 3c pale pink, red & ultra .25 .25
448C A142 4c rose, red & ultra .25 .25
Nos. 448-448C,C292-C294 (7) 3.30 2.70

Meeting of Central American Presidents with Pres. John F. Kennedy, San José, Mar. 18-20, 1963.

Vasco Nuñez de Balboa — A143

1964, Jan. 22 Photo. ***Perf. 13***
449 A143 4c green, *pale rose* .25 .25

450th anniv. of Balboa's discovery of the Pacific Ocean. See No. C295.

No. C231 Surcharged "Correos B/.0.10" in Red

Wmk. 311

1964, Feb. 25 Litho. ***Perf. 12½***
450 AP74 10c on 21c lt bl .30 .25

Type of 1962 Overprinted "HABILITADA" in Red

1964, Oct. 20 Wmk. 343
451 A138 1b red, bl & blk 2.50 2.50

1964 Summer Olympics, Tokyo — A144

1964, Mar. 4 ***Perf. 13½x14***
452 A144 ½c shown .25 .25
452A A144 1c Torch bearer .25 .25

Perf. 14x13½

452B A144 5c Olympic stadium .30 .25
452C A144 10c like No. 452B .55 .30
452D A144 21c like No. 452B 1.10 .60
452E A144 50c like No. 452B 2.25 1.25
f. Souv. sheet of 1, perf. 13½x14 17.50 16.00
Nos. 452-452E (6) 4.70 2.90

Nos. 452B-452E are airmail. No. 452Ef exists imperf. with different colors. Value, $17.50.

Space Conquest — A145

½c, Projected Apollo spacecraft. 1c, Gemini, Agena spacecraft. 5c, Astronaut Walter M. Schirra. 10c, Astronaut L. Gordon Cooper. 21c, Schirra's Mercury capsule. 50c, Cooper's Mercury capsule.

1964, Apr. 24 ***Perf. 14x14x13½***
453 A145 ½c bl grn & multi .25 .25
453A A145 1c dk blue & multi .25 .25
453B A145 5c yel bis & multi .35 .35
453C A145 10c lil rose & multi .55 .45
453D A145 21c blue & multi 1.25 1.00
453E A145 50c violet & multi 5.75 5.00
f. Souvenir sheet of 1 22.50 22.50
Nos. 453-453E (6) 8.40 7.30

Nos. 453B-453E are airmail. No. 453Ef exists imperf. with different colors. Value, $22.50.

Aquatic Sports A146

Perf. 14x13½, 13½x14

1964, Jun3. 17
454 A146 ½c Water skiing .25 .25
454A A146 1c Skin diving .25 .25
454B A146 5c Fishing .35 .25
454C A146 10c Sailing, vert. 1.75 .50
454D A146 21c Hydroplane racing 3.25 1.00
454E A146 31c Water polo 4.00 1.25
f. Souvenir sheet of 1 20.00 20.00
Nos. 454-454E (6) 9.85 3.50

Nos. 454B-454E are airmail.
Nos. 454-454Ef exist imperf in different colors. Value imperf, Nos. 454-454E $20. Value imperf, No. 454Ef $20.

Eleanor Roosevelt — A147

Perf. 12x12½

1964, Oct. 9 Litho. Unwmk.
455 A147 4c car & blk, *grnsh* .30 .25

Issued to honor Eleanor Roosevelt (1884-1962). See Nos. C330-C330a.

Canceled to Order

Canceled sets of new issues have been sold by the government. Postally used examples are worth more.

1964 Winter Olympics, Innsbruck — A147a

Olympic medals and winners: ½c, Women's slalom. 1c, Men's 500-meter speed skating. 2c, Four-man bobsled. 3c, Women's figure skating. 4c, Ski jumping. 5c, 15km cross country skiing. 6c, 50km cross country skiing. 7c, Women's 3000-meter speed skating. 10c, Men's figure skating. 21c, Two-man bobsled. 31c, Men's downhill skiing.

Litho. & Embossed

Perf. 13½x14

1964, Oct. 14 Unwmk.
456 A147a ½c bl grn & multi .25 .25
456A A147a 1c dk bl & multi .25 .25
456B A147a 2c brn vio & multi .25 .25
456C A147a 3c lil rose & multi .45 .25
456D A147a 4c brn lake & multi .70 .25
456E A147a 5c brt vio & multi .55 .30
456F A147a 6c grn bl & multi .70 .40
456G A147a 7c dp vio & multi 1.10 .65
456H A147a 10c emer grn & multi 1.75 1.00
456I A147a 21c ver & multi 2.00 1.10
456J A147a 31c ultra & multi 3.50 2.00
k. Souv. sheet of 3, #456H-456J 17.50 16.00
Nos. 456-456J (11) 11.50 6.70

Nos. 456E-456J are airmail.
No. 456Jk exists imperf. Value $17.50.
See Nos. 458-458J.

Satellites — A147b

Designs: ½c, Telstar 1. 1c, Transit 2A. 5c, OSO 1 Solar Observatory. 10c, Tiros 2 weather satellite. 21c, Weather station. 50c, Syncom 3.

1964, Dec. 21 ***Perf. 14x14x13½***
457 A147b ½c ver & multi .55 .25
457A A147b 1c vio & multi .55 .25
457B A147b 5c lil rose & multi .55 .40
457C A147b 10c blue & multi .70 .25
457D A147b 21c bl grn & multi 2.00 1.25

457E A147b 50c green & multi 3.00 1.75
f. Souvenir sheet of 1 17.50 16.00
Nos. 457-457E (6) 7.35 4.15

Nos. 457B-457E are airmail. No. 457Ef exists imperf in different colors. Value, $20.
For overprints see Nos. 489-489b.

1964 Olympic Medals Type

Summer Olympic Medals and Winners: ½c, Parallel bars. 1c, Dragon-class sailing. 2c, Individual show jumping. 3c, Two-man kayak. 4c, Team road race cycling. 5c, Individual dressage. 6c, Women's 800-meter run. 7c, 3000-meter steeplechase. 10c, Men's floor exercises. 21c, Decathlon. 31c, Men's 100-meter freestyle swimming.

Litho. & Embossed

1964, Dec. 28 ***Perf. 13½x14***

458 A147a ½c org & multi .25 .25
458A A147a 1c plum & multi .25 .25
458B A147a 2c bl grn & multi .25 .25
458C A147a 3c red brn & multi .25 .25
458D A147a 4c lilac rose & multi .30 .25
458E A147a 5c dull grn & multi .60 .25
458F A147a 6c blue & multi .70 .25
458G A147a 7c dk vio & multi .85 .30
458H A147a 10c ver & multi 1.25 .40
458I A147a 21c dl vio & multi 1.90 .65
458J A147a 31c dk bl grn & multi 3.25 1.00
k. Souv. sheet of 3, #458H-458J 22.50 17.50
Nos. 458-458J (11) 9.85 4.10

#458E-458J are airmail. #458Jk exists imperf. Value, $25.

John F. Kennedy & Cape Kennedy — A147c

Designs: 1c, Launching of Titan II rocket, Gemini capsule. 2c, Apollo lunar module. 3c, Proposed Apollo command and service modules. 5c, Gemini capsule atop Titan II rocket. 6c, Soviet cosmonauts Komarov, Yegorov, Feoktistov. 11c, Ranger VII. 31c, Lunar surface.

1965, Feb. 25 **Litho.** ***Perf. 14***

459 A147c ½c vio bl & multi .55 .25
459A A147c 1c blue & multi .55 .25
459B A147c 2c plum & multi .55 .25
459C A147c 3c ol grn & multi .70 .30
459D A147c 5c lilac rose & multi .70 .40
459E A147c 10c dull grn & multi 1.25 .70
459F A147c 11c brt vio & multi 2.00 1.10
459G A147c 31c grn & multi 3.50 2.00
h. Souvenir sheet of 1 20.00 20.00
Nos. 459-459G (8) 9.80 5.25

Nos. 459D-459G are airmail. No. 459Gh exists imperf. in different colors. Value, $20.
For overprints see Nos. 491-491b.

Atomic Power for Peace — A147d

Designs: ½c, Nuclear powered submarine *Nautilus.* 1c, Nuclear powered ship *Savannah.* 4c, First nuclear reactor, Calderhall, England. 6c, Nuclear powered icebreaker *Lenin.* 10c, Nuclear powered observatory. 21c, Nuclear powered space vehicle.

1965, May 12

460 A147d ½c blue & multi
460A A147d 1c grn & multi
460B A147d 4c red & multi
460C A147d 6c dl bl grn & multi
460D A147d 10c blue grn & multi
460E A147d 21c dk vio & multi
f. Souv. sheet of 2, #460D-460E 12.50 12.50
Set, #460-460E 6.75 3.50

Nos. 460C-460E are airmail.
Nos. 460-460Ef exists imperf in different colors. Value imperf, Nos. 460-460E $12.50. Value imperf, No. 460Ef $12.50.

John F. Kennedy Memorial A147e

Kennedy and: ½c, PT109. 1c, Space capsule. 10c, UN emblem. 21c, Winston Churchill. 31c, Rocket launch at Cape Kennedy.

1965, Aug. 23 ***Perf. 13½x13***

461 A147e ½c multicolored
461A A147e 1c multicolored
461B A147e 10c + 5c, multi
461C A147e 21c + 10c, multi
461D A147e 31c + 15c, multi
e. Souv. sheet of 2, #461A, 461D, perf. 12½x12 20.00 20.00
Set, #461-461D 6.00 1.50

Nos. 461B-461D are airmail semipostal.
Nos. 461-461De exist imperf in different colors. Value $15.
For overprints see Nos. C367A-C367B.

Keel-billed Toucan A148

Song Birds: 2c, Scarlet macaw. 3c, Red-crowned woodpecker. 4c, Blue-gray tanager, horiz.

1965, Oct. 27 **Unwmk.** ***Perf. 14***

462 A148 1c brt pink & multi .65 .25
462A A148 2c multicolored .65 .25
462B A148 3c brt vio & multi 1.00 .25
462C A148 4c org yel & multi 1.00 .25
Nos. 462-462C,C337-C338 (6) 7.20 1.50

Snapper — A149

1965, Dec. 7 **Litho.**

463 A149 1c shown .35 .25
463A A149 2c Dorado .35 .25
Nos. 463-463A,C339-C342 (6) 3.95 1.60

Pope Paul VI, Visit to UN — A149a

Designs: ½c, Pope on Balcony of St. Peters, Vatican City. 1c, Pope Addressing UN General Assembly. 5c, Arms of Vatican City, Panama, UN emblem. 10c, Lyndon Johnson, Pope Paul VI, Francis Cardinal Spellman. 21c, Ecumenical Council, Vatican II. 31c, Earlybird satellite.

1966 Apr. 4 ***Perf. 12x12½***

464 A149a ½c multicolored
464A A149a 1c multicolored
464B A149a 5c multicolored
464C A149a 10c multicolored
464D A149a 21c multicolored
464E A149a 31c multicolored
f. Souv. sheet of 2, #464B, 464E, perf. 13x13½ 20.00 20.00
Set, #464-464E 8.00 3.00

Nos. 464B-464E are airmail. No. 464Ef exists imperf. with different margin color. Value $20.
For overprints see Nos. 490-490B.

Famous Men — A149b

Designs: ½c, William Shakespeare. 10c, Dante Alighieri. 31c, Richard Wagner.

1966, May 26 ***Perf. 14***

465 A149b ½c multicolored
465A A149b 10c multicolored
465B A149b 31c multicolored
c. Souv. sheet of 2, #465A-465B, perf. 13½x14 15.00 15.00
Set, #465-465B 6.75 3.25

Nos. 465A-465B are airmail. No. 465Bc exists imperf. with different margin color. Value $20.

Works by Famous Artists A149c

Paintings: ½c, Elizabeth Tucher by Durer. 10c, Madonna of the Rocky Grotto by Da Vinci. 31c, La Belle Jardiniere by Raphael.

1966, May 26

466 A149c ½c multicolored
466A A149c 10c multicolored
466B A149c 31c multicolored
c. Souv. sheet of 2, #466-466B 15.00 15.00
Set, #466-465B 7.00 2.25

Nos. 466A-466B are airmail.
No. 466Bc exists imperf. with different margin color. Value $30.

No. 441H Surcharged

1966, June 27 **Wmk. 343** ***Perf. 12½***

467 A138 13c on 25c grn & pink .40 .25

The "25c" has not been obliterated.

A149d

No. 468A, Uruguay, 1930, 1950. No. 468B, Italy, 1934, 1938. No. 468C, Brazil, 1958, 1962. No. 468D, Germany, 1954. No. 468E, Great Britain.

1966, July 11 ***Perf. 14***

468 A149d ½c multi
468A A149d .005b multi
468B A149d 10c multi
468C A149d 10c multi
468D A149d 21c multi
468E A149d 21c multi
f. Souv. sheet of 2, #468B, 468D 15.00 15.00
g. Souv. sheet of 2, #468, 468E, imperf. 12.50 11.00
Set, #468-465E 6.00 2.25

World Cup Soccer Championships, Great Britain. Nos. 468B-468E are airmail.
Nos. 468-468E exist imperf in different colors. Value, $22.50.
For overprints see Nos. 470-470g.

A149e

Italian Contributions to Space Research: ½c, Launch of Scout rocket, San Marco satellite. 1c, San Marco in orbit, horiz. 5c, Italian scientists, rocket. 10c, Arms of Panama, Italy, horiz. 21c, San Marco boosted into orbit, horiz.

Perf. 12x12½, 12½x12

1966, Aug. 12

469 A149e ½c multicolored
469A A149e 1c multicolored
469B A149e 5c multicolored
469C A149e 10c multicolored
469D A149e 21c multicolored
e. Souv. sheet of 2, #469C-469D, imperf. 15.00 15.00
Set, #469-469D 7.25 4.00

Nos. 469B-469D are airmail.

Nos. 468-468g Ovptd.

1966, Nov. 21 ***Perf. 14***

470 A149d ½c on #468
470A A149d .005b on #468A
470B A149d 10c on #468B
470C A149d 10c on #468C
470D A149d 21c on #468D
470E A149d 21c on #468E
f. on #468Ef 30.00 30.00
g. on #468Eg, imperf. 30.00 30.00
Set, #470-470E 13.50 3.75

Nos. 470B-470E are airmail.

A149f

Religious Paintings
A149g

Paintings: ½c, Coronation of Mary. 1c, Holy Family with Angel. 2c, Adoration of the Magi. 3c, Madonna and Child. No. 471D, The Annunciation. No. 471E, The Nativity. No. 471Fh, Madonna and Child.

1966, Oct. 24 *Perf. 11*

Size of No. 471D: 32x34mm

471 A149f ½c Velazquez
471A A149f 1c Saraceni
471B A149g 2c Durer
471C A149f 3c Orazio
471D A149g 21c Rubens
471E A149f 21c Boticelli

Souvenir Sheet

Perf. 14

471F Sheet of 2
g. A149f 21c like No. 471E, black inscriptions 12.50 11.00
h. A149f 31c Mignard 18.00 18.00
Set, #471-471E 9.00 1.25

Nos. 471D-471F are airmail.
Nos. 471-471F exist imperf in different colors. Value imperf, Nos. 471-471E $10. Value imperf, No. 471F $17.50.

Sir Winston Churchill, British Satellites — A149h

Churchill and: 10c, Blue Streak, NATO emblem. 31c, Europa 1, rocket engine.

1966, Nov. 25 *Perf. 12x12½*

472 A149h ½c shown
472A A149h 10c org & multi
472B A149h 31c dk bl & multi
c. Souv. sheet of 2, #472A-472B, perf. 13½x14 11.50 11.50
Set, #472-472B 6.25 2.00

Nos. 472A-472B are airmail.
No. 472Bc exists imperf in different colors. Value $12.50.
For overprints see Nos. 492-492B.

John F. Kennedy, 3rd Death Anniv. — A149i

10c, Kennedy, UN building. 31c, Kennedy, satellites & map.

1966, Nov. 25 *Perf. 14*

473 A149i ½c shown
473A A149i 10c multi
473B A149i 31c multi
c. Souv. sheet of 2, #473A-473B 18.00 18.00
Set, #473-473B 5.75 2.00

Nos. 473A-473B are airmail.
No. 473Bc exists imperf in different colors. Value $17.50.

Jules Verne (1828-1905), French Space Explorations — A149j

Designs: ½c, Earth, A-1 satellite. 1c, Verne, submarine. 5c, Earth, FR-1 satellite. 10c, Verne, telescope. 21c, Verne, capsule heading toward Moon. 31c, D-1 satellite over Earth.

1966, Dec. 28 *Perf. 13½x14*

474 A149j ½c bl & multi
474A A149j 1c bl grn & multi
474B A149j 5c ultra & multi
474C A149j 10c lil, blk & red
474D A149j 21c vio & multi
f. Souv. sheet of 2, #474C, 474D, imperf. 12.50 12.50
474E A149j 31c dl bl & multi
g. Souvenir sheet of 1 15.00 15.00
Set, #474-474E 8.50 2.00

Nos. 474B-474E are airmail.
Nos. 474-474Eg exist imperf in different colors. Value imperf. Nos. 474-474E $10. Value imperf, No. 474Eg $17.50.

Hen and Chicks
A150

Domestic Animals: 3c, Rooster. 5c, Pig, horiz. 8c, Cow, horiz.

1967, Feb. 3 **Unwmk.** *Perf. 14*

475 A150 1c multi .25 .25
475A A150 3c multi .25 .25
475B A150 5c multi .25 .25
475C A150 8c multi .25 .25
Nos. 475-475C,C353-C356 (8) 4.25 2.60

Easter
A150a

Paintings: ½c, Christ at Calvary. 1c, The Crucifixion. 5c, Pieta, horiz. 10c, Body of Christ. 21c, The Arisen Christ. No. 476E, ChristAscending into Heaven. No. 476F, Christ on the Cross. No. 476G, Madonna and Child.

1967, Mar. 13 *Perf. 14x13½, 13½x14*

476 A150a ½c Giambattista Tiepolo
476A A150a 1c Rubens
476B A150a 5c Sarto
476C A150a 10c Raphael Santi
476D A150a 21c Multscher
476E A150a 31c Grunewald
Set, #476-476E 7.50 3.00

Souvenir Sheets

Perf. 12½x12x12½x13½

476F A150a 31c Van der Weyden 20.00 20.00

Imperf

476G A150a 31c Rubens 20.00 20.00

Nos. 476B-476G are airmail.

1968 Summer Olympics, Mexico City — A150b

Indian Ruins at: ½c, Teotihuacan. 1c, Tajin. 5c, Xochicalco. 10c, Monte Alban. 21c, Palenque. 31c, Chichen Itza.

1967, Apr. 18 *Perf. 12x12½*

477 A150b ½c plum & multi
477A A150b 1c red lil & multi
477B A150b 5c blue & multi
477C A150b 10c ver & multi
477D A150b 21c grn bl & multi
477E A150b 31c grn & multi
Set, #477-477E 8.00 3.00

Souvenir Sheet

Perf. 12x12½x14x12½

477F A150a 31c multi 18.00 18.00

Nos. 477B-477E are airmail.

New World Anhinga
A151

Birds: 1c, Quetzals. 3c, Turquoise-browed motmot. 4c, Double-collared aracari, horiz. 5c, Macaw. 13c, Belted kingfisher. 50c, Hummingbird.

1967, July 20 *Perf. 14*

478 A151 ½c lt bl & multi 1.00 .25
478A A151 1c lt gray & multi 1.00 .25
478B A151 3c pink & multi 1.10 .25
478C A151 4c lt grn & multi 1.40 .25
478D A151 5c buff & multi 1.75 .25
478E A151 13c yel & multi 6.75 .75
Nos. 478-478E (6) 13.00 2.00

Souvenir Sheet

Perf. 14½

478F A151 50c Sheet of 1 15.00 15.00

No. 478A exists imperf. with blue background. Value $17.50.

Works of Famous Artists
A151a

Paintings: No. 479, Maiden in the Doorway. No. 479A, Blueboy. No. 479B, The Promise of Louis XIII. No. 479C, St. George and the Dragon. No. 479D, The Blacksmith's Shop, horiz. No. 479E, St. Hieronymus. Nos. 479F-479K, Self-portraits.

Perf. 14x13½, 13½x14

1967, Aug. 23

479 A151a 5c Rembrandt
479A A151a 5c Gainsborough
479B A151a 5c Ingres
479C A151a 21c Raphael
479D A151a 21c Velazquez
479E A151a 21c Durer
Set, #479-479E 7.25 2.00

Souvenir Sheets

Various Compound Perfs.

479F A151a 21c Gainsborough 8.50 5.00
479G A151a 21c Rembrandt 8.50 5.00
479H A151a 21c Ingres 8.50 5.00
479I A151a 21c Raphael 8.50 5.00
479J A151a 21c Velazquez 8.50 5.00
479K A151a 21c Durer 8.50 5.00

Nos. 479C-479K are airmail.

Red Deer, by Franz Marc — A152

Animal Paintings by Franz Marc: 3c, Tiger, vert. 5c, Monkeys. 8c, Blue Fox.

1967, Sept. 1 *Perf. 14*

480 A152 1c multicolored .25 .25
480A A152 3c multicolored .25 .25
480B A152 5c multicolored .25 .25
480C A152 8c multicolored .25 .25
Nos. 480-480C,C357-C360 (8) 3.80 2.20

Paintings by Goya
A152a

Designs: 2c, The Water Carrier. 3c, Count Floridablanca. 4c, Senora Francisca Sebasa y Garcia. 5c, St. Bernard and St. Robert. 8c, Self-portrait. 10c, Dona Isabel Cobos de Porcel. 13c, Clothed Maja, horiz. 21c, Don Manuel Osoria de Zuniga as a child. 50c, Cardinal Luis of Bourbon and Villabriga.

1967, Oct. 17 *Perf. 14x13½, 13½x14*

481 A152a 2c multicolored
481A A152a 3c multicolored
481B A152a 4c multicolored
481C A152a 5c multicolored
481D A152a 8c multicolored
481E A152a 10c multicolored
481F A152a 13c multi, horiz.
481G A152a 21c multicolored
Set, #481-481G 9.00 2.25

Souvenir Sheet

481H A152a 50c multicolored 20.00 20.00

Nos. 481C-481H are airmail.

Life of Christ
A152b

Paintings: No. 482, The Holy Family. No. 482A, Christ Washing Feet. 3c, Christ's Charge to Peter. 4c, Christ and the Money Changers in the Temple, horiz. No. 482D, Christ's Entry into Jerusalem, horiz. No. 482E, The Last Supper.

No. 482Fl, Pastoral Adoration. No. 482Fm, The Holy Family. No. 482Gn, Christ with Mary and Martha. No. 482Go, Flight from Egypt. No. 482Hp, St. Thomas. No. 482Hq, The Tempest. No. 482Ir, The Transfiguration. No. 482Is, The Crucification.

No. 482J, The Baptism of Christ, by Guido Reni. No. 482K, Christ at the Sea of Galilee, by Tintoretto, horiz.

1968, Jan. 10 ***Perf. 14x13½x13½x14***

482 A152b 1c Michaelangelo
482A A152b 1c Brown
482B A152b 3c Rubens
482C A152b 4c El Greco
482D A152b 21c Van Dyck
482E A152b 21c do Juanes
Set, #482-482E 7.00 3.00

Souvenir Sheets

Various Perfs.

482F Sheet of 2 13.50 13.50
l. A152b 1c Schongauer
m. A152b 21c Raphael
482G Sheet of 2 13.50 13.50
n. A152b 3c Tintoretto
o. A152b 21c Caravaggio
482H Sheet of 2 13.50 13.50
p. A152b 21c Anonymous, 12th cent.
q. A152b 31c multicolored
482I Sheet of 2 13.50 13.50
r. A152b 21c Raphael
s. A152b 31c Montanez
482J A152b 22c Sheet of 1 13.50 13.50
482K A152b 24c Sheet of 1 13.50 13.50

Nos. 482C-482K are airmail.
Nos. 482J-482K also exist imperf.

Butterflies — A152c

½c, Apodemia albinus. 1c, Caligo ilioneus, vert. 3c, Meso semia tenera. 4c, Pamphila epictetus. 5c, Entheus peleus. 13c, Tmetoglene drymo.
50c, Thymele chalco, vert.

1968, Feb. 23 ***Perf. 14***

483 A152c ½c multi
483A A152c 1c multi
483B A152c 3c multi
483C A152c 4c multi
483D A152c 5c multi
483E A152c 13c multi
Set, #483-483E 22.00 4.00

Souvenir Sheet

Perf. 14½

483F A152c 50c multi 15.00 15.00

Nos. 483D-483F are airmail.
No. 483F exists imperf with pink margin. Value $15.

10th Winter Olympics, Grenoble — A152d

½c, Emblem, vert. 1c, Ski jumper. 5c, Skier. 10c, Mountain climber. 21c, Speed skater. 31c, Two-man bobsled.

1968, Feb. 2 ***Perf. 14x13½, 13½x14***

484 A152d ½c multi
484A A152d 1c multi
484B A152d 5c multi
484C A152d 10c multi
484D A152d 21c multi
484E A152d 31c multi
Set, #484-484E 7.00 1.50

Souvenir Sheets

Perf. 14

484F Sheet of 2 16.00 16.00
h. A152d 10c Emblem, snowflake
i. A152d 31c Figure skater
484G Sheet of 2 16.00 16.00
j. A152d 31c Biathlon
k. A152d 10c Skier on ski lift

Nos. 484B-484G are airmail.

Sailing Ships — A152e

Paintings by: ½c, Gamiero, vert. 1c, Lebreton. 3c, Anonymous Japanese. 4c, Le Roi. 5c, Van de Velde. 13c, Duncan. 50c, Anonymous Portuguese, vert.

1968, May 7 ***Perf. 14***

485 A152e ½c multicolored
485A A152e 1c multicolored
485B A152e 3c multicolored
485C A152e 4c multicolored
485D A152e 5c multicolored
485E A152e 13c multicolored
Set, #485-485E 7.50 2.00

Souvenir Sheet

Perf. 14½

485F A152e 50c multicolored 9.00 9.00

Nos. 485D-485E are airmail. No. 485F exists imperf. with light blue margin. Value $9.

Tropical Fish — A152f

½c, Balistipus undulatus. 1c, Holacanthus ciliaris. 3c, Chaetodon ephippium. 4c, Epinephelus elongatus. 5c, Anisotremus virginicus. 13c, Balistoides conspicillum.
50c, Raja texana, vert.

1968, June 26 ***Perf. 14***

486 A152f ½c multi
486A A152f 1c multi
486B A152f 3c multi
486C A152f 4c multi
486D A152f 5c multi
486E A152f 13c multi
Set, #486-486E 6.75 2.00

Souvenir Sheet

Perf. 14½

486F A152f 50c multi 15.00 15.00

Nos. 486D-486F are airmail. No. 486F exists imperf. with pink margin. Value $15.

Olympic Medals and Winners, Grenoble — A152g

Olympic Medals and Winners: 1c, Men's giant slalom. 2c, Women's downhill. 3c, Women's figure skating. 4c, 5000-meter speed skating. 5c, 10,000-meter speed skating. 6c, Women's slalom. 8c, Women's 1000-meter speed skating. 13c, Women's 1500-meter speed skating. 30c, Two-man bobsled. 70c, Nordic combined.

Litho. & Embossed

1968, July 30 ***Perf. 13½x14***

487 A152g 1c pink & multi
487A A152g 2c vio & multi
487B A152g 3c grn & multi
487C A152g 4c plum & multi
487D A152g 5c red brn & multi
487E A152g 6c brt vio & multi
487F A152g 8c Prus bl & multi
487G A152g 13c bl & multi
487H A152g 30c rose lil & multi
Set, #487-487H 6.75 2.00

Souvenir Sheet

487I A152g 70c red & multi 18.00 18.00

Nos. 487G-487H are airmail.

Miniature Sheet

Music — A152h

Paintings of Musicians, Instruments: 5c, Mandolin, by de la Hyre. 10c, Lute, by Caravaggio. 15c, Flute, by ter Brugghen. 20c, Chamber ensemble, by Tourmer. 25c, Violin, by Caravaggio. 30c, Piano, by Vermeer. 40c, Harp, by Memling.

1968, Sept. 11 Litho. ***Perf. 13½x14***

488 A152h Sheet of 6 10.00 2.00
a. 5c multicolored
b. 10c multicolored
c. 15c multicolored
d. 20c multicolored
e. 25c multicolored
f. 30c multicolored

Souvenir Sheet

Perf. 14

488A A152h 40c multicolored 18.00 18.00

Nos. 457, 457E Ovptd. in Black

1968, Oct. 17

489 A147b ½c on No. 457 2.50 .75
489A A147b 50c on No. 457E 2.50 .75
b. Souv. sheet of 1, on No. 457Ef 22.50 22.50

Nos. 489-489A exist with gold overprint. Overprint differs on No. 489Ab.

Nos. 464, 464D & 464Ef Ovptd. in Black or Gold

1968, Oct. 18 ***Perf. 12x12½***

490 A149a ½c on No. 464 6.75
490A A149a 21c on No. 464D 6.75

Souvenir Sheet

Perf. 13x13½

490B on No. 464Ef (G) 27.50 27.50

Nos. 490A-490B are airmail. No. 490B exists imperf. with different colored border. Value same as No. 490B. Overprint differs on No. 490B.

Nos. 459, 459G-459Gh Ovptd. in Black

1968, Oct. 21 ***Perf. 14***

491 A147c ½c on No. 459 6.75
491A A147c 31c on No. 459G 6.75
b. on souv. sheet, No. 459Gh 9.00 9.00

Nos. 491A-491Ab are airmail.
Nos. 491-491A exist overprinted in gold, and imperf., overprinted in gold. No. 491Ab exists imperf in different colors and black or gold overprints. Values, black $9, gold $90.

Nos. 472-472A, 472Bc Overprinted in Black or Gold

1968, Oct. 22 ***Perf. 12x12½***

492 A149h ½c (#472) 2.00
492A A149h 10c (#472A) 2.00

Souvenir Sheet

Perf. 13½x14

492B on No. 472Bc 13.50 13.50

Nos. 492A-492B are airmail.
No. 492B exists imperf in different colors.

Hunting on Horseback — A152i

Paintings and Tapestries: 1c, Koller. 3c, Courbet. 5c, Tischbein, the Elder. 10c, Gobelin, vert. 13c, Oudry. 30c, Rubens.

1968, Oct. 29 ***Perf. 14***

493 A152i 1c multicolored
493A A152i 3c multicolored
493B A152i 5c multicolored
493C A152i 10c multicolored
493D A152i 13c multicolored
493E A152i 30c multicolored
Set, #493-493E 5.75 2.00

Nos. 493D-493E are airmail.

Miniature Sheet

Famous Race Horses — A152j

Horse Paintings: a, 5c, Lexington, by Edward Troye. b, 10c, American Eclipse, by Alvan Fisher. c, 15c, Plenipotentiary, by Abraham Cooper. d, 20c, Gimcrack, by George Stubbs. e, 25c, Flying Childers, by James Seymour. f, 30c, Eclipse, by Stubbs.

1968, Dec. 18 ***Perf. 13½x14***

494 A152j Sheet of 6, #a.-f. 15.00 12.50

1968 Summer Olympics, Mexico City — A152k

Mexican art: 1c, Watermelons, by Diego Rivera. 2c, Women, by Jose Clemente Orozco. 3c, Flower Seller, by Miguel Covarrubias, vert. 4c, Nutall Codex, vert. 5c, Mayan statue, vert. 6c, Face sculpture, vert. 8c, Seated figure, vert. 13c. Ceramic angel, vert. 30c, Christ, by David Alfaro Siqueiros. 70c, Symbols of Summer Olympic events.

1968, Dec. 23 ***Perf. 13½x14, 14x13½***

495	A152k	1c multicolored		
495A	A152k	2c multicolored		
495B	A152k	3c multicolored		
495C	A152k	4c multicolored		
495D	A152k	5c multicolored		
495E	A152k	6c multicolored		
495F	A152k	8c multicolored		
495G	A152k	13c multicolored		
495H	A152k	30c multicolored		
	Set, #495-495H		10.50	2.25

Souvenir Sheet

Perf. 14

495I	A152k	70c multicolored	16.00	16.00

Nos. 495G-495H are airmail.

First Visit of Pope Paul VI to Latin America A152l

Paintings: 1c-3c, 5c-6c, Madonna and Child. 4c, The Annunciation. 7c-8c, Adoration of the Magi. 10c, Holy Family. 50c, Madonna and Child, angel.

1969, Aug. 5 ***Perf. 14***

496	A152l	1c Raphael		
496A	A152l	2c Ferruzzi		
496B	A152l	3c Bellini		
496C	A152l	4c Portuguese School, 17th cent.		
496D	A152l	5c Van Dyck		
496E	A152l	6c Albani		
496F	A152l	7c Viennese master		
496G	A152l	8c Van Dyck		
496H	A152l	10c Portuguese School, 16th cent.		
	Set, #496-496H		10.00	2.75

Souvenir Sheet

Perf. 14½

496I	A152l	50c Del Sarto	15.00	7.50

Nos. 496E-496I are airmail.

Map of Americas and People — A153

5c, Map of Panama, People and Houses, horiz.

1969, Aug. 14 Photo. Wmk. 350

500	A153	5c violet blue	.25	.25
501	A153	10c bright rose lilac	.30	.25

Issued to publicize the 1970 census.

Cogwheel A154

1969, Aug. 14

502	A154	13c yel & dk bl gray	.35	.25

50th anniv. of Rotary Intl. of Panama.

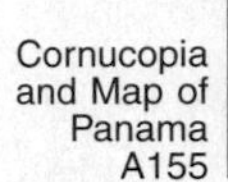

Cornucopia and Map of Panama A155

Perf. 14½x15

1969, Oct. 10 Litho. Unwmk.

503	A155	10c lt bl & multi	.35	.25

1st anniv. of the October 11 Revolution.

Map of Panama and Ruins — A156

Natá Church — A157

Designs: 5c, Farmer, wife and mule. 13c, Hotel Continental. 20c, Church of the Virgin of Carmen. 21c, Gold altar, San José Church. 25c, Del Rey bridge. 30c, Dr. Justo Arosemena monument. 34c, Cathedral of Panama. 38c, Municipal Palace. 40c, French Plaza. 50c, Thatcher Ferry Bridge (Bridge of the Americas). 59c, National Theater.

Perf. 14½x15, 15x14½

1969-70 Litho. Unwmk.

504	A156	3c org & blk	.25	.25
505	A156	5c lt bl grn ('70)	.25	.25
506	A157	8c dl brn ('70)	.25	.25
507	A156	13c emer & blk	.35	.25
508	A157	20c vio brn ('70)	.50	.25
509	A157	21c yellow ('70)	.50	.40
510	A156	25c lt bl grn ('70)	.65	.25
511	A157	30c black ('70)	.80	.40
512	A156	34c org brn ('70)	1.00	.50
513	A156	38c brt bl ('70)	1.00	.40
514	A156	40c org yel ('70)	1.25	.60
515	A156	50c brt rose lil & blk	1.40	.70
516	A156	59c brt rose lil ('70)	2.00	.90
	Nos. 504-516 (13)		10.20	5.40

Issued: Nos. 504, 507, 515, 10/10/69. Others, 1/28/70.

For surcharges see Nos. 541, 543, 545-547, RA78-RA80.

Stadium and Discus Thrower A158

Flor del Espiritu Santo — A159

Wmk. 365

1970, Jan. 6 Litho. ***Perf. 13½***

517	A158	1c ultra & multi	.25	.25
518	A158	2c ultra & multi	.25	.25
519	A158	3c ultra & multi	.25	.25
520	A158	5c ultra & multi	.25	.25
521	A158	10c ultra & multi	.30	.25
522	A158	13c ultra & multi	.35	.25
523	A159	13c pink & multi	.40	.25
524	A158	25c ultra & multi	.85	.50
525	A158	30c ultra & multi	1.00	.75
	Nos. 517-525,C368-C369 (11)		6.15	4.05

11th Central American and Caribbean Games, Feb. 28-Mar. 14.

Office of Comptroller General, 1970 — A160

Designs: 5c, Alejandro Tapia and Martin Sosa, first Comptrollers, 1931-34, horiz. 8c, Comptroller's emblem. 13c, Office of Comptroller General, 1955-70, horiz.

1971, Feb. 25 Litho. Wmk. 365

526	A160	3c yel & multi	.25	.25
527	A160	5c brn, buff & gold	.25	.25
528	A160	8c gold & multi	.25	.25
529	A160	13c blk & multi	.25	.25
	Nos. 526-529 (4)		1.00	1.00

Comptroller General's Office, 40th anniv.

Indian Alligator Design A161

1971, Aug. 18 Wmk. 343 ***Perf. 13½***

530	A161	8c multicolored	.80	.25

SENAPI (Servicio Nacional de Artesania y Pequeñas Industrias), 5th anniv.

Education Year Emblem, Map of Panama A162

1971, Aug. 19 Litho.

531	A162	1b multicolored	3.50	2.50

International Education Year, 1970.

For surcharge see No. 542.

Congress Emblem — A163

1972, Aug. 25

532	A163	25c multicolored	1.00	.60

9th Inter-American Conference of Saving and Loan Associations, Panama City, Jan. 23-29, 1971.

UPU Headquarters, Bern — A164

Design: 30c, UPU Monument, Bern, vert.

1971, Dec. 14 Wmk. 343

533	A164	8c multicolored	.25	.25
534	A164	30c multicolored	1.00	.60

Inauguration of Universal Postal Union Headquarters, Bern, Switzerland.

For surcharge see No. RA77.

Cow, Pig and Produce A165

1971, Dec. 15

535	A165	3c yel, brn & blk	.25	.25

3rd agricultural census.

Map of Panama and "4-S" Emblem A166

1971, Dec. 16

536	A166	2c multicolored	.25	.25

Rural youth 4-S program.

UNICEF Emblem, Children A167

Wmk. 365

1972, Sept. 12 Litho. ***Perf. 13½***

537	A167	1c yel & multi	.25	.25
	Nos. 537,C390-C392 (4)		2.00	1.30

25th anniv. (in 1971) of UNICEF. See No. C392a.

Tropical Fruits A168

1972, Sept. 13

538	A168	1c shown	.25	.25
539	A168	2c Isla de Noche	.25	.25
540	A168	3c Carnival float, vert.	.25	.25
	Nos. 538-540,C393-C395 (6)		2.05	1.70

Tourist publicity.

For surcharges see Nos. RA75-RA76.

Nos. 516, 531 and 511 Surcharged in Red

Perf. 14½x15, 15x14½, 13½
Wmk. 343, Unwmkd.

1973, Mar. 15

541	A156	8c on 59c brt rose lil	.25	.25
542	A162	10c on 1b multi	.25	.25
543	A157	13c on 30c blk	.25	.25
		Nos. 541-543,C402 (4)	1.10	1.05

UN Security Council Meeting, Panama City, Mar. 15-21. Surcharges differ in size and are adjusted to fit shape of stamp.

José Daniel Crespo, Educator A169

Wmk. 365

1973, June 20 Litho. *Perf. 13½*

544	A169	3c lt bl & multi	.25	.25
		Nos. 544,C403-C413 (12)	7.95	4.35

For overprints and surcharges see Nos. C414-C416, C418-C421, RA81-RA82, RA84.

Nos. 511-512 and 509 Surcharged in Red

Perf. 15x14½, 14½x15

1974, Nov. 11 Unwmk.

545	A157	5c on 30c blk	.25	.25
546	A156	10c on 34c org brn	.25	.25
547	A157	13c on 21c yel	.25	.25
		Nos. 545-547,C417-C421 (8)	2.00	2.00

Surcharge vertical on No. 546.

Bolivar, Bridge of the Americas, Men with Flag — A170

Perf. 12½

1976, Mar. 30 Litho. Unwmk.

548	A170	6c multicolored	.25	.25
		Nos. 548,C426-C428 (4)	2.90	1.40

150th anniversary of Congress of Panama.

Evibacus Princeps A171

Marine life: 3c, Ptitosarcus sinuosus, vert. 4c, Acanthaster planci. 7c, Starfish. 1b, Mithrax spinossimus.

Perf. 12½x13, 13x12½

1976, May 6 Litho. Wmk. 377

549	A171	2c multi	.65	.25
550	A171	3c multi	.65	.25
551	A171	4c multi	.65	.25
552	A171	7c multi	.65	.25
		Nos. 549-552,C429-C430 (6)	6.45	2.15

Souvenir Sheet

Imperf

553	A171	1b multi	7.00	

Bolivar from Bolivar Monument A172

Bolivar and Argentine Flag A173

Stamps of design A172 show details of Bolivar Monument, Panama City; design A173 shows head of Bolivar and flags of Latin American countries.

Perf. 13½

1976, June 22 Unwmk. Litho.

554	A173	20c shown	.50	.50
555	A173	20c shown	.50	.50
556	A173	20c Bolivia	.50	.50
557	A173	20c Brazil	.50	.50
558	A173	20c Chile	.50	.50
559	A172	20c Battle scene	.50	.50
560	A173	20c Colombia	.50	.50
561	A173	20c Costa Rica	.50	.50
562	A173	20c Cuba	.50	.50
563	A173	20c Ecuador	.50	.50
564	A173	20c El Salvador	.50	.50
565	A173	20c Guatemala	.50	.50
566	A173	20c Guyana	.50	.50
567	A173	20c Haiti	.50	.50
568	A172	20c Assembly	.50	.50
569	A172	20c Liberated people	.50	.50
570	A173	20c Honduras	.50	.50
571	A173	20c Jamaica	.50	.50
572	A173	20c Mexico	.50	.50
573	A173	20c Nicaragua	.50	.50
574	A173	20c Panama	.50	.50
575	A173	20c Paraguay	.50	.50
576	A173	20c Peru	.50	.50
577	A173	20c Dominican Rep.	.50	.50
578	A172	20c Bolivar and flag bearer	.50	.50
579	A173	20c Surinam	.50	.50
580	A173	20c Trinidad-Tobago	.50	.50
581	A173	20c Uruguay	.50	.50
582	A173	20c Venezuela	.50	.50
583	A172	20c Indian delegation	.50	.50
a.		Sheet of 30, #554-583	25.00	25.00

Souvenir Sheet

584		Sheet of 3	3.50	3.50
a.		A172 30c Bolivar and flag bearer	.65	.65
b.		A172 30c Monument, top	.65	.65
c.		A172 40c Inscription tablet	.80	.80

Amphictyonic Congress of Panama, sesquicentennial. No. 584 comes perf. and imperf. Values the same.

Nicanor Villalaz, Designer of Coat of Arms — A174

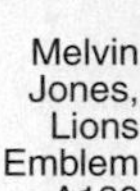

National Lottery Building, Panama City — A175

1976, Nov. 12 Litho. *Perf. 12½*

585	A174	5c dk blue	.25	.25
586	A175	6c multicolored	.25	.25

Contadora Island — A176

1976, Dec. 29 *Perf. 12½*

587	A176	3c multicolored	.25	.25

Pres. Carter and Gen. Omar Torrijos Signing Panama Canal Treaties — A177

Design: 23c, like No. 588. Design includes Alejandro Orfila, Secretary General of OAS.

1978, Jan. 3 Litho. *Perf. 12*

Size: 90x40mm

588	A177	50c Strip of 3	8.00	8.00
a.		3c multicolored	.25	.25
b.		40c multicolored	1.00	1.00
c.		50c multicolored	1.25	*1.25*

Perf. 14

Size: 36x26mm

589	A177	23c multicolored	.45	.25

Signing of Panama Canal Treaties, Washington, DC, Sept. 7, 1977.

Pres. Carter and Gen. Torrijos Signing Treaties — A178

1978, Nov. 13 Litho. *Perf. 12*

590	A178	Strip of 3	7.00	7.00
a.		5c multi (30x40mm)	.25	.25
b.		35c multi (30x40mm)	1.00	.35
c.		41c multi (45x40mm)	1.00	.40

Size: 36x26mm

591	A178	3c Treaty signing	.25	.25

Signing of Panama Canal Treaties ratification documents, Panama City, Panama, June 6, 1978.

World Commerce Zone, Colon A179

1978, Nov. 13 Litho. *Perf. 12*

592	A179	6c multicolored	.25	.25

Free Zone of Colon, 30th anniversary.

Melvin Jones, Lions Emblem A180

1978, Nov. 13

593	A180	50c multicolored	1.25	.75

Birth centenary of Melvin Jones, founder of Lions International.

Torrijos with Children, Ship, Flag A181

"75," Coat of Arms A182

Rotary Emblem, "75" A183

Gen. Torrijos and Pres. Carter, Flags, Ship A184

UPU Emblem, Globe — A185

Boy and Girl Inside Heart — A186

1979, Oct. 1 Litho. *Perf. 14*

594	A181	3c multicolored	.25	.25
595	A182	6c multicolored	.25	.25
596	A183	17c multicolored	.35	.30
597	A184	23c multicolored	.45	.25
598	A185	35c multicolored	.70	.60
599	A186	50c multicolored	1.00	.50
		Nos. 594-599 (6)	3.00	2.15

Return of Canal Zone to Panama, Oct. 1 (3c, 23c); Natl. Bank, 75th anniv.; Rotary Intl., 75th anniv.; 18th UPU Cong., Rio, Sept.-Oct., 1979; Intl. Year of the Child.

Colon Station, St. Charles Hotel, Engraving A187

Postal Headquarters, Balboa, Inauguration — A188

Return of Canal Zone to Panama, Oct. 1, 1979 — A189

Census of the Americas A190

Panamanian Tourist and Convention Center Opening — A191

Inter-American Development Bank, 25th Anniversary — A192

Canal Centenary A193

Olympic Stadium, Moscow '80 Emblem A194

1980, May 21 Litho. *Perf. 12*

600	A187	1c rose violet	.25	.25
601	A188	3c multicolored	.25	.25
602	A189	6c multicolored	.25	.25
603	A190	17c multicolored	.35	.25
604	A191	23c multicolored	.45	.25
605	A192	35c multicolored	.70	.30
606	A193	41c pale rose & blk	.90	.45
607	A194	50c multicolored	1.00	.50
		Nos. 600-607 (8)	4.15	2.50

Transpanamanian Railroad, 130th anniv. (1c); 22nd Summer Olympic Games, Moscow, July 19-Aug. 3 (50c).

La Salle Congregation, 75th Anniv. (1979) — A195

1981, May 15 Litho. *Perf. 12*

608 A195 17c multicolored .50 .25

Louis Braille — A196

1981, May 15

609 A196 23c multicolored .45 .25

Intl. Year of the Disabled.

Bull's Blood — A197

1981, June 26 Litho. *Perf. 12*

610	A197	3c shown	1.00	.25
611	A197	6c Lory, vert.	1.00	.25
612	A197	41c Hummingbird, vert.	4.25	.50
613	A197	50c Toucan	5.25	.40
		Nos. 610-613 (4)	11.50	1.40

Apparition of the Virgin to St. Catherine Laboure, 150th Anniv. — A198

1981, June 26 Litho. *Perf. 12*

614 A198 35c multicolored .90 .35

Gen. Torrijos and Bayano Dam A199

Wmk. 311

1982, Mar. 22 Litho. *Perf. 10½*

615 A199 17c multicolored .35 .25

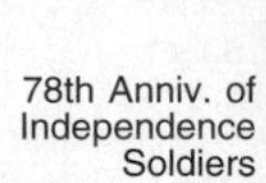

78th Anniv. of Independence Soldiers Institute — A200

1981, Mar. 17 Litho. *Perf. 10½*

616 A200 3c multicolored .25 .25

First Death Anniv. of Gen. Omar Torrijos Herrera A201

1982, May 14 Litho. *Perf. 10½*

617	A201	5c Aerial view	.25	.25
618	A201	6c Army camp	.25	.25
619	A201	50c Felipillo Engineering Works	1.00	.40
		Nos. 617-619,C433-C434 (5)	3.60	1.70

Ricardo J. Alfaro (1882-1977), Statesman A202

1982, Aug. 18 Wmk. 382

620 A202 3c multicolored .25 .25

See Nos. C436-C437.

1982 World Cup A203

1982, Dec. 27 Litho. *Perf. 10½*

621 A203 50c Italian team 1.40 .50

See Nos. C438-C440.

Expo Comer '83, Panama Intl. Commerce Exposition, Jan. 12-16 A204

Wmk. 382

1983, Jan. 12 Litho. *Perf. 10½*

622 A204 17c multicolored .40 .30

Visit of Pope John Paul II — A205

Various portraits of the Pope. 35c airmail.

Perf. 12x11

1983, Mar. 1 Litho. Wmk. 382

623	A205	6c multicolored	.45	.25
624	A205	17c multicolored	.80	.25
625	A205	35c multicolored	1.75	.25
		Nos. 623-625 (3)	3.00	.75

Bank Emblem — A206

1983, Mar. 18

626 A206 50c multicolored 1.25 .40

24th Council Meeting of Inter-American Development Bank, Mar. 21-23.

Simon Bolivar (1783-1830) A207

1983, July 25 Litho. *Perf. 12*

627 A207 50c multicolored 1.25 .50

Souvenir Sheet

Imperf

628 A207 1b like 50c 4.00 1.25

World Communications Year — A208

1983, Oct. 9 Litho. *Perf. 14*

629	A208	30c UPAE emblem	.80	.25
630	A208	40c WCY emblem	1.00	.35
631	A208	50c UPU emblem	1.25	.45
632	A208	60c Dove in flight	1.60	.55
		Nos. 629-632 (4)	4.65	1.60

Souvenir Sheet

Imperf

633 A208 1b multicolored 2.75 2.75

No. 633 contains designs of Nos. 629-632 without denominations.

Freedom of Worship A209

1983, Oct. 21 Litho. *Perf. 11½*

634	A209	3c Panama Mosque	.25	.25
635	A209	5c Bahai Temple	.25	.25
636	A209	6c St. Francis Church	.25	.25
637	A209	17c Kol Shearit Israel Synagogue	.70	.25
		Nos. 634-637 (4)	1.45	1.00

No. 637 incorrectly inscribed.

Ricardo Miro (1883-1940), Poet — A210

Famous Men: 3c, Richard Newman (1883-1946), educator. 5c, Cristobal Rodriguez (1883-1943), politician. 6c, Alcibiades Arosemena (1883-1958), industrialist and financier. 35c, Cirilo Martinez (1883-1924), linguist.

1983, Nov. 8 Litho. *Perf. 14*

638 A210 1c multicolored .25 .25
639 A210 3c multicolored .25 .25
640 A210 5c multicolored .25 .25
641 A210 6c multicolored .25 .25
642 A210 35c multicolored 1.00 .35
Nos. 638-642 (5) 2.00 1.35

The Prophet, by Alfredo Sinclair — A211

#643, Village House, by Juan Manuel Cedeno. #644, Large Nude, by Manuel Chong Neto. 3c, On Another Occasion, by Spiros Vamvas. 6c, Punta Chame Landscape, by Guillermo Trujillo. 28c, Neon Light, by Alfredo Sinclair. 41c, Highland Girls, by Al Sprague. 1b, Bright Morning, by Ignacio Mallol Pibernat. Nos. 643-647, 650 horiz.

1983, Dec. 12 *Perf. 12*

643 A211 1c multicolored .25 .25
644 A211 1c multicolored .25 .25
645 A211 3c multicolored .25 .25
646 A211 6c multicolored .25 .25
647 A211 28c multicolored .70 .25
648 A211 35c multicolored .90 .35
649 A211 41c multicolored 1.00 .40
650 A211 1b multicolored 2.75 1.00
Nos. 643-650 (8) 6.35 3.00

Double Cup, Indian Period A212

Pottery: 40c, Raised dish, Tonosi period. 50c, Jug with face, Canazas period, vert. 60c, Bowl, Conte, vert.

1984, Jan. 16 Litho. *Perf. 12*

651 A212 30c multicolored 1.10 .25
652 A212 40c multicolored 1.25 .30
653 A212 50c multicolored 1.60 .40
654 A212 60c multicolored 2.00 .55
Nos. 651-654 (4) 5.95 1.50

Souvenir Sheet

Imperf

655 A212 1b like 30c 4.50 4.50

Pre-Olympics — A213

1984, Mar. 15 Litho. *Perf. 14*

656 A213 19c Baseball .90 .35
657 A213 19c Basketball, vert. .90 .35
658 A213 19c Boxing .90 .35
659 A213 19c Swimming, vert. .90 .35
Nos. 656-659 (4) 3.60 1.40

Roberto Duran — A214

1984, June 14 Litho. *Perf. 14*

660 A214 26c multicolored .60 .25

1st Panamanian to hold 3 boxing championships.

1984 Olympic Games — A214a

1984, July, 12 Litho. *Perf. 14*

660A A214a 6c Shooting .25 .25
660B A214a 30c Weight lifting .90 .30
660C A214a 37c Wrestling 1.00 .40
660D A214a 1b Long jump 3.00 1.50
Nos. 660A-660D (4) 5.15 2.45

Souvenir Sheet

660E A214a 1b Running 4.75 4.75

Nos. 660B-660D are airmail. No. 660E contains one 45x45x64mm stamp.

Paintings — A215

Paintings by Panamanian artists: 1c, Woman Thinking, by Manuel Chong Neto. 3c, The Child, by Alfredo Sinclair. 6c, A Day in the Life of Rumalda, by Brooke Alfaro. 30c, Highlands People, by Al Sprague. 37c, Intermission during the Dance, by Roberto Sprague. 44c, Punta Chame Forest, by Guillermo Trujillo. 50c, The Blue Plaza, by Juan Manuel Cedeno. 1b, Ira, by Spiros Vamvas.

1984, Sept. 17 Litho. *Perf. 14*

661 A215 1c multi .25 .25
662 A215 3c multi, horiz. .25 .25
663 A215 6c multi, horiz. .25 .25
664 A215 30c multi .90 .30
665 A215 37c multi, horiz. 1.00 .40
666 A215 44c multi, horiz. 1.25 .50
667 A215 50c multi, horiz. 1.50 .55
668 A215 1b multi, horiz. 3.00 1.50
Nos. 661-668 (8) 8.40 4.00

Postal Sovereignty — A216

1984, Oct. 1 Litho. *Perf. 12*

669 A216 19c Gen. Torrijos, canal .80 .30

Fauna A217

1984, Dec. 5 Engr. *Perf. 14*

670 A217 3c Manatee .25 .25
671 A217 30c Gato negro 1.40 .50
672 A217 44c Tigrillo congo 2.00 .75
673 A217 50c Puerco de monte 2.25 .90
Nos. 670-673 (4) 5.90 2.40

Souvenir Sheet

674 A217 1b Perezoso de tres dedos, vert. 5.00 5.00

Nos. 671-673 are airmail.

Coins A218

Perf. 11x12

1985, Jan. 17 Litho. Wmk. 353

675 A218 3c 1935 1c .25 .25
676 A218 3c 1904 10c .25 .25
677 A218 6c 1916 5c .25 .25
678 A218 30c 1904 50c 1.25 .50
679 A218 37c 1962 half-balboa 1.60 .60
680 A218 44c 1953 balboa 2.00 .70
Nos. 675-680 (6) 5.60 2.55

Nos. 678-680 are airmail.

Contadora Type of 1985

Souvenir Sheet

Perf. 13½x13

1985, Oct. 1 Litho. Unwmk.

680A AP108 1b Dove, flags, map 4.50 4.50

Cargo Ship in Lock A219

1985, Oct. 16 *Perf. 14*

681 A219 19c multicolored 1.10 .30

Panama Canal, 70th anniv. (1984).

UN 40th Anniv. A220

1986, Jan. 17 Litho. *Perf. 14*

682 A220 23c multicolored .80 .35

Intl. Youth Year A221

1986, Jan. 17

683 A221 30c multicolored .90 .35

Waiting Her Turn, by Al Sprague (b.1938) — A222

Oil paintings: 5c, Aerobics, by Guillermo Trujillo (b. 1927). 19c, Cardboard House, by Eduardo Augustine (b. 1954). 30c, Door to the Homeland, by Juan Manuel Cedeno (b. 1914). 36c, Supper for Three, by Brooke Alfaro (b. 1949). 42c, Tenderness, by Alfredo Sinclair (b. 1915). 50c, Woman and Character, by Manuel Chong Neto (b. 1927). 60c, Calla lillies, by Maigualida de Diaz (b. 1950).

1986, Jan. 21

684 A222 3c multicolored .25 .25
685 A222 5c multicolored .25 .25
686 A222 19c multicolored .80 .30
687 A222 30c multicolored 1.25 .50
688 A222 36c multicolored 1.50 .55
689 A222 42c multicolored 1.75 .65
690 A222 50c multicolored 2.25 .80
691 A222 60c multicolored 2.75 1.00
Nos. 684-691 (8) 10.80 4.30

Miss Universe Pageant A223

1986, July 7 Litho. *Perf. 12*

692 A223 23c Atlapa Center .80 .30
693 A223 60c Emblem, vert. 2.10 .80

Halley's Comet A224

30c, Old Panama Cathedral tower, vert.

1986, Oct. 30 Litho. *Perf. 13½*

694 A224 23c multicolored .80 .35
695 A224 30c multicolored 1.00 .35

Size: 75x86mm

Imperf

695A A224 1b multicolored 8.00

A225

1986 World Cup Soccer Championships, Mexico: Illustrations from Soccer History, by Sandoval and Meron.

1986, Oct. 30

696 A225 23c Argentina, winner .90 .35
697 A225 30c Fed. Rep. of Germany, 2nd 1.00 .35
698 A225 37c Argentina, Germany 1.25 .60
Nos. 696-698 (3) 3.15 1.30

Souvenir Sheet

698A A225 1b Argentina, diff. 4.00

A226

1986, Nov. 21

699 A226 20c shown .65 .25
700 A226 23c Montage of events .70 .35

15th Central American and Caribbean Games, Dominican Republic.

Christmas A227

1986, Dec. 18 Litho.

701 A227 23c shown .70 .30
702 A227 36c Green tree 1.10 .50
703 A227 42c Silver tree 1.25 .55
Nos. 701-703 (3) 3.05 1.35

Intl. Peace Year — A228

1986, Dec. 30 *Perf. 13½*

704	A228	8c multicolored	.25	.25
705	A228	19c multicolored	.65	.25

Tropical Carnival, Feb.-Mar. A229

1987, Jan. 27 **Litho.** *Perf. 13½*

706	A229	20c Diablito Sucio mask	.65	.30
707	A229	35c Sun	1.25	.50

Size: 74x84mm

Imperf

708	A229	1b like 35c	3.25	1.50
		Nos. 706-708 (3)	5.15	2.30

1st Panamanian Eye Bank — A230

1987, Feb. 17 **Litho.** *Perf. 14*

709	A230	37c multicolored	1.25	.75

Panama Lions Club, 50th Anniv. (in 1985). Dated 1986.

Flowering Plants — A231

Birds A232

3c, Brownea macrophylla. 5c, Thraupis episcopus. 8c, Solandra grandiflora. 15c, Tyrannus melancholicus. 19c, Barleria micans. 23c, Pelecanus occidentalis. 30c, Cordia dentata. 36c, Columba cayennensis.

1987, Mar. 5

710	A231	3c multicolored	.25	.25
711	A232	5c multicolored	.25	.25
712	A231	8c multicolored	.25	.25
713	A232	15c multicolored	.55	.25
714	A231	19c multicolored	.70	.35
715	A232	23c multicolored	.80	.35
716	A231	30c multicolored	1.10	.45
717	A232	36c multicolored	1.50	.55
		Nos. 710-717 (8)	5.40	2.70

Dated 1986.

Monument and Octavio Mendez Pereira, Founder A233

1987, Mar. 26 **Litho.** *Perf. 14*

718	A233	19c multicolored	.65	.30

University of Panama, 50th anniv. (in 1985). Stamp dated "1986."

UNFAO, 40th Anniv. (in 1985) A234

1987, Apr. 9 *Perf. 13½*

719	A234	10c blk, pale ol & yel org	.25	.25
720	A234	45c blk, dk grn & yel grn	1.50	.70

Natl. Theater, 75th Anniv. A235

Baroque composers: 19c, Schutz (1585-1672). 37c, Bach. 60c, Handel. Nos. 721, 723-724 vert.

1987, Apr. 28 *Perf. 14*

721	A235	19c multicolored	.55	.30
722	A235	30c shown	.90	.50
723	A235	37c multicolored	1.00	.60
724	A235	60c multicolored	1.75	1.00
		Nos. 721-724 (4)	4.20	2.40

A236

1987, May 13 **Litho.** *Perf. 14*

725	A236	23c multicolored	.70	.45

Inter-American Development Bank, 25th anniv.

A237

25c, Fire wagon, 1887, and modern ladder truck. 35c, Fireman carrying victim.

1987, Nov. 28 **Litho.** *Perf. 14*

726	A237	25c multicolored	1.25	.40
727	A237	35c multicolored	1.75	.60

Panama Fire Brigade, cent.

A238

1987, Dec. 11

728	A238	15c Wrestling, horiz.	.70	.25
729	A238	23c Tennis	1.00	.40
730	A238	30c Swimming, horiz.	1.25	.50
731	A238	41c Basketball	1.75	.70
732	A238	60c Cycling	2.50	1.00
		Nos. 728-732 (5)	7.20	2.85

Souvenir Sheet

733	A238	1b Weight lifting	3.75	3.75

10th Pan American Games, Indianapolis. For surcharges see Nos. 813, 817.

A239

Christmas (Religious paintings): 22c, Adoration of the Magi, by Albrecht Nentz (d. 1479). 35c, Virgin Adored by Angels, by Matthias Grunewald (d. 1528). 37c, The Virgin and Child, by Konrad Witz (c. 1400-1445).

1987, Dec. 17

734	A239	22c multicolored	.70	.35
735	A239	35c multicolored	1.10	.60
736	A239	37c multicolored	1.10	.60
		Nos. 734-736 (3)	2.90	1.55

Intl. Year of Shelter for the Homeless A240

45c, by A. Sinclair. 50c, Woman, boy, girl, shack, housing in perspective by A. Pulido.

1987, Dec. 29 *Perf. 14*

737	A240	45c multicolored	1.25	.75
738	A240	50c multicolored	1.40	.80

For surcharge see No. 814.

Reforestation Campaign — A241

1988, Jan. 14 **Litho.** *Perf. 14½x14*

739	A241	35c dull grn & yel grn	1.10	.55
740	A241	40c red & pink	1.25	.70
741	A241	45c brn & lemon	1.50	.75
		Nos. 739-741 (3)	3.85	2.00

Dated 1987. For surcharge see No. 816.

Say No to Drugs — A242

1988, Jan. 14

742	A242	10c org lil rose	.25	.25
743	A242	17c yel grn & lil rose	.65	.30
744	A242	25c pink & sky blue	1.00	.40
		Nos. 742-744 (3)	1.90	.95

Child Survival Campaign A243

20c, Breast-feeding. 31c, Universal immunization. 45c, Growth and development, vert.

1988, Feb. 29 **Litho.** *Perf. 14*

745	A243	20c multicolored	.65	.35
746	A243	31c multicolored	1.10	.60
747	A243	45c multicolored	1.75	.90
		Nos. 745-747 (3)	3.50	1.85

For surcharge see No. 816A.

Fish A244

7c, Myripristis jacobus. 35c, Pomacanthus paru. 60c, Holocanthus tricolor. 1b, Equetus punctatus.

1988, Mar. 14

748	A244	7c multicolored	.25	.25
749	A244	35c multicolored	1.10	.60
750	A244	60c multicolored	2.00	1.00
751	A244	1b multicolored	3.50	1.60
		Nos. 748-751 (4)	6.85	3.45

The 7c actually shows the Holocanthus tricolor, the 60c the Myripristis jacobus.

For surcharge see No. 819.

Girl Guides, 75th Anniv. — A245

1988, Apr. 14

752	A245	35c multicolored	1.00	.60

Christmas A246

Paintings: 17c, *Virgin and Gift-givers.* 45c, *Virgin of the Rosary and St. Dominic.*

1988, Dec. 29 **Litho.** *Perf. 12*

753	A246	17c multicolored	.65	.30
754	A246	45c multicolored	1.50	.75

See No. C446.

St. John Bosco (1815-1888) A247

1989, Jan. 31

755	A247	10c Portrait	.25	.25
756	A247	20c Minor Basilica	.65	.35

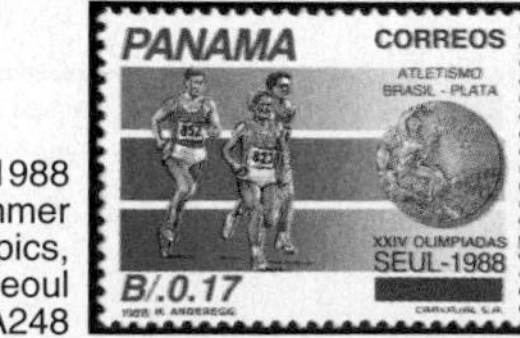

1988 Summer Olympics, Seoul A248

Athletes and medals.

1989, Mar. 17 **Litho.** *Perf. 12*

757	A248	17c Running	.55	.30
758	A248	25c Wrestling	.80	.40
759	A248	60c Weight lifting	2.00	1.00
		Nos. 757-759 (3)	3.35	1.70

Souvenir Sheet

760	A248	1b Swimming, vert.	3.75	3.75

See No. C447.

A249

1b, Emergency and rescue services.

1989, Apr. 12 Litho. *Perf. 12*

761 A249 40c red, blk & blue 1.25 .75
762 A249 1b multicolored 3.25 1.75

Intl. Red Cross and Red Crescent organizations, 125th annivs.

A250

America Issue: Pre-Columbian artifacts.

1989, Oct. 12 Litho. *Perf. 12*

767 A250 20c Monolith of Barriles 1.25 .50
768 A250 35c Vessel 2.75 1.25

French Revolution, Bicent. A251

1989, Nov. 14 *Perf. 13½*

769 A251 25c multicolored 1.10 .50
Nos. 769,C450-C451 (3) 4.95 2.00

Christmas — A252

17c, Holy family in Panamanian costume. 35c, Creche. 45c, Holy family, gift givers.

1989, Dec. 1

770 A252 17c multicolored .70 .30
771 A252 35c multicolored 1.50 .65
772 A252 45c multicolored 2.00 .85
Nos. 770-772 (3) 4.20 1.80

A253

1990, July 3

773 A253 23c brown .70 .45

Rogelio Sinan (b. 1902), writer.

A254

1990, Nov. 20 Litho. *Perf. 13½*

774 A254 25c blue & black 1.00 .45
775 A254 35c Experiment 1.25 .60
776 A254 45c Beakers, test tubes, books 1.60 .75
Nos. 774-776 (3) 3.85 1.80

Dr. Guillermo Patterson, Jr., chemist.

Fruits A255

20c, Byrsonima crassifolia. 35c, Bactris gasipaes. 40c, Anacardium occidentale.

1990, May 18 *Perf. 13½*

777 A255 20c multicolored .55 .35
778 A255 35c multicolored 1.10 .60
779 A255 40c multicolored 1.50 .70
Nos. 777-779 (3) 3.15 1.65

Tortoises A256

35c, Pseudemys scripta. 45c, Lepidochelys olivacea. 60c, Geochelone carbonaria.

1990, Sept. 11

780 A256 35c multicolored 1.40 .60
781 A256 45c multicolored 1.75 .75
782 A256 60c multicolored 2.50 1.00
Nos. 780-782 (3) 5.65 2.35

For surcharges see Nos. 815, 818.

Native American A257

1990, Oct. 12

783 A257 20c shown 1.40 .40
784 A257 35c Native, vert. 2.25 .85

Discovery of Isthmus of Panama, 490th Anniv. — A258

1991, Nov. 19 Litho. *Perf. 12*

785 A258 35c multicolored 1.75 1.25

St. Ignatius of Loyola, 500th Birth Anniv. — A259

No. 786, St. Ignatius of Loyola.
No. 786B: c, St. Ignatius' seal over map of Panama (horiz.); d, 5c stamp, Panama Scott No. C119 in black (horiz.).

1991, Nov. 29

786 A259 20c multicolored .65 .30
a. Tete beche pair 1.25 1.25

Souvenir Sheet

786B Sheet of 2, #a.-b. — —
c. A259 25c multi — —
d. A259 25c multi — —

Society of Jesus, 450th anniv.

Christmas A260

1991, Dec. 2

787 A260 35c Luke 2:14 1.10 .65
788 A260 35c Nativity scene 1.10 .65
a. Pair, #787-788 2.25 2.25

Social Security Administration, 50th Anniv. — A261

Design: No. 790, Dr. Arnulfo Arias Madrid (1901-1988), Constitution of Panama, 1941.

1991, Feb. 20 Litho. *Perf. 12*

789 A261 10c multicolored .35 .25
790 A261 10c multicolored .35 .25

Women's citizenship rights, 50th anniv. (No. 790).

Epiphany — A262

1992, Feb. 5 Litho. *Perf. 12*

791 A262 10c multicolored .25 .25
a. Tete beche pair .50 .30

New Life Housing Project — A263

1992, Feb. 17

792 A263 5c multicolored .25 .25
a. Tete beche pair .50 .50

Border Treaty Between Panama and Costa Rica, 50th Anniv. — A264

a, 20c, Hands clasped. b, 40c, Map. c, 50c, Pres. Rafael A. Calderon, Costa Rica, Pres. Arnulfo Arias Madrid, Panama.

1992, Feb. 20

793 A264 Strip of 3, #a.-c. 3.25 3.25

Causes of Hole in Ozone Layer — A265

1992, Feb. 24

794 A265 40c multicolored 1.75 .70
a. Tete beche pair 3.50 3.50

Expocomer '92, Intl. Commercial Exposition — A266

1992, Mar. 11

795 A266 10c multicolored .25 .25

A267

Margot Fonteyn (1919-91), ballerina: a, 35c, Wearing dress. b, 45c, In costume.

1992, Mar. 13

796 A267 Pair, #a.-b. 4.50 4.50

A268

1992, June 22 Litho. *Perf. 12*

797 A268 10c multicolored .25 .25
a. Tete beche pair .50 .30

Maria Olimpia de Obaldia (1891-1985), poet.

1992 Summer Olympics, Barcelona — A269

1992, June 22 Litho. *Perf. 12*

798	A269 10c multicolored	.25	.25
a.	Tete-beche pair	.50	.35

Zion Baptist Church, Bocas del Toro, 1892 — A270

1992, Oct. 1 Litho. *Perf. 12*

799	A270 20c multicolored	.65	.35
a.	Tete beche pair	1.25	1.25

Baptist Church in Panama, Cent.

Discovery of America, 500th Anniv. — A271

a, 20c, Columbus' fleet. b, 35c, Coming ashore.

1992, Oct. 12

800	A271 Pair, #a.-b.	3.00	3.00

Endangered Wildlife — A272

a, 5c, Agouti paca. b, 10c, Harpia harpyja. c, 15c, Felis onca. d, 20c, Iguana iguana.

1992, Sept. 23

801	A272 Strip of 4, #a.-d.	6.25	6.25

A273

1992, Dec. 21 Litho. *Perf. 12*

802	A273 10c multicolored	.25	.25
a.	Tete beche pair	.50	.30

Expo '92, Seville.

A274

1992, Dec. 21

803	A274 15c multicolored	.45	.30
a.	Tete beche pair	1.00	1.00

Worker's Health Year.

A275

1992, Dec. 21 Litho. *Perf. 12*

804	A275 10c multi + label	.35	.25

Unification of Europe.

Christmas — A276

a, 20c, Angel announcing birth of Christ. b, 35c, Mary and Joseph approaching city gate.

1992, Dec. 21

805	A276 Pair, #a.-b.	1.75	1.75

Evangelism in America, 500th Anniv. (in 1992) — A277

1993, Apr. 13 Litho. *Perf. 12*

806	A277 10c multicolored	.25	.25
a.	Tete beche pair	.50	.30

Natl. Day for the Disabled A278

1993, May 10

807	A278 5c multicolored	.35	.25
a.	Tete beche pair	.50	.50

Dr. Jose de la Cruz Herrera (1876-1961), Humanitarian A279

1993, May 26

808	A279 5c multicolored	.25	.25
a.	Tete beche pair	.50	.50

1992 Intl. Conference on Nutrition, Rome — A280

1993, June 22 Litho. *Perf. 12*

809	A280 10c multicolored	.25	.25
a.	Tete beche pair	.50	.50

Columbus' Exploration of the Isthmus of Panama, 490th Anniv. — A281

1994, June 2 Litho. *Perf. 12*

810	A281 50c multicolored	1.50	.95
a.	Tete beche pair + 2 labels	3.00	3.00

Dated 1993.

Greek Community in Panama, 50th Anniv. A282

Designs: 20c, Greek influences in Panama, Panamanian flag, vert. No. 812a, Parthenon. No. 812b, Greek Orthodox Church.

1995, Feb. 16 Litho. *Perf. 12*

811	A282 20c multicolored	.45	.30

Souvenir Sheet

812	A282 75c Sheet of 2, #a.-b.	4.00	2.50

Nos. 729, 731, 737, 741, 747, 750, 781-782 Surcharged

1995 *Perfs., Etc. as Before*

813	A238	20c on 23c #729	.75	.35
814	A240	25c on 45c #737	1.10	.50
815	A256	30c on 45c #781	1.25	.65
816	A241	35c on 45c #741	1.40	.75
816A	A243	35c on 45c No. 747	1.60	.85
817	A238	40c on 41c #731	1.90	.90
818	A256	50c on 60c #782	3.00	1.25
819	A244	1b on 60c No. 750	5.00	2.50
		Nos. 813-819 (8)	16.00	7.75

Issued: #816A, 819, 5/6; Others, 3/3.

First Settlement of Panama, 475th Anniv. (in 1994) — A283

Designs: 15c, Horse and wagon crossing bridge. 20c, Arms of first Panama City, vert. 25c, Model of an original cathedral. 35c, Ruins of cathedral, vert.

1996, Oct. 11 Litho. *Perf. 14*

820	A283 15c beige, blk & brn	.45	.30
821	A283 20c multicolored	.65	.40
822	A283 25c beige, blk & brn	.80	.45
823	A283 35c beige, blk & brn	1.25	.70
	Nos. 820-823 (4)	3.15	1.85

Endangered Species — A284

1996, Oct. 18 Litho. *Perf. 14*

824	A284 20c Tinamus major	1.25	.60

Mammals A285

a, Nasua narica. b, Tamandua mexicana. c, Cyclopes didactylus. d, Felis concolor.

1996, Oct. 18

825	A285 25c Block of 4, #a.-d.	4.75	4.75

A286

1996, Oct. 22 Litho. *Perf. 14*

826	A286 40c multicolored	1.25	.75

Kiwanis Clubs of Panama, 25th anniv. (in 1993.)

A287

1996, Oct. 15

827	A287 5b multicolored	15.00	9.50

Rotary Clubs of Panama, 75th anniv. (in 1994).

A288

1996, Oct. 21

828	A288 45c multicolored	1.40	.85

UN, 50th anniv. (in 1995).

A289

Design: Ferdinand de Lesseps (1805-94), builder of Suez Canal.

1996, Oct. 21

829	A289 35c multicolored	1.10	.70

Andrés Bello Covenant, 25th Anniv. (in 1995) — A290

1996, Oct. 23
830 A290 35c multicolored 1.25 .70

Chinese Presence in Panama A291

1996, June 10 ***Perf. 14½***
831 A291 60c multicolored 2.25 1.10

Litho.
Imperf
Size: 80x68mm

Patterns depicting four seasons: 1.50b, Invierno, Primavera, Verano, Otono.

832 A291 1.50b multicolored 5.00 5.00

Radiology, Cent. (in 1995) — A292

1996, Oct. 24 Litho. ***Perf. 14***
833 A292 1b multicolored 3.00 1.90

University of Panama, 60th Anniv. A293

1996, Oct. 14
834 A293 40c multicolored 1.25 .75

Christmas — A295

1996, Oct. 24 Litho. ***Perf. 14***
836 A295 35c multicolored 1.10 .70

Mail Train A296

1996, Dec. 10 Litho. ***Perf. 14***
837 A296 30c multicolored 2.00 .60

America issue.

Universal Congress of the Panama Canal — A297

No. 838: a, Pedro Miguel Locks. b, Miraflores Double Locks.
1.50b, Gatún Locks.

1997, Sept. 9 Litho. ***Perf. 14½x14***
838 A297 45c Pair, #a.-b. 2.75 2.75

Imperf
839 A297 1.50b multicolored 5.00 5.00

Perforated portion of No. 839 is 76x31mm.

Torrijos-Carter Panama Canal Treaties, 20th Anniv. — A298

Designs: 20c, Painting, "Panama, More Than a Canal," by C. Gonzalez P. 30c, "Curtain of Our Flag," by A. Siever M., vert. 45c, "Huellas Perpetuas," by R. Marinez R. 50c, 1.50b, #588.

1997, Sept. 9 ***Perf. 14***

840	A298	20c multicolored	.65	.50
841	A298	30c multicolored	1.00	.75
842	A298	45c multicolored	1.40	1.10
843	A298	50c multicolored	1.60	1.25
		Nos. 840-843 (4)	4.65	3.60

Imperf
844 A298 1.50b multicolored *5.00* *5.00*

Perforated portion of No. 844 is 114x50mm.

India's Independence, 50th Anniv. — A299

1997, Oct. 2 ***Perf. 14x14½***
845 A299 50c Mahatma Gandhi 1.60 1.25

Crocodylus Acutus A300

World Wildlife Fund: a, Heading right. b, Looking left. c, One in distance, one up close. d, With mouth wide open.

1997, Nov. 18 ***Perf. 14½x14***
846 A300 25c Block of 4, #a.-d. 5.50 5.50

Christmas A301

1997, Nov. 18 Litho. ***Perf. 14x14½***
847 A301 35c multicolored 1.75 .70

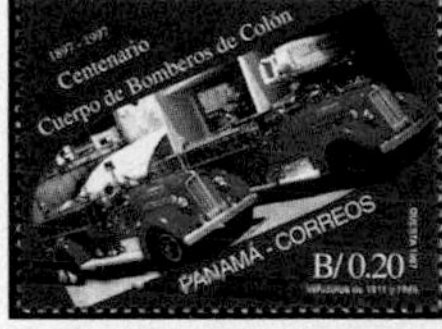
Colon Fire Brigade, Cent. A302

1997, Nov. 21 Litho. ***Perf. 14½x14***
848 A302 20c multicolored .65 .50

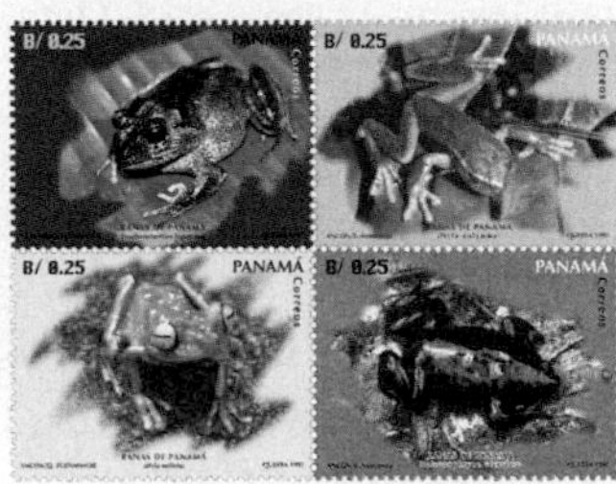
Frogs — A303

Designs: a, Eleutherodactylus biporcatus. b, Hyla colymba. c, Hyla rufitela. d, Nelsonphryne aterrima.

1997, Nov. 21
849 A303 25c Block of 4, #a.-d. 3.25 3.25

National Costumes A304

1997, Nov. 25
850 A304 20c multicolored 1.00 .75

America issue.

Colon Chamber of Commerce, Agriculture and Industry, 85th Anniv. — A305

1997, Nov. 27 ***Perf. 14x14½***
851 A305 1b multicolored 3.25 2.50

Justo Arosemena, Lawyer, Politician, Death Cent. (in 1996) — A306

1997, Nov. 27
852 A306 40c multicolored 1.25 1.00

Panamanian Aviation Co., 50th Anniv. — A307

Designs: a, Douglas DC-3. b, Martin-404. c, Avro HS-748. d, Electra L-168. e, Boeing B727-100. f, Boeing B737-200 Advanced.

1997, Dec. 3 ***Perf. 14½x14***
853 A307 35c Block of 6, #a.-f. 6.75 6.75

Jerusalem, 3000th Anniv. — A308

20c, Jewish people at the Wailing Wall. 25c, Christians being led in worship at Church of the Holy Sepulchre. 60c, Muslims at the Dome of the Rock.

1997, Dec. 29 ***Perf. 14x14½***

854	A308	20c multicolored	.65	.50
855	A308	25c multicolored	.80	.65
856	A308	60c multicolored	1.75	1.50
		Nos. 854-856 (3)	3.20	2.65

Imperf
857 A308 1.50b like #854-856 5.00 5.00

Perforated portion of No. 857 is 90x40mm.

Tourism A309

10c, Old center of town, Panama City. 20c, Soberania Park. 25c, Panama Canal. 35c, Panama Bay. 40c, Fort St. Jerónimo. 45c, Rafting on Chagres River. 60c, Beach, Kuna Yala Region.

Perf. 14x14½, 14½x14
1998, July 7 **Litho.**

858	A309	10c multi, vert	.25	.25
859	A309	20c multi, vert	.65	.40
860	A309	25c multi	.80	.50
861	A309	35c multi	1.10	.70
862	A309	40c multi	1.25	.80
863	A309	45c multi	1.50	.90
864	A309	60c multi	2.00	1.25
		Nos. 858-864 (7)	7.55	4.80

Organization of American States (OAS), 50th Anniv. — A310

1998, Apr. 30 ***Perf. 14½x14***
865 A310 40c multicolored 1.25 .80

Colón Free Trade Zone, 50th Anniv. — A311

Perf. 14x14½

1998, Feb. 2 Litho. Unwmk.
866 A311 15c multi .70 .40

Protection of the Harpy Eagle — A312

Contest-winning art by students: a, Luis Mellilo. b, Jorvisis Jiménez. c, Samuel Castro. d, Jorge Ramos.

1998, Jan. 20
867 A312 20c Block of 4, #a.-d. 4.50 4.50

Universal Declaration of Human Rights, 50th Anniv. — A313

1998, Feb. 10
868 A313 15c multi .70 .30

Panamanian Assoc. of Business Executives, 40th Anniv. — A314

1998, Jan. 28 ***Perf. 14½x14***
869 A314 50c multi 2.25 1.00

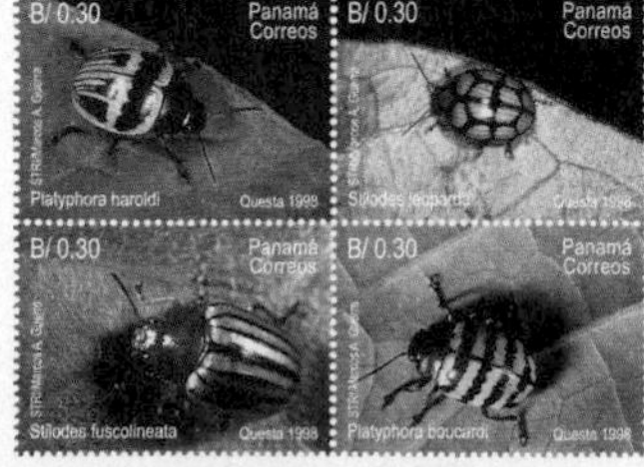
Beetles — A315

Designs: a, Platyphora haroldi. b, Stilodes leoparda. c, Stilodes fuscolineata. d, Platyphora boucardi.

1998, Feb. 10
870 A315 30c Block of 4, #a.-d. 6.75 6.75

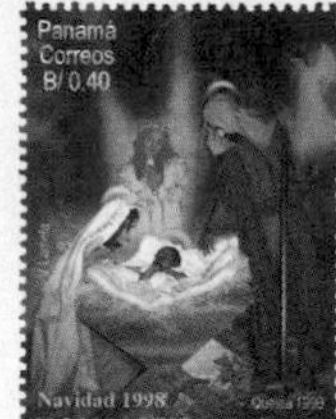
Christmas — A316

1998, Jan. 14 Litho. ***Perf. 14x14½***
871 A316 40c multi 1.40 .80

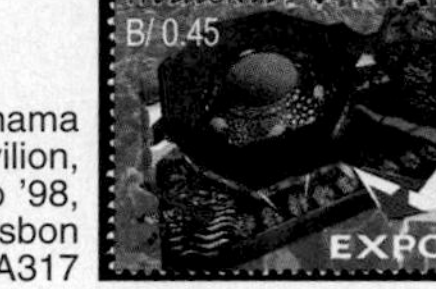
Panama Pavilion, Expo '98, Lisbon A317

1998, Jan. 14 Litho. ***Perf. 14½x14***
872 A317 45c multi 1.60 .90

Panama Canal, 85th Anniv. (in 1999) — A318

No. 873: a, Canal builders and crane on train trestle. b, Partially built structures, construction equipment.

2000, Sept. 7 Litho. ***Perf. 14½x14***
873 A318 40c Pair, #a-b 4.00 4.00

Souvenir Sheet

874 A318 1.50b Valley 7.50 7.50

No. 874 contains one label.

Reversion of Panama Canal to Panama (in 1999) A319

Various ships. Denominations: 20c, 35c, 40c, 45c.

2000, Sept. 7 ***Perf. 14½x14***
875-878 A319 Set of 4 6.25 3.50

Pres. Arnulfo Arias Madrid (1901-88) — A320

No. 879: a, 20c, Arias as medical doctor, with people. b, 20c, Arias giving speech, holding glasses.

No. 880, a, 30c, Arias in 1941, 1951 and 1969, Panamanian flag. b, 30c, Arias giving speech, crowd.

2001, Aug. 14 Litho. ***Perf. 13x13½***
Horiz. pairs, #a-b
879-880 A320 Set of 2 4.50 4.50

Christmas — A321

2001, Dec. 4 Litho. ***Perf. 14x14½***
881 A321 35c multi .80 .70

Dated 1999.

Holy Year (in 2000) A322

2001, Dec. 4 ***Perf. 14½x14***
882 A322 20c multi .90 .50

Dated 2000.

18th UPAEP Congress (in 2000) A323

2001, Dec. 4
883 A323 5b multi 22.50 12.50

Dated 2000.

Dreaming of the Future — A324

Children's art by: No. 884, 20c, I. Guerra. No. 885, 20c, D. Ortega.

No. 886, horiz.: a, J. Aguilar P. b, S. Sittón.

2001, Dec. 4 ***Perf. 14x14½***
884-885 A324 Set of 2 1.75 1.00

Souvenir Sheet
Perf. 14½x14

886 A324 75c Sheet of 2, #a-b 6.75 6.75

Dated 2000.

Architecture of the 1990s — A325

Designs: No. 887, 35c, Los Delfines Condominium, by Edwin Brown. No. 888, 35c, Banco General Tower, by Carlos Medina.

No. 889, horiz.: a, Building with round sides, by Ricardo Moreno. b, Building with three peaked roofs, by Moreno.

2001, Dec. 4 ***Perf. 14x14½***
887-888 A325 Set of 2 3.25 1.75

Souvenir Sheet
Perf. 14½x14

889 A325 75c Sheet of 2, #a-b 6.75 6.75

Dated 2000.

Orchids A326

Designs: No. 890, 35c, Cattleya dowiana. No. 891, 35c, Psychopsis krameriana.

No. 892: a, Peristeria clata. b, Miltoniopsis roezlii.

2001, Dec. 4 ***Perf. 14½x14***
890-891 A326 Set of 2 3.25 1.75

Souvenir Sheet

892 A326 75c Sheet of 2, #a-b 6.75 6.75

Dated 2000.

San Fernando Hospital, 50th Anniv. (in 1999) A327

2001, Dec. 21 Litho. ***Perf. 14½x14***
893 A327 20c multi .90 .50

Dated 2000.

Pres. Mireya Moscoso A328

2002, Mar. 25
894 A328 35c multi 1.60 .90

Dated 2000.

Independence From Spain, 180th Anniv. — A329

Details from mural by Roberto Lewis: No. 895, 15c, "180" at L. No. 896, 15c, "180" at R.

2002, Apr. 30 ***Perf. 13¼x13***
895-896 A329 Set of 2 1.25 .70

Dated 2001.

Discovery of the Isthmus, 500th Anniv. A330

Designs: 50c, Natives, ship. 5b, Native, European, crucifix, ships.

2002, Apr. 30 ***Perf. 13x13¼***
897-898 A330 Set of 2 21.00 12.00

Dated 2001. No. 898 is airmail.

America Issue — UNESCO World Heritage — A331

No. 899, 15c: a, Castle of San Lorenzo. b, Salón Bolivar, Panama City.

No. 900, 1.50b, horiz.: a, Cathedral, Panama City. b, Portobelo Fortifications.

2002, May 30 ***Perf. 13¼x13, 13x13¼***
Horiz. Pairs, #a-b

899-900	A331 Set of 2	14.50	8.00

Dated 2001. No. 900 is airmail.

Murals by Roberto Lewis in Palacio de las Garzas A332

No. 901: a, Heron, flagbearer and natives. b, Battle with natives. c, Woman, horse, men. d, Heron, woman in dress, woman picking fruit.

2002, June 19 ***Perf. 13x13¼***

901	Horiz. strip of 4	1.60	1.60
a.-d.	A332 5c Any single	.40	.25

Dated 2001.

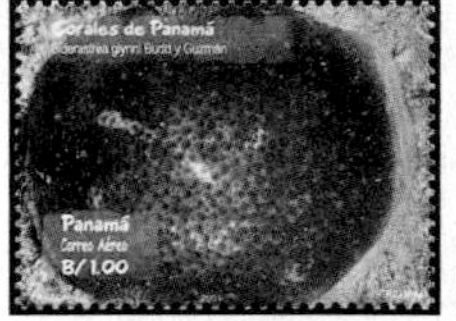

Corals A333

No. 902: a, Montastraea annularis. b, Pavona chiriquiensis.

1b, Siderastrea glynni. 2b, Pociliopora.

2002, June 28

902	A333 10c Horiz. pair, #a-b	.70	.40
903	A333 1b multi	4.00	2.00
904	A333 2b multi	8.00	4.00
	Nos. 902-904 (3)	12.70	6.40

Dated 2001. Nos. 903-904 are airmail.

Butterflies and Caterpillars A334

Designs: No. 905, 10c, Ophioderes materna. No. 906, 10c, Rhuda focula. 1b, Morpho peleides. 2b, Tarchon felderi.

2002, June 28 Litho. ***Perf. 13x13¼***

905-908	A334 Set of 4	14.50	8.00

Dated 2001. Nos. 907-908 are airmail.

Christmas 2002 A335

2003, June 16 Litho. ***Perf. 14***

909	A335 15c multi	.60	.60

Dated 2002.

America Issue — Youth, Education and Literacy A336

2003, June 23

910	A336 45c multi	1.40	.90

Dated 2002.

Clara González de Behringer, First Female Lawyer in Panama — A337

2003, July 10 ***Perf. 13½x13***

911	A337 30c multi	1.00	.60

Dated 2002.

Colón, 150th Anniv. (in 2002) — A338

2003, July 17

912	A338 15c multi	.55	.30

Dated 2002.

Luis C. Russell (b. 1902), Jazz Musician A339

2003, Aug. 6 ***Perf. 14***

913	A339 10c multi	.50	.25

Dated 2002.

Artwork in the National Theater — A340

Designs: No. 914, 5c, Statue of Erato (holding lyre). No. 915, 5c, Statue of Melpomene (holding mask). 50c, Decoration on front of theater box, horiz. 60c, Theater facade and painting, horiz.

Perf. 13½x13, 14 (50c), 13x13½ (60c)
2003, Aug. 12

914-917	A340 Set of 4	4.00	2.40

Dated 2002. Nos. 916-917 are airmail.

St. Josemaría Escrivá de Balaguer (1902-75) — A341

2003, Aug. 13 ***Perf. 14***

918	A341 10c multi	.50	.25

Dated 2002.

Republic of Panama, Cent. A342

Designs: 5c, National arms. 10c, First national flag. No. 921a, Manuel Amador Guerrero, first president. No. 921b, Pres. Mireya Moscoso. 25c, Declaration of Independence. No. 923a, Sterculia apetala. No. 923b, Peristeria elata. 35c, Revolutionary junta. 45c, Flag, Constitution of 1904, Constituent Delegates.

2003, Nov. 26 ***Perf. 12***

919	A342 5c multi	.25	.25
920	A342 10c multi	.25	.25
921	A342 15c Horiz. pair, #a-b	.95	.95
922	A342 25c multi	.80	.80
923	A342 30c Horiz. pair, #a-b	2.10	2.10
924	A342 35c multi	1.10	1.10
925	A342 45c multi	1.40	1.40
	Nos. 919-925 (7)	6.85	6.85

Nos. 924-925 are airmail.

Republic of Panama, Cent. Type of 2003 Redrawn

2003, Nov. 26 Litho. ***Perf. 12***

925A	Souvenir booklet	10.00	
b.	Booklet pane, #f-g	.80	—
c.	Booklet pane, #h-i	1.60	—
d.	Booklet pane, #j, m	3.50	—
e.	Booklet pane, #k-l	3.50	—
f.	A342 5c Similar to #919	.35	.25
g.	A342 10c Similar to #920	.35	.25
h.	A342 15c Similar to #921a	.75	.30
i.	A342 15c Similar to #921b	.75	.30
j.	A342 25c Similar to #922	1.60	.50
k.	A342 30c Similar to #923a	1.60	.60
l.	A342 30c Similar to #923b	1.60	.60
m.	A342 35c Similar to #924	1.60	.70

The text "1903 — Centenario de lar República de Panamá - 2003" is inscribed across the se-tenant pair stamps in each booklet pane. Other differences in text are also on each of Nos. 925Af-925Am.

Christmas A343

2003, Nov. 28

926	A343 10c multi	.50	.50

Panama, 2003 Iberoamerican Cultural Capital — A344

2003, Dec. 4

927	A344 5c multi	.25	.25

For surcharges, see Nos. 945-948.

Pres. Mireya Moscoso A345

2004, Aug. 10 Litho. ***Perf. 14½x14***

928	A345 35c multi	1.60	1.60

Compare with Type A328. Dated 2000.

Publication of Don Quixote, by Miguel de Cervantes, 400th Anniv. (in 2005) A346

2007, Apr. 23 Litho. ***Perf. 12***

929	A346 45c multi	1.40	1.40

St. Augustine High School, Panama, 50th Anniv. A347

2007, May 7

930	A347 35c multi	1.25	1.25

A348

A349

A350

Worldwide Fund for Nature (WWF) A351

2007, June 27

931	Horiz. strip of 4	3.25	3.25
a.	A348 20c multi	.75	.75
b.	A349 20c multi	.75	.75
c.	A350 20c multi	.75	.75
d.	A351 20c multi	.75	.75

Popes — A352

No. 932: a, Pope John Paul II (1920-2005). b, Pope Benedict XVI.

Imperf. x Perf. 12 on 1 Side

2007, June 29

932 A352 50c Horiz. pair, #a-b 3.25 3.25

Tourism A353

2007, July 10 ***Perf. 12***

933 A353 5c multi .25 .25

See Nos. 936-941.

Panama Canal Railway Company, 150th Anniv. (in 2005) A354

Designs: 20c, Emblem, Diesel and steam trains. 30c, Emblem, Diesel and steam trains, Diesel train in foreground.

2007, Nov. 27 Litho. ***Perf. 12***

934-935 A354 Set of 2 1.00 1.00

Tourism Type of 2007

Designs: 15c, Devil's mask. 20c, Chorrera Waterfalls, vert. 25c, Sarigua National Park. 35c, Pottery from Barilles archaeological site. 45c, San Fernando Fort, Portobelo. 60c, Colonial era buildings, vert.

2008, Feb. 27 Litho. ***Perf. 12***

936-941 A353 Set of 6 4.00 4.00

Dated 2007.

Carter-Torrijos Panama Canal Treaty, 30th Anniv. — A355

2008, Nov. 11 Litho. ***Perf. 14***

942 A355 35c multi .70 .70

Souvenir Sheet

Various Airplanes of Copa Airlines — A356

2010, July 30 ***Perf. 14 on 3 Sides***

943 A356 1b multi 2.00 2.00

Copa Airlines, 60th anniv.

Miniature Sheet

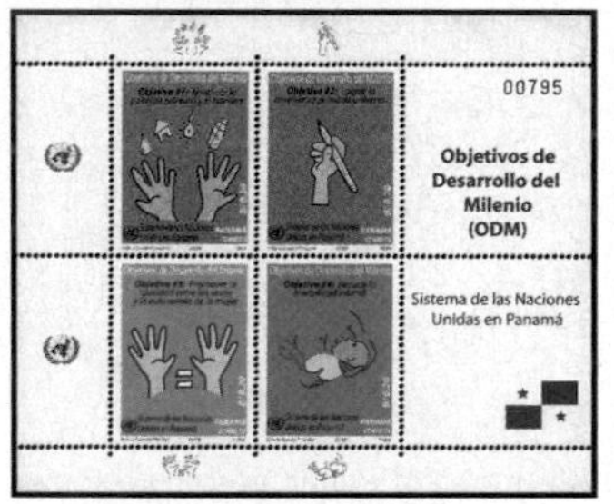

United Nations Millennium Objectives — A357

No. 944: a, Objective #1, Eradication of extreme poverty and hunger. b, Objective #2, Universal primary education. c, Objective #3, Promotion of equality of the sexes and women's rights. d, Objective #4, Reduction of infant mortality.

2010, Aug. 18 ***Perf. 14***

944 A357 20c Sheet of 4, #a-d — —

Dated 2008.

No. 927 Surcharged in Black or Blue

No. 945

No. 946

No. 947

No. 948

Methods and Perfs. As Before

2014, June 1

945 A344 10c on 5c #927 (Bl) .25 .25
946 A344 20c on 5c #927 (Bl) .40 .40
947 A344 25c on 5c #927 (Bl) .50 .50
948 A344 35c on 5c #927 .70 .70
Nos. 945-948 (4) 1.85 1.85

AIR POST STAMPS

Special Delivery Stamp No. E3 Srchd. in Dark Blue

1929, Feb. 8 Unwmk. ***Perf. 12½***

C1 SD1 25c on 10c org 1.00 .80
a. Inverted surcharge 22.50 22.50

Nos. E3-E4 Overprinted in Blue

1929, May 22

C2 SD1 10c orange .50 .50
a. Inverted overprint 20.00 17.50
b. Double overprint 20.00 17.50

Some specialists claim the red overprint is a proof impression.

With Additional Surcharge of New Value

C3 SD1 15c on 10c org .50 .50
C4 SD1 25c on 20c dk brn 1.10 1.00
a. Double surcharge 20.00 20.00
Nos. C2-C4 (3) 2.10 2.00

No. E3 Surcharged in Blue

1930, Jan. 25

C5 SD1 5c on 10c org .50 .50

No. 219 Overprinted in Red

1930, Feb. 28 ***Perf. 12***

C6 A39 1b dk vio & blk 16.00 12.50

AP5

1930-41 Engr. ***Perf. 12***

C6A AP5 5c blue ('41) .25 .25
C6B AP5 7c rose car ('41) .25 .25
C6C AP5 8c gray blk ('41) .25 .25
C7 AP5 15c dp grn .30 .25
C8 AP5 20c rose .35 .25
C9 AP5 25c deep blue .65 .65
Nos. C6A-C9 (6) 2.05 1.90

Issued: Nos. C7-C9, 1/20; Nos. C6A-C6C, 7/1/41. See No. C112.

For surcharges and overprints see Nos. 353, C16-C16A, C53B, C69, C82-C83, C109, C122, C124.

Airplane over Map of Panama — AP6

1930, Aug. 4 ***Perf. 12½***

C10 AP6 5c ultra .25 .25
C11 AP6 10c orange .30 .25
C12 AP6 30c dp vio 5.50 4.00
C13 AP6 50c dp red 1.50 .50
C14 AP6 1b black 5.50 4.00
Nos. C10-C14 (5) 13.05 9.00

For surcharge and overprints see Nos. C53A, C70-C71, C115.

Amphibian AP7

1931, Nov. 28 **Typo.**

Without Gum

C15 AP7 5c deep blue .80 1.00
a. 5c gray blue .80 1.00
b. Horiz. pair, imperf. btwn. 50.00

For the start of regular airmail service between Panama City and the western provinces, but valid only on Nov. 28-29 on mail carried by hydroplane "3 Noviembre."

Many sheets have a papermaker's watermark "DOLPHIN BOND" in double-lined capitals.

No. C9 Surcharged in Red 19mm long

1932, Dec. 14 ***Perf. 12***

C16 AP5 20c on 25c dp bl 6.25 .70

Surcharge 17mm long

C16A AP5 20c on 25c dp bl 200.00 2.50

Special Delivery Stamp No. E4 Overprinted in Red or Black

1934 ***Perf. 12½***

C17 SD1 20c dk brn 1.00 .50
C17A SD1 20c dk brn (Bk) 100.00 55.00

Issued: No. C17, 7/31.

Surcharged In Black

1935, June

C18 SD1 10c on 20c dk brn .80 .50

Same Surcharge with Small "10"

C18A SD1 10c on 20c dk brn 40.00 5.00
b. Horiz. pair, imperf. vert. 100.00

Nos. 234 and 242 Surcharged in Blue

1936, Sept. 24

C19 A53 5c on ½c org 400.00 250.00
C20 A53 5c on 50c org 1.00 .80
a. Double surcharge 60.00 60.00

Centenary of the birth of President Pablo Arosemena.

It is claimed that No. C19 was not regularly issued. Counterfeits of No. C19 exist.

Urracá Monument AP8

Palace of Justice AP9

10c, Human Genius Uniting the Oceans. 20c, Panama City. 30c, Balboa Monument. 50c, Pedro Miguel Locks.

1936, Dec. 1 Engr. *Perf. 12*

C21 AP8 5c blue .65 .40
C22 AP9 10c yel org .85 .60
C23 AP9 20c red 3.00 1.50
C24 AP8 30c dk vio 3.50 2.50
C25 AP9 50c car rose 8.00 5.75
C26 AP9 1b black 9.50 6.00
Nos. C21-C26 (6) 25.50 16.75

4th Postal Congress of the Americas and Spain.

Nos. C21-C26 Overprinted in Red or Blue

1937, Mar. 9

C27 AP8 5c blue (R) .55 .30
a. Inverted overprint 50.00
C28 AP9 10c yel org (Bl) .75 .45
C29 AP9 20c red (Bl) 1.75 1.00
a. Double overprint 50.00
C30 AP8 30c dk vio (R) 4.50 3.25
C31 AP8 50c car rose (Bl) 18.00 13.00
a. Double overprint 175.00
C32 AP9 1b black (R) 22.50 13.00
Nos. C27-C32 (6) 48.05 31.00

Regular Stamps of 1921-26 Surcharged in Red

1937, June 30 *Perf. 12, 12½*

C33 A55 5c on 15c ultra .75 .75
C34 A55 5c on 20c brn .75 .75
C35 A47 10c on 10c vio 1.75 1.50

Regular Stamps of 1920-26 Surcharged in Red

C36 A56 5c on 24c blk vio .75 .75
C37 A39 5c on 1b dk vio & blk .75 .50
C38 A56 10c on 50c blk 2.25 2.00
a. Inverted surcharge 30.00

No. 248 Overprinted in Red

C39 A54 5c dark blue .75 .75
a. Double overprint 18.00
Nos. C33-C39 (7) 7.75 7.00

Fire Dept. Badge AP14

Florencio Arosemena AP15

José Gabriel Duque — AP16

Perf. 14x14½

1937, Nov. 25 Photo. Wmk. 233

C40 AP14 5c blue 3.50 .60
C41 AP15 10c orange 5.00 1.00
C42 AP16 20c crimson 7.25 .75
Nos. C40-C42 (3) 15.75 2.35

50th anniversary of the Fire Department.

Basketball — AP17

Baseball AP18

1938, Feb. 12 *Perf. 14x14½, 14½x14*

C43 AP17 1c shown 2.25 .25
C44 AP18 2c shown 2.25 .25
C45 AP18 7c Swimming 3.00 .25
C46 AP18 8c Boxing 3.00 .25
C47 AP17 15c Soccer 5.00 1.25
a. Souv. sheet of 5, #C43-C47 18.00 18.00
b. As "a," No. C43 omitted 3,500.
Nos. C43-C47 (5) 15.50 2.25

4th Central American Caribbean Games.

US Constitution Type

Engr. & Litho.

1938, Dec. 7 Unwmk. *Perf. 12½*

Center in Black, Flags in Red and Ultramarine

C49 A83 7c gray .35 .25
C50 A83 8c brt ultra .55 .35
C51 A83 15c red brn .70 .45
C52 A83 50c orange 8.00 5.75
C53 A83 1b black 8.00 5.75
Nos. C49-C53 (5) 17.60 12.55

Nos. C12 and C7 Surcharged in Red

1938, June 5 *Perf. 12½, 12*

C53A AP6 7c on 30c dp vio .40 .40
c. Double surcharge 27.50
d. Inverted surcharge 27.50
C53B AP5 8c on 15c dp grn .40 .40
e. Inverted surcharge 22.50

Opening of the Normal School at Santiago, Veraguas Province, June 5, 1938. The 8c surcharge has no bars.

Belisario Porras AP23

Designs: 2c, William Howard Taft. 5c, Pedro J. Sosa. 10c, Lucien Bonaparte Wise. 15c, Armando Reclus. 20c, Gen. George W. Goethals. 50c, Ferdinand de Lesseps. 1b, Theodore Roosevelt.

1939, Aug. 15 Engr.

C54 AP23 1c dl rose .40 .25
C55 AP23 2c dp bl grn .40 .25
C56 AP23 5c indigo .65 .25
C57 AP23 10c dk vio .70 .25
C58 AP23 15c ultra 1.60 .35
C59 AP23 20c rose pink 4.00 1.40
C60 AP23 50c dk brn 5.00 .70
C61 AP23 1b black 7.25 3.75
Nos. C54-C61 (8) 20.00 7.00

Opening of Panama Canal, 25th anniv.

For surcharges see Nos. C63, C65, G1, G3.

Flags of the 21 American Republics AP31

1940, Apr. 15 Unwmk.

C62 AP31 15c blue .40 .35

Pan American Union, 50th anniversary.

For surcharge see No. C66.

Stamps of 1939-40 Surcharged in Black

a

b

c

d

1940, Aug. 12

C63 AP23 (a) 5c on 15c lt ultra .25 .25
a. "7 AEREO 7" on 15c 60.00 60.00
C64 A84 (b) 7c on 15c ultra .40 .25
C65 AP23 (c) 7c on 20c rose pink .40 .25
C66 AP31 (d) 8c on 15c blue .40 .25
Nos. C63-C66 (4) 1.45 1.00

Stamps of 1924-30 Overprinted in Black or Red

e

f

g

1941, Jan. 2 *Perf. 12½, 12*

C67 SD1 (e) 7c on 10c org 1.00 1.00
C68 A53 (f) 15c on 24c yel brn (R) 2.50 2.50
C69 AP5 (g) 20c rose 2.00 2.00
C70 AP6 (g) 50c deep red 6.00 4.00
C71 AP6 (g) 1b black (R) 13.50 10.00
Nos. C67-C71 (5) 25.00 19.50

New constitution of Panama which became effective Jan. 2, 1941.

Liberty — AP32

Black Overprint

1942, Feb. 19 Engr. *Perf. 12*

C72 AP32 20c chestnut brn 4.00 2.50

Costa Rica - Panama Type

Engr. & Litho.

1942, Apr. 25 Unwmk.

C73 A94 15c dp grn, dk bl & dp rose .70 .25

Swordfish AP34

J. D. Arosemena Normal School — AP35

Designs: 8c, Gate of Glory, Portobelo. 15c, Taboga Island, Balboa Harbor. 50c, Firehouse. 1b, Gold animal figure.

1942, May 11 Engr. *Perf. 12*

C74 AP34 7c rose carmine .90 .25
C75 AP34 8c dk ol brn & blk .25 .25
C76 AP34 15c dark violet .45 .25
C77 AP35 20c red brown .65 .25
C78 AP34 50c olive green 1.10 .40
C79 AP34 1b blk & org yel 2.75 .80
Nos. C74-C79 (6) 6.10 2.20

See Nos. C96-C99, C113, C126. For surcharges and overprints see Nos. 354-355, C84-C86, C108, C110-C111, C114, C116, C118, C121, C123, C127-C128, C137.

Alejandro Meléndez G. — AP40

Design: 5b, Ernesto T. Lefevre.

1943, Dec. 15

C80 AP40 3b dk olive gray 6.00 4.75
C81 AP40 5b dark blue 9.00 7.50

For overprint & surcharge see #C117, C128A.

Catalogue values for unused stamps in this section, from this point to the end of the section, are for Never Hinged items.

Nos. C6C and C7 Surcharged in Carmine

1947, Mar. 8 *Perf. 12*

C82 AP5 5c on 8c gray blk .25 .25
a. Double overprint 25.00 22.50
C83 AP5 10c on 15c dp grn .55 .40

Nos. C74 to C76 Surcharged in Black or Carmine

C84 AP34 5c on 7c rose car (Bk) .25 .25
a. Double surcharge *500.00*
b. Pair, one without surcharge 75.00
C85 AP34 5c on 8c dk ol brn & blk .25 .25
C86 AP34 10c on 15c dk vio .25 .25
a. Double surcharge 30.00 30.00
Nos. C82-C86 (5) 1.55 1.40

National Theater — AP42

1947, Apr. 7 Engr. Unwmk.

C87 AP42 8c violet .40 .25

Natl. Constitutional Assembly of 1945, 2nd anniv.

For surcharge see No. 356.

Manuel Amador Guerrero AP43

Manuel Espinosa B. — AP44

5c, José Agustin Arango. 10c, Federico Boyd. 15c, Ricardo Arias. 50c, Carlos Constantino Arosemena. 1b, Nicanor de Obarrio. 2b, Tomas Arias.

1948, Feb. 20 *Perf. 12½*

Center in Black

C88 AP43 3c blue .45 .25
C89 AP43 5c brown .45 .25
C90 AP43 10c orange .45 .25
C91 AP43 15c deep claret .45 .25
C92 AP44 20c deep carmine .80 .55
C93 AP44 50c dark gray 1.40 .80
C94 AP44 1b green 4.50 2.50
C95 AP44 2b yellow 10.00 6.00
Nos. C88-C95 (8) 18.50 10.85

Members of the Revolutionary Junta of 1903.

Types of 1942

1948, June 14 *Perf. 12*

C96 AP34 2c carmine .90 .25
C97 AP34 15c olive gray .45 .25
C98 AP35 20c green .45 .25
C99 AP34 50c rose carmine 7.25 3.00
Nos. C96-C99 (4) 9.05 3.75

Franklin D. Roosevelt and Juan D. Arosemena AP45

Four Freedoms AP46

Monument to F. D. Roosevelt — AP47

Map showing Boyd-Roosevelt Trans-Isthmian Highway — AP48

Franklin D. Roosevelt — AP49

1948, Sept. 15 *Perf. 12½*

C100 AP45 5c dp car & blk .25 .25
C101 AP46 10c yellow org .35 .30
C102 AP47 20c dull green .45 .35
C103 AP48 50c dp ultra & blk .70 .60
C104 AP49 1b gray black 1.75 1.25
Nos. C100-C104 (5) 3.50 2.75

Franklin Delano Roosevelt (1882-1945).
For surcharges see Nos. RA28-RA29.

Monument to Cervantes AP50

10c, Don Quixote attacking windmill.

1948, Nov. 15

C105 AP50 5c dk blue & blk .55 .25
C106 AP50 10c purple & blk .90 .25

400th anniv. of the birth of Miguel de Cervantes Saavedra, novelist, playwright and poet.

No. C106 Ovptd. in Carmine

1949, Jan. 18

C107 AP50 10c purple & blk .60 .40
a. Inverted overprint *50.00*

José Gabriel Duque (1849-1918), newspaper publisher and philanthropist.

Nos. C96, C6A, C97 and C99 Overprinted in Black or Red

h

i

1949, May 26

C108 AP34(h) 2c carmine .25 .25
a. Double overprint 7.50 7.00
b. Inverted surcharge 20.00 20.00
c. On No. C74 (error) 70.00
C109 AP5(i) 5c blue (R) .25 .25
C110 AP34(h) 15c ol gray (R) .65 .65
C111 AP34(h) 50c rose car 2.25 2.25
Nos. C108-C111 (4) 3.35 3.35

Centenary of the incorporation of Chiriqui Province.

Types of 1930-42

Design: 10c, Gate of Glory, Portobelo.

1949, Aug. 3 *Perf. 12*

C112 AP5 5c orange .25 .25
C113 AP34 10c dk blue & blk .25 .25

For surcharge see No. C137.

Stamps of 1943-49 Overprinted or Surcharged in Black, Green or Red

1949, Sept. 9

C114 AP34 2c carmine .25 .25
a. Inverted overprint 24.00
b. Double overprint 32.50
c. Double overprint, one inverted 37.50 35.00
C115 AP5 5c orange (G) .90 .35
a. Inverted overprint 12.50
b. Double overprint 30.00 30.00
c. Double ovpt., one inverted 30.00 30.00
C116 AP34 10c dk bl & blk (R) .90 .40
C117 AP40 25c on 3b dk ol gray (R) 1.25 .70
C118 AP34 50c rose carmine 4.00 2.10
Nos. C114-C118 (5) 7.30 3.75

75th anniv. of the UPU.

No. C115 has small overprint, 15½x12mm, like No. 368. Overprint on Nos. C114, C116 and C118 as illustrated. Surcharge on No. C117 is arranged vertically, 29x18mm.

University of San Javier AP51

1949, Dec. 7 Engr. *Perf. 12½*

C119 AP51 5c dk blue & blk .35 .25

See note after No. 371.

Mosquito — AP52

1950, Jan. 12 *Perf. 12*

C120 AP52 5c dp ultra & gray blk 1.60 .65

See note after No. 372.

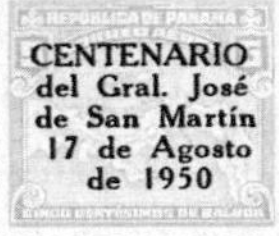

Nos. C96, C112, C113 and C9 Overprinted in Black or Carmine (5 or 4 lines)

1950, Aug. 17 Unwmk.

C121 AP34 2c carmine .55 .25
C122 AP5 5c orange .65 .35
C123 AP34 10c dk bl & blk (C) .65 .40
C124 AP5 25c deep blue (C) 1.00 .75

Same on No. 362, Overprinted "AEREO"

C125 A105 50c pur & blk (C) 2.00 1.25
Nos. C121-C125 (5) 4.85 3.00

Gen. José de San Martin, death cent.

Firehouse Type of 1942

1950, Oct. 30 Engr.

C126 AP34 50c deep blue 3.50 1.00

Nos. C113 and C81 Surcharged in Carmine or Orange

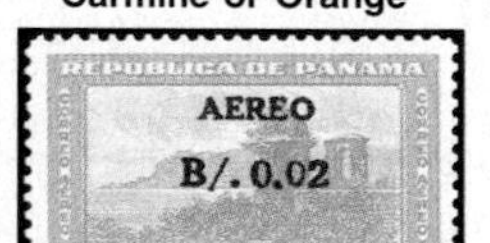

1952, Feb. 20

C127 AP34 2c on 10c .25 .25
a. Pair, one without surch. 375.00
C128 AP34 5c on 10c (O) .25 .25
b. Pair, one without surch. 375.00
C128A AP40 1b on 5b 29.00 20.00

The surcharge on No. C128A is arranged to fit stamp, with four bars covering value panel at bottom, instead of crosses.

Nos. 376 and 380 Srchd. "AEREO 1952" and New Value in Carmine or Black

1952, Aug. 1

C129 A97 5c on 2c ver & blk (C) .25 .25
a. Inverted surcharge 32.50
C130 A99 25c on 10c pur & org 1.00 1.00

Isabella Type of Regular Issue

Perf. 12½

1952, Oct. 20 Unwmk. Engr.

Center in Black

C131 A110 4c red orange .45 .25
C132 A110 5c olive green .45 .25
C133 A110 10c orange .65 .25
C134 A110 25c gray blue 1.75 .30
C135 A110 50c chocolate 2.50 .65
C136 A110 1b black 7.50 3.00
Nos. C131-C136 (6) 13.30 4.60

Queen Isabella I of Spain, 500th birth anniv.

No. C113 Surcharged "5 1953" in Carmine

1953, Apr. 22 ***Perf. 12***

C137 AP34 5c on 10c dk bl & blk .35 .25

Masthead of La Estrella — AP54

1953, July 15

C138 AP54 5c rose carmine .25 .25
C139 AP54 10c blue .45 .25

Panama's 1st newspaper, La Estrella de Panama, cent.
For surcharges see Nos. C146-C147.

Act of Independence AP55

Senora de Remon and Pres. José A. Remon Cantera AP56

Designs: 7c, Pollera. 25c, National flower. 50c, Marcos A. Salazar, Esteban Huertas and Domingo Diaz A. 1b, Dancers.

1953, Nov. 2

C140 AP55 2c deep ultra .45 .25
C141 AP56 5c deep green .45 .25
C142 AP56 7c gray .55 .25
C143 AP56 25c black 3.50 .65
C144 AP56 50c dark brown 2.25 .75
C145 AP56 1b red orange 5.75 1.50
Nos. C140-C145 (6) 12.95 3.65

Founding of republic, 50th anniversary.
For overprints see Nos. C227-C229.

Nos. C138-C139 Surcharged with New Value in Black or Red

1953-54

C146 AP54 1c on 5c rose car ('54) .25 .25
C147 AP54 1c on 10c blue (R) .25 .25

Gen. Herrera at Conference Table AP57

Design: 1b, Gen. Herrera leading troops.

1954, Dec. 4 Litho. ***Perf. 12½***

C148 AP57 6c deep green .25 .25
C149 AP57 1b scarlet & blk 4.00 2.25

Death of Gen. Tomas Herrera, cent.
For surcharge see No. C198.

Rotary Emblem and Map — AP58

1955, Feb. 23

C150 AP58 6c rose violet .25 .25
C151 AP58 21c red .70 .35
C152 AP58 1b black 5.50 2.50
a. 1b violet black 6.75 3.75
Nos. C150-C152 (3) 6.45 3.10

Rotary International, 50th anniv.
For surcharge see No. C154.

Cantera Type

1955, June 1

C153 A115 6c rose vio & blk .25 .25

Issued in tribute to Pres. José Antonio Remon Cantera, 1908-1955.
For surcharge see No. C188.

No. C151 Surcharged

1955, Dec. 7

C154 AP58 15c on 21c red .40 .35

Pedro J. Sosa — AP60

First Barge Going through Canal and de Lesseps AP61

Perf. 12½

1955, Nov. 22 Unwmk. Litho.

C155 AP60 5c grn, *lt grn* .35 .25
C156 AP61 1b red lilac & blk 5.00 2.50

150th anniversary of the birth of Ferdinand de Lesseps. Imperforates exist.

Pres. Dwight D. Eisenhower — AP62

Statue of Bolivar — AP63

Bolivar Hall AP64

Portraits-Presidents: C158, Pedro Aramburu, Argentina. C159, Dr. Victor Paz Estenssoro, Bolivia. C160, Dr. Juscelino Kubitschek O., Brazil. C161, Gen. Carlos Ibanez del Campo, Chile. C162, Gen. Gustavo Rojas Pinilla, Colombia. C163, Jose Figueres, Costa Rica. C164, Gen. Fulgencio Batista y Zaldivar, Cuba. C165, Gen. Hector B. Trujillo Molina, Dominican Rep. C166, José Maria Velasco Ibarra, Ecuador. C167, Col. Carlos Castillo Armas, Guatemala. C168, Gen. Paul E. Magloire, Haiti. C169, Julio Lozano Diaz, Honduras. C170, Adolfo Ruiz Cortines, Mexico. C171, Gen. Anastasio Somoza, Nicaragua. C172, Ricardo Arias Espinosa, Panama. C173, Gen. Alfredo Stroessner, Paraguay. C174, Gen. Manuel Odria, Peru. C175, Col. Oscar Osorio, El Salvador. C176, Dr. Alberto F. Zubiria, Uruguay. C177, Gen. Marcos Perez Jimenez, Venezuela. 1b, Simon Bolivar.

1956, July 18

C157 AP62 6c rose car & vio bl .45 .35
C158 AP62 6c brt grnsh bl & blk .45 .25
C159 AP62 6c bister & blk .45 .25
C160 AP62 6c emerald & blk .45 .25
C161 AP62 6c lt grn & brn .45 .25
C162 AP62 6c yellow & grn .45 .25
C163 AP62 6c brt vio & grn .45 .25
C164 AP62 6c dl pur & vio bl .45 .25
C165 AP62 6c red lil & sl grn .45 .25
C166 AP62 6c citron & vio bl .45 .25
C167 AP62 6c ap grn & brn .45 .25
C168 AP62 6c brn & vio bl .45 .25
C169 AP62 6c brt car & grn .45 .25
C170 AP62 6c red & brn .45 .25
C171 AP62 6c lt bl & grn .45 .25
C172 AP62 6c vio bl & grn .45 .25
C173 AP62 6c orange & blk .45 .25
C174 AP62 6c bluish gray & brn .45 .25
C175 AP62 6c sal rose & blk .45 .25
C176 AP62 6c dk grn & vio bl .45 .25
C177 AP62 6c dk org brn & dk grn .45 .25
C178 AP63 20c dk bluish gray 1.10 .55
C179 AP64 50c green 2.00 1.00
C180 AP63 1b brown 5.00 1.75
Nos. C157-C180 (24) 17.55 8.65

Pan-American Conf., Panama City, July 21-22, 1956, and 130th anniv. of the 1st Pan-American Conf. Imperforates exist.

Ruins of First Town Council Building — AP65

Design: 50c, City Hall, Panama City.

1956, Aug. 17

C181 AP65 25c red .65 .35
C182 AP65 50c black 1.25 .90
a. Souv. sheet of 3, #404, C181-C182, imperf. 2.40 2.40

6th Inter-American Congress of Municipalities, Panama City, Aug. 14-19, 1956.
No. C182a sold for 85c.
For overprint see No. C187a.

Monument — AP66

St. Thomas Hospital AP67

1956, Nov. 27 Wmk. 311

C183 AP66 5c green .25 .25
C184 AP67 15c dk carmine .45 .25

Centenary of the birth of Pres. Belisario Porras.

Highway Construction AP68

20c, Road through jungle, Darien project. 1b, Map of Americas showing Pan-American Highway.

Wmk. 311

1957, Aug. 1 Litho. ***Perf. 12½***

C185 AP68 10c black .25 .25
C186 AP68 20c lt blue & blk .65 .55
C187 AP68 1b green 2.75 2.25
a. AP65 Souvenir sheet of 3, unwmkd. 16.00 16.00
Nos. C185-C187 (3) 3.65 3.00

7th Pan-American Highway Congress.
No. C187a is No. C182a overprinted in black: "VII degree CONGRESSO INTER-AMERICANO DE CARRETERAS 1957."

No. C153 Surcharged "1957" and New Value

1957, Aug. 13 Unwmk.

C188 A115 10c on 6c rose vio & blk .25 .25

Remon Polyclinic — AP69

Customs House, Portobelo AP70

Buildings: #C191, Portobelo Castle. #C192, San Jeronimo Castle. #C193, Remon Hippodrome. #C194, Legislature. #C195, Interior & Treasury Department. #C196, El Panama Hotel. #C197, San Lorenzo Castle.

Wmk. 311

1957, Nov. 1 Litho. ***Perf. 12½***

Design in Black

C189 AP69 10c lt blue .25 .25
C190 AP70 10c lilac .25 .25
C191 AP70 10c gray .25 .25
C192 AP70 10c lilac rose .25 .25
C193 AP70 10c ultra .25 .25
C194 AP70 10c brown ol .25 .25
C195 AP70 10c orange yel .25 .25
C196 AP70 10c yellow grn .25 .25
C197 AP70 1b red 2.25 1.60
Nos. C189-C197 (9) 4.25 3.60

No. C148 Surcharged with New Value and "1958" in Red

1958, Feb. 11 Unwmk.

C198 AP57 5c on 6c dp grn .25 .25

United Nations Emblem — AP71

Flags of Panama and UN AP72

1958, Mar. 5 Litho. Wmk. 311
C199 AP71 10c brt green .25 .25
C200 AP71 21c lt ultra .45 .25
C201 AP71 50c orange 1.10 .85
C202 AP72 1b gray, ultra & car 2.25 1.60
  a. Souv. sheet of 4, #C199-C202, imperf. 5.25 5.25
  Nos. C199-C202 (4) 4.05 2.95

10th anniv. of the UN (in 1955).
The sheet also exists with the 10c and 50c omitted.

OAS Type of Regular Issue, 1958

Designs: 10c, 1b, Flags of 21 American Nations. 50c, Headquarters in Washington.

1958, Aug. 12 Unwmk. *Perf. 12½*
Center yellow and black; flags in national colors
C203 A124 5c lt blue .25 .25
C204 A124 10c carmine rose .25 .25
C205 A124 50c gray .70 .60
C206 A124 1b black 2.25 1.60
  Nos. C203-C206 (4) 3.45 2.60

Type of Regular Issue

Pavilions: 15c, Vatican City. 50c, United States. 1b, Belgium.

1958, Sept. 8 Wmk. 311 *Perf. 12½*
C207 A125 15c gray & lt vio .25 .25
C208 A125 50c dk gray & org brn .70 .65
C209 A125 1b brt vio & bluish grn 1.60 1.40
  a. Souv. sheet of 7, #418-421, C207-C209 5.25 5.25
  Nos. C207-C209 (3) 2.55 2.25

No. C209a sold for 2b.

Pope Type of Regular Issue

Portraits of Pius XII: 5c, As cardinal. 30c, Wearing papal tiara. 50c, Enthroned.

1959, Jan. 21 Litho. Wmk. 311
C210 A126 5c violet .25 .25
C211 A126 30c lilac rose .65 .40
C212 A126 50c blue gray .90 .65
  a. Souv. sheet of 4, #422, C210-C212, imperf. 2.25 2.25
  Nos. C210-C212 (3) 1.80 1.25

#C212a is watermarked sideways and sold for 1b. The sheet also exists with 30c omitted. #C212a with C.E.P.A.L. overprint is listed as #C221a.

Human Rights Issue Type

Designs: 5c, Humanity looking into sun. 10c, 20c, Torch and UN emblem. 50c, UN Flag. 1b, UN Headquarters building.

1959, Apr. 14 *Perf. 12½*
C213 A127 5c emerald & bl .25 .25
C214 A127 10c gray & org brn .25 .25
C215 A127 20c brown & gray .25 .25
C216 A127 50c green & ultra .80 .65
C217 A127 1b red & blue 1.75 1.40
  Nos. C213-C217 (5) 3.30 2.65

Nos. C213-C215, C212a Overprinted and C216 Surcharged in Red or Dark Blue

1959, May 16
C218 A127 5c emer & bl (R) .25 .25
C219 A127 10c gray & org brn (Bl) .25 .25
C220 A127 20c brown & gray (R) .45 .25
C221 A127 1b on 50c grn & ultra (R) 2.25 1.90
  a. Souvenir sheet of 4 7.00 7.00
  Nos. C218-C221 (4) 3.20 2.55

8th Reunion of the Economic Commission for Latin America.
This overprint also exists on Nos. C216-C217. These were disavowed by Panama's postmaster general.
No. C221a is No. C212a with two-line black overprint at top of sheet: "8a. REUNION DE LA C.E.P.A.L. MAYO 1959."

Type of Regular Issue, 1959

Portraits: 5c, Justo A. Facio, Rector. 10c, Ernesto de la Guardia, Jr., Pres. of Panama.

Wmk. 311
1959, Aug. 5 Litho. *Perf. 12½*
C222 A128 5c black .25 .25
C223 A128 10c black .25 .25

Type of Regular Issue, 1959

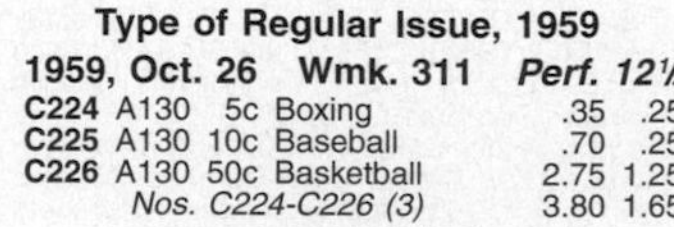

1959, Oct. 26 Wmk. 311 *Perf. 12½*
C224 A130 5c Boxing .35 .25
C225 A130 10c Baseball .70 .25
C226 A130 50c Basketball 2.75 1.25
  Nos. C224-C226 (3) 3.80 1.65

For surcharge see No. C349.

Nos. C143-C145 Overprinted in Vermilion, Red or Black

Unwmk.
1960, Feb. 6 Engr. *Perf. 12*
C227 AP56 25c black (V) .90 .25
C228 AP56 50c dk brown (R) 1.25 .40
C229 AP56 1b red orange 2.00 1.25
  Nos. C227-C229 (3) 4.15 1.90

World Refugee Year, July 1, 1959-June 30, 1960.
The revenues from the sale of Nos. C227-C229 went to the United Nations Refugee Fund.

Administration Building, National University — AP74

Designs: 21c, Humanities building. 25c, Medical school. 30c, Dr. Octavio Mendez Pereira first rector of University.

Wmk. 311
1960, Mar. 23 Litho. *Perf. 12½*
C230 AP74 10c brt green .25 .25
C231 AP74 21c lt blue .55 .25
C232 AP74 25c ultra .80 .35
C233 AP74 30c black 1.00 .40
  Nos. C230-C233 (4) 2.60 1.25

National University, 25th anniv.
For surcharges see Nos. 450, C248, C253, C287, C291.

Olympic Games Type

5c, Basketball. 10c, Bicycling, horiz. 25c, Javelin thrower. 50c, Athlete with Olympic torch.

1960, Sept. 22 Wmk. 343 *Perf. 12½*
C234 A131 5c orange & red .25 .25
C235 A131 10c ocher & blk .55 .25
C236 A131 25c lt bl & dk bl 1.10 .55
C237 A131 50c brown & blk 2.25 1.00
  a. Souv. sheet of 2, #C236-C237 4.50 4.50
  Nos. C234-C237 (4) 4.15 1.95

For surcharges see Nos. C249-C250, C254, C266-C270, C290, C350, RA40.

Citizens' Silhouettes AP75

10c, Heads and map of Central America.

1960, Oct. 4 Litho. Wmk. 229
C238 AP75 5c black .25 .25
C239 AP75 10c brown .25 .25

6th census of population and the 2nd census of dwellings (No. C238), Dec. 11, 1960, and the All America Census, 1960 (No. C239).

Boeing 707 Jet Liner AP76

1960, Dec. 1 Wmk. 343 *Perf. 12½*
C240 AP76 5c lt grnsh blue .25 .25
C241 AP76 10c emerald .25 .25
C242 AP76 20c red brown .45 .25
  Nos. C240-C242 (3) .95 .75

1st jet service to Panama. For surcharge see No. RA41.

Souvenir Sheet

UN Emblem — AP77

Wmk. 311
1961, Mar. 7 Litho. *Imperf.*
C243 AP77 80c blk & car rose 2.25 2.25

15th anniv. (in 1960) of the UN.
Counterfeits without control number exist.

No. C243 Overprinted in Blue with Large Uprooted Oak Emblem and "Ano de los Refugiados"

1961, June 2
C244 AP77 80c blk & car rose 2.50 2.50

World Refugee Year, July 1, 1959-June 30, 1960.

Lions International Type

Designs: 5c, Helen Keller School for the Blind. 10c, Children's summer camp. 21c, Arms of Panama and Lions emblem.

1961, May 2 Wmk. 311 *Perf. 12½*
C245 A133 5c black .25 .25
C246 A133 10c emerald .25 .25
C247 A133 21c ultra, yel & red .40 .25
  Nos. C245-C247 (3) .90 .75

For overprints see Nos. C284-C286.

Nos. C230 and C236 Surcharged in Black or Red

1961 Wmk. 311 (1c); Wmk. 343
C248 AP74 1c on 10c .25 .25
C249 A131 1b on 25c (Bk) 2.10 2.00
C250 A131 1b on 25c (R) 2.10 2.00
  Nos. C248-C250 (3) 4.45 4.25

Issued: Nos. C248-C249, 7/6; No. C250, 9/5.

Pres. Roberto F. Chiari and Pres. Mario Echandi AP78

Wmk. 343
1961, Oct. 2 Litho. *Perf. 12½*
C251 AP78 1b black & gold 2.75 1.60

Meeting of the Presidents of Panama and Costa Rica at Paso Canoa, Apr. 21, 1961.

Dag Hammarskjold AP79

1961, Dec. 27 *Perf. 12½*
C252 AP79 10c black .25 .25

Dag Hammarskjold, UN Secretary General, 1953-61.

No. C230 Surcharged

1962, Feb. 21 Wmk. 311
C253 AP74 15c on 10c brt grn .30 .25

No. C236 Surcharged

Wmk. 343
C254 A131 1b on 25c 2.75 1.25

City Hall, Colon AP80

1962, Feb. 28 Litho. Wmk. 311
C255 AP80 5c vio bl & blk .25 .25

Issued to publicize the third Central American Municipal Assembly, Colon, May 13-17.

Church Type of Regular Issue, 1962

Designs: 5c, Church of Christ the King. 7c, Church of San Miguel. 8c, Church of the Sanctuary. 10c, Saints Church. 15c, Church of St. Ann. 21c, Canal Zone Synagogue (Now used as USO Center). 25c, Panama Synagogue. 30c, Church of St. Francis. 50c, Protestant Church, Canal Zone. 1b, Catholic Church, Canal Zone.

Wmk. 343
1962-64 Litho. *Perf. 12½*
Buildings in Black
C256 A138 5c purple & buff .25 .25
C257 A138 7c lil rose & brt pink .25 .25
C258 A139 8c purple & bl .25 .25
C259 A139 10c lilac & sal .25 .25
C259A A139 10c grn & dl red brn ('64) .25 .25
C260 A139 15c red & buff .35 .25
C261 A138 21c brown & blue .55 .40
C262 A138 25c blue & pink .65 .35
C263 A139 30c lil rose & bl .70 .40
C264 A138 50c lilac & lt grn 1.10 .65
  a. Souv. sheet of 4, #441H-441I, C262, C264, imperf. 5.75 5.75
C265 A139 1b bl & sal 2.25 1.40
  Nos. C256-C265 (11) 6.85 4.70

Freedom of religion in Panama. Issue dates: #C259A, 6/4/64; others, 7/20/62.
For overprints and surcharges see Nos. C288, C296-C297, C299.

Nos. C234, C236 Overprinted & Surcharged in Black, Green, Orange or Red

1962, July 27 Wmk. 343 *Perf. 12½*

C266 A131 5c org & red .25 .25
C267 A131 10c on 25c (G) .65 .35
C268 A131 15c on 25c (O) .80 .45
C269 A131 20c on 25c (R) .90 .50
C270 A131 25c lt bl & dk bl 1.00 .55
Nos. C266-C270 (5) 3.60 2.10

Ninth Central American and Caribbean Games, Kingston, Jamaica, Aug. 11-25.

Nos. CB1-CB2 Surcharged

1962, May 3 Wmk. 311

C271 SPAP1 10c on 5c + 5c 1.40 .75
C272 SPAP1 20c on 10c + 10c 2.10 1.50

Type of Regular Issue, 1962

Design: 10c, Canal bridge completed.

1962, Oct. 12 Wmk. 343

C273 A140 10c blue & blk .25 .25

John H. Glenn, "Friendship 7" Capsule — AP81

Designs: 10c, "Friendship 7" capsule and globe, horiz. 31c, Capsule in space, horiz. 50c, Glenn with space helmet.

1962, Oct. 19 Wmk. 311 *Perf. 12½*

C274 AP81 5c rose red .25 .25
C275 AP81 10c yellow .35 .25
C276 AP81 31c blue 1.50 .80
C277 AP81 50c emerald 1.75 1.00
a. Souv. sheet of 4, #C274-C277, imperf. 4.50 4.50
Nos. C274-C277 (4) 3.85 2.30

1st orbital flight of US astronaut Lt. Col. John H. Glenn, Jr., Feb. 20, 1962. No. C277a sold for 1b.

For surcharges see Nos. C290A-C290D, C367, CB4-CB7.

UPAE Emblem — AP82

1963, Jan. 8 Litho. Wmk. 343

C278 AP82 10c multi .35 .25

50th anniversary of the founding of the Postal Union of the Americas and Spain, UPAE.

Type of Regular Issue

10c, Fire Engine "China", Plaza de Santa Ana. 15c, 14th Street team. 21c, Fire Brigade emblem.

1963, Jan. 22 Wmk. 311 *Perf. 12½*

C279 A141 10c orange & blk .35 .25
C280 A141 15c lilac & blk .45 .25
C281 A141 21c gold, red & ultra .90 .50
Nos. C279-C281 (3) 1.70 .90

"FAO" and Wheat Emblem — AP83

1963, Mar. 21 Litho.

C282 AP83 10c green & red .35 .25
C283 AP83 15c ultra & red .45 .25

FAO "Freedom from Hunger" campaign.

No. C245 Ovptd. in Yellow, Orange or Green

1963, Apr. 18 Wmk. 311 *Perf. 12½*

C284 A133 5c black (Y) .70 .25
C285 A133 5c black (O) .70 .25
C286 A133 5c black (G) .70 .25
Nos. C284-C286 (3) 2.10 .60

22nd Central American Lions Congress, Panama, Apr. 18-21.

No. C230 Surcharged

1963, June 11

C287 AP74 4c on 10c brt grn .25 .25

Nos. 445 and 432 Overprinted Vertically

1963 Wmk. 343 *Perf. 12½*

C288 A139 10c green, yel & blk .25 .25

Wmk. 311

C289 A130 20c emerald & red brn .65 .25

No. C234 Overprinted

1963, Aug. 20 Wmk. 343

C290 A131 5c orange & red .25 .25

Freedom of Press Day, Aug. 20, 1963.

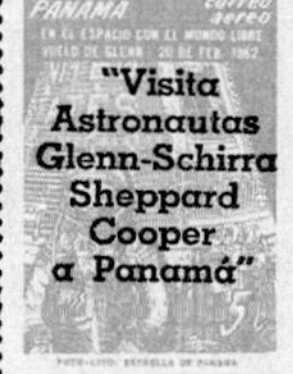

Nos. C274, C277a Overprinted or Surcharged — a

No. C274 Surcharged in Black — b

Wmk. 311

1963, Aug. 22 Litho. *Perf. 12½*

C290A AP81(a) 5c on #C274 3.25
C290B AP81(a) 10c on 5c #C274 7.25
C290C AP81(b) 10c on 5c #C274 0.00

Souvenir Sheet

Imperf.

C290D AP81(a) Sheet of 4, #C277a 50.00

Overprint on No. C290D has names in capital letters and covers all four stamps.

No. C232 Surcharged in Red

1963, Oct. 9 Wmk. 311 *Perf. 12½*

C291 AP74 10c on 25c ultra .25 .25

Type of Regular Issue, 1963

Flags and Presidents: 5c, Julio A. Rivera, El Salvador. 10c, Miguel Ydigoras F., Guatemala. 21c, John F. Kennedy, US.

Perf. 12½x12

1963, Dec. 18 Litho. Unwmk.

Portrait in Slate Green

C292 A142 5c yel, red & ultra .30 .25
C293 A142 10c bl, red & ultra .50 .35
C294 A142 21c org yel, red & ultra 1.50 1.10
Nos. C292-C294 (3) 2.30 1.70

Balboa Type of Regular Issue, 1964

1964, Jan. 22 Photo. *Perf. 13*

C295 A143 10c dk vio, *pale pink* .25 .25

No. C261 Srchd. in Red

1964 Wmk. 343 Litho. *Perf. 12½*

C296 A138 50c on 21c brn, bl & blk 1.00 .70

Type of 1962 Overprinted

C297 A139 1b emer, yel & blk 2.00 2.00

Issued. No. C296, 2/25; No. C297, 2/20.

Nos. 434 and 444 Surcharged

1964 Wmk. 343 *Perf. 12½*

C298 A131 10c on 5c bl grn & emer .25 .25
C299 A139 10c on 5c rose, lt grn & blk .25 .25

Issued: No. C298, 4/6; No. C299, 3/30.

St. Patrick's Cathedral, New York — AP84

Cathedrals: #C301, St. Stephen's, Vienna. #C302, St. Sofia's, Sofia. #C303, Notre Dame, Paris. #C304, Cologne. #C305, St. Paul's, London. #C306, Metropolitan, Athens. #C307, St. Elizabeth's, Kosice, Czechoslovakia (inscr. Kassa, Hungary). #C308, New Delhi. #C309, Milan. #C310, Guadalupe Basilica. #C311, New Church, Delft, Netherlands. #C312, Lima. #C313, St. John's Poland. #C314, Lisbon. #C315, St. Basil's, Moscow. #C316, Toledo. #C317, Stockholm. #C318, Basel. #C319, St. George's Patriarchal Church, Istanbul. 1b, Panama City. 2b, St. Peter's Basilica, Rome.

Unwmk.

1964, Feb. 17 Engr. *Perf. 12*

Center in Black

C300 AP84 21c olive 1.40 .90
C301 AP84 21c chocolate 1.40 .90
C302 AP84 21c aqua 1.40 .90
C303 AP84 21c red brown 1.40 .90
C304 AP84 21c magenta 1.40 .90
C305 AP84 21c red 1.40 .90
C306 AP84 21c orange red 1.40 .90
C307 AP84 21c blue 1.40 .90
C308 AP84 21c brown 1.40 .90
C309 AP84 21c green 1.40 .90
C310 AP84 21c violet bl 1.40 .90
C311 AP84 21c dk slate grn 1.40 .90
C312 AP84 21c violet 1.40 .90
C313 AP84 21c black 1.40 .90
C314 AP84 21c emerald 1.40 .90
C315 AP84 21c dp violet 1.40 .90
C316 AP84 21c olive grn 1.40 .90
C317 AP84 21c carmine rose 1.40 .90
C318 AP84 21c Prus green 1.40 .90
C319 AP84 21c dark brown 1.40 .90
C320 AP84 1b dark blue 7.50 5.00
C321 AP84 2b yellow green 14.50 9.00
a. Souv. sheet of 6 15.00 15.00
Nos. C300-C321 (22) 50.00 32.00

Vatican II, the 21st Ecumenical Council of the Roman Catholic Church.

No. C321a contains 6 imperf. stamps similar to Nos. C300, C303, C305, C315, C320 and C321. Size: 198x138mm. Sold for 3.85b.

For overprints, see Nos. C329C-C329i.

World's Fair, New York AP84a

5c, 10c, 15c, Various pavilions. 21c, Unisphere.

1964, Sept. 14 Wmk. 311 *Perf. 12½*

C322 AP84a 5c yellow & blk
C323 AP84a 10c red & blk
C324 AP84a 15c green & blk
C325 AP84a 21c ultra & blk
Set, #C322-C325 7.25 3.00

Souvenir Sheet

Perf. 12

C326 AP84a 21c ultra & blk 6.00 6.00

No. C326 contains one 49x35mm stamp. Exists imperf. Value, same as No. C326.

AP84b

Hammarskjold Memorial, UN Day: No. C327, C329a, Dag Hammarskjold. No. C328, C329b, UN emblem.

Perf. 13½x14

1964, Sept. 1 — Unwmk.

C327 AP84b 21c black & blue 1.00 .60
C328 AP84b 21c black & blue 1.00 .60

Souvenir Sheet

Imperf

C329 Sheet of 2 6.75 6.75
a.-b. AP84b 21c blk & grn, any single 1.25 1.25

Nos. C327-C328 exist imperf in black and green. Value $4.50.

Nos. C300//C321a Overprinted "1964"

1964, Sept. 28

C329C AP84 21c olive (#C300) 1.25 .75
C329D AP84 21c red (#C305) 1.25 .75
C329E AP84 21c grn (#C309) 1.25 .75
C329F AP84 21c dk brn (#C319) 1.25 .75
C329G AP84 1b dk blue (#C320) 4.50 3.25
C329H AP84 2b yel grn (#C321) 9.50 7.50
i. Souv. sheet of 6 (#C321a) 80.00 80.00
Nos. C329C-C329H (6) 19.00 13.75

Vatican II, the 21st Ecumenical Council of the Roman Catholic Church, Third Period.

On No. C329i, the original dates are obliterated by a bar, with "1964" and papal arms overprinted below.

The overprint is olive bister on the stamps, yellow on the souvenir sheet. The overprint also exists in yellow gold on the same six stamps and in olive bister on the souvenir sheet. Values: set, $400; souvenir sheet $325.

Roosevelt Type of Regular Issue

Perf. 12x12½

1964, Oct. 9 — Litho. — Unwmk.

C330 A147 20c grn & blk, *buff* .40 .30
a. Souv. sheet of 2, #455, C330, imperf. .55 .55

AP84c

1964, Sept. 1 — *Perf. 13½x14*

C331 AP84c 21c shown .75 .50
C332 AP84c 21c Papal coat of arms .75 .50
a. Souv. sheet of 2, #C331-C332 6.00 5.00

Pope John XXIII (1881-1963). Nos. C331-C332 exist imperf in different colors. Value $20.

Galileo, 400th Birth Anniv. — AP84d

21c, Galileo, studies of gravity.

1965, May 12 — *Perf. 14*

C333 AP84d 10c blue & multi 2.00 .75
C334 AP84d 21c green & multi 2.00 .75
a. Souv. sheet of 2, #C333-C334 15.00 15.00

Nos. C333-C334a exist imperf in different colors. Value, $11.

Alfred Nobel (1833-1896), Founder of Nobel Prize — AP84e

1965, May 12 — Litho. & Embossed

C335 AP84e 10c Peace Medal, rev. 2.25 .75
C336 AP84e 21c Peace Medal, obv. 2.25 .75
a. Souv. sheet of 2, #C335-C336 15.00 15.00

Nos. C335-C336a exist imperf in different colors. Value, $4.50.

Bird Type of Regular Issue, 1965

Song Birds: 5c, Common troupial, horiz. 10c, Crimson-backed tanager, horiz.

1965, Oct. 27 — Unwmk. — *Perf. 14*

C337 A148 5c dp org & multi 1.40 .25
C338 A148 10c brt blue & multi 2.50 .25
a. Souv. sheet of 6, #462-462C, C337-C338 22.50 22.50

No. C338a exists imperf. Value, $22.50.

Fish Type of Regular Issue

Designs: 8c, Shrimp. 12c, Hammerhead. 13c, Atlantic sailfish. 25c, Seahorse, vert.

1965, Dec. 7 — Litho.

C339 A149 8c multi .45 .25
C340 A149 12c multi .70 .25
C341 A149 13c multi .70 .25
C342 A149 25c multi 1.40 .35
Nos. C339-C342 (4) 3.25 1.00

English Daisy and Emblem — AP85

Junior Chamber of Commerce Emblem and: #C344, Hibiscus. #C345, Orchid. #C346, Water lily. #C347, Gladiolus. #C348, Flor del Espiritu Santo.

1966, Mar. 16

C343 AP85 30c brt pink & multi .90 .35
C344 AP85 30c salmon & multi .90 .35
C345 AP85 30c pale yel & multi .90 .35
C346 AP85 40c lt grn & multi 1.25 .35
C347 AP85 40c blue & multi 1.25 .35
C348 AP85 40c pink & multi 1.25 .35
Nos. C343-C348 (6) 6.45 2.10

50th anniv. of the Junior Chamber of Commerce.

Nos. C224 and C236 Surcharged

1966, June 27 — Wmk. 311 — *Perf. 12½*

C349 A130 3c on 5c blk & red brn .25 .25

Wmk. 343

C350 A131 13c on 25c lt & dk bl .35 .25

The old denominations are not obliterated on Nos. C349-C350.

ITU Cent. — AP85a

1966, Aug. 12 — *Perf. 13½x14*

C351 AP85a 31c multicolored 4.50 —

Souvenir Sheet

Perf. 14

C352 AP85a 31c multicolored 15.00 15.00

No. C352 exists imperf. with blue green background. Value $15.

Animal Type of Regular Issue, 1967

Domestic Animals: 10c, Pekingese dog. 13c, Zebu, horiz. 30c, Cat. 40c, Horse, horiz.

1967, Feb. 3 — Unwmk. — *Perf. 14*

C353 A150 10c multi .45 .25
C354 A150 13c multi .55 .25
C355 A150 30c multi 1.00 .50
C356 A150 40c multi 1.25 .60
Nos. C353-C356 (4) 3.25 1.50

Young Hare, by Durer AP86

10c, St. Jerome and the Lion, by Albrecht Durer. 20c, Lady with the Ermine, by Leonardo Da Vinci. 30c, The Hunt, by Delacroix, horiz.

1967, Sept. 1

C357 AP86 10c black, buff & car .35 .25
C358 AP86 13c lt yellow & multi .55 .25
C359 AP86 20c multicolored .80 .25
C360 AP86 30c multicolored 1.10 .45
Nos. C357-C360 (4) 2.80 1.10

Panama-Mexico Friendship — AP86a

Designs: 1b, Pres. Gustavo Diaz Ordaz of Mexico and Pres. Marco A. Robles of Panama, horiz.

1968, Jan. 20 — *Perf. 14*

C361 AP86a 50c shown 2.00 .60
C361A AP86a 1b multi 4.00 1.10
b. Souv. sheet of 2, #C361-C361A, imperf. 8.00 8.00

For overprints see Nos. C364-C364B.

Souvenir Sheet

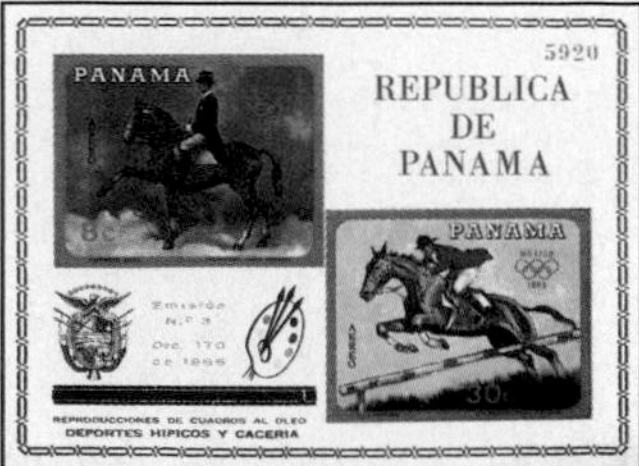

Olympic Equestrian Events — AP86b

1968, Oct. 29 — *Imperf.*

C362 AP86b Sheet of 2 45.00 45.00
a. 8c Dressage 1.50 1.00
b. 30c Show jumping 5.00 3.50

Intl. Human Rights Year — AP86c

1968, Dec. 18 — *Perf. 14*

C363 AP86c 40c multicolored 11.50 7.50
a. Miniature sheet of 1 30.00 30.00

Nos. C361-C361b Ovptd. in Red or Black

1969, Jan. 31

C364 AP86a 50c on #C361 (R) 6.25 1.50
C364A AP86a 1b on #C361A (B) 6.25 1.50

Souvenir Sheet

C364B on #C361b (R) 11.50 11.50

Intl. Philatelic and Numismatic Expo.

Overprint larger on No. C364A, larger and in different arrangement on No. C364B.

Intl. Space Exploration — AP86d

1969, Mar. 14

C365 Sheet of 6 18.00 18.00
a. AP86d 5c France, Diadem I .50 .25
b. AP86d 10c Italy, San Marco II 1.00 .40
c. AP86d 15c Great Britain, UK 3 1.50 .50
d. AP86d 20c US, Saturn V/Apollo 7 2.00 .75
e. AP86d 25c US, Surveyor 7 3.00 1.00
f. AP86d 30c Europe/US, Esro 2 4.00 1.25

Satellite Transmission of Summer Olympics, Mexico, 1968 — AP86e

1969, Mar. 14 *Perf. 14½*

C366 AP86e 1b multi 3.00 1.00
a. Miniature sheet of 1 10.00 2.00

Nos. CB4, 461B & 461C Surcharged

1969, Apr. 1 *Perf. 13½x13*

C367 AP81 5c on 5c+5c 3.50 .50
C367A A147e 5c on 10c+5c 3.50 .50
C367B A147e 10c on 21c+10c 3.50 .50

Games Type of Regular Issue and

San Blas Indian Girl — AP87

Design: 13c, Bridge of the Americas.

1970, Jan. 6 **Litho.** *Perf. 13½*

C368 A158 13c multi 1.00 .30
C369 AP87 30c multi 1.25 .75
a. "AEREO" omitted *50.00 50.00*

See notes after No. 525.

Juan D. Arosemena and Arosemena Stadium — AP88

Designs: 2c, 3c, 5c, like 1c. No. C374, Basketball. No. C375, New Panama Gymnasium. No. C376, Revolution Stadium. No. C377, Panamanian man and woman in Stadium. 30c, Stadium, eternal flame, arms of Mexico, Puerto Rico and Cuba.

1970, Oct. 7 **Wmk. 365** *Perf. 13½*

C370 AP88 1c pink & multi .25 .25
C371 AP88 2c pink & multi .25 .25
C372 AP88 3c pink & multi .25 .25
C373 AP88 5c pink & multi .25 .25
C374 AP88 13c lt blue & multi .45 .25
C375 AP88 13c lilac & multi .45 .25
C376 AP88 13c yellow & multi .45 .25
C377 AP88 13c pink & multi .45 .25
C378 AP88 30c yellow & multi 1.25 .50
a. Souv. sheet of 1, imperf. 2.00 2.00
Nos. C370-C378 (9) 4.05 2.50

11th Central American and Caribbean Games, Feb. 28-Mar. 14.

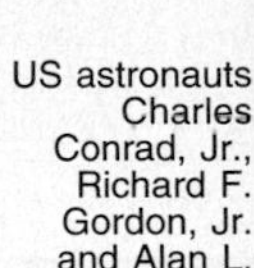
US astronauts Charles Conrad, Jr., Richard F. Gordon, Jr. and Alan L. Bean. — AP89

No. C379, Astronaut on Moon.

1971, Aug. 20 **Wmk. 343** *Perf. 13½*

C379 AP89 13c gold & multi .50 .35
C380 AP89 13c lt green & multi .50 .35

Man's first landing on the moon, Apollo 11, July 20, 1969 (No. C379) and Apollo 12 moon mission, Nov. 14-24, 1969.

EXPO '70 Emblem and Pavilion AP90

1971, Aug. 24 **Litho.**

C381 AP90 10c pink & multi .25 .25

EXPO '70 International Exposition, Osaka, Japan, Mar. 15-Sept. 13.

Flag of Panama AP91

Design: 13c, Map of Panama superimposed on Western Hemisphere, and tourist year emblem.

1971, Dec. 11 **Wmk. 343**

C382 AP91 5c multi .25 .25
C383 AP91 13c multi .25 .25

Proclamation of 1972 as Tourist Year of the Americas.

Mahatma Gandhi AP92

1971, Dec. 17

C384 AP92 10c black & multi *60.00 25.00*

Centenary of the birth of Mohandas K. Gandhi (1869-1948), leader in India's fight for independence.

Central American Independence Issue

Flags of Central American States AP92a

1971, Dec. 20

C385 AP92a 13c multi .35 .25

160th anniv. of Central America independence.

AP93

1971, Dec. 21

C386 AP93 8c Panama #4 .25 .25

2nd National Philatelic and Numismatic Exposition, 1970.

AP94

1972, Sept. 7 **Wmk. 365**

C387 AP94 40c Natá Church .80 .60

450th anniversary of the founding of Natá.
For surcharges see Nos. C402, RA85.

Telecommunications Emblem — AP95

1972, Sept. 8

C388 AP95 13c lt bl, dp bl & blk .40 .40

3rd World Telecommunications Day (in 1971).

Apollo 14 AP96

1972, Sept. 11

C389 AP96 13c tan & multi .90 .50

Apollo 14 US moon mission, 1/1-2/9/71.

Shoeshine Boy Counting Coins — AP97

1972, Sept. 12

C390 AP97 5c shown .25 .25
C391 AP97 8c Mother & Child .25 .25
C392 AP97 50c UNICEF emblem 1.25 .55
a. Souv. sheet of 1, imperf. 1.75 1.75
Nos. C390-C392 (3) 1.70 1.00

25th anniv. (in 1971) of the UNICEF.

San Blas Cloth, Cuna Indians AP98

8c, Beaded necklace, Guaymi Indians. 25c, View of Portobelo.

1972, Sept. 13

C393 AP98 5c multicolored .25 .25
C394 AP98 8c multicolored .25 .25
C395 AP98 25c multicolored .80 .45
a. Souv. sheet of 2, #C393, C395, imperf. 3.50 3.50
Nos. C393-C395 (3) 1.25 .85

Tourist publicity.
For surcharges see Nos. C417, RA83.

Baseball and Games' Emblem AP99

Games' Emblem and: 10c, Basketball, vert. 13c, Torch, vert. 25c, Boxing. 50c, Map and flag of Panama, Bolivar. 1b, Medals.

Perf. 12½

1973, Feb. 10 **Litho.** **Unwmk.**

C396 AP99 8c rose red & yel .25 .25
C397 AP99 10c black & ultra .25 .25
C398 AP99 13c blue & multi .35 .25
C399 AP99 25c blk, yel grn & red .70 .25
C400 AP99 50c green & multi 1.50 .60
C401 AP99 1b multicolored 3.00 1.00
Nos. C396-401 (1) .25 .25

7th Bolivar Games, Panama City, 2/17-3/3.

No. C387 Surcharged in Red Similar to No. 542

1973, Mar. 15 **Wmk. 365** *Perf. 13½*

C402 AP94 13c on 40c multi .35 .30

UN Security Council Meeting, Panama City, Mar. 15-21.

Portrait Type of Regular Issue 1973

Designs: 5c, Isabel Herrera Obaldia, educator. 8c, Nicolas Victoria Jaén, educator. 10c, Forest Scene, by Roberto Lewis. No. C406, Portrait of a Lady, by Manuel E. Amador. No. C407, Ricardo Miró, poet. 20c, Portrait, by Isaac Benitez. 21c, Manuel Amador Guerrero, statesman. 25c, Belisario Porras, statesman. 30c, Juan Demostenes Arosemena, statesman. 34c, Octavio Mendez Pereira, writer. 38c, Ricardo J. Alfaro, writer.

1973, June 20 **Litho.** *Perf. 13½*

C403 A169 5c pink & multi .25 .25
C404 A169 8c pink & multi .25 .25
C405 A169 10c gray & multi .35 .25
C406 A169 13c pink & multi .55 .25
C407 A169 13c pink & multi .55 .25
C408 A169 20c blue & multi .70 .40
C409 A169 21c yellow & multi .80 .40
C410 A169 25c pink & multi .90 .40
C411 A169 30c gray & multi 1.00 .45

C412 A169 34c lt blue & multi 1.10 .60
C413 A169 38c lt blue & multi 1.25 .60
Nos. C403-C413 (11) 7.65 3.85

Famous Panamanians.
For overprints and surcharges see Nos. C414-C416, C418-C421.

Nos. C403, C410, and C412 Overprinted in Black or Red

1973, Sept. 14 Litho. *Perf. 13½*

C414 A169 5c pink & multi .25 .25
C415 A169 25c pink & multi .90 .45
C416 A169 34c bl & multi (R) 1.10 .75
Nos. C414-C416 (3) 2.25 1.45

50th anniversary of the Isabel Herrera Obaldia Professional School.

Nos. C395, C408, C413, C412 and C409 Surcharged in Red

1974, Nov. 11 Litho. *Perf. 13½*

C417 AP98 1c on 25c multi .25 .25
C418 A169 3c on 20c multi .25 .25
C419 A169 8c on 38c multi .25 .25
C420 A169 10c on 34c multi .25 .25
C421 A169 13c on 21c multi .25 .25
Nos. C417-C421 (5) 1.00 1.00

Women's Hands, Panama Map, UN and IWY Emblems AP100

Perf. 12½

1975, May 6 Litho. Unwmk.

C422 AP100 17c blue & multi .70 .25
a. Souv. sheet, typo., imperf., no gum 1.50 1.50

International Women's Year 1975.

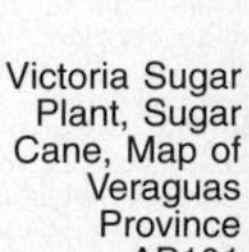

Victoria Sugar Plant, Sugar Cane, Map of Veraguas Province AP101

Designs: 17c, Bayano electrification project and map of Panama, horiz. 33c, Tocumen International Airport and map, horiz.

1975, Oct. 9 Litho. *Perf. 12½*

C423 AP101 17c bl, buff & blk .70 .30
C424 AP101 27c ultra & yel grn 1.00 .35
C425 AP101 33c bl & multi 1.10 .45
Nos. C423-C425 (3) 2.80 1.10

Oct. 11, 1968, Revolution, 7th anniv.

Bolivar Statue and Flags — AP102

Bolivar Hall, Panama City AP103

Design: 41c, Bolivar with flag of Panama, ruins of Old Panama City.

1976, Mar.

C426 AP102 23c multi .65 .25
C427 AP103 35c multi 1.00 .30
C428 AP102 41c multi 1.00 .60
Nos. C426-C428 (3) 2.65 1.10

150th anniversary of Congress of Panama. Issued: 23c, Mar. 5; others Mar. 30.

Marine Life Type of 1976

Marine life: 17c, Diodon hystrix, vert. 27c, Pocillopora damicornis.

Perf. 13x12½, 12½x13

1976, May 6 Litho. Wmk. 377

C429 A171 17c multi 1.60 .50
C430 A171 27c multi 2.25 .65

Cerro Colorado — AP104

1976, Nov. 12 Litho. *Perf. 12½*

C431 AP104 23c multi .55 .25

Cerro Colorado copper mines, Chiriqui Province.

Gen. Omar Torrijos Herrera (1929-1981) AP105

1982, Feb. 13 Litho. *Perf. 10½*

C432 AP105 23c multi .65 .25

Torrijos Type of 1982

Wmk. 311

1982, May 14 Litho. *Perf. 10½*

C433 A201 35c Security Council reunion, 1973 1.00 .30
C434 A201 41c Torrijos Airport 1.10 .50

Souvenir Sheet

Imperf

C435 A201 23c like #C432 3.00 3.00

No. C435 sold for 1b.

Alfaro Type of 1982

Photos by Luiz Gutierrez Cruz.

1982, Aug. 18 Wmk. 382

C436 A202 17c multi .45 .25
C437 A202 23c multi .65 .25

World Cup Type of 1982

1982, Dec. 27 Litho. *Perf. 10½*

C438 A203 23c Map .70 .25
C439 A203 35c Pele, vert. 1.00 .30
C440 A203 41c Cup, vert. 1.25 .40
Nos. C438-C440 (3) 2.95 .95

1b imperf. souvenir sheet exists in design of 23c; black control number. Size; 85x75mm. Value $13.50.

Nicolas A. Solano (1882-1943), Tuberculosis Researcher AP106

Wmk. 382 (Stars)

1983, Feb. 8 Litho. *Perf. 10½*

C441 AP106 23c brown .50 .25

World Food Day — AP107

1984, Oct. 16 Litho. *Perf. 12*

C442 AP107 30c Hand grasping fork 1.25 .50

Contadora Group for Peace — AP108

1985, Oct. 1 Litho. *Perf. 14*

C443 AP108 10c multi .45 .25
C444 AP108 20c multi .90 .30
C445 AP108 30c multi 1.25 .50
Nos. C443-C445 (3) 2.60 1.05

See No. 680A.

Christmas Type of 1988

1988, Dec. 29 Litho. *Perf. 12*

C446 A246 35c St. Joseph and the Infant 1.10 .40

Olympics Type of 1989

1989, Mar. 17 Litho. *Perf. 12*

C447 A248 35c Boxing 1.10 .40

Opening of the Panama Canal, 75th Anniv. AP109

35c, Ancon in lock, 1914. 60c, Ship in lock, 1989.

1989, Sept. 29 Litho. *Perf. 13½*

C448 AP109 35c multicolored 1.25 .65
C449 AP109 60c multicolored 2.00 1.10

Revolution Type of 1989

1989, Nov. 14 Litho.

C450 A251 35c Storming of the Bastille 1.75 .65
C451 A251 45c Anniv. emblem 2.10 .85

French revolution, bicent.

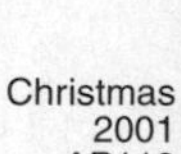

Christmas 2001 AP110

Designs: 60c, Man, woman, drums. 1b, Guitar, drum, candle. 2b, Pots, potted plant.

2002, Apr. 30 Litho. *Perf. 13x13¼*

C452-C454 AP110 Set of 3 14.50 14.50

Dated 2001.

La Salle Schools in Panama, Cent. (in 2002) AP111

2003, May 15 Litho. *Perf. 13x13½*

C455 AP111 5b multi 16.00 10.00

Dated 2002.

Natá, 480th Anniv. (in 2002) AP112

2003, May 20

C456 AP112 1b multi 3.25 2.00

Dated 2002.

Trains AP113

Designs: 40c, Colón locomotive. 50c, Panama Railroad, vert.

Perf. 13x13½, 14 (50c)

2003, July 17

C457-C458 AP113 Set of 2 4.00 2.50

Dated 2002.

Santa María de Belén, 500th Anniv. AP114

2003, July 31 *Perf. 14*

C459 AP114 1.50b multi 5.00 3.00

Dated 2002.

Fourth Voyage of Christopher Columbus, 500th Anniv. (in 2002) AP115

2003, July 31 *Perf. 13x13½*

C460 AP115 2b multi 6.75 4.00

Dated 2002.

Kuna Indians
AP116

Designs: No. C461, 50c, Village, people in canoe, woman. No. C462, 50c, Man and woman, vert. No. C463, 60c, Woman sewing. No. C464, 60c, Dancers.
1.50b, Fish.

Perf. 14 (#C461), 13½x13 (#C462), 13x13½

2003, Aug. 13
C461-C464 AP116 Set of 4 7.00 4.50

Souvenir Sheet

Perf. 13½x14

C465 AP116 1.50b multi 5.75 5.75

Dated 2002. No. C465 contains one 50x45mm stamp.

Medicine in Panama
AP117

Designs: No. C466, 50c, Santo Tomás de Villanueva Hospital, 300th anniv. No. C467, 50c, Gorgas Memorial Institute of Tropical and Preventative Medicine, 75th anniv.

2003 ***Perf. 12***
C466-C467 AP117 Set of 2 3.25 3.25

Issued: No. C466, 12/17; No. C467, 11/17.

Jewelry
AP118

Designs: 45c, Necklaces. 60c, Brooches.

2003, Nov. 24
C468-C469 AP118 Set of 2 3.50 3.50

For surcharges, see Nos. C474-C475.

America Issue - Endangered Species — AP119

2003, Nov. 26
C470 AP119 2b multi 6.25 6.25

La Estrella de Panama Newspaper, 150th Anniv. — AP120

2003, Dec. 3
C471 AP120 40c multi 1.25 1.25

Scouting, Cent.
AP121

2010, Sept. 3 **Litho.** ***Perf. 14***
C472 AP121 20c multi .40 .40

Printed in sheets of 4.

Salesian Order in Panama, Cent. — AP122

2010, Aug. 27
C473 AP122 20c multi .40 .40

No. C468 Surcharged

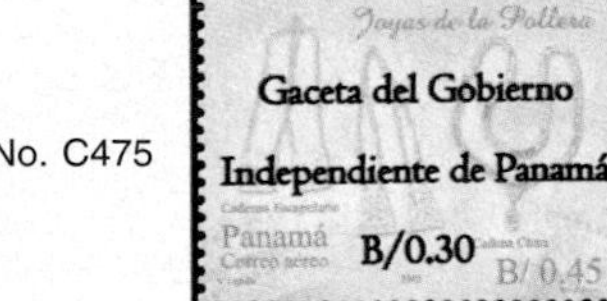

No. C474

No. C475

Methods and Perfs. As Before

2014, June 1
C474 AP118 15c on 45c #C468 .30 .30
C475 AP118 30c on 45c #C468 .60 .60

AIR POST SEMI-POSTAL STAMPS

Catalogue values for unused stamps in this section are for Never Hinged items.

"The World Against Malaria" — SPAP1

Wmk. 311

1961, Dec. 20 **Litho.** ***Perf. 12½***
CB1 SPAP1 5c + 5c car rose .50 .50
CB2 SPAP1 10c + 10c vio bl .50 .50
CB3 SPAP1 15c + 15c dk grn .50 .50
Nos. CB1-CB3 (3) 1.50 1.50

WHO drive to eradicate malaria.
For surcharges see Nos. C271-C272.

Nos. C274-C276 Surcharged in Red

Wmk. 311

1963, Mar. 4 **Litho.** ***Perf. 12½***
CB4 AP81 5c +5c on #C274 1.00 .75
CB5 AP81 10c +10c on #C275 2.00 1.50
CB6 AP81 15c +31c on #C276 2.00 1.50

Surcharge on No. CB4 differs to fit stamp. See No. CB7.

No. CB4 Surcharged in Black

1963, Aug. 22
CB7 AP81 10c on 5c+5c 6.00 5.00

Intl. Red. Cross cent.

SPECIAL DELIVERY STAMPS

Nos. 211-212 Overprinted in Red

1926 **Unwmk.** ***Perf. 12***
E1 A31 10c org & blk 7.50 3.25
a. "EXRPESO" 40.00
E2 A32 20c brn & blk 10.00 3.25
a. "EXRPESO" 40.00
b. Double overprint 35.00 35.00

Bicycle Messenger
SD1

1929, Feb. 8 **Engr.** ***Perf. 12½***
E3 SD1 10c orange 1.25 1.00
E4 SD1 20c dk brn 4.75 2.50

For surcharges and overprints see Nos. C1-C5, C17-C18A, C67.

REGISTRATION STAMPS

Issued under Colombian Dominion

R1

1888 **Unwmk.** **Engr.** ***Perf. 13½***
F1 R1 10c black, *gray* 8.00 5.25

Imperforate and part-perforate copies without gum and those on surface-colored paper are reprints.

Magenta, Violet or Blue Black Handstamped Overprint

1898 ***Perf. 12***
F2 A4 10c orange 7.00 6.50

The handstamp on No. F2 was also used as a postmark.

R3

1900 **Litho.** ***Perf. 11***
F3 R3 10c blk, *lt bl* 4.00 3.50

1901
F4 R3 10c brown red 30.00 20.00

R4

1902 **Blue Black Surcharge**
F5 R4 20c on 10c brn red 20.00 16.00

Issues of the Republic Issued in the City of Panama

Registration Stamps of Colombia Handstamped in Blue Black or Rose

1903-04 ***Imperf.***
F6 R9 20c red brn, *bl* 45.00 42.50
F7 R9 20c blue, *blue* (R) 45.00 42.50

For surcharges and overprints see Nos. F8-F11, F16-F26.

Reprints exist of Nos. F6 and F7; see note after No. 64.

With Additional Surcharge in Rose

F8 R9 10c on 20c red brn, *bl* 60.00 55.00
b. "10" in blue black 60.00 55.00
F9 R9 10c on 20c bl, *bl* 60.00 45.00

Handstamped in Rose

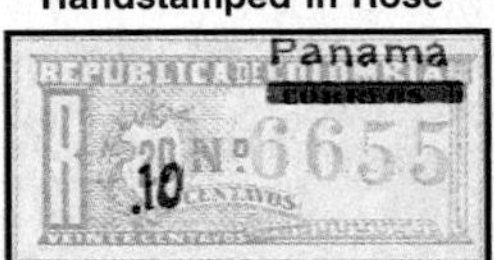

F10 R9 10c on 20c red brn, *bl* 60.00 55.00
F11 R9 10c on 20c blue, *blue* 45.00 42.50

Issued in Colon

Regular Issues Handstamped "R/COLON" in Circle (as on F2) Together with Other Overprints and Surcharges

Handstamped

1903-04 ***Perf. 12***
F12 A4 10c orange 3.00 2.50

Handstamped

F13 A4 10c orange 22.50

Overprinted in Red

F14 A4 10c orange 3.00 2.50

Overprinted in Black

F15 A4 10c orange 7.50 5.00

The handstamps on Nos. F12 to F15 are in magenta, violet or red; various combinations of these colors are to be found. They are struck in various positions, including double, inverted, one handstamp omitted, etc.

Colombia No. F13 Handstamped Like No. F12 in Violet

Imperf

F16 R9 20c red brn, *bl* 60.00 55.00

Overprinted Like No. F15 in Black

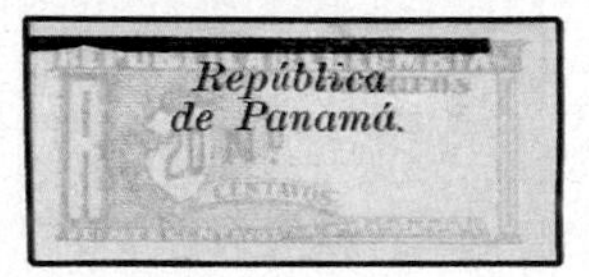

F17 R9 20c red brn, *bl* 6.00 5.75

No. F17 Surcharged in Manuscript

F18 R9 10c on 20c red brn, *bl* 60.00 55.00

No. F17 Surcharged in Purple **10**

F19 R9 10c on 20c 82.50 80.00

No. F17 Surcharged in Violet

F20 R9 10c on 20c 82.50 80.00

The varieties of the overprint which are described after No. 138 are also to be found on the Registration and Acknowledgment of Receipt stamps. It is probable that Nos. F17 to F20 inclusive owe their existence more to speculation than to postal necessity.

Issued in Bocas del Toro

Colombia Nos. F17 and F13 Handstamped in Violet

R DE PANAMA

1903-04

F21 R9 20c blue, *blue* 125.00 125.00
F22 R9 20c red brn, *bl* 125.00 125.00

No. F21 Surcharged in Manuscript in Violet or Red

F23 R9 10c on 20c bl, *bl* 150.00 140.00

Colombia Nos. F13, F17 Handstamped in Violet

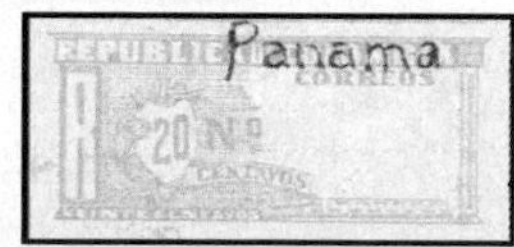

Surcharged in Manuscript (a) "10" (b) "10cs" in Red

F25 R9 10 on 20c red brn, *bl* 70.00 65.00
F26 R9 10cs on 20c bl, *bl* 55.00 50.00
Nos. F21-F26 (5) 525.00 505.00

No. F25 without surcharge is bogus, according to leading experts.

General Issue

R5

1904, Aug. 1 **Engr.** ***Perf. 12***

F27 R5 10c green 1.00 .50

Nos. 190 and 213 Surcharged in Red

#F29-F30 #F29b

1916-17

F29 A11 5c on 8c pur & blk 3.00 2.25
- *a.* "5" inverted 75.00
- *b.* Large, round "5" 50.00
- *c.* Inverted surcharge 12.50 11.00
- *d.* Tête bêche surcharge
- *e.* Pair, one without surcharge 10.00

F30 A33 5c on 8c vio & blk 3.50 .80
- *a.* Inverted surcharge 13.00 8.25
- *b.* Tête bêche surcharge
- *c.* Double surcharge 60.00

Issued: No. F29, 1/1/16; No. F30, 1/28/17.

Stamps similar to No. F30, overprinted in green were unauthorized.

INSURED LETTER STAMPS

Stamps of 1939 Surcharged in Black

1942, Nov. 14 **Unwmk.** ***Perf. 12½***

G1 AP23 5c on 1b blk .50 .50
G2 A84 10c on 1b dk brn .80 .80
G3 AP23 25c on 50c dk brn 2.00 2.00
Nos. G1-G3 (3) 3.30 3.30

ACKNOWLEDGMENT OF RECEIPT STAMPS

Issued under Colombian Dominion

Experts consider this handstamp-"A.R. / COLON / COLOMBIA"-to be a cancellation or a marking intended for a letter to receive special handling. It was applied at Colon to various stamps in 1897-1904 in different colored inks for philatelic sale. It exists on cover, usually with the bottom line removed by masking the handstamp.

Nos. 17-18 Handstamped in Rose

1902

H4 A4 5c blue 5.00 5.00
H5 A4 10c yellow 10.00 10.00

This handstamp was also used as a postmark.

Issues of the Republic Issued in the City of Panama

Colombia No. H3 Handstamped in Rose

1903-04 **Unwmk.** ***Imperf.***

H9 AR2 10c blue, *blue* 10.00 8.00

Reprints exist of No. H9, see note after No. 64.

No. H9 Surcharged

H10 AR2 5c on 10c bl, *bl* 5.00 5.00

Colombia No. H3 Handstamped in Rose

H11 AR2 10c blue, *blue* 17.50 14.00

Issued in Colon

Handstamped in Magenta or Violet

Imperf

H17 AR2 10c blue, *blue* 15.00 15.00

Handstamped

H18 AR2 10c blue, *blue* 82.50 70.00

Overprinted in Black

H19 AR2 10c blue, *blue* 11.00 8.00

No. H19 Surcharged in Manuscript

H20 AR2 10c on 5c on 10c 100.00 82.50

Issued in Bocas del Toro

Colombia No. H3 Handstamped in Violet and Surcharged in Manuscript in Red Like Nos. F25-F26

1904

H21 AR2 5c on 10c blue, *blue*

No. H21, unused, without surcharge is bogus.

General Issue

AR3

1904, Aug. 1 **Engr.** ***Perf. 12***

H22 AR3 5c blue 1.00 .80

No. 199 Overprinted in Violet

1916, Jan. 1

H23 A20 2½c red orange 1.00 .80
- *a.* "R.A." for "A.R." 50.00
- *b.* Double overprint 8.00
- *c.* Inverted overprint 8.00

LATE FEE STAMPS

Issues of the Republic Issued in the City of Panama

Colombia No. I4 Handstamped in Rose or Blue Black

LF3

REPUBLICA DE
PANAMA

1903-04 **Unwmk.** ***Imperf.***

I1 LF3 5c pur, *rose* 12.50 9.00
I2 LF3 5c pur, *rose* (Bl Blk) 17.50 12.50

Reprints exist of #I1-I2; see note after #64.

General Issue

LF4

1904 **Engr.** ***Perf. 12***

I3 LF4 2½c lake 1.00 .65

No. 199 Overprinted with Typewriter

1910, Aug. 12

I4 A20 2½c red orange 125.00 100.00

Used only on Aug. 12-13.
Counterfeits abound.

Handstamped

1910

I5 A20 2½c red orange 60.00 50.00

Counterfeits abound.

No. 195 Surcharged in Green

1917, Jan. 1

I6 A17 1c on ½c orange .80 .80
a. "UN CENTESIMO" inverted 50.00
b. Double surcharge 10.00
c. Inverted surcharge 6.50 6.50

No. 196 Surcharged in Green

1921

I7 A17 1c on ½c rose 25.00 20.00

POSTAGE DUE STAMPS

San Lorenzo Castle Gate, Mouth of Chagres River D1

Statue of Columbus D2

Pedro J. Sosa — D4

Design: 4c, Capitol, Panama City.

Unwmk.

1915, Mar. 25 Engr. *Perf. 12*

J1 D1 1c olive brown 3.50 .75
J2 D2 2c olive brown 5.25 .65
J3 D1 4c olive brown 7.25 1.25
J4 D4 10c olive brown 5.25 1.75
Nos. J1-J4 (4) 21.25 4.40

Type D1 was intended to show a gate of San Lorenzo Castle, Chagres, and is so inscribed.

D5

1930, Dec. 30 *Perf. 12½*

J5 D5 1c emerald 1.00 .60
J6 D5 2c dark red 1.00 .60
J7 D5 4c dark blue 1.60 .80
J8 D5 10c violet 1.60 .80
Nos. J5-J8 (4) 5.20 2.80

POSTAL TAX STAMPS

Pierre and Marie Curie — PT1

Unwmk.

1939, June 15 Engr. *Perf. 12*

RA1 PT1 1c rose carmine .65 .25
RA2 PT1 1c green .65 .25
RA3 PT1 1c orange .65 .25
RA4 PT1 1c blue .65 .25
Nos. RA1-RA4 (4) 2.60 1.00

See Nos. RA6-RA18, RA24-RA27, RA30.

Stamp of 1924 Overprinted in Black

1940, Dec. 20

RA5 A53 1c dark green 1.40 .75

1941, Jan. 30 Inscribed 1940

RA6 PT1 1c rose carmine .65 .25
RA7 PT1 1c green .65 .25
RA8 PT1 1c orange .65 .25
RA9 PT1 1c blue .65 .25
Nos. RA6-RA9 (4) 2.60 1.00

1942 Inscribed 1942

RA10 PT1 1c violet .40 .25

1943 Inscribed 1943

RA11 PT1 1c rose carmine .40 .25
RA12 PT1 1c green .40 .25
RA13 PT1 1c orange .40 .25
RA14 PT1 1c blue .40 .25
Nos. RA11-RA14 (4) 1.60 1.00

1945 Inscribed 1945

RA15 PT1 1c rose carmine .90 .25
RA16 PT1 1c green .90 .25
RA17 PT1 1c orange .90 .25
RA18 PT1 1c blue .90 .25
Nos. RA15-RA18 (4) 3.60 1.00

Nos. 234 and 235 Surcharged in Black or Red

1946 Unwmk. *Perf. 12*

RA19 A53 1c on ½c orange .60 .25
RA20 A53 1c on 1c dk grn (R) .60 .25

Catalogue values for unused stamps in this section, from this point to the end of the section, are for Never Hinged items.

Same Surcharged in Black on Nos. 239 and 241

1947, Apr. 7

RA21 A53 1c on 12c ol grn 1.00 .30
RA22 A53 1c on 24c yel brn 1.00 .30

Surcharged in Red on No. 342

RA23 A95 1c on ½c dl vio, bl & car 1.00 .25

Type of 1939 Inscribed 1947

1947, July 21

RA24 PT1 1c rose carmine 1.25 .25
RA25 PT1 1c green 1.25 .25
RA26 PT1 1c orange 1.25 .25
RA27 PT1 1c blue 1.25 .25
Nos. RA24-RA27 (4) 5.00 1.00

Nos. C100 and C101 Surcharged in Black

a

b

1949, Feb. 16 Unwmk. *Perf. 12½*

RA28 AP45 (a) 1c on 5c .65 .25
a. Inverted surcharge 15.00
RA29 AP46 (b) 1c on 10c yel org .65 .25
a. Inverted surcharge —

Type of 1939

1949 Inscribed 1949 *Perf. 12*

RA30 PT1 1c brown 2.00 .25

The tax from the sale of Nos. RA1-RA30 was used for the control of cancer.

Juan D. Arosemena Stadium PT2

Torch Emblem — PT3

No. RA33, Adan Gordon Olympic Swimming Pool.

1951 Unwmk. Engr. *Perf. 12½*

RA31 PT2 1c carmine & blk 1.60 .25
RA32 PT3 1c dk bl & blk 1.60 .25
RA33 PT2 1c grn & blk 1.60 .25
Nos. RA31-RA33 (3) 4.80 .75

Issued: No. RA31, 2/21; No. RA32, 7/12; No. RA33, 12/13.

Discobolus — PT4

No. RA34, Turners' emblem.

1952

RA34 PT3 1c org & blk 1.60 .25
RA35 PT4 1c pur & blk 1.60 .25

Issued: No. RA34, 4/18; No. RA35, 9/10.

The tax from the sale of Nos. RA31-RA35 was used to promote physical education.

Boys Doing Farm Work PT5

Wmk. 311

1958, Jan. 24 Litho. *Perf. 12½*

Size: 35x24mm

RA36 PT5 1c rose red & gray .25 .25

Type of 1958 Inscribed 1959

1959 Size: 35x24mm

RA37 PT5 1c gray & emerald .25 .25
RA38 PT5 1c vio bl & gray .25 .25

Type of 1958 Inscribed 1960

Wmk. 334

1960, July 20 Litho. *Perf. 13½*

Size: 32x23mm

RA39 PT5 1c carmine & gray .25 .25

Nos. C235 and C241 Surcharged in Black or Red

1961, May 24 Wmk. 343 *Perf. 12½*

RA40 A131 1c on 10c ocher & blk .25 .25
RA41 AP76 1c on 10c emer (R) .25 .25

Girl at Sewing Machine PT6

Wmk. 343

1961, Nov. 24 Litho. *Perf. 12½*

RA42 PT6 1c brt vio .25 .25
RA43 PT6 1c rose lilac .25 .25
RA44 PT6 1c yellow .25 .25
RA45 PT6 1c blue .25 .25
RA46 PT6 1c emerald .25 .25
Nos. RA42-RA46 (5) 1.25 1.25

1961, Dec. 1

Design: Boy with hand saw.

RA47 PT6 1c red lilac .25 .25
RA48 PT6 1c rose .25 .25
RA49 PT6 1c orange .25 .25
RA50 PT6 1c blue .25 .25
RA51 PT6 1c gray .25 .25
Nos. RA47-RA51 (5) 1.25 1.25

Boy Scout — PT7

Designs: Nos. RA57-RA61, Girl Scout.

1964, Feb. 7 Wmk. 343

RA52 PT7 1c olive .25 .25
RA53 PT7 1c gray .25 .25
RA54 PT7 1c lilac .25 .25
RA55 PT7 1c carmine rose .25 .25
RA56 PT7 1c blue .25 .25
RA57 PT7 1c bluish green .25 .25
RA58 PT7 1c violet .25 .25
RA59 PT7 1c orange .25 .25
RA60 PT7 1c yellow .25 .25
RA61 PT7 1c brn org .25 .25
Nos. RA52-RA61 (10) 2.50 2.50

The tax from Nos. RA36-RA61 was for youth rehabilitation.

Map of Panama, Flags — PT8

1973, Jan. 22 Unwmk.

RA62 PT8 1c black .25 .25

7th Bolivar Sports Games, Feb. 17-Mar. 3, 1973. The tax was for a new post office in Panama City.

Post Office — PT9

Designs: No. RA63, Farm Cooperative. No. RA64, 5b silver coin. No. RA65, Victoriano

Lorenzo. No. RA66, RA69, Cacique Urraca. No. RA67, RA70, Post Office.

1973-75

RA63	PT9	1c brt yel grn & ver	.45	.25
RA64	PT9	1c gray & red	.45	.25
RA65	PT9	1c ocher & red	.45	.25
RA66	PT9	1c org & red	.45	.25
RA67	PT9	1c bl & red	.45	.25
RA68	PT9	1c blue ('74)	.45	.25
RA69	PT9	1c orange ('74)	.45	.25
RA70	PT9	1c vermilion ('75)	.45	.25
		Nos. RA63-RA70 (8)	3.60	2.00

Issued: No. RA63, 3/19; No. RA64, 6/4; No. RA65, 6/6; No. RA66, 8/16; No. RA67, 8/17; Nos. RA68-RA69, 4/9/74; No. RA70, 11/24/75.

The tax was for a new post office in Panama City.

Stamps of 1969-1973 Surcharged in Violet Blue, Yellow, Black or Carmine

1975, Sept. 3

RA75	A168	1c on 1c (#538; VB)	.25	.25
RA76	A168	1c on 2c (#539; Y)	.25	.25
RA77	A164	1c on 30c (#534; B)	.25	.25
RA78	A157	1c on 30c (#511; B)	.25	.25
RA79	A156	1c on 40c (#514; B)	.25	.25
RA80	A156	1c on 50c (#515; B)	.25	.25
RA81	A169	1c on 20c (#C408; C)	.25	.25
RA82	A169	1c on 25c (#C410; B)	.25	.25
RA83	AP98	1c on 25c (#C395; B)	.25	.25
RA84	A169	1c on 30c (#C411; B)	.25	.25
RA85	AP94	1c on 40c (#C387; C)	.25	.25
		Nos. RA75-RA85 (11)	2.75	2.75

The tax was for a new post office in Panama City. Surcharge vertical, reading down on No. RA75 and up on Nos. RA76, RA78 and RA83. Nos. RA75-RA85 were obligatory on all mail.

PT10

1980, Dec. 3 Litho. *Perf. 12*

RA86	PT10	2c Boys	.25	.25
RA87	PT10	2c Boy and chicks	.25	.25
RA88	PT10	2c Working in fields	.25	.25
RA89	PT10	2c Boys feeding piglet	.25	.25
a.		Souv. sheet of 4, #RA86-RA89	11.25	
b.		Block of 4, #RA86-RA89	1.00	

Tax was for Children's Village (Christmas 1980). #RA89a sold for 1b.

PT11

1981, Nov. 1 Litho. *Perf. 12*

RA90	PT11	2c Boy, pony	.25	.25
RA91	PT11	2c Nativity	.25	.25
RA92	PT11	2c Tree	.25	.25
RA93	PT11	2c Church	.25	.25
a.		Block of 4, #RA90-RA93	1.00	

Souvenir Sheet

RA94	Sheet of 4	12.50
a.-d.	PT11 2c, Children's drawings	

Tax was for Children's Village. No. RA94 sold for 5b.

PT12

1982, Nov. 1 Litho. *Perf. 13½x12½*

RA95	PT12	2c Carpentry	.25	.25
RA96	PT12	2c Beekeeping	.25	.25
a.		Pair, #RA95-RA96	.20	
RA97	PT12	2c Pig farming, vert.	.25	.25
RA98	PT12	2c Gardening, vert.	.25	.25
a.		Pair, #RA97-RA98	.20	

Tax was for Children's Village (Christmas 1982).

Two imperf souvenir sheets solf for 2B each. Value, each $16.

Children's Drawings PT13

No. RA99, Annunciation. No. RA100, Bethlehem and Star. No. RA101, Church and Houses. No. RA102, Flight into Egypt.

1983, Nov. 1 Litho. *Perf. 14½*

RA99	PT13	2c multicolored	.25	.25
RA100	PT13	2c multicolored	.25	.25
RA101	PT13	2c multicolored	.25	.25
RA102	PT13	2c multicolored	.25	.25
		Nos. RA99-RA102 (4)	1.00	1.00

Nos. RA100-RA102 are vert.

Souvenir sheets exist showing undenominated designs of Nos. RA99, RA101 and Nos. RA100, RA102 respectively. They sold for 2b each. Value $7.50 each.

Boy — PT14

1984, Nov. 1 Litho. *Perf. 12x12½*

RA103	PT14	2c White-collared shirt	.25	.25
RA104	PT14	2c T-shirt	.25	.25
RA105	PT14	2c Checked shirt	.25	.25
RA106	PT14	2c Scout uniform	.25	.25
a.		Block of 4, #RA103-RA106	1.00	

Tax was for Children's Village. An imperf. souvenir sheet sold for 2b, with designs similar to Nos. RA103-RA106, exists. Value $7.50.

Christmas 1985 — PT15

Inscriptions: No. RA107, "Ciudad del Nino es . . . mi vida." No. RA108, "Feliz Navidad." No. RA109, "Feliz Ano Nuevo." No. RA110, "Gracias."

1985, Dec. 10 Litho. *Perf. 13½x13*

RA107	PT15	2c multi	.25	.25
RA108	PT15	2c multi	.25	.25
RA109	PT15	2c multi	.25	.25
RA110	PT15	2c multi	.25	.25
a.		Block of 4, #RA107-RA110	1.00	

Tax for Children's Village. A souvenir sheet, perf. and imperf., sold for 2b, with designs of Nos. RA107-RA110. Value, each $14.

Children's Village, 20th Anniv. — PT16

Inscriptions and Embera, Cuna, Embera and Guaymies tribal folk figures: No. RA111, "1966-1986." No. RA112, "Ciudad del Nino es . . . mi vida." No. RA113, "20 anos de fundacion." No. RA114, "Gracias."

1986, Nov. 1 Litho. *Perf. 13½*

RA111	PT16	2c multi	.40	.40
RA112	PT16	2c multi	.40	.40
RA113	PT16	2c multi	.40	.40
RA114	PT16	2c multi	.40	.40
		Nos. RA111-RA114 (4)	1.60	1.60

Nos. RA111-RA114 obligatory on all mail through Nov., Dec. and Jan.; tax for Children's Village. Printed se-tenant. Sheets of 4 exist perf. and imperf. Sold for 2b. Sheet exists, perf and imperf, with one 58x68mm 2b stamp showing similar characters. Value $6.75 each.

PAPUA NEW GUINEA

'pa-pyə-wə 'nü 'gi-nē

LOCATION — Eastern half of island of New Guinea, north of Australia

GOVT. — Independent state in British Commonwealth.

AREA — 185,136 sq. mi.

POP. — 4,705,126 (1999 est.)

CAPITAL — Port Moresby

In 1884 a British Protectorate was proclaimed over this part of the island, called "British New Guinea." In 1905 the administration was transferred to Australia and in 1906 the name was changed to Territory of Papua.

In 1949 the administration of Papua and New Guinea was unified, as the 1952 issue indicates. In 1972 the name was changed to Papua New Guinea. In 1973 came self-government, followed by independence on September 16, 1975.

Issues of 1925-39 for the mandated Territory of New Guinea are listed under New Guinea.

12 Pence = 1 Shilling
20 Shillings = 1 Pound
100 Cents = 1 Dollar (1966)
100 Toea = 1 Kina (1975)

Catalogue values for unused stamps in this country are for Never Hinged items, beginning with Scott 122 in the regular postage section and Scott J1 in the postage due section.

Watermarks

Wmk. 13 — Crown and Double-Lined A

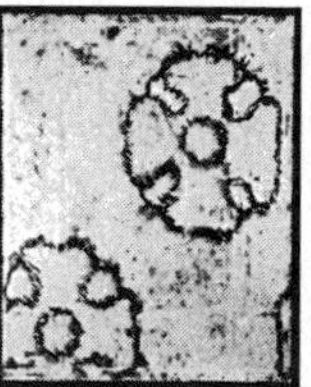

Wmk. 47 — Multiple Rosette

Wmk. 74 — Crown and Single-Lined A Sideways

Wmk. 228 — Small Crown and C of A Multiple

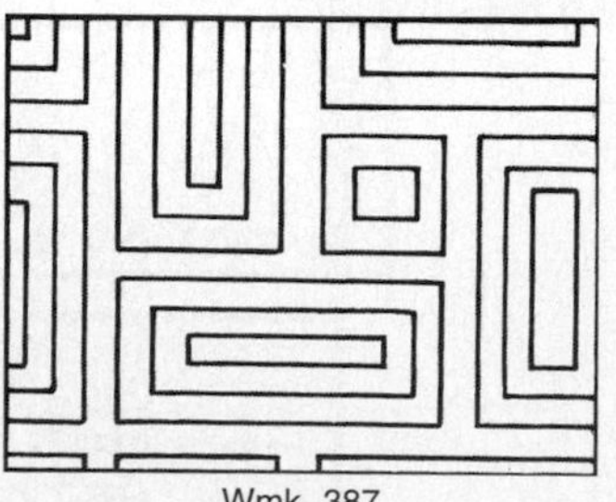

Wmk. 387

British New Guinea

Lakatoi — A1

Wmk. 47

1901, July 1 Engr. *Perf. 14*

Center in Black

1	A1	½p yellow green	24.00	6.00
2	A1	1p carmine	11.00	5.50
3	A1	2p violet	13.50	7.50
4	A1	2½p ultra	32.50	12.00
5	A1	4p black brown	40.00	40.00
6	A1	6p dark green	65.00	40.00
7	A1	1sh orange	65.00	*75.00*
8	A1	2sh6p brown ('05)	700.00	*700.00*
		Nos. 1-8 (8)	951.00	*886.00*

The paper varies in thickness and the watermark is found in two positions, with the greater width of the rosette either horizontal or vertical.

For overprints see Nos. 11-26.

Papua

Stamps of British New Guinea, Overprinted

Large Overprint

1906, Nov. 8 Wmk. 47 *Perf. 14*

Center in Black

11	A1	½p yellow green	10.00	*25.00*
12	A1	1p carmine	20.00	*22.50*
13	A1	2p violet	16.00	5.00
14	A1	2½p ultra	10.00	*18.00*
15	A1	4p black brown	250.00	160.00
16	A1	6p dark green	47.50	*50.00*
17	A1	1sh orange	30.00	*50.00*
18	A1	2sh6p brown	225.00	*240.00*
		Nos. 11-18 (8)	608.50	*570.50*

Small Overprint

1907 Center in Black

19	A1	½p yel grn	22.50	*27.50*
a.		Double overprint	3,500.	
20	A1	1p carmine	10.00	*7.50*
a.		Vertical overprint, up	7,500.	4,500.
21	A1	2p violet	7.00	4.00
a.		Double overprint	4,250.	
22	A1	2½p ultra	19.00	*24.00*
a.		Double overprint		
23	A1	4p blk brn	50.00	*70.00*
24	A1	6p dk grn	50.00	*55.00*
a.		Double overprint	6,500.	*12,000.*
25	A1	1sh orange	50.00	*60.00*
a.		Double overprint	*20,000.*	*13,000.*
26	A1	2sh6p brown	60.00	*75.00*
b.		Vert. ovpt., down	*8,500.*	
d.		Double horiz. ovpt.		4,500.
		Nos. 19-26 (8)	273.50	*323.00*

A2

Small "PAPUA"

Perf. 11, 12½

1907-08 Litho. Wmk. 13

Center in Black

28	A2	1p carmine ('08)	7.50	*5.75*
29	A2	2p violet ('08)	25.00	8.00
30	A2	2½p ultra ('08)	16.00	*9.00*
31	A2	4p black brown	9.00	*15.00*
32	A2	6p dk green ('08)	17.50	*18.50*
33	A2	1sh orange ('08)	50.00	*32.50*
		Nos. 28-33 (6)	125.00	*88.75*

Perf. 12½

30a	A2	2½p	180.00	*190.00*
31a	A2	4p	13.00	*13.00*
33a	A2	1sh	77.50	*100.00*
		Nos. 30a-33a (3)	270.50	*303.00*

1909-10 Wmk. Sideways

Center in Black

34	A2	½p yellow green	5.50	*6.50*
a.		Perf. 11x12½	5,000.	*5,000.*
b.		Perf. 11	6.00	*7.50*
35	A2	1p carmine	10.00	*14.00*
a.		Perf. 11	11.00	9.25
36	A2	2p violet ('10)	8.50	*15.00*
a.		Perf. 11x12½	1,700.	
b.		Perf. 11	25.00	*10.50*
37	A2	2½p ultra ('10)	7.00	*26.00*
a.		Perf. 12½	13.00	*45.00*
38	A2	4p black brn ('10)	8.50	*12.00*
a.		Perf. 11x12½	15,000.	
39	A2	6p dark green	15.00	22.50
a.		Perf. 12½	5,500.	*13,000.*
40	A2	1sh orange ('10)	30.00	*60.00*
a.		Perf. 11	85.00	*95.00*
		Nos. 34-40 (7)	84.50	*156.00*

One stamp in each sheet has a white line across the upper part of the picture which is termed the "rift in the clouds."

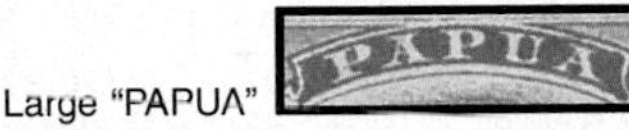

Large "PAPUA"

2sh6p:

Type I — The numerals are thin and irregular. The body of the "6" encloses a large spot of color. The dividing stroke is thick and uneven.

Type II — The numerals are thick and well formed. The "6" encloses a narrow oval of color. The dividing stroke is thin and sharp.

1910 Wmk. 13

Center in Black

41	A2	½p yellow green	7.00	*13.00*
42	A2	1p carmine	15.00	13.00
43	A2	2p violet	12.50	*9.00*
44	A2	2½p blue violet	10.00	*22.50*
45	A2	4p black brown	13.50	*14.00*
46	A2	6p dark green	11.00	*11.00*
47	A2	1sh orange	18.00	*22.50*
48	A2	2sh6p brown, type II	70.00	*75.00*
a.		Type I	55.00	*60.00*
		Nos. 41-48 (8)	157.00	*180.00*

Wmk. Sideways

49	A2	2sh6p choc, type I	85.00	*100.00*

1911 Typo. Wmk. 74 Perf. 12½

50	A2	½p yellow green	1.25	*4.00*
51	A2	1p lt red	1.50	2.00
52	A2	2p lt violet	3.50	2.00
53	A2	2½p ultra	6.50	*11.00*
54	A2	4p olive green	4.75	*18.00*
55	A2	6p orange brown	5.00	*6.50*
56	A2	1sh yellow	14.00	*20.00*
57	A2	2sh6p rose	46.00	*50.00*
		Nos. 50-57 (8)	82.50	*113.50*

For surcharges see Nos. 74-79.

1915, June Perf. 14

59	A2	1p light red	18.00	3.00

A3

1916-31

60	A3	½p pale yel grn & myr grn ('19)	1.50	2.00
61	A3	1p rose red & blk	3.50	1.50
62	A3	1½p yel brn & gray bl ('25)	2.50	1.00
63	A3	2p red vio & vio brn ('19)	3.75	1.50
64	A3	2p red brn & vio brn ('31)	4.00	1.50
a.		2p cop red & vio brn ('31)	29.00	2.25
65	A3	2½p ultra & dk grn ('19)	6.25	*17.50*
66	A3	3p emerald & blk	4.75	4.00
a.		3p dp bl grn & blk	5.75	9.25
67	A3	4p org & lt brn ('19)	5.75	7.00
68	A3	5p ol brn & sl ('31)	6.25	*20.00*
69	A3	6p vio & dl vio ('23)	6.00	*12.00*
70	A3	1sh ol grn & dk brn ('19)	10.00	*12.00*
71	A3	2sh6p rose & red brn ('19)	27.50	*47.50*
72	A3	5sh dp grn & blk	55.00	*60.00*
73	A3	10sh gray bl & grn ('25)	175.00	*200.00*
		Nos. 60-73 (14)	311.75	*387.50*

Type A3 is a redrawing of type A2. The lines of the picture have been strengthened, making it much darker, especially the sky and water.

See Nos. 92-93. For surcharges & overprints see Nos. 88-91, O1-O10.

Stamps of 1911 Surcharged

1917 Perf. 12½

74	A2	1p on ½p yellow grn	1.75	*1.90*
75	A2	1p on 2p lt violet	14.50	*17.50*
76	A2	1p on 2½p ultra	1.50	*4.50*
77	A2	1p on 4p olive green	2.10	*5.25*
78	A2	1p on 6p org brn	10.00	*20.00*
79	A2	1p on 2sh6p rose	2.25	*7.00*
		Nos. 74-79 (6)	32.10	*56.15*

No. 62 Surcharged

1931, Jan. 1 Perf. 14

88	A3	2p on 1½p yellow brn & gray blue	1.75	*2.75*

Nos. 70, 71 and 72 Surcharged in Black

1931

89	A3	5p on 1sh #70	2.50	*4.25*
90	A3	9p on 2sh6p #71	10.00	*18.00*
91	A3	1sh3p on 5sh #72	6.00	*10.50*
		Nos. 89-91 (3)	18.50	*32.75*

Type of 1916 Issue

1932 Wmk. 228 Perf. 11

92	A3	9p dp violet & gray	9.50	*37.50*
93	A3	1sh3p pale bluish grn & grayish vio	14.50	*37.50*

For overprints see Nos. O11-O12.

Motuan Girl — A5

Bird of Paradise and Boar's Tusk — A6

Mother and Child — A7

Papuan Motherhood — A8

Dubu (Ceremonial Platform) — A9

Fire Maker — A10

Designs: 1p, Steve, son of Oala. 1½p, Tree houses. 3p, Papuan dandy. 5p, Masked dancer. 9p, Shooting fish. 1sh3p, Lakatoi. 2sh, Delta art. 2sh6p, Pottery making. 5sh, Sgt.-Major Simoi. £1, Delta house.

Unwmk.

1932, Nov. 14 Engr. Perf. 11

94	A5	½p orange & blk	3.50	3.75
95	A5	1p yel grn & blk	3.00	.70
96	A5	1½p red brn & blk	3.50	*9.25*
97	A6	2p light red	12.50	.35
98	A5	3p blue & blk	3.75	*7.50*
99	A7	4p olive green	9.00	*11.00*
100	A5	5p grnsh sl & blk	6.00	3.50
101	A8	6p bister brown	8.50	6.25
102	A5	9p lilac & blk	11.50	*24.00*
103	A9	1sh bluish gray	8.00	*9.75*
104	A5	1sh3p brown & blk	19.00	*29.00*
105	A5	2sh bluish slate & blk	19.00	*26.00*
106	A5	2sh6p rose lilac & blk	29.00	*42.50*
107	A5	5sh olive & blk	70.00	62.50
108	A10	10sh gray lilac	150.00	120.00
109	A5	£1 lt gray & black	275.00	180.00
		Nos. 94-109 (16)	631.25	*536.05*

For overprints see Nos. 114-117.

Hoisting Union Jack at Port Moresby A21

H. M. S. "Nelson" at Port Moresby A22

1934, Nov. 6

110	A21	1p dull green	2.00	*3.50*
111	A22	2p red brown	2.00	*3.00*
112	A21	3p blue	2.00	*3.00*
113	A22	5p violet brown	12.00	*20.00*
		Nos. 110-113 (4)	18.00	*29.50*
		Set, never hinged	27.50	

Declaration of British Protection, 50th anniv.

Silver Jubilee Issue

Stamps of 1932 Issue Overprinted in Black

a

b

1935, July 9 Glazed Paper

114	A5(a)	1p yellow grn & blk	1.20	*4.00*
115	A6(b)	2p light red	3.50	*5.00*
116	A5(a)	3p lt blue & blk	2.25	*4.00*
117	A5(a)	5p grnsh slate & blk	2.25	*4.00*
		Nos. 114-117 (4)	9.20	*17.00*
		Set, never hinged	16.50	

25th anniv. of the reign of George V.

Coronation Issue

King George VI — A22a

Unwmk.

1937, May 14 Engr. Perf. 11

118	A22a	1p green	.40	.25
119	A22a	2p salmon rose	.40	*1.50*
120	A22a	3p blue	.40	*1.50*
121	A22a	5p brown violet	.40	*2.00*
		Nos. 118-121 (4)	1.60	*5.25*
		Set, never hinged	2.50	

Catalogue values for unused stamps in this section, from this point to the end of the section, are for Never Hinged items.

Papua and New Guinea

Tree-climbing Kangaroo A23

Kiriwina Chief's House A24

Copra Making A25

Designs: 1p, Buka head-dress. 2p, Youth. 2½p, Bird of paradise. 3p, Policeman. 3½p, Chimbu headdress. 7½p, Kiriwina yam house. 1sh, Trading canoe. 1sh6p, Rubber tapping. 2sh, Shields and spears. 2sh6p, Plumed shepherd. 10sh, Map. £1, Spearing fish.

Unwmk.

1952, Oct. 30 Engr. Perf. 14

122	A23	½p blue green	.30	.25
123	A23	1p chocolate	.25	.25
124	A23	2p deep ultra	.75	.25
125	A23	2½p orange	3.50	.60
126	A23	3p dark green	.85	.25
127	A23	3½p dk carmine	.85	.25
128	A24	6½p vio brown	2.25	.25
129	A24	7½p dp ultra	5.00	2.50
130	A25	9p chocolate	4.75	.75
131	A25	1sh yellow green	3.50	.25
132	A24	1sh6p dark green	8.50	1.50
133	A24	2sh deep blue	7.50	.25
134	A25	2sh6p dk red brown	7.00	.75
135	A25	10sh gray black	50.00	16.00
136	A24	£1 chocolate	65.00	20.00
		Nos. 122-136 (15)	160.00	44.10
		Set, hinged	85.00	

See #139-141. For surcharges & overprints see #137-138, 147, J1-J3, J5-J6.

Nos. 125 and 131 Surcharged with New Values and Bars

1957, Jan. 29 Perf. 14

137	A23	4p on 2½p orange	.85	.35
138	A25	7p on 1sh yellow green	1.75	.45

Type of 1952 and

Klinki Plymill A26

Designs: 3½p, Chimbu headdress. 4p, 5p, Cacao. 8p, Klinki Plymill. 1sh7p, Cattle. 2sh5p, Cattle. 5sh, Coffee, vert.

1958-60 Engr. Perf. 14

139	A23	3½p black	7.00	2.00
140	A23	4p vermilion	1.25	.25
141	A23	5p green ('60)	1.50	.25

142 A26 7p gray green 11.00 .25
143 A26 8p dk ultra ('60) 2.50 2.00
144 A26 1sh7p red brown 30.00 16.00
145 A26 2sh5p vermilion ('60) 6.00 2.50
146 A26 5sh gray olive & brn red 11.00 2.10
Nos. 139-146 (8) 70.25 25.35

Issued: June 2, 1958, Nov. 10, 1960.
For surcharge see No. J4.

No. 122 Surcharged with New Value

1959, Dec. 1
147 A23 5p on ½p blue green .85 .25

Council Chamber and Frangipani Flowers A27

1961, Apr. 10 Photo. *Perf. 14½x14*
148 A27 5p green & yellow .80 .35
149 A27 2sh3p grn & salmon 8.00 4.00

Reconstitution of the Legislative Council.

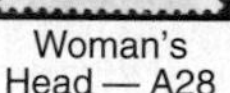

Woman's Head — A28

Red-plumed Bird of Paradise — A29

Port Moresby Harbor A30

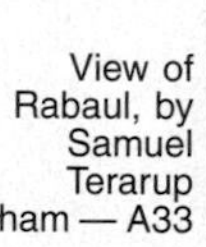

Constable Ragas Amis Matia, Port Moresby A32

View of Rabaul, by Samuel Terarup Cham — A33

Woman Dancer A31

Elizabeth II A34

Designs: 3p, Man's head. 6p, Golden opossum. 2sh, Male dancer with drum. 2sh3p, Piaggio transport plane landing at Tapini.

Perf. 14 (A28, A31, A32), 11½ (A29, A33), 14x13½ (A30), 14½ (A34)

1961-63 Engr. Unwmk.
153 A28 1p dk carmine .70 .25
154 A28 3p bluish black .45 .25

Photo.

155 A29 5p lt brn, red brn, blk & yel .50 .25
156 A29 6p gray, ocher & slate .75 1.25

Engr.

157 A30 8p green .30 .25
158 A31 1sh gray green 4.75 .90
159 A31 2sh rose lake 1.50 .45
160 A30 2sh3p dark blue .90 .40
161 A32 3sh green 2.25 2.00

Photo.

162 A33 10sh multicolored 16.50 13.00
163 A34 £1 brt grn, blk & gold 9.00 8.50
Nos. 153-163 (11) 37.60 27.50

The 5p and 6p are on granite paper.
Issued: 3sh, 9/5/62; 10sh, 2/13/63: 5p, 6p, 3/27/63; 8p, 2sh3p, 5/8/63; £1, 7/3/63; others, 7/26/61.

Malaria Eradication Emblem — A35

1962, Apr. 7 Litho. *Perf. 14*
164 A35 5p lt blue & maroon 1.25 .50
165 A35 1sh lt brown & red 2.25 .75
166 A35 2sh yellow green & blk 2.75 *3.25*
Nos. 164-166 (3) 6.25 4.50

WHO drive to eradicate malaria.

Map of Australia and South Pacific A36

1962, July 9 Engr. Unwmk.
167 A36 5p dk red & lt grn 1.75 .30
168 A36 1sh6p dk violet & yel 2.75 1.00
169 A36 2sh6p green & lt blue 2.75 2.25
Nos. 167-169 (3) 7.25 3.55

5th So. Pacific Conf., Pago Pago, July 1962.

High Jump — A37

1962, Oct. 24 Photo. *Perf. 11½*
Size: 26x21mm
Granite Paper

171 A37 5p shown .50 .30
172 A37 5p Javelin .50 .30

Size: 32½x22½mm

173 A37 2sh3p runners 2.50 2.00
Nos. 171-173 (3) 3.50 2.60

British Empire and Commonwealth Games, Perth, Australia, Nov. 22-Dec. 1.
Nos. 171 and 172 printed in alternating horizontal rows in sheet.

Red Cross Centenary Emblem — A38

1963, May 1 *Perf. 13½*
174 A38 5p blue grn, gray & red .60 .25

Games Emblem — A38a

1963, Aug. 14 Engr. *Perf. 13½x14*
176 A38a 5p olive bister .25 .25
177 A38a 1sh green .75 .25

So. Pacific Games, Suva, Aug. 29-Sept. 7.

Top of Wooden Shield — A39

Various Carved Heads.

Perf. 11½

1964, Feb. 5 Unwmk. Photo.
Granite Paper

178 A39 11p multicolored .60 .25
179 A39 2sh5p multicolored .65 *1.75*
180 A39 2sh6p multicolored .75 .25
181 A39 5sh multicolored .90 .25
Nos. 178-181 (4) 2.90 2.50

Casting Ballot — A40

1964, Mar. 4 Unwmk. *Perf. 11½*
Granite Paper

182 A40 5p dk brn & pale brn .25 .25
183 A40 2sh3p dk brn & lt bl .80 .50

First Common Roll elections.

A41

Designs: 5p, Patients at health center clinic. 8p, Dentist and school child patient. 1sh, Nurse holding infant. 1sh2p, Medical student using microscope.

1964, Aug. 5 Engr. *Perf. 14*
184 A41 5p violet .25 .25
185 A41 8p green .25 .25
186 A41 1sh deep ultra .25 .25
187 A41 1sh2p rose brown .40 .40
Nos. 184-187 (4) 1.15 1.15

Territorial health services.

A42

Designs: 1p, Striped gardener bower birds. 3p, New Guinea regent bower birds. 5p, Blue birds of paradise. 6p, Lawes six-wired birds of paradise. 8p, Sickle-billed birds of paradise. 1sh, Emperor birds of paradise. 2sh, Brown sickle-billed bird of paradise. 2sh3p, Lesser bird of paradise. 3sh, Magnificent bird of paradise. 5sh, Twelve-wired bird of paradise. 10sh, Magnificent rifle birds.

Birds in Natural Colors
Size: 21x26mm

1964-65 Unwmk. Photo. *Perf. 11½*
188 A42 1p brt cit & dk brn .55 .25
189 A42 3p gray & dk brn .65 .25
190 A42 5p sal pink & blk .70 .25
191 A42 6p pale grn & sep 1.05 .25
192 A42 8p pale lil & dk brn 1.50 .35

Size: 25x36mm

193 A42 1sh salmon & blk 1.50 .25
194 A42 2sh blue & dk brn 1.05 .40
195 A42 2sh3p lt grn & dk brn 1.05 1.10
196 A42 3sh yel & dk brn 1.05 *1.50*
197 A42 5sh lt ultra & dk brn 11.00 2.25
198 A42 10sh gray & dk blue 4.75 *11.00*
Nos. 188-198 (11) 24.85 17.85

Issued: 6p, 8p, 1sh, 10sh, 10/28/64; others, 1/20/65.

Carved Crocodile's Head — A43

Designs: Wood carvings from Sepik River Region used as ship's prows and as objects of religious veneration.

1965, Mar. 24 Photo. *Perf. 11½*
199 A43 4p multicolored .55 .25
200 A43 1sh2p gray brown, bister & dk brown 1.75 1.75
201 A43 1sh6p lil, dk brn & buff .55 .25
202 A43 4sh bl, dk vio & mar .85 .55
Nos. 199-202 (4) 3.70 2.80

"Simpson and His Donkey" by Wallace Anderson — A43a

1965, Apr. 14 *Perf. 13½x13*
203 A43a 2sh3p brt grn, sep & blk .75 .50

ANZAC issue. See note after Australia No. 387.

Urbanized Community and Stilt House — A44

Design: 1sh, Stilt house at left.

1965, July 7 Photo. *Perf. 11½*
204 A44 6p multicolored .25 .25
205 A44 1sh multicolored .25 .25

6th South Pacific Conf., Lae, July, 1965.

UN Emblem, Mother and Child A45

UN Emblem and: 1sh, Globe and orbit, vert. 2sh, Four globes in orbit, vert.

1965, Oct. 13 Unwmk. *Perf. 11½*
206 A45 6p brown, grnsh bl & dp bl .25 .25
207 A45 1sh dull pur, blue & org .25 .25
208 A45 2sh dp blue, pale grn & grn .25 .25
Nos. 206-208 (3) .75 .75

20th anniversary of the United Nations.

New Guinea Birdwing A46

Butterflies: 1c, Blue emperor, vert. 3c, White-banded map butterfly, vert. 4c, Mountain swallowtail, vert. 5c, Port Moresby terinos, vert. 12c, Blue crow. 15c, Euchenor butterfly. 20c, White-spotted parthenos. 25c, Orange Jezebel. 50c, New Guinea emperor. $1, Blue-spotted leaf-wing. $2, Paradise birdwing.

1966 Photo. *Perf. 11½*
Granite Paper

209	A46	1c sal, blk & aqua	.40	*1.00*
210	A46	3c gray grn, brn & org	.40	*1.00*
211	A46	4c multicolored	.40	*1.00*
212	A46	5c multicolored	.45	.25
213	A46	10c multicolored	.55	.30
214	A46	12c salmon & multi	2.75	2.25
215	A46	15c pale vio, dk brn & buff	1.75	.80
216	A46	20c yel bister, dk brn & yel org	.65	.25
217	A46	25c gray, blk & yel	1.40	1.25
218	A46	50c multicolored	12.00	2.00
219	A46	$1 pale blue, dk brn & dp org	3.50	2.75
220	A46	$2 multicolored	6.25	*9.00*
		Nos. 209-220 (12)	30.50	*21.85*

In 1967 Courvoisier made new plates for the $1 and $2. Stamps from these plates show many minor differences and slight variations in shade.

Issued: 12c, 10/10; others, 2/14.

Molala Harai and Paiva Streamer — A47

Myths of Elema People: 7c, Marai, the fisherman. 30c, Meavea Kivovia and the Black Cockatoo. 60c, Toivita Tapaivita (symbolic face decorations).

1966, June 8 Photo. *Perf. 11½*
Granite Paper

221	A47	2c black & carmine	.30	.25
222	A47	7c blue, blk & yel	.30	.25
223	A47	30c blk, yel grn & car	.35	.25
224	A47	60c blk, org & car	.90	.60
		Nos. 221-224 (4)	1.85	1.35

Discus — A48

1966, Aug. 31 *Perf. 11½*
Granite Paper

225	A48	5c shown	.25	.25
226	A48	10c Soccer	.30	.25
227	A48	20c Tennis	.40	.35
		Nos. 225-227 (3)	.95	.85

Second South Pacific Games, Noumea, New Caledonia, Dec. 8-18.

d'Albertis' Creeper — A49

Flowers: 10c, Tecomanthe dendrophila. 20c, Rhododendron macgregoriae. 60c, Rhododendron konori.

1966, Dec. 7 Photo. *Perf. 11½*

228	A49	5c multicolored	.30	.25
229	A49	10c multicolored	.30	.25
230	A49	20c multicolored	.75	.25
231	A49	60c multicolored	1.90	1.50
		Nos. 228-231 (4)	3.25	2.25

Book and Pen ("Fine Arts") — A50

3c, "Surveying," transit, view finder, pencil. 4c, "Civil Engineering," buildings, compass. 5c, "Science," test tubes, chemical formula. 20c, "Justice," Justitia, scales.

1967, Feb. 8 Photo. *Perf. 12½x12*

232	A50	1c orange & multi	.25	.25
233	A50	3c blue & multi	.25	.25
234	A50	4c brown & multi	.25	.25
235	A50	5c green & multi	.25	.25
236	A50	20c pink & multi	.25	.25
		Nos. 232-236 (5)	1.25	1.25

Issued to publicize the development of the University of Papua and New Guinea and the Institute of Higher Technical Education.

Leaf Beetle — A51

Beetles: 10c, Eupholus schoenherri. 20c, Sphingnotus albertisi. 25c, Cyphogastra albertisi.

1967, Apr. 12 Unwmk. *Perf. 11½*

237	A51	5c blue & multi	.40	.26
238	A51	10c lt green & multi	.55	.25
239	A51	20c rose & multi	.85	.35
240	A51	25c yellow & multi	1.20	.45
		Nos. 237-240 (4)	3.00	1.30

Hydroelectric Power — A52

Designs: 10c, Pyrethrum (Chrysanthemum cinerariaefolium). 20c, Tea. 25c, like 5c.

1967, June 28 Photo. *Perf. 12x12½*

241	A52	5c multicolored	.25	.25
242	A52	10c multicolored	.25	.25
243	A52	20c multicolored	.35	.25
244	A52	25c multicolored	.35	.25
		Nos. 241-244 (4)	1.20	1.00

Completion of part of the Laloki River Hydroelectric Works near Port Moresby, and the Hydrological Decade (UNESCO), 1965-74.

Battle of Milne Bay — A53

Designs: 5c, Soldiers on Kokoda Trail, vert. 20c, The coast watchers. 50c, Battle of the Coral Sea.

1967, Aug. 30 Unwmk. *Perf. 11½*

245	A53	2c multicolored	.25	*.45*
246	A53	5c multicolored	.25	.25
247	A53	20c multicolored	.35	.25
248	A53	50c multicolored	.90	.75
		Nos. 245-248 (4)	1.75	1.70

25th anniv. of the battles in the Pacific, which stopped the Japanese from occupying Papua and New Guinea.

Pesquet's Parrot — A54

Parrots: 5c, Fairy lory. 20c, Dusk-orange lory. 25c, Edward's fig parrot.

1967, Nov. 29 Photo. *Perf. 12*

249	A54	5c multicolored	.60	.25
250	A54	7c multicolored	.75	.90
251	A54	20c multicolored	1.15	.25
252	A54	25c multicolored	1.40	.25
		Nos. 249-252 (4)	3.90	1.65

Chimbu District Headdress — A55

Headdress from: 10c, Southern Highlands District, horiz. 20c, Western Highlands District. 60c, Chimbu District (different from 5c).

Perf. 12x12½, 12½x12
1968, Feb. 21 Photo. Unwmk.

253	A55	5c multi	.25	.25
254	A55	10c multi	.35	.25
255	A55	20c multi, horiz.	.35	.25
256	A55	60c multi	1.10	.80
		Nos. 253-256 (4)	2.05	1.55

Frogs — A56

1968, Apr. 24 Photo. *Perf. 11½*

257	A56	5c Tree	.60	.45
258	A56	10c Tree, diff.	.60	.25
259	A56	15c Swamp	.60	.25
260	A56	20c Tree, diff.	.80	.55
		Nos. 257-260 (4)	2.60	1.50

Human Rights Flame and Headdress A57

Symbolic Designs: 10c, Human Rights Flame surrounded by the world. 20c, 25c, "Universal Suffrage" in 2 abstract designs.

1968, June 26 Litho. *Perf. 14x13*

261	A57	5c black & multi	.25	.25
262	A57	10c black & multi	.25	.25
263	A57	20c black & multi	.30	.30
264	A57	25c black & multi	.30	.30
		Nos. 261-264 (4)	1.10	1.10

Issued for Human Rights Year, 1968, and to publicize free elections.

Sea Shells — A58

Designs: 1c, Ovula ovum. 3c, Strombus sinuatus. 4c, Conus litoglyphus. 5c, Conus marmoreus. 7c, Mitra mitra. 10c, Cymbiola rutila ruckeri. 12c, Phalium areola. 15c, Lambis scorpius. 20c, Tridacna squamosa. 25c, Lioconcha castrensis. 30c, Murex ramosus. 40c, Nautilus pompilius. 60c, Charonia tritonis. $1, Papustyla pulcherrima. $2, Conus gloriamaris, vert.

1968-69 Photo. *Perf. 12½x12*
Granite Paper
Size: 30x22½mm

265	A58	1c multicolored	.25	.25
266	A58	3c multicolored	.40	*1.40*
267	A58	4c multicolored	.25	*1.40*
268	A58	5c multicolored	.35	.25
269	A58	7c multicolored	.45	.25
270	A58	10c multicolored	.60	.25
271	A58	12c multicolored	1.75	*2.25*
272	A58	15c multicolored	1.80	*1.25*
273	A58	20c multicolored	1.00	.25

Size: 30x25mm
Perf. 11

274	A58	25c multicolored	1.00	*1.75*
275	A58	30c multicolored	1.00	*1.10*
276	A58	40c multicolored	1.10	*1.40*
277	A58	60c multicolored	1.00	.60
278	A58	$1 multicolored	1.60	1.00

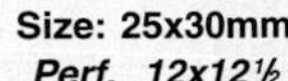

Size: 25x30mm
Perf. 12x12½

279	A58	$2 multicolored	16.00	5.50
		Nos. 265-279 (15)	28.55	18.90

Issued: 5c, 20c, 25c, 30c, 60c, 8/28/68; 3c, 10c, 15c, 40c, $1, 10/30/68; others, 1/29/69.

Legend of Tito-Iko — A59

Myths of Elema People: No. 281, 5c inscribed "Iko." No. 282, 10c inscribed "Luvuapo." No. 283, 10c inscribed "Miro."

Nos. 280, 282: Perf. 12½x13½xRoul. 9xPerf. 13½
Nos. 281, 283: Roul. 9 x Perf. 13½x12½x13½

1969, Apr. 9 Litho. Unwmk.

280		5c black, yellow & red	.25	.25
281		5c black, yellow & red	.25	.25
a.		A59 Vert. pair, #280-281	.55	*.75*
282		10c black, gray & red	.25	.25
283		10c black, gray & red	.25	.25
a.		Vert. pair, #282-283	.60	*.90*
		Nos. 280-283 (4)	1.00	1.00

Nos. 281a, 283a have continuous designs, rouletted between.

Fireball Class Sailboat, Port Moresby Harbor — A60

Designs: 10c, Games' swimming pool, Boroko, horiz. 20c, Main Games area, Konedobu, horiz.

Perf. 14x14½, 14½x14
1969, June 25 Engr.

284	A60	5c black	.25	.25
285	A60	10c bright violet	.25	.25
286	A60	20c green	.40	.30
		Nos. 284-286 (3)	.90	.80

3rd S. Pacific Games, Port Moresby, Aug. 13-23.

Dendrobium Ostrinoglossum A61

Orchids: 10c, Dendrobium lawesii. 20c, Dendrobium pseudofrigidum. 30c, Dendrobium conanthum.

1969, Aug. 27 Photo. *Perf. 11½*
Granite Paper

287	A61	5c multicolored	.70	.25
288	A61	10c multicolored	.80	.50
289	A61	20c multicolored	1.00	.80
290	A61	30c multicolored	1.10	.85
		Nos. 287-290 (4)	3.60	2.40

Issued to publicize the 6th World Orchid Conference, Sydney, Australia, Sept. 1969.

Potter — A62

1969, Sept. 24 Photo. *Perf. 11½*
Granite Paper

291 A62 5c multicolored .35 .25

50th anniv. of the ILO.

Bird of Paradise — A63

Coil Stamps

1969-71 *Perf. 14½ Horiz.*

291A A63 2c red, dp blue & blk .30 .25
292 A63 5c orange & emerald .30 .25

Issue dates: 5c, Sept. 24, 2c, Apr. 1, 1971.

Seed Pod Rattle (Tareko) — A64

Musical Instruments: 10c, Hand drum (garamut). 25c, Pan pipes (iviliko). 30c, Hourglass drum (kundu).

1969, Oct. 29 Photo. *Perf. 12½*

293 A64 5c multicolored .25 .25
294 A64 10c multicolored .25 .25
295 A64 25c multicolored .40 .35
296 A64 30c multicolored .80 .40
Nos. 293-296 (4) 1.70 1.25

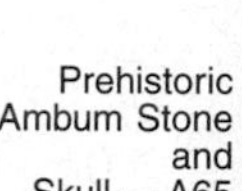

Prehistoric Ambum Stone and Skull — A65

Designs: 10c, Masawa canoe of the Kula Circuit. 25c, Map of Papua and New Guinea made by Luis Valez de Torres, 1606. 30c, H.M.S. Basilisk, 1873.

1970, Feb. 11 Photo. *Perf. 12½*

297 A65 5c violet brown & multi .25 .25
298 A65 10c ocher & multi .25 .25
299 A65 25c org brn & multi .50 .35
300 A65 30c olive green & multi 1.10 .40
Nos. 297-300 (4) 2.10 1.25

King of Saxony Bird of Paradise — A66

Birds of Paradise: 10c, King. 15c, Augusta Victoria. 25c, Multi-crested.

1970, May 13 Photo. *Perf. 11½*

301 A66 5c tan & multi .90 .25
302 A66 10c multicolored 1.10 .60
303 A66 15c lt blue & multi 1.50 1.00
304 A66 25c multicolored 2.25 .75
Nos. 301-304 (4) 5.75 2.60

Canceled to Order

Starting in 1970 or earlier, the Philatelic Bureau at Port Moresby began to sell new issues canceled to order at face value.

Douglas DC-3 and Matupi Volcano — A67

Aircraft: No. 305, DC-6B and Mt. Wilhelm. No. 306, Lockheed Mark II Electra and Mt. Yule. No. 307, Boeing 727 and Mt. Giluwe. No. 308, Fokker F27 Friendship and Manam Island Volcano. 30c, Boeing 707 and Hombom's Bluff.

1970, July 8 Photo. *Perf. 14½x14*

305 A67 5c "TAA" on tail .30 .25
306 A67 5c Striped tail .30 .25
307 A67 5c "T" on tail .30 .25
308 A67 5c Red tail .30 .25
a. Block of 4, #305-308 1.60 *2.00*
309 A67 25c multicolored .75 .40
310 A67 30c multicolored .75 .55
Nos. 305-310 (6) 2.70 1.95

Development of air service during the last 25 years between Australia and New Guinea.

Nicolaus N. de Miklouho-Maclay, Explorer, and Mask — A68

Designs: 10c, Bronislaw Kaspar Malinowski, anthropologist, and hut. 15c, Count Tommaso Salvadori, ornithologist, and cassowary. 20c, Friedrich R. Schlechter, botanist, and orchid.

1970, Aug. 19 Photo. *Perf. 11½*

311 A68 5c brown, blk & lilac .25 .25
312 A68 10c multicolored .25 .25
313 A68 15c dull lilac & multi .80 .35
314 A68 20c slate & multi .80 .35
Nos. 311-314 (4) 2.10 1.20

42nd Cong. of the Australian and New Zealand Assoc. for the Advancement of Science, Port Moresby, Aug. 17-21.

Wogeo Island Food Bowl — A69

National Handicraft: 10c, Lime pot. 15c, Aibom sago storage pot. 30c, Manus Island bowl, horiz.

1970, Oct. 28 Photo. *Perf. 12½*

315 A69 5c multicolored .30 .25
316 A69 10c multicolored .40 .25
317 A69 15c multicolored .40 .25
318 A69 30c multicolored .60 .50
Nos. 315-318 (4) 1.70 1.25

Eastern Highlands Round House — A70

Local Architecture: 7c, Milne Bay house. 10c, Purari Delta house. 40c, Sepik or Men's Spirit House.

1971, Jan. 27 Photo. *Perf. 11½*

319 A70 5c dark olive & multi .30 .25
320 A70 7c Prus blue & multi .35 *.60*
321 A70 10c deep org & multi .35 .25
322 A70 40c brown & multi .80 .75
Nos. 319-322 (4) 1.80 1.85

Spotted Cuscus — A71

Animals: 10c, Brown and white striped possum. 15c, Feather-tailed possum. 25c, Spiny anteater, horiz. 30c, Good-fellow's tree-climbing kangaroo, horiz.

1971, Mar. 31 Photo. *Perf. 11½*

323 A71 5c blue green & multi .45 .25
324 A71 10c multicolored .50 .25
325 A71 15c multicolored .75 .90
326 A71 25c dull yellow & multi 1.05 .90
327 A71 30c olive & multi 1.05 .60
Nos. 323-327 (5) 3.80 2.90

Basketball A72

1971, June 9 Litho. *Perf. 14*

328 A72 7c shown .30 .25
329 A72 14c Yachting .45 .25
330 A72 21c Boxing .45 .30
331 A72 28c Field events .45 .35
Nos. 328-331 (4) 1.65 1.15

Fourth South Pacific Games, Papeete, French Polynesia, Sept. 8-19.

Bartering Fish for Coconuts and Taro — A73

Primary industries: 9c, Man stacking yams and taro. 14c, Market scene. 30c, Farm couple tending yams.

1971, Aug. 18 Photo. *Perf. 11½*

332 A73 7c multicolored .30 .25
333 A73 9c multicolored .35 .25
334 A73 14c multicolored .50 .25
335 A73 30c multicolored .70 .50
Nos. 332-335 (4) 1.85 1.25

Siaa Dancer — A74

Designs: 9c, Urasena masked dancer. 20c, Two Siassi masked dancers, horiz. 28c, Three Siaa dancers, horiz.

1971, Oct. 27 Photo. *Perf. 11½*

336 A74 7c orange & multi .30 .25
337 A74 9c yel green & multi .35 .25
338 A74 20c bister & multi .90 .80
339 A74 28c multicolored 1.25 .95
Nos. 336-339 (4) 2.80 2.25

Papua New Guinea and Australia Arms — A75

#341, Papua New Guinea & Australia flags.

1972, Jan. 26 *Perf. 12½x12*

340 A75 7c gray blue, org & blk .30 .30
341 A75 7c gray blue, blk, red & yel .30 .30
a. Pair, #340-341 .75 .75

Constitutional development for the 1972 House of Assembly elections.

Papua New Guinea Map, South Pacific Commission Emblem — A76

#343, Man's head, So. Pacific Commission flag.

1972, Jan. 26

342 A76 15c brt green & multi .55 .40
343 A76 15c brt green & multi .55 .40
a. Pair, #342-343 1.50 1.50

South Pacific Commission, 25th anniv.

Pitted-shelled Turtle — A77

Designs: 14c, Angle-headed agamid. 21c, Green python. 30c, Water monitor.

1972, Mar. 15 Photo. *Perf. 11½*

344 A77 7c multicolored .40 .25
345 A77 14c car rose & multi 1.10 1.00
346 A77 21c yellow & multi 1.10 1.10
347 A77 30c yel green & multi 1.40 1.00
Nos. 344-347 (4) 4.00 3.35

Curtiss Seagull MF 6 and Ship — A78

14c, De Havilland 37 & porters from gold fields. 20c, Junkers G 31 & heavy machinery. 25c, Junkers F 13 & Lutheran mission church.

1972, June 7 Granite Paper

348 A78 7c dp yellow & multi .25 .25
349 A78 14c dp orange & multi .65 1.00
350 A78 20c olive & multi 1.10 1.00
351 A78 25c multicolored 1.25 1.00
Nos. 348-351 (4) 3.25 3.25

50th anniv. of aviation in Papua New Guinea.

National Day Unity Emblem — A79

Designs: 10c, Unity emblem and kundu (drum). 30c, Unity emblem and conch.

1972, Aug. 16 *Perf. 12x12½*

352 A79 7c violet blue & multi .30 .25
353 A79 10c orange & multi .40 .30
354 A79 30c vermilion & multi .60 .55
Nos. 352-354 (3) 1.30 1.10

National Day, Sept. 15, 1972.

Rev. Copland King — A80

Pioneering Missionaries: No. 356, Pastor Ruatoka. No. 357, Bishop Stanislaus Henry Verjus. No. 358, Rev. Dr. Johannes Flierl.

1972, Oct. 25 Photo. *Perf. 11½*

355	A80	7c dark blue & multi	.35	.35
356	A80	7c dark red & multi	.35	.35
357	A80	7c dark green & multi	.35	.35
358	A80	7c dark olive bister & multi	.35	.35
		Nos. 355-358 (4)	1.40	1.40

Christmas 1972.

Relay Station on Mt. Tomavatur — A81

1973, Jan. 24 Photo. *Perf. 12½*

359		7c shown	.30	.25
360		7c Mt. Kerigomna	.30	.25
361		7c Sattelburg	.30	.25
362		7c Wideru	.30	.25
a.	A81	Block of 4, #359-362	1.40	1.40
		Complete booklet, 3 each #359, 361, 2 each #360, 362	—	
363	A81	9c Teleprinter	.35	.25
364	A81	30c Map of network	1.25	.85
		Nos. 359-364 (6)	2.80	2.10

Telecommunications development 1968-1972. No. 362a has a unifying frame.

Queen Carol's Bird of Paradise — A82

Birds of Paradise: 14c, Goldie's. 21c, Ribbon-tailed astrapia. 28c, Princess Stephanie's.

1973, Mar. 30 Photo. *Perf. 11½*

Size: 22½x38mm

365	A82	7c citron & multi	1.00	.45
366	A82	14c dull green & multi	2.50	1.25

Size: 17x48mm

367	A82	21c lemon & multi	3.00	1.75
368	A82	28c lt blue & multi	4.00	2.50
		Nos. 365-368 (4)	10.50	5.95

Wood Carver, Milne Bay — A83

Designs: 3c, Wig makers, Southern Highlands. 5c, Bagana Volcano, Bougainville. 6c, Pig Exchange, Western Highlands. 7c, Coastal village, Central District. 8c, Arawe mother, West New Britain. 9c, Fire dancers, East New Britain. 10c, Tifalmin hunter, West Sepik District. 14c, Crocodile hunters, Western District. 15c, Mt. Elimbari, Chimbu. 20c, Canoe racing, Manus District. 21c, Making sago, Gulf District. 25c, Council House, East Sepik. 28c, Menyamya bowmen, Morobe. 30c, Shark snaring, New Ireland. 40c, Fishing canoes, Madang. 60c, Women making tapa cloth, Northern District. $1, Asaro mudmen, Eastern Highlands. $2, Sing festival, Enga District.

1973-74 Photo. *Perf. 11½*

Granite Paper

369	A83	1c multicolored	.25	.25
370	A83	3c multi ('74)	.35	.25
371	A83	5c multicolored	.75	.25
372	A83	6c multi ('74)	1.00	*2.00*
373	A83	7c multicolored	.30	.25
374	A83	8c multi ('74)	.35	.30
375	A83	9c multicolored	.40	.25
376	A83	10c multi ('74)	.60	.25
377	A83	14c multicolored	.45	*.90*
378	A83	15c multicolored	.75	.35
379	A83	20c multi ('74)	1.00	.45
380	A83	21c multicolored	.50	*1.25*
381	A83	25c multicolored	.50	*.60*
382	A83	28c multicolored	.50	*1.25*
383	A83	30c multicolored	.60	.60
385	A83	40c multicolored	.50	.50
386	A83	60c multi ('74)	.60	.75
387	A83	$1 multi ('74)	.85	1.50
388	A83	$2 multi ('74)	3.50	*6.50*
		Nos. 369-383,385-388 (19)	13.75	18.45

Issued: 1c, 7c, 9c, 15c, 25c, 40c, 6/13; 5c, 14c, 21c, 28c, 30c, Aug.; 3c, 8c, 10c, 20c, 60c, $1, 1/23/74.

Papua New Guinea No. 7 — A84

1c, Ger. New Guinea #1-2. 6c, Ger, New Guinea #17. 7c, New Britain #43. 25c, New Guinea #1. 30c, Papua New Guinea #108.

Litho. (1c, 7c); Litho. & Engr. (others)

1973, Oct. 24 *Perf. 13½x14*

Size: 54x31mm

389	A84	1c gold, brn, grn & blk	.25	.25
390	A84	6c silver, blue & indigo	.30	.25
391	A84	7c gold, red, blk & buff	.30	.25

Perf. 14x14½

Size: 45x38mm

392	A84	9c gold, org, blk & brn	.40	.35
393	A84	25c gold & orange	.75	*.90*
394	A84	30c silver & dp lilac	.80	*1.00*
		Nos. 389-394 (6)	2.80	3.00

75th anniv. of stamps in Papua New Guinea.

Masks — A85

1973, Dec. 5 Photo. *Perf. 12½*

Granite Paper

395	A85	7c multicolored	.35	.25
396	A85	10c violet blue & multi	.65	.65

Self-government.

Queen Elizabeth II A86

1974, Feb. 22 Photo. *Perf. 14x14½*

397	A86	7c dp carmine & multi	.35	.25
398	A86	30c vio blue & multi	.90	.90

Visit of Queen Elizabeth II and the Royal Family, Feb. 22-27.

Wreathed Hornbill — A87

Size of No. 400, 32½x48mm.

Perf. 12, 11½ (10c)

1974, June 12 Photo.

Granite Paper

399	A87	7c shown	1.50	.75
400	A87	10c Great cassowary	2.50	*3.25*
401	A87	30c Kapul eagle	5.50	*7.50*
		Nos. 399-401 (3)	9.50	*11.50*

Dendrobium Bracteosum — A88

Orchids: 10c, Dendrobium anosmum. 20c, Dendrobium smillieae. 30c, Dendrobium insigne.

1974, Nov. 20 Photo. *Perf. 11½*

Granite Paper

402	A88	7c dark green & multi	.95	.25
403	A88	10c dark blue & multi	.75	.60
404	A88	20c bister & multi	1.25	1.25
405	A88	30c green & multi	1.60	1.60
		Nos. 402-405 (4)	4.55	3.70

Motu Lakatoi A89

Traditional Canoes: 10c, Tami two-master morobe. 25c, Aramia racing canoe. 30c, Buka Island canoe.

1975, Feb. 26 Photo. *Perf. 11½*

Granite Paper

406	A89	7c multicolored	.30	.25
407	A89	10c orange & multi	.50	.50
408	A89	25c apple green & multi	1.00	*2.00*
409	A89	30c citron & multi	1.10	*1.25*
		Nos. 406-409 (4)	2.90	4.00

Paradise Birdwing Butterfly, 1t Coin — A90

Ornate Butterfly Cod on 2t and Plateless Turtle on 5t — A91

New coinage: 10t, Cuscus on 10t. 20t, Cassowary on 20t. 1k, River crocodiles on 1k coin with center hole; obverse and reverse of 1k.

Perf. 11, 11½ (A91)

1975, Apr. 21 Photo.

Granite Paper

410	A90	1t green & multi	.25	.25
411	A91	7t brown & multi	.40	.40
412	A90	10t violet blue & multi	.40	.40
413	A90	20t carmine & multi	.80	.80
414	A91	1k dull blue & multi	2.40	2.40
		Nos. 410-414 (5)	4.25	4.25

Ornithoptera Alexandrae — A92

Birdwing Butterflies: 10t, O. victoriae regis. 30t, O. allottei. 40t, O. chimaera.

1975, June 11 Photo. *Perf. 11½*

Granite Paper

415	A92	7t multicolored	.40	.25
416	A92	10t multicolored	.50	.50
417	A92	30t multicolored	1.60	1.60
418	A92	40t multicolored	2.00	*3.25*
		Nos. 415-418 (4)	4.50	5.60

Boxing and Games' Emblem — A93

1975, Aug. 2 Photo. *Perf. 11½*

Granite Paper

419	A93	7t shown	.35	.25
420	A93	20t Track and field	.60	.45
421	A93	25t Basketball	.65	.60
422	A93	30t Swimming	.70	*.75*
		Nos. 419-422 (4)	2.30	2.05

5th South Pacific Games, Guam, Aug. 1-10.

Map of South East Asia and Flag of PNG — A94

Design: 30t, Map of South East Asia and Papua New Guinea coat of arms.

1975, Sept. 10 Photo. *Perf. 11½*

Granite Paper

423	A94	7t red & multi	.25	.25
424	A94	30t blue & multi	.65	.65
a.		Souvenir sheet of 2, #423-424	1.40	1.40

Papua New Guinea independence, Sept. 16, 1975.

M. V. Bulolo A95

Ships of the 1930's: 15t, M.V. Macdhui. 25t, M.V. Malaita. 60t, S.S. Montoro.

1976, Jan. 21 Photo. *Perf. 11½*

Granite Paper

425	A95	7t multicolored	.25	.25
426	A95	15t multicolored	.35	.30
427	A95	25t multicolored	.65	.50
428	A95	60t multicolored	1.50	*2.00*
		Nos. 425-428 (4)	2.75	3.05

Rorovana Carvings A96

Bougainville Art: 20t, Upe hats. 25t, Kapkaps (tortoise shell ornaments). 30t, Carved canoe paddles.

1976, Mar. 17 Photo. *Perf. 11½*

Granite Paper

429	A96	7t multicolored	.30	.25
430	A96	20t blue & multi	.50	.45
431	A96	25t dp orange & multi	.60	*.90*
432	A96	30t multicolored	.75	.75
		Nos. 429-432 (4)	2.15	2.35

Houses
A97

1976, June 9 Photo. *Perf. 11½*
Granite Paper

433 A97 7t Rabaul .25 .25
434 A97 15t Aramia .30 .25
435 A97 30t Telefomin .65 .60
436 A97 40t Tapini .70 *1.25*
Nos. 433-436 (4) 1.90 2.35

Boy Scouts and Scout Emblem A98

De Havilland Sea Plane, Map of Pacific — A99

Designs: 15t, Sea Scouts on outrigger canoe, Scout emblem. 60t, Plane on water.

1976, Aug. 18 Photo. *Perf. 11½*
Granite Paper

437 A98 7t multicolored .35 .25
438 A99 10t lilac & multi .35 .25
439 A98 15t multicolored .45 .45
440 A99 60t multicolored 1.10 *1.75*
Nos. 437-440 (4) 2.25 2.70

50th anniversaries: Papua New Guinea Boy Scouts; 1st flight from Australia.

Father Ross and Mt. Hagen A100

1976, Oct. 28 Photo. *Perf. 11½*
Granite Paper

441 A100 7t multicolored .50 .25

Rev. Father William Ross (1896-1973), American missionary in New Guinea.

Clouded Rainbow Fish — A101

Tropical Fish: 15t, Imperial angelfish. 30t, Freckled rock cod. 40t, Threadfin butterflyfish.

1976, Oct. 28 Granite Paper

442 A101 5t multicolored .25 .25
443 A101 15t multicolored .70 .50
444 A101 30t multicolored 1.40 .80
445 A101 40t multicolored 1.90 1.90
Nos. 442-445 (4) 4.25 3.45

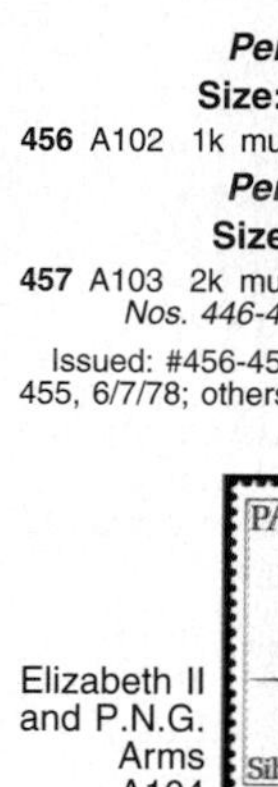

Kundiawa Man — A102

Mekeo Headdress A103

Headdresses: 5t, Masked dancer, East Sepik Province. 10t, Dancer, Koiari area. 15t, Hanuabada woman. 20t, Young woman, Orokaiva. 25t, Haus Tambaran dancer, East Sepik Province. 30t, Asaro Valley man. 35t, Garaina man, Morobe. 40t, Waghi Valley man. 50t, Trobriand dancer, Milne Bay. 1k, Wasara.

Sizes: 25x30mm (1, 5, 20t), 26x26mm (10, 15, 25, 30, 50t), 23x38mm (35, 40t)

Perf. 12 (15, 25, 30t), 11½ (others)

1977-78 Photo.

446 A102 1t multicolored .25 .25
447 A102 5t multicolored .25 .25
448 A102 10t multicolored .30 .25
449 A102 15t multicolored .30 .25
450 A102 20t multicolored .55 .25
451 A102 25t multicolored .35 .30
452 A102 30t multicolored .40 .40
453 A102 35t multicolored .65 .50
454 A102 40t multicolored .60 .30
455 A102 50t multicolored .85 *.90*

Litho.
Perf. 14½x14
Size: 28x35½mm

456 A102 1k multicolored 1.50 *1.75*

Perf. 14½x15
Size: 33x23mm

457 A103 2k multicolored 2.00 *3.25*
Nos. 446-457 (12) 8.00 8.65

Issued: #456-457, 1/12/77; #448, 450, 453, 455, 6/7/78; others, 3/29/78.

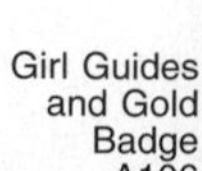

Elizabeth II and P.N.G. Arms A104

Designs: 7t, Queen and P.N.G. flag. 35t, Queen and map of P.N.G.

1977, Mar. 16 Photo. *Perf. 15x14*

462 A104 7t multicolored .35 .25
a. Silver omitted *500.00*
463 A104 15t multicolored .45 .45
464 A104 35t multicolored .75 *.90*
Nos. 462-464 (3) 1.55 1.60

25th anniv. of the reign of Elizabeth II.

Whitebreasted Ground Dove — A105

Protected Birds: 7t, Victoria crowned pigeon. 15t, Pheasant pigeon. 30t, Orange-fronted fruit dove. 50t, Banded imperial pigeon.

1977, June 8 Photo. *Perf. 11½*
Granite Paper

465 A105 5t multicolored .55 .25
466 A105 7t multicolored .55 .25
467 A105 15t multicolored .90 .85
468 A105 30t multicolored 1.25 1.25
469 A105 50t multicolored 1.75 *3.25*
Nos. 465-469 (5) 5.00 *5.85*

Girl Guides and Gold Badge A106

Designs (Girl Guides): 15t, Mapping and blue badge. 30t, Doing laundry in brook and red badge. 35t, Wearing grass skirts, cooking and green badge.

1977, Aug. 10 Litho. *Perf. 14½*

470 A106 7t multicolored .25 .25
471 A106 15t multicolored .30 .25
472 A106 30t multicolored .60 .60
473 A106 35t multicolored .60 .60
Nos. 470-473 (4) 1.75 1.70

Papua New Guinea Girl Guides, 50th anniv.

Legend of Kari Marupi — A107

Myths of Elema People: 20t, Savoripi Clan. 30t, Oa-Laea. 35t, Oa-Iriarapo.

1977, Oct. 19 Litho. *Perf. 13½*

474 A107 7t black & multi .25 .25
475 A107 20t black & multi .50 .35
476 A107 30t black & multi .65 .65
477 A107 35t black & multi .65 .65
Nos. 474-477 (4) 2.05 1.90

Blue-tailed Skink A108

Lizards: 15t, Green tree skink. 35t, Crocodile skink. 40t, New Guinea blue-tongued skink.

1978, Jan. 25 Photo. *Perf. 11½*
Granite Paper

478 A108 10t blue & multi .30 .25
479 A108 15t lilac & multi .40 .25
480 A108 35t olive & multi .60 *.75*
481 A108 40t orange & multi .85 .85
Nos. 478-481 (4) 2.15 2.10

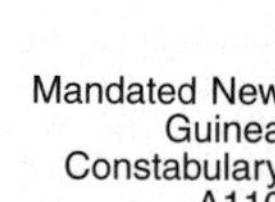

Roboastra Arika — A109

Sea Slugs: 15t, Chromodoris fidelis. 35t, Flabellina macassarana. 40t, Chromodoris trimarginata.

1978, Aug. 29 Photo. *Perf. 11½*

482 A109 10t multicolored .30 .25
483 A109 15t multicolored .40 .40
484 A109 35t multicolored .65 .65
485 A109 40t multicolored .90 *1.15*
Nos. 482-485 (4) 2.25 2.45

Mandated New Guinea Constabulary A110

Constabulary and Badge: 10t, Royal Papua New Guinea. 20t, Armed British New Guinea. 25t, German New Guinea police. 30t, Royal Papua and New Guinea.

1978, Oct. 26 Photo. *Perf. 14½x14*

486 A110 10t multicolored .25 .25
487 A110 15t multicolored .35 .35
488 A110 20t multicolored .40 .40
489 A110 25t multicolored .45 .45
490 A110 30t multicolored .55 .55
Nos. 486-490 (5) 2.00 2.00

Ocarina, Chimbu Province — A111

Musical Instruments: 20t, Musical bow, New Britain, horiz. 28t, Launut, New Ireland. 35t, Nose flute, New Hanover, horiz.

Perf. 14½x14, 14x14½

1979, Jan. 24 Litho.

491 A111 7t multicolored .30 .25
492 A111 20t multicolored .40 .30
493 A111 28t multicolored .60 .60
494 A111 35t multicolored .70 .70
Nos. 491-494 (4) 2.00 1.85

Prow and Paddle, East New Britain — A112

Canoe Prows and Paddles: 21t, Sepik war canoe. 25t, Trobriand Islands. 40t, Milne Bay.

1979, Mar. 28 Litho. *Perf. 14½*

495 A112 14t multicolored .30 .25
496 A112 21t multicolored .40 .25
497 A112 25t multicolored .55 .55
498 A112 40t multicolored .70 .70
Nos. 495-498 (4) 1.95 1.75

Belt of Shell Disks — A113

Traditional Currency: 15t, Tusk chest ornament. 25t, Shell armband. 35t, Shell necklace.

1979, June 6 Litho. *Perf. 12½x12*

499 A113 7t multicolored .25 .25
500 A113 15t multicolored .35 .30
501 A113 25t multicolored .55 .55
502 A113 35t multicolored .65 .65
Nos. 499-502 (4) 1.80 1.75

Oenetus A114

Moths: 15t, Celerina vulgaris. 20t, Alcidis aurora, vert. 25t, Phyllodes conspicillator. 30t, Nyctalemon patroclus, vert.

1979, Aug. 29 Photo. *Perf. 11½*

503 A114 7t multicolored .25 .25
504 A114 15t multicolored .40 .35
505 A114 20t multicolored .45 .45
506 A114 25t multicolored .50 *.75*
507 A114 30t multicolored .65 *.90*
Nos. 503-507 (5) 2.25 2.70

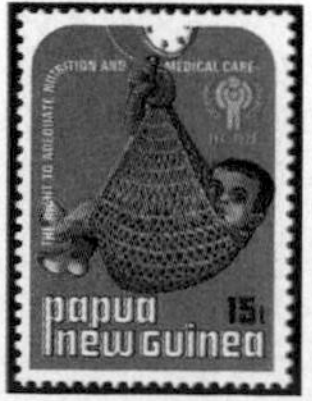

Baby in String Bag Scale — A115

IYC (Emblem and): 7t, Mother nursing baby. 30t, Boy playing with dog and ball. 60t, Girl in classroom.

1979, Oct. 24 Litho. *Perf. 14x13½*

508 A115 7t multicolored .30 .25
509 A115 15t multicolored .35 .25
510 A115 30t multicolored .45 .45
511 A115 60t multicolored .80 .80
Nos. 508-511 (4) 1.90 1.75

Mail Sorting, Mail Truck
A116

UPU Membership: 25t, Wartime mail delivery. 35t, UPU monument, airport and city. 40t, Hand canceling, letter carrier.

1980, Jan. 23 Litho. *Perf. 13½x14*

512 A116 7t multicolored .30 .25
513 A116 25t multicolored .40 .30
514 A116 35t multicolored .50 .50
515 A116 40t multicolored .65 .65
Nos. 512-515 (4) 1.85 1.70

Male Dancer, Betrothal Ceremony — A117

Third South Pacific Arts Festival, Port Moresby (Minj Betrothal Ceremony Mural): a, One dancer, orange and yellow. b, Two dancers, red, yellow & blk. c, Two dancers side by side, orange, black. d, Two dancers, one in front of the other one. e, One dancer, yellow and red.

No. 516 has continuous design.

1980, Mar. 26 Photo. *Perf. 11½*
Granite Paper

516 A117 Strip of 5 2.00 2.00
a.-e. 20t any single .30 .30

National Census — A118

1980, June 4 Litho. *Perf. 14*

517 A118 7t shown .25 .25
518 A118 15t Population symbol .25 .25
519 A118 40t P. N. G. map .55 .55
520 A118 50t Faces .75 .75
Nos. 517-520 (4) 1.80 1.80

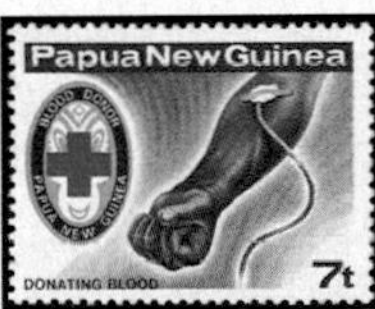

Blood Transfusion, Donor's Badge — A119

15t, Donating blood. 30t, Map of donation centers. 60t, Blood components and types.

1980, Aug. 27 Litho. *Perf. 14½*

521 A119 7t shown .25 .25
522 A119 15t multicolored .25 .25
523 A119 30t multicolored .50 .50
524 A119 60t multicolored .85 .85
Nos. 521-524 (4) 1.85 1.85

Dugong
A120

30t, Native spotted cat, vert. 35t, Tube-nosed bat, vert. 45t, Raffray's bandicoot.

1980, Oct. 29 Photo. *Perf. 11½*

525 A120 7t shown .25 .25
526 A120 30t multicolored .60 .60
527 A120 35t multicolored .70 .70
528 A120 45t multicolored .95 .95
Nos. 525-528 (4) 2.50 2.50

Beach Kingfisher — A121

1981, Jan. 21 Photo. *Perf. 12*
Granite Paper

529 A121 3t shown .30 *.45*
530 A121 7t Forest kingfisher .30 .25
531 A121 20t Sacred kingfisher .50 .50

Size: 26x45½mm

532 A121 25t White-tailed paradise kingfisher .60 .60

Size: 26x36mm

533 A121 60t Blue-winged kookaburra 1.60 *2.50*
Nos. 529-533 (5) 3.30 4.30

Mask — A122

Coil Stamps

Perf. 14½ Horiz.

1981, Jan. 21 Photo.

534 A122 2t shown .25 .25
535 A122 5t Hibiscus .25 .25

Defense Force Soldiers Firing Mortar — A123

1981, Mar. 25 Photo. *Perf. 13½x14*

536 A123 7t shown .25 .25
537 A123 15t DC-3 military plane .30 .25
538 A123 40t Patrol boat Eitape .65 .65
539 A123 50t Medics treating civilians .80 .80
Nos. 536-539 (4) 2.00 1.95

For surcharge see No. 615.

Missionary Aviation Fellowship Plane — A124

Planes of Missionary Organizations: 15t, Holy Ghost Society. 20t, Summer Institute of Linguistics. 30t, Lutheran Mission. 35t, Seventh Day Adventist.

1981, June 17 Litho. *Perf. 14*

540 A124 10t multicolored .25 .25
541 A124 15t multicolored .30 .25
542 A124 20t multicolored .40 .30
543 A124 30t multicolored .50 .50
544 A124 35t multicolored .60 .60
Nos. 540-544 (5) 2.05 1.90

Scoop Net Fishing
A125

1981, Aug. 26

545 A125 10t shown .25 .25
546 A125 15t Kite fishing .30 .30
547 A125 30t Rod fishing .55 .55
548 A125 60t Scissor net fishing 1.00 1.00
Nos. 545-548 (4) 2.10 2.10

Forcartia Buhleri
A126

15t, Naninia citrina. 20t, Papuina adonis, papuina hermione. 30t, Papustyla hindei, papustyla novaepommeraniae. 40t, Rhynchotrochus strabo.

1981, Oct. 28 Photo. *Perf. 12*
Granite Paper

549 A126 5t multicolored .25 .25
550 A126 15t multicolored .30 .30
551 A126 20t multicolored .40 .40
552 A126 30t multicolored .60 .60
553 A126 40t multicolored .75 .75
Nos. 549-553 (5) 2.30 2.30

75th Anniv. of Boy Scouts
A127

1982, Jan. 20 Photo. *Perf. 11½*
Granite Paper

554 A127 15t Lord Baden-Powell, flag raising .25 .25
555 A127 25t Leader, campfire .45 .45
556 A127 35t Scout, hut building .60 .60
557 A127 50t Percy Chatterton, first aid .90 .90
Nos. 554-557 (4) 2.20 2.20

Wanigela Pottery
A128

1982, Mar. 24 Litho. *Perf. 14*

Size: 29x29mm

558 A128 10t Boiken, East Sepik .25 .25
559 A128 20t Gumalu, Madang .40 .40

Perf. 14½

Size: 36x23mm

560 A128 40t shown .70 .70
561 A128 50t Ramu Valley, Madang .90 .90
Nos. 558-561 (4) 2.25 2.25

Nutrition
A129

1982, May 5 Litho. *Perf. 14½x14*

562 A129 10t Mother, child .25 .25
563 A129 15t Protein .35 .35
564 A129 30t Fruits, vegetables .65 .65
565 A129 40t Carbohydrates .85 .85
Nos. 562-565 (4) 2.10 2.10

Coral
A130

1982, July 21 Photo. *Perf. 11½*
Granite Paper

566 A130 1t Stylophora sp. .35 .25
567 A130 5t Acropora humilis .35 .25
568 A130 15t Distichopora sp. .75 .40
569 A130 1k Xenia sp. 3.75 2.75
Nos. 566-569 (4) 5.20 3.65

See Nos. 575-579, 588-591, 614.

Centenary of Catholic Church in Papua New Guinea — A131

a, Ship and Men, one dog. b, Men and three dogs. c, Men and tree.

1982, Sept. 15 Photo. *Perf. 11½*

570 A131 Strip of 3 1.00 1.00
a.-c. 10t any single .30 .30

12th Commonwealth Games, Brisbane, Australia, Sept. 30-Oct. 9 — A132

1982, Oct. 6 Litho. *Perf. 14½*

571 A132 10t Running .25 .25
572 A132 15t Boxing .25 .25
573 A132 45t Shooting .90 .90
574 A132 50t Lawn bowling 1.00 1.00
Nos. 571-574 (4) 2.40 2.40

Coral Type of 1982

1983, Jan. 12 Photo. *Perf. 11½*
Granite Paper

575 A130 3t Dendrophyllia .70 *1.25*
576 A130 10t Dendronephthya .90 .90
577 A130 30t Dendronephthya, diff. 1.40 .90
578 A130 40t Antipathes 1.50 1.50
579 A130 3k Distichopora 6.50 6.50
Nos. 575-579 (5) 11.00 11.05

Nos. 575-579 vert.

Commonwealth Day — A133

1983, Mar. 9 Litho. *Perf. 14*

580 A133 10t Flag, arms .25 .25
581 A133 15t Youth, recreation .25 .25
582 A133 20t Technical assistance .40 .40
583 A133 50t Export assistance .90 .90
Nos. 580-583 (4) 1.80 1.80

World Communications Year — A134

1983, Sept. 7 Litho. *Perf. 14*

584 A134 10t Mail transport .30 .25
585 A134 25t Writing & receiving letter .50 .40
586 A134 30t Telephone calls .55 .45
587 A134 60t Family reunion 1.20 .95
Nos. 584-587 (4) 2.55 2.05

Coral Type of 1982

1983, Nov. 9 Photo. *Perf. 11½*

588 A130 20t Isis sp. 1.10 .70
589 A130 25t Acropora sp. .90 .90
590 A130 35t Stylaster elegans 1.60 1.40
591 A130 45t Turbinarea sp. 2.50 1.75
Nos. 588-591 (4) 6.10 4.75

Nos. 588-591 vert.

Turtles A135

5t, Chelonia depressa. 10t, Chelonia mydas. 15t, Eretkmochelys imbricata. 20t, Lepidochelys olivacea. 25t, Caretta caretta. 40t, Dermochelys coriacea.

1984, Feb. 8 **Photo.**
Granite Paper

592 A135 5t multicolored .25 .25
593 A135 10t multicolored .30 .30
594 A135 15t multicolored .50 .50
595 A135 20t multicolored .65 .60
596 A135 25t multicolored 1.10 1.10
597 A135 40t multicolored 1.30 1.30
Nos. 592-597 (6) 4.10 4.05

Papua-Australia Airmail Service, 50th Anniv. — A136

Mail planes — 20t, Avro X VH-UXX. 25t, DH86B VH-UYU Carmania. 40t, Westland Widgeon. 60t, Consolidated Catalina NC777.

1984, May 9 **Litho.** ***Perf. 14½x14***

598 A136 20t multicolored .45 .45
599 A136 25t multicolored .55 .55
600 A136 40t multicolored 1.00 1.00
601 A136 60t multicolored 1.40 1.40
Nos. 598-601 (4) 3.40 3.40

Parliament House Opening — A137

1984, Aug. 7 **Litho.** ***Perf. 13½x14***

602 A137 10t multicolored .40 .40

Bird of Paradise A138

1984, Aug. 7 **Photo.** ***Perf. 11½***
Granite Paper

603 A138 5k multicolored 10.00 10.00

Ceremonial Shield — A139

1984, Sept. 21

604 A139 10t Central Province .25 .25
605 A139 20t West New Britain .55 .55
606 A139 30t Madang .85 .85
607 A139 50t East Sepik .90 .90
Nos. 604-607 (4) 2.55 2.55

See Nos. 677-680.

British New Guinea Proclamation Centenary — A140

1984, Nov. 6 **Litho.** ***Perf. 14½x14***

608 A140 Pair .50 .50
a. 10t Nelson, Port Moresby, 1884 .25 .25
b. 10t Port Moresby, 1984 .25 .25
609 A140 Pair 2.50 2.50
a. 45t Rabaul, 1984 1.10 1.10
b. 45t Elizabeth, Rabaul, 1884 1.10 1.10

Chimbu Gorge A142

1985, Feb. 6 **Photo.** ***Perf. 11½***

610 A142 10t Fergusson Island, vert. .25 .25
611 A142 25t Sepik River, vert. .70 .70
612 A142 40t shown 1.15 1.15
613 A142 60t Dali Beach, Vanimo 1.90 1.90
Nos. 610-613 (4) 4.00 4.00

Coral Type of 1982

1985, May 29 **Photo.** ***Perf. 11½***

614 A130 12t Dendronephthya sp. 4.50 4.50

For surcharge see No. 686.

No. 536 Surcharged

1985, Apr. 1 **Litho.** ***Perf. 13½x14***

615 A123 12t on 7t multi .75 *1.00*
a. Inverted surcharge —

Ritual Structures A143

Designs: 15t, Dubu platform, Central Province. 20t, Tamuniai house, West New Britain. 30t, Yam tower, Trobriand Island. 60t, Huli grave, Tari.

1985, May 1 ***Perf. 13x13½***

616 A143 15t multicolored .45 .45
617 A143 20t multicolored .65 .65
618 A143 30t multicolored .95 .95
619 A143 60t multicolored 1.50 1.50
Nos. 616-619 (4) 3.55 3.55

Indigenous Birds of Prey — A144

1985, Aug. 26 ***Perf. 14x14½***

620 12t Accipiter brachyurus .75 .75
621 12t In flight .75 .75
a. A144 Pair, #629-621 1.75 1.75
622 30t Megatriorchis doriae 1.25 1.25
623 30t In Flight 1.25 1.25
a. A144 Pair, #622-623 3.00 3.00
624 60t Henicopernis longicauda 2.50 2.50
625 60t In flight 2.50 2.50
a. A144 Pair, #624-625 6.00 6.00
Nos. 620-625 (6) 9.00 9.00

Flag and Gable of Parliament House, Port Moresby — A145

1985, Sept. 11 ***Perf. 14½x15***

626 A145 12t multicolored .60 .60

Post Office Centenary A146

Designs: 12t, No. 631a, 1901 Postal card, aerogramme, spectacles and inkwell. 30t, No. 631b, Queensland Type A15, No. 628. 40t, No. 631c, Plane and news clipping, 1885. 60t, No. 631d, 1892 German canceler, 1985 first day cancel.

1985, Oct. 9 ***Perf. 14½x14***

627 A146 12t multicolored .70 .70
628 A146 30t multicolored 1.75 1.75
629 A146 40t multicolored 2.40 2.40
630 A146 60t multicolored 3.00 3.00
Nos. 627-630 (4) 7.85 7.85

Souvenir Sheet

631 Sheet of 4 9.00 9.00
a. A146 12t multicolored .90 .90
b. A146 30t multicolored 1.60 1.60
c. A146 40t multicolored 2.00 2.00
d. A146 60t multicolored 3.00 3.00

Nombowai Cave Carved Funerary Totems — A147

12t, Bird Rulowlaw, headman. 30t, Barn owl Raus, headman. 60t, Melerawuk. 80t, Cockerel, woman.

1985, Nov. 13 ***Perf. 11½***

632 A147 12t multicolored .70 .30
633 A147 30t multicolored 1.40 .80
634 A147 60t multicolored 2.25 2.25
635 A147 80t multicolored 2.75 *3.75*
Nos. 632-635 (4) 7.10 7.10

Conch Shells — A148

15t, Cypraea valentia. 35t, Oliva buelowi. 45t, Oliva parkinsoni. 70t, Cypraea aurantium.

1986, Feb. 12 ***Perf. 11½***

636 A148 15t multicolored .80 .45
637 A148 35t multicolored 1.90 1.50
638 A148 45t multicolored 2.25 2.25
639 A148 70t multicolored 3.00 *4.25*
Nos. 636-639 (4) 7.95 8.45

Common Design Types pictured following the introduction.

Queen Elizabeth II 60th Birthday
Common Design Type

Designs: 15t, In ATS officer's uniform, 1945. 35t, Silver wedding anniv. portrait by Patrick Lichfield, Balmoral, 1972. 50t, Inspecting troops, Port Moresby, 1982. 60t, Banquet aboard Britannia, state tour, 1982. 70t, Visiting Crown Agents' offices, 1983.

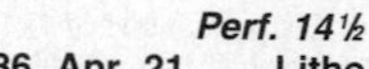
Perf. 14½

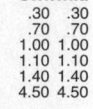

1986, Apr. 21 **Litho.** **Unwmk.**

640 CD337 15t scar, blk & sil .30 .30
641 CD337 35t ultra & multi .70 .70
642 CD337 50t green & multi 1.00 1.00
643 CD337 60t violet & multi 1.10 1.10
644 CD337 70t rose vio & multi 1.40 1.40
Nos. 640-644 (5) 4.50 4.50

AMERIPEX '86 A149

Small birds — 15t, Pitta erythrogaster. 35t, Melanocharis striativentris. 45t, Rhipidura rufifrons. 70t, Poecilodryas placens, vert.

1986, May 22 **Photo.** ***Perf. 12½***
Granite Paper

645 A149 15t multicolored 1.10 .70
646 A149 35t multicolored 2.25 1.60
647 A149 45t multicolored 2.50 2.10
648 A149 70t multicolored 3.75 3.75
Nos. 645-648 (4) 9.60 8.15

Lutheran Church, Cent. — A150

1986, July 7 **Litho.** ***Perf. 14x15***

649 A150 15t Monk, minister .60 .55
650 A150 70t Churches from 1886, 1986 2.75 2.75

Indigenous Orchids — A151

15t, Dendrobium vexillarius. 35t, Dendrobium lineale. 45t, Dendrobium johnsoniae. 70t, Dendrobium cuthbertsonii.

1986, Aug. 4 **Litho.** ***Perf. 14***

651 A151 15t multicolored 1.25 .75
652 A151 35t multicolored 2.50 1.60
653 A151 45t multicolored 2.75 2.10
654 A151 70t multicolored 3.50 3.50
Nos. 651-654 (4) 10.00 7.95

Folk Dancers — A152

1986, Nov. 12 **Litho.** ***Perf. 14***

655 A152 15t Maprik .95 .65
656 A152 35t Kiriwina 1.75 1.50
657 A152 45t Kundiawa 2.00 1.90
658 A152 70t Fasu 3.50 *3.75*
Nos. 655-658 (4) 8.20 7.80

Fish A153

17t, White-cap anemonefish. 30t, Black anemonefish. 35t, Tomato clownfish. 70t, Spine-cheek anemonefish.

Unwmk.

1987, Apr. 15 Litho. *Perf. 15*

659 A153 17t multicolored 1.00 .35
660 A153 30t multicolored 1.50 1.75
661 A153 35t multicolored 2.00 1.40
662 A153 70t multicolored 3.00 *4.00*
Nos. 659-662 (4) 7.50 7.50

For surcharges see Nos. 720, 823, 868.

Ships — A154

1t, La Boudeuse, 1768. 5t, Roebuck, 1700. 10t, Swallow, 1767. 15t, Fly, 1845. 17t, like No. 666. 20t, Rattlesnake, 1849. 30t, Vitiaz, 1871. 35t, San Pedrico, Zabre, 1606. 40t, L'Astrolabe, 1827. 45t, Neva, 1876. 60t, Caravel of Jorge De Meneses, 1526. 70t, Eendracht, 1616. 1k, Blanche, 1872. 2k, Merrie England, 1889. 3k, Samoa, 1884.

1987-88 Photo. Unwmk. *Perf. 11½*
Granite Paper

663 A154 1t multicolored .55 *1.25*
664 A154 5t multicolored 1.10 *1.50*
665 A154 10t multicolored 1.40 1.40
666 A154 15t multicolored 2.00 1.00
667 A154 17t multicolored 2.00 .75
668 A154 20t multicolored 2.00 1.00
669 A154 30t multicolored 2.00 2.00
670 A154 35t multicolored .75 *.90*
671 A154 40t multicolored 2.25 2.25
672 A154 45t multicolored .90 .90
673 A154 60t multicolored 2.75 2.75
674 A154 70t multicolored 2.25 2.25
675 A154 1k multicolored 2.75 2.75
676 A154 2k multicolored 4.25 4.25
676A A154 3k multicolored 5.25 *7.50*
Nos. 663-676A (15) 32.20 32.45

Issued: 5, 35, 45, 70t, 2k, 6/15/87; 15, 20, 40, 60t, 2/17/88; 17t, 1k, 3/1/88; 1, 10, 30t, 3k, 11/16/88.

See Nos. 960-963. For surcharge see No. 824.

Shield Type of 1984

War shields — 15t, Elema shield, Gulf Province, c. 1880. 35t, East Sepik Province. 45t, Simbai region, Madang Province. 70t, Telefomin region, West Sepik.

Perf. 11½x12

1987, Aug. 19 Photo. Unwmk.

677 A139 15t multicolored .30 .30
678 A139 35t multicolored .70 .70
679 A139 45t multicolored .90 .90
680 A139 70t multicolored 1.40 1.40
Nos. 677-680 (4) 3.30 3.30

Starfish A156

17t, Protoreaster nodosus. 35t, Gomophia egeriae. 45t, Choriaster granulatus. 70t, Neoferdina ocellata.

1987, Sept. 30 Litho. *Perf. 14*

682 A156 17t multicolored .75 .40
683 A156 35t multicolored 1.50 .90
684 A156 45t multicolored 1.75 1.10
685 A156 70t multicolored 2.25 *3.50*
Nos. 682-685 (4) 6.25 5.90

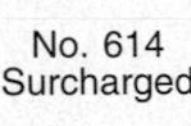

No. 614 Surcharged

1987, Sept. 23 Photo. *Perf. 11½*
Granite Paper

686 A130 15t on 12t multi 1.60 1.25

Aircraft A157

Designs: 15t, Cessna Stationair 6, Rabaraba Airstrip. 35t, Britten-Norman Islander over Hombrum Bluff. 45t, DHC Twin Otter over the Highlands. 70t, Fokker F28 over Madang.

Unwmk.

1987, Nov. 11 Litho. *Perf. 14*

687 A157 15t multicolored 1.25 .45
688 A157 35t multicolored 1.75 1.00
689 A157 45t multicolored 2.00 1.25
690 A157 70t multicolored 3.00 *4.25*
Nos. 687-690 (4) 8.00 6.95

Royal Papua New Guinea Police Force, Cent. — A158

Historic and modern aspects of the force: 17t, Motorcycle constable and pre-independence officer wearing a lap-lap. 35t, Sir William McGregor, Armed Native Constabulary founder, 1890, and recruit. 45t, Badges. 70t, Albert Hahl, German official credited with founding the island's police movement in 1888, and badge, early officer.

Perf. 14x15

1988, June 15 Litho. Unwmk.

691 A158 17t multicolored .60 .45
692 A158 35t multicolored 1.10 .85
693 A158 45t multicolored 1.40 1.10
694 A158 70t multicolored 2.00 2.00
Nos. 691-694 (4) 5.10 4.40

Sydney Opera House and a Lakatoi (ship) — A159

Fireworks and Globes — A160

1988, July 30 Litho. *Perf. 13½*

695 A159 35t multicolored .90 .90
696 A160 Pair 2.00 2.00
a.-b. 35t any single .90 .90
c. Souvenir sheet of 2, #a.-b. 2.75 2.75

SYDPEX '88, Australia (No. 695); Australia bicentennial (No. 696).

World Wildlife Fund A161

Metamorphosis of a Queen Alexandra's birdwing butterfly — 5t, Courtship. 17t, Ovipositioning and larvae, vert. 25t, Emergence from pupa, vert. 35t, Adult male on leaf.

1988, Sept. 19 *Perf. 14½*

697 A161 5t multicolored *2.50* *2.00*
698 A161 17t multicolored *3.75* *1.25*
699 A161 25t multicolored *4.25* *3.50*
700 A161 35t multicolored *5.50* *4.50*
Nos. 697-700 (4) *16.00* *11.25*

1988 Summer Olympics, Seoul A162

1988, Sept. 19 Litho. *Perf. 13½*

701 A162 17t Running .75 .75
702 A162 45t Weight lifting 1.50 1.50

Rhododendrons A163

Wmk. 387

1989, Jan. 25 Litho. *Perf. 14*

703 A163 3t R. zoelleri .25 .25
704 A163 20t R. cruttwellii .65 .65
705 A163 60t R. superbum 1.60 1.60
706 A163 70t R. christianae 2.00 2.00
Nos. 703-706 (4) 4.50 4.50

Intl. Letter Writing Week — A164

1989, Mar. 22 *Perf. 14½*

707 A164 20t Writing letter .40 .40
708 A164 35t Mailing letter .70 .60
709 A164 60t Stamping letter 1.15 1.15
710 A164 70t Reading letter 1.35 1.35
Nos. 707-710 (4) 3.60 3.50

Thatched Dwellings — A165

20t, Buka Is., 1880s. 35t, Koiari tree houses. 60t, Lauan, New Ireland, 1890s. 70t, Basilaki, Milne Bay Province, 1930s.

1989, May 17 Wmk. 387 *Perf. 15*

711 A165 20t multicolored .45 .40
712 A165 35t multicolored .95 .75
713 A165 60t multicolored 1.50 1.50
714 A165 70t multicolored 1.75 1.75
Nos. 711-714 (4) 4.65 4.40

Small Birds — A166

No. 715, Oreocharis arfaki female, shown. No. 716, Male. No. 717, Ifrita kowaldi. No. 718, Poecilodryas albonotata. No. 719, Sericornis nouhuysi.

1989, July 12 Unwmk. *Perf. 14½*

715 A166 20t multicolored 1.40 1.40
716 A166 20t multicolored 1.40 1.40
a. Pair, #715-716 3.25 3.25
717 A166 35t multicolored 1.90 1.40
718 A166 45t multicolored 1.90 1.60
719 A166 70t multicolored 2.75 2.75
Nos. 715-719 (5) 9.35 8.55

No. 659 Surcharged

1989, July 12 Unwmk. *Perf. 15*

720 A153 20t on 17t multi 1.00 1.00
a. Double surcharge 180.00

Traditional Dance — A167

Designs: 20t, Motumotu, Gulf Province. 35t, Baining, East New Britain Province. 60t, Vailala River, Gulf Province. 70t, Timbunke, East Sepik Province.

Perf. 14x14½

1989, Sept. 6 Litho. Wmk. 387

721 A167 20t multicolored .80 .65
722 A167 35t multicolored 1.40 1.10
723 A167 60t multicolored 2.40 2.40
724 A167 70t multicolored 2.75 2.75
Nos. 721-724 (4) 7.35 6.90

For surcharge see No. 860.

Christmas A168

Designs: 20t, Hibiscus, church and symbol from a gulf gope board, Kavaumai. 35t, Rhododendron, madonna and child, and mask, Murik Lakes region. 60t, D'Albertis creeper, candle, and shield from Oksapmin, West Sepik highlands. 70t, Pacific frangipani, peace dove and flute mask from Chungrebu, a Rao village in Ramu.

Perf. 14x14½

1989, Nov. 8 Litho. Unwmk.

725 A168 20t multicolored .55 .50
726 A168 35t multicolored .85 .85
727 A168 60t multicolored 1.75 1.75
728 A168 70t multicolored 1.90 1.90
Nos. 725-728 (4) 5.05 5.00

Waterfalls — A169

Unwmk.

1990, Feb. 1 Litho. *Perf. 14*

729 A169 20t Guni Falls .75 .55
730 A169 35t Rouna Falls 1.10 .90
731 A169 60t Ambua Falls 2.10 2.10
732 A169 70t Wawoi Falls 2.40 2.40
Nos. 729-732 (4) 6.35 5.95

For surcharges see Nos. 866, 870.

Natl. Census A170

1990, May 2 ***Perf. 14½x15***

No.	Type	Description	Unused	Used
733	A170	20t Three youths, form	.60	.60
734	A170	70t Man, woman, child, form	2.50	2.50

For surcharge see No. 869.

Gogodala Dance Masks — A171

1990, July 11 **Litho.** ***Perf. 13½***

No.	Type	Description	Unused	Used
735	A171	20t shown	1.25	.50
736	A171	35t multi, diff.	1.75	.90
737	A171	60t multi, diff.	2.75	*4.00*
738	A171	70t multi, diff.	3.00	*4.00*
		Nos. 735-738 (4)	8.75	9.40

For surcharges see Nos. 867, 871.

Waitangi Treaty, 150th Anniv. — A172

Designs: 20t, Dwarf Cassowary, Great Spotted Kiwi. No. 740, Double Wattled Cassowary, Brown Kiwi. No. 741, Sepik mask and Maori carving.

1990, Aug. 24 **Litho.** ***Perf. 14½***

No.	Type	Description	Unused	Used
739	A172	20t multicolored	1.25	.90
740	A172	35t multicolored	1.75	.90
741	A172	35t multicolored	2.10	1.40
		Nos. 739-741 (3)	5.10	3.20

No. 741 for World Stamp Exhibition, New Zealand 1990.

For surcharges see Nos. 862-863.

Birds A173

1990, Sept. 26 **Litho.** ***Perf. 14***

No.	Type	Description	Unused	Used
742	A173	20t Whimbrel	1.25	.70
743	A173	35t Sharp-tailed sandpiper	1.90	1.10
744	A173	60t Ruddy turnstone	3.00	*4.00*
745	A173	70t Terek sandpiper	3.75	*4.00*
		Nos. 742-745 (4)	9.90	9.80

Musical Instruments A174

1990, Oct. 31 **Litho.** ***Perf. 13***

No.	Type	Description	Unused	Used
746	A174	20t Jew's harp	.90	.75
747	A174	35t Musical bow	1.40	1.25
748	A174	60t Wantoat drum	2.75	2.75
749	A174	70t Gogodala rattle	3.00	3.00
		Nos. 746-749 (4)	8.05	7.75

For surcharge see No. 861.

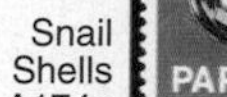

Snail Shells A174a

Designs: 21t, Rhynchotrochus weigmani. 40t, Forcartia globula, Canefriula azonata. 50t, Planispira deaniana. 80t, Papuina chancel, Papuina xanthocheila.

1991, Mar. 6 **Litho.** ***Perf. 14x14½***

No.	Type	Description	Unused	Used
750	A174a	21t multicolored	1.00	.65
751	A174a	40t multicolored	1.60	1.10
752	A174a	50t multicolored	2.25	2.25
753	A174a	80t multicolored	3.25	3.25
		Nos. 750-753 (4)	8.10	7.25

For surcharge see No. 864.

A175

A176

1t, Ptiloris magnificus. 5t, Loria loriae. 10t, Cnemophilus macgregorii. 20t, Parotia wahnesi. 21t, Manucodia chalybata. 30t, Paradisaea decora. 40t, Loboparadisea sericea. 45t, Cicinnurus regius. 50t, Paradigalla brevicauda. 60t, Parotia carolae. 90t, Paradisaea guilielmi. 1k, Diphyllodes magnificus. 2k, Lophorina superba. 5k, Phonygammus keraudrenii. 10k, Paradisaea minor.

1991-94 **Litho.** ***Perf. 14½***

No.	Type	Description	Unused	Used
755	A175	1t multicolored	.25	.25
756	A175	5t multicolored	.25	.25
757	A175	10t multicolored	.25	.25
758	A175	20t multicolored	.45	.45
759	A175	21t multicolored	.50	.50
760	A175	30t multicolored	.70	.70
761	A175	40t multicolored	.90	.90
762	A175	45t multicolored	2.25	1.10
763	A175	50t multicolored	1.25	1.25
764	A175	60t multicolored	3.75	1.40
765	A175	90t multicolored	3.75	2.10
766	A175	1k multicolored	2.25	2.25
767	A175	2k multicolored	4.10	4.50
a.		Strip of 4, #761, 763, 766-767 + label	9.00	9.00
768	A175	5k multicolored	10.00	10.00
		Perf. 13		
769	A176	10k multicolored	20.00	20.00
		Nos. 755-769 (15)	50.65	45.90

No. 767a for Hong Kong '94 and sold for 4k.

Stamps in No. 767a do not have "1992 BIRD OF PARADISE" at bottom of design.

Issued: 21t, 45t, 60t, 90t, 3/25/92; 5t, 40t, 50t, 1k, 2k, 9/2/92; 1t, 10t, 20t, 30t, 5k, 1993; 10k, 5/1/91; No. 767a, 2/18/94.

For surcharges see #878A, 878C.

Large T — A176a

1993 **Litho.** ***Perf. 14½***

No.	Type	Description	Unused	Used
770A	A176a	21T like #759	1.50	.75
770B	A176a	45T like #762	3.00	1.60
770C	A176a	60T like #764	3.50	3.50
770D	A176a	90T like #765	4.25	*5.25*
		Nos. 770A-770D (4)	12.25	11.10

Originally scheduled for release on Feb. 19, 1992, #770A-770D were withdrawn when the denomination was found to have an upper case "T." Corrected versions with a lower case "T" are #759, 762, 764-765. A quantity of the original stamps appeared in the market and to prevent speculation in these items, the Postal Administration of Papua New Guinea released the stamps with the upper case "T."

For surcharges see #878B, 878D.

1991 South Pacific Games A177

1991, June 26 **Litho.** ***Perf. 13***

No.	Type	Description	Unused	Used
771	A177	21t Cricket	2.50	.80
772	A177	40t Running	2.10	1.60
773	A177	50t Baseball	2.50	2.50
774	A177	80t Rugby	4.75	*6.00*
		Nos. 771-774 (4)	11.85	10.90

Anglican Church in Papua New Guinea, Cent. A178

Churches: 21t, Cathedral of St. Peter & St. Paul, Dogura. 40t, Kaieta Shrine, Anglican landing site. 80t, First thatched chapel, modawa tree.

1991, Aug. 7 **Litho.** ***Perf. 14½***

No.	Type	Description	Unused	Used
775	A178	21t multicolored	1.00	.70
776	A178	40t multicolored	2.00	2.00
777	A178	80t multicolored	3.50	3.50
		Nos. 775-777 (3)	6.50	6.20

Traditional Headdresses A179

Designs: 21t, Rambutso, Manus Province. 40t, Marawaka, Eastern Highlands. 50t, Tufi, Oro Province. 80t, Sina Sina, Simbu Province.

1991, Oct. 16 **Litho.** ***Perf. 13***

No.	Type	Description	Unused	Used
778	A179	21t multicolored	.95	.60
779	A179	40t multicolored	1.75	1.75
780	A179	50t multicolored	2.00	2.00
781	A179	80t multicolored	2.75	*4.25*
		Nos. 778-781 (4)	7.45	8.60

Discovery of America, 500th Anniv. A180

1992, Apr. 15 **Litho.** ***Perf. 14***

No.	Type	Description	Unused	Used
782	A180	21t Nina	.70	.50
783	A180	45t Pinta	1.75	1.10
784	A180	60t Santa Maria	2.10	2.10
785	A180	90t Columbus, ships	3.00	*3.50*
a.		Souvenir sheet of 2, #784-785	7.00	7.00
		Nos. 782-785 (4)	7.55	7.20

World Columbian Stamp Expo '92, Chicago. Issue date: No. 785a, June 3.

A181

Papuan Gulf Artifacts: 21t, Canoe prow shield, Bamu. 45t, Skull rack, Kerewa. 60t, Ancestral figure, Era River. 90t, Gope (spirit) board, Urama.

1992, June 3 **Litho.** ***Perf. 14***

No.	Type	Description	Unused	Used
786	A181	21t multicolored	.75	.55
787	A181	45t multicolored	1.50	1.25
788	A181	60t multicolored	1.75	1.60
789	A181	90t multicolored	2.75	2.75
		Nos. 786-789 (4)	6.75	6.15

A182

Soldiers from: 21t, Papuan Infantry Battalion. 45t, Australian Militia. 60t, Japanese Nankai Force. 90t, US Army.

1992, July 22 **Litho.** ***Perf. 14***

No.	Type	Description	Unused	Used
790	A182	21t multicolored	.95	.60
791	A182	45t multicolored	1.90	1.25
792	A182	60t multicolored	2.75	2.10
793	A182	90t multicolored	3.50	3.50
		Nos. 790-793 (4)	9.10	7.45

World War II, 50th anniv.

Flowering Trees — A183

21t, Hibiscus tiliaceus. 45t, Castanospermum australe. 60t, Cordia subcordata. 90t, Acacia auriculiformis.

1992, Oct. 28 **Litho.** ***Perf. 14***

No.	Type	Description	Unused	Used
794	A183	21t multicolored	1.00	.60
795	A183	45t multicolored	2.10	1.25
796	A183	60t multicolored	3.50	2.40
797	A183	90t multicolored	4.25	4.25
		Nos. 794-797 (4)	10.85	8.50

Mammals A184

21t, Myoictis melas. 45t, Microperoryctes longicauda. 60t, Mallomys rothschildi. 90t, Pseudocheirus forbesi.

1993, Apr. 7 **Litho.** ***Perf. 14***

No.	Type	Description	Unused	Used
798	A184	21t multicolored	.70	.50
799	A184	45t multicolored	1.30	1.20
800	A184	60t multicolored	1.90	1.90
801	A184	90t multicolored	2.60	2.60
		Nos. 798-801 (4)	6.50	6.20

Small Birds — A185

21t, Clytomyias insignis. 45t, Pitta superba. 60t, Rhagologus leucostigma. 90t, Toxorhamphus poliopterus.

1993, June 9 **Litho.** ***Perf. 14***

No.	Type	Description	Unused	Used
802	A185	21t multicolored	.85	.50
803	A185	45t multicolored	1.40	1.10
804	A185	60t multicolored	2.00	2.00
805	A185	90t multicolored	2.75	2.75
		Nos. 802-805 (4)	7.00	6.35

Nos. 802-805 Redrawn with Taipei '93 emblem in Blue and Yellow

1993, Aug. 13 Litho. *Perf. 14*

No.	Type	Description	Unused	Used
806	A185	21t multicolored	1.10	.45
807	A185	45t multicolored	2.10	1.15
808	A185	60t multicolored	2.40	2.40
809	A185	90t multicolored	2.75	*4.50*
		Nos. 806-809 (4)	8.35	8.50

Freshwater Fish A186

Designs: 21t, Iriatherina werneri. 45t, Tateurndina ocellicauda. 60t, Melanotaenia affinis. 90t, Pseudomugil connieae.

1993, Sept. 29 Litho. *Perf. 14x14½*

No.	Type	Description	Unused	Used
810	A186	21t multicolored	1.10	.70
811	A186	45t multicolored	2.10	1.40
812	A186	60t multicolored	2.50	2.50
813	A186	90t multicolored	3.50	3.50
		Nos. 810-813 (4)	9.20	8.10

For surcharges see Nos. 876-878.

Air Niugini, 20th Anniv. A187

1993, Oct. 27 *Perf. 14*

No.	Type	Description	Unused	Used
814	A187	21t DC3	1.10	.65
815	A187	45t F27	2.50	1.25
816	A187	60t Dash 7	3.00	3.00
817	A187	90t Airbus A310-300	3.50	*4.75*
		Nos. 814-817 (4)	10.10	9.65

Souvenir Sheet

Paradisaea Rudolphi — A188

1993, Sept. 29 Litho. *Perf. 14*

No.	Type	Description	Unused	Used
818	A188	2k multicolored	11.50	11.50

Bangkok '93.

Huon Tree Kangaroo — A189

1994, Jan. 19 Litho. *Perf. 14½*

No.	Type	Description	Unused	Used
819	A189	21t Domesticated joey	.75	.65
820	A189	45t Adult male	1.60	1.25
821	A189	60t Female, joey in pouch	2.25	2.25
822	A189	90t Adolescent	3.25	*3.75*
		Nos. 819-822 (4)	7.85	7.90

No. 661 Surcharged

No. 671 Surcharged

Perfs. and Printing Methods as Before

1994, Mar. 23

No.	Type	Description	Unused	Used
823	A153	21t on 35t multi	*15.00*	.80
824	A154	1.20k on 40t multi	*4.50*	1.75

No. 824 exists with double surcharge. Other varieties may exist.

Artifacts — A190

Designs: 1t, Hagen ceremonial axe, Western Highlands. 2t, Telefomin war shield, West Sepik. 20t, Head mask, Gulf of Papua. 21t, Kanganaman stool, East Sepik. 45t, Trobriand lime gourd, Milne Bay. 60t, Yuat River flute stopper, East Sepik. 90t, Tami island dish, Morobe. 1k, Kundu drum, Ramu River estuary. 5k, Gogodala dance mask, Western Province. 10k, Malanggan mask, New Ireland.

1994-95 Litho. *Perf. 14½*

No.	Type	Description	Unused	Used
825	A190	1t multicolored	.25	.25
826	A190	2t multicolored	.25	.25
828	A190	20t multicolored	.35	.35
829	A190	21t multicolored	.35	.35
833	A190	45t multicolored	.80	.80
835	A190	60t multicolored	1.10	1.10
836	A190	90t multicolored	1.65	1.65
837	A190	1k multicolored	5.00	3.00
839	A190	5k multicolored	9.00	9.00
840	A190	10k multicolored	15.00	15.00
		Nos. 825-840 (10)	33.75	31.75

Issued: 21, 45, 60, 90t, 3/23; 1, 2, 20t, 5k, 6/29/94; 1k, 10k, 4/12/95.

This is an expanding set. Numbers may change.

Classic Cars A191

1994, May 11 Litho. *Perf. 14*

No.	Type	Description	Unused	Used
841	A191	21t Model T Ford	.80	.65
842	A191	45t Chevrolet 490	1.50	1.15
843	A191	60t Baby Austin	2.25	2.25
844	A191	90t Willys Jeep	3.00	3.00
		Nos. 841-844 (4)	7.55	7.05

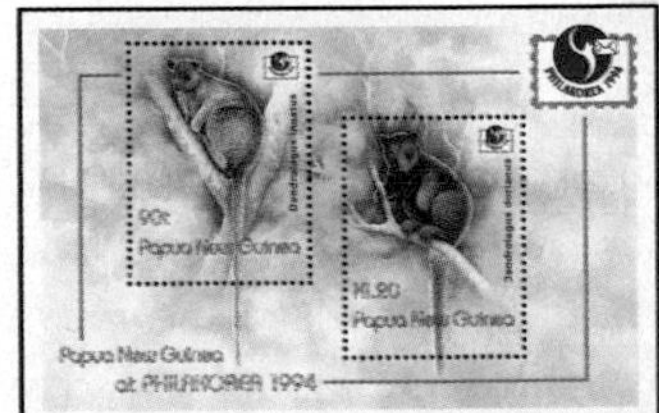

PHILAKOREA '94 — A192

Tree kangaroos: 90t, Dendrolagus inustus. 1.20k, Dendrolagus dorianus.

1994, Aug. 10 Litho. *Perf. 14*

No.	Type	Description	Unused	Used
845	A192	Sheet of 2, #a.-b.	8.00	8.00

Moths A193

Designs: 21t, Daphnis hypothous pallescens. 45t, Tanaorhinus unipuncta. 60t, Neodiphthera sciron. 90t, Parotis maginata.

1994, Oct. 26 Litho. *Perf. 14*

No.	Type	Description	Unused	Used
846	A193	21t multicolored	.60	.50
847	A193	45t multicolored	1.50	1.00
848	A193	60t multicolored	1.75	1.75
849	A193	90t multicolored	3.00	3.00
		Nos. 846-849 (4)	6.85	6.25

Beatification of Peter To Rot — A194

1995, Jan. 11 Litho. *Perf. 14*

No.	Type	Description	Unused	Used
850	A194	21t Peter To Rot	.80	.80
851	A194	1k on 90t Pope John Paul II	4.50	4.50
a.		Pair, #850-851 + label	6.50	6.50

No. 851 was not issued without surcharge.

For surcharge see No. 1008.

Tourism A195

#852, Cruising. #853, Handicrafts. #854, Jet. #855, Resorts. #856, Trekking adventure. #857, White-water rafting. #858, Boat, diver. #859, Divers, sunken plane.

1995, Jan. 11

No.	Type	Description	Unused	Used
852	A195	21t multicolored	.80	.80
853	A195	21t multicolored	.80	.80
a.		Pair, #852-853	2.25	2.25
854	A195	50t on 45t multi	2.00	2.00
855	A195	50t on 45t multi	2.00	2.00
a.		Pair, #854-855	5.00	5.00
856	A195	65t on 60t multi	2.60	2.60
a.		"65t" omitted	37.50	
857	A195	65t on 60t multi	2.60	2.60
a.		Pair, #856-857	6.00	6.00
858	A195	1k on 90t multi	4.00	4.00
859	A195	1k on 90t multi	4.00	4.00
a.		Pair, #858-859	9.25	9.25
		Nos. 852-859 (8)	18.80	18.80

Nos. 854-859 were not issued without surcharge.

Nos. 662, 722, 730, 732, 734, 736, 738, 740-741, 747, 753, 762, 765, 770B, 770D Surcharged

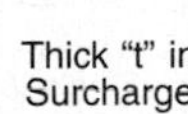

Thick "t" in Surcharge

1994 *Perfs., Etc. as Before*

No.	Type	Description	Unused	Used
860	A167	5t on 35t #722	5.75	1.00
861	A174	5t on 35t #747	*27.50*	*17.50*
862	A172	10t on 35t #740	*24.00*	*16.00*
863	A172	10t on 35t #741	*17.50*	*6.50*
864	A174a	21t on 80t #753	*75.00*	*3.50*
866	A169	50t on 35t #730	*35.00*	*17.50*
867	A171	50t on 35t #736	*80.00*	*50.00*
a.		Inverted surcharge	650.00	
868	A153	65t on 70t #662	4.00	1.75
869	A170	65t on 70t #734	4.00	1.75
870	A169	1k on 70t #732	*20.00*	*6.50*
871	A171	1k on 70t #738	27.50	2.50
		Nos. 860-871 (11)	*320.25*	*124.50*

Size, style and location of surcharge varies.

No. 861 exists in pair, one without surcharge. Other varieties exist.

Issued: #862, 8/23/94; #864, 8/28/94; #861, 863, 864, 10/3/94; #860, 871, 10/6/94; #866-868, 869-870, 11/28/94.

Mushrooms A196

25t, Lentinus umbrinus. 50t, Amanita hemibapha. 65t, Boletellus emodensis. 1k, Ramaria zippellii.

1995, June 21 Litho. *Perf. 14*

No.	Type	Description	Unused	Used
872	A196	25t multicolored	.80	.60
		Complete booklet, 10 #872	15.00	
873	A196	50t multicolored	1.50	1.50
		Complete booklet, 10 #873	22.50	
874	A196	65t multicolored	1.90	1.90
875	A196	1k multicolored	3.00	3.00
		Nos. 872-875 (4)	7.20	7.00

1996 Litho. *Perf. 12*

No.	Type	Description	Unused	Used
875A	A196	25t like #872	2.25	2.25

No. 875A has a taller vignette, a smaller typeface for the description, denomination, and country name and does not have a date inscription like #872.

Nos. 876-878 Surcharged Thick "t"
Nos. 878A-878D Surcharged Thin "t"

Thin "t" in Srch.

See illustration above #860.

1995 Litho. *Perf. 14x14½*

No.	Type	Description	Unused	Used
876	A186	21t on 45t #811	1.00	.35
877	A186	21t on 60t #812	3.00	1.75
878	A186	21t on 90t #813	1.00	.70
878A	A175	21t on 45t #762	4.00	.70
878B	A176a	21t on 45T #770B	11.00	1.75
878C	A175	21t on 90t #765	4.00	.70
878D	A176a	21t on 90T #770D	11.00	1.75
		Nos. 876-878D (7)	35.00	7.70

Nos. 878A-878D exist with thick surcharge. This printing of 3200 each does not seem to have seen much, if any, public sale. Value, $10 to $150 each.

Nos. 878A, 878C dated 1993. Nos. 878B, 878D dated 1992. Nos. 878A, 878C exist dated 1992.

Issued: Nos. 876-878, 6/20; Nos. 878A-878B, 5/16; No. 878C, 3/27; No. 878D, 4/25.

Independence, 20th Anniv. — A197

Designs: 50t, 1k, "20" emblem.

1995, Aug. 30 *Perf. 14*

No.	Type	Description	Unused	Used
879	A197	21t shown	.65	.65
880	A197	50t blue & multi	1.40	1.40
881	A197	1k green & multi	2.75	2.75
		Nos. 879-881 (3)	4.80	4.80

Souvenir Sheet

Singapore '95 — A198

Orchids: a, 21t, Dendrobium rigidifolium. b, 45t, Dendrobium convolutum. c, 60t, Dendrobium spectabile. d, 90t, Dendrobium tapiniense.

1995, Aug. 30 Litho. *Perf. 14*

882 A198 Sheet of 4, #a.-d. 6.00 6.00

No. 882 sold for 3k.

Souvenir Sheet

New Year 1995 (Year of the Boar) — A199

1995, Sept. 14

883 A199 3k multicolored 7.50 7.50

Beijing '95.

Eruption of Rabaul Volcano, 1st Anniv. A200

1995, Sept. 19

884 A200 2k multicolored 4.00 4.00

Crabs A201

1995, Oct. 25 Litho. *Perf. 14*

885 A201 21t Zosimus aeneus .70 .55
886 A201 50t Cardisoma carnifex 1.40 1.40
887 A201 65t Uca tetragonon 1.90 1.90
888 A201 1k Eriphia sebana 2.75 2.75
Nos. 885-888 (4) 6.75 6.60

For surcharge see #939B.

Parrots — A202

Designs: 25t, Psittrichas fulgidas. 50t, Trichoglossus haemotodus. 65t, Alisterus chloropterus. 1k, Aprosmictus erythropterus.

1996, Jan. 17 Litho. *Perf. 12*

889 A202 25t multicolored 1.75 .60
890 A202 50t multicolored 2.50 1.05
891 A202 65t multicolored 3.00 2.25
892 A202 1k multicolored 3.75 3.75
Nos. 889-892 (4) 11.00 7.65

Beetles — A203

Designs: 25t, Lagriomorpha indigacea. 50t, Eupholus geoffroyi. 65t, Promechus pulcher. 1k, Callistola pulchra.

1996, Mar. 20 Litho. *Perf. 12*

893 A203 25t multicolored .65 .65
894 A203 50t multicolored 1.30 1.30
895 A203 65t multicolored 1.70 1.70
896 A203 1k multicolored 2.60 2.60
Nos. 893-896 (4) 6.25 6.25

Souvenir Sheet

Zhongshan Memorial Hall, Guangzhou, China — A204

1996, Apr. 22 Litho. *Perf. 14*

897 A204 70t multicolored 2.50 2.50

CHINA '96, 9th Asian Intl. Philatelic Exhibition.

1996 Summer Olympics, Atlanta A205

1996, July 24 Litho. *Perf. 12*

898 A205 25t Shooting .45 .45
899 A205 50t Track .85 .85
900 A205 65t Weight lifting 1.50 1.50
901 A205 1k Boxing 2.10 2.10
Nos. 898-901 (4) 4.90 4.90

Olymphilex '96.

Radio, Cent. A206

25t, Air traffic control. 50t, Commercial broadcasting. 65t, Gerehu earth station. 1k, 1st transmission in Papua New Guinea.

1996, Sept. 11 Litho. *Perf. 12*

902 A206 25t multicolored .40 .40
903 A206 50t multicolored .85 .85
904 A206 65t multicolored 1.10 1.10
905 A206 1k multicolored 1.60 1.60
Nos. 902-905 (4) 3.95 3.95

Souvenir Sheet

Taipei '96, 10th Asian Intl. Philatelic Exhibition — A207

a, Dr. Sun Yat-sen (1866-1925). b, Dr. John Guise (1914-91).

1996, Oct. 16 Litho. *Perf. 14*

906 A207 65t Sheet of 2, #a.-b. 4.50 4.50

Flowers A208

Designs: 1t, Hibiscus rosa-sinensis. 5t, Bougainvillea spectabilis. 65t, Plumeria rubra. 1k, Mucuna novo-guineensis.

1996, Nov. 27 Litho. *Perf. 14*

907 A208 1t multicolored .40 .25
908 A208 5t multicolored .40 .25
909 A208 65t multicolored 1.40 1.40
910 A208 1k multicolored 2.10 2.10
Nos. 907-910 (4) 4.30 4.00

Souvenir Sheet

Oxen and Natl. Flag — A209

1997, Feb. 3 Litho. *Perf. 14*

911 A209 1.50k multicolored 3.75 3.75

Hong Kong '97.

Boat Prows A210

1997, Mar. 19 Litho. *Perf. 14½x14*

912 A210 25t Gogodala .35 .35
913 A210 50t East New Britain .75 .75
914 A210 65t Trobriand Island 1.10 1.10
915 A210 1k Walomo 1.60 1.60
Nos. 912-915 (4) 3.80 3.80

Queen Elizabeth II and Prince Philip, 50th Wedding Anniv. — A211

#916, Princess Anne, polo players. #917, Queen up close. #918, Prince in riding attire. #919, Queen, another person riding horses. #920, Grandsons riding horses, Prince waving. #921, Queen waving, riding pony.

2k, Queen, Prince riding in open carriage.

1997, June 25 Litho. *Perf. 13½*

916 A211 25t multicolored .50 .50
917 A211 25t multicolored .50 .50
a. Pair, #916-917 1.25 1.25
918 A211 50t multicolored 1.00 1.00
919 A211 50t multicolored 1.00 1.00
a. Pair, #918-919 2.50 2.50
920 A211 1k multicolored 1.75 1.75
921 A211 1k multicolored 1.75 1.75
a. Pair, #920-921 4.00 4.00
Nos. 916-921 (6) 6.50 6.50

Souvenir Sheet

922 A211 2k multicolored 3.75 3.75

Souvenir Sheet

Air Niugini, First Flight, Port Moresby-Osaka — A212

1997, July 19 Litho. *Perf. 12*

923 A212 3k multicolored 6.00 6.00

1997 Pacific Year of Coral Reef A213

Designs: 25t, Pocillopora woodjonesi. 50t, Subergorgia mollis. 65t, Oxypora glabra. 1k, Turbinaria reinformis.

1997, Aug. 27 Litho. *Perf. 12*

924 A213 25t multicolored .50 .50
925 A213 50t multicolored 1.00 1.00
926 A213 65t multicolored 1.50 1.50
927 A213 1k multicolored 1.90 1.90
Nos. 924-927 (4) 4.90 4.90

Flowers — A214

Designs: 10t, Thunbergia fragrans. 20t, Caesalpinia pulcherrima. 25t, Hoya. 30t, Heliconia. 50t, Amomum goliathensis.

1997, Nov. 26 Litho. *Perf. 12*

928 A214 10t multicolored .60 .40
929 A214 20t multicolored .80 .70
930 A214 25t multicolored 1.00 .90
931 A214 30t multicolored 1.25 1.25
932 A214 50t multicolored 2.00 1.40
Nos. 928-932 (5) 5.65 4.65

Birds A215

Designs: 25t, Tyto tenebricosa. 50t, Aepypodius arfakianus. 65t, Accipiter poliocephalus. 1k, Zonerodius heliosylus.

1998, Jan. 28 Litho. *Perf. 12*

933 A215 25t multicolored 1.40 .75
934 A215 50t multicolored 1.75 1.40
935 A215 65t multicolored 2.75 2.75
936 A215 1k multicolored 3.75 *4.25*
Nos. 933-936 (4) 9.65 9.15

Diana, Princess of Wales (1961-97)

Common Design Type

Designs: a, In beige colored dress. b, In violet dress with lace collar. c, Wearing plaid jacket. d, Holding flowers.

1998, Apr. 29 Litho. *Perf. 14½x14*

937 CD355 1k Sheet of 4, #a.-d. 6.50 6.50

No. 937 sold for 4k + 50t with surtax from international sales being donated to the Princess Diana Memorial fund and surtax from national sales being donated to designated local charity.

Mother Teresa (1910-97) A216

1998, Apr. 29 *Perf. 14½*

938 A216 65t With child 1.25 1.25
939 A216 1k shown 1.90 1.90
a. Pair, #938-939 4.00 4.00

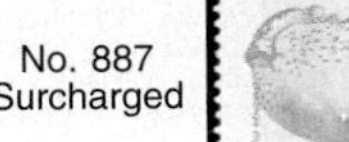

No. 887 Surcharged

1998, May 28 **Litho.** *Perf. 14*

939B A201 25t on 65t multi 1.10 1.10

Moths A217

25t, Daphnis hypothous pallescens. 50t, Theretra polistratus. 65t, Psilogramma casurina. 1k, Meganoton hyloicoides.

1998, June 17 **Litho.** *Perf. 14*

940 A217 25t multicolored .55 .55
941 A217 50t multicolored .90 .90
942 A217 65t multicolored 1.40 1.40
943 A217 1k multicolored 1.90 1.90
Nos. 940-943 (4) 4.75 4.75

A218

First Orchid Spectacular '98: 25t, Coelogyne fragrans. 50t, Den. cuthbertsonii. 65t, Den. vexillarius. 1k, Den. finisterrae.

1998, Sept. 15 **Litho.** *Perf. 14*

944 A218 25t multicolored .60 .60
945 A218 50t multicolored 1.00 1.00
946 A218 65t multicolored 1.50 1.50
947 A218 1k multicolored 2.25 2.25
Nos. 944-947 (4) 5.35 5.35

A219

Sea Kayaking World Cup, Manus Island: 25t, Couple in kayak. 50t, Competitor running through Loniu Caves. 65t, Man standing in boat with sail, man seated in kayak. 1k, Competitor in kayak, bird of paradise silhouette.

1998, Oct. 5 **Litho.** *Perf. 14*

948 A219 25t multicolored .60 .60
949 A219 50t multicolored 1.00 1.00
950 A219 65t multicolored 1.50 1.50
951 A219 1k multicolored 2.25 2.25
Nos. 948-951 (4) 5.35 5.35

1998 Commonwealth Games, Kuala Lumpur — A220

1998, Sept. 30 **Litho.** *Perf. 14*

952 A220 25t Weight lifting .40 .40
953 A220 50t Lawn bowls .70 .70
954 A220 65t Rugby .95 .95
955 A220 1k Squash 1.40 1.40
Nos. 952-955 (4) 3.45 3.45

Christmas A221

Designs: 25t, Infant in manger. 50t, Mother breastfeeding infant. 65t, "Wise men" in traditional masks, headdresses looking at infant. 1k, Map of Papua New Guinea.

1998, Nov. 18 **Litho.** *Perf. 14*

956 A221 25t multicolored .35 .35
957 A221 50t multicolored .70 .70
958 A221 65t multicolored .95 .95
959 A221 1k multicolored 1.60 1.60
Nos. 956-959 (4) 3.60 3.60

Australia '99, World Stamp Expo — A222

Ships: 25t, "Boudeuse," 1768. 50t, "Neva," 1876. 65t, "Merrir England," 1889. 1k, "Samoa," 1884.

#964: a, 5t, Rattlesnake, 1849. b, 10t, Swallow, 1767. c, 15t, Roebeck, 1700. d, 20t, Blanche, 1872. e, 30t, Vitiaz, 1871. f, 40t, San Pedrico and Eabre, 1606. g, 60t, Jorge de Menesis, 1526. h, 1.20k, L'Astrolabe, 1827.

1999, Mar. 17

960 A222 25t multicolored .30 .30
961 A222 50t multicolored .65 .65
962 A222 65t multicolored 1.05 1.05
963 A222 1k multicolored 1.25 1.25
Nos. 960-963 (4) 3.25 3.25

Sheet of 8

964 A222 #a.-h. 5.50 5.50

No. 964a is incorrectly inscribed "Simpson Blanche '1872."

IBRA '99, World Philatelic Exhibition, Nuremberg — A223

Exhibition emblem and: a, German New Guinea #17. b, German New Guinea #1, #2.

1999 **Litho.** *Perf. 14*

965 A223 1k Pair, #a.-b. 3.00 3.00

Millennium A224

Map and: 25t, Stopwatch, computer keyboard. 50t, Concentric circles. 65t, Internet page, computer user. 1k, Computers, satellite dish.

1999 **Litho.** *Perf. 12¾*

966 A224 25t multicolored .45 .25
967 A224 50t multicolored .65 .40
968 A224 65t multicolored 1.10 .90
969 A224 1k multicolored 1.60 *1.75*
Nos. 966-969 (4) 3.80 3.30

For surcharge see No. 1010.

PhilexFrance '99 — A225

Frenchmen with historical ties to Papua New Guinea: 25t, Father Jules Chevalier. 50t, Bishop Alain-Marie. 65t, Chevalier D'Entrecasteaux. 1k, Count de Bougainville.

1999, Mar. 2 **Litho.** *Perf. 12¾*

970 A225 25t multicolored .30 .25
971 A225 50t multicolored .55 .55
972 A225 65t multicolored .85 .85
973 A225 1k multicolored 1.25 *1.40*
Nos. 970-973 (4) 2.95 3.05

For surcharge see No. 1011.

Hiri Moale Festival A226

Designs: 25t, Clay pots, native. 50t, Hanenamo, native. 65t, Lakatoi, native. #977, 1k, Sorcerer, native.

No. 978: a, Sorcerer. b, Clay pots. c, Lakatoi.

1999, Sept. 8 *Perf. 12¾*

974 A226 25t multicolored .35 .30
975 A226 50t multicolored .55 .55
976 A226 65t multicolored .85 .85
977 A226 1k multicolored 1.25 1.25
Nos. 974-977 (4) 3.00 2.95

Souvenir Sheet

978 A226 1k Sheet of 3, #a.-c. 3.50 3.50

For surcharge see No. 1012.

Souvenir Sheet

Year of the Rabbit (in 1999) — A227

Color of rabbit: a, Gray. b, Tan. c, White. d, Pink.

2000, Apr. 21 **Litho.** *Perf. 12¾*

979 A227 65t Sheet of 4, #a-d 3.75 3.75

Queen Mother, 100th Birthday A228

Various photos. Color of frame: 25t, Yellow. 50t, Lilac. 65t, Green. 1k, Dull orange.

2000, Aug. 4 *Perf. 14*

980-983 A228 Set of 4 3.25 3.25

Shells A229

Designs: 25t, Turbo petholatus. 50t, Charonia tritonis. 65t, Cassis cornuta. 1k, Ovula ovum.

2000, Feb. 23 **Litho.** *Perf. 14*

984-987 A229 Set of 4 3.75 3.75

Independence, 25th Anniv. — A230

Designs: 25t, Shell. 50t, Bird of Paradise. 65t, Ring. 1k, Coat of arms.

2000, June 21 *Perf. 14*

Stamps with se-tenant label

988-991 A230 Set of 4 3.75 3.75
991a Souvenir sheet, #988-991, no labels 3.75 3.75

Strips with two stamps alternating with two different labels exist for Nos. 989 and 990.

2000 Summer Olympics, Sydney A231

Designs: 25t, Running. 50t, Swimming. 65t, Boxing. 1k, Weight lifting.

2000, July 12

992-995 A231 Set of 4 3.50 3.50

For surcharge see No. 1009.

Souvenir Sheet

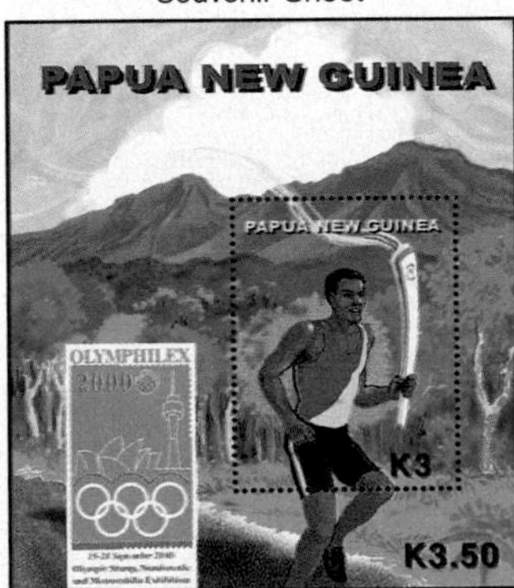

Olymphilex 2000, Sydney — A232

2000, July 12 *Perf. 14¼*

996 A232 3k multi 3.75 3.75

Sold for 3.50k.

Birds A233

Designs: 35t, Comb-crested jacana. 70t, Masked lapwing. 90t, White ibis. 1.40k, Black-tailed godwit.

2001, Mar. 21 **Litho.** *Perf. 14*

997-1000 A233 Set of 4 5.00 5.00

Mission Aviation Fellowship, 50th Anniv. in Papua New Guinea — A234

Designs: 35t, Cessna 170, pig, bird, Bibles. 70t, Harry Hartwig (1916-51), Auster Autocar. 90t, Pilot and Cessna 260. 1.40k, Twin Otter and plane mechanics.

2001, Oct. 17 ***Perf. 13¼x13¾***
1001-1004 A234 Set of 4 4.50 4.50

Papua New Guinea — People's Republic of China Diplomatic Relations, 25th Anniv. A235

Designs: 10t, Flags, world map. 50t, Dragon, bird of paradise. 2k, Tien An Men Square, Papua New Guinea Parliament Building.

2001, Oct. 12 **Litho.** ***Perf. 12***
1005-1007 A235 Set of 3 4.75 4.75

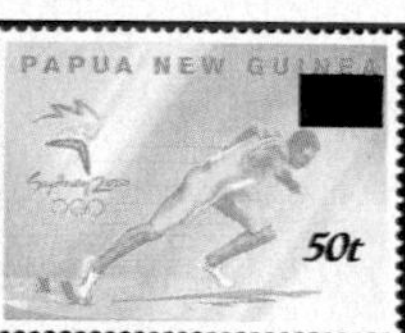
Nos. 850, 968, 972, 976 and 992 Srchd.

Methods and Perfs As Before
2001, Dec. 1

1008	A194	50t on 21t #850	2.50	1.25
a.		Horiz. pair, 1008, 851 + central label	6.00	4.00
1009	A231	50t on 25t #992	1.00	.50
a.		Obliterator present, missing new denomination		—
1010	A224	50t on 65t #968	1.00	.50
1011	A225	2.65k on 65t #972	4.00	4.00
1012	A226	2.65k on 65t #976	4.00	4.00
		Nos. 1008-1012 (5)	12.50	10.25

Provincial Flags A236

2001, Dec. 12 **Litho.** ***Perf. 14***

1013	A236	10t Enga	.45	.25
1014	A236	15t Simbu	.45	.25
1015	A236	20t Manus	.45	.25
1016	A236	50t Central	1.10	.40
1017	A236	2k New Ireland	3.50	2.25
1018	A236	5k Sandaun	4.75	4.75
		Nos. 1013-1018 (6)	10.70	8.15

For surcharge see No. 1113.

Reign Of Queen Elizabeth II, 50th Anniv. Issue
Common Design Type

Designs: Nos. 1019, 1023a, 1.25k, Princess Elizabeth with Queen Mother and Princess Margaret, 1941. Nos. 1020, 1023b, 1.45k, Wearing tiara, 1975. Nos. 1021, 1023c, 2k, With Princes Philip and Charles, 1951. Nos. 1022, 1023d, 2.65k, Wearing red hat. No. 1023e, 5k, 1955 portrait by Annigoni (38x50mm).

Perf. 14¼x14½, 13¾ (#1023e)
2002, Feb. 6 **Litho.** **Wmk. 373**
With Gold Frames

1019	CD360	1.25k multicolored	1.20	1.20
1020	CD360	1.45k multicolored	1.40	1.40
1021	CD360	2k multicolored	1.90	1.90
1022	CD360	2.65k multicolored	2.50	2.50
		Nos. 1019-1022 (4)	7.00	7.00

Souvenir Sheet
Without Gold Frames
1023 CD360 Sheet of 5, #a-e 7.50 7.50

Lakatoi Type of 1901 Inscribed "Papua New Guinea"

Frame colors: 5t, Red. 15t, Brown violet. 20t, Light blue. 1.25k, Brown. 1.45k, Green. 10k, Orange.

Perf. 14½x14
2002, June 5 **Litho.** **Unwmk.**
Center in Brown Black
1024-1029 A1 Set of 6 13.00 13.00
a. Souvenir sheet, #1024-1029 15.00 15.00

British New Guinea stamps, cent. (in 2001).

Orchids — A237

Designs: 5t, Cadetia taylori. 30t, Dendrobium anosmum. 45t, Dendrobium bigibbum. 1.25k, Dendrobium cuthbertsonii. 1.45k, Sprianthes sinensis. 2.65k, Thelymitra carnea.

No. 1036, horiz.: a, Dendrobium bracteosum. b, Calochilus campestris. c, Anastomus oscitans. d, Thelymitra carnea, diff. e, Dendrobium macrophyllum. f, Dendrobium johnsoniae.

7k, Bulbophyllum graveolens, horiz.

2002, Aug. 28 ***Perf. 14***
1030-1035 A237 Set of 6 8.00 8.00
1036 A237 2k Sheet of 6, #a-f 12.00 12.00

Souvenir Sheet
1037 A237 7k multi 9.00 9.00

Protected Butterflies A238

Designs: No. 1038, 50t, Ornithoptera chimaera. No. 1039, 50t, Ornithoptera goliath. 1.25k, Ornithoptera meridionalis. 1.45k, Ornithoptera paradisea. 2.65k, Ornithoptera victoriae. 5k, Ornithoptera alexandrae.

2002, Oct. 16
1038-1043 A238 Set of 6 15.00 15.00

Queen Mother Elizabeth (1900-2002) — A239

No. 1044, horiz.: a, With Queen Elizabeth II (28x23mm). b, With Elizabeth and two other women (28x23mm). c, With pearl necklace visible at left (26x29mm). d, Color photograph (40x29mm). e, With pearl necklace visible at right (26x29mm). f, With man in top hat at right (28x23mm). g, With King George VI (28x23mm).

No. 1045, blue shading in UR of stamps : a, 3k, As child. b, 3k, Wearing black hat.

No. 1046, blue shading in UL of stamps: a, 3k, Wearing white hat. b, 3k, Wearing hat and brooch.

Perf. 13¼x14¼ (#1044d), Compound x 14¼ (#1044c, 1044e) 13¼x10¾
2002
1044 A239 2k Sheet of 7, #a-g 14.00 14.00

Souvenir Sheets
Perf. 14¾
1045-1046 A239 Set of 2 14.00 14.00

A240

United We Stand A241

2002, Nov. 20 **Litho.** ***Perf. 14***
1047 A240 50t multi 1.25 1.25
1048 A241 50t multi 1.25 1.25

No. 1048 was printed in sheets of 4.

Intl. Year of Mountains A242

Designs: 50t, Mt. Wilhelm, Papua New Guinea. 1.25k, Matterhorn, Switzerland. 1.45k, Mt. Fuji, Japan. 2.65k, Massif des Aravis, France.

2002, Nov. 20
1049-1052 A242 Set of 4 6.50 6.50

Clay Pots — A243

Designs: 65t, Sago storage pot. 1k, Smoking pot. 1.50k, Water jar. 2.50k, Water jar, diff. 4k, Ridge pot.

2003, Jan. 22
1053-1057 A243 Set of 5 9.50 9.50

20th World Scout Jamboree, Thailand — A244

Designs: 50t, Group of scouts. 1.25k, Two scouts seated. 1.45k, Scouts on tower. 2.65k, Two scouts standing.

2003, Feb. 12
1058-1061 A244 Set of 4 8.50 8.50

A245

Various portraits of Queen Elizabeth II with background colors of: No. 1062, 65t, Purple. No. 1063, 65t, Olive green. 1.50k, Dark blue. No. 1065, 2k, Red. 2.50k, Dull green. 4k, Orange.

No. 1068, 2k — Yellow orange background with Queen: a, Without hat. b, Wearing crown and sash. c, Wearing hat with blue flowers. d, Wearing tiara. e, Wearing red dress. f, Wearing black hat.

8k, Wearing black robe, gray green background.

2003, Apr. 30 **Litho.** ***Perf. 14***
1062-1067 A245 Set of 6 9.50 9.50
1068 A245 2k Sheet of 6, #a-f 10.00 10.00

Souvenir Sheet
1069 A245 8k multi 7.00 7.00

Coronation of Queen Elizabeth, 50th anniv.

A246

Prince William: No. 1070, 65t, Wearing colored sports shirt. No. 1071, 65t, Wearing white shirt. 1.50k, As child. No. 1073, 2k, Wearing suit and tie, gray green background. 2.50k, Wearing plaid shirt. 4k, On polo pony.

No. 1076, 2k — Lilac background: a, As toddler. b, Wearing sunglasses. c, Wearing suit and tie (full face). d, Wearing suit and tie (profile). e, Wearing deep blue shirt. f, Wearing yellow shirt with black collar.

8k, Wearing suit and tie, gray green background, diff.

2003, June 18
1070-1075 A246 Set of 6 8.50 8.50
1076 A246 2k Sheet of 6, #a-f 9.50 9.50

Souvenir Sheet
1077 A246 8k multi 7.00 7.00

Prince William, 21st birthday.

Coastal Villages A247

Designs: No. 1078, 65t, Gabagaba. No. 1079, 65t, Wanigela (Koki). 1.50k, Tubuserea. 2k, Hanuabada. 2.50k, Barakau. 4k, Porebada.

2003, July 24
1078-1083 A247 Set of 6 9.50 9.50

For surcharges see Nos. 1114-1115.

Powered Flight, Cent. A248

Designs: 65t, Orville Wright circles plane over Fort Myer, Va., 1908. 1.50k, Orville Wright pilots "Baby Grand" Belmont, 1910. No. 1086, 2.50k, Wilbur Wright holding anemometer, Pau, France, 1909. 4k, Wilbur Wright pilots Model A, Pau, France, 1909.

No. 1088, 2.50k — 1903 photos from Kitty Hawk: a, Untried airplane outside hangar. b, Rollout of airplane from hangar. c, Preparing airplane for takeoff. d, Airplane takes off.

10k, Airplane takes off, diff.

2003, Aug. 27

1084-1087 A248 Set of 4 8.00 8.00
1088 A248 Sheet of 4, #a-d 9.00 9.00

Souvenir Sheet

1089 A248 10k multi 9.00 9.00

Worldwide Fund for Nature (WWF) A249

Tree kangaroos: Nos. 1090a, 1091a, Dendrolagus inustus. Nos. 1090b, 1091b, Dendrolagus matschiei. Nos. 1090c, 1091c, Dendrolagus dorianus. Nos. 1090d, 1091d, Dendrolagus goodfellowi.

2003, Oct. 15 *Perf. 14½x14¾*

With White Frames

1090 Horiz. strip of 4 8.00 8.00
a. A249 65t multi .75 .75
b. A249 1.50k multi 1.40 1.40
c. A249 2.50k multi 2.25 2.25
d. A249 4k multi 3.25 3.25

Without White Frames

1091 Sheet, 2 each #a-d 14.00 14.00
a. A249 65t multi .65 .65
b. A249 1.50k multi 1.25 1.25
c. A249 2.50k multi 2.00 2.00
d. A249 4k multi 2.75 2.75

Endangered Dolphins — A250

Designs: No. 1092, 65t, Humpback dolphin. No. 1093, 65t, Bottlenose dolphins. No. 1094, 1.50k, Bottlenose dolphin, with frame line. 2k, Irrawaddy dolphin. 2.50k, Humpback dolphin and fishermen. 4k, Irrawaddy dolphin and diver.

No. 1098, 1.50k: a, Humpback dolphin and sailboat. b, Bottlenose dolphin, without frame line. c, Bottlenose dolphins, diff. d, Irrawaddy dolphin and diver, diff. e, Irrawady dolphin, diff. f, Humpback dolphin underwater.

2003, Nov. 19 *Perf. 13½*

1092-1097 A250 Set of 6 10.00 10.00
1098 A250 1.50k Sheet of 6, #a-f 8.00 8.00

For surcharges see Nos. 1116-1117.

Freshwater Fish — A251

Designs: No. 1099, 70t, Lake Wanam rainbowfish. No. 1100, 70t, Kokoda mogurnda. 1k, Sepik grunter. 2.70k, Papuan black bass. 4.60k, Lake Tebera rainbowfish. 20k, Wichmann's mouth almighty.

2004, Jan. 30 *Perf. 14¼*

1099-1104 A251 Set of 6 25.00 25.00
Complete booklet, 10 #1099 6.00
Complete booklet, 10 #1100 6.00

For surcharges see Nos. 1154-1155.

Dinosaurs A252

Designs: 70t, Ankylosaurus. 1k, Oviraptor. 2k, Tyrannosaurus. 2.65k, Gigantosaurus. 2.70k, Centrosaurus. 4.60k, Carcharodontosaurus.

No. 1111: a, Edmontonia. b, Struthiomimus. c, Psittacosaurus. d, Gastonia. e, Shunosaurus. f, Iguanodon.

7k, Afrovenator.

2004, Feb. 25 *Perf. 14*

1105-1110 A252 Set of 6 11.00 11.00
1111 A252 1.50k Sheet of 6, #a-f 8.75 8.75

Souvenir Sheet

1112 A252 7k multi 6.25 6.25

Nos. 1015, 1078, 1079, 1092 and 1093 Surcharged

a

b

Methods and Perfs As Before

2004

1113 A236(a) 5t on 20t #1015 .65 .65
1114 A247(b) 70t on 65t #1078 1.25 1.25
1115 A247(b) 70t on 65t #1079 1.50 1.50
1116 A250(a) 70t on 65t #1092 1.50 1.50
1117 A250(a) 70t on 65t #1093 1.25 1.25
Nos. 1113-1117 (5) 6.15 6.15

Issued: Nos. 1114-1115, 1/20; others, 6/2.

Orchids A253

Designs: 70t, Phalaenopsis amabilis. 1k, Phaius tankervilleae. No. 1120, 2k, Bulbophyllum macranthum. 2.65k, Dendrobium rhodostictum. 2.70k, Diplocaulobium ridleyanum. 4.60k, Spathoglottis papuana.

No. 1124, 2k: a, Dendrobium cruttwellii. b, Dendrobium coeloglossum. c, Dendrobium alaticaulinum. d, Dendrobium obtusisepalum. e, Dendrobium johnsoniae. f, Dendrobium insigne.

7k, Dendrobium biggibum.

2004, May 19 **Litho.** *Perf. 14*

1118-1123 A253 Set of 6 11.00 11.00
1124 A253 2k Sheet of 6, #a-f 10.50 10.50

Souvenir Sheet

1125 A253 7k multi 6.50 6.50

Headdresses — A254

Province of headdress: No. 1126, 70t, Simbu. No. 1127, 70t, East Sepik. 2.65k, Southern Highlands. 2.70k, Western Highlands. 4.60k, Eastern Highlands. 5k, Central.

2004, June 2

1126-1131 A254 Set of 6 14.00 14.00
Complete booklet, 10 #1126 6.00
Complete booklet, 10 #1127 6.00

For surcharges see Nos. 1156-1157.

2004 Summer Olympics, Athens — A255

Designs: 70t, Swimming. 2.65k, Weight lifting, vert. 2.70k, Torch race, vert. 4.60k, Poster for 1952 Helsinki Olympics, vert.

2004, Aug. 11 *Perf. 13¼*

1132-1135 A255 Set of 4 10.50 10.50

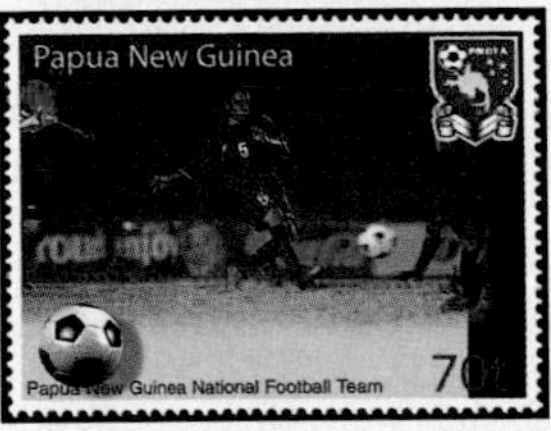

National Soccer Team — A256

Various players in action: 70t, 2.65k, 2.70k, 4.60k.

2004, Sept. 8 *Perf. 14¼*

1136-1139 A256 Set of 4 12.00 12.00

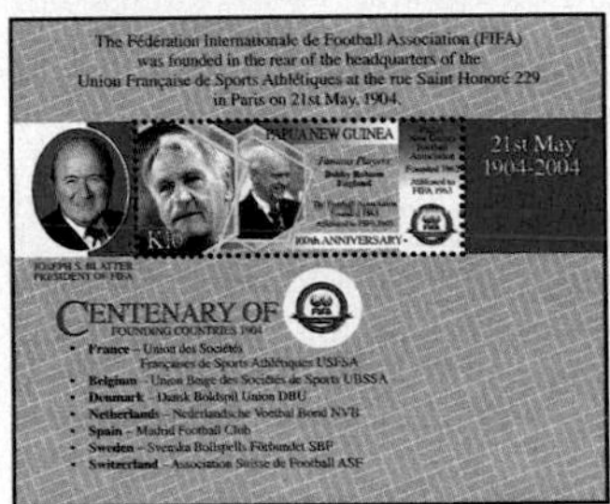

FIFA (Fédération Internationale de Football Association), Cent. — A257

No. 1140: a, Bruno Conti. b, Oliver Kahn. c, Mario Kempes. d, Bobby Moore.

10k, Bobby Robson.

2004, Sept. 8 *Perf. 13¼x13½*

1140 A257 2.50k Sheet of 4, #a-d 12.00 12.00

Souvenir Sheet

1141 A257 10k multi 10.00 10.00

Provincial Flags A258

Province: No. 1142, 70t, East New Britain. No. 1143, 70t, Madang. 2.65k, Eastern Highlands. 2.70k, Morobe. 4.60k, Milne Bay. 10k, East Sepik.

2004, Oct. 20 *Perf. 14*

1142-1147 A258 Set of 6 20.00 20.00

Shells A259

Designs: No. 1148, 70t, Phalium areola. No. 1149, 70t, Conus auratus. 2.65k, Oliva miniacea. 2.70k, Lambis chiragra. 4.60k, Conus suratensis. 10k, Architectonica perspectiva.

2004, Nov. 17

1148-1153 A259 Set of 6 18.00 18.00

For surcharges see Nos. 1223-1224.

Nos. 1099, 1100, 1126, 1127 Surcharged

Methods and Perfs as Before

2005, Jan. 3

1154 A251 75t on 70t #1099 1.10 1.10
1155 A251 75t on 70t #1100 1.10 1.10
1156 A254 75t on 70t #1126 1.10 1.10
1157 A254 75t on 70t #1127 1.10 1.10
Nos. 1154-1157 (4) 4.40 4.40

Birds A260

Designs: 5t, Little egret. No. 1159, 75t, White-faced heron. No. 1160, 75t, Nankeen night heron. 3k, Crested tern. 3.10k, Bar-tailed godwit. 5.20k, Little pied heron.

2005, Jan. 26 **Litho.** *Perf. 14*

1158-1163 A260 Set of 6 10.50 10.50

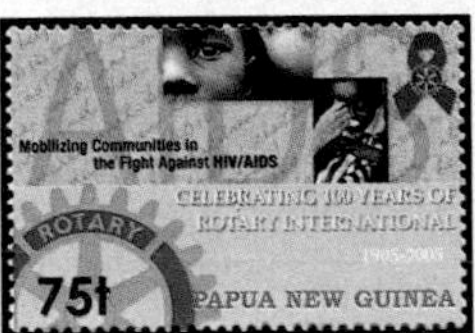

Rotary International, Cent. — A261

Designs: 75t, Mobilizing communities in the fight against HIV and AIDS. 3k, Barefoot child, PolioPlus and Rotary centennial emblems. 3.10k, Co-founders of first Rotary Club. 5.20k, Chicago skyline.

No. 1168, vert.: a, Silvester Schiele (1870-1945), first Rotary President. b, Paul Harris, founder. c, Children.

10k, Emblem and globe, vert.

2005, Feb. 23 **Litho.** *Perf. 14*

1164-1167 A261 Set of 4 9.00 9.00
1168 A261 4k Sheet of 3, #a-c 9.00 9.00

Souvenir Sheet

1169 A261 10k multi 7.50 7.50

Frangipani Varieties — A262

Designs: No. 1170, 75t, Evergreen. No. 1171, 75t, Lady in Pink. 1k, Carmine Flush. 3k, Cultivar acutifolia. 3.10k, American Beauty. 5.20k, Golden Kiss.

2005, Apr. 6 *Perf. 12¾*

1170-1175 A262 Set of 6 10.50 10.50

Mushrooms A263

Designs: No. 1176, 75t, Gymnopilus spectabilis. No. 1177, 75t, Melanogaster ambiguus. 3.10k, Microporus xanthopus. 5.20k, Psilocybe subcubensis.

No. 1180: a, Amanita muscaria. b, Amanita rubescens. c, Suillus luteus. d, Stropharia cubensis. e, Aseroes rubra. f, Psilocybe aucklandii.
10k, Mycena pura.

2005, May 18
1176-1179 A263 Set of 4 7.50 7.50
1180 A263 2k Sheet of 6, #a-f 9.50 9.50

Souvenir Sheet

1181 A263 10k multi 7.50 7.50

Beetles A264

Designs: No. 1182, 75t, Promechus pulcher. No. 1183, 75t, Callistola pulchra. 1k, Lagriomorpha indigacea. 3k, Hellerhinus papuanus. 3.10k, Aphorina australis. 5.20k, Bothricara pulchella.

2005, June 29 ***Perf. 14***
1182-1187 A264 Set of 6 10.00 10.00

Souvenir Sheet

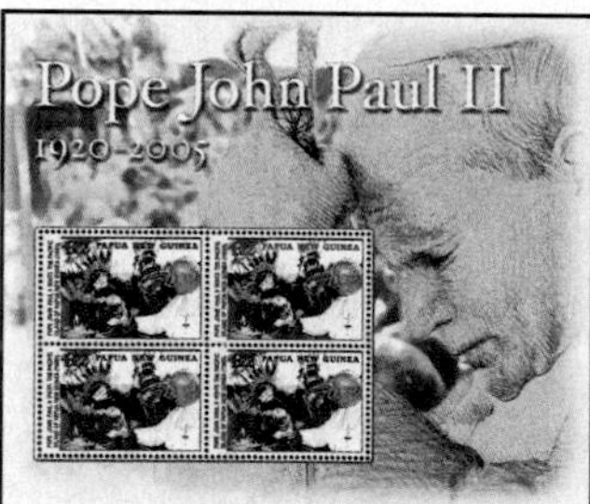

Pope John Paul II (1920-2005) — A265

No. 1188 — Denomination and country name in: a, Blue. b, Green. c, Orange. d, Red violet.

2005, Aug. 10 **Litho.** ***Perf. 12¾***
1188 A265 2k Sheet of 4, #a-d 6.50 6.50

Provincial Flags A266

Province: No. 1189, 75t, Gulf. No. 1190, 75t, Southern Highlands. 1k, North Solomons. 3k, Oro. 3.10k, Western Highlands. 5.20k, Western.

2005, Sept. 21 ***Perf. 14***
1189-1194 A266 Set of 6 10.00 10.00

Cats and Dogs — A267

Designs: No. 1195, 75t, Somali Rudy cat. No. 1196, 75t, Balinese Seal Lynx Point cat. 3k, Sphynx Brown Mackerel Tabby and White cat. 3.10k, Korat Blue cat. 5.20k, Bengal Brown Spotted Tabby cat.
No. 1200: a, Yorkshire terrier. b, Basenji. c, Neapolitan mastiff. d, Poodle.
10k, Boston terrier, horiz.

2005, Nov. 2 ***Perf. 12¾***
1195-1199 A267 Set of 5 10.00 10.00
1200 A267 2.50k Sheet of 4, #a-d 8.00 8.00

Souvenir Sheet

1201 A267 10k multi 8.00 8.00

Summer Institute of Languages in Papua New Guinea, 50th Anniv. — A268

Designs: No. 1202, 80t, Postal services. No. 1203, 80t, Literacy. 1k, Jim Dean, first director. 3.20k, Tokples preschools. 3.25k, Aviation. 5.35k, Community development.

2006, Jan. 4 **Litho.** ***Perf. 13¼***
1202-1207 A268 Set of 6 15.00 15.00

Miniature Sheets

Queen Elizabeth II, 80th Birthday — A269

No. 1208, 2.50k: a, Wearing polka dot dress. b, Engraving in brown from Canadian bank note. c, Engraving in blue from banknote. d, With Queen Mother.
No. 1209: a, 80t, With Pres. Bill Clinton. b, 3.20k, Dancing with Pres. Gerald Ford. c, 3.25k, With Pres. Ronald Reagan. d, 5.35k, With Pres. George W. Bush.

2006, Feb. 22 **Litho.** ***Perf. 13½***
Sheets of 4, #a-d
1208-1209 A269 Set of 2 17.00 17.00

Contemporary Art — A270

Designs: 5t, Shown. No. 1211, 80t, One head. No. 1212, 80t, Two heads. 3.20k, Man wearing headdress. 3.25k, Man and woman. 5.35k, Man with beads and man with painted face.

2006, Apr. 12 ***Perf. 13¼x13½***
1210-1215 A270 Set of 6 11.00 11.00

Miniature Sheet

2006 World Cup Soccer Championships, Germany — A271

No. 1216 — Player and uniform from: a, 80t, England. b, 3.20k, Germany. c, 3.25k, Argentina. d, 5.35k, Australia.

2006, May 17 ***Perf. 12***
1216 A271 Sheet of 4, #a-d 10.00 10.00

Salvation Army in Papua New Guinea, 50th Anniv. A272

Designs: 5t, Salvation Army emblem. 80t, Emblem, flags of Papua New Guinea and Salvation Army Papua New Guinea Territory. 1k, Lt. Ian Cutmore and Senior Major Keith Baker. 3.20k, Colonels, Andrew and Julie Kalai. 3.25k, Kei Geno. 5.35k, Lt. Dorothy Elphick holding baby.

2006, June 14 ***Perf. 13¼***
1217-1222 A272 Set of 6 10.00 10.00

Nos. 1148-1149 Surcharged

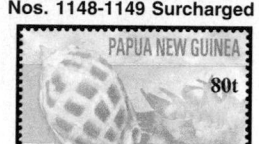

2006, July 5 **Litho.** ***Perf. 14***
1223 A259 80t on 70t #1148 .85 .85
1224 A259 80t on 70t #1149 .85 .85

Butterflies A273

Designs: 80t, Delias iltis. 3.20k, Ornithoptera paradisea. 3.25k, Taenaris catops. 5.35k, Papilio ulysses autolycus.

2006, Aug. 30 ***Perf. 13¼***
1225-1228 A273 Set of 4 11.00 11.00

Snakes A274

Designs: 5t, Black whip snake. 80t, Papuan taipan. 2k, Smooth-scaled death adder. 3.20k, Papuan black snake. 3.25k, New Guinea small-eyed snake. 5.35k, Eastern brown snake.

2006, Sept. 13 ***Perf. 14¼x14***
1229-1234 A274 Set of 6 12.00 12.00

A275

Elvis Presley (1935-77) — A276

Designs: 80t, Wearing white jacket and pants. 3.20k, Wearing red shirt. 3.25k, Wearing white jacket and black bow tie. 5.35k, With guitar.
No. 1239 — Record covers: a, 80t, 50,000 Elvis Fans Can't Be Wrong. b, 3.20k, Elvis Country. c, 3.25k, His Hand in Mine. d, 5.35k, King Creole.
10k, Holding teddy bears.

Perf. 13½, 13¼ (#1239)
2006, Nov. 15 **Litho.**
1235-1238 A275 Set of 4 10.00 10.00
1239 A276 Sheet of 4, #a-d 9.00 9.00

Souvenir Sheet

1240 A275 10k multi 8.75 8.75

Tropical Fruits A277

Designs: 5t, Mangos. No. 1242, 85t, Watermelons. No. 1243, 85t, Pineapples. No. 1244, 3.35t, Guavas. No. 1245, 3.35t, Pawpaws (papaya). 5.35t, Lemons.

2007, Jan. 2 ***Perf. 14x14¼***
1241-1246 A277 Set of 6 10.00 10.00

Endangered Turtles — A278

Designs: 10t, Hawksbill turtle. 35t, Flatback turtle. No. 1249, 85t, Loggerhead turtle. No. 1250, 3k, Leatherback turtle (blue violet panel). No. 1251, 3.35k, Green turtle (emerald panel). No. 1252, 5.35k, Olive Ridley turtle (tan panel).
No. 1253: a, 85t, Flatback turtle, diff. b, 3k, Leatherback turtle, diff. (olive green panel). c, 3.35k, Green turtle, diff. (olive green panel). d, 5.35k, Olive Ridley turtle, diff. (emerald panel).

2007, Mar. 23 **Litho.** ***Perf. 13¼***
1247-1252 A278 Set of 6 12.00 12.00

Souvenir Sheet

1253 A278 Sheet of 4, #a-d 12.00 12.00

Scouting, Cent. A279

Designs: 10t, Scouts standing at attention. 85t, Scouts carrying flag. 3.35k, Scouts and leaders at campsite. 5.35k, Scouts and leader.
10k, Lord Robert Baden-Powell, vert.

2007, May 23 Litho. *Perf. 14x14¼*

1254-1257	A279	Set of 4	8.00	8.00
1257a		Souvenir sheet, #1254-1257	6.50	6.50

Souvenir Sheet

1257B	A279	10k multi	6.75	6.75

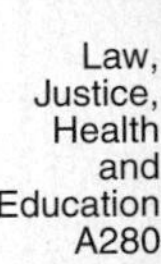

Law, Justice, Health and Education A280

Inscriptions: 5t, "A Just, Safe & Secure Society for All." 30t, "Prosperity Through self-reliance." 85t, "HIV/AIDS." 3k, "Crime Reduction." 3.35k, "Infant Care & Child Immunization." 5.35k, "Minimizing Illiteracy."

2007, July 25 *Perf. 13¼*

1258-1263	A280	Set of 6	8.75	8.75

A281

A282

A283

A284

A285

A286

A287

A288

A289

A290

A291

Orchids — A292

2007, Aug. 3 Litho. *Perf. 14*

1264		Sheet of 12 +12 labels	12.00	12.00
a.	A281	1k multi + label	1.00	1.00
b.	A282	1k multi + label	1.00	1.00
c.	A283	1k multi + label	1.00	1.00
d.	A284	1k multi + label	1.00	1.00
e.	A285	1k multi + label	1.00	1.00
f.	A286	1k multi + label	1.00	1.00
g.	A287	1k multi + label	1.00	1.00
h.	A288	1k multi + label	1.00	1.00
i.	A289	1k multi + label	1.00	1.00
j.	A290	1k multi + label	1.00	1.00
k.	A291	1k multi + label	1.00	1.00
l.	A292	1k multi + label	1.00	1.00

Labels could not be personalized.

Dendrobium Conanthum, Dendrobium Lasianthera — A293

Dendrobium Conanthum — A294

Dendrobium Lasianthera "May River Red" — A295

Dendrobium Wulaiense — A296

2007, Aug. 21 Litho. *Perf. 14*

1265	A293	85t multi + label	.60	.60
1266	A294	3k multi + label	2.10	2.10
1267	A295	3.35k multi + label	2.40	2.40
1268	A296	5.35k multi + label	3.75	3.75
		Nos. 1265-1268 (4)	8.85	8.85

Nos. 1265-1268 were each issued in sheets of 20 + 20 labels. The labels illustrated are generic labels. Labels could be personalized for an additional fee.

Rotary International in Papua New Guinea, 50th Anniv. — A297

Inscriptions: 85t, Rotary's humanitarian service. 3.35k, Rotary against malaria. 5k, Rotary clubs in Papua New Guinea. 5.35k, Donations in kind.

2007, Sept. 5 Litho. *Perf. 13¼*

1269-1272	A297	Set of 4	10.00	10.00
1272a		Souvenir sheet, #1269-1272	10.00	10.00

A298

Wedding of Queen Elizabeth II and Prince Philip, 60th Anniv. — A299

No. 1273: a, Couple, pink background. b, Queen, pink background. c, Queen, lilac background. d, Couple, lilac background. e, Couple, pale yellow background. f, Queen, pale yellow background.

2007, Oct. 31 Litho. *Perf. 14*

1273	A298	2k Sheet of 6, #a-f	8.50	8.50

Souvenir Sheet

1274	A299	10k multi	7.25	7.25

A300

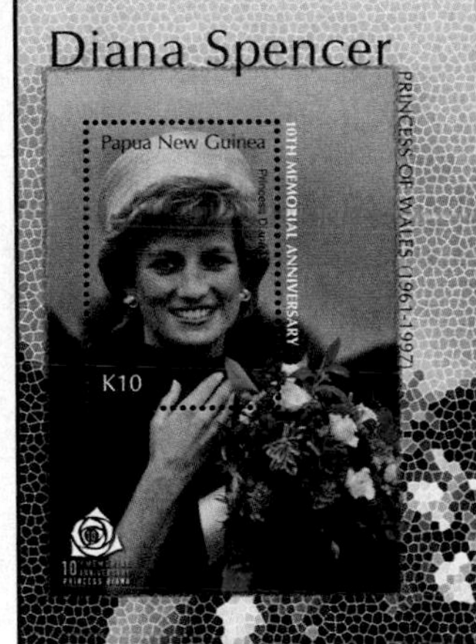

Princess Diana (1961-97) — A301

No. 1275 — Photographs of Diana from: a, 85t, 1965. b, 2.45k, 1971. c, 3.35k, 1981. d, 5.35k, 1983.

2007, Oct. 31

1275	A300	Sheet of 4, #a-d	8.50	8.50

Souvenir Sheet

1276	A301	10k multi	7.00	7.00

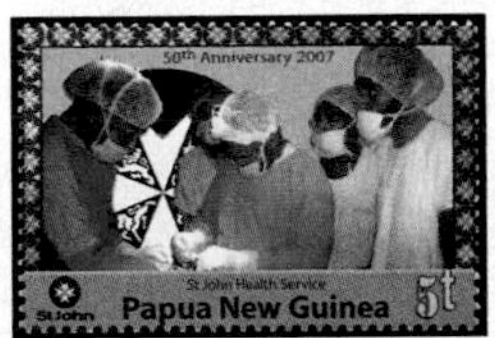

St. John Ambulance in Papua New Guinea, 50th Anniv. — A302

Inscriptions: 5t, St. John Health Service. 20t, St. John Blood Service. 85t, St. John Blind Service. 1k, St. John Ambulance Service. 3.35k, St. John Volunteer Service. 5.35k, Order of St. John.

2007, Nov. 30 *Perf. 14¼*

1277-1282	A302	Set of 6	8.00	8.00
1282a		Miniature sheet, #1277-1282	8.00	8.00

Contemporary Art — A303

Designs: 5t, Oro Gagara. 30t, Western Province tribesman. 85t, Sorcerer. 3k, Hewa wigman. 3.35k, Pigs Into Python Legend. 5.35k, Tolai masks.

2007, Dec. 12

1283-1288 A303 Set of 6 9.50 9.50
1288a Miniature sheet, #1283-1288 9.50 9.50

Protected Birds A304

Designs: 10t, Papuan hornbill. 50t, Osprey. 85t, New Guinea harpy eagle. 3k, Victoria crowned pigeon.
No. 1293: a, 1k, Palm cockatoo. b, 5.35k, Great white egret.
10k, Like #1293a.

2008, Jan. 25 Litho. *Perf. 14x14¼*

1289-1292 A304 Set of 4 4.00 4.00
1293 A304 Sheet of 6, #1289-1292, 1293a, 1293b 9.00 9.00

Souvenir Sheet

1294 A304 10k multi 8.50 8.50

Asaro Mudmen Legend A305

Designs: 85t, Two Mudmen, large skull. 3k, Three Mudmen scouting for enemies in forest. 3.35k, Mudmen attacking enemies. 5.35k, Retreat of enemies.
10k, Similar to 85t.

2008, Feb. 27 *Perf. 13¼*

1295-1298 A305 Set of 4 9.50 9.50
1298a Miniature sheet, #1295-1298 9.50 9.50

Souvenir Sheet

1299 A305 10k multi 8.00 8.00

Marine Life A306

Designs: No. 1300, 85t, Leather coral. No. 1301, 3k, Kunei's chromodoris. No. 1302, 3.35k, Scorpion spider snail. No. 1303, 5.35k, Veined sponge.
No. 1304: a, 85t, Radiant sea urchin. b, 3k, Varicose. c, 3.35k, Sea squirt. d, 5.35k, Heffernan's sea star.
10k, White grape coral.

2008, Mar. 21 *Perf. 14x14¼*

1300-1303 A306 Set of 4 12.00 12.00
1304 A306 Sheet of 4, #a-d 15.00 15.00

Souvenir Sheet

1305 A306 10k multi 10.00 10.00

Miniature Sheet

2008 Summer Olympics, Beijing — A307

No. 1306: a, Weight lifting. b, Diving. c, Hurdles. d, Boxing.

2008, Apr. 16 *Perf. 12¾*

1306 A307 1.40k Sheet of 4, #a-d 4.50 4.50

Papua New Guinea Partnership With European Union, 30th Anniv. — A308

Flags of Papua New Guinea and European Union, bird of paradise, circle of stars and background color of: Nos. 1307, 1311a, 85t, Gray. Nos. 1308, 1311b, 3k, Yellow. Nos. 1309, 1311c, 3.35k, Rose pink. Nos. 1310, 1311d, 5.35k, Light blue.
10k, Gray, without blue panel at bottom.

2008, May 9 *Perf. 13x13¼*

Stamps With Blue Panel With Bold White Drawings

1307-1310 A308 Set of 4 10.00 10.00

Stamps With Blue Panel With Faint White Drawings

1311 A308 Sheet of 4, #a-d 10.00 10.00

Souvenir Sheet

1312 A308 10k multi 8.00 8.00

Art by Timothy Akis (1944-84) — A309

Designs: No. 1313, 85t, Long Hair. No. 1314, 3k, Alone. No. 1315, 3.35k, Woman with Cassowary and Child. No. 1316, 5.35k, Man Shooting Cassowary.
No. 1317: a, 85t, Five Men in Their Gardens (top half). b, 3k, The Crocodile Woman and Two Headed Man (top half). c, 3.35k, As "a," bottom half. d, 5.35k, As "b," bottom half.
10k, Flying Fox.

2008, June 25 Litho. *Perf. 14¼x14*

1313-1316 A309 Set of 4 9.75 9.75
1317 A309 Sheet of 4, #a-d 9.75 9.75

Souvenir Sheet

1318 A309 10k multi 7.75 7.75

Headdresses A310

Headdresses of: No. 1319, 85t, Central Province (person showing shoulder). No. 1320, 3k, Western Highlands Province. No. 1321, 3.35k, Oro Province. No. 1322, 5.35k, Western Highlands Province, diff.
No. 1323: a, 85t, Central Province (headdress with yellow side tassels). b, 3k, Central Province, diff. c, 3.35k, Southern Highlands Province, diff. d, 5.35k, Oro Province, diff.
10k, Central Province, diff.

2008, July 31

1319-1322 A310 Set of 4 10.00 10.00
1323 A310 Sheet of 4, #a-d 10.00 10.00

Souvenir Sheet

1324 A310 10k multi 8.00 8.00

Marilyn Monroe (1926-62), Actress — A311

No. 1325, horiz. — Various photographs of Monroe: a, 85t. b, 3k. c, 3.35k. d, 5.35k
10k, Monroe in automobile.

2008, Aug. 6 Litho. *Perf. 13¼*

1325 A311 Sheet of 4, #a-d 9.50 9.50

Souvenir Sheet

1326 A311 10k multi 7.50 7.50

Birds of Paradise — A312

Designs: No. 1327, 85t, Paradisaea guilielmi. No. 1328, 3k, Parotia lawesi. No. 1329, 3.35k, Epimachus meyeri. No. 1330, 5.35k, Diphyllodes magnificus.
No. 1331: a, 85t, Astrapia stephaniae. b, 3k, Cnemophilus macgregorii. c, 3.35k, Pteridophora alberti. d, 5.35k, Astrapia meyeri.
10k, Cicinnurus regius.

2008, Sept. 3 Litho. *Perf. 14¼x14*

1327-1330 A312 Set of 4 10.00 10.00
1331 A312 Sheet of 4, #a-d 11.00 11.00

Souvenir Sheet

1332 A312 10k multi 8.00 8.00

Gold Mining A313

Designs: No. 1333, 85t, Tunnel drilling. No. 1334, 3k, Logistics. No. 1335, 3.35k, Refinery. No. 1336, 5.35k, Gold bars.
No. 1337: a, 85t, Open pit mining. b, 3k, Conveyor belt. c, 3.35k, Plant site. d, 5.35k, Refinery.
10k, Gold bar.

2008, Oct. 31 *Perf. 14¼*

1333-1336 A313 Set of 4 10.00 10.00
1337 A313 Sheet of 4, #a-d 10.00 10.00

Souvenir Sheet

1338 A313 10k multi 8.00 8.00

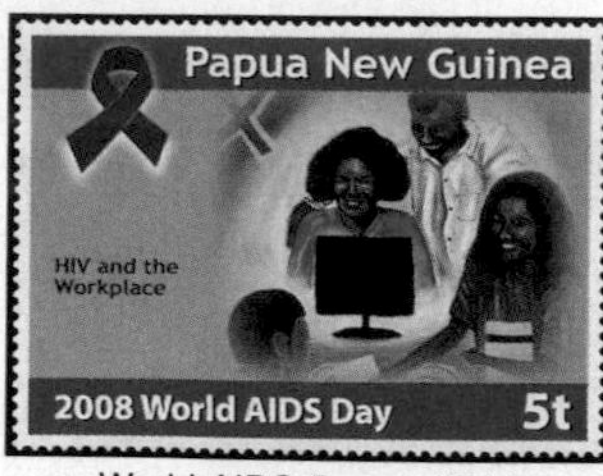

World AIDS Day — A314

Red ribbon and inscription: 5t, HIV and the workplace. 10t, Voluntary counseling and testing. 50t, Role of men and women. Nos. 1342, 1348a, 85t, Education. 1k, 10k, Eradicating stigma and discrimination. 2k, Living with the virus. Nos. 1345, 1348b, 3k, Care, support and the role of family. Nos. 1346, 1348c, 3.70k, Building leadership. Nos. 1347, 1348d, 6k, Health and nutrition.

2008, Dec. 1 Litho. *Perf. 14¼*

1339-1347 A314 Set of 9 14.00 14.00
1348 A314 Sheet of 4, #a-d 13.00 13.00

Souvenir Sheet

1349 A314 10k multi 9.00 9.00

No. 1348 contains four 42x28 stamps; No. 1349 contains one 42x28mm stamp.

Christmas — A315

Designs: No. 1350, 85t, Holy Family. No. 1351, 3k, Santa Claus on reindeer. No. 1352, 3.35k, Book and candle. No. 1353, 5.35k, Bell and book.
No. 1354: a, 85t, Journey to Bethlehem. b, 3k, Silent night. c, 3.35k, Behold that star. d, 5.35k, Three wise men.
10k, Gift and map of Papua New Guinea.

2008, Dec. 3 *Perf. 14¼*

1350-1353 A315 Set of 4 9.75 9.75
1354 A315 Sheet of 4, #a-d 9.75 9.75

Souvenir Sheet

1355 A315 10k multi 8.00 8.00

Plants A316

Designs: No. 1356, 85t, Bixa. No. 1357, 3k, Perfume tree. No. 1358, 3.70k, Beach kalofilum. No. 1359, 6k, Macaranga.
No. 1360: a, 85t, Native frangipani. b, 3k, Ten cent flower. c, 3.70k, Beach terminali. d, 6k, Red beech.
10k, Beach convolvulus (morning glory).

2009, Jan. 14 *Perf. 14¼*

1356-1359 A316 Set of 4 10.00 10.00
1360 A316 Sheet of 4, #a-d 10.00 10.00

Souvenir Sheet

1361 A316 10k multi 7.75 7.75

For surcharge, see No. 1732K.

Worldwide Fund for Nature (WWF) — A317

Designs: No. 1362, 85t, Albericus siegfriedi. No. 1363, 3k, Cophixalus nubicola. No. 1364, 3.70k, Nyctimystes pulcher. No. 1365, 6k, Sphenophryne cornuta.

No. 1366: a, 85t, Litoria sauroni. b, 3k, Litoria prora. c, 3.70k, Litoria multiplica. d, 6k, Litoria pronimia.

10k, Oreophryne sp.

2009, Feb. 18 Litho. *Perf. 13¼*

1362-1365 A317 Set of 4 10.00 10.00
1366 A317 Sheet of 4, #a-d 10.00 10.00

Souvenir Sheet

1367 A317 10k multi 7.50 7.50

Art by David Lasisi — A318

Designs: No. 1368, 85t, Chota. No. 1369, 3k, Stability. No. 1370, 3.70k, Taumimir. No. 1371, 6k, The Moieties.

No. 1372: a, 85t, Like a Log Being Adrifted. b, 3k, Lasisi. c, 3.70k, Lupa. d, 6k, In Memory of Marker Craftsman.

10k, Trapped by Cobweb of Stinging Pain.

2008, Mar. 11 *Perf. 13½*

1368-1371 A318 Set of 4 9.50 9.50
1372 A318 Sheet of 4, #a-d 9.50 9.50

Souvenir Sheet

1373 A318 10k multi 7.00 7.00

A319

China 2009 World Stamp Exhibition, Luoyang — A320

2009, Apr. 10 *Perf. 12¾x12½*

1374 A319 1k multi .90 .90

Souvenir Sheet

1375 A320 6k multi 5.00 5.00

Chinese Antiquities A321

Designs: Nos. 1376, 1382a, 5t, Vessel with design of deities, animals and masks. Nos. 1377, 1382b, 10t, Evening in the Peach and Plum Garden, by Li Bai. Nos. 1378, 1382c, 85t, Reliquary with Buddhist figures. Nos. 1379, 1382d, 3k, Brick relief figure. Nos. 1380, 1382e, 3.70k, Round tray with scroll designs. Nos. 1381, 1382f, 6k, Plate in the shape of two poach halves with design of two foxes.

2009, Apr. 10 *Perf. 14¼x14¾*

With Inscription "World Stamp Exhibition / China 2009" At Left

1376-1381 A321 Set of 6 9.50 9.50

Stamps Without Inscription "World Stamp Exhibition / China 2009" At Left

1382 A321 Sheet of 6, #a-f 9.50 9.50

Assets of Coral Triangle A322

Designs: No. 1383, 85t, Fish. No. 1384, 3k, Marine turtle (blue green frame). No. 1385, 3.70k, Mangroves. No. 1386, 6k, Coral reefs.

No. 1387: a, 85t, Dolphins. b, 3k, Marine turtle (no frame). c, 3.70k, Reef fish. d, 6k, Killer whale.

10k, Grouper.

2009, May 22 Litho. *Perf. 14½x14¼*

1383-1386 A322 Set of 4 10.00 10.00
1387 A322 Sheet of 4, #a-d 10.00 10.00

Souvenir Sheet

1388 A322 10k multi 7.50 7.50

Kokoda Trail A323

Designs: No. 1389, 85t, Guides assisting a trekker. No. 1390, 3k, Crossing Vabuyavi River. No. 1391, 3.70k, Waterfall near Abuari. No. 1392, 6k, Crossing Lake Myola 1.

No. 1393: a, 85t, Crossing Emune River. b, 3k, Entering Imita Ridge. c, 3.70k, Crossing Alo Creek. d, 6k, Templeton's Crossing No. 2.

10k, Golden Staircase, Imita Ridge.

2009, June 23 *Perf. 14¼*

1389-1392 A323 Set of 4 10.50 10.50
1393 A323 Sheet of 4, #a-d 10.50 10.50

Souvenir Sheet

1394 A323 10k multi 7.75 7.75

Bats A324

Designs: No. 1395, 85t, Black-bellied bat. No. 1396, 3k, Least blossom bat. No. 1397, 3.70k, Sanborn's broad-nosed bat. No. 1398, 6k, Mantled mastiff bat.

No. 1399: a, 85t, Trident leaf-nosed bat. b, 3k, Flower-faced bat. c, 3.70k, Eastern horse-shoe bat. d, 6k, Greater tube-nosed bat.

10k, Bougainville's fruit bat.

2009, July 15

1395-1398 A324 Set of 4 10.50 10.50
1399 A324 Sheet of 4, #a-d 10.50 10.50

Souvenir Sheet

1400 A324 10k multi 7.75 7.75

For surcharge, see No. 1732I.

Intl. Day of Non-violence A325

Doves and: No. 1401, 85t, Abraham Lincoln. No. 1402, 3k, Princess Diana. No. 1403, 3.70k, Nelson Mandela. No. 1404, 6k, Barack Obama.

No. 1405: a, 85t, Obama. b, 3k, Dr. Martin Luther King, Jr. c, 3.70k, Mohandas K. Gandhi. d, 6k, Princess Diana.

10k, Obama, diff.

2009, Aug. 6 *Perf. 13¼*

1401-1404 A325 Set of 4 10.50 10.50
1405 A325 Sheet of 4, #a-d 10.50 10.50

Souvenir Sheet

1406 A325 10k multi 7.75 7.75

No. 1406 contains one 38x51mm stamp.

Volcanoes — A326

Designs: No. 1407, 85t, Mount Vulcan. No. 1408, 3k, Mount Tavurvur. No. 1409, 3.70k, Mount Bagana. No. 1410, 6k, Manam Island.

No. 1411: a, 85t, Mount Tavurvur, diff. b, 3k, Manam Island, diff. c, 3.70k, Mount Tavurvur, diff. d, 6k, Mount Ulawun.

10k, Mount Tavurvur, diff.

2009, Sept. 9 *Perf. 14¼*

1407-1410 A326 Set of 4 10.50 10.50
1411 A326 Sheet of 4, #a-d 10.50 10.50

Souvenir Sheet

1412 A326 10k multi 7.75 7.75

Palm Oil Production — A327

Designs: No. 1413, 85t, Oil palm fruitlets. No. 1414, 3k, Oil palm nursery. No. 1415, 3.70k, Oil palm bunches. No. 1416, 6k, Fruit collection.

No. 1417: a, 85t, Irrigation. b, 3k, Oil palm bunches. c, 3.70k, Loose fruits. d, 6k, Mill.

10k, Oil palm fruitlets in hand.

2009, Oct. 7 Litho. *Perf. 14¼*

1413-1416 A327 Set of 4 10.50 10.50
1417 A327 Sheet of 4, #a-d 10.50 10.50

Souvenir Sheet

1418 A327 10k multi 7.75 7.75

For surcharge, see No. 1732P.

Canoes — A328

Canoe from: No. 1419, 85t, Mortlock Island. No. 1420, 3k, Manus Province. No. 1421, 3.70k, Bilbil. No. 1422, 6k, Central Province.

No. 1423: a, 85t, Kimbe. b, 3k, Vuvulu Island. c, 3.70k, Suau Island. d, 6k, Mailu.

10k, Gogodala.

2009, Nov. 4 Litho. *Perf. 12¾*

1419-1422 A328 Set of 4 10.50 10.50
1423 A328 Sheet of 4, #a-d 10.50 10.50

Souvenir Sheet

1424 A328 10k multi 7.50 7.50

Traditional Dances — A329

Designs: No. 1425, 1k, Engagement dance, Western Highlands Province. No. 1426, 3k, Bride price dance, Central Province. No. 1427, 4.65k, Engagement dance, Manus Province. No. 1428, 6.30k, Trobriand love dance, Milne Bay Province.

No. 1429: a, 1k, Courtship dance, Chimbu Province. b, 3k, Engagement dance, Enga Province. c, 4.65k, Engagement Dance, Central Province. d, 6.30k, Womanhood dance, Central Province.

10k, Trobriand love dance, Milne Bay Province, diff.

2009, Dec. 2 *Perf. 14¼*

1425-1428 A329 Set of 4 11.50 11.50
1429 A329 Sheet of 4, #a-d 11.50 11.50

Souvenir Sheet

1430 A329 10k multi 7.50 7.50

Pioneer Art A330

Paintings by Jakupa Ako: No. 1431, 1k, Fish Man. No. 1432, 3k, Story Board. No. 1433, 4.65k, Hunting Trip. No. 1434, 6.30k, Warrior.

No. 1435: a, 1k, Bird Art. b, 3k, Bird Eating. c, 4.65k, Bird Nest. d, 6.30k, Marsupial.

10k, Spirit Mask.

2010, Jan. 1 *Perf. 14¼*

1431-1434 A330 Set of 4 11.00 11.00
1435 A330 Sheet of 4, #a-d 11.00 11.00

Souvenir Sheet

1436 A330 10k multi 7.50 7.50

Beche-de-Mer Industry — A331

Edible sea cucumbers: No. 1437, 1k, Chalkfish. No. 1438, 3k, Elephant trunk fish. No. 1439, 4.65k, Curryfish. No. 1440, 6.30k, Tigerfish.

No. 1441: a, 1k, Surf redfish. b, 3k, Lollyfish. c, 4.65k, Brown sandfish. d, 6.30k, Sandfish.

10k, Pinkfish.

2010, Feb. 8 Litho. *Perf. 14x14¼*

1437-1440 A331 Set of 4 11.00 11.00
1441 A331 Sheet of 4, #a-d 11.00 11.00

Souvenir Sheet

1442 A331 10k multi 7.50 7.50

For surcharge, see No. 1732M.

Carteret Atoll
A332

Designs: No. 1443, 1k, Huene Island divided. No. 1444, 3k, Upsurge of water through man-made barriers. No. 1445, 4.65k, Salt water intrusion No. 1446, 6.30k, Tree killed by salt water.

No. 1447: a, 1k, Dwindling island. b, 3k, Tree killed by salt water, diff. c, 4.65k, Storm surge and erosion. d, 6.30k, Man-made barriers.

10k, Divided atolls.

2010, Mar. 18

1443-1446	A332	Set of 4	11.50	11.50
1447	A332	Sheet of 4, #a-d	11.50	11.50

Souvenir Sheet

1448	A332	10k multi	7.75	7.75

Girl Guides, Cent.
A333

Designs: No. 1449, 1k, Guides learning cooking for badge work, 1970. No. 1450, 3k, Guide creating a wash bowl for badge work. No. 1451, 4.65k, Trainer teaching knot tying. No. 1452, 6.30k, Brownies displaying badge work.

No. 1453: a, 1k, Lady Kala Olewale, Second Papua New Guinea Chief Commissioner. b, 3k, Lady Christian Chartterton, founder of Papua New Guinea Girl Guides. c, 4.65k, Princess Anne visiting Papua New Guinea Girl Guides. d, 6.30k, Enny Moaitz, First Papua New Guinea Chief Commissioner.

10k, Lady Olave Baden-Powell.

2010, Apr. 10 Litho. *Perf. 14x14¼*

1449-1452	A333	Set of 4	11.00	11.00
1453	A333	Sheet of 4, #a-d	11.00	11.00

Souvenir Sheet

1454	A333	10k multi	7.50	7.50

For surcharges, see Nos. 1732O, 1732R.

Kokoda Campaigns, 68th Anniv. — A334

No. 1455: a, Soldiers in battle. b, Injured Australian soldier, Papuan natives. c, Tourists at Kokoda.

No. 1456: a, Veterans at Kokoda Campaign Memorial, Isurava. b, Veterans of Kokoda Campaign, Papuan houses.

2010, Apr. 20 Litho. *Perf. 14¾x14*

1455	A334	Horiz. strip of 3	2.40	2.40
a.-c.		1k Any single	.80	.80
1456	A334	Horiz. pair	7.50	7.50
a.-b.		4.65k Either single	3.75	3.75
c.		Souvenir sheet, #1455a-1455c, 1456a-1456b	10.00	10.00

See Australia Nos. 3244-3252.

National Population and Housing Census — A335

Inscriptions: No. 1457, 1k, Young and old. No. 1458, 1k, Youths. No. 1459, 3k, Infants. No. 1460, 3k, Villagers.

No. 1461: a, 1k, School kids. b, 1k, Elderly men. c, 3k, Elderly women. d, 3k, All walks of life.

2010, May 3 *Perf. 14x14¼*

1457-1460	A335	Set of 4	6.00	6.00
1461	A335	Sheet of 4, #a-d	6.00	6.00

For surcharge, see No. 1732Q.

Expo 2010, Shanghai — A336

Designs: 1k, Summer Palace, Wenchang Tower. No. 1463, 3k, Dancer, Shanghai Intl. Culture and Art Festival. 4.65k, Oriental Pearl Tower, Pudong, Shanghai. 6.30k, Male Chinese acrobatic performers.

No. 1466: a, 5t, Like 1k. b, 10t, Like #1463. c, 85t, Like 4.65k. d, 3k, Female Chinese acrobatic performers. e, 3.70k, Like 6.30k. f, 6k, Ancient Chinese building.

10k, Tower, Suzhou.

2010, May 21 *Perf. 11¼x11½*

1462-1465	A336	Set of 4	11.00	11.00
1466	A336	Sheet of 6, #a-f	10.00	10.00

Souvenir Sheet

1467	A336	10k multi	9.00	9.00

Sport Fishing — A337

Inscriptions: No. 1468, 1k, Female angler. No. 1469, 3k, Team effort. No. 1470, 4.65k, 25kg Sailfish. No. 1471, 6.30k, 10kg Barramundi.

No. 1472: a, 1k, Game fishing boat. b, 3k, Male angler. c, 4.65k, 14kg Wahoo. d, 6.30k, 11kg Barramundi.

10k, Irene Robinson's world record catch blue fin trevally (92.6kg) on a 4kg line.

2010, June 11 *Perf. 13½*

1468-1471	A337	Set of 4	11.00	11.00
1472	A337	Sheet of 4, #a-d	11.00	11.00

Souvenir Sheet

1473	A337	10k multi	7.25	7.25

Coffee
A338

Designs: 15t, Coffee tree with cherries. No. 1475, 1k, Budding beans. No. 1476, 4.65k, Green coffee cherries. No. 1477, 6.30k, Red coffee cherries.

No. 1478: a, 1k, Man harvesting cherries. b, 3k, Fermentation. c, 4.65k, Drying parchment. d, 6.30k, Man holding green coffee beans.

10k, Green and red coffee cherries.

2010, July 7 Litho. *Perf. 14¼*

1474-1477	A338	Set of 4	9.00	9.00
1478	A338	Sheet of 4, #a-d	11.00	11.00

Souvenir Sheet

1479	A338	10k multi	7.25	7.25

Bowerbirds
A339

Designs: 5t, Macgregor's gardener bowerbird. No. 1481, 1k, Flame bowerbird. No. 1482, 4.65k, Archbold's bowerbird. No. 1483, 6.30k, Adelbert regent bowerbird.

No. 1484: a, 1k, Pair of Flame bowerbirds. b, 3k, Yellow-fronted gardener bowerbird. c, 4.65k, Vogelkop gardener bowerbird. d, 6.30k, Lauterbach's bowerbird.

10k, Head of Flame bowerbird.

2010, Aug. 4

1480-1483	A339	Set of 4	9.00	9.00
1484	A339	Sheet of 4, #a-d	11.50	11.50

Souvenir Sheet

1485	A339	10k multi	7.50	7.50

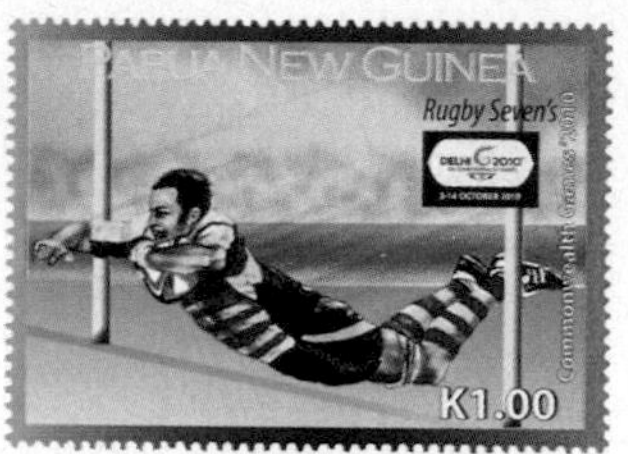

2010 Commonwealth Games, Delhi — A340

Designs: No. 1486, 1k, Rugby sevens. No. 1487, 3k, Boxing. No. 1488, 4.65k, Netball. No. 1489, 6.30k, Hurdles.

No. 1490: a, 1k, Weight lifting. b, 3k, Swimming. c, 4.65k, Lawn bowling. d, 6.30k, Sprinting.

10k, Tennis.

2010, Sept. 3 *Perf. 13½*

1486-1489	A340	Set of 4	11.50	11.50
1490	A340	Sheet of 4, #a-d	11.50	11.50

Souvenir Sheet

1491	A340	10k multi	7.75	7.75

Orchids
A341

Designs: No. 1492, 1k, Dendrobium lasianthera May River Red. No. 1493, 3k, Dendrobium violaceoflavens J.J. Smith. No. 1494, 4.65k, Dendrobium mirbelianum var. Vanimo. No. 1495, 6.30k, Dendrobium helix.

No. 1496: a, 1k, Dendrobium nindii W. Hill. b, 3k, Dendrobium sp. off. D. gouldii Reichb. f. c, 4.65k, Dendrobium gouldii Reichb. f. var. Bougainville White. d, 6.30k, Dendrobium discolor var. pink Bensbach.

10k, Dendrobium lasianthera var. Sepik Blue.

2010, Sept. 28 *Perf. 14¼*

1492-1495	A341	Set of 4	11.50	11.50
1496	A341	Sheet of 4, #a-d	11.50	11.50

Souvenir Sheet

1497	A341	10k multi	7.75	7.75

For surcharge, see No. 1732L.

Mother Teresa (1910-97)
A342

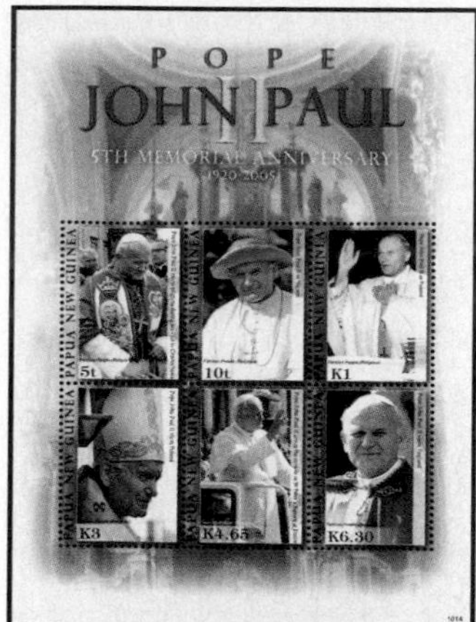

Pope John Paul II (1920-2005) — A343

Pope Benedict XVI — A344

Photographs of Mother Teresa from: 1k, 1997. 3k, 1971. 4.65k, 1988. 6.30k, 1984.

No. 1502 — Photographs of Pope John Paul II: a, 5t, Meeting with pilgrims at Czestochowa. b, 10t, In Nigeria. c, 1k, In Poland, as young man (without miter). d, 3k, In Poland (wearing miter). e, 4.65k, Greeting crowds in St. Peter's Square. f, 6.30k, In England.

2010, Oct. 13 *Perf. 12*

1498-1501	A342	Set of 4	12.00	12.00
1502	A343	Sheet of 6, #a-f	12.00	12.00

Souvenir Sheet

1503	A344	10k multi	8.00	8.00

Spiders
A345

Designs: No. 1504, 1k, Nephila pilipes. No. 1505, 3k, Argiope aemula. No. 1506, 4.65k, Gasterocantha (blue violet color at UL). No. 1507, 6.30k, Cyrtophora moluccensis.

No. 1508: a, 1k, Leucauge celebesiana. b, 3k, Holconia. c, 4.65k, Gasterocantha (red background color at UL). d, 6.30k, Ocrisiona.

10k, Nephila pilipes, diff.

2010, Nov. 3 Litho. *Perf. 14½*

1504-1507	A345	Set of 4	12.00	12.00
1508	A345	Sheet of 4, #a-d	12.00	12.00

Souvenir Sheet

1509	A345	10k multi	8.00	8.00

War Dances — A346

Designs: 50t, Warrior with bow and arrow, Western Highlands Province. 1.05k, Simbu warrior with spear, Chimbu Province. 5k, Warrior with spear and shield, Western Highlands Province. 7k, Mudman with bow and arrow, Eastern Highlands Province.

10k, Tasman Island knife dancer, North Solomons Province.

2010, Dec. 1 Litho. *Perf. 14¼x14*
1510-1513 A346 Set of 4 11.00 11.00

Souvenir Sheet

1514 A346 10k multi 8.00 8.00

Monitor Lizards A347

Designs: No. 1515, 1.05k, Emerald tree monitor. No. 1516, 5k, Papuan argus monitor. No. 1517, 5k, Papuan monitor. 7k, Blue-tailed monitor.

No. 1519: a, 1.05k, Blue-tailed monitor, diff. b, 2k, Spotted tree monitor. c, 5k, Mangrove monitor. d, 5k, Peach-throat monitor.

No. 1520, Papuan argus monitor with tongue extended.

2011, Jan. 5 Litho. *Perf. 14x14¼*
1515-1518 A347 Set of 4 14.50 14.50
1519 A347 Sheet of 4, #a-d 10.50 10.50

Souvenir Sheet

1520 A347 5k multi 4.00 4.00

Chinese Zodiac Animals A348

Designs: No. 1521, 5t, Dragon. No. 1522, 50t, Tiger. No. 1523, 1.05k, Horse. 2k, Monkey. No. 1525, 5k, Snake. No. 1526, 5k, Dog.

No. 1527: a, 5t, Ox. b, 50t, Rooster. c, 55t, Sheep. d, 1.05k, Rat. e, 5k, Boar. f, 7k, Rabbit.

2011, Feb. 8 *Perf. 13 Syncopated*
1521-1526 A348 Set of 6 11.00 11.00
1527 A348 Sheet of 6 #a-f 11.00 11.00

Paintings by Mathias Kauage (1944-2003) — A349

Designs: No. 1528, 1.05k, Pailet Draivim Balus (Pilot Flying an Airplane). No. 1529, 5k, Fes Misineri (First Missionary). No. 1530, 5k, Pailet i Trein Long Draivim Balus (Trainee Pilot at Training). No. 1531, 7k, Eia Bas (Airbus).

No. 1532 — Details from Eia Bas Bilong Eiu Gini (Air New Guinea's Airbus): a, 1.05k, Wing at top. b, 5k, Bird at top. c, 5k, Wing at bottom. 7k, Rear wheel.

10k, Barasut Man (Parachute Man).

2011, Mar. 18 Litho. *Perf. 13¼*
1528-1531 A349 Set of 4 14.50 14.50
1532 A349 Sheet of 4, #a-d 14.50 14.50

Souvenir Sheet

1533 A349 10k multi 8.00 8.00

Fish A350

Designs: No. 1534, 1.05k, Cephalopholis miniata. No. 1535, 1.05k, Cromileptes altivelis. 5k, Plectropomus areolatus. 7k, Epinephelus lanceolatus.

10k, Epinephelus polyphekadion.

2011, Apr. 6 *Perf. 14¼*
1534-1537 A350 Set of 4 11.50 11.50

Souvenir Sheet

1538 A350 10k multi 8.00 8.00

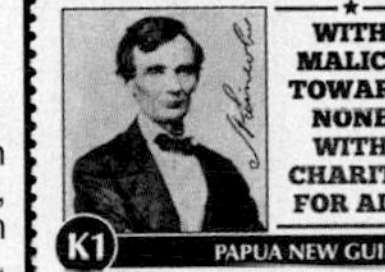

American Civil War, 150th Anniv. A351

Designs: 1k, Pres. Abraham Lincoln, text "With malice toward none, with charity for all." No. 1540, 1.05k, Lincoln, text "Of the people, by the people, for the people." No. 1541, 5k, Slave and banner. No. 1542, 7k, Lincoln, Confederate States Pres. Jefferson Davis, US and Confederate flags, eagle, banner.

No. 1543: a, 5t, The Peacemakers, painting by George P. A. Healy. b, 50t, Battle of Fort Sumter. c, 55t, Lincoln and his Cabinet. d, 1.05k, Lincoln, Generals Ulysses S. Grant and Robert E. Lee. e, 5k, Lincoln, slave, text "If slavery is not wrong, nothing is wrong." f, 7k, Battle of Gettysburg.

10k, Lincoln, text "A house divided cannot stand."

2011, Apr. 20 *Perf. 12*
1539-1542 A351 Set of 4 12.00 12.00

13 Syncopated

1543 A351 Sheet of 6, #a-f 12.00 12.00

Souvenir Sheet

1544 A351 10k multi 8.50 8.50

Butterflies A352

Designs: No. 1545, 1.05k, Orange birdwing. No. 1546, 1.05k, Green birdwing. 5k, Blue birdwing. 7k, Goliath birdwing.

10k, Pair of Queen Alexandra's birdwings.

2011, May 3 Litho. *Perf. 14x14¼*
1545-1548 A352 Set of 4 12.00 12.00

Souvenir Sheet

1549 A352 10k multi 8.50 8.50

Pineapples — A353

Pineapple slices and: No. 1550, 1.05k, African Queen pineapples sliced. No. 1551, 1.05k, African Queen and Hawaiian pineapples sliced. No. 1552, 5k, One Hawaiian and Two African Queen pineapples, one basket. No. 1553, 7k, One Hawaiian and two African Queen pineapples, two baskets.

No. 1554 — Popular pineapple varieties found in Papua New Guinea: a, 10t. b, 2k. c, 5k. d, 7k.

10k, African pineapple species cut.

2011, May 25 *Perf. 14x14¼*
1550-1553 A353 Set of 4 12.00 12.00
1554 A353 Sheet of 4, #a-d 12.00 12.00

Souvenir Sheet

1555 A353 10k multi 8.25 8.25

Nos. 1550-1555 are impregnated with a pineapple scent.

Urban Safety and Crime Prevention A354

Designs: 5t, National Capital District Commission emblem. No. 1557, 1.05k, No guns emblem. No. 1558, 5k, Meri SEIF Ples emblem. No. 1559, 7k, UN-Habitat certificate of recognition.

No. 1560: a, 1.05k, Shelter for women and children. b, 1.05k, Krismas SEIF Kempan members. c, 5k, Meri SEIF Ples members. d, 7k, Port Moresby Chamber of Commerce and Industry emblem.

10k, National Capital District Commission emblem, diff.

2011, June 15 *Perf. 14¼x14*
1556-1559 A354 Set of 4 11.50 11.50
1560 A354 Sheet of 4, #a-d 12.00 12.00

Souvenir Sheet

1561 A354 10k multi 8.75 8.75

For surcharge, see No. 1732J.

Cacao Production — A355

Designs: 5t, Harvesting cocoa pods. No. 1563, 1.05k, Breaking cocoa pod. No. 1564, 5k, Drying cocoa. No. 1565, 7k, Exporting cocoa bags.

No. 1566: a, 1.05k, Cocoa seedling. b, 1.05k, Cocoa flower. c, 5k, Pruning cocoa treas. d, 7k, Cocoa pods.

10k, Exporting cocoa bags, diff.

2011, July 7 *Perf. 14x14¼*
1562-1565 A355 Set of 4 11.50 11.50
1566 A355 Sheet of 4, #a-d 12.00 12.00

Souvenir Sheet

1567 A355 10k multi 8.75 8.75

Tattoos — A356

Designs: No. 1568, 1.05k, Face tattoo from Tufi. No. 1569, 1.05k, Face tattoo from Nondugl-Banz. No. 1570, 5k, Face tattoo from Asaro. No. 1571, 7k, Face tattoo from Kudjip.

No. 1572: a, 1.05k, Arm tattoo from Kairuku. b, 1.05k, Chest tattoo from Gumine. c, 5k, Leg tattoo from South Whagi. d, 7k, Minei tribe arm tattoo, Manus.

10k, Face tattoo from Tufi, diff.

2011, Aug. 4 *Perf. 14¼x14*
1568-1571 A356 Set of 4 13.00 13.00
1572 A356 Sheet of 4, #a-d 13.00 13.00

Souvenir Sheet

1573 A356 10k multi 9.00 9.00

Southern Cassowaries A357

Designs: No. 1574, 1.05k, Two newly-weaned chicks feeding. No. 1575, 1.05k, One weaned chick feeding. No. 1576, 5k, Adult feeding. No. 1577, 7k, Heads of two adults.

No. 1578: a, 1.05k, Head and shoulder of adult. b, 1.05k, Back rump of adult. c, 5k, Full view of chick. d, 7k, Legs of adult.

10k, Cassowary in natural habitat.

2011, Aug. 25
1574-1577 A357 Set of 4 13.00 13.00
1578 A357 Sheet of 4, #a-d 13.00 13.00

Souvenir Sheet

1579 A357 10k multi 9.25 9.25

Waterfalls A358

Designs: No. 1580, 1.05k, Kesesoru Falls. No. 1581, 1.05k, Mageni Falls aerial view. No. 1582, 5k, Mageni Falls outlet. No. 1583, 7k, Waghi Falls.

No. 1584: a, 1.05k, Sogeri Falls. b, 1.05k, Beaver Falls. c, 5k, Wawoi Falls. d, 7k, Remote Island Falls.

10k, Ambua Falls.

2011, Sept. 22 *Perf. 14x14¼*
1580-1583 A358 Set of 4 13.00 13.00
1584 A358 Sheet of 4, #a-d 13.00 13.00

Souvenir Sheet

1585 A358 10k multi 9.25 9.25

Wedding of Prince William and Catherine Middleton A359

Badge of the House of Windsor and: No. 1586, 1.05k, Catherine Middleton (at right). No. 1587, 1.05k, Middleton and sister, Pippa. No. 1588, 5k, Prince William. No. 1589, 7k, Couple.

No. 1590 — Badge of the House of Windsor and: a, 1.05k, Middleton (at left). b, 1.05k, Couple waving. c, 5k, Couple holding hands. d, 7k, Prince William, diff.

10k, Couple and badge of the House of Windsor.

2011, Oct. 19 *Perf. 12, 14 (#1590)*
1586-1589 A359 Set of 4 13.50 13.50
1590 A359 Sheet of 4, #a-d 13.50 13.50

Souvenir Sheet

1591 A359 10k multi 9.50 9.50

World War II Relics A360

Designs: No. 1592, 1.05k, American B-17E 41-2446. No. 1593, 1.05k, Japanese Ki-21 Sally. No. 1594, 5k, American P-38F 12647-S. No. 1595, 7k, American B17E 41-9234.

No. 1596: a, 1.05k, Japanese 95 Ha Go tank. b, 1.05k, Australian Hudson A16-91. c, 5k, New Zealand PV-1 Ventura NZ4613 Tail 13. d, 7k, Japanese 120mm dual purpose gun.

10k, American B-17F "Black Jack."

2011, Nov. 16 *Perf. 13¼*
1592-1595 A360 Set of 4 13.50 13.50
1596 A360 Sheet of 4, #a-d 13.50 13.50

Souvenir Sheet

1597 A360 10k multi 9.50 9.50

Victory Dancers — A361

Designs: No. 1598, 1.05k, Kiriwina woman. No. 1599, 1.05k, Oro man. No. 1600, 5k, Kandep woman. No. 1601, 7k, Siasi man.

No. 1602: a, 1.05k, Kerowagi man. b, 1.05k, Tolai man. c, 5k, Rigo man. d, 7k, Huli man.

10k, Baining fire dancer.

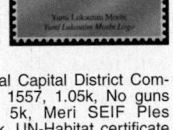

2011, Dec. 1 *Perf. 14¼x14*

1598-1601 A361 Set of 4 13.50 13.50
1602 A361 Sheet of 4, #a-d 13.50 13.50

Souvenir Sheet

1603 A361 10k multi 9.50 9.50

For surcharge, see No. 1732S.

Fish A362

Designs: No. 1604, 1.20k, Emperor angelfish. No. 1605, 1.20k, Yellow-mask angelfish. No. 1606, 6k, Meyer's butterflyfish. No. 1607, 8k, Barrier Reef anemonefish.

No. 1608: a, 1.20k, Clown anemonefish. b, 1.20k, Clown triggerfish. c, 6k, Clark's anemonefish. d, 8k, Spotfin lionfish.

10k, Bearded scorpionfish.

2012, Jan. 5 *Perf. 14x14¼*

1604-1607 A362 Set of 4 15.50 15.50
1608 A362 Sheet of 4, #a-d 15.50 15.50

Souvenir Sheet

1609 A362 10k multi 9.25 9.25

A363

A364

A365

A366

Paintings by Philip Yobale (1968-2009) — A367

Designs: No. 1610, Fish Berserk. No. 1611, Facing Faces. No. 1612, Regiana Bird of Paradise and Its Four Captors. No. 1613, Face Without Eye.

No. 1614 — Untitled works with: a, 1.20k, Faces. b, 1.20k, Head with headband. c, 6k, Eye at UL. d, 8k, Mask at UR.

10k, On-looking Eyes.

2012, Feb. 22 *Perf. 14¼x14*

1610 A363 1.20k multi 1.10 1.10
1611 A364 1.20k multi 1.10 1.10
1612 A365 6k multi 5.75 5.75
1613 A366 8k multi 7.50 7.50
Nos. 1610-1613 (4) 15.45 15.45
1614 A367 Sheet of 4, #a-d 15.50 15.50

Souvenir Sheet

1615 A367 10k multi 9.50 9.50

Blessed Peter To Rot (1912-45), Christian Martyr — A368

Designs: No. 1616, 1.20k, Beatification ceremony, 1995. No. 1617, 1.20k, To Rot baptizing child. No. 1618, 6k, Beatification ceremony, diff. No. 1619, 8k, To Rot giving holy communion.

No. 1620: a, 1.20k, To Rot in Taliligap Catechist School. b, 1.20k, To Rot officiating a marriage. c, 6k, To Rot leading worship and devotion. d, 8k, Murder of To Rot in cell in Japanese concentration camp.

10k, Statue of To Rot.

2012, Mar. 14 *Perf. 14x14¼*

1616-1619 A368 Set of 4 16.50 16.50

Perf. 14

1620 A368 Sheet of 4, #a-d 16.50 16.50

Souvenir Sheet

1621 A368 10k multi 10.00 10.00

Traditional Clay Cooking Pots — A369

Cooking pots from: No. 1622, 1.20k, Central Province. No. 1623, 1.20k, Mapang Province. No. 1624, 6k, Autonomous Region of Bougainville. No. 1625, 8k, East Sepik Province.

No. 1626: a, 1.20k, Milne Bay Province (brown pot). b, 1.20k, Milne Bay Province (black pot). c, 6k, East Sepik Province, diff. d, 8k, Manus Province.

10k, West Sepik Province.

2012, Apr. 11 *Perf. 14x14¼*

1622-1625 A369 Set of 4 15.50 15.50

Perf. 14

1626 A369 Sheet of 4, #a-d 15.50 15.50

Souvenir Sheet

1627 A369 10k multi 9.50 9.50

For surcharges, see Nos. 1732A 1732B.

Marsupials — A370

Designs: No. 1628, 1.20k, Common gray cuscus. No. 1629, 1.20k, Common spotted cuscus. No. 1630, 6k, Black spotted cuscus. No. 1631, 8k, Woodlark cuscus.

No. 1632: a, 1.20k, Sugar glider. b, 1.20k, Feather-tail possum. c, 6k, Striped possum. d, 8k, Northern glider.

10k, Common spotted cuscus, diff.

2012, May 7 *Perf. 13¼*

1628-1631 A370 Set of 4 15.50 15.50
1632 A370 Sheet of 4, #a-d 15.50 15.50

Souvenir Sheet

1633 A370 10k multi 9.50 9.50

For surcharges, see Nos. 1732C, 1732D.

Sports Legends A371

Designs: No. 1634, 1.20k, Iamo Launa, track and field. No. 1635, 1.20k, Martin Beni, boxer. No. 1636, 6k, Stanley Nandex, kick boxer. No. 1637, 8k, Will Genia, rugby player.

No. 1638: a, 1.20k, Tau John, track. b, 1.20k, Iwila Jacobs, weight lifter. c, 6k, Takale Tuna, track. d, 8k, John Aba, boxer.

10k, Genia, diff.

2012, June 18

1634-1637 A371 Set of 4 15.50 15.50
1638 A371 Sheet of 4, #a-d 15.50 15.50

Souvenir Sheet

1639 A371 10k multi 9.50 9.50

For surcharge, see No. 1732E.

Orchids A372

Designs: No. 1640, 1.20k, Dendrobium macrophyllum. No. 1641, 1.20k, Dendrobium williamsianum. No. 1642, 6k, Pink Dendrobium bracteosum. No. 1643, 8k, Phalaenopsis amabilis.

No. 1644: a, 1.20k, White Dendrobium bracteosum. b, 1.20k, Dendrobium bifalce. c, 6k, Dendrobium strepsiceros. d, 8k, Vanda hindsii.

10k, Dendrobium spectabile.

2012, July 2 *Perf. 14x14¼*

1640-1643 A372 Set of 4 15.50 15.50

Perf. 14

1644 A372 Sheet of 4, #a-d 15.50 15.50

Souvenir Sheet

1645 A372 10k multi 9.50 9.50

For surcharges, see Nos. 1732F, 1732G.

2012 Summer Olympics, London — A373

No. 1646: a, 50t, Weight lifting. b, 55t, Swimming. c, 1k, Relay race.

5k, Boxing.

2012, July 27 *Perf. 12*

1646 A373 Sheet of 3, #a-c 2.00 2.00

Souvenir Sheet

1647 A373 5k multi 4.75 4.75

New Year 2012 (Year of the Snake) — A374

Flags of Papua New Guinea and People's Republic of China and snake with background color of: No. 1648, 1.20k, Pink. No. 1649, 1.20k, Blue. No. 1650, 6k, Yellow orange. No. 1651, 8k, Green.

No. 1652: a, 1.20k, Green. b, 1.20k, Yellow orange. c, 6k, Pink. d, 8k, Blue.

10k, Yellow.

2012, Aug. 1 *Perf. 14, 12 (#1652)*

1648-1651 A374 Set of 4 15.50 15.50
1652 A374 Sheet of 4, #a-d 15.50 15.50

Souvenir Sheet

1653 A374 10k multi 9.50 9.50

Traditional Costumes — A375

Designs: No. 1654, 1.20k, Man from Telefomin, Sandaun Province. No. 1655, 1.20k, Woman from Pomio, East New Britain Province. No. 1656, 6k, Women from Hanuabada, National Capital District. No. 1657, 8k, Woman and child from Duna, Southern Highlands Province.

No. 1658: a, 1.20k, Bride from Mendi, Southern Highlands Province. b, 1.20k, Woman from Tari, Southern Highlands Province. c, 6k, Family from Trobriand Islands, Milne Bay Province. d, 8k, Women from Mukawa, Milne Bay Province.

10k, Woman from Popondetta, Oro Province.

2012, Sept. 5 *Perf. 14¼*

1654-1657 A375 Set of 4 15.50 15.50
1658 A375 Sheet of 4, #a-d 15.50 15.50

Souvenir Sheet

1659 A375 10k multi 9.50 9.50

For surcharge, see No. 1732H.

Reign of Queen Elizabeth II, 60th Anniv. A376

Profile of Queen Elizabeth II, Diamond Jubilee emblem, and: 25t, Duchess of Cornwall and Prince of Wales. 50t, Prince of Wales. 1k, Prince of Wales, Duchess of Cornwall, Queen Elizabeth II and Prince Philip. 1.25k, Prince of Wales with sword. 6k, Queen Elizabeth II and Prince of Wales. 8k, Queen Elizabeth II and Prince Philip.

10k, Queen Elizabeth II, vert.

2012, Nov. 4 *Perf. 14¼*

1660-1665 A376 Set of 6 16.50 16.50

Souvenir Sheet

1666 A376 10k multi 9.75 9.75

Public Transportation — A377

Designs: No. 1667, 1.30k, Passenger truck. No. 1668, 1.30k, Banana boat. No. 1669, 6k, Remote service airplane. No. 1670, 8.70k, Trading canoe.

No. 1671: a, 1.30k, Taxi. b, 1.30k, Passenger bus. c, 6k, Domestic and international airplane. d, 8k, Ship.

10k, Dugout canoe.

2013, Jan. 2 *Perf. 13¾x13¼*

1667-1670 A377 Set of 4 17.00 17.00
1671 A377 Sheet of 4, #a-d 17.00 17.00

Souvenir Sheet

1672 A377 10k multi 9.75 9.75

Sculptures by Gigmai Kundun — A378

Designs: No. 1673, 1.30k, Hiri Trade Canoe (Lakatoi). No. 1674, 1.30k, Kundu Slit Gong. No. 1675, 6k, Hiri Moale Queen. No. 1676, 8.70k, Bird of Paradise.

No. 1677: a, 1.30k, Follow the Leader. b, 1.30k, Walking Together. c, 6k, Relieving Education Burden. d, 8k, Inherited Believe System.

10k, Indo-Pacific Lionfish (Pterois).

2013, Feb. 20 ***Perf. 12***

1673-1676 A378 Set of 4 16.50 16.50

1677 A378 Sheet of 4, #a-d 16.50 16.50

Souvenir Sheet

1678 A378 10k multi 9.50 9.50

In 2012, Papua New Guinea postal officials permitted customers who wished to purchase personalized stamps to work with them in designing the stamps and labels, instead of only providing the image for the attached label, as had been done with previous personalized stamp issues. Some of the items produced by customers are known to lack the country name on the stamp and label. These stamps are known to have a number of different denominations. Beyond Nos. 1264-1268, Papua New Guinea postal officials have not provided any information on other personalizable stamps that are available to any customer.

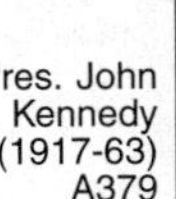

Pres. John F. Kennedy (1917-63) A379

Designs: No. 1679, 1.30k, Pres. Kennedy seated. No. 1680, 1.30k, Pres. Kennedy, wife, Jacqueline, and Vice-president Lyndon B. Johnson. No. 1681, 6k, Pres. Kennedy in limousine. No. 1682, 8.70k, Honor guard holding flag over Pres. Kennedy's casket.

No. 1683: a, 1.30k, Pres. Kennedy and flag. b, 1.30k, Pres. Kennedy and wife at Love Field, Dallas, Texas. c, 6k, Flag-draped coffin of Pres. Kennedy. d, 8.70k, Johnson being sworn in as President.

10k, Pres. Kennedy, vert.

2013, Mar. 13 **Litho.** ***Perf. 14***

1679-1682 A379 Set of 4 16.00 16.00

1683 A379 Sheet of 4, #a-d 16.00 16.00

Souvenir Sheet

Perf. 12

1684 A379 10k multi 9.25 9.25

Root Crops A380

Designs: No. 1685, 1.30k, Cassava. No. 1686, 1.30k, Chinese taro. No. 1687, 6k, Sweet potatoes. No. 1688, 8.70k, Taro.

No. 1689: a, 1.30k, Five-leaflet yam. b, 1.30k, Lesser yam. c, 6k, Greater yam. d, 8.70k, Nummularia yam.

10k, Queensland arrowroot.

2013, Apr. 10 **Litho.** ***Perf. 12***

1685-1688 A380 Set of 4 16.00 16.00

1689 A380 Sheet of 4, #a-d 16.00 16.00

Souvenir Sheet

1690 A380 10k multi 9.25 9.25

Orchids A381

Designs: No. 1691, 1.30k, Dendrobium gouldii. No. 1692, 1.30k, Dendrobium lineale. No. 1693, 6k, Dendrobium mirbelianum. No. 1694, 8.70k, Dendrobium sp. aff. D. cochiliodes.

No. 1695: a, 1.30k, Dendrobium sp. aff. D. gouldii. b, 1.30k, Dendrobium sp. aff. D. conanthum. c, 6k, Dendrobium lineale, diff. d, 8.70k, Dendrobium carronii.

10k, Dendrobium mussauense.

2013, May 24 **Litho.** ***Perf. 12***

1691-1694 A381 Set of 4 15.50 15.50

1695 A381 Sheet of 4, #a-d 15.50 15.50

Souvenir Sheet

1696 A381 10k multi 9.00 9.00

Spacecraft and Space Stations A382

Designs: No. 1697, 1.30k, Skylab. No. 1698, 1.30k, Salyut 6 Space Station. No. 1699, 6k, Spacehab. No. 1700, 8.70k, Mir Space Station.

No. 1701: a, 1.30k, Skylab, diff. b, 1.30k, Salyut 6 Space Station, diff. c, 6k, Space shuttle re-entering atmosphere. d, 8.70k, Mir Space Station, diff.

10k, Space shuttle as seen from International Space Station window.

2013, July 15 **Litho.** ***Perf. 14***

1697-1700 A382 Set of 4 15.50 15.50

Perf. 12

1701 A382 Sheet of 4, #a-d 15.50 15.50

Souvenir Sheet

1702 A382 10k multi 9.00 9.00

Launch of the International Space Station, 15th anniv.

Woven Baskets A383

Designs: No. 1703, 1.30k, Common "Tolai" carry basket, East New Britain Province. No. 1704, 1.30k, Pepeni (yam basket), Kitava Island, Milne Bay Province. No. 1705, 6k, Carry basket, Milne Bay Province. No. 1706, 8.70k, Carry baskets, Ialibu, Southern Highlands Province.

No. 1707: a, 1.30k, Common Sepik basket, East Sepik Province. b, 1.30k, Carry basket, Milne Bay Province, diff. c, 6k, Carry basket, Gulf Province. d, 8.70k, Manus carry basket, Manus Province.

10k, Temporary palm leaf basket, Coastal and Island Provinces.

2013, Aug. 9 **Litho.** ***Perf. 12***

1703-1706 A383 Set of 4 15.00 15.00

1707 A383 Sheet of 4, #a-d 15.00 15.00

Souvenir Sheet

1708 A383 10k multi 8.75 8.75

Coconuts A384

Designs: 4k, Green coconuts. No. 1710, 6k, Coconut husking. No. 1711, 8.70k, Coconut juice. 12k, Coconut meat.

No. 1713: a, 1k, Dry coconut. b, 1.30k, Inner shell. c, 6k, Meat. d, 8.70k, Apple.

10k, Inner shell.

2013, Aug. 21 **Litho.** ***Perf. 12***

1709-1712 A384 Set of 4 25.00 25.00

1713 A384 Sheet of 4, #a-d 14.00 14.00

Souvenir Sheet

1714 A384 10k multi 8.25 8.25

Birth of Prince George of Cambridge A385

Designs (inscribed "22nd of July 2013" at top: No. 1715, 1.30k, Duke and Duchess of Cambridge, Prince George. No. 1716, 1.30k, Duke of Cambridge, Prince George. No. 1717, 6k, Duchess of Cambridge, Prince George. No. 1718, 8.70k, Duke and Duchess of Cambridge, Prince George, diff.

No. 1719 (stamps without "22nd of July 2013" inscription at top): a, 1.30k, Like #1715. b, 1.30k, Like #1716. c, 6k, Like #1717. d, 8.70k, Like #1718.

10k, Prince George in arms of Duchess of Cambridge.

Perf. 13¼x12½

2013, Sept. 11 **Litho.**

1715-1718 A385 Set of 4 14.00 14.00

Perf. 12x12½

1719 A385 Sheet of 4, #a-d 14.00 14.00

Souvenir Sheet

1720 A385 10k multi 8.25 8.25

Cooking Methods A386

Designs: No. 1721, 1.30k, Boiling. No. 1722, 1.30k, Drying. No. 1723, 6k, Drying, diff. No. 1724, 8.70k, Roasting.

No. 1725: a, 1.30k, Dug out mumu pit. b, 1.30k, Stones being heated in mumu pit. c, 6k, Food placed in mumu pit. d, 8.70k, Covered mumu pit.

10k, Hot stones steaming in pot.

2013, Nov. 6 **Litho.** ***Perf. 12***

1721-1724 A386 Set of 4 13.50 13.50

1725 A386 Sheet of 4, #a-d 13.50 13.50

Souvenir Sheet

1726 A386 10k multi 7.75 7.75

New Year 2014 (Year of the Horse) A387

Various horses with background colors of: No. 1727, 1.70k, Grayish lilac. No. 1728, 1.70k, Tan. No. 1729, 6k, Red. No. 1730, 8.70k, Blue violet.

No. 1731 — Various horses with background colors of: a, 1.30k, Violet. b, 1.30k, Olive bister. c, 6k, Grayish lilac. d, 8.70k, Blue green.

10k, Horse with greenish gray background.

2014, Jan. 2 **Litho.** ***Perf. 12***

1727-1730 A387 Set of 4 14.50 14.50

1731 A387 Sheet of 4, #a-d 14.00 14.00

Souvenir Sheet

1732 A387 10k multi 8.00 8.00

For surcharges, see Nos. 1733-1734.

Nos. 1358, 1395, 1416, 1440, 1451, 1452, 1460, 1494, 1512, 1557, 1601, 1622, 1623, 1628, 1629, 1634, 1640, 1641, 1654 Surcharged in Black or Black and Red

Serifed "K"

Sans-serif "K"

Methods and Perfs. As Before

2014, Jan.

Serifed "K" Surcharges

1732A	A369	1.30k on 1.20k #1622		—
1732B	A369	1.30k on 1.20k #1623	—	—
1732C	A370	1.30k on 1.20k #1628	—	—
1732D	A370	1.30k on 1.20k #1629		—
1732E	A371	1.30k on 1.20k #1634	—	—
1732F	A372	1.30k on 1.20k #1640 (Bk&R)	—	—
1732G	A372	1.30k on 1.20k #1641	—	—

Sans-serif "K" Surcharges

1732H	A375	1.30k on 1.20k #1654		—
1732I	A324	15k on 85t #1395	—	—
1732J	A354	15k on 1.05k #1557	—	—
1732K	A316	15k on 3.70k #1358		—
1732L	A341	25k on 4.65k #1494	—	—
1732M	A331	25k on 6.30k #1440	—	—
1732O	A333	40k on 4.65k #1451	—	—
1732P	A327	40k on 6k #1416	—	—
1732Q	A335	90k on 3k #1460	—	—
1732R	A333	90k on 6.30k #1452	—	—
1732S	A361	90k on 7k #1601	—	—
1732T	A346	25k on 5k #1512	—	—
1732U	A361	90k on 7k #1601	—	—

Obliterators and sizes of surcharges vary.

Nos. 1727-1728 Surcharged in Black and Red

2014, Feb. 12 **Litho.** ***Perf. 12***

1733 A387 5k on 1.70k #1727 4.50 4.50

1734 A387 5k on 1.70k #1728 4.50 4.50

Nelson Mandela (1918-2013), President of South Africa — A388

Various photographs of Mandela (stamps with white frames): No. 1735, 1.30k. No. 1736, 3k. No. 1737, 6k. No. 1738, 8k.

No. 1739 — Various photographs of Mandela (stamps with green frames): a, 1.30k. b, 3k. c, 6k. d, 8k.
10k, Mandela, diff. (stamp without frame).

2014, Mar. 31 Litho. *Perf. 12*

1735-1738	A388	Set of 4	13.50	13.50
1739	A388	Sheet of 4, #a-d	13.50	13.50

Souvenir Sheet

1740	A388	10k multi	7.25	7.25

Spirit of Hela Liquified Natural Gas Tanker A389

Various photographs of Spirit of Hela with side panel color of: 1.30k, Pale green, 3k, Beige. 6k, Light blue green. 8k, Lilac.
10k, Spirit of Hela, light blue panel.

2014, Apr. 7 Litho. *Perf. 13½*

1741-1744	A389	Set of 4	13.00	13.00
1744a		Souvenir sheet of 4, #1741-1744	13.00	13.00

Souvenir Sheet

1745	A389	10k multi	7.25	7.25

World War I, Cent. — A390

Designs: No. 1746, 1.30k, Russian soldier. No. 1747, 5k, American bugler. No. 1748, 6k, French airplanes. No. 1749, 8k, German observation balloon.
No. 1750: a, 1.30k, French lancers. b, 5k, British Army. c, 6k, American National Guard. 8k, French battleship.
10k, British soldier.

2014, Apr. 24 Litho. *Perf. 13¼x12½*

1746-1749	A390	Set of 4	14.50	14.50

Perf. 12x12½

1750	A390	Sheet of 4, #a-d	14.50	14.50

Souvenir Sheet

1751	A390	10k multi	7.25	7.25

Pope Francis — A391

Coat of arms of Pope Francis and various photographs with frame color of: No. 1752, 1.30k, Red violet. No. 1753, 5k, Green. No. 1754, 6k, Blue. No. 1755, 8k, Vermilion.
No. 1756 — Coat of arms of Pope Francis and photographs with bister frame: a, 1.30k, Photo like #1753. b, 5k, Photo like #1754. c, 6k, Photo like #1755. d, 8k, Photo like #1752
10k, Pope Francis, coat of arms.

2014, July 28 Litho. *Perf. 13¼x12½*

1752-1755	A391	Set of 4	16.00	16.00

Perf. 12x12½

1756	A391	Sheet of 4, #a-d	16.00	16.00

Souvenir Sheet

1757	A391	10k multi	8.00	8.00

Bank of Papua New Guinea, 40th Anniv. A393

Artifacts — A392

Designs: No. 1758, 1.30k, Trobriand Islands lime pot. No. 1759, 5k, Manus Island bowl. No. 1760, 6k, Wogeo Island food bowl. No. 1761, 8k, Sepik Region pan pipes.
No. 1762, horiz. — Various Sepik River canoe prows: a, 1.30k. b, 5k. c, 6k. d, 8k.
10k, Kiriwina lime pot.

Perf. 13¼x13¾, 13¾x13¼ (#1762)

2014, Aug. 28 Litho.

1758-1761	A392	Set of 4	16.50	16.50
1762	A392	Sheet of 4, #a-d	16.50	16.50

Souvenir Sheet

1763	A392	10k multi	8.25	8.25

Bank building, 40th anniv. emblem and bank governors: No. 1764, 1.30k, Loi M. Bakani. No. 1765, 4k, Sir Mekere Morauta. No. 1766, 6k, Sir Henry ToRobert. No. 1767, 8k, Sir Wilson Kamit.
No. 1768 — 40th anniv. emblem and: a, 1.30k, Bank building, bank governor John Vulupindi. b, 4k, Bank building, bank governor Koiari Tarata. c, 6k, Bank building. d, 8k, Bank building, bank governor Morea Vele.
10k, 40th anniv. emblem, native costume, vert.

Litho. With Foil Application

2014, Sept. 15 *Perf. 13¾x13¼*

1764-1767	A393	Set of 4	15.50	15.50
1768	A393	Sheet of 4, #a-d	15.50	15.50

Souvenir Sheet

Perf. 13¼x13¾

1769	A393	10k multi	8.00	8.00

A394

A395

A396

New Year 2015 (Year of the Ram) — A397

No. 1774: a, 1.35k, Ram in circle. b, 1.35k, Ram in rectangle. c, 6.20k, Ram on pot. d, 8.95, Ram in circle, flowers at top.
10k, Ram and Chinese characters.

2015, Jan. 5 Litho. *Perf. 13¼x12½*

1770	A394	1.35k multi	1.00	1.00
1771	A395	1.35k multi	1.00	1.00
1772	A396	6.20k multi	4.75	4.75
1773	A397	8.95k multi	6.75	6.75
		Nos. 1770-1773 (4)	13.50	13.50

Miniature Sheet

1774	A397	Sheet of 4, #a-d	13.50	13.50

Souvenir Sheet

1775	A397	10k multi	7.75	7.75

Traditional Paintings — A398

Designs: No. 1776, 1.35k, Arawe Mother and Child. No. 1777, 1.35k, Motuan Village Totem Pole. No. 1778, 6.20k, Baining Fire Dancers. No. 1779, 8.95k, Crocodile Hunters.
No. 1780: a, 1.35k, Mount Elimbari. b, 1.35k, Wig Makers. c, 6.20k, Tifalmin Hunter. d, 8.95k, Wood Carver.
10k, Like No. 1777.

2015, Mar. 9 Litho. *Perf. 14½x14*

1776-1779	A398	Set of 4	13.50	13.50
1780	A398	Sheet of 4, #a-d	13.50	13.50

Souvenir Sheet

1781	A398	10k multi	7.50	7.50

Christian Leaders' Training College, 50th Anniv. — A399

Designs: No. 1782, 1.35k, College founder Dr. Gilbert J. McArthur and student leader, Jezreel Flora. No. 1783, 1.35k, Students of 1967. No. 1784, 6.20k, Graduates. No. 1785, 8.95k, Aerial view of Banz Campus.
No. 1786: a, 1.35k, Banz Campus, 1965. b, 1.35k, Banz Campus, 2015. c, 6.20k, Port Moresby Campus. d, 8.95k, Lae Campus.
10k, Graduation ceremony.

Litho. With Foil Application

2015, Mar. 30 *Perf. 14½x14*

1782-1785	A399	Set of 4	13.50	13.50
1786	A399	Sheet of 4, #a-d	13.50	13.50

Souvenir Sheet

1787	A399	10k multi	7.50	7.50

Traditional Headdresses — A400

Headdress from: No. 1788, 1.35k, Central Province. No. 1789, 1.35k, Eastern Highlands Province. 6.20k, Central Province, diff. 8.95k, East Sepik Province.
10k, Headdress from Simbu Province.

2015, June 22 Litho. *Perf. 14¼x14*

1788-1791	A400	Set of 4	13.00	13.00
1791a		Souvenir sheet of 4, #1788-1791	13.00	13.00

Souvenir Sheet

1792	A400	10k multi	7.25	7.25

2015 Pacific Games, Port Moresby — A401

Emblem, mascot and: No. 1793, 1.35k, Dika Toua, weight lifting. No. 1794, 1.35k, Toea Wisil, running. No. 1795, 6.20k, Ryan Pini, swimming. No. 1796, 8.95k, Jack Biyufa, body building.
No. 1797: a, 1.35k, Abigail Tere Apisah, tennis. b, 1.35k, Betty Burua, running. c, 6.20k, Linda Pulsan, powerlifting. d, 8.95k, Steven Kari, weight lifting.
10k, Emblem and mascot.

2015, June 22 Litho. *Perf. 14¼x14*

1793-1796	A401	Set of 4	13.00	13.00
1797	A401	Sheet of 4, #a-d	13.00	13.00

Souvenir Sheet

1798	A401	10k multi	7.25	7.25

Queen Elizabeth II, Longest Reigning British Monarch — A402

Designs: No. 1799, 1.35k, Princesses Elizabeth and Margaret as children. No. 1800, 1.35k, Color photograph of Queen Elizabeth II. 6.20k, Queen Elizabeth II wearing crown. 8.95k, Queen Elizabeth II and Prince Philip.
10k, Queen Elizabeth II wearing crown, diff.

2015, July 6 Litho. *Perf. 14*

1799-1802	A402	Set of 4	13.00	13.00
1802a		Souvenir sheet of 4, #1799-1802, perf. 12	13.00	13.00

Souvenir Sheet

Perf. 12

1803	A402	10k multi	7.25	7.25

Birth of Princess Charlotte of Cambridge A403

Designs: No. 1804, 1.35k, Princess Charlotte in arms of Duchess of Cambridge. No. 1805, 1.35k, Duke and Duchess of Cambridge, Princess Charlotte. 6.20k, Duke and Duchess of Cambridge, Princess Charlotte, diff. 8.95k, Duke and Duchess of Cambridge, Princess Charlotte, diff.
10k, Duchess of Cambridge holding Princess Charlotte.

2015, Aug. 3 Litho. *Perf. 14*

1804-1807	A403	Set of 4	13.00	13.00
1807a		Souvenir sheet of 4, #1804-1807	13.00	13.00

Souvenir Sheet

1808	A403	10k multi	7.25	7.25

Singapore 2015 Intl. Stamp Exhibition — A404

Designs: No. 1809, 3.75k, Bird of paradise. No. 1810, 3.75k, Merlion.
No. 1811: a, Bird of paradise. b, Merlion.

2015, Aug. 14 Litho. *Perf. 12*
1809-1810 A404 Set of 2 5.25 5.25

Embossed With Foil Application, Litho. Sheet Margin

Souvenir Sheet

1811 A404 20k Sheet of 2, #a-b 28.00 28.00

Nos. 1809-1810 were each printed in sheets of 4.

AIR POST STAMPS

Regular Issue of 1916 Overprinted

1929 Wmk. 74 *Perf. 14*
C1 A3 3p blue grn & dk gray 2.00 *12.50*
b. Vert. pair, one without ovpt. *6,000.*
c. Horiz. pair, one without ovpt. *6,500.*
d. 3p blue grn & sepia blk 57.50 *75.00*
e. Overprint on back, vert. *5,000.*

No. C1 exists on white and on yellowish paper, No. C1d on yellowish paper only.

Regular Issues of 1916-23 Overprinted in Red

1930, Sept. 15 Wmk. 74
C2 A3 3p blue grn & blk 2.00 *7.00*
a. Yellowish paper 2,200. *3,750.*
b. Double overprint 1,500.
C3 A3 6p violet & dull vio 8.00 *12.00*
a. Yellowish paper 5.00 *19.00*
C4 A3 1sh ol grn & ol brn 6.00 *17.50*
a. Inverted overprint *14,500.*
b. Yellowish paper 10.00 26.00
Nos. C2-C4 (3) 16.00 *36.50*

Port Moresby AP1

Unwmk.

1938, Sept. 6 Engr. *Perf. 11*
C5 AP1 2p carmine 2.75 3.25
C6 AP1 3p ultra 2.75 2.50
C7 AP1 5p dark green 2.75 *3.50*
C8 AP1 8p red brown 6.50 *21.00*
C9 AP1 1sh violet 17.50 22.50
Nos. C5-C9 (5) 32.25 *52.75*
Set, never hinged 65.00

Papua as a British possession, 50th anniv.

Papuans Poling Rafts — AP2

1939-41
C10 AP2 2p carmine 3.00 6.00
C11 AP2 3p ultra 3.00 *11.00*
C12 AP2 5p dark green 3.00 2.25
C13 AP2 8p red brown 7.50 3.25
C14 AP2 1sh violet 9.00 9.00
C15 AP2 1sh6p lt olive ('41) 27.50 *40.00*
Nos. C10-C15 (6) 53.00 *71.50*
Set, never hinged 90.00

POSTAGE DUE STAMPS

Catalogue values for unused stamps in this section are for Never Hinged items.

Nos. 128, 122, 129, 139 and 125 Surcharged in Black, Blue, Red or Orange

1960 Unwmk. Engr. *Perf. 14*
J1 A24 1p on 6½p 7.00 *7.00*
J2 A23 3p on ½p (Bl) 8.25 5.00
a. Double surcharge 600.00
J3 A24 6p on 7½p (R) 25.00 12.00
a. Double surcharge 600.00
J4 A23 1sh3p on 3½p (O) 9.50 *7.50*
J5 A23 3sh on 2½p 25.00 15.00
Nos. J1-J5 (5) 74.75 46.50

No. 129 Surcharged with New Value in Red

J6 A24 6p on 7½p 1,100. 775.
a. Double surcharge 4,000. 2,200.

Surcharge forgeries exist.

D1

Perf. 13½x14

1960, June 2 Litho. Wmk. 228
J7 D1 1p orange .50 .55
J8 D1 3p ocher .55 .55
J9 D1 6p light ultra .55 .35
J10 D1 9p vermilion .55 1.25
J11 D1 1sh emerald .55 .30
J12 D1 1sh3p bright violet .80 1.40
J13 D1 1sh6p light blue 4.00 4.00
J14 D1 3sh yellow 3.50 .70
Nos. J7-J14 (8) 11.00 9.10

OFFICIAL STAMPS

Nos. 60-63, 66-71, 92-93 Overprinted

1931 Wmk. 74 *Perf. 14½*
O1 A3 ½p #60 2.50 *5.50*
O2 A3 1p #61 5.00 *13.00*
O3 A3 1½p #62 2.00 *14.00*
O4 A3 2p #63 4.50 *14.00*
O5 A3 3p #66 3.00 *25.00*
O6 A3 4p #67 3.00 *21.00*
O7 A3 5p #68 7.00 *42.50*
O8 A3 6p #69 5.00 *9.75*
O9 A3 1sh #70 11.00 *35.00*
O10 A3 2sh6p #71 47.50 *97.50*

1932 Wmk. 228 *Perf. 11½*
O11 A3 9p #92 37.50 *55.00*
O12 A3 1sh3p #93 37.50 *55.00*
Nos. O1-O12 (12) 165.50 *387.25*

PARAGUAY

'par-ə-,gwī

LOCATION — South America, bounded by Bolivia, Brazil and Argentina
GOVT. — Republic
AREA — 157,042 sq. mi.
POP. — 5,434,095 (1999 est.)
CAPITAL — Asuncion

10 Reales = 100 Centavos = 1 Peso
100 Centimos = 1 Guarani (1944)

Catalogue values for unused stamps in this country are for Never Hinged items, beginning with Scott 430 in the regular postage section, Scott B11 in the semi-postal section, and Scott C154 in the airpost section.

Watermarks

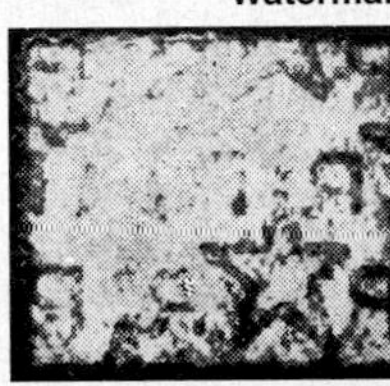

Wmk. 319 — Stars and R P Multiple

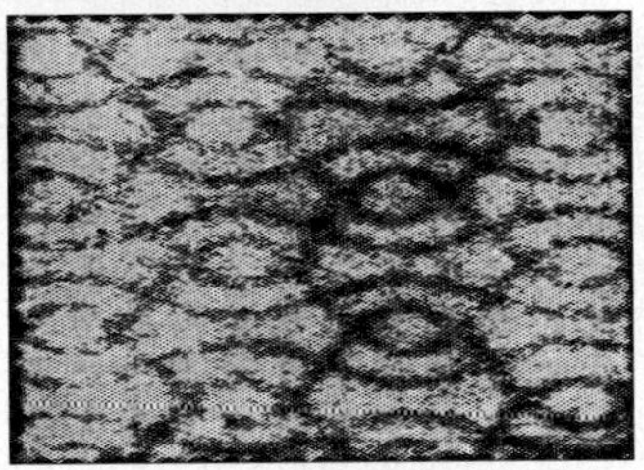

Wmk. 320 — Interlacing Lines

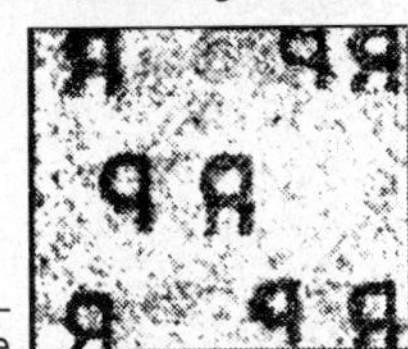

Wmk. 347 — RP Multiple

Vigilant Lion Supporting Liberty Cap

A1 A2

A3

1870, Aug. Unwmk. Litho. *Imperf.*
1 A1 1r rose 9.00 *16.50*
2 A2 2r blue 100.00 *150.00*
3 A3 3r black 225.00 225.00
Nos. 1-3 (3) 334.00 391.50

Counterfeits of 2r in blue and other colors are on thicker paper than originals. They show a colored dot in upper part of "S" of "DOS" in upper right corner.

For surcharges see Nos. 4-9, 19.

Handstamp Surcharged

1878 Black Surcharge
4 A1 5c on 1r rose 80. *110.*
5 A2 5c on 2r blue 325. 300.
5E A3 5c on 3r black 450. 450.
Nos. 4-5E (3) 855.00 860.00

Blue Surcharge
5F A1 5c on 1r rose 80. *110.*
5H A2 5c on 2r blue *1,000. 1,000.*
6 A3 5c on 3r black 425. 425.
Nos. 5F-6 (3) 1,505. 1,535.

The surcharge may be found inverted, double, sideways and omitted.

Remainders of Nos. 4 and 5F were placed on sale at Post Offices during 1892. Covers dated 1892 are worth about $7,500.

The originals are surcharged in dull black or dull blue. The reprints are in intense black and bright blue. The reprint surcharges are over-inked and show numerous breaks in the handstamp.

Handstamp Surcharged

Black Surcharge
7 A2 5c on 2r blue 500.00 425.00
8 A3 5c on 3r black 425.00 425.00

Blue Surcharge
9 A3 5c on 3r black 250.00 250.00
a. Dbl. surch., large & small "5" —
Nos. 7-9 (3) 1,175. 1,100.

The surcharge on Nos. 7, 8 and 9 is usually placed sideways. It may be found double or inverted on Nos. 8 and 9.

Nos. 4 to 9 have been extensively counterfeited.

Two examples recorded of No. 9a, one without gum, the other with full but disturbed original gum.

A4

1879 Litho. *Perf. 12½*

Thin Paper

10 A4 5r orange 1.25
11 A4 10r red brown 1.50
a. Imperf.
b. Horiz. pair, imperf. vert. 60.00

Nos. 10 and 11 were never placed in use.
For surcharges see Nos. 17-18.

A4a

1879-81 Thin Paper
12 A4a 5c orange brown 2.50 2.00
13 A4a 10c blue grn ('81) 3.50 3.00
a. Imperf., pair 10.00 *12.00*

Reprints of Nos. 10-13 are imperf., perf. 11½, 12, 12½ or 14. They have yellowish gum and the 10c is deep green.

A5

A6

A7

1881, Aug. Litho. *Perf. 11½-13½*

14 A5 1c blue .80 .70
a. Imperf., pair —
b. Horiz. pair, imperf. btwn. —
15 A6 2c rose red .80 *.70*
a. 2c dull orange red 1.00 .90
b. Imperf., pair —
c. Horiz. pair, imperf. vert. 25.00 25.00
d. Vert. pair, imperf. horiz. 25.00 25.00
16 A7 4c brown .80 *.70*
a. Imperf., pair —
b. Horiz. pair, imperf. vert. 25.00 25.00
c. Vert. pair, imperf. horiz. 25.00 25.00

No. 11 Handstamped Surcharge in Black or Gray

1881, July *Perf. 12½*

17 A4 1c on 10c blue grn 15.00 10.00
18 A4 2c on 10c blue grn 15.00 10.00

Gray handstamps sell for 10 times more than black as many specialists consider the black to be reprints.

No. 1 Handstamped Surcharge in Black

1884, May 8 *Imperf.*

19 A1 1c on 1r rose 10.00 8.00

The surcharges on Nos. 17-19 exist double, inverted and in pairs with one omitted. Counterfeits exist.

Seal of the Treasury — A11

1884, Aug. 3 Litho. *Perf. 12½*

20 A11 1c green 1.00 .80
21 A11 2c rose pink, thin paper 1.00 .80

Perf. 11½

22 A11 5c pale blue, yellowish paper 1.00 .80
Nos. 20-22 (3) 3.00 2.40

There are two types of each value differing mostly in the shape of the numerals. In addition, there are numerous small flaws in the lithographic transfers.

For overprints see Nos. O1, O8, O15.

Imperf., Pairs

20a A11 1c green 12.50
21a A11 2c rose red 16.00
22a A11 5c blue 16.00
Nos. 20a-22a (3) 44.50

Seal of the Treasury — A12

Perf. 11½, 11½x12, 12½x11½

1887 Typo.

23 A12 1c green .30 .25
24 A12 2c rose .30 .25
25 A12 5c blue .50 .35
26 A12 7c brown .90 .50
27 A12 10c lilac .60 .35
28 A12 15c orange .60 .35
29 A12 20c pink .60 .35
Nos. 23-29 (7) 3.80 2.40

See #42-45. For surcharges & overprints see #46, 49-50, 71-72, 167-170A, O20-O41, O49.

Symbols of Liberty from Coat of Arms — A13

1889, Feb. Litho. *Perf. 11½*

30 A13 15c red violet 2.50 2.00
a. Imperf., pair 10.00 8.00

For overprints see Nos. O16-O19.

Overprint Handstamped in Violet

1892, Oct. 12 *Perf. 12x12½*

31 A15 10c violet blue 10.00 5.00

Discovery of America by Columbus, 400th anniversary. Overprint reads: "1492 / 12 DE OCTUBRE / 1892." Sold only on day of issue.

Cirilo A. Rivarola — A15

Designs: 2c, Salvador Jovellanos. 4c, Juan B. Gil. 5c, Higinio Uriarte. 10c, Cándido Bareiro. 14c, Gen. Bernardino Caballero. 20c, Gen. Patricio Escobar. 30c, Juan G. González.

1892-96 Litho. *Perf. 12x12½*

32 A15 1c gray (centavos) .25 .25
33 A15 1c gray (centavo) ('96) .25 .25
34 A15 2c green .25 .25
a. Chalky paper ('96) .25 .25
35 A15 4c carmine .25 .25
a. Chalky paper ('96) .25 .25
36 A15 5c violet ('93) .25 .25
a. Chalky paper ('96) .25 .25
37 A15 10c vio bl (punched) ('93) .25 .25
Unpunched ('96) 5.00
38 A15 10c dull blue ('96) .25 .25
39 A15 14c yellow brown .75 .50
40 A15 20c red ('93) 1.25 .50
41 A15 30c light green 2.00 .80
Nos. 32-41 (10) 5.75 3.55

The 10c violet blue (No. 37) was, until 1896, issued punched with a circular hole in order to prevent it being fraudulently overprinted as No. 31.

Nos. 33 and 38 are on chalky paper.

For surcharge see No. 70.

Seal Type of 1887

1892 Typo.

42 A12 40c slate blue 3.00 1.25
43 A12 60c yellow 1.50 .50
44 A12 80c light blue 1.40 .50
45 A12 1p olive green 1.40 .50
Nos. 42-45 (4) 7.30 2.75

For surcharges see Nos. 71-72.

No. 26 Surcharged in Black

1895, Aug. 1 *Perf. 11½x12*

46 A12 5c on 7c brown .75 .75

Telegraph Stamps Surcharged

1896, Apr. Engr. *Perf. 11½*

Denomination in Black

47 5c on 2c brown & gray .90 .60
a. Inverted surcharge 10.00 10.00
48 5c on 4c yellow & gray .90 .60
a. Inverted surcharge 7.50 7.50

Nos. 28, 42 Surcharged

1898-99 Typo.

49 A12 10c on 15c org ('99) .75 .45
a. Inverted surcharge 17.50 17.50
b. Double surcharge 11.00 11.00
50 A12 10c on 40c slate bl .35 .25

Surcharge on No. 49 has small "c."

Telegraph Stamps Surcharged

1900, May 14 Engr. *Perf. 11½*

50A 5c on 30c grn, gray & blk 2.75 1.50
50B 10c on 50c dl vio, gray & blk 6.00 3.75

The basic telegraph stamps are like those used for Nos. 47-48, but the surcharges on Nos. 50A-50B consist of "5 5" and "10 10" above a blackout rectangle covering the engraved denominations.

A 40c red, bluish gray and black telegraph stamp (basic type of A24) was used provisionally in August, 1900, for postage. Value, postally used, $5.

Seal of the Treasury — A25

1900, Sept. Engr. *Perf. 11½, 12*

51 A25 2c gray .40 .30
52 A25 3c orange brown .40 .30
53 A25 5c dark green .40 .30
54 A25 8c dark brown .40 .30
55 A25 10c carmine rose 1.00 .30
56 A25 24c deep blue 1.20 .30
Nos. 51-56 (6) 3.80 1.80

See Nos. 57-67. For surcharges see Nos. 69, 74, 76, 156-157.

Small Figures

1901, Apr. Litho. *Perf. 11½*

57 A25 2c rose .25 .25
58 A25 5c violet brown .25 .25
59 A25 40c blue .85 .30
Nos. 57-59 (3) 1.35 .80

1901-02 Larger Figures

60 A25 1c gray green ('02) .30 .30
61 A25 2c gray .30 .30
a. Half used as 1c on cover 10.00
62 A25 4c pale blue .30 .30
63 A25 5c violet .30 .30
64 A25 8c gray brown ('02) .30 .30
65 A25 10c rose red ('02) .75 .30
66 A25 28c orange ('02) 1.50 .30
67 A25 40c blue .75 .30
Nos. 60-67 (8) 4.50 2.40

For surcharges see Nos. 74, 76.

J. B. Egusquiza — A26

Chalky Paper

1901, Sept. 24 Typo. *Perf. 12x12½*

68 A26 1p slate .30 .25

For surcharge see No. 73.

No. 56 Surcharged in Red

1902, Aug.

69 A25 20c on 24c dp blue .50 .40
a. Inverted surcharge 6.25

Counterfeit surcharges exist.

Nos. 39, 43-44 Surcharged

1902, Dec. 22 *Perf. 12x12½*

70 A15 1c on 14c yellow brn .25 .25
a. No period after "cent" .90 .75
b. Comma after "cent" .65 .50
c. Accent over "Un" .65 .50

1903 *Perf. 11½*

71 A12 5c on 60c yellow .35 .30
72 A12 5c on 80c lt blue .30 .30

Nos. 68, 64, 66 Surcharged

No. 73

No. 74

No. 76

1902-03 *Perf. 12*

73 A26 1c on 1p slate ('03) .40 .40
a. No period after "cent" 3.25 3.00

Perf. 11½

74 A25 5c on 8c gray brown .50 .40
a. No period after "cent" 1.75 1.50
b. Double surcharge 7.00 6.00
76 A25 5c on 28c orange .50 .40
a. No period after "cent" 1.75 1.50
b. Comma after "cent" .80 .60
Nos. 73-76 (3) 1.40 1.20

The surcharge on Nos. 73 and 74 is found reading both upward and downward.

Sentinel Lion with Right Paw Ready to Strike for "Peace and Justice" — A32

Perf. 11½

1903, Feb. 28 Litho. Unwmk.

77 A32 1c gray .30 .30
78 A32 2c blue green .45 .30
79 A32 5c blue .60 .30
80 A32 10c orange brown .75 .30
81 A32 20c carmine .75 .30
82 A32 30c deep blue .90 .30
83 A32 60c purple 2.10 1.00
Nos. 77-83 (7) 5.85 2.80

For surcharges and overprints see Nos. 139-140, 166, O50-O56.

Sentinel Lion with Right Paw Ready to Strike for "Peace and Justice" — A33

1903, Sept.

84 A33 1c yellow green .30 .30
85 A33 2c red orange .30 .30
86 A33 5c dark blue .45 .30
87 A33 10c purple .45 .30
88 A33 20c dark green 5.00 .45
89 A33 30c ultramarine 1.50 .30
90 A33 60c ocher 1.75 .75
Nos. 84-90 (7) 9.75 2.70

Nos. 84-90 exist imperf. Value for pairs, $3 each for 1c-20c, $4 for 30c, $5 for 60c.

The three-line overprint "Gobierno provisorio Ago. 1904" is fraudulent.

Sentinel Lion at Rest — A35

Perf. 11½, 12, 11½x12

1905-10 **Engr.**

Dated "1904"

91 A35 1c orange .30 .25
92 A35 1c vermilion ('07) .30 .25
93 A35 1c grnsh bl ('07) .30 .25
94 A35 2c vermilion ('06) .30 .25
95 A35 2c olive grn ('07) 60.00
96 A35 2c car rose ('08) .45 .25
97 A35 5c dark blue .30 .25
98 A35 5c slate blue ('06) .30 .25
99 A35 5c yellow ('06) .30 .25
100 A35 10c bister ('06) .30 .25
101 A35 10c emerald ('07) .30 .25
102 A35 10c dp ultra ('08) .30 .25
103 A35 20c violet ('06) .45 .25
104 A35 20c bister ('07) .45 .25
105 A35 20c apple grn ('07) .45 .25
106 A35 30c turq bl ('06) .65 .25
107 A35 30c blue gray ('07) .65 .25
108 A35 30c dull lilac ('08) .90 .25
109 A35 60c chocolate ('07) .60 .25
110 A35 60c org brn ('07) 5.25 1.60
111 A35 60c salmon pink ('10) 5.25 1.60
Nos. 91-111 (21) 78.10
Nos. 91-94,96-111 (20) 18.10 7.70

All but Nos. 92 and 104 exist imperf. Value for pair, $10 each, except No. 95 at $35.00 and Nos. 109-111 at $15.00 each pair.

For surcharges and overprints see Nos. 129-130, 146-155, 174-190, 266.

Sentinel Lion at Rest — A36

1904, Aug. **Litho.** ***Perf. 11½***

112 A36 10c light blue .50 .40
a. Imperf., pair 6.00

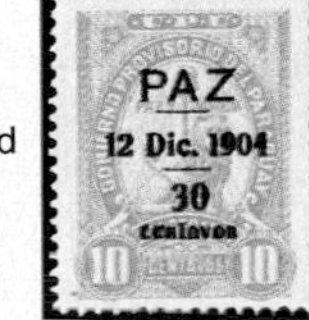

No. 112 Surcharged in Black

1904, Dec.

113 A36 30c on 10c light blue .80 .50

Peace between a successful revolutionary party and the government previously in power.

Governmental Palace, Asunción — A37

Dated "1904"
Center in Black

1906-10 **Engr.** ***Perf. 11½, 12***

114 A37 1p bright rose 2.50 1.50
115 A37 1p brown org ('07) 1.00 .50
116 A37 1p ol gray ('07) 1.00 .50
117 A37 2p turquoise ('07) .50 .40
118 A37 2p lake ('09) .50 .40
119 A37 2p brn org ('10) .60 .40
120 A37 5p red ('07) 1.50 1.00
121 A37 5p ol grn ('10) 1.50 1.00
122 A37 5p dull bl ('10) 1.50 1.00
123 A37 10p brown org ('07) 1.40 1.00
124 A37 10p dp blue ('10) 1.40 1.00
125 A37 10p choc ('10) 1.50 1.00
126 A37 20p olive grn ('07) 3.50 3.25
127 A37 20p violet ('10) 3.50 3.25
128 A37 20p yellow ('10) 3.50 3.25
Nos. 114-128 (15) 25.40 19.45

Nos. 94 and 95 Surcharged

1907

129 A35 5c on 2c vermilion .45 .30
a. "5" omitted 1.50 1.50
b. Inverted surcharge 5.25 5.25
c. Double surcharge
d. Double surcharge, one inverted 1.50 1.50
e. Double surcharge, both invtd. 9.00 9.00
130 A35 5c on 2c olive grn .60 .30
a. "5" omitted 1.50 1.50
b. Inverted surcharge 1.50 1.50
c. Double surcharge 3.00 3.00
d. Bar omitted 3.00 3.00

Official Stamps of 1906-08 Surcharged

1908

131 O17 5c on 10c bister .45 .30
a. Double surcharge 4.50 4.50
132 O17 5c on 10c violet .45 .30
a. Inverted surcharge 3.50 3.50
133 O17 5c on 20c emerald .45 .30
134 O17 5c on 20c violet .45 .30
a. Inverted surcharge 3.50 3.50
135 O17 5c on 30c slate bl 1.50 1.00
136 O17 5c on 30c turq bl 1.50 1.00
a. Inverted surcharge
b. Double surcharge 9.00 9.00
137 O17 5c on 60c choc .45 .30
a. Double surcharge 9.00 9.00
138 O17 5c on 60c red brown .90 .30
a. Inverted surcharge 1.60 1.60
Nos. 131-138 (8) 6.15 3.80

Same Surcharge on Official Stamps of 1903

139 A32 5c on 30c dp blue 3.75 3.25
140 A32 5c on 60c purple 1.50 .90
a. Double surcharge 7.50 7.50

Official Stamps of 1906-08 Overprinted

141 O17 5c deep blue .40 .40
a. Inverted overprint 3.00 3.00
b. Bar omitted 9.00 9.00
c. Double overprint 4.00 4.00
142 O17 5c slate blue .50 .40
a. Inverted overprint 4.00 4.00
b. Double overprint 3.50 3.50
c. Bar omitted 9.00 9.00
143 O17 5c greenish blue .40 .40
a. Inverted overprint 2.50 2.50
b. Bar omitted 7.50 7.50
144 O18 1p brown org & blk .50 .50
a. Double overprint 2.00 2.00
b. Double overprint, one inverted 2.50 2.50
c. Triple overprint, two inverted 4.50 4.50
145 O18 1p brt rose & blk .90 .70
a. Bar omitted
Nos. 141-145 (5) 2.70 2.40

Regular Issues of 1906-08 Surcharged

1908

146 A35 5c on 1c grnsh bl .30 .30
a. Inverted surcharge 1.50 1.50
b. Double surcharge 2.25 2.25
c. "5" omitted 2.25 2.25
147 A35 5c on 2c car rose .30 .30
a. Inverted surcharge 2.50 2.50
b. "5" omitted 3.00 3.00
c. Double surcharge 5.25 5.25
d. Double surcharge, one invtd.
148 A35 5c on 60c org brn .30 .30
a. Inverted surcharge 3.75 3.75
b. "5" omitted 1.50 1.50
149 A35 5c on 60c sal pink .30 .30
a. Double surcharge .75 .75
b. Double surcharge, one invtd. 5.25 5.25
150 A35 5c on 60c choc .30 .30
a. Inverted surcharge 7.50 7.50
151 A35 20c on 1c grnsh bl .30 .30
a. Inverted surcharge 2.25 2.25
152 A35 20c on 2c ver 9.00 7.50
153 A35 20c on 2c car rose 5.25 4.50
a. Inverted surcharge 19.00
154 A35 20c on 30c dl lil .30 .30
a. Inverted surcharge 2.25 2.25
b. Double surcharge
155 A35 20c on 30c turq bl 2.25 2.25
Nos. 146-155 (10) 18.60 16.35

Same Surcharge on Regular Issue of 1901-02

156 A25 5c on 28c org 1.90 1.60
157 A25 5c on 40c dk bl .60 .45
a. Inverted surcharge 6.00 6.00

Same Surcharge on Official Stamps of 1908

158 O17 5c on 10c emer .40 .40
a. Double surcharge 14.00
159 O17 5c on 10c red lil .40 .40
a. Double surcharge 4.00 4.00
b. "5" omitted 3.00 3.00
160 O17 5c on 20c bis .80 .60
a. Double surcharge 2.50 2.50
161 O17 5c on 20c sal pink .80 .60
a. "5" omitted 3.50 3.50
162 O17 5c on 30c bl gray .40 .40
163 O17 5c on 30c yel .40 .40
a. "5" omitted 3.00 3.00
b. Inverted surcharge 2.50 2.50
164 O17 5c on 60c org brn .40 .40
a. Double surcharge 12.00 12.00
165 O17 5c on 60c dp ultra .40 .40
a. Inverted surcharge 5.00 5.00
b. "5" omitted 3.00
Nos. 158-165 (8) 4.00 3.60

Same Surcharge on No. O52

166 A32 20c on 5c blue 2.50 2.00
a. Inverted surcharge 6.00 7.50

Stamp of 1887 Surcharged

1908 **On Stamp of 1887**

167 A12 20c on 2c car 6.50 3.00
a. Inverted surcharge 22.50

On Official Stamps of 1892

168 A12 5c on 15c org 7.50 5.25
169 A12 5c on 20c pink 120.00 95.00
170 A12 5c on 50c gray 52.50 37.50
170A A12 20c on 5c blue 4.50 3.75
b. Inverted surcharge 25.00 25.00
Nos. 167-170A (5) 191.00 144.50

Nos. 151, 152, 153, 155, 167, 170A, while duly authorized, all appear to have been sold to a single individual, and although they paid postage, it is doubtful whether they can be considered as ever having been placed on sale to the public.

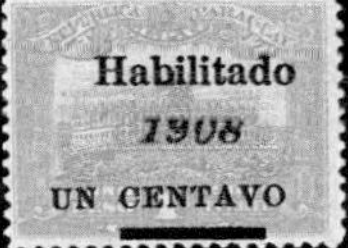

Nos. O82-O84 Surcharged (Date in Red)

1908-09

171 O18 1c on 1p brt rose & blk .50 .50
172 O18 1c on 1p lake & blk .50 .50
173 O18 1c on 1p brn org & blk ('09) 5.00 5.00
Nos. 171-173 (3) 6.00 6.00

Varieties of surcharge on Nos. 171-173 include: "CETTAVO"; date omitted, double or inverted; third line double or omitted.

Types of 1905-1910 Overprinted

1908, Mar. 5 ***Perf. 11½***

174 A35 1c emerald .30 .30
175 A35 5c yellow .30 .30
176 A35 10c lilac brown .30 .30
177 A35 20c yellow orange .30 .30
178 A35 30c red .40 .30
179 A35 60c magenta .30 .30
180 A37 1p light blue .30 .30
Nos. 174-180 (7) 2.20 2.10

Overprinted

1909, Sept.

181 A35 1c blue gray .40 .40
182 A35 1c scarlet .40 .40
183 A35 5c dark green .40 .40
184 A35 5c deep orange .40 .40
185 A35 10c rose .40 .40
186 A35 10c bister brown .40 .40
187 A35 20c yellow .40 .40
188 A35 20c violet .40 .40
189 A35 30c orange brown .60 .40
190 A35 30c dull blue .60 .40
Nos. 181-190 (10) 4.40 4.00

Counterfeits exist.

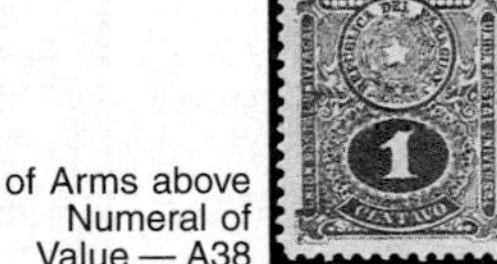

Coat of Arms above Numeral of Value — A38

1910-21 **Litho.** ***Perf. 11½***

191 A38 1c brown .40 .25
192 A38 5c bright violet .40 .25
a. Pair, imperf. between 2.00 2.00
193 A38 5c blue grn ('19) .40 .25
194 A38 5c lt blue ('21) .40 .25
195 A38 10c yellow green .40 .25
196 A38 10c dp vio ('19) .40 .25
197 A38 10c red ('21) .40 .25
198 A38 20c red .40 .25
199 A38 50c car rose .60 .25
200 A38 75c deep blue .40 .25
a. Diag. half perforated ('11) .40 .25
Nos. 191-200 (10) 4.20 2.50

Nos. 191-200 exist imperforate.

No. 200a was authorized for use as 20c.

For surcharges see Nos. 208, 241, 261, 265.

"The Republic" — A39

1911 **Engr.**

201 A39 1c olive grn & blk .30 .30
202 A39 2c dk blue & blk .45 .30
203 A39 5c carmine & indigo .45 .30
204 A39 10c dp blue & brn .45 .30
205 A39 20c olive grn & ind .60 .30
206 A39 50c lilac & indigo .75 .30
207 A39 75c ol grn & red lil .75 .30
Nos. 201-207 (7) 3.75 2.10

Centenary of National Independence.

The 1c, 2c, 10c and 50c exist imperf. Value for pairs, $2.25 each.

No. 199 Surcharged

1912

208 A38 20c on 50c car rose .30 .30
a. Inverted surcharge 1.90 1.90
b. Double surcharge 1.90 1.90
c. Bar omitted 2.50 2.50

National Coat of Arms — A40

1913 **Engr.** ***Perf. 11½***

209 A40 1c gray .30 .25
210 A40 2c orange .30 .25
211 A40 5c lilac .30 .25
212 A40 10c green .30 .25
213 A40 20c dull red .30 .25
214 A40 40c rose .30 .25
215 A40 75c deep blue .30 .25
216 A40 80c yellow .30 .25
217 A40 1p light blue .45 .25
218 A40 1.25p pale blue .45 .25
219 A40 3p greenish blue .45 .25
Nos. 209-219 (11) 3.75 2.75

For surcharges see Nos. 225, 230-231, 237, 242, 253, 262-263, L3-L4.

Nos. J7-J10 Overprinted

1918

220 D2 5c yellow brown .25 .25
221 D2 10c yellow brown .25 .25
222 D2 20c yellow brown .25 .25
223 D2 40c yellow brown .25 .25

Nos. J10 and 214 Surcharged

224 D2 5c on 40c yellow brn .25 .25
225 A40 30c on 40c rose .25 .25
Nos. 220-225 (6) 1.50 1.50

Nos. 220-225 exist with surcharge inverted, double and double with one inverted.

The surcharge "Habilitado-1918-5 cents 5" on the 1c gray official stamps of 1914, is bogus.

No. J11 Overprinted

1920

229 D2 1p yellow brown .25 .25
a. Inverted overprint .65 .65
e. As "g," "AABILITADO" .75 .75
f. As "g," "1929" for "1920" .75 .75
g. Overprint lines 8mm apart .25 .25

Nos. 216 and 219 Surcharged

230 A40 50c on 80c yellow .25 .25
231 A40 1.75p on 3p grnsh bl .75 .65

Same Surcharge on No. J12

232 D2 1p on 1.50p yel brn .25 .25
Nos. 229-232 (4) 1.50 1.40

Nos. 229-232 exist with various surcharge errors, including inverted, double, double inverted and double with one inverted. Those that were issued are listed.

Parliament Building A41

1920 **Litho.** ***Perf. 11½***

233 A41 50c red & black .35 .30
a. "CORRLOS" 5.00 5.00
234 A41 1p lt blue & blk 1.00 .45
235 A41 1.75p dk blue & blk .30 .30
236 A41 3p orange & blk 1.50 .30
Nos. 233-236 (4) 3.15 1.35

50th anniv. of the Constitution.

All values exist imperforate and Nos. 233, 235 and 236 with center inverted. It is doubtful that any of these varieties were regularly issued.

No. 215 Surcharged

1920

237 A40 50c on 75c deep blue .60 .40

Nos. 200, 215 Surcharged

1921

241 A38 50c on 75c deep blue .40 .40
242 A40 50c on 75c deep blue .40 .40

A42

1922, Feb. 8 **Litho.** ***Perf. 11½***

243 A42 50c car & dk blue .40 .40
a. Imperf. pair 2.00
b. Center inverted 25.00 25.00
244 A42 1p dk blue & brn .40 .40
a. Imperf. pair 2.00
b. Center inverted 30.00 30.00
c. As "b," imperf. pair *110.00*

For overprints see Nos. L1-L2.

Rendezvous of Conspirators A43

1922-23

245 A43 1p deep blue .40 .40
246 A43 1p scar & dk bl ('23) .40 .40
247 A43 1p red vio & gray ('23) .40 .40
248 A43 1p org & gray ('23) .40 .40
249 A43 5p dark violet 1.20 .40
250 A43 5p dk bl & org brn ('23) 1.20 .40
251 A43 5p dl red & lt bl ('23) 1.20 .40
252 A43 5p emer & blk ('23) 1.20 .40
Nos. 245-252 (8) 6.40 3.20

National Independence.

No. 218 Surcharged "Habilitado en $1:-1924" in Red

1924

253 A40 1p on 1.25p pale blue .40 .40

This stamp was for use in Asunción. Nos. L3 to L5 were for use in the interior, as is indicated by the "C" in the surcharge.

Map of Paraguay — A44

1924 **Litho.** ***Perf. 11½***

254 A44 1p dark blue .40 .40
255 A44 2p carmine rose .40 .40
256 A44 4p light blue .40 .40
a. Perf. 12 .80 .40
Nos. 254-256 (3) 1.20 1.20

#254-256 exist imperf. Value $3 each pair.

For surcharges and overprint see Nos. 267, C5, C15-C16, C54-C55, L7.

Gen. José E. Díaz — A45

1925-26 ***Perf. 11½, 12***

257 A45 50c red .25 .25
258 A45 1p dark blue .25 .25
259 A45 1p emerald ('26) .25 .25
Nos. 257-259 (3) .75 .75

#257-258 exist imperf. Value $1 each pair.

For overprints see Nos. L6, L8, L10.

Columbus — A46

1925 ***Perf. 11½***

260 A46 1p blue .50 .40
a. Imperf., pair 3.00

For overprint see No. L9.

Nos. 194, 214-215, J12 Surcharged in Black or Red

1926

261 A38 1c on 5c lt blue .25 .25
262 A40 7c on 40c rose .25 .25
263 A40 15c on 75c dp bl (R) .25 .25
264 D2 1.50p on 1.50p yel brn .25 .25
Nos. 261-264 (4) 1.00 1.00

Nos. 194, 179 and 256 Surcharged "Habilitado" and New Values

1927

265 A38 2c on 5c lt blue .25 .25
266 A35 50c on 60c magenta .25 .25
a. Inverted surcharge 2.00
267 A44 1.50p on 4p lt blue .25 .25

Official Stamp of 1914 Surcharged "Habilitado" and New Value

268 O19 50c on 75c dp bl .25 .25
Nos. 265-268 (4) 1.00 1.00

National Emblem — A47

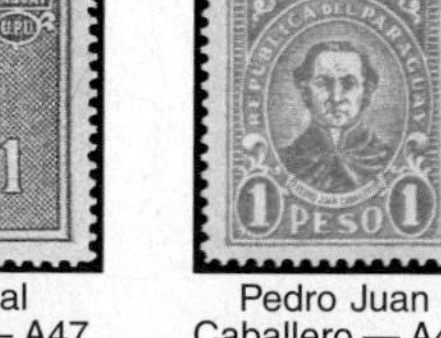

Pedro Juan Caballero — A48

Map of Paraguay — A49

Fulgencio Yegros — A50

Ignacio Iturbe — A51

Oratory of the Virgin, Asunción — A52

Perf. 12, 11, 11½, 11x12

1927-38 **Typo.**

269 A47 1c lt red ('31) .25 .25
270 A47 2c org red ('30) .25 .25
271 A47 7c lilac .25 .25
272 A47 7c emerald ('29) .25 .25
273 A47 10c gray grn ('28) .25 .25
a. 10c light green ('31) .25 .25
274 A47 10c lil rose ('30) .25 .25
275 A47 10c light bl ('35) .25 .25
276 A47 20c dull bl ('28) .25 .25
277 A47 20c lil brn ('30) .25 .25
278 A47 20c lt vio ('31) .25 .25
279 A47 20c rose ('35) .25 .25
280 A47 50c ultramarine .25 .25
281 A47 50c dl red ('28) .25 .25
282 A47 50c orange ('30) .25 .25
283 A47 50c gray ('31) .25 .25
284 A47 50c brn vio ('34) .25 .25
285 A47 50c rose ('36) .25 .25
286 A47 70c ultra ('28) .25 .25
287 A48 1p emerald .25 .25
288 A48 1p org red ('30) .25 .25
289 A48 1p brn org ('34) .25 .25
290 A49 1.50p brown .25 .25
291 A49 1.50p lilac ('28) .25 .25
292 A49 1.50p rose red ('32) .25 .25
293 A50 2.50p bister .25 .25
294 A51 3p gray .25 .25
295 A51 3p rose red ('36) .25 .25
296 A51 3p brt vio ('36) .25 .25
297 A52 5p chocolate .25 .25
298 A52 5p violet ('36) .25 .25
299 A52 5p pale org ('38) .25 .25
300 A49 20p red ('29) 7.00 5.50
301 A49 20p emerald ('29) 7.00 5.50
302 A49 20p vio brn ('29) 7.00 5.50
Nos. 269-302 (34) 28.75 24.25

No. 281 is also known perf. 10½x11½.

Papermaker's watermarks are sometimes found on No. 271 ("GLORIA BOND" in double-lined circle) and No. 280 ("Extra Vencedor Bond" or "ADBANCE/M M C").

For surcharges and overprints see Nos. 312, C4, C6, C13-C14, C17-C18, C25-C32, C34-C35, L11-L30, O94-O96, O98.

Arms of Juan de Salazar de Espinosa — A53

1928, Aug. 15 ***Perf. 12***

303 A53 10p violet brown 3.00 2.00

Juan de Salazar de Espinosa, founder of Asunción.

A papermaker's watermark ("INDIAN BOND EXTRA STRONG S.&C") is sometimes found on Nos 303, 305-307.

Columbus — A54

1928 **Litho.**

304 A54 10p ultra 2.40 1.50
305 A54 10p vermilion 2.40 1.50
306 A54 10p deep red 2.40 1.50
Nos. 304-306 (3) 7.20 4.50

For surcharge and overprint see Nos. C33, L37.

President Rutherford B. Hayes of US and Villa Occidental — A55

1928, Nov. 20 *Perf. 12*

307	A55	10p	gray brown	10.00	3.50
308	A55	10p	red brown	10.00	3.50

50th anniv. of the Hayes' Chaco decision.

Portraits of Archbishop Bogarin — A56

1930, Aug. 15

309	A56	1.50p	lake	2.00	1.50
310	A56	1.50p	turq blue	2.00	1.50
311	A56	1.50p	dull vio	2.00	1.50
			Nos. 309-311 (3)	6.00	4.50

Archbishop Juan Sinforiano Bogarin, first archbishop of Paraguay.

For overprints see Nos. 321-322.

No. 272 Surcharged

1930

312	A47	5c	on 7c emer	.25	.25

A57

1930-39 **Typo.** *Perf. 11½, 12*

313	A57	10p	brown	1.00	.40
314	A57	10p	brn red, *bl* ('31)	1.00	.40
315	A57	10p	dk bl, *pink* ('32)	1.00	.40
316	A57	10p	gray brn ('36)	.80	.40
317	A57	10p	gray ('37)	.80	.40
318	A57	10p	blue ('39)	.40	.40
			Nos. 313-318 (6)	5.00	2.40

1st Paraguayan postage stamp, 60th anniv.

For overprint see No. L31.

Gunboat "Humaitá" — A58

1931 *Perf. 12*

319	A58	1.50p	purple	.80	.50
			Nos. 319,C39-C53 (16)	25.75	18.05

Constitution, 60th anniv.

For overprint see No. L33.

View of San Bernardino — A59

1931, Aug.

320	A59	1p	light green	.50	.40

Founding of San Bernardino, 50th anniv.

For overprint see No. L32.

Nos. 309-310 Overprinted in Blue or Red

1931, Dec. 31

321	A56	1.50p	lake (Bl)	3.00	3.00
322	A56	1.50p	turq blue (R)	3.00	3.00

Map of the Gran Chaco — A60

1932-35 **Typo.** *Perf. 12*

323	A60	1.50p	deep violet	.40	.40
324	A60	1.50p	rose ('35)	.40	.40

For overprints see Nos. L34-L36, O97.

Nos. C74-C78 Surcharged

1933 **Litho.**

325	AP18	50c	on 4p ultra	.50	.40
326	AP18	1p	on 8p red	1.00	.80
327	AP18	1.50p	on 12p bl grn	1.00	.80
328	AP18	2p	on 16p dk vio	1.00	.80
329	AP18	5p	on 20p org brn	2.25	1.75
			Nos. 325-329 (5)	5.75	4.55

Flag of the Race Issue

Flag with Three Crosses: Caravels of Columbus — A61

1933, Oct. 10 **Litho.** *Perf. 11*

330	A61	10c	multicolored	.60	.40
331	A61	20c	multicolored	.60	.40
332	A61	50c	multicolored	.60	.40
333	A61	1p	multicolored	.60	.40
334	A61	1.50p	multicolored	.60	.40
335	A61	2p	multicolored	1.25	.50
336	A61	5p	multicolored	1.25	1.00
337	A61	10p	multicolored	1.25	1.00
			Nos. 330-337 (8)	6.75	4.50

441st anniv. of the sailing of Christopher Columbus from the port of Palos, Aug. 3, 1492, on his first voyage to the New World.

Nos. 332, 334 and 335 exist with Maltese crosses omitted.

Monstrance — A62

1937, Aug. **Unwmk.** *Perf. 11½*

338	A62	1p	dk blue, yel & red	.40	.40
339	A62	3p	dk blue, yel & red	.40	.40
340	A62	10p	dk blue, yel & red	.40	.40
			Nos. 338-340 (3)	1.20	1.20

1st Natl. Eucharistic Congress, Asuncion.

Arms of Asunción — A63

1937, Aug.

341	A63	50c	violet & buff	.60	.40
342	A63	1p	bis & lt grn	.60	.40
343	A63	3p	red & lt bl	.60	.40
344	A63	10p	car rose & buff	.60	.40
345	A63	20p	blue & drab	.60	.40
			Nos. 341-345 (5)	3.00	2.00

Founding of Asuncion, 400th anniv.

Oratory of the Virgin, Asunción — A64

1938-39 **Typo.** *Perf. 11, 12*

346	A64	5p	olive green	.60	.40
347	A64	5p	pale rose ('39)	.60	.40
348	A64	11p	violet brown	.80	.50
			Nos. 346-348 (3)	2.00	1.30

Founding of Asuncion, 400th anniv.

Carlos Antonio Lopez — A65

José Eduvigis Diaz — A66

1939 *Perf. 12*

349	A65	2p	lt ultra & pale brn	.90	.60
350	A66	2p	lt ultra & brn	.90	.60

Reburial of ashes of Pres. Carlos Antonio Lopez (1790-1862) and Gen. José Eduvigis Diaz in the National Pantheon, Asuncion.

Pres. Patricio Escobar and Ramon Zubizarreta A67

Design: 5p, Pres. Bernardino Caballero and Senator José S. Decoud.

1939-40 **Litho.** *Perf. 11½*

Heads in Black

351	A67	50c	dull org ('40)	.60	.60
352	A67	1p	lt violet ('40)	.60	.60
353	A67	2p	red brown ('40)	.60	.60
354	A67	5p	lt ultra	.75	.60
			Nos. 351-354,C122-C123,O99-O104 (12)	27.55	26.20

Founding of the University of Asuncion, 50th anniv.

Varieties of this issue include inverted heads (50c, 1p, 2p); doubled heads; Caballero and Decoud heads in 50c frame: imperforates and part-perforates. Examples with inverted heads were not officially issued.

Coats of Arms — A69

Flags of Paraguay, United States — A70

Designs: 1p, Pres. Baldomir, flags of Paraguay, Uruguay. 2p, Pres. Benavides, flags of Paraguay, Peru. 5p, Pres. Alessandri, flags of Paraguay, Chile. 6p, Pres. Vargas, flags of Paraguay, Brazil. 10p, Pres. Ortiz, flags of Paraguay, Argentina.

1939 **Engr.; Flags Litho.** *Perf. 12*

Flags in National Colors

355	A69	50c	violet blue	.30	.30
356	A70	1p	olive	.30	.30
357	A70	2p	blue green	.30	.30
358	A70	3p	sepia	.35	.35
359	A70	5p	orange	.30	.30
360	A70	6p	dull violet	.75	.60
361	A70	10p	bister brn	.60	.35
			Nos. 355-361,C113-C121 (16)	42.30	28.25

First Buenos Aires Peace Conference.

For overprint and surcharge, see Nos. 387, B10.

Coats of Arms of New York and Asunción A76

1939, Nov. 30

362	A76	5p	scarlet	.80	.80
363	A76	10p	deep blue	1.20	.80
364	A76	11p	dk blue grn	1.20	1.20
365	A76	22p	olive blk	2.00	1.60
			Nos. 362-365,C124-C126 (7)	33.95	31.40

New York World's Fair.

Paraguayan Soldier — A77

Paraguayan Woman — A78

Cowboys — A79

Plowing — A80

View of Paraguay River — A81

Oxcart A82

Pasture A83

Pirareta Falls — A84

1940, Jan. 1 Photo. *Perf. 12½*

366	A77	50c deep orange	.40	.25
367	A78	1p brt red violet	.40	.25
368	A79	3p bright green	.40	.25
369	A80	5p chestnut	.40	.25
370	A81	10p magenta	.40	.25
371	A82	20p violet	1.00	.30
372	A83	50p cobalt blue	2.00	.45
373	A84	100p black	4.00	1.40
		Nos. 366-373 (8)	9.00	3.40

Second Buenos Aires Peace Conference.
For surcharge see No. 386.

Map of the Americas — A85

1940, May Engr. *Perf. 12*

374	A85	50c red orange	.30	.25
375	A85	1p green	.30	.25
376	A85	5p dark blue	.50	.25
377	A85	10p brown	1.00	.50
		Nos. 374-377,C127-C130 (8)	12.20	9.20

Pan American Union, 50th anniversary.

Reproduction of Type A1 — A86

Sir Rowland Hill — A87

Designs: 6p, Type A2. 10p, Type A3.

1940, Aug. 15 Photo. *Perf. 13½*

378	A86	1p aqua & brt red vio	.50	.25
379	A87	5p dp yel grn & red brn	.65	.30
380	A86	6p org brn & ultra	1.50	.65
381	A86	10p ver & black	1.50	1.00
		Nos. 378-381 (4)	4.15	2.20

Postage stamp centenary.

Dr. José Francia
A90 A91

1940, Sept. 20 Engr. *Perf. 12*

382	A90	50c carmine rose	.30	.25
383	A91	50c plum	.30	.25
384	A90	1p bright green	.30	.25
385	A91	5p deep blue	.30	.25
		Nos. 382-385 (4)	1.20	1.00

Centenary of the death of Dr. Jose Francia (1766-1840), dictator of Paraguay, 1814-1840.

No. 366 Surcharged in Black

1940, Sept. 7 *Perf. 12½*

386	A77	5p on 50c dp org	.40	.25

In honor of Pres. Jose F. Estigarribia who died in a plane crash Sept. 7, 1940.

No. 360 Overprinted in Black

1941, Aug. *Perf. 12*

387	A70	6p multi	.40	.40

Visit to Paraguay of Pres. Vargas of Brazil.

Nos. C113-C115 Overprinted in Blue or Red

1942, Jan. 17 *Perf. 12½*

388	A69	1p multi (Bl)	.30	.25
389	A69	3p multi (R)	.30	.25
390	A70	5p multi (R)	.30	.25
		Nos. 388-390 (3)	.90	.75

Coat of Arms — A92

1942-43 Litho. *Perf. 11, 12, 11x12*

391	A92	1p light green	.50	.25
392	A92	1p orange ('43)	.50	.25
393	A92	7p light blue	.50	.25
394	A92	7p yel brn ('43)	.50	.25
		Nos. 391-394 (4)	2.00	1.00

Values are for examples perforated 11. Stamps perforated 12 and 11x12 are worth more. Nos. 391-394 exist imperf.

The Indian Francisco — A93

Domingo Martinez de Irala and His Vision A94

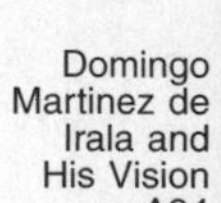

Arms of Irala — A95

1942, Aug. 15 Engr. *Perf. 12*

395	A93	2p green	.75	.30
396	A94	5p rose	.75	.30
397	A95	7p sapphire	.75	.30
		Nos. 395-397,C131-C133 (6)	10.75	5.90

400th anniversary of Asuncion.

Pres. Higinio Morinigo, Scenes of Industry & Agriculture — A96

1943, Aug. 15 Unwmk.

398	A96	7p blue	.25	.25

For surcharges see Nos. 404, 428.

Christopher Columbus — A97

1943, Aug. 15

399	A97	50c violet	.25	.25
400	A97	1p gray brn	.25	.25
401	A97	5p dark grn	.50	.25
402	A97	7p brt ultra	.25	.25
		Nos. 399-402 (4)	1.25	1.00

Discovery of America, 450th anniv.
For surcharges see Nos. 405, 429.

No. 296 Surcharged in Black

1944 *Perf. 12, 11, 11½, 11x12*

403	A51	1c on 3p brt vio	.50	.25

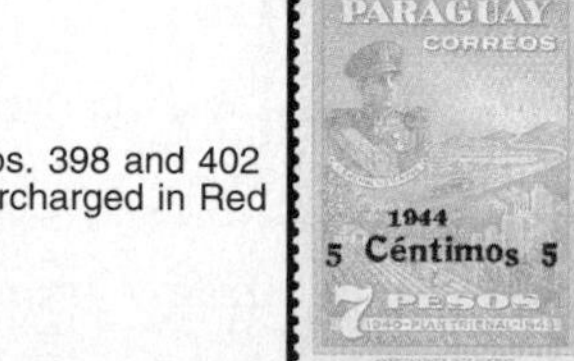

Nos. 398 and 402 Surcharged in Red

1944 *Perf. 12*

404	A96	5c on 7p blue	.50	.25
405	A97	5c on 7p brt ultra	.50	.25

Imperforates
Starting with No. 406, many Paraguayan stamps exist imperf.

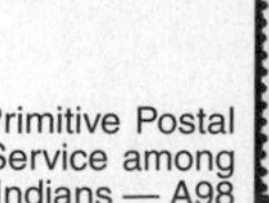

Primitive Postal Service among Indians — A98

Ruins of Humaitá Church — A99

Locomotive of early Paraguayan Railroad — A100

Marshal Francisco S. Lopez — A101

Early Merchant Ship — A102

Port of Asunción — A103

Birthplace of Paraguay's Liberation — A104

Monument to Heroes of Itororó — A105

1944-45 Unwmk. Engr. *Perf. 12½*

406	A98	1c black	.25	.25
407	A99	2c copper brn ('45)	.25	.25
408	A100	5c light olive	1.00	.25
409	A101	7c light blue ('45)	.40	.25
410	A102	10c green ('45)	.50	.25
411	A103	15c dark blue ('45)	.50	.30
412	A104	50c black brown	.65	.40
413	A105	1g dk rose car ('45)	1.90	1.00
		Nos. 406-413 (8)	5.45	2.95
		Nos. 406-413,C134-C146 (21)	26.55	14.35

See #435, 437, 439, 441, C158-C162.
For surcharges see #414, 427.

No. 409 Surcharged in Red

1945

No.	Type	Description	Unused	Used
414	A101	5c on 7c light blue	.50	.25

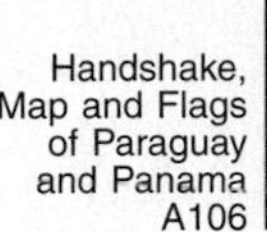

Handshake, Map and Flags of Paraguay and Panama A106

Designs: 3c, Venezuela Flag. 5c, Colombia Flag. 2g, Peru Flag.

Engr.; Flags Litho. in Natl. Colors

1945, Aug. 15 Unwmk. *Perf. 12½*

No.	Type	Description	Unused	Used
415	A106	1c dark green	.25	.25
416	A106	3c lake	.25	.25
417	A106	5c blue blk	.25	.25
418	A106	2g brown	1.10	.75
		Nos. 415-418,C147-C153 (11)	21.40	21.05

Goodwill visits of Pres. Higinio Morinigo during 1943.

Nos. B6 to B9 Surcharged in Black

1945 Engr. *Perf. 12*

No.	Type	Description	Unused	Used
419	SP4	2c on 7p + 3p red brn	.40	.40
420	SP4	2c on 7p + 3p purple	.40	.40
421	SP4	2c on 7p + 3p car rose	.40	.40
422	SP4	2c on 7p + 3p saph	.40	.40
423	SP4	5c on 7p + 3p red brn	.40	.40
424	SP4	5c on 7p + 3p purple	.40	.40
425	SP4	5c on 7p + 3p car rose	.40	.40
426	SP4	5c on 7p + 3p saph	.40	.40
		Nos. 419-426 (8)	3.20	3.20

Similar Surcharge in Red on Nos. 409, 398 and 402

Perf. 12½, 12

No.	Type	Description	Unused	Used
427	A101	5c on 7c lt blue	.40	.40
428	A96	5c on 7p blue	.40	.40
429	A97	5c on 7p brt ultra	.40	.40
		Nos. 427-429 (3)	1.20	1.20

Nos. 427-429 exist with black surcharge.

Catalogue values for unused stamps in this section, from this point to the end of the section, are for Never Hinged items.

Coat of Arms ("U.P.U." at bottom) — A110

1946 Litho. *Perf. 11, 12*

No.	Type	Description	Unused	Used
430	A110	5c gray	.40	.25

See Nos. 459-463, 478-480, 498-506, 525-536, 646-658.
For overprints see Nos. 464-466.

Nos. B6 to B9 Surcharged "1946" and New Value in Black

1946 *Perf. 12*

No.	Type	Description	Unused	Used
431	SP4	5c on 7p + 3p red brn	2.00	1.50
432	SP4	5c on 7p + 3p purple	2.00	1.50
433	SP4	5c on 7p + 3p car rose	2.00	1.50
434	SP4	5c on 7p + 3p saph	2.00	1.50
		Nos. 431-434 (4)	8.00	6.00

Types of 1944-45 and

First Telegraph in South America A111

Monument to Antequera A112

Colonial Jesuit Altar — A113

1946, Sept. 21 Engr. *Perf. 12½*

No.	Type	Description	Unused	Used
435	A102	1c rose car	.40	.40
436	A111	2c purple	.40	.40
437	A98	5c ultra	.40	.40
438	A112	10c org yel	.40	.40
439	A105	15c brn olive	.40	.40
440	A113	50c deep grn	.70	.40
441	A104	1g brt ultra	1.25	.80
		Nos. 435-441 (7)	3.95	3.20

See Nos. C135-C138, C143.

Marshal Francisco Solano Lopez — A114

1947, May 15 *Perf. 12*

No.	Type	Description	Unused	Used
442	A114	1c purple	.30	.25
443	A114	2c org red	.30	.25
444	A114	5c green	.30	.25
445	A114	15c ultra	.30	.25
446	A114	50c dark grn	1.00	.65
		Nos. 442-446,C163-C167 (10)	11.25	10.70

Juan Sinforiano Bogarin, Archbishop of Asunción — A115

Archbishopric Coat of Arms — A116

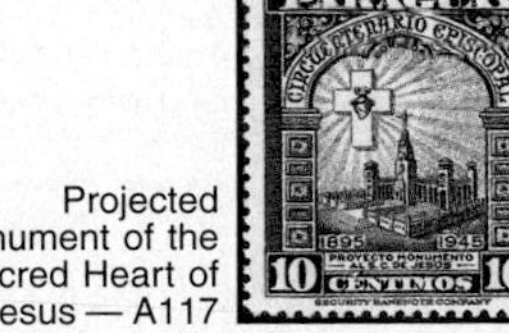

Projected Monument of the Sacred Heart of Jesus — A117

Vision of Projected Monument A118

1948, Jan. 6 Engr. *Perf. 12½*

No.	Type	Description	Unused	Used
447	A115	2c dark blue	.40	.25
448	A116	5c deep car	.40	.25
449	A117	10c gray blk	.40	.25
450	A118	15c green	.70	.25
		Nos. 447-450,C168-C175 (12)	19.10	10.00

Archbishopric of Asunción, 50th anniv.

"Political Enlightenment" A119

1948, Sept. 11 Engr. & Litho.

No.	Type	Description	Unused	Used
451	A119	5c car red	.30	.30
452	A119	15c red org	.30	.30
		Nos. 451-452,C176-C177 (4)	9.50	9.50

Issued to honor the Barefeet, a political group.

C. A. Lopez, J. N. Gonzalez and Freighter Paraguari A120

Centers in Carmine, Black, Ultramarine and Blue

1949 Litho.

No.	Type	Description	Unused	Used
453	A120	2c orange	.25	.25
454	A120	5c blue vio	.25	.25
455	A120	10c black	.25	.25
456	A120	15c violet	.25	.25
457	A120	50c blue grn	.25	.25
458	A120	1g dull vio brn	.30	.25
		Nos. 453-458 (6)	1.55	1.50

Paraguay's merchant fleet centenary.

Arms Type of 1946

1950 Unwmk. *Perf. 10½*

No.	Type	Description	Unused	Used
459	A110	5c red	.50	.25
460	A110	10c blue	.50	.25
461	A110	50c rose lilac	.75	.25
462	A110	1g pale violet	.75	.25

1951 Coarse Impression

No.	Type	Description	Unused	Used
463	A110	30c green	.75	.25
		Nos. 459-463 (5)	3.25	1.25

Nos. 459, 460 and 463 Overprinted in Various Colors

1951, Apr. 18

No.	Type	Description	Unused	Used
464	A110	5c red (Bk), block	1.00	1.00
465	A110	10c blue (R), block	2.00	2.00
466	A110	30c green (V), block	3.00	3.00
		Nos. 464-466 (3)	6.00	6.00

1st Economic Cong. of Paraguay, 4/18/51.

Columbus Lighthouse — A121

1952, Feb. 11 *Perf. 10*

No.	Type	Description	Unused	Used
467	A121	2c org brn	.40	.25
468	A121	5c light ultra	.40	.25
469	A121	10c rose	.40	.25
470	A121	15c light blue	.40	.25
471	A121	20c lilac	.40	.25
472	A121	50c orange	.40	.25
473	A121	1g bluish grn	.40	.25
		Nos. 467-473 (7)	2.80	1.75

Silvio Pettirossi, Aviator — A122

1954, Mar. Litho. *Perf. 10*

No.	Type	Description	Unused	Used
474	A122	5c blue	.55	.25
475	A122	20c rose pink	.55	.25
476	A122	50c vio brn	.55	.25
477	A122	60c lt vio	.55	.25
		Nos. 474-477,C201-C204 (8)	4.40	2.00

Arms Type of 1946

1954 *Perf. 11*

No.	Type	Description	Unused	Used
478	A110	10c vermilion	2.00	.25

Perf. 10

No.	Type	Description	Unused	Used
478A	A110	10c ver, redrawn	.75	.25
479	A110	10g orange	5.00	2.00
480	A110	50g vio brn	9.00	7.00
		Nos. 478-480 (4)	16.75	9.50

No. 478A measures 20½x24mm, has 5 frame lines at left and 6 at right. No. 478 measures 20x24½mm, has 6 frame lines at left and 5 at right.

Three National Heroes — A123

1954, Aug. 15 Litho. *Perf. 10*

No.	Type	Description	Unused	Used
481	A123	5c light vio	.25	.25
482	A123	20c light blue	.25	.25
483	A123	50c rose pink	.25	.25
484	A123	1g org brn	.25	.25
485	A123	2g blue grn	.35	.25
		Nos. 481-485,C216-C220 (10)	17.35	10.10

Marshal Francisco S. Lopez, Pres. Carlos A. Lopez and Gen. Bernardino Caballero.

Pres. Alfredo Stroessner and Pres. Juan D. Peron — A124

Photo. & Litho.

1955, Apr. Wmk. 90 *Perf. 13x13½*

No.	Type	Description	Unused	Used
486	A124	5c multicolored	.25	.25
487	A124	10c multicolored	.25	.25
488	A124	50c multicolored	.25	.25
489	A124	1.30g multicolored	.25	.25
490	A124	2.20g multicolored	.35	.25
		Nos. 486-490,C221-C224 (9)	3.75	4.45

Visit of Pres. Juan D. Peron of Argentina.

Jesuit Ruins, Trinidad Belfry
A125

Santa Maria Cornice — A126

Jesuit Ruins: 20c, Corridor at Trinidad. 2.50g, Tower of Santa Rosa. 5g, San Cosme gate. 15g, Church of Jesus. 25g, Niche at Trinidad.

Perf. 12½x12, 12x12½

1955, June 19 Engr. Unwmk.

491 A125 5c org yel .40 .25
492 A125 20c olive bister .40 .25
493 A126 50c lt red brn .40 .25
494 A126 2.50g olive .40 .25
495 A125 5g yel brn .40 .25
496 A125 15g blue grn .40 .25
497 A126 25g deep grn .90 .25
Nos. 491-497,C225-C232 (15) 7.25 3.80

25th anniv. of the priesthood of Monsignor Rodriguez.

For surcharges see Nos. 545-551.

Arms Type of 1946

Perf. 10, 11 (No. 500)

1956-58 Litho. Unwmk.

498 A110 5c brown ('57) 1.00 .50
499 A110 30c red brn ('57) 2.00 .50
500 A110 45c gray olive 3.00 .50
500A A110 90c lt vio bl 5.00 .75
501 A110 2g ocher 5.00 .25
502 A110 2.20g lil rose 2.00 .25
503 A110 3g ol bis ('58) 3.00 .25
503A A110 4.20g emer ('57) 6.00 .25
504 A110 5g ver ('57) 10.00 5.00
505 A110 10g lt grn ('57) 10.00 5.00
506 A110 20g blue ('57) 10.00 5.00
Nos. 498-506 (11) 57.00 18.25

No. 500A exists with four-line, carmine overprint: "DIA N. UNIDAS 24 Octubre 1945-1956". It was not regularly issued and no decree authorizing it is known.

Soldiers, Angel and Asuncion Cathedral — A127

#513-519, Soldier & nurse in medallion & flags.

Perf. 13½

1957, June 12 Photo. Unwmk.

Granite Paper

Flags in Red and Blue

508 A127 5c bl grn .25 .25
509 A127 10c carmine .25 .25
510 A127 15c ultra .25 .25
511 A127 20c dp claret .25 .25
512 A127 25c gray blk .25 .25
513 A127 30c lt blue .25 .25
514 A127 40c gray blk .25 .25
515 A127 50c dark car .25 .25
516 A127 1g bluish grn .25 .25
517 A127 1.30g ultra .25 .25
518 A127 1.50g dp claret .25 .25
519 A127 2g brt grn .25 .25
Nos. 508-519 (12) 3.00 3.00

Heroes of the Chaco war. See #C233-C245.

Statue of St. Ignatius (Guarani Carving) — A128

Blessed Roque Gonzales and St. Ignatius
A129

A129a

1.50g, St. Ignatius and San Ignacio Monastery.

Wmk. 319

1958, Mar. 15 Litho. *Perf. 11*

520 A128 50c dk red brn .80 *1.25*
521 A129 50c lt bl grn .80 *1.25*
522 A129a 1.50g brt vio .80 *1.25*
523 A128 3g light bl .80 .50
524 A129 6.25g rose car .80 .25
Nos. 520-524 (5) 4.00 4.50

St. Ignatius of Loyola (1491-1556).

See Nos. 935-942.

On designs A129a text under Paraguay is different from those of design A185b (Nos. 939-942).

Arms Type of 1946

1958-64 Litho. *Perf. 10, 11*

525 A110 45c gray olive 2.00 1.00
526 A110 50c rose vio 1.25 1.00
527 A110 70c lt brn ('59) 2.00 1.00
527A A110 90c vio blue 2.00 1.00
528 A110 1g violet 1.00 .50
529 A110 1.50g lilac ('59) 1.50 1.00
529A A110 2g bister ('64) 5.00 3.00
530 A110 3g ol bis ('59) 5.00 3.00
531 A110 4.50g lt ultra ('59) 2.00 2.00
531A A110 5g rose red ('59) 1.00 1.00
531B A110 10g bl grn ('59) 2.00 1.00
532 A110 12.45g yel green 3.00 3.00
533 A110 15g dl orange 10.00 2.00
534 A110 30g citron 3.00 2.00
535 A110 50g brown red 2.00 1.00
536 A110 100g gray vio 3.00 2.00
Nos. 525-536 (16) 45.75 25.50

Pres. Alfredo Stroessner
A130

Wmk. 320

1958, Aug. 15 Litho. *Perf. 13½*

Center in Slate

537 A130 10c sal pink .25 *.30*
538 A130 15c violet .25 *.30*
539 A130 25c yel grn .25 *.30*
540 A130 30c light fawn .25 *.30*
541 A130 50c rose car .30 .30
542 A130 75c light ultra .30 .30
543 A130 5g lt bl grn .50 .50
544 A130 10g brown 1.00 .50
Nos. 537-544,C246-C251 (14) 24.10 17.80

Re-election of President General Alfredo Stroessner.

Nos. 491-497 Srchd. in Red

Perf. 12½x12, 12x12½

1959, May 14 Engr. Unwmk.

545 A125 1.50g on 5c org yel .25 *.50*
546 A125 1.50g on 20c ol bis .25 *.50*
547 A126 1.50g on 50c lt red brn .25 *.50*
548 A126 3g on 2.50g ol .25 *.50*
549 A125 6.25g on 5g yel brn .25 *.50*
550 A125 20g on 15g bl grn .70 *.80*
551 A126 30g on 25g dp grn 1.00 *1.00*
Nos. 545-551,C252-C259 (15) 15.45 12.30

The surcharge is made to fit the stamps.

Counterfeits of surcharge exist.

Goalkeeper Catching Soccer Ball — A131

1960, Mar. 18 Photo. *Perf. 12½*

556 A131 30c brt red & bl grn .30 .30
557 A131 50c plum & dk bl .30 .30
558 A131 75c ol grn & org .30 .30
559 A131 1.50g dk vio & bl grn .30 .30
Nos. 556-559,C262-C264 (7) 2.25 2.25

Olympic Games of 1960.

WRY Emblem — A132

1960, Apr. 7 Litho. *Perf. 11*

560 A132 25c sal & yel grn .60 .25
561 A132 50c lt yel grn & red org .60 .25
562 A132 70c lt brn & lil rose .75 .25
563 A132 1.50g lt bl & ultra .75 .25
564 A132 3g gray & bis brn 1.40 .45
Nos. 560-564,C265-C268 (9) 9.90 4.75

World Refugee Year, July 1, 1959-June 30, 1960 (1st issue).

UN Emblem and Dove — A133

UN Declaration of Human Rights: 3g, Hand holding scales. 6g, Hands breaking chains. 20g, Flame.

1960, Apr. 21 *Perf. 12½x13*

565 A133 1g dk car & bl .30 .25
566 A133 3g blue & org .30 .25
567 A133 6g gray grn & sal .40 .25
568 A133 20g ver & yel .55 .25
Nos. 565-568,C269-C271 (7) 2.75 2.20

Miniature sheets exist, perf. and imperf., containing one each of Nos. 565-568, all printed in purple and orange. Values: perf. $4; imperf. $15.

Flags of UN and Paraguay and UN Emblem
A134

Perf. 13x13½

1960, Oct. 24 Photo. Unwmk.

569 A134 30c lt bl, red & bl .30 .30
570 A134 75c yel, red & bl .30 .30
571 A134 90c pale lil, red & bl .30 .30
Nos. 569-571,C272-C273 (5) 1.70 1.50

15th anniversary of the United Nations.

International Bridge, Arms of Brazil, Paraguay — A135

1961, Jan. 26 Litho. *Perf. 14*

572 A135 15c green .50 .50
573 A135 30c dull blue .50 .50
574 A135 50c orange .50 .50
575 A135 75c vio blue .50 .50
576 A135 1g violet .50 .50
Nos. 572-576,C274-C277 (9) 6.75 6.75

Inauguration of the International Bridge between Paraguay and Brazil.

Truck Carrying Logs — A136

90c, 2g, Logs on river barge. 1g, 5g, Radio tower.

Unwmk.

1961, Apr. 10 Photo. *Perf. 13*

577 A136 25c yel grn & rose car .25 .25
578 A136 90c blue & yel .25 .25
579 A136 1g car rose & org .25 .25
580 A136 2g ol grn & sal .25 .25
581 A136 5g lilac & emer .25 .25
Nos. 577-581,C278-C281 (9) 4.05 3.70

Paraguay's progress, "Paraguay en Marcha."

P. J. Caballero, José G. R. Francia, F. Yegros, Revolutionary Leaders — A137

1961, May 16 Litho. *Perf. 14½*

582 A137 30c green .40 .25
583 A137 50c lil rose .40 .25
584 A137 90c violet .40 .25
585 A137 1.50g Prus bl .40 .25
586 A137 3g olive bis .40 .25
587 A137 4g ultra .40 .25
588 A137 5g brown .40 .25
Nos. 582-588,C282-C287 (13) 9.95 7.90

150th anniv. of Independence (1st issue).

"Chaco Peace" — A138

1961, June 12 *Perf. 14x14½*

589 A138 25c vermilion .40 .40
590 A138 30c green .40 .40
591 A138 50c red brn .40 .40
592 A138 1g bright vio .40 .40
593 A138 2g dk bl gray .40 .40
Nos. 589-593,C288-C290 (8) 7.80 7.10

Chaco Peace; 150th anniv. of Independence (2nd issue).

Puma — A139

1961, Aug. 16 Unwmk. *Perf. 14*

594 A139 75c dull vio 1.00 1.00
595 A139 1.50g brown 1.00 1.00
596 A139 4.50g green 1.00 1.00
597 A139 10g Prus blue 1.00 1.00
Nos. 594-597,C291-C293 (7) 15.50 13.00

150th anniv. of Independence (3rd issue).

University Seal — A140

1961, Sept. 18 *Perf. 14x14½*

598 A140 15c ultra .30 .30
599 A140 25c dk red .30 .30
600 A140 75c bl grn .30 .30
601 A140 1g orange .30 .30
Nos. 598-601,C294-C296 (7) 3.20 2.80

Founding of the Catholic University in Asuncion; 150th anniv. of Independence (4th issue).

Hotel Guarani A141

1961, Oct. 14 **Litho.** *Perf. 15*

602 A141 50c slate bl .50 *1.00*
603 A141 1g green .50 *1.00*
604 A141 4.50g lilac .50 *1.00*
Nos. 602-604,C297-C300 (7) 11.00 10.25

Opening of the Hotel Guarani; 150th anniv. of Independence (5th issue).

Tennis Racket and Balls in Flag Colors — A142

1961, Oct. 16 **Litho.** *Perf. 11*

605 A142 35c multi .25 .25
606 A142 75c multi .25 .25
607 A142 1.50g multi .25 .25
608 A142 2.25g multi .25 .25
609 A142 4g multi .25 .25
Nos. 605-609 (5) 1.25 1.25

28th South American Tennis Championships, Asuncion, Oct. 15-23 (1st issue). Some specialists question the status of this issue. See Nos. C301-C303.

Imperforates exist in changed colors as well as two imperf. souvenir sheets with stamps in changed colors. Values: stamps, set $25; souvenir sheets, pair $40.

Alan B. Shepard, First US Astronaut A143

18.15g, 36g, 50g, Shepard, Saturn, horiz.

1961, Dec. 22 **Litho.** *Perf. 11*

610 A143 10c blue & brown .25 .25
611 A143 25c blue & car rose .25 .25
612 A143 50c blue & yel org .25 .25
613 A143 75c blue & green .25 .25
614 A143 18.15g green & blue *10.50* *6.50*
615 A143 36g orange & blue *10.50* *6.50*
616 A143 50g car rose & blue *14.00* *9.75*
a. Souvenir sheet of 1 37.50
Nos. 610-616 (7) 36.00 23.75

Nos. 614-616a are airmail.

Also exist imperf in different colors. Value, set $36, souvenir sheet $210.

Uprooted Oak Emblem — A145

1961, Dec. 30 **Unwmk.** *Perf. 11*

619 A145 10c ultra & lt bl .25 .25
620 A145 25c maroon & org .25 .25
621 A145 50c car rose & pink .25 .25
622 A145 75c dk bl & yel grn .25 .25
Nos. 619-622 (4) 1.00 1.00

World Refugee Year, 1959-60 (2nd issue). Imperforates in changed colors and souvenir sheets exist. Values: imperf. set of 7, $5; souvenir sheet, perf. or imperf., each $15. Some specialists question the status of this issue.

See Nos. C307-C309.

Europa A146

Design: 20g, 50g, Dove.

1961, Dec. 31

623 A146 50c multicolored .35 .35
624 A146 75c multicolored .35 .35
625 A146 1g multicolored .35 .35
626 A146 1.50g multicolored .35 .35
627 A146 4.50g multicolored .80 .75
a. Souvenir sheet of 5, #623-627 21.00
628 A146 20g multicolored 21.00
629 A146 50g multicolored 25.00
a. Souvenir sheet of 1 90.00
Nos. 623-629 (7) 48.20 2.15

Nos. 628-629 are airmail.

Imperforates in changed colors exist. Values: set, $30; souvenir sheets, pair, $90.

Tennis Player — A147

1962, Jan. 5 *Perf. 15x14½*

630 A147 35c Prussian bl .60 .25
631 A147 75c dark vio .60 .25
632 A147 1.50g red brn .60 .25
633 A147 2.25g emerald .60 .25
634 A147 4g carmine 2.00 .25
635 A147 12.45g red lil 2.00 .25
636 A147 20g bl grn 2.00 .40
637 A147 50g org brn 2.00 .65
Nos. 630-637 (8) 10.40 2.55

28th South American Tennis Championships, 1961 (2nd issue) and the 150th anniv. of Independence (6th issue).

Nos. 634-637 are airmail.

Scout Bugler — A148

Lord Baden-Powell A148a

1962, Feb. 6 *Perf. 11*

Olive Green Center

638 A148 10c dp magenta .25 .25
639 A148 20c red orange .25 .25
640 A148 25c dk brown .25 .25
641 A148 30c emerald .25 .25
642 A148 50c indigo .25 .25
643 A148a 12.45g car rose & bl .85 .85
644 A148a 36g car rose & emer 2.40 2.40
645 A148a 50g car rose & org yel 3.25 3.25
Nos. 638-645 (8) 7.75 7.75

Issued to honor the Boy Scouts. Imperfs in changed colors exist and imperf souvenir sheets exist. Value, set $22, souvenir sheet $95. Some specialists question the status of this issue.

Nos. 643-645 are airmail.

Arms Type of 1946

1962-68 **Litho.** **Wmk. 347**

646 A110 50c steel bl ('63) 3.00 2.00
647 A110 70c dull lil ('63) 3.00 2.00
648 A110 1.50g violet ('63) 3.00 1.00
649 A110 3g dp bl ('68) 5.00 2.00
650 A110 4.50g redsh brn ('67) 5.00 1.00
651 A110 5g lilac ('64) 5.00 2.00
652 A110 10g car rose ('63) 10.00 3.00
653 A110 12.45g ultra 7.00 3.00
654 A110 15.45g org ver 10.00 2.00
655 A110 18.15g lilac 10.00 2.00
656 A110 20g lt brn ('63) 10.00 2.00
657 A110 50g dl red brn ('67) 10.00 3.00
658 A110 100g bl gray ('63) 3.00 2.00
Nos. 646-658 (13) 84.00 27.00

Map and Laurel Branch — A149

Design: 20g, 50g, Hands holding globe.

Perf. 14x14½

1962, Apr. 14 **Unwmk.**

659 A149 50c ocher .30 .30
660 A149 75c vio blue .30 .30
661 A149 1g purple .30 .30
662 A149 1.50g brt grn .30 .30
663 A149 4.50g vermilion .30 .30
664 A149 20g lil rose .30 .30
665 A149 50g orange .90 .90
Nos. 659-665 (7) 2.70 2.70

Day of the Americas; 150th anniv. of Independence (7th issue).

Nos. 664-665 are airmail.

UN Emblem A150

Design: #670-673, UN Headquarters, NYC.

1962, Apr. 23 *Perf. 15*

666 A150 50c bister brn .40 .25
667 A150 75c dp claret .40 .25
668 A150 1g Prussian bl .40 .25
669 A150 2g orange brn 2.00 .25
670 A150 12.45g dl vio 2.00 .35
671 A150 18.15g ol grn 2.00 .65
672 A150 23.40g brn red 2.00 .95
673 A150 30g carmine 2.00 1.10
Nos. 666-673 (8) 11.20 4.05

UN; Independence, 150th anniv. (8th issue).

Nos. 670-673 are airmail.

Malaria Eradication Emblem and Mosquito A151

Design: 75c, 1g, 1.50g, Microscope, anopheles mosquito and eggs. 3g, 4g, Malaria eradication emblem. 12.45g, 18.15g, 36g, Mosquito, UN emblem and microscope.

Perf. 14x13½

1962, May 23 **Wmk. 346**

674 A151 30c pink, ultra & blk .30 .30
675 A151 50c bis, grn & blk .30 .30
676 A151 75c rose red, blk & bis .30 .30
677 A151 1g brt grn, blk & bis .30 .30
678 A151 1.50g dl red brn, blk & bis .30 .30
679 A151 3g bl, red & blk .30 .30
680 A151 4g grn, red & blk .30 .30
681 A151 12.45g ol bis, grn & blk .30 .30
682 A151 18.15g rose lil, red & blk .60 .45
683 A151 36g rose red, vio bl & blk 1.50 1.10
Nos. 674-683 (10) 4.50 3.95

WHO drive to eradicate malaria.

Imperforates exist in changed colors. Value, $10. Also, two souvenir sheets exist, one containing one copy of No. 683, the other an imperf 36g in blue, red & black. Value, each $20.

Some specialists question the status of this issue.

Nos. 679-683 are airmail.

Stadium — A152

Soccer Players and Globe A152a

Perf. 13½x14

1962, July 28 **Litho.** **Wmk. 346**

684 A152 15c yel & dk brn .25 .25
685 A152 25c brt grn & dk brn .25 .25
686 A152 30c lt vio & dk brn .25 .25
687 A152 40c dl org & dk brn .25 .25
688 A152 50c brt yel grn & dk brn .25 .25
689 A152a 12.45g brt rose, blk & vio .70 .35
690 A152a 18.15g lt red brn, blk & vio 1.00 .45
691 A152a 36g gray grn, blk & brn 2.25 .80
Nos. 684-691 (8) 5.20 2.85

World Soccer Championships, Chile, May 30-June 17.

Imperfs exist. Value $10. A souvenir sheet containing one No. 691 exists, both perforated and imperf. Value, $24 and $60, respectively.

Some specialists question the status of this issue.

Nos. 689-691 are airmail.

Freighter A153

Ship's Wheel — A153a

Designs: Various merchantmen. 44g, Like 12.45g with diagonal colorless band in background.

Perf. 14½x15

1962, July 31 **Unwmk.**

692 A153 30c bister brn .25 .25
693 A153 90c slate bl .25 .25
694 A153 1.50g brown red .25 .25
695 A153 2g green .25 .25
696 A153 4.20g vio blue .30 .25

Perf. 15x14½

697 A153a 12.45g dk red 5.00 .25
698 A153a 44g blue 5.00 .35
Nos. 692-698 (7) 11.30 1.85

Issued to honor the merchant marine.
Nos. 697-698 are airmail.

Friendship 7 over South America — A154

Lt. Col. John H. Glenn, Jr., Lt. Cmdr. Scott Carpenter A154a

Perf. 13½x14

1962, Sept. 4 **Litho.** **Wmk. 346**

699 A154 15c dk bl & bis .55 .45
700 A154 25c vio brn & bis .55 .45
701 A154 30c dk sl grn & bis .55 .45
702 A154 40c dk gray & bis .55 .45
703 A154 50c dk vio & bis .55 .45
704 A154a 12.45g car lake & gray .55 .45
705 A154a 18.15g red lil & gray .55 .45
706 A154a 36g dl cl & gray .95 .80
Nos. 699-706 (8) 4.80 3.95

U.S. manned space flights. A souvenir sheet containing one No. 706 exists. Value $20.
Imperfs. in changed colors exist. Values: set, $14; souvenir sheet $60. Some specialists question the status of this issue.
Nos. 704-706 are airmail.

Discus Thrower — A155

Olympic flame &: 12.45g, Melbourne, 1956. 18.15g, Rome, 1960. 36g, Tokyo, 1964.

1962, Oct. 1 **Litho.**

707 A155 15c blk & yel .75 .25
708 A155 25c blk & lt grn .75 .25
709 A155 30c blk & pink .75 .25
710 A155 40c blk & pale vio .75 .25
711 A155 50c blk & lt bl .75 .25
712 A155 12.45g brt grn, lt grn & choc .85 .75
713 A155 18.15g ol brn, yel & choc .85 .75
714 A155 36g rose red, pink & choc 1.50 1.00
Nos. 707-714 (8) 6.95 3.75

Olympic Games from Amsterdam 1928 to Tokyo 1964. Each stamp is inscribed with date and place of various Olympic Games. A souvenir sheet containing one No. 714 exists. Value $12.
Imperfs. in changed colors exist. Values: set, $27.50; souvenir sheet $125.
Some specialists question the status of this issue.
Nos. 712-714 are airmail.

Peace Dove and Cross A156

Dove Symbolizing Holy Ghost — A156a

Perf. 14½

1962, Oct. 11 **Litho.** **Unwmk.**

715 A156 50c olive .25 .25
716 A156 70c dark blue .25 .25
717 A156 1.50g bister .25 .25
718 A156 2g violet .25 .25
719 A156 3g brick red .25 .25
720 A156a 5g vio bl 1.00 .25
721 A156a 10g brt grn 1.00 .25
722 A156a 12.45g lake 1.00 .25
723 A156a 18.15g orange 1.00 .30
724 A156a 23.40g violet 1.00 .40
725 A156a 36g rose red 1.00 .50
Nos. 715-725 (11) 7.25 3.20

Vatican II, the 21st Ecumenical Council of the Roman Catholic Church, which opened Oct. 11, 1962.
Nos. 720-725 are airmail.

Europa A157

1962, Dec. 17 *Perf. 11*

726 A157 4g yel, red & brn .50 .50
727 A157 36g multi, diff. 10.00 3.00
a. Souvenir sheet of 2, #726-727 *25.00*
Nos. 726-727 (2) 10.50 3.50

No. 727 is airmail.
Exist imperf. in changed colors. Values: set, $45; souvenir sheet, $70.

Solar System A158

12.45g, 36g, 50g, Inner planets, Jupiter & rocket.

Perf. 14x13½

1962, Dec. 17 **Wmk. 346**

728 A158 10c org & purple .35 .35
729 A158 20c org & brn vio .35 .35
730 A158 25c org & dark vio .35 .35
731 A158 30c org & ultra .35 .35
732 A158 50c org & dull green .35 .35
733 A158 12.45g org & brown 2.25 1.25
734 A158 36g org & blue 4.25 2.00
735 A158 50g org & green 8.50 4.25
a. Souvenir sheet of 1 17.50
Nos. 728-735 (8) 16.75 9.25

Nos. 733-735 are airmail.
Exist imperf. in changed colors. Values: set, $25; souvenir sheet, $80.

The following stamps exist imperf. in different colors: Nos. 736-743a, 744-751a, 752-759a, 760-766a, 775-782a, 783-790a, 791-798a, 799-805a, 806-813a, 814-821a, 828-835a, 836-843, 841a, 850-857a, 858-865a, 871-878, 876a, 887-894a, 895-902, 900a, 903-910a, 911-918a, 919-926a, 927-934a, 943-950a, 951-958a, 959-966a, 978-985a, 986-993a, 994-1001a, 1002-1003, 1003d, 1004-1007a, 1051-1059, B12-B19.

Pierre de Coubertin (1836-1937), Founder of Modern Olympic Games — A159

Summer Olympic Games sites and: 15c, Athens, 1896. 25c, Paris, 1900. 30c, St. Louis, 1904. 40c, London, 1908. 50c, Stockholm, 1912. 12.45g, No games, 1916. 18.15g, Antwerp, 1920. 36g, Paris, 1924.
12.45g, 18.15g, 36g, Torch bearer & stadium.

Perf. 14x13½

1963, Feb. 16 **Wmk. 346**

736 A159 15c multicolored .25 .25
737 A159 25c multicolored .25 .25
738 A159 30c multicolored .25 .25
739 A159 40c multicolored .25 .25
740 A159 50c multicolored .25 .25
741 A159 12.45g multicolored 3.50 3.50
742 A159 18.15g multicolored 3.50 3.50
743 A159 36g multicolored 4.50 4.50
a. Souvenir sheet of 1 45.00
Nos. 736-743 (8) 12.75 12.75

Nos. 741-743a are airmail.
Exist imperf. in changed colors. Values: set, $30; souvenir sheet $150.

Walter M. Schirra, US Astronaut — A160

Design: 12.45g, 36g, 50g, Schirra.

1963, Mar. 16 *Perf. 13½x14*

744 A160 10c brn org & blk .25 .25
745 A160 20c car & blk .25 .25
746 A160 25c lake & blk .25 .25
747 A160 30c ver & blk .25 .25
748 A160 50c mag & blk .25 .25
749 A160 12.45g bl blk & lake 4.25 4.25
750 A160 36g dl gray vio & lake 4.25 4.25
751 A160 50g dk grn bl & lake 5.25 5.25
a. Souvenir sheet of 1 15.00
Nos. 744-751 (8) 15.00 15.00

Nos. 749-751a are airmail.
Exist imperf. in changed colors. Values: set, $25; souvenir sheet, $125.

Winter Olympics A161

Games sites and: 10c, Chamonix, 1924. 20c, St. Moritz, 1928. 25c, Lake Placid, 1932. 30c, Garmisch-Partenkirchen, 1936. 50c, St. Moritz, 1948. 12.45g, Oslo, 1952. 36g, Cortina d'Ampezzo, 1956. 50g, Squaw Valley, 1960.
12.45g, 36g, 50g, Snowflake.

1963, May 16 *Perf. 14x13½*

752 A161 10c multicolored .25 .25
753 A161 20c multicolored .25 .25
754 A161 25c multicolored .25 .25
755 A161 30c multicolored .25 .25
756 A161 50c multicolored .25 .25
757 A161 12.45g multicolored 3.75 3.75
758 A161 36g multicolored 3.75 3.75
759 A161 50g multicolored 4.50 4.50
a. Souvenir sheet of 1 13.00 13.00
Nos. 752-759 (8) 13.25 13.25

Nos. 757-759a are airmail.
Exist imperf. in changed colors. Values: set, $17.50; souvenir sheet, $140.

Freedom from Hunger A162

1963, May 31 *Perf. 13½x14, 14x13½*

760 A162 10c yel grn & brn .25 .25
761 A162 25c lt bl & brn .25 .25
762 A162 50c lt grn bl & brn .25 .25
763 A162 75c lt lil & brn .25 .25
764 A162 18.15g yel org & brn 2.00 1.75
765 A162 36g lt bl grn & brn 2.00 1.75
766 A162 50g bis & brn 2.00 1.75
a. Souvenir sheet of 1 17.00
Nos. 760-766 (7) 7.00 6.25

Nos. 760-763 are vert. Nos. 764-766a are airmail.
Exist imperf. in changed colors. Values: set, $17; souvenir sheet, $22.50.

Pres. Alfredo Stroessner A163

1963, Aug. 6 **Wmk. 347** *Perf. 11*

767 A163 50c ol gray & sep 1.00 *2.50*
768 A163 75c buff & sepia 1.00 *2.50*
769 A163 1.50g lt lil & sep 1.00 *2.50*
770 A163 3g emer & sepia 1.00 1.00
771 A163 12.45g pink & claret 5.00 1.00
772 A163 18.15g pink & grn 5.00 1.00
773 A163 36g pink & vio 5.00 1.00
Nos. 767-773 (7) 19.00 11.50

Third presidential term of Alfredo Stroessner. A 36g imperf. souvenir sheet exists.
Nos. 771-773 are airmail.

MUESTRA
Some illustrated stamps show the word "MUESTRA" ("SPECIMEN"). This overprint is not on the actual stamps. The editors would like to borrow examples without the overprint so that replacement illustrations can be made.

Souvenir Sheet

Dag Hammarskjold, UN Secretary General — A164

1963, Aug. 21 **Unwmk.** ***Imperf.***

774 A164 2g Sheet of 2 25.00 25.00

Project Mercury Flight of L. Gordon Cooper
A165

12.45g, 18.15g, 50g, L. Gordon Cooper, vert.

Perf. 14x13½, 13½x14

1963, Aug. 23 Litho. Wmk. 346

775	A165	15c brn & orange	.25	.25
776	A165	25c brn & blue	.25	.25
777	A165	30c brn & violet	.25	.25
778	A165	40c brn & green	.25	.25
779	A165	50c brn & red vio	.25	.25
780	A165	12.45g brn & bl grn	3.50	2.50
781	A165	18.15g brn & blue	3.50	2.50
782	A165	50g brn & pink	3.50	2.50
a.		Souvenir sheet of 1	25.00	
		Nos. 775-782 (8)	11.75	8.75

Nos. 780-782 are airmail.

Exist imperf. in changed colors. Values: set, $22.50; souvenir sheet, $30.

1964 Winter Olympics, Innsbruck
A166

Design: 12.45g, 18.15g, 50g, Innsbruck Games emblem, vert.

Perf. 14x13½, 13½x14

1963, Oct. 28 Unwmk.

783	A166	15c choc & red	.25	.25
784	A166	25c gray grn & red	.25	.25
785	A166	30c plum & red	.25	.25
786	A166	40c sl grn & red	.25	.25
787	A166	50c dp bl & red	.25	.25
788	A166	12.45g sep & red	3.75	1.75
789	A166	18.15g grn bl & red	3.75	1.75
790	A166	50g tan & red	3.75	1.75
a.		Souvenir sheet of 1	19.00	
		Nos. 783-790 (8)	12.50	6.50

Nos. 788-790 are airmail.

Exist imperf. in changed colors. Values: set, $25; souvenir sheet, $25.

1964 Summer Olympics, Tokyo — A167

12.45g, 18.15g, 50g, Tokyo games emblem.

1964, Jan. 8 *Perf. 13½x14*

791	A167	15c blue & red	.25	.25
792	A167	25c org & red	.25	.25
793	A167	30c tan & red	.25	.25
794	A167	40c vio brn & red	.25	.25
795	A167	50c grn bl & red	.25	.25
796	A167	12.45g vio & red	2.00	1.60
797	A167	18.15g brn & red	2.00	1.60
798	A167	50g grn bl & red	2.00	1.60
a.		Souvenir sheet of 1	25.00	
		Nos. 791-798 (8)	7.25	6.05

Nos. 796-798 are airmail.

Exist imperf. in changed colors. Values: set, $20; souvenir sheet, $37.50.

Intl. Red Cross, Cent.
A168

Designs: 10c, Helicopter. 25c, Space ambulance. 30c, Red Cross symbol, vert. 50c, Clara Barton, founder of American Red Cross, vert. 18.15g, Jean Henri Dunant, founder of Intl. Red Cross, vert. 36g, Red Cross space hospital, space ambulance. 50g, Plane, ship, ambulance, vert.

1964, Feb. 4 *Perf. 14x13½, 13½x14*

799	A168	10c vio brn & red	.25	.25
800	A168	25c bl grn & red	.25	.25
801	A168	30c dk bl & red	.25	.25
802	A168	50c ol blk & red	.25	.25
803	A168	18.15g choc, red, & pink	1.60	.80
804	A168	36g grn bl & red	2.25	1.10
805	A168	50g vio & red	3.50	2.00
a.		Souvenir sheet of 1	14.00	11.00
		Nos. 799-805 (7)	8.35	4.90

Nos. 803-805 are airmail.

Exist imperf. in changed colors. Values: set, $50; souvenir sheet, $20.

Space Research
A169

15c, 25c, 30c, Gemini spacecraft rendezvous with Agena rocket. 40c, 50c, Future Apollo and Lunar Modules, vert. 12.45g, 18.15g, 50g, Telstar communications satellite, Olympic rings, vert.

1964, Mar. 11

806	A169	15c vio & tan	.25	.25
807	A169	25c grn & tan	.25	.25
808	A169	30c bl & tan	.25	.25
809	A169	40c brt bl & red	.25	.25
810	A169	50c sl grn & red	.25	.25
811	A169	12.45g dk bl & tan	3.00	2.00
812	A169	18.15g dk grn bl & tan	3.00	2.00
813	A169	50g dp vio & tan	3.00	2.00
a.		Souvenir sheet of 1	25.00	19.00
		Nos. 806-813 (8)	10.25	7.25

1964 Summer Olympic Games, Tokyo (Nos. 811-813a). Nos. 811-813a are airmail.

Exist imperf. in changed colors. Values: set, $25; souvenir sheet, $17.

Rockets and Satellites
A170

15c, 25c, Apollo command module mockup. 30c, Tiros 7 weather satellite, vert. 40c, 50c, Ranger 6. 12.45g, 18.15g, 50g, Saturn I lift-off, vert.

1964, Apr. 25

814	A170	15c brn & tan	.25	.25
815	A170	25c vio & tan	.25	.25
816	A170	30c Prus bl & lake	.25	.25
817	A170	40c ver & tan	.25	.25
818	A170	50c ultra & tan	.25	.25
819	A170	12.45g grn bl & choc	1.40	.85
820	A170	18.15g bl & choc	2.25	1.60
821	A170	50g lil rose & choc	3.50	2.50
a.		Souvenir sheet of 1	12.00	
		Nos. 814-821 (8)	8.40	6.20

Nos. 819-821a are airmail.

Exist imperf. in changed colors. Values: set, $15; souvenir sheet, $17.

Popes Paul VI, John XXIII and St. Peter's, Rome
A171

Design: 12.45g, 18.15g, 36g, Asuncion Cathedral, Popes Paul VI and John XXIII.

1964, May 23 Wmk. 347

822	A171	1.50g claret & org	.25	.25
823	A171	3g claret & dk grn	.25	.25
824	A171	4g claret & bister	.25	.25
825	A171	12.45g sl grn & lem	1.00	1.00
826	A171	18.15g pur & lem	1.00	1.00
827	A171	36g vio bl & lem	2.00	2.00
		Nos. 822-827 (6)	4.75	4.75

National holiday of St. Maria Auxiliadora (Our Lady of Perpetual Help).

Nos. 825-827 are airmail.

United Nations
A172

Designs: 15c, John F. Kennedy. 25c, 12.45g, Pope Paul VI and Patriarch Atenagoras. 30c, Eleanor Roosevelt, Chairman of UN Commission on Human Rights. 40c, Relay, Syncom and Telstar satellites. 50c, Echo 2 satellite. 18.15g, U Thant, UN Sec. Gen. 50g, Rocket, flags of Europe, vert.

Perf. 14x13½, 14 (15c, 25c, 12.45g)

1964, July 30 Unwmk.

Size: 35x35mm (#830, 834), 40x29mm (#831-832, 835)

828	A172	15c blk & brn	.25	.25
829	A172	25c blk, bl & red	.25	.25
830	A172	30c blk & ver	.25	.25
831	A172	40c dk bl & sep	.25	.25
832	A172	50c vio & car	.25	.25
833	A172	12.45g blk, grn & red	.75	.75
834	A172	18.15g blk & grn	.75	.75

Perf. 13½x14

835	A172	50g multicolored	1.75	1.75
a.		Souvenir sheet of 1	32.50	
		Nos. 828-835 (8)	4.50	4.50

Nos. 833-835a are airmail.

Exist imperf. in changed colors. Values: set, $15; souvenir sheet, $32.50.

Space Achievements — A173

Designs: 10c, 30c, Ranger 7, Moon, vert. 15c, 12.45+6g, Wernher von Braun looking through telescope, vert. 20c, 20+10g, John F. Kennedy, rockets, vert. 40c, 18.15+9g, Rockets, von Braun.

1964, Sept. 12 *Perf. 12½x12*

836	A173	10c bl & blk	.25	.25
837	A173	15c yel grn & brt pink	.25	.25
838	A173	20c yel org & bl	.25	.25
839	A173	30c mag & blk	.25	.25
840	A173	40c yel org, bl & blk	.25	.25
841	A173	12.45g +6g red & bl	2.40	1.60
a.		Souvenir sheet of 2, #840-841	24.00	
842	A173	18.15g +9g grn bl, brn & blk	2.40	1.60
843	A173	20g +10g red & bl	3.25	2.40
		Nos. 836-843 (8)	9.30	6.85

Nos. 841-843 are airmail.

Exist imperf. in changed colors. Values: set, $22.50; souvenir sheet, $37.50.

Coats of Arms of Paraguay and France
A174

Designs: 3g, 12.45g, 36g, Presidents Stroessner and de Gaulle. 18.15g, Coats of Arms of Paraguay and France.

1964, Oct. 6 Wmk. 347

844	A174	1.50g brown	.30	.30
845	A174	3g ultramarine	.30	.30
846	A174	4g gray	.30	.30
847	A174	12.45g lilac	.40	.40
848	A174	18.15g bl grn	.60	.60
849	A174	36g magenta	2.50	1.75
		Nos. 844-849 (6)	4.40	3.65

Visit of Pres. Charles de Gaulle of France.

Nos. 847-849 are airmail.

Boy Scout Jamborees — A175

Boy Scout Emblem — A175a

Designs: 10c, Argentina, 1961. 15c, Peru, canceled. 20c, Chile, 1959. 30c, Brazil, 1954. 50c, Uruguay, 1957. 12.45g, Brazil, 1960. 18.15g, Venezuela, 1964. 36g, Brazil, 1963.

15c, 18.15g, Lord Robert Baden-Powell (1857-1941), Boy Scouts founder.

1965, Jan. 15 Unwmk. *Perf. 14*

850	A175	10c multicolored	.25	.25
851	A175	15c multicolored	.25	.25
852	A175a	20c multicolored	.25	.25
853	A175a	30c multicolored	.25	.25
854	A175	50c multicolored	.25	.25
855	A175a	12.45g multicolored	1.50	1.50
856	A175	18.15g multicolored	1.60	1.40
857	A175	36g multicolored	3.00	2.50
a.		Souvenir sheet of 1, perf. 12x12½	17.00	
		Nos. 850-857 (8)	7.35	6.65

Nos. 855-857a are airmail.

Exist imperf. in changed colors. Values: set, $9; souvenir sheet, $22.50.

A176

Olympic and Paraguayan Medals: 25c, John F. Kennedy. 30c, Medal of Peace and Justice, reverse. 40c, Gens. Stroessner and DeGaulle, profiles. 50c, 18.15g, DeGaulle and Stroessner, in uniform. 12.45g, Medal of Peace and Justice, obverse.

Litho. & Embossed

1965, Mar. 30 *Perf. 13½x13*

858	A176	15c multicolored	.25	.25
859	A176	25c multicolored	.25	.25
860	A176	30c multicolored	.25	.25

Perf. 12½x12

861	A176	40c multicolored	.25	.25
862	A176	50c multicolored	.25	.25
863	A176	12.45g multicolored	2.25	1.50
864	A176	18.15g multicolored	2.75	1.75
865	A176	50g multicolored	4.25	1.75
a.		Souv. sheet of 1, perf. 13½x13	35.00	
		Nos. 858-865 (8)	10.50	6.25

Nos. 863-865a are airmail. Medal on No. 865a is gold foil.

Exist imperf. in changed colors. Values: set, $20; souvenir sheet, $60.

Overprinted in Black — A177

Design: Map of Americas.

1965, Apr. 26 Wmk. 347 *Perf. 11*

866 A177 1.50g dull grn .40 .40
867 A177 3g car red .40 .40
868 A177 4g dark blue .40 .40
869 A177 12.45g brn & blk .40 .40
870 A177 36g brt lil & blk 1.00 .70
Nos. 866-870 (5) 2.60 2.30

Centenary of National Epic. Not issued without overprint.
Nos. 869-870 are airmail.

Scientists — A178

Unwmk.

1965, June 5 Litho. *Perf. 14*

871 A178 10c Newton .25 .25
872 A178 15c Copernicus .25 .25
873 A178 20c Galileo .25 .25
874 A178 30c like #871 .25 .25
875 A178 40c Einstein .25 .25
876 A178 12.45g +6g like #873 1.00 .50
a. Souvenir sheet of 2, #875-876 12.50
877 A178 18.15g +9g like #875 1.50 1.00
878 A178 20g +10g like #872 1.75 1.50
Nos. 871-878 (8) 5.50 4.25

Nos. 876-878 are airmail.
Exist imperf. in changed colors. Values: set, $12; souvenir sheet, $12.50.

Cattleya Warscewiczii A179

Ceibo Tree — A179a

1965, June 28 Unwmk. *Perf. 14½*

879 A179 20c purple .25 .25
880 A179 30c blue .25 .25
881 A179 90c bright mag .25 .25
882 A179 1.50g green .25 .25
883 A179a 3g brn red 1.40 .90
884 A179a 4g green 1.75 .90
885 A179 4.50g orange 1.75 .90
886 A179a 66g brn org 3.50 1.40
Nos. 879-886 (8) 9.40 5.10

150th anniv. of Independence (1811-1961).
Nos. 883-884, 886 are airmail.

John F. Kennedy and Winston Churchill — A180

Designs: 15c, Kennedy, PT 109. 25c, Kennedy family. 30c, 12.45g, Churchill, Parliament building. 40c, Kennedy, Alliance for Progress emblem. 50c, 18.15g, Kennedy, rocket launch at Cape Canaveral. 50g, John Glenn, Kennedy, Lyndon Johnson examining Friendship 7.

1965, Sept. 4 *Perf. 12x12½*

887 A180 15c bl & brn .25 .25
888 A180 25c red & brn .25 .25
889 A180 30c vio & blk .25 .25
890 A180 40c org & sep .25 .25
891 A180 50c bl grn & sep .25 .25
892 A180 12.45g yel & blk 1.40 .75
893 A180 18.15g car & blk 2.00 1.20
894 A180 50g grn & blk 3.50 1.75
a. Souvenir sheet of 1 20.00
Nos. 887-894 (8) 8.15 4.95

Nos. 892-894a are airmail.
Exist imperf. in changed colors. Values: set, $20; souvenir sheet, $20.

ITU, Cent. — A181

Satellites: 10c, 40c, Ranger 7 transmitting to Earth. 15c, 20g+10g, Syncom, Olympic rings. 20c, 18.15g+9g, Early Bird. 30c, 12.45g+6g, Relay, Syncom, Telstar, Echo 2.

1965, Sept. 30

895 A181 10c dull bl & sep .25 .25
896 A181 15c lilac & sepia .25 .25
897 A181 20c ol grn & sep .25 .25
898 A181 30c blue & sepia .25 .25
899 A181 40c grn & sep .25 .25
900 A181 12.45g +6g ver & sep 1.20 .50
a. Souvenir sheet of 2, #899-900 22.50
901 A181 18.15g +9g org & sep 1.75 .75
902 A181 20g +10g vio & sep 3.00 1.25
Nos. 895-902 (8) 7.20 3.75

Nos. 900-902 are airmail.
Exist imperf. in changed colors. Values: set, $17.50; souvenir sheet, $27.50.

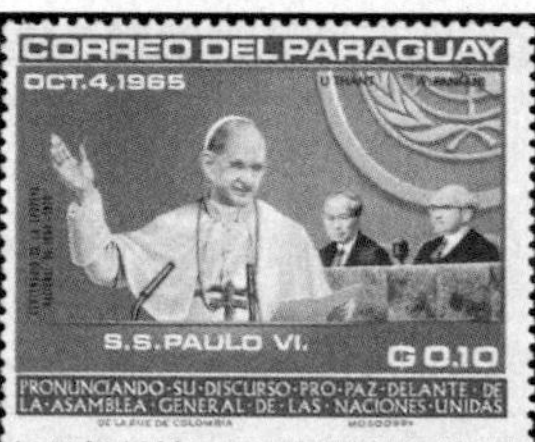

Pope Paul VI, Visit to UN A182

Designs: 10c, 50c, Pope Paul VI, U Thant, A. Fanfani. 15c, 12.45g, Pope Paul VI, Lyndon B. Johnson. 20c, 36g, Early Bird satellite, globe, papal arms. 30c, 18.15g, Pope Paul VI, Unisphere.

1965, Nov. 19

903 A182 10c multicolored .25 .25
904 A182 15c multicolored .25 .25
905 A182 20c multicolored .25 .25
906 A182 30c multicolored .25 .25
907 A182 50c multicolored .25 .25
908 A182 12.45g multicolored .75 .50
909 A182 18.15g multicolored 1.25 1.25
910 A182 36g multicolored 2.50 1.75
a. Souvenir sheet of 1 22.50
Nos. 903-910 (8) 5.75 4.75

Nos. 908-910a are airmail.
Exist imperf. in changed colors. Values: set, $25; souvenir sheet, $32.50.

Astronauts and Space Exploration — A183

15c, 50g, Edward White walking in space, 6/3/65. 25c, 18.15g, Gemini 7 & 8 docking, 12/16-18/65. 30c, Virgil I. Grissom, John W. Young, 3/23/65. 40c, 50c, Edward White, James McDivitt, 6/3/65. 12.45g, Photographs of lunar surface.

1966, Feb. 19 *Perf. 14*

911 A183 15c multicolored .25 .25
912 A183 25c multicolored .25 .25
913 A183 30c multicolored .25 .25
914 A183 40c multicolored .25 .25
915 A183 50c multicolored .25 .25
916 A183 12.45g multicolored 1.10 1.10
917 A183 18.15g multicolored 1.90 1.90
918 A183 50g multicolored 3.25 3.25
a. Souvenir sheet of 1 25.00
Nos. 911-918 (8) 7.50 7.50

Nos. 916-918a are airmail.
Exist imperf. in changed colors. Values: set, $12; souvenir sheet, $25.

Events of 1965 — A184

10c, Meeting of Pope Paul VI & Cardinal Spellman, 10/4/65. 15c, Intl. Phil. Exposition, Vienna. 20c, OAS, 75th anniv. 30c, 36g, Intl. Quiet Sun Year, 1964-65. 50c, 18.15g, Saturn rockets at NY World's Fair. 12.45g, UN Intl. Cooperation Year.

1966, Mar. 9

919 A184 10c multicolored .25 .25
920 A184 15c multicolored .25 .25
921 A184 20c multicolored .25 .25
922 A184 30c multicolored .25 .25
923 A184 50c multicolored .25 .25
924 A184 12.45g multicolored 1.10 .75
925 A184 18.15g multicolored 1.90 1.50
926 A184 36g multicolored 3.75 1.25
a. Souvenir sheet of 1 20.00
Nos. 919-926 (8) 8.00 4.75

Nos. 924-926a are airmail.
Exist imperf. in changed colors. Values: set, $25; souvenir sheet, $25.

1968 Summer Olympics, Mexico City — A185

Perf. 12½x12 (Nos. 927, 929, 931, 933), 13½x13

1966, Apr. 1

927 A185 10c shown .25 .25
928 A185 15c God of Death .25 .25
929 A185 20c Aztec calendar stone .25 .25
930 A185 30c like No. 928 .25 .25
931 A185 50c Zapotec deity .25 .25
932 A185 12.45g like No. 931 1.25 .75
933 A185 18.15g like No. 927 1.90 1.25
934 A185 36g like No. 929 4.50 3.00
a. Souvenir sheet of 1 15.00
Nos. 927-934 (8) 8.90 6.25

Nos. 932-934a are airmail.
Exist imperf. in changed colors. Values: set, $15; souvenir sheet, $30.

A185a

St. Ignatius and San Ignacio Monastery A185b

1966, Apr. 20 Wmk. 347 *Perf. 11*

935 A185a 15c ultramarine 1.00 .50
936 A185a 25c ultramarine 1.00 .50
937 A185a 75c ultramarine 1.00 .50
938 A185a 90c ultramarine 1.00 .50
939 A185b 3g brown 1.00 .50
940 A185b 12.45g sepia 1.00 .50
941 A185b 18.15g sepia 1.00 .50
942 A185b 23.40g sepia 1.00 .50
Nos. 935-942 (8) 8.00 4.00

350th anniv. of the founding of San Ignacio Guazu Monastery.
Nos. 939-942 are airmail.
On designs A185b text under Paraguay is different from that of design A129a (No. 522)

German Contributors in Space Research — A186

Designs: 10c, 36g, Paraguay #835, C97, Germany #C40. 15c, 50c, 18.15g, 3rd stage of Europa 1 rocket, vert. 20c, 12.45g, Hermann Oberth, jet propulsion engineer, vert. 30c, Reinhold K. Tiling, builder of 1st German rocket, 1931, vert.

Perf. 12x12½ (Nos. 943, 950), 12½x12 (Nos. 945, 947, 949), 13½x13

1966, May 16 Unwmk.

943 A186 10c multicolored .25 .25
944 A186 15c multicolored .25 .25
945 A186 20c multicolored .25 .25
946 A186 30c multicolored .25 .25
947 A186 50c multicolored .25 .25
948 A186 12.45g multicolored 1.50 .50
949 A186 18.15g multicolored 1.90 1.00
950 A186 36g multicolored 3.75 2.25
a. Souvenir sheet of 1, perf. 12x13½x13x13½ 35.00
Nos. 943-950 (8) 8.40 5.00

Nos. 948-950a are airmail.
Exist imperf. in changed colors. Values: set, $25; souvenir sheet, $40.

Writers — A187

1966, June 11 *Perf. 12x12½*

951 A187 10c Dante .25 .25
952 A187 15c Moliere .25 .25
953 A187 20c Goethe .25 .25
954 A187 30c Shakespeare .25 .25
955 A187 50c like #952 .25 .25
956 A187 12.45g like #953 1.90 1.50
957 A187 18.15g like #954 2.25 1.50
958 A187 36g like #951 3.75 1.50
a. Souvenir sheet of 1, perf. 13½x14 14.00
Nos. 951-958 (8) 9.15 5.75

Nos. 956-958a are airmail.
Exist imperf. in changed colors. Values: set, $12; souvenir sheet, $20.

Italian Contributors in Space Research — A188

10c, 36g, Italian satellite, San Marco 1. 15c, 18.15g, Drafting machine, Leonardo Da Vinci. 20c, 12.45g, Map, Italo Balbo (1896-1940), aviator. 30c, 50c, Floating launch & control facility, satellite.

1966, July 11

959 A188 10c multicolored .25 .25
960 A188 15c multicolored .25 .25
961 A188 20c multicolored .25 .25
962 A188 30c multicolored .25 .25
963 A188 50c multicolored .25 .25
964 A188 12.45g multicolored 1.50 .50
965 A188 18.15g multicolored 2.60 .50
966 A188 36g multicolored 4.50 3.00
a. Souvenir sheet of 1, perf. 13x13½ 15.00
Nos. 959-966 (8) 9.85 5.25

Nos. 964-966a are airmail.
Exist imperf. in changed colors. Values: set, $20; souvenir sheet, $20.

Rubén Dario — A189

"Paraguay de Fuego" by Dario — A189a

1966, July 16 **Wmk. 347**

967 A189 50c ultramarine .50 .40
968 A189 70c bister brn .50 .40
969 A189 1.50g rose car .50 .40
970 A189 3g violet .50 .40
971 A189 4g greenish bl .50 .40
972 A189 5g black .50 .40
973 A189a 12.45g blue 1.50 .40
974 A189a 18.15g red lil 1.50 .40
975 A189a 23.40g org brn 1.50 .40
976 A189a 36g brt grn 1.50 .90
977 A189a 50g rose car 1.50 1.20
Nos. 967-977 (11) 10.50 5.70

50th death anniv. of Ruben Dario (pen name of Felix Rubén Garcia Sarmiento, 1867-1916), Nicaraguan poet, newspaper correspondent and diplomat.
Nos. 973-977 are airmail.

Space Missions — A190

1966, Aug. 25 **Unwmk.**

978 A190 10c Gemini 8 .25 .25
979 A190 15c Gemini 9 .25 .25
980 A190 20c Surveyor 1 on moon .25 .25
981 A190 30c Gemini 10 .25 .25
982 A190 50c like #981 .25 .25
983 A190 12.45g like #980 2.25 1.25
984 A190 18.15g like #979 2.25 1.25
985 A190 36g like #978 12.50 6.00
a. Souvenir sheet of 1, perf. 13x13½ 20.00
Nos. 978-985 (8) 18.25 9.75

Nos. 983-985a are airmail.
Exist imperf. in changed colors. Values: set, $25; souvenir sheet, $25.

1968 Winter Olympics, Grenoble — A191

1966, Sept. 30 ***Perf. 14***

986 A191 10c Figure skating .25 .25
987 A191 15c Downhill skiing .25 .25
988 A191 20c Speed skating .25 .25
989 A191 30c 2-man luge .25 .25
990 A191 50c like #989 .25 .25
991 A191 12.45g like #988 1.00 .50
992 A191 18.15g like #987 1.25 .50
993 A191 36g like #986 2.50 2.50
a. Souvenir sheet of 1 15.00
Nos. 986-993 (8) 6.00 4.75

Nos. 987, 992, World Skiing Championships, Portillo, Chile, 1966. Nos. 991-993a are airmail.
Exist imperf. in changed colors. Values: set, $12.50; souvenir sheet, $27.50.

Pres. John F. Kennedy, 3rd Death Anniv. — A192

Perf. 12x12½, 13½x14 (#997-998, 1001)

1966, Nov. 7

994 A192 10c Echo 1 & 2 .25 .25
995 A192 15c Telstar 1 & 2 .25 .25
996 A192 20c Relay 1 & 2 .25 .25
997 A192 30c Syncom 1, 2 & 3, Early Bird .25 .25
998 A192 50c like #997 .25 .25
999 A192 12.45g like #996 1.25 .50
1000 A192 18.15g like #995 1.50 .50
1001 A192 36g like #994 5.00 3.50
a. Souvenir sheet of 1, perf. 13x14x13½x14 20.00
Nos. 994-1001 (8) 9.00 5.75

Nos. 999-1001a are airmail.
Exist imperf. in changed colors. Values: set, $20; souvenir sheet, $24.

Paintings A193

Portraits of women by: No. 1002a, 10c, De Largilliere. b, 15c, Rubens. c, 20c, Titian. d, 30c, Hans Holbein. e, 50c, Sanchez Coello.
Paintings: No. 1003a, 12.45g, Mars and Venus with United by Love by Veronese. b, 18.15g, Allegory of Prudence, Peace and Abundance by Vouet. c, 36g, Madonna and Child by Andres Montegna.

1966, Dec. 10 ***Perf. 14x13½***

1002 A193 Strip of 5, #a.-e. 1.25 1.25
1003 A193 Strip of 3, #a.-c. 4.50 4.50
d. Souvenir sheet of 1, #1003c 16.00
Nos. 1002-1003 (2) 5.75 5.75

Nos. 1003a-1003d are airmail. No. 1003d has green pattern in border and is perf. 12½x12.
Exist imperf. in changed colors. Values: set, $15; souvenir sheet, $16.

Holy Week Paintings A194

Life of Christ by: No. 1004a, 10c, Raphael. b, 15c, Rubens. c, 20c, Da Ponte. d, 30c, El Greco. e, 50c, Murillo, horiz.
12.45g, G. Reni. 18.15g, Tintoretto. 36g, Da Vinci, horiz.

1967, Feb. 28 ***Perf. 14x13½, 13½x14***

1004 A194 Strip of 5, #a.-e. 1.25 1.25
1005 A194 12.45g multicolored .55 .50
1006 A194 18.15g multicolored .55 .50
1007 A194 36g multicolored 5.75 5.00
a. Souvenir sheet of 1 15.00
Nos. 1004-1007 (4) 8.10 7.25

Nos. 1005-1007a are airmail. No. 1007a has salmon pattern in border and contains one 60x40mm, perf. 14 stamp.
Exist imperf. in changed colors. Values: set, $15; souvenir sheet, $15.

Birth of Christ by Barocci A195

16th Cent. Paintings: 12.45g, Madonna and Child by Caravaggio. 18.15g, Mary of the Holy Family (detail) by El Greco. 36g, Assumption of the Virgin by Vasco Fernandes.

1967, Mar. 10 ***Perf. 14½***

1008 A195 10c lt bl & multi .25 .25
1009 A195 15c lt grn & multi .25 .25
1010 A195 20c lt brn & multi .25 .25
1011 A195 30c lil & multi .25 .25
1012 A195 50c pink & multi .25 .25
1013 A195 12.45g lt bl grn & multi .50 .50
1014 A195 18.15g brt pink & multi .50 .50
1015 A195 36g lt vio & multi 6.00 4.00
a. Souv. sheet of 1, sep & multi 17.00
Nos. 1008-1015 (8) 8.25 6.25

Nos. 1013-1015a are airmail.
Exist imperf. with changed borders. Values: set, $15; souvenir sheet, $17.

Globe and Lions Emblem — A196

Medical Laboratory "Health" A196a

Designs: 1.50g, 3g, Melvin Jones. 4g, 5g, Lions' Headquarters, Chicago. 12.45g, 18.15g, Library "Education."

1967, May 9 **Litho.** **Wmk. 347**

1016 A196 50c light vio 1.00 .50
1017 A196 70c blue 1.00 .50
1018 A196 1.50g ultra 1.00 .50
1019 A196 3g brown 1.00 .50
1020 A196 4g Prussian grn 1.00 .50
1021 A196 5g ol gray 2.00 .50
1022 A196a 12.45g dk brn 2.00 .50
1023 A196a 18.15g violet 2.00 .50
1024 A196a 23.40g rose cl 2.00 .50
1025 A196a 36g Prus blue 2.00 .50
1026 A196a 50g rose car 2.00 .50
Nos. 1016-1026 (11) 17.00 5.50

50th anniversary of Lions International.
Nos. 1022-1026 are airmail.

Vase of Flowers by Chardin A197

Still Life Paintings by: No. 1027b, 15c, Fontanesi, horiz. c, 20c, Cezanne. d, 30c, Van Gogh. e, 50c, Renoir.
Paintings: 12.45g, Cha-U-Kao at the Moulin Rouge by Toulouse-Lautrec. 18.15g, Gabrielle with Jean Renoir by Renoir. 36g, Patience Escalier, Shepherd of Provence by Van Gogh.

1967, May 16 ***Perf. 12½x12***

1027 A197 Strip of 5, #a.-e. 1.25 1.25
1028 A197 12.45g multicolored .50 .50
1029 A197 18.15g multicolored .50 .50
1030 A197 36g multicolored 4.00 4.00
a. Souvenir sheet of 1, perf. 14x12x14x13½ 20.00
Nos. 1027-1030 (4) 6.25 6.25

Nos. 1028-1030a are airmail. No. 1030a has a green pattern in border.
Exist imperf. with changed borders. Values: set, $15; souvenir sheet, $20.

Famous Paintings — A198

10c, Jan Steen. 15c, Frans Hals, vert. 20c, Jordaens. 25c, Rembrandt. 30c, de Marees, vert. 50c, Quentin, vert. 12.45g, Nicolaes Maes, vert. 18.15g, Vigee-Lebrun, vert. 36g, Rubens, vert.
50g, G. B. Tiepolo.

1967, July 16 ***Perf. 12x12½***

1031 A198 10c multicolored .25 .25

Perf. 14x13½, 13½x14

1032 A198 15c multicolored .25 .25
1033 A198 20c multicolored .25 .25
1034 A198 25c multicolored .25 .25
1035 A198 30c multicolored .25 .25
1036 A198 50c multicolored .25 .25
1037 A198 12.45g multicolored .60 .50
1038 A198 18.15g multicolored .60 .50
1039 A198 36g multicolored 6.00 4.00
Nos. 1031-1039 (9) 8.70 6.50

Souvenir Sheet

Perf. 12x12½

1040 A198 50g multicolored 10.00

Nos. 1037-1039 are airmail. An imperf. souvenir sheet of 3, Nos. 1037-1039 exists with dark green pattern in border. Value $15.

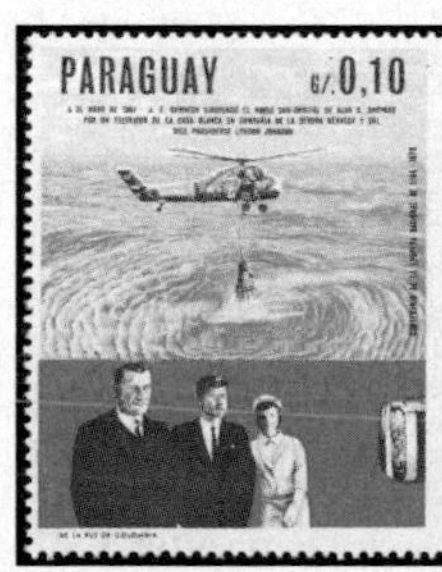

John F. Kennedy, 50th Birth Anniv. A199

Kennedy and: 10c, Recovery of Alan Shepard's capsule, Lyndon Johnson, Mrs. Kennedy. 15c, John Glenn. 20c, Mr. and Mrs. M. Scott Carpenter. 25c, Rocket 2nd stage, Wernher Von Braun. 30c, Cape Canaveral, Walter Schirra. 50c, Syncom 2 satellite, horiz. 12.45g, Launch of Atlas rocket. 18.15g, Theorized lunar landing, horiz. 36g, Portrait of Kennedy by Torres. 50g, Apollo lift-off, horiz.

Perf. 14x13½, 13½x14

1967, Aug. 19

1041 A199 10c multicolored .25 .25
1042 A199 15c multicolored .25 .25
1043 A199 20c multicolored .25 .25
1044 A199 25c multicolored .25 .25
1045 A199 30c multicolored .25 .25
1046 A199 50c multicolored .25 .25
1047 A199 12.45g multicolored 1.50 .75
1048 A199 18.15g multicolored 2.00 1.00
1049 A199 36g multicolored 7.50 4.00
Nos. 1041-1049 (9) 12.50 7.25

Souvenir Sheet

1050 A199 50g multicolored 22.50

Nos. 1047-1050 are airmail. An imperf. souvenir sheet of 3 containing Nos. 1047-1049 exists with violet border. Value $30.

Sculptures A200

10c, Head of athlete. 15c, Myron's Discobolus. 20c, Apollo of Belvedere. 25c, Artemis. 30c, Venus De Milo. 50c, Winged Victory of Samothrace. 12.45g, Laocoon Group. 18.15g, Moses. 50g, Pieta.

1967, Oct. 16 *Perf. 14x13½*

1051 A200 10c multicolored .25 .25
1052 A200 15c multicolored .25 .25
1053 A200 20c multicolored .25 .25
1054 A200 25c multicolored .25 .25
1055 A200 30c multicolored .25 .25
1056 A200 50c multicolored .25 .25
1057 A200 12.45g multicolored .75 .40
1058 A200 18.15g multicolored 1.10 .40
1059 A200 50g multicolored 5.00 3.00
Nos. 1051-1059 (9) 8.35 5.30

Nos. 1057-1059 are airmail.

Exist imperf. in changed colors. Value, set $8.

Mexican Art — A201

Designs: 10c, Bowl, Veracruz. 15c, Knobbed vessel, Colima. 20c, Mixtec jaguar pitcher. 25c, Head, Veracruz. 30c, Statue of seated woman, Teotihuacan. 50c, Vessel depicting a woman, Aztec. 12.45g, Mixtec bowl, horiz. 18.15g, Three-legged vessel, Teotihuacan, horiz. 36g, Golden mask, Teotihuacan, horiz. 50g, The Culture of the Totonac by Diego Rivera, 1950, horiz.

1967, Nov. 29 *Perf. 14x13½*

1060 A201 10c multicolored .25 .25
1061 A201 15c multicolored .25 .25
1062 A201 20c multicolored .25 .25
1063 A201 25c multicolored .25 .25
1064 A201 30c multicolored .25 .25
1065 A201 50c multicolored .25 .25

Perf. 13½x14

1066 A201 12.45g multicolored 1.25 .60
1067 A201 18.15g multicolored 1.50 .60
1068 A201 36g multicolored 7.50 6.00
Nos. 1060-1068 (9) 11.75 8.70

Souvenir Sheet

Perf. 14

1069 A201 50g multicolored 19.00

1968 Summer Olympics, Mexico City (#1065-1069).

Nos. 1066-1069 are airmail. An imperf. souvenir sheet of 3 containing #1066-1068 exists with green pattern in border. Value $30.

Paintings of the Madonna and Child A202

1968, Jan. 27 *Perf. 14x13½,13½x14*

1070 A202 10c Bellini .25 .25
1071 A202 15c Raphael .25 .25
1072 A202 20c Corregio .25 .25
1073 A202 25c Luini .25 .25
1074 A202 30c Bronzino .25 .25
1075 A202 50c Van Dyck .25 .25
1076 A202 12.45g Vignon, horiz. .60 .40
1077 A202 18.15g de Ribera .60 .40
1078 A202 36g Botticelli 6.25 3.00
Nos. 1070-1078 (9) 8.95 5.30

Nos. 1076-1078 are airmail and also exist as imperf. souvenir sheet of 3 with olive brown pattern in border. Value $37.50.

Paintings of Winter Scenes — A203

1968 Winter Olympics Emblem A204

10c, Pissarro. 15c, Utrillo, vert. 20c, Monet. 25c, Breitner, vert. 30c, Sisley. 50c, Brueghel, vert. 12.45g, Avercampe, vert. 18.15g, Brueghel, diff. 36g, P. Limbourg & brothers, vert.

1968, Apr. 23 *Perf. 13½x14, 14x13½*

1079 A203 10c multi .25 .25
1080 A203 15c multi .25 .25
1081 A203 20c multi .25 .25
1082 A203 25c multi .25 .25
1083 A203 30c multi .25 .25
1084 A203 50c multi .25 .25
1085 A203 12.45g multi .75 .40
1086 A203 18.15g multi 1.10 .40
1087 A203 36g multi 3.75 2.00
Nos. 1079-1087 (9) 7.10 4.30

Souvenir Sheet

1088 Sheet of 2 25.00
a. A204 50g multicolored

Nos. 1087-1088, 1088a are airmail. No. 1088 contains #1088a and #1087 with red pattern.

Paraguayan Stamps, Cent. (in 1970) — A205

Perf. 13½x14, 14x13½

1968, June 3 **Litho.**

1089 A205 10c #1, 4 .25 .25
1090 A205 15c #C21, 310, vert. .25 .25
1091 A205 20c #203, C140 .25 .25
1092 A205 25c #C72, C61, vert. .25 .25
1093 A205 30c #638, 711 .25 .25
1094 A205 50c #406, C38, vert. .25 .25
1095 A205 12.45g #B2, B7 .90 .45
1096 A205 18.15g #C10, C11, vert. .90 .45
1097 A205 36g #828, C76, 616 9.00 4.50
Nos. 1089-1097 (9) 12.30 6.90

Souvenir Sheet

Perf. 14

1098 Sheet of 2 25.00 25.00
a. A205 50g #929 & #379

Nos. 1095-1098a are airmail. No. 1098 contains No. 1098a and No. 1097 with light brown pattern in border.

Paintings A206

#1099-1106, paintings of children. #1107-1108, paintings of sailboats at sea.

1968, July 9 *Perf. 14x13½, 13½x14*

1099 A206 10c Russell .25 .25
1100 A206 15c Velazquez .25 .25
1101 A206 20c Romney .25 .25
1102 A206 25c Lawrence .25 .25
1103 A206 30c Caravaggio .25 .25
1104 A206 50c Gentileschi .25 .25
1105 A206 12.45g Renoir .65 .45
1106 A206 18.15g Copley .65 .45
1107 A206 36g Sessions, horiz. 6.75 3.00
Nos. 1099-1107 (9) 9.55 5.40

Souvenir Sheet

Perf. 14

1108 Sheet of 2 15.00 15.00
a. A206 50g Currier & Ives, horiz.

1968 Summer Olympics, Mexico City (Nos. 1107-1108).

Nos. 1106-1108a are airmail. No. 1108 contains No. 1108a and No. 1107 with a red pattern in border.

A207

WHO Emblem — A207a

1968, Aug. 12 **Wmk. 347** *Perf. 11*

1109 A207 3g bluish grn .50 .40
1110 A207 4g brt pink .50 .40
1111 A207 5g bister brn .50 .40
1112 A207 10g violet .50 .40
1113 A207a 36g blk brn 2.00 .40
1114 A207a 50g rose claret 2.00 .50
1115 A207a 100g brt bl 2.00 1.20
Nos. 1109-1115 (7) 8.00 3.70

WHO, 20th anniv.; cent. of the natl. epic. Nos. 1113-1115 are airmail.

39th Intl. Eucharistic Congress A208

Paintings of life of Christ by various artists (except No. 1125a).

Perf. 14x13½

1968, Sept. 25 **Litho.** **Unwmk.**

1116 A208 10c Caravaggio .25 .25
1117 A208 15c El Greco .25 .25
1118 A208 20c Del Sarto .25 .25
1119 A208 25c Van der Weyden .25 .25
1120 A208 30c De Patinier .25 .25
1121 A208 50c Plockhorst .25 .25
1122 A208 12.45g Bronzino .75 .40
1123 A208 18.15g Raphael .75 .40
1124 A208 36g Correggio 8.00 3.00
Nos. 1116-1124 (9) 11.00 5.30

Souvenir Sheet

Perf. 14

1125 Sheet of 2 15.00
a. A208 36g Pope Paul VI
b. A208 50g Tiepolo

Pope Paul VI's visit to South America (No. 1125). Nos. 1122-1125b are airmail.

Events of 1968 — A209

Designs: 10c, Mexican 25p Olympic coin. 15c, Rentry of Echo 1 satellite. 20c, Visit of Pope Paul VI to Fatima, Portugal. 25c, Dr. Christian Barnard, 1st heart transplant. 30c, Martin Luther King, assasination. 50c, Pres. Alfredo Stroessner laying wreath at grave of Pres. Kennedy, vert. 12.45g, Pres. Stroessner, Pres. Lyndon B. Johnson. 18.15g, John F. Kennedy, Abraham Lincoln, Robert Kennedy. 50g, Summer Olympics, Mexico City, satellite transmissions, vert.

1968, Dec. 21 *Perf. 13½x14, 14x13½*

1126 A209 10c multicolored .25 .25
1127 A209 15c multicolored .25 .25
1128 A209 20c multicolored .25 .25
1129 A209 25c multicolored .25 .25
1130 A209 30c multicolored .25 .25
1131 A209 50c multicolored .25 .25
1132 A209 12.45g multicolored 1.10 .40
1133 A209 18.15g multicolored 1.50 .40
1134 A209 50g multicolored 7.50 3.00
Nos. 1126-1134 (9) 11.60 5.30

Nos. 1132-1134 are airmail. Set exists imperf. in sheets of 3 in changed colors. Value, set of 3 sheets $35.

1968 Summer Olympics, Mexico City A210

Olympic Stadium A210a

Gold Medal Winners: 10c, Felipe Munoz, Mexico, 200-meter breast stroke. 15c, Daniel Rebillard, France, 4000-meter cycling. 20c, David Hemery, England, 400-meter hurdles. 25c, Bob Seagren, US, pole vault. 30c, Francisco Rodriguez, Venezuela, light flyweight boxing. 50c, Bjorn Ferm, Sweden, modern pentathlon. 12.45g, Klaus Dibiasi, Italy, platform diving. 50g, Ingrid Becker, West Germany, fencing, women's pentathlon.

1969, Feb. 13 *Perf. 14x13½*

1135 A210 10c multicolored .25 .25
1136 A210 15c multicolored .25 .25
1137 A210 20c multicolored .25 .25
1138 A210 25c multicolored .25 .25
1139 A210 30c multicolored .25 .25
1140 A210 50c multicolored .25 .25
1141 A210 12.45g multicolored .70 .30
1142 A210a 18.15g multicolored 1.00 .40
1143 A210 50g multicolored 5.50 3.00
Nos. 1135-1143 (9) 8.70 5.20

Nos. 1141-1143 are airmail. Set exists imperf. in sheets of 3 in changed colors. Value, set of 3 sheets $30.

Space Missions — A211

Designs: 10c, Apollo 7, John F. Kennedy. 15c, Apollo 8, Kennedy. 20c, Apollo 8, Kennedy, diff. 25c, Study of solar flares, ITU emblem. 30c, Canary Bird satellite. 50c, ESRO satellite. 12.45g, Wernher von Braun, rocket launch. 18.15g, Global satellite coverage, ITU emblem. 50g, Otto Lilienthal, Graf Zeppelin, Hermann Oberth, evolution of flight.

1969, Mar. 10 *Perf. 13½x14*

1144 A211 10c multicolored .25 .25
1145 A211 15c multicolored .25 .25
1146 A211 20c multicolored .25 .25
1147 A211 25c multicolored .25 .25
1148 A211 30c multicolored .25 .25
1149 A211 50c multicolored .25 .25
1150 A211 12.45g multicolored .60 .40
1151 A211 18.15g multicolored .90 .40
1152 A211 50g multicolored 3.25 2.00
Nos. 1144-1152 (9) 6.25 4.30

Nos. 1150-1152 are airmail. Set exists imperf. in sheets of 3 in changed colors. Value, set of 3 sheets $50.

"World United in Peace" — A212

1969, June 28 **Wmk. 347** *Perf. 11*

1153 A212 50c rose .50 .50
1154 A212 70c ultra .50 .50
1155 A212 1.50g light brn .50 .50
1156 A212 3g lil rose .50 .50
1157 A212 4g emerald .75 .50
1158 A212 5g violet .90 .50
1159 A212 10g brt lilac 2.50 .50
Nos. 1153-1159 (7) 6.15 3.50

Peace Week.

Birds A213

Designs: 10c, Pteroglossus viridis. 15c, Phytotoma rutila. 20c, Porphyrula martinica. 25c, Oxyrunchus cristatus. 30c, Spizaetus ornatus. 50c, Phoenicopterus ruber. 75c, Amazona ochrocephala. 12.45g, Ara ararauna, Ara macao. 18.15g, Colibri coruscans.

Perf. 13½x14, 14x13½

1969, July 9 **Unwmk.**

1160 A213 10c multicolored .90 .25
1161 A213 15c multicolored .90 .25
1162 A213 20c multicolored .90 .25
1163 A213 25c multicolored .90 .25
1164 A213 30c multicolored .90 .25
1165 A213 50c multicolored .90 .25
1166 A213 75c multicolored .90 .25
1167 A213 12.45g multicolored 2.75 .50
1168 A213 18.15g multicolored 6.50 1.00
Nos. 1160-1168 (9) 15.55 3.25

Nos. 1167-1168 are airmail. Nos. 1161, 1164-1168 are vert.

Fauna — A214

1969, July 9

1169 A214 10c Porcupine .25 .25
1170 A214 15c Lemur, vert. .25 .25
1171 A214 20c 3-toed sloth, vert. .25 .25
1172 A214 25c Puma .25 .25
1173 A214 30c Alligator .25 .25
1174 A214 50c Jaguar .25 .25
1175 A214 75c Anteater .25 .25
1176 A214 12.45g Tapir .50 .25
1177 A214 18.15g Capybara 1.50 1.00
Nos. 1169-1177 (9) 3.75 3.00

Nos. 1176-1177 are airmail.

Olympic Soccer Champions, 1900-1968 A215

Designs: 10c, Great Britain, Paris, 1900. 15c, Canada, St. Louis, 1904. 20c, Great Britain, London, 1908 and Stockholm, 1912. 25c, Belgium, Antwerp, 1920. 30c, Uruguay, Paris, 1924 and Amsterdam, 1928. 50c, Italy, Berlin, 1936. 75c, Sweden, London, 1948; USSR, Melbourne, 1956. 12.45g, Yugoslavia, Rome, 1960. 18.15g, Hungary, Helsinki, 1952, Tokyo, 1964 and Mexico, 1968.

No. 1187, Soccer ball, Mexico 1968 emblem. No. 1188, Soccer player and ball.

1969, Nov. 26 *Perf. 14*

1178 A215 10c multicolored .25 .25
1179 A215 15c multicolored .25 .25
1180 A215 20c multicolored .25 .25
1181 A215 25c multicolored .25 .25
1182 A215 30c multicolored .25 .25
1183 A215 50c multicolored .25 .25
1184 A215 75c multicolored .25 .25
1185 A215 12.45g multicolored .70 .40
1186 A215 18.15g multicolored 6.75 2.50
Nos. 1178-1186 (9) 9.20 4.65

Souvenir Sheet

1187 A215 23.40g multicolored 7.50 7.50
1188 A215 23.40g multi 15.00 15.00

Nos. 1185-1188 are airmail. No. 1187 contains one 49x60mm stamp. No. 1188 contains one 50x61mm stamp.

A216

World Cup or South American Soccer Champions: 10c, Paraguay, 1953. 15c, Uruguay, 1930. 20c, Italy, 1934. 25c, Italy, 1938. 30c, Uruguay, 1950. 50c, Germany, 1954, horiz. 75c, Brazil, 1958. 12.45g, Brazil, 1962. 18.15g, England, 1966. No. 1198, Trophy. No. 1199, Soccer player, satellite.

1969, Nov. 26 *Perf. 14*

1189 A216 10c multicolored .25 .25
1190 A216 15c multicolored .25 .25
1191 A216 20c multicolored .25 .25
1192 A216 25c multicolored .25 .25
1193 A216 30c multicolored .25 .25
1194 A216 50c multicolored .30 .25
1195 A216 75c multicolored .45 .25
1196 A216 12.45g multicolored 2.00 .25
1197 A216 18.15g multicolored 4.50 1.50
Nos. 1189-1197 (9) 8.50 3.50

Souvenir Sheets

Perf. 13½, Imperf(#1199)

1198 A216 23.40g multicolored 27.50 27.50
1199 A216 23.40g multicolored 15.00 15.00

Nos. 1196-1199 are airmail. No. 1198 contains one 50x60mm stamp. No. 1199 contains one 45x57mm stamp.

Paintings by Francisco de Goya (1746-1828) — A217

Designs: 10c, Miguel de Lardibazal. 15c, Francisca Sabasa y Gracia. 20c, Don Manuel Osorio. 25c, Young Women with a Letter. 30c, The Water Carrier. 50c, Truth, Time and History. 75c, The Forge. 12.45g, The Spell. 18.15g, Duke of Wellington on Horseback. 23.40g, "La Maja Desnuda."

1969, Nov. 29 **Litho.** *Perf. 14x13½*

1200 A217 10c multicolored .25 .25
1201 A217 15c multicolored .25 .25
1202 A217 20c multicolored .25 .25
1203 A217 25c multicolored .25 .25
1204 A217 30c multicolored .25 .25
1205 A217 50c multicolored .25 .25
1206 A217 75c multicolored .30 .25
1207 A217 12.45g multicolored 2.00 .60
1208 A217 18.15g multicolored 4.50 1.25
Nos. 1200-1208 (9) 8.30 3.60

Souvenir Sheet

Perf. 14

1209 A217 23.40g multicolored 20.00 20.00

Nos. 1207-1209 are airmail.

Christmas A218

Various paintings of The Nativity or Madonna and Child.

1969, Nov. 29 *Perf. 14x13½*

1210 A218 10c Master Bertram .25 .25
1211 A218 15c Procaccini .25 .25
1212 A218 20c Di Crediti .25 .25
1213 A218 25c De Flemalle .25 .25
1214 A218 30c Correggio .25 .25
1215 A218 50c Borgianni .25 .25
1216 A218 75c Botticelli .25 .25
1217 A218 12.45g El Greco 1.50 .60
1218 A218 18.15g De Morales 3.25 1.50
Nos. 1210-1218 (9) 6.50 3.85

Souvenir Sheet

Perf. 13½

1219 A218 23.40g Isenheimer Altar 12.00 12.00

Nos. 1217-1219 are airmail.

Souvenir Sheet

European Space Program — A219

1969, Nov. 29 **Litho.** *Perf. 14*

1220 A219 23.40g ESRO 1B 15.00 15.00

Imperf

1221 A219 23.40g Ernst Stuhlinger 20.00 20.00

Francisco Solano — A220

1970, Mar. 1 **Wmk. 347** *Perf. 11*

1222 A220 1g bis brn 1.00 1.00
1223 A220 2g violet 1.00 1.00
1224 A220 3g brt pink 1.00 .50
1225 A220 4g rose claret 1.00 1.00
1226 A220 5g blue 1.00 1.00
1227 A220 10g bright grn 1.00 .75
1228 A220 15g lt Prus bl 1.00 *2.00*
1229 A220 20g org brn 1.00 *2.00*
1230 A220 30g gray grn 1.00 1.00
1231 A220 40g gray brn 1.00 3.00
Nos. 1222-1231 (10) 10.00 13.25

Marshal Francisco Solano Lopez (1827-1870), President of Paraguay. Nos. 1226-1231 are airmail.

1st Moon Landing, Apollo 11 — A221

Designs: 10c, Wernher von Braun, lift-off. 15c, Eagle and Columbia in lunar orbit. 20c, Deployment of lunar module. 25c, Landing on Moon. 30c, First steps on lunar surface. 50c, Gathering lunar soil. 75c, Lift-off from Moon. 12.45g, Rendevouz of Eagle and Columbia. 18.15g, Pres. Kennedy, von Braun, splashdown. No. 1241, Gold medal of Armstrong, Aldrin and Collins. No. 1242, Moon landing medal, Kennedy, von Braun. No. 1243, Apollo 12 astronauts Charles Conrad and Alan Bean on moon, and Dr. Kurt Debus.

1970, Mar. 11 Unwmk. *Perf. 14*

1232	A221	10c multicolored	.25	.25
1233	A221	15c multicolored	.25	.25
1234	A221	20c multicolored	.25	.25
1235	A221	25c multicolored	.25	.25
1236	A221	30c multicolored	.25	.25
1237	A221	50c multicolored	.25	.25
1238	A221	75c multicolored	.25	.25
1239	A221	12.45g multicolored	1.50	.60
1240	A221	18.15g multicolored	3.00	1.25
		Nos. 1232-1240 (9)	6.25	3.60

Souvenir Sheets

1241	A221	23.40g multicolored	14.00	11.00

Imperf

1242	A221	23.40g multicolored	17.00	15.00
1243	A221	23.40g multicolored	14.00	11.00

Nos. 1239-1243 are airmail. Nos. 1241-1242 contain one 50x60mm stamp, No. 1243 one 60x50mm stamp.

Easter — A222

Designs: 10c, 15c, 20c, 25c, 30c, 50c, 75c, Stations of the Cross. 12.45g, Christ appears to soldiers, vert. 18.15g, Christ appears to disciples, vert. 23.40g, The sad Madonna, vert.

1970, Mar. 11

1244	A222	10c multicolored	.25	.25
1245	A222	15c multicolored	.25	.25
1246	A222	20c multicolored	.25	.25
1247	A222	25c multicolored	.25	.25
1248	A222	30c multicolored	.25	.25
1249	A222	50c multicolored	.25	.25
1250	A222	75c multicolored	.30	.25
1251	A222	12.45g multicolored	1.25	.50
1252	A222	18.15g multicolored	3.25	1.50
		Nos. 1244-1252 (9)	6.30	3.75

Souvenir Sheet

Perf. 13½

1253	A222	23.40g multicolored	10.00

Nos. 1251-1253 are airmail. No. 1253 contains one 50x60mm stamp.

Paraguay No. 2 — A223

Designs (First Issue of Paraguay): 2g, 10g, #1. 3g, #3. 5g, #2. 15g, #3. 30g, #2. 36g, #1.

1970, Aug. 15 Litho. Wmk. 347

1254	A223	1g car rose	1.00	1.00
1255	A223	2g ultra	1.00	1.00
1256	A223	3g org brn	1.00	1.00
1257	A223	5g violet	1.00	1.00
1258	A223	10g lilac	1.00	1.00
1259	A223	15g vio brn	2.00	2.00
1260	A223	30g dp grn	2.00	2.00
1261	A223	36g brt pink	2.00	2.00
		Nos. 1254-1261 (8)	11.00	11.00

Centenary of stamps of Paraguay. #1259-1261 are airmail.

1972 Summer Olympics, Munich A224

No. 1262: a, 10c, Discus. b, 15c, Cycling. c, 20c, Men's hurdles. d, 25c, Fencing. e, 30c, Swimming, horiz.

50c, Shotput. 75c, Sailing. 12.45, Women's hurdles, horiz. 18.15g, Equestrian, horiz. No. 1267, Flags, Olympic coins. No. 1268, Frauenkirche Church, Munich. No. 1269, Olympic Village, Munich, horiz.

1970, Sept. 28 Unwmk. *Perf. 14*

1262	A224	Strip of 5, #a.-e.	1.25	1.25
1263	A224	50c multicolored	.25	.25
1264	A224	75c multicolored	.30	.25
1265	A224	12.45g multicolored	1.40	.45
1266	A224	18.15g multicolored	3.50	1.25
		Nos. 1262-1266 (5)	6.70	3.45

Souvenir Sheets

Perf. 13½

1267	A224	23.40g multicolored	12.50	

Imperf

1268	A224	23.40g multicolored	60.00	
1269	A224	23.40g multicolored	20.00	20.00

Nos. 1265-1269 are airmail. Nos. 1267-1269 each contain one 50x60mm stamp.

Paintings, Pinakothek, Munich, 1972 A225

Nudes by: No. 1270a, 10c, Cranach. b, 15c, Baldung. c, 20c, Tintoretto. d, 25c, Rubens. e, 30c, Boucher, horiz. 50c, Baldung, diff. 75c, Cranach, diff.

12.45g, Self-portrait, Durer. 18.15g, Alterpiece, Altdorfer. 23.40g, Madonna and Child.

1970, Sept. 28 *Perf. 14*

1270	A225	Strip of 5, #a.-e.	1.75	1.25
1271	A225	50c multicolored	.40	.25
1272	A225	75c multicolored	.40	.25
1273	A225	12.45g multicolored	1.75	.50
1274	A225	18.15g multicolored	2.25	1.50
		Nos. 1270-1274 (5)	6.55	3.75

Souvenir Sheet

Perf. 13½

1275	A225	23.40g multicolored	20.00	20.00

Nos. 1273-1275 are airmail. No. 1275 contains one 50x60mm stamp.

Apollo Space Program — A226

No. 1276: a, 10c, Ignition, Saturn 5. b, 15c, Apollo 1 mission emblem, vert. c, 20c, Apollo 7, Oct. 1968. d, 25c, Apollo 8, Dec. 1968. e, 30c, Apollo 9, Mar. 1969.

50c, Apollo 10, May 1969. 75c, Apollo 11, July 1969. 12.45g, Apollo 12, Nov. 1969. 18.15g, Apollo 13, Apr. 1970. No. 1281, Lunar landing sites. No. 1282, Wernher von Braun, rockets. No. 1283, James A. Lovell, John L. Swigert, Fred W. Haise.

1970, Oct. 19 *Perf. 14*

1276	A226	Strip of 5, #a.-e.	1.25	1.25
1277	A226	50c multicolored	.25	.25
1278	A226	75c multicolored	.25	.25
1279	A226	12.45g multicolored	1.00	.50
1280	A226	18.15g multicolored	3.50	1.50
		Nos. 1276-1280 (5)	6.25	3.75

Souvenir Sheets

Perf. 13½

1281	A226	23.40g multicolored	10.00

Imperf

1282	A226	23.40g multicolored	50.00
1283	A226	23.40g multicolored	20.00

Nos. 1279-1283 are airmail. Nos. 1281-1283 each contain one 60x50mm stamp.

1970, Oct. 19 *Perf. 14*

Future Space Projects: No. 1284a, 10c, Space station, 2000. b, 15c, Lunar station, vert. c, 20c, Space transport. d, 25c, Lunar rover. e, 30c, Skylab.

50c, Space station, 1971. 75c, Lunar vehicle. 12.45g, Lunar vehicle, diff., vert. 18.15g, Vehicle rising above lunar surface. 23.40g, Moon stations, transport.

1284	A226	Strip of 5, #a.-e.	1.25	1.25
1285	A226	50c multicolored	.25	.25
1286	A226	75c multicolored	.25	.25
1287	A226	12.45g multicolored	1.25	.50
1288	A226	18.15g multicolored	2.50	1.00
		Nos. 1284-1288 (5)	5.50	3.25

Souvenir Sheet

Perf. 13½

1289	A226	23.40g multicolored	12.50	12.50

Nos. 1287-1289 are airmail. No. 1289 contains one 50x60mm stamp. For overprints see Nos. 2288-2290, C653.

EXPO '70, Osaka, Japan A228

Paintings from National Museum, Tokyo: No. 1288a, 10c, Buddha. b, 15c, Fire, people. c, 20c, Demon, Ogata Korin. d, 25c, Japanese play, Hishikawa Moronobu. e, 30c, Birds.

50c, Woman, Utamaro. 75c, Samurai, Wantabe Kazan. 12.45c, Women Beneath Tree, Kano Hideroi. 18.15g, Courtesans, Torrii Kiyonaga. 50g, View of Mt. Fuji, Hokusai, horiz. No. 1296, Courtesan, Kaigetsudo Ando. No. 1297, Emblem of Expo '70. No. 1298, Emblem of 1972 Winter Olympics, Sapporo.

1970, Nov. 26 Litho. *Perf. 14*

1290	A228	Strip of 5, #a.-e.	1.25	1.25
1291	A228	50c multicolored	.25	.25
1292	A228	75c multicolored	.25	.25
1293	A228	12.45g multicolored	.50	.50
1294	A228	18.15g multicolored	.60	.60
1295	A228	50g multicolored	3.50	1.50
		Nos. 1290-1295 (6)	6.35	4.35

Souvenir Sheets

Perf. 13½

1296	A228	20g multicolored	10.00
1297	A228	20g multicolored	17.50
1298	A228	20g multicolored	30.00

Nos. 1293-1298 are airmail. Nos. 1296-1298 each contain one 50x60mm stamp.

Flower Paintings A229

Artists: No. 1299a, 10c, Von Jawlensky. b, 15c, Purrmann. c, 20c, De Vlaminck. d, 25c, Monet. e, 30c, Renoir.

50c, Van Gogh. 75, Cezanne. 12.45g, Van Huysum. 18.15g, Ruysch. 50g, Walscappelle. 20g, Bosschaert.

1970, Nov. 26 *Perf. 14*

1299	A229	Strip of 5, #a.-e.	1.25	1.25
1300	A229	50c multicolored	.25	.25
1301	A229	75c multicolored	.25	.25
1302	A229	12.45g multicolored	.90	.40
1303	A229	18.15g multicolored	1.20	.40
1304	A229	50g multicolored	2.50	1.00
		Nos. 1299-1304 (6)	6.35	3.55

Souvenir Sheet

Perf. 13½

1305	A229	20g multicolored	7.50	7.50

Nos. 1302-1305 are airmail. No. 1305 contains one 50x60mm stamp.

Paintings from The Prado, Madrid — A230

Nudes by: No. 1306a, 10c, Titian. b, 15c, Velazquez. c, 20c, Van Dyck. d, 25c, Tintoretto. e, 30c, Rubens.

50c, Venus and Sleeping Adonis, Veronese. 75c, Adam and Eve, Titian. 12.45g, The Holy Family, Goya. 18.15g, Shepherd Boy, Murillo. 50g, The Holy Family, El Greco.

1970, Dec. 16 *Perf. 14*

1306	A230	Strip of 5, #a.-e.	1.25	1.25
1307	A230	50c multicolored	.25	.25
1308	A230	75c multicolored	.25	.25
1309	A230	12.45g multicolored	.50	.25
1310	A230	18.15g multicolored	.50	.25
1311	A230	50g multicolored	2.50	1.50
		Nos. 1306-1311 (6)	5.25	3.75

Nos. 1309-1311 are airmail. Nos. 1307-1311 are vert.

1970, Dec. 16

Paintings by Albrecht Durer (1471-1528): No. 1312a, 10c, Adam and Eve. b, 15c, St. Jerome in the Wilderness. c, 20c, St. Eustachius and George. d, 25c, Piper and drummer. e, 30c, Lucretia's Suicide.

50c, Oswald Krel. 75c, Stag Beetle. 12.45g, Paul and Mark. 18.15g, Lot's Flight. 50g, Nativity.

1312	A230	Strip of 5, #a.-e.	1.25	1.25
1313	A230	50c multicolored	.25	.25
1314	A230	75c multicolored	.25	.25
1315	A230	12.45g multicolored	.60	.40
1316	A230	18.15g multicolored	1.20	.40
1317	A230	50g multicolored	3.50	1.25
		Nos. 1312-1317 (6)	7.05	3.80

Nos. 1315-1317 are airmail. See No. 1273.

Christmas A232

Paintings: No. 1318a, 10c, The Annunciation, Van der Weyden. b, 15c, The Madonna, Zeitblom. c, 20c, The Nativity, Von Soest. d, 25c, Adoration of the Magi, Mayno. e, 30c, Adoration of the Magi, Da Fabriano.

50c, Flight From Egypt, Masters of Martyrdom. 75c, Presentation of Christ, Memling. 12.45g, The Holy Family, Poussin, horiz. 18.15g, The Holy Family, Rubens. 20g, Adoration of the Magi, Giorgione, horiz. 50g, Madonna and Child, Batoni.

1971, Mar. 23

1318 A232 Strip of 5, #a.-e. 1.25 1.25
1319 A232 50c multicolored .25 .25
1320 A232 75c multicolored .25 .25
1321 A232 12.45g multicolored .60 .40
1322 A232 18.15g multicolored 1.25 .40
1323 A232 50g multicolored 3.50 1.25
Nos. 1318-1323 (6) 7.10 3.80

Souvenir Sheet

Perf. 13½

1324 A232 20g multicolored 10.00 10.00

Nos. 1321-1324 are airmail. No. 1324 contains one 60x50mm stamp.

1972 Summer Olympics, Munich A233

Olympic decathlon gold medalists: No. 1325a, 10c, Hugo Wieslander, Stockholm 1912. b, 15c, Helge Lovland, Antwerp 1920. c, 20c, Harold M. Osborn, Paris 1924. d, 25c, Paavo Yrjola, Amsterdam 1928. e, 30c, James Bausch, Los Angeles 1932.

50c, Glenn Morris, Berlin 1936. 75c, Bob Mathias, London 1948, Helsinki 1952. 12.45g, Milton Campbell, Melbourne 1956. 18.15g, Rafer Johnson, Rome 1960. 50g, Willi Holdorf, Tokyo 1964. No. 1331, Bill Toomey, Mexico City 1968.

No. 1332, Pole vaulter, Munich, 1972.

1971, Mar. 23 ***Perf. 14***

1325 A233 Strip of 5, #a.-e. 1.25 1.25
1326 A233 50c multicolored .25 .25
1327 A233 75c multicolored .25 .25
1328 A233 12.45g multicolored .60 .40
1329 A233 18.15g multicolored 1.25 .40
1330 A233 50g multicolored 3.50 1.25
Nos. 1325-1330 (6) 7.10 3.80

Souvenir Sheets

Perf. 13½

1331 A233 20g multicolored 12.00 8.00
1332 A233 20g multicolored 12.00 8.00

Nos. 1328-1332 are airmail. Nos. 1331-1332 each contain one 50x60mm stamp.

Art — A234

Paintings by: No. 1333a, 10c, Van Dyck. b, 15c, Titian. c, 20c, Van Dyck, diff. d, 25c, Walter. e, 30c, Orsi.

50c, 17th cent. Japanese artist, horiz. 75c, David. 12.45g, Huguet. 18.15g, Perugino. 20g, Van Eyck. 50g, Witz.

1971, Mar. 26 ***Perf. 14***

1333 A234 Strip of 5, #a.-e. 1.25 1.25
1334 A234 50c multicolored .25 .25
1335 A234 75c multicolored .25 .25
1336 A234 12.45g multicolored .75 .40
1337 A234 18.15g multicolored 1.25 .40
1338 A234 50g multicolored 3.00 1.25
Nos. 1333-1338 (6) 6.75 3.80

Souvenir Sheet

Perf. 13½

1339 A234 20g multicolored 15.00 15.00

Nos. 1336-1339 are airmail. No. 1339 contains one 50x60mm stamp.

Paintings from the Louvre, Paris

Portraits of women by: No. 1340a, 10c, De la Tour. b, 15c, Boucher. c, 20c, Delacroix. d, 25c, 16th cent. French artist. e, 30c, Ingres.

50c, Ingres, horiz. 75c, Watteau, horiz. 12.45g, 2nd cent. artist. 18.15g, Renoir. 20g, Mona Lisa, Da Vinci. 50g, Liberty Guiding the People, Delacroix.

1971, Mar. 26 ***Perf. 14***

1340 A234 Strip of 5, #a.-e. 1.25 1.25
1341 A234 50c multicolored .25 .25
1342 A234 75c multicolored .25 .25
1343 A234 12.45g multicolored .60 .40
1344 A234 18.15g multicolored .75 .40
1345 A234 50g multicolored 2.00 1.00
Nos. 1340-1345 (6) 5.10 3.55

Souvenir Sheet

Perf. 13½

1346 A234 20g multicolored 9.00 9.00

Nos. 1343-1346 are airmail. No. 1346 contains one 50x60mm stamp.

Paintings A236

Artist: No. 1347a, 10c, Botticelli. b, 15c, Titian. c, 20c, Raphael. d, 25c, Pellegrini. e, 30c, Caracci.

50c, Titian, horiz. 75c, Ricci, horiz. 12.45g, Courtines. 18.15g, Rodas. 50g, Murillo.

1971, Mar. 29 ***Perf. 14***

1347 A236 Strip of 5, #a.-e. 1.25 1.25
1348 A236 50c multicolored .25 .25
1349 A236 75c multicolored .25 .25
1350 A236 12.45g multicolored .75 .40
1351 A236 18.15g multicolored 1.25 .40
1352 A236 50g multicolored 3.00 1.00
Nos. 1347-1352 (6) 6.75 3.55

Nos. 1350-1352 are airmail.

Hunting Scenes — A237

Different Paintings by: No. 1353a, 10c, Gozzoli, vert. b, 15c, Velazquez, vert. c, 20c, Brun. d, 25c, Fontainebleau School, 1550, vert. e, 30c, Uccello, vert.

50c, P. De Vos. 75c, Vernet. 12.45g, 18.15g, 50g, Alken & Sutherland. No. 1359, Paul & Derveaux. No. 1360, Degas.

1971, Mar. 29

1353 A237 Strip of 5, #a.-e. 1.25 1.25
1354 A237 50c multicolored .25 .25
1355 A237 75c multicolored .25 .25
1356 A237 12.45g multicolored .60 .40
1357 A237 18.15g multicolored .75 .40
1358 A237 50g multicolored 3.00 1.00
Nos. 1353-1358 (6) 6.10 3.55

Souvenir Sheets

Perf. 13½

1359 A237 20g multicolored 10.00 10.00
1360 A237 20g multicolored 10.00 10.00

Nos. 1356-1360 are airmail. Nos. 1359-1360 each contain one 60x50mm stamp.

Philatokyo '71 — A238

Designs: Nos. 1361a-1361e, 10c, 15c, 20c, 25c, 30c, Different flowers, Gukei. 50c, Birds, Lu Chi. 75c, Flowers, Sakai Hoitsu. 12.45g, Man and Woman, Utamaro. 18.15g, Tea Ceremony, from Tea museum. 50g, Bathers, Utamaro. No. 1367, Woman, Kamakura Period. No. 1368, Japan #1, #821, #904, #1023.

1971, Apr. 7 ***Perf. 14***

1361 A238 Strip of 5, #a.-e. 1.25 1.25
1362 A238 50c multicolored .25 .25
1363 A238 75c multicolored .25 .25
1364 A238 12.45g multicolored .65 .40
1365 A238 18.15g multicolored .65 .40
1366 A238 50g multicolored 3.50 1.00
Nos. 1361-1366 (6) 6.55 3.55

Souvenir Sheets

Perf. 13½

1367 A238 20g multicolored 12.50 12.50
1368 A238 20g multicolored 12.50 12.50

Nos. 1364-1368 are airmail. Nos. 1367-1368 each contain one 50x60mm stamp.

See Nos. 1375-1376.

1972 Winter Olympics, Sapporo A239

Paintings of women by: No. 1369a, 10c, Harunobu. b, 15c, Hosoda. c, 20c, Harunobu, diff. d, 25c, Uemura Shoen. e, 30c, Ketao.

50c, Three Women, Torii. 75c, Old Man, Kakizahi. 12.45g, 2-man bobsled. 18.15g, Ice sculptures, horiz. 50g, Mt. Fuji, Hokusai, horiz. No. 1375, Skier, horiz. No. 1376, Sapporo Olympic emblems.

1971, Apr. ***Perf. 14***

1369 A239 Strip of 5, #a.-e. 1.25 1.25
1370 A239 50c multicolored .25 .25
1371 A239 75c multicolored .25 .25
1372 A239 12.45g multicolored .60 .40
1373 A239 18.15g multicolored 1.25 .40
1374 A239 50g multicolored 3.50 1.00
Nos. 1369-1374 (6) 7.10 3.55

Souvenir Sheets

Perf. 14½

1375 A239 20g multicolored 14.00 14.00

Perf. 13½

1376 A239 20g multicolored 20.00 20.00

Nos. 1372-1376 are airmail. No. 1375 contains one 35x25mm stamp with PhilaTokyo 71 emblem. No. 1376 contains one 50x60mm stamp.

For Japanese painting stamps with white border and Winter Olympics emblem see #1409-1410.

UNESCO and Paraguay Emblems, Globe, Teacher and Pupil A240

Wmk. 347

1971, May 18 **Litho.** ***Perf. 11***

1377 A240 3g ultra 1.00 1.00
1378 A240 5g lilac 1.00 1.00
1379 A240 10g emerald 1.00 1.00
1380 A240 20g claret 2.00 2.00
1381 A240 25g brt pink 2.00 2.00
1382 A240 30g brown 2.00 2.00
1383 A240 50g gray olive 2.00 2.00
Nos. 1377-1383 (7) 11.00 11.00

International Education Year.

Nos. 1380-1383 are airmail.

Paintings, Berlin-Dahlem Museum — A241

Artists: 10c, Caravaggio. No. 1385: a, 15c, b, 20c, Di Cosimo. 25c, Cranach. 30c, Veneziano. 50g, Holbein. 75c, Baldung. 12.45g, Cranach, diff. 18.15g, Durer. 50g, Schongauer.

1971, Dec. 24 **Unwmk.** ***Perf. 14***

1384 A241 10c multicolored .25 .25
1385 A241 Pair, #a.-b. .25 .25
1386 A241 25c multicolored .25 .25
1387 A241 30c multicolored .25 .25
1388 A241 50c multicolored .25 .25
1389 A241 75c multicolored .25 .25
1390 A241 12.45g multicolored .90 .40
1391 A241 18.15g multicolored .90 .40
1392 A241 50g multicolored 3.50 1.00
Nos. 1384-1392 (9) 6.80 3.30

Nos. 1390-1392 are airmail. No. 1385 has continuous design.

Napoleon I, 150th Death Anniv. A242

Paintings: No. 1393a, 10c, Desiree Clary, Gerin. b, 15c, Josephine de Beauharnais, Gros. c, 20c, Maria Luisa, Gerard. d, 25c, Juliette Recamier, Gerard. e, 30c, Maria Walewska, Gerard.

50c, Victoria Kraus, unknown artist, horiz. 75c, Napoleon on Horseback, Chabord. 12.45g, Trafalgar, A. Mayer, horiz. 18.15g, Napoleon Leading Army, Gautherot, horiz.

50g, Napoleon's tomb.

1971, Dec. 24

1393 A242 Strip of 5, #a.-e. 1.25 1.25
1394 A242 50c multicolored .25 .25
1395 A242 75c multicolored .25 .25
1396 A242 12.45g multicolored .75 .40
1397 A242 18.15g multicolored .90 .40
1398 A242 50g multicolored 3.50 1.00
Nos. 1393-1398 (6) 6.90 3.55

Nos. 1396-1398 are airmail.

Locomotives — A243

Designs: No. 1399a, 10c, Trevithick, Great Britain, 1804. b, 15c, Blenkinsops, 1812. c, 20c, G. Stephenson #1, 1825. d, 25c, Marc Seguin, France, 1829. e, 30c, "Adler," Germany, 1835.

50c, Sampierdarena #1, Italy, 1854. 75c, Paraguay #1, 1861. 12.45g, "Munich," Germany, 1841. 18.15g, US, 1875. 20g, Japanese locomotives, 1872-1972. 50g, Mikado D-50, Japan, 1923.

1972, Jan. 6

1399 A243 Strip of 5, #a.-e. 1.25 1.25
1400 A243 50c multicolored .25 .25
1401 A243 75c multicolored .25 .25
1402 A243 12.45g multicolored .90 .40
1403 A243 18.15g multicolored .90 .40
1404 A243 50g multicolored 3.50 .90
Nos. 1399-1404 (6) 7.05 3.45

Souvenir Sheet

Perf. 13½

1405 A243 20g multicolored 30.00 30.00

Nos. 1402-1405 are airmail. No. 1405 contains one 60x50mm stamp.

See Nos. 1476-1480.

1972 Winter Olympics, Sapporo — A244

Designs: Nos. 1406a, 10c, Hockey player. b, 15c, Jean-Claude Killy. c, 20c, Gaby Seyfert. d, 25c, 4-Man bobsled. e, 30c, Luge.

50c, Ski jumping, horiz. 75c, Slalom skiing, horiz. 12.45g, Painting, Kuniyoshi. 18.15g, Winter Scene, Hiroshige, horiz. 50g, Ski lift, man in traditional dress.

1972, Jan. 6 ***Perf. 14***

1406 A244 Strip of 5, #a.-e. 1.25 1.25
1407 A244 50c multicolored .25 .25
1408 A244 75c multicolored .25 .25
1409 A244 12.45g multicolored 1.25 .40
1410 A244 18.15g multicolored 1.25 .40
1411 A244 50g multicolored 4.75 1.25
Nos. 1406-1411 (6) 9.00 3.80

Souvenir Sheet

Perf. 13½

1412 A244 20g Skier 14.00 14.00
1413 A244 20g Flags 20.00 20.00

Nos. 1409-1413 are airmail. Nos. 1412-1413 each contain one 50x60mm stamp. For overprint see Nos. 2295-2297. For Winter Olympic stamps with gold border, see Nos. 1372-1373.

UNICEF, 25th Anniv. (in 1971) — A245

1972, Jan. 24 **Granite Paper**

1414 A245 1g red brn 1.00 1.00
1415 A245 2g ultra 1.00 1.00
1416 A245 3g lil rose 1.00 1.00
1417 A245 4g violet 1.00 1.00
1418 A245 5g emerald 1.00 1.00
1419 A245 10g claret 2.00 *3.00*
1420 A245 20g brt bl 2.00 *3.00*
1421 A245 25g lt ol 2.00 *3.00*
1422 A245 30g dk brn 2.00 *3.00*
Nos. 1414-1422 (9) 13.00 17.00

Nos. 1420-1422 are airmail.

Race Cars A246

No. 1423: a, 10c, Ferrari. b, 15c, B.R.M. c, 20c, Brabham. d, 25c, March. e, 30c, Honda.

50c, Matra-Simca MS 650. 75c, Porsche. 12.45g, Maserati-8 CTF, 1938. 18.15g, Bugatti 35B, 1929. 20g, Lotus 72 Ford. 50g, Mercedes, 1924.

1972, Mar. 20 **Unwmk.** ***Perf. 14***

1423 A246 Strip of 5, #a.-e. 2.25 1.25
1424 A246 50c multicolored .35 .25
1425 A246 75c multicolored .35 .25
1426 A246 12.45g multicolored 1.00 .45
1427 A246 18.15g multicolored 1.00 .45
1428 A246 50g multicolored 5.25 5.25
Nos. 1423-1428 (6) 10.20 7.90

Souvenir Sheet

Perf. 13½

1429 A246 20g multicolored 22.50

Nos. 1426-1429 are airmail. No. 1429 contains one 60x50mm stamp.

Sailing Ships — A247

Paintings: No. 1430a, 10c, Holbein. b, 15c, Nagasaki print. c, 20c, Intrepid, Roux. d, 25c, Portuguese ship, unknown artist. e, 30c, Mount Vernon, US, 1798, Corne.

50c, Van Eertvelt, vert. 75c, Santa Maria, Van Eertvelt, vert. 12.45g, Royal Prince, 1679, Van Beecq. 18.15g, Van Bree. 50g, Book of Arms, 1497, vert.

1972, Mar. 29 ***Perf. 14***

1430 A247 Strip of 5, #a.-e. 1.25 1.25
1431 A247 50c multicolored .30 .25
1432 A247 75c multicolored .40 .25
1433 A247 12.45g multicolored 1.00 .35
1434 A247 18.15g multicolored 1.40 .40
1435 A247 50g multicolored 3.00 .75
Nos. 1430-1435 (6) 7.35 3.25

Nos. 1433-1435 are airmail.

Paintings in Vienna Museum A248

Nudes by: No. 1436a, 10c, Rubens. b, 15c, Bellini. c, 20c, Carracci. d, 25c, Cagnacci. e, 30c, Spranger.

50c, Mandolin Player, Strozzi. 75c, Woman in Red Hat, Cranach the elder. 12.45g, Adam and Eve, Coxcie. 18.15g, Legionary on Horseback, Poussin. 50g, Madonna and Child, Bronzino.

1972, May 22

1436 A248 Strip of 5, #a.-e. 1.25 1.25
1437 A248 50c multicolored .25 .25
1438 A248 75c multicolored .25 .25
1439 A248 12.45g multicolored .70 .40
1440 A248 18.15g multicolored .70 .40
1441 A248 50g multicolored 2.75 1.25
Nos. 1436-1441 (6) 5.90 3.80

Nos. 1439-1441 are airmail.

Paintings in Asuncion Museum A249

No. 1442: a, 10c, Man in Straw Hat, Holden Jara. b, 15c, Portrait, Tintoretto. c, 20c, Indians, Holden Jara. d, 25c, Nude, Bouchard. e, 30c, Italian School.

50c, Reclining Nude, Berisso, horiz. 75c, Carracci, horiz. 12.45g, Reclining Nude, Schiaffino, horiz. 18.15g, Reclining Nude, Lostow, horiz. 50g, Madonna and Child, 17th cent. Italian School.

1972, May 22

1442 A249 Strip of 5, #a.-e. 1.25 1.25
1443 A249 50c multicolored .25 .25
1444 A249 75c multicolored .25 .25
1445 A249 12.45g multicolored .70 .40
1446 A249 18.15g multicolored .70 .40
1447 A249 50g multicolored 2.75 1.25
Nos. 1442-1447 (6) 5.90 3.80

Nos. 1445-1447 are airmail.

Presidential Summit — A250

No. 1448: a, 10c, Map of South America. b, 15c, Brazil natl. arms. c, 20c, Argentina natl. arms. d, 25c, Bolivia natl. arms. e, 30c, Paraguay natl. arms.

50c, Pres. Emilio Garrastazu, Brazil. 75c, Pres. Alejandro Lanusse, Argentina. 12.45g, Pres. Hugo Banzer Suarez, Bolivia. 18.15, Pres. Stroessner, Paraguay, horiz. 23.40g, Flags.

1972, Nov. 18

1448 A250 Strip of 5, #a.-e. 1.25 1.25
1449 A250 50c multicolored .25 .25
1450 A250 75c multicolored .25 .25
1451 A250 12.45g multicolored 1.40 .25
1452 A250 18.15g multicolored 1.75 .30
Nos. 1448-1452 (5) 4.90 2.30

Souvenir Sheet

Perf. 13½

1453 A250 23.40g multicolored 2.50

Nos. 1451-1453 are airmail. No. 1453 contains one 50x60mm stamp. For overprint see No. 2144.

Pres. Stroessner's Visit to Japan — A251

No. 1454: a, 10c, Departure of first Japanese mission to US & Europe, 1871. b, 15c, First railroad, Tokyo-Yokahama, 1872. c, 20c, Samurai. d, 25c, Geishas. e, 30c, Cranes, Hiroshige.

50c, Honda race car. 75c, Pres. Stroessner, Emperor Hirohito, Mt. Fuji, bullet train, horiz. 12.45g, Rocket. 18.15g, Stroessner, Hirohito, horiz. No. 1459, Mounted samurai, Masanobu, 1740. No. 1460, Hirohito's speech, state dinner, horiz. No. 1461, Delegations at Tokyo airport, horiz.

1972, Nov. 18 ***Perf. 14***

1454 A251 Strip of 5, #a.-e. 1.25 1.25
1455 A251 50c multicolored .25 .25
1456 A251 75c multicolored .25 .25
1457 A251 12.45g multicolored 2.00 2.00
1458 A251 18.15g multicolored 2.50 2.50
Nos. 1454-1458 (5) 6.25 6.25

Souvenir Sheets

Perf. 13½

1459 A251 23.40g multicolored 7.50 7.50
1460 A251 23.40g multicolored 17.50 17.50

Imperf

1461 A251 23.40g multicolored 15.00 15.00

Nos. 1457-1461 are airmail. Nos. 1459-1460 each contain one 50x60mm stamp. No. 1461 contains one 85x42mm stamp with simulated perforations. For overprints see Nos. 2192-2194, 2267.

Wildlife A252

Paintings — #1462: a, 10c, Cranes, Botke. b, 15c, Tiger, Utamaro. c, 20c, Horses, Arenys. d, 25c, Pheasant, Dietzsch. e, 30c, Monkey, Brueghel, the Elder. All vert.

50c, Deer, Marc. 75c, Crab, Durer. 12.45g, Rooster, Jakuchu, vert. 18.15g, Swan, Asselyn.

1972, Nov. 18 ***Perf. 14***

1462 A252 Strip of 5, #a.-e. 1.25 1.25
1463 A252 50c multicolored .25 .25
1464 A252 75c multicolored .25 .25
1465 A252 12.45g multicolored 1.50 .75
1466 A252 18.15g multicolored 1.75 1.00
Nos. 1462-1466 (5) 5.00 3.50

Nos. 1465-1466 are airmail.

Acaray Dam A253

Designs: 2g, Francisco Solano Lopez monument. 3g, Friendship Bridge. 5g, Tebicuary River Bridge. 10g, Hotel Guarani. 20g, Bus and car on highway. 25g, Hospital of Institute for Social Service. 50g, "Presidente Stroessner" of state merchant marine. 100g, "Electra C" of Paraguayan airlines.

Perf. 13½x13

1972, Nov. 16 **Wmk. 347**

Granite Paper

1467 A253 1g sepia 2.00 1.00
1468 A253 2g brown 2.00 1.00
1469 A253 3g brt ultra 2.00 1.00
1470 A253 5g brt pink 2.00 1.00
1471 A253 10g dl grn 3.00 2.00
1472 A253 20g rose car 3.00 2.00
1473 A253 25g gray 3.00 2.00
1474 A253 50g violet 3.00 2.00
1475 A253 100g brt lil 3.00 2.00
Nos. 1467-1475 (9) 23.00 14.00

Tourism Year of the Americas.
Nos. 1472-1475 are airmail.

Locomotives Type

No. 1476: a, 10c, Stephenson's Rocket, 1829. b, 15c, First Swiss railroad, 1847. c, 20c, 1st Spanish locomotive, 1848. d, 2c, Norris, US, 1850. e, 30c, Ansaldo, Italy, 1859.

50c, Badenia, Germany, 1863. 75c, 1st Japanese locomotive, 1895. 12.45g, P.L.M., France, 1924. 18.15g, Stephenson's Northumbrian.

1972, Nov. 25 **Unwmk.** ***Perf. 14***

1476 A243 Strip of 5, #a.-e. 1.25 1.25
1477 A243 50c multicolored .25 .25
1478 A243 75c multicolored .25 .25
1479 A243 12.45g multicolored 3.50 .40
1480 A243 18.15g multicolored 5.00 1.00
Nos. 1476-1480 (5) 10.25 3.15

Nos. 1479-1480 are airmail.

South American Wildlife — A254

No. 1481: a, 10c, Tetradactyla. b, 15c, Nasua socialis. c, 20c, Priodontes giganteus. d, 25c, Blastocerus dichotomus. e, 30c, Felis pardalis.

50c, Aotes, vert. 75c, Rhea americana. 12.45g, Desmodus rotundus. 18.15g, Urocyon cinereo-argenteus.

1972, Nov. 25

1481	A254	Strip of 5, #a.-e.	1.25	1.25
1482	A254	50c multicolored	.35	.25
1483	A254	75c multicolored	.35	.25
1484	A254	12.45g multicolored	3.75	.75
1485	A254	18.15g multicolored	5.00	1.25
		Nos. 1481-1485 (5)	10.70	3.75

Nos. 1484-1485 are airmail.

OAS Emblem A255

Perf. 13x13½

1973 Litho. Wmk. 347

Granite Paper

1486	A255	1g multi	1.00	1.00
1487	A255	2g multi	1.00	1.00
1488	A255	3g multi	1.00	1.00
1489	A255	4g multi	1.00	1.00
1490	A255	5g multi	1.00	1.00
1491	A255	10g multi	1.00	1.00
1492	A255	20g multi	2.00	1.00
1493	A255	25g multi	2.00	1.00
1494	A255	50g multi	3.00	1.00
1495	A255	100g multi	5.00	1.00
		Nos. 1486-1495 (10)	18.00	10.00

Org. of American States, 25th anniv. Nos. 1492-1495 are airmail.

Paintings in Florence Museum A256

Artists: No. 1496: a, 10c, Cranach, the Elder. b, 15c, Caravaggio. c, 20c, Fiorentino. d, 25c, Di Credi. e, 30c, Liss. f, 50c, Da Vinci. g, 75c, Botticelli.

No. 1497: a, 5g, Titian, horiz. b, 10g, Del Piombo, horiz. c, 20g, Di Michelino, horiz.

1973, Mar. 13 Unwmk. *Perf. 14*

1496	A256	Strip of 7, #a.-g.	1.75	1.00
1497	A256	Strip of 3, #a.-c.	3.75	2.50
		Nos. 1496-1497 (2)	5.50	3.50

No. 1497 is airmail.

Butterflies — A257

#1498: a, 10c, Catagramma patazza. b, 15c, Agrias narcissus. c, 20c, Papilio zagreus. d, 25c, Heliconius chestertoni. e, 30c, Metamorphadido. f, 50c, Catagramma astarte. g, 75c, Papilio brasiliensis.

No. 1499a, 5g, Agrias sardanapalus. b, 10g, Callithea saphhira. c, 20g, Jemadia hospita.

1973, Mar. 13

1498	A257	Strip of 7, #a.-g.	1.75	1.00
1499	A257	Strip of 3, #a.-c.	6.25	3.50
		Nos. 1498-1499 (2)	8.00	4.50

No. 1499 is airmail.

Cats A258

Faces of Cats: No. 1500: a, 10c, b, 15c. c, 20c, d, 25c, e, 30c. f, 50c. g, 75c.

No. 1501a, 5g, Cat under rose bush, by Desportes. b, 10g, Two cats, by Marc, horiz. c, 20g, Man with cat, by Rousseau.

1973, June 29

1500	A258	Strip of 7, #a.-g.	1.75	1.00
1501	A258	Strip of 3, #a.-c.	7.25	3.50
		Nos. 1500-1501 (2)	9.00	4.50

No. 1500 is airmail. For other cat designs, see type A287.

Flemish Paintings A259

Nudes by: No. 1502: a, 10c, Spranger. b, 15c, Jordaens. c, 20c, de Clerck. d, 25c, Spranger, diff. e, 30c, Goltzius. f, 50c, Rubens. g, 75c, Vase of flowers, J. Brueghel.

No. 1503a, 5g, Nude, de Clerck, horiz. b, 10g, Woman with mandolin, de Vos. c, 20g, Men, horses, Rubens, horiz.

1973, June 29 Litho. *Perf. 14*

1502	A259	Strip of 7, #a.-g.	1.75	1.00
1503	A259	Strip of 3, #a.-c.	4.25	3.00
		Nos. 1502-1503 (2)	6.00	4.00

No. 1503 is airmail.

Hand Holding Letter — A260

Wmk. 347

1973, July 10 Litho. *Perf. 11*

1504	A260	2g lil rose & blk	5.00	1.50

No. 1504 was issued originally as a nonobligatory stamp to benefit mailmen, but its status was changed to regular postage.

EXPOPAR 73, Paraguayan Industrial Exhib. — A261

1973, Aug. 11 *Perf. 13x13½*

Granite Paper

1505	A261	1g org brn	2.00	2.00
1506	A261	2g vermilion	2.00	2.00
1507	A261	3g blue	2.00	2.00
1508	A261	4g emerald	2.00	2.00
1509	A261	5g lilac	2.00	2.00
1510	A261	20g lilac rose	7.50	3.00
1511	A261	25g rose claret	7.50	3.00
		Nos. 1505-1511 (7)	25.00	16.00

Nos. 1510-1511 are airmail.

1974 World Cup Soccer Championships, Munich — A262

No. 1512: a, 10c, Uruguay vs. Paraguay. b, 15c, Crerand, England and Eusebio, Portugal. c, 20c, Bobby Charlton, England. d, 25c, Franz Beckenbauer, Germany. e, 30c, Erler, Germany and McNab, England. f, 50c, Pele, Brazil and Willi Schulz, Germany. g, 75c, Arsenio Erico, Paraguay.

5g, Brian Labone, Gerd Mueller, Bobby Moore. No. 1514a, 10g, Luigi Riva, Italy. No. 1514b, 20g, World Cup medals. No. 1515, World Cup trophy. 25g, Player scoring goal.

1973 Litho. Unwmk. *Perf. 14*

1512	A262	Strip of 7, #a.-g.	1.75	1.00
1513	A262	5g multicolored	5.00	1.50
1514	A262	Pair, #a.-b.	2.25	1.00
		Nos. 1512-1514 (3)	9.00	3.50

Souvenir Sheets

Perf. 13½

1515	A262	25g multicolored	25.00	25.00
1516	A262	25g multicolored	22.50	22.50

Nos. 1513-1516 are airmail. Issue dates: Nos. 1512-1514, 1516, Oct. 8. No. 1515, June 29. For overprint see No. 2131.

Paintings A263

Details from paintings, artist: No. 1517a, 10c, Lion of St. Mark, Carpaccio. b, 15c, Venus and Mars, Pittoni. c, 20c, Rape of Europa, Veronese. d, 25c, Susannah and the Elders, Tintoretto. e, 30c, Euphrosyne, Amigoni. f, 50c, Allegory of Moderation, Veronese. g, 75c, Ariadne, Tintoretto.

5g, Pallas and Mars, Tintoretto. No. 1519a, 10g, Portrait of Woman in Fur Hat, G.D. Tiepolo. b, 20g, Dialectic of Industry, Veronese.

1973, Oct. 8 *Perf. 14*

1517	A263	Strip of 7, #a.-g.	1.75	1.00
1518	A263	5g multicolored	2.50	.75
1519	A263	Pair, #a.-b.	3.00	1.25
		Nos. 1517-1519 (3)	7.25	3.00

Nos. 1518-1519 are airmail.

Birds A264

No. 1520: a, 10c, Tersina viridis. b, 15c, Pipile cumanensis. c, 20c, Pyrocephalus rubinus. d, 25c, Andigona laminirostris. e, 30c, Xipholena punicea. f, 50c, Tangara chilensis. g, 75c, Polytmus guainumbi.

5g, Onychorhynchus mexicanus, vert. No. 1522a, 10g, Rhinocrypta lanceolata, vert. b, 20g, Trogon collaris, vert. 25g, Colibri florisuga mellivora, vert.

1973, Nov. 14

1520	A264	Strip of 7, #a.-g.	1.10	1.10
1521	A264	5g multicolored	3.00	1.50
1522	A264	Pair, #a.-b.	2.00	.50
		Nos. 1520-1522 (3)	6.10	3.10

Souvenir Sheet

Perf. 13½

1523	A264	25g multicolored	10.00	10.00

Nos. 1521-1523 are airmail. No. 1523 contains one 50x60mm stamp.

Space Exploration — A265

No. 1524a, 10c, Apollo 11. b, 15c, Apollo 12. c, 20c, Apollo 13. d, 25c, Apollo 14. e, 30c, Apollo 15. f, 50c, Apollo 16. g, 75c, Apollo 17.

5g, Skylab. No. 1526a, 10g, Space shuttle. b, 20g, Apollo-Soyuz mission. No. 1527, Pioneer 11, Jupiter. No. 1528, Pioneer 10, Jupiter, vert.

1973, Nov. 14 *Perf. 14*

1524	A265	Strip of 7, #a.-g.	1.10	1.10
1525	A265	5g multicolored	3.50	1.50
1526	A265	Pair, #a.-b.	1.40	1.00
		Nos. 1524-1526 (3)	6.00	3.60

Souvenir Sheet

Perf. 14½

1527	A265	25g multicolored	17.00	12.00

Perf. 13½

1528	A265	25g multicolored	15.00	10.00

#1525-1528 are airmail. #1527 contains on 35x25mm stamp, #1528 one 50x60mm stamp.

Souvenir Sheet

Women of Avignon, Pablo Picasso — A266

1973, Nov. 14 *Perf. 13½*

1529	A266	25g multicolored	11.00	11.00

Traditional Costumes A267

No. 1530: a, 25c, Indian girl. b, 50c, Bottle dance costume. c, 75c, Dancer balancing vase on head. d, 1g, Dancer with flowers. e, 1.50g, Weavers. f, 1.75g, Man, woman in dance costumes. g, 2.25g, Musicians in folk dress, horiz.

1973, Dec. 30 *Perf. 14*

1530	A267	Strip of 7, #a.-g.	2.00	1.00

Flowers A268

Designs: No. 1531a, 10c Passion flower. b, 20c, Dahlia. c, 25c, Bird of paradise. d, 30c, Freesia. e, 40c, Anthurium. f, 50c, Water lily. g, 75c, Orchid.

1973, Dec. 31

1531	A268	Strip of 7, #a.-g.	6.00	2.50

Roses A269

Designs: No. 1532a, 10c, Hybrid perpetual. b, 15c, Tea scented. c, 20c, Japanese rose. d, 25c, Bouquet of roses and flowers. e, 30c, Rose of Provence. f, 50c, Hundred petals rose. g, 75c, Bouquet of roses, dragonfly.

1974, Feb. 2

1532	A269	Strip of 7, #a.-g.	7.00	3.00

Paintings in Gulbenkian Museum A270

Designs and artists: No. 1533a, 10c, Cupid and Three Graces, Boucher. b, 15c, Bath of Venus, Burne-Jones. c, 20c, Mirror of Venus, Burne-Jones. d, 25c, Two Women, Natoire. e, 30c, Fighting Cockerels, de Vos. f, 50c, Portrait of a Young Girl, Bugiardini. g, 75c, Madonna and Child, J. Gossaert.

5g, Outing on Beach at Enoshima, Utamaro. No. 1535: a, 10g, Woman with Harp, Lowrence. b, 20g, Centaurs Embracing, Rubens.

1974, Feb. 4

1533	A270	Strip of 7, #a.-g.	1.10	1.10
1534	A270	5g multicolored	2.50	1.75
1535	A270	Pair, #a.-b.	3.50	3.50
		Nos. 1533-1535 (3)	7.10	6.35

Nos. 1534-1535 are airmail.

UPU Cent. A271

Horse-drawn mail coaches: No. 1536a, 10c, London. b, 15c, France. c, 20c, England. d, 25c, Bavaria. e, 30c, Painting by C.C. Henderson. f, 50c, Austria, vert. g, 75c, Zurich, vert.

5g, Hot air balloon, Apollo spacecraft, airplane, Graf Zeppelin. No. 1538a, 10g, Steam locomotive. b, 20g, Ocean liner, sailing ship. No. 1539, Airship, balloon. No. 1540, Mail coach crossing river.

1974, Mar. 20 *Perf. 14*

1536	A271	Strip of 7, #a.-g.	1.25	1.25
1537	A271	5g multicolored	1.40	.65
1538	A271	Pair, #a.-b.	5.50	3.50
		Nos. 1536-1538 (3)	8.15	5.40

Souvenir Sheets

Perf. 14½

1539	A271	15g multicolored	25.00	25.00

Perf. 13½

1540	A271	15g multicolored	25.00	25.00

Nos. 1537-1540 are airmail. No. 1539 contains one 50x35mm stamp, No. 1540 one 60x50mm stamp. Nos. 1539-1540 each include a 5g surtax for a monument to Francisco Solano Lopez. For overprint see No. 2127.

Paintings — A272

Details from works, artist: No. 1541a, 10c, Adam and Eve, Mabuse. b, 15c, Portrait, Piero di Cosimo. c, 20c, Bathsheba in her Bath, Cornelisz. d, 25c, Toilet of Venus, Boucher. e, 30c, The Bathers, Renoir. f, 50c, Lot and his Daughters, Dix. g, 75c, Bouquet of Flowers, van Kessel.

5g, King's Pet Horse, Seele. No. 1543a, 10g, Woman with Paintbrushes, Batoni. b, 20g, Three Musicians, Flemish master.

1974, Mar. 20

1541	A272	Strip of 7, #a.-g.	1.25	1.25
1542	A272	5g multicolored	1.40	.40
1543	A272	Pair, #a.-b.	6.50	3.00
		Nos. 1541-1543 (3)	9.15	4.65

Nos. 1542-1543 are airmail.

Sailing Ships — A272a

Designs: No. 1544a, 5c, Ship, map. b, 10c, English ship. c, 15c, Dutch ship. d, 20c, Whaling ships. e, 25c, Spanish ship. f, 35c, USS Constitution. g, 40c, English frigate. h, 50c, "Fanny," 1832.

1974, Sept. 13 *Perf. 14½*

1544	A272a	Strip of 8, #a.-h.	3.00	1.00

Strip price includes a 50c surtax.

Paintings in Borghese Gallery, Rome A273

Details from works and artists: No. 1545a, 5c, Portrait, Romano. b, 10c, Boy Carrying Fruit, Caravaggio. c, 15c, A Sybil, Domenichino. d, 20c, Nude, Titian. e, 25c, The Danae, Correggio. f, 35c, Nude, Savoldo. g, 40c, Nude, da Vinci. h, 50c, Nude, Rubens. 15g, Christ Child, Piero di Cosimo.

1975, Jan. 15 *Perf. 14*

1545	A273	Strip of 8, #a.-h.	3.00	1.50

Souvenir Sheet

Perf. 14½

1546	A273	15g multicolored	10.00	5.00

No. 1546 is airmail and price includes a 5g surtax used for a monument to Francisco Solano Lopez.

Christmas A274

Paintings, artists: No. 1547a, 5c, The Annunciation, della Robbia. b, 10c, The Nativity, G. David. c, 15c, Madonna and Child, Memling. d, 20c, Adoration of the Shepherds, Giorgione. e, 25c, Adoration of the Magi, French school, 1400. f, Madonna and Child with Saints, 35c, Pulzone. g, 40c, Madonna and Child, van Orley. h, 50c, Flight From Egypt, Pacher.

15g, Adoration of the Magi, Raphael.

1975, Jan. 17 *Perf. 14*

1547	A274	Strip of 8, #a.-h.	3.00	1.50

Souvenir Sheet

Perf. 14½

1548	A274	15g multicolored	10.00	5.00

No. 1548 is airmail and price includes a 5g surtax for a monument to Francisco Solano Lopez.

"U.P.U.," Pantheon, Carrier Pigeon, Globe — A275

1975, Feb. **Wmk. 347** *Perf. 13½x13*

1549	A275	1g blk & lilac	.25	.25
1550	A275	2g blk & rose red	.25	.25
1551	A275	3g blk & ultra	.25	.25
1552	A275	5g blk & blue	.25	.25
1553	A275	10g blk & lil rose	.50	.25
1554	A275	20g blk & brn	1.50	.25
1555	A275	25g blk & emer	1.50	.25
		Nos. 1549-1555 (7)	4.50	1.75

Centenary of Universal Postal Union.
Nos. 1554-1555 are airmail.

Paintings in National Gallery, London A276

Details from paintings, artist: 5c, The Rokeby Venus, Velazquez, horiz. 10c, The Range of Love, Watteau. 15c, Venus (The School of Love), Correggio. 20c, Mrs. Sarah Siddons, Gainsborough. 25c, Cupid Complaining to Venus, L. Cranach the Elder. 35c, Portrait, Lotto. 40c, Nude, Rembrandt. 50c, Origin of the Milky Way, Tintoretto. 15g, Rider and Hounds, Pisanello.

1975, Apr. 25 **Unwmk.** *Perf. 14*

1556	A276	5c multicolored	.25	.25
1557	A276	10c multicolored	.30	.25
1558	A276	15c multicolored	.40	.25
1559	A276	20c multicolored	.45	.25
1560	A276	25c multicolored	.50	.25
1561	A276	35c multicolored	.65	.25
1562	A276	40c multicolored	.70	.25
1563	A276	50c multicolored	.80	.25
		Nos. 1556-1563 (8)	4.05	2.00

Souvenir Sheet

Perf. 13½

1564	A276	15g multicolored	10.00	10.00

No. 1564 is airmail, contains one 50x60mm stamp and price includes a 5g surtax for a monument to Francisco Solano Lopez.

Dogs A277

1975, June 7 *Perf. 14*

1565	A277	5c Boxer	.25	.25
1566	A277	10c Poodle	.25	.25
1567	A277	15c Basset hound	.25	.25
1568	A277	20c Collie	.25	.25
1569	A277	25c Chihuahua	.35	.25
1570	A277	35c German shepherd	.50	.25
1571	A277	40c Pekinese	.55	.25
1572	A277	50c Chow	.70	.25
		Nos. 1565-1572 (8)	3.10	2.00

Souvenir Sheet

Perf. 13½

1573	A277	15g Fox hound, horse	15.00	8.00

No. 1573 is airmail, contains one 39x57mm stamp and price includes a 5g surtax for a monument to Francisco Solano Lopez.

South American Fauna — A278

Designs: No. 1574a, 5c, Piranha (Pirana). b, 10c, Anaconda. c, 15c, Turtle (Tortuga). d, 20c, Iguana. e, 25c, Mono, vert. f, 35c, Mara. g, 40c, Marmota, vert. h, 50c, Peccary.

1975, Aug. 20 **Litho.** *Perf. 14*

1574	A278	Strip of 8, #a.-h.	3.00	1.50

Souvenir Sheet

Perf. 13½

1575	A278	15g Aguara guazu	10.00	7.50

No. 1575 is airmail, contains and one 60x50mm stamp, and price includes a 5g surtax for a monument to Francisco Solano Lopez.

For overprints see Nos. 2197.

Michelangelo (1475-1564), Italian Sculptor and Painter — A279

No. 1583: Statues, a, 5c, David. b, 10c, Aurora.

Paintings, c, 15c, Original Sin. d, 20c, The Banishment. e, 25c, The Deluge. f, 35c, Eve. g, 40c, Mary with Jesus and John. h, 50c, Judgement Day.

4g, Adam Receiving Life from God, horiz. No. 1585a, 5g, Libyan Sybil. b, 10g, Delphic Sybil. No. 1586, God Creating the Heaven and the Earth, horiz. No. 1587, The Holy Family.

1975, Aug. 23 Litho. *Perf. 14*

No.	Design	Description	Unused	Used
1583	A279	Strip of 8, #a.-h.	1.50	1.50
1584	A279	4g multicolored	4.00	2.75
1585	A279	Pair, #a.-b.	1.00	.75

Souvenir Sheets

Perf. 12

No.	Design	Description	Unused	Used
1586	A279	15g multicolored	15.00	7.50

Perf. 13½

No.	Design	Description	Unused	Used
1587	A279	15g multicolored	15.00	12.00

Nos. 1586-1587 sold for 20g with surtax for a monument to Francisco Solano Lopez. Nos. 1584-1587 are airmail.

Winter Olympics, Innsbruck, 1976 — A280

No. 1596, Luge. No. 1599, 4-Man bobsled.

No. 1597a, 2g, Slalom skier. b, 3g, Cross country skier. c, 4g, Pair figure skating. d, 5g, Hockey.

No. 1598a, 10g, Speed skater. b, 15g, Downhill skier.

No. 1600, Ski jumper. No. 1601, Woman figure skater.

1975, Aug. 27 Litho. *Perf. 14*

No.	Design	Description	Unused	Used
1596	A280	1g multi	.25	.25
1597	A280	Strip of 4, #a.-d.	2.00	1.00
1598	A280	Pair, #a.-b.	2.50	.80
1599	A280	20g multi	3.00	1.50
		Nos. 1596-1599 (4)	7.75	3.55

Souvenir Sheet

Perf. 13½

No.	Design	Description	Unused	Used
1600	A280	25g multi	22.50	22.50
1601	A280	25g multi	14.00	14.00

Nos. 1596, 1598-1601 are horiz. Nos. 1598-1601 are airmail. Nos. 1600-1601 each contain one 60x50mm stamp.

Summer Olympics, Montreal, 1976 — A281

No. 1606: a, 1g, Weightlifting. b, 2g, Kayak. c, 3g, Hildegard Flack, 800 meter run. d, Lasse Viren, 5,000 meter run.

No. 1607: a, 5g, Dieter Kottysch, boxing. b, 10g, Lynne Evans, archery. c, 15g, Akinori Nakayama, balance rings. 20g, Heide Rosendahl, broad jump. No. 1609, Decathlon. No. 1610, Liselott Linsenhoff, dressage, horiz.

1975, Aug. 28 *Perf. 14*

No.	Design	Description	Unused	Used
1606	A281	Strip of 4, #a.-d.	.80	.80
1607	A281	Strip of 3, #a.-c.	3.25	1.00
1608	A281	20g multicolored	4.00	1.50
		Nos. 1606-1608 (3)	8.05	3.30

Souvenir Sheets

Perf. 14½

No.	Design	Description	Unused	Used
1609	A281	25g multicolored	15.00	15.00
1610	A281	25g multicolored	15.00	15.00

Nos. 1607b-1610 are airmail.

US, Bicent. — A282

Ships: 5c, Sachem, vert. 10c, Reprisal, Lexington. 15c, Wasp. 20c, Mosquito, Spy. 25c, Providence, vert. 35c, Yankee Hero, Milford. 40c, Cabot, vert. 50c, Hornet, vert. 15g, Montgomery.

Unwmk.

1975, Oct. 20 Litho. *Perf. 14*

No.	Design	Description	Unused	Used
1616	A282	5c multicolored	.25	.25
1617	A282	10c multicolored	.35	.25
1618	A282	15c multicolored	.35	.25
1619	A282	20c multicolored	.35	.25
1620	A282	25c multicolored	.35	.25
1621	A282	35c multicolored	.50	.25
1622	A282	40c multicolored	.55	.25
1623	A282	50c multicolored	.75	.30
		Nos. 1616-1623 (8)	3.45	2.05

Souvenir Sheet

No.	Design	Description	Unused	Used
1624	A282	15g multicolored	15.00	15.00

No. 1624 is airmail and contains one 50x70mm stamp.

US, Bicent. — A283

Details from paintings, artists: No. 1625a, 5c, The Collector, Kahill. b, 10c, Morning Interlude, Brackman, vert. c, 15c, White Cloud, Catlin, vert. d, 20c, Man From Kentucky, Benton, vert. e, 25c, The Emigrants, Remington. f, 35c, Spirit of '76, Willard, vert. g, John Paul Jones capturing Serapis, unknown artist. h, 50c, Declaration of Independence, Trumbull. 15g, George Washington, Stuart and Thomas Jefferson, Peale.

1975, Nov. 20 *Perf. 14*

No.	Design	Description	Unused	Used
1625	A283	Strip of 8, #a.-h.	4.00	1.50

Souvenir Sheet

Perf. 13½

No.	Design	Description	Unused	Used
1625A	A283	15g multicolored	15.00	15.00

No. 1625A is airmail, contains one 60x50mm stamp and price includes a 5g surtax for a monument to Francisco Solano Lopez.

Institute of Higher Education — A284

Perf. 13½x13

1976, Mar. 16 Litho. Wmk. 347

No.	Design	Description	Unused	Used
1626	A284	5g vio, blk & red	1.10	.50
1627	A284	10g ultra, blk & red	2.00	1.50
1628	A284	30g brn, blk & red	2.00	1.50
		Nos. 1626-1628 (3)	5.10	3.50

Inauguration of Institute of Higher Education, Sept. 23, 1974.

No. 1628 is airmail.

Rotary Intl., 70th Anniv. — A285

1976, Mar. 16 *Perf. 13x13½*

No.	Design	Description	Unused	Used
1629	A285	3g blk, bl & citron	1.00	.75
1630	A285	4g car, bl & citron	1.00	.75
1631	A285	25g emer, bl & lemon	3.00	2.00
		Nos. 1629-1631 (3)	5.00	3.50

No. 1631 is airmail.

IWY Emblem, Woman's Head — A286

1976, Mar. 16

No.	Design	Description	Unused	Used
1632	A286	1g ultra & brn	1.00	.75
1633	A286	2g car & brn	1.00	.75
1634	A286	20g grn & brn	3.00	2.00
		Nos. 1632-1634 (3)	5.00	3.50

Intl Women's Year (1975).

No. 1634 is airmail.

Cats A287

Various cats: No. 1635a, 5c. b, 10c. c, 15c. d, 20c. e, 25c. f, 35c. g, 40c. h, 50c. 15g.

1976, Apr. 2 Unwmk. *Perf. 14*

No.	Design	Description	Unused	Used
1635	A287	Strip of 8, #a.-h.	3.00	1.00

Souvenir Sheet

Perf. 13½

No.	Design	Description	Unused	Used
1636	A287	15g multicolored	15.00	5.00

No. 1636 is airmail, contains one 50x60mm stamp and price includes a 5g surtax for a monument to Francisco Solano Lopez.

See Nos. 2132-2133, 2201-2202, 2274-2275. For overprint see No. 2212.

Railroads, 150th Anniv. (in 1975) — A288

Locomotives: 1g, Planet, England, 1830. 2g, Koloss, Austria, 1844. 3g, Tarasque, France, 1846. 4g, Lawrence, Canada, 1853. 5g, Carlsruhe, Germany, 1854. 10g, Great Sagua, US, 1856. 15g, Berga, Spain. 20g, Encarnacion, Paraguay. 25g, English locomotive, 1825.

1976, Apr. 2 *Perf. 13x13½*

No.	Design	Description	Unused	Used
1637	A288	1g multicolored	.25	.25
1638	A288	2g multicolored	.25	.25
1639	A288	3g multicolored	.25	.25
1640	A288	4g multicolored	.25	.25
1641	A288	5g multicolored	.25	.25
1642	A288	10g multicolored	1.50	.40
1643	A288	15g multicolored	2.40	.60
1644	A288	20g multicolored	3.00	1.00
		Nos. 1637-1644 (8)	8.15	3.25

Souvenir Sheet

No.	Design	Description	Unused	Used
1645	A288	25g multicolored	32.50	32.50

Nos. 1642-1645 are airmail. No. 1645 contains one 40x27mm stamp.

Painting by Spanish Artists — A289

Paintings: 1g, The Naked Maja by Goya. 2g, Nude by J. de Torres. 3g, Nude holding oranges by de Torres, vert. 4g, Woman playing piano by Z. Velazquez, vert. 5g, Knight on white horse by Esquivel, vert. 10g, The Shepherd by Murillo, vert. 15g, The Immaculate Conception by Antolinez, vert. 20g, Nude by Zuloaga. 25g, Prince Baltasar Carlos on Horseback by D. Velasquez.

1976, Apr. 2 *Perf. 13x13½,13½x13*

No.	Design	Description	Unused	Used
1646	A289	1g multicolored	.25	.25
1647	A289	2g multicolored	.25	.25
1648	A289	3g multicolored	.25	.25
1649	A289	4g multicolored	.25	.25
1650	A289	5g multicolored	.30	.25
1651	A289	10g multicolored	.75	.40
1652	A289	15g multicolored	1.10	.50
1653	A289	20g multicolored	1.50	.60
		Nos. 1646-1653 (8)	4.65	2.75

Souvenir Sheet

No.	Design	Description	Unused	Used
1654	A289	25g multicolored	9.00	5.00

Nos. 1651-1654 are airmail. No. 1654 contains one 58x82mm stamp.

Butterflies — A290

No. 1655: a, 5c, Prepona praeneste. b, 10c, Prepona proschion. c, 15c, Pereute leucodrosime. d, 20c, Agrias amydon. e, 25c, Morpho aegea gynandromorphe. f, 35c, Pseudatteria leopardina. g, 40c, Morpho helena. h, 50c, Morpho hecuba.

1976, May 12 Unwmk. *Perf. 14*

No.	Design	Description	Unused	Used
1655	A290	Strip of 8, #a.-h.	5.00	1.50

Farm Animals — A291

1976, June 15

No.	Design	Description	Unused	Used
1656	A291	1g Rooster, vert.	.25	.25
1657	A291	2g Hen, vert.	.35	.25
1658	A291	3g Turkey, vert.	.35	.25
1659	A291	4g Sow	.40	.25
1660	A291	5g Donkeys	.50	.25
1661	A291	10g Brahma cattle	.55	.35
1662	A291	15g Holstein cow	.65	.35
1663	A291	20g Horse	.80	.50
		Nos. 1656-1663 (8)	3.85	2.45

Nos. 1661-1663 are airmail.

US and US Post Office, Bicent. — A292

Designs: 1g, Pony Express rider. 2g, Stagecoach. 3g, Steam locomotive, vert. 4g, American steamship, Savannah. 5g, Curtiss Jenny biplane. 10g, Mail bus. 15g, Mail car, rocket train. 20g, First official missile mail, vert. No. 1672, First flight cover, official missile mail. No. 1673, US #C76 tied to cover by moon landing cancel.

1976, June 18

No.	Design	Description	Unused	Used
1664	A292	1g multicolored	.25	.25
1665	A292	2g multicolored	.35	.25
1666	A292	3g multicolored	.40	.25
1667	A292	4g multicolored	.50	.25
1668	A292	5g multicolored	.65	.25

1669 A292 10g multicolored .85 .50
1670 A292 15g multicolored 1.60 .70
1671 A292 20g multicolored 2.50 1.00
Nos. 1664-1671 (8) 7.10 3.45

Souvenir Sheets

Perf. 14½

1672 A292 25g multicolored 15.00 15.00
1673 A292 25g multicolored 15.00 15.00

Nos. 1669-1673 are airmail and each contain one 50x40mm stamp.

Mythological Characters — A293

Details from paintings, artists: No. 1674a, 1g, Jupiter, Ingres. b, 2g, Saturn, Rubens. c, 3g, Neptune, Tiepolo. d, 4g, Uranus and Aphrodite, Medina, horiz. e, 5g, Pluto and Prosperpine, Giordano, horiz. f, 10g, Venus, Ingres. g, 15g, Mercury, de la Hyre. 20g, Mars and Venus, Veronese.

25g, Viking Orbiter descending to Mars, horiz.

1976, July 18 ***Perf. 14***

1674 A293 Strip of 7, #a.-g. 4.50 3.00
1675 A293 20g multicolored 2.50 1.50
Nos. 1674-1675 (2) 7.00 4.50

Souvenir Sheet

Perf. 14½

1676 A293 25g multicolored 40.00 40.00

Nos. 1674f-1674g, 1675-1676 are airmail.

Sailing Ships — A294

Paintings: No. 1677a, 1g, Venice frigate of the Spanish Armada, vert. b, 2g, Swedish war ship, Vasa, 1628, vert. c, 3g, Spanish galleon being attacked by pirates by Puget. d, 4g, Combat by Dawson. e, 5g, European boat in Japan, vert. f, 10g, Elizabeth Grange in Liverpool by Walters. g, 15g, Prussen, 1903, by Holst. 20g, Grand Duchess Elizabeth, 1902, by Bohrdt.

1976, July 15 ***Perf. 14***

1677 A294 Strip of 7, #a.-g. 4.00 2.50
1678 A294 20g multicolored 2.00 .50
Nos. 1677-1678 (2) 6.00 3.00

Nos. 1677f-1678 are airmail.

German Sailing Ships — A295

Ship, artist: 1g, Bunte Kuh, 1402, Zeeden. 2g, Arms of Hamburg, 1667, Wichman, vert. 3g, Kaiser Leopold, 1667, Wichman, vert. 4g, Deutschland, 1848, Pollack, vert. 5g, Humboldt, 1851, Fedeler. 10g, Borussia, 1855, Seitz. 15g, Gorch Fock, 1958, Stroh, vert. 20g, Grand Duchess Elizabeth, 1902, Bohrdt. 25g, SS Pamir, Zeytline, vert.

Unwmk.

1976, Aug. 20 **Litho.** ***Perf. 14***

1685 A295 1g multicolored .35 .25
1686 A295 2g multicolored .50 .25
1687 A295 3g multicolored .65 .25
1688 A295 4g multicolored .80 .25
1689 A295 5g multicolored .90 .30
1690 A295 10g multicolored 1.00 .45
1691 A295 15g multicolored 1.75 .80
1692 A295 20g multicolored 2.25 1.00
Nos. 1685-1692 (8) 8.20 3.55

Souvenir Sheet

Perf. 14½

1693 A295 25g multicolored 14.00 14.00

Intl. German Naval Exposition, Hamburg; NORDPOSTA '76 (No. 1693). Nos. 1690-1693 are airmail.

US Bicentennial — A296

Western Paintings by: No. 1694a, 1g, E. C. Ward. b, 2g, William Robinson Leigh. c, 3g, A. J. Miller. d, 4g, Charles Russell. e, 5g, Frederic Remington. f, 10g, Remington, horiz. g, 15g, Carl Bodmer.

No. 1695, A. J. Miller. No. 1696, US #1, 2, 245, C76.

Unwmk.

1976, Sept. 9 **Litho.** ***Perf. 14***

1694 A296 Strip of 7, #a.-g. 5.25 2.00
1695 A296 20g multicolored 2.75 1.00
Nos. 1694-1695 (2) 8.00 3.00

Souvenir Sheet

Perf. 13x13½

1696 A296 25g multicolored 40.00 40.00

Nos. 1694f-1694g, 1695-1696 are airmail. No. 1696 contains one 65x55mm stamp.

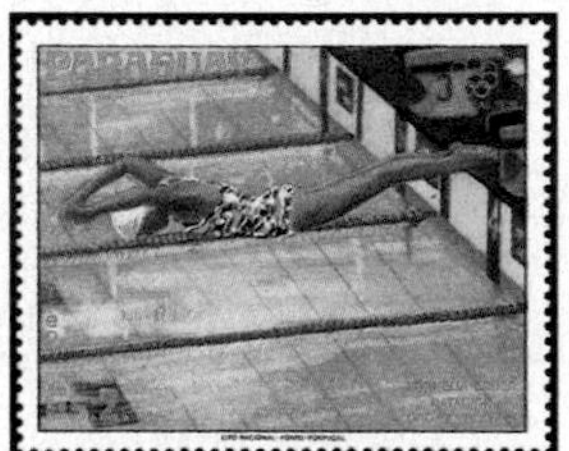

1976 Summer Olympics, Montreal — A297

Gold Medal Winners: No. 1703a, 1g, Nadia Comaneci, Romania, gymnastics, vert. b, 2g, Kornelia Ender, East Germany, swimming. c, 3g, Luann Ryan, US, archery, vert. d, 4g, Jennifer Chandler, US, diving. e, 5g, Shirley Babashoff, US, swimming. f, 10g, Christine Stuckelberger, Switzerland, equestrian. g, 15g, Japan, volleyball, vert.

20g, Annegret Richter, W. Germany, running, vert. No. 1705, Bruce Jenner, US, decathlon. No. 1706, Alwin Schockemohle, equestrian. No. 1707, Medals list, vert.

Unwmk.

1976, Dec. 18 **Litho.** ***Perf. 14***

1703 A297 Strip of 7, #a.-g. 5.00 2.00
1704 A297 20g multicolored 2.00 .75
Nos. 1703-1704 (2) 7.00 2.75

Souvenir Sheets

Perf. 14½

1705 A297 25g multicolored 25.00 25.00
1706 A297 25g multicolored 25.00 25.00
1707 A297 25g multicolored 25.00 25.00

Nos. 1703f-1703g, 1705-1707 are airmail. Nos. 1705-1706 each contain one 50x40mm stamp. No. 1707 contains one 50x70mm stamp.

Titian, 500th Birth Anniv. A298

Details from paintings: No. 1708a, 1g, Venus and Adonis. b, 2g, Diana and Callisto. c, 3g, Perseus and Andromeda. d, 4g, Venus of the Mirror. e, 5g, Venus Sleeping, horiz. f, 10g, Bacchanal, horiz. g, 15g, Venus, Cupid and the Lute Player, horiz. 20g, Venus and the Organist, horiz.

1976, Dec. 18 ***Perf. 14***

1708 A298 Strip of 7, #a.-g. 6.00 2.50
1709 A298 20g multicolored 2.00 1.00
Nos. 1708-1709 (2) 8.00 3.50

No. 1708f-1708g, 1709 are airmail.

Peter Paul Rubens, 400th Birth Anniv. A299

Paintings: No. 1710a, 1g, Adam and Eve. b, 2g, Tiger and Lion Hunt. c, 3g, Bathsheba Receiving David's Letter. d, 4g, Susanna in the Bath. e, 5g, Perseus and Andromeda. f, 10g, Andromeda Chained to the Rock. g, 15g, Shivering Venus. 20g, St. George Slaying the Dragon. 25g, Birth of the Milky Way, horiz.

1977, Feb. 18

1710 A299 Strip of 7, #a.-g. 5.50 2.00
1711 A299 20g multicolored 2.50 1.00
Nos. 1710-1711 (2) 8.00 3.00

Souvenir Sheet

Perf. 14½

1712 A299 25g multicolored 30.00 30.00

Nos. 1710f-1710g, 1711-1712 are airmail.

US, Bicent. — A300

Space exploration: No. 1713a, 1g, John Glenn, Mercury 7. b, 2g, Pres. Kennedy, Apollo 11. c, 3g, Wernher von Braun, Apollo 17. d, 4g, Mercury, Venus, Mariner 10. e, 5g, Jupiter, Saturn, Jupiter 10/11. f, 10g, Viking, Mars. g, 15g, Viking A on Mars. 20g, Viking B on Mars. No. 1715, Future space projects on Mars, vert. No. 1716, Future land rover on Mars.

1976, Mar. 3 ***Perf. 14***

1713 A300 Strip of 7, #a.-g. 4.00 2.00
1714 A300 20g multicolored 2.00 1.20
Nos. 1713-1714 (2) 6.00 3.20

Souvenir Sheets

Perf. 13½

1715 A300 25g multicolored 25.00 25.00
1716 A300 25g multicolored 20.00 20.00

Nos. 1713f-1713g, 1714-1716 are airmail. No. 1715 contains one 50x60mm stamp, No. 1716 one 60x50mm stamp.

Olympic History A301

Designs: 1g, Spiridon Louis, marathon 1896, Athens, Pierre de Coubertin. 2g, Giuseppe Delfino, fencing 1960, Rome, Pope John XXIII. 3g, Jean Claude Killy, skiing 1968, Grenoble, Charles de Gaulle. 4g, Ricardo Delgado, boxing 1968, Mexico City, G. Diaz Ordaz. 5g, Hayata, gymnastics 1964, Tokyo, Emperor Hirohito. 10g, Klaus Wolfermann, javelin 1972, Munich, Avery Brundage. 15g, Michel Vaillancourt, equestrian 1976, Montreal, Queen Elizabeth II. 20g, Franz Klammer, skiing 1976, Innsbruck, Austrian national arms.

25g, Emblems of 1896 Athens games and 1976 Montreal games.

1977, June 7 ***Perf. 14***

1717 A301 1g multicolored .25 .25
1718 A301 2g multicolored .25 .25
1719 A301 3g multicolored .40 .25
1720 A301 4g multicolored .60 .25
1721 A301 5g multicolored .80 .40
1722 A301 10g multicolored 1.00 .50
1723 A301 15g multicolored 1.20 .50
1724 A301 20g multicolored 2.00 1.00
Nos. 1717-1724 (8) 6.50 3.40

Souvenir Sheet

Perf. 13½

1725 A301 25g multicolored 22.50 15.00

Nos. 1722-1725 are airmail. No. 1725 contains one 49x60mm stamp.

LUPOSTA '77, Intl. Stamp Exibition, Berlin A302

Graf Zeppelin 1st South America flight and: 1g, German girls in traditional costumes. 2g, Bull fighter, Seville. 3g, Dancer, Rio de Janeiro. 4g, Gaucho breaking bronco, Uruguay. 5g, Like #1530b. 10g, Argentinian gaucho. 15g, Ceremonial indian costume, Bolivia. 20g, Indian on horse, US.

No. 1734, Zeppelin over sailing ship. No. 1735, Ferdinand Von Zeppelin, zeppelin over Berlin, horiz.

1977, June 9 ***Perf. 14***

1726 A302 1g multicolored .25 .25
1727 A302 2g multicolored .25 .25
1728 A302 3g multicolored .30 .25
1729 A302 4g multicolored .50 .25
1730 A302 5g multicolored .65 .30
1731 A302 10g multicolored .80 .40
1732 A302 15g multicolored 1.00 .45
1733 A302 20g multicolored 1.60 .75
Nos. 1726-1733 (8) 5.35 2.90

Souvenir Sheets

Perf. 13½

1734 A302 25g multicolored 50.00 50.00
1735 A302 25g multicolored 20.00 20.00

#1731-1735 are airmail. #1734 contains one 49x60mm stamp, #1735 one 60x49mm stamp.

Mburucuya Flowers A303

Weaver with Spider Web Lace — A304

Designs: 1g, Ostrich feather panel. 2g, Black palms. 20g, Rose tabebuia. 25g, Woman holding ceramic pot.

Perf. 13x13½

1977 Litho. Wmk. 347

1736	A304	1g multicolored	2.00	1.50
1737	A303	2g multicolored	2.00	1.50
1738	A303	3g multicolored	2.00	1.50
1739	A304	5g multicolored	2.00	1.50
1740	A303	20g multicolored	3.00	2.00
1741	A304	25g multicolored	3.00	2.50
		Nos. 1736-1741 (6)	14.00	10.50

Issued: 2g, 3g, 20g, 4/25; 1g, 5g, 25g, 6/27.
Nos. 1740-1741 are airmail.

Aviation History — A305

Designs: No. 1742a, 1g, Orville and Wilbur Wright, Wright Flyer, 1903. b, 2g, Alberto Santos-Dumont, Canard, 1906. c, 3g, Louis Bleriot, Bleriot 11, 1909. d, 4g, Otto Lilienthal, Glider, 1891. e, 5g, Igor Sikorsky, Avion le Grande, 1913. f, 10g, Juan de la Cierva, Autogiro. g, 15g, Silvio Pettirossi, Deperdussin acrobatic plane. No. 1743, Concorde jet. No. 1744, Lindbergh, Spirit of St. Louis, Statue of Liberty, Eiffel Tower. No. 1745, Design of flying machine by da Vinci.

1977, July 18 Unwmk. *Perf. 14*

1742	A305	Strip of 7, #a.-g.	5.00	2.25
1743	A305	20g multicolored	2.50	1.25
		Nos. 1742-1743 (2)	7.50	3.50

Souvenir Sheet

Perf. 14½

1744	A305	25g multicolored	25.00	25.00
1745	A305	25g multicolored	27.50	27.50

Nos. 1742f-1745 are airmail. No. 1745 contains one label.

Francisco Solano Lopez — A306

Perf. 13x13½

1977, July 24 Litho. Wmk. 347

1752	A306	10g brown	1.50	*2.00*
1753	A306	50g dk vio	3.00	1.50
1754	A306	100g green	5.00	3.00
		Nos. 1752-1754 (3)	9.50	6.50

Marshal Francisco Solano Lopez (1827-1870), President of Paraguay.
Nos. 1753-1754 are airmail.

Paintings — A307

Paintings by: No. 1755a, 1g, Gabrielle Rainer Istvanffy. b, 2g, L. C. Hoffmeister. c, 3g, Frans Floris. d, 4g, Gerard de Lairesse. e, 5g, David Teniers I. f, 10g, Jacopo Zucchi. g, 15g, Pierre Paul Prudhon. 20g, Francois Boucher. 25g, Ingres. 5g-25g vert.

1977, July 25 *Perf. 14*

1755	A307	Strip of 7, #a.-g.	3.75	1.25
1756	A307	20g multicolored	1.25	.50
		Nos. 1755-1756 (2)	5.00	1.75

Souvenir Sheet

Perf. 14½

1757	A307	25g multicolored	15.00	15.00

Nos. 1755f-1757 are airmail.

German Sailing Ships — A308

Designs: No. 1764a, 1g, De Beurs van Amsterdam. b, 2g, Katharina von Blankenese. c, 3g, Cuxhaven. d, 4g, Rhein. e, 5g, Churprinz and Marian. f, 10g, Bark of Bremen, vert. g, 15g, Elbe II, vert. 20g, Karacke. 25g, Admiral Karpeanger.

Unwmk.

1977, Aug. 27 Litho. *Perf. 14*

1764	A308	Strip of 7, #a.-g.	4.75	2.00
1765	A308	20g multicolored	2.25	1.25
		Nos. 1764-1765 (2)	7.00	3.25

Souvenir Sheet

Perf. 13½

1766	A308	25g multicolored	12.00	12.00

Nos. 1764f-1766 are airmail. No. 1766 contains one 40x30mm stamp.

Nobel Laureates for Literature — A309

Authors and scenes from books: No. 1773a, 1g, John Steinbeck, Grapes of Wrath, vert. b, 2g, Ernest Hemingway, Death in the Afternoon. c, 3g, Pearl S. Buck, The Good Earth, vert. d, 4g, George Bernard Shaw, Pygmalion, vert. e, 5g, Maurice Maeterlinck, Joan of Arc, vert. f, 10g, Rudyard Kipling, The Jungle Book. g, Henryk Sienkiewicz, Quo Vadis. 20g, C. Theodor Mommsen, History of Rome. 25g, Nobel prize medal.

1977, Sept. 5 *Perf. 14*

1773	A309	Strip of 7, #a.-g.	5.25	2.00
1774	A309	20g multicolored	2.75	1.25
		Nos. 1773-1774 (2)	8.00	3.25

Souvenir Sheet

Perf. 14½

1775	A309	25g multicolored	35.00	35.00

Nos. 1773f-1775 are airmail.

1978 World Cup Soccer Championships, Argentina — A310

Posters and World Cup Champions: No. 1782a, 1g, Uruguay, 1930. b, 2g, Italy, 1934. c, 3g, Italy, 1938. d, 4g, Uruguay, 1950. e, 5g, Germany, 1954. f, 10g, Soccer player by Fritz Genkinger. g, 15g, Soccer player, orange shirt by Genkinger.

No. 1783a, 1g, Brazil, 1958. b, 2g, Brazil, 1962. c, 3g, England, 1966. d, 4g, Brazil, 1970. e, 5g, Germany, 1974. f, 10g, Player #4 by Genkinger. g, 15g, Player #1 by Genkinger, horiz.

No. 1784, World Cup Trophy. No. 1785, German players, Argentina '78. No. 1786, The Loser, by Genkinger. No. 1787, The Defender, (player #11) by Genkinger.

1977, Oct. 28 Unwmk. *Perf. 14*

1782	A310	Strip of 7, #a.-g.	5.50	2.25
1783	A310	Strip of 7, #a.-g.	5.25	2.25
1784	A310	20g multicolored	1.60	.65
1785	A310	20g multicolored	1.60	.65
		Nos. 1782-1785 (4)	13.95	5.80

Souvenir Sheets

Perf. 14½

1786	A310	25g red & multi	30.00	30.00
1787	A310	25g black & multi	30.00	30.00

Nos. 1782f-1782g, 1783f-1783g, 1784-1787 are airmail.

Peter Paul Rubens, 400th Birth Anniv. A312

Details from paintings: No. 1788a, 1g, Rubens and Isabella Brant under Honeysuckle Bower. b, 2g, Judgment of Paris. c, 3g, Union of Earth and Water. d, 4g, Daughters of Kekrops Discovering Erichthonius. e, 5g, Holy Family with the Lamb. f, 10c, Adoration of the Magi. g, 15c, Philip II on Horseback.

20g, Education of Marie de Medici, horiz. 25g, Triumph of Eucharist Over False Gods.

1978, Jan. 19 Unwmk. *Perf. 14*

1788	A312	Strip of 7, #a.-g.	5.00	2.50
1789	A312	20g multicolored	2.75	1.40
		Nos. 1788-1789 (2)	7.75	3.90

Souvenir Sheet

Perf. 14½

1790	A312	25g multi, gold	12.00	12.00
1790A	A312	25g multi, silver	17.50	17.50

Nos. 1788f-1788g, 1789-1790 are airmail. No. 1790 contains one 50x70mm stamp and exists inscribed in gold or silver.

1978 World Chess Championships, Argentina — A313

Paintings of chess players: No. 1791a, 1g, De Cremone. b, 2g, L. van Leyden. c, 3g, H. Muehlich. d, 4g, Arabian artist. e, 5g, Benjamin Franklin playing chess, E. H. May. f, 10g, G. Cruikshank. g, 15g, 17th cent. tapestry. 20g, Napoleon playing chess on St. Helena. 25g, Illustration from chess book, Shah Name.

1978, Jan. 23 *Perf. 14*

1791	A313	Strip of 7, #a.-g.	20.00	7.50
1792	A313	20g multicolored	10.00	3.50
		Nos. 1791-1792 (2)	30.00	11.00

Souvenir Sheet

Perf. 14½

1793	A313	25g multicolored	40.00	40.00

Nos. 1791f-1791g, 1792-1793 are airmail. No. 1793 contains one 50x40mm stamp.

Jacob Jordaens, 300th Death Anniv. A314

Paintings: No. 1794a, 3g, Satyr and the Nymphs. b, 4g, Satyr with Peasant. c, 5g, Allegory of Fertility. d, 6g, Upbringing of Jupiter. e, 7g, Holy Family. f, 8g, Adoration of the Shepherds. g, 20g, Jordaens with his family. 10g, Meleagro with Atalanta, horiz. No. 1796, Feast for a King, horiz. No. 1797, Holy Family with Shepherds.

1978, Jan. 25 *Perf. 14*

1794	A314	Strip of 7, #a.-g.	8.50	2.75
1795	A314	10g multicolored	2.00	.75
1796	A314	25g multicolored	4.00	1.40
		Nos. 1794-1796 (3)	14.50	4.90

Souvenir Sheet

Perf. 14½

1797	A314	25g multicolored	14.00	14.00

Nos. 1795-1797 are airmail. No. 1797 contains one 50x70mm stamp.

Albrecht Durer, 450th Death Anniv. A315

Monograms and details from paintings: No. 1804a, 3g, Temptation of the Idler. b, 4g, Adam and Eve. c, 5g, Satyr Family. d, 6g, Eve. e, 7g, Adam. f, 8g, Portrait of a Young Man. g, 20g, Squirrels and Acorn. 10g, Madonna and Child. No. 1806, Brotherhood of the Rosary (Lute-playing Angel). No. 1807, Soldier on Horseback with a Lance.

1978, Mar. 10 *Perf. 14*

1804	A315	Strip of 7, #a.-g.	5.00	2.25
1805	A315	10g multicolored	1.60	.50
1806	A315	25g multicolored	3.25	1.20
		Nos. 1804-1806 (3)	9.85	3.95

Souvenir Sheet

Perf. 13½

1807	A315	25g blk, buff & sil	25.00	25.00

Nos. 1805-1807 are airmail. No. 1807 contains one 30x40mm stamp.

Francisco de Goya, 150th Death Anniv. A316

Paintings: No. 1814a, 3g, Allegory of the Town of Madrid. b, 4g, The Clothed Maja. c, 5g, The Parasol. d, 6g, Dona Isabel Cobos de Porcel. e, 7g, The Drinker. f, 8g, The 2nd of May 1908. g, 20g, General Jose Palafox on Horseback. 10g, Savages Murdering a Woman. 25g, The Naked Maja, horiz.

1978, May 11		*Perf. 14*	
1814 A316	Strip of 7, #a.-g.	5.00	1.60
1815 A316	10g multicolored	1.25	.40
1816 A316	25g multicolored	2.00	.80
	Nos. 1814-1816 (3)	8.25	2.80

Nos. 1815-1816 are airmail.

Future Space Projects — A317

Various futuristic space vehicles and imaginary creatures: No. 1816a, 3g. b, 4g. c, 5g. d, 6g. e, 7g. f, 8g. g, 20g.

1978, May 16			
1817 A317	Strip of 7, #a.-g.	4.50	2.25
1818 A317	10g multicolored	1.00	.50
1819 A317	25g multi, diff.	2.50	1.00
	Nos. 1817-1819 (3)	8.00	3.75

Nos. 1818-1819 are airmail.

Racing Cars — A318

No. 1820: a, 3g, Tyrell Formula I. b, 4g, Lotus Formula 1, 1978. c, 5g, McLaren Formula 1. d, 6g, Brabham Alfa Romeo Formula 1. e, 7g, Renault Turbo Formula 1. f, 8g, Wolf Formula 1. g, 20g, Porsche 935. 10g, Bugatti. 25g, Mercedes Benz W196, Stirling Moss, driver. No. 1823, Ferrari 312T.

1978, June 28		*Perf. 14*	
1820 A318	Strip of 7, #a.-g.	3.75	1.90
1821 A318	10g multicolored	.60	.25
1822 A318	25g multicolored	1.60	.80
	Nos. 1820-1822 (3)	5.95	2.95

Souvenir Sheet

Perf. 14½

1823 A318	25g multicolored	16.00	16.00

Nos. 1821-1823 are airmail. No. 1823 contains one 50x35mm stamp.

Paintings by Peter Paul Rubens A319

3g, Holy Family with a Basket. 4g, Amor Cutting a Bow. 5g, Adam & Eve in Paradise. 6g, Crown of Fruit, horiz. 7g, Kidnapping of Ganymede. 8g, The Hunting of Crocodile & Hippopotamus. 10g, The Reception of Marie de Medici at Marseilles. 20g, Two Satyrs. 25g, Felicity of the Regency.

1978, June 30		*Perf. 14*	
1824 A319	3g multicolored	.30	.25
1825 A319	4g multicolored	.50	.25
1826 A319	5g multicolored	.65	.25
1827 A319	6g multicolored	.70	.25
1828 A319	7g multicolored	.85	.30
1829 A319	8g multicolored	1.00	.40
1830 A319	10g multicolored	2.40	.80
1831 A319	20g multicolored	3.50	1.10
1832 A319	25g multicolored	4.75	1.60
	Nos. 1824-1832 (9)	14.65	5.20

Nos. 1830, 1832 are airmail.

National College A320

Perf. 13½x13

1978	**Litho.**	**Wmk. 347**	
1833 A320	3g claret	2.00	2.00
1834 A320	4g violet blue	2.00	2.00
1835 A320	5g lilac	2.00	2.00
1836 A320	20g brown	2.00	2.00
1837 A320	25g violet black	3.00	2.00
1838 A320	30g bright green	3.00	2.00
	Nos. 1833-1838 (6)	14.00	12.00

Centenary of National College in Asuncion.
Nos. 1836-1838 are airmail.

José Estigarribia, Bugler, Flag of Paraguay A321

1978	**Litho.**	***Perf. 13x13½***	
1839 A321	3g multi	3.00	2.00
1840 A321	5g multi	3.00	2.00
1841 A321	10g multi	3.00	2.00
1842 A321	20g multi	5.00	3.00
1843 A321	25g multi	5.00	3.00
1844 A321	30g multi	5.00	3.00
	Nos. 1839-1844 (6)	24.00	15.00

Induction of Jose Felix Estigarribia (1888-1940), general and president of Paraguay, into Salon de Bronce (National Heroes' Hall of Fame).
Nos. 1842-1844 are airmail.

Queen Elizabeth II Coronation, 25th Anniv. A322

Flowers and: 3g, Barbados #234. 4g, Tristan da Cunha #13. 5g, Bahamas #157. 6g, Seychelles #172. 7g, Solomon Islands #88. 8g, Cayman Islands #150. 10g, New Hebrides #77. 20g, St. Lucia #156. 25g, St. Helena #139.
No. 1854, Solomon Islands #368a-368c, Gilbert Islands #312a-312c. No. 1855, Great Britain #313-316.

1978, July 25	**Unwmk.**	*Perf. 14*	
1845 A322	3g multicolored	.30	.25
1846 A322	4g multicolored	.50	.25
1847 A322	5g multicolored	.65	.25
1848 A322	6g multicolored	.70	.25
1849 A322	7g multicolored	.85	.30
1850 A322	8g multicolored	1.00	.40
1851 A322	10g multicolored	2.40	.80
1852 A322	20g multicolored	3.50	1.20
1853 A322	25g multicolored	4.75	1.60
	Nos. 1845-1853 (9)	14.65	5.30

Souvenir Sheets

Perf. 13½

1854 A322	25g multicolored	25.00	25.00
1855 A322	25g multicolored	25.00	25.00

Nos. 1851, 1853-1855 are airmail. Nos. 1854-1855 each contain one 60x40mm stamp.

Intl. Philatelic Exhibitions A323

Various paintings, ship, nudes, etc. for: No. 1856a, 3g, Nordposta '78. b, 4g, Riccione '78. c, 5g, Uruguay '79. d, 6g, ESSEN '78. e, 7g, ESPAMER '79. f, 8g, London '80. g, 20g, PRAGA '78. 10g, EUROPA '78. No. 1858, Eurphila '78.
No. 1859, Francisco de Pinedo, map of his flight.

1978, July 19		*Perf. 14*	
1856 A323	Strip of 7, #a.-g.	6.00	1.25
1857 A323	10g multicolored	1.40	.40
1858 A323	25g multicolored	2.10	.70
	Nos. 1856-1858 (3)	9.50	2.35

Souvenir Sheet

Perf. 13½x13

1859 A323	25g multicolored	25.00	25.00

No. 1859 for Riccione '78 and Eurphila '78 and contains one 54x34mm stamp. Nos. 1857-1859 are airmail. Nos. 1856b-1858 are vert.

Intl. Year of the Child A324

Grimm's Snow White and the Seven Dwarfs: No. 1866a, 3g, Queen pricking her finger. b, 4g, Queen and mirror. c, 5g, Man with dagger, Snow White. d, 6g, Snow White in forest. e, 7g, Snow White asleep, seven dwarfs. f, 8g, Snow White dancing with dwarfs. g, 20g, Snow White being offered apple. 10g, Snow White in repose. 25g, Snow White, Prince Charming on horseback.

1978, Oct. 26			
1866 A324	Strip of 7, #a.-g.	4.50	2.25
1867 A324	10g multicolored	1.00	.50
1868 A324	25g multicolored	2.40	1.00
	Nos. 1866-1868 (3)	7.90	3.75

Nos. 1867-1868 are airmail.
See Nos. 1893-1896, 1916-1919.

Mounted South American Soldiers A325

No. 1869a, 3g, Gen. Jose Felix Bogado (1771-1829). b, 4g, Colonel, First Volunteer Regiment, 1806. c, 5g, Colonel wearing dress uniform, 1860. d, 6g, Soldier, 1864-1870. e, 7g, Dragoon, 1865. f, 8g, Lancer. g, 20g, Soldier, 1865. 10g, Gen. Bernardo O'Higgins, 200th birth anniv. 25g, Jose de San Martin, 200th birth anniv.

1978, Oct. 31			
1869 A325	Strip of 7, #a.-g.	4.25	1.75
1870 A325	10g multicolored	.70	.25
1871 A325	25g multicolored	2.00	.45
	Nos. 1869-1871 (3)	6.95	2.45

Nos. 1870-1871 are airmail.

1978 World Cup Soccer Championships, Argentina — A326

Soccer Players: No. 1872a, 3g, Paraguay, vert. b, 4g, Austria, Sweden. c, 5g, Argentina, Poland. d, 6g, Italy, Brazil. e, 7g, Netherlands, Austria. f, 8g, Scotland, Peru. g, 20g, Germany, Italy. 10g, Argentina, Holland. 25g, Germany, Tunisia.
No. 1875, Stadium.

1979, Jan. 9		*Perf. 14*	
1872 A326	Strip of 7, #a.-g.	5.00	2.00
1873 A326	10g multicolored	.70	.25
1874 A326	25g multicolored	2.00	.50
	Nos. 1872-1874 (3)	7.70	2.75

Souvenir Sheet

Perf. 13½

1875 A326	25g multicolored	40.00	40.00

Nos. 1873-1875 are airmail. No. 1875 contains one 60x40mm stamp.
For overprint see No. C610.

Christmas A327

Paintings of the Nativity and Madonna and Child by: No. 1876a, 3g, Giorgione, horiz. b, 4g, Titian. c, 5g, Titian, diff. d, 6g, Raphael. e, 7g, Schongauer. f, 8g, Muratti. g, 20g, Van Oost. 10g, Memling. No. 1878, Rubens.
No. 1879, Madonna and Child Surrounded by a Garland and Boy Angels, Rubens.

1979, Jan. 10	**Litho.**	*Perf. 14*	
1876 A327	Strip of 7, #a.-g.	3.50	1.40
1877 A327	10g multicolored	.70	.25
1878 A327	25g multicolored	1.40	.50
	Nos. 1876-1878 (3)	5.60	2.15

Souvenir Sheet

Photo. & Engr.

Perf. 12

1879 A327	25g multicolored	60.00	60.00

Nos. 1877-1879 are airmail.

First Powered Flight, 75th Anniv. (in 1978) — A328

Airplanes: No. 1880a, 3g, Eole, C. Ader, 1890. b, 4g, Flyer III, Wright Brothers. c, 5g, Voisin, Henri Farman, 1908. d, 6g, Curtiss, Eugene Ely, 1910. e, 7g, Etrich-Taube A11. f, 8g, Fokker EIII. g, 20g, Albatros C, 1915. 10g, Boeing 747 carrying space shuttle. No. 1882, Boeing 707. No. 1883, Zeppelin flight commemorative cancels.

1979, Apr. 24 Litho. *Perf. 14*

1880 A328 Strip of 7, #a.-g. 5.50 1.40
1881 A328 10g multicolored .85 .25
1882 A328 25g multicolored 2.00 .50
Nos. 1880-1882 (3) 8.35 2.15

Souvenir Sheet

Perf. 14½

1883 A328 25g blue & black 45.00 45.00

Nos. 1881-1883 are airmail. Nos. 1880-1883 incorrectly commemorate 75th anniv. of ICAO. No. 1883 contains one 50x40mm stamp.

Albrecht Durer, 450th Death Anniv. (in 1978) A329

Paintings: No. 1884a, 3g, Virgin with the Dove. b, 4g, Virgin Praying. c, 5g, Mater Dolorosa. d, 6g, Virgin with a Carnation. e, 7g, Madonna and Sleeping Child. f, 8g, Virgin Before the Archway. g, 20g, Flight Into Egypt. No. 1885, Madonna of the Haller family. No. 1886, Virgin with a Pear.

No. 1887, Lamentation Over the Dead Christ for Albrecht Glimm. No. 1888, Space station, horiz., with Northern Hemisphere of Celestial Globe in margin.

1979, Apr. 28 *Perf. 14*

1884 A329 Strip of 7, #a.-g. 3.75 2.00
1885 A329 10g multicolored .85 .50
1886 A329 25g multicolored 2.50 1.00
Nos. 1884-1886 (3) 7.10 3.50

Souvenir Sheets

Perf. 13½

1887 A329 25g multicolored 17.00 17.00
1888 A329 25g multicolored 25.00 25.00

Intl. Year of the Child (#1885-1886).

Nos. 1885-1886, 1888 are airmail. No. 1887 contains one 30x40mm stamp, No. 1888 one 40x30mm stamp.

Sir Rowland Hill, Death Cent. — A330

Hill and: No. 1889a, 3g, Newfoundland #C1, vert. b, 4g, France #C14. c, 5g, Spain #B106. d, 6g, Similar to Ecuador #C2, vert. e, 7g, US #C3a. f, 8g, Gelber Hund inverted overprint, vert. g, 20g, Switzerland #C20a.

10g, Privately issued Zeppelin stamp. No. 1891, Paraguay #C82, #C96, vert. No. 1892, Italy #C49. No. 1892A, France #C3-C4.

1979, June 11 *Perf. 14*

1889 A330 Strip of 7, #a.-g. 4.50 1.50
1890 A330 10g multicolored 1.20 .50
1891 A330 25g multicolored 3.50 1.20
Nos. 1889-1891 (3) 9.20 3.20

Souvenir Sheet

Perf. 13½x13

1892 A330 25g multicolored 25.00 25.00

Perf. 14½

1892A A330 25g multicolored 17.50 17.50

Issue dates: No. 1892A, Aug. 28. Others, June 11. Nos. 1890-1892A are airmail.

Grimm's Fairy Tales Type of 1978

Cinderella: No. 1893a, 3g, Two stepsisters watch Cinderella cleaning. b, 4g, Cinderella, father, stepsisters. c, 5g, Cinderella with birds while working. d, 6g, Finding dress. e, 7g, Going to ball. f, 8g, Dancing with prince. g, 20g, Losing slipper leaving ball.

10g, Prince Charming trying slipper on Cinderella's foot. No. 1895, Couple riding to castle. No. 1896, Couple entering ballroom.

1979, June 24 *Perf. 14*

1893 A324 Strip of 7, #a.-g. 4.25 2.25
1894 A324 10g multicolored 1.00 .55
1895 A324 25g multicolored 2.75 1.20
Nos. 1893-1895 (3) 8.00 4.00

Souvenir Sheet

Perf. 13½

1896 A324 25g multicolored 15.00 15.00

Intl. Year of the Child.

Congress Emblem A331

1979, Aug. Litho. *Perf. 13x13½*

1897 A331 10g red, blue & black 5.00 2.00
1898 A331 50g red, blue & black 5.00 2.00

22nd Latin-American Tourism Congress, Asuncion. No. 1898 is airmail.

1980 Winter Olympics, Lake Placid — A332

#1899: a, 3g, Monica Scheftschik, luge. b, 4g, E. Deufl, Austria, downhill skiing. c, 5g, G. Thoeni, Italy, slalom skiing. d, 6g, Canada Two-man bobsled. e, 7g, Germany vs. Finland, ice hockey. f, 8g, Hoenl, Russia, ski jump. g, 20g, Dianne De Leeuw, Netherlands, figure skating, vert.

10g, Hanni Wenzel, Liechtenstein, slalom skiing. No. 1901, Frommelt, Liechtenstein, slalom skiing, vert. No. 1902, Kulakova, Russia, cross country skier. No. 1903, Dorothy Hamill, US, figure skating, vert. No. 1904, Brigitte Totschnig, skier.

1979 Unwmk. *Perf. 14*

1899 A332 Strip of 7, #a.-g. 4.25 2.25
1900 A332 10g multicolored 1.00 .55
1901 A332 25g multicolored 2.75 1.20
Nos. 1899-1901 (3) 8.00 4.00

Souvenir Sheets

Perf. 13½

1902 A332 25g multicolored 17.50 17.50
1903 A332 25g multicolored 17.50 17.50
1904 A332 25g multicolored 45.00 45.00

#1900-1904 are airmail. #1902-1903 each contain one 40x30mm stamp, #1904, one 25x36mm stamp.

Issued: #1899-1902, 8/22; #1903, 6/11; #1904, 4/24.

Sailing Ships — A333

No. 1905: a, 3g, Caravel, vert. b, 4g, Warship. c, 5g, Warship, by Jan van Beeck. d, 6g, H.M.S. Britannia, vert. e, 7g, Salamis, vert. f, 8g, Ariel, vert. g, 20g, Warship, by Robert Salmon.

1979, Aug. 28 *Perf. 14*

1905 A333 Strip of 7, #a.-g. 4.50 2.00
1906 A333 10g Lisette .70 .25
1907 A333 25g Holstein, vert. 2.00 .50
Nos. 1905-1907 (3) 7.20 2.75

Nos. 1906-1907 are airmail.

Intl. Year of the Child A334

Various kittens: No. 1908a, 3g. b, 4g. c, 5g. d, 6g. e, 7g. f, 8g. g, 20g.

1979, Nov. 29 *Perf. 14*

1908 A334 Strip of 7, #a.-g. 4.75 1.25
1909 A334 10g multicolored 1.90 .25
1910 A334 25g multicolored 1.60 .45
Nos. 1908-1910 (3) 8.25 1.95

Nos. 1909-1910 are airmail.

Grimm's Fairy Tales Type of 1978

Little Red Riding Hood: No. 1916a, 3g, Leaving with basket. b, 4g, Meets wolf. c, 5g, Picks flowers. d, 6g, Wolf puts on Granny's gown. e, 7g, Wolf in bed. f, 8g, Hunter arrives. g, 20g, Saved by the hunter.

10g, Hunter enters house. No. 1918, Hunter leaves. No. 1919, Overall scene.

1979, Dec. 4 *Perf. 14*

1916 A324 Strip of 7, #a.-g. 4.25 2.25
1917 A324 10g multicolored 1.00 .55
1918 A324 25g multicolored 2.75 1.20
Nos. 1916-1918 (3) 8.00 4.00

Souvenir Sheet

Perf. 14½

1919 A324 25g multicolored 20.00 20.00

Intl. Year of the Child. No. 1919 contains one 50x70mm stamp.

Greek Athletes A335

Paintings on Greek vases: No. 1926a, 3g, 3 runners. b, 4g, 2 runners. c, 5g, Throwing contest. d, 6g, Discus. e, 7g, Wrestlers. f, 8g, Wrestlers, diff. g, 20g, 2 runners, diff.

10g, Horse and rider, horiz. 25g, 4 warriors with shields, horiz.

1979, Dec. 20 *Perf. 14*

1926 A335 Strip of 7, #a.-g. 4.00 1.60
1927 A335 10g multicolored .65 .25
1928 A335 25g multicolored 1.60 .55
Nos. 1926-1928 (3) 6.25 2.40

Nos. 1927-1928 are airmail.

Electric Trains — A336

No. 1929: a, 3g, First electric locomotive, Siemens, 1879, vert. b, 4g, Switzerland, 1897. c, 5g, Model E71 28, Germany. d, 6g, Mountain train, Switzerland. e, 7g, Electric locomotive used in Benelux countries. f, 8g, Locomotive "Rheinpfeil," Germany. g, 20g, Model BB-9004, France.

10g, 200-Km/hour train, Germany. 25g, Japanese bullet train.

1979, Dec. 24 Litho. *Perf. 14*

1929 A336 Strip of 7, #a.-g. 5.00 2.00
1930 A336 10g multicolored 3.00 1.10
1931 A336 25g multicolored 3.00 1.10
Nos. 1929-1931 (3) 11.00 4.20

Nos. 1930-1931 are airmail.

Sir Rowland Hill, Death Cent. — A337

Hill and: No. 1938a, 3g, Spad S XIII, 1917-18. b, 4g, P-51 D Mustang, 1944-45. c, 5g, Mitsubishi A6M6c Zero-Sen, 1944. d, 6g, Deperdussin float plane, 1913. e, 7g, Savoia Marchetti SM 7911, 1936. f, 8g, Messerschmitt Me 262B, 1942-45. g, 20g, Nieuport 24bis, 1917-18.

10g, Zeppelin LZ 104-/l59, 1917. No. 1940, Fokker Dr-1 Caza, 1917. No. 1941, Vickers Supermarine "Spitfire" Mk.IX, 1942-45.

1980, Apr. 8 *Perf. 14*

1938 A337 Strip of 7, #a.-g. 5.00 2.00
1939 A337 10g multicolored .90 .55
1940 A337 25g multicolored 3.00 1.10
Nos. 1938-1940 (3) 8.90 3.65

Souvenir Sheet

Perf. 13½

1941 A337 25g multicolored 20.00 20.00

Incorrectly commemorates 75th anniv. of ICAO. Nos. 1939-1941 are airmail. No. 1941 contains one 37x27mm stamp.

Sir Rowland Hill, Paraguayan Stamps — A338

Hill and: No. 1948a, 3g, #1. b, 4g, #5. c, 5g, #6. d, 6g, #379. e, 7g, #381. f, 8g, #C384. g, 20g, #C389.

10g, #C83, horiz. No. 1950, #C92, horiz. No. 1951, #C54, horiz. No. 1952, #C1, horiz.

1980, Apr. 14 Litho. *Perf. 14*

1948 A338 Strip of 7, #a.-g. 5.25 2.50
1949 A338 10g multicolored 1.10 .60
1950 A338 25g multicolored 3.50 1.40
Nos. 1948-1950 (3) 9.85 4.50

Souvenir Sheets

Perf. 14½

1951 A338 25g multicolored 25.00 22.50
1952 A338 25g multicolored 25.00 22.50

#1949-1952 are airmail. #1951 contains one 50x40mm stamp. #1952 one 50x35mm stamp.

1980 Winter Olympics, Lake Placid
A339

No. 1953: a, 3g, Thomas Wassberg, Sweden, cross country skiing. b, 4g, Scharer & Benz, Switzerland, 2-man bobsled. c, 5g, Annemarie Moser-Proll, Austria, women's downhill skiing. d, 6g, Hockey team, US. e, 7g, Leonhard Stock, Austria, men's downhill skiing. f, 8g, Anton (Toni) Innauer, Austria, ski jump. g, 20g, Christa Kinshofer, Germany, slalom skiing.

10g, Ingemar Stenmark, slalom, Sweden. No. 1955, Robin Cousins, figure skating, Great Britain. No. 1956, Eric Heiden, speed skating, US, horiz.

1980, June 4 ***Perf. 14***

1953	A339	Strip of 7, #a.-g.	5.25	3.00
1954	A339	10g multi, horiz.	1.10	.60
1955	A339	25g multi, horiz.	3.50	1.40
		Nos. 1953-1955 (3)	9.85	5.00

Souvenir Sheet

Perf. 13½

1956	A339	25g multicolored	17.50	17.50

Nos. 1954-1956 are airmail. No. 1956 contains one 60x49mm stamp.

Composers and Paintings of Young Ballerinas
A340

Paintings of ballerinas by Cydney or Degas and: No. 1957a, 3g, Gioacchino Rossini. b, 4g, Johann Strauss, the younger. c, 5g, Debussy. d, 6g, Beethoven. e, 7g, Chopin. f, 8g, Richard Wagner. g, 20g, Johann Sebastian Bach, horiz. 10g, Robert Stoltz. 25g, Verdi.

1980, July 1 ***Perf. 14***

1957	A340	Strip of 7, #a.-g.	4.75	2.50
1958	A340	10g multicolored	1.10	.60
1959	A340	25g multicolored	3.25	1.40
		Nos. 1957-1959 (3)	9.10	4.50

Birth and death dates are incorrectly inscribed on 4g, 8g, 10g. No. 1957f is incorrectly inscribed "Adolph" Wagner. Nos. 1958-1959 are airmail. For overprints see Nos. 1998-1999.

Pilar City Bicentennial — A341

Perf. 13½x13

1980, July 17 Litho. Wmk. 347

1966	A341	5g multi	5.00	2.00
1967	A341	25g multi	5.00	2.00

No. 1967 is airmail.

Christmas, Intl. Year of the Child
A342

No. 1968: a, 3g, Christmas tree. b, 4g, Santa filling stockings. c, 5g, Nativity scene. d, 6g, Adoration of the Magi. e, 7g, Three children, presents. f, 8g, Children, dove, fruit. g, 20g, Children playing with toys. 10g, Madonna and Child, horiz. No. 1970, Children blowing bubbles, horiz. No. 1971, Five children, horiz.

1980, Aug. 4 Unwmk. ***Perf. 14***

1968	A342	Strip of 7, #a.-g.	4.25	2.00
1969	A342	10g multicolored	.65	.25
1970	A342	25g multicolored	1.20	.55
		Nos. 1968-1970 (3)	6.10	2.80

Souvenir Sheet

1971	A342	25g multicolored	17.50	17.50

Nos. 1969-1970 are airmail.

Ships
A343

Emblems and ships: No. 1972a, 3g, ESPAMER '80, Spanish Armada. b, 4g, NORWEX '80, Viking longboat. c, 5g, RICCIONE '80, Battle of Lepanto. d, 6g, ESSEN '80, Great Harry of Cruickshank. e, 7g, US Bicentennial, Mount Vernon. f, 8g, LONDON '80, H.M.S. Victory. g, 20g, ESSEN '80, Hamburg III, vert. 10g, ESSEN '80, Gorch Fock. 25g, PHILATOKYO '81, Nippon Maru, horiz.

1980, Sept. 15 ***Perf. 14***

1972	A343	Strip of 7, #a.-g.	4.75	2.25
1973	A343	10g multicolored	1.20	.55
1974	A343	25g multicolored	3.25	1.40
		Nos. 1972-1974 (3)	9.20	4.20

Nos. 1973-1974 are airmail. For overprint see No. 2278.

Souvenir Sheet

King Juan Carlos — A344

1980, Sept. 19 ***Perf. 14½***

1975	A344	25g multicolored	15.00	15.00

Paraguay Airlines Boeing 707 Service Inauguration — A345

Perf. 13½x13

1980, Sept. 17 Litho. Wmk. 347

1976	A345	20g multi	2.50	1.50
1977	A345	100g multi	2.50	1.50

No. 1977 is airmail.

A346

World Cup Soccer Championships, Spain — A346a

Various soccer players, winning country: No. 1978a, 3g, Uruguay 1930, 1950. b, 4g, Italy 1934, 1938. c, 5g, Germany 1954, 1974. d, 6g, Brazil 1958, 1962, 1970. e, 7g, England, 1966. f, 8g, Argentina, 1978. g, 20g, Espana '82 emblem.

10g, World Cup trophy, flags. 25g, Soccer player from Uruguay.

1980, Dec. 10 Unwmk. ***Perf. 14***

1978	A346	Strip of 7, #a.-g.	5.25	1.75
1979	A346	10g multicolored	1.60	.50
1980	A346	25g multicolored	5.25	1.75
		Nos. 1978-1980 (3)	12.10	4.00

Souvenir Sheet

Perf. 14½

1981	A346a	25g Sheet of 1 + 2 labels	19.00	19.00

Nos. 1979-1981 are airmail.

1980 World Chess Championships, Mexico — A347

Illustrations from The Book of Chess: No. 1982a, 3g, Two men, chess board. b, 4g, Circular chess board, players. c, 5g, Four-person chess match. d, 6g, King Alfonso X of Castile and Leon. e, 7g, Two players, chess board, horiz. f, 8g, Two veiled women, chess board, horiz. g, 20g, Two women in robes, chess board, horiz.

10g, Crusader knights, chess board, horiz. 25g, Three players, chess board, horiz.

1980, Dec. 15 Litho. ***Perf. 14***

1982	A347	Strip of 7, #a.-g.	9.50	2.50
1983	A347	10g multicolored	1.75	.35
1984	A347	25g multicolored	2.10	.70
		Nos. 1982-1984 (3)	13.35	3.55

Nos. 1983-1984 are airmail.

See Nos. C506-C510. Compare with illustration AP199.

1980 Winter Olympics, Lake Placid
A348

Olympic scenes, gold medalists: No. 1985a, 25c, Lighting Olympic flame. b, 50c, Hockey team, US. c, 1g, Eric Heiden, US, speed skating. d, 2g, Robin Cousins, Great Britain, figure skating. e, 3g, Thomas Wassberg, Sweden, cross country skiing. f, 4g, Annie Borckinck, Netherlands, speed skating. g, 5g, Gold, silver, and bronze medals.

No. 1986, Irene Epple, silver medal, slalom, Germany. 10g, Ingemar Stenmark, slalom, giant slalom, Sweden. 30g, Annemarie Moser-Proll, downhill, Austria. 25g, Baron Pierre de Coubertin.

1981, Feb. 4 Litho. ***Perf. 14***

1985	A348	Strip of 7, #a.-g.	3.00	1.90
1986	A348	5g multicolored	.80	.35
1987	A348	10g multicolored	1.10	.50
1988	A348	30g multicolored	2.40	1.00
		Nos. 1985-1988 (4)	7.30	3.75

Souvenir Sheet

Perf. 13½

1988A	A348	25g multicolored	16.00	16.00

No. 1985 exists in strips of 4 and 3. Nos. 1986-1988A are airmail. No. 1988A contains one 30x40mm stamp.

Locomotives — A349

No. 1989, 25c, Electric model 242, Germany. b, 50c, Electric, London-Midlands-Lancashire, England. c, 1g, Electric, Switzerland. d, 2g, Diesel-electric, Montreal-Vancouver, Canada. e, 3g, Electric, Austria. f, 4g, Electric inter-urban, Lyons-St. Etienne, France, vert. g, 5g, First steam locomotive in Paraguay.

No. 1991, Steam locomotive, Japan. 10g, Stephenson's steam engine, 1830 England. No. 1993, Crocodile locomotive, Switzerland. 30g, Stephenson's Rocket, 1829, England, vert.

1981, Feb. 9 Litho. ***Perf. 14***

1989	A349	Strip of 7, #a.-g.	2.10	1.10
1990	A349	5g multicolored	1.00	.35
1991	A349	10g multicolored	1.75	.65
1992	A349	30g multicolored	5.50	2.00
		Nos. 1989-1992 (4)	10.35	4.10

Souvenir Sheet

Perf. 13½x13

1993	A349	25g multicolored	25.00	25.00

Electric railroads, cent. (#1989a-1989f), steam-powered railway service, 150th anniv. (#1989g, 1990-1991), Liverpool-Manchester Railway, 150th anniv. (#1992). Swiss Railways, 75th anniv. (#1993).

Nos. 1990-1993 are airmail. No. 1993 contains one 54x34mm stamp.

Intl. Year of the Child
A350

Portraits of children with assorted flowers: No. 1994a, 10g. b, 25g. c, 50g. d, 100g. e, 200g. f, 300g. g, 400g.

1981, Apr. 13 Litho. *Perf. 14*

1994 A350 Strip of 7, #a.-g. 16.00 8.25
1995 A350 75g multicolored 1.50 .70
1996 A350 500g multicolored 8.00 4.00
1997 A350 1000g multicolored 16.00 8.00
Nos. 1994-1997 (4) 41.50 20.95

Nos. 1995-1997 are airmail.

Nos. 1957b and 1958 Overprinted in Red

1981, May 22

1998 A340 4g on #1957b 1.00 .60
1999 A340 10g on #1958 2.00 1.00

No. 1999 is airmail.

The following stamps were issued in sheets of 8 with 1 label: Nos. 2001, 2013, 2037, 2044, 2047, 2055, 2140.

The following stamp was issued in sheets of 10 with 2 labels: No. 1994a.

The following stamps were issued in sheets of 6 with 3 labels: Nos. 2017, 2029, 2035, 2104, 2145.

The following stamps were issued in sheets of 3 with 6 labels: 2079, 2143.

The following stamps were issued in sheets of 5 with 4 labels: Nos. 2050-2051, 2057, 2059, 2061, 2067, 2069, 2077, 2082, 2089, 2092, 2107, 2117, 2120, 2121, 2123, 2125, 2129, 2135, 2138, 2142, 2146, 2148, 2151, 2160, 2163, 2165, 2169, 2172, 2176, 2179, 2182, 2190, 2196, 2202, 2204, 2214, 2222, 2224, 2232, 2244, 2246, 2248, 2261, 2263, 2265, 2271, 2273, 2275, 2277.

The following stamps were issued in sheets of 4 with 5 labels: Nos. 2307, 2310, 2313, 2316, 2324, 2329.

Royal Wedding of Prince Charles and Lady Diana Spencer — A351

Prince Charles, sailing ships: No. 2000a, 25c, Royal George. b, 50c, Great Britain. c, 1g, Taeping. d, 2g, Star of India. e, 3g, Torrens. f, 4g, Loch Etive. No. 2001, Medway.

No. 2002, Charles, flags, and Concorde. 10g, Flags, flowers, Diana, Charles. 25g, Charles, Diana, flowers, vert. 30g, Coats of arms, flags.

1981, June 27

2000 A351 Strip of 6, #a.-f. 4.25 1.40
2001 A351 5g multicolored 1.40 .35
2002 A351 5g multicolored .85 .45
2003 A351 10g multicolored 2.75 .75
2004 A351 30g multicolored 4.50 2.25
Nos. 2000-2004 (5) 13.75 5.20

Souvenir Sheet

Perf. 13½

2005 A351 25g multicolored 17.50 17.50

Nos. 2002-2005 are airmail. No. 2005 contains one 50x60mm stamp. For overprint see No. 2253.

No. 2005 has an orange margin. It also exists with gray margin. Same value.

Traditional Costumes and Itaipu Dam A352

Women in various traditional costumes: a, 10g. b, 25g. c, 50g. d, 100g. e, 200g. f, 300g. g, 400g, President Stroessner, Itaipu Dam.

1981, June 30 *Perf. 14*

2006 A352 Strip of 7, #a.-g. 25.00 8.00

For overprints see No. 2281.

UPU Membership Centenary — A353

1981, Aug. 18 Litho. *Perf. 13½x13*

2007 A353 5g rose lake & blk 2.00 1.00
2008 A353 10g lil & blk 2.00 1.00
2009 A353 20g grn & blk 2.00 1.00
2010 A353 25g lt red brn & blk 2.00 1.00
2011 A353 50g bl & blk 3.00 2.00
Nos. 2007-2011 (5) 11.00 6.00

Peter Paul Rubens, Paintings A354

Details from paintings: No. 2012: a, 25c, Madonna Surrounded by Saints. b, 50c, Judgment of Paris. c, 1g, Duke of Buckingham Conducted to the Temple of Virtus. d, 2g, Minerva Protecting Peace from Mars. e, 3g, Henry IV Receiving the Portrait of Marie de Medici. f, 4g, Triumph of Juliers. 5g, Madonna and Child Reigning Among Saints (Cherubs).

1981, July 9 Litho. *Perf. 14*

2012 A354 Strip of 6, #a.-f. 2.25 .75
2013 A354 5g multicolored .65 .25
Nos. 2012-2013 (2) 2.90 1.00

Jean Auguste-Dominique Ingres (1780-1867), Painter — A355

Details from paintings: No. 2014: a, 25c, c, 1g, d, 2g, f, 4g, The Turkish Bath. b, 50c, The Water Pitcher. e, 3g, Oedipus and the Sphinx. g, 5g, The Bathing Beauty.

1981, Oct. 13

2014 A355 Strip of 7, #a.-g. 2.50 1.50

A horiz. strip of 5 containing Nos. 2014a-2014e exists.

No. 2014f and 2014g exist in sheet of 8 (four each) plus label.

For overprints see No. 2045.

Pablo Picasso, Birth Cent. — A356

Designs: No. 2015: a, 25c, Women Running on the Beach. b, 50c, Family on the Beach.

No. 2016: a, 1g, Still-life. b, 2g, Bullfighter. c, 3g, Children Drawing. d, 4g, Seated Woman. 5g, Paul as Clown.

1981, Oct. 19

2015 A356 Pair, #a.-b. .50 .50
2016 A356 Strip of 4, #a.-d. 5.00 1.50
2017 A356 5g multicolored 1.25 .40
Nos. 2015-2017 (3) 6.75 2.40

Nos. 2015-2016 Ovptd. in Silver

1981, Oct. 22

2018 A356 on #2015a-2015b .50 .50
2019 A356 on #2016a-2016d 1.90 1.00
Nos. 2018-2019 (2) 2.40 1.50

Philatelia '81, Frankfurt.

Nos. 2015-2016 Ovptd. in Gold

1981, Oct. 25

2020 A356 on #2015a-2015b .50 .50
2021 A356 on #2016a-2016d 1.90 1.00
Nos. 2020-2021 (2) 2.40 1.50

Espamer '81 Philatelic Exhibition.

Royal Wedding of Prince Charles and Lady Diana A357

Designs: No. 2022a-2022c, 25c, 50c, 1g, Diana, Charles, flowers. d, 2g, Couple. e, 3g, Couple leaving church. f, 4g, Couple, Queen Elizabeth II waving from balcony. 2022G, 5g, Diana. No. 2023, Wedding party, horiz. 10g, Riding in royal coach, horiz. 30g, Yeomen of the guard, horiz.

1981, Dec. 4 Litho. *Perf. 14*

2022 A357 Strip of 6, #a.-f. 1.50 1.50
2022G A357 5g multicolored .25 .25
2023 A357 5g multicolored 2.25 .70
2024 A357 10g multicolored 4.25 1.40
2025 A357 30g multicolored 13.00 4.50
Nos. 2022-2025 (5) 21.25 8.35

Souvenir Sheets

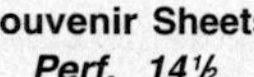

Perf. 14½

2026 A357 25g like #2022d 30.00 30.00
2027 A357 25g Wedding portrait 30.00 30.00

No. 2022g exists in sheets of 8 plus label. Nos. 2023-2027 are airmail. Nos. 2026-2027 contain one each 50x70mm stamp.

Christmas A358

Designs: No. 2028a, 25c, Jack-in-the-box. b, 50c, Jesus and angel. c, 1g, Santa, angels. d, 2g, Angels lighting candle. e, 3g, Christmas plant. f, 4g, Nativity scene. 5g, Children singing by Christmas tree.

1981, Dec. 17 *Perf. 14*

2028 A358 Strip of 6, #a.-f. 4.00 1.00

Size: 28x45mm

Perf. 13½

2029 A358 5g multicolored 2.00 .55

Intl. Year of the Child (Nos. 2028-2029). For overprints see No. 2042.

Intl. Year of the Child A359

Story of Puss 'n Boots: No. 2030a, 25c, Boy, Puss. b, 50c, Puss, rabbits.

1g, Puss, king. 2g, Prince, princess, king. 3g, Giant ogre, Puss. 4g, Puss chasing mouse. 5g, Princess, prince, Puss.

1982, Apr. 16 Litho. *Perf. 14*

2030 A359 Pair, #a.-b. .50 .50
2031 A359 1g multicolored .25 .25
2032 A359 2g multicolored .50 .25
2033 A359 3g multicolored .70 .25
2034 A359 4g multicolored 1.20 .25
2035 A359 5g multicolored 4.50 1.50
Nos. 2030-2035 (6) 7.65 3.00

Nos. 2031-2034 printed se-tenant with label.

Scouting, 75th Anniv. and Lord Baden-Powell, 125th Birth Anniv. — A360

No. 2036: a, 25c, Tetradactyla, Scout hand salute. b, 50c, Nandu (rhea), Cub Scout and trefoil. c, 1g, Peccary, Wolf's head totem. d, 2g, Coatimundi, emblem on buckle. e, 3g, Mara, Scouting's Intl. Communications emblem. f, 4g, Deer, boy scout.

No. 2037, Aotes, Den mother, Cub Scout. No. 2038, Ocelot, scouts cooking. 10g, Collie, boy scout. 30g, Armadillo, two scouts planting tree. 25g, Lord Robert Baden-Powell, founder of Boy Scouts.

1982, Apr. 21

2036 A360 Strip of 6, #a.-f. 1.75 1.00
2037 A360 5g multicolored 1.40 .40
2038 A360 5g multicolored 1.40 .40

2039	A360	10g multicolored	2.00	.45
2040	A360	30g multicolored	2.50	.40
		Nos. 2036-2040 (5)	9.05	2.65

Souvenir Sheet

Perf. 14½

2041	A360	25g multicolored	12.50	12.50

Nos. 2038-2041 are airmail. For overprint see No. 2140.

No. 2028 Overprinted with ESSEN 82 Emblem

1982, Apr. 28 ***Perf. 14***

2042	A358	on #2028a-2028f	2.50	1.75

Essen '82 Intl. Philatelic Exhibition.

Cats and Kittens — A361

Various cats or kittens: No. 2043a, 25c. b, 50c. c, 1g. d, 2g. e, 3g. f, 4g.

1982, June 7 ***Perf. 14***

2043	A361	Strip of 6, #a.-f.	2.00	1.00
2044	A361	5g multi, vert.	.75	.35
		Nos. 2043-2044 (2)	2.75	1.35

For overprints see Nos. 2054-2055.

Nos. 2014a-2014e Ovptd. PHILEXFRANCE 82 Emblem ans "PARIS 11-21.6.82" in Blue

1982, June 11

2045	A355	Strip of 5, #a.-e.	2.00	1.00

Philexfrance '82 Intl. Philatelic Exhibition. Size of overprint varies.

World Cup Soccer Championships, Spain — A362

Designs: 2046a, 25c, Brazilian team. b, 50c, Chilean team. c, 1g, Honduran team. d, 2g, Peruvian team. e, 3g, Salvadoran team. f, 4g, Globe as soccer ball, flags of Latin American finalists. No. 2047, Ball of flags. No. 2048, Austrian team. No. 2049, Players from Brazil, Austria. No. 2050, Spanish team. No. 2051, Two players from Argentina, Brazil, vert. No. 2052, W. German team. No. 2053, Players from Argentina, Brazil. No. 2053A, World Cup trophy, world map on soccer balls. No. 2053B, Players from W. Germany, Mexico, vert.

1982 **Litho.** ***Perf. 14***

2046	A362	Strip of 6, #a.-f.	3.75	1.25
2047	A362	5g multicolored	.35	.25
2048	A362	5g multicolored	1.95	1.40
2049	A362	5g multicolored	3.25	1.00
2050	A362	10g multicolored	.90	.25
2051	A362	10g multicolored	.50	.50
2052	A362	30g multicolored	2.25	.25
2053	A362	30g multicolored	.25	.25
		Nos. 2046-2053 (8)	13.20	5.15

Souvenir Sheets

Perf. 14½

2053A	A362	25g multicolored	14.00	14.00
2053B	A362	25g multicolored	14.00	14.00

Issued: #2049, 2051, 2053, 2053A, 4/19; others, 6/13.

Nos. 2047 exists in sheets of 8 plus label. Nos. 2048-2053B are airmail.

For overprints see Nos. 2086, 2286, C593.

Nos. 2043-2044 Overprinted in Silver With PHILATECIA 82 and Intl. Year of the Child Emblems

1982, Sept. 12 ***Perf. 14***

2054	A361	Strip of 5, #a.-e.	2.25	1.25
2055	A361	5g on #2044	.90	.40
		Nos. 2054-2055 (2)	3.15	1.65

Philatelia '82, Hanover, Germany and Intl. Year of the Child.

Raphael, 500th Birth Anniv. A363

Details from paintings: No. 2056a, 25c, Adam and Eve (The Fall). b, 50c, Creation of Eve. c, 1g, Portrait of a Young Woman (La Fornarina). d, 2g The Three Graces. e, 3g, f, 4g, Cupid and the Three Graces. 5g. Leda and the Swan.

1982, Sept. 27

2056	A363	Strip of 6, #a.-f.	4.00	1.50
2057	A363	5g multicolored	3.00	1.00
		Nos. 2056-2057 (2)	7.00	2.50

Nos. 2056e-2056f have continuous design.

Christmas A364

Entire works or details from paintings by Raphael: No. 2058a, 25c, The Belvedere Madonna. b, 50c, The Ansidei Madonna. c, 1g, La Belle Jardiniere. d, 2g, The Aldobrandini (Garvagh) Madonna. e, 3g, Madonna of the Goldfinch. f, 4g, The Alba Madonna. No. 2059, Madonna of the Grand Duke. No. 2060, Madonna of the Linen Window. 10g, The Alba Madonna, diff. 25g, The Holy Family with St. Elizabeth and the Infant St. John and Two Angels. 30g, The Canigiani Holy Family.

1982 ***Perf. 14, 13x13½ (#2061)***

2058	A364	Strip of 6, #a.-f.	3.50	1.50
2059	A364	5g multicolored	1.40	.50
2060	A364	5g multicolored	3.25	1.00
2061	A364	10g multicolored	1.50	.50
2062	A364	30g multicolored	.75	.25
		Nos. 2058-2062 (5)	10.40	3.75

Souvenir Sheet

Perf. 14½

2063	A364	25g multicolored	15.00	15.00

Issued: #2058-2059, 9/30; others, 12/17.

Nos. 2058a-2058f and 2059 exist perf. 13. Nos. 2060-2063 are airmail and have silver lettering. For overprint see No. 2087.

Life of Christ, by Albrecht Durer A365

Details from paintings: No. 2064a, 25c, The Flight into Egypt. b, 50c, Christ Among the Doctors. c, 1g, Christ Carrying the Cross. d, 2g, Nailing of Christ to the Cross. e, 3g, Christ on the Cross. f, 4g, Lamentation Over the Dead Christ. 5g, The Circumcision of Christ.

1982, Dec. 14 ***Perf. 14***

2064	A365	Strip of 6, #a.-f.	5.50	2.75

Perf. 13x13½

2065	A365	5g multicolored	2.50	.75
		Nos. 2064-2065 (2)	8.00	3.50

For overprint see No. 2094.

South American Locomotives — A366

Locomotives from: No. 2066a, 25c, Argentina. b, 50c, Uruguay. c, 1g, Ecuador. d, 2g, Bolivia. e, 3g, Peru. f, 4g, Brazil. 5g, Paraguay.

1983, Jan. 17 **Litho.** ***Perf. 14***

2066	A366	Strip of 6, #a.-f.	2.50	1.00
2067	A366	5g multicolored	2.00	.75
		Nos. 2066-2067 (2)	4.50	1.75

For overprint see No. 2093.

Race Cars A367

No. 2068: a, 25c, ATS-Ford D 06. b, 50c, Ferrari 126 C 2. c, 1g, Brabham-BMW BT 50. d, 2g, Renault RE 30 B. e, 3g, Porsche 956. f, 4g, Talbot-Ligier-Matra JS 19. 5g, Mercedes Benz C-111.

1983, Jan. 19 ***Perf. 14***

2068	A367	Strip of 6, #a.-f.	3.25	1.00

Perf. 13½x13

2069	A367	5g multicolored	1.50	.50
		Nos. 2068-2069 (2)	4.75	1.50

For overprint see No. 2118.

Itaipua Dam, Pres. Stroessner — A368

1983, Jan. 22 **Litho.** **Wmk. 347**

2070	A368	3g multi	2.00	1.00
2071	A368	5g multi	2.00	1.00
2072	A368	10g multi	2.00	1.00
2073	A368	20g multi	2.00	1.00
2074	A368	25g multi	2.00	1.00
2075	A368	50g multi	2.00	1.00
		Nos. 2070-2075 (6)	12.00	6.00

25th anniv. of Stroessner City.

Nos. 2073-2075 airmail.

1984 Winter Olympics, Sarajevo — A369

Ice skaters: No. 2076a, 25c, Marika Kilius, Hans-Jurgens Baumler, Germany, 1964. b, 50c, Tai Babilonia, Randy Gardner, US, 1976. c, 1g, Anett Poetzsch, E. Germany, 1980, vert. d, 2g, Tina Riegel, Andreas Nischwitz, Germany, 1980, vert. e, Dagmar Lurz, Germany, 1980, vert. f, 4g, Trixi Schuba, Austria, 1972, vert. 5g, Peggy Fleming, US, 1968, vert.

Perf. 13½x13, 13x13½

1983, Feb. 23 **Unwmk.**

2076	A369	Strip of 6, #a.-f.	1.40	1.00
2077	A369	5g multicolored	2.10	.75
		Nos. 2076-2077 (2)	3.50	1.75

For overprints see Nos. 2177, 2266.

Pope John Paul II A370

#2078: a, 25c, Virgin of Caacupe. b, 50c, Cathedral of Caacupe. c, 1g, Cathedral of Asuncion. d, 2g, Pope holding crucifix. e, 3g, Our Lady of the Assumption. f, 4g, Pope giving blessing. 5g, Pope with hands clasped. 25g, Madonna & child.

1983, June 11 **Litho.** ***Perf. 14***

2078	A370	Strip of 6, #a.-f.	3.75	2.00
2079	A370	5g multicolored	1.75	.80
		Nos. 2078-2079 (2)	5.50	2.80

Souvenir Sheet

Perf. 14½

2080	A370	25g multicolored	14.00	14.00

No. 2080 is airmail. For overprint see No. 2143.

Antique Automobiles — A371

No. 2081: a, 25c, Bordino Steamcoach, 1854. b, 50c, Panhard & Levassor, 1892. c, 1g, Benz Velo, 1894. d, 2g, Peugeot-Daimler, 1894. e, 3g, 1st car with patented Lutzmann system, 1898. f, 4g, Benz Victory, 1891-92. No. 2082, Ceirano 5CV. No. 2083, Mercedes Simplex PS 32 Turismo, 1902. 10g, Stae Electric, 1909. 25g, Benz Velocipede, 1885. 30g, Rolls Royce Silver Ghost, 1913.

1983, July 18 ***Perf. 14***

2081	A371	Strip of 6, #a.-f.	1.75	1.25
2082	A371	5g multicolored	1.10	.40
2083	A371	5g multicolored	4.00	1.10
2084	A371	10g multicolored	.75	.25
2085	A371	30g multicolored	1.50	.25
		Nos. 2081-2085 (5)	9.10	3.25

Souvenir Sheet

Perf. 14½

2085A	A371	25g Sheet of 1 + label	14.00	14.00

Nos. 2083-2085A are airmail.

No. 2046 Ovptd. in Red, No. 2058 Ovptd. in Black with "52o CONGRESO F.I.P." and Brasiliana 83 Emblem

1983, July 27 ***Perf. 14***

2086	A362	Strip of 6, #a.-f.	5.00	5.00
2087	A364	Strip of 6, #a.-f.	5.00	5.00

Brasiliana '83, Rio de Janiero and 52nd FIP Congress. No. 2087 exists perf. 13.

Aircraft Carriers — A372

Carriers and airplanes: No. 2088a, 25c, 25 de Mayo, A-4Q Sky Hawk, Argentina. b, 50c, Minas Gerais, Brazil. c, 1g, Akagi, A6M3 Zero, Japan. d, 2g, Guiseppe Miraglia, Italy. e, 3g, Enterprise, S-3A Viking, US. f, 4g, Dedalo, AV-8A Matador, Spain. No. 2089, 5g, Schwabenland, Dornier DO-18, Germany.
No aircraft on Nos. 2088b, 2088d.
25g, US astronauts Donn Eisele, Walter Schirra & Walt Cunningham, Earth & Apollo 7.

1983, Aug. 29 *Perf. 14*
2088 A372 Strip of 6, #a.-f. 3.50 1.50
2089 A372 5g multicolored 1.50 .75
Nos. 2088-2089 (2) 5.00 2.25

Souvenir Sheet
Perf. 13½
2090 A372 25g multicolored 15.00 15.00

No. 2090 is airmail and contains one 55x45mm stamp.

Birds A373

#2091: a, 25c, Pulsatrix perspicillata. b, 50c, Ortalis ruficauda. c, 1g, Chloroceryle amazona. d, 2g, Trogon violaceus. e, 3g, Pezites militaris. f, 4g, Bucco capensis. 5g, Cyanerpes cyaneus.

1983, Oct. 22 *Perf. 14*
2091 A373 Strip of 6, #a.-f. 4.25 1.00
Perf. 13
2092 A373 5g multicolored 1.75 .40
Nos. 2091-2092 (2) 6.00 1.40

No. 2066 Ovptd. for PHILATELICA 83 in Silver

1983, Oct. 28
2093 A366 Strip of 6, #a.-f. 3.00 2.00

Philatelia '83, Dusseldorf, Germany.

No. 2064 Overprinted in Silver for EXFIVIA - 83

1983, Nov. 5
2094 A365 Strip of 6, #a.-f. 4.50 2.00

Exfivia '83 Philatelic Exhibition, La Paz, Bolivia.

Re-election of President Stroessner — A374

10g, Passion flower, vert. 25g, Miltonia phalaenopsis, vert. 50g, Natl. arms, Chaco soldier. 75g, Acaray hydroelectric dam. 100g, Itaipu hydroelectric dam. 200g, Pres. Alfredo Stroessner, vert.

1983, Nov. 24 *Perf. 14*
2095 A374 10g multicolored .25 .25
2096 A374 25g multicolored .40 .25
2097 A374 50g multicolored .80 .25
2098 A374 75g multicolored .65 .25
Perf. 13
2099 A374 100g multicolored .80 .25
2100 A374 200g multicolored 1.60 .80
Nos. 2095-2100 (6) 4.50 2.05

Nos. 2099-2100 are airmail. No. 2096 exists perf 13. For overprint see No. C577.

Montgolfier Brothers' 1st Flight, Bicent. — A375

No. 2101: a, 25c, Santos-Dumont's Biplane, 1906. b, 50c, Airship. c, 1g, Paulhan's biplane over Juvisy. d, 2g, Zeppelin LZ-3, 1907. e, 3g, Biplane of Henri Farman. f, 4g, Graf Zeppelin over Friedrichshafen. 5g, Lebaudy's dirigible. 25g, Detail of painting, Great Week of Aviation at Betheny, 1910.

1984, Jan. 7 *Perf. 13*
2101 A375 Strip of 6, #a.-f. 2.25 1.25
Perf. 14
2104 A375 5g multicolored 3.75 .75
Nos. 2101-2104 (2) 6.00 2.00

Souvenir Sheet
Perf. 13½
2105 A375 25g multicolored 15.00 15.00

No. 2105 is airmail and contains one 75x55mm stamp. For overprint see No. 2145.

Dogs A376

#2106: a, 25c, German Shepherd. b, 50c, Great Dane, vert. c, 1g, Poodle, vert. d, 2g, Saint Bernard. e, 3g, Greyhound. f, 4g, Dachshund. 5g, Boxer.

1984, Jan. 11 **Litho.** *Perf. 14*
2106 A376 Strip of 6, #a.-f. 3.00 1.25
2107 A376 5g multicolored 1.50 .50
Nos. 2106-2107 (2) 4.50 1.75

Animals, Anniversaries — A377

1984, Jan. 24 *Perf. 13*
2108 A377 10g Puma .25 .25
2109 A377 25g Alligator .65 .25
2110 A377 50g Jaguar 1.25 .40
2111 A377 75g Peccary 1.90 .60
2112 A377 100g Simon Bolivar, vert. 2.90 .90
2113 A377 200g Girl scout, vert. 5.50 1.75
Nos. 2108-2113 (6) 12.45 4.15

Simon Bolivar, birth bicent. and Girl Scouts of Paraguay, 76th anniv.
Nos. 2112-2113 are airmail.

Christmas A378

Designs: No. 2114a, 25c, Pope John Paul II. b, 50c, Christmas tree. c, 1g, Children. d, 2g, Nativity Scene. e, 3g, Three Kings. f, 4g, Madonna and Child. No. 2115, Madonna and Child by Raphael.

1984, Mar. 23 *Perf. 13x13½*
2114 A378 Strip of 6, #a.-f. 7.50 1.50
2115 A378 5g multicolored 3.50 1.00
Nos. 2114-2115 (2) 11.00 2.50

Troubadour Knights A379

Illustrations of medieval miniatures: No. 2116a, 25c, Ulrich von Liechtenstein. b, 50c, Ulrich von Gutenberg. c, 1g, Der Putter. d, 2g, Walther von Metz. e, 3g, Hartman von Aue. f, 4g, Lutok von Seuen. 5g, Werner von Teufen.

1984, Mar. 27 *Perf. 14*
2116 A379 Strip of 6, #a.-f. 3.50 1.25
Perf. 13
2117 A379 5g multicolored 2.00 .75
Nos. 2116-2117 (2) 5.50 2.00

For overprint see No. 2121.

No. 2068 Ovptd. in Silver with ESSEN 84 Emblem

1984, May 10
2118 A367 Strip of 6, #a.-f. 2.50 1.25

Essen '84 Intl. Philatelic Exhibition.

Endangered Animals — A380

#2119: a, 25c, Priodontes giganteus. b, 50c, Catagonus wagneri. c, 1g, Felis pardalis. d, 2g, Chrysocyon brachyurus. e, 3g, Burmeisteria retusa. f, 4g, Myrmecophaga tridactyla. 5g, Caiman crocodilus.

1984, June 16 *Perf. 14*
2119 A380 Strip of 6, #a.-f. 4.50 2.00
Perf. 13
2120 A380 5g multicolored 2.00 .50
Nos. 2119-2120 (2) 6.50 2.50

A canceled-to-order perf. 13 strip of seven stamps containing Nos. 2119a-2119g and 2120 exists. For overprint see No. 2129.

No. 2117 Ovptd. in Silver with Emblems, etc., for U.P.U. 19th World Congress, Hamburg

1984, June 19 *Perf. 13*
2121 A379 5g on #2117 2.50 1.25

UPU Congress, Hamburg '84 — A381

Sailing ships: No. 2122a, 25c, Admiral of Hamburg. b, 50c, Neptune. c, 1g, Archimedes. d, 2g, Passat. e, 3g, Finkenwerder cutter off Heligoland. f, 4g, Four-masted ship. 5g, Deutschland.

1984, June 19 *Perf. 13*
2122 A381 Strip of 6, #a.-f. 4.50 1.50
2123 A381 5g multicolored 1.75 .50
Nos. 2122-2123 (2) 6.25 2.00

For overprints see Nos. 2146, 2279-2280.

British Locomotives — A382

No. 2124: a, 25c, Pegasus 097, 1868. b, 50c, Pegasus 097, diff. c, 1g, Cornwall, 1847. d, 2g, Cornwall, 1847, diff. e, 3g, Patrick Stirling #1, 1870. f, 4g, Patrick Stirling #1, 1870, diff. 5g, Stepney Brighton Terrier, 1872.

1984, June 20 *Perf. 14*
2124 A382 Strip of 6, #a.-f. 4.25 1.50
Perf. 13
2125 A382 5g multicolored 1.75 .50
Nos. 2124-2125 (2) 6.00 2.00

No. C486 Overprinted in Blue on Silver with UN emblem and "40o Aniversario de la / Fundacion de las / Naciones Unidas 26.6.1944"

1984, Aug. 1 **Litho.** *Perf. 14½*
2126 AP161 25g on No. C486 15.00 15.00

No. 1536 Ovptd. in Orange (#a.-d.) or Silver (#e.-g.)

and

B

A383

1984, Aug. 21 *Perf. 14*
2127 A271 Strip of 7, #a.-g. 8.00 1.75

Souvenir Sheet

Perf. 14½

2128 A383 25g multicolored 14.00 14.00

Ausipex '84 Intl. Philatelic Exhibition, Melbourne, Australia. No. 2128 is airmail.

Nos. 2120 and C551 Ovptd. in Black and Red

1984 *Perf. 13*
2129 A380 5g on #2120 2.00 2.00

Perf. 14

2130 AP178 30g on #C551 4.00 4.00

Issued: #2129, Sept. 20; #2130, Aug. 30. No. 2130 is airmail.

No. 1512 Ovptd. "VER STUTTGART CAMPEON NACIONAL DE FUTBOL DE ALEMANIA 1984" and Emblem

1984, Sept. 5 *Perf. 14*
2131 A263 Strip of 7, #a.-g. 2.50 1.25

VFB Stuttgart, 1984 German Soccer Champions.

Cat Type of 1976

Various cats: No. 2132: a, 25c. b, 50c. c, 1g. d, 2g. e, 3g. f, 4g.

1984, Sept. 10 *Perf. 13x13½*
2132 A287 Strip of 6, #a.-f. 3.00 1.50
2133 A287 5g multicolored 2.50 .75
Nos. 2132-2133 (2) 5.50 2.25

1984 Summer Olympics, Los Angeles — A384

Gold medalists: No. 2134a, 25c Michael Gross, W. Germany, swimming. b, 50c, Peter Vidmar, US, gymnastics. c, 1g, Fredy Schmidtke, W. Germany, cycling. d, 2g, Philippe Boisse, France, fencing. e, 3g, Ulrike Meyfarth, W. Germany, women's high jump. f, 4g, Games emblem. 5g, Mary Lou Retton, US, women's all-around gymnastics, vert. 30g, Rolf Milser, W. Germany, weight lifting, vert.

1985, Jan. 16 **Litho.** *Perf. 13*
2134 A384 Strip of 6, #a.-f. 2.00 1.25
2135 A384 5g multicolored 3.00 .75
Nos. 2134-2135 (2) 5.00 2.00

Souvenir Sheet

Perf. 13½

2136 A384 30g multicolored 15.00 15.00

No. 2136 is airmail and contains one 50x60mm stamp. For overprints see Nos. 2174, 2199, 2200. Compare with type A399.

Mushrooms A385

#2137: a, 25c, Boletus luteus. b, 50c, Agaricus campester. c, 1g, Pholiota spectabilis. d, 2g, Tricholoma terreum. e, 3g, Laccaria laccata. f, 4g, Amanita phalloides. 5g, Scleroderna verrucosum.

1985, Jan. 19 *Perf. 14*
2137 A385 Strip of 6, #a.-f. 9.00 3.00
2138 A385 5g multicolored 8.00 3.00
Nos. 2137-2138 (2) 17.00 6.00

See Nos. 2166-2167.

World Wildlife Fund — A386

Endangered or extinct species: No. 2139a, 25c, Capybara. b, 50c, Mono titi, vert. c, 1g, Rana cornuda adornada. d, 2g, Priodontes giganteus, digging. e, 3g, Priodontes giganteus, by water. f, 4g, Myrmecophaga tridactyla. g, 5g, Myrmecophaga tridactyla, with young.

1985, Mar. 13 *Perf. 14*
2139 A386 Strip of 7, #a.-g. 47.50 10.00

See No. 2252.

No. 2037 Ovptd. in Red with ISRAPHIL Emblem

1985, Apr. 10
2140 A360 5g on No. 2037 2.00 1.00

Israel '85 Intl. Philatelic Exhibition.

John James Audubon, Birth Bicent. A387

Birds: No. 2141a, 25c, Piranga flava. b, 50c, Polyborus plancus. c, 1g, Chiroxiphia caudata. d, 2g, Xolmis irupero. e, 3g, Phloeoceastes leucopogon. f, 4g, Thraupis bonariensis. 5g, Parula pitiayumi, horiz.

1985, Apr. 18 *Perf. 13*
2141 A387 Strip of 6, #a.-f. 3.75 1.25
2142 A387 5g multicolored 1.75 .50
Nos. 2141-2142 (2) 5.50 1.75

No. 2079 Ovptd. in Silver with Italia '85 Emblem

1985, May 20 *Perf. 14*
2143 A370 5g on #2079 4.00 1.50

Italia '85 Intl. Philatelic Exhibition.

No. 1448e Ovptd. in Red on Silver

1985, June 12
2144 A250 30c on #1448e 1.50 .75

No. 2104 Ovptd. in Silver and Blue with LUPO 85 Congress Emblem

1985, July 5
2145 A375 5g on No. 2104 1.00 .50

LUPO '85, Lucerne, Switzerland.

No. 2123 Ovptd. in Silver and Blue with MOPHILA 85 Emblem and "HAMBURGO 11-12. 9. 85"

1985, July 5 *Perf. 13*
2146 A381 5g on #2123 1.00 .50

Mophila '85 Intl. Philatelic Exhibition, Hamburg.

Intl. Youth Year A388

Scenes from Tom Sawyer and Huckleberry Finn: No. 2147a, 25c, Mississippi riverboat. b, 50c, Finn. c, 1g, Finn and friends by campfire. d, 2g, Finn and Joe, sinking riverboat. e, 3g, Finn, friends, riverboat. f, 4g, Cemetery. 5g, Finn, Sawyer. 25g, Raft, riverboat.

1985, Aug. 5 *Perf. 13½x13*
2147 A388 Strip of 6, #a.-f. 3.50 1.50
2148 A388 5g multicolored 3.00 .75
Nos. 2147-2148 (2) 6.50 2.25

Souvenir Sheet

Perf. 14½

2149 A388 25g multicolored 12.00 12.00

No. 2149 is airmail. For overprint see No. C612.

German Railroads, 150th Anniv. — A389

Locomotives: No. 2150a, 25c, T3, 1883. b, 50c, T18, 1912. c, 1g, T16, 1914. d, 2g, #01 118, Historic Trains Society, Frankfurt. e, 3g, #05 001 Express, Nuremberg Transit Museum. f, 4g, #10 002 Express, 1957. 5g, Der Adler, 1835. 25g, Painting of 1st German Train, Dec. 7, 1835.

1985, Aug. 8 *Perf. 14*
2150 A389 Strip of 6, #a.-f. 4.50 1.50

Perf. 13

2151 A389 5g multicolored 1.75 .50
Nos. 2150-2151 (2) 6.25 2.00

Souvenir Sheet

Perf. 13½

2152 A389 25g multicolored 14.00 14.00

No. 2152 is airmail and contains one 75x53mm stamp. For overprint see No. 2165.

Development Projects — A390

Pres. Stroessner and: 10g, Soldier, map, vert. 25g, Model of Yaci Reta Hydroelectric Project. 50g, Itaipu Dam. 75g, Merchantman Lago Ipoa. 100g, 1975 Coin, vert. 200g, Asuncion Intl. Airport.

1985, Sept. 17 **Litho.** *Perf. 13*
2153 A390 10g multicolored .25 .25
2154 A390 25g multicolored .25 .25
2155 A390 50g multicolored .50 .25
2156 A390 75g multicolored .75 .25
2157 A390 100g multicolored 1.00 .25
2158 A390 200g multicolored 2.00 .50
Nos. 2153-2158 (6) 4.75 1.75

Chaco Peace Agreement, 50th Anniv. (#2153, 2157). Nos. 2157-2158 are airmail. For overprints see Nos. 2254-2259.

Nudes by Peter Paul Rubens A391

Details from paintings: No. 2159a, 25c, b, 50c, Venus in the Forge of Vulcan. c, 1g, Cimon and Iphigenia, horiz. d, 2g, The Horrors of War. e, 3g, Apotheosis of Henry IV and the Proclamation of the Regency. f, 4g, The Reception of Marie de Medici at Marseilles. 5g, Union of Earth and Water. 25g, Nature Attended by the Three Graces.

1985, Oct. 18 *Perf. 14*
2159 A391 Strip of 6, #a.-f. 4.50 1.50

Perf. 13x13½

2160 A391 5g multicolored 2.00 .50
Nos. 2159-2160 (2) 6.50 2.00

Souvenir Sheet

Perf. 14

2161 A391 25g multicolored 17.50 15.00

No. 2161 is airmail.

1986, Jan. 16 *Perf. 14*

Nudes by Titian: details from paintings. No. 2162a, 25c, Venus, an Organist, Cupid and a Little Dog. b, 50c, c, 1g, Diana and Actaeon. d, 2g, Danae. e, 3g, Nymph and a Shepherd. f, 4g, Venus of Urbino. 5g, Cupid Blindfolded by Venus, vert. 25g, Diana and Callisto, vert.

2162 A391 Strip of 6, #a.-f. 6.00 2.00

Perf. 13

2163 A391 5g multicolored 2.50 1.00
Nos. 2162-2163 (2) 8.50 3.00

Souvenir Sheet

Perf. 13½

2164 A391 25g multicolored 15.00 15.00

No. 2164 is airmail and contains one 50x60mm stamp.

Nos. 2150 Ovptd. in Red

1986, Feb. 25 *Perf. 14*
2165 A389 Strip of 6, #a.-f. 2.00 1.00

Essen '86 Intl. Philatelic Exhibition.

Mushrooms Type of 1985

Designs: No. 2166a, 25g, Lepiota procera. b, 50c, Tricholoma albo-brunneum. c, 1g, Clavaria. d, 2g, Volvaria. e, 3g, Licoperdon perlatum. f, 4g, Dictyophora duplicata. 5g, Polyporus rubrum.

1986, Mar. 17 *Perf. 14*
2166 A385 Strip of 6, #a.-f. 6.00 1.50

Perf. 13

2167 A385 5g multicolored 2.50 .50
Nos. 2166-2167 (2) 8.50 2.00

Automobile, Cent. — A393

No. 2168: a, 25c, Wolseley, 1904. b, 50c, Peugeot, 1892. c, 1g, Panhard, 1895. d, 2g, Cadillac, 1903. e, 3g, Fiat, 1902. f, 4g, Stanley Steamer, 1898. 5g, Carl Benz Velocipede, 1885. 25g, Carl Benz (1844-1929), automotive engineer.

1986, Apr. 28 Litho. ***Perf. 13½x13***

2168 A393 Strip of 6, #a.-f. 2.75 1.50
2169 A393 5g multicolored 3.25 1.25
Nos. 2168-2169 (2) 6.00 2.75

Souvenir Sheet

Perf. 13½

2170 A393 25g multicolored 15.00 15.00

No. 2170 is airmail and contains one 30x40mm stamp.

World Cup Soccer Championships, Mexico City — A394

Various match scenes, Paraguay vs.: No. 2171a, 25c, b, 50c, US, 1930. c, 1g, d, 2g, Belgium, 1930. e, 3g, Bolivia, 1985. f, 4g, Brazil, 1985.
5g, Natl. Team, 1986. 25g, Player, vert.

1986, Mar. 12 ***Perf. 13½x13***

2171 A394 Strip of 6, #a.-f. 3.25 1.50
2172 A394 5g multicolored 3.75 1.00
Nos. 2171-2172 (2) 7.00 2.50

Souvenir Sheet

Perf. 14½

2173 A394 25g multicolored 15.00 15.00

No. 2173 is airmail. For overprints see Nos. 2283, 2287.

No. 2135 Ovptd. in Silver "JUEGOS / PANAMERICANOS / INDIANAPOLIS / 1987"

1986, June 9 ***Perf. 13***

2174 A384 5g on No. 2135 2.50 1.25

1987 Pan American Games, Indianapolis.

Maybach Automobiles — A395

#2175: a, 25c, W-6, 1930-36. b, 50c, SW-38 convertible. c, 1g, SW-38 hardtop, 1938. d, 2g, W-6/DSG, 1933. e, 3g, Zeppelin DS-8, 1931. f, 4g, Zeppelin DS-8, 1936. 5g, Zeppelin DS-8 aerodynamic cabriolet, 1936.

1986, June 19 ***Perf. 13½x13***

2175 A395 Strip of 6, #a.-f. 2.25 1.25
2176 A395 5g multicolored 3.75 1.25
Nos. 2175-2176 (2) 6.00 2.50

No. 2077 Overprinted in Bright Blue with Olympic Rings and "CALGARY 1988"

1986, July 9 ***Perf. 13***

2177 A369 5g on #2077 2.50 1.25

1988 Winter Olympics, Calgary.

Statue of Liberty, Cent. — A396

Passenger liners: No. 2178a, 25c, City of Paris, England, 1867. b, 50c, Mauretania, England. c, 1g, Normandie, France, 1932. d, 2g, Queen Mary, England, 1938. e, 3g, Kaiser Wilhelm the Great II, Germany, 1897. f, 4g, United States, US, 1952. 5g, Bremen, Germany, 1928. 25g, Sailing ship Gorch Fock, Germany, 1976, vert.

1986, July 25 ***Perf. 13***

2178 A396 Strip of 6, #a.-f. 2.50 1.50
2179 A396 5g multicolored 2.50 .60
Nos. 2178-2179 (2) 5.00 2.10

Souvenir Sheet

Perf. 14½

2180 A396 25g multicolored 13.00 13.00

No. 2180 is airmail and contains one 50x70mm stamp.

Dog Type of 1984

#2181: a, 25c, German shepherd. b, 50c, Icelandic shepherd. c, 1g, Collie. d, 2g, Boxer. e, 3g, Scottish terrier. f, 4g, Welsh springer spaniel. 5g, Painting of Labrador retriever by Ellen Krebs, vert.

1986, Aug. 28 ***Perf. 13x13½***

2181 A376 Strip of 6, #a.-f. 2.50 1.00

Perf. 13½x13

2182 A376 5g multicolored 1.50 .50
Nos. 2181-2182 (2) 4.00 1.50

Paraguay Official Stamps, Cent. — A397

#2183-2185, #O1. #2186-2188, #O4.

1986, Aug. 28 Litho. ***Perf. 13x13½***

2183 A397 5g multi 1.50 1.50
2184 A397 15g multi 1.50 1.50
2185 A397 40g multi 1.50 1.50
2186 A397 65g multi 1.50 1.50
2187 A397 100g multi 1.50 1.50
2188 A397 150g multi 1.50 1.50
Nos. 2183-2188 (6) 9.00 9.00

Nos. 2186-2188 are airmail.

Tennis Players A398

Designs: No. 2189a, Victor Pecci, Paraguay. b, 50c, Jimmy Connors, US. c, 1g, Gabriela Sabatini, Argentina. d, 2g, Boris Becker, W. Germany. e, 3g, Claudia Kohde, E. Germany. f, 4g, Sweden, 1985 Davis Cup team champions, horiz. 5g, Steffi Graf, W. Germany. 25g, 1986 Wimbledon champions Martina Navratilova and Boris Becker, horiz.

Perf. 13x13½, 13½x13

1986, Sept. 17 **Unwmk.**

2189 A398 Strip of 6, #a.-f. 3.00 1.25
2190 A398 5g multicolored 1.50 .50
Nos. 2189-2190 (2) 4.50 1.75

Souvenir Sheet

Perf. 13½

2191 A398 25g multicolored 12.00 12.00

No. 2191 is airmail and contains one 75x55mm stamp. For overprints see No. 2229.

Nos. 1454-1456 Ovptd. in Red or Silver (#2192c, 2192d): "Homenage a la visita de Sus Altezas Imperiales los Principes Hitachi --28.9-3.10.86"

1986, Sept. 28 ***Perf. 14***

2192 A251 Strip of 5, #a.-e. 1.50 1.00
2193 A251 50c on #1455 .60 .50
2194 A251 75c on #1456 .90 .75
Nos. 2192-2194 (3) 3.00 2.25

1988 Summer Olympics, Seoul A399

Athletes, 1984 Olympic medalists: No. 2195a, 25c, Runner. b, 50c, Boxer. c, 1g, Joaquim Cruz, Brazil, 800-meter run. d, 2g, Mary Lou Retton, US, individual all-around gymnastics. e, 3g, Carlos Lopes, Portugal, marathon. f, 4g, Fredy Schmidtke, W. Germany, 1000-meter cycling, horiz. 5g, Joe Fargis, US, equestrian, horiz.

1986, Oct. 29 ***Perf. 13x13½,13½x13***

2195 A399 Strip of 6, #a.-f. 1.75 1.25
2196 A399 5g multicolored 2.50 1.75
Nos. 2195-2196 (2) 4.25 3.00

For overprints see Nos. 2227-2228, 2230.

Nos. 1574c-1574g Ovptd. in Silver, Ship Type of 1983 Ovptd. in Red

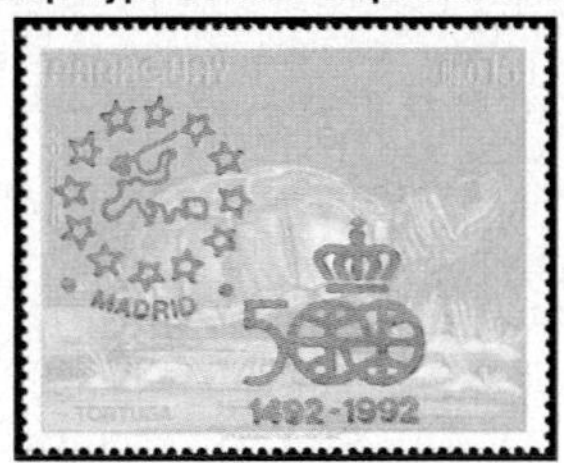

1987, Mar. 20 Litho. ***Perf. 14***

2197 A278 Strip of 5, #a.-e. 3.50 3.00
2198 AP176 10g multicolored 1.50 1.50
Nos. 2197-2198 (2) 5.00 4.50

500th Anniv. of the discovery of America and the 12th Spanish-American Stamp & Coin Show, Madrid.

Olympics Type of 1985 Overprinted in Silver with Olympic Rings and 500th Anniv. of the Discovery of America Emblems and "BARCELONA 92 / Sede de las Olimpiadas en el ano del 500o Aniversario del Descubrimiento de America"

Designs like Nos. 2134a-2134f.

1987, Apr. 24 ***Perf. 14***

2199 A384 Strip of 6, #a.-f. 8.00 8.00

1992 Summer Olympics, Barcelona and discovery of America, 500th anniv. in 1992.

No. 2135 Overprinted in Silver "ROMA / OLYMPHILEX" / Olympic Rings / "SEOUL / CALGARY / 1988"

1987, Apr. 30 ***Perf. 13***

2200 A384 5g on No. 2135 2.50 2.50

Olymphilex '87 Intl. Philatelic Exhibition, Rome.

Cat Type of 1976

Various cats and kittens: No. 2201: a, 1g. b, 2g. c, 3g. d, 5g. 60g, Black cat.

1987, May 22 ***Perf. 13x13½***

2201 A287 Strip of 4, #a.-d. 1.60 .75
2202 A287 60g multicolored 1.10 .95
Nos. 2201-2202 (2) 2.70 1.70

No. 2202 also exists perf. 14. For overprint see No. 2212.

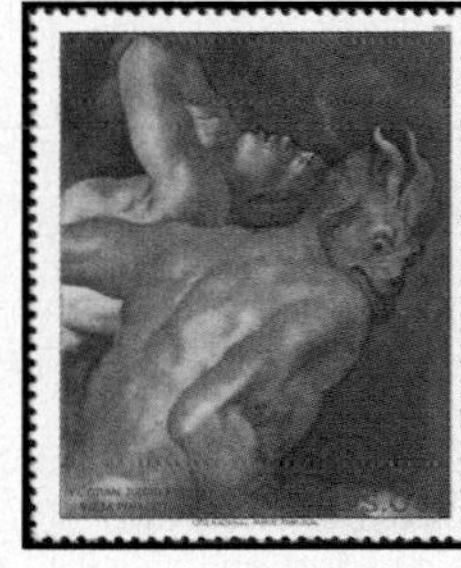
Paintings by Rubens A400

No. 2203: a, 1g, The Four Corners of the World, horiz. b, 2g, Jupiter and Calisto. c, 3g, Susanna and the Elders. d, 5g, Marriage of Henry IV and Marie de Medici in Lyon.
60g, The Last Judgment. 100g, The Holy Family with St. Elizabeth and John the Baptist. No. 2205A, War and Peace.

1987 Litho. ***Perf. 13x13½, 13½x13***

2203 A400 Strip of 4, #a.-d. 1.50 1.00
2204 A400 60g multicolored 2.00 1.50
Nos. 2203-2204 (2) 3.50 2.50

Souvenir Sheets

2205 A400 100g multicolored 14.00 14.00
2205A A400 100g multicolored 14.00 14.00

Christmas 1986 (#2205).
Issued: #2204, May 25; #2205, May 26.
Nos. 2205-2205A are airmail and contain one 54x68mm stamp.

Places and Events — A401

10g, ACEPAR Industrial Plant. 25g, Franciscan monk, native, vert. 50g, Yaguaron Church altar, vert. 75g, Founding of Asuncion, 450th anniv. 100g, Paraguay Airlines passenger jet. 200g, Pres. Stoessner, vert.

1987, June 2 Litho. ***Perf. 13***

2206 A401 10g multicolored .25 .25
2207 A401 25g multicolored .25 .25
2208 A401 50g multicolored .25 .25
2209 A401 75g multicolored .50 .25
2210 A401 100g multicolored .75 .30
2211 A401 200g multicolored 1.00 .50
Nos. 2206-2211 (6) 3.00 1.80

Nos. 2210-2211 are airmail. For overprints see Nos. 2225-2226, C685, C722.

No. 2201 Ovptd. in Blue

1987, June 12 ***Perf. 13x13½***

2212 A287 Strip of 4, #a.-d. 1.50 1.50

Discovery of America, 500th Anniv. (in 1992) — A402

Discovery of America anniv. emblem and ships: No. 2213a, 1g, Spanish galleon, 17th cent. b, 2g, Victoria, 1st to circumnavigate the globe, 1519-22. c, 3g, San Hermenegildo. 5g, San Martin, c.1582. 60g, Santa Maria, c.1492, vert.

1987, Sept. 9 *Perf. 14*
2213 A402 Strip of 4, #a.-d. 4.50 1.50

Perf. 13x13½
2214 A402 60g multicolored 1.60 1.60
Nos. 2213-2214 (2) 6.10 3.10

Colorado Party, Cent. — A403

Bernardino Caballero (founder), President Stroessner and: 5g, 10g, 25g, Three-lane highway. 150g, 170g, 200g, Power lines.

Perf. 13½x13
1987, Sept. 11 **Wmk. 347**

2215	A403	5g multi	3.00	2.00
2216	A403	10g multi	3.00	2.00
2217	A403	25g multi	3.00	2.00
2218	A403	150g multi	3.00	2.00
2219	A403	170g multi	3.00	2.00
2220	A403	200g multi	3.00	2.00
		Nos. 2215-2220 (6)	18.00	12.00

Nos. 2218-2220 are airmail.

Berlin, 750th Anniv. — A404

Berlin Stamps and Coins: No. 2221: a, 1g, #9NB145. b, 2g, #9NB154. c, 3g, #9N57, vert. d, 5g, #9N170, vert. 60g, 1987 Commemorative coin, vert.

Perf. 13½x13, 13½x13
1987, Sept. 12 **Unwmk.**
2221 A404 Strip of 4, #a.-d. 6.50 2.00
2222 A404 60g multicolored 3.50 3.00
Nos. 2221-2222 (2) 10.00 5.00

For overprints see Nos. 2239, 2294.

Race Cars A405

No. 2223: a, 1g, Audi Sport Quattro. b, 2g, Lancia Delta S 4. c, 3g, Fiat 131. d, 5g, Porsche 911 4x4. 60g, Lancia Rally.

1987, Sept. 27 *Perf. 13*
2223 A405 Strip of 4, #a.-d. 1.50 1.00

Perf. 14
2224 A405 60g multicolored 1.50 1.00
Nos. 2223-2224 (2) 3.00 2.00

Nos. 2209-2210 Ovptd. in Blue

1987, Sept. 30 *Perf. 13*
2225 A401 75g on #2209 .70 .70
2226 A401 100g on #2210 .80 .80
Nos. 2225-2226 (2) 1.50 1.50

EXFIVIA '87 Intl. Philatelic Exhibition, LaPaz, Bolivia. No. 2226 is airmail. No. 2225 surcharge is in dark blue; and No. 2226 surcharge is bright blue.

Nos. 2195d-2195f, 2196 Overprinted in Black or Silver

1987, Oct. 1 *Perf. 13½x13*
2227 A399 Strip of 3, #a.-c. 3.00 3.00
2228 A399 5g on No. 2196 (S) 2.00 2.00
Nos. 2227-2228 (2) 5.00 5.00

Olymphilex '87 Intl. Phil. Exhib., Seoul.

No. 2189 Ovptd. with Emblem and "PHILATELIA '87," etc.

1987, Oct. 15 *Perf. 13x13½, 13½x13*
2229 A398 Strip of 6, #a.-f. 3.00 3.00

PHILATELIA '87 Intl. Phil. Exhib., Cologne. Size and configuration of overprint varies.

Nos. 2195a-2195b Ovptd. in Bright Blue for EXFILNA '87 and BARCELONA 92

1987, Oct. 24 *Perf. 13x13½*
2230 A399 Pair, #a.-b. 4.00 4.00

Exfilna '87 Intl. Philatelic Exhibition.

Ship Paintings — A406

No. 2231: a, 1g, San Juan Nepomuceno. b, 2g, San Eugenio. c, 3g, San Telmo. d, 5g, San Carlos. 60g, Spanish galleon, 16th cent. 100g, One of Columbus' ships.

1987 **Litho.** *Perf. 14*
2231 A406 Strip of 4, #a.-d. 7.00 2.50

Perf. 13x13½
2232 A406 60g multicolored 3.00 1.50
Nos. 2231-2232 (2) 10.00 4.00

Souvenir Sheet

Perf. 13½
2233 A406 100g multicolored 13.00 13.00

Discovery of America, 500th anniv. in 1992 (#2233). Issue dates: Nos. 2231-2232, Dec. 10. No. 2233, Dec. 12.

No. 2233 is airmail and contains one 54x75mm stamp.

1988 Winter Olympics, Calgary — A407

#2237: a, 5g, Joel Gaspoz. b, 60g, Peter Mueller.

1987, Dec. 31 *Perf. 14*
2234 A407 1g Maria Walliser 3.50 1.25
2235 A407 2g Erika Hess 3.50 1.25
2236 A407 3g Pirmin Zurbriggen 3.50 1.25
Nos. 2234-2236 (3) 10.50 3.75

Miniature Sheet

Perf. 13½x13
2237 A407 Sheet of 4 each #2237a, 2237b+label 20.00 20.00

Souvenir Sheet

Perf. 14½
2238 A407 100g Walliser, Zurbriggen 12.00 12.00

No. 2238 is airmail. For overprints see Nos. 2240-2242.

No. 2221 Ovptd. in Silver "AEROPEX 88 / ADELAIDE"

1988, Jan. 29 *Perf. 13*
2239 A404 Strip of 4, #a.-d. 8.00 4.00

Aeropex '88, Adelaide, Australia.

Nos. 2234-2236 Ovptd. in Gold with Olympic Rings and "OLYMPEX / CALGARY 1988"

1988, Feb. 13 *Perf. 14*
2240 A407 1g on #2234 .75 .75
2241 A407 2g on #2235 1.50 1.50
2242 A407 3g on #2236 2.00 2.00
Nos. 2240-2242 (3) 4.25 4.25

Olympex '88, Calgary. Size and configuration of overprint varies.

1988 Summer Olympics, Seoul — A408

Equestrians: No. 2243a, 1g, Josef Neckermann, W. Germany, on Venetia. b, 2g, Henri Chammartin, Switzerland. c, 3g, Christine Stueckelberger, Switzerland, on Granat. d, 5g, Liselott Linsenhoff, W. Germany, on Piaff. 60g, Hans-Guenter Winkler, W. Germany.

1988, Mar. 7 *Perf. 13*
2243 A408 Strip of 4, #a.-d. 5.50 2.00

Perf. 13½x13
2244 A408 60g multicolored 2.50 2.00
Nos. 2243-2244 (2) 8.00 4.00

For overprint see No. 2291.

Berlin, 750th Anniv. — A409

Paintings: No. 2245a, 1g, Virgin and Child, by Jan Gossaert. b, 2g, Virgin and Child, by Rubens. c, 3g, Virgin and Child, by Hans Memling. d, 5g, Madonna, by Albrecht Durer. 60g, Adoration of the Shepherds, by Martin Schongauer.

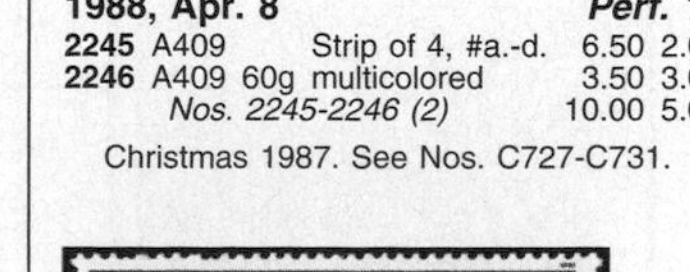

1988, Apr. 8 *Perf. 13*
2245 A409 Strip of 4, #a.-d. 6.50 2.00
2246 A409 60g multicolored 3.50 3.00
Nos. 2245-2246 (2) 10.00 5.00

Christmas 1987. See Nos. C727-C731.

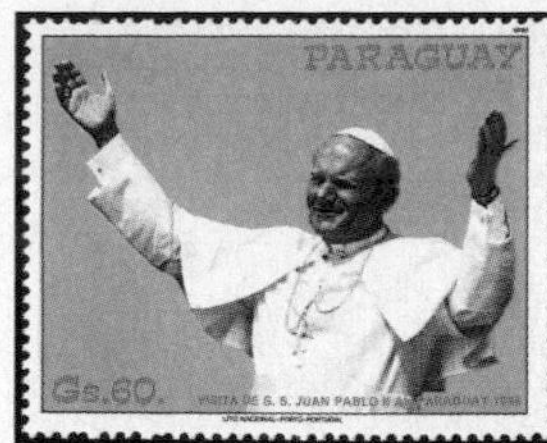

Visit of Pope John Paul II A410

Religious art: No. 2247a, 1g, Pope John Paul II, hands clasped. b, 2g, Statue of the Virgin. c, 3g, Czestochowa Madonna. d, 5g, Our Lady of Caacupe. Nos. 2247a-2247d are vert.

1988, Apr. 11 *Perf. 13*
2247 A410 Strip of 4, #a.-d. 2.50 1.00
2248 A410 60g multicolored 1.50 1.00
Nos. 2247-2248 (2) 4.00 2.00

Visit of Pope John Paul II — A411

Rosette window and crucifix.

1988, May 5 **Litho.** *Perf. 13x13½*
2249 A411 10g blue & blk 2.00 .75
2250 A411 20g blue & blk 2.00 .75
2251 A411 50g blue & blk 2.00 .75
Nos. 2249-2251 (3) 6.00 2.25

World Wildlife Fund Type of 1985

Endangered Animals: No. 2252a, 1g, like #2139g. b, 2g, like #2139f. c, 3g, like #2139d. d, 5g, like #2139e.

1988, June 14 **Unwmk.** *Perf. 14*
2252 A386 Strip of 4, #a.-d. 10.00 2.00

Nos. 2252a-2252d have denomination and border in blue.

Nos. 2000a-2000d Ovptd. in Gold with Emblem and "Bicentenario de / AUSTRALIA / 1788-1988"

1988, June 17
2253 A351 Strip of 4, #a.-d. 3.50 3.50

Australia, bicent.

Types of 1985 Overprinted in 2 or 4 Lines in Gold "NUEVO PERIODO PRESIDENCIAL CONSTITUCIONAL 1988-1993"

1988, Aug. 12 *Perf. 14*

2254	A390	10g like #2153	.25	.25
2255	A390	25g like #2154	.25	.25
2256	A390	50g like #2155	.40	.40
2257	A390	75g like #2156	.75	.75
2258	A390	100g like #2157	.90	.90
2259	A390	200g like #2158	1.50	1.50
		Nos. 2254-2259 (6)	4.05	4.05

Pres. Stroessner's new term in office. Nos. 2258-2259 are airmail.

Olympic Tennis, Seoul — A412

Designs: No. 2260a, 1g, Steffi Graf, W. Germany. b, 2g, Olympic gold medal, horiz. c, 3g, Boris Becker, W. Germany. d, 5g, Emilio Sanchez, Spain. 60g, Steffi Graf, diff.

1988, Aug. 16 *Perf. 13*
2260 A412 Strip of 4, #a.-d. 10.00 3.25
2261 A412 60g multicolored 2.50 2.50
Nos. 2260-2261 (2) 12.50 5.75

1992 Summer Olympics, Barcelona — A413

Olympic medalists from Spain: No. 2262a, 1g, Ricardo Zamora, soccer, Antwerp, 1920, vert. b, 2g, Equestrian team, Amsterdam, 1928. c, 3g, Angel Leon, shooting, Helsinki, 1952. d, 5g, Kayak team, Montreal, 1976. 60g, Francisco Fernandez Ochoa, slalom, Sapporo, 1972, vert. 100g, Olympic Stadium, Barcelona, vert.

1989, Jan. 5 *Perf. 14*

2262 A413 Strip of 4, #a.-d. 6.00 3.25

Perf. 13

2263 A413 60g multicolored 1.50 1.25
Nos. 2262-2263 (2) 7.50 4.50

Souvenir Sheet

Perf. 13½

2264 A413 100g multicolored 12.00 12.00

Discovery of America 500th anniv. (in 1992). No. 2264 is airmail and contains one 50x60mm stamp. For overprint see No. 2293.

Columbus Space Station A414

1989, Jan. 7 **Litho.** *Perf. 13x13½*

2265 A414 60g multicolored 4.00 2.00

Discovery of America 500th anniv. (in 1992). Printed in sheets of 4 + 5 labels.

No. 2076 Overprinted in Silver, Red and Blue with Olympic Rings, "1992" and Emblem

1989, Jan. 10 *Perf. 13½x13, 13x13½*

2266 A369 Strip of 6, #a.-f. 5.00 5.00

1992 Winter Olympics, Albertville. Location and configuration of overprint varies.

No. 1454 Ovptd. in Silver "HOMENAJE AL EMPERADOR HIROITO DE JAPON 29.IV,1901-6.1.1989"

1989, Feb. 8 *Perf. 14*

2267 A251 Strip of 5, #a.-e. 3.00 3.00

Death of Emperor Hirohito of Japan.

Formula 1 Drivers, Race Cars — A415

No. 2268: a, 1g, Stirling Moss, Mercedes W196. b, 2g, Emerson Fittipaldi, Lotus. c, 3g, Nelson Piquet, Lotus. d, 5g, Niki Lauda, Ferrari 312 B. 60g, Juan Manuel Fangio, Maserati 250F.

1989, Mar. 6 *Perf. 13*

2268 A415 Strip of 4, #a.-d. 6.50 2.00
2269 A415 60g multicolored 2.50 2.50
Nos. 2268-2269 (2) 9.00 4.50

Paintings by Titian A416

No. 2270: a, 1g, Bacchus and Ariadne (Bacchus). b, 2g, Bacchus and Ariadne (tutelary spirit). c, 3g, Death of Actaeon. d, 5g, Portrait of a Young Woman with a Fur Cape. 60g, Concert in a Field. 100g, Holy Family with Donor.

1989, Apr. 17 *Perf. 13x13½*

2270 A416 Strip of 4, #a.-d. 5.50 1.75
2271 A416 60g multicolored 2.50 .75
Nos. 2270-2271 (2) 8.00 2.50

Souvenir Sheet

Perf. 13½

2271A A416 100g multicolored 12.00 12.00

No. 2271A is airmail and contains one 60x49mm stamp. Issue date: May 27.

1994 Winter Olympics, Lillehammer — A417

Athletes: No. 2272a, 1g, Torbjorn Lokken, 1987 Nordic combined world champion. b, 2g, Atle Skardal, skier, Norway. c, 3g, Geir Karlstad, Norway, world 10,000-meter speed skating champion, 1987. d, 5g, Franck Piccard, France, 1988 Olympic medalist, skiing. 60g, Roger Ruud, ski jumper, Norway.

1989, May 23 *Perf. 13½x13*

2272 A417 Strip of 4, #a.-d. 12.00 4.00
2273 A417 60g multicolored 5.50 3.50
Nos. 2272-2273 (2) 17.50 7.50

Cat Type of 1976

Various cats: #2274a, 1g. b, 2g. c, 3g. d, 5g.

1989, May 25 *Perf. 13*

2274 A287 Strip of 4, #a.-d. 6.50 2.00
2275 A287 60g Siamese 2.00 2.00
Nos. 2274-2275 (2) 8.50 4.00

Federal Republic of Germany, 40th Anniv. — A418

Famous men and automobiles: No. 2276a, 1g, Konrad Adenauer, chancellor, 1949-1963, Mercedes. b, 2g, Ludwig Erhard, chancellor, 1963-1966, Volkswagen Beetle. c, 3g, Felix Wankel, engine designer, 1963 NSU Spider. d, 5g, Franz Josef Strauss, President of Bavarian Cabinet, BMW 502. 60g, Pres. Richard von Weizsacker and Dr. Josef Neckermann.

1989, May 27 *Perf. 13½x13*

2276 A418 Strip of 4, #a.-d. 8.00 2.50
2277 A418 60g multicolored 3.00 3.00
Nos. 2276-2277 (2) 11.00 5.50

For overprints see No. 2369.

Ship Type of 1980 Overprinted with Discovery of America, 500th Anniv. Emblem in Red on Silver

1989, May 29 *Perf. 14½*

Miniature Sheet

2278 A343 Sheet of 7+label, like #1972 18.00 18.00

Discovery of America 500th anniv. (in 1992).

No. 2122a Overprinted with Hamburg Emblem and Nos. 2122b-2122f, 2123 Ovptd. with Diff. Emblem in Red on Silver

1989, May 30 **Litho.** *Perf. 13½x13*

2279 A381 Strip of 6, #a.-f. 12.00 12.00
2280 A381 5g on #2123 3.00 3.00
Nos. 2279-2280 (2) 15.00 15.00

City of Hamburg, 800th anniv.

Nos. 2006a-2006b Ovptd. "BRASILIANA / 89"

1989, July 5 *Perf. 14*

2281 A352 Pair, #a.-b. 4.00 2.00

No. 2171 Overprinted in Metallic Red and Silver with FIFA and Italia 90 Emblems and "PARAGUAY PARTICIPO EN 13 CAMPEONATOS MUNDIALES"

1989, Sept. 14 **Litho.** *Perf. 13½x13*

2283 A394 Strip of 6, #a.-f. 4.00 4.00

Size and configuration of overprint varies.

Nos. C738, C753 Ovptd. in metallic red with Italia '90 emblem & "SUDAMERICA-GRUPO 2 / PARAGUAY-COLOMBIA / PARAGUAY-ECUADOR / COLOMBIA-PARAGUAY / ECUADOR-PARAGUAY" and in metallic red on silver with FIFA emblem

1989, Sept. 14 **Litho.** *Perf. 13*

2284 AP228 25g on #C738 7.50 3.50
2285 AP232 25g on #C753 7.50 3.50
Nos. 2284-2285 (2) 15.00 7.00

Nos. 2046, 2172 Overprinted in Metallic Red and Silver "PARAGUAY CLASIFICADO EN 1930, 1950, 1958 Y 1986" and Emblems or "ITALIA '90"

1989, Sept. 15 **Litho.** *Perf. 14*

2286 A362 Strip of 6, #a.-f. 15.00 4.50

Perf. 13½x13

2287 A394 5g multicolored 5.00 3.00
Nos. 2286-2287 (2) 20.00 7.50

1990 World Cup Soccer Championships, Italy. Location and size of overprint varies.

Nos. 1284-1286 Ovptd. in Gold "...BIEN ESTUVIMOS EN LA LUNA AHORA NECESITAMOS LOS MEDIOS PARA LLEGAR A LOS PLANETAS" Wernher von Braun's Signature and UN and Space Emblems

1989, Sept. 16 *Perf. 14*

2288 A226 Strip of 5, #a.-e. 5.50 5.50
2289 A226 50c multicolored 2.50 2.50
2290 A226 75c multicolored 4.00 4.00
Nos. 2288-2290 (3) 12.00 12.00

Location, size and configuration of overprint varies.

Nos. 2243, C764 Overprinted in Silver or Gold with Emblem and "ATENAS 100 ANOS DE LOS JUEGOS OLIMPICOS 1896-1996"

1989, Sept. 18 *Perf. 13*

2291 A408 Strip of 4, #a.-d. 3.00 3.00
2292 AP233 25g on #C764 (G) 7.00 7.00
Nos. 2291-2292 (2) 10.00 10.00

1992 Summer Olympics Barcelona, Spain. Size and location of overprint varies.

Nos. 2262a-2262d Ovptd. in Silver with Heads of Steffi Graf or Boris Becker and: "WIMBLEDON 1988 / SEUL 1988 / WIMBLEDON 1989 / EL TENIS NUEVAMENTE EN / LAS OLIMPIADAS 1988-1992" or Similar

1989, Sept. 19 *Perf. 14*

2293 A413 Strip of 4, #a.-d. 8.00 8.00

Addition of tennis as an Olympic sport in 1992. Size and configuration of overprint varies.

No. 2221 Ovptd. in Gold and Blue "PRIMER AEROPUERTO PARA / /COHETES, BERLIN 1930 OBERTH, / NEBEL, RITTER, VON BRAUN" space emblem and "PROF. DR. HERMANN / OBERTH 95o ANIV. / NACIMIENTO 25.6.1989"

Perf. 13½x13, 13x13½

1989, Sept. 20

2294 A404 Strip of 4, #a.-d. 18.00 6.00

Dr. Hermann Oberth, rocket scientist, 95th birth anniv. Overprint size, etc, varies.

Nos. 1406-1408 Ovptd. in Metallic Red and Silver with Emblems and "OLIMPIADAS / DE INVIERNO / ALBERTVILLE 1992" in 2 or 3 Lines

1989, Sept. 21 *Perf. 14*

2295 A244 Strip of 5, #a.-e. 9.00 3.00
2296 A244 50c multicolored 4.50 2.50
2297 A244 75c multicolored 6.50 4.00
Nos. 2295-2297 (3) 20.00 9.50

1992 Winter Olympics, Albertville. Size and configuration of overprint varies.

Nos. 2251, C724 Overprinted

Perf. 13½, 13½x13

1989, Oct. 9 **Litho.** **Wmk. 347**

2298 A411 50g on #2251 10.00 7.50
2299 AP226 120g on #C724 10.00 8.00

Parafil '89, Paraguay-Argentina philatelic exhibition.

Birds Facing Extinction — A419

50g, Ara chloroptera. 100g, Mergus octosetaceus. 300g, Rhea americana. 500g, Ramphastos toco. 1000g, Crax fasciolata. 2000g, Ara ararauna.

Perf. 13½x13

1989, Dec. 19 **Litho.** **Wmk. 347**

2300 A419 50g multicolored .30 .30
2301 A419 100g multicolored .30 .30
2302 A419 300g multicolored .75 .75
2303 A419 500g multicolored 1.20 1.20
2304 A419 1000g multicolored 2.25 2.25
2305 A419 2000g multicolored 4.25 4.25
Nos. 2300-2305 (6) 9.05 9.05

Nos. 2302-2305 airmail. Nos. 2300 & 2305 vert. Frames and typestyles vary greatly. Watermark on 50g, 100g, 300g is 8mm high.

1992 Summer Olympics, Barcelona — A420

Athletes: No. 2306a, 1g, A. Fichtel and S. Bau, W. Germany, foils, 1988. b, 2g, Spanish basketball team, 1984. c, 3g, Jackie Joyner-Kersee, heptathalon and long jump, 1988, horiz. d, 5g, L. Beerbaum, W. Germany, show jumping, team, 1988. 60g, W. Brinkmann, W. Germany, show jumping, team, 1988. 100g, Emilio Sanchez, tennis.

Unwmk.

1989, Dec. 26 Litho. *Perf. 14*
2306 A420 Strip of 4, #a.-d. 6.00 2.00

Perf. 13
2307 A420 60g multicolored 6.50 3.50
Nos. 2306-2307 (2) 12.50 5.50

Souvenir Sheet

Perf. 13½
2308 A420 100g multicolored 20.00 15.00

No. 2308 is airmail and contains one 47x57mm stamp.

World Cup Soccer Championships, Italy — A421

1986 World Cup soccer players in various positions: No. 2309a, 1g, England vs. Paraguay. b, 2g, Spain vs. Denmark. c, 3g, France vs. Italy. d, 5g, Germany vs. Morocco. 60g, Mexico vs. Paraguay. 100g, Germany vs. Argentina.

1989, Dec. 29 *Perf. 14*
2309 A421 Strip of 4, #a.-d. 8.50 2.50

Perf. 13½
2310 A421 60g multicolored 5.50 2.50
Nos. 2309-2310 (2) 14.00 5.00

Souvenir Sheet

Perf. 14½
2311 A421 100g multicolored 20.00 15.00

No. 2311 is airmail and contains one 40x50mm stamp.
For overprints see Nos. 2355-2356.

1992 Summer Olympics, Barcelona — A422

Barcelona '92, proposed Athens '96 emblems and: No. 2312a, 1g, Greece #128. b, 2g, Greece #126, vert. c, 3g, Greece #127, vert. d, 5g, Greece #123, vert. 60g, Paraguay #736. 100g, Horse and rider, vert.

1990, Jan. 4 *Perf. 13½x13, 13x13½*
2312 A422 Strip of 4, #a.-d. 6.00 2.00
2313 A422 60g multicolored 11.00 4.00
Nos. 2312-2313 (2) 17.00 6.00

Souvenir Sheet

Perf. 13½
2314 A422 100g multicolored 15.00 15.00

No. 2314 is airmail and contains one 50x60mm stamp and exists with either white or yellow border, same value. Stamps inscribed 1989.
For overprints see No. 2357.

Swiss Confederation, 700th Anniv. — A423

#2315: a, 3g, Monument to William Tell. b, 5g, Manship Globe, UN Headquarters, Geneva. 60g, 15th cent. messenger, Bern. #2317, 1st Swiss steam locomotive, horiz. #2318, Jean Henri Dunant, founder of the Red Cross, horiz.

1990, Jan. 25 *Perf. 14*
2315 A423 Pair, #a.-b. 5.50 2.00

Perf. 13
2316 A423 60g multicolored 5.00 3.50
Nos. 2315-2316 (2) 10.50 5.50

Souvenir Sheets

Perf. 14½
2317 A423 100g multicolored 25.00 25.00
2318 A423 100g multicolored 20.00 20.00

Nos. 2317-2318 are airmail. For overprints see Nos. 2352-2354.

Wood Carving — A424

Discovery of America, 500th anniv. emblem &: #2319: a, 1g, 1st cathechism in Guarani. b, 2g, shown. #2319 has continuous design.

1990, Jan. 26 *Perf. 14*
2319 A424 Pair, #a.-b. + label 4.00 1.40

Organization of American States, Cent. — A425

Perf. 13½x13

1990, Feb. 9 Litho. Wmk. 347
2320 A425 50g multicolored .30 .30
2321 A425 100g multicolored .45 .35
2322 A425 200g Map of Paraguay .90 .65
Nos. 2320-2322 (3) 1.65 1.30

1992 Winter Olympics, Albertville — A426

Calgary 1988 skiers: No. 2323a, 1g, Alberto Tomba, Italy, slalom and giant slalom. b, 2g, Vreni Schneider, Switzerland, women's slalom and giant slalom, vert. c, 3g, Luc Alphand, France, skier, vert. d, 5g, Matti Nykaenen, Finland, ski-jumping.
60g, Marina Kiehl, W. Germany, women's downhill. 100g, Frank Piccard, France, super giant slalom.

1990, Mar. 7 Unwmk. *Perf. 14*
2323 A426 Strip of 4, #a.-d. 5.75 2.25

Perf. 13
2324 A426 60g multicolored 2.25 2.25
Nos. 2323-2324 (2) 8.00 4.50

Souvenir Sheet

Perf. 14½
2325 A426 100g multicolored 15.00 15.00

No. 2325 is airmail, contains one 40x50mm stamp and exists with either white or yellow border.

Pre-Columbian Art, Customs A427

UPAE Emblem and: 150g, Pre-Columbian basket. 500g, Aboriginal ceremony.

1990, Mar. 8 Wmk. 347 *Perf. 13*
2326 A427 150g multicolored 1.50 1.10
2327 A427 500g multicolored 3.75 2.25

No. 2327 is airmail.
For overprints see Nos. 2345-2346.

First Postage Stamp, 150th Anniv. — A428

Penny Black, Mail Transportation 500th anniv. emblem and: No. 2328a, 1g, Penny Black on cover. b, 2g, Mauritius #1-2 on cover. c, 3g, Baden #4b on cover. d, 5g, Roman States #4 on cover. 60g, Paraguay #C38 and four #C54 on cover.

1990, Mar. 12 Unwmk. *Perf. 14*
2328 A428 Strip of 4, #a.-d. 5.50 2.25

Perf. 13½x13
2329 A428 60g multicolored 2.25 2.25

Postal Union of the Americas and Spain (UPAE) A429

1990, July 2 *Perf. 13x13½*
2330 A429 200g Map, flags .90 .45
2331 A429 250g Paraguay #1 1.10 .50
2332 A429 350g FDC of #2326-2327, horiz. 2.40 .65
Nos. 2330-2332 (3) 4.40 1.60

National University, Cent. (in 1989) — A430

1990, Sept. 8
2333 A430 300g Future site 1.25 1.00
2334 A430 400g Present site 1.60 1.25
2335 A430 600g Old site 2.50 2.00
Nos. 2333-2335 (3) 5.35 4.25

Franciscan Churches — A431

Perf. 13½x13

1990, Sept. 25 Litho. Wmk. 347
2336 A431 50g Guarambare .30 .30
2337 A431 100g Yaguaron .45 .35
2338 A431 200g Ita .90 .65
Nos. 2336-2338 (3) 1.65 1.30

For overprints see Nos. 2366-2368.

Democracy in Paraguay — A432

Designs: 100g, State and Catholic Church, vert. 200g, Human rights, vert. 300g, Freedom of the Press, vert. 500g, Return of the exiles. 3000g, People and democracy.

Perf. 13½x13, 13x13½

1990, Oct. 5 Litho. Wmk. 347
2339 A432 50g multicolored .30 .30
2340 A432 100g multicolored .30 .30
2341 A432 200g multicolored .60 .50
2342 A432 300g multicolored .90 .80
2343 A432 500g multicolored 11.00 1.40
2344 A432 3000g multicolored 8.00 7.50
Nos. 2339-2344 (6) 21.10 10.80

Nos. 2343-2344 are airmail.

Nos. 2326-2327 Overprinted in Magenta

1990 Litho. Wmk. 347 *Perf. 13*
2345 A427 150g multicolored 1.25 .60
2346 A427 500g multicolored 4.00 1.90

No. 2346 is airmail.

UN Development Program, 40th Anniv. — A433

Designs: 50m, Human Rights, sculpture by Hugo Pistilli. 100m, United Nations, sculpture by Hermann Guggiari. 150m, Miguel de Cervantes Literature Award, won by Augusto Roa Bastos.

1990, Oct. 26
2347 A433 50g lilac & multi .45 .30
2348 A433 100g gray & multi .65 .35
2349 A433 150g green & multi 1.00 .60
Nos. 2347-2349 (3) 2.10 1.25

America A434

50g, Paraguay River banks. 250g, Chaco land.

Perf. 13½x13

1990, Oct. 31 **Wmk. 347**

2350	A434	50g multicolored		10.00	5.00
2351	A434	250g multicolored		20.00	10.00

No. 2351 is airmail.

Nos. 2315-2316, 2318 Ovptd. in Metallic Red and Silver

Unwmk.

1991, Apr. 2 **Litho.** ***Perf. 14***

2352	A423	Pair, #a.-b.	4.00	4.00

Perf. 13

2353	A423	60g on #2316	3.50	3.50
		Nos. 2352-2353 (2)	7.50	7.50

Souvenir Sheet

Perf. 14½

2354	A423	100g on #2318	17.00	17.00

Swiss Confederation, 700th anniv. and Red Cross, 125th anniv. No. 2354 is airmail. No. 2352 exists perf. 13. Location of overprint varies.

Nos. 2309-2310 Ovptd. in Silver

1991, Apr. 4 ***Perf. 14***

2355	A421	Strip of 4, #a.-d.	6.25	6.25

Perf. 13x13½

2356	A421	60g on #2310	3.75	3.75
		Nos. 2355-2356 (2)	10.00	10.00

1994 World Cup Soccer Championships. Location of overprint varies.

Nos. 2312, C822, C766 Ovptd. in Silver

1991, Apr. 4 ***Perf. 13***

2357	A422	Strip of 4, #a.-d.	7.00	5.00
2358	AP246	25g on #C822	4.50	3.00

Perf. 13x13½

2359	AP233	30g on #C766	6.00	4.00

Participation of reunified Germany in 1992 Summer Olympics. Nos. 2358-2359 are airmail. Location of overprint varies.

Professors A435

Designs: 50g, Julio Manuel Morales, gynecologist. 100g, Carlos Gatti, clinician. 200g, Gustavo Gonzalez, geologist. 300g, Juan Max Boettner, physician and musician. 350g, Juan Boggino, pathologist. 500g, Andres Barbero, physician, founder of Paraguayan Red Cross.

Perf. 13x13½

1991, Apr. 5 **Wmk. 347**

2360	A435	50g multicolored	.30	.30
2361	A435	100g multicolored	.30	.30
2362	A435	200g multicolored	.60	.50
2363	A435	300g multicolored	.90	.80
2364	A435	350g multicolored	1.00	.90
2365	A435	500g multicolored	1.50	1.40
		Nos. 2360-2365 (6)	4.60	4.20

Nos. 2364-2365 are airmail.

Nos. 2336-2338 Ovptd. in Black and Red

1991 **Wmk. 347** ***Perf. 13½x13***

2366	A431	50g on #2336	.50	.50
2367	A431	100g on #2337	.60	.60
2368	A431	200g on #2338	.90	.90
		Nos. 2366-2368 (3)	2.00	2.00

Espamer '91 Philatelic Exhibition.

Nos. 2276a-2276b Ovptd. in Silver

Nos. 2276c-2276d Ovptd. in Silver

1991 **Unwmk.** ***Perf. 13***

2369	A418	Strip of 4, #a.-d.	5.25	5.00

Writers and Muscians — A436

Designs: 50g, Ruy Diaz de Guzman, historian. 100g, Maria Talavera, war correspondent, vert. 150g, Augusto Roa Bastos, writer, vert. 200g, Jose Asuncion Flores, composer, vert. 250g, Felix Perez Cardozo, harpist. 300g, Juan Carlos Moreno Gonzalez, composer.

Perf. 13½x13,13x13½

1991, Aug. 27 **Litho.** **Wmk. 347**

2373	A436	50g multicolored	.30	.30
2374	A436	100g multicolored	.35	.35
2375	A436	150g multicolored	.60	.50
2376	A436	200g multicolored	.75	.65
2377	A436	250g multicolored	.90	.80
2378	A436	300g multicolored	1.10	1.00
		Nos. 2373-2378 (6)	4.00	3.60

Nos. 2376-2378 are airmail.

America A437

100g, War of Tavare. 300g, Arrival of Spanish explorer Domingo Martinez de Irala in Paraguay.

Perf. 13x13½

1991, Oct. 9 **Litho.** **Wmk. 347**

2379	A437	100g multicolored	1.50	.35
2380	A437	300g multicolored	1.75	.90

No. 2380 is airmail.

Paintings A438

Designs: 50g, Compass of Life, by Alfredo Moraes. 100g, The Lighted Alley, by Michael Burt. 150g, Earring, by Lucy Yegros. 200g, Migrant Workers, by Hugo Bogado Barrios. 250g, Passengers Without a Ship, by Bernardo Ismachoviez. 300g, Native Guarani, by Lotte Schulz.

Perf. 13x13½

1991, Nov. 12 **Litho.** **Wmk. 347**

2381	A438	50g multicolored	.30	.30
2382	A438	100g multicolored	.35	.35
2383	A438	150g multicolored	.60	.50
2384	A438	200g multicolored	.75	.65
2385	A438	250g multicolored	.90	.80
2386	A438	300g multicolored	1.10	1.00
		Nos. 2381-2386 (6)	4.00	3.60

Nos. 2384-2386 are airmail.

Endangered Species — A439

Perf. 13x13½, 13½x13

1992, Jan. 28 **Litho.** **Wmk. 347**

2387	A439	50g Catagonus wagneri, vert.	.30	.30
2388	A439	100g Felis pardalis	.35	.35
2389	A439	150g Tapirus terrestri	.60	.50
2390	A439	200g Chrysocyon brachyurus	.75	.65
		Nos. 2387-2390 (4)	2.00	1.80

Tile Designs of Christianized Indians A440

Perf. 13x13½

1992, Mar. 2 **Litho.** **Wmk. 347**

2391	A440	50g Geometric	.35	.30
2392	A440	100g Church	.35	.30
2393	A440	150g Missionary ship	.50	.35
2394	A440	200g Plant	.65	.50
		Nos. 2391-2394 (4)	1.85	1.45

Discovery of America, 500th anniv.

Leprosy Society of Paraguay, 60th Anniv. — A441

Designs: 50g, Society emblem, Malcolm L. Norment, founder. 250g, Gerhard Henrik Armauer Hansen (1841-1912), discoverer of leprosy bacillus.

Perf. 13x13½

1992, Apr. 28 **Litho.** **Wmk. 347**

2395	A441	50g multicolored	.30	.30
2396	A441	250g multicolored	.90	.80

Earth Summit, Rio de Janeiro A442

Earth Summit emblem, St. Francis of Assisi, and: 50g, Hands holding symbols of clean environment. 100g, Butterfly, industrial pollution. 250g, Globe, calls for environmental protection.

1992, June 9

2397	A442	50g multicolored	.30	.30
2398	A442	100g multicolored	.35	.35
2399	A442	250g multicolored	.80	.80
		Nos. 2397-2399 (3)	1.45	1.45

For overprints see Nos. 2422-2424.

PARAGUAY
ACTIVIDAD ECONOMICA
₲. 50
CENSO NACIONAL DE POBLACION Y VIVIENDAS 1992

Natl. Census A443

1992, July 30 ***Perf. 13½x13, 13x13½***

2400	A443	50g Economic activity	.30	.30
2401	A443	200g Houses, vert.	.65	.65
2402	A443	250g Population, vert.	.90	.80
2403	A443	300g Education	1.10	1.00
		Nos. 2400-2403 (4)	2.95	2.75

1992 Summer Olympics, Barcelona — A444

1992, Sept. 1 *Perf. 13x13½, 13½x13*

2404 A444 50g Soccer, vert. .30 .30
2405 A444 100g Tennis, vert. .35 .35
2406 A444 150g Running, vert. .60 .50
2407 A444 200g Swimming .75 .60
2408 A444 250g Judo, vert. .90 .80
2409 A444 350g Fencing 1.25 1.10
Nos. 2404-2409 (6) 4.15 3.65

Evangelism in Paraguay, 500th Anniv. — A445

Designs: 50g, Friar Luis Bolanos. 100g, Friar Juan de San Bernardo. 150g, San Roque Gonzalez de Santa Cruz. 200g, Father Amancio Gonzalez. 250g, Monsignor Juan Sinforiano Bogarin, vert.

Rough Perf. 13½x13, 13x13½

1992, Oct. 9 **Unwmk.**

2410 A445 50g multicolored .30 .30
2411 A445 100g multicolored .35 .35
2412 A445 150g multicolored .60 .50
2413 A445 200g multicolored .75 .65
2414 A445 250g multicolored .90 .80
Nos. 2410-2414 (5) 2.90 2.60

For overprints see Nos. 2419-2421.

America A446

Designs: 150g, Columbus, fleet arriving in New World. 350g, Columbus, vert.

Rough Perf. 13½x13, 13x13½

1992, Oct. 12

2415 A446 150g multicolored 1.00 .50
2416 A446 350g multicolored 1.50 1.10

No. 2416 is airmail.

Ovptd. "PARAFIL 92" in Blue

1992, Nov. 9

2417 A446 150g multicolored 1.00 .50
2418 A446 350g multicolored 1.50 1.10

No. 2418 is airmail.

Nos. 2410-2412 Ovptd. in Green

1992, Nov. 6 ***Rough Perf. 13½x13***

2419 A445 50g multicolored .30 .30
2420 A445 100g multicolored .35 .35
2421 A445 150g multicolored .60 .50
Nos. 2419-2421 (3) 1.25 1.15

Nos. 2397-2399 Ovptd. in Blue

Perf. 13x13½

1992, Oct. 24 **Wmk. 347**

2422 A442 50g multicolored .30 .30
2423 A442 100g multicolored .35 .35
2424 A442 250g multicolored .85 .85
Nos. 2422-2424 (3) 1.50 1.50

Inter-American Institute for Cooperation in Agriculture, 50th Anniv. — A447

Designs: 50g, Field workers. 100g, Test tubes, cattle in pasture. 200g, Hands holding flower. 250g, Cows, corn, city.

Perf. 13x13½

1992, Nov. 27 **Unwmk.**

2425 A447 50g multicolored .50 .30
2426 A447 100g multicolored .60 .35
2427 A447 200g multicolored .90 .75
2428 A447 250g multicolored 1.25 .90
Nos. 2425-2428 (4) 3.25 2.30

For overprints see Nos. 2461-2462.

Notary College of Paraguay, Cent. — A448

Designs: 50g, Yolanda Bado de Artecona. 100g, Jose Ramon Silva. 150g, Abelardo Brugada Valpy. 200g, Tomas Varela. 250g, Jose Livio Lezcano. 300g, Francisco I. Fernandez.

1992, Nov. 29 ***Rough Perf. 13½x13***

2429 A448 50g multicolored .30 .30
2430 A448 100g multicolored .35 .35
2431 A448 150g multicolored .60 .60
2432 A448 200g multicolored .75 .75
2433 A448 250g multicolored .90 .90
2434 A448 300g multicolored 1.00 1.00
Nos. 2429-2434 (6) 3.90 3.90

Opening of Lopez Palace, Cent. A449

Paintings of palace by: 50g, Michael Burt. 100g, Esperanza Gill. 200g, Emili Aparici. 250g, Hugo Bogado Barrios, vert.

1993, Mar. 9 ***Perf. 13½x13, 13x13½***

2435 A449 50g multicolored .30 .30
2436 A449 100g multicolored .35 .35
2437 A449 200g multicolored .75 .75
2438 A449 250g multicolored .90 .90
Nos. 2435-2438 (4) 2.30 2.30

For overprints see Nos. 2453-2456.

Treaty of Asuncion, 1st Anniv. — A450

Rough Perf. 13x13½

1993, Mar. 10 **Wmk. 347**

2439 A450 50g Flags, map .50 .30
2440 A450 350g Flags, globe 1.50 1.25

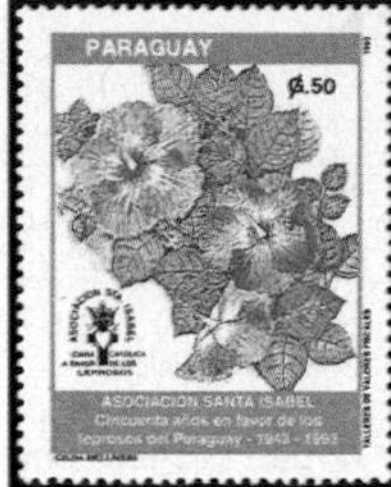

Santa Isabel Leprosy Assoc., 50th Anniv. — A451

Various flowers.

Perf. 13x13½

1993, May 24 **Unwmk.**

2441 A451 50g multicolored .30 .30
2442 A451 200g multicolored .75 .75
2443 A451 250g multicolored .90 .90
2444 A451 350g multicolored 1.25 1.25
Nos. 2441-2444 (4) 3.20 3.20

Goethe College, Cent. — A452

Designs: 50g, Goethe, by Johann Heinrich Lips, inscription. 100g, Goethe (close-up), by Johann Heinrich Wilhelm Tischbein.

1993, June 18

2445 A452 50g multicolored .30 .30
2446 A452 200g multicolored .75 .75

For overprints see Nos. 2451-2452.

World Friendship Crusade, 35th Anniv. — A453

Designs: 50g, Stylized globe. 100g, Map, Dr. Ramon Artemio Bracho. 200g, Children. 250g, Two people embracing.

1993, July 1

2447 A453 50g multicolored .40 .30
2448 A453 100g multicolored .40 .35
2449 A453 200g multicolored .80 .75
2450 A453 250g multicolored 1.00 .90
Nos. 2447-2450 (4) 2.60 2.30

For overprint see No. 2486.

Nos. 2445-2446 Ovptd. "BRASILIANA 93"

1993, July 12

2451 A452 50g multicolored .30 .30
2452 A452 200g multicolored .85 .85

Nos. 2435-2438 Ovptd.

Perf. 13½x13, 13x13½

1993, Aug. 13

2453 A449 50g multicolored .30 .30
2454 A449 100g multicolored .40 .35
2455 A449 200g multicolored .80 .75
2456 A449 250g multicolored 1.00 .90
Nos. 2453-2456 (4) 2.50 2.30

Size of overprint varies.

Church of the Incarnation, Cent. — A454

Design: 50g, Side view of church, vert.

Unwmk.

1993, Oct. 8 **Litho.** ***Perf. 13***

2457 A454 50g multicolored .30 .30
2458 A454 350g multicolored 1.20 .60

Endangered Animals — A455

America: 50g, Myrmecophaga tridactyla. 250g, Speothos venaticus.

1993, Oct. 27

2459 A455 50g multicolored 2.50 .60
2460 A455 250g multicolored 1.50 .75

No. 2459 is airmail.

Nos. 2426-2427 Ovptd.

1993, Nov. 16 ***Perf. 13x13½***

2461 A447 100g multicolored .30 .30
2462 A447 200g multicolored .60 .30

Christmas A456

1993, Nov. 24

2463 A456 50g shown .30 .30
2464 A456 250g Stars, wise men .70 .30

Scouting in Paraguay, 80th Anniv. A457

50g, Girl scouts watching scout instuctor. 100g, Boy scouts learning crafts. 200g, Lord Robert Baden-Powell. 250g, Girl scout with flag.

1993, Dec. 30

2465 A457 50g multicolored .30 .30
2466 A457 100g multicolored .30 .30
2467 A457 200g multicolored .60 .30
2468 A457 250g multicolored .80 .50
Nos. 2465-2468 (4) 2.00 1.40

First Lawyers to Graduate from Natl. University of Ascuncion, Cent. — A458

50g, Cecilio Baez. 100g, Benigno Riquelme, vert. 250g, Emeterio Gonzalez. 500g, J. Gaspar Villamayor.

1994, Apr. 8 ***Perf. 13***

2469 A458 50g multicolored .40 .30
2470 A458 100g multicolored .50 .30
2471 A458 250g multicolored .60 .45
2472 A458 500g multicolored 1.00 .75
Nos. 2469-2472 (4) 2.50 1.80

Phoenix Sports Corporation, 50th Anniv. — A459

Designs: 50g, Basketball player, vert. 200g, Soccer players, vert. 250g, Pedro Andrias Garcia Arias, founder, tennis player.

1994, May 20 Litho. ***Perf. 13***

2473 A459 50g multicolored .30 .30
2474 A459 200g multicolored .35 .35
2475 A459 250g multicolored .50 .45
Nos. 2473-2475 (3) 1.15 1.10

1994 World Cup Soccer Championships, U.S. — A460

Various soccer plays.

1994, June 2

2476 A460 250g multicolored .50 .45
2477 A460 500g multicolored 1.00 .75
2478 A460 1000g multicolored 1.75 1.50
Nos. 2476-2478 (3) 3.25 2.70

For overprints see Nos. 2483-2485.

Intl. Olympic Committee, Cent. — A461

Unwmk.

1994, June 23 Litho. ***Perf. 13***

2479 A461 350g Runner .60 .60
2480 A461 400g Lighting Olympic flame .65 .65

World Congress on Physical Education, Asuncion — A462

Designs: 1000g, Stylized family running to break finish line, vert.

Perf. 13½x13, 13x13½

1994, July 19 Litho.

2481 A462 200g multicolored .60 .45
2482 A462 1000g multicolored 2.75 2.25

Nos. 2476-2478 Ovptd.

1994, Aug. 2 ***Perf. 13***

2483 A460 250g multicolored .65 .65
2484 A460 500g multicolored 1.40 1.40
2485 A460 1000g multicolored 2.75 2.25
Nos. 2483-2485 (3) 4.80 4.30

No. 2448 Ovptd.

1994, Aug. 3 ***Perf. 13x13½***

2486 A453 100g multicolored .50 .30

Agustin Pio Barrios Mangore (1885-1944), Musician A463

1994, Aug. 5 ***Perf. 13x13½***

2487 A463 250g In tuxedo .60 .50
2488 A463 500g In traditional costume 1.25 1.00

Paraguayan Police, 151st Anniv. — A464

50g, 1913 Guardsman on horseback. 250g, Pedro Nolasco Fernandez, 1st capital police chief; Carlos Bernadino Cacabelos, 1st commissioner.

1994, Aug. 26 ***Perf. 13x13½***

2489 A464 50g multicolored .30 .30
2490 A464 250g multicolored .65 .60

For overprint see Nos. 2569-2570.

Parafil '94 A465

Birds: 100g, Ciconia maquari. 150g, Paroaria capitata. 400g, Chloroceryle americana, vert. 500g, Jabiru mycteria, vert.

1994, Sept. 9 ***Perf. 13***

2491 A465 100g multicolored .50 .30
2492 A465 150g multicolored .75 .40
2493 A465 400g multicolored 1.90 .90
2494 A465 500g multicolored 2.75 1.10
Nos. 2491-2494 (4) 5.90 2.70

Solar Eclipse A466

Designs: 50g, Eclipse, Copernicus. 200g, Sundial, Johannes Kepler.

Unwmk.

1994, Sept. 23 Litho. ***Perf. 13***

2495 A466 50g multicolored .30 .30
2496 A466 200g multicolored .60 .45

America Issue A467

100g, Derelict locomotive. 1000g, Motorcycle.

1994, Oct. 11 ***Perf. 13½***

2497 A467 100g multicolored .60 .45
2498 A467 1000g multicolored 4.50 3.00

Intl. Year of the Family — A468

1994, Oct. 25 ***Perf. 13x13½***

2499 A468 50g Mother, child .40 .30
2500 A468 250g Family faces .80 .60

Christmas — A469

Ceramic figures: 150g, Nativity. 700g, Joseph, infant Jesus, Mary, vert.

1994, Nov. 4 ***Perf. 13½***

2501 A469 150g multicolored .45 .35
2502 A469 700g multicolored 2.10 1.60

Paraguayan Red Cross, 75th Anniv. — A470

Designs: 150g, Boy Scouts, Jean-Henri Dunant. 700g, Soldiers, paramedics, Dr. Andres Barbero.

1994, Nov. 25 ***Perf. 13½x13***

2503 A470 150g multicolored .60 .45
2504 A470 700g multicolored 3.00 2.40

A 500g showing "75" inside a red cross, with ambulance and emblem with black cross in center was part of this set. When it was discovered that the emblem contained a black instead of a red cross it was withdrawn. Value $200.

San Jose College, 90th Anniv. — A471

Pope John Paul II and: 200g, Eternal flame. 250g, College entrance.

1994, Dec. 4

2505 A471 200g multicolored .60 .45
2506 A471 250g multicolored .75 .60

Louis Pasteur (1822-95) A472

1995, Mar. 24 Litho. ***Perf. 13½***

2507 A472 1000g multicolored 3.00 2.10

Fight Against AIDS — A473

1995, May 4

2508	A473	500g	Faces	1.50	.75
2509	A473	1000g	shown	3.00	1.50

FAO, 50th Anniv. A474

1995, June 23

2510	A474	950g	Bread, pitcher	2.10	1.50
2511	A474	2000g	Watermelon	4.50	3.00

Fifth Neotropical Ornithological Congress — A475

100g, Parula pitiayumi. 200g, Chirroxiphia caudata. 600g, Icterus icterus. 1000g, Carduelis magellanica.

1995, July 6

2512	A475	100g	multicolored	.60	.45
2513	A475	200g	multicolored	.75	.45
2514	A475	600g	multicolored	2.75	1.20
2515	A475	1000g	multicolored	3.00	2.10
			Nos. 2512-2515 (4)	7.10	4.20

Fifth Intl. Symposium on Municipalities, Ecology & Tourism A476

Designs: 1150g, Rio Monday rapids. 1300g, Areguá Railroad Station.

1995, Aug. 4 Litho. *Perf. 13½*

2516	A476	1150g	multicolored	1.90	1.25
2517	A476	1300g	multicolored	2.10	1.40

Volleyball, Cent. — A477

1995, Sept. 28

2518	A477	300g	shown	.55	.30
2519	A477	600g	Ball, net	1.10	.60
2520	A477	1000g	Hands, ball, net	1.60	1.00
			Nos. 2518-2520 (3)	3.25	1.90

America Issue A478

Preserve the environment: 950g, Macizo Monument, Achay. 2000g, Tinfunique Reserve, Chaco, vert.

1995, Oct. 12

2521	A478	950g	multicolored	3.00	1.00
2522	A478	2000g	multicolored	5.00	2.10

UN, 50th Anniv. — A479

Designs: 200g, Flags above olive branch. 3000g, UN emblem, stick figures.

1995, Oct. 20

2523	A479	200g	multicolored	.30	.30
2524	A479	3000g	multicolored	4.50	3.00

Christmas A480

1995, Nov. 7

2525	A480	200g	shown	.50	.30
2526	A480	1000g	Nativity	2.00	1.00

Jose Marti (1853-95) — A481

Designs: 200g, Hedychium coronarium, Marti, vert. 1000g, Hedychium coronarium, map & flag of Cuba, Marti.

1995, Dec. 19 Litho. *Perf. 13½*

2527	A481	200g	multicolored	.50	.30
2528	A481	1000g	multicolored	2.50	1.10

Lion's Clubs of South America & the Caribbean, 25th Anniv. — A482

1996, Jan. 11

2529	A482	200g	Railway station	.40	.30
2530	A482	1000g	Viola House	1.75	1.10

Orchids A483

Designs: 100g, Cattleya nobilior. 200g, Oncidium varicosum. 1000g, Oncidium jonesianum, vert. 1150g, Sophronitis cernua.

Perf. 13½x13, 13x13½

1996, Apr. 22 Litho.

2531	A483	100g	multicolored	.50	.45
2532	A483	200g	multicolored	.50	.45
2533	A483	1000g	multicolored	2.25	1.20
2534	A483	1150g	multicolored	2.50	1.40
			Nos. 2531-2534 (4)	5.75	3.50

1996 Summer Olympic Games, Atlanta A484

1996, June 6 *Perf. 13½x13*

2535	A484	500g	Diving	1.00	.45
2536	A484	1000g	Running	2.00	.90

Founding of Society of Salesian Fathers in Paraguay, Cent. — A485

Pope John Paul II, St. John Bosco (1815-88), and: 200g, Men, boys from Salesian Order, natl. flag. 300g, Madonna and Child, vert. 1000g, Map of Paraguay, man following light.

1996, July 22 *Perf. 13½x13, 13x13½*

2537	A485	200g	multicolored	.40	.30
2538	A485	300g	multicolored	.50	.30
2539	A485	1000g	multicolored	1.60	.90
			Nos. 2537-2539 (3)	2.50	1.50

UNICEF, 50th Anniv. — A486

Children's paintings: 1000g, Outdoor scene, by S. Báez, 1300g, Four groups of children, by C. Pérez.

1996, Sept. 27 *Perf. 13½x13*

2540	A486	1000g	multicolored	2.25	.90
2541	A486	1300g	multicolored	2.50	1.25

Visit of Pope John Paul II to Caacupe, Site of Apparition of the Virgin — A487

Design: 200g, Pope John Paul II, church, Virgin of Caacupe, vert.

1996, Oct. 4 *Perf. 13x13½, 13½x13*

2542	A487	200g	multicolored	.35	.35
2543	A487	1300g	multicolored	2.10	1.50

Traditional Costumes A488

America issue: 500g, Woman in costume. 1000g, Woman, man, in costumes.

1996, Oct. 11 *Perf. 13x13½*

2544	A488	500g	multicolored	1.25	.45
2545	A488	1000g	multicolored	3.00	.90

UN Year for Eradication of Poverty — A489

1996, Oct. 17 *Perf. 13½x13, 13x13½*

2546	A489	1000g	Food products	1.60	.90
2547	A489	1150g	Boy, fruit, vert.	1.75	1.10

Christmas A490

Madonna and Child, by: 200g, Koki Ruíz. 1000g, Hernán Miranda.

1996, Nov. 7 *Perf. 13x13½*

2548	A490	200g	multicolored	.75	.30
2549	A490	1000g	multicolored	1.75	.90

Butterflies A491

Designs: 200g, Eryphanis automedon. 500g, Dryadula phaetusa. 1000g, Vanessa myrinna. 1150g, Heliconius ethilla.

1997, Mar. 5 Litho. *Perf. 13x13½*

2550	A491	200g	multicolored	.60	.30
2551	A491	500g	multicolored	1.75	.45
2552	A491	1000g	multicolored	3.00	.80
2553	A491	1150g	multicolored	3.50	.95
			Nos. 2550-2553 (4)	8.85	2.50

Official Buildings — A492

200g, 1st Legistlature. 1000g, Postal Headquarters.

1997, May 5 *Perf. 13½x13*

2554 A492 200g multicolored .75 .30
2555 A492 1000g multicolored 1.75 .90

1997, Year of Jesus Christ — A493

1000g, Crucifix, Pope John Paul II.

1997, June 10 *Perf. 13x13½*

2556 A493 1000g multi 2.00 .75

11th Summit of the Rio Group Chiefs of State, Asunción — A494

1997, Aug. 23 *Perf. 13½x13*

2557 A494 1000g multicolored 2.00 1.00

Environmental and Climate Change — A495

Flowers: 300g, Opunita elata. 500g, Bromelia balansae, 1000g, Monvillea kroenlaini.

Perf. 13½x13, 13x13½

1997, Aug. 25

2558 A495 300g multi .60 .30
2559 A495 500g multi, vert. .80 .50
2560 A495 1000g multi 1.75 1.00
Nos. 2558-2560 (3) 3.15 1.80

1st Philatelic Exposition of MERCOSUR Countries, Chile and Bolivia — A496

Fauna: 200g, Felis tigrina. 1000g, Alouatta caraya, vert. 1150g, Agouti paca.

Perf. 13½x13, 13x13½

1997, Aug. 29

2561 A496 200g multicolored .50 .25
2562 A496 1000g multicolored 2.00 1.00
2563 A496 1150g multicolored 2.25 1.10
Nos. 2561-2563 (3) 4.75 2.35

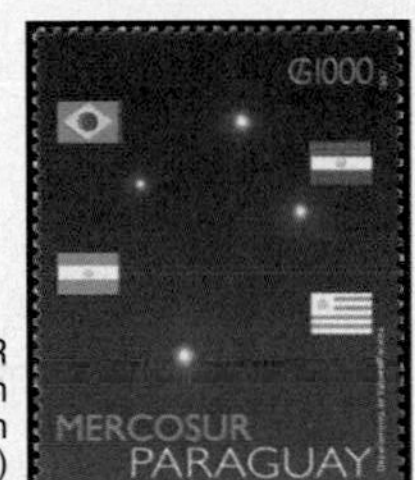

MERCOSUR (Common Market of Latin America) A497

1997, Sept. 26 *Perf. 13x13½*

2564 A497 1000g multicolored 2.00 .90

See Argentina #1975, Bolivia #1019, Brazil #2646, Urugray #1681.

America Issue — A498

Life of a postman: 1000g, Postman, letters going around the world, vert. 1150g, Window with six panes showing weather conditions, different roads, postman.

1997, Oct. 10 *Perf. 13x13½, 13½x13*

2565 A498 1000g multicolored 2.50 1.00
2566 A498 1150g multicolored 2.50 1.25

Natl. Council on Sports, 50th Anniv. — A499

200g, Neri Kennedy throwing javelin. 1000g, Ramón Milciades Giménez Gaona throwing discus.

1997, Oct. 16 *Perf. 13x13½*

2567 A499 200g multicolored .50 .30
2568 A499 1000g multicolored 2.00 1.10

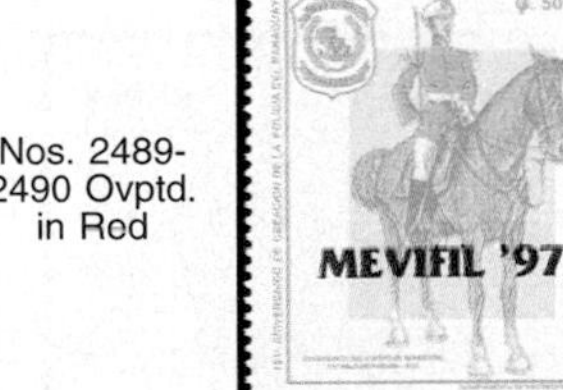

Nos. 2489-2490 Ovptd. in Red

1997, Nov. 14

2569 A464 50g multicolored 1.00 .45
2570 A464 250g multicolored 3.50 2.00

Christmas A500

Paintings of Madonna and Child: 200g, By Olga Blinder. 1000g, By Hermán Miranda.

1997, Nov. 17

2571 A500 200g multicolored .50 .30
2572 A500 1000g multicolored 2.00 1.00

UN Fund for Children of the World with AIDS — A501

Children's paintings: 500g, Boy. 1000g, Girl.

1997, Dec. 5

2573 A501 500g multicolored 1.00 .45
2574 A501 1000g multicolored 1.75 .90

Rotary Club of Asunción, 70th Anniv. — A502

1997, Dec. 11

2575 A502 1150g multicolored 2.00 1.00

1998 World Cup Soccer Championships, France — A503

200g, Julio César Romero, vert. 500g, Carlos Gamarra, vert. 1000g, 1998 Paraguayan team.

1998, Jan. 22 **Litho.** *Perf. 13*

2576 A503 200g multicolored .30 .25
2577 A503 500g multicolored .90 .45
2578 A503 1000g multicolored 1.80 .90
Nos. 2576-2578 (3) 3.00 1.60

Fish A504

Designs: 200g, Tetrogonopterus argenteus. 300g, Pseudoplatystoma coruscans. 500g, Salminus brasiliensis. 1000g, Acestrorhynchus altus.

1998, Apr. 17 **Litho.** *Perf. 13½*

2579 A504 200g multicolored .70 .30
2580 A504 300g multicolored .90 .30
2581 A504 500g multicolored 1.25 .45
2582 A504 1000g multicolored 2.75 .90
Nos. 2579-2582 (4) 5.60 1.95

Contemporary Paintings — A505

200g, Hands, geometric shape, by Carlos Colombino. 300g, Mother nursing infant, by Félix Toranzos. 400g, Flowers, by Edith Giménez. 1000g, Woman lifting tray of food, by Ricardo Migliorisi.

1998, June 5

2583 A505 200g multi, vert. .30 .25
2584 A505 300g multi, vert. .60 .30
2585 A505 400g multi, vert. .70 .30
2586 A505 1000g multi 1.60 .75
Nos. 2583-2586 (4) 3.20 1.60

Mushrooms A506

400g, Boletus edulis. 600g, Macrolepiota procera. 1000g, Geastrum triplex.

1998, June 26

2587 A506 400g multicolored .75 .30
2588 A506 600g multicolored 1.00 .50
2589 A506 1000g multicolored 1.75 .90
Nos. 2587-2589 (3) 3.50 1.70

Organization of American States (OAS), 50th Anniv. — A507

Designs: 500g, Home of Carlos A. López, botantical and zooligical gardens, Asunción. 1000g, Palmerola Villa, Areguá.

1998, July 16

2590 A507 500g multicolored 1.00 .40
2591 A507 1000g multicolored 2.00 .90

Episcopacy of Hernando de Trejo y Sanabria, 400th Anniv. — A508

Pope John Paul II and: 400g, Sacrarium doors, Caazapá Church, vert. 1700g, Statue of St. Francis of Assisi, Atyrá Church.

Perf. 13x13½, 13½x13

1998, Sept. 5 **Litho.**

2592 A508 400g multi 1.00 .40
2593 A508 1700g multi 3.00 1.75

Ruins of Jesuit Mission Church A509

1998, Sept. 16 **Litho.** *Perf. 13½x13*

2594 A509 5000g multicolored 8.00 5.00

Flowers A510

Designs: 100g, Acacia caven. 600g, Cordia trichotoma. 1900g, Glandularia sp.

1998, Sept. 16 Litho. ***Perf. 13x13½***

2595	A510	100g	multi	.30	.25
2596	A510	600g	multi	1.20	.50
2597	A510	1900g	multi	3.25	1.75
	Nos. 2595-2597 (3)			4.75	2.50

America Issue A511

Famous women and buildings: 1600g, Serafina Davalos (1883-1957), first woman lawyer, National College building. 1700g, Adela Speratti (1865-1902), director of Normal School.

1998, Oct. 12 Litho. ***Perf. 13½x13***

2598	A511	1600g	multi	3.50	1.50
2599	A511	1700g	multi	4.00	1.75

Universal Declaration of Human Rights, 50th Anniv. — A512

Artwork by: 500g, Carlos Colombino. 1000g, Jose Filártiga.

1998, Oct. 23 ***Perf. 13x13½***

2600	A512	500g	multi	1.00	.50
2601	A512	1000g	multi	1.90	1.00

Christmas Creche Figures — A513

Perf. 13½x13, 13x13½

1998, Sept. 16 Litho.

2602	A513	300g	shown	1.00	.25
2603	A513	1600g	Stable, vert.	3.00	1.75

Reptiles A514

Designs: 100g, Micrurus frontalis. 300g, Ameiva ameiva. 1600g, Geochelone carbonaria. 1700g, Caiman yacare.

1999, May 13 Litho. ***Perf. 13½x13***

2604-2607	A514	Set of 4	6.00	4.00

Paintings — A515

Paintings by: 500g, Ignacio Nuñez Soler. 1600g, Modesto Delgado Rodas. 1700g, Jaime Bestard.

1999, June 23 Litho. ***Perf. 13½x13***

2608	A515	500g	multi	.65	.40
2609	A515	1600g	multi	2.00	1.40
2610	A515	1700g	multi	2.25	1.40
	Nos. 2608-2610 (3)			4.90	3.20

America Soccer Cup A516

Designs: 300g, Carlos Humberto Paredes, vert. 500g, South American Soccer Confederation Building, Luque. 1900g, Feliciano Cáceres Stadium, Luque.

Perf. 13x13½, 13½x13

1999, June 24

2611	A516	300g	multi	.40	.25
2612	A516	500g	multi	.70	.35
2613	A516	1900g	multi	2.75	1.50
	Nos. 2611-2613 (3)			3.85	2.10

SOS Children's Villages, 50th Anniv. — A517

1999, July 16 ***Perf. 13½x13, 13x13½***

2614	A517	1700g	Toucan	2.50	1.10
2615	A517	1900g	Toucan, vert.	3.50	1.40

Protests of Assassination of Vice-President Luis Maria Argaña — A518

Designs: 100g, Protest at Governmental Palace. 500g, Argaña, vert. 1500g, Protest at National Congress.

1999, Aug. 26

2616	A518	100g	multi	.25	.25
2617	A518	500g	multi	.70	.40
2618	A518	1500g	multi	1.90	1.25
	Nos. 2616-2618 (3)			2.85	1.90

Medicinal Plants — A519

Designs: 600g, Cochlospermum regium. 700g, Borago officinalis. 1700g, Passiflora cincinnata.

1999, Sept. 8 ***Perf. 13x13½***

2619	A519	600g	multi	.75	.35
2620	A519	700g	multi	.75	.45
2621	A519	1700g	multi	2.00	1.00
	Nos. 2619-2621 (3)			3.50	1.80

America Issue, A New Millennium Without Arms — A520

Various artworks by Ricardo Migliorisi.

Perf. 13½x13, 13x13½

1999, Oct. 12 Litho.

2622	A520	1500g	multi	2.00	1.10
2623	A520	3000g	multi, vert.	3.50	2.25

Intl. Year of the Elderly A521

Artwork by: 1000g, Olga Blinder. 1900g, Maria de los Reyes Omella Herrero, vert.

Perf. 13½x13, 13x13½

1999, Oct. 20 Litho.

2624-2625	A521	Set of 2	3.50	2.00

Christmas A522

Artwork by: 300g, Manuel Viedma. 1600g, Federico Ordiñana.

1999, Nov. 11 Litho. ***Perf. 13x13½***

2626	A522	300g	multi	.75	.25
2627	A522	1600g	multi	2.25	1.00

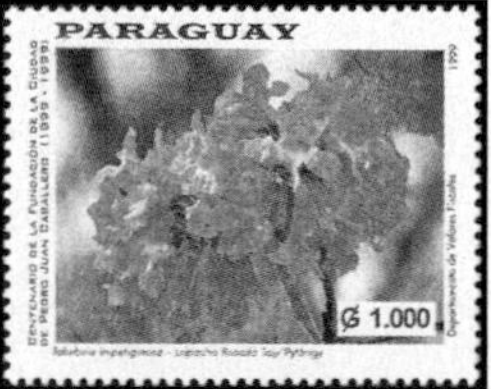

City of Pedro Juan Caballero, Cent. — A523

Flowers: 1000g, Tabebuia impetiginosa. 1600g, Tabebuia pulcherrima, vert.

Perf. 13½x13, 13x13½

1999, Dec. 1 Litho.

2628	A523	1000g	multi	1.25	.70
2629	A523	1600g	multi	1.75	1.00

Inter-American Development Bank, 40th Anniv. — A524

Designs: 600g, Oratory of Our Lady of Asuncion and Pantheon of Heroes, Asuncion. 700g, Governmental Palace.

1999, Dec. 6 ***Perf. 13½x13***

2630	A524	600g	multi	1.00	.35
2631	A524	700g	multi	1.25	.45

Intl. Women's Day — A525

Carmen Casco de Lara Castro and sculpture: 400g, Conjunction, by Domingo Rivarola. 2000g, Violation, by Gustavo Beckelmann.

2000, Apr. 7 Litho. ***Perf. 13x13½***

2632-2633	A525	Set of 2	3.00	3.00

Expo 2000, Hanover A526

Designs: 500g, Yacyreta Dam and deer. 2500g, Itaipú Dam, tapir.

2000, May 5 ***Perf. 13½x13***

2634-2635	A526	Set of 2	4.00	3.50

Salesians in Paraguay, Cent. — A527

Madonna and Child, Pope John Paul II and: 600g, Salesians, vert. 2000g, College building.

Perf. 13x13½, 13½x13

2000, May 19 Litho.

2636-2637	A527	Set of 2	3.00	3.00

2000 Summer Olympics, Sydney — A528

Designs: 2500g, Soccer, vert. 3000g, Runner Francisco Rojas Soto.

2000, July 28 ***Perf. 13x13½, 13½x13***

2638-2639	A528	Set of 2	7.50	7.50

Rights of the Child A529

Designs: 1500g, Child between hands, vert. 1700g, Handprints.

Perf. 13x13½, 13½x13

2000, Aug. 16
2640-2641 A529 Set of 2 4.50 4.50

Fire Fighters A530

Designs: 100g, Fire fighters, white truck, vert. 200g, Fire fighter in old uniform, emblem, vert. 1500g, Fire fighters at fire. 1600g, Fire fighters, yellow truck.

Perf. 13x13½, 13½x13

2000, Sept. 28
2642-2645 A530 Set of 4 5.00 4.50

Roads and Flowers — A531

Designs: 500g, Paved road between San Bernardino and Altos, Rosa banksiae. 3000g, Gaspar Rodriguez de Francia Highway, Calliandra brevicaulis.

2000, Oct. 5 Litho. *Perf. 13½x13¼*
2646-2647 A531 Set of 2 5.00 5.00

America Issue, Fight Against AIDS — A532

Designs: 1500g, Signs with arrows. 2500g, Tic-tac-toe game.

2000, Oct. 19 *Perf. 13x13½*
2648-2649 A532 Set of 2 5.50 5.50

Intl. Year of Culture and Peace A533

Sculptures by: 500g, Hugo Pistilli. 2000g, Herman Guggiari.

2000, Oct. 27 Litho. *Perf. 13¼x13½*
2650-2651 A533 Set of 2 3.25 3.25

Christmas A534

Designs: 100g, Holy Family, sculpture by Hugo Pistilli. 500g, Poem by José Luis Appleyard. 2000g, Creche figures, horiz.

Perf. 13x13½, 13½x13

2000, Nov. 17 Litho.
2652-2654 A534 Set of 3 3.50 3.50

Artisan's Crafts — A535

Designs: 200g, Campesina Woman, by Behage. 1500g, Cattle horns, by Quintin Velazquez, horiz. 2000g, Silver filigree orchid, by Quirino Torres.

Perf. 13¼x13½, 13½x13¼

2000, Nov. 28 Litho.
2655-2657 A535 Set of 3 5.25 5.25

Guarania Music, 75th Anniv. — A536

Designs: 100g, José Asunción Flores (1904-72), composer. 1500g, Violin. 2500g, Trombone.

2000, Dec. 20 *Perf. 13¼x13½*
2658-2660 A536 Set of 3 5.00 5.00

Signing of Asunción Treaty, 10th Anniv. A537

Designs: 500g, Delegates signing treaty. 2500g, Map of South America with signatory nations colored, vert.

Perf. 13½x13¼, 13¼x13½

2001, June 20
2661-2662 A537 Set of 2 3.50 3.50

Cacti — A538

Designs: 2000g, Opuntia sp. 2500g, Cereus stenogonus.

2001, June 29 *Perf. 13¼x13½*
2663-2664 A538 Set of 2 6.00 6.00

Second Paz del Chaco Philatelic Exhibition.

Under 20 Soccer Championships, Argentina — A539

Designs: 2000g, Players. 2500g, Players, diff., vert.

Perf. 13½x13¼, 13¼x13½

2001, June 29
2665-2666 A539 Set of 2 6.00 6.00

Cattle A540

Designs: 200g, Holando-Argentino. 500g, Nelore. 1500g, Pampa Chaqueño.

2001, July 20 *Perf. 13½x13¼*
2667-2669 A540 Set of 3 3.50 3.50

Engravings — A541

Woodcuts by: No. 2670, 500g, Josefina Plá. No. 2671, 500g, Leonor Cecotto, vert. 1500g, Jacinto Rivero. 2000g, Livio Abramo.

Perf. 13½x13¼, 13¼x13½

2001, Aug. 28
2670-2673 A541 Set of 4 6.00 6.00

Mythological Heavens of the Guarani — A542

Designs: 100g, Eichu (Pleiades). 600g, Mborevi Rape (Milky Way). 1600g, Jagua Ho'u Jasy (lunar eclipse).

2001, Sept. 24 *Perf. 13½x13¼*
2674-2676 A542 Set of 3 3.25 3.25

America Issue — UNESCO World Heritage Sites — A543

No. 2677: a, 500g, St. Ignatius of Loyola, Jesuit Mission Ruins, Trinidad. b, 2000g, Jesuit Mission Ruins.

2001, Oct. 9 *Perf. 13¼x13½*
2677 A543 Horiz. pair, #a-b, + 2 flanking labels 3.50 3.50

World Teachers' Day — A544

Designs: 200g, Children studying, school blackboard, J. Inocencio Lezcano (1889-1935), educator. 1600g, Symbols of education, Ramón I. Cardozo (1876-1943), educator.

2001, Oct. 9 *Perf. 13½x13¼*
2678-2679 A544 Set of 2 2.50 2.50

Year of Dialogue Among Civilizations — A545

2001, Oct. 23 *Perf. 13¼x13½*
2680 A545 3000g multi + 2 flanking labels 4.25 4.25

Christmas — A546

Nativity scenes by: 700g, Gladys and Maria de Feliciangeli. 4000g, Mercedes Servin.

2001, Nov. 29 *Perf. 13½x13¼*
2681-2682 A546 Set of 2 5.00 5.00

No to Terrorism A547

Designs: 700g, Statue of Liberty, World Trade Center, vert. 5000g, Flags of Paraguay and U.S., chain becoming doves.

Perf. 13¼x13½, 13½x13¼

2001, Dec. 19 Litho.
2683-2684 A547 Set of 2 8.50 8.50

Passiflora Caerulea A548

2001, Dec. 21 *Perf. 13¼x13½*
2685 A548 4000g multi 4.50 4.00

Paraguayan, Bolivian, and Argentinian Scout Jamboree, Boquerón Province A549

2002, Jan. 24
2686 A549 6000g multi 9.50 9.50

El Mbiguá Social Club, Asunción, Cent. — A550

2002, May 3 ***Perf. 13½x13¼***
2687 A550 700g multi 1.10 1.10

Juan de Salazar Spanish Cultural Center, 25th Anniv. — A551

Jesuit wood carvings, 18th cent.: 2500g, Pieta. 5000g, St. Michael Archangel.

2002, May 7 ***Perf. 13¼x13½***
2688-2689 A551 Set of 2 11.00 11.00

2002 World Cup Soccer Championships, Japan and Korea — A552

Designs: 3000g, Paraguay team. 5000g, Players in action, vert.

Perf. 13½x13¼, 13¼x13½
2002, May 18
2690-2691 A552 Set of 2 12.00 12.00

For overprint see No. 2705.

Arrival of Mennonites in Paraguay, 75th Anniv. — A553

Cross, plow, Menno Simons (1496-1561), Religious Leader, and: 2000g, Mennonite Church, Filadelfia. 4000g, Mennonite Church, Loma Plata.

2002, June 25 ***Perf. 13½x13¼***
2692-2693 A553 Set of 2 7.50 7.50

Horses A554

Designs: 700g, Criollo. 1000g, Cuarto de Milla (quarterhorse). 6000g, Arabian.

2002, July 12
2694-2696 A554 Set of 3 9.50 9.50

Olimpia Soccer Team, Cent. — A555

2002, July 24
2697 A555 700g multi + 2 flanking labels 2.00 2.00

Pan-American Health Organization, Cent. — A556

Medicinal plants: 4000g, Stevia rebaudiana bertoni. 5000g, Ilex paraguayensis.

2002, Sept. 16 ***Perf. 13¼x13½***
2698-2699 A556 Set of 2 13.00 13.00

International Forum on Postal Service Modernization and Reform — A557

Forum emblem and statues by Serafin Marsal: 1000g, Campesina. 4000g, Quygua-vera.

2002, Sept. 30 ***Perf. 13½x13¼***
2700-2701 A557 Set of 2 7.00 7.00

Paraguay — Republic of China Diplomatic Relations, 45th Anniv. — A558

2002, Oct. 10 ***Perf. 13¼x13½***
2702 A558 4000g multi + 2 flanking labels 6.00 6.00

America Issue — Youth, Education and Literacy — A559

Designs: 3000g, Classroom. 6000g, Children playing.

2002, Oct. 12 ***Perf. 13½x13¼***
2703-2704 A559 Set of 2 12.00 12.00

No. 2690 Overprinted

2002
2705 A552 3000g on #2690 4.00 4.00

Christmas — A560

Various creche figures: a, 1000g. b, 4000g. c, 700g.

2002, Dec. 2 **Litho.** ***Perf. 13¼***
2706 A560 Horiz. strip of 3, #a-c 7.00 7.00

Church, Areguá — A561

2002, Dec. 18
2707 A561 4000g multi 4.50 4.50

District of San Antonio, Cent. — A562

2003, Apr. 21 **Litho.** ***Perf. 13¼***
2708 A562 700g multi .50 .50

Josefina Plá (1903-99), Artist — A563

Designs: 700g, Plate. 6000g, Carving.

2003, May 30 **Litho.** ***Perf. 13¼***
2709-2710 A563 Set of 2 5.00 5.00

Parrots — A564

Designs: 1000g, Amazona aestiva. 2000g, Myiopsitta monachus. 4000g, Aratinga leucophtalmus.

2003, June 9
2711-2713 A564 Set of 3 6.50 6.50

Paraguay Philatelic Center, 90th anniv. (#2711), Paz del Chaco Bi-national Philatelic Exhibition (#2712), PARAFIL Bi-national Philatelic Exhibition (#2713).

Legislative Palace — A565

2003, June 24 ***Perf. 13½x13¼***
2714 A565 4000g multi + label 3.50 3.50

Printed in sheets of 12 stamps and 18 labels.

Pontificate of Pope John Paul II, 25th Anniv. — A566

2003, June 27 ***Perf. 13¼***
2715 A566 6000g multi + label 3.50 3.50

Farm Animals A567

Designs: 1000g, Pig. 3000g, Sheep. 8000g, Goat.

2003, July 18
2716-2718 A567 Set of 3 8.50 8.50

Foods A568

Designs: 700g, Peanuts, honey and nougat. 2000g, Sopa Paraguaya. 3000g, Chipá.

2003, July 25
2719-2721 A568 Set of 3 4.00 4.00

Folk Artists A569

Designs: 700g, Julio Correa (1890-1953), playwright. 1000g, Emiliano Rivarola Fernández (1894-1949), singer. 2000g, Manuel Ortiz Guerrero (1894-1933), poet.

2003, Sept. 12
2722-2724 A569 Set of 3 2.75 2.75

Dances A570

Designs: 700g, Golondriana. 3000g, Polka. 4000g, Galopera.

2003, Sept. 23
2725-2727 A570 Set of 3 5.50 5.50

Guaraní Soccer Team, Cent. — A571

2003, Oct. 9
2728 A571 700g multi + label .50 .50

Native Clothing A572

Designs: 4000g, Sixty-strip poncho, Para'i. 5000g, Shirt, Ao Poí.

2003, Oct. 22
2729-2730 A572 Set of 2 6.00 6.00

Christmas A573

Designs: 700g, Journey to Egypt. 1000g, Adoration of the Shepherds. 4000g, Nativity.

2003, Nov. 12
2731-2733 A573 Set of 3 4.00 4.00

Indoor Soccer World Cup Championships, Paraguay — A574

No. 2734 — Various players: a, 4000g. b, 5000g.

2003, Nov. 14
2734 A574 Horiz. pair, #a-b 5.50 5.50

Printed in sheets with two columns of five pairs separated by a column of labels.

No. 2734 Overprinted "PARAGUAY / CAMPEON MUNDIAL" in Silver

No. 2734C: d, On #2734a. e, On #2734b.

2003 Litho. *Perf. 13¼*
2734C A574 Horiz. pair, #d-e 5.50 5.50

America Issue - Flowers A575

Designs: 1000g, Cordia bordasii. No. 2736, 5000g, Bulnesia sarmientoi. No. 2737, 5000g, Chorisia insignis.

2003, Nov. 26
2735-2737 A575 Set of 3 7.50 7.50

For overprints see Nos. 2797-2798.

Comics by Robin Wood — A576

Designs: 1000g, Anahí. 3000g, Nippur de Lagash. 5000g, Dago.

2004, May 24 Litho. *Perf. 13¼*
2738-2740 A576 Set of 3 7.00 7.00

National Soccer Team, Cent. — A577

2004, June 25
2741 A577 700g multi + label .50 .50

San José College, Cent. — A578

2004, July 2 Litho. *Perf. 13¼*
2742 A578 700g multi .65 .65

Pablo Neruda (1904-73), Poet — A579

2004, July 6 Litho. *Perf. 13¼*
2743 A579 5000g multi 3.50 3.50

World of the Guaranís — A580

Designs: 700g, Monday Waterfalls. 6000g, Entrance to Ciudad de Tobati.

2004, July 7
2744-2745 A580 Set of 2 4.00 4.00

Nos. 2744 and 2745 were issued in sheets of 15 stamps and 10 labels.

Independence House — A581

Dr. Carlos Pussineri and: 700g, Mural by José Laterza Parodi. 5000g, Independence House.

2004, Aug. 13 Litho. *Perf. 13¼*
2746-2747 A581 Set of 2 4.00 4.00

José Asunción Flores (1904-72), Composer A582

2004, Aug. 24 Litho. *Perf. 13¼*
2748 A582 5000g multi 3.50 3.50

Museo del Barro, 25th Anniv. A583

Designs: 2000g, Painting by Enrique Careaga. 3000g, Anthropomorphic jug, vert. 4000g, Christ of the Column, vert.

2004, Aug. 26
2749-2751 A583 Set of 3 6.00 6.00

For overprint see No. 2799.

Paraguayan Railroads, 150th Anniv. — A584

Designs: 2000g, Locomotive No. 151, Camello. 3000g, Locomotive No. 104, El Coqueto, horiz.
6000g, Locomotiove No. 10, Sapucai, horiz.

2004, Sept. 22 *Perf. 13¼*
2752-2753 A584 Set of 2 3.00 3.00

Souvenir Sheet
Rouletted 5¼

2754 A584 6000g multi 5.00 5.00

No. 2754 contains one 50x40mm stamp.

America Issue — Environmental Protection — A585

Designs: No. 2755, Procnias nudicollis. No. 2756, Ceratophrys cranwelli.

2004, Oct. 11 Litho. *Perf. 13¼*
2755 A585 6000g multi 3.50 3.50

Souvenir Sheet
Rouletted 5¼

2756 A585 6000g multi 5.00 5.00

Water Conservation — A586

Designs: 3000g, Felis pardalis, storks, telephone poles. 4000g, Myrmecophaga tridactyla, Hydrochoerus hydrochaeris, Chauna torquata.

2004, Oct. 22
2757-2758 A586 Set of 2 7.00 7.00

Crops — A587

Designs: 2000g, Corn. 4000g, Cotton. 6000g, Soybeans.

2004, Oct. 22 Litho. *Perf. 13¼*
2759-2761 A587 Set of 3 6.50 6.50

Christmas — A588

Paintings by Ricardo Migliorisi: 3000g, Madonna and Child. 5000g, Angel, vert.

2004, Nov. 12
2762-2763 A588 Set of 2 5.50 5.50

Latin American Parliament, 40th Anniv. — A589

2004, Nov. 16
2764 A589 4000g multi + label 2.50 2.50

For overprint, see No. 3006.

Itaipú Dam, 30th Anniv. A590

Designs: 4000g, Dam and spillway. 5000g, Aerial view of dam, vert.

2004, Dec. 10 **Litho.** ***Perf. 13¼***
2765-2766 A590 Set of 2 5.00 5.00

Rotary International, Cent. — A591

Jesuit Mission ruins, Trinidad: 3000g, Building ruins. 4000g, Religious statue, vert.

2005, Feb. 23 **Litho.** ***Perf. 13¼***
2767-2768 A591 Set of 2 4.50 4.50

Castelvi House, Asunción, 200th Anniv. — A592

2005, Mar. 14
2769 A592 5000g multi 3.00 3.00

Herminio Giménez (1905-91), Conductor — A593

2005, Apr. 22
2770 A593 700g multi .50 .50

Cabildo Cultural Center, Asunción, 1st Anniv. — A594

2005, May 19
2771 A594 1000g multi .70 .70

Fernheim Colony, 75th Anniv. — A595

Designs: 5000g, Pioneer's Monument. 6000g, Cross, cactus, oxcart.

2005, June 15 ***Perf. 13¼***
2772 A595 5000g multi 3.50 3.50

Souvenir Sheet

Rouletted 5¼

2773 A595 6000g multi 3.50 3.50

Libertad Soccer Team, Cent. — A596

Illustration reduced.

2005, July 20 ***Perf. 13¼***
2774 A596 700g multi + label .50 .50

Publication of Don Quixote, 400th Anniv. A597

2005, July 26
2775 A597 8000g multi 5.00 5.00

Writers A598

Designs: 3000g, Herib Campos Cervera (1905-53), poet. 5000g, Gabriel Casaccia (1907-80), novelist.

2005, July 27
2776-2777 A598 Set of 2 5.00 5.00

Pope John Paul II (1920-2005) A599

2005, Aug. 18
2778 A599 2000g multi 2.00 2.00

Truth and Justice A600

2005, Aug. 23
2779 A600 8000g multi 4.50 4.50

America Issue, Fight Against Poverty A601

Designs: 5000g, Women selling vegetables. 6000g, Cobbler.

2005, Aug. 31
2780-2781 A601 Set of 2 6.50 6.50

Dogs and Cats A602

Designs: No. 2782, 2000g, Samoyed. No. 2783, 2000g, Three European cats. No. 2784, 3000g, Doberman pinscher. No. 2785, 3000g, White European cat.

2005, Oct. 7
2782-2785 A602 Set of 4 6.00 6.00

Anthropologists — A603

Designs: 1000g, Branislava Susnik, bracelet. 2000g, Miguel Chase-Sardi, poncho. 8000g, León Cadogan, basket.

2005, Oct. 26
2786-2788 A603 Set of 3 6.50 6.50

Intl. Year of Sports and Physical Education — A604

Designs: 5000g, Lucy Aguero throwing hammer and javelin. 6000g, Golfer Carlos Franco.

2005, Nov. 9 ***Perf. 13¼***
2789 A604 5000g multi 3.00 3.00

Souvenir Sheet

Rouletted 5¼

2790 A604 6000g multi 5.00 5.00

Christmas A605

Designs: 700g, Angels, people celebrating Christmas, rooftops. 5000g, Nativity scene.

2005, Nov. 22 ***Perf. 13¼***
2791-2792 A605 Set of 2 3.50 3.50

Yacyreta Dam — A606

Various views of dam: 3000g, 5000g.

2005, Nov. 28
2793-2794 A606 Set of 2 4.75 4.75

Ministry of Defense, 150th Anniv. A607

Designs: 700g, Monument to the Residents, by Javier Báez Rolón. 1000g, Defense Ministry Building, Marshal Francisco Solano López.

2005, Dec. 21
2795-2796 A607 Set of 2 1.25 1.25

Nos. 2736-2737 Overprinted

2005, Dec. 28 ***Perf. 13¼***
2797 A575 5000g On #2736 3.00 3.00
2798 A575 5000g On #2737 3.00 3.00

No. 2751 Overprinted

2005, Dec. 28 *Perf. 13¼*
2799 A583 4000g On #2751 2.40 2.40

Paraguay — Germany Chamber of Commerce and Industry, 50th Anniv. — A608

2006, Mar. 14
2800 A608 8000g multi 5.00 5.00

2006 World Cup Soccer Championships, Germany — A609

Emblem and: 3000g, Paraguayan team. 5000g, World Cup.

2006, May 17 **Litho.** *Perf. 13¼*
2801-2802 A609 Set of 2 5.00 5.00

French Alliance of Asuncion, 50th Anniv. — A610

2006, June 20
2803 A610 8000g multi + label 5.00 5.00

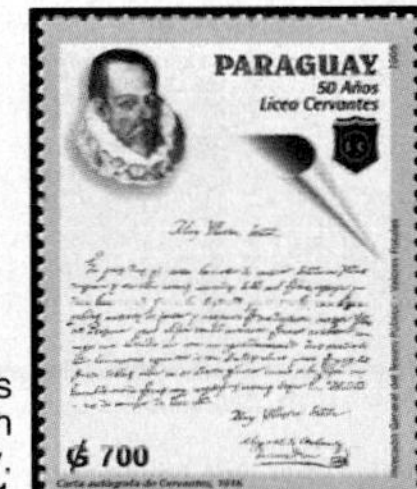

Cervantes Club, 50th Anniv. A611

2006, June 27
2804 A611 700g multi .60 .60

Paraguayan Soccer Association, Cent. — A612

2006, Aug. 1
2805 A612 1000g multi .75 .75

National Commerce School, Cent. — A613

2006, Sept. 7
2806 A613 700g multi .65 .65

Japanese Emigration to Paraguay, 70th Anniv. — A614

Flags of Paraguay and Japan and butterflies: 1000g, Junonia evarete. 2000g, Anartia jatrophae. 3000g, Agraulis vanillae. 6000g, Danaus plexippus.

2006, Sept. 8 *Perf. 13¼*
2807-2809 A614 Set of 3 4.00 4.00

Souvenir Sheet
Rouletted 5¼

2810 A614 6000g multi 5.00 5.00

No. 2810 contains one 50x40mm stamp.

OPEC Intl. Development Fund, 30th Anniv. — A615

2006, Sept. 18 *Perf. 13¼*
2811 A615 8000g multi 5.00 5.00

Tuparenda Shrine, 25th Anniv. — A616

2006, Oct. 9
2812 A616 700g multi .50 .50

America Issue, Energy Conservation — A617

Designs: 5000g, Windmills. 6000g, Solar collector.

2006, Oct. 11
2813-2814 A617 Set of 2 6.50 6.50

Agronomy and Veterinary Medicine Faculties of Asuncion National University, 50th Anniv. A618

Designs: No. 2815, 4000g, Symbols of agronomy. No. 2816, 4000g, Livestock.

2006, Oct. 20
2815-2816 A618 Set of 2 5.00 5.00

South American Soccer Confederation, 90th Anniv. — A619

2006, Nov. 6
2817 A619 8000g multi 5.00 5.00

Musical Instruments A620

Designs: 5000g, Harp. 6000g, Guitar.

2006, Nov. 10
2818-2819 A620 Set of 2 6.50 6.50

Christmas A621

Designs: 4000g, Our Lady of Asuncion Cathedral. 6000g, Holy Trinity Church, horiz.

2006, Nov. 17
2820-2821 A621 Set of 2 6.00 6.00

First Lieutenant Adolfo Rojas Silva (1906-27), Military Hero — A622

Designs: 4000g, Rojas Silva and hut. 6000g, Rojas Silva, vert.

2007, Feb. 27 **Litho.**
2822-2823 A622 Set of 2 6.50 6.50

B'nai B'rith of Paraguay, 50th Anniv. — A623

2007, Mar. 29 *Perf. 13¼*
2824 A623 8000g multi 5.00 5.00

Junior Chamber International Conference, Asuncion — A624

2007, Apr. 18
2825 A624 8000g multi 5.00 5.00

World Tobacco-Free Day — A625

Emblem and: 5000g, Person wearing gas mask. 6000g, Map of Paraguay with umbrella, vert.

2007, May 30
2826-2827 A625 Set of 2 6.50 6.50

Arlequin Theater, Asuncion, 25th Anniv. A626

2007, June 11
2828 A626 700g multi .60 .60

Paz del Chaco 07 Philatelic Exhibition, Asuncion — A627

Exhibition emblem and: 700g, Felis pardalis. 8000g, Chaco War postman riding cow.

2007, June 11
2829-2830 A627 Set of 2 5.00 5.00

Diplomatic Relations Between Paraguay and South Korea, 45th Anniv. — A628

Flags of Paraguay and South Korea and: 1000g, Open horse-drawn wagon. 2000g, Covered horse-drawn carriage. 3000g, Ox cart, vert.
6000g, Mugungfa flower.

2007, June 15 ***Perf. 13¼***
2831-2833 A628 Set of 3 3.50 3.50

Souvenir Sheet
Rouletted 7¼

2834 A628 6000g multi 5.00 5.00

No. 2834 contains one 50x40mm stamp.

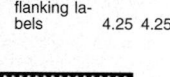

Friendship Between Paraguay and Republic of China, 50th Anniv. — A628a

2007, July 8 ***Perf. 13¼***
2834A A628a 7000g multi + 2 flanking labels 4.25 4.25

Diplomatic Relations Between Paraguay and Indonesia, 25th Anniv. — A629

2007, July 9
2835 A629 11,000g multi 6.50 6.50

Official Veterinary Service, 40th Anniv. A630

Designs: 5000g, Prize-winning cow. 7000g, Veterinarian inspecting cow, cattle herd, prize-winning cow, horiz.

2007, June 11
2836-2837 A630 Set of 2 7.00 7.00

Peace Corps in Paraguay, 40th Anniv. A631

2007, Sept. 19
2838 A631 7000g multi 4.50 4.50

Scouting, Cent. — A632

Designs: 700g, Scouts near campfire. 6000g, Lord Robert Baden-Powell, female Scouts.

2007, Oct. 11
2839-2840 A632 Set of 2 4.00 4.00

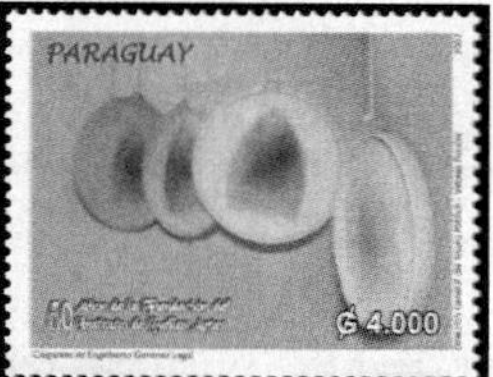

Institute of Fine Arts, 50th Anniv. A633

Designs: 4000g, Pendants, by Engelberto Giménez Legal. 8000g, Sculpture by Hugo Pistilli, vert.

2007, Nov. 20
2841-2842 A633 Set of 2 7.00 7.00

Gabriel Casaccia Bibolini (1907-80), Writer — A634

2007, Nov. 23
2843 A634 8000g multi 5.00 5.00

Marco Aguayo Foundation, 15th Anniv. — A635

Designs: 1000g, Dr. Marco Aguayo (1956-92), red ribbon. 8000g, Red ribbon and geometrical design.

2007, Dec. 11
2844-2845 A635 Set of 2 5.50 5.50

Dr. Nicolas Leoz Stadium — A636

2007, Oct. 22
2846 A636 700g multi 1.00 1.00

Gen. Martin T. McMahon (1838-1906), US Minister to Paraguay A637

2007, Sept. 19
2847 A637 700g multi .50 .50

Intl. Day of Deserts and Desertification (in 2006) — A638

2007, Nov. 28
2848 A638 7000g multi 4.00 4.00

Parks and Reserves — A639

Designs: 3000g, Nú Guazú Park, Luque. 6000g, Monkey.

2007, Nov. 27 ***Perf. 13¼***
2849 A639 3000g multi 1.90 1.90

Souvenir Sheet
Rouletted 7¼

2850 A639 6000g multi 4.00 4.00

No. 2850 contains one 50x40mm stamp.

America Issue, Education for All — A640

Teachers and school children in class: 5000g, 6000g.

2007, Sept. 3 ***Perf. 13¼***
2851-2852 A640 Set of 2 6.50 6.50

Architecture A641

Designs: 6000g, Nautilus Building, by Genaro Pindú. 7000g, Museo del Barro, by Carlos Colombino.

2007, Sept. 3
2853-2854 A641 Set of 2 8.00 8.00

Christmas — A642

Designs: 700g, Coconut flower. 8000g, Creche figures.

2007, Nov. 29 **Litho.** ***Perf. 13¼***
2855-2856 A642 Set of 2 5.00 5.00

Paraguayan Atheneum, 125th Anniv. — A643

2008, July 28
2857 A643 700g multi .60 .60

America Issue, Traditional Celebrations — A644

2008, July 30
2858 A644 11,000g multi 7.50 7.50

Nasta Publicity Agency, 40th Anniv. A645

Designs: 700g, Flower. 5000g, Flower, vert.

2008, Apr. 1
2859-2860 A645 Set of 2 3.50 3.50

Scouting in Paraguay, 70th Anniv. — A646

Designs: 3000g, Three scouts, tent. 4000g, Scout troop.

2008, Oct. 11
2861-2862 A646 Set of 2 4.75 4.75

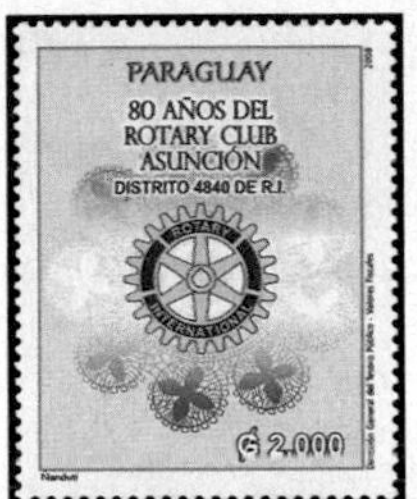

Asuncion Rotary Club, 80th Anniv. A647

Rotary International emblem and: 2000g, Stylized gearwheels. 8000g, Forest path, horiz.

2008, Apr. 4
2863-2864 A647 Set of 2 6.50 6.50

Birds — A648

Designs: 5000g, Coryphospingus cucullatus. 6000g, Pitangus sulphuratus.

2008, July 28
2865-2866 A648 Set of 2 7.50 7.50

Christmas A649

Paintings: 700g, Madonna and Child, by unknown artist. 5000g, Madonna and Child, by José Laterza Parodi.

2008, Oct. 9
2867-2868 A649 Set of 2 4.00 4.00

Carter-Torrijos Treaty, 30th Anniv. (in 2007) — A650

Designs: 700g, Signing ceremony. 7000g, Panamanian General Omar Torrijos, U.S. President Jimmy Carter, ship in Panama Canal.

2008, Aug. 5
2869-2870 A650 Set of 2 5.00 5.00

City of Coronel Oviedo, 250th Anniv. A651

Cotton boll and: 3000g, Cathedral. 7000g, Road.

2008, Oct. 28
2871-2872 A651 Set of 2 7.00 7.00

SOS Children's Village, Asuncion, 25th Anniv. — A653

SOS Children's Village emblem and: 2000g, Children and flower. 7000g, Red, white and blue ribbon.

2008, Nov. 18 **Litho.** ***Perf. 13¼***
2874-2875 A653 Set of 2 6.50 6.50

Year of the Harp — A654

2008, Oct. 20 ***Perf. 13¼x13½***
2876 A654 5000g multi 3.50 3.50

Schoenstatt Movement in Paraguay, 50th Anniv. — A655

2009, Oct. 18 ***Perf. 13¼***
2877 A655 3000g multi 1.90 1.90

Christmas A656

Designs: 800g, Our Lady of Caacupé. 5000g, Our Lady of Asunción.

2009, Dec. 1
2878-2879 A656 Set of 2 3.75 3.75

Dr. José Segundo Decoud (1848-1909), Politician and Journalist — A657

2009, Dec. 3
2880 A657 7000g multi 5.00 5.00

Exports A658

Designs: 2000g, Nelore cow. 5000g, Stevia rebaudiana.

2009, Dec. 18
2881-2882 A658 Set of 2 4.50 4.50

Arsenio Erico (1915-77), Soccer Player — A659

Erico: 700g, Kicking soccer ball. 1000g, Holding four soccer balls, vert.

2009, Dec. 22
2883-2884 A659 Set of 2 1.20 1.20

Ceryle Torquata — A660

2009
2885 A660 7000g multi 3.00 3.00

Charles Darwin (1809-82), naturalist. Printed in sheets of 15 + 10 labels.

Diplomatic Relations Between Paraguay and Russia, Cent. — A661

2009
2886 A661 7000g multi 3.00 3.00

Printed in sheets of 15 + 10 labels.

America Issue, Children's Games A662

Children: 4000g, Spinning top. 7000g, Playing marbles, horiz.

2010, Jan. 2
2887-2888 A662 Set of 2 7.50 7.50

Independence, Bicent. — A663

Designs: 700g, Governor's House. 2000g, Painting by Jaime Bestard.

2010, Feb. 23
2889-2890 A663 Set of 2 2.10 2.10

Astronomy Aided By Telescopes, 400th Anniv. A664

2010, Mar. 3
2891 A664 2500g multi 1.90 1.90

Printed in sheets of 15 + 10 labels.

2010 World Cup Soccer Championships, South Africa — A665

Designs: 700g, Paraguayan players. 6000g, Team, crowd holding Paraguayan flags.

2010, July 2 **Litho.** ***Perf. 13¼***
2892 A665 700g multi + label — —
2893 A665 6000g multi — —

America Issue — A666

National symbols: 5000g, National anthem. 6000g, Flag and emblems, horiz.

2010, Oct. 9 **Litho.** ***Perf. 13¼***
2894-2895 A666 Set of 2 7.00 7.00

Christmas — A667

Designs: 700g, Magi following Star of Bethlehem. 6000g, Nativity, vert. 11,000g, Journey to Bethlehem.

2010, Nov. 19
2896-2898 A667 Set of 3 11.50 11.50

Road Safety Day A668

2010
2899 A668 700g multi .60 .60

Famous Paraguayan Buildings — A669

Designs: 700g, Venancio López Palace. 2000g, Residencia Patri.

2010, Dec. 17
2900-2901 A669 Set of 2 1.75 1.75

2010 Youth Olymmpics, Singapore — A670

Emblem and: 2000g, Diego Galeano Harrison, tennis player. 5000g, Paraguayan athletes.

2010, Dec. 31
2902-2903 A670 Set of 2 5.00 5.00

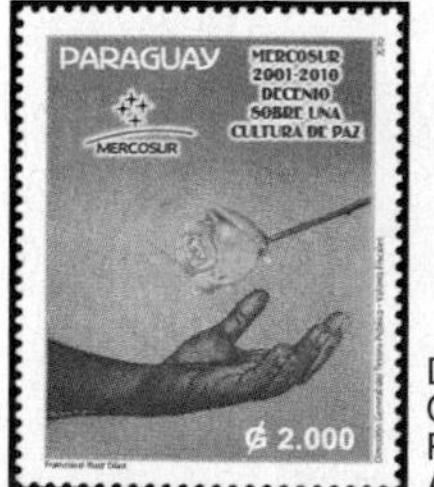

Decade for Culture of Peace A671

Designs: 2000g, Hand below rose. 6000g, Hand holding rose.

2010, Dec. 31
2904-2905 A671 Set of 2 5.25 5.25

Postal Union of the Americas, Spain and Portugal (UPAEP), Cent. — A672

Designs: 6000g, Map of South and Central America, Spain and Portugal with flags. 11,000g, Building and flags, horiz.

2011, Mar. 18
2906-2907 A672 Set of 2 11.00 11.00

Dated 2010.

National Development Bank, 50th Anniv. — A673

2011, Apr. 12 ***Perf. 13¼***
2908 A673 700g multi + label .60 .60

Republic of China, Cent. — A674

No. 2909: a, National Pantheon of Heroes, Paraguay. b, Pantheon of the Martyrs of the National Revolution, Taiwan.

2011, Apr. 24 **Litho.**
2909 A674 6000g Horiz. pair, #a-b, + central label 8.50 8.50

Asunción Buildings A675

No. 2910: a, Asunción, Cathedral. b, Train station. c, Governmental Palace. d, Municipal Theater. e, Town Hall (Cabildo).

11,000g, Independence House, horiz.

2011, May 6 ***Perf. 13¼***
2910 Horiz. strip of 5 + flanking label 3.50 3.50
a.-e. A675 1000g Any single .65 .65

Souvenir Sheet

Rouletted

2911 A675 11,000g multi 7.75 7.75

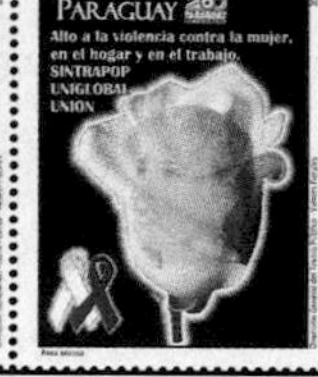

Marie Curie (1867-1934), Chemist and Physicist — A676

2011, May 9 ***Perf. 13¼***
2912 A676 2000g multi + label 1.75 1.75

Intl. Year of Chemistry.

Campaign Against Violence Towards Women — A677

2011, Apr. 29 **Litho.** ***Perf. 13¼***
2913 A677 700g multi + label .60 .60

Souvenir Sheet

Beatification of Pope John Paul II — A678

2011, May 9 **Litho.** ***Rouletted 1¼***
2914 A678 10,000g multi 7.25 7.25

Masons in Paraguay, 140th Anniv. — A679

2011, May 25 **Litho.** ***Perf. 13¼***
2915 A679 11,000g multi + label 8.00 8.00

Intl. Friendship Day — A680

2011, Nov. 8 **Litho.** ***Perf. 13¼***
2916 A680 700g multi + label .60 .60

Radio Cáritas, 75th Anniv. — A681

2011, Nov. 21 **Litho.** ***Perf. 13¼***
2917 A681 700g multi + label .55 .55

San José Academy, Cent. — A682

2011, Nov. 29 **Litho.** ***Perf. 13¼***
2918 A682 700g multi + label .55 .55

America Issue — A683

No. 2919: a, 5000g, Red mailbox. b, 6000g, Green mailbox.

2011, Dec. 13 **Litho.** ***Perf. 13¼***
2919 A683 Horiz. pair, #a-b 8.25 8.25

Campaign Against AIDS, 30th Anniv. — A684

2011, Dec. 13 **Litho.** ***Perf. 13¼***
2920 A684 1000g multi + label .85 .85

Intl. Year of Forests A685

Designs: 5000g, Animals and forest. 6000g, Trees and map of North and South America.

2011, Dec. 13 **Litho.** ***Perf. 13¼***
2921 A685 5000g multi 4.00 4.00

Souvenir Sheet

Rouletted 4

2922 A685 6000g multi 4.75 4.75

Actors and Actresses — A686

Designs: 2000g, Map of Paraguay, Perlita Fernández (1951-2002), César Alvarez Blanco (1927-2003), Máxima Lugo (1925-91), José Olitte (1937-2000). 6000g, Edda de los Rios (1942-2007).

2011, Dec. 13 Litho. *Perf. 13¼*

2923 A686 2000g multi + label 1.60 1.60

Souvenir Sheet

Rouletted 5

2924 A686 6000g multi 4.75 4.75

A687

Christmas A688

Designs: 700g, Star of Bethlehem and Magi. 5000g, Star of Bethlehem and manger. 11,000g, Holy Family and lambs.

2011, Dec. 13 Litho. *Perf. 13¼*

2925 A687 700g multi	.50	.50
2926 A687 5000g multi	3.25	3.25
2927 A688 11,000g multi	6.50	6.50
Nos. 2925-2927 (3)	10.25	10.25

Campaign Against Terrorism — A689

No. 2928 — Handprint in: a, 2000g, Black. b, 5000g, White.

2011, Dec. 30 Litho. *Perf. 13¼*

2928 A689 Horiz. pair, #a-b 5.50 5.50

A690

2011 Copa America Soccer Tournament, Argentina — A691

2011, Dec. 30 Litho. *Perf. 13¼*

2929 A690 700g multi + label	.55	.55
2930 A691 6000g multi	4.75	4.75

José Luis Chilavert, Soccer Player, Estaban Casarino, Squash Player, Olegario Farrés, Shooter, Juan Carlos Giménez, Boxer — A692

Benjamin Hockin Brusquetti, Swimmer — A693

2011, Dec. 30 Litho. *Perf. 13¼*

2931 A692 700g multi + label .55 .55

Souvenir Sheet

Rouletted 5x6

2932 A693 6000g multi 4.75 4.75

Miniature Sheet

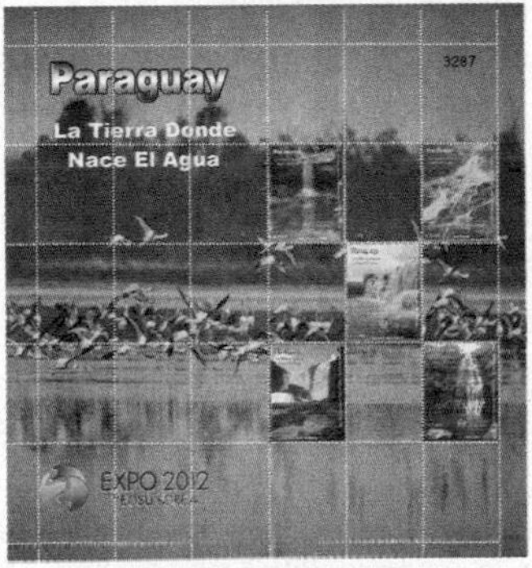

Expo 2012, Yeosu, South Korea — A694

No. 2933, 2000g — Expo 2012 emblem and: a, Small waterfall in Ybycuí National Park. b, Karapa Waterfall. c, Large waterfall in Ybycuí National Park. d, Monday Waterfall. e, Cristal Waterfall,

2012, May 28 Litho. *Perf. 13¼*

2933 A694 2000g Sheet of 5, #a-e, + 25 labels 7.75 7.75

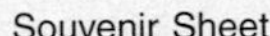

Souvenir Sheet

National Police Band, Cent. — A695

2012, June 1 Litho. *Rouletted 5*

2934 A695 7000g multi 5.50 5.50

Myths and Legends — A696

No. 2935 — Guarani monsters: a, Teju Jagua. b, Moñai. c, Jasy Jatere. d, Luisón. e, Kurupi. f, Ao Ao. g, Mbói Tui.

7000p, Kerana, horiz.

2012, June 7 Litho. *Perf. 13¼*

2935 A696 1000g Sheet of 7, #a-g, + 23 labels 5.50 5.50

Souvenir Sheet

Rouletted 5

2936 A696 7000g multi 5.50 5.50

America Issue.

Souvenir Sheets

Korean and Paraguayan Dancers — A697

Paraguayan Dancers — A698

Korean Dancers — A699

2012, June 26 Litho. *Rouletted 5*

2937 A697 2000g multi	1.75	1.75
2938 A698 2000g multi	1.75	1.75
2939 A699 2000g multi	1.75	1.75
Nos. 2937-2939 (3)	5.25	5.25

Diplomatic relations between Paraguay and South Korea, 50th anniv.

Authentic Radical Liberal Party, 125th Anniv. — A700

Party flag and: 2000g, Anodorhynchus hyacinthinus. 16,000g, Morpho peleides.

2012, July 14 Litho. *Perf. 13¼*

Stamp + Label

2940-2941 A700 Set of 2 14.00 14.00

2012 Summer Olympics, London A701

No. 2942 — Paraguayan flag, emblem of Paraguayan Olympic Committee and: a, Judo. b, Javelin. c, Running. d, Tennis. e, Table tennis. f, Rowing and swimming.

No. 2943, 4000g, Paraguayan flag, emblem of Paraguayan Olympic Committee, Marcelo Aguirre, table tennis player, and Benjamin Hockin Busquetti, swimmer. No. 2944, 4000g, Paraguayan flag, emblem of Paraguayan Olympic Committee and various athletes.

2012, Aug. 9 Litho. *Perf. 13¼*

2942 Horiz. strip of 6	5.50	5.50
a.-f. A701 1000g Any single	.90	.90

Souvenir Sheets

Rouletted 5

2943-2944 A701 Set of 2 7.50 7.50

Paraguayan Academy of History, 75th Anniv. — A702

No. 2945 — Academy emblem, building and: a, Ruy Díaz de Guzmán (c. 1558-1692), conquistador and historian. b, Dr. Manuel Domínguez (1868-1935), Vice-President of Paraguay and writer. c, Dr. Fulgencio R. Moreno (1872-1933), historian. d, Dr. Efraím Cardozo (1906-73), historian. e, Dr. Rafael E. Velázquez (1926-94), historian.

2012, Aug. 10 Litho. *Perf. 13¼*

2945 Horiz. strip of 5	5.50	5.50
a.-e. A702 1400g Any single	1.10	1.10

Souvenir Sheet

Asunción, 475th Anniv. — A703

2012, Aug. 14 Litho. *Rouletted 5*
2946 A703 10,000g multi 7.00 7.00

Souvenir Sheet

Locomotive — A704

2012, Aug. 14 Litho. *Rouletted 5*
2947 A704 8000g multi 6.00 6.00

Carlos Antonio López (1792-1862), first President of Paraguay.

National University of Asunción Economic Sciences Faculty, 75th Anniv. — A705

2012, Aug. 22 Litho. *Perf. 13¼*
2948 A705 1400g multi 1.10 1.10

Technical Planning Ministry, 50th Anniv. — A706

2012, Sept. 17 Litho. *Perf. 13¼*
2949 A706 8000g multi + label 6.00 6.00

Cerro Porteño Basketball Team — A707

Cerro Porteño Soccer Team — A708

2012, Oct. 1 Litho. *Perf. 13¼*
2950 A707 1000g multi .80 .80
2951 A708 6000g multi + label 4.25 4.25

Cerro Porteño Sports Club, cent.

Independence of Slovakia, 20th Anniv. — A709

2012, Nov. 13 Litho. *Perf. 13¼*
2952 A709 11,000g multi + label 8.25 8.25

No. 2952 was printed in sheets of 10 stamps + 15 labels.

First National Eucharistic Congress, 75th Anniv. — A710

2012, Nov. 19 Litho. *Perf. 13¼*
2953 A710 3000g multi + label 2.25 2.25

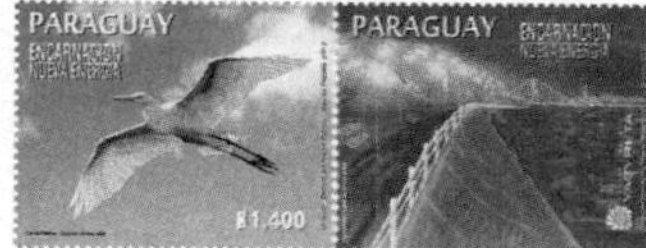

Ardea Alba — A711

2012, Nov. 20 Litho. *Perf. 13¼*
2954 A711 1400g multi + label 1.10 1.10

Completion of new dam near Encarnacion. No. 2954 was printed in sheets containing 10 stamps + 15 labels.

Radio Nanduti, 50th Anniv. — A712

2012, Nov. 29 Litho. *Perf. 13¼*
2955 A712 1400g multi + label 1.10 1.10

United Nations Environmental Program, 40th Anniv. — A713

Designs: 3000g, Butorides striatus. 16,000g, Platalea ajaja.

2012, Dec. 18 Litho. *Perf. 13¼*
2956 A713 3000g multi 2.25 2.25

Souvenir Sheet

Rouletted 5

2957 A713 16,000g multi 12.00 12.00

Christmas — A714

No. 2958 — Various creche figures: a, 1000g. b, 5000g. c, 11,000g.

2012, Dec. 18 Litho. *Perf. 13¼*
2958 A714 Vert. strip of 3, #a-c 13.00 13.00

National Library, 125th Anniv. A715

2012, Dec. 27 Litho. *Perf. 13¼*
2959 A715 1400g multi 1.10 1.10

Alternative Energy Sources A716

No. 2960: a, Wind energy (wind turbines). b, Solar energy (solar collector). c, Biodiesel (jatropha tree). d, Biomass (hay roll). e, Biodiesel (corn).
3000g, Biodiesel (sunflower), horiz.

2012, Dec. 27 Litho. *Perf. 13¼*
2960 Horiz. strip of 5 6.00 6.00
a.-e. A716 1500g Any single 1.20 1.20

Souvenir Sheet

Rouletted 5

2961 A716 3000g multi 2.25 2.25

Paraguayan-Japanese Center, Asuncion — A718

No. 2964: a, Building exterior and flags. b, Cherry blossoms.

2013, Aug. 19 Litho. *Perf. 13¼*
2964 Horiz. pair + central label 8.75 8.75
a. A718 1400g multi 1.00 1.00
b. A718 11,000g multi 7.75 7.75

Birds — A719

No. 2965: a, Dendrocygna viduata. b, Amazona aestiva. c, Chlorostilbon aureoventris. d, Jabiru mycteria. e, Zenaida auriculata. f, Athene cunicularia. g, Aramides ypecaha. h, Dendrocygna autumnalis. i, Caracara plancus. j, Vanellus chilensis.

2013, Aug. 19 Litho. *Perf. 13¼*
2965 Block of 10 15.00 15.00
a.-j. A719 2000g Any single 1.50 1.50

Mammals — A720

No. 2966: a, Lycalopex gymnocercus. b, Myrmecophaga tridactyla. c, Cebus apella paraguayanus. d, Tayassu pecari. e, Nasua nasua.
6000g, Panthera onca, vert.

2013, Aug. 19 Litho. *Perf. 13¼*
2966 Horiz. strip of 5 10.00 10.00
a.-e. A720 3000g Any single 2.00 2.00

Souvenir Sheet

Rouletted 5

2967 A720 6000g multi 4.50 4.50

Scouting in Paraguay, Cent. — A721

No. 2968: a, Group of Scouts. b, Scouts running.

2013, Aug. 23 Litho. *Perf. 13¼*
2968 Horiz. pair + central label 9.50 9.50
a. A721 5000g multi 3.75 3.75
b. A721 8000g multi 5.75 5.75

Rubio Nú Soccer Team, Cent. A722

Designs: 1400g, Six palyers celebrating. 6000g, Team photograph.

2013, Aug. 24 Litho. *Perf. 13¼*
2969-2970 A722 Set of 2 5.50 5.50

Flowers A723

No. 2971 — Inscriptions at LL: a, Azahar. b, Aguape. c, Agosto Poty. d, Chivato Poty. e, Santa Lucia. f, Ceibo.

No. 2972, 10,000g, Samu'u (yellow flower), horiz. No. 2973, 10,000g, Mburucuja (blue flower), horiz.

2013, Sept. 17 Litho. *Perf. 13¼*

2971 Horiz. strip of 6 21.00 21.00
a.-f. A723 5000g Any single 3.50 3.50

Souvenir Sheets

Rouletted 5

2972-2973 A723 Set of 2 16.00 16.00

Agustín Barboza (1913-98), Musician A724

Barboza: 1400g, Holding neck of guitar. 4000g, Playing guitar.

2013, Oct. 9 Litho. *Perf. 13¼*

2974-2975 A724 Set of 2 4.00 4.00

Campaign Against Discrimination A725

Paintings by Juan de Dios Valdez depicting: 5000g, Old man. 10,000g, Old woman.

2013, Oct. 9 Litho. *Perf. 13¼*

2976 A725 5000g multi 3.50 3.50

Souvenir Sheet

Rouletted 5

2977 A725 10,000g multi 7.00 7.00

America Issue.

Republic of Paraguay, 200th Anniv. — A726

200th Anniv. emblem and: 1000g, Map of Asuncion, 1809. 8000g, Consuls Fulgencio Yegros (1780-1821) and Dr. José Gaspar de Francia (1766-1840), vert.

2013, Oct. 12 Litho. *Perf. 13¼*

2978 A726 1000g multi + label .75 .75

Souvenir Sheet

Rouletted 5

2979 A726 8000g multi 5.75 5.75

National Pantheon of Heroes and Oratory of Our Lady of Asuncion, 150th Anniv. — A727

2013, Nov. 1 Litho. *Perf. 13¼*

2980 A727 11,000g multi 8.00 8.00

Paraguayan Atheneum, 130th Anniv. — A728

2013, Dec. 5 Litho. *Perf. 13¼*

2982 A728 1400g multi 1.00 1.00

Philatelic Center of Paraguay, Cent. — A729

2013, Dec. 6 Litho. *Perf. 13¼*

2983 A729 1400g multi 1.00 1.00

Christmas A730

Designs: 3000g, Virgin Mary and St. Joseph. 8000g, Holy Family creche figurines. 16,000g, Creche figurines, horiz.

2013, Dec. 6 Litho. *Perf. 13¼*

2984-2986 A730 Set of 3 19.00 19.00

Encarnación, 400th Anniv. (in 2015) — A731

Designs: 3000g, Mirador San José, Virgin of Itacuá. 11,000g, Woman in Carnaval costume, vert.

2014, Feb. 6 Litho. *Perf. 13¼*

2987 A731 3000g multi 2.10 2.10

Souvenir Sheet

Rouletted 5

2988 A731 11,000g multi 8.00 8.00

Asuncion Tennis Club, Cent. — A732

2014, Mar. 4 Litho. *Perf. 13¼*

2989 A732 1400g multi 1.00 1.00

Villeta, 300th Anniv. — A733

2014, Mar. 5 Litho. *Perf. 13¼*

2990 A733 1400g multi + label 1.00 1.00

Campaign Against Violence Towards Women A734

2014, Mar. 7 Litho. *Perf. 13¼*

2991 A734 700g multi .50 .50

Vice-President Domingo F. Sánchez National College, 50th Anniv. — A735

2014, Mar. 28 Litho. *Perf. 13¼*

2992 A735 1400g multi 1.00 1.00

Jorge Castro, Singer — A736

Castro: 1400g, On horse. 5000g, With orchestra.

2014, Apr. 25 Litho. *Perf. 13¼*

2993 A736 1400g multi 1.00 1.00

Souvenir Sheet

Rouletted 5

2994 A736 5000g multi 3.50 3.50

Cabildo Cultural Center, Asuncion, 10th Anniv. — A737

2014, May 13 Litho. *Perf. 13¼*

2995 A737 1400g multi 1.00 1.00

Itaipu Dam and Speothos Venaticus — A738

2014, May 20 Litho. *Perf. 13¼*

2996 A738 16,000g multi 11.00 11.00

Itaipu Binacional, 40th anniv.

44th General Assembly of the Organization of American States, Asuncion — A739

2014, June 5 Litho. *Perf. 13¼*

2997 A739 5000g multi + label 3.50 3.50

Pope Francis and Map of South America A740

2014, June 27 Litho. *Perf. 13¼*

2998 A740 9000g multi 6.00 6.00

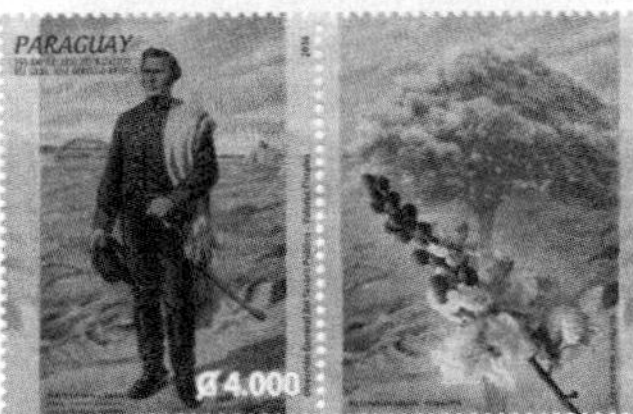

Gen. José Gervasio Artigas (1764-1850), National Hero of Uruguay — A741

2014, July 18 Litho. *Perf. 13¼*

2999 A741 4000g multi + label 2.75 2.75

Salvador Cabañas and Emblem of 12 de Octubre Soccer Team — A742

2014, Aug. 8 Litho. *Perf. 13¼*

3000 A742 1400g multi + label 1.00 1.00

12 de Octubre Soccer Team, cent.

Apostolic Movement of Schoenstatt, Cent. — A743

2014, Oct. 6 Litho. *Perf. 13¼*

3001 A743 3000g multi + label 2.00 2.00

Paraguayan Presidents A744

Designs: 1400g, José Félix Estigarribia (1888-1940). 4000g, Bernardino Caballero (1839-1912)

2014, Oct. 9 Litho. *Perf. 13¼*
3002-3003 A744 Set of 2 3.75 3.75

America issue.

Telecommunications in Paraguay, 150th Anniv. — A745

2014, Oct. 9 Litho. *Perf. 13¼*
3004 A745 9000g multi + label 6.00 6.00

Asuncion Zoo and Botanical Gardens, Cent. — A746

No. 3005: a, Ara ararauna. b, Rhea americana.

2014, Oct. 15 Litho. *Perf. 13¼*
3005 Horiz. pair + central label 9.00 9.00
a. A746 3000g multi 2.00 2.00
b. A746 10,000g multi 7.00 7.00

No. 2764 Overprinted

Method and Perf. As Before
2014, Oct. 16
3006 A589 4000g multi + label 2.75 2.75

Latin American Parliament, 50th anniv.

Asuncion, Green Capital — A747

2014, Nov. 6 Litho. *Perf. 13¼*
3007 A747 1400g multi + label 1.00 1.00

Carlos Miguel Jiménez (1914-70), Musician — A748

2014, Nov. 10 Litho. *Perf. 13¼*
3008 A748 2000g black + label 1.75 1.75

Silvio Pettirossi (1887-1916), Aviator — A749

No. 3009: a, Pettirossi, airplane inverted in flight, note written by Pettirossi. b, Pettirossi in airplace cockpit.

2014, Nov. 17 Litho. *Perf. 13¼*
3009 Horiz. pair + central label 8.00 8.00
a. A749 2500g multi 1.75 1.75
b. A749 9000g multi 6.25 6.25

Spanish Academy, 300th Anniv. — A750

Designs: No. 3010, Flowers. No. 3011, Emblem of Paraguayan Spanish Language Academy.

2014, Nov. 21 Litho. *Perf. 13¼*
3010 A750 11,000g multi 8.00 8.00

Souvenir Sheet
Rouletted 5
3011 A750 11,000g multi 8.00 8.00

Christmas A751

Designs: 1400g, Star, pottery, angel. 5000g, Star, pottery, melons, grapes.

2014, Dec. 5 Litho. *Perf. 13¼*
3012-3013 A751 Set of 2 4.50 4.50

Campaign Against Discrimination — A752

Designs: 1000g, Three empty chairs of different heights. 10,000g, Handicapped child with other children.

2015, Jan. 7 Litho. *Perf. 13¼*
3014-3015 A752 Set of 2 7.50 7.50

Dated 2014.

Visit of United Nations Secretary General Ban Ki-moon — A753

2015, Feb. 25 Litho. *Perf. 13¼*
3016 A753 10,000g multi + label 7.00 7.00

Paraguayan postal officials declared as "illegal" two blocks of nine stamps and two souvenir sheets of four dated 2013 and inscribed "Winter War."

Encarnación, 400th Anniv. — A754

No. 3017: a, Municipal Building, horse-drawn carriage. b, San Roque González de Santa Cruz Basilica, St. Roque González de Santa Cruz (1576-1628).

2015, Mar. 25 Litho. *Perf. 13¼*
3017 Horiz. pair + central label 6.00 6.00
a. A754 1000g multi .50 .50
b. A754 10,000g multi 5.50 5.50

Lorenzo Prieto, Record-Setting Bicyclist — A755

2015, Apr. 24 Litho. *Perf. 13¼*
3018 A755 2000g multi + label 1.40 1.40

Efrén Echeverría, Guitarist — A756

2015, Apr. 24 Litho. *Perf. 13¼*
3019 A756 5000g multi + label 3.25 3.25

Secretary of Social Action, 20th Anniv. — A757

2015, May 7 Litho. *Perf. 13¼*
3020 A757 10,000g multi + label 5.50 5.50

Instruments of the Recycled Orchestra of Catuera — A758

2015, May 25 Litho. *Perf. 13¼*
3021 A758 5000g Trumpet 2.75 2.75

Souvenir Sheet
Rouletted 5
3022 A758 2000g Saxophone, vert. .80 .80

Santa Teresa de Jesus College, Cent. — A759

2015, May 25 Litho. *Perf. 13¼*
3023 A759 13,000g multi + label 7.25 7.25

Animals — A760

No. 3024: a, 1000g, Azara's night monkey (ka'i pyhare). b, 1400g, Geoffroy's cat (gato montés). c, 3000g, Capybara (carpincho).
No. 3025, 3000g, Blue-fronted Amazons (loro hablador).

2015, June 12 Litho. *Perf. 13¼*
3024 A760 Block of 3, #a-c, + label 3.00 3.00

Souvenir Sheet
Rouletted 5
3025 A760 3000g multi 2.40 2.40

Junior Chamber International in Paragauy, cent.

Visit of Pope Francis to Paraguay — A762

Designs: 5000g, Pope Francis, map and flag of Paraguay.
6000g, Pope Francis, church.

2015, July 6 Litho. *Perf. 13¼*
3027 A762 5000g multi + label 2.75 2.75

Souvenir Sheet
Rouletted 8
3028 A762 6000g multi 3.50 3.50

St. John Bosco (1815-88) — A763

2015, Aug. 12 Litho. *Perf. 13¼*
3029 A763 2000g multi + label 1.40 1.40

Postal Headquarters — A764

No. 3030 — Postal Headquarters in: a, 5000g, Guatemala (denomination at left). b, 10,000g, Paraguay (denomination at right).

2015, Aug. 13 Litho. *Perf. 13¼*
3030 A764 Horiz. pair, #a-b 6.50 6.50

See Guatemala No. 708.

Luis Alberto del Paraná (1926-74) and Los Paraguayos, Musical Group — A765

No. 3031: a, 2000g, Three band members. b, 5000g, Del Paraná.

2015, Sept. 15 **Litho.** ***Perf. 13¼***

3031 A765 Horiz. pair, #a-b, + flanking label 1.40 1.40

SEMI-POSTAL STAMPS

Red Cross Nurse SP1

Unwmk.

1930, July 22 **Typo.** ***Perf. 12***

B1 SP1 1.50p + 50c gray violet 2.00 1.20
B2 SP1 1.50p + 50c deep rose 2.00 1.20
B3 SP1 1.50p + 50c dark blue 2.00 1.20
Nos. B1-B3 (3) 6.00 3.60

The surtax was for the benefit of the Red Cross Society of Paraguay.

College of Agriculture — SP2

1930

B4 SP2 1.50p + 50c blue, *pale pink* .60 .50

Surtax for the Agricultural Institute.

The sheet of No. B4 has a papermaker's watermark: "Vencedor Bond."

A 1.50p+50c red on pale yellow was prepared but not regularly issued. Value, 40 cents.

Red Cross Headquarters SP3

1932

B5 SP3 50c + 50c rose .60 .60

Our Lady of Asunción — SP4

1941 **Engr.**

B6 SP4 7p + 3p red brown .40 .35
B7 SP4 7p + 3p purple .40 .35
B8 SP4 7p + 3p carmine rose .40 .35
B9 SP4 7p + 3p sapphire .40 .35
Nos. B6-B9 (4) 1.60 1.40

For surcharges see Nos. 419-426, 431-434.

No. 361 Surcharged in Black

1944

B10 A70 10c on 10p multicolored .70 .50

The surtax was for the victims of the San Juan earthquake in Argentina.

Catalogue values for unused stamps in this section, from this point to the end of the section, are for Never Hinged items.

No. C169 Surcharged in Carmine "AYUDA AL ECUADOR 5 + 5"

1949 **Unwmk.** ***Perf. 12½***

B11 A117 5c + 5c on 30c dk blue .30 .30

Surtax for the victims of the Ecuador earthquake.

38th Intl. Eucharistic Congress, Bombay — SP5

Various coins and coat of arms.

Litho. & Engr.

1964, Dec. 11 ***Perf. 12x12½***

B12 SP5 20g +10g multi 6.50 6.50
B13 SP5 30g +15g multi 6.50 6.50
B14 SP5 50g +25g multi 6.50 6.50
B15 SP5 100g +50g multi 6.50 6.50
a. Souvenir sheet of 4, #B12-B15 26.00 26.00
Nos. B12-B15 (4) 26.00 26.00

Buildings and Coats of Arms of Popes John XXIII & Paul VI — SP6

#B16, Dome of St. Peters. #B17, Site of Saint Peter's tomb. #B18, Saint Peter's Plaza. #B19,Taj Mahal.

1964, Dec. 12

B16 SP6 20g +10g multi 6.50 6.50
B17 SP6 30g +15g multi 6.50 6.50
B18 SP6 50g +25g multi 6.50 6.50
B19 SP6 100g +50g multi 6.50 6.50
a. Souvenir sheet of 4, #B16-B19 140.00 140.00
Nos. B16-B19 (4) 26.00 26.00

AIR POST STAMPS

Official Stamps of 1913 Surcharged

1929, Jan. 1 **Unwmk.** ***Perf. 11½***

C1 O19 2.85p on 5c lilac 2.25 1.50
C2 O19 5.65p on 10c grn 1.25 1.50
C3 O19 11.30p on 50c rose 2.00 1.25
Nos. C1-C3 (3) 5.50 4.25

Counterfeits of surcharge exist.

Regular Issues of 1924-27 Surcharged

1929, Feb. 26 ***Perf. 12***

C4 A51 3.40p on 3p gray 4.50 4.00
a. Surch. "Correo / en $3.40 / Habilitado / Aereo" 8.75
b. Double surcharge 8.75
c. "Aéro" instead of "Aéreo"
C5 A44 6.80p on 4p lt bl 4.50 3.25
a. Surch. "Correo / Aereo / en $6.80 / Habilitado" 8.75
C6 A52 17p on 5p choc 4.50 3.25
a. Surch. "Correo / Habilitado / Habilitado / en 17p" 4.50
b. Double surcharge 25.00 25.00
Nos. C4-C6 (3) 13.50 10.50

Wings AP1

Pigeon with Letter AP2

Airplanes — AP3

1929-31 **Typo.** ***Perf. 12***

C7 AP1 2.85p gray green 1.75 1.25
a. Imperf., pair 37.50
C8 AP1 2.85p turq grn ('31) .50 .50
C9 AP2 5.65p brown 2.00 1.25
C10 AP2 5.65p scar ('31) 1.00 .50
C11 AP3 11.30p chocolate 1.75 1.25
a. Imperf., pair 37.50
C12 AP3 11.30p dp blue ('31) .50 .50
Nos. C7-C12 (6) 7.50 5.25

Sheets of these stamps sometimes show portions of a papermaker's watermark "Indian Bond C. Extra Strong."

Excellent counterfeits are plentiful.

Regular Issues of 1924-28 Surcharged in Black or Red

1929 ***Perf. 11½, 12***

C13 A47 95c on 7c lilac .35 .30
C14 A47 1.90p on 20c dull bl .35 .30
C15 A44 3.40p on 4p lt bl (R) .45 .30
a. Double surcharge 3.00
C16 A44 4.75p on 4p lt bl (R) .90 .75
a. Double surcharge 3.00
C17 A51 6.80p on 3p gray 1.00 .90
a. Double surcharge 4.50
C18 A52 17p on 5p choc 3.00 3.00
a. Horiz. pair, imperf. between 37.50
Nos. C13-C18 (6) 6.05 5.55

Six stamps in the sheet of No. C17 have the "$" and numerals thinner and narrower than the normal type.

Airplane and Arms — AP4

Cathedral of Asunción AP5

Airplane and Globe — AP6

1930 ***Perf. 12***

C19 AP4 95c dp red, *pink* 1.50 .90
C20 AP4 95c dk bl, *blue* 1.50 .90
C21 AP5 1.90p lt red, *pink* 1.50 .90
C22 AP5 1.90p violet, *blue* 1.50 .90
C23 AP6 6.80p blk, *lt bl* 1.50 .90
C24 AP6 6.80p green, *pink* 1.50 .90
Nos. C19-C24 (6) 9.00 5.40

Sheets of Nos. C19-C24 have a papermaker's watermark: "Extra Vencedor Bond."

Counterfeits exist.

Stamps and Types of 1927-28 Overprinted in Red

1930

C25 A47 10c olive green .60 .40
a. Double overprint 6.00
C26 A47 20c dull blue .60 .40
a. "CORREO CORREO" instead of "CORREO AEREO" 5.00
b. "AEREO AEREO" instead of "CORREO AEREO" 5.00
C27 A48 1p emerald 1.40 1.40
C28 A51 3p gray 1.40 1.40
Nos. C25-C28 (4) 4.00 3.60

Counterfeits of Nos. C26a and C26b exist.

Nos. 273, 282, 286, 288, 300, 302, 305 Surcharged in Red or Black

#C29-C30, C32

#C31

#C33

#C34-C35

1930 **Red or Black Surcharge**

C29 A47 5c on 10c gray grn (R) .50 .50
a. "AEREO" omitted 30.00
C30 A47 5c on 70c ultra (R) .50 .50
a. Vert. pair, imperf. between 40.00
C31 A48 20c on 1p org red .60 .50
a. "CORREO" double 6.00 6.00
b. "AEREO" double 6.00 6.00

C32 A47 40c on 50c org (R) .60 .50
a. "AEREO" omitted 9.00 9.00
b. "CORREO" double 6.00 6.00
c. "AEREO" double 6.00 6.00
C33 A54 6p on 10p red 2.50 2.00
C34 A49 10p on 20p red 10.00 10.00
C35 A49 10p on 20p vio brn 10.00 10.00
Nos. C29-C35 (7) 24.70 24.00

Declaration of Independence AP11

1930, May 14 **Typo.**
C36 AP11 2.85p dark blue .70 .50
C37 AP11 3.40p dark green .70 .40
C38 AP11 4.75p deep lake .70 .40
Nos. C36-C38 (3) 2.10 1.30

Natl. Independence Day, May 14, 1811.

Gunboat Type

Gunboat "Paraguay."

1931-39 ***Perf. 11½, 12***
C39 A58 1p claret .60 .60
C40 A58 1p dk blue ('36) .60 .60
C41 A58 2p orange .60 .60
C42 A58 2p dk brn ('36) .60 .60
C43 A58 3p turq green .75 .75
C44 A58 3p lt ultra ('36) .90 .75
C45 A58 3p brt rose ('39) .60 .60
C46 A58 6p dk green 1.20 .90
C47 A58 6p violet ('36) 1.40 .90
C48 A58 6p dull bl ('39) 1.20 .75
C49 A58 10p vermilion 3.00 1.75
C50 A58 10p bluish grn ('35) 4.50 3.00
C51 A58 10p yel brn ('36) 3.25 2.25
C52 A58 10p dk blue ('36) 2.75 1.50
C53 A58 10p lt pink ('39) 3.00 2.00
Nos. C39-C53 (15) 24.95 17.55

1st constitution of Paraguay as a Republic and the arrival of the "Paraguay" and "Humaita."

Counterfeits of #C39-C53 are plentiful.

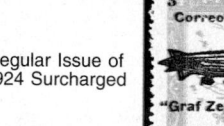

Regular Issue of 1924 Surcharged

1931, Aug. 22
C54 A44 3p on 4p lt bl 17.50 17.50

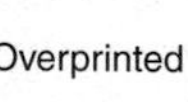

Overprinted

C55 A44 4p lt blue 15.00 15.00

On Nos. C54-C55 the Zeppelin is handstamped. The rest of the surcharge or overprint is typographed.

War Memorial AP13

Orange Tree and Yerba Mate — AP14

Yerba Mate — AP15

Palms — AP16

Eagle — AP17

1931-36 **Litho.**
C56 AP13 5c lt blue .25 *.40*
a. Horiz. pair, imperf. btwn. 6.25
C57 AP13 5c dp grn ('33) .25 *.40*
C58 AP13 5c lt red ('33) .30 *.40*
C59 AP13 5c violet ('35) .25 *.40*
C60 AP14 10c dp violet .25 *.40*
C61 AP14 10c brn lake ('33) .25 *.40*
C62 AP14 10c yel brn ('33) .25 *.40*
C63 AP14 10c ultra ('35) .25 *.40*
a. Imperf., pair 5.50
C64 AP15 20c red .25 *.40*
C65 AP15 20c dl blue ('33) .30 *.40*
C66 AP15 20c emer ('33) .25 *.40*
C67 AP15 20c yel brn ('35) .25 *.40*
a. Imperf., pair 3.75
C68 AP16 40c dp green .25 *.40*
C69 AP16 40c slate bl ('35) .25 *.40*
C70 AP16 40c red ('36) .30 *.40*
C71 AP17 80c dull blue .25 *.40*
C72 AP17 80c dl grn ('33) .50 *.40*
C73 AP17 80c scar ('33) .30 *.40*
Nos. C56-C73 (18) 4.95 7.20

Airship "Graf Zeppelin" — AP18

1932, Apr. **Litho.**
C74 AP18 4p ultra 3.75 3.75
a. Imperf., pair *35.00*
C75 AP18 8p red 6.25 5.00
C76 AP18 12p blue grn 5.00 5.00
C77 AP18 16p dk violet 8.75 6.25
C78 AP18 20p orange brn 8.75 6.25
Nos. C74-C78 (5) 32.50 26.25

For surcharges see Nos. 325-329.

"Graf Zeppelin" over Brazilian Terrain AP19

"Graf Zeppelin" over Atlantic — AP20

1933, May 5
C79 AP19 4.50p dp blue 4.00 3.00
C80 AP19 9p dp rose 7.00 5.00
a. Horiz. pair, imperf. between 150.00
C81 AP19 13.50p blue grn 8.00 6.00
C82 AP20 22.50p bis brn 18.00 14.00
C83 AP20 45p dull vio 24.00 24.00
Nos. C79-C83 (5) 61.00 52.00

Excellent counterfeits are plentiful.
For overprints see Nos. C88-C97.

Posts and Telegraph Building, Asunción — AP21

1934-37 ***Perf. 11½***
C84 AP21 33.75p ultra 6.00 5.25
C85 AP21 33.75p car ('35) 6.00 5.25
a. 33.75p rose ('37) 5.25 4.50
C86 AP21 33.75p emerald ('36) 7.50 6.00
C87 AP21 33.75p bis brn ('36) 2.25 2.25
Nos. C84-C87 (4) 21.75 18.75

Excellent counterfeits exist.
For surcharge see No. C107.

Nos. C79-C83 Overprinted in Black

1934, May 26
C88 AP19 4.50p deep bl 3.00 2.25
C89 AP19 9p dp rose 3.75 3.00
C90 AP19 13.50p blue grn 10.50 7.50
C91 AP20 22.50p bis brn 9.00 6.00
C92 AP20 45p dull vio 13.50 10.50
Nos. C88-C92 (5) 39.75 29.25

Types of 1933 Issue Overprinted in Black

1935
C93 AP19 4.50p rose red 3.50 2.50
C94 AP19 9p lt green 4.50 3.00
C95 AP19 13.50p brown 9.50 7.00
C96 AP20 22.50p violet 7.50 5.50
C97 AP20 45p blue 22.50 13.00
Nos. C93-C97 (5) 47.50 31.00

Tobacco Plant — AP22

1935-39 **Typo.**
C98 AP22 17p lt brown 12.50 12.50
C99 AP22 17p carmine 21.00 21.00
C100 AP22 17p dark blue 15.00 15.00
C101 AP22 17p pale yel grn ('39) 8.00 8.00
Nos. C98-C101 (4) 56.50 56.50

Excellent counterfeits are plentiful.

Church of Incarnation AP23

1935-38
C102 AP23 102p carmine 7.50 5.00
C103 AP23 102p blue 7.50 5.00
C103A AP23 102p indigo ('36) 4.50 4.50
C104 AP23 102p yellow brn 5.50 4.75
a. Imperf., pair 30.00
C105 AP23 102p violet ('37) 2.50 2.50
C106 AP23 102p brn org ('38) 2.25 2.25
Nos. C102-C106 (6) 29.75 24.00

Excellent counterfeits are plentiful.
For surcharges see Nos. C108-C109.

Types of 1934-35 Surcharged in Red

1937, Aug. 1
C107 AP21 24p on 33.75p sl bl 1.00 .70
C108 AP23 65p on 102p ol bis 2.50 1.75
C109 AP23 84p on 102p bl grn 2.50 1.50
Nos. C107-C109 (3) 6.00 3.95

Plane over Asunción AP24

1939, Aug. 3 **Typo.** ***Perf. 10½, 11½***
C110 AP24 3.40p yel green 1.00 1.00
C111 AP24 3.40p orange brn .60 .50
C112 AP24 3.40p indigo .60 .50
Nos. C110-C112 (3) 2.20 2.00

Buenos Aires Peace Conference Type and

Map of Paraguay with New Chaco Boundary AP28

Designs: 1p, Flags of Paraguay and Bolivia. 3p, Coats of Arms. 5p, Pres. Ortiz of Argentina, flags of Paraguay, Argentina. 10p, Pres. Vargas, Brazil. 30p, Pres. Alessandri, Chile. 50p, US Eagle and Shield. 100p, Pres. Benavides, Peru. 200p, Pres. Baldomir, Uruguay.

Engr.; Flags Litho.
1939, Nov. ***Perf. 12½***
Flags in National Colors
C113 A69 1p red brown .60 .60
C114 A69 3p dark blue .60 .60
C115 A70 5p olive blk .60 .60
C116 A70 10p violet .60 .60
C117 A70 30p orange .60 .60
C118 A70 50p black brn .90 .60
C119 A70 100p brt green 1.25 .90
C120 A70 200p green 6.75 3.75
C121 AP28 500p black 27.50 17.50
Nos. C113-C121 (9) 39.40 25.75

For overprints see Nos. 388-390.

University of Asuncion Type

Pres. Bernardino Caballero and Senator José S. Decoud.

1939, Sept. **Litho.** ***Perf. 12***
C122 A67 28p rose & blk 10.00 10.00
C123 A67 90p yel grn & blk 12.00 12.00

Map with Asunción to New York Air Route — AP35

1939, Nov. 30 **Engr.**
C124 AP35 30p brown 7.75 6.00
C125 AP35 80p orange 9.00 9.00
C126 AP35 90p purple 12.00 12.00
Nos. C124-C126 (3) 28.75 27.00

New York World's Fair.

Pan American Union Type

1940, May ***Perf. 12***

C127	A85	20p rose car	.60	.60
C128	A85	70p violet bl	1.25	.60
C129	A85	100p Prus grn	1.50	1.50
C130	A85	500p dk violet	6.75	5.25
		Nos. C127-C130 (4)	10.10	7.95

Asuncion 400th Anniv. Type

1942, Aug. 15

C131	A93	20p deep plum	1.00	.40
C132	A94	70p fawn	2.00	1.10
C133	A95	500p olive gray	5.50	3.50
		Nos. C131-C133 (3)	8.50	5.00

Imperforates
Starting with No. C134, many Paraguayan air mail stamps exist imperforate.

Port of Asunción AP40

First Telegraph in South America AP41

Early Merchant Ship — AP42

Birthplace of Paraguay's Liberation AP43

Monument to Antequera AP44

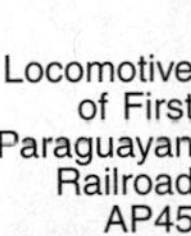

Locomotive of First Paraguayan Railroad AP45

Monument to Heroes of Itororó — AP46

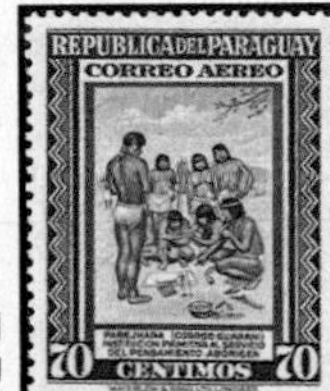

Primitive Postal Service among Indians — AP48

Government House AP47

Colonial Jesuit Altar — AP49

Ruins of Humaitá Church — AP50

Oratory of the Virgin — AP51

Marshal Francisco S. Lopez — AP52

1944-45 **Unwmk.** ***Perf. 12½***

C134	AP40	1c blue	.40	.25
C135	AP41	2c green	.40	.25
C136	AP42	3c brown vio	.40	.25
C137	AP43	5c brt bl grn	.40	.25
C138	AP44	10c dk violet	.40	.25
C139	AP45	20c dk brown	.40	.25
C140	AP46	30c lt blue	.40	.25
C141	AP47	40c olive	.40	.25
C142	AP48	70c brown red	.50	.30
C143	AP49	1g orange yel	1.50	.60
C144	AP50	2g copper brn	2.00	.90
C145	AP51	5g black brn	4.00	2.75
C146	AP52	10g indigo	10.00	5.00
		Nos. C134-C146 (13)	21.20	11.15

See Nos. C158-C162. For surcharges see Nos. C154-C157.

Flags Type

20c, Ecuador. 40c, Bolivia. 70c, Mexico. 1g, Chile. 2g, Brazil. 5g, Argentina. 10g, US.

Engr.; Flags Litho. in Natl. Colors

1945, Aug. 15

C147	A106	20c orange	.60	.60
C148	A106	40c olive	.60	.60
C149	A106	70c lake	.60	.60
C150	A106	1g slate bl	1.00	1.00
C151	A106	2g blue vio	1.50	1.50
C152	A106	5g green	4.25	4.25
C153	A106	10g brown	11.00	11.00
		Nos. C147-C153 (7)	19.55	19.55

Sizes: Nos. C147-C151, 30x26mm; 5g, 32x28mm; 10g, 33x30mm.

Catalogue values for unused stamps in this section, from this point to the end of the section, are for Never Hinged items.

Nos. C139-C142 Surcharged "1946" and New Value in Black

1946 **Engr.** ***Perf. 12½***

C154	AP45	5c on 20c dk brn	.80	.80
C155	AP46	5c on 30c lt blue	.80	.80
C156	AP47	5c on 40c olive	.80	.80
C157	AP48	5c on 70c brn red	.80	.80
		Nos. C154-C157 (4)	3.20	3.20

Types of 1944-45

1946, Sept. 21 **Engr.**

C158	AP50	10c dp car	.40	.40
C159	AP40	20c emerald	.40	.40
C160	AP47	1g brown org	.70	.70
C161	AP52	5g purple	2.00	2.00
C162	AP51	10g rose car	10.00	10.00
		Nos. C158-C162 (5)	13.50	13.50

Marshal Francisco Solano Lopez Type

1947, May. 15 ***Perf. 12***

C163	A114	32c car lake	.30	.30
C164	A114	64c orange brn	.45	.45
C165	A114	1g Prus green	.90	.90
C166	A114	5g Prus grn & brn vio	2.40	2.40
C167	A114	10g dk car rose & dk yel grn	5.00	5.00
		Nos. C163-C167 (5)	9.05	9.05

Archbishopric of Asunción Types

1948, Jan. 6 **Unwmk.** ***Perf. 12½***

Size: 25½x31mm

C168	A116	20c gray blk	.40	.25
C169	A117	30c dark blue	.40	.25
C170	A118	40c lilac	.70	.35
C171	A115	70c orange red	.90	.45
C172	A112	1g brown red	.90	.45
C173	A118	2g red	1.90	1.25

Size: 25½x34mm

C174	A115	5g brt car & dk bl	4.50	2.25
C175	A116	10g dk grn & brn	7.50	3.75
		Nos. C168-C175 (8)	17.20	8.90

For surcharges see Nos. B11, C178.

Type of Regular Issue of 1948 Inscribed "AEREO"

1948, Sept. 11 **Engr. & Litho.**

C176	A119	69c dk grn	1.40	1.40
C177	A119	5g dk blue	7.50	7.50

The Barefeet, a political group.

No. C171 Surcharged in Black

1949, June 29

C178	A115	5c on 70c org red	.30	.25

Archbishop Juan Sinforiano Bogarin (1863-1949).

Symbols of UPU — AP65

1950, Sept. 4 **Engr.** ***Perf. 13½x13***

C179	AP65	20c green & violet	.60	.25
C180	AP65	30c rose vio & brn	.90	.40
C181	AP65	50c gray & green	1.20	.50
C182	AP65	1g blue & brown	1.50	.65
C183	AP65	5g rose & black	3.50	1.00
		Nos. C179-C183 (5)	7.70	2.80

UPU, 75th anniv. (in 1949).

Franklin D. Roosevelt AP66

Engr.; Flags Litho.

1950, Oct. 2 ***Perf. 12½***

Flags in Carmine & Violet Blue.

C184	AP66	20c red	.30	.25
C185	AP66	30c black	.30	.25
C186	AP66	50c claret	.30	.25
C187	AP66	1g dk gray grn	.40	.25
C188	AP66	5g deep blue	.50	.40
		Nos. C184-C188 (5)	1.80	1.40

Franklin D. Roosevelt (1882-1945).

Urn Containing Remains of Columbus AP67

1952, Feb. 11 **Litho.** ***Perf. 10***

C189	AP67	10c ultra	.40	.25
C190	AP67	20c green	.40	.25
C191	AP67	30c lilac	.40	.25
C192	AP67	40c rose	.40	.25
C193	AP67	50c bister brn	.40	.25
C194	AP67	1g blue	.40	.25
C195	AP67	2g orange	.40	.25
C196	AP67	5g red brown	.60	.30
		Nos. C189-C196 (8)	3.40	2.05

Queen Isabella I — AP68

1952, Oct. 12

C197	AP68	1g vio blue	.30	.25
C198	AP68	2g chocolate	.40	.30
C199	AP68	5g dull green	.80	.50
C200	AP68	10g lilac rose	1.60	1.00
		Nos. C197-C200 (4)	3.10	2.05

500th birth anniv. of Queen Isabella I of Spain (in 1951).

Pettirossi Type

1954, Mar.

C201	A122	40c brown	.55	.25
C202	A122	55c green	.55	.25
C203	A122	80c ultra	.55	.25
C204	A122	1.30g gray blue	.55	.25
		Nos. C201-C204 (4)	2.20	1.00

Church of San Roque AP70

1954, June 20 **Engr.** ***Perf. 12x13***

C205	AP70	20c carmine	.30	.25
C206	AP70	30c brown vio	.30	.25
C207	AP70	50c ultra	.30	.25
C208	AP70	1g red brn & bl grn	.35	.25
C209	AP70	1g red brn & lil rose	.35	.25
C210	AP70	1g red brn & blk	.35	.25
C211	AP70	1g red brn & org	.35	.25
a.		Min. sheet of 4, #C208-C211, perf. 12x12½	14.00	7.00
C212	AP70	5g dk red brn & vio	.70	.30
C213	AP70	5g dk red brn & ol grn	.70	.30
C214	AP70	5g dk red brn & org yel	.70	.30
C215	AP70	5g dk red brn & yel org	.70	.30
a.		Min. sheet of 4, #C212-C215, perf. 12x12½	14.00	7.00
		Nos. C205-C215 (11)	5.10	2.95

Centenary (in 1953) of the establishment of the Church of San Roque, Asuncion.

Nos. C211a and C215a issued without gum.

Heroes Type

Unwmk.

1954, Aug. 15 **Litho.** ***Perf. 10***

C216	A123	5g violet	.50	.25
C217	A123	10g olive green	1.00	.40
C218	A123	20g gray brown	1.75	.70

C219	A123	50g vermilion	2.75	1.75
C220	A123	100g blue	10.00	5.75
		Nos. C216-C220 (5)	16.00	8.85

Peron Visit Type

Photo. & Litho.

1955, Apr. Wmk. 90 *Perf. 13x13½*

Frames & Flags in Blue & Carmine

C221	A124	60c ol grn & cream	.60	.80
C222	A124	2g bl grn & cream	.60	.80
C223	A124	3g brn org & cream	.60	.80
C224	A124	4.10g brt rose pink & cr	.60	.80
		Nos. C221-C224 (4)	2.40	3.20

Monsignor Rodriguez Type

Jesuit Ruins: 3g, Corridor at Trinidad. 6g, Tower of Santa Rosa. 10g, San Cosme gate. 20g, Church of Jesus. 30g, Niche at Trinidad. 50g, Sacristy at Trinidad.

Perf. 12½x12, 12x12½

1955, June 19 Engr. Unwmk.

C225	A125	2g aqua	.40	.25
C226	A125	3g olive grn	.40	.25
C227	A126	4g lt blue grn	.40	.25
C228	A126	6g brown	.40	.25
C229	A125	10g rose	.40	.25
C230	A126	20g brown ol	.40	.25
C231	A126	30g dk green	.70	.25
C232	A126	50g dp aqua	.85	.30
		Nos. C225-C232 (8)	3.95	2.05

For surcharges see Nos. C252-C259.

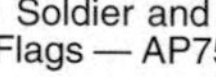

Soldier and Flags — AP75

"Republic" and Soldier — AP76

1957, June 12 Photo. *Perf. 13½*

Granite Paper

Flags in Red and Blue

C233	AP75	10c ultra	.25	.25
C234	AP75	15c dp claret	.25	.25
C235	AP75	20c red	.25	.25
C236	AP75	25c light blue	.25	.25
C237	AP75	50c bluish grn	.25	.25
C238	AP75	1g rose car	.30	.25
C239	AP76	1.30g dp claret	.30	.25
C240	AP76	1.50p light blue	.30	.25
C241	AP76	2g emerald	.30	.25
C242	AP76	4.10g red	.30	.25
C243	AP76	5g gray black	.30	.25
C244	AP76	10g bluish grn	.35	.25
C245	AP76	25g ultra	.30	.25
		Nos. C233-C245 (13)	3.70	3.25

Heroes of the Chaco war.

Stroessner Type of Regular Issue

1958, Aug. 16 Litho. Wmk. 320

Center in Slate

C246	A130	12g rose lilac	1.00	1.00
C247	A130	18g orange	1.25	1.00
C248	A130	23g orange brn	1.25	1.00
C249	A130	36g emerald	2.50	2.00
C250	A130	50g citron	5.00	4.00
C251	A130	65g gray	10.00	6.00
		Nos. C246-C251 (6)	21.00	15.00

Re-election of Pres. General Alfredo Stroessner.

Nos. C225-C232 Surcharged like #545-551 in Red

Perf. 12½x12, 12x12½

1959, May 26 Engr. Unwmk.

C252	A125	4g on 2g aqua	.50	*1.00*
C253	A125	12.45g on 3g ol grn	.50	.50
C254	A126	18.15g on 6g brown	.70	.50
C255	A125	23.40g on 10g rose	.80	.50
C256	A125	34.80g on 20g brn ol	1.00	1.00
C257	A126	36g on 4g lt bl grn	2.00	1.00
C258	A126	43.95g on 30g dk grn	2.00	1.00
C259	A126	100g on 50g deep aqua	5.00	2.50
		Nos. C252-C259 (8)	12.50	8.00

The surcharge is made to fit the stamps. Counterfeits of surcharge exist.

UN Emblem AP77

Unwmk.

1959, Aug. 27 Typo. *Perf. 11*

C260	AP77	5g ocher & ultra	1.00	.80

Visit of Dag Hammarskjold, Secretary General of the UN, Aug. 27-29.

Map and UN Emblem — AP78

1959, Oct. 24 Litho. *Perf. 10*

C261	AP78	12.45g blue & salmon	.50	.25

United Nations Day, Oct. 24, 1959.

Olympic Games Type of Regular Issue

Design: Basketball.

1960, Mar. 18 Photo. *Perf. 12½*

C262	A131	12.45g red & dk bl	.30	.30
C263	A131	18.15g lilac & gray ol	.30	.30
C264	A131	36g bl grn & rose car	.45	.45
		Nos. C262-C264 (3)	1.05	1.05

The Paraguayan Philatelic Agency reported as spurious the imperf. souvenir sheet reproducing one of No. C264. Value, $10.

Uprooted Oak Emblem — AP79

1960, Apr. 7 Litho. *Perf. 11*

C265	AP79	4g green & pink	.70	.40
C266	AP79	12.45g bl & yel grn	1.25	.65
C267	AP79	18.15g car & ocher	1.75	.75
C268	AP79	23.40g red org & bl	2.10	1.50
		Nos. C265-C268 (4)	5.80	3.30

World Refugee Year, July 1, 1959-June 30, 1960 (1st issue).

Human Rights Type of Regular Issue, 1960

Designs: 40g, UN Emblem. 60g, Hands holding scales. 100g, Flame.

1960, Apr. 21 *Perf. 12½x13*

C269	A133	40g dk ultra & red	.25	.25
C270	A133	60g grnsh bl & org	.30	.30
C271	A133	100g dk ultra & red	.65	.65
		Nos. C269-C271 (3)	1.20	1.20

An imperf. miniature sheet exists, containing one each of Nos. C269-C271, all printed in green and vermilion. Value, $15.

UN Type of Regular Issue

Perf. 13x13½

1960, Oct. 24 Photo. Unwmk.

C272	A134	3g orange, red & bl	.40	.30
C273	A134	4g pale grn, red & bl	.40	.30

International Bridge, Paraguay-Brazil AP80

1961, Jan. 26 Litho. *Perf. 14*

C274	AP80	3g carmine	.50	.50
C275	AP80	12.45g brown lake	.75	.75
C276	AP80	18.15g Prus grn	1.00	1.00
C277	AP80	36g dk blue	2.00	2.00
	a.	Souv. sheet of 4, #C274-C277, imperf.	15.00	15.00
		Nos. C274-C277 (4)	4.25	4.25

Inauguration of the International Bridge between Paraguay and Brazil.

"Paraguay en Marcha" Type of 1961

12.45g, Truck carrying logs. 18.15g, Logs on river barge. 22g, Radio tower. 36g, Jet plane.

1961, Apr. 10 Photo. *Perf. 13*

C278	A136	12.45g yel & vio bl	.45	.35
C279	A136	18.15g pur & ocher	.60	.50
C280	A136	22g ultra & ocher	.65	.60
C281	A136	36g brt grn & yel	1.10	1.00
		Nos. C278-C281 (4)	2.80	2.45

Declaration of Independence — AP81

1961, May 16 Litho. *Perf. 14½*

C282	AP81	12.45g dl red brn	.60	.40
C283	AP81	18.15g dk blue	.70	.60
C284	AP81	23.40g green	1.00	.90
C285	AP81	30g lilac	1.25	1.00
C286	AP81	36g rose	1.60	1.50
C287	AP81	44g olive	2.00	1.75
		Nos. C282-C287 (6)	7.15	6.15

150th anniv. of Independence (1st issue).

"Paraguay" and Clasped Hands — AP82

1961, June 12 *Perf. 14x14½*

C288	AP82	3g vio blue	.60	.50
C289	AP82	4g rose claret	.70	.60
C290	AP82	100g gray green	4.50	4.00
		Nos. C288-C290 (3)	5.80	5.10

Chaco Peace; 150th anniv. of Independence (2nd issue).

South American Tapir — AP83

1961, Aug. 16 Unwmk. *Perf. 14*

C291	AP83	12.45g claret	3.00	2.00
C292	AP83	18.15g ultra	3.00	2.50
C293	AP83	34.80g red brown	5.50	4.50
		Nos. C291-C293 (3)	11.50	9.00

150th anniv. of Independence (3rd issue).

Catholic University Type of 1961

1961, Sept. 18 *Perf. 14x14½*

C294	A140	3g bister brn	.50	.40
C295	A140	12.45g lilac rose	.50	.40
C296	A140	36g blue	1.00	.80
		Nos. C294-C296 (3)	2.00	1.60

Hotel Guarani Type of 1961

Design: Hotel Guarani, different view.

1961, Oct. 14 Litho. *Perf. 15*

C297	A141	3g dull red brn	1.75	1.75
C298	A141	4g ultra	1.75	1.75
C299	A141	18.15g orange	2.00	1.75
C300	A141	36g rose car	4.00	2.00
		Nos. C297-C300 (4)	9.50	7.25

Tennis Type

1961, Oct. 16 Unwmk. *Perf. 11*

C301	A142	12.45g multi	.65	.65
C302	A142	20g multi	1.25	1.25
C303	A142	50g multi	3.00	3.00
		Nos. C301-C303 (3)	4.90	4.90

Some specialists question the status of this issue.

Two imperf. souvenir sheets exist containing four 12.45g stamps each in a different color with simulated perforations and black marginal inscription.

WRY Type

Design: Oak emblem rooted in ground, wavy-lined frame.

1961, Dec. 30

C307	A145	18.15g brn & red	.50	.50
C308	A145	36g car & emer	1.25	1.25
C309	A145	50g emer & org	1.60	1.60
		Nos. C307-C309 (3)	3.35	3.35

Imperforates in changed colors and souvenir sheets exist. Some specialists question the status of this issue.

Pres. Alfredo Stroessner and Prince Philip AP84

1962, Mar. 9 Litho.

Portraits in Ultramarine

C310	AP84	12.45g grn & buff	3.00	2.00
C311	AP84	18.15g red & pink	3.00	2.00
C312	AP84	36g brn & yel	3.00	2.00
		Nos. C310-C312 (3)	9.00	6.00

Visit of Prince Philip, Duke of Edinburgh, perf. and imperf. souvenir sheets exist. Values: each $5.

Illustrations AP85-AP89, AP92-AP94, AP96-AP97, AP99-AP105, AP107-AP110, AP113-AP115, AP117, AP123, AP127a, AP132-AP133, AP136, AP138, AP140, AP142, AP144-AP145, AP149-AP150, AP152-AP153, AP156, AP158-AP159, AP165, AP167, AP171, AP180, AP183-AP184, AP187, AP196, AP202, AP205, AP208, AP211, AP221-AP222, AP224-AP225, AP229, AP234-AP235, AP237 and AP240 are reduced.

Souvenir Sheet

Abraham Lincoln (1809-1865), 16th President of U.S. — AP85

1963, Aug. 21 Litho. *Imperf.*

C313	AP85	36g gray & vio brn	10.00	10.00

Souvenir Sheet

1960 Summer Olympics, Rome — AP86

1963, Aug. 21 **Litho. & Engr.**
C314 AP86 50g lt bl, vio brn & sep 50.00 50.00

MUESTRA

Illustrations may show the word "MUESTRA." This means specimen and is not on the actual stamps.

Souvenir Sheet

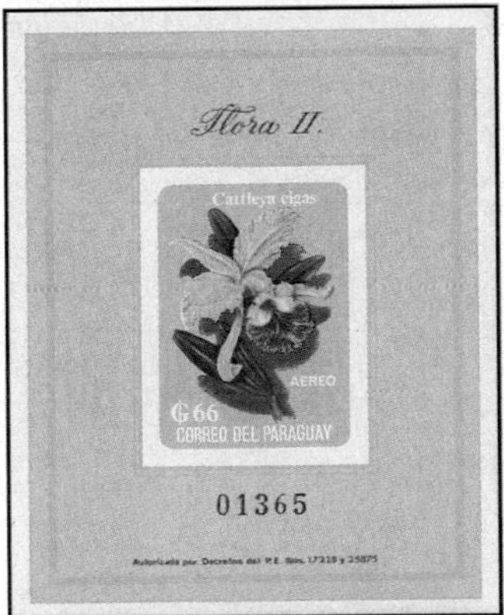

Cattleya Cigas — AP87

1963, Aug. 21 **Litho.**
C315 AP87 66g multicolored 60.00 60.00

Souvenir Sheet

Pres. Alfredo Stroessner — AP88

1964, Nov. 3
C316 AP88 36g multicolored 8.00 7.00

Souvenir Sheet

Saturn V Rocket, Pres. John F. Kennedy — AP89

1968, Jan. 27 ***Perf. 14***
C317 AP89 50g multicolored 20.00 20.00

Pres. Kennedy, 4th death anniv. (in 1967).

Torch, Book, Houses — AP90

1969, June 28 **Wmk. 347** ***Perf. 11***
C318 AP90 36g blue 2.00 1.00
C319 AP90 50g bister brn 4.00 2.00
C320 AP90 100g rose car 6.00 3.00
Nos. C318-C320 (3) 12.00 6.00

National drive for teachers' homes.

Souvenir Sheets

U.S. Space Program — AP91

John F. Kennedy, Wernher von Braun, moon and: No. C321, Apollo 11 en route to moon. No. C322, Saturn V lift-off. No. C323, Apollo 9. No. C324, Apollo 10.

1969, July 9 ***Perf. 14***
C321 AP91 23.40g multi 15.00 15.00
C322 AP91 23.40g multi 22.50 22.50

Imperf

C323 AP91 23.40g multi 22.50 22.50
C324 AP91 23.40g multi 27.50 27.50

Nos. C323-C324 each contain one 56x46mm stamp.

Souvenir Sheets

Events and Anniversaries — AP92

#C325, Apollo 14. #C326, Dwight D. Eisenhower, 1st death anniv. #C327, Napoleon Bonaparte, birth bicent. #C328, Brazil, winners of Jules Rimet World Cup Soccer Trophy.

1970, Dec. 16 ***Perf. 13½***
C325 AP92 20g multicolored 22.50 22.50
C326 AP92 20g multicolored 12.00 12.00
C327 AP92 20g multicolored 15.00 15.00
C328 AP92 20g multicolored 15.00 15.00
Nos. C325-C328 (4) 64.50 64.50

Souvenir Sheets

Paraguayan Postage Stamps, Cent. — AP93

No. C329, Marshal Francisco Solano Lopez, Pres. Alfredo Stroessner, Paraguay #1. No. C330, #3, 1014, 1242. No. C331, #1243, C8, C74.

1971, Mar. 23
C329 AP93 20g multicolored 7.50 7.50
C330 AP93 20g multicolored 14.00 14.00
C331 AP93 20g multicolored 14.00 14.00
Nos. C329-C331 (3) 35.50 35.50

Issued: #C329, 3/23; #C330-C331, 3/29.

Souvenir Sheets

Emblems of Apollo Space Missions — AP94

Designs: No. C332, Apollo 7, 8, 9, & 10. No. C333, Apollo 11, 12, 13, & 14.

1971, Mar. 26
C332 AP94 20g multicolored 13.00 13.00
C333 AP94 20g multicolored 13.00 13.00

Souvenir Sheet

Charles de Gaulle — AP95

1971, Dec. 24 ***Perf. 14***
C334 AP95 20g multicolored 17.50 17.50

Souvenir Sheet

Taras Shevchenko (1814-1861), Ukrainian Poet — AP96

1971, Dec. 24 ***Perf. 13½***
C335 AP96 20g multicolored 7.50 7.50

Souvenir Sheets

Johannes Kepler (1571-1630), German Astronomer — AP97

Kepler and: No. C336, Apollo lunar module over moon. No. C337, Astronaut walking in space.

1971, Dec. 24
C336 AP97 20g multicolored 17.00 17.00
C337 AP97 20g multicolored 17.00 17.00

Souvenir Sheet

10 years of U.S. Space Program — AP98

1972, Jan. 6 ***Perf. 13½***
C338 AP98 20g multicolored 17.00 17.00

Souvenir Sheet

Apollo 16 Moon Mission — AP99

1972, Mar. 29 **Litho.** ***Perf. 13½***
C339 AP99 20g multicolored 17.00 17.00

Souvenir Sheets

History of the Olympics — AP100

Designs: No. C340, Pierre de Coubertin (1863-1937), founder of modern Olympics. No. C341, Skier, Garmisch-Partenkirchen, 1936. No. C342, Olympic flame, Sapporo, 1972. No. C343, French, Olympic flags. No. C344, Javelin thrower, Paris, 1924. No. C345, Equestrian event.

1972, Mar. 29 ***Perf. 14½***

C340 AP100 20g multicolored 15.00 12.00
C341 AP100 20g multicolored 15.00 12.00
C342 AP100 20g multicolored 15.00 15.00
C343 AP100 20g multicolored 15.00 15.00
C344 AP100 20g multicolored 15.00 15.00
C345 AP100 20g multicolored 15.00 15.00
Nos. C340-C345 (6) 90.00 84.00

Souvenir Sheet

Medal Totals, 1972 Winter Olympics, Sapporo — AP101

1972, Nov. 18 ***Perf. 13½***

C346 AP101 23.40g multi 15.00 15.00

Souvenir Sheets

French Contributions to Aviation and Space Exploration — AP102

Georges Pompidou, Charles de Gaulle and: No. C347, Concorde. No. C348, Satellite D2A, Mirage G 8 jets.

1972, Nov. 25

C347 AP102 23.40g multi 50.00 50.00
C348 AP102 23.40g multi 45.00 45.00

Souvenir Sheets

Summer Olympic Gold Medals, 1896-1972 — AP103

No. C349, 9 medals, 1896-1932, vert. No. C350, 8 medals, 1936-1972.

1972, Nov. 25

C349 AP103 23.40g multi 15.00 15.00
C350 AP103 23.40g multi 15.00 15.00

Souvenir Sheet

Adoration of the Shepherds by Murillo — AP104

1972, Nov. 25

C351 AP104 23.40g multi 15.00 15.00

Christmas.

Souvenir Sheet

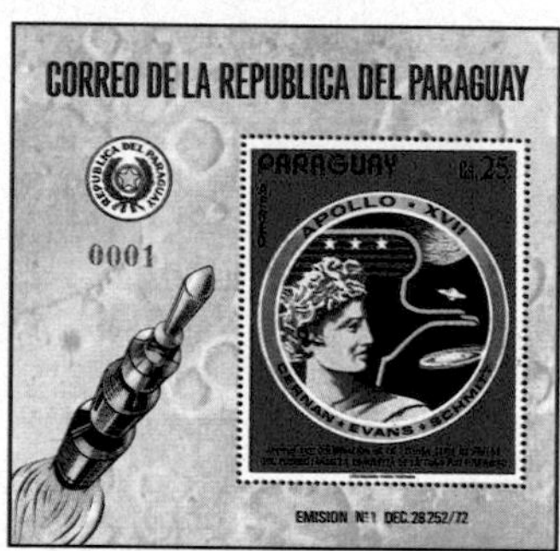

Apollo 17 Moon Mission — AP105

1973, Mar. 13

C352 AP105 25g multicolored 20.00 20.00

Souvenir Sheet

Medal Totals, 1972 Summer Olympics, Munich — AP106

1973, Mar. 15 ***Perf. 13½***

C353 AP106 25g multicolored 25.00 25.00

Souvenir Sheets

The Holy Family by Peter Paul Rubens — AP107

Design: No. C355, In the Forest at Pierrefonds by Alfred de Dreux.

1973, Mar. 15

C354 AP107 25g multicolored 20.00 20.00
C355 AP107 25g multicolored 15.00 15.00

Souvenir Sheet

German Championship Soccer Team F.C. Bayern, Bavaria #2 — AP108

1973, June 29 ***Imperf.***

C356 AP108 25g multicolored 15.00 15.00

IBRA '73 Intl. Philatelic Exhibition, Munich,

Souvenir Sheet

Copernicus, 500th Birth Anniv. and Space Exploration — AP109

#C357, Lunar surface, Apollo 11. #C358, Copernicus, position of Earth at soltices and equinoxes, vert. #C359, Skylab space laboratory.

1973, June 29 ***Perf. 13½***

C357 AP109 25g multicolored 30.00 30.00
C358 AP109 25g multicolored 30.00 30.00
C359 AP109 25g multicolored 20.00 20.00
Nos. C357-C359 (3) 80.00 80.00

Souvenir Sheets

Exploration of Mars — AP110

1973, Oct. 8

C360 AP110 25g Mariner 9 20.00 20.00
C361 AP110 25g Viking probe, horiz. 30.00 30.00

Pres. Stroessner's Visit to Europe and Morocco — AP111

Designs: No. C362a, 5g, Arms of Paraguay, Spain, Canary Islands. b, 10g, Gen. Franco, Stroessner, vert. c, 25g, Arms of Paraguay, Germany. d, 50g, Stroessner, Giovanni Leone, Italy, vert. No. C363, Itaipu Dam between Paraguay and Brazil.

1973, Dec. 30 ***Perf. 14***

C362 AP111 Strip of 4, #a.-d. 2.00 1.25
C363 AP111 150g multicolored 2.50 1.75
Nos. C362-C363 (2) 4.50 3.00

Souvenir Sheet

Imperf

C364 AP111 100g Country flags 15.00 15.00

No. C364 contains one 60x50mm stamp. See Nos. C375-C376.

1974 World Cup Soccer Championships, Munich — AP112

Abstract paintings of soccer players: No. C366a, 10g, Player seated on globe. b, 20g, Player as viewed from under foot. No. C367, Player kicking ball. No. C368, Goalie catching ball, horiz.

1974, Jan. 31 ***Perf. 14***

C365 AP112 5g shown 10.00 3.50
C366 AP112 Pair, #a.-b. 2.00 1.00
Nos. C365-C366 (2) 12.00 4.50

Souvenir Sheets

Perf. 13½

C367 AP112 25g multicolored 15.00 15.00
C368 AP112 25g multicolored 15.00 15.00

Nos. C367-C368 each contain one 50x60mm stamp.

Souvenir Sheets

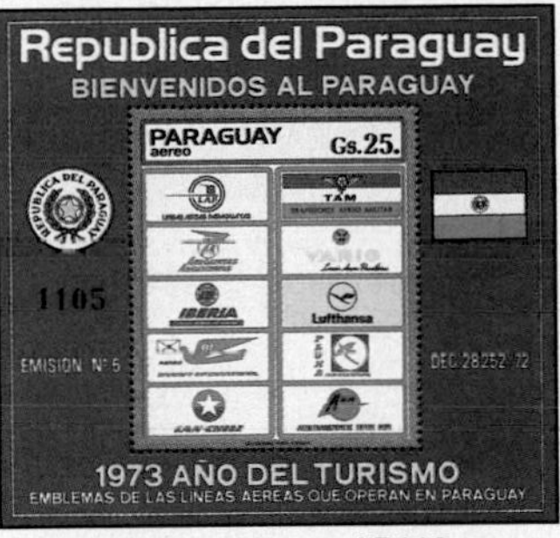

Tourism Year — AP113

Design: No. C370, Painting, Birth of Christ by Louis le Nain (1593-1648), horiz.

1974, Feb. 4 ***Perf. 13½***

C369	AP113	25g multicolored	12.00	12.00
C370	AP113	25g multicolored	7.00	7.00

Christmas (No. C370).

Souvenir Sheets

Events and Anniversaries — AP114

No. C371, Rocket lift-off. No. C372, Solar system, horiz. No. C373, Skylab 2 astronauts, horiz. No. C374, Olympic Flame.

1974, Mar. 20

C371	AP114	25g multicolored	20.00	20.00
C372	AP114	25g multicolored	20.00	20.00
C373	AP114	25g multicolored	12.00	12.00
C374	AP114	25g multicolored	12.00	12.00
		Nos. C371-C374 (4)	64.00	64.00

UPU centennial (#C371-C372). 1976 Olympic Games (#C374).

President Stroessner Type of 1973

100g, Stroessner, Georges Pompidou. 200g, Stroessner and Pope Paul VI.

1974, Apr. 25 ***Perf. 14***

C375 AP111 100g multicolored 2.00 1.00

Souvenir Sheet

Perf. 13½

C376 AP111 200g multicolored 5.00 5.00

No. C376 contains one 60x50mm stamp.

Souvenir Sheet

Lufthansa Airlines Intercontinental Routes, 40th Anniv. — AP115

1974, July 13 ***Perf. 13½***

C377 AP115 15g multicolored 15.00 15.00

No. C377 face value was 15g plus 5g extra for a monument to Francisco Solano Lopez.

Souvenir Sheet

Hermann Oberth, 80th Anniv. of Birth — AP115a

1974, July 13 **Litho.** ***Perf. 13½***

C378 AP115a 15g multi 25.00 25.00

No. C378 face value was 15g plus 5g extra for a monument to Francisco Solano Lopez.

1974 World Cup Soccer Championships, West Germany — AP116

1974, July 13 ***Perf. 14***

C379	AP116	4g Goalie	10.00	5.00
C380	AP116	5g Soccer ball	2.50	1.10
C381	AP116	10g shown	3.50	1.50
		Nos. C379-C381 (3)	16.00	7.60

Souvenir Sheet

Perf. 13½

C382 AP116 15g Soccer ball, diff. 22.50 22.50

No. C382 contains one 53x46mm stamp. No. C382 face value was 15g plus 5g extra for a monument for Francisco Solano Lopez.

Souvenir Sheet

First Balloon Flight over English Channel — AP117

1974, Sept. 13 ***Imperf.***

C383 AP117 15g multicolored 24.00 24.00

No. C383 face value was 15g plus 5g extra for a monument for Francisco Solano Lopez.

Anniversaries and Events — AP118

Designs: 4g, US #C76 on covers that went to Moon. No. C385a, 5g, Pres. Pinochet of Chile. No. C385b, 10g, Pres. Stroessner's visit to South Africa. No. C386, Mariner 10 over Mercury, horiz.

1974, Dec. 2 ***Perf. 14***

C384	AP118	4g multicolored	5.00	5.00
C385	AP118	Pair #a.-b.	1.25	1.00
		Nos. C384-C385 (2)	6.25	6.00

Souvenir Sheets

Perf. 13½

C386 AP118 15g multicolored 15.00 15.00

Nos. C386 contains one 60x50mm stamp, Face value was 15g plus 5g extra for a monument to Francisco Solano Lopez. Compare No. C386 with No. C392.

Anniversaries and Events — AP119

Designs: 4g, UPU, cent. 5g, 17th Congress, UPU, Lausanne. 10g, Intl. Philatelic Exposition, Montevideo, Uruguay. No. C392, Mariner 10 orbiting Mercury, horiz. No. C393, Figure skater, horiz. No. C394, Innsbruck Olympic emblem.

1974, Dec. 7 ***Perf. 14***

C389	AP119	4g multicolored	3.00	2.00
C390	AP119	5g multicolored	1.10	.75
C391	AP119	10g multicolored	1.10	.75
		Nos. C389-C391 (3)	5.20	3.50

Souvenir Sheets

Perf. 13½

C392	AP119	15g bl & multi	15.00	15.00
C393	AP119	15g multicolored	15.00	15.00
C394	AP119	15g multicolored	15.00	15.00

UPU centennial (#C389). Nos. C392-C394 each contain one 60x50mm stamp and face value was 15g plus 5g extra for a monument to Francisco Solano Lopez.

German World Cup Soccer Champions — AP120

4g, Holding World Cup trophy, vert. 5g, Team on field. 10g, Argentina '78 emblem, vert.

No. C398, Players holding trophy, vert. No. C399, Hemispheres, emblems of 1974 and 1978 World Cup championships.

1974, Dec. 20 ***Perf. 14***

C395	AP120	4g multicolored	5.00	3.25
C396	AP120	5g multicolored	.75	.35
C397	AP120	10g multicolored	1.50	.35
		Nos. C395-C397 (3)	7.25	3.95

Souvenir Sheets

Perf. 13½

C398	AP120	15g multicolored	20.00	20.00
C399	AP120	15g multicolored	20.00	20.00

No. C398 contains one 50x60mm stamp, and No. C399 contains one 60x50mm stamp. Face value of each sheet was 15g plus 5g extra for a monument to Francisco Solano Lopez.

Souvenir Sheet

Apollo-Soyuz — AP121

1974, Dec. 20 ***Perf. 13½***

C400 AP121 15g multicolored 17.50 17.50

Expo '75 — AP122

4g, Ryukyumurasaki, vert. 5g, Hibiscus. 10g, Ancient sailing ship.

15g, Expo emblem, vert.

1975, Feb. 24 ***Perf. 14***

C401	AP122	4g multicolored	3.00	1.10
C402	AP122	5g multicolored	.75	.25
C403	AP122	10g multicolored	1.50	.25
		Nos. C401-C403 (3)	5.25	1.60

Souvenir Sheet

Perf. 14½

C404 AP122 15g multicolored 10.00 10.00

No. C404 face value was 15g plus 5g extra for a monument to Francisco Solano Lopez.

Souvenir Sheets

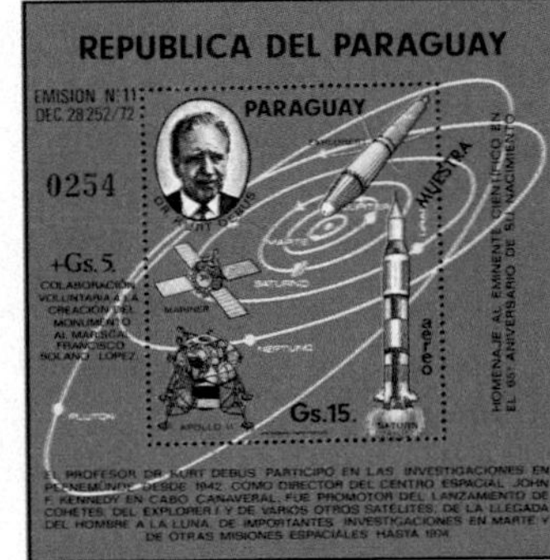

Anniversaries and Events — AP123

Designs: No. C405, Dr. Kurt Debus, space scientist, 65th birth anniv. No. C406, 1976 Summer Olympics, Montreal, horiz.

1975, Feb. 24 ***Perf. 13½***

C405	AP123	15g multicolored	17.00	17.00
C406	AP123	15g multicolored	17.00	17.00

Nos. C405-C406 face value was 15g plus 5g extra for a monument to Francisco Solano Lopez.

GEOS Satellite AP124

No. C408a, 5g, ESPANA 75. b, 10g, Mother and Child, Murillo.

No. C409, Spain #1139, 1838, C167, charity stamp. No. C410, Zeppelin, plane, satellites. No. C411, Jupiter.

1975, Aug. 21 *Perf. 14*

C407	AP124	4g shown	3.00	1.90
C408	AP124	Pair, #1.-b.	2.25	.50
		Nos. C407-C408 (2)	5.25	2.40

Souvenir Sheet

Perf. 13½

C409	AP124	15g multicolored	30.00	30.00
C410	AP124	15g multicolored	40.00	40.00

Perf. 14½

C411	AP124	15g multicolored	15.00	15.00

Nos. C409-C411 face value was 15g plus 5g extra for a monument to Francisco Solano Lopez.

Size of stamps: No. C409, 45x55mm; C410, 55x45mm; C411, 32x22mm.

Souvenir Sheets

Anniversaries and Events — AP125

#C413, UN emblem, Intl. Women's Year, vert. #C414, Helios space satellite.

1975, Aug. 26 *Perf. 13½*

C413	AP125	15g multicolored	15.00	15.00
C414	AP125	15g multicolored	15.00	15.00

Nos. C413-C414 face value was 15g plus 5g extra for a monument to Francisco Solano Lopez.

Anniversaries and Events — AP125a

Designs: 4g, First Zeppelin flight, 75th anniv. 5g, Emblem of 1978 World Cup Soccer Championships, Argentina, vert. 10g, Emblem of Nordposta 75, statue.

1975, Oct. 13 **Litho.** *Perf. 14*

C415-C417	AP125a	Set of 3	6.00	3.00

Souvenir Sheets

Anniversaries and Events — AP126

No. C418, Zeppelin, boats. No. C419, Soccer, Intelsat IV, vert. No. C420, Viking Mars landing.

1975, Oct. 13 *Perf. 13½*

C418	AP126	15g multicolored	17.50	17.50
C419	AP126	15g multicolored	17.50	17.50
C420	AP126	15g multicolored	17.50	17.50
		Nos. C418-C420 (3)	52.50	52.50

Nos. C418-C420 face value was 15g plus 5g extra for a monument to Francisco Solano Lopez.

United States, Bicent. — AP127

#C421: a, 4g, Lunar rover. b, 5g, Ford Elite, 1975. c, 10g, Ford, 1896. No. C422, Airplanes and spacecraft. No. C423, Arms of Paraguay & US.

1975, Nov. 28 **Litho.** *Perf. 14*

C421	AP127	Strip of 3, #a.-c.	6.00	3.00

Souvenir Sheets

Perf. 13½

C422	AP127	15g multicolored	22.50	22.50
C423	AP127	15g multicolored	22.50	22.50

Nos. C422-C423 each contain one 60x50mm stamp and face value was 15g plus 20g with 5g surtax for a monument to Francisco Solano Lopez.

Souvenir Sheet

La Musique by Francois Boucher — AP127a

1975, Nov. 28 *Perf. 13½*

C424	AP127a	15g multicolored	7.50	7.50

No. C424 face value was 15g plus 5g extra for a monument to Francisco Solano Lopez.

Anniversaries and Events — AP128

Designs: 4g, Flight of Concorde jet. 5g, JU 52/3M, Lufthansa Airlines, 50th anniv. 10g, EXFILMO '75 and ESPAMER '75. No. C428, Concorde, diff. No. C429, Dr. Albert Schweitzer, missionary and Konrad Adenauer, German statesman. No. C430, Ferdinand Porsche, auto designer, birth cent., vert.

1975, Dec. 20 *Perf. 14*

C425	AP128	4g multicolored	4.00	2.50
C426	AP128	5g multicolored	.40	.40
C427	AP128	10g multicolored	.40	.40
		Nos. C425-C427 (3)	4.80	3.30

Souvenir Sheets

Perf. 13½

C428	AP128	15g multicolored	27.50	25.00
C429	AP128	15g multicolored	15.00	12.00
C430	AP128	15g multicolored	40.00	40.00

Nos. C428-C430 face value was 15g plus 5g extra for a monument to Francisco Solano Lopez. No. C428 contains one 54x34mm stamp, No. C429 one 60x50mm stamp, No. C430 one 30x40mm stamp.

Anniversaries and Events — AP129

Details: 4g, The Transfiguration by Raphael, vert. 5g, Nativity by Del Mayno. 10g, Nativity by Vignon. No. C434, Detail from Adoration of the Shepherds by Ghirlandaio. No. C435, Austria, 1000th anniv., Leopold I, natl. arms, vert. No. C436, Sepp Herberger and Helmut Schon, coaches for German soccer team.

1976, Feb. 2 **Litho.** *Perf. 14*

C431	AP129	4g multicolored	4.00	2.00
C432	AP129	5g multicolored	.80	.40
C433	AP129	10g multicolored	.80	.40
		Nos. C431-C433 (3)	5.60	2.80

Souvenir Sheets

Perf. 13½

C434	AP129	15g multicolored	10.00	10.00
C435	AP129	15g multicolored	40.00	40.00

Perf. 13½x13

C436	AP129	15g multicolored	75.00	75.00

Nos. C434-C436 face value was 15g plus 5g extra for a monument to Francisco Solano Lopez. No. C434 contains one 40x30mm stamp, No. C435 one 30x40mm stamp, No. C436 one 54x34mm stamp.

Souvenir Sheet

Apollo-Soyuz — AP130

1976, Apr. 2 *Perf. 13½x13*

C437	AP130	25g multicolored	17.00	17.00

Souvenir Sheet

Lufthansa, 50th Anniv. — AP131

1976, Apr. 7 *Perf. 13½x13*

C438	AP131	25g multicolored	14.00	14.00

Souvenir Sheet

Interphil '76 — AP132

1976, May 12 *Perf. 13½*

C439	AP132	15g multicolored	9.00	9.00

No. C439 face value was 15g plus 5g extra for a monument to Francisco Solano Lopez.

Souvenir Sheets

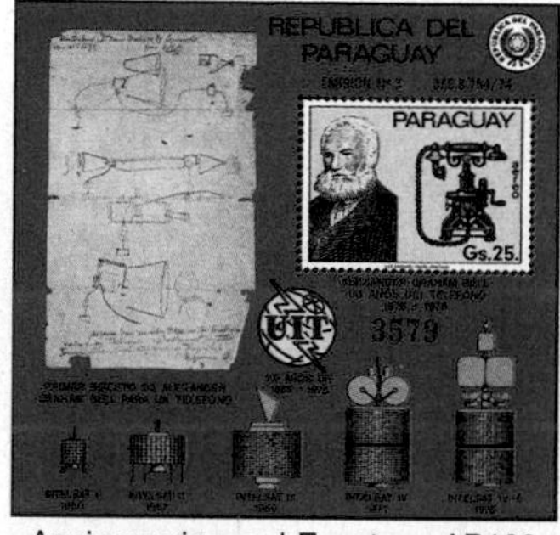

Anniversaries and Events — AP133

Designs: No. C440, Alexander Graham Bell, telephone cent. No. C441, Gold, silver, and bronze medals, 1976 Winter Olympics, Innsbruck. No. C442, Gold medalist Rosi Mittermaier, downhill and slalom, vert. No. C443, Viking probe on Mars. No. C444, UN Postal Administration, 25th anniv. and UPU, cent., vert. No. C445, Prof. Hermanm Oberth, Wernher von Braun. No. C446, Madonna and Child by Durer, vert.

1976 *Perf. 13½*

C440	AP133	25g multi	30.00	30.00
C441	AP133	25g multi	17.50	17.50
C442	AP133	25g multi	125.00	125.00

Perf. 14½

C443	AP133	25g multi	15.00	15.00
C444	AP133	25g multi	30.00	30.00
C445	AP133	25g multi	60.00	60.00
C446	AP133	25g multi	60.00	60.00
		Nos. C440-C446 (7)	337.50	337.50

No. C442 contains one 35x54mm stamp, No. C443 one 46x36mm stamp, No. C444 one 25x35mm stamp.

Issued: #C440-C441, 6/15; #C443, 7/8; #C442, C444, 7/15; #C445, 8/20; #C446, 9/9.

Souvenir Sheet

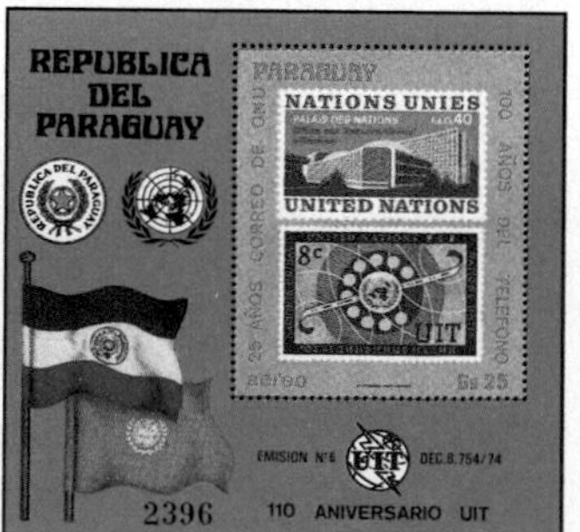

UN Offices in Geneva #22, UN #42 — AP136

1976, Dec. 18 *Perf. 13½*

C447	AP136	25g multicolored	14.00	14.00

UN Postal Administration, 25th anniv. and telephone, cent.

Souvenir Sheet

Ludwig van Beethoven (1770-1827) — AP137

1977, Feb. 28 Litho. *Perf. 14¼*
C448 AP137 25g multi 6.00 6.00

Souvenir Sheet

Alfred Nobel, 80th Death Anniv. and First Nobel Prize, 75th Anniv. — AP138

1977, June 7 *Perf. 13½*
C449 AP138 25g multicolored 22.50 22.50

Souvenir Sheet

Coronation of Queen Elizabeth II, 25th Anniv. — AP139

1977, July 25 *Perf. 14½*
C450 AP139 25g multicolored 20.00 20.00

Souvenir Sheet

Uruguay '77 Intl. Philatelic Exhibition — AP140

1977, Aug. 27 Litho. *Perf. 13½*
C451 AP140 25g multicolored 14.00 14.00

Souvenir Sheets

Exploration of Mars — AP141

No. C452, Martian craters. No. C453, Wernher von Braun. No. C454, Projected Martian lander.

1977, Sept. 5 *Perf. 13½*
C452 AP141 25g multicolored 35.00 35.00

Perf. 14¼x14½

1977, Nov. 28 Litho.
C453 AP141 25g multicolored 40.00 40.00

1977, Oct. 28 Litho. *Perf. 13½*
C454 AP141 25g multicolored 60.00 60.00

Souvenir Sheet

Sepp Herberger, German Soccer Team Coach — AP142

1978, Jan. 23 Litho. *Perf. 13½*
C455 AP142 25g multicolored 35.00 35.00

Souvenir Sheet

Austria #B331, Canada #681, US #716, Russia #B66 — AP143

1978, Mar. 10 Litho. *Perf. 14½*
C456 AP143 25g multicolored 25.00 25.00

Inner perforations are simulated.

Souvenir Sheet

Alfred Nobel — AP144

1978, Mar. 15 Litho. *Perf. 13½*
C457 AP144 25g multicolored 35.00 35.00

Souvenir Sheets

Anniversaries and Events — AP145

Designs: No. C458, Queen Elizabeth II wearing St. Edward's Crown, holding orb and scepter. No. C459, Queen Elizabeth II presenting World Cup Trophy to English team captain. No. C460, Flags of nations participating in 1978 World Cup Soccer Championships. No. C461, Soccer action. No. C462, Argentina, 1978 World Cup Champions.

1978 *Perf. 14½, 13½ (#C461)*
C458 AP145 25g multi 15.00 15.00
C459 AP145 25g multi 25.00 25.00
C460 AP145 25g multi 30.00 30.00
C461 AP145 25g multi 25.00 25.00
C462 AP145 25g multi 25.00 25.00
Nos. C458-C462 (5) 120.00 120.00

Coronation of Queen Elizabeth II, 25th Anniv. (#C458-C459). 1978 World Cup Soccer Championships, Argentina (#C460-C462).

No. C460 contains one 70x50mm stamp, No. C461 one 39x57mm stamp.

Issued: #C458, 5/11; #C459-C460, 5/16; #C461, 6/30; #C462, 10/26.

Souvenir Sheet

Jean-Henri Dunant, 150th Birth Anniv. — AP146

1978, June 28 *Perf. 14½*
C463 AP146 25g multicolored 20.00 20.00

Souvenir Sheet

Capt. James Cook, 250th Birth Anniv. — AP147

1978, July 19 *Perf. 13½*
C464 AP147 25g multicolored 15.00 15.00

Discovery of Hawaii, Death of Capt. Cook, bicentennial; Hawaii Statehood, 20th anniv.

Aregua Satellite Communication Station — AP148

Coat of Arms — AP148a

Pres. Alfredo Stroessner — AP148b

1978, Aug. 15 Litho. *Perf. 14*
C465 AP148 75g multi 1.60 .30
C466 AP148a 500g multi 6.50 2.00
C467 AP148b 1000g multi 12.00 4.00
Nos. C465-C467 (3) 20.10 6.30

Souvenir Sheet

Adoration of the Magi by Albrecht Durer — AP149

1978, Oct. 31 *Perf. 13½*
C468 AP149 25g multicolored 15.00 15.00

Souvenir Sheet

Prof. Hermann Oberth, 85th Birth Anniv. — AP150

1979, Aug. 28 *Perf. 14½*
C469 AP150 25g multicolored 20.00 20.00

Souvenir Sheet

World Cup Soccer Championships — AP151

1979, Nov. 29
C470 AP151 25g multicolored 25.00 25.00

Souvenir Sheet

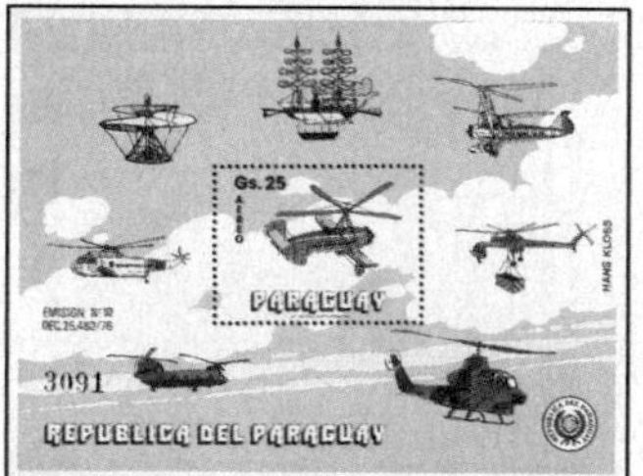

Helicopters — AP152

1979, Nov. 29 Litho. *Perf. 13½*
C471 AP152 25g multicolored 20.00 20.00

Souvenir Sheet

1980 Summer Olympics, Moscow — AP153

1979, Dec. 20 *Perf. 14½*
C472 AP153 25g Two-man canoe 30.00 30.00

Souvenir Sheet

1982 World Cup Soccer Championships, Spain — AP154

1979, Dec. 24 Litho. *Perf. 13x13½*
C473 AP154 25g Sheet of 1 + label 25.00 25.00

Souvenir Sheet

Maybach DS-8 "Zeppelin" — AP155

1980, Apr. 8 *Perf. 14½*
C474 AP155 25g multicolored 30.00 30.00

Wilhelm Maybach, 50th death anniv. Karl Maybach, 100th birth anniv.

Souvenir Sheet

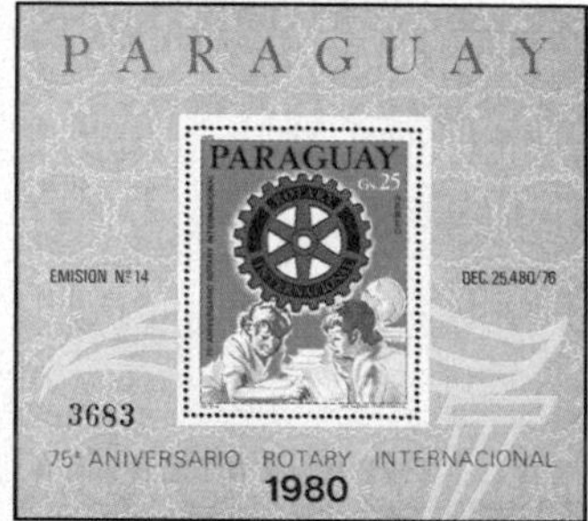

Rotary Intl., 75th Anniv. — AP156

1980, July 1 Litho. *Perf. 14½*
C475 AP156 25g multicolored 20.00 20.00

Apollo 11 Type of 1970
Souvenir Sheet

Design: 1st steps on lunar surface.

1980, July 30 *Perf. 13½*
Size: 36x26mm
C476 A221 25g multicolored 17.50 17.50

Souvenir Sheet

Virgin Surrounded by Animals by Albrecht Durer — AP158

Photo. & Engr.
1980, Sept. 24 *Perf. 12*
C477 AP158 25g multi 125.00 125.00

Souvenir Sheet

1980 Olympic Games — AP159

1980, Dec. 15 Litho. *Perf. 14*
C478 AP159 25g multi 20.00 20.00

Metropolitan Seminary Centenary — AP160

1981, Mar. 26 Litho. Wmk. 347
C479 AP160 5g ultra 1.50 1.00
C480 AP160 10g red brn 1.50 1.00
C481 AP160 25g green 1.50 1.00
C482 AP160 50g gray 3.00 1.00
Nos. C479-C482 (4) 7.50 4.00

Anniversaries and Events — AP161

5g, George Washington, 250th birth anniv. (in 1982). 10g, Queen Mother Elizabeth, 80th birthday (in 1980). 30g, Phila Tokyo '81.
No. C486, Emperor Hirohito, 80th birthday. No. C487, Washington Crossing the Delaware.

1981, July 10 Unwmk. *Perf. 14*
C483 AP161 5g multicolored 6.50 2.25
C484 AP161 10g multicolored 1.25 .45
C485 AP161 30g multicolored 1.50 .55
Nos. C483-C485 (3) 9.25 3.25

Souvenir Sheets
Perf. 14½
C486 AP161 25g multicolored 17.50 17.50
C487 AP161 25g multicolored 17.50 17.50

No. C484 issued in sheets of 8 plus label. For overprints see Nos. 2126, C590-C591, C611.

First Space Shuttle Mission — AP162

Pres. Ronald Reagan and: 5g, Columbia in Earth orbit. 10g, Astronauts John Young and Robert Crippen. 30g, Columbia landing.

George Washington and: No. C491, Columbia re-entering atmosphere. No. C492, Columbia inverted above Earth.

1981, Oct. 9 *Perf. 14*
C488 AP162 5g multicolored 6.50 3.25
C489 AP162 10g multicolored 1.25 .80
C490 AP162 30g multicolored 2.00 1.00
Nos. C488-C490 (3) 9.75 5.05

Souvenir Sheets
Perf. 13½
C491 AP162 25g multicolored 17.50 17.50
C492 AP162 25g multicolored 17.50 17.50

Nos. C491-C492 each contain one 60x50mm stamp. Inauguration of Pres. Reagan, George Washington, 250th birth anniv. (in 1982) (#C491-C492).

World Cup Soccer, Spain, 1982 AP163

1981, Oct. 15 *Perf. 14*
Color of Shirts
C493 AP163 5g yellow, green 4.00 2.00
C494 AP163 10g blue, white 1.10 .50
C495 AP163 30g white & blk, org .60 .30
Nos. C493-C495 (3) 5.70 2.80

Souvenir Sheet
Perf. 14½
C496 AP163 25g Goalie 17.50 17.50

No. C494 exists in sheets of 5 plus 4 labels.

Christmas AP164

Paintings: 5g, Virgin with the Child by Stefan Lochner. 10g, Our Lady of Caacupe. 25g, Altar of the Virgin by Albrecht Durer. 30g, Virgin and Child by Matthias Grunewald.

1981, Dec. 21 *Perf. 14*
C497 AP164 5g multicolored 1.25 .40
C498 AP164 10g multicolored 2.50 .85
C499 AP164 30g multicolored 6.75 2.10
Nos. C497-C499 (3) 10.50 3.35

Souvenir Sheet
Perf. 13½
C500 AP164 25g multicolored 20.00

No. C500 contains one 54x75mm stamp.

Souvenir Sheet

Graf Zeppelin's First Flight to South America, 50th Anniv. — AP165

1981, Dec. 28 *Perf. 14½*
C501 AP165 25g multicolored 24.00 24.00

Mother Maria Mazzarello (1837-1881), Co Founder of Daughters of Mary
AP166

Perf. 13x13½

1981, Dec. 30 Litho. Wmk. 347

C502	AP166 20g blk & grn	1.00	1.00
C503	AP166 25g blk & red brn	1.00	1.00
C504	AP166 50g blk & gray vio	1.00	1.00
	Nos. C502-C504 (3)	3.00	3.00

Souvenir Sheet

The Magus (Dr. Faust) by Rembrandt — AP167

Litho. & Typo.

1982, Apr. 23 Unwmk. *Perf. 14½*

C505	AP167 25g blk, buff & gold	20.00	20.00

Johann Wolfgang von Goethe, 150th death anniv.

The following stamps were issued 4 each in sheets of 8 with 1 label: Nos. C590-C591, C669-C670, C677-C678, C682-C683, C690-C691, C699-C700, C718-C719, C747-C748.

The following stamps were issued in sheets of 4 with 5 labels: Nos. C765-C766, C774, C779-C780, C785, C803, C813, C818, C823.

The following stamps were issued in sheets of 3 with 6 labels: Nos. C739, C754.

The following stamps were issued in sheets of 5 with 4 labels: Nos. C507, C512, C515, C519, C524, C529, C535, C539, C542, C548, C550, C559, C569, C572, C579, C582, C585, C588, C596, C598, C615, C622, C626, C634, C642, C647, C650, C656, C705, C711, C731, C791, C798, C808.

The following stamp was issued in sheets of 7 with 2 labels: No. C660.

World Chess Championships Type of 1980

Illustrations from The Book of Chess: 5g, The Game of the Virgins. 10g, Two gothic ladies. 30g, Chess game at apothecary shop.

No. C509, Christians and Jews preparing to play in garden. No. C510, Indian prince introducing chess to Persia.

1982, June 10 Litho. *Perf. 14*

C506	A347 5g multicolored	3.50	1.10
C507	A347 10g multicolored	1.60	.55
C508	A347 30g multicolored	.80	.25
	Nos. C506-C508 (3)	5.90	1.90

Souvenir Sheets

Perf. 13½

C509	A347 25g multicolored	15.00	15.00

Perf. 14½

C510	A347 25g multicolored	20.00	20.00

No. C509 contains one 50x60mm stamp, No. C510 one 50x70mm stamp. For overprint see No. C665.

Italy, Winners of 1982 World Cup Soccer Championships — AP168

Players: 5g, Klaus Fischer, Germany. 10g, Altobelli holding World Cup Trophy. 25g, Forster, Altobelli, horiz. 30g, Fischer, Gordillo.

1982, Oct. 20 *Perf. 14*

C511	AP168 5g multicolored	5.50	1.20
C512	AP168 10g multicolored	1.60	.55
C513	AP168 30g multicolored	.80	.25
	Nos. C511-C513 (3)	7.90	2.00

Souvenir Sheet

C513A	AP168 25g multicolored	14.00	14.00

Christmas — AP169

Paintings by Peter Paul Rubens: 5g, The Massacre of the Innocents. 10g, The Nativity, vert. 25g, The Madonna Adored by Four Penitents and Saints. 30g, The Flight to Egypt.

1982, Oct. 23

C514	AP169 5g multicolored	3.50	1.20
C515	AP169 10g multicolored	1.60	.55
C516	AP169 30g multicolored	.80	.25
	Nos. C514-C516 (3)	5.90	2.00

Souvenir Sheet

Perf. 14½

C517	AP169 25g multicolored	14.00	14.00

No. C517 contains one 50x70mm stamp.

The Sampling Officials of the Draper's Guild by Rembrandt — AP170

Details from Rembrandt Paintings: 10g, Self portrait, vert. 25g, Night Watch, vert. 30g, Self portrait, diff., vert.

1983, Jan. 21 *Perf. 14, 13 (10g)*

C518	AP170 5g multicolored	3.50	1.20
C519	AP170 10g multicolored	1.60	.55
C520	AP170 30g multicolored	.80	.25
	Nos. C518-C520 (3)	5.90	2.00

Souvenir Sheet

Perf. 13½

C521	AP170 25g multicolored	15.00	15.00

No. C521 contains one 50x60mm stamp.

Souvenir Sheet

1982 World Cup Soccer Championships, Spain — AP171

1983, Jan. 21 *Perf. 13½*

C522	AP171 25g Fuji blimp	16.00	16.00

German Rocket Scientists — AP172

Designs: 5g, Dr. Walter R. Dornberger, V2 rocket ascending. 10g, Nebel, Ritter, Oberth, Riedel, and Von Braun examining rocket mock-up. 30g, Dr. A. F. Staats, Cyrus B research rocket.

No. C526, Dr. Eugen Sanger, rocket design. No. C527, Fritz Von Opel, Opel-Sander rocket plane. No. C528, Friedrich Schmiedl, first rocket used for mail delivery.

1983 *Perf. 14*

C523	AP172 5g multicolored	4.00	1.25
C524	AP172 10g multicolored	1.75	.60
C525	AP172 30g multicolored	.80	.25
	Nos. C523-C525 (3)	6.55	2.10

Souvenir Sheets

Perf. 14½

C526	AP172 25g multicolored	35.00	35.00
C527	AP172 25g multicolored	35.00	35.00
C528	AP172 25g multicolored	35.00	35.00

Issued: No. C528, Apr. 13; others, Jan. 24.

First Manned Flight, 200th Anniv.
AP173

Balloons: 5g, Montgolfier brothers, 1783. 10g, Baron von Lutgendorf's, 1786. 30g, Adorne's, 1784.

No. C532, Montgolfier brothers, diff. No. C533, Profiles of Montgolfier Brothers. No. C534, Bicentennial emblem, nova.

1983 *Perf. 14, 13 (10g)*

C529	AP173 5g multicolored	4.00	1.25
C530	AP173 10g multicolored	2.50	.65
C531	AP173 30g multicolored	1.60	.25
	Nos. C529-C531 (3)	8.10	2.15

Souvenir Sheets

Perf. 13½

C532	AP173 25g multicolored	17.00	17.00
C533	AP173 25g multicolored	17.00	17.00
C534	AP173 25g multicolored	17.00	17.00

Nos. C532-C533 each contain one 50x60mm stamp, No. C534 one 30x40mm stamp.

Issued: #C529-C533, 2/25; #C534, 10/19.

1984 Summer Olympics, Los Angeles
AP174

1932 Gold medalists: 5g, Wilson Charles, US, 100-meter dash. 10g, Ellen Preis, Austria, fencing. 25g, Rudolf Ismayr, Germany, weight lifting. 30g, John Anderson, US, discus.

1983, June 13 *Perf. 14*

C535	AP174 5g multicolored	.80	.30
C536	AP174 10g multicolored	1.25	.40
C537	AP174 30g multicolored	3.25	.55
	Nos. C535-C537 (3)	5.30	1.25

Souvenir Sheet

Perf. 14½

C538	AP174 25g Sheet of 1 + label	20.00	20.00

No. C535 incorrectly credits Charles with gold medal.

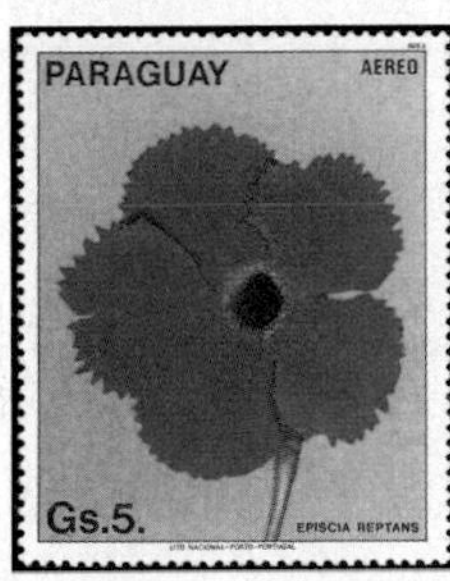

Flowers
AP175

1983, Aug. 31 *Perf. 14*

C539	AP175 5g Episcia reptans	1.60	.40
C540	AP175 10g Lilium	.80	.25
C541	AP175 30g Heliconia	1.60	.25
	Nos. C539-C541 (3)	4.00	.90

Intl. Maritime Organization, 25th Anniv. — AP176

5g, Brigantine Undine. 10g, Training ship Sofia, 1881, horiz. 30g, Training ship Stein, 1879.

No. C545, Santa Maria. No. C546, Santa Maria and Telstar communications satellite.

Perf. 14, 13½x13 (10g)

1983, Oct. 24 Litho.

C542	AP176 5g multicolored	2.50	.55
C543	AP176 10g multicolored	1.25	.40
C544	AP176 30g multicolored	1.50	.25
	Nos. C542-C544 (3)	5.25	1.20

Souvenir Sheets

Perf. 14½

C545	AP176 25g multicolored	20.00	15.00

Perf. 13½

C546	AP176 25g multicolored	20.00	15.00

No. C546 contains one 90x57mm stamp. Discovery of America, 490th Anniv. (in 1982) (#C545-C546). For overprint see No. 2198.

Space Achievements — AP177

Designs: 5g, Space shuttle Challenger. 10g, Pioneer 10, vert. 30g, Herschel's telescope, Cerro Tololo Obervatory, Chile, vert.

1984, Jan. 9 *Perf. 14*

C547	AP177	5g multicolored	2.75	.90
C548	AP177	10g multicolored	2.75	.90
C549	AP177	30g multicolored	.95	.35
	Nos. C547-C549 (3)		6.45	2.15

Summer Olympics, Los Angeles AP178

5g, 400-meter hurdles. 10g, Small bore rifle, horiz. 25g, Equestrian, Christine Stuckleberger. 30g, 100-meter dash.

1984, Jan. *Perf. 14*

C550	AP178	5g multicolored	2.75	.80
C551	AP178	10g multicolored	2.75	.55
C552	AP178	30g multicolored	1.20	.25
	Nos. C550-C552 (3)		6.70	1.60

Souvenir Sheet

Perf. 14½

C553	AP178	25g multicolored	25.00	25.00

For overprint see No. 2130.

1984 Winter Olympics, Sarajevo AP179

No. C554, Steve Podborski, downhill. No. C555, Olympic Flag. No. C556, Gaetan Boucher, speed skating.

Perf. 14, 13x13½ (10g)

1984, Mar. 24

C554	AP179	5g multicolored	2.40	.55
C555	AP179	10g multicolored	1.60	.40
C556	AP179	30g multicolored	1.60	.25
	Nos. C554-C556 (3)		5.60	1.20

No. C555 printed se-tenant with label.

Souvenir Sheets

Cupid and Psyche by Peter Paul Rubens — AP180

Design: No. C558, Satyr and Maenad (copy of Rubens' Bacchanal) by Jean-Antoine Watteau (1684-1721).

1984, Mar. 26 *Perf. 13½*

C557	AP180	25g multicolored	15.00	15.00
C558	AP180	25g multicolored	17.00	17.00

No. C558 contains one 78x57mm stamp.

1982, 1986 World Cup Soccer Championships, Spain, Mexico City — AP181

Soccer players: 5g, Tardelli, Breitner. 10g, Zamora, Stielke. 30g, Walter Schachner, player on ground.

No. C562, Player from Paraguay. No. C563, World Cup Trophy, Spanish, Mexican characters, horiz.

1984, Mar. 29 *Perf. 14, 13 (10g)*

C559	AP181	5g multicolored	2.40	.55
C560	AP181	10g multicolored	1.50	.55
C561	AP181	30g multicolored	1.50	.25
	Nos. C559-C561 (3)		5.40	1.35

Souvenir Sheets

Perf. 14½

C562	AP181	25g multicolored	15.00	15.00
C563	AP181	25g multicolored	15.00	15.00

Souvenir Sheet

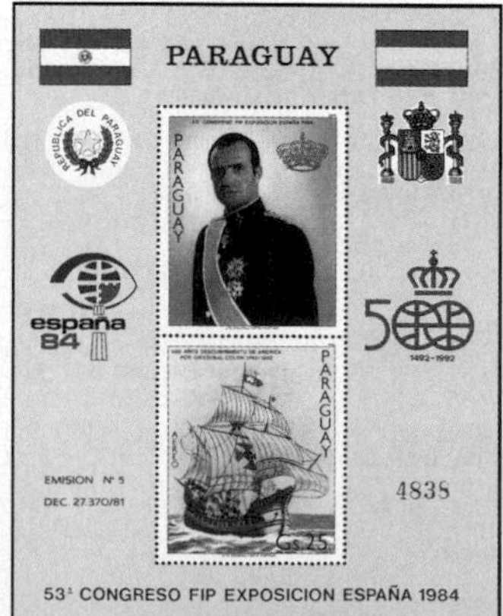

ESPANA '84 — AP182

1984, Mar. 31

C564	AP182	25g multicolored	20.00	20.00

No. C564 has one stamp and a label.

Souvenir Sheets

ESPANA '84 — AP183

No. C565, Holy Family of the Lamb by Raphael. No. C566, Adoration of the Magi by Rubens.

1984, Apr. 16 *Perf. 13½*

C565	AP183	25g multicolored	15.00	12.00
C566	AP183	25g multicolored	15.00	12.00

Souvenir Sheet

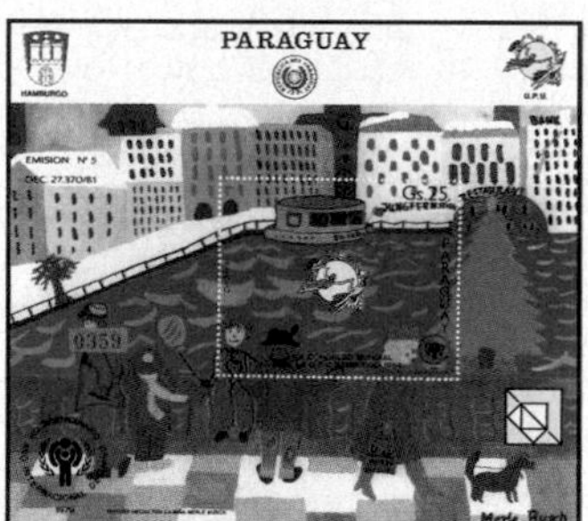

19th UPU Congress — AP184

1984, June 9

C567	AP184	25g multicolored	15.00	12.00

Intl. Chess Federation, 60th Anniv. AP185

10g, Woman holding chess piece. 30g, Bishop, knight.

Perf. 14, 13x13½ (10g)

1984, June 18

C568	AP185	5g shown	3.75	1.20
C569	AP185	10g multicolored	3.00	.80
C570	AP185	30g multicolored	2.25	.25
	Nos. C568-C570 (3)		9.00	2.25

First Europe to South America Airmail Flight by Lufthansa, 50th Anniv. — AP186

Designs: 5g, Lockheed Superconstellation. 10g, Dornier Wal. 30g, Boeing 707.

Perf. 14, 13½x13 (10g)

1984, June 22

C571	AP186	5g multicolored	2.75	.75
C572	AP186	10g multicolored	1.50	.30
C573	AP186	30g multicolored	1.10	.25
	Nos. C571-C573 (3)		5.35	1.30

For overprint see No. C592.

Souvenir Sheets

First Moon Landing, 15th Anniv. — AP187

No. C574, Apollo 11 lunar module. No. C575, Prof. Hermann Oberth.

1984, June 23 *Perf. 14½*

C574	AP187	25g multicolored	35.00	35.00
C575	AP187	25g multicolored	35.00	35.00

Hermann Oberth, 90th Birthday (#C575).

Souvenir Sheet

The Holy Family with John the Baptist — AP188

Photo. & Engr.

1984, Aug. 3 *Perf. 14*

C576	AP188	20g multicolored	45.00	45.00

Raphael, 500th birth anniv. (in 1983).

No. 2099 Overprinted ANIVERSARIO GOBIERNO CONSTRUCTIVO Y DE LA PAZ DEL PRESIDENTE CONSTITUCIONAL GRAL. DE EJERCITO ALFREDO STROESSNER 15 / 8 / 1964 in Red

1984, Aug. 15 *Perf. 13*

C577	A374	100g on No. 2099	1.50	1.50

1984 Winter Olympics, Sarajevo — AP189

Gold medalists: 5g, Max Julen, giant slalom, Switzerland. 10g, Hans Stanggassinger, Franz Wembacher, luge, West Germany. 30g, Peter Angerer, biathlon, Germany.

Perf. 14, 13½x13 (10g)

1984, Sept. 12

C578 AP189 5g multicolored 2.75 .80
C579 AP189 10g multicolored 3.50 1.20
C580 AP189 30g multicolored 1.25 .25
Nos. C578-C580 (3) 7.50 2.25

For overprint see No. C596.

Motorcycles, Cent. — AP190

5g, Reitwagen, Daimler-Maybach, 1885. 10g, BMW, 1980. 30g, Opel, 1930.

1984, Nov. 9 *Perf. 14, 13½x13 (10g)*

C581 AP190 5g multicolored 2.50 .50
C582 AP190 10g multicolored 1.90 .60
C583 AP190 30g multicolored 1.10 .25
Nos. C581-C583 (3) 5.50 1.35

Christmas AP191

10g, Girl playing guitar. 30g, Girl, candle, basket.

1985, Jan. 18 *Perf. 13*

C584 AP191 5g shown 1.90 .45
C585 AP191 10g multicolored 1.10 .30
C586 AP191 30g multicolored .80 .25
Nos. C584-C586 (3) 3.80 1.00

1986 World Cup Soccer Championships, Mexico — AP192

Various soccer players.

1985, Jan. 21 *Perf. 13x13½, 13½x13*

Color of Shirt

C587 AP192 5g red & white 2.25 .80
C588 AP192 10g white & black, horiz. 1.50 .40
C589 AP192 30g blue 1.50 .25
Nos. C587-C589 (3) 5.25 1.45

No. C484 Ovptd. in Silver

No. C590, INTERPEX / 1985. No. C591, STAMPEX / 1985.

1985, Feb. 6 *Perf. 14*

C590 AP161 10g multicolored 1.50 .75
C591 AP161 10g multicolored 1.50 .75

No. C572 Ovptd. in Vermilion

1985, Feb. 16 *Perf. 13½x13*

C592 AP186 10g on No. C572 4.00 1.50

No. 2053A Ovptd. "FINAL / ALEMANIA 1 : 3 ITALIA"

1985, Mar. 7 *Perf. 14½*

C593 A362 25g multicolored 14.00 14.00

Souvenir Sheets

Rotary Intl., 80th Anniv. — AP193

Designs: No. C594, Paul Harris, founder of Rotary Intl. No. C595, Rotary Intl. Headquarters, Evanston, IL, horiz.

1985, Mar. 11

C594 AP193 25g multicolored 30.00 30.00
C595 AP193 25g multicolored 30.00 30.00

No. C579 Ovptd. "OLYMPHILEX 85" in Black and Olympic Rings in Silver

1985, Mar. 18 *Perf. 13½x13*

C596 AP189 10g on No. C579 3.00 1.50

Music Year — AP194

Designs: 5g, Agustin Barrios (1885-1944), musician, vert. 10g, Johann Sebastian Bach, composer, score. 30g, Folk musicians.

Perf. 14, 13½x13 (10g)

1985, Apr. 16

C597 AP194 5g multicolored 1.75 .75
C598 AP194 10g multicolored 1.00 .70
C599 AP194 30g multicolored 1.25 .55
Nos. C597-C599 (3) 4.00 2.00

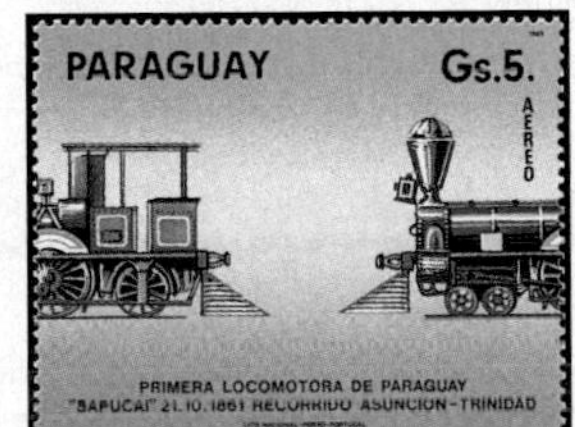

1st Paraguayan Locomotive, 1861 — AP195

10g, Transrapid 06, Germany. 30g, TGV, France.

1985, Apr. 20 *Perf. 14*

C600 AP195 5g shown 10.00 3.50
a. Horiz. Pair 40.00 *40.00*
C601 AP195 10g multi 2.50 .75
C602 AP195 30g multi 2.50 .75
Nos. C600-C602 (3) 15.00 5.00

Souvenir Sheet

Visit of Pope John Paul II to South America — AP196

1985, Apr. 22 **Litho.** *Perf. 13½*

C603 AP196 25g silver & multi 17.00 17.00

No. C603 also exists with gold inscriptions.

Inter-American Development Bank, 25th Anniv. — AP197

1985, Apr. 25 **Litho.** **Wmk. 347**

C604 AP197 3g dl red brn, org & yel 1.00 1.00
C605 AP197 5g vio, org & yel 1.00 1.00
C606 AP197 10g rose vio, org & yel 1.00 1.00
C607 AP197 50g sep, org & yel 1.00 1.00
C608 AP197 65g bl, org & yel 1.00 1.00
C609 AP197 95g pale bl grn, org & yel 1.00 1.00
Nos. C604-C609 (6) 6.00 6.00

No. 1875 Ovptd. in Black

1985, May 24 **Unwmk.** *Perf. 13½*

C610 A326 25g on No. 1875 12.00 12.00

No. C485 Ovptd. in Dark Blue with Emblem and: "Expo '85/TSUKUBA"

1985, July 5 *Perf. 14*

C611 AP161 30g on No. C485 3.00 1.50

No. 2149 Ovptd. in Dark Blue in Margin with UN emblem and "26.6.1905 — 40-ANIVERSARIO DE LA / FUNDACION DE LAS NACIONES UNIDAS"

1985, Aug. 5 *Perf. 14½*

C612 A388 25g on No. 2149 12.00 12.00

Jean-Henri Dunant, Founder of Red Cross, 75th Death Anniv. — AP198

Dunant and: 5g, Enclosed ambulance. 10g, Nobel Peace Prize, Red Cross emblem. 30g, Open ambulance with passengers.

1985, Aug. 6 *Perf. 13*

C614 AP198 5g multicolored 5.25 1.60
C615 AP198 10g multicolored 4.75 1.60
C616 AP198 30g multicolored 2.00 .60
Nos. C614-C616 (3) 12.00 3.80

World Chess Congress, Austria — AP199

5g, The Turk, copper engraving, Book of Chess by Racknitz, 1789. 10g, King seated, playing chess, Book of Chess, 14th cent. 25g, Margrave Otto von Brandenburg playing chess with his wife, Great Manuscript of Heidelberg Songs, 13th cent. 30g, Three men playing chess, Book of Chess, 14th cent.

1985, Aug. 9 **Litho.** *Perf. 13*

C617 AP199 5g multicolored 6.25 2.10
C618 AP199 10g multicolored 1.50 .50
C619 AP199 30g multicolored 1.50 .50
Nos. C617-C619 (3) 9.25 3.10

Souvenir Sheet

Perf. 13½

C620 AP199 25g multicolored 25.00 25.00

No. C620 contains one 60x50mm stamp.

Discovery of America 500th Anniv. AP200

Explorers, ships: 5g, Marco Polo and ship. 10g, Vicente Yanez Pinzon, Nina, horiz. 25g, Christopher Columbus, Santa Maria. 30g, James Cook, Endeavor.

Perf. 14, 13½x13 (10g)

1985, Oct. 19 **Litho.**

C621 AP200 5g multicolored 2.50 .60
C622 AP200 10g multicolored .85 .40
C623 AP200 30g multicolored 1.25 .45
Nos. C621-C623 (3) 4.60 1.45

Souvenir Sheet

Perf. 14½

C624 AP200 25g multicolored 22.00 22.00

Year of Cook's death is incorrect on No. C623. For overprint see No. C756.

ITALIA '85 — AP201

Nudes (details): 5g, La Fortuna, by Guido Reni, vert. 10g, The Triumph of Galatea, by Raphael. 25g, The Birth of Venus, by Botticelli, vert. 30g, Sleeping Venus, by Il Giorgione.

1985, Dec. 3 *Perf. 14*

C625 AP201 5g multicolored 4.50 1.50
C626 AP201 10g multicolored 2.00 .60
C627 AP201 30g multicolored 1.75 .40
Nos. C625-C627 (3) 8.25 2.50

Souvenir Sheet

Perf. 13½

C628 AP201 25g multicolored 35.00 35.00

No. C628 contains one 49x60mm stamp.

Souvenir Sheet

Maimonides, Philosopher, 850th Birth Anniv. — AP202

1985, Dec. 31 *Perf. 13½*

C629 AP202 25g multicolored 22.50 22.50

UN, 40th Anniv. AP203

1986, Feb. 27 **Wmk. 392**

C630 AP203 5g bl & sepia 1.00 1.00
C631 AP203 10g bl & gray 1.00 1.00
C632 AP203 50g bl & grysh brn 1.00 1.00
Nos. C630-C632 (3) 3.00 3.00

For overprint see No. C726.

AMERIPEX '86 AP204

Discovery of America 500th anniv. emblem and: 5g, Spain #424. 10g, US #233. 25g, Spain #426, horiz. 30g, Spain #421.

Perf. 14, 13½x13 (10g)

1986, Mar. 19 **Unwmk.**

C633 AP204 5g multicolored 5.00 1.75
C634 AP204 10g multicolored 2.00 .70
C635 AP204 30g multicolored 1.75 .60
Nos. C633-C635 (3) 8.75 3.05

Souvenir Sheet

Perf. 13½

C636 AP204 25g multicolored 12.00 *12.00*

No. C636 contains one 60x40mm stamp. For overprint see No. C755.

Souvenir Sheet

1984 Olympic Gold Medalist, Dr. Reiner Klimke on Ahlerich — AP205

1986, Mar. 20 *Perf. 14½*

C637 AP205 25g multicolored 20.00 20.00

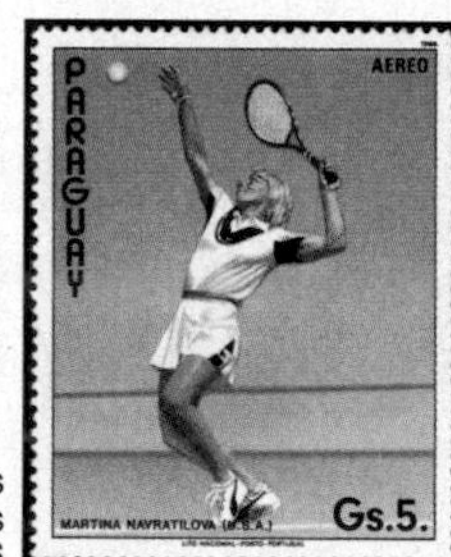

Tennis Players AP206

Designs: 5g, Martina Navratilova, US. 10g, Boris Becker, W. Germany. 30g, Victor Pecci, Paraguay.

1986, Mar. 26 *Perf. 14, 13 (10g)*

C638 AP206 5g multicolored 4.25 1.25
C639 AP206 10g multicolored 2.25 .55
C640 AP206 30g multicolored .50 .25
Nos. C638-C640 (3) 7.00 2.05

Nos. C638-C640 exist with red inscriptions, perf. 13. For overprints see Nos. C672-C673.

Halley's Comet — AP207

5g, Bayeux Tapestry, c. 1066, showing comet. 10g, Edmond Halley, comet. 25g, Comet, Giotto probe. 30g, Rocket lifting off, Giotto probe, vert.

Perf. 14, 13½x13 (10g)

1986, Apr. 30

C641 AP207 5g multicolored 5.50 2.00
C642 AP207 10g multicolored 3.50 1.10
C643 AP207 30g multicolored 2.50 .65
Nos. C641-C643 (3) 11.50 3.75

Souvenir Sheet

Perf. 14½

C644 AP207 25g multicolored 20.00 20.00

Souvenir Sheet

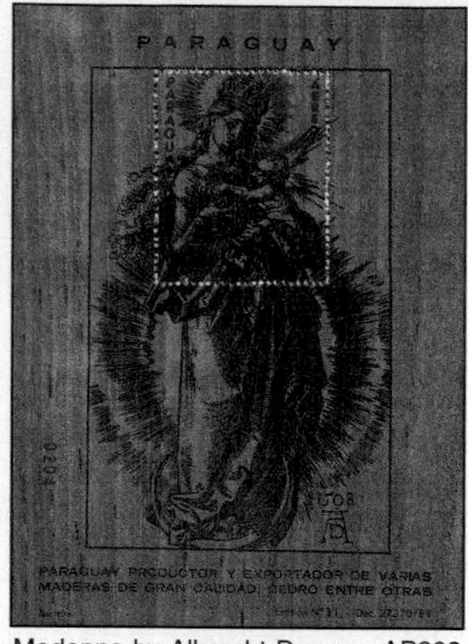

Madonna by Albrecht Durer — AP208

1986, June 4 Typo. ***Rough Perf. 11***

Self-Adhesive

C645 AP208 25g black & red 20.00 20.00

No. C645 was printed on cedar.

Locomotives — AP209

5g, #3038. 10g, Canadian Pacific A1E, 1887. 30g, 1D1 #483, 1925.

1986, June 23 Litho. *Perf. 13*

C646 AP209 5g multi 2.25 .50
C647 AP209 10g multi 1.50 .50
C648 AP209 30g multi 2.25 .50
Nos. C646-C648 (3) 6.00 1.50

1986 World Cup Soccer Championships — AP210

Paraguay vs.: 5g, Colombia. 10g, Chile. 30g, Chile, diff.
25g, Paraguay Natl. team.

Perf. 13, 13½x13 (10g)

1986, June 24

C649 AP210 5g multicolored 2.25 .50
C650 AP210 10g multicolored 1.50 .50
C651 AP210 30g multicolored 2.50 .45
Nos. C649-C651 (3) 6.25 1.45

Souvenir Sheet

Perf. 14½

C652 AP210 25g multicolored 13.00 13.00

No. C652 contains one 81x75mm stamp. For overprints see Nos. C693-C695.

No. 1289 Ovptd. in Silver on Dark Blue with Mercury Capsule and "MERCURY / 5-V-1961 / 25 Anos Primer / Astronauta / Americano / Alan B. Shepard / 1986"

1986, July 11 *Perf. 13½*

C653 A226 23.40g on No. 1289 13.00 13.00

Souvenir Sheet

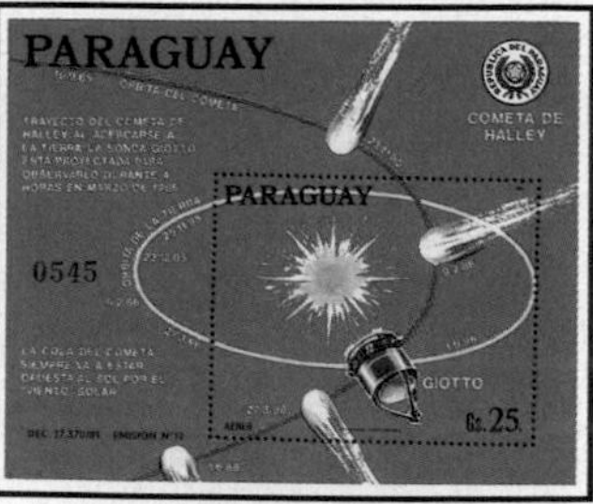

Trajectory Diagram of Halley's Comet, Giotto Probe — AP211

1986, July 28

C654 AP211 25g multicolored 15.00 15.00

German Railroads, 150th Anniv. — AP212

5g, VT 10 501DB, 1954. 10g, 1st Electric, 1879. 30g, Hydraulic diesel, class 218.
25g, Christening of the 1st German Train, 1835, by E. Schilling & B. Goldschmitt.

1986, Sept. 1 *Perf. 13½x13*

C655 AP212 5g multicolored 4.50 1.50
C656 AP212 10g multicolored 1.75 .50
C657 AP212 30g multicolored 2.00 2.00
Nos. C655-C657 (3) 8.25 4.00

Souvenir Sheet

Perf. 13½

C658 AP212 25g multicolored 18.00 18.00

No. C658 contains one 54x75mm stamp.

Intl. Peace Year AP213

Details from The Consequences of War by Rubens: 5g, Two women. 10g, Woman nursing child. 30g, Two men.

1986, Oct. 27 *Perf. 13*

C659 AP213 5g multicolored 5.00 1.75
C660 AP213 10g multicolored 2.60 2.60
C661 AP213 30g multicolored 1.75 .40
Nos. C659-C661 (3) 9.35 4.75

Japanese Emigrants in Paraguay, 50th Anniv. — AP214

5g, La Colemna Vineyard. 10g, Cherry, lapacho flowers. 20g, Integration monument, vert.

1986, Nov. 6 *Perf. 13½x13, 13x13½*

C662 AP214 5g multicolored 2.00 2.00
C663 AP214 10g multicolored 2.00 2.00
C664 AP214 20g multicolored 2.00 2.00
Nos. C662-C664 (3) 6.00 6.00

No. C507 Ovptd. in Silver "XXVII-DUBAI / Olimpiada de / Ajedrez - 1986"

1986, Dec. 30	**Unwmk.**	***Perf. 14***		
C665	A347 10g on No. C507		6.00	2.00

1986 World Cup Soccer Championships, Mexico — AP214a

Match scenes — 5g, England vs. Paraguay. 10g, Larios catching ball. 20g, Trejo, Ferreira. 25g, Torales, Flores, Romero. 30g, Mendoza. 100g, Romero.

1987, Feb. 19		***Perf. 14***		
C666	AP214a	5g multicolored	.60	.25
C667	AP214a	10g multicolored	4.50	1.50
C668	AP214a	20g multicolored	1.25	.40
		Perf. 13½x13		
C669	AP214a	25g multicolored	1.20	1.20
C670	AP214a	30g multicolored	1.50	1.50
		Nos. C666-C670 (5)	9.05	4.85

Souvenir Sheet

Perf. 14½

C671	AP214a	100g multi	15.00	13.00

Nos. C669-C670 are horiz. No. C671 contains one 40x50mm stamp.

Nos. C639-C640 Ovptd. in Silver including Olympic Rings and "NUEVAMENTE EL / TENIS EN LAS / OLYMPIADAS 1988 / SEOUL COREA"

1987, Apr. 15		***Perf. 13***		
C672	AP206	10g on No. C639	*4.50*	*3.00*
C673	AP206	30g on No. C640	*4.50*	*3.00*

Automobiles — AP215

5g, Mercedes 300 SEL 6.3. 10g, Jaguar Mk II 3.8. 20g, BMW 635 CSI. 25g, Alfa Romeo GTA. 30g, BMW 1800 Tisa.

1987, May 29	**Litho.**	***Perf. 13½***		
C674	AP215	5g multicolored	.60	.25
C675	AP215	10g multicolored	4.50	1.50
C676	AP215	20g multicolored	1.25	.40
C677	AP215	25g multicolored	1.50	1.50
C678	AP215	30g multicolored	1.50	1.50
		Nos. C674-C678 (5)	9.35	5.15

1988 Winter Olympics, Calgary — AP216

Gold medalists or Olympic competitors: 5g, Michela Figini, Switzerland, downhill, 1984, vert. 10g, Hanni Wenzel, Liechtenstein, slalom and giant slalom, 1980. 20g, 4-Man bobsled, Switzerland, 1956, 1972. 25g, Markus Wasmeier, downhill. 30g, Ingemar Stenmark, Sweden, slalom and giant slalom, 1980. 100g, Pirmin Zurbriggen, Switzerland, vert. (downhill, 1988).

1987, Sept. 10		***Perf. 14***		
C679	AP216	5g multicolored	.75	.25
C680	AP216	10g multicolored	4.50	1.40
C681	AP216	20g multicolored	1.50	.40
		Perf. 13½x13		
C682	AP216	25g multicolored	1.40	1.10
C683	AP216	30g multicolored	1.60	1.40
		Nos. C679-C683 (5)	9.75	4.55

Souvenir Sheet

Perf. 13½

C684	AP216	100g multicolored	14.00	14.00

No. C684 contains one 45x57mm stamp.

Nos. 2211 and C467 Ovptd. in Red on Silver "11.IX.1887 - 1987 / Centenario de la fundacion de / la A.N.R. (Partido Colarado) / Bernardino Caballero Fundador / General de Ejercito / D. Alfredo Stroessner Continuador"

1987, Sept. 11		***Perf. 13, 14***		
C685	A401	200g on No. 2211	.50	.50
C686	AP148	1000g on No. C467	2.75	2.75
		Nos. C685-C686 (2)	3.25	3.25

1988 Summer Olympics, Seoul — AP217

Medalists and competitors: 5g, Sabine Everts, West Germany, javelin. 10g, Carl Lewis, US, 100 and 200-meter run, 1984. 20g, Darrell Pace, US, archery, 1976, 1984. 25g, Juergen Hingsen, West Germany, decathlon, 1984. 30g, Claudia Losch, West Germany, shot put, 1984. 100g, Fredy Schmidtke, West Germany, cycling, 1984.

1987, Sept. 22		***Perf. 14***		
C687	AP217	5g multi	.50	.25
C688	AP217	10g multi, vert.	2.00	.55
C689	AP217	20g multi	1.20	.40
		Perf. 13½x13		
C690	AP217	25g multi, vert.	1.10	1.10
C691	AP217	30g multi, vert.	1.40	1.40
		Nos. C687-C691 (5)	6.20	3.70

Souvenir Sheet

Perf. 14½

C692	AP217	100g multi, vert.	13.00	13.00

Nos. C650-C652 Ovptd. in Violet or Blue (#C694) with Soccer Ball and "ZURICH 10.VI.87 / Lanzamiento ITALIA '90 / Italia 3 - Argentina 1"

Perf. 13½x13, 13

1987, Oct. 19		**Litho.**		
C693	AP210	10g on No. C650	2.00	2.00
C694	AP210	30g on No. C651	3.00	3.00
		Nos. C693-C694 (2)	5.00	5.00

Souvenir Sheet

Perf. 14½

C695	AP210	25g on No. C652	12.00	12.00

Paintings by Rubens AP218

Details from: 5g, The Virtuous Hero Crowned. 10g, The Brazen Serpent, 1635. 20g, Judith with the Head of Holofernes, 1617. 25g, Assembly of the Gods of Olympus. 30g, Venus, Cupid, Bacchus and Ceres.

1987, Dec. 14		***Perf. 13***		
C696	AP218	5g multicolored	.80	.25
C697	AP218	10g multicolored	4.50	1.60
C698	AP218	20g multicolored	1.40	.40
		Perf. 13x13½		
C699	AP218	25g multicolored	1.10	1.10
C700	AP218	30g multicolored	1.25	1.25
		Nos. C696-C700 (5)	9.05	4.60

Christmas AP219

Details from paintings: 5g, Virgin and Child with St. Joseph and St. John the Baptist, anonymous. 10g, Madonna and Child under the Veil with St. Joseph and St. John, by Marco da Siena. 20g, Sacred Conversation with the Donors, by Titian. 25g, The Brotherhood of the Rosary, by Durer. 30g, Madonna with Standing Child, by Rubens. 100g, Madonna and Child, engraving by Albrecht Durer.

1987	**Litho.**	***Perf. 14***		
C701	AP219	5g multicolored	.40	.25
C702	AP219	10g multicolored	1.40	.55
C703	AP219	20g multicolored	.80	.25
C704	AP219	25g multicolored	1.20	.40
		Perf. 13x13½		
C705	AP219	30g multicolored	2.00	2.00
		Nos. C701-C705 (5)	5.80	3.45

Souvenir Sheet

Perf. 14½

C706	AP219	100g multi	20.00	20.00

Issued: #C701-C705, 12/16; #C706, 12/17.

Austrian Railways, Sesquicentennial — AP220

Locomotives: 5g, Steam #3669, 1899. 10g, Steam #GZ 44074. 20g, Steam, diff. 25g, Diesel-electric. 30g, Austria No. 1067. 100g, Steam, vert.

1988, Jan. 2		***Perf. 14***		
C707	AP220	5g multicolored	.75	.25
C708	AP220	10g multicolored	3.25	1.00
C709	AP220	20g multicolored	1.00	.30
C710	AP220	25g multicolored	1.75	.45
		Perf. 13½x13		
C711	AP220	30g multicolored	2.75	2.75
		Nos. C707-C711 (5)	9.50	4.75

Souvenir Sheet

Perf. 13½

C712	AP220	100g multicolored	25.00	25.00

No. C712 contains one 50x60mm stamp.

Souvenir Sheet

Christmas — AP221

1988, Jan. 4		***Perf. 13½***		
C713	AP221	100g Madonna, by Rubens	20.00	20.00

Souvenir Sheet

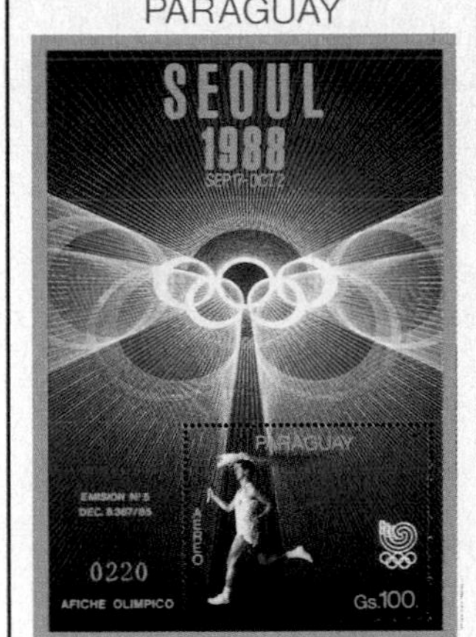

1988 Summer Olympics, Seoul — AP222

1988, Jan. 18		***Perf. 14½***		
C714	AP222	100g gold & multi	12.00	12.00

Exists with silver lettering and frame. Same value.

Colonization of Space — AP223

5g, NASA-ESA space station. 10g, Eurospace module Columbus docked at space station. 20g, NASA space sation. 25g, Ring section of space station, vert. 30g, Space station living quarters in central core, vert.

1988, Mar. 9	**Litho.**	***Perf. 13½x13***		
C715	AP223	5g multicolored	.55	.25
C716	AP223	10g multicolored	2.60	.90
C717	AP223	20g multicolored	1.00	.35
		Perf. 13x13½		
C718	AP223	25g multicolored	1.40	.50
C719	AP223	30g multicolored	2.25	2.25
		Nos. C715-C719 (5)	7.80	4.25

Souvenir Sheet

Berlin, 750th Anniv. — AP224

1988, Mar. 10 Litho. *Perf. 14½*
C720 AP224 100g multicolored 25.00 25.00

LUPOSTA '87.

Souvenir Sheet

Apollo 15 Launch, 1971 — AP225

1988, Apr. 12
C721 AP225 100g multicolored 20.00 20.00

No. 2210 Ovptd. in Metallic Red

1988, Apr. 28 *Perf. 13*
C722 A401 100g on No. 2210 2.00 2.00

Caacupe Basilica and Pope John Paul II — AP226

Perf. 13½x13

1988, May 5 Litho. Wmk. 347
C723 AP226 100g multi 2.00 2.00
C724 AP226 120g multi 2.00 2.00
C725 AP226 150g multi 2.00 2.00
Nos. C723-C725 (3) 6.00 6.00

Visit of Pope John Paul II.

No. C631 Overprinted

Perf. 13x13½

1988, June 15 Wmk. 392
C726 AP203 10g blue & gray .40 .25

Paraguay Philatelic Center, 75th Anniv.

Berlin, 750th Anniv. Paintings Type of 1988

5g, Venus and Cupid, 1742, by Francois Boucher. 10g, Perseus Liberates Andromeda, 1662, by Rubens. 20g, Venus and the Organist by Titian. 25g, Leda and the Swan by Correggio. 30g, St. Cecilia by Rubens.

1988, June 15 Unwmk. *Perf. 13*
C727 A409 5g multi, horiz. *.35 .25*
C728 A409 10g multi, horiz. *.75 .35*
C729 A409 20g multi, horiz. *1.10 .50*
C730 A409 25g multi, horiz. *1.60 .80*

Perf. 13x13½

C731 A409 30g multicolored *2.50 2.50*
Nos. C727-C731 (5) 6.30 4.40

Founding of "New Germany" and 1st Cultivation of Herbal Tea, Cent. — AP227

Perf. 13x13½, 13½x13

1988, June 18 Litho. Wmk. 347
C732 AP227 90g Cauldron, vert. 3.00 2.50
C733 AP227 105g Farm workers carrying crop 3.00 2.50
C734 AP227 120g like 105g 3.00 2.50
Nos. C732-C734 (3) 9.00 7.50

1990 World Cup Soccer Championships, Italy — AP228

5g, Machine slogan cancel from Montevideo, May 21, 1930. 10g, Italy #324, vert. 20g, France #349. 25g, Brazil #696, vert. 30g, Paraguayan commemorative cancel for ITALIA 1990.

1988, Aug. 1 Unwmk. *Perf. 13*
C735 AP228 5g multicolored .85 .25
C736 AP228 10g multicolored 2.60 .90
C737 AP228 20g multicolored 1.60 .50
C738 AP228 25g multicolored 1.40 .95

Perf. 13½x13

C739 AP228 30g multicolored 1.60 1.20
Nos. C735-C739 (5) 8.05 3.80

For overprint see No. 2284.

Souvenir Sheet

Count Ferdinand von Zeppelin, Airship Designer, Birth Sesquicentennial — AP229

1988, Aug. 3 *Perf. 14½*
C740 AP229 100g multicolored 20.00 20.00

Government Palace and Pres. Stroessner — AP230

Wmk. 347

1988, Aug. 5 Litho. *Perf. 13½*
C741 AP230 200g multi .60 .50
C742 AP230 500g multi 1.40 1.40
C743 AP230 1000g multi 2.50 2.50
Nos. C741-C743 (3) 4.50 4.40

Pres. Stroessner's new term in office, 1988-1993. Size of letters in watermark on 200g, 1000g: 5mm. On 500g, 10mm.

1988 Winter Olympics, Calgary — AP231

Gold medalists: 5g, Hubert Strolz, Austria, Alpine combined. 10g, Alberto Tomba, Italy, giant slalom and slalom. 20g, Franck Piccard, France, super giant slalom. 25g, Thomas Muller, Hans-Peter Pohl and Hubert Schwarz, Federal Republic of Germany, Nordic combined team, vert. 30g, Vreni Schneider, Switzerland, giant slalom and slalom, vert. 100g, Marina Kiehl, Federal Republic of Germany, downhill, vert.

Perf. 13½x13

1988, Sept. 2 Unwmk.
C744 AP231 5g multicolored .85 .25
C745 AP231 10g multicolored 2.60 .90
C746 AP231 20g multicolored 1.60 .50

Perf. 13x13½

C747 AP231 25g multicolored 1.40 .95
C748 AP231 30g multicolored 1.60 1.20
Nos. C744-C748 (5) 8.05 3.80

Souvenir Sheet

Perf. 14½

C749 AP231 100g multicolored 13.00 13.00

1990 World Cup Soccer Championships, Italy — AP232

Designs: 5g, Mexico #C350. 10g, Germany #1146. 20g, Argentina #1147, vert. 25g, Spain #2211. 30g, Italy #1742.

1988, Oct. 4 *Perf. 13*
C750 AP232 5g multicolored .55 .25
C751 AP232 10g multicolored 2.50 .85
C752 AP232 20g multicolored .95 .30
C753 AP232 25g multicolored 1.40 .50

Perf. 14

C754 AP232 30g multicolored 1.60 1.20
Nos. C750-C754 (5) 7.00 3.10

For overprint see No. 2285.

No. C635 Ovptd. in Metallic Red

1988, Nov. 25 *Perf. 14*
C755 AP204 30g on No. C635 4.00 4.00

No. C623 Ovptd. in Gold

1988, Nov. 25 *Perf. 14*
C756 AP200 30g on No. C623 2.00 2.00

1988 Summer Olympics, Seoul — AP233

Gold medalists: No. C757, Nicole Uphoff, individual dressage. No. C758, Anja Fichtel, Sabine Bau, Zita Funkenhauser, Anette Kluge and Christine Weber, team foil. No. C759, Silvia Sperber, smallbore standard rifle. No. C760, Mathias Baumann, Claus Erhorn, Thies Kaspareit and Ralph Ehrenbrink, equestrian team 3-day event. No. C761, Anja Fichtel, individual foil, vert. No. C762, Franke Sloothaak, Ludger Beerbaum, Wolfgang Brinkmann and Dirk Hafemeister, equestrian team jumping. No. C763, Arnd Schmitt, individual epee, vert. No. C764, Jose Luis Doreste, Finn class yachting. No. C765, Steffi Graf, tennis. No. C766, Michael Gross, 200-meter butterfly, vert. No. C767, West Germany, coxed eights. No. C768, Nicole Uphoff, Monica Theodorescu, Ann Kathrin Linsenhoff and Reiner Klimke, team dressage.

1989 *Perf. 13*
C757 AP233 5g multicolored .55 .25
C758 AP233 5g multicolored .55 .25
C759 AP233 10g multicolored 2.60 .25
C760 AP233 10g multicolored 2.60 .25
C761 AP233 20g multicolored .95 .40
C762 AP233 20g multicolored .95 .40
C763 AP233 25g multicolored 1.40 .60
C764 AP233 25g multicolored 1.40 .60

Perf. 13½x13

C765 AP233 30g multicolored 2.60 2.60
C766 AP233 30g multicolored 2.60 2.60
Nos. C757-C766 (10) 16.20 8.20

Souvenir Sheets

Perf. 14½

C767 AP233 100g multicolored 10.00 10.00
C768 AP233 100g multicolored 10.00 10.00

Nos. C767-C768 each contain one 80x50mm stamp.

Issue dates: Nos. C757, C759, C761, C763, C765, and C767, Mar. 3. Others, Mar. 20.

For overprints see Nos. 2292, 2359.

Souvenir Sheet

Intl. Red Cross, 125th Anniv. (in 1988) — AP234

1989, Apr. 17 Litho. ***Perf. 13½***

C769 AP234 100g #803 in changed colors 10.00 10.00

No. C769 has perforated label picturing Nobel medal.

Olympics Type of 1989

1988 Winter Olympic medalists or competitors: 5g, Pirmin Zurbriggen, Peter Mueller, Switzerland, and Franck Piccard, France, Alpine skiing. 10g, Sigrid Wolf, Austria, super giant slalom, vert. 20g, Czechoslovakia vs. West Germany, hockey, vert. 25g, Piccard, skiing, vert. 30g, Piccard, wearing medal, vert.

1989, Apr. 17 ***Perf. 13½x13***

C770 AP233 5g multicolored .80 .25

Perf. 13x13½

C771 AP233 10g multicolored 1.60 .55
C772 AP233 20g multicolored 1.20 .40
C773 AP233 25g multicolored 1.40 .50
C774 AP233 30g multicolored 2.60 2.60
Nos. C770-C774 (5) 7.60 4.30

Souvenir Sheet

1990 World Cup Soccer Championships, Italy — AP235

1989, Apr. 21 ***Perf. 14½***

C775 AP235 100g Sheet of 1 + label 10.00 10.00

1st Moon Landing, 20th Anniv. — AP236

Designs: 5g, Wernher von Braun, Apollo 11 launch, vert. 10g, Michael Collins, lunar module on moon. 20g, Neil Armstrong, astronaut on lunar module ladder, vert. 25g, Buzz Aldrin, solar wind experiment, vert. 30g, Kurt Debus, splashdown of Columbia command module, vert.

1989, May 24 ***Perf. 13***

C776 AP236 5g multicolored .55 .25
C777 AP236 10g multicolored 4.00 1.40
C778 AP236 20g multicolored 2.40 .80
C779 AP236 25g multicolored 1.40 1.40
C780 AP236 30g multicolored 1.60 1.60
Nos. C776-C780 (5) 9.95 5.45

Souvenir Sheet

Luis Alberto del Parana and the Paraguayans — AP237

1989, May 25 ***Perf. 14½***

C780A AP237 100g multi 30.00 30.00

A clear plastic phonograph record is affixed to the souvenir sheet.

Hamburg, 800th Anniv. — AP238

Hamburg anniv. emblem, SAIL '89 emblem, and: 5g, Galleon and Icarus, woodcut by Pieter Brueghel. 10g, Windjammer, vert. 20g, Bark in full sail. 25g, Old Hamburg by A.E. Schliecker, vert. 30g, Commemorative coin issued by Federal Republic of Germany. 100g, Hamburg, 13th cent. illuminated manuscript, vert.

1989, May 26 ***Perf. 13½x13, 13x13½***

C781 AP238 5g multicolored .80 .25
C782 AP238 10g multicolored 3.50 1.10
C783 AP238 20g multicolored 1.20 .40
C784 AP238 25g multicolored 1.60 .50
C785 AP238 30g multicolored 3.00 3.00
Nos. C781-C785 (5) 10.10 5.25

Souvenir Sheet

Perf. 14½

C786 AP238 100g multicolored 20.00 20.00

No. C786 contains one 40x50mm stamp.

French Revolution, Bicent. — AP239

Details from paintings: 5g, Esther Adorns Herself for her Presentation to King Ahasuerus, by Theodore Chasseriau, vert. 10g, Olympia, by Manet, vert. 20g, The Drunker Erigone with a Panther, by Louis A. Reisener. 25g, Anniv. emblem and natl. coats of arms. 30g, Liberty Leading the People, by Delacroix, vert. 100g, The Education of Maria de Medici, by Rubens, vert.

1989, May 27 ***Perf. 13x13½, 13½x13***

C787 AP239 5g multicolored .80 .25
C788 AP239 10g multicolored 3.50 1.20
C789 AP239 20g multicolored 1.20 .40
C790 AP239 25g multicolored 1.60 .50
C791 AP239 30g multicolored 2.40 2.40
Nos. C787-C791 (5) 9.50 4.75

Souvenir Sheet

Perf. 14½

C792 AP239 100g multicolored 14.00 14.00

Souvenir Sheet

Railway Zeppelin, 1931 — AP240

1989, May 27 Litho. ***Perf. 13½***

C793 AP240 100g multicolored 18.00 18.00

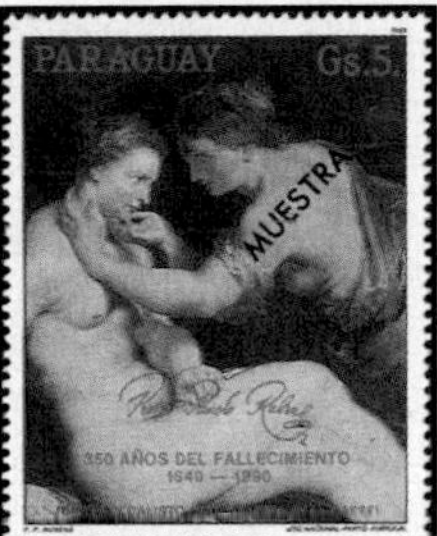

Jupiter and Calisto by Rubens AP241

Details from paintings by Rubens: 10g, Boreas Abducting Oreithyia (1619-20). 20g, Fortuna (1625). 25g, Mars with Venus and Cupid (1625). 30g, Virgin with Child (1620).

1989, Dec. 27 Litho. ***Perf. 14***

C794 AP241 5g multicolored .50 .25
C795 AP241 10g multicolored .80 .25
C796 AP241 20g multicolored 1.75 .55
C797 AP241 25g multicolored 2.25 .75

Perf. 13

C798 AP241 30g multicolored 2.10 2.10
Nos. C794-C798 (5) 7.40 3.90

Death of Rubens, 350th anniversary.

Penny Black, 150th Anniv. AP242

Penny Black, 500 years of postal services emblem, Stamp World '90 emblem and: 5g, Brazil #1. 10g, British Guiana #2. 20g, Chile #1. 25g, Uruguay #1. 30g, Paraguay #1.

1989, Dec. 30 ***Perf. 14***

C799 AP242 5g multicolored .40 .25
C800 AP242 10g multicolored .80 .25
C801 AP242 20g multicolored 1.60 .50
C802 AP242 25g multicolored 2.00 .65

Perf. 13

C803 AP242 30g multicolored 2.75 2.75
Nos. C799-C803 (5) 7.55 4.40

Animals AP243

Designs: 5g, Martucha. 10g, Mara. 20g, Lobo de crin. 25g, Rana cornuda tintorera, horiz. 30g, Jaguar, horiz. Inscribed 1989.

1990, Jan. 8 ***Perf. 13x13½, 13½x13***

C804 AP243 5g multicolored .75 .25
C805 AP243 10g multicolored 1.60 .50
C806 AP243 20g multicolored 2.00 .65
C807 AP243 25g multicolored 2.60 .90
C808 AP243 30g multicolored 2.75 1.75
Nos. C804-C808 (5) 9.70 4.05

Columbus' Fleet AP244

Discovery of America 500th anniversary emblem and: 10g, Olympic rings, stylized basketball player, horiz. 20g, Medieval nave, Expo '92 emblem. 25g, Four-masted barkentine, Expo '92 emblem, horiz. 30g, Similar to Spain Scott 2571, Expo '92 emblem.

1990, Jan. 27 ***Perf. 14***

C809 AP244 5g multicolored .55 .25
C810 AP244 10g multicolored 1.10 .35
C811 AP244 20g multicolored 1.20 .40
C812 AP244 25g multicolored 1.40 .55

Perf. 13½x13

C813 AP244 30g multicolored 1.75 1.75
Nos. C809-C813 (5) 6.00 3.30

Postal Transportation, 500th Anniv. — AP245

500th Anniv. Emblem and: 5g, 10g, 20g, 25g, Penny Black and various post coaches, 10g, vert. 30g, Post coach.

1990, Mar. 9 ***Perf. 13½x13, 13x13½***

C814 AP245 5g multicolored .50 .25
C815 AP245 10g multicolored .90 .35
C816 AP245 20g multicolored 2.00 .65
C817 AP245 25g multicolored 2.60 .85
C818 AP245 30g multicolored 3.50 3.50
Nos. C814-C818 (5) 9.50 5.60

Fort and City of Arco by Durer — AP246

Paintings by Albrecht Durer, postal transportation 500th anniversary emblem and: 10g, Trent Castle. 20g, North Innsbruck. 25g, Fort yard of Innsbruck, vert. 30g, Virgin of the Animals. No. C824, Madonna and Child, vert. No. C825, Postrider, vert.

1990, Mar. 14 ***Perf. 14***

C819 AP246 5g multicolored .50 .25
C820 AP246 10g multicolored .95 .35
C821 AP246 20g multicolored 2.00 .65
C822 AP246 25g multicolored 2.75 1.00

Perf. 13

C823 AP246 30g multicolored 3.75 3.75
Nos. C819-C823 (5) 9.95 6.00

Souvenir Sheets

Perf. 14½

C824 AP246 100g multicolored 17.00 17.00
C825 AP246 100g multicolored 17.00 17.00

Nos. C824-C825 each contain one 40x50mm stamp.

For overprint see No. 2358.

AP247

Wmk. 347

1986-88?	Photo.	*Perf. 11*		
C826 AP247	40g red lilac		1.00	.85
C827 AP247	60g bright green ('88)		1.50	1.25

POSTAGE DUE STAMPS

D1

1904	Unwmk.	Litho.	*Perf. 11½*	
J1 D1	2c green		1.00	*2.00*
J2 D1	4c green		1.00	*2.00*
J3 D1	10c green		1.00	*2.00*
J4 D1	20c green		1.00	*2.00*
	Nos. J1-J4 (4)		4.00	8.00

D2

1913		Engr.		
J5 D2	1c yellow brown		1.00	1.00
J6 D2	2c yellow brown		1.00	1.00
J7 D2	5c yellow brown		1.00	1.00
J8 D2	10c yellow brown		1.00	1.00
J9 D2	20c yellow brown		1.00	1.00
J10 D2	40c yellow brown		1.00	1.00
J11 D2	1p yellow brown		1.00	1.00
J12 D2	1.50p yellow brown		1.00	1.00
	Nos. J5-J12 (8)		8.00	8.00

For overprints and surcharges see Nos. 220-224, 229, 232, 264, L5.

INTERIOR OFFICE ISSUES

The "C" signifies "Campana" (rural). These stamps were sold by Postal Agents in country districts, who received a commission on their sales. These stamps were available for postage in the interior but not in Asunción or abroad.

Nos. 243-244 Overprinted in Red

1922			
L1 A42	50c car & dk bl	.50	.50
L2 A42	1p dk bl & brn	.50	.50

The overprint on Nos. L2 exists double or inverted. Counterfeits exist. Double or inverted overprints on No. L1 and all overprints in black are counterfeit.

Nos. 215, 218, J12 Surcharged

1924			
L3 A40	50c on 75c deep bl	.50	.50
L4 A40	1p on 1.25p pale bl	.50	.50
L5 D2	1p on 1.50p yel brn	.50	.50
	Nos. L3-L5 (3)	1.50	1.50

Nos. L3-L4 exist imperf.

Nos. 254, 257-260 Overprinted in Black or Red

1924-26			
L6 A45	50c red ('25)	1.00	1.00
L7 A44	1p dk blue (R)	1.00	1.00
L8 A45	1p dk bl (R) ('25)	1.00	1.00
L9 A46	1p blue (R) ('25)	1.00	1.00
L10 A45	1p emerald ('26)	2.00	.75
	Nos. L6-L10 (5)	6.00	4.75

Nos. L6, L8-L9 exist imperf. Value $2.50 each pair.

Same Overprint on Stamps and Type of 1927-36 in Red or Black

1927-39			
L11 A47	50c ultra (R)	.50	.50
L12 A47	50c dl red ('28)	.50	.50
L13 A47	50c orange ('29)	.50	.50
L14 A47	50c lt bl ('30)	.50	.50
L15 A47	50c gray (R) ('31)	.50	.50
L16 A47	50c bluish grn (R) ('33)	.50	.50
L17 A47	50c vio (R) ('34)	.50	.50
L18 A48	1p emerald	.50	.50
L19 A48	1p org red ('29)	.50	.50
L20 A48	1p lil brn ('31)	.50	.50
L21 A48	1p dk bl (R) ('33)	.50	.50
L22 A48	1p brt vio (R) ('35)	.50	.50
L23 A49	1.50p brown	.50	.50
a.	Double overprint	3.00	
L24 A49	1.50p lilac ('28)	.50	.50
L25 A49	1.50p dull bl (R)	.50	.50
L26 A50	2.50p bister ('28)	.50	.50
L27 A50	2.50p vio (R) ('36)	.50	.50
L28 A51	3p gray (R)	.50	.50
L29 A51	3p rose red ('39)	.50	.50
L30 A52	5p vio (R) ('36)	.50	.50
L31 A57	10p gray brn (R) ('36)	5.00	3.00
	Nos. L11-L31 (21)	15.00	13.00

Types of 1931-35 and No. 305 Overprinted in Black or Red

1931-36			
L32 A59	1p light red	2.00	1.00
L33 A58	1.50p dp bl (R)	1.00	.75
L34 A60	1.50p bis brn ('32)	2.00	1.00
L35 A60	1.50p grn (R) ('34)	2.00	1.00
L36 A60	1.50p bl (R) ('36)	2.00	1.00
L37 A54	10p vermilion	8.00	2.50
	Nos. L32-L37 (6)	17.00	7.25

OFFICIAL STAMPS

O1

O2

O3

O4

O5

O6

O7

Unwmk.

1886, Aug. 20	Litho.	*Imperf.*	
O1 O1	1c orange	7.00	7.00
O2 O2	2c violet	7.00	7.00
O3 O3	5c red	7.00	7.00
O4 O4	7c green	7.00	7.00
O5 O5	10c brown	7.00	7.00
O6 O6	15c slate blue	7.00	7.00
a.	Wavy lines on face of stamp		
b.	"OFICIAL" omitted	1.25	
O7 O7	20c claret	7.00	7.00
	Nos. O1-O7 (7)	49.00	49.00

Nos. O1 to O7 have the date and various control marks and letters printed on the back of each stamp in blue and black.

The overprints exist inverted on all values.

Nos. O1 to O7 have been reprinted from new stones made from slightly retouched dies.

Types of 1886 With Overprint

1886		*Perf. 11½*	
O8 O1	1c dark green	1.50	1.50
O9 O2	2c scarlet	1.50	1.50
O10 O3	5c dull blue	1.50	1.50
O11 O4	7c orange	1.50	1.50
O12 O5	10c lake	1.50	1.50
O13 O6	15c brown	1.50	1.50
O14 O7	20c blue	1.50	1.50
	Nos. O8-O14 (7)	10.50	10.50

The overprint exists inverted on all values. Value, each $1.50.

No. 20 Overprinted

1886, Sept. 1			
O15 A11	1c dark green	4.00	4.00

Types of 1889 Regular Issue Surcharged

Handstamped Surcharge in Black

1889		*Imperf.*	
O16 A13	3c on 15c violet	3.75	2.75
O17 A13	5c on 15c red brn	3.75	2.25
	Perf. 11½		
O18 A13	1c on 15c maroon	4.00	2.25
O19 A13	2c on 15c maroon	4.00	2.25
	Nos. O16-O19 (4)	15.50	9.50

Counterfeits of Nos. O16-O19 abound.

Regular Issue of 1887 Handstamp Overprinted in Violet

Perf. 11½-12½ & Compounds

1890		Typo.	
O20 A12	1c green	.35	.30
O21 A12	2c rose red	.35	.30
O22 A12	5c blue	.35	.30
O23 A12	7c brown	10.00	8.00
O24 A12	10c lilac	.35	.35
O25 A12	15c orange	.75	.45
O26 A12	20c pink	.65	.45
	Nos. O20-O26 (7)	12.80	10.15

Nos. O20-O26 exist with double overprint and all but the 20c with inverted overprint.

Nos. O20-O22, O24-O26 exist with blue overprint. The status is questioned. Value, set $15.

Stamps and Type of 1887 Regular Issue Overprinted in Black

1892			
O33 A12	1c green	.30	.30
O34 A12	2c rose red	.30	.30
O35 A12	5c blue	.30	.30
O36 A12	7c brown	4.00	1.75
O37 A12	10c lilac	1.25	.55
O38 A12	15c orange	.35	.30
O39 A12	20c pink	.65	.35
O40 A12	50c gray	.75	.35
	Nos. O33-O40 (8)	7.90	4.20

No. 26 Overprinted

1893			
O41 A12	7c brown	17.50	8.00

Counterfeits of No. O41 exist.

O16

1901, Feb.	Engr.	*Perf. 11½, 12½*	
O42 O16	1c dull blue	.75	.50
O43 O16	2c rose red	.75	.50
O44 O16	4c dark brown	.75	.50
O45 O16	5c dark green	.75	.50
O46 O16	8c orange brn	.75	.50
O47 O16	10c car rose	2.50	1.00
O48 O16	20c deep blue	2.50	1.00
	Nos. O42-O48 (7)	8.75	4.50

A 12c deep green, type O16, was prepared but not issued.

No. 45 Overprinted

1902		*Perf. 12x12½*	
O49 A12	1p olive grn	2.00	2.00
a.	Inverted overprint	10.00	

Counterfeits of No. O49a exist.

Regular Issue of 1903 Overprinted

1903		*Perf. 11½*	
O50 A32	1c gray	.90	.35
O51 A32	2c blue green	.90	.35
O52 A32	5c blue	.90	.35
O53 A32	10c orange brn	.90	.35
O54 A32	20c carmine	.90	.35

O55 A32 30c deep blue .90 .35
O56 A32 60c purple .90 .35
Nos. O50-O56 (7) 6.30 2.45

O17

1905-08 Engr. *Perf. 11½, 12*

O57 O17 1c gray grn .50 .30
O58 O17 1c ol grn ('05) .90 .30
O59 O17 1c brn org ('06) .80 .30
O60 O17 1c ver ('08) .50 .30
O61 O17 2c brown org .35 .30
O62 O17 2c gray grn ('05) .35 .30
O63 O17 2c red ('06) 2.00 .75
O64 O17 2c gray ('08) 1.00 .50
O65 O17 5c deep bl ('06) .50 .35
O66 O17 5c gray bl ('08) 4.00 2.00
O67 O17 5c grnsh bl ('08) 2.00 1.50
O68 O17 10c violet ('06) .35 .50
O69 O17 20c violet ('08) 2.00 1.25
Nos. O57-O69 (13) 15.25 8.65

O18

1908

O70 O17 10c bister 10.50
O71 O17 10c emerald 10.50
O72 O17 10c red lilac 13.50
O73 O17 20c bister 9.00
O74 O17 20c salmon pink 10.50
O75 O17 20c green 10.50
O76 O17 30c turquoise bl 10.50
O77 O17 30c blue gray 10.50
O78 O17 30c yellow 4.50
O79 O17 60c chocolate 12.00
O80 O17 60c orange brn 15.00
O81 O17 60c deep ultra 12.00
O82 O18 1p brt rose & blk 72.50
O83 O18 1p lake & blk 72.50
O84 O18 1p brn org & blk 75.00
Nos. O70-O84 (15) 349.00

Nos. O70-O84 were not issued, but were surcharged or overprinted for use as regular postage stamps. See Nos. 131-138, 141-145, 158-165, 171-173.

O19

1913 *Perf. 11½*

O85 O19 1c gray .30 .35
O86 O19 2c orange .30 .35
O87 O19 5c lilac .30 .35
O88 O19 10c green .30 .35
O89 O19 20c dull red .30 .35
O90 O19 50c rose .30 .35
O91 O19 75c deep blue .30 .35
O92 O19 1p dull blue 1.00 .50
O93 O19 2p yellow 1.00 .50
Nos. O85-O93 (9) 4.10 3.45

For surcharges see Nos. 268, C1-C3.

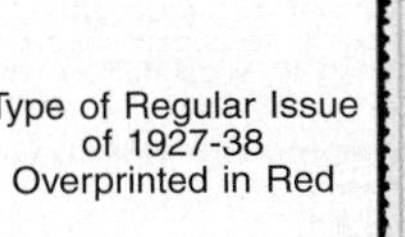

Type of Regular Issue of 1927-38 Overprinted in Red

1935

O94 A47 10c light ultra .35 .30
O95 A47 50c violet .35 .30
O96 A48 1p orange .35 .30
O97 A60 1.50p green .35 .30
O98 A50 2.50p violet .35 .30
Nos. O94-O98 (5) 1.75 1.50

Overprint is diagonal on 1.50p.

University of Asunción Type

1940 Litho. *Perf. 12*

O99 A67 50c red brn & blk .50 .30
O100 A67 1p rose pink & blk .50 .30
O101 A67 2p lt bl grn & blk .50 .30
O102 A67 5p ultra & blk .50 .30
O103 A67 10p lt vio & blk .50 .30
O104 A67 50p dp org & blk .50 .30
Nos. O99-O104 (6) 3.00 1.80

PENRHYN ISLAND

pen-'rin 'ī-lənd

(Tongareva)

AREA — 3 sq. mi.
POP. — 395 (1926)

Stamps of Cook Islands were used in Penrhyn from 1932 until 1973.

12 Pence = 1 Shilling

Catalogue values for unused stamps in this country are for Never Hinged items, beginning with Scott 35 in the regular postage section, Scott B1 in the semi-postal section and Scott O1 in the officials section.

Watermarks

Wmk. 61 — N Z and Star Close Together

Wmk. 63 — Double-lined N Z and Star

On watermark 61 the margins of the sheets are watermarked "NEW ZEALAND POSTAGE" and parts of the double-lined letters of these words are frequently found on the stamps. It occasionally happens that a stamp shows no watermark whatever.

Stamps of New Zealand Surcharged in Carmine, Vermilion, Brown or Blue

½ pence

1 pence

2 ½ pence

1902 Wmk. 63 *Perf. 14*

1 A18 ½p green (C) 1.00 *14.00*
a. No period after "ISLAND" 175.00 *325.00*
2 A35 1p carmine (Br) 3.75 *27.50*
a. Perf. 11 1,000. *1,200.*
b. Perf. 11x14 1,200. *1,400.*

Wmk. 61 *Perf. 14*

5 A18 ½p green (V) 4.25 *14.00*
a. No period after "ISLAND" 180.00 *375.00*
6 A35 1p carmine (Bl) 1.50 *9.50*
a. No period after "ISLAND" 60.00 *170.00*
b. Perf. 11x14 15,000. *8,500.*

Unwmk. *Perf. 11*

8 A22 2½p blue (C) 14.50 13.00
a. "½" and "PENI" 2mm apart 30.00 *35.00*
9 A22 2½p blue (V) 14.50 13.00
a. "½" and "PENI" 2mm apart 30.00 *35.00*
Nos. 1-9 (6) 39.50 *91.00*

Stamps with compound perfs. also exist perf. 11 or 14 on one or more sides.

d

e

f

1903 Wmk. 61

10 A23(d) 3p yel brn (Bl) 11.50 *42.50*
11 A26(e) 6p rose (Bl) 17.50 *50.00*
12 A29(f) 1sh org red (Bl) 65.00 *65.00*
a. 1sh bright red (Bl) 47.50 *47.50*
b. 1sh brown red (Bl) 65.00 *65.00*
Nos. 10-12 (3) 94.00 *157.50*

1914-15 *Perf. 14, 14x14½*

13 A41(a) ½p yel grn (C) .90 *12.00*
a. No period after "ISLAND" 29.00 *110.00*
b. No period after "PENI" 110.00 *350.00*
14 A41(a) ½p yel grn (V) ('15) .90 *9.25*
a. No period after "ISLAND" 11.50 *65.00*
b. No period after "PENI" 55.00 *190.00*
15 A41(e) 6p car rose (Bl) 27.50 *82.50*
16 A41(f) 1sh ver (Bl) 50.00 *110.00*
Nos. 13-16 (4) 79.30 *213.75*

New Zealand Stamps of 1915-19 Overprinted in Red or Dark Blue

Perf. 14x13½, 14x14½

1917-20 Typo.

17 A43 ½p yel grn (R) ('20) 1.10 *2.25*
18 A47 1½p gray black (R) 7.50 *27.50*
19 A47 1½p brn org (R) ('19) .70 *27.50*
20 A43 3p choc (Bl) ('19) 4.00 *45.00*

Engr.

21 A44 2½p dull bl (R) ('20) 2.25 *10.00*
22 A45 3p vio brn (Bl) ('18) 12.00 *80.00*
23 A45 6p car rose (Bl) ('18) 5.75 *21.00*
24 A45 1sh vermilion (Bl) 14.00 *37.50*
Nos. 17-24 (8) 47.30 *250.75*

Landing of Capt. Cook A10

Avarua Waterfront A11

Capt. James Cook — A12

Coconut Palm — A13

Arorangi Village, Rarotonga — A14

Avarua Harbor — A15

1920 Unwmk. *Perf. 14*

25 A10 ½p emerald & blk 1.25 *23.00*
a. Center inverted 1,000.
26 A11 1p red & black 2.00 *19.00*
a. Center inverted 1,000.
27 A12 1½p violet & blk 7.75 *24.00*
28 A13 3p red org & blk 3.25 *15.00*
29 A14 6p dk brn & red brn 4.00 *24.00*
30 A15 1sh dull bl & blk 12.00 *32.50*
Nos. 25-30 (6) 30.25 *137.50*

Rarotongan Chief (Te Po) — A16

1927 Engr. Wmk. 61

31 A16 2½p blue & red brn 17.50 *47.50*

Types of 1920 Issue

1928-29

33 A10 ½p yellow grn & blk 6.50 *25.00*
34 A11 1p carmine rose & blk 6.50 *22.50*

PENRHYN

Northern Cook Islands

POP. — 606 (1996).

The Northern Cook Islands include six besides Penrhyn that are inhabited: Nassau, Palmerston (Avarua), Manihiki (Humphrey), Rakahanga (Reirson), Pukapuka (Danger) and Suwarrow (Anchorage).

100 Cents = 1 Dollar

Catalogue values for unused stamps in this section are for Never Hinged items.

Cook Islands Nos. 200-201, 203, 205-208, 211-212, 215-217 Overprinted

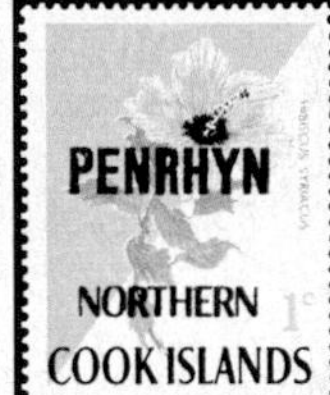

1973 Photo. Unwmk. *Perf. 14x13½*

35 A34 1c gold & multi .25 .25
36 A34 2c gold & multi .25 .25
37 A34 3c gold & multi .25 .25
38 A34 4c gold & multi .25 .25
a. Overprinted on #204 38.00 38.00
39 A34 5c gold & multi .25 .25
40 A34 6c gold & multi .25 .35
41 A34 8c gold & multi .25 .45
42 A34 15c gold & multi .35 .60
43 A34 20c gold & multi 1.25 1.00
44 A34 50c gold & multi .90 2.00
45 A35 $1 gold & multi .90 2.25
46 A35 $2 gold & multi .90 4.50
Nos. 35-46 (12) 6.05 12.40

Nos. 45-46 are overprinted "Penrhyn" only. Overprint exists with broken "E" or "O."

Issued with and without fluorescent security underprinting.

Issued: #35-45, Oct. 24; #46, Nov. 14.

Cook Islands Nos. 369-371 Overprinted in Silver: "PENRHYN / NORTHERN"

1973, Nov. 14 Photo. *Perf. 14*

47 A60 25c Princess Anne .35 .25
48 A60 30c Mark Phillips .35 .25
49 A60 50c Princess and Mark Phillips .35 .25
Nos. 47-49 (3) 1.05 .75

Wedding of Princess Anne and Capt. Mark Phillips.

Fluorescence

Starting with No. 50, stamps carry a "fluorescent security underprinting" in a multiple pattern combining a sailing ship, "Penrhyn Northern Cook Islands" and stars.

Ostracion A17

Aerial View of Penrhyn Atoll — A18

Designs: ½c-$1, Various fish of Penrhyn. $5, Map showing Penrhyn's location.

1974-75 Photo. Perf. 13½x14

50	A17	½c multicolored	.25	.25
51	A17	1c multicolored	.25	.25
52	A17	2c multicolored	.25	.25
53	A17	3c multicolored	.25	.25
54	A17	4c multicolored	.25	.25
55	A17	5c multicolored	.25	.25
56	A17	8c multicolored	.25	.25
57	A17	10c multicolored	.25	.25
58	A17	20c multicolored	.75	.40
59	A17	25c multicolored	.80	.45
60	A17	60c multicolored	2.00	1.10
61	A17	$1 multicolored	3.25	1.75
62	A18	$2 multicolored	6.50	*10.00*
63	A18	$5 multicolored	8.50	3.50
		Nos. 50-63 (14)	23.80	19.20

Issued: $2, 2/12/75; $5, 3/12/75; others 8/15/74.

For surcharges and overprints see Nos. 72, 352-353, O1-O12.

Map of Penrhyn and Nos. 1-2 — A19

UPU, cent.: 50c, UPU emblem, map of Penrhyn and Nos. 27-28.

1974, Sept. 27 Perf. 13

64	A19	25c violet & multi	.30	.30
65	A19	50c slate grn & multi	.60	.60

Adoration of the Kings, by Memling — A20

Christmas: 10c, Adoration of the Shepherds, by Hugo van der Goes. 25c, Adoration of the Kings, by Rubens. 30c, Holy Family, by Orazio Borgianni.

1974, Oct. 30

66	A20	5c multicolored	.25	.25
67	A20	10c multicolored	.25	.25
68	A20	25c multicolored	.30	.30
69	A20	30c multicolored	.40	.40
		Nos. 66-69 (4)	1.20	1.20

Churchill Giving "V" Sign — A21

1974, Nov. 30 Photo.

70	A21	30c shown	.35	*.80*
71	A21	50c Portrait	.45	*.90*

Winston Churchill (1874-1965).

No. 63 Overprinted

1975, July 24 Perf. 13½x13

72	A18	$5 multicolored	2.25	2.75

Safe splashdown of Apollo space capsule.

Madonna, by Dirk Bouts — A22

Madonna Paintings: 15c, by Leonardo da Vinci. 35c, by Raphael.

1975, Nov. 21 Photo. Perf. 14½x13

73	A22	7c gold & multi	.45	.25
74	A22	15c gold & multi	.75	.30
75	A22	35c gold & multi	1.10	.45
		Nos. 73-75 (3)	2.30	1.00

Christmas 1975.

Pietà, by Michelangelo A23

1976, Mar. 19 Photo. Perf. 14x13

76	A23	15c gold & dark brown	.25	.25
77	A23	20c gold & deep purple	.40	.30
78	A23	35c gold & dark green	.55	.35
a.		Souvenir sheet of 3, #76-78	1.60	1.60
		Nos. 76-78 (3)	1.20	.90

Easter and for the 500th birth anniv. of Michelangelo Buonarroti (1475-1564), Italian sculptor, painter and architect.

The Spirit of '76, by Archibald M. Willard — A24

No. 79, Washington Crossing the Delaware, by Emmanuel Leutze.

1976, May 20 Photo. Perf. 13½

79	A24	Strip of 3	1.00	1.00
a.		30c Boatsman	.30	.30
b.		30c Washington	.30	.30
c.		30c Men in boat	.30	.30
80	A24	Strip of 3	2.00	2.00
a.		50c Drummer boy	.50	.50
b.		50c Old drummer	.50	.50
c.		50c Fifer	.50	.50
d.		Souvenir sheet, #79-80	3.25	3.25

American Bicentennial. Nos. 79-80 printed in sheets of 15, 5 strips of 3 and 3-part corner labels.

For overprint see No. O13.

Running A25

Montreal Olympic Games Emblem and: 30c, Long jump. 75c, Javelin.

1976, July 9 Photo. Perf. 13½

81	A25	25c multicolored	.30	.25
82	A25	30c multicolored	.35	.30
83	A25	75c multicolored	.75	.50
a.		Souvenir sheet of 3, #81-83, perf. 14½x13½	1.40	1.40
		Nos. 81-83 (3)	1.40	1.05

21st Olympic Games, Montreal, Canada, July 17-Aug. 1. Nos. 81-83 printed in sheets of 6 (2x3).

Flight into Egypt, by Dürer A26

Etchings by Albrecht Dürer: 15c, Adoration of the Shepherds. 35c, Adoration of the Kings.

1976, Oct. 20 Photo. Perf. 13x13½

84	A26	7c silver & dk brown	.25	.25
85	A26	15c silver & slate grn	.25	.25
86	A26	35c silver & purple	.45	.35
		Nos. 84-86 (3)	.95	.85

Christmas. Nos. 84-86 printed in sheets of 8 (2x4) with decorative border.

Elizabeth II and Westminster Abbey — A27

$1, Elizabeth II & Prince Philip. $2, Elizabeth II.

1977, Mar. 24 Photo. Perf. 13½x13

87	A27	50c silver & multi	.25	.25
88	A27	$1 silver & multi	.30	.30
89	A27	$2 silver & multi	.45	.45
a.		Souvenir sheet of 3, #87-89	1.25	1.25
		Nos. 87-89 (3)	1.00	1.00

25th anniversary of reign of Queen Elizabeth II. Nos. 87-89 issued in sheets of 4.

For overprints see Nos. O14-O15.

Annunciation A28

Designs: 15c, Announcement to Shepherds. 35c, Nativity. Designs from "The Bible in Images," by Julius Schnorr von Carolsfeld (1794-1872).

1977, Sept. 23 Photo. Perf. 13½

90	A28	7c multicolored	.25	.25
91	A28	15c multicolored	.65	.65
92	A28	35c multicolored	1.10	1.10
		Nos. 90-92 (3)	2.00	2.00

Christmas. Issued in sheets of 6.

A29

No. 93a, Red Sickle-bill (I'wii). No. 93b, Chief's Feather Cloak. No. 94a, Crimson creeper (apapane). No. 94b, Feathered head of Hawaiian god. No. 95a, Hawaiian gallinule (alae). No. 95b, Chief's regalia: feather cape, staff (kahili) and helmet. No. 96a, Yellow-tufted bee-eater (o'o). No. 96b, Scarlet feathered image (head).

Birds are extinct; their feathers were used for artifacts shown.

1978, Jan. 19 Photo. Perf. 12½x13

93	A29	20c Pair, #a.-b.	1.40	.70
94	A29	30c Pair, #a.-b.	1.75	.90
95	A29	35c Pair, #a.-b.	1.90	1.00
96	A29	75c Pair, #a.-b.	3.00	1.60
c.		Souv. sheet, #93a, 94a, 95a, 96a	4.25	4.25
d.		Souv. sheet, #93b, 94b, 95b, 96b	4.25	4.25
		Nos. 93-96 (4)	8.05	4.20

Bicentenary of Capt. Cook's arrival in Hawaii. Printed in sheets of 8 (4x2).

A31

Rubens' Paintings: 10c, St. Veronica by Rubens. 15c, Crucifixion. 35c, Descent from the Cross.

1978, Mar. 10 Photo. Perf. 13½x13

Size: 25x36mm

101	A31	10c multicolored	.25	.25
102	A31	15c multicolored	.25	.25
103	A31	35c multicolored	.50	.50
a.		Souvenir sheet of 3	1.10	1.10
		Nos. 101-103 (3)	1.00	1.00

Easter and 400th birth anniv. of Peter Paul Rubens (1577-1640). Nos. 101-103 issued in sheets of 6. No. 103a contains one each of Nos. 101-103 (27x36mm).

Miniature Sheet

A32

1978, May 24 Photo. Perf. 13

104	A32	Sheet of 6	1.75	1.75
a.		90c Arms of United Kingdom	.35	.25
b.		90c shown	.35	.25
c.		90c Arms of New Zealand	.35	.25
d.		Souvenir sheet of 3, #104a-104c	1.40	1.40

25th anniv. of coronation of Elizabeth II.

No. 104 contains 2 horizontal se-tenant strips of Nos. 104a-104c, separated by horizontal gutter showing coronation.

A33

Paintings by Dürer: 30c, Virgin and Child. 35c, Virgin and Child with St. Anne.

1978, Nov. 29 Photo. *Perf. 14x13½*

105 A33 30c multicolored .60 .60
106 A33 35c multicolored .65 .65
a. Souvenir sheet of 2, #105-106 1.25 1.25

Christmas and 450th death anniv. of Albrecht Dürer (1471-1528), German painter. Nos. 105-106 issued in sheets of 6.

A34

#107a, Penrhyn #64-65. #107b, Rowland Hill, Penny Black. #108a, Penrhyn #104b. #108b, Hill portrait.

1979, Sept. 26 Photo. *Perf. 14*

107 A34 75c Pair, #a.-b. 1.00 1.00
108 A34 90c Pair, #a.-b. 1.25 1.25
c. Souvenir sheet of 4, #107-108 2.25 2.25

Sir Rowland Hill (1795-1879), originator of penny postage. Issued in sheets of 8.

Max and Moritz, IYC Emblem — A35

IYC: Scenes from Max and Moritz, by Wilhelm Busch (1832-1908).

1979, Nov. 20 Photo. *Perf. 13x12½*

111 Sheet of 4 1.00
a. A35 12c shown .25
b. A35 12c Looking down chimney .25
c. A35 12c With stolen chickens .25
d. A35 12c Woman and dog, empty pan .25
112 Sheet of 4 1.00
a. A35 15c Sawing bridge .25
b. A35 15c Man falling into water .25
c. A35 15c Broken bridge .25
d. A35 15c Running away .25
113 Sheet of 4 1.00
a. A35 20c Baker .25
b. A35 20c Sneaking into bakery .25
c. A35 20c Falling into dough .25
d. A35 20c Baked into breads .25
Nos. 111-113 (3) 3.00

Sheets come with full labels at top and bottom showing text from stories or trimmed with text removed. Values of 3 sheets with full labels $11.

A36

Easter (15th Century Prayerbook Illustrations): 12c, Jesus Carrying the Cross. 20c, Crucifixion, by William Vreland. 35c, Descent from the Cross.

1980, Mar. 28 Photo. *Perf. 13x13½*

114 A36 12c multicolored .25 .25
115 A36 20c multicolored .25 .25
116 A36 35c multicolored .40 .40
a. Souvenir sheet of 3, #114-116 .75 .75
Nos. 114-116 (3) .90 .90

See Nos. B4-B6.

A37

1980, Sept. 17 Photo. *Perf. 13*

117 A37 $1 multicolored 1.10 1.10

Souvenir Sheet

118 A37 $2.50 multicolored 2.10 2.10

Queen Mother Elizabeth, 80th birthday.

A38

Platform diving: #119a, Falk Hoffman, DDR. #119b, Martina Jaschke.
Archery: #120a, Tomi Polkolainen. #120b, Kete Losaberidse.
Soccer: #121a, Czechoslovakia, gold. #121b, DDR, silver.
Running: #122a, Barbel Wockel. #122b, Pietro Mennea.

1980, Nov. 14 Photo. *Perf. 13½*

119 A38 10c Pair, #a.-b. .25 .25
120 A38 20c Pair, #a.-b. .45 .45
121 A38 30c Pair, #a.-b. .70 .70
122 A38 50c Pair, #a.-b. 1.10 1.10
Nos. 119-122 (4) 2.50 2.50

Souvenir Sheet

123 A38 Sheet of 8 2.50 2.50

22nd Summer Olympic Games, Moscow, July 19-Aug. 3.
No. 123 contains #119-122 with gold borders and white lettering at top and bottom.

A39

Christmas (15th Century Virgin and Child Paintings by): 20c, Virgin and Child, by Luis Dalmau. 35c, Serra brothers. 50c, Master of the Porciuncula.

1980, Dec. 5 Photo. *Perf. 13*

127 A39 20c multicolored .25 .25
128 A39 35c multicolored .30 .30
129 A39 50c multicolored .45 .45
a. Souvenir sheet of 3, #127-129 2.40 2.40
Nos. 127-129 (3) 1.00 1.00

See Nos. B7-B9.

A40

A41

Cutty Sark, 1869 A42

#160a, 165a, Amatasi. #160b, 165b, Ndrua. #160c, 165c, Waka. #160d, 165d, Tongiaki. #161a, 166a, Va'a teu'ua. #161b, 166b, Victoria, 1500. #161c, 166c, Golden Hinde, 1560. #161d, 166d, Boudeuse, 1760. #162a, 167a, Bounty, 1787. #162b, 167b, Astrolabe, 1811. #162c, 167c, Star of India, 1861. #162d, 167d, Great Rep., 1853. #163a, 168a, Balcutha, 1886. #163b, 168b, Coonatto, 1863. #163c, 168c, Antiope, 1866. #163d, 168d, Teaping, 1863. #164a, 169a, Preussen, 1902. #164b, 169b, Pamir, 1921. #164c, 169c, Cap Hornier, 1910. #164d, 169d, Patriarch, 1869.

1981 Photo. *Perf. 14*

160 A40 1c Block of 4, #a.-d. .30 .30
161 A40 3c Block of 4, #a.-d. .50 .50
162 A40 4c Block of 4, #a.-d. .65 .65
163 A40 6c Block of 4, #a.-d. 1.00 1.00
164 A40 10c Block of 4, #a.-d. 1.25 1.25

Perf. 13½x14½

165 A41 15c Block of 4, #a.-d. 1.40 1.40
166 A41 20c Block of 4, #a.-d. 1.60 1.60
167 A41 30c Block of 4, #a.-d. 2.75 2.75
168 A41 50c Block of 4, #a.-d. 4.50 4.50
169 A41 $1 Block of 4, #a.-d. 11.00 11.00

Perf. 13½

170 A42 $2 shown 5.00 5.00
171 A42 $4 Mermerus, 1872 10.00 10.00
172 A42 $6 Resolution, Discovery, 1776 17.00 17.00
Nos. 160-172 (13) 56.95 56.95

Issued: 1c-10c, Feb. 16; 15c-50c, Mar. 16; $1, May 15; $2, $4, June 26; $6, Sept. 21.
For surcharges and overprints see Nos. 241-243, 251, 254, 395, O35, O37, O39.

Christ with Crown of Thorns, by Titian — A44

Easter: 30c, Jesus at the Grove, by Paolo Veronese. 50c, Pieta, by Van Dyck

1981, Apr. 5 *Perf. 14*

173 A44 30c multicolored .40 .30
174 A44 40c multicolored .60 .45
175 A44 50c multicolored .75 .60
a. Souv. sheet, #173-175, perf 13½ 3.00 3.00
Nos. 173-175 (3) 1.75 1.35

See Nos. B10-B12.

A45

Designs: Portraits of Prince Charles.

1981, July 10 Photo. *Perf. 14*

176 A45 40c multicolored .25 .25
177 A45 50c multicolored .25 .25
178 A45 60c multicolored .25 .25
179 A45 70c multicolored .30 .30
180 A45 80c multicolored .35 .35
a. Souv. sheet of 5, #176-180+label 2.00 2.00
Nos. 176-180 (5) 1.40 1.40

Royal wedding. Nos. 176-180 each issued in sheets of 5 plus label showing couple.
For overprints and surcharges see Nos. 195-199, 244-245, 248, 299-300, B13-B18.

A46

Shirts: No. 181: a, Red. b, Striped. c, Blue. No. 182: a, Blue. b, Red. c, Striped. No. 183: a, Orange. b, Purple. c, Black

1981, Dec. 7 Photo. *Perf. 13*

181 A46 15c Strip of 3, #a.-c. 1.00 1.00
182 A46 35c Strip of 3, #a.-c. 1.75 1.75
183 A46 50c Strip of 3, #a.-c. 2.75 2.75
Nos. 181-183 (3) 5.50 5.50

1982 World Cup Soccer. See No. B19.

Christmas — A47

Dürer Engravings: 30c, Virgin on a Crescent, 1508. 40c, Virgin at the Fence, 1503. 50c, Holy Virgin and Child, 1505.

1981, Dec. 15 Photo. *Perf. 13x13½*

184 A47 30c multicolored .75 .75
185 A47 40c multicolored 1.25 1.25
186 A47 50c multicolored 1.50 1.50
a. Souvenir sheet of 3 3.25 3.25
Nos. 184-186 (3) 3.50 3.50

Souvenir Sheets

Perf. 14x13½

187 A47 70c + 5c like #184 1.10 1.10
188 A47 70c + 5c like #185 1.10 1.10
189 A47 70c + 5c like #186 1.10 1.10

No. 186a contains Nos. 184-186 each with 2c surcharge. Nos. 187-189 each contain one 25x40mm stamp. Surtaxes were for childrens' charities.

21st Birthday of Princess Diana — A48

Designs: Portraits of Diana.

1982, July 1 Photo. *Perf. 14*

190 A48 30c multicolored .75 .75
191 A48 50c multicolored 1.00 1.00
192 A48 70c multicolored 1.25 1.25
193 A48 80c multicolored 1.50 1.50
194 A48 $1.40 multicolored 3.25 3.25
a. Souv. sheet, #190-194 + label 7.75 7.75
Nos. 190-194 (5) 7.75 7.75

For new inscriptions, overprints and surcharges, see Nos. 200-204, 246-247, 249-250, 301-302.

Nos. 176-180a Overprinted

1982, July 30

195 A45 40c multicolored .45 .45
196 A45 50c multicolored .60 .60
197 A45 60c multicolored .65 .65
198 A45 70c multicolored .75 .75
199 A45 80c multicolored .80 .80
a. Souv. sheet, #195-199 + label 6.00 6.00
Nos. 195-199 (5) 3.25 3.25

Nos. 190-194a Inscribed in Silver

1982 Photo. *Perf. 14*

200 A48 30c Pair, #a.-b. .70 .70
201 A48 50c Pair, #a.-b. .90 .90
202 A48 70c Pair, #a.-b. 1.60 1.60
203 A48 80c Pair, #a.-b. 1.75 1.75
204 A48 $1.40 Pair, #a.-b. 3.00 3.00
c. Souv. sheet, #200a, 201a, 202a, 203a, 204a + label 6.50 6.50
Nos. 200-204 (5) 7.95 7.95

Miniature sheets of each denomination were issued containing 2 "21 JUNE 1982...," 3 "COMMEMORATING...," and a label. Value, set of 5 sheets, $21.

Se-tenant pairs come with or without label.

For surcharges see Nos. 247, 250, 253.

A49

Christmas — Virgin and Child Paintings: 35c, Joos Van Cleve (1485-1540). 48c, Filippino Lippi (1457-1504). 60c, Cima Da Conegliano (1459-1517).

1982, Dec. 10 Photo. *Perf. 14*

205 A49 35c multicolored .50 .50
206 A49 48c multicolored .70 .70
207 A49 60c multicolored .80 .80
a. Souvenir sheet of 3 3.00 3.00
Nos. 205-207 (3) 2.00 2.00

Souvenir Sheets

208 A49 70c + 5c like 35c 1.60 1.60
209 A49 70c + 5c like 48c 1.60 1.60
210 A49 70c + 5c like 60c 1.60 1.60

Nos. 205-207 were printed in sheets of five plus label. No. 207a contains Nos. 205-207 each with 2c surcharge. Nos. 208-210 each contain one stamp, perf. 13½. Surtaxes were for childrens' charities.

A50

#a, Red coral. #b, Aerial view. #c, Eleanor Roosevelt, grass skirt. #d, Map.

1983, Mar. 14 *Perf. 13½x13*

211 A50 60c Block of 4, #a.-d. 2.25 2.25

Commonwealth day.

For surcharges see No. O27-O30.

Scouting Year A51

Emblem and various tropical flowers.

1983, Apr. 5 *Perf. 13½x14½*

215 A51 36c multicolored 1.75 .75
216 A51 48c multicolored 2.25 1.00
217 A51 60c multicolored 2.50 1.25
Nos. 215-217 (3) 6.50 3.00

Souvenir Sheet

218 A51 $2 multicolored 3.50 3.50

Nos. 215-218 Overprinted: "XV / WORLD JAMBOREE / CANADA / 1983"

1983, July 8 Photo. *Perf. 13½x14½*

219 A51 36c multicolored 1.60 .65
220 A51 48c multicolored 2.10 1.25
221 A51 60c multicolored 2.50 1.25
Nos. 219-221 (3) 6.20 3.15

Souvenir Sheet

222 A51 $2 multicolored 3.50 3.50

15th World Boy Scout Jamboree.

Save the Whales Campaign A52

Various whale hunting scenes.

1983, July 29 Photo. *Perf. 13*

223 A52 8c multicolored .80 .70
224 A52 15c multicolored 1.20 1.00
225 A52 35c multicolored 2.40 1.40
226 A52 60c multicolored 3.75 2.00
227 A52 $1 multicolored 5.75 2.75
Nos. 223-227 (5) 13.90 7.85

World Communications Year — A53

Designs: Cable laying Vessels.

1983, Sept. Photo. *Perf. 13*

228 A53 36c multicolored 1.00 .50
229 A53 48c multicolored 1.25 .70
230 A53 60c multicolored 1.50 .90
Nos. 228-230 (3) 3.75 2.10

Souvenir Sheet

231 Sheet of 3 2.75 2.75
a. A53 36c + 3c like No. 228 .65 .65
b. A53 48c + 3c like No. 229 .85 .85
c. A53 60c + 3c like No. 230 1.00 1.00

Surtax was for local charities.

Nos. 164, 166-167, 170, 172, 178-180, 192-194, 202-204 Surcharged

Blocks of 4, #a.-d. (#241-243)
Pairs, #a.-b. (#247, 250, 253)

Perf. 14, 13½x14½, 13½

1983 Photo.

241 A40 18c on 10c #164 4.00 4.00
242 A41 36c on 20c #166 5.00 5.00
243 A41 36c on 30c #167 5.00 5.00
244 A45 48c on 60c multi 1.25 1.25
245 A45 72c on 70c multi 1.75 1.75
246 A48 72c on 70c #192 1.75 1.75
247 A48 72c on 70c #202 4.00 3.75
248 A45 96c on 80c multi 3.50 2.25
249 A48 96c on 80c #193 3.75 2.25
250 A48 96c on 80c #203 4.75 4.00
251 A42 $1.20 on $2 multi 5.00 3.00
252 A48 $1.20 on $1.40 #194 4.00 3.00
253 A48 $1.20 on $1.40 #204 7.00 5.00
254 A42 $5.60 on $6 multi 21.00 15.00
Nos. 241-254 (14) 71.75 57.00

Issued: #241-243, 245, 251, Sept. 26; #244, 246, 249, 252, 254, Oct. 28; others Dec. 1.

First Manned Balloon Flight, 200th Anniv. — A54

Designs: 36c, Airship, Sir George Cayley (1773-1857). 48c, Man-powered airship, Dupuy de Lome (1818-1885). 60c, Brazilian Aviation Pioneer, Alberto Santos Dumont (1873-1932). 96c, Practical Airship, Paul Lebaudy (1858-1937). $1.32, L-Z 127 Graf Zeppelin.

1983, Oct. 31 Litho. *Perf. 13*

255 A54 36c multicolored 1.00 1.00
256 A54 48c multicolored 1.50 1.50
257 A54 60c multicolored 1.75 1.75
258 A54 96c multicolored 2.25 2.25
259 A54 $1.32 multicolored 3.50 3.50
a. Souvenir sheet of 5, #255-259 9.00 9.00
Nos. 255-259 (5) 10.00 10.00

Nos. 255-259 se-tenant with labels. Sheets of 5 for each value exist.

Nos. 255-259 are misspelled "ISLANS." For correcting overprints see Nos. 287-291.

Christmas A55

Raphael Paintings: 36c, Madonna in the Meadow. 42c, Tempi Madonna. 48c, Small Cowper Madonna. 60c, Madonna Della Tenda.

1983, Nov. 30 Photo. *Perf. 13x13½*

260 A55 36c multicolored .75 .45
261 A55 42c multicolored 1.00 .55
262 A55 48c multicolored 1.25 .60
263 A55 60c multicolored 1.50 .80
a. Souvenir sheet of 4 4.50 4.50
Nos. 260-263 (4) 4.50 2.40

Souvenir Sheets

Perf. 13½

264 A55 75c + 5c like #260 1.20 1.20
265 A55 75c + 5c like #261 1.20 1.20
266 A55 75c + 5c like #262 1.20 1.20
267 A55 75c + 5c like #263 1.20 1.20

No. 263a contains Nos. 260-263 each with 3c surcharge. Nos. 264-267 each contain one 29x41mm stamp. Issued Dec. 28. Surtaxes were for children's charities.

Waka Canoe — A56

4c, Amatasi fishing boat. 5c, Ndrua canoe. 8c, Tongiaki canoe. 10c, Victoria, 1500. 18c, Golden Hind, 1560. 20c, Boudeuse, 1760. 30c, Bounty, 1787. 36c, Astrolabe, 1811. 48c, Great Republic, 1853. 50c, Star of India, 1861. 60c, Coonatto, 1863. 72c, Antiope, 1866. 80c, Balcutha, 1886. 96c, Cap Hornier, 1910. $1.20, Pamir, 1921. $3, Mermerus, 1872. $5, Cutty Sark, 1869. $9.60, Resolution, Discovery.

1984 Photo. *Perf. 14½*

268 A56 2c multicolored .25 .25
269 A56 4c multicolored .25 .25
270 A56 5c multicolored .25 .25
271 A56 8c multicolored .25 .25
272 A56 10c multicolored .40 .40
273 A56 18c multicolored 1.00 .55
274 A56 20c multicolored .65 .65
275 A56 30c multicolored 1.25 .90
276 A56 36c multicolored 1.10 1.10
277 A56 48c multicolored 1.50 1.50
278 A56 50c multicolored 1.60 1.60
279 A56 60c multicolored 1.75 1.75
280 A56 72c multicolored 2.25 2.25
281 A56 80c multicolored 2.50 2.50
282 A56 96c multicolored 3.25 3.25
283 A56 $1.20 multicolored 1.60 1.60

Perf. 13

Size: 42x34mm

284 A56 $3 multicolored 6.25 6.25
285 A56 $5 multicolored 10.00 10.00
286 A56 $9.60 multicolored 20.00 20.00
Nos. 268-286 (19) 56.10 55.30

Issue dates: Nos. 268-277, Feb. 8. Nos. 278-283, Mar. 23. Nos. 284-286 June 15.

For overprints and surcharges see Nos. O16-O26, O31-O34, O36, O38, O40.

Nos. 255-259a Overprinted

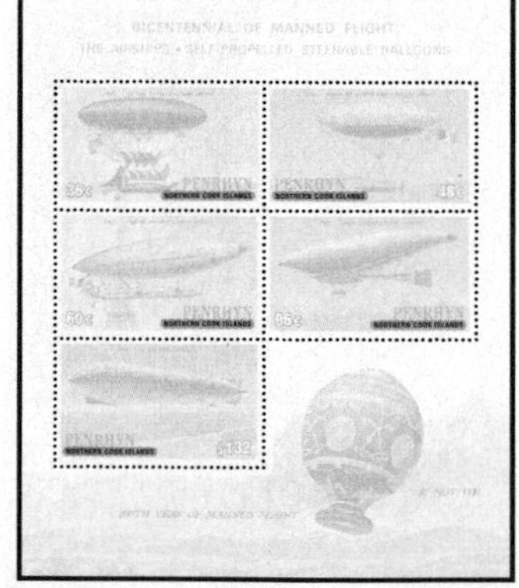

1984 Litho. *Perf. 13*

287 A54 36c multicolored .85 .85
288 A54 48c multicolored 1.10 1.10
289 A54 60c multicolored 1.40 1.40
290 A54 96c multicolored 2.25 2.25
291 A54 $1.32 multicolored 3.00 3.00
a. Souvenir sheet of 5, #287-291 7.50 8.75
Nos. 287-291 (5) 8.60 8.60

1984 Los Angeles Summer Olympic Games A57

35c, Olympic flag. 60c, Torch, flags. $1.80, Classic runners, Memorial Coliseum.

1984, July 20 Photo. *Perf. 13½x13*

292 A57 35c multicolored .45 .45
293 A57 60c multicolored .80 .80
294 A57 $1.80 multicolored 2.00 2.00
Nos. 292-294 (3) 3.25 3.25

Souvenir Sheet

295 Sheet of 3 + label 3.00 3.00
a. A57 35c + 5c like #292 .35 .35
b. A57 60c + 5c like #293 .50 .50
c. A57 $1.80 + 5c like #294 1.75 1.75

Surtax for amateur sports.

AUSIPEX '84 — A57a

60c, Nos. 161c, 107b, 180, 104b. $1.20, Map of South Pacific.

1984, Sept. 20

296 A57a 60c multicolored .85 .85
297 A57a $1.20 multicolored 1.75 1.75

Souvenir Sheet

298 Sheet of 2 3.00 3.00
a. A57a 96c like #296 1.50 1.50
b. A57a 96c like #297 1.50 1.50

For surcharge see No. 345.

Nos. 176-177, 190-191 Ovptd. "Birth of/Prince Henry/15 Sept. 1984" and Surcharged in Black or Gold

1984, Oct. 18 *Perf. 14*

299 A45 $2 on 40c 1.75 1.75
300 A45 $2 on 50c 1.75 1.75
301 A48 $2 on 30c 1.75 1.75
302 A48 $2 on 50c 1.75 1.75
Nos. 299-302 (4) 7.00 7.00

Nos. 209-302 printed in sheets of 5 plus one label each picturing a portrait of the royal couple or an heraldic griffin.

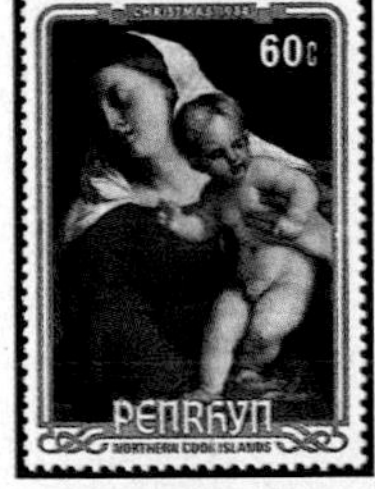

Christmas 1984 — A58

Paintings: 36c, Virgin and Child, by Giovanni Bellini. 48c, Virgin and Child, by Lorenzo di Credi. 60c, Virgin and Child, by Palma, the Older. 96c, Virgin and Child, by Raphael.

1984, Nov. 15 Photo. *Perf. 13x13½*

303 A58 36c multicolored .55 .55
304 A58 48c multicolored .90 .90
305 A58 60c multicolored 1.00 1.00
306 A58 96c multicolored 1.75 1.75
a. Souvenir sheet of 4 4.25 4.25
Nos. 303-306 (4) 4.20 4.20

Souvenir Sheets

307 A58 96c + 10c like #303 1.60 1.60
308 A58 96c + 10c like #304 1.60 1.60
309 A58 96c + 10c like #305 1.60 1.60
310 A58 96c + 10c like #306 1.60 1.60

No. 306a contains Nos. 303-306, each with 5c surcharge. Nos. 307-310 issued Dec. 10. Surtax for children's charities.

Audubon Bicentenary — A59

1985, Apr. 9 Photo. *Perf. 13*

311 A59 20c Harlequin duck 1.50 1.50
312 A59 55c Sage grouse 4.00 4.00
313 A59 65c Solitary sandpiper 4.75 4.75
314 A59 75c Red-backed sandpiper 5.25 5.25
Nos. 311-314 (4) 15.50 15.50

Souvenir Sheets

Perf. 13½x13

315 A59 95c Like #311 3.00 2.00
316 A59 95c Like #312 3.00 2.00
317 A59 95c Like #313 3.00 2.00
318 A59 95c Like #314 3.00 2.00

For surcharges see Nos. 391-394.

Queen Mother, 85th Birthday — A60

75c, Photograph, 1921. 95c, New mother, 1926. $1.20, Coronation day, 1937. $2.80, 70th birthday.
$5, Portrait, c. 1980.

1985, June 24 Photo. *Perf. 13x13½*

319 A60 75c multicolored .55 *.65*
320 A60 95c multicolored .70 *.80*
321 A60 $1.20 multicolored 1.00 *1.00*
322 A60 $2.80 multicolored 2.25 *2.50*
a. Souvenir sheet of 4, #319-322 15.00 15.00
Nos. 319-322 (4) 4.50 *4.95*

Souvenir Sheet

323 A60 $5 multicolored 3.75 3.75

No. 322a issued on 8/4/86, for 86th birthday.

Intl. Youth Year — A61

Grimm Brothers' fairy tales: 75c, House in the Wood. 95c, Snow White and Rose Red. $1.15, Goose Girl.

1985, Sept. 10 *Perf. 13x13½*

324 A61 75c multicolored 2.25 2.25
325 A61 95c multicolored 3.25 3.25
326 A61 $1.15 multicolored 4.50 4.50
Nos. 324-326 (3) 10.00 10.00

Christmas 1985 A62

Paintings (details) by Murillo: 75c, No. 330a, The Annunciation. $1.15, No. 330b, Adoration of the Shepherds. $1.80, No. 330c, The Holy Family.

1985, Nov. 25 Photo. *Perf. 14*

327 A62 75c multicolored 1.50 1.50
328 A62 $1.15 multicolored 2.25 2.25
329 A62 $1.80 multicolored 3.75 3.75
Nos. 327-329 (3) 7.50 7.50

Souvenir Sheets

Perf. 13½

330 Sheet of 3 4.25 4.25
a.-c. A62 95c any single 1.30 1.30
331 A62 $1.20 like #327 1.75 1.75
332 A62 $1.45 like #328 2.00 2.00
333 A62 $2.75 like #329 3.25 3.25

Halley's Comet — A63

Fire and Ice, by Camille Rendal. Nos. 334-335 se-tenant in continuous design.

1986, Feb. 4 *Perf. 13½x13*

334 A63 $1.50 Comet head 3.50 3.50
335 A63 $1.50 Comet tail 3.50 3.50
a. Pair, #334-335 7.00 7.00

Size: 109x43mm

Imperf

336 A63 $3 multicolored 6.00 6.00
Nos. 334-336 (3) 13.00 13.00

Elizabeth II, 60th Birthday A64

1986, Apr. 21 *Perf. 14*

337 A64 95c Age 3 1.25 1.25
338 A64 $1.45 Wearing crown 1.60 1.60

Size: 60x34mm

Perf. 13½x13

339 A64 $2.50 Both portraits 2.75 2.75
Nos. 337-339 (3) 5.60 5.60

A65

Statue of Liberty, Cent.: 95c, Statue, scaffolding. $1.75 Removing copper facade. $3, Restored statue on Liberty Island.

1986, June 27 Photo. *Perf. 13½*

340 A65 95c multicolored .85 .85
341 A65 $1.75 multicolored 1.75 1.75
342 A65 $3 multicolored 3.00 3.00
Nos. 340-342 (3) 5.60 5.60

A66

1986, July 23 *Perf. 13x13½*

343 A66 $2.50 Portraits 3.00 3.00
344 A66 $3.50 Profiles 3.75 3.75

Wedding of Prince Andrew and Sarah Ferguson. Nos. 343-344 each printed in sheets of 4 plus 2 center decorative labels.

No. 298 Surcharged with Gold Circle, Bar, New Value in Black and Exhibition Emblem in Gold and Black

1986, Aug. 4

345 Sheet of 2 8.75 8.75
a. A57a $2 on 96c #298a 4.25 4.25
b. A57a $2 on 96c #298b 4.25 4.25

STAMPEX '86, Adelaide, Aug. 4-10.

Christmas A67

Engravings by Rembrandt: 65c, No. 349a, Adoration of the Shepherds. $1.75, No. 349b, Virgin and Child. $2.50, No. 349c, The Holy Family.

1986, Nov. 20 Litho. *Perf. 13x13½*

346 A67 65c multicolored 2.50 2.50
347 A67 $1.75 multicolored 3.50 3.50
348 A67 $2.50 multicolored 5.00 5.00
Nos. 346-348 (3) 11.00 11.00

Souvenir Sheet

Perf. 13½x13

349 Sheet of 3 13.00 13.00
a.-c. A67 $1.50 any single 4.00 4.00

Corrected inscription is black on silver.
For surcharges see Nos. B20-B23.

Souvenir Sheets

Statue of Liberty, Cent. — A68

Photographs: No. 350a, Workmen, crown. No. 350b, Ellis Is., aerial view. No. 350c, Immigration building, Ellis Is. No. 350d, Buildings, opposite side of Ellis Is. No. 350e, Workmen inside torch structure. No. 351a, Liberty's head and torch. No. 351b, Torch. No. 351c, Workmen on scaffold. No. 351d, Statue, full figure. No. 351e, Workmen beside statue. Nos. 351a-351e vert.

1987, Apr. 15 Litho. *Perf. 14*

350 A68 Sheet of 5 + label 5.75 5.75
a.-e. 65c any single 1.05 1.05
351 A68 Sheet of 5 + label 5.75 5.75
a.-e. 65c any single 1.05 1.05

Nos. 62-63 Ovptd. "Fortieth Royal Wedding / Anniversary 1947-87" in Lilac Rose

1987, Nov. 20 Photo. *Perf. 13½x14*

352 A18 $2 multicolored 2.00 2.00
353 A18 $5 multicolored 5.50 5.50

Christmas A69

Paintings (details) by Raphael: 95c, No. 357a, The Garvagh Madonna, the National Gallery, London. $1.60, No. 357b, The Alba Madonna, the National Gallery of Art, Washington. $2.25, No. 357c, $4.80, The Madonna of the Fish, Prado Museum, Madrid.

1987, Dec. 11 Photo. *Perf. 13½*

354 A69 95c multicolored 2.40 2.40
355 A69 $1.60 multicolored 3.00 3.00
356 A69 $2.25 multicolored 4.75 4.75
Nos. 354-356 (3) 10.15 10.15

Souvenir Sheets

357 Sheet of 3 + label 16.00 16.00
a.-c. A69 $1.15 any single 4.75 4.75
358 A69 $4.80 multicolored 16.00 16.00

No. 358 contains one 31x39mm stamp.

1988 Summer Olympics, Seoul — A70

Events and: 55c, $1.25, Seoul Games emblem. 95c, Obverse of a $50 silver coin issued in 1987 to commemorate the participation of Cook Islands athletes in the Olympics for the 1st time. $1.50, Coin reverse.

Perf. 13½x13, 13x13½

1988, July 29 **Photo.**
359 A70 55c Running 1.20 1.20
360 A70 95c High jump, vert. 2.40 2.40
361 A70 $1.25 Shot put 2.75 2.75
362 A70 $1.50 Tennis, vert. 4.50 4.50
Nos. 359-362 (4) 10.85 10.85

Souvenir Sheet

363 Sheet of 2 10.00 10.00
a. A70 $2.50 like 95c 4.75 4.75
b. A70 $2.50 like $1.50 4.75 4.75

Nos. 359-363 Ovptd. for Olympic Gold Medalists

a. "CARL LEWIS / UNITED STATES / 100 METERS"
b. "LOUISE RITTER / UNITED STATES / HIGH JUMP"
c. "ULF TIMMERMANN / EAST GERMANY / SHOT-PUT"
d. "STEFFI GRAF / WEST GERMANY / WOMEN'S TENNIS"
e. "JACKIE / JOYNER-KERSEE / United States / Heptathlon"
f. "STEFFI GRAF / West Germany / Women's Tennis / MILOSLAV MECIR / Czechoslovakia / Men's Tennis"

Perf. 13½x13, 13x13½

1988, Oct. 14 **Photo.**
364 A70(a) 55c on No. 359 1.20 1.20
365 A70(b) 95c on No. 360 2.40 2.40
366 A70(c) $1.25 on No. 361 2.75 2.75
367 A70(d) $1.50 on No. 362 4.50 4.50
Nos. 364-367 (4) 10.85 10.85

Souvenir Sheet

368 Sheet of 2 10.00 10.00
a. A70(e) $2.50 on No. 363a 4.75 4.75
b. A70(f) $2.50 on No. 363b 4.75 4.75

Christmas A71

Virgin and Child paintings by Titian.

1988, Nov. 9 *Perf. 13x13½*
369 A71 70c multicolored 1.40 1.40
370 A71 85c multi, diff. 1.75 1.75
371 A71 95c multi, diff. 2.25 2.25
372 A71 $1.25 multi, diff. 2.50 2.50
Nos. 369-372 (4) 7.90 7.90

Souvenir Sheet

Perf. 13

373 A71 $6.40 multi, diff. 10.00 10.00

No. 373 contains one diamond-shaped stamp, size: 55x55mm.

1st Moon Landing, 20th Anniv. A72

Apollo 11 mission emblem, US flag and: 55c, First step on the Moon. 75c, Astronaut carrying equipment. 95c, Conducting experiment. $1.25, Crew members Armstrong, Collins and Aldrin. $1.75, Armstrong and Aldrin aboard lunar module.

1989, July 24 **Photo.** *Perf. 14*
374-378 A72 Set of 5 12.00 12.00

Christmas A73

Details from *The Nativity*, by Albrecht Durer, 1498, center panel of the Paumgartner altarpiece: 55c, Madonna. 70c, Christ child, cherubs. 85c, Joseph. $1.25, Attendants. $6.40, Entire painting.

1989, Nov. 17 **Photo.** *Perf. 13x13½*
379-382 A73 Set of 4 6.25 6.25

Souvenir Sheet

383 A73 $6.40 multicolored 10.00 10.00

No. 383 contains one 31x50mm stamp.

Queen Mother, 90th Birthday — A74

1990, July 24 **Photo.** *Perf. 13½*
384 A74 $2.25 multicolored 3.50 3.50

Souvenir Sheet

385 A74 $7.50 multicolored 17.00 17.00

Christmas — A75

Paintings: 55c, Adoration of the Magi by Veronese. 70c, Virgin and Child by Quentin Metsys. 85c, Virgin and Child Jesus by Van Der Goes. $1.50, Adoration of the Kings by Jan Gossaert. $6.40, Virgin and Child with Saints Francis, John the Baptist, Zenobius and Lucy by Domenico Veneziano.

1990, Nov. 26 **Litho.** *Perf. 14*
386-389 A75 Set of 4 9.50 9.50

Souvenir Sheet

390 A75 $6.40 multicolored 11.00 11.00

Nos. 311-314 Surcharged in Red or Black

1990, Dec. 5 **Photo.** *Perf. 13*
391 A59 $1.50 on 20c (R) 2.75 2.75
392 A59 $1.50 on 55c 2.75 2.75
393 A59 $1.50 on 65c 2.75 2.75
394 A59 $1.50 on 75c (R) 2.75 2.75
Nos. 391-394 (4) 11.00 11.00

Birdpex '90, 20th Intl. Ornithological Cong., New Zealand. Surcharge appears in various locations.

No. 172 Overprinted "COMMEMORATING 65th BIRTHDAY OF H.M. QUEEN ELIZABETH II"

1991, Apr. 22 **Photo.** *Perf. 13½*
395 A42 $6 multicolored 13.00 13.00

Christmas A76

Paintings: 55c, Virgin and Child with Saints, by Gerard David. 85c, The Nativity, by Tintoretto. $1.15, Mystic Nativity, by Botticelli. $1.85, Adoration of the Shepherds, by Murillo. $6.40, Madonna of the Chair, by Raphael.

1991, Nov. 11 **Litho.** *Perf. 14*
396-399 A76 Set of 4 9.25 9.25

Souvenir Sheet

400 A76 $6.40 multicolored 16.00 16.00

1992 Summer Olympics, Barcelona — A77

1992, July 27 **Litho.** *Perf. 14*
401 A77 75c Runners 2.25 2.25
402 A77 95c Boxing 2.60 2.60
403 A77 $1.15 Swimming 3.00 3.00
404 A77 $1.50 Wrestling 3.25 3.25
Nos. 401-404 (4) 11.10 11.10

6th Festival of Pacific Arts, Rarotonga — A78

Festival poster and: $1.15, Marquesan canoe. $1.75, Statue of Tangaroa. $1.95, Manihiki canoe.

1992, Oct. 16 **Litho.** *Perf. 14x15*
405 A78 $1.15 multicolored 2.75 2.75
406 A78 $1.75 multicolored 3.25 3.25
407 A78 $1.95 multicolored 3.75 3.75
Nos. 405-407 (3) 9.75 9.75

For overprints see Nos. 455-457.

Overprinted "ROYAL VISIT"

1992, Oct. 16
408 A78 $1.15 on #405 3.00 3.00
409 A78 $1.75 on #406 3.75 3.75
410 A78 $1.95 on #407 4.25 4.25
Nos. 408-410 (3) 11.00 11.00

Christmas A79

Paintings by Ambrogio Bergognone: 55c, $6.40, Virgin with Child and Saints. 85c, Virgin on Throne. $1.05, Virgin on Carpet. $1.85, Virgin of the Milk.

1992, Nov. 18 **Litho.** *Perf. 13½*
411-414 A79 Set of 4 8.25 8.25

Souvenir Sheet

415 A79 $6.40 multicolored 11.50 11.50

No. 415 contains one 38x48mm stamp.

Discovery of America, 500th Anniv. — A80

Designs: $1.15, Vicente Yanez Pinzon, Nina. $1.35, Martin Alonso Pinzon, Pinta. $1.75, Columbus, Santa Maria.

1992, Dec. 4 *Perf. 15x14*
416 A80 $1.15 multicolored 2.75 2.75
417 A80 $1.35 multicolored 3.00 3.00
418 A80 $1.75 multicolored 4.25 4.25
Nos. 416-418 (3) 10.00 10.00

Coronation of Queen Elizabeth II, 40th Anniv. — A81

1993, June 4 **Litho.** *Perf. 14x14½*
419 A81 $6 multicolored 9.50 9.50

Marine Life — A82

Marine Life — A82a

5c, Helmet shell. 10c, Daisy coral. 15c, Hydroid coral. 20c, Feather star. 25c, Sea star. 30c, Nudibranch. 50c, Smooth sea star. 70c, Black pearl oyster. 80c, Pyjama nudibranch. 85c, Prickly sea cucumber. 90c, Organ pipe coral. $1, Aeolid nudibranch. $2, Textile cone shell.

1993-98 **Litho.** *Perf. 14*
420 A82 5c multi .25 .25
421 A82 10c multi .25 .25
422 A82 15c multi .25 .25
423 A82 20c multi .25 .25
424 A82 25c multi .30 .30
425 A82 30c multi .35 .35
426 A82 50c multi .55 .55
427 A82 70c multi .85 .80
428 A82 80c multi .95 .90
429 A82 85c multi 1.05 .95
430 A82 90c multi 1.05 1.00
431 A82 $1 multi 1.25 1.10
432 A82 $2 multi 3.50 2.25
433 A82a $3 pink & multi 5.00 3.25
434 A82a $5 lilac & multi 8.50 5.50

Perf. 14x13½

435 A82a $8 blue & multi 12.00 11.00
435A A82a $10 grn & multi 13.00 12.00
Nos. 420-435A (17) 49.35 40.95

For overprints see #O41-O53.

Issued: 80c, 85c, 90c, $1, $2, 12/3/93; $3, $5, 11/21/94; $8, 11/17/97; $10, 10/1/98; others, 10/18/93.

Christmas — A83

Details from Virgin on Throne with Child, by Cosimo Tura: 55c, Madonna and Child. 85c, Musicians. $1.05, Musicians, diff. $1.95, Woman. $4.50, Entire painting.

1993, Nov. 2 Litho. *Perf. 14*

436	A83	55c multicolored	1.40	1.40
437	A83	85c multicolored	2.10	2.10
438	A83	$1.05 multicolored	2.50	2.50
439	A83	$1.95 multicolored	3.75	3.75

Size: 32x47mm

Perf. 13½

440	A83	$4.50 multicolored	6.25	6.25
		Nos. 436-440 (5)	16.00	16.00

First Manned Moon Landing, 25th Anniv. A84

1994, July 20 Litho. *Perf. 14*

441 A84 $3.25 multicolored 10.00 10.00

Christmas — A85

Details or entire paintings: No. 442a, Virgin and Child with Saints Paul & Jerome, by Vivarini. b, The Virgin and Child with St. John, by B. Luini. c, The Virgin and Child with Saints Jerome & Dominic, by F. Lippi. d, Adoration of Shepherds, by Murillo.

No. 443a, Adoration of the Kings, by Reni. b, Madonna & Child with the Infant Baptist, by Raphael. c, Adoration of the Kings, by Reni, diff. d, Virgin and Child, by Bergognone.

1994, Nov. 30 Litho. *Perf. 14*

442	A85	90c Block of 4, #a.-d.	5.75	5.75
443	A85	$1 Block of 4, #a.-d.	6.25	6.25

End of World War II, 50th Anniv. — A86

Designs: a, Battleships on fire, Pearl Harbor, Dec. 7, 1941. b, B-29 bomber Enola Gay, A-bomb cloud, Aug. 1945.

1995, Sept. 4 Litho. *Perf. 13*

444 A86 $3.75 Pair, #a.-b. 22.00 22.00

Queen Mother, 95th Birthday A87

1995, Sept. 14 Litho. *Perf. 13½*

445 A87 $4.50 multicolored 12.00 12.00

No. 445 was issued in sheets of 4.

UN, 50th Anniv. — A88

1995, Oct. 20 Litho. *Perf. 13½*

446 A88 $4 multicolored 5.75 5.75

No. 446 was issued in sheets of 4.

1995, Year of the Sea Turtle — A89

No. 447: a, Loggerhead. b, Hawksbill.
No. 448: a, Olive ridley. b, Green.

1995, Dec. 7 Litho. *Perf. 13½*

447	A89	$1.15 Pair, #a.-b.	4.75	4.75
448	A89	$1.65 Pair, #a.-b.	7.25	7.25

Queen Elizabeth II, 70th Birthday A90

1996, June 20 Litho. *Perf. 14*

449 A90 $4.25 multicolored 7.50 7.50

No. 449 was issued in sheets of 4.

1996 Summer Olympic Games, Atlanta A91

1996, July 12 Litho. *Perf. 14*

450 A91 $5 multicolored 10.00 10.00

Queen Elizabeth II and Prince Philip, 50th Wedding Anniv. A92

1997, Nov. 20 Litho. *Perf. 14*

451 A92 $3 multicolored 4.50 4.50

Souvenir Sheet

452 A92 $4 multicolored 5.50 5.50

No. 452 is a continuous design.

Diana, Princess of Wales (1961-97) — A93

1998, May 7 Litho. *Perf. 14*

453 A93 $1.50 multicolored 3.00 3.00

Souvenir Sheet

454 A93 $3.75 like #453 6.00 6.00

No. 453 was issued in sheets of 5 + label. For surcharge see #B24.

Nos. 405-407 Ovptd. "KIA ORANA / THIRD MILLENNIUM"

Methods and Perfs as before

1999, Dec. 31

455	A78	$1.15 multi	1.30	1.30
456	A78	$1.75 multi	2.10	2.10
457	A78	$1.95 multi	2.60	2.60
		Nos. 455-457 (3)	6.00	6.00

Queen Mother, 100th Birthday — A94

No. 458: a, With King George VI. b, With Princess Elizabeth. c, With King George VI, Princesses Elizabeth and Margaret. d, With Princesses.

2000, Oct. 20 Litho. *Perf. 14*

458 A94 $2.50 Sheet of 4, #a-d 11.00 11.00

Souvenir Sheet

459 A94 $10 Portrait 11.00 11.00

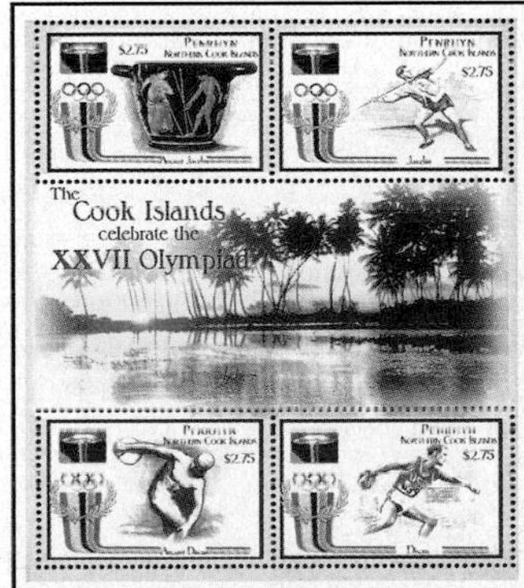

2000 Summer Olympics, Sydney — A95

No. 460, horiz.: a, Ancient javelin. b, Javelin. c, Ancient discus. d, Discus.

2000, Dec. 14

460 A95 $2.75 Sheet of 4, #a-d 11.50 11.50

Souvenir Sheet

461 A95 $3.50 Torch relay 5.00 5.00

Worldwide Fund for Nature (WWF) A96

Various photos of ocean sunfish: 80c, 90c, $1.15, $1.05.

2003, Feb. 24

462-465 A96 Set of 4 6.50 6.50

Each printed in sheets of 4.

United We Stand — A97

2003, Sept. 30

466 A97 $1.50 multi 2.00 2.00

Printed in sheets of 4.

Pope John Paul II (1920-2005) A98

2005, Nov. 11

467 A98 $1.45 multi 2.75 2.75

Printed in sheets of 5 + label.

Worldwide Fund for Nature (WWF) — A99

Pacific reef egret: 80c, Male and female. 90c, Bird at water's edge. $1.15, Bird in flight. $1.95, Adult and chicks.

2008, Oct. 16 *Perf. 13½*

468-471 A99 Set of 4 5.75 5.75

Nos. 468-471 each were printed in sheets of 4.

Worldwide Fund for Nature — A100

Striped dolphin: 80c, Breaching. 90c Pair underwater. $1.10, Breaching, diff. $1.20, Pod breaching.

2010, Dec. 9 *Perf. 14*

472-475 A100	Set of 4	6.00	6.00

Nos. 472-475 each were printed in sheets of 4.

A101

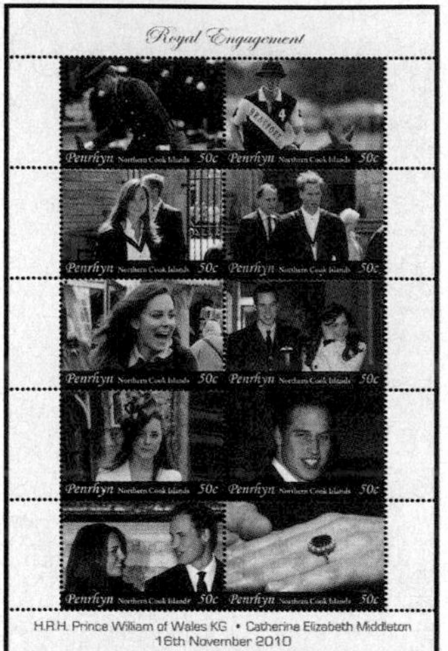

Engagement of Prince William and Catherine Middleton — A102

Designs: Nos. 476, 479a, 481, Prince. Nos. 477, 479b, 482, Middleton.

No. 478: a, Prince in military uniform. b, Prince playing polo. c, Middleton, fence. d, Prince, man and woman in background. e, Middleton, woman in background. f, Couple, Prince at left. g, Middleton with black hat. h, Prince. i, Couple, Middleton at left. j, Hands of couple, engagement ring.

$8.10, Couple, Prince in uniform at left.

2011, Jan. 14 *Perf. 14*

476 A101	$2 multi	3.25	3.25
477 A101	$2 multi	3.25	3.25

Miniature Sheets

478 A102	50c Sheet of 10, #a-j	7.75	7.75

Perf. 13¾x13½

479 A101	$2 Sheet of 2, #a-b	6.25	6.25

Souvenir Sheets

Perf. 14¼

480 A101	$8.10 multi	12.50	12.50
481 A101	$11 multi	17.00	17.00
482 A101	$11 multi	17.00	17.00
	Nos. 480-482 (3)	46.50	46.50

No. 479 contains two 28x44mm stamps. Nos. 480-482 each contain one 38x50mm stamp.

A103

Peonies — A104

2011, Apr. 8 **Litho.** *Perf. 13¼*

483 A103	$1.10 multi	1.75	1.75

Souvenir Sheet

Perf. 14¾x14

484 A104	$7.20 multi	11.50	11.50

Miniature Sheets

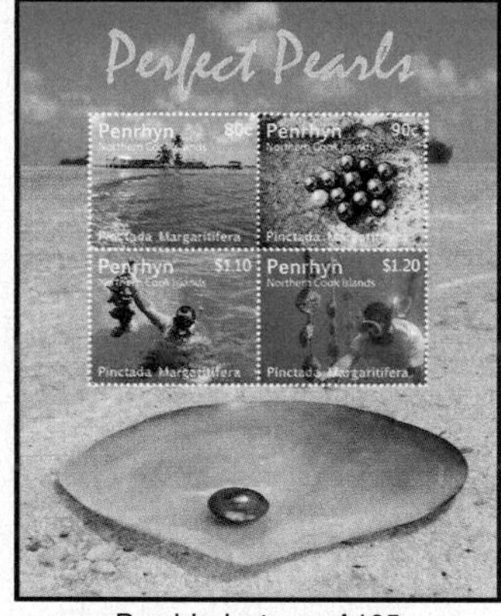

Pearl Industry — A105

No. 485 — Inscription "Pinctada Margaritifera" and: a, 80c, Buildings near shore. b, 90c, Pearls. c, $1.10, Diver at surface holding string of oysters. d, $1.20, Diver tending string of oysters underwater.

No. 486 — Inscription "Pearl Industry" and: a, 20c, Shark. b, 30c, Diver at surface. c, 50c, Pearls, diff. d, $1, Pearl in tongs. e, $2, Pearl oysters.

2011, May 5 *Perf. 13¾*

485 A105	Sheet of 4, #a-d	6.50	6.50
486 A105	Sheet of 5, #a-e	6.50	6.50

Tourism A106

Designs: 10c, Birds flying over ocean. 20c, Ray. 30c, Buildings on shore. 40c, Rocky coastline. 50c, Road in forest. 60c, Sharks. 70c, Aerial view of island. 80c, Clouds over ocean. 90c, Palm trees near shore. $1, Sharks, diff. $1.10, Saab 340 airplane, aerial view of island. $1.20, Pearls. $1.50, Sea turtle. $2, Aerial view of island, diff. $3, Sun and clouds above island.

2011, May 6 *Perf. 14*

487 A106	10c multi	.25	.25
488 A106	20c multi	.35	.35
489 A106	30c multi	.50	.50
490 A106	40c multi	.65	.65
491 A106	50c multi	.80	.80
492 A106	60c multi	.95	.95
493 A106	70c multi	1.10	1.10
494 A106	80c multi	1.25	1.25
495 A106	90c multi	1.50	1.50
496 A106	$1 multi	1.60	1.60
497 A106	$1.10 multi	1.75	1.75
498 A106	$1.20 multi	1.90	1.90
499 A106	$1.50 multi	2.40	2.40
500 A106	$2 multi	3.25	3.25
501 A106	$3 multi	4.75	4.75
a.	Miniature sheet of 15, #487-501	23.00	23.00
	Nos. 487-501 (15)	23.00	23.00

Souvenir Sheet

Wedding of Prince William and Catherine Middleton — A107

No. 502 — Couple in wedding procession: a, $1. b, $1.20.

2011, July 15 *Perf. 15x14¼*

502 A107	Sheet of 2, #a-b	3.75	3.75

Christmas A108

No. 503: a, Partridge in a pear tree. b, Two turtle doves. c, Three French hens. d, Four calling birds.

2011, Dec. 24 *Perf. 13¼*

503	Horiz. strip of 4	6.00	6.00
a.	A108 30c multi	.50	.50
b.	A108 50c multi	.80	.80
c.	A108 90c multi	1.40	1.40
d.	A108 $2 multi	3.25	3.25
e.	Souvenir sheet of 4, #503a-503d	6.00	6.00

Beatification of Pope John Paul II — A109

No. 504: a, $1.20, Pope Benedict XVI. b, $5, Pope John Paul II.

2012, Jan. 10 *Perf. 13¾*

504 A109	Horiz. pair, #a-b	10.50	10.50

Christ Taking Leave of His Mother, by Correggio A110

Deposition, by Correggio A111

The Martyrdom of Four Saints, by Correggio A112

Mystic Marriage of St. Catherine and St. Sebastian, by Correggio A113

Nativity, by Correggio, c. 1510 A114

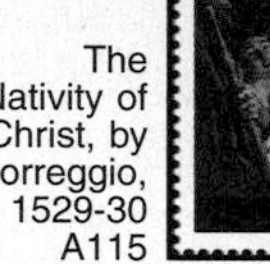

The Nativity of Christ, by Correggio, c. 1529-30 A115

Perf. 14¾x14¼

2012, Nov. 16 **Litho.**

Stamps With White Frames

505	Horiz. pair	2.80	2.80
a.	A110 80c multi	1.40	1.40
b.	A111 80c multi	1.40	1.40
506	Horiz. pair	3.00	3.00
a.	A112 90c multi	1.50	1.50
b.	A113 90c multi	1.50	1.50
507	Horiz. pair	10.00	10.00
a.	A114 $3 multi	5.00	5.00
b.	A115 $3 multi	5.00	5.00
	Nos. 505-507 (3)	15.80	15.80

Miniature Sheet

Stamps With Colored Frames

508	Sheet of 6	16.00	16.00
a.	A110 80c multi	1.40	1.40
b.	A111 80c multi	1.40	1.40
c.	A112 90c multi	1.50	1.50
d.	A113 90c multi	1.50	1.50
e.	A114 $3 multi	5.00	5.00
f.	A115 $3 multi	5.00	5.00

Fish — A116

Nos. 509 and 512: a, 80c, Myripristis hexagonia. b, 90c, Scarus psittacus. c, $1.10, Zanclus cornutus. d, $1.20, Acanthurus guttatus.

Nos. 510 and 513: a, $2, Pygoplites diacanthus. b, $2.25, Chaetodon flavirostris. c, $4, Pseudanthias pleurotaenia. d, $5, Chaetodon ornatissimus.

Nos. 511 and 514: a, $6, Chaetodon melanotus. b, $8, Gymnothorax rueppellii. c, $10, Synchiropus ocellatus. d, $20, Kyphosus sandwichensis.

2012, Nov. 27 **Litho.** *Perf. 14*

Stamps With White Frames

509 A116	Block of 4, #a-d	6.75	6.75
510 A116	Block of 4, #a-d	22.00	22.00
511 A116	Block of 4, #a-d	72.50	72.50
	Nos. 509-511 (3)	101.25	101.25

Stamps Without White Frames

512 A116	Sheet of 4, #a-d	6.75	6.75
513 A116	Sheet of 4, #a-d	22.00	22.00
514 A116	Sheet of 4, #a-d	72.50	72.50
e.	Sheet of 12, #512a-512d, 513a-513d, 514a-514d	102.00	102.00
	Nos. 512-514 (3)	101.25	101.25

Personalizable Stamp — A117

2012, Dec. 21 Litho. *Perf. 14x14¾*
515 A117 $4 multi 6.75 6.75

Miniature Sheet

New Year 2013 (Year of the Snake) — A118

No. 516 — Various snakes with background color of: a, Blue. b, Bright rose. c, Green. d, Yellow.

Perf. 14¾x14¼
2013, Feb. 21 Litho.
516 A118 $1.20 Sheet of 4, #a-d 8.00 8.00

Souvenir Sheet

Duchess of Cambridge — A119

No. 517 — Various photographs of pregnant Duchess of Cambridge: a, $1.30. b, $1.50. c, $1.70.

2013, Aug. 1 Litho. *Perf. 13¾x13½*
517 A119 Sheet of 3, #a-c 7.25 7.25

Birth of Prince George of Cambridge.

Souvenir Sheet

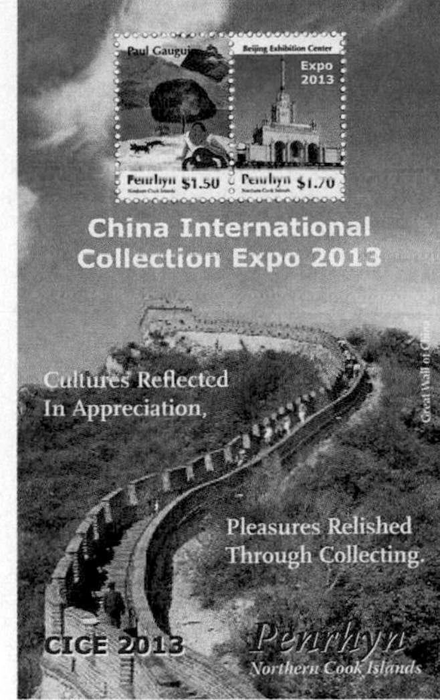

China International Collection Expo 2013, Beijing — A120

No. 518: a, $1.50, Painting by Paul Gauguin. b, $1.70, Beijing Exhibition Center.

2013, Sept. 26 Litho. *Perf. 12*
518 A120 Sheet of 2, #a-b 5.50 5.50

Pres. John F. Kennedy (1917-63) A121

Designs: $2, Photograph of Kennedy. $3, Photograph of Kennedy and crowd, quote from Kennedy.

2013, Nov. 8 Litho. *Perf. 14x14¼*
519-520 A121 Set of 2 8.25 8.25

Fish A122

Designs: 30c, Chaetodon ornatissimus. 50c, Kyphosus pacificus. $1, Acanthurus guttatus. $1.30, Chaetodon flavirostris. $1.50, Myripristis murdjan. $1.70, Pygoplites diacanthus. $2.40, Zanclus cornutus. $2.50, Scarus psittacus. $3, Rhinomuraena quaesita. $4.50, Synchiropus ocellatus. $7.50, Gymnothorax rueppelliae. $12.90, Hoplolatilus starcki.

2013, Nov. 11 Litho. *Perf. 14*

Stamps With White Frames

521	A122	30c multi	.50	.50
522	A122	50c multi	.85	.85
523	A122	$1 multi	1.75	1.75
524	A122	$1.30 multi	2.25	2.25
525	A122	$1.50 multi	2.50	2.50
526	A122	$1.70 multi	2.75	2.75
527	A122	$2.40 multi	4.00	4.00
528	A122	$2.50 multi	4.25	4.25
529	A122	$3 multi	5.00	5.00
530	A122	$4.50 multi	7.50	7.50
531	A122	$7.50 multi	12.50	12.50
532	A122	$12.90 multi	21.50	21.50
		Nos. 521-532 (12)	65.35	65.35

Stamps Without White Frames

533	Sheet of 12	66.00	66.00
a.	A122 30c multi	.50	.50
b.	A122 50c multi	.85	.85
c.	A122 $1 multi	1.75	1.75
d.	A122 $1.30 multi	2.25	2.25
e.	A122 $1.50 multi	2.50	2.50
f.	A122 $1.70 multi	2.75	2.75
g.	A122 $2.40 multi	4.00	4.00
h.	A122 $2.50 multi	4.25	4.25
i.	A122 $3 multi	5.00	5.00
j.	A122 $4.50 multi	7.50	7.50
k.	A122 $7.50 multi	12.50	12.50
l.	A122 $12.90 multi	21.50	21.50

Christmas — A123

Paintings by: $1, Peter Paul Rubens. $1.30, Albrecht Dürer.

No. 536 — Paintings by: a, $2, Sandro Botticelli. b, $2.40, William Brassey Hole. c, $2.60, Gerard von Honthorst.

2013, Nov. 18 Litho. *Perf. 13¼*
534-535 A123 Set of 2 3.75 3.75

Souvenir Sheet

536 A123 Sheet of 3, #a-c 11.50 11.50

Miniature Sheet

New Year 2014 (Year of the Horse) — A124

No. 537 — Background color: a, $1, Yellow. b, $1.30, Red. c, $1.50, Blue. d, $1.70, Green.

2014, Jan. 10 Litho. *Perf. 13¾*
537 A124 Sheet of 4, #a-d 9.00 9.00

Easter — A125

No. 538 — Religious paintings by: a, 50c, Peter Paul Rubens. b, $1, Lambert Lombard. c, $1.30, Titian. d, $1.50, Paolo Veronese. e, $1.70, Raphael.

$9.50, Painting by Dirck Bouts.

2014, Apr. 9 Litho. *Perf. 13¼*
538 A125 Sheet of 5, #a-e, + label 10.50 10.50

Souvenir Sheet

539 A125 $9.50 multi 16.50 16.50

Worldwide Fund for Nature (WWF) A126

Pacific green turtle: Nos. 540, 544a, $1, On beach. Nos. 541, 544b, $1.70, Swimming. Nos. 542, 544c, $2, Swimming, diff. Nos. 543, 544d, $2.40, Pair on seafloor.

$7.50, Turtle swimming, diff.

Perf. 14¾x14¼
2014, Nov. 28 Litho.

Stamps With White Frames

540-543 A126 Set of 4 11.00 11.00

Stamps Without White Frames

544 A126 Strip of 4, #a-d 11.00 11.00

Souvenir Sheet

545 A126 $7.50 multi 12.00 12.00

Souvenir Sheet

Christmas — A127

No. 546 — Religious paintings by: a, Antonio da Correggio. b, Piero della Francesca. c, Sandro Botticelli.

Perf. 14¾x14¼
2014, Dec. 14 Litho.
546 A127 $1.50 Sheet of 3, #a-c 7.00 7.00

Souvenir Sheet

New Year 2015 (Year of the Sheep) — A128

No. 547: a, $3.80, Red sheep. b, $4.10, Green sheep.

2015, Jan. 5 Litho. *Perf. 13½*
547 A128 Sheet of 2, #a-b 11.50 11.50

Miniature Sheet

Easter — A129

No. 548 — Details from religious paintings by: a, Peter Paul Rubens. b, Edouard Manet. c, Carl Heinrich Bloch. d, Jacopo Tintoretto.

2015, Mar. 31 Litho. *Perf. 14*
548 A129 $2 Sheet of 4, #a-d 12.50 12.50

Souvenir Sheet

Birth of Princess Charlotte of Cambridge — A130

No. 549: a, Duke and Duchess of Cambridge, Princess Charlotte. b, Duke of Cambridge holding Prince George.

Perf. 14¾x14¼

2015, June 23 **Litho.**

549 A130 $4.50 Sheet of 2, #a-b 12.00 12.00

New Year 2016 (Year of the Monkey) A131

Monkey with: $2.60, Both arms raised. $3, One arm raised.

No. 552 — Monkey with: a, $3.80, Both arms raised. b, $4.10, One arm raised.

2015, Sept. 25 **Litho.** ***Perf. 13¼***

550-551 A131 Set of 2 7.25 7.25

Souvenir Sheet

552 A131 Sheet of 2, #a-b 10.50 10.50

No. 552 contains two 50x50mm diamond-shaped stamps.

Miniature Sheet

Queen Elizabeth II, Longest-Reigning British Monarch — A132

No. 553 — Various photographs of Queen Elizabeth II: a, $1.30. b, $1.50. c, $1.70. d, $2.

2015, Nov. 20 **Litho.** ***Perf. 14***

553 A132 Sheet of 4, #a-d 8.75 8.75

Souvenir Sheet

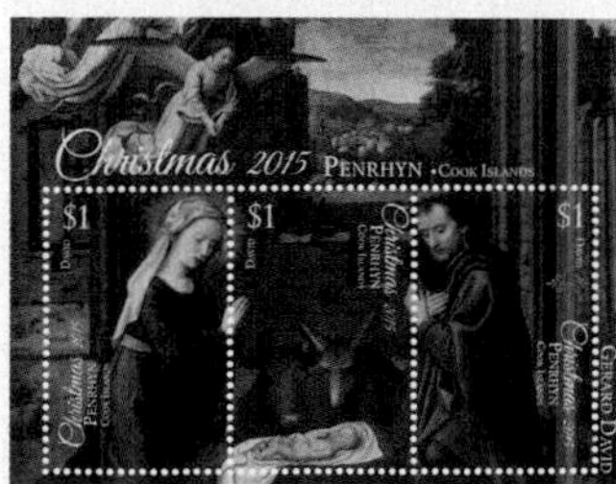

Christmas — A133

No. 554 — Nativity, by Gerard David (details): a, Virgin Mary. b, Infant Jesus and animals. c, St. Joseph.

2015, Dec. 9 **Litho.** ***Perf. 13¼***

554 A133 $1 Sheet of 3, #a-c 4.25 4.25

SEMI-POSTAL STAMPS

Catalogue values for unused stamps in this section are for Never Hinged items.

Easter Type of 1978

Souvenir Sheets

Rubens Paintings: No. B1, like #101. No. B2, like #102. No. B3, like #103.

1978, Apr. 17 **Photo.** ***Perf. 13½x13***

B1 A31 60c + 5c multi .50 .50
B2 A31 60c + 5c multi .50 .50
B3 A31 60c + 5c multi .50 .50
Nos. B1-B3 (3) 1.50 1.50

Surtax was for school children.

Easter Type of 1980

Souvenir Sheets

1980, Mar. 28 **Photo.** ***Perf. 13x13½***

B4 A36 70c + 5c like #114 .45 .45
B5 A36 70c + 5c like #115 .45 .45
B6 A36 70c + 5c like #116 .45 .45
Nos. B4-B6 (3) 1.35 1.35

Surtax was for local charities.

Christmas Type of 1980

Souvenir Sheets

1980, Dec. 5 **Photo.** ***Perf. 13***

B7 A39 70c + 5c like #127 1.00 1.00
B8 A39 70c + 5c like #128 1.00 1.00
B9 A39 70c + 5c like #129 1.00 1.00
Nos. B7-B9 (3) 3.00 3.00

Surtax was for local charities.

Easter Type of 1981

Souvenir Sheets

1981, Apr. 5 **Photo.** ***Perf. 13½***

B10 A44 70c + 5c like #173 1.00 1.00
B11 A44 70c + 5c like #174 1.00 1.00
B12 A44 70c + 5c like #175 1.00 1.00
Nos. B10-B12 (3) 3.00 3.00

Surtax was for local charities.

Nos. 176-180a Surcharged

1981, Nov. 30 **Photo.** ***Perf. 14***

B13 A45 40c + 5c like #176 .25 .25
B14 A45 50c + 5c like #177 .25 .25
B15 A45 60c + 5c like #178 .25 .25
B16 A45 70c + 5c like #179 .30 .30
B17 A45 80c + 5c like #180 .30 .30
Nos. B13-B17 (5) 1.35 1.35

Souvenir Sheet

B18 Sheet of 5 1.50 1.50
a. A45 40c + 10c like #176 .25 .25
b. A45 50c + 10c like #177 .25 .25
c. A45 60c + 10c like #178 .25 .25
d. A45 70c + 10c like #179 .25 .25
e. A45 80c + 10c like #180 .25 .25

Intl. Year of the Disabled. Surtax was for the disabled.

Soccer Type of 1981

1981, Dec. 7 ***Perf. 13***

B19 A46 Sheet of 9 5.75 4.75

No. B19 contains Nos. 181-183. Surtax was for local sports.

Nos. 346-349 Surcharged ".SOUTH PACIFIC PAPAL VISIT . 21 TO 24 NOVEMBER 1986" in Metallic Blue

1986, Nov. 24 **Litho.** ***Perf. 13x13½***

B20 A67 65c + 10c multi 4.50 4.50
B21 A67 $1.75 + 10c multi 6.50 6.50
B22 A67 $2.50 + 10c multi 8.00 8.00
Nos. B20-B22 (3) 19.00 19.00

Souvenir Sheet

Perf. 13½x13

B23 Sheet of 3 23.00 23.00
a.-c. A67 $1.50 + 10c on #349a-349c 7.00 7.00

No. B23 inscribed "COMMEMORATING FIRST PAPAL VISIT TO SOUTH PACIFIC / VISIT OF POPE JOHN PAUL II . NOVEMBER 1986."

No. 454 Surcharged "CHILDREN'S CHARITIES" in Silver

Souvenir Sheet

1998, Nov. 19 **Litho.** ***Perf. 14***

B24 A93 $3.75 +$1 multi 6.00 6.00

OFFICIAL STAMPS

Catalogue values for unused stamps in this section are for Never Hinged items.

Nos. 51-60, 80, 88-89 Overprinted or Surcharged in Black, Silver or Gold

Perf. 13½x14, 13½, 13½x13

1978, Nov. 14 **Photo.**

O1 A17 1c multi .25 .25
O2 A17 2c multi .25 .25
O3 A17 3c multi .30 .25
O4 A17 4c multi .30 .25
O5 A17 5c multi .40 .25
O6 A17 8c multi .45 .25
O7 A17 10c multi .50 .25
O8 A17 15c on 60c multi .55 .35
O9 A17 18c on 60c multi .60 .35
O10 A17 20c multi .60 .35
O11 A17 25c multi (S) .65 .40
O12 A17 30c on 60c multi .70 .60
O13 A24 Strip of 3, multi 4.25 2.75
a. 50c, No. 80a (G) 1.25 .80
b. 50c, No. 80b (G) 1.25 .80
c. 50c, No. 80c (G) 1.25 .80
O14 A27 $1 multi (S) 2.75 .65
O15 A27 $2 multi (G) 5.25 .70
Nos. O1-O15 (15) 17.80 7.90

Overprint on No. O14 diagonal.

Nos. 268-276, 278, 277, 211-214, 280, 282, 281, 283, 170, 284, 171, 285, 172, 286 Surcharged with Bar and New Value or Ovptd. "O.H.M.S." in Silver or Metallic Red

1985-87 **Photo.** ***Perfs. as before***

O16 A56 2c multi .25 .25
O17 A56 4c multi .25 .25
O18 A56 5c multi .25 .25
O19 A56 8c multi .25 .25
O20 A56 10c multi .25 .25
O21 A56 18c multi .25 .25
O22 A56 20c multi .25 .25
O23 A56 30c multi .25 .25
O24 A56 40c on 36c .35 .35
O25 A56 50c multi .40 .40
O26 A56 55c on 48c .45 .45
O27 A50 65c on 60c #211a .55 .55
O28 A50 65c on 60c #211b .55 .55
O29 A50 65c on 60c #211c .55 .55
O30 A50 65c on 60c #211d .55 .55
O31 A56 75c on 72c 1.05 .65
O32 A56 75c on 96c 1.05 .65
O33 A56 80c multi 1.05 .65
O34 A56 $1.20 multi 1.25 .85
O35 A42 $2 multi (R) 1.75 1.25
O36 A56 $3 multi 3.50 2.10
O37 A42 $4 multi (R) 4.00 3.50
O38 A56 $5 multi 6.50 4.00
O39 A42 $6 multi (R) 9.25 6.50
O40 A56 $9.60 multi 12.00 10.00
Nos. O16-O40 (25) 46.80 35.55

Issued: #O16-O30, 8/15; #O31-O37, 4/29/86; #O38-O40, 11/2/87.

Nos. 420-432 Ovptd. "O.H.M.S." in Silver

1998 **Litho.** ***Perf. 14***

O41 A82 5c multicolored .30 .30
O42 A82 10c multicolored .30 .30
O43 A82 15c multicolored .30 .30
O44 A82 20c multicolored .30 .30
O45 A82 25c multicolored .30 .30
O46 A82 30c multicolored .40 .40
O47 A82 50c multicolored .55 .55
O48 A82 70c multicolored .70 .70
O49 A82 80c multicolored .95 .95
O50 A82 85c multicolored 1.10 1.10
O51 A82 90c multicolored 1.20 1.20
O52 A82 $1 multicolored 1.30 1.30
O53 A82 $2 multicolored 4.00 4.00
Nos. O41-O53 (13) 11.70 11.70

Nos. O41-O52 were not sold unused to local customers.

Issued: $2, 9/30; others, 7/20.

GET YOUR COLLECTION IN ORDER WITH THE NEW MINKUS GLOBAL ALBUM!

KEEP UP-TO-DATE WITH THE NEWEST GLOBAL PAGES

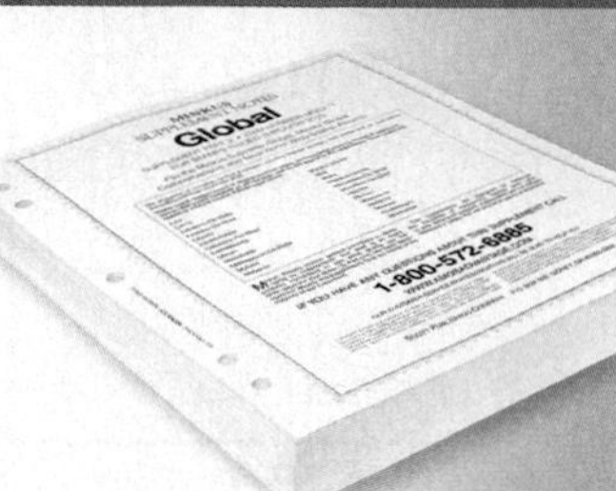

MINKUS: WORLDWIDE GLOBAL 2015 SUPPLEMENT PT. 1

ITEM	RETAIL	AA
MGL115	$135.00	$99.99

MINKUS: WORLDWIDE GLOBAL 2015 SUPPLEMENT PT. 2

ITEM	RETAIL	AA
MGL215	$135.00	$99.99

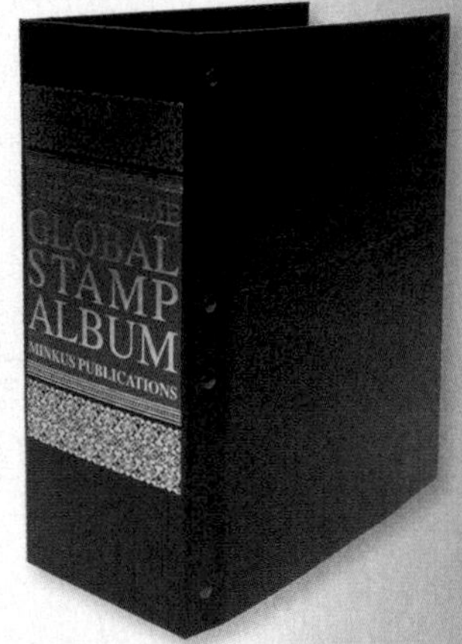

BINDERS

4" MASTER GLOBAL BINDER

ITEM	RETAIL	AA
MNMB	$44.99	$40.99

4" SUPREME GLOBAL BINDER

ITEM	RETAIL	AA
MNSB	$44.99	$40.99

Get yours today by visiting
AmosAdvantage.com
Or call 1-800-572-6885
Outside U.S. & Canada Call:
1-937-498-0800
P.O. Box 4129, Sidney, OH 45365

PERU

pə-'rü

LOCATION — West coast of South America
GOVT. — Republic
AREA — 496,093 sq. mi.
POP. — 24,800,768 (1998 est.)
CAPITAL — Lima

8 Reales = 1 Peso (1857)
100 Centimos = 8 Dineros = 4 Pesetas = 1 Peso (1858)
100 Centavos = 1 Sol (1874)
100 Centimos = 1 Inti (1985)
100 Centimos = 1 Sol (1991)

Catalogue values for unused stamps in this country are for Never Hinged items, beginning with Scott 426 in the regular postage section, Scott B1 in the semi-postal section, Scott C78 in the airpost section, Scott CB1 in the airpost semi-postal section, and Scott RA31 in the postal tax section.

Watermark

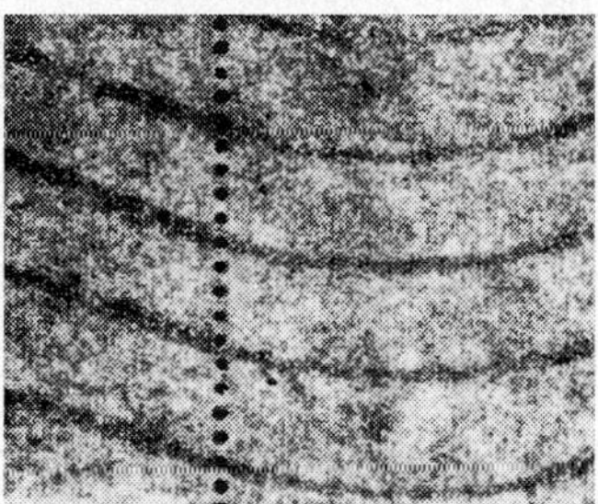

Wmk. 346 — Parallel Curved Lines

ISSUES OF THE REPUBLIC

Sail and Steamship — A1

Design: 2r, Ship sails eastward.

Unwmk.

1857, Dec. 1 Engr. *Imperf.*

1 A1 1r blue, *blue* 1,700. 2,250.
2 A1 2r brn red, *blue* 1,900. 3,000.

The Pacific Steam Navigation Co. gave a quantity of these stamps to the Peruvian government so that a trial of prepayment of postage by stamps might be made.

Stamps of 1 and 2 reales, printed in various colors on white paper, laid and wove, were prepared for the Pacific Steam Navigation Co. but never put in use. Value $50 each on wove paper, $400 each on laid paper.

Coat of Arms
A2 A3

A4

Wavy Lines in Spandrels

1858, Mar. 1 Litho.

3 A2 1d deep blue 275.00 47.50
4 A3 1p rose red 1,100. 160.00
5 A4 ½ peso rose red *6,500. 4,750.*
6 A4 ½ peso buff *2,750.* 375.00
a. ½ peso orange yellow *2,750.* 375.00

A5 A6

Large Letters

1858, Dec. Double-lined Frame

7 A5 1d slate blue 450.00 45.00
8 A6 1p red 450.00 65.00

A7 A8

1860-61

Zigzag Lines in Spandrels

9 A7 1d blue 175.00 10.50
a. 1d Prussian blue 175.00 20.00
b. Cornucopia on white ground 375.00 80.00
c. Zigzag lines broken at angles 225.00 22.50
10 A8 1p rose 450.00 42.50
a. 1p brick red 450.00 42.50
b. Cornucopia on white ground 450.00 42.50

Retouched, 10 lines instead of 9 in left label

11 A8 1p rose 250.00 27.50
a. Pelure paper 425.00 32.50
Nos. 9-11 (3) 875.00 80.50

A9 A10

1862-63 Embossed

12 A9 1d red 14.50 4.50
a. Arms embossed sideways 550.00 150.00
b. Thick paper 120.00 37.50
c. Diag. half used on cover 350.00
13 A10 1p brown ('63) 120.00 37.50
a. Diag. half used on cover 1,000.

Counterfeits of Nos. 13 and 15 exist.

A11

1868-72

14 A11 1d green 19.00 3.75
a. Arms embossed inverted *2,250. 1,200.*
b. Diag. half used on cover *2,000.*
15 A10 1p orange ('72) 150.00 55.00
a. Diag. half used on cover *1,100.*

Nos. 12-15, 19 and 20 were printed in horizontal strips. Stamps may be found printed on two strips of paper where the strips were joined by overlapping.

Llamas — A12 A13

A14

1866-67 Engr. *Perf. 12*

16 A12 5c green 10.50 .95
17 A13 10c vermilion 10.50 2.25
18 A14 20c brown 35.00 7.00
a. Diagonal half used on cover 675.00
Nos. 16-18 (3) 56.00 10.20

See Nos. 109, 111, 113.

Locomotive and Arms — A15

1871, Apr. Embossed *Imperf.*

19 A15 5c scarlet 125.00 42.50
a. 5c pale red 125.00 42.50

20th anniv. of the first railway in South America, linking Lima and Callao.

The so-called varieties "ALLAO" and "CALLA" are due to over-inking.

Llama — A16

1873, Mar. *Rouletted Horiz.*

20 A16 2c dk ultra 50.00 *325.00*

Counterfeits are plentiful.

Sun God of the Incas — A17

Coat of Arms
A18 A19

A20 A21

A22 A23

Embossed with Grill

1874-84 Engr. *Perf. 12*

21 A17 1c orange ('79) .90 .65
22 A18 2c dk violet 1.25 .95
23 A19 5c blue ('77) 1.40 .45
24 A19 5c ultra ('79) 13.00 3.25
25 A20 10c green ('76) .45 .30
a. Imperf., pair 35.00
26 A20 10c slate ('84) 2.00 .45
a. Diag. half used as 5c on cover —
27 A21 20c brown red 3.50 1.10
28 A22 50c green 15.00 4.25
29 A23 1s rose 2.40 2.40
Nos. 21-29 (9) 39.90 13.80

No. 25a lacks the grill.

No. 26 with overprint "DE OFICIO" is said to have been used to frank mail of Gen. A. A. Caceres during the civil war against Gen. Miguel Iglesias, provisional president. Experts question its status.

1880

30 A17 1c green 2.50
31 A18 2c rose 2.50

Nos. 30 and 31 were prepared for use but not issued without overprint.

See Nos. 104-108, 110, 112, 114-115.

For overprints see Nos. 32-103, 116-128, J32-J33, O2-O22, N11-N23, 1N1-1N9, 3N11-3N20, 5N1, 6N1-6N2, 7N1-7N2, 8N7, 8N10-8N11, 9N1-9N3, 10N3-10N8, 10N10-10N11, 11N1-11N5, 12N1-12N3, 13N1, 14N1-14N10, 15N5-15N8, 15N13-15N18, 16N1-16N22.

Stamps of 1874-80 Overprinted in Red, Blue or Black

1880, Jan. 5

32 A17 1c green (R) .90 .65
a. Inverted overprint 10.00 10.00
b. Double overprint 13.50 13.50
33 A18 2c rose (Bl) 1.75 1.10
a. Inverted overprint 10.00 10.00
b. Double overprint 14.00 12.00
34 A18 2c rose (Bk) 75.00 60.00
a. Inverted overprint
b. Double overprint
35 A19 5c ultra (R) 3.50 1.75
a. Inverted overprint 10.00 10.00
b. Double overprint 14.00 14.00
36 A22 50c green (R) 45.00 27.50
a. Inverted overprint 45.00 45.00
b. Double overprint 55.00 55.00
37 A23 1s rose (Bl) 70.00 50.00
a. Inverted overprint 110.00 110.00
b. Double overprint 110.00 110.00
Nos. 32-37 (6) 196.15 141.00

Stamps of 1874-80 Overprinted in Red or Blue

1881, Jan. 28

38 A17 1c green (R) 1.25 .95
a. Inverted overprint 8.25 8.25
b. Double overprint 14.00 14.00
39 A18 2c rose (Bl) 24.00 15.00
a. Inverted overprint 17.50 15.00
b. Double overprint 25.00 20.00
40 A19 5c ultra (R) 2.75 1.25
a. Inverted overprint 14.00 14.00
b. Double overprint 20.00 20.00
41 A22 50c green (R) 750.00 425.00
a. Inverted overprint 850.00
42 A23 1s rose (Bl) 140.00 90.00
a. Inverted overprint 175.00

Reprints of Nos. 38 to 42 were made in 1884. In the overprint the word "PLATA" is 3mm high instead of 2½mm. The cross bars of the letters "A" of that word are set higher than on the original stamps. The 5c is printed in blue instead of ultramarine.

For stamps of 1874-80 overprinted with Chilean arms or small UPU "horseshoe," see Nos. N11-N23.

Stamps of 1874-79 Handstamped in Black or Blue

1883

65 A17 1c orange (Bk) 1.25 1.10
66 A17 1c orange (Bl) 50.00 50.00
68 A19 5c ultra (Bk) 13.00 7.00
69 A20 10c green (Bk) 1.25 1.10
70 A20 10c green (Bl) 5.00 4.00
71 A22 50c green (Bk) 7.00 4.25
73 A23 1s rose (Bk) 10.00 8.00
Nos. 65-73 (7) 87.50 75.45
Nos. 65,68-73 (6) 37.50 25.45

This overprint is found in 11 types.

The 1c green, 2c dark violet and 20c brown red, overprinted with triangle, are fancy varieties made for sale to collectors and never placed in regular use.

Overprinted Triangle and "Union Postal Universal Peru" in Oval

1883

77 A22 50c grn (R & Bk) 210.00 110.00
78 A23 1s rose (Bl & Bk) 250.00 160.00

The 1c green, 2c rose and 5c ultramarine, over printed with triangle and "U. P. U. Peru" oval, were never placed in regular use.

Overprinted Triangle and "Union Postal Universal Lima" in Oval

1883

79 A17 1c grn (R & Bl) 70.00 70.00
80 A17 1c grn (R & Bk) 7.00 7.00
a. Oval overprint inverted
b. Double overprint of oval
81 A18 2c rose (Bl & Bk) 7.00 7.00
82 A19 5c ultra (R & Bk) 11.00 10.00
83 A19 5c ultra (R & Bl) 17.00 10.00
84 A22 50c grn (R & Bk) 250.00 150.00
85 A23 1s rose (Bl & Bk) 275.00 275.00
Nos. 79-85 (7) 637.00 529.00

Some authorities question the status of No. 79.

Nos. 80, 81, 84, and 85 were reprinted in 1884. They have the second type of oval overprint with "PLATA" 3mm high.

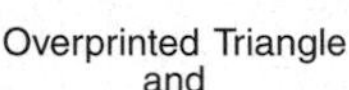

Overprinted Triangle and

86 A17 1c grn (Bk & Bk) 1.75 1.25
a. Horseshoe inverted 10.00
87 A17 1c grn (Bl & Bk) 5.00 3.50
88 A18 2c ver (Bk & Bk) 1.75 1.25
89 A19 5c bl (Bk & Bk) 2.25 1.60
90 A19 5c bl (Bl & Bk) 12.00 10.50
91 A19 5c bl (R & Bk) *1,500. 1,100.*

Overprinted Horseshoe Alone

1883, Oct. 23

95 A17 1c green 2.25 2.25
96 A18 2c vermilion 2.25 *6.50*
a. Double overprint
97 A19 5c blue 3.50 3.50
98 A19 5c ultra 20.00 15.00
99 A22 50c rose 57.50 57.50
100 A23 1s ultra 55.00 22.50
Nos. 95-100 (6) 140.50 107.25

The 2c dark violet overprinted with the above design in red and triangle in black also the 1c green overprinted with the same combination plus the horseshoe in black, are fancy varieties made for sale to collectors.

No. 23 Overprinted in Black

1884, Apr. 28

103 A19 5c blue .65 .40
a. Double overprint 5.00 5.00

Stamps of 1c and 2c with the above overprint, also with the above and "U. P. U. LIMA" oval in blue or "CORREOS LIMA" in a double-lined circle in red, were made to sell to collectors and were never placed in use.

Without Overprint or Grill

1886-95

104 A17 1c dull violet .90 .30
105 A17 1c vermilion ('95) .65 .30
106 A18 2c green 1.25 .30
107 A18 2c dp ultra ('95) .55 .30
108 A19 5c orange 1.00 .45
109 A12 5c claret ('95) 2.25 .85
110 A20 10c slate .65 .30
111 A13 10c orange ('95) 1.00 .55
112 A21 20c blue 8.75 1.10
113 A14 20c dp ultra ('95) 10.50 2.25
114 A22 50c red 2.75 1.10
115 A23 1s brown 2.25 .85
Nos. 104-115 (12) 32.50 8.65

Overprinted Horseshoe in Black and Triangle in Rose Red

1889

116 A17 1c green .75 .75
a. Horseshoe inverted 7.50

Nos. 30 and 25 Overprinted "Union Postal Universal Lima" in Oval in Red

1889, Sept. 1

117 A17 1c green 2.00 1.60
117A A20 10c green 2.00 2.00

The overprint on Nos. 117 and 117A is of the second type with "PLATA" 3mm high.

Stamps of 1874-80 Overprinted in Black

Pres. Remigio Morales Bermúdez

1894, Oct. 23

118 A17 1c orange 1.00 .65
a. Inverted overprint 7.00 7.00
b. Double overprint 7.00 7.00
119 A17 1c green .65 .55
a. Inverted overprint 3.50 3.50
b. Dbl. inverted ovpt. 5.00 5.00
120 A18 2c violet .65 .55
a. Diagonal half used as 1c
b. Inverted overprint 7.00 7.00
c. Double overprint 7.00 7.00
121 A18 2c rose .65 .55
a. Double overprint 7.00 7.00
b. Inverted overprint 9.75 7.00
122 A19 5c blue 4.50 2.75
122A A19 5c ultra 7.25 3.50
b. Inverted overprint 10.00 10.00
123 A20 10c green .65 .55
a. Inverted overprint 7.00 7.00
124 A22 50c green 2.40 2.00
a. Inverted overprint 10.00 10.00
Nos. 118-124 (8) 17.75 11.10

Same, with Additional Ovpt. of Horseshoe

125 A18 2c vermilion .55 .45
a. Head inverted 2.50 2.50
b. Head double 5.00 5.00
126 A19 5c blue 1.75 .85
a. Head inverted 7.00 7.00
127 A22 50c rose 70.00 42.50
a. Head double 55.00 45.00
b. Head inverted 75.00 60.00
128 A23 1s ultra 175.00 150.00
a. Both overprints inverted 200.00 110.00
b. Head double 200.00 110.00
Nos. 125-128 (4) 247.30 193.80

A23a

Vermilion Surcharge

1895 ***Perf. 11½***

129 A23a 5c on 5c grn 18.00 13.00
130 A23a 10c on 10c ver 13.00 10.00
131 A23a 20c on 20c brn 14.00 10.00
132 A23a 50c on 50c ultra 18.00 13.00
133 A23a 1s on 1s red brn 18.00 13.00
Nos. 129-133 (5) 81.00 59.00

Nos 129-133 were used only in Tumbes. The basic stamps were prepared by revolutionaries in northern Peru.

A23b

"Liberty" — A23c

1895, Sept. 8 **Engr.**

134 A23b 1c gray violet 1.90 1.10
135 A23b 2c green 1.90 1.10
136 A23b 5c yellow 1.90 1.10
137 A23b 10c ultra 1.90 1.10
138 A23c 20c orange 1.90 1.25
139 A23c 50c dark blue 10.00 7.00
140 A23c 1s car lake 55.00 35.00
Nos. 134-140 (7) 74.50 47.65

Success of the revolution against the government of General Caceres and of the election of President Pierola.

Manco Capac, Founder of Inca Dynasty — A24

Francisco Pizarro Conqueror of the Inca Empire — A25

General José de La Mar — A26

1896-1900

141 A24 1c ultra .90 .30
a. 1c blue (error) 70.00 60.00
142 A24 1c yel grn ('98) .90 .30
143 A24 2c blue .90 .30
144 A24 2c scar ('99) .90 .30
145 A25 5c indigo 1.25 .30
146 A25 5c green ('97) 1.25 .30
147 A25 5c grnsh bl ('99) .90 .55
148 A25 10c yellow 1.75 .45
149 A25 10c gray blk ('00) 1.75 .30
150 A25 20c orange 3.50 .45
151 A26 50c car rose 8.75 1.60
152 A26 1s orange red 13.00 1.60
153 A26 2s claret 3.50 1.25
Nos. 141-153 (13) 39.25 8.00

The 5c in black is a chemical changeling.

For surcharges and overprints see Nos. 187-188, E1, O23-O26.

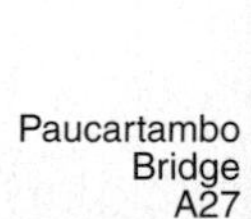
Paucartambo Bridge A27

Post and Telegraph Building, Lima — A28

Pres. Nicolás de Piérola — A29

1897, Dec. 31

154 A27 1c dp ultra 1.25 .60
155 A28 2c brown 1.25 .40
156 A29 5c bright rose 1.75 .60
Nos. 154-156 (3) 4.25 1.60

Opening of new P.O. in Lima.

No. J1 Overprinted in Black

1897, Nov. 8

157 D1 1c bister .90 .75
a. Inverted overprint 4.50 4.50
b. Double overprint 17.50 17.50

A31

1899

158 A31 5s orange red 2.75 2.75
159 A31 10s blue green 850.00 600.00

For surcharge see No. J36.

Pres. Eduardo de Romaña — A32

1900 **Frame Litho., Center Engr.**

160 A32 22c yel grn & blk 13.00 1.40

Admiral Miguel L. Grau — A33

2c, Col. Francisco Bolognesi. 5c, Pres. Romaña.

1901, Jan.

161 A33 1c green & blk 1.75 .75
162 A33 2c red & black 1.75 .75
163 A33 5c dull vio & blk 1.75 .75
Nos. 161-163 (3) 5.25 2.25

Advent of 20th century.

A34

1902 **Engr.**

164 A34 22c green .55 .30

Municipal Hygiene Institute Lima — A35

1905

165 A35 12c dp blue & blk 1.75 .50

For surcharges see Nos. 166-167, 186, 189.

Same Surcharged in Red or Violet

1907

No.	Type	Description	Unused	Used
166	A35	1c on 12c (R)	.35	.30
a.		Inverted surcharge	8.00	8.00
b.		Double surcharge	8.00	8.00
167	A35	2c on 12c (V)	.65	.45
a.		Double surcharge	8.00	8.00
b.		Inverted surcharge	8.00	8.00

Monument of Bolognesi — A36

Admiral Grau — A37

Llama — A38

Statue of Bolivar — A39

City Hall, Lima, formerly an Exhibition Building — A40

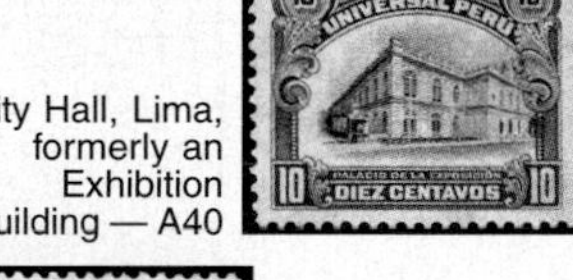
School of Medicine, Lima — A41

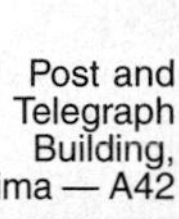

Post and Telegraph Building, Lima — A42

Grandstand at Santa Beatrix Race Track — A43

Columbus Monument — A44

1907

No.	Type	Description	Unused	Used
168	A36	1c yel grn & blk	.55	.30
169	A37	2c red & violet	.55	.30
170	A38	4c olive green	9.25	1.25
171	A39	5c blue & blk	1.00	.30
172	A40	10c red brn & blk	1.75	.45
173	A41	20c dk grn & blk	40.00	.75
174	A42	50c black	40.00	1.60
175	A43	1s purple & grn	200.00	3.75
176	A44	2s dp bl & blk	200.00	160.00
		Nos. 168-176 (9)	493.10	168.70

For surcharges and overprint see #190-195, E2.

Manco Capac A45

Columbus A46

Pizarro A47

San Martin A48

Bolívar A49

La Mar A50

Ramón Castilla A51

Grau A52

Bolognesi — A53

1909

No.	Type	Description	Unused	Used
177	A45	1c gray	.35	.25
178	A46	2c green	.35	.25
179	A47	4c vermilion	.45	.30
180	A48	5c violet	.35	.25
181	A49	10c deep blue	.75	.30
182	A50	12c pale blue	1.75	.30
183	A51	20c brown red	1.90	.45
184	A52	50c yellow	8.25	.55
185	A53	1s brn red & blk	17.00	.65
		Nos. 177-185 (9)	31.15	3.30

See types A54, A78-A80, A81-A89.
For surcharges and overprint see Nos. 196-200, 208, E3.

No. 165 Surcharged in Red

1913, Jan.

No.	Type	Description	Unused	Used
186	A35	8c on 12c dp bl & blk	.90	.35

Stamps of 1899-1908 Surcharged in Magenta

a

b

c

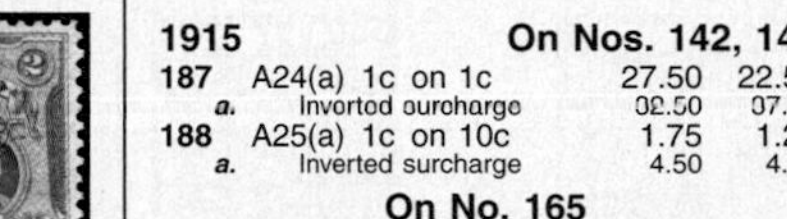

1915 — On Nos. 142, 149

No.	Type	Description	Unused	Used
187	A24(a)	1c on 1c	27.50	22.50
a.		Inverted surcharge	32.50	27.50
188	A25(a)	1c on 10c	1.75	1.25
a.		Inverted surcharge	4.50	4.50

On No. 165

No.	Type	Description	Unused	Used
189	A35(c)	2c on 12c	.45	.30
a.		Inverted surcharge	7.75	7.75

On Nos. 168-170, 172-174

No.	Type	Description	Unused	Used
190	A36(a)	1c on 1c	1.10	1.10
a.		Inverted surcharge	3.50	3.50
191	A37(a)	1c on 2c	1.75	1.60
a.		Inverted surcharge	4.50	4.50
192	A38(b)	1c on 4c	3.25	2.75
a.		Inverted surcharge	10.50	10.50
193	A40(b)	1c on 10c	1.75	1.25
a.		Inverted surcharge	3.75	3.75
193C	A40(c)	2c on 10c	175.00	125.00
b.		Inverted surcharge	175.00	
194	A41(c)	2c on 20c	22.50	21.00
a.		Inverted surcharge	45.00	45.00
195	A42(c)	2c on 50c	3.25	3.25
a.		Inverted surcharge	13.00	13.00
		Nos. 187-195 (10)	238.30	180.00

Nos. 182-184, 179, 185 Surcharged in Red, Green or Violet

d

e

f

1916

No.	Type	Description	Unused	Used
196	A50(d)	1c on 12c (R)	.35	.25
a.		Double surcharge	5.00	5.00
b.		Green surcharge	7.50	7.50
197	A51(d)	1c on 20c (G)	.35	.25
198	A52(d)	1c on 50c (G)	.35	.25
a.		Inverted surcharge	5.00	5.00
199	A47(e)	2c on 4c (V)	.35	.25
a.		Green surcharge	1.60	1.25
200	A53(f)	10c on 1s (G)	1.10	.25
a.		"VALF"	10.50	10.50
		Nos. 196-200 (5)	2.50	1.25

Official Stamps of 1909-14 Ovptd. or Srchd. in Green or Red

g

h

1916

No.	Type	Description	Unused	Used
201	O1(g)	1c red (G)	.25	.25
202	O1(h)	2c on 50c ol grn (R)	.35	.25
203	O1(g)	10c bis brn (G)	.35	.25

Postage Due Stamps of 1909 Surcharged in Violet-Black

No.	Type	Description	Unused	Used
204	D7	2c on 1c brown	.65	.65
205	D7	2c on 5c brown	.25	.25
206	D7	2c on 10c brown	.25	.25
207	D7	2c on 50c brown	.25	.25
		Nos. 201-207 (7)	2.35	2.15

Many copies of Nos. 187 to 207 have a number of pin holes. It is stated that these holes were made at the time the surcharges were printed.

The varieties which we list of the 1915 and 1916 issues were sold to the public at post offices. Many other varieties which were previously listed are now known to have been delivered to one speculator or to have been privately printed by him from the surcharging plates which he had acquired.

No. 179 Surcharged in Black

1917

No.	Type	Description	Unused	Used
208	A47	1c on 4c ver	.55	.55
a.		Double surcharge	8.25	8.25
b.		Inverted surcharge	8.25	8.25

San Martin — A54

Columbus at Salamanca — A62

Funeral of Atahualpa — A63

Battle of Arica, "Arica, the Last Cartridge" A64

Designs: 2c, Bolívar. 4c, José Gálvez. 5c, Manuel Pardo. 8c, Grau. 10c, Bolognesi. 12c, Castilla. 20c, General Cáceres.

1918 — Centers in Black — Engr.

No.	Type	Description	Unused	Used
209	A54	1c orange	.35	.25
210	A54	2c green	.35	.25
211	A54	4c lake	.45	.30
212	A54	5c dp ultra	.45	.30
213	A54	8c red brn	1.25	.45
214	A54	10c grnsh bl	.55	.30
215	A54	12c dl vio	1.75	.30
216	A54	20c ol grn	2.10	.30
217	A62	50c vio brn	8.25	.55
218	A63	1s greenish bl	21.00	.75
219	A64	2s deep ultra	35.00	1.10
		Nos. 209-219 (11)	71.50	4.85

For surcharges see Nos. 232-233, 255-256.

Augusto B. Leguía — A65

1919, Dec. — Litho.

No.	Type	Description	Unused	Used
220	A65	5c bl & blk	.35	.30
a.		Imperf.	.35	.35
b.		Center inverted	15.00	15.00
221	A65	5c brn & blk	.35	.30
a.		Imperf.	.35	.35
b.		Center inverted	15.00	15.00

Constitution of 1919.

San Martín — A66

Thomas Cochrane — A70

Oath of Independence — A69

Designs: 2c, Field Marshal Arenales. 4c, Field Marshal Las Heras. 10c, Martin Jorge Guisse. 12c, Vidal. 20c, Leguia. 50c, San Martin monument. 1s, San Martin and Leguia.

1921, July 28 — Engr.; 7c Litho.

No.	Type	Description	Unused	Used
222	A66	1c ol brn & red brn	.45	.25
a.		Center inverted	600.00	600.00
223	A66	2c green	.55	.30
224	A66	4c car rose	1.90	.90
225	A69	5c ol brn	.60	.25

No.	Type	Denomination	Color	Unused	Used
226	A70	7c	violet	1.90	.65
227	A66	10c	ultra	1.90	.65
228	A66	12c	blk & slate	4.50	.90
229	A66	20c	car & gray blk	4.50	1.10
230	A66	50c	vio brn & dl vio	13.00	3.75
231	A69	1s	car rose & yel grn	19.00	8.00
			Nos. 222-231 (10)	48.30	16.75

Centenary of Independence.

Nos. 213, 212 Surcharged in Black or Red Brown

1923-24

No.	Type	Description	Unused	Used
232	A54	5c on 8c No. 213	.75	.55
233	A54	4c on 5c (RB) ('24)	.55	.25
a.		Inverted surcharge	5.00	5.00
b.		Double surcharge, one inverted	6.00	6.00

A78

A79

Simón Bolívar — A80

Perf. 14, 14x14½, 14½, 13½

1924 Engr.; Photo. (4c, 5c)

No.	Type	Denomination	Color	Unused	Used
234	A78	2c	olive grn	.40	.25
235	A79	4c	yellow grn	.65	.25
236	A79	5c	black	2.25	.25
237	A80	10c	carmine	.80	.25
238	A78	20c	ultra	2.25	.30
239	A78	50c	dull violet	5.50	1.10
240	A78	1s	yellow brn	13.00	4.25
241	A78	2s	dull blue	35.00	18.00
			Nos. 234-241 (8)	59.85	24.65

Centenary of the Battle of Ayacucho which ended Spanish power in South America.

No. 237 exists imperf.

José Tejada Rivadeneyra A81

Mariano Melgar A82

Iturregui A83

Leguía A84

José de La Mar — A85

Monument of José Olaya — A86

Statue of María Bellido — A87

De Saco — A88

José Leguía — A89

1924-29 Engr. *Perf. 12*

Size: 18½x23mm

No.	Type	Denomination	Color	Unused	Used
242	A81	2c	olive gray	.35	.25
243	A82	4c	dk grn	.35	.25
244	A83	8c	black	3.25	3.25
245	A84	10c	org red	.35	.25
245A	A85	15c	dp bl ('28)	1.00	.30
246	A86	20c	blue	1.75	.30
247	A86	20c	yel ('29)	2.75	.30
248	A87	50c	violet	8.25	.45
249	A88	1s	bis brn	15.00	1.60
250	A89	2s	ultra	40.00	8.00
			Nos. 242-250 (10)	73.05	14.95

See Nos. 258, 260, 276-282.

For surcharges and overprint see Nos. 251-253, 257-260, 262, 268-271, C1.

No. 246 Surcharged in Red

a

b

1925

No.	Type	Description	Unused	Used
251	A86(a)	2c on 20c blue	*550.00*	*550.00*
252	A86(b)	2c on 20c blue	1.75	1.10
a.		Inverted surcharge	50.00	50.00
b.		Double surch., one inverted	50.00	50.00

No. 245 Overprinted

1925

No.	Type	Description	Unused	Used
253	A84	10c org red	1.75	1.75
a.		Inverted overprint	21.00	21.00

This stamp was for exclusive use on letters from the plebiscite provinces of Tacna and Arica, and posted on the Peruvian transport "Ucayali" anchored in the port of Arica.

No. 213 Surcharged

a

b

1929

No.	Type	Description	Unused	Used
255	A54(a)	2c on 8c	1.25	1.25
256	A54(b)	2c on 8c	1.25	1.25

No. 247 Surcharged

No.	Type	Description	Unused	Used
257	A86	15c on 20c yellow	1.25	1.25
a.		Inverted surcharge	13.00	13.00
		Nos. 255-257 (3)	3.75	3.75

Types of 1924 Coil Stamps

1929 *Perf. 14 Horizontally*

No.	Type	Denomination	Color	Unused	Used
258	A81	2c	olive gray	65.00	40.00
260	A84	10c	orange red	70.00	37.50

Postal Tax Stamp of 1928 Overprinted

1930 *Perf. 12*

No.	Type	Description	Unused	Used
261	PT6	2c dark violet	.55	.55
a.		Inverted overprint	3.25	3.25

No. 247 Surcharged

No.	Type	Description	Unused	Used
262	A86	2c on 20c yellow	.55	.55

Air Post Stamp of 1928 Surcharged

No.	Type	Description	Unused	Used
263	AP1	2c on 50c dk grn	.55	.55
a.		"Habitada"	2.10	2.10

Coat of Arms — A91

Lima Cathedral A92

10c, Children's Hospital. 50c, Madonna & Child.

Perf. 12x11½, 11½x12

1930, July 5 Litho.

No.	Type	Denomination	Color	Unused	Used
264	A91	2c	green	1.75	.95
265	A92	5c	scarlet	3.75	2.10
266	A92	10c	dark blue	2.25	1.60
267	A91	50c	bister brown	30.00	19.00
			Nos. 264-267 (4)	37.75	23.65

6th Pan American Congress for Child Welfare. By error the stamps are inscribed "Seventh Congress."

Type of 1924 Overprinted in Black, Green or Blue

1930, Dec. 22 Photo. *Perf. 15x14*

Size: 18¼x22mm

No.	Type	Description	Unused	Used
268	A84	10c orange red (Bk)	1.00	.80
a.		Inverted overprint	14.00	14.00
b.		Without overprint	8.50	8.50
c.		Double surcharge	7.00	7.00

Same with Additional Surcharge of Numerals in Each Corner

No.	Type	Description	Unused	Used
269	A84	2c on 10c org red (G)	.35	.25
a.		Inverted surcharge	17.00	
270	A84	4c on 10c org red (G)	.35	.25
a.		Double surcharge	12.50	12.50

Engr.

Perf. 12

Size: 19x23½mm

No.	Type	Description	Unused	Used
271	A84	15c on 10c org red (Bl)	.35	.25
a.		Inverted surcharge	14.00	14.00
b.		Double surcharge	14.00	14.00
		Nos. 268-271 (4)	2.05	1.55

Bolívar — A95

1930, Dec. 16 Litho.

No.	Type	Denomination	Color	Unused	Used
272	A95	2c	buff	.55	.55
273	A95	4c	red	.90	.75
274	A95	10c	blue green	.45	.30
275	A95	15c	slate gray	.90	.90
			Nos. 272-275 (4)	2.80	2.50

Death cent. of General Simón Bolivar.

For surcharges see Nos. RA14-RA16.

Types of 1924-29 Issues

Size: 18x22mm

1931 Photo. *Perf. 15x14*

No.	Type	Denomination	Color	Unused	Used
276	A81	2c	olive green	.45	.30
277	A82	4c	dark green	.45	.30
279	A85	15c	deep blue	1.25	.30
280	A86	20c	yellow	2.10	.30
281	A87	50c	violet	2.10	.45
282	A88	1s	olive brown	3.25	.55
			Nos. 276-282 (6)	9.60	2.20

Pizarro — A96

Old Stone Bridge, Lima — A97

1931, July 28 Litho. *Perf. 11*

No.	Type	Denomination	Color	Unused	Used
283	A96	2c	slate blue	2.10	1.75
284	A96	4c	deep brown	2.10	1.75
285	A96	15c	dark green	2.10	1.75
286	A97	10c	rose red	2.10	1.75
287	A97	10c	mag & lt grn	2.10	1.75
288	A97	15c	yel & bl gray	2.10	1.75
289	A97	15c	dk slate & red	2.10	1.75
			Nos. 283-289 (7)	14.70	12.25

1st Peruvian Phil. Exhib., Lima, July, 1931.

Manco Capac A99

Oil Refinery A100

Sugar Cane Field A102

Picking Cotton A103

Guano Deposits A104

Mining A105

Llamas — A106

1931-32 *Perf. 11, 11x11½*

292	A99	2c olive black	.35	.25
293	A100	4c dark green	.65	.30
295	A102	10c red orange	1.75	.25
a.		Vertical pair, imperf. between	30.00	
296	A103	15c turq blue	2.00	.30
297	A104	20c yellow	8.25	.30
298	A105	50c gray lilac	8.25	.30
299	A106	1s brown olive	20.00	1.40
		Nos. 292-299 (7)	41.25	3.10

Arms of Piura — A107

1932, July 28 *Perf. 11½x12*

300	A107	10c dark blue	8.25	8.00
301	A107	15c deep violet	8.25	8.00
		Nos. 300-301,C3 (3)	42.50	38.50

400th anniv. of the founding of the city of Piura. On sale one day. Counterfeits exist. See No. C7.

Parakas A108

Chimu A109

Inca — A110

1932, Oct. 15 *Perf. 11½, 12, 11½x12*

302	A108	10c dk vio	.35	.25
303	A109	15c brn red	.65	.30
304	A110	50c dk brn	1.50	.30
		Nos. 302-304 (3)	2.50	.85

4th cent. of the Spanish conquest of Peru.

Arequipa and El Misti — A111

President Luis M. Sánchez Cerro — A112

Monument to Simón Bolívar at Lima — A115

1932-34 **Photo.** *Perf. 13½*

305	A111	2c black	.25	.25
306	A111	2c blue blk	.25	.25
307	A111	2c grn ('34)	.25	.25
308	A111	4c dk brn	.25	.25
309	A111	4c org ('34)	.25	.25
310	A112	10c vermilion	27.50	16.00
311	A115	15c ultra	.60	.25
312	A115	15c mag ('34)	.60	.25
313	A115	20c red brn	1.25	.25
314	A115	20c vio ('34)	1.25	.25
315	A115	50c dk grn ('33)	1.25	.25
316	A115	1s dp org	11.00	1.60
317	A115	1s org brn	12.00	1.10
		Nos. 305-317 (13)	56.70	21.20

For overprint see No. RA24.

Statue of Liberty — A116

1934

318	A116	10c rose	.75	.25

The Inca — A119

Pizarro — A117

Coronation of Huascar — A118

1934-35 *Perf. 13*

319	A117	10c crimson	.40	.25
320	A117	15c ultra	1.10	.25
321	A118	20c deep bl ('35)	2.00	.25
322	A118	50c dp red brn	1.60	.25
323	A119	1s dark vio	11.00	1.10
		Nos. 319-323 (5)	16.10	2.10

For surcharges and overprint see Nos. 354-355, J54, O32.

Pizarro and the Thirteen A120

Belle of Lima — A122

Francisco Pizarro — A123

4c, Lima Cathedral. 1s, Veiled woman of Lima.

1935, Jan. 18 *Perf. 13½*

324	A120	2c brown	.55	.30
325	A120	4c violet	.60	.45
326	A122	10c rose red	.60	.30
327	A123	15c ultra	1.10	.75
328	A120	20c slate gray	2.25	.95
329	A122	50c olive grn	3.25	1.90
330	A122	1s Prus bl	6.00	3.75
331	A123	2s org brn	14.50	10.00
		Nos. 324-331,C6-C12 (15)	91.05	60.50

Founding of Lima, 4th cent.

View of Ica — A125

Lake Huacachina, Health Resort — A126

Grapes — A127

Cotton Boll — A128

Zuniga y Velazco and Philip IV — A129

Supreme God of the Nazcas — A130

Engr.; Photo. (10c)

1935, Jan. 17 *Perf. 12½*

332	A125	4c gray blue	.45	1.25
333	A126	5c dark car	.45	1.25
334	A127	10c magenta	6.50	3.25
335	A126	20c green	2.25	2.25
336	A128	35c dark car	11.00	8.00
337	A129	50c org & brn	7.75	7.00
338	A130	1s pur & red	22.50	17.00
		Nos. 332-338 (7)	50.90	40.00

Founding of the City of Ica, 300th anniv.

Pizarro and the Thirteen — A131

1935-36 **Photo.** *Perf. 13½*

339	A131	2c dp claret	.25	.25
340	A131	4c bl grn ('36)	.25	.25

For surcharge and overprints see Nos. 353, J53, RA25-RA26.

"San Cristóbal," First Peruvian Warship — A132

Naval College at Punta A133

Independence Square, Callao — A134

Aerial View of Callao A135

Plan of Walls of Callao in 1746 A137

Grand Marshal José de La Mar — A138

Packetboat "Sacramento" — A139

Viceroy José Antonio Manso de Velasco — A140

Centenary Cedar, Main Square, Pomabamba — A188

Unwmk.

1962, Sept. 7 Engr. *Perf. 13*
482 A188 1s red & green .55 .30

Cent. (in 1961) of Pomabamba province.

Types of 1952-53

Designs: 20c, Vicuña. 30c, Port of Matarani. 40c, Gunboat. 50c, Contour farming. 60c, Tourist hotel, Tacna. 1s, Paramonga, Inca fortress.

Imprint: "Thomas De La Rue & Co. Ltd."

Perf. 13x13½, 13½x13, 12 (A184)

1962, Nov. 19 Litho. Wmk. 346
483 A183 20c rose claret .25 .25
484 A182 30c dark blue .25 .25
485 AP49 40c orange .25 .25
486 A184 50c lt bluish grn .25 .25
487 A182 60c grnsh blk .55 .25
488 A184 1s rose .80 .25
Nos. 483-488 (6) 2.35 1.50

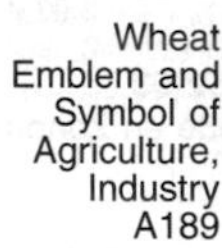

Wheat Emblem and Symbol of Agriculture, Industry A189

1963, July 23 Unwmk. *Perf. 12½*
489 A189 1s red org & ocher .25 .25

FAO "Freedom from Hunger" campaign. See No. C190.

Alliance for Progress Emblem — A190

1964, June 22 Litho. *Perf. 12x12½*
490 A190 40c multi .25 .25
Nos. 490,C192-C193 (3) 1.25 1.10

Alliance for Progress. See note after US No. 1234.

Pacific Fair Emblem — A191

1965, Oct. 30 Litho. *Perf. 12x12½*
491 A191 1.50s multi .35 .25
492 A191 2.50s multi .35 .25
493 A191 3.50s multi .60 .30
Nos. 491-493 (3) 1.30 .80

4th Intl. Pacific Fair, Lima, Oct. 30-Nov. 14.

Santa Claus and Letter A192

1965, Nov. 2 *Perf. 11*
494 A192 20c red & blk .25 .25
495 A192 50c grn & blk .45 .30
496 A192 1s bl & blk .80 .55
Nos. 494-496 (3) 1.50 1.10

Christmas. Valid for postage for one day, Nov. 2. Used Nov. 3, 1965-Jan. 31, 1966, as voluntary seals for the benefit of a fund for postal employees. See #522-524. For surcharges see #641-643.

Types of 1952-62

20c, Vicuña. 30c, Port of Matarani. 40c, Gunboat. 50c, Contour farming. 1s, Paramonga, Inca fortress.

Imprint: "I.N.A."

Perf. 12, 13½x14 (A184)

1966, Aug. 8 Litho. Unwmk.
497 A183 20c brn red .35 .30
498 A182 30c dk bl .35 .30
499 AP49 40c orange .35 .30
500 A184 50c gray grn .35 .30
501 A184 1s rose .35 .30
Nos. 497-501 (5) 1.75 1.50

Postal Tax Stamps Nos. RA40, RA43 Surcharged

a

b

Perf. 14x14½, 12½x12

1966, May 9 Litho.
501A PT11 (a) 10c on 2c lt brn .25 .25
501B PT14 (b) 10c on 3c lt car .25 .25

Map of Peru, Cordillera Central and Pelton Wheel A193

1966, Nov. 24 Photo. *Perf. 13½x14*
502 A193 70c bl, blk & vio bl .35 .25

Opening of the Huinco Hydroelectric Center. See No. C205.

Inca Wind Vane and Sun — A194

Perf. 13½x14

1967, Apr. 18 Photo. Unwmk.
503 A194 90c dp lil rose, blk & gold .35 .25

6-year building program. See No. C212.

Pacific Fair Emblem — A195

1967, Oct. 9 Photo. *Perf. 12*
504 A195 1s gold, dk grn & blk .30 .25

5th Intl. Pacific Fair, Lima, Oct. 27-Nov. 12. See No. C216.

Gold Alligator, Mochica Culture A196

Designs (gold sculptures of the pre-Inca Yunca tribes): 2.60s, Bird, vert. 3.60s, Lizard. 4.60s, Bird, vert. 5.60s, Jaguar.

Sculptures in Gold Yellow and Brown

1968, Aug. 16 Photo. *Perf. 12*
505 A196 1.90s dp magenta 1.50 .45
506 A196 2.60s black 2.00 .55
507 A196 3.60s dp magenta 2.50 .65
508 A196 4.60s black 3.50 .65
509 A196 5.60s dp magenta 4.50 .95
Nos. 505-509 (5) 14.00 3.25

See Nos. B1-B5. For surcharge see No. 685.

Indian and Wheat — A197

Designs: 3s, 4s, Farmer digging in field.

Black Surcharge

1969, Mar. 3 Litho. *Perf. 11*
510 A197 2.50s on 90c brn & yel .25 .25
511 A197 3s on 90c lil & brn .40 .25
512 A197 4s on 90c rose & grn .55 .30
Nos. 510-512,C232-C233 (5) 2.50 1.50

Agrarian Reform Law.

#510-512 were not issued without surcharge.

Flag, Worker Holding Oil Rig and Map A198

1969, Apr. 9 Litho. *Perf. 12*
513 A198 2.50s multi .35 .25
514 A198 3s gray & multi .35 .25
515 A198 4s lil & multi .65 .30
516 A198 5.50s lt bl & multi 1.00 .30
Nos. 513-516 (4) 2.35 1.10

Nationalization of the Brea Parinas oilfields, Oct. 9, 1968.

Kon Tiki Raft, Globe and Jet — A199

1969, June 17 Litho. *Perf. 11*
517 A199 2.50s dp bl & multi .55 .30
Nos. 517,C238-C241 (5) 2.85 2.10

1st Peruvian Airlines (APSA) flight to Europe.

Capt. José A. Quiñones Gonzales (1914-41), Military Aviator — A200

1969, July 23 Litho. *Perf. 11*
518 A200 20s red & multi 2.75 1.25

See No. C243.

Freed Andean Farmer A201

1969, Aug. 28 Litho. *Perf. 11*
519 A201 2.50s dk bl, lt bl & red .25 .25
Nos. 519,C246-C247 (3) 1.15 .95

Enactment of the Agrarian Reform Law of June 24, 1969.

Adm. Miguel Grau A202

1969, Oct. 8 Litho. *Perf. 11*
520 A202 50s dk bl & multi 5.50 3.25

Issued for Navy Day.

Flags and "6" — A203

1969, Nov. 14
521 A203 2.50s gray & multi .55 .30
Nos. 521,C251-C252 (3) 1.65 .80

6th Intl. Pacific Trade Fair, Lima, Nov. 14-30.

Santa Claus Type of 1965

Design: Santa Claus and letter inscribed "FELIZ NAVIDAD Y PROSPERO AÑO NUEVO."

1969, Dec. 1 Litho. *Perf. 11*
522 A192 20c red & blk .35 .25
523 A192 20c org & blk .35 .25
524 A192 20c brn & blk .35 .25
Nos. 522-524 (3) 1.05 .75

Christmas. Valid for postage for one day, Dec. 1, 1969. Used after that date as postal tax stamps.

Gen. Francisco Bolognesi and Soldier — A204

1969, Dec. 9
525 A204 1.20s lt ultra, blk & gold .40 .25

Army Day, Dec. 9. See No. C253.

Puma-shaped Jug, Vicus Culture — A205

1970, Feb. 23 Litho. *Perf. 11*
526 A205 2.50s buff, blk & brn .75 .25
Nos. 526,C281-C284 (5) 8.45 2.80

Ministry of Transport and Communications A206

1970, Apr. 1 Litho. *Perf. 11*

527	A206 40c org & gray	.30	.25
528	A206 40c gray & lt gray	.30	.25
529	A206 40c brick red & gray	.30	.25
530	A206 40c brt pink & gray	.30	.25
531	A206 40c org brn & gray	.30	.25
	Nos. 527-531 (5)	1.50	1.25

Ministry of Transport and Communications, 1st anniv.

Anchovy A207

Fish: No. 533, Pacific hake.

1970, Apr. 30 Litho. *Perf. 11*

532	A207 2.50s vio bl & multi	2.00	.30
533	A207 2.50s vio bl & multi	2.00	.30
a.	Strip of 5, #532-533, C285-C287	11.00	11.00

Composite Head; Soldier and Farmer A208

1970, June 24 Litho. *Perf. 11*

534	A208 2.50s gold & multi	.55	.45
	Nos. 534,C290-C291 (3)	2.20	.95

"United people and army building a new Peru."

Cadets, Chorrillos College, and Arms — A209

Coat of Arms and: No. 536, Cadets of La Punta Naval College. No. 537, Cadets of Las Palmas Air Force College.

1970, July 27 Litho. *Perf. 11*

535	A209 2.50s blk & multi	.90	.30
536	A209 2.50s blk & multi	.90	.30
537	A209 2.50s blk & multi	.90	.30
a.	Strip of 3, #535-537	5.00	4.50

Peru's military colleges.

Courtyard, Puruchuco Fortress, Lima — A210

1970, Aug. 6

538	A210 2.50s multi	.80	.25
	Nos. 538,C294-C297 (5)	6.10	1.85

Issued for tourist publicity.

Nativity, Cuzco School A211

Christmas paintings: 1.50s, Adoration of the Kings, Cuzco School. 1.80s, Adoration of the Shepherds, Peruvian School.

1970, Dec. 23 Litho. *Perf. 11*

539	A211 1.20s multi	.30	.25
540	A211 1.50s multi	.35	.25
541	A211 1.80s multi	.40	.25
	Nos. 539-541 (3)	1.05	.75

St. Rosa of Lima — A212

1971, Apr. 12 Litho. *Perf. 11*

542	A212 2.50s multi	.35	.25

300th anniv. of the canonization of St. Rosa of Lima (1586-1617), first saint born in the Americas.

Tiahuanacoide Cloth — A213

Design: 2.50s, Chancay cloth.

1971, Apr. 19

543	A213 1.20s bl & multi	.30	.25
544	A213 2.50s yel & multi	.55	.25
	Nos. 543-544,C306-C308 (5)	4.65	2.05

Nazca Sculpture, 5th Century, and Seriolella A214

1971, June 7 Litho. *Perf. 11*

545	A214 1.50s multi	.50	.25
	Nos. 545,C309-C312 (5)	4.75	2.40

Publicity for 200-mile zone of sovereignty of the high seas.

Mateo Garcia Pumacahua A215

#547, Mariano Melgar. #548, Micaela Bastidas. #549, Jose Faustino Sanchez Carrion. #550, Francisco Antonio de Zela. #551, Jose Baquijano y Carrillo. #552, Martin Jorge Guise.

1971

546	A215 1.20s ver & blk	.25	.25
547	A215 1.20s gray & multi	.25	.25
548	A215 1.50s dk bl & multi	.25	.25
549	A215 2s dk bl & multi	.25	.25
550	A215 2.50s ultra & multi	.35	.25
551	A215 2.50s gray & multi	.35	.25
552	A215 2.50s dk bl & multi	.35	.25
	Nos. 546-552,C313-C325 (20)	8.20	5.80

150th anniv. of independence, and to honor the heroes of the struggle for independence. Issue dates: Nos. 546, 550, May 10; Nos. 547, 551, July 5; Nos. 548-549, 552, July 27.

Gongora Portentosa A216

Designs: Various Peruvian orchids.

1971, Sept. 27 *Perf. 13½x13*

553	A216 1.50s pink & multi	.90	.25
554	A216 2s pink & multi	1.10	.25
555	A216 2.50s pink & multi	1.10	.25
556	A216 3s pink & multi	1.25	.25
557	A216 3.50s pink & multi	2.25	.25
	Nos. 553-557 (5)	6.60	1.25

"Progress of Liberation," by Teodoro Nuñez Ureta A217

3.50s, Detail from painting by Nuñez Ureta.

1971, Nov. 4 *Perf. 13x13½*

558	A217 1.20s multi	.25	.25
559	A217 3.50s multi	.55	.25
	Nos. 558-559,C331 (3)	7.30	2.75

2nd Ministerial meeting of the "Group of 77."

Plaza de Armas, Lima, 1843 A218

3.50s, Plaza de Armas, Lima, 1971.

1971, Nov. 6

560	A218 3s pale grn & blk	.65	.30
561	A218 3.50s lt brick red & blk	.65	.30

3rd Annual Intl. Stamp Exhibition, EXFILIMA '71, Lima, Nov. 6-14.

Army Coat of Arms — A219

1971, Dec. 9 Litho. *Perf. 13½x13*

562	A219 8.50s multi	1.25	.55

Sesquicentennial of Peruvian Army.

Flight into Egypt A220

Old Stone Sculptures of Huamanga: 2.50s, Three Kings. 3s, Nativity.

1971, Dec. 18 *Perf. 13x13½*

563	A220 1.80s multi	.35	.30
564	A220 2.50s multi	.55	.30
565	A220 3s gray & multi	.65	.30
	Nos. 563-565 (3)	1.55	.90

Christmas. See Nos. 597-599.

Fisherman, by J. M. Ugarte Elespuru — A221

Paintings by Peruvian Workers: 4s, Threshing Grain in Cajamarca, by Camilo Blas. 6s, Huanca Highlanders, by José Sabogal.

1971, Dec. 30 *Perf. 13½x13*

566	A221 3.50s blk & multi	1.10	.25
567	A221 4s blk & multi	1.10	.25
568	A221 6s blk & multi	1.60	.25
	Nos. 566-568 (3)	3.80	.75

To publicize the revolution and change of order.

Gold Statuette, Chimu, c. 1500 — A222

Ancient Jewelry: 4s, Gold drummer, Chimu. 4.50s, Quartz figurine, Lambayeque culture, 5th century. 5.40s, Gold necklace and pendant, Mochiqua, 4th century. 6s, Gold insect, Lambayeque culture, 14th century.

1972, Jan. 31 Litho. *Perf. 13½x13*

569	A222 3.90s red, blk & ocher	.55	.25
570	A222 4s red, blk & ocher	.55	.25
571	A222 4.50s brt bl, blk & ocher	1.25	.25
572	A222 5.40s red, blk & ocher	1.25	.25
573	A222 6s red, blk & ocher	1.90	.25
	Nos. 569-573 (5)	5.50	1.25

Popeye Catalufa A223

Fish: 1.50s, Guadara. 2.50s, Jack mackerel.

1972, Mar. 20 ***Perf. 13x13½***

574 A223 1.20s lt bl & multi .60 .25
575 A223 1.50s lt bl & multi .60 .25
576 A223 2.50s lt bl & multi 1.25 .25
Nos. 574-576,C333-C334 (5) 5.95 2.25

Seated Warrior, Mochica — A224

Painted pottery jugs of Mochica culture, 5th cent.: 1.50s, Helmeted head. 2s, Kneeling deer. 2.50s, Helmeted head. 3s, Kneeling warrior.

1972, May 8 ***Perf. 13½x13***

Emerald Background

577 A224 1.20s multi .60 .25
578 A224 1.50s multi .75 .25
579 A224 2s multi 1.25 .25
580 A224 2.50s multi 1.25 .25
581 A224 3s multi 1.90 .25
Nos. 577-581 (5) 5.75 1.25

"Bringing in the Harvest" (July) — A225

Monthly woodcuts from Calendario Incaico.

1972-73 **Litho.** ***Perf. 13½x13***

Black Vignette & Inscriptions

582 A225 2.50s red brn *(July)* 1.90 .30
583 A225 3s grn *(Aug.)* 1.90 .30
584 A225 2.50s rose *(Sept.)* 1.90 .30
585 A225 3s lt bl *(Oct.)* 1.90 .30
586 A225 2.50s org *(Nov.)* 1.90 .30
587 A225 3s lil *(Dec.)* 1.90 .30
588 A225 2.50s brn *(Jan.)* ('73) 1.90 .30
589 A225 3s pale grn *(Feb.)* ('73) 1.90 .30
590 A225 2.50s bl *(Mar.)* ('73) 1.90 .30
591 A225 3s org *(Apr.)* ('73) 1.90 .30
592 A225 2.50s lil rose *(May)* ('73) 1.90 .30
593 A225 3s yel & blk *(June)* ('73) 1.90 .30
Nos. 582-593 (12) 22.80 3.60

400th anniv. of publication of the Calendario Incaico by Felipe Guaman Poma de Ayala.

Family Tilling Field — A226

Sovereignty of the Sea (Inca Frieze) — A227

Oil Derricks — A228

Perf. 13½x13, 13x13½

1972, Oct. 31 **Litho.**

594 A226 2s multi .50 .30
595 A227 2.50s multi .50 .30
596 A228 3s gray & multi .50 .30
Nos. 594-596 (3) 1.50 .90

4th anniversaries of land reforms and the nationalization of the oil industry and 15th anniv. of the claim to a 200-mile zone of sovereignty of the sea.

Christmas Type of 1971

Sculptures from Huamanga, 17-18th cent.: 1.50s, Holy Family, wood, vert. 2s, Holy Family with lambs, stone. 2.50s, Holy Family in stable, stone, vert.

1972, Nov. 30

597 A220 1.50s buff & multi .35 .25
598 A220 2s buff & multi .35 .25
599 A220 2.50s buff & multi .35 .25
Nos. 597-599 (3) 1.05 .75

Morning Glory — A228a

1972, Dec. 29 **Litho.** ***Perf. 13***

600 A228a 1.50s shown .55 .25
601 A228a 2.50s Amaryllis .65 .25
602 A228a 3s Liabum excelsum .90 .25
603 A228a 3.50s Bletia (orchid) 1.10 .25
604 A228a 5s Cantua buxifolia 1.75 .55
Nos. 600-604 (5) 4.95 1.55

Mayor on Horseback, by Fierro — A229

Paintings by Francisco Pancho Fierro (1803-1879): 2s, Man and Woman, 1830. 2.50s, Padre Abregu Riding Mule. 3.50s, Dancing Couple. 4.50s, Bullfighter Estevan Arredondo on Horseback.

1973, Aug. 13 **Litho.** ***Perf. 13***

605 A229 1.50s salmon & multi .30 .25
606 A229 2s salmon & multi .50 .25
607 A229 2.50s salmon & multi .70 .25
608 A229 3.50s salmon & multi 1.00 .25
609 A229 4.50s salmon & multi 1.25 .60
Nos. 605-609 (5) 3.75 1.60

Presentation in the Temple — A230

Christmas Paintings of the Cuzqueña School: 2s, Holy Family, vert. 2.50s, Adoration of the Kings.

Perf. 13x13½, 13½x13

1973, Nov. 30 **Litho.**

610 A230 1.50s multi .25 .25
611 A230 2s multi .35 .25
612 A230 2.50s multi .40 .30
Nos. 610-612 (3) 1.00 .80

Peru No. 20 — A231

1974, Mar. 1 **Litho.** ***Perf. 13***

613 A231 6s gray & dk bl .90 .40

Peruvian Philatelic Assoc., 25th anniv.

Non-ferrous Smelting Plant, La Oroya A232

Colombia Bridge, San Martin A233

Designs: 8s, 10s, Different views, Santiago Antunez Dam, Tayacaja.

1974 **Litho.** ***Perf. 13x13½***

614 A232 1.50s blue .25 .25
615 A233 2s multi .25 .25
616 A232 3s rose claret .55 .25
617 A232 4.50s green .90 .45
618 A233 8s multi 1.10 .55
619 A233 10s multi 1.10 .55
Nos. 614-619 (6) 4.15 2.30

"Peru Determines its Destiny."

Issued: 2s, 8s, 10s, 7/1; 1.50s, 3s, 4.50s, 12/6.

Battle of Junin, by Felix Yañez A234

2s, 3s, Battle of Ayacucho, by Felix Yañez.

1974 **Litho.** ***Perf. 13x13½***

620 A234 1.50s multi .25 .25
621 A234 2s multi .25 .25
622 A234 2.50s multi .35 .30
623 A234 3s multi .35 .30
Nos. 620-623 (4) 1.20 1.10

Sesquicentennial of the Battles of Junin and Ayacucho.

Issued: 1.50s, 2.50s, Aug. 6; 2s, 3s, Oct. 9.

See Nos. C400-C404.

Indian Madonna — A235

1974, Dec. 20 **Litho.** ***Perf. 13½x13***

624 A235 1.50s multi .25 .25

Christmas. See No. C417.

Maria Parado de Bellido A236

International Women's Year Emblem — A237

IWY Emblem, Peruvian Colors and: 2s, Micaela Bastidas. 2.50s, Juana Alarco de Dammert.

Perf. 13x13½, 13½x13

1975, Sept. 8 **Litho.**

625 A236 1.50s bl grn, red & blk .25 .25
626 A237 2s blk & red .35 .25
627 A236 2.50s pink, blk & red .35 .25
628 A237 3s red, blk & ultra .65 .25
Nos. 625-628 (4) 1.60 1.00

International Women's Year.

St. Juan Macias — A238

1975, Nov. 14 ***Perf. 13½x13***

629 A238 5s blk & multi .55 .25

Canonization of Juan Macias in 1975.

Louis Braille A239

1976, Mar. 2 **Litho.** ***Perf. 13x13½***

630 A239 4.50s gray, red & blk .55 .45

Sesquicentennial of the invention of Braille system of writing for the blind by Louis Braille (1809-1852).

Peruvian Flag A240

1976, Aug. 29 **Litho.** ***Perf. 13x13½***

631 A240 5s gray, blk & red .35 .25

Revolutionary Government, phase II, 1st anniv.

St. Francis, by El Greco — A241

1976, Dec. 9 Litho. ***Perf. 13½x13***

632 A241 5s gold, buff & brn .75 .25

St. Francis of Assisi, 750th death anniv.

Indian Mother — A242

1976, Dec. 23

633 A242 4s multi .65 .25

Christmas.

Chasqui Messenger A243

1977 Litho. ***Perf. 13½x13***

634 A243 6s grnsh bl & blk .55 .25
635 A243 8s red & blk .55 .25
636 A243 10s ultra & blk .55 .50
637 A243 12s lt grn & blk .55 .50
Nos. 634-637,C465-C467 (7) 8.45 4.10

For surcharge see No. C502.

"X" over Flags — A244

1977, Nov. 25 Litho. ***Perf. 13½x13***

638 A244 10s multi .35 .25

10th Intl. Pacific Fair, Lima, Nov. 16-27.

Republican Guard Badge — A245

1977, Dec. 1

639 A245 12s multi .55 .30

58th anniversary of Republican Guard.

Indian Nativity — A246

1977, Dec. 23

640 A246 8s multi .45 .35

Christmas. See No. C484.

Nos. 495, 494, 496 Surcharged with New Value and Bar in Red, Dark Blue or Black: "FRANQUEO / 10.00 / RD-0161-77"

1977, Dec. ***Perf. 11***

641 A192 10s on 50c (R) .45 .30
642 A192 20s on 20c (DB) .90 .55
643 A192 30s on 1s (B) 1.25 .75
Nos. 641-643 (3) 2.60 1.60

Inca Head — A247

1978 Litho. ***Perf. 13½x13***

644 A247 6s bright green .25 .25
645 A247 10s red .25 .25
646 A247 16s red brown .45 .30
Nos. 644-646,C486-C489 (7) 6.60 4.30

For surcharges see Nos. C498-C499, C501.

Flags of Germany, Argentina, Austria, Brazil A248

Argentina '78 Emblem and Flags of Participants: No. 648, 652, Hungary, Iran, Italy, Mexico. No. 649, 653, Scotland, Spain, France, Netherlands. No. 650, 654, Peru, Poland, Sweden and Tunisia. No. 651, like No. 647.

1978 Litho. ***Perf. 13x13½***

647 A248 10s blue & multi .65 .30
648 A248 10s blue & multi .65 .30
649 A248 10s blue & multi .65 .30
650 A248 10s blue & multi .65 .30
a. Block of 4, #647-650 3.00 3.00
651 A248 16s blue & multi .65 .40
652 A248 16s blue & multi .65 .40
653 A248 16s blue & multi .65 .40
654 A248 16s blue & multi .65 .40
a. Block of 4, #651-654 4.00 4.00
Nos. 647-654 (8) 5.20 2.80

11th World Soccer Cup Championship, Argentina, June 1-25.
Issued: #647-650, 6/28; #651-654, 12/4.

Thomas Faucett, Planes of 1928, 1978 A249

1978, Oct. 19 Litho. ***Perf. 13***

655 A249 40s multicolored .90 .50

Faucett Aviation, 50th anniversary.

Nazca Bowl, Huaco A250

1978-79 Litho. ***Perf. 13x13½***

656 A250 16s violet bl ('79) .45 .25
657 A250 20s green ('79) .45 .25
658 A250 25s lt green ('79) .55 .55
659 A250 35s rose red ('79) .90 .30
660 A250 45s dk brown 1.10 .55
661 A250 50s black 1.25 .65
662 A250 55s car rose ('79) 1.25 .65
663 A250 70s lilac rose ('79) 1.50 1.10
664 A250 75s blue 1.75 1.00
665 A250 80s salmon ('79) 1.75 1.00
667 A250 200s brt vio ('79) 4.25 3.25
Nos. 656-667 (11) 15.20 9.55

For surcharges see Nos. 715, 731.

Peruvian Nativity — A252

1978, Dec. 28 Litho. ***Perf. 13½x13***

672 A252 16s multicolored .55 .50

Ministry of Education, Lima — A253

1979, Jan. 4

673 A253 16s multicolored .45 .35

National Education Program.

Nos. RA40, B1-B5 and 509 Surcharged in Various Colors

a

b

c

1978, July-Aug.

674 PT11(a) 2s on 2c (O) .25 .25
675 PT11(b) 3s on 2c (Bk) .25 .25
676 PT11(a) 4s on 2c (G) .25 .25
677 PT11(a) 5s on 2c (V) .25 .25
678 PT11(b) 6s on 2c (DBl) .25 .25
679 SP1 20s on 1.90s + 90c (G) 1.25 1.25
680 SP1 30s on 2.60s + 1.30s (Bl) 1.25 1.25
681 PT11(c) 35s on 2c (C) 1.60 1.60
682 PT11(c) 50s on 2c (LtBl) 5.50 5.50
683 SP1 55s on 3.60s + 1.80s (VBl) 1.75 1.75
684 SP1 65s on 4.60s + 2.30s (Go) 1.75 1.75
685 A196 80s on 5.60s (VBl) 1.40 1.40
686 SP1 85s on 20s + 10s (Bk) 2.75 2.75
Nos. 674-686 (13) 18.50 18.50

Surcharge on Nos. 679-680, 683-684, 686 includes heavy bar over old denomination.

Battle of Iquique A254

Heroes' Crypt — A255

Col. Francisco Bolognesi A256

War of the Pacific: No. 688, Col. Jose J. Inclan. No. 689, Corvette Union running Arica blockade. No. 690, Battle of Angamos, Aguirre, Miguel Grau (1838-1879), Perre. No. 690A, Lt. Col. Pedro Ruiz Gallo. 85s, Marshal Andres A. Caceres. No. 692, Naval Battle of Angamos. No. 693, Battle of Tarapaca. 115s, Adm. Miguel Grau. No. 697, Col. Bolognesi's Reply, by Angeles de la Cruz. No. 698, Col. Alfonso Ugarte on horseback.

Perf. 13½x13, 13x13½

1979-80 Litho.

687 A254 14s multicolored .35 .35
688 A256 25s multicolored .55 .25
689 A254 25s multicolored .90 .35
690 A254 25s multicolored .90 .35
690A A256 25s multi ('80) .45 .25
691 A256 85s multicolored .90 .65
692 A254 100s multicolored 1.00 .65
693 A254 100s multicolored 1.10 .65
694 A256 115s multicolored 2.00 1.10
695 A255 200s multicolored 11.00 7.00
696 A256 200s multicolored 2.00 1.60
697 A254 200s multicolored 2.00 1.60
698 A254 200s multicolored 2.75 1.60
Nos. 687-698 (13) 25.90 16.40

For surcharges see Nos. 713, 732.

Peruvian Red Cross, Cent. A257

1979, May 4 ***Perf. 13x13½***

699 A257 16s multicolored .40 .40

Billiard Balls — A258

1979, June 4 ***Perf. 13½x13***

700 A258 34s multicolored .50 .25

For surcharge see No. 714.

Arms of Cuzco — A259

1979, June 24

701 A259 50s multicolored 1.20 .35

Inca Sun Festival, Cuzco.

Peru Colors, Tacna Monument A260

1979, Aug. 28 Litho. *Perf. 13½x13*

702 A260 16s multicolored .55 .35

Return of Tacna Province to Peru, 50th anniv.

For surcharge see No. 712.

Telecom 79 — A261

1979, Sept. 20

703 A261 15s multicolored .35 .35

3rd World Telecommunications Exhibition, Geneva, Sept. 20-26.

Caduceus A262

1979, Nov. 13

704 A262 25s multicolored .55 .35

Stomatology Academy of Peru, 50th anniv.; 4th Intl. Congress.

World Map, "11," Fair Emblem A263

1979, Nov. 24

705 A263 55s multicolored .65 .45

11th Pacific Intl. Trade Fair, Lima, 11/14-25.

Gold Jewelry — A264

1979, Dec. 19 *Perf. 13½x13*

706 A264 85s multicolored 2.75 1.25

Larco Herrera Archaeological Museum.

Christmas A265

1979, Dec. 27 Litho. *Perf. 13x13½*

707 A265 25s multicolored .55 .35

Queen Sofia and King Juan Carlos I, Visit to Peru A266

1979, Feb. 7 Litho. *Perf. 13x13½*

708 A266 75s multicolored .90 .25

No. RA40 Surcharged in Black, Green or Blue

No. 709

No. 710

No. 711

1979, Oct. 8

709 PT11 7s on 2c brown .40 .40
710 PT11 9s on 2c brown (G) .40 .40
711 PT11 15s on 2c brown (B) .40 .40
Nos. 709-711 (3) 1.20 1.20

Nos. 702, 687, 700, 663 Surcharged

Perf. 13½x13, 13x13½

1980, Apr. 14 Litho.

712 A260 20s on 16s multi .40 .40
713 A254 25s on 14s multi .50 .40
714 A258 65s on 34s multi .90 .70
715 A250 80s on 70s lilac rose 1.25 .50
Nos. 712-715,C501-C502 (6) 4.20 2.95

Liberty Holding Arms of Peru — A267

Civic duties: 15s, Respect the Constitution. 20s, Honor country. 25s, Vote. 30s, Military service. 35s, Pay taxes. 45s, Contribute to national progress. 50s, Respect rights.

1980 Litho.

716 A267 15s greenish blue .30 .30
717 A267 20s salmon pink .30 .30
718 A267 25s ultra .30 .30
719 A267 30s lilac rose .30 .30
720 A267 35s black .50 .35
721 A267 45s light blue green .55 .50
722 A267 50s brown 1.00 .50
Nos. 716-722 (7) 3.25 2.55

Chimu Cult Cup — A268

1980, July 9 Litho.

723 A268 35s multicolored 1.50 .80

Map of Peru and Liberty — A269

Return to Civilian Government — A270

Perf. 13½x13, 13x13½

1980, Sept. 9 Litho.

724 A269 25s multicolored .50 .40
725 A270 35s multicolored .75 .40

For surcharge see No. 730.

Machu Picchu A271

1980, Nov. 10 Litho. *Perf. 13x13½*

726 A271 25s multicolored 2.00 2.00

World Tourism Conf., Manila, Sept. 27.

Tupac Amaru Rebellion Bicent. — A272

1980, Dec. 22 Litho. *Perf. 13½x13*

727 A272 25s multicolored .45 .35

Christmas A273

1980, Dec. 31 Litho. *Perf. 13*

728 A273 15s multicolored .65 .55

150th Death Anniv. of Simon Bolivar (in 1980) — A274

1981, Jan. 28 Litho. *Perf. 13½x13*

729 A274 40s multicolored .50 .25

Nos. 725, 667, 694 Surcharged

1981 Litho. *Perf. 13x13½*

730 A270 25s on 35s multi .30 .25
731 A250 85s on 200s brt violet 1.10 .80
732 A256 100s on 115s multi 1.25 .95
Nos. 730-732 (3) 2.65 2.00

Return to Constitutional Government, July 28, 1980 — A275

1981, Mar. 26 Litho. *Perf. 13½x13*

733 A275 25s multicolored .60 .40

For surcharges see Nos. 736-737, 737C.

Tupac Amaru and Micaela Bastidas, Bronze Sculptures, by Miguel Baca-Rossi A276

1981, May 18 Litho. *Perf. 13x13½*

734 A276 60s multicolored .70 .50

Rebellion of Tupac Amaru and Micaela Bastidas, bicentenary.

Nos. 733, RA41 and Voluntary Postal Tax Stamps of 1965 Surcharged in Black, Dull Brown or Lake and

Cross, Unleavened Bread, Wheat A276a

Chalice, Host A276b

Perf. 13½x13, Rouletted 11 (#735, 737B), 11½ (#737A)

1981 Litho., Photo. (#737A-737B)

735 PT17 40s on 10c #RA41 .30 .25
736 A275 40s on 25s #733 .90 .55
737 A275 130s on 25s #733 (DB) .90 .55
737A A276a 140s on 50c brn, yel & red .55 .40
737B A276b 140s on 1s multi .55 .40
737C A275 140s on 25s #733 (L) .90 .55
Nos. 735-737C (6) 4.10 2.70

Issued: #735, Apr. 12; #736, 737, 737C, Apr. 6; #737A, Apr. 15; #737B, Apr. 28.

Carved Stone Head, Pallasca Tribe A277

#739, 742, 749 Pottery vase, Inca, vert. #740, Head, diff., vert. #743, 749A-749B, Huaco idol (fish), Nazca. 100s, Pallasca, vert. 140s, Puma.

Perf. 13½x13, 13x13½

1981-82 **Litho.**

738	A277	30s dp rose lilac	.60	.60
739	A277	40s orange ('82)	.70	.25
740	A277	40s ultra	.70	.25
742	A277	80s brown ('82)	2.00	1.50
743	A277	80s red ('82)	2.00	1.40
745	A277	100s lilac rose	1.75	1.50
748	A277	140s lt blue grn	2.50	2.10
749	A277	180s green ('82)	4.50	3.75
749A	A277	240s grnsh blue ('82)	2.75	2.10
749B	A277	280s violet ('82)	3.75	2.75
		Nos. 738-749B (10)	21.25	16.20

For surcharges see #789, 798-799, 1026.

A278

1981, May 31 *Perf. 13½x13*
750 A278 130s multicolored .90 .90

Postal and Philatelic Museum, 50th anniv.

A279

1981, Oct. 7 **Litho.** *Perf. 13½x13*
751 A279 30s purple & gray .40 .40

1979 Constitution Assembly President Victor Raul Haya de la Torre.

Inca Messenger, by Guaman Poma (1526-1613) A280

1981 **Litho.** *Perf. 12*

752	A280	30s lilac & blk	1.25	1.00
753	A280	40s vermilion & blk	1.00	2.00
754	A280	130s brt yel grn & blk	2.50	2.00
755	A280	140s brt blue & blk	2.50	2.50
756	A280	200s yellow brn & blk	4.50	4.50
		Nos. 752-756 (5)	11.75	12.00

Christmas. Issue dates: 30s, 40s, 200s, Dec. 21; others, Dec. 31.

Intl. Year of the Disabled A280a

1981 **Litho.** *Perf. 13½x13*
756A A280a 100s multicolored 1.25 .85

Nos. 377, C130, C143, J56, O33, RA36, RA39, RA40, RA42, RA43 Surcharged in Brown, Black, Orange, Red, Green or Blue

1982

757	PT11	10s on 2c (#RA40, Br)	.40	.40
758	A155	10s on 10c (#377)	.30	.30
758A	AP60	40s on 1.25s (#C143)	.30	.30
758B	PT15	70s on 5c (#RA36, R)	.40	.40
759	D7	80s on 10c (#J56)	.30	.30
760	O1	80s on 10c (#O33)	.30	.30
761	PT14	80s on 3c (#RA43, O)	.30	.30
762	PT17	100s on 10c (#RA42, R)	.40	.40
763	AP57	100s on 2.20s (#C130, R)	.50	.50
764	PT14	150s on 3c (#RA39, G)	.60	.60
765	PT14	180s on 3c (#RA43, R)	.60	.60
766	PT14	200s on 3c (#RA43, Bl)	.70	.70
767	AP60	240s on 1.25s (#C143, R)	1.25	1.25
768	PT15	280s on 5c (#RA36)	1.10	1.10
		Nos. 757-768 (14)	7.45	7.45

Nos. 758A, 763, 767 airmail. Nos. 759 and 760 surcharged "Habilitado / Franq. Postal / 80 Soles".

Jorge Basadre (1903-1980), Historian — A281

Julio C. Tello (1882-1947), Archaeologist — A282

Perf. 13½x13, 13x13½

1982, Oct. 13 **Litho.**
769 A281 100s pale green & blk .40 .30
770 A282 200s lt green & dk bl .80 .55

9th Women's World Volleyball Championship, Sept. 12-26 — A283

1982, Oct. 18 *Perf. 12*
771 A283 80s black & red .30 .25

For surcharge see No. 791.

Rights of the Disabled — A284

1982, Oct. 22
772 A284 200s blue & red .90 .30

Brena Campaign Centenary A285

1982, Oct. 26 *Perf. 13x13½*
773 A285 70s Andres Caceres medallion .30 .25

For surcharge see No. 790.

1982 World Cup — A286

1982, Nov. 2 *Perf. 12*
774 A286 80s multicolored .80 .30

For surcharge see No. 800.

16th Intl. Congress of Latin Notaries, Lima, June — A287

1982, Nov. 6
775 A287 500s Emblem 1.25 .85

Handicrafts Year A288

1982, Nov. 24 *Perf. 13x13½*
776 A288 200s Clay bull figurine .60 .30

Christmas A289

1982 *Perf. 13½x13*
777 A289 280s Holy Family .70 .70

For surcharge see No. 797.

Pedro Vilcapaza A290

1982, Dec. 2 *Perf. 13½x13*
778 A290 240s black & lt brn .65 .50

Death centenary of Indian leader against Spanish during Andes Rebellion.
For surcharges see Nos. 792.

Jose Davila Condemarin (1799-1882), Minister of Posts (1849-76) — A291

1982, Dec. 10 *Perf. 13x13½*
779 A291 150s blue & blk .40 .35

10th Anniv. of Intl. Potato Study Center, Lima A292

1982, Dec. 27 *Perf. 13x13½*
780 A292 240s multicolored .65 .45

For surcharge see No. 793.

450th Anniv. of City of San Miguel de Piura A293

1982, Dec. 31 *Perf. 13x13½*
781 A293 280s Arms .90 .65

For surcharge see No. 795.

TB Bacillus Centenary A294

1983, Jan. 18 *Perf. 12*
782 A294 240s Microscope, slide .70 .70

For surcharge see No. 794.

St. Teresa of Jesus of Avila (1515-1582), by Jose Espinoza de los Monteros, 1682 — A295

1983, Mar. 1
783 A295 100s multicolored .30 .25

10th Anniv. of State Security Service A296

1983, Mar. 8
784 A296 100s blue & orange .30 .25

Horseman's Ornamental Silver Shoe, 19th Cent.
A297

1983, Mar. 18

785 A297 250s multicolored .65 .45

30th Anniv. of Santiago Declaration
A298

1983, Mar. 25

786 A298 280s Map 1.00 .60

For surcharge see No. 796.

25th Anniv. of Lima-Bogota Airmail Service — A299

1983, Apr. 8

787 A299 150s Jet .60 .25

75th Anniv. of Lima and Callao State Lotteries — A300

1983, Apr. 26

788 A300 100s multicolored .30 .25

Nos. 739, 773, 771, 778, 780, 782, 781, 786, 777, 749, 774 Srchd. in Black or Green

1983 Litho.

789 A277 100s on 40s orange 1.25 .25
790 A285 100s on 70s multi 1.25 .25
791 A283 100s on 80s blk & red 1.25 .25
792 A290 100s on 240s multi 1.25 .25
793 A292 100s on 240s multi 1.25 .25
794 A294 100s on 240s ol grn 1.25 .25
795 A293 150s on 280s multi (G) 1.50 .50
796 A298 150s on 280s multi 1.50 .50
797 A289 200s on 280s multi 2.25 .60
798 A277 300s on 180s green 3.50 1.00
799 A277 400s on 180s green 4.50 1.25
800 A286 500s on 80s multi 1.25 1.25
Nos. 789-800 (12) 22.00 6.60

Military Ships
A301

150s, Cruiser Almirante Grau, 1907; 350s, Submarine Ferre, 1913.

1983, May 2 *Perf. 12*

801 A301 150s multicolored .75 .25
802 A301 350s multicolored 2.00 .50

Simon Bolivar Birth Bicentenary
A302

1983, Dec. 13 Litho. *Perf. 14*

803 A302 100s black & lt bl .70 .25

Christmas
A303

1983, Dec. 16

804 A303 100s Virgin and Child 1.00 .25

25th Anniv. of Intl. Pacific Fair — A304

1983

805 A304 350s multicolored .90 .50

World Communications Year (in 1983) — A305

1984, Jan. 27 Litho. *Perf. 14*

806 A305 700s multicolored 2.00 1.00

Col. Leoncio Prado (1853-83)
A306

1984, Feb. 3 Litho. *Perf. 14*

807 A306 150s ol & ol brn .60 .25

Postal Building
A307

Pottery — A308

Shipbuilding and Repair — A309

Arms of City of Callao — A310

Peruvian Flora — A311

Peruvian Fauna — A312

50s, Ministry of Posts, Lima. 100s, Water jar. 150s, Llama. 200s, Painted vase. 300s, Mixed cargo ship. 400s, Arms of Cajamarca. 500s, Arms of Ayacucho. 700s, Canna edulis ker. 1000s, Lagothrix flavicauda.

1984 Litho. *Perf. 14*

808 A307 50s multi .25 .25
809 A308 100s multi .70 .25
810 A308 150s multi .70 .25
811 A308 200s multi .70 .25
812 A309 250s shown .70 .25
813 A309 300s multi 1.00 .25
814 A310 350s shown .55 .25
815 A310 400s multi 1.25 .25
816 A310 500s multi 1.60 .25
817 A311 700s multi 1.00 .40
818 A312 1000s multi 2.00 .60
Nos. 808-818 (11) 10.45 3.25

Issued: 50s, 8/29; 100s-200s, 5/9; 250s-300s, 2/22; 350s, 4/23; 400s, 6/21; 500s, 6/22; 700s, 9/12; 1000s, 7/3.

See Nos. 844-853, 880-885.

A313

Designs: 50s, Hipolito Unanue (1758-1833). 200s, Ricardo Palma (1833-1919), Writer.

1984 Litho. *Perf. 14*

819 A313 50s dull green .50 .30
820 A313 200s purple .50 .30

Issue dates: 50s, Nov. 14; 200s, Mar. 20.

See No. 828.

A315

1984, Mar. 30

821 A315 500s Shooting .80 .40
822 A315 750s Hurdles 1.20 .60

1984 Summer Olympics.

Independence Declaration Act — A316

1984, July 18 Litho. *Perf. 14*

823 A316 350s Signing document .50 .25

Admiral Grau — A317

Naval Battle — A318

1984, Oct. 8 Litho. *Perf. 12½*

824 Block of 4 4.00 3.00
a. A317 600s Knight of the Seas, by Pablo Muniz .90 .25
b. A318 600s Battle of Angamos .90 .25
c. A317 600s Congressional seat .90 .25
d. A318 600s Battle of Iquique .90 .25

Admiral Miguel Grau, 150th birth anniv.

Peruvian Naval Vessels
A319

250s, Destroyer Almirante Guise, 1934. 400s, Gunboat America, 1905.

1984, Dec. Litho. *Perf. 14*

825 A319 250s multicolored .75 .25
826 A319 400s multicolored .75 .25

Christmas A320

1984, Dec. 11 Litho. *Perf. 13x13½*
827 A320 1000s multi .70 .50

Famous Peruvians Type of 1984

1984, Dec. 14 Litho. *Perf. 14*
828 A313 100s brown lake .40 .25

Victor Andres Belaunde (1883-1967), Pres. of UN General Assembly, 1959-60.

450th Anniv., Founding of Cuzco — A322

1984, Dec. 20 Litho. *Perf. 13½x13*
829 A322 1000s Street scene .80 .40

15th Pacific Intl. Fair, Lima A323

1984, Dec. 28 Litho. *Perf. 13x13½*
830 A323 1000s Llama .80 .40

450th Anniv., Lima — A324

The Foundation of Lima, by Francisco Gamarra

1985, Jan. 17 Litho. *Perf. 13½x13*
831 A324 1500s multicolored 3.00 .50

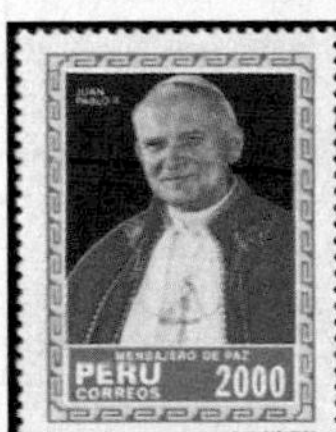

Visit of Pope John Paul II — A325

1985, Jan. 31 Litho. *Perf. 13½x13*
832 A325 2000s Portrait 2.50 .40

Microwave Tower — A326

1985, Feb. 28 Litho. *Perf. 13½x13*
833 A326 1100s multi 1.00 .30

ENTEL Peru, Natl. Telecommunications Org., 15th anniv.

Jose Carlos Mariategui (1894-1924), Author — A327

Designs: 500s, Francisco Garcia Calderon (1832-1905), president. No. 838, Oscar Miro Quesada (1884-1981), jurist. No. 839, Cesar Vallejo (1892-1938), author. No. 840, Jose Santos Chocano (1875-1934), poet.

1985-86 Photo. *Perf. 13½x13*

836	A327	500s lt olive grn	.50	.25
837	A327	800s dull red	.50	.25
838	A327	800s dk olive grn	.50	.25
839	A327	800s Prus blue ('86)	.50	.25
840	A327	800s dk red brn ('86)	.50	.25
		Nos. 836-840 (5)	2.50	1.25

See Nos. 901-905.

American Air Forces Cooperation System, 25th Anniv. — A328

1985, Apr. 16
842 A328 400s Member flags, emblem .50 .25

Jose A. Quinones Gonzales (1914-1941), Air Force Captain — A329

1985, Apr. 22 *Perf. 13x13½*
843 A329 1000s Portrait, bomber 1.10 .45

Types of 1984

Design: 200s, Entrance arch and arcade, Central PO admin. building, vert. No. 845, Spotted Robles Moqo bisque vase, Pacheco, Ica. No. 846, Huaura bisque cat. No. 847, Robles Moqo bisque llama head. No. 848, Huancavelica city arms. No. 849, Huanuco city arms. No. 850, Puno city arms. No. 851, Llama wool industry. No. 852, Hymenocallis amancaes. No. 853, Penguins, Antarctic landscape.

1985-86 Litho. *Perf. 13½x13*

844	A307	200s	slate blue	.60	.60
845	A308	500s	bister brn	.35	.30
846	A308	500s	dull yellow brn	.35	.30
847	A308	500s	black brn	.35	.30
848	A310	700s	brt org yel	.80	.70
849	A310	700s	brt bl ('86)	.80	.70
850	A310	900s	brown ('86)	1.10	.70
851	A309	1100s	multicolored	.80	.50
852	A311	1100s	multicolored	.80	.50
853	A312	1500s	multicolored	1.10	.60
			Nos. 844-853 (10)	7.05	5.20

Natl. Aerospace Institute Emblem, Globe A330

1985, May 24 *Perf. 13x13½*
858 A330 900s ultra .70 .25

14th Inter-American Air Defense Day.

Founding of Constitution City — A333

1985, July Litho. *Perf. 13½x13*
859 A333 300s Map, flag, crucifix .70 .35

Natl. Radio Society, 55th Anniv. A334

1985, July 24 *Perf. 13x13½*
860 A334 1300s bl & brt org 1.00 .35

San Francisco Convent Church — A335

1985, Oct. 12 *Perf. 13½x13*
861 A335 1300s multicolored .60 .25

Doctrina Christiana Frontispiece, 1585, Lima — A336

1985, Oct. 23
862 A336 300s pale buff & blk .70 .25

1st printed book in South America, 400th anniv.

Intl. Civil Aviation Org., 40th Anniv. A337

1100s, 1920 Curtis Jenny.

1985, Oct. 31 *Perf. 13x13½*
863 A337 1100s multicolored .80 .35

Christmas A338

2.50i, Virgin and child, 17th cent.

1985, Dec. 30 Litho. *Perf. 13½x13*
864 A338 2.50i multi 1.00 .25

Postman, Child — A338a

1985, Dec. 30 Litho. *Perf. 13½x13*
864A A338a 2.50i multi .65 .35

Christmas charity for children's and postal workers' funds.

Founding of Trujillo, 450th Anniv. — A339

1986, Mar. 5 Litho. *Perf. 13½x13*
865 A339 3i City arms 1.00 .35

Restoration of Chan Chan Ruins, Trujillo Province A340

1986, Apr. 5 Litho. *Perf. 13x13½*
866 A340 50c Bas-relief 1.00 .30

Saint Rose of Lima, Birth Quadricent. A341

1986, Apr. 30 Litho. *Perf. 13½x13*
867 A341 7i multicolored 2.50 1.25

16th Intl. Pacific Fair — A342

1i, Natl. products symbols.

1986, May 20
868 A342 1i multicolored .70 .40

Intl. Youth Year A343

1986, May 23 *Perf. 13x13½*
869 A343 3.50i multicolored .65 .45

A344

1986, June 27 Litho. *Perf. 13½x13*
870 A344 50c brown .50 .45

Pedro Vilcapaza (1740-81), independence hero.

A345

1986, Aug. 8 Litho. *Perf. 13x13½*
871 A345 3.50i multi 1.10 .75

UN, 40th anniv.

A346

1986, Aug. 11 *Perf. 13½x13*
872 A346 50c grysh brown .50 .25

Fernando and Justo Albujar Fayaque, Manuel Guarniz Lopez, natl. heroes.

Peruvian Navy A347

1986, Aug. 19 *Perf. 13x13½*
873 A347 1.50i R-1, 1926 .75 .35
874 A347 2.50i Abtao, 1954 1.40 .35

Flora Type of 1984

1986 Litho. *Perf. 13½x13*
880 A311 80c Tropaeolum majus .45 .45
881 A311 80c Datura candida .45 .45
884 A312 2i Canis nudus 1.10 1.00
885 A312 2i Penelope albipennis 1.25 1.10
Nos. 880-885 (4) 3.25 3.00

Canchis Province Folk Costumes A348

1986, Aug. 26 Litho. *Perf. 13½x13*
890 A348 3i multicolored 1.10 .75

Tourism Day A349

1986, Aug. 29 *Perf. 13x13½*
891 A349 4i Sacsayhuaman 1.60 1.00

1986, Oct. 12 Litho. *Perf. 13x13½*
891A A349 4i Intihuatana, Cuzco 2.25 1.75

Interamerican Development Bank, 25th Anniv. — A350

1986, Sept. 4
892 A350 1i multicolored .45 .45

Beatification of Sr. Ana de Los Angeles — A351

6i, Sr. Ana, Pope John Paul II.

1986, Sept. 15
893 A351 6i multicolored 3.00 1.50

Jorge Chavez (1887-1910), Aviator, and Bleriot XI 1M — A352

1986, Sept. 23 *Perf. 13½x13*
894 A352 5i multicolored 1.50 .75

Chavez's flight over the Alps, 75th anniv.

VAN '86 — A353

1986, Sept. 26
895 A353 50c light blue .40 .40

Ministry of Health vaccination campaign, Sept. 27-28, Oct. 25-26, Nov. 22-23.

Natl. Journalism Day — A354

1986, Oct. 1
896 A354 1.50i multi .50 .25

Peruvian Navy A355

No. 897, Brigantine Gamarra, 1848. No. 898, Monitor Manco Capac, 1880.

1986, Oct. 7 Litho. *Perf. 13x13½*
897 A355 1i multicolored .80 .35
898 A355 1i multicolored .80 .35

Institute of Higher Military Studies, 35th Anniv. A356

1986, Oct. 31 Litho. *Perf. 13x13½*
899 A356 1i multicolored .40 .25

Boy, Girl — A357

1986, Nov. 3 *Perf. 13½x13*
900 A357 2.50i red, brn & blk .70 .50

Christmas charity for children and postal workers' funds.

Famous Peruvians Type of 1985

1986-87
901 A327 50c Carrion .45 .35
902 A327 50c Barrenechea .45 .35
904 A327 80c Jose de la Riva Aguero .55 .45
905 A327 80c Barrenechea .45 .35
Nos. 901-905 (4) 1.90 1.50

Issued: #904, 10/22/87; #905, 11/9/87.

Christmas A358

1986, Dec. 3
908 A358 5i St. Joseph and Child 2.00 1.00

SENATI, 25th Anniv. — A359

1986, Dec. 19 *Perf. 13½x13*
909 A359 4i multicolored 1.10 .75

Shipibo Tribal Costumes A360

1987, Apr. 24 Litho. *Perf. 13½x13*
910 A360 3i multicolored 1.00 .50

World Food Day — A361

1987, May 26
911 A361 50c multicolored .60 .25

Preservation of the Nazca Lines — A362

Design: Nazca Lines and Dr. Maria Reiche (b. 1903), archaeologist.

1987, June 13 Litho. *Perf. 13x13½*
912 A362 8i multicolored 3.00 1.25

A363

1987, July 15 Litho. *Perf. 13½x13*
913 A363 50c violet .55 .25

Mariano Santos (1850-1900), "The Hero of Tarapaca," 1879, Chilean war. Dated 1986.

A364

1987, July 19 *Perf. 13x13½*
914 A364 3i multicolored .80 .50

Natl. Horse Club, 50th anniv. Dated 1986.

A365

1987, Aug 13 ***Perf. 13½x13***
915 A365 2i multicolored .70 .35

Gen. Felipe Santiago Salaverry (1806-1836), revolution leader. Dated 1986.

Colca's Canyon — A366

1987, Sept. 8 Litho. ***Perf. 13½x13***
916 A366 6i multicolored 1.00 .60

10th Natl. Philatelic Exposition, Arequipa. Dated 1986.

AMIFIL '87 — A367

1987, Sept. 10
917 A367 1i Nos. 1-2 .45 .45

Dated 1986.

Jose Maria Arguedas (b. 1911), Anthropologist, Author — A368

1987, Sept. 19
918 A368 50c brown .45 .45

Arequipa Chamber of Commerce & Industry A369

1987, Sept. 23 ***Perf. 13x13½***
919 A369 2i multicolored .45 .30

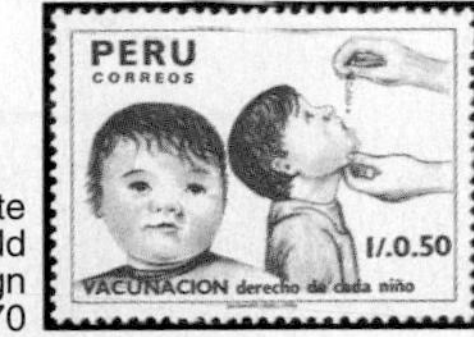

Vaccinate Every Child Campaign A370

1987, Sept. 30 Litho. ***Perf. 13x13½***
920 A370 50c orange brown .45 .45

Argentina, Winner of the 1986 World Cup Soccer Championships — A371

1987, Nov. 18
921 A371 4i multicolored .90 .45

Restoration of Chan Chan Ruins, Trujillo Province A372

Chimu culture (11th-15th cent.) bas-relief.

1987, Nov. 27
922 A372 50c multicolored 1.10 .55

See No. 936.

Halley's Comet A373

4i, Comet, Giotto satellite.

1987, Dec. 7
923 A373 4i multicolored 1.50 1.10

Jorge Chavez Dartnell (1887-1910), Aviator — A374

1987, Dec. 15 ***Perf. 13½x13***
924 A374 2i yel bis, claret brn & gold .60 .25

Founding of Lima, 450th Anniv. (in 1985) — A375

1987, Dec. 18 Litho. ***Perf. 13½x13***
925 A375 2.50i Osambela Palace .60 .25

Dated 1985.

Discovery of the Ruins at Machu Picchu, 75th Anniv. (in 1986) A376

1987, Dec. ***Perf. 13x13½***
926 A376 9i multicolored 3.25 2.00

Dated 1986.

St. Francis's Church, Cajamarca A377

1988, Jan. 23 Litho. ***Perf. 13x13½***
927 A377 2i multicolored .55 .25

Cultural Heritage. Dated 1986.

Participation of Peruvian Athletes in the Olympics, 50th Anniv. — A378

Design: Athletes on parade, poster publicizing the 1936 Berlin Games.

1988, Mar. 1 Litho. ***Perf. 13½x13***
928 A378 1.50i multicolored .65 .25

Dated 1986.

Ministry of Education, 150th Anniv. A379

1988, Mar. 10 ***Perf. 13x13½***
929 A379 1i multicolored .70 .30

Coronation of the Virgin of the Evangelization by Pope John Paul II — A380

1988, Mar. 14 Litho. ***Perf. 13x13½***
930 A380 10i multicolored 1.25 .60

Dated 1986.

Rotary Intl. Involvement in Anti-Polio Campaign A381

1988, Mar. 16
931 A381 2i org, gold & dark blue .55 .55

Postman, Cathedral A382

1988, Apr. 29 Litho. ***Perf. 13½x13***
932 A382 9i brt blue 1.00 .60

Christmas charity for children and postal workers' funds.

Meeting of 8 Latin-American Presidents, Acapulco, 1st Anniv. — A383

1988, May 4 ***Perf. 13x13½***
933 A383 9i multicolored 1.25 .75

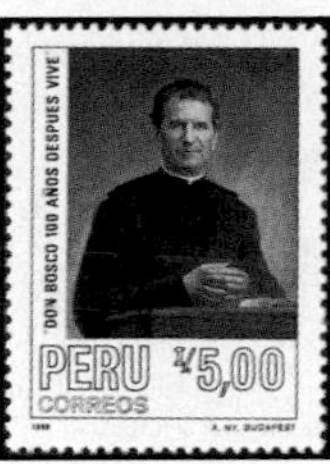

St. John Bosco (1815-1888), Educator — A384

1988, June 1 ***Perf. 13½x13***
934 A384 5i multicolored .45 .45

1st Peruvian Scientific Expedition to the Antarctic A385

7i, Ship Humboldt, globe.

1988, June 2 ***Perf. 13x13½***
935 A385 7i multicolored .65 .55

Restoration of Chan-Chan Ruins, Trujillo Province A386

1988, June 7
936 A386 4i Bas-relief .55 .25

Cesar Vallejo (1892-1938), Poet — A387

1988, June 15 ***Perf. 13½x13***
937 A387 25i buff, blk & brn 1.25 .55

Journalists' Fund — A388

1988, July 12 Litho. ***Perf. 13½x13***
938 A388 4i buff & deep ultra .45 .45

Type A44 — A389

1988, Sept. 1 Litho. ***Perf. 13½x13***
939 A389 20i blk, lt pink & ultra .50 .50

EXFILIMA '88, discovery of America 500th anniv.

17th Intl. Pacific Fair A390

1988, Sept. 6 ***Perf. 13x13½***
940 A390 4i multicolored 1.00 1.00

Painting by Jose Sabogal (1888-1956) — A391

1988, Sept. 7
941 A391 12i multicolored .45 .45

Peru Kennel Club Emblem, Dogs — A392

1988, Sept. 9 ***Perf. 13½x13***
942 A392 20i multicolored 1.60 .90

CANINE '88 Intl. Dog Show, Lima.

Alfonso de Silva (1902-1934), Composer, and Score to Esplendido de Flores — A393

1988, Sept. 27 Litho. ***Perf. 13x13½***
943 A393 20i multicolored .65 .30

2nd State Visit of Pope John Paul II — A394

1988, Oct. 10 ***Perf. 13½x13***
944 A394 50i multicolored .75 .30

1988 Summer Olympics, Seoul — A395

1988, Nov. 10 Litho. ***Perf. 13½x13***
945 A395 25i Women's volleyball 1.00 .35

Women's Volleyball Championships (1982) — A396

Surcharged in Red

1988, Nov. 16 ***Perf. 12***
946 A396 95i on 300s multi 1.40 .70

No. 946 not issued without overprint. Christmas charity for children's and postal workers' funds.

Chavin Culture Ceramic Vase — A397

Surcharged in Henna or Black

1988 Litho. ***Perf. 12***
947 A397 40i on 100s red brn 1.50 1.10
948 A397 80i on 10s blk 2.25 1.10

Nos. 947-948 not issued without surcharge. Issue dates: 40i, Dec. 15. 80i, Dec. 22.

Rain Forest Border Highway — A398

Surcharged in Black

1989, Jan. 27 Litho. ***Perf. 12***
949 A398 70i on 80s multi .60 .45

Not issued without surcharge.

Codex of the Indian Kings, 1681 — A399

Surcharged in Olive Brown

1989, Feb. 10
950 A399 230i on 300s multi 1.25 .60

Not issued without surcharge.

Credit Bank of Peru, Cent. A400

500i, Huari Culture weaving.

1989, Apr. 9 Litho. ***Perf. 13x13½***
951 A400 500i multicolored 1.50 .75

Postal Services A401

1989, Apr. 20 ***Perf. 13***
952 A401 50i SESPO, vert. .45 .35
953 A401 100i CAN .55 .40

El Comercio, 150th Anniv. — A402

1989, May 15
954 A402 600i multicolored 1.00 .50

Garcilaso de la Vega (1539-1616), Historian Called "The Inca" — A403

1989, July 11 Litho. ***Perf. 12½***
955 A403 300i multicolored .60 .30

Express Mail Service A404

1989, July 12
956 A404 100i dark red, org & dark blue .45 .35

Federation Emblem and Roca — A405

1989, Aug. 29 Litho. ***Perf. 13***
957 A405 100i multicolored .45 .35

Luis Loli Roca (1925-1988), founder of the Federation of Peruvian Newspaper Publishers.

Restoration of Chan Chan Ruins, Trujillo Province A406

Chimu culture (11th-15th cent.) bas-relief.

1989, Sept. 17 ***Perf. 12½***
958 A406 400i multicolored 2.50 1.10

Geographical Society of Lima, Cent. — A407

1989, Sept. 18 ***Perf. 13***
959 A407 600i Early map of So. America 2.50 1.25

Founders of Independence Soc. — A408

1989, Sept. 28 Litho. ***Perf. 12½***
960 A408 300i multicolored .60 .35

3rd Meeting of the Presidential Consultation and Planning Board — A409

1989, Oct. 12 ***Perf. 13***
961 A409 1300i Huacachina Lake 2.50 1.25

For surcharge see No. 1027.

Children Mailing Letters — A410

1989, Nov. 29 Litho. ***Perf. 12½***
962 A410 1200i multicolored .65 .25

Christmas charity for children's and postal workers' funds.

Cacti A411

No. 963, Loxanthocereus acanthurus. No. 964, Corryocactus huincoensis. No. 965, Haageocereus clavispinus. No. 966,

Trichocereus pervianus. No. 967, Matucana cereoides.

1989, Dec. 21 Litho. *Perf. 13*

963	A411	500i multicolored	.70	.25
964	A411	500i multicolored	.70	.25
965	A411	500i multicolored	.70	.25
966	A411	500i multicolored	.70	.25
967	A411	500i multicolored	.70	.25
		Nos. 963-967 (5)	3.50	1.25

Nos. 965-967 vert. For surcharges see Nos. 1028-1031

America Issue — A412

UPAE emblem and pre-Columbian medicine jars.

1989, Dec. 28 *Perf. 12½*

968	A412	5000i shown	7.00	2.50
969	A412	5000i multi, diff.	7.00	2.50

Belen Church, Cajamarca A413

1990, Feb. 1 Litho. *Perf. 12½*

970	A413	600i multicolored	1.60	.25

Historic patrimony of Cajamarca and culture of the Americas.

Huascaran Natl. Park — A414

No. 971, Llanganuco Lagoons. No. 972, Mountain climber, Andes, vert. No. 973, Alpamayo mountain. No. 974, Puya raimondi, vert. No. 975, Condor and Quenual. No. 976, El Huascaran.

1990, Feb. 4 *Perf. 13*

971	A414	900i multicolored	.60	.25
972	A414	900i multicolored	.60	.25
973	A414	1000i multicolored	.65	.25
974	A414	1000i multicolored	.65	.25
975	A414	1100i multicolored	.80	.25
976	A414	1100i multicolored	.80	.25
		Nos. 971-976 (6)	4.10	1.50

Pope and Icon of the Virgin — A415

1990, Feb. 6 *Perf. 12½*

977	A415	1250i multicolored	1.25	.35

Visit of Pope John Paul II. For surcharge see No. 1039.

Butterflies — A416

No. 978, Amydon. No. 979, Agrias beata, female. No. 980, Sardanapalus, male. No. 981, Sardanapalus, female. No. 982, Agrias beata, male.

1990, Feb. 11 *Perf. 13*

978	A416	1000i multi	1.75	.25
979	A416	1000i multi	1.75	.25
980	A416	1000i multi	1.75	.25
981	A416	1000i multi	1.75	.25
982	A416	1000i multi	1.75	.25
		Nos. 978-982 (5)	8.75	1.25

For surcharges see Nos. 1033-1037.

A417

Victor Raul Haya de La Torre and Seat of Government.

1990, Feb. 24 *Perf. 12½*

983	A417	2100i multicolored	.90	.40

Return to constitutional government, 10th anniv.

A418

1990, May 24 Litho. *Perf. 12½*

984	A418	300i multicolored	.60	.35

Peruvian Philatelic Assoc., 50th anniv. Dated 1989. For surcharge see No. 1038.

Prenfil '88 A419

1990, May 29

985	A419	300i multicolored	.35	.25

World Exposition of Stamp & Literature Printers, Buenos Aires. Dated 1989. For surcharge see No. 1032.

French Revolution, Bicentennial A420

#986, Liberty. #987, Storming the Bastille. #988, Lafayette celebrating the Republic. #989, Rousseau & symbols of the Revolution.

1990, June 5

986	A420	2000i multicolored	.85	.45
987	A420	2000i multicolored	.85	.45
988	A420	2000i multicolored	.85	.45
989	A420	2000i shown	.85	.45
a.		Strip of 4, #986-989 + label	5.50	5.50

Dated 1989.

Arequipa, 450th Anniv. — A421

1990, Aug. 15 Litho. *Perf. 13*

990	A421	50,000i multi	.90	.45

Lighthouse A422

Design: 230,000i, Hospital ship Morona.

Surcharged in Black

1990, Sept. 19 *Perf. 12½*

991	A422	110,000i on 200i blue	1.50	.75
992	A422	230,000i on 400i blue	3.00	1.50

Not issued without surcharge. No. 991 exists with albino surcharge.

A423

110,000i, Torch bearer. 280,000i, Shooting. 290,000i, Running, horiz. 300,000i, Soccer. 560,000i, Swimming, horiz. 580,000i, Equestrian. 600,000i, Sailing. 620,000i, Tennis.

1990-91 Litho. *Perf. 13*

993	A423	110,000i multi	1.00	.50
994	A423	280,000i multi	2.25	1.10
995	A423	290,000i multi	2.25	1.10
996	A423	300,000i multi	2.50	1.25
997	A423	560,000i multi	3.50	1.75
998	A423	580,000i multi	4.00	2.00
999	A423	600,000i multi	4.25	2.00
1000	A423	620,000i multi	4.25	2.00
		Nos. 993-1000 (8)	24.00	11.70

4th South American Games, Lima. Issue dates: #993-996, Oct. 19. #997-1000, Feb. 5, 1991.

A424

1990, Nov. 22 Litho. *Die Cut*

Self-Adhesive

1001	A424	250,000i No. 1	2.50	1.25
1002	A424	350,000i No. 2	3.50	1.75

Pacific Steam Navigation Co., 150th anniv.

Postal Workers' Christmas Fund — A425

1990, Dec. 7 Litho. *Perf. 12½*

1003	A425	310,000i multi	3.00	1.40

Maria Jesus Castaneda de Pardo, First Woman President of Peruvian Red Cross A426

1991, May 15 Litho. *Perf. 12½*

1004	A426	.15im on 2500i red & blk	1.10	.60

Dated 1990. Not issued without surcharge.

2nd Peruvian Scientific Expedition to Antarctica — A427

.40im, Penguins, man. .45im, Peruvian research station, skua. .50im, Whale, map, research station.

1991, June 20

1005	A427	.40im on 50,000i	3.50	1.60
1006	A427	.45im on 80,000i	3.75	1.75
1007	A427	.50im on 100,000i	4.75	2.10
		Nos. 1005-1007 (3)	12.00	5.45

Not issued without surcharge.

A428

St. Anthony Natl. Univ., Cuzco, 300th Anniv.: 10c, Siphoonandra ellipitica. 20c, Don Manuel de Mollinedo y Angulo, founder. 1s, University coat of arms.

1991, Sept. 26 Litho. *Perf. 13½x13*

1008	A428	10c multicolored	.40	.25
1009	A428	20c multicolored	.80	.40
1010	A428	1s multicolored	4.00	2.00
		Nos. 1008-1010 (3)	5.20	2.65

A429

Paintings: No. 1011, Madonna and child. No. 1012, Madonna with lambs and angels.

1991, Dec. 3 Litho. ***Perf. 13½x13***

1011 A429 70c multicolored 3.50 1.75
1012 A429 70c multicolored 3.50 1.75

Postal Workers' Christmas fund.

America Issue A430

No. 1013, Mangrove swamp. No. 1014, Gera waterfall, vert.

1991, Dec. 23 ***Perf. 13***

1013 A430 .50im multi 2.50 1.50
1014 A430 .50im multi 2.50 1.50

Dated 1990.

Sir Rowland Hill and Penny Black A431

1992, Jan. 15 Litho. ***Perf. 13***

1015 A431 .40im gray, blk & bl 1.75 .70

Penny Black, 150th anniv. (in 1990).

A432

1992, Jan. 28

1016 A432 .30im multicolored 1.10 .50

Our Lady of Guadalupe College, 150th anniv. (in 1990)

A433

1992, Jan. 30 ***Perf. 13½x13***

1017 A433 10c multicolored .35 .25

Entre Nous Society, 80th anniv.

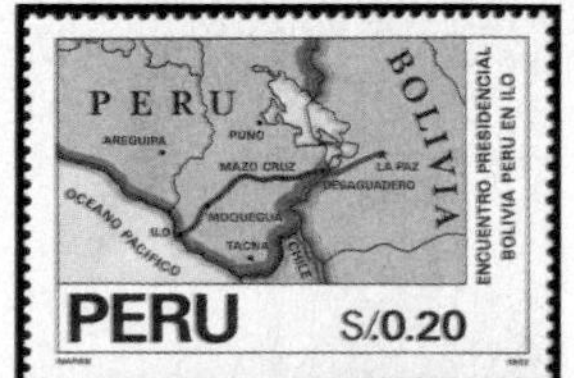

Peru-Bolivia Port Access Agreement — A434

1992, Feb. 25 Litho. ***Perf. 12½***

1018 A434 20c multicolored .80 .40

Restoration of Chan-Chan Ruins — A435

1992, Mar. 17

1019 A435 .15im multicolored 1.25 .60

Dated 1990.

Antonio Raimondi, Naturalist and Publisher, Death Cent. — A436

1992, Mar. 31

1020 A436 .30im multicolored 1.40 .75

Dated 1990.

Newspaper "Diario de Lima", Bicent. (in 1990) — A437

1992, May 22 Litho. ***Perf. 13***

1021 A437 .35im pale yel & black 1.10 .55

Dated 1990.

Mariano Melgar (1790-1815), Poet — A438

1992, Aug. 5 Litho. ***Perf. 12½x13***

1022 A438 60c multicolored 2.25 1.10

8 Reales, 1568, First Peruvian Coinage A439

1992, Aug. 7 ***Perf. 13x12½***

1023 A439 70c multicolored 2.00 1.00

Catholic Univeristy of Peru, 75th Anniv. — A440

1992, Aug. 18 ***Perf. 12½***

1024 A440 90c black & tan 2.75 1.25

Pan-American Health Organization, 90th Anniv. — A441

1992, Dec. 2 Litho. ***Die Cut***
Self-Adhesive

1025 A441 3s multicolored 6.00 4.50

Nos. 749, 961 Surcharged

Perf. 13½x13, 13

1992, Nov. 18 Litho.

1026 A277 50c on 180s #749 1.00 .60
1027 A409 1s on 1300i #961 2.50 1.40

Nos. 963, 965-967, 977-982, & 984-985 Surcharged

Perfs. as Before

1992, Dec. 24 Litho.

1028 A411 40c on 500i #963 10.50 4.25
1029 A411 40c on 500i #965 10.50 4.25
1030 A411 40c on 500i #966 10.50 4.25
1031 A411 40c on 500i #967 10.50 4.25
1032 A419 50c on 300i #985 10.50 4.25
1033 A416 50c on 1000i #978 10.50 4.25
1034 A416 50c on 1000i #979 10.50 4.25
1035 A416 50c on 1000i #980 10.50 4.25
1036 A416 50c on 1000i #981 10.50 4.25
1037 A416 50c on 1000i #982 10.50 4.25
1038 A418 1s on 300i #984 21.00 4.25
1039 A415 1s on 1250i #977 21.00 4.25
Nos. 1028-1039 (12) 147.00 51.00

Virgin with a Spindle, by Urbina — A442

1993, Feb. 10 Litho. ***Die Cut***
Self-Adhesive

1040 A442 80c multicolored 2.50 1.25

Sican Culture A443

Various artifacts.

1993, Feb. 10 Self-Adhesive

1041 A443 2s multicolored 4.50 2.25
1042 A443 5s multi, vert. 10.50 5.25

Evangelization in Peru, 500th Anniv. — A444

1993, Feb. 12 Self-Adhesive

1043 A444 1s multicolored 3.00 1.40

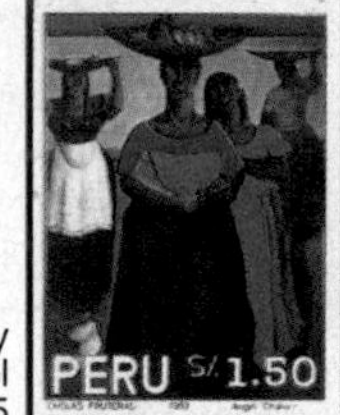

Fruit Sellers, by Angel Chavez — A445

Dancers, by Monica Rojas — A446

1993, Feb. 12 Self-Adhesive

1044 A445 1.50s multicolored 4.00 1.75
1045 A446 1.50s multicolored 4.00 1.75

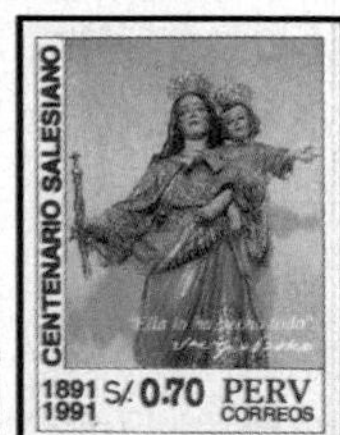

Statue of Madonna and Child — A447

1993, Feb. 24 Litho. ***Die Cut***
Self-Adhesive

1046 A447 70c multicolored 1.90 .95

Salesian Brothers in Peru, cent. (in 1991).

America Issue — A448

UPAEP: No. 1047a, 90c, Francisco Pizarro, sailing ship. b, 1s, Sailing ship, map of northwest coast of South America.

1993, Mar. 19 ***Perf. 12½***

1047 A448 Pair, #a.-b. 5.00 2.50

Sipan Gold Head — A449

1993, Apr. 1
1048 A449 50c multicolored 10.00 10.00

Beatification of Josemaria Escriva, 1st Anniv. — A450

1993, July 7 Litho. *Die Cut*
Self-Adhesive
1049 A450 30c multicolored 1.00 .50

Peru-Japan Treaty of Peace and Trade, 120th Anniv. — A451

Designs: 1.50s, Flowers. 1.70s, Peruvian, Japanese children, mountains.

1993, Aug. 21 Litho. *Perf. 11*
1050 A451 1.50s multicolored 3.25 1.60
1051 A451 1.70s multicolored 3.50 1.75

Sea Lions — A452

1993, Sept. 20 Litho. *Perf. 11*
1052 A452 90c shown 2.00 1.00
1053 A452 1s Parrot, vert. 2.40 1.25

Amifil '93 (#1052). Brasiliana '93 (#1053).

A453

1993, Nov. 9 Litho. *Die Cut*
Self-Adhesive
1054 A453 50c olive brown 2.00 1.00

Honorio Delgado, Physician and Author, Birth Cent. (in 1992).

A454

1993, Nov. 12 Self-Adhesive
1055 A454 80c orange brown 2.75 1.00

Rosalia De LaValle De Morales Macedo, Social Reformer, Birth Cent.

A455

Sculptures depicting Peruvian ethnic groups.

1993, Nov. 22 Self-Adhesive
1056 A455 2s Quechua 8.00 4.00
1057 A455 3.50s Orejon 9.00 4.00

Intl. Pacific Fair, Lima — A456

1993, Nov. 25 Litho. *Perf. 11*
1058 A456 1.50s multicolored 5.50 2.50

Christmas — A457

Design: 1s, Madonna of Loreto.

1993, Nov. 30 *Perf. 11*
1059 A457 1s multicolored 3.00 1.50

Cultural Artifacts — A458

2.50s, Sican artifacts. 4s, Sican mask. 10s, Chancay ceramic statue, vert. 20s, Chancay textile.

Self-Adhesive

1993, Nov. 30 *Die Cut*
1060 A458 2.50s multicolored 10.00 6.00
1061 A458 4s multicolored 12.50 8.75
1062 A458 10s multicolored 35.00 20.00
1063 A458 20s multicolored 72.50 40.00
Nos. 1060-1063 (4) 130.00 74.75

See Nos. 1079-1082.

Prevention of AIDS — A459

1993, Dec. 1 Litho. *Perf. 11*
1064 A459 1.50s multicolored 4.25 2.50

A460

1994, Mar. 4 Litho. *Die Cut*
Self-Adhesive
1065 A460 1s multicolored 2.75 1.40

Natl. Council on Science and Technology (Concytec), 25th Anniv. Dated 1993.

A461

20c, 30c, 40c, 50c, Bridge of Huaman Poma de Ayala.

1994 Self-Adhesive
1066 A461 20c blue .85 .40
1067 A461 40c orange 1.60 .80
1068 A461 50c purple 2.25 1.10
Nos. 1066-1068 (3) 4.70 2.30

Litho.
Perf. 12x11
1073 A461 30c brown 1.10 .55
1074 A461 40c black 1.75 .85
1075 A461 50c vermilion 2.00 1.00
Nos. 1073-1075 (3) 4.85 2.40

Issued: Nos. 1066-1068, 3/11/94; Nos. 1073-1075, 5/13/94.

Cultural Artifacts Type of 1993

No. 1079, Engraved silver container, vert. No. 1080, Engraved medallion. No. 1081, Carved bull, Pucara. No. 1082, Plate with fish designs.

1994, Mar. 25 Self-Adhesive
1079 A458 1.50s multicolored 4.00 2.00
1080 A458 1.50s multicolored 4.00 2.00
1081 A458 3s multicolored 7.00 3.50
1082 A458 3s multicolored 7.00 3.50
Nos. 1079-1082 (4) 22.00 11.00

Dated 1993.

Sipan Artifacts A464

1994, May 19 Litho. *Perf. 11*
1083 A464 3s Peanut-shaped beads 9.00 4.50
1084 A464 5s Mask, vert. 15.00 7.50

El Brujo Archaelogical Site, Trujillo — A465

1994, Nov. 3 Litho. *Perf. 14*
1085 A465 70c multicolored 1.75 .85

Christmas A466

Ceramic figures: 1.80s, Christ child. 2s, Nativity scene. Dated 1994.

1995, Mar. 17 Litho. *Perf. 13x13½*
1086 A466 1.80s multicolored 4.00 2.00
1087 A466 2s multicolored 4.25 2.10

1994 World Cup Soccer Championships, U.S. — A467

1995, Mar. 20 *Perf. 13½x13*
1088 A467 60c shown 1.00 .55
1089 A467 4.80s Mascot, flags 8.00 4.25

Dated 1994.

Ministry of Transportation, 25th Anniv. — A468

1995, Mar. 22 *Perf. 13x13½*
1090 A468 20c multicolored .35 .30

Dated 1994.

Cultural Artifacts A469

Mochican art: 40c, Pitcher with figures beneath blanket. 80c, Jeweled medallion. 90c, Figure holding severed head.

1995, Mar. 27 *Perf. 14*
1091 A469 40c multicolored 1.10 .55
1092 A469 80c multicolored 2.00 .90
1093 A469 90c multicolored 2.25 1.10
Nos. 1091-1093 (3) 5.35 2.55

Dated 1994.

Juan Parra del Riego, Birth Cent. — A470

No. 1095, Jose Carlos Mariategui, birth cent.

1995, Mar. 28 *Perf. 14*
1094 A470 90c multicolored 3.00 1.40
Perf. 13½x13
1095 A470 90c multicolored 3.00 1.40

Dated 1994.

Las Carmelitas Monastery, 350th Anniv. A471

1995, Mar. 31 Litho. *Perf. 13*
1096 A471 70c multicolored 2.00 1.00

Dated 1994.

Peru's Volunteer Fireman's Assoc. A472

Fire trucks: 50c, Early steam ladder. 90c, Modern aerial ladder.

1995, Apr. 12 ***Perf. 14***

1097	A472	50c multicolored	1.50	.75
1098	A472	90c multicolored	2.50	1.25

Dated 1994.

Musical Instruments A473

1995, Apr. 10 **Litho.** ***Perf. 13½x13***

1099	A473	20c Cello	.60	.30
1100	A473	40c Drum	1.10	.55

Union Club, Fountain, Plaza of Arms A474

Design: 1s, Santo Domingo Convent, Lima.

1995, Apr. 19 **Litho.** ***Perf. 14***

1101	A474	90c multicolored	4.00	2.00
1102	A474	1s multicolored	4.50	2.25

Cultural history of Lima.

Ethnic Groups — A475

1995, Apr. 26 ***Perf. 13½x13***

1103	A475	1s Bora girl	2.75	1.40
1104	A475	1.80s Aguaruna man	4.75	2.40

World Food Program, 30th Anniv. A476

1995, May 3 ***Perf. 13x13½***

1105	A476	1.80s multicolored	4.75	2.40

Solanum Ambosinum A477

Design: 2s, Mochica ceramic representation of papa flower.

1995, May 8 ***Perf. 13½x13***

1106	A477	1.80s multicolored	4.75	2.40
1107	A477	2s multicolored	5.25	2.50

Reed Boat, Lake Titicaca — A478

1995, May 12

1108	A478	2s multicolored	5.50	2.75

Fauna A479

1995, May 18 ***Perf. 13½x13, 13x13½***

1109	A479	1s American owl, vert.	2.75	1.40
1110	A479	1.80s Jaguar	4.75	2.40

Andes Development Corporation, 25th Anniv. — A480

1995, Aug. 29 **Litho.** ***Perf. 14***

1111	A480	5s multicolored	12.50	6.25

World Tourism Day A481

1995, Sept. 27 ***Perf. 13x13½***

1112	A481	5.40s multicolored	17.50	8.75

Dated 1994.

World Post Day A482

1995, Oct. 9 ***Perf. 14***

1113	A482	1.80s Antique mail box	4.50	2.25

Dated 1994.

America Issue A483

Perf. 13½x14, 14x13½ (#1115)

1995, Oct. 12

1114	A483	1.50s Landing of Columbus	3.50	1.75
1115	A483	1.70s Guanaco, vert.	4.00	2.00
1116	A483	1.80s Early mail cart	4.00	2.00
1117	A483	2s Postal trucks	4.50	2.25
		Nos. 1114-1117 (4)	16.00	8.00

No. 1116-1117 are dated 1994.

UN, 50th Anniv. A484

Design: 90c, Peruvian delegates, 1945.

1995, Oct. 28 ***Perf. 14***

1118	A484	90c multicolored	2.25	1.10

Entries, Lima Cathedrals A485

Designs: 30c, St. Apolonia. 70c, St. Louis, side entry to St. Francis.

1995, Oct. 20

1119	A485	30c multicolored	.75	.40
1120	A485	70c multicolored	1.75	.90

Dated 1994.

Artifacts from Art Museums A486

Carvings and sculptures: No. 1121, St. James on horseback, 19th cent. No. 1122, Church. 40c, Woman on pedestal. 50c, Archangel.

1995, Oct. 31 ***Perf. 14½x14***

1121	A486	20c multicolored	.70	.40
1122	A486	20c multicolored	.70	.40
1123	A486	40c multicolored	1.25	.70
1124	A486	50c multicolored	1.75	.80
		Nos. 1121-1124 (4)	4.40	2.30

Dated 1994.

Scouting — A487

Designs: a, 80c, Lady Olave Baden-Powell. b, 1s, Lord Robert Baden-Powell.

1995, Nov. 9 **Litho.** ***Perf. 13½x13***

1125	A487	Pair, #a.-b.	4.00	2.00

Dated 1994.

A488

Folk Dances: 1,80s, Festejo. 2s, Marinera limeña, horiz.

1995, Nov. 16 ***Perf. 14***

1126	A488	1.80s multicolored	3.75	1.75
1127	A488	2s multicolored	4.25	2.10

Dated 1994.

A489

Biodiversity: 50c, Manu Natl. Park. 90c, Anolis punctatus, horiz.

1995, Nov. 23

1128	A489	50c multicolored	4.00	2.00
1129	A489	90c multicolored	7.00	3.50

Dated 1994.

A490

Electricity for Development: 20c, Toma de Huinco. 40c, Antacoto Lake.

1995, Nov. 27

1130	A490	20c multicolored	.45	.25
1131	A490	40c multicolored	.90	.45

Dated 1994.

A491

Peruvian Saints: 90c, St. Toribio de Mogrovejo. 1s, St. Francisco Solano.

1995, Dec. 4

1132	A491	90c multicolored	1.90	.90
1133	A491	1s multicolored	2.10	1.00

Dated 1994.

FAO, 50th Anniv. A492

1996, Apr. 24 **Litho.** ***Perf. 14***

1134	A492	60c multicolored	1.25	.75

Christmas 1995 A493

Local crafts: 30c, Nativity scene with folding panels, vert. 70c, Carved statues of three Magi.

1996, May 2

1135	A493	30c multicolored	.60	.30
1136	A493	70c multicolored	1.60	.80

America Issue A494

Designs: 30c, Rock formations of Lachay. 70c, Coastal black crocodile.

1996, May 9
1137 A494 30c multicolored 1.25 .60
1138 A494 70c multicolored 2.50 1.10

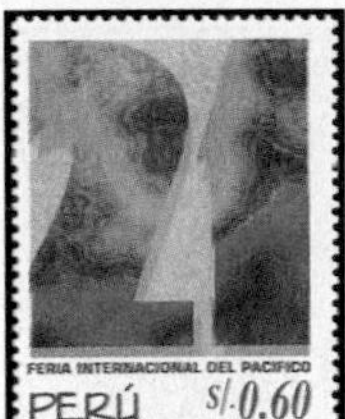
Intl. Pacific Fair — A495

1996, May 16
1139 A495 60c multicolored 1.25 .75

1992 Summer Olympic Games, Barcelona A496

a, 40c Shooting. b, 40c Tennis. c, 60c Swimming. d, 60c Weight lifting.

1996, June 10 **Litho.** ***Perf. 12½***
1140 A496 Block of 4, #a.-d. 5.00 2.50

Dated 1992.
For surcharges see #1220-1223.

Expo '92, Seville A497

1996, June 17
1141 A497 1.50s multicolored 5.75 3.50

Dated 1992.

Cesar Vallejo (1892-1938), Writer — A498

1996, June 25
1142 A498 50c black & gray 1.60 .95

Dated 1992.

Lima, City of Culture — A499

1996, July 1
1143 A499 30c brown & tan .80 .40

Dated 1992.
For surcharge see No. 1219.

Kon-Tiki Expedition, 50th Anniv. A500

1997, Apr. 28 **Litho.** ***Perf. 12½***
1144 A500 3.30s multicolored 5.50 4.00

Beginning with No. 1145, most stamps have colored lines printed on the back creating a granite paper effect.

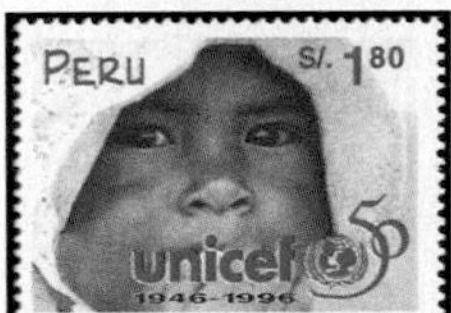
UNICEF, 50th Anniv. (in 1996) A501

1997, Aug. 7 **Litho.** ***Perf. 13½x14***
1145 A501 1.80s multicolored 3.50 2.50

Mochica Pottery — A502

Designs: 20c, Owl. 30c, Ornamental container. 50c, Goose jar. 1s, Two monkeys on jar. 1.30s, Duck pitcher. 1.50s, Cat pitcher.

1997, Aug. 18 **Litho.** ***Perf. 14½***

1146	A502	20c	green	.60	.30
1147	A502	30c	lilac	.95	.45
1148	A502	50c	black	1.50	.75
1149	A502	1s	red brown	3.00	2.10
1150	A502	1.30s	red	4.00	3.00
1151	A502	1.50s	brown	4.75	3.50
	Nos. 1146-1151 (6)			14.80	10.10

See Nos. 1179-1183, 1211-1214.

1996 Summer Olympics, Atlanta — A503

a, Shooting. b, Gymnastics. c, Boxing. d, Soccer

1997, Aug. 25 ***Perf. 14x13½***
1152 A503 2.70s Strip of 4, #a.-d. 16.00 12.00

College of Biology, 25th Anniv. — A504

1997, Aug. 26
1153 A504 5s multicolored 7.25 5.50

Scouting, 90th Anniv. — A505

1997, Aug. 29
1154 A505 6.80s multicolored 10.00 7.75

8th Intl. Conference Against Corruption, Lima A506

1997, Sept. 7 ***Perf. 13½x14***
1155 A506 2.70s multicolored 3.50 2.50

Montreal Protocol on Substances that Deplete Ozone Layer, 10th Anniv. — A507

1997, Sept. 16 ***Perf. 14x13½***
1156 A507 6.80s multicolored 13.50 9.50

Lord of Sipan Artifacts A508

Designs: 2.70s, Animal figure with large hands, feet. 3.30s, Medallion with warrior figure, vert.
10s, Tomb of Lord of Sipan, vert.

1997, Sept. 22 **Litho.** ***Perf. 13½x14***
1157 A508 2.70s multicolored 5.25 4.00
1158 A508 3.30s multicolored 6.50 4.75

Souvenir Sheet

1159 A508 10s multicolored 18.00 13.50

Peruvian Indians — A509

1997, Oct. 12 **Litho.** ***Perf. 14x13½***
1160 A509 2.70s Man 5.50 3.75
1161 A509 2.70s Woman 5.50 3.75

America Issue. Nos. 1160-1161 are dated 1996.

Heinrich von Stephan (1831-97) A510

1997, Oct. 9
1162 A510 10s multicolored 19.00 13.50

America Issue — A511

No. 1163, Early post carrier. No. 1164, Modern letter carrier.

1997, Oct. 12
1163 A511 2.70s multicolored 6.50 3.75
1164 A511 2.70s multicolored 6.50 3.75

13th Bolivar Games — A512

a, Tennis. b, Soccer. c, Basketball. d, Shot put.

1997, Oct. 17 **Litho.** ***Perf. 14x13½***
1165 A512 2.70s Block of 4, #a.-d. 22.50 15.75

Marshal Ramon Castilla (1797-1867) A513

1997, Oct. 17
1166 A513 1.80s multicolored 4.00 3.00

Treaty of Tlatelolco Banning Nuclear Weapons in Latin America, 30th Anniv. — A514

1997, Nov. 3
1167 A514 20s multicolored 37.50 29.00

Manu Natl. Park — A515

Birds: a, Kingfisher. b, Woodpecker. c, Crossbill. d, Eagle. e, Jabiru. f, Owl.

1997, Oct. 24 **Sheet of 6**
1168 A515 3.30s #a.-f. + label 40.00 27.50

8th Peruvian Antarctic Scientific Expedition A516

1997, Nov. 10
1169 A516 6s multicolored 12.00 8.25

Christmas A517

1997, Nov. 26
1170 A517 2.70s multicolored 5.00 3.75

Hipolito Unanue Agreement, 25th Anniv. — A518

1997, Dec. 18 Litho. ***Perf. 14x13½***
1171 A518 1s multicolored 2.00 1.25

Souvenir Sheet

Peruvian Gold Libra, Cent. — A519

1997, Dec. 18
1172 A519 10s multicolored 25.00 18.00

Dept. of Post and Telegraph, Cent. — A520

1997, Dec. 31
1173 A520 1s multicolored 1.75 1.25

Organization of American States (OAS), 50th Anniv. — A521

1998, Apr. 30 Litho. ***Perf. 14x13½***
1174 A521 2.70s multicolored 5.25 5.25

Chorrillos Military School, Cent. A522

1998, Apr. 29 ***Perf. 13½x14***
1175 A522 2.70s multicolored 5.25 5.25

Tourism — A523

1998, June 22 Litho. ***Perf. 14x13½***
1176 A523 5s multicolored 9.00 9.00

Peruvian Horse — A524

1998, June 5
1177 A524 2.70s pale violet & violet 5.75 5.75

1998 World Cup Soccer Championships, France — A525

a, 2.70s, Goalie. b, 3.30s, Two players. 10s, Player kicking ball.

1998, June 26
1178 A525 Pair, #a.-b. 10.00 10.00

Souvenir Sheet

Perf. 13½x14

1178C A525 10s multicolored 18.00 18.00

Mochica Pottery Type of 1997

1s, like #1149. 1.30s, like #1146. 1.50s, like #1151. 2.70s, like #1148. 3.30s, like #1150.

1998, June 19 Litho. ***Perf. 14½***
1179 A502 1s slate 3.00 3.00
1180 A502 1.30s violet 3.75 3.75
1181 A502 1.50s pale blue 4.50 4.50
1182 A502 2.70s bister 8.25 8.25
1183 A502 3.30s black brown 9.50 9.50
Nos. 1179-1183 (5) 29.00 29.00

Aero Peru, 25th Anniv. A526

1.50s, Cuzco Cathedral. 2.70s, Airplane.

1998, May 22 ***Perf. 13½x14***
1184 A526 1.50s multicolored 2.75 2.75
1185 A526 2.70s multicolored 5.25 5.25

Restoration of the Cathedral of Lima, Cent. — A527

1998, June 15 ***Perf. 14x13½***
1186 A527 2.70s multicolored 5.00 5.00

Inca Rulers — A528

No. 1187, Lloque Yupanqui. No. 1188, Sinchi Roca. No. 1189, Manco Capac.

1998, July 17 Litho. ***Perf. 14x13½***
1187 A528 2.70s multicolored 7.00 7.00
1188 A528 2.70s multicolored 7.00 7.00
1189 A528 9.70s multicolored 22.50 22.50
Nos. 1187-1189 (3) 36.50 36.50

See Nos. 1225-1228.

Intl. Year of the Ocean A529

1998, Aug. 8 ***Perf. 13½x14***
1190 A529 6.80s multicolored 13.00 13.00

Natl. Symphony Orchestra, 60th Anniv. — A530

1998, Aug. 11 ***Perf. 14x13½***
1191 A530 2.70s multicolored 5.00 5.00

Mother Teresa (1910-97) A531

1998, Sept. 5
1192 A531 2.70s multicolored 6.00 6.00

Peruvian Children's Foundation A532

1998, Sept. 17
1193 A532 8.80s multicolored 16.00 16.00

Souvenir Sheet

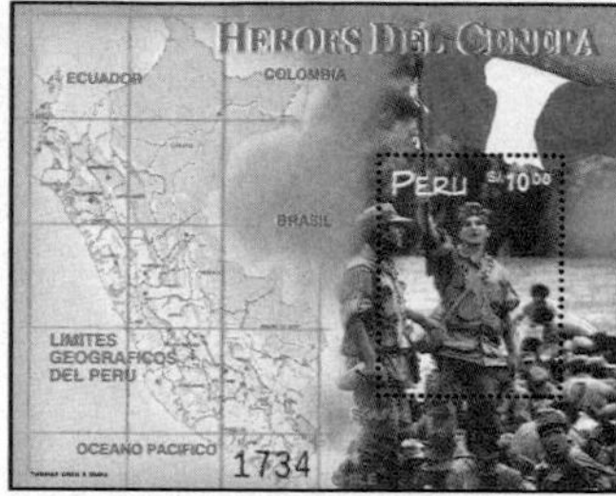

Heroes of the Cenepa River — A533

1998, June 5
1194 A533 10s multicolored 18.00 18.00

Souvenir Sheet

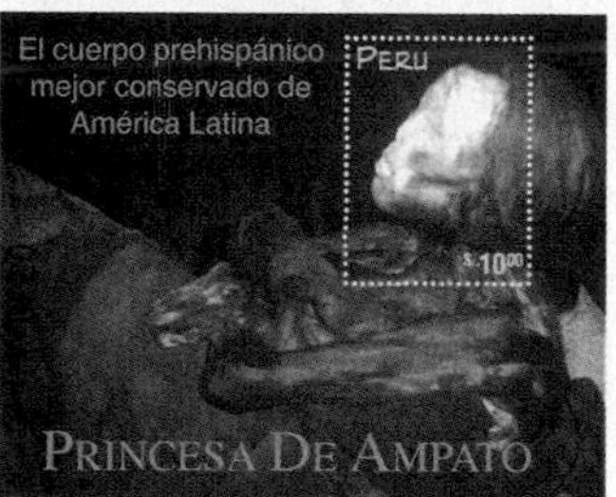

Princess De Ampato — A534

1998, Sept. 8
1195 A534 10s multicolored 18.00 18.00

Fauna of Manu Natl. Park — A535

1998, Sept. 27 Litho. ***Perf. 14x13½***
1196 A535 1.50s multicolored 3.50 3.50

America Issue — A536

1998, Oct. 12
1197 A536 2.70s Chabuca 5.00 5.00

Stamp Day — A537

1998, Oct. 9
1198 A537 6.80s No. 3 11.00 11.00

Frogs — A538

No. 1199: a, Agalychnis craspedopus. b, Ceratophrys cornuta. c, Epipedobates macero. d, Phyllomedusa vaillanti. e, Dendrobates biolat. f, Hemiphractus proboscideus.

1998, Oct. 23 Litho. ***Perf. 14x13½***
1199 A538 3.30s Block of 6, #a.-f. + label *32.50 32.50*

Christmas A539

1998, Nov. 16 ***Perf. 13½x14***
1200 A539 3.30s multicolored 3.75 3.75

Universal Declaration of Human Rights, 50th Anniv. A540

1998, Dec. 10 Litho. ***Perf. 13½x14***
1201 A540 5s multicolored 5.00 5.00

Peru-Ecuador Peace Treaty — A541

1998, Nov. 26 Litho. ***Perf. 13½x14***
1202 A541 2.70s multicolored 3.75 3.75

Brasilia '98.

19th World Scout Jamboree, Chile — A542

Designs: a, Scouting emblem, stylized tents. b, Emblem, tents, "SIEMPRE LISTO."

1999, Jan. 5 Litho. ***Perf. 14x13½***
1203 A542 5s Pair, #a.-b. 10.00 10.00

Peruvian Philatelic Assoc., 50th Anniv. — A543

1999, Jan. 10
1204 A543 2.70s No. 19 2.75 2.75

Paintings by Pancho Fierro (1809-79) — A544

Designs: 2.70s, Once Upon Time in a Shaded Grove. 3.30s, Sound of the Devil.

1999, Jan. 16
1205 A544 2.70s multicolored 2.50 2.50
1206 A544 3.30s multicolored 3.25 3.25

Regional Dance — A545

1999, Feb. 10 Litho. ***Perf. 14x13½***
1207 A545 3.30s multicolored 3.25 3.25

CENDAF, 25th Anniv. A546

1999, Mar. 1 ***Perf. 13½x14***
1208 A546 1.80s multicolored 1.90 1.90

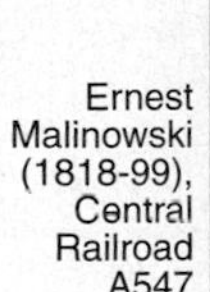

Ernest Malinowski (1818-99), Central Railroad A547

1999, Mar. 3
1209 A547 5s multicolored 5.00 5.00

Peruvian Foundation for Children's Heart Disease A548

1999, Mar. 6
1210 A548 2.70s multicolored 2.75 2.75

Mochica Pottery Type of 1997

Designs: 1s, like #1151. 1.50s, like #1148. 1.80s, like #1146. 2s, like #1150.

1999, Feb. 16 Litho. ***Perf. 14½***
1211 A502 1s lake .95 .95
1212 A502 1.50s dark blue blk 1.75 1.75
1213 A502 1.80s brown 1.90 1.90
1214 A502 2s orange 2.10 2.10
Nos. 1211-1214 (4) 6.70 6.70

Fauna of the Peruvian Rain Forest — A549

1999, Apr. 23 ***Perf. 14x13½***
1215 A549 5s multicolored 5.50 5.50

Souvenir Sheet

Fauna of Manu Natl. Park — A550

1999, Apr. 23 ***Perf. 13½x14***
1216 A550 10s multicolored 13.00 13.00

Milpo Mining Co., 50th Anniv. A551

1999, Apr. 6 ***Perf. 13½x14***
1217 A551 1.50s multicolored 1.60 1.60

See note after No. 1145.

Japanese Immigration to Peru, Cent. — A552

1999, Apr. 3 ***Perf. 14x13½***
1218 A552 6.80s multicolored 7.00 7.00

Nos. 1140, 1143 Surcharged in Black, Brown, Dark Blue, Red or Green

1999 Litho. ***Perf. 12½***
1219 A499 2.40s on 30c (Br) multi 2.50 2.50

Blocks of 4

1220 A496 1s on each value, #a.-d. 4.25 4.25
1221 A496 1.50s on each value, #a.-d. 6.00 6.00
1222 A496 2.70s on each value, #a.-d. 11.50 11.50
1223 A496 3.30s on each value, #a.-d. 13.00 13.00

Size and location of surcharge varies.

Antarctic Treaty, 40th Anniv. A553

1999, May 24 ***Perf. 13½x14***
1224 A553 6.80s multicolored 8.50 8.50

Inca Rulers Type of 1998

1999, June 24 Litho. ***Perf. 14x13½***
1225 A528 3.30s Capac Yupanqui 3.25 3.25
1226 A528 3.30s Yahuar Huaca 3.25 3.25
1227 A528 3.30s Inca Roca 3.25 3.25
1228 A528 3.30s Maita Capac 3.25 3.25
Nos. 1225-1228 (4) 13.00 13.00

Souvenir Sheet

Nazca Lines — A554

1999, June 8
1229 A554 10s multicolored 10.00 10.00

Margin shows Maria Reiche (1903-98), expert in Nazca Lines.

Minerals A555

Designs: 2.70s, Galena. 3.30s, Scheelite. 5s, Virgotrigonia petersení.

1999, July 3 ***Perf. 13½x14***
1230 A555 2.70s multicolored 2.50 2.50
1231 A555 3.30s multicolored 3.25 3.25
1232 A555 5s multicolored 5.25 5.25
Nos. 1230-1232 (3) 11.00 11.00

See Nos. 1339-1341.

Virgin of Carmen — A556

1999, July 16 ***Perf. 14x13½***
1233 A556 3.30s multicolored 4.50 4.50

Santa Catalina Monastery, Arequipa — A557

1999, Aug. 15 Litho. ***Perf. 14x13½***
1234 A557 2.70s multicolored 2.75 2.75

Chinese Immigration to Peru, 150th Anniv. A558

1999 Litho. ***Perf. 13½x14***
1235 A558 1.50s red & black 2.75 2.75

Peruvian Medical Society, 25th Anniv. — A559

1999 Litho. ***Perf. 14x13½***
1236 A559 1.50s multicolored 1.60 1.60

UPU, 125th Anniv. A560

1999, Oct. 9 Litho. ***Perf. 13½x14***
1237 A560 3.30s multicolored 3.25 3.25

America Issue, A New Millennium Without Arms A561

1999, Oct. 12 ***Perf. 14x13½, 13½x14***
1238 A561 2.70s Earth, sunflower, vert. 2.50 2.50
1239 A561 3.30s shown 3.25 3.25

Señor de los Milagros Religious Procession A562

1999, Oct. 18 ***Perf. 14x13½***
1240 A562 1s Incense burner 1.10 1.10
1241 A562 1.50s Procession 1.50 1.50

Inter-American Development Bank, 40th Anniv. — A563

1999, Oct. 22 ***Perf. 13½x14***
1242 A563 1.50s multicolored 1.50 1.50

Butterflies — A564

Designs: a, Pterourus zagreus chrysomelus. b, Asterope buckleyi. c, Parides chabrias. d, Mimoides pausanias. e, Nessaea obrina. f, Pterourus zagreus zagreus.

1999, Oct. 23 ***Perf. 14x13½***
Block of 6 + Label
1243 A564 3.30s #a.-f. 22.00 22.00

Border Disputes Settled by Brasilia Peace Accords A565

Maps of regions from: No. 1244, Cusumasa Bumbuiza to Yaupi Santiago. No. 1245, Lagatococha to Güeppi, vert. No. 1246, Cunhuime Sur to 20 de Noviembre, vert.

1999, Oct. 26 ***Perf. 13½x14, 14x13½***
1244 A565 1s multicolored 1.00 1.00
1245 A565 1s multicolored 1.00 1.00
1246 A565 1s multicolored 1.00 1.00
Nos. 1244-1246 (3) 3.00 3.00

See Nos. 1282-1286.

Peruvian Postal Services, 5th Anniv. — A566

1999, Nov. 22 ***Perf. 14x13½***
1247 A566 2.70s multicolored 2.75 2.75

Christmas A567

1999, Dec. 1 Litho. ***Perf. 14x13½***
1248 A567 2.70s multicolored 3.75 3.75

Ricardo Bentín Mujica (1899-1979), Businessman — A568

1999, Dec. 29 Litho. ***Perf. 13½x14***
1249 A568 2.70s multicolored 2.75 2.75

Souvenir Sheet

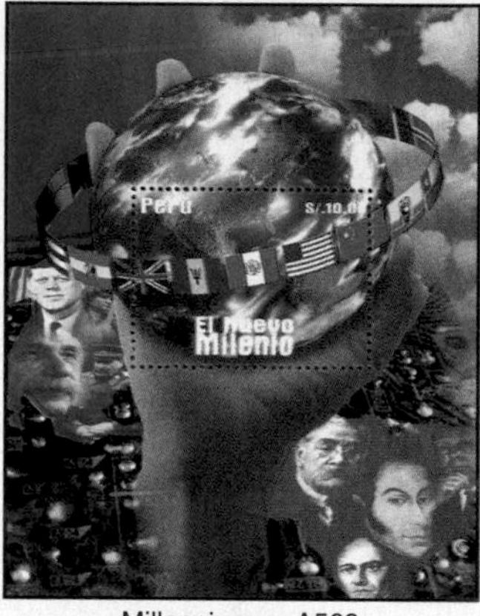

Millennium — A569

2000, Jan. 1
1250 A569 10s multicolored 11.00 11.00

Ricardo Cillóniz Oberti, Businessman A570

2000, Jan. 17 ***Perf. 14x13½***
1251 A570 1.50s multicolored 1.50 1.50

Printed se-tenant with label.

Alpaca Wool Industry — A571

a, Alpacas at right. b, Alpacas at left.

2000, Jan. 27 Litho. ***Perf. 14x13½***
1252 A571 1.50s Pair, #a.-b. 3.25 3.25

Nuclear Energy Institute — A572

2000, Feb. 4
1253 A572 4s multicolored 4.00 4.00

Retamas S.A. Gold Mine — A573

Miner, mine and buildings: a, Text in white. b, Text in blue violet.

2000, Feb. 7
1254 A573 1s Pair, #a.-b. 2.00 2.00

Comptroller General, 70th Anniv. A574

2000, Feb. 28 ***Perf. 13½x14***
1255 A574 3.30s multicolored 3.25 3.25

Emilio Guimoye, Field of Flowers A575

2000, Mar. 19 Litho. ***Perf. 13½x14***
Granite Paper
1256 A575 1.50s multicolored 1.75 1.75

1999 Natl. Scholastic Games — A576

2000, May 3 ***Perf. 14x13½***
Granite Paper
1257 A576 1.80s multi + label 2.25 2.25

Machu Picchu A577

2000, July 20 ***Perf. 13½x14***
Granite Paper
1258 A577 1.30s multicolored 2.00 2.00

Campaign Against Domestic Violence A578

2000, Aug. 22 Litho. ***Perf. 13½x14***
Granite Paper
1259 A578 3.80s multicolored 4.50 4.50

Holy Year 2000
A579

2000, Aug. 23 **Granite Paper**
1260 A579 3.20s multicolored 3.50 3.50

Children's Drawing Contest Winners
A580

Designs: No. 1261, 3.20s, Lake Yarinacocha, by Mari Trini Ramos Vargas. No. 1262, 3.20s, Ahuashiyacu Falls, by Susan Hidalgo Bacalla, vert. 3.80s, Arequipa Countryside, by Anibal Lajo Yañez.

Perf. 13½x14, 14x13½
2000, Aug. 25 **Granite Paper**
1261-1263 A580 Set of 3 12.00 12.00

"Millennium Assembly" of UN General Assembly
A581

2000, Aug. 28 ***Perf. 13½x14***
Granite Paper
1264 A581 3.20s multi 3.50 3.50

Gen. José de San Martín (1777-1850) — A582

2000, Sept. 1 **Granite Paper**
1265 A582 3.80s multi 4.00 4.00

Ormeño Bus Co., 30th Anniv. — A583

No. 1266: a, 1s, Bus and map of South America. b, 2.70s, Bus and map of North America.

2000, Sept. 3 ***Perf. 14x13½***
Granite Paper
1266 A583 Pair, #a-b 5.00 5.00

Intl. Cycling Union, Cent.
A584

2000, Sept. 11 ***Perf. 13½x14***
Granite Paper
1267 A584 3.20s multi 4.00 4.00

World Meteorological Organization, 50th Anniv. — A585

2000, Sept. 13 **Granite Paper**
1268 A585 1.50s multi 1.75 1.75

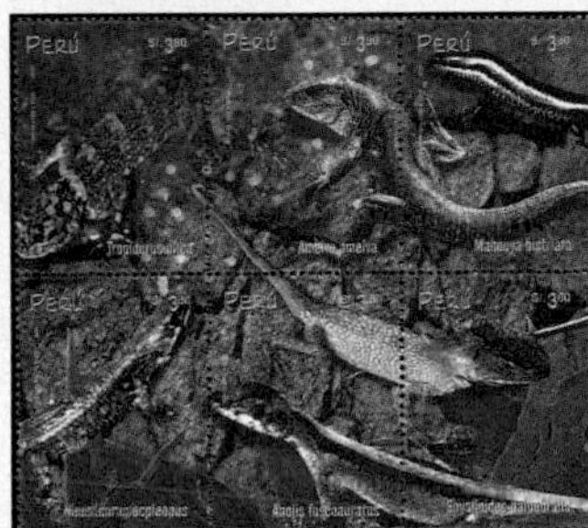

Lizards of Manu Natl. Park — A586

No. 1269: a, Tropidurus plica. b, Ameiva ameiva. c, Mabouya bistriata. d, Neusticurus ecpleopus. e, Anolis fuscoauratus. f, Enyalioides palpebralis.

2000, Sept. 15 ***Perf. 14x13½***
Granite Paper
1269 A586 3.80s Block of 6, #a-f 26.50 26.50

Matucana Madisoniorum — A587

2000, Sept. 18 ***Perf. 13½x14***
Granite Paper
1270 A587 3.80s multi 4.50 4.50

Carlos Noriega, First Peruvian Astronaut
A588

2000, Sept. 20 **Granite Paper**
1271 A588 3.80s multi 4.50 4.50

Toribio Rodríguez de Mendoza (1750-1825), Theologian
A589

2000, Sept. 21 ***Perf. 14x13½***
Granite Paper
1272 A589 3.20s multi 4.00 4.00

Ucayali Province, Cent.
A590

2000, Sept. 25 ***Perf. 13½x14***
Granite Paper
1273 A590 3.20s multi 4.00 4.00

Pisco Wine
A591

2000, Sept. 27 **Granite Paper**
1274 A591 3.80s multi 4.50 4.50

Latin American Integration Association, 20th Anniv. — A592

2000, Sept. 29 ***Perf. 14x13½***
Granite Paper
1275 A592 10.20s multi 12.50 12.50

Peruvian Journalists Federation, 50th Anniv. — A593

2000, Sept. 30 **Granite Paper**
1276 A593 1.50s multi 2.10 2.10

Sexi Petrified Forest
A594

2000, Oct. 3 ***Perf. 13½x14***
Granite Paper
1277 A594 1.50s multi 2.25 2.25

America Issue, Campaign Against AIDS
A595

2000, Oct. 12 **Granite Paper**
1278 A595 3.80s multi 5.00 5.00

Supreme Court
A596

2000, Oct. 16 **Granite Paper**
1279 A596 1.50s multi 1.75 1.75

Salvation Army in Peru, 90th Anniv. — A597

2000, Nov. 3 ***Perf. 14x13½***
Granite Paper
1280 A597 1.50s multi 2.10 2.10

Peruvian Cancer League's Fight Against Cancer, 50th Anniv.
A598

2000, Nov. 9 ***Perf. 13½x14***
Granite Paper
1281 A598 1.50s multi 2.00 2.00

Border Map Type of 1999

Flags and maps of border separating Peru and: 1.10s, Chile, vert. 1.50s, Brazil, vert. 2.10s, Colombia. 3.20s, Ecuador. 3.80s, Bolivia, vert.

Perf. 14x13½, 13½x14
2000, Nov. 27 **Granite Paper**
1282-1286 A565 Set of 5 14.50 14.50

Railroads in Peru, 150th Anniv.
A599

2000, Nov. 27 ***Perf. 13½x14***
Granite Paper
1287 A599 1.50s multi 1.75 1.75

Luis Alberto Sanchez (1900-94), Politician — A600

2000, Nov. 27 ***Perf. 14x13½***
Granite Paper
1288 A600 3.20s multi 4.00 4.00

National Congress
A601

2000, Dec. 7 ***Perf. 13½x14***
Granite Paper
1289 A601 3.80s multi 4.50 4.50

Caretas Magazine, 50th Anniv.
A602

2000, Dec. 15 **Granite Paper**
1290 A602 3.20s multi 4.00 4.00

Cacti A603

Designs: 1.10s, Haageocereus acranthus, vert. 1.50s, Cleistocactus xylorhizus, vert. No. 1293, 2.10s, Mila caespitosa, vert. No. 1294, 2.10s, Haageocereus setosus, vert. 3.20s, Opuntia pachypus. 3.80s, Haageocereus tenuis.

Perf. 13½x13¾, 13¾x13½

2001, Aug. 24 **Litho.**
1291-1296 A603 Set of 6 16.00 16.00

San Marcos University, 450th Anniv. — A604

2001, Sept. 4 *Perf. 13½x13¾*
1297 A604 1.50s multi 1.75 1.75

Alianza Lima Soccer Team, Cent. — A605

No. 1298: a, Players. b, Players, ball.

2001, Sept. 6
1298 A605 3.20s Horiz. pair, #a-b 7.50 7.50

Anti-Drug Campaign — A606

2001, Sept. 7 *Perf. 13¾x13½*
1299 A606 1.10s multi 1.50 1.50

Gen. Roque Sáenz Peña (1851-1914), Pres. of Argentina — A607

2001, Sept. 7
1300 A607 3.80s multi 4.50 4.50

Lurín River Valley A608

2001, Sept. 10
1301 A608 1.10s multi 1.25 1.25

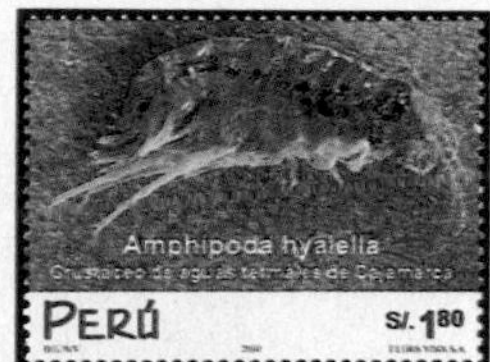

Amphipoda Hyalella — A609

2001, Sept. 10
1302 A609 1.80s multi 2.50 2.50

Postal and Philatelic Museum, 70th Anniv. — A610

2001, Oct. 9 *Perf. 13½x13¾*
1303 A610 3.20s multi 3.75 3.75

9th Iberoamerican Summit of Heads of State — A611

Country names and: a, 1.10s, Rectangle. b, 2.70s, Angled line.

2002, Mar. 6 **Litho.** *Perf. 14x13½*
1304 A611 Horiz. pair, #a-b 4.50 4.50

Dated 2001.

Peru — Costa Rica Diplomatic Relations, 150th Anniv. — A612

Flags, handshake and: a, 1.10s, Ruins. b, 2.70s, Grassland.

2002, Mar. 12
1305 A612 Horiz. pair, #a-b 4.50 4.50

Dated 2001.

World Conference Against Racism, Durban, South Africa A613

2002, Mar. 13 *Perf. 13½x14*
1306 A613 3.80s multi 4.50 4.50

Dated 2001.

Intl. Day of Indigenous People — A614

2002, Mar. 13 *Perf. 14x13½*
1307 A614 5.80s multi 6.75 6.75

Dated 2001.

Intl. Organization for Migration, 50th Anniv. — A615

2002, Apr. 2
1308 A615 3.80s multi 4.50 4.50

Dated 2001.

Pan-American Health Organization, Cent. — A616

2002, Apr. 8 *Perf. 13½x14*
1309 A616 3.20s multi 3.75 3.75

Dated 2001.

La Molina Agricultural University, Cent. — A617

Arms and: a, 1.10s, Sepia photograph of building. b, 2.70s, Color photograph of building.

2002, Apr. 16 *Perf. 14x13½*
1310 A617 Horiz. pair, #a-b 5.00 5.00

Dated 2001.

Pisco Distilling A618

Designs: 3.20s, Alembics. 3.80s, Jugs.

10s, La Fiesta de la Chicha y el Pisco, by José Sabogal.

2002, Apr. 18 *Perf. 13½x14*
1311-1312 A618 Set of 2 8.00 8.00

Souvenir Sheet

1313 A618 10s multi 12.00 12.00

Dated 2001.

Orchids — A619

Designs: 1.50s, Stanhopea sp. 3.20s, Chloraea pavoni. 3.80s, Psychopsis sp.

2002, Apr. 30 *Perf. 14x13½*
1314-1316 A619 Set of 3 10.00 10.00

Dated 2001.

Flowers of Tuber Plants A620

Designs: 1.10s, Solanum stenotomum. 1.50s, Ipomoea batatas. 2.10s, Ipomoea purpurea.

2002, May 7 *Perf. 13½x14*
1317-1319 A620 Set of 3 5.25 5.25

America Issue — UNESCO World Heritage Sites — A621

Balconies of Lima buildings: 2.70s, Palacio de Osambela. 5.80s, Palacio de Torre Tagle.

2002, May 14 **Litho.** *Perf. 14x13½*
1320-1321 A621 Set of 2 10.00 10.00

Dated 2001.

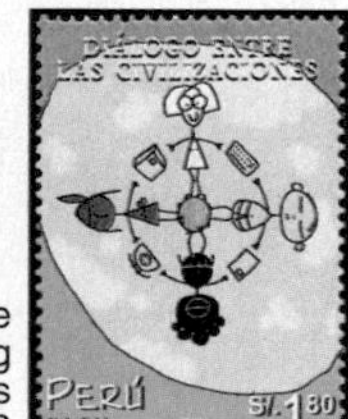

Year of Dialogue Among Civilizations A622

Designs: 1.50s, Flower. 1.80s, shown.

2002, May 16
1322-1323 A622 Set of 2 4.25 4.25

Dated 2001.

Paracas National Reserve A623

Designs: 1.10s, Sula dactilatra, vert. 1.50s, Sula variegata. 3.20s, Haematopus palliatus. 3.80s, Grapsus grapsus.

2002, May 21 ***Perf. 14x13½, 13½x14***
1324-1327 A623 Set of 4 11.00 11.00

Dated 2001.

Souvenir Sheet

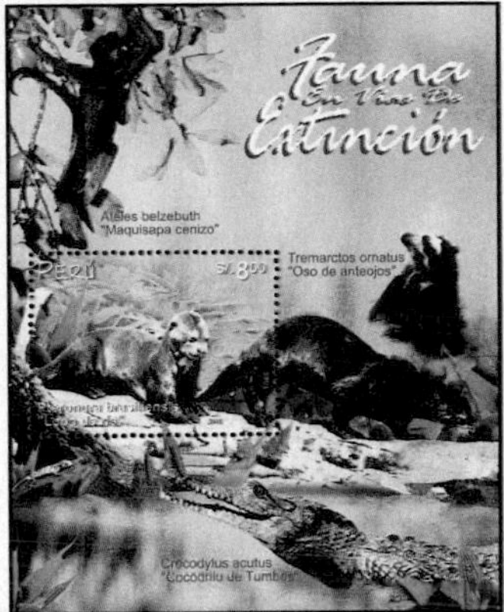

Endangered Animals — A624

2002, May 22 ***Perf. 13½x14***
1328 A624 8s multi 10.00 10.00

Dated 2001.

Scouting in Peru, 90th Anniv. — A625

No. 1329: a, Lord Robert Baden-Powell. b, Juan Luis Rospigliosi.
10.20s, First Peruvian Scouts.

2002, June 4 ***Perf. 14x13½***
1329 A625 3.20s Horiz. pair, #a-b 7.50 7.50

Souvenir Sheet

1330 A625 10.20s multi 12.00 12.00

Dated 2001.

Folk Dances — A626

Designs: 2.10s, Zamacueca. 2.70s, Alcatraz.

2002, June 4
1331-1332 A626 Set of 2 5.50 5.50

Dated 2001.

International Express Service A627

2002, June 10 ***Perf. 13½x14***
1333 A627 20s multi 22.50 22.50

Dated 2001.

Inca Rulers — A628

Designs: 1.50s, Viracocha. 2.70s, Pachacutec. 3.20s, Inca Yupanqui. 3.80s, Tupac Inca Yupanqui.

2002, June 24 **Litho.** ***Perf. 14x13½***
1334-1337 A628 Set of 4 13.50 13.50

Dated 2001.

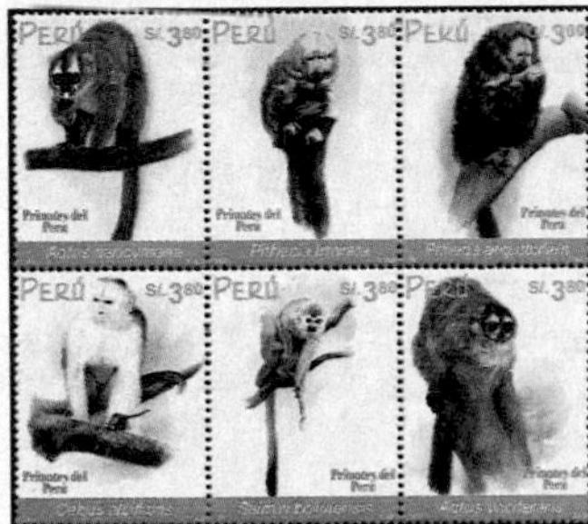

Primates — A629

No. 1338: a, Aotus nancymaea. b, Pithecia irrorata. c, Pithecia aequatorialis. d, Cebus albifrons. e, Saimiri boliviensis. f, Aotus vociferans.

2002, June 25
1338 A629 3.80s Block of 6, #a-f 26.50 26.50

Dated 2001.

Minerals Type of 1999

Designs: 1.80s, Chalcopyrite. No. 1340, 3.20s, Sphalerite. No. 1341, 3.20s, Pyrargyrite.

2002, July 3 ***Perf. 13½x14***
1339-1341 A555 Set of 3 9.00 9.00

Dated 2001.

Pre-Columbian Artifacts — A630

Designs: 1.50s, Crab-like man, Sipán. 3.20s, Warrior, Sicán. 3.80s, Gold breastplate, Kuntur Wasi, horiz.
10.20s, Pinchudo, Gran Pajatén, horiz.

2002, July 3 ***Perf. 14x13½, 13½x14***
1342-1344 A630 Set of 3 10.00 10.00

Souvenir Sheet

1345 A630 10.20s multi 12.00 12.00

Dated 2001.

Admiral Miguel Grau A631

2002, July 23 ***Perf. 13½x14***
1346 A631 3.80s multi 4.50 4.50

Dated 2001.

Peruvian — Spanish Business Meeting A632

2002, Aug. 7
1347 A632 3.80s multi 4.50 4.50

Dated 2001.

National Fisheries Society, 50th Anniv. A633

Perf. 13½x13¾

2002, Nov. 12 **Litho.**
1348 A633 3.20s multi 3.75 3.75
a. Tete beche pair 7.50 7.50

Alexander von Humboldt's Visit to Peru, Bicent. — A634

2002, Nov. 20 ***Perf. 13¾x13½***
1349 A634 3.20s multi + label 3.75 3.75
a. Tete beche strip, 2 #1349 +2 central labels 8.00 8.00

Peru - Bolivia Integration for Development — A635

2002, Nov. 29 ***Perf. 13½x14***
1350 A635 3.20s multi 3.75 3.75

Natl. Commission on Andean and Amazonian Peoples A636

2002, Dec. 12
1351 A636 1.50s multi 1.75 1.75

Hydrography and Navigation Dept., Cent. — A637

2003, June 13 **Litho.** ***Perf. 14x13½***
1352 A637 1.10s multi 1.50 1.50

Manuela Ramos Movement, 25th Anniv. — A638

2003, July 1
1353 A638 3.80s multi 4.00 4.00

Radioprogramas del Peru Network, 40th Anniv. — A639

2003, Oct. 1 **Litho.** ***Perf. 13½x14***
1354 A639 4s multi 4.00 4.00

Pres. Fernando Belaunde Terry (1912-2002) A640

2003, Oct. 7 ***Perf. 14x13½***
1355 A640 1.60s multi 1.60 1.60

Canonization of St. Josemaría Escrivá de Balaguer — A641

2003, Oct. 11 ***Perf. 13½x14***
1356 A641 1.20s multi 1.60 1.60

Sister Teresa de la Cruz Candamo (1875-1953), Founder of Canonesas de la Cruz — A642

2003, Nov. 3
1357 A642 4s multi 4.50 4.50

Treaty of Friendship, Commerce and Navigation Between Peru and Italy, 150th Anniv. — A643

No. 1358: a, Maps of Peru and Western Hemisphere. b, Map of Italy and Eastern Hemisphere.

2003, Nov. 13 ***Perf. 14x13½***
1358 A643 2s Horiz. pair, #a-b 4.25 4.25

Water Snake Bilingual Education Project — A644

No. 1359: a, Head of snake, project emblem. b, Tail of snake, children's drawing.

2003, Nov. 28
1359 A644 2s Horiz. pair, #a-b 4.25 4.25

UNESCO Associated Schools Project Network, 50th Anniv. A645

2003, Nov. ***Perf. 13½x14***
1360 A645 1.20s multi 1.50 1.50

America Issue - Fauna — A646

No. 1361: a, Four Rupicola peruviana and butterfly. b, One Rupicola peruviana.

2003, Dec. 1 ***Perf. 14x13½***
1361 A646 2s Horiz. pair, #a-b 4.50 4.50

Peru — Panama Diplomatic Relations, Cent. — A647

2003, Dec. 12
1362 A647 4r multi 4.50 4.50

Powered Flight, Cent. — A648

2003, Dec. 17 ***Perf. 13½x14***
1363 A648 4.80s multi + label 4.50 4.50

Cajón A649

2003, Dec. 18
1364 A649 4.80s multi 4.50 4.50

Chess A650

2004, Jan. 5
1365 A650 1.20s multi 1.50 1.50

Dated 2003.

National Rehabilitation Institute — A651

2004, Jan. 5
1366 A651 1.20s multi 2.10 2.10

Dated 2003.

Swimming A652

2004, Jan. 5 ***Perf. 14x13½***
1367 A652 1.20s multi 1.00 1.00

Dated 2003.

National Civil Defense System, 30th Anniv. (in 2002) — A653

2004, Jan. 14
1368 A653 4.80s multi 4.75 4.75

Dated 2002.

Christmas 2003 A654

2004, Jan. 14 ***Perf. 13½x14***
1369 A654 4.80s multi 3.75 3.75

Dated 2002.

Cebiche A655

2004, Jan. 14
1370 A655 4.80s multi 4.75 4.75

Dated 2003.

Viceroys — A656

No. 1371: a, 1.20s, Antonio de Mendoza (1495-1552). b, 1.20s, Andres Hurtado de Mendoza (1500-61). c, 1.20s, Diego Lopez de Zúñiga y Velasco (d. 1564). d, 4.80s, Blasco Nuñez de Vela (d. 1546).

2004, Jan. 14 ***Perf. 14x13½***
1371 A656 Block of 4, #a-d 8.00 8.00

Dated 2003.

Minerals A657

Designs: 1.20s, Orpiment. 4.80s, Rhodochrosite.

2004, Jan. 21 ***Perf. 13½x14***
1372-1373 A657 Set of 2 4.75 4.75

Dated 2002.

Peruvian Saints A658

Designs: No. 1374, 4.80s, St. Rose of Lima (1586-1617). No. 1375, 4.80s, St. Martin de Porres (1579-1639), vert.

2004, Jan. 21 ***Perf. 13½x14, 14x13½***
1374-1375 A658 Set of 2 7.00 7.00

Dated 2002.

Orchids A659

Designs: 1.20s, Chaubardia heteroclita, vert. 2.20s, Cochleanther amazonica, vert. 4.80s, Sobralia sp.

2004, Jan. 21 ***Perf. 14x13½, 13½x14***
1376-1378 A659 Set of 3 6.50 6.50

Dated 2002.

Jorge Basadre (1903-80), Historian — A660

2004, Jan. 30 Engr. ***Perf. 14x13½***
1379 A660 4.80s blue 4.00 4.00

Dated 2003.

Trains A661

Designs: 1.20s, Locomotive and train station. 4.80s, Train on Galeras Bridge.

2004, Jan. 30 Litho. ***Perf. 13½x14***
1380-1381 A661 Set of 2 5.00 5.00

Dated 2002.

Endangered Species — A662

Designs: No. 1382, 1.80s, Londra felina. No. 1383, 1.80s, Ara couloni, vert.

2004, Jan. 30 ***Perf. 13½x14, 14x13½***
1382-1383 A662 Set of 2 3.75 3.75

Dated 2002.

Fire Fighting A663

Designs: No. 1384, 2.20s, Firefighters with hose. No. 1385, 2.20s, Fire truck.

2004, Jan. 30 ***Perf. 13½x14***
1384-1385 A663 Set of 2 6.00 6.00

Dated 2002.

Incan Emperors A664

Designs: No. 1386, 1.20s, Huáscar (d. 1533). No. 1387, 1.20s, Atahualpa (d. 1533). 4.80s, Huayna Cápac (d. 1525).

2004, Jan. 30 ***Perf. 14x13½***
1386-1388 A664 Set of 3 6.00 6.00

Dated 2002.

Rubén Vargas Ugarte, Historian A665

2004, Feb. 4 ***Perf. 13½x14***
1389 A665 4.80s multi 4.00 4.00

Dated 2002.

2002 World Cup Soccer Championships, Japan and Korea — A666

2004, Feb. 4
1390 A666 4.80s multi 4.00 4.00

Dated 2002.

National Stadium, 50th Anniv. (in 2002) A667

2004, Feb. 4
1391 A667 4.80s multi 4.00 4.00

Dated 2002.

National Day of Biological Diversity, May 22, 2002 A668

2004, Feb. 4
1392 A668 4.80s multi 4.00 4.00

Dated 2002.

World Population Day A669

2004, Feb. 4
1393 A669 4.80s multi 4.00 4.00

Dated 2002.

José Jiménez Borja (1901-82), Writer — A670

2004, Feb. 4 ***Perf. 14x13½***
1394 A670 4.80s multi 4.00 4.00

Dated 2002.

Cacti — A671

Designs: No. 1395, 1.20s, Eriosyce islayensis. No. 1395, 1.20s, Matucana haynei. 4.80s, Pigmaeocereus bylesianus.

2004, Feb. 4
1395-1397 A671 Set of 3 9.00 9.00

Dated 2002.

Antarctic Fauna A672

Designs: No. 1398, 1.80s, Leucocarbo atriceps. No. 1399, 1.80s, Pygosceles papua, vert. No. 1400, 1.80s, Asteroidea sp., vert.

2004, Feb. 4 ***Perf. 13½x14, 14x13½***
1398-1400 A672 Set of 3 6.00 6.00

Dated 2002.

Pisco Sour A673

2004, Feb. 10 ***Perf. 13½x14***
1401 A673 4.80s multi 4.25 4.25

Daniel Alcides Carrión (1857-1885), Medical Martyr — A674

2004, Feb. 19 Litho. ***Perf. 14x13½***
1402 A674 4.80s multi 4.25 4.25

Dated 2002.

Souvenir Sheet

Foundation of Jauja, by Wenceslao Hinostroza — A675

2004, Feb. 20 ***Perf. 13½x14***
1403 A675 7s multi 6.00 6.00

Dated 2002.

Animals — A676

2004, Feb. 23 ***Perf. 14x14½***
1404 A676 20c Alpaca .30 .25
1405 A676 30c Vicuna .30 .25
1406 A676 40c Guanaco .40 .25
1407 A676 50c Llama .50 .30
Nos. 1404-1407 (4) 1.50 1.05

Dated 2002.

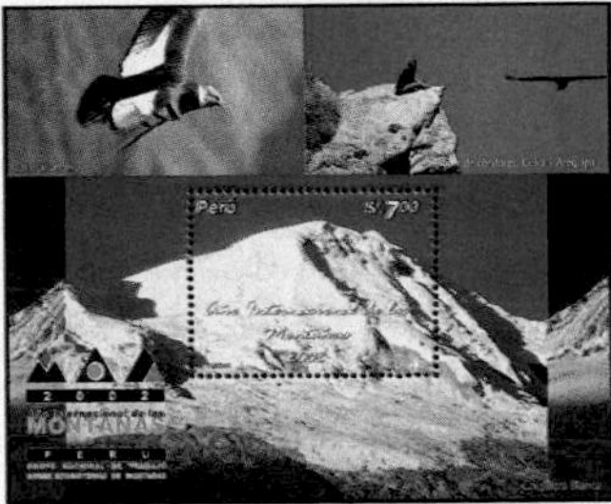

Vipers — A677

No. 1408: a, Bothrops roedingeri. b, Micrurus lemniscatus. c, Bothrops atrox. d, Bothrops microphtalmus. e, Micrurus surinamensis. f, Bothrops barnetti.

2004, Feb. 23 ***Perf. 14x13½***
1408 A677 1.80s Block of 6, #a-f, + label 10.00 10.00

Dated 2003.

Souvenir Sheet

Intl. Year of Mountains (in 2002) — A678

2004, Feb. 23 ***Perf. 13½x14***
1409 A678 7s multi 6.00 6.00

Dated 2002.

Royal Tombs of Sipán Museum A679

2004, Feb. 24
1410 A679 4.80s multi 3.75 3.75

Dated 2003.

Lighthouses — A680

No. 1411: a, Punta Capones Lighthouse. b, Chincha Islands Lighthouse.

2004, Feb. 26 ***Perf. 14x13½***
1411 A680 2s Horiz. pair, #a-b 7.00 7.00

Dated 2003.

Volunteer Firefighters of Peru, 130th Anniv. — A681

2004, Mar. 2
1412 A681 4.80s multi 6.00 6.00

Miniature Sheet

Fish — A682

No. 1413: a, Trachurus murphyi. b, Mugil cephalus. c, Engraulis ringens. d, Odontesthes regia regia. e, Merluccius gayi peruanus.

2004, Mar. 3 ***Perf. 13½x14***
1413 A682 1.60s Sheet of 5, #a-e 7.50 7.50

Dated 2002.

Souvenir Sheet

Arequipa Department — A683

No. 1414: a, Cathedral tower. b, Misti Volcano, horiz.

Perf. 14x13½, 13½x14 (#1414b)
2004, Mar. 18
1414 A683 4s Sheet of 2, #a-b 6.50 6.50

Dated 2002.

Machu Picchu — A684

No. 1415: a, 1.20s, Sundial. b, 1.20s, Temple of the Three Windows. c, 1.20s, Waterfall, Huayna Picchu. d, 4.80s, Aerial view of Machu Picchu.

2004, Mar. 20 ***Perf. 14x13½***
1415 A684 Block of 4, #a-d 7.50 7.50

Dated 2003.

Medicinal Plants A685

Designs: No. 1416, 4.80s, Uncaria tomentosa. No. 1417, 4.80s, Myrciaria dubia. No. 1418, 4.80s, Lepidium meyenii.

2004, Mar. 26 ***Perf. 13½x14***
1416-1418 A685 Set of 3 10.00 10.00

Annual Assembly of Governors of the Inter-American Development Bank — A686

2004, Mar. 29
1419 A686 4.80s multi 4.00 4.00

Dogs — A687

No. 1420: a, Italian Volpino. b, Peruvian hairless dog. c, Beauceron. d, Italian Spinone.

2004, Apr. 2 ***Perf. 14x13½***
1420 A687 4.80s Block of 4, #a-d 15.00 15.00

Dated 2003.

Dances — A688

Designs: No. 1421, 1.20s, Huaylash. No. 1422, 1.20s, Huayno.

2004
1421-1422 A688 Set of 2 2.25 2.25

Issued: No. 1421, 4/16; No. 1422, 5/28. Dated 2003.

Preparation for "El Niño" — A689

2004, Apr. 21 ***Perf. 13½x14***
1423 A689 4.80s multi 4.00 4.00

Dated 2002.

Tourism A690

Designs: No. 1424, 4.80s, Lake Paca, Jauja. No. 1425, 4.80s, Ballestas Islands, Ica, vert. No. 1426, 4.80s, Inca Baths, Cajamarca, vert. No. 1427, 4.80s, Huanchaco, Trujillo, vert.

2004 ***Perf. 13½x14, 14x13½***
1424-1427 A690 Set of 4 17.00 17.00

Issued: No. 1424, 4/22; No. 1425, 4/29; No. 1426, 5/6; No. 1427, 6/10. Dated 2002 (#1425-1427) or 2003 (#1424).

Santiago Apostol Temple, Puno A691

2004, July 2 ***Perf. 13½x14***
1428 A691 1.80s multi 1.75 1.75

Dated 2003.

America Issue — Youth, Education and Literacy — A692

Designs: 1.20s, Children, stylized flower. 4.80s, Computer operator, horiz.

2004, July 5 ***Perf. 14x13½, 13½x14***
1429-1430 A692 Set of 2 4.00 4.00

Dated 2002 (#1429) or 2003 (#1430).

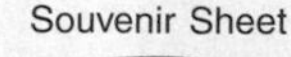
Souvenir Sheet

2004 Copa America Soccer Tournament, Peru — A693

2004, July 9 ***Perf. 14x14½***
1431 A693 5s multi 5.00 5.00

Horses — A694

No. 1432: a, 1.20s, White horse. b, 1.20s, Black horse, rider with raised hand. c, 1.20s, Black horse, rider with white poncho. d, 4.80s, Horse's head.

2004, Aug. 6 ***Perf. 14x13½***
1432 A694 Block of 4, #a-d, + label 6.50 6.50

Dated 2002.

Miniature Sheet

Worldwide Fund for Nature (WWF) — A695

No. 1433 — Pteronura brasiliensis: a, 30c. Looking. b, 50c, With mouth open. c, 1.50s, Eating. d, 1.50s, Sleeping.

2004, Oct. 15 **Litho.**
1433 A695 Sheet of 4, #a-d 4.00 4.00

America Issue — Environmental Protection — A696

2004, Oct. 25 ***Perf. 13½x14***
1434 A696 4.50s multi 3.25 3.25

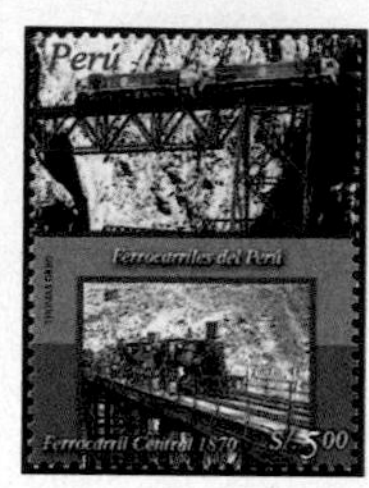
Railroads A697

Designs: 5s, Modern train on bridge, 1870 train on bridge. 10s, Train on Infiernillo Bridge, horiz.

2004, Oct. 29 ***Perf. 14x13½***
1435 A697 5s multi 4.00 4.00

Souvenir Sheet

Perf. 13½x14
1436 A697 10s multi 7.50 7.50

Peruvian Song Day, 60th Anniv. A698

2004, Oct. 31 ***Perf. 13½x14***
1437 A698 5s multi 4.00 4.00

FIFA (Fédération Internationale de Football Association), Cent. — A699

2004, Nov. 2
1438 A699 5s multi 4.00 4.00

Election of Pope John Paul II, 25th Anniv. (in 2003) A700

2004, Nov. 2
1439 A700 5s multi 4.00 4.00

Canonization of Mother Teresa — A701

2004, Nov. 2 ***Perf. 14x13½***
1440 A701 5s multi 4.00 4.00

Miniature Sheet

Musicians — A702

No. 1441: a, Juan Diego Flórez. b, Susana Baca. c, Gianmarco. d, Eva Ayllón, horiz. e, Libido, horiz.

Perf. 14x13½, 14x14x13½x14 (#1441d, 1441e)

2004, Nov. 12
1441 A702 2s Sheet of 5, #a-e 7.50 7.50

Flora Tristan Women's Center, 25th Anniv. — A703

2004, Nov. 9 Litho. *Perf. 14*
1442 A703 5s multi 4.00 4.00

Exporter's Day — A704

2004, Nov. 9
1443 A704 5s multi 4.00 4.00

Latin American Parliament, 40th Anniv. — A705

No. 1444: a, Parliament emblem. b, Andrés Townsend Escurra, first President of Latin American Parliament, and flags.

2004, Nov. 16 *Perf. 13½x14*
1444 A705 2.50s Horiz. pair, #a-b 4.00 4.00

Lima Bar Association, 200th Anniv. — A706

2004, Nov. 17
1445 A706 5s multi 4.00 4.00

Serpost, 10th Anniv. A707

2004, Nov. 22
1446 A707 5s multi 4.00 4.00

Jungle River Fauna A708

Designs: 2s, Serrasalmus. 4.50s, Pontoporia blainvillei. 5s, Arapaima gigas, vert.

Perf. 13½x14, 14x13½

2004, Nov. 30
1447-1449 A708 Set of 3 9.00 9.00

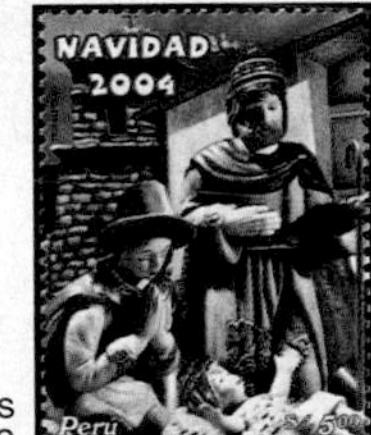

Christmas A709

2004, Dec. 2 *Perf. 14x13½*
1450 A709 5s multi 4.00 4.00

Antarctica A710

Designs: 1.50s, Machu Picchu Scientific Base, King George Island. 2s, Megaptera novaeangliae, horiz. 4.50s, Orcinus orca, horiz.

2004, Dec. 3 *Perf. 14x13½, 13½x14*
1451-1453 A710 Set of 3 6.00 6.00

Prehistoric Animals — A711

No. 1454: a, 1.80s, Drawings of Smilodon neogaeus and Toxodon platensis Owen. 3.20s, Fossils, depiction of body of Toxodon platensis.

2004, Dec. 6 *Perf. 14x13½*
1454 A711 Horiz. pair, #a-b 4.00 4.00

Mochica Ceramics — A712

Various ceramic pieces with background colors of: No. 1455, 4.50s, Dark blue. No. 1456, 4.50s, Red violet. 5s, Blue, horiz.

2004, Dec. 6 *Perf. 14x14½, 14½x14*
1455-1457 A712 Set of 3 10.00 10.00

Third Meeting of South American Presidents A713

2004, Dec. 8 *Perf. 14x13½*
1458 A713 5s multi 4.00 4.00

Lima Museum of Art, 50th Anniv. — A714

2004, Dec. 9 Litho.
1459 A714 5s multi 4.00 4.00

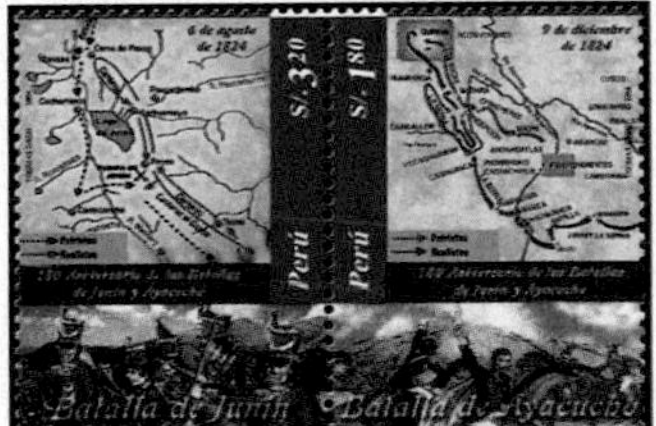

Battles, 180th Anniv. — A715

No. 1460: a, 1.80s, Map and scene of Battle of Ayacucho. b, 3.20s, Map and scene of Battle of Junín.

2004, Dec. 9
1460 A715 Horiz. pair, #a-b 4.00 4.00

Lighthouses — A716

No. 1461: a, Pijuayal Lighthouse, Amazon River. b, Suana Lighhouse, Lake Titicaca.

2004, Dec. 10
1461 A716 4.50s Horiz. pair, #a-b 7.00 7.00

Souvenir Sheet

Sacred City of Caral — A717

2004, Dec. 15 *Perf. 13½x14*
1462 A717 10s multi 7.50 7.50

Parque de las Leyendes, 40th Anniv. — A718

No. 1463: a, Cantua buxifolia. b, Puma concolor.

2005, Jan. 14 *Perf. 14x13½*
1463 A718 5s Horiz. pair, #a-b 7.50 7.50

Dated 2004.

Championship Trophies Won By Cienciano Soccer Team — A719

2005, Jan. 22
1464 A719 5s multi 4.00 4.00

Dated 2004.

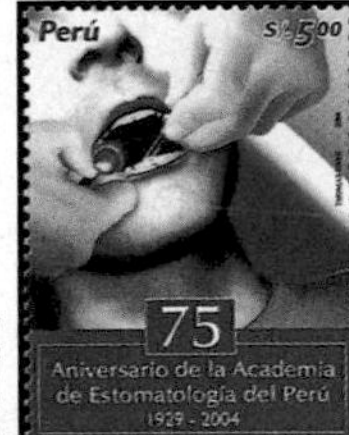

Stomatology Academy of Peru, 75th Anniv. — A720

2005, Jan. 24
1465 A720 5s multi 4.00 4.00

Dated 2004.

National Health Crusade — A721

2005, Feb. 2 *Perf. 14*
1466 A721 2s multi + label 1.50 1.50

Dated 2004.

Houses of Worship A722

Designs: 4.50s, San Cristóbal Church, Huamanga. 5s, Huancayo Cathedral.

2005, Feb. 7 Litho. *Perf. 13½x14*
1467-1468 A722 Set of 2 7.00 7.00

Abolition of Slavery, 150th Anniv. A723

2005, Feb. 25 Engr.
1469 A723 5s claret 4.00 4.00

Armed Forces — A724

No. 1470: a, 1.80s, Army tank. b, 1.80s, Navy submarine. c, 1.80s, Air Force Mirage jets. d, 3.20s, Air Force Sukhoi jet. e, 3.20s, Army soldiers. f, 3.20s, Navy frigate.

2005, Feb. 28 **Litho.**
1470 A724 Block of 6, #a-f, + label 10.00 10.00

Fruit A725

Designs: No. 1471, 4.50s, Eugenia stipitata. No. 1472, 4.50s, Mauritia flexuosa. 5s, Solanum sessiflorum dunal, vert.

2005, Mar. 4 ***Perf. 13½x14, 14x13½***
1471-1473 A725 Set of 3 10.00 10.00

Opera Singer Luis Alva Talledo, Founder of Prolirica A726

2005, Mar. 10 ***Perf. 13½x14***
1474 A726 1.50s multi 1.10 1.10

Allpahuayo Reserve Wildlife — A727

No. 1475: a, Hormiguero norteño de cola castaña. b, Tiranuelo de Mishana. c, Rana arboricola. d, Sacha runa.

2005, Mar. 21 ***Perf. 14x13½***
1475 A727 4.50s Block of 4, #a-d, + label 13.00 13.00

Paintings — A728

No. 1476 — Unidentified paintings by: a, Pancho Fierro. b, Ignacio Moreno. c, Daniel Hernández. d, Camilo Blas. e, Ricardo Grau. f, Fernando de Szyszlo.

2005, Apr. 4
1476 A728 2s Block of 6, #a-f, + label 9.00 9.00

Science of Antonio Raimondo — A729

No. 1477: a, 1.80s, Sculptures, Chavín de Huántar. b, 3.20s, Bird and bat. c, 4.50s, Stanophea. d, 5s, Fossil of N. C. Roemoceras Subplanum Hyatt.

2005, Apr. 18
1477 A729 Block of 4, #a-d, + label 11.00 11.00

Souvenir Sheet

Penelope Albipennis — A730

2005, May 2
1478 A730 10s multi 8.00 8.00

Architecture — A731

Designs: a, 4.50s, Government Palace. b, 4.50s, Italian Art Museum. c, 5s, Larco Mar. d, 5s, Mega Plaza.

2005, May 18 ***Perf. 13½x14***
1479 A731 Block of 4, #a-d, + label 14.00 14.00

Postal Money Orders A732

2005, May 30
1480 A732 5s multi 4.00 4.00

Pope John Paul II (1920-2005) — A733

2005, Nov. 24 **Litho.** ***Perf. 13½***
1481 A733 1.80s multi 1.75 1.75

Souvenir Sheet

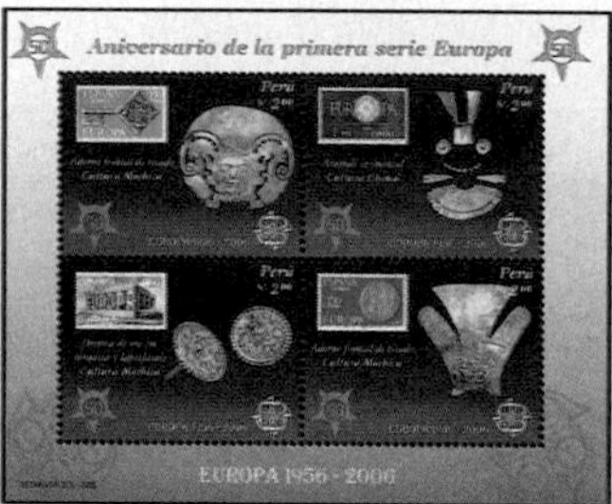
Europa Stamps, 50th Anniv. (in 2006) — A734

No. 1482: a, Mochica headdress and Spain #1526. b, Chimú ceremonial jewelry and Spain #941. c, Mochica earrings and Spain #1567. d, Mochica headdress and Spain #1607.

2005, Nov. 24 **Litho.** ***Perf. 14***
1482 A734 2s Sheet of 4, #a-d 6.00 6.00

Miniature Sheet

Naval Victories — A735

No. 1483: a, Battle of Punta Malpelo. b, Battle of Callao. c, Sinking of the Covadonga. d, Battle of Abtao. e, Battle of Iquique. f, Battle of Pedrera.

2005, Dec. 21 **Litho.** ***Perf. 13½x14***
1483 A735 2s Sheet of 6, #a-f 8.50 8.50

Medical College of Peru, 35th Anniv. A736

2005, Dec. 29
1484 A736 5.50s multi 4.00 4.00

Christmas 2005 A737

2006, Jan. 9
1485 A737 5.50s multi 4.00 4.00
Dated 2005.

Eighth Cultural Patrimony Colloquium, Cuzco — A738

2006, Jan. 9 ***Perf. 14x13½***
1486 A738 5.50s multi 4.00 4.00
Dated 2005.

Sister Ana de los Angeles Monteagudo (1602-86) — A739

2006, Jan. 10 ***Perf. 13½x14***
1487 A739 5.50s multi 4.00 4.00
Dated 2005.

Publication of Don Quixote, 400th Anniv. (in 2005) A740

2006, Jan. 11
1488 A740 5s multi 4.00 4.00
Dated 2005.

Pope Benedict XVI — A741

No. 1489: a, Profile. b, With arms raised.

2006, Jan. 11 ***Perf. 14x13½***
1489 A741 2.50s Horiz. pair, #a-b 4.00 4.00
Dated 2005.

Rotary International, Cent. (in 2005) — A742

2006, Jan. 13 ***Perf. 13½x14***
1490 A742 5.50s multi 4.00 4.00
Dated 2005.

America Issue, Fight Against Poverty — A743

2006, Jan. 16 ***Perf. 14x13½***
1491 A743 5.50s multi 4.00 4.00
Dated 2005.

Natl. Academy of History, Cent. (in 2005) A744

2006, Jan. 20 ***Perf. 13½x14***
1492 A744 5.50s multi 4.00 4.00
Dated 2005.

St. Peter's Church, Lima — A745

No. 1493: a, Exterior. b, Interior.

2006, Jan. 20 ***Perf. 14x13½***
1493 A745 2.50s Horiz. pair, #a-b 3.50 3.50
Dated 2005.

Volcanoes — A746

No. 1494: a, Pichupichu. b, Chachani. c, Misti.

2006, Jan. 20
1494 A746 Horiz. strip of 3 5.00 5.00
a.-c. 2.50s Any single 1.60 1.60
Dated 2005.

YMCA in Peru, 85th Anniv. (in 2005) — A747

2006, Jan. 23 **Litho.**
1495 A747 5.50s multi 4.00 4.00
Dated 2005.

Dr. Julio C. Tello (1880-1947), Anthropologist and Archaeologist — A748

2006, Jan. 26 ***Perf. 13½x14***
1496 A748 5s multi 3.50 3.50
Dated 2005.

Cáritas, 50th Anniv. (in 2005) A749

2006, Jan. 28
1497 A749 5.50s multi 4.00 4.00
Dated 2005.

Comptroller General, 75th Anniv. (in 2005) — A750

2006, Feb. 6 ***Perf. 14x13½***
1498 A750 5.50s multi 4.00 4.00
Dated 2005.

Creation of Cajamarca Department, 150th Anniv. (in 2005) — A751

2006, Feb. 11 ***Perf. 13½x14***
1499 A751 6s multi 4.25 4.25
Dated 2005.

Traditional Foods — A752

No. 1500: a, Chupe de camarones. b, Juane. c, Arroz con pato (duck and rice). d, Rocoto relleno.

2006, Feb. 16
1500 A752 2s Block of 4, #a-d, + label 5.50 5.50
Dated 2005.

Butterflies — A753

No. 1501: a, Heliconius sara. b, Morpho achilles. c, Dryas iulia. d, Caligo eurilochus.

2006, Feb. 17
1501 A753 2s Block of 4, #a-d, + label 6.00 6.00
Dated 2005.

12th Panamerican Scout Jamboree, Argentina — A754

No. 1502: a, Scout in foreground. b, Flag in foreground.

2006, Feb. 20 ***Perf. 14x13½***
1502 A754 2s Horiz. pair, #a-b 2.75 2.75
Dated 2005.

Pre-Columbian Cultures — A755

Artifacts of: No. 1503, 6s, Paracas culture, c. 500. No. 1504, 6s, Chavin culture, c. 1200.

2006, Feb. 22 ***Perf. 13½x14***
1503-1504 A755 Set of 2 7.50 7.50
Dated 2005.

See also Nos. 1602-1603, 1648-1649, 1700-1701, 1740-1741, 1774-1775.

Legend of the Ayar Brothers, Incan Creation Myth A756

2006, Feb. 24
1505 A756 6s multi 4.00 4.00
Dated 2005.

National Symbols — A757

No. 1506: a, Flag. b, Coat of arms. c, National anthem.

2006, Feb. 27 ***Perf. 14x13½***
1506 A757 Horiz. strip of 3 4.00 4.00
a.-c. 2s Any single 1.25 1.25
Dated 2005.

Fruit A758

Designs: No. 1507, 6s, Pouteria lucuma. No. 1508, 6s, Annona cherimola.

2006, Mar. 1 ***Perf. 13½x14***
1507-1508 A758 Set of 2 8.00 8.00
Dated 2005.

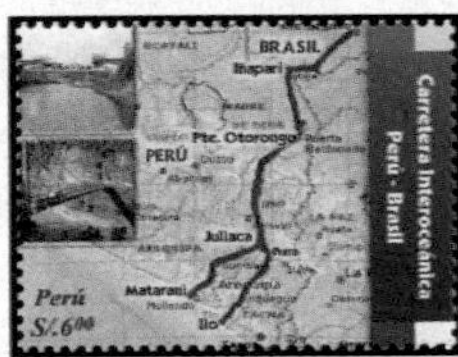
Peru to Brazil Interoceanic Highway — A759

2006, Mar. 3
1509 A759 6s multi 4.00 4.00
Dated 2005.

Writers — A760

Designs: No. 1510, 6s, Mario Vargas Llosa. No. 1511, 6s, Alfredo Bryce Echenique.

2006, Mar. 28 **Engr.** ***Perf. 14x13½***
1510-1511 A760 Set of 2 8.00 8.00
Dated 2005.

Health Ministry, 70th Anniv. (in 2005) A761

2006, Apr. 7 Litho. ***Perf. 13½x14***
1512 A761 6s multi 4.00 4.00

Dated 2005.

Latin American Integration Association, 25th Anniv. (in 2005) — A762

2006, Apr. 7
1513 A762 6s multi 4.00 4.00

Dated 2005.

Hubnerite A763

2006, Apr. 28
1514 A763 6s multi 4.00 4.00

Compare with type A657.

Purple Corn Chicha Beverage A764

2006, Apr. 28
1515 A764 6s multi 4.00 4.00

Fauna of Lake Titicaca — A765

No. 1516: a, Orestias spp. b, Plegadis ridgwayi. c, Phoenicoparrus andinus. d, Telmatobius culeus.

2006, May 2 ***Perf. 14x13½***
1516 A765 5.50s Block of 4, #a-d, + label 14.50 14.50

Parrots — A766

No. 1517: a, Pionopsitta barrabandi. b, Tovit huetii. c, Pionites melanocephala. d, Ara severa. e, Amazona festiva. f, Ara ararauna.

2006, May 5
1517 A766 5.50s Block of 6, #a-f, + label 22.50 22.50

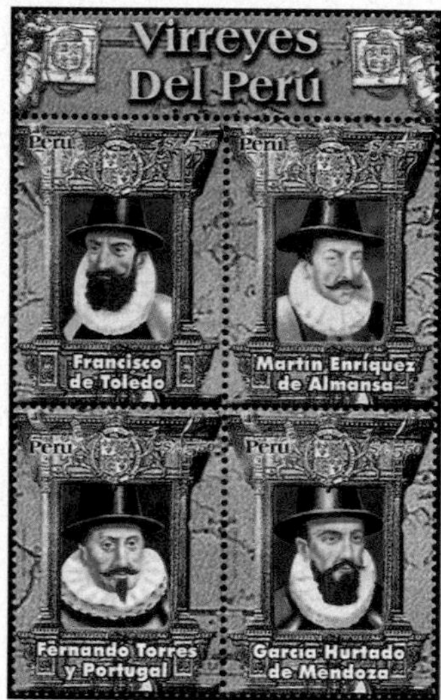

Viceroys of Peru — A767

No. 1518: a, Francisco de Toledo (1515-82). b, Martín Enríquez de Almansa (c. 1525-83). c, Fernando Torres y Portugal. d, García Hurtado de Mendoza (1535-1609).

2006, May 8
1518 A767 5.50s Block of 4, #a-d, + label 14.50 14.50

See Nos. 1569, 1575, 1622, 1681, 1737, 1776, 1858.

Souvenir Sheet

Lighthouses — A768

No. 1519: a, Isla Lobos de Tierra Lighthouse. b, Isla Blanca Lighthouse.

2006, May 10
1519 A768 6s Sheet of 2, #a-b 8.00 8.00

Birds A769

Designs: No. 1520, 6s, Perlita de Iquitos. No. 1521, 6s, Tortolita moteada (turtledove). No. 1522, 6s, Ganse Andino (Andean geese), vert.

2006, May 15 ***Perf. 13½x14, 14x13½***
1520-1522 A769 Set of 3 12.00 12.00

El Peruano Newspaper, 180th Anniv. — A770

2006, May 16 ***Perf. 13½x14***
1523 A770 6s multi 4.00 4.00

Surfing — A771

No. 1524: a, Surfers on waves. b, Sofía Mulanovich, 2004 Surfing World Champion.

2006, May 16 ***Perf. 14x13½***
1524 A771 5.50s Horiz. pair, #a-b 7.50 7.50

Souvenir Sheet

Lima-Callao Railway, 150th Anniv. — A772

2006, May 16 ***Perf. 13½x14***
1525 A772 6s multi 4.00 4.00

Miniature Sheet

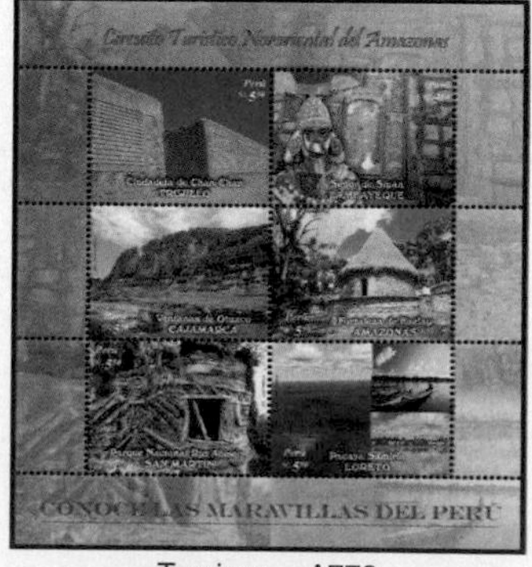

Tourism — A773

No. 1526: a, Chan Chan. b, Sipán man. c, Ventanas de Otuzco. d, Kuelap Fort. e, Río Abiseo Natl. Park. f, Pacaya Samiria.

2006, May 17
1526 A773 5.50s Sheet of 6, #a-f 22.50 22.50

Miniature Sheet

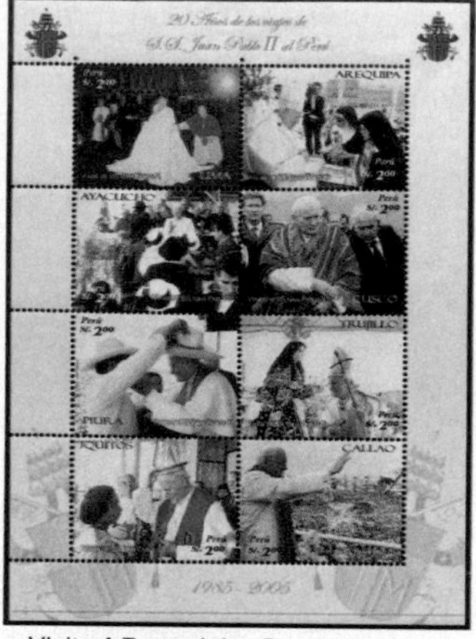

Visit of Pope John Paul II to Peru, 20th Anniv. — A774

No. 1527 — Pope in: a, Lima. b, Arequipa. c, Ayacucho. d, Cuzco. e, Piura. f, Trujillo. g, Iquitos. h, Callao.

2006, May 19
1527 A774 2s Sheet of 8, #a-h 10.50 10.50

Peruvian Air Force — A775

No. 1528: a, Air Force emblem. b, Airplanes and pilot.

2006, May 22
1528 A775 6s Horiz. pair, #a-b 8.00 8.00

Carnival Participants A776

Participants in carnivals from: No. 1529, 6s, Cajamarca. No. 1530, 6s, Arequipa. No. 1531, 6s, Puno.

2006, May 22 ***Perf. 14x13½***
1529-1531 A776 Set of 3 12.00 12.00

Precursors of Independence — A777

No. 1532: a, Micaela Bastidas. b, Plaza Mayor, Cuzco.

2006, May 31
1532 A777 2s Horiz. pair, #a-b 2.75 2.75

Intl. Year of Deserts and Desertification — A778

2006, Dec. 22 Litho. ***Perf. 13½x14***
1533 A778 2s multi 1.50 1.50

Christmas A779

2006, Dec. 22
1534 A779 2s multi 1.50 1.50

Wolfgang Amadeus Mozart (1756-91), Composer A780

2006, Dec. 22
1535 A780 5.50s multi 3.75 3.75

2006 World Cup Soccer Championships, Germany — A781

2006, Dec. 22 ***Perf. 14x13½***
1536 A781 8.50s multi 5.75 5.75

Christopher Columbus (1451-1506), Explorer — A782

2006, Dec. 27 ***Perf. 13½x14***
1537 A782 6s multi 4.00 4.00

First International Philatelic Exhibition in Peru, 75th Anniv. — A783

Litho. With Foil Application

2006, Dec. 29 ***Perf. 13½x14***
1538 A783 8.50s #286 5.75 5.75

America Issue, Energy Conservation — A784

No. 1539: a, 3s, Solar panels. b, 5.50s, Natural gas.

2006, Dec. 29 Litho. ***Perf. 14x13½***
1539 A784 Horiz. pair, #a-b 5.75 5.75

Diplomatic Relations Between Peru and People's Republic of China, 35th Anniv. — A785

No. 1540: a, Giant panda. b, Guanaco. c, Machu Picchu. d, Great Wall of China.

2006, Dec. 29
1540 A785 2s Block of 4, #a-d, + label 5.25 5.25

"The Pirates of Callao," First Peruvian 3-D Animated Film A786

Parrot and: No. 1541, 2s, Boy with sword. No. 1542, 2s, Captain with sword.

Litho. With Foil Application

2007, Jan. 5 ***Perf. 13½x14***
1541-1542 A786 Set of 2 2.75 2.75

Dated 2006.

Peruvian Art A787

Designs: No. 1543, 2.20s, Sculpture of horse by Victor Delfin. No. 1544, 2.20s, Painting by Fernando de Szyszlo.

2007, Jan. 9 Litho.
1543-1544 A787 Set of 2 3.00 3.00

Dated 2006.

Souvenir Sheet

Purussaurus Fossil — A788

Litho. (Foil Application on Sheet Margin)

2007, Jan. 16
1545 A788 8.50s multi 5.75 5.75

Dated 2006.

Flutes A789

Designs: No. 1546, 5.50s, Antara. No. 1547, 5.50s, Quena. No. 1548, 5.50s, Zampoña.

2007, Jan. 23 Litho.
1546-1548 A789 Set of 3 11.00 11.00

Dated 2006.

St. Toribio de Mogrovejo (1538-1606), Founder of First Seminary in Americas A790

2007, Jan. 27 Engr. ***Perf. 14x13½***
1549 A790 2s chocolate 1.40 1.40

Dated 2006.

Miniature Sheet

Religious Festivals — A791

No. 1550: a, Señor de los Milagros. b, Virgen de las Mercedes. c, Virgen de la Candelaria. d, Señor de Muruhuay.

2007, Jan. 30 Litho.
1550 A791 5.50s Sheet of 4, #a-d 14.50 14.50

Dated 2006.

Peruvian Film, "Dragones Destino de Fuego" — A792

Designs: No. 1551, 2s, Flying dragons. No. 1552, 2s, Head of dragon.

Litho. With Foil Application

2007, Feb. 5
1551-1552 A792 Set of 2 2.75 2.75

Dated 2006.

National Board of Elections, 75th Anniv. (in 2006) — A793

2007, Feb. 13 Engr.
1553 A793 2.20s brown 1.50 1.50

Dated 2006.

Desserts — A794

No. 1554: a, Suspiro de limeña. b, Picarones. c, Mazamorra morada.

2007, Mar. 12 Litho. ***Perf. 13½x14***
1554 A794 Horiz. strip of 3 5.00 5.00
a.-c. 2.50s Any single 1.60 1.60

Dated 2006.

Dogs — A795

No. 1555: a, Perro sin pelo (hairless dog). b, Dachshund. c, Samoyed. d, Siberian husky.

2007, Mar. 26 Litho. ***Perf. 13½x14***
1555 A795 6s Block of 4, #a-d, + label 16.00 16.00

Dated 2006.

Miniature Sheet

Architecture of the Viceregal Era in Lima — A796

No. 1556: a, St. Augustine Church. b, Sacristy of St. Francis. c, St. Apollonia Gate. d, Metropolitan Cathedral

2007, Apr. 2 Litho. *Perf. 14x13½*
1556 A796 5.50s Sheet of 4, #a-d 14.50 14.50

Dated 2006.

Incan Temples A797

Designs: No. 1557, 6s, Tambo Colorado, Ica. No. 1558, 6s, Pachacamac, Lima. No. 1559, 6s, Tambo Machay, Cusco.

2007, Apr. 23 Litho. *Perf. 13½x14*
1557-1559 A797 Set of 3 12.00 12.00

Dated 2006.

Felipe Pinglo Alva (1899-1936), Composer — A798

No. 1560: a, Photographs of Pinglo Alva and buildings. b, Guitar, photograph of Pinglo Alva.

2007, May 7 *Perf. 14x13½*
1560 A798 3s Horiz. pair, #a-b 4.00 4.00

Dated 2006.

Pre-Columbian Cultures — A799

Artifacts and maps of: No. 1561, 6s, Vicús culture, 500 B.C. No. 1562, 6s, Salinar culture, 200 B.C.

2007, May 21 *Perf. 13½x14*
1561-1562 A799 Set of 2 8.00 8.00

Dated 2006.

Dances and Costumes — A800

No. 1563: a, Danza de los Negritos. b, Danza de las Tijeras. c, Danza Cápac Colla. d, Danza La Diablada.

2007, June 4 *Perf. 14x13½*
1563 A800 2.50s Block of 4, #a-d, + label 6.75 6.75

Dated 2006.

Exports A801

Designs: No. 1564, 6s, Alpaca yarn. No. 1565, 6s, Mangos. No. 1566, 6s, Asparagus.

2007, June 18 *Perf. 13½x14*
1564-1566 A801 Set of 3 12.00 12.00

Dated 2006.

Adventure Sports — A802

No. 1567: a, Rafting. b, Cycling. c, Rock climbing.

2007, July 2
1567 A802 Horiz. strip of 3 12.00 12.00
a.-c. 6s Any single 4.00 4.00

Dated 2006.

Miniature Sheet

First Peruvian Congress, 185th Anniv. — A803

No. 1568: a, Exposition Palace. b, Painting of Francisco González Gamarra. c, Tribunal of the Inquisition Building. d, Statue of Simón Bolívar. e, Legislative Palace at night. f, Pasos Perdidos Hall. g, Stained-glass window. h, Legislative Palace sculpture.

Litho., Foil Application on Margin and Label

2007, July 12 *Perf. 14x13½*
1568 A803 2.50s Sheet of 8, #a-h, + central label 13.50 13.50

Viceroys Type of 2006

No. 1569: a, Luis de Velasco (c. 1534-1617). b, Gaspar de Zuniga y Acevedo (1560-1606). c, Juan de Mendoza y Luna (1571-1628). d, Francisco de Borja y Aragon (1581-1658).

2007, July 16 Litho.
1569 A767 6s Block of 4, #a-d, + label 16.00 16.00

Giuseppe Garibaldi (1807-82), Italian Leader A804

2007, July 26 *Perf. 13½x14*
1570 A804 6s multi 4.00 4.00

Scouting, Cent. — A805

No. 1571: a, Scouting emblem, pictures of Scouts. b, Lord Robert Baden-Powell blowing kudu horn, flags.

2007, July 30 *Perf. 14x13½*
1571 A805 3s Horiz. pair, #a-b 4.00 4.00

Endangered Animals — A806

No. 1572: a, 3s, Oncifelis colocolo. b, 3s, Lontra felina. c, 6s, Harpia harpyja. d, 6s, Odocoileus virginianus.

2007, July 30 *Perf. 13½x14*
1572 A806 Block of 4, #a-d, + label 12.00 12.00

Medicinal Plants — A807

No. 1573: a, Bixa orellana. b, Cestrum auriculatum. c, Brugmansia suaveolens. d, Anacardium occidentale. e, Caesalpinia spinosa. f, Croton lechleri.

2007, Aug. 6 Litho.
1573 A807 2.50s Block of 6, #a-f, + label 10.00 10.00

Raul Maria Pereira, Architect, and Postal Headquarters, Lima — A808

2007, Aug. 10
1574 A808 2s multi 1.50 1.50

See Portugal No. 2940.

Viceroys Type of 2006

No. 1575: a, Diego Fernández de Cordoba (1578-1630). b, Luis Jerónimo de Cabrera (1589-1647). c, Pedro de Toledo y Leiva (c. 1585-1654). d, Garcia Sarmiento de Sotomayor (c. 1595-1659).

2007, Aug. 20 *Perf. 14x13½*
1575 A767 6s Block of 4, #a-d, + label 16.00 16.00

Souvenir Sheet

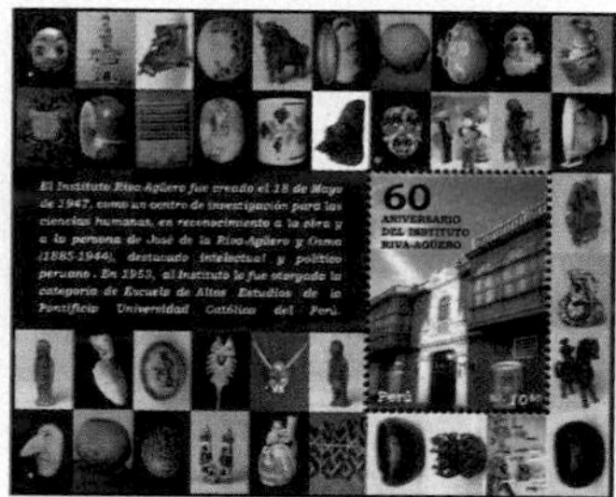

Riva-Agüero Institute, 60th Anniv. — A809

2007, Sept. 10
1576 A809 10.50s multi 7.00 7.00

Peruvian National Police Band, Cent. (in 2006) A810

Band: 2s, On steps of building. 8.50s, In parade.

2007, Sept. 15 *Perf. 13½x14*
1577-1578 A810 Set of 2 7.00 7.00

Birds A811

Designs: No. 1579, 5.50s, Coeraba flaveola. No. 1580, 5.50s, Mimus longicaudatus. No. 1581, 5.50s, Pyrocephalus rubinus. No. 1582, 5.50s, Sarcoramphus papa.

Litho. With Foil Application

2007, Sept. 15
1579-1582 A811 Set of 4 15.00 15.00

Grand Masonic Lodge of Peru, 125th Anniv. — A812

2007, Sept. 17 Litho. *Perf. 14x13½*
1583 A812 6.50s multi 4.50 4.50

Souvenir Sheet

Joint Command of the Armed Forces, 50th Anniv. — A813

2007, Sept. 24 *Perf. 13½x14*
1584 A813 14s multi 9.50 9.50

Children's Art A814

Winning pictures in children's art contest: No. 1585, 2s, River Scene, by Juana Chuquipiondo Mesía. No. 1586, 2s, Crane on Stump, by Rubén Saavedra Cobeñas, vert.

Perf. 13½x14, 14x13½
2007, Sept. 28
1585-1586 A814 Set of 2 2.75 2.75

Miniature Sheet

Automobiles — A815

No. 1587: a, 1935 Auburn Speedster 851 SC. b, 1903 Clément Brass Phaeton 9 CV. c, 1926 Dodge Special Pickup truck. d, 1928 Stutz BB Sedan Convertible Victoria. e, 1936 Pierce Arrow 1603 Touring D 700.

2007, Sept. 28 *Perf. 13½x14*
1587 A815 3s Sheet of 5, #a-e 10.00 10.00

Santa Clara Monastery, Cusco, 450th Anniv. — A816

2007, Oct. 1 *Perf. 14x13½*
1588 A816 5.50s multi 3.75 3.75

Cats — A817

No. 1589: a, Angora. b, Persian. c, Bengal. d, Siamese.

2007, Oct. 1 **Litho.**
1589 A817 6s Block of 4, #a-d, + label 16.00 16.00

Miniature Sheet

Insects — A818

No. 1590: a, Macrodontia cervicornis. b, Dynastes hercules. c, Titanus giganteus. d, Megasoma sp.

2007, Oct. 1 *Perf. 13½x14*
1590 A818 5.50s Sheet of 4, #a-d 15.00 15.00

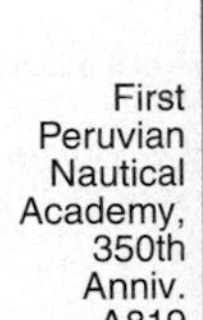

First Peruvian Nautical Academy, 350th Anniv. A819

2007, Oct. 8
1591 A819 5.50s multi 3.75 3.75

America Issue, Education for All — A820

Designs: No. 1592, 5.50s, Two boys reading. No. 1593, 5.50s, Two girls reading.

2007, Oct. 9 *Perf. 14x13½*
1592-1593 A820 Set of 2 7.50 7.50

Daniel Alcides Carrión (1857-85), Describer of Carrion's Disease A821

2007, Oct. 13 **Engr.** *Perf. 13½x14*
1594 A821 3s brown 2.00 2.00

Miniature Sheet

Mushrooms — A822

No. 1595: a, Dyctiophora indusiata. b, Sepultaria arenicola. c, Marasmius haematocephalus. d, Marasmiellus volvatus.

Litho., Foil Application in Margin
2007, Oct. 15 *Perf. 14x13½*
1595 A822 2.50s Sheet of 4, #a-d 6.75 6.75

Peru No. 18 Volunteer Fire Brigade, Cent. — A823

No. 1596 — Fire trucks: a, 1908 Merry Weather. b, 1969 Mack.

2007, Nov. 4 **Litho.** *Perf. 13½x14*
1596 A823 3s Horiz. pair, #a-b 4.50 4.50

Víctor Raúl Haya de la Torre (1895-1979), Politician — A824

2007, Aug. 16 **Engr.** *Perf. 14x13½*
1597 A824 3s claret 2.10 2.10

Souvenir Sheet

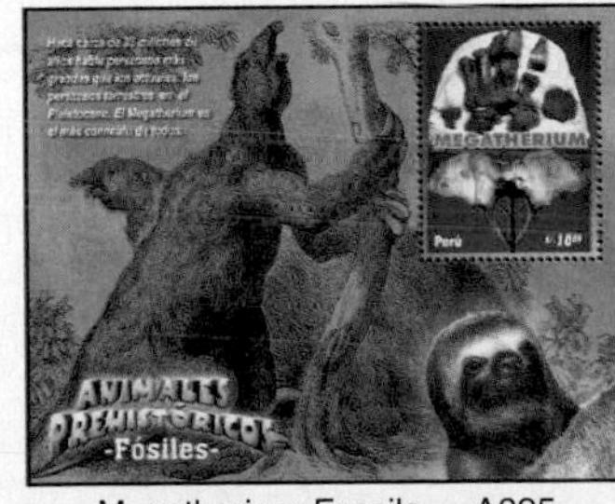

Megatherium Fossils — A825

2007, Sept. 28 **Litho.**
1598 A825 10s multi 7.25 7.25

Miniature Sheet

Bush Dog — A826

No. 1599: a, 2s, Two dogs. b, 2s, One dog. c, 5.50s, One dog, facing right. d, 5.50s, One dog, facing left.

2007, Oct. 19 *Perf. 13½x14*
1599 A826 Sheet of 4, #a-d 11.00 11.00

Souvenir Sheet

Real Felipe Fort, Callao — A827

2007, Oct. 29
1600 A827 6s multi 4.50 4.50

Familia Serrana, by Camilo Blas (1910-85) — A828

2007, Nov. 5 *Perf. 14x13½*
1601 A828 6s multi 4.50 4.50

Pre-Columbian Cultures Type of 2006

Artifacts of: 6s, Nasca culture, A.D. 600. 7s, Mochica culture, 700 B.C.-A.D. 200.

2007, Nov. 12 *Perf. 13½x14*
1602-1603 A755 Set of 2 9.50 9.50

Souvenir Sheet

Cahuachi Archaeological Site — A829

2007, Nov. 12
1604 A829 14.50s multi 10.50 10.50

Founders of Independence Society, 150th Anniv. — A830

2007, Dec. 1
1605 A830 6s multi 4.50 4.50

Christmas A831

2007, Dec. 1 ***Perf. 14x13½***
1606 A831 6.50s multi 5.00 5.00

First Peruvian Postage Stamps, 150th Anniv. — A832

No. 1607: a, Peru #1. b, Peru #2.

2007, Dec. 1
1607 A832 2.50s Horiz. pair, #a-b 3.75 3.75

Altars in Lima Churches A833

Altar from: 6s, Carmelite Church. 8.50s, Lima Cathedral.

2007, Dec. 1
1608-1609 A833 Set of 2 10.50 10.50

Asia-Pacific Economic Cooperation Forum — A834

2007, Dec. 3
1610 A834 6s multi 4.50 4.50

Roots — A835

Designs: No. 1611, 6s, Smallanthus sonchifolius. No. 1612, 6s, Manihot esculenta.

2007, Dec. 17
1611-1612 A835 Set of 2 8.50 8.50

Launch of First Peruvian Rocket, 1st Anniv. — A836

No. 1613 — Emblem of National Space Commission and: a, Pedro Paulet Mostajo (1874-1945), aeronautical pioneer and Paulet I rocket in flight. b, Paulet I rocket on launch pad and civil ensign.

Litho., Litho. With Foil Application (#1613b)

2007, Dec. 27 ***Perf. 13½x14***
1613 A836 3s Horiz. pair, #a-b 4.50 4.50

Souvenir Sheet

First Peruvian Scientific Expedition to the Antarctic, 20th Anniv. — A837

No. 1614: a, Ship "Humboldt." b, Expedition members, horiz.

Perf. 13½x14, 14x13½ (#1614b)
Litho. With Foil Application

2008, Feb. 22
1614 A837 10s Sheet of 2, #a-b 14.00 14.00

Arms Stamps of 1858, 150th Anniv. — A838

Designs: No. 1615, 5.50s, Peru #3. No. 1616, 5.50s, Peru #4. No. 1617, 5.50s, Peru #6.

2008, Mar. 10 **Litho.** ***Perf. 14x13½***
1615-1617 A838 Set of 3 12.50 12.50

Santa Rosa de Santa María Monastery, 300th Anniv. A839

2008, June 3 ***Perf. 13½x14***
1618 A839 5.50s multi 4.00 4.00

Lima Philharmonic Society, Cent. — A840

No. 1619 — Emblem and: a, Violin. b, Musicians.

2008, June 8 ***Perf. 14x13½***
1619 A840 3s Horiz. pair, #a-b 4.25 4.25

Lima General Cemetery, Bicent. A841

Designs: No. 1620, 6.50s, Statue of angel and cross. No. 1621, 6.50s, Statue of praying woman, vert.

Perf. 13½x14, 14x13½

2008, June 17
1620-1621 A841 Set of 2 8.75 8.75

Viceroys Type of 2006

No. 1622: a, Luis Enríquez de Guzmán (c. 1605-61). b, Diego de Benavides y de la Cueva (1607-66). c, Pedro Antonio Fernandez de Castro (1634-72). d, Baltasar de la Cueva Enríquez (1626-86).

2008, June 24 ***Perf. 14x13½***
1622 A767 6s Block of 4, #a-d, + label 16.50 16.50

ExportaFacil Package Service — A842

2008, June 24
1623 A842 10s multi 6.75 6.75

America Issue — A843

No. 1624: a, Inti Raymi (Festival of the Sun), Cuzco. b, Grape Harvest Festival, Ica.

2008, June 24 ***Perf. 13½x14***
1624 A843 6.50s Horiz. pair, #a-b 8.75 8.75

Latin American, Caribbean and European Union Heads of State Summit, Lima — A844

2008, July 1 ***Perf. 14x13½***
1625 A844 6.50s red & black 4.50 4.50

2008 Summer Olympics, Beijing — A845

No. 1626 — Olympic mascots and places in Peru: a, Beibei, Máncora. b, Jingjing, Lima Cathedral. c, Yingying, Machu Picchu. d, Nini, Tambopata.

2008, July 1 ***Perf. 13½x14***
1626 A845 1.40s Block of 4, #a-d, + label 4.00 4.00

Latin American and European Parliamentary Summit, Lima — A846

2008, July 2
1627 A846 6.50s multi 4.50 4.50

Aurelio Miró Quesada Sosa (1907-98), Lawyer and Writer A847

2008, July 3
1628 A847 2.50s multi 1.75 1.75

National Literacy Program A848

2008, July 4
1629 A848 2.50s multi 1.75 1.75

Exports Type of 2007

Designs: No. 1630, 5.50s, Olives (aceituna). No. 1631, 5.50s, Cotton (algodón). No. 1632, 5.50s, Avocados (palta).

2008, July 8
1630-1632 A801 Set of 3 12.00 12.00

Miniature Sheet

River Fish — A849

No. 1633: a, Phractocephalus hemioliopterus. b, Mylossoma duriventre. c, Piaractus braphypomus. d, Ageneiosus ucayalensis. e, Brycon melanopterus.

2008, July 18
1633 A849 3s Sheet of 5, #a-e 11.00 11.00

A850

A851

A852

Judgment Day Paintings, Lima Cathedral A853

2008, Aug. 5

1634	A850	6.50s multi	4.50	4.50
1635	A851	6.50s multi	4.50	4.50
1636	A852	6.50s multi	4.50	4.50
1637	A853	6.50s multi	4.50	4.50
		Nos. 1634-1637 (4)	18.00	18.00

Edwin Vásquez Cam (1922-93), First Peruvian Olympic Gold Medalist A854

2008, Aug. 6

1638 A854 6s multi 4.25 4.25

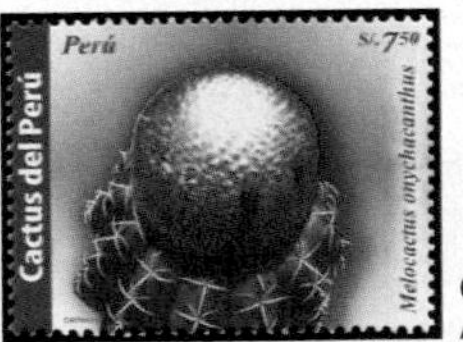

Cacti A855

Designs: No. 1639, 7.50s, Melocactus onychacanthus. No. 1640, 7.50s, Matucana oreodoxa. No. 1641, 7.50s, Espostoa mirabilis.

2008, Aug. 13

1639-1641 A855 Set of 3 15.50 15.50

Dr. Javier Arias Stella, Pathologist A856

2008, Aug. 22 ***Perf. 14x13½***

1642 A856 2s multi 1.40 1.40

Miniature Sheet

Seven Wonders of the Modern World — A857

No. 1643: a, 2.50s, Petra, Jordan. b, 2.50s, Machu Picchu, Peru. c, 2.50s, Great Wall of China. d, 2.50s, Statue of Christ the Redeemer, Brazil. e, 7.50s, Chichén Itzá, Mexico. f, 10s, Roman Colosseum, Italy. g, 10.50s, Taj Mahal, India.

2008, July 7 Litho. ***Perf. 13½x14***

1643 A857 Sheet of 7, #a-g 27.00 27.00

Intl. Year of the Potato A858

Litho. With Foil Application

2008, Sept. 3

1644 A858 5.50s multi 3.75 3.75

Orchids — A859

Designs: No. 1645, 7s, Cattleya rex. No. 1646, 7s, Cattleya máxima.

2008, Sept. 3 Litho. ***Perf. 14x13½***

1645-1646 A859 Set of 2 9.50 9.50

Souvenir Sheet

Crypt of the Heroes, Cent. — A860

2008, Sept. 8

1647 A860 10.50s multi 7.00 7.00

Pre-Columbian Cultures Type of 2006

Artifacts of: 2s, Tiahuanaco culture, 100 B.C.-A.D. 1200. 6s, Recuay culture, A.D. 1-600.

2008, Sept. 10 ***Perf. 13½x14***

1648-1649 A755 Set of 2 5.50 5.50

Performing Arts Productions A861

Designs: No. 1650, 6.50s, Play *Na Catita.* No. 1651, 6.50s, Ballet *Huatyacuri.*

Litho. with Foil Application

2008, Sept. 21 ***Perf. 14x13½***

1650-1651 A861 Set of 2 8.75 8.75

National University of Trujillo Medical School, 50th Anniv. — A862

2008, Oct. 3 Litho.

1652 A862 6s multi 4.00 4.00

Miniature Sheet

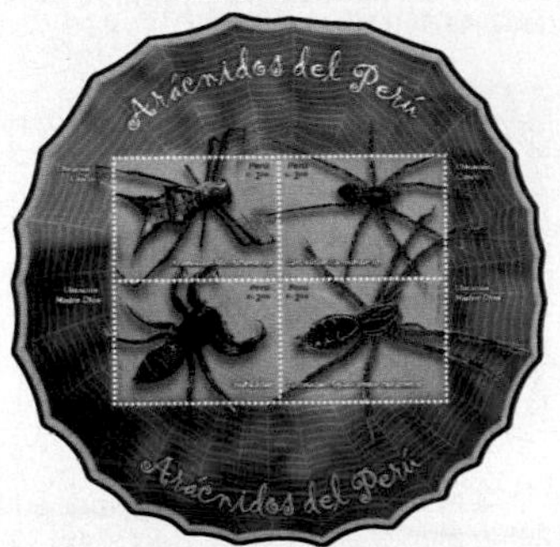

Spiders — A863

No. 1653: a, Micrathena sp. b, Lycosinae sp. c, Salticidae. d, Aglaoctenus castaneus.

2008, Oct. 3 ***Perf. 13½x14***

1653 A863 2s Sheet of 4, #a-d 5.50 5.50

Souvenir Sheet

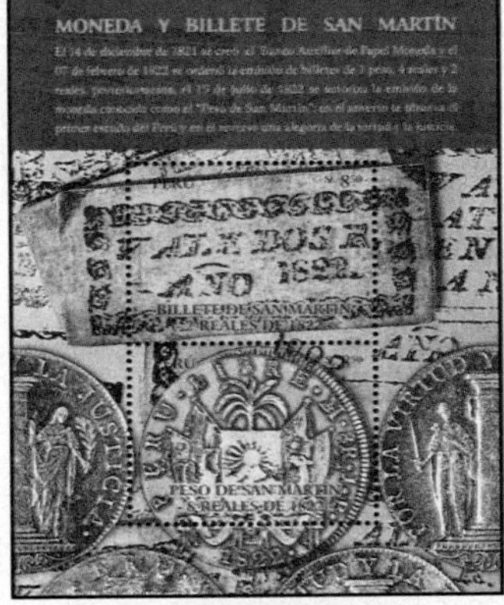

1822 José de San Martín Currency — A864

No. 1654: a, 2-real note. b, 1-peso coin.

Litho. & Engr. (Foil Application in Margin)

2008, Oct. 13

1654 A864 8.50s Sheet of 2, #a-b 11.00 11.00

Souvenir Sheet

Choquequirao Ruins — A865

2008, Oct. 21 Litho. ***Perf. 14x13½***

1655 A865 10.50s multi 7.00 7.00

Museum of the Inquisition and Congress, Lima, 40th Anniv. — A866

No. 1656: a, Museum building (old National Senate Building). b, Inquisitors.

2008, Oct. 28

1656 A866 6s Horiz. pair, #a-b 8.00 8.00

Traffic Policeman and Road Signs A867

2008, Oct. 29 ***Perf. 13½x14***

1657 A867 6.50s multi 4.25 4.25

Campaign for obeying traffic signs.

Edgardo Rebagliati National Hospital, 50th Anniv. A868

2008, Nov. 3

1658 A868 2s multi 1.40 1.40

Paracas Mantles — A869

No. 1659: a, Unbordered mantle with white and illustrated squares. b, Fringed mantle with hexagons in design. c, Fringed mantle with black squares. d, Mantle with illustrated border.

2008, Nov. 5 ***Perf. 14x13½***

1659 A869 6s Block of 4 #a-d, + label 15.50 15.50

Xenoglaux Loweryi A870

2008, Nov. 19 ***Perf. 13½x14***

1660 A870 7.50s multi 5.00 5.00

Campaign Against Drug Abuse A871

Winning art in children's stamp design contest depicting: No. 1661, 2s, Boys and Hand, by Diego Gutierrez. No. 1662, 2s, Crossed bones and marijuana leaves, by Carolina Luna Polo, vert.

Perf. 13½x14, 14x13½

2008, Nov. 21
1661-1662 A871 Set of 2 2.60 2.60

Christmas A872

2008, Dec. 1 ***Perf. 13½x14***
1663 A872 8.50s multi 5.50 5.50

Free Trade Agreement Between Peru and United States, 1st Anniv. A873

2008, Dec. 4
1664 A873 6s multi 4.00 4.00

Jerónimo de Loayza Gonzáles (1498-1575), First Archbishop of Lima — A874

2008, Dec. 10
1665 A874 2s multi 1.40 1.40

Souvenir Sheet

Inca God Wiracocha — A875

No. 1666 — Wiracocha: a, Breathing. b, With arm extended. c, Walking.

2008, Dec. 10
1666 A875 2.50s Sheet of 3, #a-c 5.00 5.00

Miniature Sheet

Intl. Polar Year — A876

No. 1667: a, Iceberg. b, Raising of Peruvian flag. c, Map of Antarctica, International Polar Year emblem. d, Quelcayya Glacier, Peru.

2009, Jan. 15
1667 A876 2.20s Sheet of 4, #a-d 5.50 5.50

College of Administrators, 30th Anniv. — A877

2009, Feb. 11 Litho. ***Perf. 13½x14***
1668 A877 6.50s multi 4.00 4.00

Intl. Heliophysical Year — A878

Litho. With Foil Application

2009, Mar. 9 ***Perf. 14x13½***
1669 A878 5.50s multi 3.50 3.50

Intl. Heliophysical Year was in 2007-08. The Intl. Year of Astronomy was in 2009.

Lighthouses A879

Designs: No. 1670, 6.50s, La Marina Lighthouse. No. 1671, 6.50s, Muelle Dársena Lighthouse and boat.

2009, Mar. 9 **Litho.**
1670-1671 A879 Set of 2 8.50 8.50

A880

Sunflowers A881

2009, Mar. 13 ***Perf. 13½x14***
1672 A880 2.50s multi 1.60 1.60
1673 A881 2.50s multi 1.60 1.60

Honesty A882

Punctuality A883

2009, Mar. 16 ***Perf. 13½x14***
1674 A882 6.50s multi 4.25 4.25

Perf. 14x13½

1675 A883 6.50s multi 4.25 4.25

Intl. Meteorology Day — A884

2009, Mar. 23 ***Perf. 14x13½***
1676 A884 2s multi 1.40 1.40

Canyons — A885

No. 1677: a, Colca Canyon. b, Cotahuasi Canyon. c, Pato Canyon.

2009, Mar. 23
1677 A885 2s Horiz. strip of 3, #a-c, + label 4.00 4.00

Parachuting — A886

No. 1678 — Skydivers with denomination in: a, UL. b, LR.

2009, Mar. 31 ***Perf. 13½x14***
1678 A886 7s Horiz. pair, #a-b 9.00 9.00

New Year 2009 (Year of the Ox) — A887

No. 1679 — Ring of Zodiac animals and: a, Rider on ox. b, Head of ox.

2009, Apr. 8 **Litho.**
1679 A887 2.50s Horiz. pair, #a-b 3.25 3.25

Earth Day A888

2009, Apr. 22
1680 A888 5.50s multi 3.75 3.75

Viceroys Type of 2006

No. 1681: a, Melchor de Liñán y Cisneros (1629-1708). b, Melchor de Navarra y Rocafull (1626-91). c, Melchor Portocarrero Lasso de la Vega (1636-1705). d, Manuel de Oms y de Santa Pau (1651-1710).

2009, Apr. 23 ***Perf. 14x13½***
1681 A767 6s Block of 4 #a-d, + label 16.00 16.00

National University of Central Peru, Huancayo, 50th Anniv. — A889

2009, Apr. 30
1682 A889 2s multi 1.40 1.40

Royal Commentaries of the Incas, 400th Anniv. — A890

Designs: No. 1683, 2s, Royal Commentaries of the Incas, book, by Garcellaso de la Vega. No. 1684, 2s, De la Vega (1539-1616), historian.

2009, Apr. 30
1683-1684 A890 Set of 2 2.75 2.75

America Issue, Children's Games — A891

Designs: No. 1685, 10.50s, Boy flying kite. No. 1686, 10.50s, Children playing ronda.

2009, Apr. 30 **Litho.**
1685-1686 A891 Set of 2 14.00 14.00

Endangered Animals — A892

No. 1687: a, Blastocerus dichotomus. b, Pelecanoides garnotii. c, Podocnemis expansa. d, Crax unicornis.

2009, May 4 ***Perf. 13½x14***
1687 A892 7.50s Block of 4, #a-d, + label 20.00 20.00

Souvenir Sheet

"Libertad Parada" Coin — A893

No. 1688: a, Obverse (arms). b, Reverse (Liberty), vert.

Perf. 13½x14 (#1688a), 14x13½ (#1688b)

2009, May 8
1688 A893 3s Sheet of 2, #a-b 4.00 4.00

Folk Art — A894

Designs: No. 1689, 6.50s, Retable, Ayacucho (Retablo Ayacuchano). No. 1690, 6.50s, Native clothing, Cusco (Muñequería Cusqueña). No. 1691, 6.50s, Decorated bull, Pucará (Torito de Pucará).

2009, May 11 ***Perf. 14x13½***
1689-1691 A894 Set of 3 13.50 13.50

Crustaceans — A895

No. 1692: a, Farfantepenaeus californiensis. b, Sicyonia aliaffnis. c, Ucides occidentalis. d, Palinurus elephas.

2009, May 15 ***Perf. 13½x14***
1692 A895 10s Block of 4, #a-d, + label 27.00 27.00

Souvenir Sheet

Peruvian Hairless Dog — A896

2009, May 15 ***Perf. 14x13½***
1693 A896 7s multi 4.75 4.75

Santiago de Surco Municipality, 80th Anniv. — A897

2009, May 21 **Litho.**
1694 A897 5.50s multi 3.75 3.75

Submarines — A898

No. 1695: a, BAP Pisagua. b, BAP Arica.

2009, May 22 ***Perf. 13½x14***
1695 A898 2.50s Vert. pair, #a-b 3.50 3.50

Cuzco as UNESCO World Heritage Site, 25th Anniv. (in 2008) A899

Litho. With Foil Application

2009, May 24
1696 A899 2.50s multi 1.75 1.75

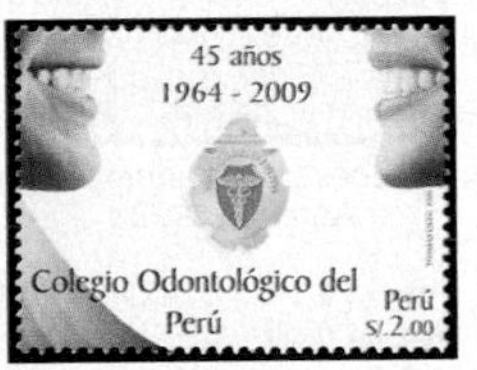

Odontological College of Peru, 45th Anniv. — A900

2009, May 29 **Litho.**
1697 A900 2s multi 1.40 1.40

Campaign Against Rabies A901

2009, June 25 **Litho.** ***Perf. 13½x14***
1698 A901 5.50s multi 3.75 3.75

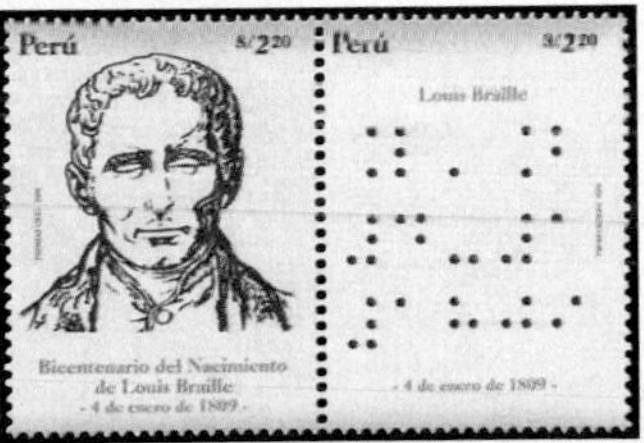

Louis Braille (1809-52), Educator of the Blind — A902

No. 1699: a, Braille. b, Braille text.

Litho. & Engr.

2009, June 30 ***Perf. 14x13½***
1699 A902 2.20s Horiz. pair, #a-b 3.00 3.00

Pre-Columbian Cultures Type of 2006

Designs: No. 1700, 2s, Huari culture, 550-900. No. 1701, 2s, Chimú culture, 1000-1400.

2009, July 3 **Litho.** ***Perf. 13½x14***
1700-1701 A755 Set of 2 2.75 2.75

Ciro Alegría (1909-67), Journalist and Politician — A903

2009, July 8 ***Perf. 14x13½***
1702 A903 2.50s multi 1.75 1.75

Peruvian Tourist Attractions A904

Designs: No. 1703, 2.50s, Amazon River, Loretio Region. No. 1704, 2.50s, Boat on Lake Titicaca, Puno Region. No. 1705, 7.50s, Cumbemayo Archaeological Site, Cajamarca Region.

2009 ***Perf. 13½x14***
1703-1705 A904 Set of 3 8.50 8.50

Issued: Nos. 1703-1704, 7/17; No. 1705, 7/10.

Peruvian Philatelic Association, 60th Anniv. — A905

2009, July 21 ***Perf. 14x13½***
1706 A905 2s multi 1.40 1.40

Víctor Raúl Haya de la Torre (1895-1975), Politician — A906

2009, Aug. 2 **Litho.** ***Perf. 13½x14***
1707 A906 2s multi 1.40 1.40

Miniature Sheet

Peruvian Cuisine — A907

No. 1708: a, Tacacho con cecina. b, Ocopa. c, Cebiche de conchas negras. d, Picante de papa con cuy frito. e, Frejoles con cabrito.

2009, Aug. 3
1708 A907 3s Sheet of 5, #a-e 10.50 10.50

Miniature Sheet

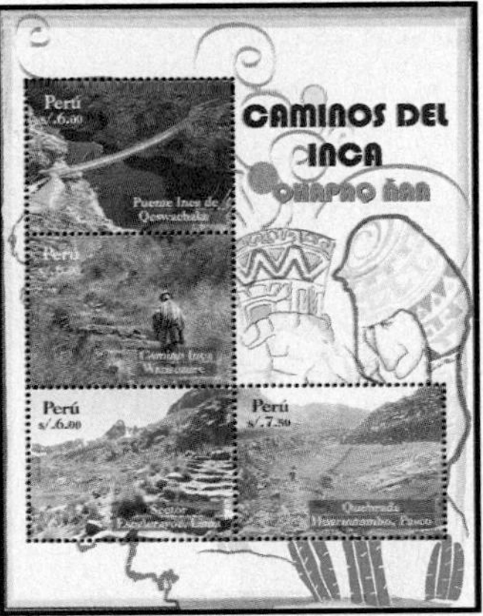

Incan Roads — A908

No. 1709: a, 6s, Inca Bridge, Qeswachaka. b, 6s, Inca Road, Wanacaure. c, 6s, Escaleraycc Sector, Lima. d, 7.50s, Quebrada Huarautambo, Pasco.

2009, Aug. 6
1709 A908 Sheet of 4, #a-d 17.50 17.50

Exports Type of 2007

Designs: No. 1710, 2.50s, Guinea pig. No. 1711, 2.50s, Coffee.

2009, Aug. 19
1710-1711 A801 Set of 2 3.50 3.50

Souvenir Sheet

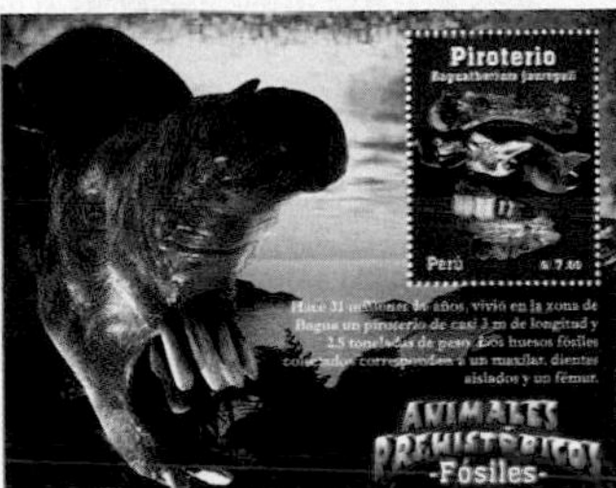

Baguatherium Jaureguii Fossil — A909

2009, Aug. 26 ***Perf. 14x13½***
1712 A909 7s multi 4.75 4.75

Miniature Sheet

Mollusks — A910

No. 1713: a, Megalobulimus popelairianus. b, Megalobulimus capillaccus. c, Scutalus versicolor. d, Scutalus proteus.

2009, Aug. 31 ***Perf. 13½x14***
1713 A910 6.50s Sheet of 4, #a-d 18.00 18.00

Free Trade Treaty Between Peru and People's Republic of China A911

2009, Sept. 10 Litho. ***Perf. 13½x14***
1714 A911 7.50s multi 5.25 5.25

Chinese Immigration to Peru, 160th Anniv. A912

2009, Oct. 12
1715 A912 8.50s multi 6.00 6.00

Natl. Museum of Archaeology, Anthropology and History of Peru — A913

2009, Oct. 13 ***Perf. 14x13½***
1716 A913 5.50s multi 4.00 4.00

Miniature Sheet

Birds — A914

No. 1717: a, Actitis macularia. b, Glaucidium brasilianum. c, Numenius phaeopus. d, Egretta caerulea.

2009, Nov. 9 ***Perf. 13½x14***
1717 A914 6s Sheet of 4, #a-d 17.00 17.00

Luciano Pavarotti (1935-2007), Singer — A915

2009, Nov. 12
1718 A915 10.50s multi 7.50 7.50

Children's Art — A916

Winning art in children's environmental protection stamp design contest: No. 1719, 2s, Orchid, parrot and hand, by Ahmed Lonia Heredia Pérez. No. 1720, 2s, Children, flora and fauna, by Scarie Estefany Rojas Reátegui.

2009, Nov. 22 ***Perf. 14x13½***
1719-1720 A916 Set of 2 3.00 3.00

Christmas A917

2009, Nov. 30 ***Perf. 13½x14***
1721 A917 2.20s multi 1.60 1.60

Souvenir Sheet

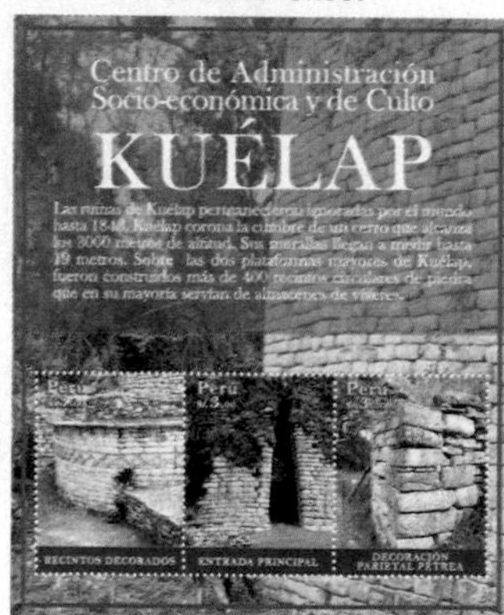

Kuélap Archaeological Site — A918

No. 1722: a, Decorated enclosures (Recintos decorados). b, Principal entrance (Entrada principal). c, Decorated stone walls (Decoración parietal petrea).

2010, June 7 Litho. ***Perf. 14x13½***
1722 A918 3s Sheet of 3, #a-c 6.50 6.50

Central Station for Lima Metropolitan Bus Line — A919

No. 1723: a, Road over tunnel. b, Bus.

2010, June 22 ***Perf. 13½x14***
1723 A919 2.20s Horiz. pair, #a-b 3.25 3.25

Javier Pérez de Cuéllar, Fifth Secretary-General of the United Nations, 90th Birthday — A920

2010, Aug. 9
1724 A920 50c multi .35 .35

St. Francis Solano (1549-1610) A921

2010, Aug. 12 ***Perf. 14x13½***
1725 A921 40c multi .30 .30

Gustavo Pons Muzzo (1916-2008), Historian — A922

2010, Aug. 12
1726 A922 50c multi .35 .35

Archdiocese of Arequipa, 400th Anniv. — A923

2010, Aug. 12 ***Perf. 13½x14***
1727 A923 2s multi 1.50 1.50

Dogs — A924

No. 1728: a, Samoyed. b, Siberian husky.

2010, Aug. 12 ***Perf. 14x13½***
1728 A924 30c Horiz. pair, #a-b .45 .45

Rebeca Carrión Cachot, Archaeologist, 50th Anniv. of Death — A925

2010, Aug. 13 **Litho.**
1729 A925 40c multi .30 .30

Afro-Peruvian Culture Day — A926

No, 1730: a, Musical instruments. b, National Afro-Peruvian Museum, Lima.

2010, Aug. 13 ***Perf. 13½x14***
1730 A926 10c Horiz. pair, #a-b .25 .25

Miniature Sheet

2010 World Cup Soccer Championships, South Africa — A927

No. 1731: a, Mascot. b, Emblem. c, World Cup trophy. d, Soccer player and ball.

2010, Aug. 13 ***Perf. 14x13½***
1731 A927 10s Sheet of 4, #a-d 29.00 29.00

Tourist Sites in Lima — A928

Designs: No. 1732, 3s, Magic Fountains. No. 1733, 3s, Lake, Huascar Park.

2010, Aug. 21
1732-1733 A928 Set of 2 4.50 4.50

Souvenir Sheet

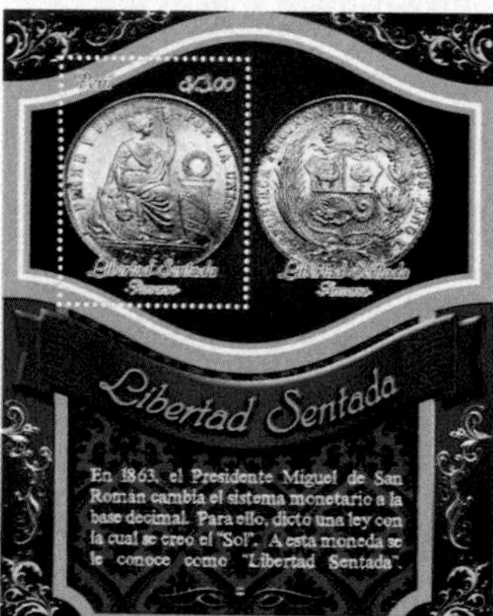

"Seated Liberty" Coin — A929

2010, Aug. 21 ***Perf. 14x13½***
1734 A929 3s multi 2.25 2.25

Mushrooms — A930

No. 1735: a, Suillus luteus. b, Pleurotus cornucopiae.

2010, Aug. 24 **Litho.**
1735 A930 6s Horiz. pair, #a-b 8.75 8.75

New Year 2010 (Year of the Tiger) A931

No. 1736: a, Tiger at left. b, Tiger at right.

2010, Aug. 26 ***Perf. 13½x14***
1736 A931 20c Vert. pair, #a-b .30 .30

Viceroys Type of 2006

No. 1737: a, Diego Ladrón de Guevara Orozco y Calderon (1641-1718). b, Carmine Nicolao Caracciolo (1671-1726). c, Diego Morcillo Rubio de Auñón (1642-1730). d, José de Armendariz (1670-1740).

2010, Sept. 1 ***Perf. 14x13½***
1737 A767 3s Block of 4, #a-d, + label 8.75 8.75

Jorge Chavez (1887-1910), Pilot — A932

Litho. & Engr.

2010, Sept. 3 ***Perf. 13½x14***
1738 A932 2s multi 1.50 1.50

Centenary of Chavez's flight over Alps, after which he crash-landed and later died.

Souvenir Sheet

Stone Heads of the Chavin Culture — A933

2010, Sept. 3 **Litho.** ***Perf. 14x13½***
1739 A933 10s multi 7.25 7.25

Pre-Columbian Cultures Type of 2006

Artifacts of: No. 1740, 50c, Chincha culture, c. 1000. No. 1741, 50c, Chancay culture, c. 1000.

2010, Sept. 7 ***Perf. 13½x14***
1740-1741 A755 Set of 2 .75 .75

Volunteer Fire Brigades in Peru, 150th Anniv. — A934

No. 1742: a, 1860 Merryweather fire carriage. b, Pierce Contender fire truck.

2010, Sept. 9
1742 A934 6s Horiz. pair, #a-b 8.75 8.75

Club Alianza Lima Soccer Team A935

2010, Sept. 10
1743 A935 3s multi 2.25 2.25

Miniature Sheet

Orchids — A936

No. 1744: a, Anguloa virginalis. b, Masdevallia pernix. c, Stanhopea marizaiana. d, Telipogon campoverdei.

2010, Sept. 16 **Litho.**
1744 A936 3s Sheet of 4, #a-d 8.75 8.75

Colegio Nacional Iquitos Soccer Team A937

2010, Sept. 17
1745 A937 3s multi 2.25 2.25

Frédéric Chopin (1810-49), Composer A938

2010, Sept. 21 **Litho. & Engr.**
1746 A938 3s multi 2.25 2.25

Windsurfing — A939

Litho. With Foil Application

2010, Sept. 21
1747 A939 3s multi 2.25 2.25

Souvenir Sheet

Thalassocnus Littoralis — A940

2010, Sept. 21 **Litho.**
1748 A940 10s multi 7.25 7.25

Melgar Soccer Team A941

2010, Sept. 24
1749 A941 3s multi 2.25 2.25

America Issue, National Symbols — A942

Peruvian: No. 1750, 5s, Arms. No. 1751, 5s, Flag.

2010, Oct. 5 ***Perf. 14x13½***
1750-1751 A942 Set of 2 7.25 7.25

Ollantaytambo Archaeological Site — A943

2010, Oct. 29 ***Perf. 13½x14***
1752 A943 5s multi 3.75 3.75

Christmas A944

2010, Nov. 2
1753 A944 10s multi 7.25 7.25

Children's Art — A945

Winning art in children's art contest by: No. 1754, 2s, Jimena P. Vega Gonzáles, 1st place. No. 1755, 2s, Bettina Paz Pinto, 2nd place.

2010, Nov. 22 ***Perf. 14x13½***
1754-1755 A945 Set of 2 3.00 3.00

Folk Art — A946

Designs: No. 1756, 2s, Virgin of Pino, statue by Antonio Olave Palomino. No. 1757, 2s, San Marcos, retable by Jesús Urbano Rojas. No. 1758, 2s, Procession of St. Peter, carving by Fidel Barrientos Bustos.

2010, Nov. 25 **Litho.**
1756-1758 A946 Set of 3 4.25 4.25

Ninth Lions International Forum of Latin America and the Caribbean, Lima — A947

2011, Jan. 15
1759 A947 7.80s multi 5.75 5.75

José María Arguedas (1911-69), Writer A948

2011, Jan. 31 ***Perf. 13½x14***
1760 A948 6.60s multi 4.75 4.75

Postal Union of the Americas, Spain and Portugal (UPAEP), Cent. A949

2011, Mar. 23
1761 A949 2s multi 1.50 1.50

Transportation Infrastructure — A950

Designs: 5s, Southern Pier, Port of Callao. 5.20s, Southern Interoceanic Highway.

2011, May 16 **Litho.**
1762-1763 A950 Set of 2 7.50 7.50

Scouting in Peru, Cent. — A951

Peruvian and Scouting flags and: No. 1764, 6.40s, Boy Scout. No. 1765, 6.40s, Girl Scout.

2011, May 25 ***Perf. 14x13½***
1764-1765 A951 Set of 2 9.25 9.25

Jicamarca Radio Observatory, 50th Anniv. — A952

2011, June 7 ***Perf. 13½x14***
1766 A952 6.60s multi 4.75 4.75

Awarding of 2010 Nobel Prize for Literature to Mario Vargas Llosa — A953

2011, June 8 ***Perf. 14x13½***
1767 A953 7.80s multi 5.75 5.75

Peruvian Submarine Force, Cent. — A954

No. 1768 — Emblem of Submarine Force, various submarines with denomination at: a, UR. b, UL.

2011, June 9 ***Perf. 13½x14***
1768 A954 7.20s Horiz. pair, #a-b 10.50 10.50

Javier Pulgar Vidal (1911-2003), Geographer A955

2011, June 13 ***Perf. 14x13½***
1769 A955 2.40s multi 1.75 1.75

Campaign Against HIV and AIDS — A956

No. 1770 — Text, AIDS ribbon and: a, Man. b, Woman.

2011, June 13 ***Perf. 13½x14***
1770 A956 5.50s Horiz. pair, #a-b 8.00 8.00

First Call for Peruvian Independence by Francisco Antonio de Zela y Arizaga, Bicent. — A957

No. 1771: a, Painting of Zela. b, Statue of Zela.

2011, June 20 **Litho.**
1771 A957 7.20s Horiz. pair, #a-b 10.50 10.50

Amazonia National University of Peru, 50th Anniv. — A958

2011, June 23 ***Perf. 14x13½***
1772 A958 2.70s multi 2.00 2.00

National Theater, Lima A959

2011, June 23 ***Perf. 13½x14***
1773 A959 5s multi 3.75 3.75

Pre-Columbian Cultures Type of 2006

Artifacts of: No. 1774, 6.40s, Chachapoya culture, 700-1500. No. 1775, 6.40s, Inca culture, 1400-1572.

2011, June 24 ***Perf. 13½x14***
1774-1775 A755 Set of 2 9.50 9.50

Viceroys Type of 2006

No. 1776: a, José Antonio de Mendoza Caamano y Sotomayor (1667-1746). b, José Antonio Manso de Velasco (1688-1767). c, Manuel de Amat y Junyent (1707-82). d, Manuel Guirior (1708-88).

2011, July 1 ***Perf. 14x13½***
1776 A767 7.80s Block of 4, #a-d, + label 23.00 23.00

Motocross Racing — A960

2011, July 5 **Litho.**
1777 A960 7.80s multi 5.75 5.75

Dances A961

Designs: No. 1778, 9s, Tijeras (scissors) dance. No. 1779, 9s, Huaconada.

2011, July 5 ***Perf. 13½x14***
1778-1779 A961 Set of 2 13.50 13.50

Year of the Rabbit — A962

No. 1780: a, Rabbit. b, Chinese character for "rabbit."

2011, July 5 ***Perf. 14x13½***
1780 A962 5.50s Horiz. pair, #a-b 8.00 8.00

Souvenir Sheet

Discovery of Machu Picchu, Cent. — A963

2011, July 5
1781 A963 7.80s multi 5.75 5.75

Electric Trains — A964

No. 1782: a, One train. b, Two trains.

2011, July 16 **Litho.**
1782 A964 5.50s Horiz. pair, #a-b 8.00 8.00

Maxillaria Pyhalae — A965

2011, July 19
1783 A965 10.50s multi 7.75 7.75

Governmental Palace and Presidents of Peru — A966

No. 1784: a, Government Palace, 18th cent. b, Marshal José de La Mar (1778-1830). c, Gen. Agustín Gamarra (1785-1841). d, Gen. Luis José de Orbegoso (1795-1847). e, Gen. Felipe Santiago Salaverry (1805-36). f, Marshal Andrés de Santa Cruz (1792-1865). g, Manuel Menéndez (1793-1847). h, Gen. Juan Crisóstomo Torrico (1808-75). i, Justo Figuerola (1771-1854). j, Government Palace, 20th cent. k, Gen. Manuel Ignacio de Vivanco (1806-73). l, Gen. Ramón Castilla (1797-1867). m, Gen. José Rufino Echenique (1808-87). n, Gen. Miguel de San Roman (1802-63). o, Gen. Juan Antonio Pezet (1809-79). p, Gen. Mariano Ignacio Prado (1826-1901). q, Col. José Balta (1814-72). r, Manuel Pardo y Lavalle (1834-78). s, Gen. Luis La Puerta (1811-96). t, Nicolás de Piérola (1839-1913). u, Francisco García Calderón (1834-1905). v, Admiral Lizardo Montero (1832-1905). w, Gen. Miguel Iglesias (1830-1909). x, Gold Room, Government Palace. y, Grand Hall, Government Palace. z, Flag and arms of Peru, Government Palace. aa, Túpac Amaru Room, Government Palace. ab, Gen. Andrés A. Cáceres (1836-1923). ac, Col. Remigio Morales Bermúdez (1836-94). ad, Eduardo López de Romaña (1847-1912). ae, Manuel Candamo (1841-1904). af, José Pardo Barreda (1864-1947). ag, Augusto B. Leguía (1863-1932). ah, Guillermo Billinghurst (1851-1915). ai, Gen. Oscar R. Benavides (1876-1945). aj, Lieutenant Colonel Luis M. Sánchez Cerro (1889-1933). ak, Manuel Prado y Ugarteche (1889-1967). al, José Luis Bustamente y Rivero (1894-1989). am, Gen. Manuel A. Odría (1897-1974). an, Gen. Ricardo Pérez Godoy (1905-82). ao, Honor Guard, Government Palace. ap, Gen. Nicolás Lindley (1908-95). aq, Fernando Belaunde Terry (1912-2002). ar, Gen. Juan Velasco Alvarado (1910-77). as, Gen. Francisco Morales Bermúdez. at, Alan García Pérez. au, Alberto Fujimori. av, Valentín Paniagua (1936-2006). aw, Alejandro Toledo Manrique. ax, Government Palace, 21st cent.

2011, July 25 ***Perf. 14x13½***
1784 A966 Sheet of 50 87.50 87.50
a.-ax. 2.40s Any single 1.75 1.75

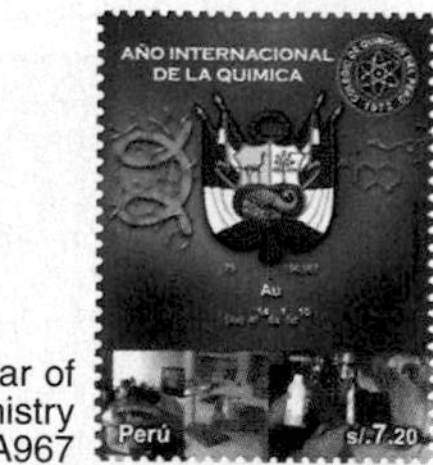

Intl. Year of Chemistry A967

2011, Aug. 1 **Litho.**
1785 A967 7.20s multi 5.25 5.25

Children's Art A968

Winning art in children's prevention of natural disasters stamp design contest: 20c, Overturned boat, hand, tornado, dead fish and flooded house, by Carlos Renato Huaynasi Calcina. 2.40s, Children at school, by Sherley Breshley Suclupe Calderon.

2011, Aug. 18 ***Perf. 13½x14***
1786-1787 A968 Set of 2 1.90 1.90

National Archives, 150th Anniv. A969

2011, Aug. 19
1788 A969 5.80s multi 4.25 4.25

Miniature Sheet

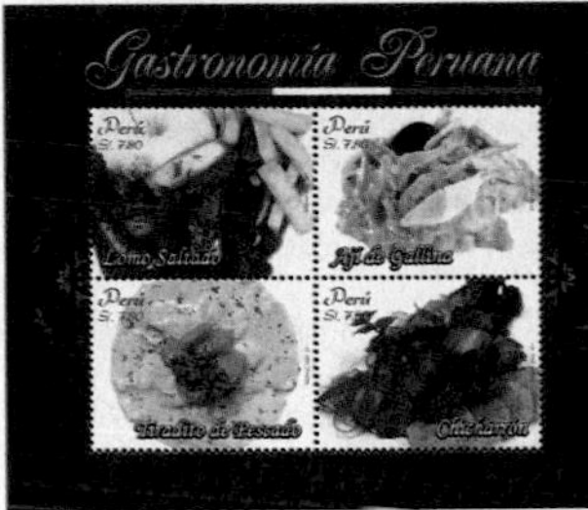

Peruvian Cuisine — A970

No. 1789: a, Lomo Saltado (beef with onions, tomatoes, rice and fried potatoes). b, Ají de Gallina (creamed chicken with chili peppers). c, Tiradito de Pescado (raw fish in spicy sauce). d, Chicharrón (fried pork rinds).

2011, Aug. 25
1789 A970 7.80s Sheet of 4, #a-d 23.00 23.00

Statue of St. Sebastian, Patron Saint of Chepén — A971

2011, Aug. 30 *Perf. 14x13½*
1790 A971 2s multi 1.50 1.50

Clorinda Matto de Turner (1852-1909), Writer — A972

2011, Sept. 9 *Perf. 13½x14*
1791 A972 3.60s multi 2.75 2.75

1838 South Peru Gold 8-Escudo Coin — A973

No. 1792: a, Reverse. b, Obverse.

2011, Sept. 12 *Perf. 14x13½*
1792 A973 5.80s Horiz. pair, #a-b 8.50 8.50

Cayetano Heredia University, 50th Anniv. A974

2011, Sept. 22 *Perf. 13½x14*
1793 A974 3.60s multi 2.75 2.75

First Airplane Flight in Peru by Juan Bielovucic Cavalie, Cent. A975

2011, Sept. 23 **Litho. & Engr.**
1794 A975 7.20p multi 5.25 5.25

Miniature Sheet

Primates — A976

No. 1795: a, Lagothrix flavicauda. b, Callicebus oenanthe. c, Aotus miconax. d, Cacajao calvus.

2011, Oct. 10 **Litho.** *Perf. 14x13½*
1795 A976 7.80s Sheet of 4, #a-d 23.00 23.00

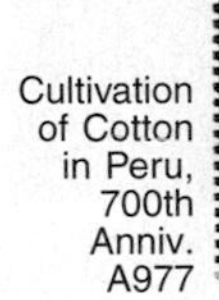
Cultivation of Cotton in Peru, 700th Anniv. A977

Gossypium barbadense with panel at bottom in: No. 1796, 8.50s, Blue. No. 1797, 8.50s, Red brown.

2011, Oc. 11 *Perf. 13½x14*
1796-1797 A977 Set of 2 12.50 12.50

Souvenir Sheet

Fossils of Livyatan Melvillei — A978

Litho. (With Foil Application in Sheet Margin)

2011, Oct. 17 *Perf. 14x13½*
1798 A978 10s multi 7.50 7.50

Franz Liszt (1811-86), Composer A979

Litho. & Engr.

2011, Oct. 22 *Perf. 14x13½*
1799 A979 5.80s multi 4.25 4.25

Endangered Birds — A980

Designs: No. 1800, 10s, Loddigesia mirabilis. No. 1801, 10s, Cinclodes palliatus.

2011, Oct. 28 **Litho.** *Perf. 13½x14*
1800-1801 A980 Set of 2 15.00 15.00

Christmas A981

2011, Nov. 1
1802 A981 5.50s multi 4.25 4.25

America Issue — A982

Designs: No. 1803, 10s, Lion's head mailbox. No. 1804, 10s, Red rectangular mailbox.

2011, Nov. 2 *Perf. 14x13½*
1803-1804 A982 Set of 2 15.00 15.00

Martín Chambi (1891-1973), Photographer A983

2011, Nov. 4
1805 A983 5.20s multi 4.00 4.00

Peruvian Coffee A984

2011, Nov. 10 *Perf. 13½x14*
1806 A984 6.60s multi 5.00 5.00

Summit of South American and Arab Countries A985

2011, Dec. 2 *Perf. 14x13½*
1807 A985 8.40s multi 6.25 6.25

Diplomatic Relations Between Peru and Australia, 50th Anniv. — A986

No. 1808: a, Sloth (oso perezoso). b, Koala.

2013, Mar. 1
1808 A986 3.30s Horiz. pair, #a-b 5.25 5.25

Diplomatic Relations Between Peru and India, 50th Anniv. — A987

No. 1809: a, Machu Picchu, Peru. b, Taj Mahal, India.

2013, Mar. 19
1809 A987 3.60s Horiz. pair, #a-b 5.75 5.75

Diplomatic Relations Between Peru and South Korea, 50th Anniv. — A988

No. 1810: a, 2.50s, Machu Picchu, Peru. b, 3s, Seongsan Ilchulbong, South Korea.

2013, Apr. 1 ***Perf. 13½x14***
1810 A988 Horiz. pair, #a-b 4.25 4.25

See South Korea No. 2399.

Service and Maintenance for Peru Air Force, 80th Anniv. — A989

2013, June 13 Litho. ***Perf. 14x13½***
1811 A989 5.50s multi 4.00 4.00

World Record Black Marlin Catch, 60th Anniv. — A990

Designs: No. 1812, 2.50s, Alfred C. Glassell, Jr. and 1,560-pound black marlin. No. 1813, 2.50s, Fishing boat "Miss Texas," horiz.

Perf. 14x13½, 13½x14
2013, Aug. 2 Litho.
Stamps + Label
1812-1813 A990 Set of 2 3.75 3.75

New Year 2013 (Year of the Dragon) — A991

No. 1814: a, Chinese Zodiac wheel and Chinese character for "dragon." b, Dragon figurine.

2013, Aug. 15 Litho. ***Perf. 14x13½***
1814 A991 6s Horiz. pair, #a-b 8.75 8.75

Diplomatic Relations Between Peru and Japan, 140th Anniv. — A992

No. 1815: a, Machu Picchu, Peru. b, Kinkaku-ji, Japan.

2013, Aug. 21 Litho. ***Perf. 14x13½***
1815 A992 6s Horiz. pair, #a-b 8.75 8.75

Santa Teresa Convent, Arequipa — A993

2013, Aug. 23 Litho. ***Perf. 14x13½***
1816 A993 6s multi 4.50 4.50

Anthropomorphic Monoliths, Ancash Archaeological Park and Museum — A994

2013, Aug. 28 Litho. ***Perf. 13½***
1817 A994 6s multi 4.50 4.50

Benavidesite — A995

2013, Aug. 29 Litho. ***Perf. 13½x14***
1818 A995 8s multi 5.75 5.75

Federico Villareal National University, 50th Anniv. — A996

2013, Sept. 5 ***Perf. 13½x14***
1819 A996 4s multi 3.00 3.00

Souvenir Sheet

Inkayacu Paracasensis and Its Fossilized Remains — A997

Litho. (With Foil Application in Sheet Margin)
2013, Sept. 12 ***Perf. 14x13½***
1820 A997 10s multi 7.25 7.25

Diocese of Cuzco, 475th Anniv. — A998

2013, Sept. 13 Litho. ***Perf. 14x13½***
1821 A998 4s multi 3.00 3.00

Intl. Year of Quinoa A999

2013, Sept. 27 Litho. ***Perf. 13½x14***
1822 A999 5.50s multi 4.00 4.00

Souvenir Sheet

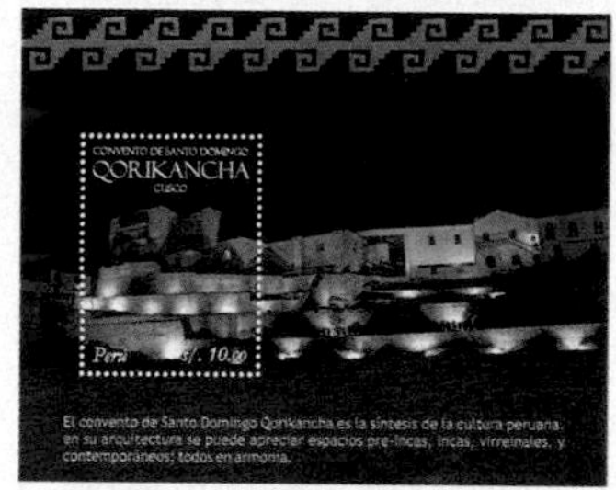

Santo Domingo Convent and Qorikancha Incan Temple, Cuzco — A1000

2013, Sept. 27 Litho. ***Perf. 14x13½***
1823 A1000 10s multi 7.25 7.25

Souvenir Sheet

Temples of the Sun and Moon Archaeological Sites — A1001

2013, Sept. 27 Litho. ***Perf. 13½x14***
1824 A1001 10s multi 7.25 7.25

Souvenir Sheet

Five-Peseta Coin of Peru From 1880 — A1002

No. 1825: a, Reverse (head of Ceres). b, Obverse (coat of arms).

2013, Oct. 1 Litho. ***Perf. 14x13½***
1825 A1002 5s Sheet of 2, #a-b 7.25 7.25

Souvenir Sheet

1863 Centavo Coins — A1003

No. 1826 — Reverse of: a, One-centavo coin. b, Two-centavo coin.

2013, Oct. 1 Litho. ***Perf. 14x13½***
1826 A1003 6s Sheet of 2, #a-b 8.75 8.75

Museum of Natural History, Lima, 95th Anniv. — A1004

2013, Oct. 4 Litho. ***Perf. 14x13½***
1827 A1004 4s multi 3.00 3.00

Souvenir Sheet

Chahuaytiri Rock Paintings — A1005

2013, Oct. 11 Litho. ***Perf. 14x13½***
1828 A1005 10s multi 7.25 7.25

Souvenir Sheet

Canaanimys Maquiensis and Its Fossilized Remains — A1006

Litho. (With Foil Application in Sheet Margin)
2013, Oct. 12 ***Perf. 14x13½***
1829 A1006 10s multi 7.25 7.25

Miniature Sheet

Eagles — A1007

No. 1830: a, Harpia harpyja. b, Morphus guianensis. c, Spizaetus ornatus. d, Spizaetus isidori.

Litho. (With Foil Application in Sheet Margin)

2013, Oct. 14 *Perf. 14x13½*
1830 A1007 3s Sheet of 4, #a-d 8.75 8.75

Miniature Sheet

Butterflies — A1008

No. 1831: a, Hypanartia splendida. b, Isanthrene flavizonata. c, Protesilaus glaucolaus. d, Histioea peruana.

2013, Oct. 24 Litho. *Perf. 13½x14*
1831 A1008 4s Sheet of 4, #a-d 11.50 11.50

Miniature Sheet

Hummingbirds — A1009

No. 1832: a, Heliangelus regalis. b, Myrtis fanny. c, Taphrolesbia griseiventris. d, Rhodopis vesper.

2013, Oct. 31 Litho. *Perf. 13½x14*
1832 A1009 6s Sheet of 4, #a-d 14.50 14.50

Canonization of St. Martin de Porres, 50th Anniv. (in 2012) — A1010

2013, Nov. 4 Litho. *Perf. 13½x14*
1833 A1010 4s multi 3.00 3.00

Diplomatic Relations Between Peru and Russia, 45th Anniv. — A1011

No. 1834: a, Machu Picchu, Peru. b, Kizhi Pogost, Russia.

2013, Nov. 4 Litho. *Perf. 13½x14*
1834 A1011 6s Horiz. pair, #a-b 8.75 8.75

America Issue — A1012

No. 1835: a, Animals and corn stalk from Myth of the Garden of Gold. b, Sun God from Myth of the Garden of Gold. c, Eyes of 14 people, face paint above 5th eye on top row. d, Eyes of 14 people, face paint below 3rd and 4th eyes on bottom row.

2013, Nov. 4 Litho. *Perf. 13½x14*
1835 A1012 4s Block of 4, #a-d, + label 11.50 11.50

Souvenir Sheet

Boat Dock on Amazon River — A1013

2013, Nov. 11 Litho. *Perf. 13½x14*
1836 A1013 8s multi 5.75 5.75

Miniature Sheet

Election of Pope Francis — A1014

No. 1837: a, Pope Francis, hands not visible. b, Pope Francis, hand visible. c, St. Peter's Square. d, Pope Benedict XVI.

2013, Nov. 13 Litho. *Perf. 14x13½*
1837 A1014 6s Sheet of 4, #a-d 17.50 17.50

Souvenir Sheet

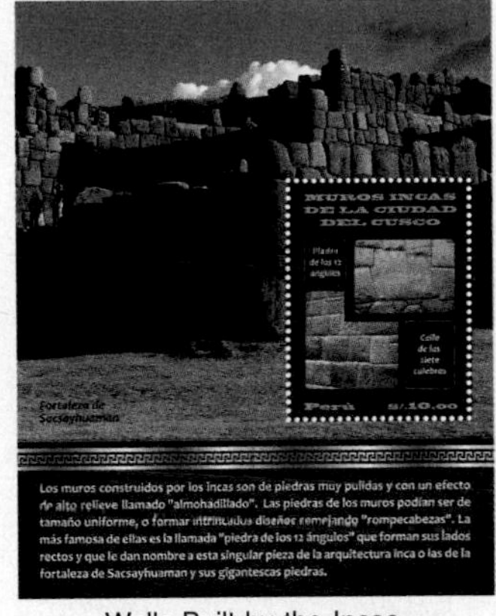

Walls Built by the Incas, Cuzco — A1015

2013, Nov. 13 Litho. *Perf. 14x13½*
1838 A1015 10s multi 7.25 7.25

A1016

Winning Designs in 6th Children's Art Contest — A1017

2013, Dec. 2 Litho. *Perf. 13½x14*
1839 A1016 4s multi 3.00 3.00

Perf. 14x13½
1840 A1017 4s multi 3.00 3.00

A1018

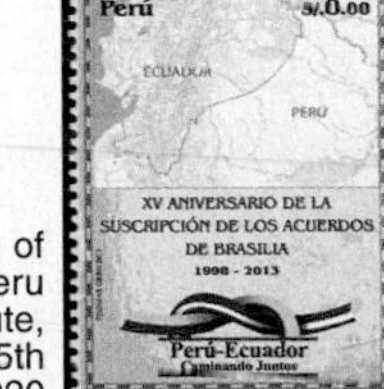

Winning Designs in 7th Children's Art Contest A1019

2013, Dec. 6 Litho. *Perf. 13½x14*
1841 A1018 4s multi 3.00 3.00
1842 A1019 4s multi 3.00 3.00

Resolution of Ecuador-Peru Border Dispute, 15th Anniv. — A1020

2014, Jan. 30 Litho. *Perf. 14x13½*
1843 A1020 8s multi 5.75 5.75

Commercial Accords Between Peru, Colombia and the European Union — A1021

2014, Feb. 28 Litho. *Perf. 14x13½*
1844 A1021 9.50s multi 6.75 6.75

Captain José Abelardo Quiñones Gonzales (1914-41), Military Hero A1022

2014, Apr. 8 Litho. *Perf. 13½x14*
1845 A1022 3.80s multi 2.75 2.75

Miguel Grau Seminario (1834-79), Admiral — A1023

2014, July 23 Litho. *Perf. 14x13½*
1846 A1023 6s multi 4.25 4.25

Peruvian Institute of the Sea, 50th Anniv. A1024

2014, Sept. 5 Litho. *Perf. 13½x14*
1847 A1024 3.80s multi 2.60 2.60

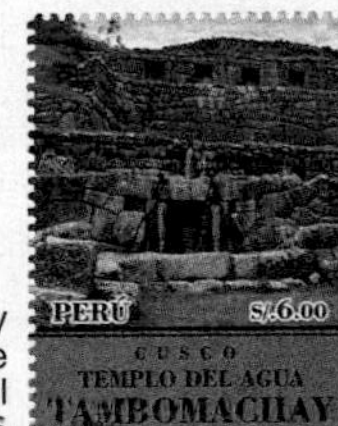

Caballito de Totoro (Traditional Reed Watercraft) A1025

2014, Sept. 17 Litho. *Perf. 14x13½*
1848 A1025 7s multi 5.00 5.00

Tambomachay Temple Archaeological Site — A1026

2014, Sept. 19 Litho. *Perf. 14x13½*
1849 A1026 6s multi 4.25 4.25

Manuel González Prada (1844-1918), Literary Critic — A1027

2014, Sept. 22 Litho. ***Perf. 13½x14***
1850 A1027 7s multi 5.00 5.00

Kotosh Temple Archaeological Site — A1028

2014, Sept. 24 Litho. ***Perf. 14x13½***
1851 A1028 6s multi 4.25 4.25

2014 Canonization of Popes — A1029

Designs: No. 1852, 7s, Pope John XXIII. No. 1853, 7s, Pope John Paul II.

2014, Sept. 26 Litho. ***Perf. 14x13½***
1852-1853 A1029 Set of 2 9.75 9.75

Musical Instruments A1030

Designs: No. 1854, 6s, Botella silbadora. No. 1855, 6s, Antara (pan flute).

2014, Sept. 30 Litho. ***Perf. 13½x14***
1854-1855 A1030 Set of 2 8.25 8.25

Souvenir Sheet

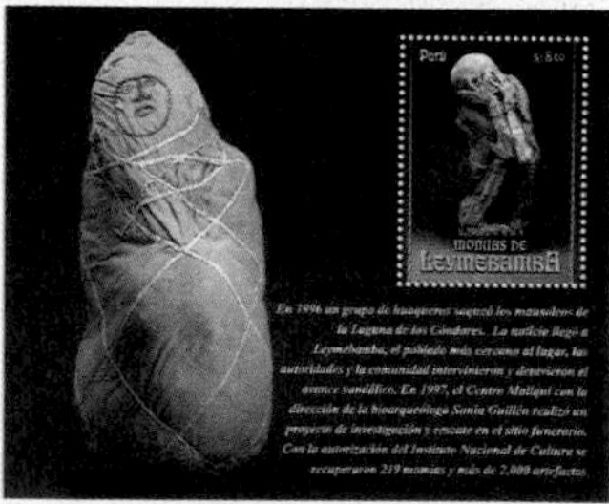

Leymebamba Mummy — A1031

2014, Sept. 30 Litho. ***Perf. 14x13½***
1856 A1031 8s multi 5.50 5.50

William Shakespeare (1564-1616), Writer — A1032

2014, Oct. 3 Litho. ***Perf. 14x13½***
1857 A1032 6s multi 4.25 4.25

Viceroys Type of 2006

No. 1858: a, Agustín de Jáuregui y Aldecoa (1711-84). b, Teodoro de Croix (1730-92). c, Francisco Gil de Taboada y Lemus (1736-1809). d, Ambrosio O'Higgins (1720-1801).

2014, Oct. 7 Litho. ***Perf. 14x13½***
1858 A767 6.50s Block of 4, #a-d, + label 18.00 18.00

Souvenir Sheet

Forensic Facial Reconstruction of the Priestess of Chornancap — A1033

2014, Oct. 13 Litho. ***Perf. 14x13½***
1859 A1033 8s multi 5.50 5.50

Dances A1034

Designs: No. 1860, 8s, La Wuallata. No. 1861, 8s, Carnaval Cusqueño.

2014, Oct. 17 Litho. ***Perf. 13½x14***
1860-1861 A1034 Set of 2 11.00 11.00

Miniature Sheet

Birds — A1035

No. 1862: a, Crotophag sulcirostris. b, Xenospingus concolor. c, Burhinus superciliaris. d, Glaucidium peruanum.

2014, Oct. 17 Litho. ***Perf. 13½x14***
1862 A1035 9s Sheet of 4, #a-d 24.50 24.50

Miniature Sheet

Trees — A1036

No. 1863: a, Swietenia macrophylla. b, Cedrela fissilis. c, Ceiba pentandra. d, Prosopis pallida.

2014, Oct. 20 Litho. ***Perf. 14x13½***
1863 A1036 9.50s Sheet of 4, #a-d 26.00 26.00

Iquitos, 150th Anniv. A1037

2014, Oct. 23 Litho. ***Perf. 13½x14***
1864 A1037 6s multi 4.25 4.25

Barranco District, 140th Anniv. — A1038

2014, Oct. 26 Litho. ***Perf. 14x13½***
1865 A1038 7s multi 4.75 4.75

Miniature Sheet

Mammals — A1039

No. 1866: a, Panthera onca. b, Dinomys branickii. c, Tapirus pinchaque. d, Leopardus jacobitus.

2014, Nov. 3 Litho. ***Perf. 14x13½***
1866 A1039 11s Sheet of 4, #a-d 30.00 30.00

The inscription on No. 1866d is incorrect. The stamp shows Leopardus colocolo.

Souvenir Sheet

Sycorax Peruensis Preserved in Amber — A1040

Litho. (With Foil Application in Sheet Margin)

2014, Nov. 5 ***Perf. 14x13½***
1867 A1040 8s multi 5.50 5.50

Minerals A1041

Designs: 6s, Quartz (Cuarzo). 8s, Jasper (Jaspe).

2014, Nov. 10 Litho. ***Perf. 13½x14***
1868-1869 A1041 Set of 2 9.50 9.50

Christmas A1042

2014, Nov. 14 Litho. ***Perf. 14x13½***
1870 A1042 6s multi 4.25 4.25

Parque de las Leyendas Zoo, 50th Anniv. — A1043

No. 1871: a, Cebuella pygmaea. b, Ateles belzebuth.

2014, Nov. 17 Litho. ***Perf. 14x13½***
1871 A1043 9.50s Horiz. pair, #a-b 13.00 13.00

Serpost (Peruvian Postal Service), 20th Anniv. A1044

2014, Nov. 22 Litho. ***Perf. 13½x14***
1872 A1044 6s multi 4.25 4.25

Miniature Sheet

2014 World Cup Soccer Championships, Brazil — A1045

No. 1873: a, Mascot Fuleco. b, Emblem. c, Soccer player and ball. d, World Cup Trophy.

2014, Nov. 28 Litho. *Perf. 13½x14*

1873 A1045 3.80s Sheet of 4, #a-d 10.50 10.50

Pancho Fierro (1807-79), Painter — A1046

No. 1874 — Paintings: a, El Soldado y la Rabona. b, Fraile de la Buena Muerte. c, El Notario Público. d, La Hermana de la Caridad.

2014, Dec. 1 Litho. *Perf. 14x13½*

1874 A1046 10s Sheet of 4, #a-d 27.50 27.50

Famous Men — A1047

Designs: No. 1875, 9s, Mariano Melgar (1790-1815), poet. No. 1876, 9s, José Olaya Balandra (1782-1823), hero in War of Independence.

2014, Dec. 3 Litho. *Perf. 14x13½*

1875-1876 A1047 Set of 2 12.00 12.00

America Issue.

Chinese Zodiac Animals — A1048

No. 1877: a, Snake. b, Horse.

2014, Dec. 5 Litho. *Perf. 14x13½*

1877 A1048 6.50s Horiz. pair, #a-b 8.75 8.75

Souvenir Sheet

1898 Gold Libra Coin — A1049

No. 1878: a, Obverse (Anverso). b, Reverse (Reverso).

2014, Dec. 9 Litho. *Perf. 14x13½*

1878 A1049 10s multi 13.50 13.50

Battle of Ayacucho, 190th Anniv. A1050

2014, Dec. 9 Litho. *Perf. 13½x14*

1879 A1050 7s multi 4.75 4.75

Archbishop Loayza National Hospital, 90th Anniv. A1051

2014, Dec. 10 Litho. *Perf. 13½x14*

1880 A1051 3.80s multi 2.60 2.60

Miniature Sheet

Carriages — A1052

No. 1881: a, Front view of covered carriage. b, Open-air carriage with red seats. c, Side view of covered carriage. d, Open-air carriage with white seats.

2014, Dec. 15 Litho. *Perf. 13½x14*

1881 A1052 11s Sheet of 4, #a-d 30.00 30.00

SEMI-POSTAL STAMPS

Catalogue values for unused stamps in this section are for Never Hinged items.

Gold Funerary Mask SP1

Designs: 2.60s+1.30s, Ceremonial knife, vert. 3.60s+1.80s, Ceremonial vessel. 4.60s+2.30s, Goblet with precious stones, vert. 20s+10s, Earplug.

Perf. 12x12½, 12½x12

1966, Aug. 16 Photo. Unwmk.

B1 SP1 1.90s + 90c multi 1.10 .90
B2 SP1 2.60s + 1.30s multi 1.25 1.10
B3 SP1 3.60s + 1.80s multi 2.00 1.75
B4 SP1 4.60s + 2.30s multi 2.75 2.25
B5 SP1 20s + 10s multi 10.00 9.00
Nos. B1-B5 (5) 17.10 15.00

The designs show gold objects of the 12th-13th centuries Chimu culture. The surtax was for tourist publicity.

For surcharges see Nos. 679-680, 683-684, 686.

AIR POST STAMPS

No. 248 Overprinted in Black

1927, Dec. 10 Unwmk. *Perf. 12*

C1 A87 50c violet 50.00 26.00
a. Inverted overprint 500.00 —

Two types of overprint: first printing, dull black ink; second printing, shiny black ink. Values are the same. No. C1a occurs in the first printing.

Counterfeits exist.

President Augusto Bernardino Leguía — AP1

1928, Jan. 12 Engr.

C2 AP1 50c dark green 1.10 .55

For surcharge see No. 263.

Coat of Arms of Piura Type

1932, July 28 Litho.

C3 A107 50c scarlet 26.00 22.50

Counterfeits exist.

Airplane in Flight — AP3

1934, Feb. Engr. *Perf. 12½*

C4 AP3 2s blue 6.50 .60
C5 AP3 5s brown 15.00 1.25

For surcharges see Nos. C14-C15.

Funeral of Atahualpa AP4

Palace of Torre-Tagle AP7

Designs: 35c, Mt. San Cristobal. 50c, Avenue of Barefoot Friars. 10s, Pizarro and the Thirteen.

1935, Jan. 18 Photo. *Perf. 13½*

C6 AP4 5c emerald .35 .25
C7 AP4 35c brown .45 .45
C8 AP4 50c orange yel .90 .75
C9 AP4 1s plum 1.75 1.25
C10 AP7 2s red orange 2.75 2.40
C11 AP4 5s dp claret 11.00 7.00
C12 AP4 10s dk blue 45.00 30.00
Nos. C6-C12 (7) 62.20 42.10

4th centenary of founding of Lima.

Nos. C6-C12 overprinted "Radio Nacional" are revenue stamps.

"La Callao," First Locomotive in South America AP9

1936, Aug. 27 *Perf. 12½*

C13 AP9 35c gray black 3.25 1.75

Founding of the Province of Callao, cent.

Nos. C4-C5 Surcharged "Habilitado" and New Value, like Nos. 353-355

1936, Nov. 4

C14 AP3 5c on 2s blue .55 .30
C15 AP3 25c on 5s brown 1.10 .55
a. Double surcharge 14.00 14.00
b. No period btwn. "O" & "25 Cts" 1.60 1.60
c. Inverted surcharge 21.00

There are many broken letters in this setting.

Mines of Peru AP10

Jorge Chávez AP14

Aerial View of Peruvian Coast AP16

View of the "Sierra" — AP17

St. Rosa of Lima — AP22

Designs: 5c, La Mar Park, Lima. 15c, Mail Steamer "Inca" on Lake Titicaca. 20c, Native Queña (flute) Player and Llama. 30c, Ram at Model Farm, Puno. 1s, Train in Mountains. 1.50s, Jorge Chavez Aviation School. 2s,

Transport Plane. 5s, Aerial View of Virgin Forests.

1936-37 Photo. *Perf. 12½*

No.	Type	Value	Color	Unused	Used
C16	AP10	5c	brt green	.35	.25
C17	AP10	5c	emer ('37)	.35	.25
C18	AP10	15c	lt ultra	.55	.25
C19	AP10	15c	blue ('37)	.35	.25
C20	AP10	20c	gray blk	1.50	.25
C21	AP10	20c	pale ol grn ('37)	1.00	.30
C22	AP14	25c	mag ('37)	.45	.25
C23	AP10	30c	henna brn	4.75	1.10
C24	AP10	30c	dk ol brn ('37)	1.50	.25
C25	AP14	35c	brown	2.75	2.25
C26	AP10	50c	yellow	.45	.30
C27	AP10	50c	brn vio ('37)	.65	.25
C28	AP16	70c	Prus grn	5.50	5.00
C29	AP16	70c	pck grn ('37)	1.00	.85
C30	AP17	80c	brn blk	6.50	5.00
C31	AP17	80c	ol blk ('37)	1.25	.55
C32	AP10	1s	ultra	4.75	.45
C33	AP10	1s	red brn ('37)	2.40	.30
C34	AP14	1.50s	red brn	7.75	6.00
C35	AP14	1.50s	org yel ('37)	4.75	.45
			Engr.		
C36	AP10	2s	deep blue	13.00	7.75
C37	AP10	2s	yel grn ('37)	9.25	.80
C38	AP16	5s	green	17.00	3.75
C39	AP22	10s	car & brn	125.00	110.00
			Nos. C16-C39 (24)	212.80	146.85

Nos. C23, C25, C28, C30, C36 Surcharged in Black or Red

1936, June 26

No.	Type	Value	Color	Unused	Used
C40	AP10	15c	on 30c hn brn	.65	.45
C41	AP14	15c	on 35c brown	.65	.45
C42	AP16	15c	on 70c Prus grn	4.50	3.50
C43	AP17	25c	on 80c brn blk (R)	4.50	3.50
C44	AP10	1s	on 2s dp bl	7.75	6.50
			Nos. C40-C44 (5)	18.05	14.40

Surcharge on No. C43 is vertical, reading down.

First Flight in Peru, 1911 — AP23

Jorge Chávez — AP24

Airport of Limatambo at Lima — AP25

Map of Aviation Lines from Peru — AP26

Designs: 10c, Juan Bielovucic (1889-?) flying over Lima race course, Jan. 14, 1911. 15c, Jorge Chavez-Dartnell (1887-1910), French-born Peruvian aviator who flew from Brixen to Domodossola in the Alps and died of plane-crash injuries.

1937, Sept. 15 Engr. *Perf. 12*

No.	Type	Value	Color	Unused	Used
C45	AP23	10c	violet	.65	.25
C46	AP24	15c	dk green	.90	.25
C47	AP25	25c	gray brn	.65	.25
C48	AP26	1s	black	3.00	2.10
			Nos. C45-C48 (4)	5.20	2.85

Inter-American Technical Conference of Aviation, Sept. 1937.

Government Restaurant at Callao — AP27

Monument on the Plains of Junin — AP28

Rear Admiral Manuel Villar — AP29

View of Tarma — AP30

Dam, Ica River — AP31

View of Iquitos AP32

Highway and Railroad Passing AP33

Mountain Road — AP34

Plaza San Martín, Lima — AP35

National Radio of Peru AP36

Stele from Chavin Temple AP37

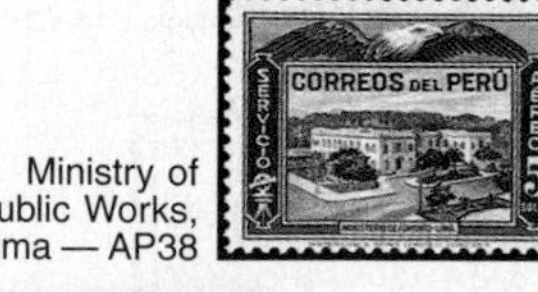

Ministry of Public Works, Lima — AP38

Crypt of the Heroes, Lima — AP39

Imprint: "Waterlow & Sons Limited, Londres."

1938, July 1 Photo. *Perf. 12½, 13*

No.	Type	Value	Color	Unused	Used
C49	AP27	5c	violet brn	.25	.25
C50	AP28	15c	dk brown	.25	.25
C51	AP29	20c	dp magenta	.55	.30
C52	AP30	25c	dp green	.25	.25
C53	AP31	30c	orange	.25	.25
C54	AP32	50c	green	.45	.30
C55	AP33	70c	slate bl	.65	.30
C56	AP34	80c	olive	1.25	.30
C57	AP35	1s	slate grn	10.00	4.25
C58	AP36	1.50s	purple	2.25	.30
			Engr.		
C59	AP37	2s	ind & org brn	3.75	.95
C60	AP38	5s	brown	18.00	1.75
C61	AP39	10s	ol grn & ind	70.00	37.50
			Nos. C49-C61 (13)	107.90	46.95

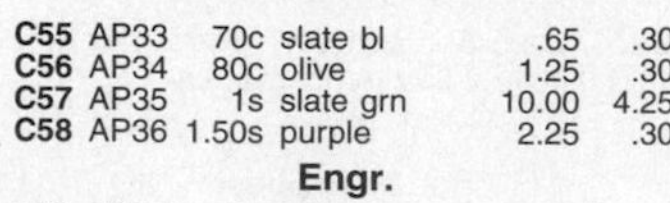

See Nos. C73-C75, C89-C93, C103.
For surcharges see Nos. C65, C76-C77, C82-C88, C108.

Torre-Tagle Palace — AP40

National Congress Building — AP41

Manuel Ferreyros, José Gregorio Paz Soldán and Antonio Arenas — AP42

1938, Dec. 9 Photo. *Perf. 12½*

No.	Type	Value	Color	Unused	Used
C62	AP40	25c	brt ultra	.90	.65
C63	AP41	1.50s	brown vio	2.40	1.90
C64	AP42	2s	black	1.50	.75
			Nos. C62-C64 (3)	4.80	3.30

8th Pan-American Conference at Lima.

No. C52 Surcharged in Black

1942 *Perf. 13*

No.	Type	Value	Color	Unused	Used
C65	AP30	15c	on 25c dp grn	1.75	.25

Types of 1938

Imprint: "Columbian Bank Note Co."

1945-46 Unwmk. Litho. *Perf. 12½*

No.	Type	Value	Color	Unused	Used
C73	AP27	5c	violet brown	.25	.25
C74	AP31	30c	orange	.25	.25
C75	AP36	1.50s	purple ('46)	.35	.30
			Nos. C73-C75 (3)	.85	.80

Nos. C73 and C54 Overprinted in Black

1947, Sept. 25 *Perf. 12½, 13*

No.	Type	Value	Color	Unused	Used
C76	AP27	5c	violet brown	.25	.25
C77	AP32	50c	green	.25	.30

1st Peru Intl. Airways flight from Lima to New York City, Sept. 27-28, 1947.

Catalogue values for unused stamps in this section, from this point to the end of the section, are for Never Hinged items.

Peru-Great Britain Air Route — AP43

Designs: 5s, Discus thrower. 10s, Rifleman.

1948, July 29 Photo. *Perf. 12½*

No.	Type	Value	Color	Unused	Used
C78	AP43	1s	blue	4.00	2.75

Basketball Players — AP44

Carmine Overprint, "AEREO"

No.	Type	Value	Color	Unused	Used
C79	AP44	2s	red brown	5.50	3.50
C80	AP44	5s	yellow green	9.25	5.75
C81	AP44	10s	yellow	11.00	7.00
a.			Souv. sheet, #C78-C81, perf 13	50.00	50.00
			Nos. C78-C81 (4)	29.75	19.00

Peru's participation in the 1948 Olympic Games held at Wembley, England, during July and August. Postally valid for four days, July 29-Aug. 1, 1948. Proceeds went to the Olympic Committee.

A surtax of 2 soles on No. C81a was for the Children's Hospital.

Remainders of Nos. C78-C81 and C81a were overprinted "Melbourne 1956" and placed on sale Nov. 19, 1956, at all post offices as "voluntary stamps" with no postal validity. Clerks were permitted to postmark them to please collectors, and proceeds were to help pay the cost of sending Peruvian athletes to Australia. On April 14, 1957, postal authorities declared these stamps valid for one day, April 15, 1957. The overprint was applied to 10,000 sets and 21,000 souvenir sheets. Value, set, $22.50; sheet, $17.50.

No. C55 Surcharged in Red

1948, Dec. *Perf. 13*

No.	Type	Value	Color	Unused	Used
C82	AP33	10c	on 70c slate blue	.35	.25
C83	AP33	20c	on 70c slate blue	.35	.25
C84	AP33	55c	on 70c slate blue	.35	.25
			Nos. C82-C84 (3)	1.05	.75

Nos. C52, C55 and C56 Surcharged in Black

1949, Mar. 25

No.	Type	Value	Color	Unused	Used
C85	AP30	5c	on 25c dp grn	.25	.25
C86	AP30	10c	on 25c dp grn	.25	.25
C87	AP33	15c	on 70c slate bl	.35	.25
C88	AP34	30c	on 80c olive	1.10	.65
			Nos. C85-C88 (4)	1.95	1.40

The surcharge reads up, on No. C87.

Types of 1938

Imprint: "Waterlow & Sons Limited, Londres."

Perf. 13x13½, 13½x13

1949-50 Photo.

No.	Type	Value	Color	Unused	Used
C89	AP27	5c	olive bister	.25	.25
C90	AP31	30c	red	.25	.25
C91	AP33	70c	blue	.45	.25
C92	AP34	80c	cerise	1.25	.45
C93	AP36	1.50s	vio brn ('50)	.90	.55
			Nos. C89-C93 (5)	3.10	1.75

Overprinted "U. P. U. 1874-1949" in Red or Black

Air View, Reserva Park, Lima — AP45

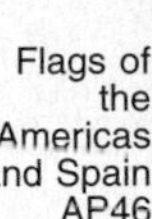

Flags of the Americas and Spain AP46

Designs: 30c, National flag. 55c, Huancayo Hotel. 95c, Blanca-Ancash Cordillera. 1.50s, Arequipa Hotel. 2s, Coal chute and dock, Chimbote. 5s, Town hall, Miraflores. 10s, Hall of National Congress, Lima.

1951, Apr. 2 Engr. *Perf. 12*

C94	AP45	5c blue grn	.25	.25
C95	AP45	30c black & car	.25	.25
a.		Inverted overprint		
C96	AP45	55c yel grn (Bk)	.25	.25
C97	AP45	95c dk green	.25	.25
C98	AP45	1.50s dp car (Bk)	.35	.30
C99	AP45	2s deep blue	.35	.30
C100	AP45	5s rose car (Bk)	4.00	3.25
C101	AP45	10s purple	5.25	4.50
C102	AP46	20s dk brn & ultra	8.75	7.00
		Nos. C94-C102 (9)	19.70	16.35

UPU, 75th anniv. (in 1949).

Nos. C94-C102 exist without overprint, but were not regularly issued. Value, set, $225.

Type of 1938

Imprint: "Inst. de Grav. Paris."

1951, May Engr. *Perf. 12½x12*

C103	AP27	5c olive bister	.25	.25

Type of 1938 Surcharged in Black

1951

C108	AP31	25c on 30c rose red	.25	.25

Thomas de San Martin y Contreras and Jerónimo de Aliaga y Ramirez — AP47

San Marcos University — AP48

Designs: 50c, Church and convent of Santo Domingo. 1.20s, P. de Peralta Barnuevo, T. de San Martin y Contreras and J. Baquijano y Carrillo de Cordova. 2s, T. Rodriguez de Mendoza, J. Hipolito Unanue y Pavon and J. Cayetano Heredia y Garcia. 5s, Arms of the University, 1571 and 1735.

Perf. 11½x12½

1951, Dec. 10 Litho.

C109	AP47	30c gray	.45	.45
C110	AP48	40c ultra	.45	.45
C111	AP48	50c car rose	.45	.45
C112	AP47	1.20s emerald	.45	.45
C113	AP47	2s slate	1.40	.45
C114	AP47	5s multicolored	3.00	.45
		Nos. C109-C114 (6)	6.20	2.70

400th anniv. of the founding of San Marcos University.

River Gunboat Marañon AP49

Peruvian Cormorants — AP50

National Airport, Lima AP51

Tobacco Plant AP52

Manco Capac Monument AP54

Garcilaso de la Vega AP53

Designs: 1.50s, Housing Unit No. 3. 2.20s, Inca Solar Observatory.

Imprint: "Thomas De La Rue & Co. Ltd."

1953-60 Unwmk. *Perf. 13, 12*

C115	AP49	40c yellow grn	.25	.25
a.		40c blue green ('57)	.25	.25
C116	AP50	75c dk brown	1.50	.30
C116A	AP50	80c pale brn red ('60)	.70	.25
C117	AP51	1.25s blue	.35	.25
C118	AP49	1.50s cerise	.45	.30
C119	AP51	2.20s dk blue	2.25	.45
C120	AP52	3s brown	1.90	.65
C121	AP53	5s bister	1.50	.30
C122	AP54	10s dull vio brn	3.75	.85
		Nos. C115-C122 (9)	12.65	3.60

See #C158-C162, C182-C183, C186-C189, C210-C211.

For surcharges see #C420-C422, C429-C433, C435-C436, C438, C442-C443, C445-C450, C455, C471-C474, C476, C478-C479, C495.

Queen Isabella I — AP55

Fleet of Columbus — AP56

Perf. 12½x11½, 11½x12½

1953, June 18 Engr. Unwmk.

C123	AP55	40c dp carmine	.25	.25
C124	AP56	1.25s emerald	.65	.25
C125	AP55	2.15s dp plum	1.10	.60
C126	AP56	2.20s black	1.50	.65
		Nos. C123-C126 (4)	3.50	1.75

500th birth anniv. (in 1951) of Queen Isabella I of Spain.

For surcharge see No. C475.

Arms of Lima and Bordeaux AP57

Designs: 50c, Eiffel Tower and Cathedral of Lima. 1.25s, Admiral Dupetit-Thouars and frigate "La Victorieuse." 2.20s, Presidents Coty and Prado and exposition hall.

1957, Sept. 16 *Perf. 13*

C127	AP57	40c claret, grn & ultra	.25	.25
C128	AP57	50c grn, blk & hn brn	.25	.25
C129	AP57	1.25s bl, ind & dk grn	.55	.45
C130	AP57	2.20s bluish blk, bl & red brn	.90	.90
		Nos. C127-C130 (4)	1.95	1.85

French Exposition, Lima, Sept. 15-Oct. 1.

For surcharges see Nos. 763, C503-C505.

Pre-Stamp Postal Markings — AP58

10c, 1r Stamp of 1857. 15c, 2r Stamp of 1857. 25c, 1d Stamp of 1860. 30c, 1p Stamp of 1858. 40c, ½p Stamp of 1858. 1.25s, José Davila Condemarin. 2.20s, Ramon Castilla. 5s, Pres. Manuel Prado. 10s, Shield of Lima containing stamps.

Perf. 12½x13

1957, Dec. 1 Engr. Unwmk.

C131	AP58	5c silver & blk	.25	.25
C132	AP58	10c lil rose & bl	.25	.25
C133	AP58	15c grn & red brn	.25	.25
C134	AP58	25c org yel & bl	.25	.25
C135	AP58	30c vio brn & org brn	.25	.25
C136	AP58	40c black & bis	.25	.25
C137	AP58	1.25s dk bl & dk brn	.75	.55
C138	AP58	2.20s red & sl bl	1.10	.75
C139	AP58	5s lil rose & mar	2.40	1.50
C140	AP58	10s ol grn & lil	4.50	2.50
		Nos. C131-C140 (10)	10.25	6.80

Centenary of Peruvian postage stamps. No. C140 issued to publicize the Peruvian Centenary Phil. Exhib. (PEREX).

Carlos Paz Soldan — AP59

Port of Callao and Pres. Manuel Prado AP60

Design: 1s, Ramon Castilla.

Perf. 14x13½, 13½x14

1958, Apr. 7 Litho. Wmk. 116

C141	AP59	40c brn & pale rose	.30	.30
C142	AP59	1s grn & lt grn	.35	.30
C143	AP60	1.25s dull pur & ind	.55	.30
		Nos. C141-C143 (3)	1.20	.90

Centenary of the telegraph connection between Lima and Callao and the centenary of the political province of Callao.

For surcharges see Nos. 758A, 767.

Flags of France and Peru — AP61

Cathedral of Lima and Lady AP62

1.50s, Horseback rider & mall in Lima. 2.50s, Map of Peru showing national products.

Perf. 12½x13, 13x12½

1958, May 20 Engr. Unwmk.

C144	AP61	50c dl vio, bl & car	.25	.25
C145	AP62	65c multi	.25	.25
C146	AP62	1.50s bl, brn vio & ol	.35	.25
C147	AP61	2.50s sl grn, grnsh bl & claret	.65	.30
		Nos. C144-C147 (4)	1.50	1.05

Peruvian Exhib. in Paris, May 20-July 10.

Bro. Martin de Porres Velasquez AP63

First Royal School of Medicine (Now Ministry of Government and Police) — AP64

Designs: 1.20s, Daniel Alcides Carrion Garcia. 1.50s, Jose Hipolito Unanue Pavon.

Perf. 13x13½, 13½x13

1958, July 24 Litho. Unwmk.

C148	AP63	60c multi	.25	.25
C149	AP63	1.20s multi	.25	.25
C150	AP63	1.50s multi	.25	.25
C151	AP64	2.20s black	.65	.65
		Nos. C148-C151 (4)	1.40	1.40

Daniel A. Carrion (1857-85), medical martyr.

Gen. Ignacio Alvarez Thomas AP65

1958, Nov. 13 ***Perf. 13x12½***

C152 AP65 1.10s brn lake, bis & ver .30 .30
C153 AP65 1.20s blk, bis & ver .55 .55

General Thomas (1787-1857), fighter for South American independence.

"Justice" and Emblem — AP66

1958, Nov. 13

Star in Blue and Olive Bister

C154 AP66 80c emerald .25 .25
C155 AP66 1.10s red orange .25 .25
C156 AP66 1.20s ultra .35 .25
C157 AP66 1.50s lilac rose .35 .25
Nos. C154-C157 (4) 1.20 1.00

Lima Bar Assoc., 150th anniv.

Types of 1953-57

Designs: 80c, Peruvian cormorants. 3.80s, Inca Solar Observatory.

Imprint: "Joh. Enschedé en Zonen-Holland"

Perf. 12½x14, 14x13, 13x14

1959, Dec. 9 **Unwmk.**

C158 AP50 80c brown red .35 .25
C159 AP52 3s lt green 1.10 .45
C160 AP51 3.80s orange 2.25 .55
C161 AP53 5s brown 1.10 .55
C162 AP54 10s orange ver 2.25 .65
Nos. C158-C162 (5) 7.05 2.45

WRY Emblem, Dove, Rainbow and Farmer — AP67

1960, Apr. 7 **Litho.** ***Perf. 14x13***

C163 AP67 80c multi .55 .55
C164 AP67 4.30s multi 1.00 1.00
a. Souv. sheet of 2, #C163-C164, imperf. 15.00 15.00

World Refugee Year, 7/1/59-6/30/60. No. C164a sold for 15s.

Peruvian Cormorant Over Ocean — AP68

1960, May 30 ***Perf. 14x13½***

C165 AP68 1s multi 3.75 1.75

Intl. Pacific Fair, Lima, 1959.

Lima Coin of 1659 AP69

1961, Jan. 19 **Unwmk.** ***Perf. 13x14***

C166 AP69 1s org brn & gray .55 .45
C167 AP69 2s Prus bl & gray .55 .45

1st National Numismatic Exposition, Lima, 1959; 300th anniv. of the first dated coin (1659) minted at Lima.

The Earth AP70

1961, Mar. 8 **Litho.** ***Perf. 13½x14***

C168 AP70 1s multicolored 1.40 .65

International Geophysical Year.

Frigate Amazonas AP71

1961, Mar. 8 **Engr.** ***Perf. 13½***

C169 AP71 50c brown & grn .30 .30
C170 AP71 80c dl vio & red org .35 .30
C171 AP71 1s green & sepia .55 .30
Nos. C169-C171 (3) 1.20 .90

Centenary (in 1958) of the trip around the world by the Peruvian frigate Amazonas.

Machu Picchu Sheet

A souvenir sheet was issued Sept. 11, 1961, to commemorate the 50th anniversary of the discovery of the ruins of Machu Picchu, ancient Inca city in the Andes, by Hiram Bingham. It contains two bi-colored imperf. airmail stamps, 5s and 10s, lithographed in a single design picturing the mountaintop ruins. The sheet was valid for one day and was sold in a restricted manner. Value $20.

Olympic Torch, Laurel and Globe — AP72

1961, Dec. 13 **Unwmk.** ***Perf. 13***

C172 AP72 5s gray & ultra .90 .60
C173 AP72 10s gray & car 2.00 1.25
a. Souv. sheet of 2, #C172-C173, imperf. 4.25 4.25

17th Olympic Games, Rome, 8/25-9/11/60.

Fair Emblem and Llama — AP73

1962, Jan. **Litho.** ***Perf. 10½x11***

C174 AP73 1s multi .35 .25

2nd International Pacific Fair, Lima, 1961.

Map Showing Disputed Border, Peru-Ecuador — AP74

1962, May 25 ***Perf. 10½***

Gray Background

C175 AP74 1.30s blk, red & car rose .35 .25
C176 AP74 1.50s blk, red & emer .35 .25
C177 AP74 2.50s blk, red & dk bl .70 .70
Nos. C175-C177 (3) 1.40 1.20

Settlement of the border dispute with Ecuador by the Protocol of Rio de Janeiro, 20th anniv.

Cahuide and Cuauhtémoc — AP75

2s, Tupac Amaru (Jose G. Condorcanqui) & Miguel Hidalgo. 3s, Pres. Manuel Prado & Pres. Adolfo Lopez Mateos of Mexico.

1962, May 25 **Engr.** ***Perf. 13***

C178 AP75 1s dk car rose, red & brt grn .25 .25
C179 AP75 2s grn, red & brt grn .45 .30
C180 AP75 3s brn, red & brt grn .70 .50
Nos. C178-C180 (3) 1.40 1.05

Exhibition of Peruvian art treasures in Mexico.

Agriculture, Industry and Archaeology AP76

1962, Sept. 7 **Litho.** ***Perf. 14x13½***

C181 AP76 1s black & gray .35 .25

Cent. (in 1961) of Pallasca Ancash province.

Types of 1953-60

1.30s, Guanayes. 1.50s, Housing Unit No. 3. 1.80s, Locomotive No. 80 (like #460). 2s, Monument to Native Farmer. 3s, Tobacco plant. 4.30s, Inca Solar Observatory. 5s, Garcilaso de la Vega. 10s, Inca Monument.

Imprint: "Thomas De La Rue & Co. Ltd."

1962-63 **Wmk. 346** **Litho.** ***Perf. 13***

C182 AP50 1.30s pale yellow .75 .25
C183 AP49 1.50s claret .55 .25
C184 A182 1.80s dark blue .55 .25

Perf. 12

C185 A184 2s emerald ('63) .55 .25
C186 AP52 3s lilac rose .60 .25
C187 AP51 4.30s orange 1.25 .45
C188 AP53 5s citron 1.25 .75

Perf. 13½x14

C189 AP54 10s vio bl ('63) 2.75 .90
Nos. C182-C189 (8) 8.25 3.35

For surcharges see Nos. C429, C432, C446, C449, C473.

Freedom from Hunger Type

1963, July 23 **Unwmk.** ***Perf. 12½***

C190 A189 4.30s lt grn & ocher 1.40 1.10

Jorge Chávez and Wing — AP77

1964, Feb. 20 **Engr.** ***Perf. 13***

C191 AP77 5s org brn, dk brn & bl .90 .45

1st crossing of the Alps by air (Sept. 23, 1910) by the Peruvian aviator Jorge Chávez, 50th anniv.

Alliance for Progress Type

Design: 1.30s, Same, horizontal.

Perf. 12½x12, 12x12½

1964, June 22 **Litho.**

C192 A190 1.30s multi .25 .25
C193 A190 3s multi .75 .60

Fair Poster — AP78

1965, Jan. 15 **Unwmk.** ***Perf. 14½***

C194 AP78 1s multi .25 .25

3rd International Pacific Fair, Lima 1963.

Basket, Globe, Pennant — AP79

1965, Apr. 19 ***Perf. 12x12½***

C195 AP79 1.30s violet & red .75 .60
C196 AP79 4.30s bis brn & red 1.75 1.40

4th Women's Intl. Basketball Championship.

For surcharge see No. C493.

St. Martin de Porres — AP80

Designs: 1.80s, St. Martin's miracle: dog, cat and mouse feeding from same dish. 4.30s, St. Martin with cherubim in Heaven.

1965, Oct. 29 **Litho.** ***Perf. 11***

C197 AP80 1.30s gray & multi .35 .25
C198 AP80 1.80s gray & multi .45 .25
C199 AP80 4.30s gray & multi .95 .95
Nos. C197-C199 (3) 1.75 1.45

Canonization of St. Martin de Porres Velasquez (1579-1639), on May 6, 1962.

For surcharges see Nos. C439, C496 and footnote below No. RA57.

Victory Monument, Lima, and Battle Scene — AP81

Designs: 3.60s, Monument and Callao Fortress. 4.60s, Monument and José Galvez.

1966, May 2 Photo. *Perf. 14x13½*

C200 AP81 1.90s multicolored .65 .50
C201 AP81 3.60s brn, yel & bis .75 .75
C202 AP81 4.60s multicolored 1.25 1.00
Nos. C200-C202 (3) 2.65 2.25

Centenary of Peru's naval victory over the Spanish Armada at Callao, May, 1866.

Civil Guard Emblem AP82

1.90s, Various activities of Civil Guard.

1966, Aug. 30 Photo. *Perf. 13½x14*

C203 AP82 90c multicolored .25 .25
C204 AP82 1.90s dp lil rose, gold & blk .55 .25

Centenary of the Civil Guard.

Hydroelectric Center Type

1966, Nov. 24 Photo. *Perf. 13½x14*

C205 A193 1.90s lil, blk & vio bl .35 .25

Sun Symbol, Ancient Carving — AP83

Designs: 3.60s, Map of Peru and spiral, horiz. 4.60s, Globe with map of Peru.

Perf. 14x13½, 13½x14

1967, Feb. 16 Litho.

C206 AP83 2.60s red org & blk .35 .25
C207 AP83 3.60s dp blue & blk .45 .45
C208 AP83 4.60s tan & multi .55 .55
Nos. C206-C208 (3) 1.35 1.25

Photography exhibition "Peru Before the World" which opened simultaneously in Lima, Madrid, Santiago de Chile and Washington, Sept. 27, 1966.

For surcharges see #C444, C470, C492.

Types of 1953-60

2.60s, Monument to Native Farmer. 3.60s, Tobacco plant. 4.60s, Inca Solar Observatory.

Imprint: "I.N.A."

1967, Jan. *Perf. 13½x14, 14x13½*

C209 A184 2.60s brt green 1.00 .30
C210 AP52 3.60s lilac rose 1.40 .45
C211 AP51 4.60s orange 1.50 .90
Nos. C209-C211 (3) 3.90 1.65

For surcharges see Nos. C433, C436-C438, C440-C442, C445, C447-C450, C454-C455, C471-C472, C474, C476, C478.

Wind Vane and Sun Type of Regular Issue

1967, Apr. 18 Photo. *Perf. 13½x14*

C212 A194 1.90s yel brn, blk & gold .45 .30

St. Rosa of Lima by Angelino Medoro — AP84

St. Rosa Painted by: 2.60s, Carlo Maratta. 3.60s, Cuzquena School, 17th century.

1967, Aug. 30 Photo. *Perf. 13½*

Black, Gold & Multi

C213 AP84 1.90s .65 .25
C214 AP84 2.60s 1.10 .30
C215 AP84 3.60s 1.25 .55
Nos. C213-C215 (3) 3.00 1.10

350th death anniv. of St. Rosa of Lima.

For surcharge see No. C477.

Fair Type of Regular Issue

1967, Oct. 27 Photo. *Perf. 12*

C216 A195 1s gold, brt red lil & blk .35 .25

Lions Emblem — AP85

1967, Dec. 29 Litho. *Perf. 14x13½*

C217 AP85 1.60s brt bl & vio bl, *grysh* .60 .30

50th anniversary of Lions International.

Decorated Jug, Nazca Culture — AP86

Painted pottery jugs of pre-Inca Nazca culture: 2.60s, Falcon. 3.60s, Round jug decorated with grain-eating bird. 4.60s, Two-headed snake. 5.60s, Marine bird.

1968, June 4 Photo. *Perf. 12*

C218 AP86 1.90s multi .65 .30
C219 AP86 2.60s multi .75 .35
C220 AP86 3.60s black & multi .75 .35
C221 AP86 4.60s brown & multi 1.10 .55
C222 AP86 5.60s gray & multi 2.25 1.10
Nos. C218-C222 (5) 5.50 2.65

For surcharges see #C451-C453, C497, C500.

Antarqui, Inca Messenger AP87

Design: 5.60s, Alpaca and jet liner.

1968, Sept. 2 Litho. *Perf. 12*

C223 AP87 3.60s multi .55 .45
C224 AP87 5.60s red, blk & brn .75 .65

12th anniv. of Peruvian Airlines (APSA).

For surcharges see Nos. C480-C482.

Human Rights Flame — AP88

1968, Sept. 5 Photo. *Perf. 14x13½*

C225 AP88 6.50s brn, red & grn .55 .30

International Human Rights Year.

Discobolus and Mexico Olympics Emblem AP89

1968, Oct. 19 Photo. *Perf. 13½*

C226 AP89 2.30s yel, brn & dk bl .35 .25
C227 AP89 3.50s yel grn, sl bl & red .35 .25
C228 AP89 5s brt pink, blk & ultra .35 .30
C229 AP89 6.50s lt bl, mag & brn .55 .40
C230 AP89 8s lil, ultra & car .55 .40
C231 AP89 9s org, vio & grn .55 .40
Nos. C226-C231 (6) 2.70 2.00

19th Olympic Games, Mexico City, 10/12-27.

Hand, Corn and Field AP90

1969, Mar. 3 Litho. *Perf. 11*

C232 AP90 5.50s on 1.90s grn & yel .55 .30
C233 AP90 6.50s on 1.90s bl, grn & yel .75 .40

Agrarian Reform Law. Not issued without surcharge.

Peruvian Silver 8-reales Coin, 1568 AP91

1969, Mar. 17 Litho. *Perf. 12*

C234 AP91 5s yellow, gray & blk .55 .45
C235 AP91 5s bl grn, gray & blk .55 .45

400th anniv. of the first Peruvian coinage.

Ramon Castilla Monument AP92

Design: 10s, Pres. Ramon Castilla.

1969, May 30 Photo. *Perf. 13½*

Size: 27x40mm

C236 AP92 5s emerald & indigo .55 .30

Perf. 12

Size: 21x37mm

C237 AP92 10s plum & brn 1.25 .65

Ramon Castilla (1797-1867), president of Peru (1845-1851 and 1855-1862), on the occasion of the unveiling of the monument in Lima.

Airline Type of Regular Issue

1969, June 17 Litho. *Perf. 11*

C238 A199 3s org & multi .45 .45
C239 A199 4s multi .55 .45
C240 A199 5.50s ver & multi .65 .45
C241 A199 6.50s vio & multi .65 .45
Nos. C238-C241 (4) 2.30 1.80

First Peruvian Airlines (APSA) flight to Europe.

Radar Antenna, Satellite and Earth — AP93

1969, July 14 Litho. *Perf. 11*

C242 AP93 20s multi 2.25 1.10
a. Souv. sheet 3.50 3.50

Opening of the Lurin satellite earth station near Lima.

No. C242a contains one imperf. stamp with simulated perforations similar to No. C242.

Gonzales Type of Regular Issue inscribed "AEREO"

1969, July 23 Litho. *Perf. 11*

C243 A200 20s red & multi 2.50 1.25

WHO Emblem AP94

1969, Aug. 14 Photo. *Perf. 12*

C244 AP94 5s gray, red brn, gold & blk .35 .30
C245 AP94 6.50s dl org, gray bl, gold & blk .45 .30

WHO, 20th anniv.

Agrarian Reform Type of Regular Issue

1969, Aug. 28 Litho. *Perf. 11*

C246 A201 3s lil & blk .35 .35
C247 A201 4s brn & buff .55 .35

Garcilaso de la Vega — AP95

Designs: 2.40s, De la Vega's coat of arms. 3.50s, Title page of "Commemtarios Reales que tratan del origen de los Yncas," Lisbon, 1609.

1969, Sept. 18 Litho. *Perf. 12x12½*

C248 AP95 2.40s emer, sil & blk .30 .30
C249 AP95 3.50s ultra, buff & blk .35 .30
C250 AP95 5s sil, yel, blk & brn .55 .30
a. Souv. sheet of 3, #C248-C250, imperf. 2.25 2.25
Nos. C248-C250 (3) 1.20 .90

Garcilaso de la Vega, called "Inca" (1539-1616), historian of Peru.

Fair Type of Regular Issue, 1969

1969, Nov. 14 Litho. *Perf. 11*

C251 A203 3s bis & multi .30 .25
C252 A203 4s multi .80 .25

Bolognesi Type of Regular Issue

1969, Dec. 9 Litho. *Perf. 11*

C253 A204 50s lt brn, blk & gold 4.00 1.90

Arms of Amazonas — AP96

1970, Jan. 6 Litho. *Perf. 11*
C254 AP96 10s multi 1.25 1.00

ILO Emblem AP97

1970, Jan. 16
C278 AP97 3s dk vio bl & lt ultra .35 .25

ILO, 50th anniv.

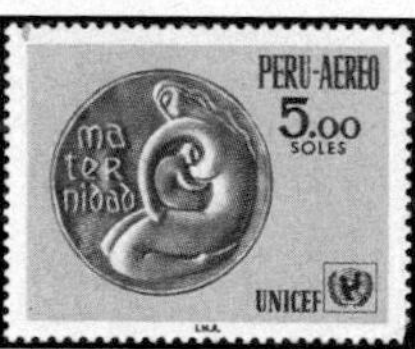

Motherhood and UNICEF Emblem AP98

1970, Jan. 16 Photo. *Perf. 13½x14*
C279 AP98 5s yel, gray & blk .45 .30
C280 AP98 6.50s brt pink, gray & blk .65 .40

Vicus Culture Type of Regular Issue

Ceramics of Vicus Culture, 6th-8th Centuries: 3s, Squatting warrior. 4s, Jug. 5.50s, Twin jugs. 6.50s, Woman and jug.

1970, Feb. 23 Litho. *Perf. 11*
C281 A205 3s buff, blk & brn 1.10 .30
C282 A205 4s buff, blk & brn 1.10 .30
C283 A205 5.50s buff, blk & brn 2.25 .85
C284 A205 6.50s buff, blk & brn 3.25 1.10
a. Vert. strip, #526, C281-C284 10.00 10.00
Nos. C281-C284 (4) 7.70 2.55

Fish Type of Regular Issue

1970, Apr. 30 Litho. *Perf. 11*
C285 A207 3s Swordfish 2.10 1.40
C286 A207 3s Yellowfin tuna 2.10 1.40
C287 A207 5.50s Wolf fish 2.10 2.10
Nos. C285-C287 (3) 6.30 4.90

Telephone — AP99

1970, June 12 Litho. *Perf. 11*
C288 AP99 5s multi .55 .25
C289 AP99 10s multi 1.10 .55

Nationalization of the Peruvian telephone system, Mar. 25, 1970.

Soldier-Farmer Type of Regular Issue

1970, June 24 Litho. *Perf. 11*
C290 A208 3s gold & multi .55 .25
C291 A208 5.50s gold & multi 1.10 .25

UN Headquarters, NY — AP100

1970 June 26
C292 AP100 3s vio bl & lt bl .35 .25

25th anniversary of United Nations.

Rotary Club Emblem — AP101

1970, July 18
C293 AP101 10s blk, red & gold 1.25 .80

Rotary Club of Lima, 50th anniversary.

Tourist Type of Regular Issue

3s, Ruins of Sun Fortress, Trujillo. 4s, Sacsayhuaman Arch, Cuzco. 5.50s, Arch & Lake Titicaca, Puno. 10s, Machu Picchu, Cuzco.

1970, Aug. 6 Litho. *Perf. 11*
C294 A210 3s multi .80 .25
C295 A210 4s multi, vert. 1.00 .25
C296 A210 5.50s multi, vert. 1.50 .35
C297 A210 10s multi, vert. 2.00 .75
a. Souvenir sheet of 5 5.50 5.50
Nos. C294-C297 (4) 5.30 1.60

No. C297a contains 5 imperf. stamps similar to Nos. 538, C294-C297 with simulated perforations.

Procession, Lord of Miracles — AP102

4s, Cockfight, by T. Nuñez Ureta. 5.50s, Altar of Church of the Nazarene, vert. 6.50s, Procession, by J. Vinatea Reinoso. 8s, Procession, by José Sabogal, vert.

1970, Nov. 30 Litho. *Perf. 11*
C298 AP102 3s blk & multi .35 .35
C299 AP102 4s blk & multi .35 .35
C300 AP102 5.50s blk & multi .65 .40
C301 AP102 6.50s blk & multi .75 .50
C302 AP102 8s blk & multi 1.10 .60
Nos. C298-C302 (5) 3.20 2.20

October Festival in Lima.

"Tight Embrace" (from ancient monolith) AP103

1971, Feb. 8 Litho. *Perf. 11*
C303 AP103 4s ol gray, yel & red .55 .30
C304 AP103 5.50s dk bl, pink & red .55 .30
C305 AP103 6.50s sl, buff & red .55 .30
Nos. C303-C305 (3) 1.65 .90

Issued to express Peru's gratitude to the world for aid after the Ancash earthquake, May 31, 1970.

Textile Type of Regular Issue

Designs: 3s, Chancay tapestry, vert. 4s, Chancay lace. 5.50s, Paracas cloth, vert.

1971, Apr. 19 Litho. *Perf. 11*
C306 A213 3s multi 1.10 .50
C307 A213 4s grn & multi 1.10 .50
C308 A213 5.50s multi 1.60 .55
Nos. C306-C308 (3) 3.80 1.55

Fish Type of Regular Issue

Fish Sculptures and Fish: 3.50s, Chimu Inca culture, 14th century and Chilean sardine. 4s, Mochica culture, 5th century, and engraulis ringens. 5.50s, Chimu culture, 13th century, and merluccios peruanos. 8.50s, Nazca culture, 3rd century, and brevoortis maculatachilcae.

1971, June 7 Litho. *Perf. 11*
C309 A214 3.50s multi .65 .25
C310 A214 4s multi .75 .25
C311 A214 5.50s multi 1.10 .55
C312 A214 8.50s multi 1.75 1.10
Nos. C309-C312 (4) 4.25 2.15

Independence Type of 1971

Paintings: No. C313, Toribio Rodriguez de Mendoza. No. C314, José de la Riva Aguero. No. C315, Francisco Vidal. 3.50s, José de San Martin. No. C317, Juan P. Viscardo y Guzman. No. C318, Hipolito Unanue. 4.50s, Liberation Monument, Paracas. No. C320, José G. Condorcanqui-Tupac Amaru. No. C321, Francisco J. de Luna Pizarro. 6s, March of the Numancia Battalion, horiz. 7.50s, Peace Tower, monument for Alvarez de Arenales, horiz. 9s, Liberators' Monument, Lima, horiz. 10s, Independence Proclamation in Lima, horiz.

1971 Litho. *Perf. 11*
C313 A215 3s brt mag & blk .25 .25
C314 A215 3s gray & multi .25 .25
C315 A215 3s dk bl & multi .25 .25
C316 A215 3.50s dk bl & multi .35 .25
C317 A215 4s emer & blk .35 .25
C318 A215 4s gray & multi .35 .25
C319 A215 4.50s dk bl & multi .35 .25
C320 A215 5.50s brn & blk .55 .25
C321 A215 5.50s gray & multi .55 .25
C322 A215 6s dk bl & multi .65 .30
C323 A215 7.50s dk bl & multi .75 .50
C324 A215 9s dk bl & multi .75 .50
C325 A215 10s dk bl & multi .75 .50
Nos. C313-C325 (13) 6.15 4.05

150th anniversary of independence, and to honor the heroes of the struggle for independence. Sizes: 6s, 10s, 45x35mm, 7.50s, 9s, 41x39mm. Others 31x49mm.

Issued: #C313, C317, C320, 5/10; #C314, C318, C321, 7/5; others 7/27.

Ricardo Palma — AP104

1971, Aug. 27 *Perf. 13*
C326 AP104 7.50s ol bis & blk 1.10 .55

Sesquicentennial of National Library. Ricardo Palma (1884-1912) was a writer and director of the library.

Weight Lifter — AP105

1971, Sept. 15
C327 AP105 7.50s brt bl & blk 1.10 .55

25th World Weight Lifting Championships, Lima.

Flag, Family, Soldier's Head — AP106

1971, Oct. 4
C328 AP106 7.50s blk, lt bl & red .90 .30
a. Souv. sheet of 1, imperf. 2.50 2.50

3rd anniv. of the revolution of the armed forces.

"Sacramento" — AP107

1971, Oct. 8
C329 AP107 7.50s lt bl & dk bl 1.10 .55

Sesquicentennial of Peruvian Navy.

Peruvian Order of the Sun AP108

1971, Oct. 8
C330 AP108 7.50s multi .60 .30

Sequicentennial of the Peruvian Order of the Sun.

Liberation Type of Regular Issue

Design: 50s, Detail from painting "Progress of Liberation," by Teodoro Nuñez Ureta.

1971, Nov. 4 Litho. *Perf. 13x13½*
C331 A217 50s multi 6.50 2.25

2nd Ministerial meeting of the "Group of 77."

Fair Emblem AP109

1971, Nov. 12 *Perf. 13*
C332 AP109 4.50s multi .55 .25

7th Pacific International Trade Fair.

Fish Type of Regular Issue

3s, Pontinus furcirhinus dubius. 5.50s, Hogfish.

1972, Mar. 20 Litho. *Perf. 13x13½*
C333 A223 3s lt bl & multi 1.25 .75
C334 A223 5.50s lt bl & multi 2.25 .75

Teacher and Children, by Teodoro Nuñez Ureta AP110

1972, Apr. 10 Litho. *Perf. 13x13½*
C335 AP110 6.50s multi .60 .30

Enactment of Education Reform Law.

White-tailed Trogon — AP111

2.50s, Amazonian umbrella bird. 3s, Peruvian cock-of-the-rock. 6.50s, Cuvier's toucan. 8.50s, Blue-crowned motmot.

1972, June 19 Litho. *Perf. 13½x13*

C336	AP111	2s	multi	2.40	1.75
C337	AP111	2.50s	multi	2.40	1.75
C338	AP111	3s	multi	2.75	1.75
C339	AP111	6.50s	multi	5.00	1.75
C340	AP111	8.50s	multi	7.50	1.75
	Nos. C336-C340 (5)			20.05	8.75

Quipu and Map of Americas AP112

1972, Aug. 21

C341	AP112	5s	blk & multi	1.00	.50

4th Interamerican Philatelic Exhibition, EXFILBRA, Rio de Janeiro, Aug. 26-Sept. 2.

Inca Runner, Olympic Rings — AP113

1972, Aug. 28

C342	AP113	8s	buff & multi	1.10	.55

20th Olympic Games, Munich, 8/26-9/11.

Woman of Catacaos, Piura — AP114

Regional Costumes: 2s, Tupe (Yauyos) woman of Lima. 4s, Indian with bow and arrow, from Conibo, Loreto. 4.50s, Man with calabash, Cajamarca. 5s, Moche woman, Trujillo. 6.50s, Man and woman of Ocongate, Cuzco. 8s, Chucupana woman, Ayacucho. 8.50s, Cotuncha woman, Junin. 10s, Woman of Puno dancing "Pandilla."

1972-73 Design AP114

C343	2s	blk & multi	.45	.45
C344	3.50s	blk & multi	1.25	.70
C345	4s	blk & multi	1.50	.80
C346	4.50s	blk & multi	.90	.90
C346A	5s	blk & multi	.90	.90
C347	6.50s	blk & multi	2.25	1.10
C347A	8s	blk & multi	1.75	1.40
C347B	8.50s	blk & multi	1.75	1.50
C348	10s	blk & multi	1.75	1.75
Nos. C343-C348 (9)			12.50	9.50

Issued: 3.50s, 4s, 6.50s, 9/29/72; 2s, 4.50s, 10s, 4/30/73; 5s, 8s, 8.50s, 10/15/73.

Funerary Tower, Sillustani, Puno — AP115

Archaeological Monuments: 1.50s, Stone of the 12 angles, Cuzco. 3.50s, Ruins of Chavin, Ancash. 5s, Wall and gate, Chavin, Ancash. 8s, Ruins of Machu Picchu.

Perf. 13½x13, 13x13½

1972, Oct. 16 Litho.

C349	AP115	1.50s	multi	.50	.25
C350	AP115	3.50s	multi, horiz.	.75	.25
C351	AP115	4s	multi	.75	.25
C352	AP115	5s	multi, horiz.	1.10	.40
C353	AP115	8s	multi, horiz.	1.75	.55
	Nos. C349-C353 (5)			4.85	1.70

AP116

Inca ponchos, various textile designs.

1973, Jan. 29 Litho. *Perf. 13½x13*

C354	AP116	2s	multi	.55	.50
C355	AP116	3.50s	multi	.75	.50
C356	AP116	4s	multi	.75	.50
C357	AP116	5s	multi	.75	.55
C358	AP116	8s	multi	1.90	.55
	Nos. C354-C358 (5)			4.70	2.60

AP117

Antique Jewelry: 1.50s, Goblets and Ring, Mochica, 10th cent. 2.50s, Golden hands and arms, Lambayeque, 12th cent. 4s, Gold male statuette, Mochica, 8th ceny. 5s, Two gold brooches, Nazca, 8th cent. 8s, Flayed puma, Mochica, 8th cent.

1973, Mar. 19 Litho. *Perf. 13½x13*

C359	AP117	1.50s	multi	1.10	.80
C360	AP117	2.50s	multi	1.10	.80
C361	AP117	4s	multi	1.10	.80
C362	AP117	5s	multi	1.50	1.25
C363	AP117	8s	multi	2.75	.80
	Nos. C359-C363 (5)			7.55	4.45

Andean Condor — AP118

Protected Animals. 5s, Vicuna. 8s, Spectacled bear.

1973, Apr. 16 Litho. *Perf. 13½x13*

C364	AP118	4s	blk & multi	.55	.25
C365	AP118	5s	blk & multi	.75	.40
C366	AP118	8s	blk & multi	1.60	.70
	Nos. C364-C366 (3)			2.90	1.35

See Nos. C372-C376, C411-C412.

Indian Guide, by José Sabogal — AP119

Peruvian Paintings: 8.50s, Portrait of a Lady, by Daniel Hernandez. 20s, Man Holding Figurine, by Francisco Laso.

1973, May 7 Litho. *Perf. 13½x13*

C367	AP119	1.50s	multi	.40	.40
C368	AP119	8.50s	multi	.80	.60
C369	AP119	20s	multi	2.50	1.10
	Nos. C367-C369 (3)			3.70	2.10

Basket and World Map AP120

1973, May 26 *Perf. 13x13½*

C370	AP120	5s	green	.65	.30
C371	AP120	20s	lil rose	2.50	1.00

1st International Basketball Festival.

Darwin's Rhea — AP121

3.50s, Giant otter. 6s, Greater flamingo. 8.50s, Bush dog, horiz. 10s, Chinchilla, horiz.

1973, Sept. 3 Litho. *Perf. 13½x13*

C372	AP121	2.50s	shown	1.75	1.00
C373	AP121	3.50s	multi	2.75	1.25
C374	AP121	6s	multi	3.50	1.25
C375	AP121	8.50s	multi	3.50	1.75
C376	AP121	10s	multi	4.50	2.50
	Nos. C372-C376 (5)			16.00	7.75

Protected animals.

Orchid — AP122

Designs: Various orchids.

1973, Sept. 27

C377	AP122	1.50s	blk & multi	1.00	.75
C378	AP122	2.50s	blk & multi	1.75	.75
C379	AP122	3s	blk & multi	2.00	.75
C380	AP122	3.50s	blk & multi	2.25	.75
C381	AP122	8s	blk & multi	5.00	.75
	Nos. C377-C381 (5)			12.00	3.75

Pacific Fair Emblem — AP123

1973, Nov. 14 Litho. *Perf. 13½x13*

C382	AP123	8s	blk, red & gray	1.10	.45

8th International Pacific Fair, Lima.

Cargo Ship ILO AP124

Designs: 2.50s, Boats of Pescaperu fishing organization. 8s, Jet and seagull.

1973, Dec. 14 Litho. *Perf. 13*

C383	AP124	1.50s	multi	.25	.25
C384	AP124	2.50s	multi	.40	.30
C385	AP124	8s	multi	1.25	.30
	Nos. C383-C385 (3)			1.90	.85

Issued to promote government enterprises.

Lima Monument AP125

1973, Nov. 27 *Perf. 13*

C386	AP125	8.50s	red & multi	1.10	.35

50th anniversary of Air Force Academy. Monument honors Jorge Chavez, Peruvian aviator.

Bridge at Yananacu, by Enrique Camino Brant AP126

Paintings: 10s, Peruvian Birds, by Teodoro Nuñez Ureta, vert. 50s, Boats of Totora, by Jorge Vinatea Reinoso.

1973, Dec. 28 *Perf. 13x13½, 13½x13*

C387	AP126	8s	multi	1.10	.30
C388	AP126	10s	multi	1.75	.65
C389	AP126	50s	multi	7.00	3.25
	Nos. C387-C389 (3)			9.85	4.20

Moral House, Arequipa AP127

2.50s, El Misti Mountain, Arequipa. 5s, Puya Raymondi (cacti), vert. 6s, Huascaran Mountain. 8s, Lake Querocochа. Views on 5s, 6s, 8s are views in White Cordilleras Range, Ancash Province.

1974, Feb. 11

C390	AP127	1.50s	multi	.25	.25
C391	AP127	2.50s	multi	.50	.25
C392	AP127	5s	multi	.75	.25
C393	AP127	6s	multi	1.10	.25
C394	AP127	8s	multi	1.75	.65
	Nos. C390-C394 (5)			4.35	1.65

San Jeronimo's, Cuzco — AP128

Churches of Peru: 3.50s, Cajamarca Cathedral. 5s, San Pedro's, Zepita-Puno, horiz. 6s, Cuzco Cathedral. 8.50s, Santo Domingo, Cuzco.

1974, May 6

C395	AP128	1.50s	multi	.75	.30
C396	AP128	3.50s	multi	.75	.30
C397	AP128	5s	multi	1.25	.30

C398 AP128 6s multi 1.25 .40
C399 AP128 8.50s multi 2.10 .50
Nos. C395-C399 (5) 6.10 1.80

Surrender at Ayacucho, by Daniel Hernandez — AP129

Designs: 6s, Battle of Junin, by Felix Yañex. 7.50s, Battle of Ayachucho, by Felix Yañez.

1974 Litho. ***Perf. 13x13½***
C400 AP129 3.50s multi .55 .25
C401 AP129 6s multi .90 .30
C402 AP129 7.50s multi .90 .30
C403 AP129 8.50s multi 1.10 .30
C404 AP129 10s multi 1.25 .60
Nos. C400-C404 (5) 4.70 1.75

Sesquicentennial of the Battles of Junin and Ayacucho and of the surrender at Ayacucho.
Issued: 7.50s, 8/6; 6s, 10/9; others, 12/9.

Chavin Stone, Ancash — AP130

Machu Picchu, Cuzco — AP131

#C407, C409, Different bas-reliefs from Chavin Stone. #C408, Baths of Tampumacchay, Cuzco. #C410, Ruins of Kencco, Cuzco.

1974, Mar. 25 ***Perf. 13½x13, 13x13½***
C405 AP130 3s multi 1.10 .25
C406 AP131 3s multi .75 .25
C407 AP130 5s multi 2.00 .65
C408 AP131 5s multi .85 .25
C409 AP130 10s multi 2.00 .65
C410 AP131 10s multi 1.75 .25
Nos. C405-C410 (6) 8.45 2.30

Cacajao Rubicundus — AP132

1974, Oct. 21 ***Perf. 13½x13***
C411 AP132 8s multi 1.10 .45
C412 AP132 20s multi 2.75 1.10

Protected animals.

Inca Gold Mask — AP133

1974, Nov. 8 ***Perf. 13x13½***
C413 AP133 8s yel & multi 1.90 .60

8th World Mining Congress, Lima.

Chalan, Horseman's Cloak — AP134

1974, Nov. 11 Litho. ***Perf. 13½x13***
C414 AP134 5s multi .55 .25
C415 AP134 8.50s multi 1.10 .55

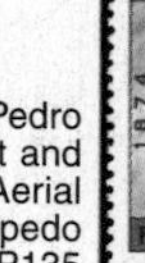

Pedro Paulet and Aerial Torpedo — AP135

1974, Nov. 28 Litho. ***Perf. 13x13½***
C416 AP135 8s bl & vio .75 .35

UPU, cent. Pedro Paulet, inventor of the mail-carrying aerial torpedo.

Christmas Type of 1974

Design: 6.50s, Indian Nativity scene.

1974, Dec. 20 ***Perf. 13½x13***
C417 A235 6.50s multi .55 .30

Andean Village, Map of South American West Coast — AP136

1974, Dec. 30
C418 AP136 6.50s multi .65 .40

Meeting of Communications Ministers of Andean Pact countries.

Map of Peru, Modern Buildings, UN Emblem — AP137

1975, Mar. 12 Litho. ***Perf. 13½x13***
C419 AP137 6s blk, gray & red .55 .45

2nd United Nations Industrial Development Organization Conference, Lima.

Nos. C187, C211 and C160 Surcharged with New Value and Heavy Bar in Dark Blue

Wmk. 346

1975, April Litho. ***Perf. 12***
C420 AP51 2s on 4.30s org .45 .25

Perf. 13½x14, 13x14

Unwmk.
C421 AP51 2.50s on 4.60s org .55 .25
C422 AP51 5s on 3.80s org .60 .40
Nos. C420-C422 (3) 1.60 .90

World Map and Peruvian Colors — AP138

1975, Aug. 25 Litho. ***Perf. 13x13½***
C423 AP138 6.50s lt bl, vio bl & red 1.10 .30

Conference of Foreign Ministers of Nonaligned Countries.

Map of Peru and Flight Route — AP139

1975, Oct. 23 Litho. ***Perf. 13x13½***
C424 AP139 8s red, pink & blk 1.00 .30

AeroPeru's first flights: Lima-Rio de Janeiro, Lima-Los Angeles.

Fair Poster — AP140

1975, Nov. 21 Litho. ***Perf. 13½x13***
C425 AP140 6s blk, bis & red .75 .30

9th International Pacific Fair, Lima, 1975.

Col. Francisco Bolognesi — AP141

1975, Dec. 23 Litho. ***Perf. 13½x13***
C426 AP141 20s multi 2.75 1.10

160th birth anniv. of Col. Bolognesi.

Indian Mother and Child — AP142

1976, Feb. 23 Litho. ***Perf. 13½x13***
C427 AP142 6s gray & multi .75 .30

Christmas 1975.

Inca Messenger, UPAE Emblem — AP143

1976, Mar. 19 Litho. ***Perf. 13½x13***
C428 AP143 5s red, blk & tan .75 .30

11th Congress of the Postal Union of the Americas and Spain, UPAE.

Nos. C187, C211, C160, C209, C210 Surcharged in Dark Blue or Violet Blue (No Bar)

1976 **As Before**
C429 AP51 2s on 4.30s org .25 .25
C430 AP51 3.50s on 4.60s org .25 .25
C431 AP51 4.50s on 3.80s org .25 .25
C432 AP51 5s on 4.30s org .35 .25
C433 AP51 6s on 4.60s org .55 .25
C434 A184 10s on 2.60s brt grn .65 .40
C435 AP52 50s on 3.60s lil rose (VB) 3.75 3.00
Nos. C429-C435 (7) 6.05 4.65

Stamps of 1962-67 Surcharged with New Value and Heavy Bar in Black, Red, Green, Dark Blue or Orange

1976-77 **As Before**
C436 AP52 1.50s on 3.60s (Bk) #C210 .35 .25
C437 A184 2s on 2.60s (R) #C209 ('77) .35 .25
C438 AP52 2s on 3.60s (G) #C210 .35 .25
C439 AP80 2s on 4.30s (Bk) #C199 .35 .25
C440 A184 3s on 2.60s (Bk) #C209 ('77) .35 .25
C441 A184 4s on 2.60s (DBl) #C209 .45 .30
C442 AP52 4s on 3.60s (DBl) #C210 ('77) .45 .30
C443 AP51 5s on 4.30s (R) #C187 .65 .30
C444 AP83 6s on 4.60s (Bk) #C208 ('77) .65 .30
C445 AP51 6s on 4.60s (DBl) #C211 ('77) .65 .30
C446 AP51 7s on 4.30s (Bk) #C187 ('77) .45 .30
C447 AP52 7.50s on 3.60s (DBl) #C210 .75 .40
C448 AP52 8s on 3.60s (O) #C210 1.00 .30
C449 AP51 10s on 4.30s (Bk) #C187 ('77) .55 .30
C450 AP51 10s on 4.60s (DBl) #C211 1.10 .30
C451 AP86 24s on 3.60s (Bk) #C220 ('77) 2.75 .95
C452 AP86 28s on 4.60s (Bk) #C221 ('77) 2.25 1.10
C453 AP86 32s on 5.60s (Bk) #C222 ('77) 2.25 1.10
C454 A184 50s on 2.60s (O) #C209 ('77) 5.00 1.75
C455 AP52 50s on 3.60s (G) #C210 4.00 2.25
Nos. C436-C455 (20) 24.70 11.50

AP144

Map of Tacna and Tarata Provinces.

1976, Aug. 28 Litho. ***Perf. 13½x13***
C456 AP144 10s multi .75 .30

Re-incorporation of Tacna Province into Peru, 47th anniversary.

AP145

Investigative Police badge.

1976, Sept. 15 Litho. ***Perf. 13½x13***
C457 AP145 20s multi 1.25 .70

Investigative Police of Peru, 54th anniv.

AP146

"Declaration of Bogota."

1976, Sept. 22

C458 AP146 10s multi .75 .30

Declaration of Bogota for cooperation and world peace, 10th anniversary.

AP147

Pal Losonczi and map of Hungary.

1976, Nov. 2 Litho. Perf. 13½x13

C459 AP147 7s ultra & blk .75 .30

Visit of Pres. Pal Losonczi of Hungary, Oct. 1976.

Map of Amazon Basin, Colors of Peru and Brazil AP148

1976, Dec. 16 Litho. Perf. 13

C460 AP148 10s bl & multi .75 .30

Visit of Gen. Ernesto Geisel, president of Brazil, Nov. 5, 1976.

Liberation Monument, Lima AP149

1977, Mar. 9 Litho. Perf. 13x13½

C461 AP149 20s red buff & blk 1.60 .65

Army Day.

Map of Peru and Venezuela, South America AP150

1977, Mar. 14

C462 AP150 12s buff & multi 1.10 .55

Meeting of Pres. Francisco Morales Bermudez Cerrutti of Peru and Pres. Carlos Andres Perez of Venezuela, Dec. 1976.

Electronic Tree — AP151

1977, May 30 Litho. Perf. 13½x13

C463 AP151 20s gray, red & blk 2.10 .75

World Telecommunications Day.

Map of Peru, Refinery, Tanker — AP152

1977, July 13 Litho. Perf. 13½x13

C464 AP152 14s multi .75 .45

Development of Bayovar oil complex.

Messenger Type of 1977

1977 Litho. Perf. 13½x13

C465 A243 24s mag & blk 1.75 .75
C466 A243 28s bl & blk 2.75 .75
C467 A243 32s rose brn & blk 1.75 1.10
Nos. C465-C467 (3) 6.25 2.60

For surcharge see No. C502.

Arms of Arequipa AP153

1977, Sept. 3 Litho. Perf. 13½x13

C468 AP153 10s multi .35 .25

Gold of Peru Exhibition, Arequipa 1977.

Gen. Jorge Rafael Videla — AP154

1977, Oct. 8 Litho. Perf. 13½x13

C469 AP154 36s multi 1.10 .40

Visit of Jorge Rafael Videla, president of Argentina.

Stamps of 1953-67 Surcharged with New Value and Heavy Bar in Black, Dark Blue or Green

1977 As Before

C470 AP83 2s on 3.60s #C207 .35 .25
C471 AP51 2s on 4.60s (DB) #C211 .35 .25
C472 AP51 4s on 4.60s (DB) #C211 .45 .25
C473 AP51 5s on 4.30s #C187 .55 .40
C474 AP52 5s on 3.60s #C210 .35 .25
C475 AP55 10s on 2.15s #C125 .75 .30
C476 AP52 10s on 3.60s (DB) #C210 1.25 .45
C477 AP84 10s on 3.60s #C215 1.10 .45
C478 AP52 20s on 3.60s (DB) #C210 1.10 .55
C479 AP51 100s on 3.80s (G) #C160 5.00 3.00
Nos. C470-C479 (10) 11.25 6.15

Nos. C223-C224 Surcharged with New Value, Heavy Bars and: "FRANQUEO"

1977 Litho. Perf. 12

C480 AP87 6s on 3.60s multi 1.10 .65
C481 AP87 8s on 3.60s multi 1.40 .90
C482 AP87 10s on 5.60s multi 1.40 1.00
Nos. C480-C482 (3) 3.90 2.55

Adm. Miguel Grau — AP155

1977, Dec. 15 Litho. Perf. 13½x13

C483 AP155 28s multi .75 .45

Navy Day. Miguel Grau (1838-1879), Peruvian naval commander.

Christmas Type of 1977

1977, Dec. 23

C484 A246 20s Indian Nativity .70 .35

Andrés Bello, Flag and Map of Participants AP156

1978, Jan. 12 Litho. Perf. 13

C485 AP156 30s multi .60 .35

8th Meeting of Education Ministers honoring Andrés Bello, Lima.

Inca Type of 1978

1978 Litho. Perf. 13½x13

C486 A247 24s dp rose lil .65 .45
C487 A247 30s salmon .75 .45
C488 A247 65s brt bl 1.75 1.00
C489 A247 95s dk bl 2.50 1.60
Nos. C486-C489 (4) 5.65 3.50

For surcharge see No. C501.

Antenna, ITU Emblem AP157

1978, July 3 Litho. Perf. 13x13½

C490 AP157 50s gray & multi 1.25 1.25

10th World Telecommunications Day.

San Martin, Flag Colors of Peru and Argentina AP158

1978, Sept. 4 Litho. Perf. 13½x13

C491 AP158 30s multi .75 .75

Gen. José de San Martin (1778-1850), soldier and statesman, protector of Peru.

Stamps of 1965-67 Surcharged "Habilitado / R.D. No. O118" and New Value in Red, Green, Violet Blue or Black

1978 Litho.

C492 AP83 34s on 4.60s multi (R) #C208 .55 .40
C493 AP79 40s on 4.30s multi (G) #C196 .65 .50
C494 A184 70s on 2.60s brt grn (VB) #C209 1.10 .85
C495 AP52 110s on 3.60s lil rose (Bk) #C210 2.25 1.10
C496 AP80 265s on 4.30s gray & multi (Bk) #C199 4.00 3.25
Nos. C492-C496 (5) 8.55 6.10

Stamps and Type of 1968-78 Surcharged in Violet Blue, Black or Red

1978 Litho.

C497 AP86 25s on 4.60s (VB) #C221 .55 .50
C498 A247 45s on 28s dk grn (Bk) 1.10 .55
C499 A247 75s on 28s dk grn (R) 1.75 1.10
C500 AP86 105s on 5.60s (R) #C222 2.50 1.75
Nos. C497-C500 (4) 5.90 3.90

Nos. C498-C499 not issued without surcharge.

Nos. C486, C467 Surcharged

1980, Apr. 14 Litho. Perf. 13½x13

C501 A247 35s on 24s dp rose lil .55 .45
C502 A243 45s on 32s rose brn & blk .60 .50

No. C130 Surcharged in Black

1981, Nov. Engr. Perf. 13

C503 AP57 30s on 2.20s multi .50 .45
C504 AP57 40s on 2.20s multi .50 .40

No. C130 Surcharged and Overprinted in Green: "12 Feria / Internacional / del / Pacifico 1981"

1981, Nov. 30

C505 AP57 140s on 2.20s multi 2.00 1.25

12th Intl. Pacific Fair.

AIR POST SEMI-POSTAL STAMPS

Catalogue values for unused stamps in this section are for Never Hinged items.

Chavin Griffin SPAP1

1.50s+1s, Bird. 3s+2.50s, Cat. 4.30s+3s, Mythological figure, vert. 6s+ 4s, Chavin god, vert.

Perf. 12½x12, 12x12½

1963, Apr. 18 Litho. Wmk. 346

Design in Gray and Brown

CB1 SPAP1 1s + 50c sal pink .35 .35
CB2 SPAP1 1.50s + 1s blue .55 .55
CB3 SPAP1 3s + 2.50s lt grn .85 .85
CB4 SPAP1 4.30s + 3s green 1.60 1.60
CB5 SPAP1 6s + 4s citron 2.00 2.00
Nos. CB1-CB5 (5) 5.35 5.35

The designs are from ceramics found by archaeological excavations of the 14th century Chavin culture. The surtax was for the excavations fund.

Henri Dunant and Centenary Emblem SPAP2

Perf. 12½x12

1964, Jan. 29 **Unwmk.**

CB6 SPAP2 1.30s + 70c multi .55 .55
CB7 SPAP2 4.30s + 1.70s multi 1.10 1.10

Centenary of International Red Cross.

SPECIAL DELIVERY STAMPS

No. 149 Overprinted in Black

1908 **Unwmk.** ***Perf. 12***

E1 A25 10c gray black 25.00 19.00

No. 172 Overprinted in Violet

1909

E2 A40 10c red brn & blk 40.00 22.50

No. 181 Handstamped in Violet

1910

E3 A49 10c deep blue 24.00 20.00

Two handstamps were used to make No. E2. Impressions from them measure 22½x6½mm and 24x6½mm.

Counterfeits exist of Nos. E1-3.

POSTAGE DUE STAMPS

Coat of Arms — D1

Steamship and Llama

D2 D3

D4 D5

With Grill

1874-79 **Unwmk.** **Engr.** ***Perf. 12***

J1 D1 1c bister ('79) .45 .30
J2 D2 5c vermilion .55 .30
J3 D3 10c orange .65 .30
J4 D4 20c blue 1.10 .55
J5 D5 50c brown 17.00 6.50
Nos. J1-J5 (5) 19.75 7.95

A 2c green exists, but was not regularly issued.

For overprints and surcharges see Nos. 157, J6-J31, J37-J38, 8N14-8N15, 14N18.

1902-07 **Without Grill**

J1a D1 1c bister .35
J2a D2 5c vermilion .55
J3a D3 10c orange .55
J4a D4 20c blue .65
Nos. J1a-J4a (4) 2.10

Nos. J1-J5 Overprinted in Blue or Red

1881 **"PLATA" 2½mm High**

J6 D1 1c bis (Bl) 6.00 5.00
J7 D2 5c ver (Bl) 12.00 11.00
a. Double overprint
b. Inverted overprint 24.00 24.00
J8 D3 10c org (Bl) 12.00 11.00
a. Inverted overprint 24.00 24.00
J9 D4 20c bl (R) 45.00 32.50
J10 D5 50c brn (Bl) 100.00 90.00
Nos. J6-J10 (5) 175.00 149.50

In the reprints of this overprint "PLATA" is 3mm high instead of 2½mm. Besides being struck in the regular colors it was also applied to the 1, 5, 10 and 50c in red and the 20c in blue.

Overprinted in Red

1881

J11 D1 1c bister 9.00 9.00
J12 D2 5c vermilion 11.00 10.00
J13 D3 10c orange 13.00 13.00
J14 D4 20c blue 55.00 37.50
J15 D5 50c brown 125.00 125.00
Nos. J11-J15 (5) 213.00 194.50

Originals of Nos. J11 to J15 are overprinted in brick-red, oily ink; reprints in thicker, bright red ink. The 5c exists with reprinted overprint in blue.

Overprinted "Union Postal Universal Lima Plata" in Oval in first named color and Triangle in second named color

1883

J16 D1 1c bis (Bl & Bk) 9.00 6.50
J17 D1 1c bis (Bk & Bl) 13.00 13.00
J18 D2 5c ver (Bl & Bk) 13.00 13.00
J19 D3 10c org (Bl & Bk) 13.00 13.00
J20 D4 20c bl (R & Bk) *850.00 850.00*
J21 D5 50c brn (Bl & Bk) 60.00 60.00

Reprints of Nos. J16 to J21 have the oval overprint with "PLATA" 3mm. high. The 1c also exists with the oval overprint in red.

Overprinted in Black

1884

J22 D1 1c bister .90 .90
J23 D2 5c vermilion .90 .90
J24 D3 10c orange .90 .90
J25 D4 20c blue 1.90 .90
J26 D5 50c brown 5.50 1.75
Nos. J22-J26 (5) 10.10 5.35

The triangular overprint is found in 11 types.

Overprinted "Lima Correos" in Circle in Red and Triangle in Black

1884

J27 D1 1c bister 42.50 42.50

Reprints of No. J27 have the overprint in bright red. At the time they were made the overprint was also printed on the 5, 10, 20 and 50c Postage Due stamps.

Postage Due stamps overprinted with Sun and "CORREOS LIMA" (as shown above No. 103), alone or in combination with the "U. P. U. LIMA" oval or "LIMA CORREOS" in double-lined circle, are fancy varieties made to sell to collectors and never placed in use.

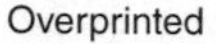

Overprinted

1896-97

J28 D1 1c bister .65 .55
a. Double overprint
J29 D2 5c vermilion .75 .45
a. Double overprint
b. Inverted overprint
J30 D3 10c orange 1.00 .65
a. Inverted overprint
J31 D4 20c blue 1.25 .85
a. Double overprint
J32 A22 50c red ('97) 1.25 .85
J33 A23 1s brown ('97) 1.90 1.25
a. Double overprint
b. Inverted overprint
Nos. J28-J33 (6) 6.80 4.60

Liberty — D6

1899 **Engr.**

J34 D6 5s yel grn 1.90 *10.50*
J35 D6 10s dl vio 1,700. 1,700.

For surcharge see No. J39.

No. J36

No. J37

1902 **On No. 159**

J36 A31 5c on 10s bl grn 1.90 1.50
a. Double surcharge 20.00 20.00

On No. J4

J37 D4 1c on 20c blue 1.10 .75
a. "DEFICIT" omitted 15.00 3.50
b. "DEFICIT" double 15.00 3.50
c. "UN CENTAVO" double 15.00 3.50
d. "UN CENTAVO" omitted 18.00 10.00

Surcharged Vertically

J38 D4 5c on 20c blue 2.75 1.75

No. J35 Surcharged Diagonally

J39 D6 1c on 10s dull vio .75 .75
Nos. J36-J39 (4) 6.50 4.75

D7

1909 **Engr.** ***Perf. 12***

J40 D7 1c red brown .90 .30
J41 D7 5c red brown .90 .30
J42 D7 10c red brown 1.10 .45
J43 D7 50c red brown 1.75 .45
Nos. J40-J43 (4) 4.65 1.50

1921 **Size: 18¼x22mm**

J44 D7 1c violet brown .45 .30
J45 D7 2c violet brown .45 .30
J46 D7 5c violet brown .65 .30
J47 D7 10c violet brown .90 .45
J48 D7 50c violet brown 2.75 1.25
J49 D7 1s violet brown 13.00 5.25
J50 D7 2s violet brown 22.50 6.50
Nos. J44-J50 (7) 40.70 14.35

Nos. J49 and J50 have the circle at the center replaced by a shield containing "S/.", in addition to the numeral.

In 1929 during a shortage of regular postage stamps, some of the Postage Due stamps of 1921 were used instead.

See Nos. J50A-J52, J55-J56. For surcharges see Nos. 204-207, 757.

Type of 1909-22

Size: 18¾x23mm

J50A D7 2c violet brown 1.25 .30
J50B D7 10c violet brown 1.75 .45

Type of 1909-22 Issues

1932 **Photo.** ***Perf. 14½x14***

J51 D7 2c violet brown 1.25 .45
J52 D7 10c violet brown 1.25 .45

Regular Stamps of 1934-35 Overprinted in Black

1935 ***Perf. 13***

J53 A131 2c deep claret 1.25 .50
J54 A117 10c crimson 1.25 .50

Type of 1909-32

Size: 19x23mm

Imprint: "Waterlow & Sons, Limited, Londres."

1936 **Engr.** ***Perf. 12½***

J55 D7 2c light brown .45 .45
J56 D7 10c gray green .90 .90

OFFICIAL STAMPS

Regular Issue of 1886 Overprinted in Red

1890, Feb. 2

O2 A17 1c dl vio 2.40 2.40
a. Double overprint 14.00 14.00
O3 A18 2c green 2.40 2.40
a. Double overprint
b. Inverted overprint 14.00 14.00
O4 A19 5c orange 3.50 2.75
a. Inverted overprint 14.00 14.00
b. Double overprint 14.00 14.00
O5 A20 10c slate 2.00 1.25
a. Double overprint 14.00 14.00
b. Inverted overprint 14.00 14.00
O6 A21 20c blue 5.50 3.50
a. Double overprint 14.00 14.00
b. Inverted overprint 14.00 14.00
O7 A22 50c red 7.25 3.25
a. Inverted overprint 20.00
b. Double overprint
O8 A23 1s brown 9.00 8.00
a. Double overprint 27.50 27.50
b. Inverted overprint 27.50 27.50
Nos. O2-O8 (7) 32.05 23.55

Nos. 118-124 (Bermudez Ovpt.) Overprinted Type "a" in Red

1894, Oct.

O9 A17 1c green 2.40 2.40
a. "Gobierno" and head invtd. 11.00 9.25
b. Dbl. ovpt. of "Gobierno"

O10 A17 1c orange 40.00 32.50
O11 A18 2c rose 2.40 2.40
a. Overprinted head inverted 17.00 17.00
b. Both overprints inverted
O12 A18 2c violet 2.40 2.40
a. "Gobierno" double
O13 A19 5c ultra 40.00 32.50
a. Both overprints inverted
O14 A19 5c blue 19.00 16.00
O15 A20 10c green 6.00 6.00
O16 A22 50c green 9.00 9.00
Nos. O9-O16 (8) 121.20 103.20

Nos. 125-126 ("Horseshoe" Ovpt.) Overprinted Type "a" in Red

O17 A18 2c vermilion 3.50 3.50
O18 A19 5c blue 3.50 3.50

Nos. 105, 107, 109, 113 Overprinted Type "a" in Red

1895, May

O19 A17 1c vermilion 13.00 13.00
O20 A18 2c dp ultra 13.00 13.00
O21 A12 5c claret 11.00 11.00
O22 A14 20c dp ultra 11.00 11.00
Nos. O19-O22 (4) 48.00 48.00

Nos. O2-O22 have been extensively counterfeited.

Nos. 141, 148, 149, 151 Overprinted in Black

1896-1901

O23 A24 1c ultra .35 .30
O24 A25 10c yellow 1.00 .50
a. Double overprint 22.50
O25 A25 10c gray blk ('01) .35 .30
O26 A26 50c brt rose 5.00 5.00
Nos. O23-O26 (4) 6.70 6.10

O1

1909-14 Engr. *Perf. 12*

Size: 18½x22mm

O27 O1 1c red .55 .30
a. 1c brown red .55 .30
O28 O1 1c orange ('14) .90 .65
O29 O1 10c bis brn ('14) .35 .30
a. 10c violet brown .90 .45
O30 O1 50c ol grn ('14) 1.25 .65
a. 50c blue green 2.00 .65

Size: 18¾x23½mm

O30B O1 10c vio brn .90 .30
Nos. O27-O30B (5) 3.95 2.20

See Nos. O31, O33-O34. For overprints and surcharge see Nos. 201-203, 760.

1933 Photo. *Perf. 15x14*

O31 O1 10c violet brown 1.25 .45

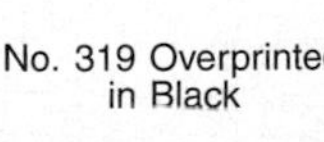

No. 319 Overprinted in Black

1935 Unwmk. *Perf. 13*

O32 A117 10c crimson .35 .25

Type of 1909-33

Imprint: "Waterlow & Sons, Limited, Londres."

1936 Engr. *Perf. 12½*

Size: 19x23mm

O33 O1 10c light brown .25 .25
O34 O1 50c gray green .65 .65

PARCEL POST STAMPS

PP1

PP2

PP3

1897 Typeset Unwmk. *Perf. 12*

Q1 PP1 1c dull lilac 4.00 3.50
Q2 PP2 2c bister 5.50 3.75
a. 2c olive 5.50 3.75
b. 2c yellow 5.50 3.75
c. Laid paper 65.00 65.00
Q3 PP3 5c dk bl 19.00 10.50
a. Tête bêche pair *375.00*
Q4 PP3 10c vio brn 24.00 18.00
Q5 PP3 20c rose red 29.00 22.50
Q6 PP3 50c bl grn 85.00 75.00
Nos. Q1-Q6 (6) 166.50 133.25

Surcharged in Black

1903-04

Q7 PP3 1c on 20c rose red 12.00 10.00
Q8 PP3 1c on 50c bl grn 12.00 10.00
Q9 PP3 5c on 10c vio brn 80.00 65.00
a. Inverted surcharge 125.00 110.00
b. Double surcharge
Nos. Q7-Q9 (3) 104.00 85.00

POSTAL TAX STAMPS

Plebiscite Issues

These stamps were not used in Tacna and Arica (which were under Chilean occupation) but were used in Peru to pay a supplementary tax on letters, etc.

It was intended that the money derived from the sale of these stamps should be used to help defray the expenses of the plebiscite.

Morro Arica — PT1

Adm. Grau and Col. Bolognesi Reviewing Troops — PT2

Bolognesi Monument PT3

1925-26 Unwmk. Litho. *Perf. 12*

RA1 PT1 5c dp bl 2.75 .75
RA2 PT1 5c rose red 1.40 .55
RA3 PT1 5c yel grn 1.25 .55
RA4 PT2 10c brown 5.50 *22.50*
RA5 PT3 50c bl grn 35.00 17.00
Nos. RA1-RA5 (5) 45.90 41.35

PT4

1926

RA6 PT4 2c orange 1.10 .30

PT5

1927-28

RA7 PT5 2c dp org 1.10 .30
RA8 PT5 2c red brn 1.10 .30
RA9 PT5 2c dk bl 1.10 .30
RA10 PT5 2c gray vio 1.10 .30
RA11 PT5 2c bl grn ('28) 1.10 .30
RA12 PT5 20c red 5.50 1.75
Nos. RA7-RA12 (6) 11.00 3.25

PT6

1928 Engr.

RA13 PT6 2c dk vio .55 .25

The use of the Plebiscite stamps was discontinued July 26, 1929, after the settlement of the Tacna-Arica controversy with Chile.

For overprint see No. 261.

Unemployment Fund Issues

These stamps were required in addition to the ordinary postage, on every letter or piece of postal matter. The money obtained by their sale was to assist the unemployed.

Nos. 273-275 Surcharged

1931

RA14 A95 2c on 4c red 1.75 .75
a. Inverted surcharge 4.25 4.25
RA15 A95 2c on 10c bl grn .75 .75
a. Inverted surcharge 4.25 4.25
RA16 A95 2c on 15c sl gray .75 .75
a. Inverted surcharge 4.25 4.25
Nos. RA14-RA16 (3) 3.25 2.25

"Labor" — PT7

Two types of Nos. RA17-RA18:
I — Imprint 15mm.
II — Imprint 13¾mm.

Perf. 12x11½, 11½x12

1931-32 Litho.

RA17 PT7 2c emer (I) .25 .25
a. Type II .25
RA18 PT7 2c rose car (I) ('32) .25 .25
a. Type II .25

Blacksmith — PT8

1932-34

RA19 PT8 2c dp gray .25 .25
RA20 PT8 2c pur ('34) .35 .25

Monument of 2nd of May — PT9

Perf. 13, 13½, 13x13½

1933-35 Photo.

RA21 PT9 2c bl vio .25 .25
RA22 PT9 2c org ('34) .25 .25
RA23 PT9 2c brn vio ('35) .25 .25
Nos. RA21-RA23 (3) .75 .75

For overprint see No. RA27.

No. 307 Overprinted in Black

1934 *Perf. 13½*

RA24 A111 2c green .25 .25
a. Inverted overprint 2.25 2.00

No. 339 Overprinted in Black

1935

RA25 A131 2c deep claret .25 .25

No. 339 Overprinted Type "a" in Black

1936 Unwmk. *Perf. 13½*

RA26 A131 2c deep claret .25 .25

No. RA23 Overprinted in Black

1936 *Perf. 13x13½*
RA27 PT9 2c brn vio .25 .25
a. Double overprint 3.50
b. Overprint reading down 3.50
c. Overprint double, reading down 3.50

St. Rosa of Lima — PT10

1937 **Engr.** *Perf. 12*
RA28 PT10 2c car rose .25 .25

Nos. RA27 and RA28 represented a tax to help erect a church.

"Protection" by John Q. A. Ward — PT11

Imprint: "American Bank Note Company"

1938 **Litho.**
RA29 PT11 2c brown .35 .25

The tax was to help the unemployed.
See Nos. RA30, RA34, RA40.

Type of 1938 Redrawn
Imprint: "Columbian Bank Note Company."

1943 *Perf. 12½*
RA30 PT11 2c dl claret brn .35 .25

See note above #RA14. See #RA34, RA40.

Catalogue values for unused stamps in this section, from this point to the end of the section, are for Never Hinged items.

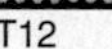

PT12 PT13

Black Surcharge

1949 *Perf. 12½, 12*
RA31 PT12 3c on 4c vio bl 1.10 .25
RA32 PT13 3c on 10c blue 1.10 .25

The tax was for an education fund.

Symbolical of Education — PT14

1950 **Typo.** *Perf. 14*
Size: 16½x21mm
RA33 PT14 3c dp car .25 .25

See Nos. RA35, RA39, RA43
For surcharges see Nos. 501B, 761, 764-766, RA45-RA48, RA58.

Type of 1938
Imprint: "Thomas De La Rue & Co. Ltd."

1951 **Litho.**
RA34 PT11 2c lt redsh brn .25 .25

Type of 1950
Imprint: "Thomas De La Rue & Company, Limited."

1952 **Unwmk.** *Perf. 14, 13*
Size: 16½x21½mm
RA35 PT14 3c brn car .25 .25

Emblem of Congress — PT15

1954 *Rouletted 13*
RA36 PT15 5c bl & red .35 .25

The tax was to help finance the National Marian Eucharistic Congress.
For surcharges see Nos. 758B, 768.

Piura Arms and Congress Emblem — PT16

1960 **Litho.** *Perf. 10½*
RA37 PT16 10c ultra, red, grn & yel .25 .25
a. Green ribbon inverted
RA38 PT16 10c ultra & red .35 .25

Nos. RA37-RA38 were used to help finance the 6th National Eucharistic Congress, Piura, Aug. 25-28. Obligatory on all domestic mail until Dec. 31, 1960. Both stamps exist imperf.

Type of 1950
Imprint: "Bundesdruckerei Berlin"

1961 **Size: 17½x22½mm** *Perf. 14*
RA39 PT14 3c dp car .25 .25

Type of 1938
Imprint: "Harrison and Sons Ltd"

1962, Apr. **Litho.** *Perf. 14x14½*
RA40 PT11 2c lt brn .25 .25

For surcharges see Nos. 501A, 674-678, 681-682, 709-711, 757.

Symbol of Eucharist — PT17

1962, May 8 *Rouletted 11*
RA41 PT17 10c bl & org .25 .25

Issued to raise funds for the Seventh National Eucharistic Congress, Huancayo, 1964. Obligatory on all domestic mail.
See No. RA42. For surcharges and overprint see Nos. 735, 762, RA44.

1962 **Imprint: "Iberia"**
RA42 PT17 10c bl & org .25 .25

Type of 1950
Imprint: "Thomas de La Rue"
Size: 18x22mm

1965, Apr. **Litho.** *Perf. 12½x12*
RA43 PT14 3c light carmine .25 .25

Type of 1962 Overprinted in Red

Imprint: "Iberia"

1966, July 2 **Litho.** *Pin Perf.*
RA44 PT17 10c vio & org .25 .25

No. RA43 Surcharged in Green or Black

b

c

d

1966-67 *Perf. 12½x12*
RA45 PT14 (b) 10c on 3c (G) 1.25 .25
RA46 PT14 (c) 10c on 3c (Bk) 1.25 .25
RA47 PT14 (c) 10c on 3c (G) .35 .25
RA48 PT14 (d) 10c on 3c (G) .35 .25
Nos. RA45-RA48 (4) 3.20 1.00

The surtax of Nos. RA44-RA48 was for the Peruvian Journalists' Fund.

Pen Made of Newspaper — PT18

1967, Dec. **Litho.** *Perf. 11*
RA49 PT18 10c dk red & blk .25 .25

The surtax was for the Peruvian Journalists' fund.
For surcharges see Nos. RA56-RA57.

Temple at Chan-Chan — PT19

Designs: No. RA51, Side view of temple. Nos. RA52-RA55, Various stone bas-reliefs from Chan-Chan.

1967, Dec. 27
RA50 PT19 20c bl & grn .25 .25
RA51 PT19 20c multi .25 .25
RA52 PT19 20c brt bl & blk .25 .25
RA53 PT19 20c emer & blk .25 .25
RA54 PT19 20c sep & blk .25 .25
RA55 PT19 20c lil rose & blk .25 .25
Nos. RA50-RA55 (6) 1.50 1.50

The surtax was for the excavations at Chan-Chan, northern coast of Peru. (Mochica-Chimu pre-Inca period).

Type of 1967 Surcharged in Red: "VEINTE / CENTAVOS / R.S. 16-8-68"

Designs: No. RA56, Handshake. No. RA57, Globe and pen.

1968, Oct. **Litho.** *Perf. 11*
RA56 PT18 20c on 50c multi .90 .90
RA57 PT18 20c on 1s multi .90 .90

Nos. RA56-RA57 without surcharge were not obligatory tax stamps.
No. C199 surcharged "PRO NAVIDAD/ Veinte Centavos/R.S. 5-11-68" was not a compulsory postal tax stamp.

No. RA43 Srchd. Similar to Type "c"

1968, Oct. *Perf. 12½x12*
RA58 PT14 20c on 3c lt car .25 .25

Surcharge lacks quotation marks and 4th line reads: Ley 17050.

OCCUPATION STAMPS

Issued under Chilean Occupation

Stamps formerly listed as Nos. N1-N10 are regular issues of Chile canceled in Peru.

Stamps of Peru, 1874-80, Overprinted in Red, Blue or Black

1881-82 *Perf. 12*
N11 A17 1c org (Bl) .50 1.00
a. Inverted overprint
N12 A18 2c dk vio (Bk) .50 4.00
a. Inverted overprint 16.50
b. Double overprint 22.50
N13 A18 2c rose (Bk) 1.60 *18.00*
a. Inverted overprint
N14 A19 5c bl (R) 55.00 62.50
a. Inverted overprint
N15 A19 5c ultra (R) 90.00 100.00
N16 A20 10c grn (R) .50 *1.60*
a. Inverted overprint 6.50 6.50
b. Double overprint 12.00 12.00
N17 A21 20c brn red (Bl) 80.00 125.00
Nos. N11-N17 (7) 228.10 312.10

Reprints of No. N17 have the overprint in bright blue; on the originals it is in dull ultramarine. Nos. N11 and N12 exist with reprinted overprint in red or yellow. There are numerous counterfeits with the overprint in both correct and fancy colors.

Same, with Additional Overprint in Black

1882
N19 A17 1c grn (R) .50 .80
a. Arms inverted 8.25 10.00
b. Arms double 5.50 6.50
c. Horseshoe inverted 12.00 13.50
N20 A19 5c bl (R) .80 .80
a. Arms inverted 13.50 15.00
b. Arms double 13.50 15.00
N21 A22 50c rose (Bk) 1.60 2.00
a. Arms inverted 10.00
N22 A22 50c rose (Bl) 1.60 2.75
N23 A23 1s ultra (R) 3.25 4.50
a. Arms inverted 13.50
b. Horseshoe inverted 16.50
c. Arms and horseshoe inverted 20.00
d. Arms double 13.50
Nos. N19-N23 (5) 7.75 10.85

PROVISIONAL ISSUES

Stamps Issued in Various Cities of Peru during the Chilean Occupation of Lima and Callao

During the Chilean-Peruvian War which took place in 1879 to 1882, the Chilean forces occupied the two largest cities in Peru, Lima & Callao. As these cities were the source of supply of postage stamps, Peruvians in other sections of the country were left without stamps and were forced to the expedient of making provisional issues from whatever material was at hand. Many of these were former canceling devices made over for this purpose. Counterfeits exist of many of the overprinted stamps.

ANCACHS

(See Note under "Provisional Issues")

Regular Issue of Peru, Overprinted in Manuscript in Black

1884 **Unwmk.** *Perf. 12*
1N1 A19 5c blue 57.50 55.00

Regular Issues of Peru, Overprinted in Black

1N2 A19 5c blue 18.00 16.50

Regular Issues of Peru, Overprinted in Black

1N3 A19 5c blue 90.00 82.50
1N4 A20 10c green 55.00 40.00
1N5 A20 10c slate 55.00 35.00

Same, with Additional Overprint "FRANCA"

1N6 A20 10c green 82.50 42.50

Overprinted

1N7 A19 5c blue 30.00 25.00
1N8 A20 10c green 30.00 25.00

Same, with Additional Overprint "FRANCA"

1N9 A20 10c green

Revenue Stamp of Peru, 1878-79, Ovptd. in Black "CORREO Y FISCAL" or "FRANCA" — A1

1N10 A1 10c yellow 37.50 37.50

APURIMAC

(See Note under "Provisional Issues")

Provisional Issue of Arequipa Overprinted in Black

Overprint Covers Two Stamps

1885 Unwmk. *Imperf.*
2N1 A6 10c gray 100.00 90.00

Some experts question the status of No. 2N1.

AREQUIPA

(See Note under "Provisional Issues")

Coat of Arms
A1 A2

Overprint ("PROVISIONAL 1881-1882") in Black

1881, Jan. Unwmk. *Imperf.*
3N1 A1 10c blue 2.50 3.50
a. 10c ultramarine 2.50 4.00
b. Double overprint 12.00 13.50
c. Overprinted on back of stamp 8.25 10.00
3N2 A2 25c rose 2.50 6.00
a. "2" in upper left corner invtd. 8.25
b. "Cevtavos" 8.25 10.00
c. Double overprint 12.00 13.50

The overprint also exists on 5s yellow.

The overprints "1883" in large figures or "Habilitado 1883" are fraudulent.

For overprints see Nos. 3N3, 4N1, 8N1, 10N1, 15N1-15N3.

With Additional Overprint Handstamped in Red

1881, Feb.
3N3 A1 10c blue 3.50 3.50
a. 10c ultramarine 13.50 11.50

A4

1883 Litho.
3N7 A4 10c dull rose 3.50 5.00
a. 10c vermilion 3.50 5.00

Overprinted in Blue like No. 3N3

3N9 A4 10c vermilion 5.00 4.00
a. 10c dull rose 5.00 4.00

See No. 3N10. For overprints see Nos. 8N2, 8N9, 10N2, 15N4.

Reprints of No. 3N9 are in different colors from the originals, orange, bright red, etc. They are printed in sheets of 20 instead of 25.

Redrawn

3N10 A4 10c brick red (Bl) 160.00

The redrawn stamp has small triangles without arabesques in the lower spandrels. The palm branch at left of the shield and other parts of the design have been redrawn.

Same Overprint in Black, Violet or Magenta On Regular Issues of Peru

1884 Embossed with Grill *Perf. 12*
3N11 A17 1c org (Bk, V or M) 6.50 6.50
3N12 A18 2c dk vio (Bk) 6.50 6.50
3N13 A19 5c bl (Bk, V or M) 2.00 1.40
a. 5c ultramarine (Bk or M) 8.25 6.50
3N15 A20 10c sl (Bk) 3.50 2.50
3N16 A21 20c brn red (Bk, V or M) 25.00 25.00
3N18 A22 50c grn (Bk or V) 25.00 25.00
3N20 A23 1s rose (Bk or V) 35.00 35.00
Nos. 3N11-3N20 (7) 103.50 101.90

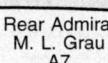

A5

A6

Rear Admiral M. L. Grau
A7

Col. Francisco Bolognesi
A8

Same Overprint as on Previous Issues

1885 *Imperf.*
3N22 A5 5c olive (Bk) 5.25 5.25
3N23 A6 10c gray (Bk) 5.25 4.75
3N25 A7 5c blue (Bk) 5.25 4.75
3N26 A8 10c olive (Bk) 5.25 3.25
Nos. 3N22-3N26 (4) 21.00 18.00

For overprints see Nos. 2N1, 8N5-8N6, 8N12-8N13, 10N9, 10N12, 15N10-15N12.

These stamps have been reprinted without overprint; they exist however with forged overprint. Originals are on thicker paper with distinct mesh, reprints on paper without mesh.

Without Overprint

3N22a A5 5c olive 5.25 5.25
3N23a A6 10c gray 4.00 3.25
3N25a A7 5c blue 4.00 3.25
3N26a A8 10c olive 4.00 3.25
Nos. 3N22a-3N26a (4) 17.25 15.00

AYACUCHO

(See Note under "Provisional Issues")

Provisional Issue of Arequipa Overprinted in Black

1881 Unwmk. *Imperf.*
4N1 A1 10c blue 150.00 125.00
a. 10c ultramarine 150.00 125.00

CHACHAPOYAS

(See Note under "Provisional Issues")

Regular Issue of Peru Overprinted in Black

1884 Unwmk. *Perf. 12*
5N1 A19 5c ultra 190.00 160.00

CHALA

(See Note under "Provisional Issues")

Regular Issues of Peru Overprinted in Black

1884 Unwmk. *Perf. 12*
6N1 A19 5c blue 17.00 13.00
6N2 A20 10c slate 22.50 16.00

CHICLAYO

(See Note under "Provisional Issues")

Regular Issue of Peru Overprinted in Black

1884 Unwmk. *Perf. 12*
7N1 A19 5c blue 29.00 18.00

Same, Overprinted **FRANCA**

7N2 A19 5c blue 65.00 37.50

CUZCO

(See Note under "Provisional Issues")

Provisional Issues of Arequipa Overprinted in Black

1881-85 Unwmk. *Imperf.*
8N1 A1 10c blue 125.00 110.00
8N2 A4 10c red 125.00 110.00

Overprinted "CUZCO" in an oval of dots

8N5 A5 5c olive 200.00 175.00
8N6 A6 10c gray 200.00 175.00

Regular Issue of Peru Overprinted in Black "CUZCO" in a Circle

Perf. 12
8N7 A19 5c blue 50.00 50.00

Provisional Issues of Arequipa Overprinted in Black

1883 *Imperf.*
8N9 A4 10c red 18.00 18.00

Same Overprint in Black on Regular Issues of Peru

1884 *Perf. 12*
8N10 A19 5c blue 29.00 18.00
8N11 A20 10c slate 29.00 18.00

Same Overprint in Black on Provisional Issues of Arequipa
Imperf

8N12 A5 5c olive 27.50 27.50
8N13 A6 10c gray 8.00 8.00

Postage Due Stamps of Peru Surcharged in Black

Perf. 12
8N14 D1 10c on 1c bis 200.00 175.00
8N15 D3 10c on 10c org 200.00 175.00

HUACHO

(See Note under "Provisional Issues")

Regular Issues of Peru Overprinted in Black

1884 Unwmk. *Perf. 12*
9N1 A19 5c blue 16.00 16.00
9N2 A20 10c green 13.00 13.00
9N3 A20 10c slate 27.50 27.50
Nos. 9N1-9N3 (3) 56.50 56.50

MOQUEGUA

(See Note under "Provisional Issues")

Provisional Issues of Arequipa Overprinted in Violet

Overprint 27mm wide.

1881-83 Unwmk. *Imperf.*
10N1 A1 10c blue 75.00 70.00
10N2 A4 10c red ('83) 75.00 70.00

Same Overprint on Regular Issues of Peru in Violet

1884 *Perf. 12*
10N3 A17 1c orange 75.00 70.00
10N4 A19 5c blue 55.00 35.00

Red Overprint

10N5 A19 5c blue 65.00 55.00

Same Overprint in Violet on Provisional Issues of Peru of 1880
Perf. 12

10N6 A17 1c grn (R) 12.00 9.75
10N7 A18 2c rose (Bl) 15.00 15.00
10N8 A19 5c bl (R) 30.00 30.00

Same Overprint in Violet on Provisional Issue of Arequipa

1885 ***Imperf.***
10N9 A6 10c gray 85.00 42.50

Regular Issues of Peru Overprinted in Violet

10N10 A19 5c blue 200.00 125.00
10N11 A20 10c slate 85.00 42.50

Same Overprint in Violet on Provisional Issue of Arequipa

Imperf
10N12 A6 10c gray 125.00 110.00

PAITA

(See Note under "Provisional Issues")

Regular Issues of Peru Overprinted

Black Overprint

1884 **Unwmk.** ***Perf. 12***
11N1 A19 5c blue 40.00 40.00
a. 5c ultramarine 40.00 40.00
11N2 A20 10c green 27.50 27.50
11N3 A20 10c slate 40.00 40.00

Red Overprint

11N4 A19 5c blue 40.00 40.00

Overprint lacks ornaments on #11N4-11N5.

Violet Overprint Letters 5½mm High

11N5 A19 5c ultra 40.00 40.00
a. 5c blue

PASCO

(See Note under "Provisional Issues")

Regular Issues of Peru Overprinted in Magenta or Black

1884 **Unwmk.** ***Perf. 12***
12N1 A19 5c blue (M) 27.50 12.50
a. 5c ultramarine (M) 42.50 22.50
12N2 A20 10c green (Bk) 65.00 55.00
12N3 A20 10c slate (Bk) 125.00 90.00
Nos. 12N1-12N3 (3) 217.50 157.50

PISCO

(See Note under "Provisional Issues")

Regular Issue of Peru Overprinted in Black

1884 **Unwmk.** ***Perf. 12***
13N1 A19 5c blue 350.00 275.00

PIURA

(See Note under "Provisional Issues")

Regular Issues of Peru Overprinted in Black

1884 **Unwmk.** ***Perf. 12***
14N1 A19 5c blue 35.00 21.00
a. 5c ultramarine 45.00 27.50
14N2 A21 20c brn red 150.00 150.00
14N3 A22 50c green 350.00 350.00

Same Overprint in Black on Provisional Issues of Peru of 1881

14N4 A17 1c grn (R) 35.00 35.00
14N5 A18 2c rose (Bl) 55.00 55.00
14N6 A19 5c ultra (R) 70.00 70.00

Regular Issues of Peru Overprinted in Violet, Black or Blue

14N7 A19 5c bl (V) 27.50 18.00
a. 5c ultramarine (V) 27.50 18.00
b. 5c ultramarine (Bk) 27.50 18.00
14N8 A21 20c brn red (Bk) 150.00 150.00
14N9 A21 20c brn red (Bl) 150.00 150.00

Same Overprint in Black on Provisional Issues of Peru of 1881

14N10 A17 1c grn (R) 35.00 35.00
14N11 A19 5c bl (R) 42.50 42.50
a. 5c ultramarine (R) 70.00 70.00

Regular Issues of Peru Overprinted in Black

14N13 A19 5c blue 7.25 6.50
14N14 A21 20c brn red 150.00 150.00

Regular Issues of Peru Overprinted in Black

14N15 A19 5c ultra 110.00 100.00
14N16 A21 20c brn red 250.00 225.00

Same Overprint on Postage Due Stamp of Peru

14N18 D3 10c orange 125.00 125.00

PUNO

(See Note under "Provisional Issues")

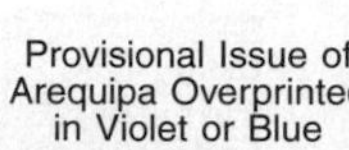

Provisional Issue of Arequipa Overprinted in Violet or Blue

Diameter of outer circle 20½mm, PUNO 11½mm wide, M 3½mm wide.
Other types of this overprint are fraudulent.

1882-83 **Unwmk.** ***Imperf.***
15N1 A1 10c blue (V) 29.00 29.00
a. 10c ultramarine (V) 35.00 35.00
15N3 A2 25c red (V) 45.00 35.00
15N4 A4 10c dl rose (Bl) 29.00 29.00
a. 10c vermilion (Bl) 29.00 29.00

The overprint also exists on 5s yellow of Arequipa.

Same Overprint in Magenta on Regular Issues of Peru

1884 ***Perf. 12***
15N5 A17 1c orange 19.00 15.00
15N6 A18 2c violet 65.00 65.00
15N7 A19 5c blue 10.00 10.00

Violet Overprint

15N8 A19 5c blue 10.00 10.00
a. 5c ultramarine 20.00 20.00

Same Overprint in Black on Provisional Issues of Arequipa

1885 ***Imperf.***
15N10 A5 5c olive 16.00 13.50
15N11 A6 10c gray 10.00 10.00
15N12 A8 10c olive 19.00 19.00

Regular Issues of Peru Overprinted in Magenta

1884 ***Perf. 12***
15N13 A17 1c orange 21.00 21.00
15N14 A18 2c violet 24.00 21.00
15N15 A19 5c blue 10.00 10.00
a. 5c ultramarine 20.00 20.00
15N16 A20 10c green 29.00 22.50
15N17 A21 20c brn red 150.00 150.00
15N18 A22 50c green

YCA

(See Note under "Provisional Issues")

Regular Issues of Peru Overprinted in Violet

1884 **Unwmk.** ***Perf. 12***
16N1 A17 1c orange 70.00 70.00
16N3 A19 5c blue 22.50 18.00

Black Overprint

16N5 A19 5c blue 19.00 9.00

Magenta Overprint

16N6 A19 5c blue 19.00 9.00
16N7 A20 10c slate 55.00 55.00

Regular Issues of Peru Overprinted in Black

16N12 A19 5c blue 275.00 225.00
16N13 A21 20c brown 350.00 275.00

Regular Issues of Peru Overprinted in Carmine

16N14 A19 5c blue 275.00 225.00
16N15 A20 10c slate 350.00 275.00

Same, with Additional Overprint

16N21 A19 5c blue 275.00 275.00
16N22 A21 20c brn red 475.00 450.00

Various other stamps exist with the overprints "YCA" and "YCA VAPOR" but they are not known to have been issued. Some of them were made to fill a dealer's order and others are reprints or merely cancellations.

PHILIPPINES

ˌfi-lə-ˈpēnz

LOCATION — Group of about 7,100 islands and islets in the Malay Archipelago, north of Borneo, in the North Pacific Ocean
GOVT. — Republic
AREA — 115,830 sq. mi.
POP. — 68,614,536 (1995)
CAPITAL — Manila

The islands were ceded to the United States by Spain in 1898. On November 15, 1935, they were given their independence, subject to a transition period. The Japanese occupation from 1942 to early 1945 delayed independence until July 4, 1946. On that date the Commonwealth became the Republic of the Philippines.

20 Cuartos = 1 Real
100 Centavos de Peso = 1 Peso (1864)
100 Centimos de Escudo = 1 Escudo (1871)
100 Centimos de Peseta = 1 Peseta (1872)
1000 Milesimas de Peso = 100 Centimos or Centavos = 1 Peso (1878)
100 Cents = 1 Dollar (1899)
100 Centavos = 1 Peso (1906)
100 Centavos (Sentimos) = 1 Peso (Piso) (1946)

Catalogue values for unused stamps in this country are for Never Hinged items, beginning with Scott 500 in the regular postage section, Scott B1 in the semi-postal section, Scott C64 in the air post section, Scott E11 in the special delivery section, Scott J23 in the postage due section, and Scott O50 in the officials section.

Watermarks

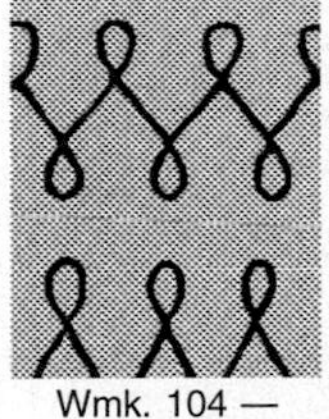

Wmk. 104 — Loops

Wmk. 257 — Curved Wavy Lines

Watermark 104: loops from different watermark rows may or may not be directly opposite each other.

Wmk. 190PI — Single-lined PIPS

Wmk. 191PI — Double-lined PIPS

Watermark 191 has double-lined USPS.

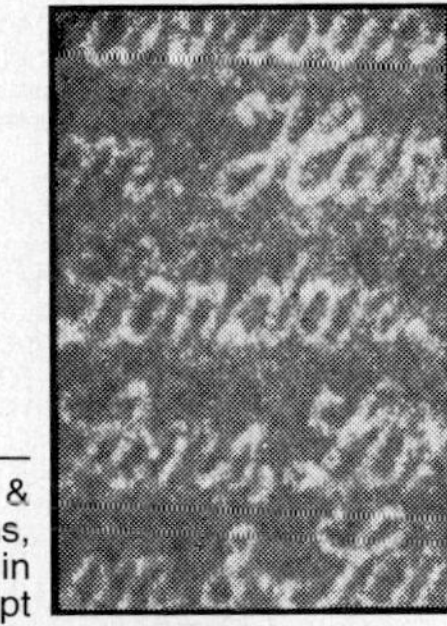

Wmk. 233 — "Harrison & Sons, London." in Script

Wmk. 372 — "K" and "P" Multiple

Wmk. 385

Wmk. 389

Wmk. 391 — Natl. Crest, Rising Sun and Eagle, with inscr. "REPUBLIKA / NG / PILIPINAS," "KAWANIHAN / NG / KOREO"

Issued under Spanish Dominion

The stamps of Philippine Islands punched with a round hole were used on telegraph receipts or had been withdrawn from use and punched to indicate that they were no longer available for postage. In this condition they sell for less, as compared to postally used copies.
Many color varieties exist of Nos. 1-88. Only major varieties are listed.

Queen Isabella II
A1 A2

1854 Unwmk. Engr. *Imperf.*

1	A1	5c orange	4,500.	350.
2	A1	10c carmine	850.	250.
d.		10c carmine, half used as 5c on cover		50,000.
4	A2	1r blue	1,000.	300.
a.		1r slate blue	800.	300.
5	A2	2r slate green	1,000.	250.

Forty varieties of each value.
A 10c black exists. This is a proof or an unissued trial color. Value about $10,000.
For overprints see Nos. 24A-25A.

A3

1855 Litho.

6	A3	5c pale red	1,600.	500.

Four varieties.

A3a

Redrawn

7	A3a	5c vermilion	*8,000.*	*1,100.*

In the redrawn stamp the inner circle is smaller and is not broken by the labels at top and bottom. Only one variety.

Queen Isabella II — A4

Blue Paper

1856 Typo. Wmk. 104

8	A4	1r green	100.00	*75.00*
9	A4	2r carmine	400.00	200.00

Nos. 8 and 9 used can be distinguished from Cuba Nos. 2 and 3 only by the cancellations.
For overprints, see Nos. 26-27.

Queen Isabella II — A5

Dot After "CORREOS"

1859, Jan. 1 Litho. Unwmk.

10	A5	5c vermilion	15.00	8.00
a.		5c scarlet	24.00	12.00
b.		5c orange	32.50	17.50
11	A5	10c lilac rose	17.00	*35.00*

Four varieties of each value, repeated in the sheet.
For overprint see No. 28.

Dot after CORREOS
A6 A7

1861-62

12	A6	5c vermilion	40.00	40.00
13	A7	5c dull red ('62)	190.00	95.00

No. 12, one variety only, repeated in the sheet.
For overprint see No. 29.

Colon after CORREOS — A8

A8a

A9

1863

14	A8	5c vermilion	13.50	8.25
15	A8	10c carmine	37.50	*250.00*
16	A8	1r violet	850.00	*3,000.*
17	A8	2r blue	650.00	*1,000.*
18	A8a	1r gray grn	500.00	140.00
20	A9	1r green	200.00	60.00
		Nos. 14-20 (6)	2,251.	4,458.

No. 18 has "CORREOS" 10½mm long, the point of the bust is rounded and is about 1mm from the circle which contains 94 pearls.
No. 20 has "CORREOS" 11mm long, and the bust ends in a sharp point which nearly touches the circle of 76 pearls.
For overprints see Nos. 30-34.

COLLECT
PHILIPPINES
IPPS
Benefits:
Quarterly
Journal, Two Yearly 350+ Lot Online
Auctions, Downloads, & Meetings
Join the:
INTERNATIONAL PHILIPPINE PHILATELIC SOCIETY (IPPS)
Information: www.theipps.info ✧ USA 1-301-834-6419

A10

1864 **Typo.**

No.	Type	Description	Unused	Used
21	A10	3 1/8c blk, *yellow*	4.75	2.00
22	A10	6 2/8c grn, *rose*	6.75	2.00
23	A10	12 4/8c blue, *sal*	9.00	1.75
24	A10	25c red, *buff*	12.00	3.75
		Nos. 21-24 (4)	32.50	9.50

For overprints see Nos. 35-38.

Preceding Issues Handstamped

1868-74

No.	Type	Description	Unused	Used
24A	A1	5c orange ('74)	*8,000.*	*6,750.*
25	A2	1r sl bl ('74)	*2,400.*	*1,050.*
25A	A2	2r grn ('74)	*3,900.*	*8,000.*
26	A4	1r grn, *bl* ('73)	180.00	80.00
27	A4	2r car, *bl* ('73)	325.00	225.00
27A	A5	5c vermilion ('74)	*6,000.*	*12,000.*
28	A5	10c rose ('74)	80.00	45.00
29	A7	5c dull red ('73)	250.00	175.00
30	A8	5c ver ('72)	115.00	35.00
30A	A8	10c car ('72)	*6,000.*	—
31	A8	1r vio ('72)	700.00	600.00
32	A8	2r bl ('72)	525.00	425.00
33	A8a	1r gray grn ('71)	175.00	85.00
34	A9	1r grn ('71)	50.00	30.00
35	A10	3 1/8c blk, *yellow*	9.50	4.75
36	A10	6 2/8c grn, *rose*	9.50	4.75
37	A10	12 4/8c bl, *salmon*	27.50	12.00
38	A10	25c red, *buff*	29.00	15.00

Reprints exist of #24A-38. These have crisp, sharp letters and usually have a broken first "A" of "HABILITADO."

Imperforates

Imperforates of designs A11-A16 probably are from proof or trial sheets.

"Spain" — A11

1871 **Typo.** ***Perf. 14***

No.	Type	Description	Unused	Used
39	A11	5c blue	95.00	9.25
40	A11	10c deep green	15.00	6.00
41	A11	20c brown	110.00	50.00
42	A11	40c rose	170.00	60.00
		Nos. 39-42 (4)	390.00	125.25

King Amadeo — A12

1872

No.	Type	Description	Unused	Used
43	A12	12c rose	20.00	5.50
44	A12	16c blue	200.00	37.50
45	A12	25c gray lilac	13.50	5.50
46	A12	62c violet	40.00	9.75
47	A12	1p25c yellow brn	85.00	42.50
		Nos. 43-47 (5)	358.50	100.75

A 12c in deep blue and a 62c in rose exist but were not issued. Value $30 each.

"Peace" — A13

1874

No.	Type	Description	Unused	Used
48	A13	12c gray lilac	22.50	5.50
49	A13	25c ultra	8.25	2.75
50	A13	62c rose	65.00	5.50
51	A13	1p25c brown	300.00	82.50
		Nos. 48-51 (4)	395.75	96.25

King Alfonso XII — A14

1875-77

No.	Type	Description	Unused	Used
52	A14	2c rose	3.50	.95
53	A14	2c dk blue ('77)	260.00	100.00
54	A14	6c orange ('77)	14.00	*16.00*
55	A14	10c blue ('77)	4.50	.85
56	A14	12c lilac ('76	4.50	.85
57	A14	20c vio brn ('76	20.00	5.00
58	A14	25c dp green ('76	25.00	5.00
		Nos. 52-58 (7)	331.50	128.65

Imperforates of type A14 are from proof or trial sheets.

Nos. 52, 63 Handstamp Surcharged in Black or Blue

1877-79

No.	Type	Description	Unused	Used
59	A14	12c on 2c rose (Bk)	85.00	22.50
a.		Surcharge inverted	*600.00*	*375.00*
b.		Surcharge double	*475.00*	*350.00*
60	A16	12c on 25m blk (Bk) ('79)	105.00	47.50
a.		Surcharge inverted	*875.00*	*650.00*
61	A16	12c on 25m blk (Bl) ('79)	350.00	225.00
		Nos. 59-61 (3)	540.00	295.00

A16

1878-79 **Typo.**

No.	Type	Description	Unused	Used
62	A16	25m black	3.50	.45
63	A16	25m green ('79)	67.50	*62.50*
64	A16	50m dull lilac	34.00	10.00
65	A16	0.0625 (62½m) gray	65.00	15.00
66	A16	100m car ('79)	110.00	37.50
67	A16	100m yel grn ('79)	10.00	2.75
68	A16	125m blue	6.00	.50
69	A16	200m rose ('79)	37.50	5.75
70	A16	200m vio rose ('79)	350.00	*900.00*
71	A16	250m bister ('79)	13.00	2.75
		Nos. 62-71 (10)	696.50	*1,037.*

Imperforates of type A16 are from proof or trial sheets.

For surcharges see Nos. 60-61, 72-75.

Stamps of 1878-79 Surcharged

a

b

1879

No.	Type	Description	Unused	Used
72	A16 (a)	2c on 25m grn	55.00	11.00
b.		Inverted surcharge	425.00	325.00
73	A16 (a)	8c on 100m car	52.50	6.50
a.		"COREROS"	150.00	80.00
b.		Surcharge double		—
74	A16 (b)	2c on 25m grn	300.00	57.50
75	A16 (b)	8c on 100m car	400.00	57.50
		Nos. 72-75 (4)	807.50	132.50

A19

Original state: The medallion is surrounded by a heavy line of color of nearly even thickness, touching the line below "Filipinas"; the opening in the hair above the temple is narrow and pointed.

1st retouch: The line around the medallion is thin, except at the upper right, and does not touch the horizontal line above it; the opening in the hair is slightly wider and rounded; the lock of hair above the forehead is shaped like a broad "V" and ends in a point; there is a faint white line below it, which is not found on the original. The shape of the hair and the width of the white line vary.

2nd retouch: The lock of hair is less pointed; the white line is much broader.

1880-86 **Typo.**

No.	Type	Description	Unused	Used
76	A19	2c carmine	.90	*.80*
77	A19	2½c brown	8.00	1.90
78	A19	2 4/8c ultra ('82)	1.25	2.25
79	A19	2 4/8c ultra, 1st retouch ('83)	.90	1.90
80	A19	2 4/8c ultra, 2nd retouch ('86)	10.50	4.25
81	A19	5c gray blue ('82)	.90	*1.90*
82	A19	6 2/8c dp grn ('82)	7.00	11.00
83	A19	8c yellow brn	36.00	6.25
84	A19	10c green	400.00	525.00
85	A19	10c brn lil ('82)	3.75	*4.25*
86	A19	12 4/8c brt rose ('82)	1.90	1.90
87	A19	20c bis brn ('82)	3.50	1.75
88	A19	25c dk brn ('82)	4.75	1.90
		Nos. 76-88 (13)	479.35	565.05

See #137-139. For surcharges see #89-108, 110-111.

Surcharges exist double or inverted on many of Nos. 89-136. Several different surcharge types exist. There are many forgeries of the surcharges.

Stamps and Type of 1880-86 Handstamp Surcharged in Black, Green or Red

c

d

e

f

Design A19

1881-88 **Black Surcharge**

No.	Type	Description	Unused	Used
89	(c)	2c on 2½c	4.25	2.25
91	(f)	10c on 2 4/8c (#80) ('87)	6.25	2.10
92	(d)	20c on 8c brn ('83)	10.00	3.25
93	(d)	1r on 2c ('83)	190.00	*325.00*
94	(d)	2r on 2 4/8c (#78; '83)	6.25	2.10
a.		On No. 79	57.50	*100.00*
b.		On No. 80	110.00	*200.00*

Most used examples of No. 93 are hole punched. Postally used examples are rare.

Green Surcharge

No.	Type	Description	Unused	Used
95	(e)	8c on 2c ('83)	11.00	2.25
95A	(d+e)	8c on 1r on 2c ('83)	200.00	*275.00*
96	(d)	10c on 2c ('83)	5.50	2.25
97	(d)	1r on 2c ('83)	190.00	150.00
98	(d)	1r on 5c gray bl ('83)	8.00	3.25
99	(d)	1r on 8c brn ('83)	10.00	3.25

Red Surcharge

No.	Type	Description	Unused	Used
100	(f)	1c on 2 4/8c (#79; '87)	1.25	*2.00*
101	(f)	1c on 2 4/8c (#80; '87)	3.50	3.00
102	(d)	16c on 2 4/8c (#78; '83)	10.00	3.25
103	(d)	1r on 2c ('83)	6.25	3.25
		On cover		550.00
104	(d)	1r on 5c bl gray ('83)	12.00	5.25

Handstamp Surcharged in Magenta

g

h

1887

No.	Type	Description	Unused	Used
105	A19 (g)	8c on 2 4/8c (#79)	1.25	.90
106	A19 (g)	8c on 2 4/8c (#80)	3.50	2.00

1888

No.	Type	Description	Unused	Used
107	A19 (h)	2 4/8c on 1c gray grn	1.75	1.00
108	A19 (h)	2 4/8c on 5c bl gray	1.90	.90
109	N1 (h)	2 4/8c on 1/8c grn	1.90	1.40
110	A19 (h)	2 4/8c on 50m bis	1.90	.80
111	A19 (h)	2 4/8c on 10c grn	1.75	.65
		Nos. 107-111 (5)	9.20	4.75

No. 109 is surcharged on a newspaper stamp of 1886-89 and has the inscriptions shown on cut N1.

On Revenue Stamps

R1

R2

R3(d)

Handstamp Surcharged in Black, Yellow, Green, Red, Blue or Magenta

j

k

m

1881-88 **Black Surcharge**

No.	Type	Description	Unused	Used
112	R1(c)	2c on 10c bis	50.00	12.50
113	R1(j)	2 4/8c on 10c bis	12.00	1.75
114	R1(j)	2 4/8c on 2r bl	200.00	140.00
115	R1(j)	8c on 10c bis	*450.00*	*6,000.*
116	R1(j)	8c on 2r bl	8.50	2.10
118	R1(d)	1r on 12 4/8c gray bl ('83)	7.75	3.75
119	R1(d)	1r on 10c bis ('82)	11.50	4.00

Yellow Surcharge

No.	Type	Description	Unused	Used
120	R2(e)	2c on 200m grn ('82)	6.25	*8.00*
121	R1(d)	16c on 2r bl ('83)	6.00	*7.00*

Green Surcharge

No.	Type	Description	Unused	Used
122	R1(d)	1r on 10c bis ('83)	11.50	4.00

Red Surcharge

No.	Type	Description	Unused	Used
123	R1(d+e)	2r on 8c on 2r blue	55.00	35.00
a.		On 8c on 2r blue (d+d)	80.00	75.00
124	R1(d)	1r on 12 4/8c gray bl ('83)	16.50	13.00
125	R1(k)	6 2/8c on 12 4/8c gray bl ('85)	5.00	*24.00*
126	R3(d)	1r on 10p bis ('83)	95.00	23.00
127	R1(m)	1r green	350.00	*700.00*
127A	R1(m)	2r blue	900.00	*1,150.*
127B	R1(d)	1r on 1r grn ('83)	700.00	*800.00*

128 R2(d) 1r on 1p grn ('83) 150.00 65.00
129 R2(d) 1r on 200m grn ('83) 500.00 *425.00*
129A R1(d) 2r on 2r blue *900.00 800.00*

The surcharge on No. 129A is pale red.

Blue Surcharge

129B R1(m) 10c bister ('81) *700.00 2,500.*

Magenta Surcharge

130 R2(h) 2⅝c on 200m grn ('88) 4.25 2.10
131 R2(h) 2⅝c on 20c brn ('88) 12.50 5.75

On Telegraph Stamps

T1

T2

Surcharged in Red, or Black

1883-88

132 T1(d) 2r on 250m ultra (R) 7.75 3.00
133 T1(d) 20c on 250m ultra *750.00* 375.00
134 T1(d) 2r on 250m ultra 10.00 4.75
135 T1(d) 1r on 20c on 250m ultra (R & Bk) 9.25 3.75

Magenta Surcharge

136 T2(h) 2⅝c on 1c bis ('88) .95 .90

Most, if not all, used stamps of No. 133 are hole-punched. Used value is for examples with hole punches.

Type of 1880-86 Redrawn

1887-89

137 A19 50m bister .65 *6.00*
138 A19 1c gray grn ('88) .65 *5.00*
a. 1c yellow green ('89) .70 *6.00*
139 A19 6c yel brn ('88) 10.00 *47.50*
Nos. 137-139 (3) 11.30 *58.50*

King Alfonso XIII — A36

1890-97 **Typo.**

140 A36 1c violet ('92) 1.00 .75
141 A36 1c rose ('94) 17.50 *40.00*
142 A36 1c bl grn ('96) 2.25 1.00
143 A36 1c claret ('97) 16.00 10.00
144 A36 2c claret ('94) .25 .25
145 A36 2c violet ('92) .25 .25
146 A36 2c dk brn ('94) .25 *3.50*
147 A36 2c ultra ('96) .35 .35
148 A36 2c gray brn ('96) .85 *2.25*
149 A36 2⅝c dull blue .55 .30
150 A36 2⅝c ol gray ('92) .30 *1.40*
151 A36 5c dark blue .50 *1.40*
152 A36 5c slate green .85 *1.40*
153 A36 5c green ('92) .80 .55
155 A36 5c vio brn ('96) 9.50 4.00
156 A36 5c blue grn ('96) 6.00 3.00
157 A36 6c brown vio ('92) .30 *1.40*
158 A36 6c red orange ('94) .95 2.25
159 A36 6c car rose ('96) 6.00 4.00
160 A36 8c yellow grn .30 .30
161 A36 8c ultra ('92) .75 .30
162 A36 8c red brn ('94) .85 .30
163 A36 10c blue grn 1.75 1.25
164 A36 10c pale cl ('91) 1.60 .40
165 A36 10c claret ('94) .75 .40
166 A36 10c yel brn ('96) .85 .30
167 A36 12⅝c yellow grn .30 .25
168 A36 12⅝c org ('92) .85 .25
169 A36 15c red brn ('92) .85 .30
170 A36 15c rose ('94) 2.10 .75
171 A36 15c bl grn ('96) 2.60 2.10
172 A36 20c pale vermilion 30.00 *45.00*
174 A36 20c gray brn ('92) 2.75 .45
175 A36 20c dk vio ('94) 15.00 8.00
176 A36 20c org ('96) 4.50 2.25
177 A36 25c brown 9.50 2.00
178 A36 25c dull bl ('91) 2.50 .50
179 A36 40c dk vio ('97) 13.50 *35.00*
180 A36 80c claret ('97) 30.00 40.00
Nos. 140-180 (39) 185.75 218.15

Many of Nos. 140-180 exist imperf and in different colors. These are considered to be proofs. Only major varieties are listed. Color varieties of most issues exist.

Stamps of Previous Issues Handstamp Surcharged in Blue, Red, Black or Violet

1897 **Blue Surcharge**

181 A36 5c on 5c green 2.00 *5.00*
182 A36 15c on 15c red brn 5.50 3.00
183 A36 20c on 20c gray brn 12.00 *12.00*

Red Surcharge

185 A36 5c on 5c green 4.50 4.75

Black Surcharge

187 A36 5c on 5c green 100.00 *300.00*
188 A36 15c on 15c rose 5.50 3.00
189 A36 20c on 20c dk vio 35.00 18.00
190 A36 20c on 25c brown 25.00 *40.00*

Violet Surcharge

191 A36 15c on 15c rose *15.00 30.00*
Nos. 181-191 (9) 204.50 415.75

Inverted, double and other variations of this surcharge exist.

The 5c on 5c blue gray (#81a) was released during US Administration. The surcharge is a mixture of red and black inks.

Impressions in violet black are believed to be reprints. The following varieties are known: 5c on 2⅝c olive gray, 5c on 5c blue green, 5c on 25c brown, 15c on 15c rose, 15c on 15c red brown, 15c on 25c brown, 20c on 20c gray brown, 20c on 20c dark violet, 20c on 25c brown. Value: each $40. These surcharges are to be found double, inverted, etc.

King Alfonso XIII — A39

1898 **Typo.**

192 A39 1m orange brown .25 *1.25*
193 A39 2m orange brown .25 *1.75*
194 A39 3m orange brown .25 *1.75*
195 A39 4m orange brown 13.00 *40.00*
196 A39 5m orange brown .25 *2.75*
197 A39 1c black violet .25 *.60*
198 A39 2c dk bl grn .25 *.60*
199 A39 3c dk brown .25 *.60*
200 A39 4c orange 20.00 *40.00*
201 A39 5c car rose .25 *.60*
202 A39 6c dk blue 1.15 *1.75*
203 A39 8c gray brown .60 .35
204 A39 10c vermilion 2.75 1.25
205 A39 15c dull ol grn 2.25 1.10
206 A39 20c maroon 2.50 1.60
207 A39 40c violet 1.25 *1.75*
208 A39 60c black 6.00 4.00
209 A39 80c red brown 8.00 5.50
210 A39 1p yellow green 20.00 *10.00*
211 A39 2p slate blue 40.00 *12.00*
Nos. 192-211 (20) 119.50 *129.20*

Nos. 192-211 exist imperf. Value, set $2,000.

Issued under U.S. Administration

Regular Issues of the United States Overprinted in Black

1899-1901 **Unwmk.** ***Perf. 12***

On U.S. Stamp No. 260

212 A96 50c orange 300. 225.
Never hinged 775.

On U.S. Stamps Nos. 279, 279B, 279Bd, 279Bj, 279Bf, 279Bc, 268, 281, 282C, 283, 284, 275, 275a

Wmk. Double-lined USPS (191)

213 A87 1c yellow green 3.50 .60
Never hinged 10.00
a. Inverted overprint *77,500.*
214 A88 2c red, type IV 1.75 .60
Never hinged 4.25
a. 2c orange red, type IV, ('01) 1.75 .60
Never hinged 4.25
b. Bklt. pane of 6, red, type IV ('00) 200.00 *300.00*
Never hinged 450.00
c. 2c reddish carmine, type IV 2.50 1.00
Never hinged 6.00
d. 2c rose carmine, type IV 3.00 1.10
Never hinged 7.25
215 A89 3c purple 9.00 1.25
Never hinged 21.50
216 A91 5c blue 9.00 1.00
Never hinged 21.50
a. Inverted overprint *6,500.*

No. 216a is valued in the grade of fine.

217 A94 10c brown, type I 35.00 4.00
Never hinged 80.00
217A A94 10c orange brown, type II 125.00 27.50
Never hinged 325.00

No. 217A was overprinted on U.S. No. 283a, vertical watermark.

218 A95 15c olive green 40.00 8.00
Never hinged 95.00
219 A96 50c orange 125.00 37.50
Never hinged 300.00
a. 50c red orange 250.00 55.00
Never hinged 600.00
Nos. 213-219 (8) 348.25 80.45

Regular Issue

Same Overprint in Black On U.S. Stamps Nos. 280b, 282 and 272

1901, Aug. 30

220 A90 4c orange brown 35.00 5.00
Never hinged 80.00
221 A92 6c lake 40.00 7.00
Never hinged 95.00
222 A93 8c violet brown 40.00 7.50
Never hinged 95.00
Nos. 220-222 (3) 115.00 19.50

Same Overprint in Red On U.S. Stamps Nos. 276, 276A, 277a and 278

223 A97 $1 black, type I 300.00 200.00
Never hinged 1,000.
223A A97 $1 black, type II 2,000. 750.00
Never hinged 5,000.
224 A98 $2 dark blue 350.00 325.00
Never hinged 1,150.
225 A99 $5 dark green 600.00 *875.00*
Never hinged 1,600.

Regular Issue

Same Overprint in Black On U.S. Stamps Nos. 300 to 310 and Shades

1903-04

226 A115 1c blue green 7.00 .40
Never hinged 15.50
227 A116 2c carmine 9.00 1.10
Never hinged 20.00
228 A117 3c bright violet 67.50 12.50
Never hinged 150.00
229 A118 4c brown 80.00 22.50
Never hinged 175.00
a. 4c orange brown 80.00 20.00
Never hinged 175.00
230 A119 5c blue 17.50 1.00
Never hinged 40.00
231 A120 6c brownish lake 85.00 22.50
Never hinged 190.00
232 A121 8c violet black 50.00 15.00
Never hinged 125.00
233 A122 10c pale red brown 35.00 2.25
Never hinged 80.00
a. 10c red brown 35.00 3.00
Never hinged 80.00
b. Pair, one without overprint *1,500.*
234 A123 13c purple black 35.00 17.50
Never hinged 80.00
a. 13c brown violet 35.00 17.50
Never hinged 80.00
235 A124 15c olive green 60.00 15.00
Never hinged 135.00
236 A125 50c orange 125.00 35.00
Never hinged 275.00
Nos. 226-236 (11) 571.00 144.75
Set, never hinged 1,285.

Same Overprint in Red On U.S. Stamps Nos. 311, 312 and 313

237 A126 $1 black 300.00 200.00
Never hinged 800.00
238 A127 $2 dark blue 550.00 *800.00*
Never hinged 1,500.
239 A128 $5 dark green 800.00 *2,750.*
Never hinged 2,000.

Same Overprint in Black On U.S. Stamp Nos. 319 and 319c

240 A129 2c carmine 8.00 2.25
Never hinged 17.50
a. Booklet pane of 6 *2,000.*
b. 2c scarlet 8.00 2.75
Never hinged 19.00
c. As "b," booklet pane of 6 —

José Rizal — A40

Designs: 4c, McKinley. 6c, Ferdinand Magellan. 8c, Miguel Lopez de Legaspi. 10c, Gen. Henry W. Lawton. 12c, Lincoln. 16c, Adm. William T. Sampson. 20c, Washington. 26c, Francisco Carriedo. 30c, Franklin. 1p-10p, Arms of City of Manila.

Wmk. Double-lined PIPS (191PI)

1906, Sept. 8 ***Perf. 12***

241 A40 2c deep green .40 .25
Never hinged 1.00
a. 2c yellow green ('10) .60 .25
Never hinged 1.50
b. Booklet pane of 6 750.00 *800.00*
Never hinged *1,500.*
242 A40 4c carmine .50 .25
Never hinged 1.25
a. 4c carmine lake ('10) 1.00 .25
Never hinged 2.50
b. Booklet pane of 6 *650.00 700.00*
Never hinged *1,250.*
243 A40 6c violet 2.50 .25
Never hinged 6.25
244 A40 8c brown 4.50 .90
Never hinged 11.00
245 A40 10c blue 3.50 .30
Never hinged 8.75
a. 10c dark blue 3.50 .30
Never hinged 8.75
246 A40 12c brown lake 9.00 2.50
Never hinged 22.50
247 A40 16c violet black 6.00 .35
Never hinged 15.00
248 A40 20c orange brown 7.00 .35
Never hinged 17.50
249 A40 26c vio brn 11.00 3.00
Never hinged 27.50
250 A40 30c olive green 6.50 1.75
Never hinged 16.00
251 A40 1p orange 50.00 7.50
Never hinged 120.00
252 A40 2p black 50.00 1.75
Never hinged 130.00
253 A40 4p dark blue 160.00 20.00
Never hinged 375.00
254 A40 10p dark green 225.00 80.00
Never hinged 575.00
Nos. 241-254 (14) 535.90 119.15
Set, never hinged 1,316.

1909-13 **Change of Colors**

255 A40 12c red orange 11.00 3.00
Never hinged 27.50
256 A40 16c olive green 6.00 .75
Never hinged 15.00
257 A40 20c yellow 9.00 1.25
Never hinged 22.50
258 A40 26c blue green 3.50 1.25
Never hinged 8.75
259 A40 30c ultramarine 13.00 3.50
Never hinged 32.50
260 A40 1p pale violet 45.00 5.00
Never hinged 110.00
260A A40 2p violet brown ('13) 100.00 12.00
Never hinged 250.00
Nos. 255-260A (7) 187.50 26.75
Set, never hinged 466.25

Wmk. Single-lined PIPS (190PI)

1911

261 A40 2c green .75 .25
Never hinged 1.80
a. Booklet pane of 6 *800.00 900.00*
Never hinged *1,400.*
262 A40 4c carmine lake 3.00 .25
Never hinged 6.75
a. 4c carmine — —
b. Booklet pane of 6 *600.00 700.00*
Never hinged *1,100.*
263 A40 6c deep violet 3.00 .25
Never hinged 6.75
264 A40 8c brown 9.50 .50
Never hinged 21.50
265 A40 10c blue 4.00 .25
Never hinged 9.00
266 A40 12c orange 4.00 .45
Never hinged 9.00
267 A40 16c olive green 4.50 .40
Never hinged 10.00
a. 16c pale olive green 4.50 .50
Never hinged 10.00
268 A40 20c yellow 3.50 .25
Never hinged 7.75
a. 20c orange 4.00 .30
Never hinged 9.00
269 A40 26c blue green 6.00 .30
Never hinged 13.50
270 A40 30c ultramarine 6.00 .50
Never hinged 13.50
271 A40 1p pale violet 27.50 .60
Never hinged 62.50
272 A40 2p violet brown 45.00 1.00
Never hinged 100.00
273 A40 4p deep blue 550.00 110.00
Never hinged 1,100.
274 A40 10p deep green 200.00 30.00
Never hinged 400.00
Nos. 261-274 (14) 866.75 145.00
Set, never hinged 1,862.

1914

275 A40 30c gray 12.00 .50
Never hinged 27.50

1914 ***Perf. 10***

276 A40 2c green 3.00 .25
Never hinged 7.00
a. Booklet pane of 6 *750.00 800.00*
Never hinged *1,250.*
277 A40 4c carmine 4.00 .30
Never hinged 9.00
a. Booklet pane of 6 *750.00*
Never hinged *1,300.*
278 A40 6c light violet 45.00 9.50
Never hinged 100.00
a. 6c deep violet 50.00 6.25
Never hinged 110.00
279 A40 8c brown 55.00 10.50
Never hinged 125.00
280 A40 10c dark blue 30.00 .25
Never hinged 67.50

281 A40 16c olive green 100.00 5.00
Never hinged 225.00
282 A40 20c orange 40.00 1.00
Never hinged 85.00
283 A40 30c gray 60.00 4.50
Never hinged 130.00
284 A40 1p pale violet 150.00 3.75
Never hinged 350.00
Nos. 276-284 (9) 487.00 35.05
Set, never hinged 1,020.

Wmk. Single-lined PIPS (190PI)

1918 ***Perf. 11***

285 A40 2c green 21.00 4.25
Never hinged 40.00
a. Booklet pane of 6 *750.00* *800.00*
Never hinged *1,300.*
286 A40 4c carmine 26.00 6.00
Never hinged 55.00
a. Booklet pane of 6 *1,350.* *2,000.*
287 A40 6c deep violet 40.00 6.00
Never hinged 90.00
287A A40 8c light brown 220.00 25.00
Never hinged 400.00
288 A40 10c dark blue 60.00 3.00
Never hinged 140.00
289 A40 16c olive green 110.00 10.00
Never hinged 250.00
289A A40 20c orange 175.00 12.00
Never hinged 400.00
289C A40 30c gray 95.00 18.00
Never hinged 215.00
289D A40 1p pale violet 100.00 25.00
Never hinged 225.00
Nos. 285-289D (9) 847.00 109.25
Set, never hinged 1,815.

1917 **Unwmk.** ***Perf. 11***

290 A40 2c yellow green .25 .25
Never hinged .55
Never hinged 25.00
a. 2c dark green .30 .25
Never hinged .65
b. Vert. pair, imperf. horiz. *2,000.*
c. Horiz. pair, imperf. between *1,500.* —
d. Vertical pair, imperf. btwn. *1,750.* *1,000.*
e. Booklet pane of 6 27.50 *30.00*
Never hinged 60.00
291 A40 4c carmine .30 .25
Never hinged .65
a. 4c light rose .30 .25
Never hinged .65
b. Booklet pane of 6 20.00 *22.50*
Never hinged 35.00
292 A40 6c deep violet .35 .25
Never hinged .70
a. 6c lilac .40 .25
Never hinged .80
b. 6c red violet .40 .25
Never hinged .70
c. Booklet pane of 6 *550.00* *800.00*
Never hinged *900.00*
293 A40 8c yellow brown .30 .25
Never hinged .50
a. 8c orange brown .30 .25
Never hinged .50
294 A40 10c deep blue .30 .25
Never hinged .65
295 A40 12c red orange .35 .25
Never hinged .75
296 A40 16c light olive green 65.00 .25
Never hinged 130.00
a. 16c olive bister 65.00 .50
Never hinged 130.00
297 A40 20c orange yellow .35 .25
Never hinged .75
298 A40 26c green .50 .45
Never hinged 1.10
a. 26c blue green .60 .25
Never hinged 1.35
299 A40 30c gray .55 .25
Never hinged 1.35
300 A40 1p pale violet 40.00 1.00
Never hinged 90.00
a. 1p red lilac 40.00 1.00
Never hinged 90.00
b. 1p pale rose lilac 40.00 1.10
Never hinged 90.00
301 A40 2p violet brown 35.00 1.00
Never hinged 77.50
302 A40 4p blue 32.50 .50
Never hinged 72.50
a. 4p dark blue 35.00 .55
Never hinged 77.50
Nos. 290-302 (13) 175.75 5.20
Set, never hinged 377.00

1923-26

Design: 16c, Adm. George Dewey.

303 A40 16c olive bister 1.00 .25
Never hinged 2.25
a. 16c olive green 1.25 .25
Never hinged 2.75
304 A40 10p dp grn ('26) 50.00 20.00
Never hinged 110.00

Legislative Palace A42

1926, Dec. 20 ***Perf. 12***

319 A42 2c green & black .50 .25
Never hinged 1.25
a. Horiz. pair, imperf. between *300.00*
b. Vert. pair, imperf. between *575.00*
320 A42 4c car & blk .55 .40
Never hinged 1.20
a. Horiz. pair, imperf. between *325.00*
b. Vert. pair, imperf. between *600.00*
321 A42 16c ol grn & blk 1.00 .65
Never hinged 2.25
a. Horiz. pair, imperf. between *350.00*
b. Vert. pair, imperf. between *625.00*
c. Double impression of center *675.00*
322 A42 18c lt brn & blk 1.10 .50
Never hinged 2.50
a. Double impression of center *1,250.*
b. Vertical pair, imperf. between *675.00*
323 A42 20c orange & black 2.00 1.00
Never hinged 4.50
a. 20c orange & brown *600.00* —
b. As No. 323, imperf., pair *575.00* *575.00*
c. As "a," imperf., pair *1,750.*
d. Vert. pair, imperf. between *700.00*
324 A42 24c gray & black 1.00 .55
Never hinged 2.25
a. Vert. pair, imperf. between *700.00*
325 A42 1p rose lil & blk 47.50 50.00
Never hinged 70.00
a. Vert. pair, imperf. between *700.00*
Nos. 319-325 (7) 53.65 53.35
Set, never hinged 83.95

Opening of the Legislative Palace.
No. 322a is valued in the grade of fine.
For overprints, see Nos. O1-O4.

Rizal Type of 1906
Coil Stamp

1928 ***Perf. 11 Vertically***

326 A40 2c green 7.50 *12.50*
Never hinged 19.00

Types of 1906-1923

1925-31 ***Imperf.***

340 A40 2c yel green ('31) .50 .50
Never hinged .90
a. 2c green ('25) .80 .75
Never hinged 1.80
341 A40 4c car rose ('31) .50 *1.00*
Never hinged 1.00
a. 4c carmine ('25) 1.20 1.00
Never hinged 2.75
342 A40 6c violet ('31) 3.00 3.75
Never hinged 5.00
a. 6c deep violet ('25) 12.00 8.00
Never hinged 26.00
343 A40 8c brown ('31) 2.00 *5.00*
Never hinged 4.00
a. 8c yellow brown ('25) 13.00 8.00
Never hinged 26.00
344 A40 10c blue ('31) 5.00 *7.50*
Never hinged 12.00
a. 10c deep blue ('25) 45.00 20.00
Never hinged 100.00
345 A40 12c dp orange ('31) 8.00 10.00
Never hinged 15.00
a. 12c red orange ('25) 60.00 35.00
Never hinged 135.00
346 A40 16c olive green 6.00 7.50
Never hinged 11.00
a. 16c bister green ('25) 42.50 18.00
Never hinged 100.00
347 A40 20c dp yel org ('31) 5.00 *7.50*
Never hinged 11.00
a. 20c yellow orange ('25) 45.00 20.00
Never hinged 100.00
348 A40 26c green ('31) 6.00 *9.00*
Never hinged 11.00
a. 26c blue green ('25) 45.00 25.00
Never hinged 110.00
349 A40 30c light gray ('31) 8.00 10.00
Never hinged 16.00
a. 30c gray ('25) 45.00 25.00
Never hinged 110.00
350 A40 1p light violet ('31) 10.00 *15.00*
Never hinged 20.00
a. 1p violet ('25) 200.00 100.00
Never hinged 425.00
351 A40 2p brn vio ('31) 30.00 *45.00*
Never hinged 80.00
a. 2p violet brown ('25) 400.00 400.00
Never hinged 675.00
352 A40 4p blue ('31) 80.00 90.00
Never hinged 150.00
a. 4p deep blue ('25) 2,200. 1,100.
Never hinged 3,500.
353 A40 10p green ('31) 175.00 *225.00*
Never hinged 300.00
a. 10p deep green ('25) 2,750. *2,950.*
Never hinged 4,250.
Nos. 340-353 (14) 339.00 436.75
Set, never hinged 636.90
Nos. 340a-353a (14) 5,859. 4,710.

Nos. 340a-353a were the original post office issue. These were reprinted twice in 1931 for sale to collectors (Nos. 340-353).

Mount Mayon, Luzon A43

Post Office, Manila A44

Pier No. 7, Manila Bay — A45

(See footnote) — A46

Rice Planting A47

Rice Terraces A48

Baguio Zigzag A49

1932, May 3 ***Perf. 11***

354 A43 2c yellow green .75 .30
Never hinged 1.25
355 A44 4c rose carmine .75 .30
Never hinged 1.25
356 A45 12c orange 1.00 .75
Never hinged 1.25
357 A46 18c red orange 50.00 15.00
Never hinged 80.00
358 A47 20c yellow 1.10 .75
Never hinged 1.75
359 A48 24c deep violet 1.75 1.00
Never hinged 3.00
360 A49 32c olive brown 1.75 1.00
Never hinged 3.00
Nos. 354-360 (7) 57.10 19.10
Set, never hinged 91.50

The 18c vignette was intended to show Pagsanjan Falls in Laguna, central Luzon, and is so labeled. Through error the stamp pictures Vernal Falls in Yosemite National Park, California.

For overprints see #C29-C35, C47-C51, C63.

Nos. 302, 302a Surcharged in Orange or Red

1932

368 A40 1p on 4p blue (O) 7.50 1.00
Never hinged 12.00
a. 1p on 4p dark blue (O) 7.50 1.00
Never hinged 12.00
369 A40 2p on 4p dark blue (R) 10.00 1.50
Never hinged 17.00
a. 2p on 4p blue (R) 10.00 1.00
Never hinged 17.00

Far Eastern Championship

Issued in commemoration of the Tenth Far Eastern Championship Games.

Baseball Players A50

Tennis Player — A51

Basketball Players — A52

1934, Apr. 14 ***Perf. 11½***

380 A50 2c yellow brown 1.50 .80
Never hinged 2.25
381 A51 6c ultramarine .25 .25
Never hinged .30
a. Vertical pair, imperf. between *700.00*
Never hinged *1,100.*
382 A52 16c violet brown .50 .50
Never hinged .75
a. Vert. pair, imperf. horiz. *950.00*
Never hinged *1,500.*
Nos. 380-382 (3) 2.25 1.55
Set, never hinged 3.30

José Rizal — A53

Woman and Carabao A54

La Filipina — A55

Pearl Fishing A56

Fort Santiago A57

Salt Spring — A58

Magellan's Landing, 1521 — A59

"Juan de la Cruz" — A60

Rice Terraces A61

"Blood Compact," 1565 — A62

Barasoain Church, Malolos A63

Battle of Manila Bay, 1898 A64

Montalban Gorge A65

George Washington A66

1935, Feb. 15 *Perf. 11*

383 A53 2c rose .25 .25
Never hinged .25
384 A54 4c yellow green .25 .25
Never hinged .25
385 A55 6c dark brown .25 .25
Never hinged .35
386 A56 8c violet .25 .25
Never hinged .35
387 A57 10c rose carmine .30 .25
Never hinged .45
388 A58 12c black .35 .25
Never hinged .50
389 A59 16c dark blue .35 .25
Never hinged .55
390 A60 20c light olive green .35 .25
Never hinged .45
391 A61 26c indigo .40 .40
Never hinged .60
392 A62 30c orange red .40 .40
Never hinged .60
393 A63 1p red org & blk 2.00 1.25
Never hinged 3.00
394 A64 2p bis brn & blk 12.00 2.00
Never hinged 16.00
395 A65 4p blue & black 12.00 4.00
Never hinged 16.00
396 A66 5p green & black 25.00 5.00
Never hinged 50.00
Nos. 383-396 (14) 54.15 15.05
Set, never hinged 74.45

For overprints & surcharges see Nos. 411-424, 433-446, 449, 463-466, 468, 472-474, 478-484, 485-494, C52-C53, O15-O36, O38, O40-O43, N2-N9, N28, NO2-NO6.

Issues of the Commonwealth

Issued to commemorate the inauguration of the Philippine Commonwealth, Nov. 15, 1935.

The Temples of Human Progress — A67

1935, Nov. 15

397 A67 2c carmine rose .25 .25
Never hinged .30
398 A67 6c deep violet .25 .25
Never hinged .30
399 A67 16c blue .25 .25
Never hinged .35
400 A67 36c yellow green .40 .30
Never hinged .60
401 A67 50c brown .60 .55
Never hinged .90
Nos. 397-401 (5) 1.75 1.60
Set, never hinged 2.45

Jose Rizal Issue

75th anniversary of the birth of Jose Rizal (1861-1896), national hero of the Filipinos.

Jose Rizal — A68

1936, June 19 *Perf. 12*

402 A68 2c yellow brown .25 .25
Never hinged .25
403 A68 6c slate blue .25 .25
Never hinged .25
a. Imperf. vertically, pair *1,000.*
Never hinged *1,500.*
404 A68 36c red brown .50 *.70*
Never hinged .75
Nos. 402-404 (3) 1.00 1.20
Set, never hinged 1.25

Commonwealth Anniversary Issue

Issued in commemoration of the first anniversary of the Commonwealth.

President Manuel L. Quezon — A69

1936, Nov. 15 *Perf. 11*

408 A69 2c orange brown .25 .25
Never hinged .30
409 A69 6c yellow green .25 .25
Never hinged .30
410 A69 12c ultramarine .25 .25
Never hinged .30
Nos. 408-410 (3) .75 .75
Set, never hinged .90

Stamps of 1935 Overprinted in Black

a

b

1936-37

411 A53(a) 2c rose .25 .25
Never hinged .25
a. Bklt. pane of 6 ('37) 2.50 2.00
Never hinged 4.00
b. Hyphen omitted 125.00 100.00
412 A54(b) 4c yel grn ('37) .50 *4.00*
Never hinged .75
413 A55(a) 6c dark brown .25 .25
Never hinged .25
414 A56(b) 8c violet ('37) .25 .25
Never hinged .35
415 A57(b) 10c rose carmine .25 .25
Never hinged .25
a. "COMMONWEALT" 20.00 —
Never hinged 30.00
416 A58(b) 12c black ('37) .25 .25
Never hinged .30
417 A59(b) 16c dark blue .30 .25
Never hinged .45
418 A60(a) 20c lt ol grn ('37) 1.00 .40
Never hinged 1.60
419 A61(b) 26c indigo ('37) .90 .35
Never hinged 1.50
420 A62(b) 30c orange red .50 .25
Never hinged .80
421 A63(b) 1p red org & blk 1.00 .25
Never hinged 1.60
422 A64(b) 2p bis brn & blk ('37) 15.00 4.00
Never hinged 25.00
423 A65(b) 4p bl & blk ('37) 50.00 8.00
Never hinged 80.00
424 A66(b) 5p grn & blk ('37) 15.00 *25.00*
Never hinged 25.00
Nos. 411-424 (14) 85.45 43.75
Set, never hinged 110.75

Eucharistic Congress Issue

Issued to commemorate the 33rd International Eucharistic Congress held at Manila, Feb. 3-7, 1937.

Map of Philippines — A70

1937, Feb. 3

425 A70 2c yellow green .25 .25
Never hinged .25
426 A70 6c light brown .25 .25
Never hinged .25
427 A70 12c sapphire .25 .25
Never hinged .25
428 A70 20c deep orange .30 .25
Never hinged .50
429 A70 36c deep violet .55 .40
Never hinged .80
430 A70 50c carmine .70 .35
Never hinged 1.10
Nos. 425-430 (6) 2.30 1.75
Set, never hinged 3.15

Arms of Manila — A71

1937, Aug. 27

431 A71 10p gray 6.00 2.00
Never hinged 8.50
432 A71 20p henna brown 5.00 1.40
Never hinged 8.00

Stamps of 1935 Overprinted in Black

a

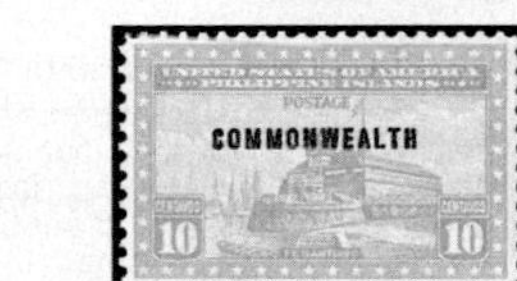
b

1938-40

433 A53(a) 2c rose ('39) .25 .25
Never hinged .25
a. Booklet pane of 6 3.50 3.50
Never hinged 5.50
b. As "a," lower left-hand stamp overprinted "WEALTH COMMON-" *2,500.*
Never hinged *4,000.*
c. Hyphen omitted 100.00 50.00
434 A54(b) 4c yel grn ('40) 3.00 *30.00*
Never hinged 4.75
435 A55(a) 6c dk brn ('39) .25 .25
Never hinged .40
a. 6c golden brown .25 .25
Never hinged .40
436 A56(b) 8c violet ('39) .25 *1.75*
Never hinged .25
a. "COMMONWEALT" (LR 31) 90.00
Never hinged 140.00
437 A57(b) 10c rose car ('39) .25 .25
Never hinged .25
a. "COMMONWEALT" (LR 31) 65.00 —
Never hinged 100.00
438 A58(b) 12c black ('40) .25 *1.00*
Never hinged .25
439 A59(b) 16c dark blue .25 .25
Never hinged .25
440 A60(a) 20c lt ol grn ('39) .25 .25
Never hinged .25
441 A61(b) 26c indigo ('40) 1.00 *2.50*
Never hinged 1.50
442 A62(b) 30c org red ('39) 3.00 .70
Never hinged 5.00
443 A63(b) 1p red org & blk .60 .25
Never hinged 1.00
444 A64(b) 2p bis brn & blk ('39) 10.00 1.00
Never hinged 15.00
445 A65(b) 4p bl & blk ('40) 175.00 250.00
Never hinged 350.00
446 A66(b) 5p grn & blk ('40) 20.00 8.00
Never hinged 35.00
Nos. 433-446 (14) 214.35 *296.45*
Set, never hinged 414.15

Overprint "b" measures 18½x1¾mm.

No. 433b occurs in booklet pane, No. 433a, position 5; all examples are straight-edged, left and bottom.

First Foreign Trade Week Issue Nos. 384, 298a and 432 Surcharged in Red, Violet or Black

a

b

c

1939, July 5

449 A54(a) 2c on 4c yel grn (R) .25 .25
Never hinged .35
450 A40(b) 6c on 26c blue grn (V) .25 .50
Never hinged .35
a. 6c on 26c green 3.00 1.00
Never hinged 5.00
451 A71(c) 50c on 20p henna brn (Bk) 1.25 1.00
Never hinged 2.00 5.00
Nos. 449-451 (3) 1.75 1.75
Set, never hinged 2.70

Commonwealth 4th Anniversary Issue (#452-460)

Triumphal Arch — A72

1939, Nov. 15

452 A72 2c yellow green .25 .25
Never hinged .25
453 A72 6c carmine .25 .25
Never hinged .25
454 A72 12c bright blue .25 .25
Never hinged .25
Nos. 452-454 (3) .75 .75
Set, never hinged .75

For overprints see Nos. 469, 476

Malacañan Palace A73

1939, Nov. 15

455 A73 2c green .25 .25
Never hinged .25

456 A73 6c orange .25 .25
Never hinged .25
457 A73 12c carmine .25 .25
Never hinged .25
Nos. 455-457 (3) .75 .75
Set, never hinged .75

For overprint, see No. 470.

Pres. Quezon Taking Oath of Office — A74

1940, Feb. 8

458 A74 2c dark orange .25 .25
Never hinged .25
459 A74 6c dark green .25 .25
Never hinged .25
460 A74 12c purple .25 .25
Never hinged .30
Nos. 458-460 (3) .75 .75
Set, never hinged .80

For overprints, see Nos. 471, 477.

José Rizal — A75

ROTARY PRESS PRINTING

1941, Apr. 14 *Perf. 11x10½*

Size: 19x22½mm

461 A75 2c apple green .25 .50
Never hinged .25

FLAT PLATE PRINTING

1941, Nov. 14 *Perf. 11*

Size: 18¾x22¼mm

462 A75 2c pale apple green 1.00 —
Never hinged 1.25
a. Booklet pane of 6 6.00 —
Never hinged 7.50

No. 461 was issued only in sheets. No. 462 was issued only in booklet panes on Nov. 14, 1941, just before the war, and only a few used stamps and covers exist. All examples have one or two straight edges. Mint booklets reappeared after the war. In August 1942, the booklet pane was reprinted in a darker shade (apple green). However, the apple green panes were available only to U.S. collectors during the war years, so no war-period used stamps from the Philippines exist. Value of apple green booklet pane, never hinged, $6.

For type A75 overprinted, see Nos. 464, O37, O39, N1 and NO1.

Philippine Stamps of 1935-41, Handstamped in Violet

1944 *Perf. 11, 11x10½*

463 A53 2c rose (On 411) *650.00* *160.00*
a. Booklet pane of 6 *12,500.*
463B A53 2c rose (On 433) *2,000.* *1,750.*
464 A75 2c apple grn (On 461) 12.50 10.00
Never hinged 22.50
a. Pair, one without ovpt. — —
465 A54 4c yel grn (On 384) 47.50 *42.50*
Never hinged 80.00
466 A55 6c dk brn (On 385) *3,250.* *2,000.*
467 A69 6c yel grn (On 409) 275.00 150.00
Never hinged *475.00*
468 A55 6c dk brn (On 413) *4,750.* *825.00*
469 A72 6c car (On 453) *350.00* *125.00*
470 A73 6c org (On 456) *1,750.* *725.00*
471 A74 6c dk grn (On 459) *275.00* *225.00*
472 A56 8c vio (On 436) 17.50 *30.00*
Never hinged 30.00
473 A57 10c car rose (On 415) *325.00* *150.00*
474 A57 10c car rose (On 437) *275.00* *200.00*
Never hinged *475.00*
475 A69 12c ultra (On 410) *1,100.* *400.00*
476 A72 12c brt bl (On 454) *7,000.* *2,500.*
477 A74 12c pur (On 460) *425.00* *275.00*
478 A59 16c dk bl (On 389) *3,000.* —
479 A59 16c dk bl (On 417) *1,500.* *1,000.*
480 A59 16c dk bl (On 439) *500.00* *200.00*
481 A60 20c lt ol grn (On 440) 125.00 35.00
Never hinged 210.00
482 A62 30c org red (On 420) *450.00* *1,500.*
483 A62 30c org red (On 442) *750.00* *375.00*
484 A63 1p red org & blk (On 443) *6,250.* *4,500.*

Nos. 463-484 are valued in the grade of fine to very fine.

No. 463 comes only from the booklet pane. All examples have one or two straight edges.

Types of 1935-37 Overprinted

a

b

Nos. 431-432 Overprinted in Black — c

1945 *Perf. 11*

485 A53(a) 2c rose .25 .25
Never hinged .25
486 A54(b) 4c yellow green .25 .25
Never hinged .25
487 A55(a) 6c golden brown .25 .25
Never hinged .25
488 A56(b) 8c violet .25 .25
Never hinged .25
489 A57(b) 10c rose carmine .25 .25
Never hinged .25
490 A58(b) 12c black .25 .25
Never hinged .25
491 A59(b) 16c dark blue .25 .25
Never hinged .30
492 A60(a) 20c lt olive green .30 .25
Never hinged .40
493 A62(b) 30c orange red .50 .35
Never hinged .75
494 A63(b) 1p red orange & black 1.10 .25
Never hinged 1.60
495 A71(c) 10p gray 55.00 13.50
Never hinged 90.00
496 A71(c) 20p henna brown 50.00 15.00
Never hinged 75.00
Nos. 485-496 (12) 108.65 31.10
Set, never hinged 169.55

José Rizal — A76

1946, May 28 *Perf. 11x10½*

497 A76 2c sepia .25 .25
Never hinged .25

For overprints see Nos. 503, O44.

Catalogue values for unused stamps in this section, from this point to the end of the section, are for Never Hinged items.

Later issues, released by the Philippine Republic on July 4, 1946, and thereafter, are listed in Scott's Standard Postage Stamp Catalogue, Vol. 5.

Republic

Philippine Girl Holding Flag of the Republic — A77

Unwmk.

1946, July 4 **Engr.** *Perf. 11*

500 A77 2c carmine .50 .25
501 A77 6c green .50 .25
502 A77 12c blue 1.25 .40
Nos. 500-502 (3) 2.25 .90

Philippine independence, July 4, 1946.

No. 497 Overprinted in Brown

1946, Dec. 30 *Perf. 11x10½*

503 A76 2c sepia .40 .25

50th anniv. of the execution of José Rizal.

Rizal Monument A78

Bonifacio Monument A79

Jones Bridge — A80

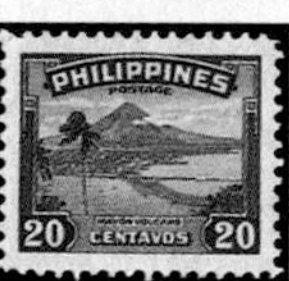

Santa Lucia Gate — A81

Mayon Volcano — A82

Avenue of Palms — A83

1947 **Engr.** *Perf. 12*

504 A78 4c black brown .40 .25
505 A79 10c red orange .40 .25
506 A80 12c deep blue .40 .25
507 A81 16c slate gray 3.00 .60
508 A82 20c red brown 3.00 .25
509 A83 50c dull green 3.00 .35
510 A83 1p violet 3.00 .35
Nos. 504-510 (7) 13.20 2.30

For surcharges see Nos. 613-614, 809. For overprints see Nos. 609, O50-O52, O54-O55.

Manuel L. Quezon — A84

1947, May 1 **Typo.**

511 A84 1c green .40 .25

See No. 515.

Pres. Manuel A. Roxas Taking Oath of Office A85

1947, July 4 **Unwmk.** *Perf. 12½*

512 A85 4c carmine rose .50 .25
513 A85 6c dk green .75 .45
514 A85 16c purple 1.25 .85
Nos. 512-514 (3) 2.50 1.55

First anniversary of republic.

Quezon Type

Souvenir Sheet

1947, Nov. 28 *Imperf.*

515 Sheet of 4 1.75 1.25
a. A84 1c bright green .25 .25

United Nations Emblem A87

1947, Nov. 24 *Perf. 12½*

516 A87 4c dk car & pink 2.40 1.40
a. Imperf. 6.00 3.75
517 A87 6c pur & pale vio 2.40 1.40
a. Imperf. 5.50 3.75
518 A87 12c dp bl & pale bl 3.50 2.10
a. Imperf. 6.00 3.75
Nos. 516-518 (3) 8.30 4.90
Nos. 516a-518a (3) 17.50 11.25

Conference of the Economic Commission in Asia and the Far East, held at Baguio.

Gen. Douglas MacArthur — A88

1948, Feb. 3 **Engr.** *Perf. 12*

519 A88 4c purple .90 .50
520 A88 6c rose car 1.25 .50
521 A88 16c brt ultra 1.60 .75
Nos. 519-521 (3) 3.75 1.75

Threshing Rice — A89

1948, Feb. 23 **Typo.** *Perf. 12½*

522 A89 2c grn & pale yel grn 1.00 .40
523 A89 6c brown & cream 1.75 .40
524 A89 18c dp bl & pale bl 3.25 1.25
Nos. 522-524 (3) 6.00 2.05

Conf. of the FAO held at Baguio. No. 524 exists imperf. See No. C67.

Manuel A. Roxas — A90

1948, July 15 **Engr.** *Perf. 12*

525 A90 2c black .25 .25
526 A90 4c black .35 .25

Issued in tribute to President Manuel A. Roxas who died April 15, 1948.

José Rizal — A91

1948, June 19 **Unwmk.**

527 A91 2c bright green .40 .25
a. Booklet pane of 6 3.00 3.00

For surcharges see Nos. 550, O56. For overprint see No. O53.

Scout Saluting — A92

1948, Oct. 31 **Typo.** ***Imperf.***

528 A92 2c chocolate & green 1.75 .55
a. Perf. 11½ 1.75 1.40
529 A92 4c chocolate & pink 3.25 .70
a. Perf. 11½ 3.00 2.00

Boy Scouts of the Philippines, 25th anniv. No. 528 exists part perforate.

Sampaguita, National Flower — A93

1948, Dec. 8 ***Perf. 12½***

530 A93 3c blk, pale grn & grn .60 .30

UPU Monument, Bern A94

Unwmk.

1949, Oct. 9 **Engr.** ***Perf. 12***

531 A94 4c green .70 .25
532 A94 6c dull violet .40 .25
533 A94 18c blue gray .40 .25
Nos. 531-533 (3) 1.50 .75

Souvenir Sheet

Imperf

534 Sheet of 3 3.00 2.00
a. A94 4c green .70 .35
b. A94 6c dull violet .70 .35
c. A94 18c blue .70 .60

75th anniv. of the UPU.

In 1960 an unofficial, 3-line overprint ("President D. D. Eisenhower /Visit to the Philippines/June 14-16, 1960") was privately applied to No. 534.

For surcharge & overprint see #806, 901.

Gen. Gregorio del Pilar at Tirad Pass — A95

1949, Dec. 2 ***Perf. 12***

535 A95 2c red brown .35 .25
536 A95 4c green .55 .25

50th anniversary of the death of Gen. Gregorio P. del Pilar and fifty-two of his men at Tirad Pass.

Globe — A96

1950, Mar. 1

537 A96 2c purple .30 .25
538 A96 6c dk green .40 .25
539 A96 18c dp blue .55 .25
Nos. 537-539,C68-C69 (5) 5.15 1.85

5th World Cong. of the Junior Chamber of Commerce, Manila, Mar. 1-8, 1950.

For surcharge see No. 825.

Red Lauan Tree — A97

1950, Apr. 14

540 A97 2c green .60 .25
541 A97 4c purple .75 .25

50th anniversary of the Bureau of Forestry.

F. D. Roosevelt with his Stamps — A98

1950, May 22

542 A98 4c dark brown 1.40 .25
543 A98 6c carmine rose .65 .45
544 A98 18c blue .65 .45
Nos. 542-544 (3) 2.70 1.15

Honoring Franklin D. Roosevelt and for the 25th anniv. of the Philatelic Association of the Philippines. See No. C70.

Lions Club Emblem — A99

1950, June 4 **Engr.**

545 A99 2c orange 1.00 .30
546 A99 4c violet 1.00 .35
Nos. 545-546,C71-C72 (4) 5.75 1.70

Convention of the Lions Club, Manila, June 1950.

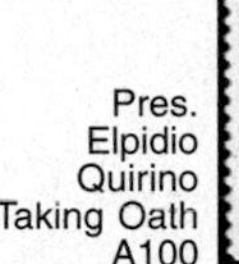

Pres. Elpidio Quirino Taking Oath A100

1950, July 4 **Unwmk.** ***Perf. 12***

547 A100 2c car rose .25 .25
548 A100 4c magenta .25 .25
549 A100 6c blue green .40 .25
Nos. 547-549 (3) .90 .75

Republic of the Philippines, 4th anniv.

No. 527 Surcharged in Black

1950, Sept. 20

550 A91 1c on 2c bright green .60 .25

Dove over Globe — A101

1950, Oct. 23

551 A101 5c green .60 .25
552 A101 6c rose carmine .45 .25
553 A101 18c ultra .45 .35
Nos. 551-553 (3) 1.50 .85

Baguio Conference of 1950.

For surcharge see No. 828.

Headman of Barangay Inspecting Harvest A102

1951, Mar. 31 **Litho.** ***Perf. 12½***

554 A102 5c dull green .75 .25
555 A102 6c red brown .40 .25
556 A102 18c violet blue .40 .30
Nos. 554-556 (3) 1.55 .80

The government's Peace Fund campaign.

Imperf., Pairs

554a A102 5c dull green 3.25 2.00
555a A102 6c red brown 1.90 .90
556a A102 18c violet blue 1.40 .75
Nos. 554a-556a (3) 6.55 3.65

Arms of Manila A103

Arms of Cebu A104

Arms of Zamboanga A105

Arms of Iloilo A106

Various Frames

1951 **Engr.** ***Perf. 12***

557 A103 5c purple 1.25 .25
558 A103 6c gray .95 .25
559 A103 18c bright ultra .60 .40

Various Frames

560 A104 5c crimson rose 1.25 .25
561 A104 6c bister brown .60 .25
562 A104 18c violet .95 .40

Various Frames

563 A105 5c blue green 1.60 .25
564 A105 6c red brown .95 .25
565 A105 18c light blue .95 .40

Various Frames

566 A106 5c bright green 1.60 .25
567 A106 6c violet .95 .25
568 A106 18c deep blue .95 .40
Nos. 557-568 (12) 12.60 3.60

Issued: A103, 2/3; A104, 4/27; A105, 6/19; A106, 8/26.

For surcharges see Nos. 634-636.

UN Emblem and Girl Holding Flag — A107

1951, Oct. 24 **Unwmk.** ***Perf. 11½***

569 A107 5c red 1.75 .30
570 A107 6c blue green 1.00 .30
571 A107 18c violet blue 1.00 .40
Nos. 569-571 (3) 3.75 1.00

United Nations Day, Oct. 24, 1951.

Liberty Holding Declaration of Human Rights — A108

1951, Dec. 10 ***Perf. 12***

572 A108 5c green 1.40 .25
573 A108 6c red orange .85 .25
574 A108 18c ultra .85 .35
Nos. 572-574 (3) 3.10 .85

Universal Declaration of Human Rights.

Students and Department Seal — A109

1952, Jan. 31

575 A109 5c orange red .75 .35

50th anniversary (in 1951) of the Philippine Educational System.

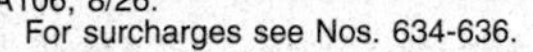

PHILIPPINE STAMPS STORE
Specializing in the Republic Period
Scott #500 & 1946 forward
Maligayang Pagdating

On-line at
PhilippineStampsStore.com

Milkfish and Map
A111

1952, Oct. 27 ***Perf. 12½***

578 A111 5c orange brown	1.60	.45
579 A111 6c deep blue	.80	.30

4th Indo-Pacific Fisheries Council Meeting, Quezon City, Oct. 23-Nov. 7, 1952.

Maria Clara — A112

1952, Nov. 16

580 A112 5c deep blue	1.00	.30
581 A112 6c brown	.75	.30
Nos. 580-581,C73 (3)	3.75	1.35

1st Pan-Asian Philatelic Exhibition, PANAPEX, Manila, Nov. 16-22.

Wright Park, Baguio City — A113

1952, Dec. 15 ***Perf. 12***

582 A113 5c red orange	1.60	.45
583 A113 6c dp blue green	1.10	.45

3rd Lions District Convention, Baguio City.

Francisco Baltazar, Poet — A114

1953, Mar. 27

584 A114 5c citron	.60	.30

National Language Week.

"Gateway to the East" — A115

1953, Apr. 30

585 A115 5c turq green	.55	.25
586 A115 6c vermilion	.45	.25

Philippines International Fair.

Presidents Quirino and Sukarno — A116

1953, Oct. 5 **Engr. & Litho.**

587 A116 5c multicolored	.65	.35
588 A116 6c multicolored	.35	.30

2nd anniversary of the visit of Indonesia's President Sukarno.

Marcelo H. del Pilar — A117

1c, Manuel L. Quezon. 2c, José Abad Santos (diff. frame). 3c, Apolinario Mabini (diff. frame). 10c, Father José Burgos. 20c, Lapu-Lapu. 25c, Gen. Antonio Luna. 50c, Cayetano Arellano. 60c, Andres Bonifacio. 2p, Graciano L. Jaena.

Perf. 12, 12½, 13, 14x13½

1952-60 **Engr.**

589 A117 1c red brn ('53)	.30	.25
590 A117 2c gray ('60)	.25	.25
591 A117 3c brick red ('59)	.30	.25
592 A117 5c crim rose	.30	.25
595 A117 10c ultra ('55)	.50	.25
597 A117 20c car lake ('55)	.80	.25
598 A117 25c yel grn ('58)	1.00	.25
599 A117 50c org ver ('59)	1.25	.25
600 A117 60c car rose ('58)	1.50	.50
601 A117 2p violet	6.00	1.00
Nos. 589-601 (10)	12.20	3.50

For overprints & surcharges see #608, 626, 641-642, 647, 830, 871, 875-877, O57-O61.

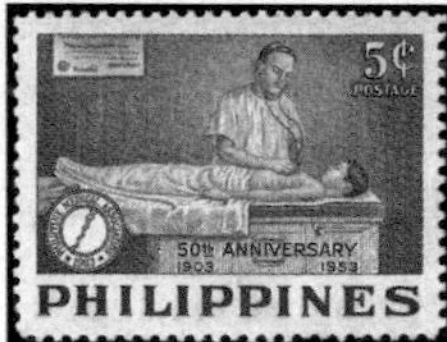

Doctor Examining Boy
A118

1953, Dec. 16

603 A118 5c lilac rose	.65	.25
604 A118 6c ultra	.60	.25

50th anniversary of the founding of the Philippine Medical Association.

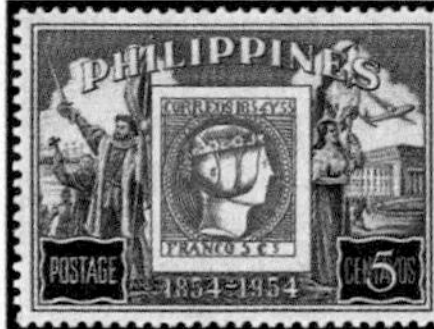

First Philippine Stamps, Magellan's Landing and Manila Scene
A119

Stamp of 1854 in Orange

1954, Apr. 25 ***Perf. 13***

605 A119 5c purple	.80	.35
606 A119 18c deep blue	1.90	1.00
607 A119 30c green	4.75	2.40
Nos. 605-607,C74-C76 (6)	22.45	9.60

Centenary of Philippine postage stamps.
For surcharge see No. 829.

Nos. 592 and 509 Overprinted or Surcharged in Black

1954, Apr. 23 ***Perf. 12***

608 A117 5c crimson rose	1.75	.90
609 A83 18c on 50c dull grn	2.50	1.40

1st National Boy Scout Jamboree, Quezon City, April 23-30, 1954.
The surcharge on No. 609 is reduced to fit the size of the stamp.

Discus Thrower and Games Emblem
A120

1954, May 31 ***Perf. 13***

610 A120 5c shown	2.75	.80
611 A120 18c Swimmer	.90	.40
612 A120 30c Boxers	2.25	1.50
Nos. 610-612 (3)	5.90	2.70

2nd Asian Games, Manila, May 1-9.

Nos. 505 and 508 Surcharged in Blue

1954, Sept. 6 ***Perf. 12***

613 A79 5c on 10c red org	.75	.45
614 A82 18c on 20c red brn	.75	.45

Manila Conference, 1954.
The surcharge is arranged to obliterate the original denomination.

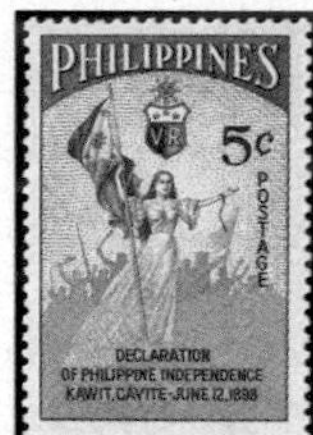

Allegory of Independence
A121

1954, Nov. 30 ***Perf. 13***

615 A121 5c dark carmine	1.00	.25
616 A121 18c deep blue	.65	.30

56th anniversary of the declaration of the first Philippine Independence.
For surcharge see No. 826.

"Immaculate Conception," by Murillo — A122

1954, Dec. 30 ***Perf. 12***

617 A122 5c blue	.65	.25

Issued to mark the end of the Marian Year.

Mayon Volcano, Moro Vinta and Rotary Emblem
A123

1955, Feb. 23 **Engr.** ***Perf. 13***

618 A123 5c dull blue	.60	.25
619 A123 18c dk car rose	1.40	.85
Nos. 618-619,C77 (3)	4.50	2.10

Rotary Intl., 50th anniv. For surcharge see #827.

Allegory of Labor — A124

1955, May 26 ***Perf. 13x12½***

620 A124 5c brown	1.75	.70

Issued in connection with the Labor-Management Congress, Manila, May 26-28, 1955.

Pres. Ramon Magsaysay
A125

1955, July 4 ***Perf. 12½***

621 A125 5c blue	.50	.25
622 A125 20c red	1.25	.50
623 A125 30c green	1.25	.50
Nos. 621-623 (3)	3.00	1.25

9th anniversary of the Republic.

Village Well
A126

1956, Mar. 16 ***Perf. 12½x13½***

624 A126 5c violet	.60	.25
625 A126 20c dull green	1.00	.40

Issued to publicize the drive for improved health conditions in rural areas.

No. 592 Overprinted

1956, Aug. 1 **Unwmk.** ***Perf. 12***

626 A117 5c crimson rose	.55	.35

5th Annual Conf. of the World Confederation of Organizations of the Teaching Profession, Manila, Aug. 1-8, 1956.

Nurse and Disaster Victims
A127

Engraved; Cross Lithographed in Red

1956, Aug. 30

627 A127 5c violet	.40	.30
628 A127 20c gray brown	1.25	.60

50 years of Red Cross Service in the Philippines.

Monument to US Landing, Leyte — A128

1956, Oct. 20 Litho. *Perf. 12½*

629 A128 5c carmine rose .65 .25
a. Imperf, pair ('57) 5.75 3.00

Landing of US forces under Gen. Douglas MacArthur on Leyte, Oct. 20, 1944.
Issue date: No. 629a, Feb. 16.

Santo Tomas University A129

1956, Nov. 13 Photo. *Perf. 11½*

630 A129 5c brown car & choc .50 .35
631 A129 60c lilac & red brn 3.25 1.60

Statue of Christ by Rizal — A130

1956, Nov. 28 Engr. *Perf. 12*

632 A130 5c gray olive .40 .25
633 A130 20c rose carmine 1.10 .60

2nd Natl. Eucharistic Cong., Manila, Nov. 28-Dec. 2, and for the centenary of the Feast of the Sacred Heart.

Nos. 561, 564 and 567 Surcharged with New Value in Blue or Black

1956 Unwmk. *Perf. 12*

634 A104 5c on 6c bis brn (Bl) .50 .25
635 A105 5c on 6c red brn (Bl) .50 .25
636 A106 5c on 6c vio (Bk) .50 .25
Nos. 634-636 (3) 1.50 .75

Girl Scout, Emblem and Tents A131

1957, Jan. 19 Litho. *Perf. 12½*

637 A131 5c dark blue .80 .40
a. Imperf, pair 9.00 5.50

Centenary of the Scout movement and for the Girl Scout World Jamboree, Quezon City, Jan. 19-Feb. 2, 1957.
Exmaples of Nos. 637 and 637a (No. 48 in sheet) exist with heavy black rectangular handstamps obliterating erroneous date at left, denomination and cloverleaf emblem.

Pres. Ramon Magsaysay (1907-57) — A132

1957, Aug. 31 Engr. *Perf. 12*

638 A132 5c black .35 .25

"Spoliarium" by Juan Luna — A133

1957, Oct. 23 *Perf. 14x14½*

639 A133 5c rose carmine .35 .25

Centenary of the birth of Juan Luna, painter.

Sergio Osmena and First National Assembly — A134

1957, Oct. 16 *Perf. 12½x13½*

640 A134 5c blue green .35 .25

1st Philippine Assembly and honoring Sergio Osmeña, Speaker of the Assembly.

Nos. 595 and 597 Surcharged in Carmine or Black

1957, Dec. 30 *Perf. 14x13½*

641 A117 5c on 10c ultra (C) .65 .25
642 A117 10c on 20c car lake .65 .30

Inauguration of Carlos P. Garcia as president and Diosdado Macapagal as vice-president, Dec. 30.

University of the Philippines — A135

1958 Engr. *Perf. 13½x13*

643 A135 5c dk carmine rose .45 .25

50th anniversary of the founding of the University of the Philippines.

Pres. Carlos P. Garcia — A136

1958 Photo. *Perf. 11½*
Granite Paper

644 A136 5c multicolored .25 .25
645 A136 20c multicolored .50 .30

12th anniversary of Philippine Republic.

Manila Cathedral — A137

1958, Dec. 8 Engr. *Perf. 13x13½*

646 A137 5c multicolored .35 .25
a. Perf 12 3.00 2.00

Issued to commemorate the inauguration of the rebuilt Manila Cathedral, Dec. 8, 1958.

No. 592 Surcharged

1959 *Perf. 12*

647 A117 1c on 5c crim rose .35 .25

Nos. B4-B5 Surcharged with New Values and Bars

1959, Feb. 3 *Perf. 13*

648 SP4 1c on 2c + 2c red .25 .25
649 SP5 6c on 4c + 4c vio .25 .25

14th anniversary of the liberation of Manila from the Japanese forces.

Philippine Flag A138

1959, Feb. 8 Unwmk. *Perf. 13*

650 A138 6c dp ultra, yel & dp car .25 .25
651 A138 20c dp car, yel & dp ultra .45 .25

Seal of Bulacan Province — A139

1959 Engr. *Perf. 13*

652 A139 6c lt yellow grn .25 .25
653 A139 20c rose red .40 .25

60th anniversary of the Malolos constitution.
For surcharge see No. 848.

1959

Design: 6c, 25c, Seal of Capiz Province and portrait of Pres. Roxas.

654 A139 6c lt brown .25 .25
655 A139 25c purple .35 .25

Pres. Manuel A. Roxas, 11th death anniv.

Seal of Bacolod City — A140

1959

656 A140 6c blue green .25 .25
657 A140 10c rose lilac .40 .25

Nos. 658-803 were reserved for the rest of a projected series showing seals and coats of arms of provinces and cities.

Camp John Hay Amphitheater, Baguio — A141

1959, Sept. 1 *Perf. 13½*

804 A141 6c bright green .25 .25
a. Perf 12 2.00 1.50
805 A141 25c rose red .35 .25

50th anniversary of the city of Baguio.

No. 533 Surcharged in Red

1959, Oct. 24 *Perf. 12*

806 A94 6c on 18c blue .40 .25

Issued for United Nations Day, Oct. 24.

Maria Cristina Falls — A142

1959, Nov. 18 Photo. *Perf. 13½*

807 A142 6c vio & dp yel grn .25 .25
a. Perf 12 2.00 1.10
808 A142 30c green & brown .75 .30
a. Perf 12 6.25 4.75

No. 504 Surcharged with New Value and Bars

1959 Engr. *Perf. 12*

809 A78 1c on 4c blk brn .35 .25

Manila Atheneum Emblem — A143

1959, Dec. 10 *Perf. 13½*

810 A143 6c ultra .25 .25
a. Perf 12 1.25 1.25
811 A143 30c rose red .55 .30
a. Perf 12 6.25 4.75

Centenary of the Manila Atheneum (Ateneo de Manila), a school, and to mark a century of progress in education.

Manuel Quezon — A144

José Rizal — A145

1959-60 Engr. *Perf. 13*

812 A144 1c olive gray ('60) .30 .25

Perf. 14x12

813 A145 6c gray blue .40 .25

For overprint see No. O62.

A146

Perf. 12½x13½

1960 Unwmk. Photo.

814 A146 6c brown & gold .65 .25

25th anniversary of the Philippine Constitution. See No. C82.

Site of Manila Pact A147

1960 Engr. *Perf. 12½*

815 A147 6c emerald .25 .25
816 A147 25c orange .40 .25

5th anniversary (in 1959) of the Congress of the Philippines establishing the South-East Asia Treaty Organization (SEATO).
For overprints see Nos. 841-842.

Sunset at Manila Bay and Uprooted Oak Emblem — A148

1960, Apr. 7 Photo. *Perf. 13½*

817 A148 6c multicolored .30 .25
818 A148 25c multicolored .70 .25

World Refugee Year, 7/1/59-6/30/60.

A149

1960, July 29 *Perf. 13½*

819 A149 5c lt grn, red & gold .30 .25
820 A149 6c bl, red & gold .30 .25

Philippine Tuberculosis Society, 50th anniv.

Basketball — A150

1960, Nov. 30 *Perf. 13x13½*

821 A150 6c shown .35 .25
822 A150 10c Runner .50 .25
Nos. 821-822,C85-C86 (4) 2.35 1.55

17th Olympic Games, Rome, 8/25-9/11.

Presidents Eisenhower and Garcia and Presidential Seals — A151

1960, Dec. 30 *Perf. 13½*

823 A151 6c multi .25 .25
824 A151 20c ultra, red & yel .60 .25

Visit of Pres. Dwight D. Eisenhower to the Philippines, June 14, 1960.

Nos. 539, 616, 619, 553, 606 and 598 Surcharged with New Values and Bars in Red or Black

1960-61 Engr. *Perf. 12, 13, 12½*

825 A96 1c on 18c dp bl (R) .30 .25
826 A121 5c on 18c dp bl (R) .55 .25
827 A123 5c on 18c dp car rose .55 .25
828 A101 10c on 18c ultra (R) .55 .25
829 A119 10c on 18c dp bl & org (R) .55 .25
830 A117 20c on 25c yel grn ('61) .55 .25
Nos. 825-830 (6) 3.05 1.50

On No. 830, no bars are overprinted, the surcharge "20 20" serving to cancel the old denomination.

Mercury and Globe — A152

1961, Jan. 23 Photo. *Perf. 13½*

831 A152 6c red brn, bl, blk & gold .95 .25

Manila Postal Conf., Jan. 10-23. See #C87.

Nos. B10, B11 and B11a Surcharged "2nd National Boy Scout Jamboree Pasonanca Park" and New Value in Black or Red

1961, May 2 Engr. *Perf. 13*

Yellow Paper

832 SP8 10c on 6c + 4c car .35 .25
833 SP8 30c on 25c + 5c bl (R) .55 .50
a. Tete beche, *wht* (10c on 6c + 4c & 30c on 25c + 5c) (Bk) 1.25 *3.00*

Second National Boy Scout Jamboree, Pasonanca Park, Zamboanga City.

De la Salle College, Manila A153

1961, June 16 Photo. *Perf. 11½*

834 A153 6c multi .25 .25
835 A153 10c multi .25 .25

De la Salle College, Manila, 50th anniv.

José Rizal as Student A154

6c, Rizal & birthplace at Calamba, Laguna. 10c, Rizal & parents. 20c, Rizal with Juan Luna & F. R. Hidalgo in Madrid. 30c, Rizal's execution.

1961 Unwmk. *Perf. 13½*

836 A154 5c multi .25 .25
837 A154 6c multi .25 .25
838 A154 10c grn & red brn .25 .25
839 A154 20c brn red & grnsh bl .30 .25
840 A154 30c vio, lil & org brn .50 .30
Nos. 836-840 (5) 1.55 1.30

Centenary of the birth of José Rizal.

Nos. 815-816 Overprinted

1961, July 4 Engr. *Perf. 12½*

841 A147 6c emerald .25 .25
842 A147 25c orange .30 .25

15th anniversary of the Republic.

Colombo Plan Emblem and Globe Showing Member Countries — A155

1961, Oct. 8 Photo. *Perf. 13x11½*

843 A155 5c multi .25 .25
844 A155 6c multi .25 .25

7th anniversary of the admission of the Philippines to the Colombo Plan.

Government Clerk — A156

1961, Dec. 9 Unwmk. *Perf. 12½*

845 A156 6c vio, bl & red .25 .25
846 A156 10c gray bl & red .50 .25

Honoring Philippine government employees.

No. C83 Surcharged

1961, Nov. 30 Engr. *Perf. 14x14½*

847 AP11 6c on 10c car .35 .25

Philippine Amateur Athletic Fed., 50th anniv.

No. 655 Surcharged with New Value and: "MACAPAGAL-PELAEZ INAUGURATION DEC. 30, 1961"

1961, Dec. 30 *Perf. 12½*

848 A139 6c on 25c pur .35 .25

Inauguration of Pres. Diosdado Macapagal and Vice-Pres. Emanuel Pelaez.

No. B8 Surcharged

1962, Jan. 23 Photo. *Perf. 13½x13*

849 SP7 6c on 5c grn & red .50 .25

Vanda Orchids — A157

Orchids: 6c, White mariposa. 10c, Sander's dendrobe. 20c, Sanggumay.

1962, Mar. 9 Photo. *Perf. 13½x14*

Dark Blue Background

850 5c rose, grn & yel .60 .25
851 6c grn & yel .60 .25
852 10c grn, car & brn .60 .25
853 20c lil, brn & grn .60 .25
a. A157 Block of 4, #850-853 2.50 2.25
b. As "a," imperf. 4.50 3.00

Apolinario Mabini — A158

Portraits: 1s, Manuel L. Quezon. 5s, Marcelo H. del Pilar. No. 857, José Rizal. No. 857A, Rizal (wearing shirt). 10s, Father José Burgos. 20s, Lapu-Lapu. 30s, Rajah Soliman. 50s, Cayetano Arellano. 70s, Sergio Osmena. No. 863, Emilio Jacinto. No. 864, José M. Panganiban.

Perf. 13½; 14 (1s); 13x12 (#857, 10s)

1962-69 Engr. Unwmk.

854 A158 1s org brn ('63) .25 .25
855 A158 3s rose red .25 .25
856 A158 5s car rose ('63) .25 .25
857 A158 6s dk red brn .25 .25
857A A158 6s pck bl ('64) .25 .25
858 A158 10s brt pur ('63) .25 .25
859 A158 20s Prus bl ('63) .30 .25
860 A158 30s vermilion .75 .25
861 A158 50s vio ('63) 1.00 .25
862 A158 70s brt bl ('63) 1.25 .25
863 A158 1p grn ('63) 3.00 .35
864 A158 1p dp org ('69) 2.00 .30
Nos. 854-864 (12) 9.80 3.15

For surcharges & overprints see #873-874, 946, 969, 1054, 1119, 1209, O63-O69.

Pres. Macapagal Taking Oath of Office — A159

1962 Photo. *Perf. 13½*
Vignette Multicolored

865 A159 6s blue .25 .25
866 A159 10s green .25 .25
867 A159 30s violet .50 .25
Nos. 865-867 (3) 1.00 .75

Swearing in of President Diosdado Macapagal, Dec. 30, 1961.

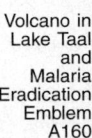

Volcano in Lake Taal and Malaria Eradication Emblem A160

1962, Oct. 24 Unwmk. *Perf. 11½*
Granite Paper

868 A160 6s multi .25 .25
869 A160 10s multi .25 .25
870 A160 70s multi 1.60 1.60
Nos. 868-870 (3) 2.10 2.10

Issued on UN Day for the WHO drive to eradicate malaria.

No. 598 Surcharged in Red

1962, Nov. 15 Engr. *Perf. 12*

871 A117 20s on 25c yel grn .50 .25

Issued to commemorate the bicentennial of the Diego Silang revolt in Ilocos Province.

No. B6 Overprinted with Sideways Chevron Obliterating Surtax

1962, Dec. 23 *Perf. 12*

872 SP6 5c on 5c + 1c dp bl .50 .25

Nos. 855, 857 Surcharged with New Value and Old Value Obliterated

1963 *Perf. 13½*

873 A158 1s on 3s rose red .25 .25

Perf. 13x12

874 A158 5s on 6s dk red brn .25 .25

No. 601 Surcharged

1963, June 12 *Perf. 12*

875 A117 6s on 2p vio .30 .25
876 A117 20s on 2p vio .45 .25
877 A117 70s on 2p vio .75 .30
Nos. 875-877 (3) 1.50 .80

Diego Silang Bicentennial Art and Philatelic Exhibition, ARPHEX, Manila, May 28-June 30.

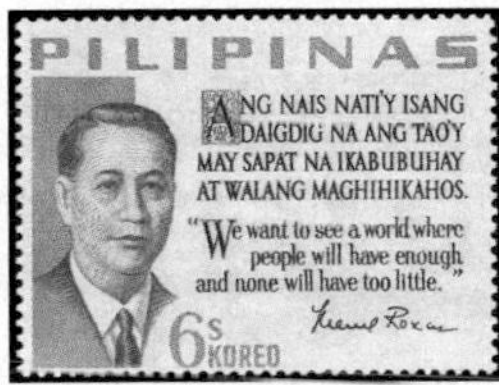

Pres. Manuel Roxas A161

1963-73 Engr. *Perf. 13½*

878 A161 6s brt bl & blk, *bluish* .35 .25
879 A161 30s brn & blk, *brownish* .80 .25

Pres. Ramon Magsaysay

880 A161 6s lil & blk .35 .25
881 A161 30s yel grn & blk .80 .25

Pres. Elpidio Quirino

882 A161 6s grn & blk ('65) .35 .25
883 A161 30s rose lil & blk ('65) .80 .25

Gen. (Pres.) Emilio Aguinaldo

883A A161 6s dp cl & blk ('66) .35 .25
883B A161 30s bl & blk ('66) .80 .25

Pres. José P. Laurel

883C A161 6s red brn & blk ('66) .35 .25
883D A161 30s bl & blk ('66) .55 .25

Pres. Manuel L. Quezon

883E A161 10s bl gray & blk ('67) .35 .25
883F A161 30s vio & blk ('67) .55 .25

Pres. Sergio Osmeña

883G A161 10s rose lil & blk ('70) .35 .25
883H A161 40s grn & blk ('70) .70 .25

Pres. Carlos P. Garcia

883I A161 10s buff & blk ('73) .35 .25
883J A161 30s pink & blk ('73) .80 .25
Nos. 878-883J (16) 8.60 4.00

Nos. 878-883J honor former presidents.
For surcharges see Nos. 984-985, 1120, 1146, 1160-1161.

Globe, Flags of Thailand, Korea, China, Philippines — A162

1963, Aug. 26 Photo. *Perf. 13½x13*

884 A162 6s dk grn & multi .25 .25
885 A162 20s dk grn & multi .35 .25

Asian-Oceanic Postal Union, 1st anniv.
For surcharge see No. 1078.

Red Cross Centenary Emblem — A163

1963, Sept. 1 *Perf. 11½*

886 A163 5s lt vio, gray & red .30 .25
887 A163 6s ultra, gray & red .30 .25
888 A163 20s grn, gray & red .30 .25
Nos. 886-888 (3) .90 .75

Centenary of the International Red Cross.

Bamboo Dance — A164

Folk Dances: 6s, Dance with oil lamps. 10s, Duck dance. 20s, Princess Gandingan's rock dance.

1963, Sept. 15 Unwmk. *Perf. 14*

889 5s multi .40 .25
890 6s multi .40 .25
891 10s multi .40 .25
892 20s multi .40 .25
a. A164 Block of 4, #889-892 2.25 1.75

For surcharges and overprints see #1043-1046.

Pres. Macapagal and Filipino Family — A165

1963, Sept. 28 *Perf. 14*

893 A165 5s bl & multi .25 .25
894 A165 6s yel & multi .25 .25
895 A165 20s lil & multi .40 .25
Nos. 893-895 (3) .90 .75

Issued to publicize Pres. Macapagal's 5-year Socioeconomic Program.
For surcharge see No. 1181.

Presidents Lopez Mateos and Macapagal — A166

1963, Sept. 28 Photo. *Perf. 13½*

896 A166 6s multi .25 .25
897 A166 30s multi .50 .25

Visit of Pres. Adolfo Lopez Mateos of Mexico to the Philippines.
For surcharge see No. 1166.

Andres Bonifacio — A167

1963, Nov. 30 Unwmk. *Perf. 12*

898 A167 5s gold, brn, gray & red .25 .25
899 A167 6s sil, brn, gray & red .35 .25
900 A167 25s brnz, brn, gray & red .50 .25
Nos. 898-900 (3) 1.10 .75

Centenary of the birth of Andres Bonifacio, national hero and poet.
For surcharges see Nos. 1147, 1162.

No. 534 Overprinted: "UN ADOPTION/DECLARATION OF HUMAN RIGHTS/15TH ANNIVERSARY DEC. 10, 1963"

1963, Dec. 10 Engr. *Imperf.*
Souvenir Sheet

901 A94 Sheet of 3 3.25 3.25

15th anniv. of the Universal Declaration of Human Rights.

Woman holding Sheaf of Rice — A168

1963, Dec. 20 Photo. *Perf. 13½x13*

902 A168 6s brn & multi .50 .25
Nos. 902,C88-C89 (3) 1.25 .80

FAO "Freedom from Hunger" campaign.

Bamboo Organ — A169

1964, May 4 *Perf. 13½*

903 A169 5s multi .25 .25
904 A169 6s multi .25 .25
905 A169 20s multi .50 .25
Nos. 903-905 (3) 1.00 .75

The bamboo organ in the Church of Las Pinas, Rizal, was built by Father Diego Cera, 1816-1822.
For surcharge see No. 1055.

Apolinario Mabini — A170

Wmk. 233

1964, July 23 Photo. *Perf. 14½*

906 A170 6s pur & gold .25 .25
907 A170 10s red brn & gold .25 .25
908 A170 30s brt grn & gold .30 .25
Nos. 906-908 (3) .80 .75

Apolinario Mabini (1864-1903), national hero and a leader of the 1898 revolution.
For surcharge see No. 1056.

Flags Surrounding SEATO Emblem — A171

Unwmk.

1964, Sept. 8 Photo. *Perf. 13*
Flags and Emblem Multicolored

909 A171 6s dk bl & yel .25 .25
910 A171 10s dp grn & yel .30 .25
911 A171 25s dk brn & yel .40 .25
Nos. 909-911 (3) .95 .75

10th anniversary of the South-East Asia Treaty Organization (SEATO).
For surcharge see No. 1121.

Pres. Macapagal Signing Code — A172

1964, Dec. 21 Wmk. 233 *Perf. 14½*

912 A172 3s multi .45 .25
913 A172 6s multi .45 .25
Nos. 912-913,C90 (3) 1.40 .75

Signing of the Agricultural Land Reform Code. For surcharges see Nos. 970, 1234.

Basketball — A173

Sport: 10s, Women's relay race. 20s, Hurdling. 30s, Soccer.

1964, Dec. 28 *Perf. 14½x14*

915 A173 6s lt bl, dk brn & gold .25 1.25
916 A173 10s gold, pink & dk brn .25 1.25
b. Gold omitted

917 A173 20s gold, dk brn & yel .45 .25
918 A173 30s emer, dk brn & gold .60 .25
Nos. 915-918 (4) 1.55 3.00

18th Olympic Games, Tokyo, Oct. 10-25.
For overprints and surcharge see Nos. 962-965, 1079.

Imperf., Pairs

915a A173 6s 1.25 1.25
916a A173 10s 1.25 1.25
917a A173 20s 2.75 1.75
918a A173 30s 2.75 1.75
Nos. 915a-918a (4) 8.00 6.00

Presidents Lubke and Macapagal and Coats of Arms — A174

1965, Apr. 19 Unwmk. *Perf. 13½*

919 A174 6s ol grn & multi .25 .25
920 A174 10s multi .30 .25
921 A174 25s dp bl & multi .40 .25
Nos. 919-921 (3) .95 .75

Visit of Pres. Heinrich Lubke of Germany, Nov. 18-23, 1964.
For surcharge see No. 1167.

Emblems of Manila Observatory and Weather Bureau — A175

1965, May 22 Photo. *Perf. 13½*

922 A175 6s lt ultra & multi .25 .25
923 A175 20s lt vio & multi .30 .25
924 A175 50s bl grn & multi .40 .25
Nos. 922-924 (3) .95 .75

Issued to commemorate the centenary of the Meteorological Service in the Philippines.
For surcharge see No. 1069.

Pres. John F. Kennedy (1917-63) — A176

Perf. 14½x14

1965, May 29 Wmk. 233

Center Multicolored

925 A176 6s gray .25 .25
926 A176 10s brt vio .30 .25
927 A176 30s ultra .40 .25
Nos. 925-927 (3) .95 .75

Nos. 925-927 exist with ultramarine of tie omitted.
The 6s and 30s exist imperf. Value, each $30.
For surcharges see Nos. 1148, 1210.

King and Queen of Thailand, Pres. and Mrs. Macapagal — A177

Perf. 12½x13

1965, June 12 Unwmk.

928 A177 2s brt bl & multi .25 .25
929 A177 6s bis & multi .30 .25
930 A177 30s red & multi .40 .25
Nos. 928-930 (3) .95 .75

Visit of King Bhumibol Adulyadej and Queen Sirikit of Thailand, July 1963.

For surcharge see No. 1122.

Princess Beatrix and Evangelina Macapagal A178

Perf. 13x12½

1965, July 4 Photo. Unwmk.

931 A178 2s bl & multi .25 .25
932 A178 6s blk & multi .25 .25
933 A178 10s multi .35 .25
Nos. 931-933 (3) .85 .75

Visit of Princess Beatrix of the Netherlands, Nov. 21-23, 1962.
For surcharge see No. 1188.

Map of Philippines, Cross and Legaspi-Urdaneta Monument — A179

Design: 3s, Cross and Rosary held before map of Philippines.

1965, Oct. 4 Unwmk. *Perf. 13*

934 A179 3s multi .25 .25
935 A179 6s multi .25 .25
Nos. 934-935,C91-C92 (4) 2.00 1.10

400th anniv. of the Christianization of the Philippines. See souvenir sheet No. C92a. For overprint see No. C108.

Presidents Sukarno and Macapagal and Prime Minister Tunku Abdul Rahman A180

1965, Nov. 25 *Perf. 13*

936 A180 6s multi .25 .25
937 A180 10s multi .30 .25
938 A180 25s multi .40 .25
Nos. 936-938 (3) .95 .75

Signing of the Manila Accord (Mapilindo) by Malaya, Philippines and Indonesia.
For surcharge see No. 1182.

Bicyclists and Globe A181

1965, Dec. 5 *Perf. 13½*

939 A181 6s multi .25 .25
940 A181 10s multi .30 .25
941 A181 25s multi .40 .25
Nos. 939-941 (3) .95 .75

Second Asian Cycling Championship, Philippines, Nov. 28-Dec. 5.

Nos. B21-B22 Surcharged

1965, Dec. 30 Engr. *Perf. 13*

942 SP12 10s on 6s + 4s .30 .25
943 SP12 30s on 30s + 5s .45 .25

Inauguration of President Ferdinand Marcos and Vice-President Fernando Lopez.

Antonio Regidor — A182

1966, Jan. 21 *Perf. 12x11*

944 A182 6s blue .25 .25
945 A182 30s brown .35 .25

Dr. Antonio Regidor, Sec. of the High Court of Manila and Pres. of Public Instruction.
For surcharges see Nos. 1110-1111.

No. 857A Overprinted in Red

1966, May 1 Engr. *Perf. 13½*

946 A158 6s peacock blue .35 .25

Anti-smuggling drive.
Exists with overprint inverted, double, double inverted and double with one inverted.
For surcharge see No. 1209.

Girl Scout Giving Scout Sign A183

1966, May 26 Litho. *Perf. 13x12½*

947 A183 3s ultra & multi .25 .25
948 A183 6s emer & multi .25 .25
949 A183 20s brn & multi .35 .25
Nos. 947-949 (3) .85 .75

Philippine Girl Scouts, 25th anniversary.
For surcharge see No. 1019.

Pres. Marcos Taking Oath of Office — A184

1966, June 12 *Perf. 12½*

950 A184 6s bl & multi .25 .25
951 A184 20s emer & multi .30 .25
952 A184 30s yel & multi .40 .25
Nos. 950-952 (3) .95 .75

Inauguration of Pres. Ferdinand E. Marcos, 12/30/65.
For overprints & surcharge see #960-961, 1050.

Seal of Manila and Historical Scenes — A185

1966, June 24

953 A185 6s multi .25 .25
954 A185 30s multi .35 .25

Adoption of the new seal of Manila.
For surcharges see Nos. 1070, 1118, 1235.

Old and New Philippine National Bank Buildings — A186

Designs: 6s, Entrance to old bank building and 1p silver coin.

1966, July 22 Photo. *Perf. 14x13½*

955 A186 6s gold, ultra, sil & blk .25 .25
956 A186 10s multi .35 .25

50th anniv. of the Philippine Natl. Bank. See #C93. For surcharges see #1071, 1100, 1236.

Post Office, Annex Three A187

1966, Oct. 1 Wmk. 233 *Perf. 14½*

957 A187 6s lt vio, yel & grn .25 .25
958 A187 10s rose cl, yel & grn .30 .25
959 A187 20s ultra, yel & grn .35 .25
Nos. 957-959 (3) .90 .75

60th anniversary of Postal Savings Bank.
For surcharges see Nos. 1104, 1112, 1189.

Nos. 950 and 952 Overprinted in Emerald or Black

Perf. 12½

1966, Oct. 24 Litho. Unwmk.

960 A184 6s multi (E) .25 .25
961 A184 30s multi .35 .25

Manila Summit Conference, Oct. 23-27.

Nos. 915a-918a Overprinted

Wmk. 233

1967, Jan. 14 Photo. *Imperf.*

962 A173 6s lt bl, dk brn & gold .35 .25
963 A173 10s gold, dk brn & pink .35 .25
964 A173 20s gold, dk brn & yel .45 .25
965 A173 30s emer, dk brn & gold .60 .40
Nos. 962-965 (4) 1.75 1.15

Lions Intl., 50th anniv. The Lions emblem is in the lower left corner on the 6s, in the upper left corner on the 10s and in the upper right corner on the 30s.

"Succor" by Fernando Amorsolo — A188

Unwmk.

1967, May 15 Litho. *Perf. 14*

966 A188 5s sepia & multi .40 .25
967 A188 20s blue & multi .85 .25
968 A188 2p green & multi 1.75 .60
Nos. 966-968 (3) 3.00 1.10

25th anniversary of the Battle of Bataan.

Nos. 857A and 913 Surcharged

1967, Aug. Engr. *Perf. 13½*

969 A158 4s on 6s pck bl .25 .25

Wmk. 233

Photo. *Perf. 14½*

970 A172 5s on 6s multi .35 .25

Issue dates: 4s, Aug. 10; 5s, Aug. 7.

Gen. Douglas MacArthur and Paratroopers Landing on Corregidor — A189

Unwmk.

1967, Aug. 31 Litho. *Perf. 14*

971 A189 6s multi .35 .25
972 A189 5p multi 5.75 3.00

25th anniversary, Battle of Corregidor.

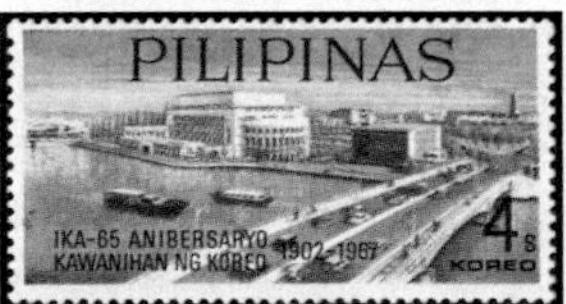

Bureau of Posts, Manila, Jones Bridge over Pasig River — A190

1967, Sept. 15 Litho. *Perf. 14x13½*

973 A190 4s multi & blk .25 .25
974 A190 20s multi & red .40 .25
975 A190 50s multi & vio .55 .30
Nos. 973-975 (3) 1.20 .80

65th anniversary of the Bureau of Posts. For overprint see No. 1015.

Philippine Nativity Scene — A191

1967, Dec. 1 Photo. *Perf. 13½*

976 A191 10s multi .30 .25
977 A191 40s multi .45 .30

Christmas 1967.

Chinese Garden, Rizal Park, Presidents Marcos and Chiang Kai-shek — A192

Presidents' heads & scenes in Chinese Garden, Rizal Park, Manila: 10s, Gate. 20s, Landing pier.

1967-68 Photo. *Perf. 13½*

978 A192 5s multi .25 .25
979 A192 10s multi ('68) .35 .25
980 A192 20s multi .70 .25
Nos. 978-980 (3) 1.30 .75

Sino-Philippine Friendship Year 1966-67.

Makati Center Post Office, Mrs. Marcos and Rotary Emblem — A193

1968, Jan. 9 Litho. *Perf. 14*

981 A193 10s bl & multi .25 .25
982 A193 20s grn & multi .30 .25
983 A193 40s multi .50 .35
Nos. 981-983 (3) 1.05 .85

1st anniv. of the Makati Center Post Office.

Nos. 882, 883C and B27 Surcharged

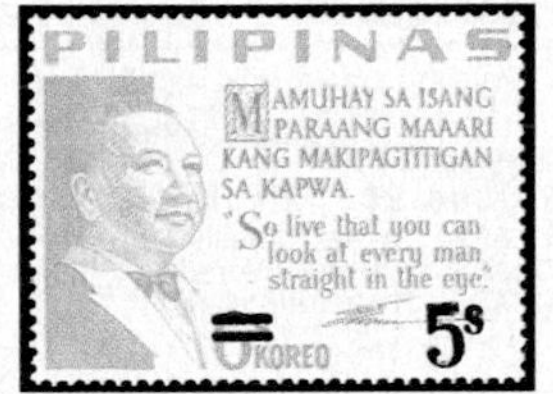

1968

984 A161 5s on 6s grn & blk .55 .25
985 A161 5s on 6s lt red brn & blk .55 .25
986 SP14 10s on 6s + 5s ultra & red .65 .25
Nos. 984-986 (3) 1.75 .75

The "1" in the surcharged value on No. 986 is serifed. For surcharge without serif on "1," see No. 1586.

Felipe G. Calderon, Barasoain Church and Malolos Constitution — A194

1968, Apr. 4 Litho. *Perf. 14*

987 A194 10s lt ultra & multi .25 .25
988 A194 40s grn & multi .60 .25
989 A194 75s multi 1.10 .60
Nos. 987-989 (3) 1.95 1.10

Calderon (1868-1909), lawyer and author of the Malolos Constitution.

Earth and Transmission from Philippine Station to Satellite — A195

1968, Oct. 21 Photo. *Perf. 13½*

990 A195 10s blk & multi .30 .25
991 A195 40s multi .60 .25
992 A195 75s multi 1.10 .30
Nos. 990-992 (3) 2.00 .80

Issued to commemorate the inauguration of the Philcomsat Station in Tany, Luzon, May 2, 1968.

Tobacco Industry and Tobacco Board's Emblem — A196

1968, Nov. 15 Photo. *Perf. 13½*

993 A196 10s blk & multi .25 .25
994 A196 40s bl & multi .65 .50
995 A196 70s crim & multi 1.10 .90
Nos. 993-995 (3) 2.00 1.65

Philippine tobacco industry.

Kudyapi A197

Philippine Musical Instruments: 20s, Ludag (drum). 30s, Kulintangan. 50s, Subing (bamboo flute).

1968, Nov. 22 Photo. *Perf. 13½*

996 A197 10s multi .25 .25
997 A197 20s multi .30 .25
998 A197 30s multi .50 .25
999 A197 50s multi .75 .45
Nos. 996-999 (4) 1.80 1.20

Concordia College A198

1968, Dec. 8 *Perf. 13x13½*

1000 A198 10s multi .25 .25
1001 A198 20s multi .35 .25
1002 A198 70s multi .65 .30
Nos. 1000-1002 (3) 1.25 .80

Centenary of the Colegio de la Concordia, Manila, a Catholic women's school. Issued Dec. 8 (Sunday), but entered the mail Dec. 9.

Singing Children — A199

1968, Dec. 16 *Perf. 13½*

1003 A199 10s multi .25 .25
1004 A199 40s multi .60 .45
1005 A199 75s multi 1.10 .80
Nos. 1003-1005 (3) 1.95 1.50

Christmas 1968.

Animals A200

1969, Jan. 8 Photo. *Perf. 13½*

1006 A200 2s Tarsier .25 .25
1007 A200 10s Tamarau .30 .25
1008 A200 20s Carabao .60 .25
1009 A200 75s Mouse deer 1.90 .75
Nos. 1006-1009 (4) 3.05 1.50

Opening of the hunting season.

Emilio Aguinaldo and Historical Building, Cavite — A201

1969, Jan. 23 Litho. *Perf. 14*

1010 A201 10s yel & multi .25 .25
1011 A201 40s bl & multi .65 .30
1012 A201 70s multi 1.00 .70
Nos. 1010-1012 (3) 1.90 1.25

Emilio Aguinaldo (1869-1964), commander of Filipino forces in rebellion against Spain.

Guard Turret, San Andres Bastion, Manila, and Rotary Emblem — A202

1969, Jan. 29 Photo. *Perf. 12½*

1013 A202 10s ultra & multi .50 .25
Nos. 1013,C96-C97 (3) 1.75 .90

50th anniv. of the Manila Rotary Club.

Senator Claro M. Recto (1890-1960), Lawyer and Supreme Court Judge — A203

1969, Feb. 10 Engr. *Perf. 13*

1014 A203 10s bright rose lilac .35 .25

No. 973 Overprinted

1969, Feb. 14 Litho. *Perf. 14x13½*

1015 A190 4s multi & blk .35 .25

Philatelic Week, Nov. 24-30, 1968.

José Rizal College, Mandaluyong — A204

1969, Feb. 19 Photo. *Perf. 13*

1016 A204 10s multicolored .25 .25
1017 A204 40s multicolored .45 .25
1018 A204 50s multicolored .95 .30
Nos. 1016-1018 (3) 1.65 .80

Founding of Rizal College, 50th anniv.

No. 948 Surcharged in Red

1969, May 12 Litho. *Perf. 13x12½*

1019 A183 5s on 6s multi .35 .25

A205

Map of Philippines, Red Crescent, Cross, Lion and Sun emblems.

1969, May 26 Photo. Perf. 12½

1020	A205	10s gray, ultra & red	.25	.25
1021	A205	40s lt ultra, dk bl & red	.45	.30
1022	A205	75s bister, brn & red	.85	.35
		Nos. 1020-1022 (3)	1.55	.90

League of Red Cross Societies, 50th anniv.

A206

Pres. and Mrs. Marcos harvesting miracle rice.

1969, June 13 Photo. Perf. 14

1023	A206	10s multicolored	.25	.25
1024	A206	40s multicolored	.45	.30
1025	A206	75s multicolored	.85	.35
		Nos. 1023-1025 (3)	1.55	.90

Introduction of IR8 (miracle) rice, produced by the International Rice Research Institute.

Holy Child of Leyte and Map of Leyte — A207

1969, June 30 Perf. 13½

1026	A207	5s emerald & multi	.25	.25
1027	A207	10s crimson & multi	.35	.25

80th anniv. of the return of the image of the Holy Child of Leyte to Tacloban. See No. C98.

Philippine Development Bank — A208

1969, Sept. 12 Photo. Perf. 13½

1028	A208	10s dk bl, blk & grn	.25	.25
1029	A208	40s rose car, blk & grn	.80	.45
1030	A208	75s brown, blk & grn	1.40	.55
		Nos. 1028-1030 (3)	2.45	1.25

Inauguration of the new building of the Philippine Development Bank in Makati, Rizal.

Common Birdwing A209

Butterflies: 20s, Tailed jay. 30s, Red Helen. 40s, Birdwing.

1969, Sept. 15 Photo. Perf. 13½

1031	A209	10s multicolored	.60	.25
1032	A209	20s multicolored	1.40	.25
1033	A209	30s multicolored	1.25	.35
1034	A209	40s multicolored	1.25	.45
		Nos. 1031-1034 (4)	4.50	1.30

World's Children and UNICEF Emblem A210

1969, Oct. 6

1035	A210	10s blue & multi	.25	.25
1036	A210	20s multicolored	.30	.25
1037	A210	30s multicolored	.40	.25
		Nos. 1035-1037 (3)	.95	.75

15th anniversary of Universal Children's Day.

Monument and Leyte Landing — A211

1969, Oct. 20 Perf. 13½x14

1038	A211	5s lt grn & multi	.25	.25
1039	A211	10s yellow & multi	.30	.25
1040	A211	40s pink & multi	.40	.25
		Nos. 1038-1040 (3)	.95	.75

25th anniv. of the landing of the US forces under Gen. Douglas MacArthur on Leyte, Oct. 20, 1944.

Philippine Cultural Center, Manila — A212

1969, Nov. 4 Photo. Perf. 13½

1041	A212	10s ultra	.30	.25
1042	A212	30s brt rose lilac	.45	.25

Cultural Center of the Philippines, containing theaters, a museum and libraries.

Nos. 889-892 Surcharged or Overprinted: "1969 PHILATELIC WEEK"

1969, Nov. 24 Photo. Perf. 14

1043	A164	5s multicolored	.40	.25
1044	A164	5s on 6s multi	.40	.25
1045	A164	10s multicolored	.40	.25
1046	A164	10s on 20s multi	.40	.25
a.		Block of 4, #1043-1046	1.75	1.25

Philatelic Week, Nov. 23-29.

Melchora Aquino — A213

1969, Nov. 30 Perf. 12½

1047	A213	10s multicolored	.25	.25
1048	A213	20s multicolored	.30	.25
1049	A213	30s dk bl & multi	.40	.25
		Nos. 1047-1049 (3)	.95	.75

Melchora Aquino (Tandang Sora; 1812-1919), the Grand Old Woman of the Revolution.

No. 950 Surcharged with New Value, 2 Bars and: "PASINAYA, IKA -2 PANUNUNGKULAN / PANGULONG FERDINAND E. MARCOS / DISYEMBRE 30, 1969"

1969, Dec. 30 Litho. Perf. 12½

1050	A184	5s on 6s multi	.55	.25

Inauguration of Pres. Marcos and Vice Pres. Fernando Lopez for 2nd term, 12/30.

Pouring Ladle and Iligan Steel Mills — A214

1970, Jan. 20 Photo. Perf. 13½

1051	A214	10s ver & multi	.25	.25
1052	A214	20s multicolored	.45	.25
1053	A214	30s ultra & multi	.55	.25
		Nos. 1051-1053 (3)	1.25	.75

Iligan Integrated Steel Mills, Northern Mindanao, the first Philippine steel mills.

Nos. 857A, 904 and 906 Surcharged with New Value and Two Bars

1970, Apr. 30 As Before

1054	A158	4s on 6s peacock bl	.50	.25
1055	A169	5s on 6s multi	.75	.25
1056	A170	5s on 6s pur & gold	.75	.25
		Nos. 1054-1056 (3)	2.00	.75

New UPU Headquarters and Monument, Bern — A215

Perf. 13½

1970, May 20 Unwmk. Photo.

1057	A215	10s bl, dk bl & yel	.30	.25
1058	A215	30s lt grn, dk bl & yel	.45	.25

Opening of the new UPU Headquarters in Bern.

Emblem, Mayon Volcano and Filipina — A216

1970, Sept. 6 Photo. Perf. 13½x14

1059	A216	10s brt blue & multi	.25	.25
1060	A216	20s multicolored	.35	.25
1061	A216	30s multicolored	.50	.25
		Nos. 1059-1061 (3)	1.10	.75

15th International Conference on Social Welfare, Manila, Sept. 6-12.

Crab, by Alexander Calder, and Map of Philippines A217

1970, Oct. 5 Perf. 13x13½

1062	A217	10s emerald & multi	.25	.25
1063	A217	40s multicolored	.45	.25
1064	A217	50s ultra & multi	.60	.45
		Nos. 1062-1064 (3)	1.30	.95

Campaign against cancer.

Scaled Tridacna A218

Sea Shells: 10s, Royal spiny oyster. 20s, Venus comb. 40s, Glory of the sea.

1970, Oct. 19 Photo. Perf. 13½

1065	A218	5s black & multi	.45	.25
1066	A218	10s dk grn & multi	1.00	.25
1067	A218	20s multicolored	.85	.25
1068	A218	40s dk blue & multi	1.60	.35
		Nos. 1065-1068 (4)	3.90	1.10

Nos. 922, 953 and 955 Surcharged

Photogravure; Lithographed

1970, Oct. 26 Perf. 13½, 12½

1069	A175	4s on 6s multi	.70	.25
1070	A185	4s on 6s multi	1.10	.25
1071	A186	4s on 6s multi	1.10	.25
		Nos. 1069-1071 (3)	2.90	.75

On No. 1070, old denomination is obliterated by two bars.

One line surcharge on No. 1071.

Map of Philippines and FAPA Emblem — A219

1970, Nov. 16 Photo. Perf. 13½

1072	A219	10s dp org & multi	.25	.25
1073	A219	50s lt violet & multi	.70	.25

Opening of the 4th General Assembly of the Federation of Asian Pharmaceutical Assoc. (FAPA) & the 3rd Asian Cong. of Pharmaceutical Sciences.

Hundred Islands of Pangasinan, Peddler's Cart — A220

20s, Tree house in Pasonanca Park, Zamboanga City. 30s, Sugar industry, Negros Island, Mt. Kanlaon, Woman & Carabao statue, symbolizing agriculture. 2p, Miagao Church, Iloilo, & horse-drawn calesa.

1970, Nov. 12 Perf. 12½x13½

1074	A220	10s multicolored	.25	.25
1075	A220	20s multicolored	.30	.25
1076	A220	30s multicolored	.75	.25
1077	A220	2p multicolored	2.50	1.00
		Nos. 1074-1077 (4)	3.80	1.75

Tourist publicity. See Nos. 1086-1097.

No. 884 Surcharged: "UPU-AOPU / Regional Seminar / Nov. 23-Dec. 5, 1970 / TEN 10s"

1970, Nov. 22 Photo. ***Perf. 13½x13***
1078 A162 10s on 6s multi .50 .50

Universal Postal Union and Asian-Oceanic Postal Union Regional Seminar, 11/23-12/5.

No. 915 Surcharged Vertically: "1970 PHILATELIC WEEK"

Perf. 14½x14
1970, Nov. 22 **Wmk. 233**
1079 A173 10s on 6s multi .35 .25

Philatelic Week, Nov. 22-28.

Pope Paul VI, Map of Far East and Australia — A221

Perf. 13½x14
1970, Nov. 27 Photo. Unwmk.
1080 A221 10s ultra & multi .35 .25
1081 A221 30s multicolored .55 .25
Nos. 1080-1081,C99 (3) 1.70 .80

Visit of Pope Paul VI, Nov. 27-29, 1970.

Mariano Ponce — A222

1970, Dec. 30 Engr. ***Perf. 14½***
1082 A222 10s rose carmine .35 .25

Mariano Ponce (1863-1918), editor and legislator. See #1136-1137. For surcharges & overprint see #1190, 1231, O70.

PATA Emblem A223

1971, Jan. 21 Photo. ***Perf. 14½***
1083 A223 5s brt green & multi .30 .25
1084 A223 10s blue & multi .45 .25
1085 A223 70s brown & multi .75 .30
Nos. 1083-1085 (3) 1.50 .80

Pacific Travel Association (PATA), 20th annual conference, Manila, Jan. 21-29.

Tourist Type of 1970

Designs: 10s, Filipina and Ang Nayong (7 village replicas around man-made lagoon). 20s, Woman and fisherman, Estancia. 30s, Pagsanjan Falls. 5p, Watch Tower, Punta Cruz, Boho.

Perf. 12½x13½
1971, Feb. 15 **Photo.**
1086 A220 10s multicolored .35 .25
1087 A220 20s multicolored .35 .25
1088 A220 30s multicolored .90 .30
1089 A220 5p multicolored 3.50 1.75
Nos. 1086-1089 (4) 5.10 2.55

1971, Apr. 19

Designs: 10s, Cultured pearl farm, Davao. 20s, Coral divers, Davao, Mindanao. 40s, Moslem Mosque, Zamboanga. 1p, Rice terraces, Banaue.

1090 A220 10s multicolored .30 .25
1091 A220 20s multicolored .45 .25
1092 A220 40s multicolored 1.00 .25
1093 A220 1p multicolored 1.75 .40
Nos. 1090-1093 (4) 3.50 1.15

1971, May 3

10s, Spanish cannon, Zamboanga. 30s, Magellan's cross, Cebu City. 50s, Big Jar monument in Calamba, Laguna. 70s, Mayon Volcano, Legaspi.

1094 A220 10s multicolored .30 .25
1095 A220 30s multicolored .45 .25
1096 A220 50s multicolored 1.00 .25
1097 A220 70s multicolored 1.25 .35
Nos. 1094-1097 (4) 3.00 1.10

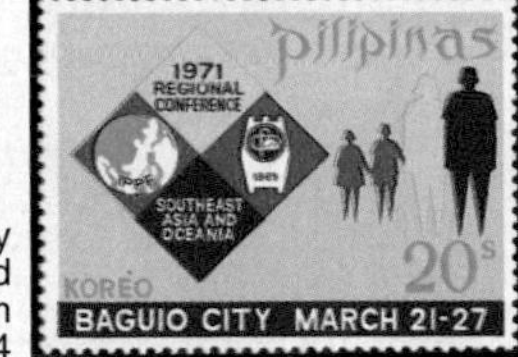

Family and Emblem A224

1971, Mar. 21 Photo. ***Perf. 13½***
1098 A224 20s lt grn & multi .25 .25
1099 A224 40s pink & multi .35 .25

Regional Conf. of the Intl. Planned Parenthood Federation for SE Asia & Oceania, Baguio City, Mar. 21-27.

No. 955 Surcharged

1971, June 10 Photo. ***Perf. 14x13½***
1100 A186 5s on 6s multi .60 .25

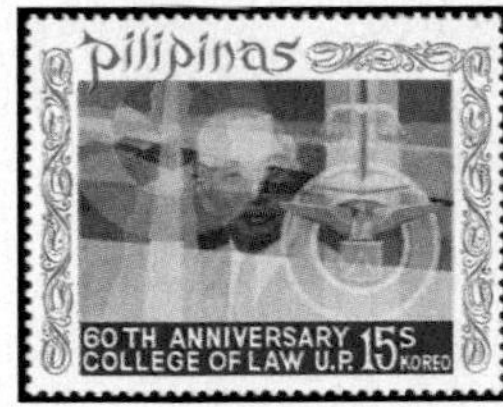

Allegory of Law A225

1971, June 15 Photo. ***Perf. 13***
1101 A225 15s orange & multi 1.50 .35

60th anniversary of the University of the Philippines Law College. See No. C100.

Manila Anniversary Emblem — A226

1971, June 24
1102 A226 10s multicolored 1.25 .35

Founding of Manila, 400th anniv. See #C101.

Santo Tomas University, Arms of Schools of Medicine and Pharmacology — A227

1971, July 8 Photo. ***Perf. 13½***
1103 A227 5s yellow & multi 1.50 .35

Centenary of the founding of the Schools of Medicine and Surgery, and Pharmacology at the University of Santo Tomas, Manila. See No. C102.

No. 957 Surcharged

1971, July 11 Wmk. 233 ***Perf. 14½***
1104 A187 5s on 6s multi .50 .25

World Congress of University Presidents, Manila.

Our Lady of Guia Appearing to Filipinos and Spanish Soldiers — A228

1971, July 8 Photo. ***Perf. 13½***
1105 A228 10s multi .25 .25
1106 A228 75s multi 1.00 .35

4th centenary of appearance of the statue of Our Lady of Guia, Ermita, Manila.

Bank Building, Plane, Car and Workers — A229

1971, Sept. 14 ***Perf. 12½***
1107 A229 10s blue & multi .30 .25
1108 A229 30s lt grn & multi .30 .25
1109 A229 1p multicolored .65 .30
Nos. 1107-1109 (3) 1.25 .80

1st Natl. City Bank in the Philippines, 70th anniv.

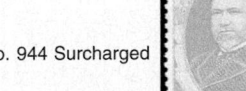

No. 944 Surcharged

Perf. 12x11
1971, Nov. 24 Engr. Unwmk.
1110 A182 4s on 6s blue .30 *.60*
1111 A182 5s on 6s blue .30 .25

No. 957 Surcharged

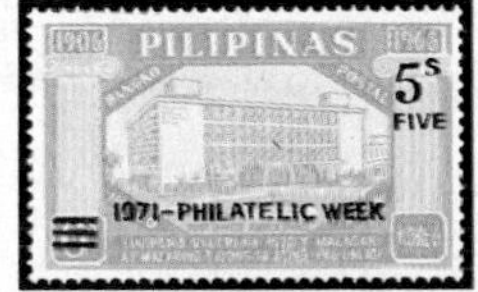

Wmk. 233
1971, Nov. 24 Photo. ***Perf. 14½***
1112 A187 5s on 6s multi .50 .25

Philatelic Week, 1971.

Radar with Map of Far East and Oceania — A230

1972, Feb. 29 Photo. ***Perf. 14x14½***
1113 A230 5s org yel & multi .30 .25
1114 A230 40s red org & multi .45 .25

Electronics Conferences, Manila, 12/1-7/71.

Fathers Gomez, Burgos and Zamora — A231

1972, Apr. 3 ***Perf. 13x12½***
1115 A231 5s gold & multi .35 .25
1116 A231 60s gold & multi .55 .25

Centenary of the deaths of Fathers Mariano Gomez, José Burgos and Jacinto Zamora, martyrs for Philippine independence from Spain.

Digestive Tract — A232

1972, Apr. 11 Photo. ***Perf. 12½x13***
1117 A232 20s ultra & multi .60 .25

4th Asian Pacific Congress of Gastroenterology, Manila, Feb. 5-12. See No. C103.

No. 953 Surcharged

1972, Apr. 20 ***Perf. 12½***
1118 A185 5s on 6s multi .90 .25

No. O69 with Two Bars over "G." and "O."

1972, May 16 Engr. ***Perf. 13½***
1119 A158 50s violet .90 .25

Nos. 883A, 909 and 929 Surcharged with New Value and 2 Bars

1972, May 29
1120 A161 10s on 6s dp cl & blk 1.10 .25
1121 A171 10s on 6s multi 1.10 .25
1122 A177 10s on 6s multi .90 .25
Nos. 1120-1122 (3) 3.10 .75

Independence Monument, Manila — A233

1972, May 31 Photo. *Perf. 13x12½*

1123 A233 5s brt blue & multi .25 .25
1124 A233 50s red & multi .80 .25
1125 A233 60s emerald & multi 1.10 .25
Nos. 1123-1125 (3) 2.15 .75

Visit ASEAN countries (Association of South East Asian Nations).

"K," Skull and Crossbones — A234

Development of Philippine Flag: No. 1126, 3 "K's" in a row ("K" stands for Katipunan). No. 1127, 3 "K's" as triangle. No. 1128, One "K." No. 1130, 3 "K's," sun over mountain on white triangle. No. 1131, Sun over 3 "K's." No. 1132, Tagalog "K" in sun. No. 1133, Sun with human face. No. 1134, Tricolor flag, forerunner of present flag. No. 1135, Present flag. Nos. 1126, 1128, 1130-1131, 1133, 1135 inscribed in Tagalog.

1972, June 12 Photo. *Perf. 13*

1126 A234 30s ultra & red 2.00 .30
1127 A234 30s ultra & red 2.00 .30
1128 A234 30s ultra & red 2.00 .30
1129 A234 30s ultra & blk 2.00 .30
1130 A234 30s ultra & red 2.00 .30
1131 A234 30s ultra & red 2.00 .30
1132 A234 30s ultra & red 2.00 .30
1133 A234 30s ultra & red 2.00 .30
1134 A234 30s ultra, red & blk 2.00 .30
1135 A234 30s ultra, yel & red 2.00 .30
a. Block of 10 25.00 10.00

Portrait Type of 1970

40s, Gen. Miguel Malvar. 1p, Julian Felipe.

1972 Engr. *Perf. 14*

1136 A222 40s rose red .40 .25
1137 A222 1p deep blue 1.00 .25

Honoring Gen. Miguel Malvar (1865-1911), revolutionary leader, and Julian Felipe (1861-1944), composer of Philippine national anthem.
Issue dates: 40s, July 10; 1p, June 26.

Parrotfish A235

1972, Aug. 14 Photo. *Perf. 13*

1138 A235 5s shown .35 .25
1139 A235 10s Sunburst butterflyfish 1.40 .25
1140 A235 20s Moorish idol 1.25 .25
Nos. 1138-1140,C104 (4) 4.60 1.20

Tropical fish.

Development Bank of the Philippines A236

1972, Sept. 12

1141 A236 10s gray blue & multi .25 .25
1142 A236 20s lilac & multi .30 .25
1143 A236 60s tan & multi .40 .25
Nos. 1141-1143 (3) .95 .75

Development Bank of the Philippines, 25th anniv.

Pope Paul VI A237

1972, Sept. 26 Unwmk. *Perf. 14*

1144 A237 10s lt green & multi .50 .25
1145 A237 50s lt violet & multi 1.00 .30
Nos. 1144-1145,C105 (3) 2.25 .90

First anniversary (in 1971) of the visit of Pope Paul VI to the Philippines, and for his 75th birthday.

Nos. 880, 899 and 925 Surcharged with New Value and 2 Bars

1972, Sept. 29 As Before

1146 A161 10s on 6s lil & blk 1.10 .25
1147 A167 10s on 6s multi 1.10 .25
1148 A176 10s on 6s multi .90 .25
Nos. 1146-1148 (3) 3.10 .75

Charon's Bark, by Resurrección Hidalgo — A238

Paintings: 10s, Rice Workers' Meal, by F. Amorsolo. 30s, "Spain and the Philippines," by Juan Luna, vert. 70s, Song of Maria Clara, by F. Amorsolo.

Perf. 14x13

1972, Oct. 16 Unwmk. Photo.

Size: 38x40mm

1149 A238 5s silver & multi .35 .25
1150 A238 10s silver & multi .35 .25

Size: 24x56mm

1151 A238 30s silver & multi .75 .25

Size: 38x40mm

1152 A238 70s silver & multi .75 .30
Nos. 1149-1152 (4) 2.20 1.05

25th anniversary of the organization of the Stamp and Philatelic Division.

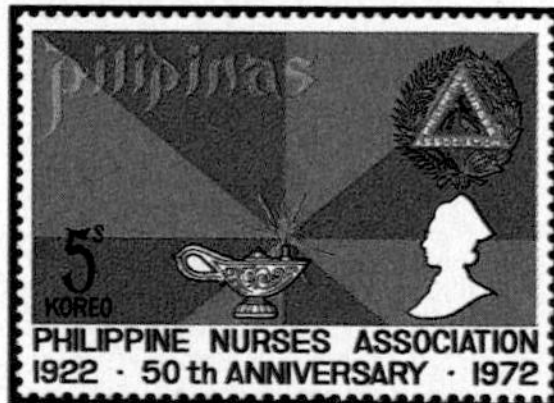

Lamp, Nurse, Emblem — A239

1972, Oct. 22 *Perf. 12½x13½*

1153 A239 5s violet & multi .25 .25
1154 A239 10s blue & multi .30 .25
1155 A239 70s orange & multi .40 .25
Nos. 1153-1155 (3) .95 .75

Philippine Nursing Association, 50th anniv.

Heart, Map of Philippines A240

1972, Oct. 24 *Perf. 13*

1156 A240 5s purple, emer & red .25 .25
1157 A240 10s blue, emer & red .30 .25
1158 A240 30s emerald, bl & red .40 .25
Nos. 1156-1158 (3) .95 .75

"Your heart is your health," World Health Month.

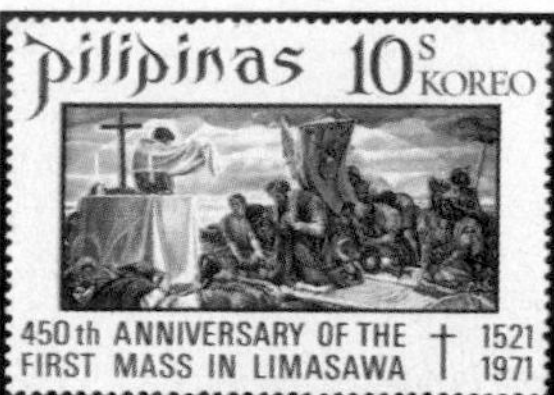

First Mass on Limasawa, by Carlos V. Francisco — A241

1972, Oct. 31 *Perf. 14*

1159 A241 10s brown & multi .90 .25

450th anniversary of the first mass in the Philippines, celebrated by Father Valderama on Limasawa, Mar. 31, 1521. See No. C106.

Nos. 878, 882, 899 Surcharged: "ASIA PACIFIC SCOUT CONFERENCE NOV. 1972"

1972, Nov. 13 As Before

1160 A161 10s on 6s bl & blk .85 .30
1161 A161 10s on 6s grn & blk 1.25 .30
1162 A167 10s on 6s multi 1.25 1.25
Nos. 1160-1162 (3) 3.35 1.85

Asia Pacific Scout Conference, Nov. 1972.

Torch, Olympic Emblems — A242

Perf. 12½x13½

1972, Nov. 15 Photo.

1163 A242 5s blue & multi .25 .25
1164 A242 10s multicolored .50 .25
1165 A242 70s orange & multi .90 .40
Nos. 1163-1165 (3) 1.65 .90

20th Olympic Games, Munich, 8/26-9/11.
For surcharges see Nos. 1297, 1758-1760.

Nos. 896 and 919 Surcharged with New Value, Two Bars and: "1972 PHILATELIC WEEK"

1972, Nov. 23 Photo. *Perf. 13½*

1166 A166 10s on 6s multi .50 *1.50*
1167 A174 10s on 6s multi .50 *1.50*

Philatelic Week 1972.

Manunggul Burial Jar, 890-710 B.C. — A243

#1169, Ngipet Duldug Cave ritual earthenware vessel, 155 B.C. #1170, Metal age chalice, 200-600 A.D. #1171, Earthenware vessel, 15th cent.

1972, Nov. 29

1168 A243 10s green & multi .40 .25
1169 A243 10s lilac & multi .40 .25
1170 A243 10s blue & multi .40 .25
1171 A243 10s yellow & multi .40 .25
Nos. 1168-1171 (4) 1.60 1.00

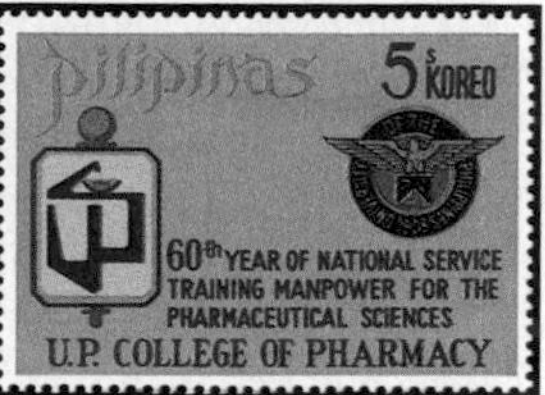

College of Pharmacy and Univ. of the Philippines Emblems — A244

1972, Dec. 11 *Perf. 12½x13½*

1172 A244 5s lt vio & multi .25 .25
1173 A244 10s yel grn & multi .25 .25
1174 A244 30s ultra & multi .40 .25
Nos. 1172-1174 (3) .90 .75

60th anniversary of the College of Pharmacy of the University of the Philippines.

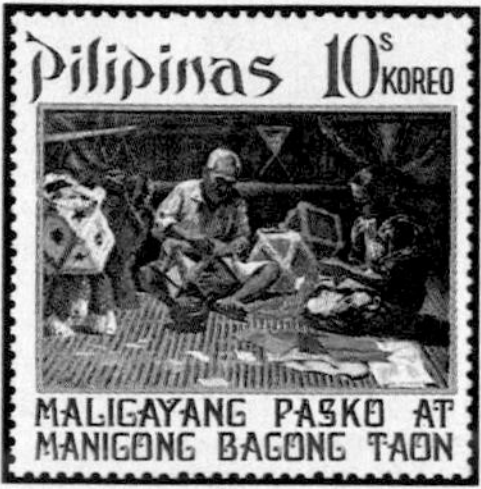

Christmas Lantern Makers, by Jorgé Pineda — A245

1972, Dec. 14 Photo. *Perf. 12½*

1175 A245 10s dk bl & multi .25 .25
1176 A245 30s brown & multi .50 .25
1177 A245 50s green & multi .75 .25
Nos. 1175-1177 (3) 1.50 .75

Christmas 1972.

Red Cross Flags, Pres. Roxas and Mrs. Aurora Quezon A246

1972, Dec. 21

1178 A246 5s ultra & multi .25 .25
1179 A246 20s multicolored .30 .25
1180 A246 30s brown & multi .40 .25
Nos. 1178-1180 (3) .95 .75

25th anniv. of the Philippine Red Cross.

Nos. 894 and 936 Surcharged with New Value and 2 Bars

1973, Jan. 22 Photo. *Perf. 14, 13*

1181 A165 10s on 6s multi .65 .25
1182 A180 10s on 6s multi .65 .25

San Luis University, Luzon — A247

1973, Mar. 1 Photo. *Perf. 13½x14*

1183 A247 5s multicolored .25 .25
1184 A247 10s yellow & multi .35 .25
1185 A247 75s multicolored .40 .25
Nos. 1183-1185 (3) 1.00 .75

60th anniversary of San Luis University, Baguio City, Luzon.
For surcharge see No. 1305.

Jesus Villamor and Fighter Planes — A248

1973, Apr. 9 Photo. *Perf. 13½x14*
1186 A248 10s multicolored .25 .25
1187 A248 2p multicolored 1.25 .70

Col. Jesus Villamor (1914-1971), World War II aviator who fought for liberation of the Philippines.
For surcharge see No. 1230.

Nos. 932, 957, O70 Surcharged with New Values and 2 Bars

1973, Apr. 23 As Before
1188 A178 5s on 6s multi 1.10 .50
1189 A187 5s on 6s multi 1.10 .50
1190 A222 15s on 10s rose car .80 .25
Nos. 1188-1190 (3) 3.00 1.25

Two additional bars through "G.O." on No. 1190.

ITI Emblem, Performance and Actor Vic Silayan — A249

1973, May 15 Photo. *Perf. 13x12½*
1191 A249 5s blue & multi .25 .25
1192 A249 10s yel grn & multi .25 .25
1193 A249 50s orange & multi .45 .25
1194 A249 70s rose & multi .60 .25
Nos. 1191-1194 (4) 1.55 1.00

1st Third World Theater Festival, sponsored by the UNESCO affiliated International Theater Institute, Manila, Nov. 19-30, 1971.
For surcharge see No. 1229.

Josefa Llanes Escoda — A250

#1196, Gabriela Silang. No. 1197, Rafael Palma. 30s, Jose Rizal. 60s, Marcela Agoncillo. 90s, Teodoro R. Yangco. 1.10p, Dr. Pio Valenzuela. 1.20p, Gregoria de Jesus. #1204, Pedro A. Paterno. #1205, Teodora Alonso. 1.80p, Edilberto Evangelista. 5p, Fernando M. Guerrero.

1973-78 Engr. *Perf. 14½*
1195 A250 15s sepia .25 .25

Litho. *Perf. 12½*
1196 A250 15s violet ('74) .25 .25
1197 A273 15s emerald ('74) .25 .25
1198 A250 30s vio bl ('78) .25 .25
1199 A250 60s dl red brn .55 .25
1200 A273 90s brt bl ('74) .75 .25
1202 A273 1.10p brt bl ('74) 1.25 .25
1203 A250 1.20p dl red ('78) .60 .25
1204 A250 1.50p lil rose 2.00 1.50
1205 A273 1.50p brown ('74) 1.50 .40
1206 A250 1.80p green 3.00 1.50
1208 A250 5p blue 6.00 3.00
Nos. 1195-1208 (12) 16.65 8.40

1973-74 *Imperf.*
1196a A250 15s violet ('74) 1.25 *2.00*
1197a A273 15s emerald ('74) 1.25 *2.00*
1199a A250 60s dull red brown 3.00 1.50
1200a A273 90s bright blue ('74) 2.75 1.60
1202a A273 1.10p bright blue ('74) 3.50 3.00
1204a A250 1.50p lilac rose 3.50 3.00
1205a A273 1.50p brown ('74) 3.75 3.50
1206a A250 1.80p green 5.00 3.50
1208a A250 5p blue 12.00 8.00
Nos. 1196a-1208a (9) 36.00 28.10

Honoring: Escoda (1898-194?), leader of Girl Scouts and Federation of Women's Clubs. Silang (1731-63), "the Ilocana Joan of Arc". Palma (1874-1939), journalist, statesman, educator. Rizal (1861-96), natl. hero. Agoncillo (1859-1946), designer of 1st Philippine flag, 1898. Yangco (1861-1939), patriot and philanthropist. Valenzuela (1869-1956), physician and newspaperman.
Gregoria de Jesus, independence leader. Paterno (1857-1911), lawyer, writer, patriot. Alonso (1827-1911), mother of Rizal. Evangelista (1862-97), army engineer, patriot. Guerrero (1873-1929), journalist, political leader.
For overprint & surcharges see #1277, 1310, 1311, 1470, 1518, 1562..

No. 946 surcharged with New Value

1973, June 4 Engr. *Perf. 13½*
1209 A158 5s on 6s peacock bl .60 .25

Anti-smuggling campaign.

No. 925 Surcharged

1973, June 4 Wmk. 233
1210 A176 5s on 6s multi .60 .25

10th anniv. of death of John F. Kennedy.

Pres. Marcos, Farm Family, Unfurling of Philippine Flag — A251

Perf. 12½x13½

1973, Sept. 24 Photo. Unwmk.
1211 A251 15s ultra & multi .25 .25
1212 A251 45s red & multi .50 .25
1213 A251 90s multi .75 .25
Nos. 1211-1213 (3) 1.50 .75

75th anniversary of Philippine independence and 1st anniversary of proclamation of martial law.

Imelda Romualdez Marcos, First Lady of the Philippines A252

1973, Oct. 31 Photo. *Perf. 13*
1214 A252 15s dl bl & multi .25 .25
1215 A252 50s multicolored .40 .25
1216 A252 60s lil & multi .60 .25
Nos. 1214-1216 (3) 1.25 .75

Presidential Palace, Manila, Pres. and Mrs. Marcos — A253

1973, Nov. 15 Litho. *Perf. 14*
1217 A253 15s rose & multi .25 .25
1218 A253 50s ultra & multi .50 .25
Nos. 1217-1218,C107 (3) 1.50 .80

INTERPOL Emblem — A254

1973, Dec. 18 Photo. *Perf. 13*
1219 A254 15s ultra & multi .30 .25
1220 A254 65s lt grn & multi .45 .25

Intl. Criminal Police Organization, 50th anniv.

Cub and Boy Scouts — A255

15s, Various Scout activities; inscribed in Tagalog.

1973, Dec. 28 Litho. *Perf. 12½*
1221 A255 15s bister & emer .65 .50
a. Imperf, pair ('74) 4.00 4.00
1222 A255 65s bister & brt bl 1.25 .50
a. Imperf, pair ('74) 6.00 6.00

50th anniv. of Philippine Boy Scouts.
Nos. 1221a-1222a issued Feb. 4, although first day covers are dated Dec. 28, 1973.

Manila, Bank Emblem and Farmers — A256

Designs: 60s, Old bank building. 1.50p, Modern bank building.

1974, Jan. 3 Photo. *Perf. 12½x13½*
1223 A256 15s silver & multi .25 .25
1224 A256 60s silver & multi .35 .25
1225 A256 1.50p silver & multi 1.10 .40
Nos. 1223-1225 (3) 1.70 .90

Central Bank of the Philippines, 25th anniv.

UPU Emblem, Maria Clara Costume — A257

Filipino Costumes: 60s, Balintawak and UPU emblem. 80s, Malong costume and UPU emblem.

1974, Jan. 15 *Perf. 12½*
1226 A257 15s multicolored .25 .25
1227 A257 60s multicolored .45 .25
1228 A257 80s multicolored .80 .35
Nos. 1226-1228 (3) 1.50 .85

Centenary of Universal Postal Union.

No. 1192 Surcharged in Red with New Value, 2 Bars and: "1973 / PHILATELIC WEEK"

1974, Feb. 4 Photo. *Perf. 13x12½*
1229 A249 15s on 10s multi .60 .25

Philatelic Week, 1973. First day covers exist dated Nov. 26, 1973.

Nos. 1186 and 1136 Overprinted and Surcharged

1974, Mar. 25 Photo. *Perf. 13½x14*
1230 A248 15s on 10s multi .60 .25

Engr. *Perf. 14*
1231 A222 45s on 40s rose red .60 .25

Lions Intl. of the Philippines, 25th anniv. The overprint on #1230 arranged to fit shape of stamp.

Pediatrics Congress Emblem and Map of Participating Countries A258

1974, Apr. 30 Litho. *Perf. 12½*
1232 A258 30s brt bl & red .50 .25
a. Imperf, pair 4.00 4.00
1233 A258 1p dl grn & red 1.00 .30
a. Imperf, pair 6.00 6.00

Asian Congress of Pediatrics, Manila, Apr. 30-May 4.

Nos. 912, 954-955 Surcharged with New Value and Two Bars

1974, Aug. 1 As Before
1234 A172 5s on 3s multi .75 .75
1235 A185 5s on 6s multi 1.00 1.00
1236 A186 5s on 6s multi 1.25 1.25
Nos. 1234-1236 (3) 3.00 3.00

WPY Emblem A259

1974, Aug. 15 Litho. *Perf. 12½*
1237 A259 5s org & bl blk .40 .25
a. Imperf, pair 2.00 2.00
1238 A259 2p lt grn & dk bl 1.60 .60
a. Imperf, pair 11.00 11.00

World Population Year, 1974.

Red Feather Community Chest Emblem A260

Wmk. 372

1974, Sept. 5 Litho. *Perf. 12½*
1239 A260 15s brt bl & red .25 .25
1240 A260 40s emer & red .65 .25
1241 A260 45s red brn & red .65 .25
Nos. 1239-1241 (3) 1.55 .75

Philippine Community Chest, 25th anniv.

Imperf. Pairs
1239a A260 15s 4.50 4.50
1240a A260 40s 2.00 2.00
1241a A260 45s 2.00 2.00
Nos. 1239a-1241a (3) 8.50 8.50

Sultan Kudarat, Flag, Order and Map of Philippines — A261

Perf. 13½x14

1975, Jan. 13 Photo. Unwmk.

1242 A261 15s multicolored .35 .25

Sultan Mohammad Dipatuan Kudarat, 16th-17th century ruler.

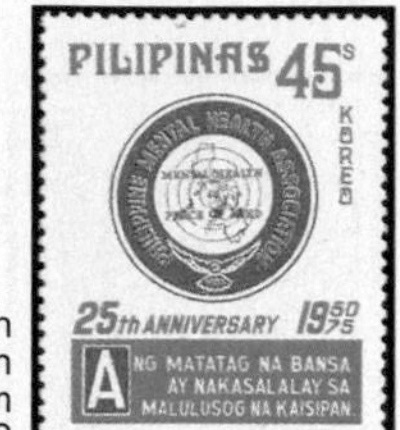
Mental Health Association Emblem A262

Wmk. 372

1975, Jan. 20 Litho. *Perf. 12½*

1243 A262 45s emer & org .35 .25
a. Imperf, pair 2.00 2.00
1244 A262 1p emer & pur .80 .30
a. Imperf, pair 4.00 4.00

Philippine Mental Health Assoc., 25th anniv.

4-Leaf Clover A263

1975, Feb. 14

1245 A263 15s vio bl & red .35 .25
a. Imperf, pair 2.50 2.50
1246 A263 50s emer & red .80 .35
a. Imperf, pair 5.00 5.00

Philippine Heart Center for Asia, inauguration.

Military Academy, Cadet and Emblem — A264

Perf. 13½x14

1975, Feb. 17 Unwmk.

1247 A264 15s grn & multi .35 .25
1248 A264 45s plum & multi .55 .25

Philippine Military Academy, 70th anniv.

Helping the Disabled — A265

Perf. 12½, Imperf.

1975, Mar. 17 Wmk. 372

1249 A265 Block of 10 7.50 *12.00*
a.-j. 45s grn, any single .55 .35

25th anniversary (in 1974) of Philippine Orthopedic Association.
For surcharge see No. 1635.
No. 1249 exists imperf. Value unused, $12.

Nos. B43, B50-B51 Surcharged with New Value and Two Bars

1975, Apr. 15 Unwmk.

1250 SP18 5s on 15s + 5s .60 *1.00*
1251 SP16 60s on 70s + 5s .90 *1.00*
1252 SP18 1p on 1.10p + 5s 1.25 *2.00*
Nos. 1250-1252 (3) 2.75 4.00

"Grow and Conserve Forests" — A266

1975, May 19 Litho. *Perf. 14½*

1253 45s "Grow" .45 .25
1254 45s "Conserve" .45 .25
a. A267 Pair, #1253-1254 .90 .75

Forest conservation.

Jade Vine — A268

1975, June 9 Photo. *Perf. 14½*

1255 A268 15s multicolored .35 .25

Imelda R. Marcos, IWY Emblem — A269

Wmk. 372

1975, July 2 Litho. *Perf. 12½*

1256 A269 15s bl & blk .35 .25
a. Imperf, pair 3.00 *2.50*
1257 A269 80s pink, bl & grn .55 .25
a. Imperf, pair 7.00 *5.00*

International Women's Year 1975.
For surcharges see Nos. 1500, 1505.

Civil Service Emblem — A270

1975, Sept. 19 Litho. *Perf. 12½*

1258 A270 15s multicolored .35 .25
a. Imperf, pair 3.00 2.25
1259 A270 50s multicolored .55 .25
a. Imperf, pair 4.50 3.75

Dam and Emblem A271

1975, Sept. 30

1260 A271 40s org & vio bl .25 .25
a. Imperf, pair 2.50 *2.00*
1261 A271 1.50p brt rose & vio bl .90 .35
a. Imperf, pair 6.00 5.50

For surcharges see Nos. 1517, 1520.

Manila Harbor, 1875 A272

1975, Nov. 4 Unwmk. *Perf. 13x13½*

1262 A272 1.50p red & multi 1.50 .40

Hong Kong and Shanghai Banking Corporation, centenary of Philippines service.

Norberto Romualdez (1875-1941), Scholar and Legislator A273

Jose Rizal Monument, Luneta Park — A273a

Noted Filipinos: No. 1264, Rafael Palma (1874-1939), journalist, statesman, educator. No. 1265, Rajah Kalantiaw, chief of Panay, author of ethical-penal code (1443). 65s, Emilio Jacinto (1875-1899), patriot. No. 1269, Gen. Gregorio del Pilar (1875-1899), military hero. No. 1270, Lope K. Santos (1879-1963), grammarian, writer. 1.60p, Felipe Agoncillo (1859-1941), lawyer, cabinet member.

Wmk. 372

1975-81 Litho. *Perf. 12½*

1264 A273 30s brn ('77) .50 .25
1265 A273 30s dp rose ('78) .50 .25
1266 A273a 40s yel & blk ('81) 1.25 .25
1267 A273 60s violet 1.50 .25
a. Imperf, pair 5.00 4.00
1268 A273 65s lilac rose 1.25 .40
a. Imperf, pair 4.00 2.50
1269 A273 90s lilac rose 2.00 .50
a. Imperf, pair 4.50 4.50
1270 A273 90s grn ('78) *1.00* .25
1272 A273 1.60p blk ('76) 3.00 .40
Nos. 1264-1272 (8) 11.00 2.55

See #1195-1208. For overprint & surcharges see #1278, 1310, 1367, 1440, 1469, 1514, 1562, 1574, 1758-1760.

A274

1975, Nov. 22 Litho. *Perf. 12½*

1275 A274 60s multicolored .75 .50
1276 A274 1.50p multicolored 1.75 .50

1st landing of the Pan American World Airways China Clipper in the Philippines, 40th anniv.

Nos. 1199 and 1205 Overprinted

1975, Nov. 22 Unwmk.

1277 A250 60s dl red brn .50 .50
1278 A273 1.50p brown 1.25 .30

Airmail Exhibition, Nov. 22-Dec. 9.

APO Emblem — A275

1975, Nov. 24 Wmk. 372

1279 A275 5s ultra & multi .25 .25
a. Imperf, pair 2.00 1.50
1280 A275 1p bl & multi .65 .25
a. Imperf, pair 7.50 6.00

Amateur Philatelists' Org., 25th anniv.
For surcharge see No. 1338.

A276

Philippine Churches: 20s, San Agustin Church. 30s, Morong Church, horiz. 45s, Basilica of Taal, horiz. 60s, San Sebastian Church.

1975, Dec. 23 Litho. *Perf. 12½*

1281 A276 20s bluish grn .50 .25
1282 A276 30s yel org & blk .50 .25
1283 A276 45s rose, brn & blk .75 .25
1284 A276 60s yel, bis & blk 1.25 .30
Nos. 1281-1284 (4) 3.00 1.05

Holy Year 1975.

Imperf. Pairs

1281a A276 20s 2.50 2.00
1282a A276 30s 2.50 2.00
1283a A276 45s 4.00 3.50
1284a A276 60s 7.00 5.00
Nos. 1281a-1284a (4) 16.00 12.50

A277

Conductor's hands.

1976, Jan. 27

1285 A277 5s org & multi .35 .25
1286 A277 50s multicolored .55 .25

Manila Symphony Orchestra, 50th anniv.

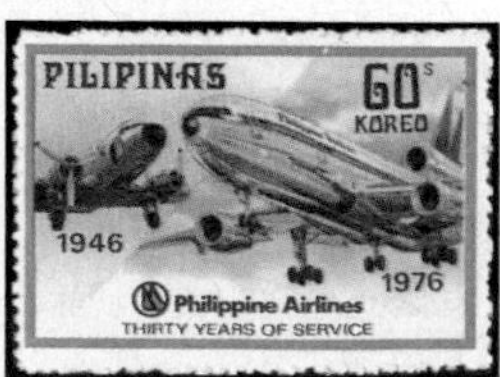
PAL Planes of 1946 and 1976 A278

1976, Feb. 14

1287 A278 60s bl & multi .60 .50
1288 A278 1.50p red & multi 1.90 .60

Philippine Airlines, 30th anniversary.

National University A279

1976, Mar. 30

1289	A279	45s bl, vio bl & yel	.40	.25
1290	A279	60s lt bl, vio bl & pink	.75	.25

National University, 75th anniversary.

Eye Exam — A280

1976, Apr. 7 Litho. *Perf. 12½*

1291	A280	15s multicolored	.50	.25

World Health Day: "Foresight prevents blindness."

Book and Emblem — A281

1976, May 24 Unwmk.

1292	A281	1.50p grn & multi	1.25	.30

National Archives, 75th anniversary.

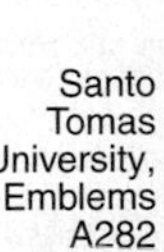

Santo Tomas University, Emblems A282

1976, June 7 Wmk. 372

1293	A282	15s yel & multi	.30	.25
1294	A282	50s multicolored	.60	.25

Colleges of Education and Science, Santo Tomas University, 50th anniversary.

Maryknoll College — A283

Wmk. 372

1976, July 26 Litho. *Perf. 12½*

1295	A283	15s lt bl & multi	.35	.25
1296	A283	1.50p bis & multi	.90	.25

Maryknoll College, Quezon City, 50th anniv.

No. 1164 Surcharged in Dark Violet

Perf. 12½x13½

1976, July 30 Photo.

1297	A242	15s on 10s multi	.75	*1.50*

21st Olympic Games, Montreal, Canada, July 17-Aug. 1.

Police College, Manila — A284

1976, Aug. 8 Litho. *Perf. 12½*

1298	A284	15s multicolored	.25	.25
a.		Imperf, pair	1.75	1.75
1299	A284	60s multicolored	.60	.25
a.		Imperf, pair	5.75	5.75

Philippine Constabulary, 75th anniversary.

Surveyors — A285

1976, Sept. 2 Wmk. 372

1300	A285	80s multicolored	1.25	.30

Bureau of Lands, 75th anniversary.

Monetary Fund and World Bank Emblems — A286

1976, Oct. 4 Litho. *Perf. 12½*

1301	A286	60s multicolored	.40	.40
1302	A286	1.50p multicolored	1.10	.60

Joint Annual Meeting of the Board of Governors of the International Monetary Fund and the World Bank, Manila, Oct. 4-8.

For surcharge see No. 1575.

Virgin of Antipollo A287

1976, Nov. 26 *Perf. 12½*

1303	A287	30s multicolored	.40	.25
1304	A287	90s multicolored	1.10	.25

Virgin of Antipolo, Our Lady of Peace and Good Voyage, 350th anniv. of arrival of statue in the Philippines and 50th anniv. of the canonical coronation.

No. 1184 Surcharged with New Value and 2 Bars and Overprinted: "1976 PHILATELIC WEEK"

Perf. 13½x14

1976, Nov. 26 Photo. Unwmk.

1305	A247	30s on 10s multi	.60	.25

Philatelic Week 1976.

People Going to Church A288

Wmk. 372

1976, Dec. 1 Litho. *Perf. 12½*

1306	A288	15s bl & multi	.50	.25
1307	A288	30s bl & multi	1.00	.25

Christmas 1976.

Symbolic Diamond and Book — A289

1976, Dec. 13

1308	A289	30s grn & multi	.50	.25
1309	A289	75s grn & multi	.75	.25

Philippine Educational System, 75th anniv.

No. 1202 and 1208 Surcharged with New Value and 2 Bars

1977, Jan. 17 Unwmk.

1310	A273	1.20p on 1.10p brt bl	1.00	.50
1311	A250	3p on 5p bl	2.50	.70

Galicano Apacible — A290

Design: 30s, José Rizal.

1977 Litho. Wmk. 372 *Perf. 12½*

1313	A290	30s multicolored	.25	.25
1318	A290	2.30p multicolored	1.25	.25

Dr. José Rizal (1861-1896) physician, poet and national hero (30s). Dr. Galicano Apacible (1864-1949), physician, statesman (2.30p).

Issue dates: 30s, Feb. 16; 2.30p, Jan. 24.

Emblem, Flags, Map of AOPU A291

1977, Apr. 1 Wmk. 372

1322	A291	50s multicolored	.40	.25
1323	A291	1.50p multicolored	1.10	.25

Asian-Oceanic Postal Union (AOPU), 15th anniv.

Cogwheels and Worker — A292

1977, Apr. 21 *Perf. 12½*

1324	A292	90s blk & multi	.50	.25
1325	A292	2.30p blk & multi	1.25	.45

Asian Development Bank, 10th anniversary.

Farmer at Work and Receiving Money A293

1977, May 14 Litho. Wmk. 372

1326	A293	30s org red & multi	.35	.75

National Commission on Countryside Credit and Collection, campaign to strengthen the rural credit system.

Solicitor General's Emblem A294

1977, June 30 Litho. *Perf. 12½*

1327	A294	1.65p multicolored	1.25	.25

Office of the Solicitor General, 75th anniv.

For surcharges see Nos. 1483, 1519.

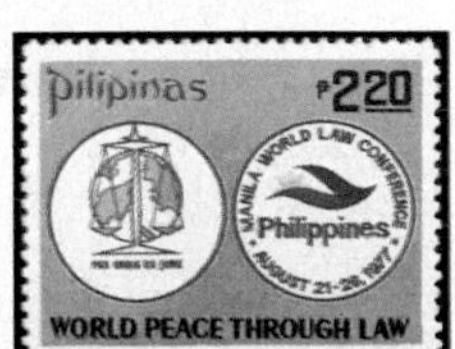

Conference Emblem A295

1977, July 29 Litho. *Perf. 12½*

1328	A295	2.20p bl & multi	1.25	.25

8th World Conference of the World Peace through Law Center, Manila, Aug. 21-26.

For surcharge see No. 1576.

ASEAN Emblem A296

1977, Aug. 8

1329	A296	1.50p grn & multi	1.25	.25

Association of South East Asian Nations (ASEAN), 10th anniversary.

For surcharge see No. 1559.

Cable-laying Ship, Map Showing Cable Route — A297

1977, Aug. 26 Litho. *Perf. 12½*
1330 A297 1.30p multicolored .85 .25

Inauguration of underwater telephone cable linking Okinawa, Luzon and Hong Kong.

President Marcos — A298

1977, Sept. 11 Wmk. 372
1331 A298 30s multicolored .30 .25
1332 A298 2.30p multicolored 1.25 .35

Ferdinand E. Marcos, president of the Philippines, 60th birthday.

People Raising Flag — A299

1977, Sept. 21 Litho. *Perf. 12½*
1333 A299 30s multicolored .35 .25
1334 A299 2.30p multicolored 1.10 .35

5th anniversary of "New Society."

Bishop Gregorio Aglipay — A300

1977, Oct. 1 Litho. *Perf. 12½*
1335 A300 30s multicolored .40 .25
1336 A300 90s multicolored 1.10 .25

Philippine Independent Aglipayan Church, 75th anniversary.

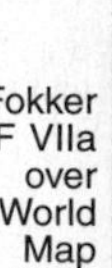
Fokker F VIIa over World Map A301

1977, Oct. 28 Wmk. 372
1337 A301 2.30p multicolored 1.90 .50

First scheduled Pan American airmail service, Havana to Key West, 50th anniversary.

No. 1280 Surcharged with New Value, 2 Bars and Overprinted in Red: "1977 / PHILATELIC / WEEK"

1977, Nov. 22 Litho. *Perf. 12½*
1338 A275 90s on 1p multi .90 *1.00*

Philatelic Week.

Children Celebrating and Star from Lantern — A302

1977, Dec. 1 Unwmk.
1339 A302 30s multicolored .30 .25
1340 A302 45s multicolored .60 .25

Christmas 1977.

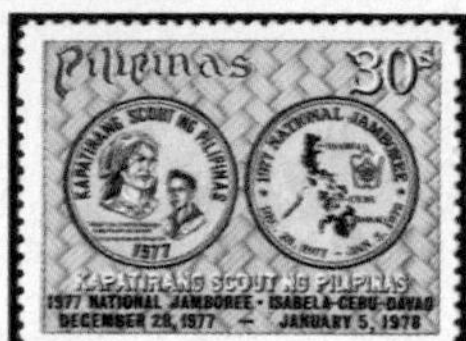

Scouts and Map showing Jamboree Locations A303

1977, Dec. 27
1341 A303 30s multicolored .50 .25

National Boy Scout Jamboree, Tumauini, Isabela; Capitol Hills, Cebu City; Mariano Marcos, Davao, Dec. 27, 1977-Jan. 5, 1978.

Far Eastern University Arms — A304

1978, Jan. 26 Litho. Wmk. 372
1342 A304 30s gold & multi .40 .25

Far Eastern University, 50th anniversary.

Sipa A305

Various positions of Sipa ball-game.

1978, Feb. 28 *Perf. 12½*
1343 A305 5s bl & multi .25 .25
1344 A305 10s bl & multi .30 .25
1345 A305 40s bl & multi .40 .25
1346 A305 75s bl & multi .75 .25
a. Block, #1343-1346 1.90 1.40

No. 1346a has continuous design.

Arms of Meycauayan A306

1978, Apr. 21 Litho. *Perf. 12½*
1347 A306 1.05p multicolored .90 .25

Meycauayan, founded 1578-1579.
For surcharge see No. 1560.

Moro Vinta and UPU Emblem — A307

2.50p, No. 1350b, Horse-drawn mail cart. No. 1350a, like 5p. No. 1350c, Steam locomotive. No. 1350d, Three-master.

1978, June 9 Litho. *Perf. 13½*
1348 A307 2.50p multi 2.50 1.50
1349 A307 5p multi 3.50 2.00
a. Pair, #1348-1349 6.00 6.00

Souvenir Sheet

Perf. 12½x13

1350 Sheet of 4 20.00 20.00
a.-d. A307 7.50p, any single 4.25 4.25
e. Sheet, imperf 20.00 20.00

CAPEX International Philatelic Exhibition, Toronto, Ont., June 9-18. No. 1350 contains 36½x25mm stamps.
No. 1350 exists imperf. in changed colors.

Andres Bonifacio Monument, by Guillermo Tolentino — A308

Wmk. 372

1978, July 10 Litho. *Perf. 12½*
1351 A308 30s multicolored .50 .25

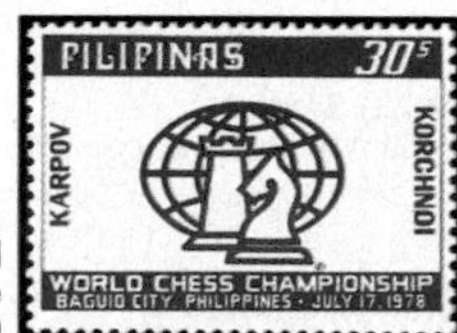

Rook, Knight and Globe A309

1978, July 17
1352 A309 30s vio bl & red .40 .25
1353 A309 2p vio bl & red 1.50 .30

World Chess Championship, Anatoly Karpov and Viktor Korchnoi, Baguio City, 1978.

Miners A310

1978, Aug. 12 Litho. *Perf. 12½*
1354 A310 2.30p multicolored 1.90 .35

Benguet gold mining industry, 75th anniv.

Manuel Quezon and Quezon Memorial A311

1978, Aug. 19
1355 A311 30s multicolored .25 .25
1356 A311 1p multicolored 1.00 .25

Manuel Quezon (1878-1944), first president of Commonwealth of the Philippines.

Law Association Emblem, Philippine Flag — A312

1978, Aug. 27 Litho. *Perf. 12½*
1357 A312 2.30p multicolored 1.25 .35

58th Intl. Law Conf., Manila, 8/27-9/2.

Pres. Sergio Osmeña (1878-1961) A313

1978, Sept. 8
1358 A313 30s multicolored .30 .25
1359 A313 1p multicolored .90 .25

For surcharge see No. 1501.

Map Showing Cable Route, Cablelaying Ship — A314

1978, Sept. 30
1360 A314 1.40p multicolored 1.25 .50

ASEAN Submarine Cable Network, Philippines-Singapore cable system, inauguration.

Basketball, Games' Emblem A315

1978, Oct. 1
1361 A315 30s multicolored .40 *1.00*
1362 A315 2.30p multicolored 1.50 .40

8th Men's World Basketball Championship, Manila, Oct. 1-15.

San Lazaro Hospital and Dr. Catalino Gavino A316

1978, Oct. 13 Litho. *Perf. 12½*
1363 A316 50s multicolored .50 .25
1364 A316 90s multicolored .75 .25

San Lazaro Hospital, 400th anniversary.
For surcharge see No. 1512.

Nurse Vaccinating Child — A317

1978, Oct. 24

1365	A317	30s multicolored	.40	.25
1366	A317	1.50p multicolored	1.50	1.00

Eradication of smallpox.

No. 1268 Surcharged

1978, Nov. 23

1367	A273	60s on 65s lil rose	.75	.25

Philatelic Week.

"The Telephone Across Country and World" — A318

Wmk. 372

1978, Nov. 28 Litho. *Perf. 12½*

1368	30s multicolored	.40	.25
1369	2p multicolored	1.40	.40
a.	A318 Pair, #1368-1369	1.90	1.90

Philippine Long Distance Telephone Company, 50th anniversary.

Traveling Family — A320

1978, Nov. 28

1370	A320	30s multicolored	.40	.25
1371	A320	1.35p multicolored	1.10	.25

Decade of Philippine children.

For surcharges see Nos. 1504, 1561.

Church and Arms of Agoo A321

1978, Dec. 7 Litho. *Perf. 12½*

1372	A321	30s multicolored	.45	.25
1373	A321	45s multicolored	.45	.25

400th anniversary of the founding of Agoo.

Church and Arms of Balayan A322

1978, Dec. 8

1374	A322	30s multicolored	.30	.25
1375	A322	90s multicolored	.60	.25

400th anniv. of the founding of Balayan.

Dr. Honoria Acosta Sison (1888-1970), 1st Philippine Woman Physician — A323

1978, Dec. 15

1376	A323	30s multicolored	.40	.25

Family, Houses, UN Emblem A324

1978, Dec. Litho. *Perf. 12½*

1377	A324	30s multicolored	.40	.25
1378	A324	3p multicolored	1.75	.50

30th anniversary of Universal Declaration of Human Rights.

Chaetodon Trifasciatus — A325

Fish: 1.20p, Balistoides niger. 2.20p, Rhinecanthus aculeatus. 2.30p, Chelmon rostratus. No. 1383, Chaetodon mertensi. No. 1384, Euxiphipops xanthometapon.

1978, Dec. 29 *Perf. 14*

1379	A325	30s multi	.30	.25
1380	A325	1.20p multi	.90	.30
1381	A325	2.20p multi	1.40	.40
1382	A325	2.30p multi	1.40	.40
1383	A325	5p multi	3.50	.90
1384	A325	5p multi	3.50	.90
		Nos. 1379-1384 (6)	11.00	3.15

Carlos P. Romulo, UN Emblem A326

1979, Jan. 14 Litho. *Perf. 12½*

1385	A326	30s multi	.40	.25
1386	A326	2p multi	1.40	.40

Carlos P. Romulo (1899-1985), pres. of UN General Assembly and Security Council.

Rotary Emblem and "60" — A327

1979, Jan. 26 Wmk. 372

1387	A327	30s multi	.35	.25
1388	A327	2.30p multi	1.25	.40

Rotary Club of Manila, 60th anniversary.

Rosa Sevilla de Alvero — A328

1979, Mar. 4 Litho. *Perf. 12½*

1389	A328	30 rose	.40	.25

Rosa Sevilla de Alvero, educator and writer, birth centenary.

For surcharges see Nos. 1479-1482.

Oil Well and Map of Palawan A329

Wmk. 372

1979, Mar. 21 Litho. *Perf. 12½*

1390	A329	30s multi	.35	*1.00*
1391	A329	45s multi	.55	.25

First Philippine oil production, Nido Oil Reef Complex, Palawan.

Merrill's Fruit Doves — A330

Birds: 1.20p, Brown tit babbler. 2.20p, Mindoro imperial pigeons. 2.30p, Steere's pittas. No. 1396, Koch's and red-breasted pittas. No. 1397, Philippine eared nightjar.

Perf. 14x13½

1979, Apr. 16 Unwmk.

1392	A330	30s multi	*.30*	.25
1393	A330	1.20p multi	*1.10*	.25
1394	A330	2.20p multi	*2.75*	.75
1395	A330	2.30p multi	*2.75*	.75
1396	A330	5p multi	*11.00*	4.00
1397	A330	5p multi	*11.00*	4.00
		Nos. 1392-1397 (6)	*28.90*	10.00

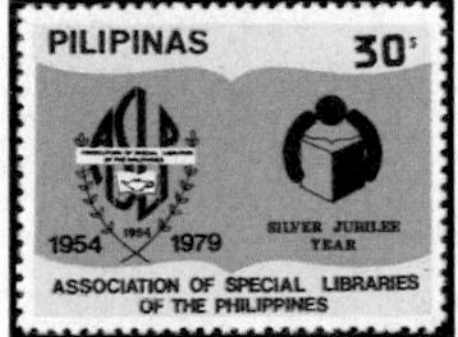

Association Emblem and Reader A331

Wmk. 372

1979, Apr. 3 Litho. *Perf. 12½*

1398	A331	30s multi	.25	.25
1399	A331	75s multi	.45	.25
1400	A331	1p multi	1.10	.30
		Nos. 1398-1400 (3)	1.80	.80

Association of Special Libraries of the Philippines, 25th anniversary.

UNCTAD Emblem A332

Wmk. 372

1979, May 3 Litho. *Perf. 12½*

1401	A332	1.20p multi	.75	.25
1402	A332	2.30p multi	1.50	.40

5th Session of UN Conference on Trade and Development, Manila, May 3-June 1.

Civet Cat A333

Philippine Animals: 1.20p, Macaque. 2.20p, Wild boar. 2.30p, Dwarf leopard. No. 1407, Asiatic dwarf otter. No. 1408, Anteater.

1979, May 14 *Perf. 14*

1403	A333	30s multi	.30	.25
1404	A333	1.20p multi	.90	.30
1405	A333	2.20p multi	1.50	.45
1406	A333	2.30p multi	1.50	.45
1407	A333	5p multi	3.25	2.50
1408	A333	5p multi	3.50	2.50
		Nos. 1403-1408 (6)	10.95	6.45

Dish Antenna — A334

1979, May 17 *Perf. 12½*

1409	A334	90s shown	1.10	.25
1410	A334	1.30p World map	1.10	.30

11th World Telecommunications Day, 5/17.

Mussaenda Donna Evangelina — A335

Philippine Mussaendas: 1.20p, Dona Esperanza. 2.20p, Dona Hilaria. 2.30p, Dona Aurora. No. 1415, Gining Imelda. No. 1416, Dona Trining.

1979, June 11 Litho. *Perf. 14*

1411	A335	30s multi	.30	.25
1412	A335	1.20p multi	.90	.30
1413	A335	2.20p multi	1.50	.45
1414	A335	2.30p multi	1.50	.45
1415	A335	5p multi	3.25	1.75
1416	A335	5p multi	3.50	1.75
		Nos. 1411-1416 (6)	10.95	4.95

Manila Cathedral, Coat of Arms — A336

1979, June 25 *Perf. 12½*

1417	A336	30s multi	.30	.25
1418	A336	75s multi	.60	.25
1419	A336	90s multi	.85	.25
		Nos. 1417-1419 (3)	1.75	.75

Archdiocese of Manila, 400th anniversary.

Patrol Boat, Naval Arms A337

1979, June 26

1420	A337	30s multi	.50	.50
1421	A337	45s multi	.75	.75

Philippine Navy Day.

Man Breaking Chains, Broken Syringe — A338

1979, July 23 Litho. *Perf. 12½*

1422 A338	30s multi		.25	.25
1423 A338	90s multi		.75	.25
1424 A338	1.05p multi		.85	.25
	Nos. 1422-1424 (3)		1.85	.75

Fight drug abuse.
For surcharge see Nos. 1480, 1513.

Afghan Hound A339

Designs: 90s, Striped tabbies. 1.20p, Dobermann pinscher. 2.20p, Siamese cats. 2.30p, German shepherd. 5p, Chinchilla cats.

1979, Aug. 6 *Perf. 14*

1425 A339	30s multi	.50	.25
1426 A339	90s multi	1.00	.30
1427 A339	1.20p multi	1.25	.40
1428 A339	2.20p multi	2.00	.45
1429 A339	2.30p multi	2.00	.45
1430 A339	5p multi	4.25	1.50
	Nos. 1425-1430 (6)	11.00	3.35

Children Playing IYC Emblem A340

Children playing and IYC emblem, diff.

1979, Aug. 31 Litho. *Perf. 12½*

1431 A340	15s multi	.25	.25
1432 A340	20s multi	.40	.25
1433 A340	25s multi	.40	.40
1434 A340	1.20p multi	.75	.50
	Nos. 1431-1434 (4)	1.80	1.40

International Year of the Child.

Hands Holding Emblem — A341

1979, Sept. 27 Litho. *Perf. 12½*

1435 A341	30s multi	.25	.25
1436 A341	1.35p multi	1.00	.25

Methodism in the Philippines, 80th anniv.

Emblem and Coins A342

Wmk. 372

1979, Nov. 15 Litho. *Perf. 12½*

1437 A342	30s multi	.50	.50

Philippine Numismatic and Antiquarian Society, 50th anniversary.

Concorde over Manila and Paris A343

Design: 2.20p, Concorde over Manila.

1979, Nov. 22

1438 A343	1.05p multi	1.00	.40
1439 A343	2.20p multi	2.50	.75

Air France service to Manila, 25th anniversary.

No. 1272 Surcharged in Red

1979, Nov. 23

1440 A273	90s on 1.60 blk	.90	.25

Philatelic Week. Surcharge similar to No. 1367.

Transport Association Emblem A344

1979, Nov. 27

1441 A344	75s multi	.60	.25
1442 A344	2.30p multi	1.75	.40

International Air Transport Association, 35th annual general meeting, Manila.

Local Government Year — A345

1979, Dec. 14 Litho. *Perf. 12½*

1443 A345	30s multi	.25	.25
1444 A345	45s multi	.45	.25

For surcharge, see No. 1481.

Mother and Children, Ornament — A346

1979, Dec. 17

1445 A346	30s shown	.30	.25
1446 A346	90s Stars	.95	.25

Christmas. For surcharges see Nos. 1482, 1515.

Rheumatic Pain Spots and Congress Emblem A347

Wmk. 372

1980, Jan. 20 Litho. *Perf. 12½*

1447 A347	30s multi	.75	.75
1448 A347	90s multi	2.25	2.00

Southeast Asia and Pacific Area League Against Rheumatism, 4th Congress, Manila, Jan. 19-24.

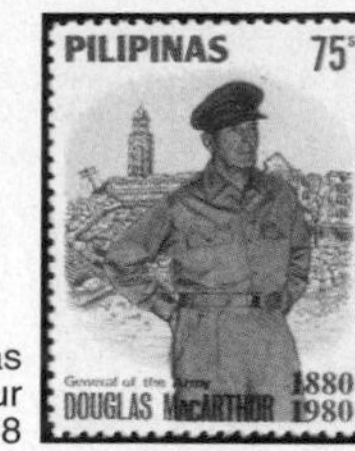

Gen. Douglas MacArthur A348

30s, MacArthur's birthplace (Little Rock, AR) & burial place (Norfolk, VA). 2.30p, MacArthur's cap, Sunglasses & pipe. 5p, MacArthur & troops wading ashore at Leyte, Oct. 20, 1944.

1980, Jan. 26 Wmk. 372 *Perf. 12½*

1449 A348	30s multi	.30	.25
1450 A348	75s multi	.50	.40
1451 A348	2.30p multi	1.75	.75
	Nos. 1449-1451 (3)	2.55	1.40

Souvenir Sheet

Imperf

1452 A348	5p multi	4.00	6.00

Gen. Douglas MacArthur (1880-1964).
For overprint see No. 2198.

Knights of Columbus of Philippines, 75th Anniversary A349

1980, Feb. 14

1453 A349	30s multi	.25	.25
1454 A349	1.35p multi	1.00	.50

Philippine Military Academy, 75th Anniversary — A350

Wmk. 372

1980, Feb. 17 Litho. *Perf. 12½*

1455 A350	30s multi	.75	.50
1456 A350	1.20p multi	2.25	1.00

Philippines Women's University, 75th Anniversary — A351

1980, Feb. 21

1457 A351	30s multi	.25	.25
1458 A351	1.05p multi	1.00	.25

A352

Disaster Relief — A352a

Rotary International, 75th Anniversary (Paintings by Carlos Botong Francisco): Nos. 1459 and 1460 each in continuous design.

1980, Feb. 23 *Perf. 12½*

1459	A352	Strip of 5	5.00	5.00
a.-e.		30s any single	.70	.70
1460	A352a	Strip of 5	12.00	12.00
a.-e.		2.30p any single	1.75	1.75

A353

Wmk. 372

1980, Mar. 28 Litho. *Perf. 12½*

1461 A353	30s multi	.75	.75
1462 A353	1.30p multi	2.00	.30

6th centenary of Islam in Philippines.

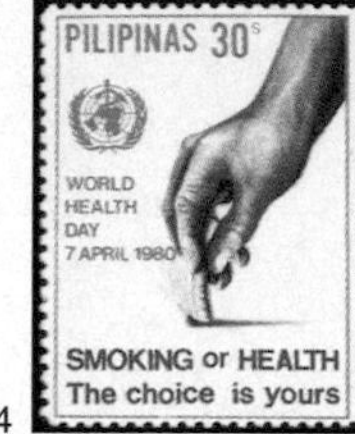

A354

Hand crushing cigarette, WHO emblem.

1980, Apr. 7

1463 A354	30s multi	.50	*1.00*
1464 A354	75s multi	2.50	2.50

World Health Day (Apr. 7); anti-smoking campaign.

Philippine Girl Scouts, 40th Anniversary A355

Wmk. 372

1980, May 26 Litho. *Perf. 12½*

1465 A355	30s multi	.40	.25
1466 A355	2p multi	1.40	.35

Jeepney (Public Jeep) A356

1980, June 24 Litho. *Perf. 12½*

1467 A356	30s Jeepney, diff.	.40	.25
1468 A356	1.20p shown	1.25	.35

For surcharge see No. 1503.

Nos. 1272, 1206 Surcharged in Red

Wmk. 372 (1.35p)

1980, Aug. 1 Litho. *Perf. 12½*

1469 A273	1.35p on 1.60p blk	1.40	.35
1470 A250	1.50p on 1.80p grn	1.90	.60

Independence, 82nd Anniversary.

Association Emblem — A357

1980, Aug. 1 **Wmk. 372**

1471 A357 30s multi .25 .25
1472 A357 2.30p multi 1.50 .40

International Association of Universities, 7th General Conference, Manila, Aug. 25-30.

Congress Emblem, Map of Philippines A358

Wmk. 372

1980, Aug. 18 **Litho.** ***Perf. 12½***

1473 A358 30s lt grn & blk .35 .35
1474 A358 75s lt bl & blk .55 .55
1475 A358 2.30p sal & blk 1.60 .40
Nos. 1473-1475 (3) 2.50 1.30

Intl. Federation of Library Associations and Institutions, 46th Congress, Manila, 8/18-23.

Kabataang Barangay (New Society), 5th Anniversary — A359

1980, Sept. 19 **Litho.** ***Perf. 12½***

1476 A359 30s multi .25 .25
1477 A359 40s multi .35 .25
1478 A359 1p multi .80 .25
Nos. 1476-1478 (3) 1.40 .75

Nos. 1389, 1422, 1443, 1445, 1327 Surcharged in Blue, Black or Red

Wmk. 372

1980, Sept. 26 **Litho.** ***Perf. 12½***

1479 A328 40s on 30s rose (Bl) 1.00 .40
1480 A338 40s on 30s multi 1.00 .25
1481 A345 40s on 30s multi 1.00 1.00
1482 A346 40s on 30s multi (R) 2.00 .25
1483 A294 2p on 1.65p multi (R) 4.00 .30
Nos. 1479-1483 (5) 9.00 2.20

Catamaran, Conference Emblem — A360

1980, Sept. 27

1484 A360 30s multi .30 .30
1485 A360 2.30p multi 1.50 .50

World Tourism Conf., Manila, Sept. 27.

Stamp Day — A361

1980, Oct. 9

1486 A361 40s multi .40 .25
1487 A361 1p multi .85 .50
1488 A361 2p multi 1.75 1.75
Nos. 1486-1488 (3) 3.00 2.50

UN, 35th Anniv. — A362

Designs: 40s, UN Headquarters and Emblem, Flag of Philippines. 3.20p, UN and Philippine flags, UN headquarters.

1980, Oct. 20

1489 A362 40s multi .35 .25
1490 A362 3.20p multi 2.25 .65

Murex Alabaster A363

1980, Nov. 2

1491 A363 40s shown 1.10 .35
1492 A363 60s Bursa bubo .80 .35
1493 A363 1.20p Homalocantha zamboi 1.10 .65
1494 A363 2p Xenophora pallidula 2.00 1.00
Nos. 1491-1494 (4) 5.00 2.35

INTERPOL Emblem on Globe — A364

1980, Nov. 5 **Litho.** **Wmk. 372**

1495 A364 40s multi .40 .25
1496 A364 1p multi .85 .25
1497 A364 3.20p multi 2.25 .75
Nos. 1495-1497 (3) 3.50 1.25

49th General Assembly Session of INTERPOL (Intl. Police Organization), Manila, Nov. 13-21.

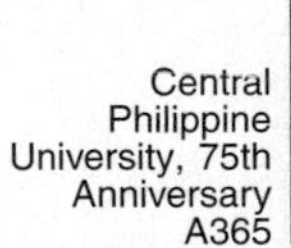
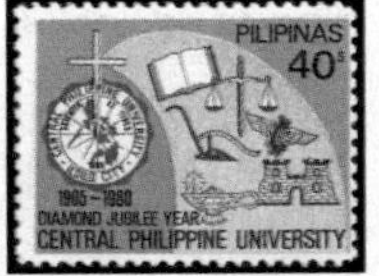

Central Philippine University, 75th Anniversary A365

1980, Nov. 17 **Unwmk.**

1498 A365 40s multi .75 .25
1499 A365 3.20p multi 2.25 1.00

No. 1257 Surcharged

Wmk. 372

1980, Nov. 21 **Litho.** ***Perf. 12½***

1500 A269 1.20p on 80s multi 1.50 .35

Philatelic Week. Surcharge similar to No. 1367.

No. 1358 Surcharged

1980, Nov. 30

1501 A313 40s on 30s multi 1.25 1.25

APO Philatelic Society, 30th anniversary.

Christmas Tree, Present and Candy Cane — A366

Perf. 12½

1980, Dec. 15 **Litho.** **Unwmk.**

1502 A366 40s multi .55 .25

Christmas 1980.

No. 1467 Surcharged

1981, Jan. 2

1503 A356 40c on 30s multi 2.00 2.00

Nos. 1370, 1257 Surcharged in Red or Black

1981

1504 A320 10s on 30s (R) multi 1.00 .50
1505 A269 85s on 80s multi 2.00 2.00

Issue dates: 10s, Jan. 12; 85s, Jan. 2.

Heinrich Von Stephan, UPU Emblem A367

1981, Jan. 30

1506 A367 3.20p multi 2.50 .75

Heinrich von Stephan (1831-1897), founder of UPU, birth sesquicentennial.

Pope John Paul II Greeting Crowd — A368

Designs: 90s, Pope, signature, vert. 1.20p, Pope, cardinals, vert. 3p, Pope giving blessing, Vatican arms, Manila Cathedral. 7.50p, Pope, light on map of Philippines, vert.

Perf. 13½x14

1981, Feb. 17 **Unwmk.**

1507 A368 90s multi .75 .25
1508 A368 1.20p multi .80 .80
1509 A368 2.30p multi 1.75 1.50
1510 A368 3p multi 2.50 2.00
Nos. 1507-1510 (4) 5.80 4.55

Souvenir Sheet

Perf. 13¾x13¼

1511 A368 7.50p multi 7.00 *8.25*

Visit of Pope John Paul, Feb. 17-22.
For surcharge, see No. 3046.

Nos. 1364, 1423, 1268, 1446, 1261, 1206, 1327 Surcharged

1981 **Litho.** ***Perf. 12½***

1512 A316 40s on 90s multi .90 .25
1513 A338 40s on 90s multi .90 .25
1514 A273 40s on 65s lil rose .90 .25
1515 A346 40s on 90s multi 1.50 1.50
1517 A271 1p on 1.50p brt rose & vio bl 1.50 .25
1518 A250 1.20p on 1.80p grn 2.10 1.00
1519 A294 1.20p on 1.65p multi 2.75 1.00
1520 A271 2p on 1.50p brt rose & vio bl 3.50 1.00
Nos. 1512-1520 (8) 14.05 5.50

A369

1981, Apr. 20 **Wmk. 372**

1521 A369 2p multi 1.40 1.00
1522 A369 3.20p multi 2.10 .75

68th Spring Meeting of the Inter-Parliamentary Union, Manila, Apr. 20-25.

Unless otherwise stated, Nos. 1523-1580 are on granite paper.

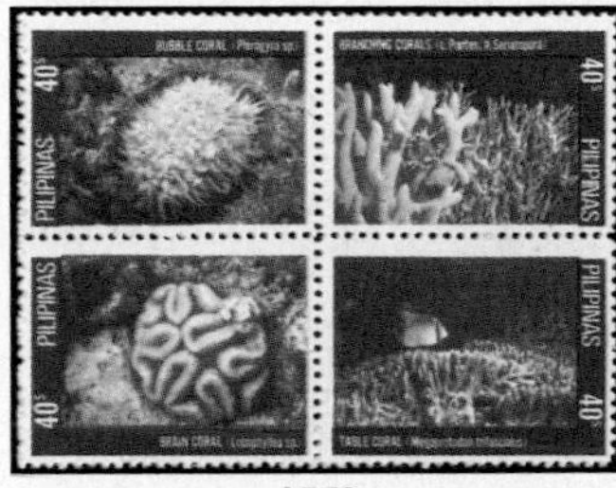

A370

Wmk. 372

1981, May 22 **Litho.** ***Perf. 12½***

1523 40s Bubble coral .90 .40
1524 40s Branching coral .90 .40
1525 40s Brain coral .90 .40
1526 40s Table coral .90 .40
a. A370 Block of 4, #1523-1526 5.00 5.00

Philippine Motor Assoc., 50th Anniv. — A371

Vintage cars.

1981, May 25

1527 40s Presidents car .80 .25
1528 40s 1930 .80 .25
1529 40s 1937 .80 .25
1530 40s shown .80 .25
a. A371 Block of 4, #1527-1530 3.50 3.50

Re-inauguration of Pres. Ferdinand E. Marcos — A372

1981, June 30

1531 A372 40s multi .50 .25

Souvenir Sheet

Imperf

1532 A372 5p multi 4.00 *5.00*

No. 1531 exists imperf. Value $1.
For overprint see No. 1753.

St. Ignatius Loyola, Founder of Jesuit Order A373

400th Anniv. of Jesuits in Philippines: No. 1534, Jose Rizal, Ateneo University. No. 1535, Father Federico Faura, Manila Observatory. No. 1536, Father Saturnino Urios, map of Philippines.

1981, July 31

1533 A373 40s multi .70 .25
1534 A373 40s multi .70 .25
1535 A373 40s multi .70 .25
1536 A373 40s multi .70 .25
a. Block of 4, #1533-1536 3.00 3.00

Souvenir Sheet

Imperf

1537 A373 2p multi 4.00 *4.75*

#1537 contains vignettes of #1533-1536. For surcharge see No. 1737.

A374

Design: 40s, Isabelo de los Reyes (1867-1938), labor union founder. 1p, Gen. Gregorio del Pilar (1875-1899). No. 1540, Magsaysay. No. 1541, Francisco Dagohoy. No. 1543, Ambrosia R. Bautista, signer of Declaration of Independence, 1898, No. 1544, Juan Sumulong (1875-1942), statesman. 2.30p, Nicanor Abelardo (1893-1934), composer. 3.20p, Gen. Vicente Lim (1888-1945), first Philippine graduate of West Point.

Wmk. 372

1981-82 Litho. *Perf. 12½*

1538 A374 40s grnsh bl ('82) .35 .25
1539 A374 1p blk & red brn .60 .25
1540 A374 1.20p blk & lt red brn .95 .25
1541 A374 1.20p brown ('82) 1.50 .35
1543 A374 2p blk & red brn 1.10 .35
1544 A374 2p rose lil ('82) 1.50 .35
1545 A374 2.30p lt red brn ('82) 1.75 .40
1546 A374 3.20p gray bl ('82) 2.25 .65
Nos. 1538-1546 (8) 10.00 2.85

See Nos. 1672-1680, 1682-1683, 1685. For surcharges see Nos. 1668-1669.

A375

1981, Sept. 2

1551 A375 40s multi .50 .25

Chief Justice Fred Ruiz Castro, 67th birth anniv.

A376

Wmk. 372

1981, Oct. 24 Litho. *Perf. 12½*

1552 A376 40s multi .40 .25
1553 A376 3.20p multi 2.10 .65

Intl. Year of the Disabled.

A376a

1981, Nov. 7

1554 A376a 40s multi .30 .25
1555 A376a 2p multi 1.40 .45
1556 A376a 3.20p multi 2.00 .60
Nos. 1554-1556 (3) 3.70 1.30

24th Intl. Red Cross Conf., Manila, 11/7-14.

Intramuros Gate, Manila — A377

1981, Nov. 13

1557 A377 40s black .50 .25

Manila Park Zoo Concert Series, Nov. 20-30 A378

1981, Nov. 20

1558 A378 40s multi .50 .25

No. 1329 Overprinted "1981 Philatelic Week" and Surcharged

Wmk. 372

1981, Nov. 23 Litho. *Perf. 12½*

1559 A296 1.20p on 1.50p multi 1.90 1.00

Nos. 1205, 1347, 1371 Surcharged

1981, Nov. 25 Litho. *Perf. 12½*

1560 A306 40s on 1.05p multi 1.25 1.25
1561 A320 40s on 1.35p multi 1.25 .75
1562 A273 1.20p on 1.50p brn 3.50 3.50
Nos. 1560-1562 (3) 6.00 5.50

11th Southeast Asian Games, Manila, Dec. 6-15 A379

40s, Running. 1p, Bicycling. 2p, Pres. Marcos, Intl. Olympic Pres. Samaranch. 2.30p, Soccer. 2.80p, Shooting. 3.20p, Bowling.

1981, Dec. 3

1563 A379 40s multi .55 .25
1564 A379 1p multi 1.10 .25
1565 A379 2p multi 2.25 .30
1566 A379 2.30p multi 2.75 .50
1567 A379 2.80p multi 3.50 1.00
1568 A379 3.20p multi 3.75 1.00
Nos. 1563-1568 (6) 13.90 3.30

Manila Intl. Film Festival, Jan. 18-29 A380

40s, Film Center. 2p, Golden trophy, vert. 3.20p, Trophy, diff., vert.

Wmk. 372

1982, Jan. 18 Litho. *Perf. 12½*

1569 A380 40s multicolored .40 .25
1570 A380 2p multicolored 1.75 .45
1571 A380 3.20p multicolored 2.50 .75
Nos. 1569-1571 (3) 4.65 1.45

Manila Metropolitan Waterworks and Sewerage System Centenary — A381

1982, Jan. 22

1572 A381 40s blue .40 .40
1573 A381 1.20p brown 1.25 .30

Nos. 1268, 1302, 1328 Surcharged

1981, Jan. 28

1574 A273 1p on 65s lil rose 2.00 .80
1575 A286 1p on 1.50p multi 1.25 .40
1576 A295 3.20p on 2.20p multi 6.00 1.00
Nos. 1574-1576 (3) 9.25 2.20

Scouting Year — A382

1982, Feb. 22

1577 A382 40s Portrait .45 .25
1578 A382 2p Scout giving salute 1.75 .55

25th Anniv. of Children's Museum and Library Foundation A383

1982, Feb. 25

1579 A383 40s Mural .30 .25
1580 A383 1.20p Children playing 1.25 .35

77th Anniv. of Philippine Military Academy A384

Wmk. 372

1982, Mar. 25 Litho. *Perf. 12½*

1581 A384 40s multi .40 .25
1582 A384 1p multi .85 .25

40th Bataan Day A385

1982, Apr. 9

1583 A385 40s Soldier .40 .25
1584 A385 2p "Reunion for Peace" 1.40 .30

Souvenir Sheet

Imperf

1585 A385 3.20p Cannon, flag 3.50 *4.00*

No. 1585 contains one 38x28mm stamp. No. 1585 comes on two different papers, the second being thicker with cream gum.
For surcharge see No. 2114.

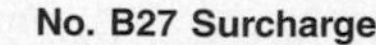

No. B27 Surcharged

1982 Photo. *Perf. 13½*

1586 SP14 10s on 6 + 5s multi 2.00 2.00

The "1" in the surcharged value of No. 1586 is unserifed. For similar surcharge with serifed "1," see No. 986.

A386

1982, Apr. 28 Litho. *Perf. 12½*

1587 A386 1p rose pink 1.50 .25

Aurora Aragon Quezon (1888-1949), former First Lady.
There are three types of No. 1587.
See Nos. 1684-1684A.

A387

1982, May 1

1588 A387 40s Man holding award .50 .25
1589 A387 1.20p Award 1.50 .25

7th Towers Awards.

UN Conf. on Human Environment, 10th Anniv. — A388

1982, June 5

1590 A388 40s Turtle .65 .25
1591 A388 3.20p Philippine eagle 3.75 1.00

75th Anniv. of Univ. of Philippines College of Medicine A389

1982, June 10

1592 A389 40s multi .50 .25
1593 A389 3.20p multi 2.00 .75

Natl. Livelihood Movement A390

1982, June 12

1594 A390 40s multi .50 .25

See #1681-1681A. For overprint see #1634.

Adamson Univ., 50th Anniv. — A391

1982, June 21

1595 A391 40s bl & multi .35 .25
1596 A391 1.20p lt vio & multi 1.10 .25

Social Security, 25th Anniv. — A392

1982, Sept. 1 ***Perf. 13½x13***

1597 A392 40s multi .30 .25
1598 A392 1.20p multi .90 .25

Pres. Marcos, 65th Birthday — A393

1982, Sept. 11 ***Perf. 13½x13***

1599 A393 40s sil & multi .50 .25
1600 A393 3.20p sil & multi 2.00 .75
a. Souv. sheet of 2, #1599-1600, imperf. 4.00 4.00

For surcharge see No. 1666.

15th Anniv. of Assoc. of Southeast Asian Nations (ASEAN) A394

1982, Sept. 22 Litho. ***Perf. 12½***

1601 A394 40s Flags .65 .25

St. Teresa of Avila (1515-1582) — A395

1982, Oct. 15 ***Perf. 13x13½***

1602 A395 40s Text .35 .25
1603 A395 1.20p Map .75 .25
1604 A395 2p like #1603 1.50 .25
Nos. 1602-1604 (3) 2.60 .75

10th Anniv. of Tenant Farmers' Emancipation Decree — A396

Perf. 13x13½

1982, Oct. 21 Litho. Wmk. 372

1605 A396 40s Pres. Marcos signing law 1.60 .25

See No. 1654.

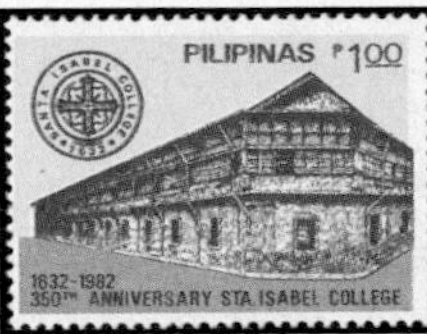
350th Anniv. of St. Isabel College A397

1982, Oct. 22

1606 A397 40s multi .30 .25
1607 A397 1p multi 1.25 .40

Reading Campaign A398

1982, Nov. 4

1608 A398 40s yel & multi .30 .25
1609 A398 2.30p grn & multi 1.50 1.00

For surcharge see No. 1713.

42nd Skal Club World Congress, Manila, Nov. 7-12 A399

1982, Nov. 7

1610 A399 40s Heads .35 .35
1611 A399 2p Chief 2.25 .60

25th Anniv. of Bayanihan Folk Arts Center A400

Designs: Various folk dances.

1982, Nov. 10 Litho. ***Perf. 13x13½***

1612 A400 40s multi .35 .25
1613 A400 2.80p multi 2.75 .65

TB Bacillus Centenary A401

1982, Dec. 7 Wmk. 372

1614 A401 40s multi .35 .25
1615 A401 2.80p multi 2.25 .75

Christmas 1982 A402

1982, Dec. 10

1616 A402 40s multi 1.00 .25
1617 A402 1p multi 2.75 .25

Philatelic Week, Nov. 22-28 A403

Perf. 13x13½

1982, Nov. 28 Litho. Wmk. 372

1618 A403 40s yel & multi .30 .25
1619 A403 1p sil & multi .90 .25

For surcharge see No. 1667.

Visit of Pres. Marcos to the US, Sept. A404

1982, Dec. 18

1620 A404 40s multi .50 *1.00*
1621 A404 3.20p multi 2.75 2.00
a. Souv. sheet of 2, #1620-1621 4.00 *4.75*

UN World Assembly on Aging, July 26-Aug. 6 — A405

1982, Dec. 24

1622 A405 1.20p Woman 1.10 .25
1623 A405 2p Man 1.50 .30

Senate Pres. Eulogio Rodriguez, Sr. (1883-1964) A406

1983, Jan. 21

1624 A406 40s grn & multi .30 .25
1625 A406 1.20p org & multi .90 .25

1983 Manila Intl. Film Festival, Jan. 24-Feb. 4 A407

1983, Jan. 24

1626 A407 40s blk & multi .35 .25
1627 A407 3.20p pink & multi 2.75 .75

Beatification of Lorenzo Ruiz (1981) — A408

Perf. 13x13½

1983, Feb. 18 Litho. Wmk. 372

1628 A408 40s multi .35 .25
1629 A408 1.20p multi 1.10 .25

400th Anniv. of Local Printing Press A409

1983, Mar. 14

1630 A409 40s blk & grn .50 .25

Safety at Sea — A410

1983, Mar. 17 ***Perf. 13½x13***

1631 A410 40s multi .50 .25

25th anniv. of Inter-Governmental Maritime Consultation Org. Convention.

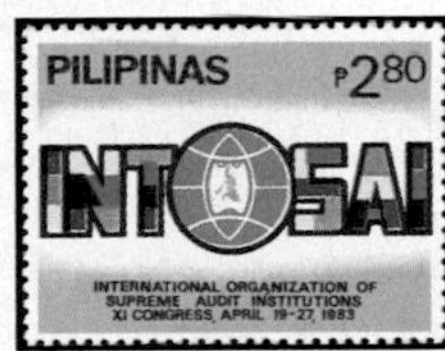
Intl. Org. of Supreme Audit Institutions, 11th Congress, Manila, Apr. 19-27 A411

Perf. 13x13½

1983, Apr. 8 Litho. Wmk. 372

1632 A411 40s Symbols .40 .25
1633 A411 2.80p Emblem 1.75 1.00
a. Souv. sheet of 2, 1632-1633, imperf. 4.25 *5.00*

No. 1633a comes on two papers: cream gum, normal watermark; white gum, watermark made up of smaller letters.

Type of 1982 Overprinted in Red: "7th BSP NATIONAL JAMBOREE 1983"

1983, Apr. 13 ***Perf. 12½***

1634 A390 40s multi 1.00 1.00

Boy Scouts of Philippines jamboree.

No. 1249 Surcharged

1983, Apr. 15

1635 Block of 10 15.00 *25.00*
a.-j. A265 40s on 45s, any single 1.00 2.00

A412

Perf. 13½x13

1983, May 9 Litho. Wmk. 372

1636 A412 40s multi .50 .25

75th anniv. of Dental Assoc.

A413

Perf. 13½x13

1983, June 17 Litho. Wmk. 372

No.	Type	Description	Unused	Used
1637	A413	40s Statue	.30	.25
1638	A413	1.20p Statue, diff., diamond	1.00	.25

75th anniv. of University of the Philippines.

Visit of Japanese Prime Minister Yasuhiro Nakasone, May 6-8 — A414

Perf. 13x13½

1983, June 20 Litho. Wmk. 372

No.	Type	Description	Unused	Used
1639	A414	40s multi	.50	.50

25th Anniv. of Natl. Science and Technology Authority A415

No. 1640, Animals, produce. No. 1641, Heart, food, pill. No. 1642, Factories, windmill, car. No. 1643, Chemicals, house, book.

1983, July 11

No.	Type	Description	Unused	Used
1640	A415	40s multicolored	.45	*.75*
1641	A415	40s multicolored	.45	*.75*
1642	A415	40s multicolored	.45	*.75*
1643	A415	40s multicolored	.45	*.75*
a.		Block of 4, #1640-1643	3.00	*6.00*

Science Week.

World Communications Year — A416

Wmk. 372

1983, Oct. 24 Litho. *Perf. 12½*

No.	Type	Description	Unused	Used
1644	A416	3.20p multi	2.25	.75

Philippine Postal System Bicentennial — A417

1983, Oct. 31

No.	Type	Description	Unused	Used
1645	A417	40s multi	.50	.25

Christmas — A418

Star of the East and Festival Scene in continuous design.

1983, Nov. 15 Litho. *Perf. 12½*

No.	Type	Description	Unused	Used
1646		Strip of 5	3.75	3.25
a.-e.		A418 40s single stamp	.75	.25
f.		Souvenir sheet	4.00	*4.75*

Xavier University, 50th Anniv. A419

1983, Dec. 1 Litho. *Perf. 14*

No.	Type	Description	Unused	Used
1647	A419	40s multi	.40	.25
1648	A419	60s multi	.90	.25

A420

1983, Dec. 8 Litho. *Perf. 12½*

No.	Type	Description	Unused	Used
1649	A420	40s brt ultra & multi	.40	.25
1650	A420	60s gold & multi	.90	.25

Ministry of Labor and Employment, golden jubilee.

A421

1983, Dec. 7

No.	Type	Description	Unused	Used
1651	A421	40s multi	.40	.40
1652	A421	60s multi	.90	.40

50th anniv. of Women's Suffrage Movement.

Philatelic Week A422

Stamp Collecting: a, Cutting. b, Sorting. c, Soaking. d, Affixing hinges. e, Mounting stamp.

1983, Dec. 20

No.	Type	Description	Unused	Used
1653		Strip of 5	*4.00*	4.00
a.-e.		A422 50s any single	.75	.75

Emancipation Type of 1982

1983 Litho. *Perf. 13*

Size: 32x22mm

No.	Type	Description	Unused	Used
1654	A396	40s multi	2.50	.45

Philippine Cockatoo — A423

40s, Philippine Cockatoo, 2.30p, Guaiabero. 2.80p, Crimson-spotted racket-tailed parrots. 3.20p, Large-billed parrot. 3.60p, Tanygnathus sumatranus. 5p, Hanging parakeets.

1984, Jan. 9 Unwmk. *Perf. 14*

No.	Type	Description	Unused	Used
1655	A423	40s multi	.55	.30
1656	A423	2.30p multi	*1.60*	.60
1657	A423	2.80p multi	*2.10*	.65
1658	A423	3.20p multi	*2.50*	.70
1659	A423	3.60p multi	*2.75*	.70
1660	A423	5p multi	*3.50*	.90
		Nos. 1655-1660 (6)	*13.00*	3.85

There were 500,000 of each value created cto with Jan 9 1984 cancel in the center of each block of 4. These were sold at a small fraction of face value. Used values are for ctos.

Princess Tarhata Kiram — A424

1984, Jan. 16 Wmk. 372 *Perf. 13*

No.	Type	Description	Unused	Used
1661	A424	3p grn & red	1.90	.35

Order of Virgin Mary, 300th Anniv. — A425

1984, Jan. 23 *Perf. 13½x13*

No.	Type	Description	Unused	Used
1662	A425	40s blk & multi	.60	.25
1663	A425	60s red & multi	1.25	.50

Dona Concha Felix de Calderon — A426

1984, Feb. 9 *Perf. 13*

No.	Type	Description	Unused	Used
1664	A426	60s blk & bl grn	.60	*1.00*
1665	A426	3.60p red & bl grn	1.75	1.50

Nos. 1546, 1599, 1618 Surcharged

1984, Feb. 20

No.	Type	Description	Unused	Used
1666	A393	60s on 40s (R)	.35	.25
1667	A403	60s on 40s	.40	.25
1668	A374	3.60p on 3.20p (R)	3.25	1.00
		Nos. 1666-1668 (3)	4.00	1.50

No. 1685 Surcharged

1985, Oct. 21 Litho. *Perf. 12½*

No.	Type	Description	Unused	Used
1669	A374	3.60p on 4.20p rose lil	5.50	3.00

Portrait Type of 1981

Designs: No. 1672, Gen. Artemio Ricarte. No. 1673, Teodoro M. Kalaw. No. 1674, Pres. Carlos P. Garcia. No. 1675, Senator Quintin Paredes. No. 1676, Dr. Deogracias V. Villadolid (1896-1976), 1st director, Bureau of Fisheries. No. 1677, Santiago Fonacier (1885-1940), archbishop. No. 1678, 2p, Vicente Orestes Romualdez (1885-1970), lawyer. 3p, Francisco Dagohoy.

Types of 3p:
Type I — Medium size "PILIPINAS," large, heavy denomination.
Type II — Large "PILIPINAS," medium denomination.

Perf. 13, 12½ (2p), 12½x13 (3p)

1984-85 Litho.

No.	Type	Description	Unused	Used
1672	A374	60s blk & lt brn	1.40	1.00
1673	A374	60s blk & pur	1.75	.40
1674	A374	60s black	1.75	.25
1675	A374	60s dull blue	.70	.25
1676	A374	60s brn blk ('85)	.70	.25
1677	A374	60s dk red ('85)	.50	.25
1678	A374	60s cobalt blue ('85)	.85	*1.00*
1679	A374	2p brt rose ('85)	3.50	.40
1680	A374	3p pale brn, type I	5.25	.30
1680A	A374	3p pale brn, type II	6.25	.30
		Nos. 1672-1680A (10)	22.65	4.40

Issued: #1672, 3/22; #1673, 3/31; #1674, 6/14; #1675, 9/12; #1676, 3/22; #1677, 5/21; #1678, 2p, 7/3; 3p, 9/7.

Types of 1982

Types of 3.60p:
Type I — Thick Frame line, large "P," "360" with line under "60."
Type II — Medium Frame line, small "p," "3.60."

1984-86

No.	Type	Description	Unused	Used
1681	A390	60s green & multi	.25	.25
1681A	A390	60s red & multi	.25	.25
1682	A374	1.80p #1546	1.10	.25
1683	A374	2.40p #1545	1.50	.25
1684	A386	3.60p Quezon, type I	1.60	.40
1684A	A386	3.60p As #1684, type II	1.75	.40
1685	A374	4.20p #1544	2.10	2.10
		Nos. 1681-1685 (7)	8.55	3.90

Issued: #1681A, 10/19; #1684A, 2/14/86; others 3/26.

Ayala Corp. Sesquicentenary — A427

Night Views of Manila.

1984, Apr. 25 Litho. *Perf. 13x13½*

No.	Type	Description	Unused	Used
1686	A427	70s multi	.50	.25
1687	A427	3.60p multi	2.25	.75

ESPANA '84 A428

Designs: 2.50p, No. 1690d, Our Lady of the Most Holy Rosary with St. Dominic, by C. Francisco. 5p, No. 1690a, Spoliarium, by Juan Luna. No. 1690b, Blessed Virgin of Manila as Patroness of Voyages, Galleon showing map of Panama-Manila. No. 1690c. Illustrations from The Monkey and the Turtle, by Rizal (first children's book published in Philippines, 1885.)

1984, Apr. 27 Unwmk. *Perf. 14*

No.	Type	Description	Unused	Used
1688	A428	2.50p multi	4.00	4.00
1689	A428	5p multi	10.00	10.00
a.		Pair, #1688-1689	16.00	16.00

Souvenir Sheet

Perf. 14½x15, Imperf.

No.	Type	Description	Unused	Used
1690		Sheet of 4, #a.-d.	25.00	25.00
a.-d.		A428 7.50p, any single	5.00	5.00

Surcharged in Black

Perf. 14½x15

No.	Type	Description	Unused	Used
1690A		Sheet of 4, #a.-d.	110.00	110.00
a.-d.		A428 7.20p on 7.50p, any single	16.00	16.00

Surcharged in Red

Imperf

No.	Type	Description	Unused	Used
1690B		Sheet of 4, #a.-d.	100.00	100.00
a.-d.		A428 7.20p on 7.50p, any single	25.00	25.00

Nos. 1690Aa-1690Ad and 1690Ba-1690Bd are each surcharged 7.20p and bear the following overprints: #1690Aa and #1690Ba, "10-5-84 NATIONAL MUSEUM WEEK" on #1690a; #1690Ab and #1690Bb, "8-3-84 PHILIPPINE-MEXICAN FRIENDSHIP 420th ANNIVERSARY" on #1690b; #1690Ac and #1690Bc, "7-17-84 NATIONAL CHILDREN'S BOOK DAY" on #1690c; #1690Ad and #1690Bd, "9-1-84 O.L. OF HOLY ROSARY PARISH 300TH YEAR" on #1690d. Nos. 1690Aa-1690Bd were released as single stamps on the dates shown in their respective overprints. A few intact sheets were sold after the release of the last of these stamps.

Maria Paz Mendoza Guazon — A429

1984, May 26 Wmk. 372 *Perf. 13*

1691	A429 60s brt blue & red	1.00	.25
1692	A429 65s brt blue, red & blk	.85	.25

Butterflies — A430

60s, Adolias amlana. 2.40p, Papilio daedalus. 3p, Prothoe frankii semperi. 3.60p, Troides magellanus. 4.20p, Yoma sabina vasuki. 5p, Chilasa idaeoides.

Unwmk.

1984, Aug. 2 Litho. *Perf. 14*

1693	A430 60s multi	.60	.80
1694	A430 2.40p multi	*1.25*	1.00
1695	A430 3p multi	*1.50*	1.00
1696	A430 3.60p multi	*1.50*	1.00
1697	A430 4.20p multi	*1.50*	*2.00*
1698	A430 5p multi	*2.10*	*3.00*
	Nos. 1693-1698 (6)	*8.45*	8.80

There were 500,000 of each value created cto with Jul 5 1984 cancel in the center of each block of 4. These were sold at a small fraction of face value. Used values are for ctos.

Summer Olympics, Los Angeles, 1984 — A431

Designs: 60s, Running (man). 2.40p, Boxing. 6p, Swimming. 7.20p, Windsurfing. 8.40p, Cycling. 20p, Running (woman).

Unwmk.

1984, Aug. 9 Litho. *Perf. 14*

1699	A431 60s multi	.25	*.50*
1700	A431 2.40p multi	1.00	1.00
1701	A431 6p multi	2.50	2.00
1702	A431 7.20p multi	3.00	3.00
1703	A431 8.40p multi	3.25	3.25
1704	A431 20p multi	8.00	8.00
	Nos. 1699-1704 (6)	18.00	17.75

Souvenir Sheet

1705	Sheet of 4	15.00	*20.00*
a.-d.	A431 6p, any single	2.50	2.50

There were 500,000 of each value created cto with Aug 8 1984 cancel in the center of each block of 4. These were sold at a small fraction of face value. Used value, set of 6 cto, $1.25.

Nos. 1699-1705 were also issued imperf, with blue, instead of red, stars at sides. Value, set of 6 stamps $100, souvenir sheet $50.

Baguio City, 75th Anniv. A432

Wmk. 372

1984, Aug. 24 Litho. *Perf. 12½*

1706	A432 1.20p The Mansion	1.25	1.25

Light Rail Transit A433

1984, Sept. 10 *Perf. 13x13½*

1707	A433 1.20p multi	1.25	.35

A similar unlisted issue shows a streecar facing left on the 1.20p.

No. 1, Australia No. 59 and Koalas A434

Perf. 14½x15

1984, Sept. 21 Unwmk.

1708	A434 3p multi	3.00	3.00
1709	A434 3.60p multi	4.00	4.00

Souvenir Sheet

1710	Sheet of 3	*30.00*	*30.00*
a.	A434 20p multi	*7.50*	*7.50*

AUSIPEX '84. No. 1710 exists imperf.

No. 1609 Surcharged with 2 Black Bars and Ovptd. "14-17 NOV. 84 / R.I. ASIA REGIONAL CONFERENCE"

Perf. 13x13½

1984, Nov. 11 Wmk. 372 Litho.

1713	A398 1.20p on 2.30p multi	2.00	*3.00*

Philatelic Week — A435

1984, Nov. 22 *Perf. 13½x13*

1714	A435 1.20p Gold medal	.50	.50
1715	A435 3p Winning stamp exhibit	1.50	1.50
a.	Pair, #1714-1715	2.75	2.75

AUSIPEX '84 and Mario Que, 1st Philippine exhibitor to win FIP Gold Award.

For overprints see Nos. 1737A and 1737B.

Ships A436

60s, Caracao canoes. 1.20p, Chinese junk. 6p, Spanish galleon. 7.20p, Casco. 8.40p, Steamboat. 20p, Cruise liner.

1984, Nov. Unwmk. Litho. *Perf. 14*

1718	A436 60s multi	.40	.25
1719	A436 1.20p multi	.40	.30
1720	A436 6p multi	1.75	.45
1721	A436 7.20p multi	2.25	.60
1722	A436 8.40p multi	2.50	1.25
1723	A436 20p multi	5.25	3.00
	Nos. 1718-1723 (6)	*12.55*	5.85

There were 500,000 of each value created cto with Oct 5 1984 cancel in the center of each block of 4. These were sold at a small fraction of face value. Value, set of 6 cto, $1.25.

For surcharge, see No. 3051.

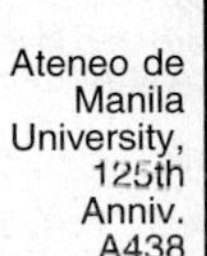

Ateneo de Manila University, 125th Anniv. A438

Perf. 13x13½

1984, Dec. 7 Wmk. 372 Litho.

1730	A438 60s ultra & gold	.55	.25
1731	A438 1.20p dk ultra & sil	1.10	.30

A438a

60s, Manila-Dagupan, 1892. 1.20p, Light rail transit, 1984. 6p, Bicol Express, 1955. 7,20p, Tranvis (1905, electric street car). 8.40, Commuter train, 1984. 20p, Early street car pulled by horses, 1898.

Perf. 14x13¾

1984, Dec. 18 Unwmk.

1731A	A438a 60s multi	.40	.25
1731B	A438a 1.20p multi	.85	.30
1731C	A438a 6p multi	2.50	.45
1731D	A438a 7.20p multi	3.25	.60
1731E	A438a 8.40p multi	3.50	.65
1731F	A438a 20p multi	7.50	6.00
	Nos. 1731A-1731F (6)	*18.00*	8.25

There were 500,000 of each value created cto with Dec 5 1984 cancel in the center of each block of 4. These were sold at a small fraction of face value. Value, set of 6 cto, $1.50.

For surcharges see #1772-1773.

Christmas A439

Perf. 13½x13

1984, Dec. 8 Wmk. 372

1732	A439 60s Madonna and Child	.75	.25
1733	A439 1.20p Holy family	2.50	1.00
a.	Pair, #1732-1733	2.25	2.25

Natl. Jaycees Awards, 25th anniv. — A440

Philippines Jaycees Commitment to Youth Development.

Abstract painting by Raoul G. Isidro.

1984, Dec. 19

1734	Strip of 10	*24.00*	*24.00*
a.-e.	A440 60s any single	.75	.75
f.-j.	A440 3p any single	3.00	3.00

Dried Tobacco Leaf and Plant A441

1985, Jan. 14 *Perf. 13x13½*

1735	A441 60s multicolored	.35	.25
1736	A441 3p multicolored	1.90	1.00

Philippine-Virginia Tobacco Admin., 25th anniv.

No. 1537 Surcharged

1985, Jan. Litho. *Imperf.*

1737	A373 3p on 2p multi	4.75	4.75

First printing had missing period ("p300"). Value $12.

Nos. 1714-1715 Overprinted "Philatelic Week 1984"

1985, Jan. *Perf. 13½x13*

1737A	A435 1.20p Gold medal	.50	.50
1737B	A435 3p Winning stamp exhibit	1.50	1.50
c.	Pair, #1737A-1737B	2.75	2.75

Natl. Research Council Emblem A442

1985, Feb. 3 Litho. *Perf. 13x13½*

1738	A442 60s bl, dk bl & blk	.30	.25
1739	A442 1.20p org, dk bl & blk	1.00	.25

Pacific Science Assoc., 5th intl. congress, Manila, Feb. 3-7.

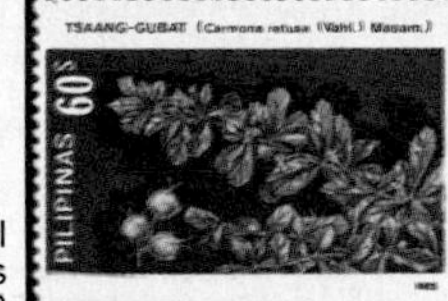

Medicinal Plants A443

60s, Carmona retusa. 1.20p, Orthosiphon aristatus. 2.40p, Vitex negundo. 3p, Aloe barbadensis. 3.60p, Quisqualis indica. 4.20p, Blumea balsamifera.

1985, Mar. 15 *Perf. 12½*

1740	A443 60s multi	1.25	.25
1741	A443 1.20p multi	2.40	.50
1742	A443 2.40p multi	3.75	.65
1743	A443 3p multi	3.75	.75
1744	A443 3.60p multi	4.75	2.00
1745	A443 4.20p multi	6.50	3.00
	Nos. 1740-1745 (6)	22.40	7.15

INTELSAT, 20th Anniv. A444

1985, Apr. 6 *Perf. 13x13½*

1746	A444 60s multicolored	.35	.25
1747	A444 3p multicolored	2.25	1.50

A444a

Philippine Horses: 60s, Pintos. 1.20p, Palomino. 6p, Bay. 7.20p, Brown. 8.40p, Gray. 20p, Chestnut.

#1747G: h, as 1.20p. i, as 7.20p. j, as 6p. k, as 20p.

Perf. 14x13¾

1984, Dec. 18 Unwmk.

1747A	A444a 60s multi	.40	1.00
1747B	A444a 1.20p multi	.85	.35
1747C	A444a 6p multi	2.00	.75
1747D	A444a 7.20p multi	2.75	.90
1747E	A444a 8.40p multi	3.25	2.00
1747F	A444a 20p multi	6.75	3.00
	Nos. 1747A-1747F (6)	16.00	8.00

Souvenir Sheet of 4

1747G	A444a 8.40p h.-k.	15.00	*20.00*

There were 500,000 each of #1747A-1747F created cto with Apr 12 1985 cancel in the center of each block of 4. These were sold at a small fraction of face value. Value, set of 6 cto, $1.50.

Tax Research Institute, 25th Anniv. — A445

Perf. 13½x13

1985, Apr. 22 Wmk. 372

1748	A445 60s multicolored	.60	.60

Intl. Rice Research Institute, 25th Anniv. A446

1985, May 27 *Perf. 13x13½*

1749	A446 60s Planting		.40	.40
1750	A446 3p Paddies		2.25	1.00

1st Spain-Philippines Peace Treaty, 420th Anniv. — A447

Designs: 1.20p, Blessed Infant of Cebu, statue, shrine and basilica. 3.60p, King Tupas of Cebu and Miguel Lopez de Legaspi signing treaty, 1565.

1985, June 4 *Perf. 12½*

1751	A447 1.20p multi	.50	.25
1752	A447 3.60p multi	1.00	.30
a.	Pair, #1751-1752 + label	4.50	4.50

No. 1532 Ovptd. "10th Anniversary Philippines and People's Republic of China Diplomatic Relations 1975-1985"

1985, June 8 *Imperf.*

1753	A372 5p multi	6.00	*7.00*

Arbor Week, June 9-15 — A448

1985, June 9 *Perf. 13½x13*

1754	A448 1.20p multi	1.25	1.00

Battle of Bessang Pass, 40th Anniv. A449

1985, June 14 *Perf. 13x13½*

1755	A449 1.20p multi	1.25	1.00

Natl. Tuberculosis Soc., 75th Anniv. — A450

1985, July 29

1756	A450 60s Immunization, research	1.00	.80
1757	A450 1.20p Charity seal	2.00	1.25
a.	Pair, #1756-1757	4.00	4.00

No. 1297 Surcharged with Bars, New Value and Scout Emblem in Gold, Ovptd. "GSP" and "45th Anniversary Girl Scout Charter" in Black

Perf. 12½x13½

1985, Aug. 19 Unwmk. Photo.

1758	A242 2.40p on 15s on 10s	1.50	1.50
1759	A242 4.20p on 15s on 10s	2.50	2.50
1760	A242 7.20p on 15s on 10s	3.50	3.50
	Nos. 1758-1760 (3)	7.50	7.50

Virgin Mary Birth Bimillennium A451

Statues and paintings.

Perf. 13½x13

1985, Sept. 8 Wmk. 372 Litho.

1761	A451 1.20p Fatima	.70	.40
1762	A451 2.40p Beaterio	1.60	.80
1763	A451 3p Penafrancia	2.25	1.50
1764	A451 3.60p Guadalupe	2.75	2.00
	Nos. 1761-1764 (4)	7.30	4.70

Intl. Youth Year A452

Prize-winning children's drawings.

1985, Sept. 23 *Perf. 13x13½*

1765	A452 2.40p Agriculture	1.00	.35
1766	A452 3.60p Education	2.00	.75

Girl and Rice Terraces A453

1985, Sept. 26

1767	A453 2.40p multi	2.25	.65

World Tourism Organization, 6th general assembly, Sofia, Bulgaria, Sept. 17-26.

Export Year — A454

1985, Oct. 8 *Perf. 13½x13*

1768	A454 1.20p multi	1.25	.35

UN, 40th Anniv. — A455

1985, Oct. 24

1769	A455 3.60p multi	2.50	.65

1st Transpacific Airmail Service, 50th Anniv. — A456

3p, China Clipper on water. 3.60p, China Clipper, map.

1985, Nov. 22 *Perf. 13x13½*

1770	A456 3p multi	2.25	1.00
1771	A456 3.60p multi	2.75	1.00

Nos. 1731C-1731D Surcharged in Black

Perf. 14x13¾

1985, Nov. 24 Unwmk.

1772	A438a 60s on 6p	.75	.75
1773	A438a 3p on 7.20p	3.25	3.25

No. 1773 is airmail.

Natl. Bible Week A457

1985, Dec. 3 Wmk. 372 *Perf. 12½*

1774	A457 60s multicolored	.40	.40
1775	A457 3p multicolored	2.25	2.25

Christmas 1985 A458

1985, Dec. 8 *Perf. 13x13½*

1776	A458 60s Panuluyan	.50	.50
1777	A458 3p Pagdalaw	2.50	1.50

Scales of Justice A459

1986, Jan. 12

1778	A459 60s lilac rose & blk	.40	.25
1779	A459 3p brt grn, lil rose & blk	2.10	1.00

University of the Philippines, College of Law, 75th anniv.

See No. 1838.

Flores de Heidelberg, by Jose Rizal — A460

Design: 60s, Noli Me Tangere.

1986 Wmk. 391 Litho. *Perf. 13*

1780	A460 60s violet	.30	.25
1781	A460 1.20p bluish grn	1.25	.25
1782	A460 3.60p redsh brn	2.25	.35
	Nos. 1780-1782 (3)	3.80	.85

Issued: 60s, 1.20p, Feb. 21; 3.60p, July 10.

For surcharges see Nos. 1834, 1913.

Philippine Airlines, 45th Anniv. — A461

Aircraft: No. 1783a, Douglas DC3, 1946. b, Douglas DC4 Skymaster, 1946. c, Douglas DC6, 1948. d, Vickers Viscount 784, 1957.

No. 1784a, Fokker Friendship F27 Mark 100, 1960. b, Douglas DC8 Series 50, 1962. c, Bac One Eleven Series 500, 1964. d, McDonnell Douglas DC10 Series 30, 1974.

No. 1785a, Beech Model 18, 1941. b, Boeing 747, 1980.

1986, Mar. 15

1783	A461 Block of 4	*4.00*	4.00
a.-d.	60s, any single	*1.00*	1.00
1784	A461 Block of 4	*7.50*	7.50
a.-d.	2.40p, any single	*1.50*	1.50
1785	A461 Pair	*5.25*	5.25
a.-b.	3.60p, any single	*2.25*	2.25
	Nos. 1783-1785 (3)	*16.75*	16.75

See No. 1842.

Bataan Oil Refining Corp., 25th Anniv. A462

Perf. 13½x13, 13x13½

1986, Apr. 12 Wmk. 372

1786	A462 60s Refinery, vert.	.40	.35
1787	A462 3p shown	2.00	1.00

EXPO '86, Vancouver A463

Perf. 13x13½

1986, May 2 Wmk. 391

1788	A463 60s multicolored	.40	.35
1789	A463 3p multicolored	2.10	1.00

Asian Productivity Organization, 25th Anniv. — A464

1986

1790	A464 60s multicolored	.40	.40
1791	A464 3p multicolored	2.25	2.00

Size: 30x22mm

1792	A464 3p pale brown	1.25	.30
	Nos. 1790-1792 (3)	3.90	2.70

Issued: #1790-1791, 5/15; #1792, 7/10.

AMERIPEX '86 — A465

1986, May 22 *Perf. 13½x13*
1793 A465 60s No. 241 .40 .25
1794 A465 3p No. 390 2.00 .70

See No. 1835.

Election of Corazon Aquino, 7th Pres. — A466

Portrait of Aquino and: 60s, Salvador Laurel, vice-president, and hands in symbolic gestures of peace and freedom. 1.20p, Symbols of communication and transportation. 2.40p, Parade. 3p, Military. 7.20p, Vice-president, parade, horiz.

1986, May 25 **Wmk. 372**
1795 A466 60s multi .25 .25
1796 A466 1.20p multi .40 .25
1797 A466 2.40p multi 1.10 .30
1798 A466 3p multi 1.25 .50
Nos. 1795-1798 (4) 3.00 1.30

Souvenir Sheet
Imperf

1799 A466 7.20p multi 4.00 *4.75*

For surcharge see No. 1939.

De La Salle University, 75th Anniv. A467

60s, Statue of St. John the Baptist de la Salle, Paco buildings, 1911, & university, 1986. 2.40p, St. Miguel Febres Cordero, buildings, 1911. 3p, St. Benilde, buildings, 1986. 7.20p, Founding fathers.

Perf. 13x13½
1986, June 16 **Wmk. 391**
1800 A467 60s grn, blk & pink .50 .50
1801 A467 2.40p grn, blk & bl 1.25 1.00
1802 A467 3p grn, blk & yel 2.00 1.50
Nos. 1800-1802 (3) 3.75 3.00

Souvenir Sheet
Imperf

1803 A467 7.20p grn & blk 5.00 *6.00*

For surcharge see No. 1940.

A468

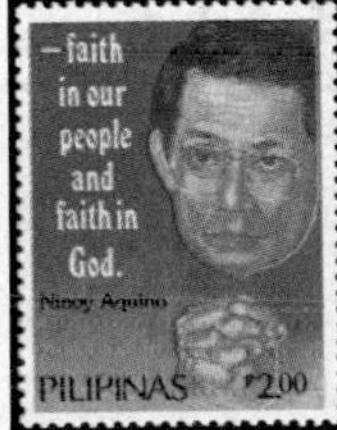

Memorial to Benigno S. Aquino, Jr. (1932-83) A469

3.60p, The Filipino is worth dying for, horiz. 10p, Hindi ka nag-iisa, horiz.

Perf. 13½x13, 13x13½
1986, Aug. 21 **Wmk. 389**
1804 A468 60s dl bluish grn .40 .25
1805 A469 2p shown 1.00 .35
1806 A469 3.60p multicolored 1.60 1.00
Nos. 1804-1806 (3) 3.00 1.60

Souvenir Sheet
Imperf

1807 A469 10p multicolored 4.75 *5.50*

See No. 1836. For surcharges see No. 1914 and 2706A.

Indigenous Orchids — A470

60s, Vanda sanderiana. 1.20p, Epigeneium lyonii. 2.40p, Paphiopedilum philippinense. 3p, Amesiella philippinensis.

1986, Aug. 28 *Perf. 13½x13*
1808 A470 60s multi *.50* .25
1809 A470 1.20p multi *1.50* 1.00
1810 A470 2.40p multi *2.75* 2.00
1811 A470 3p multi *3.50* 3.00
Nos. 1808-1811 (4) *8.25* 6.25

For surcharge see No. 1941.

Quiapo District, 400th Anniv. — A471

60s, Our Lord Jesus the Nazarene, statue, Quiapo church. 3.60p, Quiapo church, 1930, horiz.

Perf. 13½x13, 13x13½
1986, Aug. 29 **Wmk. 391**
1812 A471 60s pink, blk & lake .35 .25
1813 A471 3.60p pale grn, blk & dk ultra 2.50 .75

For surcharge see No. 1915.

General Hospital, 75th Anniv. — A472

1986, Sept. 1 *Perf. 13½x13*
1814 A472 60s bl & multi .30 *1.00*
1815 A472 3p grn & multi 1.75 *2.00*

See No. 1841. For surcharge see No. 1888.

Halley's Comet A473

Perf. 13x13½
1986, Sept. 25 **Wmk. 389**
1816 A473 60s Comet, Earth .50 .25
1817 A473 2.40p Comet, Earth, Moon 2.00 .50

For surcharge see No. 1942.

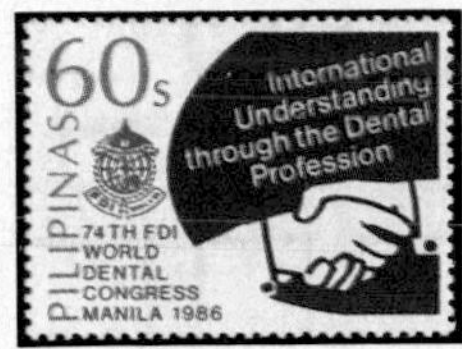

74th FDI World Dental Congress, Manila A474

1986, Nov. 10 **Litho.** *Perf. 13x13½*
1818 A474 60s Handshake .75 .25
1819 A474 3p Jeepney bus *4.25* 1.00

See Nos. 1837, 1840.

Insects A475

Intl. Peace Year — A476

Perf. 13x13½, 13½x13
1986, Nov. 21
1820 A475 60s Butterfly, beetles *1.00* .30
1821 A476 1p blue & blk *2.00* .80
1822 A475 3p Dragonflies *3.00* 1.00
Nos. 1820-1822 (3) *6.00* 2.10

Philately Week.

Manila YMCA, 75th Anniv. — A477

Perf. 13x13½
1986, Nov. 28 **Wmk. 391**
1823 A477 2p blue *1.25* .40
1824 A477 3.60p red *3.25* .60

See No. 1839. For surcharge see No. 1916.

Philippine Normal College, 85th Anniv. A478

Various arrangements of college crest and buildings, 1901-1986.

1986, Dec. 12 **Wmk. 389**
1825 A478 60s multi *1.00* 1.00
1826 A478 3.60p buff, ultra & gldn brn 2.75 2.00

For surcharge see No. 1917.

Christmas A479

No. 1827, Holy family. No. 1828, Mother and child, doves. No. 1829, Child touching mother's face. No. 1830, Adoration of the shepherds. No. 1831, Mother, child signaling peace. No. 1832, Holy family, lamb. No. 1833, Mother, child blessing food.

1986, Dec. 15 *Perf. 13½x13, 13x13½*
1827 A479 60s multicolored *.50* .25
1828 A479 60s multicolored *.50* .25
1829 A479 60s multicolored *.50* .25
1830 A479 1p multicolored *.75* .50
1831 A479 1p multicolored *.75* .50
1832 A479 1p multicolored *.75* .50
1833 A479 1p multicolored *.75* .50
Nos. 1827-1833 (7) *4.50* 2.75

Nos. 1827-1829, vert.

No. 1780 Surcharged
Wmk. 391

1987, Jan. 6 **Litho.** *Perf. 13*
1834 A460 1p on 60s vio 1.00 .25

Types of 1986

Designs: 75s, No. 390, AMERIPEX '86. 1p, Benigno S. Aquino, Jr. 3.25p, Handshake, 74th World Dental Congress. 3.50p, Scales of Justice. 4p, Manila YMCA emblem. 4.75p, Jeepney bus. 5p, General Hospital. 5.50p, Boeing 747, 1980.

Types of 4p
Type I — "4" is taller than "0's."
Type II — "4" is same height as "0's."

1987 **Litho.** *Perf. 13*
Size: 22x31mm, 31x22mm
1835 A465 75s brt yel grn .75 .25
1836 A468 1p blue .75 .25
1837 A474 3.25p dull grn 1.50 .75
1838 A459 3.50p dark car 2.00 .40
1839 A477 4p blue, type I 3.00 .40
1839A A477 4p blue, type II 6.00 5.00
1840 A474 4.75p dl yel grn 3.00 2.50
1841 A472 5p olive bister 3.00 2.50
1842 A461 5.50p dk bl gray 3.00 3.00
Nos. 1835-1842 (9) 23.00 15.05

All No. 1839 dated "1-1-87."
Issued: #1839A, 12/16; others, 1/16.

Manila Hotel, 75th Anniv. A480

Perf. 13x13½
1987, Jan. 30 **Wmk. 389**
1843 A480 1p Hotel, c. 1912 .50 .40
1844 A480 4p Hotel, 1987 2.10 1.00
1845 A480 4.75p Lobby 2.50 1.25
1846 A480 5.50p Foyer 4.00 1.50
Nos. 1843-1846 (4) 9.10 4.15

Intl. Eucharistic Congress, Manila, 50th Anniv. A481

1987, Feb. 7 *Perf. 13½x13, 13x13½*
1847 A481 75s Emblem, vert. .50 .25
1848 A481 1p shown .70 .40

Pres. Aquino Taking Oath A482

Text — A483

1987, Mar. 4 *Perf. 13½x13, 13x13½*
1849 A482 1p multi .40 .10
1850 A483 5.50p bl & deep bis 2.40 .65

Ratification of the new constitution.
See No. 1905. For surcharge see No. 2005.

Lyceum College and Founder, Jose P. Laurel A484

1987, May 7 Litho. *Perf. 13x13½*
1851 A484 1p multi .50 .25
1852 A484 2p multi 1.25 1.00

Lyceum of the Philippines, 35th anniv.

Government Service Insurance System — A485

1p, Salary and policy loans. 1.25p, Disability, medicare. 2p, Retirement benefits. 3.50p, Life insurance.

1987, June 1 *Perf. 13½x13*
1853 A485 1p multi .45 .25
1854 A485 1.25p multi .65 .40
1855 A485 2p multi 1.10 .80
1856 A485 3.50p multi 1.60 1.00
Nos. 1853-1856 (4) 3.80 2.45

Davao City, 50th Anniv. A486

1p, Falconer, woman planting, city seal.

1987, Mar. 16 Litho. *Perf. 13x13½*
1857 A486 1p multicolored .75 .30

Salvation Army in the Philippines, 50th Anniv. — A487

1987, June 5 Photo. *Perf. 13½x13*
1858 A487 1p multi 1.25 1.25

Natl. League of Women Voters, 50th Anniv. — A488

1987, July 15
1859 A488 1p pink & blue .75 .75

A489

#1861, Gen. Vicente Lukban (1860-1916). #1862, Wenceslao Q. Vinzons (1910-1942). #1863, Brig.-gen. Mateo M. Capinpin (1887-1958). #1864, Jesus Balmori (1882-1948).

Perf. 13x13½, 12½ (#1862)
1987 Litho. Wmk. 391
1861 A489 1p olive grn .50 .25
1862 A489 1p dull greenish blue .60 .25
1863 A489 1p dull red brn .60 .25
1864 A489 1p rose red & rose claret .50 .25
Nos. 1861-1864 (4) 2.20 1.00

Issued: #1861, 7/31; #1862, 9/9; #1863, 10/15; #1864, 12/17.

A490

Nuns (1862-1987), children, Crucifix, Sacred Heart.

Perf. 13½x13
1987, July 22 Litho. Wmk. 389
1881 A490 1p multi .90 .90

Daughters of Charity of St. Vincent de Paul in the Philippines, 125th anniv.

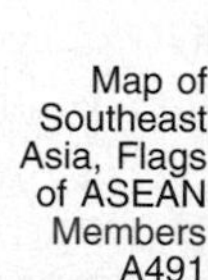

Map of Southeast Asia, Flags of ASEAN Members A491

1987, Aug. 7 *Perf. 13x13½*
1882 A491 1p multi .90 .90

ASEAN, 20th anniv.

Exports Campaign A492

1987, Aug. 11 Wmk. 391 *Perf. 13*
1883 A492 1p shown .40 .25
1884 A492 2p Worker, gearwheel .85 .25

See No. 1904.

Canonization of Lorenzo Ruiz by Pope John Paul II, Oct. 18 — A493

First Filipino saint: 1p, Ruiz, stained glass window showing Crucifixion. 5.50p, Ruiz at prayer, execution in 1637.

Perf. 13½x13
1987, Oct. 10 Litho. Wmk. 389
1885 A493 1p multi .75 .25
1886 A493 5.50p multi 3.00 1.00

Size: 57x57mm

Imperf
1887 A493 8p like 5.50p 4.50 4.50
Nos. 1885-1887 (3) 8.25 5.75

No. 1887 has denomination at LL.

No. 1841 Surcharged

1987, Oct. 12 Wmk. 391 *Perf. 13*
1888 A472 4.75p on 5p olive bis 1.90 .90

Order of the Good Shepherd Sisters in Philippines, 65th Anniv. A494

Perf. 13x13½
1987, Oct. 27 Wmk. 389
1889 A494 1p multi 1.50 1.00

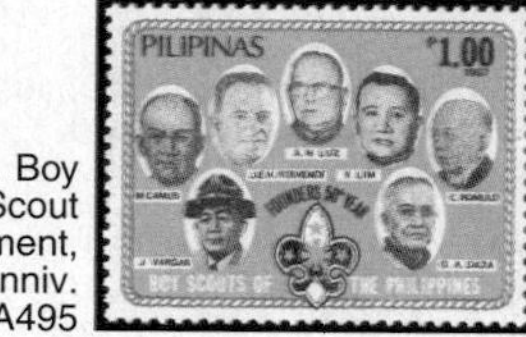

Natl. Boy Scout Movement, 50th Anniv. A495

Founders: J. Vargas, M. Camus, J.E.H. Stevenot, A.N. Luz, V. Lim, C. Romulo and G.A. Daza.

1987, Oct. 28 Litho. *Perf. 13x13½*
1890 A495 1p multi 1.25 1.00

Philippine Philatelic Club, 50th Anniv. A496

1987, Nov. 7 *Perf. 13x13½*
1891 A496 1p multi 1.25 1.00

Order of the Dominicans in the Philippines, 400th Anniv. A497

Designs: 1p, First missionaries shipwrecked, church and image of the Virgin, vert. 4.75p, J.A. Jeronimo Guerrero, Br., Diego de St. Maria and Letran Dominican College. 5.50p, Pope with Dominican representatives.

Perf. 13½x13, 13x13½
1987, Nov. 11
1892 A497 1p multi .30 .25
1893 A497 4.75p multi 1.75 1.00
1894 A497 5.50p multi 2.50 2.50
Nos. 1892-1894 (3) 4.55 3.75

3rd ASEAN Summit Meeting, Dec. 14-15 A498

1987, Dec. 5 *Perf. 13x13½*
1895 A498 4p multicolored 2.50 2.50

Christmas 1987 — A499

No. 1896, Postal service. No. 1897, 5-Pointed stars. No. 1898, Procession, church. No. 1899, Gift exchange. No. 1900, Bamboo cannons. No. 1901, Pig, holiday foods. No. 1902, Traditional foods. No. 1903, Serving meal.

1987, Dec. 8 *Perf. 13½x13*
1896 A499 1p multicolored .45 .45
1897 A499 1p multicolored .45 .45
1898 A499 4p multicolored 2.25 2.25
1899 A499 4.75p multicolored 2.25 2.25
1900 A499 5.50p multicolored 3.00 3.00
1901 A499 8p multicolored 4.00 4.00
1902 A499 9.50p multicolored 4.50 4.50
1903 A499 11p multicolored 5.25 5.25
Nos. 1896-1903 (8) 22.15 22.15

Exports Type of 1987

Design: Worker, gearwheel.

Wmk. 391
1987, Dec. 16 Litho. *Perf. 13*
1904 A492 4.75p lt blue & blk 1.40 .25

Constitution Ratification Type of 1987

1987, Dec. 16 *Perf. 13*
Size: 22x31½mm
1905 A483 5.50p brt yel grn & fawn 1.60 .45

Grand Masonic Lodge of the Philippines, 75th Anniv. A500

Perf. 13x13½
1987, Dec. 19 Wmk. 389
1906 A500 1p multi 1.50 .50

United Nations Projects A501

Designs: a, Intl. Fund for Agricultural Development (IFAD). b, Transport and Communications Decade for Asia and the Pacific. c, Intl. Year of Shelter for the Homeless (IYSH). d, World Health Day, 1987.

1987, Dec. 22 Litho. *Perf. 13x13½*
1907 Strip of 4 + label *9.00* 9.00
a.-d. A501 1p, any single 2.00 2.00

Label pictures UN emblem. Exists imperf. Value $30.

7th Opening of Congress A502

Designs: 1p, Official seals of the Senate and Quezon City House of Representatives, gavel, vert. 5.50p, Congress in session.

1988, Jan. 25 *Perf. 13½x13, 13x13½*
1908 A502 1p multi .75 .25
1909 A502 5.50p multi 3.00 .85

St. John Bosco (1815-1888), Educator — A503

1988, Jan. 31 *Perf. 13x13½*
1910 A503 1p multi .30 .25
1911 A503 5.50p multi 2.40 .60

Buy Philippine Goods — A504

1988, Feb. 1 Litho. *Perf. 13½x13*

1912 A504 1p buff, ultra, blk & scar .60 .25

Nos. 1782, 1806, 1813, 1824, 1826 Surcharged

Wmk. 389 (#1914, 1917), 391 (#1913, 1915, 1916)

Perf. 13 (#1782), 13x13½

1988, Feb. 14

1913 A460 3p on 3.60p redsh brn 2.50 2.00
1914 A469 3p on 3.60p multi 2.50 .40
1915 A471 3p on 3.60p pale grn, blk & dark ultra 3.00 2.00
1916 A477 3p on 3.60p red 3.50 .50
1917 A478 3p on 3.60p buff, ultra & golden brn 3.50 2.00
Nos. 1913-1917 (5) 15.00 6.90

Use Zip Codes — A505

1988, Feb. 25 Wmk. 391 *Perf. 13*

1918 A505 60s multi .35 .25
1919 A505 1p multi .55 .25

Insects That Prey on Other Insects — A506

1p, Vesbius purpureus. 5.50p, Campsomeris aurulenta.

1988, Mar. 11 *Perf. 13*

1920 A506 1p multi .40 .25
1921 A506 5.50p multi 2.25 .65

Solar Eclipse 1988 A507

Perf. 13x13½

1988, Mar. 18 Unwmk.

1922 A507 1p multi .50 .25
1923 A507 5.50p multi 2.50 .50

Toribio M. Teodoro (1887-1965), Shoe Manufacturer A508

Wmk. 391

1988, Apr. 27 Litho. *Perf. 13*

1924 A508 1p multicolored .60 .25
1925 A508 1.20p multicolored .90 .25

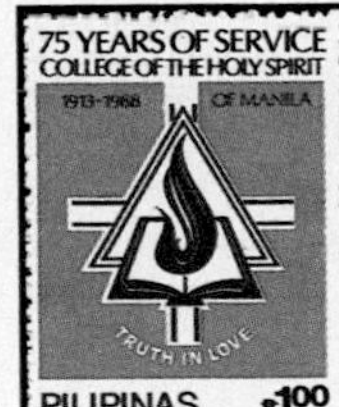

A509

College of the Holy Spirit, 75th anniv.: 1p, Emblem and motto "Truth in Love." 4p, Arnold Janssen, founder, and Sr. Edelwina, director 1920-1947.

Perf. 13½x13

1988, May 22 Unwmk.

1926 A509 1p blk, mar & gold .35 .25
1927 A509 4p blk, ol grn & mar 2.00 1.75

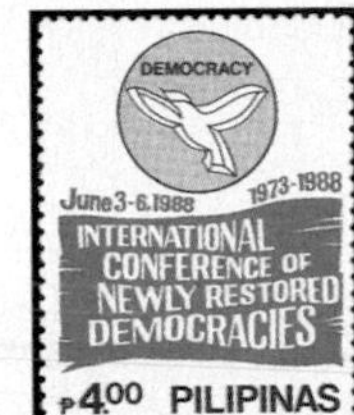

A510

Perf. 13½x13

1988, June 4 Litho. Unwmk.

1928 A510 4p dark ultra, brt blue & blk 2.25 .65

Intl. Conf. of Newly Restored Democracies.

A511

Juan Luna and Felix Hidalgo.

1988, June 15 Wmk. 391 *Perf. 13*

1929 A511 1p multi .40 .25
1930 A511 5.50p multi 1.90 .55

First Natl. Juan Luna and Felix Resurreccion Hidalgo Commemorative Exhibition, June 15-Aug. 15. Artists Luna and Hidalgo won medals at the 1884 Madrid Fine Arts Exhibition.

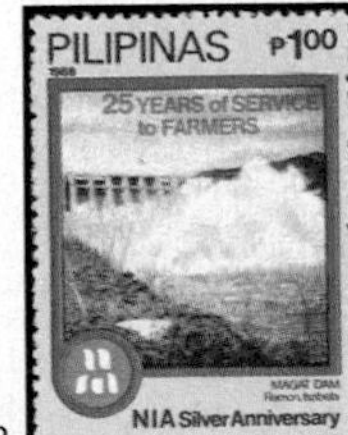

A512

Perf. 13½x13

1988, June 22 Litho. Wmk. 372

1931 A512 1p multi .50 .25
1932 A512 5.50p multi 2.50 .75

Natl. Irrigation Administration, 25th anniv.

Natl. Olympic Committee Emblem and Sporting Events A513

Designs: 1p, Scuba diving, Siquijor Is. 1.20p, Big game fishing, Aparri, Cagayan Province. 4p, Yachting, Manila Central. 5.50p, Climbing Mt. Apo. 8p, Golf, Cebu, Cebu Is. 11p, Cycling through Marawi, Mindanao Is.

1988, July 11 *Perf. 13x13½*

1933 A513 1p multi .40 .25
1934 A513 1.20p multi .40 .40
1935 A513 4p multi 1.60 1.00
1936 A513 5.50p multi 2.00 1.50
1937 A513 8p multi 2.75 2.00
1938 A513 11p multi 3.75 3.00
Nos. 1933-1938 (6) *10.90* 8.15

Exist imperf. 4p, 8p, 1p and 5.50p also exist in strips of 4 plus center label, perf and imperf, picturing torch and inscribed "Philippine Olympic Week, May 1-7, 1988."

Nos. 1797, 1801, 1810 and 1817 Surcharged with 2 Bars and New Value in Black or Gold (#1942)

1988, Aug. 1 As Before

1939 A466 1.90p on 2.40p #1797 1.25 .60
1940 A467 1.90p on 2.40p #1801 1.25 .60
1941 A470 1.90p on 2.40p #1810 1.25 .60
1942 A473 1.90p on 2.40p #1817 1.25 .60
Nos. 1939-1942 (4) 5.00 2.40

Land Bank of the Philippines, 25th Anniv. A514

Philippine Intl. Commercial Bank, 50th Anniv. A515

Perf. 13x13½

1988, Aug. 8 Litho. Wmk. 372

1943 A514 1p shown .40 .40
1944 A515 1p shown .40 .40
1945 A514 5.50p like No. 1943 2.75 .80
1946 A515 5.50p like No. 1944 2.75 .80
Nos. 1943-1946 (4) 6.30 2.40

Nos. 1943-1944 and 1945-1946 exist in se-tenant pairs from center rows of the sheet.

Profile of Francisco Balagtas Baltasar (b. 1788), Tagalog Language Poet, Author — A516

Wmk. 391

1988, Aug. 8 Litho. *Perf. 13*

1947 A516 1p Facing right .35 .25
1948 A516 1p Facing left .35 .25
a. Pair, #1947-1948 1.25 1.25

Quezon Institute, 50th Anniv. A517

Perf. 13x13½

1988, Aug. 18 Litho. Wmk. 372

1949 A517 1p multi .50 .25
1950 A517 5.50p multi 3.25 .65

Philippine Tuberculosis Soc.

Mushrooms — A518

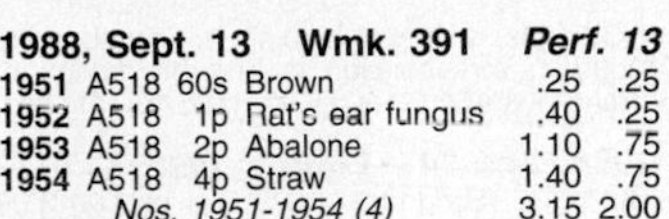

1988, Sept. 13 Wmk. 391 *Perf. 13*

1951 A518 60s Brown .25 .25
1952 A518 1p Rat's ear fungus .40 .25
1953 A518 2p Abalone 1.10 .75
1954 A518 4p Straw 1.40 .75
Nos. 1951-1954 (4) 3.15 2.00

1988 Summer Olympics, Seoul — A519

1p, Women's archery. 1.20p, Women's tennis. 4p, Boxing. 5.50p, Women's running. 8p, Swimming. 11p, Cycling.

Perf. 13½x13

1988, Sept. 19 Wmk. 372

1955 A519 1p multi .45 .45
1956 A519 1.20p multi .50 .50
1957 A519 4p multi 1.40 1.40
1958 A519 5.50p multi 1.90 1.90
1959 A519 8p multi 2.00 2.00
1960 A519 11p multi 2.75 2.75
Nos. 1955-1960 (6) 9.00 9.00

Souvenir Sheet

Imperf

1961 Sheet of 4 15.00 15.00
a. A519 5.50p Weight lifting 3.25 2.75
b. A519 5.50p Basketball, horiz. 3.25 2.75
c. A519 5.50p Judo 3.25 2.75
d. A519 5.50p Shooting, horiz. 3.25 2.75

Nos. 1955-1960 exist imperf. Value $25.

Department of Justice, Cent. A520

1988, Sept. 26 *Perf. 13x13½*

1962 A520 1p multi .60 .25

Intl. Red Cross and Red Crescent Organizations, 125th Annivs. — A521

1988, Sept. 30 *Perf. 13½x13*

1963 A521 1p multi .50 .25
1964 A521 5.50p multi 2.50 .70

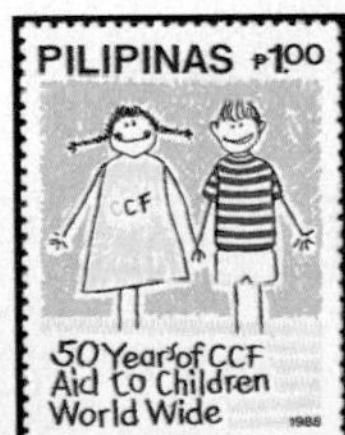

Christian Children's Fund, 50th Anniv. — A522

1988, Oct. 6

1965 A522 1p multi .00 .25

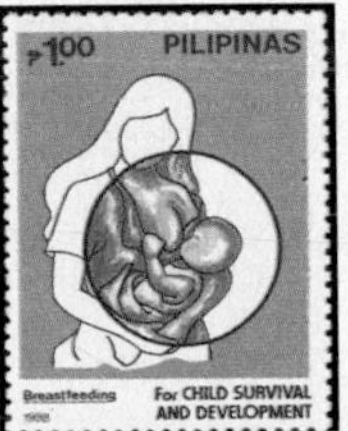

UN Campaigns A523

Designs: a, Breast-feeding. b, Growth monitoring. c, Immunization. d, Oral rehydration. e, Oral rehydration therapy. f, Youth on crutches.

1988, Oct. 24 Litho. *Perf. 13½x13*
1966 Strip of 5 *3.00* 3.00
a.-e. A523 1p any single .60 .60

Child Survival Campaign (Nos. 1966a-1966d); Decade for Disabled Persons (No. 1966e).

Bacolod City Charter, 50th Anniv. A524

1988, Oct. 19 Litho. *Perf. 13x13½*
1967 A524 1p multi .60 .25

UST Graduate School, 50th Anniv. — A525

1988, Dec. 20 Litho. *Perf. 13½x13*
1968 A525 1p multi .60 .25

Dona Aurora Aragon Quezon (b. 1888) — A526

1988, Nov. 7 Wmk. 391 *Perf. 13*
1969 A526 1p multi .30 .25
1970 A526 5.50p multi 2.00 .55

Malate Church, 400th Anniv. — A527

a, Church, 1776. b, Statue & anniv. emblem. c, Church, 1880. d, Church, 1988. Continuous design.

1988, Dec. 16 Wmk. 391
1971 A527 Block of 4 1.50 1.50
a.-d. 1p any single .35 .35

UN Declaration of Human Rights, 40th Anniv. A528

Perf. 13½x13
1988, Dec. 9 Wmk. 372
1972 A528 1p shown .45 .25
1973 A528 1p Commission on human rights .45 .25
a. Pair, Nos. 1972-1973 1.00 1.00

Long Distance Telephone Company A529

1988, Nov. 28
1974 A529 1p Communications tower .60 .25

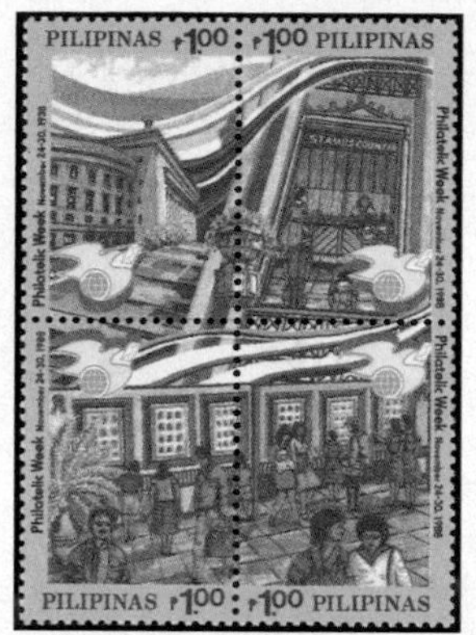

Philatelic Week, Nov. 24-30 — A530

Emblem and: a, Post Office. b, Stamp counter. c, Framed stamp exhibits, four people. d, Exhibits, 8 people. Has a continuous design.

1988, Nov. 24 Wmk. 391 *Perf. 13*
1975 A530 Block of 4 2.50 2.50
a.-d. 1p any single .55 .55
e. As "a," dated "1938" (error) 10.00 10.00

Christmas A531

Designs: 75s, Handshake, peave dove, vert. 1p, Children making ornaments. 2p, Boy carrying decoration. 3.50p, Tree, vert. 4.75p, Candle, vert. 5.50p, Man, star, heart.

1988, Dec. 2
1976 A531 75s multi .50 .25
1977 A531 1p multi .50 .25
1978 A531 2p multi 1.00 .25
1979 A531 3.50p multi 1.50 .35
1980 A531 4.75p multi 2.00 .35
1981 A531 5.50p multi 2.50 .50
Nos. 1976-1981 (6) 8.00 1.95

Gen. Santos City, 50th Anniv. A532

Perf. 13x13½
1989, Feb, 27 Litho. Wmk. 372
1982 A532 1p multi .60 .25

Guerrilla Fighters — A533

Emblem and: No. 1983, Miguel Z. Ver (1918-42). No. 1984, Eleuterio L. Adevoso (1922-75). Printed in continuous design.

1989, Feb. 18 Wmk. 391
1983 1p multi .40 .25
1984 1p multi .40 .25
a. A533 Pair, #1983-1984 1.25 1.25

Oblates of Mary Immaculate, 50th Anniv. — A534

Perf. 13½x13
1989, Feb. 17 Wmk. 372
1985 A534 1p multicolored .60 .25

Fiesta Islands '89 — A535

No. 1986, Turumba. No. 1987, Pahiyas. No. 1988, Pagoda Sa Wawa. No. 1989, Masskara. No. 1990, Independence Day. No. 1990A, like #1995. No. 1991, Sinulog. No. 1992, Cagayan de Oro. No. 1993, Grand Canao. No. 1994, Lenten festival. No. 1995, Penafrancia. No. 1996, Fireworks. No. 1997, Iloilo Paraw regatta.

Perf. 13 (Nos. 1991, 1994, 1997), 13½x14
1989-90 Litho. Wmk. 391
1986 A535 60s multicolored .25 .25
1987 A535 75s multicolored .30 .25
1988 A535 1p multicolored .25 .25
1989 A535 1p multicolored .35 .25
1990 A535 3.50p multicolored .95 .25
1990A A535 4p multicolored 2.25 .40
1991 A535 4.75p multicolored 1.10 .25
1992 A535 4.75p multicolored 1.10 .25
1993 A535 4.75p multicolored 1.10 .35
1994 A535 5.50p multicolored 1.10 .60
1995 A535 5.50p multicolored 1.40 .55
1996 A535 5.50p multicolored 1.50 .70
1997 A535 6.25p multicolored 1.90 1.00
Nos. 1986-1997 (13) 13.55 5.35

Issued: #1991, 1994, 6.25p, 3/1/89; 60s, 75s, 3.50p, 6/28/89; #1988, 1992, 1995, 9/1/89; #1989, 1993, 1996, 12/1/89; 4p, 8/6/90.

Great Filipinos — A536

Men and women: a, Don Tomas B. Mapua (1888-), educator. b, Camilo O. Osias (1889-), educator. c, Dr. Olivia D. Salamanca (1889-), physician. d, Dr. Francisco S. Santiago (1889-), composer. e, Leandro H. Fernandez (1889-), educator.

Perf. 14x13½
1989, May 18 Litho. Unwmk.
1998 Strip of 5 3.00 3.00
a.-e. A536 1p any single .35 .35

See Nos. 2022, 2089, 2151, 2240, 2307, 2360, 2414, 2486, 2536.

26th World Congress of the Intl. Federation of Landscape Architects — A537

Designs: a, Adventure Pool. b, Paco Park. c, Beautification of Malacanang area streets. d, Erosion control at an upland farm.

1989, May 31 Wmk. 391
1999 A537 Block of 4 2.00 2.00
a.-d. 1p any single .35 .35

Printed in continuous design.

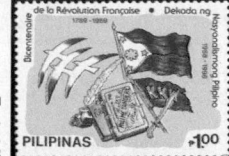

French Revolution, Bicent. A538

1989, July 1 *Perf. 14*
2000 A538 1p multi .30 .25
2001 A538 5.50p multi 1.90 .60

Supreme Court — A539

1989, June 11 Wmk. 372
2002 A539 1p multi .60 .25

Natl. Science and Technology Week — A540

1989, July 14
2003 1p GNP chart .40 .25
2004 1p Science High School emblem .40 .25
a. A540 Pair, #2003-2004 .90 .90

No. 1905 Surcharged
Wmk. 391
1989, Aug. 21 Litho. *Perf. 13*
2005 A483 4.75p on 5.50p 1.25 .35

Philippine Environment Month — A542

No. 2006, Palawan peacock pheasant. No. 2007, Palawan bear cat.

1989, June 5 Litho. *Perf. 14*
2006 1p multicolored .60 .25
2007 1p multicolored .60 .25
a. A542 Pair, #2006-2007 2.00 2.00

Asia-Pacific Telecommunity, 10th Anniv. — A544

Wmk. 372
1989, Oct. 30 Litho. *Perf. 14*
2008 A544 1p multicolored .60 .25

Dept. of Natl. Defense, 50th Anniv. — A545

1989, Oct. 23
2009 A545 1p multicolored .60 .25

Intl. Maritime Organization — A546

1989, Nov. 13 ***Perf. 14***
2010 A546 1p multicolored .60 .25

World Stamp Expo '89 A546a

1989, Nov. 17 **Litho.** ***Perf. 14***
2010A A546a 1p #1, Y1 .60 *2.00*
2010B A546a 4p #219, 398 2.00 *4.00*
2010C A546a 5.50p #N1, 500 3.00 *6.00*
Nos. 2010A-2010C (3) 5.60 *12.00*

Nos. 2010A-2010C withdrawn from sale week of release.

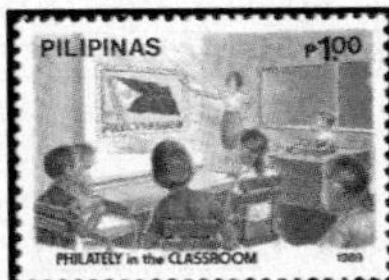

Teaching Philately in the Classroom, Close-up of Youth Collectors A547

1989, Nov. 20 ***Perf. 14x13½***
2011 A547 1p shown .50 .40
2012 A547 1p Class, diff. .50 .40

Christmas — A548

60s, Annunciation. 75s, Visitation. 1p, Journey to Bethlehem. 2p, Search for the inn. 4p, Appearance of the star. 4.75p, Birth of Jesus Christ.

1989 ***Perf. 13½x14***
2013 A548 60s multi .25 .25
2014 A548 75s multi .30 .25
2015 A548 1p multi .35 .25
2016 A548 2p multi .65 .25
2017 A548 4p multi 1.00 1.00
2018 A548 4.75p multi 1.25 1.25
Nos. 2013-2018 (6) 3.80 3.25

11th World Cardiology Congress A549

Wmk. 391

1990, Feb. 12 **Photo.** ***Perf. 14***
2019 A549 5.50p black, dark red & deep blue 1.25 .35

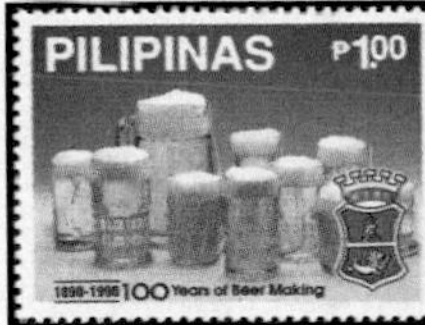

Beer Production, Cent. A550

1990, Apr. 16
2020 A550 1p multicolored .25 .25
2021 A550 5.50p multicolored 1.25 .35

Great Filipinos Type of 1989

Designs: a, Claro M. Recto (1890-1960), politician. b, Manuel H. Bernabe. c, Guillermo E. Tolentino. d, Elpidio R. Quirino (1890-1956), politician. e, Bienvenido Ma. Gonzalez.

Perf. 14x13½

1990, June 1 **Litho.** **Unwmk.**
2022 Strip of 5, #a.-e. 3.00 3.00

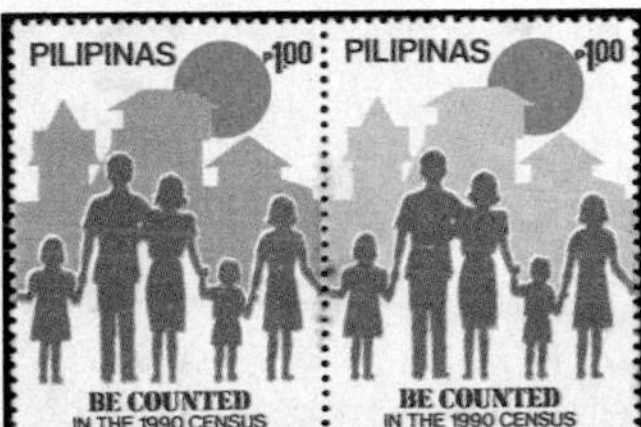

1990 Census — A551

Wmk. 391

1990, Apr. 30 **Photo.** ***Perf. 14***
Color of Buildings
2023 1p light blue .45 .25
2024 1p beige .45 .25
a. A551 Pair, #2023-2024 1.00 1.00

Legion of Mary, 50th Anniv. — A552

1990, July 21 **Photo.** ***Perf. 14***
2025 A552 1p multicolored .60 .25

Girl Scouts of the Philippines, 50th Anniv. A553

1990, May 21
2026 A553 1p yellow & multi .30 .25
2027 A553 1.20p lt lilac & multi .45 .25

Asian Pacific Postal Training Center, 20th Anniv. A554

Wmk. 391

1990, Sept. 10 **Photo.** ***Perf. 14***
2028 A554 1p red & multi .30 .25
2029 A554 4p blue & multi 1.25 .35

Natl. Catechetical Year — A555

1990, Sept. 28
2030 A555 1p blk & multi .25 .25
2031 A555 3.50p grn & multi 1.00 .30

Intl. Literacy Year A556

1990, Oct. 24 **Photo.** ***Perf. 14***
2032 A556 1p blk, org & grn .25 .25
2033 A556 5.50p blk, yel & grn 1.60 .40

UN Development Program, 40th Anniv. — A557

1990, Oct. 24
2034 A557 1p yel & multi .25 .25
2035 A557 5.50p orange & multi 1.60 .40

Flowers — A558

1990 **Photo.** **Wmk. 391** ***Perf. 14***
2036 A558 1p Waling waling .50 .25
2037 A558 4p Sampaguita 1.75 .50

29th Orient and Southeast Asian Lions forum.
Issued: 1p, Oct. 3; 4p, Oct. 18.

A559

Christmas A560

Drawings of the Christmas star: a, Yellow star, pink beading. b, Yellow star, white beading. c, Green, blue, yellow and orange star. d, Red star, white outlines.

1990, Dec. 3
2038 A559 Strip of 4 2.00 2.00
a.-d. 1p any single .30 .25
2039 A560 5.50p multicolored 1.75 .50

Blind Safety Day A561

1990, Dec. 7 **Photo.** ***Perf. 14***
2040 A561 1p bl, blk & yel .50 .25

Publication of Rizal's "Philippines After 100 Years," Cent. A562

1990, Dec.17
2041 A562 1p multicolored .50 .25

Philatelic Week A563

Paintings: 1p, Family by F. Amorsolo. 4.75p, The Builders by V. Edades. 5.50p, Laughter by A. Magsaysay-Ho.

1990, Nov. 16
2042 A563 1p multicolored .25 .25
2043 A563 4.75p multi, vert. 1.25 .40
2044 A563 5.50p multi, vert. 1.50 .50
Nos. 2042-2044 (3) 3.00 1.15

A564

1991, Jan. 30
2045 A564 1p multicolored .50 .25

2nd Plenary Council of the Philippines.

A565

1991, Mar. 15 **Litho.** ***Perf. 14***
2046 A565 1p multicolored .25 .25
2047 A565 5.50p multicolored 1.40 .35

Philippine Airlines, 50th anniv. No. 2047 is airmail.

Flowers — A566

Flowers: 1p, 2p, Plumeria. 4p, 6p, Ixora. 4.75p, 7p, Bougainvillea. 5.50p, 8p, Hibiscus.

1991 **Photo.** ***Perf. 14x13½***
"1991" Below Design
2048 A566 60s Gardenia .35 .25
2049 A566 75s Allamanda *.35* .25
2050 A566 1p yellow *.40* .25
2051 A566 1p red *.40* .25

2052 A566 1p salmon *.40* .25
2053 A566 1p white *.40* .25
a. Block of 4, #2050-2053 *1.75* 1.75
2054 A566 1.20p Nerium *.50* .25
2055 A566 1.50p like #2048 *.75* .25
2056 A566 2p yellow *1.00* .30
2057 A566 2p red *1.00* .30
2058 A566 2p rose & yel *1.00* .30
2059 A566 2p white *1.00* .30
a. Block of 4, #2056-2059 *4.25* 4.25
2060 A566 3p like #2054 *1.40* .35
2061 A566 3.25p Cananga *1.50* .40
2062 A566 4p dull rose *1.75* .50
2063 A566 4p pale yellow *1.75* .50
2064 A566 4p orange yel *1.75* .50
2065 A566 4p scarlet *1.75* .50
a. Block of 4, #2062-2065 *8.25* 8.25
2066 A566 4.75p vermilion *2.10* .70
2067 A566 4.75p brt rose lil *2.10* .70
2068 A566 4.75p white *2.10* .70
2069 A566 4.75p lilac rose *2.10* .70
a. Block of 4, #2066-2069 *9.00* 9.00
2070 A566 5p Canna *2.50* .80
2071 A566 5p like #2061 *2.50* .80
2072 A566 5.50p red *2.50* .85
2073 A566 5.50p yellow *2.50* .85
2074 A566 5.50p white *2.50* .85
2075 A566 5.50p pink *2.50* .85
a. Block of 4, #2072-2075 *11.00* 11.00
2076 A566 6p dull rose *3.00* 1.00
2077 A566 6p pale yellow *3.00* 1.00
2078 A566 6p orange yel *3.00* 1.00
2079 A566 6p scarlet *3.00* 1.00
a. Block of 4, #2076-2079 *13.00* 13.00
2080 A566 7p vermilion *3.50* 1.10
2081 A566 7p brt rose lil *3.50* 1.10
2082 A566 7p white *3.50* 1.10
2083 A566 7p dp lil rose *3.50* 1.10
a. Block of 4, #2080-2083 *14.50* 14.50
2084 A566 8p red *3.75* 1.25
2085 A566 8p yellow *3.75* 1.25
2086 A566 8p white *3.75* 1.25
2087 A566 8p deep pink *3.75* 1.25
a. Block of 4, #2084-2087 *16.00* 16.00
2088 A566 10p like #2070 *5.00* *6.00*
Nos. 2048-2088 (41) *86.85* 33.15

Issued: #2053a, 2075a, 4/1/91. #2048, 2049, 2061, 4/11. #2054, 2065a, 2069a, 2070, 6/7. #2059a, 2079a, 2083a, 2087a, 12/1. #2055, 2060, 2071, 2088, 12/13.

1992-93 "1992" Below Design

2048a A566 60s Gardenia .50 .50
2050a A566 1p yellow *.75* .50
2051a A566 1p red *.75* .50
2052a A566 1p salmon *.75* .50
2053c A566 1p white *.90* .60
d. Block of 4, #2050a-2052a, 2053c *4.00* 4.00
2053B A566 1p like #2049 *.75* .50
2055a A566 1.50p like #2048 *.40* .25
2056a A566 2p yellow *1.25* .50
2057a A566 2p red *1.25* .45
2058a A566 2p rose & yel *1.25* .45
2059b A566 2p white *1.25* .45
c. Block of 4, , #2056a-2058a, 2059b *6.00* 6.00
2060a A566 3p like #2054 *1.00* .80
2071a A566 5p like #2061 *2.00* 2.00
2076a A566 6p dull rose *3.00* 2.00
2077a A566 6p pale yellow *3.00* 2.00
2078a A566 6p orange yel *3.00* 2.00
2079b A566 6p scarlet *3.00* 2.00
c. Block of 4, #2076a-2078a, 2079b *16.00* 16.00
2080a A566 7p vermilion *3.00* 2.00
2081a A566 7p brt rose lil *3.00* 2.00
2082a A566 7p white *3.00* 3.00
2083b A566 7p dp lil rose *3.00* 3.00
c. Block of 4, #2080a-2082a, 2083b *14.00* 14.00
2084a A566 8p red *3.00* 2.40
2085a A566 8p yellow *3.00* 2.40
2086a A566 8p white *3.00* 2.40
2087b A566 8p deep pink *3.00* 2.40
c. Block of 4, #2084a-2086a, 2087b *14.00* 14.00
2088a A566 10p like #2070 *7.00* *8.00*
Nos. 2048a-2088a (26) *55.80* 43.60

Issued: 2059c, 1/24/92. 2053d, 2060a, 2/10. #2079c, 2/12. #2083c, 2/27. #2048a, 3/4. #2071a, 3/24. #2087c, 3/25. #2088a, 9/22. #2053B, 1/23/93.

No. 2053B, although issued in 1993, is inscribed "1992."

Great Filipinos Type of 1989

Designs: a, Jorge B. Vargas (1890-1980). b, Ricardo M. Paras (1891-1984). c, Jose P. Laurel (1891-1959), politician. d, Vicente Fabella (1891-1959). e, Maximo M. Kalaw (1891-1954).

1991, June 3 Litho. ***Perf. 14x13½***
2089 A536 1p Strip of 5, #a.-e. 3.00 3.00

12th Asia-Pacific Boy Scout Jamboree A567

1p, Square knot. 4p, Sheepshank knot. 4.75p, Figure 8 knot.

1991, Apr. 22 ***Perf. 14x13½***
2090 A567 1p multicolored .30 .25
2091 A567 4p multicolored .90 .25
2092 A567 4.75p multicolored 1.10 .30
a. Souv. sheet of 3, #2090-2092, imperf. 4.50 4.50
Nos. 2090-2092 (3) 2.30 .80

No. 2092a sold for 16.50p and has simulated perfs.

Antipolo by Carlos V. Francisco A568

1991, June 23 Litho. ***Perf. 14***
Granite Paper
2093 A568 1p multicolored .60 .25

Pithecophaga Jefferyi — A569

1991, July 31 **Photo.**
2094 A569 1p Head *1.00* .30
2095 A569 4.75p Perched on limb *2.25* .50
2096 A569 5.50p In flight *3.50* 1.00
2097 A569 8p Feeding young *5.00* 2.00
Nos. 2094-2097 (4) *11.75* 3.80

World Wildlife Fund.

Philippine Bar Association, Cent. — A570

Wmk. 391
1991, Aug. 20 Photo. ***Perf. 14***
2098 A570 1p multicolored .50 .25

A571

1991, Aug. 29
2099 A571 1p multicolored .70 .25
Size: 82x88mm
Imperf
2100 A571 16p like #2099 6.00 6.00

Induction of Filipinos into USAFFE (US Armed Forces in the Far East), 50th Anniv. For overprint see No. 2193.

A572

Independence Movement, cent.: a, Basil at graveside. b, Simon carrying lantern. c, Father Florentino, treasure chest. d, Sister Juli with rosary.

1991, Sept. 18
2101 A572 1p Block of 4, #a.-d. 4.00 4.00

A573

Wmk. 391
1991, Oct. 15 Photo. ***Perf. 14***
2102 A573 1p multicolored .50 .25
Size: 60x60mm
Imperf
2103 A573 16p multicolored 6.00 6.00

St. John of the Cross, 400th death anniv.

United Nations Agencies A574

Designs: 1p, UNICEF, children. 4p, High Commissioner for Refugees, hands supporting boat people. 5.50p, Postal Administration, 40th anniv., UN #29, #C3.

1991, Oct. 24 ***Perf. 14***
2104 A574 1p multicolored .25 .25
2105 A574 4p multicolored .90 .25
2106 A574 5.50p multicolored 1.40 .65
Nos. 2104-2106 (3) 2.55 1.15

Philatelic Week A575

Paintings: 2p, Bayanihan by Carlos Francisco. 7p, Sari-sari Vendor by Mauro Malang Santos. 8p, Give Us This Day by Vicente Manansala.

1991, Nov. 20
2107 A575 2p multicolored .35 .25
2108 A575 7p multicolored 1.50 .40
2109 A575 8p multicolored 1.90 .50
Nos. 2107-2109 (3) 3.75 1.15

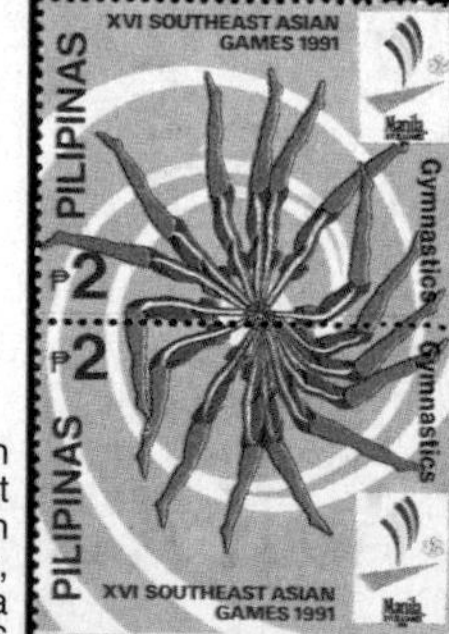

16th Southeast Asian Games, Manila A576

#2110, Gymnastics, games emblem at UR. #2111, Gymnastics, games emblem at LR. #2112, Martial arts, games emblem at LL, vert. #2113, Martial arts, games emblem at LR, vert.

Wmk. 391
1991, Nov. 22 Photo. ***Perf. 14***
2110 2p multicolored .35 .35
2111 2p multicolored .35 .35
a. A576 Pair, #2110-2111 1.00 1.00
2112 6p multicolored 1.00 .50
2113 6p multicolored 1.00 .50
a. A576 Pair, #2112-2113 2.75 2.75
b. Souv. sheet of 2, #2112-2113, imperf. 3.00 *3.50*
c. Souv. sheet of 4, #2110-2113 4.00 *4.75*
Nos. 2110-2113 (4) 2.70 1.70

No. 2113b has simulated perforations.

No. 1585 Surcharged in Red
Souvenir Sheet

1991, Nov. 27 Wmk. 372 ***Imperf.***
2114 A385 4p on 3.20p 3.00 *3.50*

First Philippine Philatelic Convention.

Children's Christmas Paintings — A577

1991, Dec. 4 Wmk. 391 ***Perf. 14***
2115 A577 2p shown .40 .25
2116 A577 6p Wrapped gift 1.10 .35
2117 A577 7p Santa, tree 1.40 .40
2118 A577 8p Tree, star 1.50 .45
Nos. 2115-2118 (4) 4.40 1.45

Insignias of Military Groups Inducted into USAFFE — A578

White background: No. 2119a, 1st Regular Div. b, 2nd Regular Div. c, 11th Div. d, 21st Div. e, 31st Div. f, 41st Div. g, 51st Div. h, 61st Div. i, 71st Div. j, 81st Div. k, 91st Div. l, 101st Div. m, Bataan Force. n, Philippine Div. o, Philippine Army Air Corps. p, Offshore Patrol.

Nos. 2120a-2120p, like #2119a-2119p with yellow background.

Perf. 14x13½
1991, Dec. 8 Photo. Wmk. 391
2119 A578 2p Block of 16, #a.-p. 15.00 *25.00*
2120 A578 2p Block of 16, #a.-p. 15.00 *25.00*
q. Block of 32, #2119-2120 *50.00* *80.00*

Induction of Filipinos into USAFFE, 50th anniv.

Nos. 2119-2120 were printed in sheets of 200 containing 5 #2120q plus five blocks of 8.

Basketball, Cent. A579

Designs: 2p, PBA Games, vert. 6p, Map, player dribbling. 7p, Early players. 8p, Men shooting basketball, vert. 16p, Tip-off.

Wmk. 391
1991, Dec. 19 Litho. ***Perf. 14***
2121 A579 2p multicolored .60 .25
2122 A579 6p multicolored 1.50 .50
2123 A579 7p multicolored 2.25 1.00
2124 A579 8p multicolored 2.50 1.25
a. Souv. sheet of 4, #2121-2124 7.25 7.25
Nos. 2121-2124 (4) 6.85 3.00

Souvenir Sheet
Imperf
2125 A579 16p multicolored 5.25 5.25

No. 2125 has simulated perforations.

New Year 1992, Year of the Monkey A580

Wmk. 391

1991, Dec. 27 **Litho.** ***Perf. 14***

2126 A580 2p violet & multi *1.25* .30
2127 A580 6p green & multi *3.25* .65

See Nos. 2459a, 2460a.

Services and Products A581

Wmk. 391

1992, Jan. 15 **Litho.** ***Perf. 14***

2128 A581 2p Mailing center .40 .25
2129 A581 6p Housing project 1.10 .35
2130 A581 7p Livestock 1.40 .75
2131 A581 8p Handicraft 1.60 1.00
Nos. 2128-2131 (4) 4.50 2.35

Medicinal Plants — A582

Wmk. 391

1992, Feb. 7 **Litho.** ***Perf. 14***

2132 A582 2p Curcuma longa .75 .25
2133 A582 6p Centella asiatica 1.60 .40
2134 A582 7p Cassia alata 2.00 .50
2135 A582 8p Ervatamia pandacaqui 2.40 .60
Nos. 2132-2135 (4) 6.75 1.75

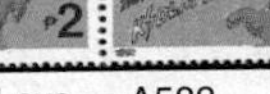

Love — A583

"I Love You" in English on Nos. 2137a-2140a, in Filipino on Nos. 2137b-2140b with designs: No. 2137, Letters, map. No. 2138, Heart, doves. No. 2139, Bouquet of flowers. No. 2140, Map, Cupid with bow and arrow.

Wmk. 391

1992, Feb. 10 **Photo.** ***Perf. 14***

2137 A583 2p Pair, #a.-b. 1.00 1.00
2138 A583 6p Pair, #a.-b. 2.75 2.75
2139 A583 7p Pair, #a.-b. 3.50 3.50
2140 A583 8p Pair, #a.-b. 8.00 8.00
Nos. 2137-2140 (4) 15.25 15.25

A584

Wmk. 391

1992, Apr. 12 **Litho.** ***Perf. 14***

2141 A584 2p blue & multi .40 .25
2142 A584 8p red vio & multi 1.90 .40

Our Lady of Sorrows of Porta Vaga, 400th anniv.

A585

Expo '92, Seville: 2p, Man and woman celebrating. 8p, Philippine discovery scenes. 16p, Pavilion, horiz.

1992, Mar. 27

2143 A585 2p multicolored .40 .25
2144 A585 8p multicolored 1.90 .40

Souvenir Sheet

Imperf

2145 A585 16p multicolored 7.50 7.50

Department of Agriculture, 75th Anniv. — A586

a, Man planting seed. b, Fish trap. c, Pigs.

1992, May 4

2146 A586 2p Strip of 3, #a.-c. 1.90 1.90

Manila Jockey Club, 125th Anniv. A588

Wmk. 391

1992, May 14 **Litho.** ***Perf. 14***

2149 A588 2p multicolored .75 .25

Souvenir Sheet

Imperf

2150 A588 8p multicolored 4.00 *4.75*

No. 2150 has simulated perfs.

Great Filipinos Type of 1989

Designs: a, Pres. Manuel A. Roxas (1892-1948). b, Justice Natividad Almeda-Lopez (1892-1977). c, Justice Roman A. Ozaeta (b. 1892). d, Engracia Cruz-Reyes (1892-1975). e, Fernando Amorsolo (1892-1972).

Perf. 14x13½

1992, June 1 **Wmk. 391**

2151 A536 2p Strip of 5, #a.-e. 3.00 3.00

30th Chess Olympiad, Manila A589

#2154: a, like #2152. b, like #2153.

1992, June 7 ***Perf. 14***

2152 A589 2p No. 1352 .40 .25
2153 A589 6p No. B21 1.40 .35

Souvenir Sheet

Imperf

2154 A589 8p Sheet of 2, #a.-b. 4.50 *5.25*

No. 2154 has simulated perfs.

World War II, 50th Anniv. — A590

2p, Bataan, cross. 6p, Insignia of defenders of Bataan & Corregidor. 8p, Corregidor, Monument. #2158, Cross, map of Bataan. #2159, Monument, map of Corregidor.

Wmk. 391

1992, June 12 **Photo.** ***Perf. 14***

2155 A590 2p multicolored .40 .25
2156 A590 6p multicolored 1.25 .35
2157 A590 8p multicolored 1.60 .45

Size: 63x76mm, 76x63mm

Imperf

2158 A590 16p multicolored 5.00 5.00
2159 A590 16p multicolored 5.00 5.00
Nos. 2155-2159 (5) 13.25 11.05

Nos. 2158-2159 have simulated perforations.

President Corazon C. Aquino and President-Elect Fidel V. Ramos — A591

1992, June 30 ***Perf. 14***

2160 A591 2p multicolored .60 .25

Anniversary of Democracy.

Jose Rizal's Exile to Dapitan, Cent. A592

1992, June 17

2161 A592 2p Dapitan shrine .95 .25
2162 A592 2p Portrait, vert. .95 .25

ASEAN, 25th Anniv. A593

Contemporary paintings: Nos. 2163, 2165, Spirit of ASEAN. Nos. 2164, 2166, ASEAN Sea.

Wmk. 391

1992, July 18 **Litho.** ***Perf. 14***

2163 A593 2p multicolored .40 .25
2164 A593 2p multicolored .40 .25
2165 A593 6p multicolored 1.25 .35
2166 A593 6p multicolored 1.25 .35
Nos. 2163-2166 (4) 3.30 1.20

Founding of Katipunan, Cent. A594

Details or entire paintings of revolutionaries, by Carlos "Botong" Francisco: No. 2167a, Preparing for battle, vert. No. 2167b, Attack leader (detail), vert. No. 2168a, Attack. No. 2168b, Signing papers.

Wmk. 391

1992, July 27 **Photo.** ***Perf. 14***

2167 A594 2p Pair, #a.-b. 1.50 1.50
2168 A594 2p Pair, #a.-b. 1.50 1.50

Philippine League, Cent. A595

Wmk. 391

1992, July 31 **Photo.** ***Perf. 14***

2169 A595 2p multicolored .75 .75

1992 Summer Olympics, Barcelona A596

Wmk. 391

1992, Aug. 4 **Litho.** ***Perf. 14***

2170 A596 2p Swimming .30 .25
2171 A596 7p Boxing 1.50 .45
2172 A596 8p Hurdling 2.00 .55
Nos. 2170-2172 (3) 3.80 1.25

Souvenir Sheet

Imperf

2172A A596 Sheet of 3, #2171-2172, 2172Ab 6.00 *6.75*
b. 1p like #2170 .65 .65

No. 2172A has simulated perforations.

Religious of the Assumption in Philippines, Cent. — A597

Cathedral of San Sebastian, Cent. — A597a

Wmk. 391

1992, Aug. 15 **Photo.** ***Perf. 14***

2173 A597 2p multicolored .60 .25
2174 A597a 2p multicolored .60 .25

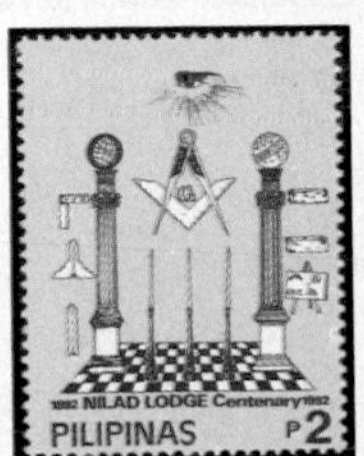

Founding of Nilad Masonic Lodge, Cent. — A598

Various Masonic symbols and: 6p, A. Luna. 8p, M.H. Del Pilar.

Wmk. 391

1992, Aug. 15 Photo. *Perf. 14*

2175 A598 2p green & black .35 .35
2176 A598 6p yellow, black & brown 1.50 .80
2177 A598 8p blue, black & violet 1.90 1.00
Nos. 2175-2177 (3) 3.75 2.15

Pres. Fidel V. Ramos Taking Oath of Office, June 30, 1992 — A599

1992, July 30

2178 A599 2p Ceremony, people .35 .25
2179 A599 8p Ceremony, flag 1.50 .60

Freshwater Aquarium Fish — A600

Designs: No. 2180a, Red-tailed guppy, b, Tiger lacetail guppy. c, Flamingo guppy. d, Neon tuxedo guppy. e, King cobra guppy.

No. 2181a, Black moor. b, Bubble eye. c, Pearl scale goldfish. d, Red cap. e, Lionhead goldfish.

No. 2182, Golden arowana.

No. 2183a, Delta topsail variatus. b, Orange spotted hi-fin platy. c, Red lyretail swordtail. d, Bleeding heart hi-fin platy.

No. 2184a, 6p, Green discus. b, 6p, Brown discus. c, 7p, Red discus. d, 7p, Blue discus.

1992, Sept. 9 *Perf. 14*

2180 A600 1.50p Strip of 5, #a.-e. 4.00 4.00
2181 A600 2p Strip of 5, #a.-e. 4.00 4.00

Imperf

Size: 65x45mm

2182 A600 8p multicolored 3.00 3.00

Souvenir Sheets of 4

Perf. 14

2183 A600 4p #a.-d. 4.75 *5.75*
2184 A600 6p, 7p #a.-d. 8.25 *9.25*

Nos. 2182 and 2184 were overprinted "PHILIPPINE STAMP EXHIBITION 1992 — TAIPEI" in margins. Most of this overprinted issue was sold to the dealer to co-sponsored the exhibit.

See Nos. 2253-2257.

Birthday Greetings — A601

1992, Sept 28 *Perf. 14*

2185 A601 2p Couple dancing .35 .25
2186 A601 6p like #2185 1.25 .50
2187 A601 7p Cake, balloons 1.25 .50
2188 A601 8p like #2187 1.60 .75
Nos. 2185-2188 (4) 4.45 2.00

Columbus' Discovery of America, 500th Anniv. — A602

Various fruits and vegetables.

1992, Oct. 14

2189 A602 2p multicolored .40 .25
2190 A602 6p multi, diff. 1.40 .35
2191 A602 8p multi, diff. 2.00 .45
Nos. 2189-2191 (3) 3.80 1.05

Intl. Conference on Nutrition, Rome — A603

1992, Oct. 27

2192 A603 2p multicolored .60 .25

No. 2100 Ovptd. in Blue "Second / National Philatelic Convention / Cebu, Philippines, Oct. 22-24, 1992"

Wmk. 391

1992, Oct. 15 Photo. *Imperf.*

2193 A571 16p multicolored 6.00 6.00

Christmas — A604

Various pictures of mother and child.

Wmk. 391

1992, Nov. 5 Litho. *Perf. 14*

2194 A604 2p multicolored .35 .25
2195 A604 6p multicolored 1.25 .35
2196 A604 7p multicolored 1.25 .40
2197 A604 8p multicolored 1.75 .45
Nos. 2194-2197 (4) 4.60 1.45

No. 1452 Ovptd. "INAUGURATION OF THE PHILIPPINE POSTAL MUSEUM / AND PHILATELIC LIBRARY, NOVEMBER 10, 1992" in Red

Wmk. 372

1992, Nov. 10 Litho. *Imperf.*

Souvenir Sheet

2198 A348 5p multicolored 2.50 *3.00*

A605

Wmk. 391

1992, Nov. 15 Litho. *Perf. 14*

2199 A605 2p People, boat .35 .25
2200 A605 8p People, boat, diff. 1.50 .45

Fight Against Drug Abuse.

A606

Paintings: 2p, Family, by Cesar Legaspi. 6p, Pounding Rice, by Nena Saguil. 7p, Fish Vendors, by Romeo V. Tabuena.

1992, Nov. 24

2201 A606 2p multicolored .35 .25
2202 A606 6p multicolored 1.25 .30
2203 A606 7p multicolored 1.40 .40
Nos. 2201-2203 (3) 3.00 .95

Philatelic Week.

Birds — A607

Designs: No. 2204a, Black shama. b, Philippine cockatoo. c, Sulu hornbill. d, Mindoro imperial pigeon. e, Blue-headed fantail.

No. 2205a, Philippine trogon, vert. b, Rufous hornbill, vert. c, White-bellied woodpecker, vert. d, Spotted wood kingfisher, vert.

No. 2206a, Brahminy kite. b, Philippine falconet. c, Pacific reef egret. d, Philippine mallard.

Wmk. 391

1992, Nov. 25 Litho. *Perf. 14*

2204 A607 2p Strip of 5, #a.-e. 3.00 3.00

Souvenir Sheets

2205 A607 2p Sheet of 4, #a.-d. 4.00 *4.00*
2206 A607 2p Sheet of 4, #a.-d. 4.00 *4.00*

No. 2204 printed in sheets of 10 with designs in each row shifted one space to the right from the preceding row. Two rows in each sheet are tete-beche.

The 1st printing of this set was rejected. The unissued stamps do not have the frame around the birds. The denominations on the sheet stamps and the 2nd souvenir sheet are larger. On the 1st souvenir sheet they are smaller.

For overprint see No. 2405.

New Year 1993, Year of the Rooster — A608

1992

2207 A608 2p Native fighting cock .40 .25
2208 A608 6p Legendary Maranao bird 1.40 .40
a. Souvenir sheet of 2, #2207-2208 + 2 labels 2.50 *3.00*
b. As "a," ovptd. in sheet margin 2.50 *3.00*

Nos. 2208a and 2208b exist imperf. Overprint on No. 2208b reads: "PHILIPPINE STAMP EXHIBIT / TAIPEI, DECEMBER 1-3, 1992" in English and Chinese.

Issued: #2207-2208, 2208a, 11/27; #2208b, 12/1.

See Nos. 2459b, 2460b.

Guerrilla Units of World War II — A609

Units: a, Bulacan Military Area, Anderson's Command, Luzon Guerrilla Army Forces. b, Marking's Fil-American Guerrillas, Hunters ROTC Guerrillas, President Quezon's Own Guerrillas. c, 61st Division, 71st Division, Cebu Area Command. d, 48th Chinese Guerrilla Squadron, 101st Division, Vinzons Guerrillas.

1992, Dec. 7

2209 A609 2p Block of 4, #a.-d. 3.50 3.50

National Symbols

Tree — A610 A610c Fish

Flower
A610a A610b

Flag
A610d A610e

Animal
A610f A610g

Bird
A610h A610i

Leaf
A610j A610k

A610l A610m Costume

Fruit
A610n A610o

A610p House A610q Various

A610r José Rizal A610s National Dance

National Sport — A610t

Nos. 2210-2236 inscribed with year of issue unless noted otherwise

Wmk. 391, except #2212A, 2214, 2215, 2216A, 2218A, 2220, 2222 (Unwmk.)

Red (R) or Blue (B) "PILIPINAS" on bottom, except #2212 (Brown (Br) "PILIPINAS" on top)

1993-98 Litho. *Perf. 14x13½*

2210	A610	60s (R)	.80	*4.00*
2211	A610b	1p (R)	.25	.25
2211A	A610b	1p (R)	.25	.25
2212	A610a	1p (Br)	.25	.25
2212A	A610b	1p (B)	.25	.25
2213	A610c	1.50p (R)	.25	.25
a.		Dated "1995"	.25	.25
2214	A610c	1.50p (B)	.25	.25

Nos. 2212A and 2214 have blue security printing.

Issued: #2210, 6/12/93; #2211, 5/3/94; #2211A, 2/6/95; #2212, 4/29/93; #2212A, 2/12/96; #2213, 6/12/3; #2213a, 2/6/95; #2214, 2/12/6.

Red "PILIPINAS" on bottom, except #2215a (Brown "PILIPINAS" on top)

Blue Security Printing

2215	2p Block of 14, #a.-n.	9.00	*15.00*
a.	A610d 2p multi	.30	.25
b.	A610r 2p multi	.30	.25
c.	A610p 2p multi	.30	.25
d.	A610m 2p multi	.30	.25
e.	A610s 2p multi	.30	.25
f.	A610t 2p multi	.30	.25
g.	A610i 2p multi	.30	.25
h.	A610e 2p multi	.30	.25
i.	A610f 2p multi	.30	.25
j.	A610b 2p multi	.30	.25
k.	A610 2p multi	.30	.25
l.	A610o 2p multi	.30	.25
m.	A610k 2p multi	.30	.25
n.	A610c 2p multi	.30	.25

Issued 11/2/95.

Red "PILIPINAS" on bottom, except #2216, 2217a (Brown "PILIPINAS" on top)

No Security Printing

2216	A610d	2p multi	.30	.25
2216A	A610e	2p multi	.30	.25
2217		2p Block of 14, #a.-n.	9.00	*15.00*
a.	A610d 2p multi		.30	.25
b.	A610r 2p multi		.30	.25
c.	A610p 2p multi		.30	.25
d.	A610m 2p multi		.30	.25
e.	A610s 2p multi		.30	.25
f.	A610t 2p multi		.30	.25
g.	A610h 2p multi		.30	.25
h.	A610e 2p multi		.30	.50
i.	A610f 2p multi		.30	.25
j.	A610b 2p multi		.30	.25
k.	A610 2p multi		.30	.25
l.	A610o 2p multi		.30	.25
m.	A610k 2p multi		.30	.25
n.	A610c 2p multi		.30	.25

Issued: #2216, 4/29/93; #2216A (dated 1993), 2/10/94; #2217, 10/28/93.

#2217a is a later printing of #2216, in which the word "watawat" is much smaller. #2217h is a later printing of #2216A, in which the date is lowered near the middle of "PILIPINAS," rather than near the top of "PILIPINAS."

Red "PILIPINAS" on bottom

2218	A610f	3p multi	.50	.35
a.		Dated "1994"	.50	.35
b.		Dated "1995"	.50	.35

Blue Security Printing at Top, Blue "PILIPINAS" on bottom

2218C	A610g	3p multi, dated "1996"	.50	.35
d.		Dated "1997"	.50	.35

"PILIPINAS" red: Nos. 2218, 2218a, 2218c. Blue security printing: Nos. 2218C, 2281d.

Issued: No. 2218, 6/12/93; No. 2218a, 4/19/94; No. 2218b, 2/1/95; No. 2218C, 3/1/96; No. 2218d, 4/18/97.

Blue "PILIPINAS" on bottom, except #2219n (Blue "PILIPINAS" on top)

Blue Security Printing

2219	4p Block of 14, #a.-n.	15.00	*25.00*
a.	A610d 4p multi	.75	.40
b.	A610r 4p multi	.75	.40
c.	A610p 4p multi	.75	.40
d.	A610m 4p multi	.75	.40
e.	A610s 4p multi	.75	.40
f.	A610t 4p multi	.75	.40
g.	A610i 4p multi	.75	.40
h.	A610d 4p multi	.75	.40
i.	A610f 4p multi	.75	.40
j.	A610b 4p multi	.75	.40
k.	A610 4p multi	.75	.40
l.	A610o 4p multi	.75	.40
m.	A610k 4p multi	.75	.40
n.	A610c 4p multi	.75	.40

Issued 1/8/96. Stamps are dated "1995."

Blue "PILIPINAS" on bottom, except #2220a (Blue "PILIPINAS" on top)

Blue Security Printing

2220	4p Block of 14, #a.-n.	15.00	*25.00*
a.	A610d 4p multi	.75	.30
b.	A610r 4p multi	.75	.30
c.	A610p 4p multi	.75	.30
d.	A610m 4p multi	.75	.30
e.	A610s 4p multi	.75	.30
f.	A610t 4p multi	.75	.30
g.	A610i 4p multi	.75	.30
h.	A610e 4p multi	.75	.30
i.	A610g 4p multi	.75	.30
j.	A610b 4p multi	.75	.30
k.	A610 4p multi	.75	.30
l.	A610o 4p multi	.75	.30
m.	A610k 4p multi	.75	.30
n.	A610c 4p multi	.75	.30

Issued 2/12/96.

Red "PILIPINAS" on bottom (R): #2221-2221b, 2223B, 2223c, 2224B, 2224c, 2226, 2226a, 2228-2228b. Blue "PILIPINAS" on bottom (B): #2222, 2223A, 2224A, 2227, 2229. Brown "PILIPINAS" on top (Br): #2223, 2224, 2225.

2221	A610h	5p (R)	1.50	.60
a.		Dated "1994"	1.50	.60
b.		Dated "1995"	1.50	.60
2222	A610i	5p (B)	1.50	.60
2223	A610j	6p (Br)	2.50	1.00
2223A	A610k	6p (B)	2.50	1.00
2223B	A610k	6p (R)	2.50	1.00
c.		Dated "1995"	2.50	1.00
2224	A610l	7p (Br)	3.00	1.25
2224A	A610m	7p (B)	3.00	1.25
2224B	A610m	7p (R)	3.00	1.25
c.		Dated "1995"	3.00	1.25
2225	A610n	8p (Br)	3.50	1.50
2226	A610o	8p (R)	3.50	1.50
a.		Dated "1995"	3.50	1.50
2227	A610o	8p (B)	3.50	1.50
2228	A610p	10p (R)	4.00	2.00
a.		Dated "1994"	4.00	2.00
b.		Dated "1995"	4.00	2.00
2229	A610p	10p (B)	4.00	2.00
	Nos. 2210-2229 (28)		89.90	103.15

Blue security printing: #2222, 2223A, 2224A, 2227, 2229.

Issued: #2221, 2228, 6/12/93; #2221a, 2228a, 4/19/94; #2221b, 2/1/95; #2222, 2/12/96; #2223, 2224, 2225, 4/29/93; #2223A, 11/21/96; #2223B, 12/1/94; #2223Bc, 2228b, 4/3/95; #2224A, 2227, 2229, 4/19/96; #2224Bc, 5/5/95; #2226, 10/4/93; #2226a, 3/14/95; #2224B, 7/6/94.

See Nos. 2463-2469A, 2544-2545.

Souvenir Sheets

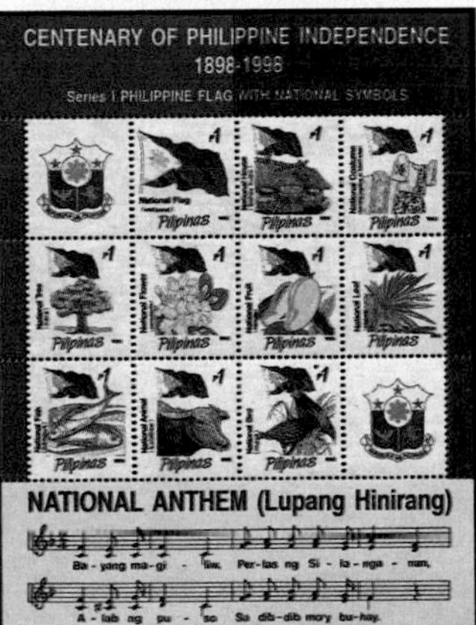

Philippine Flag with National Symbols — A610u

Unwmk. *Perf. 13½*

2231	A610u	1p, Sheet of 12, #a.-j.+2 labels	15.00	*25.00*
a.	A610e 1p multi		1.00	2.00
b.	A610p 1p multi		1.00	2.00
c.	A610m 1p multi		1.00	2.00
d.	A610 1p multi		1.00	2.00
e.	A610b 1p multi		1.00	2.00
f.	A610o 1p multi		1.00	2.00
g.	A610k 1p multi		1.00	2.00
h.	A610c 1p multi		1.00	2.00
i.	A610f 1p multi		1.00	2.00
j.	A610h 1p multi		1.00	2.00

No. 2231e does not have the blue security printing, present on No. 2212A.

Issued: 6/12/93.

Philippine Flag with National Landmarks — A610v

Designs: a, Aquinaldo Shrine; b, Rizal Shrine; c, Barasoian Shrine; d, Mabini Shrine.

2232	A610v	2p, 3p, #a.-d.	8.00	*12.00*
a.	A610q 2p multi		1.00	2.00
b.	A610q 3p multi		1.00	2.00
c.	A610q 2p multi		1.00	2.00
d.	A610q 3p multi		1.00	2.00

Issued 6/12/94.

1872 Cavite Mutiny — A610w

Designs: a, Cavite Arsenal; b, La Fuerza de San Felipe-Cavite; c, Commemorative marker; d, Cristanto de Los Reyes y Mendoza.

2233	A610w	2p, 3p, Sheet of 4, #a.-d.	8.00	*15.00*
a.	A610q 2p multi		1.00	2.00
b.	A610q 3p multi		1.00	2.00
c.	A610q 2p multi		1.00	2.00
d.	A610q 3p multi		1.00	2.00

Issued 6/12/95.

1896 Philippine Revolution — A610x

Designs: a, Cry of Pudgadlawin; b, Battle of Pinaglabanan; c, Cry of Nueca Ecija; d, Battle of Binakayan.

Nos. 2234a-2234d have blue security printing.

2234	A610x	4p, Sheet of 4, #a.-d.	8.00	*15.00*
a.	A610q 4p multi		1.00	2.00
b.	A610q 4p multi		1.00	2.00
c.	A610q 4p multi		1.00	2.00
d.	A610q 4p multi		1.00	2.00

Issued 6/12/96.

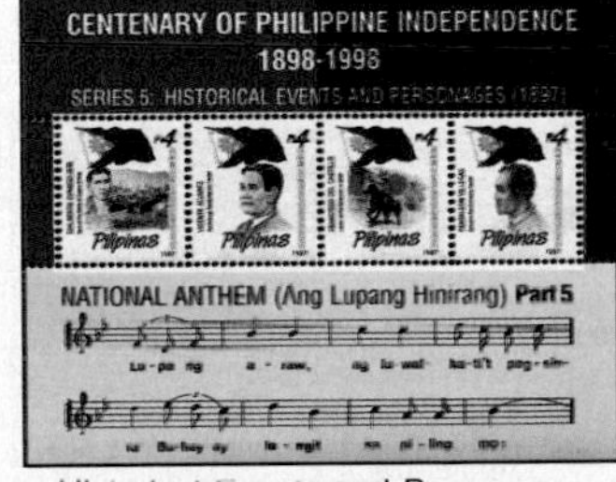

Historical Events and Personages (1897) — A610y

Designs: a, Edilberto Evangelista; b, Vicente Alvarez; c, Francisco Del Castillo; d, Pantaleon Vallegas.

Nos. 2235a-2235d have blue security printing.

2235	A610y	4p, Sheet of 4, #a.-d.	8.00	*15.00*
a.	A610y 4p multi		1.00	2.00
b.	A610q 4p multi		1.00	2.00
c.	A610q 4p multi		1.00	2.00
d.	A610q 4p multi		1.00	2.00

Issued 6/12/97.

Historical Events of 1898 — A610z

Designs: a, Tres de Abril Uprising in Cebu; b, Negros Uprising, 1898; c, Iligan Uprising, 1898; d, Philippine Centennial Logo, Kalayaan.

Nos. 2236a-2236d have blue security printing.

2236	A610z	4p, Sheet of 4, #a.-d.	8.00	*15.00*
a.	A610q 4p multi		1.00	2.00
b.	A610q 4p multi		1.00	2.00
c.	A610q 4p multi		1.00	2.00
d.	A610q 4p multi		1.00	2.00

Issued 6/12/98.

Butterflies A611

Designs: No. 2237a, Euploea mulciber. b, Cheritra orpheus. c, Delias henningia. d, Mycalesis ita. e, Delias diaphana.

No. 2238a, Papilio rumanzobia. b, Papilio palinurus. c, Trogonoptera trojana. d, Graphium agamemnon.

No. 2239, Papilio lowi, Valeria boebera, Delias themis.

1993 Litho. Wmk. 391 *Perf. 14*

2237	A611	2p Strip of 5, #a.-e.	4.50	4.50

Souvenir Sheets

2238	A611	2p Sheet of 4, #a.-d.	5.25	*6.25*
e.		Ovptd. in sheet margin	6.00	*7.25*
2239	A611	10p multicolored	7.50	*9.00*
a.		Ovptd. in sheet margin	6.00	*7.25*
b.		Ovptd. in blue in sheet margin	*14.00*	*15.00*

Issue dates: Nos. 2237-2239, May 28. Nos. 2238e, 2239a, May 29. No. 2239b, July 1.

Nos. 2238a-2238d are vert. No. 2239 contains one 116x28mm stamp.

Overprint on Nos. 2238e, 2239a reads "INDOPEX '93 / INDONESIA PHILATELIC EXHIBITION 1993" and "6th ASIAN INTERNATIONAL PHILATELIC EXHIBITION / 29th MAY-4th JUNE 1993 SURABAYA-INDONESIA."

Overprint on No. 2239b reads "Towards the Year 2000 / 46th PAF Anniversary 1 July 1993" and includes Philippine Air Force emblem and jet.

Great Filipinos Type of 1989

Designs: a, Nicanor Abelardo, composer. b, Pilar Hidalgo-Lim, mathematician, educator. c, Manuel Viola Gallego, lawyer, educator. d, Maria Ylagan Orosa (1893-1943), pharmacist, health advocate. e, Eulogio B. Rodriguez, historian.

1993, June 10 *Perf. 13½*

2240	A536	2p Strip of 5, #a.-e.	3.00	3.00

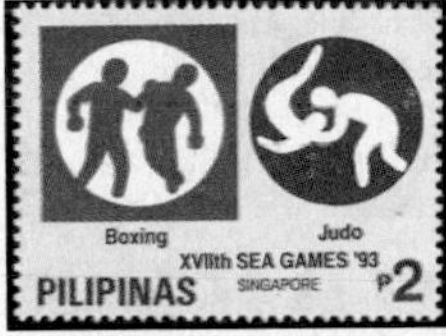

17th South East Asia Games, Singapore A612

No. 2241: a, Weight lifting, archery, fencing, shooting. b, Boxing, judo. c, Track, cycling, gymnastics, golf.

No. 2242: a, Table tennis, soccer, volleyball, badminton. b, Billiards, bowling. c, Swimming, water polo, yachting, diving.
No. 2243, Basketball, vert.

1993, June 18 *Perf. 13*

2241 A612 2p Strip of 3, #a.-c. 2.00 1.25
2242 A612 6p Strip of 3, #a.-c. 5.00 3.75

Souvenir Sheet

2243 A612 10p multicolored 5.00 *6.00*

#2241a, 2241c, 2242a, 2242c are 80x30mm. No. 2243 contains one 30x40mm stamp. No. 2242a exists inscribed "June 13-20, 1993."

Orchids — A613

No. 2244: a, Spathoglottis chrysantha. b, Arachnis longicaulis. c, Phalaenopsis mariae. d, Coelogyne marmorata. e, Dendrobium sanderae.
No. 2245: a, Dendrobium serratilabium. b, Phalaenopsis equestris. c, Vanda merrillii. d, Vanda luzonica. e, Grammatophyllum martae.
No. 2246, Aerides quinquevulnera. No. 2247, Vanda lamellata.

1993, Aug. 14 **Unwmk.** *Perf. 14*

2244 A613 2p Block of 5, #a.-e. 3.50 3.50
2245 A613 3p Block of 5, #a.-e. 4.75 4.75

Souvenir Sheets

2246 A613 8p multicolored 2.50 *3.00*
a. With additional inscription 3.25 *3.75*

Imperf

2247 A613 8p multicolored 2.50 *3.00*
a. With additional inscription 3.25 *3.75*

No. 2246 contains one 27x78mm stamp.
Nos. 2246a, 2247a inscribed in sheet margin with Taipei '93 emblem in blue and yellow. Additional black inscription in English and Chinese reads: "ASIAN INTERNATIONAL INVITATION STAMP EXHIBITION / TAIPEI '93."

Greetings — A614

"Thinking of You" in English on Nos. 2248a-2251a, in Filipino on Nos. 2248b-2251b with designs: 2p, Flowers, dog at window. 6p, Dog looking at alarm clock. 7p, Dog looking at calendar. 8p, Dog with slippers.

Wmk. 391

1993, Aug. 20 **Litho.** *Perf. 14*

2248 A614 2p Pair, #a.-b. 1.00 1.00
2249 A614 6p Pair, #a.-b. 3.25 3.25
2250 A614 7p Pair, #a.-b. 3.25 3.25
2251 A614 8p Pair, #a.-b. 4.25 4.25
Nos. 2248-2251 (4) 11.75 11.75

A615

1993, Aug. 24

2252 A615 2p multicolored .60 .25

Natl. Coconut Week.

Fish Type of 1992

No. 2253: a, Paradise fish. b, Pearl gourami. c, Red-tailed black shark. d, Tiger barb. e, Cardinal tetra.
No. 2254: a, Albino ryukin goldfish. b, Black oranda goldfish. c, Lionhead goldfish. d, Celestial-eye goldfish. e, Pompon goldfish.
No. 2255: a, Pearl-scale angelfish. b, Zebra angelfish. c, Marble angelfish. d, Black angelfish.
No. 2256: a, Neon betta. b, Libby betta. c, Split-tailed betta. d, Butterfly betta.
No. 2257, Albino oscar.

1993 **Unwmk.** *Perf. 14*

2253 A600 2p Strip of 5, #a.-e. 4.00 4.00
2254 A600 2p Strip of 5, #a.-e. 4.00 4.00

Souvenir Sheets

Perf. 14

2255 A600 2p Sheet of 4, #a.-d. 5.25 *6.50*
2256 A600 3p Sheet of 4, #a.-d. 5.25 *6.00*
e. Ovptd. in margin 5.25 *6.25*

Imperf

Stamp Size: 70x45mm

2257 A600 6p multicolored 5.25 5.25
a. Ovptd. in margin 5.25 5.25

Nos. 2256e, 2257a overprinted in black "QUEEN SIRIKIT NATIONAL CONVENTION CENTER / 1-10 OCTOBER 1993," "BANGKOK WORLD PHILATELIC EXHIBITION 1993" with Bangkok '93 show emblem in purple in margin.
Nos. 2255a-2255d are vert.
Issued: #2256e, 2257a, 9/20; others, 9/9.

A616

Wmk. 391

1993, Sept. 20 **Photo.** *Perf. 14*

2258 A616 2p multicolored .50 .25

Basic Petroleum and Minerals, Inc., 25th anniv.

16th World Law Conference, Manila — A617

6p, Globe on scales, gavel, flag, vert. 7p, Justice holding scales, courthouse. 8p, Fisherman, vert.

Unwmk.

1993, Sept. 30 **Litho.** *Perf. 14*

2259 A617 2p multicolored .30 .25
2260 A617 6p multicolored 1.00 .30
2261 A617 7p multicolored 1.10 .35
2262 A617 8p multicolored 1.40 .40
Nos. 2259-2262 (4) 3.80 1.30

Our Lady of the Rosary of la Naval, 400th Anniv. A618

1993, Oct. 18 **Wmk. 391**

2263 A618 2p multicolored .50 .25

Intl. Year of Indigenous People — A619

People wearing traditional costumes.

1993, Oct. 24 **Unwmk.**

2264 A619 2p multicolored .45 .25
2265 A619 6p multicolored 1.40 .35
2266 A619 7p multicolored 1.40 .40
2267 A619 8p multicolored 1.75 .50
Nos. 2264-2267 (4) 5.00 1.50

Environmental Protection — A620

Paintings: 2p, Trees. 6p, Marine life. 7p, Bird, trees. 8p, Man and nature.

1993, Nov. 22

2268 A620 2p multicolored .45 .25
2269 A620 6p multicolored 1.40 .35
2270 A620 7p multicolored 1.40 .40
2271 A620 8p multicolored 1.75 .50
Nos. 2268-2271 (4) 5.00 1.50

Philately Week.

A621

a, Lunar buggy. b, Floating power tiller.

Unwmk.

1993, Nov. 30 **Litho.** *Perf. 14*

2272 A621 2p Pair, #a.-b. .90 .90

Filipino Inventors Society, Inc., 50th Anniv.

A622

1993, Nov. 30

2273 A622 2p multicolored .50 .25

Printing of Doctrina Christiana in Spanish and Tagalog, 400th anniv.

A623

Christmas: 2p, Nativity scene. 6p, Church, people. 7p, Water buffalo carrying fruits, vegetables, sea food. 8p, Christmas lantern, carolers.

1993, Dec. 1

2274 A623 2p multicolored .35 .25
2275 A623 6p multicolored 1.00 .30
2276 A623 7p multicolored 1.25 .60
2277 A623 8p multicolored 1.40 .45
Nos. 2274-2277 (4) 4.00 1.60

A624

Maps, Philippine guerrilla units of World War II: a, US Army Forces in the Philippines Northern Luzon. b, Bohol Area Command. c, Leyte Area Command. d, Palawan Special Battalion, Sulu Area Command.

1993, Dec. 10

2278 A624 2p Block or strip of 4, #a.-d. 4.00 4.00

Philippines 2000 A625

Designs: 2p, Peace and Order. 6p, Transportation, communications. 7p, Infrastructure, industry. No. 2282, People empowerment. No. 2283, Transportation, communications, buildings, people.

Unwmk.

1993, Dec. 14 **Litho.** *Perf. 14*

2279 A625 2p multicolored .25 .25
2280 A625 6p multicolored .90 .30
2281 A625 7p multicolored 1.10 .50
2282 A625 8p multicolored 1.25 .60
Nos. 2279-2282 (4) 3.50 1.65

Souvenir Sheet

Imperf

Size: 110x85mm

2283 A625 8p multicolored 3.00 3.00

New Year 1994 (Year of the Dog) A626

Unwmk.

1993, Dec. 15 **Litho.** *Perf. 14*

2284 A626 2p Manigong bagong taon .40 .25
2285 A626 6p Happy new year 1.40 .40
a. Souvenir sheet of 2, #2284-2285 + 2 labels 3.75 3.75

No. 2285a exists imperf.
See Nos. 2459c, 2460c.

First ASEAN Scout Jamboree, Mt. Makiling — A627

2p, Flags of ASEAN countries, Boy Scout emblem. 6p, Flags, Boy Scout, emblem.

1993, Dec. 28

2286 A627 2p multicolored .35 .25
2287 A627 6p multicolored 1.10 .60
a. Souv. sheet of 2, #2286-2287 3.50 3.50

Rotary Club of Manila, 75th Anniv. A628

Unwmk.

1994, Jan. 19 **Litho.** *Perf. 14*

2288 A628 2p multicolored .50 .25

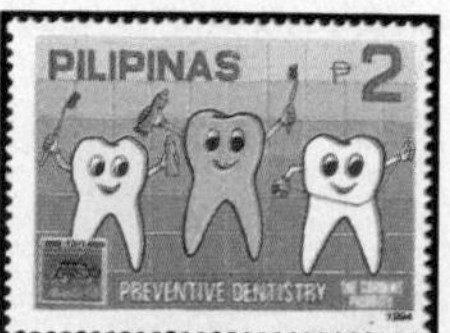

17th Asian Pacific Dental Congress, Manila A629

2p, Healthy teeth. 6p, Globe, flags, teeth.

1994, Feb. 3

2289 A629 2p multicolored .50 .25
2290 A629 6p multicolored 1.50 .35

Corals — A630

#2291: a, Acropora micropthalma. b, Serlatopora hystrix. c, Acropora latistella. d, Millepora tenella. e, Millepora tenella, up close. f, Pachyseris valenciennesi. g, Pavona decussata. h, Galaxea fascicularis. i, Acropora formosa. j, Acropora humilis.

#2292: a, Isis. b, Plexaura. c, Dendronepthya. d, Heteroxenia.

#2293: a, Xenia puertogalerae. b, Plexaura, diff. c, Dendrophyllia gracilis. d, Plerogyra sinuosa.

1994, Feb. 15 Litho. *Perf. 14*

2291 A630 2p Block of 10, #a.-j. 9.00 *15.00*

Souvenir Sheets

2292 A630 2p Sheet of 4, #a.-d. 5.75 *7.00*
2293 A630 3p Sheet of 4, #a.-d. 5.75 *6.50*
e. With added inscription 12.50 *14.00*

No. 2293e is inscribed in sheet margin "NAPHILCON '94 / 1ST NATIONAL / PHILATELIC CONGRESS / 21 FEBRUARY - 5 MARCH 1994 / PHILATELY 2000."

Issued: No. 2293e, 2/21.

Hong Kong '94 — A631

2p, Nos. 2126, 2207. 6p, Nos. 2284, 2285.

1994, Feb. 18

2294 A631 2p multicolored .35 .25
2295 A631 6p multicolored 1.10 .35
a. Souv. sheet of 2, #2294-2295, blue 2.50 *3.00*
b. As "a," green 2.50 *3.00*

Backgrounds differ on Nos. 2295a, 2295b.

A632

1994, Feb. 20

2296 A632 2p multicolored .50 .25

Philippine Military Academy Class of 1944, 50th Anniv.

A633

1994, Mar. 1

2297 A633 2p multicolored .50 .25

Federation of Filipino-Chinese Chambers of Commerce and Industry, 40th Anniv.

A634

"Congratulations" in English on Nos. 2298a-2301a, in Tagalog on Nos. 2298b-2301b with designs: No. 2298, Books, diploma, mortarboard. No. 2299, Baby carried by stork. No. 2300, Valentine bouquet with portraits in heart. No. 2301, Bouquet.

1994, Apr. 15

2298 A634 2p Pair, #a.-b. 1.00 1.00
2299 A634 2p Pair, #a.-b. 1.00 1.00
2300 A634 2p Pair, #a.-b. 1.00 1.00
2301 A634 2p Pair, #a.-b. 1.00 1.00
Nos. 2298-2301 (4) 4.00 4.00

A635

1994 Miss Universe Pageant, Manila: Nos. 2302a (2p), 2304a, Gloria Diaz, 1969 winner. No. 2302b (6p), Crown, Philippine jeepney. Nos. 2303a (2p), 2304b, Margie Moran, 1973 winner. No. 2303b (7p), Pageant participant, Kalesa horse-drawn cart.

1994, May 5 Litho. *Perf. 14*

2302 A635 Pair, #a.-b. 1.00 1.00
2303 A635 Pair, #a.-b. 1.50 1.50

Souvenir Sheet

2304 A635 8p Sheet of 2, #a.-b. 3.50 *4.25*

Great Filipinos Type of 1989

Designs: a, Antonio J. Molina, musician. b, Jose Yulo, politician. c, Josefa Jara-Martinez, social worker. d, Nicanor Reyes, Sr., accountant. e, Sabino B. Padilla, lawyer.

1994, June 10

2307 A536 2p Strip of 5, #a.-e. 2.25 2.25

Philippine Export Processing Zones — A637

No. 2308: a, Baguio City. b, Bataan. c, Mactan. d, Cavite.

No. 2309a, 7p, Map of Philippines, export products. b, 8p, Export products flowing around world map.

Unwmk.

1994, July 4 Litho. *Perf. 14*

2308 A637 2p Block of 4, #a.-d. 1.75 1.75
2309 A637 Pair, #a.-b. 2.75 2.75

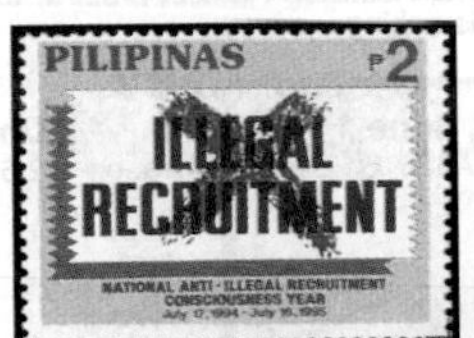

Fight Illegal Recruitment Year — A638

1994, July 15

2310 A638 2p multicolored .50 .25

Wildlife — A639

a, Palawan bearcat. b, Philippine tarsier. c, Scaly anteater. d, Palawan porcupine.

12p, Visayan spotted deer.

1994, Aug. 12 Litho. *Perf. 14*

2311 A639 6p Block of 4, #a.-d. 5.75 5.75

Souvenir Sheet

2312 A639 12p multicolored 7.00 8.50
a. Ovptd. in margin 11.00 13.50

No. 2312a overprinted in white, black and red in sheet margin with "SINGPEX '94 / 31 August-3 September 1994" and show emblem.

PHILAKOREA '94 — A640

Shells: a, Conus gloriamaris. b, Conus striatus. c, Conus geographus. d, Conus textile.

No. 2314a, Conus marmoreus. No. 2314b, Conus geographus, diff. No. 2315a, Conus striatus, diff. No. 2315b, Conus marmoreus, diff.

1994, Aug. 16

2313 A640 2p Block of 4, #a.-d. 4.25 4.25

Souvenir Sheets

2314 A640 6p Sheet of 2, #a.-b. 4.50 *5.50*
2315 A640 6p Sheet of 2, #a.-b. 4.50 *5.50*

Landings at Leyte Gulf, 50th Anniv. A641

Designs: a, Pres. Sergio Osmena, Sr. b, Gen. MacArthur wading ashore. c, Dove of Peace. d, Carlos P. Romulo.

1994, Sept. 15

2316 A641 2p Block of 4, #a.-d. 2.25 2.25

See Nos. 2391a-2391d.

Intl. Anniversaries & Events — A642

Unwmk.

1994, Oct. 24 Litho. *Perf. 14*

2317 A642 2p Family .30 .25
2318 A642 6p Labor workers .90 .35
2319 A642 7p Feather, clouds 1.10 .50
Nos. 2317-2319 (3) 2.30 1.10

Intl. Year of the Family (#2317). ILO, 75th anniv. (#2318). ICAO, 50th anniv. (#2319).

Visit of US Pres. Bill Clinton A643

1994, Nov. 12

2320 A643 2p green & multi .40 .25
2321 A643 8p blue & multi 1.60 .45

East Asean Business Convention, Davao — A644

1994, Nov. 15

2322 A644 2p violet & multi .30 .25
2323 A644 6p brown & multi .90 .50

Nos. 2322-2323 not issued without overprint "Nov. 15-20, 1994" and obliterator covering original date at lower left.

Philatelic Week — A645

Portraits by Philippine artists: 2p, Soteranna Puson Y Quintos de Ventenilla, by Dionisio de Castro. 6p, Quintina Castor de Sadie, by Simon Flores y de la Rosa. 7p, Artist's mother, by Felix Eduardo Resurreccion Hidalgo y Padilla. 8p, Una Bulaquena, by Juan Luna y Novicio.

12p, Cirilo and Severina Quiason Family, by Simon Flores y de la Rosa.

1994, Nov. 21

2324 A645 2p multicolored .35 .25
2325 A645 6p multicolored 1.00 .40
2326 A645 7p multicolored 1.10 .55
2327 A645 8p multicolored 1.25 .65
Nos. 2324-2327 (4) 3.70 1.85

Souvenir Sheet

2328 A645 12p multicolored 3.00 *3.75*

No. 2328 contains one 29x80mm stamp.

Christmas A646

1994, Nov. 25

2329 A646 2p Wreath .25 .25
2330 A646 6p Angels .90 .30
2331 A646 7p Bells 1.10 .35
2332 A646 8p Basket 1.50 .40
Nos. 2329-2332 (4) 3.75 1.30

ASEANPEX '94 — A647

Souvenir Sheet

Philippine-American Friendship Day, Republic Day, 50th Anniv. — A716

1997, May 29

2475 A716 16p multicolored		4.25	4.25

PACIFIC 97.

Wild Animals — A717

World Wildlife Fund: No. 2476, Visayan spotted deer. No. 2477, Visayan spotted deer (doe & fawn). No. 2478, Visayan warty pig. No. 2479, Visayan warty pig (adult, young).

1997, July 24

2476 4p multicolored	1.00	.50
a. Sheet of 8	8.50	8.50
2477 4p multicolored	1.00	.50
a. Sheet of 8	8.50	8.50
2478 4p multicolored	1.00	.50
a. Sheet of 8	8.50	8.50
2479 4p multicolored	1.00	.50
a. Sheet of 8	8.50	8.50
b. A717 Block or strip of 4, #2476-2479	4.25	4.25
Set of 4 sheets, #2476a-2479a	34.00	34.00

No. 2479b was issued in sheets of 16 stamps.

ASEAN, 30th Anniv. — A718

Founding signatories: No. 2480, Adam Malik, Indonesia, Tun Abdul Razak, Malaysia, Narciso Ramos, Philippines, S. Rajaratnam, Singapore, Thanat Khoman, Thailand. No. 2481, Natl. flags of founding signatories. No. 2482, Flags of current ASEAN countries. No. 2483, Flags of ASEAN countries surrounding globe.

1997, Aug. 7 ***Perf. 14***

2480 4p multicolored	.40	.40
2481 4p multicolored	.40	.40
a. A718 Pair, #2480-2481	1.75	1.75
2482 6p multicolored	.70	.70
2483 6p multicolored	.70	.70
a. A718 Pair, #2482-2483	2.50	2.50
Nos. 2480-2483 (4)	2.20	2.20

World Scout Parliamentary Union, 2nd General Assembly A719

1997, Aug. 17

2484 A719 4p multicolored	.60	.25

Manuel L. Quezon University, 50th Anniv. A720

1997, Aug. 19

2485 A720 4p multicolored	.60	.25

Great Filipinos Type of 1989

Famous people: a, Justice Roberto Regala (1897-1979). b, Doroteo Espiritu, dental surgeon, inventor (b. 1897). c, Elisa R. Ochoa (1897-1978), nurse, tennis champion. d, Mariano Marcos (1897-1945), lawyer, educator. e, Jose F. Romero (1897-1978), editor.

Perf. 14x13½

1997, June 1 **Litho.** **Unwmk.**

2486 A536 4p Strip of 5, #a.-e.	3.50	3.50

Battle of Candon, 1898 A721

4p, Don Federico Isabelo Abaya, revolutionary leader against Spanish. 6p, Soldier on horseback.

1997, Sept. 24 ***Perf. 14***

2487 A721 4p multi, vert.	.65	.35
2488 A721 6p multi	1.00	.60

St. Therese of Lisieux (1873-97) A722

1997, Oct. 16

2489 A722 6p multicolored	1.00	.50

Stamp and Philatelic Division, 50th Anniv. A723

Abstract art: 4p, Homage to the Heroes of Bessang Pass, by Hernando Ruiz Ocampo. 6p, Jardin III, by Fernando Zobel. 7p, Abstraction, by Nena Saguil, vert. 8p, House of Life, by Jose Joya, vert.

16p, Dimension of Fear, by Jose Joya.

1997, Oct. 16

2490 A723 4p multicolored	.60	.35
2491 A723 6p multicolored	.90	.60
2492 A723 7p multicolored	1.10	.75
2493 A723 8p multicolored	1.25	.80
Nos. 2490-2493 (4)	3.85	2.50

Souvenir Sheet

2494 A723 16p multicolored	5.25	5.25

No. 2494 contains one 80x30mm stamp.

Heinrich von Stephan (1831-97) A724

1997, Oct. 24 **Litho.** ***Perf. 14***

2495 A724 4p multicolored	.60	.25

Asian and Pacific Decade of Disabled Persons A725

1997, Oct. 24 **Litho.** ***Perf. 14***

2496 A725 6p multicolored	.90	.45

Intl. Year of the Reef — A726

1997, Oct. 24 **Litho.** ***Perf. 14***

2497 A726 8p multicolored	1.25	.50

Souvenir Sheet

2498 A726 16p multicolored	4.25	4.25

No. 2498 is a continuous design.

Natl. Stamp Collecting Month A726a

Paintings: 4p, Dalagang Bukid, by Fernando Amorsolo, vert. 6p, Bagong Taon, by Arturo Luz, vert. 7p, Jeepneys, by Vincente Manansala. 8p, encounter of the Nuestra Sra. de Cavadonga and the Centurion, by Alfredo Carmelo.

16p, Pista sa Nayon, by Carlos Francisco.

1997, Nov. 4 **Litho.** ***Perf. 14***

2498A A726a 4p multicolored	.60	.35
2498B A726a 6p multicolored	.90	.60
2498C A726a 7p multicolored	1.10	.65
2498D A726a 8p multicolored	1.25	.75
Nos. 2498A-2498D (4)	3.85	2.35

Souvenir Sheet

2498E A726a 16p multicolored	3.50	3.50

No. 2498E contains one 80x30mm stamp.

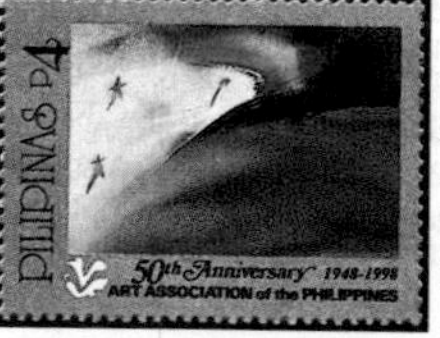

Christmas A727

Various stained glass windows.

1997, Nov. 7

2499 A727 4p multicolored	.40	.25
2500 A727 6p multicolored	.85	.40
2501 A727 7p multicolored	1.10	.55
2502 A727 8p multicolored	1.40	.65
Nos. 2499-2502 (4)	3.75	1.85

Independence, Cent. — A728

Various monuments to Andres Bonifacio (1863-97), revolutionary, founder of the Katipunan: a, red & multi. b, yellow & multi. c, blue & multi.

1997, Nov. 30

2503 A728 4p Strip of 3, #a.-c.	1.75	1.75

New Year 1998 (Year of the Tiger) A729

1997, Dec. 1

2504 A729 4p shown	.70	.30
2505 A729 6p Tigers, diff.	1.10	.45
a. Souvenir sheet, #2504-2505 + 2 labels	3.25	3.25

No. 2505a exists imperf. Value, $5.00.

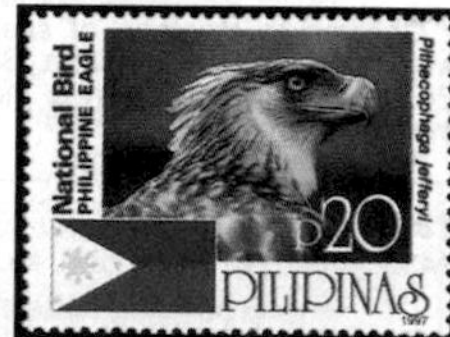

Philippine Eagle A730

1997, Dec. 5

2506 A730 20p Looking right	2.75	1.25
2507 A730 30p Looking forward	4.25	2.00
2508 A730 50p On cliff	7.00	3.50
Nos. 2506-2508 (3)	14.00	6.75

Game Cocks — A731

No. 2509: a, Hatch grey. b, Spangled roundhead. c, Racey mug. d, Silver grey.

No. 2510, vert: a, Grey. b, Kelso. c, Bruner roundhead. d, Democrat.

No. 2511, Cock fight, vert. No. 2512, Cocks facing each other ready to fight.

1997, Dec. 18

2509 A731 4p Block of 4, #a.-d.	2.25	2.25
2510 A731 4p Block of 4, #a.-d.	2.25	2.25

Souvenir Sheets

2511 A731 12p multicolored	2.75	2.75
2512 A731 16p multicolored	3.75	3.75

No. 2512 contains one 80x30mm stamp.

Art Association of the Philippines, 50th Anniv. A732

Stylized designs: No. 2513, Colors of flag, sunburst. No. 2514, Association's initials, clenched fist holding artist's implements.

Unwmk.

1998, Feb. 14 **Litho.** ***Perf. 14***

2513 A732 4p multicolored	.65	.25
2514 A732 4p multicolored	.65	.25
a. Pair, #2513-2514	1.50	1.50

Club Filipino Social Organization, Cent. — A733

1998, Feb. 25
2515 A733 4p multicolored .60 .25

Blessed Marie Eugenie (1817-98) A734

1998, Feb. 25
2516 A734 4p multicolored .60 .25

Fulbright Educational Exchange Program in the Philippines, 50th Anniv. — A735

1998, Feb. 25
2517 A735 4p multicolored .60 .40

Heroes of the Revolution — A736

National flag and: 4p, Melchora Aquino (1812-1919). 11p, Andres Bonifacio (1863-97). 13p, Apolinario Mabini (1864-1903). 15p, Emilio Aguinaldo (1869-1964).

1998 Litho. Unwmk. ***Perf. 13½***
Inscribed "1998"
2518 A736 4p multicolored .60 .30
2519 A736 11p multicolored 1.50 .65
a. Inscribed "1999" 3.00 .65
2520 A736 13p multicolored 1.60 .80
a. Inscribed "1999" 3.25 .80
2521 A736 15p multicolored 1.90 .90
a. Inscribed "1999" 3.75 .90
Nos. 2518-2521 (4) 5.60 2.65

Issued: 4p, 3/3/98. 11p, 13p, 15p, 3/24/98.
See Nos. 2528, 2546-2550, 2578-2597, 2607.

Apo View Hotel, 50th Anniv. — A737

1998, Mar. 20 ***Perf. 14***
2522 A737 4p multicolored .60 .30

Philippine Cultural High School, 75th Anniv. — A738

1998, May 5
2523 A738 4p multicolored .60 .40

Victorino Mapa High School, 75th Anniv. A739

1998, May 5
2524 A739 4p multicolored .60 .30

Philippine Navy, Cent. A740

1998, May 5
2525 A740 4p multicolored .60 .30

University of Baguio, 50th Anniv. A741

1998, May 5
2526 A741 4p multicolored .60 .60

Philippine Maritime Institute, 50th Anniv. A742

1998, May 5
2527 A742 4p multicolored .60 .60

Heroes of the Revolution Type of 1998

Design: Gen. Antonio Luna (1866-99).

Perf. 13½
1998, Apr. 30 Litho. Unwmk.
2528 A736 5p multicolored .60 .30

Expo '98, Lisbon A743

4p, Boat on lake, vert. 15p, Vinta on water. 15p, Main lobby, Philippine Pavilion.

1998, May 22 ***Perf. 14***
2529 A743 4p multicolored .50 .25
2530 A743 15p multicolored 2.00 1.00

Souvenir Sheet

2531 A743 15p multicolored 3.50 3.50

No. 2531 contains one 80x30mm stamp.

Clark Special Economic Zone — A744

1998, May 28
2532 A744 15p multicolored 1.90 1.00

Flowers — A745

#2533: a, Artrabotrys hexapetalus. b, Hibiscus rosa-sinensis. c, Nerium oleander. d, Jasminum sambac.
#2534, vert: a, Gardenia jasminoides. b, Ixora coccinea. c, Erythrina indica. d, Abelmoschus moschatus.
#2535, Medinilla magnifica.

1998, May 29
2533 A745 4p Block of 4, #a.-d. 2.25 2.25
2534 A745 4p Block of 4, #a.-d. 2.25 2.25

Souvenir Sheet

2535 A745 15p multicolored 4.00 4.00

Great Filipinos Type of 1989

Designs: a, Andres R. Soriano (1898-1964). b, Tomas Fonacier (1898-1991). c, Josefa L. Escoda (1898-1945). d, Lorenzo M. Tañada (1898-1992). e, Lazaro Francisco (1898-1980).

1998, June 1 ***Perf. 14x13½***
2536 A536 4p Strip of 5, #a.-e. 3.00 3.00

Philippine Indepencence, Cent. — A746

No. 2537, Mexican flag, sailing ship. No. 2538, Woman holding Philippine flag, monument, sailing ship, map of Philippines. No. 2539, Spanish flag, Catholic Church, religious icon, Philippine flag.

1998, June 3 ***Perf. 14***
2537 A746 15p multicolored 1.40 .40
2538 A746 15p multicolored 1.40 .40
2539 A746 15p multicolored 1.40 .40
a. Strip of 3, #2537-2539 4.50 4.50
b. Souvenir sheet, #2537-2539 + 3 labels 5.00 5.00

See Mexico #2079-2080, Spain #2949. For overprint see #2629.

Philippine Independence, Cent. — A747

Patriots of the revolution: a, Melchora Aquino. b, Nazaria Lagos. c, Agueda Kahabagan.

Unwmk.
1998, June 9 Litho. ***Perf. 14***
2540 A747 4p Strip of 3, #a.-c. 1.50 1.50

Pasig River Campaign for Waste Management — A748

1998, June 19
2541 A748 4p multicolored .60 .25

MARINE MAMMALS FOUND IN PHILIPPINE WATERS

Marine Mammals — A749

No. 2542: a, Bottlenose dolphin. b, Humpback whale. c, Fraser's dolphin. d, Melon-headed whale. e, Minke whale. f, Striped dolphin. g, Sperm whale. h, Pygmy killer whale. i, Cuvier's beaked whale. j, Killer whale. k, Bottlenose dolphin. l, Long-snouted pinner dolphin. m, Risso's dolphin. n, Finless porpoise. o, Pygmy sperm whale. p, Pantropical spotted dolphin. q, False killer whale. r, Blainville's beaked whale. s, Rough-toothed dolphin. t, Bryde's whale.
15p, Dugong.

1998, June 19
2542 A749 4p Sheet of 20, #a.-t. 15.00 *40.00*

Souvenir Sheet

2543 A749 15p multicolored 4.00 4.00

Nos. 2218a, 2218b, 2220 Ovptd. in Gold with Philippine Independence Centennial Emblem

1998 Litho. Unwmk. ***Perf. 14x13½***
2544 A610f 3p multi, dated "1995" (#2218b) .40 .25
2544A A610f 3p multi, dated "1994" (#2218a) 75.00 *85.00*
2545 A610g 4p Block of 14, #a.-n. 15.00 25.00
a. A610d 4p multi .75 .75
b. A610r 4p multi .75 .75
c. A610p 4p multi .75 .75
d. A610m 4p multi .75 .75
e. A610s 4p multi .75 .75
f. A610t 4p multi .75 .75
g. A610i 4p multi .75 .75
h. A610e 4p multi .75 .75
i. A610g 4p multi .75 .75
j. A610b 4p multi .75 .75
k. A610 4p multi .75 .75
l. A610o 4p multi .75 .75
m. A610k 4p multi .75 .75
n. A610c 4p multi .75 .75

Issued: No. 2544, 7/7/98; 2545, 6/12/98.
No. 2544A, dated "1994," was overprinted in error.

Heroes of the Revolution Type of 1998

2p, Emilio Jacinto. 4p, Jose P. Rizal. 8p, Marcelo H. del Pilar. 10p, Gregorio del Pilar. 18p, Juan Luna.

1998 Inscribed "1998" ***Perf. 13½***
2546 A736 2p multicolored .60 .25
2547 A736 4p multicolored .60 .30
2548 A736 8p multicolored 1.00 .50
a. Inscribed "1999" 2.00 .50
2549 A736 10p multicolored 1.25 .70
a. Inscribed "1999" 2.50 .70
2550 A736 18p multicolored 2.50 1.25
Nos. 2546-2550 (5) 5.95 3.00

Issued: 4p, 10p, 18p, 5/18/98. 2p, 8p, 7/20/98.
For surcharges, see Nos. 2879-2882.

Philippine Centennial — A749a

No. 2550A: b, Spoliarium, by Juan Luna. c, 1st display of Philippine flag, 1898. d, Execution of Jose Rizal, 1896. e, Andres Bonifacio. f, Church, Malolos.

1998, July *Perf. 14*

2550A	Souv. booklet	*32.50*	*32.50*
b.	A749a 4p multicolored	.55	*.55*
c.	A749a 8p multicolored	1.10	*1.10*
d.-e.	A749a 16p multicolored	4.00	*4.00*
f.	A749a 20p multicolored	2.75	*2.75*

No. 2550A contains panes of 4 each of Nos. 2550Ab-2550Ac and one pane of 1 each of Nos. 2550Ad-2550Af.

For surcharges, see Nos. 2879-2882.

Philippine Coconut Industry, Cent. A750

1998, Oct. 9 *Perf. 14*

2551	A750 4p multicolored	1.00	.60

Holy Spirit Adoration Sisters in Philippines, 75th Anniv. A751

1998, Oct. 9

2552	A751 4p multicolored	1.25	.30

Universal Delclaration of Human Rights, 50th Anniv. — A752

1998, Oct. 24

2553	A752 4p multicolored	.90	.90

Intl. Year of the Ocean — A753

1998, Oct. 24

2554	A753 15p multicolored	2.60	1.10
a.	Souvenir sheet, #2554	4.50	4.50

No. 2554a is a continuous design.

A754

Philippine Postal Service, Cent. — #2555: a, Child placing envelope into mailbox, globe. b, Arms encircling globe, envelopes, Philippine flag as background. c, Airplane, globe, various stamps over building. d, Child holding up hands, natl. flag colors, envelopes.

15p, Child holding envelope as it crisscrosses globe.

1998, Nov. 4

2555	A754 6p Block of 4, #a.-d.	3.00	3.00

Souvenir Sheet

2556	A754 15p multicolored	4.00	4.00

No. 2556 contains one 76x30mm stamp.

A755

Christmas: Various star lanterns.

1998, Nov. 5

2557	A755 6p multicolored	.65	.35
2558	A755 11p multicolored	1.25	.70
2559	A755 13p multicolored	1.60	.85
2560	A755 15p multicolored	1.75	1.00
	Nos. 2557-2560 (4)	5.25	2.90

Pasko '98.

Souvenir Sheets

Philippines '98, Philippine Cent. Invitational Intl. Philatelic Exhibition — A756

Revolutionary scenes, stamps of revolutionary govt.: No. 2561, Soldiers celebrating, #Y1-Y2. No. 2562, Signing treaty, telegraph stamps. No. 2563, Waving flag from balcony, #YF1, "Recibos" (Offical receipt) stamps. No. 2564, Procession, #Y3, perf. and imperf. examples of #YP1. No. 2565, New government convening, "Trans de Ganades" (cattle transfer) stamp, Libertad essay.

1998

2561	A756 15p multicolored	5.50	5.50
2562	A756 15p multicolored	5.50	5.50
2563	A756 15p multicolored	5.50	5.50
2564	A756 15p multicolored	5.50	5.50
2565	A756 15p multicolored	5.50	5.50
	Nos. 2561-2565 (5)	27.50	27.50

No. 2561 exists imperf. The first printing has varying amounts of black offset on the reverse. Value, $60. The second printing does not have the offset. Value, $12.50.

Nos. 2561-2565 were issued one each day from 11/5-11/9.

Pres. Joseph Ejercito Estrada A757

1998, Nov. 10

2566	A757 6p Taking oath	.75	.40
2567	A757 15p Giving speech	1.75	1.00

Shells — A758

No. 2568: a, Mitra papalis. b, Vexillum citrinum. c, Vexillum rugosum. d, Volema carinifera.

No. 2569: a, Teramachia dalli. b, Nassarius vitiensis. c, Cymbiola imperialis. d, Cymbiola aulica.

No. 2570: a, Nassarius papillosus. b, Fasciolaria trapezium.

Unwmk.

1998, Nov. 6 **Litho.** *Perf. 14*

2568	A758 4p Block of 4, #a.-d.	3.00	3.00
2569	A758 4p Block of 4, #a.-d.	3.00	3.00

Souvenir Sheet

2570	A758 8p Sheet of 2, #a.-b.	5.00	5.00
c.	Souvenir sheet, Type II	10.00	10.00

Cloud in sheet margin touches "s" of Shells on #2570. On #2570c, cloud does not touch "s" of Shells. Colors are dark on #2570c, lighter on #2570.

Natl. Stamp Collecting Month — A759

Motion picture, director: 6p, "Dyesebel," Gerardo de Leon. 11p, "Ang Sawa Sa Lumang Simboryo," Gerardo de Leon. 13p, "Prinsipe Amante," Lamberto V. Avellana. No. 2574, "Anak Dalita," Lamberto V. Avellana.

No. 2575, "Siete Infantes de Lara," costume design by Carlos "Botong" Francisco.

1998, Nov. 25

2571	A759 6p black & blue	.60	.40
2572	A759 11p black & brown	1.25	.70
2573	A759 13p black & lilac	1.40	.80
2574	A759 15p black & green	1.75	.95
	Nos. 2571-2574 (4)	5.00	2.85

Souvenir Sheet

2575	A759 15p black	3.25	3.25

No. 2575 contains one 26x76mm stamp.

Philippine Centennial — A759a

Pride, various women and: No. 2575A, Eagle (Resources). No. 2575B, Costume (Heritage). No. 2575C, Flag (Filipino People). No. 2575D, Artifacts with text (Literature). No. 2575E, Rice terraces (Engineering). No. 2575F, "Noli Me Tangere" (Citizenry).

Unwmk.

1998, Nov. 20 **Litho.** *Imperf.*

2575A	A759a 15p multi	3.00	3.00
2575B	A759a 15p multi	3.00	3.00
2575C	A759a 15p multi	3.00	3.00
2575D	A759a 15p multi	3.00	3.00
2575E	A759a 15p multi	3.00	3.00
2575F	A759a 15p multi	3.00	3.00
	Nos. 2575A-2575F (6)	18.00	18.00

Nos. 2575A-2575F have simulated perforations.

New Year 1999 (Year of the Rabbit) A760

1998, Dec. 1

2576	A760 4p shown	.50	.40
2577	A760 11p Two rabbits	1.50	.70
a.	Souvenir sheet, #2576-2577	3.75	3.75

No. 2577a exists imperf. Value, $5.

Heroes of the Revolution Type of 1998

1998, Dec. 15 **Litho.** *Perf. 13½*

Booklet Stamps

Yellow Background

2578	A736 6p like #2518	.70	.40
2579	A736 6p like #2519	.70	.40
2580	A736 6p like #2520	.70	.40
2581	A736 6p like #2521	.70	.40
2582	A736 6p like #2528	.70	.40
2583	A736 6p like #2547	.70	.40
2584	A736 6p like #2549	.70	.40
2585	A736 6p like #2550	.70	.40
2586	A736 6p like #2546	.70	.40
2587	A736 6p like #2548	.70	.40
a.	Booklet pane, #2578-2587	8.00	8.00
	Complete booklet, #2587a	8.00	8.00

Green Background

2588	A736 15p like #2546	2.00	1.00
2589	A736 15p like #2518	2.00	1.00
2590	A736 15p like #2547	2.00	1.00
2591	A736 15p like #2528	2.00	1.00
2592	A736 15p like #2548	2.00	1.00
2593	A736 15p like #2549	2.00	1.00
2594	A736 15p like #2519	2.00	1.00
2595	A736 15p like #2520	2.00	1.00
2596	A736 15p like #2521	2.00	1.00
a.	Booklet pane, 2c #2546, 8c #2548, 2 each 11c, 13c, #2519-2520, 6c #2583, #2596	13.00	13.00
	Complete booklet, #2596a	13.00	13.00
2597	A736 15p like #2550	2.00	1.00
a.	Booklet pane, #2588-2597	19.00	19.00
	Complete booklet, #2597a	19.00	19.00

Nos. 2587a, 2596a, 2597a were made available to collectors unattached to the booklet cover.

Philippine Central Bank, 50th Anniv. A761

1999, Jan. 3 Litho. *Perf. 14*

2598 A761 6p multicolored .90 .30

Philippine Centennial — A762

Designs: a, Centennial emblem. b, Proclamation of Independence. c, Malolos Congress. d, Nov. 5th uprising. e, Cry of Santa Barbara Iloilo. f, Victory over colonial forces. g, Flag raising, Butuan City. h, Ratification of Malolos Constitution. i, Philippine Republic formed. j, Barasoain Church.

1999, Jan. 11

2599 A762 6p Sheet of 10, #a.-j. 10.00 *25.00*

Scouting — A762a

Designs: No. 2599K, Girl Scout, boys planting tree. No. 2599L, Boy Scout, Girl Scout, flag, people representing various professions.

Perf. 13½

1999, Jan. 16 Litho. Unwmk.

2599K A762a 5p multicolored 1.50 .30
2599L A762a 5p multicolored 1.50 .30

Nos. 2599K-2599L are dated 1995, are inscribed "THRIFT STAMP," and were valid for postage due to stamp shortage.

Dept. of Transportation and Communications, Cent. — A763

Emblem and: a, Ship. b, Jet. c, Control tower. d, Satellite dish, bus.

15p, Philpost Headquarters, truck, motorcycle on globe.

1999, Jan. 20

2600 A763 6p Block of 4, #a.-d. 4.00 *6.00*

Souvenir Sheet

2601 A763 15p multicolored 3.00 *4.00*

No. 2601 contains one 80x30mm stamp.

Filipino-American War, Cent. — A764

1999, Feb. 4

2602 A764 5p multicolored .60 .30

Philippine Military Academy, Cent. A765

1999-2001 *Perf. 14*

2603 A765 5p multicolored .60 .30
a. Small "P" in denomination ('01) 1.25 .65

"P" in denomination is 1¾mm tall on No. 2603, 1½mm tall on No. 2603a.

Issue dates: No. 2603, 2/4/99. No. 2063a, 2001.

Birds — A766

#2604: a, Greater crested tern. b, Ruddy turnstone. c, Green-backed heron. d, Common tern.

#2605: a, Black-winged stilt. b, Asiatic dowitcher. c, Whimbrel. d, Reef heron.

#2606: a, Spotted greenshank. b, Tufted duck.

1999 Litho. *Perf. 14*

2604 A766 5p Block of 4, #a.-d. 3.00 3.00
2605 A766 5p Block of 4, #a.-d. 3.00 3.00

Souvenir Sheets

2606 A766 8p Sheet of 2, #a.-b. 5.75 5.75
c. As #2606, diff. sheet margin, inscription 5.75 5.75

Issued: #2604-2606, 2/22; #2606c, 3/19.

No. 2606c contains inscription, emblem for Australia '99 World Stamp Expo.

Heroes of the Revolution Type

Perf. 13½

1999, Mar. 12 Litho. Unwmk.

Pink Background

2607 A736 5p like #2547 .55 .30

Manila Lions Club, 50th Anniv. A767

Design: Emblem, Francisco "Paquito" Ortigas, Jr., first president.

1999, Mar. 20 *Perf. 14*

2608 A767 5p multicolored .60 .30

Philippine Orthopedic Assoc., 50th Anniv. — A768

1999, Mar. 20

2609 A768 5p multicolored .60 .30

La Union Botanical Garden, San Fernando — A769

Designs: No. 2610, Entrance sign, birdhouse. No. 2611, Ticket booth at entrance.

1999, Mar. 20

2610 5p multicolored .60 .50
2611 5p multicolored .60 .50
a. A769 Pair, #2610-2611 2.00 2.00

Frogs — A770

#2612: a, Woodworth's frog. b, Giant Philippine frog. c, Gliding tree frog. d, Common forest frog.

#2613: a, Spiny tree frog. b, Truncate-toed chorus frog. c, Variable-backed frog.

1999, Apr. 5

2612 A770 5p Block of 4, #a.-d. 3.00 3.00

Sheet of 3

2613 A770 5p #a.-c. + label 5.00 5.00

Marine Life — A771

No. 2614: a, Sea squirt. b, Banded sea snake. c, Manta ray. d, Painted rock lobster.

No. 2615: a, Sea grapes. b, Branching coral. c, Sea urchin.

1999, May 11 Litho. *Perf. 14*

2614 A771 5p Block of 4, #a.-d. 3.00 3.00

Sheet of 3

2615 A771 5p #a.-c. + label 5.75 5.75

Juan F. Nakpil, Architect, Birth Cent. A772

1999, May 25

2616 A772 5p multicolored .65 .40

UPU, 125th Anniv. A773

Designs: 5p, Globe, boy writing letter. 15p, Globe, girl looking at stamp collection.

1999, May 26 Litho. *Perf. 14*

2617 A773 5p multicolored .65 .40
2618 A773 15p multicolored 1.90 1.00

Philippines-Thailand Diplomatic Relations, 50th Anniv. — A774

Orchids: 5p, 11p, Euanthe sanderiana, cattleya Queen Sirikit.

1999, June 13 Litho. *Perf. 14*

2619 A774 5p multicolored .65 .30
2620 A774 11p multicolored 1.40 .70

Order of flowers from top is reversed on 11p value.

Issued in sheets of 20 (10 of each denomination in two rows of 5, separated by a central gutter). Most sheets of 20 were cut in half through the central gutter.

See #2623-2624, 2640-2641, 2664-2666, 2719-2721, 2729-2731.

Masonic Charities for Crippled Children, Inc., 75th Anniv. A775

1999, July 5

2621 A775 5p multicolored .65 .30

Production of Eberhard Faber "Mongol" Pencils, 150th Anniv. — A776

1999, July 5

2622 A776 5p multicolored .65 .30

Diplomatic Relations Type of 1999

Philippines-Korea diplomatic relations, 50th anniv., flowers: 5p, 11p, Jasminum sambac, hibiscus synacus.

1999, Aug. 9 **Litho.** ***Perf. 14***

2623 A774 5p multicolored .70 .35
2624 A774 11p multicolored 1.50 .75

Order of flowers from top is reversed on 11p value.

issued in sheets of 20 (10 of each denomination in two rows of 5, separated by a central gutter). Most sheets of 20 were cut in half through the central gutter.

Community Chest, 50th Anniv. A777

1999, Aug. 30
2625 A777 5p multicolored .80 .25

A778

1999, Aug. 30
2626 A778 5p multicolored .80 .25

Philippine Bible Society, cent.

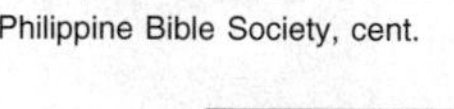

A779

1999, Sept. 3
2627 A779 5p multicolored .80 .25

St. Francis of Assisi Parish, Sariaya, 400th anniv.

National Anthem, Cent. A780

1999, Sept. 3
2628 A780 5p multicolored .80 .25

No. 2539b Overprinted in Silver "25th ANNIVERSARY IPPS"

Souvenir Sheet

1999, Sept. 24 **Litho.** ***Perf. 14***

2629 A746 15p Sheet of 3, #a.-c., + 3 labels 4.50 4.50

Ovpt. in sheet margin has same inscription twice, "25th ANNIVERSARY INTERNATIONAL PHILIPPINE PHILATELIC SOCIETY 1974-99" and two society emblems.

Senate — A781

1999, Oct. 15
2630 A781 5p multi .80 .25

A782

1999, Oct. 20
2631 A782 5p multi .80 .25

New Building of Chiang Kai-shek College, Manila.

Issued in sheets of 10.

Tanza National Comprehensive High School, 50th Anniv. — A783

1999, Oct. 24
2632 A783 5p multi .80 .40

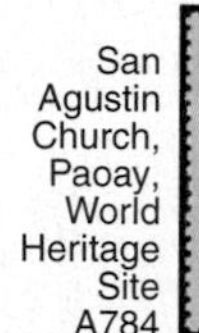

San Agustin Church, Paoay, World Heritage Site A784

Intl. Year of Older Persons A785

World Teachers' Day A786

1999, Oct. 24

2633 A784 5p multi .80 .50
2634 A785 11p multi 1.75 .80
2635 A786 15p multi 2.50 1.50
Nos. 2633-2635 (3) 5.05 2.80

United Nations Day.

Christmas A787

1999, Oct. 27

Color of Angel's Gown

2636 A787 5p red violet 1.00 .25
2637 A787 11p yellow 2.00 .45
2638 A787 13p blue 2.25 .55
2639 A787 15p green 2.75 .65
a. Sheet of 4, #2636-2639 8.00 8.00
Nos. 2636-2639 (4) 8.00 1.90

Nos. 2636-2639 each issued in sheets of 10 stamps with two central labels.

Diplomatic Relations Type of 1999

Philippines-Canada diplomatic relations, 50th anniv., mammals: 5p, 15p, Tamaraw, polar bear.

1999, Nov. 15 ***Perf. 14***

2640 A774 5p multi .75 .25
2641 A774 15p multi 2.75 .75

Order of mammals from top is reversed on 15p value.

Issued in sheets of 20 (10 of each denomination in two rows of 5, separated by a central gutter). Most sheets of 20 were cut in half through central gutter.

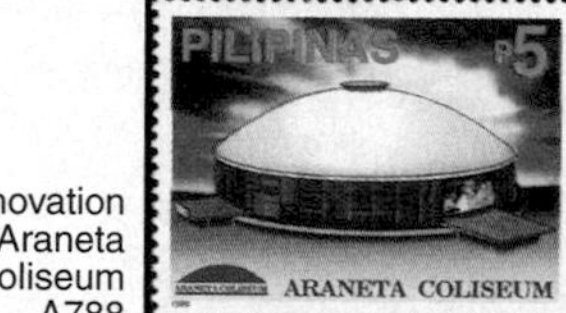

Renovation of Araneta Coliseum A788

1999, Nov. 19 **Litho.**
2642 A788 5p multi 1.00 .25

A789

1999, Nov. 19 **Color of Sky**

2643 A789 5p dark blue .75 .25
2644 A789 11p blue green 2.25 .50

3rd ASEAN Informal Summit.

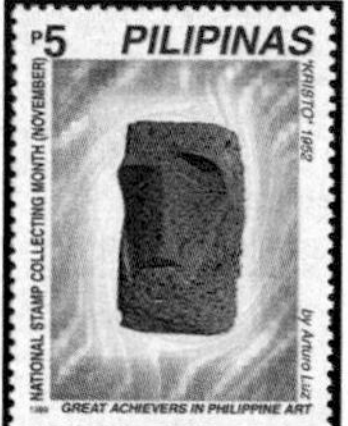

A790

Sculptures: No. 2645, Kristo, by Arturo Luz. 11p, Homage to Dodgie Laurel, by J. Elizalde Navarro. 13p, Hilojan, by Napoleon Abueva. No. 2648, Mother and Child, by Abueva.

No. 2649: a, 5p, Mother's Revenge, by José Rizal, horiz. b, 15p, El Ermitano, by Rizal, horiz.

1999, Nov. 29

2645 A790 5p multi 1.00 .25
2646 A790 11p multi 2.00 .45
2647 A790 13p multi 2.25 .55
2648 A790 15p multi 2.75 .65
Nos. 2645-2648 (4) 8.00 1.90

Souvenir Sheet

2649 A790 Sheet of 2, #a.-b. 4.00 4.00

Natl. Stamp Collecting Month.

New Year 2000 (Year of the Dragon) A791

1999, Dec. 1 ***Perf. 14***

2650 A791 5p Dragon in water .75 .25
2651 A791 11p Dragon in sky 2.75 .75
a. Sheet of 2, #2650-2651 2.25 2.25
b. As "a," imperf. 5.75 5.75

Battle of Tirad Pass, Cent. A792

1999, Dec. 2 ***Perf. 14***
2652 A792 5p multi .80 .25

Orchids — A793

No. 2653: a, Paphiopedilum urbanianum. b, Phalaenopsis schilleriana. c, Dendrobium amethystoglossum. d, Paphiopedilum barbatum.

No. 2654, horiz.: a, Paphiopedilum haynaldianum. b, Phalaenopsis stuartiana. c, Trichoglottis brachiata. d, Ceratostylis rubra.

1999, Dec. 3 **Litho.**
2653 A793 5p Block of 4, #a.-d. 4.00 4.00

Souvenir Sheet

2654 A793 5p Sheet of 4, #a.-d. 5.00 5.00

Battle of San Mateo, Cent. A794

1999, Dec. 19
2655 A794 5p multicolored .80 .25

People Power — A795

People and: a, Tank. b, Tower. c, Crucifix.

1999, Dec. 31
2656 A795 5p Strip of 3, #a.-c. 3.50 3.50

Natl. Commission on the Role of Filipino Women — A796

2000, Jan. 7 **Litho.** ***Perf. 14***
2657 A796 5p multi .80 .25

Manila Bulletin, Cent. A797

2000, Feb. 2 Litho. *Perf. 14*

2658 A797 5p multi .50 .25
a. Year at LR .50 .25

Issued: No. 2658a, 6/7.

La Union Province, 150th Anniv. — A798

Arms of province and: a, Sailboat, golfer. b, Tractor, worker, building. c, Building, flagpole. d, Airplane, ship, telephone tower, people on telephone, computer.

2000, Mar. 2

2659 A798 5p Block of 4, #a.-d. 2.50 2.50

Civil Service Commission, Cent. — A799

2000, Mar. 20

2660 A799 5p multi .50 .25

Millennium — A800

Designs: a, Golden Garuda of Palawan. b, First sunrise of the millennium, Pusan Point. c, Golden Tara of Agusan.

2000, Mar. 31

2661 A800 5p Strip of 3, #a.-c. 3.50 3.50

GMA Radio and Television Network, 50th Anniv. A802

2000, Mar. 1 Litho. *Perf. 14*

2662 A802 5p multi .60 .25

Philippine Presidents — A803

No. 2662A: b, Manuel Roxas. c, Elpidio Quirino. No. 2663: a, Presidential seal. b, Joseph Ejercito Estrada. c, Fidel V. Ramos. d, Corazon C. Aquino. e, Ferdinand E. Marcos. f, Diosdado Macapagal. g, Carlos P. Garcia. h, Ramon Magsaysay. i, Elpidio Quirino. j, Manuel Roxas.

2000 *Perf. 13½*

2662A Pair 1.25 1.25
b.-c. A803 5p Any single .55 .25
2663 Block of 10 7.50 7.50
a.-j. A803 5p Any single .60 .25

Nos. 2662b-2662c have presidential seal but lack blue lines at bottom. No. 2663a has denomination at left. Nos. 2663b-2663j have small Presidential seal at bottom.

Issued: No. 2662A, 2/6. No. 2663, 3/16.

See Type A828 for stamps showing Presidential seal with colored background.

See Nos. 2672-2676, 2786.

Diplomatic Relations Type of 1999

5p, Sarimanok, Great Wall of China. 11p, Phoenix, Banaue rice terraces.

No. 2666: a, 5p, Great Wall, horiz. b, 11p, Rice terraces, horiz.

2000, May 8 *Perf. 14*

2664-2665 A774 Set of 2 2.00 2.00

Souvenir Sheet

2666 A774 Sheet of 2, #a-b 3.00 3.00

Issued in sheets of 20 (10 of each denomination in two rows of 5, separated by a central gutter). Most sheets of 20 were cut in half through central gutter.

St. Thomas Aquinas Parish, Mangaldan, 400th Anniv. A805

2000, June 1

2667 A805 5p multi .60 .45

Battle Centenaries — A806

Battles in Philippine Insurrection: #2668, Mabitac. #2669, Paye, vert. #2670, Makahambus Hill, vert. #2671, Pulang Lupa.

2000, June 19

2668-2671 A806 5p Set of 4 2.00 2.00

Presidents Type of 2000 Redrawn

No. 2672: a, Presidential seal. b, Joseph Ejercito Estrada. c, Fidel V. Ramos. d, Corazon C. Aquino. e, Ferdinand E. Marcos. f, Diosdado Macapagal. g, Carlos P. Garcia. h, Ramon Magsaysay. i, Elpidio Quirino. j, Manuel Roxas.

No. 2673: a, Magsaysay. b, Garcia.
No. 2674: a, Macapagal. b, Marcos.
No. 2675: a, Aquino. b, Ramos.
No. 2676: a, Estrada. b, Presidential seal.

2000 Litho. *Perf. 13½*

Blue Lines at Bottom

2672 Block of 10 *9.50 9.50*
a.-j. A803 5p Any single *.75 .75*
2673 Pair *3.75 3.75*
a.-b. A803 10p Any single *1.25 1.25*
2674 Pair *4.25 4.25*
a.-b. A803 11p Any single *1.50 1.50*
2675 Pair *4.75 4.75*
a.-b. A803 13p Any single *1.75 1.75*
2676 Pair *5.50 5.50*
a.-b. A803 15p Any single *2.00 2.00*
Nos. 2672-2676 (5) 27.75 27.75

Issued: No. 2672, 7/3; Nos. 2673-2674, 8/4. Nos. 2675-2676, 6/19.

No. 2672a has denomination at R, while No. 2663a has denomination at L. Nos. 2672b-2672j have no presidential seal, while Nos. 2662Ab-2662Ac, 2663b-2663j have seal.

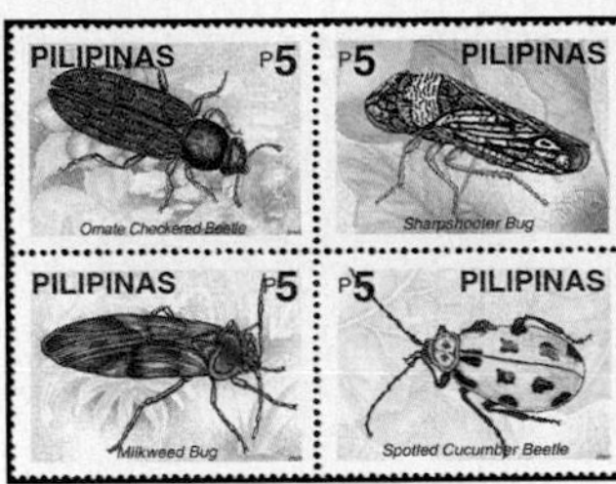

Insects — A807

No. 2677: a, Ornate checkered beetle. b, Sharpshooter bug. c, Milkweed bug. d, Spotted cucumber beetle.

No. 2678: a, Green June beetle. b, Convergent ladybird. c, Eastern Hercules beetle. d, Harlequin cabbage bug.

2000, July 21 *Perf. 14*

2677 A807 5p Block of 4, #a-d 4.00 4.00
e. Souevnir sheet, #2677 6.00 6.00
2678 A807 5p Block of 4, #a-d 4.00 4.00
e. Souevnir sheet, #2678 6.00 6.00

Occupational Health Nurses Association, 50th Anniv. — A808

2000, Aug. 30

2679 A808 5p multi .65 .25

Diocese of Lucena, 50th Anniv. A809

2000. Aug. 30

2680 A809 5p multi .65 .25

Millennium — A810

Boats: a, Balanghai. b, Vinta. c, Caracoa.

2000, Sept. 21

2681 A810 Horiz. strip of 3 4.00 4.00
a.-c. 5p Any single *.75 .25*

Equitable PCI Bank, 50th Anniv. A811

2000, Sept. 26

2682 A811 5p multi .50 .25

Year of the Overseas Filipino Worker A812

2000, Sept. 29 Litho.

2683 A812 5p multi .65 .50

2000 Olympics, Sydney — A813

No. 2684: a, Running. b, Archery. c, Shooting. d, Diving.

No. 2685, horiz.: a, Boxing. b, Equestrian. c, Rowing. d, Taekwondo.

2000, Sept. 30

2684 A813 5p Block of 4, #a-d 3.00 3.00

Souvenir Sheet

2685 A813 5p Sheet of 4, #a-d 5.00 5.00

Teresian Association in the Philippines, 50th Anniv. A814

2000, Oct. 10

2686 A814 5p multi .65 .50

House of Representatives A815

2000, Oct. 15 *Perf. 14*

2687 A815 5p multi .60 .45

Marine Corps, 50th Anniv. A816

2000, Oct. 18

2688 A816 5p multi .60 .25

Souvenir Sheet

Postal Service, Cent. (in 1998) — A817

2000, Nov. 6

2689 A817 15p multi 3.00 3.00

Clothing Exhibit at Metropolitan Museum of Manila — A818

No. 2690, 5p: a, Kalinga / Gaddang cotton loincloth. b, Portrait of Leticia Jimenez, by unknown artist.

No. 2691, 5p, horiz.: a, B'laan female upper garment. b, T'boli T'nalak abaca cloth.

No. 2692: a, 5p, Portrait of Teodora Devera Ygnacio, by Justiniano Asunción. b, 15p, Detail of Tawsug silk sash.

2000, Nov. 15 **Pairs, #a-b**

2690-2691 A818 Set of 2 4.00 4.00
#2690a-b, 2691a-b, any single .50 .25

Souvenir Sheet

2692 A818 Sheet of 2, #a-b 4.00 4.00

Natl. Stamp Collecting Month A819

Designs: 5p, Portrait of an Unkown Lady, by Juan Luna, vert. 11p, Nude, by José Joya. 13p, Lotus Odalisque, by Rodolfo Paras-Perez. No. 2696, 15p, Untitled Nude, by Fernando Amorsolo.

No. 2697, The Memorial, by Cesar Legaspi.

2000, Nov. 20 ***Perf. 14***

2693-2696 A819 Set of 4 6.50 6.50

Souvenir Sheet

2697 A819 15p multi 4.00 4.00

No. 2697 contains one 80x29 stamp and label.

Christmas A820

Angels: No. 2698, 5p, In pink robe, with bouquet of flowers. No. 2699, 5p, As #2698, with Holy Year 2000 emblem and inscription. 11p, In green robe. 13p, In orange robe. 15p, In red robe, with garland of flowers.

2000, Nov. 22 **Litho.**

2698-2702 A820 Set of 5 6.00 6.00

APO Philatelic Society, 50th Anniv. — A821

Emblem and stamps: No. 2703, 5p, #620 (yellow background). No. 2704, 5p, #639 (light blue background), horiz. No. 2705, 5p, #850 (dull green background). No. 2706, 5p, #B21 (pink background), horiz.

2000, Nov. 23

2703-2706 A821 Set of 4 2.75 1.50

No. 1806 Handstamp Surcharged in Red

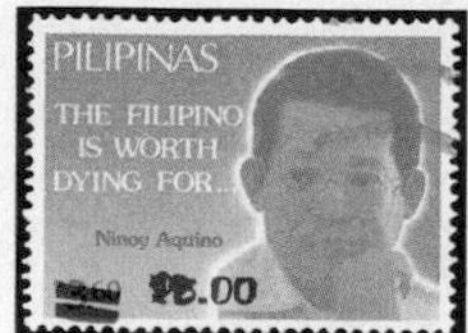

Perf. 13x13½

2000, Nov. 24 **Litho.** **Wmk.**

2706A A469 5p on 3.60p multi *7.50 7.50*

Nine varieties of the surcharge on No. 2706A exist.

New Year 2001 (Year of the Snake) A822

Snakes with inscription in: 5p, Tagalog. 11p, English.

2000, Dec. 20 **Unwmk.** ***Perf. 14***

2707-2708 A822 Set of 2 2.50 2.50
2708a Souvenir sheet, #2707-2708 + 2 labels 7.00 7.00

No. 2708a exists imperf.

Millennium A823

No. 2709: a, Trade and progress. b, Education and knowledge. c, Communication and information.

2000, Dec. 28

2709 Horiz. strip of 3 4.00 4.00
a.-c. A823 5p Any single .50 .50

Bank of the Philippine Islands, 150th Anniv. A824

2001, Jan. 30 **Litho.**

2710 A824 5p multi .50 .25

Hong Kong 2001 Stamp Exhibition A825

Designs: No. 2711a, 5p, No. 2712, 11p, Tamaraw. No. 2711b, 5p, No. 2713, 11p, Agila. No. 2711c, 5p, No. 2714, 11p, Tarsier. No. 2711d, 5p, No. 2715, 11p, Talisman Cove orchid. No. 2711e, 5p, No. 2716, 11p, Pawikan.

2001, Feb. 1

2711 Horiz. strip of 5 4.00 4.00
a.-e. A825 5p Any single .60 .60

Souvenir Sheets

2712-2716 A825 Set of 5 12.50 12.50
2713a Ovptd. in margin in red 3.75 3.75
2715a Ovptd. in margin in red 3.75 3.75

Nos. 2712-2716 have show emblem on sheet margin instead of on stamp.

Issued: Nos. 2713a, 2715a, 6/30/01. Overprint in margin on Nos. 2713a, 2715a has Chinese inscriptions and English text "PHILIPPINE-CHINESE PHILATELIC SOCIETY / 1951 GOLDEN JUBILEE 2001."

Gen. Paciano Rizal (1851-1930) A826

2001, Mar. 7 **Litho.** ***Perf. 14***

2717 A826 5p multi .50 .25

San Beda College, Cent. A827

2001, Mar. 9

2718 A827 5p multi .50 .25

Diplomatic Relations Type of 1999

Philippines-Vatican City diplomatic relations, 50th anniv., main altars at: 5p, St. Peter's Basilica, Vatican City. No. 2720, 15p, San Agustin Church, Manila.

No. 2721: a, Adam, from Creation of Adam, by Michelangelo. b, God, from Creation of Adam.

2001, Mar. 14

2719-2720 A774 Set of 2 2.50 2.50

Souvenir Sheet

2721 A774 15p Sheet of 2, #a-b 4.50 4.50

Nos. 2719-2720 issued in sheets of 20 (10 of each denomination in two rows of 5, separated by a central gutter). Most sheets of 20 were cut in half through central gutter.

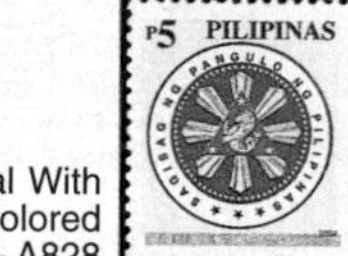

Presidential Seal With Colored Background — A828

2001, Apr. 5 ***Perf. 13¾***

Background Colors

2722 A828 5p yellow .50 .25
2723 A828 15p blue 1.50 .45

Stamps of the same denomination showing the Presidential seal with white backgrounds are listed as Nos. 2663a, 2672a and 2676b.

See Nos. 2746-2748. For surcharges, see Nos. 2834-2836. For overprints, see Nos. 2865-2866.

Tourist Spots A829

No. 2724: a, El Nido, Palawan Province. b, Vigan House, Ilocos Sur Province. c, Boracay, Aklan Province. d, Chocolate Hills, Bohol Province.

15p, Banaue Rice Terraces, Ifugao Province.

2000, Apr. 14 ***Perf. 14***

2724 Horiz. strip of 4 2.00 2.00
a.-d. A829 5p Any single .50 .50

Souvenir Sheet

2725 A829 15p multi 3.00 3.00

No. 2725 contains one 80x30mm stamp.

No. 2725 exists with washed-out colors and a larger year date.

Canonical Coronation of Our Lady of Manaoag, 75th Anniv. — A830

2001, Apr. 22

2726 A830 5p multi .50 .40

Pres. Gloria Macapagal-Arroyo A831

Pres. Macapagal-Arroyo: No. 2727, 5p, Waving. No. 2728, 5p, Taking oath of office.

2001, Apr. 29

2727-2728 A831 Set of 2 1.00 1.00

Diplomatic Relations Type of 1999

Philippines-Australia diplomatic relations, landmarks: 5p, Nos. 2730-2731, 13p, Sydney Opera House, Cultural Center of the Philippines. No. 2731 is horiz.

2001, May 21

2729-2730 A774 Set of 2 2.00 .75

Souvenir Sheet

2731 A774 13p multi 3.50 3.50

No. 2731 contains one 80x30mm stamp.

Supreme Court, Cent. A832

2001, May 31

2732 A832 5p multi .50 .40

Silliman University, Dumaguete City, Cent. A833

2001, June 1

2733 A833 5p multi .50 .25

Philippine Normal University, Cent. A834

2001, June 1

2734 A834 5p multi .50 .40

Joaquin J. Ortega (1870-1943), First Civil Governor of La Union Province — A835

2001, July 12

2735 A835 5p multi .35 .40

Eugenio Lopez (1901-75), Businessman A836

2001, July 12
2736 A836 5p multi .35 .25

Illustrations from Boxer Codex, c. 1590 — A837

No. 2737: a, Visayan couple. b, Tagalog couple. c, Moros of Luzon (multicolored frame). d, Moros of Luzon (blue frame).
No. 2738: a, Pintados (denomination at left). b, Pintados (denomination at right). c, Cagayan female. d, Zambal.

2001, Aug. 1
2737 A837 5p Block of 4, #a-d 2.50 2.50

Souvenir Sheet

2738 A837 5p Sheet of 4, #a-d 3.00 3.00
e. Sheet of 4, #a-d, with Phila Nippon '01 margin 3.00 3.00

Arrival of American Educators (Thomasites), Cent. — A838

Designs: 5p, Thomasite teachers, US transport ship Thomas. 15p, Philippine students.

2001, Aug. 23
2739-2740 A838 Set of 2 2.00 1.00

Technological University of the Philippines, Cent. — A839

2001, Aug. 20 **Litho.** ***Perf. 14***
2741 A839 5p multi .60 .25

National Museum of the Philippines, Cent. — A840

2001, Sept. 3
2742 A840 5p multi .60 .25

Lands Management Bureau, Cent. — A841

2001, Sept. 17
2743 A841 5p multi .60 .25

Colegio de San Jose and San Jose Seminary, 400th Anniv. — A842

2001, Oct. 1
2744 A842 5p multi .60 .25

Makati City Financial District A843

2001, Oct. 1
2745 A843 5p multi .60 .25

Presidential Seal With Colored Background Type of 2001

2001, Oct. 5 ***Perf. 13¾***

Background Colors

2746 A828 10p green .60 .30
2747 A828 11p pink .65 .30
2748 A828 13p gray .75 .40
Nos. 2746-2748 (3) 2.00 1.00

Musical Instruments — A844

No. 2749: a, Trumpet. b, Tuba. c, French horn. d, Trombone.
No. 2750, vert.: a, Bass drum. b, Clarinet, oboe. c, Xylophone. d, Sousaphone.

2001, Oct. 8 ***Perf. 14***
2749 A844 5p Block of 4, #a-d 2.50 2.50

Souvenir Sheet

2750 A844 5p Sheet of 4, #a-d 4.00 *5.00*

Malampaya Deep Water Gas Power Project A845

Frame colors: 5p, Silver. 15p, Gold.

2001, Oct. 16
2751-2752 A845 Set of 2 2.25 2.25

Intl. Volunteers Year A846

2001, Oct. 24
2753 A846 5p multi .60 .25

Year of Dialogue Among Civilizations A847

2001, Oct. 24
2754 A847 15p multi 1.60 .80

Christmas A848

Designs: 5p, Herald Angels. 11p, Kumukutikutitap. 13p, Pasko ni Bitoy. 15p, Pasko na naman.

2001, Oct. 30
2755-2758 A848 Set of 4 4.50 4.50

Philippines — Switzerland Relations, 150th Anniv. — A849

Monument statues by Richard Kissling: 5p, William Tell. No. 2760, 15p, Jose P. Rizal.
No. 2761, 15p, Mayon Volcano, Philippines, and Matterhorn, Switzerland.

2001, Nov. 26
2759-2760 A849 Set of 2 2.25 1.25

Souvenir Sheet

2761 A849 15p multi 2.50 2.50

No. 2761 contains one 79x29mm stamp. Nos. 2759-2760 issued in sheets of 20 (10 of each denomination in two rows of 5, separated by a central gutter). Most sheets of 20 were cut in half through central gutter.

Drawings of Manila Inhabitants, c. 1840 — A850

Designs: 17p, Woman with hat, man with green pants. 21p, Woman with veil, man with brown pants. 22p, Man, woman at mortar and pestle.

2001, Dec. 1 ***Perf. 13¾***

Inscribed "2001"

2762 A850 17p multi 1.75 .85
a. Inscribed "2002" 1.75 .85
b. Inscribed "2003" 1.75 .85
2763 A850 21p multi 2.10 1.00
a. Inscribed "2002" 2.10 1.00
2764 A850 22p multi 2.40 1.10
a. Inscribed "2002" 2.40 1.10
Nos. 2762-2764 (3) 6.25 2.95

See No. 2779.

Solicitor General, Cent. — A851

2001, Dec. 7 ***Perf. 14***
2765 A851 5p multi .60 .25

Natl. Stamp Collecting Month A852

Art: 5p, PUJ, by Antonio Austria. 17p, Hesus Nazareno, by Angelito Antonio. 21p, Three Women with Basket, by Anita Magsaysay-Ho, vert. No. 2769, 22p, Church with Yellow Background, by Mauro "Malang" Santos, vert.
No. 2770, 22p, Komedya ng Pakil, by Danilo Dalena.

2001, Dec. 7 **Litho.**
2766-2769 A852 Set of 4 6.75 6.75

Souvenir Sheet

2770 A852 22p multi 2.50 2.50

No. 2770 contains one 79x29mm stamp.

New Year 2002 (Year of the Horse) A853

Horse color: 5p, Red. 17p, White.

2001, Dec. 14 ***Perf. 14***
2771-2772 A853 Set of 2 2.50 1.10
2772a Souvenir sheet, #2771-2772, + 2 labels 5.00 5.00

No. 2772a exists imperf. Value $8.

Josemaria Escrivá (1902-75), Founder of Opus Dei — A854

2002, Jan. 9
2773 A854 5p multi .60 .25

World Heritage Sites A855

Vigan City sites: 5p, St. Paul's Metropolitan Cathedral. 22p, Calle Crisologo.

2002, Jan. 22
2774-2775 A855 Set of 2 3.00 3.00

Salvador Z. Araneta, Statesman, Birth Cent. — A856

2002, Jan. 31
2776 A856 5p multi .60 .25

Customs Service, Cent. A857

2002, Feb. 1
2777 A857 5p multi .60 .25

Valentine's Day — A858

No. 2778: a, Envelope. b, Man and woman. c, Cat and dog. d, Balloon.

2002, Feb. 8
2778 A858 5p Block of 4, #a-d 2.50 2.50

Drawings of Manila Inhabitants Type of 2001

2002, Mar. 1 Litho. ***Perf. 13¾***

Inscribed "2002"

2779 A850 5p Man, woman on horses .30 .25
a. Inscribed "2003" .30 .25

Baguio General Hospital and Medical Center, Cent. A859

2002, Mar. 22 ***Perf. 14***
2780 A859 5p multi .60 .25

Beatification of Blessed Pedro Calungsod A860

Designs: 5p, Calungsod with palm frond. 22p, Map of Guam, ship, Calungsod with cross.

2002, Apr. 2 ***Perf. 14***
2781 A860 5p multi .60 .25

Size: 102x72mm

Imperf

2782 A860 22p multi 2.00 2.00

Negros Occidental High School, Cent. — A861

2002, Apr. 12 ***Perf. 14***
2783 A861 5p multi .60 .25

La Consolacion College, Manila, Cent. A862

2002, Apr. 12
2784 A862 5p multi .60 .25

Vesak Day — A863

2002, May 26
2785 A863 5p multi .60 .25

Presidents Type of 2000 Redrawn Without Years of Service

No. 2786: a, Gloria Macapagal-Arroyo. b, Joseph Ejercito Estrada. c, Fidel V. Ramos. d, Corazon C. Aquino. e, Ferdinand E. Marcos. f, Diosdado Macapagal. g, Carlos P. Garcia. h, Ramon Magsaysay. i, Elpidio Quirino. j, Manuel Roxas.

2002, June 12 ***Perf. 13½***

Without Presidential Seal

Blue Lines at Bottom

2786 Block of 10 6.00 6.00
a.-j. A803 5p Any single .50 .40

Cavite National High School, Cent. A864

2002, June 19 ***Perf. 14***
2787 A864 5p multi .60 .25

Mangroves A865

Fish A866

Fish A867

Hands and Small Fish A868

No. 2792: a, Monitors in boats at marine sanctuary. b, Mangrove reforestation. c, Monitors checking reefs. d, Seaweed farming.

Unwmk.

2002, June 24 Litho. ***Perf. 14***
2788 A865 5p multi .60 .25
2789 A866 5p multi .60 .25
2790 A867 5p multi .60 .25
2791 A868 5p multi .60 .25
Nos. 2788-2791 (4) 2.40 1.00

Souvenir Sheet

2792 A865 5p Sheet of 4, #a-d 3.00 3.00

Coastal resources conservation.

Iglesia Filipina Independiente, Cent. — A869

2002, July 4
2793 A869 5p multi .60 .25

Souvenir Sheet

Philakorea 2002 World Stamp Exhibition, Seoul — A870

No. 2794: a, 5p, Mangrove. b, 17p, Buddhist, temple and flower.

2002, Aug. 2 **Unwmk.**
2794 A870 Sheet of 2, #a-b 2.50 2.50

No. 2794 exists imperf. with changed background color. Value $7.

No. 2210 Surcharged

Method & Perf. as Before

2002, Aug. 15 **Wmk. 391**
2795 A610 3p on 60s multi .45 .25

Telecommunications Officials Meetings, Manila — A870a

2002, Aug. 22 Litho. ***Perf. 14***
2795A A870a 5p multi .60 .25

Second Telecommunications Ministerial Meeting, Third ASEAN Telecommunications Senior Officials Meeting, Eighth ASEAN Telecommunications Regulators Council Meeting.

Marikina, Shoe Capital of the Philippines A871

Unwmk.

2002, Oct. 15 Litho. ***Perf. 14***
2796 A871 5p multi .50 .25

Souvenir Sheet

Intl. Year of Mountains — A872

2002, Oct. 28
2797 A872 22p multi 2.00 2.00

Christmas — A873

Various holiday foods: 5p, 17p, 21p, 22p.

2002, Nov. 5
2798-2801 A873 Set of 4 6.50 3.25

Stamp Collecting Month A874

Designs: 5p, Gerardo de Leon (1913-81), movie director. 17p, Francisca Reyes Aquino (1899-1983), founder of Philippine Folk Dance Society. 21p, Pablo S. Antonio (1901-75), architect. No. 2805, 22p, Jose Garcia Villa (1912-97), writer.

No. 2806, 22p, Honorata de la Rama (1902-91), singer and actress.

2002, Nov. 2 ***Perf. 14***
2802-2805 A874 Set of 4 6.50 6.50

Size: 99x74mm

Imperf

2806 A874 22p multi 2.25 2.25

First Circumnavigation of the World, 480th Anniv. — A875

No. 2807 — Ship and: a, Antonio Pigafetta. b, Ferdinand Magellan. c, King Charles I of Spain. d, Sebastian Elcano.
22p, World Map and King Charles I of Spain.

2002, Nov. 11 ***Perf. 14***

2807 A875 5p Vert. strip of 4, #a-d 3.00 3.00

Size: 104x85mm

Imperf

2808 A875 22p multi 3.00 3.00

Fourth World Meeting of Families — A876

Designs: 5p, Sculpture of Holy Family. 11p, Family, crucifix, Holy Spirit.

2002, Nov. 23 ***Perf. 14***

2809-2810 A876 Set of 2 1.40 1.40

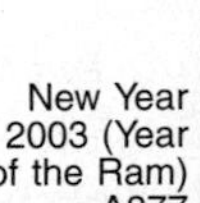

New Year 2003 (Year of the Ram) A877

Ram facing: 5p, Left. 17p, Right.

2002, Dec. 1

2811-2812 A877 Set of 2 2.25 2.25

a. Souvenir sheet, #2811-2812 + 2 labels 3.00 3.00

No. 2812a exists imperf.

Lyceum of the Philippines, 50th Anniv. — A878

2002, Dec. 5 ***Perf. 14***

2813 A878 5p multi .50 .25

Orchids — A879

No. 2814: a, Luisia teretifolia. b, Dendrobium victoria-reginae, horiz. c, Gedorum densiflorum. d, Nervilia plicata, horiz.
22p, Grammatophyllum scriptum, horiz.

2002, Dec. 19 ***Perf. 14***

2814 A879 5p Block of 4, #a-d 2.00 2.00

Souvenir Sheet

Imperf

2815 A879 22p multi 3.00 3.00

No. 2815 contains one 69x40mm stamp.
No. 2814 was reprinted with a larger "2002" date.

La Union National High School, Cent. A880

2003, Jan. 22 ***Perf. 14***

2816 A880 5p multi .40 .25

St. Luke's Medical Center, Cathedral Heights, Cent. A881

2003, Jan. 23

2817 A881 5p multi .40 .25

Far Eastern University, 75th Anniv. A882

2003, Jan. 28

2818 A882 5p multi .40 .25

Manila Electric Railroad and Light Company, Cent. A883

2003, Jan. 31

2819 A883 5p multi .40 .25

St. Valentine's Day — A884

Mailman and: 5p, Heart-shaped strawberry. 17p, Hearts and mountains. 21p, Hearts and clouds. 22p, Butterflies and heart-shaped flowers.

2003, Feb. 11

2820-2823 A884 Set of 4 6.00 4.00

Souvenir Sheets

Summer Institute of Linguistics, 50th Anniv. in Philippines — A885

No. 2824: a, 5p, Yakan weaving. b, 6p, Ifugao weaving. c, 5p, Kagayanen weaving. d, Bagobo Abaca weaving.
No. 2825, 11p: a, Ayta bow and arrows. b, Ibatan baskets. c, Palawano gong. d, Mindanao instruments.
No. 2826: a, 17p, Tboli cross-stitch. b, 5p, Aklanon Piña weaving. c, Kalinga weaving. d, Manobo beadwork.

2003, Feb. 28 **Litho.**

Sheets of 4, #a-d

2824-2826 A885 Set of 3 15.00 *30.00*

Intl. Decade of the World's Indigenous People.

Arrival of Japanese Workers for Construction of Kennon Road, Cent. A886

2003, Feb. 20 ***Perf. 14***

2827 A886 5p multi .40 .25

National Heroes A887

Designs: No. 2828, 6p, Apolinario Mabini (1864-1903), Independence advocate. No. 2829, 6p, Luciano San Miguel (1875-1903), military leader.

2003, May 13 **Litho.** ***Perf. 14***

2828-2829 A887 Set of 2 1.25 .70

Orchids — A888

Designs (no flower names shown): 6p, Dendrobium uniflorum. 9p, Paphiopedilum urbanianum. 17p, Epigeneium lyonii. 21p, Thrixspermum subulatum.

2003, May 16 ***Perf. 14½, 13¾ (9p)***

2830 A888 6p multi .50 .25
2831 A888 9p multi .70 .35
2832 A888 17p multi 1.40 .70
2833 A888 21p multi 1.75 .85
Nos. 2830-2833 (4) 4.35 2.15

See Nos. 2849-2853, 2904-2912 for stamps with flower names.

No. 2722 Surcharged in Black or Red

2003 ***Perf. 13¾***

2834 A828 1p on 5p multi .25 .25
2835 A828 1p on 5p multi (R) .25 .25
2836 A828 6p on 5p multi .50 .25
Nos. 2834-2836 (3) 1.00 .75

Issued: Nos. 2834-2835, 5/19; No. 2836, 6/4.

Philippine Medical Association, Cent. — A889

2003, May 21 ***Perf. 14***

2837 A889 6p multi .60 .30

Rural Banking, 50th Anniv. — A890

2003, May 22

2838 A890 6p multi .60 .30

Mountains — A891

No. 2839: a, Mt. Makiling. b, Mt. Kanlaon. c, Mt. Kitanglad. d, Mt. Mating-oy.
No. 2840: a, Mt. Iraya. b, Mt. Hibok-Hibok. c, Mt. Apo. d, Mt. Santo Tomas.

2003, June 16

2839 A891 6p Block of 4, #a-d 2.50 2.50

Souvenir Sheet

2840 A891 6p Sheet of 4, #a-d 4.00 4.00

Chinese Roots of José Rizal A892

Designs: 6p, Rizal Monument, Rizal Park, Jinjiang, People's Republic of China, vert. 17p, Rizal and Pagoda, Jinjiang.

2003, June 19

2841-2842 A892 Set of 2 2.25 2.25

Waterfalls — A893

No. 2843: a, Maria Cristina Falls. b, Katibawasan Falls. c, Bagongbong Falls. d, Pagsanjan Falls.
No. 2844: a, Casiawan Falls. b, Pangi Falls. c, Tinago Falls. d, Kipot Twin Falls.

2003, June 27

2843 A893 6p Block of 4, #a-d 2.50 2.50

Souvenir Sheet

2844 A893 6p Sheet of 4, #a-d 4.00 4.00

Philippine — Spanish Friendship Day — A894

Designs: 6p, Poster for Madoura Exhibit, by Pablo Picasso. 22p, Flashback, by José T. Joya.

2003, June 30

2845-2846 A894 Set of 2 2.75 2.75

Philippines Chamber of Commerce, Cent. A895

2003, July 15

2847 A895 6p multi .60 .30

Benguet Corporation, Cent. A896

2003, Aug. 12

2848 A896 6p multi .60 .30

Orchid Type of 2003 With Plant Names and

A897

Designs: 6p, Dendrobium uniflorum. 9p, Paphiopedilum urbanianum. 10p, Kingidium philippinense. 17p, Epigeneium lyonii. 21p, Thrixspermum subulatum. 22p, Trichoglottis philippinensis. 30p, Mariposa. 50p, Sanggumay. 75p, Lady's slipper. 100p, Waling-waling.

2003-04 *Perf. 14½*

2849 A888 6p multi .50 .25
2849A A888 9p multi .70 .35
2850 A888 10p multi .80 .40
a. With space between "P" and "10," dated 2004 ('04) .80 .80
2851 A888 17p multi 1.25 .70
a. Base of "P" even with base of "17," dated 2004 ('04) 1.40 1.40
2852 A888 21p multi 2.10 1.00
a. Base of "P" even with base of "21," dated 2004 ('04) 1.75 1.75
2853 A888 22p multi 2.10 1.10
a. Base of "P" even with base of "22," dated 2004, plant name 14mm long ('04) 1.75 1.75
b. As "a," plant name 12½mm long ('04) 1.75 .90

Perf. 14

2854 A897 30p multi 2.75 1.50
2855 A897 50p multi 4.75 2.40
2856 A897 75p multi 7.25 3.50
2857 A897 100p multi 9.50 4.75
Nos. 2849-2857 (10) 31.70 15.95

Issued: 6p, 10p, 17p, 21p, 22p, 8/8; 30p, 100p, 8/21; 50p, 75p, 9/9. 9p, 11/4.
No. 2850a, 6/2/04; No. 2851a, 8/2/04; No. 2852a, 7/21/04; No. 2853a, 6/10/04. No, 2853b, 2004.
See Nos. 2904-2912.

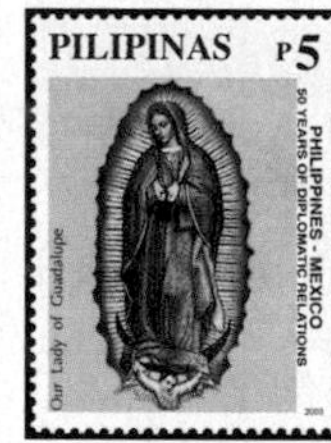

Philippines — Mexico Diplomatic Relations, 50th Anniv. — A898

Designs: 5p, Our Lady of Guadalupe. No. 2859, 22p, Miraculous Image of the Black Nazarene.
No. 2860, 22p, Crowd around church.

2003, Apr. 23 *Perf. 14*

2858-2859 A898 Set of 2 2.75 2.75

Souvenir Sheet

2860 A898 22p multi 3.00 3.00

No. 2860 contains one 80x30mm stamp.

Our Lady of Caysasay, 400th Anniv. — A899

2003, Sept. 8

2861 A899 6p multi .60 .30

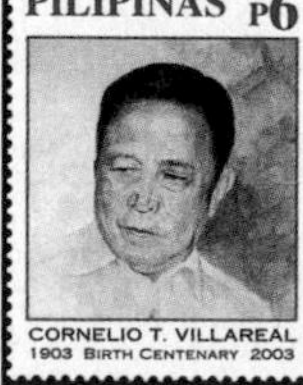

Cornelio T. Villareal, Sr., House Speaker, Birth Cent. — A900

2003, Sept. 11

2862 A900 6p multi .60 .30

National Teachers College, 75th Anniv. — A901

2003, Sept. 15

2863 A901 6p multi .60 .30

Sanctuary of San Antonio Parish, 50th Anniv. — A902

2003, Oct. 4 **Litho.**

2864 A902 6p multi .60 .30

Nos. 2722-2723 Overprinted in Red

2003, Oct. 17 *Perf. 13¾*

2865 A828 5p multi .50 .25
2866 A828 15p multi 1.50 .70

Souvenir Sheet

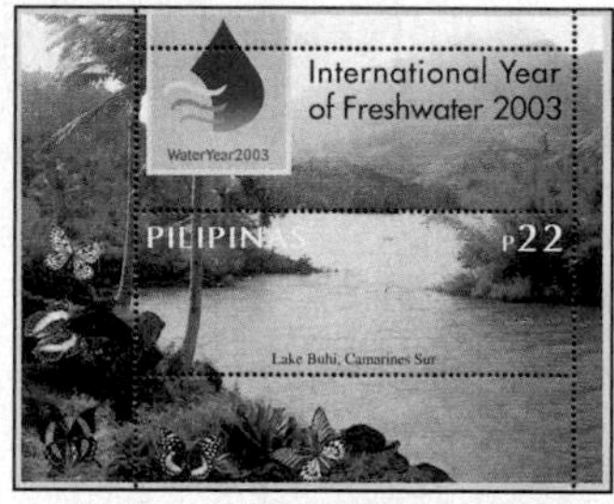

Intl. Year of Fresh Water — A903

2003, Oct. 24 *Perf. 14*

2867 A903 22p multi + label 2.00 2.00

Federation of Free Farmers, 50th Anniv. — A904

2003, Oct. 25

2868 A904 6p multi .60 .30

Christmas A905

Inscriptions: 6p, Mano po ninong ii. 17p, Himig at kulay ng Pasko, vert. 21p, Noche buena, vert. 22p, Karoling sa jeepney.

2003, Oct. 28

2869-2872 A905 Set of 4 6.50 6.50

National Stamp Collecting Month A906

Cartoon art: 6p, Kenkoy, by Tony Velasquez, vert. 17p, Ikabod, by Nonoy Marcelo, vert. 21p, Sakay N'Moy, by Hugo C. Yonzon, Jr. No. 2876, 22p, Kalabong en Bosyo, by Larry Alcala.
No. 2877, 22p, Hugo, the Sidewalk Vendor, by Rodolfo Y. Ragodon.

2003, Nov. 1

2873-2876 A906 Set of 4 6.50 3.25

Souvenir Sheet

2877 A906 22p multi 3.00 3.00

No. 2877 contains one 80x30mm stamp.

Winning Children's Art in National Anti-Drug Stamp Design Contest — A907

No. 2878: a, Globe, child with broom, by Nicole Fernan L. Caminian. b, Children, "No Drugs" symbol, by Jairus Cabajar. c, Children painting over "Drug Addiction" picture, by Genevieve V. Lazarte. d, Child chopping tree with hatchet, by Martin F. Rivera.

2003, Nov. 3

2878 A907 6p Block of 4, #a-d 2.50 2.50

Nos. 2550Ab, 2550Ac, 2550Ad and 2550Ae Surcharged

2003, Nov. 11 *Perf. 14*

2879 A749a 17p on 4p #2550Ab 2.25 1.10
2880 A749a 17p on 8p #2550Ac 2.25 1.10
2881 A749a 22p on 16p #2550Ad 3.00 1.40
2882 A749a 22p on 16p #2550Ae 3.00 1.40
Nos. 2879-2882 (4) 10.50 5.00

Nos. 2879-2882 were sold removed from the booklet the basic stamps were in.

Souvenir Sheet

First Philippine Stamps, 150th Anniv. — A908

2003, Nov. 14

2883 A908 22p Nos. 1, 2, 4 & 5, org to yellow background 2.00 2.00

Filipinas 2004 Stamp Exhibition, Mandaluyong City.

See Nos. 2891-2897.

Camera Club of the Philippines, 75th Anniv. A909

2003, Dec. 1		**Litho.**
2884 A909 6p multi	.60	.30

New Year 2004 (Year of the Monkey) A910

Monkey: 6p, Perched on branch. 17p, Hanging from branch.

2003, Dec. 1

2885-2886 A910	Set of 2	2.25	1.10
2886a	Souvenir sheet, #2885-2886 + 2 labels	3.00	3.00

No. 2886a exists imperf. Value $5.

Succulent Plants — A911

No. 2887: a, Mammilaria spinosissima (yellow frame). b, Epithelantha bokei. c, Rebutia spinosissima. d, Turbinicarpus alonsoi.

No. 2888, horiz.: a, Aloe humilis. b, Euphorbia golisana. c, Gymnocalycium spinosissima. d, Mammilaria spinossisima (green frame).

2003, Dec. 5

2887 A911 6p Block of 4, #a-d	2.50	2.50

Souvenir Sheet

2888 A911 6p Sheet of 4, #a-d	4.00	4.00

Powered Flight, Cent. — A911a

No. 2888E — Do24TT: f, Green background. g, Yellow background.

2003, Dec. 17	**Litho.**	***Perf. 14***
2888E A911a 6p Horiz. pair, #f-g	1.00	1.00

Architecture — A912

No. 2889: a, Luneta Hotel. b, Hong Kong Shanghai Bank. c, El Hogar. d, Regina Building.

No. 2890, horiz.: a, Pangasinan Capitol. b, Metropolitan Theater. c, Philtrust. d, University of Manila.

2003, Dec. 22

2889 A912 6p Block of 4, #a-d	2.50	2.50

Souvenir Sheet

2890 A912 6p Sheet of 4, #a-d	4.00	4.00

First Philppine Stamps, 150th Anniv. Type of 2003

No. 2891 (36x26mm each): a, Blue to lilac background, #1. b, Orange to yellow background, #2. c, Light to dark green background, #4. d, Dark to light pink background, #5.

Nos. 2892-2897: Like #2883.

2003-04	**Litho.**	***Perf. 14***	
2891	Horiz. strip of 4	2.00	2.00
a.-d.	A908 6p Any single	.50	.25

Souvenir Sheets

Background Colors

2892 A908 22p dk to lt rose	1.75	1.75
2893 A908 22p dk to lt blue	1.75	1.75
2894 A908 22p blue to lt grn	1.75	1.75
2895 A908 22p dk to lt pink	1.75	1.75
2896 A908 22p brn to yellow	1.75	1.75
2897 A908 22p white	1.75	1.75
a. With Postpex 2004 inscription added in red and black in sheet margin	2.00	2.00

Filipinas 2004 Stamp Exhibition, Mandaluyong City.

Issued: No. 2892, 12/15/03, No. 2893, 1/15/04; No. 2894, 1/30/04; No. 2895, 1/31/04; Nos. 2891, 2896, 2897, 2/1/04. No. 2897a, 4/19/04.

A sheet containing a block of four of perf. and imperf. examples of Nos. 2891a-2891d sold for 100p.

Arrival in Philippines of Sisters of St. Paul of Chartres, Cent. A913

2004, Jan. 22		***Perf. 14***
2898 A913 6p multi	.50	.25

Polytechnic University of the Philippines, Cent. — A914

2004, Jan. 22

2899 A914 6p multi	.50	.25

Tanduay Distillers, Inc., 150th Anniv. — A915

2004, Jan. 22

2900 A915 6p multi	.50	.25

Grepalife Life Insurance Co., 50th Anniv. — A916

2004, Jan. 22

2901 A916 6p multi	.50	.25

2003 State Visit of U.S. Pres. George W. Bush A917

Flags of U.S. and Philippines, George W. Bush and: 6p, Crowd. 22p, Philippines Pres. Gloria Macapagal-Arroyo, Malacañang Palace.

2004, Feb. 23	**Litho.**	***Perf. 13x13½***	
2902-2903 A917	Set of 2	2.25	1.10

Orchid Type of 2003 With Plant Names

Designs: 1p, Liparis latifolia. 2p, Cymbidium finlaysonianum. 3p, Phalaenopsis philippinensis. 4p, Phalaenopsis fasciata. 5p, Spathoglottis plicata.

No. 2909: a, Phalaenopsis fuscata. b, Phalaenopsis stuartiana. c, Renanthera monachia. d, Aerides quinquevulnera.

8p, Phalaenopsis schilleriana. 9p, Phalaenopsis pulchra. 20p, Phaius tankervilleae.

Two types of 1p and 5p:

I — Denomination and year date not touching edges of background color, digits of year date touching.

II — Denomination and year date touch edges of background color, digits of year date spaced.

Three types of 2p:

I — Plant name 13½mm long and 1mm from year date, denomination and year date not touching edges of background color.

II — Plant name 13½ mm long and 2mm from year date, denomination and year date touching edges of background color.

III — Plant name 14mm long and 1½mm from year date, denomination and year date touching edges of background color.

2004	**Litho.**	***Perf. 14½***	
2904 A888	1p multi, type I	.25	.25
a.	Type II	.40	.40
2905 A888	2p multi, type I	.25	.25
a.	Type II	.25	.25
b.	Type III	.25	.25
2906 A888	3p multi	.25	.25
2907 A888	4p multi	.30	.25
2908 A888	5p multi, type I	.40	.25
a.	Type II	.60	.60
2909	Block of 4	2.00	2.00
a.-d.	A888 6p Any single	.50	.25
2910 A888	8p multi	.65	.30
2911 A888	9p multi	.70	.35
2912 A888	20p multi	1.60	.80
	Nos. 2904-2912 (9)	6.40	4.70

Issued: Nos. 2904, 2908, 3/9; Nos. 2904a, 2905, 2905b, 2910, 4/1; Nos. 2905a, 2908a, 4/28; Nos. 2906, 2907, 2911, 2912, 6/11; No. 2909, 12/20.

Pfizer Pharmaceuticals, 50th Anniv. in Philippines A918

2004, Apr. 30		***Perf. 14***
2913 A918 6p multi	.50	.25

Our Lady of Piat, 400th Anniv. — A919

2004, June 21

2914 A919 6p multi	.50	.25

Bonsai A920

No. 2915, vert. — Orange to yellow background: a, Bantigue. b, Kamuning Binangonan with thick trunk, dark brown pot. c, Balete. d, Mulawin aso. e, Kamuning Binangonan with root-like trunk, dark brown pot. f, Logwood. g, Kamuning Binangonan, orange clay pot. h, Bantolinao.

No. 2916 — Purple to white background: a, Bantigue with thick trunk, brown pot. b, Chinese elm. c, Bantigue with two trunks, brown pot. d, Bantigue, white pot. e, Balete with many green leaves, black and brown pot. f, Balete with few green leaves, brown pot. g, Bantigue, light brown rectangular pot. h, Mansanita.

Nos. 2917a, 2918a, Lomonsito. Nos. 2917b, 2918b, Bougainvillea, pot on table. Nos. 2917c, 2918c, Bougainvillea, orange brown pot. Nos. 2917d, 2918d, Kalyos.

2004		***Perf. 14***	
2915	Block of 8	6.00	*8.00*
a.-h.	A920 6p Any single	.50	.50
2916	Block of 8	6.00	*8.00*
a.-h.	A920 6p Any single	.50	.50

Souvenir Sheets

Solid Blue Background

2917	Sheet of 4	4.00	4.00
a.-d.	A920 6p Any single	1.00	.50

Blue to White Background

2918	Sheet of 4	4.00	4.00
a.-d.	A920 6p Any single	1.00	.50

Issued: Nos. 2915-2917, 7/27; No. 2918, 8/28. 2004 World Stamp Championship, Singapore (No. 2918).

2004 Summer Olympics, Athens A921

Designs: 6p, Shooting. 17p, Taekwondo. 21p, Swimming. No. 2922, 22p, Archery.

No. 2923, 22p, Boxing.

2004, Aug. 13

2919-2922 A921	Set of 4	5.50	2.75

Souvenir Sheet

2923 A921 22p multi	2.00	2.00

Miguel Lopez de Legazpi (c. 1510-72), Founder of Manila — A922

2004, Aug. 20 **Litho.**
2924 A922 6p multi .50 .50

Admiral Tomas A. Cloma, Sr. (1904-96) A923

2004, Aug. 20
2925 A923 6p multi .50 .50

Animals of the Lunar New Year Cycle — A924

Designs: Nos. 2926a, 2927a, Rat. Nos. 2926b, 2927b, Ox. Nos. 2926c, 2927c, Tiger. Nos. 2926d, 2927d, Rabbit. Nos. 2926e, 2927e, Dragon. Nos. 2926f, 2927f, Snake. Nos. 2926g, 2928a, Horse. Nos. 2926h, 2928b, Goat. Nos. 2926i, 2928c, Monkey. Nos. 2926j, 2928d, Cock. Nos. 2926k, 2928e, Dog. Nos. 2926l, 2928f, Pig.

2004, Sept. 9 ***Perf. 14***

English Inscriptions at Left

2926 A924 6p Sheet of 12, #a-l, + 3 labels 10.00 10.00

Chinese Inscriptions at Left

2927 A924 6p Sheet of 6, #a-f, + 6 labels 4.00 4.00
2928 A924 6p Sheet of 6, #a-f, + 6 labels 4.00 4.00

Manila Central University, Cent. A925

2004, Sept. 21
2929 A925 6p multi .50 .25
a. Miniature sheet of 8 6.00 6.00

Christmas A926

Various Christmas trees: 6p, 17p, 21p, 22p.

2004, Oct. 1
2930-2933 A926 Set of 4 5.50 5.50

Filipino-Chinese General Chamber of Commerce, Cent. — A927

No. 2934: a, Intramuros, Philippines. b, Great Wall of China.

2004, Oct. 12
2934 A927 6p Horiz. pair, #a-b 1.00 1.00

Winning Designs in Rice Is Life National Stamp Design Contest — A928

No. 2935, 6p: a, By Maria Enna T. Alegre. b, By Lady Fatima M. Velasco.
No. 2936, 6p: a, By Sean Y. Pajaron. b, By Ljian B. Delgado.
No. 2937, 6p: a, By Michael O. Villadolid. b, By Gary M. Manalo.

2004, Oct. 15 **Litho.**

Horiz. Pairs, #a-b

2935-2937 A928 Set of 3 5.00 5.00
2937c Miniature sheet, #2935a-2935b, 2936a-2936b, 2937a-2937b 7.00 7.00

Intl. Year of Rice.

Natl. Stamp Collecting Month A929

Comic strip and comic book illustrations: No. 2938, 6p, Darna, by Nestor P. Redondo. No. 2939, 6p, Kulafu, by Francisco Reyes. No. 2940, 6p, El Vibora, by Federico C. Javinal, vert. No. 2941, 6p, Lapu-Lapu, by Francisco V. Coching, vert.
22p, Darna, by Mars Ravelo, vert

2004 ***Perf. 14***
2938-2941 A929 Set of 4 2.00 1.25

Souvenir Sheet

2942 A929 22p multi 3.00 3.00

No. 2942 contains one 30x80mm stamp.

San Agustin Church, Manila, 400th Anniv. — A930

No. 2943: a, Denomination at left. b, Denomination at right.

2004, Nov. 13
2943 A930 6p Horiz. pair, #a-b 1.00 1.00

New Year 2005 (Year of the Rooster) A931

Designs: 6p, Rooster's head. 17p, Rooster.

2004, Dec. 1
2944-2945 A931 Set of 2 1.90 1.90
2945a Souvenir sheet, 2 each #2944-2945 4.00 4.00

Worldwide Fund for Nature (WWF) — A932

Owls: No. 2946, 6p, Giant Scops owl. No. 2947, 6p, Philippine eagle owl. No. 2948, 6p, Negros Scops owl. No. 2949, 6p, West Visayan hawk owl.

2004, Dec. 22
2946-2949 A932 Set of 4 3.25 2.50
2949a Block of 4, #2946-2949 3.75 3.75

Liceo de Cagayan University A933

2005, Feb. 5 **Litho.** ***Perf. 14***
2950 A933 6p multi .50 .25

Seventh-Day Adventist Church in the Philippines, Cent. — A934

2005, Feb. 18
2951 A934 6p multi .50 .25

Baguio Country Club, Cent. — A935

No. 2952: a, Club in 1905. b, Club in 2005.

2005, Feb. 18
2952 A935 6p Horiz. pair, #a-b 1.00 1.00

Butterflies — A936

Designs: 1p, Arisbe decolor stratos.
No. 2954: a, Parantica noeli. b, Chilasa osmana osmana. c, Graphium sandawanum joreli. d, Papilio xuthus benguetanus.

2005 **Litho.** ***Perf. 14½***
2953 A936 1p multi .25 .25
a. Butterfly redrawn with two antennae .25 .25
2954 Block of 4 7.00 7.00
a.-d. A936 22p Any single 1.75 1.75

Issued: 1p, 4/12; No. 2954, 3/3.

See Nos. 2978-2981.

Shells — A937

No. 2955: a, Chicoreus saulii. b, Spondylus varians. c, Spondylus linquaefelis. d, Melo broderipii.
No. 2956: a, Chlamys senatoria. b, Siphonofusus vicdani. c, Epitonium scalare. d, Harpa harpa.
No. 2957: a, Siliquaria armata. b, Argonauta argo. c, Perotrochus vicdani. d, Corculum cardissa.

2005, Apr. 15 ***Perf. 14***
2955 A937 Block of 4 2.00 2.00
a.-d. 6p Any single .50 .50
2956 A937 Block of 4 2.00 2.00
a.-d. 6p Any single .50 .50

Souvenir Sheet

2957 A937 Sheet of 4 + 2 labels 6.00 6.00
a.-d. 6p Any single 1.25 1.25

State Visit of Hu Jintao, Pres. of People's Republic of China A938

Flags of Philippines and People's Republic of China, Philippines Pres. Gloria Macapagal-Arroyo and: 6p, Pres. Hu at right. 17p, Pres. Hu at left.

2005, Apr. 27
2958-2959 A938 Set of 2 1.90 .95
2959a Souvenir sheet, #2958-2959 2.00 2.00

Architecture — A939

No. 2960: a, Ernesto de la Cruz Ancestral House. b, Limjoco Residence. c, Pelaez Ancestral House. d, Vergara House.
No. 2961: a, Gliceria Marella Villavicencio. b, Lasala-Guarin House. c, Claparols House. d, Ilagan Ancestral House.

2005, May 7
2960 A939 Block of 4 2.00 2.00
a.-d. 6p Any single .50 .50

Souvenir Sheet

2961 A939 Sheet of 4 2.00 2.00
a.-d. 6p Any single .50 .50

Central Philippine University, Cent. A940

2005, May 13
2962 A940 6p multi .50 .25

Rotary International, Cent. — A941

Denomination: 6p, At left, in blue. 22p, At right, in rod.

2005, May 31

2963-2964	A941	Set of 2	1.90	.95
2964a		Miniature sheet, 6 #2963, 2 #2964	6.00	6.00

San Bartolome Parish, 400th Anniv. A942

2005, July 25 **Litho.** ***Perf. 14***

2965	A942 6p multi	.50	.25

Senator Blas F. Ople (1927-2003) A943

2005, July 28

2966	A943 6p multi	.50	.25

Shells — A944

No. 2967, 6p: a, Chrysallis fischeri. b, Helicostyla bicolorata. c, Helicostyla dobiosa. d, Helicostyla portei.

No. 2968, 6p: a, Cochlostyla imperator. b, Helicostyla turbinoides. c, Helicostyla lignaria. d, Amphidromus dubius.

No. 2969, horiz.: a, Calocochlia depressa. b, Cochlostyla sarcinosa. c, Calocochlia schadenbergi. d, Helicostyla pulcherrina.

2005 **Blocks of 4, #a-d** ***Perf. 14***

2967-2968	A944 Set of 2	8.00	8.00

Souvenir Sheets

2969	A944 6p Sheet of 4, #a-d, + 2 labels	4.00	4.00
2970	Sheet, #2969a, 2969b, 2970a, 2970b	4.00	4.00
a.	A944 2p Like #2969c	.25	.25
b.	A944 3p Like #2969d	.25	.25

Issued: Nos. 2967-2969, 8/8; No. 2970, 8/19. Upper left label on No. 2970 has Taipei 2005 Stamp Exhibition emblem, lower right label has "Greetings from the Philippines" inscription.

Intl. Year of the Eucharist A945

Winning pictures in stamp design contest by: No. 2971, 6p, Carlos Vincent H. Ruiz. No. 2972, 6p, Rommer A. Fajardo. No. 2973, 6p, Telly Farolan-Somera. No. 2974, 6p, Allen A. Moran. No. 2975, 6p, Elouiza Athena Tentativa. No. 2976, 6p, Jianina Marishka C. Montealto.

2005, Sept. 8

2971-2976	A945	Set of 6	3.00	2.00
2976a		Souvenir sheet, #2971-2976, + 6 labels	3.00	*6.00*

No. 1887 Surcharged in Red

Souvenir Sheet

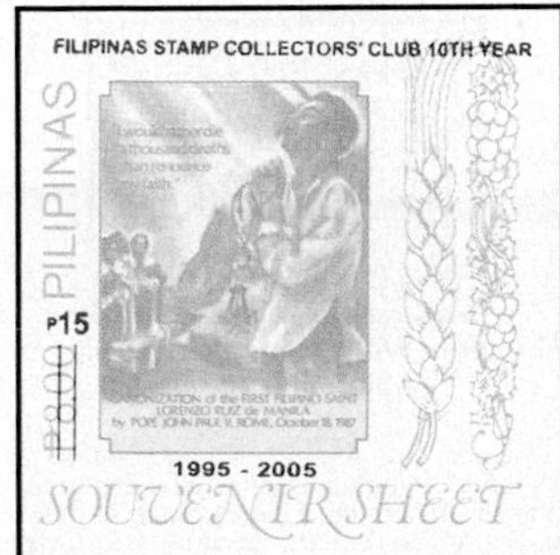

Wmk. 389

2005, Sept. 14 **Litho.** ***Imperf.***

2977	A493 15p on 8p multi	2.00	2.00

Butterflies Type of 2005 and

A946

A947

Designs: 5p, Parantica danatti danatti.

No. 2979: a, Hebemoia glaucippe philippinensis. b, Moduza urdaneta aynii. c, Lexias satrapes hiwaga. d, Cheritra orpheus orpheus. e, Achillides chikae chikae. f, Arisbe ideaoiedes ideaoiedes. g, Dellas schoenigi hermeli. h, Achillides palinurus daedalus. i, Dellas levicki justini. j, Troides magellanus magellanus.

No. 2980: a, Idea electra electra. b, Charaxes bajula adoracion. c, Tanaecia calliphorus calliphorus. d, Trogonoptera trojana. e, Charaxes bajula adoracion, diff.

No. 2981: a, Cethosia biblis barangingi. b, Menalaides polytes ledebouria. c, Appias nero palawanica. d, Udara tyotaroi.

2005 **Unwmk.** ***Perf. 14½***

2978	A936 5p multi	.40	.25
2979	Block of 10	8.00	8.00
a.-j.	A936 6p Any single	.50	.25
2980	Block of 4, #a-d	5.50	5.50
a.	A936 17p multi	1.25	.60
b.	A946 17p multi	1.25	.60
c.	A936 17p multi	1.25	.60
d.	A936 17p multi	1.25	.60
e.	A947 17p multi	—	—
f.	Block of 4, #2980a, 2980c, 2980d, 2980e	*65.00*	—
2981	Block of 4	6.75	6.75
a.-d.	A936 21p Any single	1.60	.80
	Nos. 2978-2981 (4)	20.65	20.50

Issued: No. 2978, 11/22; No. 2979, 10/12; No. 2980, 12/9. No. 2981, 12/2.

Intl. Year of Sports and Physical Education — A948

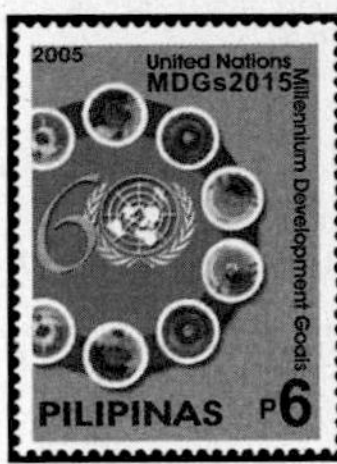

UN Millennium Development Goals — A949

No. 2982: a, Dove, open book, Philippines flag, basketball, emblem at LL. b, Torch, sports equipment, people with joined hands, dove flying to right, emblem at LR. c, Torch, sports equipment, people with joined hands, dove flying to left, emblem at LL.

2005, Oct. 19 ***Perf. 14***

2982	A948 6p Horiz. pair, #a-b	1.00	1.00
c.	6p multi	.50	.50
d.	Horiz. pair, #2982a, 2982c	1.00	2.00
2983	A949 6p multi	.50	.50

Souvenir Sheet

2984	Sheet, #2982a, 2982b, 2984a	2.00	2.00
a.	A949 10p multi	.75	.40
b.	Sheet, #2982a, 2982c, 2984a	2.25	2.25

United Nations, 60th anniv.

Bureau of Corrections, Cent. — A950

2005, Nov. 4

2985	A950 6p multi	.50	.25

Inauguration of Pres. Gloria Macapagal-Arroyo — A951

Pres. Macapagal-Arroyo: 6p, Taking oath. 22p, Giving inaugural speech.

2005, Nov. 9

2986-2987	A951	Set of 2	2.25	1.10

Christmas A952

Various department store window Christmas displays: 6p, 17p, 21p, 22p.

2005, Nov. 16

2988-2991	A952	Set of 4	5.50	2.75

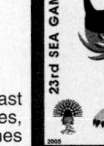

23rd Southeast Asia Games, Philippines A953

No. 2992: a, Boxing. b, Cycling. c, Wushu. d, Dowling. c, Badminton. f, Billiards. Eagle has black beak on all stamps.

No. 2993, horiz.: a, Track. b, Soccer. c, Taekwondo. d, Judo. e, Chess. f, Karate. g, Gymnastics. h, Pencaksilat. i, Dragon boat racing. j, Swimming.

No. 2994: a, Baseball. b, Shooting. c, Archery. d, Bowling (eagle with brown beak). e, Volleyball. f, Boxing (eagle with brown beak). g, Cycling (eagle with brown beak). h, Badminton (eagle with brown beak).

No. 2995: a, Archery. b, Shooting. c, Equestrian.

No. 2996, horiz.: a, Arnis. b, Chess. c, Dragon boat racing.

2005, Nov. 22 **Red Frames**

2992	Block of 6	6.00	*8.00*
a.-f.	A953 6p Any single	.60	.60
2993	Sheet of 10 + 8 labels	15.00	*20.00*
a.-j.	A953 6p Any single	.75	.75
2994	Sheet of 10, #2992c, 2992f, 2994a-2994h, + 20 labels	15.00	*20.00*
a.-h.	A953 6p Any single	.75	.75

Blue Frames

2995	Sheet of 3	4.00	*6.00*
a.	A953 5p multi	.40	.25
b.-c.	A953 6p Either single	.50	.25
2996	Sheet of 3	4.00	*6.00*
a.	A953 5p multi	.40	.25
b.-c.	A953 6p Either single	.50	.25

No. 2992 was printed in sheets containing two blocks. Nos. 2993a-2993j lack perforations between the stamp and the adjacent labels that are the same size as the stamp. There are perforations between the stamps and labels on No. 2994. The labels to the right of the stamps could be personalized. Nos. 2993 and 2994 each sold for 99p with generic flag labels, and for 350p with personalized labels.

National Stamp Collecting Month — A954

Prints: No. 2997, 6p, Pinoy Worker Abr'd., by Ben Cab. No. 2998, 6p, Bulbs, by M. Parial. No. 2999, 6p, The Fourth Horseman, by Tequi. No. 3000, 6p, Breaking Ground, by R. Olazo. 22p, Form XV, by Brenda Fajardo, horiz.

2005, Nov. 28

2997-3000	A954	Set of 4	2.00	1.00

Souvenir Sheet

3001	A954 22p multi	2.00	2.00

No. 3001 contains one 80x30mm stamp.

New Year 2006 (Year of the Dog) A955

Dog and inscription: a, 6p, "Manigong Bagong Taon." b, 17p, "Happy New Year."

2005, Dec. 1

3002-3003	A955	Set of 2	1.90	.95
3003a		Souvenir sheet, 2 each #3002-3003	4.00	4.00

Third Asian Para Games — A956

Designs: 6p, Runner with amputated arm. 17p, Wheelchair racer.

2005, Dec. 6

3004-3005 A956 Set of 2 1.90 .95

Pope John Paul II (1920-2005) A957

Pope John Paul II, Vatican arms and text: 6p, "Mahal Namin Kayo!" 22p, "We Love You!"

2005, June 28 Litho. *Perf. 14*

3006-3007 A957 Set of 2 2.25 1.10

Lighthouses — A958

No. 3008: a, Cape Santiago Lighthouse, Calatagan. b, Bacagay Lighthouse, Liloan. c, Malabrigo Lighthouse, Lobo. d, Capones Lighthouse, San Antonio.

No. 3009: a, Tubbataha Lighthouse, Cagayancillo. b, Cape Bojeador Lighthouse, Burgos. c, Cape Bolinao Lighthouse, Bolinao. d, San Fernando Point Lighthouse, San Fernando.

2005, Dec. 22

3008 A958 6p Block of 4, #a-d 2.00 2.00

Souvenir Sheet

3009 A958 6p Sheet of 4, #a-d 2.00 2.00

St. Scholastica's College, Manila, Cent. — A959

2006, Jan. 3

3010 A959 6p multi .50 .25

Filipinos in Hawaii, Cent. — A960

Contest-winning designs: 6p, Filipinos in Hawaii, by Allen A. Moran. 22p, Filipinos and flags, by Crisanto S. Umali.

No. 3013: a, Like 6p. b, Like 22p.

2006, Jan. 5

3011-3012 A960 Set of 2 2.25 1.10

Souvenir Sheet

3013 A960 11p Sheet of 2, #a-b 2.00 2.00

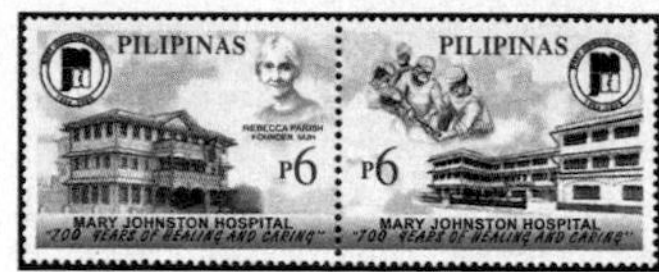

Mary Johnston Hospital, Manila, Cent. — A961

No. 3014: a, Hospital building and founder Rebecca Parish. b, Surgeons, hospital building.

2006, Jan. 20

3014 A961 6p Horiz. pair, #a-b 1.00 1.00

Love — A962

No. 3015 — Angel with: a, Letter. b, Flower.

2006, Feb. 8

3015 A962 7p Horiz. pair, #a-b 1.10 1.10

Jaime Cardinal Sin (1928-2005), Archbishop of Manila — A963

Sin and: 7p, Cathedral. 22p, Statue.

2006, Feb. 25

3016-3017 A963 Set of 2 2.40 1.25

3017a Souvenir sheet, 2 each #3016-3017 4.80 4.80

Marine Turtles — A964

No. 3018: a, Olive Ridley turtle. b, Hawksbill turtle. c, Loggerhead turtle. d, Leatherback turtle.

26p, Green turtle.

2006, Mar. 31

3018 A964 Horiz. strip of 4 2.25 2.25

a.-d. 7p Any single .55 .45

Souvenir Sheet

3019 A964 26p multi 2.10 2.10

No. 3019 contains one 80x30mm stamp.

Butterfly Type of 2005 and

Butterfly With Fully-colored Background A965

Butterfly With Blue Lines At Bottom A966

Butterfly With Partially-colored Background — A967

Butterfly With Framed and Colored Background — A968

Designs: 1p, Arisbe decolor stratos. 2p, Arhopala anthelus impar. 3p, Zophoessa dataensis nihrai. 4p, Liphyra brassolis justini. 5p, Parantica danatti danatti. 9p, Lexias satrapes amlana. 10p, Tanaecia aruna pallida. 30p, Appias nero domitia. 100p, Cepora aspasia olga.

Nos. 3030 and 3031: a, Hebemoia glaucippe philippensis. b, Moduza urdaneta aynii. c, Lexias satrapes hiwaga. d, Cheritra orpheus orpheus. e, Achillides chikae chikae. f, Arisbe ideaoiedes ideaoiedes. g, Delias schoenigi hermeli. h, Achillides palinurus daedalus. i, Delias levicki justini. j, Troides magellanus magellanus.

Nos. 3036 and 3037: a, Idea electra electra. b, Charaxes bajula adoracion. c, Tanaecia calliphorus calliphorus. d, Trogonoptera trojana.

Nos. 3038 and 3039: a, Cethosia biblis barangingi. b, Menalaides polytes ledebouria. c, Appias nero palawanica. d, Udara tyotaroi.

Nos. 3040 and 3041: a, Parantica noeli. b, Chilasa osmana osmana. c, Graphium sandawanum joreli. d, Papilio xuthus benguetanus.

Perf. 14½ (A936, A965), 13¾ (A966), 13x13¼ (A967), 14 (A968)

2006 Inscribed "2006"

3020 A965 1p multi .25 .25
3021 A966 1p multi .25 .25
a. Inscribed "2007" .25 .25
3022 A965 2p multi .25 .25
3023 A966 2p multi .25 .25
a. Inscribed "2007" .25 .25
3024 A936 3p multi .25 .25
3025 A966 3p multi .25 .25
a. Inscribed "2007" .25 .25
3026 A936 4p multi .35 .25
3027 A966 4p multi .35 .25
a. Inscribed "2007" .35 .25
3028 A965 5p multi .40 .25
3029 A966 5p multi .40 .25
a. Inscribed "2007" .40 .25
3030 Block of 10 5.75 5.75
a.-j. A965 7p Any single .55 .25
3031 Block of 10 5.75 5.75
a.-j. A966 7p Any single .55 .25
k. Block of 10, inscr. "2007" 5.75 5.75
l.-u. A966 7p Any single, inscr. "2007" .55 .25
3032 A936 9p multi .75 .35
3033 A966 9p multi .75 .35
a. Inscribed "2007" .75 .35
3034 A936 10p multi .80 .40
3035 A966 10p multi .80 .40
a. Inscribed "2007" .80 .40
3036 Block of 4 6.50 6.50
a.-d. A965 20p Any single 1.60 .80
3037 Block of 4 6.50 6.50
a.-d. A966 20p Any single 1.60 .80
e. Block of 4, inscr. "2007" 6.50 6.50
f.-i. A966 20p Any single, inscr. "2007" 1.60 .80
3038 Block of 4 7.75 7.75
a.-d. A965 24p Any single 1.90 .95
3039 Block of 4 7.75 7.75
a.-d. A966 24p Any single 1.90 .95
e. Block of 4, inscr. "2007" 7.75 7.75
f.-i. A966 24p Any single, inscr. "2007" 1.90 .95
3040 Block of 4 8.50 8.50
a.-d. A965 26p Any single 2.10 1.00
3041 Block of 4 8.50 8.50
a.-d. A966 26p Any single 2.10 1.00
e. Block of 4, inscr. "2007" 8.50 8.50
f.-i. A966 26p Any single, inscr. "2007" 2.10 1.00
3042 A967 30p multi 2.40 1.25
3043 A968 30p multi 2.40 1.25
3044 A967 100p multi 8.00 4.00
3045 A968 100p multi 8.00 4.00
Nos. 3020-3045 (26) 83.90 71.50

Issued: Nos. 3020, 3030, 4/28; Nos. 3021, 3029, 7/3; Nos. 3022, 3028, 5/10; No. 3023, 12/27; Nos. 3024, 3034, 11/10; Nos. 3025, 3027, 3033, 3035, 12/26; Nos. 3026, 3032, 9/9; No. 3031, 12/14; No. 3036, 6/7; Nos. 3037, 3039, 3041, 12/21; No. 3038, 6/15; No. 3040, 6/9; No. 3042, 9/18; Nos. 3043, 3045, 12/29; No. 3044, 9/26.

See Nos. 3101-3102.

No. 1511 Surcharged

2006, May 2 Litho. *Perf. 13¾x13¼*

3046 A368 26p on 7.50p #1511 2.10 2.10

Lighthouses — A969

No. 3047: a, Punta Bugui Lighthouse, Aroroy. b, Capul Island Lighthouse, Samar del Norte. c, Corregidor Island Lighthouse, Cavite. d, Pasig River Lighthouse, Manila.

No. 3048: a, Cabo Engaño Lighthouse, Santa Ana. b, Punta Cabra Lighthouse, Lubang. c, Cabo Melville Lighthouse, Balabac Island. d, Gintotolo Island Lighthouse, Balud.

2006, May 17 *Perf. 14*

3047 A969 7p Block of 4, #a-d 2.25 2.25

Souvenir Sheet

3048 A969 7p Sheet of 4, #a-d 2.25 2.25

Xavier School, Manila, 50th Anniv. — A970

No. 3049: a, Emblems. b, School building. c, Paul Hsu Kuang-ch'i, Chinese Christian convert. d, St. Francis Xavier (1506-52).

2006, June 6
3049 A970 7p Block of 4, #a-d 2.25 2.25

Air Materiel Wing Savings and Loan Association, Inc., 50th Anniv. — A971

No. 3050 — Emblem and: a, Soldier's family, piggy bank. b, Building.

2006, June 13
3050 A971 7p Horiz. pair, #a-b 1.10 1.10

No. 1721 Surcharged in Blue Violet

2006, July 4 Litho. *Perf. 14*
3051 A436 26p on 7.20p multi 2.10 1.10

Knights of Columbus, 100th Anniv. in Philippines A972

2006, July 7
3052 A972 7p multi .55 .30

Ortigas & Company, 75th Anniv. A973

Anniversary emblem and: 7p, Map of Mandaloyon. 26p, Building.

2006, July 10
3053-3054 A973 Set of 2 2.75 1.40
3054a Souvenir sheet, 2 each #3053-3054 5.50 5.50

Ozamiz Cotta Military Fort, 250th Anniv. A974

2006, July 16
3055 A974 7p multi .55 .30

Friendship Between Philippines and Japan, 50th Anniv. A975

José P. Rizal and: 7p, Mt. Fuji and cherry blossoms. 20p, Mt. Mayon and flowers.

2006, July 23
3056-3057 A975 Set of 2 2.25 1.10
3057a Souvenir sheet, 2 each #3056-3057 4.50 4.50

Roque B. Ablan, (1906-43) Politician, Military Hero A976

2006, Aug. 9
3058 A976 7p multi .55 .30

No. 1809 Surcharged in Gold

Perf. 13½x13
2006, Aug. 15 Litho. Wmk. 389
3059 A470 7p on 1.20p multi .55 .30

Chan-Cu Association, Cent. — A977

No. 3060: a, Centennial emblem. b, Figurine of Chan-Tze, Chinese scholar.

2006, Aug. 28 Unwmk. *Perf. 14*
3060 A977 7p Horiz. pair, #a-b 1.10 1.10

Cats — A978

No. 3061: a, Himalayan cat. b, Maine Coon cat. c, Red point Siamese cat. d, Persian cat.
No. 3062: a, Japanese bobtail cat. b, Ragdoll cat. c, Egyptian mau cat. d, Abyssinian cat.

2006, Sept. 29
3061 A978 7p Block of 4, #a-d 2.25 2.25

Souvenir Sheet

3062 A978 7p Sheet of 4, #a-d 2.25 2.25

United Nations Month A979

Text in: 7p, Tagalog and English. 26p, English.

2006, Oct. 19
3063-3064 A979 Set of 2 2.75 1.40

Philippines Postal Service, 108th Anniv. — A980

No. 3065: a, Ruins of Manila Post Office after Battle of Manila. b, Manila Central Post Office, 2006.

2006, Nov. 6 *Perf. 13¾*
3065 A980 Horiz. pair 1.10 1.10
a.-b. 7p Either single .55 .30

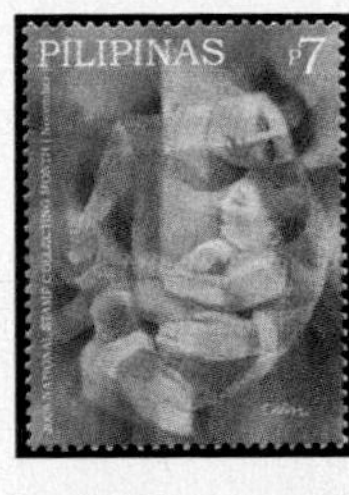

National Stamp Collecting Month — A981

Designs: No. 3066, 7p, Mother and child. No. 3067, 7p, Fish and fruit, horiz.. No. 3068, 7p, Oranges and grapes, horiz. No. 3069, 7p, Watermelon and coconut, horiz.
26p, Roses.

2006, Nov. 15
3066-3069 A981 Set of 4 2.25 1.10

Souvenir Sheet

3070 A981 26p multi 2.10 2.10

No. 3070 contains one 30x80mm stamp.

Ascent of Mt. Everest by Filipino Climbers — A982

Designs: No. 3071, 7p, Climbers ascending mountain. No. 3072, 20p, No. 3074a, 10p, Climbers ascending mountain and Philippines flag. No. 3073, 26p, No. 3074b, 7p, Climbers at summit with flag.

2006, Nov. 23 *Perf. 13¾*
3071-3073 A982 Set of 3 4.25 2.10

Souvenir Sheet

3074 A982 Sheet of 3, #3071, 3074a, 3074b 2.00 2.00

Christmas A983

Stars and: 7p, Manila Cathedral. 20p, Paoay Church. 24p, Miagao Church. 26p, Barasoain Church.

Litho. with Hologram Affixed
2006 *Perf. 14*
3075-3078 A983 Set of 4 6.25 6.25

Issued: 7p, 20p, 12/15; 24p, 26p, 12/19.

New Year 2007 (Year of the Pig) A984

Designs: 7p, Head of pig. 20p, Pig.

2006, Dec. 27 Litho.
3079-3080 A984 Set of 2 2.25 1.10
3080a Souvenir sheet, 2 each #3079-3080 4.50 4.50

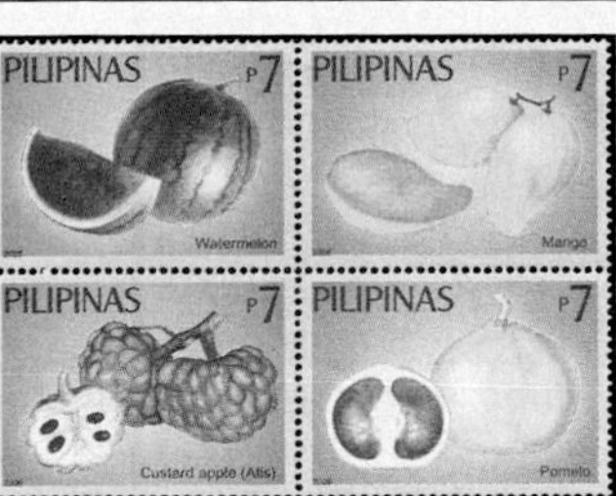

Fruit — A985

No. 3081: a, Watermelons. b, Mangos. c, Custard apples. d, Pomelos.
No. 3082: a, Jackfruit. b, Lanzones. c, Coconuts. d, Bananas.

2006, Dec. 15
3081 A985 7p Block or strip of 4, #a-d 2.25 2.25

Souvenir Sheet

3082 A985 7p Sheet of 4, #a-d 2.25 2.25

Graciano Lopez Jaena (1856-96), Journalist A986

2006, Dec. 18
3083 A986 7p multi .55 .30

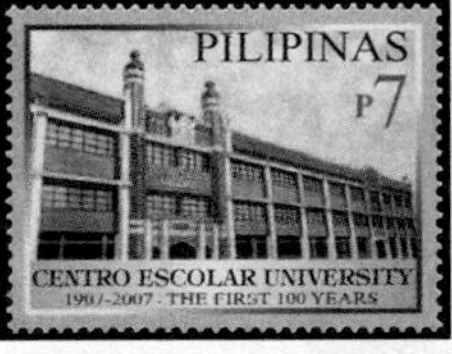

Centro Escolar University, Cent. A987

2007, Jan. 18 Litho. *Perf. 14*
3084 A987 7p multi .55 .30

Philippine School of the Deaf, Cent. A988

2007, Jan. 19
3085 A988 7p multi .55 .30

Rare Flowers — A989

No. 3086: a, Medinilla magnifica. b, Strongylodon elmeri. c, Amyema incarnatiflora. d, Dillenia monantha. e, Xanthostemon fruticosus. f, Plumeria acuminata. g, Paphiopedilum adductum. h, Rafflesia manillana.
26p, Rafflesia manillana and man, horiz.

2007, Mar. 30
3086 A989 7p Sheet of 8, #a-h 4.50 *8.00*

Souvenir Sheet

3087 A989 26p multi 2.10 2.10

No. 3087 contains one 120x30mm stamp.

Manulife Philippines Insurance, Cent. — A990

2007, Apr. 26

3088 A990 7p multi .55 .30
a. Souvenir sheet of 4 2.25 2.25

Colonial Era Bridges — A991

No. 3089: a, Isabel II Bridge, Imus, Cavite. b, Dampol Bridge, Dupax, Nueva Viscaya. c, Barit Bridge, Laoad, Ilocos Norte. d, Blanco Bridge, Binondo, Manila.

No. 3090: a, Malagonlong Bridge, Tayabas, Quezon. b, Fort Santiago Bridge. c, Mahacao Bridge, Maragondon, Cavite. d, Busay Bridge, Guinobatan, Albay.

2007, May 16

3089 A991 7p Block of 4, #a-d 2.25 2.25

Souvenir Sheet

3090 A991 7p Sheet of 4, #a-d 2.25 2.25

Diplomatic Relations Between Philippines and France, 60th Anniv. — A992

Symbols of France and Philippines including: 7p, Eiffel Tower. No. 3092, 26p, Castle.

No. 3093, 26p, Flags of France and Philippines, symbols of countries.

2007, June 26

3091-3092 A992 Set of 2 2.75 1.40

Souvenir Sheet

3093 A992 26p multi 2.10 2.10

No. 3093 contains one 30x80mm stamp.

Bureau of Fisheries and Aquatic Resources, 60th Anniv. — A993

No. 3094: a, Diana. b, Giant trevally. c, Skipjack tuna. d, Yellowfin tuna.

No. 3095: a, Cuttlefish. b, Bigfin reef squid and sacol (80x30mm).

2007, July 2

3094 A993 Horiz. strip of 4 2.25 2.25
a.-d. 7p Any single .55 .30

Souvenir Sheet

3095 Sheet of 2 2.25 2.25
a. A993 7p multi .55 .30
b. A993 20p multi 1.60 .80

Scouting, Cent. — A994

Designs: No. 3096, 7p, Scouting flag, hand giving scout sign. No. 3097, 7p, Scouting and Scouting Centenary emblems.

2007, Aug. 1

3096-3097 A994 Set of 2 1.10 .60
3097a Souvenir sheet, 2 each #3096-3097 + label 2.25 2.25

A995

Ducks and Geese — A996

No. 3098: a, Mallards. b, Green-winged teal. c, Tufted ducks. d, Cotton pygmy geese.

Nos. 3099 and 3100: a, Northern pintails. b, Common shelducks. c, Northern shovelers. d, Greater scaups.

2007, Aug. 3

3098 A995 7p Block of 4, #a-d 2.25 2.25

Souvenir Sheets

3099 A996 7p Sheet of 4, #a-d 2.25 2.25

With Bangkok 2007 Emblem Added to Stamps

3100 A996 7p Sheet of 4, #a-d 4.00 4.00

No. 3100 sold for 50p.

Butterfly Type of 2006

Designs: 8p, Troidaes magellanus magellanus. 17p, Achillides palinurus daedalus.

2007, Aug. 7 *Perf. 13¾x13½*

3101 A966 8p multi .65 .30
3102 A966 17p multi 1.40 .70

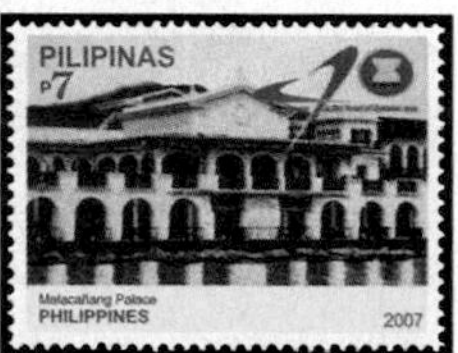

Association of South East Asian Nations (ASEAN), 40th Anniv. — A997

Designs: 7p, Malacañang Palace, Philippines.

No. 3104: a, Secretariat Building, Bandar Seri Begawan, Brunei. b, National Museum, Cambodia. c, Fatahillah Museum, Jakarta, Indonesia. d, Typical house, Laos. e, Malayan Railway Headquarters Building, Kuala Lumpur, Malaysia. f, Yangon Post Office, Myanmar (Burma). g, Malacañang Palace, Philippines. h, National Museum, Singapore. i, Vimanmek Mansion, Bangkok, Thailand. j, Presidential Palace, Hanoi, Viet Nam.

No. 3105, Malacañang Palace, Philippines (80x30mm).

2007, Aug. 8 *Perf. 14*

3103 A997 7p multi .55 .30
3104 A997 20p Sheet of 10, #a-j 16.00 16.00

Souvenir Sheet

3105 A997 20p multi 1.60 1.60

See Brunei No. 607, Burma No. 370, Cambodia No. 2339, Indonesia Nos. 2120-2121, Laos Nos. 1717-1718, Malaysia No. 1170, Singapore No. 1265, Thailand No. 2315, and Viet Nam Nos. 3302-3311.

Pres. Ramon F. Magsaysay (1907-57) A998

2007, Aug. 31 **Litho.**

3106 A998 7p multi .55 .30

Social Security System, 50th Anniv. — A999

Nos. 3107 and 3108 — Anniversary emblem and: a, Family and building. b, Pres. Ramon Magsaysay. c, Pres. Magsaysay signing Social Security Act of 1954. d, Building.

2007, Sept. 1 *Perf. 14*

Stamps With White Margins

3107 A999 7p Block of 4, #a-d 2.25 2.25

Souvenir Sheet

Stamps With Gray Margins

3108 A999 7p Sheet of 4, #a-d 2.25 2.25

First Philippine Assembly, Cent. A1000

Designs: No. 3109, 7p, People in front of Manila Opera House. No. 3110, 7p, Manila municipal building.

2007, Oct. 16

3109-3110 A1000 Set of 2 1.10 .60

United Nations Month A1001

Text in: 7p, Tagalog and English. 26p, English.

2007, Oct. 24

3111-3112 A1001 Set of 2 2.75 1.40

Nos. 3111-3112 were printed in a sheet of 20 stamps containing ten of each stamp separated by a central gutter.

Paintings by Juan Luna (1857-99) A1002

Designs: No. 3113, 7p, El Violinista. No. 3114, 7p, Indio Bravo. No. 3115, 7p, Old Man With a Pipe. No. 3116, 7p, La Bulakeña.

No. 3117a, Picnic in Normandy, horiz. (60x40mm).

No. 3118, horiz. — Parisian Life, with background color of: a, Light yellow and blue. b, Yellow orange and green. c, Yellow orange and red. d, Yellow orange and purple.

2007 *Perf. 14*

3113-3116 A1002 Set of 4 2.25 1.25
3117 Sheet of 4, #3113-3115, 3117a 2.25 2.25
a. A1002 7p brown & multi, imperf. .55 .30
3118 Sheet of 4 2.25 2.25
a. A1002 7p Imperf. (73x48mm) .55 .30
b.-d. A1002 7p Any single .55 .30

Issued: Nos. 3113-3116, 10/24; No. 3117, 11/23; No. 3118, 12/21. No. 3116 was issued in sheets of 6.

Birds — A1003

Designs: 1p, Black-naped oriole. 2p, Asian fairy bluebird. 3p, Writhed hornbill. 4p, Crimson sunbird. 5p, Barn swallow. 8p, Hoopoe. 9p, Short-eared owl. 10p, Blue-winged pita. 50p, Head of Philippine eagle. 100p, Philippine eagle on tree branch.

No. 3124: a, Mindanao bleeding heart pigeon. b, Nicobar pigeon. c, Black-chinned fruit dove. d, Metallic pigeon. e, Pink-necked green pigeon. f, Amethyst brown dove. g, Gray imperial pigeon. h, Red turtle dove. i, Pied imperial pigeon. j, Spotted imperial pigeon.

No. 3128: a, Dwarf kingfisher. b, Blue-capped wood kingfisher. c, White-throated kingfisher. d, White-collared kingfisher.

No. 3129: a, Green-faced parrotfinch. b, Java sparrow. c, Yellow-breasted bunting. d, White-cheeked bullfinch.

No. 3130: a, Great-billed parrot. b, Philippine cockatoo. c, Blue-naped parrot. d, Blue-backed parrot.

2007 *Perf. 13¾x13½*

Inscribed "2007"

3119 A1003 1p multi .25 .25
a. Inscribed "2008" .25 .25
b. Inscribed "2008A" .25 .25
c. Inscribed "2008B" .25 .25
3120 A1003 2p multi .25 .25
a. Inscribed "2008" .25 .25
b. Inscribed "2008A" .25 .25
c. Inscribed "2008B" .25 .25
3121 A1003 3p multi .25 .25
3122 A1003 4p multi .35 .25
a. Inscribed "2008" .35 .25
3123 A1003 5p multi .40 .25
a. Inscribed "2008" .40 .25
3124 Block of 10 6.00 6.00
a.-j. A1003 7p Any single .55 .30
k. Block of 10, inscr. "2008" 6.00 6.00
l.-u. A1003 7p Any single, inscr. "2008" .55 .30
3125 A1003 8p multi .65 .30
3126 A1003 9p multi .75 .35
3127 A1003 10p multi .80 .40
a. Inscribed "2008" .80 .40
b. Inscribed "2008A" .40 .25
3128 Block of 4 6.50 6.50
a.-d. A1003 20p Any single 1.60 .80
3129 Block of 4 7.75 7.75
a.-d. A1003 24p Any single 1.90 .95
3130 Block of 4 8.50 8.50
a.-d. A1003 26p Any single 2.10 1.10
e. Block of 4, inscr. "2008" 8.50 8.50
f.-i. A1003 26p Any single, inscr. "2008" 2.10 1.10
j. Block of 4, inscr. "2008A" 8.50 8.50
k.-n. A1003 26p Any single, inscr. "2008A" 2.10 1.10

Size: 30x40mm

Perf. 14

3131 A1003 50p multi 4.00 2.00
a. Inscribed "2008" 4.00 2.00
b. Inscribed "2008A" 4.00 2.00
3132 A1003 100p multi 8.00 4.00
a. Inscribed "2008" 8.00 4.00
b. Inscribed "2008A" 8.00 4.00
Nos. 3119-3132 (14) 44.45 37.05

Issued: 1p, 100p, 10/30; 2p, 20p, 11/15; 3p, 4p, 8p, 26p, 12/12; 5p, 50p, 11/5; 7p, 12/10; 9p, 10p, 24p, 12/19.

For stamps without blue lines at bottom, see No. 3151.

Manila Central Post Office, 1926 A1004

No. 3133: a, Shown. b, Manila Central Post Office and architect Juan Marcos Arellano (80x30mm).

2007, Nov. 5 *Perf. 14*

3133 Horiz. pair 2.25 2.25
a. A1004 7p multi .55 .30
b. A1004 20p multi 1.60 .80

San Diego de Alcala Cathedral, Cumaca, 425th Anniv. — A1005

2007, Nov. 13 *Perf. 13¾x13½*

3134 A1005 7p multi .55 .30

Sacred Heart School, Cebu, 50th Anniv. — A1006

No. 3135: a, School building and Philippines flag. b, School building and statue. c, Nun, school crest. d, Nun, school building.

2007, Nov. 16 *Perf. 14*

Stamps With White Margins

3135 A1006 7p Block of 4, #a-d 2.25 2.25

Souvenir Sheet

3136 Sheet of 4, #3135a, 3135b, 3135d, 3136a 2.25 2.25

a. A1006 7p As #3135c, with greenish gray tint in margin at LL .55 .30

Development Bank of the Philippines, 60th Anniv. — A1007

No. 3137: a, Ship emblem, blue background. b, Bank building, brown background. c, Bank building at left, dark green background. d, Bank building at right, olive green background.

2007, Nov. 26

3137 A1007 7p Block of 4, #a-d 2.25 2.25

e. Souvenir sheet, #3137a-3137d 2.25 2.25

Christmas A1008

Designs: 7p, Teddy bear. 20p, Toy train. 24p, Toy truck. 26p, Angel with candle decoration.

2007, Nov. 28

3138-3141 A1008 Set of 4 6.25 3.25

New Year 2008 (Year of the Rat) A1009

Designs: 7p, Head of rat. 20p, Rat.

2007, Dec. 3

3142-3143 A1009 Set of 2 2.25 1.10

3143a Souvenir sheet, 2 each #3142-3143 4.50 4.50

World Vision in Philippines, 50th Anniv. — A1010

Designs: 7p, Pres. Ramon F. Magsaysay and World Vision founder, Rev. Bob Pierce. 20p, World Vision anniversary emblem, horiz.

2007, Dec. 5

3144-3145 A1010 Set of 2 2.25 1.10

No. 1810 Surcharged in Silver

Methods, Perfs and Watermark As Before

2007, Dec. 14

3146 A470 7p on 2.40p #1810 .55 .30

Dominican School, Manila, 50th Anniv. — A1011

No. 3147: a, St. Dominic de Guzman. b, St. Dominic, school, emblem. c, Two emblems. d, School, emblem.

Unwmk.

2008, Feb. 1 **Litho.** *Perf. 14*

3147 A1011 7p Block of 4, #a-d 2.25 2.25

Valentine's Day — A1012

No. 3148: a, Roses in heart. b, Cupid, hearts.

2008, Feb. 6

3148 A1012 7p Pair, #a-b 1.10 1.10

c. Sheet of 10, 5 each #3148a-3148b 8.00 8.00

No. 3148c sold for 100p.

Missionary Catechists of St. Therese of the Infant Jesus, 50th Anniv. A1013

Designs: No. 3149, 7p, Emblem and nuns. No. 3150, 7p, 50th anniv. emblem, St. Therese of the Infant Jesus, Bishop Alfredo Obviar.

2008, Feb. 23

3149-3150 A1013 Set of 2 1.10 .55

3150a Pair, #3149-3150 1.10 .55

Bird Type of 2007 Without Blue Lines at Bottom

Miniature Sheet

No. 3151: a, Mindanao bleeding heart pigeon. b, Nicobar pigeon. c, Black-chinned fruit dove. d, Metallic pigeon. e, Pink-necked green pigeon. f, Amethyst brown dove. g, Gray imperial pigeon. h, Red turtle dove. i, Pied imperial pigeon. j, Spotted imperial pigeon. k, Philippine eagle. l, Philippine cockatoo. m, Java sparrow. n, Blue-capped wood kingfisher.

2008, Mar. 7 *Perf. 13¾x13½*

3151 A1003 7p Sheet of 14, #a-n, + label 10.00 10.00

2008 Taipei Intl. Stamp Exhibition. No. 3151 sold for 125p.

Rodents of Luzon Island — A1014

No. 3152: a, Luzon furry-tailed rat. b, Cordillera striped earth rat. c, Cordillera forest mouse. d, Cordillera shrew mouse.

No. 3153: a, 7p, Northern giant cloud rat. b, 7p, Lesser dwarf cloud rat. c, 20p, Bushy-tailed cloud rat, vert. (40x70mm).

2008, Mar. 7 *Perf. 14*

3152 A1014 7p Block of 4, #a-d 2.25 2.25

Souvenir Sheet

Perf. 14, Imperf. (20p)

3153 A1014 Sheet of 3, #a-c 2.75 2.75

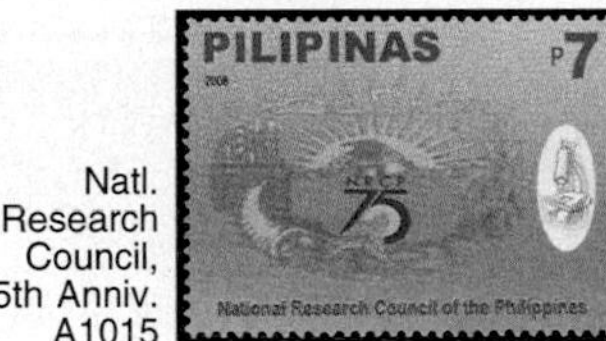

Natl. Research Council, 75th Anniv. A1015

2008, Mar. 12 *Perf. 14*

3154 A1015 7p multi .55 .30

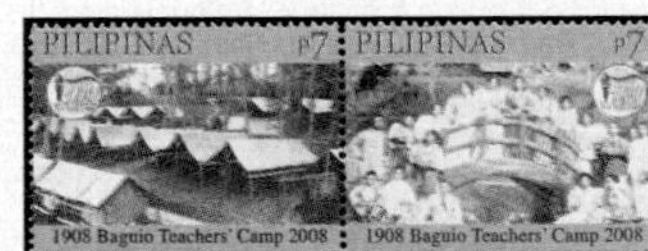

Baguio Teachers Camp, Cent. — A1016

No. 3155: a, Camp. b, Teachers, bridge.

2008, May 10

3155 A1016 7p Horiz. pair, #a-b 1.10 1.10

Bridges of the American Era — A1017

No. 3156: a, Gasan Bridge, Gasan, Marinduque. b, Hinigaran Bridge, Hinigaran, Negros Occidental. c, Wahig Bridge, Dagoboy, Bohol. d, Pan-ay Bridge, Pan-ay, Capiz.

No. 3157: a, Quezon Bridge, Quiapo, Manila. b, Governor Reynolds Bridge, Guinobatan, Albay. c, Mauca Railway Bridge, Ragay, Camarines Sur. d, Balucuan Bridge, Dao, Capiz.

Illustration reduced.

2008, May 16

3156 A1017 7p Block of 4, #a-d 2.25 2.25

Miniature Sheet

3157 A1017 7p Sheet of 4, #a-d 2.25 2.25

Miniature Sheet

Manny Pacquiao, World Boxing Council Lightweight Champion — A1018

No. 3158 — Pacquiao: a, With hands taped. b, Wearing robe and gloves. c, Wearing championship belt. d, Wearing gloves.

2008, May 30

3158 A1018 7p Sheet of 4, #a-d 2.25 2.25

Dept. of Science and Technology, 50th Anniv. — A1019

Philippine Nuclear Research Institute, 50th Anniv. A1020

2008, June 4

3159 A1019 7p multi .55 .30

3160 A1020 7p multi .55 .30

Liong Tek Go Family Association, Cent. — A1021

No. 3161: a, Association centenary emblem. b, Tai Bei Kong.

2008, June 11

3161 A1021 7p Pair, #a-b 1.10 1.10

University of the Philippines, Cent. — A1022

Designs: Nos. 3162a, 3163c, 3164c, Emblem (with eagle). Nos. 3162b, 3163a, 3164a, Carillon. Nos. 3162c, 3163d, 3164d, Oblation sculpture. Nos. 3162d, 3163b, 3164b, Centenary emblem (with Oblation sculpture).

2008 ***Perf. 13¾x13½***

3162 A1022 7p Block of 4, #a-d 2.25 2.25

Stamp Size: 40x30mm

Perf. 14

3163 A1022 7p Block of 4, #a-d 2.25 2.25
e. Souvenir sheet, #3163a-3163d 2.25 2.25

Litho. With Foil Application

3164 A1022 7p Block of 4, #a-d 3.25 3.25
e. Souvenir sheet, #3164a-3164d 4.00 4.00

No. 3164 was printed in sheets containing four blocks that sold for 160p. No. 3164e sold for 50p.

Friar Andres de Urdaneta (c. 1608-1568), Navigator A1023

2008, June 26 ***Perf. 14***

3165 A1023 7p multi .55 .30

Philippine-Spanish Friendship Day.

Xavier University, Ateneo de Cagayan, 75th Anniv. — A1024

No. 3166: a, Immaculate Conception Chapel. b, Statue of St. Francis Xavier. c, Archbishop James T. G. Hayes. d, Science Center.

2008, June 26

3166 A1024 7p Block of 4, #a-d 2.25 2.25

Ateneo de Davao University, 60th Anniv. — A1025

No. 3167: a, College building. b, High school building, statue. c, Grade school building, flags. d, Assumption (stained glass).

2008, July 31

3167 A1025 7p Block of 4, #a-d 2.25 2.25
e. Souvenir sheet, #3167a-3167d 2.25 2.25

2008 Summer Olympics, Beijing A1026

Designs: 7p, Archery. 20p, Judo. 24p, Equestrian. 26p, Weight lifting.

2008, Aug. 11 **Litho.**

3168-3171 A1026 Set of 4 6.25 6.25

Se Jo Lim Family Association, Cent. — A1027

Designs: Nos. 3172a, 3173a, Pi Kan, Lim family ancestor. Nos. 3172b, 3173b, Senator Roselier T. Lim, Gen. Vicente P. Lim. Nos. 3172c, 3173c, Binondo Church, Chinese gate. Nos. 3172d, 3173d, Association centenary emblem, sun, stars and colors of Philippines flag.

2008, Aug. 22 ***Perf. 14***

3172 A1027 7p Block of 4, #a-d 2.25 2.25

Souvenir Sheet

Perf. 14 on 3 Sides

3173 A1027 7p Sheet of 4, #a-d, + 2 labels 2.25 2.25

Philippine Bonsai Society, 35th Anniv. A1028

No. 3174: a, Pemphis acidula (on short-legged table), red background. b, Ficus microcarpa. c, Serissa foetida. d, Pemphis acidula, violet background. e, Pemphis acidula, blue background. f, Triphasia trifolia. g, Pemphis acidula (on piece of wood), cerise background. h, Bougainville sp.

No. 3175, vert.: a, Murraya sp. b, Pemphis acidula, tan background. c, Pemphis acidula, gray blue background. d, Pemphis acidula, violet background. e, Pemphis acidula, blue background. f, Antidesma bunius. g, Maba buxifolia. h, Ficus concina.

No. 3176: a, Lagerstroemia indica. b, Pemphis acidula, yellow green background. c, Vitex sp. d, Ixora chinensis.

2008, Oct. 17 ***Perf. 14***

3174 Block of 8 4.50 4.50
a.-h. A1028 7p Any single .55 .30
3175 Block of 8 4.50 4.50
a.-h. A1028 7p Any single .55 .30

Souvenir Sheet

3176 Sheet of 4 2.25 2.25
a.-d. A1028 7p Any single .55 .30

Miniature Sheet

Jakarta 2008 Intl. Stamp Exhibition — A1029

No. 3177 — Birds: a, Brahminy kite. b, Olive-backed sunbird. c, Purple-throated sunbird. d, Metallic-winged sunbird. e, Gray-headed fish eagle. f, Plain-throated sunbird. g, Lina's sunbird. h, Apo sunbird. i, Copper-throated sunbird. j, Flaming sunbird. k, Gray-hooded sunbird. l, Lovely sunbird. m, Crested serpent eagle. n, Philippine hawk eagle. o, Blue-crowned racquet-tail. p, Philippine eagle owl. q, Common flameback.

2008, Oct. 23 ***Perf. 13¾x13½***

3177 A1029 7p Sheet of 17, #a-q, + 13 labels 12.00 *40.00*

No. 3177 sold for 150p.

Visit of Ban Ki-moon, United Nations Secretary General A1030

Ban Ki-moon and: 7p, UN emblem. 26p, Philippines President Gloria Macapagal-Arroyo.

2008, Oct. 29 ***Perf. 14***

3178-3179 A1030 Set of 2 2.75 2.75

Tourism — A1031

No. 3180: a, Boracay Beach, Aklan. b, Intramuros, Manila. c, Banaue Rice Terraces, Mountain Province. d, Mayon Volcano, Bicol.

20p, Puerto Princesa Underground River, Palawan. 24p, Chocolate Hills, Bohol. 26p, Tubbataha Reef, Palawan.

2008, Nov. 3 ***Perf. 13½x13¾***

3180 Block of 4 2.25 2.25
a.-d. A1031 7p Any single .55 .30
3181 A1031 20p multi 1.60 .80
3182 A1031 24p multi 2.00 1.00
3183 A1031 26p multi 2.10 1.10
Nos. 3180-3183 (4) 7.95 5.15

Philippine Postal Service, 110th anniv.

Christmas A1032

Designs: 7p, Mother with brown hair, and child. 20p, Mother nursing child. 24p, Mother, child, dove. 26p, Mother with child in sling.

No. 3188: a, 7p, Madonna and Child. b, 26m, Mother with sleeping child.

2008, Nov. 10 ***Perf. 14***

3184-3187 A1032 Set of 4 6.25 4.00

Souvenir Sheet

3188 A1032 Sheet of 2, #a-b 2.75 2.75

Comic Book Superheroes of Carlo J. Caparas — A1033

No. 3189, 7p: a, Joaquin Bordado. b, Totoy Bato. c, Gagambino. d, Pieta.

No. 3190: a, 7p, Ang Panday (with hammer). b, 20p, Ang Panday (holding sword).

2008, Nov. 17

3189 A1033 7p Block of 4, #a-d 2.25 2.25

Souvenir Sheet

3190 A1033 Sheet of 2, #a-b 2.25 2.25

Natl. Stamp Collecting Month.

Senator Benigno S. Aquino, Jr. (1932-83) — A1034

No. 3191: a, 7p, Photograph. b, 26p, Drawing.

2008, Nov. 27

3191 A1034 Horiz. pair, #a-b 2.75 2.75

Fernando G. Bautista (1908-2002), Founder of University of Baguio — A1035

2008, Dec. 8

3192 A1035 7p multi .55 .30

New Year 2009 (Year of the Ox) A1036

Designs: 7p, Ox head. 20p, Ox.

2008, Dec. 10

3193-3194 A1036 Set of 2 2.25 1.25
3194a Souvenir sheet of 4, 2 each #3193-3194 4.50 4.50

Crabs — A1037

No. 3195: a, Goneplacid crab. b, Largo's spider crab. c, Fuzzy sponge crab. d, Daniele's deepwater porter crab.

No. 3196: a, Stimpson's intricate spider crab. b, Spider crab.

2008, Dec. 19

3195 A1037 7p Block of 4, #a-d 2.25 2.25

Souvenir Sheet

3196 A1037 20p Sheet of 2, #a-b, + 2 labels 4.00 4.00

No. 3196 sold for 50p.

Dr. Manuel Sarmiento Enverga (1909-81), Educator and Politician A1038

2009, Jan. 1 **Litho.** ***Perf. 14***

3197 A1038 7p multi .55 .30

Love — A1039

No. 3198: a, Roses and heart. b, Hearts and envelope.

2009, Feb. 2

3198 A1039 7p Pair, #a-b 1.10 1.10

Philippine Intl. Arts Festival — A1040

Emblem and: a, Painting. b, Theater masks and book of poetry. c, Cymbal and dancers. d, Theater and movie poster.

2009, Feb. 16

3199 A1040 7p Block of 4, #a-d 2.25 2.25

Diplomatic Relations Between Philippines and Republic of Korea, 60th Anniv. — A1041

No. 3200: a, Panagbenga Flower Festival, Philippines. b, Cow Play, Hangawi, Republic of Korea.

2009, Mar. 3

3200 A1041 7p Horiz. pair, #a-b 1.10 1.10

See Republic of Korea Nos. 2304-2305.

Birds — A1042

Designs: 1p, Mugimaki flycatcher. 2p, Narcissus flycatcher.3p, Mountain verditer-flycatcher. 4p, Blue rock thrush. 5p, Brown shrike. 8p, Apo myna. 9p, Crested serpent-eagle. 10p, Blue-crowned racquet-tail. 17p, Common flameback. 50p, Gray-headed fish-eagle. 100p, Philippine hawk-eagle.

No. 3206: a, Olive-backed sunbird. b, Metallic-winged sunbird. c, Plain-throated sunbird. d, Lina's sunbird. e, Purple-throated sunbird. f, Apo sunbird. g, Copper-throated sunbird. h, Flaming sunbird. i, Gray-hooded sunbird. j, Lovely sunbird.

No. 3211: a, Palawan flowerpecker. b, Fire-breasted flowerpecker. c, Cebu flowerpecker. d, Red-keeled flowerpecker.

No. 3212: a, Philippine tailorbird. b, Mountain tailorbird. c, Black-headed tailorbird. d, Ashy tailorbird.

2009 **Litho.** ***Perf. 13¾x13½***

3201	A1042	1p multi	.25	.25
3202	A1042	2p multi	.25	.25
3203	A1042	3p multi	.25	.25
3204	A1042	4p multi	.35	.25
3205	A1042	5p multi	.40	.25
3206		Block of 10	5.75	*6.00*
a.-j.		A1042 7p Any single	.55	.30
3207	A1042	8p multi	.65	.30
3208	A1042	9p multi	.75	.35
3209	A1042	10p multi	.80	.40
3210	A1042	17p multi	1.40	.70
3211		Block of 4	6.50	*7.00*
a.-d.		A1042 20p Any single, dated "2009"	1.60	.80
3212		Block of 4	8.50	*9.00*
a.-d.		A1042 26p Any single, dated "2009"	2.10	1.00

Size: 30x40mm

Perf. 14

3213	A1042	50p multi	4.00	2.00
3214	A1042	100p multi	8.00	4.00
		Nos. 3201-3214 (14)	37.85	31.00

Issued: 1p, 2p, No. 3206, 3/9; 3p, 4p, No. 3211, 6/2; 5p, 100p, 3/13; 8p, 9p, 10p, 17p, 50p, 3/23; No. 3212, 5/25.

See No. 3258.

2009-10 **Litho.** ***Perf. 13¾x13½***

3201a	Dated "2009A"	.25	.25
3201b	Dated "2009B"	.25	.25
3201c	Dated "2009C"	.25	.25
3202a	Dated "2009A"	.25	.25
3202b	Dated "2009B"	.25	.25
3202c	Dated "2009C"	.25	.25
3203a	Dated "2009A"	.25	.25
3203b	Dated "2009B"	.25	.25
3203c	Dated "2009C"	.25	.25
3204a	Dated "2009A"	.35	.25
3204b	Dated "2009B"	.35	.25
3204c	Dated "2009C"	.35	.25
3205a	Dated "2009A"	.40	.25
3205b	Dated "2009B"	.40	.25
3205c	Dated "2009C"	.40	.25
3206k	Block of 10, #3206l-3206u, dated "2009A"	5.75	*6.00*
3206l-3206u	Like Nos. 3206a-3206j, any single, dated "2009A"	.55	.30
3207a	Dated "2009A"	.65	.30
3207b	Dated "2009B"	.65	.30
3207c	Dated "2009C"	.65	.30
3208a	Dated "2009A"	.75	.35
3208b	Dated "2009B"	.75	.35
3208c	Dated "2009C"	.75	.35
3208d	Dated "2009D"	.75	.35
3209a	Dated "2009A"	.80	.40
3209b	Dated "2009B"	.80	.40
3210a	Dated "2009A"	1.40	.70
3210b	Dated "2009B"	1.40	.70
3210c	Dated "2009C"	1.40	.70
3211e	Block of 4, #3211f-3211i, dated "2009A"	6.50	6.50
3211f-3211i	Like Nos. 3211a-3211d, any single, dated "2009A"	1.60	.80
3212e	Block of 4, #3212f-3212i, dated "2009A"	8.50	8.50
3212f-3212i	Like Nos. 3212a-3212d, any single, dated "2009A"	2.10	1.00
3212j	Block of 4, #3212k-3212n, dated "2009B"	8.50	8.50
3212k-3212n	Like Nos. 3212a-3212d, any single, dated "2009B"	2.10	1.00

Size: 30x40mm

Perf. 14

3213a	Dated "2009A"	4.00	2.00
3213b	Dated "2009B"	4.00	2.00
3213c	Dated "2009C"	4.00	2.00
3213d	Dated "2009D"	4.00	2.00
3214a	Dated "2009A"	8.00	4.00
3214b	Dated "2009B"	8.00	4.00
3214c	Dated "2009C"	8.00	4.00
3214d	Dated "2009D"	8.00	4.00

Issued: No. 3206k, 5/13; No. 3205a, 5/25; Nos. 3201a, 3202a, 6/2; Nos. 3207a, 3208a, 3213a, 3214a, 6/8; Nos. 3201b, 3202b, 3205b, 8/6; No. 3208b, 8/10; Nos. 3203a, 3204a, 3210a, 8/13; Nos. 3207b, 3212e, 8/17; Nos. 3213b, 3214b, 9/1; Nos. 3209a, 3211e, 9/9; Nos. 3213c, 3214c, 11/24; No. 3201c, 12/11; Nos. 3209b, 3212j, 12/28; Nos. 3202c, 3204b, 3205c, 3210b, 1/11/10; Nos. 3203b, 3207c, 3208c, 1/12/10; Nos. 3213d, 3214d, 1/28/10; Nos. 3203c, 3204c, 3208d, 3210c, 2/5/10.

Minerals — A1043

No. 3215: a, Quartz. b, Rhodochrosite. c, Malachite. d, Nickel.

No. 3216: a, Cinnabar. b, Native gold. c, Native copper. d, Magnetite.

2009, Mar. 25 ***Perf. 14***

3215 A1043 7p Block of 4, #a-d 2.25 2.25

Souvenir Sheet

3216 A1043 7p Sheet of 4, #a-d 2.25 2.25

Mothers Dionisia (1691-1732) and Cecilia Rosa Talangpaz (1693-1731), Founders of Augustinian Recollect Sisters — A1044

2009, Apr. 28

3217 A1044 7p multi .55 .30

Art Deco Theaters — A1045

No. 3218: a, King's Theater. b, Capitol Theater. c, Joy Theater. d, Scala Theater.

No. 3219, horiz.: a, Life Theater. b, Times Theater. c, Bellevue Theater. d, Pines Theater.

2009, May 8

3218 A1045 7p Block of 4, #a-d 2.25 2.25

Souvenir Sheet

3219 A1045 7p Sheet of 4, #a-d 2.25 2.25

Rodolfo S. Cornejo (1909-91), Composer A1046

2009, May 15

3220 A1046 7p multi .55 .30

Tourist Attractions in Taguig — A1047

No. 3221: a, City Hall. b, Global City. c, Santa Ana Church. d, Blue Mosque.

2009, June 5 **Litho.**

3221 A1047 7p Block of 4, #a-d 2.25 2.25

Diplomatic Relations Between Philippines and Thailand, 60th Anniv. — A1048

No. 3222 — Dances: a, Tinikling, Philippines. b, Ten Krathop Sark, Thailand.

2009, June 14 ***Perf. 14***

3222 A1048 7p Horiz. pair, #a-b 1.10 1.10

Ateneo de Manila University, 150th Anniv. — A1049

No. 3223: a, Sesquicentennial emblem. b, Blue eagle. c, St. Ignatius of Loyola. d, José Rizal.

2009, June 14

3223 A1049 7p Block of 4, #a-d 2.25 2.25

e. Souvenir sheet, #3223a-3223d, + 2 labels 3.25 3.25

No. 3223e sold for 40p.

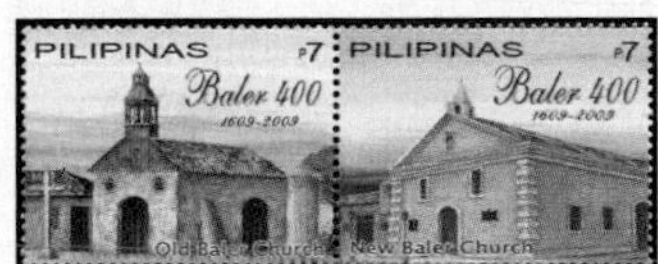

Baler, 400th Anniv. — A1050

No,. 3224: a, Old church. b, New church.

2009, June 30 **Litho.**

3224 A1050 7p Horiz. pair, #a-b 1.10 1.10

Che Yong Cua and Chua Family Association, Cent. — A1051

No. 3225: a, Chua Tiong. b, Chua Siok To.

2009, July 15 ***Perf. 14***
3225 A1051 7p Horiz. pair, #a-b 1.10 1.10

Souvenir Sheet

3226 A1051 Sheet of 4, #3225a-3225b, 3226a-3226b, + 2 labels 2.25 2.25
a. 7p Like #3225a, perf. 14 at left .55 .25
b. 7p Like #3225b, perf. 14 at right .55 .25

See Nos. 3239-3240.

Pheepoy, Mascot of Philippine Postal Corporation — A1052

2009, July 27 ***Perf. 13½x13¾***
3227 A1052 7p multi .55 .30

See No. 3336.

Knights of Columbus in Philippines, 50th Anniv. A1053

Color of denomination outline: 7p, Red. 9p, Dark blue.

2009, July 31 ***Perf. 14***
3228-3229 A1053 Set of 2 1.40 .70

Agricultural Cooperation Agreement Between Philippines and Brunei — A1054

2009, Aug. 3
3230 A1054 7p multi .55 .30

Diplomatic Relations Between Philippines and Singapore, 40th Anniv. — A1055

No. 3231: a, Bamban Bridge, Philippines. b, Marcelo B. Fernan Bridge, Philippines. c, Cavenagh Bridge, Singapore. d, Henderson Waves and Alexandra Arch, Singapore.

2009, Aug. 29 **Litho.**
3231 A1055 7p Block of 4, #a-d 2.25 2.25
e. Souvenir sheet, #3231a-3231d 2.25 2.25

See Singapore Nos. 1398-1401.

Baguio, Cent. — A1056

No. 3232 — Butterfly on posters and Baguio landmarks: a, Mansion House. b, Mines View Park. c, Baguio Cathedral. d, Kennon Road.

2009, Sept. 1 ***Perf. 13¾x13½***
3232 A1056 7p Horiz. strip of 4, #a-d 2.25 2.25
e. Souvenir sheet, #3232a-3232d 2.25 2.25

Pres. Corazon Aquino (1933-2009) — A1057

No. 3233: a, With raised arm, denomination at UL. b, Head and signature, denomination at UR.

No. 3234: a, With raised arm, denomination at UR. b, Head and signature, denomination at UL.

2009 **Litho.** ***Perf. 14***
3233 A1057 7p Horiz. pair, #a-b 1.10 1.10
3234 A1057 7p Horiz. pair, #a-b 1.10 1.10

Issued: No. 3233, 9/8; No. 3234, 9/18.

Intl. Year of Natural Fibers A1058

No. 3235: a, Ananas comosus, clothing made from pineapple fibers. b, Musa textilis, bags and hats made from abaca fibers. c, Musa textilis, Philippines bank notes made from abaca fibers. d, Musa textilis, abaca rope.

2009, Sept. 10
3235 Horiz. strip of 4 2.25 2.25
a.-d. A1058 7p Any single .55 .30

Lobsters — A1059

No. 3236: a, Locust lobster. b, Blind lobster. c, Northwest Reef lobster. d, Two-spot locust lobster.

No. 3237: a, Neptune Reef lobster. b, Fan lobster. c, Blue-back locust lobster. d, Banded whip lobster.

2009, Sept. 30
3236 A1059 7p Block of 4, #a-d 2.25 2.25

Souvenir Sheet

3237 A1059 7p Sheet of 4, #a-d 2.25 2.25

Quezon City, 70th Anniv. — A1060

No. 3238: a, Statue of Pres. Manuel L. Quezon, Philippines flag. b, City Hall. c, Araneta Center. d, Eastwood City.

2009, Oct. 12
3238 A1060 7p Block of 4, #a-d 2.25 2.25
e. Souvenir sheet, #3238a-3238d 2.25 2.25

Che Yong Cua and Chua Family Association, Cent. — A1061

No. 3239 — Philippines flag, emblem and: a, Cua Lo.

2009, Oct. 15 ***Perf. 14***
3239 A1061 7p Horiz. pair, #3225a, 3239a. 1.10 1.10

Souvenir Sheet

3240 A1061 Sheet of 4, #3225a, 3226a, 3239a, 3240a + 2 labels 2.25 2.25
a. 7p Like #3239a, perf. 14 at right .55 .25

Alpha Phi Beta Fraternity of the University of the Philippines, 70th Anniv. — A1062

No. 3241 — Fraternity emblem and: a, 70th anniv. emblem. b, Quezon Hall Oblation. c, Malcolm Hall. d, Founding fathers of fraternity.

2009, Oct. 17 ***Perf. 14***
3241 A1062 7p Block of 4, #a-d 2.25 2.25

A1063

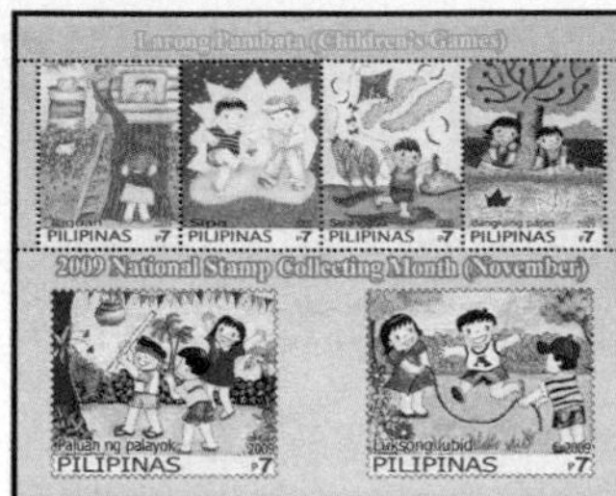

Children's Games and Activities — A1064

No. 3242: a, Tumbang preso. b, Luksong tinik. c, Holen (marbles). d, Sungka.

No. 3243: a, Taguan (hide-and seek) (30x40mm). b, Sipa (30x40mm). c, Sarang-gola (kite flying) (30x40mm). d, Bangkang papel (paper boat racing) (30x40mm). e, Paluan ng palayok (piñata) (48x38mm). f, Luksong lubid (rope jumping) (48x38mm).

Illustrations reduced.

2009, Nov. 9 ***Perf. 14***
3242 A1063 7p Block of 4, #a-d 2.25 2.25

Souvenir Sheet

Perf. 14, Imperf. (#3243e-3243f)

3243 A1064 7p Sheet of 6, #a-f 3.50 3.50

Natl. Stamp Collecting Month.

Christmas A1065

No. 3244 — Lyrics from Christmas carol "Ang Pasko ay Sumapit" and: a, Four children caroling. b, Nativity. c, Magi on camels. d, Angels and baby Jesus. e, Christmas decorations.

2009, Nov. 18 ***Perf. 14***
3244 Horiz. strip of 5 2.75 2.75
a.-e. A1065 7p Any single .55 .25

Cecilia Muñoz Palma (1913-2006), First Female Supreme Court Justice — A1066

2009, Nov. 22
3245 A1066 7p multi .55 .25

Diplomatic Relations Between the Philippines and India, 60th Anniv. — A1067

Endangered marine mammals: Nos. 3246a, 3247a, Whale shark. No. 3246b, Gangetic dolphin.

2009, Nov. 27 **Litho.**

3246 A1067 7p Horiz. pair, #a-b 1.10 1.10

Souvenir Sheet

3247 A1067 Sheet of 2, #3246b, 3247a + 2 labels 2.25 2.25

a. 20p multi 1.60 .80

See India No. 2374.

New Year 2010 (Year of the Tiger) A1068

Designs: 7p, Tiger's head. 20p, Tiger.

2009, Dec. 1 ***Perf. 14***

3248-3249 A1068 Set of 2 2.25 2.25

3249a Souvenir sheet, 2 each #3248-3249 4.50 4.50

Nudibranchs — A1069

No. 3250: a, Hypselodoris apolegma. b, Glossodoris colemani. c, Chromodoris sp. d, Chromodoris elizabethina.

No. 3251: a, Jorunna funebris. b, Chromodoris lochi. c, Noumea alboannulata. d, Chromodoris hintuanesis. e, Risbechi tryoni. f, Chromodoris leopardus.

2009, Dec. 4

3250 A1069 7p Block of 4, #a-d 2.25 2.25

Souvenir Sheet

3251 A1069 7p Sheet of 6, #a-f, + 2 labels 3.50 3.50

Stamp Collage Depicting Daedalus A1070

Designs: No. 3252, Entire collage.

No. 3253 — Quadrants of entire collage: a, UL. b, UR. c, LL. d, LR.

2009, Dec. 7

3252 A1070 7p multi .55 .25

Souvenir Sheet

3253 A1070 7p Sheet of 4, #a-d 2.25 2.25

Intl. Civil Aviation Organization, 65th anniv.

Return of Olongapo to the Philippines, 50th Anniv. — A1071

No. 3254 — Official seals of the Philippines and US and: a, Turnover ceremony. b, Parade of flags of the Philippines and US.

2009, Dec. 7 ***Perf. 14***

3254 A1071 7p Horz. pair, #a-b 1.10 1.10

Pheepoy Delivering Mail — A1072

2009, Dec. 10 ***Perf. 13½x13¾***

3255 A1072 7p multi .55 .25

See No. 3336.

Philippine Charity Sweepstakes Office, 75th Anniv. — A1073

No. 3256 — 75th anniv. emblem and: a, Charity Sweepstakes Office Building, Presidents Manuel L. Quezon and Gloria Macapagal Arroyo. b, Building. c, Building and family. d, Building and employees.

2009, Dec. 18 ***Perf. 14***

3256 A1073 7p Block of 4, #a-d 2.25 2.25

e. Souvenir sheet, #3256a-3256d 2.25 2.25

Potter From San Nicolas — A1074

2009, Dec. 21

3257 A1074 7p multi .55 .25

San Nicolas, Ilocos Norte Province, cent.

Birds Type of 2009

No. 3258: a, Philippine eagle owl. b, Luzon Scops owl. c, Philippine Scops owl. d, Spotted wood owl.

2010 **Litho.** ***Perf. 13¾x13½***

3258 Block of 4 7.75 *8.00*

a.-d. A1042 24p Any single 1.90 .95

e. Block of 4, #3258f-3258i, dated "2009A" 7.75 *8.00*

f.-i. Like #3258a-3258d, any single, dated "2009A" 1.90 .95

Nos. 3258a-3258d are dated "2009." Issued: No. 3258, 1/11; No. 3258e, 2/8.

St. Valentine's Day — A1075

No. 3259 — Cupid: a, With bow and arrow. b, Blowing flower petals.

2010, Jan. 25 ***Perf. 14***

3259 A1075 7p Horiz. pair, #a-b 1.10 1.10

Pheepoy on Motorcycle — A1076

2010, Feb. 12 ***Perf. 13½x13¾***

3260 A1076 7p multi .55 .25

See No. 3336.

Rotary International in the Philippines, 90th Anniv. — A1077

Nos. 3261 and 3262: a, Peace dove above people. b, Construction workers. c, Child receiving polio vaccine. d, Rizal Monument, map of the Philippines. No. 3262 has Rotary International emblem instead of "Service Above Self" slogan.

2010, Feb. 23 ***Perf. 14***

3261 A1077 7p Block of 4, #a-d 2.25 2.25

Souvenir Sheet

Imperf

3262 A1077 7p Sheet of 4, #a-d 2.25 2.25

Beetles — A1078

No. 3263: a, Agestra luconica. b, Glycyphana. c, Paraplectrone crassa. d, Astrea.

No. 3264: a, Agestra semperi. b, Heterorhina. c, Agestra antoinei. d, Clerota rodriguezi.

2010, Mar. 29 **Litho.** ***Perf. 14***

3263 A1078 7p Block of 4, #a-d 2.25 2.25

Souvenir Sheet

3264 A1078 7p Sheet of 4, #a-d 2.25 2.25

Marine Life — A1079

Designs: No. 3265, Christmas tree worm. No. 3266, Yellow seahorse. No. 3267, Manta ray. No. 3268, Sea slug. No. 3269, Pencil urchin. No. 3270, Daisy coral. No. 3271, Magnificent sea anemone. No. 3272, Striped surgeonfish. No. 3273, Sundial. No. 3274, Blue linkia sea star. No. 3275, Sea hare. No. 3276, Giant clam. No. 3277, Green sea turtle. No. 3278, Sacoglossan sea slug. No. 3279, Lionfish. No. 3280, True clownfish. 8p, Harlequin shrimp. No. 3282, Coral beauty. No. 3283, Blue-ringed angelfish. No. 3284, Mandarinfish. No. 3285, Ribbon eel. 15p, Bowmouth guitarfish. No. 3287, Bigfin reef squid. No. 3288, Blue-spotted fantail stingray. No. 3289, Blue sea squirts. No. 3290, Scarlet-fringed flatworm. 24p, Branching anemone. 25p, Boxer crab. 26p, Spotted porcelain crab. 30p, Chambered nautilus. No. 3295, Red grouper. No. 3296, Giant moray eel. 40p, Textile cone. No. 3298, Marble sea star. No. 3299, Upside-down jellyfish. No. 3300, Bottlenose dolphin. No. 3301, Blue-ringed octopus.

2010-11 **Litho.** ***Perf. 13½x13¾***

3265 A1079 1p multi .25 .25
3266 A1079 1p multi .25 .25
3267 A1079 1p multi .25 .25
3268 A1079 2p multi .25 .25
3269 A1079 2p multi .25 .25
3270 A1079 3p multi .25 .25
3271 A1079 3p multi .25 .25
3272 A1079 3p multi .25 .25
3273 A1079 4p multi .35 .25
3274 A1079 4p multi .35 .25
3275 A1079 5p multi .40 .25
3276 A1079 5p multi .40 .25
3277 A1079 5p multi .40 .25
3278 A1079 5p multi .40 .25
3279 A1079 7p multi .55 .25
3280 A1079 7p multi .55 .25
3281 A1079 8p multi .65 .30
3282 A1079 9p multi .75 .35
3283 A1079 9p multi .75 .35
3284 A1079 10p multi .80 .40
3285 A1079 10p multi .80 .40
3286 A1079 15p multi 1.25 .60
3287 A1079 17p multi 1.40 .70
3288 A1079 17p multi 1.40 .70
3289 A1079 20p multi 1.60 .80
3290 A1079 20p multi 1.60 .80
3291 A1079 24p multi 1.90 .95
3292 A1079 25p multi 2.00 1.00
3293 A1079 26p multi 2.10 1.10
3294 A1079 30p multi 2.40 1.25
3295 A1079 35p multi 2.75 1.40
3296 A1079 35p multi 2.75 1.40
3297 A1079 40p multi 3.25 1.60

Size: 40x30mm

Perf. 14

3298 A1079 50p multi 4.00 2.00
3299 A1079 50p multi 4.00 2.00
3300 A1079 100p multi 8.00 4.00
3301 A1079 100p multi 8.00 4.00
Nos. 3265-3301 (36) 57.30 29.85

Nos. 3275 and 3278 have the same vignette; No. 3275 has an incorrect inscription and No. 3278 has the corrected inscription.

Issued: Nos. 3265, 3284, 3293, 3/29; Nos. 3266, 3276, 3290, 6/15; Nos. 3267, 3277, 3297, 11/18; Nos. 3268, 3275, 4/16; Nos. 3269, 3295, 7/15; Nos. 3270, 3273, 3298, 5/17; Nos. 3271, 3274, 3299, 12/3; Nos. 3278, 3292, 12/22; Nos. 3279, 3300, 5/13; Nos. 3280, 3296, 12/17; Nos. 3281, 3289, 4/21; Nos. 3282, 3287, 3291, 5/21; Nos. 3283, 3288, 12/13; No. 3285, 11/8; Nos. 3286, 3294, 7/23; No. 3301, 12/1; No. 3272, 1/20/11.

See Nos. 3357-3368, 3389-3403, 3447-3450, 3471-3481.

Intl. Rice Research Institute, 50th Anniv. — A1080

No. 3302: a, 50th anniversary emblem. b, Buildings. c, Rice field, water, mountains. d, Rice plants.

2010, Apr. 14 ***Perf. 14***

3302 A1080 7p Block of 4, #a-d 2.25 2.25

e. Souvenir sheet of 4 #3302a-3302d 2.25 2.25

Eraño G. Manalo (1925-2009), Executive Minister of Iglesia ni Cristo — A1081

Manalo, church and: No. 3303, Country name in brown, "2010" at left under "P." No. 3304, Like #3303, "2010" under denomination. No. 3305, Like #3303, country name in black. No. 3306, Like #3305, "2010" under denomination.

2010

3303 A1081 7p multi .55 .25
3304 A1081 7p multi .55 .25
3305 A1081 7p multi .55 .25
3306 A1081 7p multi .55 .25
Nos. 3303-3306 (4) 2.20 1.00

Issued: No. 3303, 4/23; No. 3304, 4/28; No. 3305, 5/11; No. 3306, 12/15.

Paintings by Vicente S. Manansala (1910-81) A1082

Designs: No. 3307, 7p, Sabungero. No. 3308, 7p, Bayanihan, horiz. No. 3309, 7p, Fish Vendor, horiz. No. 3310, 7p, Nipa Hut, horiz. 20p, Planting of the First Cross, horiz. (80x30mm).

No. 3312: a, Rooster. b, Mamimintakasi. c, I Believe in God, horiz. d, Three Carabaos, horiz.

2010, May 20 ***Perf. 14***
3307-3311 A1082 Set of 5 4.00 2.00

Perf. 14, Imperf. (#3312c-3312d)
3312 A1082 7p Sheet of 4, #a-d 2.25 2.25

No. 3311 was printed in sheets of 4.

Philippine Centennial Tree and Emblem of Municipality of Magallanes A1083

Tree at: 7p, Right. 9p, Left.

2010, May 28 ***Perf. 14***
3313-3314 A1083 Set of 2 1.40 .70

Bukidnon State University, 86th Anniv. — A1084

No. 3315 — University emblem and: a, Main building and sign. b, Education building and flagpole.

2010, June 18
3315 A1084 7p Horiz. pair, #a-b 1.10 1.10

Veterans Federation of the Philippines, 50th Anniv. — A1085

No. 3316 — Soldiers and: a, Emblem at left. b, Emblem at right.

2010, June 18
3316 A1085 7p Horiz. pair, #a-b 1.10 1.10

Light Rail Transit Authority, 30th Anniv. — A1086

Nos. 3317 and 3318: a, Train on curved bridge. b, Train, domed building at right. c, Train, pink and blue buildings. d, Cars on road below train.

2010, July 12 ***Perf. 14***
3317 A1086 7p Block of 4, #a-d 2.25 2.25

Souvenir Sheet

Imperf

3318 A1086 10p Sheet of 4, #a-d 3.25 3.25

Inauguration of Pres. Benigno S. Aquino III — A1087

Pres. Aquino: 7p, Taking oath. 40p, Giving inaugural speech, vert.

2010, July 26 ***Perf. 14***
3319-3320 A1087 Set of 2 3.75 1.90

Philippine Tuberculosis Society, Cent. — A1088

Society emblem and health care workers with inscription at bottom in: 7p, Tagalog. 9p, English.

26p, Emblem and 1935 Manuel L. Quezon birthday seal.

2010, July 29 ***Perf. 14***
3321-3322 A1088 Set of 2 1.40 .70

Souvenir Sheet

3323 A1088 26p multi 2.10 2.10

No. 3323 contains one 120x30mm stamp.

Devotion to Our Lady of Peñafrancia, 300th Anniv. — A1089

No. 3324: a, Our Lady of Peñafrancia, red panel. b, Our Lady of Peñafrancia, green panel. c, Our Lady of Peñafrancia Shrine, blue panel. d, Our Lady of Peñafrancia Basilica, yellow panel.

20p, Our Lady of Peñafrancia Shrine, Naga City, horiz.

2010, Sept. 8 ***Perf. 14***
3324 A1089 7p Block of 4, #a-d 2.25 2.25

Souvenir Sheet

3325 A1089 28p multi 2.25 2.25

No. 3325 contains one 80x30mm stamp.

Dogs — A1090

No. 3326: a, Chow chow. b, Bull terrier. c, Labrador retriever. d, Beagle.

No. 3327: a, American Eskimo dog. b, Black and tan coonhound. c, Afghan hound. d, Mastiff.

2010, Sept. 9 ***Perf. 14***
3326 A1090 7p Block of 4, #a-d 2.25 2.25

Souvenir Sheet

3327 A1090 7p Sheet of 4, #a-d 2.25 2.25

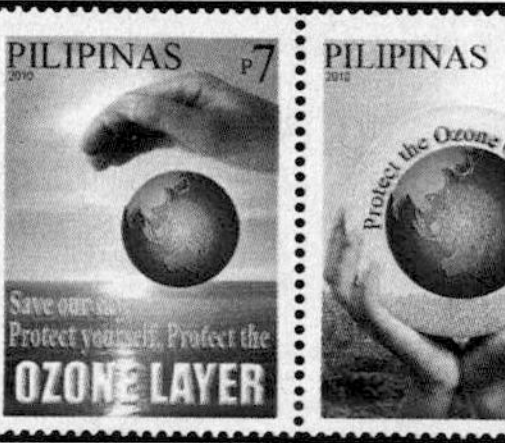

Ozone Layer Protection — A1091

No. 3328: a, Hand over globe. b. Hands below globe.

2010, Sept. 16
3328 A1091 7p Horiz. pair, #a-b 1.10 1.10

Central Mindanao University, Cent. — A1092

No. 3329 — University emblem and: a, Administration Building and lamp poles. b, University building.

2010, Sept. 17
3329 A1092 7p Horiz. pair, #a-b 1.10 1.10

Pres. Diosdado Macapagal (1910-97) A1093

2010, Sept. 28
3330 A1093 7p multi .55 .25

Day of the Galleon — A1094

No. 3331 — Galleon and map of: a, Pacific Ocean, East Asia, Western North America. b, Atlantic Ocean, Eastern North America, Western Europe and West Africa.

40p, Like #3331b.

2010, Oct. 8
3331 A1094 7p Horiz. pair, #a-b 1.10 1.10
c. Souvenir sheet of 2, #3331a-3331b 1.10 1.10

Souvenir Sheet

3332 Sheet of 2, #3331a, 3332a 3.75 3.75
a. A1094 40p multi 3.25 3.25

Intl. Year of Biodiversity — A1095

No. 3333 — Children's art by: a, Krysten Alarice Tan. b. Justen Paul Tolentino.

2010, Oct. 26
3333 A1095 7p Horiz. pair, #a-b 1.10 1.10

Philippine Rice Research Institute, 25th Anniv. — A1096

No. 3334: a, Building. b, Plants in test tubes. c, Farmer in field. d, Farm workers and tractor.

2010, Nov. 5 **Litho.** ***Perf. 14***
3334 A1096 7p Block of 4, #a-d 2.25 2.25

Pheepoy Types of 2009-10 Redrawn and

Pheepoy in Mail Van — A1097

2010, Nov. 8 ***Perf. 13½x13¾***
3335 A1097 7p multi, "Pheepoy" 7mm wide .55 .25

Souvenir Sheet

3336 Sheet of 4 2.25 2.25
a. A1052 7p multi, "Pheepoy" 6mm wide, dated "2010" .55 .25
b. A1072 7p multi, dark blue sky, dated "2010" .55 .25
c. A1076 7p multi, "Pheepoy" at bottom center .55 .25
d. A1097 7p multi, "Pheepoy" 6mm wide .55 .25
e. Sheet of 4, #3336f-3336i, imperf. 2.25 2.25
f. As "a," imperf. .55 .25
g. As "b," imperf. .55 .25
h. As "c," imperf. .55 .25
i. As "d," imperf. .55 .25

A1098

National Stamp Collecting Month — A1099

No. 3337: a, Levi Celerio (1910-2002), composer. b, Leonor Orosa Goquingco (1917-2005), dancer. c, Carlos L. Quirino (1910-99), historian. d, Nick Joaquin (1917-2004), writer.

No. 3338 — Fernando Poe, Jr. (1939-2004), actor: a, Scene from film *Ang Panday Ikatlong Yugto* (The Blacksmith, Part 3). b, Scene from film *Umpisahan Mo. . . Tatapusin Ko!* (You Start. . . I'll Finish). c, Scene from *Pepeng Kaliwete* (Pepe Lefty). d, Portrait.

2010 ***Perf. 14***

3337 A1098 7p Block of 4, #a-d 2.25 2.25
3338 A1099 7p Block of 4, #a-d 2.25 2.25
e. Souvenir sheet of 3, #3338a-3338c, + label 1.75 *2.00*

Issued: Nos. 3337, 3338e, 11/10; No. 3338, 11/25.

Inauguration of Vice-President Jejomar C. Binay — A1100

2010, Nov. 11 **Litho.** ***Perf. 14***

3339 A1100 7p multi .55 .25

Christmas — A1101

No. 3340: a, Holy Family in Filipino clothing, St. Peter's Basilica. b, Holy Family. c, Holy Family on jar. d, Adoration of the Shepherds.

2010, Nov. 23

3340 A1101 7p Block of 4, #a-d 2.25 2.25

Ateneo de Manila Class of 1960, 50th Anniv. — A1102

No. 3341: a, Ateneo de Manila emblems, "Fabilioh!" b, Eagle, cross on steeple, bell. c, Man, boy, statue of Virgin Mary. d, Bell.

2010, Dec. 2

3341 A1102 7p Block of 4, #a-d 2.25 2.25

New Year 2011 (Year of the Rabbit) A1103

Designs: 7p, Head of rabbit. 30p, Rabbit.

2010, Dec. 6

3342-3343 A1103 Set of 2 3.00 1.50
3343a Souvenir sheet of 4, 2 each #3342-3343 6.00 6.00

Senator Ambrosio B. Padilla (1910-90) — A1104

No. 3344 — Portrait of Padilla and: a, Padilla at microphone. b, Padilla playing basketball.

2010, Dec. 7

3344 A1104 7p Horiz. pair, #a-b 1.10 1.10

SyCip, Salazar, Hernandez & Gatmaitan Law Firm, 65th Anniv. A1105

2010, Dec. 10

3345 A1105 7p multi .55 .25

Grace Christian College, Manila, 60th Anniv. — A1106

No. 3346: a, Emblem and building. b, Emblem, "Grace at 60." c, Building, Chinese characters. d, Building, Chinese characters, founders Julia L. Tan, Dr. and Mrs. Edward Spahr.

2010, Dec. 16 ***Perf. 14***

3346 A1106 7p Block of 4, #a-d 2.25 2.25
e. Souvenir sheet of 4 #3346a-3346d 2.25 2.25
f. Block of 4, #3346g-3346j 2.25 2.25
g.-j. Like #3346a-3346d with "2010" date inside of frames, any single .55 .25
k. Souvenir sheet, #3346g-3346j 2.25 2.25

The "2010" year dates on Nos. 3346a-3346d and 3346e are below the frame lines at the lower right of each stamp. Issued: Nos. 3346f, 3346k, 5/10/11.

Valentine's Day — A1107

No. 3347 — Earth, hearts and Philippine Postal Corporation mascot Pheepoy: a, Carrying flowers. b, Driving postal van.

2011, Jan. 14 **Litho.** ***Perf. 14***

3347 A1107 7p Horiz. pair, #a-b 1.10 1.10

Kiwanis Club of Manila, 47th Anniv. — A1108

2011, Jan. 21

3348 A1108 7p multi .55 .25

University of Santo Tomas, Manila, 400th Anniv. — A1109

No. 3349: a, Main Building. b, Central Seminary. c, Arch of the Centuries. d, The foundation of the University of Santo Tomas by Archbishop Miguel de Benavides.

No. 3350, vert.: a, 7p, Statue of Archbishop Benavides. b, 30p, Quattro Mondial Monument.

2011, Jan. 25

3349 A1109 7p Block of 4, #a-d 2.25 2.25

Souvenir Sheet

3350 A1109 Sheet of 2, #a-b, + central label 3.00 3.00

Hoyas — A1110

No. 3351: a, Mindoro hoya. b, Grandmother's wax plant. c, Summer hoya. d, Benito Tan's hoya.

No. 3352: a, Siar's hoya. b, Shooting star hoya. c, Imperial hoya. d, Buot's hoya.

2011, Mar. 8

3351 A1110 7p Block of 4, #a-d 2.25 2.25

Souvenir Sheet

3352 A1110 7p Sheet of 4, #a-d, + 2 labels 2.25 2.25

University of the Philippines College of Law, Cent. — A1111

No. 3353 — Building and emblem with: a, Scales. b, Lady Justice (centennial emblem).

2011, Apr. 11

3353 A1111 7p Horiz. pair, #a-b 1.10 1.10

Center for Agriculture and Rural Development Mutually Reinforcing Institutions, 25th Anniv. — A1112

2011, Apr. 25

3354 A1112 7p multi .55 .25

Department of Budget and Management, 75th Anniv. — A1113

2011, Apr. 25 ***Perf. 13½***

3355 A1113 7p multi .55 .25

Wenceslao Q. Vinzons (1910-42), Leader of Resistance Forces in World War II — A1114

2011, May 3 ***Perf. 14***

3356 A1114 7p multi .55 .25

Dated 2010.

Marine Life Type of 2010

Designs: 1p, Dendronephthya soft coral. 2p, Yellowstripe snapper. 4p, Branded vexillum. 5p, Sea apple. 7p, Spotted boxfish. 9p, Broadclub cuttlefish. 10p, Mushroom coral. 17p, Cowfish. 20p, Two-banded anemone fish. 30p, Lipstick tang. 40p, Yellow-backed damselfish. 100p, Pink tube sponge.

2011 ***Perf. 13½x13¾***

3357	A1079	1p multi	.25	.25
3358	A1079	2p multi	.25	.25
3359	A1079	4p multi	.35	.25
3360	A1079	5p multi	.40	.25
3361	A1079	7p multi	.55	.25
3362	A1079	9p multi	.75	.35
3363	A1079	10p multi	.80	.40
3364	A1079	17p multi	1.40	.70
3365	A1079	20p multi	1.60	.80
3366	A1079	30p multi	2.40	1.25
3367	A1079	40p multi	3.25	1.60

Size: 40x30mm

Perf. 14

3368	A1079	100p multi	8.00	4.00
	Nos. 3357-3368 (12)		20.00	10.35

Issued: 1p, 5p, 7p, 9p, 8/17; 2p, 20p, 30p, 40p, 5/5; 4p, 10p, 17p, 100p, 5/12.

Worldwide Fund for Nature (WWF) A1115

Philippine crocodile: No. 3369, Hatchling and eggs (yellow and brown frame). No. 3370, Juvenile on log (olive green and yellow green frame). No. 3371, Adult on rock (blue green and blue frame). No. 3372, Adult with open mouth (orange and green frame).

2011, May 16 ***Perf. 14***

3369 A1115 7p multi .55 .25
3370 A1115 7p multi .55 .25
3371 A1115 7p multi .55 .25
3372 A1115 7p multi .55 .25
a. Block of 4, #3369-3372 2.25 2.25
Nos. 3369-3372 (4) 2.20 1.00

Nos. 3369-3372 each were printed in sheets of 8 and in sheets of 16 containing four of each stamp.

Arnis — A1116

No. 3373 — Arnis fighters wearing: a, Protective gear. b, White robes.

2011, May 23

3373 A1116 7p Horiz. pair, #a-b 1.10 1.10
c. Sheet of 4, 2 each #a-b 2.25 2.25

Beatification of Pope John Paul II — A1117

No. 3374 — Pope John Paul II and: a, Grandstand, Rizal Park (denomination in green at UL). b, University of Santo Tomas (denomination in red at UR). c, Philippine International Convention Center (denomination in red at UL). d, Popemobile (denomination in green at UR).

40p, Pope with crucifix, vert.

2011, May 30

3374 A1117 7p Block of 4, #a-d 2.25 2.25

Souvenir Sheet

3375 A1117 40p multi + 2 labels 3.25 3.25

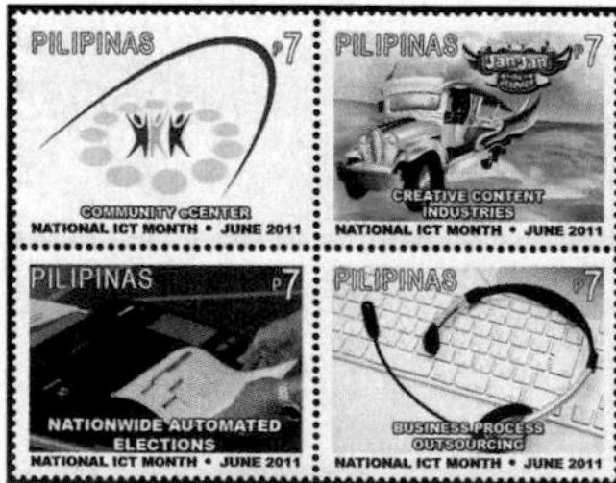

National Information and Communications Technology Month — A1118

No. 3376 — Inscriptions: a, Community eCenter. b, Creative content industries. c, Nationwide automated elections. d, Business process outsourcing.

2011, June 13

3376 A1118 7p Block of 4, #a-d 2.25 2.25

Security Bank Corporation, 60th Anniv. — A1119

No. 3377: a, Corporate Headquarters in 1951 and 2011. b, Company emblems.

2011, June 18

3377 A1119 10p Horiz. pair, #a-b 1.60 1.60

Goethe Institute in the Philippines, 50th Anniv. — A1120

No. 3378: a, José Rizal Statue, Wilhelmsfeld, Germany. b, Fountain from Wilhelmsfeld in Luneta Park. c, Residence of Rizal, Wilhelmsfeld. d, Anniversary emblem.

2011, June 19

3378 A1120 7p Block of 4, #a-d 2.25 2.25

A1121

A1122

José Rizal (1861-96), Patriot — A1123

No. 3379 — Rizal, anniversary emblem and: a, Dove, cover of *Noli Me Tangere*. b, Philippines flag elements.

No. 3380 — Annivesary emblem and Rizal in: a, Blue. b, Red.

No. 3381 — Philippines stamps depicting Rizal and monuments: a, 7p, #241, monument in Daet. b, 7p, #383, monument in Guinobatan. c, 7p, #461, monument in Santa Barbara. d, 7p, #497, monument in Biñan. e, 7p, #527, monument in Zamboanga. f, 12p, #813, monument in San Fernando. g, 13p, #857, monument in Lucban. h, 20p, #857A, monument in Romblon. i, 30p, #1313, monument in Jinjiang, China. j, 40p, #1198, monument in Illinois.

2011, June 19 ***Perf. 14***

3379 A1121 7p Horiz. pair, #a-b 1.10 1.10
3380 A1122 7p Horiz. pair, #a-b 1.10 1.10

Perf. 13¾

3381 A1123 Sheet of 10, #a-j 12.00 *20.00*

Yuchengco Group of Companies, Cent. — A1124

2011, July 20 ***Perf. 14***

3382 A1124 7p multi .55 .25

People Power Revolution, 25th Anniv. — A1125

No. 3383: a, Pres. Corazon C. Aquino (1933-2009), with collar visible, person with raised arm at LL, small helicopter at UL. b, Jaime Cardinal Sin (1928-2005), wearing biretta, helicopter at UR. c, Sin, without biretta, wearing black vestments, people with raised arms at left, helicopter at UL. d, Aquino, nun at LR.

No. 3384: a, Aquino, without collar visible, background like #3383a. b, Aquino, backgrond like #3383b. c, Aquino, background like #3383c. d, Sin, without biretta like #3383c, crowds in background. e, Sin, wearing white vestments, people carrying crucifix at right. f, Sin, wearing rosary around neck, crowds in background. g, Sin, wearing biretta like #3383b, religious statue at left.

2011, Aug. 1 **Litho.**

3383 A1125 7p Block of 4, #a-d 2.25 2.25
3384 A1125 7p Sheet of 8, #3383d, 3384a-3384g 4.50 4.50

Holy Cross of Davao College, 60th Anniv. — A1126

No. 3385: a, Bajada Campus facade. b, Grade school and high school buildings. c, Palma Gil and Mabutas Halls. d, Babak and Camudmud Campuses.

2011, Aug. 15 ***Perf. 14***

3385 A1126 7p Block of 4, #a-d 2.25 2.25

Mother Francisca del Espiritu Santo de Fuentes (1647-1711), Founder of Dominican Sisters of St. Catherine of Siena — A1127

2011, Aug. 24

3386 A1127 7p multi .55 .25

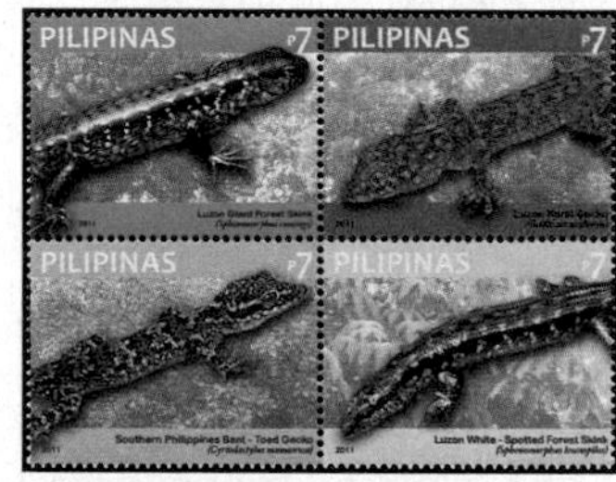

Lizards — A1128

No. 3387: a, Luzon giant forest skink. b, Luzon karst gecko. c, Southern Philippines bent-toed gecko. d, Luzon white-spotted forest skink.

No. 3388: a, Philippine forest dragon. b, Philippine spiny stream skink. c, Philippine sailfin lizard. d, Cordilleras slender skink.

2011, Aug. 30 ***Perf. 14***

3387 A1128 7p Block of 4, #a-d 2.25 2.25
3388 A1128 7p Sheet of 4, #a-d, + 2 labels 2.25 2.25

Marine Life Type of 2010 With Optical Code at Lower Right

Designs: 1p, Picasso triggerfish. 2p, Marmorated cone shell. 4p, Blue-faced angelfish. 5p, Copper-band butterflyfish. 7p, Murex shell. 9p, Polyclad flatworm. 10p, Triton trumpet shell. 13p, Valentine puffer. 17p, Polka-dot grouper. 20p, Bennett's feather star. 25p, Oriental sweetlips. 30p, Eibl's angelfish. 35p, Kunie's chromodoris. 40p, Royal empress angelfish. 100p, Regal tang.

2011 **Litho.** ***Perf. 14½***

3389	A1079	1p multi	.25	.25
3390	A1079	2p multi	.25	.25
3391	A1079	4p multi	.35	.25
3392	A1079	5p multi	.40	.25
3393	A1079	7p multi	.55	.25
3394	A1079	9p multi	.75	.35
3395	A1079	10p multi	.80	.40
3396	A1079	13p multi	1.10	.55
3397	A1079	17p multi	1.40	.70
3398	A1079	20p multi	1.60	.80
3399	A1079	25p multi	2.00	1.00
3400	A1079	30p multi	2.40	1.25
3401	A1079	35p multi	2.75	1.40
3402	A1079	40p multi	3.25	1.60

Size: 40x30mm

Perf. 13x13½

3403 A1079 100p multi 8.00 4.00
Nos. 3389-3403 (15) 25.85 13.30

Issued: 1p, 2p, 5p, 10p, 20p, 30p, 10/17; 4p, 7p, 100p, 10/25; 9p, 25p, 35p, 11/4; 13p, 17p, 40p, 11/11.

Intl. Year of Forests — A1129

No. 3404: a, Batlag Falls, Tanay. b, Tree, Pansol.

2011, Oct. 24 ***Perf. 13½x13***
3404 A1129 7p Horiz. pair, #a-b 1.10 1.10

Day of the Galleon A1130

Nos. 3405 and 3406: a, Galleon at right, map of East Asia. b, Galleon at left, map of Central and North America. c, Galleon at center, map of Atlantic Ocean, Europe and Africa.

2011, Nov. 10 ***Perf. 13x13½***
3405 Horiz. strip of 3 1.75 1.75
a.-c. A1130 7p Any single .55 .25

Souvenir Sheet

Perf. 13x13½ on 2 or 3 Sides

3406 Sheet of 3 + label 1.75 1.75
a.-c. A1130 7p Any single .55 .25

Adjacent stamps in No. 3406 are separated by simulated perforations.

Paintings by Hernando R. Ocampo (1911-78) — A1131

No. 3407: a, Homage to José Rizal. b, Break of Day. c, Summer in September. d, Mother and Child.

No. 3408, horiz.: a, Fiesta. b, Abstraction #15, 17. c, Kasaysayan ng Lahi. d, Abstraction #22, 26.

2011, Nov. 11 ***Perf. 13½x13***
3407 A1131 7p Block of 4, #a-d 2.25 2.25

Perf. 13x13½

3408 A1131 7p Sheet of 4, #a-d 2.25 2.25

Stamp Collecting Month.

National Bureau of Investigation, 75th Anniv. — A1132

No. 3409: a, Emblem of National Bureau of Investigation. b, Justice José Yulo and Pres. Manuel L. Quezon. c, Pres. Manuel A. Roxas signing bill, J. Pardo de Tavera, first director of National Bureau of Investigation. d, Fingerprint under magnifying glass, laptop computer, "Justice."

2011, Nov. 14 ***Perf. 13½x13***
3409 A1132 7p Block of 4, #a-d 2.25 2.25

Christmas — A1133

No. 3410: a, Bells. b, Poinsettias. c, Toys and gifts. d, Parol (Christmas star lantern).

2011, Nov. 26
3410 A1133 7p Block of 4, #a-d 2.25 2.25

New Year 2012 (Year of the Dragon) A1134

Designs: 7p, Head of dragon. 30p, Dragon.

2011, Dec. 5 ***Perf. 13x13½***
3411-3412 A1134 Set of 2 3.00 1.50
3412a Sheet of 4, 2 each #3411-3412 6.00 6.00

See Nos. 3435-3436.

Office of the Solicitor General, 110th Anniv. — A1135

2011, Dec. 15 ***Perf. 13½x13***
3413 A1135 7p multi .55 .25

Frogs — A1136

No. 3414: a, Philippine spiny cinnamon frog. b, Philippine pygmy forest frog. c, Philippine flat-headed frog. d, Luzon limestone forest frog.

No. 3415: a, Gliding tree frog. b, Northern Luzon tree-hole frog. c, Taylor's igorot frog. d, Mary Inger's wart frog.

2011, Dec. 15 ***Perf. 13x13½***
3414 A1136 7p Block of 4, #a-d 2.25 2.25
3415 A1136 7p Sheet of 4, #a-d + 2 labels 2.25 2.25

Lyceum of the Philippines University, 60th Anniv. — A1137

2012, Jan. 2 **Litho.** ***Perf. 12***
3416 A1137 7p multi .55 .25

Grand Lodge of Free and Accepted Masons of the Philippines, Cent. — A1138

No. 3417 — Centenary emblem and: a, Grand Lodge, Pres. Manuel L. Quezon. b, José Rizal, Marcelo H. del Pilar, Mariano Ponce, Plaridel Masonic Temple.

2012, Jan. 19
3417 A1138 7p Horiz. pair, #a-b 1.10 1.10

Diocese of Malolos, 50th Anniv. — A1139

No. 3418 — Centenary emblem and: a, Virgin of the Immaculate Conception of Malolos. b, Immaculate Conception Cathedral and Basilica.

40p, Virgin of the Immaculate Conception of Malolos, vert.

2012, Jan. 25
3418 A1139 7p Horiz. pair, #a-b 1.10 1.10

Souvenir Sheet

3419 A1139 40p multi + 2 labels 3.25 3.25

Davao, 75th Anniv. — A1140

No. 3420: a, Davao City Hall. b, Kadayawan Festival. c, Waling-waling orchids. d, Mt. Apo, Philippine eagle.

2012, Mar. 16 **Litho.** ***Perf. 14***
3420 A1140 7p Block of 4, #a-d 2.25 2.25

Ateneo de Zamboanga University, Cent. — A1141

No. 3421 — Centenary emblem and: a, Fort Pilar Shrine. b, Father William H. Kreutz, S.J. Campus. c, Ateneo Brebeuf Gymnasium. d, St. Ignatius of Loyola.

2012, Mar. 19
3421 A1141 7p Block of 4, #a-d 2.25 2.25
e. Souvenir sheet of 4, #3421a-3421d 2.25 2.25

St. Agnes Academy, Legazpi City, Cent. — A1142

No. 3422 — Centenary emblem and Main Building: a, Facade (denomination at UR). b, In ruins after World War II (denomination at UL). c, Facade, with flag at right (denomination at UR). d, Facade, flowers and flagpole in front (denomination at UL).

2012, Mar. 21
3422 A1142 7p Block of 4, #a-d 2.25 2.25

Maria Makiling, Mythical Forest Guardian — A1143

2012, Mar. 30 ***Perf. 13½x13¾***
3423 A1143 7p multi .55 .25

Asian-Pacific Postal Union, 50th Anniv. — A1144

Designs: 7p, Emblem and flags. 30p, Emblem, flags, Philippines #1323 (80x30mm).

2012, Apr. 1 ***Perf. 14***
3424-3425 A1144 Set of 2 3.00 1.50

Philippine Postal Corporation, 20th Anniv. — A1145

No. 3426: a, Pres. Corazon Aquino, Postal Service Act of 1992. b, Main Post Office, Manila.

2012, Apr. 10
3426 A1145 7p Horiz. pair, #a-b 1.10 1.10

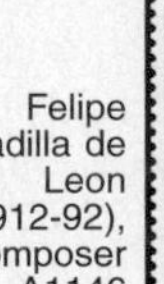

Felipe Padilla de Leon (1912-92), Composer
A1146

2012, May 1
3427 A1146 7p multi .55 .25

Churches — A1147

No. 3428: a, La Immaculada Concepcion Parish Church, Guiuan. b, San Joaquin Parish Church, San Joaquin. c, Nuestra Señora de la Porteria Parish Church, Daraga. d, San Isidro Labrador Parish Church, Lazi.

No. 3429: a, Santiago Apostol Parish Church, Betis. b, La Immaculada Concepcion Parish Church, Jasaan. c, Our Lady of Light Parish Church, Loon. d, San Gregorio Magno Parish Church, Majayjay.

2012, May 1
3428 A1147 7p Block of 4, #a-d 2.25 2.25

Souvenir Sheet

3429 A1147 7p Sheet of 4, #a-d 2.25 2.25

45th Annual Meeting of Asian Development Bank Board of Governors, Manila — A1148

2012, May 2 ***Perf. 14***
3430 A1148 7p multi .55 .25

Day of Valor, 70th Anniv.
A1149

Designs: 7p, Soldiers in Bataan Death March. 10p, Battery Hearn, Corregidor Island. 30p, Shrine of Valor, Mt. Samat, Bataan.

2012, May 6 **Litho.**
3431-3433 A1149 Set of 3 3.75 1.90

Government Service Insurance System, 75th Anniv. — A1150

No. 3434 — Emblem and: a, Head office in Solano, 1937 (25x22mm). b, Head office in Arroceros, 1957 (25x22mm). c, Financial Center, Pasay City (50x22mm).

2012, May 28 ***Perf. 13½x13¾***
3434 Horiz. strip of 3 4.50 4.50
a. A1150 7p multi .55 .25
b. A1150 9p multi .70 .35
c. A1150 40p multi 3.25 1.60

Year of the Dragon Type of 2011 Redrawn Without Line To Right of "Pilipinas" and Dated "2012"

Designs as before.

2012, June 8 ***Perf. 14***
3435-3436 A1134 Set of 2 3.00 1.50
3436a Souvenir sheet of 4, 2 each #3435-3436 6.00 6.00

Whitewater Rafters, Cagayan de Oro — A1151

2012, June 15
3437 A1151 9p multi .70 .35

Winning Design in Intl. Year of Forests Children's Art Contest — A1152

2012, June 18
3438 A1152 9p multi .70 .35

Bonifacio Monument, Caloocan
A1153

2012, June 25
3439 A1153 7p multi .55 .25

Habagat, God of Winds — A1154

2012, June 28 ***Perf. 13½x13¾***
3440 A1154 7p multi .55 .25

2012 Summer Olympics, London — A1155

No. 3441: a, Athletics. b, Shooting. c, Swimming. d, Boxing.

2012, July 27 ***Perf. 14***
3441 A1155 7p Block of 4, #a-d 2.25 2.25

Metrobank, 50th Anniv. — A1156

No. 3442: a, Binondo Branch, 1962. b, Metrobank Plaza, Makati City, 1977. c, GT International Tower, Makati City, 2004. d, Metrobank Plaza, Shanghai, People's Republic of China, 2001.

2012, Aug. 25 **Litho.**
3442 A1156 7p Block of 4, #a-d 2.25 2.25

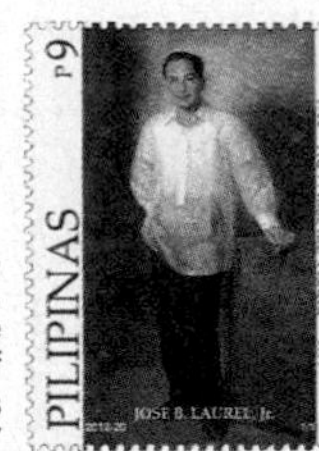

José B. Laurel, Jr. (1912-98), Speaker of the House of Representatives
A1157

2012, Aug. 27 ***Perf. 14***
3443 A1157 9p multi .70 .35

Ramon O. Valera (1912-72), Fashion Designer
A1158

2012, Aug. 31
3444 A1158 7p multi .55 .25

Amihan, Goddess of Monsoon Weather — A1159

2012, Sept. 28 ***Perf. 13½x13¾***
3445 A1159 7p multi .55 .25

Manila Hotel, Cent. — A1160

No. 3446: a, Facade. b, Maynila Ballroom. c, MacArthur Suite. d, Grand Lobby.

2012, Oct. 5 ***Perf. 14***
3446 A1160 7p Block of 4, #a-d 2.25 2.25

Marine Life Type of 2010-11

Designs: 1p, Twin-spot wrasse. 5p, Pearl-scale butterflyfish. 40p, Tassle filefish. 100p, Koran angelfish.

2012 ***Perf. 13½x13¾***
3447 A1079 1p multi .25 .25
3448 A1079 5p multi .40 .25
3449 A1079 40p multi 3.25 1.60

Size: 40x30mm

Perf. 14

3450 A1079 100p multi 8.00 4.00
Nos. 3447-3450 (4) 11.90 6.10

Issued: 1p, 5p, 40p, 10/18; 100p, 11/16.

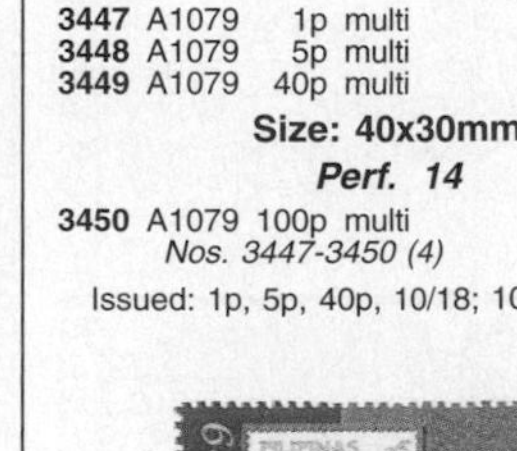

Canonization of Blessed Pedro Calungsod (1654-72) — A1161

2012, Oct. 21 ***Perf. 14***
3451 A1161 9p multi .70 .35

Carlos "Botong" Francisco (1912-69), Painter
A1162

2012, Nov. 4
3452 A1162 7p multi .55 .25

Christmas — A1163

No. 3453: a, Nativity. b, People arriving at church for dawn mass.

2012, Nov. 20 **Litho.**
3453 A1163 10p Horiz. pair, #a-b 1.60 1.60

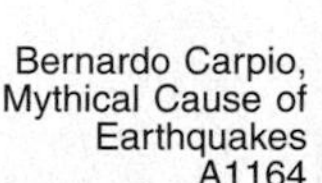

Bernardo Carpio, Mythical Cause of Earthquakes
A1164

2012, Nov. 28 ***Perf. 13½x13¾***
3454 A1164 7p multi .55 .25

Lepanto Consolidated Mining Corporation, 75th Anniv. — A1165

No. 3455: a, Reforestation. b, Miners in mine entrance.

2012, Dec. 7 **Litho.** ***Perf. 14***
3455 A1165 7p Horiz. pair, #a-b 1.10 1.10

New Year 2013 (Year of the Snake)
A1166

Designs: 10p, Head of snake. 30p, Coiled snake.

2012, Dec. 12 **Litho.** ***Perf. 14***
3456-3457 A1166 Set of 2 3.25 1.60
3457a Souvenir sheet of 4, 2 each #3456-3457 6.50 6.50

Miniature Sheet

Paintings of People Holding Roses — A1167

No. 3458 — Paintings by various artists numbered at LR: a, 1/10. b, 2/10. c, 3/10. d, 4/10. e, 5/10. f, 6/10. g, 7/10. h, 8/10. i, 9/10. j, 10/10.

2012, Dec. 14 ***Perf. 14***

3458 A1167 10p Sheet of 10, #a-j 8.00 8.00

Valentine's Day — A1168

2013, Jan. 14 **Litho.** ***Perf. 14***

3459 A1168 10p multi .80 .40

Far Eastern University Save the Tamaraw Project A1169

Designs: No. 3460, 10p, Tamaraw. No. 3461, 10p, Tamerarw, vert.

2013, Jan. 25 **Litho.** ***Perf. 14***

3460-3461 A1169 Set of 2 1.60 .80

Lucio D. San Pedro (1913-2002), Composer — A1170

2013, Feb. 11 **Litho.** ***Perf. 14***

3462 A1170 10p multi .80 .40

Teresita "Mama Sita" Reyes (1917-98), Restauranteur A1171

2013, Feb. 11 **Litho.** ***Perf. 14***

Stamp With Pink Shading at Top and Bottom

3463 A1171 10p multi .80 .40

Souvenir Sheet

Stamp with White Frame at Top and Bottom

3464 A1171 10p multi + 2 labels 1.00 1.00

Pitcher Plants — A1172

No. 3465: a, Nepenthes peltata. b, Nepenthes truncata. c, Nepenthes burkei. d, Nepenthes attenboroughii.

No. 3466: a, Nepenthes mindanaoensis. b, Nepenthes sibuyanensis. c, Nepenthes mira. d, Nepenthes mantalingajanensis.

2013, Mar. 13 **Litho.** ***Perf. 14***

3465 A1172 10p Block of 4, #a-d 3.25 3.25

Souvenir Sheet

Imperf

3466 A1172 10p Block of 4, #a-d 3.25 3.25

No. 3466 has simulated perforations.

University of the Philippines Alumni Association, Cent. — A1173

No. 3467: a, Emblem and Oblation, purple panel. b, Emblem and Carillon Tower, blue panel. c, Emblem and Ang Bahay Ng Building, green panel. d, Emblem, orange panel.

2013, Apr. 2 **Litho.** ***Perf. 14***

3467 A1173 10p Block of 4, #a-d 3.25 3.25

Diplomatic Relations Between Italy and the Philippines, 65th Annv. — A1174

No. 3468 — Flags of the Philippines and Italy and: a, Cinque Terre National Park, Italy. b, Banaue Rice Terraces, Philippines.

2013, Apr. 4 **Litho.** ***Perf. 14***

3468 A1174 40p Pair, #a-b 6.50 3.25

Edible Nuts and Seeds — A1175

No. 3469: a, Cashews. b, Pili nuts. c, Watermelon seeds. d, Peanuts.

No. 3470: a, Sunflower seeds. b, Mung beans. c, Coffee beans. d, Squash seeds.

2013, Apr. 15 **Litho.** ***Perf. 14***

3469 A1175 10p Block of 4, #a-d 3.25 3.25

Souvenir Sheet

3470 A1175 10p Sheet of 4, #a-d 3.25 3.25

Marine Life Type of 2010-11

Designs: 1p, Pinecone fish. 3p, Purple firefish. 5p, Pyjama cardinalfish. No. 3474, Long-nosed butterflyfish. No. 3475, Longnose filefish. 13p, Raccoon butterflyfish. 20p, Fire clown. 25p, Two-lined monocle bream. 30p, Green chromis. 40p, Common squirrelfish. 100p, Black-backed butterflyfish.

2013 **Litho.** ***Perf. 13½x13¾***

3471	A1079	1p	multi	.25	.25
3472	A1079	3p	multi	.25	.25
3473	A1079	5p	multi	.40	.25
3474	A1079	10p	multi	.80	.40
3475	A1079	10p	multi	.80	.40
3476	A1079	13p	multi	1.10	.55
3477	A1079	20p	multi	1.60	.80
3478	A1079	25p	multi	2.00	1.00
3479	A1079	30p	multi	2.40	1.25
3480	A1079	40p	multi	3.25	1.60

Size: 40x30mm

Perf. 14

3481	A1079	100p	multi	8.00	4.00
	Nos. 3471-3481 (11)			20.85	10.75

Issued: 1p, 100p, 12/6; 3p, 5p, #3475, 13p, 12/10; #3474, 4/23; 20p, 40p, 12/13; 25p, 30p, 12/16.

Jesse M. Robredo (1958-2012), Interior Secretary A1176

2013, May 27 **Litho.** ***Perf. 14***

3482 A1176 10p multi .80 .40

Philpost Emblem and Manila Central Post Office — A1177

Philpost Emblem A1178

2013, May 29 **Litho.** ***Perf. 13½x13¼***

Denomination Color

3483	A1177	1p	brown	.25	.25
3484	A1177	7p	blue gray	.55	.30
3485	A1177	9p	org brn	.75	.35
3486	A1177	12p	yel org	.95	.50
3487	A1177	30p	orange	2.40	1.25
3488	A1177	35p	violet	2.75	1.40
3489	A1177	40p	green	3.25	1.60
3490	A1177	45p	lilac	3.75	1.00

Perf. 14

3491	A1178	100p	dull vio brn	8.00	4.00
	Nos. 3483-3491 (9)			22.65	11.55

See Nos. 3593-3594.

Malacañan Palace, Manila, 150th Anniv. — A1179

Perf. 13½x13¾

2013, June 11 **Litho.**

3492 A1179 10p multi .80 .40

Miniature Sheet

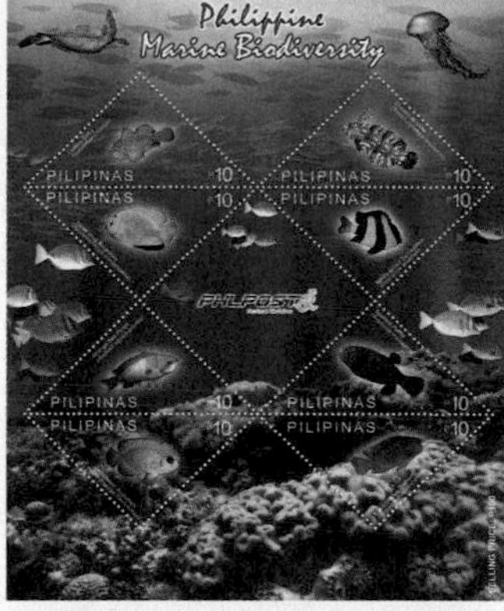

Marine Biodiversity — A1180

No. 3493: a, Lemon goby. b, Dragon wrasse. c, Three-spot angelfish. d, White-tailed damselfish. e, Orange sea perch. f, Spotted puffer. g, Lemonpeel angelfish. h, Electric blue damsel.

2013, Aug. 2 **Litho.** ***Perf. 12***

3493 A1180 10p Sheet of 8, #a-h, + central label 8.00 8.00

i. As #3493, with Thailand 2013 World Stamp Exhibition emblem on center label 8.00 8.00

Nos. 3493 and 3493i each sold for 100p.

Shrimp — A1181

No. 3494: a, Banded deep-sea spiny shrimp. b, Deep-sea shrimp. c, Huxley's scissor-foot shrimp. d, Deep-sea armored shrimp.

2013, Aug. 8 **Litho.** ***Perf. 14***

3494 A1181 10p Block of 4, #a-d 3.25 3.25

e. Souvenir sheet of 4, #3494a-3494d 3.25 3.25

Mariano Ponce (1863-1918), Writer — A1182

2013, Sept. 5 **Litho.** ***Perf. 14***

3495 A1182 10p multi .80 .40

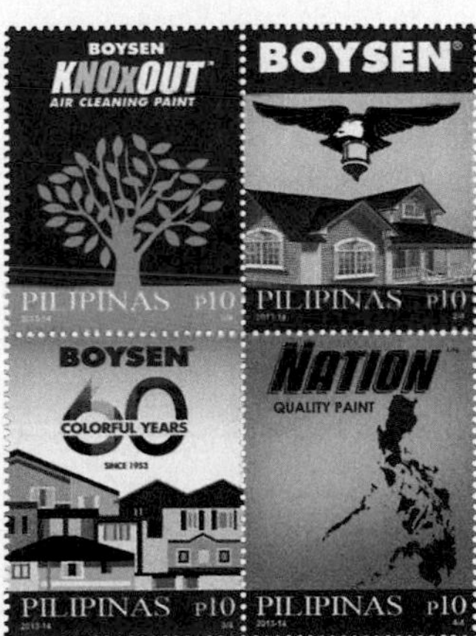

Boysen Paints, 60th Anniv. — A1183

No. 3496: a, Tree, logo for Knoxout Air Cleaning Paint. b, Boysen logo, eagle with paint can, house. c, Houses, anniversary emblem. d, Map of Philippines, logo for Nation Quality Paint.
40p, Eagle with paint can, horiz.

2013, Sept. 9 Litho. *Perf. 14*
3496 A1183 10p Block of 4, #a-d 3.25 3.25

Souvenir Sheet

3497 A1183 40p multi + 2 labels 3.25 3.25

No. 3497 contains one 80x30mm stamp.

Gerardo "Gerry" De León (1913-81), Film Actor and Director A1184

2013, Sept. 12 Litho. *Perf. 14*
3498 A1184 10p multi .80 .40

50th Fish Conservation Week — A1185

No. 3499 — Winning paintings of endangered species in Bureau of Fisheries and Aquatic Resources art contest: a, Green Sea Turtle with Giant Manta Ray and Hammerhead Sharks, by Jaylord G. Aligway. b, Tabios (dwarf pygmy goby), by Jon Carlos A. Tabios. c, Butanding (whale shark), by Bernardo V. Vergara, Jr.
40p, Tabios, by Tabios, diff.

2013, Oct. 14 Litho. *Perf. 14*
3499 Horiz. strip of 3 2.40 2.40
a.-c. A1185 10p Any single .80 .40

Souvenir Sheet

3500 A1185 40p multi + label 3.25 3.25

Motorized Tricycles — A1186

No. 3501 — Tricycle from: a, Cabadbaran. b, Puerto Princesa. c, Ozamiz City. d, Bukidnon.

2013, Nov. 13 Litho. *Perf. 14*
3501 A1186 10p Block of 4, #a-d 3.25 3.25
e. Souvenir sheet of 4, #3501a-3501d 3.25 3.25

Souvenir Sheet

Rodolfo "Dolphy" Vera Quizon (1928-2012), Comedian — A1187

Litho. With Foil Application

2013, Nov. 23 *Perf. 14*
3502 A1187 100p multi + label 8.00 8.00

A1188

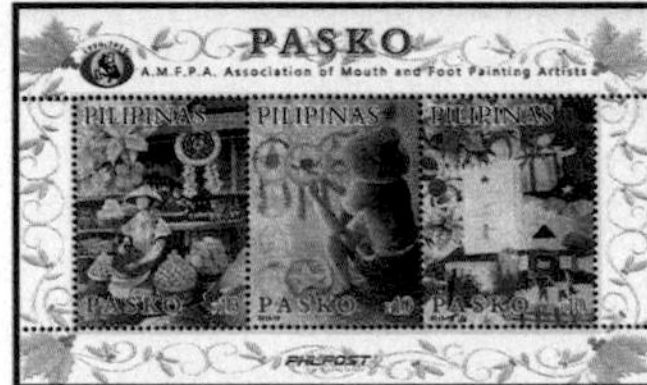

Christmas — A1189

No. 3503 — Paintings by Filipino members of Association of Mouth and Foot Painting Artists: a, The Family, by Jovita Sasutona (1/4). b, The Nativity Star, by Sasutona (2/4). c, Christmas Lantern, by Amado Dulnuan (3/4). d, Christmas at the Lake, by Bernard Pesigan (4/4).
No. 3504: a, Fruit Stand, by Sasutona. b, Lantern Maker, by Sasutona. c, Season Delight, by Sasutona.

2013, Nov. 25 Litho. *Perf. 14*
3503 A1188 10p Block of 4, #a-d 3.25 3.25

Souvenir Sheet

3504 A1189 10p Sheet of 3, #a-c 2.40 2.40

Andrés Bonifacio (1863-97), Founder of Katipunan Revolutionary Movement — A1190

No. 3505 — Winning designs in art contest: a, Dangal at Kabayanihan, by Roderick C. Macutay (1/4). b, Bonifacio Monument, by Marrion Dabalos (2/4). c, Dangal at Kabayanihan, by John Mark Nathaniel Trancales (3/4). d, Bonifacio, the Great Plebeian, by Julius R. Satparam (4/4).
No. 3506 — 150th anniversary emblem and vignette of: a, 30p, #3505a. b, 35p, #3505b. c, 40p, #3505d. d, 45p, #3505c.

2013, Nov. 30 Litho. *Perf. 14*
3505 A1190 10p Block of 4, #a-d 3.25 3.25

Miniature Sheet

3506 A1190 Sheet of 4, #a-d 12.00 12.00

No. 3506 contains four 30x80mm stamps.

New Year 2014 (Year of the Horse) A1191

Chinese characters and: 10p, Horse's head. 30p, Horse.

2013, Dec. 2 Litho. *Perf. 14*
3507-3508 A1191 Set of 2 3.25 1.60
3508a Souvenir sheet of 4, 2 each #3507-3508 6.50 6.50

Philippine Deposit Insurance Corporation, 50th Anniv. — A1192

2013, Dec. 5 Litho. *Perf. 14*
3509 A1192 10p multi .80 .40

National Parks Development Committee, 50th Anniv. — A1193

2013, Dec. 5 Litho. *Perf. 14*
3510 A1193 20p multi 1.60 .80

Parts of the design are covered with ink that glows in the dark.

Diplomatic Relations Between Nigeria and the Philippines, 50th Anniv. — A1194

No. 3511 — Flags of Philippines and Nigeria and: a, 10p, Coat of arms of Nigeria, daisies. b, 45p, Coat of arms of the Philippines, sampaguita flowers.

2013, Dec. 20 Litho. *Perf. 14*
3511 A1194 Horiz. pair, #a-b 4.50 4.50

See Nigeria Nos. 853-854.

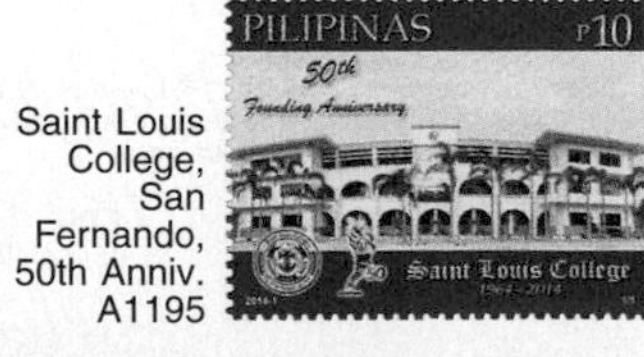

Saint Louis College, San Fernando, 50th Anniv. A1195

2014, Jan. 20 Litho. *Perf. 14*
3512 A1195 10p multi .80 .40

Valentine's Day A1196

2014, Jan. 27 Litho. *Perf. 14*
3513 A1196 10p multi .80 .40

Souvenir Sheet

New Year 2014 (Year of the Horse) — A1197

No. 3514: a, 50p, Snake (40x30mm). b, 50p, Goat (40x30mm). c, 100p, Horse (50x40mm).

Perf. 13¼x13x13¼x13¼ (#3514a), 13¼x13¼x13¼x13 (#3514b), 13 (#3514c)

Litho., Litho. & Embossed With Foil Application (100p)

2014, Jan. 31
3514 A1197 Sheet of 3, #a-c 16.00 16.00

Selection of Megan Lynne Young as Miss World 2013 — A1198

No. 3515 — Young with: a, 30p, Arms not visible. b, 40p, Arms visible.
No. 3516: a, Like #3515a. b, Like #3515b.

2014, Feb. 24 Litho. *Perf. 14*
3515 A1198 Horiz. pair, #a-b 5.75 5.75

Souvenir Sheet

Litho. & Embossed With Foil Application

3516 A1198 50p Sheet of 2, #a-b 8.00 8.00

Main Post Office, Manila — A1199

2014, Feb. 24 Litho. *Perf. 14*
3517 A1199 35p multi 2.75 2.75

No. 3517 was printed in sheets of six that sold for 250p. The right half of the stamp could be personalized.

Alpha Phi Beta Fraternity at University of Philippines, 75th Anniv. — A1200

No. 3518: a, 75th anniv. emblem (1/4). b, 75th anniv. emblem, University of the Philippines emblem, statue (2/4). c, Statue, University building and emblem, fraternity members,

75th anniv. emblem (3/4). d, Silhouettes of statues, 75th anniv. emblem (4/4).

2014, Mar. 8 Litho. *Perf. 14*
3518 A1200 10p Block of 4, #a-d 3.25 3.25

Election of Pope Francis, 1st Anniv. — A1201

2014, Mar. 21 Litho. *Perf. 14*
3519 A1201 40p multi 3.25 1.60

See Vatican City Nos. 1553-1556.

Beach on Boracay Island — A1202

2014, Mar. 28 Litho. *Perf. 14*
3520 A1202 15p multi *3.50 3.50*

No. 3520 was printed in sheets of six that sold for 250p. The right half of the stamp could be personalized.

Watchtowers — A1203

No. 3521 — Watchtower at: a, Luna, La Union Province. b, Panglao, Bohol Province. c, Oslob, Cebu Province. d, Narvacan, Ilocos Sur Province.

No. 3522, vert. — Watchtower at: a, Boljoon, Cebu Province. b, Bantay, Ilocos Sur Province. c, Samboan, Cebu Province. d, Tabaco, Albay Province.

Litho. & Silk-Screened

2014, Mar. 28 *Perf. 14*
3521 A1203 25p Block of 4, #a-d 8.00 8.00

Miniature Sheet

3522 A1203 25p Sheet of 4, #a-d 8.00 8.00

Central Luzon State University, 50th Anniv. — A1204

No. 3523 — 50th anniv. emblem and: a, Science and Technology Centrum. b, José Rizal.

2014, Apr. 4 Litho. *Perf. 14*
3523 A1204 10p Horiz. pair, #a-b 1.60 1.60

Souvenir Sheets

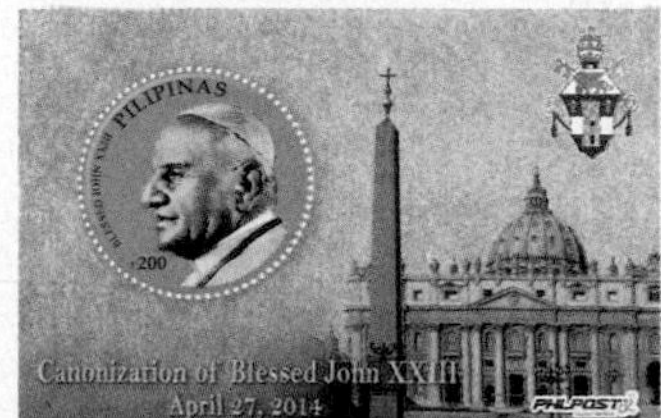

2014 Canonization of Popes — A1205

Designs: No. 3524, 200p, Pope John XXIII. No. 3525, 200p, Pope John Paul II.

Litho. & Embossed

2014, Apr. 27 *Perf.*
3524-3525 A1205 Set of 2 32.00 16.00

Philippine Charity Sweepstakes Office, 80th Anniv. — A1206

No. 3526: a, People at Lotto office (1/2). b, Family, sweepstakes office vehicle (2/2).

2014, Apr. 28 Litho. *Perf. 14*
3526 A1206 10p Horiz. pair, #a-b 1.60 1.60

Minister Felix Y. Manalo (1886-1963) and Iglesia ni Cristo Central Temple, Quezon City — A1207

2014, May 10 Litho. *Perf. 13½*
3527 A1207 10p multi .80 .40

Iglesia ni Cristo, cent.

Teresita "Mama Sita" Reyes (1917-98), Restauranteur — A1208

No. 3528 — Reyes, various foods, with background colors of: a, Orange (1/4). b, Lilac (2/4). c, Blue green (3/4). d, Orange and red (4/4).

2014, May 11 Litho. *Perf. 14*
3528 A1208 10p Block of 4, #a-d 3.25 3.25

San Bartolome Parish, 400th Anniv. — A1209

2014, May 17 Litho. *Perf. 14*
3529 A1209 20p multi 1.60 .80

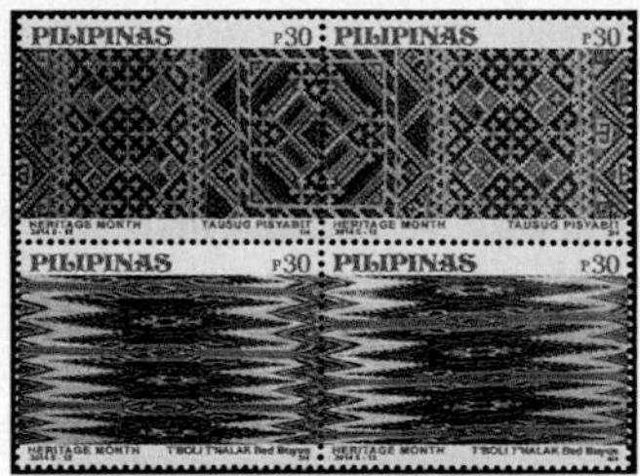

Heritage Month — A1210

No. 1210 — Various textile designs numbered: a, (1/4). b, (2/4). c, (3/4). d, (4/4). 100p, Weaver.

Litho. & Silk-Screened

2014, May 30 *Perf. 14*
3530 A1210 30p Block of 4, #a-b 9.75 9.75

Souvenir Sheet

Perf. 13½x13¾

3531 A1210 100p multi 8.00 8.00

No. 3531 contains one 50x35mm stamp.

Diplomatic Relations Between the Philippines and Germany, 60th Anniv. — A1211

No. 3532 — Flags of the Philippines and Germany and: a, 20p, Brandenburg Gate, Berlin. b, 40p, People Power Revolution Monument, Quezon City.

2014, June 25 Litho. *Perf. 14*
3532 A1211 Horiz. pair, #a-b 5.00 5.00

Aquatic Flowers — A1212

No. 3533: a, Lotus. b, Amazon lily. c, Water lily. d, Water hyacinth.
40p, Marsh marigold, horiz.

2014, June 27 Litho. *Perf. 14*
3533 A1212 10p Block of 4, #a-d 3.25 3.25

Souvenir Sheet

3534 A1212 40p multi 3.25 3.25

Kapatagan Municipal Building, Seal of Kapatagan, Cathedral Falls A1213

2014, July 5 Litho. *Perf. 14*
3535 A1213 10p multi .80 .40

Kapatagan, Lanao del Norte Province, 65th anniv.

DZRH Radio Station, 75th Anniv. — A1214

2014, July 15 Litho. *Perf. 14*
3536 A1214 25p multi 2.00 1.00

Apolinario Mabini (1864-1903), Prime Minister — A1215

No. 3537 — 150th anniv. emblem and depiction of Mabini by: a, Pinky Ludovice. b, Kenneth V. Cantimbuhan. c, Julius R. Satparam.
40p, Mabini, by Dylan Ray A. Talon.

2014, July 23 Litho. *Perf. 14*
3537 Horiz. strip of 3 2.40 2.40
a.-c. A1215 10p Any single .80 .80

Souvenir Sheet

3538 A1215 40p multi + label 3.25 3.25

ISO 9001: 2008 Certification of University of Mindanao — A1216

No. 3539: a, Bolton Campus. b, University emblem and check mark.

2014, July 27 Litho. *Perf. 14*
3539 A1216 10p Horiz. pair, #a-b 1.60 1.60

Paintings by Pres. Corazon C. Aquino (1933-2009) — A1217

No. 3540: a, Enchanting Blossoms. b, Overflowing with Good Wishes. c, Blooms of Unity. d, Fifth Painting.
100p, Rosary and Roses.

2014, Aug. 1 Litho. *Perf. 14*
3540 A1217 25p Block of 4, #a-d 8.00 8.00

Souvenir Sheet

Perf. 13½x13¾

3541 A1217 100p multi 8.00 8.00

Nos. 3540-3541 are impregnated with a rose scent. No. 3541 contains one 50x35mm stamp.

Scouting in the Philippines, Cent. — A1218

No. 3542 — Centennial emblem and emblem of Philippines Scouting and: a, Boy Scout in Action Monument. b, Old and new Boy Scout National Headquarters.

30p, Emblems, Boy Scout in Action Monument, map of Philippines, vert.

2014, Aug. 30 Litho. *Perf. 14*
3542 A1218 10p Horiz. pair, #a-b 1.60 1.60

Souvenir Sheet

3543 A1218 30p multi 2.40 2.40

No. 3543 contains one 30x80mm stamp.

National Teachers' Month — A1219

2014, Sept. 5 Litho. *Perf. 14*
3544 A1219 10p multi .80 .40

University of San Carlos College of Engineering, 75th Anniv. — A1220

2014, Sept. 8 Litho. *Perf. 14*
3545 A1220 10p multi .80 .40

Waterfalls — A1221

No. 3546: a, Balagbag Falls. b, Merloquet Falls. c, Tinago Falls. d, Asik-asik Falls.
40p, Tinuy-an Falls.

Perf. 13½x13¾
2014, Sept. 22 Litho.
3546 A1221 10p Block of 4, #a-d 3.25 3.25

Souvenir Sheet

3547 A1221 40p multi 3.25 3.25

No. 3547 contains one 100x35mm stamp.

National Family Week — A1222

No. 3548 — Winning art in stamp design contest by: a, Leah Anne Rulloda. b, Maria Joannes R. Puno.

2014, Sept. 26 Litho. *Perf. 14*
3548 A1222 10p Horiz. pair, #a-b 1.60 1.60

Quezon City, 75th Anniv. — A1223

No. 3549: a, Tandang Sora Shrine. b, Emilio Jacinto Shrine. c, North EDSA Shopping Mall. d, University of Philippines Ayala Techno Hub.
100p, Quezon Memorial Circle, horiz.

2014, Oct. 12 Litho. *Perf. 13¾x13½*
3549 A1223 10p Block of 4, #a-d 3.25 3.25

Litho. & Silk-Screened (Margin With Foil Application)

Souvenir Sheet

Perf. 13¾ Horiz.

3550 A1223 100p multi 8.00 8.00

No. 3550 contains one 86x50mm stamp.

Leyte Gulf Landing, 70th Anniv. — A1224

2014, Oct. 20 Litho. *Perf. 14*
3551 A1224 10p multi .80 .40

Christmas — A1225

No. 3552: a, Holy Family (1/4). b, Carolers (2/4). c, Respect for elders (3/4). d, Christmas Eve feast (4/4).

2014, Oct. 30 Litho. *Perf. 14*
3552 A1225 10p Block of 4, #a-d 3.25 3.25

Growing Plant — A1226

2014, Nov. 8 Litho. *Perf. 14*
3553 A1226 10p multi .80 .40

Philippine recovery after Typhoon Haiyan.

First Philippine Postage Stamps, 160th Anniv. — A1227

No. 3554 and 3555
Philippines #1-2, 4-5, with large illustration of: a, #1. b, #2. c, #4. d, #5.

Perf. 13½x13¾
2014, Nov. 10 Litho.
3554 A1227 10p Block of 4, #a-d 3.25 1.60
3555 A1227 20p Sheet of 4, #a-d 6.50 3.25

National Stamp Collecting Month.

Filipino-Chinese General Chamber of Commerce, 110th Anniv. — A1228

No. 3556: a, Traders, ship, abacuses (1/2). b, People with computer, city skyline, airplane (2/2).

2014, Nov. 19 Litho. *Perf. 14*
3556 A1228 10p Horiz. pair, #a-b 1.60 1.60

Festival Masks and Facial Decorations A1229

No. 3557: a, Moriones Festival mask. b, Higantes Festival mask. c, Pintados Festival face decoration.
100p, Masskara Festival mask, horiz.

2014, Nov. 22 Litho. *Perf. 14*
3557 Horiz. strip of 3 2.40 2.40
a.-c. A1229 10p Any single .80 .80

Litho. & Silk-Screened

Souvenir Sheet

3558 A1229 100p multi 8.00 8.00

No. 3558 contains one 80x30mm stamp.

New Year 2015 (Year of the Goat) — A1229a

Designs: 10p, Head of goat. 30p, Goat.

2014, Nov. 24 Litho. *Perf. 14*
3558A-3558B A1229a Set of 2 3.25 1.60
3558Bc Souvenir sheet of 4, 2 each #3558A-3558B 6.50 3.25

Claudio Teehankee (1918-89), Chief Justice — A1230

2014, Nov. 27 Litho. *Perf. 14*
3559 A1230 10p multi .80 .40

St. Paul University, Dumaguete City, 110th Anniv. — A1231

2014, Dec. 8 Litho. *Perf. 14*
3560 A1231 10p multi .80 .40

National Anti-Corruption Day — A1232

2014, Dec. 9 Litho. *Perf. 14*
3561 A1232 10p multi .80 .40

Shell Oil in the Philippines, Cent. — A1233

No. 3562: a. Shell Tabangao Refinery, 1960s (1/4). b, Shell Tabangao Refinery, 2014 (2/4). c, Shell retail station, 1930s (3/4). d, Shell retail station, 2014 (4/4).

Litho. With Foil Application

2014, Dec. 13 *Perf. 13½x13¼*
3562 A1233 25p Block of 4, #a-d 8.00 8.00

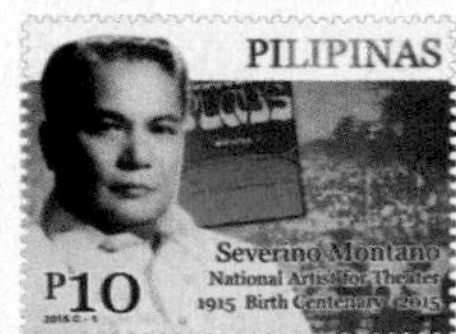

Severino Montano (1915-80), Playwright A1234

2015, Jan. 3 Litho. *Perf. 14*
3563 A1234 10p multi .80 .40

A1235

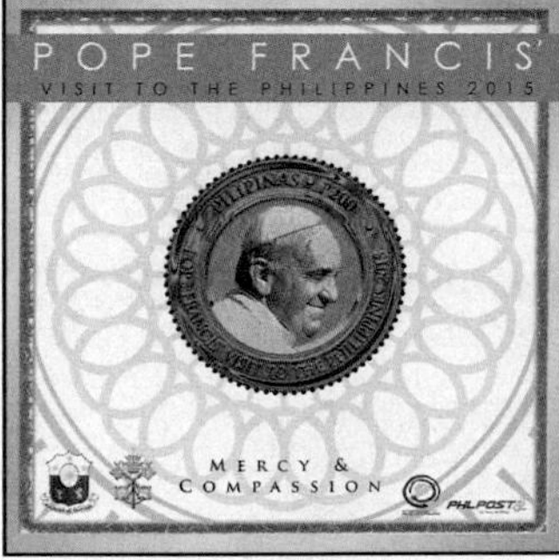

Visit of Pope Francis to the Philippines — A1236

No. 3564 — Winning art in Pope Francis stamp design contest by: a, Bryan Michael Bunag (1/4). b, Dave Arjay Tan (2/4). c, Salvador Banares, Jr. (3/4). d, Mark Leo Maac (4/4).
100p, Pope Francis.

2015 Litho. *Perf. 14*

3564 A1235 10p Block of 4, #a-d 3.25 3.25

Litho. & Embossed With Foil Application

Souvenir Sheet

Perf.

3565 A1236 200p multi 16.00 8.00

Issued: No. 3564, 1/8; No. 3565, 1/12.

St. Valentine's Day A1237

No. 3566 — Hearts and: a, Cupid (1/4). b, Boy and girl (2/4). c, Bride and groom (3/4). d, Elderly couple (4/4).

2015, Jan. 14 Litho. *Perf. 14*

3566 Horiz. strip of 4 3.25 3.25
a.-d. A1237 10p Any single .80 .80

Open Doors Monument, Rishon LeZion, Israel, Flags of Philippines and Israel — A1238

2015, Jan. 27 Litho. *Perf. 14*

3567 A1238 35p multi 3.00 1.50

See Israel No. 2048.

Laua-an, Cent. — A1239

2015, Jan. 31 Litho. *Perf. 14*

3568 A1239 10p multi .80 .40

Fruit — A1240

Designs: No. 3569, Bananas. No. 3570, Black plums. 3p, Mangos. No. 3572, Papayas. No. 3573, Aratiles fruit. No. 3574, Pineapples. No. 3575, Rose apples. 13p, Lanzones. No. 3577, Santols. No. 3578, Strawberries. 25p, Custard apples. No. 3580, Soursops. No. 3581, Ramboutaniers. No. 3582, Avocados. No. 3583, Jocotes. No. 3584, Cashew fruit. No. 3585, Johey oaks.

Perf. 13½, 12¾ (#3570, 3573, 3575, 3578, 3581, 3583, 3585)

2015 Litho.

3569	A1240	1p	multi	.25	.25
3570	A1240	1p	multi	.25	.25
3571	A1240	3p	multi	.25	.25
3572	A1240	5p	multi	.40	.25
3573	A1240	5p	multi	.40	.25
3574	A1240	10p	multi	.80	.40
3575	A1240	10p	multi	.80	.40
3576	A1240	13p	multi	1.10	.55
3577	A1240	20p	multi	1.60	.80
3578	A1240	20p	multi	1.60	.80
3579	A1240	25p	multi	2.00	1.00
3580	A1240	30p	multi	2.40	1.25
3581	A1240	30p	multi	2.40	1.25
3582	A1240	40p	multi	3.25	1.60
3583	A1240	40p	multi	3.25	1.60

Size: 43x43mm

3584	A1240	100p	multi	8.00	4.00
3585	A1240	100p	multi	8.00	4.00
	Nos. 3569-3585 (17)			36.75	18.90

Issued: Nos. 3569, 3584, 3/12; Nos. 3570, 3585, 12/15; 3p, 13p, 25p, No. 3580, 2/10; Nos. 3572, 3577, 2/6; Nos. 3573, 3575, 3578, 12/10; Nos. 3574, 3582, 2/4; Nos. 3581, 3583, 12/11.

Salud S. Tesoro (1915-2000), Business Entrepreneur A1241

2015, Feb. 6 Litho. *Perf. 13¾x13½*

3586 A1241 10p multi .80 .40

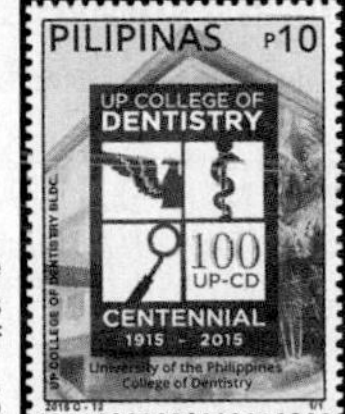

University of the Philippines College of Dentistry, Cent. — A1242

2015, Feb. 6 Litho. *Perf. 14*

3587 A1242 10p multi .80 .40

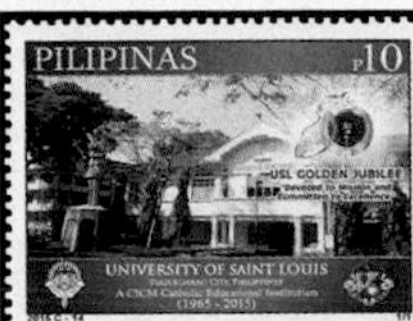

University of Saint Louis, Baguio, 50th Anniv. A1243

2015, Feb. 11 Litho. *Perf. 14*

3588 A1243 10p multi .80 .40

Lamberto V. Avellana (1915-91), Film Director A1244

2015, Feb. 12 Litho. *Perf. 14*

3589 A1244 10p multi .80 .40

Philippine Health Insurance Corporation, 20th Anniv. — A1245

2015, Feb. 14 Litho. *Perf. 14*

3590 A1245 10p multi .80 .40

Souvenir Sheet

New Year 2015 (Year of the Goat) — A1246

No. 3514: a, 50p, Horse (40x30mm). b, 50p, Monkey (40x30mm). c, 100p, Goat (50x40mm).

Perf. 13¼x13x13¼x13¼ (#3591a), 13¼x13¼x13¼x13 (#3591b), 13 (#3591c)

Litho., Litho. & Embossed With Foil Application (100p)

2015, Feb. 19

3591 A1246 Sheet of 3, #a-c 16.00 8.00

Liceo de Cagayan University, Cagayan de Oro City, 60th Anniv. — A1247

2015, Feb. 24 Litho. *Perf. 14*

3592 A1247 10p multi .80 .40

Philpost Type of 2013

Perf. 13½x13¼

2015, Mar. 20 Litho.

Denomination Color

3593	A1177	10p	brown	.80	.40
3594	A1177	15p	gray olive	1.25	.60

Visit the Philippines Year — A1248

Perf. 13¾x13½

2015, Mar. 25 Litho.

3595 A1248 10p multi .80 .40

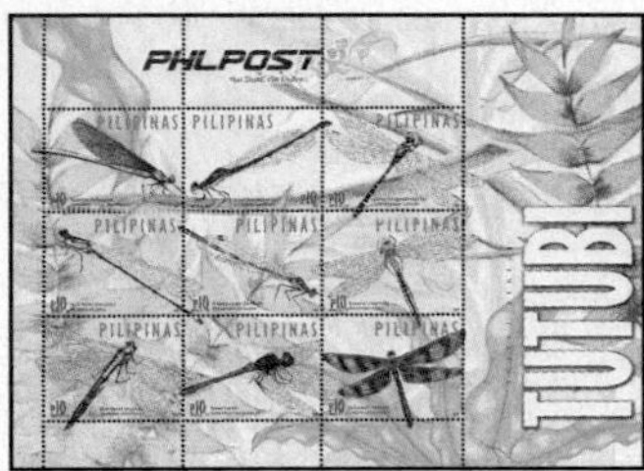

Dragonflies — A1249

No. 3596: a, Beautiful demoiselle. b, Small red damselfly. c, Golden-ringed dragonfly. d, Blue-tailed damselfly, e, White-legged damselfly. f, Emperor dragonfly. g, Club-tailed dragonfly. h, Ruddy darter. i, Halloween pennant.
40p, Broad-bodied chaser.

2015, Mar. 27 Litho. *Perf. 14*

3596 A1249 10p Sheet of 9, #a-i 7.25 3.75

Souvenir Sheet

Perf. 13½x13¾

3597 A1249 40p multi + label 3.25 1.60

No. 3597 contains one 50x35mm stamp.

A1250

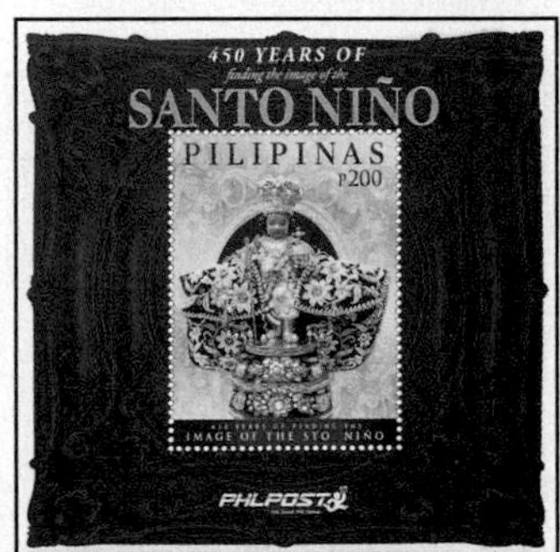

Discovery of Santo Niño Icon of Cebu, 450th Anniv. — A1251

2015, Apr. 20 Litho. *Perf. 14*

3598 A1250 10p multi .80 .40

Souvenir Sheet

Litho. & Embossed, Sheet Margin Litho. & Embossed With Foil Application

Perf. 13¼

3599 A1251 200p multi 16.00 8.00

Philippine Econonic Zone Authority, 20th Anniv. — A1252

2015, Apr. 20 Litho. *Perf. 14*
3600 A1252 10p multi .80 .40

Souvenir Sheet

Litho. & Embossed With Foil Application

Perf.

3601 A1252 200p Emblem, diff. 16.00 8.00

No. 3601 contains one 38mm diameter stamp.

Emmanuel "Manny" Pacquiao, Boxer and Politician A1253

2015, Apr. 20 Litho. *Perf. 14*
3602 A1253 10p multi .80 .40

Souvenir Sheet

Perf. 13½x13¾

3603 A1253 40p Pacquiao, diff. 3.25 1.60

No. 3603 contains one 50x35mm stamp.

Miniature Sheet

Mythical Creatures — A1255

No. 3605: a, Nuno sa Punso. b, Sirena. c, Si Malakas at Si Maganda. d, Diwata (Maria Sinukuan).

2015, Apr. 24 Litho. *Perf. 14*
3605 A1255 10p Sheet of 4, #a-d 3.25 1.60

Taipei 2015 Intl. Stamp Exhibition.

City of San Pablo, 75th Anniv. of Chartering — A1256

No. 3606: a, Municipal Building. b, Sampaloc Lake.

2015, May 7 Litho. *Perf. 14*
3606 A1256 10p Horiz. pair, #a-b 1.60 .80

Hibiscus Varieties — A1257

No. 3607 — Variety named: a, Goria. b, Nay Isa. c, Tandang Sora. d, Nazaria.

No. 3608 — Variety named: a, Emerita V. de Guzman. b, Helen L. Valmayor. c, Gelia T. Castillo. d, Dolores A. Ramirez.

2015, May 12 Litho. *Perf. 14*
3607 A1257 10p Block of 4, #a-d 3.25 1.60
3608 A1257 10p Sheet of 4, #a-d, + 2 labels 3.25 1.60

Romblon State University, Cent. A1258

2015, May 22 Litho. *Perf. 14*
3609 A1258 10p multi .80 .40

Archdiocese of Jaro, 150th Anniv. — A1259

No. 3610: a, Jaro Cathedral. b, Nuestra Señora de la Candelaria icon.

2015, May 27 Litho. *Perf. 14*
3610 A1259 10p Horiz. pair, #a-b 1.60 .80

Bilateral Relations Between the Philippines and Finland, 60th Anniv. — A1260

No. 3611 — Flags of the Philippines and Finland and: a, 10p, Brown bear. b, 40p, Philippine tamaraw.

2015, June 3 Litho. *Perf. 14*
3611 A1260 Horiz. pair, #a-b 4.00 2.00

Ateneo de Naga University, Naga City, 75th Anniv. — A1261

No. 3612: a, Emblem. b, University building.

2015, June 5 Litho. *Perf. 14*
3612 A1261 10p Horiz. pair, #a-b 1.60 .80

Kites — A1263

No. 3614 — Various kites numbered: a, 1/10. b, 2/10. c, 3/10. d, 4/10. e, 5/10. f, 6/10. g, 7/10. h, 8/10. i, 9/10. j, 10/10.
40p, Kites.

2015, June 23 Litho. *Perf. 14*
3614 A1263 10p Sheet of 10, #a-j 8.00 4.00

Souvenir Sheet

Perf. 13¾x13½

3615 A1263 40p multi 3.25 1.60

No. 3615 contains one 35x50mm stamp.

City of San Carlos, 55th Anniv. of Chartering — A1264

No. 3616: a, City Hall. b, Pinta Flores Festival.

2015, July 1 Litho. *Perf. 14*
3616 A1264 15p Horiz. pair, #a-b 2.40 1.25

Paintings of Flowers by Pres. Corazon A. Aquino (1933-2009) — A1265

No. 3617: a, Harmony of Flowers (1/4). b, Blue and Green Sea of Flowers (2/4). c, Valley of Flowers (3/4). d, Flowers by Forest Hills (4/4).
120p, Pink Flowers in a Vase, vert.

2015, July 28 Litho. *Perf. 13½x13¾*
3617 A1265 30p Block of 4, #a-d 9.75 5.00

Souvenir Sheet

Perf. 13¾x13½

3618 A1265 120p multi + label 9.75 5.00

Flags and Emblem of Association of Southeast Asian Nations — A1266

2015, Aug. 8 Litho. *Perf. 13¼*
3619 A1266 13p multi 1.10 .55

See Brunei No. , Burma No. , Cambodia No. , Indonesia No. 2428, Laos No. , Malaysia No. 1562; Singapore No. , Thailand No., Viet Nam No.

Teresita "Mama Sita" Reyes (1917-98), Restauranteur — A1267

No. 3620 — Reyes and: a, Fish, fruit and vegetables (2/3). b, Basket and blue swirls (3/3). c, Foods and stars (1/3).

Perf. 13¾x13½

2015, Aug. 24 Litho.
3620 A1267 10p Strip of 3, #a-c 2.40 1.25

Bureau of Immigration, 75th Anniv. — A1268

2015, Sept. 4 Litho. *Perf. 13½x13¾*
3621 A1268 30p multi 2.40 1.25

Pres. Elpidio Quirino (1890-1956) A1269

2015, Sept. 5 Litho. *Perf. 13¾x13½*
3622 A1269 15p multi 1.25 .60

N. V. M. Gonzales (1915-99), Writer A1270

2015, Sept. 8 Litho. *Perf. 14*
3623 A1270 10p multi .80 .40

Bandera Newspaper, 25th Anniv. A1271

Perf. 13¾x13½

2015, Sept. 10 Litho.
3624 A1271 15p multi 1.25 .60

Manila Observatory, 150th Anniv. — A1272

2015, Sept. 25 Litho. *Perf. 14*
3625 A1272 15p multi 1.25 .60

General Miguel Malvar (1865-1911) — A1273

2015, Sept. 27 Litho. *Perf. 14*
3626 A1273 10p multi .80 .40

San Miguel Brewery, 125th Anniv. — A1274

No. 3627: a, Brewery building. b, 125th anniversary emblem.

40p, 125th anniversary emblem, vert.

2015, Sept. 29 Litho. *Perf. 14*
3627 A1274 15p Horiz. pair, #a-b 2.40 1.25

Souvenir Sheet

Perf. 13¾x13½

3628 A1274 40p multi 3.25 1.60

No. 3628 contains one 35x50mm stamp.

Western Union in the Philippines, 25th Anniv. — A1275

No. 3629 — Western Union emblem and: a, Various Filipinos. b, Text, "25 Years of Moving the Filipino for Better."

Perf. 13½x13¾

2015, Sept. 30 Litho.
3629 A1275 25p Horiz. pair, #a-b 4.00 2.00

Mahaguyog Festival A1276

2015, Oct. 2 Litho. *Perf. 14*
3630 A1276 10p multi .80 .40

Manuel Conde (1915-85), Film Director A1277

2015, Oct. 15 Litho. *Perf. 14*
3631 A1277 10p multi .80 .40

2015 Asian-Pacific Economic Cooperation Summit, Manila — A1278

Perf. 13¾x13½

2015, Nov. 10 Litho.
3632 A1278 30p multi 2.40 1.25

Miniature Sheet

National Stamp Collecting Month — A1279

No. 3633: a, Boy holding stamp. b, Boy holdind stamp album. c, Girl holding stamps. d, Man holding stamps and magnifying glass.

2015, Nov. 10 Litho. *Perf. 14*

Self-Adhesive

3633 A1279 15p Sheet of 4, #a-d 5.00 2.50

Miniature Sheet

Wildlife — A1280

No. 3634: a, Vizaysa flowerpecker. b, Philippine sail-fin lizard. c, Philippine pangolin anteater. d, Freshwater purple crab.

2015, Nov. 11 Litho. *Perf. 14*
3634 A1280 15p Sheet of 4, #a-d 5.00 2.50

Christmas — A1281

No. 3635 — Children's art depicting Christmas tree by: a, Kobie Trambulo (2/4). b, Vernice Prado (3/4). c, Lomi Capili (4/4). d, Javee Fua (1/4).

No. 3636 — Children's art depicting Christmas lanterns by: a, Cedric Chua. b, Julius Cabuang. c, Thridy Cabading.

2015, Nov. 25 Litho. *Perf. 14*
3635 A1281 10p Block or strip of 4, #a-d 3.25 1.60

Souvenir Sheet

3636 A1281 10p Sheet of 3, #a-c 2.40 1.25

Office of the Government Corporate Counsel, 80th Anniv. — A1282

2015, Dec. 1 Litho. *Perf. 13½x13¾*
3637 A1282 10p multi .80 .40

New Year 2016 (Year of the Monkey) A1283

Designs: 10p, Head of monkey. 30p, Monkey.

2015, Dec. 1 Litho. *Perf. 14*
3638-3639 A1283 Set of 2 3.25 1.60
3639a Souvenir sheet of 4, 2 each #3638-3639 6.50 3.25

Philippine Daily Inquirer Newspaper, 30th Anniv. — A1284

Litho. & Embossed With Foil Application

2015, Dec. 5 *Perf. 13¼*
3640 A1284 30p multi 2.40 1.25

51st Intl. Eucharistic Congress, Cebu City — A1285

Design: 15p, Emblem. 40p, Emblem and dove's wing.

2015, Dec. 8 Litho. *Perf. 14*
3641 A1285 15p multi 1.25 .60

Souvenir Sheet

Perf. 13¾x13½

3642 A1285 40p multi + label 3.25 1.60

No. 3642 contains one 35x50mm stamp.

Cagayan Economic Zone Authority, 20th Anniv. A1286

2015, Dec. 18 Litho. *Perf. 14*
3643 A1286 15p multi 1.25 .60

Commission on Elections, 75th Anniv. A1287

2015, Dec. 18 Litho. *Perf. 14*
3644 A1287 15p multi 1.25 .60

Liberty City Center, 70th Anniv. A1288

2015, Dec. 21 Litho. *Perf. 14*
3645 A1288 15p multi 1.25 .60

Pacita Madrigal Gonzalez (1915-2008), Senator — A1289

2015, Dec. 22 Litho. *Perf. 14*
3646 A1289 15p multi 1.25 .60

SEMI-POSTAL STAMPS

Catalogue values for unused stamps in this section are for Never Hinged items.

Republic

Epifanio de los Santos, Trinidad H. Pardo and Teodoro M. Kalaw — SP1

Doctrina Christiana, Cover Page — SP2

"Noli Me Tangere," Cover Page — SP3

Unwmk.

1949, Apr. 1 Engr. *Perf. 12*

B1	SP1	4c + 2c sepia	1.50	1.50
B2	SP2	6c + 4c violet	5.00	5.00
B3	SP3	18c + 7c blue	6.00	6.00
		Nos. B1-B3 (3)	12.50	12.50

The surtax was for restoration of war-damaged public libraries.

War Widow and Children — SP4

Disabled Veteran — SP5

1950, Nov. 30

B4	SP4	2c + 2c red	.30	.25
B5	SP5	4c + 4c violet	.40	.30

The surtax was for war widows and children and disabled veterans of World War II.

For surcharges see Nos. 648-649.

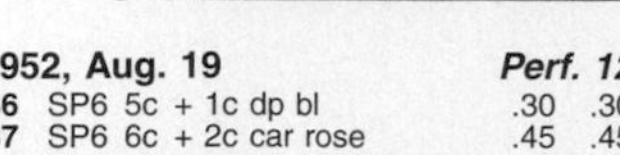

Mrs. Manuel L. Quezon SP6

1952, Aug. 19 *Perf. 12*

B6	SP6	5c + 1c dp bl	.30	.30
B7	SP6	6c + 2c car rose	.45	.45

The surtax was used to encourage planting and care of fruit trees among Philippine children. For surcharge see No. 872.

Quezon Institute SP7

1958, Aug. 19 Photo. *Perf. 13½, 12*

Cross in Red

B8	SP7	5c + 5c grn	.25	.25
B9	SP7	10c + 5c dp vio	.30	.30

These stamps were obligatory on all mail from Aug. 19-Sept. 30.

For surcharges see Nos. 849, B12-B13, B16.

The surtax on all semi-postals from Nos. B8-B9 onward was for the Philippine Tuberculosis Society unless otherwise stated.

Scout Cooking — SP8

1959 Engr. *Perf. 13*

Yellow Paper

B10	SP8	6c + 4c shown	.40	*1.50*
B11	SP8	25c + 5c Archery	.55	*2.00*
	a.	Nos. B10-B11 tête bêche, *white*	1.00	*6.00*
		Nos. B10-B11,CB1-CB3 (5)	2.95	*9.50*

10th Boy Scout World Jamboree, Makiling National Park, July 17-26. The surtax was to finance the Jamboree.

For souvenir sheet see No. CB3a. For surcharges see Nos. 832-833, C111.

Nos. B8-B9 Surcharged in Red

1959 Photo. *Perf. 13½, 12*

B12	SP7	3c + 5c on 5c + 5c	.25	.25
	a.	"3 + 5" and bars omitted		
B13	SP7	6c + 5c on 10c + 5c	.35	.25

Bohol Sanatorium — SP9

1959, Aug. 19 Engr. *Perf. 12*

Cross in Red

B14	SP9	6c + 5c yel grn	.25	.25
B15	SP9	25c + 5c vio bl	.40	.30

No. B8 Surcharged "Help Prevent TB" and New Value

1960, Aug. 19 Photo. *Perf. 13½, 12*

B16	SP7	6c + 5c on 5c + 5c	.50	.25

Roxas Memorial T.B. Pavilion SP10

Perf. 11½

1961, Aug. 19 Unwmk. Photo.

B17	SP10	6c + 5c brn & red	.50	.25

Emiliano J. Valdes T.B. Pavilion SP11

1962, Aug. 19 Cross in Red

B18	SP11	6s + 5s dk vio	.25	.25
B19	SP11	30s + 5s ultra	.35	.25
B20	SP11	70s + 5s brt bl	.70	.50
		Nos. B18-B20 (3)	1.30	1.00

José Rizal Playing Chess SP12

Design: 30s+5s, Rizal fencing.

1962, Dec. 30 Engr. *Perf. 13*

B21	SP12	6s + 4s grn & rose lil	.35	*1.00*
B22	SP12	30s + 5s brt bl & cl	.90	*2.00*

Surtax for Rizal Foundation.

For surcharges see Nos. 942-943.

Map of Philippines and Cross — SP13

1963, Aug. 19 Unwmk. *Perf. 13*

B23	SP13	6s + 5s vio & red	.25	.25
B24	SP13	10s + 5s grn & red	.30	.25
B25	SP13	50s + 5s brn & red	.75	.35
		Nos. B23-B25 (3)	1.30	.85

Negros Oriental T.B. Pavilion SP14

1964, Aug. 19 Photo. *Perf. 13½*

Cross in Red

B26	SP14	5s + 5s brt pur	.25	.25
B27	SP14	6s + 5s ultra	.25	.25
B28	SP14	30s + 5s brown	.30	.25
B29	SP14	70s + 5s green	.55	.50
		Nos. B26-B29 (4)	1.35	1.25

For surcharges see Nos. 986, 1586.

No. B27 Surcharged in Red with New Value and Two Bars

1965, Aug. 19 Cross in Red

B30	SP14	1s + 5s on 6s + 5s	.25	.25
B31	SP14	3s + 5s on 6s + 5s	.35	.25

Stork-billed Kingfisher — SP15

Birds: 5s+5s, Rufous hornbill. 10s+5s, Monkey-eating eagle. 30s+5s, Great-billed parrot.

1967, Aug. 19 Photo. *Perf. 13½*

B32	SP15	1s + 5s multi	.25	.25
B33	SP15	5s + 5s multi	.30	.25
B34	SP15	10s + 5s multi	.60	.25
B35	SP15	30s + 5s multi	2.40	.70
		Nos. B32-B35 (4)	3.55	1.45

1969, Aug. 15 Litho. *Perf. 13½*

Birds: 1s+5s, Three-toed woodpecker. 5s+5s, Philippine trogon. 10s+5s, Mt. Apo lorikeet. 40s+5s, Scarlet minivet.

B36	SP15	1s + 5s multi	.25	.25
B37	SP15	5s + 5s multi	.50	.25
B38	SP15	10s + 5s multi	1.00	.30
B39	SP15	40s + 5s multi	2.00	.60
		Nos. B36-B39 (4)	3.75	1.40

Julia V. de Ortigas and Tuberculosis Society Building — SP16

1970, Aug. 3 Photo. *Perf. 13½*

B40	SP16	1s + 5s multi	.25	.25
B41	SP16	5s + 5s multi	.30	.25
B42	SP16	30s + 5s multi	1.00	.45
B43	SP16	70s + 5s multi	1.25	.55
		Nos. B40-B43 (4)	2.80	1.50

Mrs. Julia V. de Ortigas was president of the Philippine Tuberculosis Soc., 1932-69.

For surcharge see No. 1251.

Mabolo, Santol, Chico, Papaya SP17

Philippine Fruits: 10s+5s, Balimbing, atis, mangosteen, macupa, bananas. 40s+5s, Susong-kalabao, avocado, duhat, watermelon, guava, mango. 1p+5s, Lanzones, oranges, sirhuelas, pineapple.

1972, Aug. 1 Litho. *Perf. 13*

B44	SP17	1s + 5s multi	.25	.25
B45	SP17	10s + 5s multi	.30	.25
B46	SP17	40s + 5s multi	.65	.25
B47	SP17	1p + 5s multi	1.60	.50
		Nos. B44-B47 (4)	2.80	1.25

Nos. B45-B46 Surcharged with New Value and 2 Bars

1973, June 15

B48	SP17	15s + 5s on 10s + 5s	.35	.25
B49	SP17	60s + 5s on 40s + 5s	.90	.35

Dr. Basilio J. Valdes and Veterans Memorial Hospital — SP18

1974, July 8 Litho. *Perf. 12½*

Cross in Red

B50	SP18	15s + 5s blue grn	.35	.25
	a.	Imperf.	.75	.75
B51	SP18	1.10p + 5s vio blue	1.50	1.50
	a.	Imperf.	4.00	4.00

Dr. Valdes (1892-1970) was president of Philippine Tuberculosis Society.

For surcharges see Nos. 1250, 1252.

AIR POST STAMPS

Madrid-Manila Flight Issue

Issued to commemorate the flight of Spanish aviators Gallarza and Loriga from Madrid to Manila.

Regular Issue of 1917-26 Overprinted in Red or Violet

Designs: Nos. C7-C8, Adm. William T. Sampson. No. C9, Adm. George Dewey.

1926, May 13 Unwmk. *Perf. 11*

C1 A40 2c green (R) 20.00 17.50
Never hinged 45.00
C2 A40 4c carmine (V) 30.00 20.00
Never hinged 55.00
a. Inverted overprint *4,000.* —
C3 A40 6c lilac (R) 75.00 75.00
Never hinged 125.00
C4 A40 8c org brn (V) 75.00 60.00
Never hinged 125.00
C5 A40 10c deep blue (R) 75.00 60.00
Never hinged 140.00
C6 A40 12c red org (V) 80.00 65.00
Never hinged 150.00
C7 A40 16c lt ol grn (V) *3,250. 3,250.*
C8 A40 16c ol bister (R) *5,000. 5,000.*
C9 A40 16c ol grn (V) 100.00 70.00
Never hinged 160.00
C10 A40 20c org ye (V) 100.00 80.00
Never hinged 160.00
C11 A40 26c blue grn (V) 100.00 80.00
Never hinged 160.00
C12 A40 30c gray (V) 100.00 80.00
Never hinged 160.00
C13 A40 2p vio brn (R) 600.00 600.00
Never hinged 1,100.
C14 A40 4p dk blue (R) 750.00 750.00
Never hinged 1,300.
C15 A40 10p dp grn (V) 1,350. 1,350.

Same Overprint on No. 269
Wmk. Single-lined PIPS (190)
Perf. 12

C16 A40 26c blue grn (V) *6,250.*

Same Overprint on No. 284
Perf. 10

C17 A40 1p pale violet (V) 300.00 225.00
Never hinged 450.00

London-Orient Flight Issue

Issued Nov. 9, 1928, to celebrate the arrival of a British squadron of hydroplanes.

Regular Issue of 1917-25 Overprinted in Red

1928, Nov. 9 *Perf. 11*

C18 A40 2c green 1.00 1.00
Never hinged 2.00
C19 A40 4c carmine 1.25 1.50
Never hinged 2.00
C20 A40 6c violet 5.00 3.00
Never hinged 10.00
C21 A40 8c orange brown 5.00 3.00
Never hinged 10.00
C22 A40 10c deep blue 5.00 3.00
Never hinged 10.00
C23 A40 12c red orange 8.00 4.00
Never hinged 12.00
C24 A40 16c ol grn (No. 303a) 8.00 4.00
Never hinged 12.00
C25 A40 20c orange yellow 8.00 4.00
Never hinged 12.00
C26 A40 26c blue green 20.00 8.00
Never hinged 35.00
C27 A40 30c gray 20.00 8.00
Never hinged 35.00

Same Overprint on No. 271
Wmk. Single-lined PIPS (190)
Perf. 12

C28 A40 1p pale violet 55.00 30.00
Never hinged 90.00
Nos. C18-C28 (11) 136.25 69.50
Set, never hinged 230.00

Von Gronau Issue

Commemorating the visit of Capt. Wolfgang von Gronau's airplane on its round-the-world flight.

Nos. 354-360 Overprinted

1932, Sept. 27 Unwmk. *Perf. 11*

C29 A43 2c yellow green .90 .60
Never hinged 1.40
C30 A44 4c rose carmine .90 .40
Never hinged 1.40
C31 A45 12c orange 1.25 .65
Never hinged 2.00
C32 A46 18c red orange 5.00 5.00
Never hinged 8.00
C33 A47 20c yellow 4.00 4.00
Never hinged 6.50
C34 A48 24c deep violet 4.00 4.00
Never hinged 6.50
C35 A49 32c olive brown 3.50 3.00
Never hinged 5.75
Nos. C29-C35 (7) 19.55 17.65
Set, never hinged 31.55

Rein Issue

Commemorating the flight from Madrid to Manila of the Spanish aviator Fernando Rein y Loring.

Regular Issue of 1917-25 Overprinted

1933, Apr. 11

C36 A40 2c green .75 .45
Never hinged 1.10
C37 A40 4c carmine .90 .45
Never hinged 1.40
C38 A40 6c deep violet 1.10 .80
Never hinged 1.75
C39 A40 8c orange brown 3.75 2.00
Never hinged 5.75
C40 A40 10c dark blue 3.75 2.25
Never hinged 5.75
C41 A40 12c orange 3.75 2.00
Never hinged 5.75
C42 A40 16c olive green 3.50 2.00
Never hinged 5.25
C43 A40 20c yellow 3.75 2.00
Never hinged 5.75
C44 A40 26c green 3.75 2.75
Never hinged 5.75
a. 26c blue green 4.00 2.00
Never hinged 6.00
C45 A40 30c gray 4.00 3.00
Never hinged 6.00
Nos. C36-C45 (10) 29.00 17.70
Set, never hinged 44.25

No. 290a Overprinted

1933, May 26

C46 A40 2c green .65 .40
Never hinged 1.00

Regular Issue of 1932 Overprinted

C47 A44 4c rose carmine .30 .25
Never hinged .45
C48 A45 12c orange .60 .25
Never hinged .90
C49 A47 20c yellow .60 .25
Never hinged .90
C50 A48 24c deep violet .65 .25
Never hinged 1.00
C51 A49 32c olive brown .85 .35
Never hinged 1.40
Nos. C46-C51 (6) 3.65 1.75
Set, never hinged 5.65

Transpacific Issue

Issued to commemorate the China Clipper flight from Manila to San Francisco, Dec. 2-5, 1935.

Nos. 387, 392 Overprinted in Gold

1935, Dec. 2

C52 A57 10c rose carmine .40 .25
Never hinged .60
C53 A62 30c orange red .60 .35
Never hinged .90

Manila-Madrid Flight Issue

Issued to commemorate the Manila-Madrid flight by aviators Antonio Arnaiz and Juan Calvo.

Regular Issue of 1917-25 Surcharged in Various Colors

1936, Sept. 6

C54 A40 2c on 4c carmine (Bl) .25 .25
Never hinged .25
C55 A40 6c on 12c red org (V) .25 .25
Never hinged .30
C56 A40 16c on 26c blue grn (Bk) .25 .25
Never hinged .40
a. 16c on 26c green 2.00 .70
Never hinged 3.00
Nos. C54-C56 (3) .75 .75
Set, never hinged .95

Air Mail Exhibition Issue

Issued to commemorate the first Air Mail Exhibition, held Feb. 17-19, 1939.

Regular Issue of 1917-37 Surcharged in Black or Red

1939, Feb. 17

C57 A40 8c on 26c blue grn (Bk) 2.00 2.00
Never hinged 4.00
a. 8c on 26c green (Bk) 10.00 4.00
Never hinged 16.00
C58 A71 1p on 10p gray (R) 8.00 4.00
Never hinged 12.00

Moro Vinta and Clipper AP1

1941, June 30

C59 AP1 8c carmine 2.00 .60
Never hinged 2.75
C60 AP1 20c ultramarine 3.00 .50
Never hinged 4.00
C61 AP1 60c blue green 3.00 1.00
Never hinged 4.00
C62 AP1 1p sepia .70 .50
Never hinged 1.00
Nos. C59-C62 (4) 8.70 2.60
Set, never hinged 11.75

For overprint see No. NO7. For surcharges see Nos. N10-N11, N35-N36.

No. C47 Hstmpd. in Violet

1944, Dec. 3

C63 A44 4c rose carmine *3,750. 2,750.*

Catalogue values for unused stamps in this section, from this point to the end of the section, are for Never Hinged items.

Republic

Manuel L. Quezon and Franklin D. Roosevelt AP2

Unwmk.

1947, Aug. 19 Engr. *Perf. 12*

C64 AP2 6c dark green .50 .50
C65 AP2 40c red orange 1.00 1.00
C66 AP2 80c deep blue 2.75 2.75
Nos. C64-C66 (3) 4.25 4.25

FAO Type

1948, Feb. 23 Typo. *Perf. 12½*

C67 A89 40c dk car & pink 10.00 6.00

Junior Chamber Type

1950, Mar. 1 Engr. *Perf. 12*

C68 A96 30c deep orange 1.40 .40
C69 A96 50c carmine rose 2.50 .70

F. D. Roosevelt Type
Souvenir Sheet

1950, May 22 *Imperf.*

C70 A98 80c deep green 3.00 2.50

Lions Club Type

1950, June 2 *Perf. 12*

C71 A99 30c emerald 1.75 .45
C72 A99 50c ultra 2.00 .60
a. Souvenir sheet of 2, #C71-C72 3.00 2.50

Maria Clara Type

1952, Nov. 16 *Perf. 12½*

C73 A112 30c rose carmine 2.00 .75

Postage Stamp Cent. Type

1954, Apr. 25 *Perf. 13*
1854 Stamp in Orange

C74 A119 10c dark brown 2.50 1.00
C75 A119 20c dark green 4.00 1.60
C76 A119 50c carmine 8.50 3.25
Nos. C74-C76 (3) 15.00 5.85

Rotary Intl. Type

1955, Feb. 23

C77 A123 50c blue green 2.50 1.00

Lt. José Gozar AP10

20c, 50c, Lt. Gozar. 30c, 70c, Lt. Basa

1955 Engr. *Perf. 13*

C78 AP10 20c deep violet .45 .25
C79 AP10 30c red .50 .25
C80 AP10 50c bluish green .70 .25
C81 AP10 70c blue 1.10 .90
Nos. C78-C81 (4) 2.75 1.65

Lt. José Gozar and Lt. Cesar Fernando Basa, Filipino aviators in World War II.

Constitution Type of Regular Issue

1960, Feb. 8 Photo. *Perf. 12½x13½*

C82 A146 30c brt bl & silver .50 .25

Air Force Plane of 1935 and Saber Jet AP11

1960, May 2 Engr. *Perf. 14x14½*

C83 AP11 10c carmine .30 .25
C84 AP11 20c ultra .45 .25

25th anniversary of Philippine Air Force.
For surcharge see No. 847.

Olympic Type of Regular Issue

30c, Sharpshooter. 70c, Woman swimmer.

1960, Nov. 30 Photo. *Perf. 13x13½*

C85 A150 30c orange & brn .50 .35
C86 A150 70c grnsh bl & vio brn 1.00 .70

Postal Conference Type

1961, Feb. 23 *Perf. 13½x13*

C87 A152 30c multicolored .50 .25

Freedom from Hunger Type

1963, Dec. 20 Photo.

C88 A168 30s lt grn & multi .30 .25
C89 A168 50s multicolored .45 .30

Land Reform Type

1964, Dec. 21 Wmk. 233 *Perf. 14½*

C90 A172 30s multicolored .50 .25

Mass Baptism by Father Andres de Urdaneta, Cebu — AP12

70s, World map showing route of the Cross from Spain to Mexico to Cebu, and two galleons.

Nos. O34 and C62 Overprinted in Black

a

b

NO6 A60(a) 20c light olive green .40 *.50*
Never hinged .60
NO7 AP1(b) 1p sepia .90 *1.00*
Never hinged 1.45
Nos. NO5-NO7 (3) 1.60 1.90
Set, never hinged 2.05

FILIPINO REVOLUTIONARY GOVERNMENT

Following the defeat of the Spanish fleet by U.S. Commodore Dewey in Manila on May 1, 1898, which essentially ended the Spanish-American War in the Philippines, postal services were disrupted throughout the Philippines. Postal service was reestablished through U.S. Army military stations, beginning in June 1898 near Manila, continuing province by province until culminating at Zamboanga and other cities in the southern areas in late 1899.

Provisional stamps were prepared for use in the central part of the island of Luzon at Malolos in late 1898 under the leadership of General Emilio Aguinaldo, who had proclaimed the Philippine Republic on June 12, 1898. Later, other provisional stamps were prepared by local Filipino insurgents at Iloilo (Panay Island), Bohol, Cebu and Negros, and Spanish period stamps were overprinted and/or surcharged for use by postal officials at Zamboanga and La Union.

The most familiar of these provisionals were the "Aguinaldo" issues of the Filipino Revolutionary Government in central Luzon near Manila. The letters "KKK," the initials of the revolutionary society, "Kataas-taasang, Kagalang-galang Katipunan nang Mañga Anak nang Bayan," meaning "Sovereign Worshipful Association of the Sons of the Country," readily identify the Aguinaldo provisionals. Hostilities broke out between the Aguinaldo regime and the occupying American administration in February 1899, and the Filipino-American War continued until the American capture of Aguinaldo on March 23, 1901.

The Aguinaldo regular postage, registration, revenue, newspaper and telegraph stamps were in use in Luzon as early as November 10, 1898, and continued in use through early 1901. Although the postal regulations specified that these stamps be used for their inscribed purpose, they were commonly used interchangeably.

The Filipino Republic was instituted by Gen. Emilio Aguinaldo on June 23, 1899. At the same time he assumed the office of President. Aguinaldo dominated the greater part of the island of Luzon and some of the smaller islands until late in 1899. He was taken prisoner by United States troops on March 23, 1901.

The devices composing the National Arms, adopted by the Filipino Revolutionary Government, are emblems of the Katipunan political secret society or of Katipunan origin. The letters "K K K" on these stamps are the initials of this society whose complete name is "Kataas-taasang, Kagalang-galang Katipunan nang Mañga Anak nang Bayan," meaning "Sovereign Worshipful Association of the Sons of the Country."

The regular postage and telegraph stamps were in use on Luzon as early as Nov. 10, 1898. Owing to the fact that stamps for the different purposes were not always available together with a lack of proper instructions, any of the adhesives were permitted to be used in the place of the other. Hence telegraph and revenue stamps were accepted for postage and postage stamps for revenue or telegraph charges. In addition to the regular postal emission, there are a number of provisional stamps, issues of local governments of islands and towns.

POSTAGE ISSUES

A1

A2

Coat of Arms — A3

1898-99 Unwmk. *Perf. 11½*

Y1 A1 2c red 175.00 125.00
a. Double impression *325.00*
Y2 A2 2c red .30 4.00
b. Double impression —
d. Horiz. pair, imperf. between —
e. Vert. pair, imperf. between *225.00*
Y3 A3 2c red 150.00 *200.00*

Imperf pairs and pairs, imperf horizontally, have been created from No. Y2e.

REGISTRATION STAMP

RS1

YF1 RS1 8c green 5.00 *30.00*
a. Imperf., pair 400.00
b. Imperf. vertically, pair —

NEWSPAPER STAMP

N1

YP1 N1 1m black 2.00 *20.00*
a. Imperf., pair 5.00 *20.00*

GET ORGANIZED

GLASSINE ENVELOPES

Perfect for organizing duplicates and sending approvals or mailing stamps. **Sold in packages of 100.**

Item	Size	Retail	AA
GE01	(1¾" x 2⅞")	$4.99	**$4.49**
GE02	(2 5/16" x 3⅝")	$5.49	**$4.99**
GE03	(2½" x 4¼")	$5.99	**$5.49**
GE04	(3¼" x 4⅞")	$6.99	**$5.99**
GE4H	(3⅛" x 5 1/16")	$7.99	**$6.50**
GE05	(3½" x 6")	$8.99	**$7.99**
GE06	(3¾" x 6¾")	$9.50	**$8.50**
GE07	(4⅛" x 6¼")	$10.00	**$9.00**
GE08	(4½" x 6⅝")	$10.50	**$9.50**
GE10	(4⅛" x 9½")	$16.99	**$14.99**
GE11	(4½" x 10⅜")	$17.99	**$16.99**

Glassine envelopes are also available in boxes of 1,000 – call for pricing.

GLASSINE BAGS

These larger glassine bags are ideal for storing panes, covers or prestige booklets. A handy accessory to keep around for all your collecting needs. Available in five different sizes. **Sold in packages of 100.**

Item	Size	Retail	AA
GB12	#12 (4¾" x 6¾")	$8.99	**$7.99**
GB13	#13 (5¾" x 7¾")	$9.99	**$8.99**
GB13A	#13A (6¾" x 9")	$10.99	**$9.99**
GB14	#14 (7¾" x 9¾")	$16.99	**$14.99**
GB15	#15 (8½" x 11")	$18.99	**$15.99**
GB16	#16 (11½" x 14")	$33.99	**$28.99**

Order yours today!
AmosAdvantage.com
1-800-572-6885
Outside U.S. & Canada call (937) 498-0800
P.O. Box 4129, Sidney OH 45365
*AA prices apply to paid subscribers of Amos Media titles, or for orders placed online. Prices, terms and product availability subject to change. Shipping and handling rates apply. Taxes will apply in CA, OH, & IL.
AMOS ADVANTAGE

PITCAIRN ISLANDS

'pit-,karn 'ī-lənds

LOCATION — South Pacific Ocean, nearly equidistant from Australia and South America

GOVT. — British colony under the British High Commissioner in New Zealand

AREA — 18 sq. mi. (includes all islands)

POP. — 43 (2007 est.)

The district of Pitcairn also includes the uninhabited islands of Ducie, Henderson and Oeno.

Postal affairs are administered by New Zealand.

12 Pence = 1 Shilling
100 Cents = 1 Dollar (1967)

Catalogue values for all unused stamps in this country are for Never Hinged items.

Watermarks

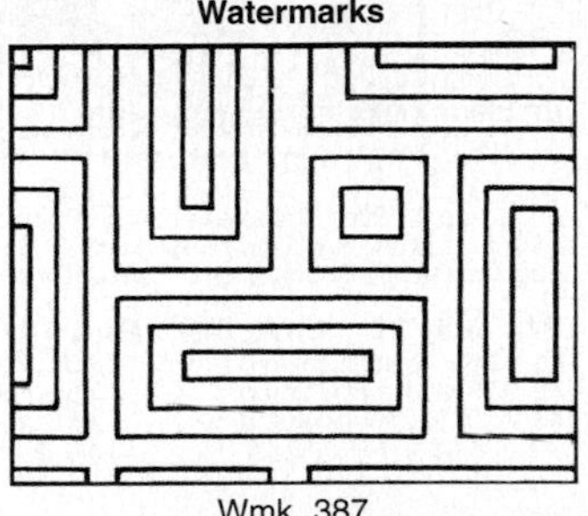

Wmk. 387

Cluster of Oranges A1

Fletcher Christian with Crew and View of Pitcairn Island — A2

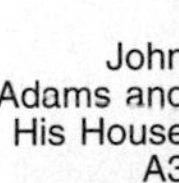

John Adams and His House A3

William Bligh and H. M. Armed Vessel "Bounty" A4

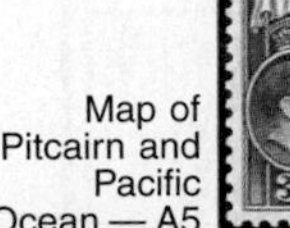

Map of Pitcairn and Pacific Ocean — A5

Bounty Bible — A6

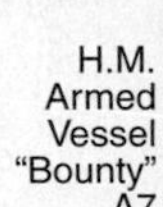

H.M. Armed Vessel "Bounty" A7

Pitcairn School, 1949 — A8

Fletcher Christian and View of Pitcairn Island — A9

Fletcher Christian with Crew and Coast of Pitcairn A10

Perf. 12½, 11½x11

1940-51 Engr. Wmk. 4

No.	Type	Value	Description	Unused	Used
1	A1	½p	blue grn & org	.75	*.95*
2	A2	1p	red lil & rose vio	.95	*.80*
3	A3	1½p	rose car & blk	.95	.50
4	A4	2p	dk brn & brt grn	2.25	1.40
5	A5	3p	dk blue & yel grn	1.25	1.25
5A	A6	4p	dk blue grn & blk	21.00	12.00
6	A7	6p	sl grn & dp brn	6.00	1.50
6A	A8	8p	lil rose & grn	22.50	8.00
7	A9	1sh	slate & vio	5.25	1.50
8	A10	2sh6p	dk brn & brt grn	15.00	4.00
			Nos. 1-8 (10)	75.90	31.90

Nos. 1-5, 6 and 7-8 exist in a booklet of eight panes of one. Value $2,750.

Issued: 4p, 8p, 9/1/51; others, 10/15/40.

Common Design Types pictured following the introduction.

Peace Issue
Common Design Type

1946, Dec. 2 ***Perf. 13½x14***

No.	Type	Value	Description	Unused	Used
9	CD303	2p	brown	.65	.65
10	CD303	3p	deep blue	.75	.75

Silver Wedding Issue
Common Design Types

1949, Aug. 1 Photo. ***Perf. 14x14½***

No.	Type	Value	Description	Unused	Used
11	CD304	1½p	scarlet	1.75	1.00

Perf. 11½x11

Engraved; Name Typographed

No.	Type	Value	Description	Unused	Used
12	CD305	10sh	purple	47.50	50.00

UPU Issue
Common Design Types

Engr.; Name Typo. on 3p & 6p

1949, Oct. 10 ***Perf. 13½, 11x11½***

No.	Type	Value	Description	Unused	Used
13	CD306	2½p	red brown	2.25	4.00
14	CD307	3p	indigo	8.00	4.00
15	CD308	6p	green	4.00	4.00
16	CD309	1sh	rose violet	4.25	4.50
			Nos. 13-16 (4)	18.50	16.50

Coronation Issue
Common Design Type

1953, June 2 ***Perf. 13½x13***

No.	Type	Value	Description	Unused	Used
19	CD312	4p	dk green & blk	2.25	2.25

Ti Plant — A11

Map — A12

Designs: 2p, John Adams and Bounty Bible. 2½p, Handicraft (Carving). 3p, Bounty Bay. 4p, School (actually Schoolteacher's House). 6p, Fiji-Pitcairn connection (Map). 8p, Inland scene. 1sh, Handicraft (Ship model). 2sh, Wheelbarrow. 2sh6p, Whaleboat.

Perf. 13x12½, 12½x13

1957, July 2 Engr. Wmk. 4

No.	Type	Value	Description	Unused	Used
20	A11	½p	lilac & green	.75	*1.00*
21	A12	1p	olive grn & blk	4.50	2.00
22	A12	2p	blue & brown	2.25	.50
23	A11	2½p	orange & brn	.65	.50
24	A11	3p	ultra & emer	.90	.50
25	A11	4p	ultra & rose red *(Pitcairn School)*	1.10	.65
26	A11	6p	indigo & buff	3.25	.65
27	A11	8p	magenta & grn	.65	*.65*
28	A11	1sh	brown & blk	2.25	.90
29	A12	2sh	dp org & grn	11.00	9.00
30	A11	2sh6p	mag & ultra	25.00	10.00
			Nos. 20-30 (11)	52.30	26.35

See Nos. 31, 38.

Type of 1957 Corrected

1958, Nov. 5 ***Perf. 13x12½***

No.	Type	Value	Description	Unused	Used
31	A11	4p	ultra & rose red *(School-teacher's House)*	5.00	2.50

Simon Young and Pitcairn A13

Designs: 6p, Maps of Norfolk and Pitcairn Islands. 1sh, Schooner Mary Ann.

Perf. 14½x13½

1961, Nov. 15 Photo. Wmk. 314

No.	Type	Value	Description	Unused	Used
32	A13	3p	yellow & black	.50	.50
33	A13	6p	blue & red brown	1.10	1.10
34	A13	1sh	brt green & dp org	1.10	1.10
			Nos. 32-34 (3)	2.70	2.70

Pitcairn Islanders return from Norfolk Island.

Freedom from Hunger Issue
Common Design Type

1963, June 4 ***Perf. 14x14½***

No.	Type	Value	Description	Unused	Used
35	CD314	2sh6p	ultra	10.00	4.50

Red Cross Centenary Issue
Common Design Type

1963, Dec. 9 Litho. ***Perf. 13***

No.	Type	Value	Description	Unused	Used
36	CD315	2p	black & red	1.00	1.00
37	CD315	2sh6p	ultra & red	5.50	4.50

Type of 1957

Perf. 13x12½

1963, Dec. 4 Engr. Wmk. 314

No.	Type	Value	Description	Unused	Used
38	A11	½p	lilac & green	1.25	2.25

Pitcairn Longboat A14

Queen Elizabeth II — A15

1p, H.M. Armed Vessel Bounty. 2p, Oarsmen rowing longboat. 3p, Great frigate bird. 4p, Fairy tern 6p, Pitcairn reed warbler. 8p, Red-footed booby. 10p, Red-tailed tropic birds. 1sh, Henderson Island flightless rail. 1sh6p, Henderson Island lory. 2sh6p, Murphy's petrel. 4sh, Henderson Island fruit pigeon.

1964-65 Photo. ***Perf. 14x14½***

No.	Type	Value	Description	Unused	Used
39	A14	½p	multicolored	.25	*.30*
a.			Blue omitted	750.00	
40	A14	1p	multicolored	.30	.30
41	A14	2p	multicolored	.30	.30
42	A14	3p	multicolored	.75	.30
43	A14	4p	multicolored	.75	.30
44	A14	6p	multicolored	.80	.35
45	A14	8p	multicolored	.85	.35
a.			Gray (beak) omitted	600.00	
46	A14	10p	multicolored	.85	.40
47	A14	1sh	multicolored	.85	.40
48	A14	1sh6p	multicolored	2.50	1.25
49	A14	2sh6p	multicolored	2.75	1.75
50	A14	4sh	multicolored	4.00	2.25
51	A15	8sh	multicolored	2.75	2.00
			Nos. 39-51 (13)	17.70	10.25

Issued: ½p-4sh, 8/5/64; 8sh, 4/5/65.

For surcharges see Nos. 72-84.

ITU Issue
Common Design Type

1965, May 17 Litho. ***Perf. 11x11½***

No.	Type	Value	Description	Unused	Used
52	CD317	1p	red lilac & org brn	1.00	.55
53	CD317	2sh6p	grnsh blue & ultra	5.25	3.75

Intl. Cooperation Year Issue
Common Design Type

1965, Oct. 25 ***Perf. 14½***

No.	Type	Value	Description	Unused	Used
54	CD318	1p	bl grn & cl	.35	.25
55	CD318	1sh6p	lt vio & grn	6.00	4.25

Churchill Memorial Issue
Common Design Type

1966, Jan. 24 Photo. ***Perf. 14***

Design in Black, Gold and Carmine Rose

No.	Type	Value	Description	Unused	Used
56	CD319	2p	brt blue	1.25	1.00
57	CD319	3p	green	2.50	1.25
58	CD319	6p	brown	3.00	1.50
59	CD319	1sh	violet	4.25	3.00
			Nos. 56-59 (4)	11.00	6.75

World Cup Soccer Issue
Common Design Type

1966, Aug. 1 Litho. ***Perf. 14***

No.	Type	Value	Description	Unused	Used
60	CD321	4p	multi	1.00	1.00
61	CD321	2sh6p	multi	4.50	4.00

WHO Headquarters Issue
Common Design Type

1966, Sept. 20 Litho. ***Perf. 14***

No.	Type	Value	Description	Unused	Used
62	CD322	8p	multi	3.00	3.00
63	CD322	1sh6p	multi	4.25	3.50

UNESCO Anniversary Issue
Common Design Type

1966, Dec. 1 Litho. ***Perf. 14***

No.	Type	Value	Description	Unused	Used
64	CD323	½p	"Education"	.35	*1.00*
65	CD323	10p	"Science"	2.25	1.00
66	CD323	2sh	"Culture"	4.50	2.75
			Nos. 64-66 (3)	7.10	4.75

Mangarevan Canoe, c. 1325, and Pitcairn Island — A16

Designs: 1p, Pedro Fernandez de Quiros and galleon, 1606. 8p, "San Pedro," 17th century Spanish brigantine, 1606. 1sh, Capt. Philip Carteret and H.M.S. Swallow. 1sh6p, "Hercules," 1819.

Wmk. 314

1967, Mar. 1 Photo. ***Perf. 14½***

No.	Type	Value	Description	Unused	Used
67	A16	½p	multicolored	.25	.25
68	A16	1p	multicolored	.25	.25
69	A16	8p	multicolored	.25	.25
70	A16	1sh	multicolored	.30	.30
71	A16	1sh6p	multicolored	.40	.40
			Nos. 67-71 (5)	1.45	1.45

Bicentenary of the discovery of Pitcairn Islands by Capt. Philip Carteret.

Nos. 39-51 Surcharged in Gold

1967, July 10 ***Perf. 14x14½***

72 A14 ½c on ½p .25 .25
a. Brown omitted 1,500.
73 A14 1c on 1p .35 *.65*
74 A14 2c on 2p .30 *.65*
75 A14 2½c on 3p .30 *.65*
76 A14 3c on 4p .35 .25
77 A14 5c on 6p .45 .75
78 A14 10c on 8p .65 .40
a. "10c" omitted *2,000.*
b. Pale blue (beak) omitted *850.00*
79 A14 15c on 10p 1.60 .55
80 A14 20c on 1sh 1.75 .70
81 A14 25c on 1sh6p 2.00 1.00
82 A14 30c on 2sh6p 2.25 1.25
83 A14 40c on 4sh 2.50 1.50
84 A15 45c on 8sh 3.00 1.75
Nos. 72-84 (13) 15.75 10.35

Size of gold rectangle and anchor varies. The anchor symbol is designed after the anchor of H.M.S. Bounty.

Admiral Bligh and Bounty's Launch — A17

Designs: 8c, Bligh and his followers adrift in a boat. 20c, Bligh's tomb, St. Mary's Cemetery, Lambeth, London.

Unwmk.

1967, Dec. 7 **Litho.** ***Perf. 13***

85 A17 1c ultra, lt blue & blk .25 .25
86 A17 8c brt rose, yel & blk .35 .35
87 A17 20c brown, yel & blk .55 .55
Nos. 85-87 (3) 1.15 1.15

150th anniv. of the death of Admiral William Bligh (1754-1817), capt. of the Bounty.

Human Rights Flame A18

Perf. 13½x13

1968, Mar. 4 **Litho.** **Wmk. 314**

88 A18 1c rose & multi .25 .25
89 A18 2c ocher & multi .25 .25
90 A18 25c multicolored .60 .45
Nos. 88-90 (3) 1.10 .95

International Human Rights Year.

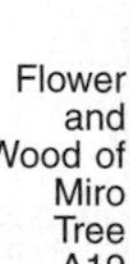

Flower and Wood of Miro Tree A19

Pitcairn Handicraft: 10c, Carved flying fish. 15c, Two "hand" vases, vert. 20c, Old and new woven baskets, vert.

Perf. 14½x14, 14x14½

1968, Aug. 19 **Photo.** **Wmk. 314**

91 A19 5c chocolate & multi .30 .30
92 A19 10c dp green & multi .30 .30
93 A19 15c brt violet & multi .40 .40
94 A19 20c black & multi .50 .50
Nos. 91-94 (4) 1.50 1.50

See Nos. 194-197.

Microscope, Cell, Germs and WHO Emblem — A20

20c, Hypodermic and jars containing pills.

1968, Nov. 25 **Litho.** ***Perf. 14***

95 A20 2c vio blue, grnsh bl & blk .25 .25
96 A20 20c black, magenta & org .60 .60

20th anniv. of WHO.

Capt. Bligh and his Larcum-Kendall Chronometer — A21

1c, Pitcairn Island. 3c, Bounty's anchor, vert. 4c, Plan of the Bounty, drawn 1787. 5c, Breadfruit and method of transporting young plants. 6c, Bounty Bay. 8c, Pitcairn longboat. 10c, Ship Landing Point and palms. 15c, Fletcher Christian's Cave. 20c, Thursday October Christian's house. 25c, "Flying Fox" cable system (for hauling cargo), vert. 30c, Radio Station at Taro Ground. 40c, Bounty Bible.

Perf. 13x12½, 12½x13

1969, Sept. 17 **Litho.** **Wmk. 314**

97 A21 1c brn, yel & gold 1.25 *1.50*
98 A21 2c brn, blk & gold .40 .25
99 A21 3c red, blk & gold .40 .25
100 A21 4c buff, brn & gold 2.00 .25
101 A21 5c gold & multi .80 .25
102 A21 6c gold & multi .45 .30
103 A21 8c gold & multi 2.00 .30
104 A21 10c gold & multi 2.00 .80
105 A21 15c gold & multi 2.25 1.50
a. Gold (Queen's head) omitted *1,100.*
106 A21 20c gold & multi .70 .45
107 A21 25c gold & multi .80 .45
108 A21 30c gold & multi .65 .55
109 A21 40c red lil, blk & gold 1.00 .75
Nos. 97-109 (13) 14.70 7.60

For overprint see No. 118.

Lantana — A22

Pitcairn Flowers: 2c, Indian shot (canna indica). 5c, Pulau (hibiscus tiliaceus). 25c, Wild gladioli.

1970, Mar. 23 **Litho.** ***Perf. 14***

110 A22 1c black & multi .25 .25
111 A22 2c black & multi .35 .35
112 A22 5c black & multi .55 .55
113 A22 25c black & multi 3.00 2.50
Nos. 110-113 (4) 4.15 3.65

Rudderfish (Dream Fish) — A23

Fish: 5c, Groupers (Auntie and Ann). 15c, Wrasse (Elwyn's trousers). 20c, Wrasse (Whistling daughter).

Perf. 14½x14

1970, Oct. 12 **Photo.** **Wmk. 314**

114 A23 5c black & multi 1.50 .75
115 A23 10c grnsh bl & blk 1.75 1.25
116 A23 15c multicolored 2.00 1.75
117 A23 20c multicolored 2.75 2.50
Nos. 114-117 (4) 8.00 6.25

No. 104 Overprinted in Silver: "ROYAL VISIT 1971"

1971, Feb. 22 **Litho.** ***Perf. 13x12½***

118 A21 10c gold & multi 2.40 2.40

Polynesian Artifacts — A24

Polynesian Art on Pitcairn: 5c, Rock carvings, vert. 15c, Making of stone fishhook. 20c, Seated deity, vert.

1971, May 3 **Litho.** ***Perf. 13½***

Queen's Head in Gold

119 A24 5c dk brown & bis 1.00 1.00
120 A24 10c ol green & blk 1.10 1.10
121 A24 15c black & lt vio 1.25 1.25
122 A24 20c black & rose red 1.60 1.60
Nos. 119-122 (4) 4.95 4.95

Health Care A25

4c, South Pacific Commission flag & Southern Cross, vert. 18c, Education (elementary school). 20c, Economy (country store).

1972, Apr. 4 **Litho.** ***Perf. 14x14½***

123 A25 4c vio bl, yel & ultra .65 .65
124 A25 8c brown & multi .75 .75
125 A25 18c yellow grn & multi .85 .85
126 A25 20c orange & multi 1.25 1.25
Nos. 123-126 (4) 3.50 3.50

So. Pacific Commission, 25th anniv.

Silver Wedding Issue, 1972

Common Design Type

Design: Queen Elizabeth II, Prince Philip, skuas and longboat.

1972, Nov. 20 **Photo.** **Wmk. 314**

127 CD324 4c slate grn & multi .30 .25
128 CD324 20c ultra & multi .60 .60

Pitcairn Coat of Arms A26

1973, Jan. 2 **Litho.** ***Perf. 14½x14***

129 A26 50c multicolored 3.00 *10.00*

Rose Apple — A27

1973, June 25 ***Perf. 14***

130 A27 4c shown .85 .85
131 A27 8c Mountain apple .95 .95
132 A27 15c Lata (myrtle) 1.25 1.25
133 A27 20c Cassia 1.40 1.40
134 A27 35c Guava 2.00 2.00
Nos. 130-134 (5) 6.45 6.45

Princess Anne's Wedding Issue

Common Design Type

1973, Nov. 14 **Litho.** ***Perf. 14***

135 CD325 10c lilac & multi .30 .25
136 CD325 25c gray grn & multi .40 .35

Miter and Horn Shells A28

1974, Apr. 15

137 A28 4c shown .70 .70
138 A28 10c Dove shells .95 .95
139 A28 18c Limpets and false limpet 1.10 1.10
140 A28 50c Lucine shells 2.00 2.00
a. Souvenir sheet of 4, #137-140 5.50 5.50
Nos. 137-140 (4) 4.75 4.75

Pitcairn Post Office, UPU Emblem A29

UPU, cent.: 20c, Stampless cover, "Posted at Pitcairn Island No Stamps Available." 35c, Longboat leaving Bounty Bay for ship offshore.

1974, July 22 **Wmk. 314** ***Perf. 14½***

141 A29 4c multicolored .40 .40
142 A29 20c multicolored .55 .55
143 A29 35c multicolored .65 .60
Nos. 141-143 (3) 1.60 1.55

Churchill: "Lift up your hearts . . ." — A30

Design: 35c, Churchill and "Give us the tools and we will finish the job."

1974, Nov. 30 **Litho.** **Wmk. 373**

144 A30 20c black & citron .40 .40
145 A30 35c black & yellow .75 .75

Sir Winston Churchill (1874-1965).

Queen Elizabeth II — A31

1975, Apr. 21 **Wmk. 314** ***Perf. 14½***

146 A31 $1 multicolored 7.00 *15.00*

Mailboats — A32

1975, July 22 **Litho.** ***Perf. 14½***

147 A32 4c Seringapatam, 1830 .50 .50
148 A32 10c Pitcairn, 1890 .60 .60
149 A32 18c Athenic, 1901 .90 .90
150 A32 50c Gothic, 1948 1.25 1.25
a. Souvenir sheet of 4, #147-150, perf. 14 12.00 12.00
Nos. 147-150 (4) 3.25 3.25

Pitcairn Wasp
A33

Insects: 6c, Grasshopper. 10c, Pitcairn moths. 15c, Dragonfly. 20c, Banana moth.

Wmk. 314

1975, Nov. 9 Litho. *Perf. 14½*

151	A33	4c blue grn & multi	.45	.45
152	A33	6c carmine & multi	.55	.55
153	A33	10c purple & multi	.75	.75
154	A33	15c black & multi	.85	.85
155	A33	20c multicolored	1.00	1.00
		Nos. 151-155 (5)	3.60	3.60

Fletcher Christian — A34 H.M.S. Bounty — A35

American Bicentennial: 30c, George Washington. 50c, Mayflower.

1976, July 4 Wmk. 373 *Perf. 13½*

156	A34	5c multicolored	.30	.30
157	A35	10c multicolored	.55	.55
158	A34	30c multicolored	.70	.70
a.		Pair, #156, 158	1.40	1.40
159	A35	50c multicolored	.85	.85
a.		Pair, #157, 159	1.75	1.75
		Nos. 156-159 (4)	2.40	2.40

Prince Philip's Arrival, 1971 Visit — A36

20c, Chair of homage. 50c, The enthronement.

1977, Feb. 6 *Perf. 13*

160	A36	8c silver & multi	.25	.25
161	A36	20c silver & multi	.30	.30
162	A36	50c silver & multi	.55	.55
		Nos. 160-162 (3)	1.10	1.10

25th anniv. of the reign of Elizabeth II.

Building Longboat — A37

Designs: 1c, Man ringing Island Bell, vert. 5c, Landing cargo. 6c, Sorting supplies. 9c, Cleaning wahoo (fish), vert. 10c, Farming. 15c, Sugar mill. 20c, Women grating coconuts and bananas. 35c, Island church. 50c, Gathering miro logs, Henderson Island. 70c, Burning obsolete stamps, vert. $1, Prince Philip and "Britannia." $2, Elizabeth II, vert.

1977-81 Litho. *Perf. 14½*

163	A37	1c multicolored	.30	*.45*
164	A37	2c multicolored	.30	*.45*
165	A37	5c multicolored	.30	*.45*
166	A37	6c multicolored	.30	*.45*
167	A37	9c multicolored	.30	*.45*
168	A37	10c multicolored	.30	*.45*
168A	A37	15c multicolored	1.10	*2.25*
169	A37	20c multicolored	.30	*.50*
170	A37	35c multicolored	.30	*.65*
171	A37	50c multicolored	.35	*.75*
171A	A37	70c multicolored	1.10	*2.50*
172	A37	$1 multicolored	.50	*.90*
173	A37	$2 multicolored	.70	*1.00*
		Nos. 163-173 (13)	6.15	*11.25*

Issued: #168A, 171A, 10/1/81; others, 9/12/77.

Building "Bounty" Model A38

Bounty Day: 20c, Bounty model afloat. 35c, Burning Bounty.

1978, Jan. 9 *Perf. 14½*

174	A38	6c yellow & multi	.40	.40
175	A38	20c yellow & multi	.55	.55
176	A38	35c yellow & multi	.70	.70
a.		Souvenir sheet of 3, #174-176	6.50	6.50
		Nos. 174-176 (3)	1.65	1.65

Souvenir Sheet

Elizabeth II in Coronation Regalia — A39

Wmk. 373

1978, Sept. Litho. *Perf. 12*

177	A39	$1.20 silver & multi	1.10	1.10

25th anniv. of coronation of Elizabeth II.

Unloading "Sir Geraint" A40

Designs: 15c, Harbor before development. 30c, Work on the jetty. 35c, Harbor after development.

Wmk. 373

1978, Dec. 18 Litho. *Perf. 13½*

178	A40	15c multicolored	.30	.30
179	A40	20c multicolored	.40	.40
180	A40	30c multicolored	.55	.55
181	A40	35c multicolored	.70	.70
		Nos. 178-181 (4)	1.95	1.95

Development of new harbor on Pitcairn.

John Adams A41

Design: 70c, John Adams' grave.

1979, Mar. 5 Litho. *Perf. 14½*

182	A41	35c multicolored	.45	.45
183	A41	70c multicolored	.75	.75

John Adams (1760-1829), founder of Pitcairn Colony, 150th death anniversary.

Pitcairn Island Seen from "Amphitrite" — A42

Engravings (c. 1850): 9c, Bounty Bay and Pitcairn Village, 20c, Lookout Ridge. 70c, Church and schoolhouse.

1979, Sept. 12 Litho. *Perf. 14*

184	A42	6c multicolored	.25	.25
185	A42	9c multicolored	.25	.25
186	A42	20c multicolored	.25	.25
187	A42	70c multicolored	.40	.40
		Nos. 184-187 (4)	1.15	1.15

Taking Presents to the Square, IYC Emblem — A43

IYC Emblem and Children's Drawings: 9c, Decorating trees with presents. 20c, Distributing presents. 35c, Carrying the presents home.

Wmk. 373

1979, Nov. 28 Litho. *Perf. 13½*

188	A43	6c multicolored	.25	.25
189	A43	9c multicolored	.25	.25
190	A43	20c multicolored	.25	.25
191	A43	35c multicolored	.35	.35
a.		Souvenir sheet of 4, #188-191	1.40	1.40
		Nos. 188-191 (4)	1.10	1.10

Christmas and IYC.

Souvenir Sheet

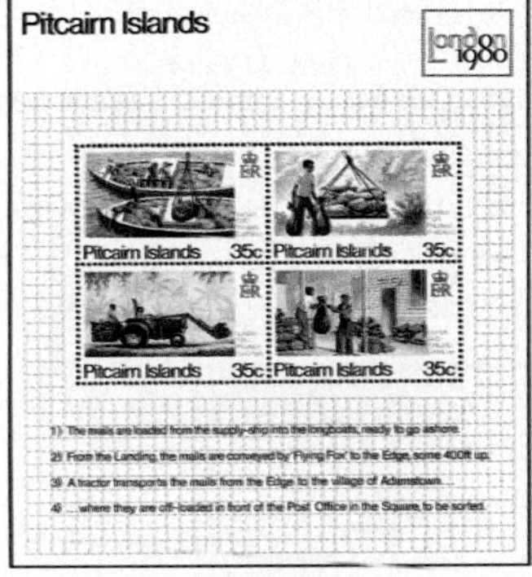

London 80 Intl. Phil. Exhibition — A44

Wmk. 373

1980, May 6 Litho. *Perf. 14½*

192	A44	Sheet of 4	1.40	1.40
a.		35c Mail Transport by Longboat	.30	.30
b.		35c Mail crane lift	.30	.30
c.		35c Tractor transport	.30	.30
d.		35c Arrival at post office	.30	.30

London 80 Intl. Phil. Exhib., May 6-14.

Queen Mother Elizabeth Birthday Issue

Common Design Type

Wmk. 373

1980, Aug. 4 Litho. *Perf. 14*

193	CD330	50c multicolored	.60	.60

Handicraft Type of 1968

Perf. 14½x14, 14x14½

1980, Sept. 29 Litho. Wmk. 373

194	A19	9c Turtles	.25	.25
195	A19	20c Wheelbarrow	.25	.25
196	A19	35c Gannet, vert.	.25	.25
197	A19	40c Bonnet and fan, vert.	.30	.30
		Nos. 194-197 (4)	1.05	1.05

Big George — A45

Wmk. 373

1981, Jan. 22 Litho. *Perf. 14*

198	A45	6c View of Adamstown	.25	.25
199	A45	9c shown	.25	.25
200	A45	20c Christian's Cave, Gannet's Ridge	.25	.25
201	A45	35c Pawala Valley Ridge	.25	.25
202	A45	70c Tatrimoa	.35	.35
		Nos. 198-202 (5)	1.35	1.35

Citizens Departing for Norfolk Island — A46

1981, May 3 Photo. *Perf. 13x14½*

203	A46	9c shown	.25	.25
204	A46	35c Norfolk Isld. from Morayshire	.35	.35
205	A46	70c Morayshire	.65	.65
		Nos. 203-205 (3)	1.25	1.25

Migration to Norfolk Is., 125th anniv.

Royal Wedding Issue

Common Design Type

Wmk. 373

1981, July 22 Litho. *Perf. 14*

206	CD331	20c Bouquet	.25	.25
207	CD331	35c Charles	.25	.25
208	CD331	$1.20 Couple	.60	.60
		Nos. 206-208 (3)	1.10	1.10

Lemon A47

1982, Feb. 23 Litho. *Perf. 14½*

209	A47	9c shown	.25	.25
210	A47	20c Pomegranate	.30	.30
211	A47	35c Avocado	.35	.35
212	A47	70c Pawpaw	.50	.50
		Nos. 209-212 (4)	1.40	1.40

Princess Diana Issue

Common Design Type

1982, July 1 Litho. *Perf. 14½x14*

213	CD333	6c Arms	.25	.25
214	CD333	9c Diana	.40	.40
215	CD333	70c Wedding	.55	.55
216	CD333	$1.20 Portrait	.95	.95
		Nos. 213-216 (4)	2.15	2.15

Christmas — A48

Designs: Various paintings of angels by Raphael. 50c, $1 vert.

1982, Oct. 19 Litho. *Perf. 14*

217	A48	15c multicolored	.30	.30
218	A48	20c multicolored	.30	.30
219	A48	50c multicolored	.40	.40
220	A48	$1 multicolored	.60	.60
		Nos. 217-220 (4)	1.60	1.60

A48a

1983, Mar. 14

221	A48a	6c Radio operator	.25	.25
222	A48a	9c Postal clerk	.25	.25
223	A48a	70c Fisherman	.40	.40
224	A48a	$1.20 Artist	.75	.75
		Nos. 221-224 (4)	1.65	1.65

Commonwealth Day.

175th Anniv. of Capt. Folger's Discovery of the Settlers A49

6c, Topaz off Pitcairn Isld. 20c, Topaz, islanders. 70c, John Adams welcoming Folger. $1.20, Presentation of Chronometer.

Wmk. 373

1983, June 14 Litho. *Perf. 14*

225 A49 6c multicolored .30 .30
226 A49 20c multicolored .45 .45
227 A49 70c multicolored .70 .70
228 A49 $1.20 multicolored 1.10 1.10
Nos. 225-228 (4) 2.55 2.55

Local Trees A50

1983, Oct. 6 Litho. *Perf. 13½*

229 Pair 1.00 1.00
a. A50 35c Hattie .40 .40
b. A50 35c Branch, wood painting .40 .40
230 Pair 1.75 1.75
a. A50 70c Pandanus .70 .70
b. A50 70c Branch, basket weaving .70 .70

See Nos. 289-290.

Pseudojuloides Atavai — A51

4c, Halichoeres melasmapomus. 6c, Scarus longipinnis. 9c, Variola louti. 10c, Centropyge hotumatua. 15c, Stegastes emeryi. 20c, Chaetodon smithi. 35c, Xanthichthys mento. 50c, Chrysiptera galba. 70c, Genicanthus spinus. $1, Myripristis tiki. $1.20, Anthias ventralis. $2, Pseudocaranx dentex.

Wmk. 373

1984, Jan. 11 Litho. *Perf. 14½*

231 A51 1c multicolored .25 .40
232 A51 4c multicolored .40 .30
233 A51 6c multicolored .40 .30
234 A51 9c multicolored .40 .30
235 A51 10c multicolored .40 .35
236 A51 15c multicolored .40 .35
237 A51 20c multicolored .50 *.50*
238 A51 35c multicolored .70 *.75*
239 A51 50c multicolored .70 *1.00*
240 A51 70c multicolored 1.00 *1.25*
241 A51 $1 multicolored 1.00 *1.50*
242 A51 $1.20 multicolored 1.20 *1.75*
243 A51 $2 multicolored 1.60 *2.00*
Nos. 231-243 (13) 8.95 10.75

See Nos. 295-296.

Constellations — A52

1984, May 14 Wmk. 373

244 A52 15c Crux Australis .30 .30
245 A52 20c Piscis Australis .40 .40
246 A52 70c Canis Minor .70 .70
247 A52 $1 Virgo 1.20 1.20
Nos. 244-247 (4) 2.60 2.60

Souvenir Sheet

AUSIPEX '84 — A53

Longboats.

1984, Sept. 21 Litho. Wmk. 373

248 Sheet of 2 2.50 2.50
a. A53 50c multicolored .50 .50
b. A53 $2 multicolored 1.75 1.75

HMS Portland off Bounty Bay, by J. Linton Palmer, 1853 — A54

Paintings by J. Linton Palmer, 1853, and William Smyth, 1825: 9c, Christian's Look Out at Pitcairn Island. 35c, The Golden Age. $2, View of Village, by Smyth.

Wmk. 373

1985, Jan. 16 Litho. *Perf. 14*

249 A54 6c multicolored .40 .40
250 A54 9c multicolored .40 .40
251 A54 35c multicolored .75 .75

Size: 48x32mm

252 A54 $2 multicolored 1.75 1.75
Nos. 249-252 (4) 3.30 3.30

Examples of No. 252 with "1835" date were not issued. Value, $85.

See Nos. 291-294.

Queen Mother 85th Birthday

Common Design Type

6c, In Dundee, 1964. 35c, At 80th birthday celebration. 70c, Queen Mother. $1.20, Holding Prince Henry.

$2, In coach at the Races, Ascot.

Perf. 14½x14

1985, June 7 Litho. Wmk. 384

253 CD336 6c multi .25 *.30*
254 CD336 35c multi .35 *.55*
255 CD336 70c multi .65 *.85*
256 CD336 $1.20 multi 1.25 *1.50*
Nos. 253-256 (4) 2.50 *3.20*

Souvenir Sheet

257 CD336 $2 multi 2.75 2.75

Act 6 — A55

Essi Gina A56

1985, Aug. 28 *Perf. 14½x14*

258 A55 50c shown 1.00 1.00
259 A55 50c Columbus Louisiana 1.00 1.00

Perf. 14

260 A56 50c shown 1.00 1.00
261 A56 50c Stolt Spirit 1.00 1.00
Nos. 258-261 (4) 4.00 4.00

See Nos. 281-284.

Christmas A57

Madonna & child paintings: 6c, by Raphael. 9c, by Krause. 35c, by Andreas Mayer. $2, by an unknown Austrian master.

1985, Nov. 26 *Perf. 14*

262 A57 6c multicolored .65 .65
263 A57 9c multicolored .65 .65
264 A57 35c multicolored 1.10 1.10
265 A57 $2 multicolored 3.50 3.50
Nos. 262-265 (4) 5.90 5.90

Turtles A58

Designs: 9c, 20c, Chelonia mydas. 70c, $1.20, Eretmochelys imbricata.

Wmk. 384

1986, Feb. 12 Litho. *Perf. 14½*

266 A58 9c multicolored 1.00 1.00
267 A58 20c multi, diff. 1.50 1.50
268 A58 70c multicolored 2.40 2.40
269 A58 $1.20 multi, diff. 3.00 3.00
Nos. 266-269 (4) 7.90 7.90

Queen Elizabeth II 60th Birthday

Common Design Type

Designs: 6c, In Royal Lodge garden, Windsor, 1946. 9c, Wedding of Princess Anne and Capt. Mark Philips, 1973. 20c, Wearing mantle and robes of Order of St. Paul's Cathedral, 1961. $1.20, Concert, Royal Festival Hall, London, 1971. $2, Visting Crown Agents' offices, 1983.

1986, Apr. 21 Litho. *Perf. 14½*

270 CD337 6c multi .25 .25
271 CD337 9c multi .25 .25
272 CD337 20c multi .35 .35
273 CD337 $1.20 multi .75 .75
274 CD337 $2 multi 1.10 1.10
Nos. 270-274 (5) 2.70 2.70

Royal Wedding Issue, 1986

Common Design Type

Designs: 20c, Informal portrait. $1.20, Andrew aboard royal navy vessel.

Wmk. 384

1986, July 23 Litho. *Perf. 14*

275 CD338 20c multi .40 .40
276 CD338 $1.20 multi 2.00 2.00

7th Day Adventist Church, Cent. — A59

Designs: 6c, First church, 1886, and John I. Tay, missionary. 20c, Second church, 1907, and mission ship Pitcairn, 1890. 35c, Third church, 1945, baptism and Down Isaac. $2, Church, 1954, and sailing ship.

1986, Oct. 18

277 A59 6c multicolored .50 .50
278 A59 20c multicolored 1.25 1.25
279 A59 35c multicolored 1.50 1.50
280 A59 $2 multicolored 4.25 4.25
Nos. 277-280 (4) 7.50 7.50

Ship Type of 1985

1987, Jan. 20 *Perf. 14x14½*

281 A55 50c Brussel 1.40 1.40
282 A55 50c Samoan Reefer 1.40 1.40

Perf. 14

283 A56 50c Australian Exporter 1.40 1.40
284 A56 50c Taupo 1.40 1.40
Nos. 281-284 (4) 5.60 5.60

Island Houses — A60

1987, May 21 Wmk. 373 *Perf. 14*

285 A60 70c lt greenish blue, bluish grn & blk .65 .65
286 A60 70c cream, yel bister & blk .65 .65
287 A60 70c lt blue, brt blue & blk .65 .65
288 A60 70c lt lil, brt vio & blk .65 .65
Nos. 285-288 (4) 2.60 2.60

Tree Type of 1983

1987, Aug. 10 Wmk. 384 *Perf. 14½*

289 Pair 1.75 1.75
a. A50 40c Leaves, blossoms .80 .80
b. A50 40c Monkey puzzle tree .80 .80
290 Pair 6.00 6.00
a. A50 $1.80 Leaves, blossoms, nuts 2.50 2.50
b. A50 $1.80 Duduinut tree 2.50 2.50

Art Type of 1985

Paintings by Lt. Conway Shipley, 1848: 20c, House and Tomb of John Adams. 40c, Bounty Bay, with H.M.S. Calypso. 90c, School House and Chapel. $1.80, Pitcairn Island with H.M.S. Calypso.

1987, Dec. 7 Litho. *Perf. 14*

291 A54 20c multi .65 .65
292 A54 40c multi 1.00 1.00
293 A54 90c multi 2.00 2.00

Size: 48x32mm

294 A54 $1.80 multi 3.00 3.00
Nos. 291-294 (4) 6.65 6.65

Fish Type of 1984

Wmk. 384

1988, Jan. 14 Litho. *Perf. 14½*

295 A51 90c Variola louti 3.50 3.50
296 A51 $3 Gymnothorax eurostus 5.00 5.00

Souvenir Sheet

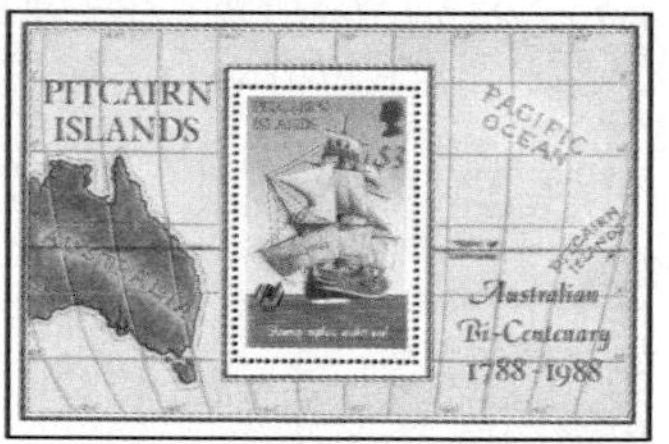

Australia Bicentennial — A61

1988, May 9 Wmk. 384 *Perf. 14*

297 A61 $3 HMS Bounty replica under sail 7.00 7.00

Visiting Ships A62

5c, HMS Swallow, 1767. 10c, HMS Pandora, 1791. 15c, HMS Briton and HMS Tagus, 1814. 20c, HMS Blossom, 1825. 30c, S.V. Lucy Anne, 1831. 35c, S.V. Charles Doggett, 1831. 40c, HMS Fly, 1838. 60c, LMS Camden, 1840. 90c, HMS Virago, 1853. $1.20, S.S. Rakaia, 1867. $1.80, HMS Sappho, 1882. $5, HMS Champion, 1893.

Wmk. 373

1988, Aug. 14 Litho. *Perf. 13½*

298 A62 5c multicolored .50 *.60*
299 A62 10c multicolored .50 *.60*
300 A62 15c multicolored .50 *.60*
301 A62 20c multicolored .60 *.70*
a. Wmk. 384 1.75 *2.00*
b. Booklet pane of 4, #301a 7.00
302 A62 30c multicolored .70 *.80*
303 A62 35c multicolored .70 *.80*
304 A62 40c multicolored .80 .80
305 A62 60c multicolored 1.00 *1.25*
306 A62 90c multicolored 1.10 *4.00*
a. Wmk. 384 3.75 *4.25*
b. Booklet pane of 4, #306a 15.00
307 A62 $1.20 multicolored 1.10 *1.50*
308 A62 $1.80 multicolored 1.50 *2.00*
309 A62 $5 multicolored 3.50 *5.00*
Nos. 298-309 (12) 12.50 *18.65*

Inscribed "1988" below design. Nos. 301a and 366a are inscribed "1990."

Issued: #301a-301b, 306a-306b, 5/3/90.

Constitution, 150th Anniv. — A63

Text and: 20c, Raising the Union Jack. 40c, Signing of the constitution aboard the H.M.S. "Fly," 1838. $1.05, Suffrage. $1.80, Equal education.

1988, Nov. 30 Wmk. 373 *Perf. 14*

315	A63	20c multicolored	.40	.40
316	A63	40c multicolored	.60	.60
317	A63	$1.05 multicolored	.95	.95
318	A63	$1.80 multicolored	1.40	1.40
		Nos. 315-318 (4)	3.35	3.35

Christmas A64

a, Angel, animals in stable. b, Holy Family. c, Two Magi. d, Magus and shepherd boy.

1988, Nov. 30 Wmk. 384 *Perf. 14*

319		Strip of 4	3.50	3.50
a.-d.	A64	90c any single	.80	.80

Miniature Sheets

Pitcairn Isls., Bicent. — A65

No. 320 (*Bounty* sets sail for the South Seas, Dec. 23, 1787): a, Fitting out the *Bounty* at Deptford. b, *Bounty* leaving Spithead. c, *Bounty* trying to round Cape Horn. d, Anchored in Adventure Bay, Tasmania. e, Ship's mates collecting breadfruit. f, Breadfruit in great cabin.

No. 321 (the mutiny, Apr. 28, 1789): a, *Bounty* leaving Mataval Bay. b, Mutineers waking Capt. Bligh. c, Confrontation between Fletcher Christian and Bligh. d, Bligh and crew members set adrift in an open boat. e, Castaways. f, Throwing breadfruit overboard.

No. 322. a, like No. 321e. b, Isle of Man #393. c, Norfolk Is. #453.

1989 Litho. Wmk. 373

320	A65	Sheet of 6	6.00	6.00
a.-f.		20c any single	.75	.75
321	A65	Sheet of 6	15.00	15.00
a.-f.		90c any single	2.00	2.25

Souvenir Sheet

Wmk. 384

322		Sheet of 3 + label	5.25	5.25
a.-c.		A65 90c any single	1.50	1.50

See #331, Isle of Man #389-394 and Norfolk Is. #452-456.

Issued: #320, Feb. 22; #321-322, Apr. 28.

Difference between #. 321e and 322a is inscription at bottom of #322a: "C. Abbott 1989 BOT."

Aircraft A66

20c, RNZAF Orion. 80c, Beechcraft Queen Air. $1.05, Navy helicopter, USS *Breton.* $1.30, RNZAF Hercules.

Wmk. 384

1989, July 25 Litho. *Perf. 14½*

323	A66	20c multicolored	1.00	1.00
324	A66	80c multicolored	2.25	2.25
325	A66	$1.05 multicolored	2.50	2.50
326	A66	$1.30 multicolored	2.75	2.75
		Nos. 323-326 (4)	8.50	8.50

Second mail drop on Pitcairn, Mar. 21, 1985 (20c); photo mission from Tahiti, Jan. 14, 1983 (80c); diesel fuel delivery by the navy, Feb. 12, 1969 ($1.05); and parachute delivery of a bulldozer, May 31, 1983 ($1.30).

The Islands A67

Wmk. 373

1989, Oct. 23 Litho. *Perf. 14*

327	A67	15c Ducie Is.	.50	.50
328	A67	90c Henderson Is.	1.50	1.50
329	A67	$1.05 Oeno Is.	2.00	2.00
330	A67	$1.30 Pitcairn Is.	2.25	2.25
		Nos. 327-330 (4)	6.25	6.25

Bicentennial Type of 1989

Miniature Sheet

Designs: a, Mutineers aboard *Bounty* anticipating landing on Pitcairn. b, Landing. c, Exploration of the island. d, Carrying goods ashore. e, Burning the *Bounty.* f, Settlement.

1990, Jan. 15 Wmk. 384 *Perf. 14*

331		Sheet of 6 + 3 labels	10.00	10.00
a.-f.		A65 40c any single	1.10	1.10

Stamp World London '90 — A68

Links with the UK: 80c, Peter Heywood and Ennerdale, Cumbria. 90c, John Adams and The Tower of St. Augustine, Hackney. $1.05, William Bligh and The Citadel Gateway, Plymouth. $1.30, Fletcher Christian and birthplace, Cockermouth.

1990, May 3 Wmk. 373 *Perf. 14*

332	A68	80c multicolored	1.00	1.00
333	A68	90c multicolored	1.10	1.10
334	A68	$1.05 multicolored	1.25	1.25
335	A68	$1.30 multicolored	1.75	1.75
		Nos. 332-335 (4)	5.10	5.10

Queen Mother 90th Birthday

Common Design Types

1990, Aug. 4 Wmk. 384 *Perf. 14x15*

336	CD343	40c Portrait, 1937	.75	.75

Perf. 14½

337	CD344	$3 King, Queen in carriage	3.50	3.50

First Pitcairn Island Postage Stamps, 50th Anniv — A69

Historical items and Pitcairn Islands stamps — 20c, Chronometer, #2. 80c, Bounty's Bible, #31. 90c, Bounty's Bell, #108. $1.05, Bounty, #172. $1.30, Penny Black, #300.

Perf. 13½x14

1990, Oct. 15 Wmk. 373

338	A69	20c multicolored	.80	.80
339	A69	80c multicolored	1.60	1.60
340	A69	90c multicolored	1.75	1.75
341	A69	$1.05 multicolored	2.00	2.00
342	A69	$1.30 multicolored	2.25	2.25
		Nos. 338-342 (5)	8.40	8.40

Birds — A70

1990, Dec. 5 Wmk. 373 *Perf. 14*

343	A70	20c Redbreast	1.00	1.00
344	A70	90c Wood pigeon	1.75	1.75
345	A70	$1.30 Sparrow	2.00	2.00
346	A70	$1.80 Flightless chicken	2.25	2.25
		Nos. 343-346 (4)	7.00	7.00

Birdpex '90, 20th Intl. Ornithological Congress, New Zealand.

Miniature Sheet

Pitcairn Islands, Bicent. — A71

Bicentennial celebrations: a, Re-enacting the landing. b, Commemorative plaque. c, Memorial church service. d, Cricket match. e, Bounty model burning. f, Fireworks.

Wmk. 384

1991, Mar. 24 Litho. *Perf. 14½*

347	A71	80c Sheet of 6, #a.-f.	12.00	12.00

Elizabeth & Philip, Birthdays

Common Design Types

Wmk. 384

1991, July 12 Litho. *Perf. 14½*

348	CD346	20c multicolored	.50	.50
349	CD345	$1.30 multicolored	2.00	2.00
a.		Pair, #348-349 + label	3.25	3.25

Cruise Ships A72

15c, Europa. 80c, Royal Viking Star. $1.30, World Discoverer. $1.80, Sagafjord.

1991, June 17

350	A72	15c multicolored	1.25	1.25
351	A72	80c multicolored	2.25	2.25
352	A72	$1.30 multicolored	2.75	2.75
353	A72	$1.80 multicolored	3.25	3.25
		Nos. 350-353 (4)	9.50	9.50

Island Vehicles A73

1991, Sept. 25 Wmk. 373 *Perf. 14*

354	A73	20c Bulldozer	.60	.60
355	A73	80c Motorcycle	1.50	1.50
356	A73	$1.30 Tractor	1.75	1.75
357	A73	$1.80 All-terrain vehicle	2.50	2.50
		Nos. 354-357 (4)	6.35	6.35

Christmas — A74

1991, Nov. 18 *Perf. 14x14½*

358	A74	20c The Annunciation	.50	.50
359	A74	80c Shepherds	1.25	1.25
360	A74	$1.30 Nativity scene	1.50	1.50
361	A74	$1.80 Three wise men	2.10	2.10
		Nos. 358-361 (4)	5.35	5.35

Queen Elizabeth II's Accession to the Throne, 40th Anniv.

Common Design Type

Wmk. 384

1992, Feb. 6 Litho. *Perf. 14*

362	CD349	20c multicolored	.50	.50
363	CD349	60c multicolored	.85	.85
364	CD349	90c multicolored	1.10	1.10
365	CD349	$1 multicolored	1.15	1.15

Wmk. 373

366	CD349	$1.80 multicolored	1.75	1.75
		Nos. 362-366 (5)	5.35	5.35

Sharks — A75

Designs: 20c, Carcharhinus galapagensis. $1, Eugomphodus taurus. $1.50, Carcharhinus melanopterus. $1.80, Carcharhinus amblyrhynchos.

Perf. 15x14½

1992, June 30 Litho. Wmk. 373

367	A75	20c multicolored	.75	.75
368	A75	$1 multicolored	2.25	2.25
369	A75	$1.50 multicolored	2.50	2.50
370	A75	$1.80 multicolored	3.00	3.00
		Nos. 367-370 (4)	8.50	8.50

Sir Peter Scott Commemorative Expedition to Pitcairn Islands, 1991-92 — A76

Designs: 20c, Montastrea, acropora coral sticks. $1, Henderson sandalwood. $1.50, Murphy's petrel. $1.80, Henderson hawkmoth.

Perf. 14x15

1992, Sept. 11 Litho. Wmk. 373

371	A76	20c multicolored	.80	.80
372	A76	$1 multicolored	1.75	1.75
373	A76	$1.50 multicolored	3.00	3.00
374	A76	$1.80 multicolored	3.50	3.50
		Nos. 371-374 (4)	9.05	9.05

Captain William Bligh, 175th Anniv. of Death A77

20c, Bligh's birthplace, St. Tudy, Cornwall, HMS Resolution. $1, On deck of HMAV Bounty, breadfruit plant. $1.50, Voyage in open boat, Bligh's answers at court martial. $1.80, Portrait by Rachel H. Combe, Battle of Camperdown, 1797.

Wmk. 373

1992, Dec. 7 Litho. *Perf. 14½*

375	A77	20c multicolored	.60	.60
376	A77	$1 multicolored	1.75	1.75
377	A77	$1.50 multicolored	2.25	2.25
378	A77	$1.80 multicolored	2.75	2.75
		Nos. 375-378 (4)	7.35	7.35

Royal Naval Vessels A78

Wmk. 384

1993, Mar. 10 Litho. *Perf. 14*

379	A78	15c HMS Chichester	.85	.85
380	A78	20c HMS Jaguar	1.00	1.00
381	A78	$1.80 HMS Andrew	4.25	4.25
382	A78	$3 HMS Warrior	6.75	6.75
		Nos. 379-382 (4)	12.85	12.85

Coronation of Queen Elizabeth II, 40th Anniv. A79

Wmk. 373

1993, June 17 Litho. *Perf. 13*

383	A79	$5 multicolored	7.00	7.00

Scenic Views A80

10c, Pawala Valley Ridge. 90c, St. Pauls. $1.20, Matt's Rocks from Water Valley. $1.50, Ridge Rope to St. Paul's Pool. $1.80, Ship Landing Point.

Wmk. 373

1993, Sept. 8 Litho. *Perf. 14*

384	A80	10c multicolored	.40	.40
385	A80	90c multicolored	1.10	1.10
386	A80	$1.20 multicolored	1.50	1.50
387	A80	$1.50 multicolored	1.60	1.60
388	A80	$1.80 multicolored	2.50	2.50
		Nos. 384-388 (5)	7.10	7.10

Lizards A81

Designs: 20c, Indopacific tree gecko. No. 390, Stump-toed gecko. No. 391, Mourning gecko. $1, Moth skink No. 393, Snake-eyed skink. No. 394, White-bellied skink.

Perf. 13x13½

1993, Dec. 14 Litho. Wmk. 373

389	A81	20c multicolored	.95	.95
390	A81	45c multicolored	1.00	1.00
391	A81	45c multicolored	1.00	1.00
a.		Pair, #390-391	2.50	2.50
392	A81	$1 multicolored	2.00	2.00
393	A81	$1.50 multicolored	2.50	2.50
394	A81	$1.50 multicolored	2.50	2.50
a.		Pair, #393-394	7.00	7.00
		Nos. 389-394 (6)	9.95	9.95

Nos. 390-391, 393-394 Ovptd. with Hong Kong '94 Emblem

Perf. 13x13½

1994, Feb. 18 Litho. Wmk. 373

395	A81	45c on #390	.80	.80
396	A81	45c on #391	.80	.80
a.		Pair, #395-396	2.00	2.00
397	A81	$1.50 on #393	2.25	2.25
398	A81	$1.50 on #394	2.25	2.25
a.		Pair, #397-398	6.00	6.00
		Nos. 395-398 (4)	6.10	6.10

Early Pitcairners — A82

Designs: 5c, Friday October Christian. 20c, Moses Young. $1.80, James Russell McCoy. $3, Rosalind Amelia Young.

1994, Mar. 7 *Perf. 14*

399	A82	5c multicolored	.30	.30
400	A82	20c multicolored	.60	.60
401	A82	$1.80 multicolored	2.50	2.50
402	A82	$3 multicolored	4.00	4.00
		Nos. 399-402 (4)	7.40	7.40

Shipwrecks A83

20c, Wildwave, Oeno Island, 1858. 90c, Cornwallis, Pitcairn Island, 1875. $1.80, Acadia, Ducie Island, 1881. $3, Oregon, Oeno Island, 1883.

Wmk. 373

1994, June 22 Litho. *Perf. 14*

403	A83	20c multicolored	.75	.75
404	A83	90c multicolored	2.00	2.00
405	A83	$1.80 multicolored	3.25	3.25
406	A83	$3 multicolored	4.75	4.75
		Nos. 403-406 (4)	10.75	10.75

Corals A84

Designs: 20c, Fire coral, vert. 90c, Cauliflower coral, arc-eye hawkfish. $1, Snubnose chub, lobe coral, vert.

$3, Coral garden, butterflyfish, vert.

Wmk. 373

1994, Sept. 15 Litho. *Perf. 14*

407	A84	20c multicolored	.90	.90
408	A84	90c multicolored	2.00	2.00
409	A84	$1 multicolored	2.50	2.50
		Nos. 407-409 (3)	5.40	5.40

Souvenir Sheet

410	A84	$3 multicolored	5.50	5.50

Christmas A85

Flowers: 20c, Morning glory. 90c, Hibiscus, vert. $1, Frangipani. $3, Ginsey, vert.

Wmk. 373

1994, Nov. 24 Litho. *Perf. 14*

411	A85	20c multicolored	.45	.45
412	A85	90c multicolored	1.50	1.50
413	A85	$1 multicolored	1.75	1.75
414	A85	$3 multicolored	3.50	3.50
		Nos. 411-414 (4)	7.20	7.20

Birds A86

Designs: 5c, Fairy tern. 10c, Red-tailed tropicbird chick, vert. 15c, Henderson rail. 20c, Red-footed booby, vert. 45c, Blue-gray noddy. 50c, Henderson reed warbler. 90c, Common noddy. $1, Masked booby, chick, vert. $1.80, Henderson fruit dove. $2, Murphy's petrel. $3, Christmas shearwater. $5, Red-tailed tropicbird juvenile.

1995, Mar. 8 *Perf. 13½*

415	A86	5c multicolored	.60	.60
416	A86	10c multicolored	.60	.60
417	A86	15c multicolored	.75	.75
418	A86	20c multicolored	.75	.75
419	A86	45c multicolored	1.00	1.00
420	A86	50c multicolored	1.25	1.25
421	A86	90c multicolored	1.50	1.50
422	A86	$1 multicolored	1.75	1.75
423	A86	$1.80 multicolored	2.50	2.50
424	A86	$2 multicolored	2.75	2.75
425	A86	$3 multicolored	3.00	3.00
426	A86	$5 multicolored	4.25	4.25
		Nos. 415-426 (12)	20.70	20.70

Oeno Island Vacation — A87

Designs: 20c, Boating. 90c, Volleyball on the beach. $1.80, Picnic. $3, Sing-a-long.

1995, June 26 *Perf. 14x15*

427	A87	20c multicolored	.50	.50
428	A87	90c multicolored	1.25	1.25
429	A87	$1.80 multicolored	2.25	2.25
430	A87	$3 multicolored	3.75	3.75
		Nos. 427-430 (4)	7.75	7.75

Souvenir Sheet

Queen Mother, 95th Birthday — A88

1995, Aug. 4 *Perf. 14½*

431	A88	$5 multicolored	7.50	7.50

Radio, Cent. — A89

Designs: 20c, Guglielmo Marconi, radio equipment, 1901. $1, Man, Pitcairn radio, 1938. $1.50, Woman, satellite earth station equipment, 1994. $3, Satellite in orbit, 1992.

1995, Sept. 5 *Perf. 13*

432	A89	20c multicolored	.45	.45
433	A89	$1 multicolored	1.25	1.25
434	A89	$1.50 multicolored	2.00	2.00
435	A89	$3 multicolored	4.00	4.00
		Nos. 432-435 (4)	7.70	7.70

UN, 50th Anniv.

Common Design Type

Designs: 20c, Lord Mayor's Show. $1, RFA Brambleleaf. $1.50, UN ambulance. $3, Royal Air Force Tristar.

Wmk. 373

1995, Oct. 24 Litho. *Perf. 14*

436	CD353	20c multicolored	.40	.40
437	CD353	$1 multicolored	1.75	1.75
438	CD353	$1.50 multicolored	2.25	2.25
439	CD353	$3 multicolored	3.75	3.75
		Nos. 436-439 (4)	8.15	8.15

Supply Ship Day — A90

1996, Jan. 30 *Perf. 14x14½*

440	A90	20c Early morning	.35	.35
441	A90	40c Meeting ship	.50	.50
442	A90	90c Unloading supplies	1.25	1.25
443	A90	$1 Landing work	1.40	1.40
444	A90	$1.50 Supply sorting	1.75	1.75
445	A90	$1.80 Last load	2.25	2.25
		Nos. 440-445 (6)	7.50	7.50

Queen Elizabeth II, 70th Birthday

Common Design Type

Various portraits of Queen, scenes from Pitcairn Islands: 20c, Bounty Bay. 90c, Jetty, Landing Point, Bounty Bay. $1.80, Matt's Rocks. $3, St. Paul's.

1996, Apr. 21 *Perf. 13½x14*

446	CD354	20c multicolored	.60	.60
447	CD354	90c multicolored	1.75	1.75
448	CD354	$1.80 multicolored	2.50	2.50
449	CD354	$3 multicolored	3.75	3.75
		Nos. 446-449 (4)	8.60	8.60

CHINA '96, 9th Asian Intl. Philatelic Exhibition — A91

#450, Chinese junk. #451, HMAV Bounty. No. 452: a, Chinese rat. b, Polynesian rat.

1996, May 17 *Perf. 14*

450	A91	$1.80 multicolored	2.75	2.75
451	A91	$1.80 multicolored	2.75	2.75

Souvenir Sheet

452	A91	90c Sheet of 2, #a.-b.	3.00	3.00

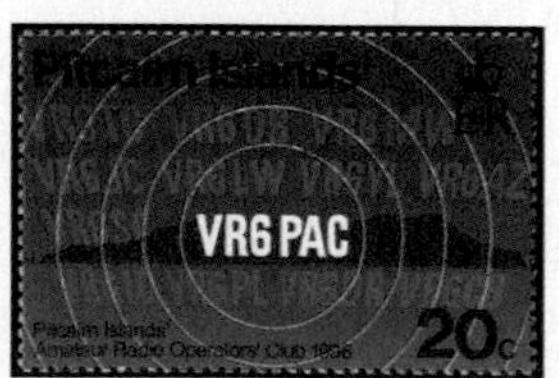

Amateur Radio — A92

Designs: 20c, Call signs of members in Amateur Radio Operator's Club, 1996. No. 454, VR6 1M calling for medical assistance. No. 455, Operator receiving transmission, physician standing by. $2.50, Andrew Young, Pitcairn's first operator, 1938.

1996, Sept. 4 Wmk. 384 *Perf. 14*

453	A92	20c multicolored	.65	.65
454	A92	$1.50 multicolored	2.50	2.50
455	A92	$1.50 multicolored	2.50	2.50
a.		Pair, #454-455	6.00	6.00
456	A92	$2.50 multicolored	3.25	3.25
		Nos. 453-456 (4)	8.90	8.90

Birds
A93

World Wildlife Fund: 5c, Henderson Island reed-warbler, vert. 10c, Stephen's lorikeet, vert. 20c, Henderson Island rail, vert. 90c, Henderson Island fruit-dove, vert. No. 461, Masked booby. No. 462, Common fairy-tern.

1996, Nov. 20 **Wmk. 373**

457	A93	5c multicolored	.65	.65
458	A93	10c multicolored	.65	.65
459	A93	20c multicolored	1.25	1.25
460	A93	90c multicolored	1.50	1.50
461	A93	$2 multicolored	2.00	2.00
462	A93	$2 multicolored	2.00	2.00
		Nos. 457-462 (6)	8.05	8.05

Nos. 461 and 462 do not include WWF emblem.

Souvenir Sheet

Coat of Arms — A94

1997, Feb. 12 ***Perf. 14½x14***

463	A94	$5 multicolored	7.25	7.25

Hong Kong '97.

South Pacific Commission, 50th Anniv. — A95

a, MV David Baker. b, MV McLachlan.

Perf. 13½x14

1997, May 26 **Litho.** **Wmk. 373**

464	A95	$2.50 Sheet of 2, #a.-b.	7.00	7.00

Health Care
A96

Designs: 20c, New Health Center. $1, Resident nurse treating patient. $1.70, Dental officer treating patient. $3, Patient being taken aboard ship.

Wmk. 373

1997, Sept. 12 **Litho.** ***Perf. 14***

465	A96	20c multicolored	.50	.50
466	A96	$1 multicolored	1.25	1.25
467	A96	$1.70 multicolored	2.00	2.00
468	A96	$3 multicolored	4.50	4.50
		Nos. 465-468 (4)	8.25	8.25

Queen Elizabeth II and Prince Philip, 50th Wedding Anniv. — A97

Designs: No. 469, Prince driving team of horses. No. 470, Queen wearing wide-brimmed hat. No. 471, Prince in formal riding attire. No. 472, Queen, horse. No. 473, Queen and Prince standing behind flowers. No. 474, Prince Charles riding horse.

Wmk. 373

1997, Nov. 20 **Litho.** ***Perf. 13***

469		20c multicolored	.40	.40
470		20c multicolored	.40	.40
a.		A97 Pair, #469-470	1.00	1.00
471		$1 multicolored	1.25	1.25
472		$1 multicolored	1.25	1.25
a.		A97 Pair, #471-472	3.00	3.00
473		$1.70 multicolored	1.75	1.75
474		$1.70 multicolored	1.75	1.75
a.		A97 Pair, #473-474	4.25	4.25
		Nos. 469-474 (6)	6.80	6.80

Christmas
A98

Flower, picture: 20c, Gardenia taitensis, view of Island at night. 80c, Bauhinia variegata, ringing public bell. $1.20, Metrosideros collina, children's baskets hanging on line. $3, Hibiscus tiliaceus, Pitcairn Church, Square at Adamstown.

Wmk. 373

1997, Dec. 1 **Litho.** ***Perf. 13½***

475	A98	20c multicolored	.50	.50
476	A98	80c multicolored	1.50	1.50
477	A98	$1.20 multicolored	1.75	1.75
478	A98	$3 multicolored	3.25	3.25
		Nos. 475-478 (4)	7.00	7.00

Views of Christian's Cave — A99

5c, Dorcas Apple, looking across Adamstown. 20c, Rocks near Betty's Edge looking past Tatinanny. 35c, Cave mouth. $5, Cave from road near where Fletcher Christian built home.

Wmk. 384

1998, Feb. 9 **Litho.** ***Perf. 13½***

479	A99	5c multi	.35	.35
480	A99	20c multi	.65	.65
481	A99	35c multi, vert.	.85	.85
482	A99	$5 multi, vert.	5.00	5.00
		Nos. 479-482 (4)	6.85	6.85

Sailing Ships
A100

Designs: 20c, HMS Bounty, 1790. 90c, HMS Swallow, 1767. $1.80, HMS Briton & HMS Tagus, 1814. $3, HMS Fly, 1838.

Perf. 14½x14

1998, May 28 **Litho.** **Wmk. 373**

483	A100	20c multicolored	.90	.90
484	A100	90c multicolored	1.50	1.50
485	A100	$1.80 multicolored	2.25	2.25
486	A100	$3 multicolored	3.25	3.25
		Nos. 483-486 (4)	7.90	7.90

Diana, Princess of Wales (1961-97)

Common Design Type

a, In evening dress. b, Wearing white hat, pearls. c, In houndstooth top. d, Wearing white hat, top.

Perf. 14½x14

1998, Aug. 31 **Litho.** **Wmk. 373**

487	CD355	90c Sheet of 4, #a.-d.	4.75	4.75

No. 487 sold for $3.60 + 40c with surtax being donated to the Princess Diana Memorial Fund.

Flowers
A101

20c, Bidens mathewsii. 90c, Hibiscus. $1.80, Osteomeles anthyllidifolia. $3, Ipomoea littoralis.

Wmk. 373

1998, Oct. 20 **Litho.** ***Perf. 14***

488	A101	20c multicolored	1.25	1.25
489	A101	90c multicolored	2.00	2.00
490	A101	$1.80 multicolored	3.50	3.50
491	A101	$3 multicolored	4.00	4.00
		Nos. 488-491 (4)	10.75	10.75

Flowers are below inscriptions on Nos. 489, 491.

Intl. Year of the Ocean
A102

Designs: 20c, Fishing. 90c, Divers, vert. $1.80, Reef fish. $3, Murphy's petrel, vert.

Unwmk.

1998, Dec. 16 **Litho.** ***Perf. 14***

492	A102	20c multicolored	1.40	1.40
493	A102	90c multicolored	2.50	2.50
494	A102	$1.80 multicolored	4.00	4.00
495	A102	$3 multicolored	5.75	5.75
a.		Souv. sheet of 4, #492-495 + label	16.00	16.00
		Nos. 492-495 (4)	13.65	13.65

Government Education on Pitcairn, 50th Anniv. — A103

Scenes on pages of books: 20c, Schoolmaster George Hunn Nobbs, students, 1828. 90c, Schoolmaster Simon Young, daughter Rosalind, teacher Hattie Andre, 1893. $1.80, Teacher Roy Clark, 1932. $3, Modern school at Palau, 1999.

Unwmk.

1999, Feb. 15 **Litho.** ***Perf. 14***

496	A103	20c multicolored	1.00	1.00
497	A103	90c multicolored	1.50	1.50
498	A103	$1.80 multicolored	3.00	3.00
499	A103	$3 multicolored	5.00	5.00
		Nos. 496-499 (4)	10.50	10.50

Archaeological Expedition to Survey Wreck of the Bounty — A104

Scenes of ship during last voyage and: a, 50c, Anchor. b, $1, Cannon. c, $1.50, Chronometer. d, $2, Copper caldron.

1999, Mar. 19

500	A104	Sheet of 4, #a.-d.	13.00	13.00

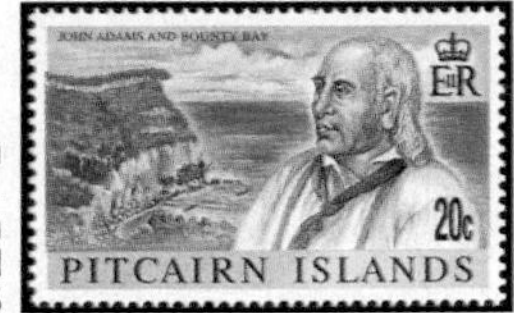

19th Cent. Pitcairn Island
A105

Designs: 20c, John Adams (d. 1829), Bounty Bay. 90c, Topaz, 1808. $1.80, George Hunn Nobbs, Norfolk Island. $3, HMS Champion, 1893.

Perf. 14½x14

1999, May 25 **Litho.** **Wmk. 373**

501	A105	20c multicolored	1.00	1.00
502	A105	90c multicolored	2.40	2.40
503	A105	$1.80 multicolored	3.00	3.00
504	A105	$3 multicolored	5.50	5.50
		Nos. 501-504 (4)	11.90	11.90

Wedding of Prince Edward and Sophie Rhys-Jones

Common Design Type

Perf. 13¾x14

1999, June 18 **Litho.** **Wmk. 384**

505	CD356	$2.50 Separate portraits	3.50	3.50
506	CD356	$2.50 Couple	3.50	3.50

Honey Bees
A106

Designs: 20c, Beekeepers, hives. $1, Bee, white and purple flower. $1.80, Bees, honeycomb. $3, Bee on flower, honey jar.

Die Cut Perf. 9

1999, Sept. 12 **Litho.**

Self-Adhesive

507	A106	20c multicolored	1.00	1.00
508	A106	$1 multicolored	2.00	2.00
a.		Souvenir sheet of 1	6.00	6.00
509	A106	$1.80 multicolored	3.25	3.25
510	A106	$3 multicolored	4.50	4.50
		Nos. 507-510 (4)	10.75	10.75

China 1999 World Philatelic Exhibition, No. 508a. Issued 8/21.

Protection of Galapagos Tortoise "Mr. Turpen"
A107

Designs: a, 5c, Arrival of the ship Yankee, 1937. b, 20c, Off-loading Mr. Turpen to a longboat. c, 35c, Mr. Turpen. d, $5, Close-up of tortoise's head.

Perf. 14¼

2000, Jan. 14 Litho. Unwmk.

511 A107 Strip of 4 + label 9.50 9.50

Flowers A108

Designs: 10c, Guettarda speciosa. 15c, Hibiscus tiliaceus. 20c, Selenicereus grandiflorus. 30c, Metrosideros collina. 50c, Alpinia zerumbet. $1, Syzygium jambos. $1.50, Commelina diffusa. $1.80, Canna indica. $2, Allamanda cathartica. $3, Calophyllum inophyllum. $5, Ipomea indica. $10, Bauhinia monandra (40x40mm).

Litho., Litho. with Foil Application ($10)

Perf. 13¾x13¼, 13¼x13¾ ($10)

2000, May 22 Unwmk.

512-523 A108 Set of 12 26.50 26.50
520a Souvenir sheet, #518, 520 8.25 8.25

The Stamp Show 2000, London (No. 520a).

Millennium — A109

Old and modern pictures: 20c, Longboat at sea. 90c, Landing and longboat house. $1.80, Transportation of crops. $3, Communications.

Wmk. 373

2000, June 28 Litho. ***Perf. 13¾***

524-527 A109 Set of 4 12.00 12.00

Souvenir Sheets

Satellite Recovery Mission — A110

No. 528: a, Surveyor, helicopter. b, Military personnel, boat, ship, helicopter.

2000, July 7 Unwmk. ***Perf. 14¼***

528 A110 $2.50 Sheet of 2, #a-b 15.00 15.00

World Stamp Expo 2000, Anaheim.

Illustration shows lower half of the entire sheet. The upper half, which has descriptive text, and is printed on the reverse, is the same size as the lower half. The entire sheet is folded where the halves meet.

Queen Mother, 100th Birthday — A111

No. 529: a, $2, Blue hat. b, $3, Maroon hat.

2000, Aug. 4 ***Perf. 14***

529 A111 Sheet of 2, #a-b 7.00 7.00

Christmas A112

Perf. 14½

2000, Nov. 22 Litho. Unwmk.

530 Strip of 4 10.00 10.00
a. A112 20c Woman .75 .75
b. A112 80c Man, boy 2.00 2.00
c. A112 $1.50 Woman, child 3.00 3.00
d. A112 $3 Three children 4.00 4.00

Cruise Ships A113

Designs: No. 531, $1.50, Bremen. No. 532, $1.50, MV Europa. No. 533, $1.50, MS Rotterdam. No. 534, $1.50, Saga Rose.

Perf. 14¾

2001, Feb. 1 Litho. Unwmk.

531-534 A113 Set of 4 12.00 12.00

Values are for stamps with surrounding selvage.

Tropical Fruit — A114

Designs: 20c, Cocos nucifera. 80c, Punica granatum. $1, Passiflora edulis. $3, Ananas comosus.

2001, Apr. 6 Litho. ***Perf. 13½x13¼***

535-538 A114 Set of 4 7.50 7.50
538a Souvenir sheet, #536, 538 5.25 5.25

Allocation of ".pn" Internet Domain Suffix — A115

CD and: 20c, Computer keyboard. 50c, Circuit board. $1, Integrated circuit. $5, Mouse.

2001, June 11 ***Serpentine Die Cut***

Self-Adhesive

539-542 A115 Set of 4 11.00 11.00

Tropical Fish — A116

Designs: 20c, Chaetodon ornatissimus. 80c, Chaetodon reticulatus. $1.50, Chaetodon lunula. $2, Henochus chrysostomus.

Perf. 13x13¼

2001, Sept. 4 Litho. Unwmk.

543-546 A116 Set of 4 9.50 9.50
546a Souvenir sheet, #543, 546 3.25 3.25

Wood Carving — A117

No. 547: a, 20c, Miro flower, man on beach carrying log. b, 50c, Toa flower, artisans carving fish. c, $1.50, Pulau flower, man using machine, woman looking at carved objects. d, $3, Ship, boat, carved objects.

2001, Oct. 11

547 A117 Horiz. strip of 4, #a-d, + central label 8.50 8.50

Cowrie Shells A118

Designs: 20c, Cypraea argus. 80c, Cypraea isabella. $1, Cypraea mappa. $3, Cypraea mauritana.

2001, Dec. 6 ***Perf. 13¼x13***

548-551 A118 Set of 4 7.75 7.75

Reign Of Queen Elizabeth II, 50th Anniv. Issue

Common Design Type

Souvenir Sheet

No. 552: a, 50c, With Queen Mother and Princess Margaret. b, $1, Wearing tiara. c, $1.20, Without hat. d, $1.50, Wearing hat. e, $2, 1955 portrait by Annigoni (38x50mm).

Perf. 14¼x14½, 13¾ (#552e)

2002, Feb. 6 Litho. Wmk. 373

552 CD360 Sheet of 5, #a-e 9.25 9.25

Famous Men — A119

Designs: No. 553, $1.50, Gerald DeLeo Bliss (1882-1957), Panamanian postmaster who expedited Pitcairn mail. No. 554, $1.50, Capt. Arthur C. Jones (1898-1987), shipper of trees to Pitcairn. No. 555, $1.50, James Russell McCoy (1845-1924), missionary. No. 556, $1.50, Adm. Sir Fairfax Moresby (1786-1877), philanthropist.

Perf. 14¼x14¾

2002, Apr. 5 Litho. Unwmk.

553-556 A119 Set of 4 12.00 12.00

Cats — A120

Local cats: 20c, Simba Christian. $1, Miti Christian. $1.50, Nala Brown. $3, Alicat Pulau.

Perf. 13¼x13

2002, June 28 Litho. Unwmk.

557-560 A120 Set of 4 8.25 8.25
a. Souvenir sheet of 2, #557, 560 5.00 5.00

Queen Mother Elizabeth (1900-2002)

Common Design Type

Designs: 40c, As child, c. 1910 (black and white photograph). Nos. 562, 565a, $1, As young woman, without hat. $1.50, Wearing flowered hat. Nos. 564, 565b, $2, Wearing blue hat.

Wmk. 373

2002, Aug. 5 Litho. ***Perf. 14¼***

With Purple Frames

561 CD361 40c multicolored 1.25 1.25
562 CD361 $1 multicolored 2.00 2.00
563 CD361 $1.50 multicolored 2.50 2.50
564 CD361 $2 multicolored 3.00 3.00
Nos. 561-564 (4) 8.75 8.75

Souvenir Sheet

Without Purple Frames

Perf. 14½x14¼

565 CD361 Sheet of 2, #a-b 6.50 6.50

Weaving — A121

No. 566: a, 40c, Woman cutting thatch. b, 80c, Woman dyeing thatch. c, $1.50, Millie Christian weaving. d, $2.50, Thelma Brown with finished products.

Perf. 13¼x12¾

2002, Oct. 18 Litho. Unwmk.

566 A121 Horiz. strip of 4, #a-d + central label 12.00 12.00

Trees A122

Designs: 40c, Dudwi nut. $1, Toa. $1.50, Miro. $3, Hulianda.

Perf. 13¼

2002, Dec. 1 Litho. Unwmk.

567-570 A122 Set of 4 9.50 9.50

Souvenir Sheet

Blue Star Line Ships — A123

2003, Jan. 8 Litho. ***Perf. 14x13¼***

571 A123 $5 multi 11.00 11.00

Cone Shells A124

Designs: 40c, Conus geographus. 80c, Conus textile. $1, Conus striatus. $1.20, Conus marmoreus. $3, Conus litoglyphus.

Perf. 13½x13¾

2003, Mar. 14 Litho. Unwmk.

572-576 A124 Set of 5 10.00 10.00

Coronation of Queen Elizabeth II, 50th Anniv.

Common Design Type

Designs: Nos. 577, 581a, 40c, Queen wearing tiara. No. 578, 80c, Carriage in procession. No. 579, $1.50, Queen wearing tiara, diff. Nos. 580, 581b, $3, Queen in procession at coronation.

Perf. 14¼x14½

2003, June 2 Litho. Wmk. 373

Vignettes Framed, Red Background

577 CD363 40c multicolored .90 .90
578 CD363 80c multicolored 1.50 1.50
579 CD363 $1.50 multicolored 2.25 2.25
580 CD363 $3 multicolored 4.00 4.00
Nos. 577-580 (4) 8.65 8.65

Souvenir Sheet

Vignettes Without Frame, Purple Panel

581 CD363 Sheet of 2, #a-b 5.75 5.75

Painted Leaves — A125

No. 582: a, 40c, Women putting leaves in earthenware jar. b, 80c, Washing leaves. c, $1.50, Leaf painter. d, $3, Leaf painter, diff.

Perf. 13¼

2003, Aug. 18 Litho. Unwmk.

582 A125 Horiz. strip of 4, #a-d, + central label 12.00 12.00

Squirrelfish A126

Designs: 40c, Sargocentron diadema. 80c, Sargocentron spiniferum. $1.50, Sargocentron caudimaculatum. $3, Neoniphon sammara.

Perf. 13¼

2003, Oct. 8 Litho. Unwmk.

583-586 A126 Set of 4 9.50 9.50
586a Souvenir sheet of 1 8.00 8.00

Christmas A127

Morning glory and: 40c, Holy Virgin in a Wreath of Flowers, by Peter Paul Rubens and Jan Brueghel. $1, Madonna della Rosa, by Raphael. $1.50, Stuppacher Madonna, by Matthias Grünewald. $3, Madonna with Cherries, by Titian.

Litho. with Foil Application

2003, Nov. 17 ***Perf. 13¾***

587-590 A127 Set of 4 9.00 9.00

Shells A128

Designs: 40c, Terebra maculata. 80c, Terebra subulata. $1.20, Terebra crenulata. $3, Terebra dimidiata.

Perf. 14x14½

2004, Jan. 21 Litho. Unwmk.

591-594 A128 Set of 4 9.00 9.00

Scenery A129

Designs: 50c, Anchor, Bounty Bay and Hill of Difficulty, vert. $1, Flower, Christian's Cave on Rock Face. $1.50, Shells, St. Paul's Pool, vert. $2.50, Bird, Ridge Rope towards St. Paul's Point.

Perf. 13¼

2004, Apr. 28 Litho. Unwmk.

595-598 A129 Set of 4 12.50 12.50

Souvenir Sheet

Commissioning of HMS Pitcairn, 60th Anniv. — A130

Perf. 13¼

2004, July 7 Litho. Unwmk.

599 A130 $5.50 multi 12.00 12.00

HMAV Bounty Replica, Sydney A131

Replica and: 60c, Sail and mast. 80c, Stern. $1, Figurehead. $3.50, Rigging.

2004, Sept. 8 ***Perf. 14¼x14***

600-603 A131 Set of 4 12.00 12.00
603a Souvenir sheet of 1 12.00 12.00

Murphy's Petrel A132

Designs: 40c, Three in flight. 50c, Adult and chicks. $1, Adult nesting, flower, vert. $2, Head of adult, vert. $2.50, In flight.

2004, Nov. 17 Litho. ***Perf. 14½***

604-608 A132 Set of 5 9.50 9.50
608a Souvenir sheet, #604-608 10.00 10.00

Views of Ducie and Oeno Islands A133

Designs: 50c, Beach, Ducie Island, lizards. 60c, Rocks off Ducie Island, starfish. 80c, Sun on horizon, Ducie Island, birds. $1, Boat off Oeno Island, palm tree. $1.50, Beach and palm trees, Oeno Island, shells. $2.50, Boat with fishermen off Oeno Island, fish.

2005, Feb. 10 Litho. ***Perf. 13¼***

609-614 A133 Set of 6 12.50 12.50

Souvenir Sheet

Blue Moon Butterfly — A134

No. 615: a, $1.50, Male. b, $4, Female.

2005, Apr. 8 Litho. ***Perf. 14½***

615 A134 Sheet of 2, #a-b 16.00 16.00

Souvenir Sheet

Apr. 8, 2005 Solar Eclipse — A135

No. 616 — Eclipse and various solar prominences: a, $1. b, $2. c, $3.

2005, Apr. 8 ***Perf.***

616 A135 Sheet of 3, #a-c 12.00 12.00

No. 616 contains three 38mm diameter stamps.

Wedding of Prince Charles and Camilla Parker Bowles A136

Litho. With Foil Application

2005, Apr. 9 ***Perf. 14x14½***

617 A136 $5 multi 18.00 18.00

HMS Bounty Replica, US A137

Replica, map, emblem for Bounty Post and: 40c, Ship's wheel. $1, Lantern. $1.20, Bell. $3, Rigging.

2005, June 21 Litho. ***Perf. 14¼x14***

618-621 A137 Set of 4 15.00 15.00
621a Souvenir sheet of 1 9.50 9.50

Bristle-thighed Curlew — A138

Designs: 60c, Curlews on rock. $1, Head of curlew. $1.50, Curlew with open beak, vert. $1.80, Head of curlew, two curlews in flight, vert. $2, Curlew on driftwood.

2005, Sept. 14 Litho. ***Perf. 14½***

622-626 A138 Set of 5 17.00 17.00
626a Souvenir sheet, #622-626 17.00 17.00

Christmas A139

Christmas ornament with: 40c, Hibiscus flower. 80c, Seabird. $1.80, Coat of arms. $2.50, HMS Bounty.

Litho. with Foil Application

2005, Nov. 23 ***Perf. 13¼***

627-630 A139 Set of 4 14.00 14.00

Henderson Island — A140

Various scenes of Henderson Island and: 50c, Insects. 60c, Parrots. $1, Sea birds. $1.20, Lobsters. $1.50, Octopi. $2, Turtles.

2006, Feb. 15 Litho. ***Perf. 13¼***

631-636 A140 Set of 6 13.00 13.00

Souvenir Sheet

Washington 2006 World Philatelic Exhibition — A141

2006, Apr. 21 Litho. ***Perf. 14½x14¾***

637 A141 $5 multi 10.00 10.00

Queen Elizabeth II, 80th Birthday A142

Queen: 40c, As young woman. 80c, Wearing tiara. No. 640, $1.80, Wearing yellow dress. No. 641, $3.50, Wearing red hat and jacket.

No. 642: a, $1.80, Wearing tiara. b, $3.50, Wearing yellow dress.

2006, Apr. 21 ***Perf. 14¼***

Stamps With White Frames

638-641 A142 Set of 4 10.00 10.00

Souvenir Sheet

Stamps Without White Frames

642 A142 Sheet of 2, #a-b 9.00 9.00

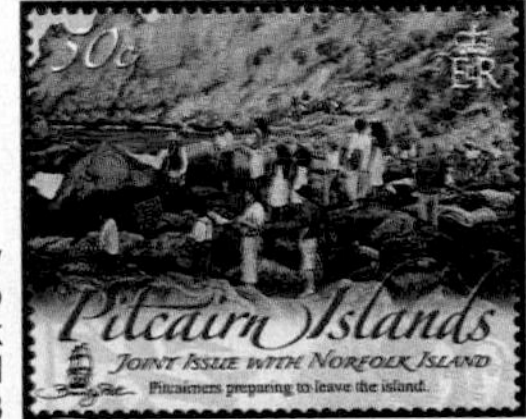

Journey to Norfolk Island A143

No. 643: a, Pitcairners preparing to leave Pitcairn Island. b, Ship, Morayshire, departing Pitcairn Island. c, Morayshire at anchor in Kingston Bay, Norfolk Island. d, Pitcairn settlers arrive in Kingston, Norfolk Island.

2006, June 7 ***Perf. 14½***

643 Horiz. strip of 4 + central label 11.00 11.00
a. A143 50c multi 1.25 1.25
b. A143 $1 multi 1.75 1.75
c. A143 $1.50 multi 2.75 2.75
d. A143 $3 multi 5.00 5.00

See Norfolk Island Nos. 875-879.

Souvenir Sheet

Cave Dwellers of Henderson Island — A144

No. 644: a, 60c, Man carrying caught fish. b, $1.20, Child, bird, boat, horiz. c, $2, Man sitting on beach, horiz. d, $2.50, Two women.

2006, Aug. 30 ***Perf. 13¼***
644 A144 Sheet of 4, #a-d 10.50 10.50

Humpback Whales A145

Designs: $1.50, Whales underwater. $3.50, Tail of whale above water.

2006, Nov. 22 ***Perf. 14½***
645-646 A145 Set of 2 10.50 10.50
646a Souvenir sheet, #645-646 10.50 10.50

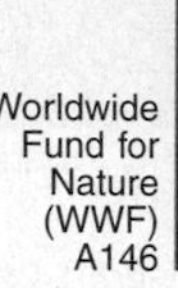

Worldwide Fund for Nature (WWF) A146

2007, Feb. 28 **Litho.** ***Perf. 14¼***
647 Horiz. strip of 4 9.00 9.00
a. A146 50c Sooty tern .70 .70
b. A146 60c Blue-gray ternlet .80 .80
c. A146 $2 Brown noddies 2.75 2.75
d. A146 $3 Black noddy 4.25 4.25
e. Miniature sheet, 2 each #647a-647d 18.00 18.00

Raising of the Anchor of the Bounty, 50th Anniv. — A147

No. 648: a, Diver approaching anchor. b, Two divers at anchor. c, Pulling anchor onto ship. d, Anchor on shore.

2007, Apr. 20 **Litho.** ***Perf. 13¼***
648 Horiz. strip of 4 + central label 12.00 12.00
a. A147 60c multi 1.50 1.50
b. A147 $1 multi 2.50 2.50
c. A147 $1.20 multi 2.75 2.75
d. A147 $2.50 multi 5.00 5.00

Souvenir Sheet

Rock Carvers of Pitcairn Island — A148

No. 649: a, 60c, Man carving on rock face. b, $1.20, Two men pounding rock, horiz. c, $2, Man near fire, horiz. d, $2.50, Man making stone ax.

2007, June 13
649 A148 Sheet of 4, #a-d 12.50 12.50

Utetheisa Pulchelloides A149

Design: $2, Moth on branch. $4, Moth in flight.

2007, Aug. 27 **Litho.** ***Perf. 14½***
650-651 A149 Set of 2 12.00 12.00
651a Souvenir sheet, #650-651 12.00 12.00

HMS Bounty Replica, United States A150

Designs: 10c, Crow's nest. 20c, Ropes and pulleys. 40c, Cannon. 50c, Compass. 80c, Captain's wheel. $1, Figurehead. $1.50, Mast. $2, Sails. $3.50, Sextant. $4, Lamp and transom. $5, Bell. $10, Chronometer.

2007, Oct. 17 **Litho.** ***Perf. 14½***
652 A150 10c multi .25 .25
653 A150 20c multi .40 .40
654 A150 40c multi .75 .75
655 A150 50c multi .85 .85
656 A150 80c multi 1.00 1.00
657 A150 $1 multi 1.25 1.25
658 A150 $1.50 multi 1.75 1.75
659 A150 $2 multi 2.25 2.25
660 A150 $3.50 multi 4.00 4.00
a. Souvenir sheet of 3, #656, 657, 660 9.50 9.50
661 A150 $4 multi 3.75 3.75
662 A150 $5 multi 4.25 4.25
663 A150 $10 multi 9.00 9.00
Nos. 652-663 (12) 29.50 29.50

Issued: No. 660a, 5/8/10. London 2010 Festival of Stamps (No. 660a).

Fish — A151

No. 664: a, Dog tooth tuna. b, Wahoo. c, Dorado-Mahimahi. d, Yellowfin tuna. e, Giant trevally. f, Bonito.

2007, Dec. 12 **Litho.** ***Perf. 14½***
664 A151 $1 Block of 6, #a-f 12.50 12.50

Pictures of Islands Taken By DigitalGlobe QuickBird Satellite A152

Islands: 60c, Oeno. $1, Pitcairn. $2, Henderson. $2.50, Ducie.

Serpentine Die Cut
2008, Feb. 27 **Litho.**
Self-Adhesive
665-668 A152 Set of 4 12.00 12.00

Longboat History — A153

No. 669 — Inscriptions: a, From 1880 Timber framed longboat. b, 1983, Last wooden longboat launched. c, 1995, Diesel powered aluminum. d, Oeno sunsets brought within reach.

2008, Apr. 24 **Litho.** ***Perf. 14x14¼***
669 Horiz. strip of 4 + central label 12.00 12.00
a. A153 50c multi 1.25 1.25
b. A153 $1 multi 1.75 1.75
c. A153 $1.50 multi 2.75 2.75
d. A153 $3.50 multi 5.00 5.00

Bees and Flowers A154

Apis mellifera ligustica and: $1, Yellow guava. $1.20, Portulaca. $1.50, Sunflower. $3, Mountain chestnut.

2008, June 25 ***Perf. 13¼***
670-673 A154 Set of 4 11.00 11.00
673a Souvenir sheet, #672-673 9.00 9.00

Sunsets — A155

Sun and various photographs of sunsets: 50c, 60c, 80c, $1, $2, $2.50.

2008, Aug. 20 **Litho.** ***Perf. 14¾***
674-679 A155 Set of 6 12.50 12.50

Souvenir Sheet

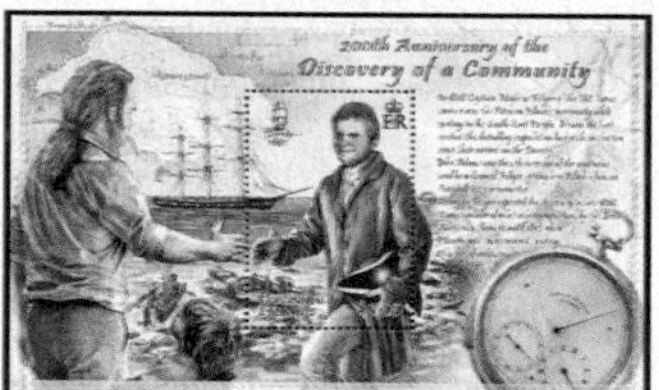

Discovery of Bounty Mutineer Community on Pitcairn by Capt. Mayhew Folger, Bicent. — A156

2008, Oct. 22 **Litho.** ***Perf. 13¼***
680 A156 $5 multi 7.75 7.75

Miniature Sheet

Green Turtles of Henderson Island — A157

No. 681: a, 60c, Head of turtle, vert. b, $1, Turtle swimming. c, $2, Turtle coming ashore. d, $2.50, Hatchlings heading toward ocean, vert.

2008, Dec. 3 **Litho.** ***Perf. 14***
681 A157 Sheet of 4, #a-d 9.00 9.00

Coconut Crab — A158

Crab: $2.80, Top view. $4, Side view.

2009, Feb. 17 ***Perf. 14½***
682-683 A158 Set of 2 11.00 11.00
683a Souvenir sheet of 2, #682-683 11.00 11.00

Return of Pitcairn Islanders to Pitcairn Island, 150th Anniv. — A159

No. 684: a, Pitcairn islanders leave Kingston Jetty on Norfolk Island. b, Passengers approach the Mary Ann. c, Pitcairn Islanders on board the Mary Ann approach Pitcairn Island. d, Arrival of Pitcairn Islanders on Pitcairn Island.

2009, Apr. 22 **Litho.** ***Perf. 14¾x13½***
684 Horiz. strip of 4 + central label 10.00 10.00
a. A159 60c multi 1.00 1.00
b. A159 $1 multi 1.75 1.75
c. A159 $2 multi 2.50 2.50
d. A159 $3.50 multi 3.75 3.75

Souvenir Sheet

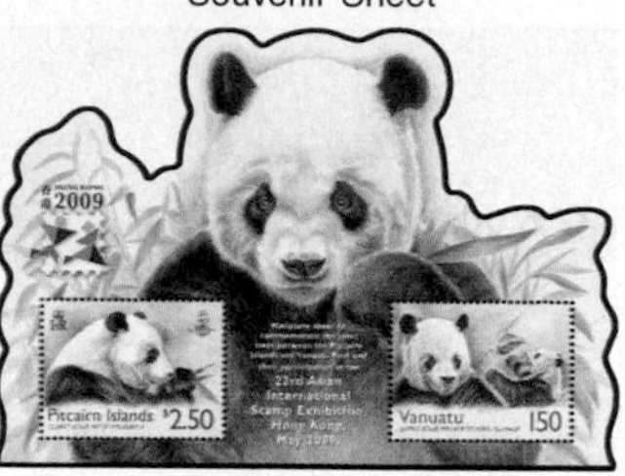

Hong Kong 2009 Intl. Stamp Exhibition — A160

2009, May 14 ***Perf. 13½***
685 A160 Sheet of 2, Pitcairn Islands #685a, Vanuatu #976a 8.50 8.50
a. $2.50 One panda 4.25 4.25

No. 685 sold for $5 and 310 Vanuatu vatus, and is identical to Vanuatu #976.

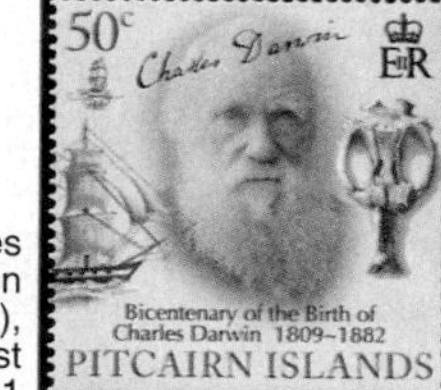

Charles Darwin (1809-82), Naturalist A161

Darwin and: 50c, Ship "Beagle" and fossil. $1.50, Tortoise and iguana. $2, Birds. $3.50, Darwin's book "On the Origin of Species by Means of Natural Selection" and ape.

2009, June 24 ***Perf. 14½***
686-689 A161 Set of 4 12.00 12.00

Wandering Glider Dragonfly A162

Dragonfly: $2.50, At flower's anthers. $4, On flower's petal.

2009, Aug. 26
690-691 A162 Set of 2 11.00 11.00
691a Souvenir sheet, #690-691 11.00 11.00

Aircraft Flying Over Pitcairn Island A163

Designs: $1, Walrus amphibious biplane. $1.50, Alouette III helicopter. $1.80, Dassault VP-BMS Falcon 900. $2.50, Piper Comanche 260C.

2009, Oct. 21
692-695 A163 Set of 4 12.00 12.00

Miniature Sheet

Visiting Royal Navy Ships — A164

No. 696: a, 80c, HMS Actaeon, 1837. b, 80c, HMS Calypso, 1860. c, 80c, HMS Juno, 1855. d, $2, HMS Sutlej, 1864. e, $2, HMS Shah, 1878. f, $2, HMS Pelican, 1886.

2009, Dec. 9 Litho. *Perf. 14*

696 A164 Sheet of 6, #a-f 12.00 12.00

See No. 711.

Children's Art A165

Island sites and children's drawings of them: 50c, Flatland, by Bradley Christian. 60c, Tedside, by Torika Warren-Peu. $1, St. Pauls, by Jayden Warren-Peu. $1.80, Isaac's Valley, by Kimiora Warren-Peu. $2, Garnets Ridge, by Ralph Warren-Peu. $2.50, Ship Landing Point, by Ariel Brown.

2010, Feb. 24 Litho. *Perf. 14¼*

697-702 A165 Set of 6 12.00 12.00

ANZAC Day — A166

No. 703 — Poppy and: a, 50c, Tank. b, $1, Airplanes.
No. 704 — Poppy and: a, $1.80, Transport ship. b, $4, Gunboat.

2010, Apr. 23 *Perf. 14½x14*
Horiz. Pairs, #a-b

703-704 A166 Set of 2 11.00 11.00

Worldwide Fund for Nature (WWF) A167

No. 705 — Fish: a, Centropyge flavissima. b, Chaetodon smithi. c, Centropyge loricula. d, Chaetodon lineolatus.

2010, June 23 *Perf. 14¼*

705 Strip or block of 4 9.50 9.50
- *a.* A167 60c multi 1.00 1.00
- *b.* A167 $1 multi 1.40 1.40
- *c.* A167 $2 multi 2.00 2.00
- *d.* A167 $2.50 multi 2.50 2.50
- *e.* Sheet of 8, 2 each #705a-705d 16.00 16.00

Exploration of Volcanic Hotspots A168

No. 706: a, Research Vessel L'Atalante. b, Submersible Nautile. c, Photographing lava tube. d, Approaching Adams Volcano.

2010, Aug. 18 *Perf. 14*

706 Horiz. strip of 4 + central label 10.00 10.00
- *a.* A168 80c multi 1.50 1.50
- *b.* A168 $1.20 multi 1.75 1.75
- *c.* A168 $1.50 multi 2.25 2.25
- *d.* A168 $3 multi 3.25 3.25

Snails A169

Designs: 80c, Orobophana solidula. $1, Philonesia filiceti. $1.80, Orobophana solidula, diff. $2.50, Philonesia filiceti, diff.

2010, Oct. 20 *Serpentine Die Cut*
Self-Adhesive

707-710 A169 Set of 4 9.50 9.50

Visiting Royal Navy Ships Type of 2009

Miniature Sheet

No. 711: a, $1, HMS Royalist, 1898. b, $1, HMS Cambrian, HMS Flora, 1906. c, $1, HMS Algerine, 1911. d, $1.80, HMS Leander, 1937. e, $1.80, HMS Monmouth, 1995. f, $1.80, HMS Sutherland, 2001.

2010, Dec. 9 *Perf. 14*

711 A164 Sheet of 6, #a-f 12.50 12.50

Yellow Fauta Flower A170

Designs: $2.50, Flower and bud. $3, Flower and three buds.

2011, Feb. 12 Litho.

712 A170 $2.50 multi 4.00 4.00
713 A170 $3 multi 4.75 4.75
- *a.* Souvenir sheet of 1 5.00 5.00

Indipex 2011 World Philatelic Exhibition, New Delhi (No. 713a).

Peonies — A171

No. 714 — Peonies with denomination color of: a, White. b, Pink.

2011, Apr. 21

714 A171 $1 Horiz. pair, #a-b 3.50 3.50

Printed in sheets containing 3 pairs.

Paper Wasp A172

Wasp on nest facing: $2.50, Right. $4, Left.

2011, Apr. 21

715-716 A172 Set of 2 10.00 10.00
- *716a* Souvenr sheet of 2, #715-716 10.50 10.50

Wedding of Prince William and Catherine Middleton A173

Litho. With Foil Application

2011, May 25 *Perf. 14½x14¾*

717 Horiz. pair + central label 14.50 14.50
- *a.* A173 $2.80 Couple 5.00 5.00
- *b.* A173 $6 Couple at wedding 7.00 7.00

Supply Ships A174

Designs: $1, Southern Salvor. $1.80, Claymore II. $2.10, Braveheart. $3, Taporo VIII.

2011, Aug. 31 Litho. *Perf. 14¼x14*

718-721 A174 Set of 4 12.50 12.50

Parkin Christian (1883-1971) A175

2011, Oct. 26 *Perf. 14½*

722 Horiz. strip of 4 + central label 12.00 12.00
- *a.* A175 $1.50 Navigator 2.00 2.00
- *b.* A175 $1.80 Goodwill ambassador 2.25 2.25
- *c.* A175 $2.10 Magistrate 2.50 2.50
- *d.* A175 $2.40 Religious leader 2.75 2.75

Christmas — A176

Designs: $1, Magus and camel. $1.50, Magus and camel, diff. $2.10, Magus and camel, diff. $3, Holy Family.

2011, Dec. 7 *Perf. 14¼*

723-726 A176 Set of 4 12.00 12.00

Henderson Island Birds — A177

Designs: 20c, Henderson crakes. 40c, Henderson fruit doves. $1.50, Henderson petrels. $2.10, Henderson reed warblers. $4.40, Henderson lorikeets.

2011, July 20 *Perf. 14¼x14*

727-731 A177 Set of 5 13.50 13.50

Souvenir Sheet

Tapa Cloth Designs — A178

No. 732: a, $1.80, Lognboat. b, $2.20, Whale. c, $4.60, HMS Bounty.

2012, Feb. 21 *Perf. 13¾x13½*

732 A178 Sheet of 3, #a-c 12.50 12.50

Dolphins A179

Designs: $1, Fraser's dolphin. $1.50, Spinner dolphin. $2.10, Spotted dolphin. $3, Bottlenose dolphin.

2012, Apr. 26 *Perf. 14¼*

733-736 A179 Set of 4 11.50 11.50
- *736a* Souvenir sheet of 2, #734, 736 7.00 7.00

Reign of Queen Elizabeth II, 60th Anniv. A180

No. 737: a, Queen in uniform. b, Queen wearing blue green hat and dress.

2012, June 1 *Perf. 14¼x14½*

737 Horiz. pair + central label 11.00 11.00
- *a.* A180 $2.80 multi 4.00 4.00
- *b.* A180 $4.40 multi 5.50 5.50

Photographs of Bounty Replicas — A181

Various photographs: 20c, $1, $2.10, $4.60

2012, July 31

738-741 A181 Set of 4 13.00 13.00
- *741a* Souvenir sheet of 1 #741 7.50 7.50

Roy P. Clark (1893-1980) A182

2012, Sept. 26 *Perf. 14½*

742 Horiz. strip of 4 + central label 12.50 12.50
- *a.* A182 $1 Teacher 2.00 2.00
- *b.* A182 $1.60 Postmaster 2.75 2.75
- *c.* A182 $2.20 Writer 3.00 3.00
- *d.* A182 $2.80 Community and church elder 3.50 3.50

Worldwide Fund for Nature (WWF) A183

Various depictions of Fluted giant clam.

2012, Oct. 31 ***Perf. 14¼x14½***

743	Strip of 4	11.50	11.50
a.	A183 20c multi	.80	.80
b.	A183 $1 multi	2.00	2.00
c.	A183 $2.10 multi	2.75	2.75
d.	A183 $3 multi	3.25	3.25
e.	Souvenir sheet of 8, 2 each #743a-743d	20.00	20.00

Charles Dickens (1812-70), Writer A184

Various photographs of Dickens and characters from his novels: $1, $1.80, $2.10, $3.

2012, Dec. 5 ***Perf. 14¾x14½***
744-747 A184 Set of 4 13.00 13.00

Books in the Bounty Trilogy, by Charles Bernard Nordhoff and James Norman Hall — A185

Designs: $1, Mutiny on the Bounty. $2.10, Men Against the Sea. $3, Pitcairn's Island.

2013, Feb. 27 ***Perf. 14½x14¾***

748-750	A185 Set of 3	9.50	9.50
750a	Souvenir sheet of 3, #748-750, perf. 14¾	9.50	9.50

Cruise Ships — A186

Designs: No. 751, $2, MV Marina. No. 752, $2, Pacific Princess. No. 753, $2, Costa Neo Romantica. No. 754, $2, Arcadia.

2013, Apr. 24 ***Perf. 14½x14***
751-754 A186 Set of 4 13.50 13.50

Souvenir Sheet

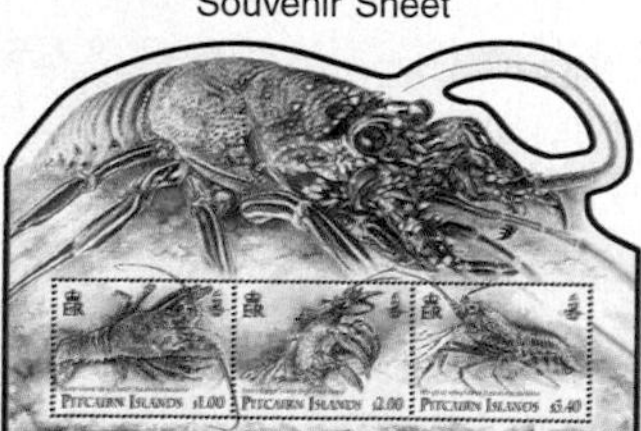

Lobsters — A187

No. 755: a, $1, Easter Island spiny lobster. b, $2, Aesop slipper lobster. c, $3.40, Pronghorn spiny lobster.

2013, May 29 ***Perf. 14***
755 A187 Sheet of 3, #a-c 10.50 10.50

Coronation of Queen Elizabeth II, 60th Anniv. — A188

Litho. & Embossed

2013, July 11 ***Perf. 14½x14***
756 A188 $6 blue 9.50 9.50

No. 756 was printed in sheets of 2 stamps.

Souvenir Sheet

Birth of Prince George of Cambridge — A189

No. 757: a, $3.40, Duke, Duchess of Cambridge, Prince George. b, $4.40, Duke of Cambridge, Pricne George.

2013, Aug. 16 **Litho.** ***Perf. 14½***
757 A189 Sheet of 2, #a-b 13.00 13.00

Lily Warren (1878-1969), Midwife A190

Varios photographs of Warren.

2013, Sept. 25

758	Horiz. strip of 4 + central label	13.00	13.00
a.	A190 $1 multi	1.75	1.75
b.	A190 $1.50 multi	2.50	2.50
c.	A190 $2.20 multi	3.75	3.75
d.	A190 $2.80 multi	4.75	4.75

Pres. John F. Kennedy (1917-63) A191

Headlines for events in Kennedy's presidency: $1, Inaugural address, Jan. 20, 1961. $1.80, Announcement of plans to put a man on the Moon, May 25, 1961. $2.10, Announcement of naval blockade of Cuba, Oct. 22, 1962. $3, "Ich bin ein Berliner" speech, June 26, 1963.

2013, Nov. 22 **Litho.** ***Perf. 14½***
759-762 A191 Set of 4 13.00 13.00

The April 18, 1962 date shown on the $2.10 stamp is incorrect for the headline. Kennedy announced plans for a nuclear disarmament treaty on April 18, 1962.

Ship Landing Point and Bounty Bay A192

Designs: 40c, Ship Landing Point as seen from Bounty Bay. No. 764, $1, Palm trees and Ship Landing Point. No. 765, $1, Bounty Bay framed by cliffs. No. 766, $2, Clouds above Ship Landing Point. No. 767, $2, Bounty Bay and rock promontory. $2.10, Aerial view of Bounty Bay.

2013, Dec. 18 **Litho.** ***Perf. 14***
763-768 A192 Set of 6 14.00 14.00

Souvenir Sheet

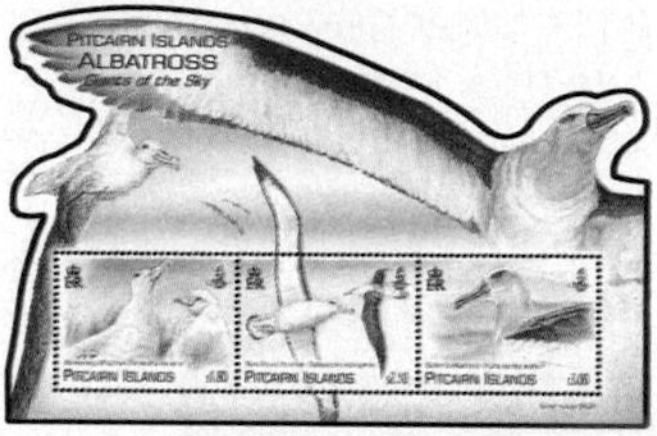

Albatrosses — A193

No. 769: a, $1.80, Wandering albatrosses. b, $2.10, Black-browed albatrosses. c, $3, Butler's albatross.

2014, Feb. 27 **Litho.** ***Perf. 13½***
769 A193 Sheet of 3, #a-c 11.50 11.50

Mutiny on the Bounty, 225th Anniv. A194

Designs: $1, Mutiny. $2, Captain Bligh and loyal crew set adrift in small boat. $2.10, Bounty leaving small boat with Captain Blight. $3, Bounty approaching Pitcairn Island.

2014, Apr. 28 **Litho.** ***Perf. 14½***
770-773 A194 Set of 4 14.00 14.00

Flora — A195

Designs: 20c, Cerbera manghas. $1, Portulaca lutea. $1.80, Canna sp. $2, Chamaesyce sparrmannii. $2.10, Coprosma benefica. $3, Pandanus tectorius.

2014, June 12 **Litho.** ***Perf. 14x14¼***
774-779 A195 Set of 6 18.00 18.00

Souvenir Sheet

World War I, Cent. — A196

No. 780 — Poppies and: a, $1, Ten soldiers hiking. b, $2.20, Three soldiers. c, $2.80, Bugler and five soldiers at attention.

2014, July 28 **Litho.** ***Perf. 14***
780 A196 Sheet of 3, #a-c 10.50 10.50

Actors Depicting Fletcher Christian in Movies — A197

Christian and actor portraying him: 20c, Wilton Power, 1916. $1, Errol Flynn, 1933. $2.10, Clark Gable, 1935. $2.80, Marlon Brando, 1962. $3, Mel Gibson, 1984.

2014, Sept. 25 **Litho.** ***Perf. 14***
781-785 A197 Set of 5 14.50 14.50

Fletcher Christian (1764-93), mutiny leader.

Nelson Mandela (1918-2013), President of South Africa — A198

Various photographs of Mandela and quote beginning with: $1, "What counts in life. . ." $1.80, "A good head. . .", vert. $2.10, "For to be free. . . .", vert. $3, "Education is the most powerful weapon. . ."

Perf. 14¼x14, 14x14¼

2014, Nov. 3 **Litho.**
786-789 A198 Set of 4 12.50 12.50

Visit to Pitcairn Islands of Richard E. Byrd Antarctic Expedition, 75th Anniv. A199

No. 790: a, Expedition members on Pitcairn, envelope cachet. b, USMS North Star, stamped cover to Philadelphia. c, USMS North Star, Snow Cruiser. d, Snow Cruiser, Admiral Byrd in parka.

Wmk. 387

2014, Dec. 11 **Litho.** ***Perf. 14½***

790	Horiz. strip of 4 + central label	12.00	12.00
a.	A199 $1 multi	1.50	1.50
b.	A199 $1.80 multi	2.75	2.75
c.	A199 $2 multi	3.25	3.25
d.	A199 $2.80 multi	4.50	4.50

Souvenir Sheet

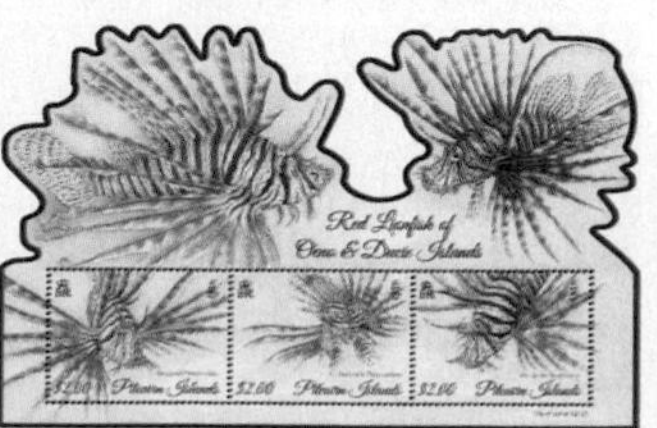

Red Lionfish — A200

No. 791: a, Denomination over fins. b, Fins above denomination. c, Fins touching "R" at UL.

Unwmk.

2015, Feb. 26 **Litho.** ***Perf. 14***
791 A200 $2 Sheet of 3, #a-c 9.25 9.25

Paintings — A201

Designs: $1, Interior of Pitcairn, 1830, by F. W. Beechey. $2, Pitcairn Island, c. 1808, by E. Low. $2.10, Christian's House, Pitcairn Island, c. 1824, by Conway Shipley. $3, Landing in Bounty Bay, 1830, by Beechey.

2015, Apr. 29 Litho. *Perf. 14¾x14¼*

792-795	A201	Set of 4	12.50	12.50

Ben Christian (1921-92), Island Secretary A202

No. 796 — Christian: a, On telephone. b, Carving wood. c, Holding caught fish. d, With medal.

2015, June 24 Litho. *Perf. 14½*

796	Horiz. strip of 4 + central label	10.50	10.50
a.	A202 $1 multi	1.40	1.40
b.	A202 $1.50 multi	2.00	2.00
c.	A202 $2.10 multi	3.00	3.00
d.	A202 $2.80 multi	3.75	3.75

Souvenir Sheet

Breadfruit — A203

No. 797: a, $1, Flower. b, $2, Breadfruit half. c, $3, Mature breadfruit.

2015, Aug. 26 Litho. *Perf. 13½*

797	A203	Sheet of 3, #a-c	7.75	7.75

First Pitcairn Islands Postage Stamps, 75th Anniv. A204

King George VI and: 10c, Cluster of oranges. 40c, Fletcher Christian with crew and view of Pitcairn Island. 60c, John Adams and his house. 80c, Map of Pitcairn and Pacific Ocean. $1, Bounty Bible. $2, H.M. Armed Vessel "Bounty." $4, William Bligh and H.M. Armed Vessel "Bounty." $5, Pitcairn School, 1949. $6, Fletcher Christian and view of Pitcairn Island. $10, Fletcher Christian with crew and coast of Pitcairn Island

2015, Oct. 15 Litho. *Perf. 14x14¼*

798	A204	10c multi	.25	.25
799	A204	40c multi	.55	.55
800	A204	60c multi	.80	.80
801	A204	80c multi	1.10	1.10
802	A204	$1 multi	1.40	1.40
803	A204	$2 multi	2.75	2.75
804	A204	$4 multi	5.50	5.50
805	A204	$5 multi	6.75	6.75
806	A204	$6 multi	8.25	8.25
807	A204	$10 multi	13.50	13.50
		Nos. 798-807 (10)	40.85	40.85

Christmas A205

Carols: $1, Hark! The Herald Angels Sing. $2, Once in Royal David's City. $2.10, Away in a Manger. $3, Silent Night.

2015, Dec. 9 Litho. *Perf. 14¼*

808-811	A205	Set of 4	11.00	11.00

Landscapes — A206

No. 812 — Inscriptions: a, Down the God from the sea. b, Rainbow over St. Paul's Pool. c, Sunset over Ship Landing Point. d, Cliff view towards Bounty Bay. e, Adamstown from inside Christian's cave. f, Tautama toward Aute Valley and Break Em Hip.

2016, Jan. 13 Litho. *Perf. 14¼x14*

812	Block of 6	16.00	16.00
a.-f.	A206 $2 Any single	2.60	2.60
	Complete booklet, #812a-812f	16.00	

Scenes from Plays by William Shakespeare (1564-1616) A207

No. 813: a, Macbeth. b, Hamlet. c, A Midsummer Night's Dream. d, Romeo and Juliet.

2016, Mar. 9 Litho. *Perf. 14¼x14½*

813	Horiz. strip of 4 + central label	9.75	9.75
a.	A207 $1 multi	1.40	1.40
b.	A207 $1.80 multi	2.50	2.50
c.	A207 $2 multi	2.75	2.75
d.	A207 $2.20 multi	3.00	3.00

POLAND

'pō-lənd

LOCATION — Europe between Russia and Germany
GOVT. — Republic
AREA — 120,628 sq. mi.
POP. — 38,608,929 (1999 est.)
CAPITAL — Warsaw

100 Kopecks = 1 Ruble
100 Fenigi = 1 Marka (1918)
100 Halerzy = 1 Korona (1918)
100 Groszy = 1 Zloty (1924)

Catalogue values for unused stamps in this country are for Never Hinged items, beginning with Scott 534 in the regular postage section, Scott B63 in the semi-postal section, Scott C28 in the airpost section, Scott CB1 in the airpost semi-postal section, and Scott J146 in the postage due section.

Watermarks

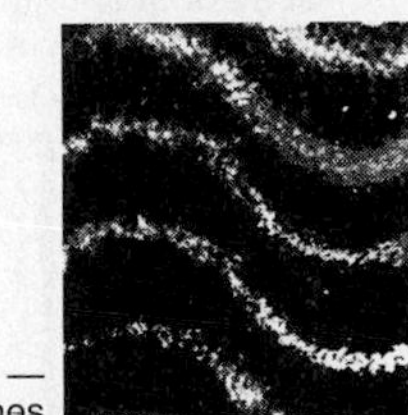
Wmk. 145 — Wavy Lines

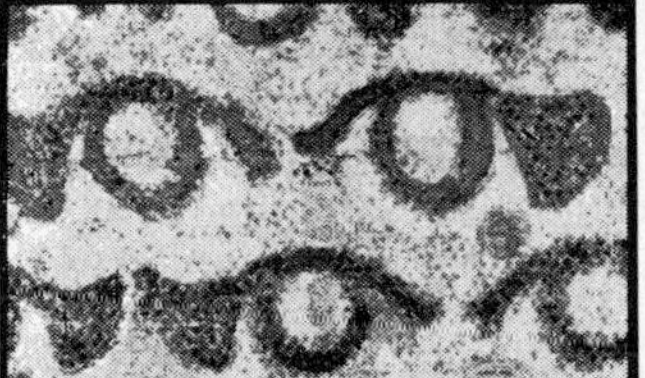
Wmk. 234 — Multiple Post Horns

Wmk. 326 — Multiple Post Horns

Issued under Russian Dominion

Coat of Arms — A1

Perf. 11½ to 12½

1860 Typo. Unwmk.

1	A1 10k blue & rose	2,400.	250.
a.	10k blue & carmine	2,500.	325.
b.	10k dark blue & rose	3,000.	350.
c.	Added blue frame for inner oval	6,000.	850.
d.	Imperf.	—	7,500.

Used for letters within the Polish territory and to Russia. Postage on all foreign letters was paid in cash.

These stamps were superseded by those of Russia in 1865.

Counterfeits exist.

Issues of the Republic

Local issues were made in various Polish cities during the German occupation.

In the early months of the Republic many issues were made by overprinting the German occupation stamps with the words "Poczta Polska" and an eagle or bars often with the name of the city.

These issues were not authorized by the Government but were made by the local authorities and restricted to local use. In 1914 two stamps were issued for the Polish Legion and in 1918 the Polish Expeditionary Force used surcharged Russian stamps. The regularity of these issues is questioned.

Numerous counterfeits of these issues abound.

Warsaw Issues

Stamps of the Warsaw Local Post Surcharged

Statue of Sigismund III — A2

Coat of Arms of Warsaw — A3

Polish Eagle A4

Sobieski Monument A5

1918, Nov. 17 Wmk. 145 *Perf. 11½*

11	A2 5f on 2gr brn & buff	1.40	1.00
a.	Inverted surcharge	200.00	200.00
12	A3 10f on 6gr grn & buff	.70	.70
a.	Inverted surcharge	15.00	15.00
13	A4 25f on 10gr rose & buff	7.00	3.50
a.	Inverted surcharge	27.50	27.50
14	A5 50f on 20gr bl & buff	8.50	7.00
a.	Inverted surcharge	350.00	350.00
	Nos. 11-14 (4)	17.60	12.20

Counterfeits exist.

Polish Philately Authentication

Photographic Certificates of Authenticity.

Andrew Sader

Specializing in Poland # 1, Poczta Polska overprints on Germania and Austria stamps,

Cracow, Gniezno, Wodzowie

2 Amboy Rd. Toronto, On M1G-3J1, Canada

e-mail: andrewsader@aol.com

Tel 416-399-4365

Occupation Stamps Nos. N6-N16 Overprinted or Surcharged

a

b

1918-19 Wmk. 125 ***Perf. 14, 14½***

No.	Type	Description	Unused	Used
15	A16	3pf brown ('19)	35.00	27.50
16	A22	5pf on 2½pf gray	1.40	.70
17	A16	5pf on 3pf brown	5.00	3.50
18	A16	5pf green	1.75	.70
19	A16	10pf carmine	1.40	.50
20	A22	15pf dark violet	1.00	.50
21	A16	20pf blue	1.40	.50
a.		20pf ultramarine	*775.00*	*2,250.*
23	A22	25pf on 7½pf org	1.00	.50
24	A16	30pf org & blk, *buff*	1.00	.50
25	A16	40pf lake & black	1.75	1.25
26	A16	60pf magenta	1.40	.50
		Nos. 15-26 (11)	52.10	36.65

There are two settings of this overprint. The first printing, issued Dec. 5, 1918, has space of 3½mm between the middle two bars. The second printing, issued Jan. 15, 1919, has space of 4mm. No. 15 comes only in the second setting; all others in both. The German overprint on No. 21a is very glossy.

Varieties of this overprint and surcharge are numerous: double; inverted; misspellings (Pocata, Poczto, Pelska); letters omitted, inverted or wrong font; 3 bars instead of 4, etc.

No. 21a requires competent expertization. A number of shades of the blue No. 21 exist. Counterfeits exist.

Lublin Issue

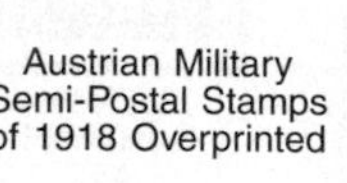
Austrian Military Semi-Postal Stamps of 1918 Overprinted

1918, Dec. 5 Unwmk. ***Perf. 12½x13***

No.	Type	Description	Unused	Used
27	MSP7	10h gray green	8.50	7.50
a.		Inverted overprint	80.00	80.00
b.		Double overprint	1,750.	700.00
c.		Double ovpt., one inverted	2,100.	850.00
28	MSP8	20h magenta	6.50	7.50
a.		Inverted overprint	50.00	50.00
b.		Double ovpt., one inverted	1,750.	500.00
29	MSP7	45h blue	6.50	7.50
a.		Inverted overprint	50.00	50.00
b.		Double ovpt., one inverted	1,750.	500.00
		Nos. 27-29 (3)	21.50	22.50

Austrian Military Stamps of 1917 Surcharged

1918-19 ***Perf. 12½***

No.	Type	Description	Unused	Used
30	M3	3hal on 3h ol gray	27.50	20.00
a.		Inverted surcharge	*3,500.*	3,500.
b.		Perf. 11½	50.00	27.50
c.		Perf. 11½x12½	30.00	27.50
31	M3	3hal on 15h brt rose	7.00	7.00
a.		Inverted surcharge	22.50	30.00

Surcharged in Black

No.	Type	Description	Unused	Used
32	M3	10hal on 30h sl grn	7.00	7.00
a.		Inverted surcharge	22.50	30.00
b.		Brown surcharge (error)	75.00	65.00
34	M3	25hal on 40h ol bis	15.00	12.00
a.		Inverted surcharge	37.50	42.50
b.		Perf. 11½	50.00	27.50
c.		As "b," inverted surcharge	175.00	175.00
35	M3	45hal on 60h rose	7.00	7.00
a.		Inverted surcharge	25.00	27.50
36	M3	45hal on 80h dl blue	8.50	8.50
a.		Inverted surcharge	35.00	35.00
37	M3	50hal on 60h rose	14.00	14.00
a.		Inverted surcharge	50.00	35.00

Similar surcharge with bars instead of stars over original value

No.	Type	Description	Unused	Used
38	M3	45hal on 80h dl blue	12.00	10.00
a.		Inverted surcharge	40.00	35.00
b.		Double srch., one inverted	1,350.	—

Overprinted

No.	Type	Description	Unused	Used
39	M3	50h deep green	27.50	27.50
a.		Inverted overprint	100.00	100.00
40	M3	90h dark violet	7.00	7.00
a.		Inverted overprint	100.00	100.00
		Nos. 30-40 (10)	132.50	120.00

Counterfeits

All Cracow issues, Nos. 41-60, J1-J12 and P1-P5, have been extensively counterfeited. Competent expertization is necessary. Prices apply only for authenticated stamps with identified plating position. Cost of certificate is not included in the catalogue value.

Cracow Issues

Austrian Stamps of 1916-18 Overprinted

1919, Jan. 17 ***Typo.***

No.	Type	Description	Unused	Used
41	A37	3h brt violet	500.00	450.00
42	A37	5h lt green	625.00	475.00
43	A37	6h deep orange	70.00	65.00
a.		Inverted overprint	*50,000.*	
44	A37	10h magenta	500.00	450.00
45	A37	12h lt blue	70.00	70.00
46	A39	40h olive green	35.00	30.00
a.		Inverted overprint	350.00	—
b.		Double overprint	*2,000.*	
47	A39	50h blue green	20.00	14.00
a.		Inverted overprint		*35,000.*
48	A39	60h deep blue	17.50	14.00
a.		Inverted overprint	*350.00*	—
49	A39	80h orange brown	14.00	14.00
a.		Inverted overprint.	*300.00*	*250.00*
b.		Double overprint	*1,750.*	—
50	A39	90h red violet	1,200.	1,000.
51	A39	1k carmine, *yel*	30.00	27.50

Engr.

No.	Type	Description	Unused	Used
52	A40	2k blue	12.00	14.00
53	A40	3k carmine rose	190.00	175.00
54	A40	4k yellow green	200.00	175.00
55	A40	10k deep violet	*12,000.*	*13,000.*

The 3k is on granite paper.

The overprint on Nos. 52-55 is litho. and slightly larger than illustration with different ornament between lines of type.

Same Overprint on Nos. 168-171

1919 ***Typo.***

No.	Type	Description	Unused	Used
56	A42	15h dull red	67.50	35.00
57	A42	20h dark green	300.00	140.00
58	A42	25h blue	*1,900.*	1,900.
59	A42	30h dull violet	550.00	350.00

Austria No. 157 Surcharged

1919, Jan. 24

No.	Type	Description	Unused	Used
60	A39	25h on 80h org brn	10.00	10.00
a.		Inverted surcharge	240.00	150.00

Excellent counterfeits of Nos. 27 to 60 exist.

Polish Eagle — A9

1919, Feb. 25 Litho. ***Imperf.***

Without gum

Yellowish Paper

No.	Type	Description	Unused	Used
61	A9	2h gray	1.75	1.40
62	A9	3h dull violet	1.00	1.00
63	A9	5h green	1.00	.70
64	A9	6h orange	17.50	20.00
65	A9	10h lake	1.00	.70
66	A9	15h brown	1.00	.70
67	A9	20h olive green	1.00	1.00

Bluish Paper

No.	Type	Description	Unused	Used
68	A9	25h carmine	.70	.70
69	A9	50h indigo	1.00	1.00
70	A9	70h deep blue	1.75	1.40
71	A9	1k ol gray & car	1.75	1.75
		Nos. 61-71 (11)	29.45	30.35

Nos. 61-71 exist with privately applied perforations.

Counterfeits exist.

For surcharges see Nos. J35-J39.

Posen (Poznan) Issue

Germany Nos. 84-85, 87, 96, 98 Overprinted in Black

Perf. 14, 14½

1919, Aug. 5 Wmk. 125

No.	Type	Description	Unused	Used
72	A22	5pf on 2pf gray	30.00	24.00
73	A22	5pf on 7½pf org	2.00	1.40
a.		Double surcharge	1,000.	
74	A16	5pf on 20pf bl vio	2.00	1.25
75	A16	10pf on 25pf org & blk, *yel*	6.00	3.50
76	A16	10pf on 40pf lake & blk	3.50	1.40
		Nos. 72-76 (5)	43.50	31.55

Counterfeits exist.

Germany Nos. 96 and 98 Surcharged in Red or Green

a

b

1919, Sept. 15

No.	Type	Description	Unused	Used
77	A22	5pf on 2pf (R)	275.00	175.00
a.		Inverted surcharge	*27,500.*	
78	A22	10pf on 7½pf (G)	400.00	125.00

Nos. 77-78 are a provisional issue for use in Gniezno. Counterfeit surcharges abound.

Eagle and Fasces, Symbolical of United Poland
A10 A11

"Agriculture"
A12

"Peace" — A13

Polish Cavalryman
A14

For Northern Poland

Denominations as "F" or "M"

1919, Jan. 27 ***Imperf.***

Wove or Ribbed Paper

No.	Type	Description	Unused	Used
81	A10	3f bister brn	.25	.35
82	A10	5f green	.25	.35
83	A10	10f red violet	.25	.35
84	A10	15f deep rose	.25	.25
85	A11	20f deep blue	.25	.50
86	A11	25f olive green	.25	.50
87	A11	50f blue green	.25	.50
88	A12	1m violet	2.50	3.75
89	A12	1.50m deep green	4.25	7.00
90	A12	2m dark brown	4.25	8.50
91	A13	2.50m orange brn	8.50	22.50
92	A14	5m red violet	17.50	40.00
		Nos. 81-92 (12)	38.75	84.55

Perf. 10, 11, 11½, 10x11½, 11½x10

1919-20

No.	Type	Description	Unused	Used
93	A10	3f bister brn	.25	.25
94	A10	5f green	.25	.25
95	A10	10f red violet	.25	.25
96	A10	10f brown ('20)	.25	.25
97	A10	15f deep rose	.25	.25
98	A10	15f vermilion ('20)	.25	.25
99	A11	20f deep blue	.25	.25
100	A11	25f olive green	.25	.25
101	A11	40f brt violet ('20)	.25	.25
102	A11	50f blue green	.25	.25
103	A12	1m violet	.70	.25
105	A12	1.50m deep green	.70	.35
106	A12	2m dark brown	1.75	.50
107	A13	2.50m orange brn	1.00	.70
108	A14	5m red violet	2.00	1.50
		Nos. 93-108 (15)	8.65	5.80

No. 108 exists in various shades of brown and violet.

Several denominations among Nos. 81-132 are found with double impression or in pairs imperf. between. See Nos. 109-132, 140-152C, 170-175. For surcharges & overprints, see Nos. 153, 199-200, B1-B14, 2K1-2K12, Eastern Silesia 41-50.

For Southern Poland

Denominations as "H" or "K"

1919, Jan. 27 ***Imperf.***

No.	Type	Description	Unused	Used
109	A10	3h red brown	.35	.35
110	A10	5h emerald	.35	.25
111	A10	10h orange	.35	.25
112	A10	15h vermilion	.35	.25
113	A11	20h gray brown	.35	.25
114	A11	25h light blue	.35	.25
115	A11	50h orange brn	.35	.70
116	A12	1k dark green	.35	1.40
117	A12	1.50k red brown	1.50	4.00
118	A12	2k dark blue	1.50	3.50
119	A13	2.50k dark violet	6.50	10.00
120	A14	5k slate blue	15.00	20.00
		Nos. 109-120 (12)	27.30	41.20

Perf. 10, 11½, 10x11½, 11½x10

No.	Type	Description	Unused	Used
121	A10	3h red brown	.25	.25
122	A10	5h emerald	.25	.25
123	A10	10h orange	.25	.25
124	A10	15h vermilion	.25	.25
125	A11	20h gray brown	.25	.25
126	A11	25h light blue	.25	.25
127	A11	50h orange brn	.25	.25
128	A12	1k dark green	.25	.25
129	A12	1.50k red brown	.35	.25
130	A12	2k dark blue	.70	.25
131	A13	2.50k dark violet	1.40	.70
132	A14	5k slate blue	1.40	1.10
		Nos. 121-132 (12)	5.85	4.30

National Assembly Issue

A20

Ignacy Jan Paderewski — A21

Adalbert Trampczynski — A22

Eagle Watching Ship — A24

25f, Gen. Josef Pilsudski. 1m, Griffin.

1919-20 *Perf. 11½*

Wove or Ribbed Paper

133 A20 10f red violet .35 .25
134 A21 15f brown red .35 .25
a. Imperf., pair 25.00
135 A22 20f dp brown (21x25mm) .35 .25
136 A22 20f dp brown (17x20mm) ('20) .75 1.60
137 A21 25f olive green .35 .25
138 A24 50f Prus blue .35 .25
139 A24 1m purple 1.00 .35
Nos. 133-139 (7) 3.50 3.20

First National Assembly of Poland.

General Issue

1919 *Perf. 9 to 14½ and Compound*

Thin Laid Paper

140 A11 25f olive green .25 .25
141 A11 50f blue green .25 .25
142 A12 1m dark gray .25 .25
143 A12 2m bister brn .25 .25
144 A13 3m red brown 2.00 .35
a. Pair, imperf. vert. 8.00 8.00
145 A14 5m red violet 1.25 .25
146 A14 6m deep rose 1.40 .25
a. Pair, imperf. vert. 8.00 8.00
147 A14 10m brown red .50 .30
a. Horizontal pair, imperf. 8.00 8.00
148 A14 20m gray green 1.40 .50
Nos. 140-148 (9) 7.55 2.65

Type of 1919 Redrawn

Perf. 9 to 14½ and Compound

1920-22 **Thin Laid or Wove Paper**

149 A10 1m red .25 .25
150 A10 2m gray green .25 .25
151 A10 3m light blue .50 .35
152 A10 4m rose red .25 .25
152A A10 5m dark violet .25 .25
b. Horiz. pair, imperf. vert. 8.00 8.00
152C A10 8m gray brown ('22) .50 .50
Nos. 149-152C (6) 2.00 1.85

The word "POCZTA" is in smaller letters and the numerals have been enlarged.

The color of No. 152A varies from dark violet to red brown.

No. 101 Surcharged

Perf. 10, 11½, 10x11½, 11½x10

1921, Jan. 25 **Thick Wove Paper**

153 A11 3m on 40f brt vio .30 .25
a. Double surcharge 25.00 25.00
b. Inverted surcharge — —

Sower and Rainbow of Hope — A27

Thin Laid or Wove Paper

Perf. 9 to 14½ and Compound

1921 **Size: 28x22mm** **Litho.**

154 A27 10m grnsh blue .50 .25
155 A27 15m light brown .25 .25
155A A27 20m red .80 .25
Nos. 154-155A (3) 1.55 .75

Signing of peace treaty with Russia.

Nos. 154-155A exist imperf. Value, unused, each $6.

See No. 191. For surcharges see Nos. 196-198.

Sun (Peace) Breaking into Darkness (Despair) — A28

"Peace" and "Agriculture" A29

"Peace" A30

Perf. 11, 11½, 12, 12½, 13 and Compound

1921, May 2

156 A28 2m green .40 9.50
157 A28 3m blue 1.50 10.00
158 A28 4m red .35 .70
a. 4m carmine rose (error) *600.00*
159 A29 6m carmine rose .35 1.50
160 A29 10m slate blue 1.25 .80
161 A30 25m dk violet 2.00 .70
162 A30 50m slate bl & buff 1.25 .70
Nos. 156-162 (7) 7.10 23.90

Issued to commemorate the Constitution.

Polish Eagle — A31

Perf. 9 to 14½ and Compound

1921-23

163 A31 25m violet & buff .80 .25
164 A31 50m carmine & buff .80 .25
a. Vert. pair, imperf. horiz.
165 A31 100m blk brn & org .80 .25
166 A31 200m black & rose ('23) .80 .25
167 A31 300m olive grn ('23) .40 .25
168 A31 400m brown ('23) .55 .25
169 A31 500m brn vio ('23) .70 .25
169A A31 1000m orange ('23) 1.25 .25
169B A31 2000m dull blue ('23) .35 .25
Nos. 163-169B (9) 6.45 2.25

For surcharge see No. 195.

Type of 1919 and

Miner — A32

Perf. 9 to 14½ and Compound

1922-23

170 A10 5f blue .25 1.00
171 A10 10f lt violet .25 1.00
172 A11 20f pale red .25 2.00
173 A11 40f violet brn .25 2.00
174 A11 50f orange .25 2.00
175 A11 75f blue green .25 3.00
176 A32 1m black .25 2.00
177 A32 1.25m dark green .25 4.50
178 A32 2m deep rose .25 2.00
179 A32 3m emerald .25 2.00
180 A32 4m deep ultra .25 4.00
181 A32 5m yellow brn .25 2.00
182 A32 6m red orange .25 8.50
183 A32 10m lilac brn .25 3.50
184 A32 20m deep violet .25 4.00
185 A32 50m olive green .25 3.50
187 A32 80m vermilion ('23) 1.00 27.50
188 A32 100m violet ('23) .60 40.00
189 A32 200m orange ('23) 2.50 40.00
190 A32 300m pale blue ('23) 6.00 60.00
Nos. 170-190 (20) 14.10 214.50

Union of Upper Silesia with Poland.

There were 2 printings of Nos. 176 to 190, the 1st being from flat plates, the 2nd from rotary press on thin paper, perf. 12½.

Nos. 173 and 175 are printed from new plates showing larger value numerals and a single "f."

Sower Type Redrawn

Size: 25x21mm

1922 **Thick or Thin Wove Paper**

191 A27 20m carmine .75 .25

In this stamp the design has been strengthened and made more distinct, especially the ground and the numerals in the upper corners.

Nicolaus Copernicus A33

Father Stanislaus Konarski — A34

1923 *Perf. 10 to 12½*

192 A33 1000m indigo .35 .35
193 A34 3000m brown .35 .70
a. "Konapski" 17.00 19.00
194 A33 5000m rose .35 .35
Nos. 192-194 (3) 1.05 1.40

Nicolaus Copernicus (1473-1543), astronomer (Nos. 192, 194); Stanislaus Konarski (1700-1773), educator, and the creation by the Polish Parliament of the Commission of Public Instruction (No. 193).

No. 163 Surcharged

1923 *Perf. 9 to 14½ and Compound*

195 A31 10000m on 25m .50 .25
a. Double surcharge 60.00
b. Inverted surcharge 35.00

Stamps of 1921 Surcharged

196 A27 25000m on 20m red 2.00 1.00
a. Double surcharge 60.00 —
b. Inverted surcharge 35.00
197 A27 50000m on 10m grnsh bl .80 .25
a. Double surcharge 60.00 —
b. Inverted surcharge 35.00 —

No. 191 Surcharged

198 A27 25000m on 20m car .60 .25
a. Double surcharge 60.00 —
b. Inverted surcharge 35.00

No. 150 Surcharged with New Value

1924

199 A10 20000m on 2m gray grn .80 .25
a. Inverted surcharge 35.00 —
b. Double surcharge 60.00 —

Type of 1919 Issue Surcharged with New Value

200 A10 100000m on 5m red brn .80 .25
a. Double surcharge 60.00 —
b. Inverted surcharge 35.00 —
Nos. 195-200 (6) 5.50 2.25

Arms of Poland — A35

Perf. 10 to 14½ and Compound

1924 **Thin Paper** **Litho.**

205 A35 10,000m lilac brn 1.10 .50
206 A35 20,000m ol grn .70 .35
207 A35 30,000m scarlet 1.25 .25
208 A35 50,000m apple grn 2.75 .25
209 A35 100,000m brn org 1.00 .25
210 A35 200,000m lt blue 1.10 .25
211 A35 300,000m red vio 2.75 1.00
212 A35 500,000m brn 2.50 1.00
213 A35 1,000,000m ple rose .35 *35.00*
214 A35 2,000,000m dk grn .35 *225.00*
Nos. 205-214 (10) 13.85 263.85
Set, never hinged 50.00

Arms of Poland A36

President Stanislaus Wojciechowski A37

Hungaria Stamp Exchange

EASTERN EUROPE DEALER

Hungary, Baltics, Czech., Greece, Poland, Romania, Russia & more...

Online Store!

(888) 868-8293

www.hungarianstamps.com

Perf. 10 to 13½ and Compound

1924

215 A36 1g orange brown .35 .50
216 A36 2g dark brown .35 .25
217 A36 3g orange .35 .25
218 A36 5g olive green .35 .25
219 A36 10g blue green .75 .25
220 A36 15g red .75 .25
221 A36 20g blue 2.50 .25
222 A36 25g red brown 6.50 .25
a. 25g indigo *12,000.* *6,000.*
223 A36 30g deep violet 10.00 .25
a. 30g gray blue *250.00* *125.00*
224 A36 40g indigo 2.50 .70
225 A36 50g magenta .50 .25

Perf. 11½, 12

226 A37 1z scarlet 17.50 1.40
Nos. 215-226 (12) 42.40 4.85
Set, never hinged 265.00

For overprints see Nos. 1K1-1K11.

Holy Gate of Wilno (Vilnius) — A38

Poznan Town Hall — A39

Sigismund Monument, Warsaw — A40

Wawel Castle at Cracow — A41

Sobieski Statue at Lwow — A42

Ship of State — A43

1925-27 ***Perf. 10 to 13***

227 A38 1g bister brown .55 .25
228 A42 2g brown olive .65 .50
229 A40 3g blue 2.00 .25
230 A39 5g yellow green 2.75 .25
231 A40 10g violet 2.00 .25
232 A41 15g rose red 3.00 .25
233 A43 20g dull red 13.00 .25
234 A38 24g gray blue 5.50 .75
235 A42 30g dark blue 1.60 .25
236 A41 40g lt blue ('27) 1.60 .25
237 A43 45g dark violet 11.00 .25
Nos. 227-237 (11) 43.65 3.50
Set, never hinged 110.00

For overprints see Nos. 1K11A-1K17.

1926-27 **Redrawn**

238 A40 3g blue .65 .25
239 A39 5g yellow green 1.00 .25
240 A40 10g violet .85 .25
241 A41 15g rose red .85 .25
Nos. 238-241 (4) 3.35 1.00
Set, never hinged 7.50

On Nos. 229-232 the lines representing clouds touch the numerals. On the redrawn stamps the numerals have white outlines, separating them from the cloud lines.

Marshal Pilsudski — A44

Frederic Chopin — A45

1927 **Typo.** ***Perf. 12½, 11½***

242 A44 20g red brown 2.00 .25
243 A45 40g deep ultra 8.50 .75
Set, never hinged 35.00

See No. 250. For overprint see No. 1K18.

President Ignacy Moscicki — A46

1927, May 4 ***Perf. 11½***

245 A46 20g red 3.00 1.00
Never hinged 10.00

Dr. Karol Kaczkowski — A47

1927, May 27 ***Perf. 11½, 12½***

246 A47 10g gray green 3.00 3.50
247 A47 25g carmine 4.50 3.50
248 A47 40g dark blue 6.00 1.75
Nos. 246-248 (3) 13.50 8.75
Set, never hinged 50.00

4th Intl. Congress of Millitary Medicine and Pharmacy, Warsaw, May 30-June 4.

Juliusz Slowacki — A48

1927, June 28 ***Perf. 12½***

249 A48 20g rose 2.75 .70
Never hinged 12.00

Transfer from Paris to Cracow of the remains of Julius Slowacki, poet.

Pilsudski Type of 1927
Design Redrawn

1928 ***Perf. 11½, 12x11½, 12½x13***

250 A44 25g yellow brown 2.00 .25
Never hinged 8.50

Souvenir Sheet

A49

1928, May 3 **Engr.** ***Perf. 12½***

251 A49 Sheet of 2 250.00 325.00
Never hinged 475.00
a. 50g black brown 25.00 85.00
b. 1z black brown 25.00 85.00

1st Natl. Phil. Exhib., Warsaw, May 3-13. Sold to each purchaser of a 1.50z ticket to the Warsaw Philatelic Exhibition. Counterfeits exist.

Marshal Pilsudski — A49a

Perf. 10½ to 14 and Compound

1928-31 **Wove Paper**

253 A49a 50g bluish slate 3.00 .25
254 A49a 50g blue grn ('31) 20.00 .35
Set, never hinged 70.00

See No. 315.

Pres. Moscicki — A50

Perf. 12x12½, 11½ to 13½ and Compound

1928 **Laid Paper**

255 A50 1z black, *cream* 15.00 .70
Never hinged 50.00
a. Horizontally laid paper ('30) 40.00 1.75
Never hinged 120.00

See Nos. 305, 316. For surcharges and overprints see Nos. J92-J94, 1K19, 1K24.

General Josef Bem — A51

Wove Paper

1928, May **Typo.** ***Perf. 12½***

256 A51 25g rose red 2.00 .35
Never hinged 8.50

Return from Syria to Poland of the ashes of General Josef Bem.

Henryk Sienkiewicz — A52

1928, Oct.

257 A52 15g ultra .75 .25
Never hinged 3.25

For overprint see No. 1K23.

Eagle Arms — A53

1928-29 ***Perf. 12x12½***

258 A53 5g dark violet .25 .25
259 A53 10g green .25 .25
260 A53 25g red brown .25 .25
Nos. 258-260 (3) .75 .75
Set, never hinged 4.00

See design A58. For overprints see Nos. 1K20-1K22.

"Swiatowid," Ancient Slav God — A54

1928, Dec. 15 ***Perf. 12½x12***

261 A54 25g brown .50 .25
Never hinged 3.50

Poznan Agricultural Exhibition.

King John III Sobieski — A55

1930, July ***Perf. 12x12½***

262 A55 75g claret 1.50 .25
Never hinged 6.00

Stylized Soldiers — A56

1930, Nov. 1 ***Perf. 12½***

263 A56 5g violet brown .35 .25
264 A56 15g dark blue 2.75 .25
265 A56 25g red brown .25 .25
266 A56 30g dull red 5.00 2.25
Nos. 263-266 (4) 8.35 3.00
Set, never hinged 25.00

Centenary of insurrection of 1830.

Kosciuszko, Washington, Pulaski — A57

Laid Paper

1932, May 3 ***Perf. 11½***

267 A57 30g brown 1.00 .35
Never hinged 3.50

200th birth anniv. of George Washington.

A58

Perf. 12x12½

1932-33 **Typo.** **Wmk. 234**

268 A58 5g dull vio ('33) .35 .25
269 A58 10g green .35 .25
270 A58 15g red brown ('33) .35 .25
271 A58 20g gray .75 .25
272 A58 25g buff .75 .25
273 A58 30g deep rose .85 .25
274 A58 60g blue 3.75 .50
Nos. 268-274 (7) 7.15 2.00
Set, never hinged 27.50

For overprints and surcharge see Nos. 280-281, 284, 292, 1K25-1K27.

Torun City Hall — A59

1933, Jan. 2 Engr. *Perf. 11½*
275 A59 60g blue 27.50 1.00
Never hinged 90.00

700th anniversary of the founding of the City of Torun by the Grand Master of the Knights of the Teutonic Order.
See No. B28.

Altar Panel of St. Mary's Church, Cracow — A60

Perf. 11½-12½ & Compound
1933, July 10 Laid Paper Unwmk.
277 A60 80g red brown 8.50 .70
Never hinged 30.00

400th death anniv. of Veit Stoss, sculptor and woodcarver.
For surcharge see No. 285.

John III Sobieski and Allies before Vienna, painted by Jan Matejko — A61

1933, Sept. 12 Laid Paper
278 A61 1.20z indigo 20.00 2.00
Never hinged 70.00

250th anniv. of the deliverance of Vienna by the Polish and allied forces under command of John III Sobieski, King of Poland, when besieged by the Turks in 1683.
For surcharge see No. 286.

Cross of Independence A62

Wmk. 234
1933, Nov. 11 Typo. *Perf. 12½*
279 A62 30g scarlet 1.75 .30
Never hinged 6.25

15th anniversary of independence.

Type of 1932 Overprinted in Red or Black

1934, May 5 *Perf. 12*
280 A58 20g gray (R) 20.00 40.00
281 A58 30g deep rose 30.00 45.00
Set, never hinged 175.00

Katowice Philatelic Exhibition. Counterfeits exist.

Josef Pilsudski — A63

Perf. 11½ to 12½ and Compound
1934, Aug. 6 Engr. Unwmk.
282 A63 25g gray blue 1.25 .70
283 A63 30g black brown 1.75 .70
Set, never hinged 17.50

Polish Legion, 20th anniversary.
For overprint see No. 293.

Nos. 274, 277-278 Surcharged in Black or Red

1934 Wmk. 234 *Perf. 12x12½*
284 A58 55g on 60g blue 1.75 .25
Perf. 11½-12½ & Compound
Unwmk.
285 A60 25g on 80g red brn 2.50 .25
286 A61 1z on 1.20z ind (R) 9.50 4.25
a. Figure "1" in surcharge 5mm high instead of 4½mm 9.50 4.25
Never hinged 50.00
Nos. 284-286 (3) 13.75 4.75
Set, never hinged 75.00

Surcharge of No. 286 includes bars.

Marshal Pilsudski — A64

1935 *Perf. 11 to 13 and Compound*
287 A64 5g black .35 .25
288 A64 15g black .35 .25
289 A64 25g black .45 .25
290 A64 45g black 2.75 .50
291 A64 1z black 5.00 3.50
Nos. 287-291 (5) 8.90 4.75
Set, never hinged 30.00

Pilsudski mourning issue.
Nos. 287-288 are typo., Nos. 290-291 litho. No. 289 exists both typo. and litho.
See No. B35b.

Nos. 270, 282 Overprinted in Blue or Red

1935 Wmk. 234 *Perf. 12x12½*
292 A58 15g red brown .75 .25
Perf. 11½, 11½x12½
Unwmk.
293 A63 25g gray blue (R) 2.00 .85
Set, never hinged 12.00

Issued in connection with the proposed memorial to Marshal Pilsudski, the stamps were sold at Cracow exclusively.

"The Dog Cliff" — A65

President Ignacy Moscicki — A75

Designs: 10g, "Eye of the Sea." 15g, M. S. "Pilsudski." 20g, View of Pieniny. 25g, Belvedere Palace. 30g, Castle in Mira. 45g, Castle at Podhorce. 50g, Cloth Hall, Cracow. 55g, Raczynski Library, Poznan. 1z, Cathedral, Wilno.

1935-36 Typo. *Perf. 12½x13*
294 A65 5g violet blue .25 .25
295 A65 10g yellow green .40 .25
296 A65 15g Prus green 1.90 .25
297 A65 20g violet black .95 .25
Engr.
298 A65 25g myrtle green .30 .30
299 A65 30g rose red .75 .25
300 A65 45g plum ('36) .25 .25
301 A65 50g black ('36) .25 .25
302 A65 55g blue ('36) 1.25 .25
303 A65 1z brown ('36) 3.50 3.50
304 A75 3z black brown 1.00 5.25
Nos. 294-304 (11) 10.80 11.05
Set, never hinged 40.00

See Nos. 308-311. For overprints see Nos. 306-307, 1K28-1K32.

Type of 1928 inscribed "1926. 3. VI. 1936" on Bottom Margin

1936, June 3
305 A50 1z ultra 2.00 4.00
Never hinged 6.50

Presidency of Ignacy Moscicki, 10th anniv.

Nos. 299, 302 Overprinted in Blue or Red

1936, Aug. 15
306 A65 30g rose red 3.50 3.50
307 A65 55g blue (R) 5.50 2.25
Set, never hinged 30.00

Gordon-Bennett Intl. Balloon Race. Counterfeits exist.

Scenic Type of 1935-36

Designs: 5g, Church at Czestochowa. 10g, Maritime Terminal, Gdynia. 15g, University, Lwow. 20g, Municipal Building, Katowice.

1937 Engr. *Perf. 12½*
308 A65 5g violet blue .25 .25
309 A65 10g green .40 .25
310 A65 15g red brown .35 .25
311 A65 20g orange brown .35 .25
Nos. 308-311 (4) 1.35 1.00
Set, never hinged 5.00

For overprints see Nos. 1K31-1K32.

Marshal Smigly-Rydz — A80

1937 *Perf. 12½x13*
312 A80 25g slate green .25 .25
313 A80 55g blue .25 .25
Set, never hinged 2.00

For surcharges see Nos. N30, N32.

Types of 1928-37

1937 Souvenir Sheets
314 Sheet of 4 14.00 20.00
a. A80 25g, dark brown 1.75 2.75
315 Sheet of 4 14.00 20.00
a. A49a 50g, deep blue 1.75 2.75
316 Sheet of 4 12.50 20.00
a. A50 1z, gray black 1.75 2.75
Set, never hinged 120.00

Visit of King Carol of Romania to Poland, June 26-July 1.
See No. B35c.

President Moscicki — A81

1938, Feb. 1 *Perf. 12½*
317 A81 15g slate green .70 .25
318 A81 30g rose violet .35 .25
Set, never hinged 3.00

71st birthday of President Moscicki.
For surcharge see No. N31.

Kosciuszko, Paine and Washington and View of New York City — A82

1938, Mar. 17 *Perf. 12x12½*
319 A82 1z gray blue 1.40 .70
Never hinged 5.00

150th anniv. of the US Constitution.

Boleslaus I and Emperor Otto III at Gnesen — A83

Marshal Pilsudski — A95

Designs: 10g, King Casimir III. 15g, King Ladislas II Jagello and Queen Hedwig. 20g, King Casimir IV. 25g, Treaty of Lublin. 30g, King Stephen Bathory commending Wielock, the peasant. 45g, Stanislas Zolkiewski and Jan Chodkiewicz. 50g, John III Sobieski entering Vienna. 55g, Union of nobles, commoners and peasants. 75g, Dabrowski, Kosciuszko and Poniatowski. 1z, Polish soldiers. 2z, Romuald Traugutt.

1938, Nov. 11 Engr. *Perf. 12½*
320 A83 5g red orange .25 .25
321 A83 10g green .25 .25
322 A83 15g fawn .25 .25
323 A83 20g peacock blue .25 .25
324 A83 25g dull violet .35 .25
325 A83 30g rose red .35 .25
326 A83 45g black .45 .25
327 A83 50g brt red vio .35 .25
328 A83 55g ultra .35 .25
329 A83 75g dull green 1.40 1.00
330 A83 1z orange 1.60 1.75
331 A83 2z carmine rose 6.50 15.00
332 A95 3z gray black 3.00 10.00
Nos. 320-332 (13) 15.35 30.00
Set, never hinged 57.50

20th anniv. of Poland's independence. See No. 339. For surcharges see Nos. N33-N47.

Souvenir Sheet

Marshal Pilsudski, Gabriel Narutowicz, President Moscicki, Marshal Smigly-Rydz — A96

1938, Nov. 11 *Perf. 12½*
333 A96 Sheet of 4 10.00 18.00
Never hinged 35.00
a. 25g dull violet (Pilsudski) 1.10 1.75
b. 25g dull violet (Narutowicz) 1.10 1.75
c. 25g dull violet (Moscicki) 1.10 1.75
d. 25g dull violet (Smigly-Rydz) 1.10 1.75

20th anniv. of Poland's independence.

Poland Welcoming Teschen People — A97

1938, Nov. 11

334 A97 25g dull violet		1.75	.50
Never hinged		5.00	

Restoration of the Teschen territory ceded by Czechoslovakia.

Skier — A98

1939, Feb. 6

335 A98 15g orange brown	.50	*.70*
336 A98 25g dull violet	.50	.70
337 A98 30g rose red	1.40	.70
338 A98 55g brt ultra	3.25	1.25
Nos. 335-338 (4)	5.65	3.35
Set, never hinged	20.00	

Intl. Ski Meet, Zakopane, Feb. 11-19.

Type of 1938

15g, King Ladislas II Jagello, Queen Hedwig.

Re-engraved

1939, Mar. 2 *Perf. 12½*

339 A83 15g redsh brown	.25	.25
Never hinged	.70	

No. 322 with crossed swords and helmet at lower left. No. 339, swords and helmet have been removed.

Marshal Pilsudski Reviewing Troops — A99

1939, Aug. 1 **Engr.**

340 A99 25g dull rose violet	.25	.90
Never hinged	1.00	

Polish Legion, 25th anniv. See No. B35a.

Polish Peoples Republic

Romuald Traugutt A100

Tadeusz Kosciuszko A101

Design: 1z, Jan Henryk Dabrowski.

Perf. 11½

1944, Sept. 7 **Litho.** **Unwmk.**

Without Gum

341 A100 25g crimson rose	37.50	50.00
342 A101 50g deep green	35.00	40.00
343 A101 1z deep ultra	35.00	45.00
Nos. 341-343 (3)	107.50	135.00

Counterfeits exist.
For surcharges see Nos. 362-363.

Polish Eagle — A103

Grunwald Monument, Cracow — A104

1944, Sept. 13 **Photo.** *Perf. 12½*

344 A103 25g deep red	.60	.35
a. 25g dull red, typo.	.85	
Never hinged	2.75	
345 A104 50g dk slate green	.45	.25
Set, never hinged	2.25	

No. 344a was not put on sale without surcharge. See Nos. 346, 349a. For surcharges see Nos. 345A-356, 364, B54, C19-C20.

No. 344 Surcharged in Black

a

b

c

1944-45

345A A103 1z on 25g	1.25	6.75
345B A103 2z on 25g ('45)	1.25	8.50
345C A103 3z on 25g ('45)	1.00	6.75
Nos. 345A-345C (3)	3.50	22.00
Set, never hinged	7.00	

Issued to honor Polish government agencies. K. R. N. — Krajowa Rada Narodowa (Polish National Council), P. K. W. N. — Polski Komitet Wyzwolenia Narodu (Polish National Liberation Committee) and R. T. R. P. — Rzad Tymczasowy Rzeczypospolitej Polskiej (Temporary Administration of the Polish Republic).
Counterfeits exist.

No. 344a Surcharged in Brown

1945, Sept. 1

346 A103 1.50z on 25g dull red	.45	.25
Never hinged	.70	
a. 1.50z on 25g deep red, #344	650.00	350.00

Counterfeits of No. 346a exist.

No. 344 Surcharged in Blue

1945, Feb. 12

347 A103 3z on 25g	5.25	22.50
348 A103 3z on 25g *(Radom, 16. I. 1945)*	1.75	5.00
349 A103 3z on 25g *(Warszawa, 17. I. 1945)*	7.25	8.50
a. 3z on 25g dull red, #344a	125.00	150.00
350 A103 3z on 25g *(Czestochowa, 17. I. 1945)*	1.75	5.00
351 A103 3z on 25g *(Krakow, 19. I. 1945)*	1.75	5.00
352 A103 3z on 25g *(Lodz, 19. I. 1945)*	1.75	5.00
353 A103 3z on 25g *(Gniezno, 22. I. 1945)*	1.75	5.00
354 A103 3z on 25g *(Bydgoszcz, 23. I. 1945)*	1.75	5.00
355 A103 3z on 25g *(Kalisz, 24. I. 1945)*	1.75	5.00
356 A103 3z on 25g *(Zakopane, 29. I. 1945)*	1.75	5.00
Nos. 347-356 (10)	26.50	71.00
Set, never hinged	50.00	

Dates overprinted are those of liberation for each city.
Counterfeits exist.

Grunwald Monument, Cracow — A105

Kosciuszko Statue, Cracow — A106

Cloth Hall, Cracow A107

Copernicus Memorial — A108

Wawel Castle — A109

1945, Apr. 10 **Photo.** *Perf. 10½, 11*

357 A105 50g dk violet brn	.25	.25
a. 50g dark brown	.35	.25
Never hinged	.75	
358 A106 1z henna brown	.30	.25
359 A107 2z sapphire	.45	.35
360 A108 3z dp red violet	.75	.30
361 A109 5z blue green	1.75	9.00
Nos. 357-361 (5)	3.50	10.15
Set, never hinged	7.00	

Liberation of Cracow Jan. 19, 1945.

Nos. 357-361 exist imperf. Value, set: unused $24; never hinged $50.

No. 357a is a coarser printing from a new plate showing designer's name (J. Wilczyk) in lower left margin. No. 357 does not show his name.

Nos. 341-342 Surcharged in Black or Red

d

e

1945 *Perf. 11½*

362 A100(d) 5z on 25g	35.00	*70.00*
363 A101(e) 5z on 50g (R)	5.00	*45.00*
Never hinged	15.00	

No. 362 was issued without gum.

No. 345 Surcharged in Brown

1945, Sept. 10 *Perf. 12½*

364 A104 1z on 50g dk sl grn	.40	.25
Never hinged	1.40	

Lodz Skyline A110

Kosciuszko Monument, Lodz A111

Flag Bearer Carrying Wounded Comrade — A112

1945, Mar. 9 **Litho.** *Perf. 11, 9 (3z)*

365 A110 1z deep ultra	.55	.25
366 A111 3z dull red violet	1.25	.25
367 A112 5z deep carmine	1.50	1.90
Nos. 365-367 (3)	3.30	2.40
Set, never hinged	5.00	

Nos. 365 and 367 commemorate the liberation of Lodz and Warsaw.

Grunwald Battle Scene — A113

1945, July 16

368 A113 5z deep blue	3.00	*15.00*
Never hinged	6.00	

Battle of Grunwald (Tannenberg), July 15, 1410.

Eagle Breaking Fetters and Manifesto of Freedom — A114

1945, July 22

369	A114	3z rose carmine	5.00	*20.00*
		Never hinged	10.00	

1st anniv. of the liberation of Poland.

Crane Tower, Gdansk — A115

Stock Tower, Gdansk — A116

Ancient High Gate, Gdansk A117

1945, Sept. 15 Photo. Unwmk.

370	A115	1z olive	.25	.25
371	A116	2z sapphire	.25	.25
372	A117	3z dark violet	.50	.50
		Nos. 370-372 (3)	1.00	1.00
		Set, never hinged	2.25	

Recovery of Poland's access to the sea at Gdansk (Danzig).
Exist imperf. Value, set $25.

Civilian and Soldiers in Rebellion — A118

1945, Nov. 29

373	A118	10z black	3.50	*20.00*
		Never hinged	7.00	

115th anniv. of the "November Uprising" against the Russians, Nov. 29, 1830.

Holy Cross Church — A119

Views of Warsaw, 1939 and 1945: 1.50z, Warsaw Castle, 1939 and 1945. 3z, Cathedral of St. John. 3.50z, City Hall. 6z, Post Office. 8z, Army General Staff Headquarters.

1945-46 Unwmk. *Imperf.*

374	A119	1.50z crimson	.25	.25
375	A119	3z dark blue	.25	.25
376	A119	3.50z lt blue grn	.50	.25
377	A119	6z gray black ('46)	.50	.25
378	A119	8z brown ('46)	1.00	.50
379	A119	10z dark violet ('46)	.80	.25
		Nos. 374-379 (6)	3.30	2.00
		Set, never hinged	6.50	

Nos. 374-379 exist with private produced rouletting.

Nos. 374-379 Overprinted in Black

1946, Jan. 17

383	A119	1.50z crimson	1.00	3.00
384	A119	3z dark blue	1.00	3.00
385	A119	3.50z lt blue grn	1.00	3.00
386	A119	6z gray black	1.00	3.00
387	A119	8z brown	1.00	3.00
388	A119	10z dark violet	1.00	3.00
		Nos. 383-388 (6)	6.00	18.00
		Set, never hinged	12.00	

Liberation of Warsaw, 1/17/45, 1st anniv. Counterfeits exist.

Polish Revolutionist A125

1946, Jan. 22 *Perf. 11*

389	A125	6z slate blue	1.75	*14.00*
		Never hinged	3.50	

Revolt of Jan. 22, 1863.

Infantry Advancing — A126

1946, May 9

390	A126	3z brown	.30	.25
		Never hinged	.50	

Polish freedom, first anniversary.

Premier Edward Osubka-Morawski Pres. Boleslaw Bierut and Marshal Michael Rola-Zymierski — A127

Perf. 11x10½

1946, July 22 Unwmk.

391	A127	3z purple	.75	*19.00*
		Never hinged	1.50	

For surcharge see No. B53.
Exists imperf., value $30.

Bedzin Castle — A128

Duke Henry IV of Silesia, from Tomb at Wroclaw — A129

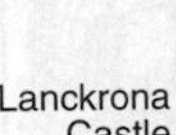

Lanckrona Castle A130

1946, Sept. 1 Photo. *Imperf.*

392	A128	5z olive gray	.25	.25
393	A128	5z brown	.25	.25

Perf. 10½

394	A129	6z gray black	.35	.35

Imperf

395	A130	10z deep blue	.65	.25
		Nos. 392-395 (4)	1.50	1.10
		Set, never hinged	2.75	

Perforated examples of Nos. 392, 393 and 395 have been privately made.
For surcharge see No. 404.

Jan Matejko, Jacek Malczewski, Josef Chelmonski — A131

Adam Chmielowski (Brother Albert) — A132

Designs: 3z, Chopin. 5z, Wojciech Boguslawski, Helena Modjeska and Stefan Jaracz. 6z, Alexander Swietochowski, Stephen Zeromski and Boleslaw Prus. 10z, Marie Sklodowska Curie. 15z, Stanislaw Wyspianski, Juliusz Slowacki and Jan Kasprowicz. 20z, Adam Mickiewicz.

1947 *Perf. 11*

396	A131	1z blue	.35	.25
397	A132	2z brown	.35	.25
398	A132	3z Prus green	.35	.25
399	A131	5z olive green	.35	.25
400	A131	6z gray green	.75	.35
401	A132	10z gray brown	.50	.25
402	A131	15z sepia	1.40	.35
403	A132	20z gray black	1.00	.25
		Nos. 396-403 (8)	5.05	2.20
		Set, never hinged	12.00	

Imperf

403A	A131	1z blue	.25	.25
403B	A132	2z brown	.25	.25
403C	A132	3z Prus green	.25	.25
403D	A131	5z olive green	.25	.25
403E	A131	6z gray green	.70	.35
403F	A132	10z gray brown	.85	.25
403G	A131	15z sepia	1.40	.35
403H	A132	20z gray black	1.75	.25
		Nos. 403A-403H (8)	5.70	2.20

No. 394 Surcharged in Red

1947, Feb. 25 *Perf. 10½*

404	A129	5z on 6z gray blk	.50	.25
		Never hinged	1.00	

Exists imperf., value $15.

Types of 1947

1947 Photo. *Perf. 11*

405	A131	1z slate gray	.25	.25
406	A132	2z orange	.25	.25
407	A132	3z olive green	.25	.35
408	A131	5z olive brown	.35	.25
409	A131	6z carmine rose	.35	.25
410	A132	10z blue	1.10	.30
411	A131	15z chestnut brn	.70	.35
412	A132	20z dark violet	1.40	.35
a.		Souv. sheet of 8, #405-412	85.00	250.00
		Never hinged	175.00	
		Nos. 405-412 (8)	4.65	2.35
		Set, never hinged	8.50	

No. 412a sold for 500z.

Imperf

412B	A131	1z slate gray	.25	.25
412C	A132	2z orange	.25	.25
412D	A132	3z olive green	.50	.25
412E	A131	5z olive brown	.75	.25
412F	A131	6z carmine rose	.35	.25
412G	A132	10z blue	.35	.25
412H	A131	15z chestnut brn	1.00	.25
412I	A132	20z dark violet	1.75	.25
		Nos. 412B-412I (8)	5.20	2.00

Laborer — A139

Farmer — A140

Fisherman A141

Miner A142

1947, Aug. 20 Engr. *Perf. 13*

413	A139	5z rose brown	.50	.25
414	A140	10z brt blue green	.25	.25
415	A141	15z dark blue	1.50	.25
416	A142	20z brown black	.35	.25
		Nos. 413-416 (4)	2.60	1.00
		Set, never hinged	6.75	

Allegory of the Revolution — A143

1948, Mar. 15 Photo. *Perf. 11*

417	A143	15z brown	.25	.25
		Never hinged	.55	

Revolution of 1848. See Nos. 430-432.

Insurgents — A144

1948, Apr. 19

418	A144	15z gray black	.60	5.00
		Never hinged	1.25	

Ghetto uprising, Warsaw, 5th anniv.
Exists imperf., value $1,700.

Decorated Bicycle Wheel A145

Krynica Spa A239

Dunajec Canyon, Pieniny Mountains A240

Designs: 80g, Morskie Oko, Tatra Mts. 2z, Windmill and framework, Ciechocinek.

1953, Dec. 16

608 A239 20g blue & rose brn .35 .25
609 A240 80g bl grn & dk vio 4.00 2.50
610 A240 1.75z ol bis & dk grn .65 .25
611 A239 2z brick red & blk .65 .25
Nos. 608-611 (4) 5.65 3.25

Electric Passenger Train — A241

Design: 80g, Electric locomotive and cars.

1954, Jan. 26 **Engr.**

612 A241 60g deep blue 6.00 3.00
613 A241 80g red brown .55 .25

Spinning Mill, Worker — A242

Designs: 40g, Woman letter carrier. 80g, Woman tractor driver.

1954, Mar. 24 **Photo.**

614 A242 20g deep green 2.00 1.00
615 A242 40g deep blue .45 .25
616 A242 80g dark brown .50 .25
Nos. 614-616 (3) 2.95 1.50

Flags and May Flowers — A243

1954, Apr. 28

617 A243 40g chocolate .60 .25
618 A243 60g deep blue 1.00 .25
619 A243 80g carmine rose .60 .25
Nos. 617-619 (3) 2.20 .75

Labor Day, May 1, 1954.

"Peace" Uniting Three Capitals — A244

No. 621, Dove, olive branch and wheel.

1954, Apr. 29 ***Perf. 12½x12***

620 A244 80g red brown .60 .25
621 A244 80g deep blue .70 .25

7th Intl. Bicycle Tour, May 2-17, 1954.

A245

1954, Apr. 30 **Engr.** ***Perf. 11½***

622 A245 25g gray 1.50 .50
623 A245 80g brown carmine .35 .25

3rd Trade Union Congress, Warsaw 1954.

Glider and Framed Clouds — A246

60g, Glider, flags. 1.35z, Glider, large cloud.

1954, May 31 **Photo.** ***Perf. 12½***

624 A246 45g dark green .65 .25
625 A246 60g purple 3.50 2.50
626 A246 60g brown 1.25 .25
627 A246 1.35z blue 2.40 .25
Nos. 624-627 (4) 7.80 3.25

Intl. Glider Championships, Leszno.

Fencing — A247

Handstand on Horizontal Bars — A248

Design: 1z, Relay racers.

1954, July 17

628 A247 25g violet brown 1.75 .25
629 A248 60g Prus blue 1.40 .30
630 A247 1z violet blue 3.50 1.75
Nos. 628-630 (3) 6.65 2.30

Javelin Throwers A249

1954, July 17 ***Perf. 12***

631 A249 60g rose brn & dk red brn .70 .70
632 A249 1.55z gray & black 1.90 .70

Nos. 628-632 were issued to publicize the second Summer Spartacist Games, 1954.

Studzianki Battle Scene — A250

Design: 1z, Soldier and flag bearer.

1954, Aug. 24 ***Perf. 12½***

633 A250 60g dark green 1.50 .30
634 A250 1z violet blue 5.50 2.75

10th anniversary, Battle of Studzianki.

Railway Signal — A251

Design: 60g, Modern train.

1954, Sept. 9

635 A251 40g dull blue 6.00 .25
636 A251 60g black 3.25 1.90

Issued to publicize Railwaymen's Day.

Ivan Michurin, Horticulturalist A252

1954, Sept. 15

637 A252 40g violet 2.00 1.60
638 A252 60g black .25 .25

Month of Polish-Soviet friendship.

View of Elblag A253

Cities: 45g, Gdansk. 60g, Torun. 1.40z, Malbork. 1.55z, Olsztyn.

1954, Oct. 16 **Engr.** ***Perf. 12x12½***

639 A253 20g dk car, *bl* 2.10 .70
640 A253 45g brown, *yel* .25 .25
641 A253 60g dk green, *cit* .25 .25
642 A253 1.40z dk blue, *pink* .35 .25
643 A253 1.55z dk vio brn, *cr* .60 .25
Nos. 639-643 (5) 3.55 1.70

Pomerania's return to Poland, 500th anniv. For overprint see No. 866.

Chopin and Piano — A254

1954, Nov. 8 **Photo.** ***Perf. 12½***

644 A254 45g dark brown .30 .25
645 A254 60g dark green .30 .25
646 A254 1z dark blue 3.00 1.60
Nos. 644-646 (3) 3.60 2.10

5th Intl. Competition of Chopin's Music.

Coal Mine — A255

Designs: 20g, Soldier, flag and map. 25g, Steel mill. 40g, Relaxing worker in deck chair. 45g, Building construction. 60g, Tractor in field. 1.15z, Lublin Castle. 1.40z, Books and publications. 1.55z, Loading ship. 2.10z, Attacking tank.

Photo.; Center Engr.

1954-55 ***Perf. 12½x12***

647 A255 10g red brn & choc .70 .25
648 A255 20g rose & grnsh blk .70 .25
649 A255 25g bister & blk 2.00 .25
650 A255 40g yel org & choc .70 .25
651 A255 45g claret & vio brn .70 .25
652 A255 60g emerald & red brn .55 .25
653 A255 1.15z brt bl grn & sep .70 .25
654 A255 1.40z orange & choc 15.00 3.50
655 A255 1.55z blue & indigo 3.50 .35
656 A255 2.10z ultra & indigo 2.75 1.75
Nos. 647-656 (10) 27.30 7.35

10th anniversary of "People's Poland." Issued: 25g, 60g, 1955; others, 12/23/54.

Photo.; Center Litho.

1954, Oct. 30

656A A255 25g bister & blk 8.25 1.75
656B A255 60g emer & red brn 2.00 .70

Insurgents Attacking Russians — A256

60g, Gen. Tadeusz Kosciuszko and insurgents. 1.40z, Kosciuszko leading attack in Cracow.

1954, Nov. 30 **Engr.** ***Perf. 12½***

657 A256 40g grnsh black .50 .25
658 A256 60g violet brown .65 .25
659 A256 1.40z dark gray 2.40 1.40
Nos. 657-659 (3) 3.55 1.90

160th anniv. of the Insurrection of 1794.

No. 658 exists in a trial color proof in black blue.

Bison — A257

60g, European elk. 1.90z, Chamois. 3z, Beaver.

Engr.; Background Photo.

1954, Dec. 22

660 A257 45g yel grn & blk brn .30 .25
661 A257 60g emerald & dk brn .30 .25
662 A257 1.90z blue & blk brn .60 .25
663 A257 3z bl grn & dk brn 3.00 1.50
Nos. 660-663 (4) 4.20 2.25

Exist imperf. Value, set: mint, $4.50, used $2.40.

Liberators Entering Warsaw — A258

60g, Allegory of freedom (Warsaw Mermaid).

1955, Jan. 17 **Photo.**

664 A258 40g red brown 1.50 1.40
665 A258 60g dull blue 1.50 .25

Liberation of Warsaw, 10th anniversary.

Frederic Chopin — A259

1955, Feb. 22 **Engr.**

666 A259 40g dark brown .25 .25
667 A259 60g indigo 1.90 .60

5th Intl. Competition of Chopin's Music, Feb. 22-Mar. 21.

Nicolaus Copernicus A260

Sigismund III A261

Warsaw monuments: 5g, Mermaid. 10g, Feliks E. Dzerzhinski. 20g, Brothers in Arms Monument. 45g, Marie Sklodowska Curie. 60g, Adam Mickiewicz. 1.55z, Jan Kilinski.

1955, May 3 Unwmk. *Perf. 12½*

668 A260	5g dk grn, *grnsh*	.25	.25
669 A260	10g vio brn, *yel*	.25	.25
670 A261	15g blk brn, *bluish*	.25	.25
671 A260	20g dk bl, *pink*	.25	.25
672 A260	40g vio, *vio*	.25	.25
673 A261	45g vio brn, *cr*	1.50	.25
674 A260	60g dk bl, *gray*	.35	.25
675 A261	1.55z sl bl, *grysh*	3.50	1.40
	Nos. 668-675 (8)	6.60	3.15

See Nos. 737-739.

Palace of Culture and Flags of Poland and USSR — A262

Design: 60g, Monument.

Perf. 12½x12, 11

1955, Apr. 21 Photo.

676 A262	40g rose red	.70	.30
677 A262	40g lt brown	.25	.25
678 A262	60g Prus blue	.25	.25
679 A262	60g dk olive brn	.25	.25
	Nos. 676-679 (4)	1.45	1.05

Polish-USSR treaty of friendship, 10th anniv.

Arms and Bicycle Wheels — A263

Design: 60g, Three doves above road.

1955, Apr. 25 *Perf. 12*

680 A263	40g chocolate	.85	.25
681 A263	60g ultra	.25	.25

8th Intl. Peace Bicycle Race, Prague-Berlin-Warsaw.

Poznan Town Hall and Fair Emblem — A264

1955, June 10 Photo. *Perf. 12½*

682 A264	40g brt ultra	.50	.25
683 A264	60g dull red	.25	.25

24th Intl. Fair at Poznan, July 3-24, 1955.

"Laikonik" Carnival Costume A265

A265a

1955, June 16 Typo. *Perf. 12*

Multicolored Centers

684 A265	20g emerald & henna	2.00	.90
685 A265a	40g brt org & lil	.25	.25
686 A265	60g blue & carmine	.30	.25
	Nos. 684-686 (3)	2.55	1.40

Cracow Celebration Days.

Pansies — A266

40g, 60g, (#690), Dove & Tower of Palace of Science & Culture. 45g, Pansies. 60g, (#691), 1z, "Peace" (POKOJ) & Warsaw Mermaid.

1955, July 13 Litho. *Perf. 12*

687 A266	25g vio brn, org & car	.25	.25
688 A266	40g gray bl & gray blk	.25	.25
689 A266	45g brn lake, yel & car	.85	.25
690 A266	60g sepia & orange	.30	.25
691 A266	60g ultra & lt blue	.30	.25
692 A266	1z purple & lt blue	1.00	.65
	Nos. 687-692 (6)	2.95	1.90

5th World Festival of Youth, Warsaw, July 31-Aug. 14, 1955.

Exist imperf. Value, set: mint, $4.50, used $3.50.

Motorcyclists A267

1955, July 20 Photo. *Perf. 12½*

693 A267	40g chocolate	.75	.25
694 A267	60g dark green	.30	.25

13th Intl. Motorcycle Race in the Tatra Mountains, Aug. 7-9, 1955.

Stalin Palace of Culture and Science, Warsaw — A268

1955, July 21

695 A268	60g ultra	.25	.25
696 A268	60g gray	.25	.25
697 A268	75g blue green	.40	.25
698 A268	75g brown	.40	.25
	Nos. 695-698 (4)	1.30	1.00

Polish National Day, July 22, 1955. Sheets contain alternating stamps of the 60g values or the 75g values respectively.

Athletes — A269

Stadium — A270

Designs: 40g, Hammer throwing. 1z, Basketball. 1.35z, Sculling. 1.55z, Swimming.

1955, July 27 Unwmk. *Perf. 12½*

699 A269	20g chocolate	.25	.25
700 A269	40g plum	.25	.25
701 A270	60g dull blue	.30	.25
702 A269	1z orange ver	.45	.25
703 A269	1.35z dull violet	.60	.25
704 A269	1.55z peacock green	.85	.50
	Nos. 699-704 (6)	2.70	1.75

2nd International Youth Games, 1955. Exist imperf. Value, set: mint or used, $3.50.

Town Hall, Szczecin (Stettin) — A271

Designs: 40g, Cathedral, Wroclaw (Breslau) 60g, Town Hall, Zielona Gora (Grunberg). 95g, Town Hall, Opole (Oppeln).

1955, Sept. 22 Engr. *Perf. 11½*

705 A271	25g dull green	.25	.25
706 A271	40g red brown	.25	.25
707 A271	60g violet blue	.45	.25
708 A271	95g dark gray	1.40	.80
	Nos. 705-708 (4)	2.35	1.55

10th anniv. of the acquisition of Western Polish Territories.

Rebels with Flag — A272

1955, Sept. 30 Photo. *Perf. 12x12½*

709 A272	40g dark brown	.95	.30
710 A272	60g dk carmine rose	.25	.25

Revolution of 1905, 50th anniversary.

Adam Mickiewicz — A273

Mickiewicz Monument, Paris — A274

60g, Death mask. 95g, Statue, Warsaw.

1955, Oct. 10 *Perf. 12x12½, 12½*

711 A273	20g dark brown	.25	.25
712 A274	40g brn org & dk brn	.25	.25
713 A274	60g green & brown	.25	.25
714 A274	95g brn red & blk	1.75	1.20
	Nos. 711-714 (4)	2.50	1.95

Death cent. of Adam Mickiewicz, poet, and to publicize the celebration of Mickiewicz year.

Teacher and Child — A275

Design: 60g, Flame and open book.

Perf. 12½x13

1955, Oct. 21 Unwmk.

715 A275	40g brown	1.25	.25
716 A275	60g ultra	1.20	.85

Polish Teachers' Trade Union, 50th anniv.

Rook and Hands — A276

Design: 60g, Chess knight and hands.

1956, Feb. 9 *Perf. 12½*

717 A276	40g dark red	2.50	2.40
718 A276	60g blue	1.40	.25

First World Chess Championship of the Deaf and Dumb, Feb. 9-23.

Captain and S. S. Kilinski A277

10g, Sailor and barges. 20g, Dock worker and S. S. Pokoj. 45g, Shipyard and worker. 60g, Fisherman, S. S. Chopin and trawlers.

1956, Mar. 16 Engr. *Perf. 12x12½*

719 A277	5g green	.25	.25
720 A277	10g carmine lake	.25	.25
721 A277	20g deep ultra	.25	.25
722 A277	45g rose brown	1.75	.70
723 A277	60g violet blue	.35	.25
	Nos. 719-723 (5)	2.85	1.70

Snowflake and Ice Skates — A278

Designs: 40g, Snowflake and Ice Hockey sticks. 60g, Snowflake and Skis.

1956, Mar. 7 Photo. *Perf. 12½*

724 A278	20g brt ultra & blk	4.50	2.40
725 A278	40g brt grn & vio bl	.70	.25
726 A278	60g lilac & lake	.55	.25
	Nos. 724-726 (3)	5.75	2.90

XI World Students Winter Sport Championship, Mar. 7-13.

Cyclist — A279

1956, Apr. 25

727 A279	40g dark blue	1.25	.60
728 A279	60g dark green	.25	.25

9th Intl. Peace Bicycle Race, Warsaw-Berlin-Prague, May 1-15.

Zakopane Mountains and Shelter — A280

40g, Map, compass & knapsack. 60g, Map of Poland & canoe. 1.15z, Skis & mountains.

1956, May 25

729 A280	30g dark green	.25	.25
730 A280	40g lt red brown	.25	.25
731 A280	60g blue	1.50	.80
732 A280	1.15z dull purple	.25	.25
	Nos. 729-732 (4)	2.25	1.55

Polish Tourist industry.

No. 593 Surcharged

1956, July 6 — Engr. — *Perf. 12½*

733	A232	10g on 80g dp plum	1.00	.45
734	A232	40g on 80g dp plum	.25	.25
735	A232	60g on 80g dp plum	.25	.25
736	A232	1.35z on 80g dp plum	1.75	.80
		Nos. 733-736 (4)	3.25	1.75

The size and type of surcharge and obliteration of old value differ for each denomination.

Type of 1955

Warsaw Monuments: 30g, Ghetto Monument. 40g, John III Sobieski. 1.55z, Prince Joseph Poniatowski.

1956, July 10

737	A260	30g black	.25	.25
738	A260	40g red brn, *grnsh*	.30	.25
739	A260	1.55z vio brn, *pnksh*	.25	.25
		Nos. 737-739 (3)	.80	.75

No. 737 measures 22½x28mm, instead of 21x27mm.

A281

Polish-Soviet Friendship Month — A281a

Designs: 40g, Polish and Russian dancers. 60g, Open book and cogwheels.

1956, Sept. 14 — Litho. — *Perf. 12*

740	A281	40g brn red & brn	.60	.30
741	A281a	60g bister & red	.25	.25

Ludwika Wawrzynska and Children — A282

1956, Sept. 17 — Photo. — *Perf. 12½*

742	A282	40g dull red brown	1.00	.25
743	A282	60g blue	.25	.25

Issued in honor of a heroic school teacher who saved three children from a burning house.

Bee on Clover and Beehive — A283

Design: 60g, Father Jan Dzierzon.

1956, Oct. 30 — Litho. — Unwmk.

744	A283	40g org yel & brn	.90	.45
745	A283	60g yellow & brn	.25	.25

50th death anniv. of Father Jan Dzierzon, the inventor of the modernized beehive.

"Lady with the Ermine" by Leonardo da Vinci A284

40g, Niobe. 60g, Madonna by Veit Stoss.

1956 — Engr. — *Perf. 11½x11*

746	A284	40g dark green	2.75	1.40
747	A284	60g dark violet	.50	.25
748	A284	1.55z chocolate	1.60	.30
		Nos. 746-748 (3)	4.85	1.95

Intl. Museum Week (UNESCO), Oct. 8-14.

Fencer A285

Designs: 20g, Boxer. 25g, Sculling. 40g, Steeplechase racer. 60g, Javelin thrower. No. 755, Woman gymnast. No. 756, Woman broad jumper.

1956 — Engr. — *Perf. 11½*

750	A285	10g slate & chnt	.25	.25
751	A285	20g lt brn & dl vio	.35	.25
a.		Center inverted	23,000.	
752	A285	25g lt blue & blk	1.20	.35
753	A285	40g brt bl grn & redsh brn	.25	.25
754	A285	60g rose car & ol brn	.25	.25
755	A285	1.55z lt vio & sepia	2.50	1.00
756	A285	1.55z orange & chnt	1.25	.50
		Nos. 750-756 (7)	6.05	2.85

16th Olympic Games, Melbourne, 11/22-12/8.

15th Century Mailman — A286

Lithographed and Engraved

1956, Nov. 30 — Unwmk. — *Perf. 12½*

757	A286	60g lt blue & blk	2.50	1.00

Reopening of the Postal Museum in Wroclaw.

Skier and Snowflake A287

Ski Jumper and Snowflake — A288

Design: 1z, Skier in right corner.

1957, Jan. 18 — Photo. — *Perf. 12½*

758	A287	40g blue	.25	.25
759	A288	60g dark green	.25	.25
760	A287	1z purple	.70	.55
		Nos. 758-760 (3)	1.20	1.05

50 years of skiing in Poland.

Globe and Tree A289

UN Emblem — A290

UN Building, NY — A291

1957, Feb. 26 — Photo. — *Perf. 12*

761	A289	5g mag & brt grnsh bl	.25	.25
762	A290	15g blue & gray	.50	.25
763	A291	40g brt bl grn & gray	.45	.45
		Nos. 761-763 (3)	1.20	.95

Issued in honor of the United Nations.

Exist imperf. Value, set: mint $4, used $3.50.

An imperf. souvenir sheet exists, containing a 1.50z stamp in a redrawn design similar to A291. The stamp is blue and bright bluish green. Value, $25 unused, $14 canceled.

Skier — A292

1957, Mar. 22 — *Perf. 12½*

764	A292	60g blue	.70	.30
765	A292	60g brown	.25	.25

12th anniv. of the death of the skiers Bronislaw Czech and Hanna Marusarzowna.

Sword, Foil and Saber on World Map — A293

Designs: No. 767, Fencer facing right. No. 768, Fencer facing left.

1957, Apr. 20 — Unwmk. — *Perf. 12½*

766	A293	40g deep plum	.55	.30
767	A293	60g carmine	.25	.25
768	A293	60g ultra	.25	.25
a.		Pair, #767-768	.75	.50

World Youth Fencing Championships, Warsaw.

No. 768a has continuous design.

Dr. Sebastian Petrycy — A294

Doctors' Portraits: 20g Wojciech Oczko. 40g, Jedrzej Sniadecki. 60g, Tytus Chalubinski. 1z, Wladyslaw Bieganski. 1.35z, Jozef Dietl. 2.50z, Benedykt Dybowski. 3z, Henryk Jordan.

Portraits Engr., Inscriptions Typo.

1957 — *Perf. 11½*

769	A294	10g sepia & ultra	.25	.25
770	A294	20g emerald & claret	.25	.25
771	A294	40g gray & org red	.25	.25
772	A294	60g blue & pale brn	.95	.40
773	A294	1z org & dk blue	.25	.25
774	A294	1.35z gray brn & grn	.25	.25
775	A294	2.50z dull vio & lil rose	.25	.25
776	A294	3z violet & ol brn	.25	.25
		Nos. 769-776 (8)	2.70	2.15

Bicycle Wheel and Carnation — A295

1957, May 4 — Photo. — *Perf. 12½*

777	A295	60g shown	.50	.25
778	A295	1.50z Cyclist	.40	.35

10th Intl. Peace Bicycle Race, Warsaw-Berlin-Prague.

Poznan Fair Emblem — A296

1957, June 8 — Litho. — Unwmk.

779	A296	60g ultramarine	.25	.25
780	A296	2.50z lt blue green	.35	.25

Issued to publicize the 26th Fair at Poznan.

Turk's Cap — A297

Flowers: No. 782, Carline Thistle. No. 783, Sea Holly. No. 784, Edelweiss. No. 785, Lady's-slipper.

1957, Aug. 12 — Photo. — *Perf. 12*

781	A297	60g bl grn & claret	.40	.25
782	A297	60g gray, grn & yel	.50	.25
783	A297	60g lt blue & grn	.50	.25
784	A297	60g gray & yel grn	2.00	.70
785	A297	60g lt grn, mar & yel	.70	.25
		Nos. 781-785 (5)	4.10	1.70

Fire Fighter — A298

60g, Child & flames. 2.50z, Grain & flames.

1957, Sept. 11 ***Perf. 12***

786 A298 40g black & red .25 .25
787 A298 60g dk grn & org red .25 .25
788 A298 2.50z violet & red .65 .30
Nos. 786-788 (3) 1.15 .80

Intl. Fire Brigade Conf., Warsaw.

Town Hall, Leipzig and Congress Emblem — A299

1957, Sept. 25 **Photo.** ***Perf. 12½***

789 A299 60g violet .25 .25

4th Intl. Trade Union Cong., Leipzig, Oct. 4-15.

"Girl Writing Letter" by Fragonard A300

1957, Oct. 9 ***Perf. 12***

790 A300 2.50z dark blue green .60 .25

Issued for Stamp Day, Oct. 9.

Karol Libelt — A301

1957, Nov. 15 **Photo.** ***Perf. 12½***

791 A301 60g carmine lake .25 .25

Centenary of the Poznan Scientific Society and to honor Karol Libelt, politician and philosopher.

Broken Chain and Flag — A302

Design: 2.50z, Lenin Statue, Poronin.

1957, Nov. 7

792 A302 60g brt blue & red .25 .25
793 A302 2.50z black & red brn .35 .25

40th anniv. of the Russian Revolution.

Jan A. Komensky (Comenius) A303

1957, Dec. 11 ***Perf. 12***

794 A303 2.50z brt carmine .35 .25

300th anniv. of the publication of "Didactica Opera Omnia."

Henri Wieniawski — A304

1957, Dec. 2 ***Perf. 12½***

795 A304 2.50z blue .25 .25

3rd Wieniawski Violin Competition in Poznan.

Andrzej Strug — A305

1957, Dec. 16 **Unwmk.** ***Perf. 12½***

796 A305 2.50z brown .35 .25

20th death anniv. of Andrzej Strug, novelist.

Joseph Conrad and "Torrens" A306

1957, Dec. 30 **Engr.** ***Perf. 12x12½***

797 A306 60g brown, *grnsh* .25 .25
798 A306 2.50z dk blue, *pink* .95 .40

Birth cent. of Joseph Conrad, Polish-born English writer.

Postilion and Stylized Plane — A307

Designs: 40g, Tomb of Prosper Prowana, globe with plane and satellite. 60g, St. Mary's Church, Cracow, mail coach and plane. 95g, Mail coach and postal bus. 2.10z, Medieval postman and train. 3.40z, Medieval galleon and modern ships.

1958 **Litho.** ***Perf. 12½***

799 A307 40g lt blue & vio brn .25 .25
800 A307 60g pale vio & blk .25 .25
801 A307 95g lemon & violet .25 .25
802 A307 2.10z gray & ultra .35 .25
803 A307 2.50z brt blue & blk .35 .25
804 A307 3.40z aqua & maroon .35 .25
Nos. 799-804 (6) 1.80 1.50

400th anniversary of the Polish posts. Imperfs. exist of all but No. 803.

Town Hall at Biecz — A308

Town Halls: 40g, Wroclaw. 60g, Tarnow, horiz. 2.10z, Danzig. 2.50z, Zamosc.

1958, Mar. 29 **Engr.** ***Perf. 12½***

805 A308 20g green .25 .25
806 A308 40g brown .25 .25
807 A308 60g dark blue .35 .25
808 A308 2.10z rose lake .50 .25
809 A308 2.50z violet .85 .35
Nos. 805-809 (5) 2.20 1.35

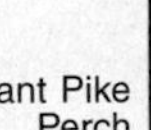

Giant Pike Perch A309

Fishes: 60g, Salmon, vert. 2.10z, Pike, vert. 2.50z, Trout, vert. 6.40z, Grayling.

1958, Apr. 22 **Photo.** ***Perf. 12***

810 A309 40g bl, blk, grn & yel .70 .30
811 A309 60g yel grn, dk grn & bl .70 .25
812 A309 2.10z dk bl, grn & yel .70 .25
813 A309 2.50z pur, blk & yel grn 2.10 .35
814 A309 6.40z bl grn, brn & red .70 .35
Nos. 810-814 (5) 4.90 1.50

Casimir Palace, Warsaw University — A310

1958, May 14 **Unwmk.** ***Perf. 12½***

815 A310 2.50z violet blue .35 .25

140th anniv. of the University of Warsaw.

Stylized Glider and Cloud — A311

Design: 2.50z, Design reversed.

1958, June 14 **Litho.**

816 A311 60g gray blue & blk .25 .25
817 A311 2.50z gray & blk .40 .25

7th Intl. Glider Competitions.

Fair Emblem — A312

1958, June 9

818 A312 2.50z black & rose .40 .25

27th Fair at Poznan.

Armed Postman and Mail Box — A313

1958, Sept. 1 **Engr.** ***Perf. 11***

819 A313 60g dark blue .30 .25

19th anniv. of the defense of the Polish post office at Danzig (Gdansk). Inscribed: "You were the first."

Letter, Quill and Postmark — A314

1958, Oct. 9 **Litho.**

820 A314 60g blk, bl grn & ver .60 .25

Issued for Stamp Day. Exists imperf., value $250.

Polar Bear — A315

Design: 2.50z, Rocket and Sputnik.

1958, Sept. 30 **Photo.** ***Perf. 12½x12***

821 A315 60g gray & black .25 .25
822 A315 2.50z blue & dark blue .50 .25

Intl. Geophysical Year.

Partisan's Cross — A316

Designs: 60g, Virtuti Militari Cross. 2.50z, Grunwald Cross.

1958, Oct. 10 ***Perf. 11***

823 A316 40g black, grn & ocher .25 .25
824 A316 60g black, blue & yel .25 .25
825 A316 2.50z multicolored .70 .30
Nos. 823-825 (3) 1.20 .80

Polish People's Army, 15th anniv.

17th Century Ship — A317

Design: 2.50z, Polish immigrants.

1958, Oct. 29 ***Perf. 11***

826 A317 60g dk slate grn .25 .25
827 A317 2.50z dk carmine rose .50 .25

350th anniversary of the arrival of the first Polish immigrants in America.

UNESCO Building, Paris — A318

1958, Nov. 3 **Unwmk.**

828 A318 2.50z yellow grn & blk .55 .25

UNESCO Headquarters in Paris, opening, Nov. 3.

Stagecoach — A319

Wmk. 326

1958, Oct. 26 Engr. *Perf. 12½*

829 A319 2.50z slate, *buff*	1.00	.35
a. Souvenir sheet of 6	10.00	10.00

Philatelic exhibition in honor of the 400th anniv. of the Polish post, Warsaw, Oct. 25-Nov. 10.

Souvenir Sheet

1958, Dec. 12 Unwmk. *Imperf.*

Printed on Silk

830 A319 50z dark blue	20.00	20.00

400th anniversary of the Polish posts.

Stanislaw Wyspianski — A320

Portrait: 2.50z, Stanislaw Moniuszko.

1958, Nov. 25 Engr. *Perf. 12½*

831 A320 60g dark violet	.30	.25
832 A320 2.50z dk slate grn	.45	.25

Stanislaw Wyspianski, painter and poet, and Stanislaw Moniuszko, composer.

Kneeling Figure — A321

1958, Dec. 10 Litho.

833 A321 2.50z lt brn & red brn	.50	.25

Signing of the Universal Declaration of Human Rights, 10th anniv.

Red Flag — A322

1958, Dec. 16 Photo.

834 A322 60g plum & red	.30	.25

Communist Party of Poland, 40th anniv.

Sailing — A323

Sports: 60g, Girl archer. 95g, Soccer. 2z, Horsemanship.

1959, Jan. 3

835 A323 40g lt bl & vio bl	.25	.25
836 A323 60g salmon & brn vio	.25	.25
837 A323 95g green & brn vio	.70	.25
838 A323 2z dp bl & lt grn	.35	.25
Nos. 835-838 (4)	1.55	1.00

Hand at Wheel — A324

Wheat, Hammer and Flag — A325

1959, Mar. 10 Wmk. 326 *Perf. 12½*

839 A324 40gr shown	.25	.25
840 A325 60gr shown	.25	.25
841 A324 1.55z Factory	.40	.25
Nos. 839-841 (3)	.90	.75

3rd Workers Congress.

Amanita Phalloides — A326

Designs: Various mushrooms.

1959, May 8 Photo. *Perf. 11½*

842 A326 20g yel, grn & brn	3.50	2.40
843 A326 30g multicolored	1.40	.50
844 A326 40g multicolored	.75	.25
845 A326 60g yel grn, brn & ocher	.75	.25
846 A326 1z multicolored	.75	.25
847 A326 2.50z blue, grn & brn	1.10	.35
848 A326 3.40z multicolored	1.75	.40
849 A326 5.60z dl yel, brn & grn	4.25	2.40
Nos. 842-849 (8)	14.25	6.80

"Storks," by Jozef Chelmonski A327

Paintings by Polish Artists: 60g, Mother and Child, Stanislaw Wyspianski, vert. 1z, Mme. de Romanet, Henryk Rodakowski, vert. 1.50z, Old Man and Death, Jacek Malczewski, vert. 6.40z, River Scene, Aleksander Gierymski.

1959 Engr. *Perf. 12, 12½x12*

850 A327 40g gray green	.25	.25
851 A327 60g dull purple	.25	.25
852 A327 1z intense black	.35	.25
853 A327 1.50z brown	.65	.25
854 A327 6.40z blue	2.25	.50
Nos. 850-854 (5)	3.75	1.50

Nos. 850 and 854 measure 36x28mm; Nos. 851 and 853, 28x36mm; No. 852, 28x37mm.

Miner and Globe — A328

1959, July 1 Litho.

855 A328 2.50z multicolored	.55	.25

3rd Miners' Conf., Katowice, July 1959.

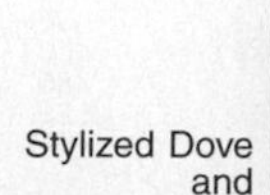

Symbol of Industry — A329

Map of Poland and: 40g, Map of Poland and Symbol of Agriculture. 1.50z, Symbol of art and science.

Perf. 12x12½

1959, July 21 Wmk. 326

856 A329 40g black, bl & grn	.25	.25
857 A329 60g black & ver	.25	.25
858 A329 1.50z black & blue	.30	.25
Nos. 856-858 (3)	.80	.75

15 years of the Peoples' Republic of Poland.

Lazarus Ludwig Zamenhof — A330

Design: 1.50z, Star, globe and flag.

1959, July 24 *Perf. 12½*

859 A330 60g blk & grn, *ol*	.25	.25
860 A330 1.50z ultra, grn & red, *gray*	.80	.25

Centenary of the birth of Lazarus Ludwig Zamenhof, author of Esperanto, and in conjunction with the Esperanto Congress in Warsaw.

Map of Austria and Flower — A331

1959, July 27 Litho.

861 A331 60g sep, red & grn, *yel*	.25	.25
862 A331 2.50z bl, red, & grn, *gray*	.60	.25

7th World Youth Festival, Vienna, July 26-Aug. 14.

Symbolic Plane — A332

1959, Aug. 24 Wmk. 326 *Perf. 12½*

863 A332 60g vio bl, grnsh bl & blk	.30	.25

30th anniv. of LOT, the Polish airline.

Sejm (Parliament) Building — A333

1959, Aug. 27 Photo. *Perf. 12x12½*

864 A333 60g lt grn, blk & red	.25	.25
865 A333 2.50z vio gray, blk & red	.50	.25

48th Interparliamentary Conf., Warsaw.

No. 640 Overprinted in Blue: "BALPEX I — GDANSK 1959"

1959, Aug. 30 Engr. Unwmk.

866 A253 45g brown, *yel*	.75	.50

Intl. Phil. Exhib. of Baltic States at Gdansk.

Stylized Dove and Globe — A334

Wmk. 326

1959, Sept. 1 Photo. *Perf. 12½*

867 A334 60g blue & gray	.30	.25

World Peace Movement, 10th anniv.

Red Cross Nurse — A335

Designs: 60g, Nurse. 2.50z, Henri Dunant.

Size: 21x26mm

1959, Sept. 21 Litho. *Perf. 12½*

868 A335 40g red, lt grn & blk	.25	.25
869 A335 60g bis brn, brn & red	.25	.25

Perf. 11

Size: 23x23mm

870 A335 2.50z red, pink & blk	.75	.35
Nos. 868-870 (3)	1.25	.85

Polish Red Cross, 40th anniv.; Red Cross, cent.

Polish-Chinese Friendship Society Emblem — A336

Wmk. 326

1959, Sept. 28 Litho. *Perf. 11*

871 A336 60g multicolored	1.20	.25
872 A336 2.50z multicolored	.50	.25

Polish-Chinese friendship.

Flower Made of Stamps — A337

1959, Oct. 9 *Perf. 12½*

873 A337 60g lt grnsh bl, grn & red	.25	.25
874 A337 2.50z red, grn & vio	.40	.25

Issued for Stamp Day, 1959.

Sputnik 3 — A338

60g, Luna I, sun. 2.50z, Earth, moon, Sputnik 2.

1959, Nov. 7 Photo. Wmk. 326

875 A338 40g Prus blue & gray	.25	.25
876 A338 60g maroon & black	.30	.25
877 A338 2.50z green & dk blue	.90	.50
Nos. 875-877 (3)	1.45	1.00

42nd anniv. of the Russian Revolution and the landing of the Soviet moon rocket.

Exist imperf. Value, set: mint $2.75, used $2.

Child Doing Homework — A339

Design: 60g, Three children leaving school.

Lithographed and Engraved

1959, Nov. 14 *Perf. 11½*

878 A339 40g green & dk brn	.25	.25
879 A339 60g blue & red	.25	.25

"1,000 Schools" campaign for the 1,000th anniversary of Poland.

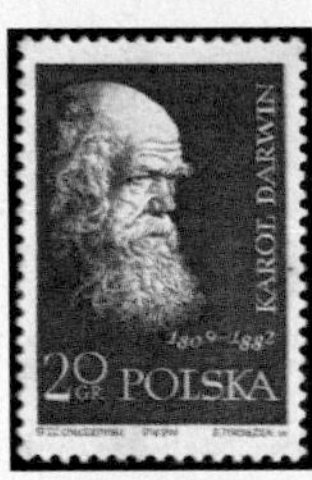

Charles Darwin — A340

Scientists: 40g, Dmitri I. Mendeleev. 60g, Albert Einstein. 1.50z, Louis Pasteur. 1.55z, Isaac Newton. 2.50z, Nicolaus Copernicus.

1959, Dec. 10 Engr. *Perf. 11*

No.	Type	Value & color	Unused	Used
880	A340	20g dark blue	.25	.25
881	A340	40g olive gray	.25	.25
882	A340	60g claret	.35	.25
883	A340	1.50z dk violet brn	.35	.25
884	A340	1.55z dark green	.35	.25
885	A340	2.50z violet	1.25	.50
		Nos. 880-885 (6)	2.80	1.75

Man from Rzeszow A341

Woman from Rzeszow A342

Regional Costumes: 40g, Cracow. 60g, Kurpiow. 1z, Silesia. 2z, Lowicz. 2.50z, Mountain people. 3.10z, Kujawy. 3.40z, Lublin. 5.60z, Szamotuli. 6.50z, Lubuski.

Engraved and Photogravure

1959-60 Wmk. 326 *Perf. 12, Imperf.*

No.	Type	Value & color	Unused	Used
886	A341	20g slate grn & blk	.25	.25
887	A342	20g slate grn & blk	.25	.25
a.		Pair, #886-887	.25	.25
888	A341	40g lt bl & rose car ('60)	.25	.25
889	A342	40g rose car & bl ('60)	.25	.25
a.		Pair, #888-889	.25	.25
890	A341	60g black & pink	.25	.25
891	A342	60g black & pink	.25	.25
a.		Pair, #890-891	.25	.25
892	A341	1z grnsh red & dk red	.25	.25
893	A342	1z grnsh bl & dk red	.25	.25
a.		Pair, #892-893	.25	.25
894	A341	2z yel & ultra ('60)	.25	.25
895	A342	2z yel & ultra ('60)	.25	.25
a.		Pair, #894-895	.40	.25
896	A341	2.50z green & rose lil	.75	.25
897	A342	2.50z green & rose lil	.75	.25
a.		Pair, #896-897	1.50	.50
898	A341	3.10z yel grn & sl grn ('60)	.25	.25
899	A342	3.10z yel grn & sl grn ('60)	.25	.25
a.		Pair, #898-899	.50	.50
900	A341	3.40z gray grn & brn ('60)	.25	.25
901	A342	3.40z gray grn & brn ('60)	.25	.25
a.		Pair, #900-901	.50	.50
902	A341	5.60z yel grn & gray bl	.75	.25
903	A342	5.60z yel grn & gray bl	.75	.25
a.		Pair, #902-903	1.50	.50
904	A341	6.50z vio & gray grn ('60)	1.50	.60
905	A342	6.50z vio & gray grn ('60)	1.50	.60
a.		Pair, #904-905	3.00	1.20
		Nos. 886-905 (20)	9.50	5.70

Nos. 886-905 exist imperf. Value, same as perf.

Piano — A343

Frederic Chopin — A344

Design: 1.50z, Musical note and manuscript.

1960, Feb. 22 Litho. *Perf. 12*

No.	Type	Value & color	Unused	Used
906	A343	60g brt violet & blk	.35	.25
907	A343	1.50z black, gray & red	.50	.25

Perf. 12½x12

Engr.

No.	Type	Value & color	Unused	Used
908	A344	2.50z black	2.00	.70
		Nos. 906-908 (3)	2.85	1.20

150th anniversary of the birth of Frederic Chopin and to publicize the Chopin music competition.

Stamp of 1860 A345

Designs: 60g, Ski meet stamp of 1939. 1.35z, Design from 1860 issue. 1.55z, 1945 liberation stamp. 2.50z, 1957 stamp day stamp.

Litho. (40g, 1.35z); Litho. and Photo.

Perf. 11½x11

1960, Mar. 21 Wmk. 326

No.	Type	Value & color	Unused	Used
909	A345	40g multicolored	.25	.25
910	A345	60g violet, ultra & blk	.25	.25
911	A345	1.35z gray, red & bl	.55	.25
912	A345	1.55z green, car & blk	.75	.25
913	A345	2.50z ap grn, dk grn & blk	1.25	.40
		Nos. 909-913 (5)	3.05	1.40

Centenary of Polish stamps. Nos. 909-913 were also issued in sheets of 4. Values, set of 4 sheets: $500 unused or used.

For overprint see No. 934.

Discus Thrower, Amsterdam 1928 — A346

Polish Olympic Victories: No. 915, Runner. No. 916, Bicyclist. No. 917, Steeplechase. No. 918, Trumpeters. No. 919, Boxers. No. 920, Olympic flame. No. 921 Woman jumper.

Lithographed and Embossed

Perf. 12x12½

1960, June 15 Unwmk.

No.	Type	Value & color	Unused	Used
914	A346	60g blue & blk	.25	.25
915	A346	60g car rose & blk	.25	.25
916	A346	60g violet & blk	.25	.25
917	A346	60g blue grn & blk	.25	.25
a.		Block of 4, #914-917	.80	.40
918	A346	2.50z ultra & blk	.55	.25
919	A346	2.50z chestnut & blk	.55	.25
920	A346	2.50z red & blk	.55	.25
921	A346	2.50z emerald & blk	.55	.25
a.		Block of 4, #918-921	2.50	1.00
		Nos. 914-921 (8)	3.20	2.00

17th Olympic Games, Rome, 8/25-9/11.

Nos. 917a and 921a have continuous design forming the stadium oval.

Nos. 914-921 exist imperf. Value, same as perf.

Tomb of King Wladyslaw II Jagiello — A347

Battle of Grunwald by Jan Matejko — A348

90g, Detail from Grunwald monument.

Perf. 11x11½

1960 Wmk. 326 Engr.

No.	Type	Value & color	Unused	Used
922	A347	60g violet brown	.35	.25
923	A347	90g olive gray	.70	.35

Size: 78x37mm

No.	Type	Value & color	Unused	Used
924	A348	2.50z dark gray	2.50	1.00
		Nos. 922-924 (3)	3.55	1.60

550th anniversary, Battle of Grunwald.

The Annunciation — A349

Carvings by Veit Stoss, St. Mary's Church, Cracow: 30g, Nativity. 40g, Adoration of the Kings. 60g, The Resurrection. 2.50z, The Ascension. 5.60z, Descent of the Holy Ghost. 10z, The Assumption of the Virgin, vert.

1960 Wmk. 326 Engr. *Perf. 12*

No.	Type	Value & color	Unused	Used
925	A349	20g Prus blue	.25	.25
926	A349	30g lt red brown	.25	.25
927	A349	40g violet	.25	.25
928	A349	60g dull green	.25	.25
929	A349	2.50z rose lake	.75	.25
930	A349	5.60z dark brown	7.50	3.25
		Nos. 925-930 (6)	9.25	4.50

Miniature Sheet

Imperf

No.	Type	Value & color	Unused	Used
931	A349	10z black	8.00	5.00

No. 931 contains one vertical stamp which measures 72x95mm.

A350

1960, Sept. 26 *Perf. 12½*

No.	Type	Value & color	Unused	Used
932	A350	2.50z black	.30	.25

Birth cent. of Ignacy Jan Paderewski, statesman and musician.

A351

Lukasiewicz and kerosene lamp.

Engr. & Photo.

1960, Sept. 14 *Perf. 11*

No.	Type	Value & color	Unused	Used
933	A351	60g citron & black	.25	.25

5th Pharmaceutical Congress; Ignacy Lukasiewicz, chemist-pharmacist.

No. 909 Overprinted: "DZIEN ZNACZKA 1960"

1960 Litho. *Perf. 11½x11*

No.	Type	Value & color	Unused	Used
934	A345	40g multicolored	.85	.45

Issued for Stamp Day, 1960.

Great Bustard A352

Birds: 20g, Raven. 30g, Great cormorant. 40g, Black stork. 50g, Eagle owl. 60g, White-tailed sea eagle. 75g, Golden eagle. 90g, Short-toed eagle. 2.50z, Rock thrush. 4z, European kingfisher. 5.60z, Wall creeper. 6.50z, European roller.

1960 Unwmk. Photo. *Perf. 11½*

Birds in Natural Colors

No.	Type	Value & color	Unused	Used
935	A352	10g gray & blk	.25	.25
936	A352	20g gray & blk	.25	.25
937	A352	30g gray & blk	.25	.25
938	A352	40g gray & blk	.25	.25
939	A352	50g pale grn & blk	.30	.25
940	A352	60g pale grn & blk	.40	.25
941	A352	75g pale grn & blk	.40	.25
942	A352	90g pale grn & blk	.65	.25
943	A352	2.50z pale ol gray & blk	6.75	3.00
944	A352	4z pale ol gray & blk	2.75	1.00
945	A352	5.60z pale ol gray & blk	4.50	1.00
946	A352	6.50z pale ol gray & blk	5.50	2.00
		Nos. 935-946 (12)	22.25	9.00

Gniezno — A353

Historic Towns: 10g, Cracow. 20g, Warsaw. 40g, Poznan. 50g, Plock. 60g, Kalisz. No. 952A, Tczew. 80g, Frombork. 90g, Torun. 95g, Puck (ships). 1z, Slupsk. 1.15z, Gdansk (Danzig). 1.35z, Wroclaw. 1.50z, Szczecin. 1.55z, Opole. 2z, Kolobrzeg. 2.10z, Legnica. 2.50z, Katowice. 3.10z, Lodz. 5.60z, Walbrzych.

1960-61 Engr. *Perf. 11½, 13x12½*

No.	Type	Value & color	Unused	Used
947	A353	5g red brown	.25	.25
948	A353	10g green	.25	.25
949	A353	20g dark brown	.25	.25
950	A353	40g vermilion	.25	.25
951	A353	50g violet	.25	.25
952	A353	60g rose claret	.25	.25
952A	A353	60g lt ultra ('61)	.50	.25
953	A353	80g blue	.25	.25
954	A353	90g brown ('61)	1.20	.25
955	A353	95g olive gray	.35	.25

Engraved and Lithographed

No.	Type	Value & color	Unused	Used
956	A353	1z orange & gray	.25	.25
957	A353	1.15z slate grn & sal	.25	.25
958	A353	1.35z lil rose & lt grn	.25	.25
959	A353	1.50z sep & pale grn	.35	.25
960	A353	1.55z car lake & buff	.25	.25
961	A353	2z dk blue & pink	.25	.25
962	A353	2.10z sepia & yel	.35	.25
963	A353	2.50z dl vio & pale grn	.35	.25
964	A353	3.10z ver & gray	1.50	.75
965	A353	5.60z sl grn & lt grn	5.00	1.75
		Nos. 947-965 (20)	12.60	7.00

Front Page of "Merkuriusz" A354

Newspapers: 60g, "Proletaryat," first issue, Sept. 15, 1883. 2.50z, "Rzeczpospolita," first issue, July 23, 1944.

Lithographed and Embossed

1961 Wmk. 326 *Perf. 12*

966 A354 40g black, ultra & emer .35 .25
967 A354 60g black, org brn & yel .35 .25
968 A354 2.50z black, violet & bl 3.25 2.25
Nos. 966-968 (3) 3.95 2.75

300th anniv. of the Polish newspaper Merkuriusz.

Ice Hockey — A355

60g, Ski jump. 1z, Soldiers on skis. 1.50z, Slalom.

1961, Feb. 1 Litho. Wmk. 326

969 A355 40g lt violet, blk & yel .30 .25
970 A355 60g lt ultra, blk & car .30 .25
971 A355 1z lt blue, ol & red 5.50 1.75
972 A355 1.50z grnsh bl, blk & yel .30 .25
Nos. 969-972 (4) 6.40 2.50

1st Winter Spartacist Games of Friendly Armies.

Part of Cogwheel — A356

1961, Feb. 11 *Perf. 12½*

973 A356 60g red & black .25 .25

Fourth Congress of Polish Engineers.

Maj. Yuri A. Gagarin A357

Design: 60g, Globe and path of rocket.

1961, Apr. 27 Photo. *Perf. 12*

974 A357 40g dark red & black .50 .25
975 A357 60g ultra, black & car .50 .25

1st man in space, Yuri A. Gagarin, Apr. 12, 1961.

Emblem of Poznan Fair — A358

1961, May 25 Litho. *Perf. 12½x12*

977 A358 40g brt bl, blk & red org .25 .25
978 A358 1.50z red org, blk & brt bl .35 .25
a. Souvenir sheet of 2 4.00 2.75

30th Intl. Fair at Poznan.

No. 978a contains two of No. 978 with simulated perforation and blue marginal inscriptions. Sold for 4.50z. Issued July 29, 1961.

Famous Poles A359

No. 979, Mieszko I. No. 980, Casimir Wielki. No. 981, Casimir Jagiello. No. 982, Nicolaus Copernicus. No. 983, Andrzej Frycz-Modrzewski. No. 984, Tadeusz Kosciuszko.

Photogravure and Engraved

1961, June 15 *Perf. 11x11½*

Black Inscriptions and Designs

979 A359 60g chalky blue .25 .25
980 A359 60g deep rose .25 .25
981 A359 60g slate .25 .25
982 A359 60g dull violet .35 .25
983 A359 60g lt brown .25 .25
984 A359 60g olive gray .70 .25
Nos. 979-984 (6) 2.05 1.50

See Nos. 1059-1064, 1152-1155.

Trawler — A360

Designs: Various Polish Cargo Ships.

Unwmk.

1961, June 24 Litho. *Perf. 11*

985 A360 60g multicolored .25 .25
986 A360 1.55z multicolored .35 .25
987 A360 2.50z multicolored .50 .25
988 A360 3.40z multicolored .65 .30
989 A360 4z multicolored 1.25 .60
990 A360 5.60z multicolored 3.50 1.50
Nos. 985-990 (6) 6.50 3.15

Polish ship industry. Sizes (width): 60g, 2.50z, 54mm; 1.55z, 3.40z, 4z, 80mm; 5.60z, 108mm.

Post Horn and Telephone Dial — A361

Post horn and: 60g, Radar screen. 2.50z, Conference emblem, globe.

1961, June 26

991 A361 40g sl, gray & red org .25 .25
992 A361 60g gray, yel & vio .25 .25
993 A361 2.50z ol bis, brt bl & vio bl .35 .25
a. Souvenir sheet of 3, #991-993 4.00 2.00
Nos. 991-993 (3) .85 .75

Conference of Communications Ministers of Communist Countries, Warsaw.

No. 993a sold for 5z.

Seal of Opole, 13th Century — A362

Cement Works, Opole A363

Designs: No. 996, Tombstone of Henry IV and seal, Wroclaw. No. 997, Apartment houses, Wroclaw. No. 998, Seal of Conrad II and Silesian eagle. No. 999, Textile mill, Gorzow. No. 1000, Seal of Prince Barnim I. No. 1001, Seaport, Szczecin. No. 1002, Seal of Princess Elizabeth. No. 1003, Factory, Szczecinek. No. 1004, Seal of Unislaw. No. 1005, Shipyard, Gdansk. No. 1005A, Copernicus Tower, Frombork. No. 1005B, Agricultural College, Kortow.

1961-62 Wmk. 326 Engr. *Perf. 11*

Western Territories

994 A362 40g brown, *grysh* .25 .25
995 A363 40g brown, *grysh* .25 .25
a. "Block," #994-995 + label .25 .25
996 A362 60g violet, *pink* .25 .25
997 A363 60g violet, *pink* .25 .25
a. "Block," #996-997 + label .25 .25
998 A362 95g green, *bluish* .50 .25
999 A363 95g green, *bluish* .50 .25
a. "Block," #998-999 + label 1.00 .25
1000 A362 2.50z ol grn, *grnsh* .50 .25
1001 A363 2.50z ol grn, *grnsh* .50 .25
a. "Block," #1000-1001 + label 1.00 .40

Northern Territories

1002 A362 60g vio bl, *bluish* .25 .25
1003 A363 60g vio bl, *bluish* .25 .25
a. "Block," #1002-1003 + label .25 .25
1004 A362 1.55z brown, *buff* .25 .25
1005 A363 1.55z brown, *buff* .25 .25
c. "Block," #1004-1005 + label .50 .35
1005A A362 2.50z slate bl, *grysh* .75 .25
1005B A363 2.50z slate bl, *grysh* .75 .25
d. "Block," #1005A-1005B + label 1.50 .40
Nos. 994-1005B (14) 5.50 3.50

Issued: #994-997, 1000-1001, 7/21; 95g, 2/23/62; #1002-1005B, 7/21/62.

Kayak Race Start and "E" — A364

Designs: 60g, Four-man canoes and "E." 2.50z, Paddle, Polish flag and "E," vert.

Wmk. 326

1961, Aug. 18 Litho. *Perf. 12½*

1006 A364 40g bl grn, yel & red .25 .25
1007 A364 60g multicolored .25 .25
1008 A364 2.50z multicolored .90 .25
Nos. 1006-1008 (3) 1.40 .75

6th European Canoe Championships, Poznan, Aug. 18-20. Exist imperf. Value, set: mint $2.25, used $2.

Maj. Gherman Titov, Star, Globe, Orbit A365

Dove and Earth A366

Perf. 12x12½

1961, Aug. 24 Photo. Unwmk.

1009 A365 40g pink, blk & red .40 .25
1010 A366 60g blue & black .40 .25

Manned space flight of Vostok 2, Aug. 6-7, in which Russian Maj. Gherman Titov orbited the earth 17 times.

Insurgents' Monument, St. Ann's Mountain A367

Design: 1.55z, Cross of Silesian Insurgents.

Wmk. 326

1961, Sept. 15 Litho. *Perf. 12*

1011 A367 60g gray & emerald .25 .25
1012 A367 1.55z gray & blue .25 .25

40th anniv. of the third Silesian uprising.

"PKO," Initials of Polish Savings Bank A368

Initials and: #1014, Bee and clover. #1015, Ant. #1016, Squirrel. 2.50z, Savings bankbook.

1961, Oct. 2 Wmk. 326 *Perf. 12*

1013 A368 40g ver, blk & org .25 .25
1014 A368 60g blue, blk & brt pink .25 .25
1015 A368 60g bis brn, blk & ocher .25 .25
1016 A368 60g brt grn, blk & dl red .50 .25
1017 A368 2.50z car rose, gray & blk 1.50 .50
Nos. 1013-1017 (5) 2.75 1.50

Issued to publicize Savings Month.

Mail Cart, by Jan Chelminski — A369

1961, Oct. 9 Engr. *Perf. 12x12½*

1018 A369 60g deep green .25 .25
1019 A369 60g violet brown .25 .25

Polish Postal Museum, 40th anniv; Stamp Day.

Congress Emblem A370

1961, Nov. 20 Wmk. 326 *Perf. 12*

1020 A370 60g black .25 .25

Issued to publicize the Fifth World Congress of Trade Unions, Moscow, Dec. 4-16.

Seal of Kopasyni Family, 1284 — A371

60g, Seal of Bytom, 14th century. 2.50z, Emblem of International Miners Congress, 1958.

1961, Dec. 4 Litho. *Perf. 11x11½*

1021 A371 40g multicolored .25 .25
1022 A371 60g bl, gray bl & vio bl .25 .25

1023 A371 2.50z yel grn, grn & blk .50 .25

Nos. 1021-1023 (3) 1.00 .75

1,000 years of the Polish mining industry.

Child and Syringe — A372

Designs: 60g, Children of three races, horiz. 2.50z, Mother, child and milk bottle.

1961, Dec. 11 ***Perf. 12½x12, 12x12½***

1024 A372 40g lt blue & blk .25 .25

1025 A372 60g orange & blk .25 .25

1026 A372 2.50z brt bl grn & blk .55 .25

Nos. 1024-1026 (3) 1.05 .75

15th anniversary of UNICEF.

Emblem A373

Design: 60g, Map with oil pipe line from Siberia to Central Europe.

1961, Dec. 12 **Wmk. 326** ***Perf. 12***

1027 A373 40g dk red, yel & vio bl .25 .25

1028 A373 60g vio bl, bl & red .25 .25

15th session of the Council of Mutual Economic Assistance of the Communist States.

Ground Beetle — A374

Black Apollo Butterfly A375

Insects: 30g, Violet runner. 40g, Alpine longicorn beetle. 50g, Great oak capricorn beetle. 60g, Gold runner. 80g, Stag-horned beetle. 1.35z, Death's-head moth. 1.50z, Tiger-striped swallowtail butterfly. 1.55z, Apollo butterfly. 2.50z, Red ant. 5.60z, Bumble bee.

Perf. 12½x12

1961, Dec. 30 **Photo.** **Unwmk.**

Insects in Natural Colors

1029 A374 20g bister brown .35 .25

1030 A374 30g pale gray grn .35 .25

1031 A374 40g pale yellow grn .35 .25

1032 A374 50g blue green .35 .25

1033 A374 60g dull rose lilac .35 .25

1034 A374 80g pale green .70 .25

Perf. 11½

1035 A375 1.15z ultra .70 .25

1036 A375 1.35z sapphire .70 .25

1037 A375 1.50z bluish green .70 .25

1038 A375 1.55z brt purple 1.00 .25

1039 A375 2.50z brt green 1.75 .85

1040 A375 5.60z orange brown 10.00 5.00

Nos. 1029-1040 (12) 17.30 8.35

Worker with Gun — A376

#1042, Worker with trowel and gun. #1043, Worker with hammer. #1044, Worker at helm. #1045, Worker with dove and banner.

Perf. 12½x12

1962, Jan. 5 **Litho.** **Unwmk.**

1041 A376 60g red, blk & green .25 .25

1042 A376 60g red, blk & slate .25 .25

1043 A376 60g blk & vio bl, *red* .25 .25

1044 A376 60g blk & bis, *red* .25 .25

1045 A376 60g blk & gray, *red* .25 .25

Nos. 1041-1045 (5) 1.25 1.25

Polish Workers' Party, 20th anniversary.

Women Skiers A377

Designs: 60g, Long distance skier. 1.50z, Ski jump, vert. 10z, FIS emblem, vert.

Lithographed and Embossed

1962, Feb. 14 ***Perf. 12***

1046 A377 40g gray, red & gray bl .25 .25

a. 40g sepia, red & dull blue .35 .25

1047 A377 60g gray, red & gray bl .25 .25

a. 60g sepia, red & dull blue .45 .25

1048 A377 1.50z gray, red & gray bl .35 .25

a. 1.50z gray, lilac & red 1.40 .70

Nos. 1046-1048 (3) .85 .75

Souvenir Sheet

Imperf

1049 A377 10z gray, red & gray bl 3.25 .85

World Ski Championships at Zakopane (FIS).

No. 1049 contains one stamp with simulated perforation. The sheet sold for 15z.

Each of Nos. 1046-1048 exists in a souvenir sheet of four. Value, set of 3, $125.

Broken Flower and Prison Cloth (Auschwitz) — A378

Majdanek Concentration Camp — A379

Design: 1.50z, Proposed memorial, Treblinka concentration camp

Wmk. 326

1962, Apr. 3 **Engr.** ***Perf. 11½***

1050 A378 40g slate blue .25 .25

1051 A379 60g dark gray .25 .25

1052 A378 1.50z dark violet .40 .25

Nos. 1050-1052 (3) .90 .75

International Resistance Movement Month to commemorate the millions who died in concentration camps, 1940-45.

Bicyclist A380

2.50z, Cyclists in race. 3.40z, Wheel & arms of Berlin, Prague & Warsaw.

Unwmk.

1962, Apr. 27 **Litho.** ***Perf. 12***

1053 A380 60g blue & blk .25 .25

1054 A380 2.50z yellow & blk .35 .25

1055 A380 3.40z lilac & blk .50 .25

Nos. 1053-1055 (3) 1.10 .75

15th Intl. Peace Bicycle Race, Warsaw-Berlin-Prague.

Size of #1053, 1055: 36x22mm, #1054: 74x22mm.

Lenin in Bialy Dunajec — A381

Designs: 60g, Lenin. 2.50z, Lenin and Cloth Hall, Cathedral, Cracow.

Engraved and Photogravure

Perf. 11x11½

1962, May 25 **Wmk. 326**

1056 A381 40g pale grn & Prus grn .25 .25

1057 A381 60g pink & dp claret .25 .25

1058 A381 2.50z yellow & dk brn .50 .25

Nos. 1056-1058 (3) 1.00 .75

50th anniv. of Lenin's arrival in Poland.

Famous Poles Type of 1961

Famous Poles: No. 1059, Adam Mickiewicz. No. 1060, Juliusz Slowacki. No. 1061, Frederic Chopin. No. 1062, Romuald Traugutt. No. 1063, Jaroslaw Dabrowski. No. 1064, Maria Konopnicka.

1962, June 20 **Engr. & Photo.**

Black Inscriptions and Designs

1059 A359 60g dull green .25 .25

1060 A359 60g brown orange .25 .25

Perf. 12x12½

Litho.

1061 A359 60g dull blue .25 .25

1062 A359 60g brown olive .25 .25

1063 A359 60g rose lilac .25 .25

1064 A359 60g blue green .25 .25

Nos. 1059-1064 (6) 1.50 1.50

Karol Swierczewski-Walter — A382

Perf. 11x11½

1962, July 14 **Engr.** **Unwmk.**

1065 A382 60g black .25 .25

15th death anniv. of General Karol Swierczewski-Walter, organizer of the new Polish army.

Crocus — A383

Flowers: No. 1067, Orchid. No. 1068, Monkshood. No. 1069, Gas plant. No. 1070, Water lily. No. 1071, Gentian. No. 1072, Daphne mezereum. No. 1073, Cowbell. No. 1074, Anemone. No. 1075, Globeflower. No. 1076, Snowdrop. No. 1077, Adonis vernalis.

Unwmk.

1962, Aug. 8 **Photo.** ***Perf. 12***

Flowers in Natural Colors

1066 A383 60g dull yel & red .75 .25

1067 A383 60g redsh brn & vio .25 .25

1068 A383 60g pink & lilac .25 .25

1069 A383 90g olive & green .25 .25

1070 A383 90g yel grn & red .25 .25

1071 A383 90g lt ol grn & red .25 .25

1072 A383 1.50z gray bl & bl .35 .25

1073 A383 1.50z yel grn & dk grn .35 .25

1074 A383 1.50z Prus grn & dk bl .35 .25

1075 A383 2.50z gray grn & dk bl .75 .35

1076 A383 2.50z dk bl grn & dk bl 1.00 .35

1077 A383 2.50z gray bl & grn 2.25 1.40

Nos. 1066-1077 (12) 7.05 4.35

The Poisoned Well by Jacek Malczewski — A384

1962, Aug. 15 **Engr.** **Wmk. 326**

1078 A384 60g black, *buff* .25 .25

Issued in sheets of 40 with alternating label for FIP Day (Federation Internationale de Philatelie), Sept. 1. Also issued in miniature sheet of 4. Value: mint $30, used $20.

Pole Vault — A385

Designs: 60g, Relay race. 90g, Javelin. 1z, Hurdles. 1.50z, High jump. 1.55z, Discus. 2.50z, 100m. dash. 3.40z, Hammer throw.

Unwmk.

1962, Sept. 12 **Litho.** ***Perf. 11***

1079 A385 40g multicolored .25 .25

1080 A385 60g multicolored .25 .25

1081 A385 90g multicolored .25 .25

1082 A385 1z multicolored .25 .25

1083 A385 1.50z multicolored .25 .25

1084 A385 1.55z multicolored .25 .25

1085 A385 2.50z multicolored .45 .25

1086 A385 3.40z multicolored .75 .25

Nos. 1079-1086 (8) 2.70 2.00

7th European Athletic Championships, Belgrade, Sept. 12-16.

Exist imperf. Value, set: mint $3.25, used $2.

Anopheles Mosquito A386

Designs: 1.50z, Malaria blood cells. 2.50z, Cinchona flowers. 3z, Anopheles mosquito.

1962, Oct. 1 **Wmk. 326** ***Perf. 13x12***

1087 A386 60g ol blk, dk brn & bl grn .25 .25

1088 A386 1.50z red, gray & brt vio .25 .25

1089 A386 2.50z multicolored .50 .25

Nos. 1087-1089 (3) 1.00 .75

Miniature Sheet

Imperf

1090 A386 3z multicolored 1.10 .50

WHO drive to eradicate malaria.

Pavel R. Popovich and Andrian G. Nikolayev — A387

Design: 2.50z, Two stars in orbit around earth. 10z, Two stars in orbit.

1962, Oct. 6 ***Perf. 12½x12***

1091 A387 60g violet, blk & citron .25 .25
1092 A387 2.50z Prus bl, blk & red .25 .25

Souvenir Sheet

Perf. 12x11

1093 A387 10z sl bl, blk & red 2.40 1.40

1st Russian group space flight, Vostoks III and IV, Aug. 11-15, 1962.

Woman Mailing Letter Warsaw — A388

1962, Oct. 9 **Engr.** ***Perf. 12½x12***

1094 A388 60g black .25 .25
1095 A388 2.50z red brown .45 .25

Stamp Day. The design is from the painting "A Moment of Decision," by Aleksander Kaminski.

Mazovian Princes' Mansion, A389

1962, Oct. 13 **Litho.**

1096 A389 60g red & black .25 .25

25th anniversary of the founding of the Polish Democratic Party.

Cruiser "Aurora" — A390

Photo. & Engr.

1962, Nov. 3 ***Perf. 11***

1097 A390 60g red & dk blue .25 .25

Russian October revolution, 45th anniv.

Janusz Korczak by K. Dunikowski A391

King on Horseback A392

Illustrations from King Matthew books: 90g, King giving watch to Island girl. 1z, King handcuffed and soldier with sword. 2.50z, King with dead bird. 5.60z, King ice skating in moonlight.

Perf. 13x12

1962, Nov. 12 **Unwmk.** **Litho.**

1098 A391 40g brn, bis & sep .25 .25
1099 A392 60g multicolored .25 .25
1100 A392 90g multicolored .35 .25
1101 A392 1z multicolored .35 .25
1102 A392 2.50z brn, yel & brt grn .55 .45
1103 A392 5.60z brn, dk bl & grn 1.60 .75
Nos. 1098-1103 (6) 3.35 2.20

20th anniversary of the death of Dr. Janusz Korczak (Henryk Goldszmit), physician, pedagogue and writer, in the Treblinka concentration camp, Aug. 5, 1942.

View of Old Warsaw — A393

1962, Nov. 26 **Wmk. 326** ***Perf. 11***

1104 A393 3.40z multicolored .50 .25
a. Sheet of 4 5.00 3.00

5th Trade Union Cong., Warsaw, 11/26-12/1.

Orphan Mary and the Dwarf — A394

Various Scenes from "Orphan Mary and the Dwarfs" by Maria Konopnicka.

Perf. 13x12

1962, Dec. 31 **Unwmk.** **Litho.**

1105 A394 40g multicolored .35 .25
1106 A394 60g multicolored 1.50 .35
1107 A394 1.50z multicolored .55 .25
1108 A394 1.55z multicolored .55 .25
1109 A394 2.50z multicolored .55 .30
1110 A394 3.40z multicolored 2.75 1.40
Nos. 1105-1110 (6) 6.25 2.80

120th anniversary of the birth of Maria Konopnicka, poet and fairy tale writer.

Romuald Traugutt A395

Perf. 11½x11

1963, Jan. 31 **Wmk. 326**

1111 A395 60g aqua, blk & pale pink .25 .25

Centenary of the 1863 insurrection and to honor its leader, Romuald Traugutt.

Tractor and Wheat A396

Designs: 60g, Man reaping and millet. 2.50z, Combine and rice.

Perf. 12x12½

1963, Feb. 25 **Litho.** **Wmk. 326**

1112 A396 40g gray, bl, blk & ocher .25 .25
1113 A396 60g brn red, blk, brn & grn .50 .25
1114 A396 2.50z yel, buff, blk & grn .70 .25
Nos. 1112-1114 (3) 1.45 .75

FAO "Freedom from Hunger" campaign.

Cocker Spaniel — A397

30g, Polish sheep dog. 40g, Boxer. 50g, Airedale terrier, vert. 60g, French bulldog, vert. 1z, Poodle, vert. 2.50z, Hunting dog. 3.40z, Sheep dog, vert. 6.50z, Great Dane.

1963, Mar. 25 **Unwmk.** ***Perf. 12½***

1115 A397 20g lil, blk & org brn .25 .25
1116 A397 30g rose car & blk .25 .25
1117 A397 40g lil, blk & yel grn .25 .25
1118 A397 50g multicolored .25 .25
1119 A397 60g lt blue & blk .30 .25
1120 A397 1z yel grn & blk .50 .25
1121 A397 2.50z org, blk & brn 1.00 .35
1122 A397 3.40z red org & blk 2.40 1.00
1123 A397 6.50z brt yel & blk 5.50 2.40
Nos. 1115-1123 (9) 10.70 5.25

Egyptian Ship — A398

Ancient Ships: 10g, Phoenician merchant ship. 20g, Greek trireme. 30g, 3rd century merchantman. 40g, Scandinavian "Gokstad." 60g, Frisian "Kogge." 1z. 14th century "Holk." 1.15z, 15th century "Caraca."

Photo. (Background) & Engr.

1963, Apr. 5 ***Perf. 11½***

1124 A398 5g brown, *tan* .25 .25
1125 A398 10g green, *gray grn* .25 .25
1126 A398 20g ultra, *gray* .25 .25
1127 A398 30g black, *gray ol* .25 .25
1128 A398 40g lt bl, *bluish* .25 .25
1129 A398 60g claret, *gray* .25 .25
1130 A398 1z black, *bl* .25 .25
1131 A398 1.15z grn, *pale rose* .35 .25
Nos. 1124-1131 (8) 2.10 2.00

See Nos. 1206-1213, 1299-1306.

Fighter and Ruins of Warsaw Ghetto — A399

Perf. 11½x11

1963, Apr. 19 **Wmk. 326**

1132 A399 2.50z gray brn & gray .35 .25

Warsaw Ghetto Uprising, 20th anniv.

Centenary Emblem — A400

Perf. 12½x12

1963, May 8 **Litho.** **Unwmk.**

1133 A400 2.50z blue, yel & red .40 .25

Intl. Red Cross, cent. Every other stamp in sheet inverted.

Sand Lizard A401

40g, Smooth snake. 50g, European pond turtle. 60g, Grass snake. 90g, Slow worm. 1.15z, European tree frog. 1.35z, Alpine newt. 1.50z, Crested newt. 1.55z, Green toad. 2.50z, Firebellied toad. 3z, Fire salamander. 3.40z, Natterjack.

Perf. 11½

1963, June 1 **Unwmk.** **Photo.**

Reptiles and Amphibians in Natural Colors

1134 A401 30g grnsh gray & blk .25 .25
1135 A401 40g gray ol & blk .25 .25
1136 A401 50g bis brn & blk .25 .25
1137 A401 60g tan & blk .25 .25
1138 A401 90g gray grn & blk .25 .25
1139 A401 1.15z gray & blk .25 .25
1140 A401 1.35z gray bl & dk bl .35 .25
1141 A401 1.50z bluish grn & blk .50 .25
1142 A401 1.55z bluish gray & blk .50 .25
1143 A401 2.50z gray vio & blk .50 .25
1144 A401 3z gray grn & blk .85 .35
1145 A401 3.40z gray & blk 2.40 1.25
Nos. 1134-1145 (12) 6.60 4.10

Foil, Saber, Sword and Helmet A402

Designs: 40g, Fencers and knights in armor. 60g, Fencers and dragoons. 1.15z, Contemporary and 18th cent. fencers. 1.55z, Fencers and old houses, Gdansk. 6.50z, Arms of Gdansk, vert.

Perf. 12x12½, 12½x12

1963, June 29 **Litho.** **Unwmk.**

1146 A402 20g brown & orange .25 .25
1147 A402 40g dk blue & blue .25 .25
1148 A402 60g red & dp org .25 .25
1149 A402 1.15z green & emer .25 .25
1150 A402 1.55z violet & lilac .35 .25

1151 A402 6.50z yel brn, mar & yel 1.10 .40
Nos. 1146-1151 (6) 2.45 1.65

28th World Fencing Championships, Gdansk, July 15-28. A souvenir sheet exists containing one each of Nos. 1147-1150. Value: mint $40, used $32.50.

Famous Poles Type of 1961

No. 1152, Ludwik Warynski. No. 1153, Ludwik Krzywicki. No. 1154, Marie Sklodowska Curie. No. 1155, Karol Swierczewski-Walter.

Perf. 12x12½

1963, July 20 Wmk. 326

Black Inscriptions and Designs

1152 A359 60g red brown .25 .25
1153 A359 60g gray brown .25 .25
1154 A359 60g blue .30 .25
1155 A359 60g green .25 .25
Nos. 1152-1155 (4) 1.05 1.00

Valeri Bykovski — A403

Designs: 60g, Valentina Tereshkova. 6.50z, Rockets "Falcon" and "Mew" and globe.

Unwmk.

1963, Aug. 26 Litho. *Perf. 11*

1156 A403 40g ultra, emer & blk .25 .25
1157 A403 60g green, ultra & blk .25 .25
1158 A403 6.50z multicolored .85 .25
Nos. 1156-1158 (3) 1.35 .75

Space flights of Valeri Bykovski June 14-19, and Valentina Tereshkova, first woman cosmonaut, June 16-19, 1963.

For overprints see Nos. 1175-1177.

Basketball A404

Designs: Various positions of ball, hands and players. 10z, Town Hall, People's Hall and Arms of Wroclaw.

1963, Sept. 16 Unwmk. *Perf. 11½*

1159 A404 40g multicolored .25 .25
1160 A404 50g fawn, grn & blk .25 .25
1161 A404 60g red, lt grn & blk .25 .25
1162 A404 90g multicolored .25 .25
1163 A404 2.50z multicolored .25 .25
1164 A404 5.60z multicolored 1.00 .25
Nos. 1159-1164 (6) 2.25 1.50

Souvenir Sheet

Imperf

1165 A404 10z multicolored 1.75 1.00

13th European Men's Basketball Championship, Wroclaw, Oct. 4-13. No. 1165 contains one stamp; inscription on margin also commemorates the simultaneous European Sports Stamp Exhibition. Sheet sold for 15z.

Eagle and Ground-to-Air Missile — A405

Eagle and: 40g, Destroyer. 60g, Jet fighter plane. 1.15z, Radar. 1.35z, Tank. 1.55z, Self-propelled rocket launcher. 2.50z, Amphibious troop carrier. 3z, Swords and medieval and modern soldiers.

1963, Oct. 1 *Perf. 12x12½*

1166 A405 20g multicolored .25 .25
1167 A405 40g violet, grn & red .25 .25
1168 A405 60g multicolored .25 .25
1169 A405 1.15z multicolored .25 .25
1170 A405 1.35z multicolored .25 .25
1171 A405 1.55z multicolored .25 .25
1172 A405 2.50z multicolored .35 .25
1173 A405 3z multicolored 1.00 .35
Nos. 1166-1173 (8) 2.85 2.10

Polish People's Army, 20th anniversary.

"Love Letter" by Wladyslaw Czachórski — A406

Perf. 11½

1963, Oct. 9 Unwmk. Engr.

1174 A406 60g dark red brown .25 .25

Issued for Stamp Day.

Nos. 1156-1158 Overprinted "23-28 X. 1963" and name of astronaut

1963 Litho. *Perf. 11*

1175 A403 40g multicolored .25 .25
1176 A403 60g multicolored .25 .25
1177 A403 6.50z multicolored 1.25 .25
Nos. 1175-1177 (3) 1.75 .75

Visit of Valentina Tereshkova and Valeri Bykovski to Poland, Oct. 23-28. The overprints are: 40g, W. F. Bykowski / w Polsce; 60g, W. W. Tierieszkowa / w Polsce; 6.50z, W. F. BYKOWSKI I W. W. TIERIESZKOWA W POLSCE.

Konstantin E. Tsiolkovsky's Rocket and Rocket Speed Formula — A407

American and Russian Spacecrafts: 40g, Sputnik 1. 50g, Explorer 1. 60g, Lunik 2. 1z, Lunik 3. 1.50z, Vostok 1. 1.55z, Friendship 7. 2.50z, Vostoks 3 & 4. 5.60z, Mariner 2. 6.50z, Mars 1.

Perf. 12½x12

1963, Nov. 11 Litho. Unwmk.

Black Inscriptions

1178 A407 30g dull bl grn & gray .25 .25
1179 A407 40g lt ol grn & gray .25 .25
1180 A407 50g violet bl & gray .25 .25
1181 A407 60g brn org & gray .25 .25
1182 A407 1z brt grn & gray .25 .25
1183 A407 1.50z org red & gray .25 .25
1184 A407 1.55z blue & gray .25 .25
1185 A407 2.50z lilac & gray .25 .25
1186 A407 5.60z brt yel grn & gray .50 .25
1187 A407 6.50z grnsh bl & gray .90 .25
Nos. 1178-1187 (10) 3.40 2.50

Conquest of space. A souvenir sheet containing 2 each of Nos. 1186-1187 exists with top and bottom perfs, value: mint $65, used $45; and with bottom perfs only, value: mint $125, used $75.

Arab Stallion "Comet" — A408

Horses from Mazury Region — A409

Horses: 30g, Tarpans (wild horses). 40g, Horse from Sokolka. 50g, Arab mares and foals, horiz. 90g, Steeplechasers, horiz. 1.55z, Arab stallion "Witez II." 2.50z, Head of Arab horse, facing right. 4z, Mixed breeds, horiz. 6.50z, Head of Arab horse, facing left.

Perf. 11½x11 (A408); 12½x12, 12

1963, Dec. 30 Photo.

1188 A408 20g black, yel & car .25 .25
1189 A408 30g multicolored .25 .25
1190 A408 40g multicolored .25 .25

Sizes: 75x26mm (50g, 90g, 4z); 28x38mm (60g, 1.55z, 2.50z, 6.50z)

1191 A409 50g multicolored .25 .25
1192 A409 60g multicolored .25 .25
1193 A409 90g multicolored .35 .25
1194 A409 1.55z multicolored .35 .25
1195 A409 2.50z multicolored .85 .30
1196 A409 4z multicolored 1.75 .75
1197 A409 6.50z yel, dl bl & blk 2.75 1.50
Nos. 1188-1197 (10) 7.30 4.30

Issued to publicize Polish horse breeding.

Ice Hockey A410

Sports: 30g, Slalom. 40g, Skiing. 60g, Speed skating. 1z, Ski jump. 2.50z, Tobogganing. 5.60z, Cross-country skiing. 6.50z, Figure skating pair.

1964, Jan. 25 Litho. *Perf. 12x12½*

1198 A410 20g multicolored .25 .25
1199 A410 30g multicolored .25 .25
1200 A410 40g multicolored .25 .25
1201 A410 60g multicolored .25 .25
1202 A410 1z multicolored .35 .25
1203 A410 2.50z multicolored .35 .25
1204 A410 5.60z multicolored .65 .25
1205 A410 6.50z multicolored 1.25 .60
Nos. 1198-1205 (8) 3.60 2.35

9th Winter Olympic Games, Innsbruck, Jan. 29-Feb. 9. A souvenir sheet contains 2 each of Nos. 1203, 1205. Value $35.

Ship Type of 1963

Sailing Ships: 1.35z, Caravel of Columbus, vert. 1.50z, Galleon. 1.55z, Polish warship. 1627, vert. 2z, Dutch merchant ship, vert. 2.10z, Line ship. 2.50z, Frigate. 3z, 19th century merchantman. 3.40z, "Dar Pomorza," 20th century school ship, vert.

1964, Mar. 19 Engr. *Perf. 12½*

1206 A398 1.35z ultra .25 .25
1207 A398 1.50z claret .25 .25
1208 A398 1.55z black .25 .25
1209 A398 2z violet .25 .25
1210 A398 2.10z green .25 .25
1211 A398 2.50z carmine rose .25 .25
1212 A398 3z olive green .40 .25
1213 A398 3.40z brown .60 .25
Nos. 1206-1213 (8) 2.50 2.00

European Cat — A411

40g, 60g, 1.55z, 2.50z, 6.50z, Various European cats. 50g, Siamese cat. 90g, 1.35z, 3.40z, Various Persian cats. 60g, 90g, 1.35z, 1.55z horiz.

1964, Apr. 30 Litho. *Perf. 12½*

Cats in Natural Colors; Black Inscriptions

1216 A411 30g yellow .25 .25
1217 A411 40g orange .25 .25
1218 A411 50g yellow .25 .25
1219 A411 60g brt green .25 .25
1220 A411 90g lt brown .35 .25
1221 A411 1.35z emerald .35 .25
1222 A411 1.55z violet blue .35 .25
1223 A411 2.50z lilac .45 .25
1224 A411 3.40z rose 2.00 .60
1225 A411 6.50z violet 3.25 1.75
Nos. 1216-1225 (10) 7.75 4.35

King Casimir III, the Great — A412

Designs: No. 1227, Hugo Kollataj. No. 1228, Jan Dlugosz. No. 1229, Nicolaus Copernicus. 2.50z, King Wladyslaw II Jagiello and Queen Jadwiga.

1964, May 5 Engr. *Perf. 11x11½*

Size: 22x35mm

1226 A412 40g dull claret .25 .25
1227 A412 40g green .25 .25
1228 A412 60g violet .25 .25
1229 A412 60g dark blue .40 .25

Size: 35½x37mm

1230 A412 2.50z gray brown .40 .25
Nos. 1226-1230 (5) 1.55 1.25

Jagiellonian University, Cracow, 600th anniv.

Lapwing A413

Waterfowl: 40g, White-spotted bluethroat. 50g, Black-tailed godwit. 60g, Osprey. 90g, Gray heron. 1.35z, Little gull. 1.55z, Shoveler. 5.60z, Arctic loon. 6.50z, Great crested grebe.

Perf. 11½

1964, June 5 Unwmk. Photo.

Birds in Natural Colors; Black Inscriptions

Size: 34x34mm

1231 A413 30g chalky blue .25 .25
1232 A413 40g bister .25 .25
1233 A413 50g brt yellow grn .25 .25

Perf. 11½x11

Size: 34x48mm

1234 A413 60g blue .25 .25
1235 A413 90g lemon .25 .25
1236 A413 1.35z green .35 .25

Perf. 11½

Size: 34x34mm

1237 A413 1.55z olive .35 .25
1238 A413 5.60z blue green .85 .25
1239 A413 6.50z brt green 1.40 .60
Nos. 1231-1239 (9) 4.20 2.60

Hands Holding Red Flag — A414

Designs: No. 1241, Red and white ribbon around hammer. No. 1242, Hammer and rye. No. 1243, Brick wall under construction and red flag.

1964, June 15 Litho. *Perf. 11*

1240 A414 60g ol bis, red, blk & pink .25 .25
1241 A414 60g red, gray & black .25 .25
1242 A414 60g magenta, blk & yel .25 .25
1243 A414 60g gray, red, sal & blk .25 .25
Nos. 1240-1243 (4) 1.00 1.00

4th congress of the Polish United Workers Party.

Symbols of Peasant-Worker Alliance — A415

Atom Symbol and Book — A416

Shipyard, Gdansk — A417

Designs: No. 1245, Stylized oak. No. 1247, Factory and cogwheel. No. 1248, Tractor and grain. No. 1249, Pen, brush, mask and ornament. No. 1251, Lenin Metal Works, Nowa Huta. No. 1252, Cement factory, Chelm. No. 1253, Power Station, Turoszow. No. 1254, Oil refinery, Plock. No. 1255, Sulphur mine, Tarnobrzeg.

1964 Litho. *Perf. 12x12½*

1244 A415 60g red, org & blk .25 .25
1245 A415 60g grn, red, ocher, bl & blk .25 .25

Photo.

Perf. 11

1246 A416 60g gray & dp vio bl .25 .25
1247 A416 60g brt blue & blk .25 .25
1248 A416 60g emerald & blk .25 .25
1249 A416 60g orange & red .25 .25

Photogravure and Engraved

1250 A417 60g dl bl grn & ultra .25 .25
1251 A417 60g brt pink & pur .25 .25
1252 A417 60g gray & gray brn .25 .25
1253 A417 60g grn & slate grn .25 .25
1254 A417 60g salmon & claret .25 .25
1255 A417 60g citron & sepia .25 .25
Nos. 1244-1255 (12) 3.00 3.00

Polish People's Republic, 20 anniv.

Warsaw Fighters, 1944 — A418

1964, Aug. 1 Litho. *Perf. 12½x12*

1256 A418 60g multicolored .25 .25

20th anniv. of the Warsaw insurrection against German occupation.

Long Jump — A419

Women's High Jump — A420

Olympic Sports — A421

Sport: 40g, Rowing (single). 60g, Weight lifting. 90g, Relay race (square). 1z, Boxing (square). 2.50z, Soccer (square). 6.50z, Diving.

Unwmk.

1964, Aug. 17 Litho. *Perf. 11*

1257 A419 20g multicolored .25 .25
1258 A419 40g grnsh bl, bl & yel .25 .25
1259 A419 60g vio bl, red & rose lil .25 .25
1260 A419 90g dk brown, red & yel .25 .25
1261 A419 1z dk violet, lil & gray .25 .25
1262 A419 2.50z multicolored .30 .25
1263 A420 5.60z multicolored .75 .30
1264 A420 6.50z multicolored 1.50 .50
Nos. 1257-1264 (8) 3.80 2.30

Souvenir Sheet

Imperf

1265 A421 Sheet of 4 2.75 1.40
a. 2.50z Sharpshooting .35 .25
b. 2.50z Canoeing .35 .25
c. 5z Fencing .35 .25
d. 5z Basketball .35 .25

18th Olympic Games, Tokyo, Oct. 10-25. Size of stamps in No. 1265: 24x24mm. A souvenir sheet containing 2 each of Nos. 1263-1264 with black marginal inscription exists. Value: mint $40, used $30.

Warsaw Mermaid and Stars — A422

1964, Sept. 7 *Perf. 12½x12*

1266 A422 2.50z violet & black .35 .25

15th Astronautical Congress, Warsaw, Sept. 7-12.

Stefan Zeromski by Monika Zeromska — A423

1964, Sept. 21 Photo. *Perf. 12½*

1267 A423 60g olive gray .25 .25

Stefan Zeromski (1864-1925), writer.

Gun and Hand Holding Hammer — A424

1964, Sept. 21 Litho. *Perf. 11*

1268 A424 60g brt grn, blk & red .25 .25

Union of Fighters for Freedom and Democracy Congress, Warsaw, 9/24-26.

Globe and Red Flag — A425

1964, Sept. 28 Photo. *Perf. 12½*

1269 A425 60g black & red org .25 .25

First Socialist International, centenary.

Stagecoach by Jozef Brodowski — A426

1964, Oct. 9 Engr. *Perf. 11½*

1270 A426 60g green .25 .25
1271 A426 60g lt brown .25 .25

Issued for Stamp Day.

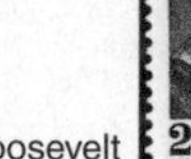

Eleanor Roosevelt (1884-1962) — A427

1964, Oct. 10 *Perf. 12½*

1272 A427 2.50z black .25 .25

Proposed Monument for Defenders of Westerplatte, 1939 — A428

Polish Soldiers Crossing Oder River, 1945 A429

Designs: No. 1274, Virtuti Military Cross. No. 1275, Nike, proposed monument for the martyrs of Bydgoszcz (woman with sword and torch). No. 1277, Battle of Studzianki, 1944.

Perf. 12x11, 11x12

1964, Nov. 16 Engr. Unwmk.

1273 A428 40g blue violet .25 .25
1274 A428 40g slate .25 .25
1275 A428 60g dark blue .25 .25
1276 A429 60g dark blue grn .25 .25
1277 A429 60g grnsh black .25 .25
Nos. 1273-1277 (5) 1.25 1.25

Struggle and martyrdom of the Polish people, 1939-45. The vertical stamps are printed in sheets of 56 stamps (8x7) with 7 labels in each outside vertical row. The horizontal stamps are printed in sheets of 50 stamps (5x10) with 10 labels in each outside vertical row. See Nos. 1366-1368.

Souvenir Sheet

Col. Vladimir M. Komarov, Boris B. Yegorov and Dr. Konstantin Feoktistov — A430

1964, Nov. 21 Litho. *Perf. 11½x11*

1278 A430 Sheet of 3 1.25 .85
a. 60g red & black (Komarov) .25 .25
b. 60g brt grn & blk (Feoktistov) .25 .25
c. 60g ultra & blk (Yegorov) .25 .25

Russian three-manned space flight in space ship Voskhod, Oct. 12-13, 1964. Size of stamps: 27x36mm.

Cyclamen A431

Garden Flowers: 30g, Freesia. 40g, Monique rose. 50g, Peony. 60g, Royal lily. 90g, Oriental poppy. 1.35z, Tulip. 1.50z, Narcissus. 1.55z, Begonia. 2.50z, Carnation. 3.40z, Iris. 5.60z, Camellia.

1964, Nov. 30 Photo. *Perf. 11*

Size: 35½x35½mm

Flowers in Natural Colors

1279 A431 20g violet .25 .25
1280 A431 30g deep lilac .25 .25
1281 A431 40g blue .25 .25
1282 A431 50g violet blue .25 .25
1283 A431 60g lilac .25 .25
1284 A431 90g deep green .25 .25

Size: 26x37½mm

1285 A431 1.35z dark blue .25 .25
1286 A431 1.50z deep carmine .40 .30
1287 A431 1.55z green .25 .25
1288 A431 2.50z ultra .40 .25
1289 A431 3.40z redsh brown .75 .30
1290 A431 5.60z olive gray 1.75 .85
Nos. 1279-1290 (12) 5.30 3.70

Future Interplanetary Spacecraft A432

Designs: 30g, Launching of Russian rocket. 40g, Dog Laika and launching tower. 60g, Lunik 3 photographing far side of the Moon. 1.55z, Satellite exploring the ionosphere. 2.50z, Satellite "Elektron 2" exploring radiation belt. 5.60z, "Mars 1" between Mars and Earth.

Perf. 12½x12

1964, Dec. 30 Litho. Unwmk.

1291 A432 20g multicolored .25 .25
1292 A432 30g multicolored .25 .25
1293 A432 40g ol grn, blk & bl .25 .25
1294 A432 60g dk bl, blk & dk red .25 .25
1295 A432 1.55z gray & multi .25 .25
1296 A432 2.50z multicolored .35 .25
1297 A432 5.60z multicolored .75 .35
Nos. 1291-1297,B108 (8) 3.60 2.20

Issued to publicize space research.

Warsaw Mermaid, Ruins and New Buildings A433

1965, Jan. 15 Engr. *Perf. 11x11½*

1298 A433 60g slate green .25 .25

Liberation of Warsaw, 20th anniversary.

Ship Type of 1963

Designs as before.

1965, Jan. 25 Engr. *Perf. 12½*

1299 A398 5g dark brown .25 .25
1300 A398 10g slate green .25 .25
1301 A398 20g slate blue .25 .25
1302 A398 30g gray olive .25 .25
1303 A398 40g dark blue .25 .25
1304 A398 60g claret .25 .25
1305 A398 1z red brown .25 .25
1306 A398 1.15z dk red brown .30 .25
Nos. 1299-1306 (8) 2.05 2.00

Edaphosaurus — A434

Dinosaurs: 30g, Cryptocleidus, vert. 40g, Brontosaurus. 60g, Mesosaurus, vert. 90g, Stegosaurus. 1.15z, Brachiosaurus, vert. 1.35z, Styracosaurus. 3.40z, Corythosaurus, vert. 5.60z, Rhamphorhynchus, vert. 6.50z, Tyrannosaurus.

1965, Mar. 5 Litho. *Perf. 12½*

1307 A434 20g multicolored .25 .25
1308 A434 30g multicolored .25 .25
1309 A434 40g multicolored .25 .25
1310 A434 60g multicolored .25 .25
1311 A434 90g multicolored .25 .25
1312 A434 1.15z multicolored .75 .25
1313 A434 1.35z multicolored .75 .25
1314 A434 3.40z multicolored .75 .25
1315 A434 5.60z multicolored 1.60 .70
1316 A434 6.50z multicolored 2.50 1.40
Nos. 1307-1316 (10) 7.60 4.10

See Nos. 1395-1403.

Symbolic Wax Seal — A435

Russian and Polish Flags, Oil Refinery-Chemical Plant, Plock — A436

1965, Apr. 21 *Perf. 12½x12, 12½*

1317 A435 60g multicolored .25 .25
1318 A436 60g multicolored .25 .25

20th anniversary of the signing of the Polish-Soviet treaty of friendship, mutual assistance and postwar cooperation.

Polish Eagle and Town Coats of Arms A437

1965, May 8 Engr. *Perf. 11½*

1319 A437 60g carmine rose .25 .25

20th anniversary of regaining the Western and Northern Territories.

Dove A438

1965, May 8 Litho. *Perf. 12x12½*

1320 A438 60g red & black .25 .25

Victory over Fascism, 20th anniversary.

ITU Emblem — A439

Perf. 12½x12

1965, May 17 Litho. Unwmk.

1321 A439 2.50z brt bl, lil, yel & blk .45 .25

ITU, cent.

"The People's Friend" and Clover — A440

Factory and Rye A441

1965, June 5 *Perf. 11*

1322 A440 40g multicolored .25 .25
1323 A441 60g multicolored .25 .25

"Popular Movement" in Poland, 70th anniv.

Finn Class Yachts — A442

Yachts: 30g, Dragon class. 40g, 5.5-m. class. 50g, Group of Finn class. 60g, V-class. 1.35z, Group of Cadet class. 4z, Group of Star class. 5.60z, Two Flying Dutchmen. 6.50z, Two Amethyst class. 15z, Finn class race. (30g, 40g, 60g, 5.60z vertical.)

1965, June 14 Litho. *Perf. 12½*

1324 A442 30g multicolored .25 .25
1325 A442 40g multicolored .25 .25
1326 A442 50g multicolored .25 .25
1327 A442 60g multicolored .25 .25
1328 A442 1.35z multicolored .25 .25
1329 A442 4z multicolored .45 .25
1330 A442 5.60z multicolored .85 .35
1331 A442 6.50z multicolored 1.40 .60
Nos. 1324-1331 (8) 3.95 2.45

Miniature Sheet

Perf. 11

1332 A442 15z multicolored 1.75 .85

World Championships of Finn Class Yachts, Gdynia, July 22-29. No. 1332 contains one stamp 48x22mm.

Marx and Lenin — A443

Photogravure and Engraved

1965, June 14 *Perf. 11½x11*

1333 A443 60g black, *ver* .25 .25

6th Conference of Ministers of Post of Communist Countries, Peking, June 21-July 15.

Warsaw's Coat of Arms, 17th Cent. — A444

Old Town Hall, 18th Cent. — A445

Designs: 10g, Artifacts, 13th century. 20g, Tombstone of last Duke of Mazovia. 60g, Barbican, Gothic-Renaissance castle. 1.50z, Arsenal, 19th century. 1.55z, National Theater. 2.50z, Staszic Palace. 3.40z, Woman with sword from Heroes' Memorial and Warsaw Mermaid seal.

Perf. 11x11½, 11½x11, 12x12½, 12½x12

1965, July 21 Engr. Unwmk.

1334 A444 5g carmine rose .25 .25
1335 A444 10g green .25 .25
1336 A445 20g violet blue .25 .25
1337 A445 40g brown .25 .25
1338 A445 60g orange .25 .25
1339 A445 1.50z black .25 .25
1340 A445 1.55z gray blue .25 .25
1341 A445 2.50z lilac .25 .25

Perf. 11½

Photogravure and Engraved

1342 A444 3.40z citron & blk .90 .50
Nos. 1334-1342 (9) 2.90 2.50

700th anniversary of Warsaw.

No. 1342 is perforated all around, with lower right quarter perforated to form a 21x26mm stamp within a stamp. It was issued in sheets of 25 (5x5).

For surcharges see Nos. 1919-1926.

IQSY Emblem A446

Designs: 2.50z, Radio telescope dish, Torun. 3.40z, Solar system.

1965, Aug. 9 Litho.

1343 A446 60g vio, ver, brt grn & blk .25 .25
a. 60g ultra, org, yel, bl & blk .25 .25
1344 A446 2.50z red, yel, pur & blk .25 .25
a. 2.50z red brn, yel, gray & blk .25 .25
1345 A446 3.40z orange & multi .35 .25
a. 3.40z ol gray & multi .35 .25
Nos. 1343-1345 (3) .85 .75
Nos. 1343a-1345a (3) .85 .75

International Quiet Sun Year, 1964-65.

Odontoglossum Grande — A447

Orchids: 30g, Cypripedium hibridum. 40g, Lycaste skinneri. 50g, Cattleya. 60g, Vanda sanderiana. 1.35z, Cypripedium hibridum. 4z, Sobralia. 5.60z, Disa grandiflora. 6.50z, Cattleya labiata.

1965, Sept. 6 Photo. *Perf. 12½x12*

1346 A447 20g multicolored .25 .25
1347 A447 30g multicolored .25 .25
1348 A447 40g multicolored .25 .25
1349 A447 50g multicolored .25 .25
1350 A447 60g multicolored .25 .25
1351 A447 1.35z multicolored .25 .25
1352 A447 4z multicolored .50 .25
1353 A447 5.60z multicolored .95 .30
1354 A447 6.50z multicolored 1.60 .75
Nos. 1346-1354 (9) 4.55 2.80

Weight Lifting — A448

Sport: 40g, Boxing. 50g, Relay race, men. 60g, Fencing. 90g, Women's 80-meter hurdles. 3.40z, Relay race, women. 6.50z, Hop, step and jump. 7.10z, Volleyball, women.

1965, Oct. 8 Photo. Unwmk.

1355	A448	30g	gold & multi	.25	.25
1356	A448	40g	gold & multi	.25	.25
1357	A448	50g	silver & multi	.25	.25
1358	A448	60g	gold & multi	.25	.25
1359	A448	90g	silver & multi	.25	.25
1360	A448	3.40z	gold & multi	.35	.25
1361	A448	6.50z	gold & multi	.65	.25
1362	A448	7.10z	bronze & multi	1.00	.35
			Nos. 1355-1362 (8)	3.25	2.10

Victories won by the Polish team in 1964 Olympic Games. Each denomination printed in sheets of eight stamps and two center labels showing medals.

Mail Coach, by Piotr Michalowski — A449

Design: 2.50z, Departure of Coach, by Piotr Michalowski.

1965, Oct. 9 Engr. *Perf. 11x11½*

1363	A449	60g	brown	.25	.25
1364	A449	2.50z	slate green	.25	.25

Issued for Stamp Day, 1965. Sheets of 50 with labels se-tenant inscribed "Dzien Znaczka 1965 R."

UN Emblem — A450

1965, Oct. 24 Litho. *Perf. 12½x12*

1365	A450	2.50z	ultra	.25	.25

20th anniversary of United Nations.

Memorial, Plaszow — A451

No. 1367, Kielce Memorial. No. 1368, Chelm Memorial.

Perf. 12x11, 11x12

1965, Nov. 29 Engr.

1366	A451	60g	grnsh gray	.25	.25
1367	A451	60g	chocolate	.25	.25
1368	A451	60g	black, horiz.	.25	.25
			Nos. 1366-1368 (3)	.75	.75

Note after #1277 applies also to #1366-1368.

Wolf A452

1965, Nov. 30 Photo. *Perf. 11½*

1369	A452	20g	shown	.25	.25
1370	A452	30g	Lynx	.25	.25
1371	A452	40g	Red fox	.25	.25
1372	A452	50g	Badger	.25	.25
1373	A452	60g	Brown bear	.25	.25
1374	A452	1.50z	Wild Boar	.35	.25
1375	A452	2.50z	Red deer	.35	.25
1376	A452	5.60z	European bison	1.00	.45
1377	A452	7.10z	Moose	1.25	.75
			Nos. 1369-1377 (9)	4.20	2.95

Gig — A453

Horse-drawn carriages, Lancut Museum: 40g, Coupé. 50g, Lady's basket. 60g, Vis-a-vis. 90g, Cab. 1.15z, Berlinka. 2.50z, Hunting break. 6.50z, Caleche à la Daumont. 7.10z, English break.

1965, Dec. 30 Litho. *Perf. 11*

Size: 50x23mm

1378	A453	20g	multicolored	.25	.25
1379	A453	40g	lilac & multi	.25	.25
1380	A453	50g	orange & multi	.25	.25
1381	A453	60g	fawn & multi	.25	.25
1382	A453	90g	yellow & multi	.25	.25

Size: 76x23mm

1383	A453	1.15z	multicolored	.25	.25
1384	A453	2.50z	olive & multi	.35	.25
1385	A453	6.50z	multicolored	1.00	.35

Size: 103x23mm

1386	A453	7.10z	blue & multi	1.40	.60
			Nos. 1378-1386 (9)	4.25	2.70

Cargo Ship (No. 1389) — A454

#1387, Supervising Technical Organization (NOT) emblem, symbols of industry. #1388, Pit head & miners' badge, vert. #1390, Chemical plant, Plock. #1391, Combine. #1392, Railroad train. #1393, Building crane, vert. #1394, Pavilion & emblem of 35th Intl. Poznan Fair.

1966 Litho. *Perf. 11*

1387	A454	60g	multicolored	.25	.25
1388	A454	60g	multicolored	.25	.25
1389	A454	60g	multicolored	.25	.25
1390	A454	60g	multicolored	.25	.25
1391	A454	60g	multicolored	.25	.25
1392	A454	60g	multicolored	.25	.25
1393	A454	60g	multicolored	.25	.25
1394	A454	60g	multicolored	.25	.25
			Nos. 1387-1394 (8)	2.00	2.00

20th anniversary of the nationalization of Polish industry. No. 1394 also commemorates the 35th International Poznan Fair. Nos. 1387-1388 issued in connection with the 5th Congress of Polish Technicians, Katowice. Printed in sheets of 20 stamps and 20 labels with commemorative inscription within cogwheel on each label.

Issued: #1387-1388, 2/10; others, 5/21.

Dinosaur Type of 1965

Prehistoric Vertebrates: 20g, Dinichthys. 30g, Eusthenopteron. 40g, Ichthyostega. 50g, Mastodonsaurus. 60g, Cynognathus. 2.50z, Archaeopteryx, vert. 3.40z, Brontotherium. 6.50z, Machairodus. 7.10z, Mammoth.

1966, Mar. 5 Litho. *Perf. 12½*

1395	A434	20g	multicolored	.25	.25
1396	A434	30g	multicolored	.25	.25
1397	A434	40g	multicolored	.25	.25
1398	A434	50g	multicolored	.25	.25
1399	A434	60g	multicolored	.25	.25
1400	A434	2.50z	multicolored	.35	.25
1401	A434	3.40z	multicolored	.50	.25
1402	A434	6.50z	multicolored	1.25	.40
1403	A434	7.10z	multicolored	2.00	1.75
			Nos. 1395-1403 (9)	5.35	3.90

Henryk Sienkiewicz A455

Photogravure and Engraved

1966, Mar. 30 *Perf. 11½*

1404	A455	60g	black, *dl yel*	.25	.25

Henryk Sienkiewicz (1846-1916), author and winner of 1905 Nobel Prize.

Soccer Game — A456

Designs: Various phases of soccer. Each stamp inscribed with the place and the result of final game in various preceding soccer championships.

1966, May 6 *Perf. 13x12*

1405	A456	20g	multicolored	.25	.25
1406	A456	40g	multicolored	.25	.25
1407	A456	60g	multicolored	.25	.25
1408	A456	90g	multicolored	.25	.25
1409	A456	1.50z	multicolored	.35	.25
1410	A456	3.40z	multicolored	.50	.25
1411	A456	6.50z	multicolored	1.00	.40
1412	A456	7.10z	multicolored	1.40	.75
			Nos. 1405-1412 (8)	4.25	2.65

World Cup Soccer Championship, Wembley, England, July 11-30. Each denomination printed in sheets of 10 (5x2).

See No. B109.

Peace Dove and War Memorial — A457

Typo. & Engr.

1966, May 9 *Perf. 11½*

1413	A457	60g	silver & multi	.25	.25

21st anniversary of victory over Fascism.

Women's Relay Race A458

20g, Start of men's short distance race. 60g, Javelin. 90g, Women's 80-meter hurdles. 1.35z, Discus. 3.40z, Finish of men's medium distance race. 6.50z, Hammer throw. 7.10z, High jump.

5z, Long distance race.

Perf. 11½x11, 11x11½

1966, June 18 Litho.

1414	A458	20g	multi, vert.	.25	.25
1415	A458	40g	multi	.25	.25
1416	A458	60g	multi, vert.	.25	.25
1417	A458	90g	multi	.25	.25
1418	A458	1.35z	multi, vert.	.25	.25
1419	A458	3.40z	multi	.40	.25
1420	A458	6.50z	multi, vert.	.65	.25
1421	A458	7.10z	multi	.65	.30
			Nos. 1414-1421 (8)	2.95	2.05

Souvenir Sheet

Imperf

1422	A458	5z	multicolored	1.25	.75

European Athletic Championships, Budapest, August, 1966. No. 1422 contains one 57x27mm stamp.

Polish Eagle — A459

Designs: Nos. 1424, 1426, Flag of Poland. No. 1425, Polish Eagle.

Photogravure and Embossed

Perf. 12½x12

1966, July 21 Unwmk.

1423	A459	60g	gold, red & blk	.25	.25
1424	A459	60g	gold, red & blk	.25	.25
1425	A459	2.50z	gold, red & blk	.25	.25
1426	A459	2.50z	gold, red & blk	.25	.25
			Nos. 1423-1426 (4)	1.00	1.00

1000th anniversary of Poland. Nos. 1423-1424 and 1425-1426 printed in 2 sheets of 10 (5x2); top row in each sheet in eagle design, bottom row in flag design.

Flowers and Farm Produce — A460

Designs: 60g, Woman holding loaf of bread. 3.40z, Farm girls holding harvest wreath.

1966, Aug. 15 Photo. *Perf. 11*

Size: 22x50mm

1427	A460	40g	gold & multi	.30	.25
1428	A460	60g	gold & multi	.30	.25

Size: 48x50mm

1429	A460	3.40z	violet bl & multi	.35	.25
			Nos. 1427-1429 (3)	.95	.75

Issued to publicize the harvest festival.

Chrysanthemum — A461

Flowers: 20g, Poinsettia. 30g, Centaury. 40g, Rose. 60g, Zinnias. 90g, Nasturtium. 5.60z, Dahlia. 6.50z, Sunflower. 7.10z, Magnolia.

1966, Sept. 1 *Perf. 11½*

Flowers in Natural Colors

1430	A461	10g	gold & black	.25	.25
1431	A461	20g	gold & black	.25	.25
1432	A461	30g	gold & black	.25	.25
1433	A461	40g	gold & black	.25	.25
1434	A461	60g	gold & black	.25	.25
1435	A461	90g	gold & black	.25	.25
1436	A461	5.60z	gold & black	.75	.25
1437	A461	6.50z	gold & black	1.00	.30
1438	A461	7.10z	gold & black	1.75	.50
			Nos. 1430-1438 (9)	5.00	2.55

Map Showing Tourist Attractions A462

Designs: 20g, Lighthouse, Hel. 40g, Amethyst yacht on Masurian Lake. No. 1442, Poniatowski Bridge, Warsaw, and sailboat. No. 1443, Mining Academy, Kielce. 1.15z, Dunajec Gorge. 1.35z, Old oaks, Rogalin. 1.55z, Planetarium, Katowice. 2z, M.S. Batory and globe.

Perf. 12½x12, 11½x12

1966, Sept. 15 Engr.

1439	A462	10g	carmine rose	.25	.25
1440	A462	20g	olive gray	.25	.25
1441	A462	40g	grysh blue	.25	.25
1442	A462	60g	redsh brown	.25	.25
1443	A462	60g	black	.25	.25
1444	A462	1.15z	green	.25	.25
1445	A462	1.35z	vermilion	.25	.25

1446 A462 1.55z violet .25 .25
1447 A462 2z dark gray .25 .25
Nos. 1439-1447 (9) 2.25 2.25

Stableman with Percherons, by Piotr Michalowski — A463

2.50z, "Horses and Dogs" by Michalowski.

1966, Sept. 8 ***Perf. 11x11½***
1448 A463 60g gray brown .25 .25
1449 A463 2.50z green .25 .25

Issued for Stamp Day, 1966.

Capital of Romanesque Column from Tyniec and Polish Flag — A464

Engraved and Photogravure
1966, Oct. 7 ***Perf. 11½***
1450 A464 60g dark brn & rose .25 .25

Polish Cultural Congress.

Soldier A465

1966, Oct. 20 **Litho.** ***Perf. 11x11½***
1451 A465 60g blk, ol grn, & dl red .25 .25

Participation of the Polish Jaroslaw Dabrowski Brigade in the Spanish Civil War.

Green Woodpecker — A466

Forest Birds: 10g, The eight birds of the set combined. 30g, Eurasian jay. 40g, European golden oriole. 60g, Hoopoe. 2.50z, European redstart. 4z, Siskin (finch). 6.50z, Chaffinch. 7.10z, Great tit.

1966, Nov. 17 **Photo.** ***Perf. 11½***
Birds in Natural Colors; Black Inscription
1452 A466 10g lt green .25 .25
1453 A466 20g dull violet bl .25 .25
1454 A466 30g dull green .35 .25
1455 A466 40g gray .35 .25
1456 A466 60g gray green .35 .25
1457 A466 2.50z lt olive grn .50 .25
1458 A466 4z dull violet 1.25 .25
1459 A466 6.50z green 1.00 .35
1460 A466 7.10z gray blue 1.75 .75
Nos. 1452-1460 (9) 6.05 2.85

Ceramic Ram, c. 4000 B.C. — A467

Designs: No. 1462, Bronze weapons and ornaments, c. 3500 B.C., horiz. No. 1463, Biskupin, settlement plan, 2500 B.C.

1966, Dec. 10 **Engr.** ***Perf. 11x11½***
1461 A467 60g dull violet blue .25 .25
1462 A467 60g brown .25 .25
1463 A467 60g green .25 .25
Nos. 1461-1463 (3) .75 .75

Polish Eagle, Hammer and Grain — A468

Designs: 60g, Eagle and map of Poland.

1966, Dec. 20 **Litho.** ***Perf. 11***
1464 A468 40g brn, red & bluish lil .25 .25
1465 A468 60g brn, red & ol grn .25 .25

Millenium of Poland.

Vostok (USSR) — A469

Spacecraft: 40g, Gemini, American Spacecraft. 60g, Ariel 2 (Great Britain). 1.35z, Proton 1 (USSR). 1.50z, FR 1 (France). 3.40z, Alouette (Canada). 6.50z, San Marco 1 (Italy). 7.10z, Luna 9 (USSR).

1966, Dec. 20 ***Perf. 11½x11***
1466 A469 20g tan & multi .25 .25
1467 A469 40g brown & multi .25 .25
1468 A469 60g gray & multi .25 .25
1469 A469 1.35z multicolored .25 .25
1470 A469 1.50z multicolored .25 .25
1471 A469 3.40z multicolored .25 .25
1472 A469 6.50z multicolored .90 .25
1473 A469 7.10z multicolored 1.25 .35
Nos. 1466-1473 (8) 3.65 2.10

Dressage — A470

Horses: 20g, Horse race. 40g, Jump. 60g, Steeplechase. 90g, Trotting. 5.90z, Polo. 6.60z, Stallion "Ofir." 7z, Stallion "Skowronek."

1967, Feb. 25 **Photo.** ***Perf. 12½***
1474 A470 10g ultra & multi .25 .25
1475 A470 20g orange & multi .25 .25
1476 A470 40g ver & multi .25 .25
1477 A470 60g multicolored .25 .25
1478 A470 90g green & multi .25 .25
1479 A470 5.90z multicolored .80 .25
1480 A470 6.60z multicolored 1.50 .50
1481 A470 7z violet & multi 2.10 .50
Nos. 1474-1481 (8) 5.65 2.50

Janov Podlaski stud farm, 150th anniv.

Memorial at Auschwitz (Oswiecim) A471

Emblem of Memorials Administration A472

Memorials at: No. 1484, Oswiecim-Monowice. No. 1485, Westerplatte (Walcz). No. 1486, Lodz-Radugoszcz. No. 1487, Stutthof. No. 1488, Lambinowice-Jencom. No. 1489, Zagan.

1967 **Engr.** ***Perf. 11½x11, 11x11½***
1482 A471 40g brown olive .25 .25
1483 A472 40g dull violet .25 .25
1484 A472 40g black .25 .25
1485 A472 40g green .25 .25
1486 A472 40g black .25 .25
1487 A471 40g ultra .25 .25
1488 A471 40g brown .25 .25
1489 A472 40g deep plum .25 .25
Nos. 1482-1489 (8) 2.00 2.00

Issued to commemorate the martyrdom and fight of the Polish people, 1939-45.

Issue dates: Nos. 1482-1484, Apr. 10. Nos. 1485-1487, Oct. 9. Nos. 1488-1489, Dec. 28.

See Nos. 1620-1624.

Striped Butterflyfish — A473

Tropical fish: 10g, Imperial angelfish. 40g, Barred butterflyfish. 60g, Spotted triggerfish. 90g, Undulate triggerfish. 1.50z, Striped triggerfish. 4.50z, Black-eye butterflyfish. 6.60z, Blue angelfish. 7z, Saddleback butterflyfish.

1967, Apr. 1 **Litho.** ***Perf. 11x11½***
1492 A473 5g multicolored .25 .25
1493 A473 10g multicolored .25 .25
1494 A473 40g multicolored .25 .25
1495 A473 60g multicolored .25 .25
1496 A473 90g multicolored .25 .25
1497 A473 1.50z multicolored .25 .25
1498 A473 4.50z multicolored .65 .25
1499 A473 6.60z multicolored 1.00 .75
1500 A473 7z multicolored 1.25 .25
Nos. 1492-1500 (9) 4.40 2.75

Bicyclists — A474

1967, May 5 **Litho.** ***Perf. 11***
1501 A474 60g multicolored .25 .25

20th Warsaw-Berlin-Prague Bicycle Race.

Men's 100-meter Race — A475

Sports and Olympic Rings: 40g, Steeplechase. 60g, Women's relay race. 90g, Weight lifter. 1.35z, Hurdler. 3.40z, Gymnast on vaulting horse. 6.60z, High jump. 7z, Boxing.

1967, May 24 **Litho.** ***Perf. 11***
1502 A475 20g multicolored .25 .25
1503 A475 40g multicolored .25 .25
1504 A475 60g multicolored .25 .25
1505 A475 90g multicolored .25 .25
1506 A475 1.35z multicolored .25 .25
1507 A475 3.40z multicolored .25 .25
1508 A475 6.60z multicolored .75 .25
1509 A475 7z multicolored .75 .25
Nos. 1502-1509 (8) 3.00 2.00

19th Olympic Games, Mexico City, 1968. Nos. 1502-1509 printed in sheets of 8, (2x4) with label showing emblem of Polish Olympic Committee between each two horizontal stamps. See No. B110.

Badge of Socialist Working Brigade A476

1967, June 2
1510 A476 60g multicolored .25 .25

6th Congress of Polish Trade Unions. Printed in sheets of 20 stamps and 20 labels and in miniature sheets of 4 stamps and 4 labels.

Mountain Arnica — A477

Medicinal Plants: 60g, Columbine. 3.40z, Gentian. 4.50z, Ground pine. 5z, Iris sibirica. 10z, Azalea pontica.

1967, June 14 ***Perf. 11½x11***
Flowers in Natural Colors
1511 A477 40g black & brn org .25 .25
1512 A477 60g black & lt blue .25 .25
1513 A477 3.40z black & dp org .35 .25
1514 A477 4.50z black & lt vio .25 .25
1515 A477 5z black & maroon .45 .25
1516 A477 10z black & bister .85 .25
Nos. 1511-1516 (6) 2.40 1.50

Monument for Silesian Insurgents A478

1967, July 21 **Litho.** ***Perf. 11½***
1517 A478 60g multicolored .25 .25

Unveiling of the monument for the Silesian Insurgents of 1919-21 at Katowice, July, 1967.

Marie Curie — A479

Designs: No. 1519, Curie statue, Warsaw. No. 1520, Nobel Prize diploma.

1967, Aug. 1 **Engr.** ***Perf. 11½x11***
1518 A479 60g dk carmine rose .25 .25
1519 A479 60g violet .25 .25
1520 A479 60g sepia .25 .25
Nos. 1518-1520 (3) .75 .75

Marie Sklodowska Curie (1867-1934), discoverer of radium and polonium.

Coal Miner — A511

Designs: No. 1666, Oil refinery-chemical plant, Plock. No. 1667, Combine harvester. No. 1668, Rebuilt Grand Theater, Warsaw. No. 1669, Marie Sklodowska-Curie Monument and University, Lublin. No. 1671, Chemical industry (sulphur) worker. No. 1672, Steel-worker. No. 1673, Ship builder and ship.

1969, July 21 Litho. & Embossed

1665	A510	60g red & multi	.25	.25
1666	A510	60g red & multi	.25	.25
1667	A510	60g red & multi	.25	.25
1668	A510	60g red & multi	.25	.25
1669	A510	60g red & multi	.25	.25
a.		Strip of 5, #1665-1669	.40	.40

Perf. 11½x11

Litho.

1670	A511	60g gray & multi	.25	.25
1671	A511	60g gray & multi	.25	.25
1672	A511	60g gray & multi	.25	.25
1673	A511	60g gray & multi	.25	.25
a.		Strip of 4, #1670-1673	.35	.35
		Nos. 1669a,1673a (2)	.75	.75

25th anniv. of the Polish People's Republic.

Landing Module on Moon, and Earth A512

1969, Aug. 21 Litho. *Perf. 12x12½*

1674	A512	2.50z multicolored	.60	.35

Man's first landing on the moon, July 20, 1969. US astronauts Neil A. Armstrong and Col. Edwin E. Aldrin, Jr., with Lieut. Col. Michael Collins piloting Apollo 11. Issued in sheets of 8 stamps and 2 tabs, with decorative border. One tab shows Apollo 11 with lunar landing module, the other shows module's take-off from moon. Value, sheet: mint, $20, used $15.

"Hamlet," by Jacek Malczewski — A513

Polish Paintings: 20g, Motherhood, by Stanislaw Wyspianski. 60g, Indian Summer (sleeping woman), by Jozef Chelmonski. 2z, Two Girls, by Olga Boznanska, vert. 2.50z, "The Sun of May" (Breakfast on the Terrace), by Jozef Mehoffer, vert. 3.40z, Woman Combing her Hair, by Wladyslaw Slewinski. 5.50z, Still Life, by Jozef Pankiewicz. 7z, The Abduction of the King's Daughter, by Witold Wojtkiewicz.

Perf. 11x11½, 11½x11

1969, Sept. 4 Photo.

1675	A513	20g gold & multi	.25	.25
1676	A513	40g gold & multi	.25	.25
1677	A513	60g gold & multi	.25	.25
1678	A513	2z gold & multi	.25	.25
1679	A513	2.50z gold & multi	.25	.25
1680	A513	3.40z gold & multi	.25	.25
1681	A513	5.50z gold & multi	.55	.30
1682	A513	7z gold & multi	1.00	.35
		Nos. 1675-1682 (8)	3.05	2.15

Issued in sheets of 4 stamps and 2 labels inscribed with painter's name. Pairs, with label, set: mint $3.50, used $2.50.

Nike — A514

1969, Sept. 19 Litho. *Perf. 11½x11*

1683	A514	60g gray, red & bister	.25	.25

4th Congress of the Union of Fighters for Freedom and Democracy.

Details from Memorial, Majdanek Concentration Camp — A515

1969, Sept. 20 *Perf. 11*

1684	A515	40g brt lil, gray & blk	.25	.25

Unveiling of a monument to the victims of the Majdanek concentration camp. The monument was designed by the sculptor Wiktor Tolkin.

Costumes from Krczonow, Lublin — A516

Regional Costumes: 60g, Lowicz, Lodz. 1.15z, Rozbark, Katowice. 1.35z, Lower Silesia, Wroclaw. 1.50z, Opoczno, Lodz. 4.50z, Sacz, Cracow. 5z, Highlanders, Cracow. 7z, Kurpiow, Warsaw.

1969, Sept. 30 Litho. *Perf. 11½x11*

1685	A516	40g multicolored	.25	.25
1686	A516	60g multicolored	.25	.25
1687	A516	1.15z multicolored	.25	.25
1688	A516	1.35z multicolored	.25	.25
1689	A516	1.50z multicolored	.25	.25
1690	A516	4.50z multicolored	.40	.25
1691	A516	5z multicolored	.55	.25
1692	A516	7z multicolored	.55	.35
		Nos. 1685-1692 (8)	2.75	2.10

"Walk at Left" — A517

Traffic safety: 60g, "Drive Carefully" (horses on road). 2.50z, "Lower your Lights" (automobile on road).

1969, Oct. 4 *Perf. 11*

1693	A517	40g multicolored	.25	.25
1694	A517	60g multicolored	.25	.25
1695	A517	2.50z multicolored	.25	.25
		Nos. 1693-1695 (3)	.75	.75

ILO Emblem and Welder's Mask — A518

1969, Oct. 20 *Perf. 11x11½*

1696	A518	2.50z violet bl & ol	.25	.25

ILO, 50th anniversary.

Bell Foundry A519

Miniatures from Behem's Code, completed 1505: 60g, Painter's studio. 1.35z, Wood carvers. 1.55z, Shoemaker. 2.50z, Cooper. 3.40z, Bakery. 4.50z, Tailor. 7z, Bowyer's shop.

1969, Nov. 12 Litho. *Perf. 12½*

1697	A519	40g gray & multi	.25	.25
1698	A519	60g gray & multi	.25	.25
1699	A519	1.35z gray & multi	.25	.25
1700	A519	1.55z gray & multi	.25	.25
1701	A519	2.50z gray & multi	.25	.25
1702	A519	3.40z gray & multi	.35	.25
1703	A519	4.50z gray & multi	.35	.25
1704	A519	7z gray & multi	.65	.35
		Nos. 1697-1704 (8)	2.60	2.10

Angel — A520

Folk Art (Sculptures): 40g, Sorrowful Christ (head). 60g, Sorrowful Christ (seated figure). 2z, Crying woman. 2.50z, Adam and Eve. 3.40z, Woman with birds.

1969, Dec. 19 Litho. *Perf. 12½*

Size: 21x36mm

1705	A520	20g lt blue & multi	.25	.25
1706	A520	40g lilac & multi	.25	.25
1707	A520	60g multicolored	.25	.25
1708	A520	2z multicolored	.25	.25
1709	A520	2.50z multicolored	.25	.25
1710	A520	3.40z multicolored	.25	.25
		Nos. 1705-1710,B118-B119 (8)	2.65	2.00

Leopold Staff (1878-1957) A521

Polish Writers: 60g, Wladyslaw Broniewski (1897-1962). 1.35z, Leon Kruczkowski (1900-1962). 1.50z, Julian Tuwim (1894-1953). 1.55z, Konstanty Ildefons Galczynski (1905-1953). 2.50z, Maria Dabrowska (1889-1965). 3.40z, Zofia Nalkowska (1885-1954).

Litho., Typo. & Engr.

1969, Dec. 30 *Perf. 11x11½*

1711	A521	40g ol grn & blk, *grnsh*	.25	.25
1712	A521	60g dp car & blk, *pink*	.25	.25
1713	A521	1.35z vio bl & blk, *grysh*	.25	.25
1714	A521	1.50z pur & blk, *pink*	.25	.25
1715	A521	1.55z dp grn & blk, *grnsh*	.25	.25
1716	A521	2.50z ultra & blk, *gray*	.25	.25
1717	A521	3.40z red brn & blk, *pink*	.25	.25
		Nos. 1711-1717 (7)	1.75	1.75

Statue of Nike and Polish Colors A522

1970, Jan. 17 Photo. *Perf. 11½*

1718	A522	60g sil, gold, red & blk	.25	.25

Warsaw liberation, 25th anniversary.

Medieval Print Shop and Modern Color Proofs — A523

1970, Jan. 20 Litho. *Perf. 11½x11*

1719	A523	60g multicolored	.25	.25

Centenary of Polish printers' trade union.

Ringnecked Pheasant — A524

Game Birds: 40g, Mallard drake. 1.15z, Woodcock. 1.35z, Ruffs (males). 1.50z, Wood pigeon. 3.40z, Black grouse. 7z, Gray partridges (cock and hen). 8.50z, Capercaillie cock giving mating call.

1970, Feb. 28 Litho. *Perf. 11½*

1720	A524	40g multicolored	.25	.25
1721	A524	60g multicolored	.25	.25
1722	A524	1.15z multicolored	.35	.25
1723	A524	1.35z multicolored	.35	.25
1724	A524	1.50z multicolored	.35	.25
1725	A524	3.40z multicolored	.75	.25
1726	A524	7z multicolored	1.00	.50
1727	A524	8.50z multicolored	1.90	.65
		Nos. 1720-1727 (8)	5.20	2.65

Lenin in his Kremlin Study, Oct. 1918, and Polish Lenin Steel Mill — A525

Designs: 60g, Lenin addressing 3rd International Congress in Leningrad, 1920, and Luna 13. 2.50z, Lenin with delegates to 10th Russian Communist Party Congress, Moscow, 1921, dove and globe.

Engr. & Typo.

1970, Apr. 22 *Perf. 11*

1728	A525	40g grnsh blk & dl red	.25	.25
1729	A525	60g sep & dp lil rose	.25	.25
a.		Souvenir sheet of 4	1.00	.50
1730	A525	2.50z bluish blk & ver	.25	.25
		Nos. 1728-1730 (3)	.75	.75

Lenin (1870-1924), Russian communist leader.

No. 1729a commemorates the Cracow Intl. Phil. Exhib.

Tourist Type of 1969

No. 1731, Townhall, Wroclaw, vert. No. 1732, Cathedral, Piast Castle tower and church towers, Opole. No. 1733, Castle, Legnica. No. 1734, Castle Tower, Bolkow. No. 1735, Town Hall, Brzeg.

1970, May 9 Litho. ***Perf. 11***

1731 A506 60g Wroclaw	.25	.25
1732 A506 60g Opole	.25	.25
1733 A506 60g Legnica	.25	.25
1734 A506 60g Bolkow	.25	.25
1735 A506 60g Brzeg	.25	.25
Nos. 1731-1735 (5)	1.25	1.25

Issued for tourist publicity. Printed in sheets of 15 stamps and 15 labels, showing coats of arms.

Polish and Russian Soldiers before Brandenburg Gate — A526

Flower, Eagle and Arms of 7 Cities — A527

Lithographed and Engraved

1970, May 9 ***Perf. 11***

1736 A526 60g tan & multi .25 .25

Perf. 11½

1737 A527 60g sil, red & sl grn .25 .25

25th anniv. of victory over Germany and of Polish administration of the Oder-Neisse border area.

Peasant Movement Flag A528

1970, May 15 Litho. ***Perf. 11½***

1738 A528 60g olive & multi .25 .25

Polish peasant movement, 75th anniv.

A529

1970, May 20

1739 A529 2.50z blue & vio bl .25 .25

Inauguration of new UPU headquarters, Bern.

A530

1970, May 30 ***Perf. 11½x11***

1740 A530 60g multicolored .25 .25

European Soccer Cup Finals. Printed in sheets of 15 stamps and 15 se-tenant labels inscribed with the scores of the games.

Lamp of Learning A531

1970, June 3 ***Perf. 11½***

1741 A531 60g black, bis & red .25 .25

Plock Scientific Society, 150th anniversary.

Cross-country Race — A532

No. 1743, Runners from ancient Greek vase. No. 1744, Archer, drawing by W. Skoczylas.

1970, June 16 Photo. ***Perf. 11x11½***

1742 A532 60g yellow & multi	.25	.25
1743 A532 60g black & multi	.25	.25
1744 A532 60g dark blue & multi	.25	.25
Nos. 1742-1744 (3)	.75	.75

10th session of the Intl. Olympic Academy. See No. B120.

Copernicus, by Bacciarelli and View of Bologna — A533

Designs: 60g, Copernicus, by W. Lesseur and view of Padua. 2.50z, Copernicus, by Zinck Nora and view of Ferrara.

Photo., Engr. & Typo.

1970, June 26 ***Perf. 11½***

1745 A533 40g orange & multi	.25	.25
1746 A533 60g olive & multi	.25	.25
1747 A533 2.50z multicolored	.35	.25
Nos. 1745-1747 (3)	.85	.75

Aleksander Orlowski (1777-1832), Self-portrait — A534

Miniatures: 40g, Jan Matejko (1838-1893), self-portrait. 60g, King Stefan Batory (1533-1586), anonymous painter. 2z, Maria Leszczynska (1703-1768), anonymous French painter. 2.50z, Maria Walewska (1789-1817), by Marie-Victoire Jaquotot. 3.40z, Tadeusz Kosciuszko (1746-1817), by Jan Rustem. 5.50z, Samuel Bogumil Linde (1771-1847), by G. Landolfi. 7z, Michal Oginski (1728-1800), by Nanette Rosenzweig-Windisch.

Litho. & Photo.

1970, Aug. 27 ***Perf. 11½***

1748 A534 20g gold & multi	.25	.25
1749 A534 40g gold & multi	.25	.25
1750 A534 60g gold & multi	.25	.25
1751 A534 2z gold & multi	.25	.25
1752 A534 2.50z gold & multi	.25	.25
1753 A534 3.40z gold & multi	.25	.25
1754 A534 5.50z gold & multi	.45	.25
1755 A534 7z gold & multi	.85	.25
Nos. 1748-1755 (8)	2.80	2.00

Nos. 1748-1755 printed in sheets of 4 stamps and 2 labels. Pairs, with label, set: mint $3.50, used $2.50. The miniatures show famous Poles and are from collections in the National Museums in Warsaw and Cracow.

Poster for Chopin Competition A535

Photogravure and Engraved

1970, Sept. 8 ***Perf. 11x11½***

1756 A535 2.50z black & vio .25 .25

8th Intl. Chopin Piano Competition, Warsaw, Oct. 7-25.

UN Emblem A536

1970, Sept. 8 Photo. ***Perf. 11½***

1757 A536 2.50z multicolored .25 .25

United Nations, 25th anniversary.

Poles — A537

Design: 60g, Family, home and Polish flag.

1970, Sept. 15 Litho. ***Perf. 11½x11***

1758 A537 40g gray & multi	.25	.25
1759 A537 60g multicolored	.25	.25

National Census, Dec. 8, 1970.

Grunwald Cross and Warship Piorun (Thunderbolt) — A538

Grunwald Cross and Warship: 60g, Orzel (Eagle). 2.50z, Garland.

1970, Sept. 25 Engr. ***Perf. 11½x11***

1760 A538 40g sepia	.25	.25
1761 A538 60g black	.25	.25
1762 A538 2.50z deep brown	.45	.25
Nos. 1760-1762 (3)	.95	.75

Polish Navy during World War II.

Cellist, by Jerzy Nowosielski A539

Paintings: 40g, View of Lodz, by Benon Liberski. 60g, Studio Concert, by Waclaw Taranczewski. 1.50z, Still Life, by Zbigniew Pronaszko. 2z, Woman Hanging up Laundry, by Andrzej Wroblewski. 3.40z, "Expressions," by Maria Jarema, horiz. 4z, Canal in the Forest, by Piotr Potworowski, horiz. 8.50z, "The Sun," by Wladyslaw Strzeminski, horiz.

1970, Oct. 9 Photo. ***Perf. 11½***

1763 A539 20g multicolored	.25	.25
1764 A539 40g multicolored	.25	.25
1765 A539 60g multicolored	.25	.25
1766 A539 1.50z multicolored	.25	.25
1767 A539 2z multicolored	.25	.25
1768 A539 3.40z multicolored	.25	.25
1769 A539 4z multicolored	.35	.25
1770 A539 8.50z multicolored	.85	.25
Nos. 1763-1770 (8)	2.70	2.00

Issued for Stamp Day.

Luna 16 Landing on Moon — A540

1970, Nov. 20 Litho. ***Perf. 11½x11***

1771 A540 2.50z multicolored .35 .25

Luna 16 Russian unmanned, automatic moon mission, Sept. 12-24. Issued in sheets of 8 stamps and 2 tabs. One tab shows rocket launching; the other, parachute landing of capsule. Value, sheet: mint $8.50, used $4.75.

Stag — A541

16th Cent. Tapestries in Wawel Castle: 1.15z, Stork. 1.35z, Leopard fighting dragon. 2z, Man's head. 2.50z, Child holding bird. 4z, God, Adam & Eve. 4.50z, Panel with monogram of King Sigismund Augustus. 5.50z, Poland's coat of arms.

1970, Dec. 23 Photo. ***Perf. 11½x12***

1772 A541 60g multicolored	.25	.25
1773 A541 1.15z purple & multi	.25	.25
1774 A541 1.35z multicolored	.25	.25
1775 A541 2z sepia & multi	.25	.25
1776 A541 2.50z dk blue & multi	.25	.25
1777 A541 4z green & multi	.45	.25
1778 A541 4.50z multicolored	.75	.35
Nos. 1772-1778 (7)	2.45	1.85

Souvenir Sheet

Imperf

1779 A541 5.50z black & multi 1.10 .65

No. 1779 contains one 48x57mm stamp. See No. B121.

School Sailing Ship Dar Pomorza — A542

Polish Ships: 60g, Transatlantic Liner Stefan Batory. 1.15z, Ice breaker Perkun. 1.35z, Rescue ship R-1. 1.50z, Freighter Ziemia Szczecinska. 2.50z, Tanker Beskidy. 5z, Express freighter Hel. 8.50z, Ferry Gryf.

1971, Jan. 30 Photo. *Perf. 11*

1780 A542 40g ver & multi .25 .25
1781 A542 60g multicolored .25 .25
1782 A542 1.15z blue & multi .25 .25
1783 A542 1.35z yellow & multi .25 .25
1784 A542 1.50z multicolored .25 .25
1785 A542 2.50z violet & multi .25 .25
1786 A542 5z multicolored .40 .25
1787 A542 8.50z blue & multi .65 .30
Nos. 1780-1787 (8) 2.55 2.05

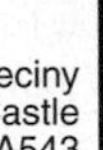

Checiny Castle A543

Polish Castles: 40g, Wisnicz. 60g, Bedzin. 2z, Ogrodzieniec. 2.50z, Niedzica. 3.40z, Kwidzyn. 4z, Pieskowa Skala. 8.50z, Lidzbark Warminski.

1971, Mar. 5 Litho. *Perf. 11*

1788 A543 20g multicolored .25 .25
1789 A543 40g multicolored .25 .25
1790 A543 60g multicolored .25 .25
1791 A543 2z multicolored .25 .25
1792 A543 2.50z multicolored .25 .25
1793 A543 3.40z multicolored .25 .25
1794 A543 4z multicolored .30 .25
1795 A543 8.50z multicolored .65 .35
Nos. 1788-1795 (8) 2.45 2.10

Fighting in Pouilly Castle, Jaroslaw Dabrowski and Walery Wroblewski — A544

1971, Mar. 3 *Perf. 12½x12½*

1796 A544 60g vio bl, brn & red .25 .25

Centenary of the Paris Commune.

Seedlings A545

1971, Mar. 30 Photo. *Perf. 11½x11*
Sizes: 26x34mm (40g, 1.50z); 26x47mm (60g)

1797 A545 40g shown .25 .25
1798 A545 60g Forest .25 .25
1799 A545 1.50z Clearing .25 .25
Nos. 1797-1799 (3) .75 .75

Proper forest management.

Bishop Marianos A546

Frescoes from Faras Cathedral, Nubia, 8th-12th centuries: 60g, St. Anne. 1.15z, 1.50z, 7z, Archangel Michael (diff. frescoes). 1.35z, Hermit Anamon of Tuna el Gabel. 4.50z, Cross with symbols of four Evangelists. 5z, Christ protecting Nubian dignitary.

1971, Apr. 20

1800 A546 40g gold & multi .25 .25
1801 A546 60g gold & multi .25 .25
1802 A546 1.15z gold & multi .25 .25
1803 A546 1.35z gold & multi .25 .25
1804 A546 1.50z gold & multi .25 .25
1805 A546 4.50z gold & multi .35 .25
1806 A546 5z gold & multi .35 .25
1807 A546 7z gold & multi .50 .25
Nos. 1800-1807 (8) 2.45 2.00

Polish archaeological excavations in Nubia.

Silesian Insurrectionists — A547

1971, May 3 Photo. *Perf. 11*

1808 A547 60g dk red brn & gold .25 .25
a. Souv. sheet of 3+3 labels 1.00 .50

50th anniversary of the 3rd Silesian uprising. Printed in sheets of 15 stamps and 15 labels showing Silesian Insurrectionists monument in Katowice.

Peacock on the Lawn, by Dorota, 4 years old — A548

Children's Drawings and UNICEF Emblem: 40g, Our Army, horiz. 60g, Spring. 2z, Cat with Ball, horiz. 2.50z, Flowers in Vase. 3.40z, Friendship, horiz. 5.50z, Clown. 7z, The Unknown Planet, horiz.

1971, May 20 *Perf. 11½x11, 11x11½*

1809 A548 20g multicolored .25 .25
1810 A548 40g multicolored .25 .25
1811 A548 60g multicolored .25 .25
1812 A548 2z multicolored .25 .25
1813 A548 2.50z multicolored .25 .25
1814 A548 3.40z multicolored .25 .25
1815 A548 5.50z multicolored .35 .25
1816 A548 7z multicolored .55 .25
Nos. 1809-1816 (8) 2.40 2.00

25th anniversary of UNICEF.

Fair Emblem — A549

1971, June 1 Photo. *Perf. 11½x11*

1817 A549 60g ultra, blk & dk car .25 .25

40th International Poznan Fair, June 13-22.

Collegium Maius, Cracow — A550

40g, Copernicus House, Torun, vert. 2.50z, Olsztyn Castle. 4z, Frombork Cathedral, vert.

1971, June Litho. *Perf. 11*

1818 A550 40g multicolored .25 .25
1819 A550 60g blk, red brn & sep .25 .25
1820 A550 2.50z multicolored .35 .25
1821 A550 4z multicolored .50 .25
Nos. 1818-1821 (4) 1.35 1.00

Nicolaus Copernicus (1473-1543), astronomer. Printed in sheets of 15 with labels showing portrait of Copernicus, page from "Euclid's Geometry," astrolabe or drawing of heliocentric system, respectively.

Paper Cut-out — A551

Designs: Various paper cut-outs (folk art).

Photo., Engr. & Typo.

1971, July 12 *Perf. 12x11½*

1822 A551 20g blk & brt grn, *bluish* .25 .25
1823 A551 40g sl grn & dk ol, *lt gray* .25 .25
1824 A551 60g brn & bl, *gray* .25 .25
1825 A551 1.15z plum & brn, *buff* .25 .25
1826 A551 1.35z dk grn & ver, *yel grn* .25 .25
Nos. 1822-1826 (5) 1.25 1.25

Worker, by Xawery Dunikowski A552

Sculptures: No. 1828, Founder, by Xawery Dunikowski. No. 1829, Miners, by Magdalena Wiecek. No. 1830, Woman harvester, by Stanislaw Horno-Poplawski.

1971, July 21 Photo. *Perf. 11½x12*

1827 A552 40g silver & multi .25 .25
1828 A552 40g silver & multi .25 .25
1829 A552 60g silver & multi .25 .25
1830 A552 60g silver & multi .25 .25
a. Souv. sheet of 4, #1827-1830 2.50 .85
Nos. 1827-1830 (4) 1.00 1.00

Punched Tape and Cogwheel — A553

1971, Sept. 2 Litho. *Perf. 11x11½*

1831 A553 60g purple & red .25 .25

6th Congress of Polish Technicians, held at Poznan, February, 1971.

Angel, by Jozef Mehoffer, 1901 — A554

Water Lilies, by Wyspianski A555

Stained Glass Windows: 60g, Detail from "The Elements" by Stanislaw Wyspianski. 1.35z, Apollo, by Wyspianski, 1904. 1.55z, Two Kings, 14th century. 3.40z, Flight into Egypt, 14th century. 5.50z, St. Jacob the Elder, 14th century.

1971, Sept. 15 Photo. *Perf. 11½x11*

1832 A554 20g gold & multi .25 .25
1833 A555 40g gold & multi .25 .25
1834 A555 60g gold & multi .25 .25
1835 A555 1.35z gold & multi .25 .25
1836 A554 1.55z gold & multi .25 .25
1837 A554 3.40z gold & multi .25 .25
1838 A554 5.50z gold & multi .35 .25
Nos. 1832-1838,B122 (8) 2.60 2.10

Mrs. Fedorowicz, by Witold Pruszkowski (1846-1896) — A556

Paintings of Women: 50g, Woman with Book, by Tytus Czyzewski (1885-1945). 60g, Girl with Chrysanthemums, by Olga Boznanska (1865-1940). 2.50z, Girl in Red Dress, by Jozef Pankiewicz (1866-1940), horiz. 3.40z, Nude, by Leon Chwistek (1884-1944), horiz. 4.50z, Strange Garden (woman), by Jozef Mehoffer (1869-1946). 5z, Artist's Wife with White Hat, by Zbiginew Pronaszko (1885-1958).

Perf. 11½x11, 11x11½

1971, Oct. 9 Litho.

1839 A556 40g gray & multi .25 .25
1840 A556 50g gray & multi .25 .25
1841 A556 60g gray & multi .25 .25
1842 A556 2.50z gray & multi .25 .25
1843 A556 3.40z gray & multi .25 .25
1844 A556 4.50z gray & multi .35 .25
1845 A556 5z gray & multi .75 .30
Nos. 1839-1845,B123 (8) 3.20 2.40

Stamp Day, 1971. Printed in sheets of 4 stamps and 2 labels inscribed "Women in Polish Paintings." Pairs, with label, set: mint $5, used $2.75.

Royal Castle, Warsaw A557

1971, Oct. 14 Photo. *Perf. 11x11½*

1846 A557 60g gold, blk & brt red .25 .25

P-11C Dive Bombers A558

Planes and Polish Air Force Emblem: 1.50z, PZL 23-A Karas fighters. 3.40z, PZL Los bomber.

1971, Oct. 14

1847	A558	90g multicolored	.25	.25
1848	A558	1.50z blue, red & blk	.25	.25
1849	A558	3.40z multicolored	.30	.25
		Nos. 1847-1849 (3)	.80	.75

Martyrs of the Polish Air Force, 1939.

Lunokhod 1 on Moon — A559

No. 1850, Lunar Rover and Astronauts.

Perf. 11x11½, 11½x11

1971, Nov. 17

1850	A559	2.50z multicolored	.40	.25
1851	A559	2.50z multicolored	.40	.25

Apollo 15 US moon exploration mission, July 26-Aug. 7 (No. 1850); Luna 17 unmanned automated USSR moon mission, Nov. 10-17 (No. 1851). Printed in sheets of 6 stamps and 2 labels, with marginal inscriptions.

Worker at Helm — A560

Shipbuilding A561

No. 1853, Worker. No. 1855, Apartment houses under construction. No. 1856, "Bison" combine harvester. No. 1857, Polish Fiat 125. No. 1858, Mining tower. No. 1859, Chemical plant.

1971, Dec. 8 ***Perf. 11½x11***

1852	A560	60g gray, ultra & red	.25	.25
1853	A560	60g red & gray	.25	.25
a.		Pair, #1852-1853 + label	.25	.25

Perf. 11x11½

1854	A561	60g red, gold & blk	.25	.25
1855	A561	60g red, gold & blk	.25	.25
1856	A561	60g red, gold & blk	.25	.25
1857	A561	60g red, gold & blk	.25	.25
1858	A561	60g red, gold & blk	.25	.25
1859	A561	60g red, gold & blk	.25	.25
a.		Souv. sheet of 6, #1854-1859	.90	.50
b.		Block of 6, #1854-1859	.60	.50
		Nos. 1853a,1859b (2)	.85	.75

6th Congress of the Polish United Worker's Party. No. 1859b has outline of map of Poland extending over the block.

Cherry Blossoms — A562

Blossoms: 20g, Niedzwiecki's apple. 40g, Pear. 60g, Peach. 1.15z, Japanese magnolia. 1.35z, Red hawthorne. 2.50z, Apple. 3.40z, Red chestnut. 5z, Acacia robinia. 8.50z, Cherry.

1971, Dec. 28 Litho. ***Perf. 12½***

Blossoms in Natural Colors

1860	A562	10g dull blue & blk	.25	.25
1861	A562	20g grnsh blue & blk	.25	.25
1862	A562	40g lt violet & blk	.25	.25
1863	A562	60g green & blk	.25	.25
1864	A562	1.15z Prus bl & blk	.25	.25
1865	A562	1.35z ocher & blk	.25	.25
1866	A562	2.50z green & blk	.25	.25
1867	A562	3.40z ocher & blk	.35	.25
1868	A562	5z tan & blk	.85	.25
1869	A562	8.50z bister & blk	1.40	.65
		Nos. 1860-1869 (10)	4.35	2.90

Fighting Worker, by J. Jarnuszkiewicz — A563

Photogravure and Engraved

1972, Jan. 5 ***Perf. 11½***

1870	A563	60g red & black	.25	.25

Polish Workers' Party, 30th anniversary.

Luge and Sapporo '72 Emblem — A564

Sapporo '72 Emblem and: 60g, Women's slalom, vert. 1.65z, Biathlon, vert. 2.50z, Ski jump.

1972, Jan. 12 Photo. ***Perf. 11***

1871	A564	40g silver & multi	.25	.25
1872	A564	60g silver & multi	.25	.25
1873	A564	1.65z silver & multi	.25	.25
1874	A564	2.50z silver & multi	.40	.25
		Nos. 1871-1874 (4)	1.15	1.00

11th Winter Olympic Games, Sapporo, Japan, Feb. 3-13. See No. B124.

Heart and Electro-cardiogram — A565

1972, Mar. 28 Photo. ***Perf. 11½x11***

1875	A565	2.50z blue, red & blk	.25	.25

"Your heart is your health," World Health Day.

Bicyclists Racing — A566

1972, May 2 ***Perf. 11***

1876	A566	60g silver & multi	.25	.25

25th Warsaw-Berlin-Prague Bicycle Race.

Berlin Monument A567

1972, May 9 Engr. ***Perf. 11½x11***

1877	A567	60g grnsh black	.25	.25

Unveiling of monument for Polish soldiers and German anti-Fascists in Berlin, May 14.

Olympic Runner — A568

Olympic Rings and "Motion" Symbol and: 30g, Archery. 40g, Boxing. 60g, Fencing. 2.50z, Wrestling. 3.40z, Weight lifting. 5z, Bicycling. 8.50z, Sharpshooting.

1972, May 20 ***Perf. 11½x11***

1878	A568	20g multicolored	.25	.25
1879	A568	30g multicolored	.25	.25
1880	A568	40g multicolored	.25	.25
1881	A568	60g gray & multi	.25	.25
1882	A568	2.50z multicolored	.25	.25
1883	A568	3.40z multicolored	.25	.25
1884	A568	5z blue & multi	.25	.25
1885	A568	8.50z multicolored	.70	.25
		Nos. 1878-1885 (8)	2.45	2.00

20th Olympic Games, Munich, Aug. 26-Sept. 10. See No. B125.

Vistula and Cracow — A569

1972, May 28 Photo. ***Perf. 11½x11***

1886	A569	60g red, grn & ocher	.25	.25

50th anniversary of Polish Immigrants Society in Germany (Rodlo).

Knight of King Mieszko I — A570

1972, June 12

1887	A570	60g gold, red brn, yel & blk	.25	.25

Millennium of the Battle of Cedynia (Cidyny).

Zoo Animals — A571

1972, Aug. 20 Litho. ***Perf. 12½***

1888	A571	20g Cheetah	.25	.25
1889	A571	40g Giraffe, vert	.25	.25
1890	A571	60g Toco toucan	.25	.25
1891	A571	1.35z Chimpanzee	.35	.25
1892	A571	1.65z Gibbon	.35	.25
1893	A571	3.40z Crocodile	.35	.25
1894	A571	4z Kangaroo	.90	.25
1895	A571	4.50z Tiger, vert	1.90	.85
1896	A571	7z Zebra	3.50	1.50
		Nos. 1888-1896 (9)	8.10	4.10

Ludwik Warynski — A572

1972, Sept. 1 Photo. ***Perf. 11***

1897	A572	60g multicolored	.25	.25

90th anniversary of Proletariat Party, founded by Ludwik Warynski. Printed in sheets of 25 stamps each se-tenant with label showing masthead of party newspaper "Proletariat."

Feliks Dzerzhinski A573

1972, Sept. 11 Litho. ***Perf. 11x11½***

1898	A573	60g red & black	.25	.25

Feliks Dzerzhinski (1877-1926), Russian politician of Polish descent.

Congress Emblem — A574

1972, Sept. 15 Photo. ***Perf. 11½x11***

1899 A574 60g multicolored .25 .25

25th Congress of the International Cooperative Union, Warsaw, Sept. 1972.

"In the Barracks," by Moniuszko A575

Scenes from Operas or Ballets by Moniuszko: 20g, The Countess. 40g, The Frightful Castle. 60g, Halka. 1.15z, A New Don Quixote. 1.35z, Verbum Nobile. 1.55z, Ideal. 2.50z, Paria.

Photogravure and Engraved

1972, Sept. 15 ***Perf. 11½***

1900 A575 10g gold & violet .25 .25
1901 A575 20g gold & dk brn .25 .25
1902 A575 40g gold & slate grn .25 .25
1903 A575 60g gold & indigo .25 .25
1904 A575 1.15z gold & dk blue .25 .25
1905 A575 1.35z gold & dk blue .25 .25
1906 A575 1.55z gold & grnsh blk .25 .25
1907 A575 2.50z gold & dk brn .30 .25
Nos. 1900-1907 (8) 2.05 2.00

Stanislaw Moniuszko (1819-72), composer.

"Amazon," by Piotr Michalowski — A576

Paintings: 40g, Ostafi Daszkiewicz, by Jan Matejko. 60g, "Summer Rain" (dancing woman), by Wojciech Gerson. 2z, Woman from Naples, by Aleksander Kotsis. 2.50z, Girl Taking Bath, by Pantaleon Szyndler. 3.40z, Count of Thun (child), by Artur Grottger. 4z, Rhapsodist (old man), by Stanislaw Wyspianski. 60g and 2.50z inscribed "DZIEN ZNACZKA 1972."

1972, Sept. 28 Photo. ***Perf. 10½x11***

1908 A576 30g gold & multi .25 .25
1909 A576 40g gold & multi .25 .25
1910 A576 60g gold & multi .25 .25
1911 A576 2z gold & multi .25 .25
1912 A576 2.50z gold & multi .25 .25
1913 A576 3.40z gold & multi .35 .25
1914 A576 4z gold & multi .85 .25
Nos. 1908-1914,B126 (8) 3.85 2.30

Stamp Day.

Copernicus, by Jacob van Meurs, 1654, Heliocentric System — A577

Portraits of Copernicus: 60g, 16th century etching and Prussian coin, 1530. 2.50z, by Jeremiah Falck, 1645, and coat of arms of King of Prussia, 1520. 3.40z, Copernicus with lily of the valley, and page from Theophilactus Simocatta's "Letters on Customs."

1972, Sept. 28 Litho. ***Perf. 11x11½***

1915 A577 40g brt blue & blk .25 .25
1916 A577 60g ocher & blk .25 .25
1917 A577 2.50z red & blk .25 .25
1918 A577 3.40z yellow grn & blk .40 .25
Nos. 1915-1918 (4) 1.15 1.00

See No. B127.

Nos. 1337-1338 Surcharged in Red or Black

a

b

1972 Engr. ***Perf. 11½x11***

1919 A445(a) 50g on 40g (R) .25 .25
1920 A445(a) 90g on 40g (R) .25 .25
1921 A445(a) 1z on 40g (R) .25 .25
1922 A445(b) 1.50z on 60g .25 .25
1923 A445(a) 2.70z on 40g (R) .25 .25
1924 A445(b) 4z on 60g .25 .25
1925 A445(b) 4.50z on 60g .25 .25
1926 A445(b) 4.90z on 60g .35 .25
Nos. 1919-1926 (8) 2.10 2.00

Issued: #1919-1920, 11/17; others, 10/2.

The Little Soldier, by E. Piwowarski A578

1972, Oct. 16 Litho. ***Perf. 11½***

1927 A578 60g rose & black .25 .25

Children's health center (Centrum Zdrowia Dzieck), to be built as memorial to children killed during Nazi regime.

Warsaw Royal Castle, 1656, by Erik J. Dahlbergh — A579

1972, Oct. 16 Photo. ***Perf. 11x11½***

1928 A579 60g violet, bl & blk .25 .25

Rebuilding of Warsaw Castle, destroyed during World War II.

Ribbons with Symbols of Trade Union Activities — A580

1972, Nov. 13 ***Perf. 11½x11***

1929 A580 60g multicolored .25 .25

7th and 13th Polish Trade Union congresses, Nov. 13-15.

Mountain Lodge, Chocholowska Valley — A581

Mountain Lodges in Tatra National Park: 60g, Hala Ornak, West Tatra, horiz. 1.55z, Hala Gasienicowa. 1.65z, Pieciu Stawow Valley, horiz. 2.50z, Morskie Oko, Rybiego Potoku Valley

1972, Nov. 13 ***Perf. 11***

1930 A581 40g multicolored .25 .25
1931 A581 60g multicolored .25 .25
1932 A581 1.55z multicolored .25 .25
1933 A581 1.65z multicolored .25 .25
1934 A581 2.50z multicolored .35 .25
Nos. 1930-1934 (5) 1.35 1.25

Japanese Azalea — A582

Flowering Shrubs: 50g, Alpine rose. 60g, Pomeranian honeysuckle. 1.65z, Chinese quince. 2.50z, Viburnum. 3.40z, Rhododendron. 4z, Mock orange. 8.50z, Lilac.

1972, Dec. 15 Litho. ***Perf. 12½***

1935 A582 40g gray & multi .25 .25
1936 A582 50g blue & multi .25 .25
1937 A582 60g multicolored .25 .25
1938 A582 1.65z ultra & multi .25 .25
1939 A582 2.50z ocher & multi .35 .25
1940 A582 3.40z multicolored .35 .25
1941 A582 4z multicolored .70 .25
1942 A582 8.50z multicolored 1.00 .45
Nos. 1935-1942 (8) 3.40 2.20

Emblem — A583

1972, Dec. 15 Photo. ***Perf. 11½***

1943 A583 60g red & multi .25 .25

5th Congress of Socialist Youth Union.

Copernicus — A584

Coil Stamps

1972, Dec. 28 Photo. ***Perf. 14***

1944 A584 1z deep claret .25 .25
1945 A584 1.50z yellow brown .25 .25

Nicolaus Copernicus (1473-1543), astronomer. Black control number on back of every 5th stamp.

Piast Knight, 10th Century A585

Polish Cavalry: 40g, Knight, 13th century. 60g, Knight of Ladislas Jagello, 15th century, horiz. 1.35z, Hussar, 17th century. 4z, National Guard Uhlan, 18th century. 4.50z, Congress Kingdom Period, 1831. 5z, Light cavalry, 1939, horiz. 7z, Light cavalry, People's Army, 1945.

1972, Dec. 28 ***Perf. 11***

1946 A585 20g violet & multi .25 .25
1947 A585 40g multicolored .25 .25
1948 A585 60g orange & multi .25 .25
1949 A585 1.35z orange & multi .25 .25
1950 A585 4z orange & multi .25 .25
1951 A585 4.50z orange & multi .35 .25
1952 A585 5z brown & multi .70 .25
1953 A585 7z multicolored 1.20 .75
Nos. 1946-1953 (8) 3.50 2.50

Man and Woman, Sculpture by Wiera Muchina — A586

Design: 60g, Globe with Red Star.

1972, Dec. 30

1954 A586 40g gray & multi .25 .25
1955 A586 60g blk, red & vio bl .25 .25

50th anniversary of the Soviet Union.

Nicolaus Copernicus, by M. Bacciarelli A587

Portraits of Copernicus: 1.50z, painted in Torun, 16th century. 2.70z, by Zinck Nor. 4z, from Strasbourg clock. 4.90z, Copernicus in his Observatory, by Jan Matejko, horiz.

Perf. 11½x11, 11x11½

1973, Feb. 18 Photo.

1956 A587 1z brown & multi .25 .25
1957 A587 1.50z multicolored .25 .25
1958 A587 2.70z multicolored .25 .25
1959 A587 4z multicolored .35 .25
1960 A587 4.90z multicolored .45 .25
Nos. 1956-1960 (5) 1.55 1.25

Piast Coronation Sword, 12th Century — A588

Polish Art: No. 1962, Kruzlowa Madonna, c. 1410. No. 1963, Hussar's armor, 17th century. No. 1964, Wawel head, wood, 16th century. No. 1965, Cock, sign of Rifle Fraternity, 16th century. 2.70z, Cover of Queen Anna Jagiellonka's prayer book (eagle), 1582. 4.90z,

Skarbimierz Madonna, wood, c. 1340. 8.50z, The Nobleman Tenczynski, portrait by unknown artist, 17th century.

1973, Mar. 28 Photo. *Perf. 11½x11*

1961 A588 50g violet & multi .25 .25
1962 A588 1z lt blue & multi .25 .25
1963 A588 1z ultra & multi .25 .25
1964 A588 1.50z blue & multi .25 .25
1965 A588 1.50z green & multi .25 .25
1966 A588 2.70z multicolored .25 .25
1967 A588 4.90z multicolored .45 .25
1968 A588 8.50z black & multi .75 .25
Nos. 1961-1968 (8) 2.70 2.00

Lenin Monument, Nowa Huta — A589

1973, Apr. 28 Litho. *Perf. 11x11½*

1969 A589 1z multicolored .25 .25

Unveiling of Lenin Monument at Nowa Huta.

Envelope Showing Postal Code A590

1973, May 5 *Perf. 11x11½*

1970 A590 1.50z multicolored .25 .25

Introduction of postal code system in Poland.

Wolf — A591

1973, May 21 Photo. *Perf. 11*

1971 A591 50g shown .25 .25
1972 A591 1z Mouflon .25 .25
1973 A591 1.50z Moose .25 .25
1974 A591 2.70z Capercaillie .35 .25
1975 A591 3z Deer .70 .25
1976 A591 4.50z Lynx 1.20 .25
1977 A591 4.90z European hart 2.00 .85
1978 A591 5z Wild boar 2.00 1.00
Nos. 1971-1978 (8) 7.00 3.35

Intl. Hunting Committee Congress and 50th anniv. of Polish Hunting Assoc.

US Satellite "Copernicus" over Earth — A592

No. 1980, USSR satellite Salyut over earth.

1973, June 20

1979 A592 4.90z multicolored .35 .25
1980 A592 4.90z multicolored .35 .25

American and Russian astronomical observatories in space. No. 1979 and No. 1980 issued in sheets of 6 stamps and 2 labels. Value: mint $14, used $7.

Flame Rising from Book — A593

1973, June 26 Litho.

1981 A593 1.50z blue & multi .25 .25

2nd Polish Science Cong., Warsaw, June 26-29.

Arms of Poznan on 14th Century Seal — A594

Polska '73 Emblem and: 1.50z, Tombstone of Nicolas Tomicki, 1524. 2.70z, Kalisz paten, 12th century. 4z, Lion knocker from bronze gate, Gniezno, 12th century, horiz.

Perf. 11½x11, 11x11½

1973, June 30

1982 A594 1z pink & multi .25 .25
1983 A594 1.50z orange & multi .25 .25
1984 A594 2.70z buff & multi .25 .25
1985 A594 4z yellow & multi .30 .25
Nos. 1982-1985 (4) 1.05 1.00

POLSKA '73 Intl. Phil. Exhib., Poznan, Aug. 19-Sept. 2. See No. B128.

Marceli Nowotko — A595

1973, Aug. 8 Litho. *Perf. 11½x11*

1986 A595 1.50z red & black .25 .25

Marceli Nowotko (1893-1942), labor leader, member of Central Committee of Communist Party of Poland.

Emblem and Orchard — A596

Human Environment Emblem and: 90g, Grazing cows. 1z, Stork's nest. 1.50z, Pond with fish and water lilies. 2.70z, Flowers on meadow. 4.90z, Underwater fauna and flora. 5z, Forest scene. 6.50z, Still life.

1973, Aug. 30 Photo. *Perf. 11*

1987 A596 50g black & multi .25 .25
1988 A596 90g black & multi .25 .25
1989 A596 1z black & multi .25 .25
1990 A596 1.50z black & multi .25 .25
1991 A596 2.70z black & multi .25 .25
1992 A596 4.90z black & multi .45 .25
1993 A596 5z black & multi 1.00 .40
1994 A596 6.50z black & multi 1.50 .70
Nos. 1987-1994 (8) 4.20 2.60

Protection of the environment.

Motorcyclist — A597

1973, Sept. 2 *Perf. 11½*

1995 A597 1.50z silver & multi .25 .25

Finals in individual world championship motorcycle race on cinder track, Chorzów, Sept. 2.

Tank — A598

1973, Oct. 12 Litho. *Perf. 12½*

1996 A598 1z shown .25 .25
1997 A598 1z Fighter plane .25 .25
1998 A598 1.50z Missile .50 .25
1999 A598 1.50z Warship .35 .25
Nos. 1996-1999 (4) 1.35 1.00

Polish People's Army, 30th anniversary.

Grzegorz Piramowicz — A599

Design: 1.50z, J. Sniadecki, Hugo Kollataj and Julian Ursyn Niemcewicz.

Photogravure and Engraved

1973, Oct. 13 *Perf. 11½x11*

2000 A599 1z buff & dk brn .25 .25
2001 A599 1.50z gray & sl grn .25 .25

Natl. Education Commission, bicent.

Henryk Arctowski, and Penguins A600

Polish Scientists: No. 2003, Pawel Edmund Strzelecki and Kangaroo. No. 2004, Benedykt Tadeusz Dybowski and Lake Baikal. No. 2005, Stefan Rogozinski, sailing ship "Lucja-Malgorzata." 2z, Bronislaw Malinowski, Trobriand Island drummers. 2.70z, Stefan Drzewiecki and submarine. 3z, Edward Adolf Strasburger and plants. 8z, Ignacy Domeyko, geological strata

1973, Nov. 30 Photo. *Perf. 10½x11*

2002 A600 1z gold & multi .25 .25
2003 A600 1z gold & multi .25 .25
2004 A600 1.50z gold & multi .25 .25
2005 A600 1.50z gold & multi .25 .25
2006 A600 2z gold & multi .25 .25
2007 A600 2.70z gold & multi .25 .25
2008 A600 3z gold & multi .40 .30
2009 A600 8z gold & multi .85 .50
Nos. 2002-2009 (8) 2.75 2.30

Polish Flag — A601

1973, Dec. 15 Photo. *Perf. 11½x11*

2010 A601 1.50z dp ultra, red & gold .25 .25

Polish United Workers' Party, 25th anniv.

Jelcz-Berliet Bus — A602

Designs: Polish automotives.

1973, Dec. 28 Photo. *Perf. 11x11½*

2011 A602 50g shown .25 .25
2012 A602 90g Jelcz 316 .35 .25
2013 A602 1z Polski Fiat 126p .25 .25
2014 A602 1.50z Polski Fiat 125p .25 .25
2015 A602 4z Nysa M-521 bus .35 .25
2016 A602 4.50z Star 660 truck .50 .25
Nos. 2011-2016 (6) 1.95 1.50

Iris — A603

Flowers: 1z, Dandelion. 1.50z, Rose. 3z, Thistle. 4z, Cornflowers. 4.50z, Clover. (Paintings by Stanislaw Wyspianski.)

1974, Jan. 22 Engr. *Perf. 12x11½*

2017 A603 50g lilac .25 .25
2018 A603 1z green .25 .25
2019 A603 1.50z red orange .25 .25
2020 A603 3z deep violet .25 .25
2021 A603 4z violet blue .30 .25
2022 A603 4.50z emerald .35 .25
Nos. 2017-2022 (6) 1.65 1.50

Cottage, Kurpie A604

Designs: 1.50z, Church, Sekowa. 4z, Town Hall, Sulmierzyce. 4.50z, Church, Lachowice. 4.90z, Windmill, Sobienie-Jeziory. 5z, Orthodox Church, Ulucz.

1974, Mar. 5 Photo. *Perf. 11x11½*

2023 A604 1z multicolored .25 .25
2024 A604 1.50z yellow & multi .25 .25
2025 A604 4z pink & multi .25 .25
2026 A604 4.50z lt blue & multi .25 .25
2027 A604 4.90z multicolored .35 .25
2028 A604 5z pink & multi .70 .25
Nos. 2023-2028 (6) 2.05 1.50

Mail Coach and UPU Emblem — A605

1974, Mar. 30 *Perf. 11½x12*

2029 A605 1.50z multicolored .25 .25

Centenary of Universal Postal Union.

Embroidery from Cracow — A606

Embroideries from: 1.50z, Lowicz. 4z, Slask.

1974, May 7 Photo. *Perf. 11½x11*

2030	A606	50g multicolored	.25	.25
2031	A606	1.50z multicolored	.25	.25
2032	A606	4z multicolored	.30	.25
a.		Souvenir sheet of 3 #2032, imperf.	1.25	1.00
b.		As "a," perf. 11½x11	5.00	5.00
		Nos. 2030-2032 (3)	.80	.75

SOCPHILEX IV International Philatelic Exhibition, Katowice, May 18-June 2.

No. 2032a sold for 17z.

No. 2032b sold for 17z plus 15z for 4 envelopes.

Association Emblem — A607

1974, May 8 Litho. *Perf. 12x11½*

2033	A607	1.50z gray & red	.25	.25

5th Congress of the Assoc. of Combatants for Liberty & Democracy, Warsaw, May 8-9.

Soldier and Dove — A608

1974, May 9 *Perf. 11½x11*

2034	A608	1.50z org, lt bl & blk	.25	.25

29th anniversary of victory over Fascism.

Comecon Building, Moscow A609

1974, May 15 *Perf. 11x11½*

2035	A609	1.50z gray bl, bis & red	.25	.25

25th anniv. of the Council of Mutual Economic Assistance.

Soccer Ball and Games' Emblem A610

Design: No. 2037, Soccer players, Olympic rings and 1972 medal.

1974, June 15 Photo. *Perf. 11x11½*

2036	A610	4.90z olive & multi	.50	.25
a.		Souv. sheet of 4 + 2 labels	4.50	2.00
2037	A610	4.90z olive & multi	.50	.25
a.		Souv. sheet, 2 each #2036-2037	12.00	7.00

World Cup Soccer Championship, Munich, June 13-July 7.

No. 2036a issued to commemorate Poland's silver medal in 1974 Championship.

Sailing Ship, 16th Century — A611

Polish Sailing Ships: 1.50z, "Dal," 1934. 2.70z, "Opty," sailed around the world, 1969. 4z, "Dar Pomorza," winner "Operation Sail," 1972. 4.90z, "Polonez," sailed around the world, 1973.

1974, June 29 Litho. *Perf. 11½x11*

2038	A611	1z multicolored	.25	.25
2039	A611	1.50z multicolored	.25	.25
2040	A611	2.70z multicolored	.25	.25
2041	A611	4z green & multi	.35	.25
2042	A611	4.90z dp blue & multi	.70	.25
		Nos. 2038-2042 (5)	1.80	1.25

Chess, by Jan Kochanowski A612

Design: 1.50z, "Education," etching by Daniel Chodowiecki.

1974, July 15 Litho. *Perf. 11½x11*

2043	A612	1z multicolored	.25	.25
2044	A612	1.50z multicolored	.30	.25

10th International Chess Festival, Lublin.

Man and Map of Poland — A613

Polish Eagle — A614

1974, July 21 Photo. *Perf. 11½x11*

2045	A613	1.50z black, gold & red	.25	.25
2046	A614	1.50z silver & multi	.25	.25
2047	A614	1.50z red & multi	.25	.25
		Nos. 2045-2047 (3)	.75	.75

People's Republic of Poland, 30th anniv.

Lazienkowska Bridge Road — A615

1974, July 21 *Perf. 11x11½*

2048	A615	1.50z multicolored	.25	.25

Opening of Lazienkowska Bridge over Vistula south of Warsaw.

Strawberries and Congress Emblem — A616

1974, Sept. 10 Photo. *Perf. 11½*

2049	A616	50g shown	.25	.25
2050	A616	90g Black currants	.25	.25
2051	A616	1z Apples	.25	.25
2052	A616	1.50z Cucumbers	.35	.25
2053	A616	2.70z Tomatoes	.35	.25
2054	A616	4.50z Peas	.35	.25
2055	A616	4.90z Pansies	.70	.35
2056	A616	5z Nasturtiums	1.25	.75
		Nos. 2049-2056 (8)	3.75	2.60

19th Intl. Horticultural Cong., Warsaw, Sept.

Civic Militia and Security Service Badge — A617

1974, Oct. 3 Photo. *Perf. 11½x11*

2057	A617	1.50g multicolored	.25	.25

30th anniv. of the Civic Militia and the Security Service.

Polish Child, by Lukasz Orlowski — A618

Polish paintings of Children: 90g, Girl with Pigeon, Anonymous artist, 19th century. 1z, Girl, by Stanislaw Wyspianski. 1.50z, The Orphan from Poronin, by Wladyslaw Slewinski. 3z, Peasant Boy, by Kazimierz Sichulski. 4.50z, Florentine Page, by Aleksander Gierymski. 4.90z, The Artist's Son Tadeusz, by Piotr Michalowski. 6.50z, Boy with Doe, by Aleksander Kotsis.

1974, Oct. 9

2058	A618	50g multicolored	.25	.25
2059	A618	90g multicolored	.25	.25
2060	A618	1z multicolored	.25	.25
2061	A618	1.50z multicolored	.25	.25
2062	A618	3z multicolored	.25	.25
2063	A618	4.50z multicolored	.30	.25
2064	A618	4.90z multicolored	.50	.25
2065	A618	6.50z multicolored	.50	.30
		Nos. 2058-2065 (8)	2.55	2.05

Children's Day. The 1z and 1.50z are inscribed "Dzien Znaczka (Stamp Day) 1974."

Cracow Manger — A619

King Sigismund Vasa — A620

Masterpieces of Polish art: 1.50z, Flight into Egypt, 1465. 4z, King Jan Olbracht.

1974, Dec. 2 Litho. *Perf. 11½x11*

2066	A619	1z multicolored	.25	.25
2067	A620	1.50z multicolored	.25	.25
2068	A620	2z multicolored	.25	.25
2069	A619	4z multicolored	.45	.25
		Nos. 2066-2069 (4)	1.20	1.00

Angler — A621

Designs: 1.50z, Hunter with bow and arrow. 4z, Boy snaring geese. 4.50z, Beekeeper. Designs from 16th century woodcuts.

1974-77 Engr. *Perf. 11½x11*

2070	A621	1z black	.25	.25
2071	A621	1.50z indigo	.25	.25
2071A	A621	4z slate green	.25	.25
2071B	A621	4.50z dark brown	.25	.25
		Nos. 2070-2071B (4)	1.00	1.00

Issued: 1z-1.50z, 12/30; 4z-4.50z, 12/12/77.

Pablo Neruda, by Osvaldo Guayasamin A622

1974, Dec. 31 Litho. *Perf. 11½x11*

2072	A622	1.50z multicolored	.25	.25

Pablo Neruda (1904-1973), Chilean poet.

Nike Monument and Opera House, Warsaw — A623

1975, Jan. 17 Photo. *Perf. 11*

2073	A623	1.50z multicolored	.25	.25

30th anniversary of the liberation of Warsaw.

Hobby Falcon — A624

No. 2074, Lesser kestrel, male. No. 2075, Lesser kestrel, female. No. 2076, Red-footed falcon, male. No. 2077, Red-footed falcon, female. No. 2079, Kestrel. No. 2080, Merlin. No. 2081, Peregrine.

1975, Jan. 23 ***Perf. 11½x12***

2074 A624 1z multi .25 .25
2075 A624 1z multi .25 .25
a. Pair, #2074-2075 .35 .25
2076 A624 1.50z multi .50 .25
2077 A624 1.50z multi .50 .25
a. Pair, #2076-2077 1.00 .25
2078 A624 2z shown .50 .25
2079 A624 3z multi 1.20 .35
2080 A624 4z multi 2.00 1.20
2081 A624 8z multi 3.50 1.40
Nos. 2074-2081 (8) 8.70 4.20

Falcons.

"Auschwitz" A625

Photogravure and Engraved

1975, Jan. 27 ***Perf. 11½x11***

2082 A625 1.50z red & black .25 .25

30th anniversary of the liberation of Auschwitz (Oswiecim) concentration camp.

Women's Hurdle Race A626

Designs: 1.50z, Pole vault. 4z, Hop, step and jump. 4.90z, Sprinting.

1975, Mar. 8 **Litho.** ***Perf. 11x11½***

2083 A626 1z multicolored .25 .25
2084 A626 1.50z olive & multi .25 .25
2085 A626 4z multicolored .25 .25
2086 A626 4.90z green & multi .35 .25
Nos. 2083-2086 (4) 1.10 1.00

6th European Indoor Athletic Championships, Katowice, Mar. 1975.

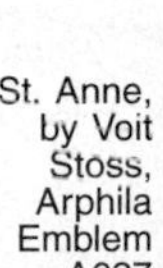

St. Anne, by Voit Stoss, Arphila Emblem A627

1975, Apr. 15 **Photo.** ***Perf. 11x11½***

2087 A627 1.50z multicolored .25 .25

ARPHILA 75, International Philatelic Exhibition, Paris, June 6-10.

Amateur Radio Union Emblem, Globe A628

1975, Apr. 15 **Litho.** ***Perf. 11½***

2088 A628 1.50z multicolored .25 .25

International Amateur Radio Union Conference, Warsaw, Apr. 1975.

Mountain Guides' Badge and Sudetic Mountains — A629

#2089, Pine, badge and Tatra Mountains, vert. #2090, Gentian and Tatra Mountains, vert. #2092, Yew branch with berries, and Sudetic Mountains. #2093, River, Beskids Mountains and badge, vert. #2094, Arnica and Beskids Mountains, vert.

1975, Apr. 30 **Photo.** ***Perf. 11***

2089 A629 1z multicolored .25 .25
2090 A629 1z multicolored .25 .25
a. Pair, #2089-2090 .25 .25
2091 A629 1.50z multicolored .25 .25
2092 A629 1.50z multicolored .25 .25
a. Pair, #2091-2092 .30 .25
2093 A629 4z multicolored .25 .25
2094 A629 4z multicolored .25 .25
a. Pair, #2093-2094 .60 .25
Nos. 2090a,2092a,2094a (3) 1.15 .75

Centenary of Polish Mountain Guides Organizations. Pairs have continuous design.

Hands Holding Tulips and Rifle — A630

1975, May 9 ***Perf. 11½x11***

2095 A630 1.50z blue & multi .25 .25

End of WWII, 30th anniv.; victory over Fascism.

Warsaw Treaty Members' Flags — A631

1975, May 14

2096 A631 1.50z blue & multi .25 .25

20th anniversary of the signing of the Warsaw Treaty (Bulgaria, Czechoslovakia, German Democratic Rep., Hungary, Poland, Romania, USSR).

Cock and Hen, Congress Emblem — A632

1975, June 23 **Photo.** ***Perf. 12x11½***

2097 A632 50g shown .25 .25
2098 A632 1z Geese .25 .25
2099 A632 1.50z Cattle .25 .25
2100 A632 2z Cow .25 .25
2101 A632 3z Arabian stallion .30 .25
2102 A632 4z Wielkopolska horses .50 .25
2103 A632 4.50z Pigs 1.25 .50
2104 A632 5z Sheep 1.75 1.40
Nos. 2097-2104 (8) 4.80 3.40

20th Congress of the European Zootechnical Federation, Warsaw.

Apollo and Soyuz Linked in Space A633

1975, July 15 ***Perf. 11x11½***

2105 A633 1.50z shown .25 .25
2106 A633 4.90z Apollo .35 .25
2107 A633 4.90z Soyuz .35 .25
a. Souv. sheet, 2 each #2105-2107 + 2 labels 5.50 2.50
b. Pair, #2106-2107 .75 .35
Nos. 2105-2107 (3) .95 .75

Apollo Soyuz space test project (Russo-American cooperation), launching July 15; link-up, July 17.

Health Fund Emblem — A634

1975, July 12 ***Perf. 11½x11***

2108 A634 1.50z silver, blk & bl .25 .25

National Fund for Health Protection.

"E" and Polich Flag A635

1975, July 30 **Litho.** ***Perf. 11x11½***

2109 A635 4z lt blue, red & blk .30 .25

European Security and Cooperation Conference, Helsinki, July 30-Aug. 1.

UN Emblem and Sunburst A636

1975, July 25

2110 A636 4z blue & multi .40 .25

30th anniversary of the United Nations.

Bolek and Lolek A637

Cartoon Characters and Children's Health Center Emblem: 1z, Jacek and Agatka. 1.50z, Reksio, the dog. 4z, Telesfor, the dragon.

1975, Aug. 30 **Photo.** ***Perf. 11x11½***

2111 A637 50g violet bl & multi .25 .25
2112 A637 1z multicolored .25 .25
2113 A637 1.50z multicolored .35 .30
2114 A637 4z multicolored .50 .35
Nos. 2111-2114 (4) 1.35 1.15

Children's television programs.

Circular Bar Graph and Institute's Emblem — A638

1975, Sept. 1 **Litho.** ***Perf. 11½x11***

2115 A638 1.50z multicolored .25 .25

International Institute of Statistics, 40th session, Warsaw, Sept. 1975.

IWY Emblem, White, Yellow and Brown Women — A639

1975, Sept. 8 **Photo.**

2116 A639 1.50z multicolored .25 .25

International Women's Year.

First Poles Arriving on "Mary and Margaret" 1608 A640

George Washington A641

Designs: 1.50z, Polish glass blower and glass works, Jamestown, 1608. 2.70z, Helena Modrzejewska (1840-1909), Polish actress, came to US in 1877. 4z, Casimir Pulaski (1747-1779), and 6.40z, Tadeusz Kosciusko (1748-1817), heroes of American War of Independence.

1975, Sept. 24 **Litho.** ***Perf. 11x11½***

2117 A640 1z black & multi .25 .25
2118 A640 1.50z black & multi .25 .25
2119 A640 2.70z black & multi .25 .25
2120 A640 4z black & multi .40 .25
2121 A640 6.40z black & multi .60 .30
Nos. 2117-2121 (5) 1.75 1.30

Souvenir Sheet

Perf. 12

2122 Sheet of 3+3 labels 1.75 .85
a. A641 4.90z shown .40 .25
b. A641 4.90z Kosciusko .40 .25
c. A641 4.90z Pulaski .40 .25

American Revolution, bicentenary.

Albatross Biplane, 1918-1925
A642

Design: 4.90z, IL 62 jet, 1975.

1975, Sept. 25 ***Perf. 11x11½***

2123 A642 2.40z buff & multi .25 .25
2124 A642 4.90z gray & multi .30 .25

50th anniversary of Polish air post stamps.

Frederic Chopin — A643

1975, Oct. 7 **Photo.**

2125 A643 1.50z gold, lt vio & blk .25 .25

9th International Chopin Piano Competition, Warsaw, Oct. 7-28.

Printed in sheets of 50 stamps with alternating labels with commemorative inscription.

Dunikowski, Self-portrait
A644

Sculptures: 1z, "Breath." 1.50z, "Maternity."

1975, Oct. 9 ***Perf. 11½x11***

2126 A644 50g silver & multi .25 .25
2127 A644 1z silver & multi .25 .25
2128 A644 1.50z silver & multi .25 .25
Nos. 2126-2128 (3) .75 .75

Stamp Day. Xawery Dunikowski (1875-1964), sculptor. See No. B131.

Town Hall, Zamosc — A645

1z, Arcades, Kazimierz Dolny, horiz.

Coil Stamps

1975, Nov. 11 **Photo.** ***Perf. 14***

2129 A645 1z olive green .25 .25
2130 A645 1.50z rose brown .25 .25

European Architectural Heritage Year. Black control number on back of every fifth stamp of Nos. 2129-2130.

Lodz, by Wladyslaw Strzeminski
A646

1975, Nov. 22 **Litho.** ***Perf. 12½***

2131 A646 4.50z multicolored .35 .25
a. Souvenir sheet .80 .40

Lodz 75, 12th Polish Philatelic Exhibition, for 25th anniv. of Polish Philatelists Union.

Piast Family Eagle
A647

1.50z, Seal of Prince Boleslaw of Legnica. 4z, Coin of Prince Jerzy Wilhelm (1660-1675).

1975, Nov. 29 **Engr.** ***Perf. 11x11½***

2132 A647 1z green .25 .25
2133 A647 1.50z brown .25 .25
2134 A647 4z dull violet .25 .25
Nos. 2132-2134 (3) .75 .75

Piast dynasty's influence on the development of Silesia.

"7" Inscribed "ZJAZD" and "PZPR" — A648

"VII ZJAZD PZPR" — A649

1975, Dec. 8 **Photo.** ***Perf. 11½x11***

2135 A648 1z lt blue & multi .25 .25
2136 A649 1.50z silver, red & ultra .25 .25

7th Cong. of Polish United Workers' Party.

Ski Jump
A650

Designs (Winter Olympic Games Emblem and): 1z, Ice hockey. 1.50z, Slalom. 2z, Speed skating. 4z, Luge. 6.40z, Biathlon.

1976, Jan. 10 ***Perf. 11x11½***

2137 A650 50g silver & multi .25 .25
2138 A650 1z silver & multi .25 .25
2139 A650 1.50z silver & multi .25 .25
2140 A650 2z silver & multi .25 .25
2141 A650 4z silver & multi .30 .25
2142 A650 6.40z silver & multi .70 .35
Nos. 2137-2142 (6) 2.00 1.60

12th Winter Olympic Games, Innsbruck, Austria, Feb. 4-15.

Engine by Richard Trevithick, 1803 — A651

Locomotives by: 1z, M. Murray and J. Blenkinsop, 1810. No. 2145, George Stephenson's Rocket, 1829. No. 2146, Polish electric locomotive, 1969. 2.70z, Stephenson, 1837. 3z, Joseph Harrison, 1840. 4.50z, Thomas Rogers, 1855. 4.90z, Chrzanow (Polish), 1922.

1976, Feb. 13 **Photo.** ***Perf. 11½x12***

2143 A651 50g multicolored .25 .25
2144 A651 1z multicolored .25 .25
2145 A651 1.50z multicolored .25 .25
2146 A651 1.50z multicolored .25 .25
2147 A651 2.70z multicolored .25 .25
2148 A651 3z multicolored .35 .25
2149 A651 4.50z multicolored .55 .25
2150 A651 4.90z multicolored .85 .35
Nos. 2143-2150 (8) 3.00 2.10

History of the locomotive.

Telephone, Radar and Satellites, ITU Emblem — A652

1976, Mar. 10 ***Perf. 11***

2151 A652 1.50z multicolored .25 .25

Centenary of first telephone call by Alexander Graham Bell, Mar. 10, 1876.

Atom Symbol and Flags of Communist Countries
A653

1976, Mar. 10 **Litho.** ***Perf. 11½***

2152 A653 1.50z multicolored .25 .25

Joint Institute of Nuclear Research, Dubna, USSR, 20th anniversary.

Ice Hockey — A654

Design: 1.50z, like 1z, reversed.

1976, Apr. 8 **Photo.** ***Perf. 11½x11***

2153 A654 1z multicolored .25 .25
2154 A654 1.50z multicolored .25 .25

Ice Hockey World Championship 1976, Katowice.

Soldier and Map of Sinai
A655

1976, Apr. 30 **Photo.** ***Perf. 11x11½***

2155 A655 1.50z multicolored .25 .25

Polish specialist troops serving with UN Forces in Sinai Peninsula.

No. 2155 printed se-tenant with label with commemorative inscription.

Sappers' Monument, by Stanislaw Kulow, Warsaw — A656

Design: No. 2157, First Polish Army Monument, by Bronislaw Koniuszy, Warsaw.

1976, May 8 ***Perf. 11½***

2156 A656 1z gold & multi .25 .25
2157 A656 1z silver & multi .25 .25

Memorials unveiled on 30th anniv. of WWII victory.

Interphil 76, Philadelphia
A657

1976, May 20 **Litho.** ***Perf. 11½x11***

2158 A657 8.40z gray & multi .45 .25

Interphil 76, Intl. Phil. Exhib., Philadelphia, May 29-June 6.

Wielkopolski Park and Owl — A658

National Parks: 1z, Wolinski Park and eagle. 1.50z, Slowinski Park and sea gull. 4.50z, Bieszczadzki Park and lynx. 5z, Ojcowski Park and bat. 6z, Kampinoski Park and elk.

1976, May 22 **Photo.** ***Perf. 12x11½***

2159 A658 90g multicolored .25 .25
2160 A658 1z multicolored .25 .25
2161 A658 1.50z multicolored .25 .25
2162 A658 4.50z multicolored .30 .25
2163 A658 5z multicolored .50 .25
2164 A658 6z multicolored .65 .25
Nos. 2159-2164 (6) 2.20 1.50

UN Headquarters, Dove-shaped Globe — A659

1976, June 29 **Litho.** ***Perf. 11x11½***

2165 A659 8.40z multicolored .45 .25

UN postage stamps, 25th anniversary.

Fencing and Olympic Rings
A660

1976, June 30 **Photo.**

2166 A660 50g shown .25 .25
2167 A660 1z Bicycling .25 .25
2168 A660 1.50z Soccer .25 .25
2169 A660 4.20z Boxing .30 .25
2170 A660 6.90z Weight lifting .40 .25
2171 A660 8.40z Running .55 .25
Nos. 2166-2171 (6) 2.00 1.50

21st Olympic Games, Montreal, Canada, July 17-Aug. 1. See No. B132.

Polish Theater, Poznan — A662

1976, July 12 Litho. *Perf. 11x11½*

2173	A662	1.50z gray olive & org	.25	.25

Polish Theater in Poznan, centenary.

Czekanowski, Lake Baikal — A663

1976, Sept. 3 Photo. *Perf. 11x11½*

2174	A663	1.50z silver & multi	.25	.25

Aleksander Czekanowski (1833-1876), geologist, death centenary.

Siren A664

Designs: 1z, Sphinx, vert. 2z, Lion. 4.20z, Bull. 4.50z, Goat. Designs from Corinthian vases, 7th century B.C.

Perf. 11x11½, 11½x11

1976, Oct. 30 Photo.

2175	A664	1z gold & multi	.25	.25
2176	A664	1.50z gold & multi	.25	.25
2177	A664	2z gold & multi	.25	.25
2178	A664	4.20z gold & multi	.25	.25
2179	A664	4.50z gold & multi	.25	.25
		Nos. 2175-2179,B133 (6)	2.05	1.55

Stamp Day.

Warszawa M20 — A665

Automobiles: 1.50z, Warszawa 223. 2z, Syrena 104. 4.90z, Polski Fiat 125.

1976, Nov. 6 Photo. *Perf. 11*

2180	A665	1z multicolored	.25	.25
2181	A665	1.50z multicolored	.25	.25
2182	A665	2z multicolored	.25	.25
2183	A665	4.90z multicolored	.30	.25
a.		Souvenir sheet of 4, #2180-2183 + 2 labels	1.50	1.00
		Nos. 2180-2183 (4)	1.05	1.00

Zeran Automobile Factory, Warsaw, 25th anniv.

Pouring Ladle — A666

1976, Nov. 26 Litho. *Perf. 11*

2184	A666	1.50z multicolored	.25	.25

First steel production at Katowice Foundry.

Virgin and Child, Epitaph, 1425 — A667

6z, The Beautiful Madonna, sculpture, c. 1410.

1976, Dec. 15

2185	A667	1z multicolored	.25	.25
2186	A667	6z multicolored	.30	.25

Polish Trade Union Emblem — A668

1976, Dec. 29

2187	A668	1.50z multicolored	.25	.25

8th Polish Trade Union Congress.

Tanker Zawrat Unloading, Gdansk — A669

Polish Ports: No. 2189, Ferry "Gryf" and cars at pier, Gdansk. No. 2190, Loading containers, Gdynia. No. 2191, "Stefan Batory" and "People of the Sea" monument, Gdynia. 2z, Barge and cargoship "Ziemia Szczecinska", Szczecin. 4.20z, Coal loading installations, Swinoujscie. 6.90z, Liner, hydrofoil and lighthouse, Kolobrzeg. 8.40z, Map of Polish Coast with ports, ships and emblem of Union of Polish Ports.

1976, Dec. 29 Photo. *Perf. 11*

2188	A669	1z multicolored	.25	.25
2189	A669	1z multicolored	.25	.25
2190	A669	1.50z multicolored	.25	.25
2191	A669	1.50z multicolored	.25	.25
2192	A669	2z multicolored	.25	.25
2193	A669	4.20z multicolored	.25	.25
2194	A669	6.90z multicolored	.45	.25
2195	A669	8.40z multicolored	.50	.30
		Nos. 2188-2195 (8)	2.45	2.05

Nurse Helping Old Woman — A670

1977, Jan. 24 Litho. *Perf. 11½x11*

2196	A670	1.50z multicolored	.25	.25

Polish Red Cross.

Civilian Defense Medal — A671

1977, Feb. 26 Litho. *Perf. 11*

2197	A671	1.50z multicolored	.25	.25

Civilian Defense.

Ball on the Road — A672

1977, Mar. 12 Photo.

2198	A672	1.50z olive & multi	.25	.25

Social Action Committee (founded 1966), "Stop, Child on the Road!"

Forest Fruits — A673

1977, Mar. 17 *Perf. 11½x11*

2199	A673	50g	Dewberry	.25	.25
2200	A673	90g	Cranberry	.25	.25
2201	A673	1z	Wild strawberry	.25	.25
2202	A673	1.50z	Bilberry	.25	.25
2203	A673	2z	Raspberry	.25	.25
2204	A673	4.50z	Blueberry	.30	.25
2205	A673	6z	Dog rose	.35	.25
2206	A673	6.90z	Hazelnut	.95	.25
			Nos. 2199-2206 (8)	2.85	2.00

Flags of USSR and Poland as Computer Tape — A674

1977, Apr. 4 Litho. *Perf. 11½x11*

2207	A674	1.50z red & multi	.25	.25

Scientific and technical cooperation between Poland and USSR, 30th anniversary.

Emblem and Graph — A675

1977, Apr. 22

2208	A675	1.50z red & multi	.25	.25

7th Congress of Polish Engineers.

Venus, by Rubens A676

Paintings by Flemish painter Peter Paul Rubens (1577-1640): 1.50z, Bathsheba. 5z, Helene Fourment. 6z, Self-portrait.

1977, Apr. 30 *Perf. 11½*

Frame in Gray Brown

2209	A676	1z multicolored	.25	.25
2210	A676	1.50z multicolored	.25	.25
2211	A676	5z multicolored	.55	.25
2212	A676	6z multicolored	.70	.25
		Nos. 2209-2212 (4)	1.75	1.00

See No. B134.

Peace Dove A677

1977, May 6 *Perf. 11x11½*

2213	A677	1.50z black, ultra & yel	.25	.25

Congress of World Council of Peace, Warsaw, May 6-11.

Bicyclist A678

1977, May 6 Photo.

2214	A678	1.50z gray & multi	.25	.25

30th International Peace Bicycling Race, Warsaw-Berlin-Prague.

Wolf — A679

Wildlife Fund Emblem and: No. 2216, Great bustard. No. 2217, Kestrel. 6z, Otter.

1977, May 12 Photo. *Perf. 11½x11*

2215	A679	1z silver & multi	.35	.25
2216	A679	1.50z silver & multi	.50	.25
2217	A679	1.50z silver & multi	.70	.25
2218	A679	6z silver & multi	1.00	.50
		Nos. 2215-2218 (4)	2.55	1.25

Wildlife protection.

Violinist, by Jacob Toorenvliet A680

1977, May 16
2219 A680 6z gold & multi .30 .25

AMPHILEX '77 Intl. Phil. Exhib., Amsterdam, May 26-June 5. No. 2219 issued in sheets of 6.

Midsummer Bonfire — A681

Folk Customs: 1z, Easter cock. 1.50z, Dousing the women on Easter Monday. 3z, Harvest festival. 6z, Christmas procession with crèche. 8.40z, Wedding dance. 1z, 1.50z, 3z, 6z vertical.

Perf. 11x11½, 11½x11
1977, June 13 **Photo.**
2220 A681 90g multicolored .25 .25
2221 A681 1z multicolored .25 .25
2222 A681 1.50z multicolored .25 .25
2223 A681 3z multicolored .25 .25
2224 A681 6z multicolored .45 .25
2225 A681 8.40z multicolored .55 .25
Nos. 2220-2225 (6) 2.00 1.50

Henryk Wieniawski and Musical Symbol — A682

1977, June 30 Litho. ***Perf. 11½x11***
2226 A682 1.50z gold, blk & red .25 .25

Wieniawski Music Festivals, Poznan: 5th Intl. Lute Competition, June 30-July 10, and 7th Intl. Violin Competition, Nov. 13-27.

Parnassius Apollo — A683

Butterflies: No. 2228, Nymphalis polychloros. No. 2229, Papilio machaon. No. 2230, Nymphalis antiopa. 5z, Fabriciana adippe. 6.90z, Argynnis paphia.

1977, Aug. 22 **Photo.** ***Perf. 11***
2227 A683 1z multicolored .25 .25
2228 A683 1z multicolored .25 .25
2229 A683 1.50z multicolored .35 .25
2230 A683 1.50z multicolored .35 .25
2231 A683 5z multicolored .90 .35
2232 A683 6.90z multicolored 2.10 1.00
Nos. 2227-2232 (6) 4.20 2.35

Arms of Slupsk, Keyboard — A684

1977, Sept. 3 ***Perf. 11½***
2233 A684 1.50z multicolored .25 .25

Slupsk Piano Festival.

Feliks Dzerzhinski A685

1977, Sept. 10 Litho. ***Perf. 11½x11***
2234 A685 1.50z olive bis & sepia .25 .25

Feliks E. Dzerzhinski (1877-1926), organizer and head of Russian Secret Police (Cheka).

Earth and Sputnik A686

1977, Oct. 1 Litho. ***Perf. 11x11½***
2235 A686 1.50z ultra & car .25 .25
a. Souvenir sheet of 3+3 labels .90 .35

60th anniv. of the Russian Revolution and 20th anniv. of Sputnik space flight. Printed in sheets of 15 stamps and 15 carmine labels showing Winter Palace, Leningrad.

Boleslaw Chrobry's Denarius, 11th Century — A687

Silver Coins: 1z, King Kazimierz Wielki's Cracow groszy, 14th century. 1.50z, Legniza-Brzeg-Wolow thaler, 17th century. 4.20z, King Augustus III guilder, Gdansk, 18th century. 4.50z, 5z (ship), 1936. 6z, 100z, Poland's millenium, 1966.

1977, Oct. 9 Photo. ***Perf. 11½x11***
2236 A687 50g silver & multi .25 .25
2237 A687 1z silver & multi .25 .25
2238 A687 1.50z silver & multi .25 .25
2239 A687 4.20z silver & multi .25 .25
2240 A687 4.50z silver & multi .35 .25
2241 A687 6z silver & multi .50 .25
Nos. 2236-2241 (6) 1.85 1.50

Stamp Day.

Monastery, Przasnysz — A688

Architectural landmarks: No. 2242, Wolin Gate, vert. No. 2243, Church, Debno, vert. No. 2245, Cathedral, Plock. 6z, Castle, Kornik. 6.90z, Palace and Garden, Wilanow.

Perf. 11½x11, 11x11½
1977, Nov. 21 **Photo.**
2242 A688 1z multicolored .25 .25
2243 A688 1z multicolored .25 .25
2244 A688 1.50z multicolored .25 .25
2245 A688 1.50z multicolored .25 .25
2246 A688 6z multicolored .45 .25
2247 A688 6.90z multicolored .50 .30
Nos. 2242-2247 (6) 1.95 1.55

Vostok (USSR) and Mercury (USA) A689

1977, Dec. 28 Photo. ***Perf. 11x11½***
2248 A689 6.90z ultra & multi .50 .30
a. Souvenir sheet of 6 4.75 2.40

20 years of space conquest. No. 2248a contains 6 No. 2248 (2 tete-beche pairs) and 2 labels, one showing Sputnik 1 and "4.X.1957," the other Explorer 1 and "31.1.1958."

DN Class Iceboats — A690

Design: No. 2250, One iceboat.

1978, Feb. 6 **Litho.** ***Perf. 11***
2249 A690 1.50z lt ultra & blk .25 .25
2250 A690 1.50z lt ultra & blk .25 .25
a. Pair, #2249-2250 + label .50 .25

6th World Iceboating Championships, Feb. 6-11.

Electric Locomotive, Katowice Station, 1957 — A691

Locomotives in Poland: No. 2252, Narrow-gauge engine and Gothic Tower, Znin. No. 2253, Pm36 and Cegielski factory, Poznan, 1936. No. 2254, Electric train and Otwock Station, 1936. No. 2255, Marki Train and Warsaw Stalow Station, 1907. 4.50z, Ty51 coal train and Gdynia Station, 1933. 5z, Tr21 and Chrzanow factory, 1920. 6z, "Cockerill" and Vienna Station, 1848.

1978, Feb. 28 Photo. ***Perf. 12x11½***
2251 A691 50g multicolored .25 .25
2252 A691 1z multicolored .25 .25
2253 A691 1z multicolored .25 .25
2254 A691 1.50z multicolored .25 .25
2255 A691 1.50z multicolored .25 .25
2256 A691 4.50z multicolored .35 .25
2257 A691 5z multicolored .40 .25
2258 A691 6z multicolored .85 .45
Nos. 2251-2258 (8) 2.85 2.20

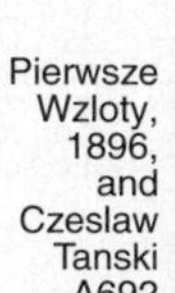

Pierwsze Wzloty, 1896, and Czeslaw Tanski A692

Polish Aviation: 1z, Zwyciezcy-Challenge, 1932, F. Zwirko and S. Wigura, vert. 1.50z, RWD-5 bis over South Atlantic, 1933, and S. Skarzynski, vert. 4.20z, Ml-2 helicopter over mountains, Pezetel emblem, vert. 6.90z, PZL-104 Wilga 35, Pezetel emblem. 8.40z, Motoszybowiec SZD-45 Ogar.

1978, Apr. 15 ***Perf. 11x11½, 11½x11***
2259 A692 50g multicolored .25 .25
2260 A692 1z multicolored .25 .25
2261 A692 1.50z multicolored .25 .25
2262 A692 4.20z multicolored .30 .25
2263 A692 6.90z multicolored .65 .40
2264 A692 8.40z multicolored .50 .40
Nos. 2259-2264 (6) 2.20 1.80

Soccer — A693

Design: 6.90z, Soccer ball, horiz.

Perf. 11½x11, 11x11½
1978, May 12 **Litho.**
2265 A693 1.50z multicolored .25 .25
2266 A693 6.90z multicolored .50 .25

11th World Cup Soccer Championships, Argentina, June 1-25.

Poster — A694

1978, June 1 ***Perf. 12x11½***
2267 A694 1.50z multicolored .25 .25

7th International Poster Biennale, Warsaw.

Fair Emblem — A695

1978, June 10 ***Perf. 11***
2268 A695 1.50z multicolored .25 .25

50th International Poznan Fair.

Polonez Passenger Car — A696

1978, June 10 **Photo.** ***Perf. 11***
2269 A696 1.50z multicolored .25 .25

Maj. Miroslaw Hermaszewski A697

6.90z, Hermaszewski, globe & trajectory.

Perf. 11½x11, 11x11½
1978, June 27 **Photo.**
2270 A697 1.50z multi .25 .25
a. Without date .25 .25
2271 A697 6.90z multi, horiz. .35 .25
a. Without date .65 .65

1st Polish cosmonaut on Russian space mission. Nos. 2270a, 2271a printed in sheets of 6 stamps and 2 labels.

Stamps and sheets showing Zenon Jankowski were prepared but not issued.

Youth Festival Emblem A698

1978, July 12 **Litho.** ***Perf. 11½***

2272 A698 1.50z multicolored .25 .25

11th Youth Festival, Havana, July 28-Aug. 5.

Souvenir Sheet

Flowers — A699

1978, July 20 ***Perf. 11½x11***

2273 A699 1.50z gold & multi .45 .25

30th anniv. of Polish Youth Movement.

Anopheles Mosquito and Blood Cells — A700

Design: 6z, Tsetse fly and blood cells.

1978, Aug. 19 **Litho.** ***Perf. 11½x11***

2274	A700	1.50z	multicolored	.25	.25
2275	A700	6z	multicolored	.35	.25

4th International Parasitological Congress.

Norway Maple, Environment Emblem — A701

Emblem and: 1z, English oak. 1.50z, White poplar. 4.20z, Scotch pine. 4.50z, White willow. 6z, Birch.

1978, Sept. 6 **Photo.** ***Perf. 14***

2276	A701	50g	gold & multi	.25	.25
2277	A701	1z	gold & multi	.25	.25
2278	A701	1.50z	gold & multi	.25	.25
2279	A701	4.20z	gold & multi	.30	.25
2280	A701	4.50z	gold & multi	.35	.25
2281	A701	6z	gold & multi	.50	.30
			Nos. 2276-2281 (6)	1.90	1.55

Protection of the environment.

Souvenir Sheet

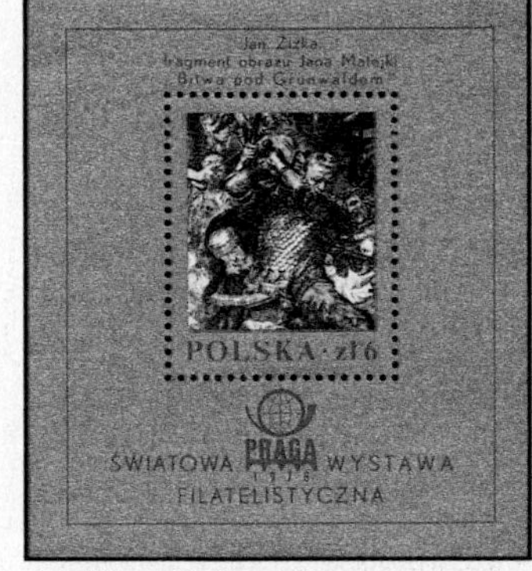

Jan Zizka, Battle of Grunwald, by Jan Matejko — A702

1978, Sept. 8 ***Perf. 11½x11***

2282 A702 6z gold & multi 1.10 .40

PRAGA '78 Intl. Phil. Exhib., Prague, Sept. 8-17.

Letter, Telephone and Satellite — A703

1978, Sept. 20 **Litho.** ***Perf. 11***

2283 A703 1.50z multicolored .25 .25

20th anniversary of the Organization of Ministers of Posts and Telecommunications of Warsaw Pact countries.

Peace, by Andre le Brun — A704

1978-79 **Litho.** ***Perf. 11½ (1z), 12½***

2284	A704	1z	violet	.25	.25
2285	A704	1.50z	steel blue ('79)	.25	.25
2286	A704	2z	brown ('79)	.25	.25
2287	A704	2.50z	ultra ('79)	.25	.25
			Nos. 2284-2287 (4)	1.00	1.00

Polish Unit, UN Middle East Emergency Force — A706

Designs: No. 2289, Color Guard, Kosziusko Division (4 soldiers). No. 2290, Color Guard, field training (3 soldiers).

1978, Oct. 6 **Photo.** ***Perf. 12x11½***

2289	A706	1.50z	multicolored	.25	.25
2290	A706	1.50z	multicolored	.25	.25
2291	A706	1.50z	multicolored	.25	.25
			Nos. 2289-2291 (3)	.75	.75

35th anniversary of People's Army.

Young Man, by Raphael A707

1978, Oct. 9 ***Perf. 11***

2292 A707 6z multicolored .30 .25

Stamp Day.

Dr. Korczak and Children — A708

1978, Oct. 11 **Litho.** ***Perf. 11½x11***

2293 A708 1.50z multicolored .25 .25

Dr. Janusz Korczak, physician, educator, writer, birth centenary.

Wojciech Boguslawski (1757-1829) — A709

Polish dramatists: 1z, Aleksander Fredro (1793-1878). 1.50z, Juliusz Slowacki (1809-1849). 2z, Adam Mickiewicz (1798-1855). 4.50z, Stanislaw Wyspianski (1869-1907). 6z, Gabriela Zapolska (1857-1921).

1978, Nov. 11 **Litho.** ***Perf. 11½***

2294	A709	50g	multicolored	.25	.25
2295	A709	1z	multicolored	.25	.25
2296	A709	1.50z	multicolored	.25	.25
2297	A709	2z	multicolored	.25	.25
2298	A709	4.50z	multicolored	.30	.25
2299	A709	6z	multicolored	.40	.25
			Nos. 2294-2299 (6)	1.70	1.50

Polish Combatants Monument, and Eiffel Tower, Paris — A710

1978, Nov. 2 **Photo.** ***Perf. 11x11½***

2300 A710 1.50z brown, red & bl .25 .25

Przewalski Mare and Colt — A711

Animals: 1z, Polar bears. 1.50z, Indian elephants. 2z, Jaguars. 4.20z, Gray seals. 4.50z, Hartebeests. 6z, Mandrills.

1978, Nov. 10

2301	A711	50g	multicolored	.25	.25
2302	A711	1z	multicolored	.25	.25
2303	A711	1.50z	multicolored	.25	.25
2304	A711	2z	multicolored	.25	.25
2305	A711	4.20z	multicolored	.40	.25
2306	A711	4.50z	multicolored	.40	.25
2307	A711	6z	multicolored	1.10	.40
			Nos. 2301-2307 (7)	2.90	1.90

Warsaw Zoological Gardens, 50th anniv.

Adolf Warski (1868-1937) A712

Party Emblem A713

#2309, Julian Lenski (1889-1937). #2310, Aleksander Zawadzki (1899-1964). #2311, Stanislaw Dubois (1901-1942).

Perf. 11½x11, 11x11½

1978, Dec. 15 **Photo.**

2308	A712	1.50z	red & brown	.25	.25
2309	A712	1.50z	red & black	.25	.25
2310	A712	1.50z	red & dk vio	.25	.25
2311	A712	1.50z	red & dk blue	.25	.25
2312	A713	1.50z	black, red & gold	.25	.25
			Nos. 2308-2312 (5)	1.25	1.25

Polish United Workers' Party, 30th anniv.

LOT Planes, 1929 and 1979 A714

1979, Jan. 2 **Photo.** ***Perf. 11x11½***

2313 A714 6.90z gold & multi .35 .25

LOT, Polish airline, 50th anniversary.

Train and IYC Emblem — A715

Children's Paintings: 1z, Children with toys. 1.50z, Children in meadow. 6z, Family.

1979, Jan. 13 ***Perf. 11***

2314	A715	50g	multicolored	.25	.25
2315	A715	1z	multicolored	.25	.25
2316	A715	1.50z	multicolored	.25	.25
2317	A715	6z	multicolored	.35	.25
			Nos. 2314-2317 (4)	1.10	1.00

International Year of the Child.

Artist's Wife, by Karol Mondral — A716

Modern Polish Graphic Arts: 50g, "Lightning," by Edmund Bartlomiejczyk, horiz. 1.50z, Musicians, by Tadeusz Kulisiewicz. 4.50z, Portrait of a Brave Man, by Wladyslaw Skoczylas.

Perf. 11½x12, 12x11½

1979, Mar. 5 **Engr.**

2318 A716 50g brt violet .25 .25
2319 A716 1z slate green .25 .25
2320 A716 1.50z blue gray .25 .25
2321 A716 4.50z violet brown .30 .25
Nos. 2318-2321 (4) 1.05 1.00

Andrzej Frycz-Modrzewski, Stefan Batory, Jan Zamoyski — A717

Photogravure and Engraved

1979, Mar. 12 *Perf. 12x11½*

2322 A717 1.50z cream & sepia .25 .25

Royal Tribunal in Piotrkow Trybunalski, 400th anniversary.

Pole Vault and Olympic Emblem — A718

Olympic Emblem and: 1.50z, High jump. 6z, Cross-country skiing. 8.40z, Equestrian.

1979, Mar. 26 Photo. *Perf. 12x11½*

2323 A718 1z multicolored .25 .25
2324 A718 1.50z multicolored .25 .25
2325 A718 6z multicolored .30 .25
2326 A718 8.40z multicolored .45 .25
Nos. 2323-2326 (4) 1.25 1.00

1980 Olympic Games.

Flounder — A720

Fish and Emblem: 90g, Perch. 1z, Grayling. 1.50z, Salmon. 2z, Trout. 4.50z, Pike. 5z, Carp. 6z, Catfish and frog.

1979, Apr. 26 Photo. *Perf. 11½x11*

2327 A720 50g multicolored .25 .25
2328 A720 90g multicolored .25 .25
2329 A720 1z multicolored .25 .25
2330 A720 1.50z multicolored .25 .25
2331 A720 2z multicolored .25 .25
2332 A720 4.50z multicolored .25 .25
2333 A720 5z multicolored .70 .25
2334 A720 6z multicolored .85 .40
Nos. 2327-2334 (8) 3.05 2.15

Polish angling, centenary, and protection of the environment.

A721

1979, Apr. 30 Litho. *Perf. 11x11½*

2335 A721 1.50z multicolored .25 .25

Council for Mutual Economic Aid of Socialist Countries, 30th anniversary.

Faces and Emblem — A722

1979, May 7 *Perf. 11*

2336 A722 1.50z red & black .25 .25

6th Congress of Association of Fighters for Liberty and Democracy, Warsaw, May 7-8.

St. George's Church, Sofia A722a

1979, May 15 Photo. *Perf. 11x11½*

2337 A722a 1.50z multicolored .25 .25

Philaserdica '79 Phil. Exhib., Sofia, Bulgaria, May 18-27.

Pope John Paul II, Cracow Cathedral A723

Designs: 8.40z, Pope John Paul II, Auschwitz-Birkenau Memorial. 50z, Pope John Paul II.

1979, June 2 Photo. *Perf. 11x11½*

2338 A723 1.50z multicolored .25 .25
2339 A723 8.40z multicolored .60 .25

Souvenir Sheet

Perf. 11½x11

2340 A723 50z multicolored & gold 5.50 3.50

Visit of Pope John Paul II to Poland, June 2-11. No. 2340 contains one 26x35mm stamp.

A variety of No. 2340 with silver margin exists. Values, unused $25, used $17.50.

Paddle Steamer Prince Ksawery and Old Warsaw — A724

Designs: 1.50z, Steamer Gen. Swierczewski and Gdansk, 1914. 4.50z, Tug Aurochs and Plock, 1960. 6z, Motor ship Mermaid and modern Warsaw, 1959.

1979, June 15 Litho. *Perf. 11*

2341 A724 1z multicolored .25 .25
2342 A724 1.50z multicolored .25 .25
2343 A724 4.50z multicolored .25 .25
2344 A724 6z multicolored .50 .25
Nos. 2341-2344 (4) 1.25 1.00

Vistula River navigation, 150th anniversary.

Kosciuszko Monument, Philadelphia A725

1979, July 1 Photo. *Perf. 11½*

2345 A725 8.40z multicolored .40 .25

Gen. Tadeusz Kosziuszko (1746-1807), Polish soldier and statesman who served in American Revolution.

Mining Machinery — A726

Design: 1.50z, Salt crystals.

1979, July 14 Photo. *Perf. 14*

2346 A726 1z lt brown & blk .25 .25
2347 A726 1.50z blue grn & blk .25 .25

Wieliczka ancient rock-salt mines.

Eagle and People — A727

No. 2349, Man with raised hand and flag.

1979, July 21 *Perf. 11½x11*

2348 A727 1.50z red, blue & gray .25 .25
2349 A727 1.50z silver, red & blk .25 .25

35 years of Polish People's Republic.

Souvenir Sheet

1979, Sept. 2 Photo. *Perf. 11½x11*

2350 A727 Sheet of 2, #2348-2349 + label .55 .30

13th National Philatelic Exhibition.

Poland No. 1, Rowland Hill (1795-1879), Originator of Penny Postage — A728

1979, Aug. 16 Litho. *Perf. 11½x11*

2351 A728 6z multicolored .30 .25

Souvenir Sheet

The Rape of Europa, by Bernardo Strozzi — A729

1979, Aug. 20 Photo. *Perf. 11x11½*

2352 A729 10z multicolored .75 .35

Europhil '79, Intl. Phil. Exhib.

Wojciech Jastrzebowski A730

1979, Aug. 27 *Perf. 11½x11*

2353 A730 1.50z multicolored .25 .25

International Ergonomics Society Congress.

Postal Workers' Monument A731

1979, Sept. 1 *Perf. 11x11½*

2354 A731 1.50z multicolored .25 .25

40th anniversary of Polish postal workers' resistance to Nazi invaders. See No. B137.

ITU Emblem, Radio Antenna A732

1979, Sept. 24 *Perf. 11x11½*

2355 A732 1.50z multicolored .25 .25

Intl. Radio Consultative Committee (CCIR) of the ITU, 50th anniv.

Violin A733

1979, Sept. 25 **Litho.**

2356 A733 1.50z dk blue, org, grn .25 .25

Henryk Wieniawski Young Violinists' Competition, Lublin.

Pulaski Monument, Buffalo — A734

1979, Oct. 1 Photo. *Perf. 11½x12*

2357	A734 8.40z multicolored		.35	.25

Gen. Casimir Pulaski (1748-1779), Polish nobleman who served in American Revolutionary War.

Gen. Franciszek Jozwiak — A735

1979, Oct. 3 *Perf. 11½x11*

2358	A735 1.50z gray blue, dk blue & gold		.25	.25

35th anniv. of Civil and Military Security Service, founded by Gen. Franciszek Jozwiak (1895-1966).

Drive-in Post Office — A736

Designs: 1.50z, Parcel sorting. 4.50z, Loading mail train. 6z, Mobile post office.

1979, Oct. 9 *Perf. 11½*

2359	A736	1z multicolored	.25	.25
2360	A736	1.50z multicolored	.25	.25
2361	A736	4.50z multicolored	.30	.25
2362	A736	6z multicolored	.40	.25
		Nos. 2359-2362 (4)	1.20	1.00

Stamp Day.

Christmas A737

Designs: 2z, Holy Family. 6.90z, Nativity, horiz.

Perf. 11½x11, 11x11½

1979, Dec. 4 Photo.

2363	A737	2z multicolored	.25	.25
2364	A737	6.90z multicolored	.35	.25

A738

Space Achievements: 1z, Soyuz 30 and Salyut 6. 1.50z, Kopernik 500 and Copernicus satellite. 2z, Lunik 2 and Ranger 7. 4.50z, Yuri Gagarin and Vostok. 6.90z, Neil Armstrong and Apollo 11.

1979, Dec. 28 Photo. *Perf. 11½x11*

2365	A738	1z multi	.25	.25
2366	A738	1.50z multi	.25	.25
2367	A738	2z multi	.25	.25
2368	A738	4.50z multi	.25	.25
2369	A738	6.90z multi	.30	.25
a.		Souvenir sheet of 5	1.50	1.00
		Nos. 2365-2369 (5)	1.30	1.25

No. 2369a contains Nos. 2365-2369, tete beche plus label.

A739

Designs: Horse Paintings.

1980, Jan. 31 Photo. *Perf. 11½x12*

2370	A739	1z Stagecoach	.25	.25
2371	A739	2z Horse, trainer	.25	.25
2372	A739	2.50z Trotters	.25	.25
2373	A739	3z Fox hunt	.25	.25
2374	A739	4z Sled	.25	.25
2375	A739	6z Hay cart	.35	.25
2376	A739	6.50z Pairs	.40	.25
2377	A739	6.90z Hurdles	.60	.35
		Nos. 2370-2377 (8)	2.60	2.10

Sierakov horse stud farm, 150th anniv.

Party Slogan on Map of Poland — A740

Worker, by Janusz Stanny — A741

1980, Feb. 11 Photo. *Perf. 11½x11*

2378	A740 2.50z multi		.25	.25
2379	A741 2.50z multi		.25	.25

Polish United Workers' Party, 8th Congress.

Equestrian, Olympic Rings — A742

1980, Mar. 31 *Perf. 12x11½*

2380	A742	2z shown	.25	.25
2381	A742	2.50z Archery	.25	.25
2382	A742	6.50z Biathlon	.35	.25
2383	A742	8.40z Volleyball	.60	.25
		Nos. 2380-2383 (4)	1.45	1.00

13th Winter Olympic Games, Lake Placid, NY, Feb. 12-24 (6.50z); 22nd Summer Olympic Games, Moscow, July 19-Aug. 3. See No. B138.

Map and Old Town Hall, 1591, Zamosc A743

1980, Apr. 3 Litho. *Perf. 11½*

2384	A743 2.50z multi		.25	.25

Zamosc, 400th anniversary.

Arms of Poland and Russia A744

1980, Apr. 21 Litho. *Perf. 11½*

2385	A744 2.50z multi		.25	.25

Treaty of Friendship, Cooperation and Mutual Assistance between Poland and USSR, 35th anniversary.

Lenin, 110th Birth Anniversary — A745

1980, Apr. 22 Photo. *Perf. 11*

2386	A745 2.50z multi		.25	.25

Workers Marching A746

1980, May 1 *Perf. 11½x11*

2387	A746 2.50z multi		.25	.25

Revolution of 1905, 75th anniversary.

Dove Over Liberation Date — A747

1980, May 9 *Perf. 11½x12*

2388	A747 2.50z multi		.25	.25

Victory over fascism, 35th anniversary.

Arms of Treaty-signing Countries A748

1980, May 14 Litho. *Perf. 11½x11*

2389	A748 2z red & blk		.25	.25

Signing of Warsaw Pact (Bulgaria, Czechoslovakia, German Democratic Rep., Hungary, Poland, Romania, USSR), 25th anniversary.

A749

No. 2390, Caverns, (1961 Expedition) Map of Cuba. No. 2391, Seals, Antarctica, 1959. No. 2392, Ethnology, Mongolia, 1963. No. 2393, Archaeology, Syria, 1959. No. 2394, Mountain climbing, Nepal, 1978. No. 2395, Paleontology, Mongolia, 1963.

1980, May 22 Photo. *Perf. 14*

2390	A749	2z multi	.25	.25
2391	A749	2z multi	.25	.25
2392	A749	2.50z multi	.25	.25
2393	A749	2.50z multi	.25	.25
2394	A749	6.50z multi	.35	.25
2395	A749	8.40z multi	.85	.35
		Nos. 2390-2395 (6)	2.20	1.60

Malachowski Lyceum Arms — A750

1980, June 7 Photo. *Perf. 11x12*

2396	A750 2z blk & dl grn		.25	.25

Malachowski Lyceum (oldest school in Plock), 800th anniversary.

A751

No. 2397, Xerocomus Parasiticus. No. 2398, Clathrus ruber. No. 2399, Phallus hadriani. No. 2400, Strobilomyces floccopus. No. 2401, Sparassis crispa. No. 2402, Langermannia gigantea.

1980, June 30 *Perf. 11½x11*

2397	A751	2z multi	.25	.25
2398	A751	2z multi	.25	.25
2399	A751	2.50z multi	.25	.25
2400	A751	2.50z multi	.25	.25
2401	A751	8z multi	.60	.25
2402	A751	10.50z multi	.70	.30
		Nos. 2397-2402 (6)	2.30	1.55

Sandomierz Millennium — A752

1980, July 12 Photo. *Perf. 11x11½*

2403	A752 2.50z dk brown		.25	.25

"Lwow," T. Ziolkowski — A753

Ships and Teachers: 2.50z, Antoni Garnuszewski, A. Garnuszewski. 6z, Zenit, A. Ledochowski. 6.50z, Jan Turlejski, K. Porebski. 6.90z, Horyzon, G. Kanski. 8.40z, Dar Pomorza, K. Maciejewicz.

1980, July 21 Litho. *Perf. 11*

2404 A753 2z multi .25 .25
2405 A753 2.50z multi .25 .25
2406 A753 6z multi .35 .25
2407 A753 6.50z multi .45 .25
2408 A753 6.90z multi .45 .25
2409 A753 8.40z multi .55 .25
Nos. 2404-2409 (6) 2.30 1.50

Training ships and teachers.

A754

Designs: Medicinal plants — No. 2410, Atropa belladonna. No. 2411, Datura innoxia. No. 2412, Valeriana. No. 2413, Mentha piperita. No. 2414, Calendula. No. 2415, Salvia officinalis.

1980, Aug. 15 Litho. *Perf. 11½x11*

2410 A754 2z multicolored .25 .25
2411 A754 2.50z multicolored .25 .25
2412 A754 3.40z multicolored .25 .25
2413 A754 5z multicolored .35 .25
2414 A754 6.50z multicolored .45 .25
2415 A754 8z multicolored .35 .30
Nos. 2410-2415 (6) 1.90 1.55

A755

1980, Aug. 20 *Perf. 11*

2416 A755 2.50z multi .25 .25

Jan Kochanowski (1530-1584), poet.

United Nations, 35th Anniversary — A756

1980, Sept. 19 Photo. *Perf. 11x11½*

2417 A756 8.40z multi .50 .25

Chopin Piano Competition — A757

1980, Oct. 2 Litho. *Perf. 11½*

2418 A757 6.90z blk & tan .45 .25

Mail Pick-up — A758

1980, Oct. 9 Photo. *Perf. 12x11½*

2419 A758 2z shown .25 .25
2420 A758 2.50z Letter sorting .25 .25
2421 A758 6z Loading mail plane .40 .25
2422 A758 6.50z Mail boxes .40 .25
a. Souvenir sheet of 4, #2419-2422 3.25 2.75
Nos. 2419-2422 (4) 1.30 1.00

Stamp Day.

Girl Embracing Dove, UN Emblem A759

1980, Nov. 21 Litho. *Perf. 11x11½*

2423 A759 8.40z multicolored .50 .25

UN Declaration on the Preparation of Societies for Life in Peace.

Battle of Olzynska Grochowska, by W. Kossak — A760

1980, Nov. 29 Photo. *Perf. 11*

2424 A760 2.50z multicolored .25 .25

Battle of Olzynska Grochowska, 1830.

Horse-drawn Fire Engine — A761

Designs: Horse-drawn vehicles.

1980, Dec. 16

2425 A761 2z shown .25 .25
2426 A761 2.50z Passenger coach .25 .25
2427 A761 3z Beer wagon .25 .25
2428 A761 5z Sled .35 .25
2429 A761 6z Bus .40 .25
2430 A761 6.50z Two-seater .65 .30
Nos. 2425-2430 (6) 2.15 1.55

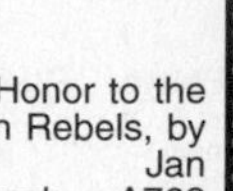

Honor to the Silesian Rebels, by Jan Borowczak — A762

1981, Jan. 22 Engr. *Perf. 11½*

2431 A762 2.50z gray grn .25 .25

Silesian uprising, 60th anniversary.

Pablo Picasso — A763

1981, Mar. 10 Photo. *Perf. 11½x11*

2432 A763 8.40z multi .40 .25
a. Miniature sheet of 2 + 2 labels 1.90 1.00

Pablo Picasso (1881-1973), artist, birth centenary. No. 2432 se-tenant with label showing A Crying Woman. Sold for 20.80z.

Balloon Flown by Pilatre de Rozier, 1783 — A764

Gordon Bennett Cup (Balloons): No. 2434, J. Blanchard, J. Jeffries, 1875. 2.50z, F. Godard, 1850. 3z, F. Hynek, Z. Burzynski, 1933. 6z, Z. Burzynski, N. Wysocki, 1935. 6.50z, B. Abruzzo, M. Anderson, L. Newman, 1978. 10.50z, Winners' names, 1933-1935, 1938.

1981, Mar. 25 Photo. *Perf. 11½x12*

2433 A764 2z multi .25 .25
2434 A764 2z multi .25 .25
2435 A764 2.50z multi .25 .25
2436 A764 3z multi .25 .25
2437 A764 6z multi .45 .25
2438 A764 6.50z multi .50 .25
Nos. 2433-2438 (6) 1.95 1.50

Souvenir Sheet

Imperf

2439 A764 10.50z multi .85 .60

Iphigenia, by Franz Anton Maulbertsch (1724-1796), WIPA '81 Emblem — A765

1981, May 11 Litho. *Perf. 11½*

2440 A765 10.50z multi .65 .25

WIPA '81 Intl. Phil. Exhib., Vienna, 5/22-31.

Wroclaw, 1493 — A766

1981, May 15 Photo. *Perf. 14*

2441 A766 6.50z brown .35 .25

See #2456-2459. For surcharge see #2526.

Gen. Wladyslaw Sikorski (1881-1943) A767

1981, May 20 *Perf. 11½x11*

2442 A767 6.50z multi .30 .25

Kwan Vase, 18th Cent. — A768

2z, Cup, saucer, 1820. 2.50z, Jug, 1820. 5z, Portrait plate, 1880. 6.50z, Vase, 1900. 8.40z, Basket, 1840.

1981, June 15

2443 A768 1z shown .25 .25
2444 A768 2z multi .25 .25
2445 A768 2.50z multi .25 .25
2446 A768 5z multi .35 .25
2447 A768 6.50z multi .45 .25
2448 A768 8.40z multi .60 .25
Nos. 2443-2448 (6) 2.15 1.50

See Nos. 2502-2507.

Intl. Architects Union, 14th Congress, Warsaw — A769

1981, July 15 Litho.

2449 A769 2.50z multi .25 .25

Moose, Rifle and Pouch — A770

1981, July 30

2450 A770 2z shown .25 .25
2451 A770 2z Boar .25 .25
2452 A770 2.50z Fox .25 .25
2453 A770 2.50z Elk .25 .25
2454 A770 6.50z Greylag goose, horiz. .55 .25
2455 A770 6.50z Fen duck .85 .25
Nos. 2450-2455 (6) 2.40 1.50

City Type of 1981

4z, Gdansk, 1652, vert. 5z, Krakow, 1493, vert. 6z, Legnica, 1744. 8z, Warsaw, 1618.

Perf. 11x11½, 11½x13

1981, July 28 **Photo.**

2456	A766 4z multicolored	.25	.25
2457	A766 5z multicolored	.30	.25
2458	A766 6z multicolored	.40	.25
2459	A766 8z multicolored	.50	.25
	Nos. 2456-2459 (4)	1.45	1.00

For surcharge see #2939.

A770a

1982, Nov. 2 **Photo.** ***Perf. 11½***

2461	A770a 12z Vistula River	.25	.25
2463	A770a 17z Kasimierz Dolny	.25	.25
2466	A770a 25z Gdansk	.35	.25
	Nos. 2461-2466 (3)	.85	.75

Wild Bison — A771

No. 2471 — Bison bonasus: a, Adult looking forward in center, adult grazing at right, tree without leaves at UR. b. Adult grazing at left, adult at center, hindquarters of juvenile at right, tree with leaves at UL. c, Adults and juvenile, inscribed "Karat-2000" at bottom. d, Juvenile suckling female. e, Two adults facing right.

1981, Aug. 27 ***Perf. 11½x11***

2471	Horiz. strip of 5	2.50	1.25
a.-e.	A771 6.50z Any single	.40	.25

60th Anniv. of Polish Tennis Federation — A772

1981, Sept. 17 **Photo.** ***Perf. 11x11½***

2472	A772 6.50z multi	.40	.25

Model Airplane — A773

1981, Sept. 24 ***Perf. 14***

2473	A773 1z shown	.25	.25
2474	A773 2z Boats	.25	.25
2475	A773 2.50z Racing cars	.25	.25
2476	A773 4.20z Gliders	.35	.25
2477	A773 6.50z Radio-controlled racing cars	.40	.25
2478	A773 8z Yachts	.60	.30
	Nos. 2473-2478 (6)	2.10	1.55

Intl. Year of the Disabled — A774

1981, Sept. 25 **Litho.** ***Perf. 11½x11***

2479	A774 8.40z multi	.50	.25

Stamp Day — A775

2.50z, Pistol, 18th cent., horiz. 8.40z, Sword, 18th cent.

1981, Oct. 9 **Photo.** ***Perf. 14***

2480	A775 2.50z multi	.25	.25
2481	A775 8.40z multi	.50	.25

A776

1981, Oct. 10 ***Perf. 11½x12***

2482	A776 2.50z multi	.25	.25

Henryk Wieniawski (1835-1880), violinist and composer.

A777

Working Movement Leaders: 50g, Bronislaw Wesolowski (1870-1919). 2z, Malgorzata Fornalska (1902-1944). 2.50z, Maria Koszutska (1876-1939). 6.50z, Marcin Kasprzak (1860-1905).

1981, Oct. 15 **Litho.**

2483	A777 50g grn & blk	.25	.25
2484	A777 2z bl & blk	.25	.25
2485	A777 2.50z brn & blk	.25	.25
2486	A777 6.50z lil rose & blk	.35	.25
	Nos. 2483-2486 (4)	1.10	1.00

World Food Day — A778

1981, Oct. 16 ***Perf. 11½x11***

2487	A778 6.90z multi	.45	.25

Old Theater, Cracow, 200th Anniv. — A779

Theater Emblem and: 2z, Helena Modrzejewska (1840-1909), actress. 2.50z, Stanislaw Kozmian (1836-1922), theater director, 1865-1885, founder of Cracow School. 6.50z, Konrad Swinarski (1929-1975), stage manager.

Photo. & Engr.

1981, Oct. 17 ***Perf. 12x11½***

2488	A779 2z multi	.25	.25
2489	A779 2.50z multi	.45	.25
2490	A779 6.50z multi	.45	.25
2491	A779 8z multi	.45	.25
	Nos. 2488-2491 (4)	1.60	1.00

Souvenir Sheet

Vistula River Project — A780

1981, Dec. 20 **Litho.** ***Perf. 11½x12***

2492	A780 10.50z multi	1.25	.75

Flowering Succulent Plants A781

No. 2493, Epiphyllopsis gaertneri. No. 2494, Cereus tonduzii. No. 2495, Cylindropuntia leptocaulis. No. 2496, Cylindroppuntia fulgida. No. 2497, Caralluma lugardi. No. 2498, Nopalea cochenillifera. No. 2499, Lithopsps helmutii. No. 2500, Cylindropuntia spinosior.

1981, Dec. 22 **Photo.** ***Perf. 13***

2493	A781 90g multicolored	.25	.25
2494	A781 1z multicolored	.25	.25
2495	A781 2z multicolored	.25	.25
2496	A781 2.50z multicolored	.25	.25
2497	A781 2.50z multicolored	.25	.25
2498	A781 6.50z multicolored	.40	.25
2499	A781 6.50z multicolored	.40	.25
2500	A781 10.50z multicolored	1.00	.45
	Nos. 2493-2500 (8)	3.05	2.20

Polish Workers' Party, 40th Anniv. — A782

1982, Jan. 5 **Photo.** ***Perf. 11½x11***

2501	A782 2.50z multi	.25	.25

Stoneware Plate, 1890 — A783

Porcelain or Stoneware: 2z, Plate, mug, 1790. 2.50z, Soup tureen, gravy dish, 1830. 6z, Salt and pepper dish, 1844, 8z, Stoneware jug, 1840. 10.50z, Stoneware figurine, 1740.

1982, Jan. 20

2502	A783 1z multi	.25	.25
2503	A783 2z multi	.25	.25
2504	A783 2.50z multi	.25	.25
2505	A783 6z multi	.40	.25
2506	A783 8z multi	.50	.25
2507	A783 10.50z multi	.75	.30
	Nos. 2502-2507 (6)	2.40	1.55

Ignacy Lukasiewicz (1822-1882), Oil Lamp Inventor — A784

Designs: Various oil lamps.

1982, Mar. 22 **Photo.** ***Perf. 11½x11***

2508	A784 1z multi	.25	.25
2509	A784 2z multi	.25	.25
2510	A784 2.50z multi	.25	.25
2511	A784 3.50z multi	.25	.25
2512	A784 9z multi	.50	.25
2513	A784 10z multi	.55	.25
	Nos. 2508-2513 (6)	2.05	1.50

Karol Szymanowski (1882-1937), Composer A785

1982, Apr. 8

2514	A785 2.50z dk brn & gold	.25	.25

Victory in Challenge Trophy Flights A786

1982, May 5 **Photo.** ***Perf. 11x11½***

2515	A786 27z RWD-6 monoplane	.75	.25
2516	A786 31z RWD-9	1.25	.25
a.	Souv. sheet of 2, #2515-2516	2.25	1.25

Henryk Sienkiewicz (1846-1916), Writer — A787

Polish Nobel Prize Winners: 15z, Wladyslaw Reymont (1867-1925), writer, 1924. 25z, Marie Curie (1867-1934), physicist 1903, 1911. 31z, Czeslaw Milosz (b. 1911), poet, 1980.

1982, May 10 Litho. *Perf. 11½x11*

2517	A787	3z black & dk grn	.25	.25
2518	A787	15z black & brown	.40	.25
2519	A787	25z black	.50	.25
2520	A787	31z black & gray	.90	.25
		Nos. 2517-2520 (4)	2.05	1.00

1982 World Cup — A788

Perf. 11½x11, 11x11½

1982, May 28 Photo.

2521	A788	25z Ball	.75	.25
2522	A788	27z Bull, ball, horiz.	.75	.25

Souvenir Sheet

Maria Kaziera Sobieska — A789

1982, June 11 Photo. *Perf. 11½x11*

2523	A789	65z multi	2.50	1.50

PHILEXFRANCE '82 Intl. Stamp Exhibition, Paris, June 11-21.

Assoc. Presidents Stanislaw Sierakowski and Boleslaw Domanski — A790

1982, July 20 Litho.

2524	A790	4.50z multi	.35	.25

Assoc. of Poles in Germany, 60th anniv.

2nd UN Conference on Peaceful Uses of Outer Space, Vienna, Aug. 9-21 — A791

1982, Aug. 9 Photo.

2525	A791	31z Globe	.75	.25

No. 2441 Surcharged

1982, Aug. 20

2526	A766	10z on 6.50z brn	.30	.25

Black Madonna of Jasna Gora, 600th Anniv. A792

2.50z, Father Augustin Kordecki (1603-1673). 25z, Siege of Jasna Gora by Swedes, 1655, horiz.

1982, Aug. 26 *Perf. 11*

2527	A792	2.50z multi	.25	.25
2528	A792	25z multi	.40	.25
2529	A792	65z multi	1.20	.35
		Nos. 2527-2529 (3)	1.85	.85

A souvenir sheet of 2 No. 2529 exists. Value: mint $10, used $9.

Workers' Movement A793

1982, Sept. 3 *Perf. 11½x11*

2530	A793	6z multicolored	.30	.25

Norbert Barlicki (1880-1941) — A794

Workers' Activists: 6z, Pawel Finder (1904-1944). 15z, Marian Buczek (1896-1939). 20z, Cezaryna Wojnarowska (1861-1911). 29z, Ignacy Daszynski (1866-1936).

1982, Sept. 10 *Perf. 12x11½*

2531	A794	5z multi	.25	.25
2532	A794	6z multi	.25	.25
2533	A794	15z multi	.25	.25
2534	A794	20z multi	.25	.25
2535	A794	29z multi	.25	.25
		Nos. 2531-2535 (5)	1.25	1.25

Carved Head, Wawel Castle — A795

1982, Sept. 25

2536	A795	60z Woman's head	.75	.25
2537	A795	100z Man's head	.75	.25

TB Bacillus Centenary A796

10z, Koch. 25z, Oko Bujwid (1857-1942), bacteriologist.

1982, Sept. 22 *Perf. 11½x11*

2538	A796	10z multicolored	.30	.25
2539	A796	25z multicolored	.50	.25

St. Maximilian Kolbe (1894-1941) A797

1982, Oct.

2540	A797	27z multi	.65	.25

50th Anniv. of Polar Research A798

1982, Oct. 25 Litho. *Perf. 11½*

2541	A798	27z multi	.65	.25

Stanislaw Zaremba (1863-1942), Mathematician — A799

Mathematicians: 6z, Waclaw Sierpinski (1882-1969). 12z, Zygmunt Janiszewski (1888-1920). 15z, Stefan Banach (1892-1945).

1982, Nov. 23 Photo. *Perf. 11x11½*

2542	A799	5z multicolored	.25	.25
2543	A799	6z multicolored	.25	.25
2544	A799	12z multicolored	.30	.25
2545	A799	15z multicolored	.40	.25
		Nos. 2542-2545 (4)	1.20	1.00

First Anniv. of Military Rule — A800

1982, Dec. 13 *Perf. 12x11½*

2546	A800	2.50z Medal obverse and reverse	.25	.25

Cracow Monuments Restoration A801

1982, Dec. 20 Litho. *Perf. 11½x11*

2547	A801	15z Deanery portal	.35	.25
2548	A801	25z Law College portal	.50	.25

Souvenir Sheet

Lithographed and Engraved

Imperf

2549	A801	65z City map	1.00	.75

No. 2549 contains one stamp 22x27mm.

See Nos. 2593-2594, 2656-2657, 2717-2718, 2809, 2847.

Map of Poland, by Bernard Wapowski, 1526 A802

Maps: 6z, Warsaw, Polish Kingdom Quartermaster, 1839. 8z, Poland, Romer's Atlas, 1908. 25z, Krakow, by A. Buchowiecki, 1703, astrolabe, 17th cent.

1982, Dec. 28 Litho. *Perf. 11½*

2550	A802	5z multicolored	.25	.25
2551	A802	6z multicolored	.25	.25
2552	A802	8z multicolored	.25	.25
2553	A802	25z multicolored	.65	.25
		Nos. 2550-2553 (4)	1.40	1.00

120th Anniv. of 1863 Uprising — A803

1983, Jan. 22 Photo. *Perf. 12x11½*

2554	A803	6z The Battle, by Arthur Grottger (1837-67)	.25	.25

Warsaw Theater Sesquicentennial — A804

1983, Feb. 24 Photo. *Perf. 11*

2555	A804	6z multicolored	.25	.25

10th Anniv. of UN Conference on Human Environment, Stockholm — A805

1983, Mar. 24 Litho. *Perf. 11½*

2556	A805	5z Wild flowers	.25	.25
2557	A805	6z Swan, carp, eel	.25	.25
2558	A805	17z Hoopoe	.40	.25
2559	A805	30z Fish	.50	.50
2560	A805	31z Deer, fawn, buffalo	.50	.50
2561	A805	38z Fruit	.75	.30
		Nos. 2556-2561 (6)	2.65	2.05

Karol Kurpinski (1785-1857), Composer A806

Famous People: 6z, Maria Jasnorzewska Pawlikowska (1891-1945), poet. 17z, Stanislaw Szober (1879-1938), linguist. 25z,

Tadeusz Banachiewicz (1882-1954), astronomer. 27z, Jaroslaw Iwaszkiewicz (1894-1980), writer. 31z, Wladyslaw Tatarkiewicz (1886-1980), philosopher, art historian.

1983, Mar. 25 Photo. ***Perf. 11½x11***

2562 A806 5z tan & brn .25 .25
2563 A806 6z pink & vio .25 .25
2564 A806 17z dk grn & lt grn .35 .25
2565 A806 25z bister & brn .60 .25
2566 A806 27z lt bl & dk bl .60 .25
2567 A806 31z violet & pur .75 .25
Nos. 2562-2567 (6) 2.80 1.50

Polish Medalists in 22nd Olympic Games, 1980 A807

1983, Apr. 5 ***Perf. 11x11½***

2568 A807 5z Steeplechase .25 .25
2569 A807 6z Equestrian .25 .25
2570 A807 15z Soccer, 1982 World Cup .35 .25
2571 A807 27z + 5z Pole vault .70 .25
Nos. 2568-2571 (4) 1.55 1.00

Warsaw Ghetto Uprising, 40th Anniv. — A808

Heroes' Monument, by Natan Rappaport.

1983, Apr. 19 Photo. ***Perf. 11½x11***

2572 A808 6z multicolored .25 .25

Se-tenant with label showing anniversary medal.

Customs Cooperation Council, 30th Anniv. — A809

1983, Apr. 28

2573 A809 5z multicolored .25 .25

Second Visit of Pope John Paul II — A810

Portraits of Pope. 31z vert.

1983, June 16 Photo. ***Perf. 11***

2574 A810 31z multicolored .80 .25
2575 A810 65z multicolored 1.50 .75
a. Souvenir sheet 1.75 1.25

Army of King John III Sobieski — A811

No. 2576, Dragoons. No. 2577, Knight in armor. No. 2578, Non-commissioned infantry officers. No. 2579, Light cavalryman. No. 2580, Hussars.

1983, July 5 ***Perf. 11½x11***

2576 A811 5z multi .25 .25
2577 A811 5z multi .25 .25
2578 A811 6z multi .25 .25
2579 A811 15z multi .35 .25
2580 A811 27z multi .70 .25
Nos. 2576-2580 (5) 1.80 1.25

750th Anniv. of Torun Municipality — A812

1983, Aug. 25 Photo. ***Perf. 11***

2581 A812 6z multicolored .25 .25
a. Souvenir sheet of 4 3.00 5.50

No. 2581a had limited distribution.

60th Anniv. of Polish Boxing Union A813

1983, Nov. 4 Litho. ***Perf. 11½x11***

2582 A813 6z multicolored .25 .25

Enigma Decoding Machine, 50th Anniv. — A813a

1983, Aug. 16 Litho. ***Perf. 11½x11***

2582A A813a 5z multicolored .25 .25

Girl Near House — A813b

1983 Photo. ***Perf. 11½x12***

2582B A813b 6z multicolored .25 .25

Public courtesy campaign.

Portrait of King John III Sobieski A814

King's Portraits by: #2584, Unknown court painter. #2585, Sobieski on Horseback, by Francesco Trevisani (1656-1746). 25z, Jerzy Eleuter Szymonowicz-Siemiginowski (1660-1711). 65z+10z, Sobieski at Vienna, by Jan Matejko (1838-1893).

1983, Sept. 12 ***Perf. 11***

2583 A814 5z multicolored .25 .25
2584 A814 6z multicolored .25 .25
2585 A814 6z multicolored .25 .25
2586 A814 25z multicolored .60 .25
Nos. 2583-2586 (4) 1.35 1.00

Souvenir Sheet

Imperf

2587 A814 65z + 10z multi 1.50 1.25

Victory over the Turks in Vienna, 300th anniv.

Polish Peoples' Army, 40th Anniv. — A815

#2588, General Zygmunt Berling (1896-1980). #2589, Wanda Wasilewska (1905-64). #2591, Troop formation.

1983, Oct. 12 Photo. ***Perf. 11***

2588 A815 5z multicolored .25 .25
2589 A815 5z multicolored .25 .25
2590 A815 6z multicolored .25 .25
2591 A815 6z multi, horiz. .25 .25
Nos. 2588-2591 (4) 1.00 1.00

World Communications Year — A816

1983, Oct. 18 Photo. ***Perf. 11***

2592 A816 15z multicolored .35 .25

Cracow Restoration Type of 1982

1983, Nov. 25 Litho. ***Perf. 11***

2593 A801 5z Cloth Hall, horiz. .25 .25
2594 A801 6z Town Hall Tower .30 .25

Traditional Hats — A818

1983, Dec. 16 Photo. ***Perf. 11½x11***

2595 A818 5z Biskupianski .25 .25
2596 A818 5z Rozbarski .25 .25
2597 A818 6z Warminsko-Mazurski .25 .25
2598 A818 6z Cieszynski .25 .25
2599 A818 25z Kurpiowski .45 .25
2600 A818 38z Lubuski .75 .25
Nos. 2595-2600 (6) 2.20 1.50

Natl. People's Council, 40th Anniv. — A819

Hand holding sword (poster).

1983, Dec. 31

2601 A819 6z multicolored .25 .25

People's Army, 40th Anniv. — A820

1984, Jan. 1 Litho. ***Perf. 11½x11***

2602 A820 5z Gen. Bem Brigade badge .25 .25

Musical Instruments A821

1984, Feb. 10 Photo.

2603 A821 5z Dulcimer .25 .25
2604 A821 6z Drum, tambourine .25 .25
2605 A821 10z Accordion .25 .25
2606 A821 15z Double bass .30 .25
2607 A821 17z Bagpipes .45 .25
2608 A821 29z Figurines by Tadeusz Zak .60 .25
Nos. 2603-2608 (6) 2.10 1.50

See Nos. 2682-2687.

Wincenty Witos (1874-1945), Prime Minister — A822

1984, Mar. 2 Litho. ***Perf. 11½x11***

2609 A822 6z green & sepia .25 .25

Local Flowers (Clematis Varieties) A823

1984, Mar. 26 Photo. ***Perf. 11x11½***

2610 A823 5z Lanuginosa .25 .25
2611 A823 6z Tangutica .25 .25
2612 A823 10z Texensis .25 .25
2613 A823 17z Alpina .40 .25
2614 A823 25z Vitalba .60 .35
2615 A823 27z Montana .75 .50
Nos. 2610-2615 (6) 2.50 1.85

The Ecstasy of St. Francis, by El Greco A824

1984, Apr. 21 *Perf. 11*
2616 A824 27z multicolored .65 .25

1984 Olympics A825

1984, Apr. 25 Litho. *Perf. 11x11½*
2617 A825 5z Handball .25 .25
2618 A825 6z Fencing .25 .25
2619 A825 15z Bicycling .35 .25
2620 A825 16z Running .40 .25
2621 A825 17z Running, diff. .45 .25
a. Souv. sheet of 2, #2620-2621 1.00 .85
2622 A825 31z Skiing .75 .30
Nos. 2617-2622 (6) 2.45 1.55

No. 2621a sold for 43z.

Battle of Monte Cassino, 40th Anniv. — A826

1984, May 18 Photo. *Perf. 11½x11*
2623 A826 15z Memorial Cross .40 .25

View of Warsaw from the Praga Bank, by Bernardo Belotto Canaletto — A827

Paintings of Vistula River views: 6z, Trumpet Festivity, by Aleksander Gierymski. 25z, The Vistula near the Bielany District, by Jozef Rapacki. 27z, Steamship Harbor in the Powisle District, by Franciszek Kostrzewski.

1984, June 20 Photo. *Perf. 11*
2624 A827 5z multicolored .25 .25
2625 A827 6z multicolored .25 .25
2626 A827 25z multicolored .60 .25
2627 A827 27z multicolored .60 .25
Nos. 2624-2627 (4) 1.70 1.00

Eastern Ruler — A828

Sculptures: 3.50z, Eastern ruler. No. 2628A, Woman wearing wreath. 10z, Man wearing hat. No. 2629, Warrior's Head, Wawel Castle.

1984-85 Photo. *Perf. 11½x12*
2628 A828 3.50z brown .25 .25
2628A A828 5z dark claret .25 .25
2628B A828 10z brt ultra .25 .25
Nos. 2628-2628B (3) .75 .75

Coil Stamp

Perf. 13½x14

2629 A828 5z dk blue grn .25 .25

Issued: 3.50z, 1/24/85; #2628A, 10z, 7/8/85; #2629, 7/10/84.

No. 2629 has black control number on back of every fifth stamp.

See Nos. 2738-2744.

Order of Grunwald Cross — A829

Designs: 6z, Order of Revival of Poland. 10z, Order of the Banner of Labor, First Class. 16z, Order of Builders of People's Poland.

1984, July 21 Photo. *Perf. 11½*
2630 A829 5z multicolored .25 .25
2631 A829 6z multicolored .25 .25
2632 A829 10z multicolored .25 .25
2633 A829 16z multicolored .25 .25
a. Sheet of 4, #2630-2633, perf. 11½x12 2.40 2.25
Nos. 2630-2633 (4) 1.00 1.00

40th anniversary of July Manifesto (Origin of Polish People's Republic).

Warsaw Uprising, 40th Anniv. A830

1984, Aug. 1
2634 A830 4z multicolored .25 .25
2635 A830 5z multicolored .25 .25
2636 A830 6z multicolored .25 .25
2637 A830 25z multicolored .75 .25
Nos. 2634-2637 (4) 1.50 1.00

Broken Heart Monument, Lodz — A831

1984, Aug. 31
2638 A831 16z multicolored .35 .25

Defense of Oksywie Holm, Col. S. Dabek — A832

6z, Bzura River battle, Gen. T. Kutrzeba.

1984, Sept. 1
2639 A832 5z shown .25 .25
2640 A832 6z multicolored .25 .25

Invasion of Poland, 45th anniversary.

See Nos. 2692-2693, 2757, 2824-2826, 2864-2866, 2922-2925.

Polish Militia, 40th Anniv. A833

6z, Militiaman at Control Center.

1984, Sept. 29 Photo. *Perf. 11½*
2641 A833 5z shown .25 .25
2642 A833 6z multicolored .25 .25

Polish Aviation A834

No. 2643, Balloon ascent, 1784. No. 2644, Powered flight, 1911. No. 2645, Balloon Polonez, 1983. No. 2646 Modern gliders. No. 2647, Wilga, 1983. No. 2648, Farman, 1914. No. 2649, Los and PZL P-7.

1984, Nov. 6 Photo. *Perf. 11x11½*
2643 A834 5z multi .25 .25
2644 A834 5z multi .25 .25
2645 A834 6z multi .25 .25
2646 A834 10z multi .25 .25
2647 A834 16z multi .35 .25
2648 A834 27z multi .60 .25
2649 A834 31z multi .65 .25
Nos. 2643-2649 (7) 2.60 1.75

Protected Animals A835

1984, Dec. 4 Photo. *Perf. 11x11½*
2650 A835 4z Mustela nivalis .25 .25
2651 A835 5z Martes foina .25 .25
2652 A835 5z Mustela erminea .25 .25

Perf. 11½x11

2653 A835 10z Castor fiber, vert. .25 .25
2654 A835 10z Lutra lutra, vert. .25 .25
2655 A835 65z Marmota marmota, vert. 1.50 .75
Nos. 2650-2655 (6) 2.75 2.00

Cracow Restoration Type of 1982

5z, Royal Cathedral, Wawel. 15z, Royal Castle, Wawel, horiz.

Perf. 11½x11, 11x11½

1984, Dec. 10 **Litho.**
2656 A801 5z multi .25 .25
2657 A801 15z multi .30 .25

Religious Buildings A837

5z, Protestant Church, Warsaw. 10z, Saint Andrew Church, Cracow. 15z, Greek Orthodox Church, Rychwald. 20z, Orthodox Church, Warsaw. 25z, Tykocin Synagogue, horiz. 31z, Tartar Mosque, Kruszyniany, horiz.

Perf. 11½x12, 12x11½

1984, Dec. 28 **Photo.**
2658 A837 5z multicolored .25 .25
2659 A837 10z multicolored .25 .25
2660 A837 15z multicolored .25 .25
2661 A837 20z multicolored .25 .25
2662 A837 25z multicolored .25 .25
2663 A837 31z multicolored .45 .25
Nos. 2658-2663 (6) 1.70 1.50

Classic and Contemporary Fire Engines — A838

Designs: 4z, Horse-drawn fire pump, 19th cent. 10z, Polski Fiat, c. 1930. 12z, Jelcz 315, 1970s. 15z, Horse-drawn hand pump, 1899. 20z, Jelcz engine, Magirus power ladder, 1970s. 30z, Hand pump, 18th cent.

1985, Feb. 25 Photo. *Perf. 11x11½*
2664 A838 4z multicolored .25 .25
2665 A838 10z multicolored .25 .25
2666 A838 12z multicolored .25 .25
2667 A838 15z multicolored .25 .25
2668 A838 20z multicolored .25 .25
2669 A838 30z multicolored .85 .25
Nos. 2664-2669 (6) 2.10 1.50

Battle of Raclawice, April, 1794, by Jan Styka, 1894 — A839

1985, Apr. 4 *Perf. 11*
2670 A839 27z multicolored .50 .25

Kosciuszko Insurrection cent.

A840

1985, Apr. 11 Litho. *Perf. 11½*
2671 A840 10z sal rose & dk vio bl .25 .25

Wincenty Rzymowski (1883-1950),Democratic Party founder.

Blue Jeans, Badge — A841

1985, Apr. 25 Photo. *Perf. 11½x11*
2672 A841 15z multicolored .25 .25

Intl. Youth Year.

Prince Boleslaw Krzywousty (1085-1138) — A842

Regional maps and: 10z, Wladyslaw Gomulka (1905-82), sec.-gen. of the Polish Workers Party, prime minister 1945-49. 20z, Piotr Zaremba (b. 1910), president of Gdansk Province 1945-50.

1985, May 8 Litho. *Perf. 11½*

2673	A842	5z multicolored	.25	.25
2674	A842	10z multicolored	.25	.25
2675	A842	20z multicolored	.35	.25
		Nos. 2673-2675 (3)	.85	.75

Restoration of the Western & Northern Territories to Polish control, 40th anniv.

Victory Berlin 1945, by Jozef Mlynarski (b. 1925) — A843

Painting: Polish and Soviet soldiers at Brandenburg Gate, May 9, 1945.

1985, May 9 Photo. *Perf. 12x11½*

2676	A843	5z multicolored	.25	.25

Liberation from German occupation, 40th anniv.

Warsaw Treaty Org., 30th Anniv. — A844

1985, May 14 Litho. *Perf. 11½x11*

2677	A844	5z Emblem, member flags	.25	.25

World Wildlife Fund A845

Endangered Wildlife: Canis lupus — No. 2678, Wolves, winter landscape. No. 2679, Female, cubs. No. 2680, Wolf. No. 2681, Wolves, summer landscape.

1985, May 25 Photo. *Perf. 11x11½*

2678	A845	5z multicolored	.25	.25
2679	A845	10z multicolored	.35	.25
2680	A845	10z multicolored	.35	.25
2681	A845	20z multicolored	1.50	.75
		Nos. 2678-2681 (4)	2.45	1.50

A846

Folk instruments.

1985, June 25 *Perf. 11½x11*

2682	A846	5z Wooden rattle	.25	.25
2683	A846	10z Jingle	.25	.25
2684	A846	12z Clay whistles	.25	.25
2685	A846	20z Wooden fiddles	.30	.25
2686	A846	25z Tuned bells	.35	.25
2687	A846	31z Shepherd's flutes, ram's horn, ocarina	.45	.25
		Nos. 2682-2687 (6)	1.85	1.50

A847

Design: O.R.P. Iskra and emblem.

Photogravure and Engraved

1985, June 29

2688	A847	5z bluish blk & yel	.25	.25

Polish Navy, 40th anniv.

Tomasz Nocznicki (1862-1944) — A848

Polish Labor Movement founders: 20z, Maciej Rataj (1884-1940).

1985, July 26 Engr. *Perf. 11x11½*

2689	A848	10z grnsh black	.25	.25
2690	A848	20z brown black	.25	.25

Natl. labor movement, 90th anniv.

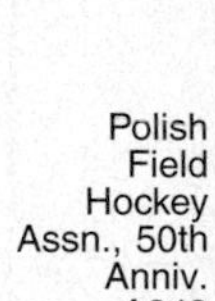

Polish Field Hockey Assn., 50th Anniv. A849

1985, Aug. 22 Litho. *Perf. 11½x11*

2691	A849	5z multicolored	.25	.25

World War II Battles Type of 1984

Designs: 5z, Defense of Wizny, Capt. Wladyslaw Raginis. 10z, Attack on Mlawa, Col. Wilhelm Andrzej Liszka-Lawicz.

1985, Sept. 1 Photo. *Perf. 12x11½*

2692	A832	5z multicolored	.25	.25
2693	A832	10z multicolored	.25	.25

Pafawag Railway Rolling Stock Co. A850

1985, Sept. 18 Litho. *Perf. 11½*

2694	A850	5z Box car	.25	.25
2695	A850	10z 201 E locomotive	.25	.25
2696	A850	17z Two-axle coal car	.25	.25
2697	A850	20z Passenger car	.50	.25
		Nos. 2694-2697 (4)	1.25	1.00

Wild Ducks A851

No. 2698, Anas crecca. No. 2699, Anas querquedula. No. 2700, Aythya fuligula. No. 2701, Bucephala clangula. No. 2702, Somateria mollissima. No. 2703, Netta rufina.

1985, Oct. 21 Photo. *Perf. 11x11½*

2698	A851	5z multicolored	.25	.25
2699	A851	5z multicolored	.25	.25
2700	A851	10z multicolored	.30	.25
2701	A851	15z multicolored	.35	.25
2702	A851	25z multicolored	.50	.25
2703	A851	29z multicolored	.65	.35
		Nos. 2698-2703 (6)	2.30	1.60

UN, 40th Anniv. A852

1985, Oct. 24 Litho. *Perf. 11½x11*

2704	A852	27z multicolored	.50	.25

Polish Ballet, 200th Anniv. — A853

1985, Dec. 4

2705	A853	5z Prima ballerina	.25	.25
2706	A853	15z Male dancer	.25	.25

Paintings by Stanislaw Ignacy Witkiewicz (1885-1939) — A854

5z, Marysia and Burek in Ceylon. No. 2708, Woman with a Fox. No. 2709, Self-portrait, 1931. 20z, Compositions, 1917. 25z, Portrait of Nena Stachurska, 1929. Nos. 2707, 2709-2711 vert.

Perf. 11½x11, 11x11½

1985, Dec. 6 Photo.

2707	A854	5z multicolored	.25	.25
2708	A854	10z multicolored	.25	.25
2709	A854	10z multicolored	.25	.25
2710	A854	20z multicolored	.25	.25
2711	A854	25z multicolored	.50	.25
		Nos. 2707-2711 (5)	1.50	1.25

Souvenir Sheet

Johann Sebastian Bach — A855

1985, Dec. 30 *Perf. 11½x11*

2712	A855	65z multicolored	1.25	.45
a.		With inscription	6.00	6.00

No. 2712a inscribed "300 Rocznica Urodzin Jana Sebastiana Bacha." Distribution was limited.

Profile, Emblem, Sigismond III Column, Royal Castle Tower — A856

1986, Jan. 16 *Perf. 11½x11*

2713	A856	10z lt ultra, brt ultra & ultra	.25	.25

Congress of Intellectuals for World Peace, Warsaw.

Halley's Comet A857

Designs: No. 2714, Michal Kamienski (1879-1973), astronomer, orbit diagram. No. 2715, Comet, Vega, Giotto, Planet-A, ICE-3 space probes.

1986, Feb. 7 Photo. *Perf. 11½*

2714	A857	25z multicolored	.40	.25
2715	A857	25z multicolored	.40	.25
a.		Pair, #2714-2715	.90	.50

Intl. Peace Year — A858

1986, Mar. 20 Photo. *Perf. 11½x11*

2716	A858	25z turq bl, yel & ultra	.35	.25

Cracow Restoration Type of 1982

Designs: 5z, Collegium Maius, Jagiellonian Museum. 10z, Town Hall, Kazimierz.

1986, Mar. 20 Litho. *Perf. 11½*

2717	A801	5z multicolored	.25	.25
2718	A801	10z multicolored	.25	.25

Wildlife A859

No. 2719, Perdix perdix. No. 2720, Oryctolagus cuniculus. No. 2721, Dama dama. No. 2722, Phasianus colchicus. No. 2723, Lepus europaeus. No. 2724, Ovis ammon.

1986, Apr. 15 Photo. *Perf. 11½x11*

2719	A859	5z multicolored	.25	.25
2720	A859	5z multicolored	.25	.25
2721	A859	10z multicolored	.25	.25
2722	A859	10z multicolored	.25	.25
2723	A859	20z multicolored	.35	.25
2724	A859	40z multicolored	.75	.50
		Nos. 2719-2724 (6)	2.10	1.75

Nos. 2719-2720, 2723-2724 vert.

Stanislaw Kulczynski (1895-1975), Scientist, Party Leader — A860

Photogravure and Engraved

1986, May 3 *Perf. 11½x11*

2725	A860	10z buff & choc	.25	.25

Warsaw Fire Brigade, 150th Anniv. — A861

Painting detail: The Fire Brigade on the Cracow Outskirts on Their Way to a Fire, 1871, by Josef Brodowski (1828-1900).

1986, May 16 ***Perf. 11***
2726 A861 10z dl brn & dk brn .25 .25

Paderewski A862

1986, May 22 ***Perf. 11½x11***
2727 A862 65z multicolored 1.00 .25

AMERIPEX'86.

1986 World Cup Soccer Championships, Mexico — A863

1986, May 26 ***Perf. 11½***
2728 A863 25z multicolored .35 .25

Ferryboats — A864

1986, June 18 **Photo.** ***Perf. 11***
2729 A864 10z Wilanow .25 .25
2730 A864 10z Wawel .25 .25
a. Souv. sheet of 2, #2729-2730 1.25 .75
2731 A864 15z Pomerania .30 .25
2732 A864 25z Rogalin .35 .25
a. Souv. sheet of 2, #2731-2732 2.50 2.50
Nos. 2729-2732 (4) 1.15 1.00

Nos. 2729-2732 printed se-tenant with labels picturing historic sites from the names of cities serviced. No. 2730a sold for 30z; No. 2732a for 55z. Surtax for the Natl. Assoc. of Philatelists.

Antarctic Agreement, 25th Anniv. — A865

Map of Antarctica and: 5z, A. B. Dobrowolski, Kopernik research ship. 40z, H. Arctowski, Professor Siedlecki research ship.

1986, June 23 **Litho.** ***Perf. 11½x11***
2733 A865 5z ver, pale grn & blk .25 .25
2734 A865 40z org, pale vio & dk vio .75 .40

Polish United Workers' Party, 10th Congress A866

1986, July 29 **Photo.** ***Perf. 11x11½***
2735 A866 10z red & dk gray bl .25 .25

Wawel Heads Type of 1984-85

Designs: 15z, Woman wearing a wreath (like No. 2628A). No. 2739, Thinker. No. 2740, Eastern ruler. 40z, Youth wearing beret. 60z, Warrior. 200z, Man's head.

Perf. 11½x12, 14 (15z, No. 2740, 60z)
Engr., Photo. (15z, No. 2740, 60z)
1986-89
2738 A828 15z rose brown .25 .25
2739 A828 20z green .25 .25
2740 A828 20z peacock blue .25 .25
2742 A828 40z gray .25 .35
2743 A828 60z dark green .25 .25
2744 A828 200z dark gray .25 .25
Nos. 2738-2744 (6) 1.50 1.60

Issued: 15z, 9/22/88; #2739, 2742, 7/30/86; #2740, 3/31/89; 60z, 12/15/89; #2744, 11/11/86.

No. 2740 and 60z are coil stamps, have black control number on back of every 5th stamp.

For surcharge see No. 2954.

Jasna Gora Monastery Collection A867

Designs: No. 2746, The Paulinite Church on Skalka in Cracow, oil painting detail, circa 1627. No. 2747, Jesse's Tree, oil on wood, 17th cent. No. 2748, Gilded chalice, 18th cent. No. 2749, Virgin Mary embroidery, 15th cent.

1986, Aug. 15 **Photo.** ***Perf. 11½x11***
2746 A867 5z multicolored .25 .25
2747 A867 5z multicolored .25 .25
2748 A867 20z multicolored .35 .25
2749 A867 40z multicolored .50 .25
Nos. 2746-2749 (4) 1.35 1.00

Victories of Polish Athletes at 1985 World Championships — A868

Designs: No. 2750, Precision Flying, Kissimmee, Florida, won by Waclaw Nycz. No. 2751, Wind Sailing, Tallinn, USSR, won by Malgorzata Palasz-Piasecka. No. 2752, Glider Acrobatics, Vienna, won by Jerzy Makula. No. 2753, Greco-Roman Wrestling (82kg), Kolboten, Norway, won by Bogdan Daras. No. 2754, Road Cycling, Giavera del Montello, Italy, won by Lech Piasecki. No. 2755, Women's Modern Pentathlon, Montreal, won by Barbara Kotowska.

1986, Aug. 21 ***Perf. 11½***
2750 A868 5z multicolored .25 .25
2751 A868 10z multicolored .25 .25
2752 A868 10z multicolored .25 .25
2753 A868 15z multicolored .25 .25
2754 A868 20z multicolored .25 .25
2755 A868 30z multicolored .50 .25
Nos. 2750-2755 (6) 1.75 1.50

STOCKHOLMIA '86 — A869

1986, Aug. 28 ***Perf. 11x11½***
2756 A869 65z multicolored 1.00 .35
a. Souvenir sheet 1.00 .50

World War II Battles Type of 1984

Design: Battle of Jordanow, Col. Stanislaw Maczek, motorized cavalry 10th brigade commander-in-chief.

1986, Sept. 1 ***Perf. 12x11½***
2757 A832 10z multicolored .25 .25

Albert Schweitzer — A870

Photogravure and Engraved
1986, Sept. 26 ***Perf. 12x11½***
2758 A870 5z pale bl vio, sep & buff .25 .25

World Post Day — A871

1986, Oct. 9 **Litho.** ***Perf. 11x11½***
2759 A871 40z org, ultra & sep .50 .25
a. Souvenir sheet of 2 8.50 8.50

No. 2759a sold for 120z.

Folk and Fairy Tale Legends A872

Designs: No. 2760, Basilisk. No. 2761, Duke Popiel, vert. No. 2762, Golden Duck. No. 2763, Boruta, the Devil, vert. No. 2764, Janosik the Thief, vert. No. 2765, Lajkonik, conqueror of the Tartars, 13th cent., vert.

1986, Oct. 28 **Photo.** ***Perf. 11½x11***
2760 A872 5z multicolored .25 .25
2761 A872 5z multicolored .25 .25
2762 A872 10z multicolored .25 .25
2763 A872 10z multicolored .25 .25
2764 A872 20z multicolored .30 .25
2765 A872 50z multicolored .80 .35
Nos. 2760-2765 (6) 2.10 1.60

Prof. Tadeusz Kotarbinski (1886-1981) — A873

1986, Nov. 19 **Litho.** ***Perf. 11½***
2766 A873 10z sepia, buff & brn blk .25 .25

17th-20th Cent. Architecture — A874

Designs: No. 2767, Church, Baczal Dolny. No. 2768, Windmill, Zygmuntow. 10z, Oravian cottage, Zubrzyca Gorna. 15z, Kashubian Arcade cottage, Wazydze. 25z, Barn, Grzawa. 30z, Water mill, Molkowice Stare.

Perf. 11x11½, 11½x11
1986, Nov. 26 **Photo.**
2767 A874 5z multicolored .25 .25
2768 A874 5z multi, vert. .25 .25
2769 A874 10z multicolored .25 .25
2770 A874 15z multicolored .25 .25
2771 A874 25z multicolored .35 .25
2772 A874 30z multicolored .65 .40
Nos. 2767-2772 (6) 2.00 1.65

Royalty A875

Photogravure and Engraved
1986, Dec. 4 ***Perf. 11***
2773 A875 10z Mieszko I .40 .25
2774 A875 25z Dobrava .50 .40

See Nos. 2838-2839, 2884-2885, 2932-2933, 3033-3034, 3068-3069, 3141-3144, 3191-3192, 3222-3225, 3309-3312, 3366-3369, 3394-3397, 3479-3482, 3553-3556.

For surcharges see Nos. 3016-3017.

New Year 1987 A876

1986, Dec. 12 **Photo.** ***Perf. 11x11½***
2775 A876 25z multicolored .35 .25

Warsaw Cyclists Soc., Cent. A877

No. 2776, First trip to Bielany, uniformed escort, 1887. No. 2777, Jan Stanislaw Skrodzki (1867-1957), 1895 record-holder. No. 2778, Dynasy Society building, 1892-1937. No. 2779, Mieczyslaw Baranski, champion, 1896. No. 2780, Karolina Kociecka (b. 1875), female competitor. No. 2781, Henryk Weiss (d. 1912), Dynasy champion, 1904-1908.

Perf. 13x12½, 12½x13
1986, Dec. 19 **Litho.**
2776 A877 5z multi .25 .25
2777 A877 5z multi, vert. .25 .25
2778 A877 10z multi, vert. .25 .25
2779 A877 10z multi, vert. .25 .25
2780 A877 30z multi, vert. .35 .25
2781 A877 50z multi, vert. .65 .25
Nos. 2776-2781 (6) 2.00 1.50

Henryk Arctowski Antarctic Station, King George Island, 10th Anniv. A878

Wildlife and ships: No. 2782, Euphausia superba, training freighter Antoni Garnuszewski. No. 2783, Notothenia rossi, Dissostichus mawsoni, Zulawy transoceanic ship. No. 2784, Fulmarus glacialoides, yacht Pogoria. No. 2785, Pigoscelis adeliae, yacht Gedania. 30z, Arctocephalus, research boat Dziunia. 40z, Hydrurga leptonyx, ship Kapitan Ledochowski.

1987, Feb. 13 Litho. *Perf. 11½*

2782 A878 5z multicolored .25 .25
2783 A878 5z multicolored .25 .25
2784 A878 10z multicolored .25 .25
2785 A878 10z multicolored .25 .25
2786 A878 30z multicolored .45 .30
2787 A878 40z multicolored .65 .35
Nos. 2782-2787 (6) 2.10 1.65

Paintings by Leon Wyczolkowski (1852-1936) — A879

No. 2788, Cineraria Flowers, 1924. No. 2789, Portrait of a Woman, 1883. No. 2790, Wood Church, 1910. No. 2791, Harvesting Beetroot, 1910. No. 2792, Wading Fishermen, 1891. No. 2793, Self-portrait, 1912.

1987, Mar. 20 Photo. *Perf. 11*

2788 A879 5z multicolored .25 .25
2789 A879 10z multicolored .25 .25
2790 A879 10z multicolored .25 .25
2791 A879 25z multicolored .35 .25
2792 A879 30z multicolored .45 .30
2793 A879 40z multicolored .75 .40
Nos. 2788-2793 (6) 2.30 1.70

Nos. 2789 and 2791 vert.

The Ravage, 1866, by Artur Grottger (1837-1867) — A880

1987, Mar. 26 Photo. *Perf. 11*

2794 A880 15z dk brown & buff .25 .25

Gen. Karol Swierczewski-Walter (1897-1947) — A881

1987, Mar. 27 Engr. *Perf. 11½x12*

2795 A881 15z olive green .25 .25

Pawel Edmund Strzelecki (1797-1873), Explorer — A882

1987, Apr. 23 Photo. *Perf. 11½x11*

2796 A882 65z olive black .60 .25

Colonization of Australia, bicentennial.

2nd PRON Congress A883

1987, May 8 Litho. *Perf. 11½*

2797 A883 10z pale gray, brn, red & brt ultra .25 .25

Patriotic Movement of the National Renaissance Congress.

Motor Vehicles — A884

No. 2798, 1936 Saurer-Zawrat. No. 2799, 1928 CWS T-1. No. 2800, 1928 Ursus-A. No. 2801, 1936 Lux-Sport. No. 2802, 1939 Podkowa 100. No. 2803, 1935 Sokol 600 RT.

1987, May 19 Photo. *Perf. 12x11½*

2798 A884 10z multicolored .25 .25
2799 A884 10z multicolored .25 .25
2800 A884 15z multicolored .25 .25
2801 A884 15z multicolored .25 .25
2802 A884 25z multicolored .35 .25
2803 A884 45z multicolored .60 .35
Nos. 2798-2803 (6) 1.95 1.60

Royal Castle, Warsaw — A885

1987, June 5

2804 A885 50z multicolored .60 .25

A souvenir sheet of 1 exists. Value $50.

A886

State Visit of Pope John Paul II — A887

1987, June 8 *Perf. 11*

2805 A886 15z shown .25 .25
2806 A886 45z Portrait, diff. .50 .30
a. Pair, #2805-2806 .75 .50

Souvenir Sheet

Perf. 12x11½

2807 A887 50z shown 1.00 1.00

No. 2806a has continuous design.

Cracow Restoration Type of 1982

1987, July 6 Litho. *Perf. 11½*

2809 A801 10z Barbican Gate, Wawel, horiz. .25 .25

Esperanto Language, Cent. — A890

1987, July 25 Litho. *Perf. 11½*

2811 A890 45z Ludwig L. Zamenhof .40 .25

A891

Poznan and Town Hall, by Stanislaw Wyspianski.

1987, Aug. 3

2812 A891 15z blk & pale salmon .25 .25

POZNAN '87, Aug. 8-16.

A892

No. 2813, Queen. No. 2814, Worker. No. 2815, Drone. No. 2816, Box hive, orchard. No. 2817, Bee collecting pollen. No. 2818, Beekeeper collecting honey.

1987, Aug. 20 Photo. *Perf. 11½x11*

2813 A892 10z multicolored .25 .25
2814 A892 10z multicolored .25 .25
2815 A892 15z multicolored .25 .25
2816 A892 15z multicolored .25 .25
2817 A892 40z multicolored .25 .50
2818 A892 50z multicolored .70 .25
Nos. 2813-2818 (6) 1.95 1.75

31st World Apiculture Congress, Warsaw.

Success of Polish Athletes at World Championship Events — A894

10z, Acrobatics, France. 15z, Kayak, Canada. 20z, Marksmanship, E. Germany. 25z, Wrestling, Hungary.

1987, Sept. 24 Litho. *Perf. 14*

2820 A894 10z multicolored .25 .25
2821 A894 15z multicolored .25 .25
2822 A894 20z multicolored .25 .25
2823 A894 25z multicolored .25 .25
Nos. 2820-2823 (4) 1.00 1.00

World War II Battles Type of 1984

Designs: No. 2824, Battle of Mokra, Julian Filipowicz. No. 2825, Battle scene near Oleszycami, Brig.-Gen. Josef Rudolf Kustron. 15z, Air battles over Warsaw, pilot Stefan Pawlikowski.

1987, Sept. 1 Photo. *Perf. 12x11½*

2824 A832 10z multicolored .25 .25
2825 A832 10z multicolored .25 .25
2826 A832 15z multicolored .35 .25
Nos. 2824-2826 (3) .85 .75

Jan Hevelius (1611-1687), Astronomer, and Constellations — A895

1987, Sept. 15 Litho. *Perf. 11½*

2827 A895 15z Hevelius, sextant, vert. .25 .25
2828 A895 40z shown .40 .30

Souvenir Sheet

1st Artificial Satellite, Sputnik, 30th Anniv. — A896

1987, Oct. 2 Photo. *Perf. 11½x11*

2829 A896 40z Stacionar 4 satellite 1.00 .75

World Post Day A897

Design: Ignacy Franciszek Przebendowski (1730-1791), postmaster general, and post office building, 19th cent., Krakowskie Przedmiescie, Warsaw.

1987, Oct. 9 Litho.

2830 A897 15z lt olive grn & rose claret .25 .25

Col. Stanislaw Wieckowski — A898

Photo. & Engr.

1987, Oct. 16 *Perf. 12x11½*

2831 A898 15z deep blue & blk .25 .25

Col. Wieckowski (1884-1942), physician and social reformer executed by the Nazis at Auschwitz.

HAFNIA '87 — A899

Fairy tales by Hans Christian Andersen (1805-1875): No. 2832, The Little Mermaid. No. 2833, The Nightingale. No. 2834, The Wild Swan. No. 2835, The Match Girl. 30z, The Snow Queen. 40z, The Brave Toy Soldier.

1987, Oct. 16 Photo. *Perf. 11x11½*

2832 A899 10z multicolored .25 .25
2833 A899 10z multicolored .25 .25
2834 A899 20z multicolored .35 .25
2835 A899 20z multicolored .35 .25
2836 A899 30z multicolored .35 .30
2837 A899 40z multicolored .50 .30
Nos. 2832-2837 (6) 2.05 1.60

Royalty Type of 1986

Photo. & Engr.

1987, Dec. 4 *Perf. 11*

2838 A875 10z Boleslaw I Chrobry .35 .25
2839 A875 15z Mieszko II .75 .25

No. 2838 exists with label. Value: mint $4, used $6.25.

New Year 1988 A900

1987, Dec. 14 Photo. *Perf. 11x11½*

2840 A900 15z multicolored .25 .25

Dragonflies — A901

No. 2841, Anax imperator. No. 2842, Libellula quadrimaculata, vert. No. 2843, Calopteryx splendens. No. 2844, Cordulegaster annulatus, vert. No. 2845, Sympetrum pedemontanum. No. 2846, Aeschna viridis, vert.

Perf. 11x11½, 11½x11

1988, Feb. 23 **Photo.**

2841 A901 10z multicolored .25 .25
2842 A901 15z multicolored .25 .25
2843 A901 15z multicolored .25 .25
2844 A901 20z multicolored .25 .25
2845 A901 30z multicolored .35 .25
2846 A901 50z multicolored .75 .40
Nos. 2841-2846 (6) 2.10 1.65

Cracow Restoration Type of 1982

1988, Mar. 8 Litho. *Perf. 11½x11*

2847 A801 15z Florianska Gate, 1300 .25 .25

Intl. Year of Graphic Design A903

1988, Apr. 28 Photo. *Perf. 11x11½*

2848 A903 40z multicolored .35 .25

Antique Clocks — A904

Clocks in the Museum of Artistic and Precision Handicrafts, Warsaw, and clockworks: No. 2849, Frisian wall clock, 17th cent., vert. No. 2850, Anniversary clock and rotary pendulum, 20th cent. No. 2851, Carriage clock, 18th cent., vert. No. 2852, Louis XV rococo bracket clock, 18th cent., vert. 20z, Pocket watch, 19th cent. 40z, Gdansk six-sided clock signed by Benjamin Zoll, 17th cent.

Perf. 11½x12, 12x11½

1988, May 19 **Photo.**

2849 A904 10z lt green & multi .25 .25
2850 A904 10z purple & multi .25 .25
2851 A904 15z dull org & multi .25 .25
2852 A904 15z brown & multi .25 .25
2853 A904 20z multicolored .35 .25
2854 A904 40z multicolored .50 .25
Nos. 2849-2854 (6) 1.85 1.50

1988 Summer Olympics, Seoul A905

1988, June 27 Photo. *Perf. 11x11½*

2855 A905 15z Triple jump .25 .25
2856 A905 20z Wrestling .25 .25
2857 A905 20z Two-man kayak .25 .25
2858 A905 25z Judo .25 .25
2859 A905 40z Shooting .40 .25
2860 A905 55z Swimming .50 .30
Nos. 2855-2860 (6) 1.90 1.55

See No. B148.

Natl. Industry A906

1988, Aug. 23 Photo. *Perf. 11x11½*

Size: 35x27mm

2861 A906 45z Los "Elk" aircraft .30 .25

State Aircraft Works, 60th anniv.
See Nos. 2867, 2871, 2881-2883.

16th European Regional FAO Conference, Cracow — A907

15z, Computers and agricultural growth. 40z, Balance between industry and nature.

1988, Aug. 22 *Perf. 11½x11*

2862 A907 15z multicolored .25 .25
2863 A907 40z multicolored .40 .25

World War II Battles Type of 1984

Battle scenes and commanders: 15z, Modlin, Brig.-Gen. Wiktor Thommee. No. 2865, Warsaw, Brig.-Gen. Walerian Czuma. No. 2866, Tomaszow Lubelski, Brig.-Gen. Antoni Szylling.

1988, Sept. 1 Photo. *Perf. 12x11½*

2864 A832 15z multicolored .25 .25
2865 A832 20z multicolored .25 .25
2866 A832 20z multicolored .25 .25
Nos. 2864-2866 (3) .75 .75

Natl. Industries Type of 1988

Design: Stalowa Wola Ironworks, 50th anniv.

1988, Sept. 5 *Perf. 11x11½*

Size: 35x27mm

2867 A906 15z multicolored .25 .25

World Post Day A909

Design: Postmaster Tomasz Arciszewski (1877-1955), Post and Telegraph Administration emblem used from 1919 to 1927.

1988, Oct. 9 Litho. *Perf. 11½x11*

2868 A909 20z multicolored .25 .25

Also printed in sheet of 12 plus 12 labels.

World War II Combat Medals — A910

No. 2869, Battle of Lenino Cross. No. 2870, On the Field of Glory Medal.

1988, Oct. 12 **Photo.**

2869 A910 20z multicolored .25 .25
2870 A910 20z multicolored .25 .25

See Nos. 2930-2931.

Natl. Industries Type of 1988

Air Force Medical Institute, 60th anniv.

1988, Oct. 12 *Perf. 11x11½*

Size: 38x27mm

2871 A906 20z multicolored .25 .25

Stanislaw Malachowski, Kazimierz Nestor Sapieha — A912

1988, Oct. 16 *Perf. 11*

2872 A912 20z multicolored .25 .25

Four Years' Sejm (Parliament) (1788-1792), bicent.

National Leaders — A913

No. 2873, Wincenty Witos. No. 2874, Ignacy Daszynski. No. 2875, Wojciech Korfanty. No. 2876, Stanislaw Wojciechowski. No. 2877, Julian Marchlewski. No. 2878, Ignacy Paderewski. No. 2879, Jozef Pilsudski. No. 2880, Gabriel Narutowicz.

1988, Nov. 11 *Perf. 12x11½*

2873 A913 15z multicolored .25 .25
2874 A913 15z multicolored .25 .25
2875 A913 20z multicolored .25 .25
2876 A913 20z multicolored .25 .25
2877 A913 20z multicolored .25 .25
2878 A913 200z multicolored .25 .25
2879 A913 200z multicolored .25 .25
2880 A913 200z multicolored .25 .25
a. Souvenir sheet of 3, #2878-2880 29.00 35.00
Nos. 2873-2880 (8) 2.00 2.00

Natl. independence, 70th anniv.

Natl. Industries Type of 1988

15z, Wharf, Gdynia. 20z, Industrialist Hipolit Cegielski, 1883 steam locomotive. 40z, Poznan fair grounds, Upper Silesia Tower.

1988 Photo. *Perf. 11x11½*

Size: 39x27mm

2881 A906 15z multicolored .25 .25
2882 A906 20z multicolored .25 .25

Size: 35x27mm

2883 A906 40z multicolored .25 .25
Nos. 2881-2883 (3) .75 .75

70th anniv. of Polish independence. Gdynia Port, 65th anniv (15z); Metal Works in Poznan, 142nd anniv. (20z); and Poznan Intl. Fair 60th anniv. (40z).

Issued: 15z, 12/12; 20z, 11/28; 40z, 12/21.

Royalty Type of 1986

10z, Rycheza. 15z, Kazimierz I Odnowiciel.

Photo. & Engr.

1988, Dec. 4 *Perf. 11*

2884 A875 10z multicolored .35 .25
2885 A875 15z multicolored .55 .25

New Year 1989 A914

1988, Dec. 9 Photo. *Perf. 11x11½*

2886 A914 20z multicolored .25 .25

Unification of Polish Workers' Unions, 40th Anniv. — A915

1988, Dec. 15 *Perf. 11½x12*

2887 A915 20z black & ver .25 .25

Fire Boats — A916

1988, Dec. 29 Litho. *Perf. 14*

2888 A916 10z Blysk .25 .25
2889 A916 15z Zar .25 .25
2890 A916 15z Plomien .25 .25
2891 A916 20z Strazak 4 .25 .25
2892 A916 20z Strazak 11 .25 .25
2893 A916 45z Strazak 25 .45 .40
Nos. 2888-2893 (6) 1.70 1.65

Horses — A917

1989, Mar. 6 Photo. *Perf. 11*

2894 A917 15z Lippizaner .25 .25
2895 A917 15z Arden, vert. .25 .25
2896 A917 20z English .25 .25
2897 A917 20z Arabian, vert. .25 .25
2898 A917 30z Wielkopolski .35 .25
2899 A917 70z Polish, vert. .75 .25
Nos. 2894-2899 (6) 2.10 1.50

Dogs — A918

No. 2900, Wire-haired dachshund. No. 2901, Cocker spaniel. No. 2902, Czech fousek pointer. No. 2903, Welsh terrier. No. 2904, English setter. No. 2905, Pointer.

1989, May 3 Photo. *Perf. 11½x11*

2900 A918 15z multicolored .25 .25
2901 A918 15z multicolored .25 .25
2902 A918 20z multicolored .25 .25
2903 A918 20z multicolored .25 .25
2904 A918 25z multicolored .35 .25
2905 A918 45z multicolored .85 .60
Nos. 2900-2905 (6) 2.20 1.85

Battle of Monte Cassino, 45th Anniv. — A919

Design: 80z, Gen. W. Anders. 165z, Battle of Falaise, General Stanislaw Maczek, horiz. 210z, Battle of Arnhem, Gen. Stanislaw Sosabowski, vert.

1989, May 18 *Perf. 11½x12*

2906 A919 80z multicolored .25 .25
2907 A919 165z multicolored .50 .25
2907A A919 210z multicolored .60 .25
Nos. 2906-2907A (3) 1.35 .75

1st Armored Division at the Battle of Falaise, 45th anniv. Battle of Arnhem, 45th anniv.

See No. 2968.

A 50z stamp for Gen. Grzegorz Korczynski was prepared but not released. Value: mint $25, cto $35.

Woman Wearing a Phrygian Cap — A920

1989, July 3 Litho. *Perf. 11½x11*

2908 A920 100z blk, dark red & dark ultra .25 .25
a. Souv. sheet of 2+2 labels 1.00 .75

French revolution bicent., PHILEXFRANCE '89. No. 2908 printed se-tenant with inscribed label picturing exhibition emblem. No. 2908a sold for 270z. Surcharge benefited the Polish Philatelic Union.

Polonia House, Pultusk — A921

1989, July 16 Photo. *Perf. 11½*

2909 A921 100z multicolored .35 .25

First Moon Landing, 20th Anniv. A922

1989, July 21 *Perf. 11x11½*

2910 A922 100z multicolored .35 .25
a. Souvenir sheet of 1 1.25 .50

No. 2910a exists imperf. Value $20.

Polish People's Republic, 45th Anniv. — A923

Winners of the Order of the Builders of People's Poland: No. 2911, Ksawery Dunikowski (1875-1964), artist. No. 2912, Stanislaw Mazur (1897-1964), agriculturist. No. 2913, Natalia Gasiorowska (1881-1964), historian. No. 2914, Wincenty Pstrowski (1904-1948), coal miner.

1989, July 21 *Perf. 11½x11*

2911 A923 35z multicolored .25 .25
2912 A923 35z multicolored .25 .25
2913 A923 35z multicolored .25 .25
2914 A923 35z multicolored .25 .25
Nos. 2911-2914 (4) 1.00 1.00

Security Service and Militia, 45th Anniv. A924

1989, July 21 *Perf. 11x11½*

2915 A924 35z dull brn & slate blue .25 .25

World Fire Fighting Congress, July 25-30, Warsaw — A925

1989, July 25 *Perf. 11½x11*

2916 A925 80z multicolored .35 .25

Daisy — A926

Designs: 60z, Juniper. 150z, Daisy. 500z, Wild rose. 1000z, Blue corn flower.

1989 Photo. *Perf. 11x12*

2917 A926 40z slate green .25 .25
2918 A926 60z violet blue .25 .25
2919 A926 150z rose lake .25 .25
2920 A926 500z bright violet .25 .25
2921 A926 1000z bright blue .25 .25
Nos. 2917-2921 (5) 1.25 1.25

Issue dates: 40z, 60z, Aug. 25. 150z, Dec. 4; 500z, 1000z, Dec. 19.

See Nos. 2978-2979, 3026. For surcharge see No. 2970.

World War II Battles Type of 1984

Battle scenes and commanders: No. 2922, Westerplatte, Capt. Franciszek Dabrowski. No. 2923, Hel, Artillery Capt. B. Przybyszewski. No. 2924, Kock, Brig.-Gen. Franciszek Kleeberg. No. 2925, Lwow, Brig.-Gen. Wladyslaw Langner.

1989, Sept. 1 *Perf. 12x11½*

2922 A832 25z multicolored .25 .25
2923 A832 25z multicolored .25 .25
2924 A832 35z multicolored .25 .25
2925 A832 35z multicolored .25 .25
Nos. 2922-2925 (4) 1.00 1.00

Nazi invasion of Poland, 50th anniv.

Caricature Museum — A927

1989, Sept. 15 Photo. *Perf. 11½x11*

2926 A927 40z multicolored .25 .25

Teaching Surgery at Polish Universities, Bicent., and Surgeon's Soc. Cent. — A928

Surgeons: 40z, Rafal Jozef Czerwiakowski (1743-1813), 1st professor of surgery and founder of the 1st surgical department, Jagellonian University, Cracow. 60z, Ludwik Rydygier (1850-1920), founder of the Polish Surgeons Society.

1989, Sept. 18 *Perf. 11½x12*

2927 A928 40z black & brt ultra .25 .25
2928 A928 60z black & brt green .25 .25

World Post Day — A929

Design: Emil Kalinski (1890-1973), minister of the Post and Telegraph from 1933-1939.

1989, Oct. 9 *Perf. 12x11½*

2929 A929 60z multicolored .35 .25

Printed se-tenant with label picturing postal emblem of the second republic.

WWII Decorations Type of 1988

Medals: No. 2930, Participation in the Struggle for Control of the Nation. No. 2931, Defense of Warsaw, 1939-45.

1989, Oct. 12 Photo. *Perf. 11½x11*

2930 A910 60z multicolored .25 .25
2931 A910 60z multicolored .25 .25

Royalty Type of 1986

20z, Boleslaw II Szczodry. 30z, Wladyslaw I Herman.

Photo. & Engr.

1989, Oct. 18 *Perf. 11*

2932 A875 20z multicolored .50 .30
2933 A875 30z multicolored .60 .50

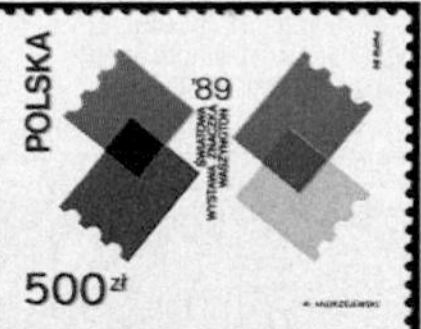

World Stamp Expo '89, Washington, DC, Nov. 17-Dec.3 — A930

1989, Nov. 14 Photo. *Perf. 11x11½*

2934 A930 500z multicolored .90 .35

Exists imperf. Value: mint $1.50, used $1.40.

Polish Red Cross Soc., 70th Anniv. — A931

1989, Nov. 17 *Perf. 11½x11*

2935 A931 200z blk, brt yel grn & scar .35 .25

Treaty of Versailles, 70th Anniv. A932

Design: State arms and representatives of Poland who signed the treaty, including Ignacy Jan Paderewski (1860-1941), pianist, composer, statesman, and Roman Dmowski (1864-1939), statesman.

1989, Nov. 21 *Perf. 11x11½*

2936 A932 350z multicolored .65 .25

Camera Shutter as the Iris of the Eye — A933

Designs: 40z, Photographer in silhouette, Maksymilian Strasz (1804-1870), pioneer of photography in Poland.

Perf. 11½x12, 12x11½

1989, Nov. 27

2937 A933 40z multicolored .25 .25
2938 A933 60z shown .25 .25

Photography, 150th anniv.

No. 2456 Surcharged

1989, Nov. 30 Photo. *Perf. 11x11½*

2939 A766 500z on 4z dark violet .25 .25

Flowers, Still-life Paintings in the National Museum, Warsaw A934

25z, Jan Ciaglinski. 30z, Wojciech Weiss. 35z, Antoni Kolasinski. 50z, Stefan Nacht-Samborski. 60z, Jozef Pankiewicz. 85z, Henryka Beyer. 110z, Wladyslaw Slewinski. 190z, Czeslaw Wdowiszewski.

1989, Dec. 18 *Perf. 13*

2940 A934 25z multicolored .25 .25
2941 A934 30z multicolored .25 .25
2942 A934 35z multicolored .25 .25
2943 A934 50z multicolored .25 .25
2944 A934 60z multicolored .25 .25
2945 A934 85z multicolored .25 .25

2946 A934 110z multicolored .25 .25
2947 A934 190z multicolored .50 .30
Nos. 2940-2947 (8) 2.25 2.05

Religious Art — A935

50z, Jesus, shroud. 60z, Two saints. 90z, Three saints. 150z, Jesus, Mary, Joseph. 200z, Madonna and Child Enthroned. 350z, Holy Family with angels.

1989, Dec. 21 ***Perf. 11½x11***
2948 A935 50z multicolored .25 .25
2949 A935 60z multicolored .25 .25
2950 A935 90z multicolored .25 .25

Perf. 11x11½
2951 A935 150z multicolored .25 .25
2952 A935 200z multicolored .30 .25
2953 A935 350z multicolored .50 .30
Nos. 2948-2953 (6) 1.80 1.55

Nos. 2951-2953 vert.

Republic of Poland

No. 2738 Surcharged

1990, Jan. 31 Photo. ***Perf. 11½x12***
2954 A828 350z on 15z rose brn .25 .25

Opera Singers — A936

Portraits: 100z, Krystyna Jamroz (1923-1986). 150z, Wanda Werminska (1900-1988). 350z, Ada Sari (1882-1968). 500z, Jan Kiepura (1902-1966).

1990, Feb. 9 ***Perf. 12x11½***
2955 A936 100z multicolored .25 .25
2956 A936 150z multicolored .25 .25
2957 A936 350z multicolored .25 .25
2958 A936 500z multicolored .35 .25
Nos. 2955-2958 (4) 1.10 1.00

Yachting A937

1990, Mar. 29 ***Perf. 11x11½***
2959 A937 100z shown .25 .25
2960 A937 200z Rugby .25 .25
2961 A937 400z High jump .25 .25
2962 A937 500z Figure skating .25 .25
2963 A937 500z Diving .25 .25
2964 A937 1000z Rhythmic gymnastics .55 .25
Nos. 2959-2964 (6) 1.80 1.50

Roman Kozlowski (1889-1977), Paleontologist — A938

1990, Apr. 17 Photo. ***Perf. 11x11½***
2965 A938 500z red & olive bis .30 .25

Pope John Paul II, 70th Birthday A939

1990, May 18 ***Perf. 11***
2966 A939 1000z multicolored .75 .35

Souvenir Sheet

First Polish Postage Stamp, 130th Anniv. — A940

Design includes No. 1 separated by simulated perforations from 1000z commemorative version at right.

1990, May 25 ***Perf. 11½***
2967 A940 1000z multicolored .75 .50

World War II Battle Type of 1989

Design: Battle of Narvik, 1940, General Z. Bohusz-Szyszko.

1990, May 28 ***Perf. 11½x12***
2968 A919 1500z multicolored .45 .25

World Cup Soccer Championships, Italy — A941

1990, June 8 ***Perf. 11½x11***
2969 A941 1000z multicolored .35 .30

No. 2918 Surcharged in Vermilion

1990, June 18 Photo. ***Perf. 11x12***
2970 A926 700z on 60z vio bl .25 .25

Memorial to Victims of June 1956 Uprising, Poznan — A942

1990, June 28 Photo. ***Perf. 12x11½***
2971 A942 1500z multicolored .30 .25

Social Insurance Institution, 70th Anniv. — A943

1990, July 5 ***Perf. 11x11½***
2972 A943 1500z multicolored .30 .25

Shells — A944

#2973, Mussel. #2974, Fresh water snail.

1990, July 16 ***11½, 14 (#2974)***
2973 A944 B (500z) dk pur .75 .25
2974 A944 A (700z) olive grn .75 .25

Katyn Forest Massacre, 50th Anniv. — A945

1990, July 20
2975 A945 1500z gray, red & blk .30 .25

Polish Meteorological Service — A946

1990, July 27 ***Perf. 11x11½***
2976 A946 500z shown .25 .25
2977 A946 700z Water depth gauge .35 .25

Flower Type of 1989

2000z, Nuphar. 5000z, German iris.

1990, Aug. 13 ***Die Cut***

Self Adhesive

2978 A926 2000z olive grn .35 .25
2979 A926 5000z violet .50 .25

World Kayaking Championships, Poznan — A947

Design: 1000z, One-man kayak.

1990, Aug. 22 Photo. ***Perf. 11x11½***
2980 A947 700z multicolored .25 .25
2981 A947 1000z multicolored .30 .25
a. Souv. sheet of 1 + label 2.50 2.50

A948

1990, Aug. 31 ***Perf. 11½x11***
2982 A948 1500z blk, red & gray .35 .25

Solidarity, 10th anniv.

A949

Flowers — No. 2983, Polemonium coeruleum. No. 2984, Nymphoides peltata. No. 2985, Dracocephalum ruyschiana. No. 2986, Helleborus purpurascens. No. 2987, Daphne cneorum. No. 2988, Dianthus superbus.

1990, Sept. 24 Photo. ***Perf. 11½x11***
2983 A949 200z multi .25 .25
2984 A949 700z multi .25 .25
2985 A949 700z multi .25 .25
2986 A949 1000z multi .25 .25
2987 A949 1500z multi .50 .35
2988 A949 1700z multi .65 .35
Nos. 2983-2988 (6) 2.15 1.70

Cmielow Porcelain Works, Bicentennial — A950

Designs: 700z, Platter, 1870-1887. 800z, Plate, 1887-1890, vert. No. 2991, Figurine, 1941-1944, vert. No. 2992, Cup, saucer, c. 1887. 1500z, Candy box, 1930-1990. 2000z, Vase, 1979, vert.

1990, Oct. 31 Photo. ***Perf. 11***
2989 A950 700z multicolored .25 .25
2990 A950 800z multicolored .25 .25
2991 A950 1000z multicolored .25 .25
2992 A950 1000z multicolored .25 .25
2993 A950 1500z multicolored .30 .25
2994 A950 2000z multicolored .75 .25
Nos. 2989-2994 (6) 2.05 1.50

Owls — A951

1990, Nov. 6 Litho. ***Perf. 14***
2995 A951 200z Athene noctua .25 .25
2996 A951 500z shown .35 .25
2997 A951 500z Strix aluco, winter .25 .25
2998 A951 1000z Asio flammeus .25 .25
2999 A951 1500z Asio otus .30 .40
3000 A951 2000z Tyto alba 1.10 .75
Nos. 2995-3000 (6) 2.50 2.15

Pres. Lech Walesa, 1983 Nobel Peace Prize Winner A952

1990, Dec. 12 Litho. ***Perf. 11x11½***
3001 A952 1700z multicolored .50 .25

A953

1990, Dec. 21 Photo. ***Perf. 11½x11***
3002 A953 1500z multicolored .30 .25

Polish participation in Battle of Britain, 50th anniv.

A954

Architecture: 700z, Collegiate Church, 12th cent., Leczyca. 800z, Castle, 14th cent., Reszel. 1500z, Town Hall, 16th cent., Chelmno. 1700z, Church of the Nuns of the Visitation, 18th cent., Warsaw.

1990, Dec. 28 Litho. ***Perf. 11½***
3003 A954 700z multicolored .25 .25
3004 A954 800z multicolored .25 .25
3005 A954 1500z multicolored .45 .25
3006 A954 1700z multicolored .45 .25
Nos. 3003-3006 (4) 1.40 1.00

No. 3006 printed with se-tenant label for World Philatelic Exhibition, Poland '93.

Art Treasures of the Natl. Gallery, Warsaw A955

Paintings: 500z, King Sigismund Augustus. 700z, The Adoration of the Magi, Pultusk Codex. 1000z, St. Matthew, Pultusk Codex. 1500z, Christ Removing the Moneychangers by Mikolaj Haberschrack. 1700z, The Annunciation. 2000z, The Three Marys by Haberschrack.

1991, Jan. 11 Photo. ***Perf. 11***
3007 A955 500z multicolored .25 .25
3008 A955 700z multicolored .25 .25
3009 A955 1000z multicolored .25 .25
3010 A955 1500z multicolored .25 .30
3011 A955 1700z multicolored .35 .25
3012 A955 2000z multicolored .60 .35
Nos. 3007-3012 (6) 1.95 1.65

Pinecones — A956

1991, Feb. 22 ***Perf. 12x11½***
3013 A956 700z Abies alba .25 .25
3014 A956 1500z Pinus strobus .30 .25

See Nos. 3163-3164, 3231-3232.

Radziwill Palace A957

1991, Mar. 3 Photo. ***Perf. 11x12***
3015 A957 1500z multicolored .85 .60

Admission to CEPT.

Royalty Type of 1986 Srchd. in Red

Designs: 1000z, Boleslaw III Krzywousty. 1500z, Wladyslaw II Wygnaniec.

Photo. & Engr.

1991, Mar. 25 ***Perf. 11***
3016 A875 1000z on 40z, grn & blk .45 .25
3017 A875 1500z on 50z, red vio & gray blk .65 .30

Not issued without surcharge.

Brother Albert (Adam Chmielowski, 1845-1916) — A958

1991, Mar. 29 Photo. ***Perf. 12x11½***
3018 A958 2000z multicolored .65 .30

Battle of Legnica, 750th Anniv. A959

Photo. & Engr.

1991, Apr. 9 ***Perf. 14½x14***
3019 A959 1500z multicolored .60 .30

See Germany No. 1635.

Polish Icons A960

Designs: 500z, 1000z, 1500z, Various paintings of Madonna and Child. 700z, 2000z, 2200z, Various paintings of Jesus.

1991, Apr. 22 Photo. ***Perf. 11***
3020 A960 500z multicolored .25 .25
3021 A960 700z multicolored .25 .25
3022 A960 1000z multicolored .25 .25
3023 A960 1500z multicolored .25 .25
3024 A960 2000z multicolored .45 .25
3025 A960 2200z multicolored .75 .35
Nos. 3020-3025 (6) 2.20 1.60

Flower Type of 1989

Design: 700z, Lily of the Valley.

1991, Apr. 26 Litho. ***Perf. 14***
3026 A926 700z dk blue green .25 .25

Royalty Type of 1986

Designs: 1000z, Boleslaw IV Kedzierzawy. 1500z, Mieszko III Stary.

Photo. & Engr.

1991, Apr. 30 ***Perf. 11x11½***
3033 A875 1000z brn red & black .60 .25
3034 A875 1500z brt bl & bluish blk .85 .40

A961

2000z, Title page of act. 2500z, Debate in the Sejm. 3000z, Adoption of Constitution, May 3, 1791, by Jan Matejko (1838-1893).

1991, May 2 Litho. ***Perf. 11½***
3035 A961 2000z brown & ver .30 .25
3036 A961 2500z brown & ver .45 .25

Souvenir Sheet

3037 A961 3000z multicolored .85 .50

May 3, 1791 Polish constitution, bicent.

A962

1991, May 6 Litho. ***Perf. 11½x11***
3038 A962 1000z multicolored 1.60 .75

Europa.

European Conference for Protection of Cultural Heritage, Cracow — A963

1991, May 27 Litho. ***Perf. 11½***
3039 A963 2000z blue & lake .45 .25

Sinking of the Bismarck, 50th Anniv. — A964

1991, May 27
3040 A964 2000z multicolored .50 .25

A965

Designs: 1000z, Pope John Paul II. 2000z, Pope wearing white.

1991, June 1 Litho. ***Perf. 11½x11***
3041 A965 1000z multicolored .40 .30
3042 A965 2000z multicolored .65 .40

A966

1991, June 21 Litho. ***Perf. 11½***
3043 A966 2000z multicolored .50 .25

Antarctic Treaty, 30th anniv.

Polish Paper Industry, 500th Anniv. A967

1991, July 8
3044 A967 2500z lake & gray .35 .25

Victims of Stalin — A968

1991, July 29 Litho. ***Perf. 11½x12***
3045 A968 2500z black & red .35 .25

Souvenir Sheet

Pope John Paul II — A969

1991, Aug. 15 Photo. ***Perf. 11½x11***

3046 A969 3500z multicolored 1.10 .50

Basketball, Cent. — A970

1991, Aug. 19 Litho. ***Perf. 11x11½***

3047 A970 2500z multicolored .45 .25

Leon Wyczolkowski (1852-1936), painter — A971

1991, Sept. 7 Photo. ***Perf. 11½x12***

3048 A971 3000z olive brown .40 .25
a. Sheet of 4 2.25 3.00

16th Polish Philatelic Exhibition, Bydgoszcz '91.

Kazimierz Twardowski (1866-1938) — A972

1991, Oct. 10 ***Perf. 11x11½***

3049 A972 2500z sepia & blk .50 .25

Butterflies — A973

No. 3050, Papilio machaon. No. 3051, Mormonia sponsa. No. 3052, Vanessa cardui. No. 3053, Iphiclides podalirius. No. 3054, Panaxia dominula. No. 3055, Nymphalis io. No. 3056, Aporia crataegi.

1991, Nov. 16 Litho. ***Perf. 12½***

3050	A973	1000z multi		.25	.25
3051	A973	1000z multi		.25	.25
3052	A973	1500z multi		.25	.25
3053	A973	1500z multi		.25	.25
3054	A973	2500z multi		.50	.30
3055	A973	2500z multi		.50	.30
a.		Block of 6, #3050-3055		2.25	1.60

Souvenir Sheet

3056 A973 15,000z multi 2.25 2.25

No. 3056 has a holographic image on the stamp and comes se-tenant with a Phila Nippon '91 label. The image may be affected by soaking in water. Varieties such as missing hologram, double and shifted images, and imperfs exist.

On Jan. 15, 1994, the Polish postal administration demonetized No. 3056.

Nativity Scene, by Francesco Solimena A974

1991, Nov. 25 Photo. ***Perf. 11***

3057 A974 1000z multicolored .45 .25

Polish Armed Forces at Tobruk, 50th Anniv. — A975

1991, Dec. 10 Photo. ***Perf. 11½***

3058 A975 2000z Gen. Stanislaw Kopanski .50 .25

A976

World War II Commanders: 2000z, Brig. Gen. Michal Tokarzewski-Karaszewicz (1893-1964). 2500z, Gen. Kazimierz Sosukowski (1885-1969). 3000z, Gen. Stefan Rowecki (1895-1944). 5000z, Gen. Tadeusz Komorowski (1895-1966). 6500z, Brig. Gen. Leopold Okulicki (1898-1946).

1991, Dec. 20 Litho.

3059	A976	2000z vermilion & blk	.35	.25
3060	A976	2500z violet bl & lake	.45	.25
3061	A976	3000z mag & dk bl	.55	.25
3062	A976	5000z olive & brn	1.00	.30
3063	A976	6500z brn org & brn	1.25	.35
		Nos. 3059-3063 (5)	3.60	1.40

A977

Boy Scouts in Poland, 80th anniv.: 1500z, Lord Robert Baden-Powell, founder of Boy Scouts. 2000z, Andrzej Malkowski (1889-1919), founder of Boy Scouts in Poland. 2500z, Scout standing guard, 1920. 3500z, Soldier scout, 1944.

1991, Dec. 30 Photo. ***Perf. 12x11½***

3064	A977	1500z multicolored	.30	.25
3065	A977	2000z multicolored	.30	.25
3066	A977	2500z multicolored	.35	.25
3067	A977	3500z multicolored	.75	.40
		Nos. 3064-3067 (4)	1.70	1.15

Royalty Type of 1986

Designs: 1500z, Kazimierz II Sprawiedliwy. 2000z, Leszek Bialy.

Photo. & Engr.

1992, Jan. 15 ***Perf. 11***

3068 A875 1500z olive green & brn .45 .25
3069 A875 2000z gray blue & blk 1.00 .35

Paintings A978

Paintings (self-portraits except for 2200z) by: 700z, Sebastien Bourdon. 1000z, Sir Joshua Reynolds. 1500z, Sir Gottfried Kneller. 2000z, Murillo. 2200z, Rubens. 3000z, Diego de Silva y Velazquez.

1992, Jan. 16 Photo.

3070	A978	700z multicolored	.25	.25
3071	A978	1000z multicolored	.25	.25
3072	A978	1500z multicolored	.25	.25
3073	A978	2000z multicolored	.25	.25
3074	A978	2200z multicolored	.50	.25
3075	A978	3000z multicolored	.55	.50
		Nos. 3070-3075 (6)	2.05	1.75

1992 Winter Olympics, Albertville A979

1992, Feb. 8 Litho. ***Perf. 11x11½***

3076 A979 1500z Skiing .35 .25
3077 A979 2500z Hockey .60 .35

See Nos. 3095-3098.

Tadeusz Manteuffel (1902-1970), Historian A980

1992, Mar. 5 Photo. ***Perf. 11½x11***

3078 A980 2500z brown .40 .25

Famous Poles A981

Designs: 1500z, Nicolaus Copernicus, astronomer. 2000z, Frederic Chopin, composer. 2500z, Henryk Sienkiewicz, novelist. 3500z, Marie Sklodowska Curie, scientist. 5000z, Casimir Funk, biochemist.

1992, Mar. 5 Litho. ***Perf. 11x11½***

3079	A981	1500z multicolored	.25	.25
3080	A981	2000z multicolored	.25	.25
3081	A981	2500z multicolored	.50	.25
3082	A981	3500z multicolored	.85	.50
		Nos. 3079-3082 (4)	1.85	1.25

Souvenir Sheet

3083 A981 5000z multicolored 2.75 .75

Expo '92, Seville (#3083).

Discovery of America, 500th Anniv. — A982

No. 3084, Columbus, chart. No. 3085, Chart, Santa Maria.

1992, May 5

3084	A982	1500z multicolored	.30	.25
3085	A982	3000z multicolored	.45	.25
a.		Pair, #3084-3085	1.50	1.10

Europa.

Waterfalls A983

2000z, Pstrag (trout). 2500z, Zimorodek (kingfisher). 3000z, Jelec (whiting). 3500z, Pluszcz.

1992, June 1 Litho. ***Perf. 11½***

3086	A983	2000z multicolored	.25	.25
3087	A983	2500z multicolored	.30	.25
3088	A983	3000z multicolored	.60	.35
3089	A983	3500z multicolored	.75	.35
		Nos. 3086-3089 (4)	1.90	1.20

Order of Virtuti Militari, Bicent. A984

Designs: 1500z, Prince Jozef Poniatowski (1763-1813). 3000z, Marshal Jozef Pilsudski (1867-1935). No. 3092, Black Madonna of Czestochowa.

1992, June 18 ***Perf. 11***

3090 A984 1500z multi .50 .25
3091 A984 3000z multi .75 .25

Souvenir Sheet

Imperf

3092 A984 20,000z multi 2.50 2.50

No. 3092 contains one 39x60mm stamp.

Children's Drawings of Love — A985

1500z, Heart between woman and man. 3000z, Butterfly, animals with sun and rain.

1992, June 26 Litho. *Perf. 11½x11*

3093 A985 1500z multicolored .25 .25
3094 A985 3000z multicolored .35 .25
a. Pair, #3093-3094 .75 .50

Olympics Type of 1992

1992, July 25 Litho. *Perf. 11x11½*

3095 A979 1500z Fencing .50 .25
3096 A979 2000z Boxing .25 .25
3097 A979 2500z Sprinting .35 .30
3098 A979 3000z Cycling .50 .35
Nos. 3095-3098 (4) 1.60 1.15

1992 Summer Olympics, Barcelona.

Souvenir Sheet

OLYMPHILEX '92, Barcelona — A986

1992, July 29

3099 A986 20,000z Runners 2.50 2.50

Exists imperf. Value: mint $6, used $7.

Janusz Korczak (1879-1942), Physician, Concentration Camp Victim — A987

1992, Aug. 5 Photo. *Perf. 11x11½*

3100 A987 1500z multicolored .35 .25

Polish Emigrants Assoc. World Meeting — A988

1992, Aug. 19 *Perf. 12x11½*

3101 A988 3000z multicolored .35 .25

World War II Combatants World Meeting — A989

1992, Aug. 14 *Perf. 11½x11*

3102 A989 3000z multicolored .35 .25

Stefan Cardinal Wyszynski (1901-1981) — A990

3000z, Pope John Paul II embracing person.

1992, Aug. 15 Litho.

3103 A990 1500z multicolored .45 .25
3104 A990 3000z multicolored .65 .50
a. Block of 2, #3103-3104 + 2 labels 1.75 1.25

6th World Youth Cong., Czestochowa (#3104).

Adampol, Polish Village in Turkey, 150th Anniv. A991

1992, Sept. 15 Photo. *Perf. 11x11½*

3105 A991 3500z multicolored .35 .25

World Post Day — A992

1992, Oct. 9 *Perf. 11½x11*

3106 A992 3500z multicolored .45 .25

Bruno Schulz (1892-1942), Author — A993

1992, Oct. 26 Litho. *Perf. 11x11½*

3107 A993 3000z multicolored .45 .25

Polish Sculptures, Natl. Museum, Warsaw A994

Designs: 2000z, Seated Girl, by Henryk Wicinski. 2500z, Portrait of Tytus Czyzewski, by Zbigniew Pronaszko. 3000z, Polish Nike, by Edward Wittig. 3500z, The Nude, by August Zamoyski.

1992, Oct. 29 *Perf. 11½*

3108 A994 2000z multicolored .25 .25
3109 A994 2500z multicolored .25 .25
3110 A994 3000z multicolored .30 .25
3111 A994 3500z multicolored .30 .25
a. Souvenir sheet of 4, #3108-3111 1.50 .75
Nos. 3108-3111 (4) 1.10 1.00

Polska '93 (#3111a).

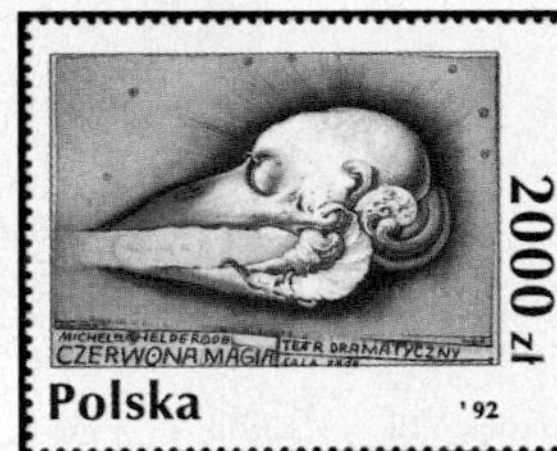

Posters — A995

Designs: 1500z, 10th Theatrical Summer in Zamosc, by Jan Mlodozeniec, vert. 2000z, Red Magic, by Franciszek Starowieyski. 2500z, Circus, by Waldemar Swierzy, vert. 3500z, Mannequins, by Henryk Tomaszewski.

1992, Oct. 30 *Perf. 13½*

3112 A995 1500z multicolored .25 .25
3113 A995 2000z multicolored .25 .25
3114 A995 2500z multicolored .35 .30
3115 A995 3500z multicolored .50 .40
Nos. 3112-3115 (4) 1.35 1.20

Illustrations by Edward Lutczyn A996

Designs: 1500z, Girl using snake as jump rope. 2000z, Boy on rocking horse with rockers reversed. 2500z, Boy using bird as arrow. 3500z, Girl with ladder, wind-up giraffe with keys on back.

1992, Nov. 16 Photo. *Perf. 11*

3116 A996 1500z multicolored .25 .25
3117 A996 2000z multicolored .25 .25
3118 A996 2500z multicolored .35 .25
3119 A996 3500z multicolored .75 .35
Nos. 3116-3119 (4) 1.60 1.10

Polska '93.

Home Army A997

1992, Nov. 20 Litho. *Perf. 13½*

3120 A997 1500z shown .30 .25
3121 A997 3500z Soldiers, diff. .30 .25
a. Pair, #3120-3121 .75 .75

Souvenir Sheet

3122 A997 20,000z +500z "WP AK," vert. 2.25 1.75

Christmas A998

1992, Nov. 25 Photo. *Perf. 11½*

3123 A998 1000z multicolored .25 .25

A999

1992, Dec. 5 Photo. *Perf. 11½x11*

3124 A999 1500z Wheat stalks .25 .25
3125 A999 3500z Food products .35 .25

Intl. Conference on Nutrition, Rome.

A1000

1992, Dec. 10 Litho.

3126 A1000 3000z multicolored .45 .30

Postal Agreement with the Sovereign Military Order of Malta, Aug. 1, 1991.

Natl. Arms — A1001

1992, Dec. 14 Photo. *Perf. 12x11½*

3127 A1001 2000z 1295 .25 .25
3128 A1001 2500z 15th cent. .25 .25
3129 A1001 3000z 18th cent. .30 .25
3130 A1001 3500z 1919 .30 .25
3131 A1001 5000z 1990 .60 .25
Nos. 3127-3131 (5) 1.70 1.25

Polish Philatelic Society, Cent. A1002

1993, Jan. 6 Photo. *Perf. 11½*

3132 A1002 1500z multicolored .35 .25

A1003

1993, Feb. 5 *Perf. 11½x11*

3133 A1003 3000z multicolored .55 .25

1993 Winter University Games, Zakopane.

A1004

Design: I Love You.

1993, Feb. 14
3134 A1004 1500z shown .30 .25
3135 A1004 3000z Heart on envelope .45 .25

Amber — A1005

Various pieces of amber.
20,000z, Necklace, map, horiz.

1993, Jan. 29 Litho. *Perf. 13½*
3136 A1005 1500z multicolored .25 .25
3137 A1005 2000z multicolored .25 .25
3138 A1005 2500z multicolored .35 .25
3139 A1005 3000z multicolored .75 .30
Nos. 3136-3139 (4) 1.60 1.05

Souvenir Sheet

3140 A1005 20,000z multi 2.25 1.40

Polska '93 (#3140).

Royalty Type of 1986

Designs: 1500z, Wladyslaw Laskonogi. 2000z, Henryk I Brodaty (1201-38). 2500z, Konrad I Mazowiecki. 3000z, Boleslaw V Wstydliwy.

Photo. & Engr.

1993, Mar. 25 *Perf. 11*
3141 A875 1500z yel grn & brn .25 .25
3142 A875 2000z red vio & ind .25 .25
3143 A875 2500z gray & black .50 .25
3144 A875 3000z yel brn & brn 1.10 .50
Nos. 3141-3144 (4) 2.10 1.25

#3144 printed with se-tenant label for Polska '93.

Battle of the Arsenal, 50th Anniv. — A1006

1993, Mar. 26 Photo. *Perf. 11½*
3145 A1006 1500z multicolored .40 .25

Intl. Medieval Knights' Tournament, Golub-Dobrzyn — A1007

Various knights on horseback.

1993, Mar. 29 *Perf. 11x11½*
3146 A1007 1500z multicolored .25 .25
3147 A1007 2000z multicolored .25 .25
3148 A1007 2500z multicolored .30 .30
3149 A1007 3500z multicolored .75 .25
Nos. 3146-3149 (4) 1.55 1.05

City of Szczecin, 750th Anniv. A1008

1993, Apr. 3 Litho. *Perf. 11½x11*
3150 A1008 1500z multicolored .40 .25

Warsaw Ghetto Uprising, 50th Anniv. — A1009

1993, Apr. 19 Litho. *Perf. 14*
3151 A1009 4000z gray, blk & yel .65 .30

See Israel No. 1163.

Europa — A1010

Contemporary art by: No. 3152, A. Szapocznikow and J. Lebenstein. No. 3153, S. Gierowski and B. Linke.

1993, Apr. 30 Photo. *Perf. 11x11½*
3152 A1010 1500z multicolored .35 .25
3153 A1010 4000z multicolored .50 .35
a. Pair, #3152-3153 .85 .50

Polish Parliament (Sejm), 500th Anniv. — A1011

1993, May 2 Photo. *Perf. 11*
3154 A1011 2000z multicolored .35 .25

Death of Francesco Nullo, 130th Anniv. — A1012

1993, May 5 Litho. *Perf. 11x11½*
3155 A1012 2500z multicolored .35 .25

Souvenir Sheet

Legend of the White Eagle — A1013

1993, May 7 Engr. *Perf. 13½*
3156 A1013 50,000z dark brn 5.50 5.50

Polska '93.

No. 3156 exists imperf., value: mint $9, used $12.

Cadets of Second Polish Republic — A1014

1993, May 21 Litho. *Perf. 11x11½*
3157 A1014 2000z multicolored .35 .25

Nicolaus Copernicus (1473-1543) — A1015

1993, May 24
3158 A1015 2000z multicolored .55 .30

Kornel Makuszymski, 40th Death Anniv. — A1016

Illustrations: 1500z, Lion, monkey. 2000z, Goat walking. 3000z, Monkey. 5000z, Goat riding bird.

1993, June 1
3159 A1016 1500z multicolored .25 .25
3160 A1016 2000z multicolored .35 .25
3161 A1016 3000z multicolored .50 .30
3162 A1016 5000z multicolored .85 .70
Nos. 3159-3162 (4) 1.95 1.50

Pine Cone Type of 1991

10,000z, Pinus cembra. 20,000z, Pinus sylvestris.

1993, June 30 Photo. *Perf. 12x11½*
3163 A956 10,000z multi .85 .25
3164 A956 20,000z multi 1.60 .30

Birds — A1017

No. 3165, Passer montanus. No. 3166, Motacilla alba. No. 3167, Dendrocopos syriacus. No. 3168, Carduelis carduelis. No. 3169, Sturnus vulgaris. No. 3170, Pyrrhula pyrrhula.

1993, July 15 Litho. *Perf. 11½*
3165 A1017 1500z multi .25 .25
3166 A1017 2000z multi .25 .25
3167 A1017 3000z multi .30 .25
3168 A1017 4000z multi .50 .30
3169 A1017 5000z multi 1.40 .90
3170 A1017 6000z multi 1.60 1.25
Nos. 3165-3170 (6) 4.30 3.20

Polish Natl. Anthem, Bicent. A1018

1993, July 20 Photo. *Perf. 11x11½*
3171 A1018 1500z multicolored .25 .25

See No. 3206.

Madonna and Child A1019

Designs: 1500z, Stone carving from Basilica, Lesna Podlaska. 2000z, Statue, Swieta Lipska.

Perf. 11x11½ Syncopated Type A
1993, Aug. 15
3172 A1019 1500z multicolored .50 .35
3173 A1019 2000z multicolored .85 .75

World Post Day — A1020

Photo. & Engr.

1993, Oct. 9 *Perf. 11½x11*
3174 A1020 2500z multicolored .55 .30

Polish Parachute Brigade A1021

Perf. 11x11½, Syncopated Type A
1993, Sept. 25 Photo.
3175 A1021 1500z multicolored .45 .25

Death of St. Hedwig (Jadwiga), 750th Anniv. — A1022

1993, Oct. 14 Litho. *Perf. 14*
3176 A1022 2500z multicolored .75 .35

See Germany No. 1816.

35th Intl. Jazz Jamboree — A1023

Perf. 11½ Syncopated Type A

1993, Sept. 27 **Litho.**

3177 A1023 2000z multicolored .50 .30

Souvenir Sheet

Election of Pope John Paul II, 15th Anniv. — A1024

1993, Oct. 16

3178 A1024 20,000z multicolored 2.25 2.00

A1025

1993, Nov. 11

3179 A1025 4000z Eagle, crown 1.10 .75

Souvenir Sheet

3180 A1025 20,000z Dove 2.25 1.75

Independence, 75th anniv. No. 3180 has a continuous design.

A1026

1993, Nov. 25

3181 A1026 1500z multicolored .45 .25

Christmas.

Posters A1027

Designs: 2000z, "Come and see Polish mountains." 5000z, Alban Berg Wozzeck.

1993, Dec. 10

3182 A1027 2000z multicolored .50 .35

3183 A1027 5000z multicolored .80 .50

See Nos. 3203-3204, 3259-3260.

"I Love You" — A1028

Perf. 11½x11 Syncopated Type A

1994, Jan. 14 **Litho.**

3184 A1028 1500z multicolored .55 .35

A1029

2500z, Cross-country skiing. 5000z, Ski jumping.

10,000z, Downhill skiing.

1994, Feb. 12 **Photo.** ***Perf. 11½x11***

3185 A1029 2500z multi .85 .35

3186 A1029 5000z multi 1.40 .70

Souvenir Sheet

3187 A1029 10,000z multi 1.90 1.40

1994 Winter Olympics, Lillehammer. Intl. Olympic Committee, cent. (#2187).

Kosciuszko Insurrection, Bicent. — A1030

Perf. 11½x11 Syncopated Type A

1994, Mar. 24 **Photo.**

3188 A1030 2000z multicolored .65 .40

Zamosc Academy, 400th Anniv. — A1031

1994, Mar. 15

3189 A1031 5000z brn, blk & gray .90 .50

Gen. Jozef Bem (1794-1850) — A1032

Perf. 11½ Syncopated Type A

1994, Mar. 14

3190 A1032 5000z multicolored .90 .50

Royalty Type of 1986 with Denomination at Bottom

Photo. & Engr.

1994, Apr. 15 ***Perf. 11***

3191 A875 2500z Leszek Czarny .75 .75

3192 A875 5000z Przemysl II 1.25 .75

Inventions A1033

Europa: 2500z, Petroleum lamp, invented by I. Lukasiewicz (1822-82). 6000z, Astronomical sighting device, with profile of Copernicus (1473-1543).

Perf. 11½x11 Syncopated Type A

1994, Apr. 30 **Litho.**

3193 A1033 2500z multicolored .50 .35

3194 A1033 6000z multicolored 1.10 .70

St. Mary's Sanctuary A1034

4000z, Our Lady of Kalwaria Zebrzydowska.

Perf. 11½x11 Syncopated Type A

1994, May 16 **Litho.**

3195 A1034 4000z multicolored 1.10 .70

Battle of Monte Cassino, 50th Anniv. A1035

Perf. 11x11½ Syncopated Type A

1994, May 18

3196 A1035 6000z multicolored .80 .40

Traditional Dances A1036

Perf. 11½ Syncopated Type A

1994, May 25

3197 A1036 3000z Mazurka .50 .35

3198 A1036 4000z Goralski .85 .75

3199 A1036 9000z Krakowiak 1.10 .75

Nos. 3197-3199 (3) 2.45 1.85

ILO, 75th Anniv. A1037

Perf. 11½x11 Syncopated Type A

1994, June 7 **Litho.**

3200 A1037 6000z multicolored .65 .30

Polish Electricians Assoc., 75th Anniv. A1038

Perf. 11x11½ Syncopated Type A

1994, June 10

3201 A1038 4000z multicolored .75 .35

1994 World Soccer Cup Championships, U.S. — A1039

Perf. 11½x11 Syncopated Type A

1994, June 17

3202 A1039 6000z multicolored .90 .50

Poster Art Type of 1993

4000z, Mr. Fabre, by Wiktor Gorka. 6000z, VIII OISTAT Congress, by Hubert Hilscher, horiz.

Perf. 11x11½, 11½x11 Syncopated Type A

1994, July 4 **Litho.**

3203 A1027 4000z multicolored .55 .35

3204 A1027 6000z multicolored .75 .50

Florian Znaniecki (1882-1958), Sociologist A1040

Perf. 11½ Syncopated Type A

1994, July 15 **Litho.**

3205 A1040 9000z multicolored .75 .45

Polish Natl. Anthem Type of 1993

Design: 2500z, Battle of Raclawice, 1794.

1994, July 20 **Photo.** ***Perf. 11x11½***

3206 A1018 2500z multicolored .40 .25

A1042

Perf. 11½x11 Syncopated Type A

1994, Aug. 1 **Litho.**

3207 A1042 2500z Natl. arms .55 .25

Warsaw Uprising, 50th anniv.

PHILAKOREA '94 — A1043

1994, Aug. 16
3208 A1043 4000z multicolored .70 .35

Stamp Day.

Basilica of St. Brigida, Gdansk A1044

1994, Aug. 28
3209 A1044 4000z multicolored 1.00 .70

Modern Olympic Games, Cent. A1045

Perf. 11x11½ Syncopated Type A
1994, Sept. 5
3210 A1045 4000z multicolored .85 .70

Krzysztof Komeda (1931-69), Jazz Muscian — A1046

Perf. 11½ Syncopated Type A
1994, Sept. 22 **Litho.**
3211 A1046 6000z multicolored .85 .50

Aquarium Fish — A1047

Designs: No. 3212a, Ancistrus dolichopterus. b, Pterophyllum scalare. c, Xiphophorus helleri, paracheirodon innesi. d, Poecilia reticulata.

Perf. 11½x11 Syncopated Type A
1994, Sept. 28 **Litho.**
3212 Strip of 4 2.40 1.75
a.-d. A1047 4000z any single .50 .40

World Post Day — A1048

1994, Oct. 9
3213 A1048 4000z Postal Arms, 1858 .85 .50

St. Maximilian Kolbe (1894-1941), Concentration Camp Victim — A1049

1994, Oct. 24 **Photo.** ***Perf. 11x11½***
3214 A1049 2500z multicolored .60 .30

Pigeons A1050

a, Mewka polska. b, Krymka biatostacka. c, Srebrniak polski. d, Sokot gdanski. 10,000z, Polski golab pocztowy.

Perf. 11x11½ Syncopated Type A
1994, Oct. 28 **Litho.**
3215 Block of 4 2.50 1.60
a.-b. A1050 4000z any single .50 .35
c.-d. A1050 6000z any single .50 .35

Souvenir Sheet
3216 A1050 10,000z multicolored 1.40 .85

Christmas A1051

Perf. 11x11½ Syncopated Type A
1994, Nov. 25 **Litho.**
3217 A1051 2500z multicolored .85 .50

European Union A1052

1994, Dec. 15
3218 A1052 6000z multicolored 1.10 .70

Love Stamp — A1053

Perf. 11½x11 Syncopated Type A
1995, Jan. 31 **Litho.**
3219 A1053 35g dk bl & rose car .85 .40

Hydro-Meteorological Service, 75th Anniv. — A1054

Perf. 11x11½ Syncopated Type A
1995, Jan. 31
3220 A1054 60g multicolored .75 .35

Poland's Renewed Access to the Sea, 75th Anniv. A1055

1995, Feb. 10
3221 A1055 45g multicolored .50 .30

Royalty Type of 1986 with Denomination at Bottom

35g, Waclaw II. 45g, Wladyslaw I Lotiek. 60g, Kazimierz III, the Great. 80g, Ludwik Wegierski.

Photo. & Engr.
1995, Feb. 28 ***Perf. 11***
3222 A875 35g multicolored .35 .25
3223 A875 45g multicolored .45 .25
3224 A875 60g multicolored .60 .30
3225 A875 80g multicolored 1.10 .50
Nos. 3222-3225 (4) 2.50 1.30

St. John of God (1495-1550), Initiator of Order — A1056

Perf. 12x11½ Syncopated Type A
1995, Mar. 8 **Litho.**
3226 A1056 60g multicolored .55 .30

Easter Eggs A1057

Each stamp showing various designs on 3 eggs.

Perf. 11½ Syncopated Type A
1995, Mar. 16 **Background Color**
3227 A1057 35g dull red .35 .25
3228 A1057 35g violet .35 .25
3229 A1057 45g bright blue .45 .35
3230 A1057 45g blue green .45 .35
Nos. 3227-3230 (4) 1.60 1.20

Pine Cone Type of 1991
1995, Mar. 27 **Photo.** ***Perf. 11½***
3231 A956 45g Larix decidua .30 .25
3232 A956 80g Pinus mugo .45 .25

Katyn Forest Massacre, 55th Anniv. A1058

Perf. 11½ Syncopated Type A
1995, Apr. 13 **Litho.**
3233 A1058 80g multicolored .50 .30

Europa A1060

Perf. 11x11½ Syncopated Type A
1995, Apr. 28 **Litho.**
3234 A1060 35g shown .40 .30
3235 A1060 80g Flowers in helmet .65 .40

Ruturn of Western Polish Territories, 50th Anniv. — A1061

Perf. 11½ Syncopated Type A
1995, May 6 **Litho.**
3236 A1061 45g multicolored .40 .25

Pope John Paul II, 75th Birthday A1062

Perf. 11½ Syncopated Type A
1995, May 18 **Litho.**
3237 A1062 80g multicolored .90 .70

Groteska Theatre of Fairy Tales, 50th Anniv. — A1063

Designs: No. 3238, Two performing. No. 3239, Stage scene. No. 3240, Puppet leaning on barrel, vert. No. 3241, Character holding flower, vert.

1995, May 25
3238 35g multicolored .35 .30
3239 35g multicolored .35 .30
a. A1063 Pair, #3238-3239 1.10 .75
3240 45g multicolored .45 .30
3241 45g multicolored .45 .30
a. A1063 Pair, #3240-3241 .90 .65
Nos. 3238-3241 (4) 1.60 1.20

Polish Railways, 150th Anniv. A1064

Designs: 35g, Warsaw-Vienna steam train, 1945. 60g, Combustion fuel powered train, 1927. 80g, Electric train, 1936. 1z, Euro City Sobieski, Warsaw-Vienna, 1992.

1995, June 9
3242 35g multicolored .35 .25
3243 60g multicolored .35 .25
a. A1064 Pair, #3242-3243 .75 .50
3244 80g multicolored .50 .35
3245 1z multicolored .85 .55
a. A1064 Pair, #3244-3245 1.50 1.00
Nos. 3242-3245 (4) 2.05 1.40

UN, 50th Anniv. A1065

Perf. 11½ Syncopated Type A

1995, June 26 **Litho.**
3246 A1065 80g multicolored .80 .35

Handlowy Bank, Warsaw, 125th Anniv. — A1066

1995, June 30
3247 A1066 45g multicolored .40 .25

Polish Peasants' Movement, Cent. A1067

Perf. 11½ Syncopated Type A

1995, July 13 **Litho.**
3248 A1067 45g multicolored .45 .25

Polish Natl. Anthem, Bicent. A1068

1995, July 20 Photo. ***Perf. 11x11½***
3249 A1068 35g multicolored .40 .25

Deciduous Trees — A1069

1995, July 31 ***Perf. 12x11½***
3250 A1069 B Quercus petraea .85 .25
3251 A1069 A Sorbus aucuparia .85 .25

On day of issue #3250 was valued at 35g; #3551at 45g.

St. Mary of Consolation, Holy Trinity and All Saints Basilica, Lezajsk A1070

Perf. 11½ Syncopated Type A

1995, Aug. 2 **Litho.**
3252 A1070 45g multicolored .35 .25

Battle of Warsaw, 75th Anniv. A1071

Design: 45g, Jósef Pilsudski (1867-1935).

1995, Aug. 14
3253 A1071 45g multicolored .40 .25

Horse-Equipage Driving World Championships, Poznan — A1072

Designs: 60g, Horses pulling carriage, men in formal attire. 80g, Marathon race through water, around pylons.

Perf. 11½ Syncopated Type A

1995, Aug. 23 **Litho.**
3254 A1072 60g multicolored .70 .35
3255 A1072 80g multicolored .70 .50
a. Pair, #3254-3255 1.50 .95

18th All Polish Philatelic Exhibition, Warsaw A1073

Designs: 35g, Warsaw Technical University, School of Architecture. 1z, Warsaw Castle Place, Old Town, horiz.

Perf. 11½ Syncopated Type A

1995, Aug. 30 **Litho.**
3256 A1073 35g multicolored .35 .25

Souvenir Sheet

3257 A1073 1z multicolored 1.40 1.10

11th World Congress of Space Flight Participants, Warsaw A1074

Perf. 11½ Syncopated Type A

1995, Sept. 10 **Litho.**
3258 A1074 80g multicolored .55 .40

Poster Art Type of 1993

35g, The Crazy Locomotive, by Jan Sawka. 45g, The Wedding, by Eugeniusz Get Stankiewicz.

Perf. 11½ Syncopated Type A

1995, Sept. 27 **Litho.**
3259 A1027 35g multicolored .30 .25
3260 A1027 45g multicolored .40 .30

13th Intl. Chopin Piano Festival A1076

Perf. 11½ Syncopated Type A

1995, Oct. 1 **Litho.**
3261 A1076 80g Polonaise score .65 .40

A1077

World Post Day 45g, Postman in uniform, Polish Kingdom. 80g, Feather, wax seal of Stanislaw II Poniatowski.

1995, Oct. 9
3262 A1077 45g multicolored .30 .25
3263 A1077 80g multicolored .40 .30

A1078

1995, Oct. 26
3264 A1078 45g multicolored .35 .25

Acrobatic Sports World Championships, Wroclaw.

Janusz Groszkowski (1898-1984), Physicist — A1079

Perf. 11½ Syncopated Type A

1995, Nov. 10 **Litho.**
3265 A1079 45g multicolored .35 .25

Christmas — A1080

1995, Nov. 27
3266 35g Nativity .30 .25
3267 45g Magi, tree .40 .25
a. A1080 Pair, Nos. 3266-3267 .75 .40

No. 3267a is a continuous design.

Songbird Chicks — A1081

Designs: a, 35g, Parus caeruleus. b, 45g, Aegithalos caudatus. c, 60g, Lanius excubitor. d, 80g, Coccothraustes.

1995, Dec. 15
3268 A1081 Block of 4, #a.-d. 2.25 1.20

See No. 3377.

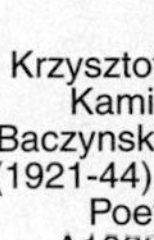

Krzysztof Kamil Baczynski (1921-44), Poet A1082

Perf. 11½ Syncopated Type A

1996, Jan. 22 **Litho.**
3269 A1082 35g multicolored .45 .25

Love — A1083

1996, Jan. 31
3270 A1083 40g Cherries .40 .25

Architecture A1084

40g, Romanesque style church, Inowlodz, 11-12th cent. 55g, Gothic syle, St. Virgin Mary's Church, Cracow, 14th cent. 70g, Renaissance period, St. Sigismundus Chapel of Cracow, Wawel Castle, 1519-33. 1z, Order of Holy Sacrament Nuns Baroque Church, Warsaw, 1688-92.

Perf. 11½ Syncopated Type A

1996, Feb. 27 **Litho.**
3271 A1084 40g multicolored .30 .25
3272 A1084 55g multicolored .35 .25
3273 A1084 70g multicolored .45 .30
3274 A1084 1z multicolored .85 .60
Nos. 3271-3274 (4) 1.95 1.40

Polish Sailing Ships — A1085

Designs: a, 40g, Topmast schooner, "Oceania," 1985. b, 55g, Staysail schooner, "Zawisza Czarny," 1961. c, 70g, Schooner, "General Zaruski," 1939. d, 75g, Brig, "Fryderyk Chopin," 1992.

1996, Mar. 11
3275 A1085 Strip of 4, #a.-d. 1.75 1.40

Warsaw, Capital of Poland, 400th Anniv. A1086

1996, Mar. 18
3276 A1086 55g multicolored .50 .25

Signs of the Zodiac — A1087

1996 Photo. *Perf. 12x11½*

3277 A1087 5g Aquarius .25 .25
3278 A1087 10g Pisces .25 .25
3279 A1087 20g Taurus .25 .25
3280 A1087 25g Gemini .25 .25
3281 A1087 30g Cancer .25 .25
3282 A1087 40g Virgo .25 .25
3283 A1087 50g Leo .35 .25
3284 A1087 55g Libra .40 .25
3285 A1087 70g Aries .50 .25
3286 A1087 1z Scorpio .70 .25
3287 A1087 2z Sagittarius 1.40 .25
3288 A1087 5z Capricorn 3.50 .30
Nos. 3277-3288 (12) 8.35 3.05

Design will dissolve when soaked on at least three denominations, 5g, 20g and 25g, from the second printing which is on fluorescent paper.

Issued: 70g, 3/21; 20g, 4/21; 25g, 5/10; 30g, 5/20; 40g, 50g, 5/31; 55g, 6/10; 1z, 6/20; 2z, 6/28; 5z, 7/10; 5g, 7/19; 10g, 7/31.

Famous Women A1088

Europa: 40g, Hanka Ordonówa (1902-50), singer. 1z, Pola Negri (1896-1987), actress.

Perf. 11½ Syncopated Type A

1996, Apr. 30 Litho.

3289 A1088 40g multicolored .35 .25
3290 A1088 1z multicolored .90 .55

3rd Silesian Uprising, 75th Anniv. A1089

Perf. 11 ½ Syncopated Type A

1996, May 2 Litho.

3291 A1089 55g multicolored .50 .25

UNICEF, 50th Anniv. — A1090

Illustrations from tales of Jan Brzechwa: No. 3292, Cat and mouse. No. 3293. Man at table, waiters. No. 3294, People with "onion heads." No. 3295, Chef, duck, vegetables at table. No. 3296, Man talking to bird with human head. No. 3297, Fox standing in front of bears.

1996, May 31

3292 A1090 40g multicolored .30 .25
3293 A1090 40g multicolored .30 .25
3294 A1090 55g multicolored .40 .25
3295 A1090 55g multicolored .40 .25
3296 A1090 70g multicolored .50 .35
3297 A1090 70g multicolored .50 .35
Nos. 3292-3297 (6) 2.40 1.70

Drawings by Stanislaw Noakowski (1867-1928) A1091

Designs: 40g, Renaissance building. 55g, Renaissance bedroom. 70g, Gothic village church. 1z, Stanislaw August Library, 18th cent.

1996, June 28

3298 A1091 40g multicolored .35 .25
3299 A1091 55g multicolored .35 .25
3300 A1091 70g multicolored .50 .25
3301 A1091 1z multicolored .90 .90
Nos. 3298-3301 (4) 2.10 1.65

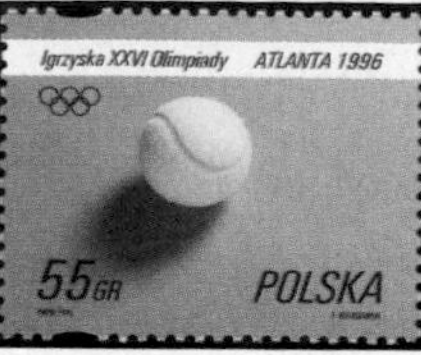

1996 Summer Olympic Games, Atlanta A1092

40g, Discus as medallion, vert. 55g, Tennis ball. 70g, Polish flag, Olympic rings. 1z, Tire & wheel of mountain bicycle, vert.

1996, July 5

3302 A1092 40g multicolored .25 .25
3303 A1092 55g multicolored .30 .25
3304 A1092 70g multicolored .50 .35
3305 A1092 1z multicolored .90 .35
Nos. 3302-3305 (4) 1.95 1.20

OLYMPHILEX '96, Atlanta — A1093

1996, July 5

3306 A1093 1z multicolored .60 .35

National Anthem, Bicent. A1094

1996, July 20 Photo. *Perf. 11x11½*

3307 A1094 40g multicolored .35 .25

Madonna and Child, St. Mary's Ascension Church, Przeczyce A1095

Perf. 11½x11 Syncopated Type A

1996, Aug. 2 Litho.

3308 A1095 40g multicolored .45 .25

Royalty Type of 1986

Designs: 40g, Jadwiga. 55g, Wladyslaw II Jagiello. 70g, Wladyslaw II Warnenczyk. 1z, Kazimierz Jagiellonczyk.

1996, Aug. 29 Engr. *Perf. 11*

3309 A875 40g olive brown & brown .35 .25
3310 A875 55g red violet & violet .35 .25
3311 A875 70g gray & black .50 .35
3312 A875 1z yellow green & green .80 .60
Nos. 3309-3312 (4) 2.00 1.45

Mountain Scenes, Tatra Natl. Park A1096

Perf. 11½ Syncopated Type A

1996, Sept. 5 Litho.

3313 A1096 40g Giewont .25 .25
3314 A1096 40g Krzesanica .25 .25
3315 A1096 55g Swinica .30 .25
3316 A1096 55g Koscielec .30 .25
3317 A1096 70g Rysy .50 .35
3318 A1096 70g Miguszowieckie Szczyty .50 .35
Nos. 3313-3318 (6) 2.10 1.70

Zbigniew Seifert (1946-79), Jazz Musician A1097

Perf. 11½ Syncopated Type A

1996, Sept. 25 Litho.

3319 A1097 70g multicolored .50 .30

Post and Telecommunications Museum, Wroclaw, 75th Anniv. — A1098

Paintings: 40g, Horse Exchange and Post Station, by M. Watorski. 1z+20g, Stagecoach in Jagniatkowo, by Prof. Täger.

1996, Oct. 9 Photo. *Perf. 12x11½*

3320 A1098 40g multicolored .35 .25

Souvenir Sheet

Perf. 11x11½

3321 A1098 1z +20g multi 1.50 .90

Nos. 3321 contains one 43x31mm stamp.

Christmas A1099

Perf. 11½ Syncopated Type A

1996, Nov. 27 Litho.

3322 A1099 40g Santa in sleigh .30 .25
3323 A1099 55g Carolers .40 .30

Bison Bonasus A1100

1996, Dec. 4

3324 A1100 55g shown .35 .25
3325 A1100 55g Facing .35 .25
3326 A1100 55g Two animals .35 .25
3327 A1100 55g Adult male .35 .25
a. Strip of 4, #3324-3327 2.00 1.40

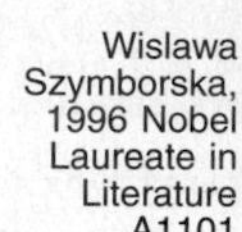

Wislawa Szymborska, 1996 Nobel Laureate in Literature A1101

1996, Dec. 10

3328 A1101 1z multicolored .70 .45

Queen of Hearts A1102

Perf. 11x11½ Syncopated Type A

1997, Jan. 14 Litho.

3329 A1102 B King of Hearts .75 .25
3330 A1102 A Queen of Hearts .75 .35
a. Pair, #3329-3330 1.60 .65
Complete booklet, 4 #3330a 6.50

Nos. 3329-3330 sold for 40g and 55g, respectively, on day of issue.

Easter Traditions A1103

50g, Man, woman in traditional costumes holding palms. 60g, Decorating eggs. 80g, Blessing the Easter meal. 1.10z, Man pouring water on woman.

Perf. 11x11½ Syncopated Type A

1997, Mar. 14 Litho.

3331 A1103 50g multicolored .35 .25
3332 A1103 60g multicolored .45 .25
3333 A1103 80g multicolored .60 .30
3334 A1103 1.10z multicolored .80 .35
Nos. 3331-3334 (4) 2.20 1.15

A1104

St. Adalbert (956-97) A1105

50g, St. Adalbert among heathen, horiz.

1997 Engr. *Perf. 11x11½x 11½x11*

3335 A1104 50g brown .35 .25
3336 A1104 60g slate .45 .25
3337 A1105 1.10z purple .80 .50
Nos. 3335-3337 (3) 1.60 1.00

See Czech Republic No. 3012, Germany No. 1964, Hungary No. 3569, Vatican City No. 1040.

Issued: #3335-3336, 4/19; #3337, 4/23.

Stories and Legends A1106

Europa: 50g, shown. 1.10z, Mermaid.

Perf. 11½ Syncopated Type A

1997, May 5

3338 A1106 50g multicolored .40 .25
3339 A1106 1.10z multicolored .85 .50

46th Eucharistic Congress — A1107

1997, May 6

3340 A1107 50g multicolored .50 .30

Souvenir Sheet

Pope John Paul II — A1108

Perf. 11x11½ Syncopated Type A

1997, May 28

3341 A1108 1.10z multicolored 2.00 1.60

City of Gdansk, 1000th Anniv. — A1109

Design: 1.10z, View of city, horiz.

Perf. 11½x11, 11x11½

1997, Apr. 18 **Engr.**

3342 A1109 50g multicolored .35 .25

Souvenir Sheet

3343 A1109 1.10z multicolored 1.75 1.40

No. 3343 exists imperf., value $12.

Polish Country Estates — A1110

1997 **Photo.** ***Perf. 11½x12***

3344 A1110 50g Lopusznej .35 .25
3345 A1110 60g Zyrzyna .45 .25
3346 A1110 1.10z Ozarowie .80 .40
3347 A1110 1.70z Tulowicach 1.20 .50
3348 A1110 2.20z Kuznocinie 1.60 .60
3349 A1110 10z Koszutach 7.00 2.25
Nos. 3344-3349 (6) 11.40 4.25

Issued: 50g, 60g, 4/26/97; 1.10z, 1.70z, 2.20z, 10z, 5/23/97.

See Nos. 3385-3390, 3463-3467, 3511-3514, 3571-3574

PACIFIC 97 — A1111

Design: San Francisco-Oakland Bay Bridge.

Perf. 11½ Syncopated Type A

1997, May 20 **Litho.**

3350 A1111 1.30z multicolored .95 .45

Bats A1113

50g, Plecotus auritus. 60g, Nyctalus noctula. 80g, Myotis myotis. 1.30z, Vespertilio murinus.

1997, May 30

3352 A1113 50g multicolored .35 .25
3353 A1113 60g multicolored .45 .25
3354 A1113 80g multicolored .55 .30
3355 A1113 1.30z multicolored .95 .65
Nos. 3352-3355 (4) 2.30 1.45

Jagiellon University School of Theology, 600th Anniv. A1114

Painting by Jan Matejko.

1997, June 6 ***Perf. 11***

3356 A1114 80g multicolored .60 .30

Polish Settlement in Argentina, Cent. — A1115

Perf. 11½ Syncopated Type A

1997, June 6

3357 A1115 1.40z multicolored 1.00 .45

Paintings, by Juliusz Kossak (1824-99) — A1116

Designs: 50g, Man on horse, woman, child. 60g, Men on galloping horses, carriage. 80g, Feeding horses in stable. 1.10z, Man with horses.

1997, July 4 **Photo.** ***Perf. 11***

3358 A1116 50g multicolored .35 .25
3359 A1116 60g multicolored .45 .25
3360 A1116 80g multicolored .65 .30
3361 A1116 1.10z multicolored .80 .50
Nos. 3358-3361 (4) 2.25 1.30

Polish Natl. Anthem, Bicent. A1117

Designs: 50g, People in city waving hats at Gen. Jan Henryk Dabrowski.
1.10z, Words to Natl. Anthem, Dabrowski.

1997, July 18 ***Perf. 11x11½***

3362 A1117 50g multicolored .35 .25

Souvenir Sheet

3363 A1117 1.10z multicolored 1.10 .70

Pawel Edmund Strzelecki (1797-1873), Geographer — A1118

Perf. 11½ Syncopated Type A

1997, July 20 **Litho.**

3364 A1118 1.50z multicolored 1.10 .50

Virgin of Consolation, Church of the Virgin of Consolation and St. Michael Archangel, Gorka Duchowna A1119

Perf. 11½x11 Syncopated Type A

1997, Aug. 28

3365 A1119 50g multicolored .50 .25

Royalty Type of 1986

Kings: 50g, Jan I Olbracht (1459-1501). 60g, Aleksander (1461-1506). 80g, Sigismundus I Stary (1467-48). 1.10z, Sigismundus II Augustus (1520-72).

1997, Sept. 22 **Engr.** ***Perf. 11***

3366 A875 50g brn & dk brn .35 .25
3367 A875 60g blue & dp brn .45 .25
3368 A875 80g grn & dk slate .55 .30
3369 A875 1.10z mag & dk mag .75 .55
Nos. 3366-3369 (4) 2.10 1.35

Mieczyslaw Kosz (1944-73), Jazz Musician — A1120

Perf. 11½ Syncopated Type A

1997, Oct. 3 **Litho.**

3370 A1120 80g multicolored .55 .30

World Post Day — A1121

1997, Oct. 9

3371 A1121 50g multicolored .50 .25

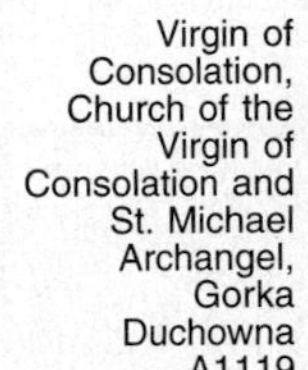

Moscow '97 Intl. Philatelic Exhibition A1122

Perf. 11½ Syncopated Type B

1997, Oct. 13

3372 A1122 80g multicolored .70 .35

Theater Poster Art — A1123

#3373, "Sam Pierze Radion," black cat becoming white cat, by T. Gronowski, 1926. #3374, "Szewcy" (Bootmakers), by R. Cieslewicz, 1971. #3375, "Goya," by W. Sadowski, 1983. #3376, "Maz i zona," by A. Pagowski, 1977.

Perf. 11x11½, 11½x11 Syncopated Type A

1997, Nov. 14 **Litho.**

3373 A1123 50g multi .35 .25
3374 A1123 50g multi, vert. .35 .25
3375 A1123 60g multi, vert. .45 .25
3376 A1123 60g multi, vert. .45 .25
Nos. 3373-3376 (4) 1.60 1.00

Chick Type of 1995

Designs: a, Tadorna tadorna. b, Mergus merganser. c, Gallinago gallinago. d, Gallinula chloropus.

Perf. 11½ Syncopated Type A

1997, Dec. 5

3377 A1081 50g Block of 4, #a.-d. 2.00 1.20

Christmas A1124

50g, Nativity. 60g, Food, candles. 80g, Outdoor winter scene, star, church. 1.10z, Carolers.

Perf. 11½x11, 11x11½ Syncopated Type A

1997, Nov. 27

3378 A1124 50g multi, vert. .35 .25
3379 A1124 60g multi .45 .25
3380 A1124 80g multi .55 .35
3381 A1124 1.10z multi, vert. .75 .35
Nos. 3378-3381 (4) 2.10 1.20

A1125

Perf. 11½ Syncopated Type A

1998, Jan. 5 **Litho.**

3382 A1125 1.40z multicolored .95 .30

1998 Winter Olympic Games, Nagano.

A1126

Love Stamps: B, Face of dog, cat on shirt. A, Face of cat, dog on shirt.

Perf. 12x11½ Syncopated Type A

1998, Jan. 14

3383	A1126	B multicolored	.70	.35
3384	A1126	A multicolored	.70	.35

Nos. 3383-3384 were valued at 55g and 65g, respectively, on day of issue.

Polish Country Estates Type of 1997

Designs: B, Gluchach. 55g, Oblegorku. A, Czarnolesie. 65g, Bronowicach. 90g, Oborach. 1.20z, Romanowie.

1998 Photo. *Perf. 11½x12*

3385	A1110	B multicolored	.70	.35
3386	A1110	55g multicolored	.40	.25
3387	A1110	A multicolored	.70	.25
3388	A1110	65g multicolored	.45	.25
3389	A1110	90g multicolored	.65	.25
3390	A1110	1.20z multicolored	.85	.30
		Nos. 3385-3390 (6)	3.75	1.65

No. 3385 was valued at 55g, and No. 3387 was valued at 65g on day of issue.

Issued: B, A, 1/15; 55g, 65g, 90g, 1.20z, 3/3.

Easter — A1127

Perf. 11½ Syncopated Type A

1998, Mar. 12 Litho.

3391	A1127	55g shown	.40	.25
3392	A1127	65g Image of Christ	.45	.25

European Revolutionary Movements of 1848, 150th Anniv. — A1128

1998, Mar. 20 Engr. *Perf. 11x11½*

3393	A1128	55g gray violet	.50	.25

Royalty Type of 1986

Designs: 55g, Henryk Walezy. 65g, Anna Jagiellonka. 80g, Stefan Batory. 90g, Zygmunt III.

1998, Mar. 31 *Perf. 11*

3394	A875	55g multicolored	.40	.25
3395	A875	65g multicolored	.45	.25
3396	A875	80g multicolored	.55	.25
3397	A875	90g multicolored	.65	.30
		Nos. 3394-3397 (4)	2.05	1.05

Protection of the Baltic Sea — A1129

Marine life: #3398, Halichoerus grypus. #3399, Pomatoschistus microps. #3400, Alosa fallax, syngnathus typhle. #3401, Acipenser sturio. #3402, Salmo salar. #3403, Phocoena phocoena. 1.20z, Halichoerus grypus.

Perf. 11½ Syncopated Type B

1998, Apr. 28 Litho.

3398	A1129	65g multicolored	.45	.25
3399	A1129	65g multicolored	.45	.25
3400	A1129	65g multicolored	.45	.25
3401	A1129	65g multicolored	.45	.25
3402	A1129	65g multicolored	.45	.25
3403	A1129	65g multicolored	.45	.25
a.		Strip of 6, #3398-3403	2.75	1.75

Souvenir Sheet

3404	A1129	1.20z multicolored	1.10	.50

Israel '98 World Philatelic Exhibition, Tel Aviv — A1130

Perf. 11½ Syncopated Type A

1998, Apr. 30

3405	A1130	90g Israel No. 8, logo	.75	.35

Natl. Holidays and Festivals A1131

Europa: 55g, Logo of Warwaw Autumn, Intl. Festival of Contemporary Music. 1.20z, First bars of song, "Welcome the May Dawn," 3rd of May Constitution Day.

1998, May 5

3406	A1131	55g multicolored	.40	.25
3407	A1131	1.20z multicolored	.85	.40
a.		Pair, #3406-3407	1.40	.85

Coronation of Longing Holy Mother — A1132

Perf. 11½x12 Syncopated Type A

1998, June 28 Litho.

3408	A1132	55g multicolored	.45	.25

Nikifor (Epifan Drowniak) (1895-1968), Artist — A1133

Paintings: 55g, "Triple Self-portrait." 65g, "Cracow Office." 1.20z, "Orthodox Church." 2.35z, "Ucrybów Station."

Perf. 11½ Syncopated Type A

1998, July 10 Litho.

3409	A1133	55g multicolored	.40	.25
3410	A1133	65g multicolored	.40	.25
3411	A1133	1.20z multicolored	.85	.30
3412	A1133	2.35z multicolored	1.60	.40
		Nos. 3409-3412 (4)	3.25	1.20

Main Board of Statistics, 80th Anniv. A1134

Perf. 11x11½ Syncopated Type A

1998, July 13

3413	A1134	55g multicolored	.45	.25

15th Cent. Statue of Madonna and Child, Sejny Basilica A1135

Perf. 11½ Syncopated Type A

1998, Aug. 14

3414	A1135	55g multicolored	.50	.25

Warsaw Diocese, Bicent. A1136

1998, Aug. 28

3415	A1136	65g multicolored	.50	.30

Souvenir Sheet

17th Polish Philatelic Exhibition, Szczecin — A1137

View of city, 1624: a, People on raft, pier. b, Sailing ships, pier.

1998, Sept. 18 Engr. *Perf. 11x11½*

3416	A1137	65g Sheet of 2, #a.-b.	1.25	.75

Discovery of Radium and Polonium, Cent. A1138

Perf. 11½ Syncopated Type A

1998, Sept. 18 Litho.

3417	A1138	1.20z Pierre, Marie Curie	.85	.30

Mazowsze Song and Dance Ensemble, 50th Anniv. — A1139

Couple dancing, denomination at: No. 3418, LL. No. 3419, LR.

1998, Sept. 22

3418		65g multicolored	.45	.25
3419		65g multicolored	.45	.25
a.	A1139	Pair, #3418-3419	1.00	.60

Mniszech Palace (Belgian Embassy), Warsaw, Bicent. A1140

Photo. & Engr.

1998, Sept. 28 *Perf. 11½*

3420	A1140	1.20z multicolored	.85	.30

See Belgium No. 1706.

Sigismund III Vasa (1566-1632), King of Sweden and Poland — A1141

1998, Oct. 3 Engr. *Perf. 11½x11*

3421	A1141	1.20z deep claret	.85	.30

See Sweden No. 2312.

World Stamp Day — A1142

Perf. 11½x11 Syncopated Type A

1998, Oct. 9 Litho.

3422	A1142	65g multicolored	.45	.25

Pontificate of John Paul II, 20th Anniv. — A1143

Perf. 11½x12 Syncopated Type A

1998, Oct. 16

3423	A1143	65g multicolored	.65	.35

Independence, 80th Anniv. — A1144

Perf. 12x11½ Syncopated Type A

1998, Nov. 11

3424	A1144	65g multicolored	.45	.25

Christmas A1145

Paintings: 55g, Nativity scene. 65g, Adoration of the Magi.

1998, Nov. 27 Photo. ***Perf. 11½x11***

3425	A1145	55g multicolored	.40	.25
3426	A1145	65g multicolored	.50	.25

Universal Declaration of Human Rights, 50th Anniv. A1146

Perf. 11x11½ Syncopated Type A

1998, Dec. 10 Litho.

3427	A1146	1.20z blue & dark blue	.85	.35

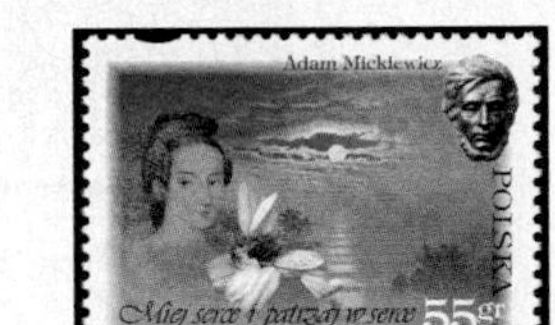

Adam Mickiewicz (1798-1855), Poet — A1147

Scenes, quotations from poems: 55g, Maryla Wereszczakówna, flower, night landscape. 65g, Cranes flying over tomb of Maria Potocka. 90g, Burning candles, cross. 1.20z, Nobleman's house, flowers, uhlan's cap. 2.45z, Bust of Mickiewicz, by Jean David d'Angers.

Perf. 12x11½ Syncopated Type A

1998, Dec. 24

3428	A1147	55g multicolored	.40	.25
3429	A1147	65g multicolored	.45	.25
3430	A1147	90g multicolored	.65	.25
3431	A1147	1.20z multicolored	.85	.35
		Nos. 3428-3431 (4)	2.35	1.10

Souvenir Sheet

3432	A1147	2.45z multicolored	1.75	.90

No. 3432 contains one 27x35mm stamp.

Polish Navy, 80th Anniv. (in 1998) A1148

No. 3433, Destroyer ORP Piorun, 1942-46. No. 3434, Frigate ORP Piorun, 1994.

Perf. 11¼x11½ Syncopated Type A

1999, Jan. 4 Litho.

3433	A1148	55g multicolored	.40	.25
3434	A1148	55g multicolored	.40	.25
a.		Pair, #3433-3434	1.00	.50

Love Stamps A1149

Perf. 11½x11¼ Syncopated Type A

1999, Feb. 5

3435	A1149	B Dominoes	.75	.30
3436	A1149	A Dominoes, diff.	.75	.30

Nos. 3535-3436 were valued at 55g and 65g, respectively, on day of issue.

Famous Polish Men A1150

Designs: 1z, Ernest Malinowski (1818-99), constructor of Central Trans-Andean Railway, Peru. 1.60z, Rudolf Modrzejewski (Ralph Modjeski) (1861-1940), bridge builder.

Perf. 11½ Syncopated Type A

1999, Feb. 12

3437	A1150	1z multicolored	.70	.30
3438	A1150	1.60z multicolored	1.10	.40

Easter — A1151

Scenes from Srudziadz Polyptych: 60g, Prayer in Ogrójec. 65g, Carrying cross. 1.40z, Resurrection.

1z, Tubadzin Pieta, 15th cent.

1999, Mar. 5 ***Perf. 11½x11¼***

3439	A1151	60g multicolored	.40	.25
3440	A1151	65g multicolored	.40	.25
3441	A1151	1z multicolored	.70	.30
3442	A1151	1.40z multicolored	.95	.40
		Nos. 3439-3442 (4)	2.45	1.20

Souvenir Sheet

China 1999, World Philatelic Exhibition — A1152

Perf. 11½x11¼ Syncopated Type A

1999, Mar. 31

3443	A1152	1.70z Ideogram, dragon	1.60	.80

Virgin Mary, Patron Saint of Soldiers A1153

Perf. 11½x11¾ Syncopated Type A

1999, Apr. 2 Litho.

3444	A1153	60g shown	.40	.25
3445	A1153	70g Katyn	.50	.25

Characters from Works by Henryk Sienkiewicz — A1154

No. 3446, Jan Skrzetuski. No. 3447, Onufry Zagloba. No. 3448, Longin Podbipieta. No. 3449, Bohun. No. 3450, Andrzej Kmicic. No. 3451, Michal Jerzy Wolodyjowski.

Perf. 11¾x11½ Syncopated Type B

1999, Apr. 6 Litho.

3446	A1154	70g multicolored	.50	.25
3447	A1154	70g multicolored	.50	.25
3448	A1154	70g multicolored	.50	.25
3449	A1154	70g multicolored	.50	.25
3450	A1154	70g multicolored	.50	.25
3451	A1154	70g multicolored	.50	.25
a.		Block of 6, # 3446-3451	3.50	1.75

Poland's Admission to NATO — A1155

Perf. 11½ Syncopated Type B

1999, Apr. 22 Litho.

3452	A1155	70g multicolored	.50	.30

Council of Europe, 50th Anniv. — A1156

Perf. 11½x11 Syncopated Type A

1999, May 5 Litho.

3453	A1156	1z multicolored	.70	.30

Europa A1157

Perf. 11½ Syncopated Type A

1999, May 5 Litho.

3454	A1157	1.40z multicolored	1.00	.70

Sports A1158

Perf. 11½ Syncopated Type B

1999, June 1 Litho.

3455	A1158	60g Cycling	.40	.25
3456	A1158	70g Snowboarding	.50	.25
3457	A1158	1z Skateboarding	.70	.30
3458	A1158	1.40z Roller blading	1.00	.35
		Nos. 3455-3458 (4)	2.60	1.15

Visit of Pope John Paul II — A1159

Pope and: 60g, Church of the Virgin Mary, Cracow, crowd with Solidarity banners. 70g, Crowd with crosses. 1z, Crowd with flags. 1.40z, Eiffel Tower, Monument to Christ the Redeemer, Rio, Shrine of Our Lady of Fatima.

Perf. 11¾x11½ Syncopated Type A

1999, June 5 Litho.

3459	A1159	60g multicolored	.40	.25
		Complete booklet, 10 #3459	4.00	
3460	A1159	70g multicolored	.50	.25
		Complete booklet, 10 #3460	5.00	
3461	A1159	1z multicolored	.70	.30
3462	A1159	1.40z multicolored	1.00	.40
		Nos. 3459-3462 (4)	2.60	1.20

Country Estates Type of 1997

Perf. 11½x11¾

1999, June 15 Photo.

3463	A1110	70g Modlnicy	.50	.25
3464	A1110	1z Krzeslawicach	.70	.30
3465	A1110	1.40z Winnej Górze	1.00	.30
3466	A1110	1.60z Potoku Zlotym	1.10	.35
3467	A1110	1.85z Kasnej Dolnej	1.25	.40
		Nos. 3463-3467 (5)	4.55	1.60

Versailles Treaty, 80th Anniv. A1159a

Perf. 11¼x11½ Syncopated Type A

1999, June 29 Litho.

3467A	A1159a	1.40z multi	1.00	.40

Depictions of the Virgin Mary — A1160

Designs: 60g, Painting from church in Rokitno. 70g, Crowned statue.

Perf. 11½x11¼ Syncopated Type A

1999, July 9 Litho.

3468	A1160	60g multi	.40	.25
3469	A1160	70g multi	.50	.25

Insects — A1161

Designs: No. 3470, Corixa punctata. No. 3471, Dytiscus marginalis. No. 3472, Perla marginata. No. 3473, Limnophilus. No. 3474, Anax imperator. No. 3475, Ephemera vulgata.

Perf. 11½x11¾ Syncopated Type B

1999, July 16 Litho.

3470	A1161	60g multi	.45	.25
3471	A1161	60g multi	.45	.25
3472	A1161	70g multi	.50	.25
3473	A1161	70g multi	.50	.25
3474	A1161	1.40z multi	1.00	.40
3475	A1161	1.40z multi	1.00	.40
		Nos. 3470-3475 (6)	3.90	1.80

Souvenir Sheet

Ksiaz Castle — A1162

Engr. (Margin Photo.)

1999, Aug. 14 *Perf. 11¼x11*

3476 A1162 1z blue 1.10 .85

Natl. Philatelic Exhibition, Walbrzych, Czeslaw Slania's 1001st stamp design.

No. 3476 exists imperf., value $10.

Polish-Ukrainian Cooperation in Nature Conservation — A1163

Designs: No. 3477, Cervus elaphus. No. 3478, Felis silvestris.

Perf. 11x11½ Syncopated Type A

1999, Sept. 22 **Litho.**

3477 A1163 1.40z multi 1.00 .50
3478 A1163 1.40z multi 1.00 .50
a. Pair, #3477-3478 2.25 1.25

See Ukraine No. 354.

Royalty Type of 1986 with Denomination at Bottom

Designs: 60g, Wladyslaw IV. 70g, Jan II Kazimierz. 1z, Michal Korybut Wisniowiecki. 1.40z, Jan III Sobieski.

Photo. & Engr.

1999, Sept. 25 *Perf. 10¾x11*

3479 A875 60g olive & black .40 .25
3480 A875 70g brn & dk brn .50 .25
3481 A875 1z blue & black .70 .30
3482 A875 1.40z lilac & claret 1.00 .35
Nos. 3479-3482 (4) 2.60 1.15

UPU, 125th Anniv., World Post Day A1164

Perf. 11¾x11½ Syncopated Type A

1999, Oct. 9 **Litho.**

3483 A1164 1.40z multi 1.00 .40

Frédéric Chopin (1810-49), Composer — A1165

1999, Oct. 17 **Engr.** *Perf. 11x11½*

3484 A1165 1.40z dark green 1.00 .50

See France No. 2744.

Jerzy Popieluszko (1947-84), Priest Murdered by Secret Police — A1166

Perf. 11½x11¼ Syncopated Type A

1999, Oct. 19 **Litho.**

3485 A1166 70g multi .50 .30

Souvenir Sheet

Memorial to Heroes of World War II — A1167

1999, Oct. 21

3486 A1167 1z multi 1.10 .85

Christmas A1168

Various angels.

Perf. 11¼x11½ Syncopated Type A

1999, Nov. 26 **Panel Color** **Litho.**

3487 A1168 60g orange .45 .25
3488 A1168 70g blue .50 .25
3489 A1168 1z red .70 .30
3490 A1168 1.40z olive green 1.00 .35
Nos. 3487-3490 (4) 2.65 1.15

Polish Cultural Buildings in Foreign Countries A1169

Designs: 1z, Polish Museum, Rapperswil, Switzerland. 1.40z, Marian Fathers' Museum at Fawley Court Historic House, United Kingdom. 1.60z, Polish History and Literary Society Library, Paris. 1.80z, Polish Institute and Sikorski Museum, London.

Perf. 11½x11¾ Syncopated Type A

1999, Dec. 6 **Litho.**

3491 A1169 1z multi .70 .30
3492 A1169 1.40z multi 1.00 .35
3493 A1169 1.60z multi 1.10 .40
3494 A1169 1.80z multi 1.25 .50
Nos. 3491-3494 (4) 4.05 1.55

New Year 2000 — A1170

Perf. 11½x11¾ Syncopated Type A

2000, Jan. 2 **Litho.**

3495 A1170 A multi .70 .25

No. 3495 sold for 70g on day of issue.

Famous Poles A1171

Designs: 1.55z, Bronislaw Malinowski (1884-1942), ethnologist. 1.95z, Józef Zwierzycki (1888-1961), geologist.

Perf. 11¼x11½ Syncopated Type A

2000, Feb. 22

3496 A1171 1.55z multi 1.10 .30
3497 A1171 1.95z multi 1.40 .40

Gniezno Summit, 1000th Anniv. — A1172

Designs: 70g, Holy Roman Emperor Otto III granting crown to Boleslaw Chrobry. 80g, Four bishops.

1.55z, Sclaunia, Germania, Gallia, Roma and Otto III, horiz.

Perf. 11½x11¼

2000, Mar. 12 **Photo.**

3498 A1172 70g multi .50 .25
3499 A1172 80g multi .55 .25

Souvenir Sheet

Perf. 11¼x11½

3500 A1172 1.55z multi 1.40 .85

Organization of Roman Catholic Church in Poland, 1000th anniv.

Easter A1173

Designs: 70g, Christ in tomb. 80g, Resurrected Christ.

Perf. 11¼x11½ Syncopated Type B

2000, Mar. 24 **Litho.**

3501 A1173 70g multi .50 .25
3502 A1173 80g multi .55 .25

Dinosaurs — A1174

#3503, Saurolophus. #3504, Gallimimus. #3505, Saichania. #3506, Protoceratops. #3507, Prenocephale. #3508, Velociraptor.

Perf. 11¾x11½ Syncopated Type A

2000, Mar. 24 **Litho.**

3503 A1174 70g multi .50 .25
3504 A1174 70g multi .50 .25
3505 A1174 80g multi .55 .25
3506 A1174 80g multi .55 .25
3507 A1174 1.55z multi 1.10 .40
3508 A1174 1.55z multi 1.10 .40
a. Souvenir sheet, #3503-3508 6.00 3.25
Nos. 3503-3508 (6) 4.30 1.80

Awarding of Honorary Academy Award to Director Andrzej Wajda A1175

2000, Mar. 26

3509 A1175 1.10z blk & gray .75 .25
a. Tete beche pair 1.75 .75

Holy Year 2000 — A1176

Perf. 11½x11¼ Syncopated Type B

2000, Apr. 7

3510 A1176 80g multi .55 .35

Country Estates Type of 1997

80g, Grabonóg. 1.55z, Zelazowa Wola. 1.65z, Sucha, Wegrów. 2.65z, Liwia, Wegrów.

Perf. 11½x11¾

2000, Apr. 14 **Photo.**

3511 A1110 80g multicolored .55 .25
3512 A1110 1.55z multicolored 1.10 .35
3513 A1110 1.65z multicolored 1.20 .40
3514 A1110 2.65z multicolored 1.75 .65
Nos. 3511-3514 (4) 4.60 1.65

Cracow, 2000 European City of Culture — A1177

70g, Jan Matejko, Franciszek Joseph, Stanislaw Wyspianski, Konstanty Ildefons Galczynski, Stanislaw Lem, Slawomir Mrozek, Piotr Skrzynecki and Cloth Hall. 1.55z, Queen Jadwiga, Józef Dietl, Krzystof Penderecki, Casimir the Great, Pope John Paul II, Jerzy Turowicz, Brother Albert, Copernicus, Collegium Maius and St. Mary's Church.

1.75z, Panorama of Cracow from 1493 wood engraving.

Perf. 11½x11¼ Syncopated Type A

2000, Apr. 26 **Litho.**

3515 A1177 70g multi .50 .25
3516 A1177 1.55z multi 1.10 .35

Souvenir Sheet

Engr.

Perf. 11¼x11½ Syncopated Type A

3517 A1177 1.75z blue 1.50 1.00

No. 3517 contains one 39x31mm stamp.

No. 3517 exists imperf. Value $10.

Fight Against Drug Addiction A1178

Perf. 11¼x11½ Syncopated Type B

2000, Apr. 28 **Litho.**

3518 A1178 70g multi .50 .25

Europa, 2000

Common Design Type

Perf. 11½x11¾ Syncopated Type B

2000, May 9

3519 CD17 1.55z multi 1.10 .50

Pope John Paul II, 80th Birthday A1179

Designs: 80g, Pope. 1.10z, Black Madonna of Jasna Gora. 1.55z, Pope's silver cross.

Engr., Litho. & Engr. (1.10z)

2000, May 9 ***Perf. 12¾***

3520 A1179 80g purple .55 .25
3521 A1179 1.10z multi .75 .35
3522 A1179 1.55z green 1.10 .45
Nos. 3520-3522 (3) 2.40 1.05

See Vatican City Nos. 1153-1155.

España 2000 Intl. Philatelic Exhibition A1180

Perf. 11½x11¼ Syncopated Type A

2000, May 26 **Litho.**

3523 A1180 1.55z multi 1.10 .50

Parenthood A1181

Perf. 11½x11¼ Syncopated Type B

2000, May 31

3524 A1181 70g multi .50 .25

Souvenir Sheet

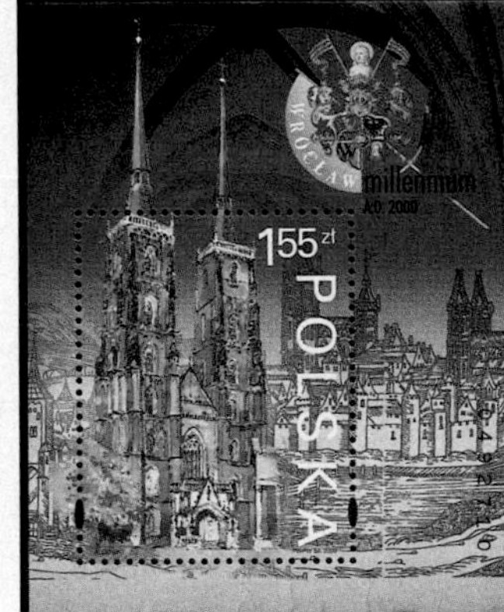

Wroclaw, 1000th Anniv. — A1182

Perf. 11¼x11½ Syncopated Type A

2000, June 15

3525 A1182 1.55z multi 1.10 .70

Social Activists A1183

70g, Karol Marcinkowski (1800-46), philantropist. 80g, Blessed Josemaría Escrivá de Balaguer, (1902-75), founder of Opus Dei.

Perf. 11¼x11½ Suncopated Type B

2000, June 23

3526-3527 A1183 Set of 2 1.10 .50

Illustrations of Characters from Pan Tadeusz, by Adam Mickiewicz A1184

No. 3528, 70g, Gerwazy & Count. No. 3529, 70g, Telimena & Judge. No. 3530, 80g, Father Robak, Judge & Gerwazy. No. 3531, 80g, Wojski. No. 3532, 1.10z, Jankiel. No. 3533, 1.10z, Zofia & Tadeusz.

2000, June 30 **Engr.** ***Perf. 11x11¼***

3528-3533 A1184 Set of 6 3.75 1.90

National Pilgrimage to Rome — A1185

Designs: 80g, Pope John Paul II, St. Peter's Basilica. 1.55z, Cross, Colosseum.

Perf. 11½x11¾ Syncopated Type B

2000, July 1 **Litho.**

3534-3535 A1185 Set of 2 1.60 .65

Piotr Michalowski (1800-55), Artist — A1186

70g, Self-portrait, vert. 80g, Portrait of Boy in a Hat, vert. 1.10z, Stableboy Bridling Percherons. 1.55z, Horses & a Horse Cart.

Perf. 11½x11¼ (no syncopation), 11¾x11½ Syncopated Type A

2000, July 2

3536-3539 A1186 Set of 4 3.00 .85

Depictions of the Virgin Mary — A1187

Designs: 70g, Rózanostok. 1.55z, Lichen.

Perf. 11½x11¼ Syncopated Type A

2000, Aug. 14

3540-3541 A1187 Set of 2 1.60 .50

St. John Bosco and Adolescents A1188

Perf. 11¼x11½ Syncopated Type B

2000, Aug. 25

3542 A1188 80g multi .55 .25

Educational work of Salesian order.

Souvenir Sheet

Solidarity Labor Union, 20th Anniv. — A1189

Perf. 11½x11¼ Syncopated Type B

2000, Aug. 31

3543 A1189 1.65z multi 1.25 .75

2000 Summer Olympics, Sydney A1190

Designs: 70g, Runners. 80g, Diving, sailing, rowing. 1.10z, High jump, weight lifting, fencing. 1.55z, Basketball, judo, runner.

Perf. 11¾x11½ Syncopated Type A

2000, Sept. 1

3544-3547 A1190 Set of 4 3.00 1.00

World Post Day — A1191

Children's art by: 70g, Tomasz Wistuba, vert. 80g, Katarzyna Chrzanowska. 1.10z, Joanna Zbik. 1.55z, Katarzyna Lonak.

Perf. 11½x11¼, 11¼x11½ All Sync. Type B

2000, Oct. 9 **Litho.**

3548-3551 A1191 Set of 4 3.00 1.00

Souvenir Sheet

Polish Philatelic Union, 50th Anniv. — A1192

Perf. 11¼x11½ Sync. Type B

2000, Oct. 12

3552 A1192 1.55z multi 1.25 .75

Royalty Type of 1986 With Denominations at Bottom

Designs: 70g, August II. 80g, Stanislaw Leszczynski. 1.10z, August III. 1.55z, Stanislaw August Poniatowski.

2000, Oct. 23 **Engr.** ***Perf. 10¾x11***

3553-3556 A875 Set of 4 3.00 1.25

Katyn Massacre, 60th Anniv. — A1193

Designs: 70g, Priest and cross. 80g, Pope John Paul II at monument in Warsaw.

Perf. 11½x11¾ Sync. Type A

2000, Nov. 15 **Litho.**

3557-3558 A1193 Set of 2 1.10 .50

Christmas A1194

Scenes from the life of Jesus: 70g, Nativity. 80g, Wedding at Cana. 1.10g, Last Supper. 1.55z, Ascension.

Perf. 11½ Sync. Type A

2000, Nov. 27

3559-3562 A1194 Set of 4 3.00 1.25

Zacheta Art Museum, Warsaw, Cent. — A1195

Perf. 11½x11¼ Sync. Type B

2000, Dec. 4

3563 A1195 70g multi .50 .25

Underground Post During Martial Law — A1196

Perf. 11½x11¼ Sync. Type A

2000, Dec. 13

3564 A1196 80g multi + label .85 .35
a. Tete beche block of 2 stamps + 2 labels 2.00 1.00

End of Holy Year 2000 — A1197

Type C Syncopation (1st stamp #3565): Like Type A Syncopation but with oval hole on shorter sides rather than longer sides.

Perf. 11¾x11½ Sync. Type C

2001, Jan. 6 **Litho.**

3565 A1197 A multi .85 .35

Sold for 1z on day of issue.

20th Winter Universiade, Zakopane — A1198

Perf. 11¼x11½ Sync. Type B

2001, Feb. 7

3566 A1198 1z multi .70 .25

Internet A1199

Perf. 11¼x11½ Sync. Type A

2001, Feb. 22

3567 A1199 1z multi .70 .25

World Ski Championships, Lahti, Finland — A1200

Perf. 11½ Sync. Type A

2001, Feb. 23

3568 A1200 1z shown .70 .25

With Inscription "Adam Malysz" in Black

3569 A1200 1z multi .70 .25

As #3569, With Inscription "Mistrzem Swiata" in Red

3570 A1200 1z multi .70 .25
Nos. 3568-3570 (3) 2.10 .75

Country Estates Type of 1997

Perf. 11½x11¾

2001, Feb. 28 **Photo.**

3571 A1110 10g Lipków .25 .25
3572 A1110 1.50z Sulejówek 1.10 .30
3573 A1110 1.90z Petrykozy 1.40 .40
3574 A1110 3z Janowiec 2.10 .65

Issued: 1.90z, 3z, 2/28. 10g, 1.50z, 6/20.

Easter A1201

Designs: 1z, Women at empty tomb. 1.90z, Resurrected Christ with apostles.

Perf. 11½ Sync. Type A

2001, Mar. 16 **Litho.**

3575-3576 A1201 Set of 2 2.00 .50

12th Salesian Youth World Championships — A1202

Perf. 11¾x11½ Sync. Type C

2001, Apr. 28

3577 A1202 1z multi .70 .30

Europa — A1203

Perf. 11½x11¼ Sync. Type A

2001, May 5

3578 A1203 1.90z multi 1.40 .65

Greetings A1204

Designs: No. 3579, 1z, All the best (couple in field of flowers). No. 3580, 1z, Vacation greetings (merman and mermaid at beach).

Perf. 11½x11¾ Syncopated Type B

2001, May 10 **Litho.**

3579-3580 A1204 Set of 2 1.40 .50

Wrzesnia Children's Strike Against German Language, Cent. — A1205

Perf. 11½x11¾ Syncopated Type A

2001, May 20

3581 A1205 1z multi .70 .30

Polish Cultural Buildings in North America A1206

Designs: 1z, Poland Scientific Institute and Wanda Stachiewicz Polish Library, Montreal. 1.90z, Josef Pilsudski Institute, New York. 2.10z, Polonia Archives, Library and Museum, Orchard Lake, Mich. 2.20z, Polish Museum, Chicago.

Perf. 11½ Syncopated Type B

2001, June 29

3582 A1206 1z multi .70 .25
a. Tete beche pair 1.40 .65
3583 A1206 1.90z multi 1.40 .30
a. Tete beche pair 2.75 .85
3584 A1206 2.10z multi 1.50 .35
a. Tete beche pair 3.00 1.00
3585 A1206 2.20z multi 1.50 .40
a. Tete beche pair 3.00 1.10
Nos. 3582-3585 (4) 5.10 1.30

Endangered Flora and Fauna — A1207

Convention on Intl. Trade in Endangered Species emblem and: No. 3586, 1z, Parnassius apollo, Orchis sambucina. No. 3587, 1z, Bubo bubo, Adonis vernalis. No. 3588, 1z, Galanthus nivalis, Lynx lynx. No. 3589, 1.90z, Orchis latifolia, Lutra lutra. No. 3590, 1.90z, Falco peregrinus, Orchis pallens. No. 3591, 1.90z, Cypripedium calceolus, Ursus arctos. 2z, World map.

Perf. 11½ Syncopated Type A

2001, July 10

3586-3591 A1207 Set of 6 6.00 1.50

Souvenir Sheet

Perf. 11¼x11½ Syncopated Type A

3592 A1207 2z multi 1.50 .95

No. 3592 contains one 39x30mm stamp.

Stefan Cardinal Wyszynski (1901-81) A1208

Perf. 11¾x11½ Syncopated Type A

2001, Aug. 3

3593 A1208 1z multi .70 .30

St. Maximilian Kolbe (1894-1941) — A1209

Perf. 11¾x11½ Syncopated Type B

2001, Aug. 14

3594 A1209 1z multi .70 .30

Depictions of the Virgin Mary — A1210

Designs: No. 3595, 1z, Pieknej Milosci, Bydgoszcz. No. 3596, 1z, Królowa Podhala, Ludzmierz. 1.90z, Mariampol, Wroclaw.

Perf. 11½x11¼ Syncopated Type A

2001, Aug. 14

3595-3597 A1210 Set of 3 2.75 .90

See Nos. 3650-3652, 3694-3696.

Extension of God's Mercy Sanctuary, Cracow — A1211

2001, Aug. 31

3598 A1211 1z multi .70 .30

Euro Cuprum 2001 Philatelic Exhibition, Lubin — A1212

Designs: 1z, Copper smelter. 1.90z, Copper engravers at work. 2z, Copying with a copper engraving press.

3z, Engraver's burin, view of Lubin, 18th cent.

Perf. 11½x11¼ Syncopated Type A

2001, Sept. 1 **Litho. & Engr.**

3599-3601 A1212 Set of 3 3.50 1.25

Souvenir Sheet

Litho.

3602 A1212 3z multi 2.25 1.10

No. 3602 exists imperf. Value: mint $6, used $11.

Premiere of Movie "Quo Vadis," Directed by Jerzy Kawalerowicz — A1213

No. 3603: a, Ligia, Vinicius, Petrinius (red and light yellow inscriptions). b, Nero singing (blue and red inscriptions). c, Apostle Peter in catacombs, baptism of Chilon Chilonides (orange and yellow inscriptions). d, Chilon Chilonides, fire in Rome (white and yellow inscriptions). e, Ligia tied to back of aurochs, Ursus holding Ligia (red and white inscriptions). f, Apostle Peter blessing Vinicius and Ligia, close-up of Peter (purple and pink inscriptions).

Perf. 11¾x11½ Syncopated Type A

2001, Sept. 1 **Litho.**

3603 A1213 1z Sheet of 6, #a-f 4.25 2.75

Exhibition on Christian Traditions in Military at Polish Army Museum A1214

Perf. 11¾x11½ Syncopated

2001, Sept. 10 **Litho.**

3604 A1214 1z multi .70 .30

Polish State Railways, 75th Anniv. — A1215

2001, Sept. 24

3605 A1215 1z multi .70 .30

Children's Stamp Design Contest Winners A1216

Art by: 1z, Marcin Kuron. 1.90z, Agata Grzyb, vert. 2z, Joanna Sadrakula.

Perf. 11½ Syncopated

2001, Sept. 28

3606-3608 A1216 Set of 3 3.50 1.40

Poland's Advancement to 2002 World Cup Soccer Championships A1217

Perf. 11½x11¾ Syncopated

2001, Oct. 6

3609 A1217 1z multi .70 .30

Year of Dialogue Among Civilizations A1218

2001, Oct. 9

3610 A1218 1.90z multi 1.40 .50

a. Tete beche pair 3.00 1.20

12th Intl. Henryk Wieniawski Violin Competition — A1219

Perf. 11¾x11½ Syncopated

2001, Oct. 13

3611 A1219 1z multi .70 .30

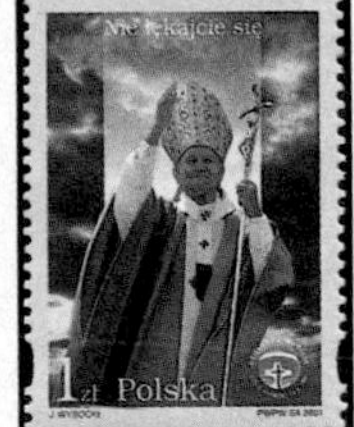

Papal Day — A1220

Perf. 11½x11¾ Syncopated

2001, Oct. 14

3612 A1220 1z multi .70 .40

Warsaw Philharmonic, Cent. — A1221

Perf. 11½x11¼ Syncopated

2001, Nov. 5

3613 A1221 1z multi .70 .30

a. Tete beche pair 1.75 .75

Millennium — A1222

No. 3614: a, Pope John Paul II, Gniezno Doors. b, Pres. Lech Walesa taking oath, cover of May 1791 Constitution. c, Covers of three magazines. d, Playwright Wojciech Boguslawski and Director Jerzy Grotowski, manuscript by Adam Mickiewicz. e, Marshal Józef Pilsudski, Solidarity posters. f, NATO emblem, Gen. Casimir Pulaski. g, Astronomers Nicolaus Copernicus and Aleksander Wolszczan, text from De Revolutionibus Orbium Coelestium, by Copernicus. h, Woodcut of mathematician Jan of Glogow, physicist Tadeusz Kotarbinski. i, Detail from 1920 poster and painting, Battle of Grunwald, by Jan Matejko. j, Four members of the Belvedere Group, masthead of Warszawa Walczy newspaper, soldiers at Warsaw Uprising of 1944, seal of Marian Langiewicz. k, Head of John the Apostle, by Veit Stoss, and self-sculpture, by Magdalena Abakanowicz. l, Composers Krzysztof Penderecki and Frederic Chopin, Mazurka No. 10, Opus 50, by Karol Szymanowski. m, Engraving of Cracow and Royal Castle, Warsaw. n, Portrait of Jan III Sobieski, flag of European Union. o, Writers Wislawa Szymborska and Mikolaj Rej. p, Runners Janusz Kusocinski and Robert Korzeniowski.

Perf. 11¼x11½ Syncopated

2001, Nov. 11

3614 A1222 1z Sheet of 16, #a-p 12.00 6.00

Christmas A1223

Creches from Lower Silesia: 1z, 1.90z.

2001, Nov. 27

3615-3616 A1223 Set of 2 2.00 .75

Radio Maryja, 10th Anniv. A1224

Designs: No. 3617, 1z, Head of Virgin Mary statue, building.

No. 3618: a, 1z, Statue of Virgin Mary praying, crowd with flag. b, 1z, Statue of crowned Virgin Mary, crowd with flag.

2001, Dec. 7

3617 A1224 1z multi .70 .30

Souvenir Sheet

3618 A1224 1z Sheet, #a-b, 3617 1.90 .95

Love A1225

Perf. 11¾x11½ Syncopated

2002, Feb. 4 **Litho.**

3619 A1225 1.10z multi .75 .30

2002 Winter Olympics, Salt Lake City — A1226

Perf. 11½x11¼ Syncopated

2002, Feb. 8

3620 A1226 1.10z multi .75 .30

a. Stamp + label .85 .40

No. 3620a was issued 2/22, and lists medals won by Adam Malysz.

Famous Poles A1227

Designs: No. 3621, 2z, Jan Czerski (1845-92), geologist. No. 3622, 2z, Bronislaw Pilsudski (1866-1918), linguist.

Perf. 11¾x11½ Syncopated

2002, Feb. 22

3621-3622 A1227 Set of 2 2.75 1.10

City Landmarks — A1228

Designs: 2z, Cathedral, St. Adalbert's coffin, Gniezno. 2.10z, Wawel Cathedral, St. Mary's Church, Lajkonik, Cracow. 3.20z, Mermaid monument, Royal Palace, Warsaw.

2002, Mar. 1 **Photo.** *Perf. 11¾x11½*

3623 A1228 2z multi 1.40 .40

3624 A1228 2.10z multi 1.50 .45

3625 A1228 3.20z multi 2.25 .75

Nos. 3623-3625 (3) 5.15 1.60

See Nos. 3643-3644, 3665-3666, 3709-3712, 3763.

Easter — A1229

Designs: 1.10z, Flowers. 2z, Chicks.

Perf. 11½x11¾ Syncopated

2002, Mar. 8 **Litho.**

3626-3627 A1229 Set of 2 2.10 .65

Mammals and Their Young — A1230

No. 3628: a, Dog (purple denomination). b, Cat (brown denomination). c, Wolf (red denomination). d, Lynx (blue denomination).

Perf. 11¾x11½ Syncopated

2002, Mar. 25

3628 Horiz. strip of 4 3.00 1.25

a.-d. A1230 1.10z Any single .75 .25

Evacuation of Gen. Wladyslaw Anders' Army from USSR, 60th Anniv. A1231

Perf. 11½ Syncopated

2002, Mar. 26

3629 A1231 1.10z multi .75 .30

Paintings by Disabled Artists A1232

Unnamed works by: No. 3630, 1.10z, Henryk Paraszczuk, vert. No. 3631, 1.10z,

Amanda Zejmis, vert. 2z, Lucjan Matula. 3.20z, Józefa Laciak.

Perf. 11½x11¼ Sync., 11¼x11½ Sync.

2002, Apr. 17 **Litho.**

3630-3633 A1232 Set of 4 5.00 1.75

Census A1233

2002, Apr. 30 *Perf. 11¼x11½ Sync.*

3634 A1233 1.10z multi .75 .30

Radio Free Europe, 50th Anniv. — A1234

2002, May 2 *Perf. 11¾x11½ Sync.*

3635 A1234 2z multi 1.40 .45

State Fire Brigade, 10th Anniv. A1235

2002, May 4 *Perf. 11¼x11½ Sync.*

3636 A1235 1.10z multi .75 .50

Europa A1236

2002, May 5

3637 A1236 2z multi 1.40 .60

Madonna With Child, St. John the Baptist and Angel, by Sandro Botticelli A1237

2002, May 18 *Perf. 11½ Sync.*

3638 A1237 1.10z multi .75 .35

National Gallery, Warsaw, 140th anniv.

Maria Konopnicka (1842-1910), Poet — A1238

Photo. & Engr.

2002, May 23 *Perf. 11½x11¼*

3639 A1238 1.10z multi .75 .35

Children's Activities — A1239

No. 3640: a, Child playing badminton. b, Child flying kite. c, Child riding scooter.

Perf. 11½x11¼ Syncopated

2002, May 31 **Litho.**

3640 A1239 1.10z Horiz. strip of 3, #a-c 2.25 1.00

2002 World Cup Soccer Championships, Japan and Korea — A1240

Soccer ball and: 1.10z, Map. 2z, Players.

2002, June 1

3641-3642 A1240 Set of 2 2.10 1.00

3642a Souvenir sheet, 2 each #3641-3642 5.00 3.50

City Landmarks Type of 2002

Designs: 1.80z, Roman paten, St. Joseph's Sanctuary, Kalisz. 2.60z, Castle, reliquary of St. Sigismund, Plock, horiz.

Perf. 11¾x11½, 11½x11¾

2002, July 1 **Photo.**

3643 A1228 1.80z multi 1.60 .80

3644 A1228 2.60z multi 2.40 1.25

Ignacy Domeyko (1802-89), Mineralogist — A1241

Perf. 11¾x11½ Syncopated

2002, July 3 **Litho.**

3645 A1241 2.60z multi 1.75 .80

See Chile No. 1389.

Philakorea 2002 and Anphilex 2002 Stamp Exhibitions — A1242

2002, July 12

3646 A1242 2z multi 1.40 .50

Seventh Visit of Pope John Paul II A1243

Pope at: 1.10z, Kalwaria Zebrzydowska. 1.80z, Lagiewniki, Cracow. 3.20z, Wawel Castle, Cracow.

Perf. 11¾x11½ Syncopated

2002 **Litho.**

3647-3648 A1243 Set of 2 2.00 .70

Souvenir Sheet

Engr.

Perf. 11x11½

3649 A1243 3.20z blue 2.25 1.25

Issued: 1.10z, 1.80z, 8/5; 3.20z, 8/16.

Depictions of the Virgin Mary Type of 2001

Designs: No. 3650, 1.10z, Holy Lady of Incessant Assistance (Matka Boza Nieustajacej Pomocy), Jaworzno. No. 3651, 1.10z, Holy Lady of Opole. 2z, Holy Lady of Trabki, Trabki Wielkie.

Perf. 11½x11¼ Syncopated

2002, Aug. 14 **Litho.**

3650-3652 A1210 Set of 3 3.00 1.00

Souvenir Sheet

23rd Polish Philatelic Association Convention, Ciechocinek — A1244

Engr. (Margin Photo. & Engr.)

2002, Sept. 1 *Perf. 11x10¾*

3653 A1244 3.20z brown 3.00 1.50

Exists imperf. Value $7.50.

Premiere of Film "Zemsta," Directed by Andrzej Wajda — A1245

No. 3654: a, Czesnik and Dyndalski reading letter. b, Klara and Waclaw kissing. c, Papkin with mandolin. d, Rejent and Papkin, in chair. e, Rejent and Czesnik shaking hands. f, Attendant and Klara.

Perf. 11¾x11½ Syncopated

2002, Sept. 12 **Litho.**

3654 A1245 1.10z Sheet of 6, #a-f 8.50 4.75

Steam Locomotives — A1246

Designs: No. 3655, 1.10z, Ok1-359. No. 3656, 1.10z, Ol49-7. No. 3657, 2z, TKi3-87. No. 3658, 2z, Pm36-2.

Perf. 11¾x11½ Syncopated

2002, Sept. 21 **Litho.**

3655-3658 A1246 Set of 4 4.25 1.50

a. Horiz. strip of 4, #3655-3658 4.50 1.75

World Post Day A1247

Perf. 11¼x11½ Syncopated

2002, Oct. 9

3659 A1247 2z multi 1.40 .50

Fight Against Cancer A1248

Perf. 11¾x11½ Syncopated

2002, Oct. 25

3660 A1248 1.10z multi .75 .30

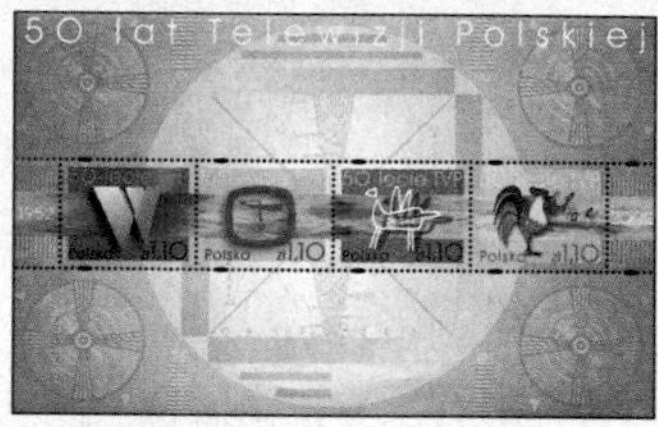

Polish Television, 50th Anniv. — A1249

No. 3661 — Programs: a, Wiadomosci (News, red background). b, Teatru Televizji (Television theater, green background). c, Pegaz (Cultural program). d, Teleranek (children's program).

Perf. 11¼x11½ Syncopated

2002, Oct. 25

3661 A1249 1.10z Sheet of 4, #a-d 3.00 1.25

Saints — A1250

No. 3662: a, St. Stanislaw of Szczepanow (1030-79). b, St. Kazimierz (1458-84). c, St. Faustyna Kowalska (1905-38). d, St. Benedict (480-547). e, Sts. Cyril (826-869) and Methodius (815-85). f, St. Catherine of Siena (1347-80).

Perf. 11½x11¼ Syncopated

2002, Nov. 8

3662 A1250 1.10z Sheet of 6, #a-f 4.50 2.00

Christmas A1251

Ornaments: 1.10z, 2z.

Perf. 11¼x11½ Syncopated

2002, Nov. 27

3663-3664 A1251 Set of 2 2.10 .70
Booklet, 10 #3663 7.50

City Landmarks Type of 2002

Designs: 1.20z, Towers of Old City Hall, Statue of Nicolaus Copernicus, Torun, horiz. 3.40z, Church and well, Kazimierz Dolny, horiz.

2003 Photo. *Perf. 11½x11¾*

3665 A1228 1.20z multi .85 .30
3666 A1228 3.40z multi 2.40 .85

Issued: 1.20z, 1/31; 3.40z, 4/10.

1998-2002 Negotiations to Join European Union A1252

2003, Feb. 18 *Perf. 11x11½*

3667 A1252 1.20z multi .85 .35

A1253

Pontificate of John Paul II, 25th Anniv. — A1254

No. 3668: a, Election as Pope, 1978. b, In Poland, 1979. c, In France, 1980. d, Assassination attempt, 1981. e, At Fatima, Portugal, 1982. f, Extraordinary Holy Year, 1983. g, At Quirinale Palace, Rome, 1984. h, World Youth Day, 1985. i, At synagogue, Rome, 1986. j, Pentecost vigil, 1987. k, At European Parliament, Strasbourg, France, 1988. l, Meeting with Mikhail Gorbachev, 1989. m, At Guinea-Bissau leper colony, 1990. n, At European Bishops' Synod, 1991. o, Publication of Catechism of the Catholic Church, 1992. p, Praying for the Balkans in Assisi, 1993. q, At Sistine Chapel, 1994. r, At UN Headquarters for 50th anniv. celebrations, 1995. s, In Germany, 1996. t, In Sarajevo, Bosnia & Herzegovina, 1997. u, In Cuba, 1998. v, Opening Holy Doors, 1999. w, World Youth Day, 2000. x, Closing Holy Doors, 2001. y, Addressing Italian Parliament, 2002.

2003, Mar. 20 Litho. *Perf. 13x13¼*

3668 Sheet of 25 21.00 12.00
a.-y. A1253 1.20z Any single .85 .30

Etched on Silver Foil
Die Cut Perf. 12½x13
Self-Adhesive

3669 A1254 10z Pope John Paul II 7.00 13.50

Cancels can be easily removed from No. 3669. See Vatican City Nos. 1236-1237.

Andrzej Frycz-Modrzewski (1503-72), Writer — A1255

2003, Mar. 28 Engr. *Perf. 11½x11*

3670 A1255 1.20z brown .85 .30

Easter — A1256

Folk representations: 1.20z, Jesus seated. 2.10z, Jesus standing.

2003, Mar. 28 Photo. *Perf. 11½x11*

3671-3672 A1256 Set of 2 2.25 .75

Granting of Municipal Rights to Poznan, 750th Anniv. — A1257

Designs: 1.20z, Old and modern skylines of Poznan.
3.40z, View of Poznan, 1626.

Perf. 11¾x11½

2003, Apr. 15 Photo.

3673 A1257 1.20z multi .85 .30

Souvenir Sheet
Photo. & Engr.
Perf. 11¼x11½

3674 A1257 3.40z brown & lt brown 2.40 .75

No. 3674 contains one 39x31mm stamp.

Signing of European Union Accession Treaty — A1257a

2003, Apr. 16 Photo. *Perf. 11x11½*

3674A A1257a 1.20z multi .85 .30

Europa A1258

2003, May 5 Photo. *Perf. 11*

3675 A1258 2.10z multi 1.50 .70

European Union Referendum — A1258a

2003, May 26 Photo. *Perf. 11x11½*

3675A A1258a 1.20z multi .85 .30

Lazienkowski Park Landmarks, Warsaw — A1259

Designs: 1.20z, Palac Na Wyspie. 1.80z, Palac Na Wyspie, diff. 2.10z, Palac Myslewicki. 2.60z, Amphitheater.

Perf. 11¼x11½

2003, May 30 Photo.

3676-3679 A1259 Set of 4 5.25 1.90

Children's Dream Vacations — A1260

Children's art by: 1.20z, Anna Golebiewska. 1.80z, Marlena Krejpcio, vert. 2.10z, Michal Korzen. 2.60z, Ewa Zajdler.

2003, June 20 *Perf. 11*

3680-3683 A1260 Set of 4 5.25 1.90

Fairy Tales A1261

Designs: 1.20z, Krak, traditional tale. 1.80z, Stupid Mateo, by Jozef Ignacy Kraszewski. 2.10z, The Princess Enchanted Into a Frog, by Antoni Jozef Glinski. 2.60z, The Crock of Gold, by Kraszewski.

2003, June 30

3684-3687 A1261 Set of 4 5.25 1.90

Souvenir Sheet

19th National Philatelic Exhibition, Katowice — A1262

Photo. & Engr.

2003, Aug. 18 *Perf. 11½x11¼*

3688 A1262 3.40z multi 2.40 .70

No. 3688 exists imperf. Value: mint $5, used $7.

Paintings of Julian Falat (1853-1929) — A1263

Designs: 1.20z, Self-portrait, vert. 1.80z, Spearmen, vert. 2.10z, Winter Landscape with River and Bird. 2.60z, On the Ship — Merchants at Ceylon.

Perf. 11½x11¼, 11¼x11½

2003, Sept. 30 Photo.

3689-3692 A1263 Set of 4 5.25 1.75

World Post Day — A1264

2003, Oct. 9 *Perf. 11½x11¼*

3693 A1264 2.10z multi 1.40 .50

Depictions of the Virgin Mary Type of 2001

Designs: 1.20z, Mother of the Redeemer. 1.80z, Holy Mother Benevolent, Krzeszowice. 2.10z, Holy Mother, Zieleniec.

2003, Oct. 14

3694-3696 A1210 Set of 3 4.75 2.40

Motorcycle Racing in Poland, Cent. — A1265

No. 3697 — Motorcycles of various eras with text in: a, Yellow. b, Green. c, Pink.

2003, Oct. 20 *Perf. 11¼x11½*

3697 Horiz. strip of 3 2.50 1.00
a.-c. A1265 1.20z Any single .85 .30

Silesian Folk Ensemble — A1266

No. 3698: a, Denomination at left. b, Denomination at right.

2003, Oct. 29 *Perf. 11½x11¼*

3698 A1266 1.20z Horiz. pair, #a-b 1.75 .55

Cranes and Polish Government Internet Address — A1267

2003, Oct. 31 *Perf. 11¼x11½*

3699 A1267 2.10z multi 1.50 .50

Worldwide Fund for Nature (WWF) — A1268

No. 3700 — Pandion haliaetus: a, On branch holding fish. b, Adult and young at nest. c, Adult hunting for prey. d, Adult flying with fish in talons.

2003, Oct. 31 *Perf. 11½x11¼*

3700	Horiz. strip of 4	3.50	1.75
a.-d.	A1268 1.20z Any single	.85	.30

Christmas — A1269

Designs: 1.20z, Nativity. 1.80z, The Magi. 2.10z, The Annunciation, vert. 2.60z, Holy Family, vert.

Perf. 11½ Syncopated

2003, Nov. 27 **Litho.**

3701-3704	A1269	Set of 4	5.25	2.00

Foreign Stamps Depicting Polish Subjects A1270

Designs: 1.20z, Sweden No. 2399a (Wislawa Szymborska), vert. 1.80z, France No. 1195 (Marie Curie). 2.10z, Sweden No. 1598 (Czeslaw Milosz), vert. 2.60z, Vatican City No. 437 (Black Madonna of Czestochowa).

2003, Dec. 12

3705-3708	A1270	Set of 4	5.25	2.00

City Landmarks Type of 2002

Designs: 5g, Town Hall, church archway, Sandomierz, horiz. 1.25z, Town Hall, Neptune Fountain, Gdansk. 1.90z, Church of the Descent of the Holy Ghost, Israel Poznanski House, Lódz, horiz. 3.45z, Union Monument, Lublin Castle, Lublin, horiz.

Perf. 11½x11¾, 11¾x11½

2004 **Photo.**

3709	A1228 5g multi	.25	.25
3710	A1228 1.25z multi	.85	.30
3711	A1228 1.90z multi	1.25	.40
3712	A1228 3.45z multi	2.40	.75
	Nos. 3709-3712 (4)	4.75	1.70

Issued: 5g, 1/1; 1.25z, 1/9; 1.90z, 5/14; 3.45z, 2/23. Sheet margins of No. 3711 served as etiquettes.

12th Concert of the Great Holiday Help Orchestra — A1271

2004, Jan. 5 *Perf. 11x11½*

3713	A1271 1.25z multi	.85	.30

LOT (Polish National Airlines), 75th Anniv. A1272

2004, Jan. 21

3714	A1272 1.25z multi	.85	.30

Love A1273

2004, Feb. 2

3715	A1273 1.25z multi	.85	.30

Famous Poles A1274

Designs: No. 3716, 2.10z, Helena Paderewska (1856-1934), chairwoman of Polish White Cross. No. 3717, 2.10z, Father Lucjan Bójnowski (1868-1960), Polish Army recruiter in US.

2004, Feb. 27

3716-3717	A1274	Set of 2	3.00	.70

Easter — A1275

Designs: 1.25z, Rabbit. 2.10z, Lamb.

2004, Mar. 12 *Perf. 11½x11¾*

3718-3719	A1275	Set of 2	2.25	.80

Flora and Fauna in Reservoirs — A1276

No. 3720: a, Beaver, frog, flowers. b, Kingfisher holding fish, crawfish holding fish, snail, beetle and water lilies. c, Grayling, leech, mussel, snail. d, Pike chasing smaller fish, grebe, snail.

Perf. 11¾x11½ Syncopated

2004, Mar. 30 **Litho.**

3720	Horiz. strip of 4	3.50	1.25
a.-d.	A1276 1.25z Any single	.85	.30

Admission to European Union — A1277

Perf. 11½x11¾ Syncopated

2004, May 1

3721	A1277 2.10z multi + label	1.50	.70

Europa A1278

2004, May 5

3722	A1278 2.10z multi	1.50	.70

Tenth Government Postage Stamp Printers' Conference, Krakow A1279

Photo. & Engr.

2004, May 7 *Perf. 11½x11¾*

3723	A1279 3.45z multi + label	2.40	.65

A1280

Visits to Poland by Pope John Paul II — A1281

No. 3724: a, Wearing red stole, hand on chin. b, Wearing red stole, praying. c, Holding crucifix with rays. d, Holding crucifix.

No. 3725: a, Wearing gold stole, holding crucifix. b, With arm raised. c, Wearing white vestments, seated. d, Wearing red stole, seated.

Litho. (Embossed Labels)

2004, June 2 *Perf. 13¼x13*

Country Name in Blue

3724	A1280 1.25z Sheet of 4, #a-d, + 8 labels	3.75	2.00

Country Name in Red

3725	A1281 1.25z Sheet of 4, #a-d, + 8 labels	3.75	2.00

See Vatican City Nos. 1264-1265.

Birds — A1282

No. 3726: a, Platycercus elegans, Platycercus eximius. b, Nymphicus hollandicus. c, Melopsittacus undulatus. d, Chloebia gouldiae, Poephila guttata, Padda oryzivora.

Perf. 11½x11¾ Syncopated

2004, June 30 **Litho.**

3726	A1282 1.25z Block of 4, #a-d	3.50	.90

Paintings by Jacek Malczewski (1854-1929) — A1283

Designs: 1.20z, Self-portrait, vert. 1.90z, Ellonai, vert. 2.10z, Tobias and Harpy. 2.60z, The Unknown Note.

Perf. 11½x11¼, 11¼x11½

2004, July 15 Photo.
3727-3730 A1283 Set of 4 5.50 1.75

Souvenir Sheet

Singapore World Stamp Championship 2004 — A1284

Perf. 11¼x11½ Syncopated

2004, July 30 Litho.
3731 A1284 3.45z multi 2.50 .70
a. Imperf. *3.50 4.00*

Miniature Sheet

2004 Summer Olympics, Athens — A1285

No. 3732: a, Boxing. b, Women's track. c, Equestrian. d, Wrestling.

Perf. 11¾x11½ Syncopated

2004, Aug. 2
3732 A1285 1.25z Sheet of 4, #a-d 3.50 .85
e. Imperf. *7.00 9.00*

Witold Gombrowicz (1904-69), Writer — A1286

Perf. 11½x11¼ Syncopated

2004, Aug. 4
3733 A1286 1.25z blue .85 .30

Depictions of the Virgin Mary — A1287

Inscriptions: No. 3734, 1.25z, Matka Boza Dzikowska. No. 3735, 1.25z, Matka Boza Fatimska. No. 3736, 1.25z, Matka Boza Jasnagórska. No. 3737, 1.25z, Matka Boza Laskawa. No. 3738, 1.25z, Matka Boza Lomzynska. No. 3739, 1.25z, Matka Boza Miedzenska. No. 3740, 1.25z, Matka Boza Nieustajacej Pomocy. No. 3741, 1.25z, Matka Boza Bolesna Oborska. No. 3742, 1.25z, Matka Boza Piekarska. No. 3743, 1.25z, Matka Boza Placzaca. No. 3744, 1.25z, Matka Boza Pokorna Rudzka. No. 3745, 1.25z, Matka Boza Rychwaldzka. No. 3746, 1.25z, Matka Boza Rywaldzka. No. 3747, 1.25z, Matka Boza Rzeszowska. No. 3748, 1.25z, Matka Boza Sianowska. No. 3749, 1.25z, Bolesna Matka Boza Skrzatuska. No. 3750, 1.25z, Matka Boza Swietorodzinna.

Perf. 11½x11¼ Syncopated

2004, Aug. 14 Litho.
3734-3760 A1287 Set of 17 15.00 6.00

Czeslaw Niemen (1939-2004), Musician — A1288

Perf. 11¾x11½ Syncopated

2004, Aug. 30 Litho.
3751 A1288 1.25z black & gray .85 .35

Dunajec River Raftsmen — A1289

2004, Sept. 3
3752 A1289 2.10z multi 1.50 .75

See Slovakia No. 463.

Motor Sports A1290

No. 3753: a, Cinder track motorcycle racing (four motorcycles). b, Auto racing. c, Go-kart racing. d, Motorcycle racing (one motorcycle).

Perf. 11¼x11½ Syncopated

2004, Sept. 11
3753 Horiz. strip of 4 3.50 1.50
a.-d. A1290 1.25z Any single .85 .30

World Post Day A1291

Perf. 11¼x11½ Syncopated

2004, Oct. 9 Litho.
3754 A1291 2.10z multi 1.50 .50

UNESCO World Heritage Sites — A1292

Designs: No. 3755, 1.25z, Castle of the Teutonic Order, Malbork. No. 3756, 1.25z, Historic Center of Warsaw. No. 3757, 1.25z, Historic Center of Cracow, vert. No. 3758, 1.25z, Medieval Town of Torun, vert. No. 3759, 1.25z, Old City of Zamosc.

2004, Oct. 20 *Perf. 11½ Syncopated*
3755-3759 A1292 Set of 5 4.25 1.40

Christmas A1293

Designs: 1.25z, Worshippers at shrine. 2.10z, Window, ornaments, candle, poinsettia.

2004, Nov. 5 Photo. *Perf. 11½x11¾*
3760-3761 A1293 Set of 2 2.25 .75

History of the Earth — A1294

No. 3762: a, Birth (narodziny). b, Infancy (dziecinstwo). c, Youth (mlodosc). d, Maturity (dojrzalosc).

Perf. 11½ Syncopated

2004, Dec. 3 Litho.
3762 A1294 1.25z Block of 4, #a-d 3.50 1.10

City Landmarks Type of 2002

Design: Monument of Hygea, Raczynski Library, Poznan.

2005, Jan. 3 Photo. *Perf. 11½x11¾*
3763 A1228 1.30z multi .90 .30

13th Concert of the Great Holiday Help Orchestra — A1295

2005, Jan. 6 *Perf. 11¼x11½*
3764 A1295 1.30z multi .90 .30

Konstanty Ildefons Galczynski (1905-53), Poet — A1296

2005, Jan. 14 *Perf. 11½x11¼*
3765 A1296 1.30z multi .90 .30

Mikolaj Rej (1505-69), Writer A1297

2005, Jan. 26 *Perf. 11¼x11½*
3766 A1297 1.30z black & red .90 .30

Love A1298

2005, Feb. 1 Photo. *Perf. 11¼x11½*
3767 A1298 1.30z multi .90 .30

Easter — A1299

Flowers and: 1.30z, Rabbit. 2.20z, Chick.

2005, Mar. 1 *Perf. 11¾x11½*
3768-3769 A1299 Set of 2 2.40 .75

Hans Christian Andersen (1805-75), Author — A1300

Designs: No. 3770, 1.30z, The Little Mermaid (Mala Syrenka), No. 3771, 1.30z, The Snow Queen (Królowa Sniegu).

Perf. 11½x11¾ Syncopated

2005, Mar. 15 Litho.
3770-3771 A1300 Set of 2 1.75 .55

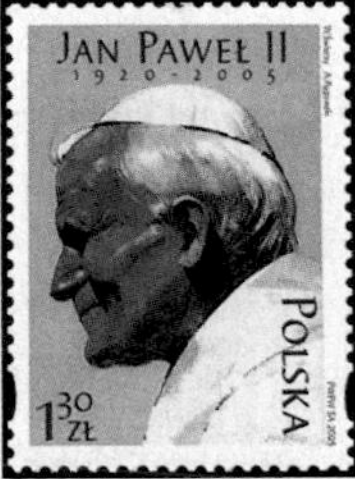

Pope John Paul II (1920-2005) A1301

Perf. 11½x11¾ Syncopated

2005, Apr. 8 Litho.
3772 A1301 1.30z multi .90 .30

Extreme Sports — A1302

No. 3773: a, Parachuting. b, Bungee jumping. c, Rock climbing. d, White water rafting.

Perf. 11¾x11½ Syncopated

2005, Apr. 15 Litho.
3773 A1302 1.30z Block of 4, #a-d 3.75 1.20

Souvenir Sheet

Pacific Explorer 2005 World Stamp Expo, Sydney — A1303

Perf. 11¼x11½ Syncopated

2005, Apr. 21

3774 A1303 3.50z multi 2.40 .85

No. 3774 exists imperf., value: mint $3.25, used $5.50.

Souvenir Sheet

Pope John Paul II (1920-2005) — A1304

Perf. 11½x11¼ Syncopated

2005, Apr. 22

3775 A1304 3.50z multi 2.40 1.10

All Saints Collegiate Church, Sieradz — A1305

Buildings, Katowice A1306

Baltic Shore, Sopot — A1307

Buildings, Szczecin A1308

St. John the Baptist Cathedral, Przemysl A1309

Perf. 11¾x11½, 11½x11¾

2005			**Photo.**	
3776 A1305	20g multi		.25	.25
3777 A1306	30g multi		.25	.25
3778 A1307	2.20z multi		1.50	.50
3779 A1308	2.80z multi		1.90	.60
3780 A1309	3.50z multi		2.40	.70
	Nos. 3776-3780 (5)		6.30	2.30

Issued: 20g, 7/29; 2.20z, 6/15; 2.80z, 5/30; 30g, 10/5; 3.50z, 4/30.

Europa A1310

Perf. 11¼x11½ Syncopated

2005, May 5 **Litho. & Embossed**

3781 A1310 2.20z multi 1.50 .85

End of World War II, 60th Anniv. — A1311

Perf. 11¾x11½ Syncopated

2005, May 6 **Litho.**

3782 A1311 1.30z multi .85 .30

Souvenir Sheet

Youth Literature — A1312

No. 3783: a, 1.30z, *Hour of the Crimson Rose*, by Maria Krüger. b, 2z, *The Little Prince*, by Antoine de Saint-Exupery. c, 2.20z, *20,000 Leagues Under the Sea*, by Jules Verne. d, 2.80z, *In Desert and Wilderness*, by Henryk Sienkiewicz.

Perf. 11½ Syncopated

2005, June 1 **Litho.**

3783 A1312 Sheet of 4, #a-d 5.75 2.25

Souvenir Sheet

Items in the Wilanow Museum — A1313

No. 3784: a, 1.30z, Portrait of Stanislaw Kostka Potocki, by Jacques Louis David, 1781. b, 2z, Nautilus wine cup, 17th cent. c, 2.20z, Porcelain figurine of flower girl, 18th cent. d, 2.80z, Decorative clock, 19th cent.

Perf. 11½x11¼

2005, June 21 **Photo.**

3784 A1313 Sheet of 4, #a-d 5.75 2.00

Embroidered Roses — A1314

Embroidered roses from: 1.30z, Podhale region. 2z, Lowicz region. 2.20z, Lowicz region, diff. 2.80z, Lowicz region, diff.

Perf. 11½x11¼ Syncopated

2005, July 15 **Litho.**

3785-3788 A1314 Set of 4 5.00 1.90

Souvenir Sheet

World Track and Field Championships, Helsinki — A1315

No. 3789: a, 1.30z, Hurdles. b, 1.30z, Shot put. c, 2z, Long jump. d, 2z, Pole vault.

Perf. 11¾x11½ Syncopated

2005, Aug. 8

3789 A1315 Sheet of 4, #a-d 4.50 1.50

Souvenir Sheet

Polish Eagle and Józef Pilsudski — A1316

Perf. 11¼x11½

2005, Aug. 12 **Photo.**

3790 A1316 3.50z multi 2.40 .85

"Miracle on the Vistula," repulse of Red Army counter-offensive, 85th anniv.

Lech Walesa and Solidarity Emblem A1317

Perf. 11½x11¼ Syncopated

2005, Aug. 17 **Litho.**

3791 A1317 2.20z red & gray 1.50 .50

Solidarity Trade Union, 25th anniv.

Polish Radio, 80th Anniv. — A1318

Perf. 11½x11¾ Syncopated

2005, Sept. 1 **Photo.**

3792 A1318 1.30z multi .90 .30

15th Frederic Chopin Piano Competition A1319

Perf. 11¼x11½ Syncopated

2005, Sept. 16 **Litho.**

3793 A1319 2.20z multi 1.50 .50

a. Souvenir sheet of 4 6.00 5.00

Zoo Animals A1320

Designs: 1.30z, Lemuridae, Opole Zoo. 2z, Panthera tigris altaica, Wroclaw Zoo. 2.20z, Ceratotherium simum, Poznan Zoo. 2.80z, Myrmecophagidae, Warsaw Zoo.

Perf. 11½x11¾ Syncopated

2005, Sept. 30

3794-3797 A1320 Set of 4 6.00 2.10

Main Post Office, Cracow A1321

Perf. 11¾x11½ Syncopated

2005, Oct. 7

3798 A1321 1.30z multi .90 .30

World Post Day.

United Nations, 60th Anniv. A1322

Perf. 11¼x11½ Syncopated

2005, Oct. 14

3799 A1322 2.20z multi 1.50 .60

Landmarks in European Union Capitals A1323

Designs: No. 3800, 1.30z, Vilnius Cathedral, Vilnius, Lithuania. No. 3801, 1.30z, St. Matthias's Church, Statue of St. Stephen, Budapest, Hungary. No. 3802, 2.20z, Government building, Dublin, Ireland. No. 3803, 2.20z, Monument, Lisbon, Portugal. 2.80z, Arc de Triomphe, Paris, France.

Perf. 11¼x11½ Syncopated

2005, Oct. 24

3800-3804 A1323 Set of 5 6.75 2.25

See Nos. 3838-3842, 3875-3879, 3914-3918, 3957-3961, 4095.

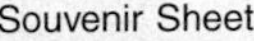

Souvenir Sheet

Paintings by Polish Impressionists — A1324

No. 3805: a, 1.30z, Plowing in the Ukraine, by L. J. Wyczolkowski. b, 1.30z, Still Life, by J. Pankiewicz. c, 2z, Flower Sellers, by O. Boznanska. d, 2z, Gooseberry Bushes, by W. Podkowinski.

2005, Nov. 3 **Photo.**

3805 A1324 Sheet of 4, #a-d, + 2 labels 4.50 2.75

Polish Doctors' Association, Bicent. — A1325

Perf. 11½x11¼ Syncopated

2005, Nov. 24 **Litho.**

3806 A1325 1.30z multi .90 .30

Christmas — A1326

Christmas trees and angel in: 1.30z, Blue. 2.20z, Rose pink.

Perf. 11¾x11½

2005, Nov. 28 **Photo.**

3807-3808 A1326 Set of 2 2.40 .75

2006 Winter Olympics, Turin — A1327

Perf. 11¾x11½ Syncopated

2006, Feb. 7 **Litho.**

3809 A1327 2.40z multi + label 1.60 .50

Love — A1328

Perf. 11½x11¼

2006, Feb. 10 **Photo.**

3810 A1328 1.30z multi .90 .30

Wolfgang Amadeus Mozart (1756-91), Composer — A1329

Perf. 11¾x11½ Syncopated

2006, Feb. 15 **Litho.**

3811 A1329 2.40z multi 1.60 .55

Independent Students Association, 25th Anniv. — A1330

2006, Feb. 17

3812 A1330 1.30z multi .90 .30

Museum of Industry, Warsaw, and Zygmunt Gloger (1845-1910), First President of Polish Touring Society — A1331

2006, Feb. 20

3813 A1331 1.30z multi .90 .30

Polish Touring Society, cent.

Endangered Flora — A1332

Designs: 1.30z, Pedicularis sudetica. 2.40z, Trapa natans.

2006, Mar. 14

3814-3815 A1332 Set of 2 2.50 .80

A1333

Sculptures by Igor Mitoraj — A1334

2006, Mar. 27

3816 A1333 1.30z Lips of Eros .90 .30

3817 A1334 1.30z Dream II .90 .30

a. Souvenir sheet, 2 each #3816-3817 3.50 4.00

Easter — A1335

Traditional customs: 1.30z, Women holding paper flower palms. 2.40z, Man dousing woman with water.

2006, Apr. 3 ***Perf. 11½x11¾***

3818-3819 A1335 Set of 2 2.50 .85

Convent of Jasna Gora, Czestochowa A1336

2006, Apr. 24 **Photo.**

3820 A1336 2.40z multi 1.60 .50

Europa — A1337

Perf. 11½x11¾ Syncopated

2006, May 5 **Litho.**

3821 A1337 2.40z multi 1.60 .50

Souvenir Sheet

Washington 2006 World Philatelic Exhibition — A1338

Perf. 11¼x11½

2006, May 19 **Photo.**

3822 A1338 2.40z multi + label 1.60 .50

Visit of Pope Benedict XVI — A1339

Perf. 11½x11¼ Syncopated

2006, May 25 **Litho.**

3823 A1339 1.30z multi .90 .30

Souvenir Sheet

Lighthouses — A1340

No. 3824: a, Stilo. b, Krynica Morska. c, Gaski. d, Niechorze.

Perf. 11½x11¼

2006, May 29 **Photo.**

3824 A1340 2.40z Sheet of 4, #a-d 6.50 2.25

Toys — A1341

Designs: No. 3825, 1.30z, Pinwheel. No. 3826, 1.30z, Top.

Perf. 11 Syncopated

2006, June 1 **Litho.**

3825-3826 A1341 Set of 2 1.75 .70

See Nos. 3896-3897.

Souvenir Sheets

Worker Uprisings — A1342

Photo. & Engr.

2006 ***Perf. 11¼x11½***

3827 A1342 3.50z Poznan, 1956 2.40 .80

3828 A1342 3.50z Radom, 1976 2.40 .80

Issued: No. 3827, 6/25; No. 3828, 6/28.

Silver and Gold Objects — A1343

No. 3829: a, Tankard with Biblical designs, by Peter Rohde, Poland. b, Jeweled Qing Dynasty cup, China.

Perf. 11½x11¼

2006, June 20 **Photo.**

3829 A1343 1.30z Horiz. pair, #a-b 1.25 .65

See People's Republic of China Nos. 3506-3507.

Jerzy Giedroyc (1906-2000), Literary Magazine Editor — A1344

2006, July 27 **Engr.**

3830 A1344 1.30z black .90 .30

Polish Society of Internal Medicine, Cent. — A1345

Doctors: No. 3831, 1.30z, Witold Eugeniusz Orlowski (1874-1966). No. 3832, 1.30z, Edward Szczeklik (1898-1985). 3z, Antoni Wladyslaw Gluzinski (1856-1935).

Perf. 11¾x11½ Syncopated

2006, Sept. 8 **Litho.**

3831-3833 A1345 Set of 3 3.75 1.25

Souvenir Sheet

19th Polish Philatelic Congress, Lubin — A1346

Photo. & Engr.

2006, Sept. 20 *Perf. 11¼x11½*

3834 A1346 3.50z multi 2.40 .75

Miniature Sheets

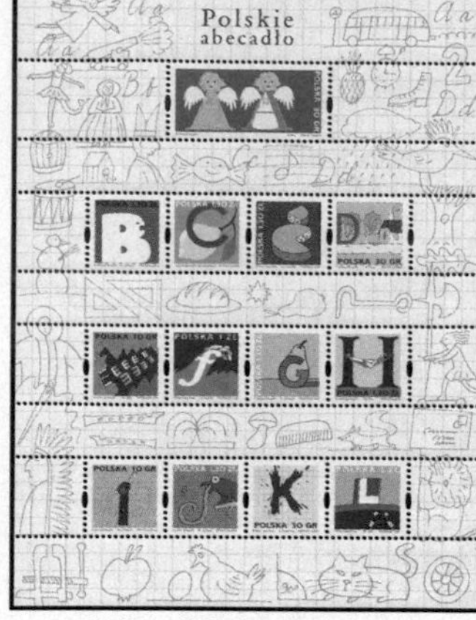
Polish Alphabet — A1347

No. 3835 — Depictions of Polish words starting with letters of the alphabet: a, 10gr, Man shouting "E". b, 10gr, Indian. c, 30gr, Angels. d, 30gr, House. e, 30gr, Ink-splattered "K." f, 1z, Wave. g, 1z, Driver and "L." h, 1.30z, Snowman. i, 1.30z, Lemon. j, 1.30z, Cake. k, 1.30z, Pear. l, 1.30z, Hammock. m, 1.30z, Lizard's tongue.

No. 3836: a, 10gr, Musical notes. b, 10gr, Child. c, 30gr, Carrots. d, 30gr, Eagle. e, 30gr, Zebra. f, 1z, Peacock. g, 1z, Strawberry. h, 1.30z, Patch on "L." i, 1.30z, Lobster. j, 1.30z, Elephant. k, 1.30z, Snail. l, 1.30z, Face with large lips. m, 1.30z, Wolf.

2006 **Litho.** *Perf. 11½ Syncopated*

Sheets of 13, #a-m

3835-3836 A1347 Set of 2 15.00 5.25

Issued: No. 3835, 9/29; No. 3836, 11/7. Nos. 3835c and 3836e are 41x19mm; other stamps are 18x19mm.

World Post Day A1348

2006, Oct. 9 **Photo.** *Perf. 11¼x11½*

3837 A1348 2.40z multi 1.60 .50

Landmarks in European Capitals Type of 2005

Designs: No. 3838, 2.40z, Brandenburg Gate, Berlin, Germany. No. 3839, 2.40z, Colosseum, Rome, Italy. No. 3840, 2.40z, Royal Dramatic Theater, Stockholm, Sweden. No. 3841, 2.40z, St. Alexander Nevski Cathedral, Tallinn, Estonia. No. 3842, 2.40z, St. Paul's Cathedral, Valletta, Malta.

Perf. 11¼x11½ Syncopated

2006, Oct. 24 **Litho.**

3838-3842 A1323 Set of 5 8.00 3.00

Dogs A1349

No. 3843: a, Ogar polski (Polish bloodhound). b, Gonczy polski (Polish hound). c, Polski owczarek nizinny (Polish Lowland sheepdog). d, Chart polski (Polish greyhound). e, Polski owczarek podhalanski (Polish Podhale sheepdog).

2006, Nov. 6

3843 Horiz. strip of 5 4.75 1.75
a.-e. A1349 1.30z Any single .90 .30

Christmas A1350

Designs: 1.30z, Nativity. 2.40z, Angel, "Christmas" in Polish, Italian, English, French and German.

Perf. 11½x11¾

2006, Nov. 30 **Photo.**

3844-3845 A1350 Set of 2 2.50 .75

Wujek Coal Mine Massacre, 25th Anniv. — A1351

Perf. 11¾ Syncopated

2006, Dec. 16 **Litho.**

3846 A1351 1.30z multi .90 .30

15th Concert of the Great Holiday Help Orchestra — A1352

2007, Jan. 4 **Photo.** *Perf. 11¼x11½*

3847 A1352 1.35z multi .95 .30

Cathedral of the Assumption, Pauksch Fountain, Gorzów Wielkopolski A1353

2007, Jan. 19 *Perf. 11¾x11½*

3848 A1353 1.35z multi .95 .30

2007 European Figure Skating Championships, Warsaw — A1354

Perf. 11¾x11½ Syncopated

2007, Jan. 22 **Litho.**

3849 A1354 2.40z multi 1.60 .50

Love — A1355

Perf. 11½x11¾ Syncopated

2007, Feb. 8 **Litho.**

3850 A1355 1.35z multi .95 .30

Easter A1356

Folk art: 1.35z, Lamb made of straw. 2.40z, Chicken made from wooden eggs.

2007, Mar. 8 **Photo.** *Perf. 11¼x11½*

3851-3852 A1356 Set of 2 2.60 .90

Treaty of Rome, 50th Anniv. — A1357

Perf. 11½x11¾ Syncopated

2007, Mar. 20 **Litho.**

3853 A1357 3.55z multi 2.50 .90

Greetings for Special Days — A1358

Designs: No. 3854, 1.35z, Birthday cake and confetti. No. 3855, 1.35z, Grapes, chalice, bread, monogram of Jesus. No. 3856, 1.35z, Wedding rings, rose.

Perf. 11½ Syncopated

2007, Mar. 30 **Litho.**

3854-3856 A1358 Set of 3 3.00 .90

Earth Day A1359

Perf. 11¾x11½ Syncopated

2007, Apr. 22 **Litho.**

3857 A1359 1.35z multi 1.00 .30

Railway Cars A1360

No. 3858: a, Type 5G postal car, 1956. b, Type Cd21b passenger car, 1924. c, Type C3Pr07 passenger car, 1909. d, Type Ci29 passenger car, 1929.

2007, Apr. 28

3858 Horiz. strip of 4 5.50 1.75
a.-b. A1360 1.35z Either single 1.00 .30
c.-d. A1360 2.40z Either single 1.75 .55

Europa A1361

2007, May 5
3859 A1361 3z multi 2.25 .85
Scouting, cent.

Little Helen with a Vase of Flowers, by Stanislaw Wyspianski — A1362

2007, May 18
3860 A1362 1.35z multi 1.00 .30
Stanislaw Wyspianski Year.

Karol Szymanowski (1882-1937), Composer A1363

2007, May 26 ***Perf. 11½x11¼***
3861 A1363 1.35z multi 1.00 .30
Karol Szymanowski Year.

Granting of Municipal Rights to Cracow, 750th Anniv. — A1364

Photo. & Engr.
2007, May 29 ***Perf. 11¾x11½***
3862 A1364 2.40z multi 1.75 .65

Souvenir Sheet

St. Petersburg Intl. Philatelic Exhibition — A1365

2007, June 12 ***Perf. 11¼x11***
3863 A1365 3z multi 2.25 .75

Nicolaus Copernicus Planetarium, Chorzów A1366

Perf. 11½x11¾
2007, June 15 **Photo.**
3864 A1366 3.55z multi 2.60 .75

Souvenir Sheet

Lighthouses — A1367

No. 3865: a, 1.35z, Gdansk Lighthouse. b, 2.40z. Rozewie Lighthouse. c, 3z, Kolobrzeg Lighthouse. d, 3.55z, Hel Lighthouse.

2007, June 15 ***Perf. 11½x11¼***
3865 A1367 Sheet of 4, #a-d 7.50 2.50

Holy Virgin of Lesniów A1368

Perf. 11½x11¼ Syncopated
2007, July 2 **Litho.**
3866 A1368 1.35z multi 1.00 .30
Lesniów Jubilee Year.

Arabian Horses — A1369

No. 3867 — Color of horse: a, Brown. b, White. c, Brown, diff. d, White, diff.

Perf. 11½x11¾ Syncopated
2007, Aug. 31
3867 Horiz. strip of 4 8.50 3.00
a. A1369 1.35z multi 1.00 .30
b. A1369 3z multi 2.25 .75
c.-d. A1369 3.55z Either single 2.60 .95

Animals in Polish Zoos — A1370

Designs: 1.35z, Saguinus imperator, Plock Zoo. 2.40z, Ciconia nigra, Lódz Zoo. 3z, Loxodonta africana, Gdansk Zoo. 3.55z, Uncia uncia, Cracow Zoo.

Perf. 11½x11¾ Syncopated
2007, Sept. 11 **Litho.**
3868-3871 A1370 Set of 4 7.75 2.50

50th Warsaw Autumn Intl. Contemporary Music Festival — A1371

Perf. 11¼x11½ Syncopated
2007, Sept. 21
3872 A1371 3z multi 2.25 .70

Theater in Katowice, Cent. A1372

Perf. 11x11½ Syncopated
2007, Oct. 5 **Litho.**
3873 A1372 1.35z multi 1.10 .30

World Post Day A1373

Perf. 11¾x11½ Syncopated
2007, Oct. 9 **Litho.**
3874 A1373 1.35z multi 1.10 .30

Landmarks in European Union Capitals Type of 2005

Designs: No. 3875, 1.35z, Statue of St. Roland and House of Blackheads, Riga, Latvia. No. 3876, 1.35z, Dragon's Bridge, Ljubljana, Slovenia. No. 3877, 3z, Plaza de Cibeles, Madrid. No. 3878, 3z, Luxembourg Philharmonic Building, Luxembourg. 3.55z, Tower Bridge, London.

Perf. 11¼x11½ Syncopated
2007, Oct. 24 **Litho.**
3875-3879 A1323 Set of 5 9.75 2.75

Pope John Paul II Foundation, 25th Anniv. A1374

2007, Oct. 30
3880 A1374 1.35z multi 1.10 .35

Self-portrait, by Jerzy Duda-Gracz (1941-2004) — A1375

2007, Nov. 5
3881 A1375 1.35z multi 1.10 .30

Teddy Bear and Christmas Tree — A1376

Adoration of the Magi, by Mikolaj Haberschrack A1377

Perf. 11½x11¼
2007, Nov. 27 **Photo.**
3882 A1376 1.35z multi .95 .30
3883 A1377 3z multi 2.00 .45

Joseph Conrad (1857-1924), Writer — A1378

2007, Dec. 3 **Engr.** ***Perf. 11¼x11½***
3884 A1378 3z black 2.00 .70

Souvenir Sheet

PostEurop Plenary Assembly, Cracow — A1379

Perf. 11½x11¼ Syncopated
2008, Jan. 15 **Litho.**
3885 A1379 3z multi 2.00 .85

Love
A1380

Perf. 11¾x11½ Syncopated

2008, Feb. 7 **Litho.**
3886 A1380 1.35z multi .95 .30

Easter — A1381

Designs: 1.35z, Easter eggs. 2.40z, Easter eggs, diff.

Perf. 11½x11¼

2008, Feb. 29 **Photo.**
3887-3888 A1381 Set of 2 2.50 .85

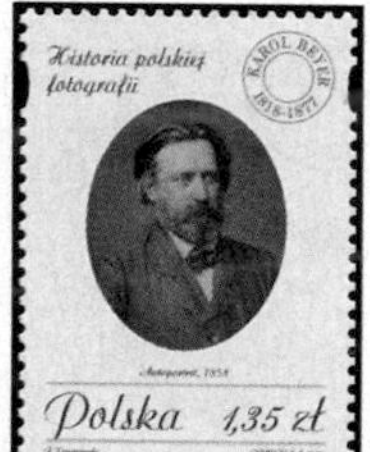
Photography by Karol Beyer (1818-77)
A1382

No. 3889: a, Self-portrait, 1858. b, Peasants from Wilanów, 1866. c, Holy Cross Church, Warsaw, 1858, d, Russian Army in Castle Square, Warsaw, 1861.

Perf. 11½x11¾ Syncopated

2008, Feb. 29 **Litho.**
3889 Horiz. strip of 4 3.75 1.50
a.-d. A1382 1.35z Any single .90 .30

Border Guards, 80th Anniv. — A1383

Perf. 11½x11¼ Syncopated

2008, Mar. 22 **Litho.**
3890 A1383 2.10z multi 1.50 .50

Military Aircraft — A1384

No. 3891: a, 3z, TS-11 Iskra (Spark). b, 3.55z, F-16 Jastrzab (Falcon).

Perf. 11½x11¾ Syncopated

2008, Mar. 31
3891 A1384 Horiz. pair, #a-b 4.50 1.75

Meteorological Phenomena — A1385

No. 3892: a, Sandstorm. b, Lightning. c, Rainbow. d, Tornado.

Perf. 11¾x11½ Syncopated

2008, Apr. 25
3892 Horiz. strip of 4 5.00 1.75
a.-b. A1385 1.35z Either single .90 .25
c.-d. A1385 2.40z Either single 1.60 .60

Europa
A1386

2008, May 5
3893 A1386 3z multi 2.00 .70

European Organization of Supreme Audit Institutions Congress, Cracow
A1387

Perf. 11½x11¾ Syncopated

2008, May 30
3894 A1387 3.55z multi 2.40 .85

UEFA Euro 2008 Soccer Championships, Austria and Switzerland
A1388

Perf. 11½x11¼ Syncopated

2008, May 30 **Photo.**
3895 A1388 1.35z multi .90 .30

Toys Type of 2006

Designs: 1.35z, Wooden train. 3z, Xylophone.

Perf. 11 Syncopated

2008, June 1 **Litho.**
3896-3897 A1341 Set of 2 3.00 .85

Boy and Iranian Rug — A1389

Perf. 11½x11¼ Syncopated

2008, June 10
3898 A1389 2.40z multi 1.60 .55

Esfahan, Iran, city of Polish exiled orphan children.

Souvenir Sheet

EFIRO 2008 Philatelic Exhibition, Bucharest, Romania — A1390

Photo. & Engr.

2008, June 20 *Perf. 11x11½*
3899 A1390 3z multi 2.00 .85

No. 3899 exists imperf. Value: mint $5, used $6.

Coronation of St. Mary of the Snow Icon, 25th Anniv. — A1391

Perf. 11½x11¼ Syncopated

2008, June 21 **Litho.**
3900 A1391 1.35z multi .90 .30

Towns — A1392

Designs: 1.45z, Tower and column, Racibórz. 3.65z, Town Hall and Neptune Fountain, Jelenia Góra.

2008 **Photo.** *Perf. 11¾x11½*
3901 A1392 1.45z multi 1.00 .30
3902 A1392 3.65z multi 2.50 .75

Issued: 1.45z, 7/1. 3.65z, 8/1.

2008 Summer Olympics, Beijing — A1393

No. 3903: a, Swimming. b, Women's volleyball. c, Women's pole vault. d, Fencing.

Perf. 11½ Syncopated

2008, Aug. 8 **Litho.**
3903 Horiz. strip of 4 2.00 .75
a.-b. A1393 10g Either single .25 .25
c.-d. A1393 1.45z Either single 1.00 .35
e. Souvenir sheet, #3903 3.00 2.50

Bridges
A1394

No. 3904: a, Siekierkowski Bridge, Warsaw. b, Poniatowski Bridge, Warsaw. c, Welded bridge over Sludwia River, Maurzyce. d, Ernest Malinowski Bridge, Torun.

Perf. 11¾x11½ Syncopated

2008, Aug. 29 **Litho. & Embossed**
3904 Horiz. strip of 4 6.00 2.00
a.-b. A1394 1.45z Either single 1.00 .35
c.-d. A1394 3z Either single 2.00 .70

Souvenir Sheet

Polish Post, 450th Anniv. — A1395

No. 3905: a, Prosper Provana, first supervisor of Krakow to Venice postal service. b, King Sigismund II August and grant to Provana (50x30mm). c, Sebastian Montelupi, administrator of royal postal service in 1564.

Photo. & Engr.

2008, Sept. 15 *Perf. 11¾x11½*
3905 A1395 1.45z Sheet of 3, #a-c 3.00 1.25

Sheet margin of No. 3905 is embossed.

Miniature Sheet

Presidents of the Republic of Poland in Exile — A1396

No. 3906: a, Wladyslaw Raczkiewicz (1885-1947), 1939-47 President. b, August Zaleeski (1883-1972), 1947-72 President. c, Stanislaw Ostrowski (1892-1982), 1972-79 President. d, Edward Raczynski (1891-1993), 1979-86 President. e, Kazimierz Sabbat (1913-89), 1986-89 President. f, Ryszard Kaczorowski, 1989-90 President.

Perf. 11¾x11½ Syncopated

2008, Sept. 24 **Litho.**
3906 A1396 1.45z Sheet of 6, #a-f 6.00 2.25

Lódz Sports Club, Cent.
A1397

Perf. 11¼x11½

2008, Sept. 30 **Photo.**
3907 A1397 1.45z red & silver 1.00 .40

Arrival of Poles in America, 400th Anniv.
A1398

Perf. 11¾x11½ Syncopated

2008, Sept. 30 **Litho.**
3908 A1398 3z multi 2.00 .90

World Post Day A1399

Perf. 11¾x11½ Syncopated

2008, Oct. 9 **Litho.**
3909 A1399 2.10z multi 1.40 .50

Composers A1400

Designs: No. 3910, 1.45z, Henryk Mikolaj Górecki. No. 3911, 1.45z, Mieczylaw Karlowicz (1876-1909). No. 3912, 1.45z, Wojciech Kilar. No. 3913, 1.45z, Witold Lutoslawski (1913-94).

Perf. 11½x11¾ Syncopated

2008, Oct. 18 **Litho.**
3910-3913 A1400 Set of 4 4.25 1.40

Landmarks in European Union Capitals Type of 2005

Designs: No. 3914, 1.45z, Rijksmuseum, Amsterdam, Netherlands. No. 3915, 1.45z, Royal Library, Copenhagen, Denmark. No. 3916, 3z, Acropolis, Athens, Greece. No. 3917, 3z, Charles Bridge, Prague, Czech Republic. 3.65z, Parliament, Vienna, Austria.

Perf. 11¼x11½ Syncopated

2008, Oct. 24
3914-3918 A1323 Set of 5 8.50 3.00

Jeremi Przybora (1915-2004) and Jerzy Wasowski (1913-84), Television Performers — A1401

Perf. 11¾x11½ Syncopated

2008, Oct. 30
3919 A1401 1.45z multi 1.10 .35

Television show, Kabaret Starszych Panów (Senior Men's Cabaret), 50th anniv.

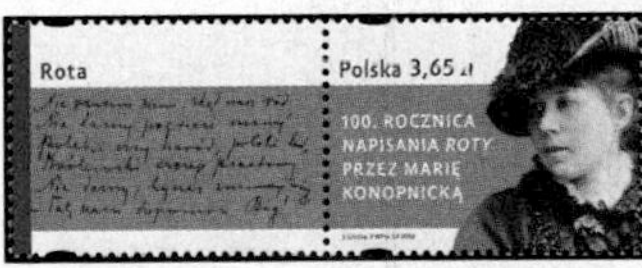
The Oath, Poem by Maria Konopnicka, Cent. — A1402

2008, Nov. 7
3920 A1402 3.65z multi + label 2.60 .85

Independence, 90th Anniv. — A1403

2008, Nov. 11 **Engr.** ***Perf. 11x11¼***
3921 A1403 1.45z carmine lake .95 .35

Election of Karol Woytyla as Pope John Paul II, 30th Anniv. — A1404

Perf. 11½x11¼

2008, Nov. 27 **Photo.**
3922 A1404 2.40z multi 1.60 .70

Christmas A1405

Stars and snowflakes with background color of: 1.45z, Blue. 3z, Red violet.

Perf. 11½x11¼

2008, Nov. 27 **Photo.**
3923-3924 A1405 Set of 2 3.00 1.00

Zbigniew Herbert (1924-98), Writer — A1406

Perf. 11½x11¼ Syncopated

2008, Dec. 1 **Litho.**
3925 A1406 2.10z multi 1.40 .50

United Nations Conference on Climate Change, Poznan A1407

2008, Dec. 1 **Photo.** ***Perf. 11½x11¼***
3926 A1407 2.40z multi 1.60 .60

Souvenir Sheet

Polish Post, 450th Anniv. — A1408

Printed On Silk
Self-Adhesive
Silk-screened

2008, Dec. 19 ***Imperf.***
3927 A1408 20z multi 13.50 9.50

Louis Braille (1809-52), Educator of the Blind — A1409

Perf. 11¾x11½ Syncopated

2009, Jan. 4 **Litho.**
3928 A1409 1.45z multi + label 1.00 .40

Concentration Camp Survivors A1410

No. 3929: a, Witold Pilecki (1901-48), organizer of resistance movement at Auschwitz. b, Józef Wladyslaw Wolski (1910-2008), historian. c, Bishop Ignacy Ludwik Jez (1914-2007). d, Stanislawa Maria Sawicka (1895-1982), art and music historian.

Perf. 11½x11¼ Syncopated

2009, Jan. 30 **Litho.**
3929 Horiz. strip of 4 5.25 2.00
a. A1410 1.45z multi 1.00 .35
b. A1410 2.10z multi 1.40 .35
c. A1410 2.40z multi 1.40 .60
d. A1410 3z multi 2.00 .70

Love — A1411

Perf. 11½x11¾ Syncopated

2009, Feb. 6
3930 A1411 1.45z multi 1.00 .35

Miniature Sheet

Sculpture and Fabric Art by Wladyslaw Hasior (1928-99) — A1412

No. 3931: a, 1.45z, Zwiastowanie (The Herald). b, 1.45z, Mucha (The Fly). c, 2.10z, Sztandar Zielonej Poetki (Banner of the Green Poet). d, 2.40z, Sztandar Rozbieranie do snu (The Night Undressing Banner).

Perf. 11½x11¾ Syncopated

2009, Mar. 6 **Litho.**
3931 A1412 Sheet of 4, #a-d 5.25 3.50

Easter — A1413

Paintings by Szymon Czechowicz (1689-1775): 1.55z, Chrystus Zmartwychwstaly (Christ Resurrected). 3z, Zlozenie do Grobu (Entombment), vert.

Perf. 11½x11¾, 11¾x11½

2009, Apr. 1 **Photo.**
3932-3933 A1413 Set of 2 3.00 .75

Souvenir Sheet

China 2009 World Philatelic Exhibition, Luoyang — A1414

Perf. 11½x11¼ Syncopated

2009, Apr. 16 **Litho.**
3934 A1414 3z multi 2.00 1.00

Souvenir Sheet

Berek Joselewicz, A Jewish Fighter for Polish Freedom's Last Battle, Kock, by Juliusz Kossak — A1415

Perf. 11¼x11½ Syncopated

2009, Apr. 22
3935 A1415 3z multi 2.00 1.00

See Israel No. 1772.

Miniature Sheet

Photographs of African Animals by Tomasz Gudzowaty — A1416

No. 3936: a, 1.55z, First Lesson of Killing (cheetahs and antelope). b, 1.95z, Zebras at Waterhole. c, 2.40z, Paradise Crossing (crocodile and gnus in water). d, 3z, Elephants.

Perf. 11¾x11½ Syncopated

2009, Apr. 30

3936 A1416 Sheet of 4, #a-d 6.00 2.40

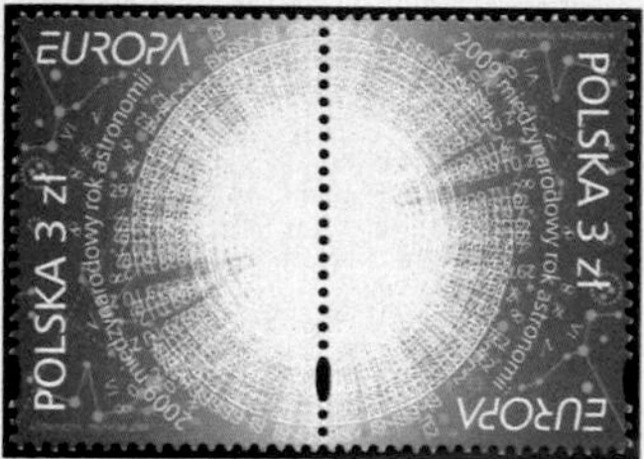

Europa — A1417

No. 3937 — Star map drawings and overlapping text with: a, Syncopation near "O" in Polska. b, Syncopation near "Europa."

Perf. 11½x11¾ Syncopated

2009, May 5

3937 A1417 3z Horiz. pair, #a-b 3.75 .75

Intl. Year of Astronomy.

Grazyna Bacewicz (1909-69), Composer A1418

2009, May 28

3938 A1418 1.55z multi .95 .40

Tytus, Romek, and A'Tomek, Comic Book Characters by Papcio Chmiel — A1419

No. 3939: a, Tytus (ape). b, Romek (boy in boots). c, A'Tomek (man in suit).

2009, May 29

3939 A1419 1.55z Horiz. strip of 3, #a-c 3.00 1.25

Souvenir Sheet

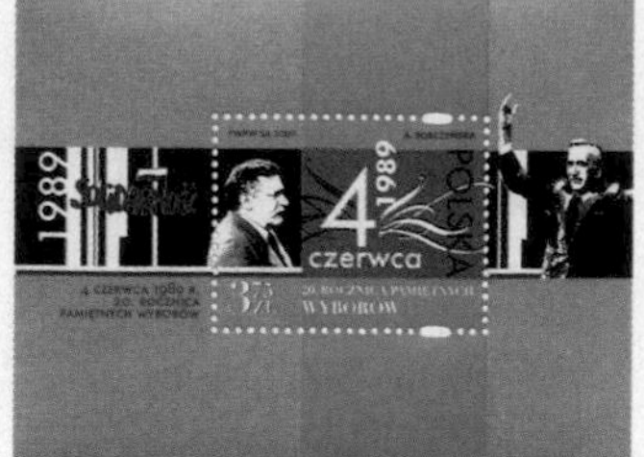

Lech Walesa — A1420

Perf. 11¼x11½ Syncopated

2009, May 30

3940 A1420 3.75z multi 2.40 .85

Victories of Solidarity candidates in June 4, 1989 parliamentary elections, 20th anniv.

St. Bruno of Querfurt (c. 974-1009) A1421

Perf. 11½x11¼

2009, June 19 **Photo.**

3941 A1421 3z multi 2.00 .65

Souvenir Sheet

Ship "Dar Mlodzilzy" — A1422

Photo. & Engr.

2009, June 30 ***Perf. 11¼x11***

3942 A1422 3.75z multi 2.40 1.00

2009 Tall Ships Race, Gdynia.

Baltic Sea Mammals A1423

No. 3943: a, Phocoena phocoena. b, Halichoerus grypus. c, Phoca vitulina. d, Phoca hispida.

Perf. 11½x11¾ Syncopated

2009, July 31 **Litho.**

3943 Horiz. strip of 4 5.00 2.00

a.-b. A1423 1.55z Either single .70 .40

c.-d. A1423 1.95z Either single .85 .60

Souvenir Sheet

Warsaw Uprising, 65th Anniv. — A1424

Photo. & Engr.

2009, Aug. 1 ***Perf. 11½x11¼***

3944 A1424 3.75z multi 2.60 1.00

Fruit and Flowers A1425

Designs: 1.95z, Cerasus avium. 3.75z, Calendula officinalis.

Perf. 11½x11¾

2009, Aug. 10 **Photo.**

3945-3946 A1425 Set of 2 4.00 1.25

See Nos. 3986, 4029, 4178-4180, 4205.

Famous Polish Emigrés A1426

Designs: No. 3947, 1.55z, Jan Czochralski (1885-1953), metallurgist. No. 3948, 1.55z, Antoni Patek (1812-77), watchmaker. No. 3949, 1.95z, Ludwik Hirszfeld (1884-1954), serologist. No. 3950, 1.95z, Jerzy Rózycki (1909-42), Marian Rejewski (1905-80) and Henryk Zygalski (1907-78), cryptologists who broke the Enigma code.

Perf. 11½x11¾ Syncopated

2009, Aug. 28 **Litho.**

3947-3950 A1426 Set of 4 5.00 2.00

Juliusz Slowacki (1809-49), Writer — A1427

Perf. 11¼x11½

2009, Aug. 31 **Photo.**

3951 A1427 1.55z multi 1.10 .40

Start of World War II, 70th Anniv. A1428

Battles of: 1.55z, Wegierska Górka. 2.40z, Wielun.

2009, Sept. 1

3952-3953 A1428 Set of 2 2.75 1.00

European Men's Basketball Championships, Poland — A1429

Perf. 11½x11¾ Syncopated

2009, Sept. 7 **Litho.**

3954 A1429 3z multi 2.10 .70

Selection of Tadeusz Mazowiecki as Prime Minister, 20th Anniv. — A1430

Perf. 11¾x11½ Syncopated

2009, Sept. 11 **Litho. & Embossed**

3955 A1430 1.55z multi 1.10 .40

European Women's Volleyball Championships, Poland — A1431

Perf. 11¾x11½ Syncopated

2009, Sept. 25 **Litho.**

3956 A1431 3z multi 2.10 .70

Landmarks in European Capitals Type of 2005

Designs: No. 3957, 1.55z, Castle, Bratislava, Slovakia. No. 3958, 1.55z, Famagusta Gate, Nicosia, Cyprus. No. 3959, 3z, Grand Place, Brussels, Belgium. No. 3960, 3z, Plac Zamkowy (Castle Square), Warsaw. 3.75z, National Museum, Helsinki, Finland.

Perf. 11¼x11½ Syncopated

2009, Oct. 6 **Litho.**

3957-3961 A1323 Set of 5 9.00 3.00

World Post Day — A1432

Photo. & Engr.

2009, Oct. 9 ***Perf. 11½x11¼***

3962 A1432 3z multi 2.10 .75

Father Jerzy Popieluszko (1947-84), Murdered Supporter of Solidarity Movement — A1433

Perf. 11¾x11½ Syncopated

2009, Oct. 19 **Litho.**

3963 A1433 1.55z multi 1.10 .40

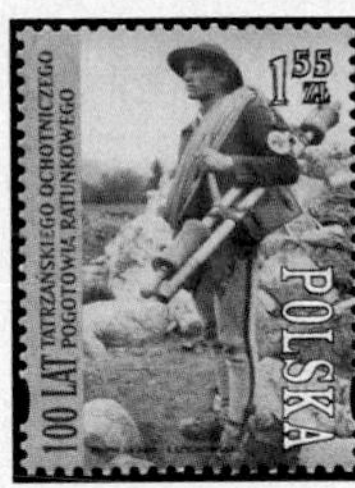

Tatra Mountain Volunteer Rescue Corps, Cent. — A1434

Perf. 11½x11¾ Syncopated

2009, Oct. 24 **Litho.**

3964 A1434 1.55z multi 1.10 .40

Pawel Jasienica (1909-70), Writer — A1435

Perf. 11½x11¼ Syncopated

2009, Nov. 10 **Photo.**

3965 A1435 1.55z blk & silver 1.10 .40

Jerzy Franciszek Kulczycki (1640-94), Hero of Battle of Vienna and Viennese Café Proprietor — A1436

2009, Nov. 16 **Litho.**

3966 A1436 1.55z multi + label 1.10 .50

Lost Artworks — A1437

No. 3967: a, Exlibris Willibald Pirckheimer, by Albrecht Dürer. b, Christ Falling Under the Cross, by Peter Paul Rubens. c, Joseph's Dream, by Rembrandt.

Perf. 11½x11¼

2009, Nov. 20 **Photo.**

3967 A1437 1.55z Horiz. strip of 3, #a-c 3.50 1.50

Christmas

A1438 A1439

2009, Nov. 27 ***Perf. 11¾x11½***

3968 A1438 1.55z multi 1.10 .35

3969 A1439 2.40z multi 1.75 .70

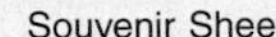

Souvenir Sheet

First Polish Postage Stamp, 150th Anniv. — A1440

Perf. 11½x11¼ Syncopated

2010, Jan. 15 **Litho.**

3970 A1440 4.15z multi 3.00 1.25

2010 Winter Olympics, Vancouver — A1441

Perf. 11¾x11½ Syncopated

2010, Jan. 27

3971 A1441 3z multi 2.10 .75

Miniature Sheet

Cats — A1442

No. 3972 — Breeds: a, 1.55z, Brytyjski krótkowlosy (British shorthair). b, 1.55z, Tajski (Siamese). c, 1.95z, Somalijski (Somali). d, 1.95z, Maine Coon. e, 3z, Pers (Persian). f, 3z, Egzotyk (Exotic).

Perf. 11½x11¾ Syncopated

2010, Feb. 17 **Litho.**

3972 A1442 Sheet of 6, #a-f 9.00 4.50

Souvenir Sheet

Frédóric Chopin (1810-49), Composer — A1443

Perf. 11¼x11½ Syncopated

2010, Feb. 22

3973 A1443 4.15z multi 3.00 1.50

Easter — A1444

Designs: 1.55z, Lamb and banner. 2.40z, Eggs in basket.

2010, Mar. 5 **Photo.** ***Perf. 11¾x11½***

3974-3975 A1444 Set of 2 2.75 1.00

Historical Photographs by Jan Bulhak (1876-1950) A1445

No. 3976: a, House of Stanislaw Stazic, Warsaw, 1920 (shown). b, 16 Poselska Street, Cracow, 1921. c, Vestibule of house in Old Town, Warsaw, 1920. d, Chapel of St. Casimir's Cathedral, Vilnius, 1912.

Perf. 11½x11¾ Syncopated

2010, Mar. 31 **Litho.**

3976 Horiz. strip of 4 5.75 2.25

a.-d. A1445 1.95z Any single 1.40 .50

Special Services of the Republic of Poland, 20th Anniv. — A1446

2010, Apr. 6

3977 A1446 1.55z multi 1.10 .55

Souvenir Sheet

Katyn Massacre Remembrance Day — A1447

Perf. 11¾x11½ Syncopated

2010, Apr. 7

3978 A1447 3z multi 2.10 1.10

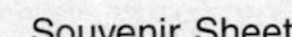

Souvenir Sheet

Portugal 2010 Intl. Philatelic Exhibition, Lisbon — A1448

Perf. 11½x11¾ Syncopated

2010, Apr. 30

3979 A1448 3z multi 2.10 1.10

Europa — A1449

2010, May 5

3980 A1449 3z multi 1.90 .95

Pope John Paul II (1920-2005) and St. Peter Apostle Church, Wadowice — A1450

Perf. 11¾x11½ Syncopated

2010, May 18 **Litho. & Embossed**

3981 A1450 1.95z multi + label 1.40 .70

Tczew Bridge — A1451

Perf. 11½x11¼

2010, May 27 **Photo.**

3982 A1451 1.55z multi 1.00 .45

Tczew, 750th anniv.

Beatification of Father Jerzy Popieluszko (1947-84) — A1452

Perf. 11¾x11½ Syncopated

2010, June 6 **Litho.**

3983 A1452 1.95z multi 1.40 .50

Dominican Convent of Ursuline Sisters, Sieradz, 750th Anniv. — A1453

Perf. 11¼x11½

2010, June 24 **Photo.**

3984 A1453 1.55z multi 1.00 .45

Souvenir Sheet

Battle of Grunwald, 600th Anniv. — A1454

2010, July 15 *Perf. 11x11¼*

3985 A1454 8.30z multi 5.50 2.75

Fruit and Flowers Type of 2009

Design: 4.15z, Myosotis arvensis.

Perf. 11½x11¾

2010, Aug. 10 **Photo.**

3986 A1425 4.15z multi 1.00 1.40

Scouting in Poland, Cent. — A1455

2010, Aug. 17 *Perf. 11½x11¼*

3987 A1455 1.95z multi 1.40 .50

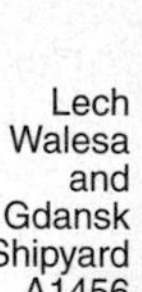

Lech Walesa and Gdansk Shipyard A1456

Perf. 11¾x11½ Syncopated

2010, Aug. 31 **Litho. & Embossed**

3988 A1456 3.75z multi 2.50 .85

Government cessions after settlement of Solidarity-led strikes, 30th anniv.

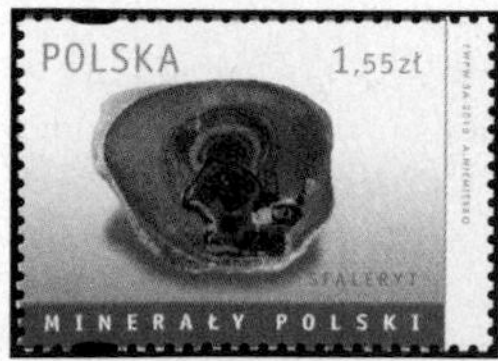

Minerals A1457

Perf. 11¾x11½ Syncopated

2010, Sept. 3 **Litho.**

3989	Vert. strip of 4	6.00	3.00
a.	A1457 1.55z Sphalerite	1.00	.40
b.	A1457 1.95z Gypsum	1.25	.55
c.	A1457 2.40z Agate	1.60	.70
d.	A1457 3z Chrysoprase	2.00	.80

World Post Day — A1458

2010, Oct. 9 Photo. *Perf. 11½x11¼*

3990 A1458 1.95z multi 1.40 .50

a. Tete-beche pair 2.80 1.40

Landmarks in European Capitals Type of 2005

Designs: 1.95z, Alexander Nevsky Cathedral, Sofia, Bulgaria. 3z, Romanian Athenaeum, Bucharest, Romania.

Perf. 11¼x11½ Syncopated

2010, Oct. 24 **Litho.**

3991-3992 A1323 Set of 2 3.75 1.90

Personalized Stamp — A1459

Perf. 11½x11¾ Syncopated

2010, Oct. 29 **Litho.**

3993 A1459 A multi + label 7.25 7.25

No. 3993 had a franking value of 1.55z on day of issue and was printed in sheets of 8 stamps + 8 labels that could be personalized for 56z.

Widzew Lódz Soccer Team, Cent. A1460

2010, Nov. 5 Photo. *Perf. 11¼x11½*

3994 A1460 1.55z multi 1.10 .55

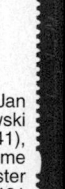

Ignacy Jan Paderewski (1860-1941), Pianist, Prime Minister A1461

Perf. 11½x11¾ Syncopated

2010, Nov. 18 **Litho.**

3995 A1461 3z multi 2.10 1.10

Christmas A1462

Star of Bethlehem, text in Polish and: 1.55z, Christmas tree. 2.40z, Night sky.

Perf. 11½x11¾

2010, Nov. 27 **Photo.**

3996-3997 A1462 Set of 2 2.75 1.40

Love — A1463

Perf. 11½x11¾

2010, Dec. 30 **Photo.**

3998 A1463 A multi 1.10 .55

No. 3998 sold for 1.55z on day of issue.

Johannes Hevelius (1611-87), Astronomer — A1464

Perf. 11¾x11½ Syncopated

2011, Jan. 28 **Litho.**

3999 A1464 3z multi + label 2.10 1.10

No. 3999 was printed in sheets of 6 + 6 labels.

Field Hockey A1465

2011, Feb. 4

4000 A1465 2.40z multi 1.75 .85

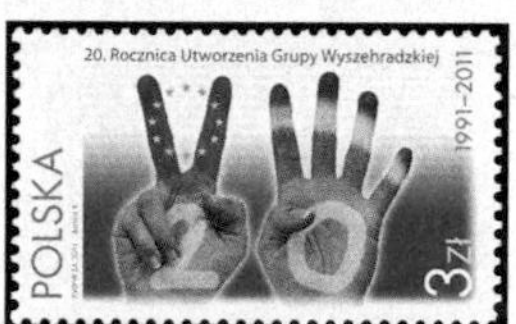

Visegrád Group, 20th Anniv. — A1466

2011, Feb. 11 *Perf. 12*

4001 A1466 3z multi 2.10 1.10

See Czech Republic No. 3490, Hungary No. 4183, Slovakia No. 611.

Governmental Registration of Lódz Independent Student's Union, 30th Anniv. — A1467

Perf. 11¼x11½ Syncopated

2011, Feb. 17

4002 A1467 1.95z multi 1.40 .70

Cystic Fibrosis Week — A1468

Perf. 11½x11¼

2011, Feb. 28 **Photo.**

4003 A1468 1.55z multi 1.10 .55

Stefan Kisielewski (1911-91), Composer and Writer — A1469

Perf. 11¾x11½ Syncopated

2011, Mar. 7 **Litho.**

4004 A1469 1.95z multi 1.40 .70

a. Tete beche pair 2.80 1.40

Easter — A1470

Flowers and: 1.55z, Chick. 2.40z, Rabbit.

Perf. 11¾x11½

2011, Mar. 25 **Photo.**

4005-4006 A1470 Set of 2 3.00 1.50

Adam Cardinal Kozlowiecki (1911-2007) — A1471

2011, Mar. 31 Photo. *Perf. 11x11½*

4007 A1471 1.95z multi 1.50 .75

Miniature Sheet

Photographs of People by Elzbieta Dzikowska — A1472

No. 4008: a, 1.95z, Monk from Myanmar (red panel). b, 1.95z, Hamer girl from Ethiopia (purple panel). c, 2.40z, Girl from Myanmar (yellow green panel). d, 2.40z, man from Palestine and camel (yellow orange panel). e, 3z, Woman from Nepal (blue panel). f, 3z, Indian woman from Peru (red violet panel).

Perf. 11½x11¾ Syncopated

2011, Apr. 18 **Litho.**

4008 A1472 Sheet of 6, #a-f 11.00 5.50

Souvenir Sheet

Beatification of Pope John Paul II — A1473

Perf. 11½x11¼ Syncopated

2011, Apr. 28

4009 A1473 8.30z multi 6.00 3.00

See Vatican City No. 1471.

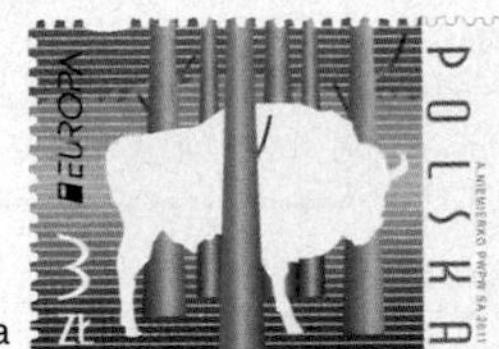

Europa A1474

Perf. 11¾x11½ Syncopated

2011, May 5

4010 A1474 3z multi 2.25 1.10

Intl. Year of Forests.

Cartoon Characters by Bohdan Butenko A1475

No. 4011: a, Cezar (blue dog). b, Gucio (brown hippopotamus). c, Kwapiszon (boy with white hat). d, Gapiszon (boy with striped stocking hat).

2011, May 27 ***Perf. 11½ Syncopated***

4011 Horiz. strip of 4 5.75 3.00
a.-b. A1475 1.55z Either single 1.10 .55
c.-d. A1475 2.40z Either single 1.75 .85

Polish Presidency of European Union Council — A1476

Perf. 11¾x11½ Syncopated

2011, June 30 **Litho.**

4012 A1476 3z multi + label 2.25 1.10

Souvenir Sheet

Czeslaw Milosz (1911-2004), 1980 Nobel Laureate in Literature — A1477

Photo. & Engr.

2011, June 30 ***Perf. 11x11½***

4013 A1477 4.15z multi 3.00 1.50

St. Maximilian Kolbe (1894-1941) A1478

Perf. 11½x11¾ Syncopated

2011, Aug. 12 **Litho.**

4014 A1478 1.95z multi 1.40 .70

Famous Poles A1479

Designs: 1.55z, Michal Sedziwój (1566-1636), chemist. 1.95z. Jan Szczepanik (1872-1926), inventor. No. 4017, 3z, Jan Józef Baranowski (1805-88), inventor. No. 4018, 3z, Rudolf Stefan Weigl (1883-1957), biologist.

Perf. 11¾x11½ Syncopated

2011, Aug. 29

4015-4018 A1479 Set of 4 6.00 3.00

Father Jan Dzierzon (1811-1906), Apiarist A1480

Perf. 11½x11¾ Syncopated

2011, Sept. 2

4019 A1480 1.55z multi 1.00 .50

Church of the Assumption of the Virgin Mary, Niegowic, First Pastoral Assignment of Pope John Paul II — A1481

Perf. 11¾x11½ Syncopated

2011, Sept. 22

4020 A1481 1.95z multi + label 1.25 .60

Souvenir Sheet

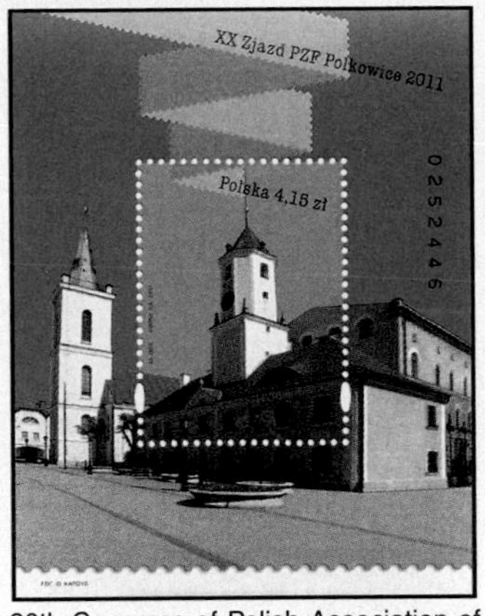

20th Congress of Polish Association of Philatelists, Polkowice — A1482

Perf. 11½x11¾ Syncopated

2011, Sept. 30

4021 A1482 4.15z multi 2.75 1.40

Lost Works of Art A1483

No. 4022: a, Double Portrait of Eliza Parenska, by Stanislaw Wyspianski. b, Scene from the Legends of Theophilus of Adana, by Veit Stoss. c, Woman Looking Backwards, by Jean-Antoine Watteau.

2011, Oct. 21 ***Perf. 11¼x11½***

4022 Horiz. strip of 3 4.75 2.40
a. A1483 1.95z multi 1.25 .60
b. A1483 2.40z multi 1.60 .80
c. A1483 3z multi 1.90 .95

Souvenir Sheet

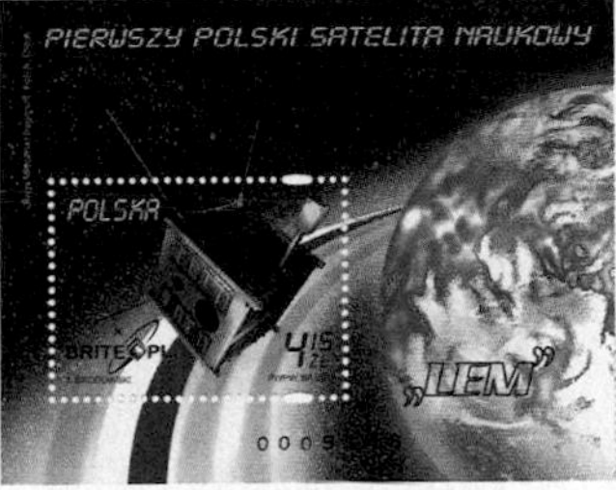

First Polish Scientific Satellite — A1484

Perf. 11¾x11½ Syncopated

2011, Nov. 4

4023 A1484 4.15z multi 2.60 1.40

Souvenir Sheet

Intl. Year of Chemistry — A1485

No. 4024: a, 3z, Nobel medal and radium (36x28mm). b, Marie Curie (1867-1934), 1911 Nobel laureate for Chemistry (40x55mm).

Perf. 12¾ (#4024a), 13x12¾ (#4024b)

2011, Nov. 17 **Litho. & Engr.**

4024 A1485 Sheet of 2, #a-b 6.50 3.25

See Sweden No. 2672.

Christmas A1486

Designs: 1.55z, Santa Claus, reindeer and sleigh. 2.40z, Nativity.

Perf. 11½x11¾

2011, Nov. 25 **Photo.**

4025 A1486 1.55z multi .95 .45

Self-Adhesive

Litho.

Die Cut Perf. 11½x11¾

4026 A1486 2.40z multi 1.50 .75

Souvenir Sheet

Military Suppression of Warsaw Fire Academy Strike, 30th Anniv. — A1487

Perf. 11½x11¾ Syncopated

2011, Dec. 2

4027 A1487 4.15z multi 2.50 1.25

Independence of Kazakhstan, 20th Anniv. — A1488

2011, Dec. 8 Photo. ***Perf. 11¼x11½***
4028 A1488 2.40z multi 1.40 .70

Fruit and Flowers Type of 2009
Perf. 11½x11¾

2011, Dec. 16 Photo.
4029 A1425 1.55z Rubus idaeus .90 .45

Souvenir Sheet

20th Concert of the Great Holiday Help Orchestra — A1489

Litho. (With Foil Application in Sheet Margin)
Perf. 11¾x11½ Syncopated

2012, Jan. 8
4030 A1489 1.95z multi 1.25 .60

National Army, 70th Anniv. — A1490

Perf. 11½x11¼

2012, Feb. 14 Photo.
4031 A1490 1.55z multi 1.00 .50

Souvenir Sheet

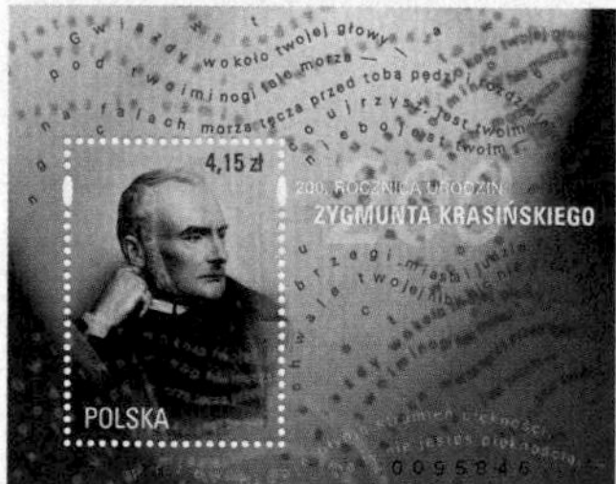

Zygmunt Krasinski (1812-59), Poet — A1491

Perf. 11½x11¾ Syncopated

2012, Feb. 19 Litho.
4032 A1491 4.15z multi 2.75 1.40

Easter — A1492

Stylized flowers and: 1.55z, Lamb. 1.95z, Easter egg. 3z, Rabbit.

2012, Mar. 9 ***Perf. 11¾x11½***
4033-4035 A1492 Set of 3 4.25 2.10

Leopold Kronenberg (1812-78), Banker and Leader of January 1863 Uprising A1493

2012, Mar. 20 Photo. ***Perf. 11½x11***
4036 A1493 2.40z multi 1.50 .75

Photographs of Warsaw by Konrad Brandel (1838-1920) — A1494

No. 4037: a, Dworzec Wiedenski (Vienna Station), c. 1890. b, Krakowskie Przedmiescie, c. 1880. c, Plac Trzech Krzyzy (Three Crosses Square), c. 1875. d, Wiadukt Pancera (Pancera Viaduct), c. 1890.

Perf. 11¾x11½ Syncopated

2012, Mar. 28 Litho.
4037 Vert. strip of 4 5.50 2.75
a.-b. A1494 1.95z Either single 1.25 .60
c.-d. A1494 2.40z Either single 1.50 .75

Suwalki, 300th Anniv. A1495

2012, Mar. 30 Photo. ***Perf. 11x11½***
4038 A1495 1.95z multi 1.25 .60

Miniature Sheet

First Polish Discoveries in Egypt, 150th Anniv. — A1496

No. 4039: a, 1.,55z, Porcelain statue. b, 1.95z, Porcelain statue, diff. c, 2.40z. Nefertem amulet. d, 3z, Michal Tyszkiewicz (1828-97), Egyptologist.

2012, Apr. 30 ***Perf. 11½x11***
4039 A1496 Sheet of 4, #a-d 5.75 3.00

Souvenir Sheet

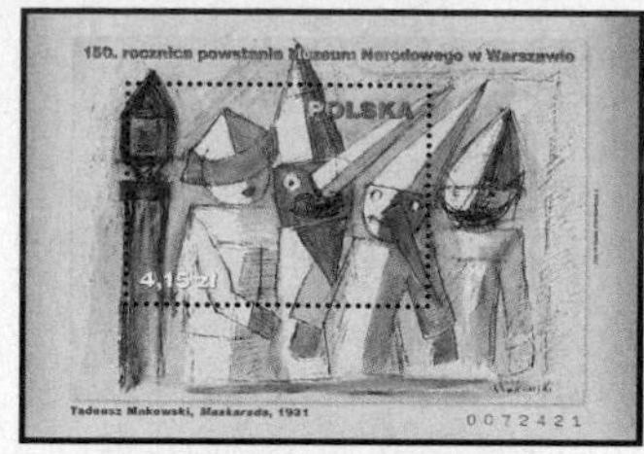

Masquerade, by Tadeusz Makowski — A1497

2012, May 17 ***Perf. 11¼x10¾***
4040 A1497 4.15z multi 2.40 1.25

National Museum, Warsaw, 150th anniv.

Europa A1498

Perf. 11½ Syncopated

2012, May 22 Litho.
4041 A1498 3z multi 1.75 .85

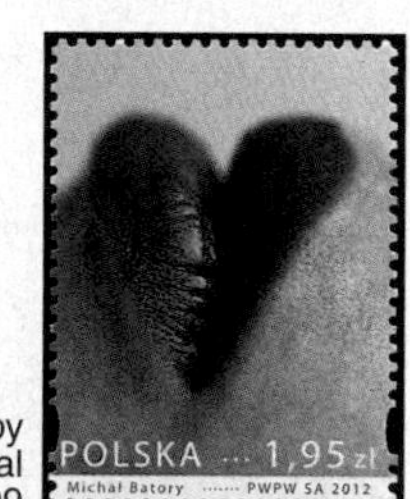

Heart, by Michal Batory — A1499

Piano, by Michal Batory A1500

2012, May 25
4042 A1499 1.95z multi 1.10 .55
4043 A1500 3z multi 1.75 .85

Souvenir Sheet

Animated Film *Parauszek the Rabbit* — A1501

2012, May 30
4044 A1501 4.15z multi 2.40 1.25

2012 European Soccer Championships, Poland and Ukraine — A1502

Tournament stadiums in Poland: 1.55z, Municipal Stadium, Poznan. 1.95z, National Stadium, Warsaw. 2.40z, PGE Arena, Gdansk. 3z, Municipal Stadium, Wroclaw.

2012, June 8
4045-4048 A1502 Set of 4 5.25 2.60
4048a Souvenir sheet of 4, #4045-4048 5.25 2.60

Nos. 4045-4048 each were printed in sheets of 8 + central label.

Soccer Ball, Flags of Ukraine and Poland A1503

2012, June 15
4049 A1503 3z multi 1.75 .85

2012 European Soccer Championships, Poland and Ukraine. No. 4049 was printed in sheets of 6. Selvage surrounding each stamp on the sheet differs. Values are for stamps with surrounding selvage.

Muzakowski Park UNESCO World Heritage Site, Poland and Germany — A1504

Perf. 11¾x11½ Syncopated

2012, July 12
4050 A1504 3z multi 1.90 .95

See Germany No. 2683.

Miniature Sheet

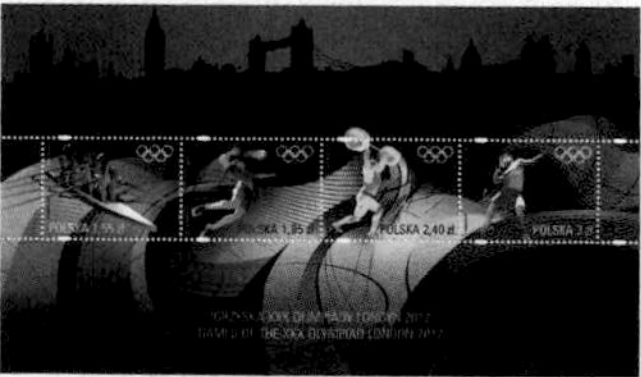

2012 Summer Olympics, London — A1505

No. 4051: a, 1.55z, Rowing. b, 1.95z, Volleyball. c, 2.40z, Weight lifting. d, 3z, Shot put.

2012, July 27
4051 A1505 Sheet of 4, #a-d 5.50 2.75

Józef Ignacy Kraszewski (1812-87), Writer — A1506

Perf. 11½x11¼

2012, July 28 **Photo.**

4052 A1506 4.15z multi + label 2.60 1.25

Miniature Sheet

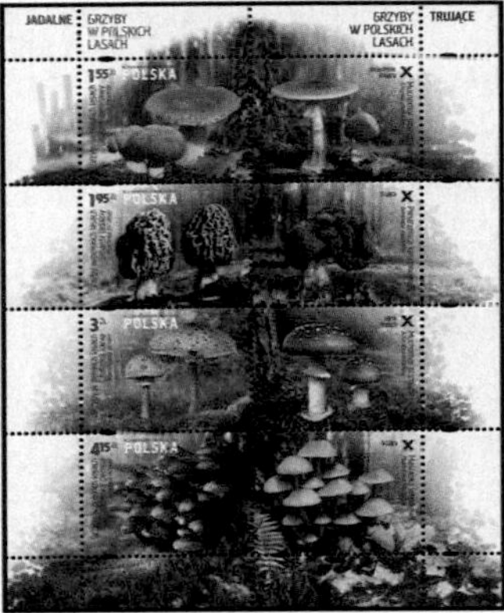
Mushrooms — A1507

No. 4053: a, 1.55z, Russula virescens. b, 1.95z, Morchella esculenta. c, 3z, Macrolepiota procera. d, 4.15z, Armillaria ostoyae.

Perf. 11¾x11½ Syncopated

2012, Aug. 31 **Litho.**

4053 A1507 Sheet of 4, #a-d, + 4 labels 6.75 3.50

2012 Polish-German Philatelic Exhibition, Kargowa A1508

Perf. 11½x11¾ Syncopated

2012, Sept. 6

4054 A1508 2.40z multi 1.50 .75

Piotr Skarga (1536-1612), Counter-reformation Preacher — A1509

Perf. 11¼x11½

2012, July 27 **Photo.**

4055 A1509 1.55z multi 1.00 .55

Piotr Kwit (1929-2002), Painter — A1510

2012, Oct. 10 ***Perf. 11½x11¼***

4056 A1510 1.55z multi .95 .50

Pope John Paul II and Wawel Cathedral — A1511

Perf. 11¾x11½ Syncopated

2012, Oct. 13 **Litho.**

4057 A1511 1.95z multi + label 1.25 .60

Stage and Film Stars — A1512

Designs: 1.55z, Jadwiga Smosarska (1898-1971). 1.95z, Aleksander Zabczynski (1900-58). 3z, Eugeniusz Bodo (1899-1943).

Perf. 11½x11¾ Syncopated

2012, Oct. 31

4058-4060 A1512 Set of 3 4.00 2.00

4060a Souvenir sheet of 3, #4058-4060 4.00 2.00

See Nos. 4098-4100, 4149-4151, 4194-4196.

Souvenir Sheet

Turczynek Villa, Milanówek — A1513

Perf. 11¾x11½ Syncopated

2012, Oct. 31

4061 A1513 4.15z multi 2.60 1.25

Christmas — A1514

Designs: A, Angels. 2.40z, Children with gifts, horiz.

Perf. 11¾x11½, 11½x11¾

2012, Nov. 30 **Photo.**

4062-4063 A1514 Set of 2 2.50 1.25

No. 4062 sold for 1.55z on day of issue.

Jerzy Turowicz (1912-99), Journalist A1515

Perf. 11½x11¾ Syncopated

2012, Dec. 10 **Litho.**

4064 A1515 1.55z multi 1.00 .50

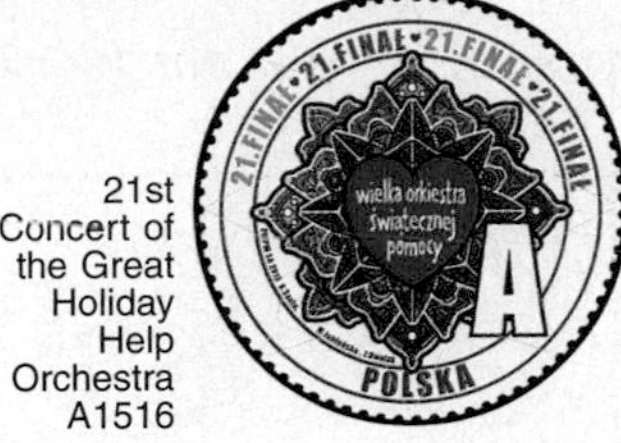
21st Concert of the Great Holiday Help Orchestra A1516

2013, Jan. 13 ***Die Cut Perf.***

Self-Adhesive

4065 A1516 A multi 1.10 .55

No. 4065 was printed in sheets of 6. Unused values are for stamps with surrounding selvage.

A1517

A1518

A1519

A1520

2013, Mar. 8 **Photo.** ***Perf. 11¾x11½***

4066 A1517 (1.60z) multi 1.00 .50

4067 A1518 (2.35z) multi 1.50 .75

4068 A1519 (3.75z) multi 2.40 1.25

4069 A1520 (5.10z) multi 3.25 1.60

Nos. 4066-4069 (4) 8.15 4.10

A1521

A1522

A1523

A1524

2013, Mar. 29

4070 A1521 (3.70z) multi 2.25 1.10

4071 A1522 (4.50z) multi 2.75 1.40

4072 A1523 (4.75z) multi 3.00 1.50

4073 A1524 (7.10z) multi 4.50 2.25

Nos. 4070-4073 (4) 12.50 6.25

Souvenir Sheet

Alcedo Atthis — A1525

Perf. 11½ Syncopated

2013, Apr. 12 **Litho.**

4074 A1525 4.55z multi 3.00 1.50

Wieslaw Chrzanowski (1923-2012), Marshal of the Sejm — A1526

2013, Apr. 16

4075 A1526 3.80z multi 2.40 1.25

Warsaw Ghetto Uprising, 70th Anniv. — A1527

2013, Apr. 19 **Photo.** ***Perf. 11½x11***

4076 A1527 3.80z multi 2.40 1.25

Flag Day A1528

Perf. 11½ Syncopated

2013, May 2 **Litho.**

4077 A1528 1.60z multi 1.00 .50

Europa A1529

2013, May 6

4078 A1529 4.60z multi 3.00 1.50

Souvenir Sheet

Disney Cartoon Characters — A1530

2013, June 1
4079 A1530 4.60z multi 3.00 1.50

Miniature Sheet

Lighthouses — A1531

No. 4080: a, 1.60z, Darlowo Lighthouse. b, 2.35z, Jaroslawiec Lighthouse. c, 3.75z, Ustka Lighthouse. d, 3.80z, Czolpino Lighthouse.

2013, June 14 Photo. ***Perf. 11½x11***
4080 A1531 Sheet of 4, #a-d 7.25 3.75

A1532

A1533

A1534

A1535

Perf. 11¾x11½

2013, June 20 **Photo.**
4081 A1532 (6.30z) multi 4.00 2.00
4082 A1533 (7.30z) multi 4.50 2.25
4083 A1534 (8.80z) multi 5.50 2.75
4084 A1535 (10.90z) multi 6.75 3.50
Nos. 4081-4084 (4) 20.75 10.50

Souvenir Sheet

Prince Boleslaw III the Wrymouthed (1086-1138) — A1536

Photo. & Engr.

2013, June 28 ***Perf. 11½x11¼***
4085 A1536 8.50z red & brn blk 5.25 2.60

Deeds of the Princes of the Poles, chronicle of Polish history by Gallus Anonymus, 900th anniv. of publication.

Strawberry — A1537

2013, July 18 Litho. ***Perf. 11¼x11½***
4086 A1537 4.60z multi 3.00 1.50

Tour de Pologne Bicycle Race — A1538

No. 4087: a, One cyclist. b, Two cyclists.

Perf. 11½ Syncopated

2013, July 30 **Litho.**
4087 A1538 Horiz. pair 4.00 2.00
a. 1.60z multi 1.00 .50
b. 4.60z multi 3.00 1.50

Souvenir Sheet

Heweliusz Satellite — A1539

Perf. 11¾x11½ Syncopated

2013, July 31 **Litho.**
4088 A1539 4.55z multi 3.00 1.50

Woodstock Festival Poland, Kostrzyn nad Odra A1540

Die Cut Perf. 11½

2013, Aug. 1 **Litho.**

Self-Adhesive

4089 A1540 2.35z multi 1.50 .75

Souvenir Sheet

Szczecin 2013 Tall Ships Regatta — A1541

Photo. & Engr.

2013, Aug. 3 ***Perf. 11¼x11***
4090 A1541 8.50z black & blue 5.50 2.75

Modernization of Polish Armed Forces — A1542

No. 4091: a, General Dynamics F-16 Block 52+ jets. b, Rosomak armored vehicle. c, ORP Kontradmiral Xawery Czernicki support ship.

Perf. 11¾x11½ Syncopated

2013, Aug. 14 **Litho.**
4091 A1542 1.60z Vert. strip of 3, #a-c 3.00 1.50

Souvenir Sheet

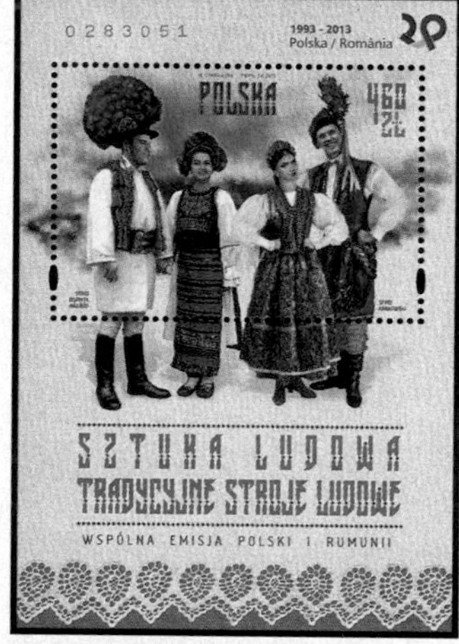

Traditional Costumes of Poland and Romania — A1543

Perf. 11½x11¾ Syncopated

2013, Sept. 11 **Litho.**
4092 A1543 4.60z multi 3.00 1.50

See Romania No. 5483.

Minerals A1544

No. 4093: a, Salt (gray violet panel). b, Malachite and azurite (blue panel). c, Marcasite (blue green panel). d, Gypsum (red panel).

Perf. 11¾x11½ Syncopated

Litho. & Silk-screened

2013, Sept. 20
4093 Vert. strip of 4 5.50 2.75
a.-b. A1544 1.60z Either single 1.10 .55
c.-d. A1544 2.35z Either single 1.60 .80

Pres. Lech Walesa, 70th Birthday A1545

Perf. 11½x11¼ Syncopated

2013, Sept. 29 **Litho.**
4094 A1545 3.80z multi 2.50 1.25

Landmarks in European Capitals Type of 2005

Design: St. Mark's Church, Zagreb, Croatia.

Perf. 11¼x11½ Syncopated

2013, Oct. 11 **Litho.**
4095 A1323 4.60z multi 3.00 1.50

World Post Day A1546

Perf. 11¼x11½

2013, Oct. 18 **Photo.**
4096 A1546 4.60z multi 3.00 1.50

Polish postal services, 455th anniv.

Lost Works of Art A1547

No. 4097 — Pastel drawings by Stanislaw Wyspianski of the actor Ludwik Solski in costume in plays: a, Treasure, by Leopold Staff. b, The Twelfth Night, by William Shakespeare. c, Varsovian Anthem, by Wyspianski.

Perf. 11¼x11½

2013, Oct. 21 **Photo.**
4097 Horiz. strip of 3 5.00 2.50
a. A1547 1.60z multi 1.00 .50
b. A1547 2.35z multi 1.50 .75
c. A1547 3.80z multi 2.50 1.25

Stage and Film Stars Type of 2012

Designs: 1.60z, Helena Grossówna (1904-94). 2.35z, Adolf Dymsza (1900-75). 3.80z, Mieczyslawa Cwiklinska (1879-1972).

Perf. 11½x11¾ Syncopated

2013, Oct. 31 **Litho.**
4098 A1512 1.60z multi 1.00 .50
4099 A1512 2.35z multi 1.50 .75
4100 A1512 3.80z multi 2.50 1.25
a. Souvenir sheet of 3, #4098-4100 5.00 2.50

Krzystof Penderecki, Composer, 80th Birthday A1548

Perf. 11½x11¼

2013, Nov. 23 **Photo.**
4101 A1548 3.80z multi 2.50 1.25

Spiders
A1549

Designs: 1.60z, Argiope bruennichi. 2.35z, Atypus muralis. 3.80z, Eresus kollari. 4.55z, Philaeus chrysops.

Perf. 11¾x11½ Syncopated
Litho. & Silk-screened

2013, Nov. 29
4102-4105 A1549 Set of 4 8.25 4.25

Nos. 4102-4105 were each printed in sheets of 8 + label.

2014 Winter Olympics, Sochi, Russia
A1550

No. 4106: a, Ski jumping. b, Cross-country skiing.

Perf. 11¾x11½ Syncopated

2014, Feb. 7 **Litho. & Embossed**
4106 A1550 Vert. pair 4.50 2.25
a. 1.75z multi 1.25 .60
b. 5z multi 3.25 1.60

No. 4106 was printed in sheets containing two pairs.

Oskar Kolberg (1814-90), Ethnologist and Composer
A1551

2014, Feb. 22 **Photo.** ***Perf. 11½x11***
4107 A1551 4.20z multi 2.75 1.40

World Indoors Track and Field Championships, Sopot — A1552

Perf. 11¼x11½ Syncopated
Litho. & Silk-Screened

2014, Mar. 7
4108 A1552 5z multi 3.50 1.75

No. 4108 was printed in sheets of 4.

Easter — A1553

Color of egg: 1.75z, Green. 5z, Purple.

Perf. 11¾x11½

2014, Mar. 26 **Photo.**
4109-4110 A1553 Set of 2 4.50 2.25

See Nos. 4162-4163.

Souvenir Sheet

Consecration of Wawel Cathedral, 650th Anniv. — A1554

No. 4111: a, 4.20z, Wawel Cathedral spires, 14th-15th cent.. b, 8.30z, Wawel Cathedral, Sigismund Bell.

Photo. & Engr.

2014, Mar. 28 ***Perf. 11***
4111 A1554 Sheet of 2, #a-b 8.25 4.25

Souvenir Sheet

Canonization of Popes John Paul II and John XXIII — A1555

No. 4112: a, Pope John Paul II. b, Pope John XXIII.

Perf. 11½x11¼ Syncopated

2014, Apr. 2 **Litho.**
4112 A1555 5z Sheet of 2, #a-b 6.75 3.25

See Vatican City No. 1558.

A1556

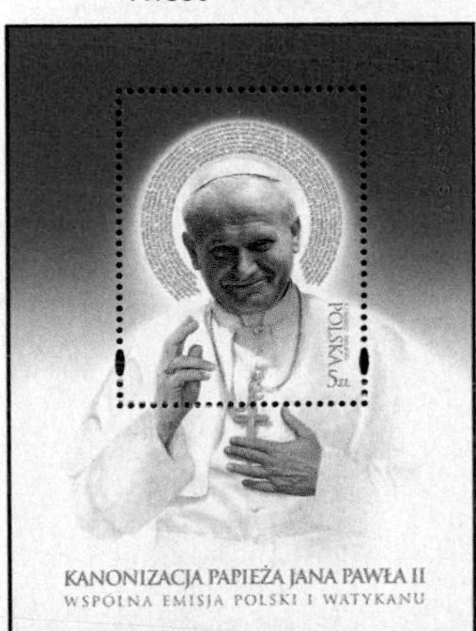
Canonization of Pope John Paul II — A1557

Perf. 11½x11¾ Syncopated

2014, Apr. 2 **Litho.**
4113 A1556 2.35z multi 1.60 .80

Souvenir Sheets

Perf. 11¼x11½ Syncopated
4114 A1557 5z multi 3.50 1.75

Engr.
4115 A1557 8.50z brown 5.75 2.75

See Vatican City Nos. 1559-1561.

Souvenir Sheet

Polish Gold Medalists at 2014 Winter Olympics — A1558

No. 4116: a, Kamil Stoch, ski jumping. b, Justyna Kowalczyk, cross-country skiing. c, Zbigniew Bródka, speed skating.

Perf. 11¾x11½ Syncopated

2014, Apr. 11 **Litho.**
4116 A1558 4.20z Sheet of 3, #a-c 8.25 4.25

Jan Karski (1914-2000), World War II Resistance Fighter — A1559

Perf. 11½x11¼

2014, Apr. 24 **Photo.**
4117 A1559 4.20z multi 2.75 1.40
a. Tete-beche pair 5.50 3.00

Admission to the European Union, 10th Anniv.
A1560

Perf. 11¼x11½ Syncopated

2014, May 1 **Litho.**
4118 A1560 5.20z multi 3.50 1.75

Bagpipes
A1561

Perf. 11½x11¾ Syncopated

2014, May 5 **Litho.**
4119 A1561 5.20z multi 3.50 1.75

Europa.

International Year of the Family — A1562

Perf. 11¼x11½

2014, May 15 **Photo.**
4120 A1562 2.35z multi 1.60 .80

Battle of Monte Cassino, 70th Anniv. — A1563

Perf. 11½x11¾ Syncopated

2014, May 18 **Litho.**
4121 A1563 1.75z multi *4.50 2.25*

Souvenir Sheet

Premiere of Animated Film *The Pirate Fairy* — A1565

Perf. 11¾x11½ Syncopated

2014, June 1 **Litho.**
4123 A1565 5.20z multi 3.50 1.75

Miniature Sheet

Coaches — A1566

No. 4124: a, Kazimierz Górski (1921-2006), soccer coach. b, Hubert Wagner (1941-2002), volleyball coach. c, Feliks Stamm (1901-76), boxing coach. d, Henryk Lasak (1932-73), cycling coach.

Perf. 11¼x11½

2014, June 27 **Photo.**
4124 A1566 2.35z Sheet of 4, #a-d 6.25 3.25

Historic Photographs by Henryk Poddebski (1890-1945) — A1567

No. 4125: a, Zinc smelter, Szopienice. b, Machinery at Kleofas colliery. c, Smokestacks and buildings, Krolewska Huta. d, Coal transport at Gdynia Harbor.

Perf. 11¾x11½ Syncopated

2014, July 11 **Litho.**

4125	Vert. strip of 4	7.75	4.00
a.	A1567 1.75z multi	1.10	.55
b.	A1567 2.35z multi	1.50	.75
c.	A1567 3.75z multi	2.40	1.25
d.	A1567 4.20z multi	2.75	1.40

Apple A1568

Perf. 11¼x11½

2014, July 18 **Photo.**

4126 A1568 5z multi 3.25 1.60

Souvenir Sheet

Merops Apiaster — A1569

Perf. 11½x11¾ Syncopated

2014, July 31 **Litho.**

4127 A1569 5.50z multi 3.50 1.75

Souvenir Sheet

Warsaw Uprising, 70th Anniv. — A1570

Perf. 11½x11¾ Syncopated

2014, Aug. 1 **Litho.**

4128 A1570 5.20z multi 3.50 1.75

Souvenir Sheet

Józef Pilsudski (1867-1935), Prime Minister, and Members of Polish Legion — A1571

Photo. & Engr.

2014, Aug. 6 *Perf. 11¼*

4129 A1571 8.50z multi 5.25 2.60

Icons A1572

Designs: 1.75z, Our Lady of Drohobycz. 4.20z. Our Lady of Kochawinskiej.

2014, Aug. 14 **Photo.** *Perf. 10¾x11*

4130-4131 A1572 Set of 2 3.75 1.90

Miniature Sheet

Mushrooms — A1573

No. 4132: a, 1.75z, Cantharellus cibarius. b, 2.35z, Agaricus campestris. c, 3.75z, Russula vesca. d, 4.20z, Boletus edulis.

Perf. 11¾x11½ Syncopated

2014, Aug. 29 **Litho.**

4132 A1573 Sheet of 4, #a-d, + 4 labels 7.50 3.75

Miniature Sheet

2014 Men's World Volleyball Championships, Poland — A1574

No. 4133 — Color of player's shirt: a, 1.75z, White. b, 1.75z, Dark blue. c, 2.35z, Green. d, 5z, Red. e, 5.10z, White. f, 5.50z, Yellow.

Perf. 11½x11¾ Syncopated

2014, Aug. 30 **Litho.**

4133 A1574 Sheet of 6, #a-f 13.50 6.75

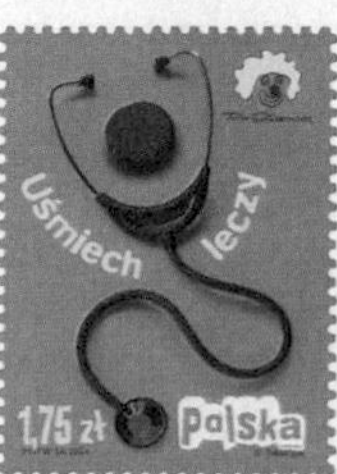

Dr. Clown Charitable Foundation — A1575

Perf. 11½x11¼

2014, Sept. 5 **Photo.**

4134 A1575 1.75z multi 1.10 .55

Souvenir Sheet

Mural by Natalia Rak — A1576

Perf. 11¾x11½ Syncopated

2014, Sept. 26 **Litho.**

4135 A1576 4.20z multi 2.60 1.25

Alternative Energy Sources — A1577

No. 4136: a, Hydroelectric dam. b, Geothermal energy. c, Wind generator. d, Solar panel.

Perf. 11½x11¼

2014, Sept. 29 **Photo.**

4136	A1577 Block of 4	7.50	3.75
a.	1.75z multi	1.10	.55
b.	2.35z multi	1.50	.75
c.	3.75z multi	2.25	1.10
d.	4.20z multi	2.60	1.25

Meteorological Phenomena — A1578

No. 4137: a, Aurora. b, Sun dog. c, Smoke. d, Frost.

Perf. 11¾x11½ Syncopated

Litho. & Silk-Screened

2014, Sept. 30

4137	Horiz. strip of 4	8.75	4.50
a.	A1578 1.75z multi	1.10	.55
b.	A1578 2.35z multi	1.50	.75
c.	A1578 4.20z multi	2.60	1.25
d.	A1578 5.50z multi	3.50	1.75

Jan Nowak-Jezioranski (1914-2005), Head of Polish Section for Radio Free Europe — A1579

2014, Oct. 2 **Photo.** *Perf. 11½x11¼*

4138 A1579 4.20z multi 2.60 1.25

Fish — A1580

Designs: 35g, Acanthurus sohal. 45g, Chaetodon capistratus. 55g, Rhinomuraena quaesita. 65g, Hippocampus sp. 1.10z, Balistoides conspicillum. 1.20z, Pomacanthus xanthometopon. 1.30z, Chelmon rostratus. 1.40z, Amphiprion ocellaris.

Perf. 11½x11¼

2014, Oct. 10 **Photo.**

4139-4146 A1580 Set of 8 4.25 2.10

2014 National Philatelic Exhibition, Warsaw. Nos. 4139-4146 each were printed in sheets of 12 + 4 labels.

Stefan Zeromski (1864-1925), Writer — A1581

Perf. 11½x11¼ Syncopated

2014, Oct. 14 **Litho.**

4147 A1581 4.20z multi 2.50 1.25

Miniature Sheet

Victory of Polish Men's Volleyball Team and 2014 World Championships — A1582

No. 4148: a, Stéphan Antiga. b, Piotr Nowakowski. c, Michal Winiarski. d, Dawid Konarski. e, Rafal Buszek. f, Pawel Zagumny. g, Karol Klos. h, Andrzej Wrona. i, Mariusz Wlazly. j, Fabian Drzyzga. k, Michal Kubiak. l, Krzysztof Ignaczak. m, Pawel Zatorski. n, Marcin Mozdzonek. o, Mateusz Mika. p, Philippe Blain.

Perf. 11¾x11½ Syncopated

2014, Oct. 18 **Litho.**

4148 A1582 1z Sheet of 16, #a-p, + 4 labels 9.50 4.75

Stage and Film Stars Type of 2012

Designs: 1.75z, Tola Mankiewiczówna (1900-85). 2.35z, Antoni Fertner (1874-1959). 4.20z, Loda Halama (1911-96).

Perf. 11½x11¾ Syncopated

2014, Oct. 31 **Litho.**

4149-4151	A1512 Set of 3	5.00	2.50
4151a	Souvenir sheet of 3, #4149-4151	5.00	2.50

Christmas — A1583

Stained-glass windows depicting: 2.35z, Holy Family. 5.20z, Adoration of the Magi.

2014, Nov. 14 Photo. ***Perf. 11¼***
4152-4153 A1583 Set of 2 4.50 2.25

William Shakespeare (1564-1616), Writer — A1584

Perf. 11½x11¾
2014, Nov. 21 Photo.
4154 A1584 4.20z multi 2.50 1.25

Souvenir Sheet

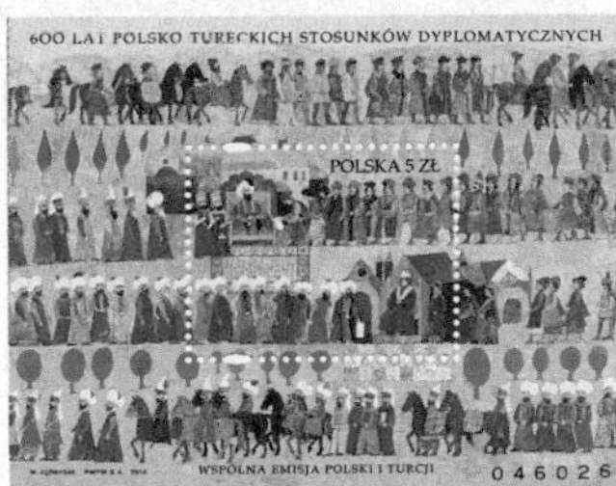

Diplomatic Relations Between Poland and Turkey, 600th Anniv. — A1585

Perf. 11¼x11½ Syncopated
2014, Nov. 28 Litho.
4155 A1585 5z multi 3.00 1.50

See Turkey No. 3416.

Ring of Youths A1586

Main Square, Cracow A1587

Perf. 11¼ Syncopated
2014, Dec. 19 Litho.
4156 A1586 1.75z multi 1.00 .50

Perf. 11½ Syncopated
4157 A1587 5z multi 3.00 1.50

Selection of Cracow as host city of 2016 World Youth Day.

23rd Concert of the Great Holiday Help Orchestra A1588

Perf. 11½x11¾ Syncopated
2015, Jan. 7 Litho.
4158 A1588 2.35z multi 1.25 .65

Love A1589

Litho. & Silk-Screened
2015, Feb. 6 ***Perf. 11½ Syncopated***
4159 A1589 2.35z multi 1.25 .65

Values are for stamps with surrounding selvage.

Kazimierz Przerwa-Tetmajer (1865-1940), Poet — A1590

Perf. 11½x11¼ Syncopated
2015, Feb. 12 Litho.
4160 A1590 1.75z multi .95 .45

Souvenir Sheet

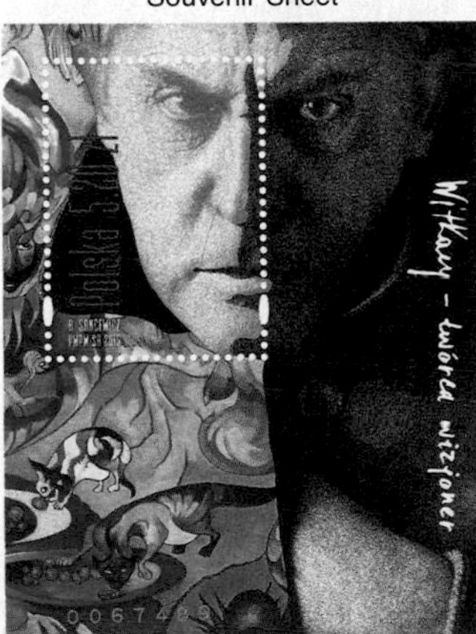

Witkacy (1885-1939), Writer and Painter — A1591

Perf. 11½x11¾ Syncopated
2015, Feb. 24 Litho.
4161 A1591 5.20z multi 2.75 1.40

Easter Type of 2014

Color of egg: 2.35z, Purplish black. 5.20z, Red.

2015, Mar. 6 Photo. ***Perf. 11¾x11½***
4162-4163 A1553 Set of 2 4.25 2.10

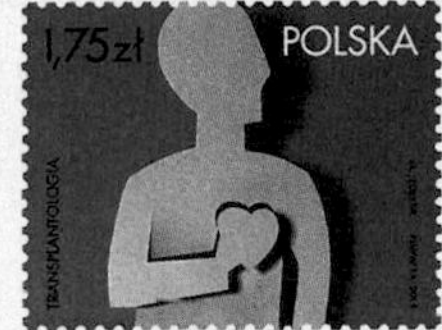

Organ Transplantation — A1592

2015, Mar. 20 Photo. ***Perf. 11x11½***
4164 A1592 1.75z multi .95 .45

Awarding of Best Foreign Film Academy Award to Polish Movie "Ida" A1593

Perf. 11½ Syncopated
2015, Mar. 31 Litho.
4165 A1593 2.35z multi 1.25 .65

No. 4165 was printed in sheets of 8 + central label.

Tadeusz Kantor (1915-90), Theater Director — A1594

Perf. 11½x11¾ Syncopated
2015, Apr. 3 Photo.
4166 A1594 1.75z multi .95 .45

Katyn Massacre, 75th Anniv. — A1595

Perf. 11½x11¼ Syncopated
2015, Apr. 7 Litho.
4167 A1595 1.75z multi 1.00 .50

2016 World Youth Day, Cracow — A1596

Emblem and: 1.75z, St. John Paul II. 5z, Map of Poland, signature of St. John Paul II.

Perf. 11½x11¼
2015, Apr. 27 Photo.
4168-4169 A1596 Set of 2 3.75 1.90

Toy Made of Nuts A1597

Perf. 11¾x11½ Syncopated
2015, May 5 Litho.
4170 A1597 5z multi 3.00 1.50

Europa.

Souvenir Sheet

End of World War II, 70th Anniv. — A1598

2015, May 8 Photo. ***Perf. 11½x11¼***
4171 A1598 2.35z multi 1.25 .65

Souvenir Sheet

Expo 2015, Milan — A1599

Perf. 11½x11¾ Syncopated
2015, May 28 Litho.
4172 A1599 5.20z multi 3.00 1.50

Father Jan Twardowski (1915-2006), Poet — A1600

Perf. 11½x11¾ Syncopated
2015, May 29 Litho.
4173 A1600 1.75z multi .95 .45

Souvenir Sheet

Characters From Animated Film *Frozen* — A1601

No. 4174: a, Anna, denomination at UL. b, Elsa, denomination at UR.

Perf. 11½ Syncopated

2015, June 1 **Litho.**

4174 A1601 2.35z Sheet of 2, #a-b 2.60 1.25

World Blood Donor Day — A1602

Perf. 11½x11¼

2015, June 14 **Photo.**

4175 A1602 1.75z multi .95 .45

Miniature Sheet

Lighthouses — A1603

No. 4176: a, Rozewie II Lighthouse. b, Kikut Lighthouse. c, Swinoujscie Lighthouse. d, Jastarnia Lighthouse. e, Gdansk North Port Lighthouse.

Perf. 11½x11¼

2015, June 19 **Photo.**

4176 A1603 2.35z Sheet of 5, #a-e, + label 6.25 3.25

Count Jan Potocki (1761-1815), Writer — A1604

Perf. 11½x11¼ Syncopated

2015, June 25 **Litho.**

4177 A1604 5z multi 2.75 1.40

Fruit and Flowers Type of 2009

2015 **Photo.** ***Perf. 11½x11¾***

4178 A1425 10g Nymphaea .25 .25
4179 A1425 1z Helianthus .55 .25
4180 A1425 5z Rose 2.75 1.40
Nos. 4178-4180 (3) 3.55 1.90

Issued: 1z, 6/26, 10g, 5z, 9/15.

Polish Presidency of Council of Baltic Sea States for 2015-16 A1605

Perf. 11½x11¼ Syncopated

2015, July 1 **Litho.**

4181 A1605 5z multi 2.75 1.40

Cows and Korycinski Cheese — A1606

Perf. 11¾x11½ Syncopated

2015, July 17 **Litho. & Embossed**

4182 A1606 5z multi 2.75 1.40

Souvenir Sheet

Pipe Organ, Cistercian Monastery Church, Jedrzejów — A1607

No. 4183: a, 4.20z, Organ pipes and balcony railing. b, 8.30z, Organ pipes and ceiling.

Perf. 11½x11¼ Syncopated

2015, July 30 **Litho. & Engr.**

4183 A1607 Sheet of 2, #a-b 6.75 3.50

Souvenir Sheet

St. John Bosco (1815-88) — A1608

Photo. & Engr.

2015, Aug. 16 ***Perf. 11x11¼***

4184 A1608 5.20z multi 2.75 1.40

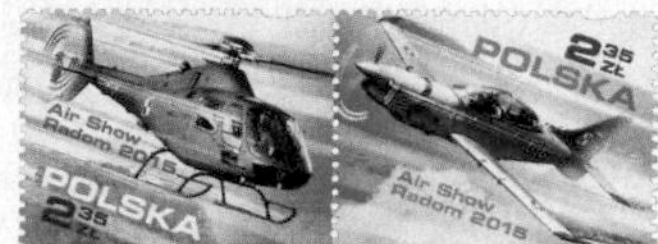

2015 Radom Air Show — A1609

No. 4185: a, Helicopter. b, Airplane.

Perf. 11¼x11½ Syncopated

2015, Aug. 22 **Litho.**

4185 A1609 2.35z Pair, #a-b 2.50 1.25

Optimist Class Sailboat World Championships — A1610

Perf. 11¾x11½ Syncopated

2015, Aug. 26 **Litho.**

4186 A1610 1.75z multi .95 .45

Miniature Sheet

Metal Crystals — A1611

No. 4187: a, 1.75fr, Cast iron (green, yellow, pink & black). b, 1.75z, Bronze (blue violet, red and orange). c, 2.35z, Iron (large crystals at top, small crystals at bottom). d, 2.35z, Iron (large round crystal).

Litho. & Silk-Screened

Perf. 11½ Syncopated

2015, Sept. 11

4187 A1611 Sheet of 4, #a-d 4.50 2.25

Warsaw Post Office, Cent. — A1612

Perf. 11½x11¾ Syncopated

2015, Sept. 23 **Litho.**

4188 A1612 2.35z multi 1.25 .60

Depictions of Quotations from Polish Literature — A1613

Designs: No. 4189, 2.35z, Woman, man holding crocodile balloon (quotation from Revenge, by Aleksander Fredro). No. 4190, 2.35z, Dogs (quotation from Ashes, by Stefan Zeromski).

Perf. 11¾x11½ Syncopated

2015, Sept. 23 **Litho.**

4189-4190 A1613 Set of 2 2.50 1.25

17th Chopin Intl. Piano Competition A1614

Perf. 11½x11¼ Syncopated

2015, Oct. 1 **Litho.**

4191 A1614 1.75z multi .95 .45

Letter of Reconciliation from Polish Bishops to German Bishops, 50th Anniv. — A1615

Perf. 11½x11¼

2015, Oct. 23 **Photo.**

4192 A1615 1.75z multi .90 .45

Miniature Sheet

Owls — A1616

No. 4193: a, Bubo bubo. b, Aegolius funereus. c, Tyto alba. d, Strix nebulosa.

Perf. 11¾x11½ Syncopated

2015, Oct. 23 **Litho. & Embossed**

4193 A1616 2.35z Sheet of 4, #a-d, + 4 labels 5.00 2.50

Stage and Film Stars Type of 2012

Designs: 1.75z, Jerzy Pichelski (1903-63). 2.35z, Hanka Bielicka (1915-2006). 4.20z, Aleksander Zelwerowicz (1877-1955).

Perf. 11½x11¾ Syncopated

2015, Oct. 30 **Litho.**

4194-4196 A1512 Set of 3 4.50 2.25
4196a Souvenir sheet of 3, #4194-4196 4.50 2.25

Christmas — A1617

Designs: 1.75z, Holy Family and animals. 2.35z, Annunciation. 5.20z, Adoration of the Magi.

Perf. 11¾x11½

2015, Nov. 16 **Photo.**

4197-4199 A1617 Set of 3 4.75 2.40

Wojciech Boguslawski (1757-1829), Director of National Theater, Warsaw A1618

Perf. 11½x11¼

2015, Nov. 19 **Photo.**

4200 A1618 1.75z multi .90 .45

National Theater, 250th anniv.

National Day of Rights of the Child — A1619

Perf. 11½x11¼

2015, Nov. 20 **Photo.**

4201 A1619 1.75z multi .90 .45

Wladyslaw Bartoszewski (1922-2015), Minister of Foreign Affairs — A1620

Perf. 11¾x11½ Syncopated

2015, Nov. 25 **Litho.**

4202 A1620 1.75z multi .90 .45

City of Cracow and Jan Dlugosz (1415-80), Diplomat and Chronicler of Polish History A1621

Perf. 11¼x11½

2015, Nov. 30 **Photo.**

4203 A1621 1.75z multi .90 .45

Beatification of Fathers Michal Tomaszek (1960-91), and Zbigniew Strzalkowski (1958-91), Murdered Missionaries to Peru — A1622

Perf. 11½x11¾ Syncopated

2015, Dec. 5 **Litho.**

4204 A1622 1.75z multi .90 .45

Fruit and Flowers Type of 2009

2015 **Photo.** *Perf. 11½x11¾*

4205 A1425 5g Lilacs .25 .25

Issued: 5g, 12/7.

St. Paraskevi Church, Kwiaton, Poland and St. George's Church, Drohobych, Ukraine — A1623

Photo. & Engr.

2015, Dec. 18 *Perf. 11x10¾*

4208 A1623 5z multi 2.60 1.25

Wooden Churches of the Carpathian Region of Poland and Ukraine UNESCO World Heritage Site. See Ukraine No.

European Men's Handball Championships, Poland — A1625

No. 4210 — Handball and: a, Player. b, Hand.

Perf. 11½ Syncopated

2016, Jan. 15 **Litho.**

4210 Vert. pair 3.75 1.90
a. A1625 2.35z multi 1.25 .60
b. A1625 5z multi 2.50 1.25

Souvenir Sheet

Wroclaw, 2016 European Capital of Culture — A1626

Perf. 11¾x11½ Syncopated

2016, Jan. 15 **Litho.**

4211 A1626 5z multi 2.50 1.25

Warsaw Mint, 250th Anniv. — A1627

Perf. 11½x11¾ Syncopated

2016, Jan. 21 **Litho.**

4212 A1627 2.35z multi 1.25 .60

SEMI-POSTAL STAMPS

Regular Issue of 1919 Surcharged in Violet

a

b

1919, May 3 **Unwmk.** *Imperf.*

B1 A10(a) 5f + 5f grn .35 .35
B2 A10(a) 10f + 5f red vio .35 .50
B3 A10(a) 15f + 5f dp red .35 .50
B4 A11(b) 25f + 5f ol grn .35 .35
B5 A11(b) 50f + 5f bl grn .35 .70

Perf. 11½

B6 A10(a) 5f + 5f grn .25 .25
B7 A10(a) 10f + 5f red vio .50 .50
B8 A10(a) 15f + 5f dp red .25 .25
B9 A11(b) 25f + 5f ol grn .25 .25
B10 A11(b) 50f + 5f bl grn .35 .35
Nos. B1-B10 (10) 3.35 4.00
Set, never hinged 15.00

First Polish Philatelic Exhibition. The surtax benefited the Polish White Cross Society.

Regular Issue of 1920 Surcharged in Red and Carmine

1921, Mar. 5 *Perf. 9*

Thin Laid Paper

B11 A14 5m + 30m red vio 1.50 8.50
B12 A14 6m + 30m dp rose 1.50 8.50
B13 A14 10m + 30m lt red 3.00 *8.50*
B14 A14 20m + 30m gray grn 65.00 *120.00*
Nos. B11-B14 (4) 71.00 145.50
Set, never hinged 125.00

Counterfeits, differently perforated, exist of Nos. B11-B14.

SP1

1925, Jan. 1 **Typo.** *Perf. 12½*

B15 SP1 1g orange brn 4.50 35.00
B16 SP1 2g dk brown 4.50 35.00
B17 SP1 3g orange 4.50 35.00
B18 SP1 5g olive grn 4.50 35.00
B19 SP1 10g blue grn 4.50 35.00
B20 SP1 15g red 4.50 35.00
B21 SP1 20g blue 4.50 35.00
B22 SP1 25g red brown 4.50 35.00
B23 SP1 30g dp violet 4.50 35.00
B24 SP1 40g indigo 110.00 35.00
B25 SP1 50g magenta 4.50 35.00
Nos. B15-B25 (11) 155.00 385.00
Set, never hinged 350.00

"Na Skarb" means "National Funds." These stamps were sold at a premium of 50 groszy each, for charity.

Light of Knowledge — SP2

1927, May 3 *Perf. 11½*

B26 SP2 10g + 5g choc & grn 6.25 7.00
B27 SP2 20g + 5g dk bl & buff 7.50 12.00
Set, never hinged 37.50

"NA OSWIATE" means "For Public Instruction." The surtax aided an Association of Educational Societies.

Torun Type of 1933

1933, May 21 **Engr.**

B28 A59 60g (+40g) red brn, *buff* 8.50 10.00
Never hinged 30.00

Philatelic Exhibition at Torun, May 21-28, 1933, and sold at a premium of 40g to aid the exhibition funds.

Souvenir Sheet

Stagecoach and Wayside Inn — SP3

1938, May 3 **Engr.** *Imperf.*

B29 SP3 Sheet of 4 52.50 100.00
Never hinged 125.00
a. 45g green 5.25 7.00
b. 55g blue 5.25 7.00

Perf. 12

B29C SP3 Sheet of 4 67.50 120.00
Never hinged 150.00
d. 45g green 6.50 8.50
e. 55g blue 6.50 8.50

5th Phil. Exhlb., Warsaw, May 3-8. The sheets each contain two 45g and two 55g stamps. Sold for 3z.

Souvenir Sheet

Stratosphere Balloon over Mountains — SP4

1938, Sept. 15 *Perf. 12½*

B31 SP4 75g dp vio, sheet 40.00 65.00
Never hinged 120.00

Issued in advance of a proposed Polish stratosphere flight. Sold for 2z.

Winterhelp Issue

SP5

1938-39

B32 SP5 5g + 5g red org .45 *.25*
B33 SP5 25g + 10g dk vio ('39) .90 *.25*
B34 SP5 55g + 15g brt ultra ('39) 1.10 *3.00*
Nos. B32-B34 (3) 2.45 *3.50*
Set, never hinged 9.50

For surcharges see Nos. N48-N50.

Souvenir Sheet

SP6

1939, Aug. 1

B35 SP6 Sheet of 3, dark blue gray 15.00 24.00
Never hinged 40.00
a. 25g Marshal Pilsudski Reviewing Troops 3.50 2.75
b. 25g Marshal Pilsudski 3.50 2.75
c. 25g Marshal Smigly-Rydz 3.50 2.75

25th anniv. of the founding of the Polish Legion. The sheets sold for 1.75z, the surtax going to the National Defense fund.

See types A64, A80, A99.

Polish People's Republic

Polish Warship SP7

Sailing Vessel — SP8

Polish Naval Ensign and Merchant Flag — SP9

Crane and Crane Tower, Gdansk SP10

1945, Apr. 24 **Typo.** ***Perf. 11***

B36 SP7 50g + 2z red 2.00 24.00
B37 SP8 1z + 3z dp bl 1.25 13.00
B38 SP9 2z + 4z dk car 1.00 13.00
B39 SP10 3z + 5z ol grn 1.00 17.00
Nos. B36-B39 (4) 5.25 67.00
Set, never hinged 15.00

Polish Maritime League, 25th anniv.

City Hall, Poznan — SP11

1945, June 16 **Photo.**

B40 SP11 1z + 5z green 4.00 27.50
Never hinged 12.00

Postal Workers' Convention, Poznan, June 16, 1945. Exists imperf. Value, never hinged $50.

Last Stand at Westerplatte — SP12

1945, Sept. 1

B41 SP12 1z + 9z steel blue 3.50 27.50
Never hinged 29.00

Polish army's last stand at Westerplatte, Sept. 1, 1939. Exists imperf. Value, $30.

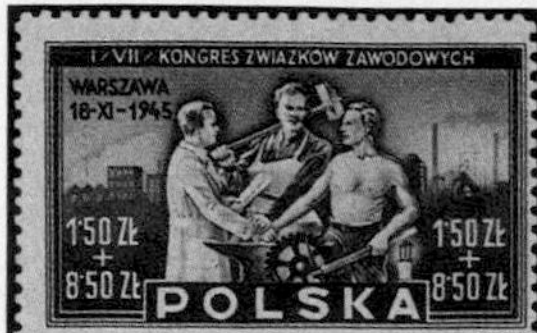

"United Industry" — SP13

1945, Nov. 18 **Unwmk.** ***Perf. 11***

B42 SP13 1.50z + 8.50z sl blk 2.00 8.50
Never hinged 6.00

Trade Unions Congress, Warsaw, Nov. 18.

Polish Volunteers in Spain — SP14

1946, Mar. 10

B43 SP14 3z + 5z red 1.00 17.00
Never hinged 2.75

Participation of the Jaroslaw Dabrowski Brigade in the Spanish Civil War.

14th Century Piast Eagle and Soldiers — SP15

1946, May 2

B44 SP15 3z + 7z brn .30 4.00
Never hinged .85

Silesian uprisings of 1919-21, 1939-45.

"Death" Spreading Poison Gas over Majdanek Prison Camp — SP16

1946, Apr. 29

B45 SP16 3z + 5z Prus grn 1.50 *18.00*
Never hinged 4.00

Issued to recall Majdanek, a concentration camp of World War II near Lublin.

Bydgoszcz (Bromberg) Canal — SP17

1946, Apr. 19 **Unwmk.** ***Perf. 11***

B46 SP17 3z + 2z ol blk 1.00 10.00
Never hinged 2.75

600th anniv. of Bydgoszcz (Bromberg).

Map of Polish Coast and Baltic Sea — SP18

1946, July 21

B47 SP18 3z + 7z dp bl .50 13.00
Never hinged 1.50

Maritime Holiday of 1946. The surtax was for the Polish Maritime League.

Salute to P.T.T. Casualty and Views of Gdansk — SP19

1946, Sept. 14

B48 SP19 3z + 12z slate .65 18.00
Never hinged 1.40

Polish postal employees killed in the German attack on Danzig (Gdansk), Sept. 1939.

School Children — SP20

Designs: 6z+24z, Courtyard of Jagiellon University, Cracow. 11z+19z, Gregor Piramowicz (1735-1801), founder of Education Commission.

1946, Oct. 10 **Unwmk.** ***Perf. 11½***

B49 SP20 3z + 22z dk red 15.00 65.00
B49A SP20 6z + 24z dk bl 15.00 65.00
B49B SP20 11z + 19z dk grn 15.00 65.00
c. Souv. sheet of 3, #B49-B49B 190.00 575.00
Never hinged 375.00
Nos. B49-B49B (3) 45.00 195.00
Never hinged 85.00

Polish educational work. Surtax was for International Bureau of Education.

No. B49Bc sold for 100z.

Stanislaw Stojalowski, Jakob Bojko, Jan Stapinski and Wincenty Witos — SP21

1946, Dec. 1

B50 SP21 5z + 10z bl grn .45 12.00
B51 SP21 5z + 10z dull blue .50 12.00
B52 SP21 5z + 10z dk olive .45 12.00
Nos. B50-B52 (3) 1.40 36.00
Never hinged 2.75

50th anniv. of the Peasant Movement. The surtax was for education and cultural improvement among the Polish peasantry.

No. 391 Surcharged in Red

1947, Feb. 4 ***Perf. 11x10½***

B53 A127 3z + 7z purple 1.75 15.00
Never hinged 3.50

Opening of the Polish Parliament, 1/19/47.

No. 344 Surcharged in Blue

1947, Feb. 21 ***Perf. 12½***

B54 A103 5z + 15z on 25g .85 5.00
Never hinged 1.75

Ski Championship Meet, Zakopane. Counterfeits exist.

Emil Zegadlowicz — SP22

1947, Mar. 1 **Photo.** ***Perf. 11***

B55 SP22 5z + 15z dl gray grn .70 13.00
Never hinged 1.40

Nurse and War Victims — SP23

1947, June 1 ***Perf. 10½***

B56 SP23 5z + 5z ol blk & red 1.50 6.75
Never hinged 3.00

The surtax was for the Red Cross.

Adam Chmielowski SP24

1947, Dec. 21 ***Perf. 11***

B57 SP24 2z + 18z dk vio .35 12.00
Never hinged .70

Zamkowy Square and Proposed Highway SP25

1948, Nov. 1

B58 SP25 15z + 5z green .30 .25

The surtax was to aid in the reconstruction of Warsaw.

Infant and TB Crosses — SP26

Various Portraits of Children

1948, Dec. 16 *Perf. 11½*

B59 SP26 3z + 2z dl grn 1.75 5.00
B60 SP26 5z + 5z brn 1.40 3.50
B61 SP26 6z + 4z vio .85 2.40
B62 SP26 15z + 10z car lake .35 1.00
Nos. B59-B62 (4) 4.35 11.90
Set, never hinged 8.50

Alternate vertical rows of stamps was ten different labels. The surtax was for anti-tuberculosis work among children.

Catalogue values for unused stamps in this section, from this point to the end of the section, are for Never Hinged items.

Workers Party Type of 1952

Perf. 12½

1952, Jan. 18 Engr. Unwmk.

B63 A195 45g + 15g Marceli Nowotko .25 .25

Women's Day Type of 1952

1952, Mar. 8 *Perf. 12½x12*

B64 A196 45g + 15g chocolate .35 .35

Swierczewski-Walter Type of 1952

1952, Mar. 28 *Perf. 12½*

B65 A197 45g + 15g chocolate .35 .30

Bierut Type of 1952

1952, Apr. 18

B66 A198 45g + 15g red .50 .25
B67 A198 1.20z + 15g ultra .50 .25

Type of Regular Issue of 1951-52 Inscribed "Plan 6," etc.

Design: 45g+15g, Electrical installation.

1952

B68 A193 30g + 15g brn red .50 .25
B69 A193 45g + 15g chocolate .90 .25
B69A A194 1.20z + 15g red org .30 .25
Nos. B68-B69A (3) 1.70 .75

Labor Day Type of Regular Issue of 1952

1952, May 1

B70 A200 45g + 15g car rose .35 .25

Similar to Regular Issue of 1952

#B71, Maria Konopnicka. #B72, Hugo Kollataj.

1952, May Different Frames

B71 A201 30g + 15g blue green .40 .60
B72 A201 45g + 15g brown .35 .40

Issued: No. B71, May 10. No. B72, May 20.

Leonardo da Vinci — SP28

1952, June 1

B73 SP28 30g + 15g ultra .95 .65

500th birth anniv. of Leonardo da Vinci.

Pres. Bierut and Children — SP29

1952, June 1 Photo. *Perf. 13½x14*

B74 SP29 45g + 15g blue 1.75 1.20

Intl. Children's Day, June 1.

Sports Type

1952, June 21 *Perf. 13*

45g+15g, Soccer players and trophy.

B75 A203 30g + 15g blue 3.50 1.00
B76 A203 45g + 15g purple 1.00 .25

Yachts SP31

"Dar Pomorza" SP32

1952, June 28 Engr. *Perf. 12½*

B77 SP31 30g + 15g dp bl grn 3.50 1.40
B78 SP32 45g + 15g dp ultra 1.75 .35

Shipbuilders' Day, 1952.

Workers on Holiday — SP33

Students SP34

1952, July 17 *Perf. 12½x12, 12x12½*

B79 SP33 30g + 15g dp grn .35 .25
B80 SP34 45g + 15g red .35 .25

Issued to publicize the Youth Festival, 1952.

Constitution Type of Regular Issue

1952, July 22 Photo. *Perf. 11*

B81 A208 45g + 15g lt bl grn & dk brn 1.90 .25

Power Plant Type of Regular Issue

1952, Aug. 7 Engr. *Perf. 12½*

B82 A209 45g + 15g red .35 .25

Ludwik Warynski SP36

1952, July 31

B83 SP36 30g + 15g dk red .35 .25
B84 SP36 45g + 15g blk brn .85 .40

70th birth anniv. of Ludwik Warynski, political organizer.

Church of Frydman — SP37

1952, Aug. 18

B85 SP37 45g + 15g vio brn 1.40 1.50

Aviator Watching Glider — SP38

Design: 45g+15g, Pilot entering plane.

1952, Aug. 23

B86 SP38 30g + 15g grn 1.25 .85
B87 SP38 45g + 15g brn red 2.75 .50

Aviation Day, Aug. 23.

Henryk Sienkiewicz — SP39

1952, Oct. 25

B88 SP39 45g + 15g vio brn .70 .35

Henryk Sienkiewicz (1846-1916), author of "Quo Vadis" and other novels, Nobel prizewinner (literature, 1905).

Revolution Type of Regular Issue

1952, Nov. 7 *Perf. 12x12½*

B92 A214 45g + 15g red brn .85 .25

Exists imperforate. See #562.

Lenin — SP42

1952, Nov. 7 *Perf. 12½*

B93 SP42 30g + 15g vio brn .50 .60
B94 SP42 45g + 15g brn .90 .25
a. "LENIN" omitted 24.00

Month of Polish Soviet friendship, Nov. 1952.

Miner — SP43

1952, Dec. 4

B95 SP43 45g + 15g blk brn .50 .25
B96 SP43 1.20z + 15g brn .80 .60

Miners' Day, Dec. 4.

Henryk Wieniawski and Violin — SP44

1952, Dec. 5 Photo.

B97 SP44 30g + 15g dk grn 1.00 .95
B98 SP44 45g + 15g purple 1.00 .40

Henryk Wieniawski; 2nd Intl. Violin Competition.

Type of Regular Issue of 1952

1952, Dec. 12 Engr.

B99 A215 45g + 15g dp grn .35 .25

Truck Factory, Lublin — SP45

1953, Feb. 20

B100 SP45 30g + 15g dp bl 1.40 .80
B101 SP45 60g + 20g vio brn .35 .25

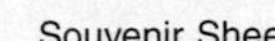

Souvenir Sheet

Town Hall in Poznan — SP46

Photo. & Litho.

1955, July 7 *Imperf.*

B102 SP46 2z pck grn & ol grn 1.75 1.00
B103 SP46 3z car rose & ol blk 24.00 10.00

6th Polish Philatelic Exhibition in Poznan. Sheets sold for 3z and 4.50z respectively.

Souvenir Sheet

"Peace" (POKOJ) and Warsaw Mermaid — SP47

Design: 1z, Pansies (A266) and inscription on map of Europe, Africa and Asia.

1955, Aug. 3

B104 SP47 1z bis, rose vio & yel 1.75 .75
B105 SP47 2z ol gray, ultra & lt bl 20.00 9.50

Intl. Phil. Exhib., Warsaw, Aug. 1-14, 1955. Sheets sold for 2z and 3z respectively.

Souvenir Sheet

Chopin and Liszt — SP48

1956, Oct. 25 Photo. *Imperf.*

B106 SP48 4z dk blue grn 30.00 16.00

Day of the Stamp; Polish-Hungarian friendship. The sheet sold for 6z.

Souvenir Sheet

Stamp of 1860 — SP49

Wmk. 326

1960, Sept. 4 Litho. *Perf. 11*
B107 SP49 Sheet of 4 50.00 42.50
a. 10z + 10z blue, red & black 9.00 9.00

Intl. Phil. Exhib. "POLSKA 60," Warsaw, 9/3-11.
Sold only with 5z ticket to exhibition.

Type of Space Issue, 1964

Design: Yuri A. Gagarin in space capsule.

Perf. 12½x12
1964, Dec. 30 Unwmk.
B108 A432 6.50z + 2z Prus grn & multi 1.25 .35

Souvenir Sheet

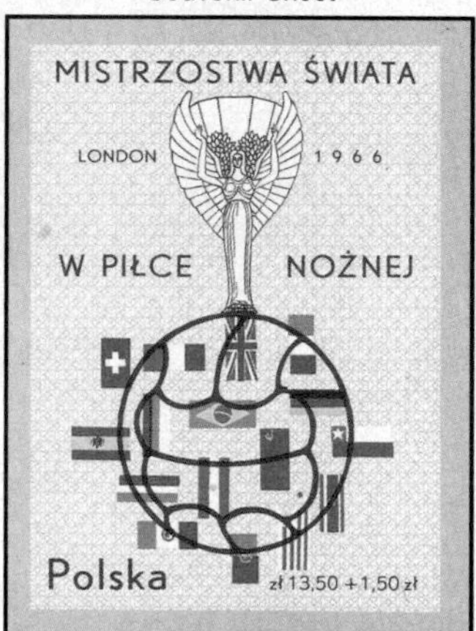

Jules Rimet Cup and Flags of Participating Countries — SP50

1966, May 9 Litho. *Imperf.*
B109 SP50 13.50z + 1.50z multi 2.00 1.00

World Cup Soccer Championship, Wembley, England, July 11-30.

Souvenir Sheet

J. Kusocinski, Olympic Winner 10,000-Meter Race, 1932 — SP51

1967, May 24 Litho. *Imperf.*
B110 SP51 10z + 5z multi 1.50 .75

19th Olympic Games, Mexico City, 1968. Simulated perforations.

Flower Type of Regular Issue

Flowers: 4z+2z, Abutilon. 8z+4z, Rosa polyantha hybr.

1968, May 15 Litho. *Perf. 11½*
B111 A492 4z + 2z vio & multi .75 .30
B112 A492 8z + 4z lt vio & multi 1.25 .40

Olympic Type of Regular Issue, 1968

Design: 10z+5z, Runner with Olympic torch and Chin cultic carved stone disc showing Mayan ball player and game's scoreboard.

1968, Sept. 2 Litho. *Perf. 11½*
Size: 56x45mm
B113 A497 10z + 5z multi 1.50 .40

19th Olympic Games, Mexico City, Oct. 12-27. The surtax was for the Polish Olympic Committee.

Olympic Type of Regular Issue, 1969

Olympic Rings and: 2.50z+50g, Women's discus. 3.40z+1z, Running. 4z+1.50z, Boxing. 7z+2z, Fencing.

1969, Apr. 25 Litho. *Perf. 11½x11*
B114 A505 2.50z + 50g multi .25 .25
B115 A505 3.40z + 1z multi .25 .25
B116 A505 4z + 1.50z multi .50 .25
B117 A505 7z + 2z multi 1.00 .35
Nos. B114-B117 (4) 2.00 1.10

Folk Art Type of Regular Issue

5.50z+1.50z, Choir. 7z+1.50z, Organ grinder.

1969, Dec. 19 Litho. *Perf. 11½x11*
Size: 24x36mm
B118 A520 5.50z + 1.50z multi .50 .25
B119 A520 7z + 1.50z multi .65 .25

Sports Type of Regular Issue
Souvenir Sheet

Design: "Horse of Glory," by Z. Kaminski.

1970, June 16 Photo. *Imperf.*
B120 A532 10z + 5z multi 1.50 .75

The surtax was for the Polish Olympic Committee. No. B120 contains one imperf. stamp with simulated perforations.

Tapestry Type of Regular Issue
Souvenir Sheet

Design: 7z+3z, Satyrs holding monogram of King Sigismund Augustus.

1970, Dec. 23 Photo. *Imperf.*
B121 A541 7z + 3z multi 1.40 .75

Type of Regular Issue

Design: 8.50z+4z, Virgin Mary, 15th century stained glass window.

1971, Sept. 15 *Perf. 11½x11*
B122 A555 8.50z + 4z multi .75 .35

Painting Type of Regular Issue

7z+1z, Nude, by Wojciech Weiss (1875-1950).

1971, Oct. 9 Litho.
B123 A556 7z + 1z multi .85 .60

Winter Olympic Type of Regular Issue
Souvenir Sheet

Slalom and Sapporo '72 emblem, vert.

1972, Jan. 12 Photo. *Imperf.*
B124 A564 10z + 5z multi 2.25 1.00

No. B124 contains one stamp with simulated perforations, 27x52mm.

Summer Olympic Type of Regular Issue
Souvenir Sheet

Design: 10z+5z, Archery (like 30g).

1972, May 20 Photo. *Perf. 11½x11*
B125 A568 10z + 5z multi 1.50 .75

Painting Type of Regular Issue, 1972

Design: 8.50z+4z, Portrait of a Young Lady, by Jacek Malczewski, horiz.

1972, Sept. 28 Photo. *Perf. 11x10½*
B126 A576 8.50z + 4z multi 1.40 .55

Souvenir Sheet

Copernicus — SP52

Engraved and Photogravure
1972, Sept. 28 *Perf. 11½*
B127 SP52 10z + 5z vio bl, gray & car 1.75 .80

Nicolaus Copernicus (1473-1543), astronomer. No. B127 shows the Ptolemaic and Copernican concepts of solar system from L'Harmonica Microcosmica, by Cellarius, 1660.

Souvenir Sheet

Poznan, 1740, by F. B. Werner — SP53

1973, Aug. 19 *Imperf.*
B128 SP53 10z + 5z ol & dk brn 1.00 .60
a. 10z + 5z pale lilac & dk brn 5.00 5.25

POLSKA 73 Intl. Phil. Exhib., Poznan, Aug. 19-Sept. 2. No. B128 contains one stamp with simulated perforations.
No. B128a was sold only in combination with an entrance ticket.

Copernicus, by Marcello Bacciarelli — SP54

1973, Sept. 27 Photo. *Perf. 11x11½*
B129 SP54 4z + 2z multi .40 .25

Stamp Day. The surtax was for the reconstruction of the Royal Castle in Warsaw.

Souvenir Sheet

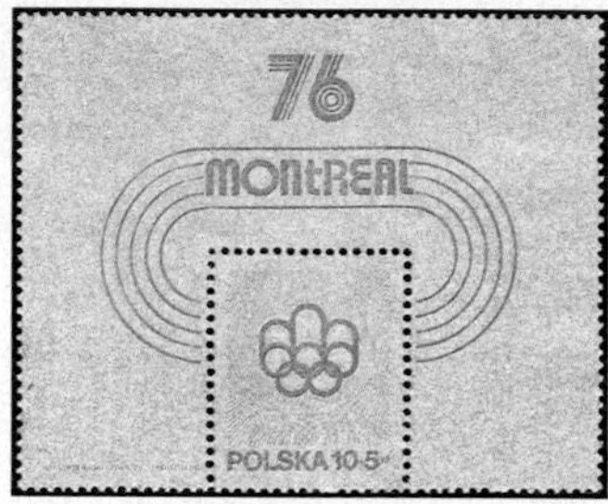

Montreal Olympic Games Emblem — SP55

Photo. & Engr.
1975, Mar. 8 *Perf. 12*
B130 SP55 10z + 5z sil & grn 1.75 .65

21st Olympic Games, Montreal, July 17-Aug. 8, 1976.
Outer edge of souvenir sheet is perforated.

Dunikowski Type of 1975

Design: 8z+4z, Mother and Child, from Silesian Insurrectionist Monument, by Dunikowski.

1975, Oct. 9 Photo. *Perf. 11½x11*
B131 A644 8z + 4z multi .50 .25

Souvenir Sheet

Volleyball — SP56

Engraved and Photogravure
1976, June 30 *Perf. 11½*
B132 SP56 10z + 5z blk & car 1.50 .75

21st Olympic Games, Montreal, Canada, July 17-Aug. 1. No. B132 contains one perf. 11½ stamp and is perf. 11½ all around.

Corinthian Art Type 1976

Design: 8z+4z, Winged Sphinx, vert.

1976, Oct. 30 Photo. *Perf. 11½x11*
B133 A664 8z + 4z multi .80 .30

Souvenir Sheet

Stoning of St. Stephen, by Rubens — SP57

1977, Apr. 30 Engr. ***Perf. 12x11½***
B134 SP57 8z + 4z sepia 1.00 .40

Peter Paul Rubens (1577-1640), Flemish painter.
Outer edge of souvenir sheet is perforated.

Souvenir Sheet

Kazimierz Gzowski — SP58

1978, June 6 Photo. ***Perf. 11½x11***
B135 SP58 8.40z + 4z multi 1.10 .60

CAPEX, '78 Canadian Intl. Phil. Exhib., Toronto, June 9-18.
K. S. Gzowski (1813-1898), Polish engineer and lawyer living in Canada, built International Bridge over Niagara River.

Souvenir Sheet

Olympic Rings — SP59

1979, May 19 Engr. ***Imperf.***
B136 SP59 10z + 5z black .90 .65

1980 Olympic Games.

Monument Type of 1979
Souvenir Sheet

1979, Sept. 1 Photo. ***Imperf.***
B137 A731 10z + 5z multi 1.00 .60

Surtax was for monument.

Summer Olympic Type of 1980
Souvenir Sheet

1980, Mar. 31 Photo. ***Perf. 11x11½***
B138 A742 10.50z + 5z Kayak 1.00 .60

No. B138 contains one stamp 42x30mm.

Souvenir Sheet

Intercosmos Cooperative Space Program — SP60

1980, Apr. 12 ***Perf. 11½x11***
B139 SP60 6.90z + 3z multi .80 .60

SP61

1970 Uprising Memorial: 2.50z + 1z, Triple Crucifix, Gdansk (27x46mm). 6.50z + 1z, Monument, Gdynia.

1981, Dec. 16 Photo. ***Perf. 11½x12***
B140 SP61 2.50 + 1z blk & red .35 .25
B141 SP61 6.50 + 1z blk & lil .40 .25

SP62

Portrait of a German Princess, by Lucas Cranach

1984, May 15 Photo. ***Perf. 11½x12***
B142 SP62 27z + 10z multi 1.25 1.00

1984 UPU Congress, Hamburg. No. B142 issued se-tenant with multicolored label showing UPU emblem and text.

Souvenir Sheet

Madonna with Child, St. John and the Angel, by Sandro Botticelli (1445-1510), Natl. Museum, Warsaw — SP63

1985, Sept. 25 Photo. ***Perf. 11***
B143 SP63 65z + 15z multi 2.25 1.25
a. Inscribed: 35 LAT POLSKIEGO . . . 5.00 5.00

ITALIA '85. Surtax for Polish Association of Philatelists.
No. B143a was for the 35th anniv. of the Polish Philatelic Union. Distribution was limited.

Joachim Lelewel (1786-1861), Historian — SP64

1986, Dec. 22 Photo. ***Perf. 11½x12***
B144 SP64 10z + 5z multi .40 .25

Surtax for the Natl. Committee for School Aid.

Polish Immigrant Settling in Kasubia, Ontario — SP65

1987, June 13 Photo. ***Perf. 12x11½***
B145 SP65 50z + 20z multi .75 .30

CAPEX '87, Toronto, Canada. Surtaxed for the Polish Philatelists' Union.

Souvenir Sheet

OLYMPHILEX '87, Rome — SP66

1987, Aug. 28 Litho. ***Perf. 14***
B146 SP66 45z + 10z like #2617 1.10 1.10

FINLANDIA '88 — SP67

1988, June 1 Photo. ***Perf. 12x11½***
B147 SP67 45z +20z Salmon, reindeer .75 .30

Souvenir Sheet

Jerzy Kukuczka, Mountain Climber Awarded Medal by the Intl. Olympic Committee for Climbing the Himalayas — SP68

1988, Aug. 17 Photo. ***Perf. 11x11½***
B148 SP68 70z +10z multi 1.00 .65

Surtax for the Polish Olympic Fund.

Aid for Victims of 1997 Oder River Flood — SP69

1997, Aug. 18 Photo. ***Perf. 11½x12***
B149 SP69 60g +30g multi .65 .40

Souvenir Sheet

Museum of Posts and Telecommunications, 80th Anniv. — SP70

2001, Oct. 9 Photo. ***Perf. 11¼x11½***
B150 SP70 3z +75g multi 2.40 1.25

AIR POST STAMPS

Biplane — AP1

Perf. 12½

1925, Sept. 10 Typo. Unwmk.

C1	AP1	1g	lt blue	.65	10.00
C2	AP1	2g	orange	.65	10.00
C3	AP1	3g	yellow brn	.65	10.00
C4	AP1	5g	dk brown	.65	.85
C5	AP1	10g	dk green	.65	.85
C6	AP1	15g	red violet	3.25	.85
C7	AP1	20g	olive grn	7.50	4.50

C8 AP1 30g dull rose 7.50 2.50
C9 AP1 45g dk violet 8.50 4.25
Nos. C1-C9 (9) 30.00 43.80
Set, never hinged 95.00

Counterfeits exist.
Nos. C1-C9 exist imperf. Value, set $125.
For overprint see No. C11.

Capt. Franciszek Zwirko and Stanislaus Wigura — AP2

Perf. 11½ to 12½ and Compound
1933, Apr. 15 Engr. Wmk. 234
C10 AP2 30g gray green 14.00 1.00
Never hinged 42.50

Winning of the circuit of Europe flight by two Polish aviators in 1932. The stamp was available for both air mail and ordinary postage.
For overprint see No. C12.

Nos. C7 and C10 Ovptd. in Red

Nos. C7 and C10 Ovptd. in Red

1934, Aug. 28 Unwmk. *Perf. 12½*
C11 AP1 20g olive green 5.00 7.00

Wmk. 234
Perf. 11½
C12 AP2 30g gray green 6.00 2.00
Set, never hinged 50.00

Polish People's Republic

Douglas Plane over Ruins of Warsaw — AP3

Unwmk.
1946, Mar. 5 Photo. *Perf. 11*
C13 AP3 5z grnsh blk .40 .25
a. Without control number 4.00 .40
Never hinged 6.00
C14 AP3 10z dk violet .40 .25
C15 AP3 15z blue 1.25 .25
C16 AP3 20z rose brn .80 .25
C17 AP3 25z dk bl grn 1.65 .40
C18 AP3 30z red 2.50 .55
Nos. C13-C18 (6) 7.00 1.95
Set, never hinged 12.00

The 10z, 20z and 30z were issued only with control number in lower right stamp margin. The 15z and 25z exist only without number. The 5z comes both ways.
Nos. C13-C18 exist imperforate. Value, set $125.

Nos. 345, 344 and 344a Surcharged in Red or Black

a

b

1947, Sept. 10 *Perf. 12½*
C19 A104(a) 40z on 50g (R) 1.75 1.00
C20 A103(b) 50z on 25g dl red 2.25 2.00
a. 50z on 25g deep red 3.00 2.75
Never hinged, #C20a 4.50 2.25
Set, never hinged 10.00

Counterfeits exist.

Centaur AP4

1948 *Perf. 11*
C21 AP4 15z dk violet 1.50 .25
C22 AP4 25z deep blue .80 .25
C23 AP4 30z brown .65 .25
C24 AP4 50z dk green 1.25 .25
C25 AP4 75z gray black 1.50 .25
C26 AP4 100z red orange 1.50 .25
Nos. C21-C26 (6) 7.20 1.50
Set, never hinged 12.50

Nos. C21-C26 exist imperf.

Pres. F. D. Roosevelt AP5

100z, Casimir Pulaski. 120z, Tadeusz Kosciusko.

1948, Dec. 30 Photo. *Perf. 11½*
Granite Paper
C26A AP5 80z blue blk 13.00 *30.00*
C26B AP5 100z purple 14.00 *30.00*
C26C AP5 120z deep blue 14.00 *30.00*
d. Souvenir sheet of 3 210.00 *400.00*
Never hinged 325.00
Nos. C26A-C26C (3) 41.00 *90.00*
Set, never hinged 75.00

Nos. C26A-C26C were issued in panes containing 16 stamps and 4 labels.
No. C26Cd contains stamps similar to Nos. C26A-C26C with colors changed: 80z ultramarine, 100z carmine rose, 120z dark green. Sold for 500z.

Airplane Mechanic and Propeller — AP5a

1950, Feb. 6 Engr. *Perf. 12½*
C27 AP5a 500z rose lake 3.75 4.25
Never hinged 6.00

Catalogue values for unused stamps in this section, from this point to the end of the section, are for Never Hinged items.

Seaport AP6

Designs: 90g, Mechanized farm. 1.40z, Warsaw. 5z, Steel mill.

1952, Apr. 10 *Perf. 12x12½*
C28 AP6 55g intense blue .50 .25
C29 AP6 90g dull green .65 .35
C30 AP6 1.40z violet brn .55 .25
C31 AP6 5z gray black .65 .35
Nos. C28-C31 (4) 2.35 1.20

Nos. C28-C31 exist imperf. Value $25.

Congress Badge — AP7

1953, Aug. 24 Photo. *Imperf.*
C32 AP7 55g brown lilac 1.75 .35
C33 AP7 75g brown org 2.50 1.40

3rd World Congress of Students, Warsaw 1953.

Souvenir Sheet

AP8

1954, May 23 Engr. *Perf. 12x12½*
C34 AP8 5z gray green 35.00 25.00

3rd congress of the Polish Phil. Assoc., Warsaw, 1954. Sold for 7.50 zlotys. A similar sheet, imperf. and in dark blue, was issued but had no postal validity. Value: mint $275; cto $325.

Paczkow Castle, Luban — AP9

80g, Kazimierz Dolny. 1.15z, Wawel castle, Cracow. 1.50z, City Hall, Wroclaw. 1.55z, Lazienki Park, Warsaw. 1.95z, Cracow gate, Lublin.

1954, July 13 *Perf. 12½*
C35 AP9 60g dk gray grn .50 .25
C36 AP9 80g red .50 .25
C37 AP9 1.15z black 3.25 1.25
C38 AP9 1.50z rose lake .50 .25
C39 AP9 1.55z dp gray bl .50 .25
C40 AP9 1.95z chocolate 1.50 .85
Nos. C35-C40 (6) 6.75 3.10

Plane over "Peace" Steelworks — AP10

Plane over: 1.50z, Castle Square, Warsaw. 3.40z, Old Market, Cracow. 3.90z, King Boleslaw Chrobry Wall, Szczecin. 4z, Karkonosze mountains. 5z, Gdansk. 10z, Ruins of Liwa Castle. 15z, Old City, Lublin. 20z, Kasprowy Wierch Peak and cable car. 30z, Porabka dam. 50z, M. S. Batory and Gdynia harbor.

Wmk. 326 ('58 Values); Unwmkd.
1957-58 Engr. & Photo. *Perf. 12½*
C41 AP10 90g black & pink .35 .25
C42 AP10 1.50z brn & salmon .35 .25
C43 AP10 3.40z sep & buff .35 .25
C44 AP10 3.90z dk brn & cit .35 .25
C45 AP10 4z ind & lt grn .35 .25
C46 AP10 5z maroon & gray .75 .25
C47 AP10 10z sepia & grn 1.40 .25
C48 AP10 15z vio bl & pale bl 1.40 .70
C49 AP10 20z vio blk & lem 1.50 .70
C50 AP10 30z ol gray & bis 4.25 3.50
C51 AP10 50z dk bl & gray 12.00 5.00
Nos. C41-C51 (11) 23.05 11.65

Issue dates: 5z, 10z, 20z, 30z, 50z, Dec. 15, 1958. Others, Dec. 6, 1957.

1959, May 23 Litho. Wmk. 326
C52 AP10 10z sepia 2.00 1.75
a. With 5z label 3.50 3.50

65th anniv. of the Polish Philatelic Society. Sheet of 6 stamps and 2 each of 3 different labels. Each label carries an added charge of 5z for a fund to build a Society clubhouse in Warsaw.

Jantar Glider — AP11

Contemporary aviation: 10z, Mi6 transport helicopter. 20z, PZL-106 Kruk, crop spraying plane. 50z, Plane over Warsaw Castle.

1976-78 Unwmk. Engr. *Perf. 11½*
C53 AP11 5z dk blue grn .25 .25
C54 AP11 10z dk brown .25 .50
C55 AP11 20z grnsh black .25 .25
C56 AP11 50z claret .25 .25
Nos. C53-C56 (4) 1.00 1.25

Issued: 5z, 10z, 3/27/76; 20z, 2/15/77; 50z, 2/2/78.

AIR POST SEMI-POSTAL STAMP

Catalogue values for unused stamps in this section are for Never Hinged items.

Polish People's Republic

Wing of Jet Plane and Letter — SPAP1

Perf. 11½
1957, Mar. 28 Unwmk. Photo.
CB1 SPAP1 4z + 2z blue 2.00 1.00
a. Souv. sheet of 1, ultra, imperf. 10.00 5.00

7th Polish National Philatelic Exhibition, Warsaw. Sheet of 12 with 4 diagonally arranged gray labels.

REGISTRATION STAMPS

Insects — R1

Designs: (3.80z), Polyommatus semiargus. (5.90z), Rosalia alpina. (6.70z), Gerris paludum. (9.30z), Sympetrum flaveolum.

Perf. 11¾x11½
2013, Aug. 16 Photo.
F1 R1 (3.80z) multi 2.40 2.40
F2 R1 (5.90z) multi 3.75 3.75
F3 R1 (6.70z) multi 4.25 4.25
F4 R1 (9.30z) multi 6.00 6.00
Nos. F1-F4 (4) 16.40 16.40

Insects — R2

Designs: (5.90z), Coccinella septempunctata. (6.70z), Chorthippus parallelus. (6.95z), Inachis io. (9.30z), Formica rufa.

Perf. 11¾x11½

2013, Sept. 30 **Photo.**

F5 R2 (5.90z) multi 4.00 4.00
F6 R2 (6.70z) multi 4.50 4.50
F7 R2 (6.95z) multi 4.50 4.50
F8 R2 (9.30z) multi 6.00 6.00
Nos. F5-F8 (4) 19.00 19.00

Insects — R3

Designs: (8.50z), Arctia caja. (9.50z), Papilio machaon caterpillar. (11z), Apis mellifera. (13.10z), Lucanus cervus.

Perf. 11¾x11½

2013, Oct. 18 **Photo.**

F9 R3 (8.50z) multi 5.50 5.50
F10 R3 (9.50z) multi 6.00 6.00
F11 R3 (11z) multi 7.00 7.00
F12 R3 (13.10z) multi 8.50 8.50
Nos. F9-F12 (4) 27.00 27.00

POSTAGE DUE STAMPS

Cracow Issues

Postage Due Stamps of Austria, 1916, Overprinted in Black or Red

1919, Jan. 10 **Unwmk.** ***Perf. 12½***

J1 D4 5h rose red 17.50 20.00
J2 D4 10h rose red *5,250.* *8,500.*
J3 D4 15h rose red 12.00 *10.00*
a. Inverted overprint 3,500. *3,000.*
J4 D4 20h rose red 825.00 *650.00*
J5 D4 25h rose red 40.00 *40.00*
J6 D4 30h rose red *1,900.* *1,500.*
J7 D4 40h rose red *400.00* *400.00*
J8 D5 1k ultra (R) *5,500.* *6,250.*
J9 D5 5k ultra (R) *5,500.* *6,250.*
J10 D5 10k ultra (R) *22,500.* *25,000.*
a. Black overprint *85,000.* *100,000.*

Overprint on Nos. J1-J7, J10a is type. Overprint on Nos. J8-J10 is slightly larger than illustration, has a different ornament between lines of type and is litho.

Type of Austria, 1916-18, Surcharged in Black

D6

1919, Jan. 10

J11 D6 15h on 36h vio *525.00* 425.00
J12 D6 50h on 42h choc 70.00 *50.00*
a. Double surcharge 3,500. *5,500.*

See note above No. 41. Counterfeits exist of Nos. J1-J12.

Regular Issues

Numerals of Value — D7

1919 **Typo.** ***Perf. 11½***

For Northern Poland

J13 D7 2f red orange .25 .25
J14 D7 4f red orange .25 .25
J15 D7 5f red orange .25 .25
J16 D7 10f red orange .25 .25
J17 D7 20f red orange .25 .25
J18 D7 30f red orange .25 .25
J19 D7 50f red orange .25 .25
J20 D7 100f red orange .50 .35
J21 D7 500f red orange 2.50 2.40

For Southern Poland

J22 D7 2h dark blue .25 .25
J23 D7 4h dark blue .25 .25
J24 D7 5h dark blue .25 .25
J25 D7 10h dark blue .25 .25
J26 D7 20h dark blue .25 .25
J27 D7 30h dark blue .25 .25
J28 D7 50h dark blue .35 .25
J29 D7 100h dark blue .45 .80
J30 D7 500h dark blue 1.40 1.60
Nos. J13-J30 (18) 8.45 8.65

Counterfeits exist.

Nos. J13-J30 never hinged valued at 4x hinged value.

1920 ***Perf. 9, 10, 11½***

Thin Laid Paper

J31 D7 20f dark blue .25 .25
J32 D7 100f dark blue .25 .25
J33 D7 200f dark blue .35 .25
J34 D7 500f dark blue .35 .25
Nos. J31-J34 (4) 1.20 1.00

Nos. J31-J34 never hinged valued at 3.5x hinged values.

Regular Issue of 1919 Surcharged

1921, Jan. 25 ***Imperf.***

Wove Paper

J35 A9 6m on 15h brown .75 .75
J36 A9 6m on 25h car .75 .75
J37 A9 20m on 10h lake 5.00 7.00
J38 A9 20m on 50h indigo 4.00 3.75
J39 A9 35m on 70h dp bl 7.00 9.00
Nos. J35-J39 (5) 17.50 21.25

Counterfeits exist.

Numerals of Value — D8

Thin Laid or Wove Paper

Size: 17x22mm

Perf. 9 to 14½ and Compound

1921-22 **Typo.**

J40 D8 1m indigo .25 .25
J41 D8 2m indigo .25 .25
J42 D8 4m indigo .25 .25
J43 D8 6m indigo .45 .25
J44 D8 8m indigo .45 .25
J45 D8 20m indigo .45 .25
J46 D8 50m indigo .45 .25
J47 D8 100m indigo .70 .35
Nos. J40-J47 (8) 3.25 2.10

Nos. J40-J47 never hinged valued at 4x hinged values.

Nos. J44-J45, J41 Surcharged

Perf. 9 to 14½ and Compound

1923, Nov.

J48 D8 10,000(m) on 8m indigo .35 .25
J49 D8 20,000(m) on 20m indigo .35 .25
J50 D8 50,000(m) on 2m indigo .45 .45
Nos. J48-J50 (3) 1.15 .95

Nos. J48-J50 never hinged valued at 5x hinged values.

Type of 1921-22 Issue

Size: 19x24mm

1923 **Typo.** ***Perf. 12½***

J51 D8 50m indigo .25 .25
J52 D8 100m indigo .25 .25
J53 D8 200m indigo .25 .25
J54 D8 500m indigo .60 .25
J55 D8 1000m indigo .35 .25
J56 D8 2000m indigo .40 .30
J57 D8 10,000m indigo .25 .25
J58 D8 20,000m indigo .35 .25
J59 D8 30,000m indigo .35 .25
J60 D8 50,000m indigo .35 .25
J61 D8 100,000m indigo .40 .25
J62 D8 200,000m indigo .40 .25
J63 D8 300,000m indigo 5.00 .35
J64 D8 500,000m indigo 1.75 .25
J65 D8 1,000,000m indigo 1.00 .30
J66 D8 2,000,000m indigo 1.75 .35
J67 D8 3,000,000m indigo 3.00 1.40
Nos. J51-J67 (17) 16.70 5.70
Set, never hinged 60.00

D9

Perf. 10 to 13½ and Compound

1924 **Size: 20x25½mm**

J68 D9 1g brown .25 .25
J69 D9 2g brown .25 .25
J70 D9 4g brown .30 .25
J71 D9 6g brown .30 .25
J72 D9 10g brown 1.25 .25
J73 D9 15g brown 4.50 .25
J74 D9 20g brown 3.25 .25
J75 D9 25g brown 6.25 .25
J76 D9 30g brown .75 .25
J77 D9 40g brown 1.00 .25
J78 D9 50g brown 1.00 .25
J79 D9 1z brown .45 .25
J80 D9 2z brown .45 .25
J81 D9 3z brown .75 1.50
J82 D9 5z brown .40 .60
Nos. J68-J82 (15) 21.15 5.35
Set, never hinged 92.50

Nos. J68-J69 and J72-J75 exist measuring 19½x24½mm.

For surcharges see Nos. J84-J91.

D10

1930, July ***Perf. 12½***

J83 D10 5g olive brown .70 .25
Never hinged 1.00

Postage Due Stamps of 1924 Surcharged

Perf. 10 to 13½ and Compound

1934-38

J84 D9 10g on 2z brown ('38) .25 .25
J85 D9 15g on 2z brown .25 .25
J86 D9 20g on 1z brown .40 .25
J87 D9 20g on 5z brown 6.00 .25
J88 D9 25g on 40g brown .85 .25
J89 D9 30g on 40g brown 1.40 .25
J90 D9 50g on 40g brown 1.40 .50
J91 D9 50g on 3z brown ('35) .85 .35
Nos. J84-J91 (8) 11.40 2.35
Set, never hinged 12.00

No. 255a Surcharged in Red or Indigo

1934-36 **Laid Paper**

J92 A50 10g on 1z (R) ('36) .80 .25
a. Vertically laid paper (No. 255) 25.00 18.00
J93 A50 20g on 1z (R) ('36) 2.50 .80
J94 A50 25g on 1z (I) .80 .30
a. Vertically laid paper (No. 255) 30.00 18.00
Nos. J92-J94 (3) 4.10 1.35
Set, never hinged 10.00

D11

1938-39 **Typo.** ***Perf. 12½x12***

J95 D11 5g dark blue green .25 .25
J96 D11 10g dark blue green .25 .25
J97 D11 15g dark blue green .25 .25
J98 D11 20g dark blue green .35 .25
J99 D11 25g dark blue green .35 .25
J100 D11 30g dark blue green .60 .25
J101 D11 50g dark blue green .95 .25
J102 D11 1z dark blue green 5.00 1.65
Nos. J95-J102 (8) 8.00 3.40
Set, never hinged 14.00

For surcharges see Nos. N51-N55.

Polish People's Republic

Post Horn with Thunderbolts D12

Size: 25½x19mm

Perf. 11x10½

1945, May 20 **Litho.** **Unwmk.**

J103 D12 1z orange brown .25 .25
J104 D12 2z orange brown .25 .25
J105 D12 3z orange brown .25 .25
J106 D12 5z orange brown .35 .30
Nos. J103-J106 (4) 1.10 1.05
Set, never hinged 2.75

Nos. J103-J106 exist imperf. Value, set $40.

Type of 1945

Perf. 11, 11½ (P) or Imperf. (I)

1946-49 **Size: 29x21½mm** **Photo.**

J106A D12 1z org brn (P) ('49) .25 .25
J107 D12 2z org brn (P,I) .25 .25
J108 D12 3z org brn (P,I) .25 .25
J109 D12 5z org brn (I) .25 .25
J110 D12 6z org brn (I) .25 .25
J111 D12 10z org brn (I) .25 .25
J112 D12 15z org brn (P,I) .55 .30
J113 D12 25z org brn (P,I) .75 .60
J114 D12 100z brn (P) ('49) 1.50 .90
J115 D12 150z brn (P) ('49) 2.00 1.00
Nos. J106A-J115 (10) 6.30 4.30
Set, never hinged 8.00

Polish Eagle — D13

1950 **Engr.** ***Perf. 12x12½***

J116 D13 5z red brown .25 .25
J117 D13 10z red brown .25 .25
J118 D13 15z red brown .25 *.25*
J119 D13 20z red brown .25 *.25*
J120 D13 25z red brown .25 .25
J121 D13 50z red brown .50 .30
J122 D13 100z red brown .50 .35
Nos. J116-J122 (7) 2.25 1.90
Set, never hinged 3.00

1951-52

J123 D13 5g red brown .25 .25
J124 D13 10g red brown .25 .25
J125 D13 15g red brown .25 .25
J126 D13 20g red brown .25 .25
J127 D13 25g red brown .25 .25
J128 D13 30g red brown .25 .25
J129 D13 50g red brown .25 .25

J130 D13 60g red brown .25 .25
J131 D13 90g red brown .50 .45
J132 D13 1z red brown .25 .25
J133 D13 2z red brown .25 .25
J134 D13 5z brown violet .60 .60
Nos. J123-J134 (12) 3.60 3.55
Set, never hinged 4.00

Without imprint

1953, Apr. **Photo.**
J135 D13 5g red brown .25 .25
J136 D13 10g red brown .25 .25
J137 D13 15g red brown .25 .25
J138 D13 20g red brown .25 .25
J139 D13 25g red brown .25 .25
J140 D13 30g red brown .25 .25
J141 D13 50g red brown .25 .25
J142 D13 60g red brown .35 .25
J143 D13 90g red brown .30 .25
J144 D13 1z red brown .25 .25
J145 D13 2z red brown .55 .55
Nos. J135-J145 (11) 3.20 3.05
Set, never hinged 3.50

Catalogue values for unused stamps in this section, from this point to the end of the section, are for Never Hinged items.

1980, Sept. 2 **Litho.** ***Perf. 12½***
J146 D13 1z lt red brown .25 .25
J147 D13 2z gray olive .25 .25
J148 D13 3z dull violet .25 .25
J149 D13 5z brown .30 .25
Nos. J146-J149 (4) 1.05 1.00

D14

1998, June 18 **Litho.** ***Perf. 14***
J150 D14 5g lilac, blk & yel .25 .25
J151 D14 10g green blue, blk & yel .25 .25
J152 D14 20g green, blk & yel .25 .25
J153 D14 50g yellow & black .30 .30
J154 D14 80g orange, blk & yel .35 .45
J155 D14 1z red, blk & yel .50 .70
Nos. J150-J155 (6) 1.90 2.20

OFFICIAL STAMPS

O1

Perf. 10, 11½, 10x11½, 11½x10
1920, Feb. 1 **Litho.** **Unwmk.**
O1 O1 3f vermilion .25 *.25*
O2 O1 5f vermilion .25 *.25*
O3 O1 10f vermilion .25 *.25*
O4 O1 15f vermilion .25 *.25*
O5 O1 25f vermilion .25 *.25*
O6 O1 50f vermilion .25 *.25*
O7 O1 100f vermilion .25 *.25*
O8 O1 150f vermilion .25 .25
O9 O1 200f vermilion .65 .45
O10 O1 300f vermilion .75 .50
O11 O1 600f vermilion 1.40 1.75
Nos. O1-O11 (11) 4.80 4.70
Set, never hinged 14.00

The stars on either side of the denomination do not appear on Nos. O7-O11. Nos. O7-O11 exist imperf. Value, set $27.50.

Numerals Larger
Stars inclined outward

1920, Nov. 20 ***Perf. 11½***
Thin Laid Paper
O12 O1 5f red .25 .25
O13 O1 10f red .25 .25
O14 O1 15f red .25 .25
O15 O1 25f red .60 .25
O16 O1 50f red .35 .25
Nos. O12-O16 (5) 1.70 1.25
Set, never hinged 5.25

Polish Eagle — O3

Perf. 12x12½
1933, Aug. 1 **Typo.** **Wmk. 234**
O17 O3 (30g) vio (Zwyczajna) .35 .25
O18 O3 (80g) red (Polecona) .35 .25
Set, never hinged 3.00

Polish Eagle — O4

1935, Apr. 1
O19 O4 (25g) bl vio (Zwyczajna) .25 .25
O20 O4 (55g) car (Polecona) .25 .25
Set, never hinged 1.40

Stamps inscribed "Zwyczajna" or "Zwykla" were for ordinary official mail. Those with "Polecona" were for registered official mail.

Polish People's Republic

Polish Eagle — O5

Perf. 11, 14
1945, July 1 **Photo.** **Unwmk.**
O21 O5 (5z) bl vio (Zwykla) .25 .25
a. Imperf. 3.50 3.50
O22 O5 (10z) red (Polecona) .25 .25
a. Imperf. 7.00 7.00
Set, never hinged, #O21, O22 1.40
Set, never hinged, #O21a, O22a 10.00

Control number at bottom right: M-01705 on No. O21; M-01706 on No. O22.

Type of 1945 Redrawn

1946, July 31
O23 O5 (5z) dl bl vio (Zwykla) .25 .25
O24 O5 (10z) dl rose red (Polecona) .25 .25
Set, never hinged 1.50

The redrawn stamps appear blurred and the eagle contains fewer lines of shading.
Control number at bottom right: M-01709 on Nos. O23-O26.

Redrawn Type of 1946

1946, July 31 ***Imperf.***
O25 O5 (60g) dl bl vio (Zwykla) .25 .25
O26 O5 (1.55z) dl rose red (Polecona) .25 .25
Set, never hinged 1.50

Type of 1945, 2nd Redrawing
No Control Number at Lower Right

Perf. 11, 11½, 11x12½
1950-53 **Unwmk.**
O27 O5 (60g) blue (Zwykla) .25 .25
O28 O5 (1.55z) red (Polecona) ('53) .25 .25
Set, never hinged 1.50

Redrawn Type of 1952

1954 ***Perf. 13x11, 11½, 14***
O29 O5 (60g) slate gray (Zwykla) 3.00 1.00
Never hinged 5.00

O6

Perf. 11x11½, 12x12½
1954, Aug. 15 **Engr.**
O30 O6 (60g) dark blue (Zwykla) .25 .25
O31 O6 (1.55z) red (Polecona) .30 .25
Set, never hinged 2.00

Polish People's Republic, 10th anniversary.

NEWSPAPER STAMPS

Austrian Newspaper Stamps of 1916 Overprinted

1919, Jan. 10 **Unwmk.** ***Imperf.***
P1 N9 2h brown 19.00 *19.00*
P2 N9 4h green 18.00 *15.00*
P3 N9 6h dark blue 15.00 *14.00*
P4 N9 10h orange 275.00 200.00
P5 N9 30h claret 19.00 17.00
Nos. P1-P5 (5) 346.00 265.00

See note above No. 41.
Counterfeits exist of Nos. P1-P5.

OCCUPATION STAMPS

Issued under German Occupation

German Stamps of 1905 Overprinted

Perf. 14, 14½
1915, May 12 **Wmk. 125**
N1 A16 3pf brown .60 .50
N2 A16 5pf green 1.25 .50
N3 A16 10pf carmine 1.25 .50
N4 A16 20pf ultra 2.50 .75
N5 A16 40pf lake & blk 7.50 3.75
Nos. N1-N5 (5) 13.10 6.00
Set, never hinged 40.00

German Stamps of 1905-17 Overprinted

1916-17
N6 A22 2½pf gray 1.25 *2.50*
N7 A16 3pf brown 1.25 *2.50*
N8 A16 5pf green 1.25 *2.50*
N9 A22 7½pf orange 1.25 *2.50*
N10 A16 10pf carmine 1.25 *2.50*
N11 A22 15pf yel brn 3.50 3.50
N12 A22 15pf dk vio ('17) 1.25 *2.50*
N13 A16 20pf ultra 1.75 *2.50*
N14 A16 30pf org & blk, *buff* 7.00 *15.00*
N15 A16 40pf lake & blk 2.50 2.50
N16 A16 60pf magenta 3.00 *3.50*
Nos. N6-N16 (11) 25.25 42.00
Set, never hinged 70.00

For overprints and surcharges see #15-26.

German Stamps of 1934 Surcharged in Black

1939, Dec. 1 **Wmk. 237** ***Perf. 14***
N17 A64 6g on 3pf bister .25 *.40*
N18 A64 8g on 4pf dl bl .25 *.40*
N19 A64 12g on 6pf dk grn .25 *.40*
N20 A64 16g on 8pf vermilion .50 1.00
N21 A64 20g on 10pf choc .25 .40
N22 A64 24g on 12pf dp car .25 .25
N23 A64 30g on 15pf maroon .50 .90
N24 A64 40g on 20pf brt bl .50 .40
N25 A64 50g on 25pf ultra .50 .75
N26 A64 60g on 30pf ol grn .50 .40
N27 A64 80g on 40pf red vio .55 .80
N28 A64 1z on 50pf dk grn & blk 1.10 1.00
N29 A64 2z on 100(pf) org & blk 2.25 *3.00*
Nos. N17-N29 (13) 7.65 10.10
Set, never hinged 25.00

Stamps of Poland 1937, Surcharged in Black or Brown

1940 **Unwmk.** ***Perf. 12½, 12½x13***
N30 A80 24g on 25g sl grn 1.25 *3.25*
N31 A81 40g on 30g rose vio .40 1.25
N32 A80 50g on 55g blue .30 *.70*

Similar Surcharge on Stamps of 1938-39
N33 A83 2g on 5g red org .25 *.40*
N34 A83 4(g) on 5g red org .25 *.40*
N35 A83 6(g) on 10g grn .25 *.40*
N36 A83 8(g) on 10g grn (Br) .25 *.40*
N37 A83 10(g) on 10g grn .25 *.40*
N38 A83 12(g) on 15g redsh brn (#339) .25 *.40*
N39 A83 16(g) on 15g redsh brn (#339) .25 *.40*
N40 A83 24g on 25g dl vio .25 *.40*
N41 A83 30(g) on 30g rose red .25 *.40*
N42 A83 50(g) on 50g brt red vio .25 *.65*
N43 A83 60(g) on 55g ultra 6.00 *17.00*
N44 A83 80(g) on 75g dl grn 6.00 *17.00*
N45 A83 1z on 1z org 6.25 *17.00*
N46 A83 2z on 2z car rose 3.00 *7.50*
N47 A95 3z on 3z gray blk 4.00 *10.00*

Similar Surcharge on Nos. B32-B34
N48 SP5 30g on 5g+5g .25 .65
N49 SP5 40g on 25g+10g .25 .65
N50 SP5 1z on 55g+15g 4.00 *10.00*

Similar Surcharge on Nos. J98-J102
Perf. 12½x12
N51 D11 50(g) on 20g 1.25 *3.25*
N52 D11 50(g) on 25g 6.00 *17.50*
N53 D11 50(g) on 30g 14.00 *37.50*
N54 D11 50(g) on 50g .75 *2.40*
N55 D11 50(g) on 1z 1.75 *4.75*
Nos. N30-N55 (26) 57.95 *154.65*
Set, never hinged 160.00

The surcharge on Nos. N30 to N55 is arranged to fit the shape of the stamp and obliterate the original denomination. On some values, "General Gouvernement" appears at the bottom. Counterfeits exist.

St. Florian's Gate, Cracow — OS1

Palace, Warsaw — OS13

Designs: 8g, Watch Tower, Cracow. 10g, Cracow Gate, Lublin. 12g, Courtyard and statue of Copernicus. 20g, Dominican Church, Cracow. 24g, Wawel Castle, Cracow. 30g, Church, Lublin. 40g, Arcade, Cloth Hall, Cracow. 48g, City Hall, Sandomierz. 50g, Court House, Cracow. 60g, Courtyard, Cracow. 80g, St. Mary's Church, Cracow.

1940-41 **Unwmk.** **Photo.** ***Perf. 14***
N56 OS1 6g brown .25 *.75*
N57 OS1 8g brn org .25 *.75*
N58 OS1 8g bl blk ('41) .45 *.50*
N59 OS1 10g emerald .25 *.25*
N60 OS1 12g dk grn 2.00 .70
N61 OS1 12g dp vio ('41) .30 *.25*
N62 OS1 20g dk ol brn .25 .25
N63 OS1 24g henna brn .25 .25
N64 OS1 30g purple .25 .25
N65 OS1 30g vio brn ('41) .30 *.25*
N66 OS1 40g slate blk .25 .25
N67 OS1 48g chnt brn ('41) .60 *1.50*
N68 OS1 50g brt bl .25 .25

N69 OS1 60g slate grn .25 *.25*
N70 OS1 80g dull pur .25 *.50*
N71 OS13 1z rose lake 2.00 1.25
N72 OS13 1z Prus grn ('41) .55 *1.00*
Nos. N56-N72 (17) 8.70 9.20
Set, never hinged 16.00

For surcharges see Nos. NB1-NB4.

Cracow Castle and City, 15th Century OS14

1941, Apr. 20 Engr. *Perf. 14½*
N73 OS14 10z red & ol blk 1.00 *2.75*
Never hinged 2.50

Printed in sheets of 8.

Rondel and Florian's Gate, Cracow OS15

Design: 4z, Tyniec Monastery, Vistula River.

1941 *Perf. 13½x14*
N74 OS15 2z dk ultra .80 *1.00*
N75 OS15 4z slate grn .80 *1.75*
Set, never hinged 3.00

Adolf Hitler — OS17

1941-43 Unwmk. Photo. *Perf. 14*
N76 OS17 2g gray blk .25 .25
N77 OS17 6g golden brn .25 .25
N78 OS17 8g slate blue .25 .25
N79 OS17 10g green .25 .25
N80 OS17 12g purple .25 .25
N81 OS17 16g org red 1.40 *1.75*
N82 OS17 20g blk brn .25 .25
N83 OS17 24g henna .25 .25
N84 OS17 30g rose vio .25 .25
N85 OS17 32g dk bl grn .50 *.50*
N86 OS17 40g brt blue .25 .25
N87 OS17 48g chestnut 1.25 *.70*
N88 OS17 50g vio bl ('43) .30 .50
N89 OS17 60g dk olive ('43) .30 .50
N90 OS17 80g dk vio ('43) .30 .50
Nos. N76-N90 (15) 6.30 6.70
Set, never hinged 10.00

A 20g black brown exists with head of Hans Frank substituted for that of Hitler. It was printed and used by Resistance movements.

Nos. N76-N90 exist imperf. Value, set unused $300.

1942-44 Engr. *Perf. 12½*
N91 OS17 50g vio bl .40 *.75*
N92 OS17 60g dk ol .40 *.75*
N93 OS17 80g dk red vio .40 *.75*
N94 OS17 1z slate grn .40 *.75*
a. Perf. 14 ('44) .80 *3.00*
N95 OS17 1.20z dk brn .60 *.90*
a. Perf. 14 ('44) 1.50 *4.00*
N96 OS17 1.60z bl vio .60 *1.25*
a. Perf. 14 ('44) 1.60 *6.00*
Nos. N91-N96 (6) 2.80 *5.15*
Set, never hinged 5.50
Set, #N94a, N95a, N96a, never hinged 7.00

Nos. N91-N96 exist imperf. Value, set unused $750.

Rondel and Florian's Gate, Cracow OS18

Designs: 4z, Tyniec Monastery, Vistula River. 6z, View of Lwow. 10z, Cracow Castle and City, 15th Century.

1943-44 *Perf. 13½x14*
N100 OS18 2z slate grn .25 .25
N101 OS18 4z dk gray vio .25 *.80*
N102 OS18 6z sepia ('44) .40 *.70*
N103 OS18 10z org brn & gray blk .40 *1.00*
Nos. N100-N103 (4) 1.30 *2.75*
Set, never hinged 2.75

OCCUPATION SEMI-POSTAL STAMPS

Issued under German Occupation

Types of 1940 Occupation Postage Stamps Surcharged in Red

Unwmk.
1940, Aug. 17 Photo. *Perf. 14*
NB1 OS1 12g + 8g olive gray 1.60 *3.50*
NB2 OS1 24g + 16g olive gray 1.60 *3.50*
NB3 OS1 50g + 50g olive gray 2.00 *4.00*
NB4 OS1 80g + 80g olive gray 2.00 *5.25*
Nos. NB1-NB4 (4) 7.20 *16.25*
Set, never hinged 15.00

German Peasant Girl in Poland OSP1

Designs: 24g+26g, Woman wearing scarf. 30g+20g, Similar to type OSP4.

1940, Oct. 26 Engr. *Perf. 14½*
Thick Paper
NB5 OSP1 12g + 38g dk sl grn 1.10 2.75
NB6 OSP1 24g + 26g cop red 1.10 2.75
NB7 OSP1 30g + 20g dk pur 2.00 *5.00*
Nos. NB5-NB7 (3) 4.20 10.50
Set, never hinged 8.50

1st anniversary of the General Government.

German Peasant OSP4

1940, Dec. 1 *Perf. 12*
NB8 OSP4 12g + 8g dk grn .50 *1.40*
NB9 OSP4 24g + 16g rose red .50 *1.75*
NB10 OSP4 30g + 30g vio brn 1.10 *2.50*
NB11 OSP4 50g + 50g ultra 1.25 *3.00*
Nos. NB8-NB11 (4) 3.35 *8.65*
Set, never hinged 7.00

The surtax was for war relief.

Adolf Hitler — OSP5

Unwmk.
1942, Apr. 20 Engr. *Perf. 11*
Thick Cream Paper
NB12 OSP5 30g + 1z brn car .40 *1.40*
NB13 OSP5 50g + 1z dk ultra .40 *1.40*
NB14 OSP5 1.20z + 1z brown .40 *1.40*
Nos. NB12-NB14 (3) 1.20 *4.20*
Set, never hinged 2.10

To commemorate Hitler's 53rd birthday. Printed in sheets of 25.

Ancient Lublin — OSP6

Designs: 24g+6g, 1z+1z, Modern Lublin.

1942, Aug. 15 Photo. *Perf. 12½*
NB15 OSP6 12g + 8g rose vio .25 *.55*
NB16 OSP6 24g + 6g henna .25 *.55*
NB17 OSP6 50g + 50g dp bl .25 *1.00*
NB18 OSP6 1z + 1z dp grn .40 *1.40*
Nos. NB15-NB18 (4) 1.15 *3.50*
Set, never hinged 1.75

600th anniversary of Lublin.

Veit Stoss — OSP8

Designs: 24g+26g, Hans Durer. 30g+30g, Johann Schuch. 50g+50g, Joseph Elsner. 1z+1z, Nicolaus Copernicus.

1942, Nov. 20 Engr. *Perf. 13½x14*
NB19 OSP8 12g + 18g dl pur .25 *.35*
NB20 OSP8 24g + 26g dl henna .25 *.35*
NB21 OSP8 30g + 30g dl rose vio .25 *.35*
NB22 OSP8 50g + 50g dl bl vio .25 *.55*
NB23 OSP8 1z + 1z dl myr grn .25 *.70*
Nos. NB19-NB23 (5) 1.25 2.30
Set, never hinged 1.40

For overprint see No. NB27.

Adolf Hitler — OSP13

1943, Apr. 20
NB24 OSP13 12g + 1z purple .25 *.65*
NB25 OSP13 24g + 1z rose car .25 *.65*
NB26 OSP13 84g + 1z myrtle grn .25 *.65*
Nos. NB24-NB26 (3) .75 1.95
Set, never hinged 1.75

To commemorate Hitler's 54th birthday.

Type of 1942 Overprinted in Black

1943, May 24
NB27 OSP8 1z + 1z rose lake .55 *1.40*
Never hinged .90

Nicolaus Copernicus. Printed in sheets of 10, with marginal inscription.

Cracow Gate, Lublin — OSP14

Designs: 24g+76g, Cloth Hall, Cracow. 30g+70g, New Government Building, Radom. 50g+1z, Bruhl Palace, Warsaw. 1z+2z, Town Hall, Lwow.

The center of the designs is embossed with the emblem of the National Socialist Party.

1943 Photogravure, Embossed
NB28 OSP14 12g + 38g dk grn .25 *.40*
NB29 OSP14 24g + 76g red .25 *.40*
NB30 OSP14 30g + 70g rose vio .25 *.40*
NB31 OSP14 50g + 1z brt bl .25 *.40*
NB32 OSP14 1z + 2z bl blk .25 *.40*
Nos. NB28-NB32 (5) 1.25 2.00
Set, never hinged 1.50

3rd anniversary of the National Socialist Party in Poland.

Adolf Hitler — OSP19

1944, Apr. 20 Photo. *Perf. 14x13½*
NB33 OSP19 12g + 1z green .25 *.80*
NB34 OSP19 24g + 1z brn red .25 *.80*
NB35 OSP19 84g + 1z dk vio .25 *.80*
Nos. NB33-NB35 (3) .75 2.40
Set, never hinged 1.10

To commemorate Hitler's 55th birthday. Printed in sheets of 25.

Conrad Celtis — OSP20

Designs: 24g+26g, Andreas Schluter. 30g+30g, Hans Boner. 50g+50g, Augustus II. 1z+1z, Georg Gottlieb Pusch.

1944, July 15 Engr. *Perf. 13½x14*
NB36 OSP20 12g + 18g dk grn .25 *1.00*
NB37 OSP20 24g + 26g dk red .25 *1.00*
NB38 OSP20 30g + 30g rose vio .25 *1.40*
NB39 OSP20 50g + 50g ultra .25 *1.75*
NB40 OSP20 1z + 1z dl red brn .25 *1.75*
Nos. NB36-NB40 (5) 1.25 6.90
Set, never hinged 1.40

Cracow Castle OSP25

1944, Oct. 26 *Perf. 14½*
NB41 OSP25 10z + 10z red & blk 7.50 *35.00*
Never hinged 15.00
a. Imperf. 12.00
Never hinged 20.00
b. 10z + 10z car & greenish blk 12.50 25.00
Never hinged 25.00
c. Horiz. pair, imperf. btwn. *65.00*
Never hinged *90.00*

5th anniv. of the General Government, Oct. 26, 1944. Printed in sheets of 8.

OCCUPATION RURAL DELIVERY STAMPS

Issued under German Occupation

OSD1

Perf. 13½
1940, Dec. 1 Photo. Unwmk.
NL1 OSD1 10g red orange .45 *1.00*
NL2 OSD1 20g red orange .45 *1.25*
NL3 OSD1 30g red orange .45 *1.25*
NL4 OSD1 50g red orange 1.10 *3.00*
Nos. NL1-NL4 (4) 2.45 *6.50*
Set, never hinged 6.00

OCCUPATION OFFICIAL STAMPS

Issued under German Occupation

Eagle and Swastika OOS1

Perf. 12, 13½x14

1940, Apr. Photo. Unwmk.

Size: 31x23mm

No.	Type	Description	Unused	Used
NO1	OOS1	6g lt brown	.60	*1.00*
NO2	OOS1	8g gray	.60	*1.00*
NO3	OOS1	10g green	.60	*1.00*
NO4	OOS1	12g dk green	.60	*1.75*
NO5	OOS1	20g dk brown	.60	*3.00*
NO6	OOS1	24g henna brn	10.00	1.75
NO7	OOS1	30g rose lake	.80	*2.75*
NO8	OOS1	40g dl violet	.80	*5.00*
NO9	OOS1	48g dl olive	3.25	*5.00*
NO10	OOS1	50g royal bl	.80	2.75
NO11	OOS1	60g dk ol grn	.60	*2.00*
NO12	OOS1	80g rose vio	.60	*2.00*

Size: 35x26mm

No.	Type	Description	Unused	Used
NO13	OOS1	1z gray blk & brn vio	1.50	*4.75*
NO14	OOS1	3z gray blk & chnt	1.50	*4.75*
NO15	OOS1	5z gray blk & org brn	2.40	*5.50*
		Nos. NO1-NO15 (15)	25.25	44.00
		Set, never hinged	70.00	

1940 Size: 21¼x16¼mm *Perf. 12*

No.	Type	Description	Unused	Used
NO16	OOS1	6g brown	.40	*1.10*
NO17	OOS1	8g slate	.50	*1.25*
NO18	OOS1	10g dp grn	1.00	*2.50*
NO19	OOS1	12g slate grn	.50	*1.25*
NO20	OOS1	20g blk brn	.50	*1.10*
NO21	OOS1	24g cop brn	1.00	*1.10*
NO22	OOS1	30g rose lake	.60	*1.25*
NO23	OOS1	40g dl pur	.60	*2.00*
NO24	OOS1	50g royal blue	.60	*2.00*
		Nos. NO16-NO24 (9)	5.70	*13.55*
		Set, never hinged	20.00	

Nazi Emblem and Cracow Castle — OOS2

1943 Photo. *Perf. 14*

No.	Type	Description	Unused	Used
NO25	OOS2	6g brown	.25	*.35*
NO26	OOS2	8g slate blue	.25	*.35*
NO27	OOS2	10g green	.25	*.50*
NO28	OOS2	12g dk vio	.25	.50
NO29	OOS2	16g red org	.40	.50
NO30	OOS2	20g dk brn	.25	.50
NO31	OOS2	24g dk red	.25	.50
NO32	OOS2	30g rose vio	.25	.50
NO33	OOS2	40g blue	.25	.50
NO34	OOS2	60g olive grn	.25	.50
NO35	OOS2	80g dull claret	.30	.50
NO36	OOS2	100g slate blk	.30	.50
		Nos. NO25-NO36 (12)	3.25	5.70
		Set, never hinged	5.00	

POLISH OFFICES ABROAD

OFFICES IN DANZIG

Poland Nos. 215-225 Overprinted

1925, Jan. 5 Unwmk. *Perf. 11½x12*

No.	Type	Description	Unused	Used
1K1	A36	1g orange brn	.35	3.75
1K2	A36	2g dk brown	.35	2.00
1K3	A36	3g orange	.35	1.40
1K4	A36	5g olive grn	12.00	2.25
1K5	A36	10g blue grn	3.50	1.25
1K6	A36	15g red	20.00	2.25
1K7	A36	20g blue	1.10	.70
1K8	A36	25g red brown	1.40	.70
1K9	A36	30g dp violet	1.40	.70
1K10	A36	40g indigo	1.40	.70
1K11	A36	50g magenta	1.75	1.00
		Nos. 1K1-1K11 (11)	43.60	16.70
		Set, never hinged	300.00	

Same Ovpt. on Poland Nos. 230-231

1926 *Perf. 11½, 12*

No.	Type	Description	Unused	Used
1K11A	A39	5g yellow grn	32.50	37.50
1K12	A40	10g violet	12.50	15.00
		Set, never hinged	125.00	

Counterfeit overprints are known on Nos. 1K1-1K32.

No. 232 Overprinted

1926-27

No.	Type	Description	Unused	Used
1K13	A41	15g rose red	42.50	50.00
		Never hinged	165.00	

Same Overprint on Redrawn Stamps of 1926-27

Perf. 13

No.	Type	Description	Unused	Used
1K14	A39	5g yellow grn	1.10	1.60
1K15	A40	10g violet	2.00	2.25
1K16	A41	15g rose red	3.50	1.60
1K17	A43	20g dull red	2.25	2.25
		Nos. 1K14-1K17 (4)	8.85	7.70
		Set, never hinged	28.00	

Same Ovpt. on Poland Nos. 250, 255a

1928-30 *Perf. 12½*

No.	Type	Description	Unused	Used
1K18	A44	25g yellow brn	3.50	2.75
		Never hinged	17.50	

Laid Paper

Perf. 11½x12, 12½x11½

No.	Type	Description	Unused	Used
1K19	A50	1z blk, *cr* ('30)	20.00	32.50
		Never hinged	55.00	

Poland Nos. 258-260 Overprinted

1929-30 *Perf. 12x12½*

No.	Type	Description	Unused	Used
1K20	A53	5g dk violet	1.00	*1.75*
1K21	A53	10g green ('30)	1.00	*1.75*
1K22	A53	25g red brown	2.00	1.75
		Nos. 1K20-1K22 (3)	4.00	*5.25*
		Set, never hinged	27.50	

Same Overprint on Poland No. 257

1931, Jan. 5 *Perf. 12½*

No.	Type	Description	Unused	Used
1K23	A52	15g ultra	2.75	*5.25*
		Never hinged	17.50	

Poland No. 255 Overprinted in Dark Blue

1933, July 1 Laid Paper *Perf. 11½*

No.	Type	Description	Unused	Used
1K24	A50	1z black, *cream*	52.50	*110.00*
		Never hinged	120.00	

Poland Nos. 268-270 Overprinted in Black

1934-36 Wmk. 234 *Perf. 12x12½*

No.	Type	Description	Unused	Used
1K25	A58	5g dl violet	2.50	5.00
1K26	A58	10g green ('36)	24.50	*90.00*
1K27	A58	15g red brown	2.50	5.00
		Nos. 1K25-1K27 (3)	29.50	*100.00*
		Set, never hinged	100.00	

Poland Nos. 294, 296, 298 Overprinted in Black in one or two lines

1935-36 Unwmk. *Perf. 12½x13*

No.	Type	Description	Unused	Used
1K28	A65	5g violet blue	2.00	4.00
1K29	A65	15g Prus green	2.00	6.00
1K30	A65	25g myrtle green	3.00	3.00
		Nos. 1K28-1K30 (3)	7.00	13.00
		Set, never hinged	30.00	

Same Overprint in Black on Poland Nos. 308, 310

1937, June 5

No.	Type	Description	Unused	Used
1K31	A65	5g violet blue	1.10	*2.50*
1K32	A65	15g red brown	1.10	*2.50*
		Set, never hinged	7.00	

Polish Merchants Selling Wheat in Danzig, 16th Century — A2

1938, Nov. 11 Engr. *Perf. 12½*

No.	Type	Description	Unused	Used
1K33	A2	5g red orange	.30	3.00
1K34	A2	15g red brown	.30	3.00
1K35	A2	25g dull violet	.70	3.00
1K36	A2	55g brt ultra	1.10	3.00
		Nos. 1K33-1K36 (4)	2.40	12.00
		Set, never hinged	10.00	

OFFICES IN THE TURKISH EMPIRE

Stamps of Poland 1919, Overprinted in Carmine

1919, May Unwmk. *Perf. 11½*

Wove Paper

No.	Type	Description	Unused	Used
2K1	A10	3f bister brn	55.00	100.00
2K2	A10	5f green	55.00	100.00
2K3	A10	10f red vio	55.00	100.00
2K4	A10	15f red	55.00	100.00
2K5	A11	20f dp blue	55.00	100.00
2K6	A11	25f olive grn	55.00	100.00
2K7	A11	50f blue grn	55.00	100.00

Overprinted

No.	Type	Description	Unused	Used
2K8	A12	1m violet	140.00	120.00
2K9	A12	1.50m dp green	140.00	120.00
2K10	A12	2m dk brown	140.00	140.00
2K11	A13	2.50m orange brn	140.00	120.00
2K12	A14	5m red violet	140.00	140.00
		Nos. 2K1-2K12 (12)	1,085.	1,340.

Counterfeit cancellations are plentiful. Counterfeits exist of Nos. 2K1-2K12.

Reissues are lighter, shiny red. Value, set $25.

Polish stamps with "P.P.C." overprint (Poste Polonaise Constantinople) were used on consular mail for a time.

Seven stamps with these overprints were not issued. Value, set: unused $10, never hinged $35.

EXILE GOVERNMENT IN GREAT BRITAIN

These stamps were issued by the Polish government in exile for letters posted from Polish merchant ships and warships.

United States Embassy Ruins, Warsaw — A1

Polish Ministry of Finance Ruins, Warsaw — A2

Destruction of Mickiewicz Monument, Cracow — A3

Polish Submarine "Orzel" — A8

Ruins of Warsaw A4

Polish Machine Gunners A5

Armored Tank A6

Polish Planes in Great Britain A7

Perf. 12½, 11½x12

1941, Dec. 15 Engr. Unwmk.

No.	Type	Description	Unused	Used
3K1	A1	5g rose violet	.75	*1.25*
3K2	A2	10g dk bl grn	1.00	*1.25*
3K3	A3	25g black	1.50	*2.00*
3K4	A4	55g dark blue	2.50	*2.00*
3K5	A5	75g olive grn	4.00	*6.50*
3K6	A6	80g dk car rose	4.00	*6.50*
3K7	A7	1z slate blue	4.00	*6.50*
3K8	A8	1.50z copper brn	4.00	*4.25*
		Nos. 3K1-3K8 (8)	21.75	*30.25*
		Set, never hinged	45.00	

These stamps were used for correspondence carried on Polish ships and, on certain days, in Polish Military camps in Great Britain.

For surcharges see Nos. 3K17-3K20.

Polish Air Force in Battle of the Atlantic — A9

Polish Army in France, 1939-40 — A11

Polish Merchant Navy A10

Polish Army in Narvik, Norway, 1940 — A12

The Homeland Fights On — A15

Polish Army in Libya, 1941-42 A13

General Sikorsky and Polish Soldiers in the Middle East, 1943 A14

The Secret Press in Poland A16

1943, Nov. 1

3K9	A9	5g rose lake	.50	*1.00*
3K10	A10	10g dk bl grn	.75	*1.10*
3K11	A11	25g dk vio	.75	*1.10*
3K12	A12	55g sapphire	1.25	*1.65*
3K13	A13	75g brn car	2.00	*3.00*
3K14	A14	80g rose car	2.50	*3.50*
3K15	A15	1z olive blk	2.50	*3.50*
3K16	A16	1.50z black	3.25	*6.50*
		Nos. 3K9-3K16 (8)	13.50	*21.35*
		Set, never hinged	22.50	

Nos. 3K5 to 3K8 Surcharged in Blue

Perf. 12½, 11½x12

1944, June 27 **Unwmk.**

3K17	A5	45g on 75g	7.50	*20.00*
3K18	A6	55g on 80g	7.50	*20.00*
3K19	A7	80g on 1z	7.50	*20.00*
3K20	A8	1.20z on 1.50z	7.50	*20.00*
		Nos. 3K17-3K20 (4)	30.00	*80.00*
		Set, never hinged	70.00	

Capture of Monte Cassino by the Poles, May 18, 1944.

EXILE GOVERNMENT IN GREAT BRITAIN SEMI-POSTAL STAMP

Heroic Defenders of Warsaw — SP1

Perf. 11½

1945, Feb. 3 **Unwmk.** **Engr.**

3KB1	SP1	1z + 2z slate green	4.25	*11.00*
		Never hinged	9.00	

Warsaw uprising, Aug. 1-Oct. 3, 1944.

PONTA DELGADA

ˌpän-tə del-ˈgä-də

LOCATION — Administrative district of the Azores comprising the islands of Sao Miguel and Santa Maria
GOVT. — A district of Portugal
AREA — 342 sq. mi.
POP. — 124,000 (approx.)
CAPITAL — Ponta Delgada

1000 Reis = 1 Milreis

King Carlos — A1

1892-93 **Typo.** **Unwmk.**
Perf. 12½, 11½ (25r), 13½ (75r, 150r)

1	A1	5r yellow	2.75	1.60
c.		Diagonal half used as 2½r on piece		17.50
2	A1	10r reddish vio	2.75	1.60
3	A1	15r chocolate	3.50	2.25
4	A1	20r lavender	5.00	2.25
a.		Perf. 13½	9.00	2.00
5d	A1	25r green	7.50	1.10
6	A1	50r ultra	9.00	3.25
7	A1	75r carmine	9.00	5.50
8	A1	80r yellow grn	11.00	9.00
9	A1	100r brn, *yel*	11.00	5.50
10	A1	150r car, *rose*	30.00	30.00
11	A1	200r dk bl, *bl*	50.00	30.00
12	A1	300r dk bl, *salmon*	50.00	30.00
		Nos. 1-12 (12)	191.50	122.05

Nos. 1, 4 and 9-12 were reprinted in 1900 (perf. 11½). Value, each $50. All values were reprinted in 1905 (perf. 13½). Value, each $25. The reprints are on paper slightly thinner than that of the originals, and unsurfaced. They have white gum and clean-cut perfs.

See the Scott Classic Specialized Catalogue for listings by perforation.

King Carlos — A2

Name and Value in Black except Nos. 25 and 34

1897-1905 ***Perf. 11½***

13	A2	2½r gray	.60	.35
14	A2	5r orange	.60	.35
15	A2	10r lt green	.60	.35
16	A2	15r brown	4.00	2.00
17	A2	15r gray grn ('99)	2.25	1.10
18	A2	20r dull violet	2.25	1.25
19	A2	25r sea green	3.00	1.25
20	A2	25r rose red ('99)	2.25	.40
21	A2	50r blue	3.00	1.25
22	A2	50r ultra ('05)	22.00	11.00
23	A2	65r slate blue ('98)	2.00	.45
24	A2	75r rose	7.00	1.25
25	A2	75r brn & car, *yel* ('05)	16.00	8.75
26	A2	80r violet	2.00	1.25
27	A2	100r dk bl, *bl*	4.25	1.25
28	A2	115r org brn, *rose* ('98)	5.00	1.60
29	A2	130r gray brn, *buff* ('98)	5.00	1.60
30	A2	150r lt brn, *buff*	5.00	2.25
31	A2	180r sl, *pnksh* ('98)	5.00	2.25
32	A2	200r red vio, *pnksh*	7.75	5.50
33	A2	300r blue, *rose*	10.00	5.50
a.		Perf. 12½	45.00	30.00
34	A2	500r blk & red, *bl*	25.00	10.00
a.		Perf. 12½	40.00	13.00
		Nos. 13-34 (22)	134.55	60.95

Imperfs are proofs.

The stamps of Ponta Delgada were superseded by those of the Azores, which in 1931 were replaced by those of Portugal.

Scott Blank Country Title Pages

Sold in convenient packs of 20 sheets.

ITEM	ITEM	RETAIL	AA
POSTBLANK	Blank Pages: Postage	$16.99	**$13.99**
USBLANK	Blank Pages: United States	$16.99	**$13.99**
101BLANK	Blank Pages: Booklet Panes	$16.99	**$13.99**
110Z000	Blank Pages: US Postal Cards	$16.99	**$13.99**
113BLANK	Blank Pages: Plate Number Coils	$16.99	**$13.99**
114BLANK	Blank Pages: Comprehensive Plate Number Coils	$16.99	**$13.99**
117BLANK	Blank Pages: Plate Numbers Coil Singles	$16.99	**$13.99**
170UNBLANK	Blank Pages: American / United Nations	$16.99	**$13.99**
180Z003	Blank Pages: Minuteman	$16.99	**$13.99**
181BLANK	Blank Pages: Minuteman UN	$16.99	**$13.99**
551BLANK	Blank Pages: United Nations	$16.99	**$13.99**
200MABLANK	Blank Pages: Great Britain Machins	$16.99	**$13.99**
200BLANK	Blank Pages: Great Britain	$16.99	**$13.99**
201BLANK	Blank Pages: Ireland	$16.99	**$13.99**
210BLANK	Blank Pages: Australia	$16.99	**$13.99**
220BLANK	Blank Pages: New Zealand	$16.99	**$13.99**
240BLANK	Blank Pages: Canada	$16.99	**$13.99**
245BLANK	Blank Pages: Master Canada	$16.99	**$13.99**
300BLANK	Blank Pages: Austria	$16.99	**$13.99**
303BLANK	Blank Pages: Belgium	$16.99	**$13.99**
CZEBLANK	Blank Pages: Czechoslovakia	$16.99	**$13.99**
310BLANK	Blank Pages: France	$16.99	**$13.99**
315BLANK	Blank Pages: Germany	$16.99	**$13.99**
320BLANK	Blank Pages: Greece	$16.99	**$13.99**
323BLANK	Blank Pages: Hungary	$16.99	**$13.99**
325BLANK	Blank Pages: Italy	$16.99	**$13.99**
355BLANK	Blank Pages: Spain	$16.99	**$13.99**
360BLANK	Blank Pages: Russia	$16.99	**$13.99**
365BLANK	Blank Pages: Switzerland	$16.99	**$13.99**
367BLANK	Blank Pages: Liechtenstein	$16.99	**$13.99**
375BLANK	Blank Pages: Vatican City	$16.99	**$13.99**
430BLANK	Blank Pages: Mexico	$16.99	**$13.99**
500BLANK	Blank Pages: Israel	$16.99	**$13.99**
510BLANK	Blank Pages: Japan	$16.99	**$13.99**

Visit AmosAdvantage.com

Or call **1-800-572-6885** Outside U.S. & Canada Call: **1-937-498-0800**

Ordering Information: *AA prices apply to paid subscribers of Amos Media publications, or orders placed online. Prices, terms and product availability subject to change. Taxes will apply in CA, OH & IL. Shipping & Handling: United States: Orders under $10 are only $3.99. 10% of order over $10 total. Minimum Freight Charge $7.99. Maximum Freight Charge $45.00. Canada: 20% of order total. Minimum Freight Charge $19.99. Maximum Freight Charge $200.00. Foreign: Orders are shipped via FedEx Economy International or USPS and billed actual freight.

PORTUGAL

ˈpōr-chi-gəl

LOCATION — Southern Europe, on the western coast of the Iberian Peninsula
GOVT. — Republic
AREA — 35,516 sq. mi.
POP. — 9,918,040 (1999 est.)
CAPITAL — Lisbon

Figures for area and population include the Azores and Madeira, which are integral parts of the republic. The republic was established in 1910. See Azores, Funchal, Madeira.

1000 Reis = 1 Milreis
10 Reis = 1 Centimo
100 Centavos = 1 Escudo (1912)
100 Cents = 1 Euro (2002)

Catalogue values for unused stamps in this country are for Never Hinged items, beginning with Scott 662 in the regular postage section, Scott C11 in the airpost section, Scott J65 in the postage due section, and Scott O2 in the officials section.

Queen Maria II
A1 A2

A3

A4

Typo. & Embossed

1853 Unwmk. *Imperf.*

No.	Type	Description	Unused	Used
1	A1	5r reddish brown	2,850.	850.00
b.		Double impression		*4,250.*
2	A2	25r blue	925.	19.00
b.		Double impression	*4,750.*	*1,500.*
3	A3	50r dp yellow grn	3,400.	875.00
a.		50r blue green	6,750.	1,650.
c.		Double impression	*14,000.*	*6,000.*
4	A4	100r lilac	31,000.	1,900.

The stamps of the 1853 issue were reprinted in 1864, 1885, 1905 and 1953. Many stamps of subsequent issues were reprinted in 1885 and 1905. The reprints of 1864 are on thin white paper with white gum. The originals have brownish gum which often stains the paper. The reprints of 1885 are on a stout, very white paper. They are usually ungummed, but occasionally have a white gum with yellowish spots. The reprints of 1905 are on creamy white paper of ordinary quality with shiny white gum.

When perforated the reprints of 1885 have a rather rough perforation 13½ with small holes; those of 1905 have a clean-cut perforation 13½ with large holes making sharp pointed teeth.

The colors of the reprints usually differ from those of the originals, but actual comparison is necessary.

The reprints are often from new dies which differ slightly from those used for the originals.

5 reis: There is a defect in the neck which makes the Adam's apple appear very large in the first reprint. The later ones can be distinguished by the paper and the shades and by the absence of the pendant curl.

25 reis: The burelage of the ground work in the original is sharp and clear, while in the 1864 reprints it is blurred in several places; the upper and lower right hand corners are very thick and blurred. The central oval is less than ½mm from the frame at the sides in the originals and fully ¾mm in the 1885 and 1905 reprints.

50 reis: In the reprints of 1864 and 1885 there is a small break in the upper right hand diagonal line of the frame, and the initials of the engraver (F. B. F.), which in the originals are plainly discernible in the lower part of the bust, do not show. The reprints of 1905 have not the break in the frame and the initials are distinct.

100 reis: The small vertical lines at top and bottom at each side of the frame are heavier in the reprints of 1864 than in the originals. The reprints of 1885 and 1905 can be distinguished only by the paper, gum and shades.

Reprints of 1953 have thick paper, no gum and dates "1853/1953" on back. Value $55 each.

Values of lowest-cost earlier reprints (1905) of Nos. 1, $100; No. 2, $120; Nos. 3, 4, $150.

King Pedro V
A5 A6

A7

A8

1855 With Straight Hair

TWENTY-FIVE REIS:
Type I — Pearls mostly touch each other and oval outer line.
Type II — Pearls are separate from each other and oval outer line.

No.	Type	Description	Unused	Used
5	A5	5r red brown	8,250.	900.00
6	A6	25r blue, type II	950.00	25.00
a.		25r blue, type I	1,150.	30.00
7	A7	50r green	600.00	70.00
b.		Double impression	1,900.	725.00
8	A8	100r lilac	800.00	90.00

1856 With Curled Hair

TWENTY-FIVE REIS:
Type I — The network is fine (single lines).
Type II — The network is coarse (double lines).

No.	Type	Description	Unused	Used
9	A5	5r brown	500.00	70.00
g.		Double impression	1,400.	375.00
10	A6	25r blue, type II	400.00	13.50
a.		25r blue, type I	*9,500.*	55.00

1858

No.	Type	Description	Unused	Used
11	A6	25r rose, type II	275.00	6.50
a.		Double impression	525.00	*275.00*

The 5r dark brown, formerly listed and sold at about $1, is now believed by the best authorities to be a reprint made before 1866. It is printed on thin yellowish white paper with yellowish white gum and is known only unused. The same remarks will apply to a 25r blue which is common unused but not known used. It is printed from a die which was not used for the issued stamps but the differences are slight and can only be told by expert comparison.

Nos. 9 and 10, also 10a in rose, were reprinted in 1885 and Nos. 9, 10, 10a and 11 in 1905. Value of lowest-cost reprints, $40 each.

See note after No. 4.

King Luiz
A9 A10

A11

A12

A13

FIVE REIS:
Type I — The distance between "5" and "reis" is 3mm.
Type II — The distance between "5" and "reis" is 2mm.

1862-64

No.	Type	Description	Unused	Used
12	A9	5r brown, type I	125.00	10.00
a.		5r brown, type II	160.00	25.00
b.		Double impression, type II	650.00	350.00
d.		Double embossing, type I	—	275.00
13	A10	10r orange	125.00	40.00
14	A11	25r rose	100.00	4.75
a.		Double impression	1,350.	375.00
b.		Double embossing, type I	1,350.	375.00
15	A12	50r yellow green	725.00	77.50
16	A13	100r lilac ('64)	900.00	90.00
		Nos. 12-16 (5)	1,975.	222.25

All values were reprinted in 1885 and all except the 25r in 1905. Value of lowest-cost reprints, $10 each.

See note after No. 4.

King Luiz — A14

1866-67 *Imperf.*

No.	Type	Description	Unused	Used
17	A14	5r black	100.00	10.00
a.		Double impression	275.00	190.00
18	A14	10r yellow	225.00	140.00
19	A14	20r bister	175.00	67.50
20	A14	25r rose ('67)	200.00	6.00
a.		Double impression		225.00
21	A14	50r green	250.00	50.00
22	A14	80r orange	250.00	50.00
23	A14	100r dk lilac ('67)	300.00	75.00
24	A14	120r blue	325.00	70.00
a.		Double impression	725.00	450.00
		Nos. 17-24 (8)	1,825.	468.50

All values were reprinted in 1885 and all except the 25r in 1905. Value of lowest-cost reprints, $10 each. Some values with unofficial percé en croix (diamond) perforation were used in Madeira.

All values were reprinted in 1885 and 1905. Value: Nos. 17-23, each $30-$40; No. 24, $100.

See note after No. 4.

Typographed & Embossed

1867-70 *Perf. 12½*

No.	Type	Description	Unused	Used
25	A14	5r black	125.00	42.50
a.		Double impression	225.00	110.00
26	A14	10r yellow	250.00	110.00
27	A14	20r bister ('69)	300.00	110.00
28	A14	25r rose	65.00	5.00
a.		Double impression	550.00	200.00
29	A14	50r green ('68)	250.00	100.00
30	A14	80r orange ('69)	350.00	100.00
31	A14	100r lilac ('69)	250.00	100.00
32	A14	120r blue	300.00	67.50
a.		Double impression	625.00	160.00
33	A14	240r pale violet ('70)	1,000.	475.00
		Nos. 25-33 (9)	2,890.	1,110.

Nos. 25-33 frequently were separated with scissors. Slightly blunted perfs on one or two sides are to be expected for stamps of this issue.

Two types each of 5r and 100r differ in the position of the "5" at upper right and the "100" at lower right in relation to the end of the label.

Nos. 25-33 were reprinted in 1885 and 1905. Some of the 1885 reprints were perforated 12½ as well as 13½. Value of the lowest-cost reprints, $40 each.

See note after No. 4.

King Luiz — A15

Typographed & Embossed

1870-84 *Perf. 12½, 13½*

No.	Type	Description	Unused	Used
34	A15	5r black	55.00	5.00
a.		Imperf	550.00	
f.		Double impression	275.00	67.50
35	A15	10r yellow ('71)	77.50	27.50
a.		Imperf	550.00	
f.		Double impression	300.00	125.00
36	A15	10r blue grn ('79)	375.00	175.00
37b	A15	10r yellow grn ('80)	110.00	24.00
		On post card		160.00
d.		Double impression	250.00	130.00
38	A15	15r lilac brn ('75)	100.00	29.00
d.		Double impression	500.00	260.00
39	A15	20r bister	72.50	25.00
a.		Imperf	550.00	
g.		Double impression	—	175.00
40	A15	20r rose ('84)	325.00	55.00
b.		Double impression	—	*1,050.*
41	A15	25r rose	30.00	3.75
a.		Imperf	550.00	
f.		Double impression	240.00	30.00
42	A15	50r pale green	140.00	40.00
43	A15	50r blue ('79)	350.00	50.00
44e	A15	80r orange	125.00	19.00
45e	A15	100r pale lilac ('71)	65.00	12.00
46	A15	120r blue ('71)	300.00	62.50
47	A15	150r pale bl ('76)	375.00	110.00
d.		Double impression	1,050.	390.00
48b	A15	150r yellow ('80)	125.00	13.50
49	A15	240r pale violet ('73)	1,700.	1,050.
50a	A15	300r dull violet ('76)	110.00	27.50
51a	A15	1000r black ('84)	400.00	77.50

Nos. 34-51 were printed on three types of paper, plain, ribbed and enamel surfaced, and with perfs gauging 11, 12½, 13½, or 14¼. Values are for the least expensive varieties. For detailed listings, see the *Scott Classic Specialized Catalogue.*

Two types each of 15r, 20r and 80r differ in the distance between the figures of value.

Imperfs probably are proofs.

For overprints and surcharges see Nos. 86-87, 94-96.

All values of the issues of 1870-84 were reprinted in 1885 and 1905. Value of the lowest-cost reprints, $10 each.

See note after No. 4.

King Luiz
A16 A17

A18

A19

1880-81 Typo. *Perf. 12½, 13½*

No.	Type	Description	Unused	Used
52	A16	5r black	40.00	4.00
53	A17	25r bluish gray	300.00	29.00
54	A18	25r gray	45.00	3.50
55	A18	25r brown vio ('81)	45.00	3.50
56	A19	50r blue ('81)	300.00	15.00
		Nos. 52-56 (5)	730.00	55.00

All values were reprinted in 1885 and 1905. Value of the lowest-cost reprints, $15 each.

See note after No. 4.

A20

A21

King Luiz
A22 A23

A24

A24a

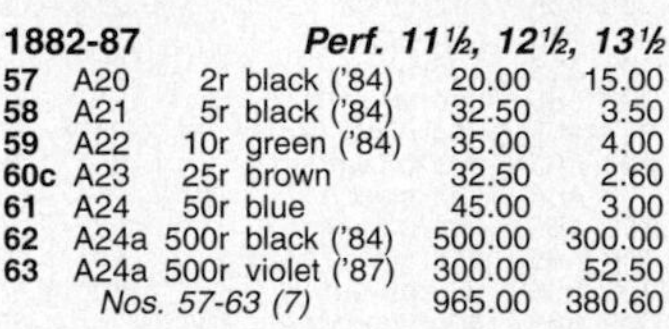

1882-87			*Perf. 11½, 12½, 13½*	
57	A20	2r black ('84)	20.00	15.00
58	A21	5r black ('84)	32.50	3.50
59	A22	10r green ('84)	35.00	4.00
60c	A23	25r brown	32.50	2.60
61	A24	50r blue	45.00	3.00
62	A24a	500r black ('84)	500.00	300.00
63	A24a	500r violet ('87)	300.00	52.50
		Nos. 57-63 (7)	965.00	380.60

Nos. 57-63 were printed on both plain and enamel surfaced papers, with one or more perf varieties for each value. Values are for the least expensive varieties. For a detailed listing, see the *Scott Classic Specialized Catalogue.*

For overprints see Nos. 79-82, 85, 88-89, 93.

The stamps of the 1882-87 issues were reprinted in 1885, 1893 and 1905. Value of the lowest-cost reprints, $5 each.

See note after No. 4.

A25

A26

1887			*Perf. 11½*	
64	A25	20r rose	50.00	17.00
65	A26	25r violet	40.00	3.00
66	A26	25r lilac rose	30.00	3.00
		Nos. 64-66 (3)	120.00	23.00

For overprints see Nos. 83-84, 90-92.

Nos. 64-66 were reprinted in 1905. Value $22.50 each. See note after No. 4.

King Carlos — A27

1892-93			*Perf. 11½, 12½, 13½*	
67	A27	5r orange	11.00	2.00
68	A27	10r redsh violet	30.00	4.00
69b	A27	15r chocolate	27.50	5.00
70	A27	20r lavender	35.00	9.25
71a	A27	25r dark green	27.50	2.00
72	A27	50r blue	35.00	9.25
73	A27	75r carmine ('93)	67.50	8.00
74a	A27	80r yellow green	85.00	42.50
75	A27	100r brn, *buff* ('93)	65.00	6.25
76	A27	150r car, *rose* ('93)	160.00	42.50
77	A27	200r dk bl, *bl* ('93)	160.00	35.00
78	A27	300r dk bl, *sal* ('93)	175.00	57.50
		Nos. 67-78 (12)	878.50	223.25

Nos. 67-78 were issued on two types of paper: enamel surfaced, which is white, with a uniform low gloss; and chalky, which bears a low-gloss application in a pattern of tiny lozenges, producing a somewhat duller appearance.

Nos. 76-78 were reprinted in 1900 (perf. 11½). Value, each $100. All values were reprinted in 1905 (perf. 13½). Value, each $50.

See note after No. 4.

Stamps and Types of Previous Issues Overprinted in Black or Red

a

b

c

1892				
79	A21 (a)	5r gray blk	16.00	8.75
a.		Double overprint	650.00	450.00
80	A22 (b)	10r green	16.00	8.75
a.		Inverted overprint	—	—
b.		Double overprint	650.00	450.00

1892-93				
81	A21 (c)	5r gray blk (R)	13.50	6.75
82	A22 (c)	10r green (R)	16.00	9.25
a.		Inverted overprint	160.00	160.00
83	A25 (c)	20r rose	42.50	22.50
a.		Inverted overprint	225.00	225.00
84	A26 (c)	25r rose lilac, perf. 11½	14.50	5.25
a.		Perf. 12½	475.00	70.00
85	A24 (c)	50r blue (R) ('93)	77.50	62.50
		Nos. 81-85 (5)	164.00	106.25

1893				
86	A15 (c)	15r bister brn (R)	20.00	12.00
87	A15 (c)	80r yellow	110.00	87.50

Nos. 86-87 are found in two types each. See note below No. 51.

Some of Nos. 79-87 were reprinted in 1900 and all values in 1905. Value of lowest-cost reprint, $10.

See note after No. 4.

Stamps and Types of Previous Issues Overprinted or Surcharged in Black or Red

d

e

1893			*Perf. 11½, 12½*	
88	A21 (d)	5r gray blk (R)	30.00	22.50
89	A22 (d)	10r grn, perf. 11½ (R)	24.00	20.00
a.		"1938"	300.00	300.00
b.		"1863"	300.00	300.00
c.		"1838"	300.00	300.00
d.		Perf. 12½	1,650.	1,100.
90	A25 (d)	20r rose	45.00	32.50
a.		Inverted overprint	125.00	100.00
b.		"1938"	300.00	300.00
91	A26 (e)	20r on 25r lil rose	55.00	47.50
92	A26 (d)	25r lilac rose	110.00	100.00
a.		Inverted overprint	275.00	275.00
93	A24 (d)	50r blue (R)	125.00	110.00
		Perf. 12½		
94	A15 (e)	50r on 80r yel	150.00	100.00
95	A15 (e)	75r on 80r yel	90.00	72.50
a.		"1893" and "50rs" double	350.00	200.00
96	A15 (d)	80r yellow	150.00	95.00
a.		"1893" double	450.00	450.00
		Nos. 88-96 (9)	779.00	600.00

Nos. 94-96 are found in two types each. See note below No. 51.

Some of Nos. 88-96 were reprinted in 1900 and all values in 1905. Value of lowest-cost reprint, $45 each.

See note after No. 4.

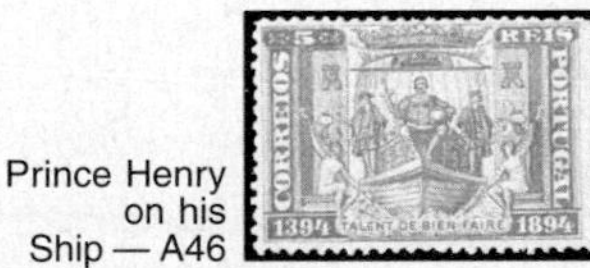
Prince Henry on his Ship — A46

Prince Henry Directing Fleet Maneuvers A47

Symbolic of Prince Henry's Studies — A48

1894		Litho.	*Perf. 14*	
97	A46	5r orange	3.75	.65
98	A46	10r magenta	3.75	.65
99	A46	15r red brown	11.00	3.25
100	A46	20r dull violet	11.00	4.00
101	A47	25r gray green	9.75	1.40
102	A47	50r blue	27.50	6.00
103	A47	75r car rose	52.50	11.50
104	A47	80r yellow grn	52.50	14.00
105	A47	100r lt brn, *pale buff*	50.00	10.00
		Engr.		
106	A48	150r lt car, *pale rose*	175.00	32.50
107	A48	300r dk bl, *sal buff*	200.00	37.50
108	A48	500r dp vio, *pale lil*	400.00	77.50
109	A48	1000r gray blk, *grysh*	600.00	110.00
		Nos. 97-109 (13)	1,596.	308.95

5th centenary of the birth of Prince Henry the Navigator.

King Carlos — A49

1895-1905 Typo. *Perf. 11½*
Value in Black or Red (#122, 500r)

No.	Type	Description	Unused	Used
110	A49	2½r gray	.25	.25
111	A49	5r orange	.25	.25
112	A49	10r lt green	.50	.25
113	A49	15r brown	90.00	3.50
114	A49	15r gray grn ('99)	47.50	2.40
115	A49	20r gray violet	.85	.35
116	A49	25r sea green	65.00	.25
117	A49	25r car rose ('99)	.40	.25
118	A49	50r blue	82.50	.40
119	A49	50r ultra ('05)	.55	.25
120	A49	65r slate bl ('98)	.55	.25
121	A49	75r rose	110.00	4.50
122	A49	75r brn, *yel* ('05)	1.75	.65
123	A49	80r violet	2.10	1.25
124	A49	100r dk bl, *bl*	1.00	.40
125	A49	115r org brn, *pink* ('98)	4.75	2.75
126	A49	130r gray brn, *straw* ('98)	3.75	1.40
127	A49	150r lt brn, *straw*	140.00	22.50
128	A49	180r sl, *pnksh* ('98)	15.00	9.00
129	A49	200r red lil, *pnksh*	5.00	1.25
130	A49	300r blue, *rose*	3.75	2.00
131	A49	500r blk, *bl* ('96)	9.75	4.50
a.		Perf. 12½	110.00	26.00
		Nos. 110-131 (22)	585.20	58.60

Several values of the above type exist without figures of value, also with figures inverted or otherwise misplaced but they were not regularly issued.

St. Anthony and his Vision — A50

St. Anthony Preaching to Fishes — A51

St. Anthony Ascends to Heaven — A52

St. Anthony, from Portrait — A53

Perf. 11½, 12½ and Compound

1895			Typo.	
132	A50	2½r black	4.00	1.10
		Litho.		
133	A51	5r brown org	4.00	1.10
134	A51	10r red lilac	13.50	8.25
135	A51	15r chocolate	14.50	8.25
136	A51	20r gray violet	14.50	8.25
137	A51	25r grn & vio	13.00	1.00
138	A52	50r blue & brn	32.50	22.50
139	A52	75r rose & brn	50.00	40.00
140	A52	80r lt grn & brn	75.00	60.00
141	A52	100r choc & blk	60.00	30.00
142	A53	150r car & bis	200.00	100.00
143	A53	200r blue & bis	200.00	125.00
144	A53	300r slate & bis	300.00	140.00
145	A53	500r vio brn & grn	500.00	300.00
146	A53	1000r vio & grn	700.00	375.00
		Nos. 132-146 (15)	2,181.	1,220.

7th centenary of the birth of Saint Anthony of Padua. Stamps have eulogy in Latin printed on the back.

Common Design Types pictured following the introduction.

Vasco da Gama Issue

Common Design Types

1898		Engr.	*Perf. 12½ to 16*	
147	CD20	2½r blue green	1.40	.35
148	CD21	5r red	1.40	.35
149	CD22	10r red violet	8.50	1.25
150	CD23	25r yel grn	5.00	.50
151	CD24	50r dark blue	10.50	3.00
152	CD25	75r violet brown	45.00	9.00
153	CD26	100r bister brown	30.00	9.00
154	CD27	150r bister	67.50	20.00
		Nos. 147-154 (8)	169.30	43.45

For overprints and surcharges see Nos. 185-192, 199-206.

Eastern Auctions Ltd.
In our Mail Auction, we offer 3000-5000 individually described and profusely illustrated lots approximately every six weeks.
There is NO BUYER'S COMMISSION.
We make every effort to present material for every collecting interest and budget.
Large lots and individual stamps from worldwide countries and areas are always offered. Contact us to receive a complimentary catalogue of our next Mail Sale.
Toll Free in North America
1(800) 667-8267
P.O. Box 250 - Bathurst - NB - E2A 3Z2 - Canada
Tel 1(506) 548-8986 - Fax 1(506)546-6627
email easternauctions@nb.aibn.com
website www.easternauctions.com

King Manuel II
A62 A63

1910 Typo. *Perf. 14½x15*

156 A62 2½r violet .25 .25
157 A62 5r black .25 .25
158 A62 10r gray green .25 .25
159 A62 15r lilac brown 2.75 1.40
160 A62 20r carmine .80 .65
161 A62 25r violet brn .60 .25
162 A62 50r dark blue 1.50 .65
163 A62 75r bister brn 9.25 5.00
164 A62 80r slate 2.50 2.25
165 A62 100r brn, *lt grn* 10.00 3.00
166 A62 200r dk grn, *sal* 6.00 4.25
167 A62 300r blk, *azure* 6.75 5.00
168 A63 500r ol grn & vio brn 13.50 11.50
169 A63 1000r dk bl & blk 30.00 24.00
Nos. 156-169 (14) 84.40 58.70

For overprint see No. RA1.

Preceding Issue Overprinted in Carmine or Green

1910

170 A62 2½r violet .25 .25
171 A62 5r black .25 .25
172 A62 10r gray green 3.50 1.25
173 A62 15r lilac brn 1.25 .85
174 A62 20r carmine (G) 4.25 1.50
175 A62 25r violet brn .80 .25
176 A62 50r dk blue 6.00 2.00
177 A62 75r bister brn 9.00 3.75
178 A62 80r slate 3.25 2.40
179 A62 100r brn, *lt grn* 2.00 .75
180 A62 200r dk grn, *sal* 2.50 1.60
181 A62 300r blk, *azure* 3.75 2.75
182 A63 500r ol grn & vio brn 9.50 8.25
183 A63 1000r dk bl & blk 24.00 24.00
Nos. 170-183 (14) 70.30 49.85

The numerous inverted and double overprints on this issue were unofficially and fraudulently made.

The 50r with blue overprint is a fraud.

Vasco da Gama Issue Overprinted or Surcharged

a

b

c

1911 *Perf. 12½ to 16*

185 CD20(a) 2½r blue grn .45 .25
a. Inverted overprint 14.00 12.00
186 CD21(b) 15r on 5r red .80 .35
a. Inverted surcharge 10.50 9.00
187 CD23(a) 25r yel grn .45 .25
188 CD24(a) 50r dk blue 3.25 1.60
a. Inverted overprint
189 CD25(a) 75r vio brn 42.50 32.50
190 CD27(b) 80r on 150r bis 8.00 4.75
191 CD26(a) 100r bis brn 8.00 3.00
a. Inverted overprint 29.00 24.00
192 CD22(c) 1000r on 10r red vio 62.50 37.50
Nos. 185-192 (8) 125.95 80.20

Postage Due Stamps of 1898 Overprinted or Surcharged for Regular Postage

d

e

1911 *Perf. 12*

193 D1(d) 5r black .85 .35
a. Double ovpt., one inverted 60.00 25.00
194 D1(d) 10r magenta 2.00 .65
195 D1(d) 20r orange 6.00 3.00
196 D1(d) 200r brn, *buff* 125.00 67.50
197 D1(e) 300r on 50r slate 90.00 42.50
198 D1(e) 500r on 100r car, *pink* 60.00 24.00
a. Inverted surcharge 125.00 87.50
Nos. 193-198 (6) 283.85 138.00

Vasco da Gama Issue of Madeira Ovptd. or Srchd. Types "a," "b" and "c"

1911 *Perf. 12½ to 16*

199 CD20(a) 2½r blue grn 11.50 8.25
a. Double overprint
200 CD21(b) 15r on 5r red 4.00 2.00
a. Inverted surcharge 12.50 11.00
201 CD23(a) 25r yellow grn 6.00 4.75
202 CD24(a) 50r dk blue 11.00 8.25
a. Inverted overprint
203 CD25(a) 75r violet brn 11.00 5.50
a. Inverted overprint 35.00 30.00
204 CD27(b) 80r on 150r bis 12.50 11.00
a. Inverted surcharge 47.50 40.00
205 CD26(a) 100r bister brn 40.00 8.25
a. Inverted overprint 125.00 100.00
206 CD22(c) 1000r on 10r red vio 40.00 50.00
Nos. 199-206 (8) 136.00 98.00

Ceres — A64

Chalky Paper With Imprint

1912-20 Typo. *Perf. 15x14*

207 A64 ¼c dark olive 8.00 5.00
208 A64 ½c black 8.00 5.00
209 A64 1c deep green 6.50 2.50
210 A64 1½c chocolate 20.00 9.00
211 A64 2c carmine 20.00 9.00
212 A64 2½c violet 9.50 9.50
213 A64 5c dp blue 5.50 .55
214 A64 7½c yellow brn 65.00 13.50
215 A64 8c slate 3.00 3.00
216 A64 10c org brn 45.00 25.00
217 A64 15c plum 300.00 75.00
218 A64 20c vio brn, *grn* 13.00 1.50
219 A64 20c brn, *buff* ('20) 15.00 3.50
220 A64 30c brn, *pink* 100.00 9.50
221 A64 30c lt brn, *yel* ('17) 8.75 1.60
222 A64 50c org, *sal* ('18) 12.00 1.10
223 A64 1e dp grn, *bl* 19.00 1.40
Nos. 207-223 (17) 658.25 175.65

1920 Typo. *Perf. 12x11½*

224 A64 14c dk bl, *yel* 3.25 1.25
225 A64 20c choc, *buff* 800.00 200.00
226 A64 50c org, *salmon* 225.00 30.00
Nos. 224-226 (3) 1,028. 231.25

1917-26 Typo. *Perf. 15x14*

Ordinary Paper

227 A64 ¼c dk ol ('18) .65 .25
228 A64 ½c black ('18) .40 .25
229 A64 1c deep green .65 .25
230 A64 1c chocolate .25 .25
231 A64 1½c chocolate 5.50 2.50
232 A64 1½c dp grn ('18) .30 .25
233 A64 2c carmine 5.50 2.50
234 A64 2c orange ('18) .25 .25
235 A64 2½c violet .25 .25
236 A64 3c car rose .25 .25
237 A64 3c ultra ('21) 200.00 80.00
238 A64 3½c lt grn ('18) .25 .25
239 A64 4c lt grn ('19) .40 .30
240 A64 5c yel brn .50 .30
240A A64 5c deep blue 2.40 .25
243 A64 7½c yellow brn 12.00 2.50
244 A64 8c slate 5.50 .75
245 A64 10c org brn 25.00 1.50
246 A64 12c bl gray ('20) 1.25 .65
247 A64 15c plum 3.25 .85
248 A64 20c choc ('20) 60.00 5.00
249 A64 30c gray brown 120.00 21.00
250 A64 36c red ('21) 4.50 1.25
251 A64 60c blue ('21) 4.00 1.90
252 A64 80c brn rose ('21) 1.40 1.10
253 A64 90c blue ('21) 5.50 4.75
254 A64 1e violet ('21) 185.00 65.00
Nos. 227-254 (27) 644.95 194.35

1920-26 *Perf. 12x11½*

Ordinary Paper

255 A64 ¼c dark olive .40 .25
256 A64 ½c black .40 .25
257 A64 1c chocolate .25 .25
258 A64 1½c dp grn .25 .25
259 A64 2c orange .70 .40
260 A64 2c yellow .55 .25
261 A64 2c choc ('26) 1.40 *8.00*
262 A64 2½c violet 4.00 2.25
263 A64 3c car rose .30 .30
264 A64 3c ultra ('21) .50 .25
265 A64 4c lt grn ('19) .25 .25
266 A64 4c org ('26) 1.40 1.60
267 A64 5c yel brn 1.00 .40
268 A64 5c ol brn ('23) .25 .25
269 A64 6c pale rose .40 .40
270 A64 6c brown ('24) .55 .25
271 A64 7½c dp blue .25 .25
272 A64 8c slate .25 .25
273 A64 8c bl grn ('22) .45 .25
274 A64 8c org ('24) .45 .45
275 A64 10c org brn .45 .25
276 A64 12c dp grn ('21) .45 .40
277 A64 13½c chlky bl 1.40 .45
278 A64 14c brt vio ('21) 1.10 .55
279 A64 15c black ('23) .40 .25
280 A64 16c brt ultra ('24) .90 .65
281 A64 20c dk brn .50 .25
282 A64 20c dp grn ('23) .45 .25
283 A64 20c gray ('24) .25 .25
284 A64 24c grnsh bl ('21) .45 .25
285 A64 25c sal pink ('23) .45 .25
286 A64 25c lt gray ('26) .45 .25
287 A64 30c gray brn ('21) .50 .25
288 A64 30c dk brn ('24) 20.00 4.00
289 A64 32c dp grn ('24) 1.10 .40
290 A64 36c red ('21) 1.75 .45
291 A64 40c dk bl ('23) .90 .55
292 A64 40c choc ('24) .45 .45
293 A64 40c green ('26) .25 .25
294 A64 48c rose ('24) 7.50 4.00
295 A64 50c yellow ('21) 1.90 .70
296 A64 60c blue ('21) 1.40 .60
297 A64 64c pale ultra ('24) 9.50 5.50
298 A64 75c dull rose ('23) 15.00 7.50
298A A64 80c brn rose ('21) 32.50 9.50
298B A64 80c violet ('24) 1.00 .55
298C A64 90c chalky bl ('21) 1.60 .85
298D A64 96c dp rose ('26) 42.50 35.00
298E A64 1e violet ('21) 4.50 1.90
298F A64 1.10e yel brn ('21) 4.50 1.60
298G A64 1.20e yel grn ('21) 2.50 1.40
298H A64 2e sl grn ('21) 45.00 5.50
Nos. 255-298H (52) 215.60 101.80

1923-26 *Perf. 12x11½*

Glazed Paper

298I A64 1e dk blue 5.00 2.25
298J A64 1e gray vio ('24) 1.50 1.10
298K A64 1.20e buff ('24) 50.00 32.50
298L A64 1.50e blk vio 17.50 3.25
298M A64 1.50e lilac ('24) 30.00 5.00
298N A64 1.60e dp bl ('24) 19.00 5.00
298O A64 2e sl grn ('24) 37.50 5.50
298P A64 2.40e ap grn ('26) 160.00 110.00
298Q A64 3e pink ('26) 160.00 100.00
298R A64 3.20e gray grn ('24) 32.50 12.00
298S A64 5e emer ('24) 35.00 9.00
298T A64 10e pink ('24) 175.00 50.00
298U A64 20e pale turq ('24) 300.00 160.00
Nos. 298I-298U (13) 1,023. 495.60

See design A85. For surcharges & overprints see Nos. 453-495, RA2.

See 496A-496R.

Presidents of Portugal and Brazil and Aviators Cabral and Coutinho A65

1923 Litho. *Perf. 14*

299 A65 1c brown .25 *.65*
300 A65 2c orange .25 *.65*
301 A65 3c ultra .25 *.65*
302 A65 4c yellow grn .25 *.65*
303 A65 5c bister brn .25 *.65*
304 A65 10c brown org .25 *.65*
305 A65 15c black .25 *.65*
306 A65 20c blue grn .25 *.65*
307 A65 25c rose .25 *.65*
308 A65 30c olive brn .60 *1.90*
309 A65 40c chocolate .25 *.65*
310 A65 50c yellow .50 *.85*
311 A65 75c violet .50 *1.00*
312 A65 1e dp blue .50 *2.00*
313 A65 1.50e olive grn .75 *2.50*
314 A65 2e myrtle grn 1.00 *6.00*
Nos. 299-314 (16) 6.35 *20.75*

Flight of Sacadura Cabral and Gago Coutinho from Portugal to Brazil.

Camoens at Ceuta A66

Camoens Saving the Lusiads — A67

Luis de Camoens — A68

First Edition of the Lusiads — A69

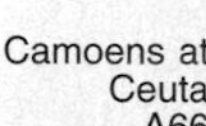

Camoens Dying — A70

Tomb of Camoens A71

Monument to Camoens — A72

Engr.; Values Typo. in Black

1924, Nov. 11 *Perf. 14, 14½*

315 A66 2c lt blue .25 .25
316 A66 3c orange .25 .25
317 A66 4c dk gray .25 .25
318 A66 5c yellow grn .25 .25
319 A66 6c lake .25 .25

320	A67	8c	orange brn	.25	.25
321	A67	10c	gray vio	.25	.25
322	A67	15c	olive grn	.25	.25
323	A67	16c	violet brn	.25	.25
324	A67	20c	dp orange	.30	.25
325	A68	25c	lilac	.30	.25
326	A68	30c	dk brown	.30	.25
327	A68	32c	dk green	.90	1.00
328	A68	40c	ultra	.30	.25
329	A68	48c	red brown	1.25	1.25
330	A69	50c	red orange	1.40	.90
331	A69	64c	green	1.40	.90
332	A69	75c	dk violet	1.40	.90
333	A69	80c	bister	1.10	.90
334	A69	96c	lake	1.10	.90
335	A70	1e	slate	1.10	.80
336	A70	1.20e	lt brown	5.25	4.75
337	A70	1.50e	red	1.25	.90
338	A70	1.60e	dk blue	1.25	.90
339	A70	2e	apple grn	5.25	4.75
340	A71	2.40e	green, *grn*	3.75	2.75
341	A71	3e	dk bl, *bl*	1.60	1.00
a.			Value double	125.00	125.00
b.			Value omitted		
342	A71	3.20e	blk, *green*	1.60	1.00
343	A71	4.50e	blk, *orange*	5.00	2.75
344	A71	10e	dk brn, *pnksh*	10.00	8.00
345	A72	20e	dk vio, *lil*	10.00	7.00
			Nos. 315-345 (31)	58.05	44.60

Birth of Luis de Camoens, poet, 400th anniv.

For overprints see Nos. 1S6-1S71.

Castello-Branco's House at Sao Miguel de Seide — A73

Castello-Branco's Study — A74

Camillo Castello-Branco A75

Teresa de Albuquerque A76

Mariana and Joao de Cruz — A77

Simao de Botelho — A78

1925, Mar. 26 ***Perf. 12½***

346	A73	2c	orange	.25	.25
347	A73	3c	green	.25	.25
348	A73	4c	ultra	.25	.25
349	A73	5c	scarlet	.25	.25
350	A73	6c	brown vio	.25	.25
a.			"6" and "C" omitted		
351	A73	8c	black brn	.25	.25
352	A74	10c	pale blue	.25	.25
353	A75	15c	olive grn	.25	.25
354	A74	16c	red orange	.30	.30
355	A74	20c	dk violet	.30	.30
356	A75	25c	car rose	.30	.30
357	A74	30c	bister brn	.30	.30
358	A74	32c	green	1.10	1.00
359	A75	40c	green & blk	.65	.65
360	A74	48c	red brn	3.00	3.00
361	A76	50c	blue green	.65	.65
362	A76	64c	orange brn	3.00	3.00
363	A76	75c	gray blk	.60	.60
364	A75	80c	brown	.60	.60
365	A76	96c	car rose	1.50	1.50
366	A76	1e	gray vio	1.50	1.50
367	A76	1.20e	yellow grn	1.50	1.50
368	A77	1.50e	dk bl, *bl*	25.00	13.50
369	A75	1.60e	indigo	4.75	3.75
370	A77	2e	dk grn, *grn*	6.25	4.25
371	A77	2.40e	red, *org*	52.50	32.50
372	A77	3e	lake, *bl*	67.50	40.00
373	A77	3.20e	*green*	32.50	32.50
374	A75	4.50e	red & blk	12.50	3.00
375	A77	10e	brn, *yel*	13.00	3.00
376	A78	20e	*orange*	13.50	3.00
			Nos. 346-376 (31)	244.80	152.70
			Set, never hinged	400.00	

Centenary of the birth of Camillo Castello-Branco, novelist.

First Independence Issue

Alfonso the Conqueror, First King of Portugal — A79

Batalha Monastery and King John I — A80

Battle of Aljubarrota A81

Filipa de Vilhena Arming her Sons A82

King John IV (The Duke of Braganza) A83

Independence Monument, Lisbon — A84

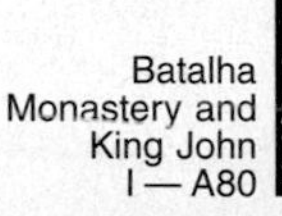

Center in Black

1926, Aug. 13 ***Perf. 14, 14½***

377	A79	2c	orange	.25	.25
378	A80	3c	ultra	.25	.25
379	A79	4c	yellow grn	.25	.25
380	A80	5c	black brn	.25	.25
381	A79	6c	ocher	.25	.25
382	A80	15c	dk green	.25	.25
383	A79	16c	dp blue	.70	.65
384	A81	20c	dull violet	.70	.65
385	A82	25c	scarlet	.70	.65
386	A81	32c	dp green	.90	.90
387	A82	40c	yellow brn	.55	.55
388	A80	46c	carmine	3.25	3.25
389	A82	50c	olive bis	3.25	3.25
390	A83	64c	blue green	4.50	4.50
391	A82	75c	red brown	4.50	4.50
392	A84	96c	dull red	6.75	6.75
393	A83	1e	black vio	7.00	7.00
394	A81	1.60e	myrtle grn	9.25	9.25
395	A84	3e	plum	27.50	27.50
396	A84	4.50e	olive grn	35.00	35.00
397	A81	10e	carmine	55.00	55.00
			Nos. 377-397 (21)	161.05	160.90
			Set, never hinged	275.00	

The use of these stamps instead of the regular issue was obligatory on Aug. 13th and 14th, Nov. 30th and Dec. 1st, 1926.

Stamps of 1926 Surcharged in Black

1926 **Center in Black** ***Perf. 13½x14***

397A	A80	2c	on 5c blk brn	1.50	1.10
397B	A80	2c	on 46c car	1.50	1.10
397C	A83	2c	on 64c bl grn	2.00	1.50
397D	A82	3c	on 75c red brn	2.00	1.50
397E	A84	3c	on 96c dull red	2.00	2.00
397F	A83	3c	on 1e blk vio	2.00	1.60
397G	A81	4c	on 1.60e myr grn	11.50	11.50
397H	A84	4c	on 3e plum	6.00	4.00
397J	A84	6c	on 4.50e ol grn	6.00	4.00
397K	A81	6c	on 10e carmine	6.00	4.00
			Nos. 397A-397K (10)	40.50	32.30
			Set, never hinged	60.00	

There are two styles of the ornaments in these surcharges.

Ceres — A85

Without Imprint

1926, Dec. 2 **Typo.** ***Perf. 13½x14***

398	A85	2c	chocolate	.25	.25
399	A85	3c	brt blue	.25	.25
400	A85	4c	dp orange	.25	.25
401	A85	5c	dp brown	.25	.25
402	A85	6c	orange brn	.25	.25
403	A85	10c	orange red	.25	.25
404	A85	15c	black	.25	.25
405	A85	16c	ultra	.25	.25
406	A85	25c	gray	.25	.25
407	A85	32c	dp green	.55	.35
408	A85	40c	blue green	.35	.25
409	A85	48c	rose	1.10	.90
410	A85	50c	ocher	2.00	1.60
411	A85	64c	deep blue	2.00	1.60
412	A85	80c	violet	3.75	.55
413	A85	96c	car rose	2.10	1.10
414	A85	1e	red brown	10.00	1.00
415	A85	1.20e	yellow brn	10.00	1.00
416	A85	1.60e	dark blue	2.40	.55
417	A85	2e	green	14.50	1.00
418	A85	3.20e	olive grn	5.50	1.00
419	A85	4.50e	yellow	5.50	1.00
420	A85	5e	brown olive	60.00	3.75
421	A85	10e	red	8.75	2.00
			Nos. 398-421 (24)	130.75	19.90
			Set, never hinged	275.00	

See design A64.

Second Independence Issue

Gonçalo Mendes da Maia — A86

Dr. Joao das Regras — A88

Guimaraes Castle — A87

Battle of Montijo — A89

Brites de Almeida — A90

Joao Pinto Ribeiro — A91

Center in Black

1927, Nov. 29 **Engr.** ***Perf. 14***

422	A86	2c	brown	.25	.25
423	A87	3c	ultra	.25	.25
424	A86	4c	orange	.25	.25
425	A88	5c	olive brn	.25	.25
426	A89	6c	orange brn	.25	.25
427	A87	15c	black brn	.45	.35
428	A88	16c	deep blue	1.00	.35
429	A86	25c	gray	1.25	1.10
430	A89	32c	blue grn	2.50	1.60
431	A90	40c	yellow grn	.65	.50
432	A86	48c	brown red	11.50	10.00
433	A87	80c	dk violet	8.25	7.00
434	A90	96c	dull red	14.50	13.50
435	A88	1.60e	myrtle grn	15.00	14.50
436	A91	4.50e	bister	22.50	22.50
			Nos. 422-436 (15)	78.85	72.65
			Set, never hinged	140.00	

The use of these stamps instead of the regular issue was compulsory on Nov. 29-30, Dec. 1-2, 1927. The money derived from their sale was used for the purchase of a palace for a war museum, the organization of an international exposition in Lisbon, in 1940, and for fêtes to be held in that year in commemoration of the 8th cent. of the founding of Portugal and the 3rd cent. of its restoration.

Third Independence Issue

Gualdim Paes — A93

The Siege of Santarem — A94

Battle of Rolica — A95

Battle of Atoleiros A96

Joana de Gouveia A97

Matias de Albuquerque A98

1928, Nov. 28 **Center in Black**

437	A93	2c	lt blue	.25	.25
438	A94	3c	lt green	.25	.25
439	A95	4c	lake	.25	.25
440	A96	5c	olive grn	.25	.25
441	A97	6c	orange brn	.25	.25
442	A94	15c	slate	.75	.75
443	A95	16c	dk violet	.75	.75
444	A93	25c	ultra	.75	.75
445	A97	32c	dk green	3.75	3.75
446	A96	40c	olive brn	.75	.75
447	A95	50c	red orange	9.25	5.75
448	A94	80c	lt gray	9.75	7.00
449	A97	96c	carmine	17.50	15.00
450	A96	1e	claret	27.50	27.50
451	A93	1.60e	dk blue	13.00	11.50
452	A98	4.50e	yellow	14.00	13.50
			Nos. 437-452 (16)	99.00	88.25
			Set, never hinged	150.00	

Obligatory Nov. 27-30. See note after No. 436.

Type and Stamps of 1912-28 Surcharged in Black

1928-29 ***Perf. 12x11½, 15x14***

453 A64 4c on 8c orange .40 .35
454 A64 4c on 30c dk brn .40 .35
455 A64 10c on ¼c dk ol .40 .35
a. Inverted surcharge 110.00 100.00
456 A64 10c on ½c blk (R) .60 .45
a. Perf. 15x14 17.50 12.50
457 A64 10c on 1c choc .60 .45
a. Perf. 15x14 *75.00* *55.00*
458 A64 10c on 4c grn .45 .35
a. Perf. 15x14 *87.50* *67.50*
459 A64 10c on 4c orange .45 .35
460 A64 10c on 5c ol brn .45 .35
461 A64 15c on 16c blue 1.10 .80
462 A64 15c on 16c ultra 1.10 .80
463 A64 15c on 20c brown 32.50 32.50
464 A64 15c on 20c gray .45 .35
465 A64 15c on 24c grnsh bl 2.10 1.60
466 A64 15c on 25c gray .45 .35
467 A64 15c on 25c sal pink .45 .35
468 A64 16c on 32c dp grn .90 .80
469 A64 40c on 2c orange .45 .35
470 A64 40c on 2c yellow 4.50 3.25
471 A64 40c on 2c choc .40 .35
472 A64 40c on 3c ultra .45 .35
473 A64 40c on 50c yellow .40 .25
474 A64 40c on 60c dull bl .90 .65
a. Perf. 15x14 10.00 8.00
475 A64 40c on 64c pale ultra .90 .80
476 A64 40c on 75c dl rose .90 .90
477 A64 40c on 80c violet .65 .55
478 A64 40c on 90c chlky bl 4.50 3.25
a. Perf. 15x14 11.50 8.75
479 A64 40c on 1e gray vio .85 .85
480 A64 40c on 1.10e yel brn .90 .80
481 A64 80c on 6c pale rose .85 .70
482 A64 80c on 6c choc .85 .70
483 A64 80c on 48c rose 1.25 1.10
484 A64 80c on 1.50e lilac 3.00 1.25
485 A64 96c on 1.20e yel grn 3.50 2.40
486 A64 96c on 1.20e buff 3.50 2.75
487 A64 1.60e on 2e slate grn 35.00 27.50
487A A64 1.60e on 2e sl grn, *glazed paper* 37.50 25.00
488 A64 1.60e on 3.20e gray grn 15.00 7.25
489 A64 1.60e on 20e pale turq 18.00 10.00
Nos. 453-489 (37) 139.55 106.55
Set, never hinged 360.00

Stamps of 1912-26 Overprinted in Black or Red

1929 ***Perf. 12x11½***

490 A64 10c orange brn .45
a. Perf. 15x14 275.00 275.00
491 A64 15c black (R) .40 .35
492 A64 40c lt green .65 .55
493 A64 40c chocolate .55 .45
494 A64 96c dp rose 5.50 4.50
495 A64 1.60e brt blue 22.50 15.00
a. Double overprint 110.00 100.00
Nos. 490-495 (6) 30.05 20.85
Set, never hinged 45.00

Liberty — A100

1929, May ***Perf. 12x11½***

496 A100 1.60e on 5c red brn 11.50 7.00

Types of 1912-20 Issues
With Imprint

1930-31 **Typo.** ***Perf. 12x11½***

496A A64 4c orange .25 .25
496B A64 5c blk brn ('31) .25 .25
496C A64 6c red brn .25 .25
496D A64 10c red ('31) .45 .25
496E A64 15c black 2.50 .50
496F A64 25c lt gray .90 .45
496G A64 25c blue grn .90 .45
496H A85 32c dp green .90 .45
496I A64 40c green 3.50 1.25
496J A64 50c bister 2.25 1.40
496K A64 50c red brn ('30) 2.25 1.40
496L A64 75c car rose 2.25 1.40
496M A64 80c dk grn 2.25 1.40
496N A64 1e brn lake 6.50 1.10
496O A64 1.20e pur brn ('31) 4.50 1.10
496P A64 1.25e dk bl ('31) 4.50 1.10
496Q A64 2e red vio ('31) 19.00 6.50
496R A64 4.50e org ('31) 65.00 45.00

Nos. 496A-496R were printed at the Lisbon Mint from new plates produced from the original dies. The paper is whiter than the paper used for earlier Ceres stamps. The gum is white.

"Portugal" Holding Volume of "Lusiads" — A101

1931-38 **Typo.** ***Perf. 14***

497 A101 4c bister brn .25 .25
498 A101 5c olive gray .25 .25
499 A101 6c lt gray .25 .25
500 A101 10c dk violet .25 .25
501 A101 15c gray blk .25 .25
502 A101 16c brt blue 1.25 .65
503 A101 25c deep green 3.00 .35
504 A101 25c brt bl ('33) 3.50 .40
505 A101 30c dk grn ('33) 1.90 .40
506 A101 40c orange red 6.25 .25
507 A101 48c fawn 1.25 .95
508 A101 50c lt brown .30 .25
509 A101 75c car rose 5.00 1.10
510 A101 80c emerald .40 .25
511 A101 95c car rose ('33) 16.00 6.75
512 A101 1e claret 30.00 .25
513 A101 1.20e olive grn 2.10 .95
514 A101 1.25e dk blue 1.90 .25
515 A101 1.60e dk blue ('33) 32.50 4.25
516 A101 1.75e dk blue ('38) .65 .25
517 A101 2e dull violet .75 .25
518 A101 4.50e orange 1.50 .25
519 A101 5e yellow grn 1.50 .25
Nos. 497-519 (23) 111.00 19.30
Set, never hinged 175.00

Birthplace of St. Anthony A102

Font where St. Anthony was Baptized A103

Lisbon Cathedral A104

St. Anthony with Infant Jesus A105

Santa Cruz Cathedral A106

St. Anthony's Tomb at Padua A107

1931, June **Typo.** ***Perf. 12***

528 A102 15c plum .65 .25

Litho.

529 A103 25c gray & pale grn 1.00 .25
530 A104 40c gray brn & buff .65 .25
531 A105 75c dl rose & pale rose 22.50 14.00
532 A106 1.25e gray & pale bl 52.50 30.00
533 A107 4.50e gray vio & lil 25.00 3.50
Nos. 528-533 (6) 102.30 48.25
Set, never hinged 190.00

7th centenary of the death of St. Anthony of Padua and Lisbon.

For surcharges see Nos. 543-548.

Nuno Alvares Pereira (1360-1431), Portuguese Warrior and Statesman — A108

1931, Nov. 1 **Typo.** ***Perf. 12x11½***

534 A108 15c black 1.00 1.10
535 A108 25c gray grn & blk 10.50 1.10
536 A108 40c orange 2.75 .50
a. Value omitted 150.00 150.00
537 A108 75c car rose 25.00 21.00
538 A108 1.25e dk bl & pale bl 30.00 20.00
539 A108 4.50e choc & lt grn 125.00 52.50
a. Value omitted 350.00 350.00
Nos. 534-539 (6) 194.25 96.20
Set, never hinged 325.00

For surcharges see Nos. 549-554.

Nos. 528-533 Surcharged

1933 ***Perf. 12***

543 A104 15c on 40c 1.00 .35
544 A102 40c on 15c 3.00 1.25
545 A103 40c on 25c 2.00 .35
546 A105 40c on 75c 20.00 5.25
547 A106 40c on 1.25e 20.00 5.25
548 A107 40c on 4.50e 20.00 5.25
Nos. 543-548 (6) 66.00 17.70
Set, never hinged 80.00

Nos. 534-539 Surcharged

1933 ***Perf. 12x11½***

549 A108 15c on 40c .65 .35
550 A108 40c on 15c 3.75 2.40
551 A108 40c on 25c 1.00 .80
552 A108 40c on 75c 17.00 4.00
553 A108 40c on 1.25e 17.00 4.00
554 A108 40c on 4.50e 17.00 4.00
Nos. 549-554 (6) 56.40 15.55
Set, never hinged 80.00

President Carmona — A109

1934, May 28 **Typo.** ***Perf. 11½***

556 A109 40c brt violet 18.00 .35
Never hinged 32.50

Head of a Colonial — A110

1934, July ***Perf. 11½x12***

558 A110 25c dk brown 3.00 1.60
559 A110 40c scarlet 19.00 .40
560 A110 1.60e dk blue 29.00 2.00
Nos. 558-560 (3) 51.00 4.00
Set, never hinged 125.00

Colonial Exposition.

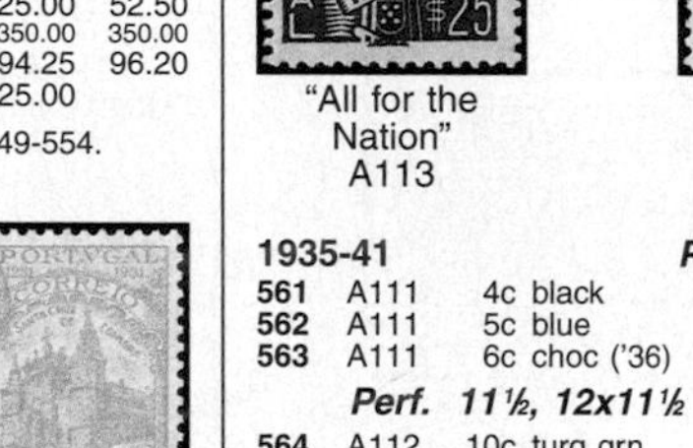

Roman Temple, Evora A111

Prince Henry the Navigator A112

"All for the Nation" A113

Coimbra Cathedral A114

1935-41 ***Perf. 11½x12***

561 A111 4c black .45 .25
562 A111 5c blue .50 .25
563 A111 6c choc ('36) .75 .35

Perf. 11½, 12x11½ (1.75e)

564 A112 10c turq grn .65 .25
565 A112 15c red brown .35 .25
a. Booklet pane of 4
566 A113 25c dp blue 6.00 .45
a. Booklet pane of 4
567 A113 40c brown 2.00 .25
a. Booklet pane of 4
568 A113 1e rose red 9.25 .50
568A A114 1.75e blue 85.00 1.25
568B A113 10e gray blk ('41) 50.00 2.50
569 A113 20e turq grn ('41) 70.00 2.10
Nos. 561-569 (11) 224.95 8.40
Set, never hinged 400.00

For overprint see No. O1.

Queen Maria — A115

Typographed, Head Embossed

1935, June 1 ***Perf. 11½***

570 A115 40c scarlet 1.40 .25
Never hinged 2.10

First Portuguese Philatelic Exhibition.

Rod and Bowl of Aesculapius — A116

1937, July 24 **Typo.** ***Perf. 11½x12***

571 A116 25c blue 8.00 .85
Never hinged 15.00

Centenary of the establishment of the School of Medicine in Lisbon and Oporto.

Gil Vicente — A117

1937

572	A117	40c dark brown	10.00	.25
573	A117	1e rose red	2.00	.25
		Set, never hinged	32.50	

400th anniversary of the death of Gil Vicente (1465-1536), Portuguese playwright. Design shows him in cowherd role in his play, "Auto do Vaqueiro."

Grapes — A118

1938 *Perf. 11½*

575	A118	15c brt purple	1.40	.55
576	A118	25c brown	3.00	1.60
577	A118	40c dp red lilac	10.00	.35
578	A118	1.75e dp blue	30.00	5.00
		Nos. 575-578 (4)	44.40	7.50
		Set, never hinged	70.00	

International Vineyard and Wine Congress.

Emblem of Portuguese Legion — A119

1940, Jan. 27 Unwmk. *Perf. 11½*

579	A119	5c dull yellow	.35	.25
580	A119	10c violet	.35	.25
581	A119	15c brt blue	.35	.25
582	A119	25c brown	22.50	1.10
583	A119	40c dk green	37.50	.40
584	A119	80c yellow grn	2.40	.55
585	A119	1e brt red	57.50	3.50
586	A119	1.75e dark blue	8.00	2.75
a.		Souv. sheet of 8, #579-586	250.00	250.00
		Never hinged	600.00	
		Nos. 579-586 (8)	128.95	9.05
		Set, never hinged	190.00	

Issued in honor of the Portuguese Legion.
No. 586a sold for 5.50e, the proceeds going to various charities.

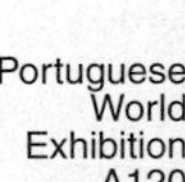

Portuguese World Exhibition A120

King John IV — A121

Discoveries Monument, Belém — A122

King Alfonso I — A123

1940 Engr. *Perf. 12x11½, 11½x12*

587	A120	10c brown violet	.25	.25
588	A121	15c dk grnsh bl	.25	.25
589	A122	25c dk slate grn	1.40	.25
590	A121	35c yellow green	1.10	.35
591	A123	40c olive bister	2.75	.25
592	A120	80c dk violet	5.25	.35
593	A122	1e dark red	12.00	1.60
594	A123	1.75e ultra	7.00	2.75
a.		Souv. sheet of 8, #587-594 ('41)	140.00	110.00
		Never hinged	275.00	
		Nos. 587-594 (8)	30.00	6.05
		Set, never hinged	50.00	

Portuguese Intl. Exhibition, Lisbon (10c, 80c); restoration of the monarchy, 300th anniv (15c, 35c); Portuguese independence, 800th anniv (40c, 1.75e).
No. 594a sold for 10e.

Sir Rowland Hill — A124

1940, Aug. 12 Typo. *Perf. 11½x12*

595	A124	15c dk violet brn	.25	.25
596	A124	25c dp org brn	.30	.25
597	A124	35c green	.30	.25
598	A124	40c brown violet	.50	.25
599	A124	50c turq green	18.00	4.25
600	A124	80c lt blue	2.10	1.10
601	A124	1e crimson	21.00	3.50
602	A124	1.75e dk blue	6.75	3.50
a.		Souv. sheet of 8, #595-602 ('41)	75.00	75.00
		Never hinged	125.00	
		Nos. 595-602 (8)	49.20	13.35
		Set, never hinged	75.00	

Postage stamp centenary.
No. 602a sold for 10e.

Fisherwoman of Nazare A126

Native of Coimbra A127

Native of Saloio — A128

Fisherwoman of Lisbon — A129

Native of Olhao — A130

Native of Aveiro — A131

Native of Madeira A132

Native of Viana do Castelo A133

Rancher of Ribatejo A134

Peasant of Alentejo A135

1941, Apr. 4 Typo. *Perf. 11½*

605	A126	4c sage green	.25	.25
606	A127	5c orange brn	.25	.25
607	A128	10c red violet	3.50	1.25
608	A129	15c lt yel grn	.25	.25
609	A130	25c rose violet	2.50	.70
610	A131	40c yellow grn	.25	.25
611	A132	80c lt blue	3.75	2.25
612	A133	1e rose red	10.00	1.60
613	A134	1.75e dull blue	11.00	4.75
614	A135	2e red orange	42.50	12.00
a.		Sheet of 10, #605-614	125.00	125.00
		Never hinged	225.00	
		Nos. 605-614 (10)	74.25	23.55
		Set, never hinged	110.00	

No. 614a sold for 10e.

Ancient Sailing Vessel — A136

1943 *Perf. 14*

615	A136	5c black	.25	.25
616	A136	10c fawn	.25	.25
617	A136	15c lilac gray	.25	.25
618	A136	20c dull violet	.25	.25
619	A136	30c brown violet	.25	.25
620	A136	35c dk blue grn	.25	.25
621	A136	50c plum	.25	.25
622	A136	1e deep rose	7.25	.25
623	A136	1.75e indigo	22.50	.25
624	A136	2e dull claret	1.60	.25
625	A136	2.50e crim rose	2.75	.25
626	A136	3.50e grnsh blue	11.00	.50
627	A136	5e dp orange	1.40	.25
628	A136	10e blue gray	3.00	.25
629	A136	15e blue green	27.50	1.00
630	A136	20e olive gray	87.50	.60
631	A136	50e salmon	250.00	1.00
		Nos. 615-631 (17)	416.25	6.35
		Set, never hinged	850.00	

See Nos. 702-710.

Farmer — A137

1943, Oct. *Perf. 11½*

632	A137	10c dull blue	.80	.30
633	A137	50c red	1.25	.35
		Set, never hinged	2.75	

Congress of Agricultural Science.

Postrider — A138

1944, May Unwmk.

634	A138	10c dk violet brn	.25	.25
635	A138	50c purple	.25	.25
636	A138	1e cerise	3.50	.65
637	A138	1.75e brt blue	3.50	1.90
a.		Sheet of 4, #634-637	32.50	35.00
		Nos. 634-637 (4)	7.50	3.05
		Set, never hinged	10.00	

3rd Philatelic Exhibition, Lisbon.
No. 637a sold for 7.50e.

Portrait of Avellar Brotero — A139

Statue of Brotero — A140

1944, Nov. 23 Typo. *Perf. 11½x12*

638	A139	10c chocolate	.25	.25
639	A140	50c dull green	1.40	.25
640	A140	1e carmine	7.50	1.60
641	A139	1.75e dark blue	6.75	2.75
a.		Sheet of 4,#638-641 ('45)	37.50	40.00
		Never hinged	57.50	
		Nos. 638-641 (4)	15.90	4.85
		Set, never hinged	21.00	

Avellar Brotero, botanist, 200th birth anniv.
No. 641a sold for 7.50e.

Gil Eannes — A141

Designs: 30c, Joao Goncalves Zarco. 35c, Bartolomeu Dias. 50c, Vasco da Gama. 1e, Pedro Alvares Cabral. 1.75e, Fernando Magellan. 2e, Goncalo Velho. 3.50e, Diogo Cao.

1945, July 29 Engr. *Perf. 13½*

642	A141	10c violet brn	.25	.25
643	A141	30c yellow brn	.25	.25
644	A141	35c blue green	.35	.25
645	A141	50c dk olive grn	1.25	.25
646	A141	1e vermilion	3.00	.65
647	A141	1.75e slate blue	3.75	2.10
648	A141	2e black	4.50	2.40
649	A141	3.50e carmine rose	8.75	4.25
a.		Sheet of 8, #642-649	32.50	40.00
		Never hinged	47.50	
		Nos. 642-649 (8)	22.10	10.40
		Set, never hinged	32.50	

Portuguese navigators of 15th and 16th centuries.
No. 649a sold for 15e.

Pres. Antonio Oscar de Fragoso Carmona — A149

Perf. 11½

1945, Nov. 12 Photo. Unwmk.

No.	Type	Denom. / Color	Unused	Used
650	A149	10c bright violet	.25	.25
651	A149	30c copper brn	.25	.25
652	A149	35c dark green	.25	.25
653	A149	50c dark olive	.40	.25
654	A149	1e dark red	10.00	1.40
655	A149	1.75e dark blue	8.25	4.00
656	A149	2e deep claret	45.00	5.00
657	A149	3.50e slate black	32.50	7.50
a.		Sheet of 8, #650-657	110.00	110.00
		Never hinged	210.00	
		Nos. 650-657 (8)	96.90	18.90
		Set, never hinged	150.00	

No. 657a sold for 15e.

Astrolabe — A150

1945, Dec. 27 Litho.

No.	Type	Denom. / Color	Unused	Used
658	A150	10c light brown	.25	.25
659	A150	50c gray green	.25	.25
660	A150	1e brown red	3.00	.75
661	A150	1.75e dull chalky bl	3.50	2.75
a.		Sheet of 4, #658-661 ('46)	26.00	27.50
		Never hinged	42.50	
		Nos. 658-661 (4)	7.00	4.00
		Set, never hinged	10.00	

Centenary of the Portuguese Naval School.
No. 661a, issued Apr. 29, sold for 7.50e.

Catalogue values for unused stamps in this section, from this point to the end of the section, are for Never Hinged items.

Silves Castle A151

Almourol Castle A152

Castles: 30c, Leiria. 35c, Feira. 50c, Guimaraes. 1.75e, Lisbon. 2e, Braganca. 3.50e, Ourem.

1946, June 1 Engr.

No.	Type	Denom. / Color	Unused	Used
662	A151	10c brown vio	.25	.25
663	A151	30c brown red	.25	.25
664	A151	35c olive grn	.25	.25
665	A151	50c gray blk	.55	.25
666	A152	1e brt carmine	25.00	1.00
667	A152	1.75e dk blue	15.00	2.40
a.		Sheet of 4	150.00	90.00
		Hinged	90.00	
668	A152	2e dk gray grn	50.00	4.50
669	A152	3.50e orange brn	27.50	5.75
		Nos. 662-669 (8)	118.80	14.65

No. 667a printed on buff granite paper, size 135x102mm, sold for 12.50e.

Figure with Tablet and Arms — A153

1946, Nov. 19 ***Perf. 12x11½***

No.	Type	Denom. / Color	Unused	Used
670	A153	50c dark blue	.75	.25
a.		Sheet of 4	140.00	100.00
		Hinged	80.00	

Establishment of the Bank of Portugal, cent.
No. 670a measures 155x143½mm and sold for 7.50e.

Madonna and Child — A154

1946, Dec. 8 Unwmk. ***Perf. 13½***

No.	Type	Denom. / Color	Unused	Used
671	A154	30c gray black	.30	.25
672	A154	50c deep green	.30	.25
673	A154	1e rose car	3.25	1.10
674	A154	1.75e brt blue	5.25	2.25
a.		Sheet of 4, #671-674 ('47)	67.50	52.50
		Nos. 671-674 (4)	9.10	3.85

300th anniv. of the proclamation making the Virgin Mary patroness of Portugal.
No. 674a sold for 7.50e.

Shepherdess, Caramullo — A155

30c, Timbrel player, Malpique. 35c, Flute player, Monsanto. 50c, Woman of Avintes. 1e, Field laborer, Maia. 1.75e, Woman of Algarve. 2e, Bastonet player, Miranda. 3.50e, Woman of the Azores.

1947, Mar. 1 Photo. ***Perf. 11½***

No.	Type	Denom. / Color	Unused	Used
675	A155	10c rose violet	.25	.25
676	A155	30c dark red	.25	.25
677	A155	35c dk olive grn	.35	.25
678	A155	50c dark brown	.60	.25
679	A155	1e red	19.00	.55
680	A155	1.75e slate blue	20.00	4.00
681	A155	2e peacock bl	65.00	4.50
682	A155	3.50e slate blk	50.00	7.50
a.		Sheet of 8, #675-682	225.00	225.00
		Hinged	150.00	
		Nos. 675-682 (8)	155.45	17.55

No. 682a sold for 15e.

Surrender of the Moors, 1147 — A163

1947, Oct. 13 Engr. ***Perf. 12½***

No.	Type	Denom. / Color	Unused	Used
683	A163	5c blue green	.25	.25
684	A163	20c dk carmine	.25	.25
685	A163	50c violet	.30	.25
686	A163	1.75e dark blue	7.25	5.00
687	A163	2.50e chocolate	11.00	6.50
688	A163	3.50e slate black	19.00	10.50
		Nos. 683-688 (6)	38.05	22.75

Conquest of Lisbon from the Moors, 800th anniv.

St. John de Britto
A164 A165

1948, May 28 ***Perf. 11½x12***

No.	Type	Denom. / Color	Unused	Used
689	A164	30c green	.25	.25
690	A165	50c dark brown	.25	.25
691	A164	1e rose carmine	10.50	1.60
692	A165	1.75e blue	13.00	2.75
		Nos. 689-692 (4)	24.00	4.85

Birth of St. John de Britto, 300th anniv.

Architecture and Engineering A166

1948, May 28 ***Perf. 13x12½***

No.	Type	Denom. / Color	Unused	Used
693	A166	50c violet brn	.65	.25

Exposition of public Works and Natl. Congress of Engineering and Architecture, 1948.

King John I — A167

Designs: 30c, Philippa of Lancaster. 35c, Prince Ferdinand. 50c, Prince Henry the Navigator. 1e, Nuno Alvarez Pereira. 1.75e, John das Regras. 2e, Fernao Lopes. 3.50e, Affonso Domingues.

Perf. 11½

1949, May 6 Unwmk. Photo.

No.	Type	Denom. / Color	Unused	Used
694	A167	10c brn vio & cr	.30	.25
695	A167	30c dk bl grn & cr	.30	.25
696	A167	35c dk ol grn & cr	.55	.25
697	A167	50c dp blue & cr	1.60	.25
698	A167	1e dk red & cr	1.60	.25
699	A167	1.75e dk gray & cr	20.00	15.00
700	A167	2e dk gray bl & cr	15.00	2.00
701	A167	3.50e dk brn & gray	40.00	17.00
a.		Sheet of 8, #694-701	80.00	80.00
		Nos. 694-701 (8)	79.35	35.25

No. 701a sold for 15e. Stamps from No. 701a differ from Nos. 694-701 in that they do not have "P. GUEDES" and "COURVOISIER S.A." below the design. Each stamp from the sheet of 8 has the same retail value.

Ship Type of 1942

1948-49 Typo. ***Perf. 14***

No.	Type	Denom. / Color	Unused	Used
702	A136	80c dp green	4.75	.45
703	A136	1e dp claret ('48)	3.25	.25
704	A136	1.20e dp carmine	4.75	.25
705	A136	1.50e olive	55.00	.40
706	A136	1.80e yellow org	47.50	2.00
707	A136	2e deep blue	7.00	.45
708	A136	4e orange	75.00	3.25
709	A136	6e yellow grn	140.00	3.75
710	A136	7.50e grnsh gray	42.50	3.50
		Nos. 702-710 (9)	379.75	14.30
		Set, hinged	250.00	

Angel, Coimbra Museum — A168

1949, Dec. 20 Engr. ***Perf. 13x14***

No.	Type	Denom. / Color	Unused	Used
711	A168	1e red brown	11.00	.25
712	A168	5e olive brown	2.75	.25

16th Intl. Congress of History and Art.

Symbols of the UPU — A169

1949, Dec. 29

No.	Type	Denom. / Color	Unused	Used
713	A169	1e brown violet	.35	.25
714	A169	2e deep blue	1.10	.25
715	A169	2.50e deep green	5.75	1.25
716	A169	4e brown red	15.00	3.50
		Nos. 713-716 (4)	22.20	5.25

75th anniv. of the UPU.

Madonna of Fatima — A170

1950, May 13 ***Perf. 11½x12***

No.	Type	Denom. / Color	Unused	Used
717	A170	50c dark green	.65	.25
718	A170	1e dark brown	3.25	.25
719	A170	2e blue	7.25	1.60
720	A170	5e lilac	100.00	29.00
		Nos. 717-720 (4)	111.15	31.10

Holy Year, 1950, and to honor "Our Lady of the Rosary" at Fatima.

St. John of God Helping Ill Man — A171

1950, Oct. 30 Engr. Unwmk.

No.	Type	Denom. / Color	Unused	Used
721	A171	20c gray violet	.30	.25
722	A171	50c cerise	.50	.25
723	A171	1e olive grn	2.00	.45
724	A171	1.50e deep orange	17.00	3.00
725	A171	2e blue	14.50	2.25
726	A171	4e chocolate	57.50	8.75
		Nos. 721-726 (6)	91.80	14.95

400th anniv. of the death of St. John of God.

Guerra Junqueiro A172

1951, Mar. 2 Litho. ***Perf. 13½***

No.	Type	Denom. / Color	Unused	Used
727	A172	50c dark brown	5.00	.35
728	A172	1e dk slate gray	1.25	.30

Birth centenary of Guerra Junqueiro, poet.

Fisherman and Catch — A173

1951, Mar. 9

No.	Type	Denom. / Color	Unused	Used
729	A173	50c gray grn, *buff*	4.00	.50
730	A173	1e rose lake, *buff*	1.00	.25

3rd National Congress of Fisheries.

Dove — A174

Pope Pius XII — A175

1951, Oct. 11
731 A174 20c dk brn & buff .40 .25
732 A174 90c dk ol grn & cr 9.00 1.75
733 A175 1e dp cl & pink 9.00 .25
734 A175 2.30e dk bl grn & bl 12.00 2.10
Nos. 731-734 (4) 30.40 4.35

End of the Holy Year.

15th Century Colonists, Terceira A176

1951, Oct. 24 ***Perf. 13x13½***
735 A176 50c dk bl, *salmon* 2.10 .45
736 A176 1e dk brn, *cream* 1.25 .35

500th anniversary (in 1950) of the colonizing of the island of Terceira.

Student, Soldiers and Workers A177

1951, Nov. 22 ***Perf. 13½x13***
737 A177 1e violet brown 7.50 .25
738 A177 2.30e dark blue 5.00 1.40

25th anniversary of the national revolution.

16th Century Coach A178

Designs: Various coaches.

Perf. 13x13½

1952, Jan. 8 Engr. Unwmk.
739 A178 10c purple .25 .25
740 A178 20c olive gray .25 .25
741 A178 50c steel blue .80 .25
742 A178 90c green 3.00 1.50
743 A178 1e red orange 2.00 .25
744 A178 1.40e rose pink 6.00 4.50
745 A178 1.50e rose brown 6.00 2.25
746 A178 2.30e deep ultra 5.00 2.00
Nos. 739-746 (8) 23.30 11.25

National Museum of Coaches.

Symbolical of NATO — A179

1952, Apr. 4 Litho. ***Perf. 12½***
747 A179 1e green & blk 13.00 .25
748 A179 3.50e gray & vio bl 325.00 15.00
Set, hinged 200.00

North Atlantic Treaty signing, 3rd anniv.

Hockey Players on Roller Skates A180

1952, June 28 ***Perf. 13x13½***
749 A180 1e dk blue & gray 4.25 .25
750 A180 3.50e dk red brown 5.75 2.25

Issued to publicize the 8th World Championship Hockey-on-Skates matches.

Francisco Gomes Teixeira — A181

1952, Nov. 25 ***Perf. 14x14½***
751 A181 1e cerise .65 .25
752 A181 2.30e deep blue 6.00 4.25

Centenary of the birth of Francisco Gomes Teixeira (1851-1932), mathematician.

St. Francis and Two Boys — A182

1952, Dec. 23 ***Perf. 13½***
753 A182 1e dark green .55 .25
754 A182 2e dp claret 1.90 .35
755 A182 3.50e chalky blue 20.00 10.00
756 A182 5e dark purple 35.00 4.00
Nos. 753-756 (4) 57.45 14.60

400th anniv. of the death of St. Francis Xavier.

Marshal Carmona Bridge A183

Designs: 1.40e, "28th of May" Stadium. 2e, University City, Coimbra. 3.50e, Salazar Dam.

1952, Dec. 10 Unwmk. ***Perf. 12½***
Buff Paper
757 A183 1e red brown .70 .25
758 A183 1.40e dull purple 13.00 5.00
759 A183 2e dark green 7.00 2.50
760 A183 3.50e dark blue 13.50 4.00
Nos. 757-760 (4) 34.20 11.75

Centenary of the foundation of the Ministry of Public Works.

Equestrian Seal of King Diniz — A184

1953-56 Litho.
761 A184 5c green, *citron* .25 .25
762 A184 10c ind, *salmon* .25 .25
763 A184 20c org red, *citron* .25 .25
763A A184 30c rose lil, *cr* ('56) .25 .25
764 A184 50c gray .25 .25
765 A184 90c dk grn, *cit* 17.50 .60
766 A184 1e vio brn, *rose* .45 .25
767 A184 1.40e rose red 18.00 1.25
768 A184 1.50e red, *cream* .65 .25
769 A184 2e gray 1.25 .25
770 A184 2.30e blue 24.00 .85
771 A184 2.50e gray blk, *sal* 2.00 .25
772 A184 5e rose vio, *cr* 2.00 .25
773 A184 10e blue, *citron* 10.00 .25
774 A184 20e bis brn, *cit* 20.00 .30
775 A184 50e rose violet 10.00 .45
Nos. 761-775 (16) 107.10 6.20

St. Martin of Braga — A185

Perf. 13x13½

1953, Feb. 26 Unwmk.
776 A185 1e gray blk & gray 1.60 .25
777 A185 3.50e dk brn & yel 10.00 4.00

14th centenary of the arrival of St. Martin of Dume on the Iberian peninsula.

Guilherme Gomes Fernandes — A186

1953, Mar. 28 ***Perf. 13***
778 A186 1e red violet 1.10 .25
779 A186 2.30e deep blue 11.00 5.50

Birth of Guilherme Gomes Fernandes, General Inspector of the Firemen of Porto.

Emblems of Automobile Club — A187

1953, Apr. 15 ***Perf. 12½***
780 A187 1e dk grn & yel grn .80 .25
781 A187 3.50e dk brn & buff 12.00 5.00

Portuguese Automobile Club, 50th anniv.

Princess St. Joanna — A188

Perf. 14½x14

1953, May 14 Litho. Unwmk.
782 A188 1e blk & gray grn 2.00 .25
783 A188 3.50e dk blue & blue 13.50 6.50

Birth of Princess St. Joanna, 500th anniv.

Queen Maria II — A189

1953, Oct. 3 Photo. ***Perf. 13½***
Background of Lower Panel in Gold
784 A189 50c red brown .25 .25
785 A189 1e claret brn .25 .25
786 A189 1.40e dk violet 2.10 .65
787 A189 2.30e dp blue 5.00 2.00
788 A189 3.50e violet blue 5.00 2.10
789 A189 4.50e dk blue grn 3.50 1.40
790 A189 5e dk ol grn 8.00 1.40
791 A189 20e red violet 60.00 5.50
Nos. 784-791 (8) 84.10 13.55

Centenary of Portugal's first postage stamp.

Allegory A190

1954, Sept. 22 ***Perf. 13***
792 A190 1e bl & dk grnsh bl .60 .25
793 A190 1.50e buff & dk brn 3.25 .65

150th anniversary of the founding of the State Secretariat for Financial Affairs.

Open Textbook A191

1954, Oct. 15 Litho.
794 A191 50c blue .40 .25
795 A191 1e red .40 .25
796 A191 2e dk green 30.00 1.40
797 A191 2.50e orange brn 25.00 1.25
Nos. 794-797 (4) 55.80 3.15

National literacy campaign.

Cadet and College Arms — A192

1954, Nov. 17
798 A192 1e choc & lt grn 1.60 .25
799 A192 3.50e dk bl & gray grn 6.50 2.50

150th anniversary of the Military College.

Manuel da Nobrega and Crucifix — A193

1954, Dec. 17 Engr. ***Perf. 14x13***
800 A193 1e brown .80 .25
801 A193 2.30e deep blue 50.00 22.50
802 A193 3.50e gray green 17.00 3.25
803 A193 5e green 45.00 4.75
Nos. 800-803 (4) 112.80 30.75

Founding of Sao Paulo, Brazil, 400th anniv.

King Alfonso I — A194

Kings: 20c, Sancho I. 50c, Alfonso II. 90c, Sancho II. 1e, Alfonso III. 1.40e, Diniz. 1.50e, Alfonso IV. 2e, Pedro I. 2.30e, Ferdinand I.

1955, Mar. 17 ***Perf. 13½x13***
804 A194 10c rose violet .25 .25
805 A194 20c dk olive grn .25 .25
806 A194 50c dk blue grn .40 .25
807 A194 90c green 3.25 1.40
808 A194 1e red brown 1.40 .25
809 A194 1.40e carmine rose 9.00 3.00
810 A194 1.50e olive brn 3.75 1.10
811 A194 2e deep orange 11.00 2.50
812 A194 2.30e violet blue 9.75 2.00
Nos. 804-812 (9) 39.05 11.00

Telegraph Pole — A195

1955, Sept. 16 Litho. ***Perf. 13½***
813 A195 1e ocher & hn brn .65 .25
814 A195 2.30e gray grn & Prus bl 20.00 3.75
815 A195 3.50e lemon & dp grn 20.00 3.25
Nos. 813-815 (3) 40.65 7.25

Centenary of the telegraph system in Portugal.

A. J. Ferreira da Silva — A196

1956, May 8 Photo. Unwmk.

816 A196 1e blue & dk blue .45 .25
817 A196 2.30e grn & dk grn 16.00 5.00

Centenary of the birth of Prof. Antonio Joaquim Ferreira da Silva, chemist.

Steam Locomotive, 1856 — A197

Design: 1.50e, 2e, Electric train, 1956.

1956, Oct. 28 Litho. *Perf. 13*

818 A197 1e lt & dk ol grn .65 .25
819 A197 1.50e Prus bl & lt grnsh bl 4.75 .35
820 A197 2e dk org brn & bis 35.00 1.40
821 A197 2.50e choc & brn 47.50 2.25
Nos. 818-821 (4) 87.90 4.25

Centenary of the Portuguese railways.

Madonna, 15th Century — A198

1956, Dec. 8 Photo.

822 A198 1e dp grn & lt ol grn .40 .25
823 A198 1.50e dk red brn & ol bis 1.00 .25

Mothers' Day, Dec. 8.

J. B. Almeida Garrett A199

1957, Mar. 7 Engr. *Perf. 13½x14*

824 A199 1e sepia .75 .25
825 A199 2.30e lt purple 40.00 11.00
826 A199 3.50e dull green 10.00 1.10
827 A199 5e rose carmine 70.00 10.50
Nos. 824-827 (4) 120.75 22.85

Issued in honor of Joao Baptista da Silva Leitao de Almeida Garrett, poet.

Cesarío Verde — A200

1957, Dec. 12 Litho. *Perf. 13½*

828 A200 1e citron & brown .40 .25
829 A200 3.30e gray grn, yel grn & dk ol 1.90 1.10

Jose Joaquim de Cesario Verde (1855-86), poet.

Exhibition Emblems — A201

1958, Apr. 7

830 A201 1e multicolored .35 .25
831 A201 3.30e multicolored 1.90 1.40

Universal & Intl. Exposition at Brussels.

Queen St. Isabel — A202

Design: 2e, 5e, St. Teotonio.

Perf. 14½x14

1958, July 10 Photo. Unwmk.

832 A202 1e rose brn & buff .25 .25
833 A202 2e dk green & buff .65 .35
834 A202 2.50e purple & buff 5.50 .85
835 A202 5e brown & buff 7.00 1.00
Nos. 832-835 (4) 13.40 2.45

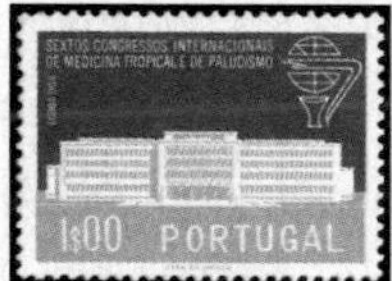

Institute for Tropical Medicine A203

1958, Sept. 4 Litho. *Perf. 13*

836 A203 1e dk grn & lt gray 2.50 .25
837 A203 2.50e bl & pale bl 7.75 1.50

6th Intl. Cong. for Tropical Medicine and Malaria, Lisbon, Sept. 1958, and opening of the new Tropical Medicine Institute.

Cargo Ship and Loading Crane — A204

1958, Nov. 27 Unwmk. *Perf. 13*

838 A204 1e brn & dk brn 6.50 .25
839 A204 4.50e vio bl & dk bl 5.00 2.25

2nd Natl. Cong. of the Merchant Marine, Porto.

Queen Leonor A205

1958, Dec. 17

840 A205 1e multi .25 .25
841 A205 1.50e bis, blk, bl & dk bis brn 4.00 .70
a. Dark bister brown omitted
842 A205 2.30e multi 3.75 1.10
843 A205 4.10e multi 3.75 1.60
Nos. 840-843 (4) 11.75 3.65

500th anniv. of the birth of Queen Leonor.

Arms of Aveiro — A206

1959, Aug. 30 Litho. *Perf. 13*

844 A206 1e ol bis, brn, gold & sil 1.75 .25
845 A206 5e grnsh gray, gold & sil 12.00 1.90

Millennium of Aveiro.

Symbols of Hope and Peace — A207

1960, Mar. 2 *Perf. 12½*

846 A207 1e lt violet & blk .35 .25
847 A207 3.50e gray & dk grn 3.25 1.75

10th anniversary (in 1959) of NATO.

Open Door to "Peace" and WRY Emblem — A208

1960, Apr. 7 Unwmk. *Perf. 13*

848 A208 20c multi .25 .25
849 A208 1e multi .50 .25
850 A208 1.80e yel grn, org & blk 1.10 .95
Nos. 848-850 (3) 1.85 1.45

World Refugee Year, 7/1/59-6/30/60.

Glider — A209

Designs: 1.50e, Plane. 2e, Plane and parachutes. 2.50e, Model plane.

1960, May 2

851 A209 1e yel, gray & bl .25 .25
852 A209 1.50e multicolored .65 .25
853 A209 2e bl grn, yel & blk 1.25 .60
854 A209 2.50e grnsh bl, ocher & red 2.50 1.10
Nos. 851-854 (4) 4.65 2.20

Aero Club of Portugal, 50th anniv. (in 1959).

Father Cruz — A210

1960, July 18 Unwmk. *Perf. 13*

855 A210 1e deep brown .25 .25
856 A210 4.30e Prus blue & blk 8.75 6.25

Father Cruz, "father of the poor."

University of Evora Seal — A211

1960, July 18 Litho.

857 A211 50c violet blue .25 .25
858 A211 1e red brn & yel .40 .25
859 A211 1.40e rose cl & rose 2.75 1.50
Nos. 857-859 (3) 3.40 2.00

Founding of the University of Evora, 400th anniv.

Arms of Prince Henry — A212

Designs: 2.50e, Caravel. 3.50e, Prince Henry. 5e, Prince Henry's motto. 8e, Prince Henry's sloop. 10e, Old chart of Sagres region of Portugal.

1960, Aug. 4 Photo. *Perf. 12x12½*

860 A212 1e gold & multi .35 .25
861 A212 2.50e gold & multi 3.00 .30
862 A212 3.50e gold & multi 4.00 1.40
863 A212 5e gold & multi 7.00 .80
864 A212 8e gold & multi 2.00 .75
865 A212 10e gold & multi 12.00 1.90
Nos. 860-865 (6) 28.35 5.40

500th anniversary of the death of Prince Henry the Navigator.

Europa Issue, 1960

Common Design Type

1960, Sept. 16 Litho. *Perf. 13*

Size: 31x21mm

866 CD3 1e ultra & gray blue .25 .25
867 CD3 3.50e brn red & rose red *2.00 1.00*
Nos. 866-867 (2) 2.25 1.25

Arms of Lisbon and Symbolic Ship — A213

1960, Nov. 17 *Perf. 13*

868 A213 1e gray ol, blk & vio bl .40 .25
869 A213 3.30e bl, blk & ultra 5.25 3.25

5th Natl. Philatelic Exhibition, Lisbon, part of the Prince Henry the Navigator festivities. (The ship in the design is in honor of Prince Henry).

Flag and Laurel — A214

1960, Dec. 20 Litho. *Perf. 13*

870 A214 1e multicolored .25 .25

50th anniversary of the Republic.

King Pedro V A215

1961, Aug. 3 Engr. *Perf. 13*

871 A215 1e gray brn & dk grn .30 .25
872 A215 6.50e dk blue & blk 3.50 .65

Centenary of the founding of the Faculty of Letters, Lisbon University.

Setubal Sea Gate and Ships A216

1961, Aug. 24 Litho. *Perf. 12x11½*

873 A216 1e gold & multi .35 .25
874 A216 4.30e gold & multi 14.00 5.00

Centenary of the city of Setubal.

Europa Issue

Clasped Hands and CEPT Emblem — A217

1961, Sept. 18 *Perf. 13½x13*
875 A217 1e blue & lt blue .25 .25
876 A217 1.50e green & brt green *1.25 .75*
877 A217 3.50e brown, pink & red *1.75 1.00*
Nos. 875-877 (3) 3.25 2.00

Tomar Castle and River Nabao — A218

1962, Jan. 26 *Perf. 11½x12*
878 A218 1e gold & multi .25 .25
879 A218 3.50e gold & multi 1.40 .85

800th anniversary of the city of Tomar.

National Guardsman — A219

1962, Feb. 20 **Unwmk.** *Perf. 13½*
880 A219 1e multi .25 .25
881 A219 2e multi 2.00 .60
882 A219 2.50e multi 2.00 .50
Nos. 880-882 (3) 4.25 1.35

Republican National Guard, 50th anniv.

Archangel Gabriel — A220

1962, Mar. 24 **Litho.** *Perf. 13*
883 A220 1e ol, pink & red brn .70 .25
884 A220 3.50e ol, pink & dk grn .50 .40

Issued for St. Gabriel's Day. St. Gabriel is patron of telecommunications.

Tents and Scout Emblem A221

1962, June 11 **Unwmk.** *Perf. 13*
885 A221 20c gray, bis, yel & blk .25 .25
a. Double impression of gray frame lettering
886 A221 50c multi .25 .25
887 A221 1e multi .60 .25
888 A221 2.50e multi 4.00 .50
889 A221 3.50e multi .90 .50
890 A221 6.50e multi 1.25 .65
Nos. 885-890 (6) 7.25 2.40

50th anniv. of the Portuguese Boy Scouts and the 18th Boy Scout World Conf., Sept. 19-24, 1961.

Children Reading A222

Designs: 1e, Vaccination. 2.80e, Children playing ball. 3.50e, Guarding sleeping infant.

1962, Sept. 10 **Litho.** *Perf. 13½*
891 A222 50c bluish grn, yel & blk .25 .25
892 A222 1e pale bl, yel & blk .90 .25
893 A222 2.80e dp org yel & blk 2.50 .90
894 A222 3.50e dl rose, yel & blk 5.00 1.40
Nos. 891-894 (4) 8.65 2.80

10th Intl. Cong. of Pediatrics, Lisbon, Sept. 9-15.

19-Cell Honeycomb A223

1962, Sept. 17
895 A223 1e bl, dk bl & gold .25 .25
896 A223 1.50e lt & dk grn & gold *1.75 .55*
897 A223 3.50e dp rose, mar & gold *2.25 1.00*
Nos. 895-897 (3) 4.25 1.80

Europa. The 19 cells represent the 19 original members of the Conference of European Postal and Telecommunications Administrations, C.E.P.T.

St. Zenon, the Courier — A224

1962, Dec. 1 **Unwmk.** *Perf. 13½*
898 A224 1e multi .25 .25
899 A224 2e multi 1.00 .55
900 A224 2.80e multi 1.90 1.40
Nos. 898-900 (3) 3.15 2.20

Issued for Stamp Day.

European Soccer Cup and Emblem — A225

1963, Feb. 5 *Perf. 13½*
901 A225 1e multi .80 .25
902 A225 4.30e multi 1.10 .90

Victories of the Benfica Club of Lisbon in the 1961 and 1962 European Soccer Championships.

Wheat Emblem A226

1963, Mar. 21 **Litho.**
903 A226 1e multi .25 .25
904 A226 3.30e multi 1.40 .80
905 A226 3.50e multi 1.25 .75
Nos. 903-905 (3) 2.90 1.80

FAO "Freedom from Hunger" campaign.

Stagecoach — A227

1963, May 7 *Perf. 12x11½*
906 A227 1e gray, lt & dk bl .25 .25
907 A227 1.50e bis, dk brn & lil rose 1.75 .40
908 A227 5e org brn, dk brn & rose lil .60 .30
Nos. 906-908 (3) 2.60 .95

1st Intl. Postal Conference, Paris, 1863.

St. Vincent de Paul by Monsaraz — A228

1963, July 10 **Photo.** *Perf. 13½x14*
Gold Inscription
909 A228 20c lt blue & ultra .25 .25
a. Gold inscription omitted 60.00
910 A228 1e gray & slate .35 .25
911 A228 2.80e green & slate 3.50 1.40
a. Gold inscription omitted 70.00
912 A228 5e dp rose car & sl 2.50 1.00
Nos. 909-912 (4) 6.60 2.90

Tercentenary of the death of St. Vincent de Paul.

Emblem of Order and Knight A229

1963, Aug. 13 **Litho.** *Perf. 11½*
913 A229 1e multi .25 .25
914 A229 1.50e multi .55 .25
915 A229 2.50e multi 1.40 .70
Nos. 913-915 (3) 2.20 1.20

800th anniv. of the Military Order of Avis.

Europa Issue

Stylized Bird — A230

1963, Sept. 16 *Perf. 13½*
916 A230 1e lt bl, gray & blk *.75 .25*
917 A230 1.50e grn, gray & blk *2.00 .60*
918 A230 3.50e red, gray & blk *3.50 .90*
Nos. 916-918 (3) *6.25* 1.75

Jet Plane — A231

1963, Dec. 1 **Unwmk.** *Perf. 13½*
919 A231 1e dk bl & lt bl .25 .25
920 A231 2.50e dk grn & yel grn 1.25 .50
921 A231 3.50e org brn & org 1.60 .85
Nos. 919-921 (3) 3.10 1.60

Transportes Aéreos Portugueses, TAP, 10th anniv.

Apothecary Jar — A232

1964, Apr. 9 **Litho.**
922 A232 50c brn ol, dk brn & blk .35 .25
923 A232 1e rose brn, dp cl & blk .35 .25
924 A232 4.30e dk gray, sl & blk 4.50 2.75
Nos. 922-924 (3) 5.20 3.25

4th centenary of the publication (in Goa, Apr. 10, 1563) of "Coloquios Dos Simples e Drogas" (Herbs and Drugs in India) by Garcia D'Orta.

Emblem of National Overseas Bank — A233

1964, May 19 **Unwmk.** *Perf. 13½*
925 A233 1e bister, yel & dk bl .25 .25
926 A233 2.50e ocher, yel & grn 2.50 .75
927 A233 3.50e bister, yel & brn 2.00 .90
Nos. 925-927 (3) 4.75 1.90

Centenary of National Overseas Bank.

Mt. Sameiro Church — A234

1964, June 5 **Litho.**
928 A234 1e red brn, bis & dl brn .25 .25
929 A234 2e brn, bis & dl brn 1.75 .60
930 A234 5e dk vio bl, bis & gray 2.25 .80
Nos. 928-930 (3) 4.25 1.65

Centenary of the Shrine of Our Lady of Mt. Sameiro, Braga.

Europa Issue
Common Design Type

1964, Sept. 14 **Unwmk.** *Perf. 13½*
Size: 19x32mm.
931 CD7 1e bl, lt bl & dk bl *1.00 .25*
932 CD7 3.50e rose brn, buff & dk brn *4.00 .50*
933 CD7 4.30e grn, yel grn & dk grn *5.00 1.25*
Nos. 931-933 (3) *10.00 2.00*

Partial Eclipse of Sun — A235

1964
934 A235 1e multicolored .25 .25
935 A235 8e multicolored 1.40 .85

International Quiet Sun Year, 1964-65.

Olympic Rings, Emblems of Portugal and Japan — A236

Black Inscriptions; Olympic Rings in Pale Yellow

1964, Dec. 1 Unwmk. *Perf. 13½*

936 A236 20c tan, red & vio bl .25 .25
937 A236 1e ultra, red & vio bl .25 .25
938 A236 1.50e yel grn, red & vio bl 2.00 .75
939 A236 6.50e rose lil, red & vio bl 3.00 1.40
Nos. 936-939 (4) 5.50 2.65

18th Olympic Games, Tokyo, Oct. 10-25.

Eduardo Coelho — A237

1964, Dec. 28 Litho. *Perf. 13½*

940 A237 1e multicolored .50 .25
941 A237 5e multicolored 5.00 .75

Centenary of the founding of Portugal's first newspaper, "Diario de Noticias," and to honor the founder, Eduardo Coelho, journalist.

Traffic Signs and Signals A238

1965, Feb. 15 Litho.

942 A238 1e yellow, red & emer .25 .25
943 A238 3.30e multicolored 5.00 3.00
944 A238 3.50e red, yellow & emer 2.00 1.10
Nos. 942-944 (3) 7.25 4.35

1st National Traffic Cong., Lisbon, 2/15-19.

Ferdinand I, Duke of Braganza — A239

1965, Mar. 16 Unwmk. *Perf. 13½*

945 A239 1e rose brown & blk .25 .25
946 A239 10e Prus green & blk 2.40 .65

500th anniv. of the city of Braganza (in 1964).

Coimbra Gate, Angel with Censer and Sword — A240

1965, Apr. 27 *Perf. 11½x12*

947 A240 1e blue & multi .25 .25
948 A240 2.50e multi 2.10 1.10
949 A240 5e multi 2.10 1.40
Nos. 947-949 (3) 4.45 2.75

9th centenary (in 1964) of the capture of the city of Coimbra from the Moors.

ITU Emblem — A241

1965, May 17 *Perf. 13½*

950 A241 1e bis brn, ol grn & ol .25 .25
951 A241 3.50e ol, rose cl & dp cl 1.60 1.00
952 A241 6.50e yel grn, dl bl & sl bl 1.40 .90
Nos. 950-952 (3) 3.25 2.15

International Telecommunication Union, cent.

Calouste Gulbenkian A242

1965, July 20 Litho. *Perf. 13½*

953 A242 1e multicolored .60 .25
954 A242 8e multicolored .55 .40

Gulbenkian (1869-1955), oil industry pioneer and sponsor of the Gulbenkian Foundation.

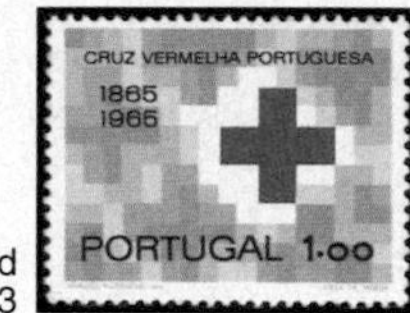

Red Cross — A243

1965, Aug. 17 Unwmk. *Perf. 13½*

955 A243 1e grn, red & blk .25 .25
956 A243 4e ol, red & blk 2.25 .90
957 A243 4.30e lt rose brn, red & blk 10.00 5.00
Nos. 955-957 (3) 12.50 6.15

Centenary of the Portuguese Red Cross.

Europa Issue
Common Design Type

1965, Sept. 27 Litho. *Perf. 13*
Size: 31x24mm

958 CD8 1e saph, grnsh bl & dk bl *2.00 .25*
959 CD8 3.50e rose brn, sal & brn *3.00 .50*
960 CD8 4.30e grn, yel grn & dk grn *5.00 2.00*
Nos. 958-960 (3) *10.00 2.75*

Military Plane — A244

1965, Oct. 20 *Perf. 13½*

961 A244 1e ol grn, red & dk grn .25 .25
962 A244 2e sepia, red & dk grn 1.40 .55
963 A244 5e chlky bl, red & dk grn 2.25 1.10
Nos. 961-963 (3) 3.90 1.90

Portuguese Air Force founding, 50th anniv.

Woman — A245

Designs: Characters from Gil Vicente Plays.

1965, Dec. 1 Litho. *Perf. 13½*

964 A245 20c ol, pale yel & blk .25 .25
965 A245 1e brn, pale yel & blk .35 .25
966 A245 2.50e dk red, buff & blk 3.25 .45
967 A245 6.50e blue, gray & blk 1.10 .55
Nos. 964-967 (4) 4.95 1.50

Gil Vicente (1465?-1536?).

Chrismon with Alpha and Omega A246

1966, Mar. 28 Litho. *Perf. 13½*

968 A246 1e ol bis, gold & blk .25 .25
969 A246 3.30e gray, gold & blk 5.00 2.75
970 A246 5e rose cl, gold & blk 4.00 .90
Nos. 968-970 (3) 9.25 3.90

Congress of the International Committee for the Defense of Christian Civilization, Lisbon.

Symbols of Peace and Labor — A247

1966, May 28 Litho. *Perf. 13½*

971 A247 1e dk bl, sl bl & lt sl bl .25 .25
972 A247 3.50e ol, ol brn, & lt ol 2.75 1.10
973 A247 4e dk brn, brn car & dl rose 2.75 .80
Nos. 971-973 (3) 5.75 2.15

40th anniversary of National Revolution.

Knight Giraldo on Horseback A248

1966, June 8

974 A248 1e multicolored .30 .25
975 A248 8e multicolored 1.10 .55

Conquest of Evora from the Moors, 800th anniv.

Salazar Bridge — A249

Designs: 2.80e, 4.30e, View of bridge, vert.

1966, Aug. 6 Litho. *Perf. 13½*

976 A249 1e gold & red .25 .25
977 A249 2.50e gold & ultra 1.40 .50
978 A249 2.80e silver & dp ultra 3.00 1.10
979 A249 4.30e silver & dk grn 4.00 1.25
Nos. 976-979 (4) 8.65 3.10

Issued to commemorate the opening of the Salazar Bridge over the Tejo River, Lisbon.

Europa Issue
Common Design Type

1966, Sept. 26 Litho. *Perf. 11½x12*
Size: 26x32mm

980 CD9 1e blue & blk *.75 .25*
981 CD9 3.50e red brn & blk *4.00 .75*
982 CD9 4.30e yel grn & blk *5.00 1.25*
Nos. 980-982 (3) *9.75* 2.25

Pestana — A250

Portraits: 20c, Camara Pestana (1863-1899), bacteriologist. 50c, Egas Moniz (1874-1955), neurologist. 1e, Antonio Pereira Coutinho (1851-1939), botanist. 1.50e, José Corrèa da Serra (1750-1823), botanist. 2e, Ricardo Jórge (1858-1938), hygienist and anthropologist. 2.50e, J. Liete de Vasconcelos (1858-1941), ethnologist. 2.80e, Maximiano Lemos (1860-1923), medical historian. 4.30e, José Antonio Serrano, anatomist.

Portrait and Inscription in Dark Brown and Bister

1966, Dec. 1 Litho. *Perf. 13½*

983 A250 20c gray green .25 .25
984 A250 50c orange .25 .25
985 A250 1e lemon .25 .25
986 A250 1.50e bister brn .35 .25
987 A250 2e brown org 1.75 .25
988 A250 2.50e pale green 2.00 .40
989 A250 2.80e salmon 2.10 1.25
990 A250 4.30e Prus blue 3.75 2.10
Nos. 983-990 (8) 10.70 5.00

Issued to honor Portuguese scientists.

Bocage — A251

1966, Dec. 28 Litho. *Perf. 11½x12*

991 A251 1e bis, grnsh gray & blk .25 .25
992 A251 2e brn org, grnsh gray & blk .90 .30
993 A251 6e gray, grnsh gray & blk 1.40 .60
Nos. 991-993 (3) 2.55 1.15

200th anniversary of the birth of Manuel Maria Barbosa du Bocage (1765-1805), poet.

Europa Issue
Common Design Type

1967, May 2 Litho. *Perf. 13*
Size: 21½x31mm

994 CD10 1e lt bl, Prus bl & blk *.50* .25
995 CD10 3.50e sal, brn red & blk *4.00 .60*
996 CD10 4.30e yel grn, ol grn & blk *5.00 1.00*
Nos. 994-996 (3) *9.50* 1.85

Apparition of Our Lady of Fatima — A252

Designs: 2.80e, Church and Golden Rose. 3.50e, Statue of the Pilgrim Virgin, with lilies and doves. 4e, Doves holding crown over Chapel of the Apparition.

1967, May 13 *Perf. 11½x12*

997 A252 1e multicolored .25 .25
998 A252 2.80e multicolored .55 .40
999 A252 3.50e multicolored .35 .25
1000 A252 4e multicolored .50 .25
Nos. 997-1000 (4) 1.65 1.15

50th anniversary of the apparition of the Virgin Mary to 3 shepherd children at Fatima.

Statues of Roman Senators — A253

1967, June 1 Litho. *Perf. 13*

1001 A253 1e gold & rose claret .25 .25
1002 A253 2.50e gold & dull blue 2.10 .85
1003 A253 4.30e gold & gray green 1.25 .85
Nos. 1001-1003 (3) 3.60 1.95

Introduction of a new civil law code.

Shipyard, Margueira, Lisbon — A254

Design: 2.80e, 4.30e, Ship's hull and map showing location of harbor.

1967, June 23

1004	A254	1e aqua & multi	.25	.25
1005	A254	2.80e multicolored	2.25	.95
1006	A254	3.50e multicolored	1.60	.85
1007	A254	4.30e multicolored	2.50	.95
		Nos. 1004-1007 (4)	6.60	3.00

Issued to commemorate the inauguration of the Lisnave Shipyard at Margueira, Lisbon.

Symbols of Healing — A255

1967, Oct. 8 **Litho.** ***Perf. 13½***

1008	A255	1e multicolored	.25	.25
1009	A255	2e multicolored	1.10	.50
1010	A255	5e multicolored	1.75	.95
		Nos. 1008-1010 (3)	3.10	1.70

Issued to publicize the 6th European Congress of Rheumatology, Lisbon, Oct. 8-13.

Flags of EFTA Nations — A256

1967, Oct. 24 **Litho.** ***Perf. 13½***

1011	A256	1e bister & multi	.25	.25
1012	A256	3.50e buff & multi	1.10	.85
1013	A256	4.30e gray & multi	3.00	2.25
		Nos. 1011-1013 (3)	4.35	3.35

Issued to publicize the European Free Trade Association. See note after Norway No. 501.

Tables of the Law — A257

1967, Dec. 27 **Litho.** ***Perf. 13½***

1014	A257	1e olive	.25	.25
1015	A257	2e red brown	1.25	.65
1016	A257	5e green	2.10	1.25
		Nos. 1014-1016 (3)	3.60	2.15

Centenary of abolition of death penalty.

Bento de Goes — A258

Perf. 13½ (#1017), 12x11½ (#1018)

1968, Feb. 14 **Engr.**

1017	A258	1e olive, indigo & dk brn	1.00	.25
1018	A258	8e org brn, dl pur & ol grn	1.50	.50

360th anniversary (in 1967) of the death of Bento de Goes (1562-1607), Jesuit explorer of the route to China.

Europa Issue

Common Design Type

1968, Apr. 29 **Litho.** ***Perf. 13***

Size: 31x21mm

1019	CD11	1e multicolored	.75	.25
1020	CD11	3.50e multicolored	*4.00*	*.60*
1021	CD11	4.30e multicolored	*5.00*	*1.25*
		Nos. 1019-1021 (3)	*9.75*	2.10

Mother's and Child's Hands — A259

1968, May 26 **Litho.** ***Perf. 13½***

1022	A259	1e lt gray, blk & red	.25	.25
1023	A259	2e salmon, blk & red	1.60	.50
1024	A259	5e lt bl, blk & red	3.00	1.10
		Nos. 1022-1024 (3)	4.85	1.85

Mothers' Organization for Natl. Education. 30th anniv.

"Victory over Disease" and WHO Emblem A260

1968, July 10 **Litho.** ***Perf. 12½***

1025	A260	1e multicolored	.25	.25
1026	A260	3.50e multicolored	1.40	.50
1027	A260	4.30e tan & multi	5.00	3.00
		Nos. 1025-1027 (3)	6.65	3.75

20th anniv. of WHO.

Madeira Grapes and Wine A261

Joao Fernandes Vieira — A262

Designs: 1e, Fireworks on New Year's Eve. 1.50e, Mountains and valley. 3.50e, Woman doing Madeira embroidery. 4.30e, Joao Gonçalves Zarco. 20e, Muschia aurea (flower.)

Perf. 12x11½, 11½x12

1968, Aug. 17 **Litho.**

1028	A261	50c multi	.25	.25
1029	A261	1e multi	.25	.25
1030	A261	1.50e multi	.35	.25
1031	A262	2.80e multi	2.40	1.25
1032	A262	3.50e multi	2.00	.85
1033	A262	4.30e multi	8.25	4.00
1034	A262	20e multi	5.00	.95
		Nos. 1028-1034 (7)	18.50	7.80

Issued to publicize Madeira and the Lubrapex 1968 stamp exhibition.

Design descriptions in Portuguese, French and English printed on back of stamps.

Pedro Alvares Cabral A263

Cabral's Fleet A264

Design: 3.50e, Cabral's coat of arms, vert.

Perf. 12x12½, 12½x12

1969, Jan. 30 **Engr.**

1035	A263	1e vio bl, bl & gray bl	.25	.25
1036	A263	3.50e deep claret	3.50	1.75

Litho.

1037	A264	6.50e green & multi	2.50	1.60
		Nos. 1035-1037 (3)	6.25	3.60

5th cent. of the birth of Pedro Alvarez Cabral (1468-1520), navigator, discoverer of Brazil. Nos. 1035-1037 have description of the designs printed on the back in Portuguese, French and English.

Europa Issue

Common Design Type

1969, Apr. 28 **Litho.** ***Perf. 13***

Size: 31x22½mm

1038	CD12	1e dp blue & multi	.85	.25
1039	CD12	3.50e multicolored	7.00	*.65*
1040	CD12	4.30e grn & multi	10.00	*1.50*
		Nos. 1038-1040 (3)	17.85	2.40

King José I and Arms of National Press — A265

1969, May 14 **Litho.** ***Perf. 11½x12***

1041	A265	1e multicolored	.25	.25
1042	A265	2e multicolored	1.10	.45
1043	A265	8e multicolored	1.00	.60
		Nos. 1041-1043 (3)	2.35	1.30

Bicentenary of the National Press.

ILO Emblem A266

1969, May 28 ***Perf. 13***

1044	A266	1e bluish grn, blk & sil	.25	.25
1045	A266	3.50e red, blk & sil	1.75	.60
1046	A266	4.30e brt bl, blk & sil	2.25	1.40
		Nos. 1044-1046 (3)	4.25	2.25

50th anniversary of the ILO.

Juan Cabrillo Rodriguez A267

1969, July 16 **Litho.** ***Perf. 11½x12***

1047	A267	1e multi	.25	.25
1048	A267	2.50e multi	1.60	.45
1049	A267	6.50e multi	1.75	.90
		Nos. 1047-1049 (3)	3.60	1.60

Bicent. of San Diego, Calif., & honoring Juan Cabrillo Rodriguez, explorer of California coast.

Backs inscribed. See note below No. 1034.

Vianna da Motta, by Columbano Bordalo Pinheiro — A268

1969, Sept. 24 **Litho.** ***Perf. 12***

1050	A268	1e multicolored	.90	.25
1051	A268	9e gray & multi	.90	.60

Centenary of the birth of Vianna da Motta (1868-1948), pianist and composer.

Gago Coutinho and 1922 Seaplane A269

Design: 2.80e, 4.30e, Adm. Coutinho and Coutinho sextant.

1969, Oct. 22

1052	A269	1e grnsh gray, dk & lt brn	.25	.25
1053	A269	2.80e yel bis, dk & lt brn	2.25	1.00
1054	A269	3.30e gray bl, dk & lt brn	2.10	1.25
1055	A269	4.30e lt rose brn, dk & lt brn	2.10	1.40
		Nos. 1052-1055 (4)	6.70	3.90

Admiral Carlos Viegas Gago Coutinho (1869-1959), explorer and aviation pioneer.

Vasco da Gama A270

Designs: 2.80e, Da Gama's coat of arms. 3.50e, Map showing route to India and compass rose, horiz. 4e, Da Gama's fleet, horiz.

Perf. 12x11½, 11½x12

1969, Dec. 30 **Litho.**

1056	A270	1e multi	.25	.25
1057	A270	2.80e multi	3.00	1.75
1058	A270	3.50e multi	2.25	.75
1059	A270	4e multi	2.10	.60
		Nos. 1056-1059 (4)	7.60	3.35

Vasco da Gama (1469-1525), navigator who found sea route to India.

Design descriptions in Portuguese, French and English printed on back of stamps.

Europa Issue

Common Design Type

1970, May 4 **Litho.** ***Perf. 13½***

Size: 31x22mm

1060	CD13	1e multicolored	*.85*	*.25*
1061	CD13	3.50e multicolored	*4.00*	*.60*
1062	CD13	4.30e multicolored	*5.00*	*1.50*
		Nos. 1060-1062 (3)	*9.85*	2.35

Distillation Plant — A271

Design: 2.80e, 6e, Catalytic cracking tower.

1970, June 5 **Litho.** ***Perf. 13***

1063	A271	1e dk bl & dl bl	.25	.25
1064	A271	2.80e sl grn & pale grn	2.50	1.40
1065	A271	3.30e dk ol grn & ol	1.60	1.00
1066	A271	6e dk brn & dl ocher	1.40	.85
		Nos. 1063-1066 (4)	5.75	3.50

Opening of the Oporto Oil Refinery.

Marshal Carmona and Oak Leaves A272

Designs: 2.50e, Carmona, Portuguese coat of arms and laurel. 7e, Carmona and ferns.

Litho. & Engr.

1970, July 1 ***Perf. 12x12½***

1067 A272 1e ol grn & blk .25 .25
1068 A272 2.50e red, ultra & blk 1.90 .60
1069 A272 7e slate bl & blk 1.60 .90
Nos. 1067-1069 (3) 3.75 1.75

Centenary of the birth of Marshal Antonio Oscar de Fragoso Carmona (1869-1951), President of Portugal, 1926-1951.

Emblem of Plant Research Station A273

1970, July 29 **Litho.**

1070 A273 1e multi .25 .25
1071 A273 2.50e multi 1.40 .40
1072 A273 5e multi 1.90 .55
Nos. 1070-1072 (3) 3.55 1.20

25th anniv. of the Plant Research Station at Elvas.

Compass Rose and EXPO Emblem — A274

Designs: 5e, Monogram of Christ (IHS) and EXPO emblem. 6.50e, "Portugal and Japan" as written in old manuscripts, and EXPO emblem.

1970, Sept. 16 **Litho.** ***Perf. 13***

1073 A274 1e gold & multi .25 .25
1074 A274 5e silver & multi 1.50 .90
1075 A274 6.50e multicolored 3.75 2.25
Nos. 1073-1075,C11 (4) 6.20 3.80

EXPO '70 International Exhibition, Osaka, Japan, Mar. 15-Sept. 13.

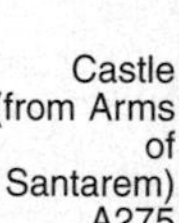

Castle (from Arms of Santarem) A275

#1077, Star & wheel, from Covilha coat of arms. 2.80e, Ram & Covilha coat of arms. 4e, Knights on horseback & Santarem coat of arms.

1970, Oct. 7 **Litho.** ***Perf. 12x11½***

1076 A275 1e multicolored .25 .25
1077 A275 1e ultra & multi .25 .25
1078 A275 2.80e red & multi 3.00 1.25
1079 A275 4e gray & multi 1.60 .70
Nos. 1076-1079 (4) 5.10 2.45

City of Santarem, cent. (#1076, 1079); City of Covilha, cent. (#1077-1078).

Paddlesteamer Great Eastern Laying Cable — A276

Designs: 2.80e, 4e, Cross section of cable.

1970, Nov. 21 **Litho.** ***Perf. 14***

1080 A276 1e multi .25 .25
1081 A276 2.50e multi 1.90 .40
1082 A276 2.80e multi 3.50 2.00
1083 A276 4e multi 1.60 .60
Nos. 1080-1083 (4) 7.25 3.25

Centenary of the Portugal-Great Britain submarine telegraph cable.

Grapes and Woman Filling Baskets A277

Designs: 1e, Worker carrying basket of grapes, and jug. 3.50e, Glass of wine, and barge with barrels on River Douro. 7e, Wine bottle and barrels.

1970, Dec. 20 **Litho.** ***Perf. 12x11½***

1084 A277 50c multi .25 .25
1085 A277 1e multi .25 .25
1086 A277 3.50e multi 1.00 .25
1087 A277 7e multi 1.00 .50
Nos. 1084-1087 (4) 2.50 1.25

Publicity for port wine export.

Mountain Windmill, Bussaco Hills — A278

Windmills: 50c, Beira Litoral Province. 1e, Estremadura Province. 2e, St. Miguel, Azores. 3.30e, Porto Santo, Madeira. 5e, Pico, Azores.

1971, Feb. 24 **Litho.** ***Perf. 13***

1088 A278 20c multicolored .25 .25
1089 A278 50c lt blue & multi .25 .25
1090 A278 1e gray & multi .25 .25
1091 A278 2e multicolored .90 .25
1092 A278 3.30e ocher & multi 2.00 1.00
1093 A278 5e multicolored 1.75 .55
Nos. 1088-1093 (6) 5.40 2.55

Backs inscribed. See note below No. 1034.

Europa Issue

Common Design Type

1971, May 3 **Photo.** ***Perf. 14***

Size: 32x22mm

1094 CD14 1e dk bl, lt grn & blk *.75* *.25*
1095 CD14 3.50e red brn, yel & blk *4.00* *.50*
1096 CD14 7.50e olive, yel & blk *5.00* *1.00*
Nos. 1094-1096 (3) *9.75* 1.75

Francisco Franco (1885-1955) A279

Portuguese Sculptors: 1e, Antonio Teixeira Lopes (1866-1942). 1.50e, Antonio Augusto da Costa Mota (1862-1930). 2.50e, Rui Roque Gameiro (1906-1935). 3.50e, José Simoes de Almeida (nephew; 1880-1950). 4e, Francisco dos Santos (1878-1930).

Perf. 11½x12½; 13½ (2.50e, 4e)

1971, July 7 **Engr.**

1097 A279 20c black .25 .25
a. Perf. 13½ 2.25 .30

1098 A279 1e claret .30 .25
1099 A279 1.50e sepia .60 .40
1100 A279 2.50e dark blue 1.00 .30
1101 A279 3.50e carmine rose 1.40 .45
1102 A279 4e gray green 2.50 1.50
Nos. 1097-1102 (6) 6.05 3.15

Pres. Antonio Salazar — A280

1971, July 27 **Engr.** ***Perf. 13½***

1103 A280 1e multicolored .25 .25
a. Perf. 12½x12 *100.00* 2.75
1104 A280 5e multicolored 1.75 .35
1105 A280 10e multicolored 2.75 .95
a. Perf. 12½x12 *40.00* 1.75
Nos. 1103-1105 (3) 4.75 1.55

Wolframite Crystals A281

Minerals: 2.50e, Arsenopyrite (gold). 3.50e, Beryllium. 6.50e, Chalcopyrite (copper).

1971, Sept. 24 **Litho.** ***Perf. 12***

1106 A281 1e multicolored .25 .25
1107 A281 2.50e carmine & multi 2.00 .40
1108 A281 3.50e green & multi .65 .30
1109 A281 6.50e blue & multi 1.25 .45
Nos. 1106-1109 (4) 4.15 1.40

Spanish-Portuguese-American Economic Geology Congress.

Town Gate, Castelo Branco — A282

Designs: 3e, Memorial column. 12.50e, Arms of Castelo Branco, horiz.

1971, Oct. 7 ***Perf. 14***

1110 A282 1e multi .25 .25
1111 A282 3e multi 1.40 .50
1112 A282 12.50e multi 1.10 .50
Nos. 1110-1112 (3) 2.75 1.25

Bicentenary of Castelo Branco as a town.

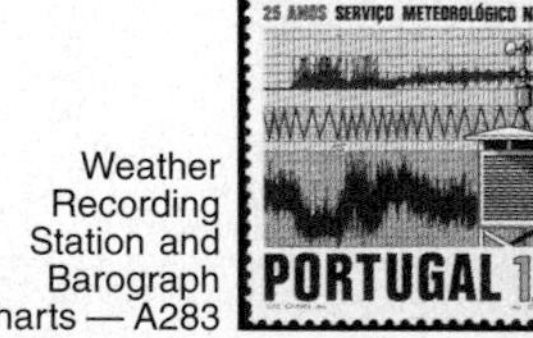

Weather Recording Station and Barograph Charts — A283

Designs: 4e, Stratospheric weather balloon and weather map of southwest Europe and North Africa. 6.50e, Satellite and aerial map of Atlantic Ocean off Portugal.

1971, Oct. 29 ***Perf. 13½***

1113 A283 1e buff & multi .25 .25
1114 A283 4e multicolored 2.25 .85
1115 A283 6.50e blk, dl red brn & org 1.50 .45
Nos. 1113-1115 (3) 4.00 1.55

25 years of Portuguese meteorological service.

Missionaries and Ship — A284

1971, Nov. 24

1116 A284 1e gray, ultra & blk .25 .25
1117 A284 3.30e dp bis, lil & blk 2.00 1.00
1118 A284 4.80e olive, grn & blk 2.10 1.10
Nos. 1116-1118 (3) 4.35 2.35

400th anniv. of the martyrdom of a group of Portuguese missionaries on the way to Brazil.

"Man" A285

Nature Conservation: 3.30e, "Earth" (animal, vegetable, mineral). 3.50e, "Air" (birds). 4.50e, "Water" (fish).

1971, Dec. 22 **Litho.** ***Perf. 12***

1119 A285 1e brown & multi .25 .25
1120 A285 3.30e lt bl, yel & grn .55 .30
1121 A285 3.50e lt bl, rose & vio .65 .25
1122 A285 4.50e lt bl, grn & ultra 2.25 1.25
Nos. 1119-1122 (4) 3.70 2.05

City Hall, Sintra — A286

Designs: 5c, Aqueduct, Lisbon. 50c, University, Coimbra. 1e, Torre dos Clerigos, Porto. 1.50e, Belem Tower, Lisbon. 2.50e, Castle, Vila da Feira. 3e, Misericordia House, Viana do Castelo. 3.50e, Window, Tomar Convent. 8e, Ducal Palace, Guimaraes. 10e, Cape Girao, Madeira. 20e, Episcopal Garden, Castelo Branco. 100e, Lakes of Seven Cities, Azores.

1972-73 **Litho.** ***Perf. 12½***

Size: 22x17½mm

1123 A286 5c gray, grn & blk .25 .25
1124 A286 50c gray bl, blk & org .25 .25
1125 A286 1e green, blk & brn .25 .25
1126 A286 1.50e blue, bis & blk .25 .25
1127 A286 2.50e brn, dk brn & gray .25 .25
1128 A286 3e yellow, blk & brn .25 .25
1129 A286 3.50e dp org, sl & brn .25 .25
1130 A286 8e blk, ol & grn 1.40 .30

Perf. 13½

Size: 31x22mm

1131 A286 10e gray & multi .50 .25
1132 A286 20e green & multi 3.75 .25
1133 A286 50e gray bl, ocher & blk 1.90 .25
1134 A286 100e green & multi 5.50 .45
Nos. 1123-1134 (12) 14.80 3.25

"CTT" and year date printed in minute gray multiple rows on back of stamps. Values are for most common dates.

Issue dates: 1e, 1.50e, 50e, 100e, Mar. 1; 50c, 3e, 10e, 20e, Dec. 6, 1972; 5c, 2.50e, 3.50e, 8e, Sept. 5, 1973.

See Nos. 1207-1214.

Tagging

Starting in 1975, phosphor (bar or L-shape) was applied to the face of most definitives and commemoratives.

Stamps issued both with and without tagging include Nos. 1124-1125, 1128, 1130-1131, 1209, 1213-1214, 1250, 1253, 1257, 1260, 1263.

Window, Pinhel Church — A287

1e, Arms of Pinhel, horiz. 7.50e, Stone lantern.

1972, Mar. 29 ***Perf. 13½***

1135 A287 1e blue & multi .25 .25
a. Perf. 11½x12½ 80.00 3.00
1136 A287 2.50e multicolored 1.75 .30
1137 A287 7.50e blue & multi 1.40 .50
Nos. 1135-1137 (3) 3.40 1.05

Bicentenary of Pinhel as a town.

Heart and Pendulum A288

Designs: 4e, Heart and spiral pattern. 9e, Heart and continuing coil pattern.

1972, Apr. 24

1138 A288 1e violet & red .25 .25
1139 A288 4e green & red 3.00 .90
1140 A288 9e brown & red 1.60 .60
Nos. 1138-1140 (3) 4.85 1.75

"Your heart is your health," World Health Day.

Europa Issue
Common Design Type

1972, May 1 ***Perf. 13½***

Size: 21x31mm

1141 CD15 1e gray & multi *.85* *.25*
1142 CD15 3.50e salmon & multi *3.00* *.35*
1143 CD15 6e grn & multi *6.00* *.90*
Nos. 1141-1143 (3) *9.85* 1.50

Trucks — A289

1972, May 17 **Litho.** ***Perf. 13½***

1144 A289 1e shown .25 .25
1145 A289 4.50e Taxi 2.10 .90
1146 A289 8e Autobus 1.75 .70
Nos. 1144-1146 (3) 4.10 1.85

13th Congress of International Union of Road Transport (I.R.U.), Estoril, May 15-18.

Soccer, Olympic Rings A290

1e, Running. 1.50e, Equestrian. 3.50e, Swimming, women's. 4.50e, Yachting. 5e, Gymnastics, women's.

1972, July 26 **Litho.** ***Perf. 14***

1147 A290 50c shown .25 .25
1148 A290 1e multicolored .25 .25
1149 A290 1.50e multicolored .45 .25
1150 A290 3.50e multicolored 1.10 .30
1151 A290 4.50e multicolored 1.50 .85
1152 A290 5e multicolored 2.75 .80
Nos. 1147-1152 (6) 6.30 2.70

20th Olympic Games, Munich, 8/26-9/11.

Marquis of Pombal — A291

2.50e, Scientific apparatus. 8e, Seal of Univ. of Coimbra.

1972, Aug. 28 ***Perf. 13½***

1153 A291 1e shown .25 .25
1154 A291 2.50e multicolored 1.60 .60
1155 A291 8e multicolored 1.75 .95
Nos. 1153-1155 (3) 3.60 1.80

Bicentenary of the Pombaline reforms of University of Coimbra.

Tomé de Sousa — A292

Designs: 2.50e, José Bonifacio. 3.50e, Dom Pedro IV. 6e, Allegory of Portuguese-Brazilian Community.

1972, Oct. 5 **Litho.** ***Perf. 13½***

1156 A292 1e gray & multi .25 .25
1157 A292 2.50e green & multi .75 .25
1158 A292 3.50e multicolored .75 .30
1159 A292 6e blue & multi 1.60 .65
Nos. 1156-1159 (4) 3.35 1.45

150th anniv. of Brazilian independence.

Sacadura Cabral, Gago Coutinho and Plane — A293

2.50e, 3.80e, Map of flight from Lisbon to Rio.

1972, Nov. 15 ***Perf. 11½x12½***

1160 A293 1e blue & multi .25 .25
a. Perf. 13½ 40.00 .95
1161 A293 2.50e multi .80 .30
1162 A293 2.80e multi 1.00 .60
1163 A293 3.80e multi 1.60 1.00
a. Perf. 13½ *125.00* *37.50*
Nos. 1160-1163 (4) 3.65 2.15

50th anniv. of the Lisbon to Rio flight by Commander Arturo de Sacadura Cabral and Adm. Carlos Viegas Gago Coutinho, Mar. 30-June 5, 1922.

Luiz Camoens A294

Designs: 3e, Hand saving manuscript from sea. 10e, Symbolic of man's questioning and discovering the unknown.

1972, Dec. 27 **Litho.** ***Perf. 13***

1164 A294 1e org brn, buff & blk .25 .25
1165 A294 3e dull bl, lt grn & blk 1.40 .50
1166 A294 10e red brn, buff & yel 1.60 .65
Nos. 1164-1166 (3) 3.25 1.40

4th centenary of the publication of The Lusiads by Luiz Camoens (1524-1580).

Graphs and Sequence Count — A295

1973, Apr. 11 **Litho.** ***Perf. 14½***

1167 A295 1e shown .25 .25
1168 A295 4e Odometer 1.40 .50
1169 A295 9e Graphs 1.25 .45
Nos. 1167-1169 (3) 2.90 1.20

Productivity Conference '72, 1/17-22/72.

Europa Issue
Common Design Type

1973, Apr. 30 ***Perf. 13***

Size: 31x29mm

1170 CD16 1e multicolored *1.00* *.25*
1171 CD16 4e brn red & multi *5.00* *.65*
1172 CD16 6e green & multi *7.00* *1.25*
Nos. 1170-1172 (3) *13.00* 2.15

Gen. Medici, Arms of Brazil and Portugal A296

2.80e, 4.80e, Gen. Medici and world map.

Lithographed and Engraved

1973, May 16 ***Perf. 12x11½***

1173 A296 1e dk grn, blk & sep .25 .25
1174 A296 2.80e olive & multi .75 .50
1175 A296 3.50e dk bl, blk & buff .85 .45
1176 A296 4.80e multicolored .90 .50
Nos. 1173-1176 (4) 2.75 1.70

Visit of Gen. Emilio Garrastazu Medici, President of Brazil, to Portugal.

Child and Birds — A297

4e, Child and flowers. 7.50e, Child.

1973, May 28 **Litho.** ***Perf. 13***

1177 A297 1e ultra & multi .25 .25
1178 A297 4e multicolored 2.00 .50
1179 A297 7.50e bister & multi 2.25 .80
Nos. 1177-1179 (3) 4.50 1.55

To pay renewed attention to children.

Transportation, Weather Map — A298

3.80e, Communications: telegraph, telephone, radio, satellite. 6e, Postal service: mailbox, truck, mail distribution diagram.

1973, June 25

1180 A298 1e multi .25 .25
1181 A298 3.80e multi .45 .30
1182 A298 6e multi 1.10 .50
Nos. 1180-1182 (3) 1.80 1.05

Ministry of Communications, 25th anniv.

Pupil and Writing Exercise — A299

Designs: 4.50e, Illustrations from 18th century primer. 5.30e, School and children, by 9-year-old Marie de Luz, horiz. 8e, Symbolic chart of teacher-pupil link, horiz.

1973, Oct. 24 **Litho.** ***Perf. 13***

1183 A299 1e blue & multi .25 .25
1184 A299 4.50e brown & multi 1.60 .40
1185 A299 5.30e lt blue & multi 1.25 .50
1186 A299 8e green & multi 2.75 1.10
Nos. 1183-1186 (4) 5.85 2.25

Primary state school education, bicent.

Oporto Streetcar, 1910 A300

Designs: 1e, Horse-drawn streetcar, 1872. 3.50e, Double-decker Leyland bus, 1972.

1973, Nov. 7 **Size: 31½x34mm**

1187 A300 1e brn, yel & blk .25 .25
1188 A300 3.50e choc & multi 1.75 1.00

Size: 37½x27mm

Perf. 12½

1189 A300 7.50e buff & multi 2.00 .90
Nos. 1187-1189 (3) 4.00 2.15

Cent. of public transportation in Oporto.

Servicemen's League Emblem — A301

Designs: 2.50e, Sailor, soldier and aviator. 11e, Military medals.

1973, Nov. 28 **Litho.** ***Perf. 13***

1190 A301 1e multi .25 .25
1191 A301 2.50e multi 2.10 .55
1192 A301 11e dk blue & multi 1.75 .45
Nos. 1190-1192 (3) 4.10 1.25

50th anniv. of the Servicemen's League.

Death of Nuño Gonzalves — A302

1973, Dec. 19

1193 A302 1e slate blue & org .30 .25
1194 A302 10e violet brn & org 1.50 .85

600th anniv. of the heroism of Nuno Gonzalves, alcaide of Faria Castle.

Damiao de Gois, by Dürer (?) A303

Designs: 4.50e, Title page of Cronica de Principe D. Joao. 7.50e, Lute and score of Dodecachordon.

1974, Apr. 5 Litho. *Perf. 12*

1195 A303 1e multi .25 .25
1196 A303 4.50e multi 2.40 .45
1197 A303 7.50e multi 1.40 .40
Nos. 1195-1197 (3) 4.05 1.10

400th anniversary of the death of Damiao de Gois (1502-1574), humanist, writer, composer.

Europa Issue

"The Exile," by Soares dos Reis — A304

1974, Apr. 29 Litho. *Perf. 13*

1198 A304 1e multicolored *1.00* .25
1199 A304 4e dk red & multi *6.00* *.50*
1200 A304 6e dk grn & multi *10.00* *1.00*
Nos. 1198-1200 (3) 17.00 1.75

Pattern of Light Emission A305

Designs: 4.50e, Spiral wave radiation pattern. 5.30e, Satellite and earth.

1974, June 26 Litho. *Perf. 14*

1201 A305 1.50e gray olive .25 .25
1202 A305 4.50e dark blue 1.25 .50
1203 A305 5.30e brt rose lilac 2.00 .75
Nos. 1201-1203 (3) 3.50 1.50

Establishment of satellite communications network via Intelsat among Portugal, Angola and Mozambique.

Diffusion of Hertzian Waves A306

Designs (Symbolic): 3.30e, Messages through space. 10e, Navigation help.

1974, Sept. 4 Litho. *Perf. 12*

1204 A306 1.50e multi .25 .25
1205 A306 3.30e multi 2.00 .60
1206 A306 10e multi 1.25 .40
Nos. 1204-1206 (3) 3.50 1.25

Guglielmo Marconi (1874-1937), Italian electrical engineer and inventor.

Buildings Type of 1972-73

Designs: 10c, Ponte do Lima (Roman bridge). 30c, Alcobaça Monastery, interior. 2e, City Hall, Bragança. 4e, New Gate, Braga. 4.50e, Dolmen of Carrazeda. 5e, Roman Temple, Évora. 6e, Leca do Balio Monastery. 7.50e, Almourol Castle.

1974, Sept. 18 Litho. *Perf. 12½*
Size: 22x17½mm

1207 A286 10c multi .25 .25
1208 A286 30c multi .25 .25
1209 A286 2e multi .25 .25
1210 A286 4e multi .55 .25
1211 A286 4.50e multi .90 .25
1212 A286 5e multi 5.75 .25
1213 A286 6e multi 2.10 .25
1214 A286 7.50e multi 1.10 .25
Nos. 1207-1214 (8) 11.15 2.00

"CTT" and year date printed in minute gray multiple rows on back of stamps. Values are for most common dates.

Postilion, Truck and Letter A307

Designs: 2e, Hand holding letter. 3.30e, Packet and steamship. 4.50e, Pigeon and letters. 5.30e, Hand holding sealed letter. 20e, Old and new locomotives.

1974, Oct. 9 Litho. *Perf. 13*

1220 A307 1.50e brown & multi .25 .25
1221 A307 2e multicolored .75 .25
1222 A307 3.30e olive & multi .40 .25
1223 A307 4.50e multicolored 1.40 .45
1224 A307 5.30e multicolored .55 .30
1225 A307 20e multicolored 2.50 .95
a. Souvenir sheet of 6 6.25 6.25
Nos. 1220-1225 (6) 5.85 2.45

Centenary of UPU. No. 1225a contains one each of Nos. 1220-1225, arranged to show a continuous design with a globe in center. Sold for 50e.

Luisa Todi, Singer (1753-1833) A308

Marcos Portugal, Composer (1762-1838) A309

Portuguese Musicians: 2e, Joao Domingos Bomtempo (1775-1842). 2.50e, Carlos Seixas (1704-1742). 3e, Duarte Lobo (1565-1646). 5.30e, Joao de Sousa Carvalho (1745-1798).

1974, Oct. 30 Litho. *Perf. 12*

1226 A308 1.50e brt pink .25 .25
1227 A308 2e vermilion 1.10 .25
1228 A308 2.50e brown .75 .25
1229 A308 3e bluish black 1.25 .30
1230 A308 5.30e slate green .75 .40
1231 A309 11e rose lake .90 .45
Nos. 1226-1231 (6) 5.00 1.90

Coat of Arms of Beja A310

2,000th Anniv. of Beja: 3.50e, Men of Beja in costumes from Roman times to date. 7e, Moorish Arches and view across plains.

1974, Nov. 13

1232 A310 1.50e multi .25 .25
1233 A310 3.50e multi 2.00 .80
1234 A310 7e multi 2.25 .95
Nos. 1232-1234 (3) 4.50 2.00

Annunciation A311

Christmas: 4.50e, Adoration of the Shepherds. 10e, Flight into Egypt. Designs show Portuguese costumes from Nazare township.

1974, Dec. 4 Litho. *Perf. 13*

1235 A311 1.50e red & multi .25 .25
1236 A311 4.50e multicolored 2.50 .45
1237 A311 10e blue & multi 2.00 .60
Nos. 1235-1237 (3) 4.75 1.30

Rainbow and Dove — A312

1974, Dec. 18 *Perf. 12*

1238 A312 1.50e multi .25 .25
1239 A312 3.50e multi 3.25 1.40
1240 A312 5e multi 1.90 .50
Nos. 1238-1240 (3) 5.40 2.15

Armed Forces Movement of Apr. 25, 1974.

Egas Moniz — A313

3.30e, Lobotomy probe and Nobel Prize medal, 1949. 10e, Cerebral angiograph, 1927.

1974, Dec. 27 Engr. *Perf. 11½x12*

1241 A313 1.50e yellow & multi .25 .25
1242 A313 3.30e brown & ocher 1.40 .35
1243 A313 10e gray & ultra 5.00 .60
Nos. 1241-1243 (3) 6.65 1.20

Egas Moniz (1874-1955), brain surgeon, birth centenary.

Soldier as Farmer, Farmer as Soldier — A314

1975, Mar. 21 Litho. *Perf. 12*

1244 A314 1.50e green & multi .25 .25
1245 A314 3e gray & multi 1.90 .50
1246 A314 4.50e multicolored 2.25 .75
Nos. 1244-1246 (3) 4.40 1.50

Cultural progress and citizens' guidance campaign.

Hands and Dove — A315

4.50e, Brown hands reaching for dove. 10e, Dove with olive branch and arms of Portugal.

1975, Apr. 23 Litho. *Perf. 13½*

1247 A315 1.50e red & multi .25 .25
1248 A315 4.50e brown & multi 2.25 .55
1249 A315 10e green & multi 3.25 .80
Nos. 1247-1249 (3) 5.75 1.60

Movement of April 25th, first anniversary. Slogans in Portuguese, French and English printed on back of stamps.

God's Hand Reaching Down — A316

Designs: 4.50e, Jesus' hand holding up cross. 10e, Dove (Holy Spirit) descending.

1975, May 13 Litho. *Perf. 13½*

1250 A316 1.50e multicolored .25 .25
1251 A316 4.50e plum & multi 3.25 .75
1252 A316 10e blue & multi 4.25 .80
Nos. 1250-1252 (3) 7.75 1.80

Holy Year 1975.

Horseman of the Apocalypse, 12th Century A317

Europa: 10e, The Poet Fernando Pessoa, by Almada Negreiros (1893-1970).

1975, May 26

1253 A317 1.50e multi *1.00* .25
1254 A317 10e multi *15.00* *1.25*

Assembly Building A318

1975, June 2 Litho. *Perf. 13½*

1255 A318 2e red, blk & yel .30 .25
1256 A318 20e emer, blk & yel 4.25 .75

Opening of Constituent Assembly.

Hikers — A319

Designs: 4.50e, Campsite on lake. 5.30e, Mobile homes on the road.

1975, Aug. 4 Litho. *Perf. 13½*

1257 A319 2e multicolored .95 .25
1258 A319 4.50e multicolored 2.75 .80
1259 A319 5.30e multicolored 1.60 .75
Nos. 1257-1259 (3) 5.30 1.80

36th Rally of the International Federation of Camping and Caravanning, Santo Andre Lake.

People and Sapling A320

Designs (UN Emblem and): 4.50e, People and dove. 20e, People and grain.

1975, Sept. 17 Litho. *Perf. 13½*

1260 A320 2e green & multi .45 .25
1261 A320 4.50e vio & multi 1.60 .40
1262 A320 20e multicolored 3.50 1.00
Nos. 1260-1262 (3) 5.55 1.65

United Nations, 30th anniversary.

Icarus and Rocket — A321

Designs: 4.50e, Apollo and Soyuz in space. 5.30e, Robert H. Goddard, Robert Esnault-Pelterie, Hermann Oberth and Konstantin Tsiolkovski. 10e, Sputnik, man in space, moon landing module.

1975, Sept. 26 Litho. *Perf. 13½*

Size: 30½x26½mm

1263 A321 2e green & multi .40 .25
1264 A321 4.50e brown & multi 2.00 .60
1265 A321 5.30e lilac & multi .95 .60

Size: 65x28mm

1266 A321 10e blue & multi 3.50 1.00
Nos. 1263-1266 (4) 6.85 2.45

26th Congress of International Astronautical Federation, Lisbon, Sept. 1975.

Land Survey A322

Designs: 8e, Ocean survey. 10e, People of many races and globe.

1975, Nov. 19 Litho. *Perf. 12x12½*

1267 A322 2e ocher & multi .25 .25
1268 A322 8e blue & multi 1.40 .55
1269 A322 10e dk vio & multi 3.00 .85
Nos. 1267-1269 (3) 4.65 1.65

Centenary of Lisbon Geographical Society.

Arch and Trees — A323

Designs: 8e, Plan, pencil and ruler. 10e, Hand, old building and brick tower.

1975, Nov. 28 *Perf. 13½*

1270 A323 2e dk bl & gray .30 .25
1271 A323 8e dk car & gray 3.25 .65
1272 A323 10e ocher & multi 3.50 .90
Nos. 1270-1272 (3) 7.05 1.80

European Architectural Heritage Year 1975.

Nurse and Hospital Ward — A324

Designs (IWY Emblem and): 2e, Farm workers. 3.50e, Secretary. 8e, Factory worker.

1975, Dec. 30 Litho. *Perf. 13½*

1273 A324 50c multicolored .25 .25
1274 A324 2e multicolored 1.50 .25
1275 A324 3.50e multicolored 1.50 .45
1276 A324 8e multicolored 2.00 .90
a. Souvenir sheet of 4 6.00 4.00
Nos. 1273-1276 (4) 5.25 1.85

International Women's Year 1975. No. 1276a contains 4 stamps similar to Nos. 1273-1276 in slightly changed colors. Sold for 25e.

Pen Nib as Plowshare A325

1976, Feb. 6 Litho. *Perf. 12*

1277 A325 3e dk bl & red org .40 .25
1278 A325 20e org, ultra & red 4.00 .90

Portuguese Soc. of Writers, 50th anniv.

Telephones, 1876, 1976 — A326

10.50e, Alexander Graham Bell & telephone.

1976, Mar. 10 Litho. *Perf. 12x12½*

1279 A326 3e yel grn, grn & blk .90 .25
1280 A326 10.50e rose, red & blk 2.50 .65

Centenary of first telephone call by Alexander Graham Bell, March 10, 1876.

Industry and Shipping — A327

1e, Garment, food and wine industries.

1976, Apr. 7 Litho. *Perf. 12½*

1281 A327 50c red brown .25 .25
1282 A327 1e slate .45 .25

Support of national production.

Carved Spoons, Olive Wood A328

Europa: 20e, Gold filigree pendant, silver box and CEPT emblem.

1976, May 3 Litho. *Perf. 12x12½*

1283 A328 3e olive & multi *2.00* .25
1284 A328 20e tan & multi *15.00 1.75*

Stamp Collectors A329

Designs: 7.50e, Stamp exhibition and hand canceler. 10e, Printing and designing stamps.

1976, May 29 Litho. *Perf. 14½*

1285 A329 3e multicolored .25 .25
1286 A329 7.50e multicolored 1.10 .45
1287 A329 10e multicolored 1.60 .50
Nos. 1285-1287 (3) 2.95 1.20

Interphil 76, International Philatelic Exhibition, Philadelphia, Pa., May 29-June 6.

King Ferdinand I — A330

Designs: 5e, Plowshare, farmers chasing off hunters. 10e, Harvest.

1976, July 2 Litho. *Perf. 12*

1288 A330 3e lt bl & multi .25 .25
1289 A330 5e yel grn & multi 1.60 .30
1290 A330 10e multicolored 1.90 .60
a. Souv. sheet of 3, #1288-1290 4.50 4.50
Nos. 1288-1290 (3) 3.75 1.15

Agricultural reform law (compulsory cultivation of uncultivated lands), 600th anniversary. No. 1290a sold for 30e.

Torch Bearer A331

7e, Women's relay race. 10.50e, Olympic flame.

1976, July 16 *Perf. 13½*

1291 A331 3e red & multi .25 .25
1292 A331 7e red & multi 1.50 .90
1293 A331 10.50e red & multi 2.10 .80
Nos. 1291-1293 (3) 3.85 1.95

21st Olympic Games, Montreal, Canada, July 17-Aug. 1.

Farm A332

1976, Sept. 15 Litho. *Perf. 12*

1294 A332 3e shown .55 .25
1295 A332 3e Ship .55 .25
1296 A332 3e City .55 .25
1297 A332 3e Factory 1.10 .25
b. Souv. sheet of 4, #1294-1297 12.50 12.50
Nos. 1294-1297 (4) 2.75 1.00

Fight against illiteracy. #1297b sold for 25e.

Perf. 13½

1294a A332 3e *24.00 .50*
1295a A332 3e *.80 .25*
1296a A332 3e *24.00 .50*
1297a A332 3e *.80 .25*
Nos. 1294a-1297a (4) 49.60 1.50

Azure-winged Magpie A333

Designs: 5e, Lynx. 7e, Portuguese laurel cherry. 10.50e, Little wild carnations.

1976, Sept. 30 Litho. *Perf. 12*

1298 A333 3e multi .25 .25
1299 A333 5e multi 1.10 .25
1300 A333 7e multi 1.25 .65
1301 A333 10.50e multi 1.40 .85
Nos. 1298-1301 (4) 4.00 2.00

Portucale 77, 2nd International Thematic Exhibition, Oporto, Oct. 29-Nov. 6, 1977.

Exhibition Hall — A334

Design: 20e, Symbolic stamp and emblem.

1976, Oct. 9 Litho. *Perf. 13½*

1302 A334 3e bl & multi .35 .25
1303 A334 20e ocher & multi 2.00 1.10
a. Souv. sheet of 2, #1302-1303 3.75 3.75

6th Luso-Brazilian Phil. Exhib., LUBRAPEX 76, Oporto, Oct. 9. #1303a sold for 30e.

Bank Emblem and Family A335

7e, Grain. 15e, Cog wheels.

1976, Oct. 29 *Perf. 12*

1304 A335 3e org & multi .25 .25
1305 A335 7e grn & multi 1.75 .60
1306 A335 15e bl & multi 2.25 .85
Nos. 1304-1306 (3) 4.25 1.70

Trust Fund Bank centenary.

Sheep Grazing on Marsh A336

Designs: 3e, Drainage ditches. 5e, Fish in water. 10e, Ducks flying over marsh.

1976, Nov. 24 Litho. *Perf. 14*

1307 A336 1e multicolored .25 .25
1308 A336 3e multicolored .90 .25
1309 A336 5e multicolored 1.50 .30
1310 A336 10e multicolored 2.75 .75
Nos. 1307-1310 (4) 5.40 1.55

Protection of wetlands.

"Liberty" — A337

1976, Nov. 30 Litho. *Perf. 13½*

1311 A337 3e gray, grn & ver .65 .25

Constitution of 1976.

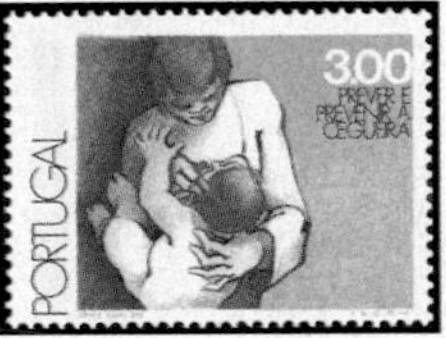

Mother Examining Child's Eyes A338

Designs: 5e, Welder with goggles. 10.50e, Blind woman reading Braille.

1976, Dec. 13

1312 A338 3e multicolored .25 .25
1313 A338 5e multicolored 2.00 .25
1314 A338 10.50e multicolored 1.60 .80
Nos. 1312-1314 (3) 3.85 1.30

World Health Day and campaign against blindness.

Hydroelectric Energy — A339

Abstract Designs: 4e, Fossil fuels. 5e, Geothermal energy. 10e, Wind power. 15e, Solar energy.

1976, Dec. 30

1315 A339 1e multicolored .25 .25
1316 A339 4e multicolored .55 .25
1317 A339 5e multicolored .70 .25
1318 A339 10e multicolored 1.50 .60
1319 A339 15e multicolored 2.40 1.10
Nos. 1315-1319 (5) 5.40 2.45

Sources of energy.

Map of Council of Europe Members A340

1977, Jan. 28 Litho. *Perf. 12*

1320 A340 8.50e multicolored 1.25 .95
1321 A340 10e multicolored 1.25 .85

Portugal's joining Council of Europe.

Alcoholic and Bottle — A341

Designs (Bottle and): 5e, Symbolic figure of broken life. 15e, Bars blotting out the sun.

1977, Feb. 4 ***Perf. 13***

1322 A341 3e multicolored .25 .25
1323 A341 5e ocher & multi .95 .30
1324 A341 15e org & multi 2.25 .95
Nos. 1322-1324 (3) 3.45 1.50

Anti-alcoholism Day and 10th anniversary of Portuguese Anti-alcoholism Society.

Trees Tapped for Resin — A342

Designs: 4e, Trees stripped for cork. 7e, Trees and logs. 15e, Trees at seashore as windbreakers.

1977, Mar. 21 **Litho.** ***Perf. 13½***

1325 A342 1e multicolored .25 .25
1326 A342 4e multicolored .70 .25
1327 A342 7e multicolored 1.50 .95
1328 A342 15e multicolored 1.50 .95
Nos. 1325-1328 (4) 3.95 2.40

Forests, a natural resource.

"Suffering" A343

6e, Man exercising. 10e, Group exercising. All designs include emblems of WHO & Portuguese Institute for Rheumatology.

1977, Apr. 13 **Litho.** ***Perf. 12x12½***

1329 A343 4e blk, brn & ocher .25 .25
1330 A343 6e blk, bl & vio 1.10 .75
1331 A343 10e blk, pur & red 1.00 .50
Nos. 1329-1331 (3) 2.35 1.50

International Rheumatism Year.

Southern Plains Landscape A344

Europa: 8.50e, Northern mountain valley.

1977, May 2

1332 A344 4e multi *.75* .25
1333 A344 8.50e multi *3.25* .60
a. Min. sheet, 3 each #1332-1333 *15.00* *14.00*

Pope John XXI Enthroned A345

Petrus Hispanus, the Physician A346

1977, May 20 **Litho.** ***Perf. 13½***

1334 A345 4e multicolored .25 .25
1335 A346 15e multicolored .60 .35

Pope John XXI (Petrus Hispanus), only Pope of Portuguese descent, 7th death centenary.

Compass Rose, Camoens Quotation A347

1977, June 8 ***Perf. 12***

1336 A347 4e multi .25 .25
1337 A347 8.50e multi 1.10 .80

Camoens Day and to honor Portuguese overseas communities.

Student, Computer and Book — A348

Designs (Book and): No. 1339, Folk dancers, flutist and boat. No. 1340, Tractor drivers. No. 1341, Atom and people.

1977, July 20 **Litho.** ***Perf. 12x12½***

1338 A348 4e multicolored .40 .25
1339 A348 4e multicolored .40 .25
1340 A348 4e multicolored .40 .25
1341 A348 4e multicolored .40 .25
a. Souv. sheet of 4, #1338-1341 4.50 4.50
Nos. 1338-1341 (4) 1.60 1.00

Continual education. #1341a sold for 20e.

Pyrites, Copper, Chemical Industry A349

Designs: 5e, Marble, statue, public buildings. 10e, Iron ore, girders, crane. 20e, Uranium ore, atomic diagram.

1977, Oct. 4 **Litho.** ***Perf. 12x11½***

1342 A349 4e multicolored .25 .25
1343 A349 5e multicolored .95 .25
1344 A349 10e multicolored 1.00 .35
1345 A349 20e multicolored 2.40 .90
Nos. 1342-1345 (4) 4.60 1.75

Natural resources from the subsoil.

Alexandre Herculano — A350

1977, Oct. 19 **Engr.** ***Perf. 12x11½***

1346 A350 4e multicolored .25 .25
1347 A350 15e multicolored 1.60 .50

Alexandre Herculano de Carvalho Araujo (1810-1877), historian, novelist, death centenary.

Maria Pia Bridge A351

4e, Arrival of first train, ceramic panel by Jorge Colaco, St. Bento railroad station.

1977, Nov. 4 **Litho.** ***Perf. 12x11½***

1348 A351 4e multicolored .25 .25
1349 A351 10e multicolored 2.25 1.25

Centenary of extension of railroad across Douro River.

Poveiro Bark A352

Coastal Fishing Boats: 3e, Do Mar bark. 4e, Nazaré bark. 7e, Algarve skiff. 10e, Xavega bark. 15e, Bateira de Buarcos.

1977, Nov. 19 ***Perf. 12***

1350 A352 2e multicolored .40 .25
1351 A352 3e multicolored .25 .25
1352 A352 4e multicolored .25 .25
1353 A352 7e multicolored .50 .25
1354 A352 10e multicolored .80 .40
1355 A352 15e multicolored 1.25 .65
a. Souv. sheet of 6, #1350-1355 4.25 4.25
Nos. 1350-1355 (6) 3.45 2.05

PORTUCALE 77, 2nd International Topical Exhibition. Oporto, Nov. 19-20. No. 1355a sold for 60e.

Nativity A353

Children's Drawings: 7e, Nativity. 10e, Holy Family, vert. 20e, Star and Christ Child, vert.

Perf. 12x11½, 11½x12

1977, Dec. 12 **Litho.**

1356 A353 4e multicolored .25 .25
1357 A353 7e multicolored 1.10 .30
1358 A353 10e multicolored 1.25 .45
1359 A353 20e multicolored 2.25 .80
Nos. 1356-1359 (4) 4.85 1.80

Christmas 1977.

Old Desk and Computer — A354

Designs: Work tools, old and new — 50c, Medical. 1e, Household. 2e, Communications. 3e, Garment making. 4e, Office. 5e, Fishing craft. 5.50e, Weaving. 6e, Plows. 6.50e, Aviation. 7e, Printing. 8e, Carpentry. 8.50e, Potter's wheel. 9e, Photography. 10e, Saws. 12.50e, Compasses ('83). 16e, Mail processing ('83). 20e, Construction. 30e, Steel industry. 40e, Transportation. 50e, Chemistry. 100e, Shipbuilding. 250e, Telescopes.

1978-83 **Litho.** ***Perf. 12½***

Size: 22x17mm

1360 A354 50c multi .25 .25
1361 A354 1e multi .25 .25
1362 A354 2e multi .25 .25
1363 A354 3e multi .25 .25
1364 A354 4e multi .25 .25
1365 A354 5e multi .25 .25
1366 A354 5.50e multi .25 .25
1367 A354 6e multi .25 .25
1368 A354 6.50e multi .25 .25
1369 A354 7e multi .25 .25
1370 A354 8e multi .25 .25
1371 A354 8.50e multi .25 .25
1372 A354 9e multi .25 .25
1373 A354 10e multi .25 .25
1373A A354 12.50e multi 1.25 .25
1373B A354 16e multi 1.50 .25

Perf. 13½

Size: 31x22mm

1374 A354 20e multi .55 .25
1375 A354 30e multi .65 .30
a. Incomplete arch 1.00 .30
1376 A354 40e multi .75 .25
1377 A354 50e multi 1.10 .25
1378 A354 100e multi 1.75 .30
1379 A354 250e multi 4.25 .60
Nos. 1360-1379 (22) 15.30 5.95

Red Mediterranean Soil — A355

Designs: 5e, Stone formation. 10e, Alluvial soil. 20e, Black soil.

1978, Mar. 6 **Litho.** ***Perf. 12***

1380 A355 4e multicolored .25 .25
1381 A355 5e multicolored .50 .25
1382 A355 10e multicolored 1.00 .45
1383 A355 20e multicolored 2.50 .60
Nos. 1380-1383 (4) 4.25 1.55

Soil, a natural resource.

Street Crossing A356

Designs: 2e, Motorcyclist. 2.50e, Children in back seat of car. 5e, Hands holding steering wheel. 9e, Driving on country road. 12.50e, "Avoid drinking and driving."

1978, Apr. 19 **Litho.** ***Perf. 12***

1384 A356 1e multi .25 .25
1385 A356 2e multi .30 .25
1386 A356 2.50e multi .70 .25
1387 A356 5e multi 1.40 .25
1388 A356 9e multi 2.00 .50
1389 A356 12.50e multi 3.00 1.25
Nos. 1384-1389 (6) 7.65 2.75

Road safety campaign.

Roman Tower, Belmonte A357

Europa: 40e, Belém Monastery of Hieronymite monks (inside).

1978, May 2

1390 A357 10e multicolored *2.00* *.25*
1391 A357 40e multicolored *4.00* *.75*
a. Souv. sheet, 2 each #1390-1391 *15.00* *12.00*

No. 1391a sold for 120e.

Trajan's Bridge — A358

Roman Tablet from Bridge — A359

1978, June 14 **Litho.** ***Perf. 13½***

1392 A358 5e multicolored .40 .25
1393 A359 20e multicolored 2.50 .80

1900th anniv. of Chaves (Aquae Flaviae).

Running
A360

1978, July 24 Litho. *Perf. 12*

1394	A360	5e	shown	.25	.25
1395	A360	10e	Bicycling	.40	.25
1396	A360	12.50e	Watersport	.95	.50
1397	A360	15e	Soccer	.95	.65
			Nos. 1394-1397 (4)	2.55	1.65

Sport for all the people.

Pedro Nunes
A361

Design: 20e, "Nonio" navigational instrument and diagram from "Tratado da Rumaçao do Globo."

1978, Aug. 9 Litho. *Perf. 12x11½*

1398	A361	5e	multicolored	.25	.25
1399	A361	20e	multicolored	1.40	.35

Nunes (1502-78), navigator and cosmographer.

Trawler, Frozen Fish Processing, Can of Sardines — A362

Fishing Industry: 9e, Deep-sea trawler, loading and unloading at dock. 12.50e, Trawler with radar and instruction in use of radar. 15e, Trawler with echo-sounding equipment, microscope and test tubes.

1978, Sept. 16 Litho. *Perf. 12x11½*

1400	A362	5e	multi	.25	.25
1401	A362	9e	multi	.65	.25
1402	A362	12.50e	multi	1.25	.70
1403	A362	15e	multi	1.90	.90
			Nos. 1400-1403 (4)	4.05	2.10

Natural resources.

Postrider
A363

Designs: No. 1405, Carrier pigeon. No. 1406, Envelopes. No. 1407, Pen.

1978, Oct. 30 Litho. *Perf. 12*

1404	A363	5e	yel & multi	.35	.25
1405	A363	5e	bl gray & multi	.35	.25
1406	A363	5e	grn & multi	.35	.25
1407	A363	5e	red & multi	.35	.25
			Nos. 1404-1407 (4)	1.40	1.00

Introduction of Postal Code.

Human Figure, Flame Emblem
A364

Design: 40e, Human figure pointing the way and flame emblem.

1978, Dec. 7 Litho. *Perf. 12*

1408	A364	14e	multicolored	.65	.30
1409	A364	40e	multicolored	1.90	.90
a.			Souv. sheet, 2 ea #1408-1409	6.25	6.25

Universal Declaration of Human Rights, 30th anniv. and 25th anniv. of European Declaration.

Sebastiao Magalhaes Lima — A365

1978, Dec. 7

1410	A365	5e	multicolored	.25	.25

Sebastiao Magalhaes Lima (1850-1928), lawyer, journalist, statesman.

Mail Boxes and Scale
A366

Designs: 5e, Telegraph and condenser lens. 10e, Portugal Nos. 2-3 and postal card printing press, 1879. 14e, Book and bookcases, 1879, 1979.

1978, Dec. 20

1411	A366	4e	multicolored	.30	.25
1412	A366	5e	multicolored	.30	.25
1413	A366	10e	multicolored	1.10	.25
1414	A366	14e	multicolored	2.50	1.25
a.			Souv. sheet of 4, #1411-1414	5.50	5.50
			Nos. 1411-1414 (4)	4.20	2.00

Centenary of Postal Museum and Postal Library; 125th anniversary of Portuguese stamps (10e). No. 1414a sold for 40e.

Emigrant at Railroad Station
A367

Designs: 14e, Farewell at airport. 17e, Emigrant greeting child at railroad station.

1979, Feb. 21 Litho. *Perf. 12*

1415	A367	5e	multicolored	.50	.25
1416	A367	14e	multicolored	1.00	.35
1417	A367	17e	multicolored	1.50	.80
			Nos. 1415-1417 (3)	3.00	1.40

Portuguese emigration.

Automobile Traffic — A368

Combat noise pollution: 5e, Pneumatic drill. 14e, Man with bull horn.

1979, Mar. 14 *Perf. 13½*

1418	A368	4e	multicolored	.25	.25
1419	A368	5e	multicolored	.70	.25
1420	A368	14e	multicolored	1.60	.50
			Nos. 1418-1420 (3)	2.55	1.00

NATO Emblem
A369

1979, Apr. 4 Litho. *Perf. 12*

1421	A369	5e	multicolored	.30	.25
1422	A369	50e	multicolored	2.75	1.60
a.			Souv. sheet, 2 ea #1421-1422	6.50	6.50

NATO, 30th anniv.

Mail Delivery, 16th Century
A370

Europa: 40e, Mail delivery, 19th century.

1979, Apr. 30 Litho. *Perf. 12*

1423	A370	14e	multicolored	*.75*	*.30*
1424	A370	40e	multicolored	*2.00*	*1.60*
a.			Souv. sheet, 2 ea #1423-1424	*10.00*	*6.00*

Mother, Infant, Dove
A371

Designs (IYC Emblem and): 5.50e, Children playing ball. 10e, Child in nursery school. 14e, Black and white boys.

1979, June 1 Litho. *Perf. 12x12½*

1425	A371	5.50e	multi	.25	.25
1426	A371	6.50e	multi	.30	.25
1427	A371	10e	multi	.45	.25
1428	A371	14e	multi	1.00	.65
a.			Souv. sheet of 4, #1425-1428	3.75	3.75
			Nos. 1425-1428 (4)	2.00	1.40

Intl. Year of the Child. No. 1428a sold for 40e.

Salute to the Flag — A372

1979, June 8

1429	A372	6.50e	multicolored	.35	.25
a.			Souvenir sheet of 9	4.50	4.50

Portuguese Day.

Pregnant Woman
A373

Designs: 17e, Boy sitting in a cage. 20e, Face, and hands using hammer.

1979, June 6 Litho. *Perf. 12x12½*

1430	A373	6.50e	multi	.35	.25
1431	A373	17e	multi	.80	.50
1432	A373	20e	multi	1.10	.60
			Nos. 1430-1432 (3)	2.25	1.35

Help for the mentally retarded.

Children Reading Book, UNESCO Emblem
A374

17e, Teaching deaf child, and UNESCO emblem.

1979, June 25

1433	A374	6.50e	multi	.35	.25
1434	A374	17e	multi	1.75	.70

Intl. Bureau of Education, 50th anniv.

Water Cart, Brasiliana '79 Emblem
A375

Brasiliana '79 Philatelic Exhibition: 5.50e, Wine sledge. 6.50e, Wine cart. 16e, Covered cart. 19e, Mogadouro cart. 20e, Sand cart.

1979, Sept. 15 Litho. *Perf. 12*

1435	A375	2.50e	multi	.25	.25
1436	A375	5.50e	multi	.25	.25
1437	A375	6.50e	multi	.50	.25
1438	A375	16e	multi	1.00	.55
1439	A375	19e	multi	1.25	.75
1440	A375	20e	multi	1.50	.30
			Nos. 1435-1440 (6)	4.75	2.35

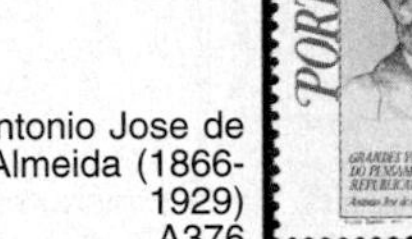

Antonio Jose de Almeida (1866-1929)
A376

Republican Leaders: 6.50e, Afonso Costa (1871-1937). 10e, Teofilo Braga (1843-1924). 16e, Bernardino Machado (1851-1944). 19.50e, Joao Chagas (1863-1925). 20e, Elias Garcia (1830-1891).

1979, Oct. 4 *Perf. 12½x12*

1441	A376	5.50e	multi	.35	.25
1442	A376	6.50e	multi	.35	.25
1443	A376	10e	multi	.55	.25
1444	A376	16e	multi	.95	.45
1445	A376	19.50e	multi	1.60	.80
1446	A376	20e	multi	1.40	.35
			Nos. 1441-1446 (6)	5.20	2.35

See Nos. 1454-1459.

Red Cross and Family
A377

20e, Doctor examining elderly man.

1979, Oct. 26 *Perf. 12x12½*

1447	A377	6.50e	multi	.35	.25
1448	A377	20e	multi	1.40	.40

National Health Service Campaign.

Holy Family, 17th Century Mosaic
A378

Mosaics, Lisbon Tile Museum: 6.50e, Nativity, 16th century. 16e, Flight into Egypt, 18th century.

1979, Dec. 5 Litho. *Perf. 12x12½*

1449	A378	5.50e	multi	.40	.25
1450	A378	6.50e	multi	.40	.25
1451	A378	16e	multi	1.10	.70
			Nos. 1449-1451 (3)	1.90	1.20

Christmas 1979.

Rotary International, 75th Anniversary — A379

1980, Feb. 22 *Perf. 12x11½*
1452 A379 16e shown 1.00 .45
1453 A379 50e Emblem, torch 2.75 1.25

Portrait Type of 1979

Leaders of the Republican Movement: 3.50e, Alvaro de Castro (1878-1928). 5.50e, Antonio Sergio (1883-1969). 6.50e, Norton de Matos (1867-1955). 11e, Jaime Cortesao (1884-1960). 16e, Teixeira Gomes (1860-1941). 20e, Jose Domingues dos Santos (1885-1958). Nos. 1454-1459 horizontal.

1980, Mar. 19
1454 A376 3.50e multi .25 .25
1455 A376 5.50e multi .30 .25
1456 A376 6.50e multi .30 .25
1457 A376 11e multi 1.50 .75
1458 A376 16e multi 1.00 .50
1459 A376 20e multi 1.00 .30
Nos. 1454-1459 (6) 4.35 2.30

Europa Issue

Serpa Pinto (1864-1900), Explorer of Africa A380

60e, Vasco da Gama.

1980, Apr. 14
1460 A380 16e shown *1.00 .30*
1461 A380 60e multicolored *3.50 .75*
a. Souv. sheet, 2 each #1460-1461 *6.50 4.50*

Barn Owl A381

1980, May 6 Litho. *Perf. 12x11½*
1462 A381 6.50e shown .30 .25
1463 A381 16e Red fox .80 .30
1464 A381 19.50e Timber wolf 1.10 .40
1465 A381 20e Golden eagle 1.10 .35
a. Souv. sheet of 4, #1462-1465 3.75 3.75
Nos. 1462-1465 (4) 3.30 1.30

European Campaign for the Protection of Species and their Habitat (Lisbon Zoo animals); London 1980 International Stamp Exhibition, May 6-14.

Luiz Camoens (1524-80) A382

Lithographed & Engraved

1980, June 9 *Perf. 11½x12*
1466 A382 6.50e multi + label .50 .25
1467 A382 20e multi + label 1.10 .75

Mendes Pinto and Chinese Men A383

1980, June 30 Litho. *Perf. 12x11½*
1468 A383 6.50e shown .35 .25
1469 A383 10e Battle at sea 1.00 .40

A Peregrinacao (The Peregrination,) by Fernao Mendes Pinto (1509-1583), written in 1580, published in 1614.

St. Vincent and Old Lisbon A384

Designs: 8e, Lantern Tower, Evora Cathedral. 11e, Jesus with top hat, Miranda do Douro Cathedral, and mountain. 16e, Our Lady of the Milk, Braga Cathedral, and Canicada Dam. 19.50e, Pulpit, Santa Cruz Monastery, Coimbra, and Aveiro River. 20e, Algarve chimney, and Rocha Beach.

1980, Sept. 17 Litho. *Perf. 12x12½*
1470 A384 6.50e multi .30 .25
1471 A384 8e multi .35 .25
1472 A384 11e multi .80 .35
1473 A384 16e multi 1.10 .55
1474 A384 19.50e multi 1.50 .65
1475 A384 20e multi 1.25 .40
Nos. 1470-1475 (6) 5.30 2.45

World Tourism Conf., Manila, Sept. 27.

Caravel, Lubrapex '80 Emblem A385

8e, Three-master Nau. 16e, Galleon. 19.50e, Paddle steam.

1980, Oct. 18 Litho. *Perf. 12x11½*
1476 A385 6.50e shown .35 .25
1477 A385 8e multicolored .70 .30
1478 A385 16e multicolored 1.40 .45
1479 A385 19.50e multicolored 1.90 .50
a. Souv. sheet of 4, #1476-1479 6.50 6.50
Nos. 1476-1479 (4) 4.35 1.50

Lubrapex '80 Stamp Exhib., Lisbon, Oct. 18-26.

Car Emitting Gas Fumes A386

1980, Oct. 31
1480 A386 6.50e Light bulbs .30 .25
1481 A386 16e shown 2.00 .55

Energy conservation.

Student, School and Sextant A387

1980, Dec. 19 Litho. *Perf. 12x11½*
1482 A387 6.50e Founder, book, emblem .30 .25
1483 A387 19.50e shown 1.40 .50

Lisbon Academy of Science bicentennial.

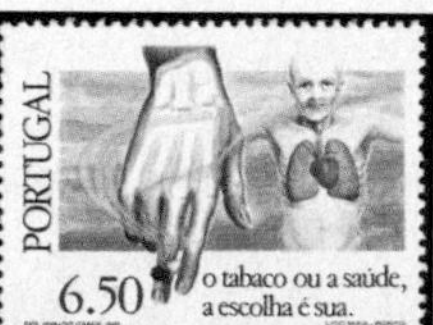

Man with Diseased Heart and Lungs, Hand Holding Cigarette A388

19.50e, Healthy man rejecting cigarette.

1980, Dec. 19 *Perf. 13½*
1484 A388 6.50e shown .30 .25
1485 A388 19.50e multicolored 1.75 .80

Anti-smoking campaign.

Census Form and Houses A389

1981, Jan. 28 Litho. *Perf. 13½*
1486 A389 6.50e Form, head .30 .25
1487 A389 16e shown 1.40 .95

Fragata on Tejo River A390

8.50e, Rabelo, Douro River. 10e, Moliceiro, Aveiro River. 16e, Barco, Lima River. 19.50e, Carocho, Minho River. 20e, Varino, Tejo River.

1981, Feb. 23 Litho. *Perf. 12x12½*
1488 A390 8e multicolored .25 .25
1489 A390 8.50e multicolored .25 .25
1490 A390 10e multicolored .50 .25
1491 A390 16e multicolored .70 .45
1492 A390 19.50e multicolored .85 .45
1493 A390 20e multicolored .85 .35
Nos. 1488-1493 (6) 3.40 2.00

Rajola Tile, Valencia, 15th Century A391

Designs: No. 1495, Moresque tile, Coimbra 16th cent. No. 1496, Arms of Duke of Braganza, 1510. No. 1497, Pisanos design, 1595.

1981 Litho. *Perf. 11½x12*
1494 A391 8.50e multi .75 .25
a. Miniature sheet of 6 5.00 5.00
1495 A391 8.50e multi .75 .25
a. Miniature sheet of 6 4.50 4.50
1496 A391 8.50e multi .75 .25
a. Miniature sheet of 6 4.50 4.50
1497 A391 8.50e multi .75 .25
a. Miniature sheet of 6 4.50 4.50
b. Souv. sheet of 4, #1494-1497 5.00 5.00
Nos. 1494-1497 (4) 3.00 1.00

Issued: #1494, 3/16; #1495, 6/13; #1496, 8/28; #1497, 12/16. See #1528-1531, 1563-1566, 1593-1596, 1617-1620.

Perdigueiro A392

7e, Cao de agua. 8.50e, Serra de aires. 22e, Podengo. 22.50e, Castro laboreiro. 33.50e, Serra da estrela.

1981, Mar. 16 *Perf. 12*
1498 A392 7e multi 3.00 .25
1499 A392 8.50e multi .45 .25
1500 A392 15e shown .80 .25
1501 A392 22e multi 1.10 .65
1502 A392 25.50e multi 1.75 1.00
1503 A392 33.50e multi 2.25 .65
Nos. 1498-1503 (6) 9.35 3.05

Portuguese Kennel Club, 50th anniversary.

Workers and Rainbow A393

25.50e, Rainbow, demonstration.

1981, Apr. 30 Litho. *Perf. 12x12½*
1504 A393 8.50e shown .30 .25
1505 A393 25.50e multi 1.40 .85

International Workers' Day.

Europa Issue

Dancer in National Costume — A394

48e, Painted boat, horiz.

1981, May 11 *Perf. 13½*
1506 A394 22e shown *1.75 .50*
1507 A394 48e multi *2.00 1.25*
a. Souv. sheet, 2 ea #1506-1507 *6.00 5.00*

St. Anthony Writing A395

St. Anthony of Lisbon, 750th Anniversary of Death: 70e, Blessing people.

1981, June 13 *Perf. 12x11½*
1508 A395 8.50e multi .50 .25
1509 A395 70e multi 3.00 1.75

500th Anniv. of King Joao II A396

27e, Joao II leading army.

1981, Aug. 28 *Perf. 12x11½*
1510 A396 8.50e shown .45 .25
1511 A396 27e multi 2.00 .95

125th Anniv. of Portuguese Railroads — A397

Designs: Locomotives — 8.50e, Dom Luis, 1862. 19e, Pacific 500, 1925. 27e, ALCO 1500, 1948. 33.50e, BB 2600 ALSTHOM, '74.

1981, Oct. 28 Litho. *Perf. 12x11½*
1512 A397 8.50e multi 1.00 .25
1513 A397 19e multi 2.00 .90
1514 A397 27e multi 2.50 1.00
1515 A397 33.50e multi 2.75 .85
Nos. 1512-1515 (4) 8.25 3.00

Pearier Pump Fire Engine, 1856 — A398

8.50e, Ford, 1927. 27e, Renault, 1914. 33.50e, Snorkel, Ford 1978.

1981, Nov. 18 Litho. *Perf. 12x12½*
1516 A398 7e shown .45 .25
1517 A398 8.50e multi .65 .25
1518 A398 27e multi 2.25 .95
1519 A398 33.50e multi 2.90 .90
Nos. 1516-1519 (4) 6.25 2.35

A399

Christmas: Clay creches.

1981, Dec. 16 ***Perf. 12½x12***
1520 A399 7e multi .55 .30
1521 A399 8.50e multi .75 .25
1522 A399 27e multi 2.25 1.40
Nos. 1520-1522 (3) 3.55 1.95

A400

8.50e, With animals. 27e, Building church.

1982, Jan. 20 Litho. ***Perf. 12½x12***
1523 A400 8.50e multi .40 .25
1524 A400 27e multi 2.00 1.40

800th birth anniv. of St. Francis of Assisi.

Centenary of Figueira da Foz A401

10e, St. Catherine Fort. 19e, Tagus Bridge, ships.

1982, Feb. 24 Litho. ***Perf. 13½***
1525 A401 10e multi .55 .25
1526 A401 19e multi 1.60 .85

25th Anniv. of European Economic Community A402

1982, Feb. 24 ***Perf. 12x11½***
1527 A402 27e multi 1.25 .65
a. Souvenir sheet of 4 5.00 5.00

Tile Type of 1981

Designs: No. 1528, Italo-Flemish pattern, 17th cent. No. 1529, Oriental fabric pattern altar frontal, 17th cent. No. 1530, Greek cross, 1630-1640. No. 1531, Blue and white design, Mother of God Convent, Lisbon, 1670.

1982 Litho. ***Perf. 12x11½***
1528 A391 10e multi .75 .25
a. Miniature sheet of 6 5.00 5.00
1529 A391 10e multi .75 .25
a. Miniature sheet of 6 4.50 4.50
1530 A391 10e multi .75 .25
a. Miniature sheet of 6 4.50 4.50
1531 A391 10e red & blue .75 .25
a. Miniature sheet of 6 4.50 4.50
b. Souv. sheet of 4, #1528-1531 4.50 4.50
Nos. 1528-1531 (4) 3.00 1.00

Issued: No. 1528, Mar. 24; No. 1529, June 11; No. 1530, Sept. 22; No. 1531, Dec. 15.

A403

Major Sporting Events of 1982: 27e, Lisbon Sail. 33.50e, 25th Roller-hockey Championships, Lisbon and Barcelos, May 1-16. 50e, Intl. 470 Class World Championships, Cascais Bay. 75e, Espana '82 World Cup Soccer.

1982, Mar. 24 ***Perf. 12x12½***
1532 A403 27e multi 1.50 .80
1533 A403 33.50e multi 2.00 1.10
1534 A403 50e multi 3.00 1.25
1535 A403 75e multi 4.75 1.50
Nos. 1532-1535 (4) 11.25 4.65

A404

1982, Apr. 14 Litho. ***Perf. 11½x12***
1536 A404 10e Phone, 1882 .45 .25
1537 A404 27e 1887 1.25 1.00

Telephone centenary.

Europa 1982 A405

Embassy of King Manuel to Pope Leo X, 1514.

1982, May 3 ***Perf. 12x11½***
1538 A405 33.50e multi *1.50 .75*
a. *Miniature sheet of 4* *8.00 8.00*

Visit of Pope John Paul II — A406

Designs: Pope John Paul and cathedrals.

1982, May 13 ***Perf. 14***
1539 A406 10e Fatima .45 .25
1540 A406 27e Sameiro 2.00 1.10
1541 A406 33.50e Lisbon 2.25 1.00
a. Min. sheet, 2 each #1539-1541 9.00 9.00
Nos. 1539-1541 (3) 4.70 2.35

Tejo Estuary Nature Reserve Birds — A407

10e, Dunlin. 19e, Red-crested pochard. 27e, Greater flamingo. 33.50e, Black-winged stilt.

1982, June 11 ***Perf. 11½x12***
1542 A407 10e multi .50 .25
1543 A407 19e multi 1.60 .55
1544 A407 27e multi 2.00 .80
1545 A407 33.50e multi 2.10 .90
Nos. 1542-1545 (4) 6.20 2.50

PHILEXFRANCE '82 Stamp Exhibition, Paris, June 11-21.

TB Bacillus Centenary — A408

1982, July 27 ***Perf. 12x11½***
1546 A408 27e Koch 1.50 1.00
1547 A408 33.50e Virus, lungs 1.60 1.10

Don't Drink and Drive! — A409

1982, Sept. 22 ***Perf. 12***
1548 A409 10e multicolored .55 .25

Boeing 747 A410

Lubrapex '82 Stamp Exhibition (Historic Flights): 10e, South Atlantic crossing, 1922. 19e, South Atlantic night crossing, 1927. 33.50e, Lisbon-Rio de Janeiro discount fare flights, 1960-1967. 50e, Portugal-Brazil service, 10th anniv.

1982, Oct. 15 ***Perf. 12x11½***
1549 A410 10e Fairey III D MK2 .30 .25
1550 A410 19e Dornier DO 1.25 .70
1551 A410 33.50e DC-7C 1.90 .70
1552 A410 50e shown 2.00 1.00
a. Souv. sheet of 4, #1549-1552 6.00 6.00
Nos. 1549-1552 (4) 5.45 2.65

Marques de Pombal, Statesman, 200th Anniv. of Death — A411

1982, Nov. 24 Litho. ***Perf. 12x11½***
1553 A411 10e multicolored .50 .25

75th Anniv. of Port Authority of Lisbon — A412

1983, Jan. 5 ***Perf. 12½***
1554 A412 10e Ships .50 .25

French Alliance Centenary A413

1983, Jan. 5 ***Perf. 12x11½***
1555 A413 27e multicolored 1.50 .70

Export Effort A414

1983, Jan. 28
1556 A414 10e multicolored .50 .25

World Communications Year — A415

1983, Feb. 23 Litho. ***Perf. 11½x12***
1557 A415 10e blue & multi .50 .25
1558 A415 33.50e lt brown & multi 1.60 1.00

Naval Uniforms and Ships — A416

12.50e, Midshipman, 1782, Vasco da Gama. 25e, Sailor, 1845, Estefania. 30e, Sergeant, 1900, Adamastor. 37.50e, Midshipman, 1892, Comandante Joao Belo

1983, Feb. 23 ***Perf. 13½***
1559 A416 12.50e multi .55 .25
1560 A416 25e multi 1.40 .35
1561 A416 30e multi 1.60 .50
1562 A416 37.50e multi 2.00 .70
a. Bklt. pane of 4, #1559-1562 5.75
Nos. 1559-1562 (4) 5.55 1.80

See Nos. 1589-1592.

Tile Type of 1981

No. 1563, Hunting scene, 1680. No. 1564, Birds, 18th cent. No. 1565, Flowers and Birds, 18th cent. No. 1566, Figurative tile, 18th cent.

1983 ***Perf. 12x11½***
1563 A391 12.50e multi .80 .25
a. Miniature sheet of 6 5.25 5.25
1564 A391 12.50e multi .80 .25
a. Miniature sheet of 6 5.00 5.00
1565 A391 12.50e multi .80 .25
a. Miniature sheet of 6 5.00 5.00
1566 A391 12.50e multi .80 .25
a. Miniature sheet of 6 5.00 5.00
b. Souv. sheet of 4, #1563-1566 4.50 4.50
Nos. 1563-1566 (4) 3.20 1.00

Issued: No. 1563, Mar. 16; No. 1564, June 16; No. 1565, Oct. 19; No. 1566, Nov. 23.

17th European Arts and Sciences Exhibition, Lisbon — A417

Portuguese Discoveries and Renaissance Europe: 11e, Helmet, 16th cent. 12.50e, Astrolabe. 25e, Ships, Flemish tapestry. 30e, Column capital, 12th cent. 37.50e, Hour glass. 40e, Chinese panel painting.

1983, Apr. 6
1567 A417 11e multi .55 .25
1568 A417 12.50e multi .75 .25
1569 A417 25e multi 1.25 .55
1570 A417 30e multi 1.50 .55
1571 A417 37.50e multi 2.00 .85
1572 A417 40e multi 2.00 .80
a. Souv. sheet of 6, #1567-1572 11.00 11.00
Nos. 1567-1572 (6) 8.05 3.25

Europa Issue

Antonio Egas Moniz (1874-1955), Cerebral Angiography and Pre-frontal Leucotomy Pioneer — A418

1983, May 5 Litho. ***Perf. 12½***

1573 A418 37.50e multi 2.00 .60
a. Souvenir sheet of 4 *8.00 8.00*

European Conference of Ministers of Transport — A419

1983, May 16

1574 A419 30e multi 2.00 .65

Endangered Sea Mammals — A420

1983, July 29 Litho. ***Perf. 12x11½***

1575 A420 12.50e Sea wolf .85 .25
1576 A420 30e Dolphin 2.00 .45
1577 A420 37.50e Killer whale 2.75 1.10
1578 A420 80e Humpback whale 4.50 1.00
a. Souv. sheet of 4, #1575-1578 12.00 12.00
Nos. 1575-1578 (4) 10.10 2.80

BRASILIANA '83 Intl. Stamp Exhibition, Rio de Janeiro, July 29-Aug. 7.

600th Anniv. of Revolution of 1383 — A421

12.50e, Death of Joao Fernandes Andeiro. 30e, Rebellion.

1983, Sept. 14 ***Perf. 13½***

1579 A421 12.50e multi .75 .25
1580 A421 30e multi 2.50 1.10

First Manned Balloon Flight A422

Designs: 16e, Bartolomeu Lourenco de Gusmao, Passarola flying machine. 51e, Montgolfier Balloon, first flight.

1983, Nov. 9 Litho. ***Perf. 12x11½***

1581 A422 16e multicolored .75 .25
1582 A422 51e multicolored 1.75 .85

Christmas 1983 — A423

Stained Glass Windows, Monastery at Batalha: 12.50e, Adoration of the Magi. 30e, Flight to Egypt.

1983, Nov. 23 ***Perf. 12½***

1583 A423 12.50e multi .65 .25
1584 A423 30e multi 2.00 .85

Lisbon Zoo Centenary — A424

1984, Jan. 18 Litho. ***Perf. 12x11½***

1585 A424 16e Siberian tigers 1.60 .25
1586 A424 16e White rhinoceros 1.60 .25
1587 A424 16e Damalisco Albifronte 1.60 .25
1588 A424 16e Cheetahs 1.60 .25
a. Strip of 4, #1585-1588 6.50 2.50

Military Type of 1983

Air Force Dress Uniforms and Planes: 16e, 1954; Hawker Hurricane II, 1943. 35e, 1960; Republic F-84G Thunderjet. 40e, Paratrooper, 1966; 2502 Nord Noratlas, 1960. 51e, 1966; Corsair II, 1982.

1984, Feb. 5 Litho. ***Perf. 13½***

1589 A416 16e multi .50 .25
1590 A416 35e multi 2.00 .55
1591 A416 40e multi 1.75 .60
1592 A416 51e multi 2.40 .85
a. Bklt. pane of 4, #1589-1592 7.00
Nos. 1589-1592 (4) 6.65 2.25

Tile Type of 1981

Design: No. 1593, Royal arms, 19th cent. No. 1594, Pombal Palace wall tile, 19th cent. No. 1595, Facade covering, 19th cent. No. 1596, Grasshoppers, by Rafael Bordallo Pinhiero, 19th cent.

1984, Mar. 8 Litho. ***Perf. 12x11½***

1593 A391 16e multi .85 .25
a. Miniature sheet of 6 5.25 5.25
1594 A391 16e multi .85 .25
a. Miniature sheet of 6 5.00 5.00
1595 A391 16e multi .85 .25
a. Miniature sheet of 6 5.00 5.00
1596 A391 16e multi .85 .25
a. Miniature sheet of 6 5.00 5.00
b. Souv. sheet of 4, #1593-1596 4.50 4.50
Nos. 1593-1596 (4) 3.40 1.00

Issued: No. 1593, Mar. 8; No. 1594, July 18; No. 1595, Aug. 3; No. 1596, Oct. 17 .

25th Lisbon Intl. Fair, May 9-13 A425

Events: 40e, World Food Day. 51e, 15th Rehabilitation Intl. World Congress, Lisbon, June 4-8, vert.

1984, Apr. 3

1597 A425 35e multicolored 1.60 .50
1598 A425 40e multicolored 1.75 .65
1599 A425 51e multicolored 2.25 .85
Nos. 1597-1599 (3) 5.60 2.00

April 25th Revolution, 10th Anniv. — A426

1984, Apr. 25 ***Perf. 13½***

1600 A426 16e multicolored 1.10 .25

Europa (1959-84) A427

1984, May 2 ***Perf. 12x11½***

1601 A427 51e multicolored *1.50 .80*
a. Souvenir sheet of 4 *7.00 5.00*

LUBRAPEX '84 and Natl. Early Art Museum Centenary — A428

Paintings: 16e, Nun, 15th cent. 40e, St. John, by Master of the Retable of Santiago, 16th cent. 51e, View of Lisbon, 17th cent. 66e, Cabeca de Jovem, by Domingos Sequeira, 19th cent.

1984, May 9 Litho. ***Perf. 12x11½***

1602 A428 16e multicolored .65 .25
1603 A428 40e multicolored 2.00 .55
1604 A428 51e multicolored 3.25 .90
1605 A428 66e multicolored 3.25 1.10
a. Souv. sheet of 4, #1602-1605 9.00 9.00
Nos. 1602-1605 (4) 9.15 2.80

1984 Summer Olympics A429

1984, June 5

1606 A429 35e Fencing 1.50 .30
1607 A429 40e Gymnastics 2.00 .55
1608 A429 51e Running 2.75 .95
1609 A429 80e Pole vault 3.00 1.00
Nos. 1606-1609 (4) 9.25 2.80

Souvenir Sheet

1610 A429 100e Hurdles 7.00 7.00

Historical Events — A430

Designs: 16e, Gil Eanes, explorer who reached west coast of Africa, 1434. 51e, King Peter I of Brazil and IV of Portugal.

1984, Sept. 24 ***Perf. 12x11½***

1611 A430 16e multicolored .45 .25
1612 A430 51e multicolored 2.00 .90

See Brazil No. 1954.

Infantry Grenadier, 1740 — A431

46e, 5th Cavalry Regiment Officer, 1810. 60e, Artillery Corporal, 1892. 100e, Engineering Soldier, 1985.

1985, Jan. 23 Litho. ***Perf. 13½***

1613 A431 20e multi .50 .25
1614 A431 46e multi 2.40 .55
1615 A431 60e multi 2.50 .70
1616 A431 100e multi 3.00 1.10
a. Bklt. pane of 4, #1613-1616 8.50
Nos. 1613-1616 (4) 8.40 2.60

Tile Type of 1981

Designs: No. 1617, Tile from entrance hall of Lisbon's Faculdade de Letras, by Jorge Barradas, 20th cent.; No. 1618, Explorer and sailing ship, detail from tile panel by Maria Keil, Avenida Infante Santo, Lisbon; No. 1619, Profile and key, detail from a 20th century tile mural by Querubim Lapa; No. 1620, Geometric designs and flowers, by Manuel Cargaleiro.

1985 Litho. ***Perf. 12x11½***

1617 A391 20e multicolored .85 .25
a. Miniature sheet of 6 5.00 5.00
1618 A391 20e multicolored .85 .25
a. Miniature sheet of 6 5.00 5.00
1619 A391 20e multicolored .85 .25
a. Miniature sheet of 6 5.00 5.00
1620 A391 20e multicolored .85 .25
a. Miniature sheet of 6 5.00 5.00
b. Souv. sheet of 4, #1617-1620 5.00 5.00
Nos. 1617-1620 (4) 3.40 1.00

Issued: No. 1617, Feb. 13; No. 1618, June 11; No. 1619, Aug. 20; No. 1620, Nov. 15.

Kiosks — A432

1985, Mar. 19 Litho. ***Perf. 11½x12***

1621 A432 20e Green kiosk 1.00 .25
1622 A432 20e Red kiosk 1.00 .25
1623 A432 20e Gray kiosk 1.00 .25
1624 A432 20e Blue kiosk 1.00 .25
a. Strip of 4, #1621-1624 6.00

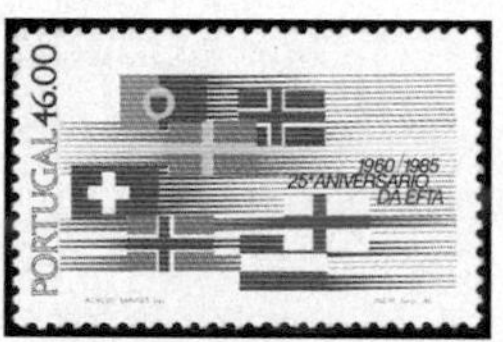

25th Anniv., European Free Trade Association — A433

1985, Apr. 10 Litho. ***Perf. 12x11½***

1625 A433 46e Flags of members 1.40 .55

Intl. Youth Year A434

60e, Heads of boy and girl.

1985, Apr. 10 **Litho.**

1626 A434 60e multicolored 1.75 .80

Europa 1985-Music A435

60e, Woman playing tambourine.

1985, May 6 Litho. ***Perf. 11½x12***

1627 A435 60e multicolored *2.00 1.00*
a. Souvenir sheet of 4 *8.00 6.00*

Historic Anniversaries — A436

20e, King John I at the Battle of Aljubarrota, 1385. 46e, Queen Leonor (1458-1525) founding the Caldas da Rainha Hospital. 60e, Cartographer Pedro Reinel, earliest Portuguese map, c. 1483.

1985, July 5 Litho. ***Perf. 12x11½***

1628 A436 20e multicolored .65 .25
1629 A436 46e multicolored 2.10 .70
1630 A436 60e multicolored 2.25 .95
Nos. 1628-1630 (3) 5.00 1.90

See Nos. 1678-1680.

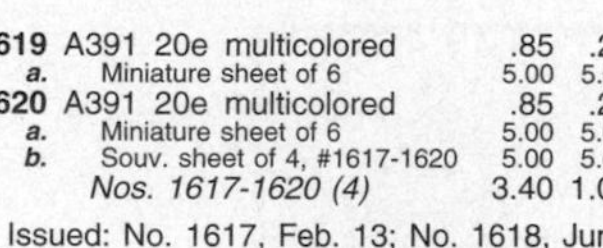

Traditional Architecture A437

50c, Saloia, Estremadura. 1e, Beira interior. 1.50e, Ribatejo. 2.50e, Transmontanas. 10e, Minho and Douro Litoral. 20e, Farm house, Minho. 22.50e, Alentejo. 25e, African Sitio, Algarve. 27e, Beira Interior. 29e, Hill country. 30e, Algarve. 40e, Beira Interior. 50e, Private home, Beira Litoral. 55e, Tras-os-Montes. 60e, Beira Litoral. 70e, Estremadura Sul and Alentejo. 80e, Estremadura. 90e, Minho. 100e, Adobe Monte, Alentejo. 500e, Algarve.

1985-89 Litho. *Perf. 12*

1631	A437	50c multi	.25	.25
1632	A437	1e multi	.25	.25
1633	A437	1.50e multi	.25	.25
1634	A437	2.50e multi	.25	.25
1635	A437	10e multi	.25	.25
1636	A437	20e multi	.30	.25
1637	A437	22.50e multi	.30	.25
1638	A437	25e multi	.35	.25
1639	A437	27e multi	.45	.25
1640	A437	29e multi	.45	.25
1641	A437	30e multi	.45	.25
1642	A437	40e multi	.60	.25
1643	A437	50e multi	.75	.25
1644	A437	55e multi	.75	.25
1645	A437	60e multi	1.00	.25
1646	A437	70e multi	1.10	.25
1647	A437	80e multi	1.10	.35
1648	A437	90e multi	1.25	.35
1649	A437	100e multi	1.50	.35
1650	A437	500e multi	6.25	.75
		Nos. 1631-1650 (20)	17.85	5.80

Issued: 20e, 25e, 50e, 100e, 8/20; 2.50e, 22.50e, 80e, 90e, 3/10/86; 10e, 40e, 60e, 70e, 3/6/87; 1.50e, 27e, 30e, 55e, 3/15/88; 50c, 1e, 29e, 500e, 3/8/89.

Aquilino Ribeiro (1885-1963), Author — A438

46e, Fernando Pessoa (1888-1935), poet.

1985, Oct. 2 Litho. *Perf. 12*

1651	A438	20e multicolored	.65	.25
1652	A438	46e multicolored	1.75	.60

Natl. Parks and Reserves A439

20e, Berlenga Island. 40e, Estrela Mountain Chain. 46e, Boquilobo March. 80e, Formosa Lagoon. 100e, St. Jacinto Dunes.

1985, Oct. 25

1653	A439	20e multi	.45	.25
1654	A439	40e multi	1.60	.55
1655	A439	46e multi	2.40	.80
1656	A439	80e multi	2.50	.85
		Nos. 1653-1656 (4)	6.95	2.45

Souvenir Sheet

1657	A439	100e multi	7.00	5.00

ITALIA '85.

Christmas 1985 — A440

Illuminated codices from The Prayer Times Book, Book of King Manuel, 1517-1538.

1985, Nov. 15 *Perf. 11½x12*

1658	A440	20e The Nativity	.50	.25
1659	A440	46e Adoration of the Magi	1.75	.65

Postrider A441

1985, Dec. 13 Litho. *Perf. 13½*

1660	A441	A(22.50e) lt yel grn & dp yel grn	.75	.25

See No. 1938 for another stamp with postrider inscribed "Serie A."

Flags of EEC Member Nations A442

Design: 57.50e, Map of EEC, flags.

1986, Jan. 7 Litho. *Perf. 12*

1661	A442	20e multi	.60	.25
1662	A442	57.50e multi	2.25	.80
a.		Souv. sheet, 2 ea #1661-1662	6.00	6.00

Admission of Portugal and Spain to the European Economic Community, Jan. 1. See Spain Nos. 2463-2466.

No. 1662a contains 2 alternating pairs of Nos. 1661-1662.

Castles A443

1986, Feb. 18 Litho. *Perf. 12*

1663	A443	22.50e Beja	.85	.25
a.		Booklet pane of 4	3.50	
1664	A443	22.50e Feira	.85	.25
a.		Booklet pane of 4	3.50	

1986, Apr. 10

1665	A443	22.50e Guimaraes	.85	.25
a.		Booklet pane of 4	3.50	
1666	A443	22.50e Braganca	.85	.25
a.		Booklet pane of 4	3.50	

1986, Sept. 18

1667	A443	22.50e Montemor-o-Velho	.85	.25
a.		Booklet pane of 4	3.50	
1668	A443	22.50e Belmonte	.85	.25
a.		Booklet pane of 4	3.50	
		Nos. 1663-1668 (6)	5.10	1.50

See Nos. 1688-1695, 1723-1726.

Intl. Peace Year A445

1986, Feb. 18 Litho. *Perf. 12*

1669	A445	75e multicolored	2.50	1.00

Automobile Centenary — A446

1986, Apr. 10 Litho. *Perf. 12*

1670		22.50e 1886 Benz	1.10	.25
1671		22.50e 1886 Daimler	1.10	.25
a.	A446	Pair, #1670-1671	2.25	2.25

Europa 1986 A447

1986, May 5 Litho.

1672	A447	68.50e Shad	3.00	1.00
a.		Souvenir sheet of 4	20.00	6.00

Horse Breeds A448

1986, May 22 Litho. *Perf. 12*

1673	A448	22.50e Alter	.60	.25
1674	A448	47.50e Lusitano	1.75	.70
1675	A448	52.50e Garrano	2.40	.90
1676	A448	68.50e Sorraia	2.75	.95
		Nos. 1673-1676 (4)	7.50	2.80

Souvenir Sheet

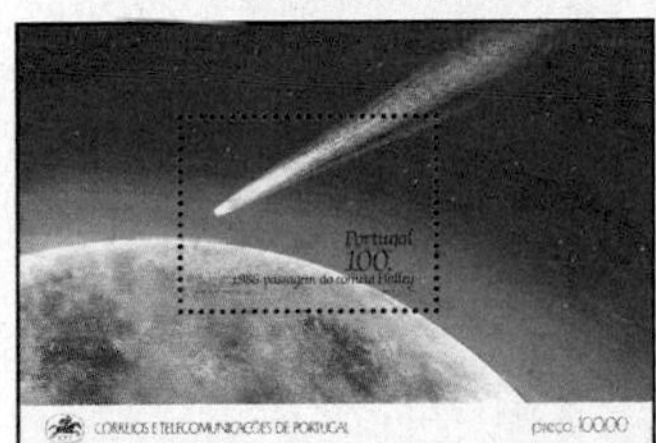

Halley's Comet — A449

1986, June 24

1677	A449	100e multi	12.00	6.00

Anniversaries Type of 1985

Designs: 22.50e, Diogo Cao, explorer, heraldic pillar erected at Cape Lobo, 1484, 1st expedition. No. 1679, Manuel Passos, Corinthian column. No. 1680, Joao Baptista Ribeiro, painter, Oporto Academy director, c. 1836, and musicians.

1986, Aug. 28 Litho.

1678	A436	22.50e multi	.55	.25
1679	A436	52.50e multi	1.60	.70
1680	A436	52.50e multi	1.60	.70
		Nos. 1678-1680 (3)	3.75	1.65

Diogo Cao's voyages, 500th anniv. Academies of Fine Art, 150th anniv.

Stamp Day — A450

Natl. Guard, 75th Anniv. — A451

Order of Engineers, 50th Anniv. — A452

No. 1681, Postal card, 100th anniv.

1986, Oct. 24 Litho.

1681	A450	22.50e multi	.85	.25
1682	A451	47.50e multi	1.50	.65
1683	A452	52.50e multi	1.60	.70
		Nos. 1681-1683 (3)	3.95	1.60

Watermills A453

1986, Nov. 7

1684	A453	22.50e Duoro	.50	.25
1685	A453	47.50e Coimbra	1.25	.85
1686	A453	52.50e Gerez	1.75	.90
1687	A453	90e Braga	2.50	.80
a.		Souv. sheet of 4, #1684-1687	9.00	7.50
		Nos. 1684-1687 (4)	6.00	2.80

LUBRAPEX '86. #1687a issued Nov. 21.

Castle Type of 1986

1987-88 Litho.

1688	A443	25e Silves	.85	.25
a.		Booklet pane of 4	3.50	
1689	A443	25e Evora Monte	.85	.25
a.		Booklet pane of 4	3.50	
1690	A443	25e Leiria	.85	.25
a.		Booklet pane of 4	3.50	
1691	A443	25e Trancoso	.85	.25
a.		Booklet pane of 4	3.50	
1692	A443	25e St. George	.90	.25
a.		Booklet pane of 4	3.75	
1693	A443	25e Marvao	.90	.25
a.		Booklet pane of 4	3.75	
1694	A443	27e Fernando's Walls of Oporto	.85	.25
a.		Booklet pane of 4	3.50	
1695	A443	27e Almourol	.85	.25
a.		Booklet pane of 4	3.50	
		Nos. 1688-1695 (8)	6.90	2.00

Issued: #1688-1689, 1/16; #1690-1691, 4/10; #1692-1693, 9/15; #1694-1695, 1/19/88.

Natl. Tourism Organization, 75th Anniv. — A454

25e, Beach houses, Tocha. 57e, Boats, Espinho. 98e, Chafariz Fountain, Arraioles.

1987, Feb. 10 Litho. *Perf. 12*

1696	A454	25e multicolored	.50	.25
1697	A454	57e multicolored	2.10	.90
1698	A454	98e multicolored	2.75	.85
		Nos. 1696-1698 (3)	5.35	2.00

European Nature Conservation Year — A455

57e, Hands, flower, map. 74.50e, Hands, star, rainbow.

1987, Mar. 20 *Perf. 12x12½*

1699	A455	25e shown	.50	.25
1700	A455	57e multicolored	1.50	.75
1701	A455	74.50e multicolored	2.00	.85
		Nos. 1699-1701 (3)	4.00	1.85

Europa 1987 A456

Modern architecture: Bank Borges and Irmao Agency, 1986, Vila do Conde.

1987, May 5 Litho. *Perf. 12*

1702 A456 74.50e multi 2.50 1.00
a. Souvenir sheet of 4 *11.00 7.50*

A457

Lighthouses

1987, June 12 *Perf. 11½x12*

1703 A457 25e Aveiro 1.00 .25
1704 A457 25e Berlenga 1.00 .25
1705 A457 25e Cape Mondego 1.00 .25
1706 A457 25e Cape St. Vincente 1.00 .25
a. Strip of 4, #1703-1706 5.00 5.00

A458

1987, Aug. 27 Litho. *Perf. 12*

1707 A458 74.50e multi 1.75 .75

Amadeo de Souza-Cardoso (1887-1919), painter.

Portgeuse Royal Library, Rio de Janeiro, 150th anniv. A459

1987, Aug. 27 *Perf. 12x11½*

1708 A459 125e multicolored 2.25 1.00

Paper Currency of Portugal, 300th Anniv. A460

1987, Aug. 27 *Perf. 12x11½*

1709 A460 100e multicolored 2.00 .75

Voyages of Bartolomeu Dias (d. 1499), 500th Anniv. — A461

No. 1710, Departing from Lisbon, 1487. No. 1711, Discovering the African Coast, 1488.

1987, Aug. 27 *Perf. 12x11½*

1710 25e multicolored 1.00 .25
1711 25e multicolored 1.00 .25
a. A461 Pair, #1710-1711 3.00 2.00

No. 1711a has continuous design. See Nos. 1721-1722.

Souvenir Sheet

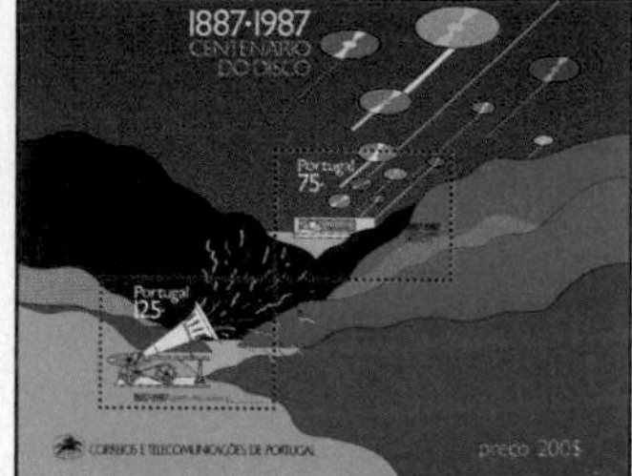

Phonograph Record, 100th Anniv. — A462

1987, Oct. 9 Litho. *Perf. 12*

1712 A462 Sheet of 2 20.00 16.00
a. 75e Compact-disc player 3.75 2.90
b. 125e Gramophone 6.00 4.50

Christmas A463

Various children's drawings, Intl. Year of the Child emblem — 25e, Angels, magi, tree. 57e, Friendship circle. 74.50e, Santa riding dove.

1987, Nov. 6

1713 A463 25e multi .60 .25
1714 A463 57e multi 1.60 .70
1715 A463 74.50e multi 2.00 1.00
a. Souv. sheet of 3, #1713-1715 5.00 5.00
Nos. 1713-1715 (3) 4.20 1.95

World Wildlife Fund A464

Lynx, Lynx pardina.

1988, Feb. 3 Litho. *Perf. 12*

1716 A464 27e Stalking 2.40 .50
1717 A464 27e Carrying prey 2.40 .50
1718 A464 27e Two adults 2.40 .50
1719 A464 27e Adult, young 2.40 .50
a. Strip of 4, Nos. 1716-1719 11.00 11.00

Printed in a continuous design.

Journey of Pero da Covilha to the East, 500th Anniv. A465

1988, Feb. 3

1720 A465 105e multi 2.50 .95

Bartolomeu Dias Type of 1987

Discovery of the link between the Atlantic and Indian Oceans by Dias, 500th Anniv.: No. 1721, Tidal wave, ship. No. 1722, Henricus Martelus Germanus's map (1489), picturing the African coast and linking the two oceans.

1988, Feb. 3

1721 A461 27e multi .85 .25
1722 A461 27e multi .85 .25
a. Bklt. pane of 4, Nos. 1710-1711, 1721-1722 6.00
b. Pair, #1721-1722 1.75 1.75

No. 1722b has continuous design.

Castle Type of 1986

No. 1723, Vila Nova de Cerveira. No. 1724, Palmela.

1988, Mar. 15 Litho. *Perf. 12*

1723 A443 27e multicolored .85 .25
a. Bklt. pane of 4 3.50
1724 A443 27e multicolored .85 .25
a. Bklt. pane of 4 3.50

1988, July 1

1725 A443 27e Chaves .85 .25
a. Bklt. pane of 4 3.50
1726 A443 27e Penedono .85 .25
a. Bklt. pane of 4 3.50
Nos. 1723-1726 (4) 3.40 1.00

Europa 1988 A466

Transportation: Mail coach, Lisbon-Oporto route, 1855-1864.

1988, Apr. 21 Litho. *Perf. 12*

1735 A466 80e multi *5.00 1.00*
a. Souv. sheet of 4 *11.00 6.50*

Jean Monnet (1888-1979), Economist — A467

1988, May 9 Litho.

1736 A467 60e multi 1.40 .55

Souvenir Sheet

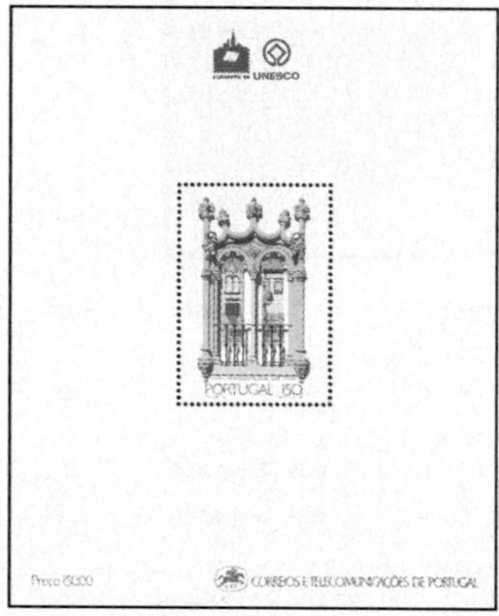

National Heritage (Patrimony) — A468

Design: 150e, Belvedere of Cordovil House and Fountain of Porta de Moura reflected in the Garcia de Resende balcony window, Evora, 16th cent.

1988, May 13 *Perf. 13½x12½*

1737 A468 150e multi 5.50 5.00

No. 1737 has inscribed margin picturing LUBRAPEX '88 and UNESCO emblems.

20th Cent. Paintings by Portuguese Artists — A469

Designs: 27e, *Viola,* c. 1916, by Amadeo de Souza-Cardoso (1887-1918). 60e, *Jugglers and Tumblers Do Not Fall,* 1949, by Jose de Almada Negreiros (1893-1970). 80e, *Still-life with Guitar,* c. 1940, by Eduardo Viana (1881-1967).

1988, Aug. 23 Litho. *Perf. 11½x12*

1738 A469 27e multi .50 .25
1739 A469 60e multi 1.50 .70
1740 A469 80e multi 1.75 .85
a. Min. sheet of 3, #1738-1740 5.50 5.50
Nos. 1738-1740 (3) 3.75 1.80

See Nos. 1748-1750, 1754-1765.

1988 Summer Olympics, Seoul A470

1988, Sept. 16 Litho. *Perf. 12x11½*

1741 A470 27e Archery .45 .25
1742 A470 55e Weight lifting 1.40 .75
1743 A470 60e Judo 1.50 .80
1744 A470 80e Tennis 2.25 .80
Nos. 1741-1744 (4) 5.60 2.60

Souvenir Sheet

1745 A470 200e Yachting 9.00 7.00

Remains of the Roman Civilization in Portugal A471

Mozaics: 27e, "Winter Image," detail of *Mosaic of the Four Seasons,* limestone and glass, 3rd cent., House of the Waterworks, Coimbra. 80e, *Fish in Marine Water,* limestone, 3rd-4th cent., cover of a tank wall, public baths, Faro.

1988, Oct. 18 Litho. *Perf. 12*

1746 A471 27e multi .55 .25
1747 A471 80e multi 1.75 .75

20th Cent. Art Type of 1988

Paintings by Portuguese artists: 27e, *Burial,* 1938, by Mario Eloy. 60e, *Lisbon Roofs,* c. 1936, by Carlos Botelho. 80e, *Avejao Lirico,* 1939, by Antonio Pedro.

1988, Nov. 18 Litho. *Perf. 11½x12*

1748 A469 27e multi .45 .25
1749 A469 60e multi 1.40 .65
1750 A469 80e multi 1.75 .75
a. Souv. sheet of 3, #1748-1750 5.50 5.50
b. Souv. sheet of 6, #1738-1740, 1748-1750 10.00 10.00
Nos. 1748-1750 (3) 3.60 1.65

Braga Cathedral, 900th Anniv. A472

1989, Jan. 20 *Perf. 12*

1751 A472 30e multi .75 .25

INDIA '89 — A473

55e, Caravel, Sao Jorge da Mina Fort, 1482. 60e, Navigator using astrolabe, 16th cent.

1989, Jan. 20

1752 A473 55e multi 1.25 .65
1753 A473 60e multi 1.75 .80

20th Cent. Art Type of 1988

Paintings by Portuguese artists: 29e, *Antithesis of Calm,* 1940, by Antonio Dacosta. 60c, *Lunch of the Unskilled Mason,* c. 1926, by Julio Pomar. 87e, *Simums,* 1949, by Vespeira.

1989, Feb. 15 Litho. *Perf. 11½x12*

1754 A469 29e multi .45 .25
1755 A469 60e multi 1.40 .60
1756 A469 87e multi 1.75 .90
a. Souv. sheet of 3, #1754-1756 5.50 5.50
Nos. 1754-1756 (3) 3.60 1.75

1989, July 7

Paintings by Portuguese artists: 29e, *046-72,* 1972, by Fernando Lanhas. 60e, *Les*

Spirales, 1954, by Nadir Afonso. 87e, *Sim,* 1987, by Carlos Calvet.

1757 A469 29e multi .45 .25
1758 A469 60e multi 1.40 .55
1759 A469 87e multi 1.75 .90
a. Souv. sheet of 3, #1757-1759 5.50 5.50
b. Souv. sheet of 6, #1754-1759 9.00 9.00
Nos. 1757-1759 (3) 3.60 1.70

1990, Feb. 14

Paintings by Portuguese artists: 32e, *Aluenda-Tordesillas* by Joaquim Rodrigo. 60e, *Pintura* by Noronha da Costa. 95e, *Pintura* by Vasco Costa (1917-1985).

1760 A469 32e multicolored .40 .25
1761 A469 60e multicolored 1.10 .50
1762 A469 95e multicolored 1.75 .85
a. Souv. sheet of 3, #1760-1762 5.50 5.50
Nos. 1760-1762 (3) 3.25 1.60

1990, Sept. 21

Paintings by Portuguese artists: 32e, Costa Pinheiro. 60e, Paula Rego. 95e, Jose De Guimaraes.

1763 A469 32e multicolored .40 .25
1764 A469 60e multicolored 1.00 .55
1765 A469 95e multicolored 1.75 .85
a. Min. sheet of 3, #1763-1765 5.50 5.50
b. Min. sheet of 6, #1760-1765 9.00 9.00
Nos. 1763-1765 (3) 3.15 1.65

A474

1989, Feb. 15 Litho. *Perf. 12*
1772 A474 29e multi .50 .25
a. Bklt. pane of 8 4.00
1773 A474 60e With love 1.00 .50
a. Bklt. pane of 8 8.00

Special occasions.

A475

1989, Mar. 8 Litho. *Perf. 11½x12*
1774 A475 60e multi 1.25 .60

European Parliament elections.

Europa 1989
A476

Children's toys.

1989, Apr. 26 Litho. *Perf. 12*
1775 A476 80e Top *1.75 1.00*

Souvenir Sheet

1776 Sheet of 4, 2 each #1775, 1776a *12.50 5.00*
a. A476 80e Tops *2.00 1.25*

Surface Transportation, Lisbon — A477

29e, Carris Co. elevated railway, Bica Street. 65e, Carris electric tram. 87e, Carmo Elevator, Santa Justa Street. 100e, Carris doubledecker bus. 250e, Transtejo Co. riverboat *Cacilheiro,* horiz.

1989, May 22 Litho.
1777 A477 29e multi .50 .25
1778 A477 65e multi 1.60 .75
1779 A477 87e multi 1.75 1.00
1780 A477 100e multi 2.25 .75
Nos. 1777-1780 (4) 6.10 2.75

Souvenir Sheet

1781 A477 250e multi 7.50 6.50

Windmills
A478

29e, Ansiao. 60e, Santiago do Cacem. 87e, Afife. 100e, Caldas da Rainha.

1989, June 14 Litho.
1782 A478 29e multicolored .50 .25
1783 A478 60e multicolored 1.60 .75
1784 A478 87e multicolored 1.75 .90
1785 A478 100e multicolored 2.00 .85
a. Bklt. pane of 4, #1782-1785 7.00
Nos. 1782-1785 (4) 5.85 2.75

Souvenir Sheet

French Revolution, 200th Anniv. — A479

1989, July 7 Litho. *Perf. 11½x12*
1786 A479 250e Drummer 6.00 6.00

No. 1786 has multicolored inscribed margin picturing the PHILEXFRANCE '89 emblem and the storming of the Bastille.

Natl. Palaces
A480

1989, Oct. 18 Litho. *Perf. 12*
1787 A480 29e Ajuda, Lisbon, and King Luiz I .35 .25
1788 A480 60e Queluz 1.40 .80

Death cent. of King Luiz.

Exhibition Emblem and Wildflowers
A481

29e, Armeria pseudarmeria. 60e, Santolina impressa. 87e, Linaria lamarckii. 100e, Limonium multiforum.

1989, Nov. 17 Litho.
1789 A481 29e multicolored .40 .25
1790 A481 60e multicolored 1.10 .60
1791 A481 87e multicolored 1.60 .85
1792 A481 100e multicolored 2.25 1.10
a. Bklt. pane of 4, #1789-1792 5.50
Nos. 1789-1792 (4) 5.35 2.80

World Stamp Expo '89, Washington, DC.

Portuguese Faience, 17th Cent.
A482

No. 1794, Nobleman (plate). No. 1795, Urn. No. 1796, Fish (pitcher). No. 1797, Crown, shield (plate). No. 1798, Lidded bowl. No. 1799, Plate.

1990, Jan. 24 Litho. *Perf. 12x11½*
1793 A482 33e shown .50 .25
1794 A482 33e multicolored .50 .25
1795 A482 35e multicolored .70 .25
1796 A482 60e multicolored 1.25 .70
1797 A482 60e multicolored 1.25 .70
1798 A482 60e multicolored 1.25 .70
Nos. 1793-1798 (6) 5.45 2.85

Souvenir Sheet

Perf. 12

1799 A482 250e multicolored 6.00 5.00

No. 1799 contains one 52x45mm stamp.
See Nos. 1829-1835, 1890-1896.

Score, Alfred Keil and Henrique Lopes de Mondonca
A483

1990, Mar. 6 *Perf. 12x11½*
1804 A483 32e multicolored .45 .25

A Portuguesa, the Natl. Anthem, cent. (32e).

University Education in Portugal, 700th Anniv. — A484

1990, Mar. 6 *Perf. 11½x12*
1805 A484 70e multicolored 1.60 .70

Europa 1990
A485

1990, Apr. 11 *Perf. 12x11½*
1806 A485 80e Santo Tirso P.O. *1.25 1.00*

Souvenir Sheet

1807 Sheet of 4, 2 each #1806, 1807a *10.00 5.00*
a. A485 80e Mala Posta P.O. *1.50 1.25*

Souvenir Sheet

Gentleman Using Postage Stamp, 1840 — A486

1990, May 3
1808 A486 250e multicolored 6.00 5.00

Stamp World London '90 and 150th anniv. of the Penny Black.

Greetings Issue
A487

"FELICITACOES" and street scenes. No. 1809, Stairway. No. 1810, Automobile. No. 1811, Man in street. No. 1812, Street scene, girl with bouquet behind mail box.

1990, June 5 Litho. *Perf. 12*
1809 A487 60e multi 1.00 .45
1810 A487 60e multi 1.00 .45
1811 A487 60e multi 1.00 .45
1812 A487 60e multi 1.00 .45
Nos. 1809-1812 (4) 4.00 1.80

Perf. 13 Vert.

1809a A487 60e 1.25 1.25
1810a A487 60e 1.25 1.25
1811a A487 60e 1.25 1.25
1812a A487 60e 1.25 1.25
b. Bklt. pane of 4, #1809a-1812a 5.00

Camilo Castelo Branco (1825-1890), Writer — A488

Designs: 70e, Friar Bartolomeu dos Martires (1514-1590), theologian.

1990, July 11 Litho. *Perf. 12x11½*
1813 A488 65e multicolored 1.10 .65
1814 A488 70e multicolored 1.25 .70

Ships
A489

1990, Sept. 21 Litho. *Perf. 12*
1815 A489 32e Barca .40 .25
1816 A489 60e Caravela Pescareza 1.10 .50
1817 A489 70e Barinel 1.25 .75
1818 A489 95e Caravela 1.75 1.00
Nos. 1815-1818 (4) 4.50 2.50

Perf. 13½ Vert.

1815a A489 32e 1.25 1.25
1816a A489 60e 1.25 1.25
1817a A489 70e 1.25 1.25
1818a A489 95e 1.25 1.25
b. Bklt. pane of 4, #1815a-1818a 5.00

National Palaces — A490

1990, Oct. 11 *Perf. 12*

1819 A490	32e Pena		.45	.25
1820 A490	60e Vila		1.10	.50
1821 A490	70e Mafra		1.25	.75
1822 A490	120e Guimaraes		1.75	1.00
	Nos. 1819-1822 (4)		4.55	2.50

Francisco Sa Carneiro (1934-1980), Politician — A491

1990, Nov. 7

1823 A491 32e ol brn & blk .55 .25

Rossio Railway Station, Cent. A492

Various locomotives.

1990, Nov. 7

1824 A492	32e Steam, 1887	.45	.25
1825 A492	60e Steam, 1891	1.10	.50
1826 A492	70e Steam, 1916	1.25	.75
1827 A492	95e Electric, 1956	1.75	1.00
	Nos. 1824-1827 (4)	4.55	2.50

Souvenir Sheet

1828 A492 200e Railway station 6.00 5.00

Ceramics Type of 1990

1991, Feb. 7 **Litho.** *Perf. 12*

1829 A482	35e Lavabo	.50	.25
1830 A482	35e Tureen and plate	.50	.25
1831 A482	35e Flower vase	.50	.25
1832 A482	60e Finger bowl	1.00	.50
1833 A482	60e Coffee pot	1.00	.50
1834 A482	60e Mug	1.00	.50
	Nos. 1829-1834 (6)	4.50	2.25

Souvenir Sheet

1835 A482 250e Plate 6.00 5.00

No. 1835 contains one 52x44mm stamp.

European Tourism Year A494

1991, Mar. 6 **Litho.** *Perf. 12*

1836 A494	60e Flamingos	.95	.50
1837 A494	110e Chameleon	1.70	.85

Souvenir Sheet

1838 A494 250e Deer 6.50 5.50

Portuguese Navigators A495

2e, Joao Goncalves Zarco. 3e, Pedro Lopes de Sousa. 4e, Duarte Pacheco Pereira. 5e, Tristao Vaz Teixeira. 6e, Pedro Alvares Cabral. 10e, Joao de Castro. 32e, Bartolomeu Perestrelo. 35e, Gil Eanes. 38e, Vasco da Gama. 42e, Joao de Lisboa. 45e, Joao Rodriques Cabrillo. 60e, Nuno Tristao. 65e, Joao da Nova. 70e, Ferdinand Magellan. 75e, Pedro Fernandes de Queiros. 80e, Diogo Gomes. 100e, Diogo de Silves. 200e, Estevao Gomes. 250e, Diogo Cao. 350e, Bartolomeu Dias.

1990-94 **Litho.** *Perf. 12x11½*

1839 A495	2e multi	.25	.25
1840 A495	3e multi	.25	.25
1841 A495	4e multi	.25	.25
1842 A495	5e multi	.25	.25
1843 A495	6e multi	.25	.25
1844 A495	10e multi	.25	.25
1845 A495	32e multi	.45	.25
1846 A495	35e multi	.40	.25
1847 A495	38e multi	.35	.25
1848 A495	42e multi	.45	.25
1849 A495	45e multi	.45	.25
1850 A495	60e multi	.90	.30
1851 A495	65e multi	.90	.25
1852 A495	70e multi	.90	.25
1853 A495	75e multi	.85	.45
1854 A495	80e multi	1.25	.50
1855 A495	100e multi	1.75	.65
1856 A495	200e multi	2.50	.60
1857 A495	250e multi	4.00	1.25
1858 A495	350e multi	4.75	1.50
	Nos. 1839-1858 (20)	21.40	8.50

Issued: 2e, 5e, 32e, 100e, 3/6; 6e, 38e, 65e, 350e, 3/6/91; 35e, 60e, 80e, 250e, 3/6/92; 4e, 42e, 70e, 200e, 4/6/93; 3e, 10e, 45e, 75e, 4/29/94.

Europa A496

1991, Apr. 11 **Litho.** *Perf. 12*

1859 A496 80e Eutelsat II *1.50 1.00*

Souvenir Sheet

1860 Sheet, 2 ea #1859, 1860a *12.00 5.00*

a. A496 80e Olympus I *2.00 1.50*

Souvenir Sheet

Princess Isabel & Philip le Bon — A497

1991, May 27 **Litho.** *Perf. 12½*

1861 A497 300e multicolored 5.50 4.50

Europalia '91. See Belgium No. 1402.

Discovery Ships A498

1991, May 27 **Litho.** *Perf. 12*

1862 A498	35e Caravel	.45	.25
1863 A498	75e Nau	1.25	.55
1864 A498	80e Nau, stern	1.25	.60
1865 A498	110e Galleon	1.75	.75
	Nos. 1862-1865 (4)	4.70	2.15

Perf. 13½ Vert.

1862a A498	35e	1.25	1.25
1863a A498	75e	1.25	1.25
1864a A498	80e	1.25	1.25
1865a A498	110e	1.25	1.25
b.	Bklt. pane of 4, #1862a-1865a	5.00	

Portuguese Crown Jewels — A499

Designs: 35e, Running knot, diamonds & emeralds, 18th cent. 60e, Royal scepter, 19th cent. 70e, Sash of the Grand Cross, ruby & diamonds, 18th cent. 80e, Court saber, gold & diamonds in hilt, 19th cent. 140e, Royal crown, 19th cent.

1991, July 8 **Litho.** *Perf. 12*

1866 A499	35e multicolored	.45	.25
1867 A499	60e multicolored	1.00	.50
1868 A499	80e multicolored	1.40	.60
1869 A499	140e multicolored	2.10	.85
	Nos. 1866-1869 (4)	4.95	2.20

Perf. 13½ Vert.

1870 A499 70e multicolored 1.25 .55

a. Booklet pane of 5 8.00

See Nos. 1898-1902.

Antero de Quental (1842-1891), Poet — A500

First Missionaries to Congo, 500th Anniv. — A501

1991, Aug. 2 *Perf. 12*

1871 A500	35e multicolored	.45	.25
1872 A501	110e multicolored	1.70	.85

Architectural Heritage — A502

Designs: 35e, School of Architecture, Oporto University, by Siza Vieira. 60e, Torre do Tombo, by Ateliers Associates of Arsenio Cordeiro. 80e, Railway Bridge over Douro River, by Edgar Cardoso. 110e, Setubal-Braga highway bridge.

1991, Sept. 4 **Litho.** *Perf. 12*

1873 A502	35e multicolored	.50	.25
1874 A502	60e multicolored	.80	.45
1875 A502	80e multicolored	1.25	.60
1876 A502	110e multicolored	1.70	.75
	Nos. 1873-1876 (4)	4.25	2.05

1992 Summer Olympics, Barcelona A503

1991, Oct. 9 **Litho.** *Perf. 12*

1877 A503	35e Equestrian	.45	.25
1878 A503	60e Fencing	.85	.40
1879 A503	80e Shooting	1.25	.60
1880 A503	110e Sailing	1.70	.75
	Nos. 1877-1880 (4)	4.25	2.00

History of Portuguese Communications — A504

Designs: 35e, King Manuel I appointing first Postmaster, 1520. 60e, Mailbox, telegraph, 1881. 80e, Automobile, telephone, 1911. 110e, Airplane, mail truck, 1991.

1991, Oct. 9

1881 A504	35e multicolored	.45	.25
1882 A504	60e multicolored	.90	.45
1883 A504	80e multicolored	1.25	.60
	Nos. 1881-1883 (3)	2.60	1.30

Souvenir Sheet

1884 A504 110e multicolored 1.90 1.40

Automobile Museum, Caramulo A505

35e, Peugeot, 1899. 60e, Rolls Royce, 1911. 80e, Bugatti 35B, 1930. 110e, Ferrari 195 Inter, 1950.

No. 1889a, Mercedes 380K, 1934. b, Hispano-Suiza, 1924.

1991, Nov. 15

1885 A505	35e multi	.45	.25
1886 A505	60e multi	.90	.45
1887 A505	80e multi	1.25	.65
1888 A505	110e multi	1.60	.70
	Nos. 1885-1888 (4)	4.20	2.05

Souvenir Sheet

1889 Sheet, 2 each #1889a-1889b 4.50 4.50

a.-b. A505 70e any single 1.10 .55

Phila Nippon '91 (#1889). See #1903-1906A.

Ceramics Type of 1990

No. 1890, Tureen with lid. No. 1891, Plate. No. 1892, Pitcher with lid. No. 1893, Violin. No. 1894, Bottle in form of woman. No. 1895, Man seated on barrel.

No. 1896, Political caricature.

1992, Jan. 24 **Litho.** *Perf. 12*

1890 A482	40e multicolored	.60	.30
1891 A482	40e multicolored	.60	.30
1892 A482	40e multicolored	.60	.30
1893 A482	65e multicolored	.95	.50
1894 A482	65e multicolored	.95	.50
1895 A482	65e multicolored	.95	.50
	Nos. 1890-1895 (6)	4.65	2.40

Souvenir Sheet

1896 A482 260e multicolored 4.00 3.00

No. 1896 contains one 51x44mm stamp.

Portuguese Presidency of the European Community Council of Ministers A506

1992, Jan. 24

1897 A506 65e multicolored .95 .45

Crown Jewels Type of 1991

Designs: 38e, Coral flowers, 19th cent. 65e, Clock of gold, enamel, ivory and diamonds, 20th cent. 70e, Tobacco box encrusted with diamonds and emeralds, 1755. 85e, Royal scepter, 1828. 125e, Eighteen star necklace with diamonds, 1863.

1992, Feb. 7 **Litho.** *Perf. 11½x12*

1898 A499	38e multicolored	.45	.25
1899 A499	70e multicolored	.85	.40
1900 A499	85e multicolored	1.10	.65
1901 A499	125e multicolored	1.50	.80

Perf. 13½ Vert.

1902 A499 65e multicolored 1.10 .50

a. Booklet pane of 5 5.00

Nos. 1898-1902 (5) 5.00 2.60

Automobile Museum Type of 1991

Designs: 38e, Citroen Torpedo, 1922. 65e, Rochet Schneider, 1914. 85e, Austin Seven, 1933. 120e, Mercedes Benz 770, 1938. No. 1906b, Renault, 1911. c, Ford Model T, 1927.

1992, Mar. 6 Litho. *Perf. 12*

1903 A505 38e multicolored .45 .25
1904 A505 65e multicolored 1.00 .50
1905 A505 85e multicolored 1.25 .65
1906 A505 120e multicolored 1.50 .75
Nos. 1903-1906 (4) 4.20 2.15

Souvenir Sheet

1906A Sheet of 2 each, #b.-c. 4.50 4.50
b.-c. A505 70e any single 1.10 .55

Automobile Museum, Oeiras.

Portuguese Arrival in Japan, 450th Anniv. A508

Granada '92: 120e, Three men with gifts, Japanese.

1992, Apr. 24 Litho. *Perf. 12*

1907 A508 38e shown .45 .25
1908 A508 120e multicolored 1.60 .75

Portuguese Pavilion, Expo '92, Seville — A509

1992, Apr. 24 Litho. *Perf. 11½x12*

1909 A509 65e multicolored .80 .40

Instruments of Navigation — A510

1992, May 9 Litho. *Perf. 12x11½*

1910 A510 60e Cross staff .80 .25
1911 A510 70e Quadrant .95 .50
1912 A510 100e Astrolabe 1.40 .55
1913 A510 120e Compass 1.50 .70
a. Souv. sheet of 4, #1910-1913 4.50 4.50
Nos. 1910-1913 (4) 4.65 2.00

Lubrapex '92 (#1913a).

Royal Hospital of All Saints, 500th Anniv. A511

1992, May 11

1914 A511 38e multicolored .60 .30

Apparitions of Fatima, 75th Anniv. A512

1992, May 11

1915 A512 70e multicolored .90 .40

Port of Leixoes, Cent. A513

1992, May 11

1916 A513 120e multicolored 1.50 .65

A514

Voyages of Columbus — A515

Designs: 85e, King John II with Columbus. No. 1918, Columbus in sight of land. No. 1919, Landing of Columbus. No. 1920, Columbus soliciting aid from Queen Isabella. No. 1921, Columbus welcomed at Barcelona. No. 1922, Columbus presenting natives. No. 1923, Columbus.

Nos. 1918-1923 are similar in design to US Nos. 230-231, 234-235, 237, 245.

1992, May 22 Litho. *Perf. 12x11½*

1917 A514 85e gold & multi *2.50 .60*

Souvenir Sheets

Perf. 12

1918 A515 260e blue *3.50 2.50*
1919 A515 260e brown violet *3.50 2.50*
1920 A515 260e brown *3.50 2.50*
1921 A515 260e violet black *3.50 2.50*
1922 A515 260e black *3.50 2.50*
1923 A515 260e black *3.50 2.50*
Nos. 1918-1923 (6) 21.00 15.00

Europa.

See US Nos. 2624-2629, Italy Nos. 1883-1888, and Spain Nos. 2677-2682.

UN Conference on Environmental Development — A516

70e, Bird flying over polluted water system. 120e, Clean water system, butterfly, bird, flowers.

1992, June 12 Litho. *Perf. 12x11½*

1924 70e multicolored 1.10 .55
1925 120e multicolored 2.00 1.00
a. A516 Pair, #1924-1925 4.00 2.00

1992 Summer Olympics, Barcelona A517

1992, July 29 Litho. *Perf. 11½x12*

1926 A517 38e Women's running .65 .30
1927 A517 70e Soccer 1.15 .60
1928 A517 85e Hurdles 1.40 .70
1929 A517 120e Roller hockey 2.00 1.00
Nos. 1926-1929 (4) 5.20 2.60

Souvenir Sheet

Perf. 12

1930 A517 250e Basketball 9.00 6.00

Olymphilex '92 (#1930).

Campo Pequeno Bull Ring, Lisbon, Cent. A518

Various scenes of picadors.

1992, Aug. 18 *Perf. 12x11½*

1931 A518 38e multicolored .65 .30
1932 A518 65e multicolored 1.10 .55
1933 A518 70e multicolored 1.25 .60
1934 A518 155e multicolored 2.50 1.25
Nos. 1931-1934 (4) 5.50 2.70

Souvenir Sheet

Perf. 13½x12½

1935 A518 250e Bull ring, vert. 6.00 4.00

No. 1935 contains one 35x50mm stamp.

Single European Market A519

1992, Nov. 4 Litho. *Perf. 12x11½*

1936 A519 65e multicolored .95 .50

European Year for Security, Hygiene and Health at Work A520

1992, Nov. 4 *Perf. 12x11½*

1937 A520 120e multicolored 1.75 .90

Postrider A521

1993, Mar. 9 Litho. *Perf. 12x12½*

1938 A521 (A) henna brown, gray & black .65 .30

No. 1938 sold for 42e on date of issue. See No. 2276A.

Almada Negreiros (1893-1970), Artist — A522

1993, Mar. 9 Litho. *Perf. 11½x12*

1939 A522 40e Portrait .60 .30
1940 A522 65e Ships .95 .50

Instruments of Navigation — A523

1993, Apr. 6 *Perf. 12x11½*

1941 A523 42e Hourglass .60 .30
1942 A523 70e Nocturlabe 1.00 .50
1943 A523 90e Kamal 1.30 .65
1944 A523 130e Backstaff 1.90 .95
Nos. 1941-1944 (4) 4.80 2.40

Contemporary Paintings by Jose Escada (1934-1980) — A524

Europa: No. 1945, Cathedral, 1979. No. 1946a, Abstract shapes, 1966.

1993, May 5 Litho. *Perf. 12x11½*

1945 A524 90e multicolored *1.25 .60*

Souvenir Sheet

1946 Sheet, 2 each #1945, 1946a *6.00 4.00*
a. A524 90e multicolored *1.50 1.00*

Assoc. of Volunteer Firemen of Lisbon, 125th Anniv. A525

1993, June 21 Litho. *Perf. 12x11½*

1947 A525 70e multicolored .90 .45

Sao Carlos Natl. Theatre, Bicent. A526

1993, June 21

1948 A526 42e Rossini .50 .25
1949 A526 70e Verdi .90 .45
1950 A526 90e Wagner 1.15 .55
1951 A526 130e Mozart 1.65 .80
Nos. 1948-1951 (4) 4.20 2.05

Souvenir Sheet

1952 A526 300e Theatre 6.00 5.00

Union of Portuguese Speaking Capitals — A527

1993, July 30 Litho. *Perf. 11½x12*

1953 A527 130e multicolored 1.60 .80
a. Miniature sheet of 4 + 2 labels 7.00 5.00

Brasiliana '93 (#1953a).

Sculpture — A528

Designs: 42e, Annunciation Angel, 12th cent. 70e, St. Mark, 16th cent., horiz. No. 1956, Virgin and Child, 17th cent. 90e, Archangel St. Michael, 18th cent. 130e, Conde de Ferreira, 19th cent. 170e, Modern sculpture, 20th cent.

No. 1960a, Head of Agrippina, the Elder, 1st cent. No. 1960b, Virgin of the Annunciation,

16th cent. No. 1960c, The Widow, 19th cent. No. 1960d, Love Ode, 20th cent.

Perf. 11½x12, 12x11½

1993, Aug. 18

1954 A528 42e multicolored .55 .30
1955 A528 70e multicolored .90 .45
1956 A528 75e multicolored .95 .50
1957 A528 90e multicolored 1.10 .60
1958 A528 130e multicolored 1.60 .80
1959 A528 170e multicolored 2.25 1.10
Nos. 1954-1959 (6) 7.35 3.75

Souvenir Sheet

1960 Sheet of 4 6.00 5.00
a.-d. A528 75e any single .95 .95

See Nos. 2001-2007, 2067-2073.

Railway World Congress A529

90e, Cars on railway overpass, train. 130e, Traffic jam, train. 300e, Train, track skirting tree.

1993, Sept. 6 *Perf. 12x11½*

1961 A529 90e multicolored 1.10 .55
1962 A529 130e multicolored 1.60 .80

Souvenir Sheet

1963 A529 300e multicolored 6.00 5.00

Portuguese Arrival in Japan, 450th Anniv. A530

Designs: 42e, Japanese using musket. 130e, Catholic priests. 350e, Exchanging items of trade.

1993, Sept. 22 **Litho.** *Perf. 12*

1964 A530 42e multicolored .55 .30
1965 A530 130e multicolored 1.60 .85
1966 A530 350e multicolored 4.50 2.25
Nos. 1964-1966 (3) 6.65 3.40

See Macao Nos. 704-706.

Trawlers A531

1993, Oct. 1 **Litho.** *Perf. 12x11½*

1967 A531 42e Twin-mast .55 .30
1968 A531 70e Single-mast .90 .45
1969 A531 90e SS Germano 3 1.10 .55
1970 A531 130e Steam-powered 1.75 .85
Nos. 1967-1970 (4) 4.30 2.15

Perf. 11½

1967a A531 42e .55 .30
1968a A531 70e .90 .45
1969a A531 90e 1.10 .55
1970a A531 130e 1.75 .85
b. Booklet pane of 4, #1967a-1970a 5.00

A532

Mailboxes: 42e, Rural mail bag, 1880. 70e, Railroad wall-mounted mailbox, 19th cent. 90e, Free-standing mailbox, 19th cent. 130e, Modern mailbox, 1992. 300e, Mailbox from horse-drawn postal vehicle, 19th cent.

1993, Oct. 9 **Litho.** *Perf. 12*

1971 A532 42e multicolored .50 .25
1972 A532 70e multicolored .80 .40
1973 A532 90e multicolored 1.00 .50
1974 A532 130e multicolored 1.50 .75
Nos. 1971-1974 (4) 3.80 1.90

Souvenir Sheet

1975 A532 300e multicolored 6.00 5.00

No. 1975 has continuous design.

A533

Endangered birds of prey.

1993, Oct. 9

1976 A533 42e Imperial eagle .50 .25
1977 A533 70e Royal eagle owl .80 .40
1978 A533 130e Peregrine falcon 1.50 .75
1979 A533 350e Hen harrier 4.00 2.00
Nos. 1976-1979 (4) 6.80 3.40

Brazil-Portugal Treaty of Consultation and Friendship, 40th Anniv. — A534

1993, Nov. 3

1980 A534 130e multicolored 1.50 .75

See Brazil No. 2430.

Souvenir Sheet

Conference of Zamora, 850th Anniv. — A535

1993, Dec. 9

1981 A535 150e multicolored 3.00 2.00

West European Union, 40th Anniv. A536

1994, Jan. 27 **Litho.** *Perf. 12*

1982 A536 85e multicolored 1.10 .55

Intl. Olympic Committee, Cent. A537

Design: No. 1984, Olympic torch, rings.

1994, Jan. 27

1983 A537 100e multicolored 1.25 .65
1984 A537 100e multicolored 1.25 .65

Issued in sheets of 8, 4 each + label.

Oliveira Martins (1845-94), Historian A538

100e, Florbela Espanca (1894-1930), poet.

1994, Feb. 21

1985 A538 45e multicolored .60 .30
1986 A538 100e multicolored 1.25 .65

Prince Henry the Navigator (1394-1460) — A539

1994, Mar. 4

1987 A539 140e multicolored 1.75 .85

See Brazil No. 2463, Cape Verde No. 664, Macao No. 719.

Transfer of Power, 20th Anniv. A540

1994, Apr. 22 **Litho.** *Perf. 12x11½*

1988 A540 75e multicolored .90 .45

Europa A541

1994, May 5 **Litho.** *Perf. 12x11½*

1989 A541 100e People of Ormuz 1.25 .65

Souvenir Sheet

1990 Sheet of 4, 2 each #1989, 1990a 4.50 3.50
a. A541 100e Ears of corn 1.00 .50

Intl. Year of the Family A542

1994, May 15 **Litho.** *Perf. 12x11½*

1991 A542 45e blk, red & brn .55 .30
1992 A542 140e blk, red & grn 1.75 .85

Treaty of Tordesillas, 500th Anniv. — A543

1994, June 7 **Litho.** *Perf. 12x11½*

1993 A543 140e multicolored 1.75 .90

1994 World Cup Soccer Championships, US — A544

1994, June 7

1994 A544 100e shown 1.25 .60
1995 A544 140e Ball, 4 shoes 1.90 .95

Lisbon '94, European Capital of Culture A545

Birds and: 45e, Music. 75e, Photography. 100e, Theater and ballet. 145e, Art.

1994, July 1

1996 A545 45e multicolored .55 .30
1997 A545 75e multicolored .95 .50
1998 A545 100e multicolored 1.25 .60
1999 A545 140e multicolored 1.90 .95
a. Souvenir sheet of 4, #1996-1999 11.00 10.00
Nos. 1996-1999 (4) 4.65 2.35

Year of Road Safety — A545a

1994, Aug. 16 **Litho.** *Perf. 11½x12*

2000 A545a 45e blk, red & grn .60 .30

Sculpture Type of 1993

Designs: 45e, Pedra Formosa, Castreja culture. No. 2002, Carved pilaster, 7th cent., vert. 80e, Capital carved with figures, 12th cent. 100e, Laying Christ in the Tomb, 16th cent. 140e, Reliquary chapel, 17th cent. 180e, Bas relief, 20th cent.

No. 2007: a, Sarcophagus of Queen Urraca, 13th cent. b, Sarcophagus of Dom Afonso. c, Tomb of Dom Joao de Noronha and Dona Isabel de Sousa, 16th cent. d, Mausoleum of Adm. Machado Santos, 20th cent.

Perf. 12x11½, 11½x12

1994, Aug. 16

2001 A528 45e multicolored .60 .30
2002 A528 75e multicolored .95 .50
2003 A528 80e multicolored 1.00 .50
2004 A528 100e multicolored 1.25 .60
2005 A528 140e multicolored 1.75 .85
2006 A528 180e multicolored 2.25 1.10
Nos. 2001-2006 (6) 7.80 3.85

Souvenir Sheet

Perf. 12x11½

2007 Sheet of 4 6.00 5.00
a.-d. A528 75e any single .95 .95

Falconry A546

Designs: 45e, Falconer, hooded bird, dog. 75e, Falcon flying after prey. 100e, Falcon, prey on ground. 140e, Three falcons on perches. 250e, Hooded falcon.

1994, Sept. 16 **Litho.** *Perf. 12*

2008 A546 45e multicolored .60 .30
2009 A546 75e multicolored .95 .50
2010 A546 100e multicolored 1.25 .60
2011 A546 140e multicolored 1.75 .85
Nos. 2008-2011 (4) 4.55 2.25

Souvenir Sheet

2012 A546 250e multicolored 6.00 5.00

Trawlers
A547

1994, Sept. 16 ***Perf. 12x11½***

2013 A547 45e Maria Arminda .60 .30
2014 A547 75e Bom Pastor .95 .50
2015 A547 100e With triplex haulers 1.25 .60
2016 A547 140e Sueste 1.75 .85
Nos. 2013-2016 (4) 4.55 2.25

Perf. 11½ Vert.

2013a A547 45e .60 .30
2014a A547 75e .95 .50
2015a A547 100e 1.25 .60
2016a A547 140e 1.75 .85
b. Booklet pane of 4, #2013a-2016a 6.00

Modern Railway Transport — A548

45e, Sintra Railway, electric multiple car unit. 75e, 5600 series locomotives. 140e, Lisbon subway cars.

1994, Oct. 10 **Litho.** ***Perf. 12***

2017 A548 45e multicolored .55 .30
2018 A548 75e multicolored .90 .45
2019 A548 140e multicolored 1.75 .90
Nos. 2017-2019 (3) 3.20 1.65

Vehicles of Postal Transportation — A549

45e, Horse-drawn mail coach, 19th cent. 75e, Railway postal ambulance, 1910. 100e, Mercedes station wagon, No. 222, 1950. 140e, Volkswagen van, 1952. 250e, DAF 2500 truck, 1983.

1994, Oct. 10

2020 A549 45e multicolored .55 .30
2021 A549 75e multicolored .90 .45
2022 A549 100e multicolored 1.25 .65
2023 A549 140e multicolored 1.75 .90
Nos. 2020-2023 (4) 4.45 2.30

Souvenir Sheet

2024 A549 250e multicolored 6.00 5.00

First Savings Bank in Portugal, 150th Anniv. A550

45e, Pelican medallion. 100e, Modern coins.

1994, Oct. 31

2025 A550 45e multicolored .55 .30
2026 A550 100e multicolored 1.25 .65

World Wide Savings Day (#2026).

American Society of Travel Agents, 64th Congress, Lisbon A551

1994, Nov. 7

2027 A551 140e multicolored 1.75 .90

Historical Inns A552

45e, S. Filipe Fort, Setubal. 75e, Obidos Castle. 100e, Dos Loios Convent, Evora. 140e, St. Marinha Guimaraes Monastery.

1994, Nov. 7

2028 A552 45e multicolored .55 .30
2029 A552 75e multicolored .90 .45
2030 A552 100e multicolored 1.25 .60
2031 A552 140e multicolored 1.75 .90
Nos. 2028-2031 (4) 4.45 2.25

Evangelization and Meeting of Cultures — A553

45e, Carving of missionary, Mozambique, 19th cent., vert. 75e, Sculpture, young Jesus ministering to the people, India, 17th cent., vert. 100e, Chalice, Macao, 17th cent., vert. 140e, Carving of native, Angola, 19th cent.

1994, Nov. 17 **Litho.** ***Perf. 12***

2032 A553 45e multicolored .55 .30
2033 A553 75e multicolored .95 .45
2034 A553 100e multicolored 1.25 .60
2035 A553 140e multicolored 1.75 .90
Nos. 2032-2035 (4) 4.50 2.25

Arrival of Portuguese in Senegal, 550th Anniv. A554

1994, Nov. 17

2036 A554 140e multicolored 1.75 .90

See Senegal No. 1083.

Souvenir Sheet

Battle of Montijo, 350th Anniv. — A555

1994, Dec. 1

2037 A555 150e multicolored 5.00 3.00

Souvenir Sheet

Christmas — A556

1994, Dec. 8

2038 A556 150e Magi 3.00 1.25

Nature Conservation in Europe — A557

Designs: 42e, Otis tarda. 90e, Pandion haliaetus. 130e, Lacerta schreiberi.

1995, Feb. 22 **Litho.** ***Perf. 12***

2039 A557 42e multicolored .60 .30
2040 A557 90e multicolored 1.25 .60
2041 A557 130e multicolored 1.75 .85
a. Souvenir sheet of 3, #2039-2041 6.00 5.00
Nos. 2039-2041 (3) 3.60 1.75

St. Joao de Deus (1495-1550), Founder of Order of Hospitalers A558

1995, Mar. 8 **Litho.** ***Perf. 12***

2042 A558 45e multicolored .60 .30

Trams & Automobiles in Portugal, Cent. — A559

Designs: 90e, 1895 Electric tram, 1895. 130e, 1895 Panhard & Levassor automobile.

1995, Mar. 8

2043 A559 90e multicolored 1.50 .60
2044 A559 130e multicolored 2.00 .95

19th Century Professions A560

Designs: 1e, Baker woman. 20e, Spinning wheel and spoon vendor. 45e, Junk dealer. 50e, Fruit vendor. 75e, Whitewasher.

1995, Apr. 20 **Litho.** ***Perf. 12***

2045 A560 1e multicolored .25 .25
2046 A560 20e multicolored .30 .25
2047 A560 45e multicolored .60 .30
Complete booklet, 10 #2047 6.00
2048 A560 50e multicolored .70 .35
2049 A560 75e multicolored 1.00 .50
Complete booklet, 10 #2049 10.00
Nos. 2045-2049 (5) 2.85 1.65

See Nos. 2088-2092, 2147-2151, 2210-2214, 2277-2281B.

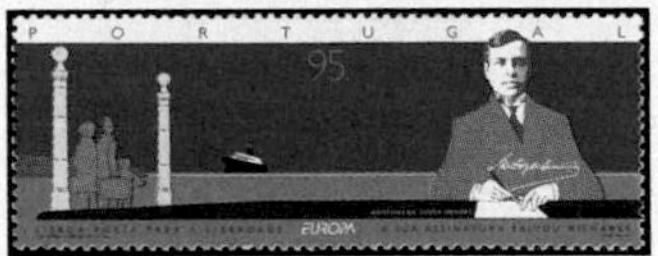

Peace & Freedom — A561

Europa: No. 2050, People awaiting ships for America, Aristides de Sousa Mendes signing entrance visas, 1940. No. 2051, Transportion of refugees from Gibraltar to Madeira, 1940.

1995, May 5 **Litho.** ***Perf. 12***

2050 A561 95e multicolored *1.25 .50*
2051 A561 95e multicolored *1.25 .50*

UN, 50th Anniv. A562

135e, like #2052, clouds in background.

1995, May 5

2052 A562 75e multicolored 1.00 .50
2053 A562 135e multicolored 1.75 .90
a. Souv. sheet, 2 ea #2052-2053 8.00 6.00

A563

St. Antony of Padua (1195-1231) A564

45e, *St. Anthony Holding Child Jesus.* 75e, St. Anthony with flowers. 135e, Statue of St. Antony holding child Jesus.

250e, Statue of St. Antony holding child Jesus, diff.

1995, June 13 **Litho.** ***Perf. 12***

2054 A563 45e multicolored .60 .30
2055 A564 75e multicolored 1.00 .50
2056 A563 135e multicolored 1.90 .95
Nos. 2054-2056 (3) 3.50 1.75

Souvenir Sheet

2057 A563 250e multicolored 6.00 4.25

See Italy Nos. 2040-2041, Brazil No. 2539.

Firemen in Portugal, 600th Anniv. A565

Designs: No. 2058, Carpenters with axes, women with pitchers, 1395. No. 2059, Dutch firemen, water pumper, 1701. 75e, Fireman of Lisbon, water wagon, 1780, firemen, 1782. 80e, Firemen pulling pumper, carrying water kegs, 1834. 95e, Fire chief directing firemen on Merryweather steam pumper, 1867. 135e, Firemen, hydrant, early fire truck, 1908.

1995, July 4 **Litho.** ***Perf. 12***

2058 A565 45e multicolored .60 .30
2059 A565 45e multicolored 2.00 .30
a. Miniature sheet of 4 8.00 1.25

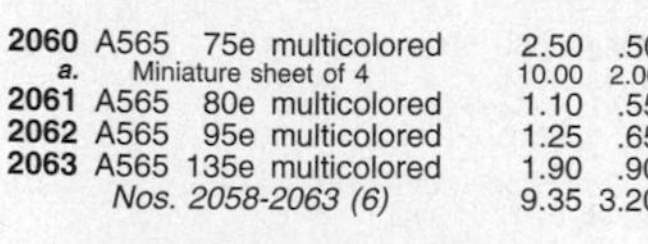

2060 A565 75e multicolored 2.50 .50
a. Miniature sheet of 4 10.00 2.00
2061 A565 80e multicolored 1.10 .55
2062 A565 95e multicolored 1.25 .65
2063 A565 135e multicolored 1.90 .90
Nos. 2058-2063 (6) 9.35 3.20

Dom Manuel I, 500th Anniv. of Acclamation — A566

1995, Aug. 4 Litho. *Perf. 12*
2064 A566 45e buff, brown & red .60 .30
a. Miniature sheet of 4 5.00 4.00

New Electric Railway Tram — A567

1995, Sept. 1
2066 A567 80e multicolored 1.10 .55
a. Booklet pane of 4 4.50
Complete booklet, No. 2066a 5.00

Sculpture Type of 1993

Designs: 45e, Warrior, Castreja culture. 75e, Two-headed fountain. 80e, Statue, "The Truth," by Texeira Lopes. 95e, Monument to the war dead. 135e, Statue of Fernão Lopes, by Martins Correia. 190e, Monument to Fernando Pessoa, by Lagoa Henriques.

Equestrian statues: No. 2073: a, Medieval cavalryman. b, D. José I. c, D. João IV. d, Vímara Peres.

1995, Sept. 27 Litho. *Perf. 11½x12*
2067 A528 45e multicolored .60 .30
2068 A528 75e multicolored 1.00 .50
2069 A528 80e multicolored 1.10 .55
2070 A528 95e multicolored 1.25 .65
2071 A528 135e multicolored 1.80 .90
2072 A528 190e multicolored 2.50 1.25
Nos. 2067-2072 (6) 8.25 4.15

Souvenir Sheet

2073 Sheet of 4 7.00 5.00
a.-d. A528 75e any single 1.00 1.00

Portuguese Expansion Period Art — A568

45e, Statue of the Guardian Angel of Portugal. 75e, Reliquary of Queen D. Leonor. 80e, Statue of Dom Manuel. 95e, Painting, St. Anthony, by Nuno Goncalves. 135e, Painting, Adoration of the Magi, by Vasco Fernandez. 190e, Painting, Christ on the Way to Mount Calvary, by Jorge Afonso.

200e, Altarpiece for Convent of St. Vincent, by Nuno Goncalves.

1995, Oct. 9 Litho. *Perf. 12*
2074 A568 45e multicolored .60 .25
2075 A568 75e multicolored 1.00 .50
2076 A568 80e multicolored 1.00 .50
2077 A568 95e multicolored 1.25 .60
2078 A568 135e multicolored 1.75 .90
2079 A568 190e multicolored 2.50 1.25
Nos. 2074-2079 (6) 8.10 4.00

Souvenir Sheet

2080 A568 200e multicolored 6.00 4.00

No. 2080 contains one 76x27mm stamp.

José Maria Eca de Queiroz (1845-1900), Writer — A569

1995, Oct. 27 Litho. *Perf. 12*
2081 A569 135e multicolored 1.75 .90

Christmas A570

1995, Nov. 14
2082 A570 80e Annunciation angel 1.00 .50
a. "PORTUGAL" omitted 1.00 .50
b. Miniature sheet, 4 #2082 4.00 4.00
c. Miniature sheet, 4 #2082a 4.00 4.00

TAP Air Portugal, 50th Anniv. A571

1995, Nov. 14
2083 A571 135e Airbus A340/300 1.75 .90

Oceanographic Voyages of King Charles I of Portugal and Prince Albert I of Monaco, Cent. — A572

95e, Ship, King Charles I holding sextant, microscope, sea life. 135e, Fish in sea, net, Prince Albert I holding binoculars, ship.

1996, Feb. 1
2084 A572 95e multicolored 1.25 .60
2085 A572 135e multicolored 1.75 .90

See Monaco Nos. 1992-1993.

Natl. Library, Bicent. A573

1996, Feb. 29
2086 A573 80e multicolored 1.00 .50

Use of Portuguese as Official Language, 700th Anniv. — A574

1996, Feb. 29
2087 A574 200e multicolored 2.50 1.25

19th Cent. Professions Type

Designs: 3e, Exchange broker. 47e, Woman selling chestnuts. 78e, Cloth seller. 100e, Black woman selling mussels. 250e, Water seller.

1996, Mar. 20 Litho. *Perf. 11½x12*
2088 A560 3e multicolored .25 .25
2089 A560 47e multicolored .60 .30
a. Booklet pane, 10 #2089 6.00
Complete booklet, #2089a 6.00
2090 A560 78e multicolored 1.00 .50
a. Booklet pane, 10 #2090 10.00
Complete booklet, #2090a 10.00
2091 A560 100e multicolored 1.25 .65
2092 A560 250e multicolored 3.20 1.60
Nos. 2088-2092 (5) 6.30 3.30

Joao de Deus (1830-96), Founder of New Method to Teach Reading A576

1996, Apr. 12 *Perf. 12*
2093 A576 78e multicolored 1.00 .50

UNICEF, 50th Anniv. — A577

1996, Apr. 12
2094 A577 78e shown 1.00 .50
2095 A577 140e Children 1.75 .90
a. Bklt. pane, 2 ea #2094-2095 5.50
Complete booklet, #2095a 5.50

Joao de Barros (1496-1570), Writer — A578

1996, Apr. 12
2096 A578 140e multicolored 1.75 .90

Helena Vieira da Silva (1908-92), Painter — A579

1996, May 3
2097 A579 98e multicolored *1.25 .60*
a. Souvenir sheet of 3 *3.75 3.75*

Europa.

Euro '96, European Soccer Championships, Great Britain — A580

1996, June 7 Litho. *Perf. 12*
2098 A580 78e Soccer players 1.00 .50
2099 A580 140e Soccer players, diff. 1.75 .90
a. Souvenir sheet, #2098-2099 2.75 2.75

Joao Vaz Corte-Real, Explorer, 500th Death Anniv. — A581

1996, June 7
2100 A581 140e multicolored 1.75 .90

Souvenir Sheet

2101 A581 315e like #2100 4.00 4.00

No. 2101 contains one 40x31 stamp with a continuous design.

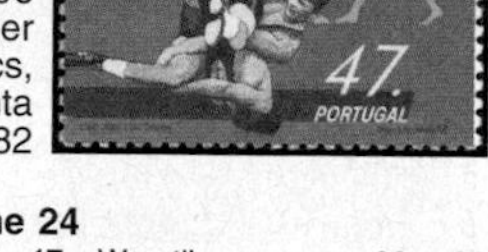

1996 Summer Olympics, Atlanta A582

1996, June 24
2102 A582 47e Wrestling .60 .30
2103 A582 78e Equestrian 1.00 .50
2104 A582 98e Boxing 1.25 .65
2105 A582 140e Running 1.75 .90
Nos. 2102-2105 (4) 4.60 2.35

Souvenir Sheet

2106 A582 300e Early track event 4.00 4.00

Olymphilex '96 (#2106).

Augusto Hilário (1864-96), Singer A583

1996, July 1 Litho. *Perf. 12x11½*
2107 A583 80e multicolored 1.00 .50

Alphonsine Condification of Statutes, 550th Anniv. — A584

1996, Aug. 7
2108 A584 350e multicolored 4.50 2.25

Motion Pictures, Cent. A585

Directors, stars of motion pictures: 47e, António Silva. 78e, Vasco Santana. 80e, Laura Alves. 98e, Aurélio Pais dos Reis. 100e, Leitao de Barros. 140e, António Lopes Ribeiro.

1996, Aug. 7
2109 A585 47e multicolored .60 .30
2110 A585 78e multicolored 1.00 .50
2111 A585 80e multicolored 1.00 .50
a. Souvenir sheet, #2109-2111 2.60 2.60
2112 A585 98e multicolored 1.25 .65
2113 A585 100e multicolored 1.25 .65
2114 A585 140e multicolored 1.75 .90
a. Souvenir sheet, #2112-2114 4.50 4.50
b. Souvenir sheet, #2109-2114 7.00 7.00
Nos. 2109-2114 (6) 6.85 3.50

Azeredo Perdigao (1896-1993), Lawyer, Chairman of Calouste Gulbenkian Foundation — A586

1996, Sept. 19 Litho. *Perf. 12*

2115 A586 47e multicolored .60 .30

Arms of the Districts of Portugal A587

1996, Sept. 27

2116 A587 47e Aveiro .60 .30
2117 A587 78e Beja 1.00 .50
2118 A587 80e Braga 1.00 .50
a. Souvenir sheet, #2116-2118 2.60 2.60
2119 A587 98e Bragança 1.25 .65
2120 A587 100e Castelo Branco 1.25 .65
2121 A587 140e Coimbra 1.75 .90
a. Souvenir sheet, #2119-2121 6.00 6.00
Nos. 2116-2121 (6) 6.85 3.50

County of Portucale, 900th Anniv. A588

1996, Oct. 9

2122 A588 47e multicolored .60 .30

Home Mail Delivery, 175th Anniv. — A589

Designs: 47e, Mail carrier, 1821. 78e, Postman, 1854. 98e, Rural mail distrubutor, 1893. 100e, Postman, 1939. 140e, Postman, 1992.

1996, Oct. 9

2123 A589 47e multicolored .60 .30
2124 A589 78e multicolored 1.00 .50
2125 A589 98e multicolored 1.25 .65
2126 A589 100e multicolored 1.25 .65
2127 A589 140e multicolored 1.75 .90
Nos. 2123-2127 (5) 5.85 3.00

Traditional Food A590

47e, Minho-style pork. 78e, Trout, Boticas. 80e, Tripe, Oporto. 98e, Baked codfish, potatoes. 100e, Eel chowder, Aveiro. 140e, Lobster, Peniche.

1996, Oct. 9

2128 A590 47e multicolored .60 .30
2129 A590 78e multicolored 1.00 .50
2130 A590 80e multicolored 1.00 .50
2131 A590 98e multicolored 1.25 .65
2132 A590 100e multicolored 1.25 .65
2133 A590 140e multicolored 1.75 .90
Nos. 2128-2133 (6) 6.85 3.50

See Nos. 2170-2175.

Bank of Portugal, 150th Anniv. A591

1996, Nov. 12 Litho. *Perf. 12*

2134 A591 78e multicolored 1.00 .50

Rights of the People of East Timor A592

1996, Nov. 12

2135 A592 140e black & red 1.75 .90

Discovery of Maritime Route to India, 500th Anniv. — A593

Voyage of Vasco da Gama: 47e, Visit of D. Manuel I to shipyards. 78e, Departure from Lisbon, July 8, 1497. 98e, Trip over Atlantic Ocean. 140e, Passing Cape of Good Hope. 315e, Dream of Manuel.

1996, Nov. 12 *Perf. 13½*

2136 A593 47e multicolored .60 .30
2137 A593 78e multicolored 1.00 .50
2138 A593 98e multicolored 1.25 .60
2139 A593 140e multicolored 1.75 .85
Nos. 2136-2139 (4) 4.60 2.25

Souvenir Sheet

2140 A593 315e multicolored 5.00 5.00

See Nos. 2191-2195, 2265-2270.

Souvenir Sheet

1996 Organization for Security and Cooperation in Europe Summit, Lisbon — A594

1996, Dec. 2 *Perf. 12*

2141 A594 200e multicolored 3.00 3.00

Ships of the Indian Shipping Line A595

Designs: 49e, Portuguese galleon, 16th cent. 80e, "Principe da Beira," 1780. 100e, Bow of Frigate "D. Fernando II e Gloria," 1843. 140e, Stern of "D. Fernando II e Gloria."

1997, Feb. 12 Litho. *Perf. 12*

2142 A595 49e multicolored .60 .30
2143 A595 80e multicolored 1.00 .50
2144 A595 100e multicolored 1.25 .65
2145 A595 140e multicolored 1.75 .90
Nos. 2142-2145 (4) 4.60 2.35

Project Life — A596

1997, Feb. 20

2146 A596 80e multicolored 1.00 .50
a. Booklet pane of 5 5.00
Complete booklet, #2146a 5.00

19th Cent. Professions Type

Designs: 2e, Laundry woman. 5e, Broom seller. 30e, Olive oil seller. 49e, Woman with cape. 80e, Errand boy.

1997, Mar. 12 Litho. *Perf. 11½x12*

2147 A560 2e multicolored .25 .25
2148 A560 5e multicolored .25 .25
2149 A560 30e multicolored .35 .25
2150 A560 49e multicolored .60 .30
a. Booklet pane of 10 6.00
Complete booklet, #2150a 6.00
2151 A560 80e multicolored 1.00 .50
a. Booklet pane of 10 10.00
Complete booklet, #2151a 10.00
Nos. 2147-2151 (5) 2.45 1.55

Managing Institute of Public Credit, Bicent. A597

1997, Mar. 12 Litho. *Perf. 12*

2152 A597 49e multicolored .60 .30

World Wildlife Fund — A598

Galemys pyreanicus: No. 2153, Looking upward. No. 2154, Paws around nose. No. 2155, Eating earthworm. No. 2156, Heading downward.

1997, Mar. 12 *Perf. 12*

2153 49e multicolored 1.25 .45
2154 49e multicolored 1.25 .45
2155 49e multicolored 1.25 .45
2156 49e multicolored 1.25 .45
a. A598 Strip of 4, #2153-2156 7.00 7.00

Stories and Legends — A599

Europa: Moorish girl watching over treasures.

1997, May 5 Litho. *Perf. 12*

2157 A599 100e multicolored 1.25 .65
a. Souvenir sheet of 3 4.50 3.25

Sports A600

#2162: a, BMX bike riding. b, Hang gliding.

1997, May 29 *Perf. 12*

2158 A600 49e Surfing .60 .30
2159 A600 80e Skate boarding 1.00 .50
2160 A600 100e Roller blading 1.25 .65
2161 A600 140e Parasailing 1.75 .90
Nos. 2158-2161 (4) 4.60 2.35

Souvenir Sheet

2162 Sheet of 2 5.00 4.00
a.-b. A600 150e any single 1.60 1.60

Capture of Lisbon and Santarém from the Moors, 850th Anniv. — A601

Designs: No. 2163, Soldier on horse, front of fortress of Lisbon. No. 2164, Soldiers climbing ladders into Santareém at night.

1997, June 9 *Perf. 12*

2163 80e multicolored 1.00 .50
2164 80e multicolored 1.00 .50
a. A601 Pair, #2163-2164 2.00 2.00
b. Souvenir sheet, 2 #2164a 4.00 4.00

Fr. Luís Fróis (1532-97), Missionary, Historian — A602

80e, Fróis on mission in Orient. #2166, Fróis holding hands across chest. #2167, Fróis, church.

1997, June 9

2165 A602 80e multi, horiz. 1.00 .50
2166 A602 140e multi 1.75 .90
2167 A602 140e multi 1.75 .90
Nos. 2165-2167 (3) 4.50 2.30

See Macao 878-879.

Fr. José de Anchieta (1534-97), Missionary in Brazil — A603

Design: No. 2169, Fr. António Vieira (1608-97), missionary in Brazil, diplomat.

1997, June 9

2168 A603 140e multicolored 1.75 .90
2169 A603 350e multicolored 4.50 2.25

See Brazil Nos. 2639-2640.

Traditional Food Type of 1996

10e, Roasted kid, Beira Baixa. 49e, Fried shad. 80e, Lamb stew. 100e, Fish chowder. 140e, Swordfish fillets with corn. 200e, Stewed octopus, Azores.

1997, July 5 Litho. *Perf. 12*

2170 A590 10e multicolored .25 .25
2171 A590 49e multicolored .60 .30
2172 A590 80e multicolored 1.00 .50
2173 A590 100e multicolored 1.25 .65
2174 A590 140e multicolored 1.75 .85
2175 A590 200e multicolored 2.50 1.25
Nos. 2170-2175 (6) 7.35 3.80

Souvenir Sheet

City of Oporto, UNESCO World Heritage Site — A605

1997, July 5 Litho. *Perf. 12*
2176 A605 350e multicolored 6.00 6.00

A606

1997, July 19 Litho. *Perf. 12*
2177 A606 100e multicolored 1.25 .65

Brotherhood of the Yeoman of Beja, 700th anniv.

A607

1997, Aug. 29 Litho. *Perf. 12*
2178 A607 50e multicolored .65 .30

Natl. Laboratory of Civil Engineering, 50th anniv.

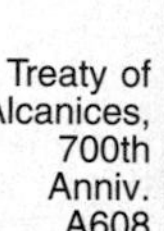

Treaty of Alcanices, 700th Anniv. A608

1997, Sept. 12
2179 A608 80e multicolored 1.00 .50

Arms of the Districts of Portugal A609

1997, Sept. 17

2180	A609	10e Evora	.25	.25
2181	A609	49e Faro	.60	.30
2182	A609	80e Guarda	1.00	.50
2183	A609	100e Leiria	1.25	.65
2184	A609	140e Lisboa	1.75	.90
a.		Souv. sheet, #2180, 2182, 2184	3.00	3.00
2185	A609	200e Portalegre	2.50	1.25
a.		Souv. sheet, #2181, 2183, 2185	4.50	4.50
		Nos. 2180-2185 (6)	7.35	3.85

See Nos. 2249-2254.

Incorporation of Postal Service in State Administration, Bicent. — A610

1997, Oct. 9
2186 A610 80e multicolored 1.00 .50

Portuguese Cartography — A611

Designs: 49e, Map from atlas of Lopo Homen-Reineis, 1519. 80e, Map from atlas of Joao Freire, 1546. 100e, Chart by Diogo Ribeiro, 1529. 140e, Anonymous map, 1630.

1997, Oct. 9

2187	A611	49e multicolored	.60	.30
2188	A611	80e multicolored	1.00	.50
2189	A611	100e multicolored	1.25	.60
2190	A611	140e multicolored	1.75	.90
a.		Souvenir sheet, #2187-2190	4.75	4.75
		Nos. 2187-2190 (4)	4.60	2.30

Discovery of Maritime Route to India Type of 1996

Voyage of Vasco da Gama: 49e, St. Gabriel's cross, Quelimane. 80e, Stop at island off Mozambique. 100e, Arrival in Mombasa. 140e, Reception for king of Melinde.
315e, Trading with natives, Natal.

1997, Nov. 5 *Perf. 13½*

2191	A593	49e multicolored	.60	.30
2192	A593	80e multicolored	1.00	.50
2193	A593	100e multicolored	1.25	.60
2194	A593	140e multicolored	1.75	.90
		Nos. 2191-2194 (4)	4.60	2.30

Souvenir Sheet

2195 A593 315e multicolored 4.00 4.00

Expo '98 — A612

Plankton: 49e, Loligo vulgaris. 80e, Scyllarus arctus. 100e, Pontellina plumata. 140e, Solea senegalensis.
No. 2200: a, Calcidiscus leptoporus. b, Tabellaria.

1997, Nov. 5 *Perf. 12*

2196	A612	49e multicolored	.60	.30
2197	A612	80e multicolored	1.00	.50
2198	A612	100e multicolored	1.25	.65
2199	A612	140e multicolored	1.75	.90
		Nos. 2196-2199 (4)	4.60	2.35

Souvenir Sheet

Perf. 12½

2200	Sheet of 2	2.50	2.50
a.-b.	A612 100e any single	1.25	1.25

See Nos. 2215-2219, 2226-2244.

Souvenir Sheet

Sintra, UNESCO World Heritage Site — A613

1997, Dec. 5 *Perf. 12*
2201 A613 350e multicolored 4.50 4.50

Portuguese Military Engineering, 350th Anniv. — A614

Engineering officer, map of fortress: 50e, Almeida. 80e, Miranda do Douro. 100e, Moncao. 140e, Elvas.

1998, Jan. 28 Litho. *Perf. 12*

2202	A614	50e multicolored	.60	.30
2203	A614	80e multicolored	1.00	.50
2204	A614	100e multicolored	1.25	.65
2205	A614	140e multicolored	1.75	.90
a.		Booklet pane, #2202-2205, perf. 12 vert.	6.00	
		Complete booklet, #2205a	6.00	
		Nos. 2202-2205 (4)	4.60	2.35

Roberto Ivens (1850-98), Naturalist A615

1998, Jan. 28
2206 A615 140e multicolored 1.75 .90

Misericórdias (Philanthropic Organizations), 500th Anniv. — A616

Sculptures: 80e, Madonna wearing crown surrounded by angels, people kneeling in praise, vert. 100e, People of antiquity gathered around another's bedside.

1998, Feb. 20

2207	A616	80e multicolored	1.00	.50
2208	A616	100e multicolored	1.25	.65

Souvenir Sheet

Aqueduct of the Free Waters, 250th Anniv. — A617

1998, Feb. 20
2209 A617 350e multicolored 4.50 2.25

19th Cent. Professions Type

10e, Fish seller. 40e, Collector of alms. 50e, Ceramics seller. 85e, Duck and eggs vendor. 250e, Queijadas (small cakes made of cheese) seller.

1998, Mar. 20 *Perf. 11½x12*

2210	A560	10e multicolored	.25	.25
2211	A560	40e multicolored	.50	.25
2212	A560	50e multicolored	.60	.30
a.		Booklet pane of 10	6.25	
		Complete booklet, #2212a	6.25	
2213	A560	85e multicolored	1.10	.55
a.		Booklet pane of 10	10.50	
		Complete booklet, #2213a	10.50	
2214	A560	250e multicolored	3.25	1.60
		Nos. 2210-2214 (5)	5.70	2.95

Expo '98 Type of 1997

Plankton: 50e, Pilumnus hirtellus. 85e, Lophius piscatorius. 100e, Sparus aurata. 140e, Cladonema radiatum.
No. 2219: a, Noctiluca miliaris. b, Dinophysis acuta.

1998, Mar. 20 *Perf. 12*

2215	A612	50e multicolored	.60	.30
2216	A612	85e multicolored	1.00	.50
2217	A612	100e multicolored	1.25	.65
2218	A612	140e multicolored	1.75	.90
		Nos. 2215-2218 (4)	4.60	2.35

Souvenir Sheet

2219	A612	100e Sheet of 2, #a.-b.	2.50	2.50
c.		Sheet of 12, #2196-2199, 2200a-2200b, 2215-2218, 2219a-2219b	15.00	15.00

Opening of the Vasco Da Gama Bridge A618

1998, Mar. 29 Litho. *Perf. 12*
2220 A618 200e multicolored 2.50 1.25

Souvenir Sheet

2221 A618 200e like #2220 2.50 2.50

Stamp in No. 2221 is a continuous design and shows bridge cables overlapping at far left.

Oporto Industrial Assoc., 150th Anniv. A619

1998, Apr. 30
2222 A619 80e multicolored 1.00 .50

Vasco da Gama Aquarium, Cent. A620

1998, May 13

2223	A620	50e Seahorse	.60	.30
2224	A620	80e Fish	1.00	.50

National Festivals A621

1998, May 21

2225 A621 100e People's Saints *1.25 .65*
a. Souvenir sheet of 3 *3.75 3.75*

Europa.

Expo '98 Type of 1997

Designs: No. 2226, Portuguese sailing ship, face on stone cliff. No. 2227, Diver, astrolabe. No. 2228, Various fish. No. 2229, Research submersible, fish. No. 2230, Mermaid swimming. No. 2231, Children under water holding globe.

No. 2232: a, Portuguese Pavilion. b, Pavilion of the Future. c, Oceans Pavilion. d, Knowledge of the Seas Pavilion. e, Pavilion of Utopia. f, Mascot putting letter into mailbox.

No. 2233, Like #2216, inscribed "Larva de Tamboril" only. No. 2234, Like #2219a, inscribed "Protozário Broluminiscente" only. No. 2235, Like #2215, inscribed "Larvas de Caranguejos" only. No. 2236, Like #2217, inscribed "Larvas de Dourada" only. No. 2237, Like #2219b, inscribed "Dinoflagolados" only. No. 2238, Like #2218, inscribed "Medusa" only.

No. 2239, like #2227. No. 2240, like #2229. No. 2241, like #2231. No. 2242, like #2226. No. 2243, like #2228. No. 2244, like #2230.

1998, May 21

2226 A612 50e multicolored .60 .30
2227 A612 50e multicolored .60 .30
2228 A612 85e multicolored 1.00 .50
2229 A612 85e multicolored 1.00 .50
2230 A612 140e multicolored 1.75 .90
2231 A612 140e multicolored 1.75 .90
a. Sheet of 6, #2226-2231 6.75 6.75
2232 Sheet of 6, #a.-f. 6.75 6.75
a. A612 50e multicolored .60 .30
b.-c. A612 85e any single 1.00 .50
d.-e. A612 140e any single 1.75 .90
f. A612 80e multicolored 1.00 .50
g. Souvenir sheet, #2232a-2232e 6.25 6.25

Die Cut 11½

Self-Adhesive Coil Stamps

Size: 29x24mm

2233 A612 50e multicolored .60 .30
2234 A612 50e multicolored .60 .30
2235 A612 50e multicolored .60 .30
2236 A612 50e multicolored .60 .30
2237 A612 50e multicolored .60 .30
2238 A612 50e multicolored .60 .30
a. Strip of 6, #2233-2238 3.75
2239 A612 85e multicolored 1.00 .45
2240 A612 85e multicolored 1.00 .45
2241 A612 85e multicolored 1.00 .45
2242 A612 85e multicolored 1.00 .45
2243 A612 85e multicolored 1.00 .45
2244 A612 85e multicolored 1.00 .45
a. Strip of 6, #2239-2244 6.00

Nos. 2233-2238 are not inscribed with Latin names.

Discovery of Radium, Cent. — A622

1998, June 1 ***Perf. 12***

2245 A622 140e Marie Curie 1.75 .90

Ferreira de Castro (1898-1974), Writer — A623

1998, June 10

2246 A623 50e multicolored .60 .30

Bernardo Marques, Artist, Birth Cent. — A624

1998, June 10

2247 A624 85e multicolored 1.00 .50

Souvenir Sheet

Universal Declaration of Human Rights, 50th Anniv. — A625

1998, June 18

2248 A625 315e multicolored 4.00 2.00

District Arms Type of 1997

1998, June 23

2249 A609 50e Vila Real .60 .30
2250 A609 85e Setubal 1.00 .50
2251 A609 85e Viana do Castelo 1.00 .50
2252 A609 100e Santarem 1.25 .65
2253 A609 100e Viseu 1.25 .65
a. Souvenir sheet of 3, #2250, 2252-2253 3.50 3.50
2254 A609 200e Porto 2.50 1.25
a. Souvenir sheet of 3, #2249, 2251, 2254 4.25 4.25
Nos. 2249-2254 (6) 7.60 3.85

Marinha Grande Glass Industry, 250th Anniv. A626

Designs: 50e, Blowing glass, furnace. 80e, Early worker heating glass, ornament. 100e, Factory, bottles. 140e, Modern worker heating glass, vases.

1998, July 7

2255 A626 50e multicolored .60 .30
2256 A626 80e multicolored 1.00 .50
2257 A626 100e multicolored 1.25 .65
2258 A626 140e multicolored 1.75 .90
Nos. 2255-2258 (4) 4.60 2.35

1998 Vasco da Gama Regatta A627

Sailing ship, country represented: 50e, Sagres, Portugal. No. 2260, Asgard II, Ireland. No. 2261, Rose, US. No. 2262, Kruzenshtern, Russia. No. 2263, Amerigo Vespucci, Italy. 140e, Creoula, Portugal.

1998, July 31

2259 A627 50e multicolored .60 .30
2260 A627 85e multicolored 1.00 .50
2261 A627 85e multicolored 1.00 .50
2262 A627 100e multicolored 1.25 .65
2263 A627 100e multicolored 1.25 .65
2264 A627 140e multicolored 1.75 .90
Nos. 2259-2264 (6) 6.85 3.50

Discovery of Maritime Route to India Type of 1996

Voyage of Vasco da Gama: No. 2265, Meeting with pilot, Ibn Madjid. 80e, Storm in the Indian Ocean. 100e, Arrival in Calicut. 140e, Meeting with the Samorin of Calicut.

No. 2269: a, like #2136. b, like #2137. c, like #2138. d, like #2139. e, like #2191. f, like #2192. g, like #2193. h, like #2194. i, like #2266. j, like #2267. k, like #2268.

315e, King of Melinde listening to narration of the history of Portugal.

1998, Sept. 4 ***Perf. 13½***

2265 A593 50e multicolored .60 .30
2266 A593 80e multicolored 1.00 .50
2267 A593 100e multicolored 1.25 .65
2268 A593 140e multicolored 1.75 .90
Nos. 2265-2268 (4) 4.60 2.35

Sheet of 12

2269 A593 50e #a.-k. + #2265 7.50 7.50

Souvenir Sheet

2270 A593 315e multicolored 4.00 4.00

Lisbon-Coimbra Mail Coach, Decree to Reorganize Maritime Mail to Brazil, Bicent. — A628

50e, Modern van delivering mail, postal emblm. 140e, Sailing ship, Postilhao da America, mail coach.

1998, Oct. 9 ***Perf. 12x11½***

2271 A628 50e multicolored .60 .30
2272 A628 140e multicolored 1.75 .90

See Brazil No. 2691.

Souvenir Sheet

8th Iberian-American Summit, Oporto — A629

1998, Oct. 18 ***Perf. 12½***

2273 A629 140e multicolored 3.00 2.00

Souvenir Sheet

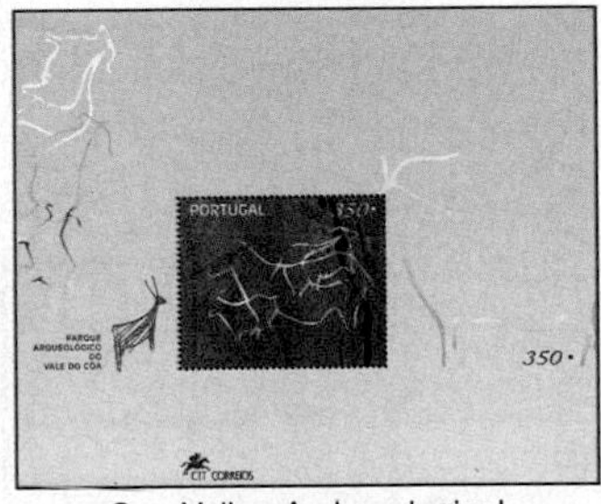

Coa Valley Archaeological Park — A630

1998, Oct. 23 ***Perf. 13½***

2274 A630 350e multicolored 4.50 2.25

Health in Portugal — A631

1998, Nov. 5 ***Perf. 12***

2275 A631 100e multicolored 1.25 .65

Souvenir Sheet

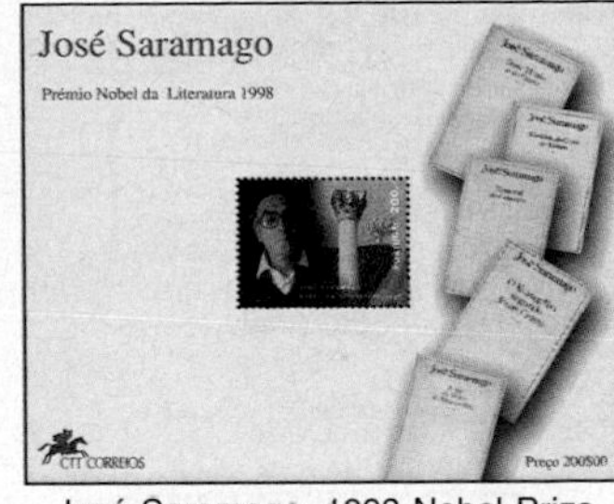

José Saramago, 1998 Nobel Prize Winner for Literature — A632

1998, Dec. 15 **Litho.** ***Perf. 12***

2276 A632 200e multicolored 2.50 1.25

Postrider Type of 1993

1999, Jan. 11 **Litho.** ***Perf. 13¼***

2276A A521 A brown, gray & black 1.00 .50

No. 2276A sold for 51e on date of issue. Inscription at LR reads "Imp: Lito Maia 99."

19th Cent. Professions Type

Designs: 51e, Knife grinder. 86e, Female bread seller. 95e, Coachman. 100e, Milkmaid. 210e, Basket seller.

1999, Feb. 26 **Litho.** ***Perf. 11½x12***

2277 A560 51e multicolored .65 .35
2278 A560 86e multicolored 1.10 .55
2279 A560 95e multicolored 1.25 .65
2280 A560 100e multicolored 1.25 .65
2281 A560 210e multicolored 2.75 1.40
Nos. 2277-2281 (5) 7.00 3.60

Booklet Stamps

Self-Adhesive

Serpentine Die Cut 11¼

2281A A560 51e like #2277 .65 .35
c. Booklet pane of 10 6.50
2281B A560 95e like #2279 1.25 .65
d. Booklet pane of 10 12.50

Nos. 2281A and 2281B were issued as coil rolls of 100 (No. 2281A) or 50 (No. 2281B) as well as in booklet form. Values the same. Used examples of each denomination are identical.

Nos. 2281Ac, 2281Bd are complete booklets. The peelable backing serves as a booklet cover.

Beginning with No. 2282 denominations are on the stamps in both escudos and euros. Listings show the value in escudos.

Introduction of the Euro — A633

1999, Mar. 15 ***Perf. 12***

2282 A633 95e multicolored 1.50 1.00

Australia '99, World Stamp Expo — A634

Portuguese in Australia: No. 2283, Sailing ship offshore, kangaroos. No. 2284, Sailing ship, natives watching.

350e, like #2283-2284.

1999, Mar. 19

2283 140e multicolored 1.75 .90
2284 140e multicolored 1.75 .90
a. A634 Pair, #2283-2284 3.50 3.50

Souvenir Sheet

2285 A634 350e multicolored 5.00 5.00

No. 2285 contains one 80x30mm stamp and is a continuous design.

Presidential Campaign of José Norton de Matos, 50th Anniv. — A635

1999, Mar. 24

2286 A635 80e multicolored 1.25 .50

Joao Almeida Garrett (1799-1854), Writer — A636

1999, Mar. 24

2287 A636 95e multicolored 1.50 .65

Souvenir Sheet

2288 A636 210e like #2287 3.00 1.40

Flight Between Portugal and Macao, 75th Anniv. A637

Airplanes: No. 2289, Breguet 16 Bn2, "Patria." No. 2290, DH9.

1999, Apr. 19

2289 A637 140e multicolored 1.75 .90
2290 A637 140e multicolored 1.75 .90
a. Souvenir sheet, #2289-2290 3.50 3.50

See Macao 979-980.

Carnation A638

Assembly building — A639

1999, Apr. 25

2291 A638 51e multicolored .65 .30
2292 A639 80e multicolored 1.00 .50
a. Souvenir sheet, #2291-2292 1.75 1.75

Revolution, 25th Anniv.

Council of Europe, 50th Anniv. A640

1999, May 5 Litho. *Perf. 12x11¾*

2293 A640 100e multicolored 1.25 .65

Europa A641

100e, Wolf, iris, Peneda-Gerês Natl. Park.

1999, May 5

2294 A641 100e multicolored *1.25 .65*
a. Souvenir sheet of 3 *3.75 3.75*

Marquis de Pombal (1699-1782), Statesman — A642

No. 2295: 80e, Portrait.
No. 2296: a, 80e, Portrait and portion of statue. b, 210e, Hand, quill pen.

1999, May 13

2295 A642 80e multicolored 1.00 1.00

Souvenir Sheet

2296 A642 Sheet of 2, #a.-b. 3.00 3.00

Meeting of Portuguese and Chinese Cultures in Macao — A643

Designs: 51e, Ship, junk, bridge. 80e, Macao dancers in Portuguese outfits. 95e, Virgin Mary statue, dragon heads. 100e, Church, temple. 140e, Statues in park, horiz.

Perf. 11¾x12, 12x11¾

1999, June 24 Litho.

2297 A643 51e multicolored .60 .30
2298 A643 80e multicolored 1.00 .50
2299 A643 95e multicolored 1.25 .60
2300 A643 100e multicolored 1.25 .65
2301 A643 140e multicolored 1.75 .90
Nos. 2297-2301 (5) 5.85 2.95

Portuguese Air Force, 75th Anniv. A644

Designs: No. 2302, De Havilland DH 82A Tiger Moth. No. 2303, Supermarine Spitfire Vb. No. 2304, Breguet Bre XIV A2. No. 2305, Spad S. VII-C1. No. 2306, Caudron G.III. No. 2307, Junkers Ju-52/3m g3e.

1999, July 1 *Perf. 12x11¾*

2302 A644 51e multicolored .60 .30
2303 A644 51e multicolored .60 .30
2304 A644 85e multicolored 1.10 .55
2305 A644 85e multicolored 1.10 .55
2306 A644 95e multicolored 1.25 .65
2307 A644 95e multicolored 1.25 .65
a. Souv. sheet of 6, #2302-2307 6.00 6.00
Nos. 2302-2307 (6) 5.90 3.00

Surrealist Group of Lisbon, 50th Anniv. A645

Sections of Painting "Cadavre Exquis" by: 51e, António Pedro (1909-66). 80e, Marcellino Vespeira (b. 1926). 95e, Joao Moniz Pereira (1920-89). 100e, Fernando de Azevedo (b. 1923). 140e, António Domingues (b. 1921).

1999, July 2 Litho. *Perf. 13¼*

2308 A645 51e multicolored .60 .30
2309 A645 80e multicolored 1.00 .50
2310 A645 95e multicolored 1.25 .60
2311 A645 100e multicolored 1.25 .65
2312 A645 140e multicolored 1.75 .90
a. Souv. sheet of 5, #2308-2312 5.75 5.75
Nos. 2308-2312 (5) 5.85 2.95

PhilexFrance 99, No. 2312a.

Inauguration of Rail Link Over 25th of April Bridge — A646

51e, No. 2315, Train, tunnel entrance. 95e, No. 2316, Train, viaduct, Tagus River.

1999, July 29 Litho. *Perf. 12x11¾*

2313 A646 51e multicolored .60 .30
2314 A646 95e multicolored 1.25 .60

Souvenir Sheets

2315 A646 350e multicolored 5.00 5.00
2316 A646 350e multicolored 5.00 5.00

Nos. 2315-2316 each contain one 80x30mm stamp.

UPU, 125th Anniv. A647

Designs: 95e, Heinrich von Stephan, earth, letter. 140e, Computer, earth, letter. 315e, Von Stephan, computer, earth, letters.

1999, Aug. 21

2317 A647 95e multicolored 1.25 .65
2318 A647 140e multicolored 1.75 .90

Souvenir Sheet

2319 A647 315e multicolored 4.00 4.00

No. 2319 contains one 80x30mm stamp.

Desserts Originating in Convents A648

Designs: 51e, Trouxas de ovos. 80e, Pudim de ovos (egg pudding). 95e, Papos de anjo. 100e, Palha de Abrantes. 140e, Castanhas de Viseu. 210e, Bolo de mel (honey cake).

1999, Aug. 30

2320 A648 51e multicolored .60 .30
2321 A648 80e multicolored 1.00 .50
2322 A648 95e multicolored 1.25 .60
2323 A648 100e multicolored 1.25 .65
2324 A648 140e multicolored 1.75 .90
2325 A648 210e multicolored 2.75 1.40
Nos. 2320-2325 (6) 8.60 4.35

See Nos. 2366-2371.

Conquest of Algarve, 750th Anniv. A649

1999, Sept. 3 Litho. *Perf. 12x11¾*

2326 A649 100e multicolored 1.25 .65

Medical Pioneers A650

#2327, Ricardo Jorge (1858-1939), Natl. Health Inst. #2328, Camara Pestana (1863-99), microscope, Pestana Bacteriological Inst. #2329, Francisco Gentil (1878-1964), Portuguese Inst. of Oncology. #2330, Egas Moniz (1874-1955), cerebral angiogram. #2331, Reynaldo dos Santos (1880-1970), arteriogram. #2332, Joao Cid dos Santos (1907-76), performer of 1st endarterectomy.

1999, Sept. 20

2327 A650 51e multicolored .60 .30
2328 A650 51e multicolored .60 .30
2329 A650 80e multicolored 1.00 .50
2330 A650 80e multicolored 1.00 .50
2331 A650 95e multicolored 1.25 .60
2332 A650 95e multicolored 1.25 .60
Nos. 2327-2332 (6) 5.70 2.80

José Diogo de Mascarenhas Neto, First Superintendent of Posts — A651

1999, Oct. 9

2333 A651 80e multicolored 1.00 .50

Postal reorganization and provisional mail regulations, bicent.

Jaime Martins Barata (1899-1970), Painter, Philatelic Art Consultant — A652

1999, Oct. 9

2334 A652 80e multicolored 1.00 .50

Christmas A653

Art by handicapped persons: 51e, Maria F. Gonçalves (Magi). 95e, Marta Silva. 140e, Luis F. Farinha. 210e, Gonçalves (Nativity).

1999, Nov. 19

2335 A653 51e multicolored .60 .30
2336 A653 95e multicolored 1.25 .60
2337 A653 140e multicolored 1.75 .90
2338 A653 210e multicolored 2.75 1.40
Nos. 2335-2338 (4) 6.35 3.20

Souvenir Sheet

Meeting of Portuguese and Chinese Cultures — A654

1999, Nov. 19 ***Perf. 11¾x12***

2339 A654 140e multicolored 2.50 1.25

See Macao No. 1009.

Souvenir Sheet

Retrospective of Macao's Portuguese History — A655

1999, Dec. 19 Litho. ***Perf. 12x11¾***

2340 A655 350e multicolored 6.00 6.00

See Macao No. 1011.

Birth of Jesus Christ, 2000th Anniv. — A656

2000, Feb. 15 Litho. ***Perf. 11¾x12***

2341 A656 52e multicolored .60 .30

The 20th Century A657

Designs: 86e, Astronaut and spacecraft.

No. 2343: a, Human rights. b, Fashions (60x30mm). c, Ecology (60x30mm). d, Transportation (old). e, Transportation (modern). f, Like No. 2342. g, Space shuttle.

No. 2344: a, Authors Marcel Proust, Thomas Mann, James Joyce, Franz Kafka, Fernando Pessoa, Jorge Luis Borges, Samuel Beckett (50x30mm). b, Musicians and composers Claude Debussy, Igor Stravinsky, Arnold Schoenberg, Béla Bartók, George Gershwin, Charlie Parker, Bill Evans (50x30mm). c, Stage. d, Stage, diff. (60x30mm). e, Art (50x30mm). f, Art (30x30mm). g. Cinema (50x30mm). h, Cinema and television (30x30mm). i, Architecture (denomination at LL). j, Architecture (denomination at LR). k, Architecture (denomination at center).

No. 2345: a, Philosophers Edmund Husserl, Ludwig Wittgenstein, Martin Heidegger. b, Mathematicians Jules Henri Poincaré, Kurt Gödel, Andrei Kolmogorov. c, Physicists Max Planck, Albert Einstein, Niels Bohr (50x30mm). d, Anthropologists Franz Boas, Claude Lévi-Strauss, Margaret Mead. e, Psychoanalyst Sigmund Freud and medical researcher Sir Alexander Fleming (30x30mm). f, Transplant pioneer Dr. Christiaan Barnard. g, Economists Joseph Schumpeter, John Maynard Keynes. h, Technology. i, Technology (30x30mm). j, Computer pioneers Alan Turing, John von Neumann. k, Radio pioneer Guglielmo Marconi. l, Information and communications (30x30mm).

2000, Feb. 18 ***Perf. 12x11¾***

2342 A657 86e multicolored 1.10 .55

Souvenir Sheets of 7, 11, 12

2343 A657 52e #a.-g.	4.50	4.50
2344 A657 52e #a.-k.	7.00	7.00
2345 A657 52e #a.-l.	7.75	7.75

Birds — A658

Designs: 52e, Golden eagle. 85e, Great crested grebe. 90e, Flamingo. 100e, Gannet. 215e, Teal.

2000, Mar. 2 Litho. ***Perf. 11¾x11½***

2346 A658 52e multi	.60	.30
2347 A658 85e multi	1.10	.55
2348 A658 90e multi	1.10	.55
2349 A658 100e multi	1.25	.65
2350 A658 215e multi	2.75	1.40
Nos. 2346-2350 (5)	6.80	3.45

Booklet Stamps

Serpentine Die Cut 11¼

Self-Adhesive

2351 A658 52e Like #2346	.60	.30
a. Booklet, 10 #2351	6.00	
2352 A658 100e Like #2349	1.25	.65
a. Booklet, 10 #2352	12.50	

See Nos. 2401-2407, 2465-2471, 2472, 2473, 2530-2535, 2537-2537A, 2621-2626, 2628.

Portuguese Presidency of Council of Europe A659

2000, Mar. 23 ***Perf. 12x11¾***

2353 A659 100e multi 1.25 .65

Discovery of Brazil, 500th Anniv. A660

Designs: 52e, Two sailors, three natives, parrot. 85e, sailor, ships, four natives. 100e, Sailors, natives, sails. 140e, Sailor and natives inspecting tree.

2000, Apr. 11 Litho. ***Perf. 12x11¾***

2354 A660 52e multi	.60	.30
2355 A660 85e multi	1.10	.55
2356 A660 100e multi	1.25	.65
2357 A660 140e multi	1.75	.90
a. Souvenir sheet, #2354-2357	4.75	2.40
Nos. 2354-2357 (4)	4.70	2.40

Lubrapex 2000 (#2357a). See Brazil No. 2738.

Europa, 2000

Common Design Type

2000, May 9 ***Perf. 11¾x12***

2358 CD17 100e multi	*1.25*	*.65*
a. Souvenir sheet of 3	*3.75*	*3.75*

Visit of Pope John Paul II A661

2000, May 12 ***Perf. 12x11¾***

2359 A661 52e multi 1.00 .40

Intl. Cycling Union, Cent. and The Stamp Show 2000, London A662

Bicycles: 52e, Draisenne, 1817. 85e, Michaux, 1868. 100e, Ariel, 1871. 140e, Rover, 1888. 215e, BTX, 2000. 350e, GT, 2000.

2000, May 22

2360 A662 52e multi	.60	.30
2361 A662 85e multi	1.10	.55
2362 A662 100e multi	1.25	.65
2363 A662 140e multi	1.75	.90
2364 A662 215e multi	2.75	1.40
2365 A662 350e multi	4.50	2.25
a. Souvenir sheet, #2360-2365	12.00	12.00
Nos. 2360-2365 (6)	11.95	6.05

Desserts Type of 1999

Designs: 52e, Fatias de Tomar. 85e, Dom rodrigos. 100e, Sericaia. 140e, Pao-de-ló. 215e, Pao de rala. 350e, Bolo real paraíso.

2000, May 30

2366 A648 52e multi	.60	.30
2367 A648 85e multi	1.10	.55
2368 A648 100e multi	1.25	.65
2369 A648 140e multi	1.75	.90
2370 A648 215e multi	2.75	1.40
2371 A648 350e multi	4.50	2.25
Nos. 2366-2371 (6)	11.95	6.05

Fishermen's Day — A663

2000, May 31

2372 A663 52e multi .60 .30

Expo 2000, Hanover — A664

Designs: 100e, Portuguese landscapes. 350e, Portuguese pavilion.

2000, June 1

2373 A664 100e multi 1.25 .65

Souvenir Sheet

2374 A664 350e multi 4.50 4.50

No. 2374 contains one 40x31mm stamp.

Constituent Assembly, 25th Anniv. A665

2000, June 2

2375 A665 85e multi 1.50 .75

Cod Fishing A666

Cod, various fishermen and boats.

2000, June 24 ***Perf. 12x11¾***

Color of Denominations

2376 A666 52e rose	.60	.30
2377 A666 85e claret	1.10	.55
2378 A666 100e green	1.25	.65
2379 A666 100e red	1.25	.65
2380 A666 140e yellow	1.75	.90
2381 A666 215e brown	2.75	1.40
a. Souvenir sheet, #2376-2381	8.75	8.75
Nos. 2376-2381 (6)	8.70	4.45

Eça de Queiroz (1845-1900), Writer — A667

2000, Aug. 16 Litho. ***Perf. 12x11¾***

2382 A667 85e multi 1.10 .55

2000 Summer Olympics, Sydney A668

Designs: 52e, Runner. 85e, Show jumping. 100e, Yachting. 140e, Diving.

No. 2387: a, 85e, Fencing. b, 215e, Beach volleyball.

2000, Sept. 15

2383-2386 A668 Set of 4 4.75 2.40

Souvenir Sheet

2387 A668 Sheet of 2, #a-b 3.75 3.75

Olymphilex 2000, Sydney (No. 2387).

Snoopy A669

Snoopy: No. 2388, 52e, At computer on dog house. No. 2389, 52e, Mailing letter. 85e, Driving mail truck. 100e, At letter sorting machine. 140e, Delivering mail. 215e, Reading letter.

2000, Oct. 6

2388-2393 A669 Set of 6	7.75	3.75
2393a Souvenir sheet, #2288-2393	7.75	7.75

Lisbon Geographic Society, 125th Anniv. — A670

No. 2394: a, 85e, African native, geographer, theodolite, sextant. b, 100e, Sextant, society emblem, map, zebras.

2000, Nov. 10

2394 A670 Horiz. pair, #a-b 2.25 1.10

Famous People — A671

No. 2395: a, Carolina Michaelis de Vasconcellos (1851-1925), teacher. b, Miguel Bombarda (1851-1910), doctor, politician. c, Bernardino Machado (1851-1944), politician. d, Tomás Alcaide (1901-67), singer. e, José Régio (1901-69), writer. f, José Rodrigues Miguéis (1901-80), writer. g, Vitorino Nemésio

(1901-78), writer. h, Bento de Jesus Caraça (1901-48), mathematician.

2001, Feb. 20 Litho. *Perf. 12x11¾*

2395	A671	Sheet of 8 + 4 labels	8.75	8.75
a.-h.		85e Any single	1.10	.55

World Indoor Track and Field Championships — A672

Designs: 85e, Runners. 90e, Pole vault. 105e, Shot put. 250e, High jump.

2001, Mar. 1

2396-2399	A672	Set of 4	6.50	3.25

Souvenir Sheet

2400	A672	350e Hurdles	4.25	2.10

Bird Type of 2000 and

A672a

Designs: 53e, Sisao. No. 2402, Caimao. 105e, Perdiz-do-mar. 140e, Peneireiro cinzento. 225e, Abutre do Egipto.

2001, Mar. 6 Litho. *Perf. 11¾x11½*

2401	A658	53e multi	.65	.35
2402	A658	85e multi	1.10	.55
2403	A658	105e multi	1.25	.65
2404	A658	140e multi	1.75	.90
2405	A658	225e multi	2.75	1.40
		Nos. 2401-2405 (5)	7.50	3.85

Serpentine Die Cut 11½x12

Self-Adhesive

2406	A658	53e multi	.65	.35
a.		Booklet of 10	6.50	
2406B	A672a	85e shown	1.10	.55
2407	A658	105e multi	1.25	.65
a.		Booklet of 10	12.50	

Arab Heritage in Portugal A673

Designs: 53e, Plate with ship design, 15th cent. 90e, Tiles, 16th cent. 105e, Tombstone, 14th cent. 140e, Gold dinar, 12th cent. 225e, container, 11th cent. 350e, Ceramic jug, 12th-13th cent.

2001, Mar. 28 Litho. *Perf. 12x11¾*

2408-2413	A673	Set of 6	12.00	6.00

Stampin' the Future Children's Stamp Design Contest Winners A674

Art by: 85e, Angela M. Lopes. 90e, Maria G. Silva, vert. 105e, Joao A. Ferreira.

Perf. 12x11¾, 11¾x12

2001, Apr. 10 Litho.

2414-2416	A674	Set of 3	3.50	1.75

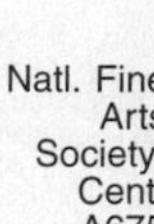

Natl. Fine Arts Society, Cent. A675

Designs: 85e, Sculpture, building, stained glass window. 105e, Artist, painting. 350p, Hen and Chicks, by Girao.

2001, Apr. 19 *Perf. 12x11¾*

2417-2418	A675	Set of 2	2.40	1.25

Souvenir Sheet

2419	A675	350e multi	4.25	4.25

Constitution, 25th Anniv. — A676

2001, Apr. 25

2420	A676	85e multi	1.10	.55

Europa A677

2001, May 9

2421	A677	105e multi	*1.25*	*.65*
a.		Souvenir sheet of 3	*3.75*	*3.75*

Congratulations A678

Designs: No. 2422, 85e, Couple, hearts. No. 2423, 85e, Birthday cake. No. 2424, 85e, Drinks. No. 2425, 85e, Flowers.

2001, May 16 *Perf. 11¾x12*

2422-2425	A678	Set of 4	4.25	2.10
2425a		Souvenir sheet, #2422-2425	4.25	4.25

Porto, European City of Culture A679

Bridge and: 53e, Open book. 85e, Globe, binary code. 105e, Piano. 140e, Stage curtain. 225e, Picture frame. 350e, Fireworks.

2001, May 23 *Perf. 12x11¾*

2426-2431	A679	Set of 6	12.00	6.00
2431a		Souvenir sheet, #2426-2431	12.00	12.00

Military Museum, 150th Anniv. A680

Designs: 85e, Shell, 1773. 105e, Suit of armor, 16th cent.

No. 2434: a, 53e, Pistol of King Joseph I, 1757. b, 53e, Cannon, 1797. c, 140e, Cannon, 1533. d, 140e, Helmet, 14th-15th cent.

2001, June 7

2432-2433	A680	Set of 2	2.40	1.25

Souvenir Sheet

2434	A680	Sheet of 4, #a-d	4.75	4.75

Animals at Lisbon Zoo A681

Designs: 53e, Bear. 85e, Monkey. 90e, Iguana. 105e, Penguin. 225e, Toucan. 350e, Giraffe.

No. 2441, vert.: a, 85e, Elephant. b, 85e, Zebra. c, 225e, Lion. d, 225e, Rhinoceros.

2001, June 11 *Perf. 12x11¾*

2435-2440	A681	Set of 6	11.50	5.75

Souvenir Sheet

2441	A681	Sheet of 4, #a-d	7.75	7.75

Belgica 2001 Intl. Stamp Exhibition, Brussels (#2441).

2001 Lions Intl. European Forum A682

2001, Sept. 6 Litho. *Perf. 12x11¾*

2442	A682	85e multi	1.10	.55

Pillars A683

No. 2443: a, Azinhoso. b, Soajo. c, Bragança. d, Linhares. e, Arcos de Valdevez. f, Vila de Rua. g, Sernancelhe. h, Frechas.

2001, Sept. 19

2443		Block of 8	5.25	2.75
a.-h.		A683 53e Any single	.65	.35

Year of Dialogue Among Civilizations A684

2001, Oct. 9

2444	A684	140e multi	1.75	.90

Walt Disney (1901-66) A685

Designs: No. 2445, Disney and sketches.

No. 2446 — Various tiles and: a, Huey, Dewey and Louie. b, Mickey Mouse. c, Minnie Mouse. d, Goofy. e, Pluto. f, Donald Duck. g, Scrooge McDuck. h, Daisy Duck.

2001, Oct. 18 Litho. *Perf. 12x11¾*

2445	A685	53e multi	.65	.35

Souvenir Sheet

2446		Sheet of 9, #a-h, 2445	6.00	6.00
a.-h.		A685 53e Any single	.65	.35

Security Services, 200th Anniv. A686

Designs: 53e, Royal police guards, Lisbon, 1801. 85e, Municipal guard, Lisbon, 1834. 90e, National infantry guard, 1911. 105e, National cavalry guard, 1911. 140e, Transit brigade guard, 1970. 350e, Fiscal brigade guard, 1993.

225e, National cavalry guard, 1911, diff.

2001, Oct. 22

2447-2452	A686	Set of 6	12.00	6.00

Souvenir sheet

2453	A686	225e multi	2.75	2.75

Sailing Ships — A687

No. 2454: a, Chinese junk, 13th cent. b, Portuguese caravel, 15th cent.

2001, Nov. 8

2454	A687	53e Horiz. pair, #a-b	1.25	1.25

See People's Republic of China No. 3146.

100 Cents = 1 Euro (€)

Introduction of the Euro A688

2002, Jan. 2 Litho. *Perf. 12x11¾*

2455	A688	1c 1c coin	.25	.25
2456	A688	2c 2c coin	.25	.25
2457	A688	5c 5c coin	.25	.25
2458	A688	10c 10c coin	.30	.25
2459	A688	20c 20c coin	.60	.25
2460	A688	50c 50c coin	2.00	.60
2461	A688	€1 €1 coin	4.00	1.25
2462	A688	€2 €2 coin	7.00	2.50
		Nos. 2455-2462 (8)	14.65	5.60

Postrider A689

2002, Jan. 2 *Perf. 13¼*

2463	A689	A multi	.85	.40

No. 2463 sold for 28c on day of issue.

Damiao de Góis (1502-74), Diplomat and Historian — A690

2002, Feb. 26 *Perf. 12x11¾*

2464	A690	45c multi	1.40	.55

Bird Type of 2000 with Euro Denominations Only and

A690a

Designs: 2c, Abelharuco. No. 2466, 28c, Andorinha do mar ana. No. 2467, 43c, Bufo real. No. 2468, 54c, Cortiçol de barriga branca. 60c, Noitibó de nuca vermelha. 70c, Cuco rabilongo. Nos. 2472A, 28c, Cuco-rabilongo. No. 2471A, 43c, Andorinha do mar ana. Nos. 2472, 2473, 54c, Bufo real.

2002, Feb. 26 *Perf. 11¾x11½*

2465	A658	2c multi	.25	.25
2466	A658	28c multi	.70	.35
2467	A658	43c multi	1.10	.55
2468	A658	54c multi	1.40	.70
2469	A658	60c multi	1.50	.75
2470	A658	70c multi	1.75	.90

Serpentine Die Cut 11½x12, 11x11½ (#2471A)

2471	A658	28c multi	.90	.35
2471A	A690a	43c multi	1.25	.55
2472	A658	54c multi	1.75	.70

Booklet Stamps

Serpentine Die Cut 11¼x11

2472A	A658	28c multi	.90	.35
b.		Booklet pane of 10	9.00	
2473	A658	54c multi	1.60	.70
a.		Booklet pane of 10	16.00	
		Nos. 2465-2473 (11)	13.10	6.15

No. 2472A has thicker numerals than No. 2471. No. 2473 lacks dot between "bufo" and "real" found on No. 2472. No. 2472A lacks dot between "cuco" and "rebilongo" found on No. 2471.

Pedro Nunes (1502-78), Mathematician and Geographer — A691

Designs: No. 2474, 28c, Ship, Earth. No. 2475, 28c, Ship, sextant. €1.15, Nunes.

2002, Mar. 6 ***Perf. 12x11¾***

2474-2476	A691	Set of 3	5.25	2.10
2476a		Souvenir sheet, #2474-2476	5.25	5.25

America Issue — Youth, Education and Literacy A692

Children and: No. 2477, 70c, Flower. No. 2478, 70c, Pencil. No. 2479, 70c, Book.

2002, Mar. 12

2477-2479	A692	Set of 3	6.25	2.75

Astronomy A693

Designs: No. 2480, 28c, Nobres College, 16th cent. astrolabe, solar eclipse. No. 2481, Polytechnic Observatory, Lisbon, telescope, Jupiter. 43c, Coimbra Observatory, quadrant, stars. No. 2483, 45c, King Pedro V, telescope, sun. No. 2484, 45c, King Luis, Cassegrain telescope, comet. 54c, Ajuda Observatory, telescope, Moon. €1.15, Porto Observatory Cassegrain telescope, Saturn. €1.75 Projector of C. Gulbenkian Planetarium, planets.

No. 2488: a, 18th cent. armillary sphere. b, 19th cent. theodolite.

2002, Apr. 23 **Litho.** ***Perf. 12x11¾***

2480-2487	A693	Set of 8	15.50	6.50

Souvenir Sheet

2488	A693	70c Sheet of 2, #a-b	4.25	3.50

Grande Oriente Lusitano Masonic Organization, Bicent. — A694

2002, May 9

2489	A694	43c multi	1.50	.75

Europa A695

2002, May 9

2490	A695	54c multi	*1.40*	*.70*
a.		Souvenir sheet of 3, perf. 12½	*4.25*	*4.25*

Portuguese Air Force, 50th Anniv. A696

Designs: 28c, F-16. 43c, SA-300 Puma helicopter. 54c, A-Jet. 70c, C-130. €1.25, P-3P. No. 2496, €1.75, Fiat G91.

No. 2497: a, €1.15, Asas de Portugal. b, €1.75, Epsilon.

2002, July 1 **Litho.** ***Perf. 12x11¾***

2491-2496	A696	Set of 6	15.00	6.00

Souvenir Sheet

2497	A696	Sheet of 2, #a-b	8.75	8.75

Sports A697

Designs: No. 2498, 28c, Race walking. No. 2499, 28c, Gymnastics. No. 2500, 45c, Basketball. No. 2501, 45c, Handball. No. 2502, 54c, Fencing. No. 2503, 54c, Women's roller hockey. No. 2504, €1.75, Golf. No. 2505, €1.75, Soccer.

No. 2506: a, €1, Soccer players. b, €2, Soccer players, diff.

2002, Aug. 2

2498-2505	A697	Set of 8	18.00	7.50

Souvenir Sheet

2506	A697	Sheet of 2, #a-b	9.00	9.00

Portuguese Gymnastics Federation, 50th anniv. (#2499), World Fencing Championships (#2502), 6th Women's Roller Hockey Championships (#2503), 2002 World Cup Soccer Championships, Japan and Korea (#2505-2506), PhilaKorea 2002 World Stamp Exhibition (#2506).

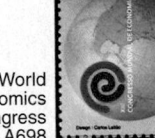

13th World Economics Congress A698

2002, Sept. 9

2507	A698	70c multi	2.10	.90

Ministry of Public Works, 150th Anniv. — A699

Designs: No. 2508, Anniversary emblem.

No. 2509: a, Port administration. b, Rail transportation. c, Air transportation. d, Infrastructure. e, Public buildings. f, Housing.

2002, Sept. 30 **Litho.** ***Perf. 12x12½***

2508	A699	43c shown	1.25	.85

Miniature Sheet

2509		Sheet of 6	7.75	7.75
a.-f.	A699	43c Any single	1.25	.85

Technical Education in Portugal, 150th Anniv. A700

2002, Oct. 9 ***Perf. 12x11¾***

2510	A700	43c multi	1.25	.85

UNESCO World Heritage Sites — A701

Various views of: No. 2511, 28c, No. 2518, 70c, No. 2519, €1.25, Alcobaça Monastery. No. 2512, 28c, No. 2517, 70c, No. 2520, €1.25, Monastery of the Hieronymites. No. 2513, 43c, No. 2516, 54c, No. 2521, €1.25, Historic Center of Guimaraes. No. 2514, 43c, No. 2515, 54c, No. 2522, €1.25, Alto Douro Wine Region.

2002, Nov. 7 ***Perf. 11¾x12, 12x11¾***

2511-2518	A701	Set of 8	12.00	8.00

Souvenir Sheets

2519-2522	A701	Set of 4	15.00	15.00

Size of Nos. 2515-2518: 80x30mm.

Portuguese Military College, Bicent. — A702

Military uniforms from: 20c, 1870. 30c, 1806. 43c, 1837. 55c, 1861. 70c, 1866. €2, 1912.

No. 2529: a, 1802. b, 1948.

2003, Feb. 22 **Litho.** ***Perf. 11¾x12***

2523-2528	A702	Set of 6	11.50	4.50

Souvenir Sheet

2529	A702	€1 Sheet of 2, #a-b	5.50	5.50

Bird Type of 2000 With Euro Denominations Only and

A703

Designs: 1c, Peto verde. 30c, Pombo das rochas. 43c, Melro azul. 55c, Toutinegra carrasqueira. 70c, Chasco ruivo.

2003, Mar. 7 ***Perf. 11¾x11½***

2530	A658	1c multi	.25	.25
2531	A658	30c multi	.85	.30
2532	A658	43c multi	1.25	.45
2533	A658	55c multi	1.50	.60
2534	A658	70c multi	2.00	.75

Self-Adhesive

Serpentine Die Cut 11¾

With Dots Between Words

2535	A658	30c multi	.85	.30
2536	A703	43c multi	1.25	.45
2537	A658	55c multi	1.50	.60
		Nos. 2530-2537 (8)	9.45	3.70

Coil Stamp

Self-Adhesive

Without Dots Between Words

2537A	A658	30c multi	—	—

Position of country name is at UL on No. 2531 but at LR on No. 2535; UR on No. 2533 but LL on No. 2537.

Nos. 2535-2537 have dots between the words in the bird's name. Two other stamps exist in this set. The editors would like to examine any examples.

European Year of Disabled People — A704

Crowd of people in design of: 30c, Person in wheelchair. 55c, Head with blue brain. 70c, Head with pink ear, eye and mouth.

2003, Mar. 12 ***Perf. 13¼***

2538-2540	A704	Set of 3	4.50	1.75

Portuguese Postage Stamps, 150th Anniv. A705

Designs: 30c, #1. 43c, #2. 55c, #3. 70c, #4.

2003, Mar. 13 ***Perf. 12x11¾***

2541-2544	A705	Set of 4	5.50	2.10

See No. 2578.

Orchids — A706

Designs: No. 2545, 46c, Aceras anthropophorum. No. 2546, 46c, Dactylorhiza maculata.

No. 2547, 30c: a, Orchis champagneuxii. b, Orchis morio. c, Serapias cordigera. d, Orchis coriophora. e, Ophrys bombyliflora. f, Ophrys vernixia. g, Ophrys speculum. h, Ophrys scolopax. i, Anacamptis pyramidalis.

No. 2548, 30c: a, Orchis italica. b, Ophrys tenthredinifera. c, Ophrys fusca fusca. d, Orchis papilionacea. e, Barlia robertiana. f, Ophrys lutea. g, Ophrys fusca. h, Ophrys apifera. i, Dactylorhiza ericetorum.

2003, Apr. 29 **Litho.** ***Perf. 11¾x12***

2545-2546	A706	Set of 2	2.75	1.10

Sheets of 9, #a-i

2547-2548	A706	Set of 2	15.00	15.00

Europa A707

Poster art by: No. 2549, 55c, Fred Kradolfer, 1931. No. 2550, 55c, Joao Machado, 1997.

2003, May 5 ***Perf. 12x12½***

2549-2550	A707	Set of 2	*3.00*	*1.25*
2550a		Souvenir sheet, #2549-2550	*3.25*	*3.00*

History of Law A708

Designs: 30c, Lawyer in black robe, lawyer in red robe, order of Portuguese lawyers. 43c, Two lawyers in black robes, national arms. 55c, Lawyer, bishop, manuscript. 70c, Lawyer in black robe, order of Portuguese lawyers, diff.

No. 2555: a, €1, Lawyer in red robe, left half of order of Portuguese lawyers. b, €2, Right half of order of Portuguese lawyers, bishop.

2003, May 13 *Perf. 12x11¾*
2551-2554 A708 Set of 4 5.50 2.40

Souvenir Sheet

2555 A708 Sheet of 2, #a-b 8.50 8.50

Traveling Exhibition on the 150th Anniv. of the First Portuguese Stamp A709

Exhibition stops: No. 2556, Viseu. No. 2557, Faro. No. 2558, Porto.

2003 *Perf. 14x13½*

Background Color

2556 A709 30c yellow		.85	.35
2557 A709 30c white		.85	.35
2558 A709 30c blue		.85	.35
	Nos. 2556-2558 (3)	2.55	1.05

Issued: No. 2556, 5/23; No. 2557, 7/21.

2004 European Soccer Championships, Portugal — A710

Emblem with background color of: 30c, White. 43c, Dark blue. 47c, Brown carmine. 55c, Green. 70c, Brown orange.

No. 2564 — Emblem and quadrant of emblem with denomination at: a, LL. b, LR. c, UL. d, UR.

2003, May 28 Litho. *Perf. 14x13½*
2559-2563 A710 Set of 5 7.00 2.75

Souvenir Sheet

2564	A710 Sheet of 4	6.75	6.75
a.-d.	55c Any single	1.50	1.25
e.	Souvenir sheet, #2559-2563, 2564a-2564d	14.00	14.00

Portuguese Automobile Club, Cent. A711

Emblems and: 30c, Driver in old automobile. 43c, Motorcyclist. €2, Driver in old automobile, blurred race car.

2003, June 24 *Perf. 12x11¾*
2565-2567 A711 Set of 3 7.75 3.25

Ricardo do Espírito Santo Silva Foundation, 50th Anniv. — A712

Designs: No. 2568, 30c, Portrait of Ricardo do Espírito Santo Silva, by Eduardo Malta. No. 2569, 30c, Chess table, 18th cent. No. 2570, 43c, Cutlery in decorated case, c. 1720-1750. No. 2571, 43c, Salver, 15th cent. No. 2572, 55c, Chinese cutlery case, c, 1700-1722. No. 2573, 55c, Wooden tub, 18th cent.

No. 2574: a, €1, Chest with drawers, 17th cent. b, €2, Carpet, 18th cent.

2003, July 9 *Perf. 11¾x12*
2568-2573 A712 Set of 6 7.25 3.00

Souvenir Sheet

2574 A712 Sheet of 2, #a-b 8.50 8.50

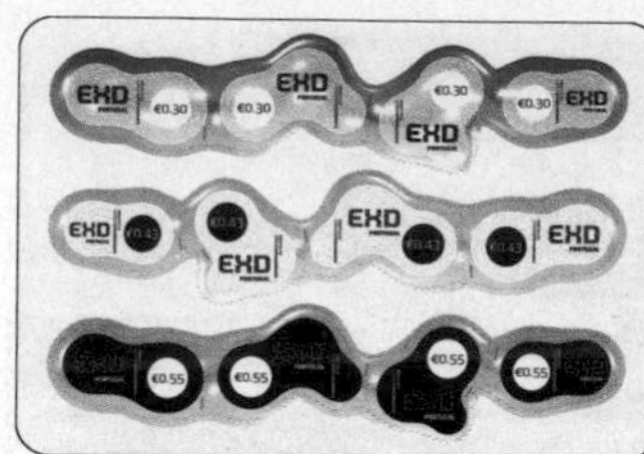

Experimental Design — A713

No. 2575: a, 2 lobes, black "EXD," white denomination circle to right. b, 3 lobes, black "EXD," white denomination circle below and to left. c, 3 lobes, black "EXD," white denomination circle above. d, 2 lobes, black "EXD," white denomination circle to left. e, 2 lobes, red "EXD," black denomination circle to right. f, 3 lobes, red "EXD," black denomination circle above. g, 3 lobes, red "EXD," black denomination circle below and to right. h, 2 lobes, red "EXD," black denomination circle to left. i, 2 lobes, red "EXD," white denomination circle to right. j, 3 lobes, red "EXD," white denomination circle below and to left. k, 3 lobes, red "EXD," white denomination circle above. l, 2 lobes, red "EXD," white denomination circle to left.

Serpentine Die Cut

2003, Sept. 17 **Litho.**

Self-Adhesive

2575	A713 Sheet of 12	15.00	15.00
a.-d.	30c Any single	.80	.35
e.-h.	43c Any single	1.10	.50
i.-l.	55c Any single	1.50	.60

Souvenir Sheet

Portuguese Stamps, 150th Anniv. — A714

Litho. & Embossed

2003, Sept. 19 *Perf. 12x11¾*
2576 A714 €3 Queen Maria II, Type A2 8.00 8.00

Souvenir Sheet

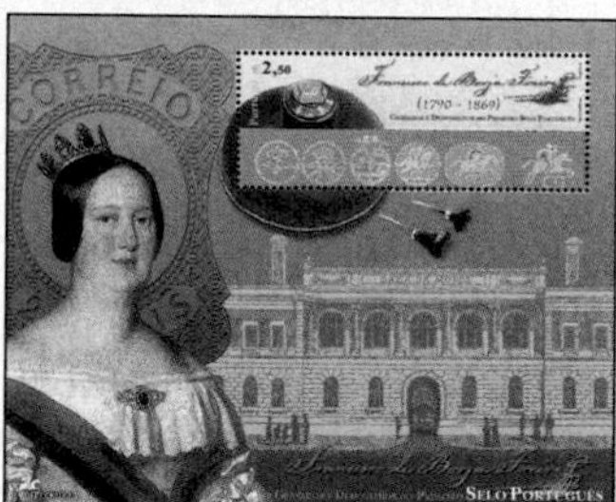

Francisco de Borja Freire (1790-1869), Designer and Engraver of First Portuguese Stamp — A715

Litho. With Hologram Applied

2003, Sept. 23 *Perf. 12x12½*
2577 A715 €2.50 multi 8.00 8.00

Souvenir Sheet

Lubrapex 2003 Philatelic Exhibition, Lisbon — A716

2003, Sept. 25 Litho. *Perf. 12x11¾*

2578	A716 Sheet, #2578a, 4 #2541	6.00	6.00
a.	30c Queen Maria II	1.00	1.00

Size of No. 2578a: 40x60mm.

Fountains A717

Designs: 30c, Sao Joao Fountain, Moucós. 43c, Fountain of Virtues, Porto. 55c, Giraldo Square Fountain, Evora. 70c, Blessed Woman Fountain, Sao Marcos de Tavira. €1, Town Fountain, Castelo de Vide. €2, Santo André Fountain, Guarda.

2003, Oct. 1 *Perf. 12x11¾*
2579-2584 A717 Set of 6 14.00 6.00

Glass — A718

Designs: 30c, Glass of King José I, 18th cent. 55c, Glass of Queen Maria II, 19th cent. 70c, Glass by Carmo Valente, 20th cent. €2, Glass by M. Helena Matos, 20th cent.

€1.50, Stained glass by Fernando Santos, 19th cent.

2003, Oct. 9 *Perf. 11¾x12*
2585-2588 A718 Set of 4 10.00 4.25

Souvenir Sheet

2589 A718 €1.50 multi 4.25 4.25

Apothecary Items A719

Designs: 30c, Persian jar, 12th-13th cent., Roman Empire medicine dropper, 1st-2nd cent. 43c, Bottle and bowl, 17th cent. 55c, Mortars and pestle, 16th and 17th cent. 70c, Alembic, 1910, and flask, 1890-1930.

2003, Oct. 23 *Perf. 12x11¾*
2590-2593 A719 Set of 4 5.50 2.40

Portuguese Design A720

Designs: No. 2594, 43c, Secretary, by Daciano da Costa, 1962. No. 2595, 43c, Chair, by António Garcia, 1970, vert. No. 2596, 43c, Drawing table, by José Espinho, 1970. No. 2597, 43c, Chairs by Leonor and António Sena da Silva, 1973. No. 2598, 43c, Telephone booth, by Pedro Silva Dias, 1998, vert. No. 2599, 43c, Cutlery, by Eduardo Afonsa Dias, 1976. No. 2600, 43c, Faucet, by Carlos Aguiar, 1998. No. 2601, 43c, Thermos bottle, by Carlos Rocha, 1982, vert. No. 2602, 43c, Tea cart, by Cruz de Carvalho, 1957.

2003, Oct. 31 *Perf. 12x11¾, 11¾x12*
2594-2602 A720 Set of 9 11.00 4.50

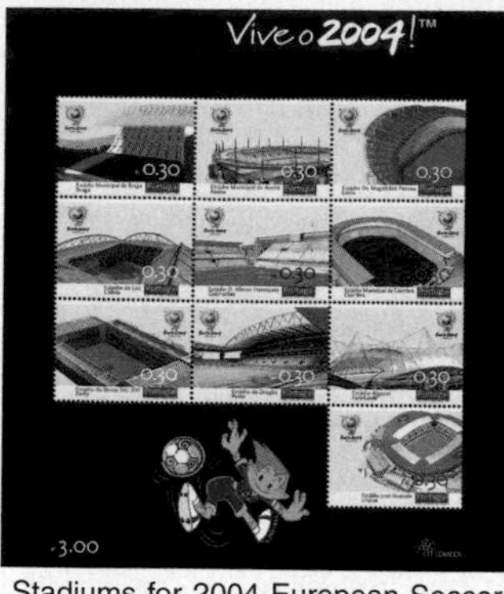

Stadiums for 2004 European Soccer Championships — A721

No. 2603: a, Braga Municipal Stadium, Braga. b, Aveiro Municpal Stadium, Aveiro. c, Dr. Magalhaes Pessoa Stadium, Leiria. d, Luz Stadium, Lisbon. e, D. Afonso Henriques Stadium, Guimaraes. f, Coimbra Municipal Stadium, Coimbra. g, Bessa 21st Century Stadium, Porto. h, Dragao Stadium, Porto. i, Algarve Stadium, Faro-Loulé. j, José Alvalade Stadium, Lisbon.

2003, Nov. 28 Litho. *Perf. 14x13½*

2603	A721 Sheet of 10	9.00	9.00
a.-j.	30c Any single	.85	.75

Souvenir Sheet

Coin Commemorating 150th Anniv. of First Portuguese Stamps, Bust and Portrait of Queen Maria II — A722

2003, Dec. 12 *Perf. 12*
2604 A722 €1 multi 2.75 2.75

Mascot of 2004 European Soccer Championships — A723

Mascot and: 45c, CorreioAzul emblem. €1.75, Priority air mail emblem.

Serpentine Die Cut 11½

2004, Mar. 16 **Litho.**

Self-Adhesive

2605	A723 45c multi	1.25	.55
2606	A723 €1.75 multi	5.00	2.10

No. 2606 is airmail.

King John IV (1604-56) — A724

No. 2607 — Vila Viçosa, birthplace and: a, 45c, Head of King. b, €1, King with sword.

2004, Mar. 19 ***Perf. 14x13½***
2607 A724 Horiz. pair, #a-b 4.00 1.75

Lisbon Oceanarium — A725

Designs: 30c, Phyllopteryx taeniolatus. 45c, Spheniscus magellanicus. 56c, Hypsypops rubicundus. 72c, Enhydra lutris. €1, Carcharias taurus. €2, Fratercula arctica.
€1.50, Eudyptes chysolophus, people at Oceanarium.

2004, Mar. 22
2608-2613 A725 Set of 6 14.00 6.25

Souvenir Sheet

2614 A725 €1.50 multi 4.25 4.25

No. 2614 contains one 80x30mm stamp.

2004 European Soccer Championships A726

Designs: Nos. 2615a, 2616, 10c, Foot kicking soccer ball. Nos. 2615b, 2617, 20c, Soccer ball in air. Nos. 2615c, 2618, 30c, Soccer ball on chalk line. Nos. 2615d, 2619, 50c, Soccer ball, corner of goal.

2004, Mar. 30 ***Perf.***

Souvenir Sheet

2615 A726 Sheet of 4, #a-d 3.25 3.25

Self-Adhesive

Serpentine Die Cut

2616-2619 A726 Set of 4 3.00 1.40

No. 2615 contains four 24mm diameter stamps.

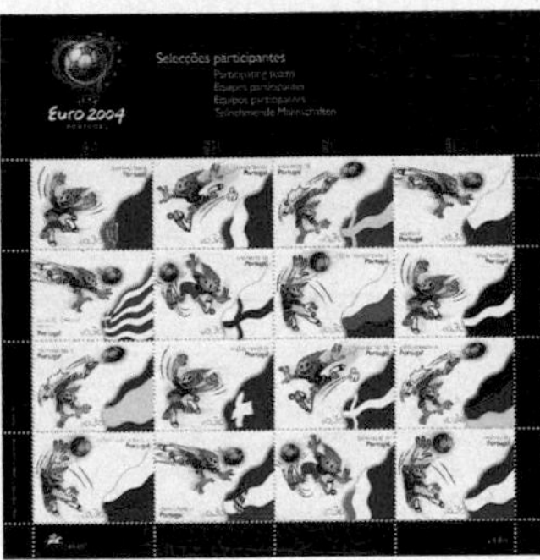

Flags of Countries in 2004 European Soccer Championships and Mascot — A727

No. 2620: a, Portugal. b, France. c, Sweden. d, Czech Republic. e, Greece. f, England. g, Bulgaria. h, Latvia. i, Spain. j, Switzerland. k, Denmark. l, Germany. m, Russia. n, Croatia. o, Italy. p, Netherlands.

2004, Apr. 6 ***Perf. 13x13¼***
2620 A727 Sheet of 16 14.00 14.00
a.-p. 30c Any single .85 .40

Bird Type of 2000 With Euro Denominations Only and

Andorinha Daurica — A728

Designs: 30c, Cruza bico comun. No. 2622, Andorinha daurica, diff. 56c, Papa figos. 58c, Cotovia montesina. 72c, Chapim de poupa.

2004, Apr. 15 ***Perf. 11¾x11½***
2621 A658 30c multi .85 .35
2622 A658 45c multi 1.25 .55
2623 A658 56c multi 1.50 .65
2624 A658 58c multi 1.60 .70
2625 A658 72c multi 2.00 .85

Self-Adhesive

Size: 26x21mm (#2626, 2628)

Serpentine Die Cut 11½, 11½x11¾ (#2627)

2626 A658 30c multi .85 .35
2627 A728 45c multi 1.25 .55
2628 A658 56c multi 1.50 .65
Nos. 2621-2628 (8) 10.80 4.65

Landmarks in Host Cities of 2004 European Soccer Championships and Players — A729

Host city: No. 2629, 30c, Aveiro. No. 2630, 30c, Braga. No. 2631, 30c, Coimbra. No. 2632, 30c, Faro-Loulé. No. 2633, 30c, Guimaraes. No. 2634, 30c, Leiria. No. 2635, 30c, Lisbon. No. 2636, 30c, Porto.

2004, Apr. 20 ***Perf. 14x13¼***
2629-2636 A729 Set of 8 6.75 3.00

Coup of Apr. 25, 1974, 30th Anniv. — A730

2004, Apr. 25 ***Perf. 13¼x13***
2637 A730 45c multi 1.25 .55

Stadiums for 2004 European Soccer Championships — A731

Designs: No. 2638, 30c, Aveiro Municipal Stadium, Aveiro. No. 2639, 30c, Braga Municipal Stadium, Braga. No. 2640, 30c, Coimbra Municipal Stadium, Coimbra. No. 2641, 30c, D. Afonso Henriques Stadium, Guimaraes. No. 2642, 30c, Algarve Stadium, Faro-Loulé. No. 2643, 30c, Dr. Magalhaes Pessoa Stadium, Leiria. No. 2644, 30c, José Alvalade Stadium, Lisbon. No. 2645, 30c, Luz Stadium, Lisbon. No. 2646, 30c, Bessa 21st Century Stadium, Porto. No. 2647, 30c, Dragao Stadium, Porto.

2004, Apr. 28 ***Perf. 14x13¼***
2638-2647 A731 Set of 10 8.50 3.50

2004 European Parliament Elections A732

2004, May 3
2648 A732 30c multi .85 .35

Expansion of the European Union — A733

Designs: 56c, Flags of newly-added nations, stars. €2, Flags of newly-added nations, flags of previous members.

2004, May 3 **Litho.**
2649 A733 56c multi 1.50 .65

Souvenir Sheet

2650 A733 €2 multi 5.75 5.75

Europa — A734

Designs: No. 2651, 56c, Woman looking at painting. No. 2652, 56c, Vacationer with gear on beach.

2004, May 10 ***Perf. 13¼x14***
2651-2652 A734 Set of 2 *3.00 1.40*
2652a Souvenir sheet, #2651-2652 *3.25 3.25*

First Telephone Line Between Lisbon and Porto, Cent. — A735

Designs: 30c, Old telephone. 45c, Telephone pole. 56c, Fiber-optic cables. 72c, Picture phone.
No. 2657: a, Old telephone, diff. b, Like 72c.

2004, May 17
2653-2656 A735 Set of 4 5.75 2.50

Souvenir Sheet

2657 A735 €1 Sheet of 2, #a-b 5.75 5.75

Jewish Heritage of Portugal — A736

Designs: 30c, Mishnah Torah of Maimonides, British Library. 45c, Star of David with lion, Cervera Bible, National Library. 56c, Menorah, Cervera Bible, National Library. 72c, Menorah carved on rock, Mértola Museum. €1, Abravanel Bible, Coimbra University Library. €2, Statue of prophet, Christ Convent, Tomar.
€1.50, Interior of Shaare Tikva Synagogue.

2004, May 20
2658-2663 A736 Set of 6 14.00 6.00

Souvenir Sheet

2664 A736 €1.50 multi 4.25 4.25

Shaare Tikva Synagogue, Cent.

Souvenir Sheet

Final Match of 2004 European Soccer Championships — A737

2004, May 27 ***Perf. 13¼x13***
2665 A737 €1 multi 2.75 2.75

Portuguese Philatelic Federation, 50th Anniv. — A738

Designs: 30c, Anniversary emblem, #761, 2652. €1.50, Handstamp and letter.

2004, June 18 ***Perf. 14x13¼***
2666 A738 30c multi .85 .35

Souvenir Sheet

2667 A738 €1.50 multi 4.25 4.25

Souvenir Sheet

UEFA (European Football Union), 50th Anniv. — A739

2004, July 29 **Litho.** ***Perf. 13x13¼***
2668 A739 €1 multi 2.75 2.75

2004 Summer Olympics, Athens A740

Designs: 30c, Hurdles. 45c, High jump.

2004, Aug. 13 ***Perf. 14x13¼***
2669-2670 A740 Set of 2 2.10 .95

2004 Paralympics, Athens — A741

Designs: 30c, Swimming. 45c, Wheelchair racing. 56c, Cycling. 72c, Running.

2004, Sept. 2 ***Perf. 13¼x14***
2671-2674 A741 Set of 4 5.75 2.50

Souvenir Sheet

Pedro Homem de Mello (1904-84), Poet — A742

2004, Sept. 6 *Perf. 14x13¼*
2675 A742 €2 multi 5.75 5.75

Opening of Presidential Museum — A743

Designs: 45c, Museum exterior. €1, Museum interior.

2004, Oct. 5
2676 A743 45c multi 1.25 .55

Souvenir Sheet

2677 A743 €1 multi 2.75 2.75

Comic Strips A744

Designs: 30c, Quim e Manecas, by Stuart de Carvalhais. 45c, Guarda Abília, by Júlio Pinto and Nuno Saraiva. 56c, Simao Infante, by Raul Correia and Eduardo Teixeira Coelho. 72c, A Pior Bando do Mundo, by José Carlos Fernandes.

No. 2682: a, O Espiao Acácio, by Relvas. b, Jim del Monaco, by Louro and Simoes. c, Tomahawk Tom, by Vitor Péon. d, Pitanga, by Arlindo Fagundes.

2004, Oct. 8
2678-2681 A744 Set of 4 6.00 2.50

Souvenir Sheet

2682 A744 50c Sheet of 4, #a-d 5.75 5.75

Viticulture A745

Designs: 30c, Sarcophagus depicting seasonal scenes, detail of mosaic of Autumn, 3rd cent. 45c, Detail of mosaic of Autumn, Apocalypse of Lorvao, 12th cent. 56c, Lorvao Missal illustration, 14th cent., detail of illustration from Book of Hours, by D. Fernando, 15th-16th cent. 72c, Detail of illustration from Book of Hours, detail of Group of the Lion, Columbano, 19th cent. €1, Detail of Group of the Lion, stained glass window, by Lino António, 20th cent.

No. 2688: a, Grapes, harvester. b, Harvester, wine jugs. c, Winery. d, Wine barrels, bottles and glasses.

2004, Oct. 15
2683-2687 A745 Set of 5 8.75 3.75

Souvenir Sheet

2688 A745 50c Sheet of 4, #a-d 5.75 5.75

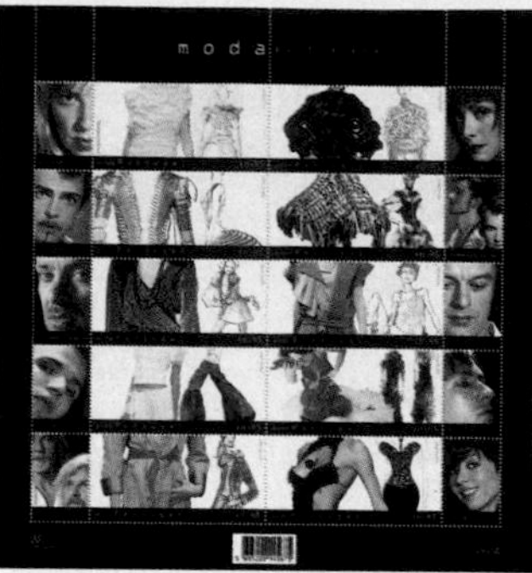

Women's Fashion — A746

No. 2689 — Clothing designed by: a, Alexandra Moura. b, Ana Salazar. c, Filipe Faisca. d, J. Branco and L. Sanchez. e, J. António Tenente. f, Luís Buchinho. g, Osvaldo Martins. h, Dino Alves. i, Alves and Gonçalves, j, Fátima Lopes. Designers names and pictures are on labels adjacent to stamps showing their clothing.

2004, Nov. 10 *Perf. 13¾x14¼*
2689 A746 45c Sheet of 10 + 10 labels 13.00 13.00

Christmas A747

Paintings: 30c, Adoration of the Magi, attributed to Jorge Afonso. 45c, Adoration of the Magi, by Flemish School. 56c, Flight into Egypt, by Francisco Vieira. 72c, Nativity, by Portuguese School.

€3, Nativity, by Josefa de Obidos.

2004, Nov. 19 *Perf. 13x13¼*
2690-2693 A747 Set of 4 5.75 2.75

Souvenir Sheet

Perf. 13½x13¼

2694 A747 €3 multi 8.50 8.50

No. 2694 contains one 50x35mm stamp.

Masks — A748

A748a

Designs: 10c, Entrudo, Lazarim. 30c Festa dos Rapazes, Salsas. 45c, Festa dos Rapazes, Salsa, different. 57c, Cardador, Vale de Ilhavo. 74c, Festa dos Rapazes, Aveleda.

Perf. 11¾x11½

2005, Feb. 17 **Litho.**

2695	A748	10c multi	.25	.25
2696	A748	30c brn red & multi	.75	.25
2697	A748	45c dk blue & multi	1.20	.60
2698	A748	57c multi	1.50	.75
2699	A748	74c multi	2.00	1.00
		Nos. 2695-2699 (5)	5.70	2.85

Self-Adhesive

Serpentine Die Cut 11½, 11 (45c)

2699A	A748	30c multi	.80	.40
2699B	A748a	45c multi	1.25	.60
2699C	A748	57c multi	1.50	.75
		Nos. 2699A-2699C (3)	3.55	1.75

See Nos. 2797-2799, 2827-2832. No. 2696 has denomination at left; No. 2829 has denomination at right.

Public Transportation — A749

Lines of people and: 30c, Train, front of trolley. 50c, Trolley, rear of train. 57c, Ferry, rear of trolley. €1, Rear of articulated bus, front of train. €2, Front of articulated bus, rear of train.

2005, Mar. 17 *Perf. 12x11¾*
2700-2704 A749 Set of 5 11.50 11.50

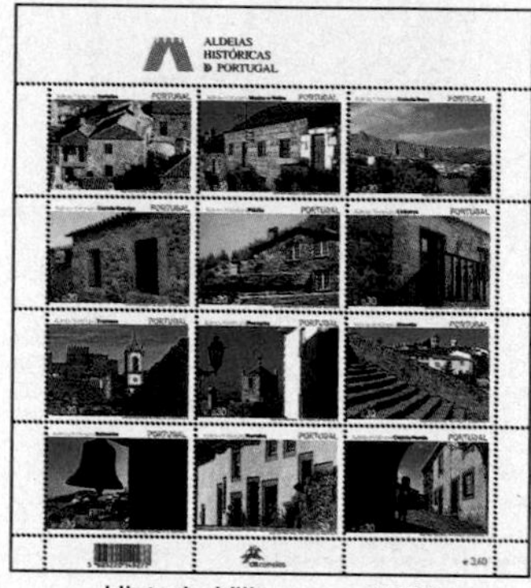

Historic Villages — A750

No. 2705: a, Sortelha. b, Idanha-a-Velha. c, Castelo Novo. d, Castelo Rodrigo. e, Piódao. f, Linhares. g, Trancoso. h, Monsanto. i, Almeida. j, Belmonte. k, Marialva. l, Castelo Mendo.

2005, Apr. 28 **Litho.** *Perf. 14x13¼*
2705 A750 Sheet of 12 9.25 9.25
a.-l. 30c Any single .75 .40

Paintings by José Malhoa (1855-1933) — A751

Designs: 30c, A Beira-Mar. 45c, The Pious Offerings.

€1.77, Conversation with a Neighbor.

2005, Apr. 28 *Perf. 12x11¾*
2706-2707 A751 Set of 2 2.00 2.00

Souvenir Sheet

2708 A751 €1.77 multi 4.50 4.50

Europa A752

Designs: No. 2709, Cozido à Portuguesa. No. 2710a, Bacalhau Assado com Batatas a Murro (dried cod and baked potatoes).

2005, May 5 *Perf. 14x13¼*
2709 A752 57c multi *1.50 .75*

Souvenir Sheet

2710 Sheet of 2 #2710a *3.00 3.00*
a. A752 57c multi *1.50 1.50*

Rotary International, Cent. — A753

2005, May 20 *Perf. 12x11¾*
2711 A753 74c Paul Harris 1.90 .95

Souvenir Sheet

2712 A753 €1.75 Harris, diff. 4.25 4.25

National Coach Museum, Cent. A754

Designs: No. 2713, 30c, Porto Covo carriage, 19th cent. No. 2714, 30c, Carriage, 19th cent. No. 2715, 45c, Coach of Francisca Sabóia, 17th cent. No. 2716, 45c, Sege "Das Plumas," 18th cent. 57c, Palanquin, 18th cent. 74c, Coche Dos Oceanos, 18th cent.

€1.75, Coaches and Queen Amelia.

2005, May 23 *Perf. 14x13¼*
2713-2718 A754 Set of 6 7.00 3.50

Souvenir Sheet

2719 A754 €1.75 multi 4.25 4.25

Era of Kings Philip I to Philip III — A755

Arms and: 5c, Pegoes Aqueduct, Tomar. 30c, Chalice from Elvas Cathedral. 45c, Tile panel of cross from Christ Convent, Tomar. 57c, Fort St. John the Baptist, Angra.€1, Armada. €2, St. Vincent of Fora Church, Lisbon.

€1.20, Cross and reliquary from Lisbon Cathedral.

2005, June 7 *Perf. 11¾x12*
2720-2725 A755 Set of 6 11.00 5.50

Souvenir Sheet

2726 A755 €1.20 multi 3.00 3.00

Miniature Sheet

Caricatures — A756

No. 2727 — Caricatures by: a, Raphael Bordallo Pinheiro. b, Sebastiao Sanhudo. c, Celso Herminio. d, Leal da Camara. e, Francisco Valença. f, Stuart Carvalhais. g, Sam. h, Joao Abel Manta. i, Augusto Cid. j, António Antunes. k, Pinheiro (Zé Povinho).

2005, June 12 *Perf. 13¼x14*
2727 A756 Sheet of 11 + label 8.00 8.00
a.-k. 30c Any single .70 .35

Souvenir Sheets

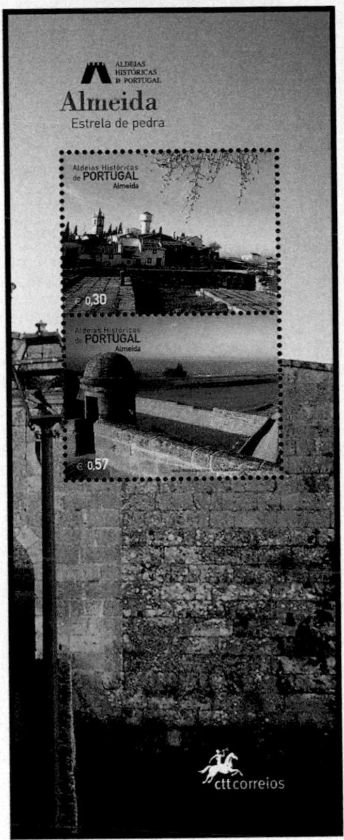

Historic Villages — A757

Various views of named villages.

2005, June 8 Litho. ***Perf. 14x13¼***
Sheets of 2, #a-b

2728	A757	Almeida	2.25	2.25
a.		30c multi	.75	.35
b.		57c multi	1.40	.70
2729	A757	Belmonte	2.25	2.25
a.		30c multi	.75	.35
b.		57c multi	1.40	.70
2730	A757	Castelo Mendo	2.25	2.25
a.		30c multi	.75	.35
b.		57c multi	1.40	.70
2731	A757	Castelo Novo	2.25	2.25
a.		30c multi	.75	.35
b.		57c multi	1.40	.70
2732	A757	Castelo Rodrigo	2.25	2.25
a.		30c multi	.75	.35
b.		57c multi	1.40	.70
2733	A757	Idanha-a-Velha	2.25	2.25
a.		30c multi	.75	.35
b.		57c multi	1.40	.70
2734	A757	Linhares da Beira	2.25	2.25
a.		30c multi	.75	.35
b.		57c multi	1.40	.70
2735	A757	Marialva	2.25	2.25
a.		30c multi	.75	.35
b.		57c multi	1.40	.70
2736	A757	Monsanto	2.25	2.25
a.		30c multi	.75	.35
b.		57c multi	1.40	.70
2737	A757	Piodao	2.25	2.25
a.		30c multi	.75	.35
b.		57c multi	1.40	.70
2738	A757	Sortelha	2.25	2.25
a.		30c multi	.75	.35
b.		57c multi	1.40	.70
2739	A757	Trancoso	2.25	2.25
a.		30c multi	.75	.35
b.		57c multi	1.40	.70
		Nos. 2728-2739 (12)	27.00	27.00

Faro, 2005 National Cultural Capital A758

Designs: 30c, Conductor's hands and baton. 45c, Broken pot. 57c, Shell. 74c, Hands applauding.

2005, June 15

2740-2743	A758	Set of 4	5.00	2.50

Tourism A759

Various scenes from: No. 2744, 45c, Lisbon. No. 2745, 45c, Porto e Norte. No. 2746, 48c, Lisbon, diff. No. 2747, 48c, Porto e Norte, diff. No. 2748, 57c, Lisbon, diff. No. 2749, 57c, Porto e Norte, diff.

2005, July 8 ***Perf. 12x11¾***

2744-2749	A759	Set of 6	7.25	3.50

Nature Conservation — A760

Designs: 30c, Man with hatchet inspecting tree. 45c, Forest fire prevention squad. 57c, Bird on branch, building in forest.

€2, Bird on fence, large trees.

2005, Aug. 19 ***Perf. 12x11¾***

2750-2752	A760	Set of 3	3.50	1.75

Souvenir Sheet

Perf. 12x12½

2753	A760	€2 multi	5.00	5.00

United Nations, 60th Anniv. A761

Intl. Day of Peace A762

Children at Risk A763

Intl. Year of Physics A764

2005, Sept. 21 ***Perf. 12x11¾***

2754	A761	30c multi	.75	.35
2755	A762	45c multi	1.10	.55
2756	A763	57c multi	1.40	.70
2757	A764	74c multi	1.90	.95
		Nos. 2754-2757 (4)	5.15	2.55

Sundials — A765

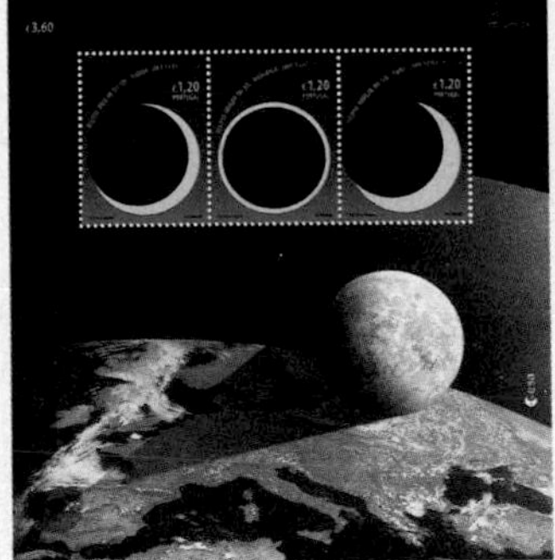

Annular Solar Eclipse, Oct. 3, 2005 — A766

Sundial from: 45c, St. John the Baptist Church, Sintra. €1, Maritime Museum, Lisbon.

No. 2760 — view of eclipsed Sun from: a, Lisbon at 9:53. b, Bragança at 9:55. c, Faro at 9:55.

2005, Oct. 3 ***Perf. 12½x12***

2758-2759	A765	Set of 2	4.00	1.75

Souvenir Sheet

Perf. 12

2760	A766	Sheet of 3	10.00	10.00
a.-c.		€1.20 multi	2.75	1.40

A767

Communications Media — A768

Designs: 30c, Press (fountain pen). 45c, Radio (microphone). 57c, Television (portable camera). 74c, Internet (globe and "@."

No. 2765: a, Press (newspaper). b, Radio (studio).

No. 2766: a, Television (studio). b, Internet (beginning of website address).

2005, Oct. 13 ***Perf. 12x12½***

2761-2764	A767	Set of 4	5.00	2.50

Souvenir Sheets

2765	A768	Sheet of 2	6.50	6.50
a.		€1.10 multi	2.75	1.40
b.		€1.55 multi	3.75	1.90
2766	A768	Sheet of 2	6.50	6.50
a.		€1.10 multi	2.75	1.40
b.		€1.55 multi	3.75	1.90

Fishing Villages — A769

No. 2767, 30c — Aldeia da Carrasquiera, Portugal: a, Denomination at R. b, Denomination at L.

No. 2768, 30c — Tai O, Hong Kong: a, Denomination at R. b, Denomination at L.

2005, Oct. 18 ***Perf. 13¼x13¾***

Horiz. Pairs, #a-b

2767-2768	A769	Set of 2	3.00	1.50

See Hong Kong Nos. 1160-1163.

Alvaro Cunhal (1913-2005), Communist Politician — A770

Designs: 30c, Cunhal in crowd. €1, Cunhal with young girl.

2005, Nov. 10 ***Perf. 12x12½***

2769	A770	30c multi	.70	.35

Souvenir Sheet

2770	A770	€1 multi	2.40	2.40

Serralves Foundation A771

Designs: No. 2771, 30c, White building. No. 2772, 45c, Silhouette of seated person. 48c, Red brown building entrance, diff. 57c, Sculpture of garden shovel. 74c, Person painting. No. 2776, €1, Walkway and hedges.

No. 2777: a, 30c, Red brown building entrance, horiz. b, 45c, Walkway and trees. c, 45c, Columns in building. d, 45c, Tower. e, 45c, Walkway and hedges, diff.

No. 2778: a, €1, White building, horiz. (80x30mm). b, €1, Art in gallery, horiz. (80x30mm). c, €1, Trees and lawn.

2005, Nov. 15 ***Perf. 13¼x14***

2771-2776	A771	Set of 6	8.50	4.25

Souvenir Sheets

2777		Sheet of 5	5.00	5.00
a.	A771	30c multi	.70	.35
b.-e.	A771	45c Any single	1.00	.50

Perf. 14x13¼

2778		Sheet of 3	7.00	7.00
a.-c.	A771	€1 Any single	2.25	1.10

Lisbon Earthquake, 250th Anniv. — A772

Designs: 45c, Fire after earthquake. €2, Victims, braced buildings.

€2.65, Victims and damaged buildings.

2005, Nov. 25 ***Perf. 14x13¼***

2779-2780	A772	Set of 2	5.75	2.75

Souvenir Sheet

2781	A772	€2.65 multi	6.25	6.25

No. 2781 contains one 40x30mm stamp.

Modernization of the Navy — A773

Designs: 45c, Navpol ship. 57c, Hydrographic ship. 74c, Ocean patrol boat and helicopter. €2, Submarine.

2005, Nov. 25 ***Perf. 12x12½***

2782-2785	A773	Set of 4	9.00	4.50

Soccer Teams A774

Players and team emblems: No. 2786, N, Sporting Clube de Portugal. No. 2787, N, Sport Lisboa e Benfica. No. 2788, N, Futebol Clube do Porto.

No. 2789, €1, Sporting Clube de Portugal, diff. No. 2790, €1, Sport Lisboa e Benfica, diff. No. 2791, €1, Player lifting trophy, Futebol Clube do Porto.

2005, Nov. 25 ***Perf. 12x12¼***

2786-2788 A774 Set of 3 2.10 1.10

Souvenir Sheets

Perf. 12x11¾

2789-2791 A774 Set of 3 7.00 7.00

Nos. 2786-2788 each sold for 30c on day of issue.

Greetings A775

Designs: No. 2792, Parabens (birthday party). No. 2793, Amote (men and women dancing and exchanging gifts, child). No. 2794, Parabens (man, woman and two children, stork with baby). No. 2795, Parabens (conductor, cocktail party). No. 2796, Parabens (man, woman, fairy, Cupid).

2006, Feb. 7 ***Perf. 12x12½***

2792	A775 N multi	.75	.35
a.	Perf. 12 vert. (from booklet pane)	.75	.35
2793	A775 N multi	.75	.35
a.	Perf. 12 vert. (from booklet pane)	.75	.35
2794	A775 N multi	.75	.35
a.	Perf. 12 vert. (from booklet pane)	.75	.35
2795	A775 N multi	.75	.35
a.	Perf. 12 vert. (from booklet pane)	.75	.35
2796	A775 N multi	.75	.35
a.	Perf. 12 vert. (from booklet pane)	.75	.35
b.	Booklet pane, #2792a-2796a	3.75	—
	Complete booklet, #2796b	3.75	
	Nos. 2792-2796 (5)	3.75	1.75

Nos. 2792-2796 each sold for 30c on day of issue.

Masks Type of 2005

Designs: N, Like No. 2696. A, "Carnaval" Lazarim, Bragança. E, "Dia de Ano Novo" Mogadouro, Bragança.

Serpentine Die Cut 11½

2006, Mar. 1 **Self-Adhesive**

2797	A748 N multi	.75	.35
2798	A748 A multi	1.10	.55
2799	A748 E multi	1.40	.70
	Nos. 2797-2799 (3)	3.25	1.60

No. 2797 sold for 30c, No. 2798 sold for 45c, and No. 2799 sold for 57c on day of issue.

Water A776

Designs: No. 2800, N, Glass of water. No. 2801, N, Water cycle. No. 2802, A, Spigot. No. 2803, A, Turbines. No. 2804, E, Sailboat. No. 2805, E, Flower.

2006, Mar. 22 Litho. ***Perf. 12x11¾***

2800-2805 A776 Set of 6 6.50 3.25

On the day of issue Nos. 2800-2801 each sold for 30c; Nos. 2802-2803 each sold for 45c, and Nos. 2804-2805 each sold for 57c.

St. Francis Xavier (1506-52), Missionary A777

St. Francis Xavier: 45c, Baptizing man. €1, Holding cross.

€2.75, Wearing black robe.

2006, Apr. 5

2806-2807 A777 Set of 2 3.50 1.75

Souvenir Sheet

2808 A777 €2.75 multi 6.75 6.75

Europa A778

No. 2810 — Children's drawings: a, Child in stroller. b, Four children.

2006, May 9 ***Perf. 12x12½***

2809 A778 60c shown 1.60 .80

Souvenir Sheet

Perf. 12x11¾

2810 A778 60c Sheet of 2, #a-b 3.25 3.25

Famous Men — A779

Designs, No. 2811, €1, Humberto Delgado (1906-65), founder of TAP Airlines. No. 2812, €1, Thomaz de Mello (Tom) (1906-90), artist. No. 2313, €1, Agostinho da Silva (1906-94), philosopher. No. 2814, €1, Fernando Lopes-Graça (1906-94), composer. No. 2815, €1, Rómulo de Carvalho (1906-97), poet.

2006, May 15 ***Perf. 11¾x12***

2811-2815 A779 Set of 5 13.00 6.50

Souvenir Sheet

UEFA Under 21 Soccer Championships, Portugal — A780

2006, May 23 ***Perf. 12x12½***

2816 A780 €2.75 multi 7.25 7.25

2006 World Cup Soccer Championships, Germany — A781

Silhouettes of soccer players in action: 45c, €1.

€2.40, World Cup.

2006, June 7 ***Perf. 12x11¾***

2817-2818 A781 Set of 2 3.75 1.90

Souvenir Sheet

2819 A781 €2.40 multi 6.25 6.25

Intl. Year of Deserts and Desertification — A782

Designs: 30c, Sand dune. 60c, Dead and living trees.

2006, June 17

2820-2821 A782 Set of 2 2.40 1.25

Roman Heritage A783

Designs: 30c, Mosaic of Oceanus. 40c, Roman temple, Evora. 50c, Patera. 60c, Two-headed sculpture.

€2.40, Mosaic of seahorse.

2006, June 21

2822-2825 A783 Set of 4 4.75 2.40

Souvenir Sheet

2826 A783 €2.40 multi 6.25 6.25

Masks Type of 2005

Designs: 3c, "Carnaval" Lazarim, Viseu. 5c, "Festa dos Rapazes," Baçal, Bragança. 30c, Like #2797. 45c, Like #2798. 60c, Like #2799. 75c, "Dia dos Diablos" Vinhais, Bragança.

2006, June 29 ***Perf. 11¾x11½***

2827	A748 3c multi	.25	.25
2828	A748 5c multi	.25	.25
2829	A748 30c dk red & multi	.75	.35
2830	A748 45c blue & multi	1.25	.60
2831	A748 60c multi	1.50	.75
2832	A748 75c multi	1.90	.95
	Nos. 2827-2832 (6)	5.90	3.15

No. 2829 has denomination at right. No. 2696 has denomination at left.

Wolfgang Amadeus Mozart (1756-91), Composer. A784

Mozart and: 60c, Musical score. €2.75, Handwritten text.

2006, July 7 ***Perf. 12x11¾***

2833 A784 60c multi 1.50 .75

Souvenir Sheet

2834 A784 €2.75 multi 7.00 7.00

Souvenir Sheet

Community of Portuguese-speaking Countries, 10th Anniv. — A785

2006, July 12 ***Perf. 12½x13***

2835 A785 €2.85 multi 7.25 7.25

Calouste Gulbenkian Foundation, 50th Anniv. — A786

Designs: 30c, Portrait of a Young Woman by Domenico Ghirlandaio. 45c, Peacock, jewelry by René Lalique. 60c, Ceramic tile from Turkey. 75c, Flora, sculpture by Jean-Baptise Carpeaux, Roman medal. €1, Jade jar from Samarkand. €2, Portrait of Calouste Gulbenkian, by C. J. Watelet.

No. 2842, vert.: a, Sculpture and "arte." b, Bookshelf and "educaçao." c, Microscope and "ciencia." d, Painting of mother and child and "caridade."

2006, July 18 Litho. ***Perf. 12½x13***

2836-2841 A786 Set of 6 13.50 6.75

Souvenir Sheet

Perf. 13x12½

2842 A786 30c Sheet of 4, #a-d 3.25 3.25

Modern Architecture — A787

Designs: No. 2843, 30c, Building, Bouça neighborhood of Porto, by Alvaro Siza. No. 2844, 30c, Apartments, Lisbon, by Teotónio Pereira, Nuno Portas, Pedro Botelho, and Joao Paciencia. No. 2845, 30c, José Gomes Ferreira School, Lisbon, by Raul Hestnes Ferreira. No. 2846, 30c, Matosinhos Town Hall, by Alcino Soutinho. No. 2847, 30c, Borges & Irmao Bank, Vila do Conde, by Siza. No. 2848, 30c, Art House, Porto, by Eduardo Souto Moura. No. 2849, 30c, University of Santiago Campus, Aveiro, by Portas. No. 2850, 30c, Social Communications School, Lisbon, by Carrilho da Graça. No. 2851, 30c, Architect's Building, Lisbon, by Manuel Graça Diaz and Egas José Vieira. No. 2852, 30c, Santa Maria Church, Marco de Canaveses, by Siza.

2006, Aug. 21 ***Perf. 12½x13***

2843-2852 A787 Set of 10 7.75 4.00

Television Broadcasting in Portugal, 50th Anniv. — A788

Men and: 30c, Camera at right. 60c, Camera at left.

2006, Sept. 4 ***Perf. 12x11¾***

2853-2854 A788 Set of 2 2.40 1.25

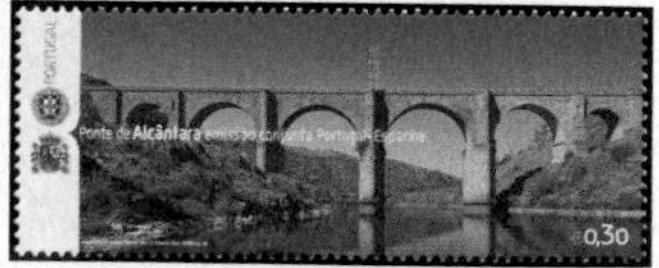

Bridges Between Portugal and Spain — A789

Designs: 30c, Alcantara Bridge. 52c, Vila Real de Santo António (Ayamonte International) Bridge.

2006, Sept. 14 **Litho.**

2855-2856 A789 Set of 2 2.10 1.10

See Spain No. 3441.

Souvenir Sheet

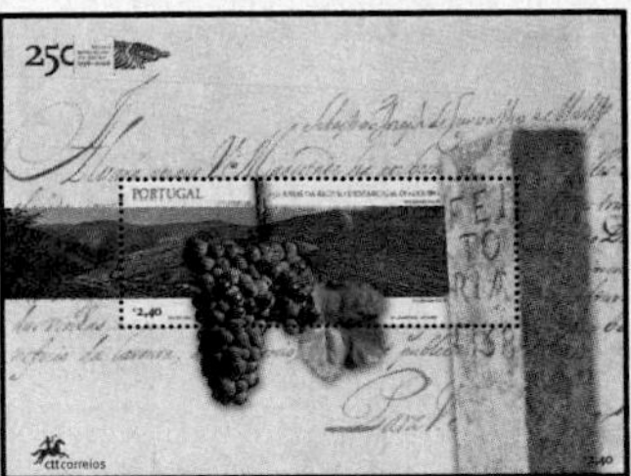

Douro Demarcated Region, 250th Anniv. — A790

2006, Sept. 14
2857 A790 €2.40 multi 6.25 6.25

Fish A791

Designs: 30c, Capros aper. 45c, Anthias anthias. 60c, Lepadogaster lepadogaster. 75c, Gobiusculus flavescens. €1, Coris julis. €2, Callionymus lyra.

No. 2864, 80c: a, Macroramphosus scolopax. b, Echlichthys vipera.

No. 2865, 80c: a, Thalassoma pavo. b, Blennius ocellaris.

2006, Oct. 7 ***Perf. 12¼x11¾***
2858-2863 A791 Set of 6 13.00 6.50

Souvenir Sheets of 2, #a-b

2864-2865 A791 Set of 2 8.00 8.00

España 06 Intl. Philatelic Exhibition, Malaga, Spain.

School Correspondence — A792

Various letters with denomination at: No. 2866, N, Upper left. No. 2867, N, Upper right.

2006, Oct. 9 ***Perf. 12½x13***
2866-2867 A792 Set of 2 1.50 .75

Portuguese Railroads, 150th Anniv. — A793

Designs: 30c, Flecha de Prata. 45c, Sud-Express. 60c, Foguete. €2, Alfa Pendular. €1.60, Inaugural ceremonies, 1856.

2006, Oct. 28 ***Perf. 12x11¾***
2868-2871 A793 Set of 4 8.50 4.25

Souvenir Sheet

2872 A793 €1.60 multi 4.25 4.25

No. 2872 contains one 80x30mm stamp.

Portuguese Arrival in Ceylon, 500th Anniv. — A794

Designs: 30c, Map. 75c, Carvings. €2.40, Map, horiz.

2006, Oct. 30 ***Perf. 13x13¼***
2873-2874 A794 Set of 2 2.75 1.40

Souvenir Sheet

Perf. 12½x13

2875 A794 €2.40 multi 6.25 6.25

Lubrapex Intl. Philatelic Exhibition, Rio.

Islamic Influences in Lisbon A795

Designs: 30c, Ceramic tile, 16th cent. 45c, Frieze, 9th-10th cent. 52c, Sousa Leal Palace. 61c, Film Museum. 75c, Casa do Alentejo. €1, Ribeiro da Cunha Palace.
€2.95, Pitcher.

2007, Feb. 15 Litho. ***Perf. 12½x13***
2876-2881 A795 Set of 6 9.75 5.00

Souvenir Sheet

2882 A795 €2.95 multi 8.00 8.00

Miniature Sheets

Regional Garments — A796

No. 2883: a, Capote and capelo, Azores. b, Campones, Beira Litoral. c, Viloa, Madeira. d, Camponesa, Ribatejo.

No. 2884: a, Lavradeira, Minho. b, Noiva, Minho. c, Capa de honras, Trás-os-Montes. d, Pauliteiro, Trás-os-Montes. e, Camisola de pescador, Douro Litoral. f, Coroça, Beiras and Trás-os-Montes. g, Saias da Nazaré, Estremadura. h, Campino, Ribatejo. i, Camponesa, Algarve. j, Capote, Alentejo.

2007, Feb. 28
2883 A796 Sheet of 4 3.25 3.25
a.-d. 30c Any single .80 .40
2884 A796 Sheet of 10 8.00 8.00
a.-j. 30c Any single .80 .40

Art by Manuel Cargaleiro A797

Designs: 30c, Carroaux Diamants. 45c, Composizione Floreale. 61c, Decoraçao Mural.

2007, Mar. 16
2885-2887 A797 Set of 3 3.75 1.90

Audit Offices in Europe, Bicent. A798

Designs: 30c, King John I Reinforces the Audit Office, by Jaime Martins Barata. 61c, Creation of Audit Tribunal, by Almada Negreiros. €2, Audit Tribunal Building.
€2.95, The Accountant, tapestry by Negreiros.

2007, Mar. 17
2888-2890 A798 Set of 3 7.75 4.00

Souvenir Sheet

2891 A798 €2.95 multi 8.00 8.00

Treaty of Rome, 50th Anniv. — A799

2007, Mar. 23 ***Perf. 13x12½***
2892 A799 61c multi 1.75 .85

Historical Urban Public Transport A800

Designs: 30c, Ox-drawn carriage, 1840. 45c, Horse-drawn streetcar, 1872. 50c, Horse-drawn streetcar, 1873. 61c, Electric trolley, 1895. 75c, Electric trolley, 1901.

2007, Mar. 30 ***Perf. 11¾x11½***
2893 A800 30c multi .80 .40
2894 A800 45c multi 1.25 .60
2895 A800 50c multi 1.40 .70
2896 A800 61c multi 1.60 .80
2897 A800 75c multi 2.00 1.00
Nos. 2893-2897 (5) 7.05 3.50

A801

Dams — A802

Designs: No. 2898, Castelo do Bode Dam. No. 2899, Aguieira Dam and Reservoir. 61c, Valeira Dam and Reservoir. 75c, Alto Lindoso Dam and Reservoir. €1, Castelo do Bode Dam and Reservoir.

2007, Apr. 19 Litho. ***Perf. 12½x13***
2898 A801 30c multi .85 .40
2899 A802 30c multi .85 .40
2900 A802 61c multi 1.75 .85
2901 A802 75c multi 2.10 1.10
2902 A802 €1 multi 2.75 1.40
Nos. 2898-2902 (5) 8.30 4.15

Europa A803

Designs: No. 2903, Lord Robert Baden-Powell.

No. 2904: a, Compass. b, Boy Scouts looking at map.

2007, May 9
2903 A803 61c multi 1.75 .85

Souvenir Sheet

2904 Sheet of 2 3.50 3.50
a.-b. A803 61c Either single 1.75 .85

Scouting, cent.

Historical Urban Public Transport Type of 2007

Designs: N, Horse-drawn streetcar, 1872. A, Electric trolley, 1895. E, Electric trolley, 1901.

Serpentine Die Cut 11½

2007, May 30 Self-Adhesive
2905 A800 N red & black .85 .40
2906 A800 A blue & black 1.25 .60
2907 A800 E brown & black 1.75 .85
Nos. 2905-2907 (3) 3.85 1.85

Nos. 2905-2907 sold for 30c, 45c and 61c, respectively, on day of issue.

Modern Architecture — A804

Designs: No. 2908, 30c, Casa dos 24, Porto, by Fernando Távora. No. 2909, 30c, Documentation and Information Center of the President of the Republic, Lisbon, by Carrilho da Graça. No. 2910, 30c, Portugal Pavilion, Lisbon, by Alvaro Siza. No. 2911, 30c, Ilhavo Maritime Museum, Ilhavo, by ARX Portugal. No. 2912, 30c, Visual Arts Center, Coimbra, by Joao Mendes Ribeiro. No. 2913, 30c, Superior School of Art and Design, Caldas da Rainha, by Vitor Figueiredo. No. 2914, 30c, VTS Tower, Lisbon, by Gonçalo Byrne. No. 2915, 30c, Braga Municipal Stadium, Braga, by Eduardo Souto Moura. No. 2916, 30c, José Saramago Library, Loures, by Fernando Martins. No. 2917, 30c, Sines Art Center, Sines, by Aires Mateus.
€1.85, Portugal Pavilion, by Siza, diff.

2007, May 31 ***Perf. 12½x13***
2908-2917 A804 Set of 10 8.50 4.25

Souvenir Sheet

2918 A804 €1.85 multi 5.00 5.00

World Sailing Championships — A805

Designs: No. 2919, 61c, Catamarans. No. 2920, 61c, Sailboats 23 and 105. No. 2921, 75c, Sailboat 75 and other sailboat. No. 2922, 75c, Sailboats CHI 34 and POR 16.
€2.95, Like #2921.

2007, June 12 ***Perf. 12x11¾***
2919-2922 A805 Set of 4 7.50 3.75

Souvenir Sheet

2923 A805 €2.95 multi 8.00 8.00

Miniature Sheets

Seven Wonders of Portugal — A806

No. 2924: a, Vila Vicosa Ducal Palace. b, Roman temple, Evora. c, Pena National Palace, Sintra. d, Queluz National Palace, Sintra. e, Jéronimos Monastery, Lisbon. f, Belem Tower, Lisbon. g, Sagres Fort, Vila do Bispo.

No. 2925: a, Christ Convent, Tomar. b, Almourol Castle, Vila Nova da Barquinha. c, Alcobaça Monastery. d, Obidos Castle. e, Mafra Convent and Basilica. f, Marvao Castle. g, Monsaraz Fortifications.

No. 2926: a, Guimaraes Castle. b, Mateus Palace, Vila Real. c, Sao Francisco Church, Porto. d, Clergymen Church and Tower, Porto. e, Coimbra University Palace. f, Conimbriga Ruins, Condeixa-a-Nova. g, Batalha Monastery.

2007, June 14 ***Perf. 12x11¾***

2924 A806 Sheet of 7 + label 6.00 6.00
a.-g. 30c Any single .85 .40
2925 A806 Sheet of 7 + label 6.00 6.00
a.-g. 30c Any single .85 .40
2926 A806 Sheet of 7 + label 6.00 6.00
a.-g. 30c Any single .85 .40
Nos. 2924-2926 (3) 18.00 18.00

Art From Berardo Museum — A807

Designs: 45c, Bridge, by Amadeo de Souza Cardoso. No. 2928, 61c, Les Baigneuses, by Niki de Saint Phalle, vert. €1, Interior with Restful Paintings, by Roy Liechtenstein, vert. €2, Femme Dans un Fauteuil, by Pablo Picasso, vert.

No. 2931, 61c, vert.: a, Le Couple, by Oscar Dominguez. b, Café Man Ray, by Man Ray. c, Néctar, by Joana Vasconcelos. d, Head, by Jackson Pollock.

2007, June 25 ***Perf. 12***

2927-2930 A807 Set of 4 11.00 5.50

Souvenir Sheet

2931 Sheet of 4 7.00 7.00
a.-d. A807 61c Any single 1.75 .85

Portuguese Presidency of European Union Council of Ministers — A808

Designs: 61c, Building, stars running from UL to LR. €2.45, Building, stars running from LL to UR.

Perf. 12x11¾ Syncopated

2007, July 1

2932 A808 61c multi 1.75 .85

Souvenir Sheet

2933 A808 €2.45 multi 6.75 6.75

Motorcycles — A809

Designs: 30c, 1935 SMC-Nacional 500cc. 52c, 1959 FAMEL Foguete. No. 2936, 61c, 1954 Vilar Cucciolo. €1, 1969, Casal Carina.

No. 2938, 61c: a, 1952 Quimera Alma. b, 1958 CINAL Pachancho. c, 1965 SIS Sachs VS. d, 1985 Casal K287.

2007, July 4

2934-2937 A809 Set of 4 6.75 3.50

Souvenir Sheet

2938 Sheet of 4 7.00 7.00
a.-d. A809 61c Any single 1.75 .85

Souvenir Sheet

New Seven Wonders of the World — A810

2007, July 7 ***Perf. 12½x13¼***

2939 A810 €2.95 multi 8.25 8.25

Raul Maria Pereira, Architect, and Postal Headquarters, Lima, Peru — A811

2007, Aug. 10 ***Perf. 12x11¾***

2940 A811 75c multi 2.10 1.10

See Peru No. 1574.

Famous Men — A812

Designs: No. 2941, 45c, Miguel Torga (1907-95), writer. No. 2942, 45c, Fialho de Almeida (1857-1911), writer. No. 2943, 45c, Columbano (1857-1929), painter.

2007, Aug. 12 ***Perf. 11¾x12***

2941-2943 A812 Set of 3 3.75 1.90

Souvenir Sheet

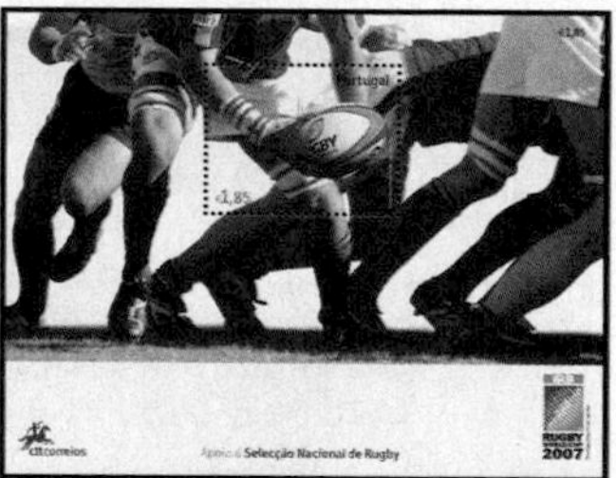

Portuguese Rugby Team — A813

2007, Aug. 22 ***Perf. 12½x13¼***

2944 A813 €1.85 multi 5.25 5.25

Art by Nadir Afonso A814

Designs: 30c, Horus. 45c, Veneza. 61c, Processao em Veneza.

2007, Sept. 5 **Litho.** ***Perf. 12½x13***

2945-2947 A814 Set of 3 3.75 1.90

Flora and Fauna of the Americas A815

Designs: No. 2948, 30c, Potatoes. No. 2949, 30c, Corn. No. 2950, 30c, Jacaranda. 45c, Cacao pods. 61c, Turkeys. 75c, Passion fruits.

€1.85, Hummingbird at passion fruit blossom, horiz.

2007, Sept. 25 ***Perf. 11¾x12***

2948-2953 A815 Set of 6 7.75 3.75

Souvenir Sheet

Perf. 12x11¾

2954 A815 €1.85 multi 5.25 5.25

Buildings — A816

Designs: 30c, Tower, Arzila, Morocco. 75c, Silves Castle, Portugal.

2007, Sept. 26 ***Perf. 13x12½***

2955-2956 A816 Set of 2 3.00 1.50

See No. 3623, Morocco Nos. 1043-1044.

Flags A817

Flag of: Nos. 2957, 2958a, Portugal.

No. 2958 — Flag of: b, Portuguese President. c, Portuguese Assembly. d, Azores. e, Madeira.

Perf. 12x11¾ Syncopated

2007, Oct. 5

2957 A817 30c multi .85 .40

Perf. 13¼x13

2958 Sheet of 5 4.25 4.25
a.-e. A817 30c Any single .85 .40

No. 2958 contains five 36x28mm stamps.

Children's Art A818

Designs: No. 2959, (30c), Children and flowers, by Ines Filipa Navrat. No. 2960, (30c), Children and globe, by Sofia Fiteiro Passeira. No. 2961, (30c), Hands and globe, by Maria Correia Borges.

Perf. 12x11¾ Syncopated

2007, Oct. 9

2959-2961 A818 Set of 3 2.60 1.25

Mafra National Reserve A819

Fauna: 30c, Cervus dama. 45c, Sus scrofa. 61c, Vulpes vulpes. 75c, Cervus elaphus. €1, Bubo bubo. €2, Hieraaetus fasciatus.

€1.25, Cervus elaphus, diff.

2007, Oct. 16 ***Perf. 12x11¾***

2962-2967 A819 Set of 6 15.00 7.50

Souvenir Sheet

2968 A819 €1.25 multi 3.75 3.75

Islamic Center, Lisbon A820

2007, Nov. 7 ***Perf. 13¼***

2969 A820 N Ground-level view .90 .45
2970 A820 I Aerial view 2.25 1.10

Reign of Aga Khan IV, 50th anniv. On day of issue, No. 2969 sold for 30c, and No. 2970 sold for 75c.

Cork Industry A821

Serpentine Die Cut 12½

2007, Nov. 28 **Litho.**

Self-Adhesive

Printed on Cork Veneer

2971 A821 €1 multi 3.00 1.50

Souvenir Sheet

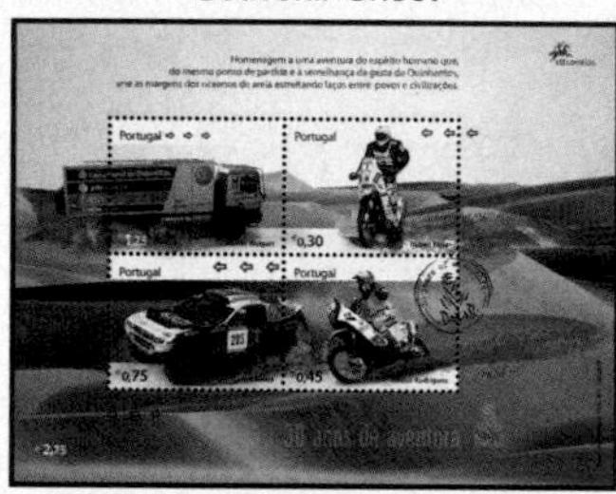

Lisbon to Dakar Rally — A822

No. 2972: a, Ruben Faria on motorcycle. b, Hélder Rodrigues on motorcycle. c, Automobile of Carlos Sousa. d, Truck of Rainer Weigart.

2008, Jan. 5 **Litho.** ***Perf. 13¼x13***

2972 A822 Sheet of 4 8.25 8.25
a. 30c multi .90 .45
b. 45c multi 1.25 .65
c. 75c multi 2.25 1.10
d. €1.25 multi 3.75 1.75

Arrival of Portuguese Royal Family in Brazil, 200th Anniv. — A823

No. 2973: a, N, Royal family and ship. b, I, King John VI and ships.

2008, Jan. 22 ***Perf. 12 Syncopated***

2973 A823 Horiz. pair, #a-b 3.25 3.25

On day of issue, Nos. 2973a and 2973b sold for 30c and 75c, respectively.

See Brazil No. 3032.

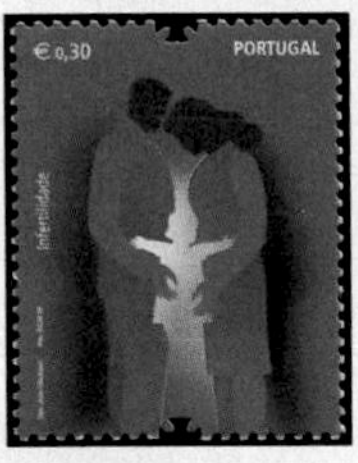
Infertility — A824

Perf. 11¾x12 Syncopated

2008, Mar. 12 **Litho.**
2974 A824 30c multi .95 .45

Intl. Year of Planet Earth A825

Designs: 30c, Forest. 45c, Clouds. 61c, Volcano. 75c, Coral reef.

Perf. 12x11¾ Syncopated

2008, Mar. 25
2975-2978 A825 Set of 4 6.75 6.75

2008 European Judo Championships, Lisbon — A826

Various action photos of judo opponents.

2008, Apr. 7
2979 A826 30c multi .95 .45
2980 A826 61c multi 2.00 1.00

Souvenir Sheet

2981 Sheet of 2 7.75 7.75
a. A826 45c multi 1.50 .75
b. A826 €2 multi 6.25 3.25

Famous People — A827

Designs: No. 2982, 30c, Maria Helena Vieira da Silva (1908-92), painter. No. 2983, 30c, Father António Vieira (1608-97), Inquisition reformer. No. 2984, 30c, Aureliano Mira Fernandes (1884-1958), mathematician. No. 2985, 30c, José Relvas (1858-1929), Prime Minister of Portugal. No. 2986, 30c, Manoel de Oliveira (b. 1908), film director. No. 2987, 30c, Ricardo Jorge (1858-1939), physician.

Perf. 11¾x12 Syncopated

2008, Apr. 18
2982-2987 A827 Set of 6 5.75 3.00

2008 Summer Olympics, Beijing A828

Emblem of 2008 Summer Olympics and: No. 2988, 30c, Runners. No. 2989, 30c, Cyclists. 75c, Triple jump.

Perf. 12x11¾ Syncopated

2008, Apr. 30
2988-2990 A828 Set of 3 4.25 2.10

Miniature Sheet

Olympex 2008, Beijing — A829

No. 2991 — Olympic athletes: a, Equestrian. b, Canoeing. c, Shooting. d, Rhythmic gymnastics.

Perf. 12x11¾ Syncopated

2008, Apr. 30
2991 A829 Sheet of 4 9.25 9.25
a.-d. 75c Any single 2.25 1.10

European Triathlon Championships — A830

Perf. 12x11¾ Syncopated

2008, May 9 **Litho.**
2992 A830 €2 multi 6.25 3.25

Europa A831

Designs: No. 2993, Man sitting on envelope, mail truck. No. 2994a, Mail truck, bull.

2008, May 9
2993 A831 61c multi 2.00 .95

Souvenir Sheet

2994 Sheet of 2, #2993, 2994a 5.00 2.00
a. A831 61c multi 2.50 .95

Historic Public Transportation A832

Designs: N, Oldsmobile taxicab, Lisbon, 1928. A, Electric trolley, Cascais, 1926. E, Bus, Lisbon, 1944.

Serpentine Die Cut 11½

2008, May 13 **Self-Adhesive**
2995 A832 N multi .95 .45
2996 A832 A multi 1.50 .75
2997 A832 E multi 2.00 1.00
Nos. 2995-2997 (3) 4.45 2.20

On day of issue, Nos. 2995-2997 sold for 30c, 45c, and 61c, respectively.
See Nos. 3026-3030.

Children's Right to Education A833

Designs: 30c, Child arriving at school. 45c, Children in classroom. 61c, Children reading and painting. 75c, Child reading with parents. €2.95, Man hugging "4," paint brushes.

Perf. 11¾x12 Suncopated

2008, June 2
2998-3001 A833 Set of 4 6.75 3.50

Souvenir Sheet

3002 A833 €2.95 multi 9.50 4.75

UEFA Euro 2008 Soccer Championships, Austria and Switzerland. A834

Silhouettes of soccer players in: 30c, Orange and red. 61c, Blue green and lilac.
No. 3005: a, Red and lilac. b, Orange and brown.

2008, June 5
3003-3004 A834 Set of 2 3.00 1.50

Souvenir Sheet

3005 Sheet of 2 9.00 4.50
a. A834 €1.20 multi 3.75 1.90
b. A834 €1.66 multi 5.25 2.60

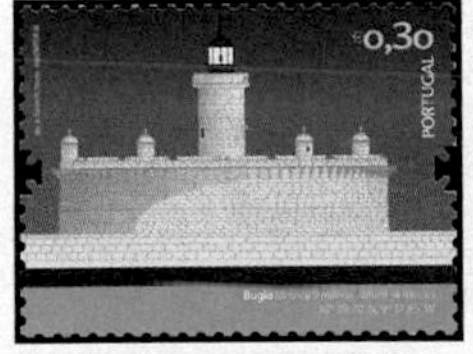
Lighthouses — A835

Designs: No. 3006, 30c, Bugio. No. 3007, 30c, Cabo de Sao Vicente. No. 3008, 30c, Cabo da Roca. No. 3009, 30c, Cabo Sardao. No. 3010, 30c, Esposende, vert. No. 3011, 30c, Santa Marta, vert. No. 3012, 30c, Cabo Espichel, vert. No. 3013, 30c, Penedo da Saudade, vert. No. 3014, 30c, Montedor, vert. No. 3015, 30c, Leça, vert.

Perf. 12x11¾, 11¾x12 Syncopated

2008, June 19
3006-3015 A835 Set of 10 9.50 4.75

International Polar Year — A836

Designs: 30c, Calidris alba. 52c, Alca torda. 61c, Oceanites oceanicus. €1, Sterna paradisea.
€2.95, Phoca hispida, Ursus maritimus.

Perf. 12x11¾ Syncopated

2008, June 23
3016-3019 A836 Set of 4 7.75 4.00

Souvenir Sheet

3020 A836 €2.95 multi 9.50 4.75

EFIRO 2008 World Philatelic Exhibition, Bucharest, Romania (#3020). No. 3020 contains one 80x30mm stamp.

Formula 1 Racing in Portugal, 50th Anniv. A837

Race cars driven by: 31c, Stirling Moss. 67c, Jack Brabham. 80c, Mark Haywood. €2, Bobby Vernon-Roe.
€2.45, 1960 Grand Prix race at Boavista Racetrack.

Perf. 12x11¾ Syncopated

2008, Sept. 11 **Litho.**
3021-3024 A837 Set of 4 10.50 5.25

Souvenir Sheet

3025 A837 €2.45 multi 6.75 3.50

No. 3025 contains one 80x30mm stamp.

Historic Public Transportation Type of 2008

Designs: 6c, Electric trolley, Porto, 1927. 31c, Oldsmobile taxicab, Lisbon, 1928. 47c, Electric trolley, Cascais, 1926. 67c, Bus, Lisbon, 1944. 80c, Electric trolley, Coimbra, 1911.

2008, Sept. 12 *Perf. 11¾x11½*
3026 A832 6c multi .25 .25
3027 A832 31c multi .85 .45
3028 A832 47c multi 1.40 .70
3029 A832 67c multi 1.90 .95
3030 A832 80c multi 2.25 1.10
Nos. 3026-3030 (5) 6.65 3.45

Souvenir Sheet

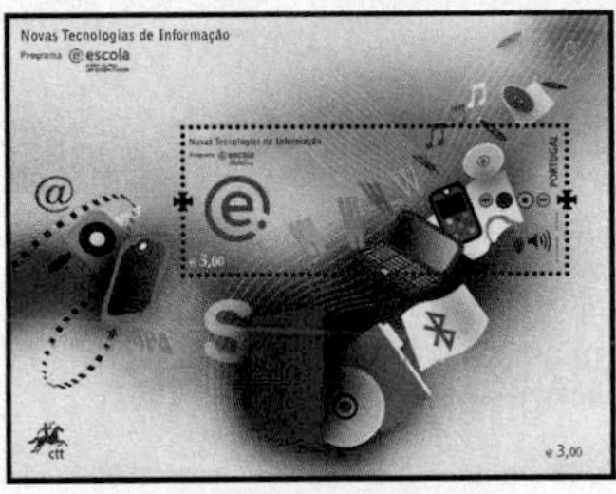
Escola School Computer Program — A838

Perf. 12x11¾ Syncopated

2008, Sept. 15
3031 A838 €3 multi 8.25 4.25

Companhia Uniao Fabril, Cent. — A839

Designs: 31c, Metalworking industry. 67c, Textile industry. €1, Naval construction industry. €2, Chemical industry.
€2.45, Alfredo da Silva, company founder, vert.

Perf. 12x11¾ Syncopated

2008, Sept. 19
3032-3035 A839 Set of 4 11.00 5.50

Perf. 11¾x12 Syncopated

3036 A839 €2.45 multi 6.75 3.50

Ceramic Pharmacy Jars A840

Designs: 31c, Two jars, 17th cent. 47c, Jar, 18th cent. 67c, Three jars, 17th-18th cent. 80c, Two jars with lids, 19th cent.
€2.48, Pharmacy, 17th-18th cent.

Perf. 12x11¾ Syncopated

2008, Sept. 26
3037-3040 A840 Set of 4 6.25 3.25

Souvenir Sheet

3041 A840 €2.48 multi 7.00 3.50

Demarcated Wine Regions, Cent. — A841

No. 3042, 31c: a, Colares vineyard and grapes. b, Carcavelos barrels and grapes.
No. 3043, 31c: a, Setúbal Muscatel bottles and grapes. b, Setúbal Muscatel vineyards and grapes.
No. 3044, 31c: a, Bucelas vineyard and grapes. b, Bucelas barrels and grapes.
No. 3045, 31c: a, Dao vineyard and grapes. b, Dao barrels and grapes.
No. 3046, 31c: a, Green Wine vineyard and grapes. b, Green Wine terraced vineyard.

Perf. 12x11¾ Syncopated

2008, Oct. 2 Litho.

Horiz. Pairs, #a-b

3042-3046 A841 Set of 5 8.75 4.50

Republican Ideas A842

Bust and: No. 3047, 31c, First Executive Republican Chamber. No. 3048, 31c, School and children. No. 3049, 47c, Row houses and family. No. 3050, 47c, Factory. 57c, Postal workers. No. 3052, 67c, Civil registry. No. 3053, 67c, Public health. 80c, Civic participation.
€2.95, Tagus River Railroad Bridge.

2008, Oct. 5

3047-3054 A842 Set of 8 11.50 5.75

Souvenir Sheet

3055 A842 €2.95 multi 8.00 4.00

No. 3055 contains one 80x30mm stamp.

Olive Oil Production A843

Designs: 31c, Olive grove. 47c, Olive pickers. 57c, Olive sorters. 67c, Olive mill. 80c, Oil vats. €2, Containers of herbed olive oil.
€1.85, Hands holding olives.

2008, Oct. 7

3056-3061 A843 Set of 6 13.00 6.50

Souvenir Sheet

3062 A843 €1.85 multi 5.00 2.50

School Correspondence — A844

Children's drawings by: 31c, Erica Bluemel Portocarrero. 47c, Eloísa O. Pereira. 67c, Joao Maria Martins Branco.

2008, Oct. 9

3063-3065 A844 Set of 3 4.00 2.00

Bridges A845

Designs: 31c, April 25th Bridge, Lisbon. 47c, Arrábida Bridge, Oporto. 57c, Arade River Bridge, Portimao. 67c, Mosteiro Bridge, Cinfães. 80c, Amizade Bridge, Vila Nova de Cerveira. €1, Santa Clara Bridge, Coimbra.
No. 3072, €1.85, April 25th Bridge, Lisbon, diff. No. 3073, €1.85, Arrábida Bridge, Oporto, diff.

2008, Oct. 16

3066-3071 A845 Set of 6 9.75 5.00

Souvenir Sheets

3072-3073 A845 Set of 2 9.50 4.75

Nos. 3072-3073 each contain one 80x30mm stamp.

European Year of Intercultural Dialogue — A846

Designs: 31c, Sculpture, tile design. 47c, Mask, bust. 67c, Window, feather headdress. 80c, African and Chinese masks.

2008, Oct. 23

3074-3077 A846 Set of 4 5.75 3.00

Waiting for Success, Painting by Henrique Pousao (1859-84) A847

Joaquim Soeiro Pereira Gomes (1909-49), Writer A848

Perf. 11¾x12 Syncopated

2009, Jan. 27 Litho.

3078 A847 32c multi .85 .40

Perf. 12x11¾ Syncopated

3079 A848 32c multi .85 .40

Creation of the Euro, 10th Anniv. A849

Euro symbols, stars and: 47c, Three stylized euro coins. €1, Two stylized euro coins.

Perf. 12x11¾ Syncopated

2009, Jan. 28

3080-3081 A849 Set of 2 3.75 1.90

Historic Public Transportation A850

Designs: 20c, Bus, 1957. Nos. 3083, 3087, Electric train, 1957. Nos. 3084, 3088, ML7 train car, 1959. Nos. 3085, 3089, Double-decker bus, 1960. 80c, Electric trolley bus, 1961.

2009 Litho. *Perf. 11¾x11½*

3082 A850 20c multi .50 .25
3083 A850 32c multi .85 .40
3084 A850 47c multi 1.25 .60
3085 A850 68c multi 1.75 .85
3086 A850 80c multi 2.10 1.10
Nos. 3082-3086 (5) 6.45 3.20

Booklet Stamps

Self-Adhesive

Serpentine Die Cut 11½

3087 A850 N multi .85 .40
a. Booklet pane of 10 8.50
Complete booklet, 10 #3087a 85.00
3088 A850 A multi 1.25 .60
a. Booklet pane of 10 12.50
Complete booklet, 5 #3088a 62.50
3089 A850 E multi 1.75 .85
a. Booklet pane of 10 17.50
Complete booklet, 5 #3089a 87.50
Nos. 3087-3089 (3) 3.85 1.85

Issued: Nos. 3082-3086, 2/9; Nos. 3087-3089, 4/30. On day of issue, Nos. 3087-3089 sold for 32c, 47c and 68c respectively.

Charles Darwin (1809-82), Naturalist A851

Darwin and: No. 3090, 32c, Finches. No. 3091, 32c, Iguana. No. 3092, 68c, Diana monkey. No. 3093, 68c, Orchids. No. 3094, 80c, Shells and fossil skull. No. 3095, 80c, Platypus.
€2.50, Darwin and finches, vert.

Perf. 12x11¾ Syncopated

2009, Feb. 12

3090-3095 A851 Set of 6 9.25 4.75

Souvenir Sheet

Perf. 11¾x12 Syncopated

3096 A851 €2.50 multi 6.50 3.25

African Heritage in Portugal A852

Africans as depicted in: 32c, Ceramic figurine, 19th cent. 47c, Santa Auta retable, 1522. 57c, Painting by José Conrado Roza, 1788. 68c, Ceramic tile, 19th cent. 80c, Portuguese faience, 18th cent. €2, Painted wood, 19th cent.
€2.50, Painting by Joaquim Marques, 1789.

Perf. 12x11¾ Syncopated

2009, Feb. 26

3097-3102 A852 Set of 6 12.50 6.25

Souvenir Sheet

3103 A852 €2.50 multi 6.50 3.25

Molecular Models A853

Multiplication Equations — A854

2009, Mar. 4

3104 A853 32c multi .85 .40
3105 A854 32c multi .85 .40

Franciscan Order, 800th Anniv. A855

Designs: 32c, St. Francis of Assisi with dog.

No. 3107, vert.: a, 50c, St. Francis receiving tonsure. b, €2, Pope Innocent III.

Perf. 12x11¾ Syncopated

2009, Mar. 11

3106 A855 32c multi .90 .45

Souvenir Sheet

Perf. 11¾x12 Syncopated

3107 A855 Sheet of 2, #a-b 6.75 3.25

Canonization of St. Nuno de Santa Maria — A856

Perf. 12x11¾ Syncopated

2009, Aug. 26

3108 A856 32c multi .85 .40

Europa A857

Designs: No. 3109, Three images from Mar. 3, 2007 lunar eclipse. No. 3110a, European Southern Observatory.

2009, May 8

3109 A857 68c multi 1.90 .95

Souvenir Sheet

3110 Sheet of 2, #3109, 3110a 4.00 2.00
a. A857 68c multi 1.90 .95

Intl. Year of Astronomy.

Ceramics A858

Designs: 32c, Faience mosque lamp, Turkey. 68c, Ceramic pot, Portugal.

2009, May 12 *Perf. 12½x13*

3111-3112 A858 Set of 2 2.75 1.40

See Turkey Nos. 3160-3161.

Cristo Rei Sanctuary, Lisbon, 50th Anniv. — A859

Designs: 32c, Statue of Christ and base. 68c, Statue of Christ.
€2.48, Head of statue and 25 de Abril Bridge.

Perf. 11¾x12 Syncopated

2009, May 17

3113-3114 A859 Set of 2 2.75 1.40

Souvenir Sheet

Perf. 12x11¾ Syncopated

3115 A859 €2.48 multi 7.00 3.50

No. 3115 contains one 80x30mm stamp.

Foods of Portuguese-speaking Areas — A860

Designs; No. 3116, 32c, Leitoa num ar de sarapatel, Brazil. No. 3117, 32c, Bebinca das sete colinas, India. No. 3118, 68c, Caldeirada de cabrito, Angola. No. 3119, 68c, Bacalhau, pao, vinho e aziete, Portugal. No. 3120, 80c, No caldeiro a tempura, Asia. No. 3121, 80c, Do cozido à cachupa, Cape Verde.

€1.85, Bacalhau, pao, vinho e aziete, diff., vert.

Perf. 12x11¾ Syncopated

2009, June 5

3116-3121	A860	Set of 6	10.00	5.00

Souvenir Sheet

Perf. 11¾x12 Syncopated

3122	A860	€1.85 multi	5.25	2.60

Lusitano Horses — A861

Designs: No. 3123, 32c, White horse with rider. No. 3124, 32c, Black horse with rider. 57c, Brown horse with rider. 68c, Brown horse rearing. 80c, Horses in team.

€2.50, Horse walking.

Perf. 11¾x12 Syncopated

2009, June 11

3123-3127	A861	Set of 5	7.50	3.75

Souvenir Sheet

3128	A861	€2.50 multi	7.00	3.50

See No. 3624.

King Afonso I (1109-85), First King of Portugal A862

Designs: 32c, Sculpture of King Afonso I €3.07, Drawing of King Afonso I on horse.

Perf. 12x11¾ Syncopated

2009, June 24

3129	A862	32c multi	.90	.45

Souvenir Sheet

3130	A862	€3.07 multi	8.75	4.50

Jazz in Portugal — A863

Inscriptions: 32c, Cascais Jazz. 47c, Jazz num Dia de Verao. 57c, Fundaçao Calouste Gulbenkian Jazz em Agosto. 68c, Jazz Europeu no Porto. 80c, Guimaraes Jazz. €1, Seixal Jazz.

€3.16, Quarteto Hot Club, horiz.

Perf. 11¾x12 Syncopated

2009, June 26

3131-3136	A863	Set of 6	11.00	5.50

Souvenir Sheet

Perf. 12x11¾ Syncopated

3137	A863	€3.16 black	9.00	4.50

Traditional Breads A864

Designs: No. 3138, 32c, Pao de Centeio (rye bread). No. 3139, 32c, Pao de Quartos. 47c, Regueifa. No. 3141, 68c, Pao de Testa. No. 3142, 68c, Pao com Chouriço (bread with sausage). 80c, Pao de Mealhada.

No. 3144, €2, Bolo de Caco. No. 3145, €2, Pao de Milho (corn bread).

Perf. 12x11¾ Syncopated

2009, July 28 **Litho.**

3138-3143	A864	Set of 6	9.25	4.75

Souvenir Sheets

3144-3145	A864	Set of 2	11.50	5.75
3144a		Booklet pane of 1	5.75	—
3145a		Booklet pane of 1	5.75	—

See No. 3667.

António Pedro (1909-66), Theater Founder A865

Designs: 32c, Pedro and stage art. €3.16, Pedro.

2009, Sept. 1

3146	A865	32c multi	.95	.45

Souvenir Sheet

3147	A865	€3.16 multi	9.00	4.50

Belém Palace (Presidential Residence), Lisbon — A866

Designs: 32c, Palace exterior, 1841-42. 47c, Decorative painting. 57c, Writing desk. 68c, Bas-relief depicting satyrs. 80c, Decorative head from Gold Room. €1, Painting from Fountain Room.

€2.50, Fountain Room.

2009, Sept. 17

3148-3153	A866	Set of 6	11.50	5.75

Souvenir Sheet

3154	A866	€2.50 multi	7.50	3.75

Birds — A867

Designs: 32c, Pandion haliaetus. 80c, Haliaeetus albicilla.

2009, Sept. 21 ***Perf. 13x12½***

3155-3156	A867	Set of 2	3.50	1.75

See Iran No. 3002.

The Senses — A868

Louis Braille (1809-52), Educator of the Blind — A869

Senses: 32c, Smell (cup of coffee). 68c, Taste (ice cream bar). 80c, Sight (eyeglasses). €1, Touch (tube of paint). €2, Hearing (file)

Perf. 11¾x12 Syncopated

2009, Oct. 2 **Litho.**

3157	A868	32c multi	.95	.45
3158	A868	68c multi	2.00	1.00

Litho. with Hologram Affixed

3159	A868	80c multi	2.40	1.25

Litho. & Embossed

3160	A868	€1 multi	3.00	1.50

Litho.

3161	A868	€2 multi	6.00	3.00
		Nos. 3157-3161 (5)	14.35	7.20

Souvenir Sheet

Litho. & Embossed

Perf. 13¼x13½

3162	A869	€2.50 multi	7.25	3.75

No. 3157 is impregnated with a coffee scent. Parts of the design of No. 3161 are covered with a gritty substance.

Famous Women — A870

Designs: No. 3163, 32c, Maria Veleda (1871-1955), teacher and writer of children's books. No. 3164, 32c, Adelaide Cabete (1867-1935), doctor and feminist leader. 57c, Ana de Castro Osório (1872-1935), writer and feminist leader. 68c, Angelina Vidal (1853-1917), teacher. 80c, Carolina Beatriz Angelo (1877-1911), surgeon and feminist leader. €1, Carolina Michaelis de Vasconcelos (1851-1925), novelist.

No. 3169: a, Virginia Quaresma (1882-1973), journalist. b, Emília de Sousa Costa (1877-1959), writer and educator.

Perf. 11¾x12 Syncopated

2009, Oct. 5 **Litho.**

3163-3168	A870	Set of 6	11.00	5.50

Souvenir Sheet

3169	A870	€1.15 Sheet of 2, #a-b	7.00	3.50

School Correspondence — A871

Children's art by: 32c, Martina Marques Teixeira Santos. 47c, Joel Filipe Silva Carmo. 68c, Manuel Pedro A. B. Paiva Martins.

Perf. 12x11¾ Syncopated

2009, Oct. 9

3170-3172	A871	Set of 3	4.50	2.25

Christmas A872

Santa Claus and: 32c, Star and hearts. 47c, Door and sack of letters. 68c, Christmas tree and gift. 80c, Reindeer and gift.

No. 3177: a, 50c, Toy reindeer, "0" and "9." b, €1, Christmas stocking

Perf. 11¾x12 Syncopated

2009, Oct. 21

3173-3176	A872	Set of 4	6.75	3.25

Souvenir Sheet

3177	A872	Sheet of 2, #a-b	4.50	2.25

Abandoned Dog — A873

Viriathus (d. 138 B.C.), Lusitanian Rebel Against Roman Empire — A874

Perf. 11¾x12 Syncopated

2010, Feb. 22 **Litho.**

3178	A873	32c multi	.90	.45
3179	A874	32c multi	.90	.45

Composers — A875

Designs: No. 3180, 68c, Frédéric Chopin (1810-49). No. 3181, 68c, Robert Schumann (1810-56).

No. 3182, €2, Chopin, diff. No. 3183, €2, Schumann, diff.

Perf. 12x11¾ Syncopated

2010, Mar. 1

3180-3181	A875	Set of 2	3.75	1.90

Souvenir Sheets

3182-3183	A875	Set of 2	11.00	5.50

Urban Transportation of the 1970s to 1990s — A876

Designs: 1c, Volvo articulated bus, Porto. Nos. 3185, 3189, Carris articulated tram, Lisbon. Nos. 3186, 3190, ML 79 subway train, Lisbon. Nos. 3187, 3191, Ferry boat Madragoa, Lisbon. 80c, CP electric train.

2010, Mar. 8 **Litho.** ***Perf. 11¾x11½***

3184	A876	1c multi	.25	.25
3185	A876	32c multi	.90	.45
3186	A876	47c multi	1.25	.65

3187 A876 68c multi 1.90 .95
3188 A876 80c multi 2.25 1.10
Nos. 3184-3188 (5) 6.55 3.40

Self-Adhesive

Serpentine Die Cut 11½

3189 A876 N multi .90 .45
3190 A876 A multi 1.25 .65
3191 A876 E multi 1.90 .95
Nos. 3189-3191 (3) 4.05 2.05

On day of isse Nos. 3189-3191 sold for 32c, 47c, and 68c, respectively.

Intl. Year of Biodiversity A877

Designs: 32c, Thunnus thynnus. 47c, Centrophorus granulosus. 68c, Ailuropoda melanoleuca. 80c, Hummingbird.
€2.50, Lion tamarin.

Perf. 12x11¾ Syncopated

2010, Mar. 8

3192-3195 A877 Set of 4 6.25 3.25

Souvenir Sheet

3196 A877 €2.50 multi 6.75 3.50

Precious Stones in Sacred Art — A878

Designs: 32c, Archdiocese of Evora bouquet pin. 68c, Bodice ornament of Virgin of Carmo. €1, Processional cross of King Sancho I.
€2.50, Crown of Our Lady of Fatima sculpture.

Perf. 12x11¾ Syncopated

2010, Mar. 22

3197-3199 A878 Set of 3 5.50 2.75

Souvenir Sheet

3200 A878 €2.50 multi 6.75 3.50

Breads A879

Designs: 32c, Broa. 47c, Padas. 68c, Broa de Avintes. 80c, Alentejano bread.
No. 3205: a, 80c, Carcaça. b, €1, Mafra bread.

Perf. 12x11¾ Syncopated

2010, Apr. 6

3201-3204 A879 Set of 4 6.25 3.25

Souvenir Sheet

3205 A879 Sheet of 2, #a-b 5.00 2.50

Famous Men A880

Designs: No. 3206, 32c, Gomes Eanes de Azurara (1410-74), royal chronicler and archive keeper. No. 3207, 32c, Fernao Mendes Pinto (1510-83), travel writer. No. 3208, 32c, Alexandre Herculano (1810-77), historian. No. 3209, 32c, Francisco Keil do Amaral (1910-75), architect.

2010, Apr. 22

3206-3209 A880 Set of 4 3.50 1.75

Europa — A881

Characters from children's story: No. 3210, Monkey. No. 3211a, Barber with razor.

Perf. 11¾x12 Syncopated

2010, May 7

3210 A881 68c multi 1.75 .85

Souvenir Sheet

3211 Sheet of 2, #3210, 3211a 3.50 1.75
a. A881 68c multi 1.75 .85

Popes A882

Designs: 68c, Pope Benedict XVI.
No. 3213, vert. — Popes who visited Portugal: a, Pope Paul VI. b, Pope John Paul II. c, Pope Benedict XVI, diff.

Perf. 12x11¾ Syncopated

2010, May 10

3212 A882 68c multi 1.75 .85

Souvenir Sheet

Perf. 11¾x12 Syncopated

3213 A882 80c Sheet of 3, #a-c 5.75 3.00

Visit of Pope Benedict XVI to Portugal.

Public Elevators and Funicular Railroads A883

Designs: 32c, Santa Justa Elevator, Lisbon. 47c, Glória Funicular, Lisbon. 57c Guindais Funicular, Porto. 68c, Bom Jesus Funicular, Braga. 80c, Santa Luiza Funicular, Viana do Castelo. €1, Nazaré Funicular, Nazaré.
No. 3220: a, Bica Funicular, Lisbon. b, Lavra Funicular, Lisbon.

Perf. 11¾x12 Syncopated

2010, May 17

3214-3219 A883 Set of 6 9.25 4.75

Souvenir Sheet

3220 A883 €1.25 Sheet of 2, #a-b 6.00 3.00

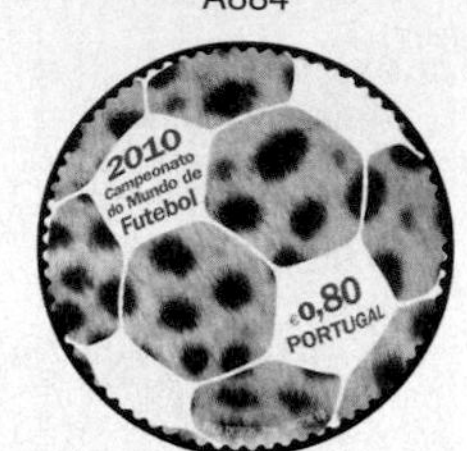

A884

2010 World Cup Soccer Championships, South Africa — A885

Perf. 12x11¾ Syncopated

2010, May 31 **Souvenir Sheet**

3221 A884 €2.50 multi 6.00 3.00

Self-Adhesive

Serpentine Die Cut

3222 A885 80c multi 1.90 .95

Theater in Portugal A886

Designs: No. 3223, 32c, Estrangeiros and Vilhalpandos, by Francisco de Sá de Miranda. No. 3224, 32c, Auto da Barca do Inferno, by Gil Vicente. 57c, A Castro, by António Ferreira. No. 3226, 68c, O Fidalgo Aprendiz, by Dom Francisco Manuel de Mello. No. 3227, 68c, El-Rei Seleuco, by Luis de Camoens. 80c, Guerras de Alecrim e Manjerona, by António José da Silva.

Perf. 12x11¾ Syncopated

2010, June 7

3223-3228 A886 Set of 6 8.25 4.25

Cheeses A887

Designs: No. 3229, 32c, Serra de Estrela. No. 3230, 32c, Rabaçal. 47c, Azeitao. 68c, Cabra Transmontano. 80c, Sao Jorge.
€2.50, Serra de Estrela, diff.

Perf. 12x11¾ Syncopated

2010, June 21

3229-3233 A887 Set of 5 6.50 3.25

Souvenir Sheet

3234 A887 €2.50 multi 6.25 3.25

Miniature Sheet

Heads of "The Republic" by Various Artists — A888

No. 3235 — Depictions by: a, 32c, Júlio Pomar. b, 32c, Francisco dos Santos. c, 32c, Costa Pinheiro. d, 32c, Bento Condado. e, 32c, Luís Maceira. f, 68c, Joao Abel Manta. g, 68c, Joao Machado. h, 80c, André Carrilho.

Perf. 11¾x12 Syncopated

2010, June 24

3235 A888 Sheet of 8, #a-h, + central label 9.50 4.75

Portugal 2010 World Philatelic Exhibition, Lisbon.

Tiles — A889

No. 3236 — Tile from: a, 68c, Portugal, 18th cent. b, 80c, Romania, 19th cent.

2010, June 30 **Litho.**

3236 A889 Pair, #a-b 3.75 1.90

See Romania Nos. 5188-5189.

Jewish Culture A890

Designs: 32c, Synagogue, Tomar. 57c, Arched doorway, Rua Nova, Lamego. 68c, Jewish neighborhood, Castelo de Vide.
€2.50, Illuminated manuscript depicting Jews building structure.

Perf. 12x11¾ Syncopated

2010, July 5

3237-3239 A890 Set of 3 4.00 2.00

Souvenir Sheet

3240 A890 €2.50 multi 6.50 3.25

Rock Music Album Covers A891

Designs: 32c, Ar de Rock, by Rui Veloso. 47c, Heróis do Mar, by Heróis do Mar. 57c, Psicopátria, by GNR. 68c, A Flor da Pele, by UHF. 80c, Compacto, by Xutos & Pontapes. €1, Wolfheart, by Moonspell.
€2.50, A Lenda de El-Rei D. Sebastiao, by Quarteto 1111.

Perf. 12x11¾ Syncopated

2010, July 10

3241-3246 A891 Set of 6 10.00 5.00

Souvenir Sheet

3247 A891 €2.50 multi 6.50 3.25

Portuguese Assembly Building (St. Benedict's Palace), Lisbon A892

Designs: 32c, Sala dos Sessoes. 68c, Senate Chambers. 80c, Sala dos Passos Perdidos.
€2, Building exterior.

Perf. 12x11¾ Syncopated

2010, Sept. 15

3247A A892 32c multi .90 .45
3248 A892 68c multi 2.00 1.00
3249 A892 80c multi 2.25 1.10

Souvenir Sheet

3250 A892 €2 multi 5.50 2.75

Portugal 2010 World Philatelic Exhibition, Lisbon (#3250).

Peninsular War, Bicent. — A893

No. 3251: a, 32c, Battle of Vimeiro. b, 68c, Battle of Buçaco.
€2.50, Battle of Pombal.

2010, Sept. 15

3251 A893 Horiz. pair, #a-b 2.75 1.40

Souvenir Sheet

3252 A893 €2.50 multi 7.00 3.50

No. 3252 contains one 80x30mm stamp.

Hydrographic Institute, 50th Anniv. — A894

No. 3253: a, 32c, Lighthouse, ship's bow. b, 68c, Ship's stern, man inspecting equipment.

2010, Sept. 22

3253 A894 Horiz. pair, #a-b 2.75 1.40

Circus Performers A895

Designs: 32c, Clown with broom. 47c, Clown on unicycle. 68c, Acrobat with hoops. 80c, Juggler with bowling pins.
€2.50, Trapeze artists.

Perf. 11¾x12 Syncopated

2010, Sept. 29

3254-3257 A895 Set of 4 6.25 3.25

Souvenir Sheet

3258 A895 €2.50 multi 7.00 3.50

No. 3258 contains one 30x80mm stamp.

Ceres — A896

Litho. & Engr.

2010, Oct. 1 *Perf. 14x13¼*

3259 A896 80c multi 2.25 1.10

Republic of Portugal, cent.

History of Freedom A897

Designs: No. 3260, 32c, Liberty with Portuguese flag. No. 3261, 32c, Man with Portuguese flag, man with rifle. 47c, Soldier with cannon, man with rifle. 68c, Liberty with French flag, French man with rifle. 80c, Uncle Sam pointing at British soldiers. €1, Bishop, king and peasant.

Perf. 12x11¾ Syncopated

2010, Oct. 2 **Litho.**

3260-3265 A897 Set of 6 10.00 5.00

Portugal 2010 World Philatelic Exhibition, Lisbon

School Correspondence — A898

Children's art by: 32c, Guilherme Pereira. 47c, Diogo Gouveia. 68c, Ana Marques.

2010, Oct. 9

3266-3268 A898 Set of 3 4.25 2.10

UN High Commissioner for Refugees, 60th Anniv. — A899

Designs: 80c, Refugees walking on road. €2.50, Refugee in framework for hut, vert.

Perf. 12x11¾ Syncopated

2010, Oct. 18

3269 A899 80c multi 2.25 1.10

Souvenir Sheet

Perf. 11¾x12 Syncopated

3270 A899 €2.50 multi 7.00 3.50

Friendship Between Portugal and Japan, 150th Anniv. — A900

No. 3271 — Detail of Japanese screen painting depicting Portuguese ship's: a, 32c, Bow. b, 80c, Stern.

2010, Oct. 22 *Perf. 13¼x12½*

3271 A900 Horiz. pair, #a-b 3.25 1.60

See Japan No. 3267.

Assoc. of Postal and Telecommunications Operators of Portuguese-Speaking Countries and Territories, 20th Anniv. — A901

Perf. 12x11¾ Syncopated

2010, Oct. 25

3272 A901 80c multi 2.25 1.10

Messenger on Horseback, Sculpture by Jorge Pé-Curto — A902

Designs: €1, Entire sculpture. €2.50, Head of sculpture, horiz.

Perf. 11¾x12 Syncopated

2010, Nov. 2

3273 A902 €1 multi 3.00 1.50

Souvenir Sheet

Perf. 12x11¾ Syncopated

3274 A902 €2.50 multi 7.00 3.50

No. 3274 contains one 80x30mm stamp.

In 2010, Portugal began issuing self-adhesive personalizable stamps as shown in the example above. These stamps, each of which were sold only in full sheets, have the inscription "Portugal CTT" at lower left, and are inscribed at the lower right with perhaps as many as 33 different denominations initially, with many more new denominations possible as postage rates change. Vignettes could be personalized or chosen from a library of stock designs.

Wind Turbines, Bridge, Buildings A903

Animals on Floating Island A904

2011, Feb. 17 *Perf. 13 Syncopated*

3275 A903 32c multi .90 .45
3276 A904 47c multi 1.40 .70

Traditional Portuguese Festivals — A905

Designs: 10c, People watching fireworks. 32c, Festa dos Tabulieros, Tomar. 47c, Festa do Sao Joao, Porto. 68c, Carneval, Loulé. 80c, Flower Festival, Madeira.

Perf. 11¾x11½

2011, Feb. 21 **Litho.**

3277 A905 10c multi .30 .25
3278 A905 32c multi .90 .45
3279 A905 47c multi 1.40 .70
3280 A905 68c multi 1.90 .95
3281 A905 80c multi 2.25 1.10
Nos. 3277-3281 (5) 6.75 3.45

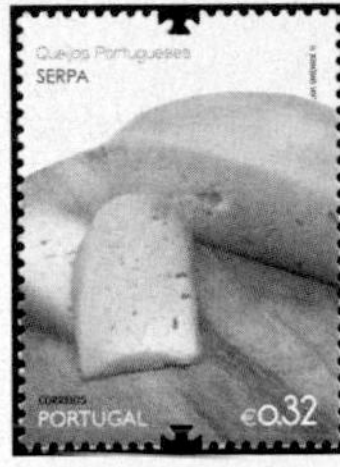

Cheeses — A906

Designs: 32c, Serpa. 47c, Castelo Branco. 68c, Pico. 80c, Nisa. €1, Terrincho.
€2.50, Castelo Branco, diff.

2011, Mar. 1 *Perf. 13 Syncopated*

3282-3286 A906 Set of 5 9.25 4.75

Souvenir Sheet

3287 A906 €2.50 multi 7.00 3.50

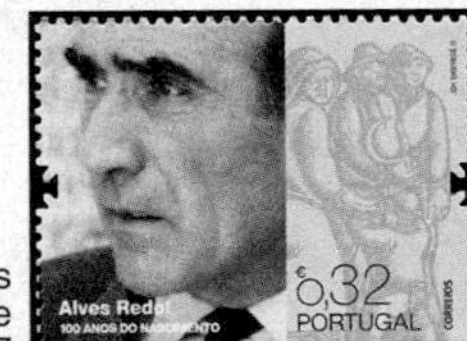

Famous People A907

Designs: 32c, Alves Redol (1911-69), writer. 47c, Manuel da Fonseca (1911-93), writer. 57c, Trindade Coelho (1861-1908), writer. 68c, Antónia Ferreira (1811-96), businesswoman. 80c, Eugénio dos Santos (1711-60), architect.

2011, Mar. 14

3288-3292 A907 Set of 5 8.25 4.25

Centenaries of Institutes of Higher Education — A908

Designs: No. 3293, 32c, University of Lisbon. No. 3294, 32c, University of Porto. No. 3295, 80c, Higher Institute of Economics and Management. No. 3296, 80c, Higher Institute of Technology.

2011, Mar. 22

3293-3296 A908 Set of 4 6.50 3.25

Crédito Agrícola, Cent. A909

Hills, plants and: No. 3297, N, Tall buildings. No. 3298, E, Small buildings.

2011, Mar. 25

3297-3298 A909 Set of 2 3.00 1.50

On day of issue, No. 3297 sold for 32c and No. 3298 sold for 68c.

Fish A910

Designs: 32c, Lampetra fluviatilis. 47c, Alosa alosa. 68c, Platichthys flesus. 80c, Liza ramada.

No. 3303, €1.80, Salmo salar. No. 3304, €1.80, Anguilla anguilla.

2011, Apr. 7

3299-3302 A910 Set of 4 6.75 3.25

Souvenir Sheets

3303-3304 A910 Set of 2 10.50 5.25

Diplomatic Relations Between Portugal and the Republic of Korea, 50th Anniv. A911

Designs: No. 3305, N, Korean turtle ship. No. 3306, I, Portuguese nau.

2011, Apr. 15 ***Perf. 12½x13***

3305-3306 A911 Set of 2 3.25 1.60

On day of issue, No. 3305 sold for 32c and No. 3306 sold for 80c. See South Korea No. 2355.

Republican National Guard, Cent. — A912

Designs: N, Hats. €3.60, Gloves, sword and uniform, horiz.

2011, Apr. 21 ***Perf. 13 Syncopated***

3307 A912 N multi .95 .45

Souvenir Sheet

3308 A912 €3.60 multi 10.50 5.25

No. 3307 sold for 32c on day of issue.

Europa A913

Designs: No. 3309, Man cutting bark from cork oak, pigs. No. 3310a, Deer at edge of forest.

Perf. 12x11¾ Syncopated

2011, May 9

3309 A913 68c multi 2.00 1.00

Souvenir Sheet

3310 Sheet of 2, #3309, 3310a 4.00 2.00

a. A913 68c multi 2.00 1.00

Intl. Year of Forests.

Postal Union of the Americas, Spain and Portugal ((UPAEP), Cent. — A914

2011, May 16 ***Perf. 13 Syncopated***

3311 A914 80c multi 2.40 1.25

Portuguese Military Academy, Cent. — A915

Designs: 32c, Shako. €1, Cadets in electronics laboratory.

€2.50, Cadet holding flag, cadet wearing shako, horiz.

2011, May 25

3312-3313 A915 Set of 2 3.75 1.90

Souvenir Sheet

3314 A915 €2.50 multi 7.25 3.75

Souvenir Sheet

Emblems of Portuguese Soccer Teams in 2010-11 UEFA Europa League Championship Match — A916

No. 3315 — Emblem of: a, Porto. b, Braga.

Perf. 11¾x12 Syncopated

2011, May 25

3315 A916 €1 Sheet of 2, #a-b 5.75 3.00

Museum of Contemporary Art, Lisbon, Cent. — A917

Designs: No. 3316, 32c, A Luva Cinzenta, by Columbano. No. 3317, 32c, Tristezas, Cabeça, by Amadeo de Souza-Cardoso. 47c, A Sesta, by Almada Negreiros. No. 3319, 68c, Cais 44, by Fernando Lanhas. No. 3320, 68c, Sombra Projectada de René Bertholo, by Lourdes Castro. 80c, A Esquiva, by Joao Maria Gusmao and Pedro Paiva.

No. 3322: a, Landscape, by Juliao Sarmento. b, Estrada da Vida, by Fernando Taborda.

2011, May 26 ***Perf. 13 Syncopated***

3316-3321 A917 Set of 6 9.50 4.75

Souvenir Sheet

3322 A917 €1.50 Sheet of 2, #a-b 8.75 4.50

Marine Training School, 50th Anniv. A918

Designs: 32c, Marine coming ashore. 80c, Marines in boat.

€2.50, Monument.

2011, June 3 **Litho.**

3323-3324 A918 Set of 2 3.25 1.60

Souvenir Sheet

3325 A918 €2.50 multi 7.25 3.75

Embroidery A919

Embroidery designs from: 32c, Vila Verde. 47c, Arraiolos. 57c, Castelo Branco. 68c, Viana. 80c, Madeira. €1, Azores.

No. 3332, €1.75, Guimaraes. No. 3333, €1.75, Ribatejo.

Perf. 11¾x12 Syncopated

2011, June 28

3326-3331 A919 Set of 6 11.00 5.50

3330a Booklet pane of 1 2.25 —

3331a Booklet pane of 1 3.00 —

Souvenir Sheets

3332-3333 A919 Set of 2 10.00 5.00

Nos. 3330a and 3331a are found in booklets listed under Azores and Madeira. See Nos. 3625, 3668.

A920

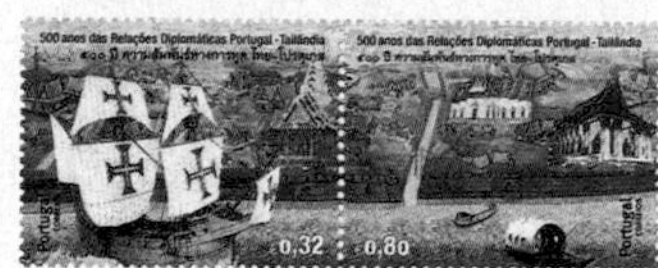

Diplomatic Relations Between Thailand and Portugal, 500th Anniv. — A921

No. 3334: a, 32c, Portuguese caravel, rowboats, Thai buildings and temples. b, 80c, Elephants and riders at dockside.

No. 3335: a, 32c, Portuguese caravel, Thai buildings. b, 80c, Thai boats and buildings.

2011, July 20 ***Perf. 13x13¼***

3334 A920 Horiz. pair, #a-b 3.25 1.60

3335 A921 Horiz. pair, #a-b 3.25 1.60

See Thailand Nos. 2617-2618.

Torre do Tombo National Archives, Cent. A922

Various historical documents and illuminations: 32c, 68c, €2.

€2.30, Torre de Tombo National Archive, document.

2011, July 27 ***Perf. 13 Syncopated***

3336-3338 A922 Set of 3 8.75 4.50

Souvenir Sheet

3339 A922 €2.30 multi 6.75 3.50

Intl. Year of Veterinary Medicine A923

Designs: 32c, Pigs in farm trailer. 68c, Horse, DNA strands. 80c, Cat, medicines. €1, Cow, milk bottles.

€2.50, Owl in tree.

2011, Sept. 7 **Litho.**

3340-3343 A923 Set of 4 7.75 4.00

Souvenir Sheet

3344 A923 €2.50 multi 7.00 3.50

Theater in Portugal A924

Actors and actresses: No. 3345, 32c, Laura Alves (1927-86). No. 3346, 32c, Amélia Rey Colaço (1898-1990). 47c, Raul Solnado (1929-2009). 68c, Armando Cortez (1928-2002). 80c, Eunice Muñoz. €1, Ruy de Carvalho.

No. 3351, €1: a, Scene from "Frei Luis de Sousa," by Almeida Garrett. b, Scene from "Os Velhos," by D. Joao da Câmara.

No. 3352, €1: a, Scene from "A Promessa," by Bernardo Santareno. b, Scene from "Bernilde ou a Virgem-Mâe," by José Régio.

2011, Sept. 14

3345-3350 A924 Set of 6 10.00 5.00

Souvenir Sheets of 2, #a-b

3351-3352 A924 Set of 2 11.00 5.50

Archaeology in Portugal — A925

Artifacts from archaeological sites in: 32c, Citânia de Briteiros. 47c, Foz Côa. 68c, Conímbriga. 80c, Milreu. €1, Alcalar.

€2.50, José Leite de Vasconcelos (1858-1941), first director of National Museum of Archaeology.

2011, Sept. 21 ***Perf. 13 Syncopated***

3353-3357 A925 Set of 5 9.00 4.50

Souvenir Sheet

3358 A925 €2.50 multi 7.00 3.50

See Nos. 3626-3627.

Protection of Water Resources and the Environment — A926

Designs: 32c, Hand holding glass under running faucet. 47c, Bandage on hose. 68c, Water bucket, filter and flowers. 80c, Recycling bins.

2011, Sept. 30

3359-3362 A926 Set of 4 6.25 3.25

Fado Musicians A927

Designs: 32c, Alfredo Marceneiro (1891-1982). 47c, Carlos Ramos (1907-69). 57c, Hermínia Silva (1907-93). 68c, Maria Teresa de Noronha (1918-93). 80c, Amália Rodrigues (1920-99). €1, Carlos do Carmo.
€2.50, O Fado, painting by José Malhoa.

2011, Oct. 3

3363-3368 A927 Set of 6 10.50 5.25

Souvenir Sheet

3369 A927 €2.50 multi 7.00 3.50

Festival of the Trays, Tomar — A928

Festival of St. John the Baptist, Porto — A929

Loulé Carnival — A930

Serpentine Die Cut 11½

2011, Oct. 3 **Self-Adhesive**

3370 A928 N multi .90 .45
3371 A929 A multi 1.40 .70
3372 A930 E multi 1.90 .95
Nos. 3370-3372 (3) 4.20 2.10

On day of issue, No. 3370 sold for 32c; No. 3371, 47c; No. 3372, 68c.

School Correspondence — A931

Children's art: 32c, Bird and fish. 68c, Earth and sun as wheels on boy's bicycle. 80c, Three girls, duck.

2011, Oct. 11 ***Perf. 13 Syncopated***

3373-3375 A931 Set of 3 5.00 2.50

Portuguese Military Academy, 175th Anniv. — A932

Designs: 32c, Academy building, Marquis de Sá da Bandeira (1795-1876). 68p, Academy crest and regalia.
€2.50, Sword and regalia, vert.

2012, Jan. 12 ***Perf. 12 Syncopated***

3376-3377 A932 Set of 2 2.75 1.40

Souvenir Sheet

3378 A932 €2.50 multi 6.75 3.25

Famous Men — A933

Designs: 32c, Marcos Portugal (1762-1830), composer. 68c, Brito Camacho (1862-1934), journalist and politician. 80c, António Vilar (1912-95), actor.

Perf. 13¼x13 Syncopated

2012, Feb. 13

3379-3381 A933 Set of 3 4.75 2.40

Art Depicting Biblical Scenes — A934

Designs: 47c, Creation of Eve (Criaçao de Eva). 68c, Moses in the Desert (Moisés no Deserto). 80c, Adoration of the Magi (Adoraçao dos Reis Magos). €1, The Last Supper (Ultima Ceia).
No. 3386, €1.50, Crucifixion (Paixao de Cristo). No. 3387, €1.50, Pentacost (Pentecostes).

2012, Feb. 23

3382-3385 A934 Set of 4 7.75 4.00

Souvenir Sheets

3386-3387 A934 Set of 2 8.00 4.00

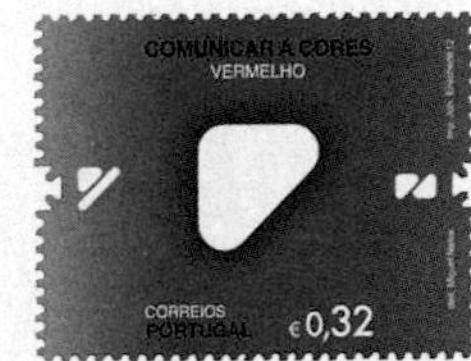
Colors and Associated Color-Blindness Shapes For Them — A935

Designs: 32c, Red (Vermelho). 47c, Blue (Azul). 68c, Yellow (Amarelo). 80c, Black (Preto). €1, White (Branco).

Perf. 13x13¼ Syncopated

2012, Mar. 20

3388-3392 A935 Set of 5 8.75 4.50

Guimares, 2012 European Capital of Culture A936

Designs: 32c, Largo da Oliveira. 47c, Vila Flor Cultural Center. 68c, Nicolinas Festival. 80c, Santa Marinha da Costa Inn.
€3, Guimaraes Castle, sculpture by Joao Cutiliero.

Perf. 12x11¾ Syncopated

2012, Apr. 10

3393-3396 A936 Set of 4 6.00 3.00

Souvenir Sheet

3397 A936 €3 multi 8.00 4.00

No. 3397 contains one 80x30mm stamp.

Erasmus Foreign Exchange Program, 25th Anniv. A937

European landmarks and: 68c, Female student on bicycle. €3, Student on motor scooter, female student.

2012, Apr. 17

3398 A937 68c multi 1.90 .95

Souvenir Sheet

3399 A937 €3 multi 8.00 4.00

No. 3399 contains one 80x30mm stamp.

Europa A938

Designs: No. 3400, Steamer Principe Perfeito. No. 3401a, Lisbon waterfront.

2012, May 9

3400 A938 68c multi 1.75 .85

Souvenir Sheet

3401 Sheet of 2, #3400, 3401a 3.50 1.75
a. A938 68c multi 1.75 .85

Cathedrals A939

Cathedrals at: No. 3402, N, Braga. No. 3403, N, Faro. No. 3404, N, Guarda. No. 3405, N, Lamego. No. 3406, N, Porto. No. 3407, N, Santarém. No. 3408, N, Silves. No. 3409, N, Viana do Castelo. No. 3410, N, Vila Real. No. 3411, N, Viseu.

2012, May 18 ***Perf. 13 Syncopated***

3402-3411 A939 Set of 10 8.00 4.00

Nos. 3402-3411 each sold for 32c on day of issue.

University of Lisbon Institute of Social Sciences, 50th Anniv. A940

Designs: N, Adérito Sedas Nunes and *Análise Social* Magazine. E, Institute of Social Sciences Building.

Perf. 12x11¾ Syncopated

2012, May 31

3412 A940 N multi .80 .40
3413 A940 E multi 1.75 .85

On day of issue, No. 3412 sold for 32c and No. 3413 sold for 68c.

2012 European Soccer Championships, Poland and Ukraine — A941

Design: 68c, Foosball figure and soccer ball.
€2.50, Foosball figures and soccer ball, horiz.

Perf. 11¾x12 Syncopated

2012, June 4

3414 A941 68c multi 1.75 .85

Souvenir Sheet

Perf. 12x11¾ Syncopated

3415 A941 €2.50 multi 6.25 3.25

2012 Summer Olympics and Paralympics, London — A942

Designs: No. 3416, N, Stylized Olympic athlete. No. 3417, N, Two stylized Paralympic athletes. No. 3418, I, Stylized Olympic fencer. No. 3419, I, Stylized athlete in wheelchair.

Perf. 11¾x12 Syncopated

2012, June 19

3416-3419 A942 Set of 4 5.50 2.75

On day of issue, Nos. 3416-3417 each sold for 32c, and Nos. 3418-3419 each sold for 80c.

Transit of Venus A943

Designs: €2, Teodoro de Almeida (1722-1804), observer of 1761 transit, Venus and Sun. €3, Diagram showing Earth, Venus and Sun.

2012, June 27 ***Perf. 13 Syncopated***

3420 A943 €2 multi 5.00 2.50

Souvenir Sheet

3421 A943 €3 multi 7.50 3.75

Souvenir Sheet

Victory of Portuguese Team at 2012 European Soccer Championships — A944

Perf. 11¾x12 Syncopated

2012, July 4

3422 A944 €1.50 multi 3.75 1.90

Traditional Portuguese Festivals A945

Designs: 5c, People watching fireworks. 32c, Festa de Santo António, Lisbon. 47c, Festas do Espírito Santo, Azores. 68c, Carnaval, Ilhavo. 90c, Golega Fair.

2012, July 20 ***Perf. 11¾x11½***

3423 A945 5c multi .25 .25
3424 A945 32c multi .80 .40
3425 A945 47c multi 1.25 .60
3426 A945 68c multi 1.75 .85
3427 A945 80c multi 2.00 1.00
Nos. 3423-3427 (5) 6.05 3.10

Compare with Types A956-A958.

Douro River A946

Designs: 32c, Riverside cliffs. 57c, Boat on river. 68c, Terraced fields and road near river. 80c, Buildings near river.
€3, Porto buildings, bridge and boats.

2012, July 30 ***Perf. 13 Syncopated***

3428-3431 A946 Set of 4 6.00 3.00

Souvenir Sheet

3432 A946 €3 multi 7.50 3.75

No. 3432 contains one 80x30mm stamp.

Training Ships — A947

Designs: 32c, NRP Sagres. 80c, NTM Creoula.
No. 3435, €1.75, Bell, silhouette of NRP Sagres. No. 3436, €1.75, Lifeboats, silhouette of NTM Creoula.

Perf. 11¾x12 Syncopated, 12x11¾ Syncopated (#3436)

2012, Aug. 3

3433-3434 A947 Set of 2 2.75 1.40

Souvenir Sheets

3435-3436 A947 Set of 2 8.75 4.25

Fernando Pessoa (1888-1935), Poet — A948

Joao da Cruz e Sousa (1861-98), Poet — A949

Perf. 11¾x12 Syncopated

2012, Sept. 7

3437 A948 80c multi + label 2.10 1.10
3438 A949 80c multi + label 2.10 1.10

See Brazil Nos. 3225-3226.

Sausages and Hams A950

Sausages: No. 3439, 32c, Guarda chouriço. No. 3440, 32c, Vinhais chouriça. No. 3441, 47c, Ponte de Lima onion chouriça. No. 3442, 47c, Barroso-Montalegre chouriça. 57c, Vinhais salpicao. No. 3444, 68c, Guarda morcela. No. 3445, 68c, Vila Real moura. No. 3446, 80c, Mirandela alheira.

No. 3447, 80c, vert. — Hams from: a, Melgaço. b, Vinhais. c, Barroso.

Perf. 12x11¾ Syncopated

2012, Sept. 25

3439-3446 A950 Set of 8 11.00 5.50

Souvenir Sheet

Perf. 11¾x12 Syncopated

3447 A950 80c Sheet of 3, #a-c 6.25 3.25

See Nos. 3483-3491.

Palaces — A951

Rooms and exterior views of: No. 3448, 32c, Pena National Palace, Sao Pedro de Penaferrim. No. 3449, 32c, Ajuda National Palace, Lisbon, Queen Consort Maria Pia of Savoy (1847-1911). No. 3450, 68c, Mafra National Palace, Mafra. No. 3451, 68c, Sintra National Palace, Sintra. No. 3452, 80c, Monserrate Palace, Sintra. No. 3453, 80c, Queluz National Palace, Queluz.

Perf. 11¾x12 Syncopated

2012, Oct. 3

3448-3453 A951 Set of 6 9.25 4.75

School Correspondence A952

Children's art by: 32c, Martim dos Santos Onofre. 68c, Matilde Amaro Nunes. 80c, Ana Carolina Marques.

Perf. 13¼x13 Syncopated

2012, Oct. 9

3454-3456 A952 Set of 3 4.75 2.40

Fado Musicians A953

Designs: No. 3457, 32c, Vicente da Câmara. No. 3458, 32c, Argentina Santos. 57c, Maria da Fé. 68c, Rodrigo. 80c, Camané. No. 3462, €1, Mariza. No. 3463, Caricature of Fado guitarist, neck of Fado guitar.

2012, Oct. 11 **Litho.**

3457-3463 A953 Set of 7 12.50 6.25

First Humorists Exhibition, Cent. — A954

Carictures and cartoon art by: No. 3464, 32c, Rafael Bordalo Pinheiro. No. 3465, 47c, Stuart Carvalhais. No. 3466, 68c, Emmerico Nunes. No. 3467, 80c, Almada Negreiros.
No. 3468: a, 32c, Francisco Valenca. b, 32c, Manuel Gustavo Bordalo Pinheiro. c, 47c, Jorge Barradas. d, 47c, Américo Amarelhe. e, 68c, Celso Herminio. f, 68c, Canto da Maya. g, 80c, Cristiano Cruz. h, 80c, Menezes Ferreira.

Perf. 13¼x13 Syncopated

2012, Oct. 16

3464-3467 A954 Set of 4 5.75 3.00

Souvenir Sheet

3468 A954 Sheet of 8, #a-h 11.50 5.75

Order of Engineers — A955

Designs: 32c, Civil, geological and mining engineering. 47c, Electrical and informational engineering. 57c, Naval and mechanical engineering. 68c, Material, chemical and biological engineering. 80c, Forestry and agronomic engineering. €1, Geographical and environmental engineering.
€3, Arch and angels.

Perf. 13x13¼ Syncopated

2012, Oct. 19

3469-3474 A955 Set of 6 10.00 5.00

Souvenir Sheet

3475 A955 €3 multi 7.75 4.00

Festa do Santo António, Lisbon — A956

Festas do Espirito Santo, Azores — A957

Carnaval, Ilhavo — A958

Serpentine Die Cut11½

2012, Nov. 13 **Self-Adhesive**

3476 A956 N multi .85 .40
3477 A957 (47c) multi 1.25 .60
3478 A958 E multi 1.75 .90
Nos. 3476-3478 (3) 3.85 1.90

Compare with type A945. On day of issue, No. 3476 sold for 32c and No. 3478 sold for 68c.

Composers A959

Designs: No. 3479, E, Giuseppe Verdi (1813-1901). No. 3480, E, Richard Wagner (1813-83).

No. 3481, €1.50, Falstaff. No. 3482, €1.50, Valkyrie.

Perf. 11¾x12 Syncopated

2013, Jan. 31

3479-3480 A959 Set of 2 3.75 1.90

Souvenir Sheets

3481-3482 A959 Set of 2 8.25 4.25

On day of issue, Nos. 3479-3480 each sold for 68c.

Sausages and Hams Type of 2012

Designs: No. 3483, N, Portalegre chouriço mouro. No. 3484, N, Estremoz and Borba farinheira. No. 3485, A, Estremoz and Borba chouriço. No. 3486, A, Monchique farinheira. No. 3487, E, Portalegre paio enguitado. No. 3488, E, Sao Miguel morcela. No. 3489, I, Serta maranhos. No. 3490, I, Portalegre paio ou lombo branco.
No. 3491, vert. — Hams from: a, Barrancos. b, Santana da Serra.

Perf. 12x11¾ Syncopated

2013, Mar. 15

3483-3490 A950 Set of 8 12.00 6.00

Souvenir Sheet

Perf. 11¾x12 Syncopated

3491 A950 €1 Sheet of 2, #a-b 5.25 2.60

On day of issue, Nos. 3483-3484 each sold for 32c, Nos. 3485-3486 each sold for 47c, Nos. 3487-3488 each sold for 68c and Nos, 3489-3490 each sold for 80c.

Falconry — A960

Designs: N, Falco peregrinus, falcon hood. A, Accipiter gentilis, pouch. E, Accipiter nisus, lure. I, Aquila chrysaetos, gauntlet.
€1.50, Royal Falconry Building, Salvaterra do Magos.

Perf. 11¾x12 Syncopated

2013, Mar. 23

3492 A960 N multi .85 .40
3493 A960 A multi 1.25 .60
3494 A960 E multi 1.75 .85
3495 A960 I multi 2.10 1.10
Nos. 3492-3495 (4) 5.95 2.95

Souvenir Sheet

3496 A960 €1.50 multi 4.00 2.00

On day of issue Nos. 3492-3495 each sold for 32c, 47c, 68c and 80c, respectively.

Famous People A961

Designs: 36c, Joao Villaret (1913-61), actor. 60c, Ilse Losa (1913-2006), writer. 70c, Joao Dos Santos (1913-87), psychiatrist. 80c, Edgar Cardoso (1913-2000), civil engineer. €1, Raúl Rego (193-2002), journalist.

Perf. 12x11¾ Syncopated

2013, Apr. 15

3497-3501 A961 Set of 5 9.00 4.50

Traditional Portuguese Festivals — A962

Designs: 3c, Icon, men in red vestments. 4c, Icon, men in blue vestments. 36c, Woman and girl, Sao Mateus Fair, Viseu. 50c, Woman, icon on boat, Feast of Our Lady of Agony, Viana do Castelo. 70c, People in costumes, Feast of Santo Estevao, Ousilhao. 80c, Men wearing hats, Feast of Our Lady of Guadalupe, Serpa. €1, Three participants,

People's Festival, Campo Maior. €1.70, Man, woman and icon, Pilgrimage of Our Lady of Almortao, Idanha-a-Nova.

2013, Apr. 30 ***Perf. 11¾x11½***

3502	A962	3c multi	.25	.25
3503	A962	4c multi	.25	.25
3504	A962	36c multi	.95	.45
3505	A962	50c multi	1.40	.70
3506	A962	70c multi	1.90	.95
3507	A962	80c multi	2.10	1.10
3508	A962	€1 multi	2.60	1.40
3509	A962	€1.70 multi	4.50	2.25
		Nos. 3502-3509 (8)	13.95	7.35

Arrival of Explorer Jorge Alvares in China, 500th Anniv. — A963

Old map of Chinese coast and: 36c, Chinese compass. 80c, Compass rose.
€3, Chinese vase, old map of Chinese coast.

Perf. 11¾x12 Syncopated

2013, May 8 **Litho.**

3510-3511	A963	Set of 2	3.25	1.60

Souvenir Sheet

3512	A963	€3 multi	8.00	4.00

No. 3512 contains one 30x80mm stamp.

Europa A964

Designs: No. 3513, Portuguese postal van facing left. No. 3514a, Postal worker and Portuguese postal van.

Perf. 12x11¾ Syncopated

2013, May 9 **Litho.**

3513	A964	70c multi	1.90	.95

Souvenir Sheet

3514		Sheet of 2, #3513, 3514a	3.80	1.90
a.	A964	70c multi	1.90	.95

Lay Missions in Africa, Cent. — A965

Designs: 36c, Eight missionaries to Angola. 80c, Seven missionaries to Mozambique.
€2.60, Colonial Missions Institute, Cernache do Bonjardim.

Perf. 11¾x12 Syncopated

2013, May 13 **Litho.**

3515-3516	A965	Set of 2	3.25	1.60

Souvenir Sheet

3517	A965	€2.60 multi	7.00	3.50

Intl. Year of Statistics A966

Graph and: 36c, Gears. €1, People carrying streamers.
€2, Graph, trees and rain clouds.

Perf. 12x11¾ Syncopated

2013, May 24 **Litho.**

3518-3519	A966	Set of 2	3.75	1.90

Souvenir Sheet

3520	A966	€2 multi	5.50	2.75

No. 3520 contains one 80x30mm stamp.

Cathedrals A967

Designs: No. 3521, 36c, Old Coimbra Cathedral (Velha). No. 3522, 36c, New Coimbra Cathedral (Nova). No. 3523, 36c, Portalegre Cathedral. No. 3524, 36c, Castelo Branco Cathedral. No. 3525, 36c, Leiria Cathedral. No. 3526, 36c, Aveiro Cathedral. No. 3527, 80c, Funchal Cathedral. No. 3528, 80c, Angra Cathedral.

Perf. 11¾x12 Syncopated

2013, June 6 **Litho.**

3521-3528	A967	Set of 8	10.00	5.00

Antique Works of Jewelers A968

Designs: 36c, Bronze Age bracelet. 70c, Iron Age earring. 80c, Roman Era phiale. €1.70, Visigoth Era fibula.
€3, Iron Age necklace, vert.

Perf. 12x11¾ Syncopated

2013, June 21 **Litho.**

3529-3532	A968	Set of 4	9.25	4.75

Souvenir Sheet

Perf. 11¾x12 Syncopated

3533	A968	€3 multi	8.00	4.00

Woman and Girl, Sao Mateus Fair, Viseu — A969

Woman, Icon on Boat, Feast of Our Lady of Agony,Viana do Castelo — A970

People in Costumes, Feast of Santo Estevao, Ousilhao — A971

Die Cut Perf. 11½

2013, July 22 **Litho.**

Self-Adhesive

3534	A969	N multi	1.00	.50
3535	A970	A multi	1.40	.70
3536	A971	E multi	1.90	.95
		Nos. 3534-3536 (3)	4.30	2.15

On day of issue, No. 3534 sold for 36c; No. 3535, 50c; No. 3536, 70c.

Catholic Missions in Africa A972

Designs: 36c, Child at blackboard (education). 50c, Nurses and patient (health care). 70c, Children at sink (building of infrastructure). 80c, Man watering plants (agricultural development). €1, Adult education. €1.70, Priest and children (evangelization).

Perf. 12x11¾ Syncopated

2013, Aug. 19 **Litho.**

3537-3542	A972	Set of 6	13.50	6.75

Compilation of the Canon of Medicine, by Avicenna, 1000th Anniv. — A973

Designs: €1.70, Avicenna taking notes.
€3.30, Avicenna examining patient, horiz.

2013, Aug. 23 **Litho.** ***Perf. 11¾x12***

3543	A973	€1.70 multi	4.50	2.25

Souvenir Sheet

3544	A973	€3.30 multi	8.75	4.50

No. 3544 contains one 61x40mm stamp.

Presentation of 12th Aga Khan Awards for Architecture — A974

Designs: 80c, Tiles. €1, Embroidery design
€3, Sao Jorge Castle, Lisbon, site of awards ceremony, vert.

2013, Sept. 6 **Litho.** ***Perf. 12x12½***

3545-3546	A974	Set of 2	4.75	2.40

Souvenir Sheet

Silk-faced Paper

Perf. 12½x12

3547	A974	€3 multi	8.00	4.00

No. 3547 contains one 30x80mm stamp.

Sculptures of Joana Vasconcelos A975

Designs: 50c, Red Independent Heart. 80c, Cinderella.

Perf. 11¾x12 Syncopated

2013, Sept. 16 **Litho.**

3548-3549	A975	Set of 2	3.50	1.75

Apiculture — A976

Designs: 36c, Bees, honeycomb, beekeeper tending hive. 50c, Bees at hive entrance and in flight. 70c, Bees in flight over field. 80c, Bees and flowers.
€1.70, Bee on flower. €1.90, Bee, beekeeper removing honey from honeycomb.

Perf. 12x11¾ Syncopated

2013, Sept. 23 **Litho.**

3550-3553	A976	Set of 4	6.50	3.25

Souvenir Sheets

3554-3555	A976	Set of 2	9.75	5.00

Papal Recognition of Sovereign Military Order of Malta, 900th Anniv. — A977

Grand Masters: 36c, Afonso of Portugal (1137-1207). 70c, Luís Mendes de Vasconcelos (c. 1542-1623). 80c, António Manoel de Vilhena (1663-1736). €1, Manuel Pinto da Fonseca (1681-1773).
€1.95, Ship of Grand Master Pinto da Fonseca.

Perf. 11¾x12 Syncopated

2013, Sept. 27 **Litho.**

3556-3559	A977	Set of 4	7.75	4.00

Souvenir Sheet

3560	A977	€1.95 multi	5.25	2.60

No. 3560 contains one 30x80mm stamp.

School Correspondence — A978

Children's art by: N, Martim Ferreira Simao. E, David Serafim Reis. I, Francisco Maria Rasquilha.

Perf. 12x11¾ Syncopated

2013, Oct. 9 **Litho.**

3561-3563	A978	Set of 3	5.00	2.50

On day of issue, No. 3561 sold for 36c; No. 3562, 70c; No. 3563, 80c.

Christmas A979

Various creche figures: N, 50c, 60c, 70c, 80c, €1.70,

Perf. 12x11¾ Syncopated

2013, Oct. 9 **Litho.**

3564-3569	A979	Set of 6	13.00	6.50

No. 3564 sold for 36c on day of issue.

Souvenir Sheet

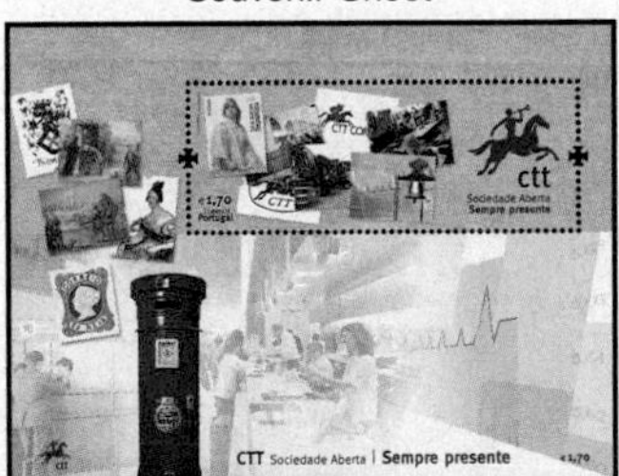

Public Trading of Shares of CTT Portugal — A980

Perf. 12x11¾ Syncopated

2014, Jan. 27 **Litho.**

3570	A980	€1.70 multi	4.75	2.40

Extreme Sports — A981

Designs: 40c, Surfing. 50c, Mountain biking. 70c, Skateboarding. 80c, Kayaking. €1.70, Paragliding.

Perf. 11¾x11½

2014, Feb. 10 **Litho.**

3571 A981 40c multi 1.10 .55
3572 A981 50c multi 1.40 .70
3573 A981 70c multi 2.00 1.00
3574 A981 80c multi 2.25 1.10
3575 A981 €1.70 multi 4.75 2.40
Nos. 3571-3575 (5) 11.50 5.75

See Nos. 3602-3604, 3669-3671, 3685-3689.

Publication of Peregrinaçao (Pilgrimage), Travel Writings of Fernao Mendes Pinto, 400th Anniv. — A982

Designs: €1, Front page of Peregrinaçao, ships, Buddhist deity on peacock, horseman. €3, Old map.

Perf. 12x11¾ Syncopated

2014, Feb. 24 **Litho.**

3576 A982 €1 multi 2.75 1.40

Souvenir Sheet

3577 A982 €3 multi 8.25 4.25

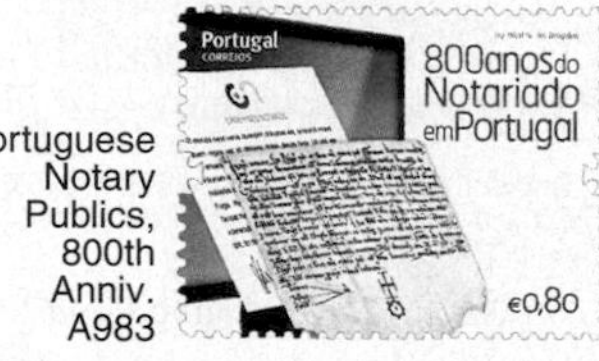

Portuguese Notary Publics, 800th Anniv. A983

Designs: 80c, Documents. €3, Notary public writing in book.

Perf. 12x11¾ Syncopated

2014, Mar. 6 **Litho.**

3578 A983 80c multi 2.25 1.10

Souvenir Sheet

3579 A983 €3 multi 8.25 4.25

No. 3579 contains one 80x30mm stamp.

Famous People — A984

Designs: 40c, Florbela Espanca (1894-1930), poet. 50c, Maria Keil (1914-2012), painter. 60c, Joaquim Namorado (1914-86), poet. 70c, Joao Hogan (1914-88), painter. 80c, António Dacosta (1914-90), painter. €1, José Sebastiao e Silva (1914-72), mathematician.

Perf. 11¾x12 Syncopated

2014, Mar. 24 **Litho.**

3580-3585 A984 Set of 6 11.00 5.50

Architects and Their Buildings — A985

Designs: No. 3586, I, Paula Rego Museum, by Eduardo Souto de Moura. No. 3587, I, Júlio Pomar Museum, by Alvaro Siza Vieira. No. 3588, I, Green Corridor of Lisbon, by Gonçalo Ribeiro Telles.

Perf. 12x11¾ Syncopated

2014, Apr. 7 **Litho.**

3586-3588 A985 Set of 3 6.75 3.50

On day of issue, Nos. 3586-3588 each sold for 80c.

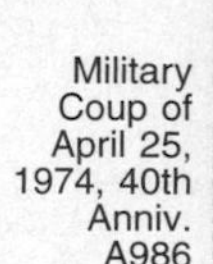

Military Coup of April 25, 1974, 40th Anniv. A986

Designs: No. 3589, N, Soldiers and vehicles in Palace Square, Lisbon. No. 3590, I, Crowd surrounding soldiers in transport vehicle. €3, Flags of Portugal, Greece and Spain.

Perf. 12x11¾ Syncopated

2014, Apr. 14 **Litho.**

3589-3590 A986 Set of 2 3.50 1.75

Souvenir Sheet

3591 A986 €3 multi 8.50 4.25

On day of issue, No. 3589 sold for 42c; No. 3590, for 80c. No. 3591 contains one 80x30mm stamp.

Miniature Sheet

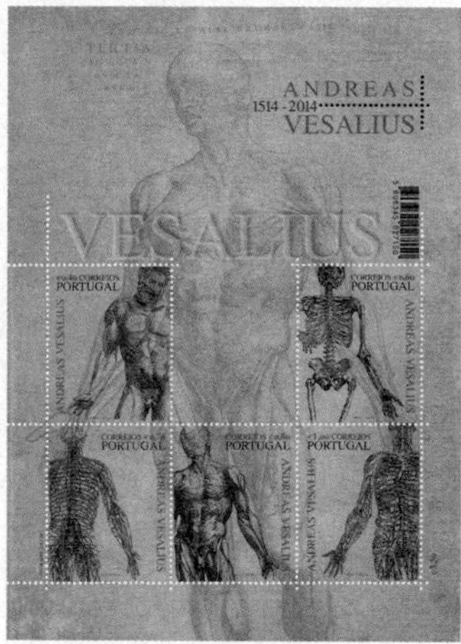

Anatomical Drawings by Andreas Vesalius (1514-64) — A987

No. 3592: a, 40c, Nude man. b, 60c, Skeleton. c, 70c, Nervous system. d, 80c, Muscular system. e, €1, Circulatory system.

Photo. & Engr.

2014, Apr. 21 *Perf. 11½*

3592 A987 Sheet of 5, #a-e 9.75 5.00

See Belgium No. 2689.

Archbishop Bartholomew of Braga (1514-90) — A988

Designs: 70c, Archbishop standing. €3, Archbishop seated.

Perf. 11¾x12 Syncopated

2014, Apr. 28 **Litho.**

3593 A988 70c multi 2.00 1.00

Souvenir Sheet

3594 A988 €3 multi 8.50 4.25

No. 3594 contains one 30x80mm stamp.

Eusébio (1942-2014), Soccer Player — A989

Designs: No. 3595, N, Eusébio chasing soccer ball. No. 3596, E, Eusébio dribbling ball. €2.50, Eusébio kicking ball.

Perf. 11¾x12 Syncopated

2014, May 2 **Litho.**

3595-3596 A989 Set of 2 3.25 1.60

Souvenir Sheet

3597 A989 €2.50 multi 7.00 3.50

On day of issue, No. 3595 sold for 42c; No. 3596, for 72c.

Portuguese Language, 800th Anniv. A990

Designs: 80c, Arms of Portugal, flags of Portuguese-speaking countries, hand with pen. €2.50, Pen nib, green and red lines, vert.

Perf. 12x11¾ Syncopated

2014, May 5 **Litho.**

3598 A990 80c multi 2.25 1.10

Souvenir Sheet

Perf. 11¾x12 Syncopated

3599 A990 €2.50 multi 7.00 3.50

Europa — A991

Designs: No. 3600, Bagpiper. No. 3601a, Bagpipes.

Perf. 11¾x12 Syncopated

2014, May 9 **Litho.**

3600 A991 E multi 2.00 1.00

Souvenir Sheet

3601 Sheet of 2, #3600, 3601a 4.00 2.00
a. A991 E multi 2.00 1.00

On day of issue Nos. 3600 and 3601a each sold for 72c.

Extreme Sports Type of 2014

Designs: N, Surfing. A, Mountain biking. E, Skateboarding.

Die Cut Perf. 11½

2014, May 27 **Litho.**

Self-Adhesive

3602 A981 N multi 1.25 .60
3603 A981 A multi 1.40 .70
3604 A981 E multi 2.00 1.00
Nos. 3602-3604 (3) 4.65 2.30

On day of issue, No. 3602 sold for 42c; No. 3603, 50c; No. 3604, 72c.

Diplomatic Relations Between Portugal and Mexico, 150th Anniv. A992

Portuguese and Mexican flags with denomination color of: 42c, Gray. 80c, White.

Perf. 12x11¾ Syncopated

2014, June 6 **Litho.**

3605-3606 A992 Set of 2 3.50 1.75

See Mexico Nos. 2876-2877.

2014 World Cup Soccer Championships, Brazil — A993

Designs: 42c, 2014 World Cup emblem and flag of Portugal. 72c, 2014 World Cup mascot and flag of Brazil. €1, Silhouettes of soccer players, World Cup trophy, flag of Portugal.

Perf. 12x11¾ Syncopated

2014, June 16 **Litho.**

3607-3608 A993 Set of 2 3.25 1.60

Souvenir Sheet

3609 A993 €1 multi 2.75 1.40

No. 3609 contains one 80x30mm stamp.

Gardens A994

Designs: No. 3610, 42c, Chalet da Condessa D'Edla, Sintra. No. 3611, 42c, Palácio Fronteira, Lisbon. 50c, Palácio Nacional de Queluz, Sintra. 62c, Parque de Serralves, Porto. No. 3614, 72c, Mosteiro de Tibaes, Braga. No. 3615, 72c, Jardim Botânico da Universidade, Coimbra. No. 3616, 80c, Quinta do Palheiro Ferreira, Madeira. No. 3617, 80c, Parque Terra Nostra, Sao Miguel, Azores.

Perf. 12x11¾ Syncopated

2014, June 26 **Litho.**

3610-3617 A994 Set of 8 14.00 7.00

See No. 3759.

Garrison Border Town of Elvas and Its Fortifications UNESCO World Heritage Site — A995

Designs: 42c, Graça Fort. 50c, Amoreira Aqueduct. 72c, Santa Luzia Fort. 80c, Pelourinho. €1.70, Olivença Gate.

Perf. 12x11¾ Syncopated

2014, June 30 **Litho.**

3618-3621 A995 Set of 4 6.75 3.50

Souvenir Sheet

3622 A995 €1.70 multi 4.75 2.40

Types of 2007-11

Die Cut Perf. 10½

2014, July 21 **Litho.**

Self-Adhesive

3623 A816 E Like #2956 2.00 1.00
3624 A861 E Like #3126 2.00 1.00
3625 A919 E Like #3327 2.00 1.00
3626 A925 E Like #3356 2.00 1.00
3627 A925 E Like #3357 2.00 1.00
Nos. 3623-3627 (5) 10.00 5.00

Nos. 3623-3627 each sold for 72c on day of issue.

Intl. Year of Crystallography — A996

Designs: 42c, Chalcopyrite. 50c, Sodium chloride. 72c, Patterson function and crystal

lattice. 80c, Caffeine molecular model, coffee beans. €1, Hemoglobin.
€1.70, Snowflake, vert.

Perf. 12x11¾ Syncopated

2014, July 21 **Litho.**
3628-3632 A996 Set of 5 9.25 4.75

Souvenir Sheet

Perf. 11¾x12 Syncopated

3633 A996 €1.70 multi 4.75 2.40

King Manuel I's Diplomatic Mission to Pope Leo X, 500th Anniv. — A997

Designs: 42c, Display of Portuguese wealth before Pope Leo X. €2, Hanno, elephant gift from King Manuel I, and crowd.

Perf. 12x11¾ Syncopated

2014, July 29 **Litho.**
3634-3635 A997 Set of 2 6.50 3.25

Cathedrals A998

Designs: No. 3636, 42c, Old Bragança Cathedral (antiga). No. 3637, 42c, New Bragança Cathedral (nova). No. 3638, 42c, Beja Cathedral. No. 3639, 42c, Elvas Cathedral. No. 3640, 42c, Evora Cathedral. No. 3641, 42c, Lisbon Cathedral. No. 3642, 42c, Miranda do Douro Cathedral. No. 3643, 42c, Setúbal Cathedral.

Perf. 12x11¾ Syncopated

2014, Aug. 18 **Litho.**
3636-3643 A998 Set of 8 9.00 4.50

University of Coimbra UNESCO World Heritage Site — A999

Designs: 42c, College of Nuestra Senhora da Graça. 50c, Joanine Library. 72c, Chemistry Laboratory. 80c, Humanities Faculties Building.
€1.70, Main courtyard.

Perf. 11¾x12 Syncopated

2014, Sept. 24 **Litho.**
3644-3647 A999 Set of 4 6.25 3.25

Souvenir Sheet

3648 A999 €1.70 multi 4.50 2.25

Coffee — A1000

Coffee bushes and plantation workers from: 42c, Timor. 62c, Angola. 72c, Brazil. 80c, St. Thomas and Prince Islands.
€3.50, Hand holding coffee bush seedling.

Perf. 11¾x12 Syncopated

2014, Sept. 29 **Litho.**
3649-3652 A1000 Set of 4 6.50 3.25

Souvenir Sheet

3653 A1000 €3.50 multi 9.00 4.50

University of Coimbra Geophysical Institute, 150th Anniv. A1001

Fields of study: 42c, Seismology. 62c, Geomagnetism. 72c, Meteorology. 80c, Planetary science.
€2.80, Geophysical Institute, vert.

Perf. 12x11¾ Syncopated

2014, Oct. 3 **Litho.**
3654-3657 A1001 Set of 4 6.50 3.25

Souvenir Sheet

Perf. 11¾x12 Syncopated

3658 A1001 €2.80 multi 7.00 3.50

No. 3658 contains one 30x80mm stamp.

Modern Portuguese Tapestries A1002

Designs: No. 3659, 42c, Ambiguous Structure, by Eduardo Nery. No. 3660, 42c, Endless Purpose, by Cruzeiro Seixas. 50c, Egypte, by Vieira da Silva. 62c, Arruto, by Júlio Pomar. 72c, Racial Integration, by Almada Negreiros. 80c, Magenta, by Joana Vasconcelos.
€1.70, Weaver at loom.

Perf. 11¾x12 Syncopated

2014, Oct. 9 **Litho.**
3659-3664 A1002 Set of 6 8.75 4.50

Souvenir Sheet

3665 A1002 €1.70 multi 4.25 2.10

Sustainable Transportation — A1003

No. 3666: a, 42c, Train, bus, man on Segway. b, 80c, Bicycle riders, electric automobile.

Perf. 12x11¾ Syncopated

2015, Jan. 27 **Litho.**
3666 A1003 Horiz. pair, #a-b 2.75 1.40

Types of 2009-11

Die Cut Perf. 10½

2015, Jan. 19 **Litho.**

Self-Adhesive

3667 A864 E Like #3144 1.75 .85
3668 A919 E Like #3330 1.75 .85

Nos. 3667-3668 each sold for 72c on day of issue.

Extreme Sports Type of 2014

Designs: N, Kitesurfing. A, Rock climbing. E, Rafting.

Die Cut Perf. 10x9½

2015, Feb. 12 **Litho.**

Self-Adhesive

3669 A981 N multi .95 .45
3670 A981 A multi 1.10 .55
3671 A981 E multi 1.60 .80
Nos. 3669-3671 (3) 3.65 1.80

On day of issue, No. 3669 sold for 42c; No. 3670, 50c; No. 3671, 72c.

Orpheu Magazine, Cent. — A1004

Cover from: 42c, First edition. 72c, Second edition.
€2.50, Painting of person reading second edition.

Perf. 11¾x12 Syncopated

2015, Feb. 20 **Litho.**
3672-3673 A1004 Set of 2 2.60 1.40

Souvenir Sheet

3674 A1004 €2.50 multi 5.50 2.75

Music Personalities A1005

Designs: 72c, Jean Sibelius (1865-1957), composer. 80c, Elisabeth Schwarzkopf (1915-2006), opera singer.
No. 3677, €1.50, Sibelius, horiz. No. 3678, €1.50, Schwarzkopf, horiz.

Perf. 11¾x12 Syncopated

2015, Mar. 26 **Litho.**
3675-3676 A1005 Set of 2 3.50 1.75

Souvenir Sheets

Perf. 12x11¾ Syncopated

3677-3678 A1005 Set of 2 6.75 3.50

Famous People A1006

Designs: N, Francisco Vieira (1765-1805), painter. A, Manuel Maria Barbosa du Bocage (1765-1805), poet. 62c, Ramalho Ortigao (1836-1915), writer. 72c, Ruy Cinatti (1915-86), poet. 80c, Agostinho Ricca (1913-2010), architect. €1, Frederico George (1915-94), architect.

Perf. 12x11¾ Syncopated

2015, Mar. 31 **Litho.**
3679-3684 A1006 Set of 6 9.25 4.75

On day of issue, No. 3679 sold for 45c; No. 3680, 55c.

Extreme Sports Type of 2014

Designs: 2c, Wingsuit flying. 45c, Kitesurfing. 55c, Rock climbing. 72c, Rafting. 80c, BMX cycling.

2015, Apr. 17 **Litho.** *Perf. 11¾x11½*

3685 A981 2c multi .25 .25
3686 A981 45c multi 1.00 .50
3687 A981 55c multi 1.25 .60
3688 A981 72c multi 1.75 .85
3689 A981 80c multi 1.90 .95
Nos. 3685-3689 (5) 6.15 3.15

Clay Figurines A1007

Figurines from: No. 3690, 45c, Barcelos. No. 3691, 45c, Vila Nova de Gaia. No. 3692, 55c, Estremoz. No. 3693, 55c, Ribolhos.

Perf. 12x11¾ Syncopated

2015, Apr. 21 **Litho.**
3690-3693 A1007 Set of 4 4.50 2.25

See Azores No. 568, Madeira No. 338.

Intl. Association of Portuguese-Speaking Countries, 25th Anniv. — A1008

Perf. 11¾x12 Syncopated

2015, Apr. 27 **Litho.**
3694 A1008 80c multi 1.75 .90

Souvenir Sheet

Perf. 12x11¾ Syncopated

3695 A1008 €2 Emblem, horiz. 4.50 2.25

See Angola No. , Brazil No. 3300, Cape Verde No. 1004, Guinea-Bissau No. , Macao No. 1440. Mozambique No. , St. Thomas and Prince Islands No. , Timor No.

Reintroduction of the Iberian Lynx to Portugal — A1009

Designs: 45c, Head of lynx. 55c, Lynx, flower. 72c, Lynx and rabbits. 80c, Lynx facing left.
€2, Pride of lynx.

Perf. 12x11¾ Syncopated

2015, Apr. 30 **Litho.**
3696-3699 A1009 Set of 4 5.75 3.00

Souvenir Sheet

3700 A1009 €2 multi 4.50 2.25

No. 3700 contains one 80x30mm stamp.

Europa A1010

Old toys: No. 3701, Helicopter. No. 3702a, Cabinet.

Perf. 12x11¾ Syncopated

2015, May 8 **Litho.**
3701 A1010 72c multi 1.60 .80

Souvenir Sheet

3702 Sheet of 2, #3701, 3702a 3.25 1.60
a. A1010 72c multi 1.60 .80

Way of St. James — A1011

Inscriptions: 45c, Sao Tiago Maior. 55c, Lisboa, Santarém. 72c, Porto, San Pedro de Rates. 80c, Viseu, Chaves.
€2, Catedral de Santiago de Compostela.

Perf. 12x11¾ Syncopated

2015, May 8 **Litho.**
3703-3706 A1011 Set of 4 5.75 3.00

Souvenir Sheet

3707 A1011 €2 multi 4.50 2.25

International Telecommunication Union, 150th Anniv. — A1012

Designs: 80c, 150th anniv. emblem. €1, 150th anniv. emblem, world map.

2015, May 18 **Litho.** ***Perf. 12x11¾***
3708-3709 A1012 Set of 2 4.00 2.00

Belém Tower, Lisbon, 500th Anniv. A1013

Designs: 45c, Drawing of tower, king. 72c, Tower, flag and boats, rhinoceros. 80c, Photograph of tower, seaplane.
€2, Photograph of tower, diff.

Perf. 12x11¾ Syncopated

2015, July 1 **Litho.**
3710-3712 A1013 Set of 3 4.50 2.25

Souvenir Sheet

3713 A1013 €2 multi 4.50 2.25

No. 3713 contains one 80x30mm stamp.

Boats of the Mediterranean — A1014

Designs: 45c, Canoa do alto. 72c, Calao. 80c, Canoa da picada.
€1.80, Caique and Galeao.

Perf. 12x11¾ Syncopated

2015, July 9 **Litho.**
3714-3716 A1014 Set of 3 4.50 2.25

Souvenir Sheet

3717 A1014 €1.80 multi 4.00 2.00

No. 3717 contains one 80x30mm stamp.

Office of the Ombudsman, 40th Anniv. — A1015

Designs: 45c, Man, woman, child, building. €2, Building, birds.

Perf. 11¾x12 Syncopated

2015, July 15 **Litho.**
3718 A1015 45c multi 1.00 .50

Souvenir Sheet

3719 A1015 €2 multi 4.50 2.25

No. 3719 contains one 30x80mm stamp.

Mediterranean Diet — A1016

Dishes: No. 3720, 45c, Sopa de beldroegas (purslane soup). No. 3721, 45c, Carapaus de escabeche (fish in vinegar sauce). 72c, Cozido do grao com peras (bean stew with pears). 80c, Broas de batata doce (sweet potato scones).
€1.80, Caldeirada de polvo (octopus stew).

Perf. 12x11¾ Syncopated

2015, July 20 **Litho.**
3720-3723 A1016 Set of 4 5.50 2.75

Souvenir Sheet

3724 A1016 €1.80 multi 4.00 2.00

Rules of Heredity, 150th Anniv. — A1017

Pea plant and: 45c, Gregor Mendel (1822-84), scientist. €1, Peas on chart.

Perf. 11¾x12 Syncopated

2015, Aug. 4 **Litho.**
3725-3726 A1017 Set of 2 3.25 1.60

Coimbra Question, 150th Anniv. — A1018

Designs: 45c, Antonio Feliciano de Castilho (1800-75), writer. 55c, Antero de Quental (1842-91), writer.
€2, Writers José Maria Eça de Queirós, Joaquim Pedro de Oliveira Martins, Antero de Quental, Ramalho Ortigao and Abilio Manuel Guerra Junqueiro, horiz.

Perf. 11¾x12 Syncopated

2015, Aug. 12 **Litho.**
3727-3728 A1018 Set of 2 2.25 1.10

Souvenir Sheet

Perf. 12x11¾ Syncopated

3729 A1018 €2 multi 4.50 2.25

No. 3729 contains one 80x30mm stamp.

Fruits and Nuts — A1019

Designs: No. 3730, 45c, Castanea sativa (chestnuts). No. 3731, 45c, Prunus avium (cherries). No. 3732, 55c, Pyrus communis (pears). No. 3733, 55c, Citrus spp. (oranges). 72c, Musa acuminata (bananas). 80c, Ananas comosus (pineapples).

Perf. 11¾x12 Syncopated

2015, Sept. 1 **Litho.**
3730-3735 A1019 Set of 6 8.00 4.00
3735a Souvenir sheet of 6, #3730-3735 8.00 4.00

St. John Bosco (1815-88) A1020

Designs: 45c, Bosco and children. €2.50, Bosco, horiz.

Perf. 11¾x12 Syncopated

2015, Sept. 3 **Litho.**
3736 A1020 45c multi 1.00 .50

Souvenir Sheet

Perf. 12x11¾ Syncopated

3737 A1020 €2.50 multi 5.75 3.00

St. Teresa of Avila (1515-82) A1021

Designs: 45c, Painting of St. Teresa. €2.50, St. Teresa, manuscript, horiz.

Perf. 11¾x12 Syncopated

2015, Sept. 11 **Litho.**
3738 A1021 45c multi 1.00 .50

Souvenir Sheet

Perf. 12x11¾ Syncopated

3739 A1021 €2.50 multi 5.75 3.00

No. 3739 contains one 80x30mm stamp.

Portugal's Use of the Sea A1022

Designs: 45c, Tourism. 62c, Fishing. 72c, Transportation. 80c, Energy.
€2, Science.

Perf. 12x11¾ Syncopated

2015, Sept. 17 **Litho.**
3740-3743 A1022 Set of 4 6.00 3.00

Souvenir Sheet

3744 A1022 €2 multi 4.50 2.25

Portuguese Capture of Ceuta, 600th Anniv. — A1023

Designs: 55c, Map, Church of Our Lady of Africa. €1, Map, Manzanna del Revellín Cultural Center.
€2.50, Royal Walls of Ceuta, 1572 depiction of Ceuta.

Perf. 11¾x12 Syncopated

2015, Sept. 28 **Litho.**
3745-3746 A1023 Set of 2 3.50 1.75

Souvenir Sheet

3747 A1023 €2.50 multi 5.75 3.00

Montepio Mutual Benefit Association, 175th Anniv. — A1024

Designs: 45c, Pelican emblem. 80c, Family and money box.
€2.50, Montepio headquarters, Lisbon, vert.

Perf. 12x11¾ Syncopated

2015, Oct. 1 **Litho.**
3748-3749 A1024 Set of 2 3.00 1.50

Souvenir Sheet

Perf. 11¾x12 Syncopated

3750 A1024 €2.50 multi 5.75 3.00

No. 3750 contains one 30x80mm stamp.

Dancers and Choreographers A1025

Designs: 45c, Francis Graça (1902-80), dancer. 55c, Margarida de Abreu (1915-2006), choreographer. 62c, Fernando Lima (1928-2005), choreographer. 72c, Agueda Sena, dancer. 80c, Isabel Santa Rosa (1931-2001), dancer. €1, Carlos Trincheiras (1937-93), dancer.

Perf. 11¾x12 Syncopated

2015, Oct. 9 **Litho.**
3751-3756 A1025 Set of 6 9.25 4.50

Intl. Year of Light — A1026

No. 3757: a, Sun, galaxy, Earth, Moon, satellite. b, Lighthouse, solar panels.

Perf. 11¾x12 Syncopated

2015, Oct. 14 **Litho.**
3757 A1026 45c Vert. pair, #a-b 2.00 1.00

Intl. Year of Soils — A1027

No. 3758: a, Earth, plant, roots, top of hourglass. b, Apple tree, apples, flowers, bottom of hourglass.

Perf. 11¾x12 Syncopated

2015, Oct. 14 **Litho.**

3758 A1027 45c Vert. pair, #a-b 2.00 1.00

Gardens Type of 2014

Die Cut Perf. 10½

2015, Oct. 23 **Litho.**

Self-Adhesive

3759 A994 E Like #3617 1.60 .80

No. 3759 sold for 72c on day of issue.

Arrival of Portuguese in Timor, 500th Anniv. — A1028

Designs: 80c, Settlement near hills, flower, woman. €1, Timorese house, Dom Aleixo Corte-Real (1886-1943), leader of revolt against Japanese occupation, Timorese sash. €2.50, Model of Timorese house, scuplture.

Perf. 12x11¾ Syncopated

2015, Oct. 28 **Litho.**

3760-3761 A1028 Set of 2 4.00 2.00

Souvenir Sheet

3762 A1028 €2.50 multi 5.50 2.25

AIR POST STAMPS

Symbol of Aviation AP1

Perf. 12x11½

1936-41 **Unwmk.** **Typo.**

C1 AP1 1.50e dark blue .45 .30
C2 AP1 1.75e red orange .75 .35
C3 AP1 2.50e rose red .85 .35
C4 AP1 3e brt blue ('41) 14.00 12.00
C5 AP1 4e dp yel grn ('41) 18.00 18.00
C6 AP1 5e car lake 1.75 1.25
C7 AP1 10e brown lake 3.00 1.25
C8 AP1 15e orange ('41) 11.50 7.00
C9 AP1 20e black brn 9.00 2.75
C10 AP1 50e brn vio ('41) 160.00 75.00
Nos. C1-C10 (10) 219.30 118.25
Set, never hinged 390.00

Nos. C1-C10 exist imperf.

Catalogue values for unused stamps in this section, from this point to the end of the section, are for Never Hinged items.

EXPO Type of Regular Issue

1970, Sept. 16 **Litho.** ***Perf. 13***

C11 A274 3.50e silver & multi .70 .40

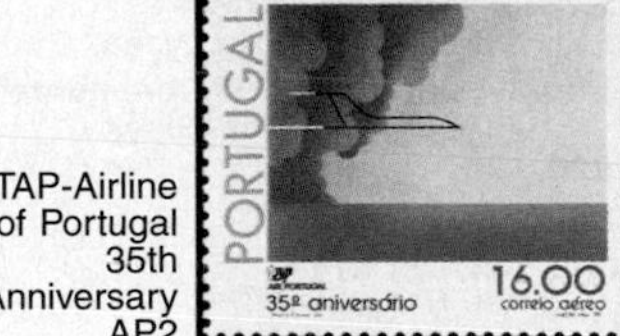

TAP-Airline of Portugal 35th Anniversary AP2

Design: 19e, Jet flying past sun.

1979, Sept. 21 **Litho.** ***Perf. 12x11½***

C12 AP2 16e multicolored 1.10 .55
C13 AP2 19e multicolored 1.25 .80

POSTAGE DUE STAMPS

Vasco da Gama Issue

The Zamorin of Calicut Receiving Vasco da Gama — D1

Unwmk.

1898, May 1 **Typo.** ***Perf. 12***

Denomination in Black

J1 D1 5r black 2.40 1.25
a. Value and "Continente" omitted 50.00 5.00
J2 D1 10r lilac & blk 4.00 1.75
J3 D1 20r orange & blk 6.50 2.50
J4 D1 50r slate & blk 50.00 11.00
J5 D1 100r car & blk, *pink* 87.50 40.00
J6 D1 200r brn & blk, *buff* 92.50 60.00

For overprints and surcharges see Nos. 193-198.

D2

1904 ***Perf. 11½x12***

J7 D2 5r brown .45 .40
J8 D2 10r orange 2.75 .90
a. Imperf.
J9 D2 20r lilac 8.00 3.75
J10 D2 30r gray green 5.75 2.75
J11 D2 40r gray violet 7.00 2.75
J12 D2 50r carmine 52.50 4.50
a. Imperf.
J13 D2 100r dull blue 8.75 6.50
a. Imperf.
Nos. J7-J13 (7) 85.20 21.55

Preceding Issue Overprinted in Carmine or Green

1910

J14 D2 5r brown .40 .25
J15 D2 10r orange .40 .25
J16 D2 20r lilac 1.40 1.00
J17 D2 30r gray green 1.25 .25
J18 D2 40r gray violet 1.40 .25
J19 D2 50r carmine (G) 6.00 4.50
J20 D2 100r dull blue 6.50 5.25
Nos. J14-J20 (7) 17.35 11.75

See note after No. 183.

D3

1915, Mar. 18 **Typo.**

J21 D3 ½c brown .60 .60
J22 D3 1c orange .60 .60
J23 D3 2c claret .60 .60
J24 D3 3c green .60 .60
J25 D3 4c gray violet .60 .60
J26 D3 5c carmine .60 .60
J27 D3 10c dark blue .60 .60
Nos. J21-J27 (7) 4.20 4.20

1921-27

J28 D3 ½c gray green ('22) .35 .35
J29 D3 4c gray green ('27) .35 .35
J30 D3 8c gray green ('23) .35 .35
J31 D3 10c gray green ('22) .35 .35
J32 D3 12c gray green .50 .50
J33 D3 16c gray green ('23) .50 .50
J34 D3 20c gray green .50 .50
J35 D3 24c gray green .50 .50
J36 D3 32c gray green ('23) .50 .50
J37 D3 36c gray green 1.50 .75
J38 D3 40c gray green ('23) 1.50 .75
J39 D3 48c gray green ('23) .65 .65
J40 D3 50c gray green .65 .65
J41 D3 60c gray green .65 .65
J42 D3 72c gray green .65 .65
J43 D3 80c gray green ('23) 7.50 7.50
J44 D3 1.20e gray green 3.00 3.00
Nos. J28-J44 (17) 20.00 18.50

D4

1932-33

J45 D4 5c buff .50 .45
J46 D4 10c lt blue .50 .45
J47 D4 20c pink 1.25 1.00
J48 D4 30c blue green 1.50 1.00
J49 D4 40c lt green 1.50 1.00
a. Figure of value inverted —
J50 D4 50c gray 1.60 1.00
J51 D4 60c rose 4.25 2.00
J52 D4 80c violet brn 10.00 4.00
J53 D4 1.20e gray ol ('33) 13.00 12.00
Nos. J45-J53 (9) 34.10 22.90

D5

1940, Feb. 1 **Unwmk.** ***Perf. 12½***

J54 D5 5c bister, perf. 14 .50 .35
J55 D5 10c rose lilac .30 .25
J56 D5 20c dk car rose .30 .25
J57 D5 30c purple .30 .25
J58 D5 40c cerise .30 .25
J59 D5 50c brt blue .30 .25
J60 D5 60c yellow grn .30 .25
J61 D5 80c scarlet .30 .25
J62 D5 1e brown .30 .25
J63 D5 2e dk rose vio .55 .45
J64 D5 5e org yel, perf. 14 11.00 9.00
a. Perf. 12½ 175.00 125.00
Nos. J54-J64 (11) 14.45 11.80

Nos. J54-J64 were first issued perf. 14. In 1955 all but the 5c were reissued in perf. 12½.

Catalogue values for unused stamps in this section, from this point to the end of the section, are for Never Hinged items.

D6

1967-84 **Litho.** ***Perf. 11½***

J65 D6 10c dp org, red brn & yel .25 .25
J66 D6 20c bis, dk brn & yel .25 .25
J67 D6 30c org, red brn & yel .25 .25
J68 D6 40c ol bis, dk brn & yel .25 .25
J69 D6 50c ultra, dk bl & bl .25 .25
J70 D6 60c grnsh bl, dk grn & lt bl .25 .25
J71 D6 80c bl, dk bl & lt bl .25 .25
J72 D6 1e vio bl, dk bl & lt bl .25 .25
J73 D6 2e grn, dk grn & lt grn .25 .25
J74 D6 3e lt grn, grn & yel ('75) .25 .25
J75 D6 4e bl grn, dk grn & yel ('75) .25 .25
J76 D6 5e cl, dp cl & pink .25 .25
J77 D6 9e vio, dk vio & pink ('75) .25 .25
J78 D6 10e lil, pur & pale vio ('75) .25 .25
J79 D6 20e red, brn & pale vio ('75) .70 .25
J80 D6 40e dp red lil, rose vio & bluish lil ('84) 1.50 .50

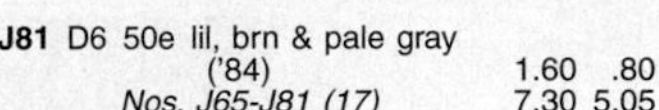

J81 D6 50e lil, brn & pale gray ('84) 1.60 .80
Nos. J65-J81 (17) 7.30 5.05

D7

1992-93 **Litho.** ***Perf. 12x11½***

J82 D7 1e multicolored .25 .25
J83 D7 2e multicolored .25 .25
J84 D7 5e multicolored .25 .25
J85 D7 10e multicolored .25 .25
J86 D7 20e multicolored .25 .25
J87 D7 50e multicolored .55 .25
J88 D7 100e multicolored 1.00 .55
J89 D7 200e multicolored 2.00 1.25
Nos. J82-J89 (8) 4.80 3.30

Issued: 1e, 2e, 5e, 200e, 10/7/92; 10e, 20e, 50e, 100e, 3/9/93.

Type D7 Inscribed "CTT CORREIOS"

1995-96

J90 D7 3e multicolored .25 .25
J91 D7 4e multicolored .25 .25
J92 D7 5e multicolored .25 .25
J93 D7 9e multicolored .25 .25
J94 D7 10e multicolored .25 .25
J95 D7 20e multicolored .25 .25
J96 D7 40e multicolored .35 .25
J97 D7 50e multicolored .55 .25
J98 D7 100e multicolored .85 .45
Nos. J90-J98 (9) 3.25 2.45

Issued: 3e, 4e, 9e, 40e, 4/20/95; 50e, 5/22/95; 5e, 10e, 20e, 100e, 5/24/96.

Numerals — D8

2002, Jan. 2 **Litho.** ***Perf. 11¾x11½***

J99 D8 1c multi .25 .25
J100 D8 2c multi .25 .25
J101 D8 5c multi .25 .25
J102 D8 10c multi .25 .25
J103 D8 25c multi .60 .25
J104 D8 50c multi 1.20 .35
J105 D8 €1 multi 2.40 .70
Nos. J99-J105 (7) 5.20 2.30

OFFICIAL STAMPS

No. 567 Overprinted in Black

1938 **Unwmk.** ***Perf. 11½***

O1 A113 40c brown .45 .25

Catalogue values for unused stamps in this section, from this point to the end of the section, are for Never Hinged items.

O1

1952, Sept. **Litho.** ***Perf. 12½***

O2 O1 black & cream .45 .25

O2

1975, June

O3	O2	black & yellow	1.00	.25

NEWSPAPER STAMPS

N1

Perf. 11½, 12½, 13½

1876 Typo. Unwmk.

P1	N1	2½r bister	9.50	1.40
a.		2½r olive green	9.50	1.40

Various shades.

PARCEL POST STAMPS

Mercury and Commerce PP1

1920-22 Unwmk. Typo. *Perf. 12*

Q1	PP1	1c lilac brown	.25	.25
Q2	PP1	2c orange	.25	.25
Q3	PP1	5c lt brown	.25	.25
Q4	PP1	10c red brown	.25	.25
Q5	PP1	20c gray blue	.30	.25
Q6	PP1	40c carmine rose	.35	.25
Q7	PP1	50c black	.50	.45
Q8	PP1	60c dk blue ('21)	.50	.45
Q9	PP1	70c gray brn ('21)	3.00	2.00
Q10	PP1	80c ultra ('21)	3.50	3.25
Q11	PP1	90c lt vio ('21)	3.50	2.25
Q12	PP1	1e lt green	4.00	2.25
Q13	PP1	2e pale lilac ('22)	11.00	3.50
Q14	PP1	3e olive ('22)	21.00	4.00
Q15	PP1	4e ultra ('22)	42.50	7.00
Q16	PP1	5e gray ('22)	55.00	4.75
Q17	PP1	10e chocolate ('22)	82.50	9.25
		Nos. Q1-Q17 (17)	228.65	40.65

Parcel Post Package PP2

1936 *Perf. 11½*

Q18	PP2	50c olive brown	.65	.50
Q19	PP2	1e bister brown	.65	.50
Q20	PP2	1.50e purple	.65	.50
Q21	PP2	2e carmine lake	2.75	.60
Q22	PP2	2.50e olive green	2.75	.60
Q23	PP2	4.50e brown lake	5.75	.65
Q24	PP2	5e violet	9.00	.75
Q25	PP2	10e orange	12.00	1.75
		Nos. Q18-Q25 (8)	34.20	5.85

POSTAL TAX STAMPS

These stamps represent a special fee for the delivery of postal matter on certain days in each year. The money derived from their sale is applied to works of public charity.

Regular Issues Overprinted in Carmine

1911, Oct. 4 Unwmk. *Perf. 14½x15*

RA1	A62	10r gray green	8.50	2.25

The 20r carmine of this type was for use on telegrams. Value, $10.

1912, Oct. 4 *Perf. 15x14½*

RA2	A64	1c deep green	6.00	1.75

The 2c carmine of this type was for use on telegrams. Value, $10.

"Lisbon" — PT1

1913, June 8 Litho. *Perf. 12x11½*

RA3	PT1	1c dark green	.95	.70

The 2c dark brown of this type was for use on telegrams. Value, $5.

"Charity" — PT2

1915, Oct. 4 Typo.

RA4	PT2	1c carmine	.35	.30

The 2c plum of this type was for use on telegrams. Value, $5.

See No. RA6.

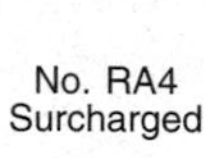

No. RA4 Surcharged

1924, Oct. 4

RA5	PT2	15c on 1c dull red	1.25	.70

The 30c on 2c claret of this type was for use on telegrams. Value, $3.

Charity Type of 1915 Issue

1925, Oct. 4 *Perf. 12½*

RA6	PT2	15c carmine	.35	.35

The 30c brown violet of this type was for use on telegrams. Value, $2.

Comrades of the Great War Issue

Muse of History with Tablet — PT3

1925, Apr. 8 Litho. *Perf. 11*

RA7	PT3	10c brown	1.10	1.10
RA8	PT3	10c green	1.10	1.10
RA9	PT3	10c rose	1.10	1.10
RA10	PT3	10c ultra	1.10	1.10
		Nos. RA7-RA10 (4)	4.40	4.40

The use of these stamps, in addition to the regular postage, was obligatory on certain days of the year. If the tax represented by these stamps was not prepaid, it was collected by means of Postal Tax Due Stamp No. RAJ1.

Pombal Issue

Common Design Types

Engraved; Value and "Continente" Typographed in Black

1925, May 8 *Perf. 12½*

RA11	CD28	15c ultra	.50	.40
RA12	CD29	15c ultra	1.00	.75
RA13	CD30	15c ultra	1.00	.75
		Nos. RA11-RA13 (3)	2.50	1.90

Olympic Games Issue

Hurdler — PT7

1928 Litho. *Perf. 12*

RA14	PT7	15c dull red & blk	10.00	*2.75*

The use of this stamp, in addition to the regular postage, was obligatory on May 22-24, 1928. 10% of the money thus obtained was retained by the Postal Administration; the balance was given to a Committee in charge of Portuguese participation in the Olympic games at Amsterdam.

POSTAL TAX DUE STAMPS

Comrades of the Great War Issue

PTD1

1925 Unwmk. Typo. *Perf. 11x11½*

RAJ1	PTD1	20c brown orange	.55	.45

See Note after No. RA10.

Pombal Issue

Common Design Types

1925 *Perf. 12½*

RAJ2	CD28	30c ultra	1.10	1.10
RAJ3	CD29	30c ultra	1.10	1.10
RAJ4	CD30	30c ultra	1.10	1.10
		Nos. RAJ2-RAJ4 (3)	3.30	3.30

When the compulsory tax was not paid by the use of stamps #RA11-RA13, double the amount was collected by means of #RAJ2-RAJ4.

Olympic Games Issue

PTD2

1928 Litho. *Perf. 11½*

RAJ5	PTD2	30c lt red & blk	8.00	1.75

FRANCHISE STAMPS

These stamps are supplied by the Government to various charitable, scientific and military organizations for franking their correspondence. This franking privilege was withdrawn in 1938.

FOR THE RED CROSS SOCIETY

F1

Perf. 11½

1889-1915 Unwmk. Typo.

1S1	F1	rose & blk ('15)	.45	.40
a.		Vermilion & black ('08)	5.75	1.25
b.		Red & black, perf. 12½	65.00	6.25

No. 1S1 Overprinted in Green

1917

1S3	F1	rose & black	90.00	77.50
a.		Inverted overprint	150.00	150.00

"Charity" Extending Hope to Invalid — F1a

1926 Litho. *Perf. 14*

Inscribed "LISBOA"

1S4	F1a	black & red	9.00	9.00

Inscribed "DELEGACOES"

1S5	F1a	black & red	9.00	9.00

No. 1S4 was for use in Lisbon. No. 1S5 was for the Red Cross chapters outside Lisbon.

For overprints see Nos. 1S72-1S73.

Camoens Issue of 1924 Overprinted in Black or Red

1927

1S6	A68	40c ultra	1.10	1.00
1S7	A68	48c red brown	1.10	1.00
1S8	A69	64c green	1.10	1.00
1S9	A69	75c dk violet	1.10	1.00
1S10	A71	4.50e blk, *org* (R)	1.10	1.00
1S11	A71	10e dk brn, *pnksh*	1.10	1.00
		Nos. 1S6-1S11 (6)	6.60	6.00

Camoens Issue of 1924 Overprinted in Red

1928

1S12	A67	15c olive grn	1.10	1.00
1S13	A67	16c violet brn	1.10	1.00
1S14	A68	25c lilac	1.10	1.00
1S15	A68	40c ultra	1.10	1.00
1S16	A70	1.20e lt brown	1.10	1.00
1S17	A70	2e apple green	1.10	1.00
		Nos. 1S12-1S17 (6)	6.60	6.00

Camoens Issue of 1924 Overprinted in Red

1929

1S18	A68	30c dk brown	1.10	1.00
1S19	A68	40c ultra	1.10	1.00
1S20	A69	80c bister	1.10	1.00
1S21	A70	1.50e red	1.10	1.00
1S22	A70	1.60e dark blue	1.10	1.00
1S23	A71	2.40e green, *grn*	1.10	1.00
		Nos. 1S18-1S23 (6)	6.60	6.00

Same Overprint Dated "1930"

1930

1S24	A68	40c ultra	1.10	1.00
1S25	A69	50c red orange	1.10	1.00
1S26	A69	96c lake	1.10	1.00
1S27	A70	1.60e dk blue	1.10	1.00
1S28	A71	3e dk blue, *bl*	1.10	1.00
1S29	A72	20e dk violet, *lil*	1.10	1.00
		Nos. 1S24-1S29 (6)	6.60	6.00

Camoens Issue of 1924 Overprinted in Red

1931

1S30	A68	25c lilac	1.25	1.10
1S31	A68	32c dk green	1.25	1.10
1S32	A68	40c ultra	1.25	1.10
1S33	A69	96c lake	1.25	1.10
1S34	A70	1.60e dark blue	1.25	1.10
1S35	A71	3.20e black, *green*	1.25	1.10
		Nos. 1S30-1S35 (6)	7.50	6.60

Same Overprint Dated "1932"

1931

1S36	A67	20c dp orange	1.75	1.75
1S37	A68	40c ultra	1.75	1.75
1S38	A68	48c red brown	1.75	1.75
1S39	A69	64c green	1.75	1.75
1S40	A70	1.60e dark blue	1.75	1.75
1S41	A71	10e dk brown, *pnksh*	1.75	1.75
		Nos. 1S36-1S41 (6)	10.50	10.50

Nos. 1S6-1S11 Overprinted in Red

1932

1S42	A68	40c ultra	1.75	1.75
1S43	A68	48c red brown	1.75	1.75
1S44	A69	64c green	1.75	1.75
1S45	A69	75c dk violet	1.75	1.75
1S46	A71	4.50e blk, *orange*	1.75	1.75
1S47	A71	10e dk brn, *pnksh*	1.75	1.75
		Nos. 1S42-1S47 (6)	10.50	10.50

1933 **Dated "1934"**

1S48	A68	40c ultra	2.25	2.25
1S49	A68	48c red brown	2.25	2.25
1S50	A69	64c green	2.25	2.25
1S51	A69	75c dark violet	2.25	2.25
1S52	A71	4.50e blk, *orange*	2.25	2.25
1S53	A71	10e dk brown, *pnksh*	2.25	2.25
		Nos. 1S48-1S53 (6)	13.50	13.50

1935 **Dated "1935"**

1S54	A68	40c ultra	2.60	2.60
1S55	A68	48c red brown	2.60	2.60
1S56	A69	64c green	2.60	2.60
1S57	A69	75c dk violet	2.60	2.60
1S58	A71	4.50e black, *orange*	2.60	2.60
1S59	A71	10e dk brn, *pnksh*	2.60	2.60
		Nos. 1S54-1S59 (6)	15.60	15.60

Camoens Issue of 1924 Overprinted in Black or Red

1935

1S60	A68	25c lilac	1.10	1.00
1S61	A68	40c ultra (R)	1.10	1.00
1S62	A69	50c red orange	1.10	1.00
1S63	A70	1e slate	1.10	1.00
1S64	A70	2e apple green	1.10	1.00
1S65	A72	20e dk violet, *lilac*	1.10	1.00
		Nos. 1S60-1S65 (6)	6.60	6.00

Camoens Issue of 1924 Overprinted in Red

1936

1S66	A68	30c dk brown	1.10	1.10
1S67	A68	32c dk green	1.10	1.10
1S68	A69	80c bister	1.10	1.10
1S69	A70	1.20e lt brown	1.10	1.10
1S70	A71	3e dk blue, *bl*	1.10	1.10
1S71	A71	4.50e black, *yel*	1.10	1.10
		Nos. 1S66-1S71 (6)	6.60	6.60

No. 1S4 Overprinted "1935"

1936 **Unwmk.** ***Perf. 14***

1S72	F1a	black & red	10.00	10.00

Same Stamp with Additional Overprint "Delegacoes"

1S73	F1a	black & red	10.00	10.00

After the government withdrew the franking privilege in 1938, the Portuguese Red Cross Society distributed charity labels which lacked postal validity.

FOR CIVILIAN RIFLE CLUBS

Rifle Club Emblem — F2

Perf. 11½x12

1899-1910 **Typo.** **Unwmk.**

2S1	F2	bl grn & car ('99)	10.00	10.00
2S2	F2	brn & yel grn ('00)	10.00	10.00
2S3	F2	car & buff ('01)	1.00	1.00
2S4	F2	bl & org ('02)	1.00	1.00
2S5	F2	grn & org ('03)	1.00	1.00
2S6	F2	lt brn & car ('04)	1.60	1.60
2S7	F2	mar & ultra ('05)	4.25	4.25
2S8	F2	ultra & buff ('06)	1.00	1.00
2S9	F2	choc & yel ('07)	1.00	1.00
2S10	F2	car & ultra ('08)	1.60	1.60
2S11	F2	bl & yel grn ('09)	1.00	1.00
2S12	F2	bl grn & brn, *pink* ('10)	4.00	4.00
		Nos. 2S1-2S12 (12)	37.45	37.45

FOR THE GEOGRAPHICAL SOCIETY OF LISBON

Coat of Arms
F3 F4

1903-34 **Unwmk.** **Litho.** ***Perf. 11½***

3S1	F3	blk, rose, bl & red	9.00	5.00
3S2	F3	bl, yel, red & grn ('09)	12.00	5.00
3S3	F4	blk, org, bl & red ('11)	5.50	4.00
3S4	F4	blk & brn org ('22)	6.75	4.75
3S5	F4	blk & bl ('24)	15.00	8.50
3S6	F4	blk & rose ('26)	6.75	4.75
3S7	F4	blk & grn ('27)	6.75	4.75
3S8	F4	bl, yel & red ('29)	4.75	3.50
3S9	F4	bl, red & vio ('30)	4.75	3.50
3S10	F4	dp bl, lil & red ('31)	4.75	3.50
3S11	F4	bis brn & red ('32)	4.75	3.50
3S12	F4	lt grn & red ('33)	4.75	3.50
3S13	F4	blue & red ('34)	4.75	3.50
		Nos. 3S1-3S13 (13)	90.25	57.75

No. 3S12 with three-line overprint, "C.I.C.I. Portugal 1933," was not valid for postage and was sold only to collectors.

No. 3S2 was reprinted in 1933. Green vertical lines behind "Porte Franco" omitted. Value $7.50.

F5

1934 **Litho.** ***Perf. 11½***

3S15	F5	blue & red	6.00	3.50

1935-38 ***Perf. 11***

3S16	F5	blue	18.00	5.25
3S17	F5	dk bl & red ('36)	4.75	4.25
3S18	F5	lil & red ('37)	3.50	2.75
3S19	F5	blk, grn & car ('38)	3.50	2.75
		Nos. 3S16-3S19 (4)	29.75	15.00

The inscription in the inner circle is omitted on No. 3S16.

FOR THE NATIONAL AID SOCIETY FOR CONSUMPTIVES

F10

Perf. 11½x12

1904, July **Typo.** **Unwmk.**

4S1	F10	brown & green	5.00	5.00
4S2	F10	carmine & yellow	5.00	5.00

AZORES

Starting in 1980, stamps inscribed Azores and Madeira were valid and sold in Portugal. See Vols. 1 and 4 for prior issues.

Azores No. 2 — A33

Design: 19.50e, Azores No. 6.

1980, Jan. 2 **Litho.** ***Perf. 12***

314	A33	6.50e multi	.25	.25
315	A33	19.50e multi	.85	.50
a.		Souvenir sheet of 2, #314-315	3.75	3.75

No. 315a exists overprinted for Capex 87.

Map of Azores A34

1980, Sept. 17 **Litho.** ***Perf. 12x11½***

316	A34	50c shown	.25	.25
317	A34	1e Cathedral	.25	.25
318	A34	5e Windmill	.40	.25
319	A34	6.50e Local women	.50	.25
320	A34	8e Coastline	.70	.25
321	A34	30e Ponta Delgada	1.60	.45
		Nos. 316-321 (6)	3.70	1.70

World Tourism Conf., Manila, Sept. 27.

Europa Issue

St. Peter's Cavalcade, St. Miguel Island A35

1981, May 11 **Litho.** ***Perf. 12***

322	A35	22e multicolored	*1.00*	*.60*
a.		Souvenir sheet of 2	*5.50*	*2.00*

Bulls Attacking Spanish Soldiers A36

Battle of Salga Valley, 400th Anniv.: 33.50e, Friar Don Pedro leading citizens.

1981, July 24 **Litho.** ***Perf. 12x11½***

323	A36	8.50e multi	.45	.25
324	A36	33.50e multi	1.60	.75

Tolpis Azorica — A37

Designs: Local flora — 8.50e, Ranunculus azoricus. 20e, Platanthera micranta. 50e, Laurus azorica.

1981, Sept. 21 **Litho.** ***Perf. 12½x12***

325	A37	7e multicolored	.25	.25
326	A37	8.50e multicolored	.35	.25
327	A37	20e multicolored	.65	.35
328	A37	50e multicolored	1.40	.75
a.		Booklet pane of 4, #325-328	5.00	
		Nos. 325-328 (4)	2.65	1.60

1982, Jan. 29

329	A37	4e Myosotis azorica	.25	.25
330	A37	10e Lactuca watsoniana	.50	.25
331	A37	27e Vicia dennesiana	1.10	.60
332	A37	33.50e Azorina vidalii	1.10	.75
a.		Booklet pane of 4	5.00	
		Nos. 329-332 (4)	2.95	1.85

See Nos. 338-341.

Europa Type of Portugal

Heroes of Mindelo embarkation, 1832.

1982, May 3 **Litho.** ***Perf. 12x11½***

333	A405	33.50e multi	*1.75*	*.65*
a.		Souvenir sheet of 3	*9.00*	*4.00*

Chapel of the Holy Ghost — A39

Various Chapels of the Holy Ghost.

1982, Nov. 24 Litho. ***Perf. 12½x12***
334 A39 27e multi 1.10 .60
335 A39 33.50e multi 1.50 .80

Europa 1983
A40

1983, May 5 Litho. ***Perf. 12½***
336 A40 37.50e Geothermal energy *2.00 .55*
a. Souvenir sheet of 3 *10.00 5.00*

Flag of the Autonomous Region — A41

1983, May 23 Litho. ***Perf. 12x11½***
337 A41 12.50e multi .65 .25

Flower Type of 1981

1983, June 16 ***Perf. 12½x12***
338 A37 12.50e St. John's wort .25 .25
339 A37 30e Prickless bramble .70 .30
340 A37 37.50e Romania bush 1.00 .55
341 A37 100e Common juniper 1.90 1.00
a. Booklet pane of 4, #338-341 6.00
Nos. 338-341 (4) 3.85 2.10

Woman Wearing Terceira Cloaks — A42

1984, Mar. 8 Litho. ***Perf. 13½***
342 A42 16e Jesters costumes, 18th cent. .50 .25
343 A42 51e shown 1.75 1.00

Europa Type of Portugal

1984, May 2 ***Perf. 12x11½***
344 A427 51e multicolored *2.50 .95*
a. Souvenir sheet of 3 *10.00 4.00*

Megabombus Ruderatus — A44

35e, Pieris brassicae azorensis. 40e, Chrysomela banksi. 51e, Phlogophora interrupta.

1984, Sept. 3 Litho. ***Perf. 12x11½***
345 A44 16e multicolored .30 .25
346 A44 35e multicolored .90 .50
347 A44 40e multicolored 1.25 .50
348 A44 51e multicolored 1.50 .80
Nos. 345-348 (4) 3.95 2.05

Perf. 12 Vert.
345a A44 16e 1.50 1.50
346a A44 35e 1.50 1.50
347a A44 40e 1.50 1.50
348a A44 51e 1.50 1.50
b. Bklt. pane of 4, #345a-348a 9.00

1985, Feb. 13 ***Perf. 12x11½***

20e, Polyspilla polyspilla. 40e, Sphaerophoria nigra. 46e, Colias croceus. 60e, Hipparchia azorina.

349 A44 20e multicolored .30 .25
350 A44 40e multicolored .90 .40
351 A44 46e multicolored 1.25 .60
352 A44 60e multicolored 1.40 .65
Nos. 349-352 (4) 3.85 1.90

Perf. 12 Vert.
349a A44 20e 1.50 1.50
350a A44 40e 1.50 1.50
351a A44 46e 1.50 1.50
352a A44 60e 1.50 1.50
b. Bklt. pane of 4, #349a-352a 9.00

Europa Type of Portugal

1985, May 6 Litho. ***Perf. 11½x12***
353 A435 60e Man playing folia drum 2.75 .80
a. Souvenir sheet of 3 24.00 6.00

Native Boats — A46

1985, June 19 Litho. ***Perf. 12x12½***
354 A46 40e Jeque 1.10 .60
355 A46 60e Bote 1.60 .70

Europa Type of Portugal

1986, May Litho.
356 A447 68.50e Pyrrhula murina *2.75 .90*
a. Souvenir sheet of 3 *12.00 5.00*

Regional Architecture A48

19th Century fountains: 22.50e, Alto das Covas, Angra do Heroismo. 52.50e, Faja de Baixo, San Miguel. 68.50e, Gates of St. Peter, Terceira. 100e, Agua d'Alto, San Miguel.

1986, Sept. 18 Litho. ***Perf. 12***
357 A48 22.50e multi .50 .25
358 A48 52.50e multi 1.50 .70
359 A48 68.50e multi 2.25 .90
360 A48 100e multi 3.00 .75
a. Booklet pane of 4, #357-360 9.00
Nos. 357-360 (4) 7.25 2.60

Traditional Modes of Transportation — A49

1986, Nov. 7 Litho.
361 A49 25e Isle of Santa Maria ox cart .50 .25
362 A49 75e Ram cart 2.25 1.10

Europa Type of Portugal

Modern architecutre: Regional Assembly, Horta, designed by Manuel Correia Fernandes and Luis Miranda.

1987, May 5 Litho. ***Perf. 12***
363 A456 74.50e multicolored *3.00 .90*
a. Souvenir sheet of 4 *12.00 4.00*

Windows and Balconies A51

51e, Santa Cruz, Graciosa. 74.50e, Ribiera Grande, San Miguel.

1987, July 1 ***Perf. 12***
364 A51 51e multicolored 1.40 .70
365 A51 74.50e multicolored 1.75 .70

Aviation History A52

Seaplanes — 25e, NC-4 Curtiss Flyer, 1919. 57e, Dornier DO-X, 1932. 74.50e, Savoia-Marchetti S 55-X, 1933. 125e, Lockheed Sirius, 1933.

1987, Oct. 9 ***Perf. 12x11½***
366 A52 25e multi .40 .25
367 A52 57e multi 1.50 .90
368 A52 74.50e multi 2.25 .85
369 A52 125e multi 2.60 1.10
Nos. 366-369 (4) 6.75 3.10

Perf. 12 Vert.
366a A52 25e 2.25 2.25
367a A52 57e 2.25 2.25
368a A52 74.50e 2.25 2.25
369a A52 125e 2.25 2.25
b. Bklt. pane of 4, #366a-369a 9.00

Europa Type of Portugal

1988, Apr. 21 Litho. ***Perf. 12***
370 A466 80e multicolored *9.00 1.20*
a. Souvenir sheet of 4 *12.00 5.00*

Birds — A54

1988, Oct. 18 Litho.
371 A54 27e Columba palumbus azorica .50 .25
372 A54 60e Scolopax rusticola 1.50 .70
373 A54 80e Sterna dougallii 1.75 .75
374 A54 100e Buteo buteo 2.10 .80
a. Booklet pane of 4, #371-374 9.00
Nos. 371-374 (4) 5.85 2.50

Coats of Arms A55

1988, Nov. 18 Litho.
375 A55 55e Dominion of Azores 1.25 .60
376 A55 80e Bettencourt family 1.75 .80

Wildlife Conservation A56

Various kinglets, Regulus regulus.

1989, Jan. 20 Litho.
377 A56 30e Adult on branch .75 .25
378 A56 30e Two adults .75 .25
379 A56 30e Adult, nest .75 .25
380 A56 30e Bird in flight .75 .25
a. Strip of 4, Nos. 377-380 3.25 3.25

See Nos. 385-388.

Europa Type of Portugal

Children's toys.

1989, Apr. 26 Litho.
381 A476 80e Tin boat *2.50 .80*

Souvenir Sheet

382 Sheet, 2 each #381, 382a *13.00 5.00*
a. A476 80e Tin boat, diff. *2.50 2.00*

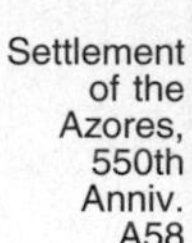

Settlement of the Azores, 550th Anniv. A58

1989, Sept. 20 Litho.
383 A58 29e Friar Goncalho Velho .45 .25
384 A58 87e Settlers farming 2.00 .90

Bird Type of 1989 With World Wildlife Fund Emblem

Various Pyrrhula murina.

1990, Feb. 14 Litho. ***Perf. 12***
385 A56 32e Adult on branch 1.25 .50
386 A56 32e Two adults 1.25 .50
387 A56 32e Brooding 1.25 .50
388 A56 32e Bird in flight 1.25 .50
a. Strip of 4, #385-388 5.75 5.75

No. 388a has continuous design.

Europa Type of Portugal

1990, Apr. 11 Litho. ***Perf. 12x11½***
389 A486 80e Vasco da Gama P.O. *2.25 .55*

Souvenir Sheet

390 Sheet of 4, 2 each #389, 390a *13.00 4.50*
a. A486 80e Maia P.O. *2.25 1.75*

Professions A61

1990, July 11 Litho. ***Perf. 12***
391 A61 5e Cart maker .25 .25
392 A61 32e Potter .45 .25
393 A61 60e Metal worker 1.25 .55
394 A61 100e Cooper 1.75 .85
Nos. 391-394 (4) 3.70 1.90

Perf. 13½ Vert.
391a A61 5e 1.50 1.50
392a A61 32e 1.50 1.50
393a A61 60e 1.50 1.50
394a A61 100e 1.50 1.50
b. Bklt. pane of 4, #391a-394a 6.00

See Nos. 397-400, 406-409.

Europa A62

1991, Apr. 11 Litho. ***Perf. 12***
395 A62 80e Hermes space shuttle *2.25 .75*

Souvenir Sheet

396 Sheet, 2 each #395, 396a *13.00 4.00*
a. A62 80e Sanger *2.25 1.75*

Professions Type of 1990

1991, Aug. 2 Litho. ***Perf. 12x11½***
397 A61 35e Tile makers .45 .25
398 A61 65e Mosaic artists 1.00 .55
399 A61 70e Quarrymen 1.10 .55
400 A61 110e Stonemasons 1.75 .65
Nos. 397-400 (4) 4.30 2.00

Perf. 13½ Vert.
397a A61 35e 1.25 1.25
398a A61 65e 1.25 1.25
399a A61 70e 1.25 1.25
400a A61 110e 1.25 1.25
b. Bklt. pane of 4, #397a-400a 5.00

Transportation in the Azores — A63

Ships and Planes: 35e, Schooner Helena, 1918. 60e, Beechcraft CS, 1947. 80e, Yacht, Cruzeiro do Canal, 1987. 110e, British Aerospace ATP, 1991.

1991, Nov. 15 Litho. *Perf. 12x11½*

401 A63 35e multicolored .45 .25
402 A63 60e multicolored .90 .45
403 A63 80e multicolored 1.25 .60
404 A63 110e multicolored 1.60 .80
Nos. 401-404 (4) 4.20 2.10

See Nos. 410-413.

Europa Type of Portugal

85e, Columbus aboard Santa Maria.

1992, May 22 Litho. *Perf. 12x11½*

405 A514 85e gold & multi *6.00 .70*

Professions Type of 1990

1992, June 12 Litho. *Perf. 12x11½*

406 A61 10e Guitar maker .25 .25
407 A61 38e Carpenter .45 .25
408 A61 85e Basket maker 1.10 .50
409 A61 120e Boat builders 1.40 .75
Nos. 406-409 (4) 3.20 1.75

Perf. 13½ Vert.

406a A61 10e 1.50 1.50
407a A61 38e 1.50 1.50
408a A61 85e 1.50 1.50
409a A61 120e 1.50 1.50
b. Bklt. pane of 4, #406a-409a 6.00

Transportation Type of 1991

Ships.

1992, Oct. 7 Litho. *Perf. 12x11½*

410 A63 38e Insulano .45 .25
411 A63 65e Carvalho Araujo .85 .50
412 A63 85e Funchal 1.10 .55
413 A63 120e Terceirense 1.40 .65
Nos. 410-413 (4) 3.80 1.95

Contemporary Paintings by Antonio Dacosta (1914-90) — A64

Europa: No. 414, Two Mermaids at the Entrance to a Cave, 1980. No. 415a, Acoriana, 1986.

1993, May 5 Litho. *Perf. 12x11½*

414 A64 90e multicolored *1.25 .60*

Souvenir Sheet

415 Sheet, 2 each #414, 415a *7.00 5.00*
a. A64 90e multicolored *1.25 .60*

Grinding Stones A64a

Designs: 42e, Animal-powered mill. 130e, Woman using hand-driven mill.

1993, May 5 Litho. *Perf. 12x11*

416 A64a 42e multicolored .45 .25
417 A64a 130e multicolored 1.75 .75

Architecture A65

Church of Praia da Vitoria: 42e, Main entry. 70e, South entry.
Church of Ponta Delgada: 90e, Main entry. 130e, South entry.

1993, Nov. 3 Litho. *Perf. 12*

418 A65 42e multicolored .45 .25
419 A65 70e multicolored .80 .40
420 A65 90e multicolored 1.00 .50
421 A65 130e multicolored 1.50 .75
Nos. 418-421 (4) 3.75 1.90

Tile Used in Religious Architecture A66

Designs: 40e, Blue and white pattern, Caloura church, Sao Miguel. 70e, Blue, white and yellow pattern, Caloura church, Sao Miguel. 100e, Drawing of Adoration of the Wise Men, by Bartolomeu Antunes, Esperanca monastery, Ponta Delgada. 150e, Drawing, frontal altar, Nossa Senhora dos Anjos chapel.

1994, Mar. 28 Litho. *Perf. 12*

422 A66 40e multicolored .40 .25
423 A66 70e multicolored .80 .35
424 A66 100e multicolored 1.10 .55
425 A66 150e multicolored 1.50 .75
Nos. 422-425 (4) 3.80 1.90

Perf. 11½ Vert.

422a A66 40e .50 .25
423a A66 70e .90 .45
424a A66 100e 1.25 .65
425a A66 150e 2.00 .50
b. Bklt. pane of 4, #422a-425a 6.00

Europa Type of Portugal

Wildlife, country: No. 426, Monkey, Brazil. No. 427a, Armadillo, Africa.

1994, May 5 Litho. *Perf. 12*

426 A541 100e multicolored *1.25 .60*

Souvenir Sheet

427 Sheet, 2 each #426, 427a *8.00 6.00*
a. A541 100e multicolored *1.25 .60*

Architecture Type of 1993

45e, Church of Santa Barbara, Manueline Entry, Cedros. 140e, Railed window, Ribeira Grande.

1994, Sept. 16 Litho. *Perf. 12*

428 A65 45e multicolored .60 .30
429 A65 140e multicolored 1.75 .85

Advocates of Local Autonomy A67

42e, Aristides Moreira da Motta (1855-1942). 130e, Gil Mont'Alverne de Sequeira (1859-1931).

1995, Mar. 2 Litho. *Perf. 12*

430 A67 42e multicolored .80 .30
431 A67 130e multicolored 1.90 .95

19th Century Architecture A68

Designs: 45e, Santana Palace, Ponta Delgada. 80e, Our Lady of Victories Chapel, Furnas Lake. 95e, Hospital of the Santa Casa da Misericórdia, Ponta Delgada. 135e, Residence of Ernesto do Canto, Myrthes Park, Furnas Lake

1995, Sept. 1 Litho. *Perf. 12*

432 A68 45e multicolored .60 .30
433 A68 80e multicolored 1.00 .50
434 A68 95e multicolored 1.25 .60
435 A68 135e multicolored 1.75 .90
Nos. 432-435 (4) 4.60 2.30

Perf. 11½ Vert.

432a A68 45e .60 .60
433a A68 80e 1.00 1.00
434a A68 95e 1.25 .60
435a A68 135e 1.75 .90
b. Bklt. pane, #432a-435a 4.75
Complete booklet, No. 435b 6.00

Natália Correia (1923-93), Writer A69

1996, May 3 Litho. *Perf. 12*

436 A69 98e multicolored *1.50 .60*
a. Souvenir sheet of 3 *6.00 5.00*

Europa.

Lighthouses — A70

Designs: 47e, Contendas, Terceira Island. 78e, Molhe, Port of Ponte Delgada, San Miguel Island. 98e, Arnel, San Miguel. 140e, Santa Clara, San Miguel. 200e, Ponta da Barca, Graciosa Island.

1996, May 3

437 A70 47e multicolored .60 .30
438 A70 78e multicolored .90 .45
439 A70 98e multicolored 1.25 .60
440 A70 140e multicolored 1.75 .90
Nos. 437-440 (4) 4.50 2.25

Souvenir Sheet

441 A70 200e multicolored 4.00 3.00

Carved Work from Church Altar Pieces A71

49e, Leaves, berries, bird, St. Peter Church, Ponta Delgada, Sao Miguel. 80e, Cherub, Church of the Convent of St. Peter de Alcântara, Sao Roque, Pico. 100e, Cherub, All Saints Church, former Jesuits' College, Ponta Delgada. 140e, Figure holding scroll above head, St. Joseph Church, Ponta Delgada.

1997, Apr. 16 Litho. *Perf. 12*

442 A71 49e multicolored .55 .30
443 A71 80e multicolored .90 .45
444 A71 100e multicolored 1.10 .60
445 A71 140e multicolored 1.60 .80
Nos. 442-445 (4) 4.15 2.15

Perf. 11½ Vert.

442a A71 49e .55 .30
443a A71 80e .90 .45
444a A71 100e 1.10 .60
445a A71 140e 1.60 .80
b. Bklt. pane, #442a-445a 5.00
Complete booklet, #445b 5.25

Stories and Legends Type of Portugal

Europa: Man on ship from "Legend of the Island of Seven Cities," horiz.

1997, May 5 Litho. *Perf. 12*

446 A599 100e multicolored *1.25 .50*
a. Souvenir sheet of 3 *4.50 1.50*

Natl. Festivals Type of Portugal

1998, May 21 Litho. *Perf. 12*

447 A621 100e Holy Spirit 1.25 .55
a. Souvenir sheet of 3 5.00 1.75

Europa.

Ocean Creatures A72

Designs: 50e, Stenella frontalis. 140e, Physeter macrocephalus.

1998, Aug. 4 Litho. *Perf. 12*

448 A72 50e multicolored 1.00 .30

Size: 80x30mm

449 A72 140e multicolored 2.00 .80

Perf. 11½ Vert.

448a A72 50e 1.00 .30
449a A72 140e 2.00 .80
b. Booklet pane, #448a-449a + label 6.00
Complete booklet, #449b 6.00

Europa Type of Portugal

100e, Flowers, Pico Mountain Natural Reserve.

1999, May 5 Litho. *Perf. 12x11¾*

450 A641 100e multi *1.25 .50*
a. Souvenir sheet of 3 *3.75 3.75*

Paintings of the Azores A73

51e, Emigrants, by Domingos Rebelo (1891-1975). 95e, Portrait of Vitorino Nemésio, by Antonio Dacosta (1914-90), vert. 100e, Espera de Gado no Alto das Covas (1939-98), by José Van der Hagen. 140e, The Vila Franca Islands, by Duarte Maia (1867-1922).

Perf. 12x11¾, 11¾x12

1999, Sept. 3 Litho.

451 A73 51e multi .60 .25
452 A73 95e multi 1.10 .45
453 A73 100e multi 1.25 .50
454 A73 140e multi 1.75 .70

Perf. 11¾ Vert., 11¾ Horiz. (#452a)

451a A73 51e multi .60 .25
452a A73 95e multi 1.10 .45
453a A73 100e multi 1.25 .50
454a A73 140e multi 1.75 .70
b. Bklt. pane of 4, #451a-454a 4.00
Complete booklet, #454b 4.75

Europa Issue
Common Design Type

2000, May 9 *Perf. 11¾x12*

455 CD17 100e multi *1.25 .50*
a. Souvenir sheet of 3 *3.75 1.50*

Mail Delivery Systems of the Past — A74

Designs: 85e, Buoy mail. 140e, Zeppelin mail, vert.

Perf. 12x11¾, 11¾x12

2000, Oct. 9 Litho.

456-457 A74 Set of 2 2.75 1.10

Europa Type of Portugal

2001, May 9 Litho. *Perf. 12x11¾*

458 A677 105e Marine life *1.25 .45*
a. Souvenir sheet of 3 *3.75 3.75*

Angra do Heroismo World Heritage Site — A75

View of town, sea and: 53e, Archway. 85e, Monument. 140e, Window.

2001, June 4

459-461 A75 Set of 3 3.25 1.25

Souvenir Sheet

462 A75 350e Map 4.25 4.25

Europa Type of Portugal

2002, May 9 Litho. *Perf. 12x11¾*

463 A695 54c Clown, diff. *1.25 .50*
a. Souvenir sheet of 3, perf. 12½ *3.75 3.75*

Flowers A76

Designs: 28c, Scabiosa nitens. 45c, Viburnum tinus. 54c, Euphorbia azorica. 70c, Lysimachia nemorum. No. 468, €1.15, Bellis azorica. No. 469, €1.75, Spergularia azorica.
No. 470: a, €1.15, Azorina vidalli. b, €1.75, Senecio malvifolius.

2002, May 20 *Perf. 12x11¾*

464-469 A76 Set of 6 11.50 4.50

Souvenir Sheet

470 A76 Sheet of 2, #a-b 7.00 7.00

Windmills — A77

Designs: 43c, Ilha do Faial windmill, Azores. 54c, Onze-Lieve-Vrouw-Lombeek windmill, Belgium.

2002, July 12 Litho. *Perf. 11¾x12*

471-472 A77 Set of 2 2.75 .95

See Belgium Nos. 1925-1926.

Europa Type of Portugal

Design: Poster art by Sebastiao Rodrigues, 1983.

2003, May 5 Litho. *Perf. 12x12½*

473 A707 55c multi *1.25 .65*
a. Souvenir sheet of 2 *2.50 2.50*

Heritage of the Azores A78

Designs: 30c, Pineapple and plants. 43c, Grapes, vines. 55c, Tea leaves and plants. 70c, Tobacco leaf and plants.
No. 478: a, €1, Carnival dancers, Terceira Island. b, €2, Festival of the Holy Spirit.

2003, June 6 *Perf. 12x11¾*

474-477 A78 Set of 4 4.75 2.40

Souvenir Sheet

478 A78 Sheet of 2, #a-b 7.00 7.00

Europa Type of Portugal

Design: People in flower garden.

2004, May 10 Litho. *Perf. 13¼x14*

479 A734 56c multi *1.40 .70*
a. Souvenir sheet of 2 *2.80 2.80*

Worldwide Fund for Nature (WWF) A79

No. 480: a, Front of Makaira nigricans. b, Rear of Makaira nigricans, fish in background. c, Front of Tetrapturus albidus. d, Rear of Tetrapturus albidus, fish in background.

2004, June 28 *Perf. 13x13¼*

480 Horiz. strip of 4 5.00 2.50
a.-d. A79 30c Any single .75 .40

Europa Type of Portugal

Designs: No. 481, Torresmos. No. 482a, Polvo Guisado (stewed octopus).

2005, May 5 *Perf. 14x13¼*

481 A752 57c multi *1.50 .75*

Souvenir Sheet

482 Sheet of 2 #482a *3.00 3.00*
a. A752 57c multi *1.50 1.50*

Tourism A80

Designs: No. 483, 30c, Cow. No. 484, 30c, Arch. No. 485, 45c, Building. No. 486, 45c, Windmill. 57c, Arm of windmill, whale, pineapple. 74c, Pineapple, volcanic lake.
No. 489: a, 30c, Statue of Jesus. b, €1.55, Embroidered dove.

2005, May 13

483-488 A80 Set of 6 7.00 3.50

Souvenir Sheet

489 A80 Sheet of 2, #a-b 4.50 4.50

Europa A81

No. 491 — Children's drawings: a, Child with one leg. b, People of many colors.

2006, May 9 Litho. *Perf. 12x12½*

490 A81 60c shown 1.60 .80
a. Booklet pane of 1, perf. 12x11¾ 1.60 —

Souvenir Sheet

Perf. 12x11¾

491 A81 60c Sheet of 2, #a-b 3.25 3.25
c. Booklet pane of 2, #491a-491b 3.25 —

Booklet panes are separated from binding stub at left by row of rouletting.

Hydrothermal Vents — A82

Designs: 20c, Crabs and mussels. 30c, Fish and mussels. 75c, Active vent. €2, Shrimp.

2006, July 22 *Perf. 12½x13*

492-495 A82 Set of 4 8.50 4.25
493a Booklet pane of 2, #492-493 1.25 —
495a Souvenir sheet of 1 5.25 5.25
495b Booklet pane of 2, #494-495 7.25 —
495c Booklet pane of 1, #495 5.25 —

Lubrapex Intl. Philatelic Exhibition, Rio (#495a). Booklet panes are separated from binding stub at left by row of rouletting.

Wines of Pico Island A83

Designs: 30c, Wine barrels, vineyard, grapes. No. 497, 60c, Grapes and vineyard. No. 498, 75c, Grape harvesters, wine barrels. No. 499, €1, Wine press, workers moving wine barrel.

No. 500: a, 45c, Vineyard, small grape vines, grapes. b, 60c, Grapes, grape harvester. c, 75c, Grapes, vats, and barrels. d, €1, Barrels, men inspecting barrels.

2006, Sept. 14

496-499 A83 Set of 4 6.75 3.50
497a Booklet pane of 2, #496-497 2.25 —
499a Booklet pane of 2, #498-499 4.50 —

Souvenir Sheet

500 A83 Sheet of 4, #a-d 7.25 7.25
500e Booklet pane of 5, #500a-500d 7.25 —
Complete booklet, #490a, 491c, 493a, 495b, 495c, 497a, 499a, 500e 33.00

Booklet panes are separated from binding stub at left by row of rouletting. Complete booklet also contains a pane of four progressive proofs of No. 490. These were not valid for postage.

Europa A84

Designs: No. 501, Scout neckerchief.
No. 502: a, Knot. b, Scouts and leader at tent.

2007, May 9 Litho. *Perf. 12½x13*

501 A84 61c multi 1.75 .85
a. Booklet pane of 1 1.75 —

Souvenir Sheet

502 Sheet of 2 3.50 3.50
a.-b. A84 61c Either single 1.75 .85
c. Booklet pane of 2, #502a-502b 3.50 —

Scouting, cent.
Booklet panes are separated from binding stub at left by a row of rouletting.

Windmills A85

Designs: 30c, Windmill with red domed roof. No. 504, 45c, Windmill with red conical roof. 61c, White windmill with metal roof. 75c, Blue windmill.
No. 507: a, 45c, Windmill with black conical roof. b, €2, Red striped windmill.

2007, May 28

503-506 A85 Set of 4 5.75 3.00
506a Booklet pane of 4, #503-506 5.75 —

Souvenir Sheet

507 Sheet of 2 6.75 6.75
a. A85 45c multi 1.25 .60
b. A85 €2 multi 5.50 2.75
c. Booklet pane of 2, #507a-507b 6.75 —

Booklet panes are separated from binding stub at left by a row of rouletting.

Sept. 27, 1957 Eruption of Capelinhos Volcano, 50th Anniv. A86

Designs: 30c, Erupting volcano, as seen from ocean. 75c, Erupting volcano and lighthouse.
€2.45, Cliff and lighthouse.

2007, Sept. 27 Litho. *Perf. 12½x13*

508-509 A86 Set of 2 3.00 1.50
509a Booklet pane of 2, #508-509 3.00 —

Souvenir Sheet

510 A86 €2.45 multi 7.00 7.00
a. Booklet pane of 1 7.00 —
Complete booklet, #501a, 502c, 506a, 507c, 509a, 510a 28.00

No. 510 contains one 80x30mm stamp.
Booklet panes are separated from binding stub at left by a row of rouletting. Complete booklet also contains a pane of four progressive proofs of No. 501. These were not valid for postage.

Europa A87

Designs: No. 511, Man in rowboat, envelope, whale. No. 512a, Windmill, envelopes.

Perf. 12x11¾ Syncopated

2008, May 9 Litho.

511 A87 61c multi 1.90 .95
a. Booklet pane of 1 1.90 —

Souvenir Sheet

512 Sheet of 2, #511, 512a 4.00 2.00
a. A87 61c multi 1.90 .95
b. Booklet pane of 2, #511, 512b 4.00 —

Booklet panes are separated from binding stub at left by a row of rouletting.

Pyrrhula Murina A88

Various depictions of Pyrrhula murina: 30c, 61c, 75c, €1.
€2.45, Pyrrhula murina feeding. €2.95, Pyrrhula murina with beak open.

2008, May 28

513-516 A88 Set of 4 8.50 4.25
514a Booklet pane of 2, #513-514 3.00 —
516a Booklet pane of 2, #515-516 5.50 —

Souvenir Sheets

517-518 A88 Set of 2 17.00 8.50
517a Booklet pane of 1 7.75 —
518a Booklet pane of 1 9.25 —

Booklet panes are separated from binding stub at left by a row of rouletting.

Lighthouse Type of Portugal of 2008

2008, June 19

519 A835 61c Arnel Lighthouse 2.00 1.00
a. Booklet pane of 1 2.00 —
Complete booklet, #511a, 512b, 514a, 516a, 517a, 518a, 519a 34.00

Booklet panes are separated from binding stub at left by a row of rouletting. Complete booklet also contains a pane of four progressive proofs of No. 511. These were not valid for postage.

Biodiversity of Lakes and Lagoons — A89

Designs: 32c, Galinhola (bird). 68c, Sátiro dos Açores (butterflies). 80c, Libélula (dragonflies). €2, Cedro-das-ilhas (tree).
No. 524, €2.50, Améijoa-boa, polvo-comun, moreia-pintada (clams, octopus, moray eel). No. 525, €2.50, Zarro, marrequinha, garça-real (ducks and kingfisher).

Perf. 12x11¾ Syncopated

2009, Apr. 22 Litho.

520-523 A89 Set of 4 10.00 5.00
521a Booklet pane of 2, #520-521 2.60 —
523a Booklet pane of 2, #522-523 7.50 —

Souvenir Sheets

524-525 A89 Set of 2 13.50 6.75
524a Booklet pane of 1 6.75 —
525a Booklet pane of 1 6.75 —

Nos. 524-525 each contain one 80x30mm stamp.
Booklet panes are separated from binding stub at left by a row of rouletting.

Europa A90

Designs: No. 526, Dish antenna of European Space Agency Satellite Tracking Center, Santa Maria Island. No. 527a, Ribeira Grande Astronomical Observatory, Sao Miguel Island.

2009, May 8
526 A90 68c multi 1.90 .95
a. Booklet pane of 1 1.90 —

Souvenir Sheet

527 Sheet of 2, #526, 527a 4.00 2.00
a. A90 68c multi 1.90 .95
b. Booklet pane of 2, #526, 527a 4.00 —
Complete booklet, #521a, 523a, 524a, 525a, 526a, 527b, Portugal #3145a 35.50

Intl. Year of Astronomy.

Booklet panes are separated from binding stub at left by a row of rouletting. Complete booklet also contains a pane of 4 progressive proofs of No. 526. These were not valid for postage.

Europa — A91

Characters from children's story: No. 528, Woman in green. No. 529a, King on horseback in blue.

Perf. 11¾x12 Syncopated

2010, May 7 **Litho.**
528 A91 68c multi 1.75 .85
a. Booklet pane of 1 1.75 —

Souvenir Sheet

529 Sheet of 2, #528, 529a 3.50 1.75
a. A91 68c multi 1.75 .85
b. Booklet pane of 2, #528, 529a 3.50 —

Issued: Nos. 528a, 529b, Nov.

Booklet panes are separated from binding stub at left by a row of rouletting.

Marine Invertebrates — A92

Designs: 32c, Dardanus callidus. 68c, Alicia mirabilis. 80c, Ophidiaster ophidianus. No. 533, €2, Sabella spallanzanii.

No. 534, €2, Grapsus adscencionis. No. 535, €2, Sphaerechinus granularis.

Perf. 12x11¾ Syncopated

2010, July 1
530-533 A92 Set of 4 9.50 4.75
531a Booklet pane of 2, #530-531 2.50 —
533a Booklet pane of 2, #532-533 7.00 —

Souvenir Sheets

534-535 A92 Set of 2 10.00 5.00
534a Booklet pane of 1 5.00 —
535a Booklet pane of 1 5.00 —
Complete booklet, #528a, 529b, 531a, 533a, 534a, 535a 25.00

Issued: Nos. 531a, 533a, 534a, 535a, Nov.

Booklet panes are separated from binding stub at left by a row of rouletting.

Europa A93

Designs: No. 536, Cows in pasture, bird in tree. No. 537a, Cows in pasture.

2011, May 9
536 A93 68c multi 2.00 1.00
a. Booklet pane of 1 2.00 —

Souvenir Sheet

537 Sheet of 2, #536, 537a 4.00 2.00
a. A93 68c multi 2.00 1.00
b. Booklet pane of 2, #536, 537a 4.00 —

Intl. Year of Forests. See No. 577.

Azores Whaling Heritage A94

Designs: 32c, Whaling boats from Azores and America. 68c, Harpooned whale, whalers. 80c, Whale hunt, whalers, whale boats. €2, Whale caught near lighthouse, whale on shore, religious statue.

No. 542, €1.75, Children, whalers and boats. No. 543, €2.30, Whalers capturing whale, whaler and boat, partially-constructed whale boat.

2011, Aug. 26
538-541 A94 Set of 4 10.50 5.25
539a Booklet pane of 2, #538-539 2.75 —
541a Booklet pane of 2, #540-541 7.75 —

Souvenir Sheets

542-543 A94 Set of 2 11.00 5.50
542a Booklet pane of 1 4.75 —
543a Booklet pane of 1 6.25 —
Complete booklet, #536a, 537b, 539a, 541a, 542a, 543a, Portugal #3331a 31.00

Europa A95

Designs: No. 544, Steamer Funchal. No. 545a, Pico waterfront.

2012, May 9
544 A95 68c multi 1.75 .85
a. Booklet pane of 1 1.75 —

Souvenir Sheet

545 Sheet of 2, #544, 545a 3.50 1.75
a. A95 68c multi 1.75 .85
b. Booklet pane of 2, #544, 545a 3.50 —

Issued: Nos. 544a, 545b, Nov.

Booklet panes are separated from binding stub at left by a row of rouletting. See No. 578.

Aerial Views of Towns — A96

Designs: 32c, Almas. 68c, D'Além Norte. 80c, Grande. €2, Sao Joao.

No. 550, €1.75, Caldeira de Santo Cristo. No. 551, €2.30, Cubres.

Perf. 11¾x12 Syncopated

2012, June 5
546-549 A96 Set of 4 9.50 4.75
547a Booklet pane of 2, #546-547 2.60 —
549a Booklet pane of 2, #548-549 7.25 —

Souvenir Sheets

550-551 A96 Set of 2 10.50 5.25
550a Booklet pane of 1 4.50 —
551a Booklet pane of 1 6.00 —
Complete booklet, #544a, 545b, 547a, 549a, 550a, 551a 26.00

Issued: Nos. 547a, 549a, 550a, 551a, Nov.

Booklet panes are separated from binding stub at left by a row of rouletting. Complete booklet contains a pane of four imperforate progressive proofs of No. 544. These were not valid for postage. See No. 579.

Europa A97

Designs: No. 552, Portuguese postal motorcycle. No. 553a, Rider on Portuguese postal motorcycle.

Perf. 12x11¾ Syncopated

2013, May 9 **Litho.**
552 A97 70c multi 1.90 .95
a. Booklet pane of 1 1.90 —

Souvenir Sheet

553 Sheet of 2, #552, 553a 3.80 1.90
a. A97 70c multi 1.90 .95
b. Booklet pane of 2, #552, 553a 3.80 —

Booklet panes are separated from binding stub at left by a row of rouletting.

Apiculture A98

Designs: 36c, Beekeepers tending hives, Sao Jorge. 70c, Beekeeper using smoker near hives, Pico. 80c, Beekeepers, bees and hives, Santa María. No. 557, €1.70, Beekeeper near hives near fruit trees, Flores.

No. 558, €1.70, Beehives on farm, Sao Miguel. €1.90, Beekeepers, hives, cattle, Terceira.

Perf. 12x11¾ Syncopated

2013, Oct. 9 **Litho.**
554-557 A98 Set of 4 9.75 5.00
555a Booklet pane of 2, #554-555 3.00 —
557a Booklet pane of 2, #556-557 6.75 —

Souvenir Sheets

558-559 A98 Set of 2 9.75 5.00
558a Booklet pane of 1 4.50 —
559a Booklet pane of 1 5.25 —
Complete booklet, #552a, 553b, 555a, 557a, 558a, 559a 25.50

Nos. 558-559 each contain one 80x30mm stamp. See No. 580.

Booklet panes are separated from binding stub at left by a row of rouletting. Complete booklet also contains a pane of 4 progressive proofs of No. 552. These were not valid for postage.

Europa — A99

Designs: No. 560, Viola da terra player. No. 561a, Viola da terra.

Perf. 11¾x12 Syncopated

2014, May 9 **Litho.**
560 A99 E multi 2.00 1.00
a. Booklet pane of 1 2.00 —

Souvenir Sheet

561 Sheet of 2, #560, 561a 4.00 2.00
a. A99 E multi 2.00 1.00
b. Booklet pane of 2, #560, 561a 4.00 —

On day of issue Nos. 560 and 561a each sold for 72c.

Booklet panes are separated from binding stub at left by a row of rouletting.

Airplanes A100

Designs: 42c, Boeing 314 Clipper. 50c, Douglas C-47. 72c, Lockheed Constellation. 80c, Hawker-Siddeley HS-748 Avro.

€1, Boeing 314 Clipper, diff. €1.70, Lockheed Super Constellation.

Perf. 12x11¾ Syncopated

2014, Sept. 4 **Litho.**
562-565 A100 Set of 4 6.25 3.25
563a Booklet pane of 2, #562-563 2.40 —
565a Booklet pane of 2, #564-565 4.00 —

Souvenir Sheets

566-567 A100 Set of 2 7.00 3.50
566a Booklet pane of 1 2.60 —
567a Booklet pane of 1 4.50 —
Complete booklet, #560a, 561b, 563a, 565a, 566a, 567a 19.50

Nos. 566-567 each contain one 80x30mm stamp.

Booklet panes are separated from binding stub at left by a row of rouletting. Complete booklet also contains a pane of 4 progressive proofs of No. 560. These were not valid for postage.

Figurines Type of Portugal of 2015

Perf. 12x11¾ Syncopated

2015, Apr. 21 **Litho.**
568 A1007 80c Azores figurines 1.90 .95

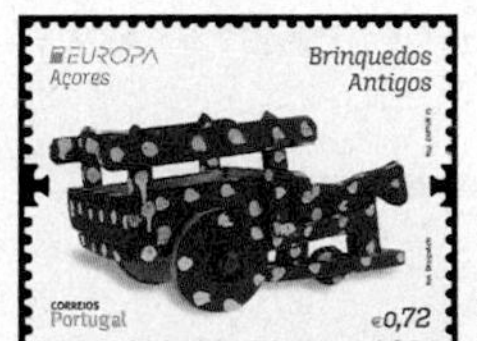

Europa A101

Old toys: No. 569, Horse-drawn cart. No. 570a, Stove.

Perf. 12x11¾ Syncopated

2015, May 8 **Litho.**
569 A101 72c multi 1.60 .80

Souvenir Sheet

570 Sheet of 2, #569, 570a 3.25 1.60
a. A101 72c multi 1.60 .80

Handicrafts A102

Designs: 45c, Ceramics. 72c, Weaving. 80c, Woodworking. €1, Lace.

€1.80, Plant fiber items. €2, Embroidery.

Perf. 11¾x12 Syncopated

2015, May 8 **Litho.**
571-574 A102 Set of 4 6.50 3.25

Souvenir Sheets

575-576 A102 Set of 2 8.50 4.25

Types of 2011-13

Die Cut Perf. 10½

2015, Oct. 23 **Litho.**

Self-Adhesive

577 A93 E Like #536 1.60 .80
578 A95 E Like #544 1.60 .80
579 A96 E Like #547 1.60 .80
580 A98 E Like #555 1.60 .80
Nos. 577-580 (4) 6.40 3.20

Nos. 577-580 each sold for 72c on day of issue.

MADEIRA

Type of Azores, 1980

6.50e, Madeira #2. 19.50e, Madeira #5.

1980, Jan. 2 **Litho.** ***Perf. 12***
66 A33 6.50e multi .25 .25
67 A33 19.50e multi .85 .55
a. Souvenir sheet of 2, #66-67 3.75 3.75

No. 67a exists overprinted for Capex 87.

Grapes and Wine — A7

1980, Sept. 17 Litho. *Perf. 12x11½*

68 A7 50c Bullock cart .25 .25
69 A7 1e shown .25 .25
70 A7 5e Produce map of Madeira .40 .25
71 A7 6.50e Basket and lace .50 .25
72 A7 8e Orchid .80 .25
73 A7 30e Madeira boat 1.60 .45
Nos. 68-73 (6) 3.80 1.70

World Tourism Conf., Manila, Sept. 27.

Europa Issue

O Bailinho Folk Dance A8

1981, May 11 Litho. *Perf. 12*

74 A8 22e multi *1.25 .65*
a. Souvenir sheet of 2 *4.00 1.50*

Explorer Ship — A9

1981, July 1 Litho. *Perf. 12x11½*

75 A9 8.50e shown .45 .25
76 A9 33.50e Map 1.60 .55

Discovery of Madeira anniv.

A10

Designs: Local flora.

1981, Oct. 6 Litho. *Perf. 12½x12*

77 A10 7e Dactylorhiza foliosa .30 .25
78 A10 8.50e Echium candicans .35 .25
79 A10 20e Geranium maderense .65 .35
80 A10 50e Isoplexis sceptrum 1.40 .75
a. Booklet pane of 4, #77-80 5.00
Nos. 77-80 (4) 2.70 1.60

See Nos. 82-85, 90-93.

Europa Type of Portugal

1982, May 3 Litho. *Perf. 12x11½*

81 A405 33.50e Sugar mills, 15th cent. 1.75 .65
a. Souvenir sheet of 3 18.00 3.00

Type of 1981

9e, Goodyera macrophylla. 10e, Armeria maderensis. 27e, Viola paradoxa. 33.50e, Scilla maderensis.

1982, Aug. 31 Litho. *Perf. 12½x12*

82 A10 9e multicolored .40 .25
83 A10 10e multicolored .45 .25
84 A10 27e multicolored 1.10 .50
85 A10 33.50e multicolored 1.10 .70
a. Booklet pane of 4, #82-85 5.00
Nos. 82-85 (4) 3.05 1.70

A12

1982, Dec. 15 Litho. *Perf. 13½*

86 A12 27e Brinco dancing dolls 1.10 .60
87 A12 33.50e Dancers 1.60 .80

Europa 1983 A13

1983, May 5 Litho. *Perf. 12½*

88 A13 37.50e Levadas irrigation system *2.00 .50*
a. Souvenir sheet of 3 *10.00 3.00*

Flag of the Autonomous Region — A14

1983, July 1 Litho. *Perf. 12x11½*

89 A14 12.50e multi .65 .25

Flower Type of 1981

1983, Oct. 19 Litho. *Perf. 12½x12*

90 A10 12.50e Matthiola maderensis .25 .25
91 A10 30e Erica maderensis .75 .25
92 A10 37.50e Cirsium latifolium .85 .55
93 A10 100e Clethra arborea 2.00 .80
a. Booklet pane of 4, #90-93 5.00
Nos. 90-93 (4) 3.85 1.85

Europa Type of Portugal

1984, May 2 Litho. *Perf. 12x11½*

94 A427 51e multi *3.00 .95*
a. Souvenir sheet of 3 *10.00 4.00*

Madeira Rally (Auto Race), 25th Anniv. — A16

Various cars.

1984, Aug. 3 Litho. *Perf. 11½x12*

95 A16 16e multicolored .45 .25
96 A16 51e multicolored 1.60 .60

Traditional Means of Transportation — A17

1984, Nov. 22 *Perf. 12*

97 A17 16e Mountain sledge .30 .25
98 A17 35e Hammock .85 .50
99 A17 40e Winebag carriers' procession 1.25 .50
100 A17 51e Carreira Boat 1.50 .65
a. Booklet pane of 4, Nos. 97-100 9.00
Nos. 97-100 (4) 3.90 1.90

See Nos. 104-107.

Europa Type of Portugal

1985, May 6 Litho. *Perf. 11½x12*

101 A435 60e Man playing guitar *2.75 .80*
a. Souvenir sheet of 3 *10.00 3.00*

Marine Life — A19

1985, July 5 Litho. *Perf. 12*

102 A19 40e Aphanopus carbo 1.10 .45
103 A19 60e Lampris guttatus 1.60 .65

See Nos. 108-109.

Transportation type of 1984

1985, Sept. 11 Litho. *Perf. 12x11½*

104 A17 20e Ox-drawn sledge .35 .25
105 A17 40e Mountain train .90 .40
106 A17 46e Fish vendors 1.25 .80
107 A17 60e Coastal steamer 1.50 .70
a. Booklet pane of 4, Nos. 104-107 5.00
Nos. 104-107 (4) 4.00 2.15

Marine Life Type of 1985

1986, Jan. 7 Litho.

108 A19 20e Thunnus obesus .55 .25
109 A19 75e Beryx decadactylus 2.50 .75

Europa Type of Portugal

1986, May 5 Litho.

110 A447 68.50e Great Shearwater *2.75 .90*
a. Souvenir sheet of 3 *12.00 3.50*

Forts in Funchal and Machico A21

22.50e, Sao Lourenco, 1583. 52.50e, Sao Joao do Pico, 1611. 68.50e, Sao Tiago, 1614. 100e, Sao do Amparo, 1706.

1986, July 1 Litho. *Perf. 12*

111 A21 22.50e multi .50 .25
112 A21 52.50e multi 1.50 .70
113 A21 68.50e multi 2.25 .90
114 A21 100e multi 3.00 .75
a. Booklet pane of 4, #111-114 7.50
Nos. 111-114 (4) 7.25 2.60

A22

Indigenous birds: 25e, Regulus ignicapillus madeirensis. 57e, Columba trocaz. 74.50e, Tyto alba schmitzi. 125e, Pterodroma madeira.

1987, Mar. 6 Litho.

115 A22 25e multi .50 .25
116 A22 57e multi 1.60 .80
117 A22 74.50e multi 2.25 1.10
118 A22 125e multi 3.00 1.25
a. Booklet pane of 4, #115-118 7.50
Nos. 115-118 (4) 7.35 3.40

See Nos. 123-126.

Europa Type of Portugal

Modern Architecture: Social Services Center, Funchal, designed by Raul Chorao Ramalho.

1987, May 5 Litho. *Perf. 12*

119 A456 74.50e multicolored *3.00 .90*
a. Souvenir sheet of 4 *11.00 4.00*

A24

Natl. Monuments — 51e, Funchal Castle, 15th cent. 74.50e, Old Town Hall, Santa Cruz, 16th cent.

1987, July 1 *Perf. 12x12½*

120 A24 51e multi 1.40 .70
121 A24 74.50e multi 1.75 .70

Europa Type of Portugal

Transportation Modern mail boat PS 13 TL.

1988, Apr. 21 Litho. *Perf. 12*

122 A466 80e multicolored *9.00 1.20*
a. Souvenir sheet of 4 *18.00 5.00*

Bird Type of 1987

1988, June 15 Litho.

123 A22 27e Erithacus rubecula .45 .25
124 A22 60e Petronia 1.40 .75
125 A22 80e Fringilla coelebs 2.00 .80
126 A22 100e Accipiter nisus 2.25 .80
a. Booklet pane of 4, #123-126 6.00
Nos. 123-126 (4) 6.10 2.60

Portraits of Christopher Columbus and Purported Residences on Madeira A27

55e, Funchal, 1480-1481, vert. 80e, Porto Santo.

1988, July 1 Litho.

127 A27 55e multicolored 1.50 .60
128 A27 80e multicolored 1.75 .70

Europa Type of Portugal

Children's toys.

1989, Apr. 26 Litho.

129 A476 80e Kite *2.50 .80*

Souvenir Sheet

130 Sheet, 2 each #129, 130a *12.00 5.00*
a. A476 80e Kite, diff. *2.50 1.75*

Monuments A29

Churches: 29e, Church of the Colegio (St. John the Evangelist Church). 87e, Santa Clara Church and convent.

1989, July 28 Litho.

131 A29 29e multi .45 .25
132 A29 87e multi 1.90 .90

Fish — A30

29e, Argyropelecus aculeatus. 60e, Pseudolepidaplois scrofa. 87e, Coris julis. 100e, Scorpaena maderensis.

1989, Sept. 20 Litho.

133 A30 29e multi .45 .25
134 A30 60e multi 1.25 .65
135 A30 87e multi 2.00 .85

136 A30 100e multi 2.00 1.25
a. Booklet pane of 4, #133-136 6.00
Nos. 133-136 (4) 5.70 3.00

Europa Type of Portugal

1990, Apr. 11 Litho. *Perf. 12x11½*
137 A486 80e Zarco P.O. *2.25 .55*

Souvenir Sheet

138 Sheet, 2 ea #137, 138a *12.00 4.00*
a. A486 80e Porto da Cruz P.O. *2.25 1.75*

Subtropical Fruits and Plants — A32

1990, June 5 Litho. *Perf. 12*
139 A32 5e Banana .25 .25
140 A32 32e Avocado .45 .25
141 A32 60e Sugar apple 1.25 .55
142 A32 100e Passion fruit 1.90 .85
Nos. 139-142 (4) 3.85 1.90

Perf. 13½ Vert.

139a A32 5e 1.50 1.50
140a A32 32e 1.50 1.50
141a A32 60e 1.50 1.50
142a A32 100e 1.50 1.50
b. Bklt. pane of 4, #139a-142a 6.00

See Nos. 153-160.

Boats of Madeira A33

1990, Aug. 24 *Perf. 12*
143 A33 32e Tuna .45 .25
144 A33 60e Desert islands 1.00 .45
145 A33 70e Maneiro 1.25 .65
146 A33 95e Chavelha 1.75 .90
Nos. 143-146 (4) 4.45 2.25

See Nos. 162-165.

Columba Trocaz Heineken — A34

1991, Jan. 23 Litho. *Perf. 12*
147 35e shown 1.10 .40
148 35e On branch 1.10 .40
149 35e In flight 1.10 .40
150 35e On nest 1.10 .40
a. A34 Strip of 4, #147-150 5.00 5.00

Europa A35

1991, Apr. 11 Litho. *Perf. 12*
151 A35 80e ERS-1 *1.25 .75*

Souvenir Sheet

152 Sheet, 2 each #151, 152a *12.00 4.00*
a. A35 80e SPOT *2.25 1.75*

Subtropical Fruits Type of 1990

1991, June 7 Litho. *Perf. 12*
153 A32 35e Mango .50 .25
154 A32 65e Surinam cherry 1.00 .50
155 A32 70e Brazilian guava 1.25 .60
156 A32 110e Papaya 1.60 .65
Nos. 153-156 (4) 4.35 2.00

Perf. 13½ Vert.

153a A32 35e 1.10 1.10
154a A32 65e 1.10 1.10
155a A32 70e 1.10 1.10
156a A32 110e 1.10 1.10
b. Bklt. pane of 4, #153a-156a 5.00

1992, Feb. 21 Litho. *Perf. 11½x12*
157 A32 10e Prickly pear .25 .25
158 A32 38e Tree tomato .45 .25
159 A32 85e Ceriman 1.30 .65
160 A32 125e Guava 1.90 .95
Nos. 157-160 (4) 3.90 2.10

Perf. 13½ Vert.

157a A32 10e .25 .25
158a A32 38e .45 .25
159a A32 85e 1.30 .65
160a A32 125e 1.90 .95
b. Bklt. pane of 4, #157a-160a 5.00

Europa Type of Portugal

Europa: 85e, Columbus at Funchal.

1992, May 22 Litho. *Perf. 12x11½*
161 A514 85e gold & multi *4.00 .70*

Ships Type of 1990

1992, Sept. 18 Litho. *Perf. 12x11½*
162 A33 38e Gaviao .65 .30
163 A33 65e Independencia 1.10 .55
164 A33 85e Madeirense 1.40 .70
165 A33 120e Funchalense 2.00 1.00
Nos. 162-165 (4) 5.15 2.55

Contemporary Paintings by Lourdes Castro — A36

Europa: No. 166, Shadow Projection of Christa Maar, 1968. No. 167a, Shadow Projection of a Dahlia, c. 1970.

1993, May 5 Litho. *Perf. 11½x12*
166 A36 90e multicolored *1.25 .60*

Souvenir Sheet

167 Sheet, 2 each #166, 167a *6.00 4.00*
a. A36 90e multicolored *1.25 .60*

Nature Preservation — A37

Monachus monachus: No. 168, Adult on rock. No. 169, Swimming. No. 170, Mother nursing pup. No. 171, Two on rocks.

1993, June 30 Litho. *Perf. 12x11½*
168 42e multicolored 1.00 .50
169 42e multicolored 1.00 .50
170 42e multicolored 1.00 .50
171 42e multicolored 1.00 .50
a. A37 Strip of 4, #168-171 4.50 2.00

Architecture A38

Designs: 42e, Window from Sao Francisco Convent, Funchal. 130e, Window of Mercy (Old Hospital), Funchal.

1993, July 30 *Perf. 11½x12*
172 A38 42e multicolored .50 .25
173 A38 130e multicolored 1.60 .80

Europa Type of Portugal

Discoveries: No. 174, Native with bow and arrows. No. 175a, Palm tree.

1994, May 5 Litho. *Perf. 12*
174 A541 100e multicolored *1.25 .60*

Souvenir Sheet

175 Sheet, 2 each, #174-175a *6.00 4.00*
a. A541 100e multicolored *1.25 .60*

Native Handicrafts A39

1994, May 5 *Perf. 12x11½*
176 A39 45e Embroidery .55 .30
177 A39 75e Tapestry .90 .45
178 A39 100e Shoes 1.25 .60
179 A39 140e Wicker work 1.60 .85
Nos. 176-179 (4) 4.30 2.20

Perf. 11½ Vert.

176a A39 45e .55 .30
177a A39 75e .90 .45
178a A39 100e 1.25 .60
179a A39 140e 1.60 .85
b. Bklt. pane of 4, #176a-179a 6.00

Arms of Madeira Districts — A40

1994, July 1 Litho. *Perf. 11½x12*
180 A40 45e Funchal .55 .30
181 A40 140e Porto Santo 1.90 .95

Traditional Arts & Crafts — A41

Designs: 45e, Chicken puppets made of flour paste. 80e, Inlaid wood furniture piece. 95e, Wicker bird cage. 135e, Knitted wool bonnet.

1995, June 30 Litho. *Perf. 11½x12*
182 A41 45e multicolored .60 .30
183 A41 80e multicolored 1.10 .55
184 A41 95e multicolored 1.25 .65
185 A41 135e multicolored 1.90 .95
Nos. 182-185 (4) 4.85 2.45

Perf. 11½ Vert.

182a A41 45e .60 .30
183a A41 80e 1.10 .55
184a A41 95e 1.25 .65
185a A41 135e 1.90 .95
b. Booklet pane, #182a-185a 6.00
Complete booklet, #185b 6.00

Famous Woman Type of Azores, 1996

Europa: Guiomar Vilhena (1705-89), entrepeneur.

1996, May 3 Litho. *Perf. 12*
186 A69 98e multicolored *1.25 .60*
a. Souvenir sheet of 3 *3.75 1.90*

Paintings from Flemish Group, Museum of Sacred Paintings of Funchal (Madeira) A42

Designs: 47e, The Adoration of the Magi, vert. 78e, St. Mary Magdalene, vert. 98e, Annunciation. 140e, St. Peter, St. Paul and St. Andrew.

Perf. 11½x12, 12x11½

1996, July 1 Litho.
187 A42 47e multicolored .60 .30
188 A42 78e multicolored 1.00 .50
189 A42 98e multicolored 1.40 .65
190 A42 140e multicolored 1.90 .90
Nos. 187-190 (4) 4.90 2.35

Perf. 11½ on 2 Sides

187a A42 47e .60 .30
188a A42 78e 1.00 .50
189a A42 98e 1.40 .65
190a A42 140e 1.90 .90
b. Booklet pane, #187a-190a 6.00
Complete booklet, #190b 6.00

Moths & Butterflies A43

Designs: 49e, Eumichtis albostigmata. 80e, Menophra maderae. 100e, Vanessa indica vulcania. 140e, Pieris brassicae wollastoni.

1997, Feb. 12 Litho. *Perf. 12*
191 A43 49e multicolored .60 .30
192 A43 80e multicolored .95 .45
193 A43 100e multicolored 1.25 .60
194 A43 140e multicolored 1.60 .80
Nos. 191-194 (4) 4.40 2.15

Perf. 11½ Vert.

191a A43 49e multicolored .60 .30
192a A43 80e multicolored .95 .45
193a A43 100e multicolored 1.25 .60
194a A43 140e multicolored 1.60 .80
b. Booklet pane, #191a-194a 6.00
Complete booklet, #194b 6.00

See Nos. 197-200.

Stories and Legends Type of Portugal

Europa: Man holding woman from "Legend of Machico," horiz.

1997, May 5 Litho. *Perf. 12*
195 A599 100e multicolored *1.25 .55*
a. Souvenir sheet of 3 *5.00 3.00*

Natl. Festivals Type of Portugal

1998, May 21 Litho. *Perf. 12*
196 A621 100e New Year's Eve *1.25 .55*
a. Souvenir sheet of 3 *5.00 3.00*

Europa.

Moths and Butterflies Type of 1997

Designs: 50e, Gonepteryx cleopatra. 85e, Xanthorhoe rupicola. 100e, Noctua teixeirai. 140e, Xenochlorodes nubigena.

1998, Sept. 6 Litho. *Perf. 12*
197 A43 50e multicolored .60 .30
198 A43 85e multicolored 1.00 .45
199 A43 100e multicolored 1.25 .55
200 A43 140e multicolored 1.60 .80
a. Booklet pane, #197-200, perf. 12 vert. 6.00
Complete booklet, #200a 6.00
Nos. 197-200 (4) 4.45 2.10

Europa Type of Portugal

100e, Flowers, Madeira Island Natural Park.

1999, May 5 Litho. *Perf. 12x11¾*
201 A641 100e multi *1.25 .50*
a. Souvenir sheet of 3 *3.75 3.75*

Glazed Tiles From Frederico de Freitas Museum, Funchal A44

Designs: 51e, Griffin, from Middle East, 13th-14th cent. 80e, Flower, from England, 19th-20th cent. 95e, Bird, from Persia, 14th cent. 100e, Geometric, from Moorish Spain, 13th cent. 140e, Ship, from Holland, 18th cent. 210e, Flowers from Syria, 13th-14th cent.

1999, July 1
202 A44 51e multicolored .60 .25
203 A44 80e multicolored .95 .40
204 A44 95e multicolored 1.10 .50
205 A44 100e multicolored 1.25 .50
206 A44 140e multicolored 1.75 .75
207 A44 210e multicolored 2.50 1.10
a. Souvenir sheet of 6, #202-207 8.50 8.50
Nos. 202-207 (6) 8.15 3.50

Europa Issue
Common Design Type

2000, May 9 *Perf. 11¾x12*
208 CD17 100e multi 1.25 .50
a. Souvenir sheet of 3 3.75 3.75

Plants from Laurissilva Forest A45

52e, Purple orchid. 85e, White orchid. No. 211, 100e, Folhado. No. 212, 100e, Laurel tree. 140e, Barbusano. 350e, Visco.

2000, July 4 Litho. *Perf. 12x11¾*
209-214 A45 Set of 6 10.00 4.00
214a Souvenir sheet, #209-214 10.00 10.00

Expansion of Madeira Airport A46

2000, Sept. 15
215 A46 140e multi 1.75 .70
a. Souvenir sheet of 1 2.50 .70

Europa Type of Portugal

2001, May 9 Litho. *Perf. 12x11¾*
216 A677 105e Signals 1.25 .45
a. Souvenir sheet of 3 5.00 3.75

Scenes of Traditional Life — A47

Designs: 53e, People retruning home. 85e, On the road to the marketplace. 105e, Traditional clothes.
350e, Leisure time.

2001, July 19 Litho. *Perf. 12x11¾*
217-219 A47 Set of 3 3.00 1.10

Souvenir Sheet

220 A47 350e multi 4.25 4.25

Europa Type of Portugal

2002, May 9 Litho. *Perf. 12x11¾*
221 A695 54c Clown, diff. 1.25 .50
a. Souvenir sheet of 3, perf. 12½ 5.00 3.00

Worldwide Fund for Nature (WWF) — A48

Streptopelia turtur: a, On nest with chicks. b, On branch, with wings extended. c, Pair on branch. d, One on branch.

2002, Aug. 30 Litho. *Perf. 11¾x12*
222 A48 28c Horiz. strip or block of 4, #a.-d. 4.50 2.50

Europa Type of Portugal

Design: Poster art by José Brandao, 1992.

2003, May 5 Litho. *Perf. 12x12½*
223 A707 55c multi 1.25 .65
a. Souvenir sheet of 2 2.50 2.50

Items in Madeira Museums A49

Designs: 30c, Funchal Bay, by W. G. James. 43c, Creche, by Manuel Orlando Noronha Gois. 55c, O Largo da Fonte, by Andrew Picken. 70c, Le Depart, by Martha Teles.

No. 228: a, €1, Photograph of Vicente Gomes da Silva. b, €2, Photograph of Jorge Bettencourt.

2003, Aug. 30 Litho. *Perf. 12x11¾*
224-227 A49 Set of 4 4.50 2.25

Souvenir Sheet

228 A49 Sheet of 2, #a-b 6.75 6.75

Europa Type of Portugal

Design: Hiker in flower garden.

2004, May 10 Litho. *Perf. 13¼x14*
229 A734 56c multi 1.40 .70
a. Souvenir sheet of 2 2.80 2.80

Flora and Fauna of the Selvagens Islands A50

Designs: 30c, Pelagodroma marina hypoleuca. 45c, Monanthes lowei. 72c, Tarentola bischoffi.

2004, May 24 *Perf. 13x13¼*
230-232 A50 Set of 3 3.50 1.75
232a Souvenir sheet, #230-232 3.50 3.50

Europa Type of Portugal

Designs: No. 233, Espetada em pau de louro. No. 234a, Filete de espada (Scabbard fish filet).

2005, May 5 *Perf. 14x13¼*
233 A752 57c multi 1.50 .75

Souvenir Sheet

234 Sheet of 2 #234a 3.00 3.00
a. A752 57c multi 1.50 1.50

Tourism A51

Designs: No. 235, 30c, Coastal village, offshore rocks, flowers. No. 236, 30c, Flowers, bird, waterfall. No. 237, 45c, Man and woman on footpath, golf course. No. 238, 45c, Windmill on beach. 57c, Horses and riders, scuba diver. 74c, Flowers, fireworks.

No. 241: a, 30c, Wicker chair, girls with flower baskets, lace. b, €1.55, Lace, clock tower.

2005, July 1 Litho. *Perf. 14x13¼*
235-240 A51 Set of 6 6.75 3.50

Souvenir Sheet

241 A51 Sheet of 2, #a-b 4.50 4.50

Flowers A52

Designs: 30c, Euphorbia pulcherrima. No. 243, 45c, Aloe arborescens. 57c, Senna didymobotrya. 74c, Anthurium andraeanum. €1, Strelitzia reginae. €2, Hydrangea macrophylla.

No. 248, 45c: a, Rosa cultivar. b, Leucospermum nutans. c, Paphiopedilum insigne. d, Hippeastrum vittatum.

No. 249, 45c: a, Bougainvillea cultivar. b, Cymbidium cultivar. c, Hibiscus rosa-sinensis. d, Erythrina crista-galli.

2006, Mar. 7 Litho. *Perf. 12x11¾*
242-247 A52 Set of 6 12.50 6.25
243a Booklet pane of 2, #242-243 1.90 —
245a Booklet pane of 2, #244-245 3.25 —
247a Booklet pane of 2, #246-247 7.50 —

Souvenir Sheets

248 Sheet of 4 4.50 4.50
a.-d. A52 45c Any single 1.10 .55
e. Booklet pane of 4, #248a-248d 4.50 —
249 Sheet of 4 4.50 4.50
a.-d. A52 45c Any single 1.10 .55
e. Booklet pane of 4, #249a-249d 4.50 —

Booklet panes are separated from binding stub at left by row of rouletting.

Europa A53

No. 251 — Children's drawings: a, Children in swimming pool. b, Boy walking dog.

2006, May 9 Litho. *Perf. 12x12½*
250 A53 60c shown 1.60 .80
a. Booklet pane of 1, perf. 12x11¾ 1.60 —

Souvenir Sheet
Perf. 12x11¾

251 A53 60c Sheet of 2, #a-b 3.25 3.25
c. Booklet pane of 2, #251a-251b 3.25 —

Booklet panes are separated from binding stub at left by row of rouletting.

Wines of Madeira A54

Designs: 30c, Wine bottles, terraces. 52c, Bottles, grape harvesters. No. 254, 60c, Bottles, barrels in cellar. No. 255, 75c, Bottles, barrels, wine glass.

No. 256: a, 45c, Vineyards. b, 60c, Grape harvester, grape masher. c, 75c, Bottles. d, €1, Bottles, barrels, grapes.

2006, July 1 *Perf. 12½x13*
252-255 A54 Set of 4 5.75 3.00
253a Booklet pane of 2, #252-253 2.25 —
255a Booklet pane of 2, #254-255 3.50 —

Souvenir Sheet

256 A54 Sheet of 4, #a-d 7.25 7.25
e. Booklet pane of 4, #256a-256d 7.25 —
Complete booklet, #243a, 245a, 247a, 248e, 249e, 250a, 251c, 253a, 255a, 256e 40.00

Booklet panes are separated from binding stub at left by row of rouletting. Complete booklet also contains a pane of four progressive proofs of No. 250. These were not valid for postage.

Marine Creatures A55

Designs: 30c Monachus monachus. 45c, Caretta caretta. No. 259, 61c, Calonectris diomedea borealis. 75c, Aphanopus carbo.

No. 261, 61c: a, Telmatactis cricoides. b, Charonia lampas. c, Patella aspera. d, Sparisoma cretense.

2007, Apr. 17 Litho. *Perf. 12½x13*
257-260 A55 Set of 4 5.75 3.00
260a Booklet pane of 4, #257-260 5.75 —

Souvenir Sheet

261 Sheet of 4 7.00 7.00
a.-d. A55 61c Any single 1.75 .85
e. Booklet pane of 4, #261a-261d 7.00 —

Booklet panes are separated from binding stub at left by a row of rouletting.

Europa A56

Designs: No. 262, Scout emblem.

No. 263: a, Lord Robert Baden-Powell. b, Scout hat.

2007, May 9
262 A56 61c multi 1.75 .85
a. Booklet pane of 1 1.75 —

Souvenir Sheet

263 Sheet of 2 3.50 3.50
a.-b. A56 61c Either single 1.75 .85
c. Booklet pane of 2, #263a-263b 3.50 —

Scouting, cent.

Booklet panes are separated from binding stub at left by a row of rouletting.

Sugar Mills A57

Designs: 30c, Man stirring syrup, man grinding cane. 75c, Oxen, man grinding cane.
€2.45, Man leading oxen, man grinding cane, man carrying cane.

2007, July 1 *Perf. 12½x13*
264-265 A57 Set of 2 3.00 1.50
265a Booklet pane of 2, #264-265 3.00 —

Souvenir Sheet
Perf. 13¼x13

266 A57 €2.45 multi 6.75 6.75
a. Booklet pane of 1 6.75 —
Complete booklet, #260a, 261e, 262a, 263c, 265a, 266a 28.00

No. 266 contains one 60x40mm stamp.

Booklet panes are separated from binding stub at left by a row of rouletting. Complete booklet also contains a pane of four progressive proofs of No. 262. These were not valid for postage.

Funchal, 500th Anniv. A58

Designs: 30c, Funchal Harbor. 61c, Map. 75c, Coat of arms. €1, Boat in harbor.

No. 271, €2.45, Boat in harbor, diff. No. 272, €2.45, Man, harbor, town.

Perf. 12x11¾ Syncopated
2008, Apr. 15 Litho.
267-270 A58 Set of 4 8.25 4.25
268a Booklet pane of 2, #267-268 2.75 —
270a Booklet pane of 2, #269-270 5.50 —

Souvenir Sheets

271-272 A58 Set of 2 15.00 15.00
271a Booklet pane of 1 7.50 —
272a Booklet pane of 1 7.50 —

Booklet panes are separated from binding stub at left by a row of rouletting.

Europa A59

Designs: No. 273, Man, envelopes. No. 274a, Houses, envelopes.

Perf. 12x11¾ Syncopated
2008, May 9 Litho.
273 A59 61c multi 1.90 .95
a. Booklet pane of 1 1.90 —

Souvenir Sheet

274 Sheet of 2, #273, 274a 4.00 2.00
a. A59 61c multi 1.90 .95
b. Booklet pane of 2, #273, 274a 4.00 —

Booklet panes are separated from binding stub at left by a row of rouletting.

Lighthouse Type of Portugal of 2008

2008, June 19

275 A835 61c Ponta do Pargo Lighthouse 2.00 1.00
a. Booklet pane of 1 2.00 —
Complete booklet, #268a, 270a, 271a, 272a, 273a, 274h, 275a 32.00

Booklet panes are separated from binding stub at left by a row of rouletting. Complete booklet also contains a pane of four progressive proofs of No. 273. These were not valid for postage.

Fruits A60

Designs: 32c, Annona cherimola. 68c, Eugenia uniflora. 80c, Persea americana. €2, Psidium guajava.

No. 280, €2.50, Dwarf Cavendish bananas. No. 281, €2.50, Passiflora edulis.

Perf. 12x11¾ Syncopated

2009, Apr. 27 **Litho.**

276-279 A60 Set of 4 10.00 5.00
277a Booklet pane of 2, #276-277 2.60 —
279a Booklet pane of 2, #278-279 7.50 —

Souvenir Sheets

280-281 A60 Set of 2 13.50 6.75
280a Booklet pane of 1 6.75 —
281a Booklet pane of 1 6.75 —

Nos. 280-281 each contain one 80x30mm stamp. See No. 316.

Booklet panes are separated from binding stub at left by a row of rouletting.

Europa A61

Designs: No. 282, M51 galaxy. No. 283a, Telescope built by astronomy student from University of Madeira.

2009, May 8

282 A61 68c multi 1.90 .95
a. Booklet pane of 1 1.90 —

Souvenir Sheet

283 Sheet of 2, #282, 283a 4.00 2.00
a. A61 68c multi 1.90 .95
b. Booklet pane of 2, #282, 283a 4.00 —
Complete booklet, #277a, 279a, 280a, 281a, 282a, 283b, Portugal #3144a 35.50

Intl. Year of Astronomy.

Booklet panes are separated from binding stub at left by a row of rouletting. Complete booklet also contains a pane of 4 progressive proofs of No. 282. These were not valid for postage.

Botanical Gardens, 50th Anniv. A62

Designs: 32c, Musschia aurea, topiary garden. 68c, Geranium maderense, path. 80c, Ranunculus cortusifolius, path and roads. No. 287, €2, Convolvulus massonii, people in gardens.

No. 288, €2, Patterned flower gardens. No. 289, €2, Building, scientist, botanist inspecting plant, seeds.

Perf. 12x11¾ Syncopated

2010, Apr. 30 **Litho.**

284-287 A62 Set of 4 10.00 5.00
285a Booklet pane of 2, #284-285 2.50 —
287a Booklet pane of 2, #286-287 7.50 —

Souvenir Sheets

288-289 A62 Set of 2 11.00 5.50
288a Booklet pane of 1 5.50 —
289a Booklet pane of 1 5.50 —

Issued: Nos. 285a, 287a, 288a, 289a, Nov.

Booklet panes are separated from binding stub at left by a row of rouletting.

See No. 317.

Europa — A63

Characters from children's story: No. 290, Woman. No. 291a, Man.

Perf. 11¾x12 Syncopated

2010, May 7 **Litho.**

290 A63 68c multi 1.75 .85
a. Booklet pane of 1 1.75 —

Souvenir Sheet

291 Sheet of 2, #290, 291a 3.50 1.75
a. A63 68c multi 1.75 .85
b. Booklet pane of 2, #290, 291a 3.50 —
Complete booklet, #285a, 287a, 288a, 289a, 290a, 291b 27.00

Issued: Nos. 290a, 291b, Nov.

Booklet panes are separated from binding stub at left by a row of rouletting.

Europa A64

Designs: No. 292, People walking on forest path, bird in tree. No. 293a, Birds in flight and on branch..

Perf. 12x11¾ Syncopated

2011, May 9

292 A64 68c multi 2.00 1.00
a. Booklet pane of 1 2.00 —

Souvenir Sheet

293 Sheet of 2, #292, 293a 4.00 2.00
a. A64 68c multi 2.00 1.00
b. Booklet pane of 2, #292, 293a 4.00 —

Intl. Year of Forests.

Country Houses A65

Designs: 32c, Quinta dos Cruzes. 68c, Quinta Jardins do Lago. 80c, Quinta Monte Palace. €2, Quinta Serra Golf.

No. 298, €1.75, Quinta do Palheiro - Casa Velha. No. 299, €2.30, Quinta Vigia.

2011, Sept. 23

294-297 A65 Set of 4 10.50 5.25
295a Booklet pane of 2, #294-295 2.75 —
297a Booklet pane of 2, #296-297 7.75 —

Souvenir Sheets

298-299 A65 Set of 2 11.00 5.50
298a Booklet pane of 1 4.75 —
299a Booklet pane of 1 6.25 —
Complete booklet, #292a, 293b, 295a, 297a, 298a, 299a, Portugal #3330a 30.00

Europa A66

Designs: No. 300, Steamer Santa Maria. No. 301a, Funchal waterfront.

2012, May 9

300 A66 68c multi 1.75 .85
a. Booklet pane of 1 1.75 —

Souvenir Sheet

301 Sheet of 2, #300, 301a 3.50 1.75
a. A66 68c multi 1.75 .85
b. Booklet pane of 2, #300, 301a 3.50 —

Issued: Nos. 300a, 301b, Nov.

Booklet panes are separated from binding stub at left by a row of rouletting.

Levadas A67

Irrigation canals at: 32c, Rei. 68c, Caldeirao Verde. 80c, Faja do Rodrigues. €2, 25 Fontes. €1.75. Cedros, vert. €2.30, Furado, vert.

2012 ***Perf. 12x11¾ Syncopated***

302-305 A67 Set of 4 10.00 5.00
303a Booklet pane of 2, #302-303 2.60 —
305a Booklet pane of 2, #304-305 7.25 —

Souvenir Sheets

Perf. 11¾x12 Syncopated

306-307 A67 Set of 2 10.50 5.25
306a Booklet pane of 1 4.50 —
307a Booklet pane of 1 6.00 —
Complete booklet, #300a, 301b, 303a, 305a, 306a, 307a 26.00

Issued: Nos. 302-307, 9/21; Nos. 303a, 305a, 306a, 307a, Nov. Nos. 306-307 each contain one 30x80mm stamp.

Booklet panes are separated from binding stub at left by a row of rouletting. Complete booklet contains a pane of four imperforate progressive proofs of No. 300. These were not valid for postage.

See No. 318.

Europa A68

Designs: No. 308, Portuguese postal all-terrain vehicle. No. 309a, Rider on Portuguese all-terrain vehicle.

Perf. 12x11¾ Syncopated

2013, May 9 **Litho.**

308 A68 70c multi 1.90 .95
a. Booklet pane of 1 1.90 —

Souvenir Sheet

309 Sheet of 2, #308, 309a 3.80 1.90
a. A68 70c multi 1.90 .95
b. Booklet pane of 2, #308, 309a 3.80 —

See No. 319.

Booklet panes are separated from binding stub at left by a row of rouletting.

Apiculture A69

Designs: 36c, Bee near water. 70c, Bee at flower. 80c, Bee at flower, diff. No. 313, €1.70, Beekeeper and bees near hives.

No. 314, €1.70, Bee approaching flower. €1.90, Hives, bee on leaf near flower.

Perf. 12x11¾ Syncopated

2013, May 17 **Litho.**

310-313 A69 Set of 4 9.75 5.00
311a Booklet pane of 2, #310-311 3.00 —
313a Booklet pane of 2, #312-313 6.75 —

Souvenir Sheets

314-315 A69 Set of 2 9.75 5.00
314a Booklet pane of 1 4.50 —
315a Booklet pane of 1 5.25 —
Complete booklet, #308a, 309b, 311a, 313a, 314a, 315a 25.50

Nos. 314-315 each contain one 80x30mm stamp. See No. 320.

Booklet panes are separated from binding stub at left by a row of rouletting. Complete booklet also contains a pane of 4 progressive proofs of No. 308. These were not valid for postage.

Types of 2009-13

Die Cut Perf. 10½

2014, Jan. 27 **Litho.**

Self-Adhesive

316 A60 E Like #277 1.90 .95
317 A62 E Like #285 1.90 .95
318 A67 E Like #303 1.90 .95
319 A68 E Like #308 1.90 .95
320 A69 E Like #311 1.90 .95
Nos. 316-320 (5) 9.50 4.75

On day of issue, Nos. 316-320 each sold for 70c.

Europa — A70

Designs: No. 321, Brinquinho player. No. 322a, Brinquinho.

Perf. 11¾x12 Syncopated

2014, May 9 **Litho.**

321 A70 E multi 2.00 1.00
a. Booklet pane of 1 2.00 —

Souvenir Sheet

322 Sheet of 2, #321, 322a 4.00 2.00
a. A70 E multi 2.00 1.00
b. Booklet pane of 2, #321, 322a 4.00 —

On day of issue Nos. 321 and 322a each sold for 72c.

Booklet panes are separated from binding stub at left by a row of rouletting.

Diocese of Funchal, 500th Anniv. — A71

Designs: 42c, Processional cross. 50c, St. James, the Lesser. 72c, Our Lady of the Mount. 80c, Pope John Paul II.

€1, Papal bull creating Diocese of Funchal. €1.70, Funchal Cathedral.

Perf. 11¾x12 Syncopated

2014, June 12 **Litho.**

323-326 A71 Set of 4 6.75 3.50
324a Booklet pane of 2, #323-324 2.60 —
326a Booklet pane of 2, #325-326 4.25 —

Souvenir Sheets

327-328 A71 Set of 2 7.50 3.75
327a Booklet pane of 1 2.75 —
328a Booklet pane of 1 4.75 —
Complete booklet, #321a, 322b, 324a, 326a, 327a, 328a 19.50

Booklet panes are separated from binding stub at left by a row of rouletting. Complete booklet also contains a pane of 4 progressive proofs of No. 321. These were not valid for postage.

Types of 2011-12

Die Cut Perf. 10½

2015, Jan. 19 **Litho.**

Self-Adhesive

329 A64 E Like #292 1.75 .85
330 A65 E Like #296 1.75 .85
331 A66 E Like #300 1.75 .85
Nos. 329-331 (3) 5.25 2.55

Nos. 329-331 each sold for 72c on day of issue.

Flower Festival A72

Designs: 45c, Flower market. 72c, Street decorations. 80c, Children in costumes carrying flowers. €1, Street garden.

€1.80, Anthurium andraeanum. €2, Heliconia rostrata.

Perf. 12x11¾ Syncopated

2015, Apr. 16 Litho.

332-335 A72 Set of 4 6.75 3.50

Souvenir Sheets

336-337 A72 Set of 2 8.75 4.25

Figurines Type of Portugal of 2015

Perf. 12x11¾ Syncopated

2015, Apr. 21 Litho.

338 A1007 72c Madeira figurines 1.75 .85

Europa A73

Old toys: No. 339, Sink, bucket and watering can. No. 340a, Taxi.

Perf. 12x11¾ Syncopated

2015, May 8 Litho.

339 A73 72c multi 1.60 .80

Souvenir Sheet

340 Sheet of 2, #339, 340a 3.25 1.60
a. A73 72c multi 1.60 .80

PORTUGUESE AFRICA

'pōr-chə-ˌgēz 'a-fri-kə

For use in any of the Portuguese possessions in Africa.

1000 Reis = 1 Milreis
100 Centavos = 1 Escudo

Common Design Types pictured following the introduction.

Vasco da Gama Issue
Common Design Types
Inscribed "Africa - Correios"

Perf. 13½ to 15½

1898, Apr. 1 Engr. Unwmk.

1	CD20	2½r blue green	.90	.90
2	CD21	5r red	.90	.90
3	CD22	10r red violet	.90	.90
4	CD23	25r yellow green	.90	.90
5	CD24	50r dark blue	1.10	1.10
6	CD25	75r violet brown	6.25	6.25
7	CD26	100r bister brown	5.00	4.50
8	CD27	150r bister	8.00	6.25
		Nos. 1-8 (8)	23.95	21.70
		Set, never hinged	32.50	

Vasco da Gama's voyage to India.

POSTAGE DUE STAMPS

D1

1945 Unwmk. Typo. *Perf. 11½x12*

Denomination in Black

J1	D1	10c claret	.80	.70
J2	D1	20c purple	.80	.70
J3	D1	30c deep blue	.80	.70
J4	D1	40c chocolate	.80	.70
J5	D1	50c red violet	1.25	*1.25*
J6	D1	1e orange brown	3.00	*4.00*
J7	D1	2e yellow green	7.50	7.00
J8	D1	3e bright carmine	12.00	12.00
J9	D1	5e orange yellow	25.00	25.00
		Nos. J1-J9 (9)	51.95	52.05
		Set, never hinged	62.50	

WAR TAX STAMPS

Liberty WT1

Overprinted in Black, Orange or Carmine

Perf. 12x11½, 15x14

1919 Typo. Unwmk.

MR1	WT1 1c green (Bk)		.75	.75
a.	Figures of value omitted		40.00	
MR2	WT1 4c green (O)		2.00	
MR3	WT1 5c green (C)		.75	.75
	Nos. MR1-MR3 (3)		3.50	1.50

Values the same for either perf.

No. MR2 used is known only with fiscal cancelation. Some authorities consider No. MR2 a revenue stamp.

PORTUGUESE CONGO

'pōr-chi-gēz 'käŋ-ˌgō

LOCATION — The northernmost district of the Portuguese Angola Colony on the southwest coast of Africa
CAPITAL — Cabinda

Stamps of Angola replaced those of Portuguese Congo.

1000 Reis = 1 Milreis
100 Centavos = 1 Escudo (1913)

King Carlos — A1

Perf. 12½

1894, Aug. 5 Typo. Unwmk.

1	A1	5r yellow	1.25	.75
b.		As "a," Perf. 13½	17.00	12.50
2	A1	10r redsh violet	2.00	.80
a.		Perf. 13½	17.50	12.50
3	A1	15r chocolate	3.00	2.00
a.		Perf. 11½	5.00	2.10
4	A1	20r lav, ordinary paper	2.50	2.00
b.		Perf. 11½	5.00	2.10
5	A1	25r green	2.00	.80
b.		Perf. 11½	3.25	.85
		Perf. 13½		
6	A1	50r light blue	5.00	2.00
a.		Perf. 11½	13.00	4.50
		Perf. 11½		
7	A1	75r rose	6.00	3.75
a.		Perf. 12½	20.00	15.00
8	A1	80r yellow green	10.00	6.00
a.		Perf. 12½	60.00	37.50
9	A1	100r brown, *yel*	6.00	3.75
a.		Perf. 13½	32.50	19.00
		Perf. 12½		
10	A1	150r carmine, *rose*	15.00	9.00
11	A1	200r dk blue, *bl*	16.00	9.00
12	A1	300r dk blue, *salmon*	18.00	11.00
		Nos. 1-12 (12)	86.75	50.85

For surcharges and overprints see Nos. 36-47, 127-131.

King Carlos — A2

Name & Value in Black except 500r

1898-1903 *Perf. 11½*

13	A2	2½r gray	.35	.30
14	A2	5r orange	.35	.30
15	A2	10r lt green	.55	.30
16	A2	15r brown	1.50	1.25
17	A2	15r gray grn ('03)	1.00	.55
18	A2	20r gray violet	1.00	.70
19	A2	25r sea green	1.40	.90
20	A2	25r car rose ('03)	.90	.45
21	A2	50r deep blue	1.60	1.25
22	A2	50r brown ('03)	2.75	1.75
23	A2	65r dull blue ('03)	30.00	6.50
24	A2	75r rose	4.00	2.25
25	A2	75r red lilac ('03)	2.75	2.25
26	A2	80r violet	3.00	2.50
27	A2	100r dk bl, *bl*	2.40	1.75
28	A2	115r org brn, *pink* ('03)	6.50	5.00
29	A2	130r brn, *straw* ('03)	30.00	11.00
30	A2	150r brown, *buff*	4.00	2.50
31	A2	200r red lilac, *pnksh*	5.00	3.00
32	A2	300r dk blue, *rose*	6.00	3.25
33	A2	400r dl bl, *straw* ('03)	15.00	9.50
34	A2	500r blk & red, *bl* ('01)	25.00	9.00
35	A2	700r vio, *yelsh* ('01)	30.00	17.50
		Nos. 13-35 (23)	175.05	83.75

For overprints and surcharges see Nos. 49-53, 60-74, 117-126, 136-138.

Surcharged in Black

Perf. 12½, 11½ (#41, 43), 13½ (#44)

1902 On Issue of 1894

36	A1	65r on 15r choc	3.50	3.00
a.		Perf. 11½	17.00	9.00
37	A1	65r on 20r lav (#4)	4.00	3.00
38	A1	65r on 25r green (#5)	4.00	3.00
a.		Perf. 11½	17.00	12.50
39	A1	65r on 300r bl, *sal*	5.00	4.50
40	A1	115r on 10r red vio	4.00	3.00
41	A1	115r on 50r lt bl	4.00	2.50
a.		Perf. 13½	4.00	2.75
42	A1	130r on 5r yellow	5.00	2.75
a.		Inverted surcharge	27.50	27.50
b.		Perf. 13½	4.00	2.75
43	A1	130r on 75r rose	5.00	3.00
a.		Perf. 12½	7.00	6.00
44	A1	130r on 100r brn, *yel*	5.00	3.75
a.		Inverted surcharge	40.00	35.00
b.		Perf. 11½	20.00	12.50
45	A1	400r on 80r yel grn	1.75	1.25
a.		Perf. 12½	5.00	3.50
46	A1	400r on 150r car, *rose*	2.25	1.90
47	A1	400r on 200r bl, *bl*	2.25	1.90

On Newspaper Stamps of 1894

48	N1	115r on 2½r brn	3.75	2.50
a.		Inverted surcharge	25.00	25.00
b.		Perf. 13½	3.75	3.25
		Nos. 36-48 (13)	49.50	36.05

Nos. 16, 19, 21 and 24 Overprinted in Black

1902 *Perf. 11½*

49	A2	15r brown	3.00	1.25
50	A2	25r sea green	3.00	1.40
51	A2	50r blue	3.00	1.40
a.		Double overprint	20.00	18.00
52	A2	75r rose	4.00	2.75
a.		Double ovpt, one albino	10.00	6.00
		Nos. 49-52 (4)	13.00	6.80

No. 23 Surcharged

1905

53 A2 50r on 65r dull blue 7.00 2.50

Angola Stamps of 1898-1903 (Port. Congo type A2) Overprinted or Surcharged

a

b

1911

54	(a)	2½r gray	1.50	.90
55	(a)	5r orange	2.00	1.25
56	(a)	10r lt green	2.00	1.25
a.		"REPUBLICA" inverted	17.50	17.50
57	(a)	15r gray green	2.00	1.25
a.		"REPUBLICA" inverted	17.50	17.50
58	(b)	25r on 200r red vio, *pnksh*	3.00	2.00
a.		"REPUBLICA" inverted	17.50	17.50
b.		"CONGO" double	17.50	17.50

Thin Bar and "CONGO" as Type "b"

59	(a)	2½r gray	1.25	.90
		Nos. 54-59 (6)	11.75	7.55

Issue of 1898-1903 Overprinted in Carmine or Green — c

1911

60	A2	2½r gray	.25	.25
61	A2	5r orange	.25	.25
62	A2	10r lt green	.25	.25
63	A2	15r gray grn	.25	.25
64	A2	20r gray vio	.45	.25
65	A2	25r car rose (G)	2.00	.90
66	A2	50r brown	.65	.35
67	A2	75r red lilac	1.10	.55
68	A2	100r dk bl, *bl*	1.00	.60
69	A2	115r org brn, *pink*	2.10	1.40
70	A2	130r brown, *straw*	2.10	1.40
71	A2	200r red vio, *pnksh*	3.00	1.90
72	A2	400r dull bl, *straw*	5.25	2.50
73	A2	500r blk & red, *bl*	5.75	2.25
74	A2	700r violet, *yelsh*	5.75	2.25
		Nos. 60-74 (15)	30.15	15.35

Numerous inverts and doubles exist. These are printer's waste or made to order.

Common Design Types pictured following the introduction.

Vasco da Gama Issue of Various Portuguese Colonies Surcharged

1913 On Stamps of Macao

75	CD20	¼c on ½a bl grn	1.50	1.25
76	CD21	½c on 1a red	1.50	1.25
77	CD22	1c on 2a red vio	1.50	1.25
78	CD23	2½c on 4a yel grn	1.50	1.25
79	CD24	5c on 8a dk blue	1.50	1.25
80	CD25	7½c on 12a vio brn	2.50	2.50
81	CD26	10c on 16a bis brn	2.00	1.75
82	CD27	15c on 24a bister	2.00	1.75
		Nos. 75-82 (8)	14.00	12.25

On Stamps of Portuguese Africa

83	CD20	¼c on 2½r bl grn	1.50	.80
84	CD21	½c on 5r red	1.50	.80
85	CD22	1c on 10r red vio	1.50	.80
86	CD23	2½c on 25r yel grn	1.50	.80
87	CD24	5c on 50r dk bl	1.50	1.10
88	CD25	7½c on 75r vio brn	1.90	1.90
89	CD26	10c on 100r bis brn	1.25	1.25
a.		Inverted surcharge	25.00	25.00
90	CD27	15c on 150r bister	2.00	1.50
		Nos. 83-90 (8)	12.65	8.95

On Stamps of Timor

91	CD20	¼c on ½a bl grn	1.50	1.25
92	CD21	½c on 1a red	1.50	1.25
93	CD22	1c on 2a red vio	1.50	1.25
94	CD23	2½c on 4a yel grn	1.50	1.25
95	CD24	5c on 8a dk blue	1.50	1.25
a.		Double surcharge	25.00	25.00
96	CD25	7½c on 12a vio brn	2.50	2.50
97	CD26	10c on 16a bis brn	2.25	2.25
98	CD27	15c on 24a bister	2.25	2.25
		Nos. 91-98 (8)	14.50	13.25
		Nos. 75-98 (24)	41.15	34.45

Ceres — A3

Name and Value in Black
Chalky Paper

1914 Typo. *Perf. 15x14*

99	A3	¼c olive brn	.35	*.50*
a.		Inscriptions inverted		
100	A3	½c black	.75	*1.00*
101	A3	1c blue grn	3.00	*4.25*
102	A3	1½c lilac brn	2.00	*1.40*
103	A3	2c carmine	2.00	*1.40*
104	A3	2½c lt violet	.75	*.90*
105	A3	5c dp blue	1.00	*1.40*
106	A3	7½c yellow brn	1.50	*1.40*

107 A3 8c slate 3.00 *3.25*
108 A3 10c orange brn 3.00 *3.25*
109 A3 15c plum 3.00 *3.25*
110 A3 20c yellow grn 3.00 *3.25*
111 A3 30c brown, *grn* 4.00 *5.00*
112 A3 40c brown, *pink* 5.00 *9.00*
113 A3 50c orange, *salmon* 9.00 9.00
114 A3 1e green, *blue* 10.00 10.00
Nos. 99-114 (16) 51.35 *58.25*

1920 **Ordinary Paper**
115 A3 ¼c olive brn .40 *.55*
116 A3 2c carmine .75 *1.15*

Issue of 1898-1903 Overprinted Locally in Green or Red

1914-18 ***Perf. 11½***
117 A2 50r brown (G) 1.00 .65
118 A2 75r rose (G) *500.00*
119 A2 75r red lilac (G) 3.00 1.50
120 A2 100r blue, *bl* (R) 1.00 .80
121 A2 200r red vio, *pink* (G) 2.00 1.25
122 A2 400r dl bl, *straw* (R) ('18) 80.00 55.00
123 A2 500r blk & red, *bl* (R) 65.00 42.50

Same on Nos. 51-52
124 A2 50r blue (R) 1.00 .70
125 A2 75r rose (G) 1.50 1.10

Same on No. 53
126 A2 50r on 65r dl bl (R) 1.25 1.10
Nos. 117,119-126 (9) 155.75 104.60

No. 118 was not regularly issued.

Provisional Issue of 1902 Overprinted Type "c" in Red

1915 ***Perf. 11½, 12½, 13½***
127 A1 115r on 10r red vio .75 .25
a. Perf. 13½ 17.00 14.00
128 A1 115r on 50r lt bl 2.00 .25
a. Perf. 11½ 2.00 .65
129 A1 130r on 5r yellow 1.00 .25
130 A1 130r on 75r rose 2.00 .65
131 A1 130r on 100r brn, *buff* 1.00 .40
135 N1 115r on 2½r brn .80 .40

Nos. 49, 51 Overprinted Type "c"
136 A2 15r brown .85 .55
137 A2 50r blue .85 .40

No. 53 Overprinted Type "c"
138 A2 50r on 65r dull blue 1.25 .40
Nos. 127-138 (9) 10.50 3.55

NEWSPAPER STAMP

N1

Perf. 12½
1894, Aug. 5 **Typo.** **Unwmk.**
P1 N1 2½r brown 1.50 .60
a. Perf. 13½ 1.50 .60

For surcharge and overprint see Nos. 48, 135.

PORTUGUESE GUINEA

'pōr-chi-gēz 'gi-nē

LOCATION — On the west coast of Africa between Senegal and Guinea
GOVT. — Portuguese Overseas Territory
AREA — 13,944 sq. mi.
POP. — 560,000 (est. 1970)
CAPITAL — Bissau

The territory, including the Bissagos Islands, became an independent republic on Sept. 10, 1974. See Guinea-Bissau in Vol. 3.

1000 Reis = 1 Milreis
100 Centavos = 1 Escudo (1913)

Catalogue values for unused stamps in this country are for Never Hinged items, beginning with Scott 273 in the regular postage section, Scott J40 in the postage due section, and Scott RA17 in the postal tax section.

Nos. 1-7 are valued with small faults such as short perfs or small thins. Completely fault-free examples of any of these stamps are very scarce and are worth more than the values given.

Stamps of Cape Verde, 1877-85 Overprinted in Black

1881 **Unwmk.** ***Perf. 12½***
Without Gum (Nos. 1-7)
1 A1 5r black *1,000.* *800.*
1A A1 10r yellow *2,000.* *800.*
2 A1 20r bister *500.* *250.*
3 A1 25r rose *1,400.* *775.*
4 A1 40r blue *1,250.* *800.*
a. Cliché of Mozambique in Cape Verde plate *16,500.* *15,250.*
4B A1 50r green *2,000.* *725.*
5 A1 100r lilac 300. 175.
6 A1 200r orange *600.* *475.*
7 A1 300r brown *600.* *475.*

Excellent forgeries exist of Nos. 1-7.

Overprinted in Red or Black

1881-85 ***Perf. 12½, 13½***
8 A1 5r black (R) 4.00 2.75
9 A1 10r yellow 160.00 160.00
10 A1 10r green ('85) 6.00 5.50
11 A1 20r bister 3.00 2.25
12 A1 20r rose ('85) 6.75 5.00
a. Double overprint
13 A1 25r carmine 2.40 1.75
a. Perf. 13½ 67.50 37.50
14 A1 25r violet ('85) 3.00 1.90
a. Double overprint
15 A1 40r blue 175.00 110.00
a. Cliché of Mozambique in Cape Verde plate *1,500.* *875.00*
16 A1 40r yellow ('85) 1.90 1.60
a. Cliché of Mozambique in Cape Verde plate 50.00 45.00
b. Imperf.
c. As "a," imperf.
g. Double overprint
17 A1 50r green 175.00 110.00
18 A1 50r blue ('85) 5.75 2.75
a. Imperf.
b. Double overprint
19 A1 100r lilac 7.75 6.00
a. Inverted overprint
20 A1 200r orange 11.50 8.00
21 A1 300r yellow brn 14.00 11.00
a. 300r lake brown 16.00 12.50

Varieties of this overprint may be found without accent on "E" of "GUINE," or with grave instead of acute accent.

Stamps of the 1881-85 issues were reprinted on a smooth white chalky paper, ungummed, and on thin white paper with shiny white gum and clean-cut perforation 13½.

See Scott Classic Catalogue for listings by perforation.

King Luiz — A3

1886 **Typo.** ***Perf. 12½, 13½***
22 A3 5r gray black 6.00 5.50
a. Imperf.
23 A3 10r green 7.25 4.00
a. Perf. 13½ 8.25 6.75
b. Imperf.
24 A3 20r carmine 10.50 4.00
25 A3 25r red lilac 10.50 6.25
a. Imperf.
26 A3 40r chocolate 8.50 6.25
a. Perf. 12½ 82.50 60.00
27 A3 50r blue 17.00 6.25
a. Imperf.
28 A3 80r gray 18.00 10.00
a. Perf. 12½ 82.50 60.00
29 A3 100r brown 18.00 10.00
a. Perf. 12½ 37.50 22.50
30 A3 200r gray lilac 40.00 20.00
31 A3 300r orange 50.00 30.00
a. Perf. 13½ 210.00 210.00
Nos. 22-31 (10) 185.75 102.25

Varieties of this overprint may be found without accent on "E" of "GUINE," or with grave instead of acute accent. For surcharges and overprints see Nos. 67-76, 180-183.

Reprinted in 1905 on thin white paper with shiny white gum and clean-cut perforation 13½.

King Carlos
A4 A5

1893-94 ***Perf. 11½***
32 A4 5r yellow 1.90 1.10
a. Perf. 12½ 2.00 1.25
33 A4 10r red violet 1.90 1.10
34 A4 15r chocolate 2.40 1.60
35 A4 20r lavender 2.40 1.60
36 A4 25r blue green 2.40 1.60
37 A4 50r lt blue 5.00 3.75
a. Perf. 12½ 17.00 12.50
38 A4 75r rose 12.00 7.50
39 A4 80r lt green 12.00 7.50
40 A4 100r brn, *buff* 12.00 7.50
41 A4 150r car, *rose* 12.00 8.00
42 A4 200r dk bl, *bl* 20.00 15.00
43 A4 300r dk bl, *sal* 20.00 15.00
Nos. 32-43 (12) 104.00 71.25

Almost all of Nos. 32-43 were issued without gum.

For surcharges and overprints see #77-88, 184-188, 203-205.

1898-1903 ***Perf. 11½***
Name & Value in Black except 500r
44 A5 2½r gray .40 .35
45 A5 5r orange .40 .35
46 A5 10r lt green .40 .35
47 A5 15r brown 3.25 2.25
48 A5 15r gray grn ('03) 1.75 1.25
49 A5 20r gray violet 1.40 1.10
50 A5 25r sea green 1.75 .90
51 A5 25r carmine ('03) 1.00 .55
52 A5 50r dark blue 2.75 1.40
53 A5 50r brown ('03) 3.25 2.25
54 A5 65r dl blue ('03) 25.00 8.75
55 A5 75r rose 20.00 8.00
56 A5 75r lilac ('03) 4.00 2.25
57 A5 80r brt violet 3.00 1.90
58 A5 100r dk bl, *bl* 2.75 1.90
a. Perf. 12½ 52.50 22.50
59 A5 115r org brn, *pink* ('03) 8.50 6.00
a. 115r orange brown, *yellowish* 8.25 5.00
60 A5 130r brn, *straw* ('03) 10.00 7.50
61 A5 150r lt brn, *buff* 11.00 3.25
62 A5 200r red lilac, *pnksh* 10.00 3.25
63 A5 300r blue, *rose* 11.00 4.25
64 A5 400r dl bl, *straw* ('03) 16.00 10.00
65 A5 500r blk & red, *bl* ('01) 18.00 7.75
66 A5 700r vio, *yelsh* ('01) 25.00 10.00
Nos. 44-66 (23) 180.60 85.55

Stamps issued in 1903 were without gum.

For overprints and surcharges see Nos. 90-115, 190-194, 197.

Issue of 1886 Surcharged in Black or Red

1902, Oct. 20 ***Perf. 12½***
67 A3 65r on 10r green 6.50 5.50
a. Inverted surcharge 30.00 25.00
68 A3 65r on 20r car 6.50 5.00
69 A3 65r on 25r red lilac 6.50 5.00
70 A3 115r on 40r choc 5.75 4.50
a. Perf. 13½ 13.00 9.50
71 A3 115r on 50r blue 5.75 4.50
a. Inverted surcharge 30.00 25.00
72 A3 115r on 300r orange 7.25 5.75
73 A3 130r on 80r gray 7.25 5.00
a. Perf. 13½ 14.00 5.75
74 A3 130r on 100r brown 7.75 5.75
a. Perf. 13½ 20.00 14.00
75 A3 400r on 200r gray lil 13.00 8.75
76 A3 400r on 5r gray blk (R) 32.50 24.00
Nos. 67-76 (10) 98.75 73.75

Reprints of No. 76 are in black and have clean-cut perforation 13½.

Same Surcharge on Issue of 1893-94

Perf. 11½, 12½ (#80)
77 A4 65r on 10r red vio 5.75 3.50
78 A4 65r on 15r choc 5.75 3.50
79 A4 65r on 20r lav 5.75 3.50
80 A4 65r on 50r lt bl 3.00 2.25
a. Perf. 13½ 3.25 2.50
81 A4 115r on 5r yel 5.50 3.00
a. Inverted surcharge 45.00 45.00
b. Perf. 12½ 55.00 40.00
82 A4 115r on 25r bl grn 6.00 3.25
83 A4 130r on 150r car, *rose* 6.00 3.25
84 A4 130r on 200r dk bl, *bl* 6.50 4.50
85 A4 130r on 300r dk bl, *sal* 6.50 4.50
86 A4 400r on 75r rose 4.50 3.00
87 A4 400r on 80r lt grn 3.00 1.60
88 A4 400r on 100r brn, *buff* 4.00 1.60

Same Surcharge on No. P1

Perf. 13½
89 N1 115r on 2½r brn 4.50 3.25
a. Inverted surcharge 30.00 25.00
b. Perf. 12½ 4.75 3.50
c. As "b," inverted surcharge 30.00 25.00
Nos. 77-89 (13) 66.75 40.70

Issue of 1898 Overprinted in Black

1902, Oct. 20 ***Perf. 11½***
90 A5 15r brown 2.50 1.25
91 A5 25r sea green 2.50 1.60
92 A5 50r dark blue 3.00 1.60
93 A5 75r rose 5.75 4.00
Nos. 90-93 (4) 13.75 8.45

No. 54 Surcharged in Black

1905
94 A5 50r on 65r dull blue 6.00 2.50

Issue of 1898-1903 Overprinted in Carmine or Green

1911 ***Perf. 11½***
95 A5 2½r gray .40 .35
a. Inverted overprint 19.00 19.00
96 A5 5r orange .40 .35
97 A5 10r lt green .70 .50
98 A5 15r gray green .70 .50
99 A5 20r gray violet .70 .50
100 A5 25r carmine (G) .70 .50
a. Double overprint 15.00 15.00
101 A5 50r brown .45 .40
102 A5 75c lilac .45 .40
103 A5 100r dk bl, *bl* 1.50 .75
104 A5 115r org brn, *pink* 1.50 1.00
105 A5 130r brn, *straw* 1.50 1.00
106 A5 200r red lil, *pink* 6.50 3.25
107 A5 400r dl bl, *straw* 2.50 1.50
108 A5 500r blk & red, *bl* 2.75 1.50
109 A5 700r vio, *yelsh* 4.25 2.25
Nos. 95-109 (15) 25.00 14.75

Issued without gum: #101-102, 104-105, 107.

Issue of 1898-1903 Overprinted in Red

1913 *Perf. 11½*

Without Gum (Nos. 110-115)

110	A5	15r gray grn	14.00	6.50
111	A5	75r lilac	14.00	6.50
a.		Inverted overprint	35.00	35.00
112	A5	100r bl, *bl*	10.00	4.50
a.		Inverted overprint	35.00	35.00
113	A5	200r red lil, *pnksh*	40.00	25.00
a.		Inverted overprint	82.50	82.50

Same Overprint on Nos. 90, 93 in Red

114	A5	15r brown	11.00	7.25
a.		"REPUBLICA" double	*35.00*	*35.00*
b.		"REPUBLICA" inverted	*30.00*	*30.00*
115	A5	75r rose	11.00	7.25
a.		"REPUBLICA" inverted	35.00	35.00
		Nos. 110-115 (6)	100.00	57.00

Vasco da Gama Issue of Various Portuguese Colonies Surcharged

1913 **On Stamps of Macao**

116	CD20	¼c on ½a bl grn	1.60	1.60
117	CD21	½c on 1a red	1.60	1.60
118	CD22	1c on 2a red vio	1.60	1.60
119	CD23	2½c on 4a yel grn	1.60	1.60
120	CD24	5c on 8a dk bl	1.60	1.60
121	CD25	7½c on 12a vio brn	3.25	3.25
122	CD26	10c on 16a bis brn	1.60	1.60
a.		Inverted surcharge	30.00	30.00
123	CD27	15c on 24a bis	2.75	2.75
		Nos. 116-123 (8)	15.60	15.60

On Stamps of Portuguese Africa

124	CD20	¼c on 2½c bl grn	1.40	1.40
125	CD21	½c on 5r red	1.40	1.40
126	CD22	1c on 10r red vio	1.40	1.40
127	CD23	2½c on 25r yel grn	1.40	1.40
128	CD24	5c on 50r dk bl	1.40	1.40
129	CD25	7½c on 75r vio brn	3.00	3.00
130	CD26	10c on 100r bis brn	1.40	1.40
131	CD27	15c on 150r bis	4.00	4.00
		Nos. 124-131 (8)	15.40	15.40

On Stamps of Timor

132	CD20	¼c on ½a bl grn	1.60	1.60
133	CD21	½c on 1a red	1.60	1.60
134	CD22	1c on 2a red vio	1.60	1.60
135	CD23	2½c on 4a yel grn	1.60	1.60
136	CD24	5c on 8a dk blue	1.60	1.60
137	CD25	7½c on 12a vio brn	3.00	3.00
138	CD26	10c on 16a bis brn	1.60	1.60
139	CD27	15c on 24a bister	3.00	3.00
		Nos. 132-139 (8)	15.60	15.60
		Nos. 116-139 (24)	46.60	46.60

Ceres — A6

Name and Value in Black

1914 **Chalky Paper** *Perf. 15x14*

140	A6	¼c olive brown	.25	.25
141	A6	½c black	.40	.30
142	A6	1c blue green	1.40	1.40
143	A6	1½c lilac brn	.60	.60
144	A6	2c carmine	.65	.65
145	A6	2½c lt violet	1.00	1.00
146	A6	5c deep blue	.65	.55
147	A6	7½c yellow brn	.95	.40
148	A6	8c slate	.65	.55
149	A6	10c orange brn	.80	.65
150	A6	15c plum	8.25	7.25
151	A6	20c yellow grn	1.15	.85
152	A6	30c brown, *grn*	7.00	6.00
153	A6	40c brown, *pink*	3.50	3.25
154	A6	50c orange, *salmon*	3.50	3.25
155	A6	1e green, *blue*	5.00	3.50
		Nos. 140-155 (16)	35.75	30.45

1919-20 **Ordinary Paper**

156	A6	¼c olive brown	.40	.35
157	A6	½c black ('20)	.25	.25
158	A6	1c blue green	2.75	2.50
159	A6	2c carmine	.65	.65
		Nos. 156-159 (4)	4.05	3.75

1921-26 *Perf. 12x11½*

160	A6	¼c olive brown	3.00	2.25
161	A6	½c black	.25	.25
162	A6	1c yellow green ('22)	.25	.25
163	A6	1½c lilac brn	.25	.25
164	A6	2c carmine	.25	.25
165	A6	2c gray ('25)	.25	*1.60*
166	A6	2½c lt violet	.25	.25
167	A6	3c orange ('22)	.25	*1.60*
168	A6	4c deep red ('22)	.25	*1.60*
169	A6	4½c gray ('22)	.25	*1.60*
170	A6	5c brt blue ('22)	.25	.25
171	A6	6c lilac ('22)	.25	*1.60*
172	A6	7c ultra ('22)	.30	*1.60*
173	A6	7½c yellow brn	.25	.25
174	A6	8c slate	.25	.25
175	A6	10c orange brn	.25	.25
176	A6	12c blue grn ('22)	.65	.50
177	A6	15c brn rose ('22)	.50	.35
178	A6	20c yellow grn	.25	.25
179	A6	24c ultra ('25)	1.90	1.60
179A	A6	25c brown ('25)	2.50	2.25
179B	A6	30c gray grn ('22)	.90	.25
179C	A6	40c turq bl ('22)	.90	.40
179D	A6	50c violet ('25)	1.90	.90
179E	A6	60c dk blue ('22)	1.90	.95
179F	A6	60c dp rose ('26)	2.50	1.75
179G	A6	80c brt rose ('22)	1.60	1.00
179H	A6	1e indigo ('26)	4.00	2.75
		Nos. 160-179H (28)	26.30	27.05

1922-25 **Glazed Paper**

179I	A6	1e pale rose	4.00	1.50
179J	A6	2e dk violet	4.00	1.50
179K	A6	5e buff ('25)	20.00	15.00
179L	A6	10e pink ('25)	40.00	20.00
179M	A6	20e pale turq ('25)	100.00	50.00
		Nos. 179I-179M (5)	168.00	88.00

For surcharges see Nos. 195-196, 211-213.

Provisional Issue of 1902 Overprinted in Carmine

1915 *Perf. 11½, 12½, 13½*

180	A3	115r on 40r choc	1.10	.65
a.		Perf. 13½	13.00	8.50
181	A3	115r on 50r blue	1.40	.75
182	A3	130r on 80r gray	4.50	1.90
a.		Perf. 12½	27.50	22.50
183	A3	130r on 100r brn	3.50	1.90
a.		Perf. 13½	14.50	11.00
184	A4	115r on 5r yellow	.80	.65
a.		Perf. 11½	5.00	4.50
185	A4	115r on 25r bl grn	.75	.65
186	A4	130r on 150r car, *rose*	1.25	.80
187	A4	130r on 200r bl, *bl*	.80	.70
188	A4	130r on 300r dk bl, *sal*	1.10	.80
189	N1	115r on 2½r brn	1.25	.90
a.		Perf. 13½	13.00	11.00
b.		Inverted overprint	22.50	22.50

On Nos. 90, 92, 94

Perf. 11½

190	A5	15r brown	.80	.70
191	A5	50r dark blue	.80	.70
192	A5	50r on 65r dl bl	.80	.70
		Nos. 180-192 (13)	18.85	11.80

Nos. 64, 66 Overprinted

1919 **Without Gum** *Perf. 11½*

193	A5	400r dl bl, *straw*	150.00	21.00
194	A5	700r vio, *yelsh*	15.00	10.00

Nos. 140, 141 and 59 Surcharged

a

b

1920, Sept. *Perf. 15x14, 11½*

Without Gum

195	A6(a)	4c on ¼c	3.25	2.75
196	A6(a)	6c on ½c	4.00	2.75
197	A5(b)	12c on 115r	8.00	5.50
		Nos. 195-197 (3)	15.25	11.00

Nos. 86-88 Surcharged

1925 *Perf. 11½*

203	A4	40c on 400r on 75r	.95	.80
204	A4	40c on 400r on 80r	.95	.80
205	A4	40c on 400r on 100r	.95	.80
		Nos. 203-205 (3)	2.85	2.40

Nos. 179F-179G, 179J Surcharged

1931 *Perf. 12x11½*

211	A6	50c on 60c dp rose	3.25	1.60
212	A6	70c on 80c pink	3.25	1.90
213	A6	1.40e on 2e dk vio	6.50	4.00
		Nos. 211-213 (3)	13.00	7.50

Ceres — A7

1933 **Wmk. 232**

214	A7	1c bister	.25	.25
215	A7	5c olive brn	.25	.25
216	A7	10c violet	.25	.25
217	A7	15c black	.25	.25
218	A7	20c gray	.25	.25
219	A7	30c dk green	.25	.25
220	A7	40c red orange	.45	.25
221	A7	45c lt blue	1.10	.80
222	A7	50c lt brown	1.10	.55
223	A7	60c olive grn	1.40	.55
224	A7	70c orange brn	2.75	.65
225	A7	80c emerald	1.50	.80
226	A7	85c deep rose	3.00	1.40
227	A7	1e red brown	1.40	.90
228	A7	1.40e dk blue	6.50	2.25
229	A7	2e red violet	4.50	1.90
230	A7	5e apple green	10.00	5.75
231	A7	10e olive bister	17.50	9.50
232	A7	20e orange	55.00	25.00
		Nos. 214-232 (19)	107.70	51.80

Common Design Types pictured following the introduction.

Common Design Types

Engr.; Name & Value Typo. in Black

1938 **Unwmk.** *Perf. 13½x13*

233	CD34	1c gray grn	.25	.25
234	CD34	5c orange brn	.25	.25
235	CD34	10c dk carmine	.25	.25
236	CD34	15c dk vio brn	.25	.25
237	CD34	20c slate	.40	.25
238	CD35	30c rose violet	.60	.25
239	CD35	35c brt green	.65	.35
240	CD35	40c brown	1.10	.35
241	CD35	50c brt red vio	1.10	.35
242	CD36	60c gray black	1.60	.35
243	CD36	70c brown vio	1.60	.35
244	CD36	80c orange	1.90	.70
245	CD36	1e red	1.50	.50
246	CD37	1.75e blue	2.10	1.00
247	CD37	2e brown car	5.00	1.40
248	CD37	5e olive grn	5.50	2.25
249	CD38	10e blue vio	7.50	2.75
250	CD38	20e red brown	22.50	4.50
		Nos. 233-250 (18)	54.05	16.35

Fort of Cacheu A8

Nuno Tristam — A9

Ulysses S. Grant — A10

Designs: 3.50e, Teixeira Pinto. 5e, Honorio Barreto. 20e, Bissau Church.

Unwmk.

1946, Jan. 12 **Litho.** *Perf. 11*

251	A8	30c gray & lt gray	.80	.70
252	A9	50c black & pink	.80	.40
253	A9	50c gray grn & lt grn	.80	.40
254	A10	1.75e blue & lt blue	9.00	1.60
255	A10	3.50e red & pink	4.75	2.75
256	A10	5e lt brn & buff	10.00	5.50
257	A8	20e vio & lt vio	14.50	7.50
a.		Sheet of 7, #251-257 ('47)	90.00	75.00
		Nos. 251-257 (7)	40.65	18.85

Discovery of Guinea, 500th anniversary. No. 257a sold for 40 escudos.

Guinea Village — A11

Designs: 10c, Crowned crane. 20c, 3.50e, Tribesman. 35c, 5e, Woman in ceremonial dress. 50c, Musician. 70c, Man. 80c, 20e, Girl. 1e, 2e, Drummer. 1.75e, Antelope.

1948, Apr. **Photo.** *Perf. 11½*

258	A11	5c chocolate	.25	.25
259	A11	10c lt violet	.65	.65
260	A11	20c dull rose	.45	.25
261	A11	35c green	.40	.25
262	A11	50c dp orange	.40	.25
263	A11	70c dp gray bl	.45	.25
264	A11	80c dk ol grn	.95	.35
265	A11	1e rose red	.95	.45
266	A11	1.75e ultra	4.00	2.25
267	A11	2e blue	8.25	1.10
268	A11	3.50e orange brn	2.75	.90
269	A11	5e slate	5.00	1.40
270	A11	20e violet	11.00	3.25
a.		Sheet of 13, #258-270 + 2 labels	75.00	67.50
		Nos. 258-270 (13)	35.50	11.60

No. 270a sold for 40 escudos.

Lady of Fatima Issue

Common Design Type

1948, Oct. **Litho.** *Perf. 14½*

271	CD40	50c deep green	3.25	3.00

UPU Symbols — A12

1949, Oct. *Perf. 14*

272	A12	2e dp org & cream	4.50	2.50

Universal Postal Union, 75th anniversary.

Catalogue values for unused stamps in this section, from this point to the end of the section, are for Never Hinged items.

Holy Year Issue

Common Design Types

1950, May *Perf. 13x13½*

273	CD41	1e brown lake	1.40	1.10
274	CD42	3e blue green	2.10	1.50

Holy Year Extension Issue
Common Design Type

1951, Oct. *Perf. 14*
275 CD43 1e choc & pale brn + label 1.00 .65

Stamps without label attached sell for less.

Medical Congress Issue
Common Design Type

Design: Physical examination.

1952 *Perf. 13½*
276 CD44 50c purple & choc .45 .35

Exhibition Entrance — A13

1953, Jan. **Litho.** *Perf. 13*
277 A13 10c brn lake & ol .25 .25
278 A13 50c dk blue & bister 1.75 .25
279 A13 3e blk, dk brn & sal 4.00 1.00
Nos. 277-279 (3) 6.00 1.50

Exhibition of Sacred Missionary Art held at Lisbon in 1951.

Stamp of Portugal and Arms of Colonies — A14

1953 **Photo.** **Unwmk.**
280 A14 50c multicolored .65 .55

Centenary of Portugal's first postage stamps.

Analeptes Trifasciata — A15

1953 *Perf. 11½*
Various Beetles in Natural Colors
281 A15 5c yellow .25 .25
282 A15 10c blue .25 .25
283 A15 30c org vermilion .25 .25
284 A15 50c yellow grn .25 .25
285 A15 70c gray brn .60 .25
286 A15 1e orange .60 .25
287 A15 2e pale ol grn 1.50 .25
288 A15 3e lilac rose 2.25 .70
289 A15 5e lt blue grn 3.75 1.10
290 A15 10e lilac 6.00 3.00
Nos. 281-290 (10) 15.70 6.55

Sao Paulo Issue
Common Design Type

1954 **Litho.** *Perf. 13½*
291 CD46 1e lil rose, bl gray & blk .35 .25

Belem Tower, Lisbon, and Colonial Arms — A16

1955, Apr. 14
292 A16 1e blue & multi .25 .25
293 A16 2.50e gray & multi .50 .25

Visit of Pres. Francisco H. C. Lopes.

Fair Emblem, Globe and Arms — A17

1958 **Unwmk.** *Perf. 12x11½*
294 A17 2.50e multicolored .65 .55

World's Fair at Brussels.

Tropical Medicine Congress Issue
Common Design Type

Design: Maytenus senegalensis.

1958 *Perf. 13½*
295 CD47 5e multicolored 2.75 1.10

Honorio Barreto — A18

1959, Apr. 29 **Litho.** *Perf. 13½*
296 A18 2.50e multicolored .40 .25

Centenary of the death of Honorio Barreto, governor of Portuguese Guinea.

Nautical Astrolabe — A19

1960, June 25 *Perf. 13½*
297 A19 2.50e multicolored .40 .25

500th anniversary of the death of Prince Henry the Navigator.

Traveling Medical Unit — A20

1960 **Unwmk.** *Perf. 14½*
298 A20 1.50e multicolored .40 .25

10th anniv. of the Commission for Technical Cooperation in Africa South of the Sahara (C.C.T.A.).

Sports Issue
Common Design Type

1962, Jan. 18 **Litho.** *Perf. 13½*
299 CD48 50c Automobile race .25 .25
300 CD48 1e Tennis 1.00 .25
301 CD48 1.50e Shot put .70 .25
302 CD48 2.50e Wrestling .70 .25
303 CD48 3.50e Trapshooting .70 .25
304 CD48 15e Volleyball 1.60 .90
Nos. 299-304 (6) 4.95 2.15

Anti-Malaria Issue
Common Design Type

Design: Anopheles gambiae.

1962 **Unwmk.** *Perf. 13½*
305 CD49 2.50e multicolored 1.25 .45

African Spitting Cobra — A21

Snakes: 35c, African rock python. 70c, Boomslang. 80c, West African mamba. 1.50e, Smythe's water snake. 2e, Common night adder, horiz. 2.50e, Green swamp snake. 3.50e, Brown house snake. 4e, Spotted wolf snake. 5e, Common puff adder. 15e, Striped beauty snake. 20e, African egg-eating snake, horiz.

1963, Jan. 17 **Litho.** *Perf. 13½*
306 A21 20c multicolored .50 .25
307 A21 35c multicolored .50 .25
308 A21 70c multicolored 1.00 .35
309 A21 80c multicolored 1.00 .35
310 A21 1.50e multicolored 1.00 .35
311 A21 2e multicolored .75 .25
312 A21 2.50e multicolored 3.25 .45
313 A21 3.50e multicolored 1.00 .45
314 A21 4e multicolored 1.50 .45
315 A21 5e multicolored 2.00 .70
316 A21 15e multicolored 4.00 .80
317 A21 20e multicolored 6.00 .80
Nos. 306-317 (12) 22.50 5.45

For overprints see Guinea-Bissau Nos. 696-703.

Airline Anniversary Issue
Common Design Type

1963 **Litho.** *Perf. 14½*
318 CD50 2.50e lt brown & multi .65 .35

National Overseas Bank Issue
Common Design Type

Design: 2.50e, Joao de Andrade Córvo.

1964, May 16 *Perf. 13½*
319 CD51 2.50e multicolored .65 .40

ITU Issue
Common Design Type

1965, May 17 **Unwmk.** *Perf. 14½*
320 CD52 2.50e lt blue & multi 1.90 .75

Soldier, 1548 — A22

40c, Rifleman, 1578. 60c, Rifleman, 1640. 1e, Grenadier, 1721. 2.50e, Fusiliers captain, 1740. 4.50e, Infantryman, 1740. 7.50e, Sergeant major, 1762. 10e, Engineers' officer, 1806.

1966, Jan. 8 **Litho.** *Perf. 13½*
321 A22 25c multicolored .25 .25
322 A22 40c multicolored .25 .25
323 A22 60c multicolored .35 .25
324 A22 1e multicolored .45 .25
325 A22 2.50e multicolored 1.25 .40
326 A22 4.50e multicolored 2.10 1.10
327 A22 7.50e multicolored 2.10 1.40
328 A22 10e multicolored 2.75 1.60
Nos. 321-328 (8) 9.50 5.50

National Revolution Issue
Common Design Type

2.50e, Berta Craveiro Lopes School and Central Pavilion of Bissau Hospital.

1966, May 28 **Litho.** *Perf. 11½*
329 CD53 2.50e multicolored .55 .35

Navy Club Issue
Common Design Type

Designs: 50c, Capt. Oliveira Muzanty and cruiser Republica. 1e, Capt. Afonso de Cerqueira and torpedo boat Guadiana.

1967, Jan. 31 **Litho.** *Perf. 13*
330 CD54 50c multicolored .40 .25
331 CD54 1e multicolored .80 .65

Sacred Heart of Jesus Monument and Chapel of the Apparition — A23

1967, May 13 *Perf. 12½x13*
332 A23 50c multicolored .35 .35

50th anniv. of the appearance of the Virgin Mary to three shepherd children at Fatima.

Pres. Rodrigues Thomaz — A24

1968, Feb. 2 **Litho.** *Perf. 13½*
333 A24 1e multicolored .25 .25

Issued to commemorate the 1968 visit of Pres. Americo de Deus Rodrigues Thomaz.

Cabral's Coat of Arms — A25

1968, Apr. 22 **Litho.** *Perf. 14*
334 A25 2.50e multicolored .55 .25

Pedro Alvares Cabral, navigator who took possession of Brazil for Portugal, 500th birth anniv.

Admiral Coutinho Issue
Common Design Type

Design: 1e, Adm. Coutinho and astrolabe.

1969, Feb. 17 **Litho.** *Perf. 14*
335 CD55 1e multicolored .35 .25

Vasco da Gama Issue

Da Gama Coat of Arms — A26

1969, Aug. 29 **Litho.** *Perf. 14*
336 A26 2.50e multicolored .35 .25

Vasco da Gama (1469-1524), navigator.

Administration Reform Issue
Common Design Type

1969, Sept. 25 **Litho.** *Perf. 14*
337 CD56 50c multicolored .25 .25

King Manuel I Issue

Arms of King Manuel I — A27

1969, Dec. 1 **Litho.** *Perf. 14*
338 A27 2e multicolored .35 .25

Pres. Ulysses S. Grant and View of Bolama — A28

1970, Oct. 25 Litho. *Perf. 13½*

339 A28 2.50e multicolored .45 .25

Centenary of Pres. Grant's arbitration in 1868 of Portuguese-English dispute concerning Bolama.

Marshal Carmona Issue

Common Design Type

Design: 1.50e, Antonio Oscar Carmona in general's uniform.

1970, Nov. 15 Litho. *Perf. 14*

340 CD57 1.50e multicolored .35 .25

Luiz Camoens — A29

1972, May 25 Litho. *Perf. 13*

341 A29 50c brn org & multi .25 .25

4th centenary of publication of The Lusiads by Luiz Camoens (1524-1580).

Olympic Games Issue

Common Design Type

Design: 2.50e, Weight lifting, hammer throw and Olympic emblem.

1972, June 20 *Perf. 14x13½*

342 CD59 2.50e multicolored .45 .25

Lisbon-Rio de Janeiro Flight Issue

Common Design Type

1e, "Lusitania" taking off from Lisbon.

1972, Sept. 20 Litho. *Perf. 13½*

343 CD60 1e multicolored .25 .25

WMO Centenary Issue

Common Design Type

1973, Dec. 15 Litho. *Perf. 13*

344 CD61 2e lt brown & multi .45 .35

AIR POST STAMPS

Common Design Type

Perf. 13½x13

1938, Sept. 19 Engr. Unwmk.

Name and Value in Black

C1	CD39	10c red orange	.60	.45
C2	CD39	20c purple	.60	.45
C3	CD39	50c orange	.65	.45
C4	CD39	1e ultra	.65	.50
C5	CD39	2e lilac brown	6.00	3.50
C6	CD39	3e dark green	2.00	1.25
C7	CD39	5e red brown	5.00	1.25
C8	CD39	9e rose carmine	7.00	3.00
C9	CD39	10e magenta	11.50	3.50
		Nos. C1-C9 (9)	34.00	14.35

No. C7 exists with overprint "Exposicao Internacional de Nova York, 1939-1940" and Trylon and Perisphere. Value $850.

POSTAGE DUE STAMPS

D1

Without Gum

1904 Unwmk. Typo. *Perf. 12*

J1	D1	5r yellow green	.60	.45
J2	D1	10r slate	.60	.45
J3	D1	20r yellow brown	.65	.55
J4	D1	30r red orange	1.90	1.60
J5	D1	50r gray brown	1.90	1.60
J6	D1	60r red brown	4.25	2.75
J7	D1	100r lilac	4.25	2.75
J8	D1	130r dull blue	3.25	2.10
J9	D1	200r carmine	6.50	5.25
J10	D1	500r violet	11.00	6.00
		Nos. J1-J10 (10)	34.90	23.50

Same Overprinted in Carmine or Green

1911 Without Gum

J11	D1	5r yellow green	.25	.25
J12	D1	10r slate	.25	.25
J13	D1	20r yellow brown	.35	.35
J14	D1	30r red orange	.35	.35
J15	D1	50r gray brown	.35	.35
J16	D1	60r red brown	1.00	.80
J17	D1	100r lilac	1.90	1.40
J18	D1	130r dull blue	1.90	1.00
J19	D1	200r carmine (G)	1.90	1.50
J20	D1	500r violet	1.10	1.00
		Nos. J11-J20 (10)	9.35	7.25

Nos. J2-J10 Overprinted

1919 Without Gum

J21	D1	10r slate	8.25	8.25
J22	D1	20r yellow brown	9.00	9.00
J23	D1	30r red orange	6.50	5.75
J24	D1	50r gray brown	2.50	2.10
J25	D1	60r red brown	800.00	500.00
J26	D1	100r lilac	2.25	1.90
J27	D1	130r dull blue	22.50	19.00
J28	D1	200r carmine	2.75	2.50
J29	D1	500r violet	24.00	20.00
		Nos. J21-J24,J26-J29 (8)	77.75	68.50

No. J25 was not regularly issued but exists on genuine covers.

D2

1921

J30	D2	½c yellow green	.25	.25
J31	D2	1c slate	.25	.25
J32	D2	2c orange brown	.25	.25
J33	D2	3c orange	.25	.25
J34	D2	5c gray brown	.25	.25
J35	D2	6c light brown	.25	.25
J36	D2	10c red violet	.60	.60
J37	D2	13c dull blue	.60	.60
J38	D2	20c carmine	.60	.60
J39	D2	50c gray	.60	.60
		Nos. J30-J39 (10)	3.90	3.90

Catalogue values for unused stamps in this section, from this point to the end of the section, are for Never Hinged items.

Common Design Type

Photogravure and Typographed

1952 Unwmk. *Perf. 14*

Numeral in Red, Frame Multicolored

J40	CD45	10c olive green	.25	.25
J41	CD45	30c purple	.25	.25
J42	CD45	50c dark green	.25	.25
J43	CD45	1e violet blue	.30	.30
J44	CD45	2e olive black	.50	.50
J45	CD45	5e brown red	1.00	1.00
		Nos. J40-J45 (6)	2.55	2.55

WAR TAX STAMPS

WT1

Perf. 11½x12

1919, May 20 Typo. Unwmk.

MR1	WT1	10r brn, buff & blk	45.00	27.50
MR2	WT1	40r brn, buff & blk	40.00	22.50
MR3	WT1	50r brn, buff & blk	42.50	25.00
		Nos. MR1-MR3 (3)	127.50	75.00

The 40r is not overprinted "REPUBLICA."

Some authorities consider Nos. MR2-MR3 to be revenue stamps.

NEWSPAPER STAMP

N1

1893 Typo. Unwmk. *Perf. 12½*

P1	N1	2½r brown	1.25	.75
a.		Perf. 13½	1.25	.90

For surcharge and overprint see Nos. 89, 189.

POSTAL TAX STAMPS

Pombal Issue

Common Design Types

1925 Unwmk. Engr. *Perf. 12½*

RA1	CD28	15c red & black	.55	.45
RA2	CD29	15c red & black	.55	.45
RA3	CD30	15c red & black	.55	.45
		Nos. RA1-RA3 (3)	1.65	1.35

Coat of Arms — PT7

Without Gum

1934, Apr. 1 Typo. *Perf. 11½*

RA4	PT7	50c red brn & grn	7.50	5.00
a.		Tête beche pair		450.00

Coat of Arms — PT8

1938-40 Without Gum

RA5	PT8	50c ol bis & citron	6.50	3.25
RA6	PT8	50c lt grn & ol brn ('40)	6.50	3.25

Coat of Arms — PT9

1942 Without Gum *Perf. 11*

RA7 PT9 50c black & yellow 1.60 1.00

1959, July Unwmk. Without Gum

RA8 PT9 30c dark ocher & blk .25 .25

See Nos. RA24-RA26.

Lusignian Cross — PT10

1967 Typo. *Perf. 11x11½*

Without Gum

RA9	PT10	50c pink, red & blk	.80	.80
RA10	PT10	1e grn, red & blk	.80	.80
RA11	PT10	5e gray, red & blk	1.10	1.10
RA12	PT10	10e lt bl, red & blk	2.25	2.25
		Nos. RA9-RA12 (4)	4.95	4.95

The tax was for national defense.

A 50e was used for revenue only.

Lusignian Cross — PT11

1967, Aug. Typo. *Perf. 11*

Without Gum

RA13	PT11	50c pink, blk & red	.55	.55
RA14	PT11	1e pale grn, blk & red	.55	.55
RA15	PT11	5e gray, blk & red	1.10	1.10
RA16	PT11	10e lt bl, blk & red	2.25	2.25
		Nos. RA13-RA16 (4)	4.45	4.45

The tax was for national defense.

Catalogue values for unused stamps in this section, from this point to the end of the section, are for Never Hinged items.

Carved Figurine — PT12

Art from Bissau Museum: 1e, Tree of Life, with 2 birds, horiz. No. RA19, Man wearing horned headgear ("Vaca Bruto"). No. RA20, as No. RA19, inscribed "Tocador de Bombolon." 2.50e, The Magistrate. 5e, Man bearing burden on head. 10e, Stylized pelican.

1968 Litho. *Perf. 13½*

RA17	PT12	50c gray & multi	.25	.25
a.		Yellow paper	.80	
RA18	PT12	1e multi	.25	.25
RA19	PT12	2e multi	.25	.25
RA20	PT12	2e multi	*6.00*	
RA21	PT12	2.50e multi	.25	.25
RA22	PT12	5e multi	.35	.35
RA23	PT12	10e multi	.75	.75
		Nos. RA17-RA19,RA21-RA23 (6)	2.10	2.10

Obligatory on all inland mail Mar. 15-Apr. 15 and Dec. 15-Jan. 15, and all year on parcels.

A souvenir sheet embracing Nos. RA17-RA19 and RA21-RA23 exists. The stamps have simulated perforations. Value $3.50.

For surcharges see Nos. RA27-RA28.

Arms Type of 1942
1968 Typo. *Perf. 11*
Without Gum
RA24 PT9 2.50e lt blue & blk .45 .45
RA25 PT9 5e green & blk .80 .80
RA26 PT9 10e dp blue & blk 1.60 1.60
Nos. RA24-RA26 (3) 2.85 2.85

No. RA20 Surcharged

1968 Litho. *Perf. 13½*
RA27 PT12 50c on 2e multi .35 .35
RA28 PT12 1e on 2e multi .35 .35

Black and White Hands Holding Sword — PT13

1968 Litho. *Perf. 13½*
RA29 PT13 50c pink & multi .25 .25
RA30 PT13 1e multicolored .25 .25
RA31 PT13 2e yellow & multi .25 .25
RA32 PT13 2.50e buff & multi .25 .25
RA33 PT13 3e multicolored .35 .35
RA34 PT13 4e gray & multi .40 .40
RA35 PT13 5e multicolored .45 .45
RA36 PT13 10e multicolored .90 .90
Nos. RA29-RA36 (8) 3.10 3.10

The surtax was for national defense. Other denominations exist: 8e, 9e, 15e. Value, $2 each.

Mother and Children — PT14

1971, June Litho. *Perf. 13½*
RA37 PT14 50c multicolored .25 .25
RA38 PT14 1e multicolored .25 .25
RA39 PT14 2e multicolored .25 .25
RA40 PT14 3e multicolored .25 .25
RA41 PT14 4e multicolored .35 .25
RA42 PT14 5e multicolored .45 .40
RA43 PT14 10e multicolored .90 .55
Nos. RA37-RA43 (7) 2.70 2.20

A 20e exists. Value $4.

POSTAL TAX DUE STAMPS

Pombal Issue
Common Design Types
1925 Unwmk. *Perf. 12½*
RAJ1 CD28 30c red & black .55 .45
RAJ2 CD29 30c red & black .55 .45
RAJ3 CD30 30c red & black .55 .45
Nos. RAJ1-RAJ3 (3) 1.65 1.35

PORTUGUESE INDIA

'pōr-chi-gēz 'in-dē-ə

LOCATION — West coast of the Indian peninsula
GOVT. — Portuguese colony
AREA — 1,537 sq. mi.
POP. — 649,000 (1958)
CAPITAL — Panjim (Nova-Goa)

The colony was seized by India on Dec. 18, 1961, and annexed by that republic.

1000 Reis = 1 Milreis
12 Reis = 1 Tanga (1881-82)
(Real = singular of Reis)
16 Tangas = 1 Rupia
100 Centavos = 1 Escudo (1959)

Catalogue values for unused stamps in this country are for Never Hinged items, beginning with Scott 490 in the regular postage section, Scott J43 in the postage due section, and Scott RA6 in the postal tax section.

Expect Nos. 1-55, 70-112 to have rough perforations. Stamps frequently were cut apart because of the irregular and missing perforations. Scissor separations that do not remove perfs do not negatively affect value.

Numeral of Value — A1

A1: Large figures of value.
"REIS" in Roman capitals. "S" and "R" of "SERVICO" smaller and "E" larger than the other letters. 33 lines in background. Side ornaments of four dashes.

A2: Large figures of value.
"REIS" in block capitals. "S," "E" and "R" same size as other letters of "SERVICO." 44 lines in background. Side ornaments of five dots.

Handstamped from a Single Die
Perf. 13 to 18 & Compound
1871, Oct. 1 Unwmk.
Thin Transparent Brittle Paper
1 A1 10r black 625.00 325.00
2 A1 20r dk carmine 1,350. 300.00
a. 20r orange vermilion 1,350. 300.00
3 A1 40r Prus blue 475.00 325.00
4 A1 100r yellow grn 550.00 375.00
5 A1 200r ocher yel 850.00 450.00

1872 Thick Soft Wove Paper
5A A1 10r black *1,500.* 350.00
6 A1 20r dk carmine *1,650.* 400.00
7 A1 20r orange ver *1,800.* 400.00
7A A1 100r yellow grn —
8 A1 200r ocher yel *1,700.* 1,000.
9 A1 300r dp red violet *3,000.*

The 600r and 900r of type A1 are bogus.
See Nos. 24-28. For surcharges see Nos. 70-71, 73, 83, 94, 99, 104, 108.

Numeral of Value — A2

Perf. 12½ to 14½ & Compound
1872
10 A2 10r black 260.00 100.00
11 A2 20r vermilion 225.00 85.00
a. "20" omitted *1,000.*
12 A2 40r blue 70.00 60.00
a. Tête bêche pair *5,750.* *5,750.*
b. 40r dark blue 85.00 60.00
13 A2 100r deep green 70.00 60.00
14 A2 200r yellow 275.00 250.00
15 A2 300r red violet 275.00 225.00
a. Imperf.
16 A2 600r red violet 175.00 140.00
a. "600" double *700.00*
17 A2 900r red violet 200.00 175.00
Nos. 10-17 (8) 1,550. 1,095.

An unused 100r blue green exists with watermark of lozenges and gray burelage on back. Experts believe it to be a proof.

White Laid Paper
18 A2 10r black 37.50 32.50
a. Tête bêche pair *14,000.* *8,500.*
b. 10r brownish black 37.50 30.00
19 A2 20r vermilion 35.00 27.50
20 A2 40r blue 70.00 57.50
a. "40" double —
b. Tête bêche pair — —
21 A2 100r green 62.50 45.00
a. "100" double *450.00*
22 A2 200r yellow 175.00 175.00
Nos. 18-22 (5) 380.00 337.50

See No. 23. For surcharges see Nos. 72, 82, 95-96, 100-101, 105-106, 109-110.

Re-issues
1873 Thin Bluish Toned Paper
23 A2 20r vermilion 200.00 160.00
24 A1 10r black 14.00 8.50
a. "1" inverted 125.00 100.00
b. "10" double 400.00
25 A1 20r vermilion 17.00 11.50
a. "20" double 400.00
b. "20" inverted
26 A1 300r dp violet 110.00 85.00
a. "300" double 475.00
27 A1 600r dp violet 140.00 100.00
a. "600" double 575.00
b. "600" inverted 575.00
28 A1 900r dp violet 140.00 100.00
a. "900" double 675.00
b. "900" triple 1,000.
Nos. 23-28 (6) 621.00 465.00

Nos. 23 to 26 are re-issues of Nos. 11, 5A, 7, and 9. The paper is thinner and harder than that of the 1871-72 stamps and slightly transparent. It was originally bluish white but is frequently stained yellow by the gum.

A3

A3: Same as A1 with small figures.

1874 Thin Bluish Toned Paper
29 A3 10r black 35.00 27.50
a. "10" and "20" superimposed 475.00 *450.00*
30 A3 20r vermilion 550.00 350.00
a. "20" double *625.00*

For surcharge see No. 84.

A4

A4: Same as A2 with small figures.

1875
31 A4 10r black 37.50 22.50
a. Value sideways 550.00
32 A4 15r rose 12.50 9.00
a. "15" inverted 475.00
b. "15" double
c. Value omitted 1,150.
33 A4 20r vermilion 70.00 42.50
a. "0" missing 850.00 575.00
b. "20" sideways *850.00*
c. "20" double
Nos. 31-33 (3) 120.00 74.00

For surcharges see Nos. 74, 78, 85.

A5

A6

A5: Re-cutting of A1.
Small figures. "REIS" in Roman capitals. Letters larger. "V" of "SERVICO" barred. 33 lines in background. Side ornaments of five dots.

A6: First re-cutting of A2.
Small figures. "REIS" in block capitals. Letters re-cut. "V" of "SERVICO" barred. 41 lines above and 43 below "REIS." Side ornaments of five dots.

Perf. 12½ to 13½ & Compound
1876
34 A5 10r black 20.00 14.00
35 A5 20r vermilion 16.00 11.50
a. "20" double —
36 A6 10r black 6.25 4.25
a. Double impression 525.00
b. "10" double 525.00
37 A6 15r rose 425.00 325.00
a. "15" omitted — *1,000.*
38 A6 20r vermilion 22.50 17.00
39 A6 40r blue 110.00 85.00
40 A6 100r green 160.00 150.00
a. Imperf.
41 A6 200r yellow 1,000. 675.00
42 A6 300r violet 550.00 450.00
a. "300" omitted
43 A6 600r violet *800.00* *675.00*
44 A6 900r violet *1,200.* *750.00*
a. "900" omitted

For surcharges see Nos. 75-76, 78C-80, 86-87, 91-92, 98, 102, 107, 111.

A7

A8

A9

A7: Same as A5 with addition of a star above and a bar below the value.
A8: Second re-cutting of A2. Same as A6 but 41 lines both above and below "REIS." Star above and bar below value.
A9: Third re-cutting of A2. 41 lines above and 38 below "REIS." Star above and bar below value. White line around central oval.

1877
45 A7 10r black 30.00 25.00
46 A8 10r black 42.50 37.50
47 A9 10r black 29.00 25.00
a. "10" omitted
48 A9 15r rose 32.50 27.50
49 A9 20r vermilion 8.50 8.00
50 A9 40r blue 17.00 16.00
a. "40" omitted 42.50 35.00
51 A9 100r green 100.00 60.00
a. "100" omitted
52 A9 200r yellow 100.00 70.00
53 A9 300r violet 150.00 85.00
54 A9 600r violet 150.00 85.00
55 A9 900r violet 150.00 85.00
Nos. 45-55 (11) 809.50 524.00

For surcharges see Nos. 77, 81, 88-90, 93, 112.
No. 47, 20r, 40r and 200r exist imperf.

Portuguese Crown — A10

1877, July 15 Typo. *Perf. 12½, 13½*
56 A10 5r black 5.00 3.50
57 A10 10r yellow 9.00 7.25
a. Imperf.
58 A10 20r bister 9.50 7.00
59 A10 25r rose 10.00 8.00
60 A10 40r blue 14.00 11.00
a. Perf. 12½ 175.00 140.00
61 A10 50r yellow grn 32.50 20.00
62 A10 100r lilac 16.00 11.50
63 A10 200r orange 22.50 17.50
64 A10 300r yel brn 29.00 25.00
Nos. 56-64 (9) 147.50 110.75

1880-81
65a A10 10r green 10.00 8.50
66 A10 25r slate 37.50 27.50
67a A10 25r violet 27.50 20.00
68a A10 40r yellow 35.00 27.50
69a A10 50r dk blue 17.50 16.00
Nos. 65a-69a (5) 127.50 99.50

For surcharges see Nos. 113-161. The 1880-81 issue exists perf 12½ and 13½ on thin paper, and 13½ on medium paper. Nos. 65a-69a above are the most common varieties. For detailed listings, see the *Scott Classic Specialized Catalogue.*

The stamps of the 1877-81 issues were reprinted in 1885, on stout very white paper, ungummed and with rough perforation 13½. They were again reprinted in 1905 on thin white paper with shiny white gum and clean-cut perforation 13½ with large holes. Value of the lowest-cost reprint, $3 each.

Stamps of 1871-77 Surcharged with New Values

1881 **Black Surcharge**

70 A1 1½r on 20r (#2) *1,500.*
71 A1 1½r on 20r (#7) *1,000.*
72 A2 1½r on 20r (#11) *800.00*
73 A1 1½r on 20r (#25) 225.00 200.00
74 A4 1½r on 20r (#33) 140.00 125.00
a. Inverted surcharge 250.00
75 A5 1½r on 20r (#35) 110.00 85.00
76 A6 1½r on 20r (#38) 125.00 110.00
77 A9 1½r on 20r (#49) 200.00 140.00
78 A4 5r on 15r (#32) 2.50 2.50
a. Double surcharge 10.00
b. Inverted surcharge 10.00
78C A6 5r on 15r (#37) 2.50 2.50
79 A5 5r on 20r (#35) 2.50
a. Double surcharge 14.00
b. Inverted surcharge —
80 A6 5r on 20r (#38) 2.75 2.50
a. Double surcharge —
b. Inverted surcharge —
81 A9 5r on 20r (#49) 5.00 4.00
a. Double surcharge —
b. Invtd. surcharge —

Red Surcharge

82 A2 5r on 10r (#18) *600.00* *350.00*
83 A1 5r on 10r (#24) *600.00* *300.00*
84 A3 5r on 10r (#29) *1,750.*
85 A4 5r on 10r (#31) *125.00* *125.00*
86 A5 5r on 10r (#34) 6.00 6.00
a. Double surcharge 17.00
87 A6 5r on 10r (#36) 9.50 7.75
a. Inverted surcharge
88 A7 5r on 10r (#45) 90.00 50.00
a. Inverted surcharge 175.00
89 A8 5r on 10r (#46) 190.00 82.50
90 A9 5r on 10r (#47) 40.00 35.00
a. Inverted surcharge 82.50
b. Double surcharge 82.50

Similar Surcharge, Handstamped Black Surcharge

1883

91 A5 1½r on 10r (#34) 1,650. *825.00*
92 A6 1½r on 10r (#36) 1,100. *825.00*
93 A9 1½r on 10r (#47) *825.00* *600.00*
94 A1 4½r on 40r (#3) 2,500. *775.00*
95 A2 4½r on 40r (#12) 35.00 35.00
96 A2 4½r on 40r (#20) 35.00 35.00
98 A6 4½r on 40r (#39) 35.00 35.00
99 A1 4½r on 100r (#4) 2,500. *775.00*
100 A2 4½r on 100r (#13) 45.00 42.50
101 A2 4½r on 100r (#21) 45.00 42.50
102 A6 4½r on 100r (#40) 40.00 42.50
104 A1 6r on 100r (#4) 2,200. *1,200.*
105 A2 6r on 100r (#13) *375.00* *275.00*
106 A2 6r on 100r (#21) *275.00* *225.00*
107 A6 6r on 100r (#40) *350.00* *275.00*
108 A1 6r on 200r (#5) *825.00* *600.00*
109 A2 6r on 200r (#14) *275.00*
110 A2 6r on 200r (#22) *275.00* *275.00*
111 A6 6r on 200r (#41) *450.00*
112 A9 6r on 200r (#52) *550.00* *500.00*

Stamps of 1877-81 Surcharged in Black

1881-82

113 A10 1½r on 5r blk 1.40 1.10
a. With additional surcharge "4½" in blue 150.00 125.00
114 A10 1½r on 10r grn 1.40 1.10
a. With additional surch. "6" 160.00 110.00
115 A10 1½r on 20r bis 11.50 8.75
a. Inverted surcharge 27.50
b. Double surcharge 27.50
c. Pair, one without surcharge —
116 A10 1½r on 25r slate 40.00 35.00
117 A10 1½r on 100r lil 60.00 47.50
118 A10 4½r on 10r grn 190.00 160.00
119 A10 4½r on 20r bis 4.00 2.75
a. Inverted surcharge 82.50 65.00
120 A10 4½r on 25r vio 11.50 11.00
121 A10 4½r on 100r lil 225.00 160.00
122 A10 6r on 10r yel 47.50 45.00
123 A10 6r on 10r grn 10.00 8.00
124 A10 6r on 20r bis 17.00 15.00
125 A10 6r on 25r slate 35.00 27.50
126 A10 6r on 25r vio 2.25 1.75
127 A10 6r on 40r blue 82.50 70.00
128 A10 6r on 40r yel 42.50 35.00
129 A10 6r on 50r grn 47.50 38.50
130 A10 6r on 50r blue 110.00 90.00
Nos. 113-130 (18) 939.05 757.95

Surcharged in Black

131 A10 1t on 10r grn 450.00 325.00
a. With additional surch. "6" 900.00 775.00
132 A10 1t on 20r bis 47.50 42.50
133 A10 1t on 25r slate 35.00 30.00
134 A10 1t on 25r vio 13.00 9.00
135 A10 1t on 40r blue 19.00 17.50
136 A10 1t on 50r grn 55.00 47.50
137 A10 1t on 50r blue 25.00 19.00
138 A10 1t on 100r lil 24.00 13.00
139 A10 1t on 200r org 47.50 42.50
140 A10 2t on 25r slate 35.00 35.00
a. Small "T" 55.00 40.00
141 A10 2t on 25r vio 14.00 11.50
142 A10 2t on 40r blue 42.50 35.00
143 A10 2t on 40r yel 52.50 42.50
144 A10 2t on 50r grn 15.00 13.00
a. Inverted surcharge 110.00 100.00
145 A10 2t on 50r blue 90.00 75.00
146 A10 2t on 100r lil 11.50 9.25
147 A10 2t on 200r org 40.00 35.00
148 A10 2t on 300r brn 35.00 30.00
149 A10 4t on 10r grn 14.00 11.50
a. Inverted surcharge 45.00 45.00
150 A10 4t on 50r grn 13.00 10.00
a. With additional surch. "2" 160.00 110.00
151 A10 4t on 200r org 40.00 35.00
152 A10 8t on 20r bis 35.00 24.00
153 A10 8t on 25r rose 190.00 160.00
154 A10 8t on 40r blue 47.50 40.00
155 A10 8t on 100r lil 40.00 35.00
156 A10 8t on 200r org 35.00 30.00
157 A10 8t on 300r brn 47.50 40.00
Nos. 131-157 (27) 1,513. 1,217.

1882 **Blue Surcharge**

158 A10 4½r on 5r black 12.00 10.50

Similar Surcharge, Handstamped

1883

159 A10 1½r on 5r black 55.00 35.00
160 A10 1½r on 10r grn 82.50 45.00
161 A10 4½r on 100r lil *400.00* *325.00*

The "2" in "½" is 3mm high, instead of 2mm as on Nos. 113, 114 and 121.

The handstamp is known double on #159-161.

A12

With or Without Accent on "E" of "REIS"

1882-83 **Typo.**

162 A12 1½r black .55 .45
a. "½" for "1½"
163 A12 4½r olive bister .95 .45
164 A12 6r green .80 .45
165 A12 1t rose .80 .45
166 A12 2t blue .80 .45
167 A12 4t lilac 3.25 2.75
168 A12 8t orange 3.25 2.75
Nos. 162-168 (7) 10.40 7.75

There were three printings of the 1882-83 issue. The first had "REIS" in thick letters with acute accent on the "E." The second had "REIS" in thin letters with accent on the "E." The third had the "E" without accent. In the first printing the "E" sometimes had a grave or circumflex accent.

The third printing may be divided into two sets, with or without a small circle in the cross of the crown.

Stamps doubly printed or with value omitted, double, inverted or misplaced are printer's waste.

Nos. 162-168 were reprinted on thin white paper, with shiny white gum and clean-cut perforation 13½. Value of lowest-cost reprint, $1 each.

"REIS" no serifs — A13

"REIS" with serifs — A14

1883 **Litho.** ***Imperf.***

169 A13 1½r black 1.40 1.10
a. Tête bêche pair
b. "1½" double *425.00* *325.00*
170 A13 4½r olive grn 14.00 11.00
a. "4½" omitted 350.00 275.00
171 A13 6r green 14.00 11.00
a. Tête bêche pair 1,200.
b. "6" omitted 400.00 300.00
172 A14 1½r black 125.00 55.00
a. "1½" omitted 350.00 325.00
173 A14 6r green 62.50 47.50
a. "6" omitted 425.00 350.00
Nos. 169-173 (5) 216.90 125.60

Nos. 169-171 exist with unofficial perf. 12.

King Luiz — A15

Perf. 12½, 13½

1886, Apr. 29 **Embossed**

174 A15 1½r black 3.00 1.40
a. Perf. 13½ 150.00 87.50
175 A15 4½r bister 4.00 1.50
a. Perf. 13½ 30.00 14.00
176 A15 6r dp green 5.00 1.75
a. Perf. 13½ 35.00 15.00
177 A15 1t brt rose 7.00 3.00
178 A15 2t deep blue 9.00 4.50
179 A15 4t gray vio 11.00 4.50
180 A15 8t orange 10.00 4.75
Nos. 174-180 (7) 49.00 21.40

For surcharges and overprints see Nos. 224-230, 277-278, 282, 317-323, 354, 397.

Nos. 178-179 were reprinted. Originals have yellow gum. Reprints have white gum and clean-cut perforation 13½. Value, $4 each.

King Carlos — A16

1895-96 **Typo.** ***Perf. 11½, 12½, 13½***

181 A16 1½r black 3.00 .65
182 A16 4½r pale orange 3.00 .65
a. Perf. 13½ 8.00 1.60
183 A16 6r green 3.00 .65
a. Perf. 12½ 3.50 1.10
184 A16 9r gray lilac 5.00 3.00
185 A16 1t lt blue 3.00 .55
a. Perf. 12½ 5.50 2.50
186 A16 2t rose 2.00 .65
a. Perf. 12½ 4.25 2.25
187 A16 4t dk blue 3.00 .80
a. Perf. 12½ 5.25 3.25
188 A16 8t brt violet 5.00 2.75
Nos. 181-188 (8) 27.00 9.70

For surcharges and overprints see Nos. 231-238,275-276, 279-281, 324-331, 352.

No. 184 was reprinted. Reprints have white gum, and clean-cut perforation 13½. Value $10.

Common Design Types pictured following the introduction.

Vasco da Gama Issue

Common Design Types

1898, May 1 **Engr.** ***Perf. 14 to 15***

189 CD20 1½r blue green 1.00 .90
190 CD21 4½r red 1.00 .90
191 CD22 6r red violet 1.25 .75
192 CD23 9r yellow green 1.50 1.00
193 CD24 1t dk blue 3.00 1.60
194 CD25 2t violet brn 3.75 1.90
195 CD26 4t bister brn 3.75 1.90
196 CD27 8t bister 5.00 4.00
Nos. 189-196 (8) 20.25 12.95

For overprints and surcharges see Nos. 290-297, 384-389.

King Carlos — A17

Name and Value in Black except No. 219

1898-1903 **Typo.** ***Perf. 11½***

197 A17 1r gray ('02) .35 .25
198 A17 1½r orange .35 .25
199 A17 1½r slate ('02) .45 .25
200 A17 2r orange ('02) .35 .25
201 A17 2½r yel brn ('02) .45 .25
202 A17 3r dp blue ('02) .45 .25
203 A17 4½r lt green .70 .55
204 A17 6r brown .70 .55
205 A17 6r gray grn ('02) .45 .25
206 A17 9r dull vio .80 .55
a. 9r gray lilac 1.75 1.75
208 A17 1t sea green .80 .50
209 A17 1t car rose ('02) .60 .25
210 A17 2t blue 1.40 .55
a. Perf. 13½ 30.00 7.75
211 A17 2t brown ('02) 3.25 2.10
212 A17 2½t dull bl ('02) 15.00 6.50
213 A17 4t blue, *blue* 3.25 2.25
214 A17 5t brn, *straw* ('02) 4.50 2.10
215 A17 8t red lil, *pnksh* 5.50 1.40
216 A17 8t red vio, *pink* ('02) 5.00 3.00
217 A17 12t blue, *pink* 10.00 2.25
218 A17 12t grn, *pink* ('02) 9.00 3.25
219 A17 1rp blk & red, *bl* 10.00 6.50
220 A17 1rp dl bl, *straw* ('02) 15.00 7.25
221 A17 2rp vio, *yelsh* 18.00 8.25
222 A17 2rp gray blk, *straw* ('03) 20.00 12.00
Nos. 197-222 (25) 126.35 61.55

Several stamps of this issue exist without value or with value inverted but they are not known to have been issued in this condition. The 1r and 6r in carmine rose are believed to be color trials.

For surcharges and overprints see Nos. 223, 239-259, 260C-274, 283-289, 300-316, 334-350, 376-383, 390-396, 398-399.

No. 210 Surcharged in Black

1900

223 A17 1½r on 2t blue 6.00 2.00
a. Inverted surcharge
b. Perf. 13½ 35.00 22.50

Stamps of 1885-96 Surcharged in Black or Red

On Stamps of 1886

1902 ***Perf. 12½, 13½***

224 A15 1r on 2t blue 1.10 .50
225 A15 2r on 4½r bis .65 .50
a. Inverted surcharge *22.50* *22.50*
b. Double surcharge
226 A15 2½r on 6r green .55 .25
227 A15 3r on 1t rose .55 .25
228 A15 2½t on 1½r blk (R) 3.00 1.40
229 A15 2½t on 4t gray vio 5.00 2.75
230 A15 5t on 8t orange 3.00 .65
a. Perf. 12½ 27.50 17.00

On Stamps of 1895-96

Perf. 11½, 12½, 13½

231 A16 1r on 6r green .50 .25
232 A16 2r on 8t brt vio .35 .25
233 A16 2½r on 9r gray vio .35 .35
234 A16 3r on 4½r yel 2.00 1.00
a. Inverted surcharge 24.00 24.00
235 A16 3r on 1t lt bl 2.00 .90
236 A16 2½t on 1½r blk (R) 3.00 .80
237 A16 5t on 2t rose 3.00 .80
a. Perf. 12½ 35.00 22.50
238 A16 5t on 4t dk bl 3.00 .80
a. Perf. 12½ 35.00 22.50
Nos. 224-238 (15) 28.05 11.45

Nos. 224, 229, 231, 233, 234, 235 and 238 were reprinted in 1905. They have whiter gum than the originals and very clean-cut perf. 13½. Value $2.50 each.

Nos. 204, 208, 210 Overprinted

1902 ***Perf. 11½***

239 A17 6r brown 3.00 1.40
a. Inverted overprint

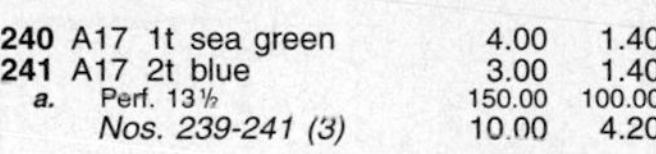

240 A17 1t sea green 4.00 1.40
241 A17 2t blue 3.00 1.40
a. Perf. 13½ 150.00 100.00
Nos. 239-241 (3) 10.00 4.20

No. 212 Surcharged in Black

1905
243 A17 2t on 2½t dull blue 2.25 1.60

Stamps of 1898-1903 Overprinted in Lisbon in Carmine or Green

1911
244 A17 1r gray .25 .25
a. Inverted overprint 11.00 11.00
245 A17 1½r slate .25 .25
a. Double overprint 11.00 11.00
246 A17 2r orange .25 .25
a. Double overprint 15.00 15.00
b. Inverted overprint 11.00 11.00
247 A17 2½r yellow brn .25 .25
248 A17 3r deep blue .25 .25
249 A17 4½r light green .35 .25
250 A17 6r gray green .25 .25
251 A17 9r gray lilac .35 .25
252 A17 1t car rose (G) .50 .25
253 A17 2t brown .50 .25
254 A17 4t blue, *blue* 1.40 1.00
255 A17 5t brn, *straw* 1.40 1.00
256 A17 8t vio, *pink* 4.25 2.50
257 A17 12t grn, *pink* 4.50 2.50
258 A17 1rp dl bl, *straw* 7.00 4.75
259 A17 2rp gray blk, *straw* 8.75 7.50
Nos. 244-259 (16) 30.50 21.75

A18

Values are for pairs, both halves.

1911 Perforated Diagonally
260 A18 1r on 2r orange .80 .70
a. Without diagonal perf. 4.50 4.00
b. Cut diagonally instead of perf. 3.50 3.25

Stamps of Preceding Issues Perforated Vertically through the Middle and Each Half Surcharged

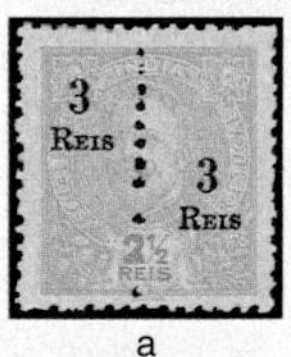
a

b

Values are for pairs, both halves of the stamp.

1912-13 On Issue of 1898-1903
260C A17(a) 1r on 2r org .25 .25
261 A17(a) 1r on 1t car .25 .25
262 A17(a) 1r on 5t brn, *straw* 300.00 225.00
263 A17(b) 1r on 5t brn, *straw* 7.75 6.00
264 A17(a) 1½r on 2½r yel brn .75 .65
264C A17(a) 1½r on 4½r lt grn 12.00 7.75
265 A17(a) 1½r on 9r gray lil .55 .45
266 A17(a) 1½r on 4t bl, *bl* .55 .45
267 A17(a) 2r on 2½r yel brn .70 .45
268 A17(a) 2r on 4t bl, *bl* 1.00 .70
269 A17(a) 3r on 2½r yel brn .70 .45
270 A17(a) 3r on 2t brown .70 .50
271 A17(a) 6r on 4½r lt grn .70 .60
272 A17(a) 6r on 9r gray lil .70 .55
273 A17(a) 6r on 9r dull vio 4.50 3.50
274 A17(b) 6r on 8t red vio, *pink* 1.60 1.00

On Nos. 237-238, 230, 226, 233
275 A16(b) 1r on 5t on 2t 20.00 17.00
276 A16(b) 1r on 5t on 4t 10.00 9.25
277 A15(b) 1r on 5t on 8t 5.00 3.25
278 A15(a) 2r on 2½r on 6r 4.25 3.25
279 A16(a) 2r on 2½r on 9r 25.00 24.00
280 A16(b) 3r on 5t on 2t 7.75 6.25
281 A16(b) 3r on 5t on 4t 7.75 6.25
282 A15(b) 3r on 5t on 8t 2.50 1.60

On Issue of 1911
283 A17(a) 1r on 1r gray .25 .25
283B A17(a) 1r on 2r org .25 .25
284 A17(a) 1r on 1t car .35 .25
285 A17(a) 1r on 5t brn, *straw* .35 .25
285A A17(b) 1r on 5t brn, *straw* 825.00 550.00
285B A17(a) 1½r on 4½r lt grn .65 .50
286 A17(a) 3r on 2t brn 11.50 8.50
289 A17(a) 6r on 9r gray lil .55 .45

There are several settings of these surcharges and many minor varieties of the letters and figures, notably a small "6." Nos. 260-289 were issued mostly without gum.

More than half of Nos. 260C-289 exist with inverted or double surcharge, or with bisecting perforation omitted. The legitimacy of these varieties is questioned. Price of inverted surcharges, $3-$15; double surcharges, $1-$4; perf. omitted, $1.50-$15.

Similar surcharges made without official authorization on stamps of type A17 are: 2r on 2½r, 3r on 2½r, 3r on 5t, and 6r on 4½r.

Vasco da Gama Issue Overprinted

1913
290 CD20 1½r blue green .35 .25
291 CD21 4½r red .35 .25
a. Double overprint 22.50
292 CD22 6r red violet .45 .40
a. Double overprint 22.50
293 CD23 9r yellow grn .45 .40
294 CD24 1t dark blue 1.00 .55
295 CD25 2t violet brown 2.25 1.25
296 CD26 4t orange brn 1.25 1.00
297 CD27 8t bister 2.25 1.40
Nos. 290-297 (8) 8.35 5.50

Issues of 1898-1913 Overprinted Locally in Red

1913-15 On Issues of 1898-1903
300 A17 2r orange 10.00 10.00
301 A17 2½r yellow brn .95 .80
302 A17 3r dp blue 19.00 17.00
303 A17 4½r lt green 1.90 1.60
304 A17 6r gray grn 25.00 20.00
305 A17 9r gray lilac 1.90 1.40
306 A17 1t sea green 45.00 35.00
307 A17 2t blue 50.00 35.00
309 A17 4t blue, *blue* 40.00 27.50
310 A17 5t brn, *straw* 55.00 35.00
311 A17 8t red vio, *pink* 65.00 45.00
312 A17 12t grn, *pink* 3.50 2.50
313 A17 1rp blk & red, *bl* 100.00 82.50
314 A17 1rp dl bl, *straw* 65.00 45.00
315 A17 2rp gray blk, *straw* 82.50 55.00
316 A17 2rp vio, *yelsh* 77.50 45.00
Nos. 300-316 (16) 642.25 458.30

Inverted or double overprints exist on 2½r, 4½r, 9r, 1rp and 2rp.

Nos. 300-316 were issued without gum except 4½r and 9r.

Nos. 302, 304, 306, 307, 310, 311 and 313 were not regularly issued. Nor were the 1½r, 2t brown and 12t blue on pink with preceding overprint.

Same Overprint In Red or Green on Provisional Issue of 1902
317 A15 1r on 2t blue 45.00 27.50
a. "REPUBLICA" inverted 140.00
318 A15 2r on 4½r bis 45.00 27.50
a. "REPUBLICA" inverted 140.00
319 A15 2½r on 6r grn .75 .65
a. "REPUBLICA" inverted 19.00 19.00
320 A15 3r on 1t rose (R) 11.00 8.75
321 A15 2½t on 4t gray vio 110.00 45.00
323 A15 5t on 8t org (G) 15.00 8.25
a. Red overprint 27.50 22.50
324 A16 1r on 6r grn 35.00 22.50
325 A16 2r on 8t vio 35.00 22.50
a. Inverted surcharge 110.00
327 A16 3r on 4½r yel 82.50 55.00
328 A16 3r on 1t lt bl 82.50 55.00
329 A16 5t on 2t rose (G) 10.00 3.00
330 A16 5t on 4t bl (G) 10.00 3.00
331 A16 5t on 4t bl (R) 10.00 4.25
a. "REPUBLICA" inverted 55.00
b. "REPUBLICA" double 55.00
Nos. 317-331 (13) 491.75 282.90

The 2½r on 1½r of types A15 and A16, the 3r on 1t (A15) and 2½r on 9r (A16) were clandestinely printed.

Some authorities question the status of No. 317-318, 320-321, 324, 327-328.

Same Overprint on Nos. 240-241

1913-15
334 A17 1t sea green 15.00 5.00
335 A17 2t blue 15.00 6.00

This overprint was applied to No. 239 without official authorization. Value $35.

On Issue of 1912-13 Perforated through the Middle

Values are for pairs, both halves of the stamp.

336 A17(a) 1r on 2r org 17.00 11.00
340 A17(a) 1½r on 4½r lt grn 17.00 11.00
341 A17(a) 1½r on 9r gray lil 20.00
342 A17(a) 1½r on 4t bl, *bl* 27.50
343 A17(a) 2r on 2½r yel brn 20.00
344 A17(a) 2r on 4t bl, *bl* 27.50 7.25
345 A17(a) 3r on 2½r yel brn 22.50
346 A17(a) 3r on 2t brn 17.00 5.25
347 A17(a) 6r on 4½r lt grn 1.10 .90
348 A17(a) 6r on 9r gray lil 1.60 1.60
350 A17(b) 6r on 8t red vio, *pink* 1.60 1.60
352 A16(b) 1r on 5t on 4t bl 110.00
354 A15(a) 2r on 2½r on 6r grn 13.00
Nos. 334-354 (15) 325.80

The 1r on 5t (A15), 1r on 1t (A17), 1½r on 2½r (A17), 3r on 5t on 8t (A15), and 6r on 9r (A17) were clandestinely printed.

Nos. 336, 347 exist with inverted surcharge.

Some authorities question the status of Nos. 341-345, 352 and 354.

Ceres — A21

Name and Value in Black
Chalky Paper

1914 Typo. *Perf. 15x14*
357 A21 1r olive brn .35 *.55*
358 A21 1½r yellow grn .35 .55
359 A21 2r black .70 .40
360 A21 2½r olive grn .70 .40
361 A21 3r lilac .70 .40
362 A21 4½r orange brn .70 .40
363 A21 5r blue green .70 .50
364 A21 6r lilac brown .70 .40
365 A21 9r ultra .70 .40
366 A21 10r carmine .95 .55
367 A21 1t lt violet 1.25 .55
368 A21 2t deep blue 1.25 .55
369 A21 3t yellow brown 1.90 .95
370 A21 4t slate 2.25 1.25
371 A21 8t plum 4.50 4.00
372 A21 12t brown, *green* 4.00 3.25
373 A21 1rp brown, *pink* 40.00 *50.00*
374 A21 2rp org, *salmon* 30.00 *60.00*
375 A21 3rp green, *blue* 40.00 60.00
Nos. 357-375 (19) 131.70 185.10

The 1r, 2r, 2½r, 3r, 4½r, 5r, 6r and 10r, 1t and 3t exist on glazed paper.

1916-20 Ordinary Paper
375A A21 1r olive brn .80 *1.25*
375B A21 1½r yellow grn .80 *1.25*
b. Imperf.
375C A21 2r black ('19) .80 *1.25*
375D A21 2½r olive grn ('19) .80 *1.25*
375E A21 3r lilac ('16) .80 *1.25*
375F A21 4½r orange brn ('19) .80 *1.25*
375G A21 6r lilac brown ('16) .80 *1.25*
375H A21 1t lt violet ('16) .80 *1.25*
375I A21 2t deep blue ('16) .80 *1.25*
Nos. 375A-375I (9) 7.20 11.25

1921-23 *Perf. 12x11½*
375J A21 1r olive brn .80 *1.25*
375K A21 1½r yellow grn .80 *1.25*
375L A21 2r black 1.50 *1.50*
375M A21 3r lilac ('22) .80 *1.25*
375N A21 4r blue ('22) 1.40 1.25
375O A21 4½r orange brn 2.75 1.60
375P A21 5r blue green 10.00 6.00
375Q A21 6r lilac brown .80 .70
375R A21 9r ultra 1.60 .95
375S A21 10r carmine 2.50 1.45
375T A21 1t lt violet 2.75 1.25
375U A21 1½t gray green ('22) 1.40 .95
375V A21 2t deep blue 2.75 1.25
375W A21 2½t turquoise blue ('22) 1.50 1.25
375X A21 3t4r yellow brown ('23) 5.50 4.50
375Y A21 4t slate 2.25 1.25
375Z A21 8t plum 7.75 5.50
Nos. 375J-375Z (17) 46.85 33.15

The 1, 2, 2½, 3, 4½r, 1, 2, and 4t exist with the black inscriptions inverted and the 2½r with them double, one inverted, but it is not known that any of these were regularly issued.

For surcharges see Nos. 400, 400A, 420, 421, 423.

Nos. 249, 251-253, 256-259 Surcharged in Black

1914
376 A17 1½r on 4½r grn .35 .25
377 A17 1½r on 9r gray lil .45 .35
378 A17 1½r on 12t grn, *pink* .55 .50
379 A17 3r on 1t car rose .45 .40
380 A17 3r on 2t brn 3.25 2.75
381 A17 3r on 8t red vio, *pink* 2.50 2.25
382 A17 3r on 1rp dl bl, *straw* 1.00 .60
383 A17 3r on 2rp gray blk, *straw* 1.10 .80

There are 3 varieties of the "2" in "1½."

Nos. 376-377 exist with inverted surcharge.

Vasco da Gama Issue Surcharged in Black

384 CD21 1½r on 4½r red .40 .35
385 CD23 1½r on 9r yel grn .50 .35
386 CD24 3r on 1t dk bl .40 .35
387 CD25 3r on 2t vio brn .60 .50
388 CD26 3r on 4t org brn .35 .25
389 CD27 3r on 8t bister 1.40 1.25
Nos. 376-389 (14) 13.30 10.95

Double, inverted and other surcharge varieties exist on Nos. 384-386, 389.

Nos. 303, 305, 312 and 315 Surcharged in Black

1915
390 A17 1½r on 4½r grn 45.00 22.50
a. "REPUBLICA" omitted *77.50 47.50*
b. "REPUBLICA" inverted 82.50
391 A17 1½r on 9r gray lil 14.00 8.25
a. "REPUBLICA" omitted 35.00
392 A17 1½r on 12t grn, *pink* 1.40 1.10
396 A17 3r on 2rp gray blk, *straw* 55.00 22.50
Nos. 390-396 (4) 115.40 54.35

Nos. 390, 390a, 390b, 391, and 391a were not regularly issued. The 3r on 2½r (A17) was surcharged without official authorization.

Preceding Issues Overprinted in Carmine

1915 On No. 230
397 A15 5t on 8t org 2.75 1.50

On Nos. 241, 243
398 A17 2t blue 2.25 1.40
399 A17 2t on 2½t dl bl 2.75 1.40
Nos. 397-399 (3) 7.75 4.30

Nos. 375C, 359 Surcharged in Carmine

1922

400 A21 1½r on 2r black (ordinary paper) .75 .60
400A A21 1½r on 2r black (chalky paper) .50 .40

No. 400 also exists on glazed paper.

Ceres Type of 1913-23 Name and Value in Black

1922 **Typo.** ***Perf. 12x11½***

Glazed Paper

407 A21 1rp gray brn 17.50 17.00
408 A21 2rp yellow 30.00 *90.00*
409 A21 3rp bluish grn 40.00 *100.00*
410 A21 5rp carmine rose 50.00 *150.00*
Nos. 407-410 (4) 137.50 357.00

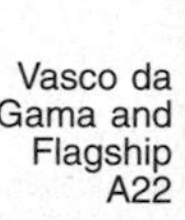

Vasco da Gama and Flagship A22

1925, Jan. 30 **Litho.**

Without Gum

411 A22 6r brown 5.00 3.25
412 A22 1t red violet 7.00 5.00

400th anniv. of the death of Vasco da Gama (1469?-1524), Portuguese navigator.

Monument to St. Francis — A23

Image of St. Francis — A25

Autograph of St. Francis A24

Image of St. Francis — A26

Tomb of St. Francis — A28

Church of Bom Jesus at Goa — A27

1931, Dec. 3 ***Perf. 14***

414 A23 1r gray green 1.00 .80
415 A24 2r brown 1.00 .80
416 A25 6r red violet 2.00 .80
417 A26 1½t yellow brn 7.00 3.50
418 A27 2t deep blue 10.00 4.75
419 A28 2½t light red 12.00 5.50
Nos. 414-419 (6) 33.00 16.15

Exposition of St. Francis Xavier at Goa, in December, 1931.

Nos. 371 and 375X Surcharged

1931-32 ***Perf. 15x14***

Chalky Paper

420 A21 1½r on 8t plum ('32) 2.25 1.60

Ordinary Paper

Perf. 12x11½

421 A21 1½r on 8t plum ('32) 1.50 1.10
423 A21 2½t on 3t4r yel brn 90.00 50.00

"Portugal" and Vasco da Gama's Flagship "San Gabriel" — A29

Perf. 11½x12

1933 **Typo.** **Wmk. 232**

424 A29 1r bister .25 .25
425 A29 2r olive brn .25 .25
426 A29 4r violet .25 .25
427 A29 6r dk green .25 .25
428 A29 8r black .40 .30
429 A29 1t gray .40 .30
430 A29 1½t dp rose .40 .30
431 A29 2t brown .40 .30
432 A29 2½t dk blue 2.25 .55
433 A29 3t brt blue 2.50 .55
434 A29 5t red orange 2.50 .55
435 A29 1rp olive grn 11.00 3.25
436 A29 2rp maroon 27.50 7.50
437 A29 3rp orange 40.00 8.75
438 A29 5rp apple grn 55.00 25.00
Nos. 424-438 (15) 143.35 48.35

For surcharges see Nos. 454-463, 472-474, J34-J36.

Common Design Types

Perf. 13½x13

1938, Sept. 1 **Engr.** **Unwmk.**

Name and Value in Black

439 CD34 1r gray grn .30 .25
440 CD34 2r orange brn .30 .25
441 CD34 3r dk vio brn .30 .25
442 CD34 6r brt green .30 .25
443 CD35 10r dk carmine .40 .30
444 CD35 1t brt red vio .55 .30
445 CD35 1½t red .90 .30
446 CD37 2t orange .90 .30
447 CD37 2½t blue .90 .30
448 CD37 3t slate 1.75 .35
449 CD36 5t rose vio 2.75 .50
450 CD36 1rp brown car 4.50 .90
451 CD36 2rp olive grn 7.75 2.75
452 CD38 3rp blue vio 13.00 6.50
453 CD38 5rp red brown 22.50 6.50
Nos. 439-453 (15) 57.10 20.00

For surcharges see Nos. 492-495, 504-505.

Stamps of 1933 Surcharged in Black

1941, June **Wmk. 232** ***Perf. 11½x12***

454 A29 1t on 1½t dp rose 2.40 2.00
455 A29 1t on 1rp olive grn 2.40 2.00
456 A29 1t on 2rp maroon 2.40 2.00
457 A29 1t on 5rp apple grn 2.40 2.00
Nos. 454-457 (4) 9.60 8.00

Nos. 430-431 Surcharged

1943

458 A29 3r on 1½t dp rose 1.60 .80
459 A29 1t on 2t brown 2.75 2.25

Nos. 434, 428, 437 and 432 Surcharged in Dark Blue or Carmine

a

b

1945-46 **Wmk. 232** ***Perf. 11½x12***

460 A29(a) 1r on 5t red org (DB) .80 .80
461 A29(b) 2r on 8r blk (C) .80 .80
462 A29(b) 3r on 3rp org (DB) ('46) 2.00 1.75
463 A29(b) 6r on 2½t dk bl (C) 2.00 1.75
Nos. 460-463 (4) 5.60 5.10

St. Francis Xavier A30

Luis de Camoens A31

Garcia de Orta — A32

St. John de Britto — A33

Arch of the Viceroy A34

Affonso de Albuquerque A35

Vasco da Gama — A36

Francisco de Almeida — A37

Perf. 11½

1946, May 28 **Litho.** **Unwmk.**

464 A30 1r black & gray blk .50 .25
465 A31 2r rose brn & pale rose brn .50 .25
466 A32 6r ocher & dl yel .50 .25
467 A33 7r vio & pale vio 3.00 *9.00*
468 A34 9r sepia & buff 3.00 .55
469 A35 1t dk sl grn & sl grn 3.00 .55
470 A36 3½t ultra & pale ultra 3.00 1.25
471 A37 1rp choc & bis brn 6.00 1.50
a. Miniature sheet of 8, #464-471 25.00 25.00
Nos. 464-471 (8) 19.50 13.60

No. 471a sold for 1½ rupias.

See #476. For surcharges see #595, J43-J46.

No. 428, 431 and 433 Surcharged in Carmine or Black

1946 **Wmk. 232** ***Perf. 11½x12***

472 A29 (c) 1r on 8r blk (C) .80 .80
473 A29 (b) 3r on 2t brn .80 .80
474 A29 (b) 6r on 3t brt bl 2.25 1.90
Nos. 472-474 (3) 3.85 3.50

Type of 1946 and

Joao de Castro — A38

José Vaz — A39

Luis de Ataide — A40

Duarte Pacheco Pereira — A41

1948 **Unwmk.** **Litho.** ***Perf. 11½***

475 A38 3r brt ultra & lt bl 1.00 .55
476 A30 1t dk grn & yel grn 1.40 .65
477 A39 1½t dk pur & dl vio 2.25 1.25
478 A40 2½t brt ver 2.50 1.75
479 A41 7½t dk brn & org brn 4.50 2.50
a. Miniature sheet of 5 30.00 25.00
Nos. 475-479 (5) 11.65 6.70

No. 476 measures 21x31mm.

No. 479a measures 106x146mm. and contains one each of Nos. 475-479. Marginal inscriptions in gray. The sheet sold for 16 tangas (1 rupia).

For surcharge see No. 591.

Lady of Fatima Issue

Common Design Type

1948 ***Perf. 14½***

480 CD40 1t dk blue green 2.50 2.25

Our Lady of Fatima — A42

1949 **Litho.** ***Perf. 14***

481 A42 1r blue .80 .55
482 A42 3r orange yel .80 .55
483 A42 9r dk car rose 1.40 .75
484 A42 2t green 3.50 1.90
485 A42 9t orange red 4.25 1.40
486 A42 2rp dk vio brn 7.00 3.00
487 A42 5rp olive grn 15.00 5.00
488 A42 8rp violet blue 35.00 13.00
Nos. 481-488 (8) 67.75 26.15

Our Lady of the Rosary at Fatima, Portugal.

UPU Symbols — A42a

1949, Oct.

489 A42a 2½t scarlet & pink 3.25 2.25

UPU, 75th anniversary.

Catalogue values for unused stamps in this section, from this point to the end of the section, are for Never Hinged items.

Holy Year Issue
Common Design Types

1950, May ***Perf. 13x13½***

490 CD41 1r olive bister 1.60 .60
491 CD42 2t dk gray green 2.00 .70

See Nos. 496-503.

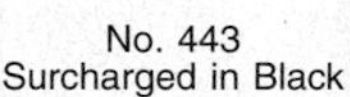

No. 443 Surcharged in Black

1950 ***Perf. 13½x13***

492 CD35 1r on 10r dk car .80 .40
493 CD35 2r on 10r dk car .80 .40

Similar Surcharge on No. 447 in Black or Red

494 CD37 1r on 2½t blue .80 .40
495 CD37 3r on 2½t blue (R) .80 .40
Nos. 492-495 (4) 3.20 1.60

Letters with serifs, small (lower case) "r" in "real" and "réis."

Holy Year Issue
Common Design Types

1951 **Litho.** ***Perf. 13½***

496 CD41 1r dp car rose .80 .30
497 CD41 2r emerald .80 .30
498 CD42 3r red brown .80 .30
499 CD41 6r gray .80 .40
500 CD42 9r brt pink 1.50 .70
501 CD41 1t blue violet 1.50 .70
502 CD42 2t yellow 1.50 .70
503 CD41 4t violet brown 1.50 .70
Nos. 496-503 (8) 9.20 4.10

No. 447 with Surcharge Similar to Nos. 492-493 in Red

1951 ***Perf. 13½x13***

504 CD37 6r on 2½t blue .80 .40
505 CD37 1t on 2½t blue .80 .40

Letters with serifs, small (lower case) "r" in "réis."

Holy Year Extension Issue
Common Design Type

1951 **Litho.** ***Perf. 14***

506 CD43 1rp bl vio & pale vio + label 1.60 1.00

Stamp without label sells for less.

José Vaz — A43

Ruins of Sancoale Church — A44

Design: 12t, Altar.

Dated: "1651-1951"

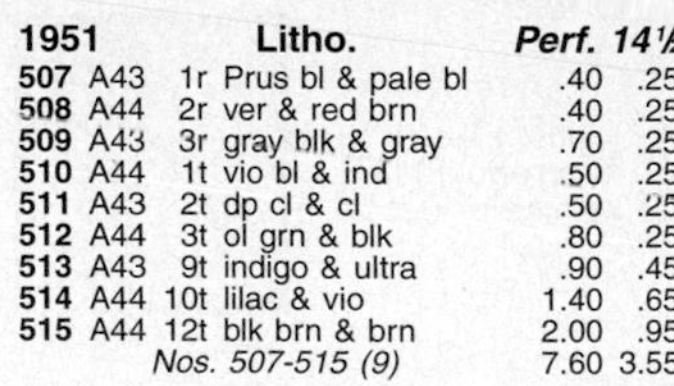

1951 **Litho.** ***Perf. 14½***

507 A43 1r Prus bl & pale bl .40 .25
508 A44 2r ver & red brn .40 .25
509 A43 3r gray blk & gray .70 .25
510 A44 1t vio bl & ind .50 .25
511 A43 2t dp cl & cl .50 .25
512 A44 3t ol grn & blk .80 .25
513 A43 9t indigo & ultra .90 .45
514 A44 10t lilac & vio 1.40 .65
515 A44 12t blk brn & brn 2.00 .95
Nos. 507-515 (9) 7.60 3.55

300th anniversary of the birth of José Vaz.

Medical Congress Issue
Common Design Type

Design: Medical School, Goa.

1952 **Unwmk.** ***Perf. 13½***

516 CD44 4½t blk & lt blue 4.75 2.00

St. Francis Xavier Issue

Statue of Saint Francis Xavier — A44a

A45

St. Francis Xavier and his Tomb, Goa — A46

Designs: 2t, Miraculous Arm of St. Francis. 4t, 5t, Tomb of St. Francis.

1952, Oct. 25 **Litho.** ***Perf. 14***

517 A44a 6r aqua & multi .55 .25
518 A44a 2t cream & multi 2.25 .60
519 A44a 5t pink & silver 4.00 1.40
Nos. 517-519 (3) 6.80 2.25

Souvenir Sheets
Perf. 13

520 A45 9t brn & dk brn 14.50 11.00
521 A46 12t Sheet of 2 14.50 11.00
  a. 4t orange buff & black 3.25 3.25
  b. 8t slate & black 3.25 3.25

400th anniv. of the death of St. Francis Xavier.

Numeral A47

St. Francis Xavier A48

1952, Dec. 4 **Litho.** ***Perf. 13½***

522 A47 3t black 9.50 9.50
523 A48 5t dk violet & blk 9.50 9.50
  a. Strip of 2 + label 25.00 25.00

Issued to publicize Portuguese India's first stamp exhibition, Goa, 1952.

No. 523a consists of a tête bêche pair of Nos. 522-523 separated by a label publicizing the exhibition.

Statue of Virgin Mary — A49

1953, Jan.

524 A49 6r dk & lt blue .65 .25
525 A49 1t brown & buff 1.40 .80
526 A49 3t dk pur & pale ol 3.25 1.50
Nos. 524-526 (3) 5.30 2.55

Exhibition of Sacred Missionary Art held at Lisbon in 1951.

For surcharge see No. 594.

Stamp Centenary Issue

Stamp of Portugal and Arms of Colonies — A49a

1953 **Typo.**

527 A49a 1t multicolored 2.00 .95

Centenary of Portugal's first postage stamps.

C. A. da Gama Pinto, Ophthalmologist and Author, Birth Cent. — A50

1954, Apr. 10 **Litho.** ***Perf. 11½***

528 A50 3r gray & ol grn .40 .25
529 A50 2t black & gray blk .80 .30

Sao Paulo Issue
Common Design Type

1954, Oct. 2 **Unwmk.** ***Perf. 13½***

530 CD46 2t dk Prus bl, bl & blk .80 .40

For surcharge see No. 593.

Affonso de Albuquerque School — A51

1955, Feb. 26

531 A51 9t multicolored 1.60 .55

Centenary (in 1954) of the founding of the Affonso de Albuquerque National School.

Msgr. Sebastiao Rodolfo Dalgado — A52

1955, Nov. 15 **Unwmk.** ***Perf. 13½***

532 A52 1r multicolored .30 .25
533 A52 1t multicolored .55 .25

Birth cent. of Msgr. Sebastiao Rodolfo Dalgado.

Francisco de Almeida — A53

Manuel Antonio de Sousa — A54

Map of Bassein by Pedro Barreto de Resendo, 1635 — A55

Portraits: 9r, Affonso de Albuquerque. 1t, Vasco da Gama. 1½t, Filipe Nery Xavier. 3t, Nuno da Cunha. 4t, Agostinho Vicente Lourenco. 8t, Jose Vaz. 9t, Manuel Godinho de Heredia. 10t, Joao de Castro. 2rp, Antonio Caetano Pacheco. 3rp, Constantino de Braganca.

Maps of ancient forts, drawn in 1635: 2½t, Mombaim (Bombay). 3½t, Damao (Daman). 5t, Diu. 12t, Cochin. 1rp, Goa.

Inscribed: "450 Aniversario da Fundacao do Estado da India 1505-1955."

Perf. 11½x12 (A53), 14½ (A54), 12½ (A55)

1956, Mar. 24 **Unwmk.**

534 A53 3r multicolored .30 .25
535 A54 6r multicolored .40 .25
536 A53 9r multicolored .40 .35
537 A53 1t multicolored .40 .35
538 A54 1½t multicolored .45 .25
539 A55 2t multicolored 4.00 2.00
540 A55 2½t multicolored 2.25 1.10
541 A53 3t multicolored .55 .25
542 A55 3½t multicolored 2.25 1.10
543 A54 4t multicolored .45 .25
544 A55 5t multicolored 2.00 .60
545 A54 8t multicolored 1.00 .45
546 A54 9t multicolored 1.00 .45
547 A53 10t multicolored .75 .40
548 A55 12t multicolored 2.00 .90
549 A55 1rp multicolored 4.00 2.00
550 A54 2rp multicolored 3.00 1.25
551 A53 3rp multicolored 3.00 1.60
Nos. 534-551 (18) 28.20 13.80

Portuguese settlements in India, 450th anniv.

For surcharges see Nos. 575-577, 579-581, 592.

Map of Damao and Nagar Aveli — A56

Map and Inscriptions in Black, Red, Ocher and Blue

1957 **Litho.** ***Perf. 11½***

552 A56 3r gray & buff .25 .25
553 A56 6r bl grn & pale lem .30 .25
554 A56 3t pink & lt gray .45 .25
555 A56 6t blue .55 .40
556 A56 11t ol bis & lt vio gray 1.20 .60
557 A56 2rp lt vio & pale gray 2.50 1.25
558 A56 3rp citron & pink 3.00 1.60
559 A56 5rp magenta & pink 3.50 1.90
Nos. 552-559 (8) 11.75 6.50

For surcharges see Nos. 571, 578, 584-585, 588-590.

Arms of Vasco da Gama — A57

Arms of: 6r, Lopo Soares de Albergaria. 9r, Francisco de Almeida. 1t, Garcia de Noronha. 4t, Alfonso de Albuquerque. 5t, Joao de Castro. 11t, Luis de Ataide. 1rp, Nuno da Cunha.

Arms in Original Colors Inscriptions in Black and Red

1958, Apr. 3 Unwmk. *Perf. 13x13½*

560	A57	2r buff & ocher	.30	.25
561	A57	6r gray & ocher	.30	.25
562	A57	9r pale blue & emer	.30	.25
563	A57	1t pale citron & brn	.40	.25
564	A57	4t pale bl grn & lil	.45	.25
565	A57	5t buff & blue	.55	.35
566	A57	11t pink & lt brn	.90	.55
567	A57	1rp pale grn & maroon	1.10	.65
		Nos. 560-567 (8)	4.30	2.80

For surcharges see Nos. 570, 572-574, 582-583, 586-587.

Exhibition Emblem and View — A58

1958, Dec. 15 Litho. *Perf. 14½*

568	A58	1rp multicolored	.95	.55

World's Fair, Brussels, Apr. 17-Oct. 19. For surcharge see No. 597.

Tropical Medicine Congress Issue

Common Design Type

Design: Holarrhena antidysenterica.

1958, Dec. 15 *Perf. 13½*

569	CD47	5t gray, brn, grn & red	1.75	.75

For surcharge see No. 596.

Stamps of 1955-58 Surcharged with New Values and Bars

1959, Jan. 1 Litho. Unwmk.

570	A57	5c on 2r (#560)	.30	.25
571	A56	10c on 3r (#552)	.30	.25
572	A57	15c on 6r (#561)	.30	.25
573	A57	20c on 9r (#562)	.30	.25
574	A57	30c on 1t (#563)	.30	.25
575	A55	40c on 2t (#539)	.65	.30
576	A55	40c on 2½t (#540)	.80	.35
577	A55	40c on 3½t (#542)	.40	.25
578	A56	50c on 3t (#554)	.40	.25
579	A53	80c on 3t (#541)	.40	.25
580	A53	80c on 10t (#547)	1.10	.80
581	A53	80c on 3rp (#551)	1.60	.95
582	A57	1e on 4t (#564)	.40	.25
583	A57	1.50e on 5t (#565)	.40	.25
584	A56	2e on 6t (#555)	.65	.35
585	A56	2.50e on 11t (#556)	.95	.25
586	A57	4e on 11t (#566)	1.10	.55
587	A57	4.50e on 1rp (#567)	1.10	.55
588	A56	5e on 2rp (#557)	1.20	.55
589	A56	10e on 3rp (#558)	2.25	1.60
590	A56	30e on 5rp (#559)	5.00	2.25
		Nos. 570-590 (21)	19.90	11.00

Types of 1946-1958 Surcharged with New Values, Old Values Obliterated

1959 Litho. Unwmk.

591	A39	40c on 1½t dl pur	.65	.25
592	A54	40c on 1½t multi	.65	.25
593	CD46	40c on 2t bl & gray	1.10	.80
594	A49	80c on 3t blk & pale cit	.65	.25
595	A36	80c on 3½t dk bl	.80	.25
596	CD47	80c on 5t gray, brn, grn & red	.80	.45
597	A58	80c on 1rp multi	2.25	.65
		Nos. 591-597 (7)	6.90	2.90

Coin, Manuel I — A59

Various Coins from the Reign of Manuel I (1495-1521) to the Republic.

Inscriptions in Black and Red

Perf. 13½x13

1959, Dec. 1 Litho. Unwmk.

598	A59	5c lt bl & gold	.30	.25
599	A59	10c pale brn & gold	.30	.25
600	A59	15c pale grn & gray	.30	.25
601	A59	30c salmon & gray	.30	.25
602	A59	40c pale yel & gray	.30	.25
603	A59	50c lilac & gray	.30	.25
604	A59	60c pale yel grn & gray	.30	.25
605	A59	80c lt bl & gray	.30	.25
606	A59	1e ocher & gray	.30	.25
607	A59	1.50e blue & gray	.30	.25
608	A59	2e pale bl & gold	.30	.25
609	A59	2.50e pale gray & gold	.35	.25
610	A59	3e citron & gray	.35	.25
611	A59	4e pink & gray	.75	.25
612	A59	4.40e pale bis & vio brn	.90	.35
613	A59	5e pale dl vio & gray	1.00	.45
614	A59	10e brt yel & gray	2.00	.80
615	A59	20e beige & gray	4.00	2.25
616	A59	30e brt yel grn & lt cop brn	5.00	3.00
617	A59	50e lt gray & gray	10.00	5.00
		Nos. 598-617 (20)	27.65	15.35

Arms of Prince Henry — A60

1960, June 25 *Perf. 13½*

618	A60	3e multicolored	.55	.55

500th anniversary of the death of Prince Henry the Navigator.

Portugal continued to print special-issue stamps for its lost colony after its annexation by India Dec. 18, 1961: Sports, six stamps issued Dec. 1961, value (set) $3; Anti-Malaria, one stamp issued April, 1962, value 75c.

Stamps of India were first used on Dec. 29. Stamps of Portuguese India remained valid until Jan. 5, 1962.

AIR POST STAMPS

Common Design Type

Perf. 13½x13

1938, Sept. 1 Engr. Unwmk.

Name and Value in Black

C1	CD39	1t red orange	.70	.40
C2	CD39	2½t purple	.80	.40
C3	CD39	3½t orange	.80	.40
C4	CD39	4½t ultra	1.60	.45
C5	CD39	7t lilac brown	1.75	.55
C6	CD39	7½t dark green	2.50	.80
C7	CD39	9t red brown	4.50	1.25
C8	CD39	11t magenta	5.00	1.25
		Nos. C1-C8 (8)	17.65	5.50

No. C4 exists with overprint "Exposicao Internacional de Nova York, 1939-1940" and Trylon and Perisphere. Value, unused $90, never hinged $125.

POSTAGE DUE STAMPS

D1

1904 Unwmk. Typo. *Perf. 11½*

Name and Value in Black

J1	D1	2r gray green	.50	.35
J2	D1	3r yellow grn	.50	.35
J3	D1	4r orange	.50	.45
J4	D1	5r slate	.50	.50
J5	D1	6r gray	.50	.50
J6	D1	9r yellow brn	.60	.60
J7	D1	1t red orange	2.25	.80
J8	D1	2t gray brown	3.25	1.60
J9	D1	5t dull blue	4.50	3.00
J10	D1	10t carmine	7.75	3.50
J11	D1	1rp dull vio	13.00	7.50
		Nos. J1-J11 (11)	33.85	19.15

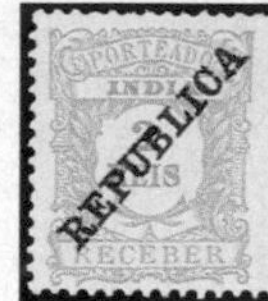

Nos. J1-J11 Overprinted in Carmine or Green

1911

J12	D1	2r gray grn	.25	.25
J13	D1	3r yellow grn	.25	.25
J14	D1	4r orange	.25	.25
J15	D1	5r slate	.25	.25
J16	D1	6r gray	.45	.25
J17	D1	9r yellow brn	.55	.35
J18	D1	1t red org	.65	.35
J19	D1	2t gray brn	.90	.55
J20	D1	5t dull blue	2.25	1.40
J21	D1	10t carmine (G)	3.25	1.90
J22	D1	1rp dull violet	7.75	3.25
		Nos. J12-J22 (11)	16.80	9.05

Nos. J1-J11 Overprinted

1914

J23	D1	2r gray grn	1.50	1.10
J24	D1	3r yellow grn	1.50	1.10
J25	D1	4r orange	1.50	1.10
J26	D1	5r slate	1.50	1.10
J27	D1	6r gray	1.60	1.10
J28	D1	9r yellow brn	1.60	1.10
J29	D1	1t red org	3.25	1.10
J30	D1	2t gray brn	20.00	3.25
J31	D1	5t dull blue	21.00	4.50
J32	D1	10t carmine	25.00	6.50
J33	D1	1rp dull violet	45.00	8.75
		Nos. J23-J33 (11)	123.45	30.70

Nos. 432, 433 and 434 Surcharged In Red or Black

1943 Wmk. 232 *Perf. 11½x12*

J34	A29	3r on 2½t dk bl (R)	.65	.45
J35	A29	6r on 3t brt bl (R)	.90	.90
J36	A29	1t on 5t red org (Bk)	1.90	1.60
		Nos. J34-J36 (3)	3.45	2.95

D2

1945 Typo. Unwmk.

Country Name and Denomination in Black

J37	D2	2r brt carmine	8.00	1.90
J38	D2	3r blue	8.00	1.90
J39	D2	4r orange yel	8.00	1.90
J40	D2	6r yellow grn	8.00	1.90
J41	D2	1t bister brn	8.00	1.90
J42	D2	2t chocolate	8.00	1.90
		Nos. J37-J42 (6)	48.00	11.40

Catalogue values for unused stamps in this section, from this point to the end of the section, are for Never Hinged items.

Nos. 467 and 471 Surcharged in Carmine or Black

1951, Jan. 1 *Perf. 11½*

J43	A33	2r on 7r vio & pale vio (C)	.60	.60
J44	A33	3r on 7r vio & pale vio (C)	.60	.60
J45	A37	1t on 1rp choc & bis brn	.60	.60
J46	A37	2t on 1rp choc & bis brn	.60	.60
		Nos. J43-J46 (4)	2.40	2.40

Common Design Type

Photogravure and Typographed

1952 *Perf. 14*

Numeral in Red; Frame Multicolored

J47	CD45	2r olive	.25	.25
J48	CD45	3r black	.40	.40
J49	CD45	6r dark blue	.55	.55
J50	CD45	1t dk carmine	.80	.80
J51	CD45	2t orange	1.10	1.10
J52	CD45	10t violet blue	3.00	3.00
		Nos. J47-J52 (6)	6.10	6.10

Nos. J47-J49 and J51-J52 Surcharged with New Value and Bars

1959, Jan.

Numeral in Red; Frame Multicolored

J53	CD45	5c on 2r olive	.25	.25
J54	CD45	10c on 3r black	.35	.45
J55	CD45	15c on 6r dk blue	.65	.80
J56	CD45	60c on 2t orange	1.00	1.40
J57	CD45	60c on 10t vio blue	2.25	2.25
		Nos. J53-J57 (5)	4.50	5.15

WAR TAX STAMPS

Overprinted in Black or Carmine

WT1

Denomination in Black

Perf. 15x14

1919, Apr. 15 Typo. Unwmk.

MR1	WT1	0:00:05,48rp grn	2.25	1.50
MR2	WT1	0:01:09,94rp grn	4.75	3.00
MR3	WT1	0:02:03,43rp grn (C)	4.75	3.00
		Nos. MR1-MR3 (3)	11.75	7.50

Some authorities consider No. MR2 a revenue stamp.

POSTAL TAX STAMPS

Pombal Issue

Common Design Types

1925 Unwmk. *Perf. 12½*

RA1	CD28	6r rose & black	.50	.50
RA2	CD29	6r rose & black	.50	.50
RA3	CD30	6r rose & black	.50	.50
		Nos. RA1-RA3 (3)	1.50	1.50

Mother and Child — PT1

1948 Litho. *Perf. 11*

RA4	PT1	6r yellow green	3.00	2.75
RA5	PT1	1t carmine	3.00	2.75

See Nos. RA7-RA7A, RA9, RA12. For surcharge and overprint see Nos. RA6, RA8.

Catalogue values for unused stamps in this section, from this point to the end of the section, are for Never Hinged items.

Type of 1948 Surcharged with New Value and Bar in Black

1951

RA6	PT1	1t on 6r carmine	3.25	2.25

Type of 1948

1952-53

RA7	PT1	1t gray	2.75	1.75
RA7A	PT1	1t red orange ('53)	3.00	2.10

No. RA5 Overprinted in Black

1953
RA8 PT1 1t carmine 8.00 6.50

Type of 1948

1954 **Typo.**
RA9 PT1 6r pale bister 4.50 4.25

Mother and Child — PT2

Surcharged in Black

1956 **Typo.** ***Perf. 11***
RA10 PT2 1t on 4t lt blue 12.00 11.00

Mother and Child — PT3

1956 **Litho.** ***Perf. 13***
RA11 PT3 1t blk, pale grn & red 1.40 1.00

See No. RA14. For surcharges see Nos. RA13, RA15-RA16.

Type of 1948 Redrawn

1956 ***Perf. 11***

Without Gum

RA12 PT1 1t bluish green 4.25 3.25

Denomination in white oval at left.

No. RA11 Surcharged with New Value and Bars in Red

1957 ***Perf. 13½***
RA13 PT3 6r on 1t 1.00 .80

Type of 1956

1958 **Unwmk.** ***Perf. 13***
RA14 PT3 1t dk bl, sal & grn .80 .65

No. RA14 Surcharged with New Values and Four Bars

1959, Jan. **Litho.** ***Perf. 13***
RA15 PT3 20c on 1t .60 .60
RA16 PT3 40c on 1t .60 .60

Arms and People Seeking Help — PT4

1960 ***Perf. 13½***
RA17 PT4 20c brown & red .25 .25

POSTAL TAX DUE STAMPS

Pombal Issue
Common Design Types

1925 **Unwmk.** ***Perf. 12½***
RAJ1 CD28 1t rose & black .65 .65
RAJ2 CD29 1t rose & black .65 .65
RAJ3 CD30 1t rose & black .65 .65
Nos. RAJ1-RAJ3 (3) 1.95 1.95

See note after Portugal No. RAJ4.

PUERTO RICO

ˌpwer-tə-ˈrē-ˌₒkō

(Porto Rico)

LOCATION — A large island in the West Indies, east of Hispaniola
GOVT. — Former Spanish Colony
AREA — 3,435 sq. mi.
POP. — 953,243 (1899)
CAPITAL — San Juan

The island was ceded to the United States by the Treaty of 1898.

100 Centimes = 1 Peseta
1000 Milesimas = 100 Centavos = 1 Peso (1881)
100 Cents = 1 Dollar (1898)

Puerto Rican stamps of 1855-73, a part of the Spanish colonial period, were also used in Cuba. They are listed as Cuba Nos. 1-4, 9-14, 18-21, 31-34, 39-41, 47-49, 51-53, 55-57.

Issued under Spanish Dominion

Values for unused stamps are for examples with original gum as defined in the catalogue introduction. Very fine examples of Nos. 1-170, MR1-MR13 will have perforations clear of the design but will be noticeably poorly centered. Extremely fine examples will be well centered; these are scarce and command substantial premiums.

Stamps of Cuba Overprinted in Black

a

b

c

d

1873 **Unwmk.** ***Perf. 14***
1 A10 (a) 25c gray 62.50 2.10
2 A10 (a) 50c brown 140.00 6.25
3 A10 (a) 1p red brown 550.00 21.00
Nos. 1-3 (3) 752.50 29.35

1874
4 A11 (b) 25c ultra 47.50 10.00
a. Double overprint 275.00
b. Inverted overprint 275.00

1875
5 A12 (b) 25c ultra 37.50 3.25
a. Inverted overprint 95.00 55.00
6 A12 (b) 50c green 45.00 3.50
a. Inverted overprint *210.00* *105.00*
7 A12 (b) 1p brown 160.00 17.50
Nos. 5-7 (3) 242.50 24.25

1876
8 A13 (c) 25c pale violet 4.25 1.90
a. 25c bluish gray 5.50 2.75
9 A13 (c) 50c ultra 10.50 3.25
10 A13 (c) 1p black 75.00 12.00
11 A13 (d) 25c pale violet 35.00 1.40
12 A13 (d) 1p black 75.00 11.00
Nos. 8-12 (5) 199.75 29.55

Varieties of overprint on Nos. 8-11 include: inverted, double, partly omitted and sideways. Counterfeit overprints exist.

King Alfonso XII — A5

1877 **Typo.**
13 A5 5c yellow brown 10.00 2.75
a. 5c carmine (error) 300.00 —
14 A5 10c carmine 40.00 7.50
a. 10c brown (error) 300.00 —
15 A5 15c deep green 60.00 15.50
16 A5 25c ultra 25.00 2.60
17 A5 50c bister 40.00 6.50
Nos. 13-17 (5) 175.00 34.85

Imperf. examples of Nos. 13-17 are from proof or trial sheets. Value, set $400.

1878 **Dated "1878"**
18 A5 5c ol bister 22.00 22.00
19 A5 10c red brown 350.00 120.00
20 A5 25c deep green 2.75 1.75
21 A5 50c ultra 9.00 3.50
22 A5 1p bister 18.00 8.50
Nos. 18-22 (5) 401.75 155.75

Imperf. examples of Nos. 18-22 are from proof or trial sheets. Value, set $600.

1879 **Dated "1879"**
23 A5 5c lake 20.00 6.50
24 A5 10c dark brown 20.00 6.50
25 A5 15c dk olive grn 20.00 6.50
26 A5 25c blue 5.00 2.25
27 A5 50c dark green 20.00 6.50
28 A5 1p gray 110.00 30.00
Nos. 23-28 (6) 195.00 58.25

Imperf, examples of Nos. 23-28 are from proof or trial sheets.

King Alfonso XII — A6

1880
29 A6 ¼c deep green 37.50 25.00
30 A6 ½c brt rose 9.00 3.25
31 A6 1c brown lilac 16.50 13.00
32 A6 2c gray lilac 8.50 5.50
33 A6 3c buff 9.50 6.00
34 A6 4c black 9.50 6.00
35 A6 5c gray green 4.75 2.50
36 A6 10c rose 5.25 3.00
37 A6 15c yellow brn 9.50 4.50
38 A6 25c gray blue 4.75 2.10
39 A6 40c gray 18.00 22.00
40 A6 50c dark brown 40.00 20.00
41 A6 1p olive bister 140.00 26.50
Nos. 29-41 (13) 312.75 139.35

1881 **Dated "1881"**
42 A6 ½m lake .55 .50
43 A6 1m violet .55 .30
44 A6 2m pale rose .75 .50
45 A6 4m brt yellowish green 1.30 .30
46 A6 6m brown lilac 1.30 .70
47 A6 8m ultra 3.25 1.75
48 A6 1c gray green 4.25 1.50
49 A6 2c lake 5.75 4.75
50 A6 3c dark brown 12.50 7.75
51 A6 5c grayish ultra 4.75 .55
52 A6 8c brown 4.75 2.25
53 A6 10c slate 75.00 11.50
54 A6 20c olive bister 90.00 21.00
Nos. 42-54 (13) 204.70 53.35

Alfonso XII — A7

1882-86
55 A7 ½m rose .30 .25
a. ½m salmon rose .55 .35
56 A7 ½m lake ('84) .90 .40
57 A7 1m pale lake .90 1.10
58 A7 1m brt rose ('84) .30 .25
59 A7 2m violet .30 .25
60 A7 4m brown lilac .30 .25
61 A7 6m brown .45 .25
62 A7 8m yellow green .45 .25
63 A7 1c gray green .30 .25
64 A7 2c rose 1.15 .25
65 A7 3c yellow 4.25 2.25
a. Cliché of 8c in plate of 3c 120.00
66 A7 3c yellow brn ('84) 4.25 .90
a. Cliché of 8c in plate of 3c 25.00
67 A7 5c gray blue 15.00 1.25
68 A7 5c gray bl, 1st retouch ('84) 15.00 3.00
69 A7 5c gray bl, 2nd retouch ('86) 115.00 5.75
70 A7 8c gray brown 3.75 .25
71 A7 10c dark green 3.75 .30
72 A7 20c gray lilac 5.50 .30
a. 20c olive brown (error) *120.00*
73 A7 40c blue 65.00 15.00
74 A7 80c olive bister 70.00 21.00
Nos. 55-74 (20) 306.85 53.50

For differences between the original and the retouched stamps see note on the 1883-86 issue of Cuba.

Alfonso XIII — A8

1890-97
75 A8 ½m black .30 .25
76 A8 ½m olive gray ('92) .25 .25
77 A8 ½m red brn ('94) .25 .25
78 A8 ½m dull vio ('96) .25 .25
79 A8 1m emerald .25 .25
80 A8 1m dk violet ('92) .25 .25
81 A8 1m ultra ('94) .25 .25
82 A8 1m dp brown ('96) .25 .25
83 A8 2m lilac rose .25 .25
84 A8 2m violet brn ('92) .25 .25
85 A8 2m red orange ('94) .25 .25
86 A8 2m yellow grn ('96) .25 .25
87 A8 4m dk olive grn 11.50 5.75
88 A8 4m ultra ('92) .25 .25
89 A8 4m yellow brn ('94) .25 .25
90 A8 4m blue grn ('96) 1.00 .35
91 A8 6m dk brown 50.00 15.00
92 A8 6m pale rose ('92) .25 .25
93 A8 8m olive bister 35.00 22.00
94 A8 8m yellow grn ('92) .25 .25
95 A8 1c yellow brown .30 .25
96 A8 1c blue grn ('91) .55 .25
97 A8 1c violet brn ('94) 6.00 .45
98 A8 1c claret ('96) .65 .25
99 A8 2c brownish violet 1.00 .85
100 A8 2c red brown ('92) .95 .25
101 A8 2c lilac ('94) 2.25 .45
102 A8 2c orange brn ('96) .65 .25
103 A8 3c slate blue 7.50 1.00
104 A8 3c orange ('92) .90 .25
105 A8 3c ol gray ('94) 6.00 .45
106 A8 3c blue ('96) 22.00 .35
107 A8 3c claret brn ('97) .30 .25
108 A8 4c slate bl ('94) 1.50 .45
109 A8 4c gray brn ('96) .70 .25
110 A8 5c brown violet 13.00 .45
111 A8 5c yellow grn ('94) 5.75 1.10
112 A8 5c blue green ('92) .90 .25
113 A8 5c blue ('96) .30 .25
114 A8 6c orange ('94) .45 .25
115 A8 6c violet ('96) .35 .25
116 A8 8c ultra 16.00 1.75
117 A8 8c gray brown ('92) .25 .25
118 A8 8c dull vio ('94) 13.00 5.00
119 A8 8c car rose ('96) 3.00 1.50
120 A8 10c rose 4.75 1.10
a. 10c salmon rose 11.50 2.75
121 A8 10c lilac rose ('92) 1.50 .35
122 A8 20c red orange 5.25 4.75
123 A8 20c lilac ('92) 2.50 .55
124 A8 20c car rose ('94) 1.50 .45
125 A8 20c olive gray ('96) 6.75 1.50
126 A8 40c orange 200.00 57.50
127 A8 40c slate blue ('92) 5.75 4.00
128 A8 40c claret ('94) 7.50 13.50
129 A8 40c salmon ('96) 7.00 1.60
130 A8 80c yellow green 750.00 240.00
131 A8 80c orange ('92) 14.50 11.50
132 A8 80c black ('97) 27.50 23.50

Imperforates of type A8 were not issued and are variously considered to be proofs or printer's waste.

Shades of No. 129 are often mistaken for No. 126. Value for No. 126 is for expertized examples.

For overprints see Nos. 154A-170, MR1-MR13.

Landing of Columbus on Puerto Rico — A9

1893 Litho. *Perf. 12*

133	A9	3c dark green	250.00	60.00

400th anniversary, landing of Columbus on Puerto Rico.

This stamp was valid for postage for only one day and for internal use only.

Counterfeits exist.

Alfonso XIII — A10

1898 Typo.

135	A10	1m orange brown	.25	.25
136	A10	2m orange brown	.25	.25
137	A10	3m orange brown	.25	.25
138	A10	4m orange brown	2.40	.75
139	A10	5m orange brown	.25	.25
140	A10	1c black violet	.25	.25
a.		Tête bêche pair	*1,700.*	
141	A10	2c dk blue green	.25	.25
142	A10	3c dk brown	.25	.25
143	A10	4c orange	2.40	1.60
144	A10	5c brt rose	.30	.25
145	A10	6c dark blue	.85	.25
146	A10	8c gray brown	.30	.25
147	A10	10c vermilion	.30	.25
148	A10	15c dull olive grn	.30	.25
149	A10	20c maroon	3.00	.75
150	A10	40c violet	2.25	2.00
151	A10	60c black	2.25	2.00
152	A10	80c red brown	8.50	7.25
153	A10	1p yellow green	18.00	14.50
154	A10	2p slate blue	50.00	22.00
		Nos. 135-154 (20)	92.60	53.85

Nos. 135-154 exist imperf. Value, set $1,300.

Stamps of 1890-97 Handstamped in Rose or Violet

1898

154A	A8	½m dull violet	19.50	11.00
155	A8	1m deep brown	1.75	1.75
156	A8	2m yellow green	.50	.50
157	A8	4m blue green	.50	.50
158	A8	1c claret	5.00	5.00
159	A8	2c orange brown	.70	*1.00*
160	A8	3c blue	42.50	18.00
161	A8	3c claret brn	3.25	3.25
162	A8	4c gray brn	.80	.80
163	A8	4c slate blue	23.00	16.50
164	A8	5c yellow grn	11.00	8.50
165	A8	5c blue	.80	.80
166	A8	6c violet	.80	.55
167	A8	8c car rose (V)	1.40	1.00
a.		Rose overprint	21.00	21.00
168	A8	20c olive gray	1.40	1.40
169	A8	40c salmon	3.25	3.25
170	A8	80c black	45.00	27.50
		Nos. 154A-170 (17)	161.15	101.30

As usual with handstamps there are many inverted, double and similar varieties. Counterfeits of Nos. 154A-170 abound.

Issued under U.S. Administration PROVISIONAL ISSUES

Ponce Issue

A11

Handstamped

1898 Unwmk. *Imperf.*

200	A11	5c violet, *yellowish*	*7,500.*	—

The only way No. 200 is known used is handstamped on envelopes. Unused stamps always have a violet control mark. Used envelopes do not have the control mark. The same handstamp used to prepare No. 200 also is known handstamped on an unused envelope, also without the control mark. Research into whether the envelopes represent prepaid postmaster provisional usage is ongoing.

Uses on 2c U.S. stamps on cover were strictly as a cancellation, not as provisional postage.

Dangerous forgeries exist.

Coamo Issue

A12

Typeset, setting of 10

1898, Aug.

201	A12	5c black	650.	*1,250.*

See the Scott U.S. Specialized Catalogue for more detailed listings.

The stamps bear the control mark "F. Santiago" in violet. About 500 were issued.

Dangerous forgeries exist.

Regular Issue

United States Nos. 279, 279Bf, 281, 272 and 282C Overprinted in Black at 36 degree angle

1899 Wmk. 191 *Perf. 12*

210	A87	1c yellow green	6.00	1.40
a.		Overprint at 25 degree angle	8.00	2.25
211	A88	2c redsh car, type IV	5.00	1.25
a.		Overprint at 25 degree angle, *Mar. 15*	6.50	2.25
212	A91	5c blue	12.50	2.50
213	A93	8c violet brown	40.00	17.50
a.		Overprint at 25 degree angle	45.00	19.00
c.		"PORTO RIC"	150.00	110.00
214	A94	10c brown, type I	22.50	6.00
		Nos. 210-214 (5)	86.00	28.65

Misspellings of the overprint on Nos. 210-214 (PORTO RICU, PORTU RICO, FORTO RICO) are actually broken letters.

United States Nos. 279 and 279B Overprinted Diagonally in Black

1900

215	A87	1c yellow green	7.50	1.40
216	A88	2c red, type IV	5.50	2.00
b.		Inverted overprint		*12,500.*

POSTAGE DUE STAMPS

United States Nos. J38, J39 and J42 Overprinted in Black at 36 degree angle

1899 Wmk. 191 *Perf. 12*

J1	D2	1c deep claret	22.50	5.50
a.		Overprint at 25 degree angle	22.50	7.50
J2	D2	2c deep claret	20.00	6.00
a.		Overprint at 25 degree angle	20.00	7.00
J3	D2	10c deep claret	180.00	55.00
a.		Overprint at 25 degree angle	160.00	75.00
		Nos. J1-J3 (3)	222.50	66.50

Stamps of Puerto Rico were replaced by those of the United States.

WAR TAX STAMPS

Stamps of 1890-94 Overprinted or Surcharged by Handstamp

1898 Unwmk. *Perf. 14*

Purple Overprint or Surcharge

MR1	A8	1c yellow brn	8.00	5.75
MR2	A8	2c on 2m orange	3.75	3.00
MR3	A8	2c on 5c blue grn	5.00	3.50
MR4	A8	2c dark violet	.95	.95
MR5	A8	2c lilac	.90	.90
MR6	A8	2c red brown	.50	.30
MR7	A8	5c blue green	1.90	1.90
MR8	A8	5c on 5c bl grn	8.75	6.00

Rose Surcharge

MR9	A8	2c on 2m orange	1.90	1.90
MR10	A8	5c on 1m dk vio	.30	.30
MR11	A8	5c on 1m dl bl	.85	.85

Magenta Surcharge

MR12	A8	5c on 1m dk vio	.50	.30
MR13	A8	5c on 1m dl bl	3.00	3.00
		Nos. MR1-MR13 (13)	36.30	28.65

Nos. MR2-MR13 were issued as War Tax Stamps (2c on letters or sealed mail; 5c on telegrams) but, during the early days of the American occupation, they were accepted for ordinary postage.

Double, inverted and similar varieties of overprints are numerous in this issue.

Counterfeit overprints exist.

MINT SHEET BINDERS & PAGES

MINT SHEET BINDERS & PAGES

Keep those mint sheets intact in a handsome, 3-ring binder. Just like the cover album, the Mint Sheet album features the "D" ring mechanism on the right hand side of binder so you don't have to worry about damaging your stamps when turning the pages.

Item	Color	Retail	AA*
BINDERS			
MBRD	Red (Burgundy)	$21.99	**$17.99**
MBBL	Blue	$21.99	**$17.99**
MBGY	Gray	$21.99	**$17.99**
MBBK	Black	$21.99	**$17.99**
MINT SHEET PAGE PACKS			
MS1	Black (25 per pack)	$16.99	**$14.99**
SSMP3C	Clear (12 per pack)	$9.95	**$8.95**

BINDER & SHEET PACK COMBOS

Item	Binder Color	Retail	AA*
MBBK3PB	Black (with 25 Black pages)	$33.97	**$29.99**
MBBK3PC	Black (with 24 Clear pages)	$33.97	**$29.99**
MBBL3PB	Blue (with 25 Black pages)	$33.97	**$29.99**
MBBL3PC	Blue (with 24 Clear pages)	$33.97	**$29.99**
MBRD3PB	Burgundy (with 25 Black pages)	$33.97	**$29.99**
MBRD3PC	Burgundy (with 24 Clear pages)	$33.97	**$29.99**
MBGY3PB	Gray (with 25 Black pages)	$33.97	**$29.99**
MBGY3PC	Gray (with 24 Clear pages)	$33.97	**$29.99**

Available from your favorite stamp dealer or direct from:

AmosAdvantage.com

1-800-572-6885

Outside U.S. & Canada call (937) 498-0800

P.O. Box 4129, Sidney OH 45365

*AA prices apply to paid subscribers of Amos Media titles, or for orders placed online. Prices, terms and product availability subject to change. Shipping and handling rates apply. Taxes will apply in CA, OH, & IL.

QATAR

'kät-ər

LOCATION — A peninsula in eastern Arabia
GOVT. — Independent state
AREA — 4,575 sq. mi.
POP. — 580,000 (1998 est.)
CAPITAL — Doha

Qatar was a British protected sheikdom until Sept. 1, 1971, when it declared its independence. Stamps of Muscat were used until 1957.

100 Naye Paise = 1 Rupee
100 Dirhams = 1 Riyal (1967)

Catalogue values for all unused stamps in this country are for Never Hinged items.

Watermarks

Wmk. 368 — JEZ Multiple

The market for Qatar stamps is extremely volatile, and dealer stocks are quite limited. All values for this country are tentative.

Great Britain Nos. 317-325, 328, 332-333 and 309-311 Surcharged "QATAR" and New Value in Black

Perf. 14½x14

1957, Apr. 1 Photo. Wmk. 308

1 A129 1np on 5p lt brn .45 .25
2 A126 3np on ½p red org .45 .25
3 A126 6np on 1p ultra .45 .25
4 A126 9np on 1½p grn .45 .25
5 A126 12np on 2p red brn .55 2.50
6 A127 15np on 2½p scarlet .50 .65
7 A127 20np on 3p dk pur .50 .25
8 A128 25np on 4p ultra .70 2.00
9 A129 40np on 6p lil rose .50 .30
10 A130 50np on 9p dp ol grn .80 2.00
11 A132 75np on 1sh3p dk grn 1.00 4.00
12 A131 1ru on 1sh6p dk bl 14.50 .65

Engr. *Perf. 11x12*

13 A133 2ru on 2sh6p dk brn 5.00 4.00
14 A133 5ru on 5sh crimson 6.75 6.50
15 A133 10ru on 10sh brt ultra 8.50 15.00
Nos. 1-15 (15) 41.10 38.85

Both typeset and stereotyped overprints were used on Nos. 13-15. The typeset have bars close together and thick, bold letters. The stereotyped have bars wider apart and thinner letters. Value, Nos. 13-15 with stereotyped overprints $95.

Great Britain Nos. 334-336 Surcharged "QATAR," New Value and Square of Dots in Black

Perf. 14½x14

1957, Aug. 1 Photo. Wmk. 308

16 A138 15np on 2½p scarlet .50 .40
17 A138 25np on 4p ultra .90 .75
18 A138 75np on 1sh3p dk grn 1.75 1.50
Nos. 16-18 (3) 3.15 2.65

50th anniv. of the Boy Scout movement and the World Scout Jubilee Jamboree, Aug. 1-12.

Great Britain Nos. 353-358, 362 Surcharged "QATAR" and New Value

1960 Wmk. 322 *Perf. 14½x14*

19 A126 3np on ½p red org .75 1.75
20 A126 6np on 1p ultra 3.00 3.00
21 A126 9np on 1½p grn .80 1.50
22 A126 12np on 2p red brn 5.00 6.50
23 A127 15np on 2½p scar 2.75 .25
24 A127 20np on 3p dk pur .60 .25
25 A129 40np on 6p lil rose 3.00 2.00
Nos. 19-25 (7) 15.90 15.25

Sheik Ahmad bin Ali al Thani — A1

Dhow — A2

Oil Derrick — A3

Designs: 40np, Peregrine Falcon. 5r, 10r, Mosque.

Perf. 14½

1961, Sept. 2 Unwmk. Photo.

26 A1 5np rose carmine .40 .35
27 A1 15np brown black .50 .35
28 A1 20np claret .50 .35
29 A1 30np deep green .50 .45
30 A2 40np red 2.75 .45
31 A2 50np sepia 3.50 .60
32 A2 75np ultra 1.75 3.00

Engr. *Perf. 13*

33 A3 1ru rose red 3.75 .50
34 A3 2ru blue 4.00 2.00
35 A3 5ru green 30.00 7.00
36 A3 10ru black 65.00 12.00
Nos. 26-36 (11) 112.65 27.05

For surcharges see Nos. 108-108J.

Nos. 31-32, 34-36 Overprinted or Surcharged

1964, Oct. 25 Photo. *Perf. 14½*

37 A2 50np sepia 3.00 2.50
38 A2 75np ultra 4.50 3.75

Engr. *Perf. 13*

39 A3 1ru on 10r black 6.00 2.00
40 A3 2ru blue 13.00 3.75
41 A3 5ru green 30.00 10.00
Nos. 37-41 (5) 56.50 22.00

18th Olympic Games, Tokyo, Oct. 10-25.
For surcharges see Nos. 110-110D.

Nos. 31-32, 34-36 with Typographed Overprint or Surcharge

1964, Nov. 22 Photo. *Perf. 14½*

42 A2 50np sepia 3.00 1.25
43 A2 75np ultra 4.50 1.75

Engr. *Perf. 13*

44 A3 1ru on 10ru blk 6.25 3.00
45 A3 2ru blue 13.00 8.00
46 A3 5ru green 32.50 13.00
Nos. 42-46 (5) 59.25 27.00

Pres. John F. Kennedy (1917-63).
For surcharges see Nos. 111-111D.

Column — A4

Designs: 2np, 1.50r, Isis Temple and Colonnade, Philae. 3np, 1r, Trajan's kiosk, Philae.

Perf. 14½x14

1965, Jan. 17 Photo. Unwmk.

47 A4 1np multicolored 2.25 .60
48 A4 2np multicolored 2.75 .60
49 A4 3np multicolored 2.75 .60
50 A4 1ru multicolored 4.00 1.50
51 A4 1.50ru multicolored 8.50 2.50
52 A4 2ru multicolored 2.75 2.00
Nos. 47-52 (6) 23.00 7.80

UNESCO world campaign to save historic monuments in Nubia. Nos. 47-52 exist imperf. Value, set $32.50.

Qatar Scout Emblem, Tents and Sheik Ahmad — A5

Scouts Saluting and Sheik Ahmad — A6

Designs: 1np, 4np, Qatar scout emblem.

Perf. 14 (A5), 14½x14 (A6)

1965, May 22 Photo. Unwmk.

53 A5 1np ol grn & dk red brn .90 .45
54 A5 2np sal & dk vio bl .90 .45
55 A5 3np dk vio bl & grn .90 .45
56 A5 4np bl & dk red brn .90 .45
57 A5 5np dk vio bl & grnsh bl .90 .45
58 A6 30np multi 8.25 3.50
59 A6 40np multi 12.50 5.00
60 A6 1ru multi 24.00 10.00
Nos. 53-60 (8) 49.25 20.75

Issued to honor the Qatar Boy Scouts. Nos. 53-60 exist imperf. Value, set $45. Perf. and imperf. souvenir sheets contain one each of Nos. 58-60 with red brown marginal inscription. Size: 108x76mm. Value, perf. $40, imperf. $60.
For surcharges see Nos. 113-113G.

Eiffel Tower, Telstar, ITU Emblem and "Qatar" in Morse Code — A7

Designs: 2np, 1ru, Tokyo Olympic Games emblem and Syncom III. 3np, 40np, Radar tracking station and Relay satellite. 4np, 50np, Post Office Tower, London, and Echo II, Syncom III, Telstar and Relay satellites around globe.

Perf. 13½x14

1965, Oct. 16 Photo. Unwmk.

61 A7 1np dk bl & red brn 1.25 .55
62 A7 2np bl & dk red brn 1.25 .55
63 A7 3np dp yel grn & brt pur 1.25 .55
64 A7 4np org brn & brt bl 1.25 .55
65 A7 5np dl vio & dk ol bis 1.25 .55
66 A7 40np dk car rose & blk 6.50 1.50
67 A7 50np sl grn & bis 10.00 1.75
68 A7 1ru emer & car 13.00 2.75
a. Souvenir sheet of 2, #67-68 40.00 40.00
Nos. 61-68 (8) 35.75 8.75

Cent. of the ITU. Nos. 61-68 exist imperf. Value, set $42.50. No. 68a exists imperf. Value $60.
For overprints and surcharges see Nos. 91-98, 114-114G, 117-117G.

Triggerfish — A8

Various Fish, including: 2np, 50np, Clown grunt. 3np, 10ru, Saddleback butterflyfish. 4np, 5ru, Butterflyfish. 15np, 3ru, Paradisefish. 20np, 1ru, Rio Grande perch. 75np, Triggerfish.

1965, Oct. 18 *Perf. 14x14½*

69 A8 1np multi & black .50 .40
70 A8 2np multi & black .50 .40
71 A8 3np multi & black .50 .40
72 A8 4np multi & black .50 .40
73 A8 5np multi & black .50 .40
74 A8 15np multi & black 1.50 .40
75 A8 20np multi & black 1.75 .40
76 A8 30np multi & black 2.50 .60
77 A8 40np multi & black 3.00 .75
78 A8 50np multi & gold 3.75 1.25
79 A8 75np multi & gold 5.00 1.75
80 A8 1ru multi & gold 6.00 —
81 A8 2ru multi & gold 16.00 4.00
82 A8 3ru multi & gold 20.00 6.50
83 A8 4ru multi & gold 30.00 8.00
84 A8 5ru multi & gold 45.00 10.00
85 A8 10ru multi & gold 90.00 14.00
Nos. 69-85 (17) 227.00 49.65

Nos. 69-85 exist imperf. Values about 25-50 percent higher.
For surcharges see Nos. 115-115P.

Basketball — A9

No. 87, Horse jumping. No. 88, Running. No. 89, Soccer. No. 90, Weight lifting.

1966, Jan. 10 Photo. *Perf. 11½*

Granite Paper

86 A9 1ru gray, blk & dk red 4.25 2.00
87 A9 1ru brn & ol grn 4.25 2.00
88 A9 1ru dull rose & blue 4.25 2.00
89 A9 1ru grn & blk 4.25 2.00
90 A9 1ru bl & brn 4.25 2.00
a. Strip of 5, #86-90 — —
Nos. 86-90 (5) 21.25 10.00

4th Pan Arab Games, Cairo, Sept. 2-11. Nos. 86-90 were printed in sheets of 25 in se-tenant horizontal rows of five. Nos. 86-90 exist imperf. Value, set $25.

Nos. 61-68 Overprinted in Black

1966, Feb. 9 Photo. *Perf. 13½x14*

91 A7 1np dk bl & red brn 1.50 .40
92 A7 2np bl & dk red brn 1.50 .40
93 A7 3np dp yel grn & brt pur 1.50 .40
94 A7 4np org brn & brt bl 1.50 .40
95 A7 5np dl vio & dk ol bis 1.50 .40

96 A7 40np dk car rose & blk 7.00 .45
97 A7 50np slate grn & bis 7.50 .55
98 A7 1ru emer & car 17.50 1.10
a. Souvenir sheet of 2, #97-98 55.00 32.50
Nos. 91-98 (8) 39.50 4.10

Issued to commemorate the rendezvous in space of Gemini 6 and 7, Dec. 15, 1965. Nos. 91-98 exist overprinted in red. Value, set $200. Nos. 96-98 also exist overprinted in blue. Value, set $150.

For surcharges see Nos. 117-117G.

Sheik Ahmad — A9a

Designs: 3np, 5np, 40np, 80np, 2ru, 10ru, Reverse of coin with Arabic inscription.

Litho. & Embossed Gold or Silver Foil

1966, Feb. 24 ***Imperf.***
99 A9a 1np ol & lil (S) .75 .40
99A A9a 3np blk & org (S) .75 .40
99B A9a 4np pur & red .75 .40
99C A9a 5np brt grn & red brn .75 .40

Diameter: 55mm

99D A9a 10np brn & brt vio (S) 2.25 .40
99E A9a 40np org red & bl (S) 3.50 .75
99F A9a 70np Prus bl & bl vio 7.25 1.60
99G A9a 80np car & grn 7.25 1.60

Diameter: 65mm

99H A9a 1ru red vio & blk (S) 10.50 2.10
99J A9a 2ru bl grn & cl (S) 18.50 4.00
99K A9a 5ru red lil & ver 40.00 9.00
99L A9a 10ru bl vio & brn car 80.00 21.00
Nos. 99-99L (12) 172.25 42.05

John F. Kennedy, UN Headquarters, NY, and ICY Emblem — A10

Designs (ICY emblem and): #100, UN emblem. #100B, Dag Hammarskjold and UN General Assembly. #100C, Jawaharlal Nehru and dove.

1966, Mar. 8 ***Perf. 11½***

Granite Paper

100 A10 40np brt bl, vio bl & red brn 5.00 2.50
100A A10 40np brt grn, vio & brn 5.00 2.50
100B A10 40np red brn, brt bl & blk 5.00 2.50
100C A10 40np dk vio & brt grn 5.00 2.50
d. Block of 4, #100-100C 27.50 25.00
Nos. 100-100C (4) 20.00 10.00

UN Intl. Cooperation Year, 1965. Printed in sheets of 16 + 9 labels in shape of a cross. Nos. 100-100C exist imperf. Value, set $30. No. 100Cd exists imperf.

An imperf. souvenir sheet of 4 contains one each of Nos. 100-100C. Value $55.

For overprints see Nos. 101E-101H. For surcharges see Nos. 117H-117K.

Telstar, Rocket — A10a

Nos. 100-100C Overprinted in Blue, Black or Red

Designs: No. 101, John F. Kennedy, "In Memoriam / John F. Kennedy / 1917-1963." No. 101A, Olive branches, Churchill quote and "In Memoriam / 1874-1965." No. 101B, like #101 portrait facing left, no overprint. No. 101C, Eternal flame, Arabic inscription. No. 101D, Telstar, Rocket.

1966, Mar. 8 **Granite Paper**

101 A10a 5np bl grn, car & blk (BL) 15.00 8.00
j. 5np Like #101, bl grn, blk & car (BL) — —
101A A10a 5np bl grn, rose & blk 15.00 8.00
k. 5np Like #101A (R) — —
101B A10a 5np bl grn, car & blk 15.00 8.00
l. 5np Like #101B, bl grn, blk & car — —
101C A10a 5np bl grn, rose & blk 15.00 8.00
m. 5np Like #101C, bl grn, blk & car (R) — —
101D A10a 5np bl grn, car & blk 15.00 8.00
n. 5np Like #101D, bl grn, blk & car (R) — —
101E A10 40np on No. 100 5.00 3.00
o. 40np Like #101E (R) — —
101F A10 40np on No. 100A 5.00 3.00
p. 40np Like #101F (R) — —
101G A10 40np on No. 100B 5.00 3.00
q. 40np Like #101G (R) — —
101H A10 40np on No. 100C 5.00 3.00
i. Sheet of 21, #101-101D, 4 ea #101E-101H+4 labels — —
r. 40np Like #101H (R) — —
s. Sheet of 21, #101j-101n, 4 ea #101o-101r+4 labels — —
Nos. 101-101H (9) 95.00 52.00

Nos. 101-101H were made from the sheets of Nos. 100-100C. The 4 outer labels and the center label were surcharged to create Nos. 101-101D. The other 4 labels were overprinted but have no denomination. Kennedy's portrait is in carmine on Nos. 101, 101B and in black on Nos. 101j and 101Bl.

The imperf. souvenir sheet exists with overprint in margin: "IN VICTORY, / MAGNANIMITY. / IN PEACE / GOODWILL / WINSTON CHURCHILL." The margin overprint overlaps onto No. 101A on upper left quarter of stamp.

Nos. 101-101H exist imperf.

For surcharges see Nos. 118-118H.

John F. Kennedy (1917-1963) — A10b

Kennedy and: No. 102c, 10np, No. 102Af, 70np, NYC. No. 102d, 30np, No. 102Ag, 80np, Rocket lifting off at Cape Kennedy. No. 102e, 60np, No. 102Ah, 1ru, Statue of Liberty. No. 102B, Statue of Liberty.

1966, July 18 ***Perf. 13½***
102 A10b Strip of 3, #c.-e. 4.00 4.00
102A A10b Strip of 3, #f.-h. 7.00 7.00

Souvenir Sheet

Imperf

102B A10b 50np multicolored 42.50 —

Nos. 102-102A exist imperf. Value, set of 2 strips $17.50.

For surcharges see Nos. 119-119B.

1968 Summer Olympics, Mexico City — A10c

Designs: #103c, 1np, #103Af, 70np, #103B, Equestrian. #103d, 4np, #103Ag, 80np, Running. #103e, 5np, #103Ah, 90np, Javelin.

1966, July 20 ***Perf. 13½***
103 A10c Strip of 3, #c.-e. 4.00 4.00
103A A10c Strip of 3, #f.-h. 10.00 15.00

Souvenir Sheet

Imperf

103B A10c 50np multicolored 42.50 —

Nos. 103-103A exist imperf. Value, set $30. For surcharges see Nos. 120-120B.

A10d

American Astronauts — A10e

Astronaut and space vehicle: No. 104c, 5np, James A. Lovell. d, 10np, Thomas P. Stafford. e, 15np, Alan B. Shepard.

No. 104Af, 20np, John H. Glenn. No. 104Ag, 30np, M. Scott Carpenter. No. 104Ah, 40np, Walter M. Schirra. No. 104Ai, 50np, Virgil I. Grissom. No. 104Aj, 60np, L. Gordon Cooper, Jr.

No. 104B, Stafford, Schirra, Frank Borman, Lovell and diagram of space rendezvous.

1966, Aug. 20 ***Perf. 12***
104 A10d Strip of 3, #c.-e. 4.00 4.00
104A A10e Strip of 5, #f.-j. 12.50 12.50

Souvenir Sheet

Imperf

Size: 115x75mm

104B A10e 50np multicolored 52.50 —

The name of James A. Lovell is spelled "Lovel" on No. 104c. Nos. 104-104A exist imperf. For surcharges see Nos. 121-121B.

A10h A10i

1966 World Cup Soccer Championships, London

Designs: 1np-4np, Jules Rimet Cup. 60np, #107H, Hands holding Cup, soccer ball. 70np, #107J, Cup, soccer ball. 80np, #107K, Soccer players, ball. 90np, #107L, Wembley Stadium.

1966, Nov. 27 **Photo.** ***Perf. 13½***
107 A10h 1np blue — —
107A A10h 2np blue — —
107B A10h 3np blue — —
107C A10h 4np blue — —
m. Block of 4, #107-107C 15.00 —
107D A10i 60np multicolored — —
107E A10i 70np multicolored — —
107F A10i 80np multicolored — —
107G A10i 90np multicolored — —
n. Block of 4, #107D-107G 50.00 —

Souvenir Sheets

Imperf

107H A10i 25np multicolored — 22.50
107J A10i 25np multicolored — 22.50
107K A10i 25np multicolored — 22.50
107L A10i 25np multicolored — 22.50

Nos. 107-107C are airmail. Issued in sheets of 36 containing 5 #107m and 4 #107n. Nos. 107-107G exist imperf.

Nos. 26-36 Surcharged with New Currency

1966, Oct. ***Perf.***
108 A1 5d on 5np rose car 11.00 7.50
108A A1 15d on 15np brn blk 11.00 7.50
108B A1 20d on 20np clar 11.00 7.50
108C A1 30d on 30np dp grn 40.00 15.00
108D A2 40d on 40np red 75.00 27.50
108E A2 50d on 50np sepia 85.00 32.50
108F A2 75d on 75np ultra 125.00 40.00
108G A3 1r on 1ru rose red 150.00 50.00
108H A3 2r on 2ru blue 160.00 110.00
108I A3 5r on 5ru green 200.00 150.00
108J A3 10r on 10ru black 300.00 225.00
Nos. 108-108J (11) 1,168. 672.50

Nos. 37-41 Surcharged with New Currency in Gray or Red

1966 **Photo.** ***Perf. 14½***
110 A2 50d on 50np #37 (G) — —
110A A2 75d on 75np #38 — —

Engr.

Perf. 13

110B A3 1r on 1ru on 10ru #39 — —
110C A3 2r on 2ru #40 — —
110D A3 5r on 5ru #41 — —
Set, #110-110D (5) 175.00 —

Nos. 42-46 Surcharged with New Currency in Gray or Red

1966 **Photo.** ***Perf. 14½***
111 A2 50d on 50np #42 (G) — —
111A A2 75d on 75np #43 — —

Engr.

Perf. 13

111B A3 1r on 1ru on 10ru #44 — —
111C A3 2r on 2ru #45 — —
111D A3 5r on 5ru #46 — —
Set, #111-111D (5) 250.00 —

Nos. 53-60 Surcharged with New Currency

Perf. 14 (A5), 14½x14 (A6)

1966 **Photo.**
113 A5 1d on 1np #53 — —
113A A5 2d on 2np #54 — —
113B A5 3d on 3np #55 — —
113C A5 4d on 4np #56 — —
113D A5 5d on 4np #57 — —
113E A6 30d on 30np #58 — —
113F A6 40d on 40np #59 — —
113G A6 1r on 1ru #60 — —
Set, #113-113G (8) 85.00 —

Exist imperf. Perf and imperf souvenir sheets contain one each of #113E-113G surcharged with new currency.

Nos. 61-68 Surcharged with New Currency in Black or Red

1966 ***Perf. 13½x14***
114 A7 1d on 1np #61 — —
114A A7 2d on 2np #62 — —
114B A7 3d on 3np #63 — —
114C A7 4d on 4np #64 — —
114D A7 5d on 5np #65 — —
114E A7 40d on 40np #66 — —
114F A7 50d on 50np #67 — —
114G A7 1r on 1ru #68 — —
Set, #114-114G (8) 85.00 —

Exist imperf.

Nos. 69-85 Surcharged with New Currency

1966, Oct.
115 A8 1d on 1np multi & black 3.00 1.75
115A A8 2d on 2np multi & black 3.00 1.75
115B A8 3d on 3np multi & black 3.00 1.75
115C A8 4d on 4np multi & black 3.00 1.75
115D A8 5d on 5np multi & black 3.00 1.75
115E A8 15d on 15np multi & black 3.50 1.75

115F A8 20d on 20np multi & black 4.00 1.75
115G A8 30d on 30np multi & black 4.00 1.75
115H A8 40d on 40np multi & black 5.00 4.50
115I A8 50d on 50np multi & gold 6.50 6.50
115J A8 75d on 75np multi & gold 7.50 20.00
115K A8 1r on 1 ru multi & gold 75.00 35.00
115L A8 2r on 2ru multi & gold 110.00 45.00
115M A8 3r on 3ru multi & gold 125.00 55.00
115N A8 4r on 4ru multi & gold 200.00 75.00
115O A8 5r on 5 ru multi & gold 225.00 100.00
115P A8 10r on 10ru multi & gold 275.00 150.00
Nos. 115-115P (17) 1,055. 505.00

Nos. 69-85 exist imperf. Value, set *$1,600.*

Nos. 91-98 Surcharged with New Currency

1966 Photo. *Perf. 13½x14*

117 A7 1d on 1np #91 — —
117A A7 2d on 2np #92 — —
117B A7 3d on 3np #93 — —
117C A7 4d on 4np #94 — —
117D A7 5d on 5np #95 — —
117E A7 40d on 40np #96 — —
117F A7 50d on 50np #97 — —
117G A7 1r on 1ru #98 — —
Set, #117-117G (8) 75.00 —

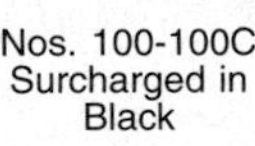

Nos. 100-100C Surcharged in Black

1966 *Perf. 11½*

Granite Paper

117H A10 40d on 40np #100 — —
117I A10 40d on 40np #100A — —
117J A10 40d on 40np #100B — —
117K A10 40d on 40np #100C — —
l. Block of 4, #117H-117K

Printed in sheets of 16 + 9 labels in shape of a cross. Nos. 117H-117K exist imperf.

Nos. 101-101H Surcharged in Black with New Currency Like Nos. 117H-117K

1966 Photo. *Perf. 11½*

Granite Paper

118 A10a 5d on 5np #101 — —
j. 5d on 5np #101j
118A A10a 5d on 5np #101A — —
k. 5d on 5np #101k
118B A10a 5d on 5np #101B — —
l. 5d on 5np #101l
118C A10a 5d on 5np #101C — —
m. 5d on 5np #101m
118D A10a 5d on 5np #101D — —
n. 5d on 5np #101n
118E A10 40d on 40np #101E — —
o. 40d on 40np #101o
118F A10 40d on 40np #101F 5.00 3.00
p. 40d on 40np #101p — —
118G A10 40d on 40np #101G — —
q. 40d on 40np #101q
118H A10 40d on 40np #101H — —
i. Sheet of 21, #118-118D, 4 ea #118E-118H+4 labels
r. 40d on 40np #101r — —
s. Sheet of 21, #118j-118n, 4 ea #118o-118r+4 labels — —

Exist imperf. Imperf. souvenir sheets mentioned after Nos. 100C, 101H exist surcharged with new currency.

Nos. 102-102B Surcharged with New Currency

1966 *Perf. 13½*

119 Strip of 3 30.00 —
c. A10b 10d on 10np #102c — —
d. A10b 30d on 30np #102d — —
e. A10b 60d on 60np #102e — —
119A Strip of 3 30.00 —
f. A10b 70d on 70np #102f — —
g. A10b 80d on 80np #102g — —
h. A10b 1r on 1ru #102h — —

Souvenir Sheet

Imperf

119B A10b 50d on 50np #102B 75.00 50.00

Nos. 119-119A exist imperf.

Nos. 103-103B Surcharged with New Currency

1966 *Perf. 13½*

120 Strip of 3 60.00 —
c. A10c 1d on 1np #103c — —
d. A10c 4d on 4np #103d — —
e. A10c 5d on 5np #103e — —
120A Strip of 3 60.00 —
f. A10c 70d on 70np #103f — —
g. A10c 80d on 80np #103g — —
h. A10c 90d on 90np #103h — —

Souvenir Sheet

Imperf

120B A10c 50d on 50np #103 75.00 —

Nos. 120-120 exist imperf.

Nos. 104-104B Surcharged with New Currency

1966 *Perf. 12*

121 Strip of 3 30.00 —
c. A10d 5d on 5np #104c — —
d. A10d 10d on 10np #104d — —
e. A10d 15d on 15np #104e — —
121A Strip of 5 45.00 —
f. A10e 20d on 20np #104f — —
g. A10e 30d on 30np #104g — —
h. A10e 40d on 40np #104h — —
i. A10e 50d on 50np #104i — —
j. A10e 60d on 60np #104j — —

Souvenir Sheet

Imperf

121B A10e 50d on 50np #104B 100.00 —

Nos. 121-121A printed se-tenant with five labels showing Arabic inscription.

Arab Postal Union Emblem — A11

1967, Apr. 15 Photo. *Perf. 11x11½*

122 A11 70d magenta & sepia 4.50 2.00
122A A11 80d dull blue & sepia 6.50 2.00

Qatar's joining the Arab Postal Union.

Apollo Project A11a

Designs: 5d, 70d, Two astronauts on Moon. 10d, 80d, Command and lunar modules in lunar orbit. 20d, 1r, Lunar module on Moon. 30d, 1.20r, Lunar module ascending from Moon. 40d, 2r, Saturn 5 rocket.

1967, May 1 *Perf. 12½*

123 A11a 5d multicolored .75 .35
123A A11a 10d multicolored .75 .35
123B A11a 20d multicolored .75 .35
123C A11a 30d multicolored 1.00 .50
123D A11a 40d multicolored 1.50 .65
123E A11a 70d multicolored 3.00 1.50
123F A11a 80d multicolored 3.25 2.25
123G A11a 1r multicolored 3.50 2.75
123H A11a 1.20r multicolored 4.25 3.00
123J A11a 2r multicolored 6.00 4.00
Nos. 123-123J (10) 24.75 15.70

#123J exists in an imperf. souv. sheet of one. Value $30.

Traffic Light and Intersection — A12

1967, May 24 Litho. *Perf. 13½*

124 A12 20d vio & multi 1.00 .40
124A A12 30d multi 2.00 .65
124B A12 50d multi 3.00 .80
124C A12 1r ultra & multi 5.00 2.50
Nos. 124-124C (4) 11.00 4.35

Issued for Traffic Day.

Boy Scouts and Sheik Ahmad A13

Designs: 1d, First Boy Scout camp, Brownsea Island, 1907, and tents, Idaho, US, 1967. 2d, Lord Baden-Powell. 5d, Boy Scout canoeing. 15d, Swimming. 75d, Mountain climbing. 2r, Boy Scout saluting flag and emblem of 12th World Jamboree. 1d and 2d lack head of Sheik Ahmad.

1967, Sept. 15 Litho. *Perf. 11½x11*

125 A13 1d multicolored .75 .45
125A A13 2d buff & multi .75 .45

Litho. and Engr.

125B A13 3d rose & multi .75 .45
125C A13 5d lilac & multi 1.00 .45
125D A13 15d multicolored 2.50 .55
125E A13 75d green & multi 5.00 1.75
125F A13 2r sepia & multi 14.00 6.00
Nos. 125-125F (7) 24.75 10.10

Nos. 125-125A for 60th anniv. of the Boy Scouts, Nos. 125B-125F for 12th Boy Scout World Jamboree, Farragut State Park, Idaho, Aug. 1-9.

Viking Ship (from Bayeux Tapestry) A14

Famous Ships: 2d, Santa Maria (Columbus). 3d, San Gabriel (Vasco da Gama). 75d, Victoria (Ferdinand Magellan). 1r, Golden Hind (Sir Francis Drake). 2r, Gipsy Moth IV (Sir Francis Chichester).

1967, Nov. 27 Litho. *Perf. 13½*

126 A14 1d org & multi .80 .35
126A A14 2d lt bl, tan & blk .90 .35
126B A14 3d lt bl & multi 1.25 .35
126C A14 75d fawn & multi 5.75 1.75
126D A14 1r gray, yel grn & red 7.50 2.75
126E A14 2r multi 14.50 3.75
Nos. 126-126E (6) 30.70 9.30

Professional Letter Writer — A15

Designs: 2d, Carrier pigeon and man releasing pigeon, vert. 3d, Postrider. 60d, Mail transport by rowboat, vert. 1.25r, Mailman riding camel, jet plane and modern buildings. 2r, Qatar No. 1, hand holding pen, paper, envelopes and inkwell.

1968, Feb. 14

127 A15 1d multicolored .75 .40
127A A15 2d multicolored .75 .40
127B A15 3d multicolored .75 .40
127C A15 60d multicolored 4.00 1.25
127D A15 1.25r multicolored 8.00 2.50
127E A15 2r multicolored 14.00 4.25
Nos. 127-127E (6) 28.25 9.20

Ten years of Qatar postal service.

Human Rights Flame and Barbed Wire A16

2d, Arab refugee family leaving concentration camp. 3d, Scales of Justice. 60d, Hands opening gates to the sun. 1.25r, Family and sun, vert. 2r, Stylized family groups.

1968, Apr. 10

128 A16 1d gray & multi .60 .30
129 A16 2d multicolored .60 .30
130 A16 3d brt grn, org & blk .75 .30
131 A16 60d org, brn & blk 4.00 2.25
132 A16 1.25r brt grn, blk & yel 5.50 4.75
133 A16 2r multicolored 11.00 6.50
Nos. 128-133 (6) 22.45 14.40

International Human Rights Year.

Nurse Attending Premature Baby — A17

Designs (WHO Emblem and): 2d, Operating room. 3d, Dentist. 60d, X-ray examination. 1.25r, Medical laboratory. 2r, State Hospital.

1968, June 20

134 A17 1d multi .75 .40
135 A17 2d multi .75 .40
136 A17 3d multi .85 .40
137 A17 60d multi 3.75 .70
138 A17 1.25r multi 8.50 2.25
139 A17 2r multi 14.00 3.25
Nos. 134-139 (6) 28.60 7.40

20th anniv. of the World Health Organization.

Olympic Rings and Gymnast A18

Designs (Olympic Rings and): 1d, Discobolus and view of Mexico City. 2d, Runner and flaming torch. 60d, Weight lifting and torch. 1.25r, Olympic flame as a mosaic, vert. 2r, Mythological bird.

1968, Aug. 24

140 A18 1d multicolored .55 .50
141 A18 2d multicolored .65 .50
142 A18 3d multicolored 1.00 .50
143 A18 60d multicolored 4.50 1.75
144 A18 1.25r multicolored 8.00 2.75
145 A18 2r multicolored 14.00 4.25
Nos. 140-145 (6) 28.70 10.25

19th Olympic Games, Mexico City, 10/12-27.

Sheik Ahmad bin Ali al Thani
A19 A21

Dhow
A20

Designs: 40d, Desalination plant. 60d, Loading platform and oil tanker. 70d, Qatar Mosque. 1r, Clock Tower, Market Place, Doha. 1.25r, Doha Fort. 1.50r, Falcon.

1968 Litho. *Perf. 13½*

No.	Type	Denomination	Unused	Used
146	A19	5d blue & green	.50	.50
147	A19	10d brt bl & red brn	.65	.50
148	A19	20d blk & vermilion	1.00	.50
149	A19	25d brt mag & brt grn	2.25	.50

Lithographed and Engraved

Perf. 13

No.	Type	Denomination	Unused	Used
150	A20	35d grn & brt pink	4.00	.50
151	A20	40d pur, lt bl & org	5.00	.50
152	A20	60d lt bl, brn & lil	6.50	.85
153	A20	70d blk, lt bl & brt grn	7.00	1.10
154	A20	1r vio bl, yel & brt grn	9.00	1.40
155	A20	1.25r ind, brt bl & ocher	10.00	1.75
156	A20	1.50r lt bl, dk grn & rose lil	12.50	2.10

Perf. 11½

No.	Type	Denomination	Unused	Used
157	A21	2r brn, ocher & bl gray	17.50	3.00
158	A21	5r grn, lt grn & pur	30.00	7.25
159	A21	10r ultra, lt bl & sep	57.50	13.50
		Nos. 146-159 (14)	*163.40*	*33.95*

UN Headquarters, NY, and Flags — A22

1d, Flags. 4d, World map and dove. 60d, Classroom. 1.50r, Farmers, wheat and tractor. 2r, Sec. Gen. U Thant and General Assembly Hall.

1968, Oct. 24 Litho. *Perf. 13½x13*

No.	Type	Denomination	Unused	Used
160	A22	1d multi	.50	.50
161	A22	4d multi	.65	.50
162	A22	5d multi	.75	.50
163	A22	60d multi	4.75	1.50
164	A22	1.50r multi	7.50	2.40
165	A22	2r multi	8.50	4.00
		Nos. 160-165 (6)	*22.65*	*9.40*

United Nations Day, Oct. 24, 1968.

Fishing Vessel Ross Rayyan A23

Progress in Qatar: 4d, Elementary School and children playing. 5d, Doha Intl. Airport. 60d, Cement factory and road building. 1.50r, Power station. 2r, Housing development.

1969, Jan. 13

No.	Type	Denomination	Unused	Used
166	A23	1d brt bl & multi	.40	.40
167	A23	4d green & multi	.40	.40
168	A23	5d dl org & multi	.75	.40
169	A23	60d lt brn & multi	4.00	1.50
170	A23	1.50r brt lil & multi	9.00	2.00
171	A23	2r buff & multi	13.00	3.00
		Nos. 166-171 (6)	*27.55*	*7.70*

Armored Cars
A24

Designs: 2d, Traffic police. 3d, Military helicopter. 60d, Military band. 1.25r, Field gun. 2r, Mounted police.

1969, May 6 Litho. *Perf. 13½*

No.	Type	Denomination	Unused	Used
172	A24	1d multicolored	.75	.45
173	A24	2d lt blue & multi	.75	.45
174	A24	3d gray & multi	.90	.50
175	A24	60d multicolored	5.00	1.50
176	A24	1.25r multi	8.50	2.25
177	A24	2r blue & multi	15.00	4.00
		Nos. 172-177 (6)	*30.90*	*9.15*

Issued to honor the public security forces.

Oil Tanker A25

2d, Research laboratory. 3d, Off-shore oil rig, helicopter. 60d, Oil rig, storage tanks. 1.50r, Oil refinery. 2r, Oil tankers, 1890-1968.

1969, July 4

No.	Type	Denomination	Unused	Used
178	A25	1d gray & multi	.65	.40
179	A25	2d olive & multi	.65	.40
180	A25	3d ultra & multi	1.00	.40
181	A25	60d lilac & multi	4.00	1.75
182	A25	1.50r red brn & multi	11.00	3.25
183	A25	2r brown & multi	16.50	4.25
		Nos. 178-183 (6)	*33.80*	*10.45*

Qatar oil industry.

Boy Scouts Building Boats A26

Designs: 2d, Scouts at work and 10 symbolic candles. 3d, Parade. 60d, Gate to camp interior. 1.25r, Main camp gate. 2r, Hoisting Qatar flag, and Sheik Ahmad.

1969, Sept. 18 Litho. *Perf. 13½x13*

No.	Type	Denomination	Unused	Used
184	A26	1d multicolored	.35	.30
185	A26	2d multicolored	.35	.30
186	A26	3d multicolored	.75	.30
187	A26	60d multicolored	6.00	1.10
a.		Souvenir sheet of 4, #184-187	40.00	20.00
188	A26	1.25r multicolored	9.50	2.25
189	A26	2r multicolored	13.00	3.50
		Nos. 184-189 (6)	*29.95*	*7.75*

10th Qatar Boy Scout Jamboree. No. 187a sold for 1r.

Neil A. Armstrong A27

Designs: 2d, Col. Edwin E. Aldrin, Jr. 3d, Lt. Col. Michael Collins. 60d, Astronaut walking on moon. 1.25r, Blast-off from moon. 2r, Capsule and raft in Pacific, horiz.

1969, Dec. 6 *Perf. 13x13½, 13½x13*

No.	Type	Denomination	Unused	Used
190	A27	1d blue & multi	.50	.50
191	A27	2d multicolored	.50	.50
192	A27	3d grn & multi	.85	.50
193	A27	60d multicolored	3.50	1.25
194	A27	1.25r pur & multi	7.00	3.00
195	A27	2r multicolored	12.50	4.75
		Nos. 190-195 (6)	*24.85*	*10.50*

See note after US No. C76.

UPU Emblem, Boeing Jet Loading in Qatar A28

2d, Transatlantic ocean liner. 3d, Mail truck and mail bags. 60d, Qatar Post Office. 1.25r, UPU Headquarters, Bern. 2r, UPU emblem.

1970, Jan. 31 Litho. *Perf. 13½x13*

No.	Type	Denomination	Unused	Used
196	A28	1d multi	.50	.50
197	A28	2d multi	.50	.50
198	A28	3d multi	.90	.50
199	A28	60d multi	3.50	1.50
200	A28	1.25r multi	6.50	2.75
201	A28	2r brt yel grn, blk & lt brn	11.00	3.50
		Nos. 196-201 (6)	*22.90*	*9.25*

Qatar's admission to the UPU.

Map of Arab League Countries, Flag and Emblem — A28a

1970, Mar. *Perf. 13x13½*

No.	Type	Denomination	Unused	Used
202	A28a	35d yellow & multi	2.25	.80
203	A28a	60d blue & multi	3.75	1.25
204	A28a	1.25r multi	7.00	2.25
205	A28a	1.50r vio & multi	9.50	4.00
		Nos. 202-205 (4)	*22.50*	*8.30*

25th anniversary of the Arab League.

VC10 Touching down for Landing A29

Designs: 2d, Hawk, and VC10 in flight. 3d, VC10 and airport. 60d, Map showing route Doha to London. 1.25r, VC10 over Gulftown. 2r, Tail of VC10 with emblem of Gulf Aviation.

1970, Apr. 5 *Perf. 13½x13*

No.	Type	Denomination	Unused	Used
206	A29	1d multi	.45	.45
207	A29	2d multi	.75	.45
208	A29	3d multi	.85	.45
209	A29	60d multi	5.50	1.50
210	A29	1.25r multi	10.00	3.00
211	A29	2r multi	17.50	4.50
		Nos. 206-211 (6)	*35.05*	*10.35*

Issued to publicize the first flight to London from Doha by Gulf Aviation Company.

Education Year Emblem, Spaceship Trajectory, Koran Quotation — A30

1970, May 24 *Perf. 13x12½*

No.	Type	Denomination	Unused	Used
212	A30	35d blue & multi	4.00	1.60
213	A30	60d blue & multi	8.00	2.50

Intl. Education Year. Translation of Koran quotation: "And say, O God, give me more knowledge."

Flowers — A31

1970, July 2 *Perf. 13x13½*

No.	Type	Denomination	Unused	Used
214	A31	1d Freesia	.80	.45
215	A31	2d Azalea	.80	.45
216	A31	3d Ixia	1.10	.45
217	A31	60d Amaryllis	5.50	1.60
218	A31	1.25r Cineraria	9.50	3.50
219	A31	2r Rose	12.50	4.50
		Nos. 214-219 (6)	*30.20*	*10.95*

For surcharges see Nos. 287-289.

EXPO Emblem and Fisherman on Shikoku Beach — A32

1d, Toyahama fishermen honoring ocean gods. 2d, Map of Japan. 60d, Mt. Fuji. 1.50r, Camphorwood torii. 2r, Tower of Motherhood, EXPO Tower and Mt. Fuji.

Perf. 13½x13, 13x13½

1970, Sept. 29

No.	Type	Denomination	Unused	Used
220	A32	1d multi, horiz.	.45	.45
221	A32	2d multi, horiz.	.60	.45
222	A32	3d multi	.90	.45
223	A32	60d multi	4.25	1.10
a.		Souvenir sheet of 4	55.00	27.50
224	A32	1.50r multi, horiz.	12.00	3.50
225	A32	2r multi	17.50	6.00
		Nos. 220-225 (6)	*35.70*	*11.95*

EXPO '70 Intl. Exhib., Osaka, Japan, Mar. 15-Sept. 13. No. 223a contains 4 imperf. stamps similar to Nos. 220-223 with simulated perforations. Sold for 1r.

Globe and UN Emblem — A33

UN, 25th anniv.: 2d, Cannon used as flower vase. 3d, Birthday cake and dove. 35d, Emblems of UN agencies forming wall. 1.50r, Trumpet and emblems of UN agencies. 2r, Two men, black and white, embracing, and globe.

1970, Dec. 7 Litho. *Perf. 14x13½*

No.	Type	Denomination	Unused	Used
226	A33	1d blue & multi	.70	.35
227	A33	2d multicolored	.70	.35
228	A33	3d brt pur & multi	1.00	.40
229	A33	35d green & multi	3.25	1.00
230	A33	1.50r multi	9.50	2.25
231	A33	2r brn red & multi	11.50	3.75
		Nos. 226-231 (6)	*26.65*	*8.10*

Al Jahiz and Old World Map A34

Designs: 2d, Sultan Saladin and palace. 3d, Al Farabi, sailboat and musical instruments. 35d, Iben al Haithum and palace. 1.50r, Al Motanabbi and camels. 2r, Avicenna and old world map.

1971, Feb. 20 ***Perf. 13½x14***

232	A34	1d brt pink & multi	.75	.40
233	A34	2d pale bl & multi	.75	.40
234	A34	3d dl yel & multi	1.25	.40
235	A34	35d lt bl & multi	5.00	.95
236	A34	1.50r yel grn & multi	20.00	3.75
237	A34	2r pale grn & multi	25.00	5.00
		Nos. 232-237 (6)	52.75	10.90

Famous men of Islam.

Cormorant — A35

Designs: 2d, Lizard and prickly pear. 3d, Flamingos and palms. 60d, Oryx and yucca. 1.25r, Gazelle and desert dandelion. 2r, Camel, palm and bronzed chenopod.

1971, Apr. 14 **Litho.** ***Perf. 11x12***

238	A35	1d multi	2.50	.45
239	A35	2d multi	2.50	.45
240	A35	3d multi	2.50	.50
241	A35	60d multi	11.00	2.00
242	A35	1.25r multi	22.50	5.00
243	A35	2r multi	30.00	7.50
		Nos. 238-243 (6)	71.00	15.90

Goonhilly Satellite Tracking Station A36

Designs: 2d, Cable ship, and section of submarine cable. 3d, 35d, London Post Office Tower, and television control room. 4d, Various telephones. 5d, 75d, Video telephone. 3r, Telex machine and tape.

1971, May 17 ***Perf. 13½x13***

244	A36	1d vio bl & multi	.40	.35
245	A36	2d multicolored	.40	.35
246	A36	3d rose red & multi	.40	.35
247	A36	4d magenta & multi	.40	.35
248	A36	5d rose red & multi	.40	.35
249	A36	35d multicolored	3.25	1.00
250	A36	75d magenta & multi	4.75	1.25
251	A36	3r ocher & multi	17.50	3.50
		Nos. 244-251 (8)	27.50	7.50

3rd World Telecommunications Day.

State of Qatar

Arab Postal Union Emblem — A37

1971, Sept. 4 ***Perf. 13***

252	A37	35d red & multi	1.25	.40
253	A37	55d blue & multi	2.25	.80
254	A37	75d brown & multi	3.25	1.25
255	A37	1.25r violet & multi	5.25	1.90
		Nos. 252-255 (4)	12.00	4.35

25th anniv. of the Conf. of Sofar, Lebanon, establishing the Arab Postal Union.

Boy Reading — A38

1971, Aug. 10 ***Perf. 13x13½***

256	A38	35d brown & multi	2.00	.40
257	A38	55d ultra & multi	4.25	.75
258	A38	75d green & multi	5.75	1.10
		Nos. 256-258 (3)	12.00	2.25

International Literacy Day, Sept. 8.

Men Splitting Racism A39

2d, 3r, People fighting racism. 3d, Soldier helping war victim. 4d, Men of 4 races rebuilding. 5d, Children on swing. 35d, Wave of racism engulfing people. 75d, like 1d.

Perf. 13½x13, 13x13½

1971, Oct. 12 **Litho.**

259	A39	1d multi	.60	.40
260	A39	2d multi	.60	.40
261	A39	3d multi	.60	.40
262	A39	4d multi, vert.	.60	.40
263	A39	5d multi, vert.	.60	.40
264	A39	35d multi	3.50	.90
265	A39	75d multi	7.50	1.75
266	A39	3r multi	17.50	3.75
		Nos. 259-266 (8)	31.50	8.40

Intl. Year Against Racial Discrimination.

UNICEF Emblem, Mother and Child — A40

UNICEF, 25th anniv.: 2d, Child's head, horiz. 3d, 75d, Child with book. 4d, Nurse and child, horiz. 5d, Mother and child, horiz. 35d, Woman and daffodil. 3r, like 1d.

1971, Dec. 6 ***Perf. 14x13½, 13½x14***

267	A40	1d blue & multi	.60	.50
268	A40	2d lil rose & multi	.60	.50
269	A40	3d blue & multi	.60	.50
270	A40	4d yellow & multi	.60	.50
271	A40	5d blue & multi	.60	.50
272	A40	35d lil rose & multi	2.50	.65
273	A40	75d yellow & multi	6.75	1.50
274	A40	3r multicolored	16.00	3.50
		Nos. 267-274 (8)	28.25	8.15

Sheik Ahmad, Flags of Arab League and Qatar A41

"International Cooperation" A42

75d, Sheik Ahmad, flags of UN and Qatar. 1.25r, Sheik Ahmad bin Ali al Thani.

1972, Jan. 17 ***Perf. 13½x13, 13x13½***

275	A41	35d black & multi	2.00	.50
276	A41	75d black & multi	3.75	1.25
277	A42	1.25r lt brn & blk	5.50	1.50
278	A42	3r multicolored	13.00	3.50
a.		Souvenir sheet	50.00	25.00
		Nos. 275-278 (4)	24.25	6.75

Independence 1971. No. 278a contains one stamp with simulated perforations.

European Roller — A43

Birds: 2d, European kingfisher. 3d, Rock thrush. 4d, Caspian tern. 5d, Hoopoe. 35d, European bee-eater. 75d, European golden oriole. 3r, Peregrine falcon.

1972, Mar. 1 **Litho.** ***Perf. 12x11***

279	A43	1d sepia & multi	2.00	.85
280	A43	2d emerald & multi	2.25	.85
281	A43	3d bister & multi	2.25	.85
282	A43	4d lt blue & multi	2.50	.85
283	A43	5d yellow & multi	2.50	.85
284	A43	35d vio bl & multi	8.00	1.00
285	A43	75d pink & multi	18.00	2.75
286	A43	3r blue & multi	47.50	11.00
		Nos. 279-286 (8)	85.00	19.00

Nos. 217-219 Surcharged

1972, Mar. 7 ***Perf. 13x13½***

287	A31	10d on 60d multi	4.00	.80
288	A31	1r on 1.25r multi	17.50	4.00
289	A31	5r on 2r multi	65.00	13.00
		Nos. 287-289 (3)	86.50	17.80

Sheik Khalifa bin Hamad al Thani
A44 A44a

1972 **Size: 23x27mm** ***Perf. 14***

290	A44	5d pur & ultra	.75	.30
291	A44	10d brn & rose red	.75	.60
291A	A44a	10d lt brn & lt red	225.00	
291B	A44a	25d vio & emer	225.00	
292	A44	35d org & dl grn	2.50	.75
293	A44	55d brt grn & lil	4.25	1.75
294	A44	75d vio & lil rose	5.50	2.00

Size: 26½x32mm

295	A44	1r bister & blk	9.50	2.50
296	A44	1.25r olive & blk	11.00	3.50
297	A44	5r blue & blk	40.00	10.00
298	A44	10r red & blk	70.00	24.00
		Nos. 290-298 (11)	594.25	
		Nos. 290-291,292-298 (9)	144.25	45.40

Issued: Type A44, Mar. 7.

Book Year Emblem A45

1972, Apr. 23 ***Perf. 13½x13***

299	A45	35d lt ultra & blk	2.50	.45
300	A45	55d lt brown & blk	3.75	.75
301	A45	75d green & blk	5.00	1.10
302	A45	1.25r violet & blk	8.25	1.75
		Nos. 299-302 (4)	19.50	4.05

International Book Year 1972.

Olympic Rings, Soccer A46

2d, 3r, Running. 3d, Bicycling. 4d, Gymnastics. 5d, Basketball. 35d, Discus. 75d, Like 1d.

1972, June 12 ***Perf. 13½x13***

303	A46	1d green & multi	.80	.40
304	A46	2d yel grn & multi	.80	.40
305	A46	3d blue & multi	.80	.40
306	A46	4d lilac & multi	.80	.40
307	A46	5d blue & multi	.90	.40
308	A46	35d gray & multi	2.25	.60
a.		Souvenir sheet of 6	37.50	25.00
309	A46	75d green & blk	4.00	1.00
310	A46	3r multicolored	15.00	4.00
		Nos. 303-310 (8)	25.35	7.60

20th Olympic Games, Munich, Aug. 26-Sept. 10. No. 308a contains stamps with simulated perforations similar to Nos. 303-308.

Installation of Underwater Pipe Line — A47

1d, Drilling for oil, vert. 5d, Drilling platform. 35d, Ship searching for oil.

1972, Aug. 8 **Litho.** ***Perf. 13x13½***

311	A47	1d multicolored	.65	.40
312	A47	4d shown	.65	.40
313	A47	5d multicolored	.65	.40
314	A47	35d multicolored	2.75	.55
315	A47	75d like 1d, vert.	5.75	1.25
316	A47	3r like 5d	27.50	6.00
		Nos. 311-316 (6)	37.95	9.00

Oil from the sea.

Government Palace — A48

Designs: 35d, Clasped hands, Qatar flag. 75d, Clasped hands, UN flag. 1.25r, Sheik Khalifa bin Hamad al-Thani, vert.

1972, Sept. 3 ***Perf. 13½x13, 13x13½***

317	A48	10d yel & multi	1.50	.50
318	A48	35d blk & multi	4.00	.65
319	A48	75d blk & multi	7.50	1.25
320	A48	1.25r gold & multi	14.00	2.00
a.		Souvenir sheet of 1	40.00	22.50
		Nos. 317-320 (4)	27.00	4.40

Independence Day, 1st anniv. of independence.

No. 320a contains one stamp with simulated perforations similar to No. 320.

Qatar Flag, Council Emblem and Flag A49

1972, Dec. 4 **Litho.** ***Perf. 14x13½***

321	A49	25d blue & multi	4.00	1.00
322	A49	30d vio bl & multi	6.00	1.50

Civil Aviation Council of Arab States, 10th session.

Tracking Station, Satellite, Telephone, ITU and UN Emblems A50

Designs (Agency and UN Emblems): 2d, Surveyor, artist; UNESCO. 3d, Tractor, helicopter, fish, grain and fruit; FAO. 4d, Reading children, teacher; UNICEF. 5d, Weather satellite and map; WMO. 25d, Workers and crane; ILO. 55d, Health clinic; WHO. 1r, Mail plane and post office; UPU.

1972, Oct. 24 *Perf. 13½x14*

No.	Type	Description	Unused	Used
323	A50	1d multicolored	.60	.35
324	A50	2d multicolored	.60	.35
325	A50	3d multicolored	.60	.35
326	A50	4d multicolored	.60	.35
327	A50	5d multicolored	.75	.50
328	A50	25d multicolored	5.75	1.00
329	A50	55d multicolored	10.00	3.00
330	A50	1r multicolored	20.00	6.00
		Nos. 323-330 (8)	38.90	11.90

United Nations Day, Oct. 24, 1972. Each stamp dedicated to a different UN agency.

Road Building — A51

3d, Housing development. 4d, Operating room. 5d, Telephone operators. 15d, School, classroom. 20d, Television studio. 35d, Sheik Khalifa. 55d, New Gulf Hotel. 1r, Fertilizer plant. 1.35r, Flour mill.

1973, Feb. 22 **Litho.** *Perf. 13x13½*

No.	Type	Description	Unused	Used
331	A51	2d multicolored	.80	.40
332	A51	3d multicolored	.80	.40
333	A51	4d multicolored	.80	.40
334	A51	5d multicolored	.80	.40
335	A51	15d multicolored	1.75	.40
336	A51	20d multicolored	2.00	.40
337	A51	35d multicolored	3.00	.50
338	A51	55d multicolored	3.75	.80
339	A51	1r multicolored	5.25	1.60
340	A51	1.35r multicolored	8.25	2.25
		Nos. 331-340 (10)	27.20	7.55

1st anniv. of the accession of Sheik Khalifa bin Hamad al Thani as Emir of Qatar.

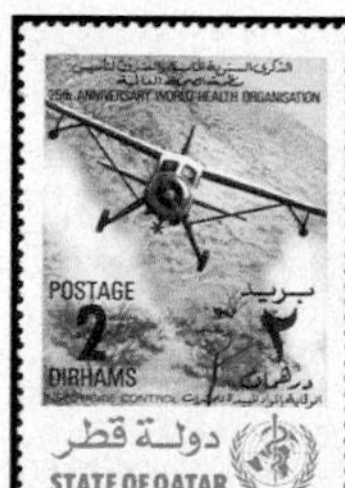

Aerial Pest Control — A52

WHO, 25th anniv.: 3d, Medicines. 4d, Poliomyelitis prevention. 5d, Malaria control. 55d, Mental health. 1r, Pollution control.

1973, May 14 **Litho.** *Perf. 14*

No.	Type	Description	Unused	Used
341	A52	2d blue & multi	.85	.50
342	A52	3d blue & multi	.85	.50
343	A52	4d blue & multi	.85	.50
344	A52	5d blue & multi	1.75	.65
345	A52	55d blue & multi	11.00	2.00
346	A52	1r blue & multi	25.00	3.75
		Nos. 341-346 (6)	40.30	7.90

Weather Ship A53

Designs (WMO Emblem and): 3d, Launching of radiosonde balloon. 4d, Plane and meteorological data checking. 5d, Cup anemometers and meteorological station. 10d, Weather plane in flight. 1r, Nimbus I weather satellite. 1.55r, Launching of rocket carrying weather satellite.

1973, July **Litho.** *Perf. 14x13*

No.	Type	Description	Unused	Used
347	A53	2d multicolored	.60	.40
348	A53	3d multicolored	.60	.40
349	A53	4d multicolored	.60	.40
350	A53	5d multicolored	.60	.40
351	A53	10d multicolored	2.00	.60
352	A53	1r multicolored	13.50	1.75
353	A53	1.55r multicolored	20.00	3.00
		Nos. 347-353 (7)	37.90	6.95

Cent. of intl. meteorological cooperation.

Sheik Khalifa — A54

Clock Tower, Doha — A55

1973-74 **Litho.** *Perf. 14*

Size: 18x27mm

No.	Type	Description	Unused	Used
354	A54	5d green & multi	1.25	.40
355	A54	10d lt bl & multi	1.75	.40
356	A54	20d ver & multi	2.25	.40
357	A54	25d org & multi	3.00	.40
358	A54	35d purple & multi	4.00	.75
359	A54	55d dk gray & multi	6.00	1.00

Engr.

Perf. 13½

No.	Type	Description	Unused	Used
360	A55	75d lil, bl & yel grn	8.50	2.00

Photo.

Perf. 13

Size: 27x32mm

No.	Type	Description	Unused	Used
360A	A54	1r multicolored	22.50	5.00
360B	A54	5r multicolored	75.00	24.00
360C	A54	10r multicolored	160.00	55.00
		Nos. 354-360C (10)	284.25	89.35

Issue dates: 20d, 75d, July 3, 1973; 1r-10r, July 1974; others, Jan. 27, 1973.

Flag of Qatar, Handclasp, Sheik Khalifa — A56

Flag, Sheik and: 35d, Harvest. 55d, Government Building. 1.35r, Market and Clock Tower, Doha. 1.55r, Illuminated fountain.

1973, Oct. 4 **Litho.** *Perf. 13*

No.	Type	Description	Unused	Used
361	A56	15d red & multi	.45	.30
362	A56	35d buff & multi	.80	.30
363	A56	55d multi	2.00	.50
364	A56	1.35r vio & multi	4.50	1.25
365	A56	1.55r multi	5.00	1.60
		Nos. 361-365 (5)	12.75	3.95

2nd anniversary of independence.

Planting Tree, Qatar and UN Flags, UNESCO Emblem — A57

Qatar and UN Flags and: 4d, UN Headquarters and flags. 5d, Pipe laying, cement mixer, helicopter and ILO emblem. 35d, Nurse, patient and UNICEF emblem. 1.35r, Telecommunications and ITU emblem. 3r, Cattle, wheat disease analysis and FAO emblem.

1973, Oct. 24

No.	Type	Description	Unused	Used
366	A57	2d multi	.50	.50
367	A57	4d multi	.50	.50
368	A57	5d multi	.60	.50
369	A57	35d multi	1.60	.50
370	A57	1.35r multi	6.50	1.75
371	A57	3r multi	15.00	5.50
		Nos. 366-371 (6)	24.70	9.25

United Nations Day.

Prison Gates Opening — A58

4d, Marchers with flags. 5d, Scales of Justice. 35d, Teacher and pupils. 1.35r, UN General Assembly. 3r, Human Rights flame, vert.

1973, Dec. **Litho.** *Perf. 13x13½*

No.	Type	Description	Unused	Used
372	A58	2d yellow & multi	.45	.40
373	A58	4d pale lil & multi	.45	.40
374	A58	5d rose & multi	.70	.40
375	A58	35d ocher & multi	2.00	.75
376	A58	1.35r lt bl & multi	7.00	3.00
377	A58	3r citron & multi	13.00	4.25
		Nos. 372-377 (6)	23.60	9.20

25th anniversary of the Universal Declaration of Human Rights.

Highway Overpass — A59

1974, Feb. 22 *Perf. 14x13½*

No.	Type	Description	Unused	Used
378	A59	2d shown	.70	.35
379	A59	3d Symbol of learning	.70	.35
380	A59	5d Oil field	.70	.35
381	A59	35d Gulf Hotel, Doha	2.25	.50
382	A59	1.55r Radar station	10.00	3.25
383	A59	2.25r Sheik Khalifa	13.00	4.00
		Nos. 378-383 (6)	27.35	8.80

Accession of Sheik Khalifa as Emir, 2nd, anniv.

Mail Truck, Camel Caravan and UPU Emblem — A60

UPU cent.: 3d, Old and new trains, Arab Postal Union emblem. 10d, Old and new ships and Qatar coat of arms. 35d, Old and new planes. 75d, Mail sorting by hand and computer, and Arab Postal Union emblem. 1.25r, Old and new post offices, and Qatar coat of arms.

1974, May 22 **Litho.** *Perf. 13½*

No.	Type	Description	Unused	Used
384	A60	2d brt yel & multi	.85	.45
385	A60	3d lt bl & multi	.85	.45
386	A60	10d dp org & multi	.85	.45
387	A60	35d slate & multi	3.25	.65
388	A60	75d yellow & multi	7.75	1.25
389	A60	1.25r lt bl & multi	11.00	2.25
		Nos. 384-389 (6)	24.55	5.50

Doha Hospital — A61

1974, July 13 **Litho.** *Perf. 13½*

No.	Type	Description	Unused	Used
390	A61	5d shown	.55	.40
391	A61	10d WPY emblem and people	.55	.40
392	A61	15d WPY emblem	.75	.40
393	A61	35d World map	1.75	.75
394	A61	1.75r Clock and infants	6.75	3.00
395	A61	2.25r Family	9.75	4.00
		Nos. 390-395 (6)	20.10	8.95

World Population Year 1974.

Television Station — A62

1974, Sept. 2 *Perf. 13½x13*

No.	Type	Description	Unused	Used
399	A62	5d shown	.45	.45
400	A62	10d Palace of Doha	.45	.45
401	A62	15d Teachers'College	.45	.45
402	A62	75d Clock Tower and Mosque	5.25	1.10
403	A62	1.55r Traffic circle, Doha	8.50	1.75
404	A62	2.25r Sheik Khalifa	13.50	2.75
		Nos. 399-404 (6)	28.60	6.95

3rd anniversary of independence.

Operating Room and WHO Emblem — A63

UN Day: 10d, Satellite earth station and ITU emblem. 20d, Tractor, UN and FAO emblems. 25d, School children, UN and UNESCO emblems. 1.75r, Open air court, UN Headquarters, emblems. 2r, UPU and UN emblems.

1974, Oct. 24 **Litho.** *Perf. 13x13½*

No.	Type	Description	Unused	Used
405	A63	5d multi	.60	.45
406	A63	10d multi	1.10	.45
407	A63	20d multi	2.25	.45
408	A63	25d multi	3.50	.55
409	A63	1.75r multi	13.50	2.00
410	A63	2r multi	16.00	2.75
		Nos. 405-410 (6)	36.95	6.65

VC-10, Gulf Aviation Airliner — A64

Arab League and Qatar Flags, Civil Aviation Emblem — A65

Design: 25d, Doha Airport.

1974, Dec. 1 **Litho.** *Perf. 13½*

No.	Type	Description	Unused	Used
411	A64	20d multi	3.00	.55
412	A64	25d yel & dk bl	4.50	.70
413	A65	30d multi	5.75	.85
414	A65	50d multi	8.50	1.00
		Nos. 411-414 (4)	21.75	3.10

Arab Civil Aviation Day.

Caspian Terns, Hoopoes and Shara'o Island — A66

Dhow by Moonlight — A67

5d, Clock Tower, Doha, vert. 15d, Zubara Fort. 35d, Gulf Hotel & sailboats. 75d, Arabian oryx. 1.25r, Khor Al-Udein. 1.75r, Ruins, Wakrah.

1974, Dec. 21 Litho. *Perf. 13½*

415	A66	5d multi	*1.25*	*.40*
416	A66	10d multi	*1.60*	*.40*
417	A66	15d multi	*2.00*	*.40*
418	A66	35d multi	*3.25*	*.40*
419	A67	55d multi	*3.75*	*.70*
420	A66	75d multi	*5.75*	*1.00*
421	A67	1.25r multi	*9.50*	*1.60*
422	A66	1.75r multi	*12.50*	*2.00*
		Nos. 415-422 (8)	*39.60*	*6.90*

Traffic Circle, Doha A68

Sheik Khalifa — A69

35d, Pipe line from offshore platform. 55d, Laying underwater pipe line. 1r, Refinery.

1975, Feb. 22 Litho. *Perf. 13½*

423	A68	10d multi	*.40*	*.40*
424	A68	35d multi	*2.10*	*.85*
425	A68	55d multi	*3.25*	*1.10*
426	A68	1r multi	*6.25*	*1.75*
427	A69	1.35r sil & multi	*7.25*	*2.50*
428	A69	1.55r gold & multi	*9.50*	*3.50*
		Nos. 423-428 (6)	*28.75*	*10.10*

Accession of Sheik Khalifa, 3rd anniv.

Qatar Flag and Arab Labor Charter Emblem — A70

1975, May 28 Litho. *Perf. 13*

429	A70	10d bl, red brn & blk	*.55*	*.55*
430	A70	35d multicolored	*4.25*	*1.00*
431	A70	1r green & multi	*11.00*	*2.75*
		Nos. 429-431 (3)	*15.80*	*4.30*

Arab Labor Charter and Constitution, 10th anniversary.

Flintlock Pistol with Ornamental Grip — A71

Designs: 3d, Ornamental mosaic. 35d, View of museum. 75d, Arch and museum, vert. 1.25r, Flint arrowheads and tool. 3r, Gold necklace, vert.

1975, June 23 *Perf. 13*

432	A71	2d multi	*.50*	*.40*
433	A71	3d ver blk & gold	*1.00*	*.40*
434	A71	35d bis & multi	*2.50*	*.50*
435	A71	75d ver & multi	*5.75*	*1.00*
436	A71	1.25r vio & multi	*9.00*	*1.75*
437	A71	3r fawn & multi	*20.00*	*3.25*
		Nos. 432-437 (6)	*38.75*	*7.30*

Opening of Qatar National Museum.

Traffic Signs, Policeman, Doha — A72

Designs: 15d, 55d, Cars, arrows, traffic lights, Doha Clock Tower. 35d, like 5d.

1975, June 24

438	A72	5d lt green & multi	*.50*	*.50*
439	A72	15d lt blue & multi	*3.25*	*.50*
440	A72	35d lemon & multi	*7.75*	*1.10*
441	A72	55d lt violet & multi	*13.00*	*1.90*
		Nos. 438-441 (4)	*24.50*	*4.00*

Traffic Week.

Constitution, Arabic Text — A73

5d, Government buildings, horiz. 15d, Museum & Clock Tower, horiz. 55d, 1.25r, Sheik Khalifa & Qatar flag. 75d, Constitution, English text.

1975, Sept. 2

442	A73	5d multi	*.40*	*.40*
443	A73	15d multi	*2.10*	*.95*
444	A73	35d multi	*2.50*	*.65*
445	A73	55d multi	*4.25*	*.95*
446	A73	75d multi	*5.75*	*1.25*
447	A73	1.25r multi	*9.00*	*2.10*
		Nos. 442-447 (6)	*24.00*	*6.30*

4th anniversary of independence.

Satellite over Globe, ITU Emblem — A74

UN, 30th anniv.: 15d, UN Headquarters, NY and UN emblem. 35d, UPU emblem over Eastern Arabia, UN emblem. 1r, Nurses and infant, WHO emblem. 1.25r, Road building equipment, ILO emblem. 2r, Students, UNESCO emblem.

1975, Oct. 25 Litho. *Perf. 13x13½*

448	A74	5d multi	*.55*	*.55*
449	A74	15d multi	*1.40*	*.55*
450	A74	35d multi	*2.10*	*.50*
451	A74	1r multi	*6.25*	*1.40*

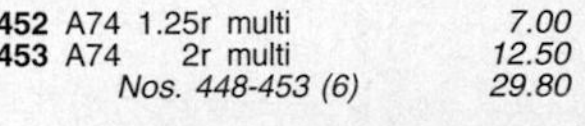

452	A74	1.25r multi	*7.00*	*1.60*
453	A74	2r multi	*12.50*	*2.75*
		Nos. 448-453 (6)	*29.80*	*7.35*

Fertilizer Plant — A75

Designs: 10d, Flour mill, vert. 35d, Natural gas plant. 75d, Oil refinery. 1.25r, Cement works. 1.55r, Steel mill.

1975, Dec. 6

454	A75	5d salmon & multi	*.50*	*.50*
455	A75	10d yellow & multi	*1.25*	*.50*
456	A75	35d multi	*2.50*	*.60*
457	A75	75d multi	*5.00*	*1.50*
458	A75	1.25r mag & multi	*10.00*	*2.50*
459	A75	1.55r multi	*15.00*	*3.50*
		Nos. 454-459 (6)	*34.25*	*9.10*

Modern Building, Doha — A76

10d, 35d, 1.55r, Various modern buildings. 55d, 75d, Sheik Khalifa & Qatar flag, diff.

1976, Feb. 22 Litho. *Perf. 13*

460	A76	5d multi	*.55*	*.55*
461	A76	10d multi	*.55*	*.55*
462	A76	35d multi	*2.25*	*.55*
463	A76	55d multi	*4.25*	*.85*
464	A76	75d multi	*5.50*	*1.25*
465	A76	1.55r multi	*11.00*	*2.50*
		Nos. 460-465 (6)	*24.10*	*6.25*

Accession of Sheik Khalifa, 4th anniv.

Satellite Earth Station — A77

Designs: 55d, 1r, Satellite. 75d, Like 35d.

1976, Mar. 1

466	A77	35d multicolored	*2.50*	*.40*
467	A77	55d dp bis & multi	*3.25*	*.50*
468	A77	75d vermilion & multi	*4.75*	*.70*
469	A77	1r violet & multi	*7.25*	*.95*
		Nos. 466-469 (4)	*17.75*	*2.55*

Inauguration of satellite earth station in Qatar.

Telephones, 1876 and 1976 — A78

1976, Mar. 10

470	A78	1r rose & multi	*4.75*	*2.00*
471	A78	1.35r lt bl & multi	*6.50*	*2.75*

Centenary of first telephone call by Alexander Graham Bell, Mar. 10, 1876.

Arabian Soccer League Emblem — A79

Designs: 10d, 1.25r, Stadium, Doha. 35d, Like 5d. 55d, Players. 75d, One player.

1976, Mar. 25 Litho. *Perf. 13½x13*

472	A79	5d lil & multi	*.45*	*.45*
473	A79	10d pink & multi	*1.25*	*.45*
474	A79	35d bl grn & multi	*2.00*	*.60*
475	A79	55d multi	*4.00*	*.95*
476	A79	75d multi	*6.75*	*1.40*
477	A79	1.25r multi	*8.75*	*2.40*
		Nos. 472-477 (6)	*23.20*	*6.25*

4th Arabian Gulf Soccer Cup Tournament, Doha, Mar. 22-Apr.

Dhow A80

Designs: Various dhows.

1976, Apr. 19 *Perf. 13½x14*

478	A80	10d blue & multi	*2.50*	*.35*
479	A80	35d blue & multi	*3.00*	*.40*
480	A80	80d blue & multi	*9.00*	*1.25*
481	A80	1.25r blue & multi	*13.00*	*2.00*
482	A80	1.50r blue & multi	*15.00*	*2.50*
483	A80	2r blue & multi	*22.50*	*4.00*
		Nos. 478-483 (6)	*65.00*	*10.50*

Soccer — A81

10d, Yachting. 35d, Steeplechase. 80d, Boxing. 1.25r, Weight lifting. 1.50r, Basketball.

1976, May 15 Litho. *Perf. 14x13½*

484	A81	5d multicolored	*.85*	*.40*
485	A81	10d blue & multi	*.85*	*.40*
486	A81	35d orange & multi	*.85*	*.40*
487	A81	80d bister & multi	*5.50*	*.85*
488	A81	1.25r lilac & multi	*9.50*	*1.60*
489	A81	1.50r rose & multi	*12.50*	*2.10*
		Nos. 484-489 (6)	*30.05*	*5.75*

21st Olympic Games, Montreal, Canada, July 17-Aug. 1.

Village and Emblems — A82

35d, Emblems. 80d, Village. 1.25r, Sheik Khalifa.

1976, May 31 *Perf. 13½x14*

490	A82	10d orange & multi	*.65*	*.30*
491	A82	35d yellow & multi	*1.75*	*.30*
492	A82	80d citron & multi	*4.25*	*.70*
493	A82	1.25r dp blue & multi	*7.25*	*2.00*
		Nos. 490-493 (4)	*13.90*	*3.30*

Habitat, UN Conf. on Human Settlements, Vancouver, Canada, May 31-June 11.

Snowy Plover A83

Birds: 10d, Great cormorant. 35d, Osprey. 80d, Flamingo. 1.25r, Rock thrush. 2r, Saker falcon. 35d, 80d, 1.25r, 2r, vertical.

Perf. 13½x14, 14x13½

1976, July 19 Litho.

494	A83	5d multi	*1.25*	*.40*
495	A83	10d multi	*3.00*	*.55*
496	A83	35d multi	*8.25*	*.90*
497	A83	80d multi	*17.50*	*2.00*
498	A83	1.25r multi	*27.50*	*3.00*
499	A83	2r multi	*30.00*	*4.00*
		Nos. 494-499 (6)	*87.50*	*10.85*

Sheik Khalifa and Qatar Flag — A84

Government Building — A85

Designs: 10d, like 5d. 80d, Government building. 1.25r, Offshore oil platform. 1.50r, UN emblem and Qatar coat of arms.

1976, Sept. 2 ***Perf. 14x13½, 13½x14***

500	A84	5d gold & multi	*.50*	*.50*
501	A84	10d silver & multi	*.50*	*.50*
502	A85	40d multicolored	*1.90*	*.60*
503	A85	80d multicolored	*3.50*	*1.25*
504	A85	1.25r multicolored	*5.50*	*1.50*
505	A85	1.50r multicolored	*7.50*	*1.75*
		Nos. 500-505 (6)	*19.40*	*6.10*

5th anniversary of independence.

Qatar Flag and UN Emblem — A86

1976, Oct. 24 Litho. ***Perf. 13½x14***

506	A86	2r multi	*7.00*	*1.75*
507	A86	3r multi	*9.50*	*2.50*

United Nations Day 1976.

Sheik Khalifa — A87

1977, Feb. 22 Litho. ***Perf. 14x13½***

508	A87	20d silver & multi	*1.50*	*.50*
509	A87	1.80r gold & multi	*11.00*	*2.50*

Accession of Sheik Khalifa, 5th anniv.

Sheik Khalifa — A88

1977, Mar. 1 Litho. ***Perf. 14x14½***

Size: 22x27mm

510	A88	5d multicolored	*.50*	*.30*
511	A88	10d aqua & multi	*.75*	*.30*
512	A88	35d orange & multi	*1.25*	*.35*
513	A88	80d multicolored	*2.50*	*.50*

Perf. 13½

Size: 25x30mm

514	A88	1r vio bl & multi	*5.00*	*.75*
515	A88	5r yellow & multi	*16.00*	*3.25*
516	A88	10r multicolored	*37.50*	*6.75*
		Nos. 510-516 (7)	*63.50*	*12.20*

Letter, APU Emblem, Flag — A89

1977, Apr. 12 ***Perf. 14x13½***

517	A89	35d blue & multi	*1.75*	*.50*
518	A89	1.35r blue & multi	*5.25*	*2.00*

Arab Postal Union, 25th anniversary.

Waves and Sheik Khalifa A90

1977, May 17 Litho. ***Perf. 13½x14***

519	A90	35d multi	*1.00*	*.45*
520	A90	1.80r multi	*6.25*	*2.50*

World Telecommunications Day.

Sheik Khalifa — A90a

Perf. 13½x13

1977, June 29 Litho. Wmk. 368

520A	A90a	5d multi	*1.00*	*1.00*
520B	A90a	10d multi	*2.00*	*2.00*
520C	A90a	35d multi	*3.00*	*3.00*
520D	A90a	80d multi	*10.00*	*10.00*
e.		Bklt. pane, 4 5d, 3 10d, 2 35d, 80d	*50.00*	*25.00*
		Nos. 520A-520D (4)	*16.00*	*16.00*

Issued in booklets only.

Parliament, Clock Tower, Minaret — A91

Designs: No. 522, Main business district, Doha. No. 523, Highway crossings, Doha.

1977, Sept. 1 Litho. ***Perf. 13x13½***

521	A91	80d multicolored	*4.25*	*1.50*
522	A91	80d multicolored	*4.25*	*1.50*
523	A91	80d multicolored	*4.25*	*1.50*
		Nos. 521-523 (3)	*12.75*	*4.50*

6th anniversary of independence.

UN Emblem, Flag — A92

1977, Oct. 24 Litho. ***Perf. 13½x14***

524	A92	20d green & multi	*1.50*	*.55*
525	A92	1r blue & multi	*6.00*	*2.25*

United Nations Day.

Surgery — A93

20d, Steel mill. 1r, Classroom. 5r, Sheik Khalifa.

1978, Feb. 22 Litho. ***Perf. 13½x14***

526	A93	20d multicolored	*1.40*	*.40*
527	A93	80d multicolored	*3.00*	*.65*
528	A93	1r multicolored	*5.00*	*1.00*
529	A93	5r multicolored	*16.00*	*3.00*
		Nos. 526-529 (4)	*25.40*	*5.05*

Accession of Sheik Khalifa, 6th anniv.

Oil Refinery — A94

80d, Office buildings, Doha. 1.35r, Traffic Circle, Doha. 1.80r, Sheik Khalifa and flag.

1978, Aug. 31 Litho. ***Perf. 13½x14***

530	A94	35d multi	*1.00*	*.40*
531	A94	80d multi	*2.50*	*.95*
532	A94	1.35r multi	*4.00*	*1.40*
533	A94	1.80r multi	*5.25*	*1.90*
		Nos. 530-533 (4)	*12.75*	*4.65*

7th anniversary of independence.

Man Learning to Read — A95

1978, Sept. 8 Litho. ***Perf. 13½x14***

534	A95	35d multicolored	*1.75*	*.50*
535	A95	80d multicolored	*5.00*	*1.60*

International Literacy Day.

Flag and UN Emblem — A96

1978, Oct. 14 ***Perf. 13x13½***

536	A96	35d multi	*1.50*	*.50*
537	A96	80d multi	*4.50*	*1.25*

United Nations Day.

Human Rights Emblem — A97

Designs: 80d, like 35d. 1.25r, 1.80r, Scales and Human Rights emblem.

1978, Dec. 10 Litho. ***Perf. 14x13½***

538	A97	35d multi	*1.00*	*.35*
539	A97	80d multi	*2.50*	*1.00*
540	A97	1.25r multi	*3.75*	*1.50*
541	A97	1.80r multi	*5.25*	*2.25*
		Nos. 538-541 (4)	*12.50*	*5.10*

30th anniversary of Universal Declaration of Human Rights.

IYC Emblem — A98

Wmk. JEZ Multiple (368)

1979, Jan. 1 Litho. ***Perf. 13½x13***

542	A98	35d multi	*1.25*	*1.00*
543	A98	1.80r multi	*4.25*	*4.00*

International Year of the Child.

A99

1979, Jan. 15 Unwmk. ***Perf. 14***

544	A99	5d multi	*.30*	*.30*
545	A99	10d multi	*.35*	*.30*
546	A99	20d multi	*.65*	*.30*
547	A99	25d multi	*1.00*	*.30*
548	A99	35d multi	*1.50*	*.55*
549	A99	60d multi	*1.90*	*.65*
550	A99	80d multi	*2.50*	*.70*

Size: 27x32mm

551	A99	1r multi	*2.75*	*1.00*
552	A99	1.25r multi	*3.00*	*1.10*
553	A99	1.35r multi	*3.25*	*1.50*
554	A99	1.80r multi	*5.00*	*1.75*
555	A99	5r multi	*12.00*	*3.25*
556	A99	10r multi	*22.50*	*7.00*
		Nos. 544-556 (13)	*56.70*	*18.70*

Sheik Khalifa — A100

1979, Feb. 22 **Wmk. 368**

557	A100	35d multi	*.80*	*.50*
558	A100	80d multi	*1.75*	*1.10*
559	A100	1r multi	*2.75*	*1.50*
560	A100	1.25r multi	*3.25*	*1.90*
		Nos. 557-560 (4)	*8.55*	*5.00*

7th anniv. of accession of Sheik Khalifa.

Cables and People — A101

1979, May 17 Litho. ***Perf. 14x13½***

561 A101 2r multi *4.75 2.00*
562 A101 2.80r multi *5.75 3.00*

World Telecommunications Day.

Children Holding Globe, UNESCO Emblem — A102

Perf. 13x13½

1979, July 15 Litho. Unwmk.

563 A102 35d multicolored *1.00 .45*
564 A102 80d multicolored *4.25 1.10*

International Bureau of Education, Geneva, 50th anniversary.

Rolling Mill — A103

Wmk. 368

1979, Sept. 2 Litho. ***Perf. 13½***

565 A103 5d shown *.75 .40*
566 A103 10d Doha, aerial view *1.10 .40*
567 A103 1.25r Qatar flag *4.50 1.25*
568 A103 2r Sheik Khalifa *6.25 1.75*
Nos. 565-568 (4) 12.60 3.80

Independence, 8th anniversary.

UN Day — A104

1979, Oct. 24 Litho. ***Perf. 13½x13***

569 A104 1.25r multi *4.25 1.25*
570 A104 2r multi *7.50 1.75*

Conference Emblem — A105

1979, Nov. 24 ***Perf. 13x13½***

571 A105 35d multi *3.25 1.00*
572 A105 1.80r multi *10.00 2.25*

Hegira (Pilgrimage Year); 3rd World Conference on Prophets.

Sheik Khalifa, 8th Anniversary of Accession — A106

1980, Feb. 22 Litho. ***Perf. 13x13½***

573 A106 20d multi *1.25 .30*
574 A106 60d multi *3.25 .65*
575 A106 1.25r multi *5.00 1.25*
576 A106 2r multi *11.00 2.10*
Nos. 573-576 (4) 20.50 4.30

Map of Arab Countries — A107

1980, Mar. 1 Litho. ***Perf. 13½x14***

577 A107 2.35r multi *8.25 1.75*
578 A107 2.80r multi *12.00 2.10*

6th Congress of Arab Town Organization, Doha, Mar. 1-4.

Oil Refinery — A108

1980, Sept. 2 Litho. ***Perf. 14½***

579 A108 10d shown *.75 .40*
580 A108 35d View of Doha *3.00 .50*
581 A108 2r Oil rig *11.00 2.50*
582 A108 2.35r Hospital *13.00 3.75*
Nos. 579-582 (4) 27.75 7.15

9th anniversary of independence.

Men Holding OPEC Emblem — A109

1980, Sept. 15 ***Perf. 14x13½***

583 A109 1.35r multi *4.75 1.40*
584 A109 2r multi *7.00 2.10*

OPEC, 20th anniversary.

United Nations Day 1980 — A110

1980, Oct. 24

585 A110 1.35r multi *3.25 1.25*
586 A110 1.80r multi *4.75 1.60*

Hegira (Pilgrimage Year) — A111

1980, Nov. 8 Litho. ***Perf. 14½***

587 A111 10d multi *.50 .50*
588 A111 35d multi *1.00 .65*
589 A111 1.25r multi *2.25 1.50*
590 A111 2.80r multi *5.50 3.75*
Nos. 587-590 (4) 9.25 6.40

International Year of the Disabled — A112

1981, Jan. 5 Photo. ***Perf. 11½***
Granite Paper

591 A112 2r multi *4.75 2.75*
592 A112 3r multi *7.25 3.25*

Education Day — A113

Perf. 14x13½

1981, Feb. 22 Litho. Wmk. 368

593 A113 2r multi *5.50 2.00*
594 A113 3r multi *6.75 2.75*

Sheik Khalifa, 9th Anniversary of Accession A114

1981, Feb. 22

595 A114 10d multi *.50 .40*
596 A114 35d multi *1.50 .40*
597 A114 80d multi *3.00 .70*
598 A114 5r multi *15.00 3.75*
Nos. 595-598 (4) 20.00 5.25

A115

1981, May 17 Litho. ***Perf. 13½x13***

599 A115 2r multi *5.00 1.25*
600 A115 2.80r multi *7.25 2.40*

13th World Telecommunications Day.

A116

Championship emblem.

1981, June 11 Litho. ***Perf. 14x13½***

601 A116 1.25r multi *6.00 1.60*
602 A116 2.80r multi *10.00 3.00*

30th Intl. Military Soccer Championship, Doha.

10th Anniv. of Independence — A117

Perf. 13½x14

1981, Sept. 2 Litho. Wmk. 368

603 A117 5d multicolored *.75 .40*
604 A117 60d multicolored *2.25 .60*
605 A117 80d multicolored *3.00 .75*
606 A117 5r multicolored *17.50 5.25*
Nos. 603-606 (4) 23.50 7.00

World Food Day A118

1981, Oct. 16 Litho. ***Perf. 13***

607 A118 2r multi *6.50 3.25*
608 A118 2.80r multi *8.50 4.00*

Red Crescent Society — A119

1982, Jan. 16 Litho. ***Perf. 14x13½***

609 A119 20d multi *1.25 .30*
610 A119 2.80r multi *7.75 3.25*

10th Anniv. of Sheik Khalifa's Accession — A120

Perf. 13½x14

1982, Feb. 22 Litho. Wmk. 368

611 A120 10d multi *1.00 .45*
612 A120 20d multi *2.00 .45*
613 A120 1.25r multi *7.00 1.40*
614 A120 2.80r multi *15.00 3.00*
Nos. 611-614 (4) 25.00 5.30

Sheik Khalifa — A121

Oil Refinery — A122

Designs: 5r, 10r, 15r, Hoda Clock Tower.

1982, Mar. 1 Photo. *Perf. 11½x12*
Granite Paper

615	A121	5d multi	.30	.30
616	A121	10d multi	.35	.30
617	A121	15d multi	.40	.30
618	A121	20d multi	.45	.30
619	A121	25d multi	.60	.30
620	A121	35d multi	.85	.30
621	A121	60d multi	1.25	.35
622	A121	80d multi	2.00	.50
623	A122	1r multi	2.25	.65
624	A122	1.25r multi	3.00	1.00
625	A122	2r multi	4.75	1.90
626	A122	5r multi	12.50	4.50
627	A122	10r multi	22.50	9.25
628	A122	15r multi	32.50	13.50
		Nos. 615-628 (14)	*83.70*	*33.45*

Hamad General Hospital — A123

1982, Mar. Litho. *Perf. 13x13½*

629	A123	10d multi	.75	.35
630	A123	2.35r multi	6.75	3.00

6th Anniv. of United Arab Shipping Co. — A124

1982, Mar. 6 Litho. *Perf. 13x13½*

631	A124	20d multi	1.25	.35
632	A124	2.35r multi	11.00	3.00

A125

1982, Apr. 12 Litho. *Perf. 13½x13*

633	A125	35d yellow & multi	1.50	.35
634	A125	2.80r blue & multi	10.50	2.25

30th anniv. of Arab Postal Union.

A126

1982, Sept. 2 Litho. *Perf. 13½x13*

635	A126	10d multi	1.00	.30
636	A126	80d multi	2.25	.60
637	A126	1.25r multi	4.00	1.50
638	A126	2.80r multi	7.75	2.25
		Nos. 635-638 (4)	*15.00*	*4.65*

11th anniv. of Independence.

World Communications Year — A127

1983, Jan. 10 Litho. *Perf. 13½x13*

639	A127	35d multi	1.75	.50
640	A127	2.80r multi	8.75	2.50

Gulf Postal Org., 2nd Conference, Doha, Apr. — A128

1983, Apr. 9 Litho. *Perf. 13½x14*

641	A128	1r multi	4.00	1.25
642	A128	1.35r multi	5.75	2.00

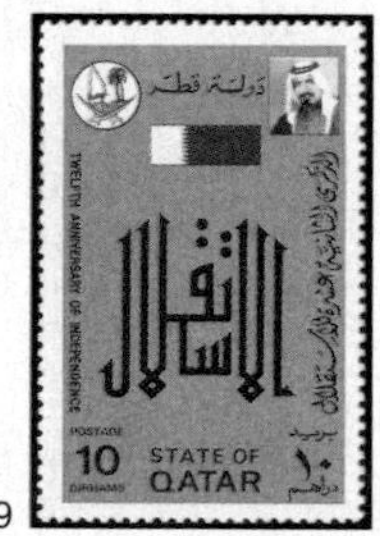

A129

1983, Sept. 2 Litho. *Perf. 14*

643	A129	10d multi	.45	.45
644	A129	35d multi	.90	.45
645	A129	80d multi	2.00	.75
646	A129	2.80r multi	6.75	2.50
		Nos. 643-646 (4)	*10.10*	*4.15*

12th anniv. of Independence.

A130

1983, Nov. 7 Litho. *Perf. 13½x14*

647	A130	35d multi	3.00	.50
648	A130	2.80r multi	10.00	3.00

GCC Supreme Council, 4th regular session.

35th Anniv. of UN Declaration of Human Rights — A131

1983, Dec. 10 Litho. *Perf. 13½x14*

649	A131	1.25r Globe, emblem	4.00	1.50
650	A131	2.80r Scale	7.75	2.50

A132

A133

1984, Mar. 1 Litho. *Perf. 13x13½*

651	A132	15d multi	.50	.25
652	A132	40d multi	1.25	.45
653	A132	50d multi	1.25	.55

Perf. 14½x13½

654	A133	1r multi	3.00	1.50
655	A133	1.50r multi	3.50	1.75
656	A133	2.50r multi	6.00	2.75
657	A133	3r multi	8.00	3.00
658	A133	5r multi	14.00	5.75
659	A133	10r multi	24.00	11.00
		Nos. 651-659 (9)	*61.50*	*27.00*

See Nos. 707-709, 792-801.

13th Anniv. of Independence — A134

1984, Sept. 2 Photo. *Perf. 12*

660	A134	15d multi	1.00	.45
661	A134	1r multi	3.00	1.00
662	A134	2.50r multi	6.00	2.25
663	A134	3.50r multi	8.75	3.25
		Nos. 660-663 (4)	*18.75*	*6.95*

Literacy Day, 1984 — A135

1984, Sept. 8 Litho. *Perf. 14x13½*

664	A135	1r lilac & multi	5.25	1.10
665	A135	1r orange & multi	5.25	1.10

40th Anniv., ICAO — A136

1984, Dec. 7 Litho. *Perf. 13½x13*

666	A136	20d multi	.50	.40
667	A136	3.50r multi	8.50	3.00

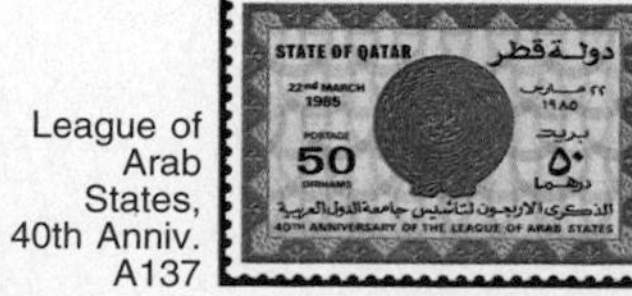

League of Arab States, 40th Anniv. A137

1985, Mar. 22 Photo. *Perf. 11½*

668	A137	50d multi	1.50	.40
669	A137	4r multi	7.75	3.00

Intl. Youth Year — A138

1985, Mar. 4 *Perf. 11½x12*
Granite Paper

670	A138	50d multi	2.25	.65
671	A138	1r multi	4.75	1.25

Traffic Crossing — A139

1985, Mar. 9 *Perf. 14x13½*

672	A139	1r lt bl & multi	4.00	1.25
673	A139	1r pink & multi	4.00	1.25

Gulf Cooperation Council Traffic Safety Week, Mar. 16-22.

Natl. Independence, 14th Anniv. — A140

1985, Sept. 2 *Perf. 11½x12*
Granite Paper

674	A140	40d Doha	1.25	.35
675	A140	50d Earth satellite station	2.00	.55
676	A140	1.50r Oil refinery	5.50	1.25
677	A140	4r Storage facility	12.50	4.00
		Nos. 674-677 (4)	*21.25*	*6.15*

Org. of Petroleum Exporting Countries, 25th Anniv. — A141

1985, Sept. 14 *Perf. 13½x14*

678	A141	1r brt yel grn & multi	5.00	1.25
679	A141	1r salmon rose & multi	5.00	1.25

UN, 40th Anniv. A142

1985, Oct. 24 Litho. *Perf. 13½x14*

680	A142	1r multi	1.75	1.25
681	A142	3r multi	5.00	3.50

Population and Housing Census — A143

1986, Mar. 1 Photo. *Perf. 11½x12*

682 A143 1r multi *3.25 1.25*
683 A143 3r multi *7.25 4.00*

United Arab Shipping Co., 10th Anniv. — A144

1986, May 30 Litho. *Perf. 13½x14*

684 A144 1.50r Qatari ibn al Fuja'a *3.00 2.75*
685 A144 4r Al Wajba *9.25 6.00*

Natl. Independence, 15th Anniv. — A145

Perf. 13x13½

1986, Sept. 2 Litho. Unwmk.

686 A145 40d multi *.75 .55*
687 A145 50d multi *1.10 .65*
688 A145 1r multi *2.25 1.25*
689 A145 4r multi *7.00 4.75*
Nos. 686-689 (4) *11.10 7.20*

Sheik Khalifa — A146

1987, Jan. 1 Photo. *Perf. 11½x12*
Granite Paper

690 A146 15r multi *19.00 12.00*
691 A146 20r multi *24.00 16.00*
692 A146 30r multi *42.50 25.00*
Nos. 690-692 (3) *85.50 53.00*

15th Anniv. of Sheik Khalifa's Accession A147

1987, Feb. 22 *Perf. 12x11½*
Granite Paper

693 A147 50d multi *.95 .50*
694 A147 1r multi *2.00 1.00*
695 A147 1.50r multi *2.75 1.40*
696 A147 4r multi *6.50 4.50*
Nos. 693-696 (4) *12.20 7.40*

Arab Postal Union, 35th Anniv. — A148

Perf. 14x13½

1987, Apr. 12 Litho. Unwmk.

697 A148 1r multi *3.00 1.25*
698 A148 1.50r multi *3.50 2.00*

Natl. Independence, 16th Anniv. — A149

1987, Sept. 2 Litho. *Perf. 13x13½*

699 A149 25d Housing complex *1.00 .35*
700 A149 75d Water tower, city *3.25 .90*
701 A149 2r Modern office building *5.00 2.25*
702 A149 4r Oil refinery *11.00 4.75*
Nos. 699-702 (4) *20.25 8.25*

A150

Perf. 13½x13

1987, Sept. 8 Litho. Unwmk.

703 A150 1.50r multicolored *2.75 1.25*
704 A150 4r multicolored *4.75 2.00*

Intl. Literacy Day.

A151

Perf. 14x13½

1987, Apr. 24 Litho. Wmk. 368

705 A151 1r multicolored *2.25 1.25*
706 A151 4r multicolored *5.75 4.00*

Gulf Environment Day.

Sheik Type of 1984

1988, Jan. 1 *Perf. 13x13½*
Size of 25d, 75d: 22x27mm

707 A133 25d multicolored *2.00 .75*
708 A133 75d multicolored *4.50 2.00*

Perf. 14½x13

709 A133 2r multicolored *15.00 4.75*

This is an expanding set. Numbers will change if necessary.

WHO, 40th Anniv. — A152

1988, Apr. 7 *Perf. 14x13½*

714 A152 1.50r multicolored *3.25 2.25*
715 A152 2r multicolored *7.00 3.50*

Independence, 17th Anniv. — A153

Perf. 11½x12

1988, Sept. 2 Litho. Unwmk.
Granite Paper

716 A153 50d multicolored *1.00 .55*
717 A153 75d multicolored *1.75 .80*
718 A153 1.50r multicolored *3.00 2.00*
719 A153 2r multicolored *3.75 2.40*
Nos. 716-719 (4) *9.50 5.75*

Opening of the Doha General P.O. — A154

1988, Sept. 3 *Perf. 13x13½*

720 A154 1.50r multicolored *2.25 2.00*
721 A154 4r multicolored *5.00 4.75*

Arab Housing Day — A155

1988, Oct. 3 *Perf. 11½x12*
Granite Paper

722 A155 1.50r multicolored *3.00 1.75*
723 A155 4r multicolored *7.75 3.75*

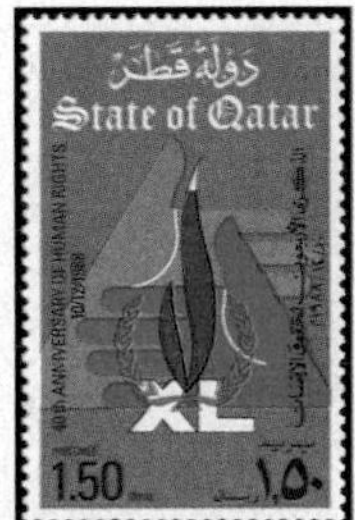

A156

Perf. 14x13½

1988, Dec. 10 Wmk. 368

724 A156 1.50r multicolored *3.25 2.50*
725 A156 2r multicolored *4.25 3.75*

Declaration of Human Rights, 40th anniv.

A157

Perf. 12x11½

1989, May 17 Unwmk.
Granite Paper

726 A157 2r multicolored *3.00 2.25*
727 A157 4r multicolored *6.00 4.00*

World Telecommunications Day.

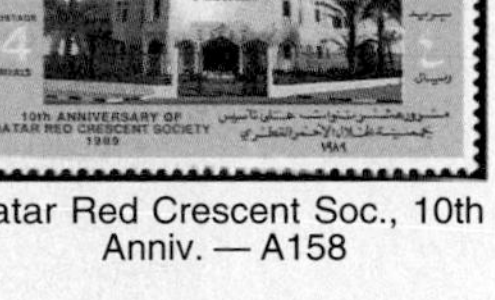

Qatar Red Crescent Soc., 10th Anniv. — A158

Perf. 13½x14

1989, Aug. 8 Wmk. 368

728 A158 4r multicolored *11.00 4.75*

Natl. Independence, 18th Anniv. — A159

Perf. 13x13½

1989, Sept. 2 Unwmk.

729 A159 75d multicolored *1.25 .85*
730 A159 1r multicolored *2.25 1.50*
731 A159 1.50r multicolored *2.75 2.00*
732 A159 2r multicolored *4.00 2.40*
Nos. 729-732 (4) *10.25 6.75*

Gulf Air, 40th Anniv. A160

1990, Mar. 24 Litho. *Perf. 13x13½*

733 A160 50d multicolored *1.25 .50*
734 A160 75d multicolored *2.00 1.00*
735 A160 4r multicolored *8.50 4.00*
Nos. 733-735 (3) *11.75 5.50*

Independence, 19th Anniv. — A161

Designs: 75d, Map, sunburst. 1.50r, 2r, Swordsman, musicians.

1990, Sept. 2 *Perf. 14x13½*

736 A161 50d multicolored *1.25 .50*
737 A161 75d multicolored *1.75 .90*
738 A161 1.50r multicolored *3.50 1.60*
739 A161 2r multicolored *5.50 2.75*
Nos. 736-739 (4) *12.00 5.75*

Organization of Petroleum Exporting Countries (OPEC), 30th Anniv. A162

1990, Sept. 14

740 A162 50d shown *2.00 .55*
741 A162 1.50r Flags *5.00 1.60*

A163

GCC Supreme Council, 11th Regular Session: 1r, Leaders of member nations. 1.50r, Flag, council emblem. 2r, State seal, emblem.

Perf. 14x13½

1990, Dec. 22 Litho. Wmk. 368

742	A163	50d multicolored	*1.50*	*.50*
743	A163	1r multicolored	*2.50*	*1.10*
744	A163	1.50r multicolored	*4.00*	*1.75*
745	A163	2r multicolored	*4.75*	*2.10*
		Nos. 742-745 (4)	*12.75*	*5.45*

A164

Plants — 10d, Glossonema edule. 25d, Lycium shawii. 50d, Acacia tortilis. 75d, Acacia ehrenbergiana. 1r, Capparis spinosa. 4r, Cymhopogon parkeri.

Perf. 12½x13½

1991, June 20 Litho. Wmk. 368

747	A164	10d multi	*1.00*	*.35*
748	A164	25d multi	*1.10*	*.40*
749	A164	50d multi	*1.25*	*1.00*
750	A164	75d multi	*2.25*	*1.25*
751	A164	1r multi	*3.25*	*2.50*
752	A164	4r multi	*13.00*	*8.50*
		Nos. 747-752 (6)	*21.85*	*14.00*

Independence, 20th Anniv. — A165

1991, Aug. 15 Litho. *Perf. 14x14½*

Granite Paper

762	A165	25d shown	*.85*	*.30*
763	A165	75d red vio & multi	*1.75*	*.65*

Perf. 14½x14

764	A165	1r Doha skyline, horiz.	*2.50*	*1.00*
765	A165	1.50r Palace, horiz.	*3.75*	*1.75*
		Nos. 762-765 (4)	*8.85*	*3.70*

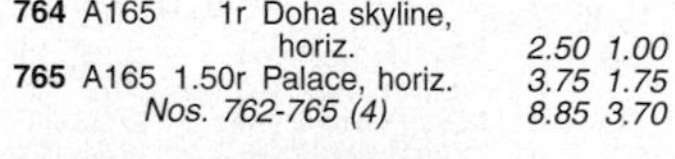

Fish A166

Various species of fish.

1991, Dec. 1 *Perf. 14x13½*

767	A166	10d multicolored	*1.00*	*.50*
768	A166	15d multicolored	*1.25*	*.55*
769	A166	25d multicolored	*2.00*	*.90*
770	A166	50d multicolored	*4.50*	*1.75*
771	A166	75d multicolored	*6.50*	*2.75*
772	A166	1r multicolored	*8.00*	*4.50*
773	A166	1.50r multicolored	*12.00*	*7.00*
774	A166	2r multicolored	*14.50*	*8.50*
		Nos. 767-774 (8)	*49.75*	*26.45*

This is an expanding set. Numbers may change.

A167

Sheik Khalifa, 20th Anniv. of Accession A168

Perf. 14x13½

1992, Feb. 22 Litho. Wmk. 368

781	A167	25d multicolored	*.75*	*.35*
782	A167	50d multicolored	*1.25*	*.50*
783	A168	75d multicolored	*2.00*	*.75*
784	A168	1.50r multicolored	*3.75*	*1.75*
		Nos. 781-784 (4)	*7.75*	*3.35*

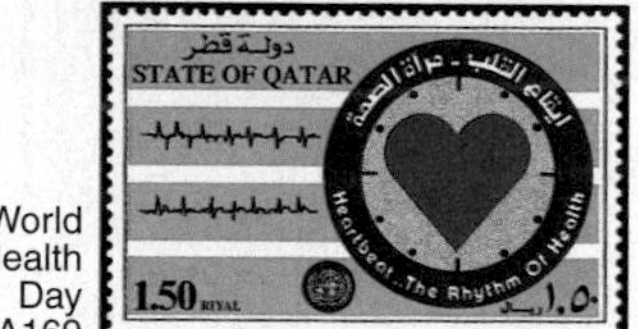

World Health Day A169

1992, Apr. 7 *Perf. 14x13½, 13½x14*

785	A169	50d Heart with face, vert.	*1.10*	*.60*
786	A169	1.50r shown	*3.00*	*2.00*

Children's Paintings A170

25d, Girls dancing. 50d, Children playing. 75d, Ships. 1.50r, Fishing from boats.

1992, June 15 Unwmk. *Perf. 11½*

787	A170	25d multi	*.75*	*.40*
788	A170	50d multi	*1.75*	*.50*
789	A170	75d multi	*3.25*	*.65*
790	A170	1.50r multi	*5.00*	*1.25*
a.		Souvenir sheet of 4, #787-790	*375.00*	*375.00*
		Nos. 787-790 (4)	*10.75*	*2.80*

Type of 1984 with Smaller Arabic Inscription and

A171

A172

Designs: 25d, 1.50r, Offshore oil field. 50d, 2r, 5r, Map. 75d, 3r, Storage tanks, horiz. 1r, 4r, 10r, Oil refinery, horiz.

1992 Litho. *Perf. 13x13½*

791	A171	10d multicolored	*.35*	*.25*
792	A132	25d multicolored	*.35*	*.25*
793	A132	50d multicolored	*.55*	*.50*

Perf. 13½x13

794	A132	75d multicolored	*.95*	*.55*
795	A132	1r multicolored	*1.25*	*.75*

Size: 25x32mm

Perf. 14½x13, 13x14½

796	A132	1.50r multicolored	*1.60*	*1.10*
797	A132	2r multicolored	*2.10*	*1.25*
798	A132	3r multicolored	*4.25*	*2.50*
799	A132	4r multicolored	*4.75*	*3.00*
800	A132	5r multicolored	*5.50*	*3.75*
801	A132	10r multicolored	*12.00*	*7.00*
802	A172	15r multicolored	*16.00*	*12.00*
803	A172	20r multicolored	*27.50*	*14.00*
804	A172	30r multicolored	*32.50*	*24.00*
		Nos. 791-804 (14)	*109.65*	*70.90*

Issued: 10-50d, 1.50, 2, 5, 15, 30r, 2/15; others, 5/14.

1992 Summer Olympics, Barcelona A174

1992, July 25 Litho. *Perf. 15*

805	A174	50d Running	*1.50*	*.40*
806	A174	1.50r Soccer	*3.75*	*1.25*

11th Persian Gulf Soccer Cup A175

1992, Nov. 27 Litho. *Perf. 14½*

807	A175	50d shown	*1.75*	*.60*
808	A175	1r Ball, net, vert.	*3.50*	*1.25*

A176

Independence, 21st Anniv. — A177

Sheik Khalifa and: No. 810, "21" in English and Arabic. No. 811, Tree, dhow in harbor. No. 812, Natural gas well, pen, dhow.

Unwmk.

1992, Sept. 2 Litho. *Perf. 12*

Granite Paper

809	A176	50d shown	*1.25*	*.55*
810	A176	50d multicolored	*1.25*	*.55*
811	A177	1r multicolored	*2.00*	*1.25*
812	A177	1r multicolored	*2.00*	*1.25*
a.		Strip of 8, 2 each #809-812	*14.00*	*9.00*
		Nos. 809-812 (4)	*6.50*	*3.60*

Intl. Conference on Nutrition, Rome — A178

50d, Globe, emblems, vert. 1r, Cornucopia.

1992, Dec. 12 *Perf. 14½*

813	A178	50d multicolored	*2.00*	*.40*
814	A178	1r multicolored	*3.25*	*.70*

Qatar Broadcasting, Silver Jubilee — A179

Designs: 25d, Man at microphone, satellite dish. 50d, Rocket lift-off, satellite. 75d, Communications building. 1r, Technicians working on books.

1993, June 25 Photo. *Perf. 12x11½*

Granite Paper

819	A179	25d multicolored	*1.00*	*.40*
820	A179	50d multicolored	*2.50*	*.75*
821	A179	75d multicolored	*3.25*	*1.00*
822	A179	1r multicolored	*4.75*	*1.25*
a.		Souvenir sheet of 4, #819-822	*225.00*	*225.00*
		Nos. 819-822 (4)	*11.50*	*3.40*

Ruins A180

Mosque with: a, Minaret (at left, shown). b, Minaret with side projections (at right). c, Minaret with catwalk, inside wall. d, Minaret at right, outside wall.

1993, May 10 Litho. *Perf. 12*

Granite Paper

823	A180	1r Strip of 4, #a.-d.	*9.00*	*3.75*

Independence, 22nd Anniv. — A181

Designs: 25c, Oil pumping station. 50d, Flag, clock tower. 75d, Coat of arms, "22." 1.50r, Flag, fortress tower.

1993, Sept. 2 Litho. *Perf. 11½*

Granite Paper

824	A181	25d multicolored	*.50*	*.30*
825	A181	50d multicolored	*1.00*	*.60*
826	A181	75d multicolored	*1.50*	*1.00*
827	A181	1.50r multicolored	*3.50*	*2.25*
		Nos. 824-827 (4)	*6.50*	*4.15*

Intl. Literacy Day — A182

Designs: 25d, Quill, paper. 50d, Papers with English letters, pen. 75d, Papers with Arabic letters, pen. 1.50r, Scroll, Arabic letters, pen.

Perf. 14x13½

1993, Sept. 2 Litho. Wmk. 368

828	A182	25d multicolored	*.50*	*.30*
829	A182	50d multicolored	*1.00*	*.60*
830	A182	75d multicolored	*1.50*	*.90*
831	A182	1.50r multicolored	*3.50*	*2.25*
		Nos. 828-831 (4)	*6.50*	*4.05*

Children's Games A183

Designs: 25d, Girls with thread and spinners. 50d, Boys with stick and disk, vert. 75r, Children guiding wheels with sticks, vert. 1.50r, Girls with jump rope.

1993, Dec. 5 Litho. *Perf. 11½*
Granite Paper

832 A183 25d multicolored .85 .35
833 A183 50d multicolored 1.75 .50
834 A183 75d multicolored 2.75 .75
a. Souvenir sheet, 2 each #833, #834 90.00 90.00
835 A183 1.50r multicolored 5.25 2.00
a. Souvenir sheet, 2 each #832, #835 90.00 90.00
Nos. 832-835 (4) 10.60 3.60

Falcons — A184

1993, Dec. 22 Granite Paper

836 A184 25d Lanner .75 .40
837 A184 50d Saker 1.25 .50
838 A184 75d Barbary 2.25 .75
839 A184 1.50r Peregrine 4.75 2.00
a. Souvenir sheet, #836-839 175.00
Nos. 836-839 (4) 9.00 3.65

A185

Society for Handicapped Welfare and Rehabilition: 75d, Hands above and below handicapped symbol.

1994, May 6 Litho. *Perf. 14*

840 A185 25d shown 1.10 .50
841 A185 75d multi 2.75 1.10

A186

Qatar Insurance Co., 30th Anniv.: 50d, Building. 1.50r, Co. arms, global tourist attractions.

Perf. 14½
1994, Mar. 11 Litho. Unwmk.

842 A186 50d gold & multi 1.50 .40
843 A186 1.50r gold & multi 4.50 1.60

A187

World Day for Water: 1r, UN emblem, hands catching water drop, tower, grain.

1994, Mar. 22 Litho. *Perf. 11½*

844 A187 25d shown 1.50 .40
845 A187 1r multicolored 2.75 1.50

A188

1994, Mar. 22 Litho. *Perf. 11½*

846 A188 75d shown 1.25 .75
847 A188 2r Scales, gavel 2.75 2.50

Intl. Law Conference.

A189

1r, Family, UN emblem.

Perf. 12x11½
1994, July 16 Litho. Unwmk.

848 A189 25d shown 1.00 .65
849 A189 1r multicolored 3.00 1.25

Intl. Year of the Family.

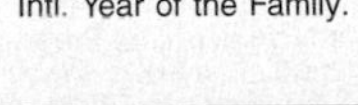

Independence, 23rd Anniv. — A190

25d, 2r, Text. 75d, Island. 1r, Oil drilling plant.

1994, Sept. 2 Photo. *Perf. 12*
Granite Paper

850 A190 25d green & multi .60 .35
851 A190 75d multicolored 1.25 .75
852 A190 1r multicolored 2.00 1.10
853 A190 2r pink & multi 4.50 2.25
Nos. 850-853 (4) 8.35 4.45

ILO, 75th Anniv. — A191

1994, May 28 *Perf. 14*

854 A191 25d salmon & multi .75 .40
855 A191 2r green & multi, diff. 4.75 1.60

ICAO, 50th Anniv. A192

1994, Dec. 7 *Perf. 13½x14*

856 A192 25d shown 1.00 .40
857 A192 75d Emblem, airplane 4.75 1.00

A193

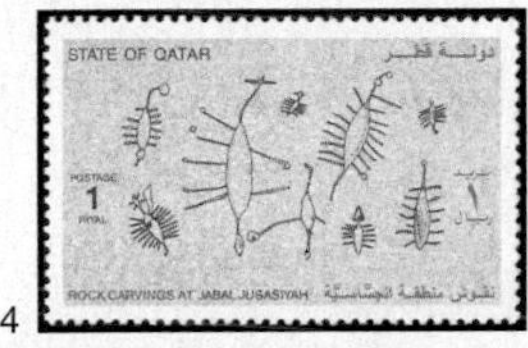
A194

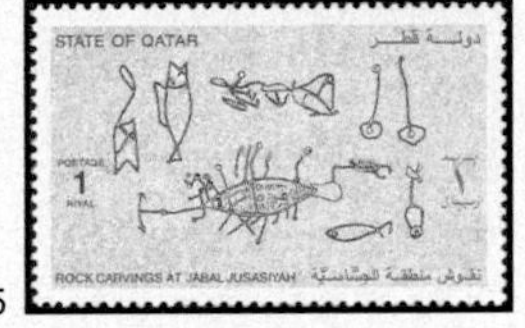
A195

A196

Rock Carvings at Jabal Jusasiyah — A197

1995, Mar. 18 Litho. *Perf. 14½x15*

858 A193 1r multicolored 1.40 .80
859 A194 1r multicolored 1.40 .80
860 A195 1r multicolored 1.40 .80
861 A196 1r multicolored 1.40 .80
862 A197 1r multicolored 1.40 .80
863 A197 1r multi, diff. 1.40 .80
a. Vert. strip of 6, #858-863 11.00 8.50
Nos. 858-863 (6) 8.40 4.80

Gulf Environment Day — A198

Shells: No. 864a, Conus pennaceus. b, Cerithidea cingulata. c, Hexaplex kuesterianus. d, Epitonium scalare.

No. 865a, Murox scolopax. b, Thais mutabilis. c, Fusinus arabicus. d, Lambis truncata sebae.

1995, Apr. 24

864 A198 75d Strip of 4, #a.-d. 5.50 4.50
865 A198 1r Strip of 4, #a.-d. 6.50 5.50

Intl. Nursing Day — A199

Designs: 1r, Nurse adjusting IV for patient. 1.50r, Injecting shot into arm of infant.

1995, May 12

866 A199 1r multicolored 2.50 1.10
867 A199 1.50r multicolored 4.25 1.60

Independence, 24th Anniv. — A200

Designs: a, 1.50r, Shipping dock, city. b, 1r, Children in classroom. c, 1.50r, Aerial view of city. d, 1r, Palm trees.

1995, Sept. 2 Litho. *Perf. 13½x14*

868 A200 Block of 4, #a.-d. 7.00 4.75

UN, 50th Anniv. — A201

1995, Oct. 24 *Perf. 13½*

869 A201 1.50r multicolored 2.50 1.25

Gazelles A202

No. 870; a, 75c, Gazella dorcas pelzelni. b, 50d, Dorcatragus megalotis. c, 25d, Gazella dama. d, 1.50r, Gazella spekei. e, 2r, Gazella soemmeringi. f, 1r, Gazella dorcas.

3r, Gazella spekei, gazella dorcas pelzelni, gazella soemmeringi.

1996, Jan. Litho. *Perf. 11½*

870 A202 Strip of 6, #a.-f. 10.00 10.00

Size: 121x81mm
Imperf

871 A202 3r multicolored 67.50 50.00

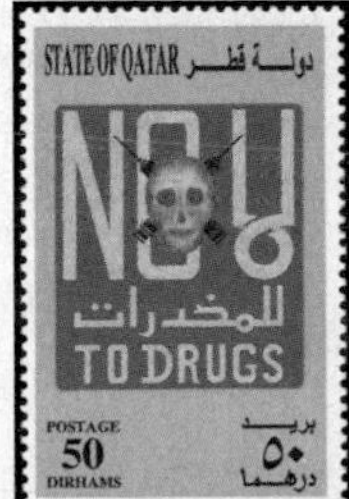
Fight Against Drug Abuse — A203

1996, June 26 Litho. *Perf. 14x13*

872 A203 50d shown *1.40 .55*

873 A203 1r "NO," needles, hand *2.50 1.00*

1996 Summer Olympic Games, Atlanta — A204

a, 10d, Olympic emblem, map of Qatar. b, 15d, Shooting. c, 25d, Bowling. d, 50d, Table tennis. e, 1r, Athletics. f, 1.50r, Yachting.

1996, July 19 Litho. *Perf. 14x13½*

874 A204 Strip of 6, #a.-f. *9.00 8.00*

Independence, 25th Anniv. — A204a

Litho. & Typo.

1996, Sept. 2 *Perf. 12*

Granite Paper

875 A204a 1.50r silver & multi *2.50 1.25*

876 A204a 2r gold & multi *4.75 1.75*

Forts A204b

25d, Al-Wajbah, vert. 75d, Al-Zubarah. 1r, Al-Kout. 3r, Umm Salal Mohammed.

1997, Jan. 15 Litho. *Perf. 14½*

877 A204b 25d multicolored *.60 .35*

878 A204b 75d multicolored *1.50 1.00*

879 A204b 1r multicolored *2.00 1.25*

880 A204b 3r multicolored *5.50 4.25*

Nos. 877-880 (4) 9.60 6.85

A205

A206

Sheik Hamad — A206a

1996-2009 (?) Photo. *Perf. 11½x12*

Granite Paper

881 A205 25d pink & multi *.40 .25*

881A A205 25d green & multi —

882 A205 50d green & multi *.65 .40*

882A A205 50d org brn & multi —

883 A205 75d bl grn & multi *1.00 .50*

884 A205 1r gray & multi *1.25 .60*

Perf. 11½

885 A206 1.50r grn bl & multi *2.25 .90*

886 A206 2r green & multi *2.50 1.00*

887 A206 4r ver & multi *4.75 2.50*

888 A206 5r purple & multi *5.75 5.00*

888A A206 5r red vio & multi —

888B A206a 5r purple & multi —

889 A206 10r brown & multi *14.50 7.00*

889A A206 10r red & multi —

889B A206a 10r brown & multi —

890 A206 20r blue & multi *25.00 14.00*

890A A206a 20r blue & multi —

891 A206 30r orange & multi *37.50 21.00*

891A A206a 30r org & multi —

Issued: Nos. 881-888, 889, 890, 891, 11/16/96; others, 2009?.

An additional stamp was issued in this set. The editors would like to examine any example.

A207

UNICEF, 50th Anniv.: No. 893, Children, open book emblem.

1996, Dec. 11 Litho. *Perf. 14½*

892 A207 75d blue & multi *1.25 .85*

893 A207 75d violet & multi *1.25 .85*

A208

17th Session of GCC Supreme Council: 1.50r, Emblem, dove with olive branch, Sheik Khalifa.

1996, Dec. 7

894 A208 1r multicolored *2.00 .75*

895 A208 1.50r multicolored *3.50 1.50*

Opening of Port of Ras Laffan — A209

1997, Feb. 24 Litho. *Perf. 13½*

896 A209 3r multicolored *8.00 3.00*

Arabian Horses A210

25d, Red horse with tan mane. 75d, Black horse. 1r, White horse. 1.50r, Red brown horse. 3r, Mares, foals.

1997, Mar. 19 Photo. *Perf. 12x11½*

897 A210 25d multi *1.00 .45*

898 A210 75d multi *1.75 .90*

899 A210 1r multi *2.25 1.25*

900 A210 1.50r multi *3.50 2.00*

Nos. 897-900 (4) 8.50 4.60

Size: 115x75mm

Imperf

901 A210 3r multi *125.00 65.00*

Independence, 26th Anniv. — A211

1997, Sept. 2 Photo. *Perf. 11½x12*

Granite Paper

902 A211 1r shown *1.75 .85*

903 A211 1.50r Oil refinery *2.75 1.25*

Doha '97, Doha-Mena Economic Conference — A212

1997, Nov. 16 Litho. *Perf. 11*

904 A212 2r multicolored *2.50 1.25*

Insects — A213

a, Nubian flower bee. b, Domino beetle. c, Seven-spot ladybird. d, Desert giant ant. e, Eastern death's-head hawkmoth. f, Arabian darkling beetle. g, Yellow digger. h, Mole cricket. i, Migratory locust. j, Elegant rhinoceros beetle. k, Oleander hawkmoth. l, American cockroach. m. Girdled skimmer. n, Sabre-toothed beetle. o, Arabian cicada. p, Pinstriped ground weevil. q, Praying mantis. r, Rufous bombardier beetle. s, Diadem. t, Shore earwing.

1998, July 20 Litho. *Perf. 11½x12*

Granite Paper

905 A213 2r Sheet of 20, #a.-t. *40.00 32.50*

u. Souvenir sheet, #905i *22.50 17.50*

v. Souvenir sheet, #905s *22.50 17.50*

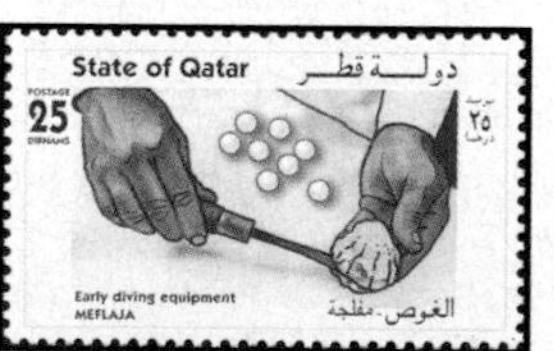

Early Diving Equipment — A214

Perf. 11½x12, 12x11½

1998, Aug. 15 Photo.

Granite Paper

906 A214 25d Meflaja *.70 .25*

907 A214 75d Mahar *1.40 .75*

908 A214 1r Dasta *2.00 1.10*

909 A214 1.50r Deyen, vert. *3.00 2.00*

Nos. 906-909 (4) 7.10 4.10

Souvenir Sheet

910 A214 2r Man seated in boat *16.00 12.00*

Qatar University, 25th Anniv. — A215

1998, Sept. 2 Litho. *Perf. 13½x13*

911 A215 1r blue & multi *1.40 .85*

912 A215 1.50r gray & muti *2.25 1.25*

Independence, 27th Anniv. — A216

1998, Sept. 2 *Perf. 14*

913 A216 1r Sheik Khalifa, vert. *1.40 .85*

914 A216 1.50r Sheik Khalifa *2.25 1.25*

Camels — A217

1999, Jan. 25 Litho. *Perf. 11½*

Granite Paper

915 A217 25d shown *.25 .25*

916 A217 75d One standing *1.50 1.25*

917 A217 1r Three standing *2.10 1.50*

918 A217 1.50r Four standing, group *3.00 2.50*

Nos. 915-918 (4) 6.85 5.50

Souvenir Sheet

919 A217 2r Adult, juvenile *24.50 20.00*

1999 FEI General Assembly Meeting, Doha — A218

1999 Litho. *Perf. 13¼x13*

920 A218 1.50r multicolored *3.50 2.00*

Ancient Coins — A219

Obverse, reverse of dirhams — #921: a, Umayyad (shown). b, Umayyad, diff. c, Abbasid (3 lines of text on obv.). d, Abbasid (6 lines of text obv.). e, Umayyad, diff. (small circles near edge at top of obv. & rev.).

Obv., rev. of dinars — #922: a, Abbasid (3 lines of text obv.). b, Umayyad. c, Abbasid (5 lines of text obv.). d, Marabitid. e, Fatimid.

Obverse and reverse of: No. 923, Arab Sasanian dirham. 3r, Umayyad dinar, diff.

1999 Litho. *Perf. 11½*

Granite Paper

921 A219 1r Strip of 5, #a.-e. *6.00 4.50*

922 A219 2r Strip of 5, #a.-e. *11.00 7.00*

Souvenir Sheets

923 A219 2r multicolored 16.00 12.00
924 A219 3r multicolored 18.00 14.00

Independence, 28th Anniv. — A220

Perf. 12¾x13¾

1999, Sept. 2 Litho. Wmk. 368

925 A220 1r violet & multi 1.40 1.25
926 A220 1.50r yellow & multi 2.00 1.75

A221

UPU, 125th anniv.: 1r, Tree with letters. 1.50r, Building, horiz.

Perf. 11½

1999, Oct. 9 Litho. Unwmk.

Granite Paper

927 A221 1r multicolored 1.40 1.25
928 A221 1.50r multicolored 2.00 1.75

A222

Fifth Stamp Exhibition for the Arab Gulf Countries: 1r, Emblem, stamps. 1.50r, Emblem, horiz.

1999, Oct. 30 Granite Paper

929 A222 1r multicolored 1.25 .75
930 A222 1.50r multicolored 1.75 1.25

National Committee for Children with Special Needs — A223

Perf. 12¾x13¼

1999, Nov. 2 Litho. Wmk. 368

931 A223 1.50r multi 2.40 2.00

Millennium A224

Photo. & Embossed

2000, Jan. 1 Unwmk. *Perf. 11¾*

Granite Paper

932 A224 1.50r red & gold 2.25 2.00
933 A224 2r blue & gold 3.00 2.50

Qatar Tennis Open — A225

Trophy and: 1r, Stadium. 1.50r, Racquet.

2000, Jan. 3 Litho. *Perf. 13¼x13½*

934 A225 1r multi 2.00 1.60
935 A225 1.50r multi 2.75 2.40

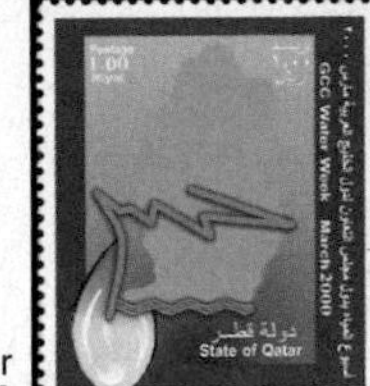

GCC Water Week — A226

2000, Mar. 1 *Perf. 13¾*

936 A226 1r Map, water drop 1.60 1.25
937 A226 1.50r Hands, water drop 2.40 1.75

15th Asian Table Tennis Championships, Doha — A227

2000, May 1 Photo. *Perf. 11¾*

Granite Paper

938 A227 1.50r multi 2.50 2.00

Independence, 29th Anniv. — A228

Sheik Hamad and: 1r, Fort. 1.50r, Oil derrick, city skyline.

Perf. 11½x11¾

2000, Sept. 2 Photo.

Granite Paper

939-940 A228 Set of 2 4.50 4.50

Post Office, 50th Anniv. A229

Monument, building and: 1.50r, Bird. 2r, Magnifying glass.

Photo. & Embossed

2000, Oct. 9 *Perf. 11¾*

Granite Paper

941-942 A229 Set of 2 5.25 5.25

9th Islamic Summit Conference — A230

No. 943: a, 1r, Emblem (size: 21x28mm). b, 1.50r, Emblem, olive branch (size: 45x28mm).

2000, Nov. 12 Photo.

Granite Paper

943 A230 Pair, #a-b 4.25 4.25

Clean Environment Day — A231

Designs: 1r, Qatar Gas emblem, tanker ship, coral reef. 1.50r, RasGas emblem, refinery, antelopes. 2r, Ras Laffan Industrial City emblem, flamingos near industrial complex. 3r, Qatar Petroleum emblem, view of Earth from space.

2001, Feb. 26 Photo. *Perf. 11½*

Granite Paper

944-947 A231 Set of 4 9.25 9.25

Independence, 30th Anniv. — A232

Background colors: 1r, Olive. 1.50r, Blue.

2001, Sept. 2 Litho. *Perf. 14x14½*

948-949 A232 Set of 2 3.75 3.75

Year of Dialogue Among Civilizations A233

Designs: 1.50r, Shown. 2r, Branch with leaves of many colors.

2001, Oct. 9 *Perf. 13¼*

950-951 A233 Set of 2 6.00 6.00

4th World Trade Organization Ministerial Conference — A234

Background colors: 1r, Yellow brown. 1.50r, Blue.

2001, Nov. 9

952-953 A234 Set of 2 5.25 5.25

Old Doors — A235

Various doors: 25d, 75d, 1.50r, 2r.

2001, Dec. 30 *Perf. 14½*

954-957 A235 Set of 4 6.00 6.00

Souvenir Sheet

958 A235 3r multi 20.00 20.00

2002 World Cup Soccer Championships, Japan and Korea — A236

No. 959 — World Cup Posters (except for #959r) from: a, 1930. b, 1934 (Italian). c, 1938. d, 1950. e, 1954. f, 1958. g, 1962. h, 1966. i, 1970. j, 1974. k, 1978. l, 1982. m, 1986. n, 1990. o, 1994. p, 1998. q, 2002. r, World Cup Trophy.

2002 Litho. *Perf. 14*

959 Sheet of 18 52.50 52.50
a.-r. A236 2r Any single 2.00 1.75
s. Souvenir sheet, #959q-959r 8.00 8.00

Asian Games Emblems — A237

No. 960: a, 1r, 2002 Asian Games emblem, Busan, South Korea. b, 3r, 2006 Asian Games Emblem, Doha, Qatar.

2002, Sept. 29 Photo. *Perf. 14¼*

Granite Paper

960 A237 Sheet of 2, #a-b 7.00 7.00

Qatar General Postal Corporation, 1st Anniv. — A238

Background colors: 1r, White. 3r, Light blue.

2002, Oct. 25 Litho. *Perf. 12½*

961-962 A238 Set of 2 5.25 5.25

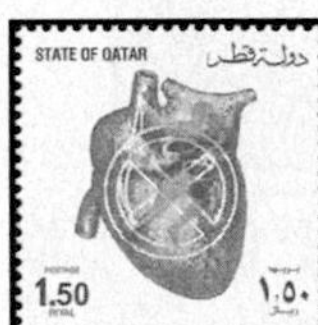

World No Tobacco Day — A239

2003, May 31 *Perf. 13¼x14*

963 A239 1.50r red 2.00 2.00

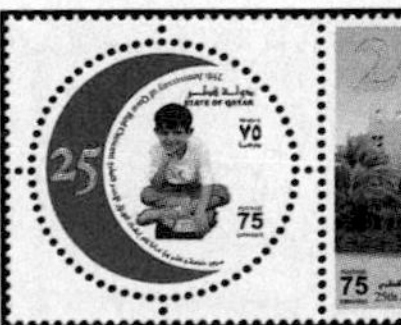

Qatar Red Crescent, 25th Anniv. — A240

No. 964: a, Red crescent, boy (30mm diameter). b, Headquarters building.

Litho. With Foil Application

2003, July 1 *Perf. 13¼*

964 A240 75d Horiz. pair, #a-b 4.25 4.25

Jewelry — A241

Designs: No. 965, 25d, Al-mashmoom. No. 966, 25d, Al-mertash. No. 967, 50d, Khatim. No. 968, 50d, Ishqab. No. 969, 1.50r, Tassa. No. 970, 1.50r, Shmailat.

Photo. & Embossed

2003, Oct. 1 ***Perf. 14½x14¼***
965-970 A241 Set of 6 *8.25 8.25*

Souvenir Sheet

Powered Flight, Cent. — A242

No. 971: a, Wright Flyer. b, Man with winged glider. c, Qatar Airways jet. d, Plane with propellers.

2003, Dec. 17 Litho. ***Perf. 13½***
971 A242 50d Sheet of 4, #a-d *5.00 5.00*

Intl. Year of the Family, 10th Anniv. A243

2004, Apr. 15 ***Perf. 14½***
972 A243 2.50r multi *4.00 4.00*

FIFA (Fédération Internationale de Football Association), Cent. — A244

2004, May 21 ***Perf. 13***
973 A244 50d multi *2.00 2.00*

Values are for stamps with selvage adjacent to diagonal sides.

Permanent Constitution — A245

2004, June 8 Litho. ***Perf. 13½x13¾***
974 A245 75d multi *2.25 2.25*

Souvenir Sheet

2004 Summer Olympics, Athens — A246

No. 975: a, Denomination at left. b, Denomination at right.

2004, Aug. 13 Litho. ***Perf. 13***
975 A246 3r Sheet of 2, #a-d *5.00 5.00*

Souvenir Sheet

MotoGP 2004 Grand Prix Motorcycle Race — A247

No. 976: a, 3r, Motorcycle, denomination at left. b, 3.50r, Two motorcycles, denomination at right. c, 3.50r, Two motorcycles, denomination at left. d, 3r, Motorcycle, denomination at right.

Perf. 13x14x14x14, 14x14x13x14

2004, Sept. 30
976 A247 Sheet of 4, #a-d *8.50 8.50*

Numeral — A248

2004, Nov. 1 Litho. ***Perf. 13½x12½***

Stamp + Label

977	A248 50d blue	.50	.50
978	A248 50d red	.50	.50
979	A248 50d orange	.50	.50
980	A248 50d blue green	.50	.50
981	A248 50d olive green	.50	.50
a.	Vert. strip, #977-981, + 5 labels	3.50	3.50
	Nos. 977-981 (5)	2.50	2.50

National Human Rights Committee — A249

2004, Nov. 11 Litho. ***Perf. 13¼x13***
982 A249 50d multi *.45 .45*

Souvenir Sheet

17th Arabian Gulf Cup — A250

No. 983: a, Mascot, emblem, stadium (35x25mm). b, Mascot, emblem, player kicking ball (25x35mm). c, Mascot, emblem (35x35mm). d, Mascot, emblem, goalie catching ball (25x35mm). e, Emblem, two mascots (35x25mm).

2004, Dec. 10 ***Perf. 12¾x13¼***
983 A250 1.50r Sheet of 5, #a-e, + 4 labels *7.50 7.50*

2006 Asian Games, Doha — A251

Mascot Orry: Nos. 984, 990a, 50d, Pointing to Doha. Nos. 985, 990b, 1r, On dhow in Doha harbor, horiz. Nos. 986, 990c, 1.50r, Counting down days on calendar, horiz. Nos. 987, 990d, 2r, Carrying torch. Nos. 988, 990e, 3r, Lighting flame. Nos. 989, 990f, Carrying Qatari flag.

Perf. 13¼x13, 13x13¼

2004, Dec. 31 Litho.
984-989 A251 Set of 6 8.00 8.00

Self-Adhesive

Serpentine Die Cut 12½

990 A251 Booklet pane of 6, #a-f 8.00 8.00

Miniature Sheet

Cars and Trucks — A252

No. 991: a, 1949 DeSoto (green car). b, 1958 Cadillac Sedan de Ville (white car facing left). c, 1938 Buick (white car facing right). d, 1953 Chrysler Windsor (black car). e, 1962 Dodge Powerwagon (red truck facing right). f, 1958 Chevrolet Pickup (orange red truck facing left). g, 1948 Chevrolet Pickup (green truck). h, 1957 Dodge Sweptside (white and red truck).

2005, Feb. 1 ***Perf. 13½x13¾***
991 A252 50d Sheet of 8, #a-h 2.75 2.75

Oryx Quest 2005 Catamaran Race — A253

Designs: No. 992, 50d, Qatar 2006. No. 993, 50d, Daedalus. No. 994, 50d, Cheyenne, vert. No. 995, 50d, Geronimo, vert.

2005, Feb. 1 ***Perf. 14½***
992-995 A253 Set of 4 1.25 1.25

Expo 2005, Aichi, Japan — A254

Designs: No. 996, 50d, Mascots. No. 997, 50d, Flag of Qatar.

2005, Mar. 25 Litho. ***Perf. 13***
996-997 A254 Set of 2 2.00 2.00

Souvenir Sheet

Doha Development Forum — A255

No. 998: a, Denomination in white. b, Denomination in maroon.

2005, Apr. 9 Litho. ***Perf. 12¼x13¼***
998 A255 6r Sheet of 2, #a-b 7.00 7.00

Souvenir Sheet

Accession of Emir Sheikh Hamad bin Khalifa Al Thani, 10th Anniv. — A256

Litho. & Embossed with Foil Application

2005, June 27 ***Perf. 13¼x13¾***
999 A256 2.50r multi 2.25 2.25

Friendship Between Doha, Qatar and Sarajevo, Bosnia and Herzegovina — A257

2005, July 13 Litho. ***Perf. 13***
1000 A257 2.50r multi 3.00 3.00

See Bosnia & Herzegovina No. 504.

National Flag — A258

Serpentine Die Cut 12¾

2005, Aug. 1 Self-Adhesive

1001 Booklet pane of 6 8.50
- *a.* A258 50d maroon .30 .30
- *b.* A258 1r maroon .65 .65
- *c.* A258 1.50r maroon .95 .95
- *d.* A258 2.50r maroon 1.60 1.60
- *e.* A258 3r maroon 1.90 1.90
- *f.* A258 3.50r maroon 2.25 2.25

Souvenir Sheet

Al Jazeera Children's Channel — A259

No. 1002: a, Children playing. b, Children and balloon. c, Children running. d, Family.

2005, Sept. 9 Litho. *Perf.*
1002 A259 50d Sheet of 4, #a-d 1.25 1.25

Souvenir Sheet

Qatar Philatelic and Numismatics Club — A260

No. 1003: a, Denomination in maroon. b, Denomination in blue.

Litho. & Embossed with Foil Application

2005, Dec. 16 *Perf. 12¾*
1003 A260 1r Sheet of 2, #a-b 1.25 1.25

11th Gulf Cooperation Council Stamp Exhibition — A261

No. 1004: a, Mascots. b, Emblems of exhibition and Qatar General Postal Corporation.

2005, Dec. 21 Litho. *Perf. 13¾*
1004 A261 1r Pair, #a-b 1.25 1.25

Intl. Civil Defense Day — A262

Fire trucks and firefighters on: 50d, Metal ladder. 2.50r, Rope ladder.

2006, Mar. 5 Litho. *Perf. 13x12¾*
1005-1006 A262 Set of 2 2.10 2.10

A263

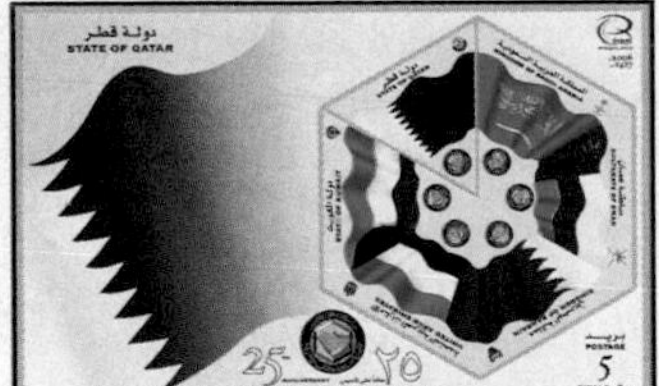

Gulf Cooperation Council, 25th Anniv. — A264

Litho. with Foil Application

2006, May 25 *Perf. 14*
1007 A263 50d multi .40 .40

Imperf

Size: 165x105mm

1008 A264 5r multi 3.25 3.25

See Bahrain Nos. 628-629, Kuwait Nos. 1646-1647, Oman Nos. 477-478, Saudi Arabia No. 1378, and United Arab Emirates Nos. 831-832.

2006 World Cup Soccer Championships, Germany — A265

2006, June 9 Litho. *Perf. 13¼*
1009 A265 2r multi + label 1.25 1.25

Printed in sheets of 8 + 8 labels.

2006 Asian Games, Doha — A266

Designs: 50d, Torch bearers. 75d, Volunteers.

2006, Oct. 8 Litho. *Perf. 13¼x13½*
1010-1011 A266 Set of 2 .80 .80

2006 Asian Games, Doha A267

Designs: No. 1012, 1.50r, Athlete's village. No. 1013, 1.50r, Khalifa Stadium. No. 1014, 1.50r, Aspire Dome. No. 1015, 1.50r, Al-Dana Club.

5r, Vignettes of Nos. 1012-1015, Khalifa Stadium, vert.

2006, Nov. 15 Litho. *Perf. 12¾*
1012-1015 A267 Set of 4 3.50 3.50

Imperf

Size: 126x179mm

1016 A267 5r multi 2.75 2.75

Sports of the 2006 Asian Games, Doha — A268

No. 1017: a, Runner breaking tape at finish line. b, Karate. c, Tennis. d, Swimming. e, Cycling.

2006, Nov. 26 Litho. *Perf. 12¾*
1017 A268 50d Vert. strip of 5, a-e, + 5 labels 5.50 5.50

Labels on Nos. 1017a-1017e could be personalized.

2006 Asian Games, Doha — A269

Designs: No. 1018, 50d, Mascot Orry playing soccer. No. 1019, 50d, Mascot Orry cycling. No. 1020, 50d, Soccer. No. 1021, 50d, Women's volleyball. No. 1022, 50d, Table tennis.

2006, Dec. 1 *Perf. 13¼*
1018-1022 A269 Set of 5 5.50 5.50

Pan-Arab Equestrian Federation General Assembly Meeting, Doha — A270

2007, Sept. 1 Litho. *Perf. 13¾x14*
1027 A270 2.50r multi 1.60 1.60

Souvenir Sheet

Doha's Bid For 2016 Summer Olympics and Paralympics — A271

No. 1029: a, Runner in starting position, denomination in red violet. b, Runner in starting position, violet denomination. c, Children with raised arms, orange denomination. d, Children with raised arms, red denomination.

2007, Oct. 25 Litho. *Perf. 14x14½*
1029 A271 50d Sheet of 4, #a-d 1.25 1.25

28th Session of Supreme Council of Gulf Cooperation Council — A272

2007, Dec. 3 Litho. *Perf. 12¾*
1030 A272 50d multi .30 .30

Miniature Sheet

Qatar Rulers and National Emblem — A273

No. 1031: a, National emblem (light blue panel, 38x28mm). b, Sheikh Hamad bin Khalifa Al Thani (38x55mm). c, National emblem (maroon panel, 38x28mm). d, Sheikh Ali bin Abdullah Al Thani (1895-1974, blue green panel, 38x28mm). e, Sheikh Abdullah bin Jassim Al Thani (1876-1957, pale green panel, 38x28mm). f, Sheikh Khalifa bin Hamad Al Thani (buff panel, 38x28mm). g, Sheikh Ahmad bin Ali Al Thani (1917-77, gray brown panel, 38x28mm).

Litho. With Foil Application

2007, Dec. 18 *Perf. 12¼*
1031 A273 2.50r Sheet of 7, #a-g, + label 9.75 9.75

Islamic Holy Sites — A274

No. 1032: a, Green Dome of the Holy Prophet, Medina (olive green frame). b, Holy Ka'aba, Mecca (yellow brown frame). c, Dome of the Rock, Jerusalem (blue frame).

Litho. & Embossed

2007, Dec. 19 *Perf. 14x13½*
1032 A274 Horiz. strip of 3 4.25 4.25
- *a.-c.* 2.50r Any single 1.40 1.40

Souvenir Sheet

Holy Ka'aba, Green Dome of the Holy Prophet, and Dome of the Rock — A274a

Litho. & Embossed

2007, Dec. 19 *Perf. 14x13½*
1033 A274a 5r multi 6.50 6.50

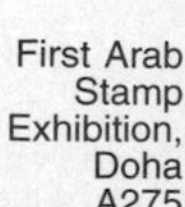

First Arab Stamp Exhibition, Doha
A275

2008, Jan. 30 Litho. ***Perf. 13x12¾***
1034 A275 50d multi .30 .30

Miniature Sheet

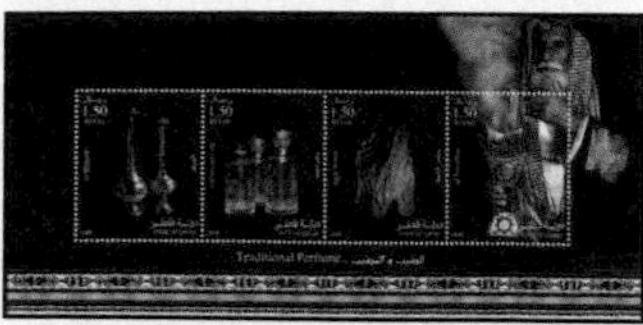

Traditional Perfumes — A276

No. 1035: a, Al Marash. b, Oud perfume oil. c, Agar wood. d, Al Mogbass.

2008, Mar. 31 ***Perf. 13¾***
1035 A276 1.50r Sheet of 4, #a-d 3.50 3.50

No. 1035 is impregnated with a sandalwood scent.

Miniature Sheet

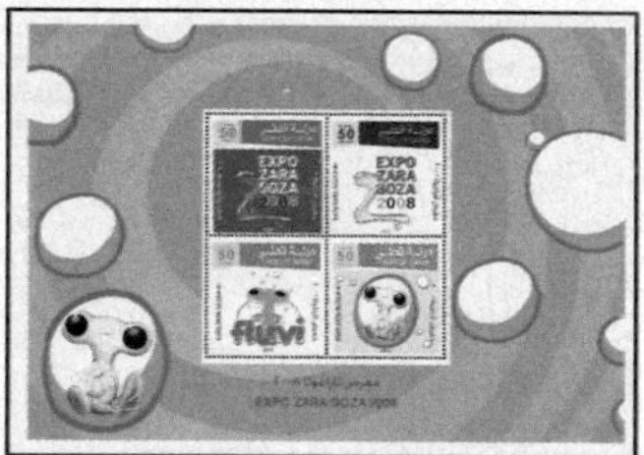

Expo Zaragoza 2008, Zaragoza, Spain — A277

No. 1036: a, Emblem, denomination in Prussian blue. b, Emblem, denomination in dark blue. c, Mascot, denomination in yellow brown. d, Mascot, denomination in gray.

2008, June 14 ***Perf. 14x14¼***
1036 A277 50d Sheet of 4, #a-d 1.10 1.10

Souvenir Sheet

Arab Post Day — A278

No. 1037 — Emblem and: a, World map, pigeon. b, Camel caravan.

Litho. & Silk-screened With Foil Application

2008, Aug. 3 ***Perf. 13½x13¼***
1037 A278 5r Sheet of 2, #a-b 5.50 5.50

Miniature Sheet

2008 Summer Olympics, Beijing — A279

No. 1038 — Beijing Olympics emblem and: a, 50d, Blue background (34x36mm). b, 50d, Green background (34x36mm). c, 3r, Stylized people (69x36mm).

2008, Aug. 8 Litho. ***Perf. 14½***
1038 A279 Sheet of 3, #a-c 2.25 2.25

14th Gulf Cooperation Council Stamp Exhibition, Doha — A280

2008, Oct. 14 ***Perf. 14x14½***
1039 A280 50d multi .30 .30

Arab Police Sporting Federation — A281

No. 1040 — Color of denomination. a, White, b, Olive green.

2008, Oct. 14 ***Perf. 13¾x13¼***
1040 A281 50d Horiz. pair, #a-b .55 .55

Museum of Islamic Art, Doha
A282

2008, Nov. 22 Litho. ***Perf. 13x13¼***
1041 A282 50d multi .30 .30

Souvenir Sheet

1042 A282 5r multi 2.75 2.75

A283

Souq Waqif
A283a

2008, Dec. 18 ***Perf. 13¾***
1043 A283 1.50r multi — —
1044 A283a 1.50r multi — —
1045 A283b 1.50r multi — —
1046 A283c 1.50r multi — —

Campaign for Responsible Media — A284

2009, Jan. 13 Litho. ***Perf. 13¼***
1047 A284 50d multi .30 .30

Tears for Gaza — A285

2009, Jan. 21 Litho. ***Perf. 12¾***
1048 A285 1r multi .55 .55

First Democratic City Council Elections, 10th Anniv. — A286

2009, Mar. 15 Litho. ***Perf. 13¾***
1050 A286 50d multi .30 .30

Jerusalem, 2009 Capital of Arab Culture
A287

2009, Aug. 3 ***Perf. 13***
1051 A287 1r multi .55 .55

Souvenir Sheet

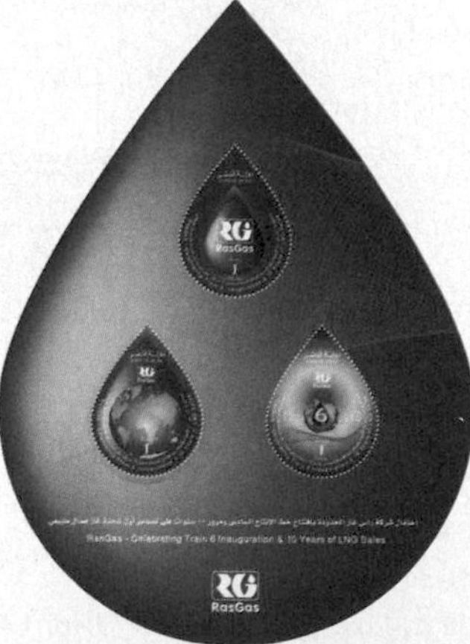

RasGas Liquified Natural Gas Sales, 10th Anniv., and Train 6 Inauguration — A288

No. 1052 — RasGas emblem and: a, Drop. b, Large globe. c, Small glove, numbers 1 to 10.

2009, Oct. 27 ***Perf.***
1052 A288 1r Sheet of 3, #a-c 1.75 1.75

Birds
A289

Designs: No. 1053, Orphean warbler. No. 1054, Woodchat shrike. No. 1055, Isabelline shrike. No. 1056, Lesser gray shrike. No. 1057, Chiffchaf. No. 1058, Yellow wagtail.

No. 1059: a, Head of Orphean warbler. b, Head of Woodchat shrike. c, Head of Isabelline shrike. d, Head of Lesser gray shrike. e, Head of Chiffchaf. f, Head of Yellow wagtail.

5r, Cream-colored courser.

2009, Dec. 18 Litho. ***Perf. 13***
1053 A289 50d multi .30 .30
1054 A289 50d multi .30 .30
1055 A289 50d multi .30 .30
1056 A289 50d multi .30 .30
1057 A289 50d multi .30 .30
1058 A289 50d multi .30 .30
Nos. 1053-1058 (6) 1.80 1.80

Booklet Stamps

1059 Booklet pane of 6 1.80 —
a.-f. A289 50d Any single .30 .30

Souvenir Sheet

1060 A289 5r multi 2.75 2.75

Organization of Petroleum Exporting Countries, 50th Anniv. — A290

2010, Jan. 28 Litho. ***Perf. 13x13¼***
1061 A290 1r multi .55 .55

Distribution of Mus-haf Qatar (Koran With Calligraphic Writing)
A291

2010, Mar. 9 ***Perf. 12¾x13***
1062 A291 3r multi 1.75 1.75

2010 Population and Housing Census
A292

2010, Apr. 20 ***Perf. 13¾***
1063 A292 1r multi .55 .55

25th Universal Postal Union Congress, Doha — A293

2010, Sept. 24 ***Perf. 13¼x13¾***
1064 A293 50d multi .30 .30

See Nos. 1076, 1084.

A294

Doha, 2010 Capital of Arab Culture — A295

No. 1065: a, Horsemen with flags. b, Masks. c, Open book. d, Stringed instrument and musical notes.
5r, Stylized peacock.

2010, Oct. 10 ***Perf. 14½***
1065 A294 1.50r Sheet of 4, #a-d 3.50 3.50

Size:60x100mm

Imperf

1066 A295 5r multi 2.75 2.75

Souvenir Sheet

2010 Aga Khan Award for Architecture — A296

2010, Nov. 24 ***Perf. 13¼x12¾***
1067 A296 1.50r multi .85 .85

Souvenir Sheets

A297

A298

A299

Qatar's Annual Production of 77 Million Tonnes of Liquified Natural Gas — A300

2010, Dec. 13 ***Perf. 14x13½***
1068 A297 1r multi .55 .55
1069 A298 1r multi .55 .55
1070 A299 1r multi .55 .55
1071 A300 1r multi .55 .55
Nos. 1068-1071 (4) 2.20 2.20

Souvenir Sheet

Qatar News Agency, 35th Anniv. — A301

2010, Dec. 18 ***Perf. 13¼***
1072 A301 1r blue & red .55 .55

Qatar Amateur Radio Society — A302

2010, Dec. 26 ***Perf. 13¾***
1073 A302 50d multi .30 .30

Arab Deaf Week — A303

2011, Apr. 20 ***Perf. 12¾x13***
1074 A303 1r multi .55 .55

First Postal Agency, 50th Anniv. — A304

Litho. With Foil Application

2011, May 17 ***Perf. 14x13¼***
1075 A304 50d multi .30 .30

25th UPU Congress Type of 2010

2011, Sept. 24 Litho. ***Perf. 14x14½***
1076 A293 1r multi .55 .55

Miniature Sheet

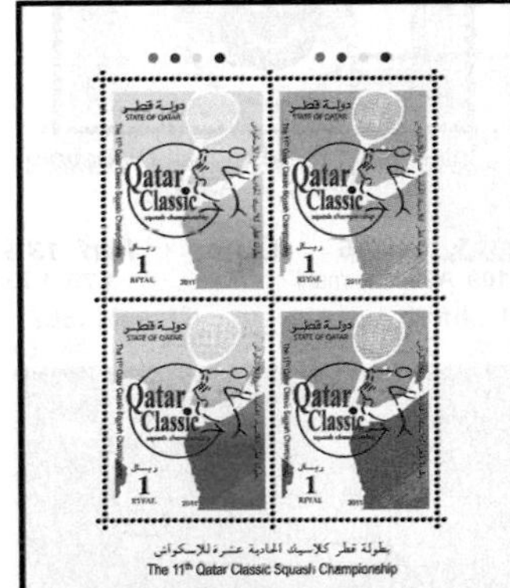

11th Qatar Classic Squash Championship — A305

No. 1077 — Color of top panel: a, Light green. b, Tan. c, Light blue. d, Rose lilac.

2011, Oct. 16 ***Perf. 14½x14¾***
1077 A305 1r Sheet of 4, #a-d 2.25 2.25

2011 Arab Games, Doha — A306

No. 1078 — Text with denomination color in: a, Orange. b, Gray. c, Yellow green.

2011, Dec. 9 ***Perf. 12½***
1078 A306 50d Vert. strip of 3, #a-c .85 .85

Qatari Endowment Deed, 90th Anniv. — A307

Designs: No. 1079, 50d, Emblem. No. 1080, 50d, Building.
3r, Scroll, vert.

2012, Mar. 4 ***Perf. 13½x13¼***
1079-1080 A307 Set of 2 .55 .55

Souvenir Sheet

Perf. 13¼x13½

1081 A307 3r multi 1.75 1.75

Arab Postal Day A308

2012, Aug. 3 ***Perf. 13¼***
1082 A308 1r multi .55 .55

25th UPU Congress Type of 2010

2012, Sept. 24 Litho. ***Perf. 14x14½***
1084 A293 2r multi 1.10 1.10

Falcon, Flags of Qatar and Morocco A310

2012, Oct. 9 ***Perf. 12¾***
1085 A310 2.50r multi 1.40 1.40

See Morocco No.

2012 United Nations Climate Change Conference, Doha — A311

2012, Nov. 1
1086 A311 2.50r blue & lt blue 1.40 1.40

Miniature Sheet

Jeemtv.net — A313

No. 1088: a, Girl, horse made of ribbons, orange panel. b, Boy, automobiles, purple panel. c, Boy in soccer uniform, red panel. d, Girl, stylized butterflies, turquoise green panel.

2013, June 23 Litho. ***Perf. 13¾***
1088 A313 2.50r Sheet of 4, #a-d 5.50 5.50

Woman's Head — A13

Woman Chemist — A14

1964 **Photo.** ***Perf. 13x12½***

47 A13 50c shown .25 .25
48 A14 1p shown .25 .25
49 A14 1.50p Logger .25 .25
Nos. 47-49 (3) .75 .75

Issued to commemorate 25 years of peace.

Goliath Beetle A15

Beetle: 1p, Acridoxena hewaniana.

1965, June 1 **Photo.** ***Perf. 12½x13***

50 A15 50c Prus green .25 .25
51 A15 1p sepia .25 .25
52 A15 1.50p black .25 .25
Nos. 50-52 (3) .75 .75

Issued for child welfare.

Ring-necked Pheasant — A16

Leopard and Arms of Rio Muni A17

Perf. 13x12½, 12½x13

1965, Nov. 23 **Photo.**

53 A16 50c grnsh gray .35 .25
54 A17 1p sepia .65 .25
55 A16 2.50p lilac 3.00 .90
Nos. 53-55 (3) 4.00 1.40

Issued for Stamp Day, 1965.

Elephant and Parrot A18

Design: 1.50p, Lion and boy.

Perf. 12½x13

1966, June 1 **Photo.** **Unwmk.**

56 A18 50c olive .25 .25
57 A18 1p dk purple .25 .25
58 A18 1.50p brt Prus blue .25 .25
Nos. 56-58 (3) .75 .75

Issued for child welfare.

Water Chevrotain A19

Designs: 40c, 4p, Tree pangolin, vert.

1966, Nov. 23 **Photo.** ***Perf. 13***

59 A19 10c brown & yel brn .25 .25
60 A19 40c brown & yellow .25 .25
61 A19 1.50p blue & rose lilac .25 .25
62 A19 4p dk bl & emerald .25 .25
Nos. 59-62 (4) 1.00 1.00

Issued for Stamp Day, 1966.

A20

Designs: 40c, 4p, Vine creeper.

1967, June 1 **Photo.** ***Perf. 13***

63 A20 10c green & yellow .25 .25
64 A20 40c blk, rose car & grn .25 .25
65 A20 1.50p blue & orange .25 .25
66 A20 4p black & green .25 .25
Nos. 63-66 (4) 1.00 1.00

Issued for child welfare.

Potto — A21

Designs: 1p, River hog, horiz. 3.50p, African golden cat, horiz.

1967, Nov. 23 **Photo.** ***Perf. 13***

67 A21 1p black & red brn .30 .30
68 A21 1.50p brown & grn .30 .30
69 A21 3.50p org brn & grn .45 .45
Nos. 67-69 (3) 1.05 1.05

Issued for Stamp Day 1967.

Zodiac Issue

Cancer — A22

1.50p, Taurus. 2.50p, Gemini.

1968, Apr. 25 **Photo.** ***Perf. 13***

70 A22 1p brt mag, *lt yel* .30 .30
71 A22 1.50p brown, *pink* .30 .30
72 A22 2.50p dk vio, *yel* .75 .75
Nos. 70-72 (3) 1.35 1.35

Issued for child welfare.

SEMI-POSTAL STAMPS

Type of Regular Issue, 1960

Designs: 10c+5c, Croton plant. 15c+5c, Flower and leaves of croton.

1960 **Unwmk.** **Photo.** ***Perf. 13x12½***

B1 A2 10c + 5c maroon .25 .25
B2 A2 15c + 5c bister brown .25 .25

The surtax was for child welfare.

Bishop Juan de Ribera — SP1

20c+5c, The clown Pablo de Valladolid by Velazquez. 30c+10c, Juan de Ribera statue.

1961 ***Perf. 13x12½***

B3 SP1 10c + 5c rose brown .25 .25
B4 SP1 20c + 5c dk slate grn .25 .25
B5 SP1 30c + 10c olive brown .25 .25
B6 SP1 50c + 20c brown .25 .25
Nos. B3-B6 (4) 1.00 1.00

Issued for Stamp Day, 1960.

Mandrill SP2

Design: 25c+10c, Elephant, vert.

Perf. 12½x13, 13x12½

1961, June 21 **Unwmk.**

B7 SP2 10c + 5c rose brown .25 .25
B8 SP2 25c + 10c gray violet .25 .25
B9 SP2 80c + 20c dark green .25 .25
Nos. B7-B9 (3) .75 .75

The surtax was for child welfare.

Statuette — SP3

Design: 25c+10c, 1p+10c, Male figure.

1961, Nov. 23 ***Perf. 13x12½***

B10 SP3 10c + 5c rose brown .25 .25
B11 SP3 25c + 10c dark purple .25 .25
B12 SP3 30c + 10c olive black .25 .25
B13 SP3 1p + 10c red orange .25 .25
Nos. B10-B13 (4) 1.00 1.00

Issued for Stamp Day 1961.

Great Britain

Don't forget our ally across the pond when collecting. Scott albums will help guide you through the thousands of stamps issued from Great Britain with easy identification using Scott numbers.

GREAT BRITAIN ALBUM SET

Save when you purchase the Great Britain Album Set that includes the complete pages through 2011, metal-hinged Scott Specialty binders and slipcases and Great Britain labels.

Item	*Description*	*Retail*	*AA**
200SET	1840-2011	$389.99	**$289.99**

GREAT BRITAIN ALBUMS

Item	*Description*	*Retail*	*AA**
200GBR1	1840-1973	$69.99	**$55.99**
200GBR2	1974-1996	$59.99	**$47.99**
200GBR3	1997-2003	$42.50	**$33.99**
200GBR4	2004-2009	$59.99	**$47.99**
200S010	2010 #64	$16.99	**$13.99**
200S011	2011 #65	$16.99	**$13.99**
200S012	2012 #66	$14.99	**$11.99**
200S013	2013 #67	$15.99	**$12.99**
200S014	2014 #68	$16.99	**$13.99**
200S015	2015 #69	$16.99	**$13.99**

GREAT BRITAIN OFFICES ABROAD

Item	*Description*	*Retail*	*AA**
200BOA0	1885-1956	$21.99	**$17.99**

GREAT BRITAIN MACHINS

Item	*Description*	*Retail*	*AA**
200GBM1	1967-2009	$28.99	**$23.99**
200M011	2011 #7	$5.99	**$4.99**
200M013	2013 #8	$5.99	**$4.99**
200M015	2015 #9	$5.99	**$4.99**

Visit
AmosAdvantage.com
Call
1-800-572-6885
Outside U.S. & Canada 937-498-0800
P.O. Box 4129, Sidney OH 45365

AMOS ADVANTAGE

TERMS & CONDITIONS

1. *AA prices apply to paid subscribers of Amos Media publications, or orders placed online. **2.** Prices, terms and product availability subject to change. Taxes will apply in CA, OH & IL. **3. Shipping & Handling: United States:** Orders under $10 are only $3.99. 10% of order over $10 total. Minimum Freight Charge $7.99; Maximum Freight Charge $45.00. **Canada:** 20% of order total. Minimum Freight Charge $19.99; Maximum Freight Charge $200.00. **Foreign:** Orders are shipped via FedEx Economy International or USPS and billed actual freight. Brokerage, Customs or duties are the responsibility of the customer.

ROMANIA

ro-'mā-nē-ə

(Rumania, Roumania)

LOCATION — Southeastern Europe, bordering on the Black Sea
GOVT. — Republic
AREA — 91,699 sq. mi.
POP. — 22,600,000 (est. 1984)
CAPITAL — Bucharest

Romania was formed in 1861 from the union of the principalities of Moldavia and Walachia in 1859. It became a kingdom in 1881. Following World War I, the original territory was considerably enlarged by the addition of Bessarabia, Bukovina, Transylvania, Crisana, Maramures and Banat. The republic was established in 1948.

40 Parale = 1 Piaster
100 Bani = 1 Leu (plural "Lei") (1868)

Catalogue values for unused stamps in this country are for Never Hinged Items, beginning with Scott 475 in the regular postage section, Scott B82 in the semi-postal section, Scott C24 in the airpost section, Scott CB1 in the airpost semi-postal section, Scott J82 in the postage due section, Scott O1 in the official section, Scott RA16 in the postal tax section, and Scott RAJ1 in the postal tax postage due section.

Watermarks

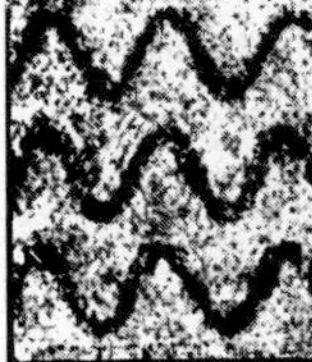

Wmk. 95 — Wavy Lines

Wmk. 163 — Coat of Arms

Wmk. 164 — PR

Wmk. 165 — PR Interlaced

Wmk. 167 — Coat of Arms Covering 25 Stamps

Wmk. 200 — PR

Wmk. 225 — Crown over PTT, Multiple

Wmk. 230 — Crowns and Monograms

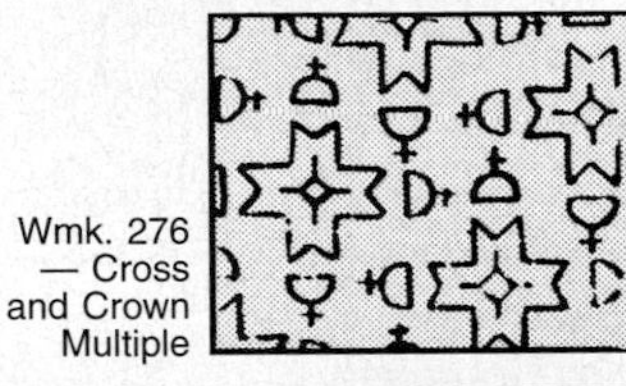

Wmk. 276 — Cross and Crown Multiple

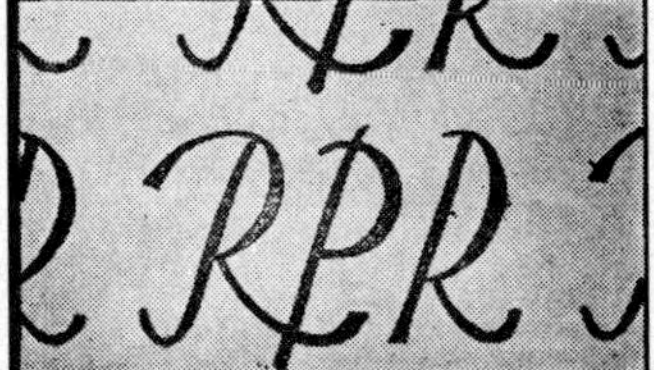

Wmk. 289 — RPR Multiple

Wmk. 358 — RPR Multiple in Endless Rows

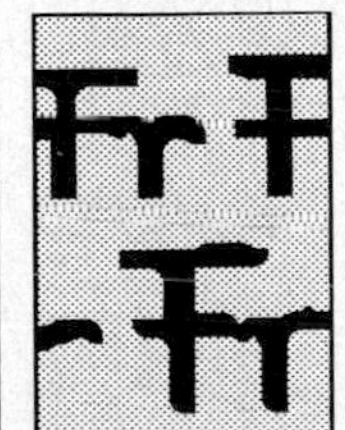

Wmk. 398 — Fr Multiple

Values for unused stamps are for examples with original gum as defined in the catalogue introduction except for Nos. 1-4 which are valued without gum.

Moldavia

Coat of Arms — A1

Laid Paper

Handstamped

1858, July Unwmk. *Imperf.*

No.	Type	Description	Unused	Used
1	A1	27pa blk, *rose*	*60,000.*	*25,000.*
a.		Tête bêche pair		
2	A1	54pa blue, *grn*	*15,500.*	*10,000.*
3	A1	108pa blue, *rose*	*35,000.*	*16,000.*

Wove Paper

No.	Type	Description	Unused	Used
4	A1	81pa blue, *bl*	*50,000.*	*55,000.*

Cut to shape or octagonally, Nos. 1-4 sell for one-fourth to one-third of these values.

Coat of Arms — A2

1858 Bluish Wove Paper

No.	Type	Description	Unused	Used
5	A2	5pa black	*15,000.*	*15,000.*
a.		Tête bêche pair		
6	A2	40pa blue	275.	225.
a.		Tête bêche pair	*1,300.*	*2,650.*
7	A2	80pa red	*7,750.*	*875.*
a.		Tête bêche pair		

1859 White Wove Paper

No.	Type	Description	Unused	Used
8	A2	5pa black	*15,000.*	*10,000.*
a.		Tête bêche pair		
b.		Frame broken at bottom	175.	
c.		As "b," tête bêche pair	600.	
9	A2	40pa blue	175.	190.
b.		Tête bêche pair	650.	*1,500.*
10	A2	80pa red	475.	300.
b.		Tête bêche pair	*1,750.*	*3,250.*

No. 8b has a break in the frame at bottom below "A." It was never placed in use.

Moldavia-Walachia

Coat of Arms — A3

Printed by Hand from Single Dies

1862 White Laid Paper

No.	Type	Description	Unused	Used
11	A3	3pa orange	300.00	*2,250.*
a.		3pa yellow	300.00	*2,250.*
12	A3	6pa carmine	300.00	475.00
13	A3	6pa red	300.00	475.00
14	A3	30pa blue	87.50	115.00
		Nos. 11-14 (4)	987.50	3,315.

White Wove Paper

No.	Type	Description	Unused	Used
15	A3	3pa orange yel	85.00	*275.00*
a.		3pa lemon	85.00	*275.00*
16	A3	6pa carmine	95.00	*275.00*
17	A3	6pa vermilion	77.50	*225.00*
18	A3	30pa blue	60.00	65.00
		Nos. 15-18 (4)	317.50	840.00

Greenish-Blue Paper

No.	Type	Description	Unused	Used
15C	A3	3pa orange yel	—	2,500.

Tête bêche pairs

No.	Type	Description	Unused	Used
11b	A3	3pa orange	1,550.	
12a	A3	6pa carmine	1,000.	1,250.
14a	A3	30pa blue	190.00	1,550.
15b	A3	3pa orange yellow	210.00	*1,600.*
16a	A3	6pa carmine	275.00	1,750.
17a	A3	6pa vermilion	190.00	1,600.
18a	A3	30pa blue	175.00	1,600.

Nos. 11-18 were printed with a hand press, one at a time, from single dies. The impressions were very irregularly placed and occasionally overlapped. Sheets of 32 (4x8). The 3rd and 4th rows were printed inverted, making the second and third rows tête bêche. All values come in distinct shades, frequently even on the same sheet. The paper of this and the following issues through No. 52 often shows a bluish, grayish or yellowish tint.

White Wove Paper

1864 Typographed from Plates

No.	Type	Description	Unused	Used
19	A3	3pa yellow	60.00	*1,500.*
a.		Tête bêche pair	350.00	
b.		Pair, one sideways	150.00	
20	A3	6pa deep rose	22.50	
a.		Tête bêche pair	52.50	
b.		Pair, one sideways	52.50	
21	A3	30pa deep blue	17.50	*100.00*
a.		Tête bêche pair	57.50	
b.		Pair, one sideways	57.50	2,650.
c.		Bluish wove paper	*150.00*	
		Nos. 19-21 (3)	100.00	

Stamps of 1862 issue range from very clear to blurred impressions but rarely have broken or deformed characteristics. The 1864 issue, though rarely blurred, usually have various imperfections in the letters and numbers. These include breaks, malformations, occasional dots at left of the crown or above the "R" of "PAR," a dot on the middle stroke of the "F," and many other bulges, breaks and spots of color.

The 1864 issue were printed in sheets of 40 (5x8). The first and second rows were inverted. Clichés in the third row were placed sideways, 4 with head to right and 4 with head to left, making one tête bêche pair. The fourth and fifth rows were normally placed.

No. 20 was never placed in use.

All values exist in shades, light to dark.

Counterfeit cancellations exist on #11-21.

Three stamps in this design- 2pa, 5pa, 20pa- were printed on white wove paper in 1864, but never placed in use. Value, set $12.

Romania

Prince Alexandru Ioan Cuza — A4

TWENTY PARALES:

Type I — The central oval does not touch the inner frame. The "I" of "DECI" extends above and below the other letters.

Type II — The central oval touches the frame at the bottom. The "I" of the "DECI" is the same height as the other letters.

1865, Jan. Unwmk. Litho. *Imperf.*

No.	Type	Description	Unused	Used
22	A4	2pa orange	70.00	*250.00*
a.		2pa yellow	77.50	*325.00*
b.		2pa ocher	325.00	*325.00*
23	A4	5pa blue	45.00	*275.00*
24	A4	20pa red, type I	35.00	47.50
a.		Bluish paper	350.00	
25	A4	20pa red, type II	35.00	40.00
a.		Bluish paper	350.00	
		Nos. 22-25 (4)	185.00	612.50

The 20pa types are found se-tenant.

White Laid Paper

No.	Type	Description	Unused	Used
26	A4	2pa orange	60.00	*275.00*
a.		2pa ocher	125.00	
27	A4	5pa blue	95.00	*450.00*

Prince Carol — A5

Type I — A6

Type II — A7

TWENTY PARALES:

Type I — A6. The Greek border at the upper right goes from right to left.

Type II — A7. The Greek border at the upper right goes from left to right.

1866-67 Thin Wove Paper

No.	Type	Description	Unused	Used
29	A5	2pa blk, *yellow*	35.00	*95.00*
a.		Thick paper	65.00	*400.00*
30	A5	5pa blk, *dk bl*	60.00	*575.00*
a.		5pa black, *indigo*	100.00	—
b.		Thick paper	70.00	*525.00*
31	A6	20pa blk, *rose*, (I)	30.00	26.50
a.		Dot in Greek border, thin paper	400.00	150.00
b.		Thick paper	175.00	87.50
c.		Dot in Greek border, thick paper	125.00	72.50
32	A7	20pa blk, *rose*, (II)	30.00	26.50
a.		Thick paper	175.00	87.50
		Nos. 29-32 (4)	155.00	723.00

The 20pa types are found se-tenant.

Faked cancellations are known on Nos. 22-27, 29-32.

The white dot of Nos. 31a and 31c occurs in extreme upper right border.

Thick paper was used in 1866, thin in 1867.

Prince Carol — A8

1868-70

33 A8 2b orange 42.50 40.00
a. 2b yellow 45.00 40.00
34 A8 3b violet ('70) 42.50 40.00
35 A8 4b dk blue 55.00 47.50
36 A8 18b scarlet 225.00 30.00
a. 18b rose 225.00 30.00
Nos. 33-36 (4) 365.00 157.50

Prince Carol — A9

1869

37 A9 5b orange yel 72.50 42.50
a. 5b deep orange 75.00 *42.50*
38 A9 10b blue 40.00 35.00
a. 10b ultramarine 77.50 52.50
b. 10b indigo 85.00 40.00
40 A9 15b vermilion 40.00 35.00
41 A9 25b orange & blue 40.00 26.50
42 A9 50b blue & red 150.00 52.50
a. 50b indigo & red 175.00 55.00
Nos. 37-42 (5) 342.50 191.50

No. 40 on vertically laid paper was not issued. Value $1,250.

Prince Carol — A10

1871-72 ***Imperf.***

43 A10 5b rose 42.50 35.00
a. 5b vermilion 45.00 45.00
44 A10 10b orange yel 55.00 35.00
a. Vertically laid paper *450.00 450.00*
45 A10 10b blue 125.00 70.00
46 A10 15b red 210.00 210.00
47 A10 25b olive brown 47.50 47.50
Nos. 43-47 (5) 480.00 397.50

1872

48 A10 10b ultra 42.50 52.50
a. Vertically laid paper 175.00 300.00
b. 10b greenish blue 150.00 175.00
49 A10 50b blue & red 225.00 240.00

No. 48 is a provisional issue printed from a new plate in which the head is placed further right.

Faked cancellations are found on No. 49.

1872 **Wove Paper** ***Perf. 12½***

50 A10 5b rose 65.00 52.50
a. 5b vermilion *1,300. 700.00*
51 A10 10b blue 57.50 52.50
a. 10b ultramarine 60.00 25.00
52 A10 25b dark brown 47.50 47.50
Nos. 50-52 (3) 170.00 152.50

No. 43a with faked perforation is frequently offered as No. 50a.

Prince Carol — A11

Paris Print, Fine Impression
Tinted Paper

1872 **Typo.** ***Perf. 14x13½***

53 A11 1½b brnz grn, *bluish* 25.00 5.00
54 A11 3b green, *bluish* 32.50 5.00
55 A11 5b bis, *pale buff* 21.00 4.50
56 A11 10b blue 21.00 5.00
57 A11 15b red brn, *pale buff* 140.00 15.00
58 A11 25b org, *pale buff* 145.00 18.50
59 A11 50b rose, *pale rose* 150.00 42.50
Nos. 53-59 (7) 534.50 95.50

Nos. 53-59 exist imperf.

Bucharest Print, Rough Impression

Perf. 11, 11½, 13½, and Compound

1876-79

60 A11 1½b brnz grn, *bluish* 6.50 4.25
61 A11 5b bis, *yelsh* 17.00 3.25
b. Printed on both sides *75.00*
62 A11 10b bl, *yelsh* ('77) 27.50 5.00
a. 10b pale bl, *yelsh* 25.00 5.00
b. 10b dark blue, *yelsh* 42.50 5.00
d. Cliché of 5b in plate of 10b ('79) 425.00 425.00
63 A11 10b ultra, *yelsh* ('77) 47.50 5.00
64 A11 15b red brn, *yelsh* 72.50 9.25
a. Printed on both sides *100.00*
65 A11 30b org red, *yelsh* ('78) 190.00 50.00
a. Printed on both sides *210.00*
Nos. 60-65 (6) 361.00 76.75

#60-65 are valued in the grade of fine.

#62d has been reprinted in dark blue. The originals are in dull blue. Value of reprint, $175.

Perf. 11, 11½, 13½ and Compound

1879

66 A11 1½b blk, *yelsh* 6.25 4.25
b. Imperf. 12.00
67 A11 3b ol grn, *bluish* 17.50 12.50
a. Diagonal half used as 1½b on cover
68 A11 5b green, *bluish* 6.75 4.25
69 A11 10b rose, *yelsh* 13.50 2.50
b. Clichê of 5b in plate of 10b 3.75.00 *475.00*
70 A11 15b rose red, *yelsh* 50.00 12.50
71 A11 25b blue, *yelsh* 140.00 25.00
72 A11 50b bister, *yelsh* 120.00 35.00
Nos. 66-72 (7) 354.00 96.00

#66-72 are valued in the grade of fine.

There are two varieties of the numerals on the 15b and 50b.

No. 69b has been reprinted in dark rose. Originals are in pale rose. Value of reprint, $40.

King Carol I — A12

1880 **White Paper**

73 A12 15b brown 12.50 2.50
74 A12 25b blue 23.50 3.25

#73-74 are valued in the grade of fine.
No. 74 exists imperf.

King Carol I — A13

Perf. 13½, 11½ & Compound

1885-89

75 A13 1½b black 3.50 1.75
a. Printed on both sides
76 A13 3b violet 5.00 1.75
a. Half used as 1½b on cover 21.00
77 A13 5b green 75.00 1.75
78 A13 15b red brown 14.50 2.50
79 A13 25b blue 17.00 6.00
Nos. 75-79 (5) 115.00 13.75

Tinted Paper

80 A13 1½b blk, *bluish* 5.00 1.75
81 A13 3b vio, *bluish* 5.00 1.75
82 A13 3b ol grn, *bluish* 5.00 1.75
83 A13 5b bl grn, *bluish* 5.00 1.75
84 A13 10b rose, *pale buff* 5.00 2.50
85 A13 15b red brn, *pale buff* 18.50 2.75
86 A13 25b bl, *pale buff* 18.50 6.00
87 A13 50b bis, *pale buff* 75.00 21.00
Nos. 80-87 (8) 137.00 39.25

Thin Pale Yellowish Paper

1889 **Wmk. 163**

88 A13 1½b black 30.00 6.00
89 A13 3b violet 21.00 6.00
90 A13 5b green 21.00 6.00
91 A13 10b rose 21.00 6.00
92 A13 15b red brown 72.50 13.00
93 A13 25b dark blue 47.50 10.00
Nos. 88-93 (6) 213.00 47.00

King Carol I — A14

1890 ***Perf. 13½, 11½ & Compound***

94 A14 1½b maroon 5.00 3.50
95 A14 3b violet 25.00 3.50
96 A14 5b emerald 12.00 3.50
97 A14 10b red 13.00 5.00
a. 10b rose 17.00 6.75
98 A14 15b dk brown 30.00 3.50
99 A14 25b gray blue 25.00 3.50
100 A14 50b orange 65.00 32.50
Nos. 94-100 (7) 175.00 55.00

1891 **Unwmk.**

101 A14 1½b lilac rose 1.75 1.25
b. Printed on both sides *65.00*
102 A14 3b lilac 2.00 1.75
a. 3b violet 2.25 2.25
b. Printed on both sides
c. Impressions of 5b on back *100.00 75.00*
103 A14 5b emerald 3.50 1.75
104 A14 10b pale red 21.00 1.75
a. Printed on both sides *140.00 110.00*
105 A14 15b gray brown 13.00 1.25
106 A14 25b gray blue 13.00 1.75
107 A14 50b orange 85.00 13.00
Nos. 101-107 (7) 139.25 22.50

Nos. 101-107 exist imperf.

King Carol I — A15

1891

108 A15 1½b claret 6.00 7.00
109 A15 3b lilac 6.00 7.00
110 A15 5b emerald 7.50 8.50
111 A15 10b red 7.50 8.50
112 A15 15b gray brown 7.50 8.50
Nos. 108-112 (5) 34.50 39.50

25th year of the reign of King Carol I.

1894 **Wmk. 164**

113 A14 3b lilac 9.25 5.00
114 A14 5b pale green 9.25 5.00
115 A14 25b gray blue 13.50 6.25
116 A14 50b orange 27.50 12.50
Nos. 113-116 (4) 59.50 28.75

King Carol I
A17 A18

A19 A20

A21 A23

1893-98 **Wmk. 164 & 200**

117 A17 1b pale brown 1.25 1.25
118 A17 1½b black .85 1.25
119 A18 3b chocolate 1.25 .85
120 A19 5b blue 1.75 .85
a. Cliché of the 25b in the plate of 5b 185.00 *200.00*
121 A19 5b yel grn ('98) 5.00 3.00
a. 5b emerald 5.00 3.00
122 A20 10b emerald 2.50 1.75
123 A20 10b rose ('98) 6.00 2.50
124 A21 15b rose 2.50 .85
125 A21 15b black ('98) 6.00 2.00
126 A19 25b violet 3.75 1.25
127 A19 25b indigo ('98) 9.25 3.25
128 A19 40b gray grn 21.00 3.50
129 A19 50b orange 12.50 2.00
130 A23 1 l bis & rose 30.00 2.00
131 A23 2 l orange & brn 35.00 3.25
Nos. 117-131 (15) 138.60 29.55

This watermark may be found in four versions (Wmks. 164, 200 and variations). The paper also varies in thickness.

A 3b orange of type A18; 10b brown, type A20; 15b rose, type A21, and 25b bright green with similar but different border, all watermarked "P R," were prepared but never issued. Value, each $15.

See Nos. 132-157, 224-229. For overprints and surcharges see Romanian Post Offices in the Turkish Empire Nos. 1-6, 10-11.

King Carol I — A24

Thin Paper, Tinted Rose on Back

Perf. 11½, 13½ and Compound

1900-03 **Unwmk.**

132 A17 1b pale brown 1.75 1.75
133 A24 1b brown ('01) 1.75 1.25
134 A24 1b black ('03) 1.75 1.25
135 A18 3b red brown 1.75 .85
136 A19 5b emerald 2.50 .85
137 A20 10b rose 3.00 1.25
138 A21 15b black 2.50 .85
139 A21 15b lil gray ('01) 2.50 .85
140 A21 15b dk vio ('03) 2.50 1.25
141 A19 25b blue 4.25 1.75
142 A19 40b gray grn 8.50 1.75
143 A19 50b orange 17.00 1.75
144 A23 1 l bis & rose ('01) 34.00 3.00
145 A23 1 l grn & blk ('03) 30.00 3.50
146 A23 2 l org & brn ('01) 30.00 3.50
147 A23 2 l red brn & blk ('03) 25.00 4.25
Nos. 132-147 (16) 168.75 29.65

#132 inscribed BANI; #133-134 BAN.

1900, July **Wmk. 167**

148 A17 1b pale brown 12.00 5.00
149 A18 3b red brown 12.00 5.50
150 A19 5b emerald 10.00 5.00
151 A20 10b rose 15.00 6.00
152 A21 15b black 17.00 7.25
153 A19 25b blue 19.00 12.50
154 A19 40b gray grn 30.00 12.50
155 A19 50b orange 30.00 12.50
156 A23 1 l bis & rose 34.00 17.00
157 A23 2 l orange & brn 42.50 21.00
Nos. 148-157 (10) 221.50 104.25

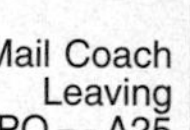

Mail Coach Leaving PO — A25

Thin Paper, Tinted Rose on Face

1903 **Unwmk.** ***Perf. 14x13½***

158 A25 1b gray brown *2.25* 1.60
159 A25 3b brown violet *3.75* 1.60
160 A25 5b pale green *7.50* 2.50
161 A25 10b rose *4.50* 2.50
162 A25 15b black *4.50* 3.25
163 A25 25b blue *22.50* 9.50
164 A25 40b dull green *32.50* 12.50
165 A25 50b orange *37.50* 16.00
Nos. 158-165 (8) *115.00* 49.45

Counterfeits are plentiful. See note after No. 172. See No. 428.

King Carol I and Façade of New Post Office — A26

Thick Toned Paper

1903 **Engr.** ***Perf. 13½x14***

166 A26 15b black 5.00 3.75
167 A26 25b blue 11.00 6.50
168 A26 40b gray grn 19.00 9.00
169 A26 50b orange 21.00 11.00
170 A26 1 l dk brown 16.00 9.00

171	A26	2 l dull red	130.00	65.00
a.		2 l orange (error)	180.00	150.00
172	A26	5 l dull violet	160.00	110.00
a.		5 l red violet	80.00	32.50
		Nos. 166-172 (7)	362.00	214.25

Opening of the new PO in Bucharest (Nos. 158-172).

Counterfeits exist.

Prince Carol Taking Oath of Allegiance, 1866 — A27

Prince in Royal Carriage A28

Prince Carol at Calafat in 1877 — A29

Prince Carol Shaking Hands with His Captive, Osman Pasha — A30

Carol I as Prince in 1866 and King in 1906 — A31

Romanian Army Crossing Danube A32

Romanian Troops Return to Bucharest in 1878 — A33

Prince Carol at Head of His Command in 1877 — A34

King Carol I at the Cathedral in 1896 — A35

King Carol I at Shrine of St. Nicholas, 1904 — A36

1906 Engr. *Perf. 12*

176	A27	1b bister & blk	.65	.45
177	A28	3b red brn & blk	1.40	.45
178	A29	5b dp grn & blk	1.75	.45
179	A30	10b carmine & blk	1.10	.45
180	A31	15b dull vio & blk	1.10	.45
181	A32	25b ultra & blk	7.00	5.25
a.		25b olive green & black	9.00	5.25
182	A33	40b dk brn & blk	1.90	1.60
183	A34	50b bis brn & blk	2.00	1.60
184	A35	1 l vermilion & blk	2.25	1.90
185	A36	2 l orange & blk	2.50	2.40
		Nos. 176-185 (10)	21.65	15.00

40 years' rule of Carol I as Prince & King.

No. 181a was never placed in use. Cancellations were by favor.

King Carol I — A37

1906

186	A37	1b bister & blk	.90	.45
187	A37	3b red brn & blk	2.25	.85
188	A37	5b dp grn & blk	1.50	.75
189	A37	10b carmine & blk	1.50	.75
190	A37	15b dl vio & blk	1.50	.75
191	A37	25b ultra & blk	13.50	7.00
192	A37	40b dk brn & blk	6.00	1.50
193	A37	50b bis brn & blk	6.00	1.50
194	A37	1 l red & blk	6.00	1.50
195	A37	2 l orange & blk	6.00	1.50
		Nos. 186-195 (10)	45.15	16.55

25th anniversary of the Kingdom.

Plowman and Angel — A38

Exposition Building — A39

Exposition Buildings
A40 A41

King Carol I — A42

Queen Elizabeth (Carmen Sylva) — A43

1906 Typo. *Perf. 11½, 13½*

196	A38	5b yel grn & blk	4.50	1.40
197	A38	10b car & blk	4.50	1.40
198	A39	15b violet & blk	6.50	2.25
199	A39	25b blue & blk	6.50	2.25
200	A40	30b red & blk brn	8.75	2.25
201	A40	40b grn & blk brn	9.50	2.75
202	A41	50b orange & blk	8.75	3.25
203	A41	75b lt brn & dk brn	7.75	3.25
204	A42	1.50 l red lil & blk brn	97.50	45.00
a.		Center inverted		
205	A42	2.50 l yellow & brn	37.50	26.00
a.		Center inverted		
206	A43	3 l brn org & brn	28.00	26.00
		Nos. 196-206 (11)	219.75	115.80

General Exposition. They were sold at post offices July 29-31, 1906, and were valid only for those three days. Those sold at the exposition are overprinted "S E" in black. Remainders were sold privately, both unused and canceled to order, by the Exposition promoters. Value, set: unused or used, $450.

A44 A45

Perf. 11½, 13½ & Compound

1908-18 Engr.

207	A44	5b pale yel grn	2.50	.25
208	A44	10b carmine	.70	.25
209	A45	15b purple	11.50	2.25
210	A44	25b deep blue	1.75	.25
211	A44	40b brt green	.85	.25
212	A44	40b dk brn ('18)	5.25	2.25
213	A44	50b orange	.65	.25
214	A44	50b lt red ('18)	2.00	.70
215	A44	1 l brown	2.00	.40
216	A44	2 l red	10.00	2.50
		Nos. 207-216 (10)	37.20	9.35

King Carol I — A46

Perf. 13½x14, 11½, 13½ & Compound

1909-18 Typo.

217	A46	1b black	.60	.25
218	A46	3b red brown	1.25	.25
219	A46	5b yellow grn	.60	.25
220	A46	10b rose	1.25	.25
221	A46	15b dull violet	21.00	12.50
222	A46	15b olive green	1.25	.25
223	A46	15b red brn ('18)	1.10	.65
		Nos. 217-223 (7)	27.05	14.40

Nos. 217-219, 222 exist imperf.

No. 219 in black is a chemical changeling.

For surcharge and overprints see Nos. 240-242, 245-247, J50-J51, RA1-RA2, RA11-RA12, Romanian Post Offices in the Turkish Empire 7-9.

Types of 1893-99

1911-19 White Paper Unwmk.

224	A17	1½b straw	1.75	.45
225	A19	25b deep blue ('18)	1.00	.85
226	A19	40b gray brn ('19)	1.25	.85
227	A19	50b dull red ('19)	1.75	.85
228	A23	1 l gray grn ('18)	2.25	.50
229	A23	2 l orange ('18)	2.25	.85
		Nos. 224-229 (6)	10.25	4.35

For overprints see Romanian Post Offices in the Turkish Empire Nos. 10-11.

Romania Holding Flag — A47

Romanian Crown and Old Fort on Danube — A48

Troops Crossing Danube — A49

View of Turtucaia — A50

Mircea the Great and Carol I — A51

View of Silistra — A52

Perf. 11½x13½, 13½x11½

1913, Dec. 25

230	A47	1b black	.85	.40
231	A48	3b ol gray & choc	2.25	.85
232	A49	5b yel grn & blk brn	1.75	.40
233	A50	10b org & gray	.85	.40
234	A51	15b bister & vio	2.25	.85
235	A52	25b blue & choc	3.00	1.25
236	A49	40b bis & red vio	6.00	4.75
237	A48	50b yellow & bl	16.00	6.50
238	A48	1 l bl & ol bis	25.00	14.50
239	A48	2 l org red & rose	40.00	20.00
		Nos. 230-239 (10)	97.95	49.90

Romania's annexation of Silistra.

No. 217 Handstamped in Red

Perf. 13½x14, 11½, 13½ & Compound

1918, May 1

240	A46	25b on 1b black	2.25	2.25

This handstamp is found inverted.

No. 219 and 220 Overprinted in Black

1918

241	A46	5b yellow green	.60	.55
a.		Inverted overprint	3.25	3.25
b.		Double overprint	3.25	3.25
242	A46	10b rose	.60	.55
a.		Inverted overprint	3.25	3.25
b.		Double overprint	3.25	3.25

Nos. 217, 219 and 220 Overprinted in Red or Black

1919, Nov. 8

245	A46	1b black (R)	.40	.25
a.		Inverted overprint	6.75	
b.		Double overprint	10.00	2.25
246	A46	5b yel grn (Bk)	.40	.25
a.		Double overprint	10.00	3.25
b.		Inverted overprint	6.75	2.00
247	A46	10b rose (Bk)	.40	.25
a.		Inverted overprint	6.75	2.00
b.		Double overprint	10.00	3.00
		Nos. 245-247 (3)	1.20	.75

Recovery of Transylvania and the return of the King to Bucharest.

King Ferdinand — A53

1920-22 **Typo.**

248	A53	1b black	.25	.25
249	A53	5b yellow grn	.25	.25
250	A53	10b rose	.25	.25
251	A53	15b red brown	.75	.25
252	A53	25b deep blue	1.50	.40
253	A53	25b brown	.75	.25
254	A53	40b gray brown	1.25	.35
255	A53	50b salmon	.35	.25
256	A53	1 l gray grn	1.25	.25
257	A53	1 l rose	.75	.25
258	A53	2 l orange	1.25	.25
259	A53	2 l dp blue	1.25	.25
260	A53	2 l rose ('22)	3.00	1.75
		Nos. 248-260 (13)	12.85	5.00

Nos. 248-260 are printed on two papers: coarse, grayish paper with bits of colored fiber, and thinner white paper of better quality.

Nos. 248-251, 253 exist imperf.

King Ferdinand — A54

Type I Type II Type III

Type I Type II Type I Type II

TWO LEI:

Type I — The "2" is thin, with tail 2½mm wide. Top of "2" forms a hook.

Type II — The "2" is thick, with tail 3mm wide. Top of "2" forms a ball.

Type III — The "2" is similar to type II. The "E" of "LEI" is larger and about 2mm wide.

THREE LEI:

Type I — Top of "3" begins in a point. Top and middle bars of "E" of "LEI" are without serifs.

Type II — Top of "3" begins in a ball. Top and middle bars of "E" of "LEI" have serifs.

FIVE LEI:

Type I — The "5" is 2½mm wide. The end of the final stroke of the "L" of "LEI" almost touches the vertical stroke.

Type II — The "5" is 3mm wide and the lines are broader than in type I. The end of the final stroke of the "L" of "LEI" is separated from the vertical by a narrow space.

Perf. 13½x14, 11½, 13½ & Compound

1920-26

261	A54	3b black	.25	.25
262	A54	5b black	.25	.25
263	A54	10b yel grn ('25)	.25	.25
a.		10b olive green ('25)	.40	
264	A54	25b bister brn	.25	.25
265	A54	25b salmon	.25	.25
266	A54	30b violet	.25	.25
267	A54	50b orange	.25	.25
268	A54	60b gray grn	1.00	.55
269	A54	1 l violet	.25	.25
270	A54	2 l rose (I)	1.25	.25
a.		2 l claret (I)	*47.50*	
271	A54	2 l lt green (II)	.70	.25
a.		2 l light green (I)	.95	.40
b.		2 l light green (III)	.80	.25
272	A54	3 l blue (I)	2.60	.80
273	A54	3 l buff (II)	2.60	.80
a.		3 l buff (I)	*12.50*	2.25
274	A54	3 l salmon (II)	.25	.25
a.		3 l salmon (I)	1.60	1.25
275	A54	3 l car rose (II)	.65	.25
276	A54	5 l emer (I)	2.10	.50
277	A54	5 l lt brn (II)	.45	.25
a.		5 l light brown (I)	1.60	.80
278	A54	6 l blue	2.60	1.25
279	A54	6 l carmine	5.75	3.25
280	A54	6 l ol grn ('26)	2.50	.80
281	A54	7½ l pale bl	2.10	.45
282	A54	10 l deep blue	2.10	.45
		Nos. 261-282 (22)	28.65	12.10

#273 and 273a, 274 and 274a, exist se-tenant. The 50b exists in three types.

For surcharge see No. Q7.

Alba Iulia Cathedral A55

King Ferdinand A56

Coat of Arms — A57

Queen Marie as Nurse — A58

Michael the Brave and King Ferdinand A59

King Ferdinand A60

Queen Marie — A61

Perf. 13½x14, 13½, 11½ & Compound

1922, Oct. 15 **Photo.** **Wmk. 95**

283	A55	5b black	.40	.30
284	A56	25b chocolate	1.25	.40
285	A57	50b dp green	1.25	.60
286	A58	1 l olive grn	1.50	.85
287	A59	2 l carmine	1.50	.85
288	A60	3 l blue	4.00	1.25
289	A61	6 l violet	11.50	8.00
		Nos. 283-289 (7)	21.40	12.25

Coronation of King Ferdinand I and Queen Marie on Oct. 15, 1922, at Alba Iulia. All values exist imperforate. Value, set $150, unused or used.

King Ferdinand
A62 A63

1926, July 1 **Unwmk.** ***Perf. 11***

291	A62	10b yellow grn	.35	.25
292	A62	25b orange	.35	.25
293	A62	50b orange brn	.35	.25
294	A63	1 l dk violet	.50	.25
295	A63	2 l dk green	.50	.25
296	A63	3 l brown car	.50	.50
297	A63	5 l black brn	.50	.50
298	A63	6 l dk olive	.50	.50
a.		6 l bright blue (error)	150.00	175.00
300	A63	9 l slate	.75	.50
301	A63	10 l brt blue	.75	.50
b.		10 l brown carmine (error)	150.00	175.00
		Nos. 291-301 (10)	5.05	3.75

60th birthday of King Ferdinand.

Exist imperf. Value, set unused $150; used $175. Imperf. examples with watermark 95 are proofs.

King Carol I and King Ferdinand A69

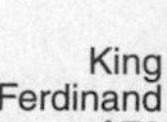

King Ferdinand A70

A71

1927, Aug. 1 ***Perf. 13½***

308	A69	25b brown vio	.50	.35
309	A70	30b gray blk	.50	.35
310	A71	50b dk green	.50	.35
311	A69	1 l bluish slate	.50	.35
312	A70	2 l dp green	.50	.45
313	A70	3 l violet	.50	.55
314	A71	4 l dk brown	.50	.65
315	A71	4.50 l henna brn	3.00	2.25
316	A70	5 l red brown	.50	.55
317	A71	6 l carmine	2.00	1.25
318	A69	7.50 l grnsh bl	.50	.55
319	A69	10 l brt blue	3.00	1.10
		Nos. 308-319 (12)	12.50	8.75

50th anniversary of Romania's independence from Turkish suzerainty.

Some values exist imperf. All exist imperf. and with value numerals omitted.

King Michael
A72 A73

Perf. 13½x14 (25b, 50b); 13½

1928-29 **Typo.** **Unwmk.**

Size: 19x25mm

320	A72	25b black	.25	.25
321	A72	30b fawn ('29)	.40	.25
322	A72	50b olive grn	.25	.25

Photo.

Size: 18½x24½mm

323	A73	1 l violet	.45	.25
324	A73	2 l dp green	.45	.25
325	A73	3 l brt rose	.90	.25
326	A73	5 l red brown	1.40	.25
327	A73	7.50 l ultra	6.25	.90
328	A73	10 l blue	5.25	.35
		Nos. 320-328 (9)	15.60	3.00

See Nos. 343-345, 353-357. For overprints see Nos. 359-368A.

Parliament House, Bessarabia — A74

Designs: 1 l, 2 l, Parliament House, Bessarabia. 3 l, 5 l, 20 l, Hotin Fortress. 7.50 l, 10 l, Fortress Cetatea Alba.

1928, Apr. 29 **Wmk. 95** ***Perf. 13½***

329	A74	1 l deep green	1.75	.65
330	A74	2 l deep brown	1.75	.65
331	A74	3 l black brown	1.75	.65
332	A74	5 l carmine lake	2.25	.80
333	A74	7.50 l ultra	2.25	.80
334	A74	10 l Prus blue	5.00	2.00
335	A74	20 l black vio	8.00	2.75
		Nos. 329-335 (7)	22.75	8.30

Reunion of Bessarabia with Romania, 10th anniv.

King Carol I and King Michael A77

View of Constanta Harbor A78

Trajan's Monument at Adam Clisi A79

Cernavoda Bridge — A80

1928, Oct. 25

336	A77	1 l blue green	1.10	.45
337	A78	2 l red brown	1.10	.45
338	A77	3 l gray black	1.40	.50
339	A79	5 l dull lilac	1.75	.60
340	A79	7.50 l ultra	2.10	.80
341	A80	10 l blue	3.25	1.90
342	A80	20 l carmine rose	5.50	3.25
		Nos. 336-342 (7)	16.20	7.95

Union of Dobruja with Romania, 50th anniv.

Michael Types of 1928-29

Perf. 13½x14

1928, Sept. 1 **Typo.** **Wmk. 95**

343	A72	25b black	.60	.25

Photo.

344	A73	7.50 l ultra	2.00	.75
345	A73	10 l blue	4.00	.60
		Nos. 343-345 (3)	6.60	1.60

Ferdinand I; Stephen the Great; Michael the Brave; Corvin and Constantine Brancoveanu — A81

Union with Transylvania A82

Avram Jancu — A83

Prince Michael the Brave — A84

Castle Bran — A85

King Ferdinand I — A86

1929, May 10 Photo. Wmk. 95

347	A81	1 l dark violet	2.25	1.75
348	A82	2 l olive green	2.25	1.75
349	A83	3 l violet brown	2.50	1.75
350	A84	4 l cerise	2.75	2.25
351	A85	5 l orange	4.00	2.25
352	A86	10 l brt blue	7.50	4.25
		Nos. 347-352 (6)	21.75	14.00

Union of Transylvania and Romania.

Michael Type of 1928

1930 Unwmk. *Perf. 14½x14*

Size: 18x23mm

353	A73	1 l deep violet	.80	.25
354	A73	2 l deep green	1.25	.25
355	A73	3 l carmine rose	2.40	.25
356	A73	7.50 l ultra	5.00	1.10
357	A73	10 l deep blue	16.00	7.00
		Nos. 353-357 (5)	25.45	8.85

Stamps of 1928-30 Overprinted

On Nos. 320-322, 326, 328

Perf. 13½x14, 13½

1930, June 8 Typo.

359	A72	25b black	.40	.25
360	A72	30b fawn	.80	.25
361	A72	50b olive green	.80	.25

Photo.

Size: 18½x24½mm

362	A73	5 l red brown	1.60	.25
362A	A73	10 l brt blue	8.25	1.50

On Nos. 353-357

Perf. 14½x14

Size: 18x23mm

363	A73	1 l deep violet	.80	.25
364	A73	2 l deep green	.80	.25
365	A73	3 l carmine rose	1.60	.25
366	A73	7.50 l ultra	4.00	.75
367	A73	10 l deep blue	3.25	.75

On Nos. 343-344

Perf. 13½x14, 13½

Typo. Wmk. 95

368	A72	25b black	1.25	.35

Photo.

Size: 18½x24½mm

368A	A73	7.50 l ultra	5.00	1.50
		Nos. 359-368A (12)	28.55	6.60

Accession to the throne by King Carol II. This overprint exists on Nos. 323, 345.

A87

A88

King Carol II — A89

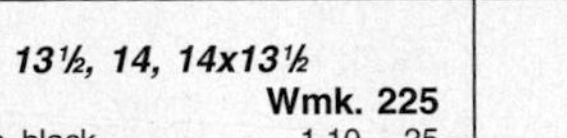

Perf. 13½, 14, 14x13½

1930 Wmk. 225

369	A87	25b black	1.10	.25
370	A87	50b chocolate	3.25	.45
371	A87	1 l dk violet	2.25	.25
372	A87	2 l gray green	2.75	.25
373	A88	3 l carmine rose	2.25	.25
374	A88	4 l orange red	3.25	.25
375	A88	6 l carmine brn	4.25	.25
376	A88	7.50 l ultra	4.25	.30
377	A89	10 l deep blue	2.25	.25
378	A89	16 l peacock grn	4.75	.25
379	A89	20 l orange	1.40	.60
		Nos. 369-379 (11)	31.75	3.35

Exist imperf. Value, unused or used, $250.

See Nos. 405-414.

A90

A91

1930, Dec. 24 Unwmk. *Perf. 13½*

380	A90	1 l dull violet	1.25	.45
381	A91	2 l green	2.25	.50
382	A91	4 l vermilion	2.50	.35
383	A91	6 l brown carmine	6.50	.45
		Nos. 380-383 (4)	12.50	1.75

First census in Romania.

King Carol II — A92

King Carol I — A93

King Ferdinand — A96

King Carol II — A94

King Carol II, King Ferdinand and King Carol I — A95

1931, May 10 Photo. Wmk. 225

384	A92	1 l gray violet	2.50	1.75
385	A93	2 l green	4.25	2.00
386	A94	6 l red brown	11.00	3.25
387	A95	10 l blue	16.00	6.00
388	A96	20 l orange	22.50	8.50
		Nos. 384-388 (5)	56.25	21.50

50th anniversary of Romanian Kingdom.

Using Bayonet — A97

Romanian Infantryman 1870 — A98

Romanian Infantry 1830 — A99

King Carol I A100

Infantry Advance A101

King Ferdinand A102

King Carol II A103

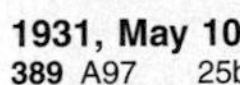

1931, May 10

389	A97	25b gray black	1.40	.75
390	A98	50b dk red brn	2.10	1.10
391	A99	1 l gray violet	2.75	1.10
392	A100	2 l deep green	4.25	1.50
393	A101	3 l carmine rose	10.00	3.50
394	A102	7.50 l ultra	13.00	9.00
395	A103	16 l blue green	16.00	4.00
		Nos. 389-395 (7)	49.50	20.95

Centenary of the Romanian Army.

Naval Cadet Ship "Mircea" A104

10 l, Ironclad. 16 l, Light cruiser. 20 l, Destroyer.

1931, May 10

396	A104	6 l red brown	7.00	4.00
397	A104	10 l blue	9.50	4.50
398	A104	16 l blue green	40.00	6.00
399	A104	20 l orange	17.50	10.00
		Nos. 396-399 (4)	74.00	24.50

50th anniversary of the Romanian Navy.

King Carol II — A108

1931 Unwmk. Engr. *Perf. 12*

400	A108	30 l ol bis & dk bl	1.75	1.00
401	A108	50 l red & dk bl	4.50	1.50
402	A108	100 l dk grn & dk bl	7.25	3.50
		Nos. 400-402 (3)	13.50	6.00

Exist imperf. Value, unused or used, $150.

Carol II, Ferdinand, Carol I — A109

Wmk. 230

1931, Nov. 1 Photo. *Perf. 13½*

403	A109	16 l Prus green	12.00	.90

Exists imperf. Value, unused or used, $300.

Carol II Types of 1930

Perf. 13½, 14, 14½ and Compound

1932 Wmk. 230

405	A87	25b black	.50	.25
406	A87	50b dark brown	1.00	.25
407	A87	1 l dark violet	1.40	.25
408	A87	2 l gray green	1.75	.25
409	A88	3 l carmine rose	2.25	.25
410	A88	4 l orange red	5.25	.25
411	A88	6 l carmine brn	12.50	.25
412	A88	7.50 l ultra	21.50	.75
413	A89	10 l deep blue	125.00	.90
414	A89	20 l orange	110.00	9.00
		Nos. 405-414 (10)	281.15	12.40

Alexander the Good — A110

1932, May *Perf. 13½*

415	A110	6 l carmine brown	12.00	6.00

500th death anniv. of Alexander the Good, Prince of Moldavia, 1400-1432.

King Carol II — A111

1932, June

416	A111	10 l brt blue	12.00	.45

Exists imperf. Value, unused or used, $200.

Cantacuzino and Gregory Ghika, Founders of Coltea and Pantelimon Hospitals — A112

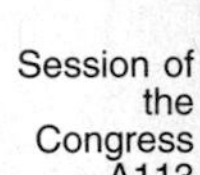

Session of the Congress A113

Aesculapius and Hygeia — A114

1932, Sept. *Perf. 13½*

417	A112	1 l carmine rose	7.50	7.50
418	A113	6 l deep orange	20.00	11.00
419	A114	10 l brt blue	34.00	18.50
		Nos. 417-419 (3)	61.50	37.00

9th Intl. History of Medicine Congress, Bucharest.

Bull's Head and Post Horn A116

Lion Rampant and Bridge A117

Dolphins A118

Eagle and Castles A119

Coat of Arms — A120

Eagle and Post Horn — A121

Bull's Head and Post Horn — A122

1932, Nov. 20 Typo. *Imperf.*

421	A116	25b black	.85	.40
422	A117	1 l violet	2.00	.70
423	A118	2 l green	2.50	.90
424	A119	3 l car rose	2.80	1.10
425	A120	6 l red brown	3.50	1.25
426	A121	7.50 l lt blue	4.25	1.75
427	A122	10 l dk blue	8.00	3.00
		Nos. 421-427 (7)	23.90	9.10

75th anniv. of the first Moldavian stamps.

Mail Coach Type of 1903

1932, Nov. 20 *Perf. 13½*

428	A25	16 l blue green	11.00	5.50

30th anniv. of the opening of the new post office, Bucharest, in 1903.

Arms of City of Turnu-Severin, Ruins of Tower of Emperor Severus — A123

Inauguration of Trajan's Bridge — A124

Prince Carol Landing at Turnu-Severin — A125

Bridge over the Danube A126

1933, June 2 Photo. *Perf. 14½x14*

429	A123	25b gray green	.75	.30
430	A124	50b dull blue	1.10	.45
431	A125	1 l black brn	1.75	.75
432	A126	2 l olive blk	3.25	1.10
		Nos. 429-432 (4)	6.85	2.60

Centenary of the incorporation in Walachia of the old Roman City of Turnu-Severin. Exist imperf. Value, unused or used, $150.

Queen Elizabeth and King Carol I — A127

Profiles of Kings Carol I, Ferdinand and Carol II — A128

Castle Peles, Sinaia A129

1933, Aug.

433	A127	1 l dark violet	2.50	2.00
434	A128	3 l olive brown	3.00	2.75
435	A129	6 l vermilion	4.25	3.25
		Nos. 433-435 (3)	9.75	8.00

50th anniversary of the erection of Castle Peles, the royal summer residence at Sinaia. Exist imperf. Value, unused or used, $125.

A130 A131

King Carol II — A132

1934, Aug. *Perf. 13½*

436	A130	50b brown	1.00	.40
437	A131	2 l gray green	2.00	.40
438	A131	4 l red	3.50	.55
439	A132	6 l deep claret	8.00	.40
		Nos. 436-439 (4)	14.50	1.75

See Nos. 446-460 for stamps inscribed "Posta." Nos. 436, 439 exist imperf. Value for both, unused or used, $100.

Child and Grapes — A133

Woman and Fruit — A134

1934, Sept. 14

440	A133	1 l dull green	5.00	2.25
441	A134	2 l violet brown	5.00	2.25

Natl. Fruit Week, Sept. 14-21. Exist imperf. Value, unused or used, $125.

Crisan, Horia and Closca A135

1935, Feb. 28

442	A135	1 l shown	.65	.50
443	A135	2 l Crisan	.90	.60
444	A135	6 l Closca	2.25	1.00
445	A135	10 l Horia	5.00	2.25
		Nos. 442-445 (4)	8.80	4.35

150th anniversary of the death of three Romanian martyrs. Exist imperf. Value, unused or used, $110.

A139

A140

A141 A142

King Carol II — A143

Wmk. 230

1935-40 Photo. *Perf. 13½*

446	A139	25b black brn	.25	.25
447	A142	50b brown	.25	.25
448	A140	1 l purple	.25	.25
449	A141	2 l green	.45	.25
449A	A141	2 l dk bl grn ('40)	.65	.25
450	A142	3 l deep rose	.70	.25
450A	A142	3 l grnsh bl ('40)	.85	.30
451	A141	4 l vermilion	1.25	.25
452	A140	5 l rose car ('40)	1.25	.80
453	A143	6 l maroon	1.60	.25
454	A140	7.50 l ultra	1.90	.30
454A	A142	8 l magenta ('40)	1.90	.70
455	A141	9 l brt ultra ('40)	2.50	.80
456	A142	10 l brt blue	1.00	.25
456A	A143	12 l slate bl ('40)	1.60	1.25
457	A139	15 l dk brn ('40)	1.60	.95
458	A143	16 l Prus blue	2.10	.25
459	A143	20 l orange	1.25	.35
460	A143	24 l dk car ('40)	2.10	.95
		Nos. 446-460 (19)	23.45	8.90

Exist imperf. Value, unused or used, $240.

Nos. 454, 456 Overprinted in Red

1936, Dec. 5

461	A140	7.50 l ultra	9.25	6.50
462	A142	10 l brt blue	9.25	6.50

16th anniversary of the Little Entente. Overprints in silver or gold are fraudulent.

Birthplace of Ion Creanga A144

Ion Creanga A145

1937, May 15

463	A144	2 l green	1.25	.80
464	A145	3 l carmine rose	1.75	.90
465	A144	4 l dp violet	2.00	1.10
466	A145	6 l red brown	5.00	2.50
		Nos. 463-466 (4)	10.00	5.30

Creanga (1837-89), writer. Exist imperf. Value, unused or used, $125.

Cathedral at Curtea de Arges — A146

1937, July 1

467	A146	7.50 l ultra	2.50	1.10
468	A146	10 l blue	3.25	.80

The Little Entente (Romania, Czechoslovakia, Yugoslavia). Exist imperf. Value, unused or used, $125.

Souvenir Sheet

A146a

Surcharged in Black with New Values

1937, Oct. 25 Unwmk. *Perf. 13½*

469	A146a	Sheet of 4	9.00	9.00
a.		2 l on 20 l orange	.35	.35
b.		6 l on 10 l bright blue	.35	.35
c.		10 l on 6 l maroon	.45	.45
d.		20 l on 2 l green	1.00	1.00

Promotion of the Crown Prince Michael to the rank of Lieutenant on his 17th birthday.

Arms of Romania, Greece, Turkey and Yugoslavia A147

Perf. 13x13½

1938, Feb. 10 Wmk. 230

470	A147	7.50 l ultra	1.50	.90
471	A147	10 l blue	2.00	.80

The Balkan Entente. Exist imperf. Value, unused or used, $100.

A148

King Carol II

A149 A150

1938, May 10 *Perf. 13½*

472	A148	3 l dk carmine	.75	.50
473	A149	6 l violet brn	1.25	.50
474	A150	10 l blue	2.00	.90
		Nos. 472-474 (3)	4.00	1.90

New Constitution of Feb. 27, 1938.
Exist imperf. Value, unused or used, $100.

Catalogue values for unused stamps in this section, from this point to the end of the section, are for Never Hinged items.

Prince Carol at Calatorie, 1866
A151

Examining Plans for a Monastery
A153

Prince Carol and Carmen Sylva (Queen Elizabeth)
A155

Sigmaringen and Peles Castles — A154

Prince Carol, Age 6 — A156

Equestrian Statue — A159

Battle of Plevna — A160

On Horseback
A161

Cathedral of Curtea de Arges
A164

King Carol I and Queen Elizabeth
A163

Designs: 50b, At Calafat. 4 l, In 1866. 5 l, In 1877. 12 l, in 1914.

Perf. 14, 13½

1939, Apr. 10 **Wmk. 230**

475	A151	25b	olive blk	.25	.25
476	A151	50b	violet brn	.25	.25
477	A153	1 l	dk purple	.25	.25
478	A154	1.50 l	green	.25	.25
479	A155	2 l	myrtle grn	.25	.25
480	A156	3 l	red orange	.25	.25
481	A156	4 l	rose lake	.25	.25
482	A156	5 l	black	.25	.25
483	A159	7 l	olive blk	.25	.25
484	A160	8 l	dark blue	.25	.25
485	A161	10 l	deep mag	.80	.25
486	A161	12 l	dull blue	1.20	.25
487	A163	15 l	ultra	1.20	.25
488	A164	16 l	Prus green	1.20	.60
			Nos. 475-488 (14)	6.90	3.85

Centenary of the birth of King Carol I.
Nos 475-488 exist imperf. Value, unused or used, $150.

Souvenir Sheets

1939 *Perf. 14x13½*

488A	Sheet of 3, #475-476, 478	3.50	3.50
d.	Imperf. ('40)	7.00	7.00

Perf. 14x15½

488B	Sheet of 4, #480-482, 486	3.50	3.50
e.	Imperf. ('40)	7.00	7.00
488C	Sheet of 4, #479, 483-485	3.50	3.50
f.	Imperf. ('40)	7.00	7.00

No. 488A sold for 20 l, Nos. 488B-488C for 50 l, the surtax for national defense.

Nos. 488A-488C and 488Ad-488Cf were overprinted "PRO-PATRIA 1940" to aid the armament fund. Value, set of 6, $100.

Nos. 488A-488C exist with overprint of "ROMA BERLIN 1940" and bars, but these are not recognized as having been officially issued.

Romanian Pavilion
A165

Romanian Pavilion
A166

1939, May 8 *Perf. 14x13½, 13½*

489	A165	6 l brown carmine	1.25	.60
490	A166	12 l brt blue	1.25	.60

New York World's Fair.
Nos 489-490 exist imperf. Value, unused or used, $250.

Mihail Eminescu
A167 A168

1939, May 22 *Perf. 13½*

491	A167	5 l olive gray	3.00	1.75
492	A168	7 l brown carmine	3.00	1.75

Mihail Eminescu, poet, 50th death anniv.
Nos 491-492 exist imperf. Value, unused or used, $300.

Three Types of Locomotives — A169

Modern Train
A170

Wood-burning Locomotive
A171

Streamlined Locomotive
A172

Railroad Terminal
A173

1939, June 10 **Typo.** *Perf. 14*

493	A169	1 l red violet	1.75	.60
494	A170	4 l deep rose	1.75	.60
495	A171	5 l gray lilac	1.75	.60
496	A171	7 l claret	1.75	.60
497	A172	12 l blue	3.50	1.75
498	A173	15 l green	3.50	2.40
		Nos. 493-498 (6)	14.00	6.55

Romanian Railways, 70th anniversary.
Nos 493-498 exist imperf. Value, unused or used, $200.

Arms of Romania, Greece, Turkey and Yugoslavia — A174

Wmk. 230

1940, May 27 **Photo.** *Perf. 13½*

504	A174	12 l lt ultra	1.25	.75
505	A174	16 l dull blue	1.25	.75

The Balkan Entente.
Nos 504-505 exist imperf. Value, unused or used, $125.

King Michael — A175

1940-42 **Wmk. 230** *Perf. 14*

506	A175	25b	Prus green	.25	.25
506A	A175	50b	dk grn ('42)	.25	.25
507	A175	1 l	purple	.25	.25
508	A175	2 l	red orange	.25	.25
508A	A175	4 l	slate ('42)	.25	.25
509	A175	5 l	rose pink	.25	.25
509A	A175	7 l	dp blue ('42)	.25	.25
510	A175	10 l	dp magenta	.40	.25
511	A175	12 l	dull blue	.25	.25
511A	A175	13 l	dk vio ('42)	.25	.25
512	A175	16 l	Prus blue	.55	.25
513	A175	20 l	brown	1.75	.25
514	A175	30 l	yellow grn	.25	.25
515	A175	50 l	olive brn	.25	.25
516	A175	100 l	rose brown	.75	.25
			Nos. 506-516 (15)	6.20	3.75

See Nos. 535A-553.

Prince Duca — A176

1941, Oct. 6 *Perf. 13½*

517	A176	6 l lt brown	.40	.40
518	A176	12 l dk violet	.80	.80
519	A176	24 l brt blue	1.10	1.10
		Nos. 517-519 (3)	2.30	2.30

Crossing of the Dniester River by Romanian forces invading Russia.

Nos. 517-519 each exist in an imperf., ungummed souvenir sheet of 4. These were prepared by the civil government of Trans-Dniestria to be sold for 300 lei apiece to aid the Red Cross, but were not recognized by the national government at Bucharest. The sheets reached philatelic channels in 1946. Value, set of 3 sheets $40.

See Nos. 554-557.

Hotin Chapel, Bessarabia
A177

Sucevita Monastery, Bucovina
A179

Designs: 50b, 9.50 l, Hotin Fortress, Bessarabia. 1.50 l, Soroca Fortress, Bessarabia. 2 l, 5.50 l, Tighina Fortress, Bessarabia. 3 l, Dragomirna Monastery, Bucovina. 6.50 l, Cetatea Alba Fortress, Bessarabia. 10 l, 130 l, Putna Monastery, Bucovina. 13 l, Milisauti Monastery, Bucovina. 26 l, St. Nicholas Monastery, Suceava, Bucovina. 39 l, Rughi Monastery, Bessarabia.

Inscribed "Basarabia" or "Bucovina" at bottom

1941, Dec. 1 *Perf. 13½*

520	A177	25b	rose car	.25	.25
521	A179	50b	red brn	.25	.25
522	A179	1 l	dp vio	.25	.25
523	A179	1.50 l	green	.25	.25
524	A179	2 l	brn org	.30	.25
525	A177	3 l	dk ol grn	.30	.25
526	A177	5 l	olive blk	.30	.25
527	A179	5.50 l	brown	.30	.25
528	A179	6.50 l	magenta	.40	.25
529	A179	9.50 l	gray blk	.40	.25
530	A179	10 l	dk vio brn	.35	.25
531	A177	13 l	slate blue	.70	.25
532	A179	17 l	brn car	1.00	.25
533	A179	26 l	gray grn	1.25	.40
534	A179	39 l	bl grn	1.75	.60
535	A179	130 l	yel org	5.00	2.75
			Nos. 520-535,B179-B187 (25)	19.50	11.75

Type of 1940-42

1943-45 **Wmk. 276** *Perf. 14*

535A	A175	25b	Prus grn ('44)	.25	.25
536	A175	50b	dk grn ('44)	.25	.25
537	A175	1 l	dk vio ('43)	.25	.25
538	A175	2 l	red org ('43)	.25	.25
539	A175	3 l	red brn ('44)	.25	.25
540	A175	3.50 l	brn ('43)	.25	.25
541	A175	4 l	slate	.25	.25
542	A175	4.50 l	dk brn ('43)	.25	.25
543	A175	5 l	rose car	.25	.25
544	A175	6.50 l	dl vio	.25	.25
545	A175	7 l	dp bl	.25	.25
546	A175	10 l	dp mag	.25	.25
547	A175	11 l	brt ultra	.25	.25
548	A175	12 l	dark blue	.25	.25
549	A175	15 l	royal blue	.25	.25
550	A175	16 l	dp blue	.25	.25
551	A175	20 l	brn ('43)	.25	.25
551A	A175	29 l	ultra ('45)	.55	.35
552	A175	30 l	yel grn	.25	.25
553	A175	50 l	olive blk	.25	.25
			Nos. 535A-553 (20)	5.30	5.10

Prince Duca Type of 1941

1943 *Perf. 13½*

554 A176 3 l red org .40 *.75*
555 A176 6 l dl brn .40 *.75*
556 A176 12 l dl vio .80 *1.10*
557 A176 24 l brt bl 1.10 *1.50*
Nos. 554-557 (4) 2.70 4.10

Andrei Saguna — A188

Andrei Muresanu A189

Transylvanians: 4.50 l, Samuel Micu. 11 l, Gheorghe Sincai. 15 l, Michael the Brave. 31 l, Gheorghe Lazar. 35 l, Avram Jancu. 41 l, Simeon Barnutiu. 55 l, Three Heroes. 61 l, Petru Maior.

1945 **Inscribed "1944"** *Perf. 14*

558 A188 25b rose red .60 *.70*
559 A189 50b orange .40 *.70*
560 A189 4.50 l brown .40 *.70*
561 A188 11 l lt ultra .40 *.70*
562 A188 15 l Prus grn .40 *.70*
563 A189 31 l dl vio .40 *.70*
564 A188 35 l bl blk .40 *.70*
565 A188 41 l olive gray 1.10 *.70*
566 A189 55 l red brown .40 *.70*
567 A189 61 l deep magenta .40 *.70*
Nos. 558-567,B251 (11) 5.40 7.75

Romania's liberation.

A198 A199

King Michael
A200 A201

1945 **Photo.**

568 A198 50b gray blue .25 .25
569 A199 1 l dl brn .25 .25
570 A199 2 l violet .25 .25
571 A198 2 l sepia .25 .25
572 A199 4 l yel grn .25 .25
573 A200 5 l dp mag .25 .25
574 A198 10 l blue .25 .25
575 A198 15 l magenta .25 .25
576 A198 20 l dl blue .25 .25
577 A200 25 l red org .25 .25
578 A200 35 l brown .25 .25
579 A200 40 l car rose .25 .25
580 A199 50 l pale ultra .25 .25
581 A199 55 l red .25 .25
582 A200 75 l Prus grn .25 .25
583 A201 80 l orange .25 .25
584 A201 100 l dp red brn .25 .25
585 A201 160 l yel grn .25 .25
586 A201 200 l dk ol grn .25 .25
587 A201 400 l dl vio .25 .25
Nos. 568-587 (20) 5.00 5.00

Nos. 571, 573, 580, 581, 585 and 587 are printed on toned paper, Nos. 576, 577, 583, 584 and 586 on both toned and white papers, others on white paper only.

See Nos. 610-624, 651-660.

Mail Carrier A202

Telegraph Operator A203

Lineman A204

Post Office, Bucharest A205

1945, July 20 **Wmk. 276** *Perf. 13*

588 A202 100 l dk brn 1.00 1.00
589 A202 100 l gray olive 1.00 1.00
590 A203 150 l brown 1.65 1.65
591 A203 150 l brt rose 1.65 1.65
592 A204 250 l lt gray ol 2.00 2.00
593 A204 250 l blue 2.00 2.00
594 A205 500 l dp mag 14.00 14.00
Nos. 588-594 (7) 23.30 23.30

Issued in sheets of 4. Value, set of 7 sheets $150.

I. Ionescu, G. Titeica, A. O. Idachimescu and V. Cristescu — A207

Allegory of Learning A208

1945, Sept. 5 *Perf. 13½*

596 A207 2 l sepia .25 .25
597 A208 80 l bl blk .55 .55

50th anniversary of "Gazeta Matematica," mathematics journal.

Cernavoda Bridge, 50th Anniv. — A209

1945, Sept. 26 *Perf. 14*

598 A209 80 l bl blk .40 .25

Blacksmith and Plowman — A210

1946, Mar. 6

599 A210 80 l blue .50 .25

Agrarian reform law of Mar. 23, 1945.

Atheneum, Bucharest A211

Numeral in Wreath A212

Georges Enescu — A213

Wmk. 276

1946, Apr. 26 **Photo.** *Perf. 13½*

600 A211 10 l dk bl .25 .25
601 A212 20 l red brn .25 .25
602 A212 55 l peacock bl .25 .25
603 A213 80 l purple .40 .25
a. Tête bêche pair .80 .80
604 A212 160 l red org .25 .25
Nos. 600-604,B330-B331 (7) 3.10 4.50

Philharmonic Society, 25th anniv.

Mechanic — A214

Labor Day: No. 606, Laborer. No. 607, Sower. No. 608, Reaper. 200 l, Students.

1946, May 1 *Perf. 13½x13*

605 A214 10 l Prus grn .75 .75
606 A214 10 l dk car rose .25 .25
607 A214 20 l dl bl .75 .75
608 A214 20 l dk red brn .25 .25
609 A214 200 l brt red .40 .40
Nos. 605-609 (5) 2.40 2.40

Michael Types of 1945

1946 **Wmk. 276** **Photo.** *Perf. 14*

Toned Paper

610 A198 10 l brt red brn .25 .25
611 A198 20 l vio brn .25 .25
612 A201 80 l blue .25 .25
613 A198 137 l yel grn .25 .25
614 A201 160 l chalky bl .25 .25
615 A201 200 l red org .25 .25
616 A201 300 l sapphire .25 .25
617 A201 360 l sepia .25 .25
618 A199 400 l red org .25 .25
619 A201 480 l brn red .25 .25
620 A201 600 l dk ol grn .25 .25
621 A201 1000 l Prus grn .25 .25
622 A198 1500 l Prus grn .25 .25
623 A201 2400 l magenta .25 .25
624 A201 3700 l dull bl .25 .25
Nos. 610-624 (15) 3.75 3.75

Demetrius Cantemir — A219

Designs: 100 l, "Cultural Ties." 300 l, "Economic Ties."

1946, Oct. 20 *Perf. 13½*

625 A219 80 l dk brn .40 .40
626 A219 100 l dp bl .40 .40
627 A219 300 l bl blk .40 .40
Nos. 625-627,B338 (4) 1.90 2.45

Romania-Soviet friendship. See No. B339.

Soccer — A222

Designs: 20 l, Diving. 50 l, Running. 80 l, Mountain climbing.

1946, Sept. 1 *Perf. 11½, Imperf.*

628 A222 10 l dp blue .40 .40
629 A222 20 l brt red .40 .40
630 A222 50 l dp violet .40 .40
631 A222 80 l chocolate .40 .40
Nos. 628-631,B340,C26,CB6 (7) 4.10 4.60

Issued in sheets of 16.

Weaving — A226

Wmk. 276

1946, Nov. 20 **Photo.** *Perf. 14*

636 A226 80 l dk ol brn .30 .30
Nos. 636,B342-B345 (5) 1.70 3.30

Democratic Women's Org. of Romania. See No. CB7.

Child Receiving Bread — A227

Transporting Relief Supplies — A228

1947, Jan. 15 *Perf. 13½x14, 14x13½*

637 A227 300 l dk ol brn .40 .40
638 A228 600 l magenta .40 .40
Nos. 637-638,B346-B347 (4) 1.40 2.00

Social relief fund. See #B348.

CGM Congress Emblem — A229

1947, Feb. 10 *Perf. 13½*

639	A229	200 l blue	.55	.55
640	A229	300 l orange	.55	.55
a.		Pair, #639-640	1.10	1.10
b.		Pair, #640-641	1.25	1.25
641	A229	600 l crimson	.70	.70
		Nos. 639-641 (3)	1.80	1.80

Congress of the United Labor Unions ("CGM").

Printed in sheets of 18 comprising 3 pairs of each denomination. Sheet yields 3 each of Nos. 640a and 640b.

Peace in Chariot A230

Peace — A231

Flags of US, Russia, GB & Romania — A232

Dove of Peace — A233

1947, Feb. 25 *Perf. 14x13½, 13½x14*

642	A230	300 l dl vio	.50	.50
643	A231	600 l dk org brn	.50	.50
644	A232	3000 l blue	.50	.50
645	A233	7200 l sage grn	.50	.50
		Nos. 642-645 (4)	2.00	2.00

Signing of the peace treaty of Feb. 10, 1947.

King Michael — A234

1947 **Size: 25x30mm** *Perf. 13½*

646	A234	3000 l blue	.25	.25
647	A234	7200 l dl vio	.25	.25
648	A234	15,000 l brt bl	.40	.25
649	A234	21,000 l magenta	.40	.25
650	A234	36,000 l violet	.75	.60
		Nos. 646-650 (5)	2.05	1.60

See Nos. 661-664.

Michael Types of 1945

1947 **Wmk. 276** **Photo.** *Perf. 14*

651	A199	10 l red brn	.25	.25
652	A200	20 l magenta	.25	.25
653	A198	80 l blue	.25	.25
654	A199	200 l brt red	.25	.25
655	A198	500 l magenta	.25	.25
656	A200	860 l vio brn	.25	.25
657	A199	2500 l ultra	.25	.25
658	A198	5000 l sl gray	.25	.25
659	A198	8000 l Prus grn	.75	.25
660	A201	10,000 l dk brn	1.00	.25

Type of 1947
Size: 18x21½mm

661	A234	1000 l gray bl	.25	.25
662	A234	5500 l yel grn	.25	.25
663	A234	20,000 l ol brn	.55	.30
664	A234	50,000 l red org	1.00	.45
		Nos. 651-664 (14)	5.80	3.75

For surcharge see No. B368.

Harvesting Wheat A235

Designs: 1 l, Log raft. 2 l, River steamer. 3 l, Resita. 5 l, Cathedral of Curtea de Arges. 10 l, View of Bucharest. 12 l, 36 l, Cernavoda Bridge. 15 l, 32 l, Port of Constantsa. 20 l, Petroleum field.

1947, Aug. 15 *Perf. 14½x14*

666	A235	50b red org	.25	.25
667	A235	1 l red brn	.25	.25
668	A235	2 l bl gray	.25	.25
669	A235	3 l rose crim	.50	.25
670	A235	5 l brt ultra	.50	.25
671	A235	10 l brt blue	.65	.30
672	A235	12 l violet	.85	.35
673	A235	15 l dp ultra	1.50	.35
674	A235	20 l dk brown	2.50	.50
675	A235	32 l violet brn	5.75	2.50
676	A235	36 l dk car rose	6.00	2.50
		Nos. 666-676 (11)	19.00	7.75

For overprints & surcharge see #684-694, B369.

Beehive, Savings Emblem — A236

1947, Oct. 31 *Perf. 13½*

677	A236	12 l dk car rose	.55	.35

World Savings Day, Oct. 31, 1947.

People's Republic

Map, Workers and Children A237

1948, Jan. 25 *Perf. 14½x14*

678	A237	12 l brt ultra	.80	.25

1948 census. For surcharge see #819A.

Government Printing Plant and Press — A238

1948 *Perf. 14½x14*

679	A238	6 l magenta	2.00	1.10
680	A238	7.50 l dk Prus grn	1.10	.25
b.		Tête bêche pair	3.25	3.25

75th anniversary of Stamp Division of Romanian State Printing Works.

Issued: No. 680, Feb. 12; No. 679, May 20.

Romanian and Bulgarian Peasants Shaking Hands A239

1948, Mar. 25 **Wmk. 276**

680A	A239	32 l red brown	1.50	.75

Romanian-Bulgarian friendship.
For surcharge see No. 696.

Allegory of the People's Republic — A240

1948, Apr. 8 **Photo.** *Perf. 14x14½*

681	A240	1 l car rose	.55	.40
682	A240	2 l dl org	.80	.55
683	A240	12 l deep blue	2.40	.90
		Nos. 681-683 (3)	3.75	1.85

New constitution.
For surcharge see No. 820.

Nos. 666 to 676 Overprinted in Black

1948, Mar. *Perf. 14½x14*

684	A235	50b red org	.30	.25
685	A235	1 l red brn	.30	.25
686	A235	2 l bl gray	.60	.25
687	A235	3 l rose crim	.60	.25
688	A235	5 l brt ultra	1.25	.30
689	A235	10 l brt bl	1.50	.30
690	A235	12 l violet	1.75	.35
691	A235	15 l dp ultra	1.75	.40
692	A235	20 l dk brn	2.50	.55
693	A235	32 l vio brn	7.50	2.50
694	A235	36 l dk car rose	7.50	2.50
		Nos. 684-694 (11)	25.55	7.90

Romanian Newspapers — A241

1948, Sept. 12

695	A241	10 l red brn	.40	.25
		Nos. 695,B396-B398 (4)	3.70	3.55

Week of the Democratic Press, Sept. 12-19.

No. 680A Surcharged with New Value in Black

1948, Aug. 17

696	A239	31 l on 32 l red brn	1.00	.35

Monument to Soviet Soldier — A242

1948, Oct. 29 **Photo.** *Perf. 14x14½*

697	A242	10 l dk red	.80	.80
		Nos. 697,B399-B400 (3)	6.30	8.30

Sheets of 50 stamps and 50 labels.

Proclamation of Islaz — A243

1948, June 1 *Perf. 14½x14*

698	A243	11 l car rose	.85	.25
		Nos. 698,B409-B412 (5)	4.30	5.05

Centenary of Revolution of 1848.
For surcharge see No. 820A.

Arms of Romanian People's Republic — A243a

1948, July 8 **Wmk. 276**

698A	A243a	50b red ("Lei 0.50")	.30	.25
698B	A243a	1 l red brn	.30	.25
698C	A243a	2 l dk grn	.30	.25
698D	A243a	3 l grnsh blk	.55	.25
698E	A243a	4 l chocolate	.55	.25
698F	A243a	5 l ultra	.70	.25
698G	A243a	10 l dp bl	.85	.25

"Bani" instead of "Lei"

698H	A243a	50b red ("Bani 0.50")	.55	.55
		Nos. 698A-698H (8)	4.10	2.30

See Nos. 712-717.

Nicolae Balcescu (1819-1852), Writer — A244

1948, Dec. 20 **Wmk. 289**

699	A244	20 l scarlet	1.00	.35

Release from Bondage — A245

1948, Dec. 30 *Perf. 13½*

700	A245	5 l brt rose	.55	.25

First anniversary of the Republic.

Lenin, 25th Death Anniv. — A246

1949, Jan. 21

701	A246	20 l black	.70	.25

Exists imperf. Value, unused or used, $1.25.

Folk Dance — A247

1949, Jan. 24 *Perf. 13½*

702	A247	10 l dp bl	.55	.30

90th anniv. of the union of the Danubian Principalities.

Ion C. Frimu and Revolutionary Scene — A248

1949, Mar. 22 *Perf. 14½x14*

703 A248 20 l red .55 .25

Exists imperf. Value, unused or used, $1.25.

Aleksander S. Pushkin, 150th Birth Anniv. — A249

1949, May 20 *Perf. 14x14½*

704 A249 11 l car rose 1.25 .75
705 A249 30 l Prus grn 1.60 .75

For surcharges see Nos. 821-822.

Globe and Post Horn — A250

Evolution of Mail Transportation — A251

Perf. 13½, 14½x14

1949, June 30 **Photo.** **Wmk. 289**

706 A250 20 l org brn 1.75 1.50
707 A251 30 l brt bl 3.50 1.00

UPU, 75th anniv.
For surcharges see Nos. C43-C44.

Russian Army Entering Bucharest, August, 1944
A252

1949, Aug. 23 *Perf. 14½x14*

708 A252 50 l choc, *bl grn* .95 .60

5th anniv. of the liberation of Romania by the Soviet army, Aug. 1944.
Exists imperf. Value, unused or used, $2.

"Long Live Romanian-Soviet Amity" — A253

1949, Nov. 1 *Perf. 13½x14½*

709 A253 20 l dp red .65 .35

Natl. week of Romanian-Soviet friendship celebration, 11/1-7/49. Exists imperf. Value, unused or used, $1.50.

Symbols of Transportation
A254

1949, Dec. 10 *Perf. 13½*

710 A254 11 l blue 1.50 1.50
711 A254 20 l crimson 1.50 1.50

Intl. Conference of Transportation Unions, Dec. 10, 1949.
Alternate vertical rows of stamps and labels in sheet. Exist imperf. Value for set, unused or used, $3.75.

Arms Type of 1948

1949-50 **Wmk. 289** *Perf. 14x13½*

712	A243a	50b red ("Lei 0.50")	.40	.25
713	A243a	1 l red brn	.40	.25
714	A243a	2 l dk grn	.40	.25
714A	A243a	3 l grnsh blk	.65	.25
715	A243a	5 l ultra	.50	.25
716	A243a	5 l rose vio ('50)	.80	.25
717	A243a	10 l dp blue	1.00	.25
		Nos. 712-717 (7)	4.15	1.75

Joseph V. Stalin — A256

1949, Dec. 21 *Perf. 13½*

718 A256 31 l olive black .65 .25

Stalin's 70th birthday. Exists imperf. Value, unused or used, $1.60.

Mihail Eminescu — A257

Poem: "Life" — A258

No. 721, "Third Letter." No. 722, "Angel and Demon." No. 723, "Emperor and Proletariat."

1950, Jan. 15 **Photo.** **Wmk. 289**

719 A257 11 l blue 1.00 .30
720 A258 11 l purple 1.75 .65
721 A258 11 l dk grn 1.00 .30
722 A258 11 l red brn 1.00 .30
723 A258 11 l rose pink 1.00 .30
Nos. 719-723 (5) 5.75 1.85

Birth cent. of Mihail Eminescu, poet.
For surcharges see Nos. 823-827.

Fair at Dragaica
A259

Ion Andreescu (Self-portrait)
A260

Village Well
A261

1950, Mar. 25 *Perf. 14½x14, 14x14½*

724 A259 5 l dk gray grn 1.00 .60
725 A260 11 l ultra 1.60 .60
726 A261 20 l brown 1.75 1.00
Nos. 724-726 (3) 4.35 2.20

Birth cent. of Ion Andreescu, painter. No. 725 also exists imperf. Value, unused or used, $3.50.
For surcharges see Nos. 827A-827B.

Graph and Factories
A262

Design: 31 l, Tractor and Oil Derricks.

Inscribed: "Planul de Stat 1950."

Perf. 14½x14

1950, Apr. 23 **Wmk. 289**

727 A262 11 l red .60 .25
728 A262 31 l violet 1.10 .50

1950 plan for increased industrial production. No. 727 exists imperf. Value, unused or used, $2.
For surcharges see Nos. 827C-827D.

Young Man Holding Flag — A263

1950, May 1 *Perf. 14x14½*

729 A263 31 l orange red .65 .25

Labor Day, May 1.
Exists imperf. Value, unused or used, $1.25.
For surcharge see No. 827E.

Canceled to Order
Canceled sets of new issues have long been sold by the government. Values in the second ("used") column are for these canceled-to-order stamps. Postally used stamps are worth more.

Arms of Republic — A264

1950 **Photo.** *Perf. 12½*

730	A264	50b black	.25	.25
731	A264	1 l red orange	.25	.25
732	A264	2 l ol gray	.25	.25
733	A264	3 l violet	.25	.25
734	A264	4 l rose lilac	.25	.25
735	A264	5 l red brn	.25	.25
736	A264	6 l dp grn	.25	.25
737	A264	7 l vio brn	.25	.25
738	A264	7.50 l blue	.40	.25
739	A264	10 l dk brn	.80	.25
740	A264	11 l rose car	.80	.25
741	A264	15 l dp bl	.40	.25
742	A264	20 l Prus grn	.40	.25
743	A264	31 l dl grn	.80	.25
744	A264	36 l dk org brn	1.25	.30
		Nos. 730-744 (15)	6.85	3.80

See Nos. 947-961 which have similar design with white denomination figures.
For overprint & surcharges see Nos. 758, 828-841.

Bugler and Drummer
A265

Designs: 11 l, Three school children. 31 l, Drummer, flag-bearer and bugler.

1950, May 25 *Perf. 14½x14*

745 A265 8 l blue 1.40 .60
746 A265 11 l rose vio 1.75 1.00
747 A265 31 l org ver 3.00 2.00
Nos. 745-747 (3) 6.15 3.60

Young Pioneers, 1st anniv.
For surcharges see Nos. 841A-841C.

Factory Worker — A266

1950, July 20 **Photo.** *Perf. 14x14½*

748 A266 11 l red brn .50 .35
749 A266 11 l red .85 .35
750 A266 11 l blue .50 .35
751 A266 11 l blk brn .85 .35
Nos. 748-751 (4) 2.70 1.40

Nationalization of industry, 2nd anniv.

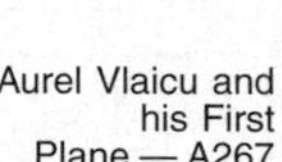

Aurel Vlaicu and his First Plane — A267

1950, July 22 **Wmk. 289** *Perf. 12½*

752 A267 3 l dk grn .40 .25
753 A267 6 l dk bl .60 .25
754 A267 8 l ultra .75 .35
Nos. 752-754 (3) 1.75 .85

Aurel Vlaicu (1882-1913), pioneer of Romanian aviation.
For surcharges see Nos. 842-844.

Mother and Child — A268

Lathe and Operator — A269

1950, Sept. 9 *Perf. 13½*

755 A268 11 l rose red .40 .25
756 A269 20 l dk ol brn .45 .25

Congress of the Committees for the Struggle for Peace.
For surcharge see No. 844A.

Statue of Soviet Soldier — A270

1950, Oct. 6 *Perf. 14x14½*

757 A270 30 l red brn .85 .35

Celebration of Romanian-Soviet friendship, Oct. 7-Nov. 7, 1950.

No. 741 Overprinted in Carmine

1950, Oct. 6 *Perf. 12½*
758 A264 15 l deep blue 1.10 .35

Romanian-Hungarian friendship.

"Agriculture," "Manufacturing" and Sports Badge — A271

5 l, Student workers & badge. 11 l, Track team & badge. 31 l, Calisthenics & badge.

1950, Oct. 30 *Perf. 14½x14*
759 A271 3 l rose car 1.40 1.40
760 A271 5 l red brn 1.00 1.00
761 A271 5 l brt bl 1.00 1.00
762 A271 11 l green 1.00 1.00
763 A271 31 l brn ol 2.50 2.50
Nos. 759-763 (5) 6.90 6.90

For surcharge see No. 845.

A272

1950, Nov. 2 *Perf. 13½*
764 A272 11 l blue .50 .35
765 A272 11 l red org .50 .35

3rd Soviet-Romanian Friendship Congress.

"Industry" — A273

"Agriculture" — A274

Perf. 14x14½, 14½x14
1951, Feb. 9 **Photo.** **Wmk. 289**
766 A273 11 l red brn .40 .25
767 A274 31 l deep bl .75 .35

Industry and Agriculture Exposition. Exist imperf. Value for set, unused or used, $2.
For surcharge see No. 846.

Ski Jump — A275

Ski Descent A276

5 l, Skating. 20 l, Hockey. 31 l, Bobsledding.

1951, Jan. 28 *Perf. 13½*
768 A275 4 l blk brn 1.50 1.50
769 A275 5 l vermilion 1.25 1.25
770 A276 11 l dp bl 1.25 1.25
771 A275 20 l org brn 1.25 1.25
772 A275 31 l dk gray grn 3.50 3.25
Nos. 768-772 (5) 8.75 8.50

9th World University Winter Games.
For surcharges see Nos. 847-848.

Medal for Work — A277

Orders: 4 l, Star of the Republic, Classes III, IV & V. 11 l, Work. 35 l, As 4 l, Classes I & II.

1951, May 1 *Perf. 13½*
773 A277 2 l ol gray .25 .25
774 A277 4 l blue .35 .25
775 A277 11 l crimson .50 .25
776 A277 35 l org brn .75 .40
Nos. 773-776 (4) 1.85 1.15

Labor Day. Exist imperf. Value for set, unused or used, $2.50.
For surcharges see Nos. 849-852.

Camp of Young Pioneers A278

Pioneers Greeting Stalin — A279

Admitting New Pioneers A280

1951, May 8 *Perf. 14x14½, 14½x14*
777 A278 1 l gray grn 1.00 .45
778 A279 11 l blue 1.00 .45
779 A280 35 l red 1.50 .70
Nos. 777-779 (3) 3.50 1.60

Romanian Young Pioneers Organization.
For surcharge see No. 853.

Woman Orator and Flags — A281

1951, Mar. 8 *Perf. 14x14½*
780 A281 11 l org brn .50 .25

Woman's Day, March 8. Exists imperf. Value, unused or used, 80c.

Ion Negulici — A282

1951, June 20 *Perf. 14x14½*
781 A282 35 l rose red 3.50 2.10

Death cent. of Ion Negulici, painter.

Bicyclists A283

1951, July 9 *Perf. 14½x14*
782 A283 11 l chnt brn 2.10 .80
a. Tête bêche pair 7.00 7.00

The 1951 Bicycle Tour of Romania.

Festival Badge — A284 Boy and Girl with Flag — A285

Youths Encircling Globe — A286

1951, Aug. 1 *Perf. 13½*
783 A284 1 l scarlet .80 .40
784 A285 5 l deep blue 1.50 .40
785 A286 11 l deep plum 2.25 .80
Nos. 783-785 (3) 4.55 1.60

3rd World Youth Festival, Berlin.

Filimon Sarbu — A287

1951, July 23 *Perf. 14x14½*
786 A287 11 l dk brn .70 .25

10th death anniv. of Filimon Sarbu, patriot.

"Romania Raising the Masses" — A288

"Revolutionary Romania" — A289

1951, July 23 *Perf. 14x14½, 14½x14*
787 A288 11 l yel brn 2.00 .75
788 A288 11 l rose vio 2.00 .75
789 A289 11 l dk grn 2.00 .75
790 A289 11 l org red 2.00 .75
Nos. 787-790 (4) 8.00 3.00

Death cent. of C. D. Rosenthal, painter.

Scanteia Building A290

1951, Aug. 16 *Perf. 14½x14*
791 A290 11 l blue .75 .35

20th anniv. of the newspaper Scanteia.

Miner in Dress Uniform — A291

Design: 11 l, Miner in work clothes.

1951, Aug. 12 *Perf. 14x14½*
792 A291 5 l blue .60 .35
793 A291 11 l plum .70 .25

Miner's Day. For surcharge see No. 854.

Order for National Defense — A293

1951, Aug. 12 *Perf. 14x14½*
794 A293 10 l crimson .55 .25

For surcharge see No. 855.

Choir — A294

Music Week Emblem — A295

Design: No. 796, Orchestra and dancers.

Wmk. 358
1951, Sept. 22 **Photo.** *Perf. 13½*
795 A294 11 l blue .50 .35
796 A294 11 l red brown .75 .40
797 A295 11 l purple .50 .35
Nos. 795-797 (3) 1.75 1.10

Music Week, Sept. 22-30, 1951.

Soldier — A296

1951, Oct. 2
798 A296 11 l blue .55 .25

Army Day, Oct. 2, 1951.

Oil Field — A297

Designs: 2 l, Coal mining. 3 l, Romanian soldier. 4 l, Smelting ore. 5 l, Agricultural machinery. 6 l, Canal construction. 7 l, Agriculture. 8 l, Self-education. 11 l, Hydroelectric production. 35 l, Manufacturing.

1951-52
799 A297 1 l black brn .70 .25
800 A297 2 l chocolate .40 .25
801 A297 3 l scarlet .75 .45
802 A297 4 l yel brn ('52) .50 .25
803 A297 5 l green .50 .25
804 A297 6 l brt bl ('52) 2.00 1.10
805 A297 7 l emerald 1.10 .50
806 A297 8 l brown ('52) .90 .50
807 A297 11 l blue .90 .25
808 A297 35 l purple 1.25 .75
Nos. 799-808,C35-C36 (12) 15.75 10.05

1951-55 Five Year Plan.
2 l and 11 l exist with wmk. 289. Values same.
For surcharges see Nos. 860-869.

Arms of Soviet Union and Romania A298

1951, Oct. 7 **Wmk. 358**
809 A298 4 l chestnut brn, *cr* .40 .25
810 A298 35 l orange red .85 .45

Month of Romanian-Soviet friendship, Oct. 7-Nov. 7.
For surcharges see Nos. 870-871.

Pavel Tcacenco — A299

1951, Dec. 15 ***Perf. 14x14½***
811 A299 10 l ol brn & dk brn .75 .40

Revolutionary, 26th death anniv.
For surcharge see No. 872.

Railroad Conductor — A300

1952, Mar. 24 ***Perf. 13½***
812 A300 55b dark brown 3.00 .40

Railroad Workers' Day, Feb. 16.

Ion L. Caragiale — A301

Announcing Caragiale Celebration — A302

Designs: No. 814, Book and painting "1907." No. 815, Bust and wreath.

Inscribed: ". . . . I. L. Caragiale."

1952, Apr. 1 ***Perf. 13½, 14½x14***
813 A301 55b chalky blue 1.50 .55
814 A302 55b scarlet 1.50 .55
815 A302 55b deep green 1.50 .55
816 A302 1 l brown 4.00 .70
Nos. 813-816 (4) 8.50 2.35

Birth cent. of Ion L. Caragiale, dramatist.
For surcharges see Nos. 817-819.

Types of 1952 Surcharged with New Value in Black or Carmine

1952-53
817 A302 20b on 11 l scar *(as #814)* 1.25 .65
818 A302 55b on 11 l dp grn *(as #815)* (C) 1.75 .80
819 A301 75b on 11 l chlky bl (C) 3.00 1.10

Various Issues Surcharged with New Values in Carmine or Black

On No. 678, Census
Perf. 14x13½
819A A237 50b on 12 l ultra 3.25 2.00

On No. 683, New Constitution
Perf. 14
820 A240 50b on 12 l dp bl 4.00 1.25

On No. 698, Revolution
820A A243 1.75 l on 11 l car rose (Bk) 18.00 5.00

On Nos. 704-705, Pushkin
1952 **Wmk. 358**
821 A249 10b on 11 l (Bk) 4.00 1.75
822 A249 10b on 30 l 4.00 1.75

On Nos. 719-723, Eminescu
Perf. 13½x13, 13x13½
823 A257 10b on 11 l blue 3.00 1.90
824 A258 10b on 11 l pur 3.00 1.90
825 A258 10b on 11 l dk grn 3.00 1.90
826 A258 10b on 11 l red brn (Bk) 3.00 1.90
827 A258 10b on 11 l rose pink (Bk) 3.00 1.90

On Nos. 724-725, Andreescu
Perf. 14
827A A259 55b on 5 l dk gray grn 10.00 3.25
827B A260 55b on 11 l ultra 10.00 3.25

On Nos. 727-728, Production Plan
Perf. 14½x14
827C A262 20b on 11 l red (Bk) 4.00 1.25
827D A262 20b on 31 l vio 4.00 1.25

On No. 729, Labor Day
Perf. 14
827E A263 55b on 31 l (Bk) 5.00 3.25

On Nos. 730-739 and 741-744, National Arms
Perf. 12½
828 A264 3b on 1 l red (Bk) 2.50 1.10
829 A264 3b on 2 l ol gray (Bk) 2.50 1.10
830 A264 3b on 4 l rose lil (Bk) 2.50 1.10
831 A264 3b on 5 l red brn (Bk) 2.50 1.10
832 A264 3b on 7.50 l bl (Bk) 2.50 1.10
833 A264 3b on 10 l dk brn (Bk) 2.50 1.10
834 A264 55b on 50b blk brn 7.00 1.90
835 A264 55b on 3 l vio 7.00 1.90
836 A264 55b on 6 l dp grn 7.00 1.90
837 A264 55b on 7 l vio brn 7.00 1.90
838 A264 55b on 15 l dp bl 9.00 1.90
839 A264 55b on 20 l Prus grn 7.00 1.90
840 A264 55b on 31 l dl grn 7.00 1.90
841 A264 55b on 36 l dk org brn 9.00 1.90

On Nos. 745-747, Young Pioneers
Perf. 14
841A A265 55b on 8 l 10.00 5.75
841B A265 55b on 11 l 10.00 5.75
841C A265 55b on 31 l (Bk) 10.00 5.75

On Nos. 752-754, Vlaicu
Perf. 12½
842 A267 10b on 3 l dk grn 3.00 1.10
843 A267 10b on 6 l dk bl 3.00 1.10
844 A267 10b on 8 l ultra 3.00 1.10

Original denomination canceled with an "X."

On No. 756, Peace Congress
Perf. 13½
844A A269 20b on 20 l 4.00 1.90

On No. 759, Sports
Perf. 14½x14
845 A271 55b on 3 l (Bk) 24.00 15.00

On No. 767, Exposition
846 A274 55b on 31 l dp bl 6.00 3.75

On Nos. 771-772, Winter Games
Perf. 13½
847 A275 55b on 20 l (Bk) 35.00 15.00
848 A275 55b on 31 l 35.00 15.00

On Nos. 773-776, Labor Medals
849 A277 20b on 2 l 5.00 2.40
850 A277 20b on 4 l 5.00 2.40
851 A277 20b on 11 l (Bk) 5.00 2.40
852 A277 20b on 35 l (Bk) 5.00 2.40

On Nov. 779, Young Pioneers
Perf. 14x14½
853 A280 55b on 35 l (Bk) 10.00 4.75

On No. 792, Miners' Day
854 A291 55b on 5 l bl 10.00 2.75

On No. 794, Defense Order
855 A293 55b on 10 l (Bk) 10.00 2.75

On Nos. B409-B412, 1848 Revolution
1952 **Wmk. 276** ***Perf. 13x13½***
856 SP280 1.75 l on 2 l + 2 l (Bk) 18.00 4.75
857 SP281 1.75 l on 5 l + 5 l 18.00 4.75
858 SP282 1.75 l on 10 l + 10 l 18.00 4.75
859 SP280 1.75 l on 36 l + 18 l 18.00 4.75

On Nos. 799-808, 5-Year Plan
Wmk. 358 ***Perf. 13½***
860 A297 35b on 1 l blk brn 2.10 .95
861 A297 35b on 2 l choc 2.50 .95
862 A297 35b on 3 l scar (Bk) 4.50 2.00
863 A297 35b on 4 l yel brn (Bk) 5.25 2.25
a. Red surcharge 25.00 15.00
864 A297 35b on 5 l grn 4.25 4.00
865 A297 1 l on 6 l brt bl 6.25 5.00
866 A297 1 l on 7 l emer 6.25 2.25
867 A297 1 l on 8 l brn 6.25 5.00
868 A297 1 l on 11 l bl 6.25 2.75
869 A297 1 l on 35 l pur 8.00 2.25

Nos. 861, 868 exist with wmk. 289.

On Nos. 809-810, Romanian-Soviet Friendship
870 A298 10b on 4 l (Bk) 2.25 1.25
871 A298 10b on 35 l (Bk) 2.25 1.25

On No. 811, Tcacenco
Perf. 13½x14
872 A299 10b on 10 l 2.25 1.00

A302a

Perf. 13½x13
1952, Apr. 14 **Photo.** **Wmk. 358**
873 A302a 1 l Ivan P. Pavlov 2.75 .40

Meeting of Romanian-Soviet doctors in Bucharest.

A303

1952, May 1
874 A303 55b Hammer & sickle medal 2.75 .25

Labor Day.

Medal for Motherhood A304

Medals: 55b, Maternal glory. 1.75 l, Mother-Heroine.

1952, Apr. 7 ***Perf. 13x13½***
875 A304 20b plum & sl gray .90 .25
876 A304 55b henna brn 2.00 .45
877 A304 1.75 l rose red & brn buff 4.25 .55
Nos. 875-877 (3) 7.15 1.25

International Women's Day.

Leonardo da Vinci — A305

1952, July 3
878 A305 55b purple 5.00 .55

500th birth anniv. of Leonardo da Vinci.

Gogol and Scene from Taras Bulba A306

Nikolai V. Gogol — A307

1952, Apr. 1 ***Perf. 13½x14, 14x13½***
879 A306 55b deep blue 2.25 .35
880 A307 1.75 l olive gray 2.75 .55

Gogol, Russian writer, death cent.

Pioneers Saluting — A308

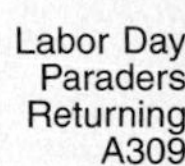

Labor Day Paraders Returning A309

Design: 55b, Pioneers studying nature.

1952, May 21 ***Perf. 14***

881	A308	20b brown	1.50	.25
882	A308	55b dp green	4.00	.25
883	A309	1.75 l blue	7.00	.55
		Nos. 881-883 (3)	12.50	1.05

Third anniversary of Romanian Pioneers.

Infantry Attack, Painting by Grigorescu A310

1.10 l, Romanian and Russian soldiers.

1952, June 7 ***Perf. 13x13½***

884	A310	50b rose brown	1.10	.25
885	A310	1.10 l blue	1.75	.50

Independence Proclamation of 1877, 75th anniv.

Miner — A311

1952, Aug. 11 **Wmk. 358**

902	A311	20b rose red	2.00	.45
903	A311	55b purple	2.00	.40

Day of the Miner.

Book and Globe — A312

Chemistry Student A313

Students in Native Dress — A314

Design: 55b, Students playing soccer.

Perf. 13½x13, 13½x14, 13x13½

1952, Sept. 5

904	A312	10b deep blue	.50	.25
905	A313	20b orange	2.75	.35
906	A312	55b deep green	2.75	.45
907	A314	1.75 l rose red	5.50	1.10
		Nos. 904-907 (4)	11.50	2.15

Intl. Student Union Congr., Bucharest, Sept.

Soldier, Sailor and Aviator — A316

1952, Oct. 2 ***Perf. 14***

909	A316	55b blue	1.75	.25

Armed Forces Day, Oct. 2, 1952.

"Russia" Leading Peace Crusade — A317

Allegory: Romanian-Soviet Friendship — A318

1952, Oct. 7 ***Perf. 13½x13, 13x13½***

910	A317	55b vermilion	1.10	.25
911	A318	1.75 l black brown	3.00	.60

Month of Romanian-Soviet friendship, Oct.

Rowing on Lake Snagov — A319

1.75 l, Athletes marching with flags.

1952, Oct. 20

912	A319	20b deep blue	5.00	.50
913	A319	1.75 l rose red	8.00	1.10

Values are for stamps with poor perforations.

Nicolae Balcescu — A320

1952, Nov. 29

914	A320	55b gray	4.00	.50
915	A320	1.75 l lemon bister	8.00	1.25

Death cent. of Nicolae Balcescu, poet.

Arms of Republic — A321

1952, Dec. 6 **Wmk. 358**

916	A321	55b dull green	1.75	.35

5th anniversary of socialist constitution.

Arms and Industrial Symbols A322

1953, Jan. 8 ***Perf. 12½x13½***

917	A322	55b blue, yellow & red	3.50	.50

5th anniv. of the proclamation of the People's Republic.

Matei Millo, Costache Caragiale and Aristita Romanescu A323

1953, Feb. **Photo.** ***Perf. 13x13½***

918	A323	55b brt ultra	3.50	.35

National Theater of I. L. Caragiale, cent.

Iron Foundry Worker — A324

Worker — A325

Design: No. 921, Driving Tractor.

1953, Feb. ***Perf. 13½x13, 13x13½***

919	A324	55b slate green	1.25	.25
920	A325	55b black brown	1.25	.25
921	A325	55b orange	1.50	.55
		Nos. 919-921 (3)	4.00	1.05

3rd Congress of the Syndicate of the Romanian People's Republic.

"Strike at Grivita," Painted by G. Miclossy A326

1953, Feb. 16 ***Perf. 13x13½***

922	A326	55b chestnut	2.75	.25

Oil industry strike, Feb. 16, 1933, 20th anniv.

Arms of Romanian People's Republic — A327

1953 ***Perf. 12½***

923	A327	5b crimson	.80	.25
924	A327	55b purple	1.40	.25

Flags of Romania and Russia, Farm Machinery A328

1953, Mar. 24 ***Perf. 14***

925	A328	55b dk brn, *bl*	2.75	.35

5th anniv. of the signing of a treaty of friendship and mutual assistance between Russia and Romania.

Map and Medal — A329

1953, Mar. 24

926	A329	55b dk gray green	10.00	1.75
927	A329	55b chestnut	10.00	1.75

20th World Championship Table Tennis Matches, Budapest, 1953.

Ceramics — A330

Folk Dance — A330a

Designs: 20b, Costume of Campulung (Muscel). 55b, Apuseni Mts. costume. 1 l, Rug.

Inscribed: "Arta Populara Romaneasca"

1953

928	A330	10b deep green	1.00	.25
929	A330	20b red brown	1.75	.25
929A	A330a	35b purple	3.00	.25
930	A330	55b violet blue	4.00	.25
931	A330	1 l brt red violet	6.00	.35
		Nos. 928-931 (5)	15.75	1.35

Romanian Folk Arts.

Karl Marx — A331

1953, May 21 ***Perf. 13½x13***

932	A331	1.55 l olive brown	3.50	.45

70th death anniv. of Karl Marx.

Children Planting Tree — A332

Physics Class A333

Design: 55b, Flying model planes.

1953, May 21 *Perf. 14*

933 A332 35b deep green 1.75 .25
934 A332 55b dull blue 2.10 .30
935 A333 1.75 l brown 4.00 .65
Nos. 933-935 (3) 7.85 1.20

Women and Flags — A334

1953, June 18 *Perf. 13½x13*

936 A334 55b red brown 2.10 .30

3rd World Congress of Women, Copenhagen, 1953.

Discus Thrower — A335

Students Offering Teacher Flowers A336

Designs: 55b, Students reaching toward dove. 1.75 l, Dance in local costumes.

1953, Aug. 2 **Wmk. 358** *Perf. 14*

937 A335 20b orange 1.00 .35
938 A335 55b deep blue 1.75 .75
939 A336 65b scarlet 2.25 1.10
940 A336 1.75 l red violet 6.50 1.75
Nos. 937-940 (4) 11.50 3.95

4th World Youth Festival, Bucharest, 8/2-16.

Waterfall — A337

Wheat Field — A338

Design: 55b, Forester holding seedling.

1953, July 29 **Photo.**

941 A337 20b violet blue 1.25 .25
942 A338 38b dull green 3.00 1.00
943 A337 55b lt brown 3.50 .35
Nos. 941-943 (3) 7.75 1.60

Month of the Forest.

Vladimir V. Mayakovsky, 60th Birth Anniv. — A339

1953, Aug. 22

944 A339 55b brown 2.50 .50

Miner Using Drill A340

1953, Sept. 19

945 A340 1.55 l slate black 4.00 .50

Miners' Day.

Arms of Republic — A342

Size: 20x24mm

1952-53 *Perf. 12½*

947 A342 3b deep orange .60 .25
948 A342 5b crimson .80 .25
949 A342 7b dk blue grn .80 .25
950 A342 10b chocolate 1.00 .25
951 A342 20b deep blue 1.25 .25
952 A342 35b black brn 2.75 .25
953 A342 50b dk gray grn 3.25 .25
954 A342 55b purple 7.25 .25

Size: 24x29mm

955 A342 1.10 l dk brown 6.50 .30
956 A342 1.75 l violet 26.00 .50
957 A342 2 l olive black 6.75 .60
958 A342 2.35 l orange brn 8.00 .40
959 A342 2.55 l dp orange 10.00 .50
960 A342 3 l dk gray grn 10.00 .40
961 A342 5 l deep crimson 13.00 .75
Nos. 947-961 (15) 97.95 5.45

Stamps of similar design with value figures in color are Nos. 730-744.

Postal Administration Building and Telephone Employees — A343

Designs: 55b, Postal Adm. Bldg. and Letter carrier. 1 l, Map and communications symbols. 1.55 l, Postal Adm. Bldg. and Telegraph employees.

1953, Oct. 20 **Wmk. 358** *Perf. 14*

964 A343 20b dk red brn .40 .25
965 A343 55b olive green .75 .25
966 A343 1 l brt blue 1.75 .25
967 A343 1.55 l rose brown 3.25 .50
Nos. 964-967 (4) 6.15 1.25

50th anniv. of the construction of the Postal Administration Building.

Liberation Medal — A344

1953, Oct. 20 *Perf. 14x13½*

968 A344 55b dark brown 1.75 .25

9th anniv. of the liberation of Romania.

Soldier and Flag — A345

1953, Oct. 2 *Perf. 13½*

969 A345 55b olive green 1.75 .25

Army Day, Oct. 2.

Girl with Model Plane A346

Civil Aviation: 20b, Parachute landing. 55b, Glider and pilot. 1.75 l, Plane in flight.

1953, Oct. 20 *Perf. 14*

970 A346 10b org & dk gray grn 3.00 .40
971 A346 20b org brn & dk ol grn 5.75 .25
972 A346 55b dk scar & rose lil 9.50 .60
973 A346 1.75 l dk rose vio & brn 12.50 .90
Nos. 970-973 (4) 30.75 2.15

Workers and Flags — A347

1.55 l, Spasski Tower, lock on Volga-Don Canal.

1953, Nov. 25 *Perf. 13x13½*

974 A347 55b brown 1.10 .25
975 A347 1.55 l rose brown 1.60 .35

Month of Romanian-Soviet friendship, Oct. 7-Nov. 7.

Hemispheres and Clasped Hands — A348

Workers, Flags and Globe — A349

1953, Nov. 25 *Perf. 14*

976 A348 55b dark olive .90 .25
977 A349 1.25 l crimson 1.75 .45

World Congress of Trade Unions.

Ciprian Porumbescu A350

1953, Dec. 16

978 A350 55b purple 8.50 .45

Ciprian Porumbescu (1853-1883), composer.

Harvesting Machine A351

Designs: 35b, Tractor in field. 2.55 l, Cattle.

Perf. 13x13½

1953, Dec. 16 **Wmk. 358**

979 A351 10b sepia .30 .25
980 A351 35b dark green .50 .25
981 A351 2.55 l orange brown 3.75 .80
Nos. 979-981 (3) 4.55 1.30

Aurel Vlaicu — A352

1953, Dec. 26 *Perf. 14*

982 A352 50b violet blue 1.75 .25

Vlaicu, aviation pioneer, 40th death anniv.

Lenin — A353

1954, Jan. 21 *Perf. 13½*

983 A353 55b dk red brn, *buff* 2.00 .25

30th death anniv. of Lenin.

Red Deer — A354

Designs: 55b, Children planting trees. 1.75 l, Mountain scene.

Yellow Surface-colored Paper

1954, Apr. 1

984 A354 20b dark brown 4.00 .45
985 A354 55b violet 3.25 .45
986 A354 1.75 l dark blue 5.75 1.00
Nos. 984-986 (3) 13.00 1.90

Month of the Forest.

Calimanesti Rest Home — A355

Workers' Rest Homes: 1.55 l, Sinaia. 2 l, Predeal. 2.35 l, Tusnad. 2.55 l, Govora.

1954, Apr. 15 ***Perf. 14***

987 A355 5b blk brn, *cream* .40 .25
988 A355 1.55 l dk vio brn, *bl* 2.00 .25
989 A355 2 l dk grn, *pink* 3.00 .30
990 A355 2.35 l ol blk, *grnsh* 3.00 .60
991 A355 2.55 l dk red brn, *cit* 4.00 .80
Nos. 987-991 (5) 12.40 2.20

Octav Bancila — A356

1954, May 26 ***Perf. 13½***

992 A356 55b red brn & dk grn 4.25 2.00

10th death anniv. of Octav Bancila, painter.

Globe, Child, Dove and Flowers A357

1954, June 1 ***Perf. 13x13½***

993 A357 55b brown 1.75 .25

Children's Day, June 1.

Girl Feeding Calf A358

Designs: 55b, Girl holding sheaf of grain. 1.75 l, Young students.

1954, July 5 ***Perf. 14***

994 A358 20b grnsh blk .45 .25
995 A358 55b blue .80 .30
996 A358 1.75 l car rose 2.50 .50
Nos. 994-996 (3) 3.75 1.05

Stephen the Great — A359

1954, July 10

997 A359 55b violet brown 2.75 .45

Stephen of Moldavia (1433?-1504).

Loading Coal on Conveyor Belt — A360

1954, Aug. 8 ***Perf. 13x13½***

998 A360 1.75 l black 3.00 .50

Miners' Day.

Victor Babes — A361

1954, Aug. 15 ***Perf. 14***

999 A361 55b rose red 2.25 .40

Birth cent. of Victor Babes, serologist.

Applicant Requesting Loan — A362

Design: 55b, Mutual aid declaration.

1954, Aug. 20

1000 A362 20b deep violet .40 .25
1001 A362 55b dk redsh brn .80 .25

5th anniv. of the Mutual Aid Organization.

Sailor and Naval Scene — A363

1954, Aug. 19 ***Perf. 13x13½***

1002 A363 55b deep blue 1.75 .35

Navy Day.

Monument to Soviet Soldier — A364

1954, Aug. 23 ***Perf. 13½x13***

1003 A364 55b scarlet & purple 1.50 .30

10th anniv. of Romania's liberation.

House of Culture A365

Academy of Music, Bucharest — A366

55b, Scanteia building. 1.55 l, Radio station.

1954, Sept. 6 ***Perf. 14, 13½x13***

1004 A365 20b violet blue .50 .25
1005 A366 38b violet 1.00 .30
1006 A365 55b violet brown 1.00 .30
1007 A366 1.55 l red brown 2.00 .30
Nos. 1004-1007 (4) 4.50 1.15

Publicizing Romania's cultural progress during the decade following liberation.

Aviator — A367

Perf. 13½x13

1954, Sept. 13 **Wmk. 358**

1008 A367 55b blue 2.75 .40

Aviation Day.

Chemical Plant and Oil Derricks A368

1954, Sept. 21 ***Perf. 13x13½***

1009 A368 55b gray 2.50 .40

Intl. Conference of chemical and petroleum workers, Bucharest, Sept. 1954.

Dragon Pillar, Peking — A369

1954, Oct. 7 ***Perf. 14***

1010 A369 55b dk ol grn, *cream* 2.50 .40

Week of Chinese Culture.

Dumitri T. Neculuta — A370

1954, Oct. 17 ***Perf. 13½x13***

1011 A370 55b purple 2.00 .30

Neculuta, poet, 50th death anniv.

ARLUS Emblem — A371

65b, Romanian & Russian women embracing.

1954, Oct. 22 ***Perf. 14***

1012 A371 55b rose carmine .70 .25
1013 A371 65b dark purple 1.00 .25

Month of Romanian-Soviet Friendship.

Gheorghe Tattarescu — A372

1954, Oct. 24 ***Perf. 13½x13***

1014 A372 55b cerise 2.50 .40

Gheorghe Tattarescu (1820-1894), painter.

Barbu Iscovescu — A373

1954, Nov. 3 ***Perf. 14***

1015 A373 1.75 l red brown 3.25 .60

Death cent. of Barbu Iscovescu, painter.

Wild Boar — A374

Month of the Forest: 65b, Couple planting tree. 1.20 l, Logging.

Perf. 13½x13

1955, Mar. 15 **Wmk. 358**

1016 A374 35b brown 1.40 .25
1017 A374 65b turq blue 1.60 .30
1018 A374 1.20 l dark red 3.50 .65
Nos. 1016-1018 (3) 6.50 1.20

Globe and Clasped Hands — A375

1955, Apr. 5 **Photo.**

1019 A375 25b carmine rose .70 .25

Intl. Conference of Universal Trade Unions (Federation Syndicale Mondiale), Vienna, Apr. 1955.

Teletype — A376

1954, Dec. 31 ***Perf. 13½x13***

1020 A376 50b lilac 1.75 .30

Romanian telegraph system, cent.

Lenin — A377

Olympic Rings and Torch — A415

Designs: 55b, Water polo. 1 l, Gymnastics. 1.55 l, Canoeing. 1.75 l, High jump.

1956, Oct. 25 ***Perf. 13½x14***

1116 A415 20b vermilion .55 .25
1117 A415 55b ultra .80 .25
1118 A415 1 l lil rose 1.60 .30
1119 A415 1.55 l lt bl grn 2.10 .30
1120 A415 1.75 l dp pur 3.00 .40
Nos. 1116-1120 (5) 8.05 1.50

16th Olympic Games, Melbourne, 11/22-12/8.

Janos Hunyadi — A416

1956, Oct. **Wmk. 358**

1121 A416 55b dp vio 1.40 .30

Janos Hunyadi (1387-1456), national hero of Hungary. No. 1121 is found se-tenant with label showing Hunyadi Castle. Value for stamp with label, unused or used, $20.

Benjamin Franklin — A417

Portraits: 35b, Sesshu (Toyo Oda). 40b, G. B. Shaw. 50b, Ivan Franco. 55b, Pierre Curie. 1 l, Henrik Ibsen. 1.55 l, Fedor Dostoevski. 1.75 l, Heinrich Heine. 2.55 l, Mozart. 3.25 l, Rembrandt.

1956 **Unwmk.**

1122 A417 20b vio bl .50 .25
1123 A417 35b rose lake .60 .25
1124 A417 40b chocolate .70 .25
1125 A417 50b brn blk .90 .25
1126 A417 55b dk ol .90 .25
1127 A417 1 l dk bl grn 1.75 .25
1128 A417 1.55 l dp pur 2.50 .25
1129 A417 1.75 l brt bl 3.25 .25
1130 A417 2.55 l rose vio 4.50 .40
1131 A417 3.25 l dk bl 4.75 .90
Nos. 1122-1131 (10) 20.35 3.30

Great personalities of the world.

George Enescu as a Boy — A418

Portrait: 1.75 l, George Enescu as an adult.

1956, Dec. 29 **Engr.**

1132 A418 55b ultramarine 1.25 .30
1133 A418 1.75 l deep claret 2.25 .40

75th birth anniv. of George Enescu, musician and composer.

A419

Fighting Peasants, by Octav Bancila.

1957, Feb. 28 **Photo.** **Wmk. 358**

1134 A419 55b dk bl gray 1.50 .30

50th anniversary of Peasant Uprising.

A420

1957, Apr. 24 ***Perf. 13½x14***

1147 A420 55b brown 1.25 .25
1148 A420 55b olive black .75 .40

Enthronement of Stephen the Great, Prince of Moldavia, 500th anniv.

Dr. George Marinescu, Marinescu Institute and Congress Emblem — A421

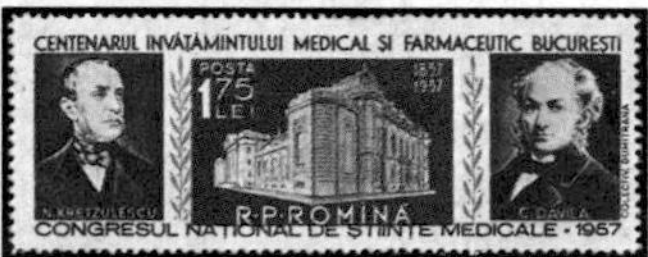

Dr. N. Kretzulescu, Medical School, Dr. C. Davila — A422

35b, Dr. I. Cantacuzino & Cantacuzino Hospital. 55b, Dr. V. Babes & Babes Institute.

1957, May 5 ***Perf. 14x13½***

1149 A421 20b dp grn .45 .25
1150 A421 35b dp red brn .60 .25
1151 A421 55b red lil 1.00 .30
1152 A422 1.75 l brt ultra & dk red 3.75 .70
Nos. 1149-1152 (4) 5.80 1.50

National Congress of Medical Science, Bucharest, May 5-6.

No. 1152 also for centenary of medical and pharmaceutical teaching in Bucharest. It measures 66x23mm.

Dove and Handle Bars — A423

1957, May 29 ***Perf. 13½x14***

1153 A423 20b shown .40 .25
1154 A423 55b Cyclist 1.25 .30

10th International Bicycle Peace Race.

Woman Watching Gymnast — A424

Woman Gymnast on Bar — A425

1957, May 21 ***Perf. 13½***

1155 A424 20b shown .60 .25
1156 A425 35b shown .90 .25
1157 A425 55b Vaulting horse 1.75 .30
1158 A424 1.75 l Acrobat 5.00 .75
Nos. 1155-1158 (4) 8.25 1.55

European Women's Gymnastic meet, Bucharest.

Slide Rule, Caliper & Atomic Symbol — A426

Wmk. 358

1957, May 29 **Photo.** ***Perf. 14***

1159 A426 55b blue 1.40 .25
1160 A426 55b brn red 1.60 .30

2nd Congress of the Society of Engineers and Technicians, Bucharest, May 29-31.

Rhododendron Hirsutum — A427

Carpathian Mountain Flowers: 10b, Daphne Blagayana. 20b, Lilium Bulbiferum L. 35b, Leontopodium Alpinum. 55b, Gentiana Acaulis L. 1 l, Dianthus Callizonus. 1.55 l, Primula Carpatica Griseb. 1.75 l, Anemone Montana Hoppe.

Light Gray Background

1957, June 22 **Litho.** **Unwmk.**

1161 A427 5b brt rose .35 .25
1162 A427 10b dk grn .45 .25
1163 A427 20b red org .50 .25
1164 A427 35b olive .90 .25
1165 A427 55b ultra 1.25 .25
1166 A427 1 l red 2.50 .25
1167 A427 1.55 l yellow 2.50 .30
1168 A427 1.75 l dk pur 4.25 .45
Nos. 1161-1168 (8) 12.70 2.25

Nos. 1161-1168 also come se-tenant with a decorative label. Value, set $50.

"Oxcart" by Grigorescu A428

Nicolae Grigorescu — A429

Painting: 1.75 l, Battle scene.

1957, June 29 **Photo.** **Wmk. 358**

1169 A428 20b dk bl grn .60 .25
1170 A429 55b deep brown 1.50 .25
1171 A428 1.75 l chalky blue 5.50 .70
Nos. 1169-1171 (3) 7.60 1.20

Grigorescu, painter, 50th death anniv.

Warship A430

1957, Aug. 3 ***Perf. 13x13½***

1172 A430 1.75 l Prus bl 2.00 .30

Navy Day.

Young Couple — A431

Festival Emblem — A432

Folk Dance — A433

Design: 55b, Girl with flags on hoop.

Perf. 14x14½, 14x14x12½ (A432), 13½x12½ (A433)

1957, July 28

1173 A431 20b red lilac .25 .25
1174 A431 55b emerald .45 .25
1175 A432 1 l red orange 1.10 .30
1176 A433 1.75 l ultra 1.75 .25
Nos. 1173-1176 (4) 3.55 1.05

Moscow 1957 Youth Festival. No. 1173 measures 23x34mm, No. 1174 22x38mm.

No. 1175 was printed in sheets of 50, alternating with 40 labels inscribed "Peace and Friendship" in 20 languages. Value for stamp with label, unused or used, $10.

Bugler — A434

1957, Aug. 30 **Wmk. 358** ***Perf. 14***

1177 A434 20b brt pur 1.50 .30

80th anniv. of the Russo-Turkish war.

Girl Holding Dove — A435

1957, Sept. 3 ***Perf. 13½***

1178 A435 55b Prus grn & red 1.75 .30

Honoring the Red Cross.

Battle Scene A436

1957, Aug. 31

1179	A436	1.75 l brown	1.75	.30

Battle of Marasesti, 40th anniv.

Jumper and Dove — A437

55b, Javelin thrower, bison. 1.75 l, Runner, stag.

1957, Sept. 14 Photo. *Perf. 13½*

1180	A437	20b brt bl & blk	.40	.25
1181	A437	55b yel & blk	1.25	.25
1182	A437	1.75 l brick red & blk	3.50	.50
		Nos. 1180-1182 (3)	5.15	1.00

International Athletic Meet, Bucharest.

Statue of Ovid, Constanta A438

1957, Sept. 20 Photo. Wmk. 358

1183	A438	1.75 l vio bl	2.75	.60

2000th anniv. of the birth of the Roman poet Publius Ovidius Naso.

Oil Field — A439

Design: 55b, Horse pulling drill, 1857.

1957, Oct. 5

1184	A439	20b dl red brn	.45	.25
1185	A439	20b indigo	.45	.25
1186	A439	55b vio blk	1.10	.30
		Nos. 1184-1186 (3)	2.00	.80

Contenary of Romanian oil industry.

Congress Emblem A440

1957, Sept. 28

1187	A440	55b ultra	1.00	.25

4th Intl. Trade Union Cong., Leipzig, 10/4 15.

Young Couple, Lenin Banner — A441

35b, Lenin & Flags. 55b, Lenin statue.

1957, Nov. 6 *Perf. 14x14½, 14½x14*

1188	A441	10b crimson	.30	.25
1189	A441	35b plum, horiz.	.60	.25
1190	A441	55b brown	.90	.25
		Nos. 1188-1190 (3)	1.80	.75

Russian Revolution, 40th anniversary.

Endre Ady — A442

1957, Dec. 5 *Perf. 14*

1191	A442	55b ol brn	1.25	.25

Ady, Hungarian poet, 80th birth anniv.

Oath of Bobilna A443

Bobilna Monument — A444

1957, Nov. 30

1192	A443	50b deep plum	.35	.25
1193	A444	55b slate blue	.50	.25

520th anniversary of the insurrection of the peasants of Bobilna in 1437.

Black-winged Stilt — A445

Animals: 10b, Great white egret. 20b, White spoonbill. 50b, Sturgeon. 55b, Ermine, horiz. 1.30 l, White pelican, horiz.

Perf. 13½x14, 14x13½

1957, Dec. 27 Photo. Wmk. 358

1194	A445	5b red brn & gray	.25	.25
1195	A445	10b emer & ocher	.25	.25
1196	A445	20b brt red & ocher	.35	.25
1197	A445	50b bl grn & ocher	.65	.25
1198	A445	55b dp cl & gray	1.00	.25
1199	A445	1.30 l pur & org	1.75	.30
		Nos. 1194-1199,C53-C54 (8)	14.00	3.80

Sputnik 2 and Laika A446

1957, Dec. 20 *Perf. 14x13½*

1200	A446	1.20 l bl & dk brn	5.00	.60
1201	A446	1.20 l grnsh bl & choc	5.00	.60

Dog Laika, "first space traveler."

Romanian Arms, Flags — A447

Designs: 55b, Arms, "Industry and Agriculture." 1.20 l, Arms, "Art, Science and Sport (soccer)."

1957, Dec. 30 *Perf. 13½*

1202	A447	25b ultra, red & ocher	.35	.25
1203	A447	55b dull yellow	.60	.25
1204	A447	1.20 l crimson rose	1.25	.30
		Nos. 1202-1204 (3)	2.20	.80

Proclamation of the Peoples' Republic, 10th anniv.

Flag and Wreath — A448

1958, Feb. 15 Unwmk. *Perf. 13½*

1205	A448	1 l dk bl & red, *buff*	.90	.25
1206	A448	1 l brn & red, *buff*	.90	.25

Grivita Strike, 25th anniversary.

Television, Radio Antennas A449

Design: 1.75 l, Telegraph pole and wires.

1958, Mar. 21 *Perf. 14x13½*

1207	A449	55b brt vio	.50	.25
1208	A449	1.75 l dp mag	1.00	.30

Telecommunications Conference, Moscow, Dec. 3-17, 1957.

Nicolae Balcescu — A450

Romanian Writers: 10b, Ion Creanga. 35b, Alexandru Vlahuta. 55b, Mihail Eminescu. 1.75 l, Vasile Alecsandri. 2 l, Barbu S. Delavrancea.

1958 Wmk. 358 *Perf. 14x14½*

1209	A450	5b bluish blk	.35	.25
1210	A450	10b int blk	.35	.25
1211	A450	35b dk bl	.35	.25
1212	A450	55b dk red brn	.60	.25
1213	A450	1.75 l blk brn	1.25	.30
1214	A450	2 l dk sl grn	2.10	.35
		Nos. 1209-1214 (6)	5.00	1.65

See Nos. 1309-1314.

Fencer in Global Mask A451

1958, Apr. 5 *Perf. 14½x14*

1215	A451	1.75 l brt pink	1.75	.30

Youth Fencing World Championships, Bucharest.

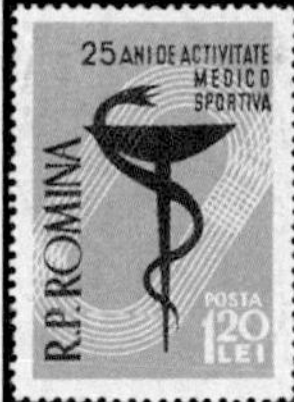

Stadium and Health Symbol — A452

1958, Apr. 16 *Perf. 14x14½*

1216	A452	1.20 l lt grn & red	1.75	.30

25 years of sports medicine.

Globe and Dove — A453

1958, May 15 Photo.

1217	A453	55b brt bl	1.10	.25

4th Congress of the Intl. Democratic Women's Federation, June 1958.

Carl von Linné — A454

Portraits: 20b, Auguste Comte. 40b, William Blake. 55b, Mikhail I. Glinka. 1 l, Henry W. Longfellow. 1.75 l, Carlo Goldoni. 2 l, Jan A. Komensky.

Perf. 14x14½

1958, May 31 Unwmk.

1218	A454	10b Prus grn	.25	.25
1219	A454	20b brown	.35	.25
1220	A454	40b dp lil	.60	.25
1221	A454	55b dp bl	.90	.25
1222	A454	1 l dp mag	1.25	.25
1223	A454	1.75 l dp vio bl	1.50	.30
1224	A454	2 l olive	2.75	.35
		Nos. 1218-1224 (7)	7.60	1.90

Great personalities of the world.

Clavaria Aurea — A456

Mushrooms: 5b, Lepiota Procera. 20b, Amanita caesarea. 30b, Lactarius deliciosus. 35b, Armillaria mellea. 55b, Coprinus comatus. 1 l, Morchella conica. 1.55 l, Psalliota campestris. 1.75 l, Boletus edulis. 2 l, Cantharellus cibarius.

1958, July Litho. Unwmk.

1225	A456	5b gray bl & brn	.25	.25
1226	A456	10b ol, ocher & brn	.25	.25
1227	A456	20b gray, red & yel	.45	.25
1228	A456	30b grn & dp org	.60	.25
1229	A456	35b lt bl & yel brn	.65	.25
1230	A456	55b pale grn, fawn & brn	.90	.25
1231	A456	1 l bl grn, ocher & brn	1.25	.25
1232	A456	1.55 l gray, lt gray & pink	2.10	.30
1233	A456	1.75 l emer, brn & buff	2.40	.35
1234	A456	2 l dl bl & org yel	3.50	.40
		Nos. 1225-1234 (10)	12.35	2.80

Antarctic Map and Emil Racovita A457

Design: 1.20 l, Cave and Racovita.

1958, July 30 Photo. *Perf. 14½x14*

1235 A457 55b indigo & lt bl 1.10 .30
1236 A457 1.20 l ol bis & dk vio 2.50 .30

90th birth anniv. of Emil Racovita, explorer and naturalist.

Armed Forces Monument — A458

Designs: 75b, Soldier guarding industry. 1.75 l, Sailor raising flag and ship.

1958, Oct. 2 *Perf. 13½x13*

1237 A458 55b orange brown .30 .25
1238 A458 75b deep magenta .45 .25
1239 A458 1.75 l bright blue 1.00 .25
Nos. 1237-1239,C55 (4) 3.35 1.25

Armed Forces Day.

Woman & Man from Oltenia — A459

Regional Costumes: 40b, Tara Oasului. 50b, Transylvania. 55b, Muntenia. 1 l, Banat. 1.75 l, Moldavia. Pairs: "a" woman, "b" man.

1958 Unwmk. Litho. *Perf. 13½x14*

1240 A459 35b Pair, #a.-b. + label .75 .25
1241 A459 40b Pair, #a.-b. + label .75 .25
1242 A459 50b Pair, #a.-b. + label .95 .25
1243 A459 55b Pair, #a.-b. + label 1.50 .25
1244 A459 1 l Pair, #a.-b. + label 3.25 .45
1245 A459 1.75 l Pair, #a.-b. + label 3.75 .55
Nos. 1240-1245 (6) 10.95 2.00

Nos. 1240-1245 exist imperf. Value, set $20, unused or used.

Printer and Hand Press A461

Moldavia Stamp of 1858 A462

55b, Scissors cutting strips of 1858 stamps. 1.20 l, Postilion, mail coach. 1.30 l, Postilion blowing horn, courier on horseback. 1.75 l, 2 l, 3.30 l, Various denominations of 1858 issue.

1958, Nov. 15 Engr. *Perf. 14½x14*

1252 A461 35b vio bl .30 .25
1253 A461 55b dk red brn .50 .25
1254 A461 1.20 l dull bl .90 .25
1255 A461 1.30 l brown vio 1.20 .25
1256 A462 1.55 l gray brn 1.50 .25
1257 A462 1.75 l rose claret 1.50 .25
1258 A462 2 l dull vio 1.90 .50
1259 A462 3.30 l dull red brn 2.50 .60
Nos. 1252-1259 (8) 10.30 2.60

Cent. of Romanian stamps. See No. C57.

Exist imperf. Value, set $25.

Bugler — A463

1958, Dec. 10 Photo. *Perf. 13½x13*

1260 A463 55b crimson rose .75 .30

Decade of teaching reforms.

Runner — A464

Perf. 13½x14

1958, Dec. 9 Wmk. 358

1261 A464 1 l deep brown 1.25 .30

Third Youth Spartacist Sports Meet. For overprint, see No. 1287.

Building and Flag — A465

1958, Dec. 16

1262 A465 55b dk car rose .80 .25

Workers' Revolution, 40th anniversary.

Prince Alexandru Ioan Cuza A466

Perf. 14x13½

1959, Jan. 27 Unwmk.

1263 A466 1.75 l dk blue 1.50 .30

Centenary of the Romanian Union.

Friedrich Handel — A467

Portraits: No. 1265, Robert Burns. No. 1266, Charles Darwin. No. 1267, Alexander Popov. No. 1268, Shalom Aleichem.

1959, Apr. 25 Photo. *Perf. 13½x14*

1264 A467 55b brown .60 .25
1265 A467 55b indigo .60 .25
1266 A467 55b slate .60 .25
1267 A467 55b carmine .60 .25
1268 A467 55b purple .60 .25
Nos. 1264-1268,C59 (6) 6.00 1.85

Various cultural anniversaries in 1959.

Corn — A468

Sheep A469

No. 1270, Sunflower and bee. No. 1271, Sugar beet and refinery. No. 1273, Cattle. No. 1274, Rooster and hens. No. 1275, Tractor and grain. No. 1276, Loaded farm wagon. No. 1277, Farm couple and "10."

Perf. 13½x14, 14x13½

1959, June 1 Photo. Wmk. 358

1269 A468 55b brt green .40 .25
1270 A468 55b red org .40 .25
1271 A468 55b red lilac .40 .25
1272 A469 55b olive grn .40 .25
1273 A469 55b red brown .40 .25
1274 A469 55b yellow brn .40 .25
1275 A469 55b blue .40 .25
1276 A469 55b brown .40 .25

Unwmk.

1277 A469 5 l dp red lilac 3.00 .60
Nos. 1269-1277 (9) 6.20 2.60

10th anniv. of collective farming. Sizes: #1272-1276 33x23mm; #1277 38x27mm.

Young Couple — A470

Design: 1.60 l, Dancer in folk costume.

Perf. 13½x14

1959, July 15 Unwmk.

1278 A470 1 l brt blue .75 .25
1279 A470 1.60 l car rose 1.00 .25

7th World Youth Festival, Vienna, 7/26-8/14.

Steel Worker and Farm Woman — A471

1959, Aug. 23 Litho. *Perf. 13½x14*

1280 A471 55b multicolored .60 .25
a. Souvenir sheet of 1 1.75 .65

15th anniv. of Romania's liberation from the Germans.

No. 1280a is ungummed and imperf. The blue, yellow and red vignette shows large "XV" and Romanian flag. Brown 1.20 l denomination and inscription in margin.

Prince Vlad Tepes and Document — A472

Designs: 40b, Nicolae Balcescu Street. No. 1283, Atheneum. No. 1284, Printing Combine. 1.55 l, Opera House. 1.75 l, Stadium.

1959, Sept. 20 Photo.

Centers in Gray

1281 A472 20b blue .95 .25
1282 A472 40b brown 1.40 .25
1283 A472 55b bister brn 1.60 .25
1284 A472 55b rose lilac 2.00 .35
1285 A472 1.55 l pale violet 4.25 .60
1286 A472 1.75 l bluish grn 4.75 .85
Nos. 1281-1286 (6) 14.95 2.55

500th anniversary of the founding of Bucharest. See No. C71.

No. 1261 Overprinted with Shield in Silver, inscribed: "Jocurile Bucaresti Balcanice 1959"

1959, Sept. 12 Wmk. 358

1287 A464 1 l deep brown 10.00 3.50

Balkan Games.

Soccer — A473

Motorcycle Race — A474

Perf. 13½

1959, Oct. 5 Unwmk. Litho.

1288 A473 20b shown .25 .25
1289 A474 35b shown .30 .25
1290 A474 40b Ice hockey .40 .25
1291 A473 55b Handball .45 .25
1292 A473 1 l Horse race .80 .25
1293 A473 1.50 l Boxing 1.40 .25
1294 A474 1.55 l Rugby 1.60 .25
1295 A474 1.60 l Tennis 2.00 .30
Nos. 1288-1295,C72 (9) 9.70 2.55

Russian Icebreaker "Lenin" A475

Perf. 14½x13½

1959, Oct. 25 Photo.

1296 A475 1.75 l blue vio 2.50 .40

First atomic ice-breaker.

Stamp Album and Magnifying Glass — A476

1959, Nov. 15 Wmk. 358 *Perf. 14*

1297 A476 1.60 l + 40b label 1.25 .40

Issued for Stamp Day.

Stamp and label were printed alternately in sheet. The 40b went to the Romanian Association of Philatelists.

Purple Foxglove — A477

1959, Dec. 15 Typo. Unwmk.
Medicinal Flowers in Natural Colors

1298	A477	20b shown	.25	.25
1299	A477	40b Peppermint	.30	.25
1300	A477	55b Cornflower	.50	.25
1301	A477	55b Daisies	.65	.25
1302	A477	1 l Autumn crocus	.90	.25
1303	A477	1.20 l Monkshood	1.00	.25
1304	A477	1.55 l Poppies	1.50	.25
1305	A477	1.60 l Linden	1.50	.30
1306	A477	1.75 l Dog rose	1.50	.30
1307	A477	3.20 l Buttercup	2.50	.50
		Nos. 1298-1307 (10)	10.60	2.85

Cuza University, Jassy, Centenary A478

1959, Nov. 26 Photo. Wmk. 358

1308	A478	55b brown	.70	.25

Romanian Writers Type of 1958

20b, Gheorghe Cosbuc. 40b, Ion Luca Caragiale. 50b, Grigore Alexandrescu. 55b, Alexandru Donici. 1 l, Costache Negruzzi. 1.55 l, Dimitrie Bolintineanu.

1960, Jan. 20 *Perf. 14*

1309	A450	20b bluish blk	.25	.25
1310	A450	40b dp lilac	.55	.25
1311	A450	50b brown	.65	.25
1312	A450	55b violet brn	.65	.25
1313	A450	1 l violet	1.10	.25
1314	A450	1.55 l dk blue	1.50	.35
		Nos. 1309-1314 (6)	4.70	1.60

Huchen (Salmon) — A480

55b, Greek tortoise. 1.20 l, Shelduck.

1960, Feb. 1 Engr. Unwmk.

1315	A480	20b blue	.30	.25
1316	A480	55b brown	.50	.25
1317	A480	1.20 l dk purple	1.25	.30
		Nos. 1315-1317,C76-C78 (6)	7.30	2.10

Woman, Dove and Globe — A481

1960, Mar. 1 Photo. *Perf. 14*

1318	A481	55b violet blue	.50	.25

50 years of Intl. Women's Day, Mar. 8.

A482

40b, Lenin. 55b, Lenin statue, Bucharest. 1.55 l, Head of Lenin.

1960, Apr. 22 Wmk. 358 *Perf. 13½*

1319	A482	40b magenta	.35	.25
1320	A482	55b violet blue	.50	.25

Souvenir Sheet

1321	A482	1.55 l carmine	3.00	2.00

90th birth anniv. of Lenin.

A483

40b, Heroes Monument. 55b, Soviet war memorial.

1960, May 9 Wmk. 358 *Perf. 14*

1322	A483	40b multicolored	.35	.25
1323	A483	55b multicolored	.45	.25
a.		Strip of 2, #1322-1323 + label	1.50	.75

15th anniversary of the liberation.

Nos. 1322-1323 exist imperf., printed in deep magenta. Value, set $3.25; label strip, $4.50.

Swimming A484

Sports: 55b, Women's gymnastics. 1.20 l, High jump. 1.60 l, Boxing. 2.45 l, Canoeing.

1960, June Unwmk. Typo. *Perf. 14*
Gray Background

1326	A484	40b blue & yel	3.00	3.00
1327	A484	55b blk, yel & emer	3.00	3.00
1328	A484	1.20 l emer & brick red	3.00	3.00
a.		Strip of 3, #1326-1328	10.00	10.00
1329	A484	1.60 l blue, yel & blk	3.00	3.00
1330	A484	2.45 l blk, emer & brick red	3.00	3.00
a.		Pair, #1329-1330 + 2 labels	10.00	10.00
		Nos. 1326-1330 (5)	15.00	15.00

17th Olympic Games, Rome, 8/25-9/11.

Nos. 1326-1330 were printed in one sheet, the top half containing No. 1328a, the bottom half No. 1330a, with gutter between. When the two strips are placed together, the Olympic rings join in a continuous design.

Exist imperf. (3.70 l replaced 2.45 l). Value, set, two strips $35.

Swimming — A485

Olympic Flame, Stadium — A486

40b, Women's gymnastics. 55b, High jump. 1 l, Boxing. 1.60 l, Canoeing. 2 l, Soccer.

1960 Photo. Wmk. 358

1331	A485	20b chalky blue	.25	.25
1332	A485	40b dk brn red	.35	.25
1333	A485	55b blue	.55	.25
1334	A485	1 l rose red	.75	.25
1335	A485	1.60 l rose lilac	1.00	.25
1336	A485	2 l dull violet	1.50	.35
		Nos. 1331-1336 (6)	4.40	1.60

Souvenir Sheets
Perf. 11½

1337	A486	5 l ultra	12.50	7.00

Imperf

1338	A486	6 l dull red	20.00	10.00

17th Olympic Games.

A487

Perf. 13½
1960, June 20 Unwmk. Litho.

1339	A487	55b red org & dk car	.50	.25

Romanian Workers' Party, 3rd congress.

A488

Portraits: 10b, Leo Tolstoy. 20b, Mark Twain. 35b, Hokusai. 40b, Alfred de Musset. 55b, Daniel Defoe. 1 l, Janos Bolyai. 1.20 l, Anton Chekov. 1.55 l, Robert Koch. 1.75 l, Frederick Chopin.

1960 Wmk. 358 Photo. *Perf. 14*

1340	A488	10b dull pur	.25	.25
1341	A488	20b olive	.30	.25
1342	A488	35b blue	.40	.25
1343	A488	40b slate green	.50	.25
1344	A488	55b dull brn vio	.75	.25
1345	A488	1 l Prus grn	1.25	.45
1346	A488	1.20 l dk car rose	1.40	.25
1347	A488	1.55 l gray blue	1.60	.25
1348	A488	1.75 l brown	2.25	.50
		Nos. 1340-1348 (9)	8.70	2.70

Various cultural anniversaries.

Students A489

Piano and Books A490

Designs: 5b, Diesel locomotive. 10b, Dam. 20b, Miner with drill. 30b, Ambulance and doctor. 35b, Textile worker. 50b, Nursery. 55b, Timber industry. 60b, Harvester. 75b, Feeding cattle. 1 l, Atomic reactor. 1.20 l, Oil derricks. 1.50 l, Coal mine. 1.55 l, Loading ship. 1.60 l, Athlete. 1.75 l, Bricklayer. 2 l, Steam roller. 2.40 l, Chemist. 3 l, Radio and television.

1960 Wmk. 358 Photo. *Perf. 14*

1349	A489	3b brt lil rose	.25	.25
1350	A489	5b olive bis	.25	.25
1351	A489	10b violet gray	.25	.25
1352	A489	20b blue vio	.25	.25
1353	A489	30b vermilion	.25	.25
1354	A489	35b crimson	.25	.25
1355	A490	40b ocher	.25	.25
1356	A489	50b bluish vio	.25	.25
1357	A489	55b blue	.25	.25
1358	A490	60b green	.25	.25
1359	A490	75b gray ol	.30	.25
1360	A489	1 l car rose	.50	.25
1361	A489	1.20 l black	.40	.25
1362	A489	1.50 l plum	.50	.25
1363	A490	1.55 l Prus grn	.50	.25
1364	A490	1.60 l dp blue	.55	.25
1365	A489	1.75 l red brown	.75	.25
1366	A489	2 l dk ol gray	1.00	.25
1367	A489	2.40 l brt lilac	1.25	.25
1368	A489	3 l grysh blue	1.75	.25
		Nos. 1349-1368,C86 (21)	11.50	5.25

Ovid Statue at Constanta A491

Black Sea Resorts: 35b, Constanta harbor. 40b, Vasile Rosita beach and vase. 55b, Ionian column and Mangalia beach. 1 l, Eforie at night. 1.60 l, Eforie and sailboat.

1960, Aug. 2 Litho. Unwmk.

1369	A491	20b multicolored	.25	.25
1370	A491	35b multicolored	.25	.25
1371	A491	40b multicolored	.25	.25
1372	A491	55b multicolored	.30	.25
1373	A491	1 l multicolored	.75	.25
1374	A491	1.60 l multicolored	1.10	.25
		Nos. 1369-1374,C87 (7)	4.40	2.00

Emblem — A492

Petrushka, Russian Puppet — A493

Designs: Various Puppets.

1960, Aug. 20 Typo.

1375	A492	20b multi	.25	.25
1376	A493	40b multi	.25	.25
1377	A493	55b multi	.25	.25
1378	A493	1 l multi	.50	.25
1379	A493	1.20 l multi	.50	.25
1380	A493	1.75 l multi	.75	.25
		Nos. 1375-1380 (6)	2.50	1.50

International Puppet Theater Festival.

Children on Sled — A494

Children's Sports: 35b, Boys playing ball, horiz. 55b, Ice skating, horiz. 1 l, Running. 1.75 l, Swimming, horiz.

Unwmk.
1960, Oct. 1 Litho. *Perf. 14*

1381	A494	20b multi	.25	.25
1382	A494	35b multi	.25	.25
1383	A494	55b multi	.30	.25
1384	A494	1 l multi	.45	.25
1385	A494	1.75 l multi	.90	.25
		Nos. 1381-1385 (5)	2.15	1.25

Globe and Peace Banner — A495

Perf. 13½x14

1960, Nov. 26 Photo. Wmk. 358

1386	A495	55b brt bl & yel	.40	.25

Intl. Youth Federation, 15th anniv.

Worker and Flags A496

Perf. 14x13

1960, Nov. 26 Litho. Unwmk.

1387	A496	55b dk car & red org	.40	.25

40th anniversary of the general strike.

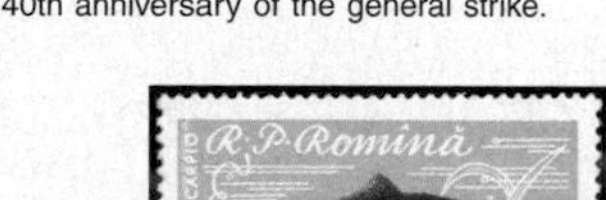

Carp A497

Fish: 20b, Pikeperch. 40b, Black Sea turbot. 55b, Allis shad. 1 l, Wels (catfish). 1.20 l, Sterlet. 1.60 l, Huchen (salmon).

1960, Dec. 5 Typo.

1388	A497	10b	multi	.25	.25
1389	A497	20b	multi	.30	.25
1390	A497	40b	multi	.35	.25
1391	A497	55b	multi	.40	.25
1392	A497	1 l	multi	1.00	.25
1393	A497	1.20 l	multi	1.10	.25
1394	A497	1.60 l	multi	1.75	.35
	Nos. 1388-1394 (7)			5.15	1.85

Kneeling Woman and Grapes — A498

Designs: 30b, Farmers drinking, horiz. 40b, Loading grapes into basket, horiz. 55b, Woman cutting grapes. 75b, Vintner with basket. 1 l, Woman filling basket with grapes. 1.20 l, Vintner with jug. 5 l, Antique wine jug.

1960, Dec. 20 Litho. *Perf. 14*

1395	A498	20b	brn & gray	.25	.25
1396	A498	30b	red org & pale grn	.30	.25
1397	A498	40b	dp ultra & gray ol	.40	.25
1398	A498	55b	emer & buff	.50	.25
1399	A498	75b	dk car rose & pale grn	.50	.25
1400	A498	1 l	Prus grn & gray ol	.65	.25
1401	A498	1.20 l	org brn & pale bl	1.00	.30
	Nos. 1395-1401 (7)			3.60	1.80

Souvenir Sheet

Imperf

1402	A498	5 l	dk car rose & bis	4.00	1.90

Each stamp represents a different wine-growing region: Dragasani, Dealul Mare, Odobesti, Cotnari, Tirnave, Minis, Murfatlar and Pietroasa.

Steelworker by I. Irimescu — A499

Modern Sculptures: 10b, G. Doja, I. Vlad. 20b, Meeting, B. Caragea. 40b, George Enescu, A. Anghel. 50b, Mihail Eminescu, C. Baraschi. 55b, Peasant Revolt, 1907, M. Constantinescu, horiz. 1 l, "Peace," I. Jalea. 1.55 l, Building Socialism, C. Medrea. 1.75 l, Birth of an Idea, A. Szobotka.

Perf. 13½x14, 14x13½

1961, Feb. 16 Photo. Unwmk.

1403	A499	5b	car rose	.25	.25
1404	A499	10b	violet	.25	.25
1405	A499	20b	ol blk	.25	.25
1406	A499	40b	ol bis	.35	.25
1407	A499	50b	blk brn	.40	.25
1408	A499	55b	org ver	.60	.25
1409	A499	1 l	dp plum	.80	.25
1410	A499	1.55 l	brt ultra	1.00	.25
1411	A499	1.75 l	green	1.40	.25
	Nos. 1403-1411 (9)			5.30	2.25

Peter Poni, and Chemical Apparatus — A500

Romanian Scientists: 20b, A. Saligny and Danube bridge, Cernavoda. 55b, C. Budeanu and electrical formula. 1.55 l, Gh. Titeica and geometrical symbol.

1961, Apr. 11 Litho. *Perf. 13½x13*

Portraits in Brown Black

1412	A500	10b	pink & vio bl	.25	.25
1413	A500	20b	citron & mar	.25	.25
1414	A500	55b	blue & red	.30	.25
1415	A500	1.55 l	ocher & lilac	1.00	.25
	Nos. 1412-1415 (4)			1.80	1.00

Freighter "Galati" A501

Ships: 40b, Passenger ship "Oltenita." 55b, Motorboat "Tomis." 1 l, Freighter "Arad." 1.55 l, Tugboat. 1.75 l, Freighter "Dobrogea."

1961, Apr. 25 Typo. *Perf. 14x13*

1416	A501	20b	multi	.25	.25
1417	A501	40b	multi	.25	.25
1418	A501	55b	multi	.40	.25
1419	A501	1 l	multi	.50	.25
1420	A501	1.55 l	multi	.75	.25
1421	A501	1.75 l	multi	1.10	.25
	Nos. 1416-1421 (6)			3.25	1.50

Marx, Lenin and Engels on Red Flag — A502

Designs: 55b, Workers. 1 l, "Industry and Agriculture" and Workers Party Emblem.

1961, Apr. 29 Litho.

1422	A502	35b red, bl & ocher	.40	.25
1423	A502	55b mar, red & gray	.60	.25

Souvenir Sheet

Imperf

1424	A502	1 l multi	1.75	.70

40th anniv. of the Romanian Communist Party. #1424 contains one 55x33mm stamp.

Roe Deer and Bronze Age Hunting Scene — A503

Lynx and Prehistoric Hunter A504

35b, Boar, Roman hunter. 40b, Brown bear, Roman tombstone. 55b, Red deer, 16th cent. hunter. 75b, Red fox, feudal hunter. 1 l, Black goat, modern hunter. 1.55 l, Rabbit, hunter with dog. 1.75 l, Badger, hunter. 2 l, Roebuck, hunter.

1961, July *Perf. 13x14, 14x13*

1425	A503	10b	multi	.25	.25
1426	A504	20b	multi	.25	.25
1427	A504	35b	multi	.35	.25
1428	A504	40b	multi	.60	.25
1429	A503	55b	multi	.75	.25
1430	A504	75b	multi	.90	.25
1431	A503	1 l	multi	1.00	.25
1432	A503	1.55 l	multi	1.25	.25
1433	A503	1.75 l	multi	1.50	.30
1434	A503	2 l	multi	1.75	.45
	Nos. 1425-1434 (10)			8.60	2.75

Georges Enescu A505

1961, Sept. 7 Litho. *Perf. 14x13*

1435	A505	3 l pale vio & vio brn	1.40	.30

2nd Intl. George Enescu Festival, Bucharest.

Peasant Playing Panpipe — A506

Peasants playing musical instruments: 20b, Alpenhorn, horiz. 40b, Flute. 55b, Guitar. 60b, Bagpipe. 1 l, Zither.

Perf. 13x14, 14x13

1961 Unwmk. Typo.

Tinted Paper

1436	A506	10b	multi	.25	.25
1437	A506	20b	multi	.25	.25
1438	A506	40b	multi	.25	.25
1439	A506	55b	multi	.45	.25
1440	A506	60b	multi	.45	.25
1441	A506	1 l	multi	.70	.25
	Nos. 1436-1441 (6)			2.35	1.50

Heraclitus — A507

Portraits: 20b, Francis Bacon. 40b, Rabindranath Tagore. 55b, Domingo F. Sarmiento. 1.35 l, Heinrich von Kleist. 1.75 l, Mikhail V. Lomonosov.

Perf. 13½x13

1961, Oct. 25 Photo. Wmk. 358

1442	A507	10b	maroon	.25	.25
1443	A507	20b	brown	.25	.25
1444	A507	40b	Prus grn	.25	.25
1445	A507	55b	cerise	.25	.25
1446	A507	1.35 l	brt bl	.75	.25
1447	A507	1.75 l	purple	1.00	.25
	Nos. 1442-1447 (6)			2.75	1.50

Swimming — A508

Gold Medal, Boxing A509

#1449, Olympic torch. #1450, Water polo, Melbourne. #1451, Women's high jump, Rome.

Perf. 14x14½

1961, Oct. 30 Photo. Unwmk.

1448	A508	20b	bl gray	.25	.25
1449	A508	20b	vermilion	.25	.25
1450	A508	55b	ultra	.60	.25
1451	A508	55b	blue	.60	.25
	Nos. 1448-1451 (4)			1.70	1.00

Perf. 10½

Size: 33x33mm

Gold Medals: 35b, Pistol shooting, Melbourne. 40b, Sharpshooting, Rome. 55b, Wrestling. 1.35 l, Woman's high jump. 1.75 l, Three medals for canoeing.

Medals in Ocher

1452	A509	10b	Prus grn	.25	.25
1453	A509	35b	brown	.40	.25
1454	A509	40b	plum	.45	.25
1455	A509	55b	org red	.60	.25
1456	A509	1.35 l	dp ultra	.90	.25

Size: 46x32mm

1457	A509	1.75 l	dp car rose	1.75	.35
	Nos. 1452-1457 (6)			4.35	1.60
	Nos. 1448-1457 (10)			6.05	2.60

Romania's gold medals in 1956, 1960 Olympics.

#1452-1457 exist imperf. Value, set: unused $5; used $3.50.

A souvenir sheet of one 4 l dark red & ocher was issued. Value, unused $5.50, canceled $4.50.

Congress Emblem — A510

1961, Dec. Litho. *Perf. 13½x14*

1458	A510	55b dk car rose	.50	.25

5th World Congress of Trade Unions, Moscow, Dec. 4-16.

Primrose A511

Designs: 20b, Sweet William. 25b, Peony. 35b, Prickly pear. 40b, Iris. 55b, Buttercup. 1 l, Hepatica. 1.20 l, Poppy. 1.55 l, Gentian. 1.75 l, Carol Davilla and Dimitrie Brindza. 20b, 25b, 40b, 55b, 1.20 l, 1.55 l, are vertical.

Perf. 14x13½, 13½x14

1961, Sept. 15

1459 A511 10b multi .25 .25
1460 A511 20b multi .25 .25
1461 A511 25b multi .25 .25
1462 A511 35b multi .30 .25
1463 A511 40b multi .30 .25
1464 A511 55b multi .35 .25
1465 A511 1 l multi .50 .25
1466 A511 1.20 l multi .65 .25
1467 A511 1.55 l multi 1.10 .25
Nos. 1459-1467 (9) 3.95 2.25

Souvenir Sheet

Imperf

1468 A511 1.75 l car, blk & grn 4.50 3.00

Bucharest Botanical Garden, cent.
No. 1459-1467 exist imperf. Value, set $12.

United Nations Emblem — A512

Designs: 20b, Map of Balkan peninsula and dove. 40b, Men of three races.

1961, Nov. 27 *Perf. 13½x14*

1469 A512 20b bl, yel & pink .25 .25
1470 A512 40b multi .55 .25
1471 A512 55b org, lil & yel .80 .25
Nos. 1469-1471 (3) 1.60 .75

UN, 15th anniv. Nos. 1469-1470 are each printed with alternating yellow labels.
Exist imperf. Value, set: unused $2.75; used $2.

Cock and Savings Book — A513

Savings Day: 55b, Honeycomb, bee and savings book.

1962, Feb. 15 **Typo.** *Perf. 13½*

1472 A513 40b multi .30 .25
1473 A513 55b multi .30 .25

Soccer Player and Map of Europe — A514

1962, Apr. 20 **Litho.** *Perf. 13x14*

1474 A514 55b emer & red brn .60 .25

European Junior Soccer Championships, Bucharest. For surcharge see No. 1510.

Wheat, Map and Tractor — A515

Designs: 55b, Medal honoring agriculture. 1.55Nl, Sheaf of wheat, hammer & sickle.

1962, Apr. 27 *Perf. 13½x14*

1475 A515 40b org & dk car .25 .25
1476 A515 55b yel, car & brn .25 .25
1477 A515 1.55 l multi .85 .25
Nos. 1475-1477 (3) 1.35 .75

Collectivization of agriculture.

Canoe Race A516

20b, Kayak. 40b, 8-man shell. 55b, 2-man skiff. 1 l, Yachts. 1.20 l, Motorboats. 1.55 l, Sailboat. 3 l, Water slalom.

1962, May 15 **Photo.** *Perf. 14x13*

Vignette in Bright Blue

1478 A516 10b lil rose .25 .25
1479 A516 20b ol gray .25 .25
1480 A516 40b red brn .25 .25
1481 A516 55b ultra .25 .25
1482 A516 1 l red .30 .25
1483 A516 1.20 l dp plum .70 .25
1484 A516 1.55 l orange 1.00 .25
1485 A516 3 l violet 1.75 .25
Nos. 1478-1485 (8) 4.75 2.00

These stamps were also issued imperf. with color of denomination and inscription changed. Value, set unused $6, canceled $2.75.

Ion Luca Caragiale — A517

40b, Jean Jacques Rousseau. 1.75 l, Aleksander I. Herzen. 3.30 l, Ion Luca Caragiale (as a young man).

1962, June 9 *Perf. 13½x14*

1486 A517 40b dk sl grn .25 .25
1487 A517 55b magenta .25 .25
1488 A517 1.75 l dp bl .75 .25
Nos. 1486-1488 (3) 1.25 .75

Souvenir Sheet

Perf. 11½

1489 A517 3.30 l brown 4.25 4.25

Rousseau, French philosopher, 250th birth anniv.; Caragiale, Romanian author, 50th death anniv.; Herzen, Russian writer, 150th birth anniv. No. 1489 contains one 32x55mm stamp.

Globes Surrounded with Flags — A518

1962, July 6 **Typo.** *Perf. 11*

1490 A518 55b multi .60 .25

8th Youth Festival for Peace and Friendship, Helsinki, July 28-Aug. 6.

Traian Vuia — A519

Portraits: 20b, Al. Davila. 35b, Vasile Pirvan. 40b, Ion Negulici. 55b, Grigore Cobilcescu. 1 l, Dr. Gheorghe Marinescu. 1.20 l, Ion Cantacuzino. 1.35 l, Victor Babes. 1.55 l, C. Levaditi.

Perf. 13½x14

1962, July 20 **Photo.** **Wmk. 358**

1491 A519 15b brown .25 .25
1492 A519 20b dl red brn .25 .25
1493 A519 35b brn mag .25 .25
1494 A519 40b bl vio .25 .25
1495 A519 55b brt bl .25 .25
1496 A519 1 l dp ultra .30 .25
1497 A519 1.20 l crimson .45 .25
1498 A519 1.35 l Prus grn .60 .25
1499 A519 1.55 l purple 1.10 .25
Nos. 1491-1499 (9) 3.70 2.25

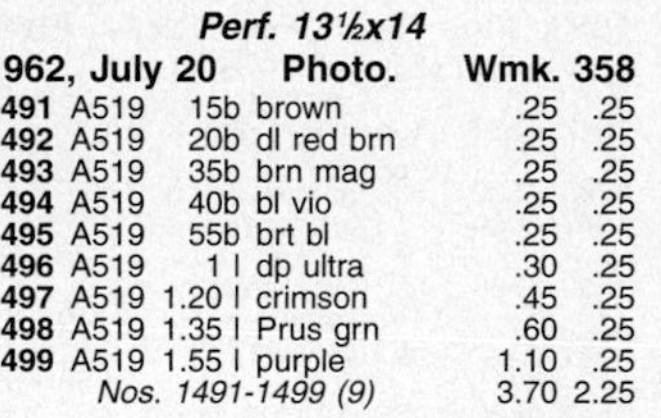

Fieldball Player and Globe — A520

Perf. 13x14

1962, May 12 **Litho.** **Unwmk.**

1500 A520 55b yel & vio 11.00 7.50

2nd Intl. Women's Fieldball Championships, Bucharest.

No. 1500 Surcharged in Violet Blue

1962, July 31

1501 A520 5 l on 55b yel & vio 5.00 2.50

Romanian victory in the 2nd Intl. Women's Fieldball Championships.

Rod Fishing A521

Various Fishing Scenes.

1962, July 25 *Perf. 14x13*

1502 A521 10b multi .25 .25
1503 A521 25b multi .25 .25
1504 A521 40b bl & brick red .25 .25
1505 A521 55b multi .25 .25
1506 A521 75b sl, gray & bl .40 .25
1507 A521 1 l multi .55 .25
1508 A521 1.75 l multi .90 .25
1509 A521 3.25 l multi 1.50 .25
Nos. 1502-1509 (8) 4.35 2.00

No. 1474 Surcharged "1962 Campioana Europeana 2 lei" in Dark Blue

1962, July 31

1510 A514 2 l on 55b 1.75 1.25

Romania's victory in the European Junior Soccer Championships, Bucharest.

Child and Butterfly — A522

Designs: 30b, Girl feeding bird. 40b, Boy and model sailboat. 55b, Children writing, horiz. 1.20 l, Girl at piano, and boy playing violin. 1.55 l, Pioneers camping, horiz.

Perf. 13x14, 14x13

1962, Aug. 25 **Litho.**

1511 A522 20b lt bl, red & brn .35 .25
1512 A522 30b org, bl & red brn .35 .25
1513 A522 40b chalky bl, dp org & Prus bl .35 .25
1514 A522 55b citron, bl & red .45 .25
1515 A522 1.20 l car, brn & dk vio .65 .25
1516 A522 1.55 l bis, red & vio 1.25 .25
Nos. 1511-1516 (6) 3.40 1.50

Handicraft — A523

Designs: 10b, Food and drink. 20b, Chemical industry. 40b, Chinaware. 55b, Leather industry. 75b, Textiles. 1 l, Furniture. 1.20 l, Electrical appliances. 1.55 l, Household goods (sewing machine and pots).

1962, Oct. 12 *Perf. 13x14*

1517 A523 5b multi .25 .25
1518 A523 10b multi .25 .25
1519 A523 20b multi .25 .25
1520 A523 40b multi .25 .25
1521 A523 55b multi .25 .25
1522 A523 75b multi .25 .25
1523 A523 1 l multi .40 .25
1524 A523 1.20 l multi .75 .25
1525 A523 1.55 l multl 1.10 .25
Nos. 1517-1525,C126 (10) 5.25 2.50

4th Sample Fair, Bucharest.

Lenin — A524

1962, Nov. 7 *Perf. 10½*

1526 A524 55b vio bl, red & bis .50 .25

Russian October Revolution, 45th anniv.

Bull — A525

Designs: 20b, Sheep, horiz. 40b, Merino ram, horiz. 1 l, York pig. 1.35 l, Cow. 1.55 l, Heifer, horiz. 1.75 l, Pigs, horiz.

1962, Nov. 20 *Perf. 14x13, 13x14*

1527 A525 20b ultra & blk .25 .25
1528 A525 40b bl, yel & sep .30 .25
1529 A525 55b ocher, buff & sl grn .50 .25
1530 A525 1 l gray, yel & brn .75 .25
1531 A525 1.35 l dl grn, choc & blk 1.25 .25
1532 A525 1.55 l org red, dk brn & blk 1.25 .25
1533 A525 1.75 l dk vio bl, yel & org 2.00 .30
Nos. 1527-1533 (7) 6.30 1.80

Arms, Factory and Harvester A526

Perf. 14½x13½

1962, Dec. 30 Litho.

1534 A526 1.55 l multi .85 .25

Romanian People's Republic, 15th anniv.

Strikers at Grivita, 1933 A527

1963, Feb. 16 ***Perf. 14x13½***

1535 A527 1.75 l red, vio & yel .80 .25

30th anniv. of the strike of railroad and oil industry workers at Grivita.

Tractor Driver and "FAO" Emblem A528

55b, Farm woman, cornfield & combine. 1.55 l, Child drinking milk & milking machine. 1.75 l, Woman with basket of grapes & vineyard.

1963, Mar. 21 Photo. ***Perf. 14½x13***

1536 A528 40b vio bl .25 .25
1537 A528 55b bis brn .25 .25
1538 A528 1.55 l rose red .50 .25
1539 A528 1.75 l green .85 .25
Nos. 1536-1539 (4) 1.85 1.00

FAO "Freedom from Hunger" campaign.

Tomatoes — A529

40b, Hot peppers. 55b, Radishes. 75b, Eggplant. 1.20 l, Mild peppers. 3.25 l, Cucumbers, horiz.

Perf. 13½x14, 14x13½

1963, Apr. 25 Litho. Unwmk.

1540 A529 35b multi .25 .25
1541 A529 40b multi .25 .25
1542 A529 55b multi .25 .25
1543 A529 75b multi .25 .25
1544 A529 1.20 l multi .70 .25
1545 A529 3.25 l multi 1.50 .30
Nos. 1540-1545 (6) 3.20 1.55

Woman Swimmer at Start — A530

Designs: 30b, Crawl, horiz. 55b, Butterfly stroke, horiz. 1 l, Backstroke, horiz. 1.35 l, Breaststroke, horiz. 1.55 l, Woman diver. 2 l, Water polo.

1963, June 15 ***Perf. 13x14, 14x13***

1546 A530 25b yel brn, emer & gray .25 .25
1547 A530 30b ol grn, gray & yel .25 .25
1548 A530 55b bl, gray & red .25 .25
1549 A530 1 l grn, gray & red .25 .25
1550 A530 1.35 l ultra, car & gray .40 .25
1551 A530 1.55 l pur, gray & org .85 .25
1552 A530 2 l car rose, gray & org .90 .35
Nos. 1546-1552 (7) 3.15 1.85

Chicks — A531

Domestic poultry: 30b, Hen. 40b, Goose. 55b, White cock. 70b, Duck. 1 l, Hen. 1.35 l, Tom turkey. 3.20 l, Hen.

Fowl in Natural Colors; Inscription in Dark Blue

1963, May 23 ***Perf. 10½***

1553 A531 20b ultra .25 .25
1554 A531 30b tan .25 .25
1555 A531 40b org brn .25 .25
1556 A531 55b brt grn .25 .25
1557 A531 70b lilac .25 .25
1558 A531 1 l blue .35 .25
1559 A531 1.35 l ocher .50 .25
1560 A531 3.20 l yel grn 1.10 .35
Nos. 1553-1560 (8) 3.20 2.10

Women and Globe A532

1963, June 15 Photo. ***Perf. 14x13***

1561 A532 55b dark blue .40 .25

Intl. Women's Cong., Moscow, June 24-29.

William M. Thackeray, Writer A533

Portraits: 50b, Eugene Delacroix, painter. 55b, Gheorghe Marinescu, physician. 1.55 l, Giuseppe Verdi, composer. 1.75 l, Stanislavski, actor and producer.

1963, July Unwmk. ***Perf. 14x13***

Portrait in Black

1562 A533 40b pale vio .25 .25
1563 A533 50b bister brn .25 .25
1564 A533 55b olive .25 .25
1565 A533 1.55 l rose brn .50 .25
1566 A533 1.75 l pale vio bl .85 .25
Nos. 1562-1566 (5) 2.10 1.25

Walnuts A534

Designs: 20b, Plums. 40b, Peaches. 55b, Strawberries. 1 l, Grapes. 1.55 l, Apples. 1.60 l, Cherries. 1.75 l, Pears.

1963, Sept. 15 Litho. ***Perf. 14x13½***

Fruits in Natural Colors

1567 A534 10b pale yel & brn ol .25 .25
1568 A534 20b pale pink & red org .25 .25
1569 A534 40b lt bl & bl .25 .25
1570 A534 55b dl yel & rose car .25 .25
1571 A534 1 l pale vio & vio .25 .25
1572 A534 1.55 l yel grn & ultra .45 .25
1573 A534 1.60 l yel & bis .75 .25
1574 A534 1.75 l lt bl & grn .75 .25
Nos. 1567-1574 (8) 3.20 2.00

Women Playing Volleyball and Map of Europe — A535

40b, 3 men players. 55b, 3 women players. 1.75 l, 2 men players. 3.20 l, Europa Cup.

1963, Oct. 22 ***Perf. 13½x14***

1575 A535 5b gray & lil rose .25 .25
1576 A535 40b gray & vio bl .25 .25
1577 A535 55b gray & grnsh bl .30 .25
1578 A535 1.75 l gray & org brn .55 .25
1579 A535 3.20 l gray & vio 1.25 .35
Nos. 1575-1579 (5) 2.60 1.35

European Volleyball Championships, Oct. 22-Nov. 4.

Pine Tree, Branch and Cone A536

Design: 1.75 l, Beech forest and branch.

Perf. 13½

1963, Dec. 5 Unwmk. Photo.

1580 A536 55b dk grn .25 .25
1581 A536 1.75 l dk bl .60 .25

Reforestation program.

Silkworm Moth — A537

Designs: 20b, Chrysalis, moth and worm. 40b, Silkworm on leaf. 55b, Bee over mountains, horiz. 60b, 1.20 l, 1.35 l, 1.60 l, Bees pollinating various flowers, horiz.

1963, Dec. 12 Litho. ***Perf. 13x14***

1582 A537 10b multi .30 .25
1583 A537 20b multi .30 .25
1584 A537 40b multi .30 .25
1585 A537 55b multi .40 .25
1586 A537 60b multi .50 .25
1587 A537 1.20 l multi .80 .25
1588 A537 1.35 l multi 1.00 .25
1589 A537 1.60 l multi 1.40 .25
Nos. 1582-1589 (8) 5.00 2.00

18th Century House, Ploesti — A538

Peasant Houses from Village Museum, Bucharest: 40b, Oltenia, 1875, horiz. 55b, Hunedoara, 19th Cent., horiz. 75b, Oltenia, 19th Cent. 1 l, Brasov, 1847. 1.20 l, Bacau, 19th Cent. 1.75 l, Arges, 19th Cent.

1963, Dec. 25 Engr. ***Perf. 13***

1590 A538 20b claret .35 .25
1591 A538 40b blue .35 .25
1592 A538 55b dl vio .35 .25
1593 A538 75b green .35 .25
1594 A538 1 l brn & mar .65 .25
1595 A538 1.20 l gray ol .80 .25
1596 A538 1.75 l dk brn & ultra 1.60 .25
Nos. 1590-1596 (7) 4.45 1.75

Ski Jump A539

20b, Speed skating. 40b, Ice hockey. 55b, Women's figure skating. 60b, Slalom. 75b, Biathlon. 1 l, Bobsledding. 1.20 l, Cross-country skiing.

1963, Nov. 25 Litho. ***Perf. 14***

1597 A539 10b red & dk bl .30 .25
1598 A539 20b ultra & red brn .30 .25
1599 A539 40b emer & red brn .30 .25
1600 A539 55b vio & red brn .40 .25
1601 A539 60b org & vio bl .65 .25
1602 A539 75b lil rose & dk bl .80 .25
1603 A539 1 l bis & vio bl 1.50 .30
1604 A539 1.20 l grnsh bl & vio 1.60 .40
Nos. 1597-1604 (8) 5.85 2.20

9th Winter Olympic Games, Innsbruck, Jan. 29-Feb. 9, 1964.

Exist imperf. in changed colors. Value, set $6.50.

A souvenir sheet contains one imperf. 1.50 l ultramarine and red stamp showing the Olympic Ice Stadium at Innsbruck and the Winter Games emblem. Value $6.50.

Elena Teodorini as Carmen — A540

Designs: 10b, George Stephanescu, founder of Romanian opera. 35b, Ion Bajenaru as Petru Rares. 40b, D. Popovici as Alberich. 55b, Hariclea Darclée as Tosca. 75b, George Folescu as Boris Godunov. 1 l, Jean Athanasiu as Rigoletto. 1.35 l, Traian Grosavescu as Duke in Rigoletto. 1.55 l, N. Leonard as Hoffmann.

1964, Jan. 20 Photo. ***Perf. 13***

Portrait in Dark Brown

1605 A540 10b olive .25 .25
1606 A540 20b ultra .25 .25
1607 A540 35b green .25 .25
1608 A540 40b grnsh bl .25 .25
1609 A540 55b car rose .30 .25
1610 A540 75b lilac .30 .25
1611 A540 1 l blue .65 .25
1612 A540 1.35 l brt vio .90 .25
1613 A540 1.55 l red org 1.00 .25
Nos. 1605-1613 (9) 4.15 2.25

Munteanu Murgoci and Congress Emblem — A541

1964, Feb. 5 Unwmk. ***Perf. 13***

1614 A541 1.60 l brt bl, ind & bis .80 .25

8th Intl. Soil Congress, Bucharest.

Asculaphid A542

Insects: 10b, Thread-waisted wasp. 35b, Wasp. 40b, Rhyparioides metelkana moth. 55b, Tussock moth. 1.20 l, Kanetisa circe butterfly. 1.55 l, Beetle. 1.75 l, Horned beetle.

1964, Feb. 20 Litho. *Perf. 14x13*

Insects in Natural Colors

1615 A542 5b pale lilac .25 .25
1616 A542 10b lt bl & red .25 .25
1617 A542 35b pale grn .25 .25
1618 A542 40b olive green .25 .25
1619 A542 55b ultra .30 .25
1620 A542 1.20 l pale grn & red .50 .25
1621 A542 1.55 l yel & brn .70 .25
1622 A542 1.75 l orange & red .75 .25
Nos. 1615-1622 (8) 3.25 2.00

Tobacco Plant — A543

Garden flowers: 20b, Geranium. 40b, Fuchsia. 55b, Chrysanthemum. 75b, Dahlia. 1 l, Lily. 1.25 l, Day lily. 1.55 l, Marigold.

1964, Mar. 25 *Perf. 13x14*

1623 A543 10b dk bl, grn & bis .25 .25
1624 A543 20b gray, grn & red .25 .25
1625 A543 40b pale grn, grn & red .25 .25
1626 A543 55b grn, lt grn & lil .30 .25
1627 A543 75b cit, red & grn .35 .25
1628 A543 1 l dp cl, rose cl, grn & org .50 .25
1629 A543 1.25 l sal, vio bl & grn .60 .25
1630 A543 1.55 l red brn, yel & grn .70 .25
Nos. 1623-1630 (8) 3.20 2.00

Jumping — A544

Horse Show Events: 40b, Dressage, horiz. 1.35 l, Jumping. 1.55 l, Galloping, horiz.

Unwmk.

1964, Apr. 25 Photo. *Perf. 13*

1631 A544 40b lt bl, rose brn & blk .25 .25
1632 A544 55b lil, red & brn .25 .25
1633 A544 1.35 l brt grn, red & dk brn .65 .25
1634 A544 1.55 l pale yel, bl & dp claret .90 .25
Nos. 1631-1634 (4) 2.05 1.00

Hogfish A545

Fish (Constanta Aquarium): 10b, Peacock blenny. 20b, Mediterranean scad. 40b, Sturgeon. 50b, Sea horses. 55b, Yellow gurnard. 1 l, Beluga. 3.20 l, Stingray.

1964, May 10 Litho. *Perf. 14*

1635 A545 5b multi .40 .25
1636 A545 10b multi .40 .25
1637 A545 20b multi .40 .25
1638 A545 40b multi .40 .25
1639 A545 50b multi .40 .25
1640 A545 55b multi .40 .25
1641 A545 1 l multi 1.10 .25
1642 A545 3.20 l multi 2.50 .25
Nos. 1635-1642 (8) 6.00 2.00

Mihail Eminescu — A546

Portraits: 20b, Ion Creanga. 35b, Emil Girleanu. 55b, Michelangelo. 1.20 l, Galileo Galilei. 1.75 l, William Shakespeare.

1964, June 20 Photo. *Perf. 13*

Portraits in Dark Brown

1643 A546 5b green .25 .25
1644 A546 20b magenta .25 .25
1645 A546 35b vermilion .25 .25
1646 A546 55b bister .35 .25
1647 A546 1.20 l ultra .60 .25
1648 A546 1.75 l violet 1.00 .25
Nos. 1643-1648 (6) 2.70 1.50

50th death anniv. of Emil Girleanu, writer; the 75th death anniversaries of Ion Creanga and Mihail Eminescu, writers; the 400th anniv. of the death of Michelangelo and the births of Galileo and Shakespeare.

Road through Gorge — A547

Tourist Publicity: 55b, Lake Bilea and cottage. 1 l, Ski lift, Polana Brasov. 1.35 l, Ceahlaul peak and Lake Bicaz, horiz. 1.75 l, Hotel Alpin.

1964, June 29 Engr.

1649 A547 40b rose brn .25 .25
1650 A547 55b dk bl .25 .25
1651 A547 1 l dl pur .40 .25
1652 A547 1.35 l pale brn .55 .25
1653 A547 1.75 l green .65 .25
Nos. 1649-1653 (5) 2.10 1.25

High Jump — A548

1964 Balkan Games: 40b, Javelin throw. 55b, Running. 1 l, Discus throw. 1.20 l, Hurdling. 1.55 l, Map and flags of Balkan countries.

Size: 23x37½mm

1964, July 28 Photo.

1654 A548 30b ver, yel & yel grn .25 .25
1655 A548 40b grn, yel, brn & vio .25 .25
1656 A548 55b gldn brn, yel & bl grn .25 .25
1657 A548 1 l brt bl, yel, brn & red .50 .25
1658 A548 1.20 l pur, yel, brn & grn .65 .25

Litho.

Size: 23x45mm

1659 A548 1.55 l multi 1.00 .25
Nos. 1654-1659 (6) 2.90 1.50

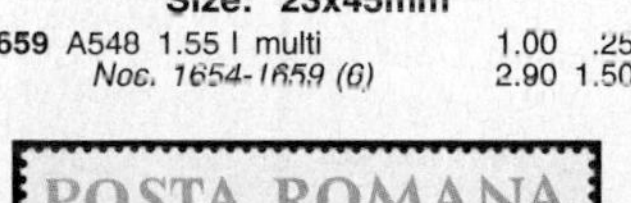

Factory — A549

55b, Flag, Coat of Arms, vert. 75b, Combine. 1.20 l, Apartment buildings. 2 l, Flag, coat of arms, industrial & agricultural scenes. 55b, 2 l, Inscribed "A XX A aniversare a eliberarii patriei!"

1964, Aug. 23 Photo. *Perf. 13*

1660 A549 55b multi .25 .25
1661 A549 60b multi .25 .25
1662 A549 75b multi .25 .25
1663 A549 1.20 l multi .60 .25
Nos. 1660-1663 (4) 1.35 1.00

Souvenir Sheet

Imperf

1664 A549 2 l multi 1.50 .50

20th anniv. of Romania's liberation. No. 1664 contains one stamp 110x70mm.

High Jump — A550

Sport: 30b, Wrestling. 35b, Volleyball. 40b, Canoeing. 55b, Fencing. 1.20 l, Women's gymnastics. 1.35 l, Soccer. 1.55 l, Sharpshooting.

Olympic Rings in Blue, Yellow, Black, Green and Red

1964, Sept. 1 Litho.

1665 A550 20b yel & blk .25 .25
1666 A550 30b lilac & blk .25 .25
1667 A550 35b grnsh bl & blk .25 .25
1668 A550 40b pink & blk .25 .25
1669 A550 55b lt yel grn & blk .45 .25
1670 A550 1.20 l org & blk .75 .25
1671 A550 1.35 l ocher & blk 1.00 .25
1672 A550 1.55 l bl & blk 1.10 .35
Nos. 1665-1672 (8) 4.30 2.10

18th Olympic Games, Tokyo, Oct. 10-25.

Nos. 1665-1669 exist imperf., in changed colors. Three other denominations exist, 1.60 l, 2 l and 2.40 l, imperf. Value, set of 8, unused $7, canceled $5.

An imperf. souvenir sheet contains a 3.25 l stamp showing a runner. Value unused $7 canceled $6.

George Enescu, Piano Keys and Neck of Violin — A551

Designs: 55b, Enescu at piano. 1.60 l, Enescu Festival medal. 1.75 l, Enescu bust by G. Anghel.

1964, Sept. 5 Engr.

1673 A551 10b bl grn .25 .25
1674 A551 55b vio blk .25 .25
1675 A551 1.60 l dk red brn .60 .25
1676 A551 1.75 l dk bl 1.00 .25
Nos. 1673-1676 (4) 2.10 1.00

3rd Intl. George Enescu Festival, Bucharest, Sept., 1964.

Black Swans A552

5b, Indian python. 35b, Ostriches. 40b, Crowned cranes. 55b, Tigers. 1 l, Lions. 1.55 l, Grevy's zebras. 2 l, Bactrian camels.

Perf. 14x13

1964, Sept. 28 Litho. Unwmk.

1677 A552 5b multi .25 .25
1678 A552 10b multi .25 .25
1679 A552 35b multi .25 .25
1680 A552 40b multi .25 .25
1681 A552 55b multi .25 .25
1682 A552 1 l multi .45 .25
1683 A552 1.55 l multi .90 .25
1684 A552 2 l multi 1.25 .25
Nos. 1677-1684 (8) 3.85 2.00

Issued to publicize the Bucharest Zoo. No. 1683 inscribed "BANI."

C. Brincoveanu, Stolnicul Cantacuzino, Gheorghe Lazar and Academy — A553

Designs: 40b, Alexandru Ioan Cuza, medal and University. 55b, Masks, curtain, harp, keyboard and palette, vert. 75b, Women students in laboratory and auditorium. 1 l, Savings Bank building.

Perf. 13x13½, 13½x13

1964, Oct. 14 Photo.

1685 A553 20b multi .25 .25
1686 A553 40b multi .25 .25
1687 A553 55b multi .25 .25
1688 A553 75b multi .25 .25
1689 A553 1 l dk brn, yel & org .50 .25
Nos. 1685-1689 (5) 1.50 1.25

No. 1685 for 250th anniv. of the Royal Academy; Nos. 1686, 1688 cent. of the University of Bucharest; No. 1687 cent. of the Academy of Art and No. 1689 cent. of the Savings Bank.

Soldier's Head and Laurel — A554

1964, Oct. 25 Litho. *Perf. 12x12½*

1690 A554 55b ultra & lt bl .40 .25

Army Day.

Canadian Kayak Singles Gold Medal, Melbourne, 1956 A555

Romanian Olympic Gold Medals: 30b, Boxing, Melbourne, 1956. 35b, Rapid Silhouette Pistol, Melbourne, 1956. 40b, Women's High Jump, Rome, 1960. 55b, Wrestling, Rome, 1960. 1.20 l, Clay Pigeon Shooting, Rome, 1960. 1.35 l, Women's High Jump, Tokyo, 1964. 1.55 l, Javelin, Tokyo, 1964.

1964, Nov. 30 Photo. *Perf. 13½*

Medals in Gold and Brown

1691 A555 20b pink & ultra .25 .25
1692 A555 30b yel grn & ultra .25 .25
1693 A555 35b bluish grn & ultra .25 .25
1694 A555 40b lil & ultra .50 .25
1695 A555 55b org & ultra .60 .25
1696 A555 1.20 l ol grn & ultra .90 .25
1697 A555 1.35 l gldn brn & ultra 1.00 .25
1698 A555 1.55 l rose lil & ultra 1.50 .35
Nos. 1691-1698 (8) 5.25 2.10

Romanian athletes who won gold medals in three Olympic Games.

Nos. 1691-1695 exist imperf., in changed colors. Three other denominations exist, 1.60 l, 2 l and 2.40 l, imperf. Value, set of 8, unused $7, canceled $5.

A 10 l souvenir sheet shows the 1964 Olympic gold medal and world map. Value unused $7, canceled $5.

Strawberries A556

Designs: 35b, Blackberries. 40b, Raspberries. 55b, Rose hips. 1.20 l, Blueberries. 1.35 l, Cornelian cherries. 1.55 l, Hazelnuts. 2.55 l, Cherries.

1964, Dec. 20 Litho. *Perf. 13½x14*

1703 A556 5b gray, red & grn .25 .25
1704 A556 35b ocher, grn & dk vio bl .25 .25
1705 A556 40b pale vio, car & grn .30 .25
1706 A556 55b yel grn, grn & red .30 .25
1707 A556 1.20 l sal pink, grn, brn & ind .50 .25
1708 A556 1.35 l lt bl, grn & red .60 .25
1709 A556 1.55 l gldn brn, grn & ocher 1.00 .25
1710 A556 2.55 l ultra, grn & red 1.25 .25
Nos. 1703-1710 (8) 4.45 2.00

Syncom 3 — A557

Space Satellites: 40b, Syncom 3 over TV antennas. 55b, Ranger 7 reaching moon, horiz. 1 l, Ranger 7 and moon close-up, horiz. 1.20 l, Voskhod. 5 l, Konstantin Feoktistov, Vladimir M. Komarov, Boris B. Yegorov and Voskhod.

Perf. 13x14, 14x13

1965, Jan. 5 Litho. Unwmk.

Size: 22x38mm, 38x22mm

1711 A557 30b multi .30 .25
1712 A557 40b multi .30 .25
1713 A557 55b multi .50 .25
1714 A557 1 l multi .60 .25
1715 A557 1.20 l multi, horiz. .90 .25

Perf. 13½x13

Size: 52x30mm

1716 A557 5 l multi 2.10 .75
Nos. 1711-1716 (6) 4.70 2.00

For surcharge see No. 1737.

UN Headquarters, NY — A558

1.60 l, Arms, flag of Romania, UN emblem.

1965, Jan. 25 *Perf. 12x12½*

1717 A558 55b ultra, red & gold .45 .25
1718 A558 1.60 l ultra, red, gold & yel .80 .25

20th anniv. of the UN and 10th anniv. of Romania's membership in the UN.

Greek Tortoise — A559

Reptiles: 10b, Bull lizard. 20b, Three-lined lizard. 40b, Sand lizard. 55b, Slow worm. 60b, Sand viper. 1 l, Desert lizard. 1.20 l, Orsini's viper. 1.35 l, Caspian whipsnake. 3.25 l, Four-lined snake.

1965, Feb. 25 Photo. *Perf. 13½*

1719 A559 5b multi .25 .25
1720 A559 10b multi .25 .25
1721 A559 20b multi .25 .25
1722 A559 40b multi .40 .25
1723 A559 55b multi .40 .25
1724 A559 60b multi .45 .25
1725 A559 1 l multi .60 .25
1726 A559 1.20 l multi .70 .25
1727 A559 1.35 l multi .90 .25
1728 A559 3.25 l multi 1.75 .25
Nos. 1719-1728 (10) 5.95 2.50

White Persian Cats — A560

Designs: 1.35 l, Siamese cat. Others; Various European cats. (5b, 10b, 3.25 l, horiz.)

1965, Mar. 20 Litho.

Size: 41x29mm, 29x41mm

Cats in Natural Colors

1729 A560 5b brn org & blk .25 .25
1730 A560 10b brt bl & blk .25 .25
1731 A560 40b yel grn, yel & blk .40 .25
1732 A560 55b rose red & blk .55 .25
1733 A560 60b yel & blk .90 .25
1734 A560 75b lt vio & blk 1.10 .25
1735 A560 1.35 l red org & blk 1.40 .25

Perf. 13x13½

Size: 62x29mm

1736 A560 3.25 l blue 2.50 .75
Nos. 1729-1736 (8) 7.35 2.50

No. 1714 Surcharged in Violet

1965, Apr. 25 *Perf. 14x13*

1737 A557 5 l on 1 l multi 14.00 14.00

Flight of the US rocket Ranger 9 to the moon, Mar. 24, 1965.

Dante Alighieri — A561

40b, Ion Bianu, philologist and historian. 55b, Anton Bacalbasa, writer. 60b, Vasile Conta, philosopher. 1 l, Jean Sibelius, Finnish composer. 1.35 l, Horace, Roman poet.

1965, May 10 Photo. *Perf. 13½*

Portrait in Black

1738 A561 40b chalky blue .25 .25
1739 A561 55b bister .25 .25
1740 A561 60b light lilac .25 .25
1741 A561 1 l dl red brn .45 .25
1742 A561 1.35 l olive .60 .25
1743 A561 1.75 l orange red 1.10 .25
Nos. 1738-1743 (6) 2.90 1.50

ITU Emblem, Old and New Communication Equipment — A562

1965, May 15 Engr.

1744 A562 1.75 l ultra .90 .40

ITU, centenary.

Iron Gate, Danube — A562a

Arms of Yugoslavia and Romania and Djerdap Dam — A562b

55b (50d), Iron Gate hydroelectric plant & dam.

Perf. 12½x12

1965, Apr. 30 Litho. Unwmk.

1745 A562a 30b (25d) lt bl & grn .25 .25
1746 A562a 55b (50d) lt bl & dk red .45 .25

Miniature Sheet

Perf. 13½x13

1747 A562b Sheet of 4 3.00 2.25
a. 80b multi .35 .35
b. 1.20 l multi .70 .70

Issued simultaneously by Romania and Yugoslavia for the start of construction of the Iron Gate hydroelectric plant and dam. Valid for postage in both countries.

No. 1747 contains one each of Nos. 1747a, 1747b and Yugoslavia Nos. 771a and 771b. Only Nos. 1747a and 1747b were valid in Romania. Sold for 4 l. See Yugoslavia Nos. 769-771.

Small-bore Rifle Shooting, Kneeling — A563

Designs: 40b, Rifle shooting, prone. 55b, Rapid-fire pistol and map of Europe. 1 l, Free pistol and map of Europe. 1.60 l, Small-bore rifle, standing, and map of Europe. 2 l, 5 l, Marksmen in various shooting positions (all horizontal).

Perf. 12x12½, 12½x12

1965, May 30 Litho. Unwmk.

Size: 23x43mm, 43x23mm

1748 A563 20b multi .25 .25
1749 A563 40b dl grn, pink & blk .25 .25
1750 A563 55b multi .25 .25
1751 A563 1 l pale grn, blk & ocher .35 .25
1752 A563 1.60 l multi .60 .25

Perf. 13½

Size: 51x28mm

1753 A563 2 l multi .70 .25
Nos. 1748-1753 (6) 2.40 1.50

European Shooting Championships, Bucharest.

Nos. 1749-1752 were issued imperf. in changed colors. Two other denominations exist, 3.25 l and 5 l, imperf. Value, set of 6, unused $5, canceled $2.

Fat-Frumos and the Giant A564

Fairy Tales: 40b, Fat-Frumos on horseback and Ileana Cosinzeana. 55b, Harap Alb and the Bear. 1 l, "The Moralist Wolf." 1.35 l, "The Ox and the Calf." 2 l, Wolf and bear pulling sled.

1965, June 25 Photo. *Perf. 13*

1756 A564 20b multi .25 .25
1757 A564 40b multi .25 .25
1758 A564 55b multi .30 .25
1759 A564 1 l multi .45 .25
1760 A564 1.35 l multi .70 .25
1761 A564 2 l multi 1.00 .25
Nos. 1756-1761 (6) 2.95 1.50

Bee and Blossoms — A565

Design: 1.60 l, Exhibition Hall, horiz.

Perf. 12x12½, 12½x12

1965, July 28 Litho. Unwmk.

1762 A565 55b org, bl & pink .35 .25
1763 A565 1.60 l multi .60 .25

20th Congress of the Intl Federation of Beekeeping Assocs. (Apimondia), Bucharest, Aug. 26-31.

Space Achievements A566

Designs: 1.75 l, Col. Pavel Belyayev, Lt. Col. Alexei Leonov and Voskhod 2. 2.40 l, Early Bird over globe. 3.20 l, Lt. Col. Gordon Cooper and Lt. Com. Charles Conrad, Gemini 3 and globe.

1965, Aug. 25 Litho. *Perf. 12x12½*

1764 A566 1.75 l dk bl, bl & ver .80 .25
1765 A566 2.40 l multi 1.10 .25
1766 A566 3.20 l dk bl, lt bl & ver 2.25 .35
Nos. 1764-1766 (3) 4.15 .85

European Quail — A567

Birds: 10b, Eurasian woodcock. 20b, Eurasian snipe. 40b, Turtle dove. 55b, Mallard. 60b, White-fronted goose. 1 l, Eurasian crane. 1.20 l, Glossy ibis. 1.35 l, Mute swan. 3.25 l, White pelican.

1965, Sept. 10 Photo. *Perf. 13½*
Size: 34x34mm
Birds in Natural Colors

1767	A567	5b red brn & rose lil	.25	.25
1768	A567	10b red brn & yel grn	.25	.25
1769	A567	20b brn & bl grn	.25	.25
1770	A567	40b lil & org brn	.25	.25
1771	A567	55b brt grn & lt brn	.25	.25
1772	A567	60b dl org & bl	.30	.25
1773	A567	1 l red & lil	.40	.25
1774	A567	1.20 l dk brn & grn	.60	.25
1775	A567	1.35 l org & ultra	.80	.25

Size: 32x73mm

1776	A567	3.25 l ultra & sep	2.10	.30
		Nos. 1767-1776 (10)	5.45	2.55

Marx and Lenin — A568

1965, Sept. 6 Photo.

1777	A568	55b red, blk & yel	.50	.25

6th Conference of Postal Ministers of Communist Countries, Peking, June 21-July 15.

Vasile Alecsandri — A569

1965, Oct. 9 Unwmk. *Perf. 13½*

1778	A569	55b red brn, dk brn & gold	.50	.25

Alecsandri (1821-1890), statesman and poet.

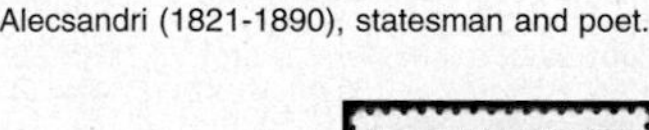

Bird-of-Paradise Flower — A570

Flowers from Cluj Botanical Gardens: 10b, Stanhope orchid. 20b, Paphiopedilum insigne. 30b, Zanzibar water lily, horiz. 40b, Ferocactus, horiz. 55b, Cotton blossom, horiz. 1 l, Hibiscus, horiz. 1.35 l, Gloxinia. 1.75 l, Victoria water lily, horiz. 2.30 l, Hibiscus, bird-of-paradise flower and greenhouse.

Perf. 12x12½, 12½x12
1965, Oct. 25 Litho.
Size: 23x43mm, 43x23mm
Flowers in Natural Colors

1779	A570	5b brown	.25	.25
1780	A570	10b green	.25	.25
1781	A570	20b dk bl	.30	.25
1782	A570	30b vio bl	.30	.25
1783	A570	40b red brn	.30	.25
1784	A570	55b dk red	.30	.25
1785	A570	1 l ol grn	.45	.25
1786	A570	1.35 l violet	.60	.25
1787	A570	1.75 l dk grn	1.00	.25

Perf. 13½
Size: 52x30mm

1788	A570	2.30 l green	1.50	.35
		Nos. 1779-1788 (10)	5.25	2.60

The orchid on No. 1780 is attached to the bottom of the limb.

Running — A571

1965, Nov. 10 Photo. *Perf. 13½*

1789	A571	55b shown	.25	.25
1790	A571	1.55 l Soccer	.50	.25
1791	A571	1.75 l Woman diver	.65	.25
1792	A571	2 l Mountaineering	.70	.25
1793	A571	5 l Canoeing, horiz.	1.60	.40
		Nos. 1789-1793 (5)	3.70	1.40

Spartacist Games. No. 1793 commemorates the Romanian victory in the European Kayak Championships.

Pigeon and Post Horn — A572

Designs: 1 l, Pigeon on television antenna and post horn, horiz. 1.75 l, Flying pigeon and post horn, horiz.

1965, Nov. 15 Engr.

1794	A572	55b + 45b label	.50	.25
1795	A572	1 l green & brown	.50	.25
1796	A572	1.75 l ol grn & sepia	1.00	.25
		Nos. 1794-1796 (3)	2.00	.75

Issued for Stamp Day. No. 1794 is printed with alternating label showing post rider and emblem of Romanian Philatelists' Association and 45b additional charge. Stamp and label are imperf. between.

Chamois and Hunting Trophy A573

Hunting Trophy and: 1 l, Brown bear. 1.60 l, Red deer. 1.75 l, Wild boar. 3.20 l, Antlers of red deer.

1965, Dec. 10 Photo. *Perf. 13½*
Size: 37x22mm

1797	A573	55b rose lil, yel & brn	.35	.25
1798	A573	1 l brt grn, red & brn	.45	.25
1799	A573	1.60 l lt vio bl, org & brn	1.25	.25
1800	A573	1.75 l rose, grn & blk	1.60	.25

Size: 48x36½mm

1801	A573	3.20 l gray, gold, blk & org	2.50	.40
		Nos. 1797-1801 (5)	6.15	1.40

Probe III Photographing Moon — A574

Designs: 5b, Proton I space station, vert. 15b, Molniya I telecommunication satellite, vert. 3.25 l, Mariner IV and Mars picture, vert. 5 l, Gemini 5.

Perf. 12x12½, 12½x12
1965, Dec. 25 Litho.

1802	A574	5b multi	.25	.25
1803	A574	10b vio bl, red & gray	.25	.25
1804	A574	15b pur, gray & org	.25	.25
1805	A574	3.25 l vio bl, blk & red	2.25	.25
1806	A574	5 l dk bl, gray & red org	3.50	.45
		Nos. 1802-1806 (5)	6.50	1.45

Achievements in space research.

Cocker Spaniel — A575

Hunting Dogs: 5b, Dachshund (triangle). 40b, Retriever. 55b, Terrier. 60b, Red setter. 75b, White setter. 1.55 l, Pointers (rectangle). 3.25 l, Duck hunter with retriever (rectangle).

1965, Dec. 28 Photo. *Perf. 13½*
Size: 30x42mm

1807	A575	5b multi	.25	.25

Size: 33½x33½mm

1808	A575	10b multi	.25	.25
1809	A575	40b multi	.30	.25
1810	A575	55b multi	.45	.25
1811	A575	60b multi	.65	.25
1812	A575	75b multi	.90	.25

Size: 43x28mm

1813	A575	1.55 l multi	1.75	.25
1814	A575	3.25 l multi	3.50	.75
		Nos. 1807-1814 (8)	8.05	2.50

Chessboard, Queen and Jester — A576

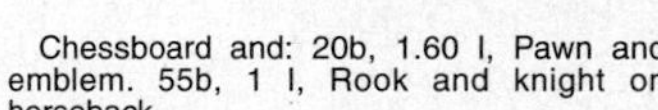

Chessboard and: 20b, 1.60 l, Pawn and emblem. 55b, 1 l, Rook and knight on horseback.

1966, Feb. 25 Litho. *Perf. 13*

1815	A576	20b multi	.25	.25
1816	A576	40b multi	.30	.25
1817	A576	55b multi	.45	.25
1818	A576	1 l multi	.75	.25
1819	A576	1.60 l multi	1.25	.25
1820	A576	3.25 l multi	2.00	1.60
		Nos. 1815-1820 (6)	5.00	2.85

Chess Olympics in Cuba.

Tractor, Grain and Sun — A577

1966, Mar. 5

1821	A577	55b lt grn & ocher	.40	.25

Founding congress of the National Union of Cooperative Farms.

Gheorghe Gheorghiu-Dej A578

1966, Mar. Photo. *Perf. 13½*

1822	A578	55b gold & blk	.60	.40
a.		5 l souvenir sheet	4.50	3.75

1st death anniv. of Pres. Gheorghe Gheorghiu-Dej (1901-65). No. 1822a contains design similar to No. 1822 with signature of Gheorghiu-Dej.

Congress Emblem — A579

1966, Mar. 21 *Perf. 13x14½*

1823	A579	55b yel & red	.40	.25

1966 Congress of Communist Youth.

Folk Dancers of Moldavia — A580

Folk Dances: 40b, Oltenia. 55b, Maramaros. 1 l, Muntenia. 1.60 l, Banat. 2 l, Transylvania.

1966, Apr. 4 Engr. *Perf. 13½*
Center in Black

1824	A580	30b lilac	.25	.25
1825	A580	40b brick red	.25	.25
1826	A580	55b brt bl grn	.30	.25
1827	A580	1 l maroon	.50	.25
1828	A580	1.60 l dk bl	1.00	.25
1829	A580	2 l yel grn	1.75	.30
		Nos. 1824-1829 (6)	4.05	1.55

Soccer Game — A581

Designs: 10b, 15b, 55b, 1.75 l, Scenes of soccer play. 4 l, Jules Rimet Cup.

1966, Apr. 25 Litho. Unwmk.

No.	Type	Value	Color	Unused	Used
1830	A581	5b	multi	.25	.25
1831	A581	10b	multi	.25	.25
1832	A581	15b	multi	.25	.25
1833	A581	55b	multi	.45	.25
1834	A581	1.75 l	multi	1.10	.25
1835	A581	4 l	gold & multi	2.50	.60
a.			10 l souv. sheet	6.00	5.50
			Nos. 1830-1835 (6)	4.80	1.85

World Cup Soccer Championship, Wembley, England, July 11-30.

No. 1835a contains one imperf. 10 l multicolored stamp in design of 4 l, but larger (32x46mm). No gum. Issued June 20.

Symbols of Industry A582

1966, May 14 Photo.

No.	Type	Value	Color	Unused	Used
1836	A582	55b	multi	.40	.25

Romanian Trade Union Congress.

Red-breasted Flycatcher A583

Song Birds: 10b, Red crossbill. 15b, Great reed warbler. 20b, European redstart. 55b, European robin. 1.20 l, White-spotted bluethroat. 1.55 l, Yellow wagtail. 3.20 l, Common penduline tit.

1966, May 25 Photo. *Perf. 13½*

No.	Type	Value	Color	Unused	Used
1837	A583	5b	gold & multi	.40	.25
1838	A583	10b	sil & multi	.40	.25
1839	A583	15b	gold & multi	.40	.25
1840	A583	20b	sil & multi	.40	.25
1841	A583	55b	sil & multi	.50	.25
1842	A583	1.20 l	gold & multi	.75	.25
1843	A583	1.55 l	sil & multi	2.25	.30
1844	A583	3.20 l	gold & multi	3.50	.50
			Nos. 1837-1844 (8)	8.60	2.30

Venera 3 (USSR) — A584

Designs: 20b, FR-1 (France). 1.60 l, Luna 9 (USSR). 5 l, Gemini 6 and 7 (US).

1966, June 25

No.	Type	Value	Color	Unused	Used
1845	A584	10b	dp vio, gray & red	.30	.25
1846	A584	20b	ultra, blk & red	.30	.25
1847	A584	1.60 l	dk bl, blk & red	.85	.25
1848	A584	5 l	bl, blk, brn & red	2.25	.40
			Nos. 1845-1848 (4)	3.70	1.15

International achievements in space.

Urechia Nestor — A585

Portraits: 5b, George Cosbuc. 10b, Gheorghe Sincai. 40b, Aron Pumnul. 55b, Stefan Luchian. 1 l, Sun Yat-sen. 1.35 l, Gottfried Wilhelm Leibnitz. 1.60 l, Romain Rolland. 1.75 l, Ion Ghica. 3.25 l, Constantin Cantacuzino.

1966, June 28

No.	Type	Value	Color	Unused	Used
1849	A585	5b	grn, blk & dk bl	.25	.25
1850	A585	10b	rose car, grn & blk	.25	.25
1851	A585	20b	grn, plum & blk	.25	.25
1852	A585	40b	vio bl, brn & blk	.25	.25
1853	A585	55b	brn org, bl grn & blk	.25	.25
1854	A585	1 l	ocher, vio & blk	.25	.25
1855	A585	1.35 l	bl & blk	.35	.25
1856	A585	1.60 l	brt grn, dl vio & blk	.55	.25
1857	A585	1.75 l	org, dl vio & blk	.55	.25
1858	A585	3.25 l	bl, dk car & blk	1.00	.25
			Nos. 1849-1858 (10)	3.95	2.50

Cultural anniversaries.

Country House, by Gheorghe Petrascu — A586

Paintings: 10b, Peasant Woman, by Nicolae Grigorescu, vert. 20b, Reapers at Rest, by Camil Ressu. 55b, Man with the Blue Cap, by Van Eyck, vert. 1.55 l, Train Compartment, by Daumier. 3.25 l, Betrothal of the Virgin, by El Greco, vert.

1966, July 25 Unwmk.

Gold Frame

No.	Type	Value	Color	Unused	Used
1859	A586	5b	Prus grn & brn org	.25	.25
1860	A586	10b	red brn & crim	.25	.25
1861	A586	20b	brn & brt grn	.30	.25
1862	A586	55b	vio bl & lil	.40	.25
1863	A586	1.55 l	dk sl grn & org	1.90	.40
1864	A586	3.25 l	vio & ultra	4.00	1.25
			Nos. 1859-1864 (6)	7.10	2.65

See Nos. 1907-1912.

Hottonia Palustris A587

Marine Flora: 10b, Ceratophyllum submersum. 20b, Aldrovanda vesiculosa. 40b, Callitriche verna. 55b, Vallisneria spiralis. 1 l, Elodea Canadensis rich. 1.55 l, Hippuris vulgaris. 3.25 l, Myriophyllum spicatum.

1966, Aug. 25 Litho. *Perf. 13½*

Size: 28x40mm

No.	Type	Value	Color	Unused	Used
1865	A587	5b	multi	.25	.25
1866	A587	10b	multi	.25	.25
1867	A587	20b	multi	.25	.25
1868	A587	40b	multi	.25	.25
1869	A587	55b	multi	.25	.25
1870	A587	1 l	multi	.45	.25
1871	A587	1.55 l	multi	.70	.25

Size: 28x50mm

No.	Type	Value	Color	Unused	Used
1872	A587	3.25 l	multi	1.40	.35
			Nos. 1865-1872 (8)	3.80	2.10

Derivation of the Meter — A588

Design: 1 l, Metric system symbols.

1966, Sept. 10 Photo. *Perf. 13½*

No.	Type	Value	Color	Unused	Used
1873	A588	55b	salmon & ultra	.30	.25
1874	A588	1 l	lt grn & vio	.40	.25

Introduction of metric system in Romania, centenary.

Statue of Ovid and Medical School Emblem — A589

Line Integral Denoting Work — A590

I. H. Radulescu, M. Kogalniceanu and T. Savulescu — A591

Design: 1 l, Academy centenary medal.

1966, Sept. 30 Size: 22x27mm

No.	Type	Value	Color	Unused	Used
1875	A589	40b	lil gray, ultra, sep & gold	.25	.25
1876	A590	55b	gray, brn, red & gold	.25	.25

Size: 22x34mm

No.	Type	Value	Color	Unused	Used
1877	A589	1 l	ultra, brn & gold	.45	.25

Size: 66x28mm

No.	Type	Value	Color	Unused	Used
1878	A591	3 l	org, dk brn & gold	1.10	.30
			Nos. 1875-1878 (4)	2.05	1.05

Centenary of the Romanian Academy.

Stone Crab A592

Molluscs and Crustaceans:5b, Crawfish. 10b, Nassa reticulata, vert. 40b, Campylaea trizona. 55b, Helix lucorum. 1.35 l, Mytilus galloprovincialis. 1.75 l, Lymnaea stagnalis. 3.25 l, Anodonta cygnaea. (10b, 40b, 55b, 1.75 l, are snails; 1.35 l, 3.25 l, are bivalves).

1966, Oct. 15

Animals in Natural Colors

No.	Type	Value	Color	Unused	Used
1879	A592	5b	dp org	.25	.25
1880	A592	10b	lt bl	.25	.25
1881	A592	20b	pale lil	.25	.25
1882	A592	40b	yel grn	.25	.25
1883	A592	55b	car rose	.25	.25
1884	A592	1.35 l	brt grn	.55	.25
1885	A592	1.75 l	ultra	.65	.25
1886	A592	3.25 l	brt org	1.60	.35
			Nos. 1879-1886 (8)	4.05	2.10

Cave Bear A593

Prehistoric Animals: 10b, Mammoth. 15b, Bison. 55b, Cave elephant. 1.55 l, Stags. 4 l, Dinotherium.

1966, Nov. 25 Size: 36x22mm

No.	Type	Value	Color	Unused	Used
1887	A593	5b	ultra, bl grn & red brn	.25	.25
1888	A593	10b	vio, emer & brn	.25	.25
1889	A593	15b	ol, grn & dk brn	.25	.25
1890	A593	55b	lil, emer & brn	.30	.25
1891	A593	1.55 l	ultra, grn & brn	.95	.25

Size: 43x27mm

No.	Type	Value	Color	Unused	Used
1892	A593	4 l	rose car, grn & brn	1.50	.50
			Nos. 1887-1892 (6)	3.50	1.75

Putna Monastery, 500th Anniv. A594

1966 Photo. *Perf. 13½*

No.	Type	Value	Color	Unused	Used
1893	A594	2 l	multi	.70	.25

Yuri A. Gagarin and Vostok 1 — A595

Russian Achievements in Space: 10b, Trajectory of Sputnik 1 around globe, horiz. 25b, Valentina Tereshkova and globe with trajectory of Vostok 6. 40b, Andrian G. Nikolayev, Pavel R. Popovich and globe with trajectory of Vostok 8. 55b, Alexei Leonov walking in space.

1967, Feb. 15 Photo. *Perf. 13½*

No.	Type	Value	Color	Unused	Used
1894	A595	10b	silver & multi	.25	.25
1895	A595	20b	silver & multi	.25	.25
1896	A595	25b	silver & multi	.25	.25
1897	A595	40b	silver & multi	.35	.25
1898	A595	55b	silver & multi	.45	.25
			Nos. 1894-1898,C163-C166 (9)	5.40	2.85

Ten years of space exploration.

Barn Owl A596

Birds of Prey: 20b, Eagle owl. 40b, Saker falcon. 55b, Egyptian vulture. 75b, Osprey. 1 l, Griffon vulture. 1.20 l, Lammergeier. 1.75 l, Cinereous vulture.

1967, Mar. 20 Photo. Unwmk.

Birds in Natural Colors

No.	Type	Value	Color	Unused	Used
1899	A596	10b	vio & olive	.30	.25
1900	A596	20b	bl & org	.35	.25
1901	A596	40b	emer & org	.30	.25
1902	A596	55b	yel grn & ocher	.35	.25
1903	A596	75b	rose lil & grn	.35	.25
1904	A596	1 l	yel org & blk	.70	.25
1905	A596	1.20 l	claret & yel	1.25	.25
1906	A596	1.75 l	sal pink & gray	1.75	.50
			Nos. 1899-1906 (8)	5.35	2.25

Painting Type of 1966

10b, Woman in Fancy Dress, by Ion Andreescu. 20b, Washwomen, by J. Al. Steriadi. 40b, Women weavers, by St. Dimitrescu, vert. 1.55 l, Venus and Amor, by Lucas Cranach, vert. 3.20 l, Hercules & the Lion of Nemea, by Rubens. 5 l, Haman Asking Esther's Forgiveness, by Rembrandt, vert.

1967, Mar. 30 *Perf. 13½*

Gold Frame

No.	Type	Value	Color	Unused	Used
1907	A586	10b	dp bl & rose red	.25	.25
1908	A586	20b	dp grn & bis	.25	.25
1909	A586	40b	carmine & bl	.25	.25
1910	A586	1.55 l	dp plum & lt ultra	.50	.25
1911	A586	3.20 l	brown & grn	.90	.25
1912	A586	5 l	ol grn & org	2.00	.45
			Nos. 1907-1912 (6)	4.15	1.70

Mlle. Pogany, by Brancusi A597

Sculptures: 5b, Girl's head. 10b, The Sleeping Muse, horiz. 20b, The Infinite Column. 40b, The Kiss, horiz. 55b, Earth Wisdom (seated woman). 3.25 l, Gate of the Kiss.

1967, Apr. 27 Photo. *Perf. 13½*

1913 A597 5b dl yel, blk brn & ver .25 .25
1914 A597 10b bl grn, blk & lil .25 .25
1915 A597 20b lt bl, blk & rose red .25 .25
1916 A597 40b pink, sep & brt grn .25 .30
1917 A597 55b yel grn, blk & ultra .35 .25
1918 A597 1.20 l bluish lil, ol blk & org .85 .25
1919 A597 3.25 l emer, blk & cer 1.50 .75
Nos. 1913-1919 (7) 3.70 2.30

Constantin Brancusi (1876-1957), sculptor.

Coins of 1867 A598

Design: 1.20 l, Coins of 1966.

1967, May 4

1920 A598 55b multicolored .25 .25
1921 A598 1.20 l multicolored 1.00 .25

Centenary of Romanian monetary system.

Infantry Soldier, by Nicolae Grigorescu A599

1967, May 9

1922 A599 55b multicolored .70 .25

90th anniv. of Romanian independence.

Peasants Marching, by Stefan Luchian — A600

Painting: 40b, Fighting Peasants, by Octav Bancila, vert.

1967, May 20 Unwmk. *Perf. 13½*

1923 A600 40b multicolored .25 .25
1924 A600 1.55 l multicolored 1.10 .70

60th anniversary of Peasant Uprising.

Centaury — A601

Carpathian Flora: 40b, Hedge mustard. 55b, Columbine. 1.20 l, Alpine violet. 1.75 l, Bell flower. 4 l, Dryas, horiz.

1967, June 10 Photo.

Flowers in Natural Colors

1925 A601 20b ocher .30 .25
1926 A601 40b violet .30 .25
1927 A601 55b bis & brn red .30 .25
1928 A601 1.20 l yel & red brn .50 .25
1929 A601 1.75 l bluish grn & car .70 .25
1930 A601 4 l lt ultra 2.00 .25
Nos. 1925-1930 (6) 4.10 1.50

Fortifications, Sibiu — A602

Map of Romania and ITY Emblem — A603

Designs: 40b, Cris Castle. 55b, Wooden Church, Plopis. 1.60 l, Ruins of Nuamtulua Fortress. 1.75 l, Mogosoaia Palace. 2.25 l, Voronet Church.

1967, June 29 Photo. *Perf. 13½*

Size: 33x33mm

1931 A602 20b ultra & multi .25 .25
1932 A602 40b vio & multi .25 .25
1933 A602 55b multi .25 .25
1934 A602 1.60 l multi .45 .25
1935 A602 1.75 l multi .60 .25

Size: 48x36mm

1936 A602 2.25 l bl & multi .90 .25
Nos. 1931-1936 (6) 2.70 1.50

Souvenir Sheet

Imperf

1937 A603 5 l lt bl, ultra & blk 3.00 1.60

International Tourist Year.

The Attack at Marasesti, by E. Stoica — A604

1967, July 24 Unwmk. *Perf. 13½*

1938 A604 55b gray, Prus bl & brn .45 .25

Battle of Marasesti & Oituz, 50th anniv.

Dinu Lipatti, Pianist — A605

Designs: 20b, Al. Orascu, architect. 40b, Gr. Antipa, zoologist. 55b, M. Kogalniceanu, statesman. 1.20 l, Jonathan Swift, writer. 1.75 l, Marie Curie, scientist.

1967, July 29 Photo. *Perf. 13½*

1939 A605 10b ultra, blk & pur .25 .25
1940 A605 20b org brn, blk & ultra .25 .25
1941 A605 40b bl grn, blk & org brn .25 .25
1942 A605 55b dp rose, blk & dk ol grn .25 .25
1943 A605 1.20 l ol, blk & brn .40 .25
1944 A605 1.75 l dl bl, blk & bl grn .80 .25
Nos. 1939-1944 (6) 2.20 1.50

Cultural anniversaries.

Wrestlers A606

Designs: 20b, 55b, 1.20 l, 2 l, Various fight scenes and world map (20b, 2 l horizontal); on 2 l maps are large and wrestlers small.

1967, Aug. 28

1945 A606 10b olive & multi .25 .25
1946 A606 20b citron & multi .25 .25
1947 A606 55b bister & multi .25 .25
1948 A606 1.20 l multi .25 .25
1949 A606 2 l ultra, gold & dp car 1.00 .30
Nos. 1945-1949 (5) 2.00 1.30

World Greco-Roman Wrestling Championships, Bucharest.

Congress Emblem — A607

1967, Aug. 28

1950 A607 1.60 l lt bl, ultra & dp car .70 .40

Intl. Linguists' Cong., Bucharest, 8/28-9/2.

Ice Skating — A608

Designs: 40b, Biathlon. 55b, 5 l, Bobsledding. 1 l, Skiing. 1.55 l, Ice Hockey. 2 l, Emblem of 10th Winter Olympic Games. 2.30 l, Ski jump.

1967, Sept. 28 Photo. *Perf. 13½x13*

1951 A608 20b lt bl & multi .25 .25
1952 A608 40b multi .25 .25
1953 A608 55b bl & multi .25 .25
1954 A608 1 l lil & multi .25 .25
1955 A608 1.55 l multi .30 .25
1956 A608 2 l gray & multi .50 .25
1957 A608 2.30 l multi .85 .35
Nos. 1951-1957 (7) 2.65 1.85

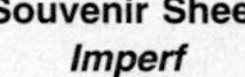

Souvenir Sheet

Imperf

1958 A608 5 l lt bl & multi 3.25 2.75

10th Winter Olympic Games, Grenoble, France, Feb. 6-18, 1968.

Nos. 1951-1957 issued in sheets of 10 (5x2) and 5 labels.

Curtea de Arges Monastery, 450th Anniv. — A609

1967, Nov. 1 Unwmk. *Perf. 13½*

1959 A609 55b multicolored .40 .25

Romanian Academy Library, Bucharest, Cent. — A610

1967, Sept. 25 Litho.

1960 A610 55b ocher, gray & dk bl .40 .25

Karl Marx and Title Page — A611

1967, Nov. 4 Photo.

1961 A611 40b rose claret, blk & yel .40 .25

Centenary of the publication of "Das Kapital" by Karl Marx.

Lenin — A612

1967, Nov. 3

1962 A612 1.20 l red, blk & gold .40 .25

Russian October Revolution, 50th anniv.

Monorail Leaving US EXPO Pavilion A613

Designs: 1 l, EXPO emblem and atom symbol. 1.60 l, Cup, world map and EXPO emblem. 2 l, EXPO emblem.

1967, Nov. 28 **Photo.**

1963	A613	55b grnsh bl, vio & blk	.25	.25
1964	A613	1 l red, blk & gray	.25	.25
1965	A613	1.60 l multicolored	.40	.25
1966	A613	2 l multicolored	.60	.25
		Nos. 1963-1966 (4)	1.50	1.00

EXPO '67 Intl. Exhib., Montreal, Apr. 28-Oct. 27. No. 1965 also for Romania's victory in the World Fencing Championships in Montreal. Issued in sheets of four.

Truck — A614

Arms of the Republic — A615

Diesel Locomotive — A616

Map Showing Telephone Network A617

Designs: 10b, Communications emblem, vert. 20b, Train. 35b, Plane. 50b, Telephone, vert. 60b, Small loading truck. 1.20 l, Autobus. 1.35 l, Helicopter. 1.50 l, Trolley bus. 1.55 l, Radio station and tower. 1.75 l, Highway. 2 l, Mail truck. 2.40 l, Television tower. 3.20 l, Jet plane. 3.25 l, Steamship. 4 l, Electric train. 5 l, World map and teletype.

Photo.; Engr. (type A615)

1967-68 ***Perf. 13½***

1967	A614	5b lt ol grn ('68)	.25	.25
1968	A614	10b henna brn ('68)	.25	.25
1969	A614	20b gray ('68)	.25	.25
1970	A614	35b bl blk ('68)	.25	.25
1971	A615	40b violet blue	.25	.25
1972	A614	50b orange ('68)	.25	.25
1973	A615	55b dull orange	.25	.25
1974	A614	60b orange brn ('68)	.25	.25

Size: 22½x28mm, 28x22½mm

1975	A616	1 l emerald ('68)	.25	.25
1976	A617	1.20 l red lil ('68)	.25	.25
1977	A617	1.35 l brt blue ('68)	.30	.25
1978	A616	1.50 l rose red ('68)	.35	.25
1979	A616	1.55 l dk brown ('68)	.35	.25
1980	A615	1.60 l rose red	.40	.25
1981	A617	1.75 l dp green ('68)	.40	.25
1982	A617	2 l citron ('68)	.60	.25
1983	A616	2.40 l dk blue ('68)	.75	.25
1984	A617	3 l grnsh blue	.75	.25
1985	A617	3.20 l ocher ('68)	1.00	.25
1986	A616	3.25 l ultra ('68)	1.00	.25
1987	A617	4 l lil rose ('68)	1.25	.25
1988	A617	5 l violet ('68)	1.40	.25
		Nos. 1967-1988 (22)	11.05	5.50

40th anniv. of the first automatic telephone exchange; introduction of automatic telephone service (No. 1984).

See Nos. 2078-2079, 2269-2284 and design A792.

Coat of Arms, Symbols of Agriculture and Industry A618

55b, Coat of arms. 1.60 l, Romanian flag. 1.75 l, Coat of arms, symbols of arts and education.

1967, Dec. 26 **Photo.** ***Perf. 13½***

Size: 27x48mm

1989	A618	40b multicolored	.25	.25
1990	A618	55b multicolored	.25	.25

Size: 33½x48mm

1991	A618	1.60 l multicolored	.50	.25

Size: 27x48mm

1992	A618	1.75 l multicolored	1.00	.55
		Nos. 1989-1992 (4)	2.00	1.30

20th anniversary of the republic.

Souvenir Sheet

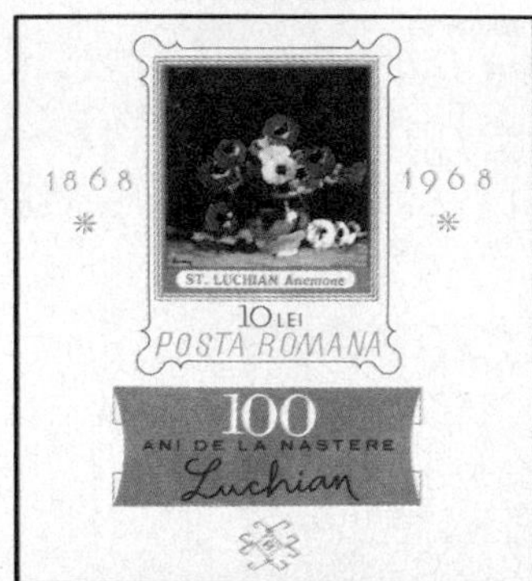

Anemones, by Stefan Luchian — A619

1968, Mar. 30 **Litho.** ***Imperf.***

1993	A619	10 l multi	6.00	6.00

Stefan Luchian, Romanian painter, birth cent.

Portrait of a Lady, by Misu Popp A620

Paintings: 10b, The Reveille of Romania, by Gheorghe Tattarescu. 20b, Composition, by Teodorescu Sionion, horiz. 35b, The Judgment of Paris, by Hendrick van Balen, horiz. 55b, Little Girl with Red Kerchief, by Nicolae Grigorescu. 60b, The Mystical Betrothal of St. Catherine, by Lamberto Sustris, horiz. 1 l, Old Nicolas, the Zither Player, by Stefan Luchian. 1.60 l, Man with a Skull, by Dierick Bouts (?). 1.75 l, Madonna and Child with Fruit Basket, by Jan van Bylert. 2.40 l, Medor and Angelica, by Sebastiano Ricci, horiz. 3 l, Summer, by Jacob Jordaens, horiz. 3.20 l, 5 l, Ecce Homo, by Titian.

Gold Frame

Size: 28x49mm

1968 **Photo.** ***Perf. 13½***

1994	A620	10b multi	.25	.25

Size: 48½x36½mm, 36x48½mm

1995	A620	20b multi	.25	.25
1996	A620	35b multi	.25	.25
1997	A620	40b multi	.25	.25
1998	A620	55b multi	.25	.25
1999	A620	60b multi	.25	.25
2000	A620	1 l multi	.65	.25
2001	A620	1.60 l multi	.80	.25
2002	A620	1.75 l multi	1.10	.25
2003	A620	2.40 l multi	1.25	.30
2004	A620	3 l multi	2.50	.50
2005	A620	3.20 l multi	2.25	.70
		Nos. 1994-2005 (12)	10.05	3.75

Miniature Sheet

Imperf

2006	A620	5 l multi	5.00	5.00

Issued: 40, 55b, 1, 1.60, 2.40, 3.20, 5 l, 3/28; others, 9/9.

See Nos. 2088-2094, 2124-2130.

Human Rights Flame — A621

1968, May 9 **Unwmk.** ***Perf. 13½***

2007	A621	1 l multicolored	.45	.25

Intl. Human Rights Year.

WHO Emblem — A622

1968, May 14 **Photo.**

2008	A622	1.60 l multi	.50	.25

WHO, 20th anniversary.

"Prince Dragos Hunting Bison," by Nicolae Grigorescu — A623

1968, May 17

2009	A623	1.60 l multi	.70	.25

15th Hunting Cong., Mamaia, May 23-29.

Pioneers and Liberation Monument — A624

Pioneers: 40b, receiving scarfs. 55b, building model planes and boat. 1 l, as radio amateurs. 1.60 l, folk dancing. 2.40 l, Girl Pioneers in camp.

1968, June 9 **Photo.** ***Perf. 13½***

2010	A624	5b multi	.25	.25
2011	A624	40b multi	.25	.25
2012	A624	55b multi	.25	.25
2013	A624	1 l multi	.30	.25
2014	A624	1.60 l multi	.50	.25
2015	A624	2.40 l multi	.70	.25
		Nos. 2010-2015 (6)	2.25	1.50

Ion Ionescu de la Brad — A625

Designs: 55b, Emil Racovita. 1.60 l, Prince Mircea of Walachia.

1968 **Size: 28x43mm**

2016	A625	40b multicolored	.25	.25
2017	A625	55b green & multi	.25	.25

Size: 28x48mm

2018	A625	1.60 l gold & multi	.55	.25
		Nos. 2016-2018 (3)	1.05	.75

Ion Ionescu de la Brad (1818-91); Emil Racovita (1868-1947), explorer and naturalist; 1.60 l, Prince Mircea (1386-1418). Issue dates: 40b, 55b, June 24; 1.60 l, June 22.

Geranium A626

Designs: Various geraniums.

1968, July 20 **Photo.** ***Perf. 13½***

2019	A626	10b multicolored	.25	.25
2020	A626	20b multicolored	.25	.25
2021	A626	40b multicolored	.25	.25
2022	A626	55b multicolored	.25	.25
2023	A626	60b multicolored	.25	.25
2024	A626	1.20 l multicolored	.25	.25
2025	A626	1.35 l multicolored	.35	.25
2026	A626	1.60 l multicolored	.75	.25
		Nos. 2019-2026 (8)	2.60	2.00

Avram Iancu, by B. Iscovescu and Demonstrating Students — A627

Demonstrating Students and: 55b, Nicolae Balcescu, by Gheorghe Tattarescu. 1.60 l, Vasile Alecsandri, by N. Livaditti.

1968, July 25

2027	A627	55b gold & multi	.25	.25
2028	A627	1.20 l gold & multi	.45	.25
2029	A627	1.60 l gold & multi	.70	.25
		Nos. 2027-2029 (3)	1.40	.75

120th anniversary of 1848 revolution.

Boxing — A628

Aztec Calendar Stone and: 10b, Javelin, Women's. 20b, Woman diver. 40b, Volleyball. 60b, Wrestling. 1.20 l, Fencing. 1.35 l, Canoeing. 1.60 l, Soccer. 5 l, Running.

1968, Aug. 28

2030	A628	10b multi	.25	.25
2031	A628	20b multi	.25	.25
2032	A628	40b multi	.25	.25
2033	A628	55b multi	.25	.25
2034	A628	60b multi	.25	.25
2035	A628	1.20 l multi	.35	.25
2036	A628	1.35 l multi	.40	.25
2037	A628	1.60 l multi	.65	.25
		Nos. 2030-2037 (8)	2.65	2.00

Souvenir Sheet

Imperf

2038	A628	5 l multi	3.00	2.00

19th Olympic Games, Mexico City, 10/12-17.

Atheneum and Harp — A629

1968, Aug. 20 Litho. *Perf. 12x12½*

2039	A629 55b multicolored		.40	.25

Centenary of the Philharmonic Orchestra.

Globe and Emblem — A630

1968, Oct. 4 Litho. *Perf. 13½*

2040	A630 1.60 l ultra & gold		.60	.25

Intl. Fed. of Photograpic Art, 20th anniv.

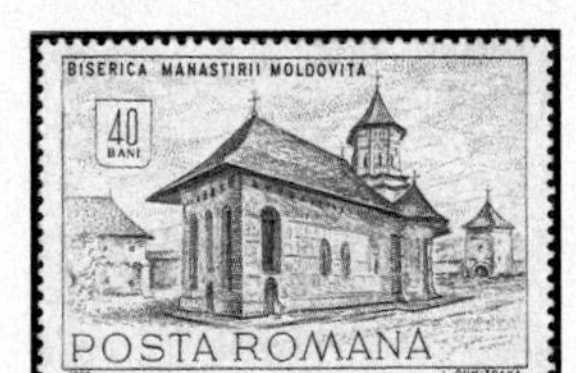
Moldovita Monastery Church — A631

Historic Monuments: 10b, "The Triumph of Trajan," Roman metope, vert. 55b, Cozia monastery church. 1.20 l, Court of Tirgoviste Palace. 1.55 l, Palace of Culture, Jassy. 1.75 l, Corvinus Castle, Hunedoara.

1968, Nov. 25 Engr. *Perf. 13½*

2041	A631	10b dk bl, ol & brn	.25	.25
2042	A631	40b rose car, bl & brn	.25	.25
2043	A631	55b ol, brn & vio	.25	.25
2044	A631	1.20 l yel, mar & gray	.30	.25
2045	A631	1.55 l vio brn, dk bl & lt grn	.50	.25
2046	A631	1.75 l org, blk & ol	1.00	.25
		Nos. 2041-2046 (6)	2.55	1.50

Mute Swan — A632

Protected Birds and Animals: 20b, European stilts. 40b, Sheldrakes. 55b, Egret feeding young. 60b, Golden eagle. 1.20 l, Great bustards. 1.35 l, Chamois. 1.60 l, Bison.

1968, Dec. 20 Photo. *Perf. 13½*

2047	A632	10b pink & multi	.30	.25
2048	A632	20b multicolored	.30	.25
2049	A632	40b lilac & multi	.30	.25
2050	A632	55b olive & multi	.30	.25
2051	A632	60b multicolored	.30	.25
2052	A632	1.20 l multicolored	.65	.25
2053	A632	1.35 l blue & multi	.75	.25
2054	A632	1.60 l multicolored	.90	.25
		Nos. 2047-2054 (8)	3.80	2.00

Michael the Brave's Entry into Alba Iulia, by D. Stoica — A633

Designs: 1 l, "The Round Dance of Union," by Theodor Aman. 1.75 l, Assembly of Alba Iulia.

1968, Dec. 1 Litho. *Perf. 13½*

2055	A633	55b gold & multi	.25	.25
2056	A633	1 l gold & multi	.40	.25
2057	A633	1.75 l gold & multi	.60	.35
a.		Souv. sheet of 3, #2055-2057, imperf.	1.75	1.50
		Nos. 2055-2057 (3)	1.25	.85

50th anniv. of the union of Transylvania and Romania. No. 2057a sold for 4 l.

Woman from Neamt — A634

Regional Costumes: 40b, Man from Neamt. 55b, Woman from Hunedoara. 1 l, Man from Hunedoara. 1.60 l, Woman from Brasov. 2.40 l, Man from Brasov.

1968, Dec. 28 *Perf. 12x12½*

2058	A634	5b orange & multi	.25	.25
2059	A634	40b blue & multi	.25	.25
2060	A634	55b multi	.25	.25
2061	A634	1 l brown & multi	.25	.25
2062	A634	1.60 l brown & multi	.50	.25
2063	A634	2.40 l multi	.95	.35
		Nos. 2058-2063 (6)	2.45	1.60

1969, Feb. 15

Regional Costumes: 5b, Woman from Dolj. 40b, Man from Dolj. 55b, Woman from Arges. 1 l, Man from Arges. 1.60 l, Woman from Timisoara. 2.40 l, Man from Timisoara.

2064	A634	5b multi	.25	.25
2065	A634	40b multi	.25	.25
2066	A634	55b lil & multi	.25	.25
2067	A634	1 l rose & multi	.25	.25
2068	A634	1.60 l multi	.55	.25
2069	A634	2.40 l brn & multi	1.00	.25
		Nos. 2064-2069 (6)	2.55	1.50

Fencing — A635

Sports: 20b, Women's javelin. 40b, Canoeing. 55b, Boxing. 1 l, Volleyball. 1.20 l, Swimming. 1.60 l, Wrestling. 2.40 l, Soccer.

1969, Mar. 10 Photo. *Perf. 13½*

Denominations Black, Athletes in Gray

2070	A635	10b pale brown	.25	.25
2071	A635	20b violet	.25	.25
2072	A635	40b blue	.25	.25
2073	A635	55b red	.25	.25
2074	A635	1 l green	.25	.25
2075	A635	1.20 l brt blue	.25	.25
2076	A635	1.60 l cerise	.45	.25
2077	A635	2.40 l dp green	.85	.25
		Nos. 2070-2077 (8)	2.80	2.00

Type of Regular Issue

1969, Jan. 10 Photo. *Perf. 13½*

2078	A614	40b Power lines, vert.	.25	.25
2079	A614	55b Dam, vert.	.25	.25

Painting Type of 1968

Paintings (Nudes): 10b, Woman Carrying Jug, by Gheorghe Tattarescu. 20b, Reclining Woman, by Theodor Pallady, horiz. 35b, Seated Woman, by Nicolae Tonitza. 60b, Venus and Amor, 17th century Flemish School. 1.75 l, 5 l, Diana and Endimion, by Marco Liberi. 3 l, The Three Graces, by Hans von Aachen.

1969, Mar. 27 Photo. *Perf. 13½*

Gold Frame

Size: 37x49mm, 49x37mm

2088	A620	10b multi	.25	.25
2089	A620	20b multi	.25	.25
2090	A620	35b multi	.25	.25
2091	A620	60b multi	.30	.25
2092	A620	1.75 l multi	.80	.25

Size: 27½x48½mm

2093	A620	3 l multi	1.75	.45
		Nos. 2088-2093 (6)	3.60	1.70

Miniature Sheet

Imperf

2094	A620	5 l multi	4.50	4.50

No. 2094 contains one stamp 36½x48½mm. with simulated perforations.

No. 2093 is incorrectly inscribed Hans von Aachen.

ILO, 50th Anniv. — A636

1969, Apr. 9 Photo. *Perf. 13½*

2095	A636 55b multicolored		.50	.25

Symbolic Head — A637

1969, Apr. 28

2096	A637	55b ultra & multi	.35	.25
2097	A637	1.50 l red & multi	1.00	.35

Romania's cultural and economic cooperation with European countries.

Communications Symbol — A638

1969, May 12 Photo. *Perf. 13½*

2098	A638	55b vio bl & bluish gray	.40	.25

7th Session of the Conference of Postal and Telecommunications Ministers, Bucharest.

Boxers, Referee and Map of Europe A639

Map of Europe and: 40b, Two boxers. 55b, Sparring. 1.75 l, Referee declaring winner.

1969, May 24

2099	A639	35b multicolored	.25	.25
2100	A639	40b multicolored	.25	.25
2101	A639	55b multicolored	.25	.25
2102	A639	1.75 l blue & multi	.60	.25
		Nos. 2099-2102 (4)	1.35	1.00

European Boxing Championships, Bucharest, May 31-June 8.

Apatura Ilia — A640

Designs: Various butterflies and moths.

1969, June 25 Photo. *Perf. 13½*

Insects in Natural Colors

2103	A640	5b yellow grn	.30	.25
2104	A640	10b rose mag	.30	.25
2105	A640	20b violet	.30	.25
2106	A640	40b blue grn	.30	.25
2107	A640	55b brt blue	.30	.25
2108	A640	1 l blue	.45	.25
2109	A640	1.20 l violet bl	.60	.25
2110	A640	2.40 l yellow bis	1.25	.25
		Nos. 2103-2110 (8)	3.80	2.00

Communist Party Flag — A641

1969, Aug. 6 Photo. *Perf. 13½*

2111	A641 55b multicolored		.40	.25

10th Romanian Communist Party Congress.

Torch, Atom Diagram and Book — A642

Designs: 40b, Symbols of agriculture, science and industry. 1.75 l, Pylon, smokestack and cogwheel.

1969, Aug. 10

2112	A642	35b multicolored	.25	.25
2113	A642	40b green & multi	.25	.25
2114	A642	1.75 l multicolored	.50	.25
		Nos. 2112-2114 (3)	1.00	.75

Exhibition showing the achievements of Romanian economy during the last 25 years.

Broken Chain — A643

55b, Construction work. 60b, Flags.

1969, Aug. 23

2115	A643	10b multicolored	.25	.25
2116	A643	55b yellow & multi	.25	.25
2117	A643	60b multicolored	.25	.25
		Nos. 2115-2117 (3)	.75	.75

25th anniversary of Romania's liberation from fascist rule.

Juggler on Unicycle — A644

Circus Performers: 20b, Clown. 35b, Trapeze artists. 60b, Dressage and woman trainer. 1.75 l, Woman in high wire act. 3 l, Performing tiger and trainer.

1969, Sept. 29 Photo. *Perf. 13½*

2118	A644	10b lt blue & multi	.25	.25
2119	A644	20b lemon & multi	.25	.25
2120	A644	35b lilac & multi	.25	.25
2121	A644	60b multicolored	.25	.25
2122	A644	1.75 l multicolored	.55	.25
2123	A644	3 l ultra & multi	.90	.35
		Nos. 2118-2123 (6)	2.45	1.60

Painting Type of 1968

10b, Venetian Senator, Tintoretto School. 20b, Sofia Kretzulescu, by Gheorghe Tattarescu. 35b, Phillip IV, by Velazquez. 60b, Man Reading and Child, by Hans Memling. 1.75 l, Doamnei d'Aguesseau, by Madame Vigée-Lebrun. 3 l, Portrait of a Woman, by Rembrandt. 5 l, The Return of the Prodigal Son, by Bernardino Licinio, horiz.

Gold Frame

1969 **Size: 36½x49mm**

2124	A620	10b multi	.25	.25
2125	A620	20b multi	.25	.25
2126	A620	35b multi	.25	.25
2127	A620	60b multi	.40	.25
2128	A620	1.75 l multi	.80	.25
2129	A620	3 l multi	1.40	.40
		Nos. 2124-2129 (6)	3.35	1.65

Miniature Sheet

Imperf

2130	A620	5 l gold & multi	3.00	2.25

No. 2130 contains one stamp with simulated perforations.

Issue dates: 5 l, July 31. Others, Oct. 1.

Masks — A645

1969, Nov. 24 **Photo.** ***Perf. 13½***

2131	A645	40b Branesti	.25	.25
2132	A645	55b Tudora	.25	.25
2133	A645	1.55 l Birsesti	.50	.25
2134	A645	1.75 l Rudaria	.60	.25
		Nos. 2131-2134 (4)	1.60	1.00

Armed Forces Memorial A646

1969, Oct. 25

2135	A646	55b red, blk & gold	.40	.25

25th anniversary of the People's Army.

Locomotives of 1869 and 1969 — A647

1969, Oct. 31

2136	A647	55b silver & multi	.40	.25

Bucharest-Filaret-Giurgevo railroad, cent.

A648

Apollo 12 landing module.

1969, Nov. 24

2137	A648	1.50 l multi	.50	.40

2nd landing on the moon, Nov. 19, 1969, astronauts Captains Alan Bean, Charles Conrad, Jr. and Richard Gordon.

Printed in sheets of 4 with 4 labels (one label with names of astronauts, one with Apollo 12 emblem and 2 silver labels with picture of landing module, Intrepid). Value, unused $2.50; used $2.25.

A649

New Year: 40b, Mother Goose in Goat Disguise. 55b, Children singing and decorated tree, Sorcova. 1.50 l, Drummer, and singer, Buhaiul. 2.40 l, Singer and bell ringer, Plugusurol.

1969, Dec. 25 **Photo.** ***Perf. 13½***

2138	A649	40b bister & multi	.25	.25
2139	A649	55b lilac & multi	.25	.25
2140	A649	1.50 l blue & multi	.60	.25
2141	A649	2.40 l multicolored	1.10	.25
		Nos. 2138-2141 (4)	2.20	1.00

The Last Judgment (detail), Voronet Monastery — A650

North Moldavian Monastery Frescoes: 10b, Stephen the Great and family, Voronet. 20b, Three prophets, Sucevita. 60b, St. Nicholas (scene from his life), Sucevita, vert. 1.75 l, Siege of Constantinople, 7th century, Moldovita. 3 l, Plowman, Voronet, vert.

1969, Dec. 15

2142	A650	10b gold & multi	.25	.25
2143	A650	20b gold & multi	.25	.25
2144	A650	35b gold & multi	.25	.25
2145	A650	60b gold & multi	.30	.25
2146	A650	1.75 l gold & multi	.50	.25
2147	A650	3 l gold & multi	1.40	.25
		Nos. 2142-2147 (6)	2.95	1.50

Ice Hockey A651

Designs: 55b, Goalkeeper. 1.20 l, Two players with puck. 2.40 l, Player and goalkeeper.

1970, Jan. 20 ***Perf. 13½***

2148	A651	20b yellow & multi	.25	.25
2149	A651	55b multicolored	.25	.25
2150	A651	1.20 l pink & multi	.50	.25
2151	A651	2.40 l lt blue & multi	1.10	.30
		Nos. 2148-2151 (4)	2.10	1.05

World Ice Hockey Championships, Bucharest and Galati, Feb. 24-Mar. 5.

Pasqueflower A652

Flowers: 10b, Adonis vernalis. 20b, Thistle. 40b, Almond tree blossoms. 55b, Iris. 1 l, Flax. 1.20 l, Sage. 2.40 l, Peony.

1970, Feb. 25 **Photo.** ***Perf. 13½***

2152	A652	5b yellow & multi	.25	.25
2153	A652	10b green & multi	.25	.25
2154	A652	20b lt bl & multi	.25	.25
2155	A652	40b violet & multi	.25	.25
2156	A652	55b ultra & multi	.25	.25
2157	A652	1 l multicolored	.25	.25
2158	A652	1.20 l red & multi	.45	.25
2159	A652	2.40 l multicolored	.95	.25
		Nos. 2152-2159 (8)	2.90	2.00

Japanese Print and EXPO '70 Emblem A653

Design: 1 l, Pagoda, EXPO '70 emblem.

1970, Mar. 23

2160	A653	20b gold & multi	.25	.25

Size: 29x92mm

2161	A653	1 l gold & multi	.50	.25

EXPO '70 Intl. Exhib., Osaka, Japan, Mar. 15-Sept. 13.

A souvenir sheet exists with perforated label in pagoda design of 1 l. Issued Nov. 28, 1970. Value $3.

Camille, by Claude Monet (Maximum Card) — A654

1970, Apr. 19 **Photo.** ***Perf. 13½***

2162	A654	1.50 l gold & multi	.55	.25

Franco-Romanian Maximafil Phil. Exhib.

Cuza, by C. Popp de Szathmary — A655

1970, Apr. 20 ***Perf. 13½***

2163	A655	55b gold & multi	.35	.25

Alexandru Ioan Cuza (1820-1866), prince of Romania.

Lenin (1870-1924) A656

1970, Apr. 21 **Photo.** ***Perf. 13½***

2164	A656	40b dk red & multi	.35	.25

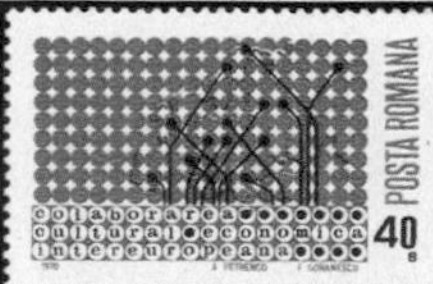

Map of Europe with Capital Cities A657

1970, Apr. 28

2165	A657	40b grn, brn org & blk	.50	.35
2166	A657	1.50 l ultra, yel brn & blk	1.00	.70

Inter-European cultural and economic cooperation.

Victory Monument, Romanian and Russian Flags — A658

1970, May 9

2167	A658	55b red & multi	.35	.25

25th anniv. of victory over the Germans.

Greek Silver Drachm, 5th Century B.C. — A659

Coins: 20b, Getic-Dacian silver didrachm, 2nd-1st centuries B.C. 35b, Emperor Trajan's copper sestertius, 106 A.D. 60b, Mircea ducat, 1400. 1.75 l, Stephen the Great's silver groschen, 1460. 3 l, Brasov klippe-taler, 1601, vert.

1970, May 15

2168	A659	10b ultra, blk & sil	.25	.25
2169	A659	20b hn brn, blk & sil	.25	.25
2170	A659	35b grn, dk brn & gold	.25	.25
2171	A659	60b brn, blk & sil	.25	.25
2172	A659	1.75 l brt bl, blk & sil	.50	.25
2173	A659	3 l dk car, blk & sil	1.00	.25
		Nos. 2168-2173 (6)	2.50	1.50

Soccer Players and Ball — A660

Soccer ball & various scenes from soccer game.

1970, May 26 ***Perf. 13½***

2174	A660	40b multi	.25	.25
2175	A660	55b multi	.25	.25
2176	A660	1.75 l blue & multi	.60	.25
2177	A660	3.30 l multi	1.00	.30
		Nos. 2174-2177 (4)	2.10	1.05

Souvenir Sheet

2178		Sheet of 4	3.00	2.00
a.	A660	1.20 l multi	.35	.25
b.	A660	1.50 l multi	.50	.25
c.	A660	1.55 l multi	.60	.25
d.	A660	1.75 l multi	.60	.25

9th World Soccer Championships for the Jules Rimet Cup, Mexico City, May 30-June 21. No. 2178 contains 4 stamps similar to Nos. 2174-2177, but with only one quarter of the soccer ball on each stamp, forming one large ball in the center of the block.

Moldovita Monastery — A661

Frescoes from North Moldavian Monasteries.

1970, June 29 *Perf. 13½*

Size: 36½x49mm

2179 A661 10b gold & multi .25 .25

Size: 27½x49mm

2180 A661 20b gold & multi .25 .25

Size: 36½x49mm, 48x37mm

2181 A661 40b gold & multi .25 .25
2182 A661 55b gold & multi .25 .25
2183 A661 1.75 l gold & multi .35 .25
2184 A661 3 l gold & multi 1.00 .35
Nos. 2179-2184 (6) 2.35 1.60

Miniature Sheet

2185 A661 5 l gold & multi 2.50 2.25

Friedrich Engels (1820-1895), German Socialist — A662

1970, July 10 **Photo.** *Perf. 13½*
2186 A662 1.50 l multi .45 .25

Aerial View of Iron Gate Power Station A663

1970, July 13
2187 A663 35b blue & multi .30 .25

Hydroelectric plant at the Iron Gate of the Danube.

Cargo Ship A664

1970, July 17
2188 A664 55b blue & multi .30 .25

Romanian merchant marine, 75th anniv.

Exhibition Hall and Oil Derrick A665

1970, July 20
2189 A665 1.50 l multi .45 .25

International Bucharest Fair, Oct. 13-24.

Opening of UPU Headquarters, Bern — A666

1970, Aug. 17 **Photo.** *Perf. 13½*
2190 A666 1.50 l ultra & slate green .45 .25

Education Year Emblem — A667

1970, Aug. 17
2191 A667 55b black, pur & red .40 .25

International Education Year.

Iceberg Rose — A668

Roses: 35b, Wiener charme. 55b, Pink luster. 1 l, Piccadilly. 1.50 l, Orange Delbard. 2.40 l, Sibelius.

1970, Aug. 21
2192 A668 20b dk red, grn & yel .25 .25
2193 A668 35b vio, yel & grn .25 .25
2194 A668 55b blue, rose & grn .25 .25
2195 A668 1 l grn, car rose & yel .40 .25
2196 A668 1.50 l dk bl, red & grn .55 .25
2197 A668 2.40 l brt bl, dp red & grn 1.00 .25
Nos. 2192-2197 (6) 2.70 1.50

Spaniel and Pheasant, by Jean B. Oudry A669

Paintings: 10b, The Hunt, by Domenico Brandi. 35b, The Hunt, by Jan Fyt. 60b, After the Chase, by Jacob Jordaens. 1.75 l, 5 l, Game Merchant, by Frans Snyders (horiz.). 3 l, The Hunt, by Adriaen de Gryeff. Sizes: 37x49mm (10b, 35b); 35x33mm (20b, 60b, 3 l); 49x37mm (1.75 l, 3 l).

1970, Sept. 20 **Photo.** *Perf. 13½*
2198 A669 10b gold & multi .25 .25
2199 A669 20b gold & multi .25 .25
2200 A669 35b gold & multi .25 .25
2201 A669 60b gold & multi .40 .25
2202 A669 1.75 l gold & multi .90 .30
2203 A669 3 l gold & multi 1.75 .60
Nos. 2198-2203 (6) 3.80 1.90

Miniature Sheet

2204 A669 5 l gold & multi 3.75 3.25

UN Emblem — A670

1970, Sept. 29
2205 A670 1.50 l lt bl, ultra & blk .60 .25

25th anniversary of the United Nations.

Mother and Child — A671

Designs: 1.50 l, Red Cross relief trucks and tents. 1.75 l, Rebuilding houses.

1970, Sept. 25
2206 A671 55b bl gray, blk & ol .25 .25
2207 A671 1.50 l ol, blk & car .45 .25
a. Strip of 3, #2206-2207, C179 1.40 .55
2208 A671 1.75 l blue & multi .70 .25
Nos. 2206-2208 (3) 1.40 .75

Plight of the Danube flood victims.

Arabian Thoroughbred — A672

Horses: 35b, American trotter. 55b, Ghidran (Anglo-American). 1 l, Northern Moravian. 1.50 l, Trotter thoroughbred. 2.40 l, Lippizaner.

1970, Oct. 10 **Photo.** *Perf. 13½*
2209 A672 20b blk & multi .25 .25
2210 A672 35b blk & multi .25 .25
2211 A672 55b blk & multi .25 .25
2212 A672 1 l blk & multi .30 .25
2213 A672 1.50 l blk & multi .50 .25
2214 A672 2.40 l blk & multi 1.10 .25
Nos. 2209-2214 (6) 2.65 1.50

Ludwig van Beethoven (1770-1827), Composer — A673

1970, Nov. 2
2215 A673 55b multicolored 1.25 .25

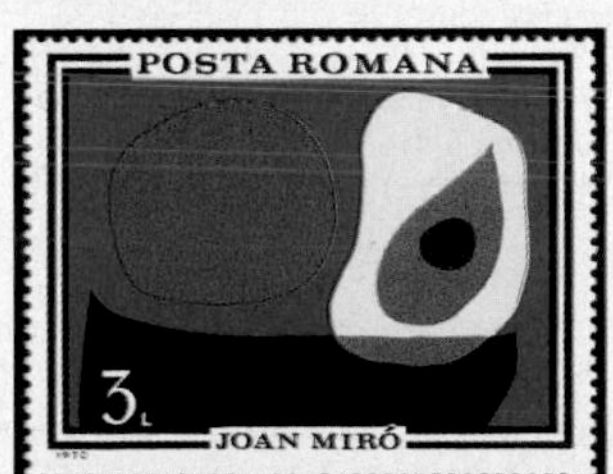

Abstract, by Joan Miró — A674

1970, Dec. 10 **Photo.** *Perf. 13½*
2216 A674 3 l ultra & multi 1.00 .70

Souvenir Sheet

Imperf

2217 A674 5 l ultra & multi 2.25 2.00

Plight of the Danube flood victims. No. 2216 issued in sheets of 5 stamps and label with signature of Miró and date of flood. No. 2217 contains one stamp with simulated perforation.

The Sense of Sight, by Gonzales Coques A675

"The Senses," paintings by Gonzales Coques (1614-1684): 20b, Hearing. 35b, Smell. 60b, Taste. 1.75 l, Touch. 3 l, Bruckenthal Museum, Sibiu. 5 l, View of Sibiu, 1808, horiz.

1970, Dec. 15 **Photo.** *Perf. 13½*
2218 A675 10b gold & multi .25 .25
2219 A675 20b gold & multi .25 .25
2220 A675 35b gold & multi .25 .25
2221 A675 60b gold & multi .25 .25
2222 A675 1.75 l gold & multi .60 .25
2223 A675 3 l gold & multi 1.00 .45
Nos. 2218-2223 (6) 2.60 1.70

Miniature Sheet

Imperf

2224 A675 5 l gold & multi 2.75 2.50

Men of Three Races A676

1971, Feb. 23 **Photo.** *Perf. 13½*
2225 A676 1.50 l multi .60 .25

Intl. year against racial discrimination.

Tudor Vladimirescu, by Theodor Aman — A677

1971, Feb. 20
2226 A677 1.50 l gold & multi .60 .25

Vladimirescu, patriot, 150th death anniv.

German Shepherd A677a

Dogs: 35b, Bulldog. 55b, Fox terrier. 1 l, Setter. 1.50 l, Cocker spaniel. 2.40 l, Poodle.

1971, Feb. 22
2227 A677a 20b blk & multi .25 .25
2228 A677a 35b blk & multi .25 .25
2229 A677a 55b blk & multi .25 .25
2230 A677a 1 l blk & multi .40 .25

No.	Type	Denom. & Color	Unused	Used
2231	A677a	1.50 l blk & multi	.65	.25
2232	A677a	2.40 l blk & multi	1.25	.40
		Nos. 2227-2232 (6)	3.05	1.65

Paris Commune — A678

1971, Mar. 15 Photo. *Perf. 13½*

No.	Type	Denom. & Color	Unused	Used
2233	A678	40b multicolored	.40	.25

Centenary of the Paris Commune.

Congress Emblem — A679

1971, Mar. 23

No.	Type	Denom. & Color	Unused	Used
2234	A679	55b multicolored	.40	.25

Romanian Trade Unions Congress.

Rock Formation A680

Designs: 10b, Bicazului Gorge, vert. 55b, Winter resort. 1 l, Danube Delta view. 1.50 l, Lakeside resort. 2.40 l, Venus, Jupiter, Neptune Hotels on Black Sea.

Size: 23x38mm, 38x23mm

1971, Apr. 15

No.	Type	Denom. & Color	Unused	Used
2235	A680	10b multi	.25	.25
2236	A680	40b multi	.25	.25
2237	A680	55b multi	.25	.25
2238	A680	1 l multi	.30	.25
2239	A680	1.50 l multi	.50	.25

Size: 76½x28mm

No.	Type	Denom. & Color	Unused	Used
2240	A680	2.40 l multi	1.00	.35
		Nos. 2235-2240 (6)	2.55	1.60

Tourist publicity.

Arrow Pattern A681

Design: 1.75 l, Wave pattern.

1971, Apr. 28 Photo. *Perf. 13½*

No.	Type	Denom. & Color	Unused	Used
2241	A681	55b multi	.75	.60
2242	A681	1.75 l multi	1.50	1.00

Inter-European Cultural and Economic Collaboration. Sheets of 10.

Historical Museum — A682

1971, May 7 Photo. *Perf. 13½*

No.	Type	Denom. & Color	Unused	Used
2243	A682	55b blue & multi	.40	.25

For Romania's Historical Museum.

Communist Party Emblem — A683

Demonstration, by A. Anastasiu — A684

35b, Reading Proclamation, by Stefan Szonyi.

1971, May 8

No.	Type	Denom. & Color	Unused	Used
2244	A684	35b multicolored	.25	.25
2245	A683	40b multicolored	.25	.25
2246	A684	55b multicolored	.25	.25
		Nos. 2244-2246 (3)	.75	.75

Romanian Communist Party, 50th anniv.

Souvenir Sheets

Motra Tone, by Kole Idromeno A685

Dancing the Hora, by Theodor Aman — A686

Designs: b, Maid by V. Dimitrov-Maystora. c, Rosa Botzaris, by Joseph Stieler. d, Woman in Costume, by Katarina Ivanovic. e, Argeseanca, by Carol Popp de Szathmary. f, Woman in Modern Dress, by Ibrahim Calli.

1971, May 25 Photo. *Perf. 13½*

No.	Type	Denom. & Color	Unused	Used
2247	A685	Sheet of 6	4.00	3.50
a.-f.		1.20 l any single	.55	.40
2248	A686	5 l multicolored	3.00	3.00

Balkanphila III Stamp Exhibition, Bucharest, June 27-July 2.

No. 2247 contains 6 stamps in 3 rows and 6 labels showing exhibition emblem and "60b."

Pomegranate Flower — A687

Flowers: 35b, Slipperwort. 55b, Lily. 1 l, Mimulus. 1.50 l, Morning-glory. 2.40 l, Leaf cactus, horiz.

1971, June 20

No.	Type	Denom. & Color	Unused	Used
2249	A687	20b ultra & multi	.25	.25
2250	A687	35b red & multi	.25	.25
2251	A687	55b ultra & multi	.25	.25
2252	A687	1 l car & multi	.45	.25
2253	A687	1.50 l car & multi	.75	.25
2254	A687	2.40 l ultra & multi	1.10	.30
		Nos. 2249-2254 (6)	3.05	1.55

Nude, by Iosif Iser A688

Paintings of Nudes: 20b, by Camil Ressu. 35b, by Nicolae Grigorescu. 60b, by Eugene Delacroix (odalisque). 1.75 l, by Auguste Renoir. 3 l, by Palma il Vecchio (Venus and Amor). 5 l, by Il Bronzino (Venus and Amor). 60b, 3 l, 5 l, horiz.

1971, July 25 Photo. *Perf. 13½*

Size: 38x50mm, 49x39mm, 29x50mm (20b)

No.	Type	Denom. & Color	Unused	Used
2255	A688	10b gold & multi	.25	.25
2256	A688	20b gold & multi	.25	.25
2257	A688	35b gold & multi	.25	.25
2258	A688	60b gold & multi	.25	.25
2259	A688	1.75 l gold & multi	.35	.25
2260	A688	3 l gold & multi	1.40	.35
		Nos. 2255-2260 (6)	2.75	1.60

Miniature Sheet

Imperf

No.	Type	Denom. & Color	Unused	Used
2261	A688	5 l gold & multi	3.25	3.25

Ships in Storm, by B. Peters — A689

Paintings of Ships by: 20b, Ludolf Backhuysen. 35b, Andries van Eertvelt. 60b, M. W. Arnold. 1.75 l, Ivan Konstantinovich Aivazovski. 3 l, Jean Steriadi. 5 l, N. Darascu, vert.

1971, Sept. 15 Photo. *Perf. 13½*

No.	Type	Denom. & Color	Unused	Used
2262	A689	10b gold & multi	.25	.25
2263	A689	20b gold & multi	.25	.25
2264	A689	35b gold & multi	.25	.25
2265	A689	60b gold & multi	.25	.25
2266	A689	1.75 l gold & multi	.45	.25
2267	A689	3 l gold & multi	1.00	.35
		Nos. 2262-2267 (6)	2.45	1.60

Miniature Sheet

No.	Type	Denom. & Color	Unused	Used
2268	A689	5 l gold & multi	2.50	2.50

Type of Regular Issue

Designs as Before and: 3.60 l, Mail collector. 4.80 l, Mailman. 6 l, Ministry of Posts.

1971 Photo. *Perf. 13½*

Size: 16½x23mm, 23x16½mm

No.	Type	Denom. & Color	Unused	Used
2269	A616	1 l emerald	.25	.25
2270	A617	1.20 l red lilac	.25	.25
2271	A617	1.35 l brt blue	.30	.25
2272	A616	1.50 l orange red	.35	.25
2273	A616	1.55 l sepia	.35	.25
2274	A617	1.75 l deep green	.40	.25
2275	A617	2 l citron	.45	.25
2276	A616	2.40 l dark blue	.55	.25
2277	A617	3 l greenish bl	.75	.25
2278	A617	3.20 l ocher	.75	.25
2279	A616	3.25 l ultra	.85	.25
2280	A616	3.60 l blue	.90	.25
2281	A617	4 l lilac rose	1.10	.25
2282	A616	4.80 l grnsh blue	1.20	.25
2283	A617	5 l violet	1.25	.25
2284	A616	6 l dp magenta	1.60	.25
		Nos. 2269-2284 (16)	11.30	4.00

Prince Neagoe Basarab A690

1971, Sept. 20 *Perf. 13½*

No.	Type	Denom. & Color	Unused	Used
2288	A690	60b gold & multi	.40	.25

450th anniversary of the death of Prince Neagoe Basarab of Walachia.

Theodor Pallady (Painter) — A691

Portraits of: 55b, Benvenuto Cellini (1500-1571), sculptor. 1.50 l, Antoine Watteau (1684-1721), painter. 2.40 l, Albrecht Dürer (1471-1528), painter.

1971, Oct. 12 Photo. *Perf. 13½*

No.	Type	Denom. & Color	Unused	Used
2289	A691	40b gold & multi	.25	.25
2290	A691	55b gold & multi	.25	.25
2291	A691	1.50 l gold & multi	.50	.25
2292	A691	2.40 l gold & multi	1.00	.25
		Nos. 2289-2292 (4)	2.00	1.00

Anniversaries of famous artists.

Proclamation of Cyrus the Great — A692

1971, Oct. 12

No.	Type	Denom. & Color	Unused	Used
2293	A692	55b multicolored	.50	.25

2500th anniversary of the founding of the Persian empire by Cyrus the Great.

Figure Skating — A693

Designs: 20b, Ice hockey. 40b, Biathlon (skier). 55b, Bobsledding. 1.75 l, Skiing. 3 l,

Sapporo '72 emblem. 5 l, Olympic flame and emblem.

1971, Oct. 25

2294 A693 10b lt bl, blk & red .25 .25
2295 A693 20b multicolored .25 .25
2296 A693 40b multicolored .25 .25
2297 A693 55b lt bl, blk & red .25 .25
2298 A693 1.75 l lt bl, blk & red .50 .25
2299 A693 3 l lt bl, blk & red .80 .25
Nos. 2294-2299 (6) 2.30 1.50

Miniature Sheet

Imperf

2300 A693 5 l multicolored 2.75 2.75

11th Winter Olympic Games, Sapporo, Japan, Feb. 3-13, 1972. Nos. 2294-2296 printed se-tenant in sheets of 15 (5x3); Nos. 2297-2298 printed se-tenant in sheets of 10 (5x2). No. 2300 contains one stamp 37x50mm.

St. George and the Dragon A694

Frescoes from North Moldavian Monasteries: 10b, 20b, 40b, Moldovita. 55b, 1.75 l, 5 l, Voronet. 3 l, Arborea, horiz.

1971, Nov. 30 Photo. *Perf. 13½*

2301 A694 10b gold & multi .25 .25
2302 A694 20b gold & multi .25 .25
2303 A694 40b gold & multi .25 .25
2304 A694 55b gold & multi .25 .25
2305 A694 1.75 l gold & multi .70 .25
2306 A694 3 l gold & multi 1.00 .40
Nos. 2301-2306 (6) 2.70 1.65

Miniature Sheet

Imperf

2307 A694 5 l gold & multi 2.50 2.50

No. 2307 contains one stamp 44x56mm.

Ferdinand Magellan A695

Designs: 55b, Johannes Kepler and observation tower. 1 l, Yuri Gagarin and rocket orbiting earth. 1.50 l, Baron Ernest R. Rutherford, atom, nucleus and chemical apparatus.

1971, Dec. 20

2308 A695 40b grn, brt rose & dk bl .25 .25
2309 A695 55b lil, bl & gray grn .25 .25
2310 A695 1 l violet & multi .35 .25
2311 A695 1.50 l red brn, grn & bl .60 .25
Nos. 2308-2311 (4) 1.45 1.00

Magellan (1480?-1521), navigator; Kepler (1571-1630), astronomer; Gagarin, 1st man in space, 10th anniv.; Ernest R. Rutherford (1871-1937), British physicist.

Matei Millo — A696

Design: 1 l, Nicolae Iorga.

1971, Dec.

2312 A696 55b blue & multi .25 .25
2313 A696 1 l purple & multi .30 .25

Millo (1814-1896), playwright; Iorga (1871-1940), historian and politician.

Young Communists Union Emblem — A697

1972, Feb.

2314 A697 55b dk bl, red & gold .40 .25

Young Communists Union, 50th anniv.

Young Animals — A698

1972, Mar. 10 Photo. *Perf. 13½*

2315 A698 20b Lynx .25 .25
2316 A698 35b Foxes .25 .25
2317 A698 55b Roe fawns .25 .25
2318 A698 1 l Wild pigs .25 .25
2319 A698 1.50 l Wolves .50 .25
2320 A698 2.40 l Bears 1.00 .25
Nos. 2315-2320 (6) 2.50 1.50

Wrestling — A699

Olympic Rings and: 20b, Canoeing. 55b, Soccer. 1.55 l, Women's high jump. 2.90 l, Boxing. 6.70 l, Field ball.

1972, Apr. 25 Photo. *Perf. 13½*

2321 A699 10b yel & multi .25 .25
2322 A699 20b multicolored .25 .25
2323 A699 55b gray & multi .25 .25
2324 A699 1.55 l grn & multi .35 .25
2325 A699 2.90 l multicolored .80 .25
2326 A699 6.70 l lil & multi 1.25 .50
Nos. 2321-2326 (6) 3.15 1.75

20th Olympic Games, Munich, Aug. 26-Sept. 10. See Nos. C186-C187.

Stylized Map of Europe and Links A700

Design: 2.90 l, Entwined arrows and links.

1972, Apr. 28

2327 A700 1.75 l dp car, gold & blk 1.10 .75
2328 A700 2.90 l grn, gold & blk 1.50 1.00
a. Pair, #2327-2328 2.60 2.00

Inter-European Cultural and Economic Collaboration.

UIC Emblem and Trains A701

1972, May 20 Photo. *Perf. 13½*

2329 A701 55b dp car rose, blk & gold .35 .25

50th anniv., Intl. Railroad Union (UIC).

Souvenir Sheet

"Summer," by Peter Brueghel, the Younger — A702

1972, May 20 *Perf. 13x13½*

2330 A702 6 l gold & multi 3.00 3.00

Belgica 72, Intl. Phil. Exhib., Brussels, June 24-July 9.

Peony — A703

Protected Flowers: 40b, Pink. 55b, Edelweiss. 60b, Nigritella rubra. 1.35 l, Narcissus. 2.90 l, Lady's slipper.

1972, June 5 Photo. *Perf. 13*

Flowers in Natural Colors

2331 A703 20b dk vio bl .25 .25
2332 A703 40b chocolate .25 .25
2333 A703 55b dp blue .25 .25
2334 A703 60b dk green .30 .25
2335 A703 1.35 l violet .65 .25
2336 A703 2.90 l dk Prus bl 1.25 .40
Nos. 2331-2336 (6) 2.95 1.65

Saligny Bridge, Cernavoda — A704

Danube Bridges: 1.75 l, Giurgeni Bridge, Vadul. 2.75 l, Friendship Bridge, Giurgiu-Ruse.

1972, June 25 Photo. *Perf. 13½*

2337 A704 1.35 l multi .35 .25
2338 A704 1.75 l multi .50 .25
2339 A704 2.75 l multi .85 .25
Nos. 2337-2339 (3) 1.70 .75

North Railroad Station, Bucharest, Cent. A705

1972, July 4

2340 A705 55b ultra & multi .35 .25

Water Polo and Olympic Rings A706

Olympic Rings and: 20b, Pistol shoot. 55b, Discus. 1.55 l, Gymnastics, women's. 2.75 l, Canoeing. 6.40 l, Fencing.

1972, July 5 Photo. *Perf. 13½*

2341 A706 10b ol, gold & lil .25 .25
2342 A706 20b red, gold & grn .25 .25
2343 A706 55b grn, gold & brn .25 .25
2344 A706 1.55 l vio, gold & ol .40 .25
2345 A706 2.75 l bl, gold & gray .70 .25
2346 A706 6.40 l pur, gold & gray 1.50 .45
Nos. 2341-2346 (6) 3.35 1.70

20th Olympic Games, Munich, Aug. 26-Sept. 11. See No. C187.

Stamp Printing Press — A707

1972, July 25

2347 A707 55b multicolored .35 .25

Centenary of the stamp printing office.

Stefan Popescu, Self-portrait — A708

1972, Aug. 10

2348 A708 55b shown .25 .25
2349 A708 1.75 l Octav Bancila .25 .25
2350 A708 2.90 l Gheorghe Petrascu .50 .25
2351 A708 6.50 l Ion Andreescu 1.25 .30
Nos. 2348-2351 (4) 2.25 1.05

Self-portraits by Romanian painters.

Runner with Torch, Olympic Rings — A709

1972, Aug. 13

2352 A709 55b sil, bl & claret .75 .25

Olympic torch relay from Olympia, Greece, to Munich, Germany, passing through Romania.

City Hall Tower, Sibiu — A710

Designs: 1.85 l, St. Michael's Cathedral, Cluj. 2.75 l, Sphinx Rock, Mt. Bucegi, horiz. 3.35 l, Heroes' Monument, Bucharest. 3.45 l, Sinaia Castle, horiz. 5.15 l, Hydroelectric Works, Arges, horiz. 5.60 l, Church of the Epiphany, Iasi. 6.20 l, Bran Castle. 6.40 l, Hunedoara Castle, horiz. 6.80 l, Polytechnic Institute, Bucharest, horiz. 7.05 l, Black

Sinaia, Carpathian Mountains — A807

Design: 2.40 l, Hotels, Aurora, Black Sea.

1977, May 17

2724 A807 2 l gold & multi 1.00 .85
2725 A807 2.40 l gold & multi 1.40 1.25

Inter-European Cultural and Economic Cooperation. Nos. 2724-2725 printed in sheets of 4 with marginal inscriptions.

Petru Rares — A808

1977, June 10 Photo. ***Perf. 13½***

2726 A808 40b multi .35 .25

450th anniversary of the elevation of Petru Rares to Duke of Moldavia.

Ion Luca Caragiale — A809

1977, June 10

2727 A809 55b multi .35 .25

Ion Luca Caragiale (1852-1912), writer.

Red Cross Nurse, Children, Emblems A810

1977, June 10

2728 A810 1.50 l multi .40 .25

23rd Intl. Red Cross Conf., Bucharest.

Arch of Triumph, Bucharest A811

1977, June 10

2729 A811 2.15 l multi .75 .25

Battles of Marasesti and Oituz, 60th anniv.

Peaks of San Marino, Exhibition Emblem — A812

1977, Aug. 28 Photo. ***Perf. 13½***

2730 A812 4 l brt bl & multi 1.20 .25

Centenary of San Marino stamps, and San Marino '77 Phil. Exhib., San Marino, 8/28-9/4.

Man on Pommel Horse — A813

Gymnasts: 40b, Woman dancer. 55b, Man on parallel bars. 1 l, Woman on balance beam. 2.15 l, Man on rings. 4.80 l, Woman on double bars.

1977, Sept. 25 Photo. ***Perf. 13½***

2731 A813 20b multi .25 .25
2732 A813 40b multi .25 .25
2733 A813 55b multi .25 .25
2734 A813 1 l multi .25 .25
2735 A813 2.15 l multi .35 .25
2736 A813 4.80 l multi 1.25 .25
Nos. 2731-2736 (6) 2.60 1.50

"Carpati" near Cazane, Iron Gate — A814

Designs: 1 l, "Mircesti" at Orsova. 1.50 l, "Oltenita" at Calafat. 2.15 l, Water bus at Giurgiu. 3 l, "Herculane" at Tulcea. 3.40 l, "Muntenia" in Nature preserve, Sulina. 4.80 l, Map of Danube Delta with Sulina Canal. 10 l, Danubius, god of Danube, from Trajan's Column, Rome, vert.

1977, Dec. 28

2737 A814 55b multi .25 .25
2738 A814 1 l multi .25 .25
2739 A814 1.50 l multi .25 .25
2740 A814 2.15 l multi .40 .25
2741 A814 3 l multi .60 .25
2742 A814 3.40 l multi .65 .25
2743 A814 4.80 l multi 1.25 .30
Nos. 2737-2743 (7) 3.65 1.80

Souvenir Sheet

2744 A814 10 l multi 2.75 2.00

European Danube Commission.

A 10 l imperf. souvenir sheet exists showing map of Danube from Regensburg to the Black Sea. Value, unused or used, $50.

Flag and Arms of Romania A815

Designs: 1.20 l, Computer production in Romania. 1.75 l, National Theater, Craiova.

1977, Dec. 30

2745 A815 55b multi .25 .25
2746 A815 1.20 l multi .25 .25
2747 A815 1.75 l multi .40 .25
Nos. 2745-2747 (3) .90 .75

Proclamation of Republic, 30th anniversary.

Dancers A816

Designs: Romanian male folk dancers.

1977, Nov. 28 Photo. ***Perf. 13½***

2748 A816 20b multi .25 .25
2749 A816 40b multi .25 .25
2750 A816 55b multi .25 .25
2751 A816 1 l multi .25 .25
2752 A816 2.15 l multi .35 .25
2753 A816 4.80 l multi 1.25 .25
Nos. 2748-2753 (6) 2.60 1.50

Souvenir Sheet

2754 A816 10 l multi 2.50 2.25

Firiza Dam A817

Hydroelectric Stations and Dams: 40b, Negovanu. 55b, Piatra Neamt. 1 l, Izvorul Muntelui-Bicaz. 2.15 l, Vidraru. 4.80 l, Iron Gate.

1978, Mar. 10 Photo. ***Perf. 13½***

2755 A817 20b multi .25 .25
2756 A817 40b multi .25 .25
2757 A817 55b multi .25 .25
2758 A817 1 l multi .25 .25
2759 A817 2.15 l multi .35 .25
2760 A817 4.80 l multi 1.00 .25
Nos. 2755-2760 (6) 2.35 1.50

Soccer and Argentina '78 Emblem A818

Various soccer scenes & Argentina '78 emblem.

1978, Apr. 15

2761 A818 55b bl & multi .25 .25
2762 A818 1 l org & multi .25 .25
2763 A818 1.50 l yel grn & multi .25 .25
2764 A818 2.15 l ver & multi .30 .25
2765 A818 3.40 l bl grn & multi .50 .25
2766 A818 4.80 l lil rose & multi 1.00 .25
Nos. 2761-2766 (6) 2.55 1.50

11th World Cup Soccer Championship, Argentina '78, June 1-25. See No. C222.

King Decebalus of Dacia Statue, Deva A819

Design: 3.40 l, King Mircea the Elder of Wallachia statue, Tulcea, and ship.

1978, May 22 Photo. ***Perf. 13½***

2767 A819 1.30 l gold & multi .90 .70
2768 A819 3.40 l gold & multi 1.60 1.25

Inter-European Cultural and Economic Cooperation. Each printed in sheet of 4.

Worker, Factory, Flag — A821

1978, June 11 Photo. ***Perf. 13½***

2770 A821 55b multi .35 .25

Nationalization of industry, 30th anniv.

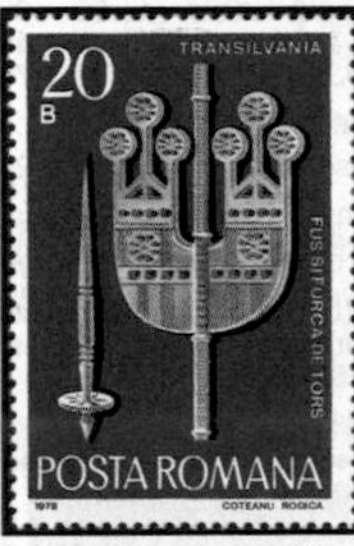

Spindle and Handle, Transylvania A822

Wood Carvings: 40b, Cheese molds, Muntenia. 55b, Spoons, Oltenia. 1 l, Barrel, Moldavia. 2.15 l, Ladle and mug, Transylvania. 4.80 l, Water bucket, Oltenia.

1978, June 20

2771 A822 20b multi .25 .25
2772 A822 40b multi .25 .25
2773 A822 55b multi .25 .25
2774 A822 1 l multi .25 .25
2775 A822 2.15 l multi .30 .25
2776 A822 4.80 l multi 1.00 .25
Nos. 2771-2776 (6) 2.30 1.50

Danube Delta — A823

Tourist Publicity: 1 l, Bran Castle, vert. 1.50 l, Monastery, Suceava, Moldavia. 2.15 l, Caves, Oltenia. 3.40 l, Ski lift, Brasov. 4.80 l, Mangalia, Black Sea. 10 l, Strehaia Fortress, vert.

1978, July 20 Photo. ***Perf. 13½***

2777 A823 55b multi .25 .25
2778 A823 1 l multi .25 .25
2779 A823 1.50 l multi .25 .25
2780 A823 2.15 l multi .30 .25
2781 A823 3.40 l multi .50 .25
2782 A823 4.80 l multi 1.00 .35
Nos. 2777-2782 (6) 2.55 1.60

Miniature Sheet

2783 A823 10 l multi 3.00 2.50

No. 2783 contains one 37x51mm stamp. Issued July 30.

Electronic Microscope A824

Designs: 40b, Hydraulic excavator. 55b, Computer center. 1.50 l, Oil derricks. 3 l, Harvester combine. 3.40 l, Petrochemical plant.

1978, Aug. 15 Photo. *Perf. 13½*

2784 A824 20b multi .25 .25
2785 A824 40b multi .25 .25
2786 A824 55b multi .25 .25
2787 A824 1.50 l multi .25 .25
2788 A824 3 l multi, horiz. .55 .25
2789 A824 3.40 l multi .70 .25
Nos. 2784-2789 (6) 2.25 1.50

Industrial development.

Polovraci Cave, Carpathians A825

Caves: 1 l, Topolnita. 1.50 l, Ponoare. 2.15 l, Ratei, Mt. Bucegi. 3.40 l, Closani, Mt. Motrului. 4.80 l, Epuran. 1 l, 1.50 l, 4.80 l, Mt. Mehedinti.

1978, Aug. 25 Photo. *Perf. 13½*

2790 A825 55b multi .25 .25
2791 A825 1 l multi .25 .25
2792 A825 1.50 l multi .25 .25
2793 A825 2.15 l multi .30 .25
2794 A825 3.40 l multi .50 .25
2795 A825 4.80 l multi 1.00 .25
Nos. 2790-2795 (6) 2.55 1.50

"Racial Equality" — A826

1978, Sept. 28

2796 A826 3.40 l multi .70 .25

Anti-Apartheid Year.

Gold Bas-relief — A827

Designs: 40b, Gold armband. 55b, Gold cameo ring. 1 l, Silver bowl. 2.15 l, Eagle from Roman standard, vert. 4.80 l, Silver armband.

1978, Sept. 25

2797 A827 20b multi .25 .25
2798 A827 40b multi .25 .25
2799 A827 55b multi .25 .25
2800 A827 1 l multi .25 .25
2801 A827 2.15 l multi .30 .25
2802 A827 4.80 l multi 1.00 .35
Nos. 2797-2802 (6) 2.30 1.60

Daco-Roman archaeological treasures. An imperf. 10 l souvenir sheet exists showing gold helmet, vert. Values: unused $10; used $6.

Woman Gymnast, Games' Emblem A828

1 l, Running. 1.50 l, Skiing. 2.15 l, Equestrian. 3.40 l, Soccer. 4.80 l, Handball.

1978, Sept. 15

2803 A828 55b multi .25 .25
2804 A828 1 l multi .25 .25
2805 A828 1.50 l multi .25 .25
2806 A828 2.15 l multi .30 .25
2807 A828 3.40 l multi .50 .25
2808 A828 4.80 l multi 1.00 .25
Nos. 2803-2808 (6) 2.55 1.50

Ptolemaic Map of Dacia A829

Designs: 55b, Meeting House of Romanian National Council, Arad. 1.75 l, Pottery vases, 8th-9th centuries, found near Arad.

1978, Oct. 21 Photo. *Perf. 13½*

2809 A829 40b multi .25 .25
2810 A829 55b multi .25 .25
2811 A829 1.75 l multi .35 .25
b. Strip of 3, #2809-2811 .50 .30

2,000th anniversary of founding of Arad.

Dacian Warrior, from Trajan's Column, Rome — A829a

1978, Nov. 5 Photo. *Perf. 13x13½*

2811A A829a 6 l + 3 l label 1.60 .85

NATIONALA '78 Phil. Exhib., Bucharest. Stamp Day.

Assembly at Alba Iulia, 1919 — A830

Design: 1 l, Open book and Romanian flag.

1978, Dec. 1

2812 A830 55b gold & multi .25 .25
2813 A830 1 l gold & multi .25 .25

60th anniversary of national unity.

Warrior, Bas-relief — A831

1.50 l, Warrior on horseback, bas-relief.

1979 Photo. *Perf. 13½*

2814 A831 55b multi .25 .25
2815 A831 1.50 l multi .25 .25

2,050 years since establishment of first centralized and independent Dacian state.

"Heroes of Vaslui" — A832

Children's Drawings: 1 l, Building houses. 1.50 l, Folk music of Tica. 2.15 l, Industrial landscape, horiz. 3.40 l, winter customs, horiz. 4.80 l, Pioneer festival, horiz.

1979, Mar. 1

2816 A832 55b multi .25 .25
2817 A832 1 l multi .25 .25
2818 A832 1.50 l multi .25 .25
2819 A832 2.15 l multi .30 .25
2820 A832 3.40 l multi .50 .25
2821 A832 4.80 l multi .75 .25
Nos. 2816-2821 (6) 2.30 1.50

International Year of the Child.

A833

1.30 l, Ice Hockey, Globe, Emblem. 3.40 l, Ice hockey players, globe & emblem.

1979, Mar. 16 Photo. *Perf. 13½*

2822 1.30 l multi .30 .25
2823 3.40 l multi .55 .25
a. A833 Pair, #2822-2823 .85 .50

European Youth Ice Hockey Championship, Miercurea-Ciuc (1.30 l) and World Ice Hockey Championship, Galati (3.40 l).

Dog's-tooth Violet — A834

Protected Flowers: 1 l, Alpine violet. 1.50 l, Linum borzaeanum. 2.15 l, Persian bindweed. 3.40 l, Primula auricula. 4.80 l, Transylvanian columbine.

1979, Apr. 25 Photo. *Perf. 13½*

2824 A834 55b multi .25 .25
2825 A834 1 l multi .25 .25
2826 A834 1.50 l multi .25 .25
2827 A834 2.15 l multi .35 .25
2828 A834 3.40 l multi .50 .25
2829 A834 4.80 l multi .75 .25
Nos. 2824-2829 (6) 2.35 1.50

Mall Coach and Post Rider, 19th Century A835

1979, May 3 Photo. *Perf. 13*

2830 A835 1.30 l multi .40 .25

Inter-European Cultural and Economic Cooperation. Printed in sheets of 4.

See No. C231.

Oil Rig and Refinery — A836

1979, May 24 Photo. *Perf. 13*

2832 A836 3.40 l multi .60 .25

10th World Petroleum Congress, Bucharest.

Girl Pioneer — A837

1979, June 20

2833 A837 55b multi .35 .25

30th anniversary of Romanian Pioneers.

Children with Flowers, IYC Emblem A838

IYC Emblem and: 1 l, Kindergarten. 2 l, Pioneers with rabbit. 4.60 l, Drummer, trumpeters, flags.

1979, July 18 Photo. *Perf. 13½*

2834 A838 40b multi .25 .25
2835 A838 1 l multi .25 .25
2836 A838 2 l multi .30 .25
2837 A838 4.60 l multi .70 .25
Nos. 2834-2837 (4) 1.50 1.00

International Year of the Child.

Stefan Gheorghiu — A840

Lady in a Garden, by Tattarescu A839

Paintings by Gheorghe Tattarescu: 40b, Mountain woman. 55b, Mountain man. 1 l, Portrait of Gh. Magheru. 2.15 l, The artist's daughter. 4.80 l, Self-portrait.

1979, June 16

2838 A839 20b multi .25 .25
2839 A839 40b multi .25 .25
2840 A839 55b multi .25 .25
2841 A839 1 l multi .25 .25
2842 A839 2.15 l multi .30 .25
2843 A839 4.80 l multi .90 .25
Nos. 2838-2843 (6) 2.20 1.50

Designs: 55b, Gheorghe Lazar monument. 2.15 l, Lupeni monument. 4.60 l, Women in front of Memorial Arch.

1979, Aug.

2844	A840	40b	multi	.25	.25
2845	A840	55b	multi	.25	.25
2846	A840	2.15 l	multi	.40	.25
2847	A840	4.60 l	multi	1.10	.25
			Nos. 2844-2847 (4)	2.00	1.00

State Theater, Tirgu-Mures — A841

Modern Architecture: 40b, University, Brasov. 55b, Political Administration Buildings, Baia Mare. 1 l, Stefan Gheorghiu Academy, Bucharest. 2.15 l, Political Administration Building, Botosani. 4.80 l, House of Culture, Tirgoviste.

1979, June 25

2848	A841	20b	multi	.25	.25
2849	A841	40b	multi	.25	.25
2850	A841	55b	multi	.25	.25
2851	A841	1 l	multi	.25	.25
2852	A841	2.15 l	multi	.25	.25
2853	A841	4.80 l	multi	.70	.25
			Nos. 2848-2853 (6)	1.95	1.50

Flags of Russia and Romania — A842

1 l, Workers' Militia, by L. Suhar, horiz.

1979, Aug. 20 Photo. *Perf. 13½*

2854	A842	55b	multi	.25	.25
2855	A842	1 l	multi	.25	.25

Liberation from Fascism, 35th anniversary.

Cargo Ship Galati A843

Romanian Ships: 1 l, Cargo ship Bucuresti. 1.50 l, Ore carrier Resita. 2.15 l, Ore carrier Tomis. 3.40 l, Tanker Dacia. 4.80 l, Tanker Independenta.

1979, Aug. 27 Photo. *Perf. 13½*

2856	A843	55b	multi	.25	.25
2857	A843	1 l	multi	.25	.25
2858	A843	1.50 l	multi	.25	.25
2859	A843	2.15 l	multi	.25	.25
2860	A843	3.40 l	multi	.45	.25
2861	A843	4.80 l	multi	.90	.25
			Nos. 2856-2861 (6)	2.35	1.50

Olympic Stadium, Melbourne, 1956, Moscow '80 Emblem — A844

Moscow '80 Emblem and Olympic Stadiums: 1 l, Rome, 1960. 1.50 l, Tokyo, 1964. 2.15 l, Mexico City, 1968. 3.40 l, Munich, 1972. 4.80 l, Montreal, 1976. 10 l, Moscow, 1980.

1979, Oct. 23 Photo. *Perf. 13½*

2862	A844	55b	multi	.25	.25
2863	A844	1 l	multi	.25	.25
2864	A844	1.50 l	multi	.25	.25
2865	A844	2.15 l	multi	.30	.25
2866	A844	3.40 l	multi	.45	.25
2867	A844	4.80 l	multi	.65	.25
			Nos. 2862-2867 (6)	2.15	1.50

Souvenir Sheet

2868	A844	10 l	multi	3.00	2.50

22nd Summer Olympic Games, Moscow, July 19-Aug. 3, 1980. No. 2868 contains one 50x38mm stamp.

No. 2868 airmail.

Imperf 10 l souvenir sheets exist for the European Sports Conference and 1980 Olympics. Value for former, unused or used, $15. Value for latter, unused or used, $20.

Arms of Alba Iulia — A845

Designs: Arms of Romanian cities.

1979, Oct. 25

2869	A845	1.20 l	shown	.30	.25
2870	A845	1.20 l	Arad	.30	.25
2871	A845	1.20 l	Bacau	.30	.25
2872	A845	1.20 l	Baia-Mare	.30	.25
2873	A845	1.20 l	Birlad	.30	.25
2874	A845	1.20 l	Botosani	.30	.25
2875	A845	1.20 l	Braila	.30	.25
2876	A845	1.20 l	Brasov	.30	.25
2877	A845	1.20 l	Buzau	.30	.25
2878	A845	1.20 l	Calarasi	.30	.25
2879	A845	1.20 l	Cluj	.30	.25
2880	A845	1.20 l	Constanta	.30	.25
2881	A845	1.20 l	Craiova	.30	.25
2882	A845	1.20 l	Dej	.30	.25
2883	A845	1.20 l	Deva	.30	.25
2884	A845	1.20 l	Turnu-Severin	.30	.25
2885	A845	1.20 l	Focsani	.30	.25
2886	A845	1.20 l	Galati	.30	.25
2887	A845	1.20 l	Gheorghe Gheorghiu-Dej	.30	.25
2888	A845	1.20 l	Giurgiu	.30	.25
2889	A845	1.20 l	Hunedoara	.30	.25
2890	A845	1.20 l	Iasi	.30	.25
2891	A845	1.20 l	Lugoj	.30	.25
2892	A845	1.20 l	Medias	.30	.25
2893	A845	1.20 l	Odorheiu Seguiesc	.30	.25

1980, Jan. 5

2894	A845	1.20 l	Oradea	.30	.25
2895	A845	1.20 l	Petrosani	.30	.25
2896	A845	1.20 l	Piatra-Neamt	.30	.25
2897	A845	1.20 l	Pitesti	.30	.25
2898	A845	1.20 l	Ploiesti	.30	.25
2899	A845	1.20 l	Resita	.30	.25
2900	A845	1.20 l	Rimnicu-Vilcea	.30	.25
2901	A845	1.20 l	Roman	.30	.25
2902	A845	1.20 l	Satu-Mare	.30	.25
2903	A845	1.20 l	Sibiu	.30	.25
2904	A845	1.20 l	Siget-Marmatiei	.30	.25
2905	A845	1.20 l	Sighisoara	.30	.25
2906	A845	1.20 l	Suceava	.30	.25
2907	A845	1.20 l	Tecuci	.30	.25
2908	A845	1.20 l	Timisoara	.30	.25
2909	A845	1.20 l	Tirgoviste	.30	.25
2910	A845	1.20 l	Tirgu-Jiu	.30	.25
2911	A845	1.20 l	Tirgu-Mures	.30	.25
2912	A845	1.20 l	Tulcea	.30	.25
2913	A845	1.20 l	Turda	.30	.25
2914	A845	1.20 l	Turnu Magurele	.30	.25
2915	A845	1.20 l	Bucharest	.30	.25
			Nos. 2869-2915 (47)	14.10	11.75

A846

Regional Costumes: 20b, Maramures Woman. 40b, Maramures man. 55b, Vrancea woman. 1.50 l, Vrancea man. 3 l, Padureni woman. 3.40 l, Padureni man.

1979, Oct. 27

2916	A846	20b	multi	.25	.25
2917	A846	40b	multi	.25	.25
2918	A846	55b	multi	.25	.25
2919	A846	1.50 l	multi	.25	.25
2920	A846	3 l	multi	.40	.25
2921	A846	3.40 l	multi	.45	.25
			Nos. 2916-2921 (6)	1.85	1.50

A847

Flower Paintings by Stefan Luchian: 40b, Snapdragons. 60b, Triple chrysanthemums. 1.55 l, Potted flowers on stairs.

1979, July 27

2922	A847	40b	multi	.25	.25
2923	A847	60b	multi	.25	.25
2924	A847	1.55 l	multi	.25	.25
			Nos. 2922-2924,B445 (4)	1.85	1.85

Socfilex, International Philatelic Exhibition, Bucharest. See No. B446.

Souvenir Sheet

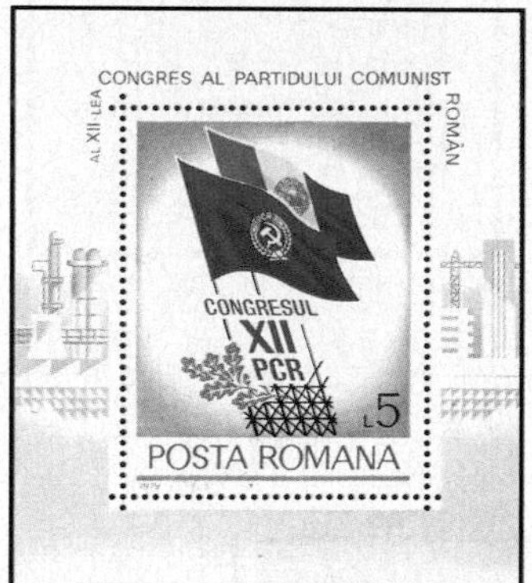

Romanian Communist Party, 12th Congress — A848

1979, Oct.

2925	A848	5 l	multi	1.75	.70

Figure Skating, Lake Placid '80 Emblem, Olympic Rings — A849

1979, Dec. 27 Photo. *Perf. 13½*

2926	A849	55b	shown	.25	.25
2927	A849	1 l	Downhill skiing	.25	.25
2928	A849	1.50 l	Biathlon	.25	.25
2929	A849	2.15 l	Two-man bobsledding	.25	.25
2930	A849	3.40 l	Speed skating	.50	.25
2931	A849	4.80 l	Ice hockey	1.00	.25
			Nos. 2926-2931 (6)	2.50	1.50

Souvenir Sheet

2932	A849	10 l	Ice hockey, diff.	3.25	2.50

13th Winter Olympic Games, Lake Placid, NY, Feb. 12-24, 1980. No. 2932 contains one 38x50mm stamp. An imperf. 10 l air post souvenir sheet exists showing four-man bobsledding. Value, unused or used, $30.

"Calugareni", Expo Emblem — A850

No. 2934, "Orleans". No. 2935, #1059, type fawn. No. 2936, #15021, type 1E. No. 2937, "Pacific". No. 2938, Electric engine 060-EA. 10 l, Diesel electric.

1979, Dec. 29

2933	A850	55b	multicolored	.25	.25
2934	A850	1 l	multicolored	.25	.25
2935	A850	1.50 l	multicolored	.25	.25
2936	A850	2.15 l	multicolored	.35	.25
2937	A850	3.40 l	multicolored	.60	.25
2938	A850	4.80 l	multicolored	.80	.25
			Nos. 2933-2938 (6)	2.50	1.50

Souvenir Sheet

2939	A850	10 l	multicolored	3.00	2.50

Intl. Transport Expo., Hamburg, June 8-July 1. #2939 contains one 50x40mm stamp.

Dacian Warrior, Trajan's Column, Rome — A851

Design: 1.50 l, Two warriors.

1980, Feb. 9 Photo. *Perf. 13½*

2940	A851	55b	multi	.25	.25
2941	A851	1.50 l	multi	.30	.25

2,050 years since establishment of first centralized and independent Dacian state.

Kingfisher — A852

1 l, Great white heron, vert. 1.50 l, Red-breasted goose. 2.15 l, Red deer, vert. 3.40 l, Roe deer. 4.80 l, European bison, vert.

1980, Mar. 25 Photo. *Perf. 13½*

2942	A852	55b	multicolored	.25	.25
2943	A852	1 l	multicolored	.25	.25
2944	A852	1.50 l	multicolored	.25	.25
2945	A852	2.15 l	multicolored	.25	.25
2946	A852	3.40 l	multicolored	.45	.25
2947	A852	4.80 l	multicolored	.90	.25
			Nos. 2942-2947 (6)	2.35	1.50

European Nature Protection Year. A 10 l imperf. souvenir sheet exists showing bears; red control number. Value, unused or used, $30.

See No. C232.

Souvenir Sheets

George Enescu — A853

1980, May 6

2948	A853		Sheet of 4	3.50	3.00
a.		1.30 l	Playing violin	.70	.25
b.		1.30 l	Conducting	.70	.25
c.		1.30 l	Playing piano	.70	.25
d.		1.30 l	Composing	.70	.25

2949 A853 Sheet of 4 3.50 3.00
a. 3.40 l Beethoven in library .70 .25
b. 3.40 l Portrait .70 .25
c. 3.40 l At piano .70 .25
d. 3.40 l Composing .70 .25

Inter-European Cultural and Economic Cooperation.

Vallota Purpurea — A854

1 l, Eichhornia crasipes. 1.50 l, Sprekelia formosissima. 2.15 l, Hypericum calycinum. 3.40 l, Camellia japonica. 4.80 l, Nelumbo nucifera.

1980, Apr. 10 Photo. *Perf. 13½*

2950 A854 55b multicolored .25 .25
2951 A854 1 l multicolored .25 .25
2952 A854 1.50 l multicolored .25 .25
2953 A854 2.15 l multicolored .40 .25
2954 A854 3.40 l multicolored .60 .25
2955 A854 4.80 l multicolored 1.00 .25
Nos. 2950-2955 (6) 2.75 1.50

Tudor Vladimirescu A855

55b, Mihail Sadoveanu. 1.50 l, Battle against Hungarians. 2.15 l, Tudor Arghezi. 3 l, Horea.

1980, Apr. 24

2956 A855 40b multicolored .25 .25
2957 A855 55b multicolored .25 .25
2958 A855 1.50 l multicolored .25 .25
2959 A855 2.15 l multicolored .40 .25
2960 A855 3 l multicolored .50 .25
Nos. 2956-2960 (5) 1.65 1.25

Anniversaries: 40b, Tudor Vladimirescu (1780-1821), leader of 1821 revolution; 55b, Mihail Sadoveanu (1880-1961), author; 1.50 l, Victory of Posada; 2.15 l, Tudor Arghezi (1880-1967), poet; 3 l, Horea (1730-1785), leader of 1784 uprising.

A856

Dacian fruit bowl and cup.

1980, May 8

2961 A856 1 l multicolored .35 .25

Petrodava City, 2000th anniversary.

A857

1980, June 20 Photo. *Perf. 13½*

2962 A857 55b Javelin .25 .25
2963 A857 1 l Fencing .25 .25
2964 A857 1.50 l Shooting .30 .25
2965 A857 2.15 l Kayak .35 .25
2966 A857 3.40 l Wrestling .55 .25
2967 A857 4.80 l Rowing .80 .25
Nos. 2962-2967 (6) 2.50 1.50

Souvenir Sheet

2968 A857 10 l Handball 2.75 2.25

22nd Summer Olympic Games, Moscow, July 19-Aug. 3. No. 2968 contains one 38x50mm stamp. An imperf. 10 l air post souvenir sheet exists showing gymnast. Value, unused or used, $27.50.

Congress Emblem — A858

1980, Aug. 10 Photo. *Perf. 13½*

2969 A858 55b multicolored .35 .25

15th Intl. Historical Sciences Congress, Bucharest.

Fireman Rescuing Child — A859

1980, Aug. 25

2970 A859 55b multicolored .35 .25

Firemen's Day, Sept. 13.

Chinese and Romanian Young Pioneers at Stamp Show — A860

1980, Sept. 18

2971 A860 1 l multicolored .35 .25

Romanian-Chinese Phil. Exhib., Bucharest.

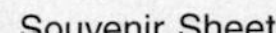

Souvenir Sheet

Parliament Building, Bucharest — A861

1980, Sept. 30

2972 A861 10 l multicolored 2.00 1.65

European Security Conference, Madrid. An imperf. 10 l air post souvenir sheet exists showing Plaza Mayor, Madrid. Value, unused or used, $20.

Knights and Chessboard — A862

1980, Oct. 1 Photo. *Perf. 13½*

2973 A862 55b shown .25 .25
2974 A862 1 l Rooks .25 .25
2975 A862 2.15 l Man .30 .25
2976 A862 4.80 l Woman 1.00 .25
Nos. 2973-2976 (4) 1.80 1.00

Chess Olympiad, Valletta, Malta, Nov. 20-Dec. 8.

Dacian Warrior — A863

40b, Moldavian soldier, 15th cent. 55b, Walachian horseman, 17th cent. 1 l, Flag bearer, 19th cent. 1.50 l, Infantryman, 19th cent. 2.15 l, Lancer, 19th cent. 4.80 l, Mounted Elite Corps Guard, 19th cent.

1980, Oct. 15

2977 A863 20b multi .25 .25
2978 A863 40b multi .25 .25
2979 A863 55b multi .25 .25
2980 A863 1 l multi .25 .25
2981 A863 1.50 l multi .25 .25
2982 A863 2.15 l multi .35 .25
2983 A863 4.80 l multi .75 .35
Nos. 2977-2983 (7) 2.35 1.85

Burebista Sculpture — A864

1980, Nov. 5 Photo. *Perf. 13½*

2984 A864 2 l multicolored .35 .25

2050 years since establishment of first centralized and independent Dacian state.

George Oprescu (1881-1969), Art Critic — A865

Famous Men: 2.15 l, Marius Bunescu (1881-1971), painter. 3.40 l, Ion Georgescu (1856-1898), sculptor.

1981, Feb. 20 Photo. *Perf. 13½*

2985 A865 1.50 l multicolored .25 .25
2986 A865 2.15 l multicolored .40 .25
2987 A865 3.40 l multicolored .70 .25
Nos. 2985-2987 (3) 1.35 .75

National Dog Show — A866

Designs: Dogs — 40b, Mountain sheepdog, horiz. 55b, Saint Bernard. 1 l, Fox terrier, horiz. 1.50 l, German shepherd, horiz. 2.15 l, Boxer. 3.40 l, Dalmatian, horiz. 4.80 l, Poodle.

1981, Mar. 15

2988 A866 40b multicolored .25 .25
2989 A866 55b multicolored .25 .25
2990 A866 1 l multicolored .25 .25
2991 A866 1.50 l multicolored .25 .25
2992 A866 2.15 l multicolored .45 .25
2993 A866 3.40 l multicolored .70 .25
2994 A866 4.80 l multicolored 1.00 .25
Nos. 2988-2994 (7) 3.15 1.75

River Steamer Stefan cel Mare — A867

1 l, Vas de Supraveghere. 1.50 l, Tudor Vladimirescu. 2.15 l, Dredger Sulina. 3.40 l, Republica Populara Romana. 4.80 l, Sulina Canal.
10 l, Galati.

1981, Mar. 25

2995 A867 55b multi .25 .25
2996 A867 1 l multi .25 .25
2997 A867 1.50 l multi .25 .25
2998 A867 2.15 l multi .25 .25
2999 A867 3.40 l multi .40 .25
3000 A867 4.80 l multi .80 .35
Nos. 2995-3000 (6) 2.20 1.60

Souvenir Sheet

3001 A867 10 l multi 2.00 2.00

European Danube Commission, 125th anniv. An imperf. 10 l souvenir sheet exists showing map of Danube. Value, unused or used, $22.50.

Carrier Pigeon A868

Various carrier pigeons and doves.

1981, Apr. 15 Photo. *Perf. 13½*

3002 A868 40b multi .25 .25
3003 A868 55b multi .25 .25
3004 A868 1 l multi .25 .25
3005 A868 1.50 l multi .25 .25
3006 A868 2.15 l multi .30 .25
3007 A868 3.40 l multi .60 .25
Nos. 3002-3007 (6) 1.90 1.50

Romanian Communist Party, 60th Anniv. — A869

1981, Apr. 22 Photo. *Perf. 13½*

3008	A869 1 l multicolored	.35	.25

Folkdance, Moldavia — A870

Designs: Regional folkdances.

1981, May 4 Photo. *Perf. 13½*

3009	Sheet of 4	2.50	2.50
a.	A870 2.50 l shown	.45	.45
b.	A870 2.50 l Transylvania	.45	.45
c.	A870 2.50 l Banat	.45	.45
d.	A870 2.50 l Muntenia	.45	.45
3010	Sheet of 4	2.50	2.50
a.	A870 2.50 l Maramures	.45	.45
b.	A870 2.50 l Dobruja	.45	.45
c.	A870 2.50 l Oltenia	.45	.45
d.	A870 2.50 l Crisana	.45	.45

Inter-European Cultural and Economic Cooperation.

Singing Romania Festival — A871

1981, July 15

3011	A871	55b Industry	.25	.25
3012	A871	1.50 l Electronics	.25	.25
3013	A871	2.15 l Agriculture	.35	.25
3014	A871	3.40 l Culture	.50	.30
		Nos. 3011-3014 (4)	1.35	1.05

University '81 Games, Bucharest — A872

1981, July 17

3015	A872	1 l Book, flag	.25	.25
3016	A872	2.15 l Emblem	.35	.25
3017	A872	4.80 l Stadium, horiz.	.75	.35
		Nos. 3015-3017 (3)	1.35	.85

Theodor Aman, Artist, Birth Sesquicentennial — A873

Aman Paintings: 40b, Self-portrait. 55b, Battle of Giurgiu. 1 l, The Family Picnic. 1.50 l, The Painter's Studio. 2.15 l, Woman in Interior. 3.40 l, Aman Museum, Bucharest. 55b, 1 l, 1.50 l, 3.40 l horiz.

1981, July 28

3018	A873	40b multi	.25	.25
3019	A873	55b multi	.25	.25
3020	A873	1 l multi	.25	.25
3021	A873	1.50 l multi	.25	.25
3022	A873	2.15 l multi	.30	.25
3023	A873	3.40 l multi	.50	.25
		Nos. 3018-3023 (6)	1.80	1.50

Thinker of Cernavoda, 3rd Cent. BC — A874

1981, July 30

3024	A874 3.40 l multi	.65	.30

16th Science History Congress.

Blood Donation Campaign — A875

1981, Aug. 15 Photo. *Perf. 13½*

3025	A875 55b multicolored	.35	.25

Bucharest Central Military Hospital Sesquicentennial — A876

1981, Sept. 1

3026	A876 55b multicolored	.35	.25

Romanian Musicians — A877

Designs: 40b, George Enescu (1881-1955). 55b, Paul Constantinescu (1909-1963). 1 l, Dinu Lipatti (1917-1950). 1.50 l, Ionel Periea (1900-1970). 2.15 l, Ciprian Porumbescu (1853-1883). 3.40 l, Mihail Jora (1891-1971).

1981, Sept. 20

3027	A877	40b multi	.25	.25
3028	A877	55b multi	.25	.25
3029	A877	1 l multi	.25	.25
3030	A877	1.50 l multi	.25	.25
3031	A877	2.15 l multi	.35	.25
3032	A877	3.40 l multi	.50	.25
		Nos. 3027-3032 (6)	1.85	1.50

Stamp Day A879

1981, Nov. 5 Photo. *Perf. 13½*

3034	A879 2 l multicolored	.35	.25

Children's Games — A880

Illustrations by Eugen Palade (40b, 55b, 1 l) and Norman Rockwell (1.50 l, 2.15 l, 3 l, 4 l).
40b, Hopscotch. 55b, Soccer. 1 l, Riding stick horse. 1.50 l, Snagging the Big One. 2.15 l, A Patient Friend. 3 l, Doggone It. 4 l, Puppy Love.

1981, Nov. 25

3035	A880	40b multicolored	.25	.25
3036	A880	55b multicolored	.25	.25
3037	A880	1 l multicolored	.25	.25
3038	A880	1.50 l multicolored	.25	.25
3039	A880	2.15 l multicolored	.30	.25
3040	A880	3 l multicolored	.40	.25
3041	A880	4 l multicolored	.45	.35
		Nos. 3035-3041,C243 (8)	2.85	2.55

A881

1981, Dec. 28

3042	A881	55b multi	.25	.25
3043	A881	1 l multi	.25	.25
3044	A881	1.50 l multi	.25	.25
3045	A881	2.15 l multi	.35	.25
3046	A881	3.40 l multi	.40	.25
3047	A881	4.80 l multi	.65	.35
		Nos. 3042-3047 (6)	2.15	1.60

Souvenir Sheet

3048	A881 10 l multi	2.00	2.00

Espana '82 World Cup Soccer.

No. 3048 contains one 38x50mm stamp. An imperf. 10 l air post souvenir sheet exists showing game. Value, unused or used, $27.50.

A882

Designs: 1 l, Prince Alexander the Good of Moldavia (ruled 1400-1432). 1.50 l, Bogdan Petriceicu Hasdeu (1838-1907), scholar. 2.15 l, Nicolae Titulescu (1882-1941), diplomat.

1982, Jan. 30 Photo. *Perf. 13½*

3049	A882	1 l multi	.25	.25
3050	A882	1.50 l multi	.25	.25
3051	A882	2.15 l multi	.40	.25
		Nos. 3049-3051 (3)	.90	.75

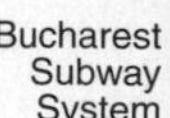

Bucharest Subway System A883

60b, Union Square station entrance. 2.40 l, Heroes' Station platform.

1982, Feb. 25

3052	A883	60b multi	.25	.25
3053	A883	2.40 l multi	.45	.25

60th Anniv. of Communist Youth Union — A884

1.20 l, Construction worker. 1.50 l, Farm workers. 2 l, Research. 2.50 l, Workers. 3 l, Musicians, dancers.

1982

3054	A884	1 l shown	.25	.25
3055	A884	1.20 l multicolored	.25	.25
3056	A884	1.50 l multicolored	.25	.25
3057	A884	2 l multicolored	.30	.25
3058	A884	2.50 l multicolored	.35	.25
3059	A884	3 l multicolored	.40	.25
		Nos. 3054-3059 (6)	1.80	1.50

Dog Sled A885

55b, Dog rescuing child. 1 l, Shepherd, dog, vert. 3 l, Hunting dog, vert. 4 l, Spitz, woman, vert. 4.80 l, Guide dog, woman, vert. 5 l, Dalmatian, girl, vert. 6 l, Saint Bernard.

1982, Mar. 28 Photo. *Perf. 13½*

3060	A885	55b multicolored	.25	.25
3061	A885	1 l multicolored	.25	.25
3062	A885	3 l multicolored	.45	.25
3063	A885	3.40 l shown	.55	.25
3064	A885	4 l multicolored	.60	.25
3065	A885	4.80 l multicolored	.70	.25
3066	A885	5 l multicolored	.75	.25
3067	A885	6 l multicolored	.90	.25
		Nos. 3060-3067 (8)	4.45	2.00

Bran Castle, Brasov, 1377 A886

1982, May 6

3068	Sheet of 4	1.75	1.75
a.	A886 2.50 l shown	.35	.35
b.	A886 2.50 l Hunedoara, Corvinilor, 1409	.35	.35
c.	A886 2.50 l Sinaia, 1873	.35	.35
d.	A886 2.50 l Iasi, 1905	.35	.35
3069	Sheet of 4	1.75	1.75
a.	A886 2.50 l Neuschwanstein	.35	.35
b.	A886 2.50 l Stolzenfels	.35	.35
c.	A886 2.50 l Katz-Loreley	.35	.35
d.	A886 2.50 l Linderhof	.35	.35

Inter-European Cultural and Economic Cooperation.

Souvenir Sheet

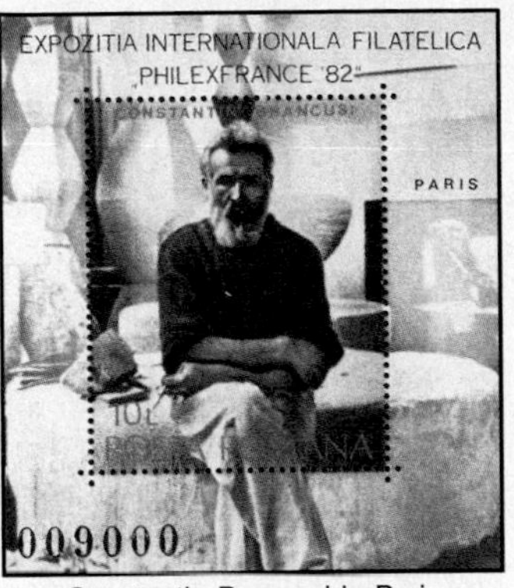

Constantin Brancusi in Paris Studio — A887

1982, June 5

3070	A887	10 l multicolored	2.50	2.00

PHILEXFRANCE '82 Intl. Stamp Exhibition, Paris, June 11-21.

Gloria C-16 Combine Harvester — A888

1982, June 29

3071	A888	50b	shown	.25	.25
3072	A888	1 l	Dairy farm	.25	.25
3073	A888	1.50 l	Apple orchard	.25	.25
3074	A888	2.50 l	Vineyard	.30	.25
3075	A888	3 l	Irrigation	.50	.25
			Nos. 3071-3075,C250 (6)	2.15	1.50

Souvenir Sheet

3076	A888	10 l Village	2.50	2.00

Agricultural modernization. No. 3076 contains one 50x38mm stamp.

A890

Resort Hotels and Beaches. 1 l, 2.50 l, 3 l, 5 l horiz.

1982, Aug. 30 Photo. *Perf. 13½*

3078	A890	50b	Baile Felix	.25	.25
3079	A890	1 l	Predeal	.25	.25
3080	A890	1.50 l	Baile Herculane	.25	.25
3081	A890	2.50 l	Eforie Nord	.40	.25
3082	A890	3 l	Olimp	.50	.25
3083	A890	5 l	Neptun	.85	.30
			Nos. 3078-3083 (6)	2.50	1.55

A891

Designs: 1 l, Legend, horiz. 1.50 l, Contrasts, horiz. 3.50 l, Relay Runner, horiz. 4 l, Genesis of Romanian People, by Sabin Balasa.

1982, Sept. 6

3084	A891	1 l	multicolored	.25	.25
3085	A891	1.50 l	multicolored	.25	.25
3086	A891	3.50 l	multicolored	.65	.25
3087	A891	4 l	multicolored	.80	.35
			Nos. 3084-3087 (4)	1.95	1.10

Souvenir Sheet

Merry Peasant Girl, by Nicolae Grigorescu (d. 1907) — A892

1982, Sept. 30 Photo. *Perf. 13½*

3088	A892	10 l multicolored	2.50	2.50

Bucharest Intl. Fair A893

1982, Oct. 2

3089	A893	2 l Exhibition Hall, flag	.40	.25

Savings Week, Oct. 25-31 — A894

1982, Oct. 25

3090	A894	1 l Girl holding bank book	.25	.25
3091	A894	2 l Poster	.35	.25

Stamp Day — A895

1982, Nov. 10

3092	A895	1 l Woman letter carrier	.25	.25
3093	A895	2 l Mailman	.35	.25

Scene from Ileana Sinziana, by Petre Ispirescu A896

Fairytales: 50b, The Youngest Child and the Golden Apples, by Petre Ispirescu. 1 l, The Bear Hoaxed by the Fox, by Ion Creanga. 1.50 l, The Prince of Tear, by Mihai Eminescu. 2.50 l, The Little Bag with Two Coins Inside, by Ion Creanga. 3 l, Ileana Simziana, by Petre Ispirescu. 5 l, Danila Prepeleac, by Ion Creanga.

1982, Nov. 30

3094	A896	50b	multicolored	.25	.25
3095	A896	1 l	multicolored	.25	.25
3096	A896	1.50 l	multicolored	.25	.25
3097	A896	2.50 l	multicolored	.40	.25
3098	A896	3 l	multicolored	.40	.25
3099	A896	5 l	multicolored	.80	.30
			Nos. 3094-3099 (6)	2.35	1.55

Arms, Colors, Book — A897

1982, Dec. 16

3100	A897	1 l Closed book	.25	.25
3101	A897	2 l Open book	.35	.25

Natl. Communist Party Conference, Bucharest, Dec. 16-18.

A898

50b, Wooden flask, Suceava. 1 l, Ceramic plate, Radauti. 1.50 l, Wooden scoop, Valea Mare, horiz. 2 l, Plate, jug, Vama. 3 l, Butter churn, wooden bucket, Moldavia. 3.50 l, Ceramic plates, Leheceni, horiz. 4 l, Wooden spoon, platter, Cluj. 5 l, Bowl, pitcher, Marginea. 6 l, Jug, flask, Bihor. 7 l, Spindle, shuttle, Transylvania. 7.50 l, Water buckets, Suceava. 8 l, Jug, Oboga; plate, Horezu. 10 l, Water buckets, Hunedoara, Suceava, horiz. 20 l, Wooden flask, beakers, Horezu. 30 l, Wooden spoons, Alba, horiz. 50 l, Ceramic dishes, Horezu.

1982, Dec. 22 Photo. *Perf. 13½*

3102	A898	50b	red orange	.25	.25
3103	A898	1 l	dark blue	.25	.25
3104	A898	1.50 l	orange brn	.25	.25
3105	A898	2 l	brt blue	.30	.25
3106	A898	3 l	olive green	.40	.25
3107	A898	3.50 l	dk green	.55	.25
3108	A898	4 l	lt brown	.60	.25
3109	A898	5 l	gray blue	.75	.25

Size: 23x29mm, 29x23mm

3110	A898	6 l	blue	.90	.25
3111	A898	7 l	lake	1.10	.25
3112	A898	7.50 l	red violet	1.25	.25
3113	A898	8 l	brt green	1.25	.25
3114	A898	10 l	red	1.50	.25
3115	A898	20 l	purple	3.25	.25
3116	A898	30 l	Prus blue	4.50	.35
3117	A898	50 l	dark brown	8.00	.65
			Nos. 3102-3117 (16)	25.10	4.50

35th Anniv. of Republic — A899

1982, Dec. 27

3118	A899	1 l Symbols of development	.25	.25
3119	A899	2 l Flag	.35	.25

Grigore Manolescu (1857-92), as Hamlet — A900

Actors or Actresses in Famous Roles: 50b, Matei Millo (1814-1896) in The Discontented. 1 l, Mihail Pascaly (1829-1882) in Director Milo. 1.50 l, Aristizza Romanescu (1854-1918), in The Dogs. 2 l, C. I. Nottara (1859-1935) in Snowstorm. 3 l, Agatha Birsescu (1857-1939) in Medea. 4 l, Ion Brezeanu (1869-1940) in The Lost Letter. 5 l, Aristide Demetriad (1872-1930) in The Despotic Prince.

1983, Feb. 28

3120	A900	50b	multi	.25	.25
3121	A900	1 l	multi	.25	.25
3122	A900	1.50 l	multi	.30	.25
3123	A900	2 l	multi	.35	.25
3124	A900	2.50 l	multi	.45	.25
3125	A900	3 l	multi	.60	.25
3126	A900	4 l	multi	.70	.25
3127	A900	5 l	multi	.90	.25
			Nos. 3120-3127 (8)	3.80	2.00

Hugo Grotius (1583-1645), Dutch Jurist — A901

1983, Apr. 30

3128	A901	2 l brown	.45	.25

Romanian-Made Vehicles — A902

50b, ARO-10. 1 l, Dacia, 1300 station wagon. 1.50 l, ARO-242 jeep. 2.50 l, ARO-244. 4 l, Dacia 1310. 5 l, OLTCIT club passenger car.

1983, May 3

3129	A902	50b	multi	.25	.25
3130	A902	1 l	multi	.25	.25
3131	A902	1.50 l	multi	.35	.25
3132	A902	2.50 l	multi	.60	.25
3133	A902	4 l	multi	.95	.35
3134	A902	5 l	multi	1.20	.40
			Nos. 3129-3134 (6)	3.60	1.75

Johannes Kepler (1571-1630) — A903

Famous Men: No. 3135: b, Alexander von Humboldt (1769-1859), explorer. c, Goethe (1749-1832). d, Richard Wagner (1813-1883), composer.

No. 3136: a, Ioan Andreescu (1850-1882), painter. b, George Constantinescu (1881-1965), engineer. c, Tudor Arghezi (1880-1967), poet. d, C.I. Parhon (1874-1969), endocrinologist.

1983, May 16

3135		Sheet of 4	2.50	2.50
a.-d.	A903	3 l multicolored	.55	.55
3136		Sheet of 4	2.50	2.50
a.-d.	A903	3 l multicolored	.55	.55

Inter-European Cultural and Economic Cooperation.

Workers' Struggle, 50th Anniv. — A904

1983, July 22 Photo. *Perf. 13½*
3137 A904 2 l silver & multi .35 .25

Birds — A905

50b, Luscinia svecica. 1 l, Sturnus roseus. 1.50 l, Coracias garrulus. 2.50 l, Merops apiaster. 4 l, Emberiza schoeniclus. 5 l, Lanius minor.

1983, Oct. 28 Photo. *Perf. 13½*
3138 A905 50b multi .25 .25
3139 A905 1 l multi .25 .25
3140 A905 1.50 l multi .35 .25
3141 A905 2.50 l multi .50 .25
3142 A905 4 l multi .80 .35
3143 A905 5 l multi 1.00 .40
Nos. 3138-3143 (6) 3.15 1.75

Water Sports A906

1983, Sept. 16 Photo. *Perf. 13½*
3144 A906 50b Kayak .25 .25
3145 A906 1 l Water polo .25 .25
3146 A906 1.50 l Canadian one-man canoes .35 .25
3147 A906 2.50 l Diving .60 .25
3148 A906 4 l Singles rowing .95 .25
3149 A906 5 l Swimming 1.20 .25
Nos. 3144-3149 (6) 3.60 1.50

Stamp Day A907

1 l, Mailman on bicycle. 3.50 l, with 3 l label, flag.
10 l, Unloading mail plane.

1983, Oct. 24
3150 A907 1 l multicolored .25 .25
3151 A907 3.50 l multicolored 1.00 .55

Souvenir Sheet

3152 A907 10 l multicolored 3.00 3.00

#3152 is airmail, contains one 38x51mm stamp.

Geum Reptans A908

Flora (No. 3154): b, Papaver dubium. c, Carlina acaulis. d, Paeonia peregrina. e, Gentiana excisa. Fauna (No. 3155): a, Sciurus vulgaria. b, Grammia quenselii. c, Dendrocopos medius. d, Lynx. e, Tichodroma muraria.

1983, Oct. 28 Photo. *Perf. 13½*
3154 Strip of 5 2.25 2.25
a.-e. A908 1 l multicolored .45 .45
3155 Strip of 5 2.25 2.25
a.-e. A908 1 l multicolored .45 .45

Issued in sheets of 15.

Lady with Feather, by Cornelius Baba — A909

1983, Nov. 3
3156 A909 1 l shown .25 .25
3157 A909 2 l Citizens .40 .25
3158 A909 3 l Farmers, horiz. .60 .25
3159 A909 4 l Resting in the Field, horiz. .80 .25
Nos. 3156-3159 (4) 2.05 1.00

A910

1983, Nov. 30
3160 A910 1 l Banner, emblem .25 .25
3161 A910 2 l Congress building, flags .40 .25

Pact with Romania, 65th anniv.

A911

Designs: 1 l, Flags of participating countries, post office, mailman. 2 l, Congress building, woman letter carrier. 10 l, Flags, Congress building.

1983, Dec. 17
3162 A911 1 l multicolored *.25 .25*
3163 A911 2 l multicolored *.45 .25*

Souvenir Sheet

3164 A911 10 l multicolored *2.25 2.25*

BALKANFILA '83 Stamp Exhibition, Bucharest. #3164 contains one 38x50mm stamp.

Souvenir Sheet

Orient Express Centenary (Paris-Istanbul) — A912

Leaving Gara de Nord, Bucharest, 1883

1983, Dec. 30
3165 A912 10 l multi 3.25 3.25

1984 Winter Olympics A913

1984, Jan. 14
3166 A913 50b Cross-country skiing .25 .25
3167 A913 1 l Biathlon .25 .25
3168 A913 1.50 l Figure skating .25 .25
3169 A913 2 l Speed skating .30 .25
3170 A913 3 l Hockey .40 .25
3171 A913 3.50 l Bobsledding .50 .25
3172 A913 4 l Luge .60 .25
3173 A913 5 l Skiing .75 .30
Nos. 3166-3173 (8) 3.30 2.05

A 10 l imperf souvenir sheet exists showing ski jumping. Value, unused or used, $27.50.

Souvenir Sheet

Prince Alexandru Ioan Cuza, Arms — A914

1984, Jan. 24 Photo. *Perf. 13½*
3174 A914 10 l multi 2.25 2.25

Union of Moldavia and Walachia Provinces, 125th anniv.

Palace of Udriste Nasturel (1596-1658), Chancery Official — A915

Miron Costin (1633-91), Poet — A916

Famous Men: 1.50 l, Crisan (Marcu Giurgiu), (1733-85), peasant revolt leader. 2 l, Simion Barnutiu (1808-64), scientist. 3.50 l, Duiliu Zamfirescu (1858-1922), poet. 4 l, Nicolas Milescu (1636-1708), Court official.

1984, Feb. 8
3175 A915 50b multi .25 .25
3176 A916 1 l multi .25 .25
3177 A916 1.50 l multi .35 .25
3178 A916 2 l multi .35 .25
3179 A916 3.50 l multi .50 .25
3180 A916 4 l multi .75 .25
Nos. 3175-3180 (6) 2.45 1.50

See Nos. 3210-3213.

Souvenir Sheet

15th Balkan Chess Match, Herculane A917

4 successive moves culminating in checkmate.

1984, Feb. 20 Photo. *Perf. 13½*
3181 Sheet of 4 4.50 4.50
a.-d. A917 3 l, any single 1.00 1.00

Orsova Bridge A918

Bridges: No. 3182b, Arges. c, Basarabi. d, Ohaba.
No. 3183: a, Kohlbrand-Germany. b, Bosfor-Turcia. c, Europa-Austria. d, Turnului-Anglia.

1984, Apr. 24
3182 Sheet of 4 2.50 2.50
a.-d. A918 3 l multi .55 .55
3183 Sheet of 4 2.50 2.50
a.-d. A918 3 l multi .55 .55

Inter-European Cultural and Economic Cooperation.

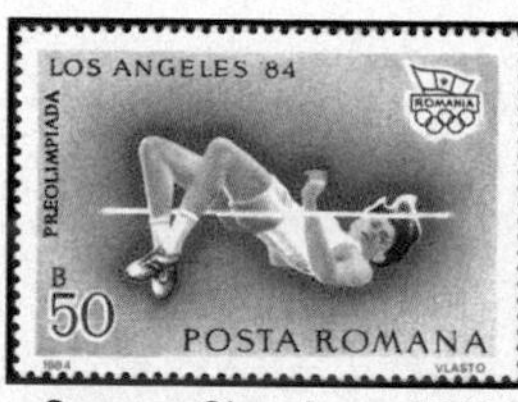

Summer Olympics — A919

1984, May 25 Photo. *Perf. 13½*
3184 A919 50b High jump .25 .25
3185 A919 1 l Swimming .25 .25
3186 A919 1.50 l Running .25 .25
3187 A919 3 l Handball .50 .30
3188 A919 4 l Rowing .70 .40
3189 A919 5 l 2-man canoe .85 .50
Nos. 3184-3189 (6) 2.80 1.95

A 10 l imperf. airmail souvenir sheet containing a vert. stamp picturing a gymnast exists. Value, unused or used, $27.50.

Environmental Protection — A920

1984, Apr. 26 Photo. *Perf. 13½*
3190 A920 1 l Sunflower .25 .25
3191 A920 2 l Stag .45 .25
3192 A920 3 l Fish .70 .25
3193 A920 4 l Bird .90 .30
Nos. 3190-3193 (4) 2.30 1.05

Danube Flowers — A921

50b, Sagittaria sagittifolia. 1 l, Iris pseudacorus. 1.50 l, Butomus umbellatus. 3 l, Nymphaea alba, horiz. 4 l, Nymphoides peltata, horiz. 5 l, Nuphar luteum, horiz.

1984, Apr. 30 Photo. *Perf. 13½*
3194 A921 50b multi .25 .25
3195 A921 1 l multi .25 .25
3196 A921 1.50 l multi .40 .25
3197 A921 3 l multi .70 .25
3198 A921 4 l multi 1.00 .30
3199 A921 5 l multi 1.10 .45
Nos. 3194-3199 (6) 3.70 1.75

45th Anniv., Youth Anti-Fascist Committee A922

1984, Apr. 30 Photo. *Perf. 13½*
3200 A922 2 l multicolored .65 .25

25th Congress, Ear, Nose and Throat Medicine — A923

1984, May 30 Photo. *Perf. 13½*
3201 A923 2 l Congress seal .40 .25

Souvenir Sheets

European Soccer Cup Championships A923a

Soccer players and flags of: c, Romania. d, West Germany. e, Portugal. f, Spain. g, France. h, Belgium. i, Yugoslavia. j, Denmark.

1984, June 7 Photo. *Perf. 13½*
3201A Sheet of 4 2.50 2.50
c.-f. A923a 3 l, any single .60 .60
3201B Sheet of 4 2.50 2.50
g.-i. A923a 3 l, any single .60 .60

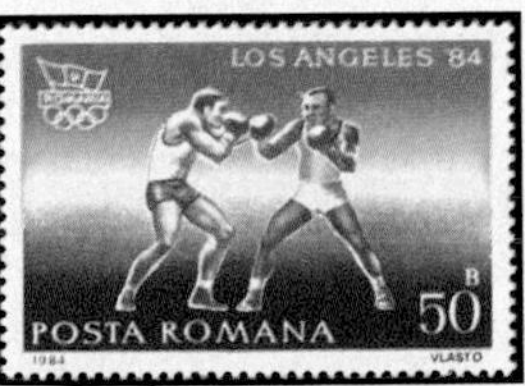

Summer Olympics — A924

1984, July 2 Photo. *Perf. 13½*
3202 A924 50b Boxing .25 .25
3203 A924 1 l Rowing .25 .25
3204 A924 1.50 l Team handball .25 .25
3205 A924 2 l Judo .25 .25
3206 A924 3 l Wrestling .40 .25
3207 A924 3.50 l Fencing .50 .25
3208 A924 4 l Kayak .65 .25
3209 A924 5 l Swimming .75 .30
Nos. 3202-3209 (8) 3.30 2.05

Two imperf. 10 l airmail souvenir sheets, showing long jumping and gymnastics exist. Value for each sheet, unused or used, $15.

Famous Romanians Type

1984, July 28 Photo. *Perf. 13½*
3210 A916 1 l Mihai Ciuca .25 .25
3211 A916 2 l Petre Aurelian .35 .25
3212 A916 3 l Alexandru Vlahuta .50 .25
3213 A916 4 l Dimitrie Leonida .70 .30
Nos. 3210-3213 (4) 1.80 1.05

40th Anniv., Romanian Revolution A925

1984, Aug. 17 Photo. *Perf. 13½*
3214 A925 2 l multicolored .40 .25

Romanian Horses — A926

1984, Aug. 30 Photo. *Perf. 13½*
3215 A926 50b Lippizaner .25 .25
3216 A926 1 l Hutul .25 .25
3217 A926 1.50 l Bucovina .30 .25
3218 A926 2.50 l Nonius .50 .25
3219 A926 4 l Arabian 1.00 .30
3220 A926 5 l Romanian Mixed-breed .80 .40
Nos. 3215-3220 (6) 3.10 1.70

1784 Uprisings, 200th Anniv. — A927

1984, Nov. 1 Photo. *Perf. 13½*
3221 A927 2 l Monument .40 .25

Children A928

Paintings: 50b, Portrait of Child, by T. Aman. 1 l, Shepherd, by N. Grigorescu. 2 l, Girl with Orange, by S. Luchian. 3 l, Portrait of Child, by N. Tonitza. 4 l, Portrait of Boy, by S. Popp. 5 l, Portrait of Girl, by I. Tuculescu.

1984, Nov. 10 Photo. *Perf. 13½*
3222 A928 50b multicolored .25 .25
3223 A928 1 l multicolored .25 .25
3224 A928 2 l multicolored .35 .25
3225 A928 3 l multicolored .50 .25
3226 A928 4 l multicolored .70 .30
3227 A928 5 l multicolored .85 .35
Nos. 3222-3227 (6) 2.90 1.65

Stamp Day A929

1984, Nov. 15 Photo. *Perf. 13½*
3228 A929 2 l + 1 l label .50 .30

Souvenir Sheet

13th Party Congress — A930

1984, Nov. 17 Photo. *Perf. 13½*
3229 A930 10 l Party symbols 4.00 4.00

Souvenir Sheets

Romanian Medalists, 1984 Summer Olympic Games — A931

No. 3230: a, Ecaterina Szabo, gymnastic floor exercise. b, 500-meter four-women kayak. c, Anisoara Stanciu, long jump. d, Greco-Roman wrestling. e, Mircea Fratica, half middleweight judo. f, Corneliu Ion, rapid fire pistol.

No. 3231: a, 1000-meter two-man scull. b, Weight lifting. c, Women's relays. d, Canoeing, pair oars without coxswain. e, Fencing, team foil. f, Ecaterina Szabo, all-around gymnastics.

1984, Oct. 29 Photo. *Perf. 13½*
3230 Sheet of 6 3.25 3.25
a.-f. A931 3 l, any single .50 .50
3231 Sheet of 6 3.25 3.25
a.-f. A931 3 l, any single .50 .50

A932

Pelicans of the Danube Delta.

1984, Dec. 15
3232 A932 50b Flying .25 .25
3233 A932 1 l On ground .55 .25
3234 A932 1 l In water .65 .25
3235 A932 2 l Nesting .95 .45
Nos. 3232-3235 (4) 2.40 1.20

A933

Famous Men: 50b, Dr. Petru Groza (1884-1958). 1 l, Alexandru Odobescu (1834-1895). 2 l, Dr. Carol Davila (1828-1884). 3 l, Dr. Nicolae G. Lupu (1884-1966). 4 l, Dr. Daniel Danielopolu (1884-1955). 5 l, Panait Istrati (1884-1935).

1984, Dec. 26
3236 A933 50b multi .25 .25
3237 A933 1 l multi .25 .25
3238 A933 2 l multi .35 .25
3239 A933 3 l multi .50 .25
3240 A933 4 l multi .70 .30
3241 A933 5 l multi .85 .35
Nos. 3236-3241 (6) 2.90 1.65

Timisoara Power Station, Electric Street Lights, Cent. A934

1984, Dec. 29
3242 A934 1 l Generator, 1884 .25 .25
3243 A934 2 l Street arc lamp, Timisoara, 1884, vert. .35 .25

Souvenir Sheets

European Music Year — A935

Composers and opera houses, No. 3244a, Moscow Theater, Tchaichovsky (1840-1893). b, Bucharest Theater, George Enescu (1881-1955). c, Dresden Opera, Wagner (1813-1883). d, Warsaw Opera, Stanislaw Moniuszko (1819-1872).

No. 3245a, Paris Opera, Gounod (1818-1893). b, Munich Opera, Strauss (1864-1949). c, Vienna Opera, Mozart (1756-1791). d, La Scala, Milan, Verdi (1813-1901).

1985, Mar. 28
3244 A935 Sheet of 4 2.50 2.50
a.-d. 3 l, any single .60 .60
3245 A935 Sheet of 4 2.50 2.50
a.-d. 3 l, any single .60 .60

August T. Laurian (1810-1881), Linguist and Historian — A936

Famous men: 1 l, Grigore Alexandrescu (1810-1885), author. 1.50 l, Gheorghe Pop de Basesti (1835-1919), politician. 2 l, Mateiu Caragiale (1885-1936), author. 3 l, Gheorghe Ionescu-Sisesti (1885-1967), scientist. 4 l, Liviu Rebreanu (1885-1944), author.

1985, Mar. 29
3246 A936 50b multi .25 .25
3247 A936 1 l multi .25 .25
3248 A936 1.50 l multi .25 .25
3249 A936 2 l multi .35 .25
3250 A936 3 l multi .50 .30
3251 A936 4 l multi .70 .40
Nos. 3246-3251 (6) 2.30 1.70

Intl. Youth Year — A937

1985, Apr. 15

3252 A937 1 l Scientific research .25 .25
3253 A937 2 l Construction .35 .25

Souvenir Sheet

3254 A937 10 l Intl. solidarity 2.50 2.25

No. 3254 contains one 54x42mm stamp.

Wildlife Conservation A938

1985, May 6

3255 A938 50b Nyctereutes procyonoides .25 .25
3256 A938 1 l Perdix perdix .25 .25
3257 A938 1.50 l Nyctea scandiaca .30 .25
3258 A938 2 l Martes martes .40 .25
3259 A938 3 l Meles meles .65 .25
3260 A938 3.50 l Lutra lutra .80 .25
3261 A938 4 l Tetrao urogallus .90 .30
3262 A938 5 l Otis tarda 1.10 .35
Nos. 3255-3262 (8) 4.65 2.15

End of World War II, 40th Anniv. — A939

War monument, natl. and party flags.

1985, May 9

3263 A939 2 l multicolored .50 .25

Union of Communist Youth, 12th Congress A940

1985, May 14

3264 A940 2 l Emblem .35 .25

Danube-Black Sea Canal Opening, May 26, 1984 — A942

1 l, Canal, map. 2 l, Bridge over lock, Cernavoda. 3 l, Bridge over canal, Medgidea. 4 l, Agigea lock, bridge.
10 l, Opening ceremony, Cernavoda, Ceaucescu.

1985, June 7 *Perf. 13½*

3266 A942 1 l multi .25 .25
3267 A942 2 l multi .50 .25
3268 A942 3 l multi .70 .25
3269 A942 4 l multi 1.00 .35
Nos. 3266-3269 (4) 2.45 1.10

Souvenir Sheet

3270 A942 10 l multi 4.50 4.00

No. 3270 contains one 54x42mm stamp.

Audubon Birth Bicentenary — A943

American bird species — 50b, Turdus migratorius. 1 l, Pelecanus occidentalis. 1.50 l, Nyctanassa violarea. 2 l, Icterus galbula. 3 l, Podiceps grisegena. 4 l, Anas platyrhynchos. Nos. 3272-3275 vert.

1985, June 26

3271 A943 50b multi .25 .25
3272 A943 1 l multi .25 .25
3273 A943 1.50 l multi .30 .25
3274 A943 2 l multi .35 .25
3275 A943 3 l multi .70 .25
3276 A943 4 l multi .95 .35
Nos. 3271-3276 (6) 2.80 1.60

20th Century Paintings by Ion Tuculescu — A944

1985, July 13

3277 A944 1 l Fire, vert. .25 .25
3278 A944 2 l Circuit, vert. .35 .25
3279 A944 3 l Interior .50 .25
3280 A944 4 l Sunset .65 .35
Nos. 3277-3280 (4) 1.75 1.10

Butterflies A945

1985, July 15

3281 A945 50b Inachis io .25 .25
3282 A945 1 l Papilio machaon .25 .25
3283 A945 2 l Vanessa atalanta .40 .25
3284 A945 3 l Saturnia pavonia .60 .30
3285 A945 4 l Ammobiota festiva .80 .40
3286 A945 5 l Smerinthus ocellatus 1.00 .50
Nos. 3281-3286 (6) 3.30 1.95

Natl. Communist Party Achievements — A946

Natl. and party flags, and: 1 l, Transfagarasan Mountain Road. 2 l, Danube-Black Sea Canal. 3 l, Bucharest Underground Railway. 4 l, Irrigation.

1985, July 29

3287 A946 1 l multicolored .25 .25
3288 A946 2 l multicolored .50 .25
3289 A946 3 l multicolored .75 .25
3290 A946 4 l multicolored 1.00 .35
Nos. 3287-3290 (4) 2.50 1.10

20th annivs.: Election of Gen.-Sec. Nicolae Ceausescu; Natl. Communist Congress.

Romanian Socialist Constitution, 20th Anniv. — A947

1985, Aug. 5

3291 A947 1 l Arms, wheat, dove .25 .25
3292 A947 2 l Arms, torch .60 .25

1986 World Cup Soccer Preliminaries — A948

Flags of participants; Great Britain, Northern Ireland, Romania, Finland, Turkey and: 50b, Sliding tackle. 1 l, Trapping the ball. 1.50 l, Heading the ball. 2 l, Dribble. 3 l, Tackle. 4 l, Scissor kick. 10 l, Dribble, diff.

1985, Oct. 15

3293 A948 50b multi .25 .25
3294 A948 1 l multi .25 .25
3295 A948 1.50 l multi .30 .25
3296 A948 2 l multi .35 .25
3297 A948 3 l multi .55 .30
3298 A948 4 l multi .70 .35
Nos. 3293-3298 (6) 2.40 1.65

An imperf airmail 10 l souvenir sheet exists, showing flags, stadium and soccer players. Value, unused or used, $13.

Souvenir Sheet

Motorcycle Centenary — A949

1985, Aug. 22 **Photo.** *Perf. 13½*

3300 A949 10 l 1885 Daimler Einspur 2.25 2.25

Retezat Natl. Park, 50th Anniv. — A950

50b, Senecio glaberrimus. 1 l, Rupicapra rupicapra. 2 l, Centaurea retezatensis. 3 l, Viola dacica. 4 l, Marmota marmota. 5 l, Aquila chrysaetos.
10 l, Lynx lynx.

1985, Aug. 29

3301 A950 50b multi .25 .25
3302 A950 1 l multi .25 .25
3303 A950 2 l multi .35 .25
3304 A950 3 l multi .55 .25
3305 A950 4 l multi .80 .35
3306 A950 5 l multi 1.00 .45
Nos. 3301-3306 (6) 3.20 1.80

Souvenir Sheet

3307 A950 10 l multi 3.00 2.75

No. 3307 contains one 42x54mm stamp.

Tractors Manufactured by Universal — A951

1985, Sept. 10

3308 A951 50b 530 DTC .25 .25
3309 A951 1 l 550 M HC .25 .25
3310 A951 1.50 l 650 Super .25 .25
3311 A951 2 l 850 .30 .25
3312 A951 3 l S 1801 IF .60 .25
3313 A951 4 l A 3602 IF .75 .30
Nos. 3308-3313 (6) 2.40 1.55

Folk Costumes — A952

Women's and men's costumes from same region printed in continuous design.

1985, Sept. 28

3314 50b Muscel woman .25 .25
3315 50b Muscel man .25 .25
a. A952 Pair, #3314-3315 .25 .25
3316 1.50 l Bistrita-Nasaud woman .25 .25
3317 1.50 l Bistrita-Nasaud man .25 .25
a. A952 Pair, #3316-3317 .50 .30
3318 2 l Vrancea woman .35 .25
3319 2 l Vrancea man .35 .25
a. A952 Pair, #3318-3319 .70 .30
3320 3 l Vilcea woman .50 .25
3321 3 l Vilcea man .50 .25
a. A952 Pair, #3320-3321 1.00 .50
Nos. 3314-3321 (8) 2.70 2.00

Admission to UN, 30th Anniv. — A953

1985, Oct. 21

3322 A953 2 l multicolored .40 .25

UN, 40th Anniv. — A954

1985, Oct. 21

3323 A954 2 l multicolored .35 .25

Mineral Flowers — A955

50b, Quartz and calcite, Herja. 1 l, Copper, Altin Tepe. 2 l, Gypsum, Cavnic. 3 l, Quartz, Ocna de Fier. 4 l, Stibium, Baiut. 5 l, Tetrahedrite, Cavnic.

1985, Oct. 28

3324 A955 50b multi .25 .25
3325 A955 1 l multi .25 .25
3326 A955 2 l multi .30 .25
3327 A955 3 l multi .60 .30
3328 A955 4 l multi .75 .40
3329 A955 5 l multi .90 .50
Nos. 3324-3329 (6) 3.05 1.95

Stamp Day — A956

1985, Oct. 29

3330 A956 2 l + 1 l label .40 .25

A Connecticut Yankee in King Arthur's Court, by Mark Twain — A957

The Three Brothers, by Jacob and Wilhelm Grimm — A958

Disney characters in classic fairy tales — No. 3331, Hank Morgan awakes in Camelot. No. 3332, Predicts eclipse of sun. No. 3333, Mounting horse. No. 3334, Sir Sagramor. No. 3335, Fencing with shadow. No. 3336, Fencing, father. No. 3337, Shoeing a horse. No. 3338, Barber, rabbit. No. 3339, Father, three sons.

No. 3340, Tournament of knights. No. 3341, Cottage.

1985, Nov. 28

3331 A957 50b multi 2.00 2.00
3332 A957 50b multi 2.00 2.00
3333 A957 50b multi 2.00 2.00
3334 A957 50b multi 2.00 2.00
3335 A958 1 l multi 4.50 4.50
3336 A958 1 l multi 4.50 4.50
3337 A958 1 l multi 4.50 4.50
3338 A958 1 l multi 4.50 4.50
3339 A958 1 l multi 4.50 4.50
Nos. 3331-3339 (9) 30.50 30.50

Souvenir Sheets

3340 A957 5 l multi 15.00 15.00
3341 A958 5 l multi 15.00 15.00

Miniature Sheets

Intereuropa 1986 — A959

Fauna & flora: #3343: a, Felis silvestris. b, Mustela erminea. c, Tetrao urogallus. d, Urso arctos.

#3344: a, Dianthus callizonus. b, Pinus cembra. c, Salix sp. d, Rose pendulina.

1986, Mar. 25 Photo. *Perf. 13½*

3343 A959 Sheet of 4 2.50 2.50
a.-d. 3 l, any single .60 .60
3344 A959 Sheet of 4 2.50 2.50
a.-d. 3 l, any single .60 .60

Inventors and Adventurers — A960

Designs: 1 l, Orville and Wilbur Wright, Wright Flyer. 1.50 l, Jacques Cousteau, research vessel Calypso. 2 l, Amelia Earhart, Lockheed Electra. 3 l, Charles Lindbergh, Spirit of St. Louis. 3.50 l, Sir Edmund Hillary (1919-), first man to reach Mt. Everest summit. 4 l, Robert Edwin Peary, Arctic explorer. 5 l, Adm. Richard Byrd, explorer. 6 l, Neil Armstrong, first man on moon.

1985, Dec. 25 Photo. *Perf. 13½*

3345 A960 1 l multi .25 .25
3346 A960 1.50 l multi .30 .25
3347 A960 2 l multi .40 .30
3348 A960 3 l multi .60 .40
3349 A960 3.50 l multi .65 .50
3350 A960 4 l multi .75 .60
3351 A960 5 l multi 1.00 .70
3352 A960 6 l multi 1.25 .85
Nos. 3345-3352 (8) 5.20 3.85

Paintings by Nicolae Tonitza — A961

1986, Mar. 12 Photo. *Perf. 13½*

3353 A961 1 l Nina in Green .25 .25
3354 A961 2 l Irina .40 .25
3355 A961 3 l Woodman's Daughter .55 .25
3356 A961 4 l Woman on the Verandah .75 .30
Nos. 3353-3356 (4) 1.95 1.05

Color Animated Films, 50th Anniv. — A962

Walt Disney characters in the Band Concert, 1935 — No. 3357, Clarabelle. No. 3358, Mickey Mouse. No. 3359, Paddy and Peter. No. 3360, Goofy. No. 3361, Donald Duck. No. 3362, Mickey Mouse, diff. No. 3363, Mickey and Donald. No. 3364, Horace. No. 3365, Donald and trombonist.

No. 3366, Finale.

1986, Apr. 10 Photo. *Perf. 13½*

3357 A962 50b multi 2.00 2.00
3358 A962 50b multi 2.00 2.00
3359 A962 50b multi 2.00 2.00
3360 A962 50b multi 2.00 2.00
3361 A962 1 l multi 4.50 4.50
3362 A962 1 l multi 4.50 4.50
3363 A962 1 l multi 4.50 4.50
3364 A962 1 l multi 4.50 4.50
3365 A962 1 l multi 4.50 4.50
Nos. 3357-3365 (9) 30.50 30.50

Souvenir Sheet

3366 A962 5 l multi 15.00 15.00

1986 World Cup Soccer Championships, Mexico — A963

Various soccer plays and flags: 50b, Italy vs. Bulgaria. 1 l, Mexico vs. Belgium. 2 l, Canada vs. France. 3 l, Brazil vs. Spain. 4 l, Uruguay vs. Germany. 5 l, Morocco vs. Poland.

1986, May 9

3367 A963 50b multi .25 .25
3368 A963 1 l multi .25 .25
3369 A963 2 l multi .30 .25
3370 A963 3 l multi .45 .25
3371 A963 4 l multi .90 .25
3372 A963 5 l multi 1.00 .35
Nos. 3367-3372 (6) 3.15 1.60

An imperf. 10 l airmail souvenir sheet exists picturing stadium, flags of previous winners, satellite and map. Value, unused or used, $22.50.

Hotels — A964

50b, Diana, Herculane. 1 l, Termal, Felix. 2 l, Delfin, Meduza and Steaua de Mare, Eforie Nord. 3 l, Caciulata, Calimanesti Caciulata. 4 l, Palas, Slanic Moldova. 5 l, Bradet, Sovata.

1986, Apr. 23 Photo. *Perf. 13½*

3373 A964 50b multi .25 .25
3374 A964 1 l multi .25 .25
3375 A964 2 l multi .35 .25
3376 A964 3 l multi .50 .25
3377 A964 4 l multi .70 .25
3378 A964 5 l multi 1.00 .35
Nos. 3373-3378 (6) 3.05 1.60

Nicolae Ceausescu, Party Flag — A965

1986, May 8 Photo. *Perf. 13½*

3379 A965 2 l multicolored 1.00 .75

Natl. Communist Party, 65th anniv.

Flowers — A966

1986, June 25 Photo. *Perf. 13½*

3380 A966 50b Tulipa gesneriana .25 .25
3381 A966 1 l Iris hispanica .25 .25
3382 A966 2 l Rosa hybrida .35 .25
3383 A966 3 l Anemone coronaria .55 .25
3384 A966 4 l Freesia refracta .80 .25
3385 A966 5 l Chrysanthemum indicum 1.00 .35
Nos. 3380-3385 (6) 3.20 1.60

Mircea the Great, Ruler of Wallachia, 1386-1418 — A967

1986, July 17 Photo. *Perf. 13½*

3386 A967 2 l multicolored .60 .30

Ascent to the throne, 600th anniv.

Open Air Museum of Historic Dwellings, Bucharest, 50th Anniv. — A968

1986, July 21

3387 A968 50b Alba .25 .25
3388 A968 1 l Arges .25 .25
3389 A968 2 l Constantia .35 .25
3390 A968 3 l Timis .55 .25
3391 A968 4 l Neamt .80 .25
3392 A968 5 l Gorj 1.00 .35
Nos. 3387-3392 (6) 3.20 1.60

Polar Research — A969

Exploration: 50b, Julius Popper, exploration of Tierra del Fuego (1886-93). 1 l, Bazil G. Assan, exploration of Spitzbergen (1896). 2 l, Emil Racovita, Antarctic expedition (1897-99). 3 l, Constantin Dumbrava, exploration of Greenland (1927-8). 4 l, Romanians with the 17th Soviet Antarctic expedition (1971-72). 5 l, Research on krill fishing (1977-80).

1986, July 23 Photo. *Perf. 13½*

3393 A969 50b multi .25 .25
3394 A969 1 l multi .25 .25
3395 A969 2 l multi .35 .25
3396 A969 3 l multi .55 .25
3397 A969 4 l multi .80 .25
3398 A969 5 l multi 1.00 .35
Nos. 3393-3398 (6) 3.20 1.60

Natl. Cycling Championships A970

Various athletes.

1986, Aug. 29

3399 A970 1 l multicolored .25 .25
3400 A970 2 l multicolored .35 .25
3401 A970 3 l multicolored .55 .25
3402 A970 4 l multicolored .75 .30
Nos. 3399-3402 (4) 1.90 1.05

Souvenir Sheet

3403 A970 10 l multicolored 2.50 1.25

No. 3403 contains one 42x54mm stamp.

Souvenir Sheet

Intl. Peace Year — A971

1986, July 25

3404 A971 5 l multicolored 1.25 .60

Fungi — A972

50b, Amanita rubescens. 1 l, Boletus luridus. 2 l, Lactarius piperatus. 3 l, Lepiota clypeolaria. 4 l, Russula cyanoxantha. 5 l, Tremiscus helvelloides.

1986, Aug. 15

3405 A972 50b multi .25 .25
3406 A972 1 l multi .25 .25
3407 A972 2 l multi .35 .25
3408 A972 3 l multi .55 .25
3409 A972 4 l multi .80 .25
3410 A972 5 l multi 1.00 .35
Nos. 3405-3410 (6) 3.20 1.60

A973

Famous Men: 50b, Petru Maior (c. 1761-1821), historian. 1 l, George Topirceanu (1886-1937), doctor. 2 l, Henri Coanda (1886-1972), engineer. 3 l, Constantin Budeanu (1886-1959), engineer.

1986, Nov. 10 Photo. *Perf. 13½*

3411 A973 50b dl cl, gold & dk bl grn .25 .25
3412 A973 1 l sl grn, gold & dk lil rose .25 .25
3413 A973 2 l rose cl, gold & brt bl .45 .25
3414 A973 3 l chlky bl, gold & choc .70 .25
Nos. 3411-3414 (4) 1.65 1.00

UNESCO, 40th Anniv. A974

1986, Nov. 10

3415 A974 4 l multicolored .75 .35

Stamp Day — A975

1986, Nov. 15

3416 A975 2 l + 1 l label 1.20 .25

Industry A976

50b, F-300 oil rigs, vert. 1 l, Promex excavator. 2 l, Pitesti refinery, vert. 3 l, 110-ton dump truck. 4 l, Coral computer, vert. 5 l, 350-megawatt turbine.

1986, Nov. 28

3417 A976 50b multi .25 .25
3418 A976 1 l multi .25 .25
3419 A976 2 l multi .40 .25
3420 A976 3 l multi .55 .25
3421 A976 4 l multi .80 .25
3422 A976 5 l multi 1.00 .35
Nos. 3417-3422 (6) 3.25 1.60

Folk Costumes — A977

1986, Dec. 26

3423 A977 50b Capra .25 .25
3424 A977 1 l Sorcova .25 .25
3425 A977 2 l Plugusorul .35 .25
3426 A977 3 l Buhaiul .55 .25
3427 A977 4 l Caiutii .80 .25
3428 A977 5 l Uratorii 1.00 .35
Nos. 3423-3428 (6) 3.20 1.60

Recycling Campaign — A978

1986, Dec. 30

3429 A978 1 l Metal .25 .25
3430 A978 2 l Trees .50 .25

Young Communists' League, 65th Anniv. — A979

1987, Mar. 18 Photo. *Perf. 13½*

3431 A979 1 l Flags, youth .25 .25
3432 A979 2 l Emblem .45 .25
3433 A979 3 l Flags, youth, diff. .65 .40
Nos. 3431-3433 (3) 1.35 .90

Miniature Sheets

Intereuropa — A980

Modern architecture: No. 3434a, Exposition Pavilion, Bucharest. b, Intercontinental Hotel, Bucharest. c, Europa Hotel, Black Sea coast. d, Polytechnic Institute, Bucharest.

No. 3435a, Administration Building, Satu Mare. b, House of Young Pioneers, Bucharest. c, Valahia Hotel, Tirgoviste. d, Caciulata Hotel, Caciulata.

1987, May 18 Photo. *Perf. 13½*

3434 A980 Sheet of 4 2.50 2.50
a.-d. 3 l, any single .60 .60
3435 A980 Sheet of 4 2.50 2.50
a.-d. 3 l, any single .60 .60

Collective Farming, 25th Anniv. — A981

1987, Apr. 25 Photo. *Perf. 13½*

3436 A981 2 l multicolored .50 .25

Birch Trees by the Lakeside, by I. Andreescu — A982

Paintings in Romanian museums: 1 l, Young Peasant Girls Spinning, by N. Grigorescu. 2 l, Washerwoman, by S. Luchian. 3 l, Inside the Peasant's Cottage, by S. Dimitrescu. 4 l, Winter Landscape, by A. Ciucurencu. 5 l, Winter in Bucharest, by N. Tonitza, vert.

1987, Apr. 28

3437 A982 50b multicolored .25 .25
3438 A982 1 l multicolored .25 .25
3439 A982 2 l multicolored .35 .25
3440 A982 3 l multicolored .50 .25
3441 A982 4 l multicolored .75 .35
3442 A982 5 l multicolored 1.00 .50
Nos. 3437-3442 (6) 3.10 1.85

Peasant Uprising of 1907, 80th Anniv. — A983

1987, May 30

3443 A983 2 l multicolored .50 .25

Men's World Handball Championships — A984

Various plays.

1987, July 15

3444 A984 50b multi, vert. .25 .25
3445 A984 1 l multi .25 .25
3446 A984 2 l multi, vert. .35 .25
3447 A984 3 l multi .50 .25
3448 A984 4 l multi, vert. .75 .35
3449 A984 5 l multi 1.00 .50
Nos. 3444-3449 (6) 3.10 1.85

A985

Natl. Currency — A986

1987, July 15

3450 A985 1 l multicolored .25 .25

Souvenir Sheet

3451 A986 10 l multicolored 2.50 2.50

Landscapes — A987

50b, Pelicans over the Danube Delta. 1 l, Transfagarasan Highway. 2 l, Hairpin curve, Bicazului. 3 l, Limestone peaks, Mt. Ceahlau.

4 l, Lake Capra, Mt. Fagaras. 5 l, Orchard, Borsa.

1987, July 31 Photo. *Perf. 13½*

3452	A987	50b multi	.25	.25
3453	A987	1 l multi	.25	.25
3454	A987	2 l multi	.35	.25
3455	A987	3 l multi	.50	.25
3456	A987	4 l multi	.70	.35
3457	A987	5 l multi	.90	.50
		Nos. 3452-3457 (6)	2.95	1.85

A988

Scenes from Fairy Tale by Peter Ispirescu (b. 1887) — A988a

1987, Sept. 25 Photo. *Perf. 13½*

3458	A988	50b shown	.25	.25
3459	A988	1 l multi, diff.	.25	.25
3460	A988	2 l multi, diff.	.35	.25
3461	A988	3 l multi, diff.	.50	.25
3462	A988	4 l multi, diff.	.70	.35
3463	A988	5 l multi, diff.	.85	.40
		Nos. 3458-3463 (6)	2.90	1.75

Souvenir Sheet

3464	A988a	10 l shown	2.50	2.50

Miniature Sheets

Flora and Fauna A989

Flora: No. 3465a, Aquilegia alpina. b, Pulsatilla vernalis. c, Aster alpinus. d, Soldanella pusilla baumg. e, Lilium bulbiferum. f, Arctostaphylos uva-ursi. g, Crocus vernus. h, Crepis aurea. i, Cypripedium calceolus. j, Centaurea nervosa. k, Dryas octopetala. l, Gentiana excisa.

Fauna: No. 3466a, Martes martes. b, Felis lynx. c, Ursus maritimus. d, Lutra lutra. e, Bison bonasus. f, Branta ruficollis. g, Phoenicopterus ruber. h, Otis tarda. i, Lyrurus tetrix. j, Gypaetus barbatus. k, Vormela peregusna. l, Oxyura leucocephala.

1987, Oct. 16 Sheets of 12

3465	A989	1 l #a.-l.	4.50	4.50
3466	A989	1 l #a.-l.	4.50	4.50

Souvenir Sheet

PHILATELIA '87, Cologne — A990

1987, Oct. 19

3467	A990	Sheet of 2 + 2 labels	2.50	2.50
a.		3 l Bucharest city seal	1.00	1.00
b.		3 l Cologne city arms	1.00	1.00

Locomotives — A991

1987, Oct. 15

3468	A991	50b L 45 H	.25	.25
3469	A991	1 l LDE 125	.25	.25
3470	A991	2 l LDH 70	.40	.25
3471	A991	3 l LDE 2100	.65	.30
3472	A991	4 l LDE 3000	.90	.40
3473	A991	5 l LE 5100	1.00	.50
		Nos. 3468-3473 (6)	3.45	1.95

Folk Costumes — A992

1987, Nov. 7

3474		1 l Tirnave (woman)	.25	.25
3475		1 l Tirnave (man)	.25	.25
a.	A992	Pair, #3474-3475	.40	.25
3476		2 l Buzau (woman)	.40	.25
3477		2 l Buzau (man)	.40	.25
a.	A992	Pair, #3476-3477	.80	.30
3478		3 l Dobrogea (woman)	.60	.30
3479		3 l Dobrogea (man)	.60	.30
a.	A992	Pair, #3478-3479	1.25	.60
3480		4 l Ilfov (woman)	.80	.40
3481		4 l Ilfov (man)	.80	.40
a.	A992	Pair, #3480-3481	1.60	.80
		Nos. 3474-3481 (8)	4.10	2.40

Postwoman Delivering Mail — A993

1987, Nov. 15 Photo. *Perf. 13½*

3482	A993	2 l + 1 l label	.75	.35

Stamp Day.

Apiculture — A994

1 l, Apis mellifica carpatica. 2 l, Bee pollinating sunflower. 3 l, Hives, Danube Delta. 4 l, Apiculture complex, Bucharest.

1987, Nov. 16 Photo. *Perf. 13½*

3483	A994	1 l multi	.25	.25
3484	A994	2 l multi	.50	.25
3485	A994	3 l multi	.75	.35
3486	A994	4 l multi	1.00	.50
		Nos. 3483-3486 (4)	2.50	1.35

1988 Winter Olympics, Calgary A995

1987, Dec. 28 Photo. *Perf. 13½*

3487	A995	50b Biathlon	.25	.25
3488	A995	1 l Slalom	.25	.25
3489	A995	1.50 l Ice hockey	.25	.25
3490	A995	2 l Luge	.25	.25
3491	A995	3 l Speed skating	.45	.25
3492	A995	3.50 l Women's figure skating	.45	.25
3493	A995	4 l Downhill skiing	.60	.25
3494	A995	5 l Two-man bob-sled	.75	.35
		Nos. 3487-3494 (8)	3.25	2.10

An imperf. 10 l souvenir sheet picturing ski jumping also exists. Value, unused or used, $20.

Traffic Safety A996

Designs: 50b, Be aware of children riding bicycles in the road. 1 l, Young Pioneer girl as crossing guard. 2 l, Do not open car doors in path of moving traffic. 3 l, Be aware of pedestrian crossings. 4 l, Observe the speed limit; do not attempt curves at high speed. 5 l, Protect small children.

1987, Dec. 10 Photo. *Perf. 13½*

3495	A996	50b multicolored	.25	.25
3496	A996	1 l multicolored	.25	.25
3497	A996	2 l multicolored	.40	.25
3498	A996	3 l multicolored	.65	.30
3499	A996	4 l multicolored	.85	.40
3500	A996	5 l multicolored	1.00	.45
		Nos. 3495-3500 (6)	3.40	1.90

October Revolution, Russia, 70th Anniv. — A997

1987, Dec. 26

3501	A997	2 l multicolored	.60	.25

40th Anniv. of the Romanian Republic — A998

1987, Dec. 30

3502	A998	2 l multicolored	.50	.25

70th Birthday of President Nicolae Ceausescu — A999

1988, Jan. 26

3503	A999	2 l multicolored	.90	.45

Pottery A1000

1988, Feb. 26 Photo. *Perf. 13½*

3504	A1000	50b Marginea	.25	.25
3505	A1000	1 l Oboga	.25	.25
3506	A1000	2 l Horezu	.35	.25
3507	A1000	3 l Curtea De Arges	.55	.25
3508	A1000	4 l Birsa	.75	.25
3509	A1000	5 l Vama	1.00	.35
		Nos. 3504-3509 (6)	3.15	1.60

Miniature Sheets

Intereuropa — A1001

Transportation and communication: No. 3510a, Mail coach. b, ECS telecommunications satellite. c, Oltcit automobile. d, ICE high-speed electric train.

No. 3511a, Santa Maria, 15th cent. b, Cheia Ground Station satellite dish receivers. c, Bucharest subway. d, Airbus-A320.

1988, Apr. 27 Photo. *Perf. 13½*

3510	A1001	Sheet of 4	2.50	2.50
a.-d.		3 l any single	.60	.60
3511	A1001	Sheet of 4	2.50	2.50
a.-d.		3 l any single	.60	.60

1988 Summer Olympics, Seoul — A1002

1988, Jun. 28

3512	A1002	50b	Gymnastics	.25	.25
3513	A1002	1.50 l	Boxing	.30	.25
3514	A1002	2 l	Tennis	.35	.25
3515	A1002	3 l	Judo	.50	.25
3516	A1002	4 l	Running	.80	.25
3517	A1002	5 l	Rowing	1.00	.40
			Nos. 3512-3517 (6)	3.20	1.65

An imperf. 10 l souvenir sheet exists. Value, unused or used, $12.

19th-20th Cent. Clocks in the Ceasului Museum, Ploesti A1003

50b, Arad Region porcelain. 1.50 l, French bronze. 2 l, French bronze, diff. 3 l, Gothic bronze. 4 l, Saxony porcelain. 5 l, Bohemian porcelain.

1988, May 20 Photo. *Perf. 13½*

3518	A1003	50b	multicolored	.25	.25
3519	A1003	1.50 l	multicolored	.25	.25
3520	A1003	2 l	multicolored	.40	.25
3521	A1003	3 l	multicolored	.55	.25
3522	A1003	4 l	multicolored	.85	.25
3523	A1003	5 l	multicolored	1.00	.35
			Nos. 3518-3523 (6)	3.30	1.60

20th cent. timepiece (50b); others 19th cent.

Miniature Sheets

European Soccer Championships, Germany — A1003a

Soccer players and flags of: c, Federal Republic of Germany. d, Spain. e, Italy. f, Denmark. g, England. h, Netherlands. i, Ireland. j, Soviet Union.

1988, June 9 Litho. *Perf. 13½*

3523A	A1003a	Sheet of 4	*3.25*	*3.25*
c.-f.		3 l any single	.80	.80
3523B	A1003a	Sheet of 4	*3.25*	*3.25*
g.-j.		3 l any single	.80	.80

Accession of Constanin Brincoveanu as Prince Regent of Wallachia, 1688-1714, 300th Anniv. — A1004

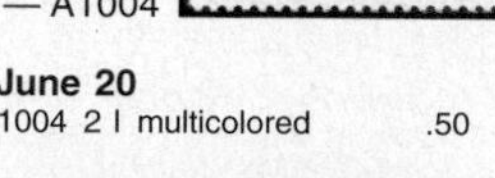

1988, June 20

3524	A1004	2 l multicolored	.50	.25

1988 Summer Olympics, Seoul — A1005

50b, Women's running. 1 l, Canoeing. 1.50 l, Women's gymnastics. 2 l, Kayaking. 3 l, Weight lifting. 3.50 l, Women's swimming. 4 l, Fencing. 5 l, Women's rowing (double).

1988, Sept. 1 Photo. *Perf. 13½*

3525	A1005	50b	multicolored	.25	.25
3526	A1005	1 l	multicolored	.25	.25
3527	A1005	1.50 l	multicolored	.25	.25
3528	A1005	2 l	multicolored	.25	.25
3529	A1005	3 l	multicolored	.40	.25
3530	A1005	3.50 l	multicolored	.50	.25
3531	A1005	4 l	multicolored	.60	.25
3532	A1005	5 l	multicolored	.75	.30
			Nos. 3525-3532 (8)	3.25	2.05

An imperf. 10 l souvenir sheet exists picturing women's gymnastics. Value, unused or used, $20.

Romania-China Philatelic Exhibition — A1006

1988, Aug. 5 Photo. *Perf. 13½*

3533	A1006	2 l multicolored	.50	.25

Souvenir Sheet

PRAGA '88 — A1007

1988, Aug. 26

3534	A1007	5 l Carnations, by Stefan Luchian	2.00	2.00

Miniature Sheets

Orchids — A1008

#3535: a, Oncidium lanceanum. b, Cattleya trianae. c, Sophronitis cernua. d, Bulbophyllum lobbii. e, Lycaste cruenta. f, Mormolyce ringens. g, Phragmipedium schlimii. h, Angraecum sesquipedale. i, Laelia crispa. j, Encyclia atropurpurea. k, Dendrobium nobile. l, Oncidium splendidum.

#3536: a, Brassavola perrinii. b, Paphiopedilum maudiae. c, Sophronitis coccinea. d, Vandopsis lissochiloides. e, Phalaenopsis lueddemanniana. f, Chysis bractescens. g, Cochleanthes discolor. h, Phalaenopsis amabilis. i, Pleione pricei. j, Sobralia macrantha. k, Aspasia lunata. l, Cattleya citrina.

1988, Oct. 24

3535	A1008	Sheet of 12	4.00	4.00
a.-l.		1 l any single	.30	.30
3536	A1008	Sheet of 12	4.00	4.00
a.-l.		1 l any single	.30	.30

Miniature Sheets

Events Won by Romanian Athletes at the 1988 Seoul Olympic Games A1009

Sporting event and medal: No. 3537a, Women's gymnastics. b, Free pistol shooting. c, Weight lifting (220 pounds). d, Featherweight boxing.

No. 3538a, Women's 1500 and 3000-meter relays. b, Women's 200 and 400-meter individual swimming medley. c, Wrestling (220 pounds). d, Rowing, coxless pairs and coxed fours.

1988, Dec. 7 Photo. *Perf. 13½*

3537		Sheet of 4	3.00	3.00
a.-d.	A1009	3 l any single	.75	.75
3538		Sheet of 4	3.00	3.00
a.-d.	A1009	3 l any single	.75	.75

Stamp Day — A1010

1988, Nov. 13 Photo. *Perf. 13½*

3539	A1010	2 l + 1 l label	.75	.35

Unitary Natl. Romanian State, 70th Anniv. A1011

1988, Dec. 29

3540	A1011	2 l multicolored	.50	.40

Anniversaries — A1012

Designs: 50b, Athenaeum, Bucharest. 1.50 l, Trajan's Bridge, Drobeta, on a Roman bronze sestertius used in Romania from 103 to 105 A.D. 2 l, Ruins, Suceava. 3 l, Pitesti municipal coat of arms, scroll, architecture. 4 l, Trajan's Column (detail), 113 A.D. 5 l, Gold helmet discovered in Prahova County.

1988, Dec. 30

3541	A1012	50b	shown	.25	.25
3542	A1012	1.50 l	multi	.25	.25
3543	A1012	2 l	multi	.35	.25
3544	A1012	3 l	multi	.50	.25
3545	A1012	4 l	multi	.80	.25
3546	A1012	5 l	multi	1.00	.35
			Nos. 3541-3546 (6)	3.15	1.60

Athenaeum, Bucharest, cent. (50b), Suceava, capital of Moldavia from 1401-1565, 600th anniv. (2 l), & Pitesti municipal charter, 600th anniv. (3 l).

Miniature Sheets

Grand Slam Tennis Championships — A1013

No. 3547: a, Men's singles, stadium in Melbourne. b, Men's singles, scoreboard. c, Mixed doubles, spectators. d, Mixed doubles, Roland Garros stadium.

No. 3548: a, Women's singles, stadium in Wimbledon. b, Women's singles, spectators. c, Men's doubles, spectators. d, Men's doubles, stadium in Flushing Meadows.

1988, Aug. 22 Photo. *Perf. 13½*

3547	A1013	Sheet of 4	3.00	3.00
a.-d.		3 l any single	.75	.75
3548	A1013	Sheet of 4	3.00	3.00
a.-d.		3 l any single	.75	.75

Australian Open (Nos. 3547a-3547b), French Open (Nos. 3547c-3547d), Wimbledon (Nos. 3548a-3548b) and US Open (Nos. 3548c-3548d).

Architecture — A1014

Designs: 50b, Zapodeni, Vaslui, 17th cent. 1.50 l, Berbesti, Maramures, 18th cent. 2 l, Voitinel, Suceava, 18th cent. 3 l, Chiojdu mic, Buzau, 18th cent. 4 l, Cimpanii de sus, Bihor, 19th cent. 5 l, Naruja, Vrancea, 19th cent.

1989, Feb. 8 Photo. *Perf. 13½*

3549	A1014	50b	multi	.25	.25
3550	A1014	1.50 l	multi	.25	.25
3551	A1014	2 l	multi	.35	.25
3552	A1014	3 l	multi	.50	.25
3553	A1014	4 l	multi	.80	.25
3554	A1014	5 l	multi	1.00	.35
			Nos. 3549-3554 (6)	3.15	1.60

Rescue and Relief Services — A1015

50b, Relief worker. 1.50 l, Fireman, child. 2 l, Fireman's carry. 3 l, Rescue team on skis. 3.50 l, Mountain rescue. 4 l, Water rescue. 5 l, Water safety.

1989, Feb. 25

3555	A1015	50b multicolored	.25	.25
3556	A1015	1 l multicolored	.25	.25
3557	A1015	1.50 l multicolored	.25	.25
3558	A1015	2 l multicolored	.30	.25
3559	A1015	3 l multicolored	.50	.25
3560	A1015	3.50 l multicolored	.60	.25
3561	A1015	4 l multicolored	.70	.30
3562	A1015	5 l multicolored	.85	.35
		Nos. 3555-3562 (8)	3.70	2.15

Nos. 3555, 3557-3558, 3560-3561 vert.

Industries — A1016

Designs: 50b, Fasca Bicaz cement factory. 1.50 l, Bridge on the Danube near Cernavoda. 2 l, MS-2-2400/450-20 synchronous motor. 3 l, Bucharest subway. 4 l, Mangalia-Constanta ferry. 5 l, *Gloria* marine platform.

1989, Apr. 10 Photo. *Perf. 13½*

3563	A1016	50b multi	.25	.25
3564	A1016	1.50 l multi	.25	.25
3565	A1016	2 l multi	.40	.25
3566	A1016	3 l multi	.55	.25
3567	A1016	4 l multi	.75	.25
3568	A1016	5 l multi	.85	.35
		Nos. 3563-3568 (6)	3.05	1.60

Anti-fascist March, 50th Anniv. — A1017

1989, May 1 Photo. *Perf. 13½*

3569	A1017	2 l shown	.50	.25

Souvenir Sheet

3570	A1017	10 l Patriots, flag	4.00	4.00

Souvenir Sheet

BULGARIA '89, Sofia, May 22-31 — A1018

1989, May 20

3571	A1018	10 l Roses	2.50	2.50

Miniature Sheets

Intereuropa 1989 — A1019

Children's activities and games: No. 3572a, Swimming. No. 3572b, Water slide. No. 3572c, Seesaw. No. 3572d, Flying kites. No. 3573a, Playing with dolls. No. 3573b, Playing ball. No. 3573c, Playing in the sand. No. 3573d, Playing with toy cars.

1989, June 15

3572	A1019	Sheet of 4	2.25	2.25
a.-d.		3 l any single	.55	.55
3573	A1019	Sheet of 4	2.25	2.25
a.-d.		3 l any single	.55	.55

Socialist Revolution in Romania, 45th Anniv. A1020

1989, Aug. 21 Photo. *Perf. 13½*

3574	A1020	2 l multicolored	.50	.25

Cartoons — A1021

50b, Pin-pin. 1 l, Maria. 1.50 l, Gore and Grigore. 2 l, Pisoiul, Balanel, Manole and Monk. 3 l, Gruia Lui Novac. 3.50 l, Mihaela. 4 l, Harap alb. 5 l, Homo sapiens.

1989, Sept. 25

3575	A1021	50b multi	.25	.25
3576	A1021	1 l multi	.25	.25
3577	A1021	1.50 l multi	.30	.25
3578	A1021	2 l multi	.35	.25
3579	A1021	3 l multi	.55	.25
3580	A1021	3.50 l multi	.60	.25
3581	A1021	4 l multi	.65	.25
3582	A1021	5 l multi	.75	.30
		Nos. 3575-3582 (8)	3.70	2.05

Famous Romanians A1022

Portraits: 1 l, Ion Creanga (1837-1889). 2 l, Mihail Eminescu (1850-1889), poet. 3 l, Nicolae Teclu (1839-1916), chemist and inventor.

1989, Aug. 18 Photo. *Perf. 13½*

3583	A1022	1 l multicolored	.25	.25
3584	A1022	2 l multicolored	.45	.25
3585	A1022	3 l multicolored	.65	.35
		Nos. 3583-3585 (3)	1.35	.85

Stamp Day — A1023

1989, Oct. 7

3586	A1023	2 l + 1 l label	.75	.30

No. 3586 has a second label picturing posthorn.

Storming of the Bastille, 1789 A1024

Emblems of PHILEXFRANCE '89 and the Revolution — A1025

Designs: 1.50 l, Gavroche. 2 l, Robespierre. 3 l, *La Marseillaise*, by Rouget de Lisle. 4 l, Diderot. 5 l, 1848 Uprising, Romania.

1989, Oct. 14

3587	A1024	50b shown	.25	.25
3588	A1024	1.50 l multicolored	.30	.25
3589	A1024	2 l multicolored	.40	.25
3590	A1024	3 l multicolored	.60	.25
3591	A1024	4 l multicolored	.80	.30
3592	A1024	5 l multicolored	1.00	.40
		Nos. 3587-3592 (6)	3.35	1.70

Souvenir Sheet

3593	A1025	10 l shown	2.50	2.50

French revolution, bicent.

14th Romanian Communist Party Congress — A1025a

1989, Nov. 20 Photo. *Perf. 13½*

3593A	A1025a	2 l multicolored	.60	.25

Souvenir Sheet

3593B	A1025a	10 l multicolored	3.50	3.50

Revolution of Dec. 22, 1989 — A1026

1990, Jan. 8 Photo. *Perf. 13½*

3594	A1026	2 l multicolored	.45	.25

For surcharge, see No. 3633.

World Cup Soccer Preliminaries, Italy — A1027

Various soccer players in action.

1990, Mar. 19 Photo. *Perf. 13½*

3595	A1027	50b multicolored	.25	.25
3596	A1027	1.50 l multicolored	.30	.25
3597	A1027	2 l multicolored	.40	.25
3598	A1027	3 l multicolored	.60	.25
3599	A1027	4 l multicolored	.80	.30
3600	A1027	5 l multicolored	1.00	.35
		Nos. 3595-3600 (6)	3.35	1.65

An imperf. 10 l airmail souvenir sheet exists. Value, $10.

Souvenir Sheet

First Postage Stamp, 150th Anniv. — A1028

1990, May 2 Litho. *Perf. 13½*

3601	A1028	10 l multicolored	3.00	3.00

Stamp World London '90. For surcharge, see No. 5681.

World Cup Soccer Championships, Italy — A1029

Various soccer players in action.

1990, May 7 Photo. *Perf. 13½*

3602	A1029	50b multicolored	.25	.25
3603	A1029	1 l multicolored	.25	.25
3604	A1029	1.50 l multicolored	.25	.25
3605	A1029	2 l multicolored	.30	.25
3606	A1029	3 l multicolored	.45	.25
3607	A1029	3.50 l multicolored	.50	.25

3608 A1029 4 l multicolored .55 .25
3609 A1029 5 l multicolored .65 .25
Nos. 3602-3609 (8) 3.20 2.00

An imperf. 10 l airmail souvenir sheet showing Olympic Stadium, Rome exists. Value, $10.

Intl. Dog Show, Brno, Czechoslovakia — A1030

50b, German shepherd. 1 l, English setter. 1.50 l, Boxer. 2 l, Beagle. 3 l, Doberman pinscher. 3.50 l, Great Dane. 4 l, Afghan hound. 5 l, Yorkshire terrier.

1990, June 6
3610 A1030 50b multicolored .25 .25
3611 A1030 1 l multicolored .25 .25
3612 A1030 1.50 l multicolored .30 .25
3613 A1030 2 l multicolored .35 .25
3614 A1030 3 l multicolored .60 .25
3615 A1030 3.50 l multicolored .75 .25
3616 A1030 4 l multicolored .80 .25
3617 A1030 5 l multicolored 1.00 .25
Nos. 3610-3617 (8) 4.30 2.00

Riccione '90, Intl. Philatelic Exhibition A1031

1990, Aug. 24
3618 A1031 2 l multicolored .50 .25

See No. 3856.

Romanian-Chinese Philatelic Exhibition, Bucharest — A1032

1990, Sept. 8 Photo. *Perf. 13½*
3619 A1032 2 l multicolored .40 .25

For surcharge see No. 4186.

Paintings Damaged in 1989 Revolution — A1033

Designs: 50b, Old Nicolas, the Zither Player, by Stefan Luchian. 1.50 l, Woman in Blue by Ion Andreescu. 2 l, The Gardener by Luchian. 3 l, Vase of Flowers by Jan Brueghel, the Elder. 4 l, Springtime by Peter Brueghel, the Elder, horiz. 5 l, Madonna and Child by G. B. Paggi.

1990. Oct. 25 Photo. *Perf. 13½*
3620 A1033 50b multicolored .25 .25
3621 A1033 1.50 l multicolored .25 .25
3622 A1033 2 l multicolored .25 .25
3623 A1033 3 l multicolored .40 .25
3624 A1033 4 l multicolored .55 .25
3625 A1033 5 l multicolored .70 .30
Nos. 3620-3625 (6) 2.40 1.55

For surcharges see #4365-4369.

Stamp Day — A1033a

1990, Nov. 10 Photo. *Perf. 13½*
3625A A1033a 2 l + 1 l label 1.00 .70

Famous Romanians A1034

Designs: 50b, Prince Constantin Cantacuzino (1640-1716). 1.50 l, Ienachita Vacarescu (c. 1740-1797), historian. 2 l, Titu Maiorescu (1840-1917), writer. 3 l, Nicolae Iorga (1871-1940), historian. 4 l, Martha Bibescu (1890-1973). 5 l, Stefan Procopiu (1890-1972), scientist.

1990, Nov. 27 Photo. *Perf. 13½*
3626 A1034 50b sepia & dk bl .25 .25
3627 A1034 1.50 l grn & brt pur .25 .25
3628 A1034 2 l claret & dk bl .30 .25
3629 A1034 3 l dk bl & brn .40 .25
3630 A1034 4 l brn & dk bl .50 .25
3631 A1034 5 l brt pur & grn .65 .25
Nos. 3626-3631 (6) 2.35 1.50

For surcharges see #4356-4360.

National Day — A1035

1990, Dec. 1 Photo. *Perf. 13½*
3632 A1035 2 l multicolored .40 .25

No. 3594 Surcharged in Brown

1990, Dec. 22 Photo. *Perf. 13½*
3633 A1026 4 l on 2 l .65 .25

Vincent Van Gogh, Death Cent. — A1036

Paintings: 50b, Field of Irises. 2 l, Artist's Room. 3 l, Night on the Coffee Terrace, vert. 3.50 l, Blossoming Fruit Trees. 5 l, Vase with Fourteen Sunflowers, vert.

1991, Mar. 29 Photo. *Perf. 13½*
3634 A1036 50b multicolored .25 .25
3635 A1036 2 l multicolored .25 .25
3636 A1036 3 l multicolored .35 .25
3637 A1036 3.50 l multicolored .40 .25
3638 A1036 5 l multicolored .60 .25
Nos. 3634-3638 (5) 1.85 1.25

For surcharges see #4371-4372.

A1037

Birds: 50b, Larus marinus. 1 l, Sterna hirundo. 1.50 l, Recurvirostra avosetta. 2 l, Stercorarius pomarinus. 3 l, Vanellus vanellus. 3.50 l, Mergus serrator. 4 l, Egretta garzetta. 5 l, Calidris alpina. 6 l, Limosa limosa. 7 l, Childonias hybrida.

1991, Apr. 3 Photo. *Perf. 13½*
3639 A1037 50b ultra .25 .25
3640 A1037 1 l blue green .25 .25
3641 A1037 1.50 l bister .25 .25
3642 A1037 2 l dark blue .25 .25
3643 A1037 3 l light green .25 .25
3644 A1037 3.50 l dark green .30 .25
3645 A1037 4 l purple .30 .25
3646 A1037 5 l brown .35 .25
3647 A1037 6 l yel brown .70 .25
3648 A1037 7 l light blue .65 .25
Nos. 3639-3648 (10) 3.55 2.50

A1038

1991, Apr. 5 Photo. *Perf. 13½*
3649 A1038 4 l multicolored .35 .25

Easter.

Europa — A1039

1991, May 10 Photo. *Perf. 13½*
3650 A1039 4.50 l Eutelsat I 2.00 .80

For surcharge see No. 4185.

Posthorn — A1040

1991, May 24 Photo. *Perf. 13½*
3651 A1040 4.50 l blue .40 .25

Gymnastics A1041

1991, June 14
3652 A1041 1 l Rings .25 .25
3653 A1041 1 l Parallel bars .25 .25
3654 A1041 4.50 l Vault .25 .25
3655 A1041 4.50 l Uneven parallel bars .25 .25
3656 A1041 8 l Floor exercise .45 .25
3657 A1041 9 l Balance beam .60 .25
Nos. 3652-3657 (6) 2.05 1.50

For surcharge on 5 l see No. 3735. For other surcharges see Nos. 3944, 3946, 4237-4238.

Monasteries — A1042

1991, July 4 Photo. *Perf. 13½*
3658 A1042 1 l Curtea de Arges, vert. .25 .25
3659 A1042 1 l Putna, vert. .25 .25
3660 A1042 4.50 l Varatec, vert. .25 .25
3661 A1042 4.50 l Agapia .25 .25
3662 A1042 8 l Golia .45 .25
3663 A1042 9 l Sucevita .60 .25
Nos. 3658-3663 (6) 2.05 1.50

For surcharges see #4354-4355.

Hotels, Lodges, and Resorts
A1043 A1044

Designs: 1 l, Hotel Continental, Timisoara, vert. 2 l, Valea Caprei Lodge, Fagaras. 4 l, Hotel Intercontinental, Bucharest, vert. 5 l, Lebada Hotel, Crisan. 6 l, Muntele Rosu Lodge, Ciucas. 8 l, Transylvania Hotel, Cluj-Napoca. 9 l, Hotel Orizont, Predeal. 10 l, Hotel Roman, Herculane, vert. 18 l, Rarau Lodge, Rarau, vert. 20 l, Alpine Hotel, Poiana Brasov. 25 l, Constanta Casino. 30 l, Miorija Lodge, Bucegi. 45 l, Sura Dacilor Lodge, Poiana Brasov. 60 l, Valea Draganului, Tourist Complex,. 80 l, Hotel Florica, Venus Health Resort. 120 l, International Hotel, Baile Felix, vert. 160 l, Hotel Egreta, Tulcea, vert. 250 l, Motel Valea de Pesti, Valea Jiului. 400 l, Tourist Complex, Baisoara. 500 l, Hotel Bradul, Covasna. 800 l, Hotel Gorj, Tirgu Jiu.

1991 Photo. *Perf. 13½*
3664 A1043 1 l blue .25 .25
3665 A1043 2 l dark green .25 .25
3666 A1043 4 l carmine .25 .25
3667 A1043 5 l violet .25 .25
3668 A1043 6 l olive brown .25 .25
3669 A1043 8 l brown .25 .25
3670 A1043 9 l red brown .60 .25
3671 A1043 10 l olive green .65 .25
3672 A1043 18 l bright red .40 .25
3673 A1043 20 l brown org .30 .25
3674 A1043 25 l bright blue .65 .25
3675 A1043 30 l magenta .85 .25
3676 A1043 45 l dark blue .75 .30
3677 A1044 60 l brown olive 1.00 .40
3678 A1044 80 l purple 1.25 .55

Size: 27x41mm, 41x27mm

3679 A1044 120 l gray bl & dk bl vio 1.50 .25
3680 A1044 160 l lt ver & dk ver 2.00 .25
3681 A1044 250 l lt bl & dk bl 2.50 .25
3682 A1044 400 l tan & dk brn 3.25 .30
3683 A1044 500 l lt bl grn & dk bl grn 3.75 .35
3684 A1044 800 l pink & dk lil rose 4.50 .40
Nos. 3664-3684 (21) 25.45 6.05

Issued: 1 l, 5 l, 9 l, 10 l, 8/27; 2 l, 4 l, 18 l, 25 l, 30 l, 10/8; 6 l, 8 l, 20 l, 45 l, 60 l, 80 l, 11/14; 120 l, 160 l, 250 l, 400 l, 500 l, 800 l, 12/5.

For surcharges see Nos. 4167-4174, 4204-4219, 4384.

Riccone '91, Intl. Philatelic Exhibition — A1045

1991, Aug. 27

3685 A1045 4 l multicolored .40 .25

A1046

Vases: a, Decorated with birds. b, Decorated with flowers.

1991, Sept. 12

3686 A1046 5 l Pair, #a.-b. .80 .35

Romanian-Chinese Philatelic Exhibition.

A1047

1991, Sept. 17

3687 A1047 1 l blue .35 .25

Romanian Academy, 125th anniv.

A1048

Balkanfila '91 Philatelic Exhibition: 4 l, Flowers, by Nicu Enea. 5 l, Peasant Girl of Vlasca, by Georghe Tattarescu. 20 l, Sports Center, Bacau.

1991, Sept. 20

3688 A1048 4 l multicolored .35 .25
3689 A1048 5 l multicolored .35 .25

Souvenir Sheet

3690 A1048 20 l multicolored 1.50 1.50

No. 3689 printed se-tenant with 2 l Romanian Philatelic Assoc. label. No. 3690 contains one 54x42mm stamp.

For surcharge see No. 4463.

Miniature Sheets

A1049

Birds: No. 3691a, Cissa erythrorhyncha. b, Malaconotus blanchoti. c, Sialia sialis. d, Sturnella neglecta. e, Harpactes fasciatus. f, Upupa epops. g, Malurus cyaneus. h, Brachypteracias squamigera. i, Leptopterus madagascariensis. j, Phoeniculus bollei. k, Melanerpes erythrocephalus. l, Pericrocotus flammeus.

No. 3692a, Melithreptus laetior. b, Rhynochetos jubatus. c, Turdus migratorius. d, Copsychus saularis. e, Monticola saxatilis. f, Xanthocephalus xanthocephalus. g, Scotopelia peli. h, Ptilogonys caudatus. i, Todus mexicanus. j, Copsychus malabaricus. k, Myzomela erythrocephala. l, Gymnostinops montezuma.

1991, Oct. 7 **Sheets of 12**

3691 A1049 2 l #a.-l. 2.50 2.50
3692 A1049 2 l #a.-l. 2.50 2.50

Natl. Census — A1050

1991, Oct. 15

3693 A1050 5 l multicolored .35 .25

Phila Nippon '91 — A1051

1991, Nov. 13 **Photo.** ***Perf. 13½***

3694 A1051 10 l Sailing ship .65 .25
3695 A1051 10 l Bridge building .65 .25

Miniature Sheets

Butterflies and Moths — A1052

Designs: No. 3696a, Ornithoptera paradisea. b, Bhutanitis lidderdalii. c, Morpho helena. d, Ornithoptera croesus. e, Phoebis avellaneda. f, Ornithoptera victoriae. g, Teinopalpus imperialis. h, Hypolimnas dexithea. i, Dabasa payeni. j, Morpho achilleana. k, Heliconius melpomene. l, Agrias claudina sardanapalus.

No. 3697a, Graellsia isabellae. b, Antocharis cardamines. c, Ammobiota festiva. d, Polygonia c-album. e, Catocala promisa. f, Rhyparia purpurata. g, Arctia villica. h, Polyommatus daphnis. i, Zerynthia polyxena. j, Daphnis nerii. k, Licaena dispar rutila. l, Pararge roxelana.

1991, Nov. 30 **Photo.** ***Perf. 13½***
Sheets of 12

3696 A1052 3 l #a.-l. 3.00 3.00
3697 A1052 3 l #a.-l. 3.00 3.00

For surcharges see #4266-4267.

A1053

1991, Nov. 21 **Photo.** ***Perf. 13½***

3698 A1053 1 l Running .25 .25
3699 A1053 4 l Long jump .25 .25
3700 A1053 5 l High jump .25 .25
3701 A1053 5 l Runner in blocks .25 .25
3702 A1053 9 l Hurdles .45 .25
3703 A1053 10 l Javelin .50 .25
Nos. 3698-3703 (6) 1.95 1.50

World Track and Field Championships, Tokyo.

A1054

Famous People: 1 l, Mihail Kogalniceanu (1817-1891), politician. 4 l, Nicolae Titulescu (1882-1941), politician. No. 3706, Andrei Mureseanu (1816-1863), author. No. 3707, Aron Pumnul (1818-1866), author. 9 l, George Bacovia (1881-1957), author. 10 l, Perpessicius (1891-1971), writer.

1991, Dec. 10 **Photo.** ***Perf. 13½***

3704 A1054 1 l multi .25 .25
3705 A1054 4 l multi .25 .25
3706 A1054 5 l multi .25 .25
3707 A1054 5 l multi .25 .25
3708 A1054 9 l multi .60 .25
3709 A1054 10 l multi .70 .25
Nos. 3704-3709 (6) 2.30 1.50

See Nos. 3759-3761, 3776-3781.
For surcharges see Nos. 4238A-4248.

Stamp Day — A1055

1991, Dec. 20

3710 A1055 8 l + 2 l label .50 .25

Central University Library, Bucharest, Cent. A1056

1991, Dec. 23

3711 A1056 8 l red brown .50 .25

Christmas A1057

1991, Dec. 25 **Photo.** ***Perf. 13½***

3712 A1057 8 l multicolored .50 .25

See No. 3874.

1992 Winter Olympics, Albertville A1058

1992, Feb. 1 **Photo.** ***Perf. 13½***

3713 A1058 4 l Biathlon .25 .25
3714 A1058 5 l Alpine skiing .25 .25
3715 A1058 8 l Cross-country skiing .25 .25
3716 A1058 10 l Two-man luge .25 .25
3717 A1058 20 l Speed skating .35 .25
3718 A1058 25 l Ski jumping .40 .25
3719 A1058 30 l Ice hockey .50 .25
3720 A1058 45 l Men's figure skating .65 .25
Nos. 3713-3720 (8) 2.90 2.00

Souvenir Sheets

3721 A1058 75 l Women's figure skating 2.50 2.50

Imperf

3722 A1058 125 l 4-Man bobsled 7.00 7.00

No. 3721 is airmail and contains one 42x54mm stamp.

For surcharge see No. 4464.

Porcelain — A1059

Designs: 4 l, Sugar and cream service. 5 l, Tea service. 8 l, Goblet and pitcher, vert. 30 l, Tea service, diff. 45 l, Vase, vert.

1992, Feb. 20 **Photo.** ***Perf. 13½***

3723 A1059 4 l multicolored .25 .25
3724 A1059 5 l multicolored .25 .25
3725 A1059 8 l multicolored .25 .25
3726 A1059 30 l multicolored .45 .25
3727 A1059 45 l multicolored .65 .35
Nos. 3723-3727 (5) 1.85 1.35

Fish A1060

Designs: 4 l, Scomber scombrus. 5 l, Tinca tinca. 8 l, Salvelinus fontinalis. 10 l, Romanichthys valsanicola. 30 l, Chondrostoma nasus. 45 l, Mullus barbatus ponticus.

1992, Feb. 28 **Photo.** ***Perf. 13½***

3728 A1060 4 l multicolored .25 .25
3729 A1060 5 l multicolored .25 .25
3730 A1060 8 l multicolored .25 .25
3731 A1060 10 l multicolored .25 .25
3732 A1060 30 l multicolored .35 .25
3733 A1060 45 l multicolored .60 .25
Nos. 3728-3733 (6) 1.95 1.50

A1060a

1992, Mar. 11 Photo. *Perf. 13½*
3734 A1060a 90 l on 5 l multi 1.50 .35

No. 3734 not issued without surcharge.

Gymnastics Type of 1991 Surcharged

1992, Mar. 11 Photo. *Perf. 13½*
3735 A1041 90 l on 5 l like #3657 1.50 .35

No. 3735 not issued without surcharge.

Horses A1061

Various stylized drawings of horses walking, running, or jumping.

1992, Mar. 17 Photo. *Perf. 13½*
3736 A1061 6 l multi, vert. .25 .25
3737 A1061 7 l multi .25 .25
3738 A1061 10 l multi, vert. .25 .25
3739 A1061 25 l multi, vert. .35 .25
3740 A1061 30 l multi .45 .25
3741 A1061 50 l multi, vert. .65 .25
Nos. 3736-3741 (6) 2.20 1.50

Miniature Sheet

Discovery of America, 500th Anniv. — A1062

Columbus and ships: a, Green background. b, Violet background. c, Blue background. d, Ship approaching island.

1992, Apr. 22 Photo. *Perf. 13½*
3742 A1062 35 l Sheet of 4, #a.-d. 17.50 17.50

Europa.

Granada '92, Philatelic Exhibition — A1063

a, 25 l, Spain No. 1 and Romania No. 1. b, 10 l, Expo emblem. c, 30 l, Building and courtyard, Granada

1992, Apr. 24 Photo. *Perf. 13½*
3743 A1063 Sheet of 3, #a.-c. 1.60 1.60

Icon of Christ's Descent into Hell, 1680 — A1064

1992, Apr. 24 Photo. *Perf. 13½*
3744 A1064 10 l multicolored .35 .25

Easter.

Fire Station, Bucharest, Cent. — A1065

1992, May 2
3745 A1065 10 l multicolored .50 .25

Chess Olympiad, Manila — A1066

No. 3747, Building, chess board. 75 l, Shore, chess board.

1992, June 7 *Perf. 13½*
3746 A1066 10 l shown .30 .25
3747 A1066 10 l multicolored .30 .25

Souvenir Sheet

3748 A1066 75 l multicolored 1.75 1.75

No. 3748 contains one 42x54mm stamp.

1992 Summer Olympics, Barcelona — A1067

1992, July 17 Photo. *Perf. 13½*
3749 A1067 6 l Shooting, vert. .25 .25
3750 A1067 7 l Weight lifting, vert. .25 .25
3751 A1067 9 l Two-man canoeing .25 .25
3752 A1067 10 l Handball, vert. .25 .25
3753 A1067 25 l Wrestling .25 .25
3754 A1067 30 l Fencing .35 .25
3755 A1067 50 l Running, vert. .40 .25
3756 A1067 55 l Boxing .50 .25
Nos. 3749-3756 (8) 2.50 2.00

Souvenir Sheets

3757 A1067 100 l Rowing 1.00 1.00

Imperf

3758 A1067 200 l Gymnastics 5.00 5.00

Nos. 3757-3758 are airmail. No. 3757 contains one 54x42mm stamp, No. 3758 one 40x53mm stamp.

Famous People Type of 1991

Designs: 10 l, Ion I. C. Bratianu (1864-1927), prime minister. 25 l, Ion Gh. Duca (1879-1933). 30 l, Grigore Gafencu (1892-1957), journalist and politician.

1992, July 27 Photo. *Perf. 13½*
3759 A1054 10 l green & violet .25 .25
3760 A1054 25 l blue & lake .25 .25
3761 A1054 30 l lake & blue .25 .25
Nos. 3759-3761 (3) .75 .75

Expo '92, Seville A1068

Designs: 6 l, The Thinker, Cernavoda. 7 l, Trajan's bridge, Drobeta. 10 l, Mill. 25 l, Railroad bridge, Cernavoda. 30 l, Trajan Vuia's flying machine. 55 l, Herman Oberth's rocket. 100 l, Prayer sculpture, by C. Brancusi.

1992, Sept. 1
3762 A1068 6 l multicolored .25 .25
3763 A1068 7 l multicolored .25 .25
3764 A1068 10 l multicolored .25 .25
3765 A1068 25 l multicolored .25 .25
3766 A1068 30 l multicolored .25 .25
3767 A1068 55 l multicolored .50 .25
Nos. 3762-3767 (6) 1.75 1.50

Souvenir Sheet

3768 A1068 100 l multicolored .75 .75

No. 3768 contains one 42x54mm stamp.

World Post Day — A1069

1992, Oct. 9
3769 A1069 10 l multicolored .35 .25

For surcharge see No. 3945.

Discovery of America, 500th Anniv. — A1070

Columbus and: 6 l, Santa Maria. 10 l, Nina. 25 l, Pinta. 55 l, Arrival in New World. 100 l, Sailing ship, vert.

1992, Oct. 30 Photo. *Perf. 13½*
3770 A1070 6 l multicolored .25 .25
3771 A1070 10 l multicolored .25 .25
3772 A1070 25 l multicolored .30 .25
3773 A1070 55 l multicolored .50 .25
Nos. 3770-3773 (4) 1.30 1.00

Souvenir Sheet

3774 A1070 100 l multicolored 1.00 1.00

No. 3774 contains one 42x54mm stamp.

Romanian Postal Reorganization, 1st Anniv. — A1071

1992, Nov. 5 Photo. *Perf. 13½*
3775 A1071 10 l multicolored .35 .25

For surcharge see No. 4113.

Famous People Type of 1991

Designs: 6 l, Iacob Negruzzi (1842-1932), author. 7 l, Grigore Antipa (1867-1944), naturalist. 9 l, Alexe Mateevici (1888-1917), poet. 10 l, Cezar Petrescu (1892-1961), author. 25 l, Octav Onicescu (1892-1983), mathematician. 30 l, Ecaterina Teodoroiu (1894-1917), World War I soldier.

1992, Nov. 9 Photo. *Perf. 13½*
3776 A1054 6 l green & violet .25 .25
3777 A1054 7 l lilac & green .25 .25
3778 A1054 9 l gray blue & pur .25 .25
3779 A1054 10 l brown & blue .25 .25
3780 A1054 25 l blue & brown .25 .25
3781 A1054 30 l slate & blue .30 .25
Nos. 3776-3781 (6) 1.55 1.50

Wild Animals — A1072

Designs: 6 l, Haliaeetus leucocephalus, vert. 7 l, Strix occidentalis, vert. 9 l, Ursus arctos, vert. 10 l, Haematopus bachmani. 25 l, Canis lupus. 30 l, Odocoileus virginianus. 55 l, Alces alces.

1992, Nov. 16 Litho. *Perf. 13½*
3782 A1072 6 l multicolored .25 .25
3783 A1072 7 l multicolored .25 .25
3784 A1072 9 l multicolored .25 .25
3785 A1072 10 l multicolored .25 .25
3786 A1072 25 l multicolored .25 .25
3787 A1072 30 l multicolored .30 .25
3788 A1072 55 l multicolored .60 .25
Nos. 3782-3788 (7) 2.15 1.75

Souvenir Sheet

3789 A1072 100 l Orcinus orca .90 .90

Romanian Anniversaries and Events — A1073

7 l, Building, Galea Victoria St., 300th anniv. 9 l, Statue, School of Commerce, 600th anniv. 10 l, Curtea de Arges Monastery, 475th anniv. 25 l, School of Architecture, Bucharest, 80th anniv.

1992, Dec. 3 Photo. *Perf. 13½*
3790 A1073 7 l multicolored .25 .25
3791 A1073 9 l multicolored .25 .25
3792 A1073 10 l multicolored .25 .25
3793 A1073 25 l multicolored .25 .25
Nos. 3790-3793 (4) 1.00 1.00

For surcharges see No. 4465-4466.

Natl. Arms — A1074

1992, Dec. 7
3794 A1074 15 l multicolored .25 .25

Christmas A1075

1992, Dec. 15

3795	A1075	15 l multicolored	.35	.25

For surcharge see No. 4249.

New Telephone Numbering System A1076

1992, Dec. 28 Photo. *Perf. 13½*

3796	A1076	15 l blue, blk & red	.35	.25

For surcharges see #4268-4272.

Souvenir Sheets

1992 Summer Olympics, Barcelona A1077

No. 3797: a, Shooting. b, Wrestling. c, Weight lifting. d, Boxing.
No. 3798: a, Women's gymnastics. b, Four-man sculls. c, Fencing. d, High jump.

1992, Dec. 30 Photo. *Perf. 13½*

3797	A1077	35 l Sheet of 4, #a.-d.	*1.00*	*1.00*
3798	A1077	35 l Sheet of 4, #a.-d.	*1.00*	*1.00*

Historic Sites, Bucharest — A1078

Designs: 10 l, Mihai Voda Monastery. 15 l, Vacaresti Monastery. 25 l, Multi-purpose hall. 30 l, Mina Minovici Medical Institute.

1993, Feb. 11 Photo. *Perf. 13½*

3799	A1078	10 l multicolored	.25	.25
3800	A1078	15 l multicolored	.25	.25
3801	A1078	25 l multicolored	.25	.25
3802	A1078	30 l multicolored	.25	.25
		Nos. 3799-3802 (4)	1.00	1.00

Easter — A1079

1993, Mar. 25

3803	A1079	15 l multicolored	.25	.25

Medicinal Plants — A1080

10 l, Crataegus monogyna. 15 l, Gentiana phlogifolia. 25 l, Hippophae rhamnoides. 30 l, Vaccinium myrtillus. 50 l, Arnica montana. 90 l, Rosa canina.

1993, Mar. 30

3804	A1080	10 l multi	.25	.25
3805	A1080	15 l multi	.25	.25
3806	A1080	25 l multi	.25	.25
3807	A1080	30 l multi	.25	.25
3808	A1080	50 l multi	.35	.25
3809	A1080	90 l multi	.65	.25
		Nos. 3804-3809 (6)	2.00	1.50

Nichita Stanescu (1933-1983), Poet — A1081

1993, Mar. 31

3810	A1081	15 l brown and blue	.25	.25

Souvenir Sheet

Polska '93 — A1082

1993, Apr. 28 Photo. *Perf. 13½*

3811	A1082	200 l multicolored	1.10	1.10

Birds A1083

5 l, Pica pica. 10 l, Aquila chrysaetos. 15 l, Pyrrhula pyrrhula. 20 l, Upupa epops. 25 l, Dendrocopos major. 50 l, Oriolus oriolus. 65 l, Loxia leucoptera. 90 l, Hirundo rustica. 160 l, Parus cyanus. 250 l, Sturnus roseus.

1993, Apr. 30

3812	A1083	5 l multi	.25	.25
3813	A1083	10 l multi	.25	.25
3814	A1083	15 l multi	.25	.25
3815	A1083	20 l multi	.25	.25
3816	A1083	25 l multi	.25	.25
3817	A1083	50 l multi	.25	.25
3818	A1083	65 l multi	.25	.25
3819	A1083	90 l multi	.30	.25
3820	A1083	160 l multi	.50	.25
3821	A1083	250 l multi	.65	.25
		Nos. 3812-3821 (10)	3.20	2.50

Nos. 3812-3813 are horiz.

Cats — A1084

Various cats.

1993, May 24 Photo. *Perf. 13½*

3822	A1084	10 l multicolored	.25	.25
3823	A1084	15 l multicolored	.25	.25
3824	A1084	30 l multicolored	.25	.25
3825	A1084	90 l multicolored	.35	.25
3826	A1084	135 l multicolored	.45	.25
3827	A1084	160 l multicolored	.60	.25
		Nos. 3822-3827 (6)	2.15	1.50

Souvenir Sheet

Europa — A1085

Paintings and sculpture by: a, Pablo Picasso. b, Constantin Brancusi. c, Ion Irimescu. d, Alexandru Ciucurencu.

1993, May 31 Photo. *Perf. 13½*

3828	A1085	280 l Sheet of 4, #a.-d.	*4.00*	*4.00*

A1086

1993, June 30 Photo. *Perf. 13½*

3829	A1086	10 l Vipera berus	.25	.25
3830	A1086	15 l Lynx lynx	.25	.25
3831	A1086	25 l Tadorna tadorna	.25	.25
3832	A1086	75 l Hucho hucho	.40	.25
3833	A1086	105 l Limenitis populi	.50	.25
3834	A1086	280 l Rosalia alpina	.75	.25
		Nos. 3829-3834 (6)	2.40	1.50

Nos. 3829, 3831-3834 are horiz.

A1087

10 l, Martes martes. 15 l, Oryctolagus cuniculus. 20 l, Sciurus vulgaris. 25 l, Rupicapra rupicapra. 30 l, Vulpes vulpes. 40 l, Ovis ammon. 75 l, Genetta genetta. 105 l, Eliomys quercinus. 150 l, Mustela erminea. 280 l, Herpestes ichneumon.

1993, June 30

3835	A1087	10 l multi	.25	.25
3836	A1087	15 l multi	.25	.25
3837	A1087	20 l multi	.25	.25
3838	A1087	25 l multi	.25	.25
3839	A1087	30 l multi	.25	.25
3840	A1087	40 l multi	.25	.25
3841	A1087	75 l multi	.25	.25
3842	A1087	105 l multi	.40	.25
3843	A1087	150 l multi	.45	.25
3844	A1087	280 l multi	1.00	.25
		Nos. 3835-3844 (10)	3.60	2.50

Nos. 3836, 3839, 3843-3844 are horiz.
For surcharges see Nos. 4427-4428.

Dinosaurs — A1088

1993, July 30 Photo. *Perf. 13½*

3845	A1088	29 l Brontosaurus	.25	.25
3846	A1088	46 l Plesiosaurus	.25	.25
3847	A1088	85 l Triceratops	.30	.25
3848	A1088	171 l Stegosaurus	.65	.25
3849	A1088	216 l Tyrannosaurus	.75	.25
3850	A1088	319 l Archaeopteryx	1.00	.25
		Nos. 3845-3850 (6)	3.20	1.50

Souvenir Sheet

Telafila '93, Israel-Romanian Philatelic Exhibition — A1089

Woman with Eggs, by Marcel Iancu.

1993, Aug. 21

3851	A1089	535 l multicolored	1.75	1.75

Icons — A1090

Designs: 75 l, St. Stephen. 171 l, Martyrs from Brancoveanu and Vacarescu families. 216 l, St. Anthony.

1993, Aug. 31

3852	A1090	75 l multicolored	.25	.25
3853	A1090	171 l multicolored	.30	.25
3854	A1090	216 l multicolored	.70	.35
		Nos. 3852-3854 (3)	1.25	.85

Rural Mounted Police, Cent. — A1091

1993, Sept. 1
3855 A1091 29 l multicolored .25 .25

No. 3618 Surcharged in Red

1993, Sept. 3
3856 A1031 171 l on 2 l multi .60 .25

Souvenir Sheet

Bangkok '93 — A1092

1993, Sept. 20
3857 A1092 535 l multicolored 1.75 1.75

Famous Men — A1093

Designs: 29 l, George Baritiu (1812-93), politician. 46 l, Horia Creanga (1892-1943), architect. 85 l, Armand Calinescu (1893-1939), politician. 171 l, Dumitru Bagdasar (1893-1946), physician. 216 l, Constantin Brailoiu (1893-1958), musician. 319 l, Iuliu Maniu (1873-1953), politician.

1993, Oct. 8
3858 A1093 29 l multicolored .25 .25
3859 A1093 46 l multicolored .25 .25
3860 A1093 85 l multicolored .25 .25
3861 A1093 171 l multicolored .30 .25
3862 A1093 216 l multicolored .35 .25
3863 A1093 319 l multicolored .60 .25
Nos. 3858-3863 (6) 2.00 1.50

For surcharge see No. 4407.

Souvenir Sheet

Romanian Entry into Council of Europe — A1094

1993, Nov. 26 Photo. *Perf. 13½*
3864 A1094 1590 l multi 3.50 3.50

Expansion of Natl. Borders, 75th Anniv. — A1095

Government leaders: 115 l, Iancu Flondor (1865-1924). 245 l, Ion I. C. Bratianu (1864-1927). 255 l, Iuliu Maniu (1873-1953). 325 l, Pantelimon Halippa (1883-1979). 1060 l, King Ferdinand I (1865-1927).

1993-94
3865 A1095 115 l multi .25 .25
3866 A1095 245 l multi .50 .25
3867 A1095 255 l multi .50 .25
3868 A1095 325 l multi .75 .35
Nos. 3865-3868 (4) 2.00 1.10

Souvenir Sheet

3869 A1095 1060 l Romania in one color 2.50 2.50
a. Romania in four colors *8.00 8.00*

No. 3869a was redrawn because of an error in the map.
Issued: No. 3869, Feb. 1994; Nos. 3865-3868, 3869a, Dec. 1, 1993.
For surcharge see No. 4472.

Anniversaries and Events A1096

Designs: 115 l, Emblem of the Diplomatic Alliance. 245 l, Statue of Johannes Honterus, founder of first Humanitarian School. 255 l, Arms, seal of Slatina, Olt River Bridge. 325 l, Map, arms of Braila.

1993, Dec. 15
3870 A1096 115 l multicolored .25 .25
3871 A1096 245 l multicolored .55 .25
3872 A1096 255 l multicolored .55 .25
3873 A1096 325 l multicolored .55 .30
Nos. 3870-3873 (4) 1.90 1.05

Diplomatic Alliance, 75th anniv. (#3870). Birth of Johannes Honterus, 450th anniv. (#3871). City of Slatina, 625th anniv. (#3872). County of Braila, 625th anniv. (#3873).
For surcharge see No. 4473.

Christmas Type of 1991

1993, Dec. 20
3874 A1057 45 l like #3712 .25 .25

Insects, Wildlife from Movile Cavern — A1097

Designs: 29 l, Clivina subterranea. 46 l, Nepa anophthalma. 85 l, Haemopis caeca. 171 l, Lascona cristiani. 216 l, Semisalsa dobrogica. 319 l, Armadilidium tabacarui. 535 l, Exploring cavern, vert.

1993, Dec. 27
3875 A1097 29 l multicolored .25 .25
3876 A1097 46 l multicolored .25 .25
3877 A1097 85 l multicolored .25 .25
3878 A1097 171 l multicolored .40 .25
3879 A1097 216 l multicolored .55 .25
3880 A1097 319 l multicolored .80 .25
Nos. 3875-3880 (6) 2.50 1.50

Souvenir Sheet

3881 A1097 535 l multicolored 1.50 1.50

Alexandru Ioan Cuza — A1098

1994, Jan. 24 Photo. *Perf. 13*
3882 A1098 45 l multicolored .25 .25

Historic Buildings, Bucharest — A1099

115 l, Opera House. 245 l, Vacaresti Monastery. 255 l, Church of St. Vineri. 325 l, Dominican House, Vacaresti Monastery.

1994, Feb. 7
3883 A1099 115 l multicolored .25 .25
3884 A1099 245 l multicolored .45 .25
3885 A1099 255 l multicolored .60 .25
3886 A1099 325 l multicolored .60 .25
Nos. 3883-3886 (4) 1.90 1.00

For surcharge see No. 4482.

1994 Winter Olympics, Lillehammer A1100

1994, Feb. 12 *Perf. 13½*
3887 A1100 70 l Speed skating .25 .25
3888 A1100 115 l Slalom skiing .25 .25
3889 A1100 125 l Bobsled .30 .25
3890 A1100 245 l Biathlon .40 .25
3891 A1100 255 l Ski jumping .40 .25
3892 A1100 325 l Figure skating .60 .25
Nos. 3887-3892 (6) 2.20 1.50

Souvenir Sheet

3893 A1100 1590 l Luge 3.00 3.00

No. 3893 contains one 43x54mm stamp.

Mills — A1101

1994, Mar. 31 *Perf. 13*
3894 A1101 70 l Sarichioi .25 .25
3895 A1101 115 l Valea Nucarilor .25 .25
3896 A1101 125 l Caraorman .30 .25
3897 A1101 245 l Romanii de Jos .40 .25
3898 A1101 255 l Enisala, horiz. .45 .25
3899 A1101 325 l Nistoresti .60 .30
Nos. 3894-3899 (6) 2.25 1.55

For surcharges see Nos. 4431-4434.

Dinosaurs — A1102

90 l, Struthiosaurs. 130 l, Megalosaurs. 150 l, Parasaurolophus. 280 l, Stenonychosaurus. 500 l, Camarasaurus. 635 l, Gallimimus.

1994, Apr. 30 Photo. *Perf. 13½*
3900 A1102 90 l multi .25 .25
3901 A1102 130 l multi .25 .25
3902 A1102 150 l multi .30 .25
3903 A1102 280 l multi .40 .25
3904 A1102 500 l multi .50 .25
3905 A1102 635 l multi .60 .30
Nos. 3900-3905 (6) 2.30 1.55

For surcharge see No. 4467.

Romanian Legends A1103

Designs: 70 l, Calin the Madman. 115 l, Ileana Cosanzeana. 125 l, Ileana Cosanzeana, diff. 245 l, Ileana Cosanzeana, diff. 255 l, Agheran the Brave. 325 l, Wolf as Prince Charming, Ileana Cosanzeana.

1994, Apr. 8 Photo. *Perf. 13½*
3906 A1103 70 l multicolored .25 .25
3907 A1103 115 l multicolored .25 .25
3908 A1103 125 l multicolored .30 .25
3909 A1103 245 l multicolored .45 .25
3910 A1103 255 l multicolored .45 .25
3911 A1103 325 l multicolored .65 .30
Nos. 3906-3911 (6) 2.35 1.55

For surcharge see No. 4474.

Easter A1104

1994, Apr. 21
3912 A1104 60 l multicolored .25 .25

Trees — A1105

No. 3913, Abies alba. No. 3914, Pinus sylvestris. No. 3915, Populus alba. No. 3916, Quercus robur. No. 3917, Larix decidua. No. 3918, Fagus sylvatica. No. 3919, Acer pseudoplatanus. No. 3920, Fraxinus excelsior. No. 3921, Picea abies. No. 3922, Tilia platyphyllos.

Wmk. 398

1994, May 27 Photo. *Perf. 13¼*

3913	A1105	15 l multi	.25	.25
3914	A1105	35 l multi	.25	.25
3915	A1105	45 l multi	.25	.25
3916	A1105	60 l multi	.25	.25
3917	A1105	70 l multi	.25	.25
3918	A1105	125 l multi	.25	.25
3919	A1105	350 l multi	.40	.25
3920	A1105	940 l multi	1.25	.25
3921	A1105	1440 l multi	1.75	.25
3922	A1105	3095 l multi	3.50	.25
		Nos. 3913-3922 (10)	8.40	2.50

For surcharges see Nos. 4221-4224, 4422-4424.

1994 World Cup Soccer Championships, US — A1106

1994, June 17 Unwmk.

3923	A1106	90 l Group A	.25	.25
3924	A1106	130 l Group B	.25	.25
3925	A1106	150 l Group C	.30	.25
3926	A1106	280 l Group D	.50	.25
3927	A1106	500 l Group E	.55	.25
3928	A1106	635 l Group F	.70	.25
		Nos. 3923-3928 (6)	2.55	1.50

Souvenir Sheet

3929	A1106	2075 l Action scene	3.00	3.00

No. 3929 is airmail and contains one 54x42mm stamp.

Intl. Olympic Committee, Cent. — A1107

Ancient Olympians: 150 l, Torchbearer. 280 l, Discus thrower. 500 l, Wrestlers. 635 l, Arbitrator.

2075 l, Runners, emblem of Romanian Olympic Committee.

1994, June 23

3930	A1107	150 l multicolored	.25	.25
3931	A1107	280 l multicolored	.45	.25
3932	A1107	500 l multicolored	.60	.25
3933	A1107	635 l multicolored	1.20	.25
		Nos. 3930-3933 (4)	2.50	1.00

Souvenir Sheet

3934	A1107	2075 l multicolored	3.00	3.00

No. 3934 contains one 54x42mm stamp. Romanian Olympic Committee, 80th anniv. (#3934).

Miniature Sheets

Mushrooms — A1108

Edible: No. 3935a, 30 l, Craterellus cornucopiodes. b, 60 l, Lepista nuda. c, 150 l, Boletus edulis. d, 940 l, Lycoperdon perlatum.

Poisonous: No. 3936a, 90 l, Boletus satanas. b, 280 l, Amanita phalloides. c, 350 l, Inocybe patonillardi. d, 500 l, Amanita muscaria.

1994, Aug. 8 Photo. *Perf. 13½*

3935	A1108	Sheet of 4, #a.-d.	2.00	2.00
3936	A1108	Sheet of 4, #a.-d.	2.00	2.00
		Complete booklet, #3935-3936	4.50	

PHILAKOREA '94 — A1109

1994, Aug. 16 *Perf. 13½*

3937	A1109	60 l Tuning fork	.30	.25

Souvenir Sheet

3938	A1109	2075 l Korean drummer	2.75	2.75

No. 3938 contains one 42x54mm stamp.

Environmental Protection in Danube River Delta — A1110

Designs: 150 l, Huso huso. 280 l, Vipera ursini. 500 l, Haliaeetus albicilla. 635 l, Mustela lutreola.

2075 l, Periploca graeca.

1994, Aug. 31

3939	A1110	150 l multicolored	.25	.25
3940	A1110	280 l multicolored	.50	.25
3941	A1110	500 l multicolored	.95	.30
3942	A1110	635 l multicolored	1.10	.35
		Nos. 3939-3942 (4)	2.80	1.15

Souvenir Sheet

3943	A1110	2075 l multi	3.00	3.00

No. 3943 contains one 54x42mm stamp.

Nos. 3654-3655 Surcharged

No. 3769 Surcharged

1994 *Perfs., Etc. as Before*

3944	A1041	150 l on 4.50 l #3654	.25	.25
3945	A1069	150 l on 10 l #3769	.30	.25
3946	A1041	525 l on 4.50 l #3655	.90	.30
		Nos. 3944-3946 (3)	1.45	.80

Issued: #3944, 3946 9/9/94; #3945, 10/7/94.

Circus Animal Acts — A1111

Designs: 90 l, Elephant. 130 l, Bear, vert. 150 l, Monkeys. 280 l, Tiger. 500 l, Tightrope walker, dogs. 635 l, Horse.

1994, Sept. 15 Photo. *Perf. 13*

3947	A1111	90 l multicolored	.25	.25
3948	A1111	130 l multicolored	.25	.25
3949	A1111	150 l multicolored	.30	.25
3950	A1111	280 l multicolored	.50	.25
3951	A1111	500 l multicolored	.65	.25
3952	A1111	635 l multicolored	.90	.25
		Nos. 3947-3952 (6)	2.85	1.50

20th Intl. Fair, Bucharest — A1112

1994, Oct. 10

3953	A1112	525 l multicolored	.90	.30

Fish — A1113

World Wildlife Fund: 150 l, Acipenser ruthenus. 280 l, Acipenser guldenstaedti. 500 l, Acipenser stellatus. 635 l, Acipenser sturio.

1994, Oct. 29 Photo. *Perf. 13½*

3954	A1113	150 l multicolored	.30	.25
3955	A1113	280 l multicolored	.50	.25
3956	A1113	500 l multicolored	.75	.25
3957	A1113	635 l multicolored	1.00	.25
		Nos. 3954-3957 (4)	2.55	1.00

Issued in sheets of 10.

Chinese-Romanian Philatelic Exhibition — A1114

1994, Oct. 29 Photo. *Perf. 13½*

3958	A1114	150 l Serpent	.30	.25
3959	A1114	1135 l Dragon	1.60	.30
a.		Pair, #3958-3959 + label	2.00	.60

Romanian State Railway, 125th Anniv. A1115

1994, Oct. 31

3960	A1115	90 l multicolored	.25	.25

Famous People A1116

Designs: 30 l, Alexandru Orascu (1817-94). 60 l, Gh. Polizu (1819-86). 90 l, Gheorghe Tattarescu (1820-94), politician, prime minister. 150 l, Iulia Hasdeu (1869-88). 280 l, S. Mehedinti (1869-1962). 350 l, Camil Petrescu (1894-1957). 500 l, N. Paulescu (1869-1931). 940 l, L. Grigorescu (1894-1965).

1994 Photo. *Perf. 13½*

3961	A1116	30 l multicolored	.25	.25
3962	A1116	60 l multicolored	.25	.25
3962A	A1116	90 l multicolored	.25	.25
3963	A1116	150 l multicolored	.30	.25
3964	A1116	280 l multicolored	.30	.25
3965	A1116	350 l multicolored	.45	.25
3966	A1116	500 l multicolored	.50	.25
3967	A1116	940 l multicolored	1.25	.25
		Nos. 3961-3967 (8)	3.55	2.00

Issued; 90 l, 12/28/94; others, 11/30/94.

Christmas — A1117

1994, Dec. 14 *Perf. 13½*

3968	A1117	60 l multicolored	.30	.25

For surcharge see No. 4250.

St. Mary's Romanian Orthodox Church, Cleveland, Ohio, 90th Anniv. — A1118

1994, Dec. 21 Photo. *Perf. 13½*

3969	A1118	610 l multicolored	.85	.30

World Tourism Organization, 20th Anniv. — A1119

1994, Dec. 22

3970	A1119	525 l multicolored	1.00	.30

Miniature Sheet

Romanian Military Decorations — A1120

Year of medal — No. 3971: a, 30 l, Distinguished Flying Cross, 1938. b, 60 l, Military Cross, 3rd class, 1916. c, 150 l, Distinguished Serivce Medal, 1st Class, 1880. d, 940 l, Order of the Romanian Star, 1877.

1994, Dec. 23
3971 A1120 Sheet of 4, #a.-d. 2.00 2.00

Baby Animals A1121

1994, Dec. 27 **Photo.** ***Perf. 13x½***

3972	A1121	90 l	Kittens	.25	.25
3973	A1121	130 l	Puppies	.25	.25
3974	A1121	150 l	Kid goat	.25	.25
3975	A1121	280 l	Foal	.30	.25
3976	A1121	500 l	Bunnies	.60	.25
3977	A1121	635 l	Lambs	.75	.25
			Nos. 3972-3977 (6)	2.40	1.50

For surcharge see No. 4468.

A1122

1995, Jan. 31 **Photo.** ***Perf. 13½***
3978 A1122 60 l dark blue .35 .25

Save the Children organization.

A1123

The Young Men of Brasov: 40 l, Tanar. 60 l, Batran. 150 l, Curcan. 280 l, Dorobant. 350 l, Brasovechean. 500 l, Rosior. 635 l, Albior.

1995, Feb. 25 **Photo.** ***Perf. 13½***

3979	A1123	40 l	multicolored	.25	.25
3980	A1123	60 l	multicolored	.25	.25
3981	A1123	150 l	multicolored	.25	.25
3982	A1123	280 l	multicolored	.30	.25
3983	A1123	350 l	multicolored	.50	.25
3984	A1123	500 l	multicolored	.60	.25
3985	A1123	635 l	multicolored	.75	.25
			Nos. 3979-3985 (7)	2.90	1.75

Liberation of Concentration Camps, 50th Anniv. — A1124

1995, Mar. 24 ***Perf. 13½***
3986 A1124 960 l black & red .85 .30

FAO & UN, 50th Anniv. A1125

Designs: 675 l, FAO emblem, grain. 960 l, "50," UN emblem. 1615 l, Hand holding pen with flags of UN Charter countries.

1995, Apr. 12 ***Perf. 13½***

3987	A1125	675 l	multicolored	.50	.25
3988	A1125	960 l	multicolored	.75	.25
3989	A1125	1615 l	multicolored	1.50	.25
			Nos. 3987-3989 (3)	2.75	.75

Easter A1126

1995, Apr. 14
3990 A1126 60 l multicolored .25 .25

Romanian Fairy Tales — A1127

Designs: 90 l, King riding horse across town. 130 l, Woman feeding animals, vert. 150 l, Man riding on winged horse. 280 l, Old man, young man. 500 l, Archer aiming at apple tree, vert. 635 l, Two people riding log pulled by galloping horses.

1995, Apr. 20 ***Perf. 13½***

3991	A1127	90 l	multicolored	.25	.25
3992	A1127	130 l	multicolored	.25	.25
3993	A1127	150 l	multicolored	.25	.25
3994	A1127	280 l	multicolored	.35	.25
3995	A1127	500 l	multicolored	.60	.25
3996	A1127	635 l	multicolored	.75	.25
			Nos. 3991-3996 (6)	2.45	1.50

For surcharge see No. 4405.

Georges Enescu (1881-1955), Composer — A1128

1995, May 5 ***Perf. 13½***
3997 A1128 960 l blk & dp yel .75 .30

Peace & Freedom A1129

Europa: 150 l, Dove carryng piece of rainbow. 4370 l, Dove under rainbow with wings forming "Europa."

1995, May 8

3998	A1129	150 l	multicolored	.25	.25
3999	A1129	4370 l	multicolored	6.00	6.00

Lucian Blaga (1895-1961), Poet — A1130

1995, May 9
4000 A1130 150 l multicolored .35 .25

See Nos. 4017-4021.

Methods of Transportation — A1131

Designs: 470 l, Bucharest Metro subway train, 1979. 675 l, Brasov aerial cable car, vert. 965 l, Sud Aviation SA 330 Puma helicopter. 2300 l, 1904 Trolleybus. 2550 l, Steam locomotive, 1869. 3410 l, Boeing 737-300.

1995, May 30 **Photo.** ***Perf. 13½***

4001	A1131	470 l	blk, gray & yel	.40	.25
4002	A1131	675 l	blk, gray & red	.55	.25
4003	A1131	965 l	bl, blk & gray	.80	.25
4004	A1131	2300 l	blk, gray & grn	2.00	.25
4005	A1131	2550 l	blk, gray & red	2.00	.25
4006	A1131	3410 l	bl, blk & gray	2.90	.25
			Nos. 4001-4006 (6)	8.65	1.50

Nos. 4003, 4006 are airmail. No. 4006, 75th anniversary of Romanian air transportation.

See Nos. 4055-4060.

Romanian Maritime Service, Cent. — A1132

Ships: 90 l, Dacia, liner, vert. 130 l, Imparatul Traian, steamer. 150 l, Romania, steamer. 280 l, Costinesti, tanker. 960 l, Caransebes, container ship. 3410 l, Tutova, car ferry.

1995, May 31 **Photo.** ***Perf. 13½***

4007	A1132	90 l	multicolored	.25	.25
4008	A1132	130 l	multicolored	.25	.25
4009	A1132	150 l	multicolored	.25	.25
4010	A1132	280 l	multicolored	.25	.25
4011	A1132	960 l	multicolored	.60	.25
4012	A1132	3410 l	multicolored	2.25	.50
			Nos. 4007-4012 (6)	3.85	1.75

For surcharge see No. 4469.

A1133

European Nature Conservation Year: 150 l, Dama dama. 280 l, Otis tarda. 960 l, Cypripedium caiceolus. 1615 l, Ghetarul scarisoara (stalagmites).

1995, June 5

4013	A1133	150 l	multicolored	.25	.25
4014	A1133	280 l	multicolored	.25	.25
4015	A1133	960 l	multicolored	.35	.50
4016	A1133	1615 l	multicolored	1.25	.50
			Nos. 4013-4016 (4)	2.10	1.50

Famous Romanians Type of 1995

Designs: 90 l, D.D. Rosca (1895-1980). 130 l, Vasile Conta (1845-1882). 280 l, Ion Barbu (1895-1961). 960 l, Iuliu Hatieganu (1885-1959). 1650 l, Dimitrie Brandza (1846-95).

1995, June 26 **Photo.** ***Perf. 13½***

4017	A1130	90 l	multicolored	.25	.25
4018	A1130	130 l	multicolored	.25	.25
4019	A1130	280 l	multicolored	.25	.25
4020	A1130	960 l	multicolored	.70	.25
4021	A1130	1650 l	multicolored	1.00	.25
			Nos. 4017-4021 (5)	2.45	1.25

For surcharge see No. 4470.

A1134

1995, July 10 **Photo.** ***Perf. 13½***
4022 A1134 1650 l multicolored 1.25 .40

European Youth Olympic days.

Stamp Day — A1135

1995, July 15
4023 A1135 960 l +715 l label 1.50 .40

Cernavoda Bridge, Cent. — A1136

1995, July 27 **Photo.** ***Perf. 13½***

4024	A1136	675 l	multicolored	.75	.40

A1137

Fowl: 90 l, Anas platyrhynchos. 130 l, Gallus gallus (hen). 150 l, Numida meleagris. 280 l, Meleagris gallopavo. 960 l, Anser anser. 1650 l, Gallus gallus (rooster).

1995, July 31 **Photo.** ***Perf. 13½***

4025	A1137	90 l	multicolored	.25	.25
4026	A1137	130 l	multicolored	.25	.25
4027	A1137	150 l	multicolored	.25	.25
4028	A1137	280 l	multicolored	.30	.25
4029	A1137	960 l	multicolored	.85	.25
4030	A1137	1650 l	multicolored	1.25	.25
			Nos. 4025-4030 (6)	3.15	1.50

For surcharge see No. 4471.

A1138

Institute of Air Medicine, 75th Anniv.: Gen. Dr. Victor Anastasiu (1886-1972).

1995, Aug. 5 **Photo.** ***Perf. 13½***

4031	A1138	960 l	multicolored	.80	.35

Battle of Calugareni, 400th Anniv. — A1139

1995, Aug. 13

4032	A1139	100 l	multicolored	.35	.25

Romanian Buildings — A1140

Structure, year completed: 250 l, Giurgiu Castle, 1395. 500 l, Neamtului Castle, 1395, vert. 960 l, Sebes-Alba Mill, 1245. 1615 l, Dorohoi Church, 1495, vert. 1650 l, Military Observatory, Bucharest, 1895, vert.

1995, Aug. 28

4033	A1140	250 l	multicolored	.25	.25
4034	A1140	500 l	multicolored	.30	.25
4035	A1140	960 l	multicolored	.50	.25
4036	A1140	1615 l	multicolored	.75	.25
4037	A1140	1650 l	multicolored	.90	.25
			Nos. 4033-4037 (5)	2.70	1.25

A1141

Buildings in Manastirea: 675 l, Moldovita Monastery. 960 l, Hurez Monastery. 1615 l, Biertan Castle, horiz.

1995, Aug. 31

4038	A1141	675 l	multicolored	.30	.25
4039	A1141	960 l	multicolored	.60	.25
4040	A1141	1615 l	multicolored	.90	.30
			Nos. 4038-4040 (3)	1.80	.80

A1142

1995, Sept. 8

4041	A1142	1020 l	multicolored	.85	.50

Romania Open Tennis Tournament, Bucharest.

Magazine "Mathematics," Cent. — A1143

Design: Ion N. Ionescu, founder.

1995, Sept. 15

4042	A1143	100 l	multicolored	.35	.25

Plants from Bucharest Botantical Garden — A1144

Designs: 50 l, Albizia julibrissin. 100 l, Taxus baccata. 150 l, Paulownia tomentosa. 500 l, Strelitzia reginae. 960 l, Victoria amazonica. 2300 l, Rhododendron indicum.

1995, Sept. 29 **Photo.** ***Perf. 13½***

4043	A1144	50 l	multicolored	.25	.25
4044	A1144	100 l	multicolored	.25	.25
4045	A1144	150 l	multicolored	.25	.25
4046	A1144	500 l	multicolored	.30	.25
4047	A1144	960 l	multicolored	.60	.25
4048	A1144	2300 l	multicolored	1.20	.30
			Nos. 4043-4048 (6)	2.85	1.55

Church of St. John — A1145

1995, Oct. 1 **Photo.** ***Perf. 13½***

4049	A1145	250 l	multi	.75	.50

City of Piatra Neamt, 600th anniv.

A1146

Emigres: 150 l, George Apostu (1934-86), sculptor. 250 l, Emil Cioran (1911-95), philosopher. 500 l, Eugen Ionescu (1909-94), writer. 960 l, Elena Vacarescu (1866-1947), writer. 1650 l, Mircea Eliade (1907-86), philosopher.

1995, Nov. 9

4050	A1146	150 l	grn, gray & blk	.25	.25
4051	A1146	250 l	bl, gray & blk	.25	.25
4052	A1146	500 l	tan, brn & blk	.40	.25
4053	A1146	960 l	lake, mag & blk	.80	.25
4054	A1146	1650 l	tan, brn & blk	1.20	.25
			Nos. 4050-4054 (5)	2.90	1.25

Transportation Type of 1995

285 l, IAR 80 fighter planes. 630 l, Training ship, Mesagerul. 715 l, IAR-316 Red Cross helicopter. 755 l, Cargo ship, Razboieni. 1575 l, IAR-818H seaplane. 1615 l, First electric tram, Bucharest, 1896, vert.

1995, Nov. 16

4055	A1131	285 l	blk, gray & grn	.25	.25
4056	A1131	630 l	bl & red	.35	.25
4057	A1131	715 l	gray bl & red	.35	.25
4058	A1131	755 l	blk, bl & gray	.40	.25
4059	A1131	1575 l	blk, grn & gray	.90	.25
4060	A1131	1615 l	blk, grn & gray	.75	.25
			Nos. 4055-4060 (6)	3.00	1.50

Nos. 4055, 4057, 4059 are air mail. For surcharges see Nos. 4475-4477.

1996 Summer Olympics, Atlanta — A1147

1995, Dec. 8

4061	A1147	50 l	Track	.25	.25
4062	A1147	100 l	Gymnastics	.25	.25
4063	A1147	150 l	Two-man canoe	.25	.25
4064	A1147	500 l	Fencing	.50	.25
4065	A1147	960 l	Rowing-eights	.85	.25
4066	A1147	2300 l	Boxing	2.00	.35
			Nos. 4061-4066 (6)	4.10	1.60

Souvenir Sheet

4067	A1147	2610 l	Gymnastics	2.50	2.50

No. 4067 contains one 42x54mm stamp.

Christmas A1148

100 l, The Holy Family.

1995, Dec. 15 **Photo.** ***Perf. 13½***

4068	A1148	100 l	multicolored	.35	.25

Folk Masks & Costumes — A1149

1996, Jan. 31

4069	A1149	250 l	Maramures	.30	.25
4070	A1149	500 l	Moldova	.50	.25
4071	A1149	960 l	Moldova, vert.	.80	.25
4072	A1149	1650 l	Moldova, diff., vert.	1.20	.25
			Nos. 4069-4072 (4)	2.80	1.00

Tristan Tzara (1896-1963), Writer — A1151

1500 l, Anton Pann (1796-1854), writer.

1996, Mar. 27 **Photo.** ***Perf. 13½***

4078	A1151	150 l	multicolored	.25	.25
4079	A1151	1500 l	multicolored	1.25	.25

Easter A1152

1996, Mar. 29

4080	A1152	150 l	multicolored	.35	.25

Romfilex '96, Romanian-Israeli Philatelic Exhibition — A1153

Paintings: a, 370 l, On the Terrace at Sinaia, by Theodor Aman. b, 150 l, The Post Office, by

M. Stoican. c, 1500 l, Old Jerusalem, by Reuven Rubin.

1996, Apr. 5

4081 A1153 Sheet of 3, #a.-c. 5.50 5.00

For surcharges see No. 4202.

Insects A1154

Designs: 70 l, Chrysomela vigintipunctata. 220 l, Cerambyx cerdo. 370 l, Entomoscelis adonidis. 650 l, Coccinella bipunctata. 700 l, Calosoma sycophanta. 740 l, Hedobia imperialis. 960 l, Oryctes nasicornis. 1000 l, Trichius fasciatus. 1500 l, Purpuricenus kaehleri. 2500 l, Anthaxia salicis.

1996

4082 A1154 70 l multicolored .25 .25
4083 A1154 220 l multicolored .25 .25
4084 A1154 370 l multicolored .25 .25
4085 A1154 650 l multicolored .30 .25
4086 A1154 700 l multicolored .30 .25
4087 A1154 740 l multicolored .45 .25
4088 A1154 960 l multicolored .60 .25
4089 A1154 1000 l multicolored .60 .25
4090 A1154 1500 l multicolored .90 .25
4091 A1154 2500 l multicolored 1.20 .30
Nos. 4082-4091 (10) 5.10 2.55

Issued: 220, 740, 960, 1000, 1500 l, 4/16/96; 70, 370, 650, 700, 2500 l, 6/10/96.

For surcharges see Nos. 4283-4289, 4375-4377.

Souvenir Sheet

Dumitru Prunariu, First Romanian Cosmonaut — A1155

1996, Apr. 22

4092 A1155 2720 l multicolored 1.50 1.50

ESPAMER '96, Aviation and Space Philatelic Exhibition, Seville, Spain.

For surcharges see Nos. 4829-4830.

1996 Summer Olympic Games, Atlanta — A1158

1996, July 12 Photo. *Perf. 13½*

4093 A1158 220 l Boxing .25 .25
4094 A1158 370 l Athletics .25 .25
4095 A1158 740 l Rowing .40 .25
4096 A1158 1500 l Judo .80 .25
4097 A1158 2550 l Gymnastics 1.75 .30
Nos. 4093-4097 (5) 3.45 1.30

Souvenir Sheet

4098 A1158 4050 l Gymnastics, diff. 2.75 2.00

No. 4098 is airmail and contains one 54x42mm stamp. Olymphilex '96 (#4098).

For surcharge see No. 4877.

UNESCO World Heritage Sites — A1159

Designs: 150 l, Arbore Church. 1500 l, Voronet Monastery. 2550 l, Humor Monastery.

1996, Apr. 24 Photo. *Perf. 13½*

4099 A1159 150 l multicolored .25 .25
4100 A1159 1500 l multicolored .80 .25
4101 A1159 2550 l multicolored 1.50 .35
Nos. 4099-4101 (3) 2.55 .85

Famous Women — A1160

Europa: 370 l, Ana Aslan (1897-1988), physician. 4140 l, Lucia Bulandra (1873-1961), actress.

1996, May 6

4102 A1160 370 l multicolored .25 .25
4103 A1160 4140 l multicolored 3.75 2.25
a. Pair, #4102-4103 + 2 labels 4.00 2.50

UNICEF, 50th Anniv. — A1161

Children's paintings: 370 l, Mother and children. 740 l, Winter Scene. 1500 l, Children and Sun over House. 2550 l, House on Stilts.

1996, May 25

4104 A1161 370 l multi .25 .25
4105 A1161 740 l multi .45 .25
4106 A1161 1500 l multi .80 .25
4107 A1161 2550 l multi, vert. 1.20 .25
Nos. 4104-4107 (4) 2.70 1.00

Habitat II (#4107).

Euro '96, European Soccer Championships, Great Britain — A1162

Designs: a, 220 l, Goal keeper, ball. b, 370 l, Player with ball. c, Two players, ball. d, 1500 l, Three players, ball. e, 2550 l, Player dribbling ball.

4050 l, Two players, four balls.

1996, May 27

4108 A1162 Strip of 5, #a.-e. 3.75 1.25

Souvenir Sheet

4109 A1162 4050 l multicolored 2.75 2.10

No. 4109 contains one 42x54mm stamp.

CAPEX '96 — A1163

Designs: 150 l, Toronto Convention Center. 4050 l, CN Tower, Skydome, Toronto skyline.

1996, May 29

4110 A1163 150 l multicolored .25 .25

Souvenir Sheet

4111 A1163 4050 l multicolored 2.75 2.10

No. 4111 contains 42x54mm stamp.

Resita Factory, 225th Anniv. A1164

1996, June 20 Photo. *Perf. 13½*

4112 A1164 150 l dark red brown .35 .25

No. 3775 Surcharged

1996, June 22

4113 A1071 150 l on 10 l multi .35 .25

Stamp Day — A1165

1996, July 15

4114 A1165 1500 l + 650 l label 1.25 .25

Conifers — A1166

70 l, Picea glauca. 150 l, Picea omorica. 220 l, Picea pungeus. 740 l, Picea sitchensis. 1500 l, Pinus sylvestris. 3500 l, Pinus pinaster.

1996, Aug. 1

4115 A1166 70 l multi .25 .25
4116 A1166 150 l multi .25 .25
4117 A1166 220 l multi .25 .25
4118 A1166 740 l multi .45 .25
4119 A1166 1500 l multi .85 .25
4120 A1166 3500 l multi 2.00 .30
Nos. 4115-4120 (6) 4.05 1.55

For surcharge see No. 4403.

Wildlife — A1167

Designs: 70 l, Natrix natrix, vert. 150 l, Testudo hermanni, vert. 220 l, Alauda arvensis. 740 l, Vulpes vulpes. 1500 l, Phocaena phocaena, vert. 3500 l, Aquila chrysaetos, vert.

1996, Sept. 12 Photo. *Perf. 13½*

4121 A1167 70 l multicolored .25 .25
4122 A1167 150 l multicolored .25 .25
4123 A1167 220 l multicolored .25 .25
4124 A1167 740 l multicolored .45 .25
4125 A1167 1500 l multicolored .85 .25
4126 A1167 3500 l multicolored 2.00 .30
Nos. 4121-4126 (6) 4.05 1.55

For surcharge see No. 4348.

Famous Men — A1168

100 l, Stan Golestan (1875-1956). 150 l, Corneliu Coposu (1914-95). 370 l, Vintila Horia (1915-92). 1500 l, Alexandru Papana (1906-46).

1996, Nov. 29

4127 A1168 100 l black & rose red .25 .25
4128 A1168 150 l black & lake .25 .25
4129 A1168 370 l blk & yel brn .35 .25
4130 A1168 1500 l black & ver 1.00 .40
Nos. 4127-4130 (4) 1.85 1.15

Madonna and Child — A1169

1996, Nov. 27

4131 A1169 150 l multicolored .35 .25

Antique Autombiles — A1170

No. 4132: a, 280 l, 1933 Mercedes Benz. b, 70 l, 1930 Ford Spider. c, 150 l, 1932 Citroen. d, 220 l, 1936 Rolls Royce.

No. 4133: a, 2550 l, 1936 Mercedes Benz 500k Roadster. b, 2500 l, 1934 Bugatti "Type 59." c. 2550 l, 1931 Alfa Romeo 8C. d, 120 l, 1937 Jaguar SS 100.

1996, Dec. 19 Photo. *Perf. 13½*

4132 A1170 Sheet of 4, #a.-d. .80 .40
4133 A1170 Sheet of 4, #a.-d. 7.00 3.50

Souvenir Sheet

Deng Xiaoping, China, and Margaret Thatcher, Great Britain — A1171

1997, Jan. 20 Photo. *Perf. 13½*
4134 A1171 1500 l multicolored .75 .75

Hong Kong '97.

Fur-Bearing Animals — A1172

Designs: 70 l, Mustela erminea. 150 l, Alopex lagopus. 220 l, Nyctereutes procyonoides. 740 l, Lutra lutra. 1500 l, Ondatra zibethica. 3500 l, Martes martes.

1997, Feb. 14

4135	A1172 70 l multicolored	.25	.25
4136	A1172 150 l multicolored	.25	.25
4137	A1172 220 l multicolored	.25	.25
4138	A1172 740 l multicolored	.25	.25
4139	A1172 1500 l multicolored	.40	.25
4140	A1172 3500 l multicolored	1.00	.25
	Nos. 4135-4140 (6)	2.40	1.50

For surcharge see No. 4349.

Greenpeace, 25th Anniv. — A1173

Various views of MV Greenpeace.

1997, Mar. 6

4141	A1173 150 l multicolored	.25	.25
4142	A1173 370 l multicolored	.25	.25
4143	A1173 1940 l multicolored	.50	.25
4144	A1173 2500 l multicolored	.75	.25
	Nos. 4141-4144 (4)	1.75	1.00

Souvenir Sheet

4145 A1173 4050 l multicolored 1.50 .85

No. 4145 contains one 49x38mm stamp.

Famous People — A1174

Designs: 200 l, Thomas A. Edison. 400 l, Franz Schubert. 3600 l, Miguel de Cervantes Saavedra (1547-1616), Spanish writer.

1997, Mar. 27 Photo. *Perf. 13½*

4146	A1174 200 l multicolored	.25	.25
4147	A1174 400 l multicolored	.25	.25
4148	A1174 3600 l multicolored	1.75	.25
	Nos. 4146-4148 (3)	2.25	.75

Inauguration of Mobile Telephone Network in Romania — A1175

1997, Apr. 7 Photo. *Perf. 13½*
4149 A1175 400 l multicolored .35 .25

Churches — A1176

1997, Apr. 21 Photo. *Perf. 13½*

4150	A1176 200 l Surdesti	.25	.25
4151	A1176 400 l Plopis	.25	.25
4152	A1176 450 l Bogdan Voda	.25	.25
4153	A1176 850 l Rogoz	.25	.25
4154	A1176 3600 l Calinesti	.80	.25
4155	A1176 6000 l Birsana	1.50	.30
	Nos. 4150-4155 (6)	3.30	1.55

A1177

Shakespeare Festival, Craiova: a, 400 l, Constantin Serghe (1819-87) as Othello, 1855. b, 200 l, Al. Demetrescu Dan (1870-1948) as Hamlet, 1916. c, 3600 l, Ion Manolescu (1881-1959) as Hamlet, 1924. d, 2400 l, Gheorghe Cozorici (1933-93) as Hamlet, 1957.

1997, Apr. 23 Photo. *Perf. 13½*
4156 A1177 Sheet of 4, #a.-d. + 4 labels 2.25 1.50

A1178

Europa (Stories and Legends): 400 l, Vlad Tepes (Vlad the Impaler), prince upon whom legend of Dracula said to be based. 4250 l, Dracula.

1997, May 5

4157	A1178 400 l multicolored	.25	.25
4158	A1178 4250 l multicolored	1.90	1.90
a.	Pair, #4157-4158 + label	2.00	2.00

A1179

Natl. Theater, Cathedral, Statue of Mihai Viteazul.

1997, June 27 Photo. *Perf. 13½*
4159 A1179 450 l multicolored .35 .25

Balcanmax '97, Maximum Cards Exhibition, Cluj-Napoca.

Cacti A1180

Designs: 100 l, Dolichothele uberiformis. 250 l, Rebutia. 450 l, Echinofossulocactus lamellosus. 500 l, Ferocactus glaucescens. 650 l, Thelocactus. 6150 l, Echinofossulocactus albatus.

1997, June 27

4160	A1180 100 l multicolored	.25	.25
4161	A1180 250 l multicolored	.25	.25
4162	A1180 450 l multicolored	.25	.25
4163	A1180 500 l multicolored	.25	.25
4164	A1180 650 l multicolored	.25	.25
4165	A1180 6150 l multicolored	2.40	.25
	Nos. 4160-4165 (6)	3.65	1.50

Stamp Day — A1181

1997, July 15 Photo. *Perf. 13½*
4166 A1181 3600 l + 1500 l label 1.75 .40

Ten different labels exist.

Nos. 3664-3670, 3672 Srchd. in Brnish Purple (#4167-4171, 4174) or Black (#4172-4173)

1997, July 17

4167	A1043 250 l on 1 l #3664	.25	.25
4168	A1043 250 l on 2 l #3665	.25	.25
4169	A1043 250 l on 4 l #3666	.25	.25
4170	A1043 450 l on 5 l #3667	.25	.25
4171	A1043 450 l on 6 l #3668	.25	.25
4172	A1043 450 l on 18 l #3672	.25	.25
4173	A1043 950 l on 9 l #3670	.25	.25
4174	A1043 3600 l on 8 l #3669	.75	.25
	Nos. 4167-4174 (8)	2.50	2.00

Castle Dracula, Sighisoara — A1181a

Designs: 650 l, Clocktower on Town Hall. 3700 l, Steps leading to castle and clocktower.

1997, July 31

4175	A1181a 250 l shown	.25	.25
4175A	A1181a 650 l multi	.25	.25
4175B	A1181a 3700 l multi	1.20	.25
	Nos. 4175-4175B (3)	1.70	.75

A1181b

Tourism Monument, Banat.

1997, Aug. 3
4175C A1181b 950 l multi .35 .25

A1181c

1997, Aug. 13
4175D A1181c 450 l multi .35 .25

Stamp Printing Works, 125th anniv.

Belgian Antarctic Expedition, Cent. — A1181d

"Belgica" sailing ship and: 450 l, Emil Racovita, biologist. 650 l, Frederick A. Cook, anthropologist, photographer. 1600 l, Roald Amundsen. 3700 l, Adrien de Gerlache, expedition commander.

1997, Aug. 18

4175E	A1181d 450 l multi	.25	.25
4175F	A1181d 650 l multi	.25	.25
4175G	A1181d 1600 l multi	.40	.25
4175H	A1181d 3700 l multi	1.50	.25
	Nos. 4175E-4175H (4)	2.40	1.00

Sports A1182

500 l, Rugby. 700 l, American football, vert. 1750 l, Baseball. 3700 l, Mountain climbing, vert.

1997, Nov. 21 Photo. *Perf. 13½*

4176	A1182 500 l multi	.25	.25
4177	A1182 700 l multi	.25	.25
4178	A1182 1750 l multi	.45	.25
4179	A1182 3700 l multi	1.40	.30
	Nos. 4176-4179 (4)	2.35	1.05

Romanian Scouts A1183

300 l, Tents at campsite. 700 l, Scouting emblem. 1050 l, Hands reaching toward each other. 1750 l, Carvings. 3700 l, Scouts seated around campfire.

1997, Oct. 25 Photo. *Perf. 13½*

4180 A1183 300 l multicolored .25 .25
4181 A1183 700 l multicolored .25 .25
4182 A1183 1050 l multicolored .30 .25
4183 A1183 1750 l multicolored .45 .25
4184 A1183 3700 l multicolored 1.10 .25
a. Strip of 5, #4180-4184 2.50 1.00

No. 3650 Surcharged in Red

1997, Sept. 27

4185 A1039 1050 l on 4.50 l .60 .25

No. 3619 Surcharged in Red

1997, Oct. 28 Photo. *Perf. 13½*

4186 A1032 500 l on 2 l multi .25 .25

Ion Mihalache (1882-1963), Politician — A1184

Design: 1050 l, King Carol I (1866-1914).

1997, Nov. 8

4187 A1184 500 l multi .25 .25
4188 A1184 1050 l pink & multi .35 .30

King Carol I Type of 1997

Designs: Nos. 4188A-4188C, King Carol I.

1997, Nov. 8 Litho. *Perf. 13½*

4188A A1184 1050 l blue & multi .35 .35
4188B A1184 1050 l clar & multi .35 .35
4188C A1184 1050 l blk & multi .35 .35

No. 4188 is pink & multi.

Chamber of Commerce and Industry, Bucharest, 130th Anniv. — A1185

1998, Jan. 29 Photo. *Perf. 13½*

4189 A1185 700 l multicolored .35 .25

No. 4189 is printed se-tenant with label.

1998 Winter Olympic Games, Nagano A1186

1998, Feb. 5

4190 A1186 900 l Skiing .30 .25
4191 A1186 3900 l Figure skating 1.25 .65

Souvenir Sheet

Flag Day — A1187

1998, Feb. 24 Photo. *Perf. 13½*

4192 A1187 900 l multicolored .60 .25

National Festivals and Holidays — A1188

1998, Feb. 26 Photo. *Perf. 13x13½*

4193 A1188 900 l 4-Leaf clover .80 1.00
4194 A1188 3900 l Heart 17.50 22.50

Europa.

Famous People and Events of the 20th Century A1189

Designs: 700 l, Alfred Nobel, creation of Nobel Foundation, 1901. 900 l, Guglielmo Marconi, first radio transmission across Atlantic, 1901. 1500 l, Albert Einstein, theory of relativity, 1905. 3900 l, Trajan Vuia, flying machine, 1906.

1998, Mar. 31 Photo. *Perf. 13½*

4195 A1189 700 l multicolored .40 .25
4196 A1189 900 l multicolored .40 .25
4197 A1189 1500 l multicolored .50 .25
4198 A1189 3900 l multicolored 1.40 .40
Nos. 4195-4198 (4) 2.70 1.15

See Nos. 4261-4265, 4312-4319, 4380-4383.

Roadside Shrines — A1190

1998, Apr. 17

4199 A1190 700 l Cluj .25 .25
4200 A1190 900 l Prahova .25 .25
4201 A1190 1500 l Arges .50 .25
Nos. 4199-4201 (3) 1.00 .75

No. 4081 Surcharged in Red

Designs: a, 900 l on 370 l. b, 700 l on 150 l, c, 3900 l on 1500 l.

1998, May 12

4202 A1153 Sheet of 3, #a.-c. 2.50 1.25

Surcharge on #4202a, 4202c does not include '98 show emblem. This appears in the selvage to the right and left of the stamps.

Romanian Surgical Society, Cent. — A1191

Thoma Ionescu (1860-1926), founder.

1998, May 18

4203 A1191 1050 l multicolored .50 .25

Nos. 3665-3669, 3672, 3676 Surcharged in Black, Red, Bright Green, Violet, Red Violet, Orange Brown, Dark Green, Violet Brown or Deep Blue

1998 Photo. *Perf. 13½*

4204 A1043 50 l on 2 l #3665 (R) .25 .25
4205 A1043 100 l on 8 l #3669 (BG) .25 .25
4206 A1043 200 l on 4 l #3666 .25 .25
4207 A1043 250 l on 45 l #3676 (Bl) .25 .25
4208 A1043 350 l on 45 l #3676 .25 .25
4209 A1043 400 l on 6 l #3668 (V) .25 .25
4210 A1043 400 l on 45 l #3676 (BG) .25 .25
4211 A1043 450 l on 45l #3676 (RV) .25 .25
4212 A1043 500 l on 18 l #3672 (Bl) .25 .25
4213 A1043 850 l on 45 l #3676 (OB) .75 .35
4214 A1043 900 l on 45 l #3676 (V) .75 .35
4215 A1043 1000 l on 45 l #3676 (DkG) .75 .35
4216 A1043 1000 l on 9 l #3670 .40 .40
4217 A1043 1500 l on 5 l #3667 (R) .40 .40
4218 A1043 1600 l on 45 l #3676 (VB) 1.75 .40
4219 A1043 2500 l on 45 l #3676 (R) 3.00 .75
Nos. 4204-4219 (16) 10.05 5.25

Obliterator varies on Nos. 4204-4219.
Issued: Nos. 4204-4206, 4209, 4212, 5/21; Nos. 4216-4217, 7/6; others, 1998.

1998 World Cup Soccer Championships, France — A1192

Various soccer plays, stadium: a, 800 l. b, 1050 l. c, 1850 l. d, 4150 l.

1998, June 10 Photo. *Perf. 13½*

4220 A1192 Sheet of 4, #a.-d. 2.25 1.10

Nos. 3913-3915, 3918 Surcharged in Red Violet, Blue, Black, or Red

Wmk. 398

1998, June 30 Photo. *Perf. 13*

Design A1105

4221 700 l on 125 l #3918 (RV) .25 .25
4222 800 l on 35 l #3914 (Bl) .25 .25
4223 1050 l on 45 l #3915 (Blk) .35 .25
4224 4150 l on 15 l #3913 (R) 1.25 .65
Nos. 4221-4224 (4) 2.10 1.40

Night Birds A1193

Designs: 700 l, Apteryx australis, vert. 1500 l, Tyto alba, vert. 1850 l, Rallus aquaticus. 2450 l, Caprimulgus europaeus.

1998, Aug. 12 Unwmk.

4225 A1193 700 l multicolored .30 .30
4226 A1193 1500 l multicolored .30 .30
a. Complete booklet, 4 each, #4225-4226 3.00
4227 A1193 1850 l multicolored .30 .30
4228 A1193 2450 l multicolored 1.10 1.10
a. Complete booklet, 4 each, #4227-4228 5.75
Nos. 4225-4228 (4) 2.00 2.00

Stamp Day A1194

1998, July Litho. *Perf. 13½*

4229 A1194 700 l Romania #4 .25 .25
4230 A1194 1050 l Romania #1 .35 .25
a. Complete booklet, #4225, 4 #4226 3.50

Souvenir Sheet

4231 A1194 4150 l +850 l Romania #2-3 1.60 .80

No. 4231 contains one 54x42mm stamp.

Natl. Uprising, 150th Anniv. — A1195

1998, Sept. 28 Photo. *Perf. 13½*

4232 A1195 1050 l multicolored .35 .25

A1196

German Personalities in Banat: 800 l, Nikolaus Lenau (1802-50). 1850 l, Stefan Jäger (1877-1962). 4150 l, Adam Müller-Guttenbrunn (1852-1923).

1998, Oct. 16

4233	A1196	800 l	multicolored	.25	.25
4234	A1196	1850 l	multicolored	.50	.25
4235	A1196	4150 l	multicolored	1.00	.50
			Nos. 4233-4235 (3)	1.75	1.00

A1197

1998, Nov. 4 Photo. *Perf. 13½*

4236	A1197	1100 l	multicolored	.40	.25

Intl. Year of the Ocean.

Nos. 3652-3653, 3704-3709, 3776-3779, 3781, 3795, 3968 Srchd. in Green, Black, Red, Red Violet or Deep Blue

1998 Photo. *Perf. 13½*

4237	A1041	50 l	on #3652 (G)	.25	.25
4238	A1041	50 l	on #3653 (Blk)	.25	.25
4238A	A1054	50 l	on 1 l #3704 (Blk)	.25	.25
4239	A1054	50 l	on #3705 (R)	.90	.25
4240	A1054	50 l	on #3706 (R)	.25	.25
4241	A1054	50 l	on #3707 (Blk)	.25	.25
4242	A1054	50 l	on #3708 (Blk)	.25	.25
4243	A1054	50 l	on #3709 (R)	.25	.25
4244	A1054	50 l	on #3776 (RV)	.25	.25
4245	A1054	50 l	on #3777 (DB)	.25	.25
4246	A1054	50 l	on #3778 (Blk)	.25	.25
4247	A1054	50 l	on #3779 (G)	.25	.25
4248	A1054	50 l	on #3781 (R)	.25	.25
4249	A1075	2000 l	on #3795 (G)	.80	.50
4250	A1117	2600 l	on #3968 (R)	.80	.50
			Nos. 4237-4250 (15)	5.50	4.25

Obliterator varies on Nos. 4237-4250.

Issued: 4237-4238, 11/10; 4238A, 11/27; 4249-4250, 12/22.

A1198

Lighthouses.

1998, Dec. 28

4251	A1198	900 l	Genovez	.25	.25
4252	A1198	1000 l	Constanta	.30	.25
4253	A1198	1100 l	Sfantu Gheorghe	.35	.25
4254	A1198	2600 l	Sulina	1.00	.40
			Nos. 4251-4254 (4)	1.90	1.15

A1199

Flowers: 350 l, Tulipa gesneriana. 850 l, Dahlia variabilis. 1100 l, Lillium martagon. 4450 l, Rosa centifolia.

1998, Nov. 25

4255	A1199	350 l	multicolored	.25	.25
4256	A1199	850 l	multicolored	.30	.25
4257	A1199	1100 l	multicolored	.30	.25
4258	A1199	4450 l	multicolored	1.00	.65
			Nos. 4255-4258 (4)	1.85	1.40

Universal Declaration of Human Rights, 50th Anniv. — A1200

1998, Dec. 10

4259	A1200	700 l	multicolored	.35	.25

Dimitrie Paciurea (1873-1932), Sculptor — A1200a

1998, Dec. 11 Photo. *Perf. 13¼*

4259A	A1200a	850 l	ocher & blk	.40	.25

Total Eclipse of the Sun, Aug. 11, 1999 — A1201

1998, Dec. 17

4260	A1201	1100 l	multi + label	.35	.25

Events of the 20th Cent. Type

Designs: 350 l, Sinking of the Titanic, 1912. 1100 l, "Coanda 1910" aircraft with air-reactive (jet) engine, 1919, by Henri Coanda (1886-1972). 1600 l, Louis Blériot's (1872-1936) Calais-Dover flight, 1909. 2000 l, Opening of the Panama Canal, 1914. 2600 l, Russian Revolution, 1917.

1998, Dec. 22 Photo. *Perf. 13½*

4261	A1189	350 l	multicolored	.25	.25
4262	A1189	1100 l	multicolored	.30	.25
4263	A1189	1600 l	multicolored	.30	.25
4264	A1189	2000 l	multicolored	.30	.30
4265	A1189	2600 l	multicolored	.75	.40
			Nos. 4261-4265 (5)	1.90	1.45

No. 3687 Surcharged in Red or Black

1999, Feb. 10 Photo. *Perf. 13½*

4266	A1047	100 l	on 1 l (R)	.30	.25
4267	A1047	250 l	on 1 l (Blk)	.30	.25

Obliterator is a guitar on #4266 and a saxophone on #4267.

No. 3796 Surcharged in Black, Red, Green, or Brown

1999, Jan. 22

4268	A1076	50 l	on 15 l (Blk)	.25	.25
4269	A1076	50 l	on 15 l (R)	.25	.25
4270	A1076	400 l	on 15 l (Grn)	.25	.25
4271	A1076	2300 l	on 15 l (Brn)	.50	.35
4272	A1076	3200 l	on 15 l (Blk)	1.00	.50
			Nos. 4268-4272 (5)	2.25	1.60

Obliterator varies on Nos. 4268-4272.

Monasteries — A1203

1999, Jan. 17

4273	A1203	500 l	Arnota	.25	.25
4274	A1203	700 l	Bistrita	.25	.25
4275	A1203	1100 l	Dintr'un Lemn	.25	.25
4276	A1203	2100 l	Govora	.50	.30
4277	A1203	4850 l	Tismana	1.40	.70
			Nos. 4273-4277 (5)	2.65	1.75

Shrub Flowers A1204

350 l, Magnolia x soulangiana. 1000 l, Stewartia malacodendron. 1100 l, Hibiscus rosa-sinensis. 5350 l, Clematis patens.

1999, Feb. 15

4278	A1204	350 l	multicolored	.25	.25
4279	A1204	1000 l	multicolored	.25	.25
4280	A1204	1100 l	multicolored	.25	.25
4281	A1204	5350 l	multicolored	1.50	.75
			Nos. 4278-4281 (4)	2.25	1.50

Easter A1205

1999, Mar. 15 Photo. *Perf. 13¼*

4282	A1205	1100 l	multi	.35	.25

No. 4082 Surcharged in Bright Pink, Red, Violet, Black, Green or Blue

1999, Mar. 22 Litho. *Perf. 13½*

4283	A1154	100 l	on 70 l (BP)	.25	.25
4284	A1154	100 l	on 70 l (R)	.25	.25
4285	A1154	200 l	on 70 l (V)	.25	.25
4286	A1154	1500 l	on 70 l	.50	.25
4287	A1154	1600 l	on 70 l (G)	.50	.25
4288	A1154	3200 l	on 70 l (Bl)	1.10	.45
4289	A1154	6000 l	on 70 l (G)	1.90	.90
			Nos. 4283-4289 (7)	4.75	2.60

Obliterators on Nos. 4283-4289 are various dinosaurs.

Jewelry — A1206

Designs: 1200 l, Keys on chain. 2100 l, Key holder. 2600 l, Necklace. 3200 l, Necklace, horiz.

1999, Mar. 29 Photo. *Perf. 13¼*

4290-4293	A1206	Set of 4	1.75	.90

Birds — A1207

Perf. 13½x13¼

1999, Apr. 26 Photo.

4294	A1207	1100 l	Ara macao	.30	.25
4295	A1207	2700 l	Pavo albus	.60	.35
4296	A1207	3700 l	Pavo cristatus	.80	.45
4297	A1207	5700 l	Cacatua galerita	1.25	.65
			Nos. 4294-4297 (4)	2.95	1.70

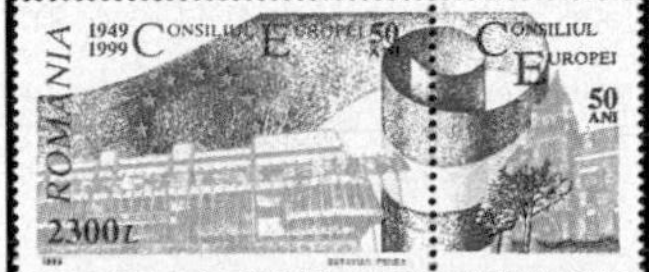

Council of Europe, 50th Anniv. — A1208

1999, May 5 Photo. *Perf. 13¼*

4298	A1208	2300 l	multi + label	.60	.35

A1209

Visit of Pope John Paul II to Romania: a, 6300 l, Pope John Paul II. b, 1300 l, St. Peter's Basilica. c, 1600 l, Patriarchal Cathedral, Bucharest. d, 2300 l, Patriarch Teoctist.

1999, May 7

4299	A1209	Sheet of 6, #a.-d.	2.50	1.90

Issued in sheets containing one strip of #4299a-4299d, 1 ea #4299a, 4299d + 2 labels.

A1210

Europa: 1100 l, Anas clypeata. 5700 l, Ciconia nigra.

1999, May 17

4300 A1210 1100 l multicolored .25 .25
4301 A1210 5700 l multicolored 1.50 1.25

Nos. 4300-4301 printed with se-tenant label.

Famous Personalities — A1211

Designs: 600 l, Gheorghe Cartan (1849-1911). 1100 l, George Calinescu (1899-1965), writer. 2600 l, Johann Wolfgang von Goethe (1749-1832), poet. 7300 l, Honoré de Balzac (1799-1850), novelist.

1999, May 31

4302 A1211 600 l multicolored .25 .25
4303 A1211 1100 l multicolored .25 .25
4304 A1211 2600 l multicolored .40 .25
4305 A1211 7300 l multicolored 1.50 .75
Nos. 4302-4305 (4) 2.40 1.50

Total Solar Eclipse, Aug. 11 — A1212

1999, June 21 Photo. *Perf. 13¼*

4306 A1212 1100 l multicolored .50 .25

No. 4306 printed se-tenant with label.

Health Dangers A1213

1999, July 29 Photo. *Perf. 13¼*

4307 A1213 400 l Smoking .25 .25
4308 A1213 800 l Alcohol .25 .25
4309 A1213 1300 l Drugs .25 .25
4310 A1213 2500 l AIDS .50 .25
Nos. 4307-4310 (4) 1.25 1.00

Luciano Pavarotti Concert in Bucharest on Day of Solar Eclipse — A1214

1999, Aug. 9

4311 A1214 8100 l multi 1.60 .80

Events of the 20th Century Type

Designs: 800 l, Alexander Fleming discovers penicillin, 1928. 3000 l, League of Nations, 1920. 7300 l, Harold C. Urey discovers heavy water, 1931. 17,000 l, First marine oil drilling platform, off Beaumont, Texas, 1934.

1999, Aug. 30

4312 A1189 800 l multi .25 .25
4313 A1189 3000 l multi .50 .40
4314 A1189 7300 l multi 1.25 .85
4315 A1189 17,000 l multi 3.50 1.90
Nos. 4312-4315 (4) 5.50 3.40

1999, Sept. 24 Photo. *Perf. 13¼*

1500 l, Karl Landsteiner (1868-1943), discoverer of blood groups. 3000 l, Nicolae C. Paulescu (1869-1931), diabetes researcher. 7300 l, Otto Hahn (1879-1968), discoverer of nuclear fission. 17,000 l, Ernst Ruska (1906-88), inventor of electron microscope.

4316 A1189 1500 l multi .30 .25
4317 A1189 3000 l multi .55 .30
4318 A1189 7300 l multi 1.40 .70
4319 A1189 17,000 l multi 3.25 1.60
Nos. 4316-4319 (4) 5.50 2.85

UPU, 125th Anniv. — A1215

1999, Oct. 9

4320 A1215 3100 l multi .70 .35

Comic Actors — A1216

Designs: 900 l, Grigore Vasiliu Birlic. 1500 l, Toma Caragiu. 3100 l, Constantin Tanase. 7950 l, Charlie Chaplin. 8850 l, Oliver Hardy and Stan Laurel, horiz.

1999, Oct. 21

4321 A1216 900 l blk & brn red .25 .25
4322 A1216 1500 l blk & brn red .25 .25
4323 A1216 3100 l blk & brn red .40 .35
4324 A1216 7950 l blk & brn red 1.20 .95
4325 A1216 8850 l blk & brn red 1.60 1.00
Nos. 4321-4325 (5) 3.70 2.80

Stavropoleos Church, 275th Anniv. — A1217

1999, Oct. 29

4326 A1217 2100 l multi .50 .25

New Olympic Sports A1218

1999, Nov. 10

4327 A1218 1600 l Snowboarding .25 .25
4328 A1218 1700 l Softball .35 .25
4329 A1218 7950 l Taekwondo 1.40 .70
Nos. 4327-4329 (3) 2.00 1.20

Christmas — A1219

Designs: 1500 l, Christmas tree, bell. 3100 l, Santa Claus.

1999, Nov. 29 Photo. *Perf. 13¼*

4330-4331 A1219 Set of 2 .80 .40

UN Rights of the Child Convention, 10th Anniv. — A1220

Children's art by: 900 l, A. Vieriu. 3400 l, A. M. Bulete, vert. 8850 l, M. L. Rogojeanu.

1999, Nov. 30 Photo. *Perf. 13¼*

4332 A1220 900 l multi .25 .25
4333 A1220 3400 l multi .60 .30
4334 A1220 8850 l multi 1.50 .75
Nos. 4332-4334 (3) 2.35 1.30

Princess Diana — A1221

1999, Dec. 2

4335 A1221 6000 l multi 1.00 .60

Issued in sheets of 4.

Ferrari Automobiles — A1222

Designs: 1500 l, 1968 365 GTB/4. 1600 l, 1970 Dino 246 GT. 1700 l, 1973 365 GT/4 BB. 7950 l, Mondial 3.2. 8850 l, 1994 F 355. 14,500 l, 1998 456M GT.

1999, Dec. 17

4336 A1222 1500 l multi .25 .25
4337 A1222 1600 l multi .30 .25
4338 A1222 1700 l multi .30 .25
4339 A1222 7950 l multi 1.40 .70
4340 A1222 8850 l multi 1.50 .75
4341 A1222 14,500 l multi 2.50 1.25
Nos. 4336-4341 (6) 6.25 3.45

Romanian Revolution, 10th Anniv. — A1223

1999, Dec. 21 *Perf. 13¼*

4342 A1223 2100 l multi .50 .25

Start of Accession Negotiations With European Union — A1224

2000, Jan. 13 Photo. *Perf. 13¼*

4343 A1224 6100 l multi 1.00 .50

Souvenir Sheet

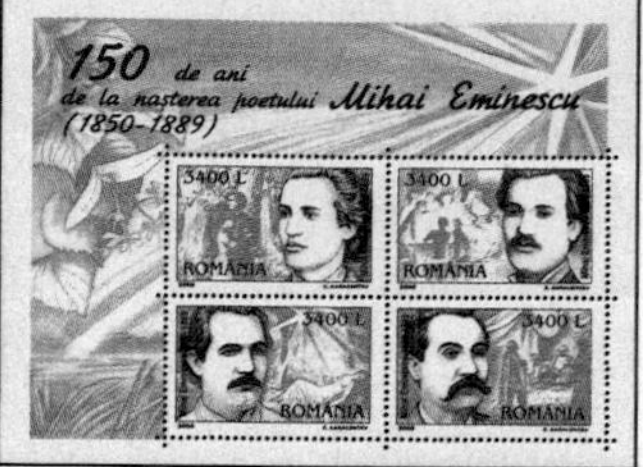

Mihail Eminescu (1850-89), Poet — A1225

Scenes from poems and Eminescu: a, At R, clean-shaven. b, At R, with mustache. c, At L, with trimmed mustache. d, At L, with handlebar mustache.

2000, Jan. 15

4344 A1225 Sheet of 4 4.75 1.10
a.-d. 3400 l Any single .55 .25

Valentine's Day — A1226

2000, Feb. 1 Photo. *Perf. 13¼*

4345 A1226 1500 l Cupid .25 .25
4346 A1226 7950 l Couple kissing 1.25 .65

Easter — A1227

2000, Feb. 29

4347 A1227 1700 l multi .35 .25

Nos. 4121, 4135 Surcharged in Red

Methods and Perfs. as Before

2000

4348 A1167 1700 l on 70 l multi .35 .25
4349 A1172 1700 l on 70 l multi .35 .25

Issued: No. 4348, 3/14; No. 4349, 3/13. Obliterator on No. 4349 is a crown.

Birds A1228

Designs: 1700 l, Paradisaea apoda. 2400 l, Diphyllodes magnificus. 9050 l, Lophorina superba. 10,050 l, Cicinnurus regius.

2000, Mar. 20 Photo. *Perf. 13¼*

4350	A1228	1700 l multi	.25	.25
4351	A1228	2400 l multi	.35	.25
4352	A1228	9050 l multi	1.40	.70
4353	A1228	10,050 l multi	1.50	.75
		Nos. 4350-4353 (4)	3.50	1.95

Nos. 3658-3659 Surcharged in Red

Methods & Perfs. as Before

2000, Mar. 31

4354	A1042	1900 l on 1 l (#3658)	.30	.25
4355	A1042	2000 l on 1 l (#3659)	.30	.25

Nos. 3626-3630 Surcharged

Methods & Perfs. as Before

2000, Apr. 12

4356	A1034	1700 l on 50b	.30	.30
4357	A1034	1700 l on 1.50 l	.30	.30
4358	A1034	1700 l on 2 l	.30	.30
4359	A1034	1700 l on 3 l	.30	.30
4360	A1034	1700 l on 4 l	.30	.30
		Nos. 4356-4360 (5)	1.50	1.50

Appearance of obliterator varies.

Flowers — A1229

Designs: 1700 l, Senecio cruentus. 3100 l, Clivia miniata. 5800 l, Plumeria rubra. 10,050 l, Fuchsia hybrida.

2000, Apr. 20 Photo. *Perf. 13¼*

4361	A1229	1700 l multi	.25	.25
4362	A1229	3100 l multi	.40	.25
4363	A1229	5800 l multi	.80	.40
4364	A1229	10,050 l multi	1.40	.70
		Nos. 4361-4364 (4)	2.85	1.60

Nos. 3620-3624 Surcharged

Methods & Perfs. as Before

2000, Apr. 24

4365	A1033	1700 l on 50b	.30	.30
4366	A1033	1700 l on 1.50 l	.30	.30
4367	A1033	1700 l on 2 l	.30	.30
4368	A1033	1700 l on 3 l	.30	.30
4369	A1033	1700 l on 4 l	.30	.30
		Nos. 4365-4369 (5)	1.50	1.50

Europa Issue

Common Design Type

2000, May 9 Photo. *Perf. 13¼*

4370 CD17 10,150 l multi 2.50 1.25

Nos. 3634, 3637 Surcharged in Red

Methods and Perfs as Before

2000, May 17

4371	A1036	1700 l on 50b	.40	.25
4372	A1036	1700 l on 3.50 l	.40	.25

Unification of Walachia, Transylvania and Moldavia by Michael the Brave, 400th Anniv. — A1230

2000, May 19 Photo. *Perf. 13¼*

4373 A1230 3800 l multi .50 .25

Printing of Bible in Latin by Johann Gutenberg, 550th Anniv. — A1231

2000, May 19

4374 A1231 9050 l multi 1.25 .60

No. 4084 Surcharged in Red

2000, May 31 Photo. *Perf. 13¼*

4375	A1154	10,000 l on 370 l	1.40	.70
4376	A1154	19,000 l on 370 l	2.50	1.25
4377	A1154	34,000 l on 370 l	4.75	2.40
		Nos. 4375-4377 (3)	8.65	4.35

Souvenir Sheet

2000 European Soccer Championships — A1232

No. 4378: a, 3800 l, Romania vs. Portugal (red and green flag). b, 3800 l, England (red and white flag) vs. Romania. c, 10,150 l, Romania vs. Germany. d, 10,150 l, Goalie.

2000, June 20

4378 A1232 Sheet of 4, #a-d 3.75 1.90

First Zeppelin Flight, Cent. A1233

2000, July 12

4379 A1233 2100 l multi .35 .25

Stamp Day.

20th Century Type of 1998

2100 l, Enrico Fermi, formula, 1st nuclear reactor, 1942. 2200 l, Signing of UN Charter, 1945. 2400 l, Edith Piaf sings "La Vie en Rose," 1947. 6000 l, 1st ascent of Mt. Everest, by Sir Edmund Hillary and Tenzing Norgay, 1953.

2000, July 12

4380-4383 A1189 Set of 4 1.60 .80

No. 3680 Surcharged in Green

Methods and Perfs as Before

2000, July 31

4384 A1044 1700 l on 160 l .30 .25

20th Century Type of 1998

Designs: 1700 l, First artificial satellite, 1957. 3900 l, Yuri Gagarin, first man in space, 1961. 6400 l, First heart transplant perfromed by Christiaan Barnard, 1967. 11,300 l, Neil Armstrong, first man on the moon, 1969.

2000, Aug. 28 Photo. *Perf. 13¼*

4385-4388 A1189 Set of 4 3.50 1.75

2000 Summer Olympics, Sydney A1234

Designs: 1700 l, Boxing. 2200 l, High jump. 3900 l, Weight lifting. 6200 l, Gymnastics.

2000, Sept. 7

4389-4392 A1234 Set of 4 2.25 1.00

Souvenir Sheet

4393 A1234 11,300 l Runner 1.40 .70

No. 4393 contains one 42x54mm stamp.

Souvenir Sheet

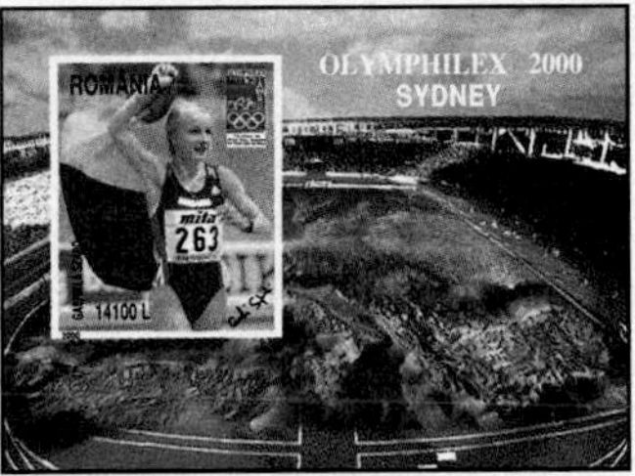
Olymphilex 2000, Sydney — A1235

2000, Sept. 7 *Imperf.*

4394 A1235 14,100 l Gabriela Szabo 2.40 .85

Bucharest Palaces A1236

Designs: 1700 l, Agricultural Ministry Palace, vert. 2200 l, Cantacuzino Palace. 2400 l, Grigore Ghica Palace. 3900 l, Stirbei Palace.

2000, Sept. 29 *Perf. 13¼*

4395-4398 A1236 Set of 4 1.60 .80

No. 4115 Surcharged in Brown

2000, Oct. 11 Photo. *Perf. 13½*

4403 A1166 300 l on 70 l multi .25 .25

No. 3664 Surcharged in Blue

2000, Oct. 26 *Perf. 13½*

4404 A1043 300 l on 1 l blue .35 .25

No. 3991 Surcharged in Red Violet

2000, Nov. 3 *Perf. 13½*

4405 A1127 2000 l on 90 l multi .35 .25

European Human Rights Convention, 50th Anniv. — A1237

2000, Nov. 3 ***Perf. 13¼***

4406 A1237 11,300 l multi 1.75 .45

No. 3858 Surcharged

2000, Nov. 28 ***Perf. 13½***

4407 A1093 2000 l on 29 l multi .60 .25

Endangered Wild Cats — A1238

Designs: 1200 l, Panthera pardus. 2000 l, Panthera uncia. 2200 l, Panthera leo. 2300 l, Lynx rufus. 4200 l, Puma concolor. 6500 l, Panthera tigris.
14,100 l, Panthera leo.

2000, Nov. 29 Photo. ***Perf. 13½***

4408	A1238	1200 l multi	.25	.25
4409	A1238	2000 l multi	.25	.25
4410	A1238	2200 l multi	.25	.25
4411	A1238	2300 l multi	.25	.25
4412	A1238	4200 l multi	.40	.25
4413	A1238	6500 l multi	1.20	.25
		Nos. 4408-4413 (6)	2.60	1.50

Souvenir Sheet

4414 A1238 14,100 l multi 2.00 .60

No. 4414 contains one 54x42mm stamp.

Self-portraits A1239

Designs: 2000 l, Camil Ressu (1880-1962), 2400 l, Jean A. Steriadi (1880-1956). 4400 l, Nicolae Tonitza (1886-1940). 15,000 l, Nicolae Grigorescu (1838-1907).

2000 Photo. ***Perf. 13½***

4415	A1239	2000 l multi	.25	.25
4416	A1239	2400 l multi	.25	.25
4417	A1239	4400 l multi	.40	.25
4418	A1239	15,000 l multi	2.00	.75
		Nos. 4415-4418 (4)	2.90	1.50

Issued: 2000 l, 12/8; others, 12/13.

Christmas — A1240

2000, Dec. 15 Photo. ***Perf. 13½***

4419 A1240 4400 l multi .35 .25

Christianity, 2000th Anniv. — A1241

Stained glass windows: 2000 l, Resurrection of Jesus. 7000 l, Holy Trinity (22x38mm).

2000, Dec. 22 Photo. ***Perf. 13¼***

4420-4421 A1241 Set of 2 1.10 .40

No. 3922 Surcharged in Red Brown

Wmk. 398

2000, Dec. 28 Photo. ***Perf. 13¼***

4422	A1105	7000 l on 3095 l multi	1.10	.30
4423	A1105	10,000 l on 3095 l multi	.75	.45
4424	A1105	11,500 l on 3095 l multi	1.10	.55
		Nos. 4422-4424 (3)	2.95	1.30

Obliterator on No. 4423 is a bear and on No. 4424 a bison.

Advent of the Third Millennium — A1242

Perf. 13½

2001, Jan. 19 Photo. Unwmk.

4425 A1242 11,500 l multi 1.90 .60

Sculptures by Constantin Brancusi (1876-1957) — A1243

No. 4426: a, 4600 l, b, 7200 l.

2001, Feb. 2

4426 A1243 Horiz. pair, #a-b 1.50 .55

No. 3844 Surcharged in Black or Red

Methods and Perfs as Before

2001, Feb. 9

4427	A1087	7400 l on 280 l multi	.75	.35
4428	A1087	13,000 l on 280 l multi (R)	1.25	.60

Obliterator on No. 4428 is snake on branch.

Valentine's Day — A1244

Designs: 2200 l, Heart of rope. 11,500 l, Rope running through heart.

2001, Feb. 15 Photo. ***Perf. 13½***

4429-4430 A1244 Set of 2 1.50 .75

Nos. 3894, 3895, 3897 Surcharged in Brown or Green

Methods and Perfs as Before

2001, Feb. 21

4431	A1101	1300 l on 245 l	.25	.25
4432	A1101	2200 l on 115 l	.25	.25
4433	A1101	5000 l on 115 l (G)	.50	.25
4434	A1101	16,500 l on 70 l	2.00	.75
		Nos. 4431-4434 (4)	3.00	1.50

Appearance of obliterators differ. Obliterators on Nos 4432-4433 are ears of corn.

Famous People A1245

Designs: 1300 l, Hortensia Papadat-Bengescu (1876-1955), writer. 2200 l, Eugen Lovinescu (1881-1943), writer. 2400 l, Ion Minulescu (1881-1944), writer. 4600 l, André Malraux (1901-76), writer. 7200 l, George H. Gallup (1901-84), pollster. 35,000 l, Walt Disney (1901-66), film producer.

2001 Photo. ***Perf. 13¼***

4435-4440 A1245 Set of 6 8.00 3.00

Issued: 2200 l, 4600 l, 7200 l, 3/9; others 3/15.

Easter — A1246

2001, Mar. 23

4441 A1246 2200 l multi .35 .25

Fruit — A1247

Designs: 2200 l, Prunus spinosa. 4600 l, Ribes rubrum. 7400 l, Ribes uva-crispa. 11,500 l, Vaccinium vitis-idaea.

2001, Apr. 12

4442-4445 A1247 Set of 4 3.00 1.25

Gheorge Hagi, Soccer Player — A1248

Designs: 2200 l, Wearing uniform. 35,000 l, Wearing team jacket.

2001, Apr. 23 ***Perf. 13¼***

4446 A1248 2200 l multi .50 .25

Souvenir Sheet

Imperf

Without Gum

4447 A1248 35,000 l multi 4.75 1.40

No. 4447 is airmail and contains one 43x28mm stamp.

Europa — A1249

2001, May 4 ***Perf. 13¼***

4448 A1249 13,000 l multi 1.75 .85

Dogs A1250

Designs: 1300 l, Collie. 5000 l, Basset hound. 8000 l, Siberian husky. 13,500 l, Sheepdog.

2001, June 16

4449-4452 A1250 Set of 4 2.75 1.40

Romanian Presidency of Organization for Security and Cooperation in Europe — A1251

2001, July 6

4453 A1251 11,500 l multi 1.25 .45

Millennium — A1252

Events of the 20th Century: 1300 l, Mariner 9, 1971. 1500 l, Telephone pioneer Augustin Maior and circuit diagram, 1906. 2400 l, Discovery of cave drawings in Ardeche, France, 1994. 5000 l, First Olympic perfect score of gymnast Nadia Comaneci, 1976. 5300 l, Pioneer 10, 1972. 8000 l, Fall of the Iron Curtain, 1989. 13,500 l, First microprocessor, 1971. 15,500 l, Hubble Space Telescope, 1990.

2001
4454-4461 A1252 Set of 8 5.50 2.75

Issued: 1300 l, 2400 l, 5000 l, 8000 l, 7/13; others, 9/25.

UN High Commissioner for Refugees, 50th Anniv. — A1253

2001, July 26
4462 A1253 13,500 l multi 1.50 .60

Nos. 3688, 3713, 3790, 3791, 3865, 3870, 3900, 3907, 3972, 4007, 4017, 4025, 4057, 4058, and 4060 Surcharged in Black, Red, Green or Blue

2001	**Photo.**	***Perf. 13½***	
4463 A1048	300 l on 4 l #3688	.40	.25
4464 A1058	300 l on 4 l #3713 (R)	.40	.25
4465 A1073	300 l on 7 l #3790 (R)	.40	.25
4466 A1073	300 l on 9 l #3791 (R)	.40	.25
4467 A1102	300 l on 90 l #3900	.40	.25
4468 A1121	300 l on 90 l #3972 (G)	.40	.25
4469 A1132	300 l on 90 l #4007	.40	.25
4470 A1130	300 l on 90 l #4017	.40	.25
4471 A1137	300 l on 90 l #4025 (G)	.40	.25
4472 A1095	300 l on 115 l #3865 (R)	.40	.25
4473 A1096	300 l on 115 l #3870 (R)	.40	.25
4474 A1103	300 l on 115 l #3907 (R)	.40	.25
4475 A1131	2500 l on 715 l #4057 (R)	.40	.25
4476 A1131	2500 l on 755 l #4058 (Bl)	.40	.25
4477 A1131	2500 l on 1615 l #4060	.40	.25
	Nos. 4463-4477 (15)	6.00	3.75

Numbers have been reserved for additional surcharges. Design and location of obliterators and new value varies.

Issued: No. 4472, 8/20; No. 4473, 8/24; Nos. 4467, 4469, 8/28; No. 4470, 8/29; Nos. 4463, 4464, 4465, 4466, Nos. 4468, 4471, 4474-4477, 8/31.

Equestrian Sports A1254

Designs: 1500 l, Harness racing. 2500 l, Dressage. 5300 l, Steeplechase. 8300 l, Racing.

2001, Aug. 21 **Photo.** ***Perf. 13¼***
4478-4481 A1254 Set of 4 2.00 1.00

No. 3883 Surcharged

2001, Aug. 29 **Photo.** ***Perf. 13½***
4482 A1099 300 l on 115 l multi .25 .25

Souvenir Sheets

Corals and Anemones — A1255

No. 4483: a, 2500 l, Porites porites. b, 8300 l, Condylactis gigantea. c, 13,500 l, Anemonia telia. 37,500 l, Gorgonia ventalina.

No. 4484: a, 9000 l, Corallium rubrum. b, 9000 l, Acropora palmata. c, 16,500 l, Actinia equina. d, 16,500 l, Metridium senile.

2001-02 **Sheets of 4, #a-d**
4483-4484 A1255 Set of 2 10.50 5.25

Issued: No. 4483, 9/27/01; No. 4484, 1/30/02.

Year of Dialogue Among Civilizations A1256

2001, Oct. 9
4485 A1256 8300 l multi .80 .40

Comic Strip A1257

No. 4486: a, Cat, bear, king. b, Fox with drum, cat. c, Fox plays drum for king. d, Cat gives drum to fox. e, Fox, exploding drum.

2001, Oct. 31
4486 Horiz. strip of 5 7.00 3.50
a.-e. A1257 13,500 l Any single 1.40 .70

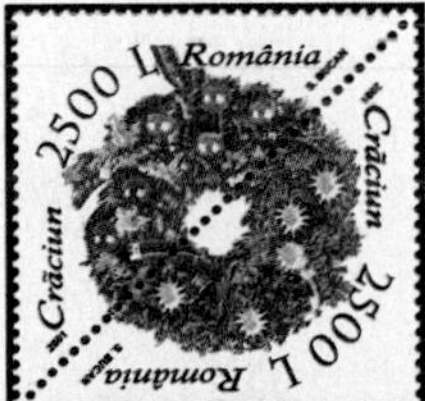

Christmas A1258

No. 4487: a, Ribbon extending from wreath. b, No ribbon extending from wreath.

2001, Nov. 5
4487 A1258 2500 l Pair, #a-b .35 .25
Booklet, 5 #4487 2.00

Zodiac Signs A1259

Designs: No. 4488, 1500 l, Scorpio. No. 4489, 1500 l, Aries. No. 4490, 2500 l, Libra. No. 4491, 2500 l, Taurus. No. 4492, 5500 l, Capricorn. No. 4493, 5500 l, Gemini. 8700 l, Cancer. No. 4495, 9000 l, Pisces. No. 4496, 9000 l, Leo. 13,500 l, Aquarius. 16,500 l, Sagittarius. 23,500 l, Virgo.

2001-02
4488-4499 A1259 Set of 12 10.00 5.00

Issued: Nos. 4488, 4490, 4492, 4495, 4497, 4498, 11/23/01; others 1/4/02.

Bucharest Post Office, Cent. — A1260

No. 4500: a, Building. b, Medal.

2001, Dec. 18 **Photo.** ***Perf. 13¼***
4500 A1260 5500 l Horiz. pair, #a-b 1.20 .55

Emanuil Gojdu (1802-70), Promoter of Romanian Orthodox Church in Hungary A1261

2002, Feb. 6
4501 A1261 2500 l multi .35 .25

Valentine's Day A1262

Designs: 5500 l, Mice. 43,500 l, Elephants.

2002, Feb. 8
4502-4503 A1262 Set of 2 4.25 2.00

Famous Men A1263

Designs: 1500 l, Ion Mincu (1852-1912), architect. 2500 l, Costin D. Nenitescu (1902-70), chemist. 5500 l, Alexandre Dumas père (1802-70), writer. 9000 l, Serban Cioculescu (1902-88), writer. 16,500 l, Leonardo da Vinci (1452-1519), artist. 34,000 l, Victor Hugo (1802-85), writer.

2002, Mar. 1
4504-4509 A1263 Set of 6 6.50 3.25

United We Stand — A1264

No. 4510: a, Statue of Liberty, US flag. b, Romanian flag.

2002, Mar. 22
4510 A1264 25,500 l Horiz. pair, #a-b 5.00 3.25

German Fortresses in Romania — A1265

Designs: 1500 l, Saschiz, vert. 2500 l, Darjiu, vert. 6500 l, Viscri. 10,500 l, Vorumloc. 13,500 l, Calnic, vert. 17,500 l, Prejmer, vert.

2002, Apr. 2
4511-4516 A1265 Set of 6 4.50 2.75

Easter — A1266

Designs: 2500 l, Crucifixion. 10,500 l, Resurrection.

2002, Apr. 12 **Photo.** ***Perf. 13¼***
4517-4518 A1266 Set of 2 1.25 .55

Souvenir Sheet

Proclamation of Independence, 125th Anniv. — A1267

2002, May 9
4519 A1267 25,500 l multi 2.50 1.75

Europa — A1268

Clown with: 17,500 l, Yellow hair. 25,500 l, Brown hair.

2002, May 9
4520-4521 A1268 Set of 2 4.50 2.00

Souvenir Sheet

Intl. Federation of Stamp Dealers' Associations, 50th Anniv. — A1269

No. 4522: a, 10,000 l, Romanian flags, #1, 2 and 4. b, 10,000 l, IFSDA emblem. c, 27,500 l, World Trade Center, Bucharest. d, 27,500 l, Romanian philatelic store.

2002, June 10
4522 A1269 Sheet of 4, #a-d 6.00 3.50

Intl. Year of Mountains A1270

2002, June 14
4523 A1270 2000 l multi .30 .25

Intl. Year of Ecotourism A1271

2002, June 14
4524 A1271 3000 l multi .40 .25

Sports A1272

Designs: 7000 l, Cricket. 11,000 l, Polo. 15,500 l, Golf. 19,500 l, Baseball.

2002, July 11
4525-4528 A1272 Set of 4 4.50 2.25

Stamp Day — A1273

No. 4529: a, Ion Luca Caragiale (1852-1912), writer. b, National Theater, Bucharest, 150th anniv.

2002, July 15
4529 A1273 10,000 l Horiz. pair, #a-b 1.75 .85

A1274

A1275

A1276

A1277

Postal Services A1278

2002, Aug. 9
4530 A1274 2000 l multi .25 .25
4531 A1275 3000 l multi .35 .25
4532 A1276 10,000 l multi .85 .40
4533 A1277 15,500 l multi 1.50 .75
4534 A1278 27,500 l multi 2.25 1.10
Nos. 4530-4534 (5) 5.20 2.75

See Nos. 4543-4545.

Souvenir Sheet

Butterflies — A1279

No. 4535: a, Boloria pales carpathomeridionalis. b, Erebia pharte romaniae. c, Peridea korbi herculana. d, Tomares nogelli dobrogensis.

2002, Sept. 2 Photo. *Perf. 13¼*
4535 A1279 44,500 l Sheet of 4, #a-d 13.00 13.00

Locomotives — A1280

Designs: 4500 l, Series 50115, 1930. 6500 l, Series 50025, 1921. 7000 l, Series 230128, 1933. 11,000 l, Series 764493, 1956. 19,500 l, Series 142072, 1939. 44,500 l, Series 704209, 1909.
72,500 l, Locomotive #1, 1872, vert.

2002, Sept. 22 Photo. *Perf. 13¼*
4536-4541 A1280 Set of 6 6.75 3.75

Souvenir Sheet

4542 A1280 72,500 l multi 5.25 3.25

No. 4542 contains one 54x41mm stamp.

A1281

A1282

Postal Services A1283

2002, Oct. 1
4543 A1281 8000 l multi .60 .35
4544 A1282 13,000 l multi .90 .55
4545 A1283 20,500 l multi 1.50 1.00
Nos. 4543-4545 (3) 3.00 1.90

Souvenir Sheet

35th Chess Olympiad, Bled, Slovenia — A1284

No. 4546: a, Knight and bishop. b, Queen and knight. c, King and rook.

2002, Oct. 23
4546 A1284 20,500 l Sheet of 3, #a-c 4.50 2.50

Fruit — A1285

Designs: 15,500 l, Cydonia oblonga. 20,500 l, Armeniaca vulgaris. 44,500 l, Cerasus vulgaris. 73,500 l, Morus nigra.

2002, Nov. 11
4547-4550 A1285 Set of 4 12.00 6.00

Christmas A1286

Santa Claus and helper: 3000 l, With gifts. 15,500 l, At computers.

2002, Nov. 19
4551-4552 A1286 Set of 2 1.40 .80

Invitation to Join NATO A1287

Litho. With Hologram Applied

2002, Nov. 22 *Perf. 12¾*
4553 A1287 131,000 l multi 10.00 10.00

Printed in sheets of 2 + central label. Value, $20.

Paintings — A1288

Designs: 4500 l, Portul Braila, by J.A. Steriadi. 6500 l, Balcic, by N. Darascu. 30,500 l, Conversatie, by N. Vermont. 34,000 l, Dalmatia, by N. Darascu. 46,500 l, Barci Pescaresti, by Steriadi. 53,000 l, Nude, by B. Pietris.
83,500 l, Femeie pe Malul Marii, by N. Grigorescu, vert.

2003, Jan. 22 Photo. *Perf. 13¼*
4554-4559 A1288 Set of 6 12.00 7.00

Souvenir Sheet

4560 A1288 83,500 l multi 6.00 3.25

No. 4560 contains one 41x54mm stamp.

Natl. Military Palace, 80th Anniv. A1289

2003, Jan. 28
4561 A1289 5000 l multi .60 .30

St. Valentine's Day A1290

Designs: 3000 l, Ladybug with heart-shaped spots. 5000 l, Man with ladder, vert.

2003, Feb. 14
4562-4563 A1290 Set of 2 .80 .40

Admission to European Union, 10th Anniv. A1291

2003, Feb. 20
4564 A1291 142,000 l multi 10.00 5.00

Famous Men — A1292

Designs: 6000 l, Ion Irimescu, sculptor, cent. of birth. 18,000 l, Hector Berlioz (1803-69), composer. 20,000 l, Vincent Van Gogh (1853-90), painter. 36,000 l, Dr. Georges de Bellio (1828-94), art collector.

2003, Feb. 27
4565-4568 A1292 Set of 4 5.00 3.00

See also Nos. 4587-4590.

Buildings in Bucharest A1293

Designs: 4500 l, Postal Palace. 5500 l, Economics House. 10,000 l, National Bank of Romania, horiz. 15,500 l, Stock Exchange. 20,500 l, Carol I University. 46,500 l, Atheneum.
73,500 l, Palace of Justice.

2003, Mar. 27 Photo. *Perf. 13¼*
4569-4574 A1293 Set of 6 7.00 4.00

Souvenir Sheet

4575 A1293 73,500 l multi 5.50 2.75

No. 4575 contains one 42x53mm stamp.

Natl. Map and Book Museum, Bucharest — A1294

No. 4576 — Map of Dacia by Petrus Kaerius: a, Northwestern Dacia. b, Northeastern Dacia. c, Southwestern Dacia. d, Southeastern Dacia.
46,500 l, Museum, vert.

2003, Apr. 4 Photo. *Perf. 13¼*
4576 A1294 30,500 l Sheet of 4, #a-d 9.00 4.50

Souvenir Sheet

4577 A1294 46,500 l multi 4.00 2.00

No. 4577 contains one 42x54mm stamp.

Easter — A1295

2003, Apr. 10
4578 A1295 3000 l multi .35 .25

Owls — A1296

Designs: 5000 l, Otus scops. 8000 l, Strix uralensis. 10,000 l, Glaucidium passerinum. 13,000 l, Asio flammeus. 15,500 l, Asio otus. 20,500 l, Aegolius funereus.

2003, Apr. 25
4579-4584 A1296 Set of 6 4.75 2.75

Europa A1297

Poster art: 20,500 l, Butterfly emerging from chrysalis. 73,500 l, Man holding framed picture.

2003, May 9
4585-4586 A1297 Set of 2 5.75 5.75

Famous Men Type of 2003

Designs: 4500 l, Dumitru Staniloae (1903-93), theologian. 8000 l, Alexandru Ciucurecu (1903-77), painter. 30,500 l, Ilarie Voronca (1903-46), writer. 46,500 l, Victor Brauner (1903-66), painter.

2003, June 6 Photo. *Perf. 13¼*
4587-4590 A1292 Set of 4 5.75 3.25

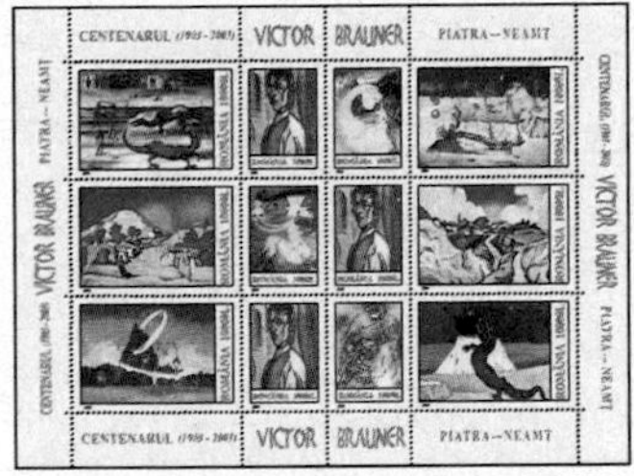
Paintings by Victor Brauner — A1298

No. 4591 — Unidentified paintings: a, Two dragons in foreground. b, White and black arcs (20x30mm). c, Spheres at left. d, Landscape with house with red roof in center. e, Abstract with fish head (20x30mm). f, Landscape with white clouds at left and right. g, Mountain with rings. h, Line drawing of man (20x30mm). i, Fire-breathing dragon. j, Man standing (20x30mm).

2003, June 24
4591 A1298 10,000 l Sheet, #a-i, 3 #j 10.00 5.00

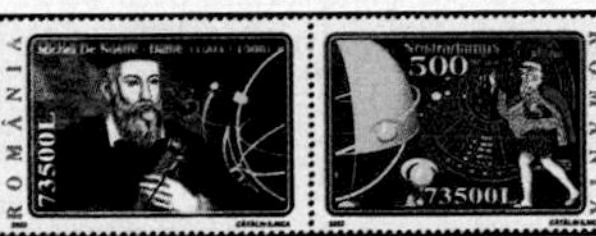
Nostradamus (1503-66), Astrologer — A1299

No. 4592: a, Nostradamus, denomination at left. b, Astrological chart, denomination at bottom.

2003, July 2
4592 A1299 73,500 l Horiz. pair, #a-b 9.00 5.00

Stamp Day A1300

2003, July 15
4593 A1300 5000 l multi .40 .25

Souvenir Sheets

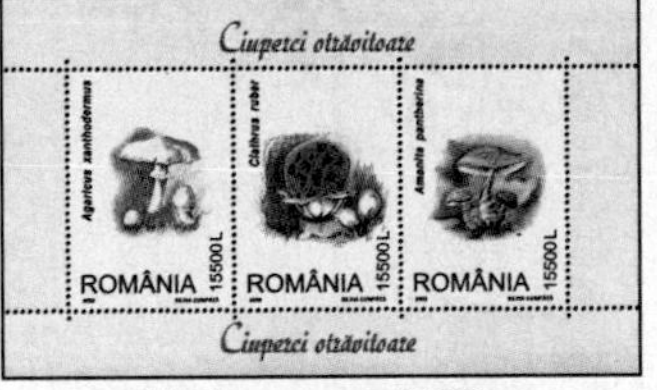
Mushrooms — A1301

No. 4594, 15,500 l: a, Agaricus xanthodermus. b, Clathrus ruber. c, Amanita pantherina.
No. 4595, 20,500 l: a, Leccinum aurantiacum. b, Laetiporus sulphureus. c, Russula xerampelina.

2003, Sept. 19 Sheets of 3, #a-c
4594-4595 A1301 Set of 2 7.50 3.75

Extreme Sports A1302

Designs: 5000 l, Skydiving, vert. 8000 l, Windsurfing. 10,000 l, Motorcycle racing. 30,500 l, Skiing, vert.

2003, Sept. 30
4596-4599 A1302 Set of 4 3.50 1.75

Reptiles and Amphibians — A1303

No. 4600: a, Lacerta viridis. b, Hyla arborea. c, Ablepharus kitaibelii stepanekii. d, Rana temporaria.

2003, Oct. 28
4600 A1303 18,000 l Sheet of 4, #a-d 6.50 3.25

Musical Instruments — A1304

Designs: 1000 l, Lute (cobza). 4000 l, Horn (bucium). 6000 l, Fiddle with horn (vioara cu goarna).

2003, Oct. 31
4601-4603 A1304 Set of 3 .80 .40

Granting of Dobruja Region to Romania, 125th Anniv. — A1305

2003, Nov. 11
4604 A1305 16,000 l multi 1.10 .55

Pope John Paul II and Patriarch Teoctist — A1306

No. 4605: a, Holding crosses. b, Embracing.

2003, Nov. 29
4605 Horiz. pair with 2 central labels 2.00 1.25
a.-b. A1306 16,000 l Either single 1.00 .60

Pontificate of Pope John Paul II, 25th anniv.

Christmas — A1307

No. 4606: a, Santa Claus. b, Snowman.

2003, Dec. 5
4606 A1307 4000 l Horiz. pair, #a-b .50 .25

Women's Fashions in the 20th Century — A1308

No. 4607, 4000 l: a, 1921-30. b, 1931-40.
No. 4608, 21,000 l: a, 1901-10. b, 1911-20.

2003, Dec. 13
Horiz. Pairs, #a-b, + Label
4607-4608 A1308 Set of 2 5.50 2.75

FIFA (Fédération Internationale de Football Association), Cent. (in 2004) — A1309

Designs: 3000 l, Women soccer players. 4000 l, Soccer players, television camera. 6000 l, Men, FIFA charter. 10,000 l, Players, equipment. 34,000 l, Rule book, field diagram.

2003, Dec. 22 Photo. *Perf. 13¼*
4609-4613 A1309 Set of 5 3.50 1.75

Miniature Sheet

Birds — A1310

No. 4614 — UPU emblem and: a, Ardea cinerea. b, Anas platyrhynchos. c, Podiceps cristatus. d, Pelecanus onocrotalus.

2004, Jan. 23 Photo. *Perf. 13¼*
4614 A1310 16,000 l Sheet of 4, #a-d 4.75 2.10

Miniature Sheet

Information Technology — A1311

No. 4615 — UPU emblem and: a, Earth, satellite, compact disc. b, Computer screen showing computer user. c, Earth, satellite dish. d, Computer keyboard, diskette.

2004, Jan. 26
4615 A1311 20,000 l Sheet of 4, #a-d 5.00 2.50

Amerigo Vespucci (1454-1512), Explorer — A1312

Designs: 16,000 l, Vespucci. 31,000 l, Ship.

2004, Jan. 31
4616-4617 A1312 Set of 2 3.00 1.50

St. Valentine's Day — A1313

2004, Feb. 10
4618 A1313 21,000 l multi 1.40 .70

23rd UPU Congress, Bucharest — A1314

No. 4619: a, UPU emblem. b, Congress emblem.

2004, Feb. 20
4619 A1314 31,000 l Horiz. pair, #a-b 4.00 2.00

Easter — A1315

2004, Mar.5
4620 A1315 4000 l multi .35 .25

High Speed Trains A1316

UPU Congress emblem and: 4000 l, Bullet Train, Japan. 6000 l, TGV, France. 10,000 l, KTX, South Korea. 16,000 l, AVE, Spain. 47,000 l, ICE, Germany. 56,000 l, Eurostar, Europe.
77,000 l, Sageata Albastra, Romania.

2004, Mar. 11
4621-4626 A1316 Set of 6 9.00 4.50

Souvenir Sheet
4627 A1316 77,000 l multi 5.00 2.50

No. 4627 contains one 54x42mm stamp.

Admission to NATO — A1317

2004, Mar. 24
4628 A1317 4000 l multi *2.00 1.00*

Women's Fashions Type of 2003

No. 4629, 5000 l: a, 1941-50. b, 1951-60.
No. 4630, 21,000 l: a, 1981-90. b, 1991-2000.
No. 4631, 31,000 l: a, 1961-70. b, 1971-80.

2004, Mar. 31
Horiz. Pairs, #a-b + Label
4629-4631 A1308 Set of 3 8.00 4.00

Intl. Council for Game and Wildlife Conservation, 51st General Assembly A1318

No. 4632 — Emblem and: a, Hunter. b, Dog and pheasant. c, Buck. d, Mountain goat. e, Bear.
No. 4633, Buck, horiz.

2004, Apr. 24
4632 Horiz. strip of 5 5.75 2.75
a.-e. A1318 16,000 l Any single 1.10 .55

Souvenir Sheet
4633 A1318 16,000 l multi 1.10 .55

No. 4633 contains one 54x42mm stamp.

Europa A1319

Stylized sun and: 21,000 l, Beach. 77,000 l, Mountains.

2004, May 7 Photo. *Perf. 13¼*
4634-4635 A1319 Set of 2 6.50 3.25

Michael the Brave (1558-1601), Prince of Walachia — A1320

2004, May 14
4636 A1320 3000 l multi .25 .25

National Philatelic and Romanian History Museum — A1321

2004, May 21
4637 A1321 4000 l multi .30 .25

Souvenir Sheet

Dracula — A1322

No. 4638: a, Bram Stoker, author of Dracula. b, Dracula and cross. c, Dracula and woman. d, Dracula in coffin.

2004, May 21
4638 A1322 31,000 l Sheet of 4, #a-d 8.50 4.25

23rd UPU Congress, Bucharest. Exists imperf.

Famous People A1323

Designs: 4000 l, Anghel Saligny (1854-1925), civil engineer. 16,000 l, Gheorge D. Anghel (1904-66), sculptor. 21,000 l, George Sand (1804-76), author. 31,000 l, Oscar Wilde (1854-1900), writer.

2004, May 27
4639-4642 A1323 Set of 4 5.00 2.25

Romanian Athenaeum — A1324

2004, May 28
4643 A1324 10,000 l multi .60 .30

Johnny Weissmuller (1904-84), Olympic Swimming Gold Medalist, Actor — A1325

2004, June 2 Photo. *Perf. 13¼*
4644 A1325 21,000 l multi 1.40 .70

TAROM Airlines, 50th Anniv. A1326

2004, June 7
4645 A1326 16,000 l multi 1.10 .55

FIFA (Fédération Internationale de Football Association), Cent. — A1327

2004, June 15
4646 A1327 31,000 l multi 2.10 1.00

Miniature Sheets

Stephen the Great (1437-1504), Prince of Moldavia — A1328

No. 4647, 10,000 l: a, Portrait of Stephen the Great, Dobrovat-Iasi Monastery Church. b, Sucevei Fortress. c, Portrait of Stephen the Great, Putna Monastery.
No. 4648, 16,000 l: a, Putna Monastery. b, Stephen the Great. c, Neamtului Fortress.

2004, June 16
Sheets of 3, #a-c
4647-4648 A1328 Set of 2 5.00 2.50

Famous Men A1329

Designs: 2000 l, Alexandru Macedonski (1854-1920), writer. 3000 l, Victor Babes (1854-1926), bacteriologist. 6000 l, Arthur Rimbaud (1854-91), writer. 56,000 l, Salvador Dali (1904-89), painter.

2004, June 30
4649-4652 A1329 Set of 4 5.00 2.25

Flight of Zeppelin LZ-127 Over Brasov, 75th Anniv. A1330

2004, July 29
4653 A1330 31,000 l multi 2.10 1.00

Savings Banks, 140th Anniv. A1331

2004, July 30
4654 A1331 5000 l multi .35 .25

Fire Fighters — A1332

No. 4655: a, Fire fighters leaving truck. b, Fire fighters in protective suits.

Horiz. pair, #a-b, + flanking label

2004, Aug. 12
4655 A1332 12,000 l multi 1.50 .75

2004 Summer Olympics, Athens — A1333

Designs: 7000 l, Rowing. 12,000 l, Fencing. 21,000 l, Swimming. 31,000 l+9000 l, Gymnastics.

2004, Aug. 20 **Litho.** ***Perf. 13¼***
4656-4659 A1333 Set of 4 5.50 2.75

Olymphilex Philatelic Exhibition (#4659).

23rd UPU Congress, Bucharest A1334

Stamps commemorating UPU Congresses: 8000 l, Romania #4619b. 10,000 l, Switzerland #590. 19,000 l, South Korea #1794, horiz. 31,000 l, People's Republic of China #2868. 47,000 l, United States #2434, horiz. 77,000 l, Brazil #1629.

2004, Sept. 10
4660-4665 A1334 Set of 6 12.50 6.25

Sculptures by Idel Ianchelevici (1909-94) A1335

Designs: 21,000 l, L'appel. 31,000 l, Perennis Perdurat Poeta.

2004, Sept. 20
4666-4667 A1335 Set of 2 3.00 1.50

Each stamp printed in sheets of 8 + 2 labels. See Belgium Nos. 2036-2037.

Chinese and Romanian Handicrafts — A1336

No. 4668: a, Drum with tigers and birds, China. b, Cucuteni pottery jar, Romania.

2004, Sept. 24
4668 A1336 5000 l Pair, #a-b .70 .35

See People's Republic of China Nos. 3390-3391.

Souvenir Sheet

23rd UPU Congress, Bucharest — A1337

No. 4669: a, Gerardus Mercator and Jodocus Hondius, cartographers. b, UPU emblem. c, Amerigo Vespucci (1454-1512), explorer.

2004, Oct. 5 ***Perf. 13½***
4669 A1337 118,000 l Sheet of 3, #a-c 24.00 12.00

for surcharge see No. 4755.

Details From Trajan's Column, Rome A1338

Various details: 7000 l, 12,000 l, 19,000 l, 21,000 l, 31,000 l, 56,000 l, 145,000 l.

2004 ***Perf. 13¼***
4670-4676 A1338 Set of 7 20.00 10.00

Issued: 7000 l, 12,000 l, 19,000 l, 56,000 l, 10/15; others, 12/4.

Roses — A1339

Designs: 8000 l, Simfonia. 15,000 l, Foc de Tabara. 25,000 l, Golden Elegance. 36,000 l, Doamna in Mov.

2004, Oct. 25
4677-4680 A1339 Set of 4 6.00 3.00
4680a Souvenir sheet, #4677-4680 6.00 3.00

Ilie Nastase, Tennis Player — A1340

2004, Nov. 16 ***Perf. 13¼***
4681 A1340 10,000 l multi .75 .35

Souvenir Sheets

Perf. 13¼x13¾

4682 A1340 72,000 l Nastase, diff. 5.25 2.60

Imperf

4683 A1340 72,000 l Like No. 4682 5.25 2.60

No. 4682 contains one 42x51mm stamp. No. 4683 contains one 37x48mm stamp.

Christmas — A1341

2004, Nov. 27 ***Perf. 13¼***
4684 A1341 5000 l multi .40 .25

Organizations A1342

Prince Dimitrie Cantemir (1673-1723), Writer — A1343

Designs: 12,000 l, Romanian Boy Scouts. 16,000 l, Lions International. 19,000 l, Red Cross and Red Crescent.

2004, Dec. 8 ***Perf. 13¼***
4685-4687 A1342 Set of 3 3.25 1.60

Souvenir Sheet

Perf. 13¼x13¾

4688 A1343 87,000 l multi 6.00 3.00

Olympic Gold Medalists A1344

Designs: 5000 l, Iolanda Balas, high jump. 33,000 l, Elisabeta Lipa, rowing. 77,000 l, Ivan Pazaichin, canoeing.

2004, Dec. 15 ***Perf. 13¼***
4689-4691 A1344 Set of 3 7.00 4.50

Values are for stamps with surrounding selvage.

Souvenir Sheets

Modern Paintings — A1345

No. 4692, 7000 l: a, Tristan Tzara, by M. H. Maxy. b, Baroness, by Merica Ramniceanu. c, Portrait of a Woman, by Jean David.

No. 4693, 12,000 l: a, Composition, by Marcel Iancu. b, Femele Care Viseaza, by Victor Brauner. c, Composition, by Hans Mattis-Teutsch.

2004, Dec. 16 **Litho.**

Sheets of 3, #a-c

4692-4693 A1345 Set of 2 4.25 2.10

Famous People — A1346

Designs: 15,000 l, Gen. Gheorghe Magheru (1804-80), politician. 25,000 l, Christian Dior (1905-57), fashion designer. 35,000 l, Henry Fonda (1905-82), actor. 72,000 l, Greta Garbo (1905-90), actress. 77,000 l, George Valentin Bibescu (1880-1941), first president of Romanian Auto Club.

2005, Jan. 20 **Litho.** ***Perf. 13¼***
4694-4698 A1346 Set of 5 15.50 7.75

See Nos. 4722-4726.

Rotary International, Cent. A1347

2005, Feb. 23
4699 A1347 21,000 l multi 1.60 .80

Printed in sheets of 4.

Pottery — A1348

Pottery from: 3000 l, Oboga, Olt. 5000 l, Sacel, Maramures. 7000 l, Romana, Olt. 8000 l, Vadul Crisului, Bihor. 10,000 l, Tara Barsei, Brasov. 12,000 l, Horezu, Valcea. 16,000 l, Corund, Harghita.

2005 **Litho.** ***Perf. 13¼***

Pottery Actual Color; Background Color:

4700 A1348 3000 l lilac .25 .25
4701 A1348 5000 l lt blue .45 .25
4702 A1348 7000 l lt green .55 .25
4703 A1348 8000 l rose brn .70 .35
4704 A1348 10,000 l orange .80 .40

4705 A1348 12,000 l green 1.00 .50
4706 A1348 16,000 l lt brown 1.40 .70
Nos. 4700-4706 (7) 5.15 2.70

Issued: 3000 l, 5000 l, 12,000 l, 16,000 l, 2/24. 7000 l, 8000 l, 10,000 l, 3/24.
See Nos. 4767-4775, 4804-4811, 4844-4847.

Dinosaurs — A1349

Designs: 21,000 l, Elopteryx nopcsai. 31,000 l, Telmatosaurus transsylvanicus. 35,000 l, Struthiosaurus transilvanicus. 47,000 l, Hatzegopteryx thambema.

2005, Feb. 25 Litho. *Perf. 13¼*
4707-4710 A1349 Set of 4 10.00 5.00
4710a Souvenir sheet, #4707-4710, + 2 labels 10.00 5.00

Fish — A1350

Designs: 21,000 l, Carassius auratus. 31,000 l, Symphysodon discus. 36,000 l, Labidochromis. 47,000 l, Betta splendens.

2005, Mar. 1 Stamp + Label
4711-4714 A1350 Set of 4 10.00 5.00
4714a Souvenir sheet, #4711-4714, + 4 labels 10.00 5.00

Jules Verne (1828-1905), Writer — A1351

Scenes from stories: 19,000 l, The Castle in the Carpathians. 21,000 l, The Danube Pilot. 47,000 l, Claudius Bombarnac. 56,000 l, Keraban, the Inflexible.

2005, Mar. 29 Litho. *Perf. 13¼*
4715-4718 A1351 Set of 4 10.50 5.25
4718a Souvenir sheet, #4715-4718, + 2 labels 10.50 5.25

Easter — A1352

No. 4719: a, Last Supper. b, Crucifixion (30mm diameter). c, Resurrection.

2005, Apr. 1
4719 A1352 Horiz. strip of 3 1.50 .55
a.-c. 5000 l Any single .40 .25

Pope John Paul II (1920-2005) — A1353

Pope John Paul II and: 5000 l, Dove, map of Romania. 21,000 l, St. Peter's Basilica.

2005, Apr. 8 Litho. *Perf. 13¼*
4720-4721 A1353 Set of 2 2.10 1.00
4721a Souvenir sheet, 2 each #4720-4721 4.50 2.25

Famous People Type of 2005

Designs: 3000 l, Hans Christian Andersen (1805-75), author. 5000 l, Jules Verne (1828-1905), writer. 12,000 l, Albert Einstein (1879-1955), physicist. 21,000 l, Dimitrie Gusti (1880-1955), sociologist. 22,000 l, George Enescu (1881-1955), composer.

2005, Apr. 18
4722-4726 A1346 Set of 5 4.75 2.40

Romanian Accession to European Union — A1354

No. 4727: a, Map in gold. b, Map in silver.

2005, Apr. 25
4727 A1354 Pair .80 .40
a.-b. 5000 l Either single .40 .25
c. Souvenir sheet, 2 each #4727a-4727b 1.75 .85

Pair of No. 3921 Surcharged in Red and Silver

No. 4728 — "Sprijin Pentru Semeni": a, In box. b, Reading up at left.

Wmk. 398
2005, May 9 Photo. *Perf. 13¼*
4728 A1105 Horiz. pair .80 .40
a.-b. 5000 l on 1440 l Either single .40 .25

Nos. 4728a-4728b also have face values expressed in revalued leu currency that was used as of July 1.

Europa — A1355

Designs: 21,000 l, Map of Dacia, archer on horseback, duck and stew pot. 77,000 l, Map, hunting dog, roasted game bird, vegetables, glass of wine.

Perf. 13¼
2005, May 9 Litho. Unwmk.
4729-4730 A1355 Set of 2 6.75 3.25
4730a Souvenir sheet, 2 each #4729-4730, #4729 at UL 13.50 6.75
4730b As "a," #4730 at UL 13.50 6.75

Miniature Sheet

Viticulture — A1356

No. 4731: a, Feteasca alba. b, Grasa de Cotnari. c, Fetesaca neagra. d, Victoria.

2005, May 27
4731 A1356 21,000 l Sheet of 4, #a-d, + 2 labels 6.50 3.25

Nos. 4731a-4731d also have face values expressed in revalued leu currency that was used as of July 1.

Scouting A1357

Designs: No. 4732, 22,000 l, Scout climbing rocks. No. 4733, 22,000 l, Scout following marked trail. No. 4734, 22,000 l, Scouts building campfire. No. 4735, 22,000 l, Scouts reading map.

2005, June 15
4732-4735 A1357 Set of 4 6.00 3.00
4735a Horiz. strip of 4, #4732-4735 6.00 3.00
4735b Souvenir sheet of 4, #4732-4735 6.00 3.00

Nos. 4732-4735 also have face values expressed in revalued leu currency that was used as of July 1.

July 1 Currency Devaluation — A1358

National Bank of Romania, new and old coins or banknotes depicting revaluation of: 30b, 100 old lei to 1 new ban. 50b, 10,000 old lei to 1 new leu. 70b, 500 old lei to 5 new bani. 80b, 50,000 old lei to 5 new lei. 1 l, 100,000 old lei to 10 new lei. 1.20 l, 500,000 old lei to 50 new lei. 1.60 l, 1,000,000 old lei to 100 new lei. 2.10 l, 1000 old lei to 10 new bani. 2.20 l, 5,000,000 old lei to 500 new lei. 3.10 l, 5000 old lei to 50 new bani.

In the pairs, the "a" stamp has the colored denomination panel on the left and shows the obverse of coins at left and reverse of coins at right, or the obverse side of banknotes. The "b" stamp has the panel on the right, shows the reverse of coins at left and obverse of coins at right, or the reverse side of banknotes.

2005, July 1 Litho.
Horiz. or Vert. Pairs, #a-b
Panel Color

4736 A1358 30b gray .40 .25
4737 A1358 50b emerald .70 .35
4738 A1358 70b blue .95 .45
4739 A1358 80b red brown 1.10 .55
4740 A1358 1 l red violet 1.40 .70
4741 A1358 1.20 l dull brown 1.60 .80
4742 A1358 1.60 l olive green 2.25 1.10
4743 A1358 2.10 l blue green 2.75 1.40
4744 A1358 2.20 l bister 3.00 1.50
4745 A1358 3.10 l purple 4.25 2.10
c. Miniature sheet of 10 horiz. pairs, #4736-4745 18.50 9.25

Military Ships — A1359

No. 4746: a, Training ship Constanta. b, Corvette Contraadmiral Horia Macellariu. c, Monitor ship Mihail Kogalniceanu. d, Frigate Marasesti.

2005, July 15 *Perf. 13¼*
4746 Vert. strip of 4 6.00 3.00
a.-d. A1359 2.20 l Any single 1.50 .75
e. Souvenir sheet of 4, #4746a-4746d 6.00 3.00

Stamp Day.

Rainbow and Genesis 1:9 — A1360

2005, Aug. 2
4747 A1360 50b multi + label .45 .25

July 2005 floods in Romania.

Election of Joseph Cardinal Ratzinger as Pope Benedict XVI — A1361

Ratzinger in vestments of: 1.20 l, Cardinal. 2.10 l, Pope.

2005, Aug. 18
4748-4749 A1361 Set of 2 2.75 1.40
4749a Souvenir sheet, #4748-4749 2.75 1.40

European Philatelic Cooperation, 50th Anniv. (in 2006) — A1362

No. 4750 — Christopher Columbus and: a, Denomination to right of face. b, Ship, denomination at lower right. c, Ship, denomination at lower left. d, Denomination to left of face.

2005, Aug. 22 *Perf. 13¼*
4750 A1362 Horiz. strip of 4 13.50 6.75
a.-d. 4.70 l Any single 3.25 1.60
e. Souvenir sheet, #4750a-4750d +2 labels 13.50 6.75

Europa stamps, 50th anniv. (in 2006). The vignettes of Nos. 4750a and 4750d are inside a 31x27mm perf. 13 hexagon. Values for singles of these stamps are for examples with surrounding selvage.
No. 4750 exists imperf.

Children's Art — A1363

Designs: 30b, Forest Mailman, by Bianca Paul. 40b, The Road to You, by Daniel Ciornei. 60b, A Messenger of Peace, by Stefan Ghiliman, horiz. 1 l, Good News for Everybody, by Adina Elena Mocanu, horiz.

2005, Aug. 31 Litho. *Perf. 13¼*
4751-4754 A1363 Set of 4 1.75 .85

No. 4669 Surcharged in Black and Blue

No. 4755: a, Gerardus Mercator and Jodocus Hondius, cartographers. b, UPU emblem. c, Amerigo Vespucci, explorer.

2005, Sept. 26 *Perf. 13½*

4755 A1337 11.80 l on 118,000

Visit of members of European Philatelic Academy to Bucharest.

Dogs — A1364

No. 4756: a, Jagd terrier. b, Rhodesian ridgeback. c, Munsterlander. d, Bloodhound. e, Transylvanian hound (Copoi ardelenesc). f, Pointer.

2005, Sept. 28 *Perf. 13¼*

4756	A1364	Block of 6	10.50	5.25
a.-f.		2.20 l Any single	1.75	.85
g.		Sheet, #4756a-4756f	10.50	5.25

Natl. Philatelic Museum, 1st Anniv. — A1365

2005, Sept. 30

4757 A1365 40b multi .40 .25

World Summit on the Information Society, Tunis — A1366

2005, Oct. 10

4758 A1366 5.60 l multi 4.75 2.25

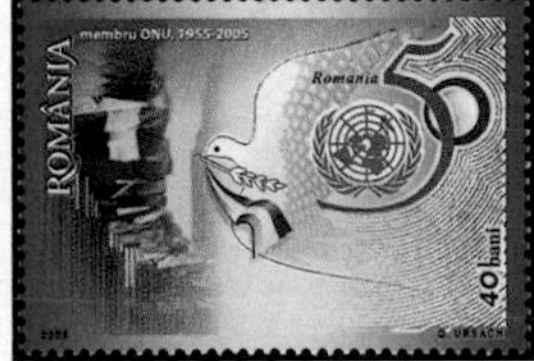

United Nations — A1367

Dove, UN emblem, Romanian flag and: 40b, Flags. 1.50 l, Security Council. 2.20 l, General Assembly building.

2005, Oct. 24

4759-4761	A1367	Set of 3	3.50	1.75
4761a		Souvenir sheet, #4759-4761	3.50	1.75

Romania's admission to UN, 50th anniv. (#4759); Romania's presidency of Security Council, 2004-05 (#4760); UN, 60th anniv. (#4761).

Birthplace of Dimitrie Butculescu, Romanian Philatelic Federation Emblem — A1368

Dimitrie Butculescu, Founder of Romanian Philatelic Society — A1369

Design: No. 4762b, Butculescu, September 1892 edition of Romanian Philatelic Society Monitor.

2005, Nov. 4 *Perf. 13¼*

4762		Horiz. pair with flanking labels	.85	.40
a.-b.	A1368	50b Either single + label	.40	.25

Souvenir Sheet

Imperf

4763 A1369 9 l multi 7.50 3.75

Central University Library, 110th Anniv. — A1370

No. 4764: a, Library building (47x32mm). b, Statue (23x32mm).

2005, Nov. 10 *Perf. 13¼*

4764	A1370	60b Horiz. pair, #a-b	1.00	.50
c.		Souvenir sheet, #4764a-4764b	1.00	.60

Souvenir Sheet

Pigeon Breeds — A1371

No. 4765: a, English Pouter (green frame). b, Parlor rollers (lilac frame). c, Standard carrier (green frame). d, Andalusian (yellow orange frame).

2005, Nov. 18 **Litho.**

4765 A1371 2.50 l Sheet of 4, #a-d 8.25 4.00

UNESCO, 60th Anniv. — A1372

2005, Nov. 21

4766 A1372 60b multi + label 1.25 .60

Pottery Type of 2005

Pottery from: 30b, Leheceni, Bihor. 50b, Vladesti, Valcea. 1 l, Curtea de Arges, Arges. 1.20 l, Vamu, Satu Mare. 2.20 l, Barsa, Arad. 2.50 l, Corund, Harghita. 4.70 l, Targu Neamt, Neamt. 5.60 l, Polana Deleni, Iasi. 14.50 l, Valea Izei, Maramures.

2005 *Perf. 13¼*

Pottery Actual Color; Background Color:

4767	A1348	30b	greenish yel	.25	.25
4768	A1348	50b	blue green	.40	.25
4769	A1348	1 l	red orange	.85	.40
4770	A1348	1.20 l	pale salmon	1.00	.50
4771	A1348	2.20 l	gray	1.75	.85
4772	A1348	2.50 l	pink	2.10	1.00
4773	A1348	4.70 l	blue violet	4.00	2.00
4774	A1348	5.60 l	red	4.75	2.25
4775	A1348	14.50 l	lt bl grn	12.00	6.00
	Nos. 4767-4775 (9)			27.10	13.50

Issued: 4.70 l, 5.60 l, 12/19; others, 11/24.

Christmas — A1373

No. 4776: a, The Annunciation (23x32mm). b, Nativity (47x32mm). c, Madonna and Child with Angels (23x32mm).

2005, Dec. 2

4776 A1373 50b Horiz. strip of 3, #a-c 1.00 .50

Modern Art — A1374

No. 4777: a, Inscriptions, by Virgil Preda. b, The Suspended Garden, by Alin Gheorghiu. c, Still Life with Bottle, by Constantin Ceraceanu. d, Monster 1, by Cristian Paleologu.

2005, Dec. 12

4777 A1374 1.50 l Block of 4, #a-d 5.00 2.50

Cats A1375

Designs: 30b, Norwegian Forest. 50b, Turkish Van. 70b, Siamese. 80b, Ragdoll. 1.20 l, Persian. 1.60 l, Birman.

2006, Jan. 20 *Perf. 13¼*

4778-4783	A1375	Set of 6	4.25	2.10
4783a		Souvenir sheet, #4778-4783, imperf.	4.25	2.10

Famous People — A1376

Designs: 50b, Wolfgang Amadeus Mozart (1756-91), composer. 1.20 l, Ion C. Bratianu (1821-91), Prime Minister. 2.10 l, Grigore Moisil (1906-73), mathematician.

2006, Jan. 27 *Perf. 13¼*

4784-4786 A1376 Set of 3 3.25 1.60

See Nos. 4825-4827.

Souvenir Sheet

2006 Winter Olympics, Turin — A1377

No. 4787: a, Figure skating. b, Downhill skiing. c, Bobsled. d, Biathlon.

2006, Feb. 1

4787 A1377 1.60 l Sheet of 4, #a-d 5.50 2.75

Gold Coins — A1378

Coin obverse and reverse: 30b, 1868 20 lei. 50b, 1906 50 lei. 70b, 1906 100 lei. 1 l, 1922 50 lei. 1.20 l, 1939 100 lei. 2.20 l, 1940 100 lei.

2006, Feb. 22

4788-4793	A1378	Set of 6	5.00	2.50
4788a		Sheet of 7 + 2 labels	1.75	.85
4789a		Sheet of 7 + 2 labels	3.00	1.50
4790a		Sheet of 7 + 2 labels	4.00	2.00
4791a		Sheet of 7 + 2 labels	6.00	3.00
4792a		Sheet of 7 + 2 labels	7.00	3.50
4793a		Sheet of 7 + 2 labels	13.00	6.50

A1379

A1380

A1381

A1382

Easter
A1383

2006, Mar. 15 Litho. *Perf. 13¼*

4794 A1379 50b multi .40 .25
4795 A1380 50b multi .40 .25
4796 A1381 50b multi .40 .25
4797 A1382 50b multi .40 .25
4798 A1383 50b multi .40 .25
a. Souvenir sheet, #4794-4798, + 4 labels, with red labels at UL and LR 2.00 1.00
b. As "a," with red labels at UR and LL 2.00 1.00
Complete booklet, 4 each #4794-4798 8.00
Nos. 4794-4798 (5) 2.00 1.25

First Flight of Traian Vuia, Cent. — A1384

Outline drawings of aircraft and: 70b, Traian Vuia. 80b, Vuia I aircraft. 1.60 l, Vuia II aircraft. 4.70 l, Vuia in airplane, vert.

2006, Mar. 18 *Perf. 13¼*

4799-4801 A1384 Set of 3 2.50 1.25
4799a Sheet of 8 + label 4.75 2.40
4800a Sheet of 8 + label 5.50 2.75
4801a Souvenir sheet, #4799-4801 + label 2.50 1.25
4801b Sheet of 8 + label 11.00 5.50

Souvenir Sheet

Perf. 13¼x14

4802 A1384 4.70 l multi 4.00 2.00

No. 4802 contains one 42x52mm stamp.

Léopold Sédar Senghor (1906-2001), First President of Senegal — A1385

2006, Mar. 20 *Perf. 13¼*

4803 A1385 2.10 l multi 1.75 .85
a. Souvenir sheet of 4 7.00 3.50

Pottery Type of 2005

Pottery from: 30b, Oboga, Olt. 40b, Radauti, Suceava. 60b, Poienita, Arges. 70b, Oboga, Olt, diff. 80b, Oboga, Olt, diff. 1.60 l, Romana, Olt. 2.50 l, Vladesti, Valcea. 3.10 l, Jupanesti, Timis.

2006 *Perf. 13¼*

Pottery Actual Color; Background Color:

4804 A1348 30b lilac .25 .25
a. Sheet of 9 2.25 1.10
4805 A1348 40b yellow .35 .25
a. Sheet of 9 3.25 1.60
4806 A1348 60b pale salmon .50 .25
a. Sheet of 9 4.50 2.25
4807 A1348 70b bister .60 .30
a. Sheet of 9 5.50 2.75
4808 A1348 80b gray blue .70 .35
a. Sheet of 9 6.25 3.00
4809 A1348 1.60 l gray 1.25 .60
a. Sheet of 9 11.50 5.75
4810 A1348 2.50 l light green 2.10 1.00
a. Sheet of 9 19.00 9.50
4811 A1348 3.10 l light blue 2.50 1.25
a. Sheet of 9 22.50 11.00
Nos. 4804-4811 (8) 8.25 4.25

Issued: 60b, 70b, 80b, 1.60 l, 3/30; others 4/20.

Tulip Varieties — A1386

Designs: 30b, Turkestanica. 50b, Ice Follies. 1 l, Cardinal. 1.50 l, Yellow Empress, horiz. (47x32mm). 2.10 l, Donna Bella. 3.60 l, Don Quixote, horiz. (47x32mm).

2006, Apr. 14 Litho. *Perf. 13¼*

4812-4817 A1386 Set of 6 7.50 3.75
a. Block of 6, #4812-4817 7.50 3.75
b. Souvenir sheet of 6, #4812-4817 7.50 3.75
c. Miniature sheet, 2 each #4812-4817 15.00 7.50

Europa — A1387

Children's drawings: 2.10 l, Children, house, sun. 3.10 l, People, house, fence.

2006, May 4

4818-4819 A1387 Set of 2 4.50 2.25
4819a Souvenir sheet, 2 each #4818-4819, #4818 at UL 9.00 4.50
4819b Souvenir sheet, 2 each #4818-4819, #4819 at UL 9.00 4.50

Romanian Stamps Depicting Royalty A1388

Crown and: 30b, Prince Carol I (#29). 1 l, King Ferdinand I (#248). 2.10 l, King Carol II (#376). 2.50 l, King Michael (#513).
4.70 l, Carol I as Prince and King (#180), horiz.

2006, May 8

4820-4823 A1388 Set of 4 5.00 2.50
4823a Miniature sheet, #4820-4823 5.00 2.50

Souvenir Sheet

Perf. 14x13¼

4824 A1388 4.70 l multi 4.00 2.00

Foundation of Romanian royal dynasty, 140th anniv., Proclamation of Romanian kingdom, 125th anniv. No. 4824 contains one 51x41mm stamp.

Famous People Type of 2006

Designs: 50b, Christopher Columbus (1451-1506), explorer. 1 l, Paul Cézanne (1839-1906), painter. 1.20 l, Henrik Ibsen (1828-1906), writer.

2006, May 17 *Perf. 13¼*

4825-4827 A1376 Set of 3 2.25 1.10

Dimitrie Gusti National Village Museum, 70th Anniv. A1389

2006, May 17

4828 A1389 2.20 l multi 1.90 .95
a. Sheet of 8 + central label 13.00 6.50

No. 4092 Surcharged in Gold or Silver

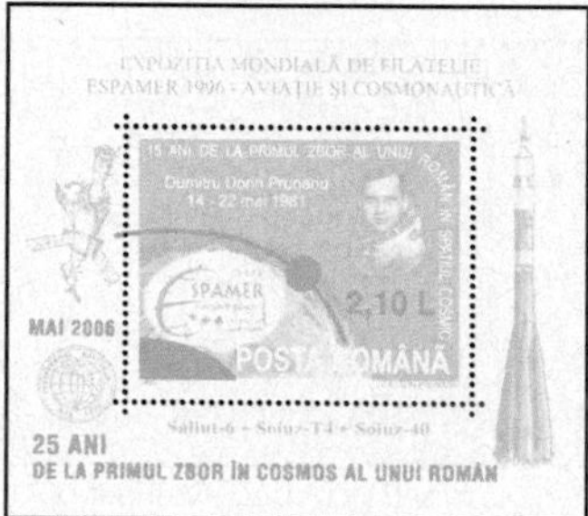

2006, May 19 *Perf. 13½*

4829 A1155 2.10 l on 2720 l #4092 (G) 1.75 .85
4830 A1155 2.10 l on 2720 l #4092 (S) 1.75 .85

First Romanian in space, 25th anniv.

1906 General Exhibition and Carol I Park, Bucharest, Cent. — A1390

Designs: 30b, Main entrance to Carol I Park. 50b, Tepes Castle. 1 l, Post Office Pavilion. 1.20 l, European Danube Commission Pavilion. 1.60 l, Industry Palace. No. 4836, 2.20 l, Roman arenas.
No. 4837, Arts Palace.

2006, June 6 *Perf. 13¼*

4831-4836 A1390 Set of 6 5.75 2.75
4836a Miniature sheet, #4831-4836 5.75 2.75

Souvenir Sheet

Perf. 14x13¼

4837 A1390 2.20 l multi 1.90 .95

No. 4837 contains one 51x41mm stamp.

Composers — A1391

No. 4838: a, Béla Bartók (1881-1945) and Hungarian flag. b, George Enescu (1881-1955) and Romanian flag.

2006, June 8 *Perf. 13¼*

4838 A1391 1.20 l Horiz. pair, #a-b 2.00 1.00
c. Souvenir sheet, #4838 2.00 1.00
d. Sheet of 6 pairs 10.50 5.25

The stamps on No. 4838d are arranged so that the stamps in the middle of the sheet are tete-beche pairs of the same stamp. No. 4838d exists with two arrangements of the stamps, one with No. 4838a as the stamps in the middle of the sheet, the other with No. 4838b as the stamps in the middle of the sheet.

2006 World Cup Soccer Championships, Germany — A1392

Designs: 30b, World Cup. 50b, Ball in goal. 1 l, Player dribbling ball. 1.20 l, Player lifting World Cup.

2006, June 9

4839-4842 A1392 Set of 4 2.50 1.25
4842a Souvenir sheet, #4839-4842 2.50 1.25

Intl. Day Against Drug Abuse and Illegal Trafficking — A1393

2006, June 26

4843 A1393 2.20 l multi 1.90 .95

Pottery Type of 2005

Pottery from: 30b, Golesti, Arges. 70b, Romana, Olt. 1 l, Oboga, Olt. 2.20 l, Vama, Satu Mare.

2006, July 10 *Perf. 13¼*

Pottery Actual Color; Background Color:

4844 A1348 30b tan .25 .25
a. Sheet of 9 2.25 1.10
4845 A1348 70b yel orange .60 .30
a. Sheet of 9 5.50 2.75
4846 A1348 1 l green .85 .40
a. Sheet of 9 7.75 3.75
4847 A1348 2.20 l blue green 1.90 .95
a. Sheet of 9 17.00 8.50
Nos. 4844-4847 (4) 3.60 1.90

Decebalus (d. 106), Dacian King — A1394

Map and: 30b, Coins and Decebalus. 50b, Head of Decebalus. 1.20 l, Dacian helmet. 3.10 l, Decebalus, diff.

2006, July 15

4848-4851 A1394 Set of 4 4.25 2.10
4851a Souvenir sheet, #4848-4851 4.25 2.10

Stamp Day.

Minerals — A1395

Designs: 30b, Fluorite. 50b, Quartz. 1 l, Agate. 1.20 l, Blende. 1.50 l, Amethyst. 2.20 l, Stibnite.

2006, Aug. 7

4852-4857 A1395 Set of 6 5.50 2.75
4857a Souvenir sheet, #4852-4857 5.50 2.75

Nos. 4852-4857 were each printed in sheets of 18 + 3 labels.

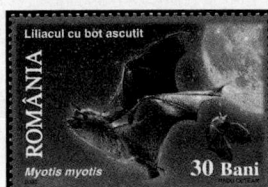

Bats — A1396

Designs: 30b, Myotis myotis. 50b, Rhinolophus hipposideros. 1 l, Plecotus auritus. 1.20 l, Pipistrellus pipistrellus. 1.60 l, Nyctalus lasiopterus. 2.20 l, Barbastella barbastellus.

2006, Aug. 15

4858-4863 A1396 Set of 6 5.50 2.75
4863a Souvenir sheet, #4858-4863 5.50 2.75

Railroads in Romania, 150th Anniv. — A1397

Locomotives: 30b, StEG111 Wartberg, 1854. 50b, D. B. S. R. 1 Ovidiu, 1860. 1 l, L. C. J. E. 56 Curierulu, 1869. 1.20 l, C. F. R. 1 Berlad, 1869. 1.50 l, B. M. 1 Unirea, 1877. 1.60 l, Fulger and King Carol I Pullman Express, 1933.
2.20 l, StEG 500 Steyerdorf.

2006, Aug. 23

4864-4869 A1397 Set of 6 5.00 2.50

Souvenir Sheet

4870 A1397 2.20 l multi 1.90 .95

No. 4870 contains one 71x32mm stamp.

EFIRO 2008 World Philatelic Exhibition, Bucharest A1398

Exhibition emblem and: 30b, Romania #1. 50b, Romania #2. 1.20 l, Romania #4. 1.60 l, Romania #3.
2.20 l, Bull and vignette of Romania #1.

2006, Aug. 30

4871-4874 A1398 Set of 4 4.00 2.00

Souvenir Sheet

Perf. 13¼x14

4875 A1398 2.20 l multi 1.90 .95

No. 4875 contains one 41x51mm stamp. Nos. 4871-4874 were each printed in sheets of 16 + 8 labels.

National Lottery, Cent. A1399

2006, Sept. 14 ***Perf. 13¼***

4876 A1399 1 l multi .85 .40

Printed in sheets of 27 + 1 label.

No. 4098 Surcharged in Gold

2006, Sept. 16 Litho. *Perf. 13½*

4877 A1159 5.60 l on 4050 l #4098 4.75 2.25

Sculptures by Constantin Brancusi (1876-1957) — A1400

Designs: 2.10 l, Sleeping Muse. 3.10 l, Sleep.

2006, Sept. 25 ***Perf. 13¼***

4878-4879 A1400 Set of 2 4.50 2.25
4878a Sheet of 12 18.00 9.00
4879a Souvenir sheet, #4878-4879 4.50 2.25
4879b Sheet of 12 27.00 13.50

The third stamp down in the middle column of Nos. 4878a and 4879b is inverted in relation to the other stamps in the sheet.
See France Nos. 3245-3246.

11th Francophone Summit, Bucharest A1401

2006, Sept. 28 ***Perf. 13¼***

4880 A1401 1.20 l multi 1.00 .50

Souvenir Sheet

Perf. 13¼x14

4881 A1401 5.60 l multi 4.75 2.25

No. 4881 contains one 41x51mm stamp.

Romanian Peasant Museum, Cent. — A1402

Designs: 40b, Headdress, 20th cent. 70b, Turkish belt, 19th cent. 1.60 l, Coin necklace, 19th cent. 3.10 l, Musuem founder Alexandru Tzgara-Samurcas.

2006, Oct. 5 ***Perf. 13¼***

4882-4885 A1402 Set of 4 5.00 2.50

Souvenir Sheet

Romanian Division of Intl. Police Association, 10th Anniv. — A1403

2006, Oct. 7

4886 A1403 8.70 l multi 7.25 3.50

Worldwide Fund for Nature (WWF) — A1404

Platalea leucorodia: No. 4887, 80b, Adult and chicks at nest. No. 4888, 80b, Birds in flight. No. 4889, 80b, Birds at water. No. 4890, 80b, Two birds.

2006, Oct. 20

4887-4890 A1404 Set of 4 3.25 2.25
4890a Souvenir sheet, #4887-4890 3.25 3.25

Nos. 4887-4890 each were printed in sheets of 10 + 2 labels.

Romanian Orders — A1405

Designs: 30b, Order of Loyal Service. 80b, Order of Romanian Star. 2.20 l, Order of Merit. 2.50 l, First Class Order of Merit in Sports.

2006, Oct. 30 ***Perf. 13¼x14***

4891-4894 A1405 Set of 4 5.00 2.50

A small star-shaped hole was punched into Nos. 4891-4894.

Actors and Actresses A1406

Designs: 40b, Radu Beligan. 1 l, Carmen Stanescu. 1.50 l, Dina Cocea. 2.20 l, Colea Rautu.

2006, Nov. 15 ***Perf. 13¼***

4895-4898 A1406 Set of 4 4.25 2.10

Christmas A1407

Designs: No. 4899, 50b, Madonna and Child (shown). No. 4900, 50b, Adoration of the Magi. No. 4901, 50b, Madonna and Child enthroned with angels.

2006, Nov. 17

4899-4901 A1407 Set of 3 1.25 .60
4901a Sheet of 9, 3 each #4899-4901 3.75 1.90

Art by Ciprian Paleologu — A1408

Designs: 30b, Ad Perpetuam Rei Memoriam. 1.50 l, Cui Bono? 3.60 l, Usqve Ad Finem.

2006, Nov. 30

4902-4904 A1408 Set of 3 4.50 2.25

2007 Admission of Romania and Bulgaria into European Union — A1409

Designs: 50b, "EU" in colors of Bulgarian and Romanian flags. 2.10 l, Flags of Bulgaria and Romania, map of Europe, European Union ballot box.

2006, Nov. 26 Litho. *Perf. 13¼*

4905-4906 A1409 Set of 2 2.00 1.00
4906a Sheet of 8, 4 each #4905-4906, + label 8.00 4.00

See Bulgaria Nos. 4412-4413.

Currency Devaluation Type of 2005

1,000,000 old lei bank notes and 200 lei note: 50b, Obverses of notes. 1.20 l, Reverses of notes.

2006, Dec. 1 Litho. *Perf. 13¼*

4907-4908 A1358 Set of 2 1.40 .70
4908a Sheet of 16, 8 each #4907-4908 11.50 5.75

UNICEF, 60th Anniv. — A1410

2006, Dec. 11

4909 A1410 3.10 l multi 2.50 1.25

Admission into European Union — A1411

2007, Jan. 3 Litho. *Perf. 13¼*

4910 A1411 2.20 l multi + label 1.75 .85
a. Sheet of 8 + 8 labels 14.00 7.00

Biospeleology, Cent. — A1412

Designs: 40b, Altar Rock Cave. 1.60 l, Emil Racovita (1868-1947), founder of Biospeleology Institute. 7.20 l, Ursus spelaeus. 8.70 l, Typhlocirolana moraguesi.

2007, Jan. 19

4911-4914 A1412 Set of 4 14.00 7.00
4914a Souvenir sheet, #4911-4914 14.00 7.00

Intl. Holocaust Remembrance Day — A1413

2007, Jan. 27

4915 A1413 3.30 l multi 2.60 1.40

Printed in sheets of 32 + 4 labels.

Black Sea Fauna A1414

Designs: 70b, Hypocampus hypocampus. 1.50 l, Delphinus delphis. 3.10 l, Caretta caretta. 7.70 l, Trigla lucerna.

2007, Feb. 9

4916-4919 A1414 Set of 4 10.50 5.25
4919a Souvenir sheet, #4916-4919 10.50 5.25

Famous People — A1415

Designs: 60b, Gustave Eiffel (1832-1923), engineer. 80b, Maria Cutarida (1857-1919), physician. 2.10 l, Virginia Woolf (1882-1941), writer. 3.50 l, Nicolae Titulescu (1882-1941), politician.

2007, Feb. 23

4920-4923 A1415 Set of 4 5.50 2.75

Easter — A1416

No. 4924: a, Decorated Easter egg, Olt (30mm diameter). b, Detail from painted glass icon. c, Decorated Easter egg, Bucovina (30mm diameter).

2007, Mar. 9

4924 A1416 50b Horiz. strip of 3, #a-c 1.25 .60
d. Miniature sheet, 3 each #4924a-4924c 3.75 1.90

Orchids A1417

Designs: 30b, Cephalanthera rubra. 1.20 l, Epipactis palustris. 1.60 l, Dactylorhiza maculata. 2.50 l, Anacamptis pyramidalis. 2.70 l, Limodorum abortivum. 6 l, Ophrys scolopax.

2007, Mar. 23

4925-4930 A1417 Set of 6 11.50 5.75
a. Souvenir sheet, #4925-4930 11.50 5.75

Nos. 4925-4930 each were printed in sheets of 21. The right column of stamps in each sheet have 3 perforation holes separating the stamp from the right selvage, which promotes the 2008 Efiro Intl. Philatelic Exhibition, Bucharest.

Peasant Plates — A1418

Plates from: 70b, Oboga, Olt. 1 l, Varna, Satu Mare. 2.10 l, Valea Izei, Maramures. 2.20 l, Fagaras, Brasov.

2007, Apr. 13

4931 A1418 70b blue & multi .60 .30
a. Miniature sheet of 6 3.75 1.90
4932 A1418 1 l fawn & multi .85 .40
a. Miniature sheet of 6 5.25 2.60
4933 A1418 2.10 l lt grn & multi 1.75 .85
a. Miniature sheet of 6 10.50 5.25
4934 A1418 2.20 l yel & multi 1.90 .95
a. Miniature sheet of 6 11.50 5.75
Nos. 4931-4934 (4) 5.10 2.50

See Nos. 4950-4957.

Birds of Prey — A1419

Designs: 50b, Accipiter nisus. 80b, Circus aeruginosus. 1.60 l, Aquila pomarina. 2.50 l, Buteo buteo. 3.10 l, Athene noctua.
4.70 l, Falco subbuteo.

2007, Apr. 19 Litho. *Perf. 13¼*

4935-4939 A1419 Set of 5 7.00 3.50

Souvenir Sheet

Perf. 13¼x14

4940 A1419 4.70 l multi 4.00 2.00

No. 4940 contains one 42x52mm stamp.

Europa A1420

Designs: 2.10 l, Scouts. 7.70 l, Lord Robert Baden-Powell.

2007, May 3 Litho. *Perf. 13¼*

4941-4942 A1420 Set of 2 8.00 4.00
4942a Souvenir sheet, 2 each #4941-4942, #4941 at UL 16.00 8.00
4942b As "a," #4942 at UL 16.00 8.00

Scouting, cent. Nos. 4941-4942 each printed in sheets of 6.

Old Bucharest — A1421

Designs: 30b, Vlad Tepes, Old Court, document mentioning Bucharest for first time. 50b, Sturdza Palace and arms. 70b, National Military Circle building and arms. 1.60 l, National Theater, Prince Alexandru Ioan Cuza. 3.10 l, I. C. Bratianu Square, King Carol I. 4.70 l, Senate Square and arms.
5.60 l, Romanian Athenaeum.

2007, May 15 *Perf. 13¼*

4943-4948 A1421 Set of 6 9.00 4.50
4948a Miniature sheet, #4943-4948, + 3 labels 9.00 4.50

Souvenir Sheet

Perf. 14x13¼

4949 A1421 5.60 l multi 4.75 2.40

No. 4949 contains one 42x42mm stamp

Peasant Plates Type of 2007

Plates from: 60b, Tirgu Lapus, Maramures. 70b, Vladesti, Valcea. No. 4952, 80b, Vistea, Brasov. No. 4953, 80b, Luncavita, Tulcea. 1.10 l, Horezu, Valcea. No. 4955, 1.60 l, Tansa, Iasi. No. 4956, 1.60 l, Radauti, Suceava. 3.10 l, Romana, Olt.

2007 *Perf. 13¼*

4950 A1418 60b gray & multi .50 .25
a. Miniature sheet of 6 3.00 1.50
4951 A1418 70b bl grn & multi .60 .30
a. Miniature sheet of 6 3.75 1.90
4952 A1418 80b org & multi .65 .35
a. Miniature sheet of 6 4.00 2.00
4953 A1418 80b pink & multi .70 .35
a. Miniature sheet of 6 4.25 2.10
4954 A1418 1.10 l gray & multi .95 .45
a. Miniature sheet of 6 5.75 2.75
4955 A1418 1.60 l grn & multi 1.40 .70
a. Miniature sheet of 6 8.50 4.25
4956 A1418 1.60 l yel org & multi 1.40 .70
a. Miniature sheet of 6 8.50 4.25
4957 A1418 3.10 l pink & multi 2.60 1.25
a. Miniature sheet of 6 16.00 8.00
Nos. 4950-4957 (8) 8.80 4.35

Issued: Nos. 4950, 4953, 4954, 4956, 8/3; Nos. 4951, 4952, 4955, 4957, 6/5.

Steaua Sports Club, 60th Anniv. — A1422

2007, June 7

4958 A1422 7.70 l multi 6.50 3.25

Printed in sheets of 8 + label.

Romanian Savings Bank Building, 110th Anniv. — A1423

Various views of building with frame color of: 4.70 l, Brown. 5.60 l, Olive green.

2007, June 8

4959 A1423 4.70 l multi 4.00 2.00

Souvenir Sheet

4960 A1423 5.60 l multi + label 4.75 2.40

No. 4959 printed in sheets of 12 with one stamp tete-beche in relation to others.

Sibiu, 2007 European Cultural Capital — A1424

Designs: 30b, Altemberger House, knights from church altar, Dupus. 50b, Liars' Bridge and Council Tower, 18th cent. Transylvanian Saxons. 60b, Parochial Evangelical Church, painting of the Crucifixion. 70b, Grand Square, 1780, 18th cent. peasants. 2.10 l, Brukenthal Palace, statue of St. Nepomuk, portrait of Samuel von Brukenthal. 5.60 l, Sibiu, 1790, Cisnadie Gate Tower.
4.70 l, Sibiu Fortress.

2007, June 11 *Perf. 13¼*

4961-4966 A1424 Set of 6 8.50 4.25
4966a Miniature sheet, #4961-4966, + 3 labels 8.50 4.25

Souvenir Sheet

Perf. 14x13¼

4967 A1424 4.70 l multi 4.25 2.10

No. 4967 contains one 52x42mm stamp.

Ducks and Geese — A1425

Designs: 40b, Anser erythropus. 60b, Branta ruficollis. 1.60 l, Anas acuta. 2.10 l, Anser albifrons. 3.60 l, Netta rufina. 4.70 l, Anas querquedula.
5.60 l, Anas clypeata.

2007, July 12 *Perf. 13¼*

4968-4973 A1425 Set of 6 11.50 5.75
4973a Miniature sheet, #4968-4973 11.50 5.75

Souvenir Sheet

Imperf

4974 A1425 5.60 l multi 5.00 2.50

Nos. 4968-4973 each printed in sheets of 10 + 5 labels. No. 4974 contains one 52x42mm stamp.

Bistra Resort Local Postage Stamps, Cent. — A1426

Designs: 50b, Carriage, Upper Colony cabins, 6 heller stamp. 2.10 l, Lower Colony cabins, postman, 2 heller stamp.

2007, July 18 *Perf. 13¼*

4975-4976 A1426 Set of 2 2.25 1.10

Teoctist (1915-2007), Patriarch of Romanian Orthodox Church A1427

2007, Aug. 3 Litho.

4977 A1427 80b multi .70 .35

Printed in sheets of 4 + 2 labels.

Pottery Baskets, Cups and Pitchers — A1428

Designs: 1.40 l, Basket, Horezu, Valcea. 1.80 l, Cup, Baia Mare, Maramures. 2.10 l, Pitcher, Transylvania. 2.90 l, Cup, Oboga, Olt. 3.10 l, Pitcher, Horezu, Valcea. 7.20 l, Cup, Obarsa, Hunedoara. 7.10 l, Cup, Baia Mare, Maramures, diff. 8.70 l, Cup, Baia Mare, Maramures, diff.

2007 ***Perf. 13¼***

4978 A1428 1.40 l gray & multi 1.25 .60
a. Miniature sheet of 4 5.00 2.50
4979 A1428 1.80 l pink & multi 1.60 .80
a. Miniature sheet of 4 6.50 3.25
4980 A1428 2.10 l blue & multi 1.75 .90
a. Miniature sheet of 4 7.00 3.75
4981 A1428 2.90 l bis & multi 2.50 1.25
a. Miniature sheet of 4 10.00 5.00
4982 A1428 3.10 l lilac & multi 2.60 1.25
a. Miniature sheet of 4 10.50 5.00
4983 A1428 7.20 l yel & multi 6.00 3.00
a. Miniature sheet of 4 24.00 12.00
4984 A1428 7.70 l gray grn & multi 6.75 3.50
a. Miniature sheet of 4 27.00 14.00
4985 A1428 8.70 l lt grn & multi 7.50 3.75
a. Miniature sheet of 4 30.00 15.00
Nos. 4978-4985 (8) 29.95 15.05

Issued: Nos. 4978, 4979, 4981, 4984, 8/10. Nos. 4980, 4982, 4983, 4985, 11/7.
See Nos. 5027-5030.

EFIRO 2008 World Philatelic Exhibition, Bucharest — A1429

EFIRO emblem and: 1.10 l, Romania #8. 2.10 l, Romania #9. 3.30 l, Romania #10. 5.60 l, Star, bull's head and post horn.

2007, Aug. 17 **Litho.** ***Perf. 13¼***

Stamp + Label

4986-4988 A1429 Set of 3 5.50 2.75

Souvenir Sheet

Perf. 13¼x13¾

4989 A1429 5.60 l multi 4.75 2.40

No. 4989 contains one 42x52mm stamp.

Famous Germans Born in Romania A1430

Designs: 1.90 l, Johannes Honterus (1498-1549), author, cartographer. 2.10 l, Hermann Oberth (1894-1989), rocket scientist. 3.90 l, Stephan Ludwig Roth (1796-1849), educator.

2007, Aug. 24 **Litho.** ***Perf. 13¼***

4990-4992 A1430 Set of 3 6.75 3.25

Nos. 4990-4992 each printed in sheets of 8 + label.

Casa Luxemburg, Sibiu — A1431

Various views of building.

2007, Sept. 3 ***Perf. 13¼***

4993 A1431 3.60 l multi 3.00 1.50

Souvenir Sheet

Perf. 14x13¼

4994 A1431 4.30 l multi 3.75 1.90

No. 4994 contains one 52x42mm stamp. See Luxembourg No. 1222.

Modern Romanian Monetary System, 140th Anniv. — A1432

Coins: 3.90 l, Reverse of 1867 1-ban coin. 5.60 l, Reverse of 1870 1-leu coin.

2007, Sept. 12 **Litho.** ***Perf. 13¼***

4995 A1432 3.90 l multi 3.25 1.60

Souvenir Sheet

Perf.

4996 A1432 5.60 l multi 4.75 2.40

Values for No. 4995 are for stamps with surrounding selvage.

2007 Rugby World Cup, France — A1433

Various players: 1.80 l, 3.10 l.

2007, Sept. 25 ***Perf. 13¼***

4997-4998 A1433 Set of 2 4.25 2.10

Nos. 4997-4998 each printed in sheets of 8 + label.

Launch of Sputnik 1, 50th Anniv. — A1434

Sputnik 1 and: 3.10 l, Earth and Moon. 5.60 l, Earth.

2007, Oct. 4 ***Perf. 13¼***

4999 A1434 3.10 l multi 2.60 1.25

Souvenir Sheet

Perf. 14x13¼

5000 A1434 5.60 l multi 4.75 2.40

No. 4999 printed in sheets of 8 + label.

Christmas — A1435

2007, Nov. 3 ***Perf. 13¼***

5001 A1435 80b multi .70 .35

Printed in sheets of 8 + label.

Support for the Blind — A1436

2007, Nov. 13 **Litho.** ***Perf. 13¼***

5002 A1436 5.60 l multi 4.75 2.40

Printed in sheets of 10 + 2 labels.

Danube River Harbors and Ships — A1437

Ships and: 1 l, Orsova, Romania. 1.10 l, Novi Sad, Serbia.
No. 5005 — Ships: a, Orsova. b, Sirona.

2007, Nov. 14

5003-5004 A1437 Set of 2 1.75 .90

Souvenir Sheet

5005 A1437 2.10 l Sheet of 2, #a-b, + 2 labels 3.50 1.75

Nos. 5003 and 5004 each were printed in sheets of 10 + 5 labels. See Serbia Nos. 412-414.

Arctic Animals — A1438

Designs: 30b, Ursus maritimus. 50b, Pagophilus groenlandicus, vert. 1.90 l, Alopex lagopus, vert. 3.30 l, Aptenodytes forsteri. 3.60 l, Balaenoptera musculus. 4.30 l, Odobenus rosmarus, vert.

2007, Dec. 12 **Litho.** ***Perf. 13¼***

5006-5011 A1438 Set of 6 11.50 5.75

Edible and Poisonous Mushrooms A1439

Designs: 1.20 l, Lepiota rhacodes. 1.40 l, Lactarius deliciosus. 2 l, Morchella esculenta. 2.40 l, Paxillus involutus. 3 l, Gyromitra exculenta. 4.50 l, Russula emetica.

2008, Jan. 18 **Litho.** ***Perf. 13¼***

5012-5017 A1439 Set of 6 11.50 5.75
5017a Miniature sheet of 6, #5012-5017 11.50 5.75

Henri Farman (1874-1958) and Voisin-Farman I Bis Airplane — A1440

2008, Jan. 25

5018 A1440 5 l multi 4.00 2.00

Printed in sheets of 8 + label. First flight of one kilometer over a circular course, cent.

Firearms in Natl. Military Museum A1441

Designs: 50b, Four-barreled flint pistol, 18th cent. 1 l, Flint pistol, 18th cent. 2.40 l, Mannlicher carbine pistol, 1903. 5 l, 8mm revolver, 1915.

2008, Feb. 8 **Litho.** ***Perf. 13¼***

5019-5022 A1441 Set of 4 7.25 3.75
5022a Souvenir sheet of 4, #5019-5022, + 2 labels 7.25 3.75

No. 5022a exists with top gun in top label pointing either left or right.

1958 Space Exploration Missions, 50th Anniv. — A1442

Designs: 1 l, Explorer 1. 2.40 l, Sputnik 3. 3.10 l, Jupiter AM-13.

2008, Feb. 22

5023-5025 A1442 Set of 3 5.00 5.00

Nos. 5023-5025 each were printed in sheets of 8 + central label.

Easter — A1443

2008, Mar. 12

5026 A1443 1 l multi .85 .40

Printed in sheets of 8 + central label.

Pottery Cups and Pitchers Type of 2007

Designs: 2 l, Cup, Cosesti, Arges. 2.40 l, Pitcher, Radauti, Suceava. 6 l, Pitcher, Baia Mare, Maramures. 7.60 l, Lidded pot, Vladesti, Valcea.

2008, Mar. 21 ***Perf. 13¼***

5027 A1428 2 l bl grn & multi 1.75 .85
a. Miniature sheet of 4 7.00 3.50
5028 A1428 2.40 l bl grn & multi 2.10 1.10
a. Miniature sheet of 4 8.50 4.50
5029 A1428 6 l bl grn & multi 5.25 2.60
a. Miniature sheet of 4 21.00 10.50
5030 A1428 7.60 l bl grn & multi 6.50 3.25
a. Miniature sheet of 4 26.00 13.00
Nos. 5027-5030 (4) 15.60 7.80

NATO Summit, Bucharest A1444

2008, Apr. 2 **Litho.**

Color of NATO Emblem

5031 A1444 6 l blue 5.25 2.60

Litho. With Foil Application

5032 A1444 6 l gold 5.25 2.60
5033 A1444 6 l silver 5.25 2.60
Nos. 5031-5033 (3) 15.75 7.80

Nos. 5032-5033 each were printed in sheets of 8 + central label.

Bears — A1445

Designs: 60b, Helarctos malayanus. 1.20 l, Ursus americanus, horiz. 1.60 l, Ailuropoda melanoleuca, horiz. 3 l, Melursus ursinus, horiz. 5 l, Tremarctos ornatus.
9.10 l, Ursus arctos.

2008, Apr. 21 **Litho.** ***Perf. 13¼***
5034-5038 A1445 Set of 5 9.75 4.50

Souvenir Sheet

Perf. 13¼x13¾

5039 A1445 9.10 l multi 7.75 3.75

Nos. 5034-5038 each were printed in sheets of 8 + label. No. 5039 contains one 42x52mm stamp.

Miniature Sheet

2008 Summer Olympics, Beijing — A1446

No. 5040: a, Track. b, Gymnastics. c, Swimming. d, Canoeing.

2008, May 1 ***Perf. 13¼***
5040 A1446 1 l Sheet of 4, #a-d 3.50 1.75

Europa — A1447

Designs: 1.60 l, Envelope, map of Europe. 8.10 l, Stamped cover, European Union flag.

2008, May 8
5041-5042 A1447 Set of 2 8.25 4.00
5042a Souvenir sheet of 4, 2 each #5041-5042, with #5041 at UL 16.50 8.25
5042b As "a," with #5042 at UL 16.50 8.25

Grigore Antipa Natl. Natural History Museum, Cent. — A1448

Designs: 2.40 l, Flora and fauna. 3 l, Grigore Antipa (1867-1944), biologist.

2008, May 20
5043-5044 A1448 Set of 2 4.75 2.40

Nos. 5043-5044 each were printed in sheets of 8 + label.

European Central Bank, 10th Anniv. — A1449

2008, May 26
5045 A1449 3.10 l multi 2.00 2.00
a. Sheet of 6 + 6 labels 14.00 14.00

No. 5045 was printed in sheets of 40 stamps + 20 labels.

A1450

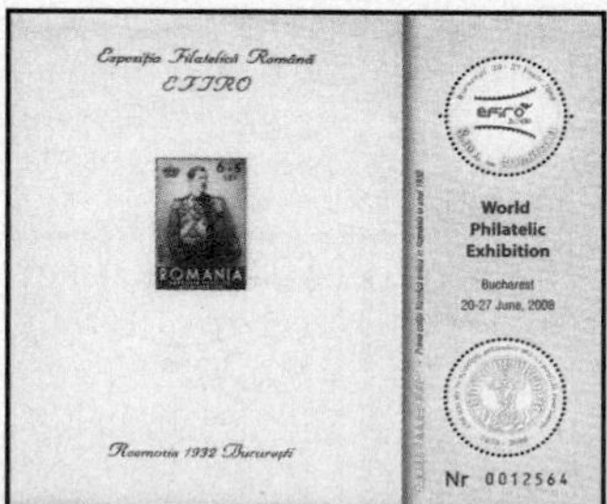

EFIRO 2008 World Philatelic Exhibition, Bucharest — A1451

Romanian stamps: 50b, #5. 1 l, #12. 2.40 l, #22. 3.10 l, #108. 4.50 l, #158. 6 l, #415.

2008, June 20 ***Perf. 13¼***
5046 A1450 50b multi + label .45 .25
a. Tete-beche pair .90 .40
5047 A1450 1 l multi + label .90 .45
a. Tete-beche pair 1.80 .90
5048 A1450 2.40 l multi + label 2.10 1.10
a. Tete-beche pair 4.20 2.20
5049 A1450 3.10 l multi + label 2.75 1.40
a. Tete-beche pair 5.50 2.80
5050 A1450 4.50 l multi + label 4.00 2.00
a. Tete-beche pair 8.00 4.00
5051 A1450 6 l multi + label 5.25 2.60
a. Tete-beche pair 10.50 5.20
b. Miniature sheet, #5046-5051, + 6 labels 15.50 7.75
Nos. 5046-5051 (6) 15.45 7.80

Souvenir Sheet

Perf.

5052 A1451 8.10 l multi 7.00 3.00

Labels of Nos. 5046-5051 are separated from stamps by two sets of three perforation holes.

Diplomatic Relations Between Romania and Kuwait, 45th Anniv. — A1452

No. 5053: a, Romanian woman weaving. b, Kuwaiti man building ship model.
3.30 l, Romanian oil well fire vehicle.

2008, June 21
5053 Horiz. pair + 2 labels 3.50 1.75
a.-b. A1452 2 l Either single 1.75 .85
c. Miniature sheet, 2 #5053 7.00 3.50

Souvenir Sheet

5054 A1452 3.30 l multi 3.00 1.50

Labels of Nos. 5053a and 5053b are separated from stamps by a partial row of perforations. The labels show the flags on top and also at the bottom. On No. 5053c, both labels are shown adjacent to the two similar stamps.
See Kuwait Nos. 1678-1679.

Selection of "7 Arts" as Best Animated Film at Tours Film Festival, 50th Anniv. — A1453

Designs: 1.40 l, Characters from film. 4.70 l, Character, award, and Ion Popescu-Gopo, director.

2008, June 22 ***Perf. 13¼***
5055-5056 A1453 Set of 2 5.25 2.60
5056a Souvenir sheet, #5055-5056 5.25 2.60

Cathedrals A1454

UNESCO World Heritage Sites: 3 l, St. George's Cathedral, Voronets Monastery, Romania, and chrismon. 4.30 l, St. Demetrius's Cathedral, Vladimir, Russia, and winged beast.

2008, June 23
5057-5058 A1454 Set of 2 6.50 3.25
5058a Souvenir sheet, #5057-5058, + 4 labels 6.50 3.25

Nos. 5057-5058 each were printed in sheets of 10 stamps + 2 labels. See Russia No. 7074.

Castles — A1455

Designs: 1 l, Fagaras Castle, Fagaras. 2.10 l, Peles Castle, Sinaia. 3 l, Huniad Castle, Hunedoara. 5 l, Bethlen Castle, Cris.

2008, June 24
5059-5062 A1455 Set of 4 9.75 4.75
5062a Miniature sheet of 4, #5059-5062 9.75 4.75

Nos. 5059-5062 each were printed in sheets of 9 stamps + 3 labels.

Printing of First Book in Romania, 500th Anniv. A1456

Designs: 4.30 l, Page from Macarie's Missal. 9.10 l, Two pages from Macarie's Missal.

2008, June 25 ***Perf. 13¼***
5063 A1456 4.30 l multi 3.75 1.90

Souvenir Sheet

Perf. 13¾x13¼

5064 A1456 9.10 l multi 8.00 4.00

No. 5063 was printed in sheets of 9 stamps + 3 labels. No. 5064 contains one 52x42mm stamp.

Iasi, 600th Anniv. of Mention in Documents — A1457

Buildings in Iasi: 1 l, Church of the Three Holy Hierarchs. 1.60 l, Metropolitan Cathedral. 2.10 l, Vasile Alecsandri National Theater. 3.10 l, Museum of Unification.
7.60 l, Palace of Culture, vert.

2008, June 26 ***Perf. 13¼***

Stamps + Label

5065-5068 A1457 Set of 4 6.75 3.25
5068a Miniature sheet of 4, #5065-5068, + 4 labels 6.75 3.25

Souvenir Sheet

Perf. 13¼x13¾

5069 A1457 7.60 l multi 6.75 3.25

Nos. 5065-5068 have labels to both the right and left of the stamp. No. 5069 contains one 42x52mm stamp.

Queen Marie (1875-1938) A1458

2008, July 15 ***Perf. 13¼***

Color of Queen

5070 A1458 1 l maroon .90 .45
a. Sheet of 8 + central label 7.25 3.75
5071 A1458 3 l gray green 2.75 1.40
a. Sheet of 8 + central label 22.00 11.50
b. Souvenir sheet of 2, #5070-5071 3.75 1.90

Nos. 5070-5071 each were printed in sheets of 16 stamps + 4 labels.

Regional Coats of Arms
A1459

Arms of: 60b, Moldavia (Moldova). 1 l, Wallachia (Tara Romaneasca). 3 l, Transylvania. 3.10 l, Bucharest.
6 l, Seal of Bucharest, vert.

2008, Sept. 4 *Perf. 13¼*

5072 A1459 60b multi .50 .25
a. Sheet of 8 + central label 4.00 2.00
5073 A1459 1 l multi .80 .40
a. Sheet of 8 + central label 6.50 3.25
5074 A1459 3 l multi 2.40 1.25
a. Sheet of 8 + central label 19.50 10.00
5075 A1459 3.10 l multi 2.50 1.25
a. Sheet of 8 + central label 20.00 10.00
b. Miniature sheet of 4, #5072-5075 6.25 3.25
Nos. 5072-5075 (4) 6.20 3.15

Souvenir Sheet

Perf. 13¼x13¾

5076 A1459 6 l multi 4.75 2.40

Nos. 5072-5075 each were printed in sheets of 16 stamps + 4 labels. No. 5076 contains one 42x52mm stamp.

Nuclearelectrica Power Company, 10th Anniv. — A1460

2008, Oct. 21 *Perf. 13¼*

5077 A1460 2.10 l multi + label 1.50 .75

Radio Romania, 80th Anniv.
A1461

2008, Oct. 28 Litho. *Perf. 13½*

5078 A1461 2.40 l multi 1.75 .85
a. Souvenir sheet of 2 3.50 1.75

No. 5078 was printed in sheets of 16 having adjacent stamps rotated 90 degrees from each other.

Christmas
A1462

2008, Nov. 5 Litho. *Perf. 13¼*

5079 A1462 1 l multi .70 .35

Flora and Fauna of Paraul Petea Nature Reserve
A1463

Designs: 1.40 l, Nymphaea lotus thermalis. 1.60 l, Scardinius racovitzai. 3.10 l, Melanopsis parreyssi.

2008, Dec. 8 Litho. *Perf. 13½*

5081-5083 A1463 Set of 3 4.25 2.10
5083a Souvenir sheet, #5081-5083 4.25 2.10

Unification of the Romanian Principalities, 150th Anniv.
A1464

Various arms of the United Romanian Principalities.

2009, Jan. 24 *Perf. 13½*

5084 A1464 2.40 l multi 1.50 .75

Souvenir Sheet

Perf.

5085 A1464 9.10 l multi 5.50 2.75

Value for No. 5084 is for stamp with surrounding selvage.

Introduction of the Euro, 10th Anniv. — A1465

2009, Jan. 30 Litho. *Perf. 13¼*

5086 A1465 3 l multi 1.90 .95

Litho. With Foil Application

5087 A1465 3 l multi 1.90 .95

Easter — A1466

No. 5088: a, Crucifixion. b, Resurrection. c, Ascension.

2009, Feb. 26 Litho. *Perf. 13½*

5088 A1466 1 l Horiz. strip of 3, #a-c 1.90 .95

Birds of the Danube Delta — A1467

Designs: 50b, Alcedo atthis atthis. 1.60 l, Himantopus himantopus, horiz. (48x33mm). 2.10 l, Egretta alba, horiz. (48x33mm). 3.10 l, Falco cherrug.
8.10 l, Haliaeetus albicilla.

2009, Feb. 28 *Perf. 13¼*

5089-5092 A1467 Set of 4 4.50 2.25
5092a Sheet of 4, #5089-5092 4.50 2.25

Souvenir Sheet

Perf. 13½

5093 A1467 8.10 l multi 4.75 2.40

No. 5093 contains one 50x50mm diamond-shaped stamp.

Preservation of Polar Regions and Glaciers
A1468

Designs: 1.60 l, Penguin, eye and teardrop. 8.10 l, Map of Antarctica, iceberg.

2009, Mar. 21 *Perf. 13¼*

5094 A1468 1.60 l multi 1.10 .55
a. Tete-beche pair 2.20 1.10
5095 A1468 8.10 l multi 5.25 2.60
a. Tete-beche pair 10.50 5.25
b. Souvenir sheet, #5094-5095 6.50 3.75

Flowers of the Rodna Mountains
A1469

Designs: 30b, Leontopodium alpinum. 60b, Aster alpinus. 1 l, Dianthus superbus. 1.20 l, Silene nivalis. 2.40 l, Campanula persicifolia. 3.10 l, Lilium martagon.

2009, Mar. 28 *Perf. 13½*

5096 A1469 30b multi .25 .25
a. Sheet of 8 + central label 1.60 .80
5097 A1469 60b multi .40 .25
a. Sheet of 8 + central label 3.25 1.60
5098 A1469 1 l multi .65 .30
a. Sheet of 8 + central label 5.25 2.60
5099 A1469 1.20 l multi .80 .40
a. Sheet of 8 + central label 6.50 3.25
5100 A1469 2.40 l multi 1.60 .80
a. Sheet of 8 + central label 13.00 6.50
5101 A1469 3.10 l multi 2.00 1.00
a. Sheet of 8 + central label 16.00 8.00
Nos. 5096-5101 (6) 5.70 3.00

Romgaz, Cent. — A1470

2009, Apr. 24 *Perf. 13¼*

5102 A1470 2.40 l multi 1.50 .75
a. Sheet of 6 + 3 central labels 9.00 4.50

Europa — A1471

Designs: 2.40 l, Galileo and his telescope, Leaning Tower of Pisa. 9.10 l, Map of constellations.

2009, May 6 **Litho.**

5103 A1471 2.40 l multi 1.60 .80
5104 A1471 9.10 l multi 6.00 3.00
a. Sheet of 4, 2 each #5103-5104, #5103 at UL 15.50 7.75
b. As "a," with #5104 at UL 15.50 7.75

Intl. Year of Astronomy. Nos. 5103-5104 were each printed in sheets of 6 with and without an illustrated margin.

Council of Europe, 60th Anniv. — A1472

2009, May 11 *Perf. 13¼*

5105 A1472 6 l multi 4.00 2.00

31st Conference of Police Agencies of European Capitals, Bucharest — A1473

Conference emblem, map of Bucharest and: 1 l, Bucharest coat of arms. 1.60 l, Emblem of Romanian Police.

2009, May 25

5106 A1473 1 l multi .70 .35
a. Tete-beche pair 1.40 .70
5107 A1473 1.60 l multi 1.10 .55
a. Tete-beche pair 2.20 1.10
b. Horiz. pair, #5106-5107 1.80 .90

Romania as Source of European Energy — A1474

Designs: 80b, Electric street light, electric tram and Timisoara Cathedral. 2.10 l, Gas street lamp and Orthodox Cathedral, Turda. 3 l, Iron Gates I Hydroelectric Station, power lines.

2009, June 2

5108-5110 A1474 Set of 3 4.00 2.00
5110a Sheet of 3, #5108-5110 4.00 2.00

First Man on the Moon, 40th Anniv.
A1475

Designs: 3 l, Astronaut stepping onto Moon. 14.50 l, Bootprint on Moon.

2009, July 20 *Perf. 13¼*

5111 A1475 3 l multi 2.00 1.00

Souvenir Sheet

Perf.

5112 A1475 14.50 l multi 9.75 5.00

No. 5111 was printed in sheets of 8 + label. Values of No. 5111 are for stamps with surrounding selvage.

Historic Center of Sigisoara, UNESCO World Heritage Site — A1476

Arms of Sigisoara and: 1 l, Church on the Hill. 1.60 l, Historic city center. 6 l, Clock Tower, vert.
7.60 l, Aerial view of Sigisoara.

2009, July 24 *Perf. 13¼*

5113-5115 A1476 Set of 3 6.00 3.00
5115a Sheet of 3 #5113-5115 6.00 3.00

Souvenir Sheet

Perf. 14x13¼

5116 A1476 7.60 l multi 5.25 2.60

Nos. 5113-5115 were each printed in sheets of 8 + central label. No. 5116 contains one 51x41mm stamp.

Stamp Day — A1477

Anghel I. Saligny (1854-1925), engineer and: 2.10 l, Cernavoda Railroad Bridge. 2.40 l, Cernavoda Railroad Bridge and statue.

2009, July 30 *Perf. 13¼*
5117-5118 A1477 Set of 2 3.00 1.50

Electric Trams of European Cities A1478

Arms and trams from: 80b, Frankfurt-am-Main, Germany. 1.20 l, Bucharest. 1.60 l, Vienna. 2.10 l, Brailia, Romania. 2.40 l, London.
8.10 l, Berlin.

2009, Aug. 14
5119-5123 A1478 Set of 5 5.50 2.75

Souvenir Sheet

5124 A1478 8.10 l multi 5.50 2.75

No. 5124 contains one 48x33mm stamp.

Protected Animals — A1479

Designs: 30b, Aquila chrysaetos. 50b, Lynx lynx, vert. 60b, Cervus elaphus. 1.40 l, Huso huso, vert. 3 l, Testudo graeca ibera. 6 l, Otis tarda, vert.

2009, Aug. 28 *Perf. 13¼*
5125-5130 A1479 Set of 6 8.00 4.00

Nos. 5125-5130 were each printed in sheets of 8 + label.

Miniature Sheet

Treasures of Romania — A1480

No. 5131: a, Dimitrie Cantemir (1673-1723), prince of Moldavia and writer. b, George Enescu (1881-1955), composer. c, Church of the Three Hierarchs, Iasi. d, Black Church, Brasov. e, Pelican and water lily, Danube Delta. f, Retezat National Park. g, Viticulture. h, Maramures pottery and wood carving.

2009, Sept. 16
5131 A1480 3 l Sheet of 8, #a-h, stamps adjacent 17.00 8.50
i. As No. 5131, stamps separated 17.00 8.50

Bucharest, 550th Anniv. — A1481

Designs: 30b, Buna Vestire Church. 80b, Coltea Hospital. 3 l, Sutu Palace. 4.70 l, School of Architecture.
8.10 l, Bucharest Patriarchal Cathedral.

2009, Sept. 18 *Perf. 13¼*
5132-5135 A1481 Set of 4 6.25 3.25
5135a Sheet of 4, #5132-5135 6.25 3.25

Souvenir Sheet

Perf. 14x13¼

5136 A1481 8.10 l multi 5.75 3.00

No. 5136 contains one 51x41mm stamp.

Intl. Day of Non-violence — A1482

2009, Oct. 6 *Perf. 13¼*
5137 A1482 3 l multi 2.10 1.10
a. Tete-beche pair 4.20 2.20
b. Sheet of 6 13.00 6.75

Transgaz, 35th Anniv. — A1483

2009, Oct. 14 **Litho.**
5138 A1483 5 l multi 3.50 1.75
a. Souvenir sheet of 3 10.50 5.25

General Staff of the Romanian Armed Forces, 150th Anniv. A1484

2009, Nov. 12
5139 A1484 7.60 l multi 5.25 2.60
a. Sheet of 6 32.00 16.00

No. 5139 was printed in sheets of 8 + central label.

Christmas A1485

2009, Nov. 20 **Litho.** *Perf. 13¼*
5140 A1485 1 l multi .70 .35
a. Sheet of 4, perf. 13¼ on 3 sides 2.80 1.40

No. 5140 was printed in sheets of 8 + central label.

University of Bucharest Law Faculty, 150th Anniv. — A1486

2009, Nov. 25
5141 A1486 9.10 l multi 6.50 3.25
a. Souvenir sheet of 2 13.00 6.50

No. 5141 was printed in sheets of 8 + central label.

First Yiddish Theater, Iasi — A1487

2009, Nov. 26
5142 A1487 3.10 l multi 2.25 1.10
a. Souvenir sheet of 2 4.50 2.25

No. 5142a contains two stamps, one with its label to the left of the stamp. The labels on No. 5142a have a complete column of perforations separating them from the adjacent stamps.
See Israel No. 1797.

Constanta Harbor, Cent. — A1488

Designs: 1 l, Ship "Mircea." 5 l, King Carol I Lighthouse.

2009, Dec. 23
5143-5144 A1488 Set of 2 4.25 2.10
5144a Sheet of 2, #5143-5144 4.25 2.10

Honeybees A1489

Designs: 50b, Apis mellifera mellifera. 2.10 l, Apis mellifera ligustica. 3.10 l, Apis mellifera carnica. 4.30 l, Apis mellifera caucasica.

2010, Jan. 22 *Perf. 13¼*
5145 A1489 50b multi .35 .25
a. Sheet of 4, perf. 13¼ on 2 or 3 sides 1.40 .70
5146 A1489 2.10 l multi 1.50 .75
a. Sheet of 4, perf. 13¼ on 2 or 3 sides 6.00 3.00
5147 A1489 3.10 l multi 2.10 1.10
a. Sheet of 4, perf. 13¼ on 2 or 3 sides 8.50 4.50
5148 A1489 4.30 l multi 3.00 1.50
a. Sheet of 4, perf. 13¼ on 2 or 3 sides 12.00 6.00
Nos. 5145-5148 (4) 6.95 3.60

2010 Winter Olympics, Vancouver A1490

Designs: 60b, Cross-country skiing. 80b, Speed skating. 1 l, Skeleton, horiz. 7.60 l, Bobsled, horiz.

2010, Feb. 12 *Perf. 13¼*
5149-5152 A1490 Set of 4 6.75 3.50

Nos. 5149-5152 each were printed in sheets of 4.

Tarantulas A1491

Designs: 50b, Brachypelma albopilosum. 80b, Haplopelma lividum. 1.20 l, Brachypelma smithi. 9.10 l, Grammostola rosea.

2010, Feb. 19
5153-5156 A1491 Set of 4 7.75 4.00

Nos. 5153-5156 each were printed in sheets of 8 + central label.

Lighthouses A1492

Designs: 60b, Genoese Lighthouse, Constanta. 80b, Old Lighthouse, Sulina. 1.20 l, Mangalia Lighthouse. 1.60 l, Landing Lighthouse, Tuzla. 8.10 l, White Lighthouse, Constanta North Harbor.

2010, Mar. 5 *Perf. 13¼*
5157-5161 A1492 Set of 5 8.25 4.25

Nos. 5157-5161 each were printed in sheets of 8 + label.

Easter A1493

2010, Mar. 12
5162 A1493 1 l multi .65 .35

Printed in sheets of 8 + central label.

Intl. Civil Aviation Organization, 65th Anniv. — A1494

2010, Mar. 29 ***Perf. 13¼x14***

5163 A1494 8.10 l multi 5.50 2.75
a. Souvenir sheet of 2 11.00 5.50

No. 5163 was printed in sheets of 8 + 2 labels

Romanian Gendarmerie, 160th Anniv. — A1495

2010, Apr. 7 ***Perf. 13¼***

5164 A1495 9.10 l multi 6.00 3.00
a. Souvenir sheet of 2 12.00 6.00

No. 5164 was printed in sheets of 8 + central label.

Souvenir Sheet

Eugeniu Carada (1836-1910), Founder of National Bank of Romania — A1496

2010, Apr. 29

5165 A1496 9.10 l multi 6.00 3.00

Europa A1497

Designs: 4.30 l, Little Red Riding Hood and Wolf. 7.60 l, Boy and Dragon.

2010, May 6

5166-5167 A1497 Set of 2 7.25 3.75
5167a Sheet of 4, 2 each #5166-5167, #5166 at UL 14.50 7.25
5167b As "a," #5167 at UL 14.50 7.25

Coats of Arms and Landmarks of Countries Along the Danube River — A1498

Mother Baar with Her Daughter, the Young Danube, Sculpture by Adolf Heer, Donaueschingen, Germany — A1499

Design on stamps and attached labels: 1.40 l, Melk Abbey, arms of Austria. 2.40 l, Bratislava Castle, arms of Slovakia. 3.10 l, Ilok Fortress, arms of Croatia. 4.30 l, Parliament Building, arms of Hungary.

2010, May 8

5168-5171 A1498 Set of 4 6.50 3.25
5171a Souvenir sheet of 4, #5168-5171 6.50 3.25

Souvenir Sheet

5172 A1499 14.50 l multi 8.25 4.25

Minerals A1500

Designs: 50b, Quartz and calcite. 1.40 l, Quartz and gold. 1.60 l, Quartz and rhodochrosite. 2.40 l, Calcite. 7.60 l, Red barite.

2010, May 21 **Litho.**

5173-5177 A1500 Set of 5 7.75 4.00

Nos. 5173-5177 each were printed in sheets of 4.

Horse Breeds — A1501

Designs: 60b, Huçul. 1 l, Arabian thoroughbred. 2 l, Lippizaner, vert. 2.10 l, Furioso North Star. 5 l, Shagya Arab.

2010, May 29 ***Perf. 13¼***

5178-5182 A1501 Set of 5 6.25 3.25

Nos. 5178-5182 each were printed in sheets of 8 + label.

Protected Fauna of the Danube Region — A1502

Designs: 1.40 l, Vipera ursinii. 1.60 l, Phalacrocorax pygmaeus. 2 l, Huso huso. 7.60 l, Pelecanus crispus.

2010, June 9

5183-5186 A1502 Set of 4 7.25 3.75
5186a Souvenir sheet of 4, #5183-5186 7.25 3.25

Nos. 5183-5186 each were printed in sheets of 8 + central label.

Save the Children Romania, 20th Anniv. A1503

2010, June 9

5187 A1503 3.10 l multi 1.75 .90

Printed in sheets of 8 + central label.

Ceramic Tiles — A1504

Tile from: 2.10 l, Portugal, 18th cent. 3.10 l, Romania, 19th cent.

2010, June 30

5188-5189 A1504 Set of 2 3.25 1.60

Nos. 5188-5189 each were printed in sheets of 8 + central label, with or without an illustrated margin. Stamps from sheets with illustrated margins are perforated on 2 or 3 sides.

See Portugal No. 3236.

Recognition of Romanian Orthodox Church Autocephaly, 125th Anniv. A1505

2010, July 15

5190 A1505 6 l multi 3.75 1.90

Stamp Day. Printed in sheets of 8 + central label.

Botanical Garden of Bucharest, 150th Anniv. — A1506

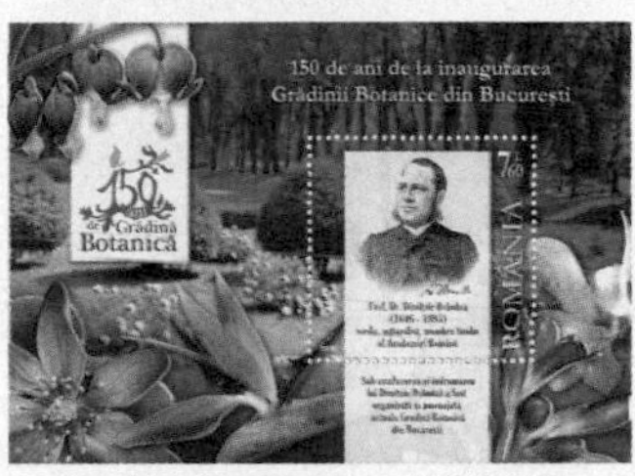

Dr. Dimitrie Brandza (1846-95), Founder of Botanical Garden — A1507

Designs: 1.60 l, Clivia miniata. 2.10 l, Magnolia kobus. 2.40 l, Strelitzia juncea. 3 l, Hepatica transsilvanica. 3.10 l, Dicentra spectabilis.

2010, July 23

5191-5195 A1506 Set of 5 7.50 3.75

Souvenir Sheet

5196 A1507 7.60 l multi 4.75 2.40

A1508

Carpathian Garden — A1509

Designs: 1 l, Tourist looking at Carpathian Sphinx. 1.60 l, Tourist looking at valley. 9.10 l, Valley.

Perf. 13¼x14 on 3 Sides

2010, July 29

Stamp + Label

5197-5198 A1508 Set of 2 1.60 .80
5198a Sheet, #5197-5198, perf. 13¼x14, + 2 labels 1.60 .80

Souvenir Sheet

Perf. 13¼x14

5199 A1509 9.10 l multi + label 5.75 2.75

Souvenir Sheet

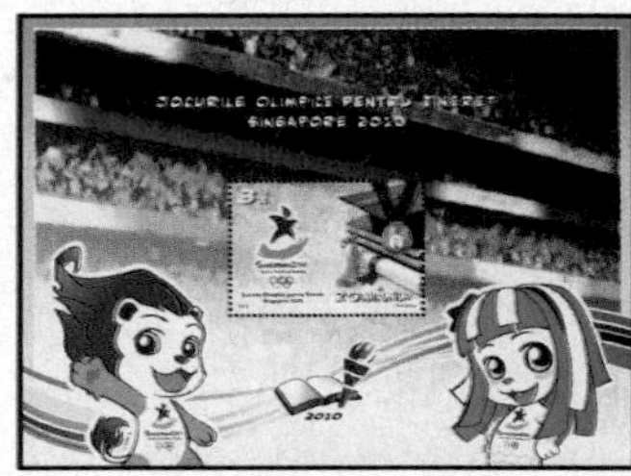

2010 Youth Olympics, Singapore — A1510

2010, Aug. 12 ***Perf. 13¼***

5200 A1510 8.10 l multi 5.00 2.50

Mountain Lakes A1511

Designs: 2.10 l, Lake Nahuel Huapi, Argentina. 3.10 l, Lake Balea, Romania.

2010, Aug. 14 ***Perf. 13¼x14***

5201-5202 A1511 Set of 2 3.25 1.60

Nos. 5201-5202 were each printed in sheets of 4. See Argentina Nos. 2588-2589.

National Bank of Romania, 130th Anniv. — A1512

100-lei banknote of 1896: 2.40 l, Obverse. 4.30 l, Reverse.

2010, Sept. 5 ***Perf. 14x13¼***

5203 A1512 2.40 l multi 1.50 .75
a. Tete-beche pair 3.00 1.50

5204 A1512 4.30 l multi 2.60 1.25
a. Tete-beche pair 5.20 2.50
b. Souvenir sheet of 2, #5203-5204 4.25 2.10

Nos. 5203-5204 each have a star punched into the paper next to denomination.

Orient Express — A1513

Locomotive and view of: 2.40 l, Salzburg, Austria. 4.70 l, Sinaia, Romania.

2010, Sept. 6 *Perf. 13¼*
5205-5206 A1513 Set of 2 4.25 2.10
5206a Souvenir sheet of 2, #5205-5206 4.25 2.10

See Austria No. 2275.

Ratification of UN Convention on the Rights of the Child, 20th Anniv. — A1514

2010, Sept. 27
5207 A1514 6 l multi 4.00 2.00

Printed in sheets of 8 + central label.

Danube River Countries Types of 2010

Designs of stamps and attached labels: 1.40 l, Ram Fortress, Serbia, arms of Serbia. 2.40 l, Sava Ognyanov Drama Theater, Ruse, Bulgaria, arms of Bulgaria. 3.10 l, Bogdan Petriceicu Hasdeu State University, Cahul, Moldova, arms of Moldova. 4.30 l, Assumption of the Virgin Church, Izmail, Ukraine, arms of Ukraine.
14.50 l, Navigation Palace, Galati, Romania.

2010, Oct. 1 Litho. *Perf. 13¼*
5208-5211 A1498 Set of 4 7.25 3.75
5211a Souvenir sheet of 4, #5208-5211 7.25 3.25

Souvenir Sheet

5212 A1499 14.50 l multi 9.50 4.75

Nos. 5208-5211 each were printed in sheets of 8 + central label. No. 5212 contains one 48x33mm stamp.

Souvenir Sheet

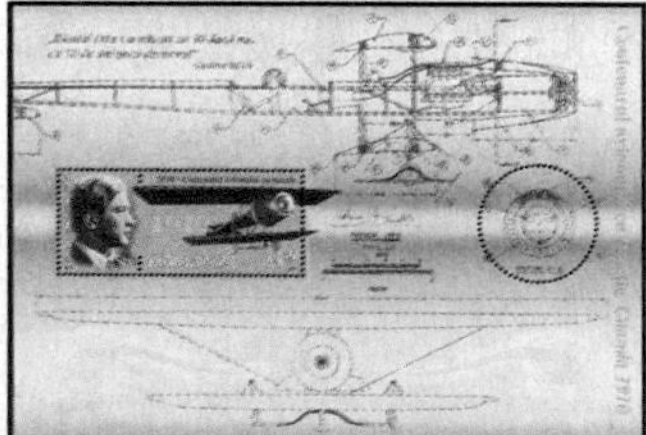

Henri Coanda (1886-1972), Aviation Pioneer and His 1910 Jet Airplane — A1515

2010, Oct. 15
5213 A1515 14.50 l multi + 2 labels 9.50 4.75

National Grand Masonic Lodge, 130th Anniv. — A1516

Designs: 3 l, Arms. 5 l, Compass and square.

2010, Nov. 4
5214-5215 A1516 Set of 2 5.25 2.60

Nos. 5214-5215 each were printed in sheets of 8 + central label.

Viticulture A1517

Designs: 2.10 l, Wine barrels, wine glass. 3.10 l, Grapes, pitcher.

2010, Nov. 10
5216-5217 A1517 Set of 2 3.50 1.75
5217a Souvenir sheet of 2, #5216-5217, perf. 13¼ on 3 sides 3.50 1.75

Nos. 5216-5217 each were printed in sheets of 8 + label. See Cyprus No. 1139.

Christmas A1518

Paintings: 1 l, The Birth of Jesus, by Gheorghe Tattarescu. 3.10 l, The Nativity and Adoration of the Shepherds, by the School of Murillo.

2010, Nov. 15 *Perf. 13¼*
5218-5219 A1518 Set of 2 2.60 1.25

Nos. 5218-5219 each were printed in sheets of 8 + central label. See Vatican City Nos. 1458-1461.

Romanian Innovations — A1519

Designs: 3 l, Brad-Barza gold mine ore car on track with switch, 16th cent. 4.30 l, Horizontal water wheel, 13th-14th cent. 5 l, Petrarche Poenaru and his fountain pen, 1827. 8.10 l, 1923 aerodynamic automobile designed by Aurel Persu.

2010, Dec. 17
5220-5223 A1519 Set of 4 13.00 6.50

Nos. 5220-5223 each were printed in sheets of 8 + central label.

Reptiles A1520

Designs: 60b, Zamenis longissimus. 2.40 l, Podarcis taurica. 3 l, Vipera ammodytes ammodytes. 9.10 l, Vipera ursinii moldavica.

2011, Jan. 19
5224 A1520 60b multi .40 .25
a. Souvenir sheet of 4 1.60 .80
5225 A1520 2.40 l multi 1.60 .80
a. Souvenir sheet of 4 6.50 3.25
5226 A1520 3 l multi 1.90 .95
a. Souvenir sheet of 4 7.75 4.00
5227 A1520 9.10 l multi 6.00 3.00
a. Souvenir sheet of 4 24.00 12.00
Nos. 5224-5227 (4) 9.90 5.00

Nos. 5224-5227 each were printed in sheets of 8 + central label.

Paintings in the National Bank of Romania Collection A1521

Designs: 1.40 l, Mercury, by George Demetrescu Mirea. 2.10 l, Marine, by Eugeniu Voinescu. 3 l, Rodica, by Nicolae Grigorescu. 7.60 l, Prometheus, by Mirea.

2011, Jan. 28 *Perf. 13¼x13¾*
5228 A1521 1.40 l multi .90 .45
a. Souvenir sheet of 4 3.75 1.90
b. Tete-beche pair 1.80 .90
5229 A1521 2.10 l multi 1.40 .70
a. Souvenir sheet of 4 5.75 3.00
b. Tete-beche pair 2.80 1.40
5230 A1521 3 l multi 1.90 .95
a. Souvenir sheet of 4 7.75 4.00
b. Tete-beche pair 3.80 1.90
5231 A1521 7.60 l multi 5.00 2.50
a. Souvenir sheet of 4 20.00 10.00
b. Tete-beche pair 10.00 5.00
Nos. 5228-5231 (4) 9.20 4.60

Nos. 5228-5231 each were printed in sheets of 8.

Caves A1522

Designs: 30b, Ursilor Cave. 50b, Closani Cave. 60b, Muierii Cave. 3 l, Meziad Cave, horiz. 3.10 l, Vantului Cave, horiz. 8.70 l, Sura Mare Cave, horiz.

2011, Feb. 17 *Perf. 13¼*
5232 A1522 30b multi .25 .25
a. Sheet of 8 + central label 1.60 .80
5233 A1522 50b multi .35 .25
a. Sheet of 8 + central label 3.00 1.50
5234 A1522 60b multi .40 .25
a. Sheet of 8 + central label 3.25 1.60
5235 A1522 3 l multi 2.00 1.00
a. Sheet of 8 + central label 16.00 8.00
5236 A1522 3.10 l multi 2.10 1.10
a. Sheet of 8 + central label 17.00 8.50
5237 A1522 8.70 l multi 5.75 3.00
a. Sheet of 8 + central label 47.50 24.00
Nos. 5232-5237 (6) 10.85 5.85

Parrots A1523

Designs: 1.60 l, Ara illiger. 2.10 l, Ara macao. 2.40 l, Primolius auricollis. 4.70 l, Platycercus eximius. 5 l, Melopsittacus undulatus.
9.10 l, Nymphicus hollandicus.

2011, Feb. 24
5238 A1523 1.60 l multi 1.10 .55
a. Sheet of 8 + label 9.00 4.50
5239 A1523 2.10 l multi 1.40 .70
a. Sheet of 8 + label 11.50 5.75
5240 A1523 2.40 l multi 1.60 .80
a. Sheet of 8 + label 13.00 6.50
5241 A1523 4.70 l multi 3.25 1.60
a. Sheet of 8 + label 26.00 13.00
5242 A1523 5 l multi 3.50 1.75
a. Sheet of 8 + label 28.00 14.00
Nos. 5238-5242 (5) 10.85 5.40

Souvenir Sheet

5243 A1523 9.10 l multi 6.00 3.00

World Down Syndrome Day — A1524

2011, Mar. 14
5244 A1524 3 l multi 2.10 1.10

Easter — A1525

2011, Mar. 24 **Litho.**
5245 A1525 1 l multi .70 .35

Printed in sheets of 8 + central label.

Peonies A1526

Designs: 1 l, Paeonia peregrina. 2.10 l, Paeonia tenuifolia.

2011, Mar. 30 *Perf. 13¼*
5246 A1526 1 l multi .70 .35

Souvenir Sheet

5247 A1526 2.10 l multi 1.50 .75

No. 5246 was printed in sheets of 4.

Butterflies and Moths — A1527

Designs: 50b, Parnassius apollo. 60b, Greta oto, vert. 2.40 l, Morpho nestira. 3 l, Papilio macahon. 4.50 l, Attacus atlas. 5 l, Inachis io.
8.10 l, Iphiclides podalirius.

2011, Apr. 12
5248 A1527 50b multi .35 .25
a. Sheet of 8 + central label 3.00 1.50
5249 A1527 60b multi .45 .25
a. Sheet of 8 + central label 3.75 1.90
5250 A1527 2.40 l multi 1.75 .85
a. Sheet of 8 + central label 14.00 7.00
5251 A1527 3 l multi 2.10 1.10
a. Sheet of 8 + central label 17.00 8.50
5252 A1527 4.50 l multi 3.25 1.60
a. Sheet of 8 + central label 26.00 13.00
5253 A1527 5 l multi 3.50 1.75
a. Sheet of 8 + central label 28.00 14.00
Nos. 5248-5253 (6) 11.40 5.80

Souvenir Sheet

5254 A1527 8.10 l multi 5.75 3.00

Palace of the Parliament, Bucharest — A1528

Designs: 30b, Exterior. 50b, Senate entrance. 60b, Senate chamber. 3 l, Human

Rights Room. 4.30 l, Chamber of Deputies. 7.60 l, Exterior, diff.

2011, Apr. 26

5255 A1528 30b multi .25 .25
a. Sheet of 8 + central label 1.60 .80
5256 A1528 50b multi .35 .25
a. Sheet of 8 + central label 3.00 1.50
5257 A1528 60b multi .45 .25
a. Sheet of 8 + central label 3.75 1.90
5258 A1528 3 l multi 2.10 1.10
a. Sheet of 8 + central label 17.00 8.50
5259 A1528 4.30 l multi 3.00 1.50
a. Sheet of 8 + central label 24.00 12.00
5260 A1528 7.60 l multi 5.50 2.75
a. Sheet of 8 + central label 45.00 22.50
b. Souvenir sheet of 6, #5255-5260, + label 12.00 6.00
Nos. 5255-5260 (6) 11.65 6.10

Europa A1529

Forest and: 2.40 l, Buck. 9.10 l, Squirrel.

2011, Apr. 27

5261 A1529 2.40 l multi 1.75 .85
a. Sheet of 6 10.50 5.25
5262 A1529 9.10 l multi 6.50 3.25
a. Sheet of 6 39.00 19.50
b. Souvenir sheet of 4, 2 each #5261-5262, #5261 at upper left 16.50 8.25
c. As "b," with #5262 at upper left 16.50 8.25

Intl. Year of Forests.

Signs of the Zodiac A1530

2011, May 5

5263 A1530 30b Aries .25 .25
a. Sheet of 8 + central label 1.60 .80
5264 A1530 50b Taurus .35 .25
a. Sheet of 8 + central label 3.00 1.50
5265 A1530 60b Gemini .45 .25
a. Sheet of 8 + central label 3.75 1.90
5266 A1530 80b Cancer .55 .25
a. Sheet of 8 + central label 4.50 2.25
5267 A1530 1.40 l Leo 1.00 .50
a. Sheet of 8 + central label 8.00 4.00
5268 A1530 14.50 l Virgo 10.00 5.00
a. Sheet of 8 + central label 80.00 40.00
b. Souvenir sheet of 6, #5263-5268 13.00 6.50
Nos. 5263-5268 (6) 12.60 6.50

See Nos. 5303-5308.

First Man in Space, 50th Anniv. — A1531

Designs: 3 l, Dumitru Dorin Prunariu, first Romanian in space, Soyuz 40 rocket on launch pad. 4.70 l, Yuri Gagarin, first man in space, Vostok 1 on launch pad.
8.70, Earth as seen from space.

2011, May 9 ***Perf. 13¼***

5269 A1531 3 l multi 2.10 1.10
a. Sheet of 8 + central label 17.00 8.50
5270 A1531 4.70 l multi 3.25 1.60
a. Sheet of 8 + central label 26.00 13.00

Souvenir Sheet

Perf.

5271 A1531 8.70 l multi 6.00 3.00

Circus A1532

Designs: 50b, Circus tent, clown's face. 8.10 l, Clown with top hat.

2011, June 1 ***Perf. 13¼***

5272 A1532 50b multi .35 .25
a. Sheet of 8 + central label 3.00 1.50
5273 A1532 8.10 l multi 5.75 3.00
a. Sheet of 8 + central label 46.00 23.00
b. Souvenir sheet of 2, #5272-5273 6.25 3.25

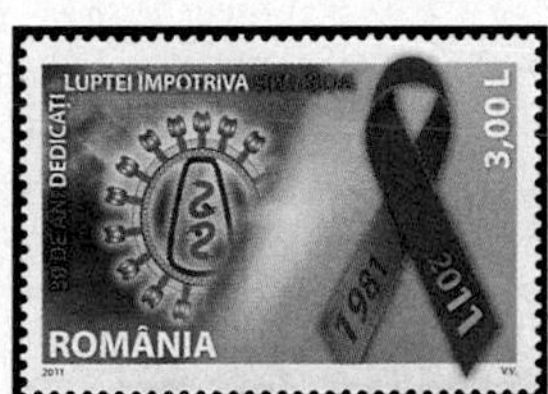

Campaign Against AIDS and HIV, 30th Anniv. — A1533

2011, June 8 **Litho.**

5274 A1533 3 l multi 2.10 1.10

Opening of Basarab Overpass, Bucharest — A1534

2011, June 21

5275 A1534 5 l multi 3.50 1.75
a. Souvenir sheet of 2 7.00 3.50
b. Sheet of 8 28.00 14.00

Peach Blossoms A1535

Blossoms of Prunus persica with denomination at: No. 5276, 50b, UL. No. 5277, 50b, UR.

2011, June 30

5276-5277 A1535 Set of 2 .70 .35

Nos. 5276-5277 were printed in sheets of 6, containing 3 of each stamp.

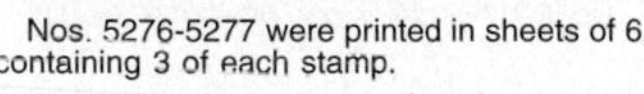

Romanian Red Cross, 135th Anniv. — A1536

2011, July 3

5278 A1536 3.10 l multi 2.10 1.10
a. Sheet of 8 + central label 17.00 8.50

Transylvanian Association for Romanian Literature and Culture of the Romanian People, 150th Anniv. — A1537

Anniversary emblem and: 3 l, Metropolitan Andrei Saguna (1808-73), first president of association. 9.10 l, Association library, Sibiu.

2011, July 15 ***Perf. 13¼***

5279 A1537 3 l multi 2.10 1.10
a. Sheet of 8 + central label 17.00 9.00
5280 A1537 9.10 l multi 6.25 3.25
a. Sheet of 8 + central label 50.00 26.00

Stamp Day.

Animals and Birds in Nature Preserves — A1538

Designs: 30b, Canis lupus. 4.50 l, Ardea purpurea. 5 l, Tetrao urogallus. 8.10 l, Nyctereutes procyonoides.

2011, July 25

5281 A1538 30b multi .25 .25
a. Sheet of 8 + label 2.00 2.00
5282 A1538 4.50 l multi 3.00 1.50
a. Sheet of 8 + label 24.00 12.00
5283 A1538 5 l multi 3.50 1.75
a. Sheet of 8 + label 28.00 14.00
5284 A1538 8.10 l multi 5.50 2.75
a. Sheet of 8 + label 44.00 22.00
b. Souvenir sheet of 4, #5281-5284 12.50 6.25
Nos. 5281-5284 (4) 12.25 6.25

Stained Glass Windows A1539

Windows in Dumitru Furnica-Minovici Western Old Art Museum of the Romanian Academy, Bucharest: 3.60 l, The Artist, 18th cent. Austrian window. 4.30 l, St. Catherine, 19th cent. Austrian window. 4.50 l, Hunter, 19th cent. Austrian window. 4.70 l, Lady in Green, 17th cent. German window.
St. Hieronymus and Resurrection of Lazarus, 15th cent. Tyrolean windows.

2011, Aug. 18

5285 A1539 3.60 l multi 2.40 1.25
a. Sheet of 8 + central label 19.50 9.75
5286 A1539 4.30 l multi 2.75 1.40
a. Sheet of 8 + central label 22.00 11.00
5287 A1539 4.50 l multi 3.00 1.50
a. Sheet of 8 + central label 24.00 12.00
5288 A1539 4.70 l multi 3.00 1.50
a. Sheet of 8 + central label 24.00 12.00
Nos. 5285-5288 (4) 11.15 5.65

Souvenir Sheet

5289 A1539 8.10 l multi 5.25 2.60

Locomotives — A1540

Designs: 2 l, CFR 103 Romania, 1869. 3 l, CFR 28 Codaesti, 1887. 3.30 l, CFR 185 Domnita Maria, 1875. 9.10 l, CFR 001 Lespezi, 1884.
8.10 l, CFR 8008, 1901.

2011, Aug. 26

5290 A1540 2 l multi 1.25 .60
a. Sheet of 8 + label 10.00 5.00
5291 A1540 3 l multi 1.90 .95
a. Sheet of 8 + label 15.50 7.75
5292 A1540 3.30 l multi 2.10 1.10
a. Sheet of 8 + label 17.00 9.00
5293 A1540 9.10 l multi 5.75 3.00
a. Sheet of 8 + label 46.00 24.00
Nos. 5290-5293 (4) 11.00 5.65

Souvenir Sheet

Perf. 14x13¼

5294 A1540 8.10 l multi 5.25 2.60

No. 5294 contains one 52x42mm stamp.

20th George Enescu Intl. Music Festival and Competition — A1541

Designs: 1.40 l, Conductor, concert hall. 3 l, Musical score, Enescu's signature, opera libretto. 7.60 l, Romanian Athenaeum.

2011, Sept. 1 ***Perf. 13¼***

5295 A1541 1.40 l multi .90 .45
a. Sheet of 8 7.25 3.75
5296 A1541 3 l multi 1.90 .95
a. Sheet of 8 15.50 7.75
5297 A1541 7.60 l multi 5.00 2.50
a. Sheet of 8 40.00 20.00
b. Souvenir sheet of 3, #5295-5297 8.00 4.00
Nos. 5295-5297 (3) 7.80 3.90

New National Arena, Bucharest — A1542

2011, Sept. 6 ***Perf. 14x13¼***

5298 A1542 5 l multi 3.25 1.60
a. Souvenir sheet of 2 6.50 3.25
b. Sheet of 10 32.50 16.00

Biertan Church Castle UNESCO World Heritage Site — A1543

2011, Sept. 15 ***Perf. 13¼***

Granite Paper

5299 A1543 2.10 l multi 1.40 .70
a. Sheet of 2 + label 2.80 1.40

See Germany No. 2638.

Franz-Joseph Müller von Reichenstein (c. 1740-1825), Discoverer of Tellurium, Diagram of Tellurium Atom — A1544

2011, Sept. 26 **Litho.**

5300 A1544 5 l multi 3.25 1.60
a. Sheet of 8 + central label 26.00 13.00

Intl. Year of Chemistry.

Diplomatic Relations Between Romania and Moldova, 20th Anniv. A1545

Designs: 1 l, Holy Gates, Chisinau, Moldova. 3.10 l, Arch of Triumph, Bucharest.

2011, Oct. 11 ***Perf. 13¼***

5301 A1545 1 l multi .65 .30
a. Sheet of 8 + central label 5.25 2.60
5302 A1545 3.10 l multi 2.00 1.00
a. Sheet of 8 + central label 16.00 8.00
b. Souvenir sheet of 2, #5301-5302 2.75 1.40

See Moldova Nos. 728-729.

Signs of the Zodiac Type of 2011

2011, Oct. 14

5303 A1530 50b Libra .35 .25
a. Sheet of 8 + central label 3.00 2.00
5304 A1530 60b Scorpio .40 .25
a. Sheet of 8 + central label 3.25 2.00
5305 A1530 80b Sagittarius .50 .25
a. Sheet of 8 + central label 4.00 2.00
5306 A1530 3 l Capricorn 1.90 .95
a. Sheet of 8 + central label 15.50 7.75
5307 A1530 6 l Aquarius 3.75 1.90
a. Sheet of 8 + central label 30.00 15.50
5308 A1530 8.10 l Pisces 5.25 2.60
a. Sheet of 8 + central label 42.00 21.00
b. Souvenir sheet of 6, #5303-5308 12.50 6.25
Nos. 5303-5308 (6) 12.15 6.20

European Day of Civil Justice — A1546

2011, Oct. 25

5309 A1546 5 l multi 3.25 1.60
a. Sheet of 8 + central label 26.00 13.00

Christmas A1547

2011, Nov. 18

5310 A1547 1 l multi .65 .30
a. Sheet of 8 + central label 5.25 2.60

Handicrafts A1548

Designs: No. 5311, Painted Easter eggs, Romania. No. 5312, Dough figurines, Hong Kong.

2011, Nov. 24

5311 A1548 2 l multi 1.25 .60
a. Sheet of 8 10.00 5.00
5312 A1548 2 l multi 1.25 .60
a. Sheet of 8 10.00 5.00
b. Souvenir sheet of 2, #5311-5312 2.50 1.25

Romanians and Their Innovations — A1549

Designs: 1.40 l, Stefan Odobleja (1902-78), neurologist, and computer chip. 1.60 l, Ioan Cantacuzino (1863-1934), discoverer of anti-cholera vaccine, bacillae and microscope. 2.10 l, Anastase Dragomir (1896-1966), inventor of airplane ejector seat. 7.60 l, Grigore Antipa (1867-1944), creator of biological dioramas for museums, and animals.

2011, Dec. 15

5313 A1549 1.40 l multi .85 .40
a. Sheet of 8 + central label 7.00 3.50
5314 A1549 1.60 l multi 1.00 .50
a. Sheet of 8 + central label 8.00 4.00
5315 A1549 2.10 l multi 1.25 .60
a. Sheet of 8 + central label 10.00 5.00
5316 A1549 7.60 l multi 4.75 2.40
a. Sheet of 8 + central label 38.00 19.50
Nos. 5313-5316 (4) 7.85 3.90

Cotroceni Palace A1550

Stained-glass windows in Union Hall: 50b, Tara Romaneasca window. 60b, Prince Basarab I window, pillar. 80b, Moldova window. 1 l, Prince Bogdan I window, pillar. 2.40 l, Transilvania window. 3.10 l, Prince Michael the Brave (Mihai Viteazul) window, pillar.

14.50 l, Cotroceni Palace.

2011, Dec. 21 ***Perf. 13¼***

5317 A1550 50b multi .30 .25
a. Sheet of 8 + central label 2.40 2.00
5318 A1550 60b multi .40 .25
a. Sheet of 8 + central label 3.25 2.00
5319 A1550 80b multi .50 .25
a. Sheet of 8 + central label 4.00 2.00
5320 A1550 1 l multi .60 .30
a. Sheet of 8 + central label 5.00 2.40
5321 A1550 2.40 l multi 1.50 .75
a. Sheet of 8 + central label 12.00 6.00
5322 A1550 3.10 l multi 1.90 .95
a. Sheet of 8 + central label 15.50 7.75
Nos. 5317-5322 (6) 5.20 2.75

Souvenir Sheet

Imperf

5323 A1550 14.50 l multi 8.75 4.50

Flowers A1551

Designs: 50b, Eritrichium nanum and snake. 60b, Amaranthus caudatus and turkey. 1 l, Pulmonaria officinalis and bear. 1.20 l, Ranunculus repens and chicken. 1.60 l, Borago officinalis and lamb. 2 l, Potentilla anserina and lobster. 3.30 l, Antirrhinum majus and lion. 3.60 l, Oxalis acetosella and rabbit. 4.70 l, Callistephus chinensis and cow. 7.60 l, Convolvulus arvensis and bird.

2012 **Litho.** ***Perf. 13¼***

5324 A1551 50b multi .30 .25
a. Sheet of 8 + central label 2.40 1.25
5325 A1551 60b multi .40 .25
a. Sheet of 8 + central label 3.25 1.60
5326 A1551 1 l multi .60 .30
a. Sheet of 8 + central label 5.00 2.50
5327 A1551 1.20 l multi .75 .35
a. Sheet of 8 + central label 6.00 3.00
5328 A1551 1.60 l multi 1.00 .50
a. Sheet of 8 + central label 8.00 4.00
5329 A1551 2 l multi 1.25 .60
a. Sheet of 8 + central label 10.00 5.00
5330 A1551 3.30 l multi 2.00 1.00
a. Sheet of 8 + central label 16.00 8.00
5331 A1551 3.60 l multi 2.25 1.10
a. Sheet of 8 + central label 18.00 9.00
5332 A1551 4.70 l multi 3.00 1.50
a. Sheet of 8 + central label 24.00 12.00
5333 A1551 7.60 l multi 4.75 2.40
a. Sheet of 8 + central label 38.00 19.50
Nos. 5324-5333 (10) 16.30 8.25

Issued: 50b, 60b, 1.60 l, 2 l, 1/19; 1 l, 1.20 l, 3.30 l, 3.60 l, 4.70 l, 7.60 l, 1/17.

Ion Luca Caragiale (1852-1912), Writer — A1552

Designs: 5 l, Caragiale. 9.10 l, Sculpture of Caragiale by Ioan Bolborea, horiz.

2012, Jan. 30 ***Perf. 13¼***

5334 A1552 5 l multi 3.00 1.50
a. Sheet of 8 + central label 24.00 12.00

Souvenir Sheet

Perf. 14x13¼

5335 A1552 9.10 l multi 5.50 2.75

No. 5335 contains one 53x42mm stamp.

Selection of Bucharest as Capital of Romania, 150th Anniv. — A1553

Designs: 14.50 l, Sutu Palace, Bucharest coat of arms.

8.10 l, Prince Alexandru Ioan Cuza.

2012, Feb. 3 ***Perf. 13¼***

5336 A1553 14.50 l multi 9.00 4.50
a. Sheet of 8 + central label 72.00 36.00

Souvenir Sheet

Perf. 14x13¼

5337 A1553 8.10 l multi 5.00 2.50

No. 5337 contains one 53x42mm stamp.

Portraits on Romanian Banknotes — A1554

Portrait of: 80b, Nicolae Iorga (1871-1940), writer. 1.40 l, George Enescu (1881-1955), composer. 2.10 l, Nicolae Grigorescu (1838-1907), painter. 2.40 l, Aurel Vlaicu (1882-1913), aviation pioneer. 3 l, Ion Luca Caragiale (1852-1912), writer. 3.10 l, Lucian Blaga (1895-1961), writer. 6 l, Mihai Eminescu (1850-89), poet.

2012, Feb. 10 ***Perf. 13¼***

5338 A1554 80b multi .50 .25
a. Souvenir sheet of 4 2.00 1.00
5339 A1554 1.40 l multi .85 .40
a. Souvenir sheet of 4 3.50 1.60
5340 A1554 2.10 l multi 1.25 .65
a. Souvenir sheet of 4 5.00 2.60
5341 A1554 2.40 l multi 1.50 .75
a. Souvenir sheet of 4 6.00 3.00
5342 A1554 3 l multi 1.90 .95
a. Souvenir sheet of 4 7.75 4.00
5343 A1554 3.10 l multi 1.90 .95
a. Souvenir sheet of 4 7.75 4.00
5344 A1554 6 l multi 3.75 1.90
a. Souvenir sheet of 4 15.00 7.75
Nos. 5338-5344 (7) 11.65 5.85

Irons A1555

Iron from: 50b, France, 18th cent. 80b, Germany, 18th cent. 1.40 l, United States, 19th cent. 4.70 l, Scotland, 19th cent. 5 l, Romania, 19th cent.

14.50 l, Romania, 20th cent.

2012, Feb. 17 ***Perf. 13¼***

5345 A1555 50b multi .30 .25
a. Sheet of 8 + central label 2.40 1.25
5346 A1555 80b multi .50 .25
a. Sheet of 8 + central label 4.00 2.00
5347 A1555 1.40 l multi .85 .40
a. Sheet of 8 + central label 7.00 3.50
5348 A1555 4.70 l multi 3.00 1.50
a. Sheet of 8 + central label 24.00 12.00
5349 A1555 5 l multi 3.00 1.50
a. Sheet of 8 + central label 24.00 12.00
Nos. 5345-5349 (5) 7.65 3.90

Souvenir Sheet

Perf. 13¼x14

5350 A1555 14.50 l multi 9.00 4.50

No. 5350 contains one 42x52mm stamp.

See Nos. 5384-5389.

Easter — A1556

2012, Mar. 16 ***Perf. 13¼***

5351 A1556 1 l multi .60 .30
a. Sheet of 8 + central label 5.00 2.50

First Mention of Timisoara in Documents, 800th Anniv. A1557

Designs: 2.10 l, Roman Catholic Cathedral. 5 l, Timisoara Fortress, horiz. 7.60 l, Hunyadi Castle, horiz. 14.50 l, Orthodox Metropolitan Cathedral.

2012, Mar. 26 **Litho.**

5352 A1557 2.10 l multi 1.25 .60
a. Sheet of 8 + central label 10.00 5.00
5353 A1557 5 l multi 3.00 1.50
a. Sheet of 8 + central label 24.00 12.00
5354 A1557 7.60 l multi 4.75 2.40
a. Sheet of 8 + central label 38.00 19.50
5355 A1557 14.50 l multi 8.75 4.25
a. Sheet of 8 + central label 70.00 35.00
b. Souvenir sheet of 1 8.75 4.25
Nos. 5352-5355 (4) 17.75 8.75

Europa
A1558

Map of Romania and: 1.40 l, Crane in Danube Delta. 8.10 l, Castle and mountains.

2012, Apr. 6

5356	A1558 1.40 l multi		.85	.40
a.	Sheet of 6		5.25	2.40
5357	A1558 8.10 l multi		5.00	2.50
a.	Sheet of 6		30.00	15.00
b.	Souvenir sheet of 4, 2 each #5356-5357, #5356 at UL		12.00	6.00
c.	As "b," with #5357 at UL		12.00	6.00

Romanian Athletic Federation, Cent. — A1559

2012, Apr. 20 *Perf. 13¼*

5358	A1559 1.40 l multi		.85	.40
a.	Sheet of 8 + central label		7.00	3.50

Ministry of Foreign Affairs, 150th Anniv. A1560

2012, Apr. 25

5359	A1560 2.10 l multi		1.25	.60
a.	Sheet of 8 + central label		10.00	5.00
b.	Souvenir sheet of 1 + label		1.25	.60

Fruits and Vegetables A1561

Designs: 50b, Grapes, peach, tomatoes, garlic. 1.60 l, Apples. 2.10 l, Peppers.

2012, May 3

5360	A1561 50b multi		.30	.25
a.	Sheet of 8 + central label		2.40	1.25
5361	A1561 1.60 l multi		.95	.50
a.	Sheet of 8 + central label		7.75	4.00
5362	A1561 2.10 l multi		1.25	.60
a.	Sheet of 8 + central label		10.00	5.00
	Nos. 5360-5362 (3)		2.50	1.35

The upper right stamp in Nos. 5360a-5362a is tete-beche in relation to the other stamps in the sheet.

Intl. Children's Day — A1562

2012, June 1

5363	A1562 2.40 l multi		1.40	.70
a.	Sheet of 8 + central label		11.50	5.75

Fish A1563

Designs: 1.40 l, Poecilia sphenops. 3 l, Eupomotis gibbosus. 3.10 l, Macropodus opercularis. 14.50 l, Thorichthys meeki.

2012, June 15

5364	A1563 1.40 l multi		.80	.40
a.	Sheet of 8 + central label		6.50	3.25
5365	A1563 3 l multi		1.60	.80
a.	Sheet of 8 + central label		13.00	6.50
5366	A1563 3.10 l multi		1.75	.85
a.	Sheet of 8 + central label		14.00	7.00
5367	A1563 14.50 l multi		8.00	4.00
a.	Sheet of 8 + central label		65.00	32.50
	Nos. 5364-5367 (4)		12.15	6.05

Birds — A1564

Designs: 1 l, Merops apiaster. 1.20 l, Egretta garzetta. 2.10 l, Ardeola ralloides. 8.10 l, Branta ruficollis. 9.10 l, Pelecanus onocrotalus.

2012, July 6 *Perf. 14x13¼*

5368	A1564 1 l multi		.55	.25
a.	Sheet of 9 + label		5.00	2.50
5369	A1564 1.20 l multi		.65	.30
a.	Sheet of 9 + label		6.00	3.00
5370	A1564 2.10 l multi		1.25	.60
a.	Sheet of 9 + label		11.50	5.50
5371	A1564 8.10 l multi		4.50	2.25
a.	Sheet of 9 + label		41.00	21.00
5372	A1564 9.10 l multi		5.00	2.50
a.	Sheet of 9 + label		45.00	22.50
b.	Souvenir sheet of 1		5.00	2.50
	Nos. 5368-5372 (5)		11.95	5.90

Eleventh meeting of the Conference of the Parties to the Convention on Wetlands of International Importance, Bucharest.

Victor Babes National Institute, 125th Anniv. — A1565

Designs: 3.10 l, Building, Bucharest. 7.60, Babes (1854-1926), physician, and flasks.

2012, July 16 *Perf. 13¼*

5373	A1565 3.10 l multi		1.75	.85
a.	Sheet of 8 + central label		14.00	7.00
5374	A1565 7.60 l multi		4.25	2.10
a.	Sheet of 8 + central label		34.00	17.00
b.	Souvenir sheet of 2, #5373-5374		6.00	3.00

2012 Summer Olympics, London — A1566

Designs: 1.20 l, Gymnastics. 1.40 l, Canoeing. 2.10 l, Fencing. 6 l, Javelin.

2012, July 27 **Litho.**

5375-5378	A1566 Set of 4		5.75	3.00

Nos. 5374-5378 each were printed in sheets of 4.

Dogs — A1567

Designs: 4.50 l, Short-haired dachshund. 5 l, Golden retriever. 8.10 l, Romanian Mioritic shepherd. 9.10 l, Romanian Carpathian shepherd.

2012, Aug. 10

5379	A1567 4.50 l multi		2.60	1.40
a.	Sheet of 8 + central label		21.00	11.50
5380	A1567 5 l multi		3.00	1.50
a.	Sheet of 8 + central label		24.00	12.00
5381	A1567 8.10 l multi		4.75	2.40
a.	Sheet of 8 + central label		38.00	19.50
5382	A1567 9.10 l multi		5.25	2.60
a.	Sheet of 8 + central label		42.00	21.00
b.	Souvenir sheet of 4, #5379-5382		16.00	8.00
	Nos. 5379-5382 (4)		15.60	7.90

Hagigadar Monastery, Moara, 500th Anniv. — A1568

2012, Aug. 11

5383	A1568 4.70 l multi		2.75	1.40
a.	Sheet of 8 + central label		22.00	11.50
b.	Souvenir sheet of 2 + 2 labels		5.50	2.75

Examples of No. 5383b with gold foil applied were printed in limited quantities and sold for 135 l. See Armenia No. 911.

Irons Type of 2012

Irons from: 80b, Burma, 19th cent. 1 l, Sweden, 18th cent. 1.20 l, Belgium, 18th cent. 1.60 l, Italy, 18th cent. 5 l, Switzerland, 19th cent. 14.50 l, United States, 19th cent.

2012, Sept. 1

5384	A1555 80b multi		.45	.25
a.	Sheet of 8 + central label		3.75	2.00
5385	A1555 1 l multi		.60	.30
a.	Sheet of 8 + central label		5.00	2.40
5386	A1555 1.20 l multi		.70	.35
a.	Sheet of 8 + central label		5.75	3.00
5387	A1555 1.60 l multi		.95	.45
a.	Sheet of 8 + central label		7.75	3.75
5388	A1555 5 l multi		3.00	1.50
a.	Sheet of 8 + central label		24.00	12.00
5389	A1555 14.50 l multi		8.50	4.25
a.	Sheet of 8 + central label		68.00	34.00
b.	Souvenir sheet of 1, imperf.		8.50	4.25
	Nos. 5384-5389 (6)		14.20	7.10

Romanian Post, 150th Anniv. — A1569

Designs: 1 l, Romania #11, 12, 14. 8.10 l, Posthorn, Postal headquarters, Bucharest.

2012, Sept. 24

5390	A1569 1 l multi		.60	.30
a.	Sheet of 8 + central label		5.00	2.40
5391	A1569 8.10 l multi		4.75	2.40
a.	Sheet of 8 + central label		38.00	19.50
b.	Souvenir sheet of 1, imperf.		4.75	2.40

A sheet containing Nos. 5390-5391 was printed in limited quantities.

Treaty Between Romania and Germany, 20th Anniv. — A1570

2012, Oct. 4

5392	A1570 2.10 l multi		1.25	.60
a.	Sheet of 8 + central label		10.00	5.00

Curtea de Arges Monastery Church, 500th Anniv. — A1571

Designs: 4.50 l, Church and icons. 14.50 l, Church.

2012, Oct. 12

5393	A1571 4.50 l multi		2.60	1.40
a.	Sheet of 8 + central label		21.00	11.50
5394	A1571 14.50 l multi		8.25	4.25
a.	Sheet of 8 + central label		66.00	34.00
b.	Souvenir sheet of 4, 2 each #5393-5394, + 2 labels		22.00	11.50

Mammals A1572

Designs: No. 5395, Capra pyrenaica. No. 5396, Cervus elaphus.

2012, Oct. 19

5395	A1572 3.10 l multi		1.75	.90
a.	Sheet of 8 + central label		14.00	7.25
5396	A1572 3.10 l multi		1.75	.90
a.	Sheet of 8 + central label		14.00	7.25

A sheet containing Nos. 5395-5396 was printed in limited quantities. See Spain No. 3878.

Christmas A1573

2012, Nov. 15

5397 A1573 1 l multi .60 .30
 a. Sheet of 8 + central label 5.00 2.40

A souvenir sheet of 2 No. 5397 was printed in limited quantities.

Stone Churches A1574

Designs: 3 l, St. Nicholas Church, Densus. 5 l, Strei Church, Hunedoara. 7.60 l, Mintia Church, Vetel. 14.50 l, Colt Church, Suseni.

2012, Nov. 16

5398 A1574 3 l multi 1.75 .85
 a. Sheet of 8 + central label 14.00 7.00
5399 A1574 5 l multi 3.00 1.50
 a. Sheet of 8 + central label 24.00 12.00
5400 A1574 7.60 l multi 4.50 2.25
 a. Sheet of 8 + central label 36.00 18.00
5401 A1574 14.50 l multi 8.25 4.25
 a. Sheet of 8 + central label 66.00 34.00
 Nos. 5398-5401 (4) 17.50 8.85

Young Animals A1575

Designs: 4.30 l, Bear cub. 5 l, Fawn. 9.10 l, Fox pup. 14.50 l, Wolf pup.

2012, Dec. 7

5402 A1575 4.30 l multi 2.50 1.25
 a. Sheet of 8 + central label 20.00 10.00
5403 A1575 5 l multi 3.00 1.50
 a. Sheet of 8 + central label 24.00 12.00
5404 A1575 9.10 l multi 5.25 2.60
 a. Sheet of 8 + central label 42.00 21.00
5405 A1575 14.50 l multi 8.25 4.25
 a. Sheet of 8 + central label 66.00 34.00
 b. Sheet of 4, #5402-5405 19.00 9.75
 Nos. 5402-5405 (4) 19.00 9.60

Seal of Mircea cel Batran and Arms of Sovereign Military Order of Malta — A1576

2012, Dec. 14

5406 A1576 8.10 l multi 5.00 2.50
 a. Sheet of 8 + central label 40.00 20.00

Romanian relations with Sovereign Military Order of Malta, 80th anniv. A souvenir sheet of two No. 5406 exists from a limited printing.

Anti-terrorist Fighter's Day — A1577

Crest of Romanian Anti-terrorist Brigade and: 1 l, Soldier. 8.10 l, Five soldiers.

2012, Dec. 21

5407 A1577 1 l multi .60 .30
 a. Sheet of 8 + 4 labels 5.00 2.40
5408 A1577 8.10 l multi 5.00 2.50
 a. Sheet of 8 + 4 labels 40.00 20.00
 b. Souvenir sheet of 1 5.00 2.50

Self-portraits A1578

Self-portrait of: 4.50 l, Stefan Luchian (1868-1916). 9.10 l, Nicolae Grigorescu (1838-1907).

2013, Jan. 18

5409 A1578 4.50 l multi 2.75 1.40
 a. Sheet of 8 + central label 22.00 11.50
5410 A1578 9.10 l multi 5.75 2.75
 a. Sheet of 8 + central label 46.00 22.00
 b. Souvenir sheet of 1 5.75 2.75

Flowers and Clocks — A1579

Designs: 60b, Papaver rhoeas, French mantel clock, 19th cent. 80b, Cichorium intybus, Austrian carriage clock, 19th cent. 1 l, Scorzonera rosea, French table clock, 19th cent. 1.60 l, Caltha palustris, German table clock, 20th cent. 2.40 l, Helianthus annuus, French portico clock, 19th cent. 5 l, Veronica chamaedrys, French table clock, 19th cent.

2013, Jan. 25

5411 A1579 60b multi .40 .25
 a. Sheet of 8 + central label 3.25 2.00
5412 A1579 80b multi .50 .25
 a. Sheet of 8 + central label 4.00 2.00
5413 A1579 1 l multi .65 .30
 a. Sheet of 8 + central label 5.25 2.40
5414 A1579 1.60 l multi 1.00 .50
 a. Sheet of 8 + central label 8.00 4.00
5415 A1579 2.40 l multi 1.50 .75
 a. Sheet of 8 + central label 12.00 6.00
5416 A1579 5 l multi 3.25 1.60
 a. Sheet of 8 + central label 26.00 13.00
 Nos. 5411-5416 (6) 7.30 3.65

A sheet of six containing Nos. 5412-5417 exists in a limited printing. See Nos. 5454-5459.

Radauti Synagogue, 130th Anniv. — A1580

Synagogue and: 8.10 l, Star of David. 14.50 l, Menorah.

2013, Feb. 8 Litho. *Perf. 13¼*

5417 A1580 8.10 l multi 5.00 2.50
 a. Sheet of 8 + central label 40.00 20.00
5418 A1580 14.50 l multi 8.75 4.50
 a. Sheet of 8 + central label 70.00 36.00

A sheet of two containing Nos. 5417-5418 exists in a limited printing.

Romanian Athenaeum. 125th Anniv. — A1581

Designs: 5 l, Stage. 9.10 l, Exterior.

Perf. 13¾x13¼

2013, Feb. 22 Litho.

5419 A1581 5 l multi 3.00 1.50
 a. Sheet of 10 30.00 15.00
5420 A1581 9.10 l multi 5.50 2.75
 a. Sheet of 10 55.00 27.50
 b. Souvenir sheet of 1 5.50 2.75

Crowns A1582

Crown of: 3.30 l, King Carol I. 4.30 l, Queen Elizabeth. 14.50 l, Queen Marie.

2013, Feb. 28 Litho. *Perf. 13¼*

5421 A1582 3.30 l multi 2.00 1.00
 a. Sheet of 6 12.00 6.00
5422 A1582 4.30 l multi 2.60 1.40
 a. Sheet of 6 16.00 8.50
5423 A1582 14.50 l multi 8.75 4.50
 a. Sheet of 6 52.50 27.00
 Nos. 5421-5423 (3) 13.35 6.90

Values are for stamps with surrounding selvage. A souvenir sheet of three containing Nos. 5421-5423 exists in a limited printing.

Tourist Attractions in Transylvania — A1583

Arms of Transylvania and: 3.30 l, Fortified Church, Viscri. 3.60 l, House, Valea Zalanului, vert. 4.30 l, Hosman, vert. 5 l, St. Michael's Church, Cluj.

2013, Mar. 15 Litho. *Perf. 13¼*

5424 A1583 3.30 l multi 1.90 .95
 a. Sheet of 8 + central label 15.50 7.75
5425 A1583 3.60 l multi 2.10 1.10
 a. Sheet of 8 + central label 17.00 9.00
5426 A1583 4.30 l multi 2.50 1.25
 a. Sheet of 8 + central label 20.00 10.00
5427 A1583 5 l multi 3.00 1.50
 a. Sheet of 8 + central label 24.00 12.00
 Nos. 5424-5427 (4) 9.50 4.80

A sheet of four containing Nos. 5424-5427 exists in a limited printing.

Cameras A1584

Designs: 50b, Goldmann camera, Austria. 80b, Suter camera, Switzerland. 1.40 l, Plaubel Makina camera, Germany. 2 l, Ernemann Tropen-Klapp camera, Germany. 2.10 l, Balda Pontina camera, Germany. 14.50 l, Welta camera, Germany.

2013, Mar. 29 Litho. *Perf. 13¼*

5428 A1584 50b multi .30 .25
 a. Sheet of 8 + central label 2.40 1.25
5429 A1584 80b multi .50 .25
 a. Sheet of 8 + central label 4.00 2.00
5430 A1584 1.40 l multi .80 .40
 a. Sheet of 8 + central label 6.50 3.25
5431 A1584 2 l multi 1.25 .60
 a. Sheet of 8 + central label 10.00 5.00
5432 A1584 2.10 l multi 1.25 .60
 a. Sheet of 8 + central label 10.00 5.00
5433 A1584 14.50 l multi 8.50 4.25
 a. Sheet of 8 + central label 68.00 34.00
 Nos. 5428-5433 (6) 12.60 6.35

Easter — A1585

2013, Apr. 5 Litho. *Perf. 13¼*

5434 A1585 1 l multi .60 .30
 a. Sheet of 8 + central label 4.80 2.40

King Carol I and Bucharest University of Economic Studies — A1586

2013, Apr. 6 Litho. *Perf. 13¼*

5435 A1586 8.10 l multi 5.00 2.50
 a. Sheet of 8 + central label 40.00 20.00

Bucharest University of Economic Studies, cent.

National Bank of Romania, Bucharest — A1587

Designs: 3.10 l, Exterior. 3.60 l, Marble Hall. 4.50 l, Main hallway. 4.70 l, Staircase.

2013, Apr. 17 Litho. *Perf. 13¼*

5436 A1587 3.10 l multi 1.90 .95
 a. Sheet of 6 11.50 5.75
5437 A1587 3.60 l multi 2.25 1.10
 a. Sheet of 6 13.50 6.75
5438 A1587 4.50 l multi 2.75 1.40
 a. Sheet of 6 16.50 8.50
5439 A1587 4.70 l multi 3.00 1.50
 a. Sheet of 6 18.00 9.00
 b. Souvenir sheet of 4, #5436-5439 10.00 5.00
 Nos. 5436-5439 (4) 9.90 4.95

Earth Day — A1588

2013, Apr. 22 Litho. *Perf. 13¼*

5440 A1588 5 l multi 3.00 1.50
 a. Sheet of 8 + central label 24.00 12.00

Famous Women — A1589

Designs: 1 l, Stefania Maracineanu (1882-1944), physicist. 3.30 l, Josephine Cochrane (1839-1913), inventor of dishwasher. 9.10 l, Rear Admiral Grace Murray Hopper (1906-92), computer scientist.

2013, Apr. 26 Litho. *Perf. 13¼*

5441	A1589	1 l multi	.60	.30
a.	Sheet of 6		3.60	1.80
5442	A1589	3.30 l multi	2.00	1.00
a.	Sheet of 6		12.00	6.00
5443	A1589	9.10 l multi	5.50	2.75
a.	Sheet of 6		33.00	16.50
	Nos. 5441-5443 (3)		8.10	4.05

Europa — A1590

Designs: 2.10 l, Biplane with airmail envelopes as wings. 14.50 l, Postman on bicycle delivering letter to driver of automobile.

2013, Apr. 30 Litho. *Perf. 13¼*

5444	A1590	2.10 l multi	1.25	.60
a.	Sheet of 6		7.50	3.75
5445	A1590	14.50 l multi	9.00	4.50
a.	Sheet of 6		54.00	27.00
b.	Souvenir sheet of 4, 2 each #5444-5445, #5444 at UL		20.50	10.50
c.	As "b," #5445 at UL		20.50	10.50

Edict of Milan, 1700th Anniv. — A1591

Emperor Constantine the Great and Empress Helen on: 4.70 l, Byzantine era icon. 9.10 l, Icon by Otilia Michail Otetelesanu from 1960s.

2013, May 21 Litho. *Perf. 13¼*

5446	A1591	4.70 l multi	3.00	1.50
a.	Sheet of 6		18.00	9.00
5447	A1591	9.10 l multi	5.50	2.75
a.	Sheet of 6		33.00	16.50

First Mention of Suceava in Documents, 625th Anniv. — A1592

Anniversary emblem and: 4.30 l, St. George's Church (Mirauti Church). 14.50 l, Suceava Fortress.

2013, May 30 Litho. *Perf. 13¼*

5448	A1592	4.30 l multi	2.60	1.40
a.	Sheet of 8 + label		21.00	11.50
5449	A1592	14.50 l multi	8.75	4.50
a.	Sheet of 8 + label		70.00	36.00

A souvenir sheet of two containing Nos. 5448-5449 was printed in limited quantities.

Healthy Foods A1593

Jar of honey and: 1 l, Walnuts, cinnamon sticks. 1.40 l, Hazelnuts. 6 l, Raspberries and blackberries. 8.10 l, Walnuts, cinnamon sticks, hazelnuts, raspberries and blackberries.

2013, June 7 Litho. *Perf. 13¼*

5450	A1593	1 l multi	.60	.30
a.	Sheet of 8 + label		5.00	2.40
5451	A1593	1.40 l multi	.85	.40
a.	Sheet of 8 + label		7.00	3.25
5452	A1593	6 l multi	3.75	1.90
a.	Sheet of 8 + label		30.00	15.50
5453	A1593	8.10 l multi	5.00	2.50
a.	Sheet of 8 + label		40.00	20.00
	Nos. 5450-5453 (4)		10.20	5.10

A souvenir sheet of four containing Nos. 5450-5453 was printed in limited quantities.

Flowers and Clocks Type of 2013

Designs: 50b, Anthericum ramosum, French table clock, 19th cent. 1.20 l, Mirabilis jalapa, German table clock, 19th cent. 1.40 l, Datura stramonium, Swiss pocket watch, 18th cent. 3 l, Silene latifolia, Austrian traveler's clock, 19th cent. 3.10 l, Nicotiana alata, French chimney clock, 19th cent. 4.70 l, Oenothera biennis, French miniature table clock, 19th cent.

2013, June 21 Litho. *Perf. 13¼*

5454	A1579	50b multi	.30	.25
a.	Sheet of 8 + central label		2.40	1.25
5455	A1579	1.20 l multi	.70	.35
a.	Sheet of 8 + central label		5.75	3.00
5456	A1579	1.40 l mulkti	.85	.40
a.	Sheet of 8 + central label		7.00	3.25
5457	A1579	3 l multi	1.75	.85
a.	Sheet of 8 + central label		14.00	7.00
5458	A1579	3.10 l multi	1.90	.95
a.	Sheet of 8 + central label		15.50	7.75
5459	A1579	4.70 l multi	2.75	1.40
a.	Sheet of 8 + central label		22.00	11.50
	Nos. 5454-5459 (6)		8.25	4.20

A sheet of six containing Nos. 5454-5459 exists in a limited printing.

Owls — A1594

Designs: 2 l, Athene noctua. 3.30 l, Asio otus. 4.50 l, Strix uralensis. 9.10 l, Strix nebulosa, horiz.

2013, June 28 Litho. *Perf. 13¼*

5460	A1594	2 l multi	1.25	.60
a.	Sheet of 6		7.50	3.75
5461	A1594	3.30 l multi	2.00	1.00
a.	Sheet of 6		12.00	6.00
5462	A1594	4.50 l multi	2.75	1.40
a.	Sheet of 6		16.50	8.50
5463	A1594	9.10 l multi	5.50	2.75
a.	Sheet of 6		33.00	16.50
	Nos. 5460-5463 (4)		11.50	5.75

Treaty of Friendly Relations and Cooperation Between Romania and Russia, 10th Anniv. — A1595

2013, July 9 Litho. *Perf. 13¾x13¼*

5464	A1595	8.10 l multi	4.75	2.40
a.	Sheet of 6 + 2 labels		28.50	14.50
b.	Souvenir sheet of 1		4.75	2.40

Sport Hunting and Fishing A1596

Designs: 2 l, Mouflon. 2.10 l, European hare. 6 l, Chamois. 7.60 l, Trout.

2013, July 9 Litho. *Perf. 13¼*

5465	A1596	2 l multi	1.25	.60
a.	Sheet of 8 + label		10.00	5.00
5466	A1596	2.10 l multi	1.25	.60
a.	Sheet of 8 + label		10.00	5.00
5467	A1596	6 l multi	3.50	1.75
a.	Sheet of 8 + label		28.00	14.00
5468	A1596	7.60 l multi	4.50	2.25
a.	Sheet of 8 + label		36.00	18.00
	Nos. 5465-5468 (4)		10.50	5.20

Antim Monastery, 300th Anniv. — A1597

Designs: 3.60 l, Monastery. 14.50 l, Bishop Antim Ivireanu (1650-1716).

2013, July 15 Litho. *Perf. 13¼*

5469	A1597	3.60 l multi	2.10	1.10
a.	Sheet of 4		8.50	4.50
5470	A1597	14.50 l multi	8.75	4.50
a.	Sheet of 4		35.00	18.00

A sheet of two containing Nos. 5469-5470 exists in a limited printing.

Romanian Gold Coins A1598

20-lei coins from: 3.30 l, 1870. 4.30 l, 1906. 4.50 l, 1922. 8.10 l, 1939.

2013, July 26 Litho. *Perf. 13¼*

5471	A1598	3.30 l multi	2.00	1.00
a.	Sheet of 6		12.00	6.00
5472	A1598	4.30 l multi	2.60	1.40
a.	Sheet of 6		16.00	8.50
5473	A1598	4.50 l multi	2.75	1.40
a.	Sheet of 6		16.50	8.50
5474	A1598	8.10 l multi	5.00	2.50
a.	Sheet of 6		30.00	15.00
	Nos. 5471-5474 (4)		12.35	6.30

Religion and Law — A1599

Designs: 1.20 l, Statue of Moses, by Michelangelo. 1.40 l, Ten Commandments. 3 l, Torahs, Great Synagogue of Bucharest. 14.50 l, St. Catherine's Monastery, Mount Sinai, Egypt.

2013, Aug. 14 Litho. *Perf. 13¼*

5475	A1599	1.20 l multi	.75	.35
a.	Sheet of 8 + central label		6.00	3.00
5476	A1599	1.40 l multi	.85	.40
a.	Sheet of 8 + central label		7.00	3.25
5477	A1599	3 l multi	1.75	.90
a.	Sheet of 8 + central label		14.00	7.25
5478	A1599	14.50 l multi	8.75	4.50
a.	Sheet of 8 + central label		70.00	36.00
	Nos. 5475-5478 (4)		12.10	6.15

A sheet of 4 containing Nos. 5475-5478 exists in a limited printing.

Mention of Oradea in Documents, 900th Anniv. — A1600

Designs: 2.10 l, Assumption of the Virgin Orthodox Cathedral. 4.30 l, Roman Catholic Cathedral. 4.70 l, Queen Marie Theater, horiz. 9.10 l, Oradea City Hall, horiz.

2013, Aug. 30 Litho. *Perf. 13¼*

5479	A1600	2.10 l multi	1.25	.60
a.	Sheet of 8 + central label		10.00	5.00
5480	A1600	4.30 l multi	2.60	1.40
a.	Sheet of 8 + central label		21.00	11.50
5481	A1600	4.70 l multi	3.00	1.50
a.	Sheet of 8 + central label		24.00	12.00
5482	A1600	9.10 l multi	5.50	2.75
a.	Sheet of 8 + central label		44.00	22.00
b.	Souvenir sheet of 1		5.50	2.75
	Nos. 5479-5482 (4)		12.35	6.25

A sheet of four containing Nos. 5479-5482 exists in a limited printing.

Traditional Costumes of Romania and Poland — A1601

Perf. 13¾x13¼

2013, Sept. 11 Litho.

5483	A1601	8.10 l multi	5.00	2.50
a.	Sheet of 10		50.00	25.00
b.	Souvenir sheet of 1		5.00	2.50

See Poland No. 4092.

Statues of the National Bank of Romania A1602

Designs: 2 l, Justice. 3.30 l, Commerce. 3.60 l, Industry. 4.50 l, Agriculture.

8.10 l, Bust of bank founder Eugeniu Carada (1836-1910), by Ioan Dolborea.

2013, Sept. 20 Litho. *Perf. 13¼*

5484	A1602	2 l multi	1.25	.60
a.	Sheet of 6		7.50	3.75
5485	A1602	3.30 l multi	2.00	1.00
a.	Sheet of 6		12.00	6.00
5486	A1602	3.60 l multi	2.25	1.10
a.	Sheet of 6		2.25	1.10
5487	A1602	4.50 l multi	2.75	1.40
a.	Sheet of 6		16.50	8.50
	Nos. 5484-5487 (4)		8.25	4.10

Souvenir Sheet

Perf. 13¼x13¾

5488	A1602	8.10 l multi	5.00	2.50

No. 5488 contains one 42x52mm stamp. A sheet of four containing Nos. 5484-5487 exists in a limited printing, as does and example of No. 5488 with gold foil.

Maria Tanase (1913-63), Singer — A1603

2013, Sept. 25 Litho. *Perf. 13¼*

5489 A1603 9.10 l multi 5.50 2.75
a. Sheet of 8 44.00 22.00
b. Souvenir sheet of 1 5.50 2.75

No. 5489a exists with two different marginal illustrations. Values are for either illustration.

Rogoz Wooden Church From Wooden Churches of Maramures UNESCO World Heritage Site — A1604

2013, Sept. 27 Litho. *Perf. 13¼*

5490 A1604 8.10 l multi 5.00 2.50
a. Sheet of 6 30.00 15.00

Rogoz Wooden Church, 350th anniv.

Transylvanian Association for Romanian Literature and Culture Museum of Traditional Folk Civilization, 50th Anniv. — A1605

2013, Oct. 4 Litho. *Perf. 13¼*

5491 A1605 14.50 l multi 9.00 4.50
a. Sheet of 4 + 2 labels 36.00 18.00

King Carol I Mosque, Constanta, Cent. A1606

2013, Oct. 10 Litho. *Perf. 13¼x13¾*

5492 A1606 8.10 l multi 5.00 2.50
a. Sheet of 6 30.00 15.00
b. Souvenir sheet of 1 5.00 2.50

No. 5492b exists with a different sheet margin on a first day cover in a limited printing.

See Turkey No. 3365.

Fauna A1607

Designs: 3.30 l, Marmota marmota. 4.30 l, Picoides tridactylus. 4.50 l, Lynx lynx. 9.10 l, Bison bonasus.

2013, Oct. 25 Litho. *Perf. 13¼*

5493 A1607 3.30 l multi 2.00 1.00
a. Sheet of 5 + label 10.00 5.00

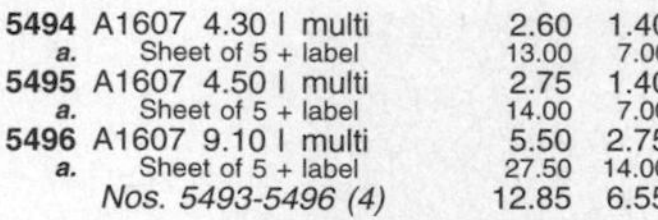

5494 A1607 4.30 l multi 2.60 1.40
a. Sheet of 5 + label 13.00 7.00
5495 A1607 4.50 l multi 2.75 1.40
a. Sheet of 5 + label 14.00 7.00
5496 A1607 9.10 l multi 5.50 2.75
a. Sheet of 5 + label 27.50 14.00
Nos. 5493-5496 (4) 12.85 6.55

Radio Romania, 85th Anniv. A1608

Designs: 1 l, Nicolae Iorga (1871-1940), writer and prime minister. 14.50 l, Elena Vacarescu (1866-1947), writer.

2013, Nov. 4 Litho. *Perf. 13¼*

5497 A1608 1 l multi .60 .30
a. Sheet of 4 2.40 1.25
5498 A1608 14.50 l multi 8.75 4.50
a. Sheet of 4 35.00 18.00
b. Sheet of 2, #5497-5498, + 14 labels 9.50 4.75

Christmas — A1609

2013, Nov. 22 Litho. *Perf. 13¼*

5499 A1609 1 l multi .60 .30
a. Sheet of 8 + central label 5.00 2.40
Complete booklet, 8 #5499 5.00

A sheet containing four No. 5499 exists in a limited printing.

Chess Pieces and Emblem of Integrated Intelligence Office — A1610

2013, Nov. 29 Litho. *Perf. 13¼*

5500 A1610 8.10 l multi 5.00 2.50
a. Sheet of 6 + 3 labels 30.00 15.00

Paintings of Roses — A1611

Designs: 1 l, Roses, by Nicolae Grigorescu. 3.60 l, Roses, by Theodor Aman. 4.50 l, Roses, by Stefan Luchian, horiz. 14.50 l, Roses, by Ion Andreescu, horiz.

2013, Dec. 12 Litho. *Perf. 13¼*

5501 A1611 1 l multi .60 .30
a. Sheet of 6 + 2 labels 3.75 1.90
5502 A1611 3.60 l multi 2.25 1.10
a. Sheet of 6 + 2 labels 13.50 6.75
5503 A1611 4.50 l multi 2.75 1.40
a. Sheet of 6 + 2 labels 16.50 8.50
5504 A1611 14.50 l multi 9.00 4.50
a. Sheet of 6 + 2 labels 54.00 27.00
Nos. 5501-5504 (4) 14.60 7.30

A sheet of four containing Nos. 5501-5504 exists in a limited printing.

Corund Ceramics A1612

Designs: 3.30 l, Plate. 3.60 l, Cup. 5 l, Bowl. 8.10 l, Vase.

2013, Dec. 20 Litho. *Perf. 13¼*

5505 A1612 3.30 l multi 2.00 1.00
a. Sheet of 6 12.00 6.00
5506 A1612 3.60 l multi 2.25 1.10
a. Sheet of 6 13.50 6.75
5507 A1612 5 l multi 3.00 1.50
a. Sheet of 6 18.00 9.00
5508 A1612 8.10 l multi 5.00 2.50
a. Sheet of 6 30.00 15.00
Nos. 5505-5508 (4) 12.25 6.10

Churches A1613

Designs: 1 l, Church of the Savior, Berestovo, Ukraine. 9.10 l, Church of the Sucevita Monastery, Romania.

2013, Dec. 21 Litho. *Perf. 13¼*

5509 A1613 1 l multi .60 .30
a. Sheet of 8 + central label 4.80 2.40
5510 A1613 9.10 l multi 5.50 2.75
a. Sheet of 8 + central label 44.00 22.00

See Ukraine No. 952.

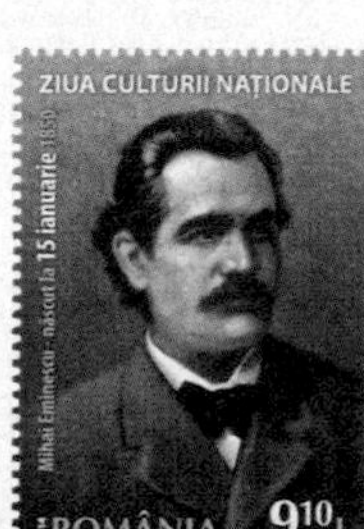

Mihai Eminescu (1850-89), Poet — A1614

2014, Jan. 15 Litho. *Perf. 13¼*

5511 A1614 9.10 l multi 5.50 2.75
a. Souvenir sheet of 1 5.50 2.75
b. Miniature sheet of 6 33.00 16.50

National Culture Day.

Buildings in Arad — A1615

Arms of Arad and: 2 l, City Hall. 2.10 l, Old Orthodox Cathedral, vert. 3.60 l, Evangelical Lutheran Church, vert. 14.50 l, Ioan Slavici Classical Theater.

2014, Jan. 23 Litho. *Perf. 13¼*

5512 A1615 2 l multi 1.25 .60
a. Sheet of 5 + label 6.25 3.00
5513 A1615 2.10 l multi 1.25 .65
a. Sheet of 5 + label 6.25 3.25
5514 A1615 3.60 l multi 2.25 1.10
a. Sheet of 5 + label 11.50 5.50
5515 A1615 14.50 l multi 8.75 4.50
a. Sheet of 5 + label 44.00 22.50
Nos. 5512-5515 (4) 13.50 6.85

Desert Flowers A1616

Designs: 1 l, Echinocereus triglochidiatus. 1.40 l, Baileya multiradiata. 8.10 l, Solanum elaeagnifolium. 14.50 l, Hibiscus denudatus.

2014, Jan. 29 Litho. *Perf. 13¼*

5516 A1616 1 l multi .60 .30
a. Sheet of 4 2.40 1.20
5517 A1616 1.40 l multi .85 .40
a. Sheet of 4 3.50 1.60
5518 A1616 8.10 l multi 5.00 2.50
a. Sheet of 4 20.00 10.00
5519 A1616 14.50 l multi 8.75 4.50
a. Sheet of 4 35.00 18.00
Nos. 5516-5519 (4) 15.20 7.70

Favorable Judgement in Black Sea Boundary Dispute With Ukraine, 5th Anniv. — A1617

2014, Feb. 3 Litho. *Perf. 13¼*

5520 A1617 9.10 l multi 5.50 2.75
a. Souvenir sheet of 1 5.50 2.75
b. Sheet of 10 + 2 labels 55.00 27.50

2014 Winter Olympics, Sochi, Russia — A1618

No. 5521: a, Biathlon. b, Bobsledding. c, Figure skating. d, Skiing.

2014, Feb. 7 Litho. *Perf. 13¼*

5521 A1618 2.10 l Block of 4, #a-d 5.25 2.60

No. 5521 was printed in sheets containing two tete-beche blocks.

Miniature Sheet

Paintings of Roma People — A1619

No. 5522 — Painting of various Roma people by: a, 3.50 l, Iosif Iser (1881-1958). b, 4.30 l, Nicolae Grigorescu (1838-1907). c, 4.50 l, Pierre Bellet (1865-1924). d, 8.10 l, Nicolae Vermont (1836-1932).

2014, Feb. 20 Litho. *Perf. 13¼x14*

5522 A1619 Sheet of 4, #a-d 12.50 6.25

Actors and Actresses A1620

Designs: No. 5523, Draga Olteanu Matei. No. 5524, Florin Piersic. No. 5525, Olga Tudorache. No. 5526, Marin Moraru. No. 5527, Mircea Albulescu. No. 5528, Ileana Stana Ionescu. No. 5529, Tamara Buciuceanu-Botez. No. 5530, Mitica Popescu. No. 5531, Sebastian Papaiani. No. 5532, Valeria Gagealov. No. 5533, George Motoi. No. 5534, Sanda Toma.

2014, Mar. 1 Litho. *Perf. 13¼*

5523 A1620 1.60 l multi 1.00 .50
a. Sheet of 4 4.00 2.00
5524 A1620 1.60 l multi 1.00 .50
a. Sheet of 4 4.00 2.00
5525 A1620 1.60 l multi 1.00 .50
a. Sheet of 4 4.00 2.00
5526 A1620 1.60 l multi 1.00 .50
a. Sheet of 4 4.00 2.00
5527 A1620 1.60 l multi 1.00 .50
a. Sheet of 4 4.00 2.00
5528 A1620 1.60 l multi 1.00 .50
a. Sheet of 4 4.00 2.00
5529 A1620 1.60 l multi 1.00 .50
a. Sheet of 4 4.00 2.00
5530 A1620 1.60 l multi 1.00 .50
a. Sheet of 4 4.00 2.00
5531 A1620 1.60 l multi 1.00 .50
a. Sheet of 4 4.00 2.00
5532 A1620 1.60 l multi 1.00 .50
a. Sheet of 4 4.00 2.00
5533 A1620 1.60 l multi 1.00 .50
a. Sheet of 4 4.00 2.00
5534 A1620 1.60 l multi 1.00 .50
a. Sheet of 4 4.00 2.00
b. Sheet of 12, #5523-5534, + 4 central labels 12.00 6.00
Nos. 5523-5534 (12) 12.00 6.00

Easter — A1621

2014, Mar. 20 Litho. *Perf. 13¼*

5535 A1621 1 l multi .65 .30
a. Sheet of 8 + central label 5.25 2.60

Ducks A1622

Designs: 1.20 l, Anas platyrhynchos. 1.40 l, Aythya fuligula. 8.10 l, Anas clypeata. 14.50 l, Anas crecca.

2014, Mar. 24 Litho. *Perf. 13¼*

5536 A1622 1.20 l multi .75 .35
a. Sheet of 5 + label 3.75 1.75
5537 A1622 1.40 l multi .85 .45
a. Sheet of 5 + label 4.25 2.25
5538 A1622 8.10 l multi 5.00 2.50
a. Sheet of 5 + label 25.00 12.50
5539 A1622 14.50 l multi 9.00 4.50
a. Sheet of 5 + label 45.00 22.50
Nos. 5536-5539 (4) 15.60 7.80

Admission to North Atlantic Treaty Organization, 10th Anniv. — A1623

2014, Apr. 2 Litho. *Perf. 13¼*

5540 A1623 9.10 l multi 5.75 3.00
a. Sheet of 6 35.00 18.00
b. Souvenir sheet of 1 5.75 3.00

No. 5540 has 13 perforation holes within stamp; No. 5540b, has 5.

Traditional Foods A1624

Designs: 1 l, Red eggs and cozonac. 3.60 l, Fish on fir tree branches. 4.50 l, Roast lamb and vegetables. 8.10 l, Cheeses and vegetables.

2014, Apr. 18 Litho. *Perf. 13¼*

5541 A1624 1 l multi .65 .30
a. Sheet of 5 + 3 labels 3.25 1.50
5542 A1624 3.60 l multi 2.25 1.10
a. Sheet of 5 + 3 labels 11.50 5.50
5543 A1624 4.50 l multi 3.00 1.50
a. Sheet of 5 + 3 labels 15.00 7.50
5544 A1624 8.10 l multi 5.00 2.50
a. Sheet of 5 + 3 labels 25.00 12.50
Nos. 5541-5544 (4) 10.90 5.40

Europa — A1625

Musicians playing: 2.10 l, Tulnics. 14.50 l, Lutes.

2014, May 5 Litho. *Perf. 13¼*

5545 A1625 2.10 l multi 1.40 .70
a. Sheet of 6 8.50 4.25
5546 A1625 14.50 l multi 9.00 4.50
a. Sheet of 6 54.00 27.00
b. Souvenir sheet of 4, 2 each #5545-5546, #5545 at UL 21.00 10.50
c. As "b," #5546 at UL 21.00 10.50

World Conference of Masonic Regular Grand Lodges, Romania A1626

Emblem and: 3.30 l, Olive branch. 9.10 l, Sever Frentiu (1931-97), painter.

2014, May 14 Litho. *Perf. 13¼*

5547 A1626 3.30 l multi 2.10 1.10
a. Sheet of 4 8.50 4.50
5548 A1626 9.10 l multi 5.75 3.00
a. Sheet of 4 23.00 12.00

Training Ship Mircea, 75th Anniv. — A1627

Designs: 1 l, Mircea with sails up. No. 5550, Mircea and military order, vert.

No. 5551, Mircea with sails down.

2014, May 24 Litho. *Perf. 13¼*

5549 A1627 1 l multi .65 .30
a. Sheet of 6 4.00 2.00
5550 A1627 14.50 l multi 9.00 4.50
a. Sheet of 6 54.00 27.00

Souvenir Sheet

5551 A1627 14.50 l multi + label 9.00 4.50

Theodor Aman (1831-91), Founder of National University of Arts, Bucharest A1628

2014, May 28 Litho. *Perf. 13¼*

5552 A1628 8.10 l multi 5.00 2.50
a. Sheet of 6 30.00 15.00
b. Souvenir sheet of 1 5.00 2.50

National University of Arts, 150th anniv.

Emblem of Court of Accounts A1630

Emblem of Court of Accounts, Prince Alexandru Ioan Cuza (1820-73) — A1631

2014, June 6 Litho. *Perf. 13¾*

5554 A1630 2.40 l multi 1.50 .75
a. Sheet of 8 + central label 12.00 6.00
5555 A1631 4.50 l gray grn & multi 3.00 1.50
a. Sheet of 8 + central label 24.00 12.00

Souvenir Sheet

5556 A1631 14.50 l beige & multi 9.00 4.50

Court of Accounts, 150th anniv.

2014 World Cup Soccer Championships, Brazil — A1632

No. 5557: a, Two players, denomination at UR. b, Goaltender, denomination at UL. c, Two players, diff., denomination at LL. d, Two players, diff. denomination at LR.

2014, June 12 Litho. *Perf. 13¼*

5557 A1632 2.40 l Block of 4, #a-d 6.00 3.00
e. Souvenir sheet of 4, #5557a-5557d 6.00 3.00

Romanian Senate, 150th Anniv. — A1633

Designs: 1 l, Senate Building and emblem. 14.50 l, Emblem.

2014, June 17 Litho. *Perf. 13¼*

5558 A1633 1 l multi .65 .30
a. Sheet of 8 + 2 labels 5.25 2.40

Souvenir Sheet

5559 A1633 14.50 l multi 9.00 4.50

No. 5559 contains one 36x36mm stamp.

Gymnastics Personalities A1634

Designs: 2.10 l, Octavian Bellu, head coach of national team. 9.10 l, Mariana Bitang, coach and trainer.

2014, June 20 Litho. *Perf. 13¼*

5560 A1634 2.10 l multi 1.40 .70
a. Sheet of 6 8.50 4.25
5561 A1634 9.10 l multi 5.75 3.00
a. Sheet of 6 35.00 18.00
b. Souvenir sheet of 2, #5560-5561 7.25 3.75

Maramures Tourist Attractions A1635

Designs: 2 l, Stephen's Tower. 3.30 l, Berbesti roadside cross. 8.10 l, Wooden church, Sugatag. 14.50 l, Cemetery with decorations, Sapanta.

2014, July 4 Litho. *Perf. 13¼*

5562 A1635 2 l multi 1.25 .60
a. Sheet of 5 + label 6.25 3.00
5563 A1635 3.30 l multi 2.00 1.00
a. Sheet of 5 + label 10.00 5.00
5564 A1635 8.10 l multi 5.00 2.50
a. Sheet of 5 + label 25.00 12.50
5565 A1635 14.50 l multi 8.75 4.50
a. Sheet of 5 + label 44.00 22.50
Nos. 5562-5565 (4) 17.00 8.60

A1636

Church of the Three Holy Hierarchs Monastery, Iasi — A1637

2014, July 15 Litho. *Perf. 13¼*

5566 A1636 14.50 l multi 8.75 4.50
a. Sheet of 8 + central label 70.00 36.00

Souvenir Sheet

5567 A1637 8.10 l multi 5.00 2.50

Stamp Day.

University of Bucharest, 150th Anniv. — A1638

Designs: 8.10 l. University building and statue.14.50 l, Watercolor depicting University Buildings by Alexandru Orascu.

2014, July 16 Litho. *Perf. 13¼*

5568 A1638 8.10 l multi 5.00 2.50
a. Sheet of 8 40.00 20.00

Souvenir Sheet

5569 A1638 14.50 l multi + label 8.75 4.50

Remembrance of National Heroes — A1639

Designs: 1 l, Order of Michael the Brave first class, King Ferdinand I, Gen. Alexandru Averescu. 3.60 l, Heroes' Cross Monument, vert. 14.50 l, Mausoleum of Marasesti.

2014, July 25 Litho. *Perf. 13¼*

5570 A1639 1 l multi .60 .30
a. Sheet of 6 3.75 1.90
5571 A1639 3.60 l multi 2.25 1.10
a. Sheet of 6 13.50 6.75
5572 A1639 14.50 l multi 8.75 4.50
a. Sheet of 6 52.50 27.00
Nos. 5570-5572 (3) 11.60 5.90

UNESCO Intangible Cultural Heritage in Romania — A1640

Designs: 3.10 l, Doina musician, sheep in pasture. 6 l, Calus dancers. No. 5575, Colindat Christmas ritual.

No. 5576, Horezu plate and potter.

2014, Aug. 7 Litho. *Perf. 13¼*

5573 A1640 3.10 l multi 1.75 .90
a. Sheet of 6 10.50 5.50
5574 A1640 6 l multi 3.75 1.90
a. Sheet of 6 22.50 11.50
5575 A1640 9.10 l multi 5.50 2.75
a. Sheet of 6 33.00 16.50
Nos. 5573-5575 (3) 11.00 5.55

Souvenir Sheet

5576 A1640 9.10 l multi 5.50 2.75

Martyrdom of the Brancoveanu Saints, 300th Anniv. — A1641

Designs: 2.40 l, Constantin Brancoveanu (1654-1714), Prince of Wallachia. 5 l, Icon depicting martyrs and Ianache Vacarescu, vert. 14.50 l, St. George's New Church, Bucharest.

2014, Aug. 16 Litho. *Perf. 13¼*

5577 A1641 2.40 l multi 1.50 .75
a. Sheet of 6 9.00 4.50
5578 A1641 5 l multi 3.00 1.50
a. Sheet of 6 18.00 9.00
5579 A1641 14.50 l multi 8.75 4.50
a. Sheet of 6 52.50 27.00
Nos. 5577-5579 (3) 13.25 6.75

An imperforate sheet of Nos. 5577-5579 was printed in a limited edition.

Paintings — A1642

Designs: 4.70 l, Spring, by Pieter Breughel the Younger. 5 l, Summer, by Breughel the Younger. 7.60 l, The Marriage of the Virgin, by El Greco, vert. 8.10 l, The Martyrdom of St. Maurice and the 10,000 Thebans, by El Greco, vert.

2014, Aug. 22 Litho. *Perf. 13¼*

5580 A1642 4.70 l multi 2.75 1.40
a. Sheet of 4 11.00 5.75
5581 A1642 5 l multi 3.00 1.50
a. Sheet of 4 12.00 6.00
5582 A1642 7.60 l multi 4.50 2.25
a. Sheet of 4 18.00 9.00
5583 A1642 8.10 l multi 5.00 2.50
a. Sheet of 4 20.00 10.00
Nos. 5580-5583 (4) 15.25 7.65

Oltenia Tourism — A1643

Arms of Oltenia and: 2.40 l, Cula Greceanu, Maldaresti Museum complex, Valcea. 3 l, Art Museum of Craiova. 3.30 l, Tismana Monastery. 4.30 l, Biserica Monastery, Hurezi. 4.50 l, Horezu ceramics. 14.50 l, Grapes and vineyard.

2014, Aug. 29 Litho. *Perf. 13¼*

5584 A1643 2.40 l multi 1.50 .75
a. Sheet of 5 + label 7.50 3.75
5585 A1643 3 l multi 1.75 .90
a. Sheet of 5 + label 8.75 4.50
5586 A1643 3.30 l multi 2.00 1.00
a. Sheet of 5 + label 10.00 5.00
5587 A1643 4.30 l multi 2.60 1.25
a. Sheet of 5 + label 13.00 6.25
5588 A1643 4.50 l multi 2.75 1.40
a. Sheet of 5 + label 14.00 7.00
5589 A1643 14.50 l multi 8.75 4.50
a. Sheet of 5 + label 44.00 22.50
Nos. 5584-5589 (6) 19.35 9.80

Animals and Their Food — A1644

Designs: 1.40 l, Squirrel and hazel nuts. 2 l, Boar and acorns, vert. 8.10 l , Bear and berries, vert. 14.50 l, Starling and grapes.

2014, Sept. 5 Litho. *Perf. 13¼*

5590 A1644 1.40 l multi .80 .40
a. Sheet of 5 + label 4.00 2.00
5591 A1644 2 l multi 1.25 .60
a. Sheet of 5 + label 6.25 3.00
5592 A1644 8.10 l multi 4.75 2.40
a. Sheet of 5 + label 24.00 12.00
5593 A1644 14.50 l multi 8.50 4.25
a. Sheet of 5 + label 42.50 21.50
Nos. 5590-5593 (4) 15.30 7.65

Romanian Olympic Committe, Cent. — A1645

"100" and: 1 l, Romanian Olympic Committee emblem. 14.50 l, Torch.

2014, Sept. 12 Litho. *Perf. 13¼*

5594 A1645 1 l multi .60 .30
a. Sheet of 8 + central label 4.80 2.40

Souvenir Sheet

5595 A1645 14.50 l multi 8.50 4.25

Bucharest, 555th Anniv. — A1646

Designs: 3.30 l, National Bank of Romania. 4.30 l, Palace of the Patriarchate. 4.50 l, Toma Stelian House. 5 l, Kretulescu Palace. 6 l, Carol Davila University of Medicine and Pharmacy. No. 5601, National Geology Museum.

No. 5602, Zodiac Fountain.

2014, Sept. 20 Litho. *Perf. 13¼*

5596 A1646 3.30 l multi 1.90 .95
a. Sheet of 5 + 5 labels 9.50 4.75
5597 A1646 4.30 l multi 2.50 1.25
a. Sheet of 5 + 5 labels 12.50 6.25
5598 A1646 4.50 l multi 2.60 1.25
a. Sheet of 5 + 5 labels 13.00 6.25
5599 A1646 5 l multi 3.00 1.50
a. Sheet of 5 + 5 labels 15.00 7.50
5600 A1646 6 l multi 3.50 1.75
a. Sheet of 5 + 5 labels 17.50 8.75
5601 A1646 9.10 l multi 5.25 2.60
a. Sheet of 5 + 5 labels 26.50 13.00
Nos. 5596-5601 (6) 18.75 9.30

Souvenir Sheet

5602 A1646 9.10 l multi 5.25 2.60

Clock Towers A1647

Designs: 3 l, Oradea City Hall. 3.10 l, Trumpeters' Tower, Medias. 3.30 l, Palace of Culture Tower, Iasi. 3.60 l, Communal Palace Tower, Buzau. 4.70 l, City Council Tower, Brasov. 14.50 l, Peles Castle Central Tower, Sinaia.

2014, Oct. 3 Litho. *Perf. 13¼*

5603 A1647 3 l multi 1.75 .85
a. Sheet of 4 7.00 3.50
5604 A1647 3.10 l multi 1.75 .85
a. Sheet of 4 7.00 3.50
5605 A1647 3.30 l multi 1.90 .95
a. Sheet of 4 7.75 4.00
5606 A1647 3.60 l multi 2.00 1.00
a. Sheet of 4 8.00 4.00
5607 A1647 4.70 l multi 2.75 1.40
a. Sheet of 4 11.00 5.75
5608 A1647 14.50 l multi 8.25 4.25
a. Sheet of 4 33.00 17.00
Nos. 5603-5608 (6) 18.40 9.30

Wild Cats — A1648

Designs; 3.30 l, Felis silvestris ocreata. 3.60 l, Felis silvestris ornata. 7.60 l, Felis silvestris. 8.10 l, Felis silvestris cafra.

2014, Oct. 10 Litho. *Perf. 13¼*

5609 A1648 3.30 l multi 1.90 .95
a. Sheet of 5 + label 9.50 4.75
5610 A1648 3.60 l multi 2.00 1.00
a. Sheet of 5 + label 10.00 5.00
5611 A1648 7.60 l multi 4.25 2.10
a. Sheet of 5 + label 21.50 10.50
5612 A1648 8.10 l multi 4.75 2.40
a. Sheet of 5 + label 24.00 12.00
Nos. 5609-5612 (4) 12.90 6.45

Coins From National Bank of Romania Numismatic Collection — A1649

Obverse and reverse of: 2 l, Dacian gold koson. 2.40 l, Istrian drachm. 8.10 l, Thaler. 14.50 l, Venetian gold ducat.

2014, Oct. 24 Litho. *Perf. 13¼*

5613 A1649 2 l multi 1.10 .55
a. Sheet of 6 6.75 3.50
5614 A1649 2.40 l multi 1.40 .70
a. Sheet of 6 8.50 4.25
5615 A1649 8.10 l multi 4.75 2.40
a. Sheet of 6 28.50 14.50
5616 A1649 14.50 l multi 8.25 4.25
a. Sheet of 6 49.50 25.50
Nos. 5613-5616 (4) 15.50 7.90

A souvenir sheet of 4 containing Nos. 5613-5616 was printed in limited quantities.

King Michael, 93rd Birthday A1650

Designs: 4.70 l, King Michael and monogram. 14.50 l, King Michael and Queen Anne.

2014, Oct. 25 Litho. *Perf. 13¼*

5617 A1650 4.70 l multi 2.75 1.40
a. Sheet of 8 + central label 22.00 11.50

Souvenir Sheet

Perf. 13¼x14

5618 A1650 14.50 l multi 8.25 4.25

No. 5618 contains one 42x52mm stamp and exists imperforate.

Tourist Attractions in Tulcea — A1651

Designs: 3 l, Independence Monument. 3.30 l, Spiru Haret College in Dobrogea, horiz. 4.30 l, Aziziye Mosque, horiz. 14.50 l, St. Nicholas Episcopal Cathedral.

2014, Oct. 31 Litho. *Perf. 13¼*

5619 A1651 3 l multi 1.75 .85
a. Sheet of 5 + label 8.75 4.25
5620 A1651 3.30 l multi 1.90 .95
a. Sheet of 5 + label 9.50 4.75
5621 A1651 4.30 l multi 2.40 1.25
a. Sheet of 5 + label 12.00 6.25
5622 A1651 14.50 l multi 8.25 4.25
a. Sheet of 5 + label 41.50 21.50
Nos. 5619-5622 (4) 14.30 7.30

Carol I University Foundation, Cent. — A1652

Designs: 9.10 l, University Library, statue of King Carol I.
14.50 l, University Foundation Palace, horiz.

2014, Nov. 7 Litho. *Perf. 13¼*

5623 A1652 9.10 l multi 5.25 2.60
a. Sheet of 4 21.00 10.50

Souvenir Sheet

Perf. 14x13¼

5624 A1652 14.50 l multi 8.25 4.25

No. 5624 contains one 52x42mm stamp. No. 5623a was printed with two different sheet margins.

Fortified Churches A1653

Designs: 1 l, St. Nicholas Church, Komiza, Croatia. 9.10 l, Evangelical Church, Cristian.

2014, Nov. 14 Litho. *Perf. 13¼*

5625 A1653 1 l multi .55 .30
a. Sheet of 8 + central label 4.50 2.40
5626 A1653 9.10 l multi 5.25 2.60
a. Sheet of 8 + central label 42.00 21.00

See Croatia No. 930.

Hammer and Sickle, "XXV" — A1654

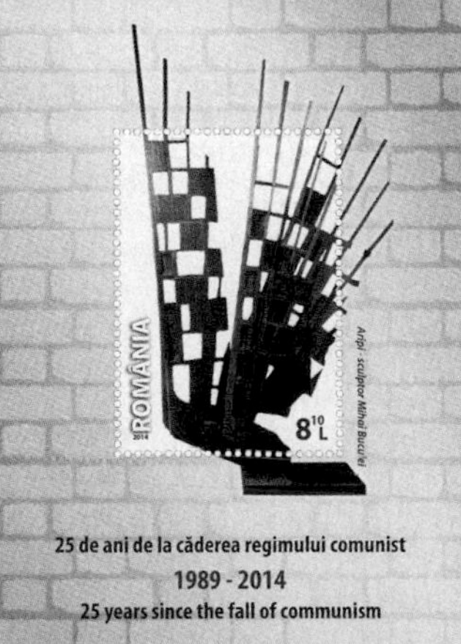

Wings Monument, by Mihai Buculei — A1655

2014, Nov. 20 Litho. *Perf. 13¼*

5627 A1654 14.50 l multi 8.25 4.25
a. Sheet of 5 + label 41.50 21.50

Souvenir Sheet

5628 A1655 8.10 l multi 4.50 2.25

Fall of Communism, 25th anniv.

Christmas A1656

2014, Nov. 21 Litho. *Perf. 13¼*

5629 A1656 1 l multi .55 .30
a. Sheet of 8 + central label 4.50 2.40

No. 5629 exists imperforate in a limited printing. A souvenir sheet of 2 was printed in limited quantities.

Romanian Savings Bank, 150th Anniv. — A1657

Designs: 8.10 l, Building. 14.50 l, Decorative frieze on Savings Bank.

2014, Nov. 28 Litho. *Perf. 13¼*

5630 A1657 8.10 l multi 4.50 2.25
a. Sheet of 8 36.00 18.00

Souvenir Sheet

5631 A1657 14.50 l multi 8.25 4.25

No. 5631 contains one 36x36mm stamp.

Writers — A1658

Writers: 3.30 l, Ion Creanga (1837-89). 4.50 l, Vasile Alecsandri (1821-90). 7.60 l, George Cosbuc (1866-1918). 8.10 l, George Bacovia (1881-1957).

2014, Dec. 5 Litho. *Perf. 14x13¼*

5632 A1658 3.30 l multi 1.75 .90
a. Sheet of 5 + label 8.75 4.50
5633 A1658 4.50 l multi 2.40 1.25
a. Sheet of 5 + label 12.00 6.25
5634 A1658 7.60 l multi 4.25 2.10
a. Sheet of 5 + label 21.50 10.50
5635 A1658 8.10 l multi 4.50 2.25
a. Sheet of 5 + label 22.50 11.50
Nos. 5632-5635 (4) 12.90 6.50

Inventors and Scientists — A1659

Designs: 3.30 l, Nikola Tesla (1856-1943), electrical engineer, induction motor. 3.60 l, Thomas Alva Edison (1847-1931), inventor, incandescent light bulb. 4.30 l, Albert Einstein (1879-1955), physicist, mass-energy equivalence equation. 14.50 l, Leonardo da Vinci (1452-1519), inventor and painter, irrigation machine.

2014, Dec. 17 Litho. *Perf. 13¼*

5636 A1659 3.30 l multi 1.75 .90
a. Sheet of 5 + label 8.75 4.50
5637 A1659 3.60 l multi 2.00 1.00
a. Sheet of 5 + label 10.00 5.00
5638 A1659 4.30 l multi 2.40 1.25
a. Sheet of 5 + label 12.00 6.25
5639 A1659 14.50 l multi 7.75 4.00
a. Sheet of 5 + label 39.00 20.00
Nos. 5636-5639 (4) 13.90 7.15

Handicrafts A1660

Rugs and: 1 l, Copper vessel from Lahich, Azerbaijan. 9.10 l, Pottery jug from Horezu, Romania.

2014, Dec. 19 Litho. *Perf. 13¼*

5640 A1660 1 l multi .55 .25
a. Sheet of 6 3.50 1.50
5641 A1660 9.10 l multi 5.00 2.50
a. Sheet of 6 30.00 15.00

See Azerbaijan No. 1075.

Wildlife A1661

Designs: 3.60 l, Antidorcas marsupialis. 4.30 l, Puma concolor. 8.10 l, Orcinus orca. 9.10 l, Acinonyx jubatus.

2015, Jan. 16 Litho. *Perf. 13¼*

5642-5645 A1661 Set fo 4 13.00 6.50
5645a Souvenir sheet of 4, #5642-5645 13.00 6.50

Paintings and Sculptures — A1662

Designs: 3.10 l, Hagar in the Desert, by Gheorghe Tattarescu (1820-94). 3.30 l, Girl with Tambourine, by Tattarescu, vert. 4.50 l, The Kiss, sculpture, by Auguste Rodin (1840-1917), vert. 14.50 l, The Spring, sculpture by Rodin.

Perf. 14x13¼, 13¼x14

2015, Jan. 23 Litho.

5646 A1662 3.10 l multi 1.60 .80
a. Sheet of 4 + 2 labels 6.50 3.25
5647 A1662 3.50 l multi 1.75 .85
a. Sheet of 4 + 2 labels 7.00 3.50
5648 A1662 4.50 l multi 2.40 1.25
a. Sheet of 4 + 2 labels 9.75 5.00
5649 A1662 14.50 l multi 7.50 3.75
a. Sheet of 4 + 2 labels 30.00 15.00
Nos. 5646-5649 (4) 13.25 6.65

Romanian Royalty A1663

Royalty and their monograms: 3.10 l, King Carol I (1839-1914), Queen Elisabeth (1843-1916). 3.30 l, King Ferdinand (1865-1927), Queen Marie (1875-1938). 6 l, King Carol II (1893-1953), Queen Helen (1896-1982). 14.50 l, King Michael, Queen Anne.

2015, Jan. 30 Litho. *Perf. 13¼x14*

5650 A1663 3.10 l multi 1.60 .80
a. Sheet of 4 + 2 labels 6.50 3.25
5651 A1663 3.30 l multi 1.75 .85
a. Sheet of 4 + 2 labels 7.00 3.50
5652 A1663 6 l multi 3.25 1.60
a. Sheet of 4 + 2 labels 13.00 6.50
5653 A1663 14.50 l multi 7.50 3.75
a. Sheet of 4 + 2 labels 30.00 15.00
Nos. 5650-5653 (4) 14.10 7.00

The royal monograms on Nos. 5650-5653 are surrounded by perforations within the stamp. A souvenir sheet of 4 containing Nos. 5650-5653 was printed in limited quantities.

Songbirds A1664

Designs: 4.50 l, Coccothraustes coccothraustes. 5 l, Emberiza citrinella. 8.10 l, Bombycilla garrulus. 9.10 l, Pyrrhula pyrrhula.

2015, Feb. 6 Litho. *Perf. 13¼*

5654 A1664 4.50 l multi 2.25 1.10
a. Sheet of 5 + label 11.50 5.50
5655 A1664 5 l multi 2.50 1.25
a. Sheet of 5 + label 12.50 6.25
5656 A1664 8.10 l multi 4.00 2.00
a. Sheet of 5 + label 20.00 10.00
5657 A1664 9.10 l multi 4.50 2.25
a. Sheet of 5 + label 22.50 11.50
Nos. 5654-5657 (4) 13.25 6.60

A souvenir sheet of 4 containing Nos. 5654-5657 was printed in a limited quantity.

Letters and Flowers A1665

Designs: 3 l, "T," roses. 3.10 l, "I," irises. 3.30 l, "M," poppies. 4.30 l, "B," begonias. 4.70 l, "R," flowering tobacco. 14.50 l, "E," purple coneflowers.

2015, Feb. 20 Litho. *Perf. 13¼*

5658 A1665 3 l multi 1.50 .75
a. Sheet of 5 + label 7.50 3.75
5659 A1665 3.10 l multi 1.60 .80
a. Sheet of 5 + label 8.00 4.00
5660 A1665 3.30 l multi 1.75 .85
a. Sheet of 5 + label 8.75 4.25
5661 A1665 4.30 l multi 2.25 1.10
a. Sheet of 5 + label 11.50 5.50
5662 A1665 4.70 l multi 2.40 1.25
a. Sheet of 5 + label 12.00 6.25
5663 A1665 14.50 l multi 7.25 3.75
a. Sheet of 5 + label 36.50 19.00
b. Souvenir sheet of 6, #5658-5663 17.00 8.50
Nos. 5658-5663 (6) 16.75 8.50

Easter A1666

Designs: 1 l, Icon depicting crucifixion from Nicula Monastery.
9.10 l, Icon depicting resurrection from Transylvanian Museum of Ethnography.

2015, Mar. 12 Litho. *Perf. 13¼*

5664 A1666 1 l multi .50 .25
a. Sheet of 4 2.00 1.00
b. Sheet of 8 + central label 4.00 2.00

Souvenir Sheet

5665 A1666 9.10 l multi 4.50 2.25

No. 5664a was printed with two different sheet margins. Two souvenir sheets of 2, one containing Nos. 5664-5665, and the other containing 2 No. 5664, were printed in limited quantities.

Archaeological Artifacts of Dinogetia — A1667

Designs: 3 l, Rings, bracelet, loop of gold wire. 4.50 l, Gold coins, chain. 9.10 l, Ring, bracelet, loop of gold wire. 14.50 l, Reliquary cross.

2015, Mar. 20 Litho. *Perf. 14x13¼*

5666 A1667 3 l multi 1.50 .75
a. Sheet of 4 6.00 3.00
5667 A1667 4.50 l multi 2.25 1.10
a. Sheet of 4 9.00 4.50
5668 A1667 9.10 l multi 4.50 2.25
a. Sheet of 4 18.00 9.00
5669 A1667 14.50 l multi 7.25 3.75
a. Sheet of 4 29.00 15.00
b. Souvenir sheet of 4, #5666-5669, + 2 labels 15.50 8.00
Nos. 5666-5669 (4) 15.50 7.85

Romanian Intelligence Service, 25th Anniv. — A1668

Designs: 8.10 l, Emblem, map of Romania. 14.50 l, Emblem.

2015, Mar. 23 Litho. *Perf. 13¼*

5670 A1668 8.10 l multi 4.00 2.00
a. Sheet of 6 24.00 12.00

Souvenir Sheet

Perf.

5671 A1668 14.50 l multi 7.25 3.75

No. 5671 contains one 30mm diameter stamp.

Pelicans — A1669

Designs: 3.60 l, Six Pelecanus onocrotalus. 5 l, Two Pelecanus crispus. 8.10 l, Two Pelecanus onocrotalus. No. 5675, 9.10 l, Two Pelecanus cripsus, close up of face.

No. 5676, 9.10 l, Head of Pelecanus crispus.

2015, Apr. 10 Litho. *Perf. 13¼*

5672 A1669 3.60 l multi 1.90 .95
a. Sheet of 5 + label 9.50 4.75
5673 A1669 5 l multi 2.60 1.40
a. Sheet of 5 + label 13.00 7.00
5674 A1669 8.10 l multi 4.25 2.10
a. Sheet of 5 + label 21.50 10.50
5675 A1669 9.10 l multi 4.75 2.40
a. Sheet of 5 + label 24.00 12.00
Nos. 5672-5675 (4) 13.50 6.85

Souvenir Sheet

Perf. 14x13¼

5676 A1669 9.10 l multi 4.75 2.40

No. 5676 contains one 52x42mm stamp. A souvenir sheet of 4 containing Nos. 5672-5675 was printed in limited quantities.

Europa A1670

Designs: 2.10 l, Wooden toys. 14.50 l, Rocking horse, tricycle.

2015, Apr. 17 Litho. *Perf. 13¼*

5677 A1670 2.10 l multi 1.10 .55
a. Sheet of 6 6.75 3.50
5678 A1670 14.50 l multi 7.50 3.75
a. Sheet of 6 45.00 22.50
b. Sheet of 4, 2 each #5677-5678, #5677 at UL 17.50 8.75
c. As "b," #5678 at UL 17.50 8.75

Quill Pen, Book, Hand Touching Tablet Screen — A1671

2015, Apr. 30 Litho. *Perf. 13¼*

5679 A1671 4.70 l multi 2.40 1.25
a. Sheet of 5 + label 12.00 6.25

The Group, 10th anniv.

Victory in World War II, 70th Anniv. — A1672

2015, May 9 Litho. *Perf. 13¼*

5680 A1672 4.30 l multi 2.25 1.10
a. Sheet of 8 + central label 18.00 9.00

No. 5680a was printed with two different central labels.

No. 3601 Surcharged in Gold

Methods and Perfs. As Before

2015, May 13

5681 A1028 9.10 l on 10 l #3601 4.50 2.25

Europhilex 2015 Intl. Stamp Exhibition, London.

University of Medicine and Pharmacy, Tirgu Mures, 70th Anniv. — A1673

Designs: 3.30 l, University building, emblem with 1945 date. 8.10 l, University building, emblem, without oval.

9.10 l, University building, emblem without oval, vert.

2015, May 15 Litho. *Perf. 13¼*

5682 A1673 3.30 l multi 1.75 .85
a. Sheet of 5 + label 8.75 4.25
5683 A1673 8.10 l multi 4.00 2.00
a. Sheet of 5 + label 20.00 10.00

Souvenir Sheet

Perf. 13¼x14

5684 A1673 9.10 l multi 4.50 2.25

No. 5684 contains one 42x52mm stamp.

Romanian Mint, 145th Anniv. — A1674

Designs: 8.10 l, Mint building, horse and carriage, 1870 1-leu coin.

14.50 l, 1870 gold 20-lei coin.

2015, May 19 Litho. *Perf. 13¼*

5685 A1674 8.10 l multi 4.00 2.00
a. Imperf. 4.00 2.00
b. Sheet of 4 #5685 + 8 labels 16.00 8.00
c. Sheet of 5, #5685a, 4 #5685 20.00 10.00

Souvenir Sheet

5686 A1674 14.50 l multi 7.25 3.75

No. 5686 contains one 36x36mm stamp. A ring of perforations surrounds the image of the coin on No. 5685. The ring of perforations is not on No. 5685a. A souvenir sheet of 2 containing Nos. 5685-5686 was produced in limited quantities.

National Institute for Research and Development in Informatics, 45th Anniv. — A1675

2015, June 5 Litho. *Perf. 14x13¼*

5687 A1675 7.60 l multi 3.75 1.90
a. Sheet of 5 + label 19.00 9.50

National Grand Masonic Lodge of Romania, 135th Anniv. — A1676

Designs: 2.10 l, Masonic and astrological symbols. 14.50 l, Lodge, horiz.

2015, June 16 Litho. *Perf. 13¼*

5688 A1676 2.10 l multi 1.10 .55
a. Sheet of 4 4.50 2.25
5689 A1676 14.50 l multi 7.25 3.75
a. Sheet of 4 29.00 15.00
b. Sheet of 2, #5688-5689, imperf. 8.50 4.25

A souvenir sheet of 2 containing perforated examples of No. 5688-5689 was produced in limited quantities.

Flowers in Botanical Gardens A1677

Designs: 1 l, Astragalus peterfii. 3.30 l, Iris brandzae. 8.10 l, Paeonia peregrina. 9.10 l, Hepatica transsilvanica.

2015, July 3 Litho. *Perf. 13¼*

5690 A1677 1 l multi .50 .25
a. Sheet of 5 + label 2.50 1.25
5691 A1677 3.30 l multi 1.60 .80
a. Sheet of 5 + label 8.00 4.00
5692 A1677 8.10 l multi 4.00 2.00
a. Sheet of 5 + label 20.00 10.00
5693 A1677 9.10 l multi 4.50 2.25
a. Sheet of 5 + label 22.50 11.50
Nos. 5690-5693 (4) 10.60 5.30

Autocephaly of Romanian Orthodox Church, 130th Anniv. — A1678

Designs: 5 l, Drawing for under-construction Romanian People's Salvation Cathedral. 8.10 l, Cathedral, arms of Patriarchate.

2015, July 15 Litho. *Perf. 13¼*

5694 A1678 5 l multi 2.50 1.25
a. Sheet of 8 + central label 20.00 10.00

Souvenir Sheet

Perf. 14x13¼

5695 A1678 8.10 l multi 4.00 2.00

No. 5695 contains one 52x42mm stamp. An souvenir sheet containing two imperforate examples of No. 5694 was printed in limited quantities.

Paintings Depicting Horses — A1679

Details of paintings: 3.60 l, The Plowing, by Ioan Andeescu (1850-82). 8.10 l, Mounted Ranger Officer, by Nicolae Grigorescu (1838-1907), vert. 9.10 l, Peasant with a Carriage, by Rudolf Schweitzer-Cumpana (1886-1975).

Perf. 14x13¼, 13¼x14

2015, July 24 Litho.

5696 A1679 3.60 l multi 1.90 .95
a. Sheet of 4 7.75 4.00
5697 A1679 8.10 l multi 4.00 2.00
a. Sheet of 4 16.00 8.00
5698 A1679 9.10 l multi 4.50 2.25
a. Sheet of 4 18.00 9.00
Nos. 5696-5698 (3) 10.40 5.20

Medicinal Plants — A1680

Designs: 1.20 l , Hypericum perforatum. 2 l, Lavandula angustifolia. 2.40 l, Calendula officinalis. 14.50 l, Matricaria chamomilla.

2015, Aug. 7 Litho. *Perf. 13¼*

5699 A1680 1.20 l multi .60 .30
a. Sheet of 5 + 4 labels 3.00 1.50
5700 A1680 2 l multi 1.00 .50
a. Sheet of 5 + 4 labels 5.00 2.50

5701 A1680 2.40 l multi 1.25 .60
a. Sheet of 5 + 4 labels 6.25 3.00
5702 A1680 14.50 l multi 7.50 3.75
a. Sheet of 5 + 4 labels 37.50 19.00
b. Souvenir sheet of 4, #5699-5702 10.50 5.25
Nos. 5699-5702 (4) 10.35 5.15

Nicula Monastery A1681

Designs: 1 l, Icon of Virgin Mary and Child. 4.50 l, Wooden church.

2015, Aug. 15 Litho. *Perf. 13¼*
5703 A1681 1 l multi .50 .25
a. Sheet of 8 + central label 4.00 2.00
5704 A1681 4.50 l multi 2.40 1.25
a. Sheet of 8 + central label 19.50 10.00

A souvenir sheet of 2 containing Nos. 5703-5704 was printed in limited quantities.

Birds A1682

Designs: 3.30 l, Sterna hirundo. 4.30 l, Larus michahellis. 4.70 l, Recurvirostra avosetta. 8.10 l, Tadorna ferruginea. 9.10 l, Cygnus olor.

2015, Aug. 21 Litho. *Perf. 13¼*
5705 A1682 3.30 l multi 1.75 .85
a. Sheet of 5 + label 8.75 4.25
5706 A1682 4.30 l multi 2.25 1.10
a. Sheet of 5 + label 11.50 5.50
5707 A1682 4.70 l multi 2.40 1.25
a. Sheet of 5 + label 12.00 6.25
5708 A1682 8.10 l multi 4.25 2.10
a. Sheet of 5 + label 21.50 10.50
Nos. 5705-5708 (4) 10.65 5.30

Souvenir Sheet

5709 A1682 9.10 l multi 4.75 2.40

A souvenir sheet of 5 containing Nos. 5705-5709 was printed in limited quantities.

Moldavian Tourist Attractions — A1683

Arms and: 3.30 l, Cucuteni Eneolithic Art Museum, Piatra Neamt, Cucuteni ceramic piece. 3.60 l, Neamt Fortress, sculpture of Stephen the Great. 6 l, St. Nicholas Church, Iasi, sculpture of Metropolitan Dosoftei. 9.10 l, Alexandru Ioan Cuza Palace, Ruginoasa, Prince Alexandru Ioan I

2015, Sept. 8 Litho. *Perf. 13¼*
5710 A1683 3.30 l multi 1.75 .85
a. Sheet of 5 + label 8.75 4.25
5711 A1683 3.60 l multi 1.90 .95
a. Sheet of 5 + label 9.50 4.75
5712 A1683 6 l multi 3.00 1.50
a. Sheet of 5 + label 15.00 7.50
5713 A1683 9.10 l multi 4.75 2.40
a. Sheet of 5 + label 24.00 12.00
Nos. 5710-5713 (4) 11.40 5.70

A souvenir sheet of 4 containing Nos. 5710-5713 was printed in limited quantities.

Dobrudja Tourist Attractions — A1684

Map and: 2 l, Tropaeum Traiani, Adamclisi. 4.70 l, Enisala Fortress ruins and coins. 7.60 l, Church of St. Andrew, St. Andrew's Cave pilgrimage site. 8.10 l, Boats and pelican in Danube Delta.

2015, Sept. 18 Litho. *Perf. 13¼*
5714 A1684 2 l multi 1.00 .50
a. Sheet of 5 + label 5.00 2.50
5715 A1684 4.70 l multi 2.40 1.25
a. Sheet of 5 + label 12.00 6.25
5716 A1684 7.60 l multi 4.00 2.00
a. Sheet of 5 + label 20.00 10.00
5717 A1684 8.10 l multi 4.25 2.10
a. Sheet of 5 + label 21.50 10.50
Nos. 5714-5717 (4) 11.65 5.85

A souvenir sheet of 4 containing Nos. 5714-5717 was printed in limited quantities.

National Bank of Romania, 135th Anniv. — A1685

Designs: 3.30 l, Obverse of 1881 20-lei banknote, Ion I. Campineanu, first governor of bank. 9.10 l, Reverse of 1881 20-lei banknote, Emil Costinescu, first director of Banknote Manufacturing and Accounting Service.

2015, Sept. 29 Litho. *Perf. 13¼*
5718 A1685 3.30 l multi 1.75 .85
a. Sheet of 4 7.00 3.50
5719 A1685 9.10 l multi 4.75 2.40
a. Sheet of 4 19.00 9.75
b. Souvenir sheet of 2, #5718-5719 6.50 3.25

A numbered souvenir sheet of 2 containing Nos. 5718-5719 with gold foil was printed in limited quantities.

Peles Castle Stained-Glass Windows — A1686

Windows depicting hunters hunting: 2 l, Boar. 3.30 l, Stags. 4.30 l, Hares. 14.50 l, Bear.

2015, Oct. 9 Litho. *Perf. 14x13¼*
5720 A1686 2 l multi 1.00 .50
a. Sheet of 4 + 2 labels 4.00 2.00
5721 A1686 3.30 l multi 1.75 .85
a. Sheet of 4 + 2 labels 7.00 3.50
5722 A1686 4.30 l multi 2.25 1.10
a. Sheet of 4 + 2 labels 9.00 4.50
5723 A1686 14.50 l multi 7.25 3.75
a. Sheet of 4 + 2 labels 29.00 15.00
Nos. 5720-5723 (4) 12.25 6.20

A souvenir sheet of 4 containing Nos. 5720-5723 was printed in limited quantities.

Ion Tiriac, Tennis Player — A1687

Designs: 2.10 l, Tiriac, tennis ball. 9.10 l, Tiriac.

2015, Oct. 16 Litho. *Perf. 13¼*
5724 A1687 2.10 l multi 1.10 .55
a. Sheet of 8 + central label 9.00 4.50

Souvenir Sheet

5725 A1687 9.10 l multi 4.50 2.25

No. 5724a was printed with two different central labels.

Flags of Romania and United States, King Carol I and Pres. Rutherford B. Hayes — A1689

2015, Nov. 18 Litho. *Perf. 13¼*
5727 A1689 3.60 l multi 1.75 .85
a. Sheet of 7 + 2 labels 12.50 6.00

Diplomatic relations between Romania and the United States, 135th anniv.

Dogs A1691

Designs: 2.40 l, German shepherd. 5 l, Malinois. 8.10 l, Labrador retriever. 9.10 l, Rottweiler.

2015, Nov. 20 Litho. *Perf. 13¼*
5729 A1691 2.40 l multi 1.25 .60
a. Sheet of 5 + label 6.25 3.00
5730 A1691 5 l multi 2.40 1.25
a. Sheet of 5 + label 12.00 6.25
5731 A1691 8.10 l multi 4.00 2.00
a. Sheet of 5 + label 20.00 10.00
5732 A1691 9.10 l multi 4.50 2.25
a. Sheet of 5 + label 22.50 11.50
Nos. 5729-5732 (4) 12.15 6.10

Alba Iulia A1692

Designs: 3 l, Roman 13th Twin Legion Fortress. 3.30 l, Third Gate. 8.10 l, St. Michael's Cathedral. 9.10 l, Coronation Cathedral, King Ferdinand.

2015, Nov. 27 Litho. *Perf. 13¼*
5733 A1692 3 l multi 1.50 .75
a. Sheet of 5 + label 7.50 3.75
5734 A1692 3.30 l multi 1.60 .80
a. Sheet of 5 + label 8.00 4.00
5735 A1692 8.10 l multi 4.00 2.00
a. Sheet of 5 + label 20.00 10.00
5736 A1692 9.10 l multi 4.50 2.25
a. Sheet of 5 + label 22.50 11.50
Nos. 5733-5736 (4) 11.60 5.80

A souvenir sheet of 4 containing Nos. 5733-5736 was printed in limited quantities.

Coins in Numismatic Collection of National Bank of Romania — A1693

Designs: 2 l, Dacian silver coins. 2.40 l, Imperial Roman gold coins. 8.10 l, Dutch ducats. 14.50 l, Polish silver coins.

2015, Dec. 4 Litho. *Perf. 13¼*
5737 A1693 2 l multi 1.00 .50
a. Sheet of 6 6.00 3.00
5738 A1693 2.40 l multi 1.25 .60
a. Sheet of 6 7.50 3.75
5739 A1693 8.10 l multi 4.00 2.00
a. Sheet of 6 24.00 12.00
5740 A1693 14.50 l multi 7.00 3.50
a. Sheet of 6 42.00 21.00
Nos. 5737-5740 (4) 13.25 6.60

A souvenir sheet of 4 containing Nos. 5737-5740 was printed in limited quantities.

Romania in United Nations, 60th Anniv. — A1694

2015, Dec. 15 Litho. *Perf. 13¼*
5741 A1694 4.50 l shown 2.25 1.10
a. Sheet of 7 + 2 labels 16.00 7.75

Souvenir Sheet

Perf.

5742 A1694 8.10 l Globe 4.00 2.00

No. 5742 contains one 30mm diameter stamp.

Sculptures Depicting Eve — A1695

Sculpture by: 1 l, Gheorghe Leonida. 9.10 l, Victor Brecheret, horiz.

2015, Dec. 21 Litho. *Perf. 13¼*
5743 A1695 1 l multi .50 .25
a. Sheet of 6 3.00 1.50
5744 A1695 9.10 l multi 4.50 2.25
a. Sheet of 6 27.00 13.50

See Brazil Nos.

Flemish Paintings in Brukenthal National Museum — A1696

Designs: 4.70 l, St. Jerome in Scriptorium, by Marinus Claeszoon van Reymerswaele. 5 l, Ceres, Bacchus and Venus, by Abraham Janssens van Nuyssen. 7.60 l, Lion in Front of the Cave, by Roelant Savery. 9.10 l, Still Life with Fruits and Parrot, by Jan Fyt.

2016, Jan. 6 Litho. *Perf. 13¼*
5745 A1696 4.70 l multi 2.25 1.10
a. Sheet of 5 + label 11.50 5.50
5746 A1696 5 l multi 2.50 1.25
a. Sheet of 5 + label 12.50 6.25
5747 A1696 7.60 l multi 3.75 1.90
a. Sheet of 5 + label 19.00 9.50
5748 A1696 9.10 l multi 4.50 2.25
a. Sheet of 5 + label 22.50 11.50
Nos. 5745-5748 (4) 13.00 6.50

Flowers A1697

Designs: 4.70 l, Dipsacus fullonum. 5 l, Centaurea solstitialis. 6 l, Echinops ruthenicus. 8.10 l, Ononis spinosa.

2016, Jan. 14 Litho. *Perf. 13¼*

5749	A1697 4.70 l multi		2.25	1.10
a.	Sheet of 4		9.00	4.50
5750	A1697 5 l multi		2.50	1.25
a.	Sheet of 4		10.00	5.00
5751	A1697 6 l multi		3.00	1.50
a.	Sheet of 4		12.00	6.00
5752	A1697 8.10 l multi		4.00	2.00
a.	Sheet of 4		16.00	8.00
	Nos. 5749-5752 (4)		11.75	5.85

SEMI-POSTAL STAMPS

Queen Elizabeth Spinning — SP1

Perf. 11½, 11½x13½

1906, Jan. 14 Typo. Unwmk.

B1	SP1	3b (+ 7b) brown	6.00	3.75
B2	SP1	5b (+ 10b) lt grn	6.00	3.75
B3	SP1	10b (+ 10b) rose red	29.00	11.00
B4	SP1	15b (+ 10b) violet	20.00	7.50
		Nos. B1-B4 (4)	61.00	26.00

The Queen Weaving — SP2

1906, Mar. 18

B5	SP2	3b (+ 7b) org brn	6.00	3.75
B6	SP2	5b (+ 10b) bl grn	6.00	3.75
B7	SP2	10b (+ 10b) car	29.00	11.00
B8	SP2	15b (+ 10b) red vio	20.00	7.50
		Nos. B5-B8 (4)	61.00	26.00

Queen as War Nurse SP3

1906, Mar. 23 *Perf. 11½, 13½x11½*

B9	SP3	3b (+ 7b) org brn	6.00	3.75
B10	SP3	5b (+ 10b) bl grn	6.00	3.75
B11	SP3	10b (+ 10b) car	29.00	11.00
B12	SP3	15b (+ 10b) red vio	20.00	7.50
		Nos. B9-B12 (4)	61.00	26.00
		Nos. B1-B12 (12)	183.00	78.00

Booklet panes of 4 exist of Nos. B1-B3, B5-B7, B9-B12.

Counterfeits of Nos. B1-B12 are plentiful. Examples of Nos. B1-B12 with smooth, even gum are counterfeits.

SP4

1906, Aug. 4 *Perf. 12*

B13	SP4	3b (+ 7b) ol brn, buff & bl	3.25	1.50
B14	SP4	5b (+ 10b) grn, rose & buff	3.25	1.50
B15	SP4	10b (+ 10b) rose red, buff & bl	5.00	3.00
B16	SP4	15b (+ 10b) vio, buff & bl	13.00	3.75
		Nos. B13-B16 (4)	24.50	9.75

Guardian Angel Bringing Poor to Crown Princess Marie SP5

1907, Feb. Engr. *Perf. 11*

Center in Brown

B17	SP5	3b (+ 7b) org brn	4.00	1.50
B18	SP5	5b (+ 10b) dk grn	4.00	1.50
B19	SP5	10b (+ 10b) dk car	4.00	1.50
B20	SP5	15b (+ 10b) dl vio	4.00	1.50
		Nos. B17-B20 (4)	16.00	6.00

Nos. B1-B20 were sold for more than face value. The surtax, shown in parenthesis, was for charitable purposes.

Map of Romania SP9

Stephen the Great SP10

Michael the Brave SP11

Kings Carol I and Ferdinand SP12

Adam Clisi Monument — SP13

1927, Mar. 15 Typo. *Perf. 13½*

B21	SP9	1 l + 9 l lt vio	4.25	1.60
B22	SP10	2 l + 8 l Prus grn	4.25	1.60
B23	SP11	3 l + 7 l dp rose	4.25	1.60
B24	SP12	5 l + 5 l dp bl	4.25	1.60
B25	SP13	6 l + 4 l ol grn	6.25	2.50
		Nos. B21-B25 (5)	23.25	8.90

50th anniv. of the Royal Geographical Society. The surtax was for the benefit of that society. The stamps were valid for postage only from 3/15-4/14.

Boy Scouts in Camp — SP15

The Rescue — SP16

Designs: 3 l+3 l, Swearing in a Tenderfoot. 4 l+4 l, Prince Nicholas Chief Scout. 6 l+6 l, King Carol II in Scout's Uniform.

1931, July 15 Photo. Wmk. 225

B26	SP15	1 l + 1 l car rose	3.75	2.50
B27	SP16	2 l + 2 l dp grn	5.00	3.00
B28	SP15	3 l + 3 l ultra	6.00	3.00
B29	SP16	4 l + 4 l ol gray	7.50	8.00
B30	SP16	6 l + 6 l red brn	10.00	8.00
		Nos. B26-B30 (5)	32.25	24.50

The surtax was for the benefit of the Boy Scout organization.

Boy Scout Jamboree Issue

Scouts in Camp SP20

Semaphore Signaling SP21

Trailing — SP22

Camp Fire — SP23

King Carol II — SP24

King Carol II and Prince Michael — SP25

1932, June 8 Wmk. 230

B31	SP20	25b + 25b pck grn	3.00	1.10
B32	SP21	50b + 50b brt bl	4.00	2.25
B33	SP22	1 l + 1 l ol grn	4.50	3.25
B34	SP23	2 l + 2 l org red	7.50	4.50
B35	SP24	3 l + 3 l Prus bl	14.00	9.00
B36	SP25	6 l + 6 l blk brn	16.00	11.50
		Nos. B31-B36 (6)	49.00	31.60

For overprints see Nos. B44-B49.

Tuberculosis Sanatorium — SP26

Memorial Tablet to Postal Employees Who Died in World War I — SP27

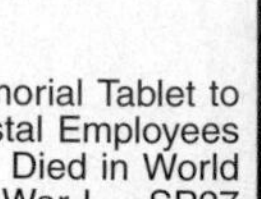

Carmen Sylva Convalescent Home — SP28

1932, Nov. 1

B37	SP26	4 l + 1 l dk grn	5.00	4.00
B38	SP27	6 l + 1 l chocolate	5.50	4.75
B39	SP28	10 l + 1 l dp bl	10.00	8.00
		Nos. B37-B39 (3)	20.50	16.75

The surtax was given to a fund for the employees of the postal and telegraph services.

Philatelic Exhibition Issue

Souvenir Sheet

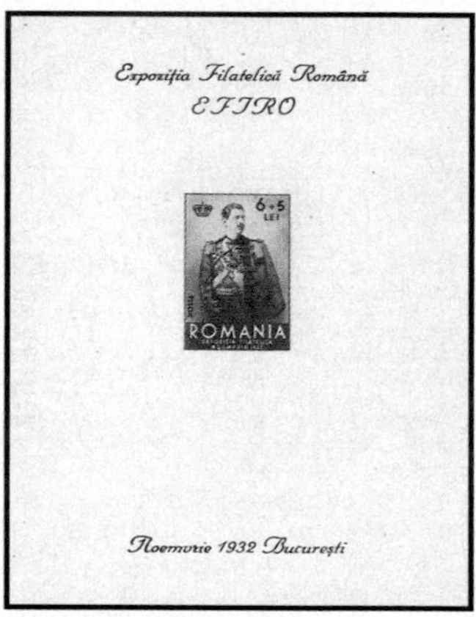

King Carol II — SP29

1932, Nov. 20 Unwmk. *Imperf.*

B40	SP29	6 l + 5 l dk ol grn	50.00	50.00

Intl. Phil. Exhib. at Bucharest, Nov. 20-24, 1932. Each holder of a ticket of admission to the exhibition could buy an example of No. B40. The ticket cost 20 lei.

Roadside Shrine — SP31

Woman Spinning — SP33

Woman Weaving SP32

1934, Apr. 16 Wmk. 230 *Perf. 13½*

B41	SP31	1 l + 1 l dk brn	1.00	.90
B42	SP32	2 l + 1 l blue	1.25	1.10
B43	SP33	3 l + 1 l slate grn	1.75	1.50
		Nos. B41-B43 (3)	4.00	3.50

Weaving Exposition.

Boy Scout Mamaia Jamboree Issue

Semi-Postal Stamps of 1932 Overprinted in Black or Gold

1934, July 8

B44	SP20	25b + 25b pck grn	3.75	2.50
B45	SP21	50b + 50b brt bl (G)	5.00	3.00
B46	SP22	1 l + 1 l ol grn	6.00	4.75
B47	SP23	2 l + 2 l org red	7.50	5.50
B48	SP24	3 l + 3 l Prus bl (G)	16.00	7.00
B49	SP25	6 l + 6 l blk brn (G)	18.00	9.50
		Nos. B44-B49 (6)	56.25	32.25

Sea Scout Saluting SP34

Scout Bugler SP35

Sea and Land Scouts SP36

King Carol II — SP37

Sea, Land and Girl Scouts — SP38

1935, June 8

B50	SP34	25b ol blk	1.25	1.00
B51	SP35	1 l violet	2.75	2.25
B52	SP36	2 l green	3.50	3.00
B53	SP37	6 l + 1 l red brn	5.00	4.50
B54	SP38	10 l + 2 l dk ultra	14.00	13.00
		Nos. B50-B54 (5)	26.50	23.75

Fifth anniversary of accession of King Carol II, and a national sports meeting held June 8. Surtax aided the Boy Scouts.

Nos. B50-B54 exist imperf. Value $250.

King Carol II — SP39

1936, May

B55	SP39	6 l + 1 l rose car	.75	.55

Bucharest Exhibition and 70th anniversary of the dynasty. Exists imperf. Value $125

Girl of Oltenia — SP40

Girl of Saliste — SP42

Youth from Gorj — SP44

Designs: 1 l+1 l, Girl of Banat. 3 l+1 l, Girl of Hateg. 6 l+3 l, Girl of Neamt. 10 l+5 l, Youth and girl of Bucovina.

1936, June 8

B56	SP40	50b + 50b brown	.60	.60
B57	SP40	1 l + 1 l violet	.60	.60
B58	SP42	2 l + 1 l Prus grn	.60	*.70*
B59	SP42	3 l + 1 l car rose	.60	*.90*
B60	SP44	4 l + 2 l red org	1.00	.90
B61	SP40	6 l + 3 l ol gray	1.00	*1.20*
B62	SP42	10 l + 5 l brt bl	2.25	*2.40*
		Nos. B56-B62 (7)	6.65	*7.30*

6th anniv. of accession of King Carol II. The surtax was for child welfare. Exist imperf. Value $300, unused or used.

Insignia of Boy Scouts SP47 SP48

Jamboree Emblem — SP49

1936, Aug. 20

B63	SP47	1 l + 1 l brt bl	3.00	*5.25*
B64	SP48	3 l + 3 l ol gray	4.50	*5.25*
B65	SP49	6 l + 6 l car rose	6.00	*5.25*
		Nos. B63-B65 (3)	13.50	*15.75*

Boy Scout Jamboree at Brasov (Kronstadt). Exist imperf. Value $350, unused or used.

Submarine "Delfinul" SP50

Designs: 3 l+2 l, Training ship "Mircea." 6 l+3 l, Steamship "S.M.R."

1936, Oct.

B66	SP50	1 l + 1 l pur	2.75	2.50
B67	SP50	3 l + 2 l ultra	2.50	*3.00*
B68	SP50	6 l + 3 l car rose	3.50	*4.25*
		Nos. B66-B68 (3)	8.75	*9.75*

Marine Exhibition at Bucharest. Exist imperf. Value $325, unused or used.

Soccer SP53

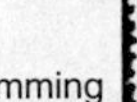

Swimming SP54

Throwing the Javelin — SP55

Skiing — SP56

King Carol II Hunting — SP57

Rowing SP58

Horsemanship SP59

Founding of the U.F.S.R. SP60

1937, June 8 Wmk. 230 ***Perf. 13½***

B69	SP53	25b + 25b ol blk	1.00	.35
B70	SP54	50b + 50b brown	1.00	.45
B71	SP55	1 l + 50b violet	1.20	.50
B72	SP56	2 l + 1 l slate grn	1.50	.55
B73	SP57	3 l + 1 l rose lake	2.20	.70
B74	SP58	4 l + 1 l red org	3.60	1.10
B75	SP59	6 l + 2 l dp claret	4.25	1.90
B76	SP60	10 l + 4 l brt blue	5.25	2.25
		Nos. B69-B76 (8)	20.00	7.80

25th anniversary of the Federation of Romanian Sports Clubs (U.F.S.R.); 7th anniversary of the accession of King Carol II.

Exist imperf. Value $200, unused or used.

Start of Race — SP61

Javelin Thrower — SP62

Designs: 4 l+1 l, Hurdling. 6 l+1 l, Finish of race. 10 l+1 l, High jump.

1937, Sept. 1 Wmk. 230 ***Perf. 13½***

B77	SP61	1 l + 1 l purple	.75	*.90*
B78	SP62	2 l + 1 l green	.95	*1.25*
B79	SP61	4 l + 1 l vermilion	1.25	*1.75*
B80	SP62	6 l + 1 l maroon	1.40	*1.90*
B81	SP61	10 l + 1 l brt bl	4.25	3.50
		Nos. B77-B81 (5)	8.60	*9.30*

8th Balkan Games, Bucharest. Exist imperf. Value $200, unused or used.

Catalogue values for unused stamps in this section, from this point to the end of the section, are for Never Hinged items.

King Carol II — SP66

1938, May 24

B82	SP66	6 l + 1 l deep magenta	1.50	.45

Bucharest Exhibition (for local products), May 19-June 19, celebrating 20th anniversary of the union of Romanian provinces.

Exists imperf. Value $200, unused or used.

Dimitrie Cantemir — SP67

Maria Doamna — SP68

Mircea the Great SP69

Constantine Brancoveanu SP70

Stephen the Great — SP71

Prince Cuza — SP72

Michael the Brave — SP73

Queen Elizabeth — SP74

King Carol II — SP75

King Ferdinand I — SP76

King Carol I — SP77

1938, June 8 ***Perf. 13½***

B83	SP67	25b + 25b ol blk	.80	.35
B84	SP68	50b + 50b brn	1.25	.35
B85	SP69	1 l + 1 l blk vio	1.25	.35
B86	SP70	2 l + 2 l dk yel grn	1.40	.35
B87	SP71	3 l + 2 l dp mag	1.40	.35
B88	SP72	4 l + 2 l scarlet	1.40	.35
B89	SP73	6 l + 2 l vio brn	1.50	.45

B90	SP74	7.50 l gray bl	1.75	.60
B91	SP75	10 l brt bl	2.25	.60
B92	SP76	16 l dk slate grn	3.50	2.00
B93	SP77	20 l vermilion	4.75	2.00
		Nos. B83-B93 (11)	21.25	7.75

8th anniv. of accession of King Carol II. Surtax was for Straja Tarii, a natl. org. for boys.
Exist imperf. Value $175, unused or used.

"The Spring" — SP78

"Escorting Prisoners" SP79

"Rodica, the Water Carrier" SP81

Nicolae Grigorescu SP82

Design: 4 l+1 l, "Returning from Market."

1938, June 23 ***Perf. 13½***

B94	SP78	1 l + 1 l brt bl	2.25	.70
B95	SP79	2 l + 1 l yel grn	2.25	1.25
B96	SP79	4 l + 1 l vermilion	2.25	1.25
B97	SP81	6 l + 1 l lake	3.00	2.25
B98	SP82	10 l + 1 l brt bl	6.75	2.50
		Nos. B94-B98 (5)	16.50	7.95

Birth centenary of Nicolae Grigorescu, Romanian painter.
Exist imperf. Value $200, unused or used.

St. George and the Dragon — SP83

1939, June 8 **Photo.**

B99	SP83	25b + 25b ol gray	.60	.45
B100	SP83	50b + 50b brn	.60	.45
B101	SP83	1 l + 1 l pale vio	.60	.45
B102	SP83	2 l + 2 l lt grn	.60	.45
B103	SP83	3 l + 2 l red vio	1.00	.45
B104	SP83	4 l + 2 l red org	1.40	.55
B105	SP83	6 l + 2 l car rose	1.50	.55
B106	SP83	8 l gray vio	1.75	.55
B107	SP83	10 l brt bl	1.90	.70
B108	SP83	12 l brt ultra	2.10	1.40
B109	SP83	16 l bl grn	2.25	1.75
		Nos. B99-B109 (11)	14.30	7.75

9th anniv. of accession of King Carol II. Exist imperf. Value $175, unused or used.

King Carol II

SP87 SP88

SP89

SP90

SP91

Wmk. 230

1940, June 8 **Photo.** ***Perf. 13½***

B113	SP87	1 l + 50b dl pur	.75	.30
B114	SP88	4 l + 1 l fawn	.75	.45
B115	SP89	6 l + 1 l blue	.75	.45
B116	SP90	8 l rose brn	1.10	.65
B117	SP89	16 l ultra	1.25	.90
B118	SP91	32 l dk vio brn	2.00	1.25
		Nos. B113-B118 (6)	6.60	4.00

10th anniv. of accession of King Carol II.
Exist imperf. Value $200, unused or used.

King Carol II

SP92 SP93

1940, June 1

B119	SP92	1 l + 50b dk grn	.25	.25
B120	SP92	2.50 l + 50b Prus grn	.25	.25
B121	SP93	3 l + 1 l rose car	.35	.25
B122	SP92	3.50 l + 50b choc	.35	.35
B123	SP93	4 l + 1 l org brn	.50	.35
B124	SP93	6 l + 1 l sapphire	.75	.25
B125	SP93	9 l + 1 l brt bl	.85	.70
B126	SP93	14 l + 1 l dk bl grn	1.10	.90
		Nos. B119-B126 (8)	4.40	3.30

Surtax was for Romania's air force. Exist imperf. Value $200, unused or used.

View of Danube SP94

Greco-Roman Ruins — SP95

Designs: 3 l+1 l, Hotin Castle. 4 l+1 l, Hurez Monastery. 5 l+1 l, Church in Bucovina. 8 l+1 l, Tower. 12 l+2 l, Village church, Transylvania. 16 l+2 l, Arch in Bucharest.

Inscribed: "Straja Tarii 8 Junie 1940"

1940, June 8 ***Perf. 14½x14, 14x14½***

B127	SP94	1 l + 1 l dp vio	.40	.25
B128	SP95	2 l + 1 l red brn	.45	.30
B129	SP94	3 l + 1 l yel grn	.50	.35
B130	SP94	4 l + 1 l grnsh blk	.55	.40
B131	SP95	5 l + 1 l org ver	.60	.45
B132	SP95	8 l + 1 l brn car	.85	.60
B133	SP95	12 l + 2 l ultra	1.75	1.10
B134	SP95	16 l + 2 l dk bl gray	3.00	2.00
		Nos. B127-B134 (8)	8.10	5.45

Issued to honor Straja Tarii, a national organization for boys. Exist imperf. Value $140, unused or used.

King Michael — SP102

1940-42 **Photo.** **Wmk. 230**

B138	SP102	1 l + 50b yel grn	.25	.25
B138A	SP102	2 l + 50b yel grn	.25	.25
B139	SP102	2.50 l + 50b dk bl grn	.25	.25
B140	SP102	3 l + 1 l pur	.25	.25
B141	SP102	3.50 l + 50b rose pink	.25	.25
B141A	SP102	4 l + 50b org ver	.25	.25
B142	SP102	4 l + 1 l brn	.25	.25
B142A	SP102	5 l + 1 l dp plum	1.25	.25
B143	SP102	6 l + 1 l lt ultra	.25	.25
B143A	SP102	7 l + 1 l sl grn	.50	.25
B143B	SP102	8 l + 1 l dp vio	.25	.25
B143C	SP102	12 l + 1 l brn vio	.50	.25
B144	SP102	14 l + 1 l brt bl	.50	.25
B144A	SP102	19 l + 1 l lil rose	1.00	.25
		Nos. B138-B144A (14)	6.00	3.50

Issue years: Nos. B138A, B141A, B142A, B143A, B143B, B143C, B144A, 1942; others, 1940.

Corneliu Codreanu — SP103

1940, Nov. 8 **Unwmk.** ***Perf. 13½***

B145	SP103	7 l + 30 l dk grn	6.00	*9.00*

13th anniv. of the founding of the Iron Guard by Corneliu Codreanu.

Vasile Marin — SP104

Design: 15 l+15 l, Ion Mota.

1941, Jan. 13

B146	SP104	7 l + 7 l rose brn	3.50	*6.00*
B147	SP104	15 l + 15 l slate bl	5.00	*9.00*

Souvenir Sheet

Imperf

B148		Sheet of 2	75.00	*125.00*
a.	SP104	7 l + 7 l Prus grn	15.00	*35.00*
b.	SP104	15 l + 15 l Prus green	15.00	*35.00*

Vasile Marin and Ion Mota, Iron Guardists who died in the Spanish Civil War.
No. B148 sold for 300 lei.

Crown, Leaves and Bible — SP107

Designs: 2 l+43 l, Library shelves. 7 l+38 l, Carol I Foundation, Bucharest. 10 l+35 l, King Carol I. 16 l+29 l, Kings Michael and Carol I.

Inscribed: "1891 1941"

Wmk. 230

1941, May 9 **Photo.** ***Perf. 13½***

B149	SP107	1.50 l + 43.50 l pur	1.60	*2.50*
B150	SP107	2 l + 43 l rose brn	1.60	*2.50*
B151	SP107	7 l + 38 l rose	1.60	*2.50*
B152	SP107	10 l + 35 l ol blk	1.60	*2.50*
B153	SP107	16 l + 29 l brown	1.60	*2.50*
		Nos. B149-B153 (5)	8.00	*12.50*

50th anniv. of the Carol I Foundation, established to endow research and stimulate the arts.

Same Overprinted in Red or Black

1941, Aug.

B154	SP107	1.50 l + 43.50 l (R)	2.00	*4.00*
B155	SP107	2 l + 43 l	2.00	*4.00*
B156	SP107	7 l + 38 l	2.00	*4.00*
B157	SP107	10 l + 35 l (R)	2.00	*4.00*
B158	SP107	16 l + 29 l	2.00	*4.00*

Occupation of Cernauti, Bucovina.

Same Overprinted in Red or Black

1941, Aug.

B159	SP107	1.50 l + 43.50 l (R)	2.00	*4.00*
B160	SP107	2 l + 43 l	2.00	*4.00*
B161	SP107	7 l + 38 l	2.00	*4.00*
B162	SP107	10 l + 35 l (R)	2.00	*4.00*
B163	SP107	16 l + 29 l	2.00	*4.00*
		Nos. B154-B163 (10)	20.00	*40.00*

Occupation of Chisinau, Bessarabia.

Romanian Red Cross — SP111

1941, Aug. ***Perf. 13½***

B164	SP111	1.50 l + 38.50 l	1.20	*2.00*
B165	SP111	2 l + 38 l	1.20	*2.00*
B166	SP111	5 l + 35 l	1.20	*2.00*
B167	SP111	7 l + 33 l	1.20	*2.00*
B168	SP111	10 l + 30 l	1.50	*2.00*
		Nos. B164-B168 (5)	6.30	*10.00*

Souvenir Sheet

Imperf

Without Gum

B169		Sheet of 2	20.00	20.00
a.	SP111	7 l + 33 l brown & red	2.75	*3.50*
b.	SP111	10 l + 30 l brt blue & red	2.75	*3.50*

The surtax on Nos. B164-B169 was for the Romanian Red Cross.
No. B169 sold for 200 l.

King Michael and Stephen the Great SP113

Hotin and Akkerman Castles SP114

Romanian and German Soldiers SP115

Soldiers SP116

SP118

1941, Oct. 11 *Perf. 14½x13½*

B170 SP113 10 l + 30 l ultra 2.25 *3.00*
B171 SP114 12 l + 28 l dl org red 2.25 *3.00*
B172 SP115 16 l + 24 l lt brn 2.50 *3.00*
B173 SP116 20 l + 20 l dk vio 2.50 *3.00*
Nos. B170-B173 (4) 9.50 *12.00*

Souvenir Sheet

Imperf

Without Gum

B174 SP118 Sheet of 2 12.00 *17.50*
a. 16 l blue gray 1.50 *4.50*
b. 20 l brown carmine 1.50 *4.50*

No. B174 sold for 200 l. The surtax aided the Anti-Bolshevism crusade.

Nos. B170-B174 Overprinted

1941, Oct. *Perf. 14½x13½*

B175 SP113 10 l + 30 l ultra 2.00 *3.00*
B176 SP114 12 l + 28 l dl org red 2.00 *3.00*
B177 SP115 16 l + 24 l lt brn 2.50 *3.00*
B178 SP116 20 l + 20 l dk vio 2.50 *3.00*
Nos. B175-B178 (4) 9.00 *12.00*

Souvenir Sheet

Imperf

Without Gum

B178A SP118 Sheet of 2 17.50 *25.00*

Occupation of Odessa, Russia.

Types of Regular Issue, 1941

Designs: 3 l+50b, Sucevita Monastery, Bucovina. 5.50 l+50b, Rughi Monastery, Soroca, Bessarabia. 5.50 l+1 l, Tighina Fortress, Bessarabia. 6.50 l+1 l, Soroca Fortress, Bessarabia. 8 l+1 l, St. Nicholas Monastery, Suceava, Bucovina. 9.50 l+1 l, Milisauti Monastery, Bucovina. 10.50 l+1 l, Putna Monastery, Bucovina. 16 l+1 l, Cetatea Alba Fortress, Bessarabia. 25 l+1 l, Hotin Fortress, Bessarabia.

1941, Dec. 1 **Wmk. 230** *Perf. 13½*

B179 A179 3 l + 50b rose brn .45 .25
B180 A179 5.50 l + 50b red org .60 .50
B181 A179 5.50 l + 1 l blk .60 .50
B182 A179 6.50 l + 1 l dk brn .75 .75
B183 A179 8 l + 1 l lt bl .60 .40
B184 A177 9.50 l + 1 l gray bl .75 .60
B185 A179 10.50 l + 1 l dk bl .80 .40
B186 A179 16 l + 1 l vio .90 .65
B187 A179 25 l + 1 l gray blk 1.00 .70
Nos. B179-B187 (9) 6.45 4.75

Titu Maiorescu SP128

1942, Oct. 5

B188 SP128 9 l + 11 l dl vio .70 *1.00*
B189 SP128 20 l + 20 l yel brn 1.75 *2.50*
B190 SP128 20 l + 30 l blue 2.00 *3.00*
Nos. B188-B190 (3) 4.45 *6.50*

Souvenir Sheet

Imperf

Without Gum

B191 SP128 Sheet of 3 9.00 *15.00*

The surtax aided war prisoners.
No. B191 contains one each of Nos. B188-B190, imperf. Sold for 200 l.

Statue of Miron Costin at Jassy — SP130

1942, Dec. *Perf. 13½*

B192 SP130 6 l + 44 l sepia 1.75 *2.75*
B193 SP130 12 l + 38 l violet 1.75 *2.75*
B194 SP130 24 l + 26 l blue 1.75 *2.75*
Nos. B192-B194 (3) 5.25 *8.25*

Anniv. of the conquest of Transdniestria, and for use only in this territory which includes Odessa and land beyond the Duiestor.

Michael, Antonescu, Hitler, Mussolini and Bessarabia Map SP131

Michael, Antonescu and (inset) Stephen of Moldavia SP132

Romanian Troops Crossing Pruth River to Retake Bessarabia — SP133

1942 **Wmk. 230** **Photo.** *Perf. 13½*

B195 SP131 9 l + 41 l red brn 2.75 *3.50*
B196 SP132 18 l + 32 l ol gray 2.75 *3.50*
B197 SP133 20 l + 30 l brt ultra 2.75 *3.50*
Nos. B195-B197 (3) 8.25 *10.50*

First anniversary of liberation of Bessarabia.

Bucovina Coats of Arms
SP134 SP135

Design: 20 l+30 l, Bucovina arms with triple-barred cross.

1942, Nov. 1

B198 SP134 9 l + 41 l brt ver 2.75 *3.50*
B199 SP135 18 l + 32 l blue 2.75 *3.50*
B200 SP135 20 l + 30 l car rose 2.75 *3.50*
Nos. B198-B200 (3) 8.25 *10.50*

First anniversary of liberation of Bucovina.

Andrei Muresanu SP137

1942, Dec. 30

B201 SP137 5 l + 5 l violet 1.00 *1.75*

80th death anniv. of Andrei Muresanu, writer.

Avram Jancu, National Hero — SP138

1943, Feb. 15

B202 SP138 16 l + 4 l brown 1.00 *1.75*

Nurse Aiding Wounded Soldier SP139

1943, Mar. 1 *Perf. 14½x14*

B203 SP139 12 l + 88 l red brn & ultra 1.00 *1.25*
B204 SP139 16 l + 84 l brt ultra & red 1.00 *1.25*
B205 SP139 20 l + 80 l ol gray & red 1.00 *1.25*
Nos. B203-B205 (3) 3.00 *3.75*

Souvenir Sheet

Imperf

B206 Sheet of 2 8.00 *9.00*
a. SP139 16 l + 84 l bright ultra & red 2.00 *2.50*
b. SP139 20 l + 80 l olive gray & red 2.00 *2.50*

Surtax on Nos. B203-B206 aided the Romanian Red Cross.
No. B206 sold for 500 l.

Sword Hilt — SP141

Sword Severing Chain — SP142

Soldier and Family, Guardian Angel — SP143

Perf. 14x14½

1943, June 22 **Wmk. 276**

B207 SP141 36 l + 164 l brn 3.75 *4.50*
B208 SP142 62 l + 138 l brt bl 3.75 *4.50*
B209 SP143 76 l + 124 l ver 3.75 *4.50*
Nos. B207-B209 (3) 11.25 *13.50*

Souvenir Sheet

Imperf

B210 Sheet of 2 20.00 20.00
a. SP142 62 l + 138 l deep blue 5.75 5.75
b. SP143 76 l + 124 l red org 5.75 5.75

2nd anniv. of Romania's entrance into WWII. No. B210 sold for 600 l.

Petru Maior — SP145

Horea, Closca and Crisan SP148

32 l+118 l, Gheorghe Sincai. 36 l+114 l, Timotei Cipariu. 91 l+109 l, Gheorghe Cosbuc.

Perf. 13½; 14½x14 (No. B214)

1943, Aug. 15 **Photo.** **Wmk. 276**

B211 SP145 16 l + 134 l red org .70 *1.40*
B212 SP145 32 l + 118 l lt bl .70 *1.40*
B213 SP145 36 l + 114 l vio .70 *1.40*
B214 SP148 62 l + 138 l car rose .70 *1.40*
B215 SP145 91 l + 109 l dk brn .70 *1.40*
Nos. B211-B215 (5) 3.50 *7.00*

See Nos. B219-B223.

King Michael and Ion Antonescu SP150

1943, Sept. 6

B216 SP150 16 l + 24 l blue 2.50 *3.50*

3rd anniv. of the government of King Michael and Marshal Ion Antonescu.

Symbols of Sports — SP151

1943, Sept. 26 *Perf. 13½*

B217 SP151 16 l + 24 l ultra .75 *1.00*
B218 SP151 16 l + 24 l red brn .75 *1.00*

Surtax for the benefit of Romanian sports.

Portrait Type of 1943

Designs: 16 l+134 l, Samuel Micu. 51 l+99 l, George Lazar. 56 l+144 l, Octavian Goga. 76 l+ 124 l, Simeon Barnutiu. 77 l+123 l, Andrei Saguna.

1943, Oct. 1

B219 SP145 16 l + 134 l red vio .60 *1.20*
B220 SP145 51 l + 99 l orange .60 *1.20*
B221 SP145 56 l + 144 l rose car .60 *1.20*
B222 SP145 76 l + 124 l slate bl .60 *1.20*
B223 SP145 77 l + 123 l brown .60 *1.20*
Nos. B219-B223 (5) 3.00 *6.00*

The surtax aided refugees.

Calatat, 1877 — SP157

Designs: 2 l +2 l, World War I scene. 3.50 l+3.50 l, Stalingrad, 1943. 4 l+4 l, Tisza, 1919. 5 l+5 l, Odessa, 1941. 6.50 l+6.50 l, Caucasus, 1942. 7 l+7 l, Sevastopol, 1942. 20 l+20 l, Prince Ribescu and King Michael.

1943, Nov. 10 **Photo.** *Perf. 13½*

B224 SP157 1 l + 1 l red brn .30 *.50*
B225 SP157 2 l + 2 l dl vio .30 *.50*
B226 SP157 3.50 l + 3.50 l lt ultra .30 *.50*
B227 SP157 4 l + 4 l mag .30 *.50*
B228 SP157 5 l + 5 l red org .70 *1.25*
B229 SP157 6.50 l + 6.50 l bl .70 *1.25*

B230 SP157 7 l + 7 l dp vio .80 *2.25*
B231 SP157 20 l + 20 l crim 1.25 *3.75*
Nos. B224-B231 (8) 4.65 *10.50*

Centenary of Romanian Artillery.

Emblem of Romanian Engineers' Association — SP165

1943, Dec. 19 ***Perf. 14***
B232 SP165 21 l + 29 l sepia 1.10 *1.75*

Society of Romanian Engineers, 25th anniv.

Motorcycle, Truck and Post Horn — SP166

Post Wagon SP167

Roman Post Chariot SP168

Post Rider — SP169

1944, Feb. 1 **Wmk. 276** ***Perf. 14***
B233 SP166 1 l + 49 l org red 2.00 *3.00*
B234 SP167 2 l + 48 l lil rose 2.00 *3.00*
B235 SP168 4 l + 46 l ultra 2.00 *3.00*
B236 SP169 10 l + 40 l dl vio 2.00 *3.00*
Nos. B233-B236 (4) 8.00 *12.00*

Souvenir Sheets

Perf. 14

B237 Sheet of 3 8.00 *12.50*
a. SP166 1 l + 49 l orange red .80 *1.20*
b. SP167 2 l + 48 l orange red .80 *1.20*
c. SP168 4 l + 46 l orange red .80 *1.20*

Imperf

B238 Sheet of 3 8.00 *12.50*
a. SP166 1 l + 49 l dull violet .80 *1.20*
b. SP167 2 l + 48 l dull violet .80 *1.20*
c. SP168 4 l + 46 l dull violet .80 *1.20*

The surtax aided communications employees.
No. B238 is imperf. between the stamps.
Nos. B237-B238 each sold for 200 l.

Nos. B233-B238 Overprinted

1944, Feb. 28
B239 SP166 1 l + 49 l org red 4.50 *6.50*
B240 SP167 2 l + 48 l lil rose 4.50 *6.50*
B241 SP168 4 l + 46 l ultra 4.50 *6.50*
B242 SP169 10 l + 40 l dl vio 4.50 *6.50*
Nos. B239-B242 (4) 18.00 *26.00*

Souvenir Sheets

Perf. 14

B243 Sheet of 3 17.50 *25.00*

Imperf

B244 Sheet of 3 17.50 *25.00*

Rugby Player — SP171

1944, Mar. 16 ***Perf. 15***
B245 SP171 16 l + 184 l crimson 4.75 *7.50*

30th anniv. of the Romanian Rugby Assoc. The surtax was used to encourage the sport.

Dr. N. Cretzulescu SP172

1944, Mar. 1 **Photo.** ***Perf. 13½***
B246 SP172 35 l + 65 l brt ultra 1.10 *1.75*

Centenary of medical teaching in Romania.

Queen Mother Helen — SP173

1945, Feb. 10
B247 SP173 4.50 l + 5.50 l multi .35 *.70*
B248 SP173 10 l + 40 l multi .45 *.90*
B249 SP173 15 l + 75 l multi .70 *1.40*
B250 SP173 20 l + 80 l multi 1.00 *2.00*
Nos. B247-B250 (4) 2.50 *5.00*

The surtax aided the Romanian Red Cross.

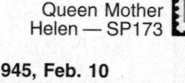

Kings Ferdinand and Michael and Map SP174

1945, Feb. ***Perf. 14***
B251 SP174 75 l + 75 l dk ol brn .50 *.75*

Romania's liberation.

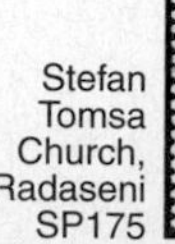

Stefan Tomsa Church, Radaseni SP175

Municipal Home SP176

Gathering Fruit — SP177

School SP178

1944 **Wmk. 276** **Photo.** ***Perf. 14***
B252 SP175 5 l + 145 l brt bl 1.00 1.00
B253 SP176 12 l + 138 l car rose 1.00 1.00
B254 SP177 15 l + 135 l red org 1.00 1.00
B255 SP178 32 l + 118 l dk brn 1.00 1.00
Nos. B252-B255 (4) 4.00 4.00

King Michael and Carol I Foundation, Bucharest — SP179

Design: 200 l, King Carol I and Foundation.

1945, Feb. 10 ***Perf. 13***
B256 SP179 20 l + 180 l dp org .50 *.75*
B257 SP179 25 l + 175 l slate .50 *.75*
B258 SP179 35 l + 165 l cl brn .50 *.75*
B259 SP179 75 l + 125 l pale vio .50 *.75*
Nos. B256-B259 (4) 2.00 *3.00*

Souvenir Sheet

Imperf

Without Gum

B260 SP179 200 l blue 7.50 *15.00*

Surtax was to aid in rebuilding the Public Library, Bucharest.
#B256-B259 were printed in sheets of 4.
No. B260 sold for 1200 l.

Ion G. Duca SP181

16 l+184 l, Virgil Madgearu. 20 l+180 l, Nikolai Jorga. 32 l+168 l, Ilie Pintilie. 35 l+165 l, Bernath Andrei. 36 l+164 l, Filimon Sarbu.

1945, Apr. 30 ***Perf. 13***
B261 SP181 12 l + 188 l dk bl .70 *1.00*
B262 SP181 16 l + 184 l cl brn .70 *1.00*
B263 SP181 20 l + 180 l blk brn .70 *1.00*
B264 SP181 32 l + 168 l brt red .70 *1.00*
B265 SP181 35 l + 165 l Prus bl .70 *1.00*
B266 SP181 36 l + 164 l lt vio .70 *1.00*
Nos. B261-B266 (6) 4.20 *6.00*

Souvenir Sheet

Imperf

B267 Sheet of 2 24.00 *40.00*
a. SP181 32 l + 168 l mag 4.75 *7.50*
b. SP181 35 l + 165 l mag 4.75 *7.50*

Honoring six victims of Nazi terrorism.
No. B267 sold for 1,000 l.

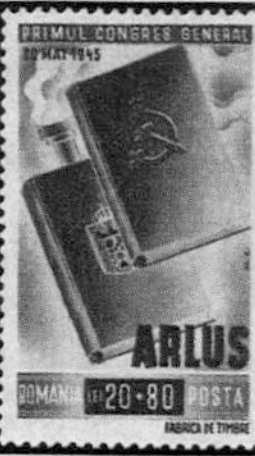

Books and Torch — SP188

Designs: #B269, Flags of Russia and Romania. #B270, Kremlin, Moscow. #B271, Tudor Vladimirescu and Alexander Nevsky.

1945, May 20 ***Perf. 14***
B268 SP188 20 l + 80 l ol grn .40 *.60*
B269 SP188 35 l + 165 l brt rose .40 *.60*
B270 SP188 75 l + 225 l blue .40 *.60*
B271 SP188 80 l + 420 l cl brn .40 *.60*
Nos. B268-B271 (4) 1.60 *2.40*

Souvenir Sheet

Imperf

Without Gum

B272 Sheet of 2 8.50 *17.50*
a. SP189 35 l + 165 l bright red 2.00 *3.50*
b. SP190 75 l + 225 l bright red 2.00 *3.50*

1st Soviet-Romanian Cong., May 20, 1945.
No. B272 sold for 900 l.

Karl Marx — SP193

120 l+380 l, Friedrich Engels. 155 l+445 l, Lenin.

1945, June 30 ***Perf. 13½***
B273 SP193 75 l + 425 l car rose 3.00 *6.00*
B274 SP193 120 l + 380 l bl 3.00 *6.00*
B275 SP193 155 l + 445 l dk vio brn 3.00 *6.00*

Imperf

B276 SP193 75 l + 425 l bl 8.50 *15.00*
B277 SP193 120 l + 380 l dk vio brn 8.50 *15.00*
B278 SP193 155 l + 445 l car rose 8.50 *15.00*
Nos. B273-B278 (6) 34.50 *63.00*

Nos. B276-B278 were printed in sheets of 4.

Woman Throwing Discus — SP196

Designs: 16 l+184 l, Diving. 20 l+180 l, Skiing. 32 l+168 l, Volleyball. 35 l+165 l, Worker athlete.

Wmk. 276

1945, Aug. 5 **Photo.** ***Perf. 13***
B279 SP196 12 l +188 l ol gray 2.00 *4.00*
B280 SP196 16 l +184 l lt ultra 2.00 *4.00*
B281 SP196 20 l +180 l dp grn 2.00 *4.00*
B282 SP196 32 l +168 l mag 2.00 *4.00*
B283 SP196 35 l +165 l brt bl 2.00 *4.00*

Imperf

B284 SP196 12 l +188 l org red 2.00 *4.00*
B285 SP196 16 l +184 l vio brn 2.00 *4.00*
B286 SP196 20 l +180 l dp vio 2.00 *4.00*
B287 SP196 32 l +168 l yel grn 2.00 *4.00*
B288 SP196 35 l +165 l dk ol grn 2.00 *4.00*
Nos. B279-B288 (10) 20.00 *40.00*

Printed in sheets of 9.

Mail Plane and Bird Carrying Letter SP201

1945, Aug. 5 ***Perf. 13½***

B289	SP201	200 l + 1000 l bl & dk bl	20.00	*40.00*
a.		With label	60.00	*150.00*

The surtax on Nos. B279-B289 was for the Office of Popular Sports.

Issued in sheets of 30 stamps and 10 labels, arranged 10x4 with second and fourth horizontal rows each having five alternating labels.

Agriculture and Industry United — SP202

King Michael SP203

1945, Aug. 23 ***Perf. 14***

B290	SP202	100 l + 400 l red	.80	*2.00*
B291	SP203	200 l + 800 l blue	.85	*2.00*

The surtax was for the Farmers' Front.

For surcharges see Nos. B318-B325.

Political Amnesty SP204

Military Amnesty SP205

Agrarian Amnesty SP206

Tudor Vladimirescu SP207

Nicolae Horia SP208

Reconstruction — SP209

1945, Aug. ***Perf. 13***

B292	SP204	20 l + 580 l choc	10.00	10.00
B293	SP204	20 l + 580 l mag	10.00	10.00
B294	SP205	40 l + 560 l blue	10.00	10.00
B295	SP205	40 l + 560 l sl grn	10.00	10.00
B296	SP206	55 l + 545 l red	10.00	10.00
B297	SP206	55 l + 545 l dk vio brn	10.00	10.00
B298	SP207	60 l + 540 l ultra	10.00	10.00
B299	SP207	60 l + 540 l choc	10.00	10.00
B300	SP208	80 l + 520 l red	10.00	10.00
B301	SP208	80 l + 520 l mag	10.00	10.00
B302	SP209	100 l + 500 l sl grn	10.00	10.00
B303	SP209	100 l + 500 l red brn	10.00	10.00
		Nos. B292-B303 (12)	120.00	120.00

1st anniv. of Romania's armistice with Russia. Issued in panes of four.

Nos. B292-B303 also exist on coarse grayish paper, ungummed (same value).

Electric Train SP210

Coats of Arms SP211

Truck on Mountain Road SP212

Oil Field SP213

"Agriculture" — SP214

1945, Oct. 1 ***Perf. 14***

B304	SP210	10 l + 490 l ol grn	.70	.70
B305	SP211	20 l + 480 l red brn	.70	.70
B306	SP212	25 l + 475 l brn vio	.70	.70
B307	SP213	55 l + 445 l ultra	.70	.70
B308	SP214	100 l + 400 l brn	.70	.70

Imperf

B309	SP210	10 l + 490 l blue	.70	.70
B310	SP211	20 l + 480 l vio	.70	.70
B311	SP212	25 l + 475 l bl grn	.70	.70
B312	SP213	55 l + 445 l gray	.70	.70
B313	SP214	100 l + 400 l dp mag	.70	.70
		Nos. B304-B313 (10)	7.00	7.00

16th Congress of the General Assoc. of Romanian Engineers.

"Brotherhood" — SP215

160 l+1840 l, "Peace." 320 l+1680 l, Hammer crushing Nazism. 440 l+2560 l, "World Unity."

1945, Dec. 5 ***Perf. 14***

B314	SP215	80 l + 920 l mag	17.50	*25.00*
B315	SP215	160 l + 1840 l org brn	17.50	*25.00*
B316	SP215	320 l + 1680 l vio	17.50	*25.00*
B317	SP215	440 l + 2560 l yel grn	17.50	*25.00*
		Nos. B314-B317 (4)	70.00	*100.00*

World Trade Union Congress at Paris, Sept. 25-Oct. 10, 1945.

Nos. B290 and B291 Surcharged in Various Colors

1946, Jan. 20

B318	SP202	10 l + 90 l (Bk)	.85	*1.75*
B319	SP203	10 l + 90 l (R)	.85	*1.75*
B320	SP202	20 l + 80 l (G)	.85	*1.75*
B321	SP203	20 l + 80 l (Bk)	.85	*1.75*
B322	SP202	80 l + 120 l (Bl)	.85	*1.75*
B323	SP203	80 l + 120 l (Bk)	.85	*1.75*
B324	SP202	100 l + 150 l (Bk)	.85	*1.75*
B325	SP203	100 l + 150 l (R)	.85	*1.75*
		Nos. B318-B325 (8)	6.80	*14.00*

Re-distribution of Land — SP219

Sower SP220

Ox Team Drawing Hay SP221

Old and New Plowing Methods SP222

1946, Mar. 6

B326	SP219	50 l + 450 l red	.40	.75
B327	SP220	100 l + 900 l purple	.40	.75
B328	SP221	200 l + 800 l orange	.40	.75
B329	SP222	400 l + 1600 l dk grn	.40	.75
		Nos. B326-B329 (4)	1.60	*3.00*

Agrarian reform law of Mar. 23, 1945.

Philharmonic Types of Regular Issue

Perf. 13, 13½x13

1946, Apr. 26 **Photo.** **Wmk. 276**

B330	A211	200 l + 800 l brt red	.80	*1.50*
a.		Sheet of 12	22.50	*25.00*
B331	A213	350 l + 1650 l dk bl	.90	*1.75*
a.		Sheet of 12	22.50	*25.00*

Issued in sheets containing 12 stamps and 4 labels, with bars of music in the margins.

Agriculture SP223

Designs: 10 l+200 l, Hurdling. 80 l+200 l, Research. 80 l+300 l, Industry. 200 l+400 l, Workers and flag.

Wmk. 276

1946, July 28 **Photo.** ***Perf. 11½***

B332	SP223	10 l + 100 l dk org brn & red	.40	.75
B333	SP223	10 l + 200 l bl & red brn	.40	.75
B334	SP223	80 l + 200 l brn vio & brn	.40	.75
B335	SP223	80 l + 300 l dk org brn & rose lil	.40	.75
B336	SP223	200 l + 400 l Prus bl & red	.40	.75
		Nos. B332-B336 (5)	2.00	*3.75*

Issued in panes of 4 stamps with marginal inscription.

Dove — SP228

1946, Oct. 20 ***Perf. 13½x13, Imperf.***

B338	SP228	300 l + 1200 l scar	.70	*1.25*

Souvenir Sheet

Perf. 14x14½

B339	SP228	1000 l scarlet	5.00	*10.00*

Romanian-Soviet friendship. No. B339 sold for 6000 lei.

Skiing — SP230

1946, Sept. 1 ***Perf. 11½, Imperf.***

B340	SP230	160 l + 1340 l dk grn	.50	.75

Surtax for Office of Popular Sports.

Spinning SP231

Reaping SP232

Riding — SP233

Water Carrier — SP234

1946, Nov. 20 *Perf. 14*
B342 SP231 80 l + 320 l brt red .35 *.75*
B343 SP232 140 l + 360 l dp org .35 *.75*
B344 SP233 300 l + 450 l brn ol .35 *.75*
B345 SP234 600 l + 900 l ultra .35 *.75*
Nos. B342-B345 (4) 1.40 *3.00*

Democratic Women's Org. of Romania.

Angel with Food and Clothing SP235

Bread for Hungry Family SP236

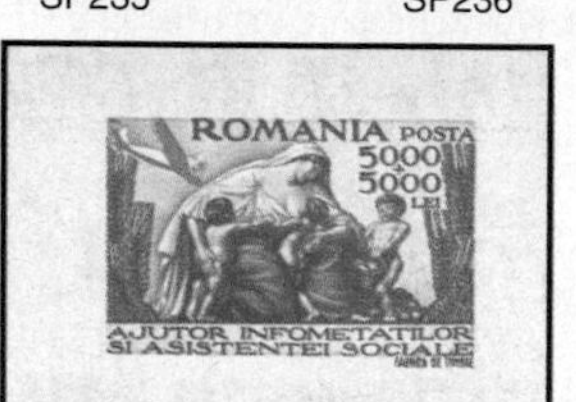

Care for Needy — SP237

1947, Jan. 15 *Perf. 13½x14*
B346 SP235 1500 l + 3500 l red org .30 *.60*
B347 SP236 3700 l + 5300 l dp vio .30 *.60*

Miniature Sheet
Imperf
Without Gum

B348 SP237 5000 l + 5000 l ultra 7.50 *15.00*

Surtax helped the social relief fund. No. B348 is miniature sheet of one.

Student Reciting SP238

Allegory of Education — SP242

SP243

#B350, Weaving class. #B351, Young machinist. #B352, Romanian school.

Perf. 14x13½

1947, Mar. 5 **Photo.** **Wmk. 276**
B349 SP238 200 l + 200 l vio bl .25 *.35*
B350 SP238 300 l + 300 l red brn .25 *.35*
B351 SP238 600 l + 600 l Prus grn .25 *.35*
B352 SP238 1200 l + 1200 l ultra .25 *.35*
B353 SP242 1500 l + 1500 l dp rose .25 *.35*
Nos. B349-B353 (5) 1.25 *1.75*

Souvenir Sheet
Imperf

B354 SP243 3700 l + 3700 l dl brn & dl bl 2.25 *5.00*

Romania's vocational schools, 50th anniv.

Victor Babes — SP244

#B356, Michael Eminescu. #B357, Nicolae Grigorescu. #B358, Peter Movila. #B359, Aleksander S. Pushkin. #B360, Mikhail V. Lomonosov. #B361, Peter I. Tchaikovsky. #B362, Ilya E. Repin.

1947, Apr. 18 *Perf. 14*
B355 SP244 1500 l + 1500 l red org .25 .25
B356 SP244 1500 l + 1500 l dk ol grn .25 .25
B357 SP244 1500 l + 1500 l dk bl .25 .25
B358 SP244 1500 l + 1500 l dp plum .25 .25
B359 SP244 1500 l + 1500 l scar .25 .25
B360 SP244 1500 l + 1500 l rose brn .25 .25
B361 SP244 1500 l + 1500 l ultra .25 .25
B362 SP244 1500 l + 1500 l choc .25 .25
Nos. B355-B362 (8) 2.00 2.00

Transportation — SP252

Labor Day: No. B364, Farmer. No. B365, Farm woman. No. B366, Scientist and Romanian Academy of Sciences. No. B367, Laborer and factory.

1947, May 1
B363 SP252 1000 l + 1000 l dk ol brn .30 *.50*
B364 SP252 1500 l + 1500 l red brn .30 *.50*
B365 SP252 2000 l + 2000 l blue .30 *.50*
B366 SP252 2500 l + 2500 l red vio .30 *.50*
B367 SP252 3000 l + 3000 l crim rose .30 *.50*
Nos. B363-B367 (5) 1.50 *2.50*

No. 650 Surcharged in Carmine

1947, Sept. 6 *Perf. 13½*
B368 A234 2 l + 3 l on 36,000 l vio 1.00 *2.00*

Balkan Games of 1947, Bucharest.

Type of 1947 Surcharged in Carmine

Design: Cathedral of Curtea de Arges.

1947, Oct. 30 ***Imperf.***
B369 A235 5 l + 5 l brt ultra .70 *1.00*

Soviet-Romanian Congress, Nov. 1-7.

Plowing — SP257

Perf. 14x14½

1947, Oct. 5 **Photo.** **Wmk. 276**
B370 SP257 1 l + 1 l shown .25 .25
B371 SP257 2 l + 2 l Sawmill .25 .25
B372 SP257 3 l + 3 l Refinery .25 .25
B373 SP257 4 l + 4 l Steel mill .25 .25
Nos. B370-B373,CB12 (5) 1.70 1.70

17th Congress of the General Assoc. of Romanian Engineers.

Allegory of Industry, Science and Agriculture — SP258

Winged Man Holding Hammer and Sickle SP259

1947, Nov. 10 *Perf. 14½x14*
B374 SP258 2 l + 10 l rose lake .30 .30
B375 SP259 7 l + 10 l bluish blk .30 .30

2nd Trade Union Conf., Nov. 10.

SP260

SP264

Designs: 1 l+1 l, Convoy of Food for Moldavia. 2 l+2 l, "Everything for the Front-Everything for Victory." 3 l+3 l, Woman, child and hospital. 4 l+4 l, "Help the Famine-stricken Regions." 5 l+5 l, "Three Years of Action."

1947, Nov. 7 *Perf. 14*
B376 SP260 1 l + 1 l dk gray bl .30 *.35*
B377 SP260 2 l + 2 l dk brn .30 *.35*
B378 SP260 3 l + 3 l rose lake .30 *.35*
B379 SP260 4 l + 4 l brt ultra .30 *.35*
B380 SP264 5 l + 5 l red .30 *.35*
Nos. B376-B380 (5) 1.50 *1.75*

Issued in sheets of eight.

Discus Thrower — SP265

Balkan Games of 1947: 2 l+2 l, Runner. 5 l+5 l, Boy and girl athletes.

Wmk. 276

1948, Feb. **Photo.** *Perf. 13½*
B381 SP265 1 l + 1 l dk brn .45 *.50*
B382 SP265 2 l + 2 l car lake .60 *.65*
B383 SP265 5 l + 5 l blue 1.00 *1.25*
Nos. B381-B383,CB13-CB14 (5) 5.05 *4.10*

Labor — SP266

Youths Following Filimon Sarbu Banner — SP269

3 l+3 l, Agriculture. 5 l+5 l, Education.

1948, Mar. 15
B384 SP266 2 l + 2 l dk sl bl .35 *.70*
B385 SP266 3 l + 3 l gray grn .40 *.70*
B386 SP266 5 l + 5 l red brn .50 *.70*

Imperf

B387 SP269 8 l + 8 l dk car rose .70 *.70*
Nos. B384-B387,CB15 (5) 3.05 *3.40*

No. B387 issued in triangular sheets of 4.

Gliders — SP270

Sailboat Race SP271

Designs: No. B389, Early plane. No. B390, Plane over farm. No. B391, Transport plane. B393, Training ship, Mircea. B394, Danube ferry. B395, S.S. Transylvania.

1948, July 26 *Perf. 14x14½*
B388 SP270 2 l + 2 l blue 1.50 1.50
B389 SP270 5 l + 5 l pur 1.50 1.50
B390 SP270 8 l + 8 l dk car rose 2.50 2.50
B391 SP270 10 l + 10 l choc 3.25 3.25
B392 SP271 2 l + 2 l dk grn 1.50 1.50
B393 SP271 5 l + 5 l slate 1.50 1.50
B394 SP271 8 l + 8 l brt bl 2.50 2.50
B395 SP271 10 l + 10 l ver 3.25 3.25
Nos. B388-B395 (8) 17.50 17.50

Air and Sea Communications Day.

Type of Regular Issue and

Torch, Pen, Ink and Flag SP272

Alexandru Sahia — SP273

Perf. 14x13½, 13½x14

1948, Sept. 12

B396 A241 5 l + 5 l crimson .70 .70
B397 SP272 10 l + 10 l violet 1.10 1.10
B398 SP273 15 l + 15 l blue 1.50 1.50
Nos. B396-B398 (3) 3.30 3.30

Week of the Democratic Press, Sept. 12-19.

Nos. B396-B398 were also issued imperf. Value, unused $4.50, used $7.

1,500 sets of Nos. 695, B396-B398 perf and B396-B398 imperf were overprinted at "The Week of the Democratic Press" exposition. These stamps were not recognized by the Romanian PTT, although some examples were used on items mailed from the exposition post office.

Romanian-Soviet Association Emblem — SP274

Design: 15 l+15 l, Spasski Tower, Kremlin.

1948, Oct. 29 ***Perf. 14***

B399 SP274 10 l + 10 l gray grn 2.50 *3.00*
B400 SP274 15 l + 15 l dp ultra 3.00 *4.50*

No. B399 was issued in sheets of 50 stamps and 50 labels.

Symbols of United Labor SP275

Agriculture SP276

Industry — SP277

1948, May 1 ***Perf. 14x13½, 13½x14***

B401 SP275 8 l + 8 l red 1.50 *2.00*
B402 SP276 10 l + 10 l ol grn 1.75 *2.50*
B403 SP277 12 l + 12 l red brn 3.00 *3.75*
Nos. B401-B403 (3) 6.25 *8.25*

Labor Day, May 1. See No. CB17.

Automatic Riflemen — SP278

Soldiers Cutting Barbed Wire SP279

No. B406, Field Artillery. No. B407, Tank. No. B408, Warship.

Flags and Dates: 23 Aug 1944-9 Mai 1945

1948, May 9

B404 SP278 1.50 l + 1.50 l shown .35 .35
B405 SP279 2 l + 2 l shown .35 .35
B406 SP279 4 l + 4 l multi .65 .65
B407 SP279 7.50 l + 7.50 l multi 1.25 1.25
B408 SP279 8 l + 8 l multi 1.40 1.40
Nos. B404-B408,CB18-CB19 (7) 18.00 18.00

Honoring the Romanian Army.

Nicolae Balcescu — SP280

Balcescu and Revolutionists SP281

Balcescu, Sandor Petöfi and Revolutionists — SP282

Revolution of 1848: #B412, Balcescu and revolutionists.

1948, June 1 ***Perf. 13x13½***

B409 SP280 2 l + 2 l car lake .40 *.60*
B410 SP281 5 l + 5 l dk vio .55 *.70*
B411 SP282 10 l + 10 l dk ol brn .75 *1.25*
B412 SP280 36 l + 18 l dp bl 1.75 *2.25*
Nos. B409-B412 (4) 3.45 *4.80*

For surcharges see Nos. 856-859.

Loading Freighter SP283

Designs: 3 l+3 l, Lineman. 11 l+11 l, Transport plane. 15 l+15 l, Railroad train.

Wmk. 289

1948, Dec. 10 Photo. ***Perf. 14***

Center in Black

B413 SP283 1 l + 1 l dk grn .65 *1.10*
B414 SP283 3 l + 3 l redsh brn .75 *1.10*
B415 SP283 11 l + 11 l dp bl 3.50 3.00
B416 SP283 15 l + 15 l red 4.00 *4.50*
a. Sheet of 4 20.00 *25.00*
Nos. B413-B416 (4) 8.90 *9.70*

No. B416a contains four imperf. stamps similar to Nos. B413-B416 in changed colors, center in brown. No gum.

Runners — SP284

Parade of Athletes SP285

1948, Dec. 31 ***Perf. 13x13½, 13½x13***

B421 SP284 5 l + 5 l grn 3.50 3.50
B422 SP285 10 l + 10 l brn vio 5.75 5.75

Imperf

B423 SP284 5 l + 5 l brown 3.50 3.50
B424 SP285 10 l + 10 l red 5.75 5.75
Nos. B421-B424,CB20-CB21 (6) 48.50 48.50

Nos. B421-B424 were issued in sheets of 4.

Souvenir Sheet

SP286

1950, Jan. 27

B425 SP286 10 l carmine 5.00 3.25

Philatelic exhib., Bucharest. Sold for 50 lei.

Crossing the Buzau, by Denis Auguste Marie Raffet — SP287

1967, Nov. 15 Engr. ***Perf. 13½***

B426 SP287 55b + 45b ocher & indigo .90 .45

Stamp Day.

Old Bucharest, 18th Century Painting — SP288

1968, Nov. 15 Photo. ***Perf. 13½***

B427 SP288 55b + 45b label 1.10 .60

Stamp Day. Simulated label has printed perforations. See Nos. 2386A, B428-B429.

1969, Nov. 15

Design: Courtyard, by M. Bouquet.

B428 SP288 55b + 45b label 1.00 .60

Stamp Day. Simulated label at right of stamp has printed perforations.

1970, Nov. 15

Mail Coach in the Winter, by Emil Volkers.

B429 SP288 55b + 45b multi 1.10 .70

Stamp Day. No simulated label.

Lady with Letter, by Sava Hentia SP289

1971, Nov. 15 Photo. ***Perf. 13½***

B430 SP289 1.10 l + 90b multi 1.25 .75

Stamp Day. Label portion below stamp has printed perforations and shows Romania No. 12.

Portrait Type of Regular Issue

Designs: 4 l+2 l, Aman at his Desk, by B. Iscovescu. 6 l+2 l, The Poet Alecsandri with his Family, by N. Livaditti.

1973, June 20 Photo. ***Perf. 13½***

B432 A728 4 l + 2 l multi 1.50 .60

Souvenir Sheet

B433 A728 6 l + 2 l multi 3.00 3.00

No. B433 contains one 38x50mm stamp.

Map of Europe with Emblem Marking Bucharest SP291

1974, June 25 Photo. ***Perf. 13½***

B435 SP291 4 l + 3 l multi 1.50 .50

EUROMAX, European Exhibition of Maximaphily, Bucharest, Oct. 6-13.

Marketplace, Sibiu — SP292

1974, Nov. 15 Photo. ***Perf. 13½***

B436 SP292 2.10 l + 1.90 l multi 1.10 .40

Stamp Day.

No. B436 Overprinted in Red: "EXPOZITIA FILATELICA 'NATIONALA '74' / 15-24 noiembrie / Bucuresti"

1974, Nov. 15

B437 SP292 2.10 l + 1.90 l multi 2.25 2.25

NATIONALA '74 Philatelic Exhibition, Bucharest, Nov. 15-24.

Post Office, Bucharest SP293

Stamp Day: 2.10 l+1.90 l, like No. B438, side view.

1975, Nov. 15 Photo. *Perf. 13½*
B438 SP293 1.50 l + 1.50 l multi .85 .45
B439 SP293 2.10 l + 1.90 l multi 1.40 .65

No. 2612 Surcharged and Overprinted "EXPOZITIA FILATELICA / BUCURESTI / 12-19.IX.1976"

1976, Sept. 12 Photo. *Perf. 13½*
B440 A787 3.60 l + 1.80 l 4.00 3.25

Philatelic Exhibition, Bucharest, Sept. 12-19.

Elena Cuza, by Theodor Aman — SP294

1976, Nov. 15 Photo. *Perf. 13½*
B441 SP294 2.10 l + 1.90 l multi 1.10 .70

Stamp Day.

Independence Type of 1977

Stamp Day: Battle of Rahova, after etching.

1977, May 9 Photo. *Perf. 13½*
B442 A806 4.80 l + 2 l multi 1.50 .40

Dispatch Rider Handing Letter to Officer — SP295

1977, Nov. Photo. *Perf. 13½*
B443 SP295 2.10 l + 1.90 l multi 1.25 .85

Socfilex Type of 1979

Flower Paintings by Luchian: 4 l+2 l, Field flowers. 10 l+5 l, Roses.

1979, July 27 Photo. *Perf. 13½*
B445 A847 4 l + 2 l multi 1.10 1.10

Souvenir Sheet

B446 A847 10 l + 5 l multi 3.00 3.00

Socfilex Intl. Phil. Exhib., Bucharest, Oct. 26-Nov. 1. #B446 contains one 50x38mm stamp.

Stamp Day SP297

1979, Dec. 12 Photo. *Perf. 13½*
B447 SP297 2.10 l + 1.90 l multi .80 .25

Souvenir Sheet

Stamp Day — SP298

1980, July 1 Photo. *Perf. 13½*
B448 SP298 5 l + 5 l multi 2.00 2.00

December 1989 Revolution — SP299

Designs: 50b+50b, Palace on fire, Bucharest. 1 l+ 1 l, Crowd, Timisoara. 1.50 l+1 l, Soldiers & crowd, Tirgu Mures. 2 l+1 l, Soldiers in Bucharest, vert. 3 l+1 l, Funeral, Timisoara. 3.50 l+1 l, Crowd celebrating, Brasov, vert. 4 l+1 l, Crowd with flags, Sibiu. No. B456, Cemetery, Bucharest. No. B457, Foreign aid.

1990, Oct. 1 Photo. *Perf. 13½*
B449 SP299 50b +50b multi .25 .25
B450 SP299 1 l +1 l multi .25 .25
B451 SP299 1.50 l +1 l multi .25 .25
B452 SP299 2 l +1 l multi .30 .25
B453 SP299 3 l +1 l multi .35 .25
B454 SP299 3.50 l +1 l multi .40 .25
B455 SP299 4 l +1 l multi .45 .25
B456 SP299 5 l +2 l multi .60 .25
Nos. B449-B456 (8) 2.85 2.00

Souvenir Sheet

B457 SP299 5 l +2 l multi 1.25 1.25

No. B457 contains one 54x42mm stamp.

Stamp Day — SP300

1992, July 15 Photo. *Perf. 13½*
B458 SP300 10 l +4 l multi .25 .25

For surcharge see No. B460.

Stamp Day — SP301

1993, Apr. 26 Photo. *Perf. 13½*
B459 SP301 15 l +10 l multi .25 .25

No. B458 Surcharged in Red

1993, Nov. 9 Photo. *Perf. 13½*
B460 SP300 70 l +45 l on 10 l+4 l .50 .50

National History Museum, Bucharest SP302

1994, July 15 Photo. *Perf. 13½*
B461 SP302 90 l +60 l multi .30 .25

Stamp Day.

Souvenir Sheet

Romanian Olympic Committee, 90th Anniv. — SP303

No. B462: a, Pierre de Coubertin. b, Greece #125 (54x42mm). c, George V. Bibescu.

2004, Mar. 25 Photo. *Perf. 13¼*
B462 SP303 16,000 l +5000 l Sheet of 3, #a-c 4.25 4.25

First Romanian Philatelic Exhibition, 80th Anniv. — SP304

2004, July 15 Photo. *Perf. 13¼*
B463 SP304 21,000 l +10,000 l multi 2.00 2.00

Litho.
Imperf

B464 SP304 21,000 l +10,000 l multi 2.00 2.00

AIR POST STAMPS

Capt. C. G. Craiu's Airplane AP1

Wmk. 95 Vertical

1928 Photo. *Perf. 13½*
C1 AP1 1 l red brown 3.00 2.50
C2 AP1 2 l brt blue 3.00 2.50
C3 AP1 5 l carmine rose 3.00 2.50

Wmk. 95 Horizontal

C4 AP1 1 l red brown 4.00 3.25
C5 AP1 2 l brt blue 4.00 3.25
C6 AP1 5 l carmine rose 4.00 3.25
Nos. C1-C6 (6) 21.00 17.25

Nos. C4-C6 also come with white gum.

Nos. C4-C6 Overprinted

1930
C7 AP1 1 l red brown 8.00 6.75
C8 AP1 2 l brt blue 8.00 6.75
a. Vert. pair, imperf. btwn. *175.00*
C9 AP1 5 l carmine rose 8.00 6.75
Nos. C7-C9 (3) 24.00 20.25

Same Overprint on Nos. C1-C3
Wmk. 95 Vertical

C10 AP1 1 l red brown 50.00 50.00
C11 AP1 2 l brt blue 50.00 50.00
C12 AP1 5 l carmine rose 50.00 50.00
Nos. C10-C12 (3) 150.00 150.00
Nos. C7-C12 (6) 174.00 170.25

Nos. C7-C12 for the accession of King Carol II.

Excellent connterfeits are known of Nos. C10-C12.

King Carol II — AP2

Bluish Paper

1930, Oct. 4 Unwmk.
C13 AP2 1 l dk violet 2.00 3.50
C14 AP2 2 l gray green 2.50 3.50
C15 AP2 5 l red brown 5.00 3.50
C16 AP2 10 l brt blue 9.00 3.50
Nos. C13-C16 (4) 18.50 14.00
Set, never hinged 36.50

Junkers Monoplane AP3

Monoplanes AP7

Designs: 3 l, Monoplane with biplane behind. 5 l, Biplane. 10 l, Monoplane flying leftward.

1931, Nov. 4 Wmk. 230
C17 AP3 2 l dull green 1.50 1.25
C18 AP3 3 l carmine 2.00 1.75
C19 AP3 5 l red brown 2.50 2.00
C20 AP3 10 l blue 6.00 4.50
C21 AP7 20 l dk violet 15.00 6.00
Nos. C17-C21 (5) 27.00 15.50
Set, never hinged 40.00

Exist imperforate. Value $350, unused or used.

Souvenir Sheets

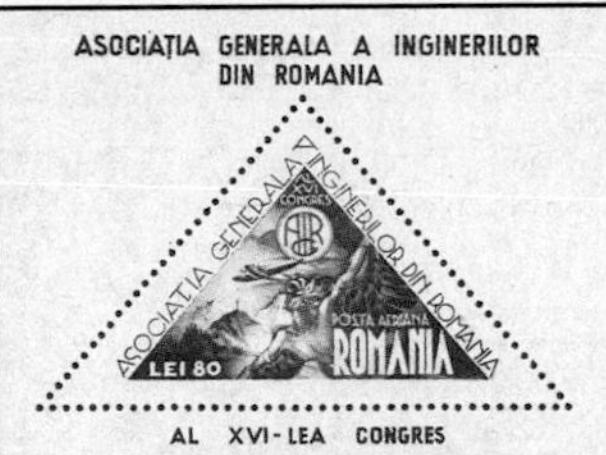
Plane over Resita — AP8

Plane over Sinaia — AP9

Wmk. 276

1945, Oct. 1 Photo. *Perf. 13*

Without Gum

C22 AP8 80 l slate green 17.50 25.00

Imperf

C23 AP9 80 l magenta 10.00 17.50

16th Congress of the General Assoc. of Romanian Engineers.

Catalogue values for unused stamps in this section, from this point to the end of the section, are for Never Hinged items.

Plane AP10

Design: 500 l, Aviator and planes.

1946, Sept. 5 *Perf. 13½x13*

C24 AP10 200 l yel grn & bl 3.00 6.00
C25 AP10 500 l org red & dl bl 3.00 6.00

Sheets of four with marginal inscription.

Lockheed 12 Electra — AP12

1946, Oct. *Perf. 11½*

C26 AP12 300 l crimson 1.00 1.00
a. Pair, #C26, CB6 2.25 2.25

Sheet contains 8 each of Nos. C26 and CB6, arranged so se-tenant or normal pairs are available.

CGM Congress Emblem — AP13

1947, Mar. Wmk. 276 *Perf. 13x14*

C27 AP13 1100 l blue .50 1.00

Congress of the United Labor Unions ("CGM"). Printed in sheets of 15.

"May 1" Supported by Parachutes AP14

Designs: No. C29, Air Force monument. No. C30, Plane over rural road.

1947, May 4 *Perf. 11½*

C28 AP14 3000 l vermilion .30 .60
C29 AP14 3000 l grnsh gray .30 .60
C30 AP14 3000 l blk brown .30 .60
Nos. C28-C30 (3) .90 1.80

Printed in sheets of four with marginal inscriptions.

Plane and Conference Banner — AP17

1947, Nov. 10 *Perf. 14*

C31 AP17 11 l bl & dp car 1.25 1.25

2nd Trade Union Conference, Nov. 10.

Emblem of the Republic and Factories AP18

Industry and Agriculture — AP19

Transportation — AP20

Perf. 14x13½

1948, Nov. 22 Wmk. 289 Photo.

C32 AP18 30 l cerise .75 .25
a. 30 l carmine ('50) .85 .45
C33 AP19 50 l dk slate grn 1.25 .50
C34 AP20 100 l ultra 3.75 1.50
Nos. C32-C34 (3) 5.75 2.25

No. C32a issued May 10. For surcharges see Nos. C37-C39.

Agriculture — AP21

Design: 50 l, Transportation.

1951-52 Wmk. 358 *Perf. 13½*

C35 AP21 30 l dk green ('52) 3.75 3.00
C36 AP21 50 l red brown 3.00 2.50

1951-55 Five Year Plan.
For surcharges see Nos. C40-C41.

Nos. C32-C36 Surcharged with New Values in Blue or Carmine

1952 Wmk. 289 *Perf. 14x13½*

C37 AP18 3b on 30 l car (Bl) 3.00 2.25
a. 3b on 30 l cerise (Bl) *12.00 8.50*
C38 AP19 3b on 50 l dk sl grn 1.00 .70
C39 AP20 3b on 100 l ultra 1.00 .70

Perf. 13½

Wmk. 358

C40 AP21 1 l on 30 l dk grn *8.00 1.50*
C41 AP21 1 l on 50 l red brn *8.00 1.50*
Nos. C37-C41 (5) 21.00 6.65

Nos. 706 and 707 Surcharged in Blue or Carmine

1953 Wmk. 289 *Perf. 13½, 14*

C43 A250 3 l on 20 l org brn *35.00 25.00*
C44 A251 5 l on 30 l brt bl (C) *45.00 32.50*

Plane facing right and surcharge arranged to fit design on No. C44.

Plane over City — AP22

Designs: 55b, Plane over Mountains. 1.75 l, over Harvest fields. 2.25 l, over Seashore.

Perf. 14½x14

1956, Dec. 15 Photo. Wmk. 358

C45 AP22 20b brt bl, org & grn .55 .80
C46 AP22 55b brt bl, grn & ocher 1.25 .80
C47 AP22 1.75 l brt bl & red org 3.75 1.25
C48 AP22 2.55 l brt bl & red org 5.25 2.00
Nos. C45-C48 (4) 10.80 4.85

Sputnik 1 and Earth — AP23

3.75 l, Sputniks 1 and 2 circling globe.

1957, Nov. 6 *Perf. 14*

C49 AP23 25b brt ultra .65 .25
C50 AP23 25b dk bl grn .65 .25
C51 AP23 3.75 l brt ultra 3.50 .60
a. Pair, #C49, C51 + label 6.00 3.75
C52 AP23 3.75 l dk bl grn 3.50 .60
a. Pair, #C50, C52 + label 6.00 3.75
Nos. C49-C52 (4) 8.30 1.70

Each sheet contains 27 triptychs with the center rows arranged tete-beche.

In 1958 Nos. C49-C52 were overprinted: 1.) "Expozitia Universal a Bruxelles 1958" and star. 2.) Large star. 3.) Small star. Value, both pairs: unused $30, used $20. Exist imperf. Value, both pairs: unused $60, used $50.

Animal Type of Regular Issue, 1957

Birds: 3.30 l, Black-headed gull, horiz. 5 l, Sea eagle, horiz.

Perf. 14x13½

1957, Dec. 27 Wmk. 358

C53 A445 3.30 l ultra & gray 4.00 1.00
C54 A445 5 l carmine & org 5.75 1.25

Armed Forces Type of Regular Issue

Design: Flier and planes.

Perf. 13½x13

1958, Oct. 2 Unwmk. Photo.

C55 A458 3.30 l brt violet 1.60 .50

Day of the Armed Forces, Oct. 2.

Earth and Sputnik 3 Orbit AP24

1958, Sept. 20 *Perf. 14x13½*

C56 AP24 3.25 l indigo & ocher 3.75 .75

Launching of Sputnik 3, May 15, 1958.

Type of Regular Issue, 1958

Souvenir Sheet

Design: Tête bêche pair of 27pa of 1858.

Perf. 11½

1958, Nov. 15 Unwmk. Engr.

C57 A462 10 l blue, bluish 35.00 35.00

A similar sheet, printed in dull red and imperf., exists. Values, unused $45; used $22.50.

No. C57 on bluish and white papers was overprinted in 1959 in vermilion to commemorate the 10th anniv. of the State Philatelic Trade. Values: unused $100; used $125.

Lunik I Leaving Earth AP25

1959, Feb. 4 Photo. *Perf. 14*

C58 AP25 3.25 l vio bl, *pnksh* 10.00 1.10

Launching of the "first artificial planet of the solar system."

For surcharge see No. C70.

Frederic Joliot-Curie — AP26

1959, Apr. 25 *Perf. 13½x14*

C59 AP26 3.25 l ultra 3.00 .60

Frederic Joliot-Curie; 10th anniv. of the World Peace Movement.

Rock Thrush AP27

Birds: 20b, European golden oriole. 35b, Lapwing. 40b, Barn swallow. No. C64, Goldfinch. No. C65, Great spotted woodpecker. No. C66, Great tit. 1 l, Bullfinch. 1.55 l, Long-tailed tit. 5 l, Wall creeper. Nos. C62-C67 vertical.

1959, June 25 Litho. *Perf. 14*

Birds in Natural Colors

C60 AP27 10b gray, *cr* .25 .25
C61 AP27 20b gray, *grysh* .25 .25
C62 AP27 35b gray, *grysh* .30 .25
C63 AP27 40b gray & red, *pnksh* .40 .25
C64 AP27 55b gray, *buff* .55 .25
C65 AP27 55b gray, *grnsh* .55 .25
C66 AP27 55b gray & ol, *grysh* .55 .25
C67 AP27 1 l gray and red, *cr* 2.00 .25
C68 AP27 1.55 l gray & red, *pnksh* 2.50 .25
C69 AP27 5 l gray, *grnsh* 6.00 2.25
Nos. C60-C69 (10) 13.35 4.50

No. C58 Surcharged in Red

1959, Sept. 14 Photo. Unwmk.

C70 AP25 5 l on 3.25 l 7.50 3.50

1st Russian rocket to reach the moon, 9/14/59.

Miniature Sheet

Prince Vlad Tepes and Document — AP28

1959, Sept. 15 Engr. *Perf. 11½x11*

C71 AP28 20 l violet brn *150.00 150.00*

500th anniv. of the founding of Bucharest.

Sport Type of Regular Issue, 1959

1959, Oct. 5 Litho. *Perf. 13½*

C72 A474 2.80 l Boating 2.50 .50

Soviet Rocket, Globe, Dog and Rabbit — AP29

Photograph of Far Side of the Moon — AP30

Design: 1.75 l, Trajectory of Lunik 3, which hit the moon.

Perf. 14, 13½ (AP30)

1959, Dec. Photo. Wmk. 358

C73 AP29	1.55 l dk blue	3.00	.35
C74 AP30	1.60 l dk vio bl, *buff*	3.50	.55
C75 AP29	1.75 l dk blue	3.50	.55
	Nos. C73-C75 (3)	10.00	1.45

Soviet conquest of space.

Animal Type of Regular Issue, 1960.

Designs: 1.30 l, Golden eagle. 1.75 l, Black grouse. 2 l, Lammergeier.

Unwmk.

1960, Mar. 3 Engr. *Perf. 14*

C76 A480 1.30 l dk blue	1.75	.40
C77 A480 1.75 l olive grn	1.75	.40
C78 A480 2 l dk carmine	1.75	.50
Nos. C76-C78 (3)	5.25	1.30

Aurel Vlaicu and Plane of 1910 AP31

Bucharest Airport and Turbo-Jet — AP32

Designs: 20b, Plane and Aurel Vlaicu. 35b, Amphibian ambulance plane. 40b, Plane spraying crops. 55b, Pilot and planes, vert. 1.75 l, Parachutes at aviation sports meet.

1960, June 15 Litho. Unwmk.

C79 AP31 10b yellow & brn	.25	.25
C80 AP31 20b red org & brn	.25	.25

Photo. Wmk. 358

C81 AP31 35b crimson	.40	.25
C82 AP31 40b violet	.55	.25
C83 AP31 55b blue	.80	.25

Litho. Unwmk.

C84 AP32 1.60 l vio bl, yel & emer	2.00	.40
C85 AP32 1.75 l bl, red, brn & pale grn	2.50	.55
Nos. C79-C85 (7)	6.75	2.20

50th anniv. of the first Romanian airplane flight by Aurel Vlaicu.

For surcharge see No. C145.

Bucharest Airport — AP33

1960 Wmk. 358 Photo. *Perf. 14*

C86 AP33 3.20 l brt ultra 1.50 .25

Type of Regular Issue, 1960

Black Sea Resort: 2 l, Beach at Mamaia.

1960, Aug. 2 Litho. Unwmk.

C87 A491 2 l grn, org & lt bl 1.50 .50

Sputnik 4 Flying into Space AP34

1960, June 8 Photo. Wmk. 358

C88 AP34 55b deep blue 2.50 .25

Launching of Sputnik 4, May 15, 1960.

Saturnia Pyri AP35

Papilio Machaon AP36

Limenitis Populi — AP37

Designs: 40b, Chrisophanus virgaureae. 1.60 l, Acherontia atropos. 1.75 l, Apatura iris.

Perf. 13, 14x12½, 14

1960, Oct. 10 Typo. Unwmk.

C89 AP35 10b multi	.25	.25
C90 AP37 20b multi	.25	.25
C91 AP37 40b multi	.35	.25
C92 AP36 55b multi	.65	.25
C93 AP36 1.60 l multi	2.00	.35
C94 AP36 1.75 l multi, horiz.	2.75	.35
Nos. C89-C94 (6)	6.25	1.70

Compass Rose and Jet — AP38

Perf. 13½x14

1960, Nov. 1 Photo. Wmk. 358

C95 AP38 55b brt bl + 45b label .50 .25

Stamp Day.

Skier AP39

Slalom — AP40

Designs: 25b, Skiers going up. 40b, Bobsled. 55b, Ski jump. 1 l, Mountain climber. 1.55 l, Long-distance skier.

Perf. 14x13½, 13½x14

1961, Mar. 18 Litho. Unwmk.

C96 AP39 10b olive & gray	.25	.25
C97 AP40 20b gray & dk red	.25	.25
C98 AP40 25b gray & bl grn	.35	.25
C99 AP40 40b gray & pur	.35	.25
C100 AP39 55b gray & ultra	.45	.25
C101 AP40 1 l gray & brn lake	.75	.25
C102 AP39 1.55 l gray & brn	1.10	.25
Nos. C96-C102 (7)	3.50	1.75

Exist imperf. with changed colors. Value, set $5.

Maj. Yuri A. Gagarin — AP41

Design: 3.20 l, Gagarin in space capsule and globe with orbit, horiz.

Perf. 14x14½, 14½x14

1961, Apr. 19 Photo. Unwmk.

C103 AP41 1.35 l brt blue	1.00	.30
C104 AP41 3.20 l ultra	2.25	.60

No. C104 exists imperf. in dark carmine rose. Value unused $7.50, canceled $3.25.

Eclipse over Republic Palace Place, Bucharest AP42

1.75 l, Total Eclipse, Scinteia House, telescope.

Perf. 14x13½

1961, June 13 Wmk. 358

C106 AP42 1.60 l ultra	1.25	.30
C107 AP42 1.75 l dk blue	1.50	.30

Total solar eclipse of Feb. 15, 1961.

Maj. Gherman S. Titov — AP43

55b, "Peace" and Vostok 2 rocket. 1.75 l, Yuri A. Gagarin and Gherman S. Titov, horiz.

Perf. 13½x14

1961, Sept. 11 Unwmk.

C108 AP43 55b dp blue	.55	.25
C109 AP43 1.35 l dp purple	.80	.25
C110 AP43 1.75 l dk carmine	1.25	.25
Nos. C108-C110 (3)	2.60	.75

Issued to honor the Russian space navigators Y. A. Gagarin and G. S. Titov.

Globe and Stamps — AP44

1961, Nov. 15 Litho. *Perf. 13½x14*

C111 AP44 55b multi + 45b label 1.00 .25

Stamp Day.

Railroad Station, Constanta AP45

Buildings: 20b, Tower, RPR Palace place, vert. 55b, Congress hall, Bucharest. 75b, Mill, Hunedoara. 1 l, Apartment houses, Bucharest. 1.20 l, Circus, Bucharest. 1.75 l, Worker's Club, Mangalia.

Perf. 13½x14, 14x13½

1961, Nov. 20 Typo.

C112 AP45 20b multi	.25	.25
C113 AP45 40b multi	.25	.25
C114 AP45 55b multi	.25	.25
C115 AP45 75b multi	.30	.25
C116 AP45 1 l multi	.40	.25
C117 AP45 1.20 l multi	.75	.25
C118 AP45 1.75 l multi	1.10	.25
Nos. C112-C118 (7)	3.30	1.75

Space Exploration Stamps and Dove AP46

Design: Each stamp shows a different group of Romanian space exploration stamps.

1962, July 27 *Perf. 14x13½*

C119 AP46 35b yellow brn	.25	.25
C120 AP46 55b green	.30	.25
C121 AP46 1.35 l blue	.60	.25
C122 AP46 1.75 l rose red	1.10	.25
a. Sheet of 4	3.00	1.50
Nos. C119-C122 (4)	2.25	1.00

Peaceful space exploration.

No. C122a contains four imperf. stamps similar to Nos. C119-C122 in changed colors and with one dove covering all four stamps. Stamps are printed together without space between.

Andrian G. Nikolayev — AP47

Designs: 1.60 l, Globe and trajectories of Vostoks 3 and 4. 1.75 l, Pavel R. Popovich.

Perf. 13½x14

1962, Aug. 20 Photo. Unwmk.

C123 AP47 55b purple .30 .25
C124 AP47 1.60 l dark blue .90 .30
C125 AP47 1.75 l rose claret 1.25 .30
Nos. C123-C125 (3) 2.45 .85

1st Russian group space flight of Vostoks 3 and 4, Aug. 11-15, 1962.

Exhibition Hall — AP48

1962, Oct. 12 Litho. *Perf. 14x13*

C126 AP48 1.60 l bl, vio bl & org 1.50 .25

4th Sample Fair, Bucharest.

The Coachmen by Szatmary — AP49

1962, Nov. 15 *Perf. 13½x14*

C127 AP49 55b + 45b label 1.25 .35

Stamp Day. Alternating label shows No. 14 on cover.

No. C127 Overprinted in Violet

1963, Mar. 30

C128 AP49 55b + 45b label 3.50 2.00

Romanian Philatelists' Assoc. meeting at Bucharest, Mar. 30.

Sighisoara Glass and Crockery Factory AP50

Industrial Plants: 40b, Govora soda works. 55b, Tirgul-Jiu wood processing factory. 1 l, Savinesti chemical plant (synthetic fibers). 1.55 l, Hunedoara metal factory. 1.75 l, Brazi thermal power station.

Perf. 14x13

1963, Apr. 10 Unwmk. Photo.

C129 AP50 30b dk bl & red .30 .25
C130 AP50 40b sl grn & pur .30 .25
C131 AP50 55b brn red & dp bl .30 .25
C132 AP50 1 l vio & brn .30 .25
C133 AP50 1.551 ver & dk bl .70 .25
C134 AP50 1.75 l dk bl & magenta 1.00 .25
Nos. C129-C134 (6) 2.90 1.50

Industrial achievements.

Lunik 4 Approaching Moon — AP51

1963, Apr. 29 *Perf. 13½x14*

C135 AP51 55b dk ultra & red .45 .25

Imperf

C136 AP51 1.75 l vio & red 1.00 .25

Moon flight of Lunik 4, Apr. 2, 1963.

Steam Locomotive AP52

Designs: 55b, Diesel locomotive. 75b, Trolley bus. 1.35 l, Passenger ship. 1.75 l, Plane.

1963, July 10 Litho. *Perf. 14½x13*

C137 AP52 40b multi .35 .25
C138 AP52 55b multi .40 .25
C139 AP52 75b multi .60 .25
C140 AP52 1.35 l multi 1.00 .30
C141 AP52 1.75 l multi 1.40 .25
Nos. C137-C141 (5) 3.75 1.30

Valeri Bykovski AP53

Designs: 1.20 l, Bykovski, vert. 1.60 l, Tereshkova, vert. 1.75 l, Valentina Tereshkova.

1963 Photo.

C142 AP53 55b blue .30 .25
C143 AP53 1.75 l rose red 1.40 .30

Souvenir Sheet

Perf. 13

C144 Sheet of 2 2.75 .80
a. AP53 1.20 l ultra .60 .30
b. AP53 1.60 l ultra .75 .40

Space flights of Valeri Bykovski, June 14-19, and Valentina Tereshkova, first woman cosmonaut, June 16-19, 1963.

No. C79 Surcharged and Overprinted "1913-1963 50 ani de la moarte"

Unwmk.

1963, Sept. 15 Litho. *Perf. 14*

C145 AP31 1.75 l on 10b 2.50 .95

50th death anniv. of Aurel Vlaicu, aviation pioneer.

Exists with "i" of "lei," missing.

Centenary Stamp of 1958 AP54

Stamps on Stamps: 40b, Sputnik 2 and Laika, No. 1200. 55b, Yuri A. Gagarin, No. C104a. 1.20 l, Nikolayev and Popovich, Nos. C123, C125. 1.55 l, Postal Administration Bldg. and letter carrier, No. 965.

1963, Nov. 15 Photo. *Perf. 14x13½*

Size: 38x26mm

C146 AP54 20b lt bl & dk brn .25 .25
C147 AP54 40b brt pink & dk bl .25 .25
C148 AP54 55b lt ultra & dk car rose .25 .25
C149 AP54 1.20 l ocher & pur .45 .25
C150 AP54 1.55 l sal pink & ol gray .65 .25
Nos. C146-C150,CB22 (6) 3.25 1.75

15th UPU Congress, Vienna.

Pavel R. Popovich AP55

Astronauts and flag: 5b, Yuri A. Gagarin. 10b, Gherman S. Titov. 20b, John H. Glenn, Jr. 35b, M. Scott Carpenter. 40b, Andrian G. Nikolayev. 60b, Walter M. Schirra. 75b, Gordon L. Cooper. 1 l, Valeri Bykovski. 1.40 l, Valentina Tereshkova. (5b, 10b, 20b, 35b, 60b and 75b are diamond shaped).

Perf. 13½

1964, Jan. 15 Litho. Unwmk.

Light Blue Background

C151 AP55 5b red, yel & vio bl .30 .25
C152 AP55 10b red, yel & pur .30 .25
C153 AP55 20b red, ultra & ol gray .30 .25
C154 AP55 35b red, ultra & sl bl .30 .25
C155 AP55 40b red, yel & ultra .30 .25
C156 AP55 55b red, yel & ultra .60 .25
C157 AP55 60b ultra, red & sep .60 .25
C158 AP55 75b red, ultra & dk bl .65 .25
C159 AP55 1 l red, yel & mar .95 .25
C160 AP55 1.40 l red, yel & mar 1.10 .25
Nos. C151-C160 (10) 5.40 2.50

Nos. C151-C160 exist imperf. in changed colors. Value, set $8 unused, $3 used.

A miniature sheet contains one imperf. horizontal 2 l ultramarine and yellow stamp. Size of stamp: 59½x43mm. Value unused $8.50, canceled $4.25.

Modern and 19th Century Post Office Buildings AP56

Engr. & Typo.

1964, Nov. 15 *Perf. 13½*

C161 AP56 1.60 l ultra + 40b label 1.25 .50

Stamp Day. Stamp and label are imperf. between.

Plane Approaching Airport and Coach Leaving Gate — AP57

Engr. & Typo.

1966, Oct. 20 *Perf. 13½*

C162 AP57 55b + 45b label .90 .50

Stamp Day.

Space Exploration Type of Regular Issue

US Achievements in Space: 1.20 l, Early Bird satellite and globe. 1.55 l, Mariner 4 transmitting pictures of the moon. 3.25 l, Gemini 6 & 7, rendezvous in space. 5 l, Gemini 8 meeting Agena rocket, and globe.

1967, Feb. 15 Photo. *Perf. 13½*

C163 A595 1.20 l silver & multi .60 .25
C164 A595 1.55 l silver & multi .75 .25
C165 A595 3.25 l silver & multi 1.00 .35
C166 A595 5 l silver & multi 1.50 .75
Nos. C163-C166 (4) 3.85 1.50

10 years of space exploration.

Plane Spraying Crops — AP58

Designs: 55b, Aerial ambulance over river, horiz. 1 l, Red Cross and plane. 2.40 l, Biplane and Mircea Zorileanu, aviation pioneer.

Perf. 12x12½, 12½x12

1968, Feb. 28 Litho. Unwmk.

C167 AP58 40b bl grn, blk & yel brn .25 .25
C168 AP58 55b multicolored .30 .25
C169 AP58 1 l ultra, pale grn & red org .30 .25
C170 AP58 2.40 l brt rose lil & multi .75 .30
Nos. C167-C170 (4) 1.60 1.05

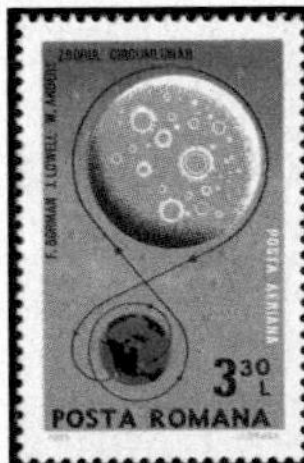

Moon, Earth and Path of Apollo 8 — AP59

Design: No. C172, Soyuz 4 and 5 over globe with map of Russia.

1969 Photo. *Perf. 13½*

C171 AP59 3.30 l multi 1.60 1.60
C172 AP59 3.30 l multi 1.60 1.60

1st manned flight around the Moon, Dec. 21-27, 1968, and the first team flights of the Russian spacecrafts Soyuz 4 and 5, Jan. 16, 1969. See note after Hungary No. C284.

Issued in sheets of 4.

Issued: #C171, Jan. 17, #C172, Mar. 28.

Apollo 9 and Lunar Landing Module over Earth AP60

Design: 2.40 l, Apollo 10 and lunar landing module over moon, vert.

1969, June 15 Photo. *Perf. 13½*

C173 AP60 60b multi .25 .25
C174 AP60 2.40 l multi 1.00 .25

US space explorations, Apollo 9 and 10.

First Man on Moon — AP61

1969, July 24 Photo. *Perf. 13½*

C175 AP61 3.30 l multi 1.90 1.90

Man's first landing on the moon July 20, 1969, US astronauts Neil A. Armstrong and Col. Edwin E. Aldrin, Jr., with Lieut. Col. Michael Collins piloting Apollo 11. Printed in sheets of 4.

1970, June 29

1.50 l, Apollo 13 capsule splashing down in Pacific.

C176 AP61 1.50 l multi .75 .60

Flight and safe landing of Apollo 13, Apr. 11-17, 1970. Printed in sheets of 4.

BAC 1-11 Jet AP62

Design: 2 l, Fuselage BAC 1-11 and control tower, Bucharest airport.

1970, Apr. 6

C177 AP62 60b multi .35 .25
C178 AP62 2 l multi .80 .25

50th anniv. of Romanian civil aviation.

Flood Relief Type of Regular Issue

Design: 60b, Rescue by helicopter.

1970, Sept. 25 Photo. *Perf. 13½*

C179 A671 60b bl gray, blk & olive .25 .25

Publicizing the plight of victims of the Danube flood. See No. 2207a.

Henri Coanda's Model Plane AP63

1970, Dec. 1

C180 AP63 60b multicolored 1.10 .30

Henri Coanda's first flight, 60th anniversary.

Luna 16 on Moon AP64

No. C182, Lunokhod 1, unmanned vehicle on moon. No. C183, US astronaut & vehicle on moon.

1971, Mar. 5 Photo. *Perf. 13½*

C181 AP64 3.30 l silver & multi 1.00 1.00
C182 AP64 3.30 l silver & multi 1.00 1.00
a. Pair, #C181-C182 + 2 labels 2.75 2.75
C183 AP64 3.30 l silver & multi 1.50 1.50
Nos. C181-C183 (3) 3.50 3.50

No. C181 commemorates Luna 16 Russian unmanned, automatic moon mission, Sept. 12-24, 1970 (labels are incorrectly inscribed Oct. 12-24). No. C182 commemorates Lunokhod 1 (Luna 17), Nov. 10-17, 1970. Nos. C181-C182 printed in sheets of 4 stamps, arranged checkerwise, and 4 labels. No. C183 commemorates Apollo 14 moon landing, Jan. 31-Feb. 9. Printed in sheets of 4 with 4 labels showing portraits of US astronauts Alan B. Shepard, Edgar D. Mitchell, Stuart A. Roosa, and Apollo 14 emblem.

Souvenir Sheet

Cosmonauts Patsayev, Dobrovolsky and Volkov — AP65

1971, July 26 Litho. *Perf. 13½*

C184 AP65 6 l black & ultra 6.50 5.00

In memory of Russian cosmonauts Viktor I. Patsayev, Georgi T. Dobrovolsky and Vladislav N. Volkov, who died during Soyuz 11 space mission, June 6-30, 1971.

No. C184 exists imperf. in black & blue green; Size: 130x90mm. Value, unused or used, $150.

Lunar Rover on Moon AP66

1971, Aug. 26 Photo.

C185 AP66 1.50 l blue & multi 1.50 1.50

US Apollo 15 moon mission, July 26-Aug. 7, 1971. No. C185 printed in sheets of 4 stamps and 4 labels showing astronauts David Scott, James Irwin, Alfred Worden and Apollo 15 emblem with dates.

No. C185 exists imperf. in green & multicolored. The sheet has a control number. Values: unused $150; used $110.

Olympics Type of Regular Issue

Souvenir Sheets

Designs: No. C186, Torchbearer and map of Romania. No. C187, Soccer.

1972 Photo. *Perf. 13½*

C186 A699 6 l pale grn & multi 7.50 7.50
C187 A699 6 l blue & multi 7.50 7.50

20th Olympic Games, Munich, Aug. 26-Sept. 11. No. C186 contains one stamp 50x38mm. No. C187 contains one stamp 48½x37mm.

Issued: #C186, Apr. 25; #C187, Sept. 29.

Two imperf. 6 l souvenir sheets exist, one showing equestrian, the other a satellite over globe. Value for either sheet, unused or used, $80.

Lunar Rover on Moon — AP67

1972, May 10 Photo. *Perf. 13½*

C188 AP67 3 l vio bl, rose & gray grn 1.10 .85

Apollo 16 US moon mission, Apr. 15-27, 1972. No. C188 printed in sheets of 4 stamps and 4 gray green and black labels showing Capt. John W. Young, Lt. Comdr. Thomas K. Mattingly 2nd, Col. Charles M. Duke, Jr., and Apollo 16 badge.

Aurel Vlaicu and Monoplane — AP68

Romanian Aviation Pioneers: 3 l, Traian Vuia and his flying machine.

1972, Aug. 15

C189 AP68 60b multicolored .25 .25
C190 AP68 3 l multicolored 1.00 .40

Olympic Medals Type of Regular Issue

Souvenir Sheet

Olympic silver and gold medals, horiz.

1972, Sept. 29 Litho. *Perf. 13½*

C191 A714 6 l multicolored 7.50 7.50

Romanian medalists at 20th Olympic Games. An imperf. 6 l souvenir sheet exists showing gold medal. Value, unused or used, $70.

Apollo Type of Regular Issue

Souvenir Sheet

Design: 6 l, Lunar rover, landing module, rocket and astronauts on moon, horiz.

1972, Dec. 27 Photo. *Perf. 13½*

C192 A715 6 l vio bl, bis & dl grn 10.00 10.00

No. C192 contains one stamp 48½x36mm.

An imperf. 6 l souvenir sheet exists showing surface of moon with landing sites of last 6 Apollo missions and landing capsule. Value, unused or used, $80.

Type of Regular Issue, 1972

Design: Otopeni Airport, horiz.

1972, Dec. 20 Photo. *Perf. 13*

Size: 29x21mm

C193 A710 14.60 l brt blue 1.50 .40

Apollo and Soyuz Spacecraft — AP69

3.25 l, Apollo and Soyuz after link-up.

1975, July 14 Photo. *Perf. 13½*

C196 AP69 1.75 l vio bl, red & ol 1.25 1.25
C197 AP69 3.25 l vio bl, red & ol 1.25 1.25

Apollo Soyuz space test project (Russo-American cooperation), launching July 15; link-up, July 17. Nos. C196-C197 printed in sheets of 4 stamps, arranged checkerwise, and 4 rose lilac labels showing Apollo-Soyuz emblem.

European Security and Cooperation Conference — AP70

1975, July 30 Photo. *Perf. 13½*

C198 AP70 Sheet of 4 2.50 2.50
a. 2.75 l Map of Europe .35 .35
b. 2.75 l Peace doves .35 .35
c. 5 l Open book .75 .75
d. 5 l Children playing .75 .75

European Security and Cooperation Conference, Helsinki, July 30-Aug. 1. No. C198b inscribed "posta aeriana."

An imperf. 10 l souvenir sheet exists showing Helsinki on map of Europe. Value, unused or used, $95.

Red Cross Type of 1976

Design: Blood donors, Red Cross plane.

1976, Apr. 20 Photo. *Perf. 13½*

C199 A790 3.35 l multi .70 .25

De Havilland DH-9 — AP71

Airplanes: 40b, I.C.A.R. Comercial. 60b, Douglas DC-3. 1.75 l, AN-24. 2.75 l, IL-62. 3.60 l, Boeing 707.

1976, June 24 Photo. *Perf. 13½*

C200 AP71 20b blue & multi .25 .25
C201 AP71 40b blue & multi .25 .25
C202 AP71 60b multi .25 .25
C203 AP71 1.75 l multi .40 .25
C204 AP71 2.75 l blue & multi .55 .25
C205 AP71 3.60 l multi .85 .30
Nos. C200-C205 (6) 2.55 1.55

Romanian Airline, 50th anniversary.

Glider I.C.A.R.-1 — AP72

Gliders: 40b, I.S.-3d. 55b, R.G.-5. 1.50 l, I.S.-11. 3 l, I.S.-29D. 3.40 l, I.S.-28B.

1977, Feb. 20 Photo. *Perf. 13*

C206 AP72 20b multi .25 .25
C207 AP72 40b multi .25 .25
C208 AP72 55b multi .25 .25
C209 AP72 1.50 l bl & multi .25 .25
C210 AP72 3 l multi .60 .25
C211 AP72 3.40 l multi .95 .25
Nos. C206-C211 (6) 2.55 1.50

Souvenir Sheet

Boeing 707 over Bucharest Airport and Pioneers — AP73

1977, June 28 Photo. *Perf. 13½*

C212 AP73 10 l multi 2.50 2.50

European Security and Cooperation Conference, Belgrade.

An imperf. 10 l souvenir sheet exists showing Boeing 707, map of Europe and buildings. Value, unused or used, $35.

Woman Letter Carrier, Mailbox AP74

30 l, Plane, newspapers, letters, packages.

1977 Photo. *Perf. 13½*

C213 AP74 20 l multicolored 3.50 1.00
C214 AP74 30 l multicolored 5.50 1.75

Issue dates: 20 l, July 25, 30 l, Sept. 10.

LZ-1 over Friedrichshafen, 1900 — AP75

Airships: 1 l, Santos Dumont's dirigible over Paris, 1901. 1.50 l, British R-34 over New York and Statue of Liberty, 1919. 2.15 l, Italia over North Pole, 1928. 3.40 l, Zeppelin LZ-127 over Brasov, 1929. 4.80 l, Zeppelin over Sibiu, 1929. 10 l, Zeppelin over Bucharest, 1929.

1978, Mar. 20 Photo. *Perf. 13½*

C215	AP75	60b multi	.25	.25
C216	AP75	1 l multi	.25	.25
C217	AP75	1.50 l multi	.35	.25
C218	AP75	2.15 l multi	.40	.25
C219	AP75	3.40 l multi	.75	.25
C220	AP75	4.80 l multi	1.10	.25
		Nos. C215-C220 (6)	3.10	1.50

Souvenir Sheet

C221	AP75	10 l multi	2.50	2.50

History of airships. No. C221 contains one 50x37½mm stamp.

Soccer Type of 1978
Souvenir Sheet

10 l, 2 soccer players, Argentina '78 emblem.

1978, Apr. 15 Photo. *Perf. 13½*

C222	A818	10 l blue & multi	3.00	3.00

11th World Cup Soccer Championship, Argentina, June 1-25. No. C222 contains one stamp 37x50mm. A 10 l imperf souvenir sheet exists showing goalkeeper. Values: unused $30; used $20.

Wilbur and Orville Wright, Flyer A — AP76

Aviation History: 1 l, Louis Blériot and his plane over English Channel, 1909. 1.50 l, Anthony Fokker and Fokker F-VII trimotor, 1926. 2.15 l, Andrei N. Tupolev and ANT-25 monoplane, 1937. 3 l, Otto Lilienthal and glider, 1891-96. 3.40 l, Traian Vuia and his plane, Montesson, France, 1906. 4.80 l, Aurel Vlaicu and 1st Romanian plane, 1910. 10 l, Henri Coanda and his "jet," 1910.

1978, Dec. 18 Photo. *Perf. 13½*

C223	AP76	55b multi	.25	.25
C224	AP76	1 l multi	.25	.25
C225	AP76	1.50 l multi	.25	.25
C226	AP76	2.15 l multi	.35	.25
C227	AP76	3 l multi	.35	.25
C228	AP76	3.40 l multi	.40	.25
C229	AP76	4.80 l multi	.45	.25
		Nos. C223-C229 (7)	2.30	1.75

Souvenir Sheet

C230	AP76	10 l multi	2.25	2.25

No. C230 contains one stamp 50x38mm.

Inter-Europa Type of 1979

3.40 l, Jet, mail truck and motorcycle.

1979, May 3 Photo. *Perf. 13*

C231	A835	3.40 l multi	.40	.40

Animal Type of 1980
Souvenir Sheet

1980, Mar. 25 Photo. *Perf. 13½*

C232	A852	10 l Pelicans	2.25	2.25

No. C232 contains one stamp 38x50mm.

Mercury AP77

1981, June 30 Photo. *Perf. 13½*

C233	AP77	55b shown	.25	.25
C234	AP77	1 l Venus, Earth, Mars	.25	.25
C235	AP77	1.50 l Jupiter	.25	.25
C236	AP77	2.15 l Saturn	.30	.25
C237	AP77	3.40 l Uranus	.60	.25
C238	AP77	4.80 l Neptune, Pluto	.75	.30
		Nos. C233-C238 (6)	2.40	1.55

Souvenir Sheet

C239	AP77	10 l Earth	2.25	2.25

No. C239 contains one stamp 37x50mm. An imperf. 10 l souvenir sheet exists showing planets in orbit. Value, unused or used, $30.

Romanian-Russian Space Cooperation — AP78

55b, Soyuz 40. 3.40 l, Salyut 6, Soyuz 40. 10 l, Cosmonauts, spacecraft.

1981 Photo. *Perf. 13½*

C240	AP78	55b multicolored	.25	.25
C241	AP78	3.40 l multicolored	.50	.25

Souvenir Sheet

C242	AP78	10 l multicolored	2.25	2.25

No. C242 contains one stamp 50x39mm. Issued: 55b, 3.40 l, May 14; 10 l, June 30.

Children's Games Type of 1981

1981, Nov. 25

C243	A880	4.80 l Flying model planes	.70	.70

Standard Glider — AP79

1982, June 20 Photo. *Perf. 13½*

C244	AP79	50b shown	.25	.25
C245	AP79	1 l Excelsior D	.25	.25
C246	AP79	1.50 l Dedal I	.25	.25
C247	AP79	2.50 l Enthusiast	.45	.25
C248	AP79	4 l AK-22	.60	.25
C249	AP79	5 l Grifrom	.75	.30
		Nos. C244-C249 (6)	2.55	1.55

Agriculture Type of 1982

1982, June 29

C250	A888	4 l Helicopter spraying insecticide	.60	.25

Vlaicu's Glider, 1909 — AP80

Aurel Vlaicu (1882-19), Aviator: 1 l, Memorial, Banesti-Prahova, vert. 2.50 l, Hero Aviators Memorial, by Kotzebue and Fekete, vert. 3 l, Vlaicu-1 glider, 1910.

1982, Sept. 27 Photo. *Perf. 13½*

C251	AP80	50b multi	.25	.25
C252	AP80	1 l multi	.25	.25
C253	AP80	2.50 l multi	.40	.25
C254	AP80	3 l multi	.45	.25
		Nos. C251-C254 (4)	1.35	1.00

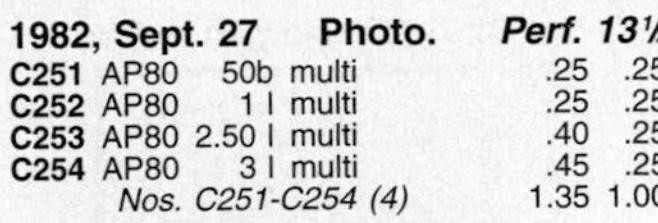

25th Anniv. of Space Flight AP81

Designs: 50b, H. Coanda, reaction motor, 1910. 1 l, H. Oberth, rocket, 1923. 1.50 l, Sputnik I, 1957. 2.50 l, Vostok I, 1961. 4 l, Apollo 11, 1969. 5 l, Columbia space shuttle, 1982. 10 l, Globe.

1983, Jan. 24

C255	AP81	50b multi	.25	.25
C256	AP81	1 l multi	.25	.25
C257	AP81	1.50 l multi	.30	.25
C258	AP81	2.50 l multi	.45	.25
C259	AP81	4 l multi	.70	.25
C260	AP81	5 l multi	.90	.25
		Nos. C255-C260 (6)	2.85	1.50

Souvenir Sheet

C261	AP81	10 l multi	2.50	2.50

No. C261 contains one stamp 41x53mm.

First Romanian-built Jet Airliner — AP82

1983, Jan. 25 Photo. *Perf. 13½*

C262	AP82	11 l Rombac 1-11	2.75	.40

World Communications Year — AP83

1983, July 25 Photo. *Perf. 13½*

C263	AP83	2 l Boeing 707, Postal van	.40	.25

40th Anniv., Intl. Civil Aviation Organization — AP84

1984, Aug. 15 Photo. *Perf. 13½*

C265	AP84	50b Lockheed L-14	.25	.25
C266	AP84	1.50 l BN-2 Islander	.35	.25
C267	AP84	3 l Rombac	.70	.25
C268	AP84	6 l Boeing 707	1.25	.35
		Nos. C265-C268 (4)	2.55	1.10

Halley's Comet — AP85

1986, Jan. 27 Photo. *Perf. 13½*

C269	AP85	2 l shown	.60	.40
C270	AP85	4 l Space probes	1.50	.65

An imperf. 10 l air post souvenir sheet exists showing comet and space probes, red control number. Value, unused or used, $10.

Souvenir Sheet

Plane of Alexandru Papana, 1936 — AP86

1986, May 15 Photo. *Perf. 13½*

C271	AP86	10 l multi	2.25	2.25

AMERIPEX '86.

Aircraft AP87

50b, Henri Auguste glider, 1909. 1 l, Sky diver, IS-28 B2 glider. 2 l, IS-29 D-2 glider. 3 l, IS-32 glider. 4 l, IAR-35 glider. 5 l, IS-28 M2, route.

1987, Aug. 10

C272	AP87	50b multi	.25	.25
C273	AP87	1 l multi	.25	.25
C274	AP87	2 l multi	.35	.25
C275	AP87	3 l multi	.55	.25
C276	AP87	4 l multi	.80	.25
C277	AP87	5 l multi	1.00	.30
		Nos. C272-C277 (6)	3.20	1.55

1st Moon Landing, 20th Anniv. — AP88

Designs: 50b, C. Haas. 1.50 l, Konstantin Tsiolkovski (1857-1935), Soviet rocket science pioneer. 2 l, H. Oberth and equations. 3 l, Robert Goddard and diagram on blackboard. 4 l, Sergei Korolev (1906-66), Soviet aeronautical engineer. 5 l, Wernher von Braun (1912-77), lunar module.

1989, Oct. 25 Photo. *Perf. 13½*

C278	AP88	50b multicolored	.25	.25
C279	AP88	1.50 l multicolored	.35	.25
C280	AP88	2 l multicolored	.45	.25
C281	AP88	3 l multicolored	.65	.25
C282	AP88	4 l multicolored	.85	.25
C283	AP88	5 l multicolored	1.10	.25
		Nos. C278-C283 (6)	3.65	1.50

A 10 l souvenir sheet picturing Armstrong and *Eagle* lunar module was also issued. Value, unused or used, $22.50.

Souvenir Sheet

World Stamp Expo '89, Washington, DC, Nov. 17-Dec. 3 — AP89

1989, Nov. 17 Photo. *Perf. 13½*

C284	AP89	5 l Postal coach	1.75	1.75

Captured Balloons — AP90

Balloons captured by Romanian army: 30 l, German balloon, Draken, 1903. 90 l, French balloon, Caquot, 1917.

1993, Feb. 26 Photo. *Perf. 13½*

C285 AP90 30 l multicolored .25 .25
C286 AP90 90 l multicolored .70 .25

Souvenir Sheet

European Inventions, Discoveries — AP91

Europa: a, 240 l, Hermann Oberth (1894-1989), rocket scientist. b, 2100 l, Henri Coanda (1886-1972), aeronautical engineer.

1994, May 25 Photo. *Perf. 13*

C287 AP91 Sheet of 2, #a.-b. + 2 labels 4.50 4.50

ICAO, 50th Anniv. AP92

Aircraft: 110 l, Traian Vuia, 1906. 350 l, Rombac 1-11. 500 l, Boeing 737-300. 635 l, Airbus A310.

1994. Aug. 12 Photo. *Perf. 13*

C288 AP92 110 l multicolored .25 .25
C289 AP92 350 l multicolored .60 .25
C290 AP92 500 l multicolored 1.00 .25
C291 AP92 635 l multicolored 1.25 .25
Nos. C288-C291 (4) 3.10 1.00

For surcharges see #C294-C297.

French-Romanian Aeronautical Agreement, 75th Anniv. — AP93

1995, Mar. 31 Photo. *Perf. 13x13¼*

C292 AP93 60 l shown .25 .25
C293 AP93 960 l Biplane Potez IX 1.25 .25

No. C291 Surcharged in Red

Methods and Perfs as Before

2000, May 19

C294 AP92 1700 l on 635 l multi .25 .25
C295 AP92 2000 l on 635 l multi .40 .25
C296 AP92 3900 l on 635 l multi .65 .25
C297 AP92 9050 l on 635 l multi 1.40 .60
Nos. C294-C297 (4) 2.70 1.35

No. C293 Surcharged in Red

2000, Oct. 27 Photo. *Perf. 13¼*

C298 AP93 2000 l on 960 l multi .25 .25
C299 AP93 4200 l on 960 l multi .45 .25
C300 AP93 4600 l on 960 l multi .45 .25
C301 AP93 6500 l on 960 l multi .65 .25
Nos. C298-C301 (4) 1.80 1.00

AIR POST SEMI-POSTAL STAMPS

Catalogue values for unused stamps in this section are for Never Hinged items.

Corneliu Codreanu SPAP1

Unwmk.

1940, Dec. 1 Photo. *Perf. 14*

CB1 SPAP1 20 l + 5 l Prus grn 4.50 3.25

Propaganda for the Rome-Berlin Axis.

No. CB1 exists with overprint "1 Mai 1941 Jamboreea Nationala." This was a private overprint, not authorized by the Romanian Postal Service.

Plane over Sinaia — SPAP2

200 l+800 l, Plane over Mountains.

1945, Oct. 1 Wmk. 276 *Imperf.*

CB2 SPAP2 80 l + 420 l gray 2.50 *2.50*
CB3 SPAP2 200 l + 800 l ultra 2.50 *2.50*

16th Congress of the General Assoc. of Romanian Engineers.

Souvenir Sheet

Re-distribution of Land — SPAP4

1946, May 4 Photo. *Perf. 14*

CB4 SPAP4 80 l blue 14.00 *25.00*

Agrarian reform law of Mar. 23, 1945. The sheet sold for 100 lei.

Souvenir Sheet

Plane Skywriting — SPAP5

1946, May 1 *Perf. 13*

CB5 SPAP5 200 l bl & brt red 12.00 *22.50*

Labor Day. The sheet sold for 10,000 lei.

Lockheed 12 Electra — SPAP6

1946, Sept. 1 *Perf. 11½*

CB6 SPAP6 300 l + 1200 l dp bl 1.00 *1.25*

For se-tenant see No. C26a and note after No. C26.

The surtax was for the Office of Popular Sports.

Miniature Sheet

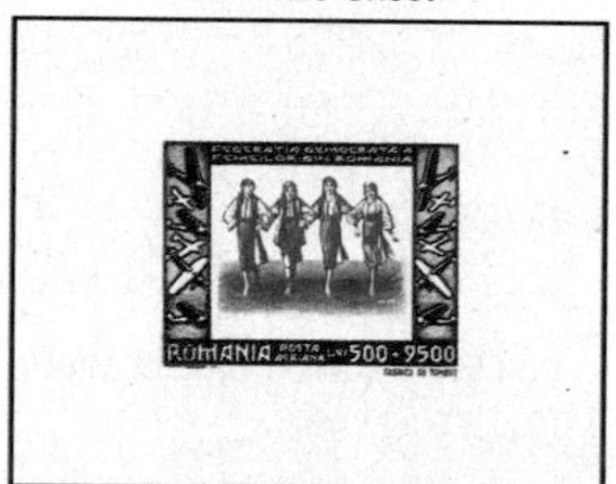

Women of Wallachia, Transylvania and Moldavia — SPAP7

1946, Dec. 20 Wmk. 276 *Imperf.*

CB7 SPAP7 500 l + 9500 l choc & red 6.00 6.00

Democratic Women's Org. of Romania.

SPAP8

1946, Oct. *Imperf.*

CB8 SPAP8 300 l deep plum 17.50 *17.50*

The surtax was for the Office of Popular Sports. Sheets of four. Stamp sold for 1300 l.

Laborer with Torch — SPAP9

1947, Mar. 1

CB9 SPAP9 3000 l + 7000 l choc .80 1.50

Sheets of four with marginal inscription.

Plane — SPAP10

1947, June 27 *Imperf.*

CB10 SPAP10 15,000 l + 15,000 l .80 .80

Sheets of four with marginal inscription.

Plane above Shore Line — SPAP11

1947, May 1 *Perf. 14x13*

CB11 SPAP11 3000 l + 12,000 l bl .60 .60

Planes over Mountains SPAP12

1947, Oct. 5 *Perf. 14x14½*

CB12 SPAP12 5 l + 5 l blue .70 .70

17th Congress of the General Assoc. of Romanian Engineers.

Plane over Athletic Field — SPAP13

Wmk. 276

1948, Feb. 20 Photo. *Perf. 13½*

CB13 SPAP13 7 l + 7 l vio 1.00 .70

Imperf

CB14 SPAP13 10 l + 10 l Prus grn 2.00 1.00

Balkan Games. Sheets of four with marginal inscription.

Swallow and Plane SPAP14

1948, Mar. 15 *Perf. 14x13½*

CB15 SPAP14 12 l + 12 l blue 1.10 .60

Bucharest-Moscow Passenger Plane, Douglas DC-3 Dakota — SPAP15

1948, Oct. 29 ***Perf. 14***

CB16 SPAP15 20 l + 20 l dp bl 10.00 10.00

Printed in sheets of 8 stamps and 16 small, red brown labels. Sheet yields 8 triptychs, each comprising 1 stamp flanked by label with Bucharest view and label with Moscow view.

Douglas DC-4 — SPAP16

1948, May 1 ***Perf. 13½x14***

CB17 SPAP16 20 l + 20 l blue 6.75 5.75

Issued to publicize Labor Day, May 1, 1948.

Pursuit Plane and Victim — SPAP17

1948, May 9 ***Perf. 13***

CB18 SPAP17 3 l + 3 l shown 6.00 6.00

CB19 SPAP17 5 l + 5 l Bomber 8.00 8.00

Issued to honor the Romanian army.

Launching Model Plane — SPAP18

1948, Dec. 31 ***Perf. 13x13½***

CB20 SPAP18 20 l + 20 l dp ultra 15.00 15.00

Imperf

CB21 SPAP18 20 l + 20 l Prus bl 15.00 15.00

Nos. CB20 and CB21 were issued in sheets of four stamps, with ornamental border and "1948" in contrasting color.

UPU Type of Air Post Issue, 1963

Design: 1.60 l+50b, Globe, map of Romania, planes and UPU monument.

Perf. 14x13½

1963, Nov. 15 **Litho.** **Unwmk.**

Size: 75x27mm

CB22 AP54 1.60 l + 50b multi 1.40 .50

Surtax for the Romanian Philatelic Federation.

POSTAGE DUE STAMPS

D1

Perf. 11, 11½, 13½ and Compound

1881 **Typo.** **Unwmk.**

J1 D1 2b brown 4.00 1.50

J2 D1 5b brown 22.50 2.50

a. Tête bêche pair *190.00 75.00*

J3 D1 10b brown 30.00 1.50

J4 D1 30b brown 32.50 1.50

J5 D1 50b brown 26.00 2.75

J6 D1 60b brown 21.00 4.00

Nos. J1-J6 (6) 136.00 13.75

1885

J7 D1 10b pale red brown 8.00 .50

J8 D1 30b pale red brown 8.00 .50

1887-90

J9 D1 2b gray green 4.00 1.00

J10 D1 5b gray green 8.00 3.50

J11 D1 10b gray green 8.00 3.50

J12 D1 30b gray green 8.00 1.00

Nos. J9-J12 (4) 28.00 9.00

1888

J14 D1 2b green, *yellowish* .90 .75

J15 D1 5b green, *yellowish* 2.25 2.25

J16 D1 10b green, *yellowish* 32.50 2.75

J17 D1 30b green, *yellowish* 17.50 1.25

Nos. J14-J17 (4) 53.15 7.00

1890-96 **Wmk. 163**

J18 D1 2b emerald 1.60 .45

J19 D1 5b emerald .80 .45

J20 D1 10b emerald 1.25 .45

J21 D1 30b emerald 2.00 .45

J22 D1 50b emerald 6.50 .95

J23 D1 60b emerald 8.75 3.25

Nos. J18-J23 (6) 20.90 6.00

1898 **Wmk. 200**

J24 D1 2b blue green .70 .45

J25 D1 5b blue green .90 .30

J26 D1 10b blue green 1.40 .30

J27 D1 30b blue green 1.90 .30

J28 D1 50b blue green 4.75 .90

J29 D1 60b blue green 5.50 1.75

Nos. J24-J29 (6) 15.15 4.00

1902-10 **Unwmk.**

Thin Paper, Tinted Rose on Back

J30 D1 2b green .85 .25

J31 D1 5b green .50 .25

J32 D1 10b green .40 .25

J33 D1 30b green .50 .25

J34 D1 50b green 2.50 .90

J35 D1 60b green 5.25 2.25

Nos. J30-J35 (6) 10.00 4.15

1908-11 **White Paper**

J36 D1 2b green .80 .50

J37 D1 5b green .60 .50

a. Tête bêche pair 12.00 12.00

J38 D1 10b green .40 .30

a. Tête bêche pair 12.00 12.00

J39 D1 30b green .50 .30

a. Tête bêche pair 12.00 12.00

J40 D1 50b green 2.00 1.25

Nos. J36-J40 (5) 4.30 2.85

D2

1911 **Wmk. 165**

J41 D2 2b dark blue, *green* .25 .25

J42 D2 5b dark blue, *green* .25 .25

J43 D2 10b dark blue, *green* .25 .25

J44 D2 15b dark blue, *green* .25 .25

J45 D2 20b dark blue, *green* .25 .25

J46 D2 30b dark blue, *green* .25 .25

J47 D2 50b dark blue, *green* .50 .30

J48 D2 60b dark blue, *green* .60 .40

J49 D2 2 l dark blue, *green* 1.00 .80

Nos. J41-J49 (9) 3.60 3.00

The letters "P.R." appear to be embossed instead of watermarked. They are often faint or entirely invisible.

The 20b, type D2, has two types, differing in the width of the head of the "2." This affects Nos. J45, J54, J58, and J63.

See Nos. J52-J77, J82, J87-J88. For overprints see Nos. J78-J81, RAJ1-RAJ2, RAJ20-RAJ21, 3NJ1-3NJ7.

Regular Issue of 1908 Overprinted

1918 **Unwmk.**

J50 A46 5b yellow green 1.40 .40

a. Inverted overprint 5.00 5.00

J51 A46 10b rose 1.40 .40

a. Inverted overprint 3.75 3.75

Postage Due Type of 1911

1920 **Wmk. 165**

J52 D2 5b black, *green* .25 .25

J53 D2 10b black, *green* .25 .25

J54 D2 20b black, *green* 4.00 .60

J55 D2 30b black, *green* 1.10 .40

J55A D2 50b black, *green* 3.00 .90

Nos. J52-J55A (5) 8.60 2.40

Perf. 11½, 13½ and Compound

1919 **Unwmk.**

J56 D2 5b black, *green* .30 .25

J57 D2 10b black, *green* .30 .25

J58 D2 20b black, *green* 1.00 .25

J59 D2 30b black, *green* .90 .25

J60 D2 50b black, *green* 2.25 .40

Nos. J56-J60 (5) 4.75 1.40

1920-26 **White Paper**

J61 D2 5b black .25 .25

J62 D2 10b black .25 .25

J63 D2 20b black .25 .25

J64 D2 30b black .25 .25

J65 D2 50b black .40 .40

J66 D2 60b black .25 .25

J67 D2 1 l black .30 .30

J68 D2 2 l black .25 .25

J69 D2 3 l black ('26) .25 .25

J70 D2 6 l black ('26) .30 .30

Nos. J61-J70 (10) 2.75 2.75

1923-24

J74 D2 1 l black, *pale green* .25 .25

J75 D2 2 l black, *pale green* .45 .25

J76 D2 3 l black, *pale green* ('24) 1.25 .60

J77 D2 6 l blk, *pale green* ('24) 1.75 .60

Nos. J74-J77 (4) 3.70 1.70

Postage Due Stamps of 1920-26 Overprinted

1930 ***Perf. 13½***

J78 D2 1 l black .25 .25

J79 D2 2 l black .25 .25

J80 D2 3 l black .35 .25

J81 D2 6 l black .60 .30

Nos. J78-J81 (4) 1.45 1.05

Accession of King Carol II.

Catalogue values for unused stamps in this section, from this point to the end of the section, are for Never Hinged items.

Type of 1911 Issue

1931 **Wmk. 225**

J82 D2 2 l black .90 .35

D3

1932-37 **Wmk. 230**

J83 D3 1 l black .25 .25

J84 D3 2 l black .25 .25

J85 D3 3 l black ('37) .25 .25

J86 D3 6 l black ('37) .25 .25

Nos. J83-J86 (4) 1.00 1.00

See Nos. J89-J98.

Type of 1911 Issue

1942 **Typo.** ***Perf. 13½***

J87 D2 50 l black .35 .25

J88 D2 100 l black .50 .25

Type of 1932

1946-47 **Unwmk.** ***Perf. 14***

J89 D3 20 l black .60 .55

J90 D3 100 l black ('47) .45 .25

J91 D3 200 l black 1.10 .55

Nos. J89-J91 (3) 2.15 1.35

1946-47 **Wmk. 276**

J92 D3 20 l black .25 .25

J93 D3 50 l black .25 .25

J94 D3 80 l black .25 .25

J95 D3 100 l black .25 .25

J96 D3 200 l black .60 .35

J97 D3 500 l black .90 .50

J98 D3 5000 l black ('47) 2.50 1.25

Nos. J92-J98 (7) 5.00 3.10

Crown and King Michael — D3a

Perf. 14½x13½

1947 **Typo.** **Wmk. 276**

J98A D3a 2 l carmine .40 .25

J98B D3a 4 l gray blue .75 .30

J98C D3a 5 l black 1.10 .45

J98D D3a 10 l violet brown 2.00 .75

Nos. J98A-J98D (4) 4.25 1.75

Nos. J98A-J98D Overprinted

1948

J98E D3a 2 l carmine .30 .25

J98F D3a 4 l gray blue .75 .25

J98G D3a 5 l black 1.00 .30

J98H D3a 10 l violet brown 1.75 .55

Nos. J98E-J98H (4) 3.80 1.35

In use, Nos. J98A-J106 and following issues were torn apart, one half being affixed to the postage due item and the other half being pasted into the postman's record book. Values are for unused and canceled-to-order pairs.

Communications Badge and Postwoman — D4

1950 **Unwmk.** **Photo.** ***Perf. 14½x14***

J99 D4 2 l orange vermilion .75 .75

J100 D4 4 l deep blue .75 .75

J101 D4 5 l dark gray green 1.25 1.25

J102 D4 10 l orange brown 1.50 1.50

Wmk. 358

J103 D4 2 l orange vermilion 7.50 7.50

J104 D4 4 l deep blue 7.50 7.50

J105 D4 5 l dark gray green 3.50 3.50

J106 D4 10 l orange brown 2.00 2.00

Nos. J99-J106 (8) 24.75 24.75

Postage Due Stamps of 1950 Surcharged with New Values in Black or Carmine

1952 **Unwmk.**

J107 D4 4b on 2 l .40 .40

J108 D4 10b on 4 l (C) .40 .40

J109 D4 20b on 5 l (C) 1.00 1.00

J110 D4 50b on 10 l 1.50 1.50

Nos. J107-J110 (4) 3.30 3.30

Wmk. 358

J111 D4 4b on 2 l

J112 D4 10b on 4 l (C)

J113 D4 20b on 5 l (C) *7.50 7.50*

J114 D4 50b on 10 l *7.50 7.50*

The existence of Nos. J111-J112 has been questioned.

See note after No. J98H.

General Post Office and Post Horn — D5

1957 **Wmk. 358** ***Perf. 14***

J115 D5 3b black .25 .25
J116 D5 5b red orange .25 .25
J117 D5 10b red lilac .25 .25
J118 D5 20b brt red .25 .25
J119 D5 40b lt bl grn .50 .25
J120 D5 1 l brt ultra 2.00 .40
Nos. J115-J120 (6) 3.50 1.65

See note after No. J98H.

General Post Office and Post Horn — D6

1967, Feb. 25 **Photo.** ***Perf. 13***

J121 D6 3b brt grn .25 .25
J122 D6 5b brt bl .25 .25
J123 D6 10b lilac rose .25 .25
J124 D6 20b vermilion .25 .25
J125 D6 40b brown .25 .25
J126 D6 1 l violet .55 .25
Nos. J121-J126 (6) 1.80 1.50

See note after No. J98H.

1970, Mar. 10 **Unwmk.**

J127 D6 3b brt grn .25 .25
J128 D6 5b brt bl .25 .25
J129 D6 10b lilac rose .25 .25
J130 D6 20b vermilion .25 .25
J131 D6 40b brown .25 .25
J132 D6 1 l violet .35 .25
Nos. J127-J132 (6) 1.60 1.50

See note after No. J98H.

Symbols of Communications — D7

Designs: 10b, Like 5b. 20b, 40b, Pigeons, head of Mercury and post horn. 50b, 1 l, General Post Office, post horn and truck.

1974, Jan. 1 **Photo.** ***Perf. 13***

J133 D7 5b brt bl .25 .25
J134 D7 10b olive .25 .25
J135 D7 20b lilac rose .25 .25
J136 D7 40b purple .25 .25
J137 D7 50b brown .25 .25
J138 D7 1 l orange .35 .25
Nos. J133-J138 (6) 1.60 1.50

See note after No. J98H.
See #J139-J144. For surcharges see #J147-J151.

1982, Dec. 23 **Photo.** ***Perf. 13½***

J139 D7 25b like #J135 .25 .25
J140 D7 50b like #J133 .25 .25
J141 D7 1 l like #J135 .25 .25
J142 D7 2 l like #J137 .45 .25
J143 D7 3 l like #J133 .70 .25
J144 D7 4 l like #J137 1.00 .25
Nos. J139-J144 (6) 2.90 1.50

See note after No. J98H.

Post Horn — D8

1992, Feb. 3 **Photo.** ***Perf. 13½***

J145 D8 4 l red .50 .25
J146 D8 8 l blue .50 .25

See note after No. J98H.

D9

1994, Dec. 10 **Photo.** ***Perf. 13¼***

J146A D9 10 l brown .25 .25
J146B D9 45 l orange .40 .25

See note after No. J98H.

Nos. J140-J142, J144 Surcharged in Green, Deep Blue, or Black

1999, Mar. 12 **Photo.** ***Perf. 13½***

J147 D7 50 l on 50b #J140 (G) .25 .25
J148 D7 50 l on 1 l #J141 (DBl) .25 .25
J149 D7 100 l on 2 l #J142 .25 .25
J150 D7 700 l on 1 l #J141 .30 .25
J151 D7 1100 l on 4 l #J144 .45 .25
Nos. J147-J151 (5) 1.50 1.25

Nos. J145, J146B Surcharged

2001, Jan. 17 **Photo.** ***Perf. 13¼***

J152 D8 500 l on 4 l red .25 .25
J153 D8 1000 l on 4 l red .25 .25
J154 D9 2000 l on 45 l org .25 .25
Nos. J152-J154 (3) .75 .75

See note after No. J98H.

OFFICIAL STAMPS

Catalogue values for unused stamps in this section are for Never Hinged items.

Eagle Carrying National Emblem — O1

1929 **Photo.** **Wmk. 95** ***Perf. 13½***

O1 O1 25b red orange .25 .25
O2 O1 50b dk brown .25 .25
O3 O1 1 l dk violet .30 .25
O4 O1 2 l olive grn .30 .25
O5 O1 3 l rose car .45 .25
O6 O1 4 l dk olive .45 .25
O7 O1 6 l Prus blue 2.50 .25
O8 O1 10 l deep blue .80 .25
O9 O1 25 l carmine brn 1.60 1.25
O10 O1 50 l purple 4.75 3.50
Nos. O1-O10 (10) 11.65 6.75

Type of Official Stamps of 1929 Overprinted

1930 **Unwmk.**

O11 O1 25b red orange .25 .25
O12 O1 50b dk brown .25 .25
O13 O1 1 l dk violet .35 .25
O14 O1 3 l rose carmine .50 .25
Nos. O11-O14 (4) 1.35 1.00

Nos. O11-O14 were not placed in use without overprint.

Same Overprint on Nos. O1-O10
Wmk. 95

O15 O1 25b red orange .25 .25
O16 O1 50b dk brown .25 .25
O17 O1 1 l dk violet .25 .25
O18 O1 2 l dp green .25 .25
O19 O1 3 l rose carmine .60 .25
O20 O1 4 l olive black .75 .25
O21 O1 6 l Prus blue 2.00 .25
O22 O1 10 l deep blue .80 .25
O23 O1 25 l carmine brown 3.00 2.50
O24 O1 50 l purple 4.00 3.50
Nos. O15-O24 (10) 12.15 8.00

Accession of King Carol II to the throne of Romania (Nos O11-O24).

Coat of Arms — O2

Perf. 13½, 13½x14½

1931-32 **Typo.** **Wmk. 225**

O25 O2 25b black .30 .25
O26 O2 1 l lilac .30 .25
O27 O2 2 l emerald .60 .40
O28 O2 3 l rose 1.00 .70
Nos. O25-O28 (4) 2.20 1.60

1932 **Wmk. 230** ***Perf. 13½***

O29 O2 25b black .30 .25
O30 O2 1 l violet .40 .35
O31 O2 2 l emerald .65 .55
O32 O2 3 l rose .80 .65
O33 O2 6 l red brown 1.25 1.00
Nos. O29-O33 (5) 3.40 2.80

PARCEL POST STAMPS

PP1

Perf. 11½, 13½ and Compound

1895 **Wmk. 163** **Typo.**

Q1 PP1 25b brown red 12.50 2.25

1896

Q2 PP1 25b vermilion 10.00 1.25

Perf. 13½ and 11½x13½

1898 **Wmk. 200**

Q3 PP1 25b brown red 7.00 1.25
a. Tête bêche pair
Q4 PP1 25b vermilion 7.00 .90

Thin Paper
Tinted Rose on Back

1905 **Unwmk.** ***Perf. 11½***

Q5 PP1 25b vermilion 7.50 1.25

1911 **White Paper**

Q6 PP1 25b pale red 7.50 1.25

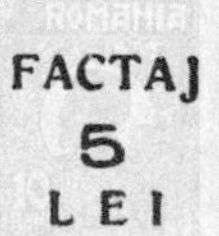

No. 263 Surcharged in Carmine

1928 ***Perf. 13½***

Q7 A54 5 l on 10b yellow green 1.50 .30

POSTAL TAX STAMPS

Regular Issue of 1908 Overprinted

Perf. 11½, 13½, 11½x13½

1915 **Unwmk.**

RA1 A46 5b green .25 .25
RA2 A46 10b rose .40 .25

The "Timbru de Ajutor" stamps represent a tax on postal matter. The money obtained from their sale was turned into a fund for the assistance of soldiers' families.

Until 1923 the only "Timbru de Ajutor" stamps used for postal purposes were the 5b and 10b. Stamps of higher values with this inscription were used to pay the taxes on railway and theater tickets and other fiscal taxes. In 1923 the postal rate was advanced to 25b.

The Queen Weaving — PT1

1916-18 **Typo.**

RA3 PT1 5b gray blk .25 .25
RA4 PT1 5b green ('18) .70 .40
RA5 PT1 10b brown .40 .25
RA6 PT1 10b gray blk ('18) 1.00 .45
Nos. RA3-RA6 (4) 2.35 1.35

For overprints see Nos. RA7-RA8, RAJ7-RAJ9, 3NRA1-3NRA8.

Stamps of 1916 Overprinted in Red or Black

1918 ***Perf. 13½***

RA7 PT1 5b gray blk (R) .70 .25
a. Double overprint 5.00
c. Black overprint 5.00
RA8 PT1 10b brn (Bk) .70 .25
a. Double overprint 5.00
b. Double overprint, one inverted 5.00
c. Inverted overprint 5.00

Same Overprint on RA1 and RA2

1919

RA11 A46 5b yel grn (R) *19.00 12.50*
RA12 A46 10b rose (Bk) *19.00 12.50*

Charity — PT3

Perf. 13½, 11½, 13½x11½

1921-24 **Typo.** **Unwmk.**

RA13 PT3 10b green .25 .25
RA14 PT3 25b blk ('24) .25 .25

Type of 1921-24 Issue

1928 **Wmk. 95**

RA15 PT3 25b black 1.00 .45

Nos. RA13, RA14 and RA15 are the only stamps of type PT3 issued for postal purposes. Other denominations were used fiscally.

Catalogue values for unused stamps in this section, from this point to the end of the section, are for Never Hinged items.

Airplane — PT4

1931 **Photo.** **Unwmk.**

RA16 PT4 50b Prus bl .45 .25
a. Double impression 15.00
RA17 PT4 1 l dk red brn .75 .25
RA18 PT4 2 l ultra 1.00 .25
Nos. RA16-RA18 (3) 2.20 .75

The use of these stamps, in addition to the regular postage, was obligatory on all postal matter for the interior of the country. The money thus obtained was to augment the National Fund for Aviation. When the stamps were not used to prepay the special tax, it was collected by means of Postal Tax Due stamps Nos. RAJ20 and RAJ21.

Nos. RA17 and RA18 were also used for other than postal tax.

Head of Aviator — PT5

1932 Wmk. 230 *Perf. 14 x 13½*

RA19 PT5 50b Prus bl .30 .25
RA20 PT5 1 l red brn .45 .25
RA21 PT5 2 l ultra .70 .25
Nos. RA19-RA21 (3) 1.45 .75

See notes after No. RA18.

After 1937 use of Nos. RA20-RA21 was limited to other than postal matter.

Nos. RA19-RA21 exist imperf.

Four stamps similar to type PT5, but inscribed "Fondul Aviatiei," were issued in 1936: 10b sepia, 20b violet, 3 l green and 5 l red. These were used for purposes other than postal tax.

Aviator — PT6

1937 *Perf. 13½*

RA22 PT6 50b Prus grn .25 .25
RA23 PT6 1 l red brn .35 .25
RA24 PT6 2 l ultra .45 .25
Nos. RA22-RA24 (3) 1.05 .75

Stamps overprinted or inscribed "Fondul Aviatiei" other than Nos. RA22, RA23 or RA24 were used to pay taxes on other than postal matters.

King Michael — PT7

1943 Wmk. 276 Photo. *Perf. 14*

RA25 PT7 50b org ver .25 .25
RA26 PT7 1 l lil rose .25 .25
RA27 PT7 2 l brown .25 .25
RA28 PT7 4 l lt ultra .25 .25
RA29 PT7 5 l dull lilac .25 .25
RA30 PT7 8 l yel grn .25 .25
RA31 PT7 10 l blk brn .25 .25
Nos. RA25-RA31 (7) 1.75 1.75

The tax was obligatory on domestic mail.

Examples of these stamps with an overprint consisting of a red cross and text are unissued franchise stamps.

Protection of Homeless Children — PT8

1945

RA32 PT8 40 l Prus bl .35 .25

PT9

Black Surcharge

1947 Unwmk. Typo. *Perf. 14x14½*

RA33 PT9 1 l on 2 l + 2 l pink .30 .25
a. Inverted surcharge 25.00 25.00
RA34 PT9 5 l on 1 l + 1 l gray grn *2.50 2.50*

"Hope" — PT10

1948 *Perf. 14*

RA35 PT10 1 l rose *.90* .35
RA36 PT10 1 l rose violet *1.00* .35

A 2 lei blue and 5 lei ocher in type PT10 were issued primarily for revenue purposes.

POSTAL TAX DUE STAMPS

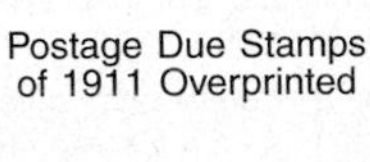

Catalogue values for unused stamps in this section are for Never Hinged items.

Postage Due Stamps of 1911 Overprinted

Perf. 11½, 13½, 11½x13½

1915 Unwmk.

RAJ1 D2 5b dk bl, *grn* .75 .25
RAJ2 D2 10b dk bl, *grn* .75 .25
a. Wmk. 165 10.00 1.00

PTD1

1916 Typo. Unwmk.

RAJ3 PTD1 5b brn, *grn* .40 .25
RAJ4 PTD1 10b red, *grn* .40 .25

See Nos. RAJ5-RAJ6, RAJ10-RAJ11. For overprint see No. 3NRAJ1.

1918

RAJ5 PTD1 5b red, *grn* .25 .25
a. Wmk. 165 1.00 .25
RAJ6 PTD1 10b brn, *grn* .25 .25
a. Wmk. 165 1.75 .25

Postal Tax Stamps of 1916, Overprinted in Red, Black or Blue

RAJ7 PT1 5b gray blk (R) .40 .25
a. Inverted overprint 7.50
RAJ8 PT1 10b brn (Bk) .80 .25
a. Inverted overprint 7.50
RAJ9 PT1 10b brn (Bl) *5.00 5.00*
a. Vertical overprint *20.00 15.00*
Nos. RAJ7-RAJ9 (3) 6.20 5.50

Type of 1916

1921

RAJ10 PTD1 5b red .50 .25
RAJ11 PTD1 10b brown .50 .25

PTD2

1922-25 Greenish Paper Typo.

RAJ12 PTD2 10b brown .25 .25
RAJ13 PTD2 20b brown .25 .25
RAJ14 PTD2 25b brown .25 .25
RAJ15 PTD2 50b brown .25 .25
Nos. RAJ12-RAJ15 (4) 1.00 1.00

1923-26

RAJ16 PTD2 10b lt brn .25 .25
RAJ17 PTD2 20b lt brn .25 .25
RAJ18 PTD2 25b brown ('26) .25 .25
RAJ19 PTD2 50b brown ('26) .25 .25
Nos. RAJ16-RAJ19 (4) 1.00 1.00

J82 and Type of 1911 Postage Due Stamps Overprinted in Red

1931 Wmk. 225 *Perf. 13½*

RAJ20 D2 1 l black .25 .25
RAJ21 D2 2 l black .25 .25

When the Postal Tax stamps for the Aviation Fund issue (Nos. RA16 to RA18) were not used to prepay the obligatory tax on letters, etc., it was collected by affixing Nos. RAJ20 and RAJ21.

OCCUPATION STAMPS

ISSUED UNDER AUSTRIAN OCCUPATION

Emperor Karl of Austria
OS1 OS2

1917 Unwmk. Engr. *Perf. 12½*

1N1 OS1 3b ol gray 2.00 3.00
1N2 OS1 5b ol grn 2.00 3.00
1N3 OS1 6b violet 2.00 3.00
1N4 OS1 10b org brn .40 .70
1N5 OS1 12b dp bl 1.50 2.50
1N6 OS1 15b brt rose 1.50 2.50
1N7 OS1 20b red brn .40 .70
1N8 OS1 25b ultra .40 .70
1N9 OS1 30b slate .70 1.00
1N10 OS1 40b olive bis .70 1.00
a. Perf. 11½ 100.00 175.00
b. Perf. 11½x12½ 100.00 175.00
1N11 OS1 50b dp grn .40 .70
1N12 OS1 60b rose .40 .70
1N13 OS1 80b dl bl .35 .65
1N14 OS1 90b dk vio .70 1.00
1N15 OS2 2 l rose, *straw* 1.10 1.60
1N16 OS2 3 l grn, *bl* 1.10 2.00
1N17 OS2 4 l rose, *grn* 1.50 2.50
Nos. 1N1-1N17 (17) 17.15 27.25

Nos. 1N1-1N14 have "BANI" surcharged in red.

Nos. 1N1-1N17 also exist imperforate. Value, set $125.

OS3 OS4

1918

1N18 OS3 3b ol gray .35 .85
1N19 OS3 5b ol grn .35 .85
1N20 OS3 6b violet .35 .85
1N21 OS3 10b org brn .35 .85
1N22 OS3 12b dp bl .35 .85
1N23 OS3 15b brt rose .35 .85
1N24 OS3 20b red brn .35 .85
1N25 OS3 25b ultra .35 .85
1N26 OS3 30b slate .35 .85
1N27 OS3 40b ol bis .35 .85
1N28 OS3 50b dp grn .35 .85
1N29 OS3 60b rose .35 .85
1N30 OS3 80b dl bl .35 .85
1N31 OS3 90b dk vio .35 .85
1N32 OS4 2 l rose, *straw* .35 .85
1N33 OS4 3 l grn, *bl* .75 2.25
1N34 OS4 4 l rose, *grn* 1.00 2.25
Nos. 1N18-1N34 (17) 7.00 17.25

Exist. imperf. Value, set $80.00.

The complete series exists with "BANI" or "LEI" inverted, also with those words and the numerals of value inverted. Neither of these sets was regularly issued.

Austrian Nos. M69-M82 Overprinted In Black

1918 Typo. *Perf. 12½*

1N35 M5 1h grnsh blue 40.00
1N36 M5 2h orange 25.00
1N37 M5 3h olive gray 47.50
1N38 M5 5h yellow green 25.00
1N39 M5 10h dark brown 70.00
1N40 M5 20h red 70.00
1N41 M5 25h blue 27.50
1N42 M5 30h bister 47.50
1N43 M5 45h dark slate 52.50
1N44 M5 50h deep green 60.00
1N45 M5 60h violet 80.00
1N46 M5 80h rose 1,000.
1N47 M5 90h brown violet 80.00
Nos. 1N35-1N47 (13) 1,625.

Nos. 1N35-1N47 were on sale at the Vienna post office for a few days before the Armistice signing. They were never issued at the Army Post Offices.

ISSUED UNDER BULGARIAN OCCUPATION

Dobruja District

Bulgarian Stamps of 1915-16 Overprinted in Red or Blue

1916 Unwmk. *Perf. 11½, 14*

2N1 A20 1s dk blue grn (R) .25 .25
2N2 A23 5s grn & vio brn (R) 3.00 1.75
2N3 A24 10s brn & brnsh blk (Bl) .30 .25
2N4 A26 25s indigo & blk (Bl) .30 .25
Nos. 2N1-2N4 (4) 3.85 2.50

Many varieties of overprint exist.

ISSUED UNDER GERMAN OCCUPATION

German Stamps of 1905-17 Surcharged

1917 Wmk. 125 *Perf. 14*

3N1 A22 15b on 15pf dk vio (R) 1.00 1.00
3N2 A16 25b on 20pf ultra (Bk) 1.00 1.00
3N3 A16 40b on 30pf org & blk, *buff* (R) 17.50 17.50
Nos. 3N1-3N3 (3) 19.50 19.50

"M.V.iR." are the initials of "Militär Verwaltung in Rumänien" (Military Administration of Romania).

German Stamps of 1905-17 Surcharged

1917-18

3N4 A16 10b on 10pf car 1.10 1.40
3N5 A22 15b on 15pf dk vio 5.50 4.50
3N6 A16 25b on 20pf ultra 3.00 4.00
3N7 A16 40b on 30pf org & blk, *buff* 1.00 1.40
a. "40" omitted 90.00 *350.00*
Nos. 3N4-3N7 (4) 10.60 11.30

German Stamps of 1905-17 Surcharged

1918

3N8	A16	5b on 5pf grn	.60	1.75
3N9	A16	10b on 10pf car	.60	1.50
3N10	A22	15b on 15pf dk vio	.25	.40
3N11	A16	25b on 20pf bl vio	.60	1.50
a.		25b on 20pf blue	2.50	8.00
3N12	A16	40b on 30pf org & blk, *buff*	.30	.35
		Nos. 3N8-3N12 (5)	2.35	5.50

German Stamps of 1905-17 Overprinted

1918

3N13	A16	10pf carmine	8.75	*40.00*
3N14	A22	15pf dk vio	13.00	*35.00*
3N15	A16	20pf blue	1.25	*1.75*
3N16	A16	30pf org & blk, *buff*	13.00	*22.50*
		Nos. 3N13-3N16 (4)	36.00	*99.25*

POSTAGE DUE STAMPS ISSUED UNDER GERMAN OCCUPATION

Postage Due Stamps and Type of Romania Overprinted in Red

Perf. 11½, 13½ and Compound

1918 **Wmk. 165**

3NJ1	D2	5b dk bl, *grn*	20.00	60.00
3NJ2	D2	10b dk bl, *grn*	20.00	60.00

The 20b, 30b and 50b with this overprint are fraudulent.

Unwmk.

3NJ3	D2	5b dk bl, *grn*	8.00	10.50
3NJ4	D2	10b dk bl, *grn*	8.00	10.50
3NJ5	D2	20b dk bl, *grn*	3.00	2.75
3NJ6	D2	30b dk bl, *grn*	3.00	2.75
3NJ7	D2	50b dk bl, *grn*	3.00	2.75
		Nos. 3NJ1-3NJ7 (7)	65.00	149.25

POSTAL TAX STAMPS ISSUED UNDER GERMAN OCCUPATION

Romanian Postal Tax Stamps and Type of 1916

Overprinted in Red or Black

Perf. 11½, 13½ and Compound

1917 **Unwmk.**

3NRA1	PT1	5b gray blk (R)	.80	2.75
3NRA2	PT1	10b brown (Bk)	.80	2.75

Same, Overprinted

1917-18

3NRA3	PT1	5b gray blk (R)	1.50	3.50
a.		Black overprint	57.00	*750.00*
3NRA4	PT1	10b brown (Bk)	9.00	19.00
3NRA5	PT1	10b violet (Bk)	1.50	5.00
		Nos. 3NRA3-3NRA5 (3)	12.00	27.50

Same, Overprinted in Red or Black

1918

3NRA6	PT1	5b gray blk (R)	*45.00*	30.00
3NRA7	PT1	10b brown (Bk)	*45.00*	30.00

Same, Overprinted

1918

3NRA8	PT1	10b violet (Bk)	.80	2.75

POSTAL TAX DUE STAMP ISSUED UNDER GERMAN OCCUPATION

Type of Romanian Postal Tax Due Stamp of 1916 Overprinted

Perf. 11½, 13½, and Compound

1918 **Wmk. 165**

3NRAJ1	PTD1	10b red, *green*	2.50	3.00

ROMANIAN POST OFFICES IN THE TURKISH EMPIRE

40 Paras = 1 Piaster

King Carol I

A1 A2

Perf. 11½, 13½ and Compound

1896 Wmk. 200 Black Surcharge

1	A1	10pa on 5b blue	32.50	30.00
2	A2	20pa on 10b emer	24.00	22.50
3	A1	1pa on 25b violet	24.00	22.50
		Nos. 1-3 (3)	80.50	75.00

Violet Surcharge

4	A1	10pa on 5b blue	17.00	15.00
5	A2	20pa on 10b emer	17.00	15.00
6	A1	1pa on 25b violet	17.00	15.00
		Nos. 4-6 (3)	51.00	45.00

Romanian Stamps of 1908-18 Overprinted in Black or Red

1919 **Typo.** **Unwmk.**

7	A46	5b yellow grn	.50	.50
8	A46	10b rose	.65	.65
9	A46	15b red brown	.75	.75
10	A19	25b dp blue (R)	1.00	1.00
11	A19	40b gray brn (R)	2.75	2.75
		Nos. 7-11 (5)	5.65	5.65

All values exist with inverted overprint.

ROMANIAN POST OFFICES IN THE TURKISH EMPIRE POSTAL TAX STAMP

Romanian Postal Tax Stamp of 1918 Overprinted

1919 Unwmk. ***Perf. 11½, 11½x13½***

RA1	PT1	5b green	2.50	2.50

ROUAD, ILE

ēl-ru-ad

(Arwad)

LOCATION — An island in the Mediterranean, off the coast of Latakia, Syria
GOVT. — French Mandate

In 1916, while a French post office was maintained on Ile Rouad, stamps were issued by France.

25 Centimes = 1 Piaster

French Offices in the Levant 1902-06 Stamps Ovptd.

Perf. 14x13½

1916, Jan. 12 **Unwmk.**

1	A2	5c green	550.00	275.00
2	A3	10c rose red	550.00	275.00
3	A5	1pi on 25c blue	550.00	275.00

Dangerous counterfeits exist.

A 40c and 2pi-on-50c exist but were not regularly issued. Most examples have favor cancels. Value so canceled, $700 each.

Stamps of French Offices in the Levant, 1902-06, Overprinted Horizontally

1916, Dec.

4	A2	1c gray	1.40	1.40
5	A2	2c lilac brown	1.50	1.50
6	A2	3c red orange	1.60	1.60
a.		Double overprint	210.00	
7	A2	5c green	1.75	1.75
8	A3	10c rose	2.00	2.00
9	A3	15c pale red	2.00	2.00
10	A3	20c brown violet	3.75	3.75
11	A5	1pi on 25c blue	2.75	2.75
12	A3	30c violet	2.50	2.50
13	A4	40c red & pale bl	6.00	6.00
14	A6	2pi on 50c bis brn & lavender	9.00	9.00
15	A6	4pi on 1fr cl & ol grn	16.00	16.00
16	A6	20pi on 5fr dk bl & buff	40.00	40.00
		Nos. 4-16 (13)	90.25	90.25

There is a wide space between the two words of the overprint on Nos. 13 to 16 inclusive. Nos. 4, 5 and 6 are on white and coarse, grayish (G. C.) papers.

(Note on G. C. paper follows France No. 184.)

RUANDA-URUNDI

rü-ˌän-də ü'rün-dē

(Belgian East Africa)

LOCATION — In central Africa, bounded by Congo, Uganda and Tanganyika
GOVT. — Former United Nations trusteeship administered by Belgium
AREA — 20,540 sq. mi.
POP. — 4,700,000 (est. 1958)
CAPITAL — Usumbura

See German East Africa in Vol. 3 for stamps issued under Belgian occupation.

In 1962 the two parts of the trusteeship became independent states, the Republic of Rwanda and the Kingdom of Burundi.

100 Centimes = 1 Franc

Catalogue values for unused stamps in this country are for Never Hinged items, beginning with Scott 151 in the regular postage section, Scott B26 in the semi-postal section, and Scott J8 in the postage due section.

Stamps of Belgian Congo, 1923-26, Overprinted

1924-26 ***Perf. 12***

6	A32	5c orange yel	.25	.25
7	A32	10c green	.25	.25
a.		Double overprint	70.00	70.00
8	A32	15c olive brn	.25	.25
9	A32	20c olive grn	.25	.25
10	A44	20c green ('26)	.25	.25
11	A44	25c red brown	.40	.25
12	A44	30c rose red	.35	.35
13	A44	30c olive grn ('25)	.25	.25
14	A32	40c violet ('25)	.35	.35
a.		Inverted overprint	95.00	95.00
15	A44	50c gray blue	.35	.35
16	A44	50c buff ('25)	.40	.35
17	A44	75c red org	.65	.60
18	A44	75c gray blue ('25)	.60	.45
19	A44	1fr bister brown	.70	.60
20	A44	1fr dull blue ('26)	.75	.50
21	A44	3fr gray brown	6.00	2.50
22	A44	5fr gray	12.00	9.00
23	A44	10fr gray black	22.50	20.00
		Nos. 6-23 (18)	46.55	36.80
		Set, never hinged	140.00	

Belgian Congo Nos. 112-113 Overprinted in Red or Black

1925-27 ***Perf. 12½***

24	A44	45c dk vio (R) ('27)	.35	.35
25	A44	60c car rose (Bk)	.60	.50
		Set, never hinged	1.75	

Stamps of Belgian Congo, 1923-1927, Overprinted

1927-29

26	A32	10c green ('29)	.65	.65
27	A32	15c ol brn ('29)	1.75	1.75
28	A44	35c green	.35	.35
29	A44	75c salmon red	.50	.45
30	A44	1fr rose red	.60	.50
31	A32	1.25fr dull blue	.95	.70
32	A32	1.50fr dull blue	.95	.65
33	A32	1.75fr dull blue	2.50	1.60

No. 32 Surcharged

34	A32	1.75fr on 1.50fr dl bl	.95	.70
		Nos. 26-34 (9)	9.20	7.35
		Set, never hinged	23.50	

Nos. 30 and 33 Surcharged

1931				
35	A44	1.25fr on 1fr rose red	3.50	2.00
36	A32	2fr on 1.75fr dl bl	5.50	3.00
		Set, never hinged	20.00	

Porter — A1

Mountain Scene — A2

Designs: 5c, 60c, Porter. 15c, Warrior. 25c, Kraal. 40c, Cattle herders. 50c, Cape buffalo. 75c, Bahutu greeting. 1fr, Urundi women. 1.25fr, Bahutu mother. 1.50fr, 2fr, Making wooden vessel. 2.50fr, 3.25fr, Preparing hides. 4fr, Watuba potter. 5fr, Mututsi dancer. 10fr, Watusi warriors. 20fr, Urundi prince.

1931-38		Engr.		Perf. 11½
37	A1	5c dp lil rose ('38)	.25	.25
38	A2	10c gray	.25	.25
39	A2	15c pale red	.25	.25
40	A2	25c brown vio	.25	.25
41	A1	40c green	.50	.50
42	A2	50c gray lilac	.25	.25
43	A1	60c lilac rose	.25	.25
44	A1	75c gray black	.25	.25
45	A2	1fr rose red	.40	.25
46	A1	1.25fr red brown	.40	.25
47	A2	1.50fr brown vio ('37)	.25	.25
48	A2	2fr deep blue	.50	.25
49	A2	2.50fr dp blue ('37)	.60	.60
50	A2	3.25fr brown vio	.65	.30
51	A2	4fr rose	.65	.45
52	A1	5fr gray	.65	.50
53	A1	10fr brown violet	.90	.90
54	A1	20fr brown	3.25	3.00
		Nos. 37-54 (18)	10.50	9.00
		Set, never hinged	25.00	

King Albert Memorial Issue

King Albert — A16

1934				Photo.
55	A16	1.50fr black	.65	.65
		Never hinged	2.50	

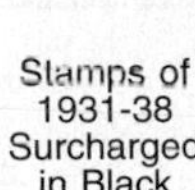

Stamps of 1931-38 Surcharged in Black

1941				
56	A1	5c on 40c green	6.50	6.50
57	A2	60c on 50c gray lil	3.50	3.50
58	A2	2.50fr on 1.50fr brn vio	3.50	3.50
59	A2	3.25fr on 2fr dp bl	15.00	15.00
		Nos. 56-59 (4)	28.50	28.50
		Set, never hinged	87.50	

Belgian Congo No. 173 Overprinted in Black

1941				Perf. 11
60	A70	10c light gray	10.00	10.00
		Never hinged	26.50	

Inverts exist. Value $45.

Belgian Congo Nos. 179, 181 Overprinted in Black

1941				
61	A70	1.75fr orange	6.00	6.00
62	A70	2.75fr vio bl	6.00	6.00
		Set, never hinged	50.00	

For surcharges see Nos. 64-65.

Belgian Congo No. 168 Surcharged in Black

1941				Perf. 11½
63	A66	5c on 1.50fr dp red brn & blk	.25	.25
		Never hinged	.35	

Inverts exist. Value $19.

Nos. 61-62 Surcharged with New Values and Bars in Black

1942				
64	A70	75c on 1.75fr org	1.75	1.75
65	A70	2.50fr on 2.75fr vio bl	5.75	5.75
		Set, never hinged	27.50	

Inverts exist. Value $50.

Belgian Congo Nos. 167, 183 Surcharged in Black

1942				Perf. 11, 11½
66	A65	75c on 90c car & brn	1.25	1.25
a.		Inverted surcharge	25.00	25.00
67	A70	2.50fr on 10fr rose red	2.50	1.90
a.		Inverted surcharge	22.00	22.00
		Set, never hinged	7.50	
		Nos. 66a-67a, never hinged	90.00	

Oil Palms — A17

Oil Palms — A18

Watusi Chief — A19

Leopard A20

Askari — A21

Zebra — A22

Askari — A23

Design: 100fr, Watusi chief.

1942-43		Engr.		Perf. 12½
68	A17	5c red	.25	.25
69	A18	10c ol grn	.25	.25
70	A18	15c brn car	.25	.25
71	A18	20c dp ultra	.25	.25
72	A18	25c brn vio	.25	.25
73	A18	30c dull blue	.25	.25
74	A18	50c dp grn	.25	.25
75	A18	60c chestnut	.25	.25
76	A19	75c dl lil & blk	.25	.25
77	A19	1fr dk brn & blk	.35	.25
78	A19	1.25fr rose red & blk	.40	.40
79	A20	1.75fr dk gray brn	1.00	.75
80	A20	2fr ocher	1.00	.50
81	A20	2.50fr carmine	1.00	.25
82	A21	3.50fr dk ol grn	.65	.35
83	A21	5fr orange	.80	.50
84	A21	6fr brt ultra	.80	.50
85	A21	7fr black	.80	.50
86	A21	10fr dp brn	1.00	.65
87	A22	20fr org brn & blk	2.50	2.00
88	A23	50fr red & blk ('43)	2.50	2.25
89	A23	100fr grn & blk ('43)	7.50	7.50
		Nos. 68-89 (22)	22.55	18.65
		Set, never hinged	45.00	

Nos. 68-89 exist imperforate, but have no franking value. Value, set never hinged $225, value set hinged $110.

Miniature sheets of Nos. 72, 76, 77 and 83 were printed in 1944 by the Belgian Government in London and given to the Belgian political review, "Message," which distributed them to its subscribers, one a month. Values, each: $55 hinged; $120 never hinged.

See note after Belgian Congo No. 225.
For surcharges see Nos. B17-B20.

Baluba Mask — A25

Carved Figures and Masks of Baluba Tribe: 10c, 50c, 2fr, 10fr, "Ndoha," figure of tribal king. 15c, 70c, 2.50fr, "Tshimanyi," an idol. 20c, 75c, 3.50fr, "Buangakokoma," statue of a kneeling beggar. 25c, 1fr, 5fr, "Mbuta," sacred double cup carved with two faces, Man and Woman. 40c, 1.25fr, 6fr, "Ngadimuashi," female mask. 1.50fr, 50fr, "Buadi-Muadi," mask with squared features (full face). 20fr, 100fr, "Mbowa," executioner's mask with buffalo horns.

1948-50		Unwmk.		Perf. 12x12½
90	A25	10c dp org	.25	.25
91	A25	15c ultra	.25	.25
92	A25	20c brt bl	.25	.25
93	A25	25c rose car	.30	.25
94	A25	40c violet	.25	.25
95	A25	50c ol brn	.25	.25
96	A25	70c yel grn	.25	.25
97	A25	75c magenta	.25	.25
98	A25	1fr yel org & dk vio	.30	.25
99	A25	1.25fr lt bl grn & mag	.30	.25
100	A25	1.50fr ol & mag ('50)	1.00	.65
101	A25	2fr org & mag	.40	.25
102	A25	2.50fr brn red & bl grn	.40	.25
103	A25	3.50fr lt bl & blk	.50	.30
104	A25	5fr bis & mag	1.00	.30
105	A25	6fr brn org & ind	1.00	.25
106	A25	10fr pale vio & red brn	1.25	.50
107	A25	20fr red org & vio brn	1.90	.80
108	A25	50fr dp org & blk	3.75	2.00
109	A25	100fr crim & blk brn	7.00	5.25
		Nos. 90-109 (20)	20.85	13.05
		Set, never hinged	80.00	

Nos. 102 and 105 Surcharged with New Value and Bars in Black

1949				
110	A25	3fr on 2.50fr	.45	.30
111	A25	4fr on 6fr	.50	.40
112	A25	6.50fr on 6fr	.65	.55
		Nos. 110-112 (3)	1.60	1.25
		Set, never hinged	3.25	

St. Francis Xavier — A26

1953, Apr. 9				Perf. 12½x13
113	A26	1.50fr ultra & gray blk	.60	.60
		Never hinged	1.00	

Death of St. Francis Xavier, 400th anniv.

Dissotis — A27

Flowers: 15c, Protea. 20c, Vellozia. 25c, Littonia. 40c, Ipomoea. 50c, Angraecum. 60c, Euphorbia. 75c, Ochna. 1fr, Hibiscus. 1.25fr, Protea. 1.50fr, Schizoglossum. 2fr, Ansellia. 3fr, Costus. 4fr, Nymphaea. 5fr, Thunborgia. 7fr, Gerbera. 8fr, Gloriosa. 10fr, Silene. 20fr, Aristolochia.

Flowers in Natural Colors

1953		Unwmk. Photo.		Perf. 11½
114	A27	10c plum & ocher	.25	.25
115	A27	15c red & yel grn	.25	.25
116	A27	20c green & gray	.25	.25
117	A27	25c dk grn & dl org	.25	.25
118	A27	40c grn & sal	.25	.25
119	A27	50c dk car & aqua	.25	.25
120	A27	60c bl grn & pink	.25	.25
121	A27	75c dp plum & gray	.25	.25
122	A27	1fr car & yel	.45	.25
123	A27	1.25fr dk grn & bl	.70	.65
124	A27	1.50fr vio & ap grn	.25	.25

No.	Type	Description	Unused	Used
125	A27	2fr ol grn & buff	2.25	.25
126	A27	3fr ol grn & pink	.70	.25
127	A27	4fr choc & lil	.70	.25
128	A27	5fr dp plum & lt bl grn	1.00	.25
129	A27	7fr dk grn & fawn	1.10	.65
130	A27	8fr grn & lt yel	1.75	.70
131	A27	10fr dp plum & pale ol	3.00	.70
132	A27	20fr vio bl & dl sal	4.75	1.25
		Nos. 114-132 (19)	18.65	7.45
		Set, never hinged	50.00	

For overprints see Burundi Nos. 1-8.

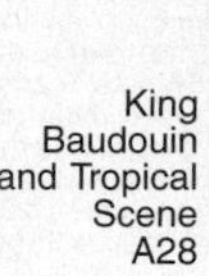

King Baudouin and Tropical Scene A28

Designs: Various African Views.

1955 Engr. & Photo.

Portrait Photo. in Black

No.	Type	Description	Unused	Used
133	A28	1.50fr rose carmine	3.00	1.25
134	A28	3fr green	3.00	1.25
135	A28	4.50fr ultra	3.00	1.25
136	A28	6.50fr deep claret	4.00	1.25
		Nos. 133-136 (4)	13.00	5.00
		Set, never hinged	30.00	

Mountain Gorilla — A29

Cape Buffaloes A30

Animals: 40c, 2fr, Black-and-white colobus (monkey). 50c, 6.50fr, Impalas. 1fr, Mountain gorilla. 3fr, 8fr, Elephants. 5fr, 10fr, Eland and Zebras. 20fr, Leopard. 50fr, Lions.

1959-61 Unwmk. Photo. *Perf. 11½*

Granite Paper

Size: 23x33mm, 33x23mm

No.	Type	Description	Unused	Used
137	A29	10c brn, crim, & blk brn	.25	.25
138	A30	20c blk, gray & ap grn	.25	.25
139	A29	40c mag, blk & gray grn	.25	.25
140	A30	50c grn, org yel & brn	.25	.25
141	A29	1fr brn, ultra & blk	.25	.25
142	A30	1.50fr blk, gray & org	.25	.25
143	A29	2fr grnsh bl, ind & brn	.25	.25
144	A30	3fr brn, dp car & blk	.25	.25
145	A30	5fr brn, dl yel, grn & blk	.25	.25
146	A30	6.50fr red, org yel & brn	.40	.45
147	A30	8fr bl, mag & blk	.50	.60
148	A30	10fr multi	.50	.60

Size: 45x26½mm

No.	Type	Description	Unused	Used
149	A30	20fr multi ('61)	.90	.90
150	A30	50fr multi ('61)	1.25	1.60
		Nos. 137-150 (14)	5.80	6.40
		Set, never hinged	7.75	

For surcharge see No. 153.
For overprints see Burundi Nos. 9-24.

Catalogue values for unused stamps in this section, from this point to the end of the section, are for Never Hinged items.

Map of Africa and Symbolic Honeycomb A31

1960, Feb.19 Unwmk. *Perf. 11½*

Inscription in French

No.	Type	Description	Unused	Used
151	A31	3fr ultra & red	.75	.25

Inscription in Flemish

No.	Type	Description	Unused	Used
152	A31	3fr ultra & red	.75	.25

10th anniversary of the Commission for Technical Co-operation in Africa South of the Sahara (C. C. T. A.).

For surcharges and overprints see Burundi Nos. 34-39.

No. 144 Surcharged with New Value and Bars

1960

No.	Type	Description	Unused	Used
153	A30	3.50fr on 3fr red, blk, brn	.40	.25

SEMI-POSTAL STAMPS

Belgian Congo Nos. B10-B11 Overprinted

1925 Unwmk. *Perf. 12½*

No.	Type	Description	Unused	Used
B1	SP1	25c + 25c car & blk	.75	.50
B2	SP1	25c + 25c car & blk	.75	.50
		Set, never hinged	3.75	

No. B2 inscribed "BELGISCH CONGO."
Commemorative of the Colonial Campaigns in 1914-1918. Nos. B1 and B2 alternate in the sheet.

Belgian Congo Nos. B12-B20 Overprinted in Blue or Red

1930 *Perf. 11½*

No.	Type	Description	Unused	Used
B3	SP3	10c + 5c ver	1.00	1.00
B4	SP3	20c + 10c dk brn	1.50	1.50
B5	SP5	35c + 15c dp grn	2.00	2.00
B6	SP5	60c + 30c dl vio	2.25	2.25
B7	SP3	1fr + 50c dk car	3.75	3.75
B8	SP5	1.75fr + 75c dp bl (R)	9.75	9.75
B9	SP5	3.50fr + 1.50fr rose lake	15.00	15.00
B10	SP5	5fr + 2.50fr red brn	15.00	15.00
B11	SP5	10fr + 5fr gray blk	16.00	16.00
		Nos. B3-B11 (9)	66.25	66.25
		Set, never hinged	170.00	

On Nos. B3, B4 and B7 there is a space of 26mm between the two words of the overprint. The surtax was for native welfare.

Queen Astrid with Native Children — SP1

1936 Photo.

No.	Type	Description	Unused	Used
B12	SP1	1.25fr + 5c dk brn	.75	.75
B13	SP1	1.50fr + 10c dl rose	.75	.75
B14	SP1	2.50fr + 25c dk bl	1.50	1.50
		Nos. B12-B14 (3)	3.00	3.00
		Set, never hinged	9.00	

Issued in memory of Queen Astrid. The surtax was for the National League for Protection of Native Children.

Lion of Belgium and Inscription "Belgium Shall Rise Again" — SP2

1942 Engr. *Perf. 12½*

No.	Type	Description	Unused	Used
B15	SP2	10fr + 40fr blue	2.50	*2.50*
B16	SP2	10fr + 40fr dark red	2.50	*2.50*
		Set, never hinged	9.00	

Nos. 74, 78, 79 and 82 Surcharged in Red

a

b

c

1945 Unwmk. *Perf. 12½*

No.	Type	Description	Unused	Used
B17	A18 (a)	50c + 50fr	2.00	1.75
B18	A19 (b)	1.25fr + 100fr	2.00	1.75
B19	A20 (c)	1.75fr + 100fr	2.00	1.75
B20	A21 (b)	3.50fr + 100fr	2.00	1.75
		Nos. B17-B20 (4)	8.00	7.00
		Set, never hinged	22.50	

Mozart at Age 7 — SP3

Queen Elizabeth and Mozart Sonata — SP4

1956 Engr. *Perf. 11½*

No.	Type	Description	Unused	Used
B21	SP3	4.50fr + 1.50fr bluish vio	1.50	*1.75*
B22	SP4	6.50fr + 2.50fr claret	3.50	*4.50*
		Set, never hinged	11.00	

200th anniv. of the birth of Wolfgang Amadeus Mozart.
Surtax for the Pro-Mozart Committee.

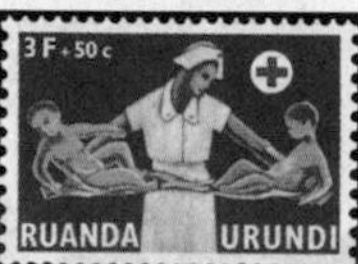

Nurse and Children — SP5

Designs: 4.50fr+50c, Patient receiving injection. 6.50fr+50c, Patient being bandaged.

1957 Photo. *Perf. 13x10½*

Cross in Carmine

No.	Type	Description	Unused	Used
B23	SP5	3fr + 50c dk blue	.30	.45
B24	SP5	4.50fr + 50c dk grn	.50	.60
B25	SP5	6.50fr + 50c red brn	.75	.75
		Nos. B23-B25 (3)	1.55	1.80
		Set, never hinged	3.25	

The surtax was for the Red Cross.

Catalogue values for unused stamps in this section, from this point to the end of the section, are for Never Hinged items.

Soccer SP6

Sports: #B26, High Jumper. #B27, Hurdlers. #B29, Javelin thrower. #B30, Discus thrower.

1960 Unwmk. *Perf. 13½*

No.	Type	Description	Unused	Used
B26	SP6	50c + 25c int bl & maroon	.40	.25
B27	SP6	1.50fr + 50c dk car & blk	.55	.25
B28	SP6	2fr + 1fr blk & dk car	.60	.25
B29	SP6	3fr + 1.25fr org ver & grn	1.90	1.25
B30	SP6	6.50fr + 3.50fr ol grn & red	2.10	1.25
		Nos. B26-B30 (5)	5.55	3.25

17th Olympic Games, Rome, Aug. 25-Sept. 11. The surtax was for the youth of Ruanda-Urundi.

Usumbura Cathedral — SP7

Designs: 1fr+50c, 5fr+2fr, Cathedral, sideview. 1.50fr+75c, 6.50fr+3fr, Stained glass window.

1961, Dec. 18 *Perf. 11½*

No.	Type	Description	Unused	Used
B31	SP7	50c + 25c brn & buff	.25	.25
B32	SP7	1fr + 50c grn & pale grn	.25	.25
B33	SP7	1.50fr + 75c multi	.25	.25
B34	SP7	3.50fr + 1.50fr lt bl & brt bl	.25	.25
B35	SP7	5fr + 2fr car & sal	.30	.30
B36	SP7	6.50fr + 3fr multi	.45	.35
		Nos. B31-B36 (6)	1.75	1.65

The surtax went for the construction and completion of the Cathedral at Usumbura.

POSTAGE DUE STAMPS

Belgian Congo Nos. J1-J7 Overprinted

1924-27 Unwmk. *Perf. 14*

No.	Type	Description	Unused	Used
J1	D1	5c black brn	.25	.25
a.		Double overprint	60.00	60.00
J2	D1	10c deep rose	.25	.25
J3	D1	15c violet	.30	.25
a.		Double overprint	60.00	60.00
J4	D1	30c green	.50	.30
J5	D1	50c ultra	.50	.40
J6	D1	50c brt blue ('27)	.80	.45
J7	D1	1fr gray	.70	.55
		Nos. J1-J7 (7)	3.30	2.45
		Set, never hinged	4.50	

Catalogue values for unused stamps in this section, from this point to the end of the section, are for Never Hinged items.

Belgian Congo Nos. J8-J12 Overprinted in Carmine

1943 *Perf. 14x14½, 12½*

J8	D2	10c	olive green	.25	.25
J9	D2	20c	dk ultra	.25	.25
J10	D2	50c	green	.25	.25
J11	D2	1fr	dark brown	.45	.45
J12	D2	2fr	yellow orange	.55	.55
			Nos. J8-J12 (5)	1.75	1.75

Nos. J8-J12 values are for stamps perf. 14x14½. Those perf. 12½ sell for about three times as much.

Belgian Congo Nos. J13-J19 Overprinted

1959 **Engr.** *Perf. 11½*

J13	D3	10c	olive brown	.25	.25
J14	D3	20c	claret	.25	.25
J15	D3	50c	green	.25	.25
J16	D3	1fr	lt blue	.25	.25
J17	D3	2fr	vermilion	.40	.40
J18	D3	4fr	purple	.80	.80
J19	D3	6fr	violet blue	.85	.85
			Nos. J13-J19 (7)	3.05	3.05

Both capital and lower-case U's are found in this overprint.

hagner

stocksheets

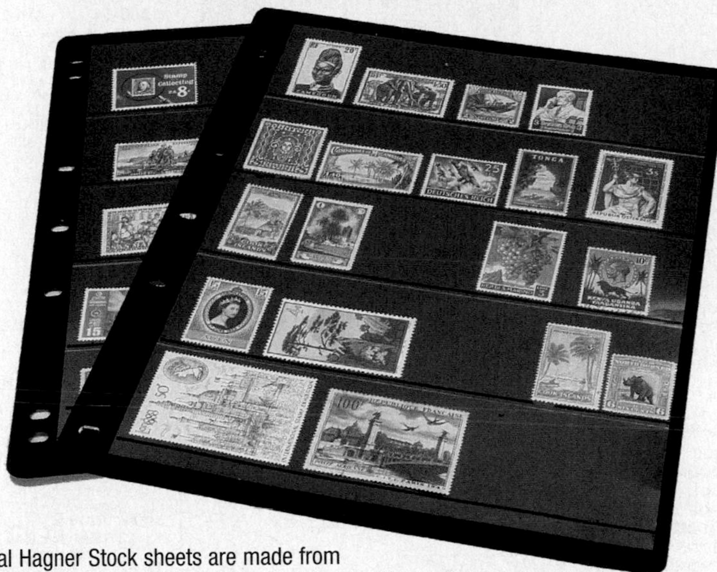

The original Hagner Stock sheets are made from archival quality pH board and feature pure polyester film pockets that are glued to each page with special chemically inert glue. For more than 40 years, collectors all over the world have come to rely on Hagner stock sheets for their long-term stamp protection. Single-sided stock sheets are available in black or white. Double-sided sheets available in black only. **Sold in packages of 5.**

	Retail	*AA**
Single Sided Sheets	$7.25	**$6.50**
Double Sided Sheets	$11.75	**$8.99**

1 Pocket 242 mm		3 Pockets 79 mm		5 Pockets 45 mm		7 Pockets 31 mm		Multi-Pockets	
HGB01	Black	HGB03	Black	HGB05	Black	HGB07	Black	HGB09	Black
HGB11*	Black	HGB33*	Black	HGB55*	Black	HGB77*	Black	HGB99*	Black
2 Pockets 119 mm		**4 Pockets 58 mm**		**6 Pockets 37 mm**		**8 Pockets 27 mm**			
HGB02	Black	HGB04	Black	HGB06	Black	HGB08	Black		
HGB22*	Black	HGB44*	Black	HGB66*	Black	HGB88*	Black		

Item #SSBSBK

Item #SSBSBL

UNIVERSAL BINDERS

We have the binders for you! Take a look at our handsome matching binder and slipcase sets. These great sets are available in your choice of blue or black. If you prefer a heavy duty binder, check out our metal-hinged, thick panel, 3-ring binder. What are you waiting for?

Item	*Description*	*Retail*	*AA*
SSBSBL	Blue 3-Ring Binder & Slipcase Set	$21.99	$17.99
SSBSBK	Black 3-Ring Binder & Slipcase Set	$21.99	$17.99
SSBMBK	Black Metal Hinged 3-Ring Binder	$24.99	$19.99

Item #SSBMBK

Call 800-572-6885

Outside U.S. & Canada call: (937) 498-0800

Visit AmosAdvantage.com

Mail to: Amos Media, P.O. Box 4129, Sidney, OH 45365

Ordering Information

***AA prices** apply to paid subscribers of Amos Media titles, or orders placed online. Prices, terms and product availability subject to change. Taxes will apply in CA, OH, & IL.

Shipping & Handling:

United States: Orders under $10 are only $3.99; Orders over $10 are 10% of order total. Minimum charge $7.99; Maximum Charge $45.00. **Canada:** 20% of order total. Minimum charge $19.99; Maximum charge $200.00. **Foreign:** Orders are shipped via FedEx Intl. or USPS and billed actual freight.

RUSSIA

'rəsh-ə

(Union of Soviet Socialist Republics)

LOCATION — Eastern Europe and Northern Asia
GOVT. — Republic
AREA — 6,592,691 sq. mi.
POP. — 147,100,000 (1999 est.)
CAPITAL — Moscow

An empire until 1917, the government was overthrown in that year and a socialist union of republics was formed under the name of the Union of Soviet Socialist Republics. The USSR includes the following autonomous republics which have issued their own stamps: Armenia, Azerbaijan, Georgia and Ukraine.

With the breakup of the Soviet Union on Dec. 26, 1991, eleven former Soviet republics established the Commonwealth of Independent States. Stamps inscribed "Rossija" are issued by the Russian Republic.

100 Kopecks = 1 Ruble

Catalogue values for unused stamps in this country are for Never Hinged items, beginning with Scott 1021 in the regular postage section, Scott B58 in the semi-postal section, and Scott C82 in the airpost section.

Watermarks

Wmk. 166 — Colorless Numerals ("1" for Nos. 1-2, "2" for No. 3, "3" for No. 4)

Wmk. 168 — Cyrillic EZGB & Wavy Lines

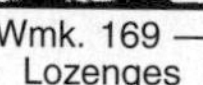

Wmk. 169 — Lozenges

Wmk. 171 — Diamonds

Wmk. 170 — Greek Border and Rosettes

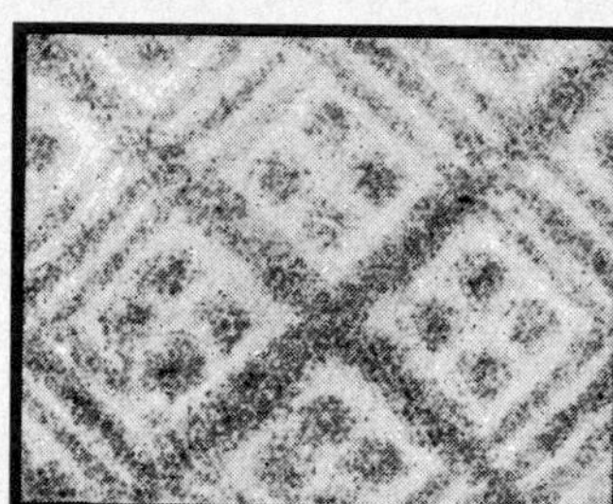

Wmk. 226 — Diamonds Enclosing Four Dots

Wmk. 293 — Hammer and Sickle, Multiple

Wmk. 383 — Cyrillic Letters in Shield

Empire

Coat of Arms — A1

Wmk. 166

1857, Dec. 10 Typo. *Imperf.*

No.		Description	Unused	Used
1	A1	10k brown & blue	62,500.	775.
		No gum	21,000.	
		Pen cancellation		475.
		Penmark & postmark		475.
		Straight line town cancellation, *from*		650.
		Circular datestamp cancellation, *from*		900.

Genuine unused examples of No. 1 are exceedingly rare. Most of those offered are used with pen cancellation removed. The unused value is for an example without gum. The very few known stamps with original gum sell for much more.

See Poland for similar stamp inscribed "ZALOT KOP. 10."

1858, Jan. 10 *Perf. 14½, 15*

No.		Description	Unused	Used
2	A1	10k brown & blue	14,000.	140.
		No gum	4,400.	
3	A1	20k blue & orange	13,000.	1,600.
		No gum	4,250.	
4	A1	30k carmine & green	18,500.	2,750.
		No gum	5,750.	

Coat of Arms — A2

Wove Paper

1858-64 Unwmk. *Perf. 12½*

No.		Description	Unused	Used
5	A2	1k blk & yel ('64)	170.00	67.50
a.		1k black & orange	340.00	55.00
6	A2	3k blk & grn ('64)	1,100.	100.00
7	A2	5k blk & lil ('64)	1,000.	90.00
8	A1	10k brown & blue	275.00	13.50
9	A1	20k blue & orange	1,000.	80.00
a.		Half used as 10k on cover		—
10	A1	30k car & grn	1,175.	125.00
		Nos. 5-10 (6)	4,720.	476.00

Coat of Arms — A3

1863

No.		Description	Unused	Used
11	A3	5k black & blue	30.00	160.00

No. 11 was issued to pay local postage in St. Petersburg and Moscow. It is known to have been used in other cities. In Aug. 1864 it was authorized for use on mail addressed to other destinations.

1865, June 2 *Perf. 14½, 15*

No.		Description	Unused	Used
12	A2	1k black & yellow	375.00	37.50
a.		1k black & orange	400.00	42.50
13	A2	3k black & green	250.00	17.50
14	A2	5k black & lilac	375.00	40.00
15	A1	10k brown & blue	925.00	3.00
a.		Thick paper	975.00	7.50
17	A1	20k blue & orange	2,750.	40.00
a.		Thick paper	3,000.	45.00
18	A1	30k car & grn	1,950.	40.00
a.		Thick paper	2,100.	45.00
		Nos. 12-18 (6)	6,625.	178.00

Horizontally Laid Paper

1866-70 Wmk. 168

No.		Description	Unused	Used
19	A2	1k blk & yel	6.50	1.10
a.		1k black & orange	12.00	1.25
b.		Imperf.		3,000.
c.		Vertically laid	315.00	45.00
d.		Groundwork inverted	5,500.	5,500.
e.		Thick paper	75.00	55.00
f.		As "c," imperf.	7,500.	7,250.
g.		As "b," "c" & "d"	11,000.	17,000.
h.		1k blk & org, vert. laid paper	350.00	42.50
20	A2	3k blk & dp grn	11.00	1.50
a.		3k black & yellow green	12.50	1.50
b.		Imperf.		3,400.
c.		Vertically laid	400.00	50.00
d.		V's in groundwork (error) ('70)	1,000.	40.00
e.		3k black & blue green	12.50	1.50
22	A2	5k black & lilac	15.00	2.00
a.		5k black & gray	240.00	32.50
b.		Imperf.		4,250.
c.		Vertically laid	10,000.	160.00
d.		As "c," imperf.	—	—
23	A1	10k brn & blue	45.00	1.75
a.		Vertically laid	525.00	16.50
b.		Center inverted		50,000.
c.		Imperf.		22,500.
24	A1	20k blue & org	105.00	15.00
a.		Vertically laid	5,250.	160.00
25	A1	30k car & grn	100.00	30.00
a.		Vertically laid	1,000.	120.00
		Nos. 19-25 (6)	282.50	51.35

Arms — A4

1875-82 Horizontally Laid Paper

No.		Description	Unused	Used
26	A2	2k black & red	25.00	1.60
a.		Vertically laid	6,750.	160.00
		No gum	1,275.	
b.		Groundwork inverted		57,500.
27	A4	7k gray & rose ('79)	16.00	1.00
a.		Imperf.		8,500.
b.		Vertically laid	2,000.	65.00
		No gum	600.00	
c.		Wmkd. hexagons ('79)		170,000.
d.		Center inverted		—
e.		Center omitted	—	—
f.		7k black & carmine ('80)	21.00	.85
g.		7k pale gray & carmine ('82)	21.00	.85
28	A4	8k gray & rose	25.00	1.60
a.		Vertically laid	2,500.	82.50
		No gum	600.00	
b.		Imperf.		22,500.
c.		"C" instead of "B" in "Bocem"	650.00	250.
29	A4	10k brn & blue	50.00	5.75
a.		Center inverted		60,000.
30	A4	20k blue & org	67.50	10.00
a.		Cross-shaped "T" in bottom word	170.00	27.50
b.		Center inverted		75,000.
c.		Center double		90,000.
d.		As "a," center inverted		—
		Nos. 26-30 (5)	183.50	19.95

The hexagon watermark of No. 27c is that of revenue stamps. No. 27c exists with Perm and Riga postmarks.

See Finland for stamps similar to designs A4-A15, which have "dot in circle" devices or are inscribed "Markka," "Markkaa," "Pen.," or "Pennia."

Imperial Eagle and Post Horns
A5 A6

Perf. 14 to 15 and Compound

1883-88 Wmk. 168

Horizontally Laid Paper

No.		Description	Unused	Used
31	A5	1k orange	7.25	1.20
a.		Imperf.		62,500.
b.		Groundwork inverted		9,000.
c.		1k yellow	6.75	1.20
32	A5	2k dark green	4.00	1.20
a.		2k yellow green ('88)	26.50	4.00
b.		Imperf.	1,100.	700.00
c.		Wove paper	—	—
d.		Groundwork inverted		31,500.
33	A5	3k carmine	7.50	1.20
a.		Imperf.	—	—
b.		Groundwork inverted		30,000.
c.		Wove paper	—	—
34	A5	5k red violet	4.00	.90
a.		Groundwork inverted		8,500.
35	A5	7k blue	7.50	.90
a.		Imperf.	800.00	475.00
b.		Groundwork inverted	1,700.	1,600.
c.		Double impression of frame and center	—	—
36	A6	14k blue & rose	85.00	2.50
a.		Imperf.	4,000.	3,000.
b.		Center inverted	—	6,250.
c.		Diagonal half surcharge "7" in red, on cover ('84)		—
37	A6	35k vio & grn	60.00	6.50
38	A6	70k brn & org	67.50	9.50
		Nos. 31-38 (8)	242.75	23.90

Before 1882 the 1, 2, 3 and 5 kopecks had small numerals in the background; beginning with No. 31 these denominations have a background of network, like the higher values.

No. 36c is handstamped. It is known with cancellations of Tiflis and Kutais, both in Georgia. It is believed to be of philatelic origin.

A7

1884 *Perf. 13½, 13½x11½*

Vertically Laid Paper

No.		Description	Unused	Used
39	A7	3.50r blk & gray	1,200.	625.
a.		Horiz. laid	175,000.	15,000.
b.		Inverted center	—	—
40	A7	7r blk & org	800.	675.

Forgeries exist, both unused and used.

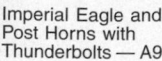

A8

Imperial Eagle and Post Horns with Thunderbolts — A9

With Thunderbolts Across Post Horns

Perf. 14 to 15 and Compound

1889, May 14

Horizontally Laid Paper

No.	Type	Description	Unused	Used
41	A8	4k rose	12.00	.45
a.		Groundwork inverted	—	—
b.		Double impression of center	—	—
c.		Double impression of frame	—	—
42	A8	10k dark blue	20.00	.45
43	A8	20k blue & carmine	21.00	1.20
a.		Groundwork inverted	—	
44	A8	50k violet & green	16.00	1.50
		Perf. 13½		
45	A9	1r lt brn, brn & org	47.50	2.50
a.		Horiz. pair, imperf. btwn.	900.00	450.00
b.		Vert. pair, imperf. btwn.	850.00	425.00
c.		Center omitted	—	—
		Nos. 41-45 (5)	116.50	6.10

See #57C, 60, 63, 66, 68, 82, 85, 87, 126, 129, 131. For surcharges see #216, 219, 223, 226.

A10

A11

A12

With Thunderbolts Across Post Horns

1889-92 *Perf. 14½x15*

Horizontally Laid Paper

No.	Type	Description	Unused	Used
46	A10	1k orange	3.25	.50
a.		Imperf.	850.00	—
47	A10	2k green	4.00	.50
a.		Imperf.	800.00	
b.		Groundwork inverted	800.00	*17,000.*
48	A10	3k carmine	8.00	.50
a.		Imperf.	425.00	350.00
49	A10	5k red vio	8.00	.60
b.		Groundwork omitted or inverted	850.00	650.00
50	A10	7k dk blue	5.25	.50
a.		Imperf.	425.00	*9,000.*
b.		Groundwork inverted	*16,000.*	*11,250.*
c.		Groundwork omitted	250.00	200.00
51	A11	14k blue & rose	16.00	.50
a.		Center inverted	*6,750.*	*4,500.*
b.		Center omitted	850.00	
52	A11	35k vio & grn	67.50	6.00
		Perf. 13½		
53	A12	3.50r blk & gray	19.00	8.00
a.		Center inverted	—	*12,750.*
54	A12	7r blk & yel	190.00	11.00
a.		Dbl. impression of black		*45,000.*
		Nos. 46-54 (9)	321.00	28.10

Perf. 14 to 15 and Compound

1902-05 **Vertically Laid Paper**

No.	Type	Description	Unused	Used
55	A10	1k orange	4.50	.35
a.		Imperf.	1,100.	*1,100.*
b.		Groundwork inverted	—	—
c.		Groundwork omitted	—	—
56	A10	2k yel grn	4.50	.35
a.		2k deep green	8.00	.70
b.		Groundwork omitted	—	—
c.		Groundwork inverted	—	—
d.		Groundwork double	*375.00*	*375.00*
57	A10	3k rose red	10.50	.35
a.		Groundwork omitted	—	—
b.		Double impression	275.00	250.00
d.		Imperf.	*1,350.*	—
e.		Groundwork inverted	—	—
f.		Groundwork double	275.00	
57C	A8	4k rose red ('04)	9.00	.85
f.		Double impression	340.00	275.00
g.		Groundwork inverted	—	—
58	A10	5k red vio	19.00	.60
a.		5k dull violet	12.50	2.25
b.		Groundwork inverted	—	—
c.		Imperf.	—	—
d.		Groundwork omitted	675.00	150.00
e.		Groundwork double	*1,350.*	100.00
59	A10	7k dk blue	10.50	.35
a.		Groundwork omitted	315.00	*275.00*
b.		Imperf.	675.00	600.00
c.		Groundwork inverted	—	—
60	A8	10k dk blue ('04)	4.00	.50
a.		Groundwork inverted	42.50	17.50
b.		Groundwork omitted	600.00	85.00
c.		Groundwork double	175.00	85.00
61	A11	14k blue & rose	22.50	.80
a.		Center inverted	—	*4,000.*
b.		Center omitted	1,100.	700.00
62	A11	15k brn vio & blue ('05)	20.00	2.00
a.		Center omitted	—	—
b.		Center inverted	*4,500.*	*4,000.*
63	A8	20k blue & car ('04)	11.00	.85
64	A11	25k dull grn & lil ('05)	45.00	2.50
a.		Center inverted	*7,250.*	6,000.
b.		Center omitted	—	—
65	A11	35k dk vio & grn	55.00	1.80
a.		Center inverted	2,500.	*2,000.*
b.		Center omitted	—	—
66	A8	50k vio & grn ('05)	35.00	1.00
67	A11	70k brn & org	45.00	3.25
		Perf. 13½		
68	A9	1r lt brn, brn & org	90.00	2.00
a.		Perf. 11½	700.00	50.00
b.		Perf. 13½x11½, 11½x13½	340.00	525.00
c.		Impert.	—	—
d.		Center inverted	—	—
e.		Center omitted	675.00	250.00
f.		Horiz. pair, imperf. btwn.	1,100.	350.00
g.		Vert. pair, imperf. btwn.	900.00	340.00
69	A12	3.50r blk & gray	55.00	4.00
a.		Center inverted		*13,000.*
b.		Imperf., pair	2,000.	2,000.
70	A12	7r blk & yel	14.00	4.75
a.		Center inverted	*7,000.*	*13,500.*
b.		Horiz. pair, imperf. btwn.	3,000.	1,450.
d.		Imperf., pair	—	—

A13

1906 *Perf. 13½*

No.	Type	Description	Unused	Used
71	A13	5r dk blue, grn & pale blue	50.00	4.50
a.		Perf. 11½	500.00	275.00
72	A13	10r car rose, yel & gray	350.00	10.50
		Nos. 55-72 (19)	854.50	41.30

The design of No. 72 differs in many details from the illustration. Nos. 71-72 were printed in sheets of 25.

See Nos. 80-81, 83-84, 86, 108-109, 125, 127-128, 130, 132-135, 137-138. For surcharges see Nos. 217-218, 220-222, 224-225, 227-229.

A14

A15

Vertical Lozenges of Varnish on Face

1909-12 **Unwmk.** *Perf. 14x14½*

Wove Paper

No.	Type	Description	Unused	Used
73	A14	1k dull org yel	.45	.45
a.		1k orange yellow ('09)	2.50	.45
c.		Double impression	90.00	—
74	A14	2k dull green	.25	.25
a.		2k green ('09)	1.60	.25
b.		Double impression	100.00	—
75	A14	3k carmine	.25	.25
a.		3k rose red ('09)	1.40	.25
76	A15	4k carmine	.25	.25
a.		4k carmine rose ('09)	1.40	.25
77	A14	5k claret	2.50	.25
a.		5k lilac ('12)	.25	.25
b.		Double impression	95.00	
78	A14	7k blue	.25	.25
a.		7k light blue ('09)	2.50	.45
b.		Imperf.	1,450.	
79	A15	10k dark blue	.25	.25
a.		10k light blue ('09)	*80.00*	*8.00*
b.		10k pale blue	8.00	2.00
80	A11	14k dk blue & car	.85	.25
a.		14k blue & rose ('09)	1.40	.25
81	A11	15k red brn & dp blue	.25	.25
a.		15k dull violet & blue ('09)	1.40	.25
c.		Center omitted	170.00	—
d.		Center double	50.00	—
82	A8	20k dull bl & dk car	.25	.25
a.		20k blue & carmine ('10)	1.40	.45
b.		Groundwork omitted	42.50	
c.		Center double	175.00	
d.		Center and value omitted	—	—
83	A11	25k dl grn & dk vio	.25	.25
a.		25k green & violet ('09)	1.40	.45
b.		Center omitted	170.00	
c.		Center double	175.00	—
84	A11	35k red brn & grn	.25	.25
a.		35k brown vio & yel green	.55	.40
b.		35k violet & green ('09)	1.40	.45
c.		Center double	25.00	—
85	A8	50k red brn & grn	.25	.25
a.		50k violet & green ('09)	3.25	.45
b.		Groundwork omitted	30.00	—
c.		Center double	175.00	—
d.		Center and value omitted	—	—
86	A11	70k brn & red org	.25	.25
a.		70k lt brown & orange ('09)	2.50	.45
b.		Center double	175.00	—
c.		Center omitted	115.00	115.00
		Perf. 13½		
87	A9	1r pale brn, dk brn & org	.50	.35
a.		1r pale brn, brn & org ('10)	1.65	.45
b.		Perf. 12½	80.00	—
c.		Groundwork inverted	25.00	—
d.		Horiz. pair, imperf. between	25.00	—
e.		Vert. pair, imperf. between	25.00	—
f.		Center inverted	40.00	—
g.		Center double	25.00	—
		Nos. 73-87 (15)	7.05	4.05

See Nos. 119-124. For surcharges see Nos. 117-118, B24-B29.

No. 87a was issued in sheets of 40 stamps, while Nos. 87 and 87b came in sheets of 50. Nos. 87g-87k are listed below No. 138a.

Nearly all values of this issue are known without the lines of varnish.

The 7k has two types:

I — The scroll bearing the top inscription ends at left with three short lines of shading beside the first letter. Four pearls extend at lower left between the leaves and denomination panel.

II — Inner lines of scroll at top left end in two curls; three pearls at lower left.

Three clichés of type II (an essay) were included by mistake in the plate used for the first printing. Value of pair, type I with type II, unused $4,500.

SURCHARGES

Russian stamps of types A6-A15 with various surcharges may be found listed under Armenia, Batum, Far Eastern Republic, Georgia, Latvia, Siberia, South Russia, Transcaucasian Federated Republics, Ukraine, Russian Offices in China, Russian Offices in the Turkish Empire and Army of the Northwest.

Peter I — A16

Alexander II — A17

Alexander III — A18

Peter I — A19

RARITAN STAMPS, INC.
International Philatelic Auction House and Dealers

QUARTERLY LIVE AUCTIONS

Rare Worldwide Stamps and Postal History
British Commonwealth, Asia,
Eastern and Western Europe

Specialized Russian Area Material:
Empire, RSFSR, Soviet Union,
Post Offices Abroad,
Locals of the Civil War Period,
Zemstvo (Rural Post).
Armenia, Azerbaijan, Georgia,
Baltic States, Russian Finland,
Poland, Tannu-Tuva and
Ukraine

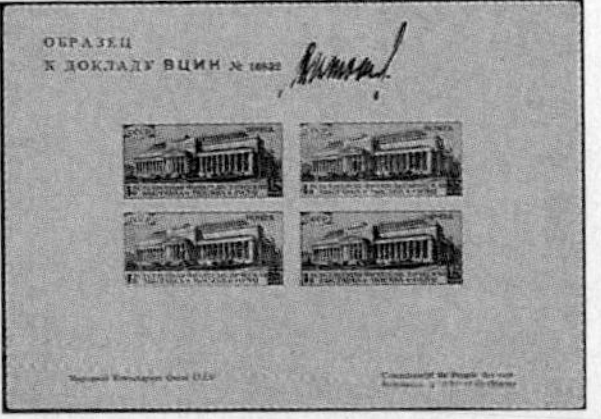

We always buy or take for consignment Collections, Accumulations, Dealer's stocks, single rare stamps and postal history of the World

RARITAN STAMPS, INC.
PO Box 557, Dayton, New Jersey 08810-0557 USA
Phone: 1.732. 422.2124 Fax: 1.732. 422.2125
E-Mail: info@raritanstamps.com
Web site: www.RaritanStamps.com

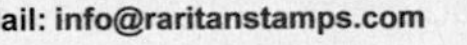

Nicholas II
A20 A21

Catherine II — A22

Nicholas I — A23

Alexander I — A24

Alexis Mikhailovich A25

Paul I A26

Elizabeth Petrovna A27

Michael Feodorovich A28

The Kremlin — A29

Winter Palace — A30

Romanov Castle — A31

Nicholas II — A32

www.russianstamps.com
The largest stock of
RUSSIAN MATERIAL

STAMPS, COVERS,
LOCALS & ZEMSTVOS,
ERRORS & VARIETIES,
RARITIES

LORAL
P.O. Box 670554
Flushing, NY 11367
Phone 718-261-6971
Fax 718-261-1838
E-Mail Lfinik@aol.com

Without Lozenges of Varnish

1913, Jan. 2 Typo. *Perf. 13½*

No.	Type	Description	Unused	Used
88	A16	1k brn org	1.60	.25
89	A17	2k yellow green	4.25	.25
90	A18	3k rose red	4.25	.25
b.		Double impression	600.00	
91	A19	4k dull red	1.60	.25
92	A20	7k brown	1.60	.25
b.		Double impression	675.00	—
93	A21	10k deep blue	4.25	.25
94	A22	14k blue green	4.25	.40
95	A23	15k yellow brown	8.00	.60
96	A24	20k olive green	26.50	.70
97	A25	25k red violet	8.00	1.10
98	A26	35k gray vio & dk grn	2.50	.70
99	A27	50k brn & slate	10.75	1.90
100	A28	70k yel grn & brn	8.00	1.90

Engr.

No.	Type	Description	Unused	Used
101	A29	1r deep green	40.00	6.25
102	A30	2r red brown	65.00	11.00
103	A31	3r dark violet	50.00	11.00
104	A32	5r black brown	40.00	19.00
		Nos. 88-104 (17)	280.55	56.05
		Set, never hinged	650.00	

Imperf

No.	Type	Description	Unused	Used
88a	A16	1k brown orange	900.00	—
89a	A17	2k yellow green	900.00	—
90a	A18	3k rose red	900.00	
91a	A19	4k dull red	2,150.	
92a	A20	7k brown	500.00	
93a	A21	10k deep blue	900.00	
94a	A22	14k blue green	2,150.	
101a	A29	1r deep green	1,750.	
102a	A30	2r red brown	900.00	
103b	A31	3r dark violet	900.00	
104a	A32	5r dark violet	2,150.	

Tercentenary of the founding of the Romanov dynasty.

See Nos. 105-107, 112-116, 139-141. For surcharges see Nos. 110-111, Russian Offices in the Turkish Empire 213-227.

Arms and 5-line Inscription on Back

Имѣетъ хожденіе наравнѣ съ размѣнной серебряной монетой.

No. 107 Back

Thin Cardboard Without Gum

1915, Oct. Typo. *Perf. 13½*

No.	Type	Description	Unused	Used
105	A21	10k blue	2.50	*32.50*
106	A23	15k brown	2.50	*32.50*
107	A24	20k olive green	2.50	*32.50*
		Nos. 105-107 (3)	7.50	*97.50*

Imperf

No.	Type	Description	Unused	Used
105a	A21	10k	550.00	
106a	A23	15k	200.00	—
107a	A24	20k	175.00	

Nos. 105-107, 112-116 and 139-141 were issued for use as paper money, but contrary to regulations were often used for postal purposes. Back inscription means: "Having circulation on par with silver subsidiary coins."

Types of 1906 Issue
Vertical Lozenges of Varnish on Face

1915 *Perf. 13½, 13½x13*

No.	Type	Description	Unused	Used
108	A13	5r ind, grn & lt blue	1.40	.50
a.		5r dk bl, grn & pale bl ('15)	13.50	1.60
b.		Perf. 12½	16.50	6.75
c.		Center double	60.00	
d.		Pair, imperf. between	*100.00*	—
109	A13	10r car lake, yel & gray	2.00	.50
a.		10r carmine, yel & light gray	2.00	.50
b.		10r rose red, yel & gray ('15)	6.75	.85
c.		10r car, yel & gray blue (error)	*2,700.*	
d.		Groundwork inverted	*450.00*	
e.		Center double	60.00	—

Nos. 108a and 109b were issued in sheets of 25. Nos. 108, 108b, 109 and 109a came in sheets of 50. Chemical forgeries of No. 109c exist. Genuine examples usually are centered to upper right.

Nos. 92, 94 Surcharged

1916

No.	Type	Description	Unused	Used
110	A20	10k on 7k brown	.85	.50
a.		Inverted surcharge	210.00	
111	A22	20k on 14k bl grn	.85	.45

Imperf

No.	Type	Description	Unused	Used
110b	A20	10k on 7k brown	*425.00*	—
111a	A22	20k on 14k bl grn	*425.00*	—

Types of 1913 Issue
Arms, Value & 4-line inscription on Back
Surcharged Large Numerals on Nos. 112-113
Thin Cardboard

1916-17 Without Gum

No.	Type	Description	Unused	Used
112	A16	1 on 1k brn org ('17)	2.50	*40.00*
113	A17	2 on 2k yel green ('17)	2.50	*40.00*

Without Surcharge

No.	Type	Description	Unused	Used
114	A16	1k brown orange	50.00	—
115	A17	2k yellow green	52.50	—
116	A18	3k rose red	2.50	*32.50*

See note after No. 107.

Nos. 78a, 80a Surcharged

a

b

1917 *Perf. 14x14½*

No.	Type	Description	Unused	Used
117	A14	10k on 7k lt blue	.85	.45
a.		Inverted surcharge	150.00	—
b.		Double surcharge	60.00	—
c.		Imperforate	*375.00*	—
118	A11	20k on 14k bl & rose	1.20	.45
a.		Inverted surcharge	250.00	—

Provisional Government
Civil War
Type of 1889-1912 Issues
Vertical Lozenges of Varnish on Face

Two types of 7r:
Type I — Single outer frame line.
Type II — Double outer frame line.

Wove Paper

1917 Typo. *Imperf.*

No.	Type	Description	Unused	Used
119	A14	1k orange	1.10	.25
120	A14	2k gray green	.25	.25
121	A14	3k red	.25	.25
122	A15	4k carmine	.85	2.50
123	A14	5k claret	.25	.25
124	A15	10k dark blue	22.50	22.50
125	A11	15k red brn & dp blue	.40	.25
a.		Center omitted	175.00	
126	A8	20k blue & car	.35	.35
a.		Groundwork omitted	42.50	—
127	A11	25k grn & gray vio	.50	1.00
128	A11	35k red brn & grn	.50	.35
129	A8	50k brn vio & grn	.45	.25
a.		Groundwork omitted	42.50	—
130	A11	70k brn & org	.45	.35
a.		Center omitted	100.00	
131	A9	1r pale brn, brn & red org	.35	.25
a.		Center inverted	25.00	—
b.		Center omitted	25.00	—
c.		Center double	25.00	—
d.		Groundwork double	150.00	—
e.		Groundwork inverted	60.00	—
f.		Groundwork omitted	60.00	—
g.		Frame double	25.00	—
132	A12	3.50r mar & lt grn	1.10	.25
133	A13	5r dk blue, grn & pale blue	1.25	.35
a.		5r dk bl, grn & yel (error)	900.00	
b.		Groundwork inverted	*3,600.*	
134	A12	7r dk grn & pink (I)	1.20	1.15
a.		Center inverted		*6,750.*
135	A13	10r scar, yel & gray	55.00	40.00
a.		10r scarlet, green & gray (error)	1,125.	
		Nos. 119-135 (17)	86.75	70.55

Beware of trimmed examples of No. 109 offered as No. 135.

Vertical Lozenges of Varnish on Face

1917 *Perf. 13½, 13½x13*

No.	Type	Description	Unused	Used
137	A12	3.50r mar & lt grn	.50	.25
138	A12	7r dk grn & pink (II)	2.50	.50
d.		Type I	40.00	6.75

Perf. 12½

No.	Type	Description	Unused	Used
137a	A12	3.50r maroon & lt grn	14.00	2.75
138a	A12	7r dk grn & pink (II)	17.00	4.75

Horizontal Lozenges of Varnish on Face

Perf. 13½x13

No.	Type	Description	Unused	Used
87g	A9	1r pale brown, brn & red orange	1.35	.30
h.		Imperf.	17.50	—
i.		As "h," center omitted	45.00	—
j.		As "h," center inverted	22.50	—
k.		As "h," center double	22.50	—
137b	A12	3.50r mar & lt green	2.50	.50
d.		Imperf.	2,250.	
138b	A12	7r dk grn & pink (II)	1.35	.25
c.		Imperf.	1,550.	

Nos. 87g, 137b and 138b often show the eagle with little or no embossing.

Types of 1913 Issue

No. 88 Surcharged Large Numeral

1
КОПѢЙКА.
Имѣетъ хожденіе наравнѣ съ мѣдной монетой.

Surcharge & 4-line Inscription on Back

1917

Thin Cardboard, Without Gum

No.	Type	Description	Unused	Used
139	A16	1 on 1k brown org	2.50	*40.00*
140	A17	2 on 2k yel green	2.50	*40.00*
a.		Imperf.	525.00	—
		Pair	*1,700.*	

Without Surcharge

No.	Type	Description	Unused	Used
141	A18	3k rose red	2.50	*40.00*
		Nos. 139-141 (3)	7.50	*120.00*

See note after No. 107.

Stamps overprinted with a Liberty Cap on Crossed Swords or with reduced facsimiles of pages of newspapers were a private speculation and without official sanction.

RUSSIAN TURKESTAN

Russian stamps of 1917-18 surcharged as above are frauds.

Russian Soviet Federated Socialist Republic

Severing Chain of Bondage — A33

1918 **Typo.** ***Perf. 13½***

149 A33 35k blue .45 *6.25*
a. Imperf., pair 1,600.
150 A33 70k brown .50 *7.25*
a. Imperf., pair *16,500.*

For surcharges see Nos. B18-B23, J1-J9 and note following No. B17.

A 15k stamp exists but was not regularly issued. Value, $30,000.

During 1918-22, the chaotic conditions of revolution and civil war brought the printing of stamps by the central government to a halt. Stocks of old tsarist Arms type stamps and postal stationery remained in use, and postal savings and various revenue stamps were authorized for postage use. During this period, stamps were sold and used at different rates at different times: 1918-20, sold at face value; from March, 1920, sold at 100 times face value; from Aug. 15, 1921, sold at 250r each, regardless of face value; from April, 1922, sold at 10,000r per 1k or 1r. In Oct. 1922, these issues were superseded by gold currency stamps.

See Nos. AR1-AR25 for fiscal stamps used as postage stamps during this period.

Symbols of Agriculture — A40

Symbols of Industry — A41

Soviet Symbols of Agriculture and Industry — A42

Science and Arts — A43

1921 **Unwmk.** **Litho.** ***Imperf.***

177 A40 1r orange .85 *140.00*
178 A40 2r lt brown .85 *140.00*
a. Double impression 800.00
179 A41 5r dull ultra 2.10 *140.00*
a. Double impression —
180 A42 20r blue 2.50 *140.00*
a. Double impression 240.00
b. Pelure paper 10.00 *175.00*
c. As "b," double impression 275.00 —
181 A40 100r orange .25 *.25*
a. Double impression 200.00
b. Pelure paper .25 .45
c. As "b," double impression 200.00
182 A40 200r lt brown .45 *.25*
a. Double impression 180.00
b. Triple impression 150.00
c. 200r gray brown 25.00
183 A43 250r dull violet .25 *.25*
a. Tête bêche pair 25.00
b. Double impression 90.00
c. Pelure paper .25 *.45*
d. As "c," tête bêche pair 32.50 —
e. As "c," double impression 100.00
f. Chalk surfaced paper 12.50 *5.00*
184 A40 300r green .50 *1.10*
a. Double impression 425.00
b. Pelure paper 8.00 22.50
185 A41 500r blue .85 .30
a. Double impression —
186 A41 1000r carmine .25 *.30*
a. Double impression 110.00
b. Triple impression 135.00
c. Pelure paper .85 *.30*
d. As "c," double impression 90.00
e. Thick paper 2.50 *2.75*
f. Chalk surfaced paper .25 *.50*
Nos. 177-186 (10) 8.85 562.45

Nos. 177-180 were on sale only in Petrograd, Moscow and Kharkov. Used values are for cancelled-to-order stamps. Postally used examples are worth substantially more.

Nos. 183a and 183d are from printings in which one of the two panes of 25 in the sheet were inverted. Thus, they are horizontal pairs, with a vertical gutter.

See Nos. 203, 205. For surcharges see Nos. 191-194, 196-199, 201, 210, B40, B43-B47, J10.

New Russia Triumphant A44

Type I — 37½mm by 23½mm.
Type II — 38½mm by 23¼mm.

1921, Aug. 10 **Wmk. 169** **Engr.**

187 A44 40r slate, type II 1.90 *160.00*
a. Type I 1.90 *160.00*

The types are caused by paper shrinkage. One type has the watermark sideways in relation to the other.

For surcharges see Nos. 195, 200.

Initials Stand for Russian Soviet Federated Socialist Republic — A45

1921 **Litho.** **Unwmk.**

188 A45 100r orange .85 .85
189 A45 250r violet .85 .85
190 A45 1000r carmine rose 1.75 1.40
Nos. 188-190 (3) 3.45 3.10

4th anniversary of Soviet Government.

A 200r was not regularly issued. Values: unused $60, never hinged $100.

Nos. 177-179 Surcharged in Black

1922

191 A40 5000r on 1r org 3.00 .80
a. Inverted surcharge 140.00 32.50
b. Double surch., red & blk 800.00 —
c. Pair, one without surcharge 250.00 —
192 A40 5000r on 2r lt brn 3.00 1.10
a. Inverted surcharge 110.00 90.00
b. Double surcharge 145.00
193 A41 5000r on 5r ultra 3.00
a. Inverted surcharge — *450.00*
b. Double surcharge 145.00

Beware of digitally created forgeries of the errors of Nos. 191-193 and 196-199.

No. 180 Surcharged

194 A42 5000r on 20r blue 2.10 2.25
a. Pelure paper 16.50 3.25
b. Pair, one without surcharge *125.00*

Nos. 177-180, 187-187a Surcharged in Black or Red

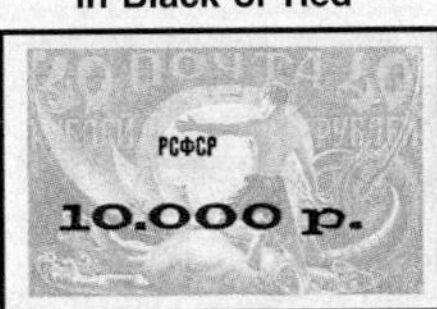

Wmk. Lozenges (169)

195 A44 10,000r on 40r, type I 95.00 50.00
a. Inverted surcharge 225.00
b. Type II 67.50 50.00
c. "1.0000" instead of "10.000" 2,750.
d. Double surcharge *8,500.*

Red Surcharge
Unwmk.

196 A40 5000r on 1r org 5.75 5.75
a. Inverted surcharge 50.00 25.00
197 A40 5000r on 2r lt brn 5.75 5.75
a. Inverted surcharge 125.00 30.00
198 A41 5000r on 5r ultra 5.75 5.75
199 A42 5000r on 20r blue 3.00 2.25
a. Inverted surcharge 200.00 50.00
b. Pelure paper 4.00 5.00

Wmk. Lozenges (169)

200 A44 10,000r on 40r, type I (R) 2.25 1.25
a. Inverted surcharge 160.00 40.00
b. Double surcharge 125.00 —
c. With periods after Russian letters 1,100. 450.00
d. Type II 2.25 2.75
e. As "a," type II 125.00 40.00
f. As "c," type II 200.00 —

No. 183 Surcharged in Black or Blue Black

1922, Mar. **Unwmk.**

201 A43 7500r on 250r (Bk) .25 .25
a. Pelure paper .25 .25
b. Chalk surfaced paper .45 .45
c. Blue black surcharge .50 .25
d. Surch. typographed 250.00 —
e. As "c," surch. lithographed 850.00 —
f. As "d," surch. inverted *3,250.* —
Nos. 191-201 (11) 128.85 75.15

Nos. 201, 201a and 201b exist with surcharge inverted (value about $20 each), and double (about $25 each).

The horizontal surcharge was prepared but not issued. Values: $11 unused, $20 never hinged. The horizontal surcharge also exists on pelure paper. Values: $70 unused, $175 never hinged.

Type of 1921 and

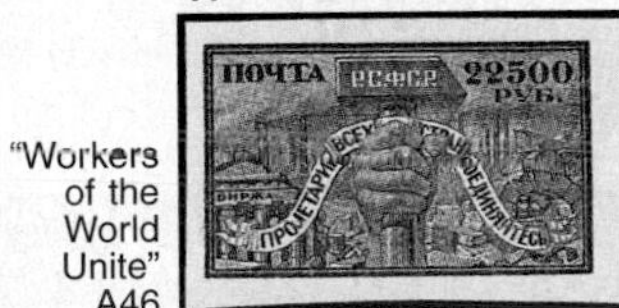

"Workers of the World Unite" A46

1922 **Litho.** **Wmk. 171**

202 A46 5000r dark violet 1.90 .60
203 A42 7500r blue .50 .50
204 A46 10,000r blue 17.50 3.00

Unwmk.

205 A42 7500r blue, *buff* .50 .50
a. Double impression 250.00
206 A46 22,500r dk violet, *buff* .50 .60
Nos. 202-206 (5) 20.90 5.20

For surcharges see Nos. B41-B42.

No. 183 Surcharged Diagonally

1922 **Unwmk.** ***Imperf.***

210 A43 100,000r on 250r .50 .50
a. Inverted surcharge 200.00 .50
b. Pelure paper .50 .50
c. Chalk surfaced paper 2.25 1.65
d. As "b," inverted surcharge 225.00 —

Marking 5th Anniversary of October Revolution — A48

1922 **Typo.**

211 A48 5r ocher & black .60 *.25*
212 A48 10r brown & black .60 *.25*
213 A48 25r violet & black 1.60 *.60*
214 A48 27r rose & black 5.50 *2.00*
215 A48 45r blue & black 3.60 *2.00*
Nos. 211-215 (5) 11.90 *5.10*

Pelure Paper

211a A48 5r ocher & black 82.50
212a A48 10r brown & black 120.00
213a A48 25r violet & black 82.50
214a A48 27r rose & black 82.50
215a A48 45r blue & black 60.00

5th anniv. of the October Revolution. Sold in the currency of 1922 which was valued at 10,000 times that of the preceding years.

For surcharges see Nos. B38-B39.

RUSSIAN STAMPS:
WANTLISTS, SPECIALIZED MATERIAL, NEW ISSUES
PHILATELIC LITERATURE:
CATALOGS, RARE PUBLICATIONS
ALWAYS BUYING:
STAMPS, LITERATURE
Dr. Greg Mirsky,
APS, IFSDA, Rossica, BSRP
stamps@gregmirsky.com
Tel. 650-320-8550
P. O. Box 50338,
Palo Alto, CA 94303, USA
www.gregmirsky.com

Nos. 81, 82a, 85-86, 125-126, 129-130 Surcharged

1922-23 *Perf. 14½x15*

216 A8 5r on 20k .45 6.00
a. Inverted surcharge 50.00 *90.00*
b. Double surcharge 100.00 —
c. Pair, one without surch. 165.00
217 A11 20r on 15k 1.90 2.00
a. Inverted surcharge 120.00 *90.00*
b. Pair, one without surch. 165.00
218 A11 20r on 70k .25 .35
a. Inverted surcharge 60.00 *45.00*
b. Double surcharge 50.00 50.00
c. Pair, one without surch. 165.00
219 A8 30r on 50k 1.75 .50
a. Inverted surcharge *67.50 67.50*
c. Groundwork omitted *50.00 50.00*
d. Double surcharge *100.00 100.00*
220 A11 40r on 15k 1.00 .35
a. Inverted surcharge 67.50 *67.50*
b. Double surcharge *90.00 90.00*
c. Pair, one without surch. 165.00
221 A11 100r on 15k 1.00 .35
a. Inverted surcharge *90.00 67.50*
b. Double surcharge *90.00 67.50*
c. Pair, one without surch. 225.00
222 A11 200r on 15k 2.75 .35
a. Inverted surcharge 57.50 *45.00*
b. Double surcharge 67.50 *45.00*
c. Pair, one without surch. 225.00

Nos. 221-222 exist with triple surcharge; No. 221 with double surcharge, one inverted. Value, each $100.

Imperf

223 A8 5r on 20k 32.50 25.00
224 A11 20r on 15k *9,500.*
225 A11 20r on 70k .90 1.75
a. Inverted surcharge 82.50
226 A8 30r on 50k brn vio & grn .50 1.00
227 A11 40r on 15k .30 .30
a. Inverted surcharge 140.00 —
b. Double surcharge 100.00 —
228 A11 100r on 15k 1.00 .50
a. Inverted surcharge 190.00 —
229 A11 200r on 15k .75 .50
a. Inverted surcharge — —
b. Double surcharge 140.00 —
Nos. 216-223,225-229 (13) 45.05 38.95

Forgeries of No. 223-229 exist, including a dangerous digital forgery of No. 224.

Worker A49

Soldier A50

1922-23 **Typo.** ***Imperf.***

230 A49 10r blue .25 .25
231 A50 50r brown .25 .25
232 A50 70r brown violet .25 .25
233 A50 100r red .25 .25
Nos. 230-233 (4) 1.00 1.00

1923 *Perf. 14x14½*

234 A49 10r dp bl, perf. 13½ .25 2.75
a. Perf. 14 32.50 4.00
b. Perf. 12½ 1.40 2.75
235 A50 50r brown .25 2.75
a. Perf. 12½ 7.50 3.25
b. Perf. 13½ 2.25 2.75
236 A50 70r brown violet .25 2.75
a. Perf. 12½ 4.00 2.75

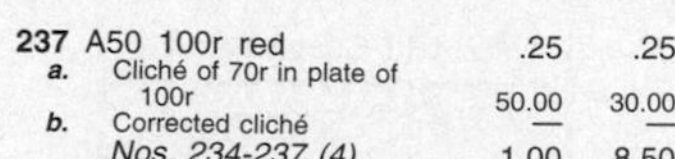

237 A50 100r red .25 .25
a. Cliché of 70r in plate of 100r 50.00 30.00
b. Corrected cliché — —
Nos. 234-237 (4) 1.00 8.50

No. 237b has extra broken line at right.

Nos. 230-233 were surcharged for use in Far Eastern Republic. See Far Eastern Republic Nos. 66-70.

Soldier — Worker — Peasant
A51 A52 A53

1923 ***Perf. 14½x15***

238 A51 3r rose .25 .25
239 A52 4r brown .25 .25
240 A53 5r light blue .25 .25
a. Double impression *82.50* —
241 A51 10r gray .25 .25
e. Double impression 95.00
241A A51 20r brown violet .50 .35
b. Double impression *140.00* —
Nos. 238-241A (5) 1.50 1.35

Imperf

238a A51 3r rose 12.50 —
239a A52 4r brown 30.00 —
b. As "a," double impression *150.00*
240b A53 5r light blue 8.00 —
241d A51 10r gray 8.00 —
f. As "d," double impression 115.00
241c A51 20r brown violet 275.00 —

Stamps of 1r buff, type A52, and 2r green, type A53, perf. 12 and imperf. were prepared but not put in use.

The imperfs of Nos. 238-241A were sold only by the philatelic bureau in Moscow.

Stamps of 20r, type A51, printed in gray black or dull violet are essays. Value, $200 each.

The stamps of this and the following issues were sold for the currency of 1923, one ruble of which was equal to 100 rubles of 1922 and 1,000,000 rubles of 1921.

Union of Soviet Socialist Republics

Reaping — A54

Sowing — A55

Fordson Tractor A56

Symbolical of the Exhibition — A57

1923, Aug. 19 **Litho.** ***Imperf.***

242 A54 1r brown & orange 4.50 2.50
243 A55 2r dp grn & pale grn 5.00 2.00
244 A56 5r dp bl & pale blue 5.00 3.75
245 A57 7r rose & pink 5.00 4.50

Perf. 12½, 13½

246 A54 1r brown & orange 5.00 *3.75*
a. Perf. 12½ 42.50 *37.50*
247 A55 2r dp grn & pale grn, perf. 12½ 6.00 *3.75*
248 A56 5r dp bl & pale bl 14.00 *3.75*
a. Perf. 13½ 13.50 *8.00*
249 A57 7r rose & pink 5.00 *6.00*
a. Perf. 12½ 24.00 *12.50*
Nos. 242-249 (8) 49.50 *30.00*

1st Agriculture and Craftsmanship Exhibition, Moscow.

Worker — Soldier — Peasant
A58 A59 A60

1923 **Unwmk.** **Litho.** ***Imperf.***

250 A58 1k orange 2.50 .45
251 A60 2k green 2.50 .45
252 A59 3k red brown 2.50 1.40
253 A58 4k deep rose 24.00 1.25
254 A58 5k lilac 2.50 .65
255 A60 6k light blue 2.75 .45
256 A59 10k dark blue 35.00 3.75
257 A58 20k yellow green 12.00 .75
258 A60 50k dark brown 19.00 2.50
259 A59 1r red & brown 50.00 5.00
Nos. 250-259 (10) 152.75 16.65

1924 ***Perf. 14½x15***

261 A58 4k deep rose 110.00 —
262 A59 10k dark blue 165.00 —
263 A60 30k violet 25.00 *4.00*
264 A59 40k slate gray 25.00 *4.00*
Nos. 261-264 (4) 325.00 *8.00*

See Nos. 273-290, 304-321. For surcharges see Nos. 349-350.

Vladimir Ilyich Ulyanov (Lenin) — A61

1924 ***Imperf.***

265 A61 3k red & black 8.25 2.40
266 A61 6k red & black 7.00 2.00
267 A61 12k red & black 5.50 2.00
268 A61 20k red & black 11.50 2.00
Nos. 265-268 (4) 32.25 8.40

Three printings of Nos. 265-268 differ in size of red frame.

Perf. 13½

269 A61 3k red & black 6.75 4.00
270 A61 6k red & black 6.75 2.00
271 A61 12k red & black 12.00 2.00
272 A61 20k red & black 8.00 2.50
Nos. 269-272 (4) 33.50 10.50
Nos. 265-272 (8) 65.75 18.90

Death of Lenin (1870-1924).
Forgeries of Nos. 265-272 exist.

Types of 1923 and

Worker — A62

There are small differences between the lithographed stamps of 1923 and the typographed of 1924-25. On a few values this may be seen in the numerals.

Type A58: Lithographed. The two white lines forming the outline of the ear are continued across the cheek. Typographed. The outer lines of the ear are broken where they touch the cheek.

Type A59: Lithographed. At the top of the right shoulder a white line touches the frame at the left. Counting from the edge of the visor of the cap, lines 5, 6 and sometimes 7 touch at their upper ends. Typographed. The top line of the shoulder does not reach the frame. On the cap lines 5, 6 and 7 run together and form a white spot.

Type A60: In the angle above the first letter "C" there is a fan-shaped ornament enclosing four white dashes. On the lithographed stamps these dashes reach nearly to the point of the angle. On the typographed stamps the dashes are shorter and often only three are visible.

On unused examples of the typographed stamps the raised outlines of the designs can be seen on the backs of the stamps.

1924-25 **Typo.** ***Imperf.***

273 A59 3k red brown 6.75 1.40
274 A58 4k deep rose 3.00 1.50
275 A59 10k dark blue 4.00 1.25
275A A60 50k brown *6,750.* 25.00

Other typographed and imperf. values include: 2k green, 5k lilac, 6k light blue, 20k green and 1r red and brown. Value, unused: $150, $100, $150, $200 and $1,000, respectively.

Nos. 273-275A were regularly issued. The 7k, 8k, 9k, 30k, 40k, 2r, 3r, and 5r also exist imperf. Value, set of 8, $75.

Perf. 14½x15
Typo.

276 A58 1k orange 160.00 8.00
277 A60 2k green 2.00 .45
278 A59 3k red brown 2.00 .45
279 A58 4k deep rose 2.00 .45
280 A58 5k lilac 160.00 5.00
281 A60 6k lt blue 2.00 .45
282 A59 7k chocolate 2.00 .45
283 A58 8k brn ol 1.80 .45
284 A60 9k orange red 4.50 .45
285 A59 10k dark blue 4.00 .45
286 A58 14k slate blue 225.00 2.50
287 A60 15k yellow *25,000. 165.00*
288 A58 20k gray green 5.25 .45
288A A60 30k violet 400.00 *4.00*
288B A59 40k slate gray 800.00 *4.00*
289 A60 50k brown 225.00 *10.00*
290 A59 1r red & brn 19.00 *1.00*
291 A62 2r grn & rose 12.00 *2.00*
Nos. 276-286,288-291 (17) 2,026. 40.55

See No. 323. Forgeries of No. 287 exist.

1925 ***Perf. 12***

276a A58 1k orange 2.50 1.00
277a A60 2k green 21.50 1.00
278a A59 3k red brown 3.50 9.00
279a A58 4k deep rose 275.00 *25.00*
280a A58 5k lilac 5.50 1.00
282a A59 7k chocolate 10.00 1.00
283a A58 8k brown olive 1,375. 5.00
284a A60 9k orange red *20.00 2.50*
285a A59 10k dark blue *5.00* 2.00
286a A58 14k slate blue 2.50 1.00
287a A60 15k yellow 6.75 1.00
288c A58 20k gray green 27.50 1.00
288d A60 30k violet 22.50 *1.50*
288e A59 40k slate gray 110.00 *2.50*
289a A60 50k brown 16.50 *1.00*
290a A59 1r red & brown *2,000. 3,000.*
Nos. 276a-290a (16) 3,903. 3,055.

Soldier — A63

Worker — A64

1924-25 ***Perf. 13½***

292 A63 3r blk brn & grn 19.00 2.50
a. Perf. 10 5,500. 145.00
b. Perf. 13½x10 *2,750.* —
293 A64 5r dk bl & gray brn 200.00 12.50
a. Perf. 10½ 70.00 —

See Nos. 324-325.

Russia, Poland, Romania & Worldwide

Extensive Stock of Mint & Used

WRITE FOR A FREE 57-PAGE PRICE LIST:

ALMAZ CO. Dept. VR
P.O. Box 100-812 • Vanderveer Station
Brooklyn, NY 11210
Phone/Fax (718) 241-6360
AlmazStamps@aol.com

Lenin Mausoleum, Moscow — A65

Wmk. 170

1925, Jan. Photo. *Imperf.*

294 A65 7k deep blue 9.00 2.50
295 A65 14k dark green 25.00 4.00
296 A65 20k carmine rose 14.00 5.00
297 A65 40k red brown 25.00 7.00
Nos. 294-297 (4) 73.00 18.50

Perf. 13½x14

298 A65 7k deep blue 5.50 4.50
299 A65 14k dark green 25.00 6.75
300 A65 20k carmine rose 20.00 5.25
301 A65 40k red brown 26.00 6.25
Nos. 298-301 (4) 76.50 22.75
Nos. 294-301 (8) 149.50 41.25

First anniversary of Lenin's death.

Nos. 294-301 are found on both ordinary and thick paper. Those on thick paper sell for twice as much, except for No. 301, which is scarcer on ordinary paper.

Lenin — A66

Wmk. 170

1925, July Engr. *Perf. 13½*

302 A66 5r red brown 40.00 6.75
a. Perf. 12½ 165.00 25.00
b. Perf. 10½ ('26) 82.50 11.00
303 A66 10r indigo 40.00 10.00
a. Perf. 12½ 1,250. 175.00
b. Perf. 10½ ('26) 200.00 11.00

Imperfs. exist. Value, set $75.

See Nos. 407-408, 621-622

Types of 1923 Issue

1925-27 Wmk. 170 Typo. *Perf. 12*

304 A58 1k orange 1.60 .35
305 A60 2k green 1.60 .35
306 A59 3k red brown 1.60 .35
307 A58 4k deep rose 1.60 .35
308 A58 5k lilac 1.60 .35
309 A60 6k lt blue 1.60 .75
310 A59 7k chocolate 3.25 .75
311 A58 8k brown olive 17.00 1.40
a. Perf. 14½x15 325.00 27.50
312 A60 9k red 6.50 .75
313 A59 10k dark blue 3.50 .75
a. 10k pale blue ('27) 9.00 4.50
314 A58 14k slate blue 4.00 1.25
315 A60 15k yellow 9.50 1.25
316 A59 18k violet 17.00 1.75
317 A58 20k gray green 9.50 1.25
318 A60 30k violet 17.00 1.25
319 A59 40k slate gray 17.00 1.75
320 A60 50k brown 17.00 1.75
321 A59 1r red & brown 19.00 4.00
a. Perf. 14½x15 325.00 50.00
323 A62 2r grn & rose red 75.00 11.00
a. Perf. 14½x15 18.00 5.00

Perf. 13½

324 A63 3r blk brn & grn 27.50 9.50
a. Perf. 12½ 475.00 82.50
325 A64 5r dk blue & gray brn 35.00 12.50
Nos. 304-325 (21) 287.35 53.40

Nos. 304-315, 317-325 exist imperf. Value, set $125.

Mikhail V. Lomonosov and Academy of Sciences — A67

1925, Sept. Photo. *Perf. 12½, 13½*

326 A67 3k orange brown 7.50 2.00
a. Perf. 12½x12 40.00 6.75
c. Perf. 13½ 50.00 9.00
327 A67 15k dk olive green 14.00 2.25
a. Perf. 12½ 20.00 5.00

Russian Academy of Sciences, 200th anniv. Exist unwatermarked, on thick paper with yellow gum, perf. 13½. These are essays, later perforated and gummed. Value, each $50.

Prof. Aleksandr S. Popov (1859-1905), Radio Pioneer — A68

1925, Oct. *Perf. 13½*

328 A68 7k deep blue 6.25 1.00
329 A68 14k green 10.00 1.50

For surcharge see No. 353.

Decembrist Exiles — A69

Street Rioting in St. Petersburg — A70

Revolutionist Leaders — A71

1925, Dec. 28 *Imperf.*

330 A69 3k olive green 5.00 *1.00*
331 A70 7k brown 32.50 *3.50*
332 A71 14k carmine lake 19.00 *5.00*

Perf. 13½

333 A69 3k olive green 4.50 1.25
a. Perf. 12½ *100.00* *50.00*
334 A70 7k brown 16.50 *3.50*
335 A71 14k carmine lake 19.50 5.50
Nos. 330-335 (6) 97.00 19.75

Centenary of Decembrist revolution.

For surcharges see Nos. 354, 357.

Revolters Parading — A72

Speaker Haranguing Mob — A73

Street Barricade, Moscow — A74

1925, Dec. 20 *Imperf.*

336 A72 3k olive green 5.00 *7.50*
337 A73 7k brown 17.50 *8.75*
338 A74 14k carmine lake 12.50 *2.75*

Perf. 12½, 12x12½

339 A72 3k olive green 5.50 *3.00*
a. Perf. 13½ 37.50 *8.00*
340 A73 7k brown 35.00 *5.00*
a. Perf. 13½ 17.50 *5.25*
b. Horiz. pair, imperf. btwn. — —
341 A74 14k carmine lake 6.75 3.75
a. Perf. 13½ 40.00 7.50
Nos. 336-341 (6) 82.25 30.75

20th anniversary of Revolution of 1905.

For surcharges see Nos. 355, 358.

Lenin — A75

1926 Wmk. 170 Engr. *Perf. 10½*

342 A75 1r dark brown 37.50 4.00
a. Perf. 12½ 2,250. —
343 A75 2r black violet 35.00 5.75
a. Perf. 12½ 2,250. —
344 A75 3r dark green 37.50 5.75
a. Perf. 12½ 4,250. —
b. Horiz. pair, imperf. btwn. — *5,000.*
Nos. 342-344 (3) 110.00 15.50

Nos. 342-343 exist imperf.

See Nos. 406, 620.

Liberty Monument, Moscow — A76

1926, July Litho. *Perf. 12x12½*

347 A76 7k blue green & red 10.00 2.75
348 A76 14k blue green & violet 12.50 2.75

6th International Esperanto Congress at Leningrad. Exist perf. 11½. Value, set $8,500.

For surcharge see No. 356.

Nos. 282, 282a and 310 Surcharged in Black

Two types of overprint: Type I, 2mm space between lines of surcharge; Type II, .7mm space between lines of surcharge.

1927, June Unwmk. *Perf. 14½x15*

349 A59 8k on 7k chocolate (I) 22.50 4.00
a. Perf. 12x12¼ 27.50 3.75
b. Inverted surcharge *300.00* —
c. Type II *2,750.* 140.00
d. As "b," surcharge inverted *275.00*

Perf. 12

Wmk. 170

350 A59 8k on 7k chocolate 8.00 2.50
a. Inverted surcharge *150.00*
b. Type II *10,500.* 70.00
c. As "b," surcharge inverted *350.00*

The surcharge on Nos. 349-350 comes in two types: With space of 2mm between lines, and with space of ¾mm. The latter is much scarcer.

Same Surcharge on Stamps of 1925-26 in Black or Red

Perf. 13½, 12½, 12x12½

353 A68 8k on 7k dp bl (R) 6.75 2.25
a. Inverted "8" 110.00 *50.00*
354 A70 8k on 7k brown 12.50 *4.75*
355 A73 8k on 7k brown 20.00 *6.25*
356 A76 8k on 7k blue green & red 21.50 8.50

Imperf

357 A70 8k on 7k brown 11.00 4.00
358 A73 8k on 7k brown 19.00 7.00
Nos. 349-350,353-358 (8) 121.25 39.25

Postage Due Stamps of 1925 Surcharged

Two settings: A's aligned (shown), bottom A to left.

Lithographed or Typographed

1927, June Unwmk. *Perf. 12*

359 D1 8k on 1k red, typo. 4.50 *2.00*
a. Litho. *2,750.* *150.00*
360 D1 8k on 2k violet 4.50 *2.00*
a. Inverted surcharge 275.00 —

Perf. 12, 14½x14

361 D1 8k on 3k lt blue 4.50 *2.00*
a. Inverted surcharge 275.00 —
362 D1 8k on 7k orange 4.25 *1.25*
363 D1 8k on 8k green 4.50 *2.00*
a. Inverted surcharge — *1,750.*
364 D1 8k on 10k dk blue 4.00 *1.25*
a. Inverted surcharge 275.00 —
365 D1 8k on 14k brown 3.75 4.00
a. Inverted surcharge 350.00 —
Nos. 359-365 (7) 30.00 14.50

Wmk. 170

1927, June Typo. *Perf. 12*

366 D1 8k on 1k red 4.50 *1.00*
367 D1 8k on 2k violet 4.50 *1.00*
368 D1 8k on 3k lt blue 4.50 *1.00*
369 D1 8k on 7k orange 4.50 *1.00*
370 D1 8k on 8k green 4.50 *1.00*
371 D1 8k on 10k dk blue 4.50 *1.00*
a. Inverted surcharge *3,500.* —
372 D1 8k on 14k brown 4.50 *1.00*
a. Inverted surcharge — *1,750.*
Nos. 366-372 (7) 31.50 *7.00*

Nos. 366, 368-370 exist with inverted surcharge.

Dr. L. L. Zamenhof A77

1927 Photo. *Perf. 10½*

373 A77 14k yel grn & brn 11.00 2.25

Unwmk.

374 A77 14k yel grn & brn 11.00 2.25
a. Perf. 10 325.00 52.50
b. Perf. 10x10½ 175.00 75.00
c. Imperf. 950.00 —
d. Vert. pair, imperf. btwn., never hinged *8,250.* —

40th anniversary of creation of Esperanto.

- Extensive selection of philatelic material for sale
- ALWAYS BUYING Russian collections, stock, individual sets and varieties.
- Custom orders
- Appraisals
- Highest prices paid for rare stamps!

www.agstamp.com

Dr. Anton Guliaev
Member of ASDA, NSDA, APS, APEX and ifsda
925-788-1859
info@agstamp.com
Martinez, CA 94553

Worker, Soldier, Peasant — A78

Worker and Sailor — A81

Lenin in Car Guarded by Soldiers A79

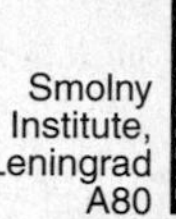

Smolny Institute, Leningrad A80

Map of the USSR A82

Men of Various Soviet Republics — A83

Workers of Different Races; Kremlin in Background — A84

Typo. (3k, 8k, 18k), Engr. (7k), Litho. (14k), Photo. (5k, 28k)

Perf. 13½, 12½x12, 11

1927, Oct.			**Unwmk.**
375	A78 3k bright rose	5.50	1.10
a.	Imperf., pair	*5,000.*	
376	A79 5k deep brown	14.00	2.25
a.	Imperf.	1,650.	*500.00*
b.	Perf. 12½	125.00	12.50
c.	Perf. 12½x10½	55.00	5.00
377	A80 7k myrtle green	14.00	4.00
a.	Perf. 11½	32.50	7.50
b.	Imperf., pair	*1,500.*	
378	A81 8k brown & black	8.00	1.50
a.	Perf. 10½x12½	*42.50*	*2.75*
379	A82 14k dull blue & red	6.75	2.75
380	A83 18k blue	4.75	1.25
a.	Imperf.	275.00	
381	A84 28k olive brown	18.00	5.00
a.	Perf. 10	45.00	8.00
	Nos. 375-381 (7)	71.00	17.85

10th anniversary of October Revolution.

The paper of No. 375 has an overprint of pale yellow wavy lines.

No. 377b exists with watermark 170. Value, $1,000.

Worker — A85

Peasant — A86

Lenin — A87

1927-28	**Typo.**		***Perf. 13½***
	Chalk Surfaced Paper		
382	A85 1k orange	1.10	.35
a.	Imperf.	1,750.	—
383	A86 2k apple green	4.25	.35
a.	Imperf.	1,750.	—
385	A85 4k bright blue	1.10	.35
386	A86 5k brown	1.10	.35
a.	Imperf.	1,750.	—
388	A86 7k dark red ('28)	1.10	.35
a.	Double impression	475.00	—
389	A85 8k green	7.00	.60
391	A85 10k light brown	5.00	.35
a.	Imperf.	1,325.	—
392	A87 14k dark green ('28)	10.75	4.00
393	A87 18k olive green	12.00	1.25
a.	Imperf.	*3,750.*	—
394	A87 18k dark blue ('28)	11.00	1.70
395	A86 20k dark gray green	16.50	.35
396	A85 40k rose red	20.00	2.00
397	A86 50k bright blue	24.00	1.10
399	A85 70k gray green	11.00	2.00
400	A86 80k orange	15.00	2.75
	Nos. 382-400 (15)	140.90	17.85

Soldier and Kremlin — A88

Sailor and Flag — A89

Cavalryman A90

Aviator A91

1928, Feb. 6			
	Chalk Surfaced Paper		
402	A88 8k light brown	4.75	.85
a.	Imperf.	1,200.	—
403	A89 14k deep blue	12.00	1.50
404	A90 18k carmine rose	6.50	1.60
a.	Imperf.	*7,000.*	
405	A91 28k yellow green	15.00	2.25
	Nos. 402-405 (4)	38.25	6.20

10th anniversary of the Soviet Army.

Lenin Types of 1925-26

Wmk. 169

1928-29	**Engr.**		***Perf. 10½***
406	A75 3r dark green ('29)	52.50	3.50
a.	Perf. 10	52.50	6.75
b.	Imperf.	3,250.	—
407	A66 5r red brown	19.00	3.75
a.	Perf. 10	105.00	14.00
b.	Imperf.	*20,000.*	—
408	A66 10r indigo	19.00	*4.50*
a.	Perf. 10	27.50	6.75
b.	Imperf.	*20,000.*	—
	Nos. 406-408 (3)	90.50	11.75

Bugler Sounding Assembly
A92 A93

Perf. 12½x12

1929, Aug. 18	**Photo.**		**Wmk. 170**
411	A92 10k olive brown	32.50	6.25
a.	Perf. 10½	140.00	27.50
b.	Perf. 12½x12x10½x12	140.00	75.00
412	A93 14k slate	5.50	2.75
a.	Perf. 12½x12x10½x12	425.00	95.00

First All-Soviet Assembly of Pioneers.

Factory Worker A95

Peasant A96

Farm Worker A97

Soldier A98

Worker, Soldier, Peasant A100

Worker A103

Lenin A104

Peasant A107

Factory Worker A109

Farm Worker A111

Perf. 12x12½

1929-31	**Typo.**		**Wmk. 170**
413	A103 1k orange	1.25	.25
a.	Perf. 10½	19.00	4.00
b.	Perf. 12x12¼	8.00	1.00
414	A95 2k yellow green	1.25	.25
415	A96 3k blue	2.75	.25
a.	Perf. 12x12¼	82.50	*25.00*
416	A97 4k claret	2.75	.45
417	A98 5k orange brown	2.75	.45
a.	Perf. 10½	190.00	*25.00*
418	A100 7k scarlet	2.75	.90
419	A103 10k olive green	2.75	.50
a.	Perf. 10½	400.00	40.00
	Unwmk.		
420	A104 14k indigo	5.50	1.00
a.	Perf. 10½	17.50	3.25
	Wmk. 170		
421	A100 15k dk ol grn ('30)	2.75	.85
422	A107 20k green	2.75	.85
a.	Perf. 10½	—	—
423	A109 30k dk violet	14.00	1.75
424	A111 50k dp brown	14.00	2.50
425	A98 70k dk red ('30)	8.00	2.50
426	A107 80k red brn ('31)	8.00	2.50
	Nos. 413-426 (14)	71.25	15.00

Nos. 422, 423, 424 and 426 have a background of fine wavy lines in pale shades of the colors of the stamps.

See Nos. 456-466, 613A-619A. For surcharge see No. 743.

Symbolical of Industry A112

Tractors Issuing from Assembly Line — A113

Iron Furnace (Inscription reads, "More Metal More Machines") A114

Blast Furnace and Chart of Anticipated Iron Production A115

1929-30			***Perf. 12x12½***
427	A112 5k orange brown	3.25	*.90*
428	A113 10k olive green	9.50	*1.80*
	Perf. 12½x12		
429	A114 20k dull green	9.50	*3.00*
a.	Perf. 10¾	*8,000.*	400.00
430	A115 28k violet black	4.25	2.00
	Nos. 427-430 (4)	26.50	7.70

Publicity for greater industrial production. No. 429 exists perf. 10½. Value *$4,000.*

Red Cavalry in Polish Town after Battle A116

Cavalry Charge A117

Staff Officers of 1st Cavalry Army A118

Plan of Action for 1st Cavalry Army — A119

1930, Feb.			***Perf. 12x12½***
431	A116 2k yellow green	3.25	*1.80*
432	A117 5k light brown	7.00	*1.80*
433	A118 10k olive gray	14.00	*2.75*
434	A119 14k indigo & red	5.50	*2.50*
	Nos. 431-434 (4)	29.75	*8.85*

1st Red Cavalry Army, 10th anniversary.

Students Preparing a Poster Newspaper A120

1930, Aug. 15			
435	A120 10k olive green	8.00	*1.80*

Educational Exhibition, Leningrad, 7/1-8/15/30.

Lenin Mausoleum, Moscow — A65

Wmk. 170

1925, Jan. Photo. ***Imperf.***
294 A65 7k deep blue 9.00 2.50
295 A65 14k dark green 25.00 4.00
296 A65 20k carmine rose 14.00 5.00
297 A65 40k red brown 25.00 7.00
Nos. 294-297 (4) 73.00 18.50

Perf. 13½x14

298 A65 7k deep blue 5.50 4.50
299 A65 14k dark green 25.00 6.75
300 A65 20k carmine rose 20.00 5.25
301 A65 40k red brown 26.00 6.25
Nos. 298-301 (4) 76.50 22.75
Nos. 294-301 (8) 149.50 41.25

First anniversary of Lenin's death.

Nos. 294-301 are found on both ordinary and thick paper. Those on thick paper sell for twice as much, except for No. 301, which is scarcer on ordinary paper.

Lenin — A66

Wmk. 170

1925, July Engr. ***Perf. 13½***
302 A66 5r red brown 40.00 6.75
a. Perf. 12½ 165.00 25.00
b. Perf. 10½ ('26) 82.50 11.00
303 A66 10r indigo 40.00 10.00
a. Perf. 12½ 1,250. 175.00
b. Perf. 10½ ('26) 200.00 11.00

Imperfs. exist. Value, set $75.
See Nos. 407-408, 621-622

Types of 1923 Issue

1925-27 Wmk. 170 Typo. ***Perf. 12***
304 A58 1k orange 1.60 .35
305 A60 2k green 1.60 .35
306 A59 3k red brown 1.60 .35
307 A58 4k deep rose 1.60 .35
308 A58 5k lilac 1.60 .35
309 A60 6k lt blue 1.60 .75
310 A59 7k chocolate 3.25 .75
311 A58 8k brown olive 17.00 1.40
a. Perf. 14½x15 325.00 27.50
312 A60 9k red 6.50 .75
313 A59 10k dark blue 3.50 .75
a. 10k pale blue ('27) 9.00 4.50
314 A58 14k slate blue 4.00 1.25
315 A60 15k yellow 9.50 1.25
316 A59 18k violet 17.00 1.75
317 A58 20k gray green 9.50 1.25
318 A60 30k violet 17.00 1.25
319 A59 40k slate gray 17.00 1.75
320 A60 50k brown 17.00 1.75
321 A59 1r red & brown 19.00 4.00
a. Perf. 14½x15 325.00 *50.00*
323 A62 2r grn & rose red 75.00 11.00
a. Perf. 14½x15 18.00 5.00

Perf. 13½

324 A63 3r blk brn & grn 27.50 9.50
a. Perf. 12½ *475.00* 82.50
325 A64 5r dk blue & gray brn 35.00 12.50
Nos. 304-325 (21) 287.35 53.40

Nos. 304-315, 317-325 exist imperf. Value, set $125.

Mikhail V. Lomonosov and Academy of Sciences — A67

1925, Sept. Photo. ***Perf. 12½, 13½***
326 A67 3k orange brown 7.50 2.00
a. Perf. 12½x12 40.00 6.75
c. Perf. 13½ 50.00 9.00
327 A67 15k dk olive green 14.00 2.25
a. Perf. 12½ 20.00 5.00

Russian Academy of Sciences, 200th anniv. Exist unwatermarked, on thick paper with yellow gum, perf. 13½. These are essays, later perforated and gummed. Value, each $50.

Prof. Aleksandr S. Popov (1859-1905), Radio Pioneer — A68

1925, Oct. ***Perf. 13½***
328 A68 7k deep blue 6.25 1.00
329 A68 14k green 10.00 1.50

For surcharge see No. 353.

Decembrist Exiles — A69

Street Rioting in St. Petersburg — A70

Revolutionist Leaders — A71

1925, Dec. 28 ***Imperf.***
330 A69 3k olive green 5.00 *1.00*
331 A70 7k brown 32.50 *3.50*
332 A71 14k carmine lake 19.00 *5.00*

Perf. 13½

333 A69 3k olive green 4.50 1.25
a. Perf. 12½ *100.00* *50.00*
334 A70 7k brown 16.50 *3.50*
335 A71 14k carmine lake 19.50 5.50
Nos. 330-335 (6) 97.00 19.75

Centenary of Decembrist revolution.
For surcharges see Nos. 354, 357.

Revolters Parading — A72

Speaker Haranguing Mob — A73

Street Barricade, Moscow — A74

1925, Dec. 20 ***Imperf.***
336 A72 3k olive green 5.00 *7.50*
337 A73 7k brown 17.50 *8.75*
338 A74 14k carmine lake 12.50 *2.75*

Perf. 12½, 12x12½

339 A72 3k olive green 5.50 *3.00*
a. Perf. 13½ 37.50 *8.00*
340 A73 7k brown 35.00 *5.00*
a. Perf. 13½ 17.50 *5.25*
b. Horiz. pair, imperf. btwn. — —
341 A74 14k carmine lake 6.75 3.75
a. Perf. 13½ 40.00 7.50
Nos. 336-341 (6) 82.25 30.75

20th anniversary of Revolution of 1905.
For surcharges see Nos. 355, 358.

Lenin — A75

1926 Wmk. 170 Engr. ***Perf. 10½***
342 A75 1r dark brown 37.50 4.00
a. Perf. 12½ 2,250. —
343 A75 2r black violet 35.00 5.75
a. Perf. 12½ 2,250. —
344 A75 3r dark green 37.50 5.75
a. Perf. 12½ 4,250. —
b. Horiz. pair, imperf. btwn. — *5,000.*
Nos. 342-344 (3) 110.00 15.50

Nos. 342-343 exist imperf.
See Nos. 406, 620.

Liberty Monument, Moscow — A76

1926, July Litho. ***Perf. 12x12½***
347 A76 7k blue green & red 10.00 2.75
348 A76 14k blue green & violet 12.50 2.75

6th International Esperanto Congress at Leningrad. Exist perf. 11½. Value, set $8,500.
For surcharge see No. 356.

Nos. 282, 282a and 310 Surcharged in Black

Two types of overprint: Type I, 2mm space between lines of surcharge; Type II, .7mm space between lines of surcharge.

1927, June Unwmk. ***Perf. 14½x15***
349 A59 8k on 7k chocolate (I) 22.50 4.00
a. Perf. 12x12¼ 27.50 3.75
b. Inverted surcharge *300.00* —
c. Type II *2,750.* 140.00
d. As "b," surcharge inverted *275.00*

Perf. 12

Wmk. 170

350 A59 8k on 7k chocolate 8.00 2.50
a. Inverted surcharge *150.00*
b. Type II *10,500.* 70.00
c. As "b," surcharge inverted *350.00*

The surcharge on Nos. 349-350 comes in two types: With space of 2mm between lines, and with space of ¾mm. The latter is much scarcer.

Same Surcharge on Stamps of 1925-26 in Black or Red

Perf. 13½, 12½, 12x12½

353 A68 8k on 7k dp bl (R) 6.75 2.25
a. Inverted "8" 110.00 *50.00*
354 A70 8k on 7k brown 12.50 *4.75*
355 A73 8k on 7k brown 20.00 *6.25*
356 A76 8k on 7k blue green & red 21.50 8.50

Imperf

357 A70 8k on 7k brown 11.00 4.00
358 A73 8k on 7k brown 19.00 7.00
Nos. 349-350,353-358 (8) 121.25 39.25

Postage Due Stamps of 1925 Surcharged

Two settings: A's aligned (shown), bottom A to left.

Lithographed or Typographed

1927, June Unwmk. ***Perf. 12***
359 D1 8k on 1k red, typo. 4.50 *2.00*
a. Litho. *2,750.* *150.00*
360 D1 8k on 2k violet 4.50 *2.00*
a. Inverted surcharge 275.00 —

Perf. 12, 14½x14

361 D1 8k on 3k lt blue 4.50 *2.00*
a. Inverted surcharge 275.00 —
362 D1 8k on 7k orange 4.25 *1.25*
363 D1 8k on 8k green 4.50 *2.00*
a. Inverted surcharge — *1,750.*
364 D1 8k on 10k dk blue 4.00 *1.25*
a. Inverted surcharge 275.00 —
365 D1 8k on 14k brown 3.75 4.00
a. Inverted surcharge 350.00 —
Nos. 359-365 (7) 30.00 14.50

Wmk. 170

1927, June Typo. ***Perf. 12***
366 D1 8k on 1k red 4.50 *1.00*
367 D1 8k on 2k violet 4.50 *1.00*
368 D1 8k on 3k lt blue 4.50 *1.00*
369 D1 8k on 7k orange 4.50 *1.00*
370 D1 8k on 8k green 4.50 *1.00*
371 D1 8k on 10k dk blue 4.50 *1.00*
a. Inverted surcharge *3,500.* —
372 D1 8k on 14k brown 4.50 *1.00*
a. Inverted surcharge — *1,750.*
Nos. 366-372 (7) 31.50 *7.00*

Nos. 366, 368-370 exist with inverted surcharge.

Dr. L. L. Zamenhof A77

1927 Photo. ***Perf. 10½***
373 A77 14k yel grn & brn 11.00 2.25

Unwmk.

374 A77 14k yel grn & brn 11.00 2.25
a. Perf. 10 325.00 52.50
b. Perf. 10x10½ 175.00 75.00
c. Imperf. 950.00 —
d. Vert. pair, imperf. btwn., never hinged *8,250.* —

40th anniversary of creation of Esperanto.

- Extensive selection of philatelic material for sale
- ALWAYS BUYING Russian collections, stock, individual sets and varieties.
- Custom orders
- Appraisals
- Highest prices paid for rare stamps!

www.agstamp.com

Dr. Anton Guliaev
Member of ASDA, NSDA, APS, APEX and ifsda
925-788-1859
info@agstamp.com
Martinez, CA 94553

Worker, Soldier, Peasant — A78

Worker and Sailor — A81

Lenin in Car Guarded by Soldiers A79

Smolny Institute, Leningrad A80

Map of the USSR A82

Men of Various Soviet Republics — A83

Workers of Different Races; Kremlin in Background — A84

Typo. (3k, 8k, 18k), Engr. (7k), Litho. (14k), Photo. (5k, 28k)

Perf. 13½, 12½x12, 11

1927, Oct. **Unwmk.**

375	A78	3k bright rose	5.50	1.10
a.		Imperf., pair	5,000.	
376	A79	5k deep brown	14.00	2.25
a.		Imperf.	1,650.	500.00
b.		Perf. 12½	125.00	12.50
c.		Perf. 12½x10½	55.00	5.00
377	A80	7k myrtle green	14.00	4.00
a.		Perf. 11½	32.50	7.50
b.		Imperf., pair	1,500.	
378	A81	8k brown & black	8.00	1.50
a.		Perf. 10½x12½	42.50	2.75
379	A82	14k dull blue & red	6.75	2.75
380	A83	18k blue	4.75	1.25
a.		Imperf.	275.00	
381	A84	28k olive brown	18.00	5.00
a.		Perf. 10	45.00	8.00
		Nos. 375-381 (7)	71.00	17.85

10th anniversary of October Revolution.

The paper of No. 375 has an overprint of pale yellow wavy lines.

No. 377b exists with watermark 170. Value, $1,000.

Worker — A85

Peasant — A86

Lenin — A87

1927-28 **Typo.** ***Perf. 13½***

Chalk Surfaced Paper

382	A85	1k orange	1.10	.35
a.		Imperf.	1,750.	—
383	A86	2k apple green	4.25	.35
a.		Imperf.	1,750.	—
385	A85	4k bright blue	1.10	.35
386	A86	5k brown	1.10	.35
a.		Imperf.	1,750.	—
388	A86	7k dark red ('28)	1.10	.35
a.		Double impression	475.00	—
389	A85	8k green	7.00	.60
391	A85	10k light brown	5.00	.35
a.		Imperf.	1,325.	—
392	A87	14k dark green ('28)	10.75	4.00
393	A87	18k olive green	12.00	1.25
a.		Imperf.	3,750.	—
394	A87	18k dark blue ('28)	11.00	1.70
395	A86	20k dark gray green	16.50	.35
396	A85	40k rose red	20.00	2.00
397	A86	50k bright blue	24.00	1.10
399	A85	70k gray green	11.00	2.00
400	A86	80k orange	15.00	2.75
		Nos. 382-400 (15)	140.90	17.85

Soldier and Kremlin — A88

Sailor and Flag — A89

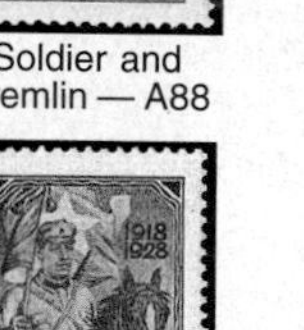
Cavalryman A90

Aviator A91

1928, Feb. 6

Chalk Surfaced Paper

402	A88	8k light brown	4.75	.85
a.		Imperf.	1,200.	—
403	A89	14k deep blue	12.00	1.50
404	A90	18k carmine rose	6.50	1.60
a.		Imperf.	7,000.	
405	A91	28k yellow green	15.00	2.25
		Nos. 402-405 (4)	38.25	6.20

10th anniversary of the Soviet Army.

Lenin Types of 1925-26

Wmk. 169

1928-29 **Engr.** ***Perf. 10½***

406	A75	3r dark green ('29)	52.50	3.50
a.		Perf. 10	52.50	6.75
b.		Imperf.	3,250.	—
407	A66	5r red brown	19.00	3.75
a.		Perf. 10	105.00	14.00
b.		Imperf.	20,000.	—
408	A66	10r indigo	19.00	4.50
a.		Perf. 10	27.50	6.75
b.		Imperf.	20,000.	—
		Nos. 406-408 (3)	90.50	11.75

Bugler Sounding Assembly
A92 A93

Perf. 12½x12

1929, Aug. 18 **Photo.** **Wmk. 170**

411	A92	10k olive brown	32.50	6.25
a.		Perf. 10½	140.00	27.50
b.		Perf. 12½x12x10½x12	140.00	75.00
412	A93	14k slate	5.50	2.75
a.		Perf. 12½x12x10½x12	425.00	95.00

First All-Soviet Assembly of Pioneers.

Factory Worker A95

Peasant A96

Farm Worker A97

Soldier A98

Worker, Soldier, Peasant A100

Worker A103

Lenin A104

Peasant A107

Factory Worker A109

Farm Worker A111

Perf. 12x12½

1929-31 **Typo.** **Wmk. 170**

413	A103	1k orange	1.25	.25
a.		Perf. 10½	19.00	4.00
b.		Perf. 12x12¼	8.00	1.60
414	A95	2k yellow green	1.25	.25
415	A96	3k blue	2.75	.25
a.		Perf. 12x12¼	82.50	25.00
416	A97	4k claret	2.75	.45
417	A98	5k orange brown	2.75	.45
a.		Perf. 10½	190.00	25.00
418	A100	7k scarlet	2.75	.90
419	A103	10k olive green	2.75	.50
a.		Perf. 10½	400.00	40.00

Unwmk.

420	A104	14k indigo	5.50	1.00
a.		Perf. 10½	17.50	3.25

Wmk. 170

421	A100	15k dk ol grn ('30)	2.75	.85
422	A107	20k green	2.75	.85
a.		Perf. 10½	—	—
423	A109	30k dk violet	14.00	1.75
424	A111	50k dp brown	14.00	2.50
425	A98	70k dk red ('30)	8.00	2.50
426	A107	80k red brn ('31)	8.00	2.50
		Nos. 413-426 (14)	71.25	15.00

Nos. 422, 423, 424 and 426 have a background of fine wavy lines in pale shades of the colors of the stamps.

See Nos. 456-466, 613A-619A. For surcharge see No. 743.

Symbolical of Industry A112

Tractors Issuing from Assembly Line — A113

Iron Furnace (Inscription reads, "More Metal More Machines") A114

Blast Furnace and Chart of Anticipated Iron Production A115

1929-30 ***Perf. 12x12½***

427	A112	5k orange brown	3.25	*.90*
428	A113	10k olive green	9.50	*1.80*

Perf. 12½x12

429	A114	20k dull green	9.50	*3.00*
a.		Perf. 10¾	*8,000.*	400.00
430	A115	28k violet black	4.25	2.00
		Nos. 427-430 (4)	26.50	7.70

Publicity for greater industrial production. No. 429 exists perf. 10½. Value *$4,000.*

Red Cavalry in Polish Town after Battle A116

Cavalry Charge A117

Staff Officers of 1st Cavalry Army A118

Plan of Action for 1st Cavalry Army — A119

1930, Feb. ***Perf. 12x12½***

431	A116	2k yellow green	3.25	*1.80*
432	A117	5k light brown	7.00	*1.80*
433	A118	10k olive gray	14.00	*2.75*
434	A119	14k indigo & red	5.50	*2.50*
		Nos. 431-434 (4)	29.75	*8.85*

1st Red Cavalry Army, 10th anniversary.

Students Preparing a Poster Newspaper A120

1930, Aug. 15

435	A120	10k olive green	8.00	*1.80*

Educational Exhibition, Leningrad, 7/1-8/15/30.

Telegraph Office, Moscow A121

Lenin Hydroelectric Power Station on Volkhov River A122

1930 Photo. Wmk. 169 *Perf. 10½*

436	A121 1r deep blue	19.00	*5.00*

Wmk. 170

437	A122 3r yel grn & blk brn	10.50	*5.00*

See Nos. 467, 469.

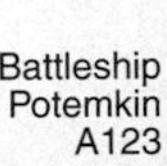

Battleship Potemkin A123

Inside Presnya Barricade A124

Moscow Barricades in 1905 — A125

1930 Typo. *Perf. 12x12½, 12½x12*

438	A123 3k red	1.75	.50
439	A124 5k blue	3.25	.70
440	A125 10k dk green & red	9.50	1.75
	Nos. 438-440 (3)	14.50	2.95

1931 *Imperf.*

452	A123 3k red	11.00	*5.00*
453	A124 5k deep blue	11.00	*9.00*
454	A125 10k dk green & red	22.00	*17.50*
	Nos. 452-454 (3)	44.00	*31.50*
	Nos. 438-454 (6)	58.50	34.45

Revolution of 1905, 25th anniversary.

Types of 1929-31 Regular Issue

1931-32 *Imperf.*

456	A103 1k orange	4.00	1.00
457	A95 2k yellow green	4.00	1.00
458	A96 3k blue	5.50	1.00
459	A97 4k claret	47.50	14.00
460	A98 5k orange brown	5.50	2.50
462	A103 10k olive green	55.00	22.50
464	A100 15k dk olive green	35.00	*25.00*
466	A109 30k dull violet	40.00	*35.00*
467	A121 1r dark blue	200.00	*35.00*
	Nos. 456-467 (9)	396.50	137.00

Nos. 459, 462-467 were sold only by the philatelic bureau.

Type of 1930 Issue

1931 Wmk. 170 *Perf. 12x12½*

469	A121 1r dark blue	8.00	1.50
	Never hinged	12.00	

Maxim Gorki — A133

1932-33 Photo.

470	A133 15k dark brown	8.00	*1.75*
a.	Imperf.	140.00	*67.50*
471	A133 35k dp ultra ('33)	35.00	*14.50*
	Set, never hinged	90.00	

40th anniversary of Gorki's literary activity.

Lenin Addressing the People A134

Revolution in Petrograd (Leningrad) A135

Dnieper Hydroelectric Power Station A136

Asiatics Saluting the Soviet Flag — A139

Designs (dated 1917 1932): 15k, Collective farm. 20k, Magnitogorsk metallurgical plant in Urals. 30k, Radio tower and heads of 4 men.

1932-33 *Perf. 12½x12; 12½ (30k)*

472	A134 3k dark violet	4.25	1.25
473	A135 5k dark brown	4.25	1.25
474	A136 10k ultra	7.00	4.25
475	A136 15k dark green	4.25	1.50
476	A136 20k lake ('33)	4.25	1.50
477	A136 30k dk gray ('33)	55.00	*15.00*
478	A139 35k gray black	95.00	*55.00*
	Nos. 472-478 (7)	174.00	79.75
	Set, never hinged	325.00	

October Revolution, 15th anniversary.

Breaking Prison Bars — A140

1932, Nov. Litho. *Perf. 12½x12*

479	A140 50k dark red	32.50	9.50
	Never hinged	67.50	

Intl. Revolutionaries' Aid Assoc., 10th anniv.

Trier, Birthplace of Marx — A141

Grave, Highgate Cemetery, London — A142

35k, Portrait & signature of Karl Marx (1818-83).

Perf. 12x12½, 12½x12

1933, Mar. Photo.

480	A141 3k dull green	4.00	1.80
481	A142 10k black brown	10.00	2.25
482	A142 35k brown violet	67.50	14.50
	Nos. 480-482 (3)	81.50	18.55
	Set, never hinged	145.00	

Fine Arts Museum, Moscow — A145

1932, Dec. *Perf. 12½*

485	A145 15k black brown	5.00	6.00
486	A145 35k ultra	90.00	52.50
a.	Perf. 10½	67.50	32.50
	Set, never hinged	240.00	

Moscow Philatelic Exhibition, 1932.

Nos. 485 and 486 were also issued in imperf. sheets of 4 containing 2 of each value, on thick paper for presentation purposes. They were not valid for postage. Value, from $25,000. Replicas of the sheet were made for Moscow 97 by the Canadian Society of Russian Philately.

Nos. 485 and 486a Surcharged

1933, Mar. *Perf. 12½*

487	A145 30k on 15k blk brn	50.00	15.00

Perf. 10½

488	A145 70k on 35k ultra	275.00	200.00
	Set, never hinged	500.00	

Leningrad Philatelic Exhibition, 1933.

Peoples of the Soviet Union

Kazaks A146

Lezghians A147

Tungus A150

Crimean Tartars A148

Jews, Birobidzhan A149

Buryats — A151

Yakuts — A156

Chechens A152

Abkhas A153

Georgians A154

Nientzians A155

Great Russians — A157

Tadzhiks — A158

Transcaucasians — A159

Turkmen — A160

Ukrainians — A161

Uzbeks — A162

Byelorussians — A163

Koryaks A164

Bashkirs A165

Chuvashes A166

Perf. 12, 12x12½, 12½x12, 11x12, 12x11

1933, Apr. Photo.

No.	Type	Description	Unused	Used
489	A146	1k black brown	9.00	2.00
490	A147	2k ultra	5.00	2.00
491	A148	3k gray green	18.00	2.00
492	A149	4k gray black	5.00	2.00
493	A150	5k brown violet	5.00	2.00
494	A151	6k indigo	5.00	2.00
495	A152	7k black brown	5.00	2.00
496	A153	8k rose red	11.00	2.00
497	A154	9k ultra	35.00	2.00
498	A155	10k black brown	5.00	2.00
499	A156	14k olive green	5.00	2.00
500	A157	15k orange	16.00	2.00
501	A158	15k ultra	13.00	2.00
502	A159	15k dark brown	13.00	2.00
503	A160	15k rose red	13.00	2.00
504	A161	15k violet brown	16.00	2.00
505	A162	15k gray black	13.00	2.00
506	A163	15k dull green	16.00	2.00
507	A164	20k dull blue	18.00	*2.00*
508	A165	30k brown violet	15.00	*3.00*
509	A166	35k black	15.00	*3.00*
		Nos. 489-509 (21)	256.00	44.00
		Set, never hinged	495.00	

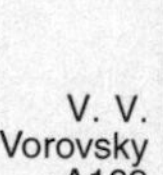

V. V. Vorovsky A169

3k, V. M. Volodarsky. 5k, M. S. Uritzky.

1933, Oct. ***Perf. 12x12½***

No.	Type	Description	Unused	Used
514	A169	1k dull green	4.00	1.00
515	A169	3k blue black	8.00	1.25
516	A169	5k olive brown	9.00	2.00
		Nos. 514-516 (3)	21.00	4.25
		Set, never hinged	42.50	

10th anniv, of the murder of Soviet Representative Vorovsky; 15th anniv. of the murder of the Revolutionists Volodarsky and Uritzky.

See Nos. 531-532, 580-582.

Order of the Red Banner, 15th Anniv. — A173

1933, Nov. 17 Unwmk. ***Perf. 14***

No.	Type	Description	Unused	Used
518	A173	20k black, red & yel	15.00	3.50
		Never hinged	40.00	

No. 518, perf. 9½, is a proof. Values: unused, $4,000; never hinged, $8,000.

Commissar Schaumyan A174

Commissar Prokofii A. Dzhaparidze A175

Commissars Awaiting Execution — A176

Designs: 35k, Monument to the 26 Commissars. 40k, Worker, peasant and soldier dipping flags in salute.

1933, Dec. 1

No.	Type	Description	Unused	Used
519	A174	4k brown	30.00	2.00
520	A175	5k dark gray	25.00	2.00
521	A176	20k purple	8.00	2.00
522	A176	35k ultra	80.00	*17.50*
523	A176	40k carmine	25.00	*7.00*
		Nos. 519-523 (5)	168.00	30.50
		Set, never hinged	440.00	

15th anniv. of the execution of 26 commissars at Baku. No. 521 exists imperf. Many part-perf varieties exist on all values of this issue, including imperf between pairs of several values.

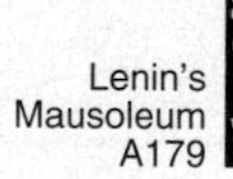

Lenin's Mausoleum A179

1934, Feb. 7 Engr. ***Perf. 14***

No.	Type	Description	Unused	Used
524	A179	5k brown	20.00	2.50
a.		Imperf.	675.00	—
525	A179	10k slate blue	90.00	10.00
a.		Imperf.	675.00	—
526	A179	15k dk carmine	32.50	7.00
527	A179	20k green	6.00	5.25
528	A179	35k dark brown	32.50	8.00
		Nos. 524-528 (5)	181.00	32.75
		Set, never hinged	360.00	

10th anniversary of Lenin's death.

Ivan Fedorov A180

1934, Mar. 5

No.	Type	Description	Unused	Used
529	A180	20k carmine rose	55.00	10.00
a.		Imperf.	675.00	—
530	A180	40k indigo	17.50	10.00
a.		Imperf.	675.00	—
		Set, never hinged	150.00	

350th anniv. of the death of Ivan Fedorov, founder of printing in Russia.

Portrait Type of 1933

Designs: 10k, Yakov M. Sverdlov. 15k, Victor Pavlovich Nogin.

1934, Mar. Photo. Wmk. 170

No.	Type	Description	Unused	Used
531	A169	10k ultra	27.50	6.00
532	A169	15k red	200.00	37.50
		Set, never hinged	475.00	

Deaths of Yakov M. Sverdlov, chairman of the All-Russian Central Executive Committee of the Soviets, 15th anniv., Victor Pavlovich Nogin, chairman Russian State Textile Syndicate, 10th anniv.

A184

Dmitri Ivanovich Mendeleev A185

1934, Sept. 15 Wmk. 170 ***Perf. 14***

No.	Type	Description	Unused	Used
536	A184	5k emerald	22.00	3.00
537	A185	10k black brown	100.00	13.00
538	A185	15k vermilion	140.00	18.00
539	A184	20k ultra	22.00	5.50
		Nos. 536-539 (4)	284.00	39.50
		Set, never hinged	525.00	

Prof. D. I. Mendeleev (1834-1907), chemist who discovered the Periodic Law of Classification of the Elements.

Imperfs. exist of 5k (value $400) and 15k (value $400).

Lenin as Child and Youth A186 A187

Demonstration before Lenin Mausoleum — A190

Designs: 5k, Lenin in middle age. 10k, Lenin the orator. 30k, Lenin and Stalin.

1934, Nov. 23 Unwmk. ***Perf. 14***

No.	Type	Description	Unused	Used
540	A186	1k indigo & black	22.00	4.00
541	A187	3k indigo & black	11.00	4.00
a.		Horiz. pair, imperf. btwn.	—	*5,000.*
542	A187	5k indigo & black	50.00	3.00
543	A187	10k indigo & black	16.50	2.50
544	A190	20k brn org & ultra	11.00	8.50
545	A190	30k brn org & car	240.00	35.00
		Nos. 540-545 (6)	350.50	57.00
		Set, never hinged	760.00	

First decade without Lenin.

See Nos. 931-935, 937.

Bombs Falling on City A192

"Before War and Afterwards" A194

Designs: 10k, Refugees from burning town. 20k, "Plowing with the sword." 35k, "Comradeship."

1935, Jan. 1 Wmk. 170 ***Perf. 14***

No.	Type	Description	Unused	Used
546	A192	5k violet black	28.00	3.00
547	A192	10k ultra	130.00	15.00
548	A194	15k green	150.00	20.00
549	A194	20k dark brown	19.00	3.75
550	A194	35k carmine	220.00	30.00
		Nos. 546-550 (5)	547.00	71.75
		Set, never hinged	1,050.	

Anti-war propaganda, the designs symbolize the horrors of modern warfare.

Subway Tunnel A197

Subway Station Cross Section A198

Subway Station A199

Train in Station — A200

1935, Feb. 25 Wmk. 170 ***Perf. 14***

No.	Type	Description	Unused	Used
551	A197	5k orange	42.50	7.50
552	A198	10k dark ultra	32.50	8.50
553	A199	15k rose carmine	300.00	32.50
554	A200	20k emerald	32.50	10.00
		Nos. 551-554 (4)	407.50	58.50
		Set, never hinged	815.00	

Completion of Moscow subway.

Friedrich Engels (1820-1895), German Socialist and Collaborator of Marx — A201

1935, May Wmk. 170 ***Perf. 14***

No.	Type	Description	Unused	Used
555	A201	5k carmine	14.00	4.00
556	A201	10k dark green	25.00	6.00
557	A201	15k dark blue	70.00	14.00
558	A201	20k brown black	13.50	6.00
		Nos. 555-558 (4)	122.50	30.00
		Set, never hinged	230.00	

Running — A202

Designs: 2k, Diving. 3k, Rowing. 4k, Soccer. 5k, Skiing. 10k, Bicycling. 15k, Tennis. 20k, Skating. 35k, Hurdling. 40k, Parade of athletes.

1935, Apr. 22 Unwmk. *Perf. 14*

559 A202 1k orange & ultra 20.00 4.25
560 A202 2k black & ultra 16.00 2.50
561 A202 3k grn & blk brn 22.00 3.00
562 A202 4k rose red & ultra 17.00 5.25
563 A202 5k pur & blk brn 20.00 2.50
564 A202 10k rose red & vio 20.00 5.25
565 A202 15k blk & blk brn 190.00 42.50
566 A202 20k blk brn & ultra 22.00 5.00
567 A202 35k ultra & blk brn 125.00 35.00
568 A202 40k blk brn & car 20.00 8.50
Nos. 559-568 (10) 472.00 113.75
Set, never hinged 925.00

International Spartacist Games, Moscow. The games never took place.

Silver Plate of Sassanian Dynasty A212

1935, Sept. 10 Wmk. 170

569 A212 5k orange red 57.50 3.50
570 A212 10k dk yel grn 22.50 5.25
571 A212 15k dark violet 22.50 8.50
572 A212 35k black brown 57.50 10.00
Nos. 569-572 (4) 160.00 27.25
Set, never hinged 300.00

3rd International Congress of Persian Art, Leningrad, Sept. 12-18, 1935.

Kalinin, the Worker — A213

Mikhail Kalinin — A216

Kalinin as: 5k, farmer. 10k, orator.

1935, Nov. 20 Unwmk. *Perf. 14*

573 A213 3k rose lilac 3.75 1.25
a. Horiz. pair, imperf. btwn. — *4,500.*
574 A213 5k green 3.75 1.25
575 A213 10k blue slate 7.50 1.75
576 A216 20k brown black 16.00 3.50
a. Imperf. *1,500.*
Nos. 573-576 (4) 31.00 7.75
Set, never hinged 52.50

60th birthday of Mikhail Kalinin, chairman of the Central Executive Committee of the USSR.

A217

Leo Tolstoy — A218

Design: 20k, Statue of Tolstoy.

1935, Dec. 4 *Perf. 14*

577 A217 3k ol black & vio 7.00 2.50
b. Horiz. pair, imperf. btwn. — *2,000.*
578 A218 10k vio blk & blk brn 11.00 1.50
b. Vert. pair, imperf. btwn. — *2,250.*
579 A217 20k dk grn & blk brn 12.50 3.00
Nos. 577-579 (3) 30.50 7.00
Set, never hinged 57.50

Perf. 11

577a A217 3k 7.00 4.00
c. Horiz. pair, imperf. btwn. *2,000. 850.00*
578a A218 10k 26.00 3.00
579a A217 20k 9.00 4.50
b. Vert. pair, imperf. btwn. *1,600. 1,100.*
Nos. 577a-579a (3) 42.00 11.50
Set, never hinged 80.00

25th anniv. of the death of Count Leo N. Tolstoy (1828-1910).

Portrait Type of 1933

Designs: 2k, Mikhail V. Frunze. 4k, N. E. Bauman. 40k, Sergei M. Kirov.

1935, Nov. Wmk. 170 *Perf. 11*

580 A169 2k purple 11.00 5.50
581 A169 4k brown violet 7.00 5.00
582 A169 40k black brown 19.00 5.00
Nos. 580-582 (3) 37.00 15.50
Set, never hinged 65.00

Perf. 14

580a A169 2k 10.00 1.50
b. Vert. pair, imperf. btwn. *2,250.* —
581a A169 4k 22.50 3.00
582a A169 40k 60.00 4.00
b. Vert. pair, imperf. btwn. — *2,750.*
Nos. 580a-582a (3) 92.50 8.50
Set, never hinged 200.00

Death of three revolutionary heroes.

Nos. 580-582 exist imperf. but were not regularly issued. Values, set: unused, $1,800; never hinged, $3,250.

Pioneers Preventing Theft from Mailbox A223

Designs: 3k, 5k, Pioneers preventing destruction of property. 10k, Helping recover kite. 15k, Girl Pioneer saluting.

1936, Apr. Unwmk. *Perf. 14*

583 A223 1k yellow green 2.00 1.00
b. Vert. pair, imperf. btwn. — *1,650.*
584 A223 2k copper red 2.50 .85
b. Vert. pair, imperf. btwn. *1,750. 1,650.*
585 A223 3k slate blue 2.75 .85
586 A223 5k rose lake 4.50 1.40
587 A223 10k gray blue 6.75 2.50
b. Horiz. pair, imperf. btwn. *2,650.* —
588 A223 15k brown olive 40.00 10.00
Nos. 583-588 (6) 58.50 16.60
Set, never hinged 135.00

Perf. 11

583a A223 1k 2.00 1.00
c. Vert. pair, imperf. btwn. — *1,200.*
584a A223 2k 2.50 1.00
c. Vert. pair, imperf. btwn. *1,750. 1,900.*
585a A223 3k 2.25 1.00
b. Vert. pair, imperf. btwn. *1,750. 1,650.*
586a A223 5k 22.50 2.25
587a A223 10k 11.50 3.00
c. Vert. pair, imperf. btwn. — *2,750.*
d. Horiz. pair, imperf. btwn. *1,750. 1,650.*
588a A223 15k 17.50 5.50
Nos. 583a-588a (6) 58.25 13.75
Set, never hinged 105.00

Nikolai A. Dobrolyubov, Writer and Critic, Birth Cent. — A227

1936, Aug. 13 Typo. *Perf. 11½*

589 A227 10k rose lake 10.50 5.50
Never hinged 20.00
a. Perf. 14 8.50 3.50
Never hinged 17.00

Aleksander Sergeyevich Pushkin — A228

Statue of Pushkin, Moscow — A229

Chalky Paper

1937, Feb. 1

Line Perf 12¼

590 A228 10k yellow brown 3.50 .75
591 A228 20k Prus green 3.50 .75
592 A228 40k rose lake 3.50 .75
593 A229 50k blue 8.25 2.00
594 A229 80k carmine rose 42.50 6.00
595 A229 1r green 82.50 8.50
Set, never hinged 120.00

Chalky or Ordinary Paper

Comb Perf 12¼x11¾

590A A228 10k yellow brown 7.00 2.00
591A A228 20k Prus green 7.00 3.00
592A A228 40k rose lake 12.00 3.00
593A A229 50k blue 21.00 7.00
594A A229 80k carmine rose 7.00 2.00
Set, never hinged 120.00

Line Perf 13¾x12¼

590B A228 10k yellow brown 9.50 .75
591B A228 20k Prus green 6.00 .75
592B A228 40k rose lake 2.00 1.75
593B A229 50k blue 27.00 4.75
594B A229 80k carmine rose 22.50 6.00
595B A229 1r green 52.50 8.50
Set, never hinged 120.00

Line Perf 11x12¼

590C A228 10k yellow brown 37.50 2.25
591C A228 20k Prus green 165.00 14.50
592C A228 40k rose lake 145.00 14.50
593C A229 50k blue 37.50 11.00
594C A229 80k carmine rose 35.00 2.25
595C A229 1r green 42.50 5.50
Set, never hinged 120.00

Line Perf 13¾

590D A228 10k yellow brown 82.50 —
591D A228 20k Prus green 60.00 —
592D A228 40k rose lake 82.50 —
Set, never hinged 120.00

Line Perf 11

590E A228 10k yellow brown 187.50 *22.50*
592E A228 40k rose lake 140.00 *22.50*
Set, never hinged 120.00

Souvenir Sheet

Imperf

596 Sheet of 2 25.00 *75.00*
Never hinged 50.00
a. A228 10k brown 4.00 *20.00*
b. A229 50k brown 4.00 *27.50*

Pushkin (1799-1837), writer and poet.

Tchaikovsky Concert Hall — A230

Designs: 5k, 15k, Telegraph Agency House. 10k, Tchaikovsky Concert Hall. 20k, 50k, Red Army Theater. 30k, Hotel Moscow. 40k, Palace of the Soviets.

Unwmk.

1937, June Photo. *Perf. 12*

597 A230 3k brown violet 5.75 .75
b. Imperf. 285.00 145.00
598 A230 5k henna brown 2.90 1.75
b. Imperf. 285.00 105.00
599 A230 10k dark brown 6.00 .75
b. Imperf. 700.00 285.00
600 A230 15k black 65.00 .75
b. Imperf. 1,050. 475.00
601 A230 20k olive green 11.50 1.75
b. Imperf. 82.50 325.00
602 A230 30k gray black 8.25 2.25
a. Perf. 11 82.50 *12.50*
b. Imperf. — —
603 A230 40k violet 11.50 1.75
a. Souv. sheet of 4, imperf. 29.00 *25.00*
b. Imperf. 1,425. —
604 A230 50k dark brown 11.50 6.00
b. Imperf. 1,650. 425.00
Nos. 597-604 (8) 122.40 15.75
Set, never hinged 450.00

First Congress of Soviet Architects. The 30k is watermarked Greek Border and Rosettes (170).

Feliks E. Dzerzhinski — A235

1937, July 27 Typo. *Perf. 12*

606 A235 10k yellow brown 3.00 1.20
a. Imperf. 1,500.
607 A235 20k Prus green 6.75 1.20
a. Imperf. 1,500.
608 A235 40k rose lake 14.00 2.25
a. Imperf. 1,500.
609 A235 80k carmine 12.00 3.75
a. Imperf. 1,500.
Nos. 606-609 (4) 35.75 8.40
Set, never hinged 80.00

Dzerzhinski, organizer of Soviet secret police, 10th death anniv.

Shota Rustaveli — A236

Line Perf 12¼

1938, Feb. Unwmk. Photo.

610 A236 20k deep green 7.25 1.00
Never hinged 13.00
a. Comb perf. 12½x12 *1,450.* 375.00
b. Imperf. *2,100.* —

750th anniversary of the publication of the poem "Knight in the Tiger Skin," by Shota Rustaveli, Georgian poet.

Statue Surmounting Pavilion A237

Soviet Pavilion at Paris Exposition A238

1938 **Typo.**

611 A237 5k red 1.25 .60
 a. Imperf. *1,650.*
612 A238 20k rose 1.75 .50
613 A237 50k dark blue 19.50 3.75
 Nos. 611-613 (3) 22.50 4.85
 Set, never hinged 42.50

USSR participation in the 1937 International Exposition at Paris.

Types of 1929-32 and Lenin Types of 1925-26

1937-52 Unwmk. ***Perf. 11½x12, 12***

613A A103 1k dull org ('40) 7.50 *2.50*
614 A95 2k yel grn ('39) 6.75 *1.00*
615 A97 4k claret ('40) 65.00 *3.50*
 b. Imperf. 950.00
615A A98 5k org brn ('46) 65.00 *10.00*
616 A109 10k blue ('38) 1.25 *.50*
 b. Imperf. 725.00
616A A103 10k olive ('40) 145.00 *12.50*
 b. Imperf. 1,875.
616B A109 10k black ('52) .25 .25
617 A97 20k dull green 1.25 .40
 b. Imperf. 2,950.
617A A107 20k green ('39) 100.00 *6.25*
 b. Imperf. 600.00
618 A109 30k claret ('39) 45.00 1.75
 b. Imperf. 600.00
619 A104 40k indigo ('38) 6.50 *.75*
 b. Imperf. 375.00
619A A111 50k dp brn ('40) 6.50 *1.00*

Engr.

620 A75 3r dk grn ('39) 2.50 .50
 a. Horiz. pair, imperf. btwn. *2,850.* —
621 A66 5r red brn ('39) 8.50 2.50
622 A66 10r indigo ('39) 3.75 1.50
 Nos. 613A-622 (15) 464.75 44.90
 Set, never hinged 800.00

No. 616B was re-issued in 1954-56 in slightly smaller format, 14½x21mm, and in gray black. See note after No. 738.

Airplane Route from Moscow to North Pole — A239

Soviet Flag and Airplanes at North Pole — A240

1938, Feb. 25 **Litho.** ***Perf. 12***

625 A239 10k brn & black 3.75 .75
626 A239 20k blue gray & blk 7.25 2.25

Typo.

627 A240 40k dl grn & car 18.00 3.75
 a. Imperf. 1,450.
628 A240 80k rose car & car 4.00 .80
 a. Imperf. 150.00
 b. Double impression of flag *2,000.*
 Nos. 625-628 (4) 33.00 7.55
 Set, never hinged 57.50

Soviet flight to the North Pole.

Infantryman A241

Soldier A242

Stalin Reviewing Cavalry A246

Chapayev and Boy — A247

Designs: 30k, Sailor, 40k, Aviator. 50k, Antiaircraft soldier.

Unwmk.

1938, Mar. **Photo.** ***Perf. 12***

629 A241 10k gray blk & dk red 5.50 .75
630 A242 20k gray blk & dk red 8.25 .80
631 A242 30k gray blk & dk red 10.50 1.20
632 A242 40k gray blk & dk red 14.50 1.90
633 A242 50k gray blk & dk red 14.50 1.90
634 A246 80k gray blk & dk red 19.00 3.75

Typo.

Perf. 12x12½

635 A247 1r black & carmine 6.00 2.00
 a. Imperf. 1,150. —
 Nos. 629-635 (7) 78.25 12.30
 Set, never hinged 140.00

Workers' & Peasants' Red Army, 20th anniv.

Aviators Chkalov, Baidukov, Beliakov and Flight Route — A248

1938, Apr. 10 **Photo.**

636 A248 10k black & red 8.25 .75
 a. Imperf. 5,250. 3,600.
637 A248 20k brn blk & red 12.00 .75
 a. Imperf. 1,050. 375.00
638 A248 40k brown & red 12.00 2.00
 a. Imperf. 1,050. 375.00
639 A248 50k brown vio & red 15.00 3.75
 a. Imperf. 1,050. 375.00
 Nos. 636-639 (4) 47.25 7.25
 Set, never hinged 95.00

First Trans-Polar flight, June 18-20, 1937, from Moscow to Vancouver, Wash.

Aviators Gromov, Danilin, Yumashev and Flight Route — A249

1938, Apr. 13

640 A249 10k claret 10.00 .75
 a. Imperf. 825.00
641 A249 20k brown black 12.00 1.75
 a. Imperf. 725.00 —
642 A249 50k dull violet 13.00 5.00
 a. Imperf. *17,500.*
 Nos. 640-642 (3) 35.00 7.50
 Set, never hinged 60.00

First Trans-Polar flight, July 12-14, 1937, from Moscow to San Jacinto, Calif.

Arrival of the Rescuing Ice-breakers Taimyr and Murmansk A250

Ivan Papanin and His Men Aboard Ice-breaker Yermak — A251

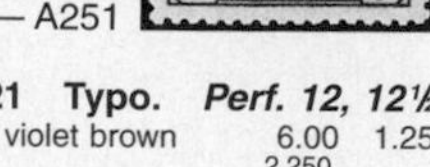

1938, June 21 **Typo.** ***Perf. 12, 12½***

643 A250 10k violet brown 6.00 1.25
 a. Imperf. 2,250.
644 A250 20k dark blue 8.25 1.50
 a. Imperf. 2,250.

Photo.

645 A251 30k olive brown 21.00 3.75
 a. Imperf. 3,250.
646 A251 50k ultra 16.50 6.00
 a. Imperf. 2,350.
 Nos. 643-646 (4) 51.75 12.50
 Set, never hinged 110.00

Rescue of Papanin's North Pole Expedition.

Arms of Armenia — A252

Arms of USSR A253

No. 650

No. 651

No. 654

No. 655

No. 656

Designs: Different arms on each stamp.

Perf. 12, 12½

1937-38 **Unwmk.** **Typo.**

647 A252 20k dp bl (Armenia) 10.50 2.00
648 A252 20k dl vio (Azerbaijan) 10.50 2.00
649 A252 20k brn org (Byelorussia) 10.50 2.00
650 A252 20k car rose (Georgia) 10.50 2.00
651 A252 20k bl grn (Kazakh) 10.50 2.00
652 A252 20k emer (Kirghiz) 10.50 2.00
653 A252 20k yel org (Uzbek) 10.50 2.00
654 A252 20k bl (R.S.F.S.R.) 10.50 2.00
655 A252 20k claret (Tadzhik) 10.50 2.00
656 A252 20k car (Turkmen) 10.50 2.00
657 A252 20k red (Ukraine) 10.50 2.00

Engr.

658 A253 40k brown red 9.25 2.00
 Nos. 647-658 (12) 124.75 24.00
 Set, never hinged 240.00

Constitution of USSR. No. 649 has inscriptions in Yiddish, Polish, Byelorussian and Russian.

Issue dates: 40k, 1937. Others, 1938. See Nos. 841-842.

Nurse Weighing Child — A264

Children at Lenin's Statue — A265

Biology Lesson A266

Health Camp A267

Young Model Builders A268

1938, Sept. 15 **Unwmk.** ***Perf. 12***

659 A264 10k dk blue green 12.00 2.00
660 A265 15k dk blue green 3.50 3.50
661 A266 20k violet brown 13.00 2.50
662 A267 30k claret 13.00 2.50
663 A266 40k light brown 13.00 2.50
664 A268 50k deep blue 12.00 *5.00*
665 A268 80k light green 13.00 *4.50*
 Nos. 659-665 (7) 79.50 22.50
 Set, never hinged 145.00

Child welfare.

View of Yalta A269

Crimean Shoreline — A272

Designs: No. 667, View along Crimean shore. No. 668, Georgian military highway. No, 670, View near Yalta. No. 671, "Swallows' Nest" Castle. 20k, Dzerzhinski Rest House for workers. 30k, Sunset in Crimea. 40k, Alupka. 50k, Gursuf. 80k, Crimean Gardens. 1r, "Swallows' Nest" Castle, horiz.

Unwmk.

1938, Sept. 21 **Photo.** ***Perf. 12***

666 A269 5k brown 4.75 *1.00*
667 A269 5k black brown 4.75 *1.00*
668 A269 10k slate green 4.75 *1.00*
669 A272 10k brown 4.75 *1.00*
670 A269 15k black brown 6.00 *1.75*
671 A272 15k black brown 6.00 *1.75*
672 A269 20k dark brown 10.00 *1.75*
673 A272 30k black brown 12.00 *1.75*
674 A269 40k brown 12.00 *1.75*
675 A272 50k slate green 12.00 *1.75*
 a. Horiz. pair, imperf. btwn. 2,175.
 b. Vert. pair, imperf. btwn. 2,175.
676 A269 80k brown 12.00 *1.75*
677 A269 1r slate green 120.00 *20.00*
 Nos. 666-677 (12) 209.00 36.25
 Set, never hinged 400.00

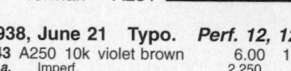

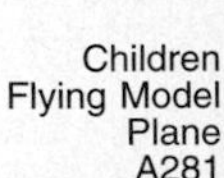

Children Flying Model Plane A281

Glider A282

Captive Balloon — A283

Dirigible over Kremlin — A284

Parachute Jumpers — A285

Hydroplane A286

Balloon in Flight — A287

Balloon Ascent — A288

Four-motor Plane A289

Unwmk.

1938, Oct. 7 Typo. *Perf. 12*

678	A281	5k violet brown	3.75	1.50
679	A282	10k olive gray	3.75	1.50
680	A283	15k pink	6.00	1.50
681	A284	20k deep blue	6.00	1.50
682	A285	30k claret	12.00	1.50
683	A286	40k deep blue	14.50	1.50
684	A287	50k blue green	12.00	2.50
685	A288	80k brown	14.50	2.50
686	A289	1r blue green	82.50	10.00
		Nos. 678-686 (9)	155.00	24.00
		Set, never hinged	270.00	

For overprints see Nos. C76-C76D.

Mayakovsky Station, Moscow Subway — A290

Sokol Terminal — A291

Kiev Station — A292

Dynamo Station A293

Train in Tunnel A294

Revolution Square Station A295

Unwmk.

1938, Nov. 7 Photo. *Perf. 12*

687	A290	10k deep red violet	3.00	2.00
a.		Vert. pair, imperf. btwn.	2,175.	—
688	A291	15k dark brown	6.00	2.00
689	A292	20k black brown	14.50	2.50
690	A293	30k dark red violet	21.00	4.75
a.		Vert. pair, imperf. btwn.	—	*3,600.*
691	A294	40k black brown	21.00	4.75
692	A295	50k dark brown	24.00	7.25
		Nos. 687-692 (6)	89.50	23.25
		Set, never hinged	155.00	

Second line of the Moscow subway opening.

Girl with Parachute A296

Young Miner A297

Harvesting A298

Designs: 50k, Students returning from school. 80k, Aviator and sailor.

1938, Dec. 7 Typo. *Perf. 12*

693	A296	20k deep blue	13.00	2.50
694	A297	30k deep claret	13.00	2.50
695	A298	40k violet brown	10.50	2.50
696	A296	50k deep rose	35.00	8.25
697	A298	80k deep blue	8.25	6.00
		Nos. 693-697 (5)	79.75	21.75
		Set, never hinged	140.00	

20th anniv. of the Young Communist League (Komsomol).

Diving — A301

Discus Thrower — A302

Designs: 15k, Tennis. 20k, Acrobatic motorcyclists. 30k, Skier. 40k, Runners. 50k, Soccer. 80k, Physical culture.

Unwmk.

1938, Dec. 28 Photo. *Perf. 12*

698	A301	5k scarlet	3.50	1.25
699	A302	10k black	3.50	1.25
700	A302	15k brown	6.00	1.75
701	A302	20k green	6.00	1.75
702	A302	30k dull violet	30.00	2.00
703	A302	40k deep green	15.00	2.00
704	A302	50k blue	82.50	10.00
705	A302	80k deep blue	10.50	5.00
		Nos. 698-705 (8)	157.00	25.00
		Set, never hinged	290.00	

Gorki Street, Moscow — A309

Dynamo Subway Station A315

Moscow scenes: 20k, Council House & Hotel Moscow. 30k, Lenin Library. 40k, Crimea Bridge. 50k, Bridge over Moscow River. 80k, Khimki River Terminal.

Paper with network as in parenthesis

1939, Mar. Typo. *Perf. 12*

706	A309	10k brn *(red brown)*	3.75	1.25
707	A309	20k dk sl grn *(lt blue)*	3.75	1.50
708	A309	30k brn vio *(red brn)*	3.75	1.50
709	A309	40k blue *(lt blue)*	12.50	2.50
710	A309	50k rose lake *(red brn)*	12.50	3.00
711	A309	80k gray ol *(lt blue)*	12.50	5.75
712	A315	1r dk blue *(lt blue)*	70.00	7.50
		Nos. 706-712 (7)	118.75	23.00
		Set, never hinged	220.00	
		Set, never hinged	250.00	

"New Moscow." On 30k, denomination is at upper right.

Foundry-man — A316

1939, Mar.

713	A316	15k dark blue	7.50	.75
		Never hinged	14.50	
a.		Imperf.	2,000.	
		Never hinged	3,000.	

Statue on USSR Pavilion — A317

USSR Pavilion A318

1939, May Photo.

714	A317	30k indigo & red	2.75	1.00
a.		Imperf. ('40)	3.00	1.00
715	A318	50k blue & bister brn	5.50	1.00
a.		Imperf. ('40)	6.00	1.25
		Set, never hinged	15.00	

Russia's participation in the NY World's Fair.

Paulina Osipenko A318a

Marina Raskova A318b

Design: 60k, Valentina Grizodubova.

1939, Mar.

718	A318a	15k green	8.25	2.00
719	A318b	30k brown violet	14.50	3.75
720	A318b	60k red	14.50	7.50
		Nos. 718-720 (3)	37.25	13.25
		Set, never hinged	65.00	

Non-stop record flight from Moscow to the Far East.

Exist imperf. Value, each unused $2,100.

Shevchenko, Early Portrait — A319

Monument at Kharkov — A321

30k, Shevchenko portrait in later years.

1939, Mar. 9

721	A319	15k black brn & blk	7.50	1.50
722	A319	30k dark red & blk	13.00	2.25
723	A321	60k green & dk brn	14.50	3.00
		Nos. 721-723 (3)	35.00	6.75
		Set, never hinged	80.00	

Taras G. Shevchenko (1814-1861), Ukrainian poet and painter.

Milkmaid with Prize Cow — A322

Tractor-plow at Work on Abundant Harvest A323

Designs: 20k, Shepherd tending sheep. No. 727, Fair pavilion. No. 728, Fair emblem. 45k, Turkmen picking cotton. 50k, Drove of horses. 60k, Symbolizing agricultural wealth. 80k, Kolkhoz girl with sugar beets. 1r, Hunter with Polar foxes.

1939, Aug.

724 A322 10k rose pink 3.50 .45
725 A323 15k red brown 3.50 .45
726 A323 20k slate black 9.50 2.00
727 A323 30k purple 5.75 1.00
728 A322 30k red orange 3.50 .45
729 A322 45k dark green 9.50 1.25
a. Horiz. pair, imperf. btwn. *1,750.*
730 A322 50k copper red 2.00 .45
a. Horiz. pair, imperf. btwn. *1,500.*
731 A322 60k bright purple 7.00 1.00
732 A322 80k dark violet 7.00 1.00
733 A322 1r dark blue 19.00 2.00
Nos. 724-733 (10) 70.25 10.05
Set, never hinged 128.00

Soviet Agricultural Fair.

Worker A331

Soldier A332

Aviator — A333

Perf. 11¾x12¼

Arms of USSR
A334 A335

Perf. 11¾x12¼

1939-43 Unwmk. Typo.

734 A331 5k red .75 .25
735 A332 15k dark green 1.25 .25
736 A333 30k deep blue 2.00 .25
737 A334 60k fawn ('43) 9.50 .75

Photo.

738 A335 60k rose carmine 2.50 .45
Nos. 734-738 (5) 16.00 1.95
Set, never hinged 15.00

No. 734 was re-issued in 1954-56 in slightly smaller format: 14x21½mm, instead of 14¾x22¼mm. Other values reissued in smaller format: 10k, 15k, 20k, 25k, 30k, 40k and 1r. (See notes following Nos. 622, 1260, 1347 and 1689.)

No. 416 Surcharged with New Value in Black

1939 Wmk. 170 *Perf. 12x12½*

743 A97 30k on 4k claret 25.00 12.50
a. Unwmkd. 250.00 37.50

M.E. Saltykov (N. Shchedrin)
A336 A337

Unwmk.

1939, Sept. Typo. *Perf. 12*

745 A336 15k claret 3.00 .75
746 A337 30k dark green 3.75 .75
747 A336 45k olive gray 8.75 1.50
748 A337 60k dark blue 8.75 2.25
Nos. 745-748 (4) 24.25 5.25
Set, never hinged 80.00

Mikhail E. Saltykov (1826-89), writer & satirist who used pen name of N. Shchedrin.

Sanatorium of the State Bank — A338

Designs: 10k, 15k, Soviet Army sanatorium. 20k, Rest home, New Afyon. 30k, Clinical Institute. 50k, 80k, Sanatorium for workers in heavy industry. 60k, Rest home, Sukhumi.

1939, Nov. Photo. *Perf. 12*

749 A338 5k dull brown 2.00 .25
750 A338 10k carmine 2.00 .25
751 A338 15k yellow green 3.50 .45
752 A338 20k dk slate green 7.00 .45
753 A338 30k bluish black 3.50 .45
a. Horiz. pair, imperf. between *2,500.*
754 A338 50k gray black 3.50 1.75
755 A338 60k brown violet 9.50 1.75
756 A338 80k orange red 7.00 1.75
Nos. 749-756 (8) 38.00 7.10
Set, never hinged 125.00

Mikhail Y. Lermontov (1814-1841), Poet and Novelist, in 1837 — A346

Portrait in 1838 — A347

Portrait in 1841 — A348

1939, Dec.

757 A346 15k indigo & sepia 8.25 1.25
a. Vert. pair, imperf. between — 1,650.
758 A347 30k dk grn & dull blk 12.00 3.00
a. Vert. pair, imperf. between — 1,650.
759 A348 45k brk red & indigo 8.25 1.25
Nos. 757-759 (3) 28.50 5.50
Set, never hinged 60.00

Nikolai Chernyshevski A349

1939, Dec. Photo.

760 A349 15k dark green 9.50 1.25
761 A349 30k dull violet 14.50 1.25
762 A349 60k Prus green 14.50 3.00
Nos. 760-762 (3) 38.50 5.50
Set, never hinged 50.00

50th anniversary of the death of Nikolai Chernyshevski, scientist and critic.

Anton Chekhov — A350

Design: 20k, 30k, Portrait with hat.

1940, Feb. Unwmk. *Perf. 12*

763 A350 10k dark yellow green 2.00 1.50
764 A350 15k ultra 3.75 1.50
765 A350 20k violet 3.75 1.50
766 A350 30k copper brown 14.50 1.50
Nos. 763-766 (4) 24.00 6.00
Set, never hinged 40.00

Chekhov (1860-1904), playwright.

Welcome to Red Army by Western Ukraine and Western Byelorussia A352

Designs: 30k, Villagers welcoming tank crew. 50k, 60k, Soldier giving newspapers to crowd. 1r, Crowd waving to tank column.

1940, Apr.

767 A352 10k deep rose 1.90 .75
768 A352 30k myrtle green 3.25 1.00
769 A352 50k gray black 3.75 1.25
770 A352 60k indigo 13.00 2.50
771 A352 1r red 9.75 2.00
Nos. 767-771 (5) 31.65 7.50
Set, never hinged 60.00

Liberation of the people of Western Ukraine and Western Byelorussia.

Ice-breaker "Josef Stalin," Captain Beloussov and Chief Ivan Papanin A356

Badigin and Papanin A358

Map of the Drift of the Sedov and Crew Members — A359

Design: 30k, Icebreaker Georgi Sedov, Captain Vadygin and First Mate Trofimov.

1940, Apr.

772 A356 15k dull yel green 3.50 .75
773 A356 30k dull purple 10.50 1.25
b. Vert. pair, imperf. between — *7,250.*
774 A358 50k copper brown 6.50 1.50
775 A359 1r dark ultra 12.50 2.50
Nos. 772-775 (4) 33.00 6.00
Set, never hinged 57.50

Heroism of the Sedov crew which drifted in the Polar Basin for 812 days.

A360

Vladimir V. Mayakovsky — A361

1940, June *Line Perf. 12¼*

776 A360 15k deep red 4.75 1.25
777 A360 30k copper brown 4.75 1.25
778 A361 60k dark gray blue 12.00 2.00
779 A361 80k bright ultra 9.50 1.25
Nos. 776-779 (4) 31.00 5.75
Set, never hinged 57.50

Mayakovsky, poet (1893-1930).

K.A. Timiryazev and Academy of Agricultural Sciences A362

In the Laboratory of Moscow University A363

Last Portrait A364

Monument in Moscow — A365

1940, June

780 A362 10k indigo 3.00 1.25
781 A363 15k purple 12.00 1.25
782 A364 30k dk violet brown 4.75 1.75
783 A365 60k dark green 4.75 2.50
Nos. 780-783 (4) 24.50 6.75
Set, never hinged 40.00

20th anniversary of the death of K. A. Timiryasev, scientist and professor of agricultural and biological sciences.

Relay Race — A366

Sportswomen Marching A367

Children's Sport Badge — A368

Skier A369

Throwing the Grenade A370

1940, July 21 ***Line Perf. 12½***

No.	Type	Description	Unused	Used
784	A366	15k carmine rose	4.25	.75
785	A367	30k sepia	8.25	3.00
786	A368	50k dk violet blue	4.75	.75
787	A369	60k dk violet blue	12.00	3.00
788	A370	1r grayish green	14.50	.75
		Nos. 784-788 (5)	43.75	8.25
		Set, never hinged	85.00	

Perf. 11¾x12¼, 12¼x11¾ (#786)

Tchaikovsky Museum at Klin — A371

Tchaikovsky & Passage from his Fourth Symphony — A372

Peter Ilich Tchaikovsky and Excerpt from Eugene Onegin — A373

Comb Perf. 12¼x11¾

1940, Aug. **Unwmk.** **Typo.**

No.	Type	Description	Unused	Used
789	A371	15k Prus green	5.50	1.50
790	A372	20k brown	6.00	1.50
791	A372	30k dark blue	5.50	2.00
792	A371	50k rose lake	14.50	3.50
793	A373	60k red	12.00	7.00
		Nos. 789-793 (5)	43.50	15.50
		Set, never hinged	65.00	

Tchaikovsky (1840-1893), composer.

Volga Provinces Pavilion A374

Northeast Provinces Pavilion — A376

ПАВИЛЬОН МОСКОВСКОЙ, РЯЗАНСКОЙ И ТУЛЬСКОЙ ОБЛ.
No. 797

ПАВИЛЬОН УКРАИНСКОЙ ССР
No. 798

ПАВИЛЬОН БЕЛОРУССКОЙ ССР
No. 799

ПАВИЛЬОН АЗЕРБАЙДЖАНСКОЙ ССР
No. 800

ПАВИЛЬОН ГРУЗИНСКОЙ ССР
No. 801

ПАВИЛЬОН АРМЯНСКОЙ ССР
No. 802

У ВХОДА В ПАВИЛЬОН УЗБЕКСКОЙ ССР
No. 803

ПАВИЛЬОН ТУРКМЕНСКОЙ ССР
No. 804

ПАВИЛЬОН ТАДЖИКСКОЙ ССР
No. 805

ПАВИЛЬОН КИРГИЗСКОЙ ССР
No. 806

ПАВИЛЬОН КАЗАХСКОЙ ССР
No. 807

ПАВИЛЬОН КАРЕЛО-ФИНСКОЙ ССР
No. 808

No. 795, Far East Provinces. No. 797, Central Regions. No. 798, Ukrainian. No. 799, Byelorussian. No. 800, Azerbaijan. No. 801, Georgian. No. 802, Armenian. No. 803, Uzbek. No. 804, Turkmen. No. 805, Tadzhik. No. 806, Kirghiz. No. 807, Kazakh. No. 808, Karelian Finnish. No. 809, Main building. No. 810, Mechanizaton Pavilion, Stalin statue.

1940, Oct. **Typo.** ***Line Perf. 12¼***

No.	Type	Description	Unused	Used
794	A374	10k shown	9.50	.55
795	A374	15k multicolored	9.50	.55
796	A376	30k shown	12.00	.55
797	A376	30k multicolored	14.50	.55
798	A376	30k multicolored	3.50	.55
799	A376	30k multicolored	3.50	.55
800	A376	30k multicolored	3.50	.55
801	A374	30k multicolored	7.00	.55
802	A376	30k multicolored	7.00	.55
803	A376	30k multicolored	3.50	.55
804	A374	30k multicolored	9.50	.55
805	A376	30k multicolored	3.50	.55
806	A376	30k multicolored	3.50	.55
807	A376	30k multicolored	3.50	.55
808	A376	30k multicolored	9.50	.55
809	A376	50k multicolored	16.50	1.50
810	A376	60k multicolored	19.00	2.50
		Nos. 794-810 (17)	138.50	12.25
		Set, never hinged	215.00	

All-Union Agricultural Fair.

Nos. 796-808 printed in three sheet formats with various vertical and horizontal se-tenant combinations.

Monument to Red Army Heroes — A391

Map of War Operations and M. V. Frunze — A393

Heroic Crossing of the Sivash A394

Designs: 15k, Grenade thrower. 60k, Frunze's headquarters, Stroganovka. 1r, Victorious soldier.

1940 ***Imperf.***

No.	Type	Description	Unused	Used
811	A391	10k dark green	2.25	.55
812	A391	15k orange ver	2.25	.55
813	A393	30k dull brown & car	6.25	1.50
814	A394	50k violet brn	3.50	1.00
815	A394	60k indigo	3.50	1.00
816	A391	1r gray black	4.25	1.50
		Nos. 811-816 (6)	22.00	6.10
		Set, never hinged	35.00	

Perf. 12

No.	Type	Description	Unused	Used
811A	A391	10k dark green	2.75	.55
812A	A391	15k orange ver	2.75	.55
813A	A393	30k dull brown & car	3.75	1.00
814A	A394	50k violet brn	2.75	.65
815A	A394	60k indigo	3.75	1.00
816A	A391	1r gray black	3.75	1.00
		Nos. 811A-816A (6)	19.50	4.75
		Set, never hinged	32.50	

20th anniversary of battle of Perekop.

Coal Miners — A397

Blast Furnace — A398

Bridge over Moscow-Volga Canal — A399

Three New Type Locomotives A400

Workers on a Collective Farm — A401

Automobiles and Planes A402

Oil Derricks — A403

1941, Jan. ***Perf. 12***

No.	Type	Description	Unused	Used
817	A397	10k deep blue	2.00	1.00
818	A398	15k dark violet	2.25	1.25
819	A399	20k deep blue	2.75	1.50
820	A400	30k dark brown	3.00	1.50
821	A401	50k olive brown	3.75	1.75
822	A402	60k olive brown	4.50	2.50
823	A403	1r dark blue green	6.75	6.00
		Nos. 817-823 (7)	25.00	15.50
		Set, never hinged	60.00	

Soviet industries.

Sailor — A405

Troops on Skis — A404

Soldiers with Cannon A406

20k, Cavalry. 30k, Machine gunners. 45k, Army horsemen. 50k, Aviator. 1r, 3r, Marshal's Star.

1941-43

No.	Type	Description	Unused	Used
824	A404	5k dark violet	2.00	.25
825	A405	10k deep blue	2.00	.25
826	A406	15k brt yellow green	1.00	.25
827	A404	20k vermilion	1.00	.25
828	A404	30k dull brown	1.00	.25
829	A406	45k gray green	4.00	.50
830	A404	50k dull blue	1.50	*.75*
831	A404	1r dull blue green	2.50	*1.00*
831A	A404	3r myrtle grn ('43)	10.00	1.75
		Nos. 824-831A (9)	25.00	5.25
		Set, never hinged	70.00	

Army & Navy of the USSR, 23rd anniv.

Battle of Ismail — A412

Field Marshal Aleksandr Suvorov — A413

1941 **Unwmk.** ***Perf. 12***

No.	Type	Description	Unused	Used
832	A412	10k dark green	3.00	.25
833	A412	15k carmine rose	3.00	.30
834	A413	30k blue black	1.00	.70
835	A413	1r olive brown	3.00	3.00
		Nos. 832-835 (4)	10.00	4.25
		Set, never hinged	25.00	

150th anniversary of the capture of the Turkish fortress, Ismail.

Kirghiz Horse Breeder A414

Kirghiz Miner A415

1941, Mar. ***Perf. 12, 12x12½***

No.	Type	Description	Unused	Used
836	A414	15k dull brown	2.50	.45
837	A415	30k dull purple	3.50	.60
		Set, never hinged	15.00	

15th anniversary of the Kirghizian Soviet Socialist Republic.

Prof. N. E. Zhukovski A416

Zhukovski Lecturing A418

Military Air Academy A417

1941, Mar.

No.	Type	Description	Unused	Used
838	A416	15k deep blue	3.50	.35
839	A417	30k carmine rose	3.00	.65
840	A418	50k brown violet	3.50	1.00
		Nos. 838-840 (3)	10.00	2.00
		Set, never hinged	20.00	

Prof. Zhukovski, scientist (1847-1921).

Arms Type of 1938

Karelian-Finnish Soviet Socialist Republic.

1941, Mar.

No.	Type	Description	Unused	Used
841	A252	30k rose	2.75	.75

842 A252 45k dark blue green 3.25 1.25
Set, never hinged 15.00

1st anniversary of the Karelian-Finnish Soviet Socialist Republic.

Spasski Tower, Kremlin — A420

Kremlin and Moscow River A421

1941, May Typo. Unwmk.

843 A420 1r dull red .75 .50
844 A421 2r brown orange 1.25 1.00
Set, never hinged 5.00

"Suvorov's March through the Alps, 1799" A422

Vasili Ivanovich Surikov, Self-portrait A424

"Stepan Rasin on the Volga" A423

1941, June Photo. *Perf. 12*

845 A422 20k black 12.00 1.25
846 A423 30k scarlet 6.00 2.75
847 A422 50k dk vio brn 45.00 8.00
848 A423 1r gray green 45.00 11.00
849 A424 2r brown 45.00 13.00
Nos. 845-849 (5) 153.00 36.00
Set, never hinged 250.00

Surikov (1848-1916), painter.

Mikhail Y. Lermontov, Poet, Death Centenary — A425

1941, July

850 A425 15k Prus green *20.00 4.00*
851 A425 30k dark violet *25.00 6.00*
Set, never hinged 125.00

Visitors in Lenin Museum A426

Lenin Museum A427

1941-42

852 A426 15k rose red 14.00 6.00
853 A427 30k dark violet ('42) 40.00 18.00
854 A426 45k Prus green 21.00 9.00
855 A427 1r org brn ('42) 45.00 17.00
Nos. 852-855 (4) 120.00 50.00
Set, never hinged 250.00

Fifth anniversary of Lenin Museum.

Mother's Farewell to a Soldier Son ("Be a Hero!") — A428

1941, Aug.

856 A428 30k carmine 15.00 15.00
Never hinged 35.00

Alisher Navoi — A429

1942, Jan.

857 A429 30k brown 90.00 25.00
858 A429 1r dark violet 60.00 25.00
Set, never hinged *300.00*

Alisher Navoi, Uzbekian poet, 500th birth anniv.

People's Militia — A430

1941, Dec. Typo.

859 A430 30k dull blue 125.00 75.00
Never hinged 300.00

Junior Lieutenant Talalikhin Ramming German Plane in Midair A431

Captain Gastello and Burning Plane Diving into Enemy Gasoline Tanks A432

Major General Dovator and Cossack Cavalry in Action A433

Shura Chekalin Fighting Nazi Soldiers A434

Nazi Soldiers Leading Zoya Kosmodemjanskaja to her Death — A435

1942-44 Unwmk. Photo. *Perf. 12*

860 A431 20k bluish black 2.50 1.75
860A A431 30k Prus grn ('44) 2.50 1.75
861 A432 30k bluish black 2.50 1.75
861A A432 30k dp ultra ('44) 2.50 1.75
862 A433 30k black 2.50 1.75
863 A434 30k black 2.50 1.75
863A A434 30k brt yel grn ('44) 2.50 1.75
864 A435 30k black 2.50 1.75
864A A435 30k rose vio ('44) 2.50 1.75
865 A434 1r slate green 32.50 11.00
866 A435 2r slate green 45.00 30.00
Nos. 860-866 (11) 100.00 56.75
Set, never hinged 200.00

Issued to honor Soviet heroes.
For surcharges see Nos. C80-C81.

Anti-tank Artillery A436

Signal Corps in Action A437

Defense of Leningrad A440

Guerrilla Fighters A438

War Worker A439

Red Army Scouts A441

1942-43

867 A436 20k black 2.50 *1.50*
868 A437 30k sappire 2.50 *1.50*
869 A438 30k Prus grn ('43) 2.50 *1.50*
870 A439 30k dull red brn ('43) 2.50 *1.50*
871 A440 60k blue black 30.00 10.00
872 A441 1r black brown 30.00 6.00
Nos. 867-872 (6) 70.00 22.00
Set, never hinged 120.00

Women Workers and Soldiers A442

Flaming Tank A443

Women Preparing Food Shipments A444

Sewing Equipment for Red Army — A445

Anti-Aircraft Battery in Action — A446

1942-43 Typo. Unwmk.

873 A442 20k dark blue 1.25 1.00
874 A443 20k dull rose violet 1.25 1.00
875 A444 30k brn vio ('43) 1.75 1.75
876 A445 45k dull rose red 7.00 5.00
877 A446 45k dp dl blue ('43) 7.00 5.00
Nos. 873-877 (5) 18.25 13.75
Set, never hinged 30.00

Manufacturing Explosives — A447

Designs: 10k, Agriculture. 15k, Group of Fighters. 20k, Storming the Palace. 30k, Lenin and Stalin. 60k, Tanks. 1r, Lenin. 2r, Revolution scene.

Inscribed: "1917 XXV 1942"

1943, Jan. Photo. *Perf. 12*

878 A447 5k black brown 1.00 .50
879 A447 10k black brown 1.00 .50
880 A447 15k blue black 1.00 .50
881 A447 20k blue black 1.50 .50
882 A447 30k black brown 2.25 .60
883 A447 60k black brown 3.50 1.50
884 A447 1r dull red brown 4.00 2.00
885 A447 2r black 11.00 3.50
Nos. 878-885 (8) 25.25 9.60
Set, never hinged 65.00

25th anniversary of October Revolution.

Mount St. Elias, Alaska A455

Bering Sea and Bering's Ship — A456

1943, Apr.

886 A455 30k chalky blue .90 .50
887 A456 60k Prus green 1.75 .65
888 A455 1r yellow green 4.00 .80
889 A456 2r bister brown 8.00 1.25
Nos. 886-889 (4) 14.65 3.20
Set, never hinged 25.00

200th anniv. of the death of Vitus Bering, explorer (1681-1741).

Medical Corpsmen and Wounded Soldier A457

Trench Mortar A458

Army Scouts A459

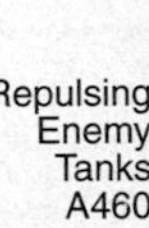

Repulsing Enemy Tanks A460

Snipers A461

1943

890 A457 30k blue gray 1.25 1.00
891 A458 30k brown bister 1.25 1.00
892 A459 30k blue gray 1.25 1.00
893 A460 60k myrtle green 2.00 1.90
894 A461 60k chalky blue 2.00 1.90
Nos. 890-894 (5) 7.75 6.80
Set, never hinged 20.00

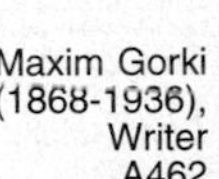

Maxim Gorki (1868-1936), Writer A462

1943, June

895 A462 30k green .80 .40
896 A462 60k slate black 1.25 .50
Set, never hinged 5.00

Patriotic War Medal A463

Order of Field Marshal Suvorov A464

1943, July **Engr.**

897 A463 1r black 1.00 1.00
898 A464 10r dk olive green 4.00 4.00
Set, never hinged 8.00

Sailors A465

Designs: 30k, Navy gunner and warship. 60k, Soldiers and tank.

1943, Oct. **Photo.**

899 A465 20k golden brown .35 .30
900 A465 30k dark myrtle green .35 .30
901 A465 60k brt yellow green .75 .60
902 A465 3r chalky blue 2.50 1.75
Nos. 899-902 (4) 3.95 2.95
Set, never hinged 7.00

25th anniv. of the Red Army and Navy.

Karl Marx — A468

1943, Sept.

903 A468 30k blue black 1.50 .25
904 A468 60k dk slate green 2.50 .25
Set, never hinged 8.00

125th anniv. of the birth of Karl Marx.

Vladimir V. Mayakovsky — A469

1943, Oct.

905 A469 30k red orange 1.50 .40
906 A469 60k deep blue 1.50 .60
Set, never hinged 6.00

Mayakovsky, poet, 50th birth anniv.

Flags of US, Britain, and USSR A470

1943, Nov.

907 A470 30k blk, dp red & dk bl .40 .30
908 A470 3r sl blue, red & lt blue 2.60 .85
Set, never hinged 5.00

The Tehran conference.

Ivan Turgenev (1818-83), Poet — A471

1943, Oct.

909 A471 30k myrtle green 20.00 20.00
910 A471 60k dull purple 25.00 25.00
Set, never hinged 125.00

Map of Stalingrad A472

Harbor of Sevastopol and Statue of Lenin A473

Leningrad A474

Odessa A475

1944, Mar. ***Perf. 12***

911 A472 30k dull brown & car 1.75 .50
912 A473 30k dark blue 1.75 .50
913 A474 30k dk slate green 1.75 .50
914 A475 30k yel green 1.75 .50
Nos. 911-914 (4) 7.00 2.00
Set, never hinged 22.50

Honoring the defenders of Stalingrad, Leningrad, Sevastopol and Odessa.

See No. 959.

No. 911 measures 33x22mm and also exists in smaller size: 32x21½mm.

USSR War Heroes A476

1944, Apr.

915 A476 30k deep ultra .50 .25
Never hinged 2.00

Sailor Loading Gun — A477

Tanks — A478

Soldier Bayoneting a Nazi A479

Infantryman A480

Soldier Throwing Hand Grenade — A481

1943-44 **Photo.**

916 A477 15k deep ultra .30 .25
917 A478 20k red orange ('44) .30 .25
918 A479 30k dull brn & dk red ('44) .30 .25
919 A480 1r brt yel green 2.00 .40
920 A481 2r blue gray ('44) 2.00 1.00
Nos. 916-920 (5) 4.90 2.15
Set, never hinged 15.00

25th anniversary of the Young Communist League (Komsomol).

Flags of US, USSR, Great Britain — A482

1944, May 30 **Unwmk.** ***Perf. 12***

921 A482 60k black, red & blue .50 .30
922 A482 3r dk bl, red & lt bl 2.75 1.10
Set, never hinged 5.00

Day of the Nations United Against Germany, June 14, 1944.

Patriotic War Order — A483

Order of Prince Alexander Nevsky — A484

Order of Field Marshal Suvorov — A485

Order of Field Marshal Kutuzov — A486

Paper with network as in parenthesis

1944 **Typo.** ***Perf. 12***

923 A483 15k dull red *(rose)* .35 .25
924 A484 20k blue *(lt blue)* .35 .25
925 A485 30k green *(green)* .50 .25
926 A486 60k dull red *(rose)* .75 .40
Nos. 923-926 (4) 1.95 1.15
Set, never hinged 10.00

Imperf

923A A483 15k dull red *(rose)* .35 .25
924A A484 20k blue *(lt blue)* .35 .25
925A A485 30k green *(green)* .50 .25
926A A486 60k dull red *(rose)* .75 .40
Nos. 923A-926A (4) 1.95 1.15
Set, never hinged 10.00

Beware of bogus perforation "errors" created from imperfs.

Order of Patriotic War — A487

Order of Prince, Alexander Nevski — A488

Order of Field Marshal Kutuzov A489

Order of Field Marshal Suvorov A490

1944, June Unwmk. Engr. *Perf. 12*

927 A487	1r black	.50	.40
928 A488	3r blue black	1.10	1.00
929 A489	5r dark olive green	1.75	1.25
930 A490	10r dark red	3.50	2.00
	Nos. 927-930 (4)	6.85	4.65
	Set, never hinged	20.00	

Types of 1934, Inscribed 1924-1944 and

Lenin's Mausoleum — A491

30k (#931), 3r, Lenin & Stalin. 50k, Lenin in middle age. 60k, Lenin, the orator.

1944, June Photo.

931 A190 30k orange & car	.30	.25
932 A186 30k slate & black	.30	.25
933 A187 45k slate & black	.50	.30
934 A187 50k slate & black	.50	.30
935 A187 60k slate & black	.50	.40
936 A491 1r indigo & brn blk	2.50	.75
937 A190 3r bl blk & dull org	3.00	1.25
Nos. 931-937 (7)	7.60	3.50
Set, never hinged	30.00	

20 years without Lenin.

Nikolai Rimski-Korsakov
A492 A493

1944, June *Perf. 12*

938 A492 30k gray black	.25	.25
939 A493 60k slate green	.25	.25
940 A492 1r brt blue green	.55	.35
941 A493 3r purple	1.25	.40
Nos. 938-941 (4)	2.30	1.25
Set, never hinged	4.00	

Imperf

938A A492 30k gray black	.25	.25
939A A493 60k slate green	.25	.25
940A A492 1r brt blue green	.55	.35
941A A493 3r purple	1.25	.40
Nos. 938A-941A (4)	2.30	1.25
Set, never hinged	5.00	

Rimski-Korsakov (1844-1909), composer.

N.A. Shchors — A494

Heroes of the 1918 Civil War: No. 943, V.I. Chapayev. No. 944, S.G. Lazo.

1944, Sept. *Perf. 12*

942 A494 30k gray black	.35	.30
943 A494 30k dark slate green	.35	.30
944 A494 30k brt yellow green	.35	.30
Nos. 942-944 (3)	1.05	.90
Set, never hinged	3.00	

See Nos. 1209-1211, 1403.

Sergei A. Chaplygin — A497

1944, Sept.

945 A497 30k gray	.50	.30
946 A497 1r lt brown	1.50	.75
Set, never hinged	3.00	

75th anniversary of the birth of Sergei A. Chaplygin, scientist and mathematician.

Khanpasha Nuradilov A498

A. Matrosov A499

F. Louzan A500

M. S. Polivanova and N. V. Kovshova A501

Pilot B. Safonov — A502

1944, July

947 A498 30k slate green	1.00	.60
948 A499 60k dull purple	1.75	.60
949 A500 60k dull blue	1.75	.60
950 A501 60k bright green	3.00	.60
951 A502 60k slate black	3.00	.60
Nos. 947-951 (5)	10.50	3.00
Set, never hinged	20.00	

Soviet war heroes.

Ilya E. Repin — A503

Ivan A. Krylov — A505

"Cossacks' Reply to Sultan Mohammed IV" — A504

1944, Nov. *Perf. 12½*

952 A503 30k slate green	.65	.30
953 A504 50k dk blue green	.75	.30
954 A504 60k chalky blue	.75	.30
955 A503 1r dk org brn	1.00	.30
956 A504 2r dark purple	2.00	.60
Nos. 952-956 (5)	5.15	1.80
Set, never hinged	14.00	

Imperf

952A A503 30k slate green	.65	.30
953A A504 50k dk blue green	.75	.30
954A A504 60k chalky blue	.75	.30
955A A503 1r dk org brn	1.00	.30
956A A504 2r dark purple	2.00	.60
Nos. 952A-956A (5)	5.15	1.80
Set, never hinged	14.00	

I. E. Repin (1844-1930), painter.

1944, Nov. *Perf. 12*

957 A505 30k yellow brown	.50	.25
958 A505 1r dk violet blue	.50	.25
Set, never hinged	3.00	

Krylov, fable writer, death centenary.

Leningrad Type of 1944
Souvenir Sheet

1944, Dec. 6 *Imperf.*

959 Sheet of 4	10.00	4.75
Never hinged	25.00	
a. Marginal inscriptions inverted		6,500.
b. Marginal inscriptions double, one inverted	30,000.	
c. A474 30k dark slate green	1.00	.60

Relief of the siege of Leningrad, Jan. 27, 1944.

Partisan Medal — A507

Order for Bravery — A508

Order of Bogdan Chmielnicki A509

Order of Victory A510

Order of Ushakov A511

Order of Nakhimov A512

Paper with network as in parenthesis

Perf. 12½

1945, Jan. Typo. Unwmk.

960 A507 15k black *(green)*	.25	.30
961 A508 30k dp blue *(lt blue)*	.35	.30
962 A509 45k dk blue	.35	.30
963 A510 60k dl rose *(pale rose)*	.45	.30
964 A511 1r dull blue *(green)*	.80	.40
965 A512 1r yel green *(blue)*	.80	.40
Nos. 960-965 (6)	3.00	2.00
Set, never hinged	7.00	

Imperf

960A A507 15k black *(green)*	.25	.30
961A A508 30k dp blue *(lt blue)*	.35	.30
962A A509 45k dk blue	.35	.30
963A A510 60k dl rose *(pale rose)*	.45	.30
964A A511 1r dull blue *(green)*	.80	.40
965A A512 1r yel green *(blue)*	.80	.40
Nos. 960A-965A (6)	3.00	2.00
Set, never hinged	5.00	

Beware of bogus perforation "errors" created from imperfs.

Aleksandr S. Griboedov — A513

1945, Jan. Photo. *Perf. 12½*

966 A513 30k dk slate green	.35	.25
967 A513 60k gray brown	.65	.30
Set, never hinged	4.00	

Griboedov (1795-1829), poet & statesman.

Red Army Soldier — A514

1945, Mar.

968 A514 60k gray blk & henna	.50	.55
969 A514 3r gray blk & henna	1.50	1.10
Set, never hinged	3.00	

Souvenir Sheet

Imperf

970 Sheet of 4	60.00	40.00
Never hinged	100.00	
a. A514 3r gray brown & henna	9.00	7.50
Never hinged	15.00	

Second anniv. of victory at Stalingrad.

Order for Bravery A516

Order of Bogdan Chmielnicki A517

Order of Victory — A518

1945 Engr. *Perf. 12*

971 A516 1r indigo	.50	.35
972 A517 2r black	1.75	.90
973 A518 3r henna	1.60	.75
Nos. 971-973 (3)	3.85	2.00
Set, never hinged	7.50	

See Nos. 1341-1342. For overprints see Nos. 992, 1709.

A519

A520

A521

A522

A523

Battle Scenes A524

1945, Apr.	Photo.	Perf. 12½	
974 A519 20k sl grn, org red & black		.75	.60
975 A520 30k bl blk & dull org		.75	.60
976 A521 30k blue black		.75	.60
977 A522 60k orange red		1.50	1.50
978 A523 1r sl grn & org red		6.00	2.75
979 A524 1r slate green		6.00	2.75
Nos. 974-979 (6)		15.75	8.80
Set, never hinged		25.00	

Red Army successes against Germany.

Parade in Red Square, Nov. 7, 1941 — A525

Designs: 60k, Soldiers and Moscow barricade, Dec. 1941. 1r, Air battle, 1941.

1945, June		
980 A525 30k dk blue violet	.30	.25
981 A525 60k olive black	.70	.35
982 A525 1r black brown	2.00	1.40
Nos. 980-982 (3)	3.00	2.00
Set, never hinged	5.00	

3rd anniversary of the victory over the Germans before Moscow.

Elite Guard Badge and Cannons — A528

1945, Apr.	Typo.	
983 A528 60k red	1.00	.50
Never hinged	4.00	

Motherhood Medal — A529

Motherhood Glory Order — A530

Mother-Heroine Order — A531

Paper with network as in parenthesis

1945	Size: 22x33¼mm	Perf. 12½	
984 A529 20k brown *(lt blue)*		.40	.40
985 A530 30k yel brown *(green)*		.50	.40
986 A531 60k dull rose *(pale rose)*		.80	.40
Imperf			
984A A529 20k brown *(lt blue)*		.40	.40
985A A530 30k yel brown *(green)*		.50	.40
986D A531 60k dull rose *(pale rose)*		.80	.40
Perf. 12½			
Engr.			
Size: 20x38mm			
986A A529 1r blk brn *(green)*		.80	.40
986B A530 2r dp bl *(lt blue)*		1.75	.70
986C A531 3r brn red *(lt blue)*		2.00	1.20
Nos. 984-986D (9)		7.95	4.70
Set, never hinged		20.00	

Academy Building, Moscow — A532

Academy at Leningrad and M. V. Lomonosov A533

1945, June	Photo.	Perf. 12½	
987 A532 30k blue violet		.50	.30
a. Horiz. pair, imperf. between		90.00	
988 A533 2r grnsh black		1.50	.65
Set, never hinged		4.00	

Academy of Sciences, 220th anniv.

Popov and his Invention A534

Aleksandr S. Popov A535

1945, July	Unwmk.	
989 A534 30k dp blue violet	.50	.25
990 A534 60k dark red	1.00	.35
991 A535 1r yellow brown	1.75	.50
Nos. 989-991 (3)	3.25	1.10
Set, never hinged	5.00	

"Invention of radio" by A. S. Popov, 50th anniv.

No. 973 Overprinted in Blue

1945, Aug.	Perf. 12	
992 A518 3r henna	2.00	1.00

Victory of the Allied Nations in Europe.

Yakovlev-3 Fighter — A536

Petliakov-2 Dive Bombers — A537

Ilyushin-2 Bombers A538

#992A, 995, Yakovlev-3 Fighter. #992B, 1000, Petliakov-2 dive bombers. #992C, 996, Ilyushin-2 bombers. #992D, 993, Petliakov-8 heavy bomber. #992E, 1001, Tupolev-2 bombers. #992F, 997, Ilyushin-4 bombers. #992G, 999, Polikarpov-2 biplane. #992H, 998, Lavochkin-7 fighters. #992I, 994, Yakovlev-3 fighter in action.

1945-46	Unwmk.	Photo.	Perf. 12	
992A	A536	5k dk violet ('46)	.40	.25
992B	A537	10k hen brn ('46)	.40	.25
992C	A538	15k hen brn ('46)	.80	.25
992D	A536	15k Prus grn ('46)	.80	.25
992E	A538	20k gray brn ('46)	.80	.50
992F	A538	30k violet ('46)	1.60	.50
992G	A538	30k brown ('46)	1.60	.50
992H	A538	50k blue vio ('46)	2.25	1.25
992I	A536	60k dl bl vio ('46)	3.00	1.50
993	A536	1r gray black	3.50	.60
994	A536	1r henna brown	3.50	.60
995	A536	1r brown	3.50	.60
996	A538	1r deep brown	3.50	.60
997	A538	1r intense black	3.50	.60
998	A538	1r orange ver	3.50	.60
999	A538	1r bright green	3.50	.60
1000	A537	1r deep brown	3.50	.60
1001	A538	1r violet blue	3.50	.60
		Nos. 992A-1001 (18)	43.15	10.65
		Set, never hinged	75.00	

Issued: #992A-992I, 3/26; #993-1001, 8/19.

A545

Lenin, 75th Birth Anniv. — A546

Various Lenin portraits.

Dated "1870-1945"

1945, Sept.	Perf. 12½	
1002 A545 30k bluish black	.60	.35
1003 A546 50k gray brown	.75	.35
1004 A546 60k orange brown	.85	.35
1005 A546 1r greenish black	2.00	.35
1006 A546 3r sepia	6.00	1.25
Nos. 1002-1006 (5)	10.20	2.65
Set, never hinged	25.00	

Prince M. I. Kutuzov — A550

1945, Sept. 16		
1007 A550 30k blue violet	.60	.40
1008 A550 60k brown	1.40	.60
Set, never hinged	4.00	

Field Marshal Prince Mikhail Illarionovich Kutuzov (1745-1813).

Aleksandr Ivanovich Herzen A551

1945, Oct. 26		
1009 A551 30k dark brown	.50	.40
1010 A551 2r black	1.50	.60
Set, never hinged	5.00	

Herzen, author, revolutionist, 75th death anniv.

Ilya Mechnikov — A552

1945, Nov. 27		
1011 A552 30k brown	.65	.40
1012 A552 1r greenish black	1.25	.60
Set, never hinged	5.00	

Ilya I. Mechnikov, zoologist and bacteriologist (1845-1916).

Friedrich Engels — A553

1945, Nov.	Unwmk.	Perf. 12½	
1013 A553 30k dark brown		1.00	.40
1014 A553 60k Prussian green		2.00	.60
Set, never hinged		5.00	

125th anniversary of the birth of Friedrich Engels, collaborator of Karl Marx.

Tank Leaving Assembly Line — A554

Designs: 30k, Harvesting wheat. 60k, Airplane designing. 1r, Moscow fireworks.

1945, Dec. 25 **Photo.**

No.	Type	Description	Unused	Used
1015	A554	20k indigo & brown	1.00	.25
1016	A554	30k blk & org brn	1.00	.40
1017	A554	60k brown & green	1.75	.60
1018	A554	1r dk blue & org	2.25	.90
		Nos. 1015-1018 (4)	6.00	2.15
		Set, never hinged	15.00	

Artillery Observer and Guns A558

Heavy Field Pieces A559

1945, Dec.

No.	Type	Description	Unused	Used
1019	A558	30k brown	1.00	.50
1020	A559	60k sepia	2.00	.75
		Set, never hinged	7.00	

Artillery Day, Nov. 19, 1945.

Catalogue values for unused stamps in this section, from this point to the end of the section, are for Never Hinged items.

Victory Medal — A560

Soldier with Victory Flag — A561

1946, Jan. 23

No.	Type	Description	Unused	Used
1021	A560	30k dk violet	.75	.25
1022	A560	30k brown	.75	.25
1023	A560	60k greenish black	1.10	.25
1024	A560	60k henna	1.10	.25
1025	A561	60k black & dull red	3.75	1.10
		Nos. 1021-1025 (5)	7.45	2.10

Arms of USSR — A562

Red Square — A563

1946, Feb. 10

No.	Type	Description	Unused	Used
1026	A562	30k henna	1.00	.25
1027	A563	45k henna	1.50	.25
1028	A562	60k greenish black	2.50	.50
		Nos. 1026-1028 (3)	5.00	1.00

Elections to the Supreme Soviet of the USSR, Feb. 10, 1946.

Artillery in Victory Parade — A564

Victory Parade A565

1946, Feb. 23

No.	Type	Description	Unused	Used
1029	A564	60k dark brown	5.00	.50
1030	A564	2r dull violet	15.00	1.00
1031	A565	3r black & red	15.00	1.50
		Nos. 1029-1031 (3)	35.00	3.00

Victory Parade, Moscow, June 24, 1945.

Order of Lenin — A566

Order of Red Star — A567

Medal of Hammer and Sickle A568

Order of Token of Veneration A569

Gold Star Medal — A570

Order of Red Banner — A571

Order of the Red Workers' Banner — A572

Paper with network as in parenthesis

1946 Unwmk. Typo. *Perf. 12½x12*

No.	Type	Description	Unused	Used
1032	A566	60k myr grn *(green)*	1.40	1.10
1033	A567	60k dk vio brn *(brown)*	1.40	1.10
1034	A568	60k plum *(pink)*	1.40	1.10
1035	A569	60k dp blue *(green)*	1.40	1.10
1036	A570	60k dk car *(salmon)*	1.40	1.10
1037	A571	60k red *(salmon)*	1.40	1.10
1038	A572	60k dk brn vio *(buff)*	1.40	1.10
		Nos. 1032-1038 (7)	9.80	7.70

See Nos. 1650-1654.

Workers' Achievement of Distinction A573

Workers' Gallantry A574

Marshal's Star — A575

Defense of Soviet Trans-Arctic Regions — A576

Meritorious Service in Battle A577

Defense of Caucasus A578

Defense of Moscow — A579

Bravery — A580

Paper with network as in parenthesis

1946

No.	Type	Description	Unused	Used
1039	A573	60k choc *(salmon)*	3.00	1.25
1040	A574	60k brown *(salmon)*	3.00	1.25
1041	A575	60k blue *(pale blue)*	3.00	1.25
1042	A576	60k dk grn *(green)*	3.00	1.25
1043	A577	60k dk blue *(green)*	3.00	1.25
1044	A578	60k dk yel grn *(grn)*	3.00	1.25
1045	A579	60k carmine *(pink)*	3.00	1.25
1046	A580	60k dk violet *(blue)*	3.00	1.25
		Nos. 1039-1046 (8)	24.00	10.00

A581

Maxim Gorki A582

1946, June 18 **Photo.**

No.	Type	Description	Unused	Used
1047	A581	30k brown	1.50	.25
1048	A582	60k dark green	2.50	.25

10th anniversary of the death of Maxim Gorki (Alexei M. Peshkov).

Kalinin — A583

1946, June

No.	Type	Description	Unused	Used
1049	A583	20k sepia	2.00	.60

Mikhail Ivanovich Kalinin (1875-1946).

Chebyshev — A584

1946, May 25

No.	Type	Description	Unused	Used
1050	A584	30k brown	1.25	.35
1051	A584	60k gray brown	1.75	.65

Pafnuti Lvovich Chebyshev (1821-94), mathematician.

View of Sukhumi A585

Sanatorium at Sochi — A587

Designs: #1053, Promenade at Gagri. 45k, New Afyon Sanatorium.

1946, June 18

No.	Type	Description	Unused	Used
1052	A585	15k dark brown	1.25	.25
1053	A585	30k dk slate green	2.50	.25
1054	A587	30k dark green	2.50	.25
1055	A585	45k chestnut brown	3.75	.50
		Nos. 1052-1055 (4)	10.00	1.25

All-Union Parade of Physical Culturists — A589

1946, July 21

No.	Type	Description	Unused	Used
1056	A589	30k dark green	6.00	2.00

Tank Divisions in Red Square A590

1946, Sept. 8

No.	Type	Description	Unused	Used
1057	A590	30k dark green	1.50	.40
1058	A590	60k brown	2.50	.60

Honoring Soviet tankmen.

Belfry of Ivan the Great, Kremlin — A591

Bolshoi Theater, Moscow — A592

Hotel Moscow A593

Red Square — A597

Spasski Tower and Statues of Minin and Pozharski — A598

Moscow scenes: 20k, Bolshoi Theater, Sverdlov Square. 45k, View of Kremlin. 50k, Lenin Museum.

1946, Sept. 5

1059 A591	5k brown		1.00	.25
1060 A592	10k sepia		1.00	.25
1061 A593	15k chestnut		1.00	.25
1062 A593	20k light brown		2.00	.25
1063 A593	45k dark green		4.50	.45
1064 A593	50k brown		4.50	.50
1065 A597	60k blue violet		10.00	.60
1066 A598	1r chestnut brown		15.00	1.00
	Nos. 1059-1066 (8)		39.00	3.55

Workers' Achievement of Distinction A599

Workers' Gallantry A600

Partisan of the Patriotic War — A601

Defense of Soviet Trans-Arctic Regions — A602

Meritorious Service in Battle A603

Defense of Caucasus A604

Defense of Moscow — A605

Bravery — A606

1946, Sept. 5 **Engr.**

1067 A599	1r dark violet brown	3.75	1.50
1068 A600	1r dark carmine	3.75	1.50
1069 A601	1r carmine	3.75	1.50
1070 A602	1r blue black	3.75	1.50
1071 A603	1r black	3.75	1.50
1072 A604	1r black brown	3.75	1.50
1073 A605	1r olive black	3.75	1.50
1074 A606	1r deep claret	3.75	1.50
	Nos. 1067-1074 (8)	30.00	12.00

See Nos. 1650-1654.

Give the Country Each Year: 127 Million Tons of Grain A607

60 Million Tons of Oil — A608

60 Million Tons of Steel — A610

500 Million Tons of Coal — A609

50 Million Tons of Cast Iron — A611

Perf. 12½x12

1946, Oct. 6 **Photo.** **Unwmk.**

1075 A607	5k olive brown	.25	.25
1076 A608	10k dk slate green	.50	.25
1077 A609	15k brown	.75	.25
1078 A610	20k dk blue violet	1.50	.25
1079 A611	30k brown	3.00	.25
	Nos. 1075-1079 (5)	6.00	1.25

Symbols of Transportation, Map and Stamps — A612

Early Soviet Stamp A613

Stamps of Soviet Russia — A614

1946, Nov. 6 ***Perf. 12½***

1080 A612	15k blk & dk red	2.00	.55
a.	Sheet of 4, imperf.	100.00	50.00
1081 A613	30k dk grn & brn	3.00	.60
a.	Sheet of 4, imperf.	100.00	50.00
1082 A614	60k dk grn & blk	5.00	.85
a.	Sheet of 4, imperf.	100.00	50.00
	Nos. 1080-1082 (3)	10.00	2.00

1st Soviet postage stamp, 25th anniv.

Lenin and Stalin — A615

1946 **Photo.** ***Perf. 12½***

1083 A615	30k dp brown org	2.00	1.00
a.	Sheet of 4, imperf.	75.00	35.00
b.	Single, imperf	6.00	1.50
1084 A615	30k dk green	2.00	1.00
a.	Single, imperf	5.00	1.50

October Revolution, 29th anniv.

Issued: #1083b-1084a, 11/6; #1083-1084, 12/18; #1083a, 6/47.

Dnieprostroy Dam and Power Station — A616

1946, Dec. 23 ***Perf. 12½***

1085 A616	30k sepia	2.00	.60
1086 A616	60k chalky blue	4.00	.90

Aleksandr P. Karpinsky — A617

1947, Jan. 17 **Unwmk.**

1087 A617	30k dark green	1.25	.75
1088 A617	50k sepia	2.75	1.00

Karpinsky (1847-1936), geologist.

Canceled to Order

Canceled sets of new issues have long been sold by the government. Values in the second ("used") column are for these canceled-to-order stamps. Postally used stamps are worth more.

Nikolai A. Nekrasov — A618

1946, Dec. 4

1089 A618	30k sepia	1.50	.25
1090 A618	60k brown	2.50	.75

Nikolai A. Nekrasov (1821-1878), poet.

Lenin's Mausoleum A619

Lenin — A620

1947, Jan. 21

1091 A619	30k slate blue	2.50	.65
1092 A619	30k dark green	2.50	.65
1093 A620	50k dark brown	5.00	1.25
	Nos. 1091-1093 (3)	10.00	2.55

23rd anniversary of the death of Lenin.

See Nos. 1197-1199.

F. P. Litke and Sailing Vessel A621

N. M. Przewalski, Mare and Foal — A622

1947, Jan. 27

1094 A621	20k blue violet	4.75	1.10
1095 A621	20k sepia	4.75	1.10
1096 A622	60k olive brown	10.50	1.40
1097 A622	60k sepia	10.50	1.40
	Nos. 1094-1097 (4)	30.50	5.00

Soviet Union Geographical Society, cent.

Nikolai E. Zhukovski (1847-1921), Scientist A623

1947, Jan. 17

1098 A623	30k sepia	1.50	.30
1099 A623	60k blue violet	2.25	.45

Stalin Prize Medal — A624

1946, Dec. 21 **Photo.**

1100 A624	30k black brown	7.50	.50

Russian Soldier A625

Military Instruction A626

Aviator, Sailor and Soldier
A627

Perf. 12x12½, 12½x12

1947, Feb. 23				**Unwmk.**	
1101	A625	20k	sepia	2.50	.50
1102	A626	30k	slate blue	3.75	.75
1103	A627	30k	brown	3.75	.75
	Nos. 1101-1103 (3)			10.00	2.00

Imperf

1101A	A625	20k	sepia	2.50	.50
1102A	A626	30k	slate blue	3.75	.75
1103A	A627	30k	brown	3.75	.75
	Nos. 1101A-1103A (3)			10.00	2.00

29th anniversary of the Soviet Army.

Reprints

From here through 1953 many sets exist in two distinct printings from different plates.

Arms of

Russian Socialist Federated Soviet Republic — A628

Armenian SSR — A629

Azerbaijan SSR — A630

Byelorussian SSR — A631

Estonian SSR — A632

Georgian SSR — A633

Karelo Finnish SSR — A634

Kazakh SSR — A635

Kirghiz SSR — A636

Latvian SSR — A637

Lithuanian SSR — A638

Moldavian SSR — A639

Tadzhkistan SSR — A640

Turkmen SSR — A641

Ukrainian SSR — A642

Uzbek SSR — A643

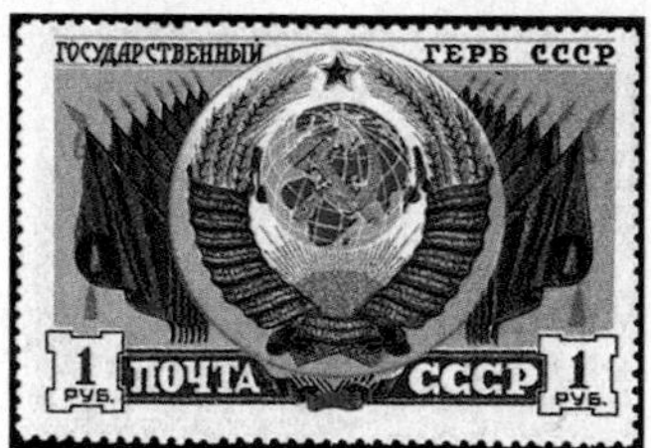

Soviet Union — A644

1947	**Unwmk.**		**Photo.**	***Perf. 12½***	
1104	A628	30k	henna brown	3.25	.50
1105	A629	30k	chestnut	3.25	.50
1106	A630	30k	olive brown	3.25	.50
1107	A631	30k	olive green	3.25	.50
1108	A632	30k	violet black	3.25	.50
1109	A633	30k	dark vio brown	3.25	.50
1110	A634	30k	dark violet	3.25	.50
1111	A635	30k	deep orange	3.25	.50
1112	A636	30k	dark violet	3.25	.50
1113	A637	30k	yellow brown	3.25	.50
1114	A638	30k	dk ol grn	3.25	.50
1115	A639	30k	dk vio brn	3.25	.50
1116	A640	30k	dark green	3.25	.50
1117	A641	30k	gray black	3.25	.50
1118	A642	30k	blue violet	3.25	.50
1119	A643	30k	brown	3.25	.50

Litho.

1120	A644	1r	dk brn, bl, gold & red	8.00	2.00
	Nos. 1104-1120 (17)			60.00	10.00

Aleksander S. Pushkin (1799-1837), Poet — A645

1947, Feb.			**Photo.**	***Perf. 12***	
1121	A645	30k	sepia	2.00	.35
1122	A645	50k	dk yellow green	3.00	.75

Classroom
A646

Parade of Women — A647

1947, Mar. 11					
1123	A646	15k	bright blue	2.00	.60
1124	A647	30k	red	3.00	.90

Intl. Day of Women, Mar. 8, 1947.

Moscow Council Building
A648

1947				***Perf. 12½***	
1125	A648	30k	sep, gray blue & brick red	3.00	1.00

30th anniversary of the Moscow Soviet. Exists imperf. The imperf. exists also with gray blue omitted.

Both perf. and imperf. stamps exist in two sizes: 40x27mm and 41x27mm.

May Day Parade in Red Square — A649

1947, June 10				***Perf. 12½***	
1126	A649	30k	scarlet	1.50	.60
1127	A649	1r	dk olive green	4.50	2.00

Labor Day, May 1, 1947.

Nos. 1062, 1064-1066 Ovptd. in Red

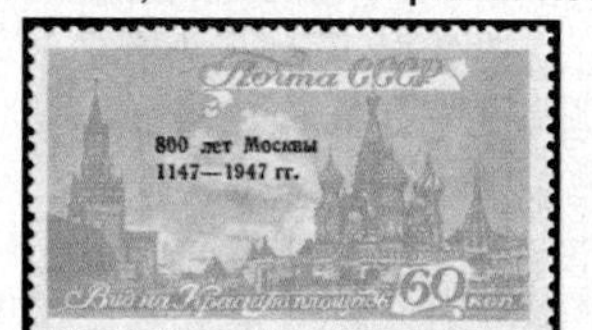

1947, Sept.				***Perf. 12½x12***	
1128	A593	20k	lt brown	2.00	.40
1129	A593	50k	brown	4.00	1.00
1130	A597	60k	blue violet	6.00	1.20
1131	A598	1r	chestnut brown	8.00	1.40
	Nos. 1128-1131 (4)			20.00	4.00

Overprint arranged in 4 lines on No. 1131.

Crimea Bridge, Moscow — A650

Gorki Street, Moscow
A651

View of Kremlin, Moscow — A652

Designs: No. 1134, Central Telegraph Building. No. 1135, Kiev Railroad Station. No. 1136, Kazan Railroad Station. No. 1137, Kaluga St. No. 1138, Pushkin Square. 50k, View of Kremlin. No. 1141, Grand Kremlin Palace. No. 1142, "Old Moscow," by Vasnetsov. No. 1143, St. Basil Cathedral. 2r, View of Kremlin. 3r, View of Kremlin. 5r, Hotel Moscow and government building.

1947			**Photo.**	***Perf. 12½***	
	Various Frames, Dated 1147-1947				
1132	A650	5k	dk bl & dk brn	*.50*	.50
1133	A651	10k	red brn & brn blk	*.50*	.50
1134	A650	30k	brown	*1.20*	.80
1135	A650	30k	dk Prus blue	*1.20*	.80
1136	A650	30k	ultra	*1.20*	.80
1137	A650	30k	dp yel green	*1.20*	.80
1138	A651	30k	yel green	*1.20*	.80
1139	A650	50k	dp yel green	*1.80*	1.00
1140	A652	60k	red brn & brn blk	*1.90*	1.20
1141	A651	60k	gray blue	*2.75*	1.50
1142	A651	1r	dark violet	*4.25*	2.50

Typo.

Colors: Blue, Yellow and Red

1143	A651	1r	multicolored	*4.25*	2.50
1144	A651	2r	multicolored	*8.50*	6.00
1145	A650	3r	multicolored	*15.00*	8.00
a.			Souv. sheet of 4, imperf.	*35.00*	20.00
1146	A650	5r	multicolored	*25.00*	16.00
	Nos. 1132-1146 (15)			*70.45*	43.70

Nos. 1128-1146 for founding of Moscow, 800th anniv.

Nos. 1143-1146 were printed in a single sheet containing a row of each denomination plus a row of labels.

Karamyshevsky Dam — A653

Map Showing Moscow-Volga Canal — A654

Designs: No. 1148, Direction towers, Yakromsky Lock. 45k, Yakromsky Pumping Station. 50k, Khimki Terminal. 1r, Lock #8.

1947, Sept. 7				**Photo.**	
1147	A653	30k	sepia	2.50	.50
1148	A653	30k	red brown	2.50	.50
1149	A653	45k	henna brown	3.25	.50
1150	A653	50k	bright ultra	3.75	.50

1151 A654 60k bright rose 4.25 .50
1152 A653 1r violet 7.75 1.00
Nos. 1147-1152 (6) 24.00 3.50

Moscow-Volga Canal, 10th anniversary.

Elektrozavodskaya Station — A655

Mayakovsky Station — A656

Moscow Subway scenes: No. 1154, Ismailovsky Station. No. 1155, Sokol Station. No. 1156, Stalinsky Station. No. 1158, Kiev Station.

1947, Sept.

1153 A655 30k sepia 2.40 .55
1154 A655 30k blue black 2.40 .55
1155 A655 45k yellow brown 3.00 .60
1156 A655 45k deep violet 3.00 .60
1157 A656 60k henna brown 4.50 .80
1158 A655 60k deep yel grn 4.50 .80
Nos. 1153-1158 (6) 19.80 3.90

Planes and Flag — A657

1947, Sept. 1

1159 A657 30k deep violet 3.00 .40
1160 A657 1r bright ultra 7.00 .60

Day of the Air Fleet. For overprints see Nos. 1246-1247.

Spasski Tower, Kremlin — A658

Perf. 12½

1947, Nov. Unwmk. Typo.

1161 A658 60k dark red 18.00 4.50

See No. 1260.

Agave Plant at Sukhumi — A659

Gullripsh Sanatorium, Sukhumi A660

Peasants', Livadia A661

New Riviera A662

Russian sanatoria: No. 1166, Abkhasia, New Afyon. No. 1167, Kemeri, near Riga. No. 1168, Kirov Memorial, Kislovodsk. No. 1169, Voroshilov Memorial, Sochi. No. 1170, Riza, Gagri. No. 1171, Zapadugol, Sochi.

1947, Nov. Photo.

1162 A659 30k dark green 3.50 .50
1163 A660 30k violet 3.50 .50
1164 A661 30k olive 3.50 .50
1165 A662 30k brown 3.50 .50
1166 A660 30k red brown 3.50 .50
1167 A660 30k black violet 3.50 .50
1168 A660 30k bright ultra 3.50 .50
1169 A660 30k dk brown violet 3.50 .50
1170 A659 30k dk yel green 3.50 .50
1171 A660 30k sepia 3.50 .50
Nos. 1162-1171 (10) 35.00 5.00

Blast Furnaces, Constantine A663

Tractor Plant, Kharkov A664

Tractor Plant, Stalingrad A665

Maxim Gorki Theater, Stalingrad A666

20k, No. 1180, Kirov foundry, Makeevka. Nos. 1175, 1179, Agricultural machine plant, Rostov.

1947, Nov. ***Perf. 12½***

1172 A663 15k yellow brown .35 .25
1173 A663 20k sepia .60 .25
1174 A663 30k violet brown .85 .25
1175 A663 30k dark green .85 .25
1176 A664 30k brown .85 .25
1177 A665 30k black brown .85 .25
1178 A666 60k violet brown 1.60 .70
1179 A663 60k yellow brown 1.60 .70
1180 A663 1r orange red 3.50 1.40
1181 A664 1r red 3.50 1.40
1182 A665 1r violet 3.50 1.40
Nos. 1172-1182 (11) 18.05 7.10

Imperf

1172A A663 15k yellow brown .35 .25
1173A A663 20k sepia .60 .25
1174A A663 30k violet brown .85 .25
1175A A663 30k dark green .85 .25
1176A A664 30k brown .85 .25
1177A A665 30k black brown .85 .25
1178A A666 60k violet brown 1.60 .70
1179A A663 60k yellow brown 1.60 .70
1180A A663 1r orange red 3.50 1.40
1181A A664 1r red 3.50 1.40
1182A A665 1r violet 3.50 1.40
Nos. 1172A-1182A (11) 18.05 7.10

Reconstruction of war-damaged cities and factories, and as Five-Year-Plan publicity.

Revolutionists — A667

Designs: 30k, No. 1185, Revolutionists. 50k, 1r, Industry. No. 1186, 2r, Agriculture.

1947, Nov. ***Perf. 12½***

Frame in Dark Red

1183 A667 30k greenish black 2.00 .30
1184 A667 50k blue black 3.00 .40
1185 A667 60k brown black 5.00 .55
1186 A667 60k brown 5.00 .55
1187 A667 1r black 8.00 .95
1188 A667 2r greenish black 15.00 1.50
Nos. 1183-1188 (6) 38.00 4.25

Imperf

1183A A667 30k greenish black 1.00 .30
1184A A667 50k blue black 1.50 .40
1185A A667 60k brown black 2.50 .55
1186A A667 60k brown 2.50 .55
1187A A667 1r black 4.00 .95
1188A A667 2r greenish black 7.50 1.50
Nos. 1183A-1188A (6) 19.00 4.25

30th anniversary of October Revolution.

Palace of the Arts (Winter Palace) A668

Peter I Monument — A669

Designs (Leningrad in 1947): 60k, Sts. Peter and Paul Fortress. 1r, Smolny Institute.

1948, Jan. 10 ***Perf. 12½***

1189 A668 30k violet 3.00 1.10
1190 A669 50k dk slate green 5.00 1.25
1191 A668 60k sepia 6.00 2.40
1192 A669 1r dk brown violet 11.00 3.25
Nos. 1189-1192 (4) 25.00 8.00

5th anniversary of the relief of the siege of Leningrad from the German blockade.

Government Building, Kiev — A670

50k, Dnieprostroy Dam. 60k, Wheat field, granary. 1r, Steel mill, coal mine.

1948, Jan. 25 ***Perf. 12½***

1193 A670 30k indigo 2.00 .40
1194 A670 50k violet 2.75 .50
1195 A670 60k golden brown 4.00 .85
1196 A670 1r sepia 6.25 2.25
Nos. 1193-1196 (4) 15.00 4.00

Ukrainian SSR, 30th anniv.

Lenin Types of 1947 Inscribed "1924-1948"

1948, Jan. 21 Unwmk.

1197 A619 30k brown violet 8.00 3.00
1198 A619 60k dark gray blue 8.00 3.00
1199 A620 60k dp yel grn 8.00 3.00
Nos. 1197-1199 (3) 24.00 9.00

24th anniversary of the death of Lenin.

Vasili I. Surikov — A672

1948, Feb. 15 Photo. ***Perf. 12***

1201 A672 30k red brown 3.50 .75
1202 A672 60k dark green 6.50 1.25

Vasili Ivanovich Surikov, artist, birth cent.

Soviet Soldier and Artillery — A675

Fliers and Planes A676

No. 1206, Soviet sailor. 60k, Military class.

1948, Feb. 23

1205 A675 30k brown 2.50 .65
1206 A675 30k gray 2.50 .65
1207 A676 30k violet blue 2.50 .65
1208 A676 60k red brown 7.50 2.00
Nos. 1205-1208 (4) 15.00 3.95

Hero Types of 1944

Designs: No. 1209, N.A. Shchors. No. 1210, V.I. Chapayev. No. 1211, S.G. Lazo.

1948, Feb. 23

1209 A494 60k deep green 6.50 1.75
1210 A494 60k yellow brown 6.50 1.75
1211 A494 60k violet blue 6.50 1.75
Nos. 1209-1211 (3) 19.50 5.25

Nos. 1205-1211 for Soviet army, 30th anniv.

Karl Marx, Friedrich Engels and Communist Manifesto A677

1948, Apr.

1212 A677 30k black 1.50 .25
1213 A677 50k henna brown 3.50 .30

Centenary of the Communist Manifesto.

Miner A678

Marine A679

Aviator A680

Woman Farmer A681

Arms of USSR A682

Scientist A683

Spasski Tower, Kremlin A684

Soldier A685

1948 **Photo.**

1214 A678 5k sepia .50 .30
1215 A679 10k violet .85 .30
1216 A680 15k bright blue 1.25 .85
1217 A681 20k brown 1.50 .75
1218 A682 30k henna brown 2.50 1.25
1219 A683 45k brown violet 5.00 1.90
1220 A684 50k bright blue 7.00 3.00
1221 A685 60k bright green 8.50 4.25
Nos. 1214-1221 (8) 27.10 12.60

See Nos. 1306, 1343-1347, 1689.

May Day Parade in Red Square — A686

1948, June 5 ***Perf. 12***

1222 A686 30k deep car rose 5.00 .80
1223 A686 60k bright blue 15.00 1.25

Labor Day, May 1, 1948.

Vissarion G. Belinski (1811-48), Literary Critic — A687

1948, June 7 **Unwmk.** ***Perf. 12***

1224 A687 30k brown 5.00 1.00
1225 A687 50k dark green 7.50 2.00
1226 A687 60k purple 15.00 2.00
Nos. 1224-1226 (3) 27.50 5.00

Aleksandr N. Ostrovski
A690 A691

1948, June 10 **Photo.** ***Perf. 12***

1227 A690 30k bright green 4.50 2.50
1228 A691 60k brown 9.00 4.50
1229 A691 1r brown violet 15.00 8.00
Nos. 1227-1229 (3) 28.50 15.00

Ostrovski (1823-1886), playwright. Exist imperf. Value, set $250.

Ivan I. Shishkin (1832-1898), Painter — A692

"Field of Rye," by Shishkin A693

60k, "Bears in a Forest," by Shishkin.

Photo. (30k, 1r), Typo. (50k, 60k)
1948, June 12

1230 A692 30k dk grn & vio brn 13.00 3.50
1231 A693 50k multicolored 20.00 7.50
1232 A693 60k multicolored 30.00 8.00
1233 A692 1r brn & bl blk 37.50 21.00
Nos. 1230-1233 (4) 100.50 40.00

Industrial Expansion A694

Public Gathering at Leningrad — A695

Photo., Frames Litho. in Carmine
1948, June 25

1234 A694 15k red brown 3.50 1.00
1235 A695 30k slate 4.50 1.50
1236 A694 60k brown black 7.00 2.75
Nos. 1234-1236 (3) 15.00 5.25

Industrial five-year plan.

Planting Crops A696

Nos. 1238, 1243, Gathering vegetables. Nos. 1239, 1241, Baling cotton. No. 1240, Planting Crops. No. 1242, Harvesting grain.

1948, July 12 **Photo.**

1237 A696 30k carmine rose .75 .30
1238 A696 30k blue green .75 .30
1239 A696 45k red brown 1.50 .70
1240 A696 50k brown black 2.25 .70
1241 A696 60k dark green 2.10 .80
1242 A696 60k dk blue green 2.10 .80
1243 A696 1r purple 5.50 1.40
Nos. 1237-1243 (7) 14.95 5.00

Agricultural five-year plan.

Arms and Citizens of USSR — A697

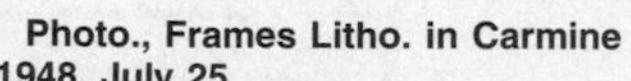

Photo., Frames Litho. in Carmine
1948, July 25

1244 A697 30k slate 10.00 2.50
1245 A697 60k greenish black 15.00 5.00

25th anniv. of the USSR.

Nos. 1159 and 1160 Overprinted in Red

1948, Aug. 24 ***Perf. 12½***

1246 A657 30k deep violet 3.00 2.50
1247 A657 1r bright ultra 10.00 2.50

Air Fleet Day, 1948. On sale one day.

Soviet Miners — A698

Miner's Day, Aug. 29: 60k, Scene in mine. 1r, Miner's badge.

1948, Aug. **Photo.** ***Perf. 12½x12***

1248 A698 30k blue 3.00 .35
1249 A698 60k purple 6.00 .45
1250 A698 1r green 11.00 1.20
Nos. 1248-1250 (3) 20.00 2.00

A. A. Zhdanov — A699

1948, Sept. 3

1251 A699 40k slate 4.00 2.00

Andrei A. Zhdanov, statesman, 1896-1948.

Soviet Sailor — A700

1948, Sept. 12 ***Perf. 12***

1252 A700 30k blue green 6.00 3.00
1253 A700 60k bright blue 14.00 5.00

Navy Day, Sept. 12.

Slalom A701

Motorcyclist — A702

Designs: No. 1254, Foot race. 30k, Soccer game. 45k, Motorboat race. 50k, Diving.

1948, Sept. 15 ***Perf. 12½x12***

1253A A701 15k dark blue 2.50 .25
1254 A702 15k violet 1.00 .25
1254A A702 20k dk slate blue 3.50 .55
1255 A701 30k brown 2.00 .25
1256 A701 45k sepia 3.00 .35
1257 A702 50k blue 3.00 .35
Nos. 1253A-1257 (6) 15.00 2.00

Tankmen Group A703

Design: 1r, Tank parade.

1948, Sept. 25

1258 A703 30k sepia 4.50 1.50
1259 A703 1r rose 10.50 3.50

Day of the Tankmen, Sept. 25.

Spasski Tower Type of 1947

1948 **Litho.** ***Perf. 12x12½***

1260 A658 1r brown red 2.00 .25

No. 1260 was re-issued in 1954-56 in slightly smaller format: 14½x21½mm, instead of 14¾x22mm and in a paler shade. See note after No. 738.

Train — A704

Transportation 5-year plan: 60k, Auto and bus at intersection. 1r, Steamships at anchor.

1948, Sept. 30 **Photo.** ***Perf. 12½x12***

1261 A704 30k brown 30.00 7.50
1262 A704 50k dark green 60.00 10.00
1263 A704 60k blue 100.00 12.50
1264 A704 1r blue violet 100.00 20.00
Nos. 1261-1264 (4) 290.00 50.00

Horses A705

Livestock 5-year plan: 60k, Dairy farm.

1948, Sept. 30 ***Perf. 12***

1265 A705 30k slate gray 11.00 4.00
1266 A705 60k bright green 19.00 6.50
1267 A705 1r brown 35.00 9.50
Nos. 1265-1267 (3) 65.00 20.00

Pouring Molten Metal A706

Designs: 60k, 1r, Iron pipe manufacture.

1948, Oct. 14 ***Perf. 12½***

1268 A706 30k purple 3.00 .75
1269 A706 50k brown 3.00 1.00
1270 A706 60k carmine 3.00 1.25
1271 A706 1r dull blue 3.00 2.00
Nos. 1268-1271 (4) 12.00 5.00

Heavy Machinery Plant
A707

Design: 60k, Pump station interior.

1948, Oct. 14

1272	A707	30k purple	10.00	.75
1273	A707	50k sepia	5.00	1.25
1274	A707	60k brown	10.00	1.40
		Nos. 1272-1274 (3)	25.00	3.40

Nos. 1268-1274 publicize the 5-year plan for steel, iron and machinery industries.

Khachatur Abovian (1809-1848), Armenian Writer and Poet — A708

1948, Oct. 16 *Perf. 12x12½*

1275	A708	40k purple	7.00	2.50
1276	A708	50k deep green	8.00	2.50

Farkhatz Hydroelectric Station
A709

Design: 60k, Zouiev Hydroelectric Station.

1948, Oct. 24 *Perf. 12½*

1277	A709	30k green	15.00	5.00
1278	A709	60k red	15.00	5.00
1279	A709	1r carmine rose	15.00	5.00
		Nos. 1277-1279 (3)	45.00	15.00

Electrification five-year plan.

Coal Mine — A710

Designs: Nos. 1282, 1283, Oil field and tank cars.

1948, Oct. 24

1280	A710	30k sepia	25.00	1.25
1281	A710	60k brown	35.00	2.50
1282	A710	60k red brown	35.00	2.50
1283	A710	1r blue green	115.00	3.75
		Nos. 1280-1283 (4)	210.00	10.00

Coal mining and oil production 5-year plan.

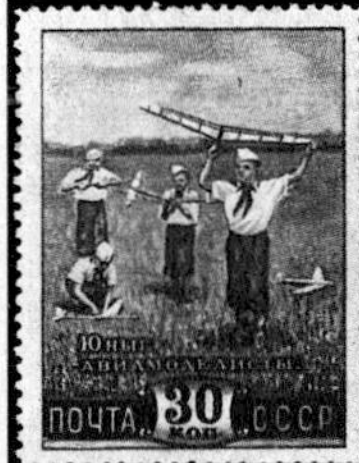
Flying Model Planes — A712

Marching Pioneers
A713

Pioneers Saluting — A714

60k, Pioneer bugler. 1r, Pioneers at campfire.

1948, Oct. 26 *Perf. 12½*

1284	A712	30k dark bl grn	30.00	4.25
1285	A713	45k dark violet	40.00	5.50
1286	A714	45k deep carmine	32.50	4.75
1287	A714	60k deep ultra	45.00	7.25
1288	A713	1r deep blue	100.00	13.00
		Nos. 1284-1288 (5)	247.50	34.75

Young Pioneers, a Soviet youth organization, and governmental supervision of children's summer vacations.

Marching Youths
A715

Farm Girl — A716

League Members and Flag — A717

Designs: 50k, Communist students. 1r, Flag and badges. 2r, Young worker.

Inscribed: "1918 1948 XXX"

1948, Oct. 29 *Perf. 12½*

1289	A715	20k violet brown	12.50	1.25
1290	A716	25k rose red	13.50	1.60
1291	A717	40k brown & red	22.50	2.00
1292	A715	50k blue green	29.00	3.25
1293	A717	1r multicolored	95.00	14.50
1294	A716	2r purple	50.00	11.00
		Nos. 1289-1294 (6)	222.50	33.60

30th anniversary of the Young Communist League (Komsomol).

Stage of Moscow Art Theater
A719

K. S. Stanislavski, V. I. Nemirovich Danchenko
A720

1948, Nov. 1 *Perf. 12½*

1295	A719	40k gray blue	6.50	3.50
1296	A720	1r violet brown	9.50	4.50

Moscow Art Theater, 50th anniv.

Flag and Moscow Buildings — A721

1948, Nov. 7 *Perf. 12½*

1297	A721	40k red	5.00	2.25
1298	A721	1r green	10.00	2.75

31st anniversary of October Revolution.

House of Unions, Moscow
A722

Player's Badge (Rook and Chessboard)
A723

1948, Nov. 20 *Perf. 12½*

1299	A722	30k greenish blue	2.50	.35
1300	A723	40k violet	6.25	.50
1301	A722	50k orange brown	6.25	.90
		Nos. 1299-1301 (3)	15.00	1.75

16th Chess Championship.

Artillery Salute
A724

1948, Nov. 19 *Perf. 12½*

1302	A724	30k blue	30.00	10.00
1303	A724	1r rose carmine	70.00	25.00

Artillery Day, Nov. 19, 1948.

Vasili Petrovich Stasov — A725

Stasov and Barracks of Paul's Regiment, Petrograd
A726

1948, Nov. 27 **Unwmk.**

1304	A725	40k brown	6.50	1.75
1305	A726	1r sepia	13.50	3.25

Stasov (1769-1848), architect.

Arms Type of 1948

1948 **Litho.** *Perf. 12x12½*

1306	A682	40k brown red	50.00	3.00

See No. 1689.

Y. M. Sverdlov Monument
A727

Design: 40k, Lenin Street, Sverdlovsk.

1948 **Photo.** *Perf. 12½*

1307	A727	30k blue	1.00	.25
1308	A727	40k purple	1.25	.35
1309	A727	1r bright green	2.50	.60
		Nos. 1307-1309 (3)	4.75	1.20

225th anniv. of the city of Sverdlovsk (before 1924, Ekaterinburg). Exist imperf. Value, set $20.00.

"Swallow's Nest," Crimea
A729

Hot Spring, Piatigorsk
A730

Shoreline, Sukhumi
A731

Tree-lined Walk, Sochi
A732

Formal Gardens, Sochi
A733

Stalin Highway, Sochi — A734

Colonnade, Kislovodsk
A735

Seascape, Gagri — A736

1948, Dec. 30 *Perf. 12½*

1310	A729	40k brown	6.25	.60
1311	A730	40k bright red violet	6.25	.60
1312	A731	40k dark green	6.25	.60
1313	A732	40k violet	6.25	.60
1314	A733	40k dark purple	6.25	.60
1315	A734	40k dark blue green	6.25	.60
1316	A735	40k bright blue	6.25	.60
1317	A736	40k dark blue green	6.25	.60
		Nos. 1310-1317 (8)	50.00	4.80

Byelorussian S.S.R. Arms — A737

1949, Jan. 4

1318	A737	40k henna brown	6.00	2.00
1319	A737	1r blue green	9.00	3.00

Byelorussian SSR, 30th anniv.

Mikhail V. Lomonosov — A738

Lomonosov Museum, Leningrad A739

1949, Jan. 10

1320	A738	40k red brown	7.00	*3.50*
1321	A738	50k green	9.00	3.50
1322	A739	1r deep blue	20.00	8.00
		Nos. 1320-1322 (3)	36.00	15.00

Cape Dezhnev (East Cape) A740

Design: 1r, Map and Dezhnev's ship.

1949, Jan. 30

1323	A740	40k olive green	12.50	5.00
1324	A740	1r gray	27.50	10.00

300th anniv. of the discovery of the strait between Asia and America by S. I. Dezhnev.

Souvenir Sheet

A741

1949, Dec. *Imperf.*

1325	A741	Sheet of 4	500.00	300.00
		Hinged	200.00	
a.		40k Stalin's birthplace, Gorki	25.00	*35.00*
b.		40k Lenin & Stalin, Leningrad, 1917	25.00	*35.00*
c.		40k Lenin & Stalin, Gorki	25.00	*35.00*
d.		40k Marshal Stalin	25.00	*35.00*

70th birthday of Joseph V. Stalin.

Lenin Mausoleum — A742

1949, Jan. 21 *Perf. 12½*

1326	A742	40k ol grn & org brn	15.00	7.50
1327	A742	1r gray blk & org brn	25.00	12.50
a.		Sheet of 4	600.00	500.00

25th anniversary of the death of Lenin.

No. 1327a exists imperf. Value $975 mint, $3,000 used.

Admiral S. O. Makarov — A743

1949, Mar. 15

1328	A743	40k blue	8.00	4.00
1329	A743	1r red brown	17.00	6.00

Centenary of the birth of Admiral Stepan Osipovich Makarov, shipbuilder.

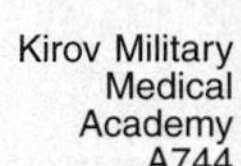

Kirov Military Medical Academy A744

Professors Botkin, Pirogov and Sechenov A745

1949, Mar. 24

1330	A744	40k red brown	6.00	3.00
1331	A745	50k blue	12.00	5.00
1332	A744	1r blue green	12.00	6.50
		Nos. 1330-1332 (3)	30.00	14.50

150th anniversary of the foundation of Kirov Military Medical Academy, Leningrad.

Soviet Soldier A746

1949, Mar. 16 **Photo.**

1333	A746	40k rose red	20.00	10.00

31st anniversary of the Soviet army.

Textile Weaving A747

Political Leadership — A748

Designs: 25k, Preschool teaching. No. 1337, School teaching. No. 1338, Farm women. 1r, Women athletes.

Inscribed: "8 МАРТА 1949г"

1949, Mar. 8 *Perf. 12½*

1334	A747	20k dark violet	.45	.25
1335	A747	25k blue	.60	.25
1336	A748	40k henna brown	.80	.25
1337	A747	50k slate gray	1.50	.35
1338	A747	50k brown	1.50	.35
1339	A747	1r green	4.00	.50
1340	A748	2r copper red	6.00	1.50
		Nos. 1334-1340 (7)	14.85	3.45

International Women's Day, Mar. 8.

Medal Types of 1945

1948-49 **Engr.**

1341	A517	2r green ('49)	12.00	5.00
1341A	A517	2r violet brown	11.00	5.25
1342	A518	3r brown car ('49)	8.00	.75
		Nos. 1341-1342 (3)	31.00	11.00

For overprint see No. 1709.

Types of 1948

1949 **Litho.** *Perf. 12x12½*

1343	A678	15k black	2.00	1.00
1344	A681	20k green	3.00	1.25
1345	A680	25k dark blue	2.50	1.00
1346	A683	30k brown	3.50	1.50
1347	A684	50k deep blue	90.00	20.00
		Nos. 1343-1347 (5)	101.00	24.75

The 20k, 25k and 30k were re-issued in 1954-56 in slightly smaller format. The 20k measures 14x21mm, instead of 15x22mm; 25k, 14½x21mm, instead of 14½x21¾mm, and 30k, 14½x21mm, instead of 15x22mm.

The smaller-format 20k is olive green, the 25k, slate blue. The 15k was reissued in 1959 (?) in smaller format: 14x21mm, instead of 14½x22mm. See note after No. 738.

Vasili R. Williams (1863-1939), Agricultural Scientist A749

1949, Apr. 18 **Photo.** *Perf. 12½*

1348	A749	25k blue green	5.00	2.75
1349	A749	50k brown	10.00	4.25

Russian Citizens and Flag — A750

1949, Apr. 30 *Perf. 12½*

1350	A750	40k scarlet	3.00	1.00
1351	A750	1r blue green	16.00	6.00

Labor Day, May 1, 1949.

A. S. Popov and Radio — A751

Popov Demonstrating Radio to Admiral Makarov — A752

1949, May **Unwmk.**

1352	A751	40k purple	8.00	3.25
1353	A752	50k brown	16.00	6.25
1354	A751	1r blue green	16.00	10.00
		Nos. 1352-1354 (3)	40.00	19.50

54th anniversary of Popov's discovery of the principles of radio.

Soviet Publications A753

Reading Pravda A754

1949, May 4

1355	A753	40k crimson	11.00	3.75
1356	A754	1r dark violet	29.00	8.00

Soviet Press Day.

Ivan V. Michurin — A755

1949, July 28

1357	A755	40k blue gray	7.00	1.50
1358	A755	1r bright green	13.00	3.50

Michurin (1855-1925), agricultural scientist.

A. S. Pushkin, 1822 — A756

Pushkin Reading Poem A757

No. 1360, Pushkin portrait by Kiprensky, 1827. 1r, Pushkin Museum, Boldino.

1949, June **Unwmk.**

1359	A756	25k indigo & sepia	3.75	.75
1360	A756	40k org brn & sep	8.75	1.75
a.		Souv. sheet of 4, 2 each #1359, 1360, imperf.	200.00	40.00
1361	A757	40k brn red & dk violet	8.75	2.00
1362	A757	1r choc & slate	21.00	4.00
1363	A757	2r brn & vio bl	32.50	6.50
		Nos. 1359-1363 (5)	74.75	15.00

150th anniversary of the birth of Aleksander S. Pushkin.

Horizontal rows of Nos. 1361 and 1363 contain alternate stamps and labels.

No. 1360a issued July 20.

River Tugboat A758

1r, Freighter, motorship "Bolshaya Volga."

1949, July, 13

1364	A758	40k slate blue	25.00	5.00
1365	A758	1r red brown	50.00	15.00

Centenary of the establishment of the Sormovo Machine and Boat Works.

VCSPS No. 3, Kislovodsk A759

State Sanatoria for Workers: No. 1367, Communications, Khosta. No. 1368, Sanatorium No. 3, Khosta. No. 1369, Electric power, Khosta. No. 1370, Sanatorium No. 1, Kislovodsk. No. 1371, State Theater, Sochi. No. 1372, Frunze Sanatorium, Sochi. No. 1373, Sanatorium at Machindzhaury. No. 1374, Clinical, Chaltubo. No. 1375, Sanatorium No. 41, Zheleznovodsk.

1949, Sept. 10 **Photo.** *Perf. 12½*

1366	A759	40k violet	1.00	.25
1367	A759	40k black	1.00	.25
1368	A759	40k carmine	1.00	.25
1369	A759	40k blue	1.00	.25
1370	A759	40k violet brown	1.00	.25
1371	A759	40k red orange	1.00	.25
1372	A759	40k dark brown	1.00	.25
1373	A759	40k green	1.00	.25
1374	A759	40k red brown	1.00	.25
1375	A759	40k blue green	1.00	.25
		Nos. 1366-1375 (10)	10.00	2.50

Regatta
A760

Sports, "1949": 25k, Kayak race. 30k, Swimming. 40k, Bicycling. No. 1380, Soccer. 50k, Mountain climbing. 1r, Parachuting. 2r, High jump.

1949, Aug. 7

1376 A760 20k bright blue .70 .25
1377 A760 25k blue green .70 .25
1378 A760 30k violet 1.20 .25
1379 A760 40k red brown 1.20 .25
1380 A760 40k green 1.20 .25
1381 A760 50k dk blue gray 1.50 .25
1382 A760 1r carmine rose 4.50 .70
1383 A760 2r gray black 8.75 1.10
Nos. 1376-1383 (8) 19.75 3.30

V. V. Dokuchayev and Fields
A761

1949, Aug. 8

1384 A761 40k brown 1.00 .30
1385 A761 1r green 2.00 .45

Vasili V. Dokuchayev (1846-1903), pioneer soil scientist.

Vasili Bazhenov and Lenin Library, Moscow
A762

1949, Aug. 14 **Photo.** ***Perf. 12½***

1386 A762 40k violet 4.00 .35
1387 A762 1r red brown 6.00 .45

Bazhenov, architect, 150th death anniv.

A. N. Radishchev — A763

1949, Aug. 31

1388 A763 40k blue green 15.00 6.00
1389 A763 1r gray 35.00 9.00

200th anniversary of the birth of Aleksandr N. Radishchev, writer.

Ivan P. Pavlov
A764

1949, Sept. 30 **Unwmk.**

1390 A764 40k deep brown 5.00 .75
1391 A764 1r gray black 10.00 1.25

Pavlov (1849-1936), Russian physiologist.

Globe Encircled by Letters
A765

1949, Oct. ***Perf. 12½***

1392 A765 40k org brn & indigo 2.50 .30
a. Imperf. 25.00 5.00
1393 A765 50k indigo & gray vio 2.50 .30
a. Imperf. 25.00 5.00

75th anniv. of the UPU.

Cultivators
A766

Map of European Russia — A767

Designs: No. 1395, Peasants in grain field. 50k, Rural scene. 2r, Old man and children.

1949, Oct. 18 ***Perf. 12½***

1394 A766 25k green 31.00 12.50
1395 A766 40k violet 7.75 2.75
1396 A767 40k gray grn & blk 9.00 5.50
1397 A766 50k deep blue 8.00 4.50
1398 A766 1r gray black 20.00 9.00
1399 A766 2r dark brown 25.00 12.50
Nos. 1394-1399 (6) 100.75 46.75

Encouraging agricultural development.
Nos. 1394, 1398, 1399 measure 33x19mm. Nos. 1395, 1397 measure 33x22mm.

Maly (Little) Theater, Moscow
A768

M. N. Ermolova, I. S. Mochalov, A. N. Ostrovski, M. S. Shchepkin and P. M. Sadovsky
A769

1949, Oct. 27

1400 A768 40k green 2.50 .25
1401 A768 50k red orange 3.75 .40
1402 A769 1r deep brown 8.75 .85
Nos. 1400-1402 (3) 15.00 1.50

125th anniversary of the Maly Theater (State Academic Little Theater).

Chapayev Type of 1944

1949, Oct. 22 **Photo.**

1403 A494 40k brown orange 75.00 30.00

30th anniversary of the death of V. I. Chapayev, a hero of the 1918 civil war.
Portrait and outer frame same as type A494. Dates "1919 1949" are in upper corners. Other details differ.

125th Anniv. of the Birth of Ivan Savvich Nikitin, Russian Poet (1824-1861) — A770

1949, Oct. 24 **Unwmk.**

1404 A770 40k brown 1.50 .25
1405 A770 1r slate blue 2.50 .35

Spasski Tower and Russian Citizens
A771

1949, Oct. 29 ***Perf. 12½***

1406 A771 40k brown orange 6.00 4.00
1407 A771 1r deep green 10.00 6.00

October Revolution, 32nd anniversary.

Sheep, Cattle and Farm Woman — A772

1949, Nov. 2

1408 A772 40k chocolate 8.00 .40
1409 A772 1r violet 12.00 .60

Encouraging better cattle breeding in Russia.

Arms and Flag of USSR — A773

1949, Nov. 30 **Engr.** ***Perf. 12***

1410 A773 40k carmine 20.00 6.00

Constitution Day.

Electric Trolley Car — A774

40k, 1r, Diesel train. 50k, Steam train.

1949, Nov. 19 **Photo.** ***Perf. 12½***

1411 A774 25k red 4.00 .50
1412 A774 40k violet 7.00 .50
1413 A774 50k brown 9.00 .75
1414 A774 1r Prus green 30.00 1.25
Nos. 1411-1414 (4) 50.00 3.00

Ski Jump — A775

Designs: 40k, Girl on rings. 50k, Ice hockey. 1r, Weight lifter. 2r, Wolf hunt.

1949, Nov. 12 **Unwmk.**

1415 A775 20k dark green 1.20 .55
1416 A775 40k orange red 2.40 .65
1417 A775 50k deep blue 3.00 .80
1418 A775 1r red 6.00 .90
1419 A775 2r violet 12.00 1.10
Nos. 1415-1419 (5) 24.60 4.00

Textile Mills — A776

Designs: 25k, Irrigation system. 40k, 1r, Government buildings, Stalinabad. 50k, University of Medicine.

1949, Dec. 7 **Photo.** ***Perf. 12***

1420 A776 20k blue 3.00 .25
1421 A776 25k green 3.00 .25
1422 A776 40k red orange 4.50 .25
1423 A776 50k violet 7.50 .40
1424 A776 1r gray black 12.00 1.00
Nos. 1420-1424 (5) 30.00 2.15

Tadzhik Republic, 20th anniv.

"Russia" versus "War" — A777

1949, Dec. 25

1425 A777 40k rose carmine 3.00 .25
1426 A777 50k blue 4.00 .75

Issued to portray Russia as the defender of world peace.

Byelorussians and Flag — A778

Design: No. 1428, Ukrainians and flag.

Inscribed: "1939 1949"

1949, Dec. 23 **Unwmk.**

1427 A778 40k orange red 37.50 5.00
1428 A778 40k deep orange 37.50 5.00

Return of western territories to the Byelorussian and Ukrainian Republics, 10th anniv.

Teachers College
A779

25k, State Theater. #1431, Government House. #1432, Navol Street, Tashkent. 1r, Fergana Canal. 2r, Kuigonyarsk Dam.

1950, Jan. 3

1429 A779 20k blue 1.00 .25
1430 A779 25k gray black 1.00 .25
1431 A779 40k red orange 2.00 .25
1432 A779 40k violet 1.50 .25
1433 A779 1r green 4.00 1.00
1434 A779 2r brown 6.00 1.00
Nos. 1429-1434 (6) 15.50 3.00

Uzbek Republic, 25th anniversary.

Lenin at Razliv — A780

Lenin's Office, Kremlin
A781

Design: 1r, Lenin Museum.

1950, Jan. **Unwmk.** **Litho.** ***Perf. 12***

1435 A780 40k dk grn & dk brn 3.00 .50
1436 A781 50k dk brn, red brn & grn 4.00 .50

1437 A781 1r dk brn, dk grn & cream 9.00 2.00
Nos. 1435-1437 (3) 16.00 3.00

26th anniversary of the death of Lenin.

Textile Factory, Ashkhabad A782

Designs: 40k, 1r, Power dam and Turkmenian arms. 50k, Rug making.

1950, Jan. 7 **Photo.**
1438 A782 25k gray black 3.50 1.00
1439 A782 40k brown 5.00 .75
1440 A782 50k green 6.50 1.25
1441 A782 1r purple 15.00 2.50
Nos. 1438-1441 (4) 30.00 5.50

Turkmen Republic, 25th anniversary.

Motion Picture Projection A783

1950, Feb.
1442 A783 25k brown 40.00 25.00

Soviet motion picture industry, 30th anniv.

Voter — A784 Kremlin — A785

1950, Mar. 8
1443 A784 40k green, *yellow* 20.00 4.00
1444 A785 1r rose carmine 40.00 6.00

Supreme Soviet elections, Mar. 12, 1950.

Morozov Monument, Moscow — A786

1950, Mar. 16 ***Perf. 12½***
1445 A786 40k black brn & red 20.00 3.25
1446 A786 1r dk green & red 30.00 7.50

Unveiling of a monument to Pavlik Morozov, Pioneer.

Globes and Communication Symbols — A787

1950, Apr. 1
1447 A787 40k deep green 10.00 4.50
1448 A787 50k deep blue 12.00 5.50

Meeting of the Post, Telegraph, Telephone and Radio Trade Unions.

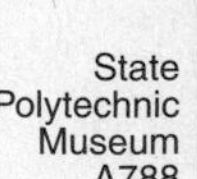

State Polytechnic Museum A788

State Museum of Oriental Cultures A789

State University Museum — A790

Pushkin Museum A791

Museums: No. 1451, Tretiakov Gallery. No. 1452, Timiryazev Biology Museum. No. 1453, Lenin Museum. No. 1454, Museum of the Revolution. No. 1456, State History Museum.

Inscribed: "MOCKBA 1949" in Top Frame

Multicolored Centers

1950, Mar. 28 **Litho.** ***Perf. 12½***
1449 A788 40k dark blue 6.00 .50
1450 A789 40k dark blue 6.00 .50
1451 A789 40k green 6.00 .50
1452 A789 40k dark brown 6.00 .50
1453 A789 40k olive brown 6.00 .50
1454 A789 40k claret 6.00 .50
1455 A790 40k red 6.00 .50
1456 A790 40k chocolate 6.00 .50
1457 A791 40k brown violet 6.00 .50
Nos. 1449-1457 (9) 54.00 4.50

Soviets of Three Races — A792

1r, 4 Russians and communist banner, horiz.

1950, May 1 **Photo.** ***Perf. 12½***
1458 A792 40k org red & gray 15.00 2.25
1459 A792 1r red & gray black 20.00 5.00

Labor Day, May 1, 1950.

A. S. Shcherbakov A793

1950, May **Unwmk.**
1460 A793 40k black, *pale blue* 8.00 1.00
1461 A793 1r dk green, *buff* 12.50 2.00

Shcherbakov, political leader (1901-1945).

Monument A794

Victory Medal A795

Perf. 12x12½

1950 **Photo.** **Wmk. 293**
1462 A794 40k dk brown & red 37.50 4.00

Unwmk.

1463 A795 1r carmine rose 37.50 8.00

5th Intl. Victory Day, May 9, 1950.

A. V. Suvorov — A796

50k, Suvorov crossing Alps, 32½x47mm. 60k, Badge, flag and marchers, 24x39½mm. 2r, Suvorov facing left, 19x33½mm.

Various Designs and Sizes

Dated "1800 1950"

1950 ***Perf. 12, 12½x12***
1464 A796 40k blue, *pink* 15.00 4.00
1465 A796 50k brown, *pink* 19.00 8.00
1466 A796 60k gray black, *pale gray* 19.00 8.00
1467 A796 1r dk brn, *lemon* 23.00 12.00
1468 A796 2r greenish blue 50.00 18.00
Nos. 1464-1468 (5) 126.00 50.00

Field Marshal Count Aleksandr V. Suvorov (1730-1800).

Farmers Studying Agronomic Techniques A797

No. 1470, 1r, Sowing on collective farm.

1950, June ***Perf. 12½***
1469 A797 40k dk grn, *pale grn* 7.50 2.00
1470 A797 40k gray black, *buff* 7.50 2.00
1471 A797 1r blue, *lemon* 15.00 4.00
Nos. 1469-1471 (3) 30.00 8.00

George M. Dimitrov — A798

1950, July 2
1472 A798 40k gray blk, *citron* 6.00 3.00
1473 A798 1r gray blk, *salmon* 14.00 6.00

Dimitrov (1882-1949), Bulgarian-born revolutionary leader and Comintern official.

Opera and Ballet Theater, Baku — A799

Designs: 40k, Azerbaijan Academy of Science. 1r, Stalin Avenue, Baku.

1950, July **Photo.** ***Perf. 12½***
1474 A799 25k dp grn, *citron* 15.00 1.50
1475 A799 40k brn, *pink* 10.00 5.00
1476 A799 1r gray blk, *buff* 15.00 8.50
Nos. 1474-1476 (3) 40.00 15.00

Azerbaijan SSR, 30th anniversary.

Victory Theater — A800

Lenin Street A801

Designs: 50k, Gorky Theater. 1r, Monument marking Stalingrad defense line.

1950, June
1477 A800 20k dark blue 5.00 1.50
1478 A801 40k green 5.00 2.25
1479 A801 50k red orange 10.00 3.50
1480 A801 1r gray 10.00 6.00
Nos. 1477-1480 (4) 30.00 13.25

Restoration of Stalingrad.

Moscow Subway Stations: "Park of Culture" A802

#1482, Kaluzskaya station. #1483, Taganskaya. #1484, Kurskaya. #1485, Paveletskaya. #1486, Park of Culture. #1487, Taganskaya.

1950, July 30 **Size: 33½x23mm**
1481 A802 40k deep carmine 5.50 .90
1482 A802 40k dk grn, *buff* 5.50 .90
1483 A802 40k deep blue, *buff* 5.50 .90
1484 A802 1r dark brn, *citron* 8.25 3.00
1485 A802 1r purple 8.25 3.00
1486 A802 1r dark grn, *citron* 8.25 3.00

Size: 33x18½mm

1487 A802 1r black, *pink* 8.25 3.25
Nos. 1481-1487 (7) 49.50 14.95

Socialist Peoples and Flags A803

1950, Aug. 4 **Unwmk.** ***Perf. 12½***
1488 A803 40k multicolored 1.75 .25
1489 A803 50k multicolored 3.50 .30
1490 A803 1r multicolored 4.75 .50
Nos. 1488-1490 (3) 10.00 1.05

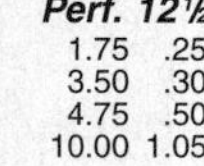

Trade Union Building, Riga — A804

Opera and Ballet Theater, Riga — A805

Designs: 40k, Latvian Cabinet building. 50k, Monument to Jan Rainis. 1r, Riga State Univ. 2r, Latvian Academy of Sciences.

1950 Photo. *Perf. 12½*

1491 A804 25k dark brown 3.00 1.50
1492 A804 40k scarlet 5.00 2.50
1493 A804 50k dark green 10.00 3.50
1494 A805 60k deep blue 12.00 4.00
1495 A805 1r lilac 15.00 6.00
1496 A804 2r sepia 30.00 10.00
Nos. 1491-1496 (6) 75.00 27.50

Latvian SSR, 10th anniv.

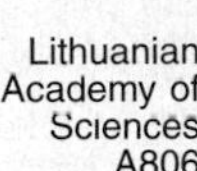

Lithuanian Academy of Sciences A806

Marite Melnik — A807

Design: 1r, Cabinet building.

1950

1497 A806 25k dp bl, *bluish* 6.00 2.50
1498 A807 40k brown 12.00 7.50
1499 A806 1r scarlet 42.00 15.00
Nos. 1497-1499 (3) 60.00 25.00

Lithuanian SSR, 10th anniv.

Stalingrad Square, Tallinn A808

Victor Kingisepp — A809

Designs: 40k, Government building, Tallinn. 50k, Estonia Theater, Tallinn.

1950

1500 A808 25k dark green 5.00 2.00
1501 A808 40k scarlet 5.00 3.00
1502 A808 50k blue, *yellow* 10.00 5.00
1503 A809 1r brown, *blue* 30.00 12.00
Nos. 1500-1503 (4) 50.00 22.00

Estonian SSR, 10th anniv.

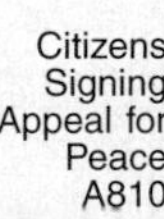

Citizens Signing Appeal for Peace A810

Children and Governess — A811

Design: 50k, Peace Demonstration.

1950, Oct. 16 Photo.

1504 A810 40k red, *salmon* 4.00 3.00
1505 A811 40k black 4.00 3.00
1506 A811 50k dark red 8.50 5.00
1507 A810 1r brown, *salmon* 24.00 9.00
Nos. 1504-1507 (4) 40.50 20.00

F. G. Bellingshausen, M. P. Lazarev and Globe — A812

Route of Antarctic Expedition — A813

Blue Paper

1950, Oct. 25 Unwmk. *Perf. 12½*

1508 A812 40k dark carmine 35.00 15.00
1509 A813 1r purple 65.00 35.00

130th anniversary of the Bellingshausen-Lazarev expedition to the Antarctic.

M. V. Frunze — A814

1950, Oct. 31

1510 A814 40k blue, *buff* 10.00 3.00
1511 A814 1r brown, *blue* 30.00 12.00

Frunze, military strategist, 25th death anniv.

M. I. Kalinin — A815

1950, Nov. 20 Engr.

1512 A815 40k deep green 10.00 1.50
1513 A815 1r reddish brown 10.00 2.50
1514 A815 5r violet 35.00 6.00
Nos. 1512-1514 (3) 55.00 10.00

75th anniversary of the birth of M. I. Kalinin, Soviet Russia's first president.

Gathering Grapes A816

Armenian Government Building A817

G. M. Sundukian — A818

1950, Nov. 29 Photo. *Perf. 12½*

1515 A816 20k dp blue, *buff* 5.00 1.00
1516 A817 40k red org, *blue* 32.50 8.50
1517 A818 1r ol gray, *yellow* 7.50 3.50
Nos. 1515-1517 (3) 45.00 13.00

Armenian Republic, 30th anniv. 1r also for birth of Sundukian, playwright.

Apartment Building, Koteljnicheskaya Quay — A819

Hotel, Kalanchevkaya Square — A820

Various Buildings
Inscribed: "Mockba, 1950"

1950, Dec. 2 Unwmk.

1518 A819 1r red brn, *buff* 57.50 22.00
1519 A819 1r gray black 57.50 22.00
1520 A819 1r brown, *blue* 57.50 22.00
1521 A819 1r dk green, *blue* 57.50 22.00
1522 A820 1r dp blue, *buff* 57.50 22.00
1523 A820 1r black, *buff* 57.50 22.00
1524 A820 1r red orange 57.50 22.00
1525 A819 1r dk grn, *yellow* 57.50 22.00
Nos. 1518-1525 (8) 460.00 176.00
Set, hinged 250.00

Skyscrapers planned for Moscow.

Spasski Tower, Kremlin — A821

1950, Dec. 4

1526 A821 1r dk grn, red brn & yel brown 75.00 5.00

October Revolution, 33rd anniversary.

Golden Autumn by Levitan A822

I. I. Levitan (1861-90), Painter A823

1950, Dec. 6 Litho. *Perf. 12½*

1527 A822 40k multicolored 10.00 .55

Perf. 12
Photo.

1528 A823 50k red brown 15.00 .55

Black Sea by Aivazovsky — A824

Ivan K. Aivazovsky (1817-1900) Painter A825

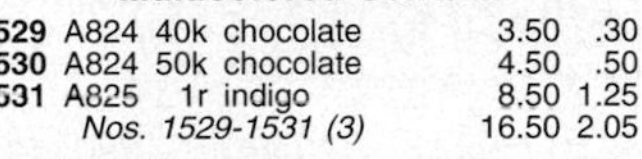

Design: 50k, "Ninth Surge."

1950, Dec. 6 Litho.
Multicolored Centers

1529 A824 40k chocolate 3.50 .30
1530 A824 50k chocolate 4.50 .50
1531 A825 1r indigo 8.50 1.25
Nos. 1529-1531 (3) 16.50 2.05

Flags and Newspapers Iskra and Pravda — A826

1r, Flag and profiles of Lenin and Stalin.

1950, Dec. 23 Photo.

1532 A826 40k gray blk & red 50.00 15.00
1533 A826 1r dk brn & red 100.00 35.00

1st issue of the newspaper Iskra, 50th anniv.

Presidium of Supreme Soviet, Alma-Ata A827

Design: 1r, Opera and Ballet Theater.

Inscribed: "ALMA-ATA" in Cyrillic

1950, Dec. 27

1534 A827 40k gray black, *blue* 10.00 7.50
1535 A827 1r red brn, *yellow* 25.00 7.50

Kazakh Republic, 30th anniversary. Cyrillic charcters for "ALMA-ATA" are above building in vignette on 40k, immediately below building on right on 1r.

Decembrists and Senatskaya Square, Leningrad — A828

1950, Dec. 30 Unwmk.

1536 A828 1r blk brn, *yellow* 30.00 10.00

Decembrist revolution of 1825.

Lenin at Razliv A829

Design: 1r, Lenin and young communists.

Multicolored Centers

1951, Jan. 21 Litho. *Perf. 12½*

1537	A829	40k olive green	7.00	.30
1538	A829	1r indigo	13.00	.70

27th anniversary of the death of Lenin.

Mountain Pasture A830

Government Building, Frunze A831

1951, Feb. 2 Photo. *Perf. 12½*

1539	A830	25k dk brown, *blue*	10.00	3.50
1540	A831	40k dp green, *blue*	20.00	6.50

Kirghiz Republic, 25th anniv.

Government Building, Tirana A832

1951, Jan. 6 Unwmk. *Perf. 12*

1541	A832	40k green, *bluish*	50.00	40.00

Honoring the Albanian People's Republic.

Bulgarians Greeting Russian Troops A833

Lenin Square, Sofia — A834

Design: 60k, Monument to Soviet soldiers.

1951, Jan. 13

1542	A833	25k gray blk, *bluish*	12.00	5.00
1543	A834	40k org red, *sal*	17.50	10.00
1544	A834	60k blk brn, *sal*	30.00	15.00
		Nos. 1542-1544 (3)	59.50	30.00

Honoring the Bulgarian People's Republic.

Choibalsan State University — A835

State Theater, Ulan Bator A836

Mongolian Republic Emblem and Flag — A837

1951, Mar. 12

1545	A835	25k purple, *salmon*	.55	.65
1546	A836	40k dp orange, *yellow*	1.25	1.00
1547	A837	1r multicolored	3.25	1.50
		Nos. 1545-1547 (3)	5.05	3.15

Honoring the Mongolian People's Republic.

D. A. Furmanov (1891-1926) Writer — A838

Furmanov at Work A839

1951, Mar. 17 *Perf. 12½*

1548	A838	40k brown	22.50	2.00
1549	A839	1r gray black, *buff*	27.50	3.00

Russian War Memorial, Berlin — A840

1951, Mar. 21 *Perf. 12*

1550	A840	40k dk gray grn & dk red	40.00	6.00
1551	A840	1r brn blk & red	50.00	14.00

Stockholm Peace Conference.

Kirov Machine Works A841

1951, May 19 Photo. *Perf. 12½*

1552	A841	40k brown, *cream*	17.50	3.00

Kirov Machine Works, 150th anniv.

Bolshoi Theater, Moscow — A842

Russian Composers A843

1951, May Unwmk.

1553	A842	40k multicolored	10.00	1.00
1554	A843	1r multicolored	10.00	1.25

Bolshoi Theater, Moscow, 175th anniv.

Liberty Bridge, Budapest A844

Monument to Liberators — A845

Budapest Buildings: 40k, Parliament. 60k, National Museum.

1951, June 9 *Perf. 12*

1555	A844	25k emerald	5.00	4.00
1556	A844	40k bright blue	5.00	4.00
1557	A844	60k sepia	10.00	6.00
1558	A845	1r sepia, *salmon*	20.00	10.00
		Nos. 1555-1558 (4)	40.00	24.00

Honoring the Hungarian People's Republic.

Harvesting Wheat A846

Designs: 40k, Apiary. 1r, Gathering citrus fruits. 2r, Cotton picking.

1951, June 25

1559	A846	25k dark green	6.50	3.50
1560	A846	40k green, *bluish*	6.50	3.50
1561	A846	1r brown, *yellow*	6.50	5.00
1562	A846	2r dk grn, *sal*	30.00	14.00
		Nos. 1559-1562 (4)	49.50	26.00

Kalinin Museum, Moscow — A847

Mikhail I. Kalinin — A848

Design: 1r, Kalinin statue.

1951, Aug. 4 *Perf. 12x12½, 12½x12*

1563	A847	20k org brn & black	1.50	.25
1564	A848	40k dp green & choc	3.00	.50
1565	A848	1r vio blue & gray	5.50	.75
		Nos. 1563-1565 (3)	10.00	1.50

5th anniv. of the death of Kalinin.

F. E. Dzerzhinski, 25th Death Anniv. — A849

Design: 1r, Profile of Dzerzhinski.

1951, Aug. 4 Engr. *Perf. 12x12½*

1566	A849	40k brown red	12.00	3.00
1567	A849	1r gray black	18.00	5.00

Aleksandr M. Butlerov — A850

A. Kovalevski A850a

P. K. Kozlov A850b

N. S. Kurnakov — A850c

P. N. Lebedev A850d

N. I. Lobachevski A850e

A. N. Lodygin A850f

A. N. Severtsov A850g

K. E. Tsiolkovsky A850h

Russian Scientists: No. 1570 Sonya Kovalevskaya. No. 1572, S. P. Krasheninnikov. No. 1577, D. I. Mendeleev. No. 1578, N. N. Miklukho-Maklai. No. 1580, A. G. Stoletov. No. 1581, K. A. Timiryasev. No. 1583, P. N. Yablochkov.

1951, Aug. 15 Photo. *Perf. 12½*

1568	A850	40k org red, *bluish*	12.50	1.25
1569	A850a	40k dk blue, *sal*	4.75	.50
1570	A850	40k pur, *salmon*	4.75	.50
1571	A850b	40k orange red	4.75	.50
1572	A850	40k purple	4.75	.50
1573	A850c	40k brn, *sal*	4.75	.50
1574	A850d	40k blue	4.75	.50
1575	A850e	40k brown	4.75	.50
1576	A850f	40k green	4.75	.50
1577	A850	40k deep blue	4.75	.50
1578	A850	40k org red, *sal*	4.75	.50
1579	A850g	40k sepia, *sal*	4.75	.50
1580	A850	40k grn, *sal*	4.75	.50
1581	A850	40k brn, *sal*	4.75	.50
1582	A850h	40k gray blk, *blue*	20.00	1.40
1583	A850	40k sepia	4.75	.50
		Nos. 1568-1583 (16)	99.00	9.65

Two printings exist in differing stamp sizes of most of this issue.

A. A. Aliabiev — A851

Design: No. 1585, V. S. Kalinnikov.

1951, Aug. 28

1584	A851	40k brown, *salmon*	50.00	15.00
1585	A851	40k gray, *salmon*	50.00	15.00

Russian composers.

Opera and Ballet Theater, Tbilisi — A852

Gathering Citrus Fruit — A853

40k, Principal street, Tbilisi. 1r, Picking tea.

1951 Unwmk. *Perf. 12½*

1586	A852	20k dp grn, *yellow*	5.00	1.60
1587	A853	25k pur, org & brn	5.00	1.60
1588	A853	40k dk brn, *blue*	22.50	3.50
1589	A853	1r red brn & dk grn	17.50	8.00
		Nos. 1586-1589 (4)	50.00	14.70

Georgian Republic, 30th anniversary.

Emblem of Aviation Society — A854

Planes and Emblem — A855

60k, Flying model planes. 1r, Parachutists.

1951, Sept. 19 Litho. *Perf. 12½*
Dated: "1951"

1590	A854	40k multicolored	3.00	.25
1591	A854	60k emer, lt bl & brn	10.00	.45
1592	A854	1r blue, sal & lilac	12.50	.45
1593	A855	2r multicolored	22.50	1.00
		Nos. 1590-1593 (4)	48.00	2.15

Promoting interest in aviation.

Victor M. Vasnetsov (1848-1926), Painter — A856

Three Heroes, by Vasnetsov — A857

1951, Oct. 15

1594	A856	40k dk bl, brn & buff	12.00	.75
1595	A857	1r multicolored	18.00	1.25

Hydroelectric Station, Lenin and Stalin — A858

Design: 1r, Spasski Tower, Kremlin.

1951, Nov. 6 Photo. *Perf. 12½*
Dated: "1917-1951"

1596	A858	40k blue vio & red	35.00	10.00
1597	A858	1r dk brown & red	65.00	35.00

34th anniversary of October Revolution.

Map, Dredge and Khakhovsky Hydroelectric Station A859

Map, Volga Dam and Tugboat — A860

Designs (each showing map): 40k, Stalingrad Dam. 60k, Excavating Turkmenian canal. 1r, Kuibyshev dam.

1951, Nov. 28 *Perf. 12½*

1598	A859	20k multicolored	*18.00*	*3.00*
1599	A860	30k multicolored	*27.00*	*4.50*
1600	A860	40k multicolored	*32.50*	*6.50*
1601	A860	60k multicolored	*55.00*	*9.50*
1602	A860	1r multicolored	*115.00*	*15.00*
		Nos. 1598-1602 (5)	*247.50*	*38.50*

Flag and Citizens Signing Peace Appeal — A861

1951, Nov. 30 *Perf. 12½*

1603	A861	40k gray & red	20.00	7.00

Third All-Union Peace Conference.

Mikhail V. Ostrogradski, Mathematician, 150th Birth Anniv. — A862

1951, Dec. 10 Unwmk.

1604	A862	40k black brn, *pink*	17.50	10.00

Monument to Jan Zizka, Prague — A863

Monument to Soviet Liberators A864

25k, Monument to Soviet Soldiers, Ostrava. 40k, Julius Fucik. 60k, Smetana Museum, Prague.

1951, Dec. 10 *Perf. 12½*

1605	A863	20k vio blue, *sal*	16.00	3.00
1606	A863	25k copper red, *yel*	35.00	12.50
1607	A863	40k red org, *sal*	60.00	7.50
1608	A863	60k brnsh gray, *buff*	35.00	6.00
1609	A864	1r brnsh gray, *buff*	30.00	9.00
		Nos. 1605-1609 (5)	176.00	38.00

Soviet-Czechoslovakian friendship.

Volkhovski Hydroelectric Station and Lenin Statue — A865

1951, Dec. 19

1610	A865	40k dk bl, gray & yel	6.00	.25
1611	A865	1r pur, gray & yel	14.00	.55

25th anniv. of the opening of the Lenin Volkhovski hydroelectric station.

Lenin as a Schoolboy A866

Horizontal Designs: 60k, Lenin among children. 1r, Lenin and peasants.

1952, Jan. 24 Photo. *Perf. 12½*
Multicolored Centers

1612	A866	40k dk blue green	2.25	.55
1613	A866	60k violet blue	3.25	.55
1614	A866	1r orange brown	4.50	.65
		Nos. 1612-1614 (3)	10.00	1.75

28th anniversary of the death of Lenin.

Semenov — A867

1952, Feb. 1

1615	A867	1r sepia, *blue*	15.00	8.00

Petr Petrovich Semenov-Tianshanski (1827-1914), traveler and geographer who explored the Tian Shan mountains.

Kovalevski — A868

1952, Mar. 3 Unwmk.

1616	A868	40k sepia, *yellow*	25.00	10.00

V. O. Kovalevski (1843-1883), biologist and palaeontologist.

Skaters A869

1952, Mar. 3

1617	A869	40k shown	4.00	.40
1618	A869	60k Skiers	6.00	.60

N. V. Gogol and Characters from "Taras Bulba" — A870

Designs: 60k, Gogol and V. G. Belinski. 1r, Gogol and Ukrainian peasants.

1952, Mar. 4 Dated: "1852-1952"

1619 A870 40k sepia, *blue* 5.00 .50
1620 A870 60k multicolored 5.00 .50
1621 A870 1r multicolored 15.00 1.00
Nos. 1619-1621 (3) 25.00 2.00

Death centenary of N. V. Gogol, writer.

G. K. Ordzhonikidze A871

1952, Apr. 23 Photo. *Perf. 12½*

1622 A871 40k dp green, *pink* 19.00 8.50
1623 A871 1r sepia, *blue* 11.00 3.50

15th anniv. of the death of Grigori K. Ordzhonikidze, Georgian party worker.

Workers and Soviet Flag — A872

Workers' Rest Home A873

No. 1626, Aged citizens. No. 1627, Schoolgirl.

1952, May 15 Unwmk.

1624 A872 40k red & blk, *cream* 40.00 10.00
1625 A873 40k red & dk grn, *pale gray* 80.00 18.00
1626 A873 40k red & brown, *pale gray* 40.00 10.00
1627 A872 40k red & black, *pale gray* 40.00 10.00
Nos. 1624-1627 (4) 200.00 48.00

Adoption of Stalin constitution., 15th anniv

A. S. Novikov-Priboy and Ship — A874

1952, June 5

1628 A874 40k blk, pale cit & bl grn 1.00 .30

Novikov-Priboy, writer, 75th birthanniv.

150th anniv. of Birth of Victor Hugo (1802-1855), French Writer — A875

1952, June 5 Unwmk. *Perf. 12½*

1629 A875 40k brn org, gray & black 2.00 .25

Julaev — A876

1952, June 28

1630 A876 40k rose red, *pink* 1.00 .25

200th anniversary of the birth of Salavat Julaev, Bashkir hero who took part in the insurrection of 1773-1775.

Sedov — A877

1952, July 4

1631 A877 40k dk bl, dk brn & blue green 37.50 8.00

Georgi J. Sedov, Arctic explorer (1877-1914).

Arms and Flag of Romania — A878

University Square, Bucharest A879

Design: 60k, Monument to Soviet soldiers.

1952, July 26

1632 A878 40k multicolored 4.50 1.00
1633 A878 60k dk green, *pink* 7.50 2.50
1634 A879 1r bright ultra 13.00 5.00
Nos. 1632-1634 (3) 25.00 8.50

Zhukovski — A880

Design: No. 1636, K. P. Bryullov.

1952, July 26 Pale Blue Paper

1635 A880 40k gray black 10.00 .50
1636 A880 40k brt blue green 10.00 .50

V. A. Zhukovski, poet, and Bryullov, painter (1799-1852).

Ogarev — A881

1952, Aug. 29

1637 A881 40k deep green .75 .25

75th anniversary of the death of N. P. Ogarev, poet and revolutionary.

Uspenski — A882

1952, Sept. 4

1638 A882 40k indigo & dk brn 2.00 .50

Gleb Ivanovich Uspenski (1843-1902), writer.

Nakhimov — A883

1952, Sept. 9

1639 A883 40k multicolored 5.00 2.00

Adm. Paul S. Nakhimov (1802-1855).

University Building, Tartu — A884

1952, Oct. 2

1640 A884 40k black brn, *sal* 20.00 *3.00*

150th anniversary of the enlargement of the University of Tartu, Estonia.

Kajum Nasyri — A885

1952, Nov. 5

1641 A885 40k brown, *yellow* 15.00 5.00

Nasyri (1825-1902), Tartar educator.

A. N. Radishchev — A886

1952, Oct. 23

1642 A886 40k blk, brn & dk red 6.00 1.00

Radishchev, writer, 150th death anniv.

M.S. Joseph Stalin at Entrance to Volga-Don Canal — A887

Design: 1r, Lenin, Stalin and red banners.

1952, Nov. 6 *Perf. 12½*

1643 A887 40k multicolored 15.00 6.00
1644 A887 1r brown, red & yel 25.00 9.00

35th anniversary of October Revolution.

Pavel Andreievitch Fedotov (1815-52), Artist — A888

1952, Nov. 26

1645 A888 40k red brn & black 2.00 .50

V. D. Polenov, Artist, 25th Death Anniv. — A889

"Moscow Courtyard" — A890

1952, Dec. 6

1646 A889 40k red brown & buff 3.50 .35
1647 A890 1r multicolored 4.50 .65

A. I. Odoyevski (1802-39) Poet — A891

1952, Dec. 8

1648 A891 40k gray blk & red org 5.00 .50

D. N. Mamin-Sibiryak — A892

1952, Dec. 15
1649 A892 40k dp green, *cream* 2.00 .50

Centenary of the birth of Dimitrii N. Mamin-Sibiryak (1852-1912), writer.

Composite Medal Types of 1946 Frames as A599-A606 Centers as Indicated

Medals: 1r, Token of Veneration. 2r, Red Star. 3r, Red Workers' Banner. 5r, Red Banner. 10r, Lenin.

1952-59 Engr. *Perf. 12½*
1650 A569 1r dark brown 9.00 7.00
1651 A567 2r red brown 1.40 .55
1652 A572 3r dp blue violet 2.00 .95
1653 A571 5r dk car ('53) 2.50 .95
1654 A566 10r bright rose 4.50 1.90
a. 10r dull red ('59) 5.00 2.00
Nos. 1650-1654 (5) 19.40 11.35

Vladimir M. Bekhterev (1857-1927), Neuropathologist A893

1952, Dec. 24 Photo.
1655 A893 40k vio bl, slate & blk 3.00 .50

Byelorusskaya Station — A894

Designs (Moscow Subway stations): 40k, Botanical Garden Station. 40k, Novoslobodskaya Station. 40k, Komsomolskaya Station.

1952, Dec. 30
Multicolored Centers
1656 A894 40k dull violet 3.50 .50
1657 A894 40k light ultra 3.50 .50
1658 A894 40k blue gray 3.50 .50
1659 A894 40k dull green 3.50 .50
a. Horiz. strip of 4, #1656-1659 15.00 4.00

USSR Emblem and Flags of 16 Union Republics — A895

1952, Dec. 30
1660 A895 1r grn, dk red & brn 25.00 4.50

30th anniversary of the USSR.

Lenin — A896

1953, Jan. 26
1661 A896 40k multicolored 10.00 4.00

29 years without Lenin.

Stalin Peace Medal — A897

1953, Apr. 30 *Perf. 12½*
1662 A897 40k red brn, bl & dull yel 12.00 6.00

Valerian V. Kuibyshev A898

1953, June 6
1663 A898 40k red brn & black 3.00 .55

Kuibyshev (1888-1935), Bolshevik leader.

A899

1953, July 21
1664 A899 40k buff & dk brown 20.00 1.25

Nikolai G. Chernyshevski (1828-1889), writer and radical leader; exiled to Siberia for 24 years.

A900

1953, July 19
1665 A900 40k ver & gray brown 8.00 2.00

60th anniv. of the birth of Vladimir V. Mayakovsky, poet.

Tsymijanskaja Dam — A901

Volga-Don Canal: No. 1666, Lock No. 9, Volga-Don Canal. No. 1667, Lock 13. No. 1668, Lock 15. No. 1669, Volga River lighthouse. No. 1671, M. S. "Joseph Stalin" in canal.

1953, Aug. 29 Litho.
1666 A901 40k multicolored 4.00 1.00
1667 A901 40k multicolored 4.00 2.00
1668 A901 40k multicolored 4.00 1.00
1669 A901 40k multicolored 4.00 2.00
1670 A901 40k multicolored 4.00 1.00
1671 A901 1r multicolored 5.00 1.00
Nos. 1666-1671 (6) 25.00 8.00

V. G. Korolenko (1853-1921), Writer — A902

1953, Aug. 29 Photo. *Perf. 12x12½*
1672 A902 40k brown 2.00 .25

Count Leo N. Tolstoy (1828-1910), Writer — A903

1953, Sept. *Perf. 12*
1673 A903 1r dark brown 15.00 5.00

Moscow University and Two Youths — A904

1r, Komsomol badge and four orders.

1953, Oct. 29 *Perf. 12½x12*
1674 A904 40k multicolored 12.50 2.00
1675 A904 1r multicolored 22.50 3.00

35th anniversary of the Young Communist League (Komsomol).

Nationalities of the Soviet Union — A905

60k, Lenin and Stalin at Smolny.

1953, Nov. 6
1676 A905 40k multicolored 30.00 10.00
1677 A905 60k multicolored 50.00 15.00

36th anniversary of October Revolution.
No. 1676 measures 25½x38mm; No. 1677, 25½x42mm.

Lenin and His Writings — A906

1r, Lenin facing left and pages of "What to Do."

1953
1678 A906 40k multicolored 8.00 4.00
1679 A906 1r dk brn, org brn & red 14.00 8.50

Communist Party formation, 50th anniv. (40k). 2nd cong. of the Russian Socialist Party, 50th anniv. (1r).
Issued: 40k, 11/12; 1r, 12/14.

Lenin Statue — A907

Peter I Statue, Decembrists' Square — A908

Leningrad Views: Nos. 1681 & 1683, Admiralty building. Nos. 1685 & 1687, Smolny Institute.

1953, Nov. 23
1680 A907 40k brn blk, *yellow* 8.00 4.00
1681 A907 40k vio brn, *yellow* 8.00 4.00
1682 A907 40k dk brn, *pink* 6.00 3.00
1683 A907 40k brn blk, *cream* 6.00 3.00
1684 A908 1r dk brn, *blue* 17.50 10.00
1685 A908 1r dk green, *pink* 17.50 10.00
1686 A908 1r violet, *yellow* 14.00 9.00
1687 A908 1r blk brn, *blue* 14.00 9.00
Nos. 1680-1687 (8) 91.00 52.00

See Nos. 1944-1945, 1943a.

"Pioneers" and Model of Lomonosov Moscow University — A909

1953, Dec. 22 Litho. *Perf. 12*
1688 A909 40k dk sl grn, dk brn & red 5.00 1.75

Arms Type of 1948

1954-57
1689 A682 40k scarlet 1.00 .50
a. 8 ribbon turns on wreath at left ('54) 4.25 1.65

No. 1689 was re-issued in 1954-56 typographed in slightly smaller format: 14½x21¾mm, instead of 14¾x21¾mm, and in a lighter shade. See note after No. 738.
No. 1689 has 7 ribbon turns on left side of wreath.

Aleksandr S. Griboedov, Writer (1795-1829) A910

1954, Mar. 4 **Photo.**
1690 A910 40k dp claret, *cream* 2.25 .75
1691 A910 1r black, *green* 5.75 2.00

Kremlin View — A911

1954, Mar. 7 **Litho.** ***Perf. 12½x12***
1692 A911 40k red & gray 12.00 3.00

1954 elections to the Supreme Soviet.

V. P. Chkalov — A912

1954, Mar. 16 ***Perf. 12***
1693 A912 1r gray, vio bl & dk brown 20.00 10.00

50th anniversary of the birth of Valeri P. Chkalov (1904-1938), airplane pilot.

Lenin — A913

Lenin at Smolny A914

Designs: No. 1696, Lenin's home (later museum), Ulyanovsk. No. 1697, Lenin addressing workers. No. 1698, Lenin among students, University of Kazan.

1954, Apr. 16 **Photo.**
1694 A913 40k multicolored 6.00 2.00

Size: 38x27½mm

1695 A914 40k multicolored 6.00 2.00
1696 A914 40k multicolored 6.00 2.00

Size: 48x35mm

1697 A914 40k multicolored 6.00 2.00
1698 A914 40k multicolored 6.00 2.00
Nos. 1694-1698 (5) 30.00 10.00

30th anniversary of the death of Lenin.
For overprint see No. 2060.

Joseph V. Stalin — A915

1954, Apr. 30 **Unwmk.** ***Perf. 12***
1699 A915 40k dark brown 15.00 2.00

First anniversary of the death of Stalin.

Supreme Soviet Buildings in Kiev and Moscow A916

T. G. Shevchenko Statue, Kharkov — A917

Designs: No. 1701, University building, Kiev. No. 1702, Opera, Kiev. No. 1703, Ukranian Academy of Science. No. 1705, Bogdan Chmielnicki statue, Kiev. No. 1706 Flags of Soviet Russia and Ukraine. No. 1707, T. G. Shevchenko statue, Kanev. No. 1708, Chmielnicki proclaming reunion of Ukraine and Russia, 1654.

1954, May 10 **Litho.**

Size: 37½x26mm, 26x37½mm

1700 A916 40k red brn, sal, cream & black 2.50 .25
1701 A916 40k ultra, vio bl & brn 2.50 .25
1702 A916 40k red brn, buff, blue brown 2.50 .25
1703 A916 40k org brn, cream & grn 2.50 .25
1704 A917 40k rose red, blk, yel & brown 2.25 .25
1705 A917 60k multicolored 3.00 .30
1706 A917 1r multicolored 5.00 .50

Size: 42x28mm

1707 A916 1r multicolored 3.50 .75

Size: 45x29½mm

1708 A916 1r multicolored, *pink* 5.00 .75

No. 1341 Overprinted in Carmine

1709 A517 2r green 9.00 1.75
Nos. 1700-1709 (10) 37.75 5.30

300th anniversary of the union between the Ukraine and Russia.

Sailboat Race A918

Basketball A919

No. 1711, Hurdle race. No. 1712, Swimmers. No. 1713, Cyclists. No. 1714, Track. No. 1715, Skier. No. 1716, Mountain climbing.

1954, May 29

Frames in Orange Brown

1710 A918 40k blue & black 2.25 .35
1711 A918 40k vio gray & blk 2.25 .35
1712 A918 40k dk blue & black 2.25 .35
1713 A918 40k dk brn & buff 2.25 .35
1714 A918 40k black brn & buff 2.25 .35
1715 A918 1r blue & black 5.50 .95
1716 A918 1r blue & black 5.50 .90
1717 A919 1r dk brn & brn 7.50 1.50
Nos. 1710-1717 (8) 29.75 5.10

For overprint see No. 2170.

Cattle A920

No. 1719, Potato planting and cultivation. No. 1720, Kolkhoz hydroelectric station.

1954, June 8
1718 A920 40k brn, cream, ind & blue gray 3.75 1.00
1719 A920 40k gray grn, buff & brown 3.75 1.00
1720 A920 40k blk, bl grn & vio bl 3.75 1.00
Nos. 1718-1720 (3) 11.25 3.00

Anton P. Chekhov, Writer, 50th Death Anniv. — A921

1954, July 15
1721 A921 40k green & black brn 5.00 .50

F. A. Bredichin, V. J. Struve, A. A. Belopolski and Observatory — A922

1954, July 26
1722 A922 40k vio bl, blk & blue 10.00 1.00

Restoration of Pulkov Observatory.

Mikhail I. Glinka, Composer, 150th Birth Anniv. — A923

Pushkin and Zhukovsky Visiting Glinka A924

1954, July 26
1723 A923 40k dp cl, pink & blk brown 6.00 1.00
1724 A924 60k multicolored 9.00 2.00

Nikolai A. Ostrovsky (1904-36), Blind Writer — A925

1954, Sept. 29 **Photo.** ***Perf. 12½x12***
1725 A925 40k brn, dark red & yel 7.00 1.00

Monument to Sunken Ships — A926

Defenders of Sevastopol — A927

Design: 1r, Admiral P. S. Nakhimov.

1954, Oct. 17 ***Perf. 12½***
1726 A926 40k blue grn, blk & ol brown 4.00 1.10
1727 A927 60k org brn, blk & brn 5.50 1.60
1728 A926 1r brn, blk & ol green 10.50 2.25
Nos. 1726-1728 (3) 20.00 4.95

Centenary of the defense of Sevastopol during the Crimean War.

Sculpture at Exhibition Entrance — A928

Agriculture Pavilion — A929

Cattle Pavilion A929a

Designs: No. 1732, Machinery pavilion. No. 1733, Main entrance. No. 1734, Main pavilion.

Perf. 12½, 12½x12, 12x12½

1954, Nov. 5 Litho.

Size: 26x37mm

1729 A928 40k multicolored 2.00 .50

Size: 40x29mm

1730 A929 40k multicolored 2.00 .50
1731 A929a 40k multicolored 2.00 .50
1732 A929 40k multicolored 2.00 .50

Size: 40½x33mm

1733 A929 1r multicolored 6.00 2.00

Size: 28½x40½mm

1734 A928 1r multicolored 6.00 2.00
Nos. 1729-1734 (6) 20.00 6.00

1954 Agricultural Exhibition.

Marx, Engels, Lenin and Stalin — A930

1954, Nov. 6 Photo. *Perf. 12½x12*

1735 A930 1r dk brn, pale org & red 6.00 2.50

37th anniversary of October Revolution.

Kazan University Building A931

1954, Nov. 11 *Perf. 12x12½*

1736 A931 40k deep blue 1.75 .50
1737 A931 60k claret 3.25 1.00

Founding of Kazan University, 150th anniv.

Salome Neris A932

1954, Nov. 17 *Perf. 12½x12*

1738 A932 40k red org & ol gray 4.00 1.50

50th anniversary of the birth of Salome Neris (1904-1945), Lithuanian poet.

Vegetables and Garden A933

Cultivating Flax — A934

Designs: No. 1741, Tractor plowing field. No. 1742, Loading ensilage.

1954, Dec. 12 Litho. *Perf. 12x12½*

1739 A933 40k multicolored 1.60 .50
1740 A934 40k multicolored 1.60 .50
1741 A933 40k multicolored 1.60 .50
1742 A934 60k multicolored 7.25 .50
Nos. 1739-1742 (4) 12.05 2.00

Joseph Stalin, 75th Birth Anniv. — A935

1954, Dec. 21 Engr. *Perf. 12½x12*

1743 A935 40k rose brown 1.50 .50
1744 A935 1r dark blue 3.50 .60

Anton G. Rubinstein (1829-94), Composer A936

1954, Dec. 30 Photo.

1745 A936 40k claret, gray & blk 4.00 1.00

Vsevolod M. Garshin (1855-1888), Writer — A937

Lithographed and Photogravure

1955, Mar. 2 Unwmk. *Perf. 12*

1746 A937 40k buff, blk brn & green 2.00 .50

K. A. Savitsky and Painting A938

1955, Mar. 21 Photo.

1747 A938 40k multicolored 3.00 .30
a. Sheet of 4, black inscription 35.00 35.00
b. As "a," red brown inscription 35.00 35.00

K. A. Savitsky (1844-1905), painter. Size: Nos. 1747a, 1747b, 152x108mm.

Globe and Clasped Hands — A939

1955, Apr. 9 Litho.

1748 A939 40k multicolored 2.00 .50

International Conference of Public Service Unions, Vienna, April 1955.

Poets Pushkin and Mickiewicz — A940

Brothers in Arms Monument, Warsaw — A941

Palace of Culture and Science, Warsaw A942

Copernicus, Painting by Jan Matejko (in Medallion) — A943

Unwmk.

1955, Apr. 22 Photo. *Perf. 12*

1749 A940 40k chalky blue, vio & black 2.50 .35
1750 A941 40k violet black 2.50 .35
1751 A942 1r brt red & gray black 5.50 1.25
1752 A943 1r multicolored 5.50 1.25
Nos. 1749-1752 (4) 16.00 3.20

Polish-USSR treaty of friendship, 10th anniv.

Lenin at Shushinskoe — A944

Lenin at Secret Printing House — A945

Design: 1r, Lenin and Krupskaya with peasants at Gorki, 1921.

1955, Apr. 22

Frame and Inscription in Dark Red

1753 A944 60k multicolored 1.50 .50
1754 A944 1r multicolored 3.00 .75
1755 A945 1r multicolored 3.00 .75
Nos. 1753-1755 (3) 7.50 2.00

85th anniversary of the birth of Lenin.

Friedrich von Schiller — A946

1955, May 10

1756 A946 40k chocolate 2.00 .50

150th anniversary of the death of Friedrich von Schiller, German poet.

A. G. Venezianov and "Spring on the Land" — A947

1955, June 21 Photo.

1757 A947 1r multicolored 5.00 .50
a. Souvenir sheet of 4 45.00 25.00

Venezianov, painter, 175th birth anniv.

Anatoli K. Liadov (1855-1914), Composer — A948

1955, July 5 Litho.

1758 A948 40k red brn, blk & lt brn 2.50 .50

Aleksandr Popov — A949

1955, Nov. 5

Portraits Multicolored

1759 A949 40k light ultra 1.75 .50
1760 A949 1r gray brown 3.25 .50

60th anniv. of the construction of a coherer for detecting Hertzian electromagnetic waves by A. S. Popov, radio pioneer.

Lenin — A950

Storming the Winter Palace — A951

Design: 1r, Lenin addressing the people.

1955, Nov. 6

1761 A950 40k multicolored 3.00 1.00
1762 A951 40k multicolored 3.00 1.00
1763 A951 1r multicolored 7.50 2.00
Nos. 1761-1763 (3) 13.50 4.00

38th anniversary of October Revolution.

Apartment Houses, Magnitogorsk — A952

1955, Nov. 29

1764 A952 40k multicolored 3.00 1.00

25th anniversary of the founding of the industrial center, Magnitogorsk.

Arctic Observation Post — A953

Design: 1r, Scientist at observation post.

1955, Nov. 29 ***Perf. 12½x12***

1765 A953 40k multicolored 6.00 2.00
1766 A953 60k multicolored 6.00 2.00
1767 A953 1r multicolored 6.00 2.00
a. Souvenir sheet of 4 ('58) 35.00 50.00
Nos. 1765-1767 (3) 18.00 6.00

Publicizing the Soviet scientific drifting stations at the North Pole.

In 1962, No. 1767a was overprinted in red "1962" on each stamp and, in the lower sheet margin, a three-line Russian inscription meaning "25 years from the beginning of the work of "NP-1" station."

Sheet value, $75 unused, $100 canceled.

Fedor Ivanovich Shubin (1740-1805), Sculptor — A954

1955, Dec. 22 ***Perf. 12***

1768 A954 40k green & multi 1.00 .35
1769 A954 1r brown & multi 1.00 .35

Federal Socialist Republic Pavilion (R.S.F.S.R.) — A955

ПАВИЛЬОН ТАДЖИКСКОЙ ССР

No. 1771

ПАВИЛЬОН БЕЛОРУССКОЙ ССР

No. 1772

ПАВИЛЬОН АЗЕРБАЙДЖАНСКОЙ ССР

No. 1773

ПАВИЛЬОН ГРУЗИНСКОЙ ССР

No. 1774

ПАВИЛЬОН АРМЯНСКОЙ ССР

No. 1775

ПАВИЛЬОН ТУРКМЕНСКОЙ ССР

No. 1776

ПАВИЛЬОН УЗБЕКСКОЙ ССР

No. 1777

ПАВИЛЬОН УКРАИНСКОЙ ССР

No. 1778

ПАВИЛЬОН КАЗАХСКОЙ ССР

No. 1779

ПАВИЛЬОН КИРГИЗСКОЙ ССР

No. 1780

ПАВИЛЬОН КАРЕЛО-ФИНСКОЙ ССР

No. 1781

ПАВИЛЬОН МОЛДАВСКОЙ ССР

No. 1782

ПАВИЛЬОН ЭСТОНСКОЙ ССР

No. 1783

ПАВИЛЬОН ЛАТВИЙСКОЙ ССР

No. 1784

ПАВИЛЬОН ЛИТОВСКОЙ ССР

No. 1785

Designs: Pavilions.

1955 Litho. Unwmk.

Centers in Natural Colors; Frames in Blue Green and Olive

1770 A955 40k shown 1.00 .50
a. Sheet of 4 15.00 15.00
1771 A955 40k Tadzhik 1.00 .50
1772 A955 40k Byelorussian 1.00 .50
a. Sheet of 4 15.00 15.00
1773 A955 40k Azerbaijan 1.00 .50
1774 A955 40k Georgian 1.00 .50
1775 A955 40k Armenian 1.00 .50
1776 A955 40k Turkmen 1.00 .50
1777 A955 40k Uzbek 1.00 .50
1778 A955 40k Ukrainian 1.00 .50
a. Sheet of 4 15.00 15.00
1779 A955 40k Kazakh 1.00 .50
1780 A955 40k Kirghiz 1.00 .50
1781 A955 40k Karelo-Finnish 1.00 .50
1782 A955 40k Moldavian 1.00 .50
1783 A955 40k Estonian 1.00 .50
1784 A955 40k Latvian 1.00 .50
1785 A955 40k Lithuanian 1.00 .50
Nos. 1770-1785 (16) 16.00 8.00

All-Union Agricultural Fair.

Nos. 1773-1785 were printed in sheets containing various stamps, providing a variety of horizontal se-tenant pairs and strips. Value, $50 per sheet.

Lomonosov Moscow State University, 200th Anniv. — A956

Design: 1r, New University buildings.

1955, June 9 ***Perf. 12***

1786 A956 40k multicolored 2.00 .25
a. Sheet of 4 ('56) 10.00 *10.00*
1787 A956 1r multicolored 4.00 .50
a. Sheet of 4 ('56) 20.00 *20.00*

Vladimir V. Mayakovsky — A957

1955, May 31

1788 A957 40k multicolored 2.00 .50

Mayakovsky, poet, 25th death anniv.

Race Horse — A958

Trotter A959

1956, Jan. 9

1789 A958 40k dark brown 3.00 .40
1790 A958 60k Prus grn & blue green 4.50 .60
1791 A959 1r dull pur & blue vio 7.50 1.00
Nos. 1789-1791 (3) 15.00 2.00

International Horse Races, Moscow, Aug. 14-Sept. 4, 1955.

Alexei N. Krylov (1863-1945), Mathematician, Naval Architect — A960

1956, Jan. 9

1792 A960 40k gray, brown & black 2.00 .50

Symbol of Spartacist Games, Stadium and Factories — A961

1956, Jan. 18

1793 A961 1r red vio & lt grn 2.00 .50

5th All-Union Spartacist Games of Soviet Trade Union sport clubs, Moscow, Aug. 12-18, 1955.

Atomic Power Station A962

Design: 60k, Atomic Reactor.

1956, Jan. 31

1794 A962 25k multicolored 1.25 .40
1795 A962 60k multicolored 3.25 1.00
1796 A962 1r multicolored 5.50 1.75
Nos. 1794-1796 (3) 10.00 3.15

Establishment of the first Atomic Power Station of the USSR Academy of Science. Inscribed in Russian: "Atomic Energy in the service of the people."

Statue of Lenin, Kremlin and Flags A963

1956, Feb.

1797 A963 40k multicolored 5.00 .50
1798 A963 1r ol, buff & red org 7.00 1.50

20th Congress of the Communist Party of the Soviet Union.

Khachatur Abovian, Armenian Writer, 150th Birth Anniv. — A964

1956, Feb. 25 Unwmk. ***Perf. 12***

1799 A964 40k black brn, *bluish* 5.00 .50

Workers with Red Flag — A965

1956, Mar. 14

1800 A965 40k multicolored 6.00 .75

Revolution of 1905, 50th anniversary.

Nikolai A. Kasatkin — A966

1956, Apr. 30

1801 A966 40k carmine lake 2.00 .50

Kasatkin (1859-1930), painter.

"On the Oka River" A967

1956, Apr. 30

Center Multicolored

1802 A967 40k bister & black 5.00 .40
1803 A967 1r ultra & black 7.00 .60

A. E. Arkhipov, painter.

I. P. Kulibin, Inventor, 220th Birth Anniv. — A968

1956, May 12

1804 A968 40k multicolored 2.00 .25

Vassili Grigorievitch Perov (1833-82), Painter — A969

"Birdcatchers" — A970

Painting: No. 1807, "Hunters at Rest."

1956, May 12

Multicolored Centers

1805 A969 40k green 3.00 .40
1806 A970 1r brown 6.00 .80
1807 A970 1r orange brown 6.00 .80
Nos. 1805-1807 (3) 15.00 2.00

Ural Pavilion A971

«ПАВИЛЬОН ТАТАРСКОЙ АССР»

No. 1809

ПАВИЛЬОН «ПОВОЛЖЬЕ»

No. 1810

ПАВИЛЬОН ЦЕНТРАЛЬНЫХ ЧЕРНОЗЕМНЫХ ОБЛАСТЕЙ

No. 1811

ПАВИЛЬОН СЕВЕРО-ВОСТОЧНЫХ ОБЛАСТЕЙ

No. 1812

ПАВИЛЬОН СЕВЕРНОГО КАВКАЗА

No. 1813

ПАВИЛЬОН БАШКИРСКОЙ АССР

No. 1814

ПАВИЛЬОН ДАЛЬНЕГО ВОСТОКА

No. 1815

ПАВИЛЬОН ЦЕНТРАЛЬНЫХ ОБЛАСТЕЙ

No. 1816

ПАВИЛЬОН ЮНЫХ НАТУРАЛИСТОВ

No. 1817

ПАВИЛЬОН «СИБИРЬ»

No. 1818

ПАВИЛЬОН «ЛЕНИНГРАД • СЕВЕРО-ЗАПАД»

No. 1819

ПАВИЛЬОН МОСКОВСКОЙ, ТУЛЬСКОЙ, КАЛУЖСКОЙ, РЯЗАНСКОЙ И БРЯНСКОЙ ОБЛАСТЕЙ

No. 1820

Pavilions: No. 1809, Tatar Republic. No. 1810, Volga District. No. 1811, Central Black Earth Area. No. 1812, Northeastern District. No. 1813, Northern Caucasus. No. 1814, Bashkir Republic. No. 1815, Far East. No. 1816, Central Asia. No. 1817, Young Naturalists. No. 1818, Siberia. No. 1819, Leningrad and Northwestern District. No. 1820, Moscow, Tula, Kaluga, Ryazan and Bryansk Districts.

1956, Apr. 25

Multicolored Centers

1808 A971 1r yel green & pale yel 3.00 .50
1809 A971 1r blue grn & pale yel 3.00 .50
1810 A971 1r dk blue grn & pale yel 3.00 .50
1811 A971 1r dk bl grn & yel grn 3.00 .50
1812 A971 1r dk blue grn & buff 3.00 .50
1813 A971 1r ol gray & pale yel 3.00 .50
1814 A971 1r olive & yellow 3.00 .50
1815 A971 1r olive grn & lemon 3.00 .50
1816 A971 1r olive brn & lemon 3.00 .50
1817 A971 1r olive brn & lemon 3.00 .50
1818 A971 1r brown & yellow 3.00 .50
1819 A971 1r redsh brown & yel 3.00 .50
1820 A971 1r dk red brn & yel 3.00 .50
Nos. 1808-1820 (13) 39.00 6.50

All-Union Agricultural Fair, Moscow.

Six of the Pavilion set were printed se-tenant in one sheet of 30 (6x5), the strip containing Nos. 1809, 1816, 1817, 1813, 1818 and 1810 in that order. Two others, Nos. 1819-1820, were printed se-tenant in one sheet of 35. Value, $50 per sheet.

Lenin — A972

1956, May 25

1821 A972 40k lilac & multi 6.00 1.00

86th anniversary of the birth of Lenin.

Lobachevski A973

1956, June 4

1822 A973 40k black brown 2.00 .25

Nikolai Ivanovich Lobachevski (1793-1856), mathematician.

Nurse and Textile Factory A974

No. 1824, First aid instruction.

1956, June 4 **Unwmk.**

1823 A974 40k lt ol grn, grnsh bl & red 3.00 .25
1824 A974 40k red brn, lt bl & red 3.00 .25

Red Cross and Red Crescent. No. 1823 measures 37x25mm; No. 1824, 40x28mm.

V. K. Arseniev (1872-1930), Explorer and Writer — A975

1956, June 15 **Litho.** ***Perf. 12***

1825 A975 40k violet, black & rose 3.00 .50

I. M. Sechenov (1829-1905), Physiologist A976

1956, June 15

1826 A976 40k multicolored 2.00 .50

A. K. Savrasov, Painter — A977

1956, June 22

1827 A977 1r dull yel & brown 3.00 .50

I. V. Michurin, Scientist, Birth Centenary A978

Design: 60k, I. V. Michurin with Pioneers.

1956, June 22

Center Multicolored

1828 A978 25k dark brown .55 .25
1829 A978 60k green & lt blue 1.10 .40
1830 A978 1r light blue 2.25 .55
Nos. 1828-1830 (3) 3.90 1.20

Nos. 1828 and 1830 measure 32x25mm. No. 1829 measures 47x26mm.

Nadezhda K. Krupskaya A979

1956, June 28

1831 A979 40k brn, lt blue & pale brown 8.00 2.00

Krupskaya (1869-1939), teacher and wife of Lenin.

See Nos. 1862, 1886, 1983, 2028.

S. M. Kirov (1886-1934), Revolutionary A980

1956, June 28

1832 A980 40k red, buff & brown 2.00 .50

Nikolai S. Leskov (1831-1895), Novelist — A981

1956, July 10

1833 A981 40k olive bister & brn 1.50 .25
1834 A981 1r green & dk brown 3.50 .75

Aleksandr A. Blok (1880-1921), Poet — A982

1956, July 10

1835 A982 40k olive & brn, *cream* 2.00 .50

Farm Machinery Factory A983

1956, July 23 ***Perf. 12½x12***

1836 A983 40k multicolored 2.00 .50

Rostov Farm Machinery Works, 25th anniv.

A984

1956, July 23 **Unwmk.**

1837 A984 40k brown & rose vio 5.00 .50

G. N. Fedotova (1846-1925), actress. See No. 2026.

P. M. Tretiakov and Art Gallery A985

"The Rooks Have Arrived" by A. K. Savrasov
A986

1956, July 31 *Perf. 12*

1838	A985 40k multicolored	5.00	1.00
1839	A986 40k multicolored	5.00	1.00

Tretiakov Art Gallery, Moscow, cent.

Relay Race
A987

Volleyball — A988

#1842, Rowing. #1843, Swimming. #1844, Medal with heads of man and woman. #1845, Tennis. #1846, Soccer. #1847, Fencing. #1848, Bicycle race. #1849, Stadium and flag. #1850, Diving. #1851, Boxing. #1852, Gymnast. 1r, Basketball.

1956, Aug. 5

1840	A987 10k carmine rose	.40	.25
1841	A988 25k dk orange brn	.60	.25
1842	A988 25k brt grnsh blue	.60	.25
1843	A988 25k grn, blue & lt brn	.60	.25
1844	A988 40k org, pink, bis & yellow	1.25	.25
1845	A988 40k orange brown	1.25	.25
1846	A987 40k brt yel grn & dk brown	1.25	.25
1847	A987 40k grn, brt grn & dk brn, *grnsh*	1.25	.25
1848	A987 40k blue green	1.25	.25
1849	A988 40k brt yel grn & red	1.25	.25
1850	A988 40k greenish blue	1.25	.25
1851	A988 60k violet	1.75	.25
1852	A987 60k brt violet	1.75	.25
1853	A987 1r red brown	2.50	.40
	Nos. 1840-1853 (14)	16.95	3.65

All-Union Spartacist Games, Moscow, Aug. 5-16.

Parachute Landing — A989

1956, Aug. 5 *Perf. 12x12½*

1854	A989 40k multicolored	2.00	1.00

Third World Parachute Championships, Moscow, July 1956.

Building under Construction
A990

Builders' Day: 60k, Building a factory. 1r, Building a dam.

1956 **Photo.** *Perf. 12*

1855	A990 40k deep orange	1.50	.50
1856	A990 60k brown carmine	1.00	.50
1857	A990 1r intense blue	2.50	.50
	Nos. 1855-1857 (3)	5.00	1.50

Ivan Franko — A991

1956, Aug. 27

1858	A991 40k deep claret	1.25	.25
1859	A991 1r bright blue	1.75	.30

Franko, writer (1856-1916).

Makhmud Aivazov — A992

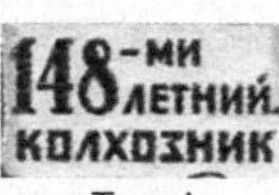

Type I Type II

Two types:
I — Three lines in panel with "148."
II — Two lines in panel with "148."

1956, Aug. 27

1860	A992 40k emerald (II)	5.00	3.00
a.	Type I	21.00	18.00

148th birthday of Russia's oldest man, an Azerbaijan collective farmer.

Robert Burns, Scottish Poet, 160th Death Anniv. — A993

1956-57 **Photo.**

1861	A993 40k yellow brown	6.00	2.00

Engr.

1861A	A993 40k lt ultra & brn ('57)	4.00	1.00

For overprint see No. 2174.

Portrait Type of 1956

Lesya Ukrainka (1871-1913), Ukrainian writer.

1956, Aug. 27 **Litho.**

1862	A979 40k olive, blk & brown	4.00	1.00

Statue of Nestor — A995

1956, Sept. 22 *Perf. 12x12½*

1863	A995 40k multicolored	1.50	.25
1864	A995 1r multicolored	3.50	.50

900th anniversary of the birth of Nestor, first Russian historian.

Aleksandr Andreevich Ivanov (1806-58), Painter — A996

1956, Sept. 22 **Unwmk.**

1865	A996 40k gray & brown	2.00	.25

I. E. Repin and "Volga River Boatmen" — A997

"Cossacks Writing a Letter to the Turkish Sultan" — A998

1956, Aug. 21
Multicolored Centers

1866	A997 40k org brn & black	7.00	1.00
1867	A998 1r chalky blue & blk	13.00	3.00

Ilya E. Repin (1844-1930), painter.

Chicken Farm
A999

Designs: No. 1869, Harvest. 25k, Harvesting corn. No. 1871, Women in corn field. No. 1872, Farm buildings. No. 1873, Cattle. No. 1874, Farm workers, inscriptions and blast furnaces.

1956, Oct. 7

1868	A999 10k multicolored	.50	.25
1869	A999 10k multicolored	.50	.25
1870	A999 25k multicolored	1.00	.25
1871	A999 40k multicolored	2.25	.50
1872	A999 40k multicolored	2.25	.50
1873	A999 40k multicolored	2.25	.50
1874	A999 40k multicolored	2.25	.50
	Nos. 1868-1874 (7)	11.00	2.75

#1868, 1872, 1873 measure 37x25½mm; #1869-1871 37x27½mm; #1874 37x21mm.

Benjamin Franklin — A1000

G. B Shaw
A1000a

Dostoevski
A1000b

Portraits: #1876 Sesshu (Toyo Oda). #1877, Rembrandt. #1879, Mozart. #1880, Heinrich Heine. #1882, Ibsen. #1883, Pierre Curie.

1956, Oct. 17 **Photo.**

Size: 25x37mm

1875	A1000 40k copper brn	3.75	1.60
1876	A1000 40k brt orange	3.75	1.60
1877	A1000 40k black	3.75	1.60
1878	A1000a 40k black	3.75	1.60

Size: 21x32mm

1879	A1000 40k grnsh blue	3.75	1.60
1880	A1000 40k violet	3.75	1.60
1881	A1000b 40k green	3.75	1.60
1882	A1000 40k brown	3.75	1.60
1883	A1000 40k brt green	3.75	1.60
	Nos. 1875-1883 (9)	33.75	14.40

Great personalities of the world.

Antarctic Bases — A1001

1956, Oct. 22 **Litho.** *Perf. 12x12½*

1884	A1001 40k slate, grnsh bl & red	2.00	.50

Soviet Scientific Antarctic Expedition.

G. I. Kotovsky (1881-1925), Military Commander A1002

1956, Oct. 30

1885	A1002 40k magenta	2.50	1.00

Portrait Type of 1956

Portrait: Julia A. Zemaite (1845-1921), Lithuanian novelist.

1956, Oct. 30 *Perf. 12*

1886	A979 40k lt ol green & brn	3.00	1.00

Fedor A. Bredichin (1831-1904), Astronomer — A1004

1956, Oct. 30

1887	A1004 40k sepia & ultra	3.00	.75

Field Marshal Count Aleksandr V. Suvorov (1730-1800)
A1005

1956, Nov. 17 **Engr.**

1888 A1005 40k org & maroon .75 .25
1889 A1005 1r ol & dk red brn 1.75 .30
1890 A1005 3r lt red brn & black 2.50 .75
Nos. 1888-1890 (3) 5.00 1.30

Shatura Power Station
A1006

1956 **Litho.** ***Perf. 12½x12***

1891 A1006 40k multicolored 6.00 .50

30th anniv. of the Shatura power station.

Kryakutni's Balloon, 1731 — A1007

1956, Nov. 17

1892 A1007 40k lt brn, sepia & yel 5.00 .50

225th anniv. of the 1st balloon ascension of the Russian inventor, Kryakutni.

A1008

1956, Dec. 3 **Unwmk.** ***Perf. 12***

1893 A1008 40k ultra & brown 1.00 .50

Yuli M. Shokalski (1856-1940), oceanographer and geodesist.

Apollinari M. Vasnetsov and "Winter Scene"
A1009

1956, Dec. 30

1894 A1009 40k multicolored 2.00 .50

Vasnetsov (1856-1933), painter.

Indian Building and Books — A1010

1956, Dec. 26

1895 A1010 40k deep carmine 2.00 .50

Kalidasa, 5th century Indian poet.

Ivan Franko, Ukrainian Writer — A1011

1956, Dec. 26 **Engr.**

1896 A1011 40k dk slate green 2.00 .50

See Nos. 1858-1859.

Leo N. Tolstoy
A1012

Portraits of Writers: No. 1898, Mikhail V. Lomonosov. No. 1899, Aleksander S. Pushkin. No. 1900, Maxim Gorki. No. 1901, Shota Rustaveli. No. 1902, Vissarion G. Belinski. No. 1903, Mikhail Y. Lermontov, poet, and Darjal Ravine in Caucasus.

1956-57 **Litho.** ***Perf. 12½x12***

Size: 37½x27½mm

1897 A1012 40k brt grnsh blue & brown 2.10 .25
1898 A1012 40k dk red, ol & brn olive 2.10 .25

Size: 35½x25½mm

1899 A1012 40k dk gray blue & brown 2.10 .25
1900 A1012 40k black & brn car 2.10 .25
1901 A1012 40k ol, brn & ol gray 2.10 .25
1902 A1012 40k bis, dl vio & brn ('57) 2.10 .25
1903 A1012 40k indigo & ol ('57) 2.10 .25
Nos. 1897-1903 (7) 14.70 1.75

Famous Russian writers.
See Nos. 1960-1962, 2031, 2112.

Fedor G. Volkov and Theater
A1013

1956, Dec. 31 **Unwmk.**

1904 A1013 40k mag, gray & yel 1.00 .30

200th anniversary of the founding of the St. Petersburg State Theater.

Vitus Bering and Map of Bering Strait
A1016

1957, Feb. 6

1905 A1016 40k brown & blue 2.00 .50

275th anniversary of the birth of Vitus Bering, Danish navigator and explorer.

Dmitri I. Mendeleev
A1017

1957, Feb. 6 ***Perf. 12x12½***

1906 A1017 40k gray & gray brn 3.00 1.00

D. I. Mendeleev (1834-1907), chemist.

Mikhail I. Glinka — A1018

Design: 1r, Scene from opera Ivan Susanin.

1957, Feb. 23 ***Perf. 12***

1907 A1018 40k dk red, buff & sep 1.50 .30
1908 A1018 1r multicolored 2.50 .50

Mikhail I. Glinka (1804-1857), composer.

All-Union Festival of Soviet Youth, Moscow — A1019

1957, Feb. 23

1909 A1019 40k dk blue, red & ocher .75 .35

23rd Ice Hockey World Championship, Moscow — A1020

Designs: 25k, Emblem. 40k, Player. 60k, Goalkeeper.

1957, Feb. 24 **Photo.**

1910 A1020 25k deep violet 1.00 .25
1911 A1020 40k bright blue 1.00 .25
1912 A1020 60k emerald 1.00 .35
Nos. 1910-1912 (3) 3.00 .85

Dove and Festival Emblem — A1021

1957 **Litho.** ***Perf. 12***

1913 A1021 40k multicolored .40 .25
1914 A1021 60k multicolored .60 .25

6th World Youth Festival, Moscow. Exist imperf. Value, each $30.

Assembly Line — A1022

1957, Mar. 15

1915 A1022 40k Prus grn & dp org 3.00 .75

Moscow Machine Works centenary.

Black Grouse
A1023

Axis Deer — A1024

No. 1916, Gray partridge. No. 1918, Polar bear. No. 1920, Bison. No. 1921, Mallard. No. 1922, European elk. No. 1923, Sable.

1957, Mar. 28

Center in Natural Colors

1916 A1024 10k yel brown .85 .35
1917 A1023 15k brown .85 .35
1918 A1023 15k slate blue .90 .35
1919 A1024 20k red orange .90 .35
1920 A1023 30k ultra .90 .35
1921 A1023 30k dk olive grn .90 .35
1922 A1023 40k dk olive grn 2.25 .40
1923 A1024 40k violet blue 2.25 .40
Nos. 1916-1923 (8) 9.80 2.90

See Nos. 2213-2219, 2429-2431.

Wooden Products, Hohloma
A1025

National Handicrafts: No. 1925, Lace maker, Vologda. No. 1926, Bone carver, North Russia. No. 1927, Woodcarver, Moscow area. No. 1928, Rug weaver, Turkmenistan. No. 1929, Painting.

1957-58 **Unwmk.**

1924 A1025 40k red org, yel & black 3.00 .80
1925 A1025 40k brt car, yel & brown 3.00 .80
1926 A1025 40k ultra, buff & gray 3.00 .80
1927 A1025 40k brn, pale yel & hn brown 3.00 .80
1928 A1025 40k buff, brn, bl & org ('58) 1.50 .90
1929 A1025 40k multicolored ('58) 1.50 .90
Nos. 1924-1929 (6) 15.00 5.00

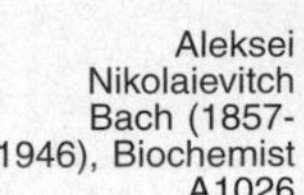

Aleksei Nikolaievitch Bach (1857-1946), Biochemist A1026

1957, Apr. 6 Litho. *Perf. 12*
1930 A1026 40k ultra, brn & buff 5.00 .30

Georgi Valentinovich Plekhanov (1856-1918), Political Philosopher A1027

1957, Apr. 6 Engr.
1931 A1027 40k dull purple .60 .30

Leonhard Euler A1028

1957, Apr. 17 Litho.
1932 A1028 40k lilac & gray 2.00 .50

Leonhard Euler (1707-1783), Swiss mathematician and physicist.

Lenin, 87th Birth Anniv. — A1029

Designs: No. 1934, Lenin talking to soldier and sailor. No. 1935, Lenin participating in a subbotnik, a voluntary neighborhood clean-up.

1957, Apr. 22
Multicolored Centers
1933 A1029 40k magenta & bis 3.00 1.00
1934 A1029 40k magenta & bis 3.00 1.00
1935 A1029 40k magenta & bis 3.00 1.00
Nos. 1933-1935 (3) 9.00 3.00

Youths of All Races Carrying Festival Banner — A1030

Design: 20k, Sculptor with motherhood statue. 40k, Young couples dancing. 1r, Festival banner and fireworks over Moscow University.

1957, May 27 *Perf. 12x12½*
1936 A1030 10k emer, pur & yel .25 .25
1937 A1030 20k multicolored .60 .25
1938 A1030 25k emer, pur & yel .90 .25
1939 A1030 40k rose, bl grn & bis brn .90 .25
1940 A1030 1r multicolored 1.40 .25
Nos. 1936-1940 (5) 4.05 1.25

6th World Youth Festival in Moscow. The 10k, 20k, and 1r exist imperf. Value: 10k, 20k, each $20; 1r $200.

Marine Museum Place and Neva — A1031

Designs: No. 1942, Lenin monument. No. 1943, Nevski Prospect and Admiralty.

1957, May 27 Photo. *Perf. 12*
1941 A1031 40k blue green 1.50 .40
1942 A1031 40k reddish brown 1.50 .40
1943 A1031 40k bluish violet 1.50 .40
a. Souv. sheet of 3, red border 35.00 20.00
Nos. 1941-1943 (3) 4.50 1.20

250th anniversary of Leningrad.

No. 1943a contains imperf. stamps similar to #1941, 1680 (in reddish brown), 1943, and is for 40th anniv. of the October Revolution. Issued Nov. 7, 1957. A similar sheet is listed as No. 2002a.

Type of 1953 Overprinted in Red

No. 1944

No. 1945

Designs: No. 1944, Peter I Statue, Decembrists' Square. No. 1945, Smolny Institute.

1957, May 27 *Perf. 12½x12*
1944 A908 1r black brn, *greenish* 1.50 .25
1945 A908 1r green, *pink* 1.50 .25

250th anniversary of Leningrad.
The overprint is in one line on No. 1945.

Henry Fielding — A1032

1957, June 20 Litho.
1946 A1032 40k multicolored 1.00 .50

Fielding (1707-54), English playwright, novelist.

William Harvey — A1033

1957, May 20 Photo.
1947 A1033 40k brown 1.00 .50

300th anniversary of the death of the English physician William Harvey, discoverer of blood circulation.

M. A. Balakirev (1836-1910), Composer A1034

1957, May 20 Engr.
1948 A1034 40k bluish black 2.00 .50

A. I. Herzen and N. P. Ogarev A1035

1957, May 20 Litho.
1949 A1035 40k blk vio & dk ol gray 1.00 .50

Centenary of newspaper Kolokol (Bell).

Kazakhstan Workers' Medal — A1036

1957, May 20
1950 A1036 40k lt blue, blk & yel 1.00 .35

A1037 A1037a A1037b

Portraits: No. 1951, A. M. Liapunov. No. 1952, V. Mickevicius Kapsukas, writer. No. 1953, G. Bashindchagian, Armenian painter. No. 1954, Yakub Kolas, Byelorussian poet. No. 1955, Carl von Linné, Swedish botanist.

1957 Various Frames Photo.
1951 A1037 40k dull red brown 6.50 1.00
1952 A1037a 40k sepia 5.00 1.00
1953 A1037 40k sepia 5.00 1.00
1954 A1037b 40k gray 5.00 1.00
1955 A1037 40k brown black 5.00 1.00
Nos. 1951-1955 (5) 26.50 5.00

See Nos. 2036-2038, 2059.

Bicyclist A1038

1957, June 20 Litho.
1956 A1038 40k claret & vio blue 1.00 .50

10th Peace Bicycle Race.

Telescope A1039

Designs: No. 1958, Comet and observatory. No. 1959, Rocket leaving earth.

1957, July 4 Size: 25½x37mm
1957 A1039 40k brn, ocher & blue 2.00 .35
1958 A1039 40k indigo, lt bl & yel 2.00 .35

Size: 14½x21mm
1959 A1039 40k blue violet 2.00 .35
Nos. 1957-1959 (3) 6.00 1.05

International Geophysical Year, 1957-58. See Nos. 2089-2091.

Folksinger A1040

1957, May 20
1960 A1040 40k multicolored 5.00 1.00

"The Song of Igor's Army," Russia's oldest literary work.

Taras G. Shevchenko, Ukrainian Poet — A1041

Design: No. 1962, Nikolai G. Chernyshevski, writer and politician.

1957, July 20
1961 A1041 40k grn & dk red brn 1.00 .35
1962 A1041 40k orange brn & grn 1.00 .35

Woman Gymnast — A1043

25k, Wrestling. No. 1965, Stadium. No. 1966, Youths of three races. 60k, Javelin thrower.

1957, July 15 Litho. *Perf. 12*
1963 A1043 20k bluish vio & org brn .60 .25
1964 A1043 25k brt grn & claret .75 .25
1965 A1043 40k Prus bl, ol & red 1.20 .25
1966 A1043 40k crimson & violet 1.20 .25
1967 A1043 60k ultra & brown 1.60 .40
Nos. 1963-1967 (5) 5.35 1.40

Third International Youth Games, Moscow.

Javelin Thrower — A1044

Designs: No. 1969, Sprinter. 25k, Somersault. No. 1971, Boxers. No. 1972, Soccer players, horiz. 60k, Weight lifter.

1957, July 20 Unwmk.
1968 A1044 20k lt ultra & ol blk .45 .25
1969 A1044 20k brt grn, red vio & black .45 .25

1970 A1044 25k orange, ultra & blk .60 .25
1971 A1044 40k rose vio & blk .90 .30
1972 A1044 40k dp pink, bl, buff & black .90 .30
1973 A1044 60k lt violet & brn 1.50 .40
Nos. 1968-1973 (6) 4.80 1.75

Success of Soviet athletes at the 16th Olympic Games, Melbourne.

Kupala — A1045

1957, July 27 **Photo.**
1974 A1045 40k dark gray 10.00 5.00

Yanka Kupala (1882-1942), poet.

Kremlin A1046

Moscow Views: No. 1976, Stadium. No. 1977, University. No. 1978, Bolshoi Theater.

Center in Black

1957, July 27 **Litho.**
1975 A1046 40k dull red brown .35 .25
1976 A1046 40k brown violet .35 .25
1977 A1046 1r red 1.10 .25
1978 A1046 1r brt violet blue 1.10 .25
Nos. 1975-1978 (4) 2.90 1.00

Sixth World Youth Festival, Moscow.

Lenin Library A1047

1957, July 27 **Photo.**
1979 A1047 40k brt grnsh blue .75 .35
a. Souvenir sheet of 2, light blue, imperf. 20.00 *20.00*

Intl. Phil. Exhib., Moscow, July 29-Aug. 11. No. 1979 exists imperf. Value $7.50.

Pierre Jean de Beranger(1780-1857), French Song Writer — A1048

1957, Aug. 9
1980 A1048 40k brt blue green .75 .35

Globe, Dove and Olive Branch — A1049

1957, Aug. 8 **Litho.**
1981 A1049 40k bl, grn & bis brn 2.50 1.00
1982 A1049 1r violet, grn & brn 5.50 2.00

Publicity for world peace.

Portrait Type of 1956

Portrait: 40k, Clara Zetkin (1857-1933), German communist.

1957, Aug. 9
1983 A979 40k gray blue, brn & blk 5.00 1.00

Krenholm Factory, Narva A1050

1957, Sept. 8 **Photo.**
1984 A1050 40k black brown 2.00 .50

Centenary of Krenholm textile factory, Narva, Estonia.

Carrier Pigeon and Globes A1051

1957, Sept. 26 **Unwmk.** ***Perf. 12***
1985 A1051 40k blue .40 .25
1986 A1051 60k lilac .60 .25

Intl. Letter Writing Week, Oct. 6-12.

Vyborzhets Factory, Lenin Statue A1052

1957, Sept. 23 **Litho.**
1987 A1052 40k dark blue 2.00 1.00

Krasny Vyborzhets factory, Leningrad, cent.

Vladimir Vasilievich Stasov (1824-1906), Art and Music Critic — A1053

1957, Sept. 23 **Engr.**
1988 A1053 40k brown .50 .25
1989 A1053 1r bluish black 1.00 .30

Congress Emblem A1054

1957, Oct. 7 **Litho.** ***Perf. 12***
1990 A1054 40k gray blue & blk, *bluish* 1.00 .35

4th International Trade Union Congress, Leipzig, Oct. 4-15.

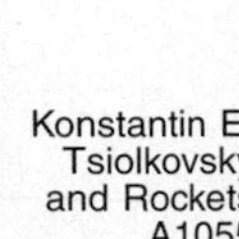

Konstantin E. Tsiolkovsky and Rockets A1055

1957, Oct. 7
1991 A1055 40k dk blue & pale brown 3.50 .50

Tsiolkovsky (1857-1935), rocket and astronautics pioneer.
For overprint see No. 2021.

Sputnik 1 Circling Globe — A1056

1957 **Photo.**
1992 A1056 40k indigo, *bluish* 1.40 .50
1993 A1056 40k bright blue 1.40 .50

Launching of first artificial earth satellite, Oct. 4. Issue dates: No. 1992, Nov. 5; No. 1993, Dec. 28.

Turbine Wheel, Kuibyshev Hydroelectric Station — A1057

1957, Nov. 20 **Litho.**
1994 A1057 40k red brown 1.00 .35

All-Union Industrial Exhib. See #2030.

Meteor — A1058

1957, Nov. 20
1995 A1058 40k multicolored 10.00 1.00

Falling of Sikhote Alinj meteor, 10th anniv.

Lenin — A1059

Design: 60k, Lenin reading Pravda, horiz.

1957, Oct. 30 **Engr.**
1996 A1059 40k blue 1.00 .25
1997 A1059 60k rose red 1.00 .25

40th anniversary of October Revolution.

Students and Moscow University — A1060

Miner and Railroad A1061

No. 1999, Red flag, Lenin. No. 2000, Lenin addressing workers and peasants. No. 2002, Harvester.

Perf. 12½x12, 12x12½, 12½

1957, Oct. 15 **Litho.**
1998 A1060 10k buff, sepia & red .40 .25
1999 A1060 40k buff, red, sep & yel .80 .25
2000 A1060 40k red, black & yel .80 .25
2001 A1061 40k red, yel & green .80 .25
2002 A1061 60k red, ocher & vio brn 1.25 .25
a. Souvenir sheet of 3, #2000-2002, imperf. 50.00 25.00
Nos. 1998-2002 (5) 4.05 1.25

40th anniv. of the October Revolution. A similar sheet is listed as No. 1943a.

Nos. 1998-2002 exist imperf. Value, set $12.50.

Federal Socialist Republic A1062

Uzbek Republic — A1063

Republic: No. 2005, Tadzhik (building, peasant girl). No. 2006, Byelorussia (truck). No. 2007, Azerbaijan (buildings). No. 2008, Georgia (valley, palm, couple). No. 2009, Armenia, (fruit, power line, mountains). No. 2010, Turkmen (couple, lambs). No. 2011, Ukraine (farmers). No. 2012, Kazakh (harvester, combine). No. 2013, Kirghiz (horseback rider, building). No. 2014, Moldavia (automatic sorting machine). No. 2015, Estonia (girl in national costume). No. 2016, Latvia (couple, sea, field). No. 2017, Lithuania (farm, farmer couple).

1957, Oct. 25
2003 A1062 40k multicolored 1.00 .35
2004 A1063 40k multicolored 1.00 .35
2005 A1062 40k multicolored 1.00 .35
2006 A1062 40k multicolored 1.00 .35
2007 A1062 40k multicolored 1.00 .35
2008 A1062 40k multicolored 1.00 .35
2009 A1062 40k multicolored 1.00 .35
2010 A1062 40k multicolored 1.00 .35
2011 A1063 40k multicolored 1.00 .35
2012 A1062 40k multicolored 1.00 .35
2013 A1062 40k multicolored 1.00 .35
2014 A1062 40k multicolored 1.00 .35
2015 A1063 40k multicolored 1.00 .35
2016 A1062 40k multicolored 1.00 .35
2017 A1062 40k multicolored 1.00 .35
Nos. 2003-2017 (15) 15.00 5.25

40th anniversary of the October Revolution.

Artists and Academy of Art — A1064

Red Army Monument, Berlin — A1065

1r, Worker and Peasant monument, Moscow.

1957, Dec. 16
2018 A1064 40k black, *pale salmon* .60 .25
2019 A1065 60k black .90 .30
2020 A1065 1r black, *pink* 1.50 .45
Nos. 2018-2020 (3) 3.00 1.00

200th anniversary of the Academy of Arts, Leningrad. Artists on 40k are K. P. Bryulov, Ilya Repin and V. I. Surikov.

No. 1991 Overprinted in Black

1957, Nov. 28
2021 A1055 40k 40.00 5.00

Launching of Sputnik 1.

Ukrainian Arms, Symbolic Figures A1066

1957, Dec. 24
2022 A1066 40k yel, red & blue .75 .35

Ukrainian Soviet Republic, 40th anniv.

Edvard Grieg — A1067

1957, Dec. 24 **Photo.**
2023 A1067 40k black, *buff* 3.00 1.00

Grieg, Norwegian composer, 50th death anniv.

Giuseppe Garibaldi — A1068

1957, Dec. 24 **Litho.**
2024 A1068 40k plum, lt grn & blk 1.00 .35

Garibaldi, (1807-1882) Italian patriot.

Vladimir Lukich Borovikovsky (1757-1825), Painter — A1069

1957, Dec. 24 **Photo.**
2025 A1069 40k brown 1.00 .50

Portrait Type of 1956

Portrait: 40k, Mariya Nikolayevna Ermolova (1853-1928), actress.

1957, Dec. 28 **Litho.**
2026 A984 40k red brn & brt vio 1.00 .30

Kuibyshev Hydroelectric Station and Dam A1070

1957, Dec. 28
2027 A1070 40k dark blue, *buff* 3.00 .50

Type of 1956

Portrait: 40k, Rosa Luxemburg (1870-1919), German socialist.

1958, Jan. 8
2028 A979 40k blue & brown 1.50 .60

Chi Pai-shih — A1070a

1958, Jan. 8 **Photo.**
2029 A1070a 40k deep violet 10.00 1.00

Chi Pai-shih (1864-1957), Chinese painter.

Flag and Symbols of Industry A1070b

1958, Jan. 8 **Litho.**
2030 A1070b 60k gray vio, red & black 2.00 .50

All-Union Industrial Exhib. Exists imperf. Value, $250.

Aleksei N. Tolstoi, Novelist & Dramatist (1883-1945) A1071

1958, Jan. 28 **Photo.** ***Perf. 12***
2031 A1071 40k brown olive 1.00 .30

See Nos. 2112, 2175-2178C.

Symbolic Figure Greeting Sputnik 2 — A1072

1957-58 **Figure in Buff** **Litho.**
2032 A1072 20k black & rose .75 .25
2033 A1072 40k black & grn ('58) 1.00 .25
2034 A1072 60k blk & lt brn ('58) 1.25 .25
2035 A1072 1r black & blue 2.00 .50
Nos. 2032-2035 (4) 5.00 1.25

Launching of Sputnik 2, Nov. 3, 1957.

Small Portrait Type of 1957

No. 2036, Henry W. Longfellow, American poet. No. 2037, William Blake, English artist, poet, mystic. No. 2038, E. Charents, Armenian poet.

1958, Mar. **Unwmk.** ***Perf. 12***
Various Frames
2036 A1037 40k gray black 5.00 2.25
2037 A1037 40k gray black 5.00 2.25
2038 A1037 40k sepia 5.00 2.25
Nos. 2036-2038 (3) 15.00 6.75

Victory at Pskov A1073

Soldier and Civilian — A1074

Designs: No. 2040, Airman, sailor and soldier. No. 2042, Sailor and soldier. 60k, Storming of Berlin Reichstag building.

1958, Feb. 21
2039 A1073 25k multicolored .50 .40
2040 A1073 40k multicolored 1.00 .40
2041 A1074 40k multicolored 1.00 .40
2042 A1074 40k multicolored 1.00 .40
2043 A1073 60k multicolored 1.50 .40
Nos. 2039-2043 (5) 5.00 2.00

40th anniversary of Red Armed Forces.

Peter Ilich Tchaikovsky A1075

Swan Lake Ballet A1076

Design: 1r, Tchaikovsky, pianist and violinist.

1958, Mar. 18
2044 A1075 40k grn, bl, brn & red .60 .25
2045 A1076 40k grn, ultra, red & yel .60 .25
2046 A1075 1r lake & emerald 2.00 .50
Nos. 2044-2046 (3) 3.20 1.00

Honoring Tchaikovsky and for the Tchaikovsky competitions for pianists and violinists. Exist imperf. Value, set $10.

Nos. 2044-2045 were printed in sheets of 30, including 15 stamps of each value and 5 se-tenant pairs. Value, pairs $10.

V. F. Rudnev — A1077

1958, Mar. 25 **Unwmk.**
2047 A1077 40k green, blk & ocher 1.00 .50

Rudnev, naval commander.

Maxim Gorki — A1078

1958, Apr. 3 **Litho.** ***Perf. 12***
2048 A1078 40k multicolored .75 .50

Gorki, writer, 90th birth anniv.

Spasski Tower — A1079

1958, Apr. 9
2049 A1079 40k dp violet, *pinkish* .75 .25
2050 A1079 60k rose red 1.25 .25

13th Congress of the Young Communist League (Komsomol).

Russian Pavilion, Brussels A1080

1958, Apr.
2051 A1080 10k multicolored .45 .25
2052 A1080 40k multicolored .55 .25

Universal and International Exhibition at Brussels. Exist imperf. Value $5.

Lenin — A1081

1958, Apr. 22 **Engr.**
2053 A1081 40k dk blue gray 1.00 .65
2054 A1081 60k rose brown 1.50 .65
2055 A1081 1r brown 2.50 .65
Nos. 2053-2055 (3) 5.00 1.95

88th anniversary of the birth of Lenin.

1958, May 5

Portrait: Nos. 2056-2058, Karl Marx.

2056 A1081 40k brown 1.00 .25
2057 A1081 60k dark blue 1.50 .25
2058 A1081 1r dark red 2.50 .40
Nos. 2056-2058 (3) 5.00 .90

140th anniversary of the birth of Marx.

Jan A. Komensky (Comenius) — A1082

1958, Apr. 17 **Photo.**
2059 A1082 40k green 3.00 1.00

No. 1695 Overprinted in Blue

1958, Apr. 22
2060 A914 40k multicolored 4.50 1.00

Academy of Arts, Moscow, 200th anniv.

Lenin Order — A1083

1958, Apr. 30 Litho.

2061 A1083 40k brn, yel & red 1.00 .50

Carlo Goldoni — A1084

1958, Apr. 28 Photo.

2062 A1084 40k blue & dk gray .75 .35

Carlo Goldoni, Italian dramatist.

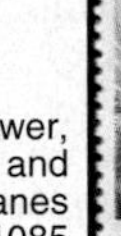

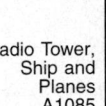

Radio Tower, Ship and Planes A1085

1958, May 7

2063 A1085 40k blue grn & red 5.00 .50

Issued for Radio Day, May 7.

Globe and Dove — A1086

1958, May 6 Litho.

2064 A1086 40k blue & black .40 .25
2065 A1086 60k ultra & black .60 .25

4th Congress of the Intl. Democratic Women's Federation, June, 1958, at Vienna.

Ilya Chavchavadze A1087

1958, May 12 Photo.

2066 A1087 40k black & blue .80 .35

50th anniversary of the death of Ilya Chavchavadze, Georgian writer.

Flags and Communication Symbols — A1088

1958-59 Litho.

2067 A1088 40k blue, red, yel & blk 8.00 3.00
a. Red half of Czech flag at bottom 8.00 3.00

Communist ministers' meeting on social problems in Moscow, Dec. 1957.

On No. 2067, the Czech flag (center flag in vertical row of five) is incorrectly pictured with red stripe on top. This error is corrected on No. 2067a.

Bugler — A1089

Pioneers: 25k, Boy with model plane.

1958, May 29 Unwmk. *Perf. 12*

2068 A1089 10k ultra, red & red brn .50 .25
2069 A1089 25k ultra, yel & red brn .50 .25

Children of Three Races — A1090

Design: No. 2071, Child and bomb.

1958, May 29

2070 A1090 40k car, ultra & brn .50 .25
2071 A1090 40k car & brn .50 .25

Intl. Day for the Protection of Children.

Soccer Players and Globe — A1091

1958, June 5

2072 A1091 40k blue, red & buff .75 .25
2073 A1091 60k blue, red & buff 2.25 .30

6th World Soccer Championships, Stockholm, June 8-29. Exist imperf. Value $5.

Rimski-Korsakov A1092

1958, June 5 Photo.

2074 A1092 40k blue & brown 3.00 .50

Nikolai Andreevich Rimski-Korsakov (1844-1908), composer.

Girl Gymnast — A1093

No. 2076, Gymnast on rings and view.

1958, June 24 Litho.

2075 A1093 40k ultra, red & buff 1.00 .25
2076 A1093 40k blue, red buff & grn 1.00 .25

14th World Gymnastic Championships, Moscow, July 6-10.

Bomb, Globe, Atom, Sputniks, Ship A1094

1958, July 1

2077 A1094 60k dk blue, blk & org 9.00 1.00

Conference for peaceful uses of atomic energy, held at Stockholm.

Street Fighters — A1095

1958, July 5

2078 A1095 40k red & violet blk 2.00 .30

Communist Party in the Ukraine, 40th anniv.

Moscow State University A1096

Congress Emblem — A1097

1958, July 8 *Perf. 12*

2079 A1096 40k red & blue .75 .25
2080 A1097 60k lt grn, blue & red 1.25 .30
a. Souvenir sheet of 2 10.00 7.00

5th Congress of the International Architects' Organization, Moscow.

No. 2080a contains Nos. 2079-2080, imperf., with background design in yellow, brown, blue and red. Issued Sept. 8, 1958.

Young Couple A1098

1958, June 25

2081 A1098 40k blue & ocher .75 .30
2082 A1098 60k yel green & ocher 1.25 .45

Day of Soviet Youth.

Sputnik 3 Leaving Earth A1099

1958, June 16

2083 A1099 40k vio blue, grn & rose 2.50 .35

Launching of Sputnik 3, May 15. Printed in sheets with alternating labels, giving details of launching.

Sadriddin Aini — A1100

1958, July 15

2084 A1100 40k rose, black & buff 3.00 .50

80th birthday of Aini, Tadzhik writer.

Emblem A1101

1958, July 21 Typo. *Perf. 12*

2085 A1101 40k lilac & blue .75 .35

1st World Trade Union Conference of Working Youths, Prague, July 14-20.

Type of 1958-59 and

TU-104 and Globe A1102

Design: 1r, Turbo-propeller liner AN-10.

1958, Aug. Litho.

2086 A1102 60k blue, red & bis .75 .25
2087 A1123 1r yel, red & black 1.25 .25

Soviet civil aviation. Exist imperf. Value, set $5.50. See Nos. 2147-2151.

L. A. Kulik A1103

1958, Aug. 12

2088 A1103 40k sep, bl, yel & claret 2.00 .50

50th anniv. of the falling of the Tungus meteor and the 75th anniv. of the birth of L. A. Kulik, meteorist.

IGY Type of 1957

Designs: No. 2089, Aurora borealis and camera. No. 2090, Schooner "Zarja" exploring's earth magnetism. No. 2091, Weather balloon and radar.

1958, July 29 Size: 25½x37mm

2089 A1039 40k blue & brt yel 1.40 .35
2090 A1039 40k blue green 1.40 .35
2091 A1039 40k bright ultra 1.40 .35
Nos. 2089-2091 (3) 4.20 1.05

International Geophysical Year, 1957-58.

Crimea Observatory A1104

Moscow University A1105

Design: 1r, Telescope.

1958, Aug. **Photo.**

2092 A1104 40k brn & brt grnsh bl 2.00 .35
2093 A1105 60k lt blue, vio & yel 2.50 .35
2094 A1104 1r dp blue & org brn 3.50 .35
Nos. 2092-2094 (3) 8.00 1.05

10th Congress of the International Astronomical Union, Moscow.

Postilion, 16th Century A1106

Designs: No. 2095, 15th cent. letter writer. No. 2097, A. L. Ordyn-Natshokin and sleigh mail coach, 17th cent. No. 2098, Mail coach and post office, 18th cent. No. 2099, Troika, 19th cent. No. 2100, Lenin stamp, ship and Kremlin. No. 2101, Jet plane and troika. No. 2102, Leningrad Communications Museum, vert. No. 2103, V. N. Podbielski and letter carriers. No. 2104, Mail train. No. 2105, Loading mail on plane. No. 2106, Ship, plane, train and globe.

1958, Aug. Unwmk. Litho. ***Perf. 12***

2095 A1106 10k red, blk, yel & lil .25 .25
2096 A1106 10k multicolored .25 .25
2097 A1106 25k ultra & slate .60 .30
2098 A1106 25k black & ultra .60 .30
2099 A1106 40k car lake & brn blk 1.20 .45
2100 A1106 40k blk, mag & brn 1.20 .45
2101 A1106 40k red, org & gray 1.20 .45
2102 A1106 40k sal & brn 1.20 .45
2103 A1106 60k grnsh blue & red lil 1.50 .35
2104 A1106 60k grnsh bl & lilac 1.50 .35
2105 A1106 1r multicolored 3.25 .70
2106 A1106 1r multicolored 3.25 .70
Nos. 2095-2106 (12) 16.00 5.00

Centenary of Russian postage stamps.

Two imperf. souvenir sheets exist, measuring 155x106mm. One contains one each of Nos. 2095-2099, with background design in red, ultramarine, yellow and brown. The other contains one each of Nos. 2100, 2103-2106, with background design in blue, gray, ocher, pink and brown. Value for both, $50 unused, $10 canceled.

Nos. 2096, 2100-2101 exist imperf. Value for both, $20 unused, $10 canceled.

M. I. Chigorin, Chess Player, 50th Death Anniv. — A1107

1958, Aug. 30 **Photo.**

2107 A1107 40k black & emerald 2.00 .50

Golden Gate, Vladimir A1108

60k, Gorki Street with trolley bus and truck.

1958, Aug. 23 **Litho.**

2108 A1108 40k multicolored .80 .40
2109 A1108 60k lt violet, yel & blk 1.20 .60

850th anniv. of the city of Vladimir.

Nurse Bandaging Man's Leg — A1109

No. 2111, Hospital, & people of various races.

1958, Sept. 15

2110 A1109 40k multicolored .75 .30
2111 A1109 40k ol, lem & red .75 .30

40 years of Red Cross-Red Crescent work.

Portrait Type of 1958

Mikhail E. Saltykov (Shchedrin), writer.

1958, Sept. 15

2112 A1071 40k brn black & mar 5.00 1.00

Rudagi — A1110

1958, Oct. 10 **Litho.** ***Perf. 12***

2113 A1110 40k multicolored 2.00 .50

1100th anniversary of the birth of Rudagi, Persian poet.

V. V. Kapnist — A1111

1958, Sept. 30

2114 A1111 40k blue & gray 1.00 .50

200th anniversary of the birth of V. V. Kapnist, poet and dramatist.

Book, Torch, Lyre, Flower A1112

1958, Oct. 4

2115 A1112 40k red org, ol & blk 2.00 .50

Conf. of Asian & African Writers, Tashkent.

Chelyabinsk Tractor Factory A1113

Designs: No. 2117, Zaporozstal foundry. No. 2118, Ural machine building plant.

1958, Oct. 20 **Photo.**

2116 A1113 40k green & yellow 1.50 .30
2117 A1113 40k brown red & yel 1.50 .30
2118 A1113 40k blue 1.50 .30
Nos. 2116-2118 (3) 4.50 .90

Pioneers of Russian Industry.

Ancient Georgian on Horseback A1114

1958, Oct. 18 **Litho.**

2119 A1114 40k ocher, ultra & red 2.00 .50

1500th anniv. of Tbilisi, capital of Georgia.

Red Square, Moscow — A1115

АЛМА-АТА • ПЛОЩАДЬ им. В. И. ЛЕНИНА

No. 2121

ТБИЛИСИ • ПРОСПЕКТ РУСТАВЕЛИ

No. 2125

ФРУНЗЕ • УНИВЕРСИТЕТСКАЯ ПЛОЩАДЬ

No. 2127

ОБЩИЙ ВИД ГОРОДА ЕРЕВАН

No. 2128

МИНСК • КРУГЛАЯ ПЛОЩАДЬ

No. 2131

Capitals of Soviet Republics: No. 2121, Lenin Square, Alma Ata. No. 2122, Lenin statue, Ashkhabad. No. 2123, Lenin statue, Tashkent. No. 2124, Lenin Square, Stalinabad. No. 2125, Rustaveli Ave., Tbilisi. No. 2126, View from Dvina River, Riga. No. 2127, University Square, Frunze. No. 2128, View, Yerevan. No. 2129, Communist Street, Baku. No. 2130, Lenin Prospect, Kishinev. No. 2131, Round Square, Minsk. No. 2132, Viru Gate, Tallinn. No. 2133, Main Street, Kiev. No. 2134, View, Vilnius.

1958 **Engr.**

2120 A1115 40k violet 1.00 .45
2121 A1115 40k brt blue green 1.00 .45
2122 A1115 40k greenish gray 1.00 .45
2123 A1115 40k dark gray 1.00 .45
2124 A1115 40k blue 1.00 .45
2125 A1115 40k violet blue 1.00 .45
2126 A1115 40k brown red 1.00 .45
2127 A1115 40k dk blue gray 1.00 .45
2128 A1115 40k brown 1.00 .45
2129 A1115 40k purple 1.00 .45
2130 A1115 40k olive 1.00 .45
2131 A1115 40k gray brown 1.00 .45
2132 A1115 40k emerald 1.00 .45
2133 A1115 40k lilac rose 1.00 .45
2134 A1115 40k orange ver 1.00 .45
Nos. 2120-2134 (15) 15.00 6.75

See No. 2836.

Young Civil War Soldier, 1919 — A1116

20k, Industrial brigade. 25k, Youth in World War II. 40k, Girl farm worker. 60k, Youth building new towns. 1r, Students, fighters for culture.

1958, Oct. 25 **Litho.**

2135 A1116 10k multicolored .40 .25
2136 A1116 20k multicolored .75 .25
2137 A1116 25k multicolored .90 .25
2138 A1116 40k multicolored 1.50 .25
2139 A1116 60k multicolored 2.25 .25
2140 A1116 1r multicolored 4.50 1.00
Nos. 2135-2140 (6) 10.30 2.25

40th anniversary of the Young Communist League (Komsomol).

Marx and Lenin — A1117

Lenin, Intellectual, Peasant and Miner A1118

1958, Oct. 31

2141 A1117 40k multicolored .50 .25
2142 A1118 1r multicolored 1.50 .30

41st anniversary of Russian Revolution.

Torch, Wreath and Family A1119

1958, Nov. 5

2143 A1119 60k blk, beige & dull bl 1.00 .50

10th anniversary of the Universal Declaration of Human Rights.

Sergei Esenin (1895-1925), Poet — A1120

1958, Nov. 29

2144 A1120 40k multicolored 1.00 .50

G. K. Ordzhonikidze A1121

1958, Dec. 12 ***Perf. 12***

2145 A1121 40k multicolored 1.00 .50

G. K. Ordzhonikidze (1886-1937), Georgian party worker.

Kuan Han-ching — A1122

1958, Dec. 5

2146 A1122 40k dk blue & gray 3.00 1.00

700th anniversary of the theater of Kuan Han-ching, Chinese dramatist.

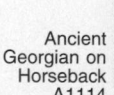

Airliner IL-14 and Globe A1123

Soviet civil aviation: No. 2148, Jet liner TU-104. No. 2149, Turbo-propeller liner TU-114. 60k, Jet liner TU-110. 2r, Turbo-propeller liner IL-18.

1958-59

2147 A1123 20k ultra, blk & red .40 .25
2148 A1123 40k bl grn, blk & red .60 .25
2149 A1123 40k brt bl, blk & red .60 .25
2150 A1123 60k rose car & black .60 .25
2151 A1123 2r plum, red & black ('59) 1.75 .25
Nos. 2147-2151 (5) 3.95 1.25

Exist imperf.; value $10.
See Nos. 2086-2087.

Eleonora Duse — A1124

1958, Dec. 26

2152 A1124 40k blue grn & gray 1.00 .50

Duse, Italian actress, birth cent.

John Milton — A1125

1958, Dec. 17

2153 A1125 40k brown 1.00 .50

John Milton (1608-1674), English poet.

K. F. Rulye — A1126

1958, Dec. 26

2154 A1126 40k ultra & black 1.00 .50

Rulye, educator, death cent.

Fuzuli — A1127

1958, Dec. 23 **Photo.**

2155 A1127 40k grnsh bl & brn 1.00 .50

400th anniv. of the death of Fuzuli (Mehmet Suleiman Oglou), Azerbaijani poet.

Census Emblem and Family — A1128

Design: No. 2157, Census emblem.

1958, Dec. **Litho.**

2156 A1128 40k multicolored .75 .25
2157 A1128 40k yel, gray, bl & red .75 .25

1959 Soviet census.

Lunik and Sputniks over Kremlin — A1129

Designs: 40k, Lenin and view of Kremlin. 60k, Workers and Lenin power plant on Volga.

1959, Jan. **Unwmk.** ***Perf. 12***

2158 A1129 40k multicolored 1.50 .25
2159 A1129 60k multicolored 2.50 .75
2160 A1129 1r red, yel & vio bl 7.00 1.50
Nos. 2158-2160 (3) 11.00 2.50

21st Cong. of the Communist Party and "the conquest of the cosmos by the Soviet people."

Lenin Statue, Minsk Buildings — A1130

1958, Dec. 20

2161 A1130 40k red, buff & brn .75 .35

Byelorussian Republic, 40th anniv.

Atomic Icebreaker "Lenin" A1131

Design: 60k, Diesel Locomotive "TE-3."

1958, Dec. 31

2162 A1131 40k multicolored 1.75 1.00
2163 A1131 60k multicolored 2.75 1.25

Shalom Aleichem — A1132

1959, Feb. 10

2164 A1132 40k chocolate .75 .35

Aleichem, Yiddish writer, birth cent.

Evangelista Torricelli — A1133

Scientists: No. 2166, Charles Darwin, English biologist. No. 2167, N. F. Gamaleya, microbiologist.

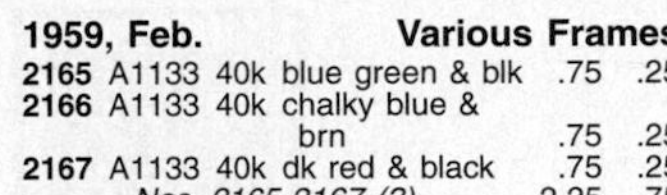

1959, Feb. **Various Frames**

2165 A1133 40k blue green & blk .75 .25
2166 A1133 40k chalky blue & brn .75 .25
2167 A1133 40k dk red & black .75 .25
Nos. 2165-2167 (3) 2.25 .75

Woman Skator — A1134

1959, Feb. 5

2168 A1134 25k ultra, black & ver .75 .25
2169 A1134 40k ultra & black 1.25 .30

Women's International Ice Skating Championships, Sverdlovsk.

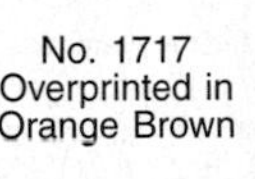
No. 1717 Overprinted in Orange Brown

1959, Feb. 12

2170 A919 1r dk brn & brn 7.50 5.00

"Victory of the USSR Basketball Team — Chile 1959." However, the 3rd World Basketball Championship honors went to Brazil when the Soviet team was disqualified for refusing to play Nationalist China.

Frederic Joliot-Curie A1135

1959, Mar. 3 **Litho.** ***Perf. 12***

2171 A1135 40k turq bl & gray brn, *beige* 1.00 .25

Joliot-Curie (1900-58), French scientist.

Selma Lagerlöf — A1136

1959, Feb. 26

2172 A1136 40k red brn & blk .75 .35

Lagerlöf (1858-1940), Swedish writer.

Peter Zwirka — A1137

1959, Mar. 3

2173 A1137 40k hn brn & blk, *yel* .75 .35

Zwirka (1909-1947), Lithuanian writer.

No. 1861A Overprinted in Red: "1759 1959"

1959, Feb. 26 **Engr.**

2174 A993 40k lt ultra & brown 10.00 10.00

200th anniversary of the birth of Robert Burns, Scottish poet.

Type of 1958

Russian Writers: No. 2175, A. S. Griboedov. No. 2176, A. N. Ostrovski. No. 2177, Anton Chekhov. No. 2178, I. A. Krylov. No. 2178A, Nikolai V. Gogol. No. 2178B, S. T. Aksakov. No. 2178C, A. V. Koltzov. poet, and reaper.

1959 **Litho.**

2175 A1071 40k buff, cl, blk & vio .75 .40
2176 A1071 40k vio & brown .75 .40
2177 A1071 40k slate & hn brn .75 .40
2178 A1071 40k ol bister & brn .75 .40
2178A A1071 40k ol, gray & bis .75 .40
2178B A1071 40k brn, vio & bis .75 .40
2178C A1071 40k violet & black .75 .40
Nos. 2175-2178C (7) 5.25 2.80

No. 2178A for the 150th birth anniv. of Nikolai V. Gogol, writer, No. 2178B the centenary of the death of S. T. Aksakov, writer.

A. S. Popov and Rescue from Ice Float A1138

60k, Radio broadcasting "Peace" in 5 languages.

1959, Mar. 13

2179 A1138 40k brn, blk & dk blue .75 .25
2180 A1138 60k multicolored 1.25 .25

Centenary of the birth of A. S. Popov, pioneer in radio research.

M.S. Rossija at Odessa A1139

Ships: 10k, Steamer, Vladivostok-Petropavlovsk-Kamchatka line. 20k, M.S. Feliks Dzerzhinski, Odessa-Latakia line. No. 2184, Ship, Murmansk-Tyksi line. 60k, M.S. Mikhail Kalinin at Leningrad. 1r, M.S. Baltika, Leningrad-London line.

1959 **Litho.** **Unwmk.**

2181 A1139 10k multicolored .30 .25
2182 A1139 20k red, lt grn & dk bl .40 .25
2183 A1139 40k multicolored .75 .25
2184 A1139 40k blue, buff & red 1.25 .25
2185 A1139 60k bl grn, red & buff 1.50 .30
2186 A1139 1r ultra, red & yel 1.75 1.00
Nos. 2181-2186 (6) 5.95 2.30

Honoring the Russian fleet.

Globe and Luna 1 A1140

Luna 1, launched Jan. 2, 1959: No. 2188, Globe and route of Luna 1.

1959, Apr. 13

2187 A1140 40k red brown & rose 2.50 .50
2188 A1140 40k ultra & blue 2.50 .50

Saadi and "Gulistan" A1141

1959, Mar. 20 **Photo.**
2189 A1141 40k dk blue & black .75 .35

Persian poet Saadi (Muslih-ud-Din) and 700th anniv. of his book, "Gulistan" (1258).

Sulhan S. Orbeliani — A1142

1959, Apr. 2
2190 A1142 40k dull rose & black .75 .35

Orbeliani (1658-1725), Georgian writer.

Drawing by Korin — A1143

1959, Apr. 10 **Litho.**
2191 A1143 40k multicolored 5.00 1.50

Ogata Korin (1653?-1716), Japanese artist.

Lenin — A1144

1959, Apr. 17 **Engr.**
2192 A1144 40k sepia 1.00 .50

89th anniversary of the birth of Lenin.

Cachin — A1146

1959, Apr. 27 **Photo.**
2194 A1146 60k dark brown 1.00 .30

Marcel Cachin (1869-1958), French Communist Party leader.

Joseph Haydn — A1147

1959, May 8
2195 A1147 40k dk bl, gray & brn black 5.00 .50

Sesquicentennial of the death of Joseph Haydn, Austrian composer.

Alexander von Humboldt — A1148

1959, May 6
2196 A1148 40k violet & brown .75 .35

Alexander von Humboldt, German naturalist and geographer, death centenary.

Three Races Carrying Flag of Peace — A1149

1959, Apr. 30 **Litho.**
2199 A1149 40k multicolored 1.00 .25

10th anniv. of World Peace Movement.

Mountain Climber — A1150

Sports and Travel: No. 2201, Tourists reading map. No. 2202, Canoeing, horiz. No. 2203, Skiers.

1959, May 15

2200	A1150	40k	multicolored	.50	.25
2201	A1150	40k	multicolored	.50	.25
2202	A1150	40k	multicolored	.50	.25
2203	A1150	40k	multicolored	.50	.25
			Nos. 2200-2203 (4)	2.00	1.00

I. E. Repin Statue, Moscow — A1151

Statues: No. 2205, Lenin, Ulyanovsk. 20k, V. V. Mayakovsky, Moscow. 25k, Alexander Pushkin, Leningrad. 60k, Maxim Gorki, Moscow. 1r, Tchaikovsky, Moscow.

1959 **Photo.** **Unwmk.**

2204	A1151	10k	ocher & sepia	.25	.25
2205	A1151	10k	red & black	.25	.25
2206	A1151	20k	violet & sepia	.35	.25
2207	A1151	25k	grnsh blue & blk	.45	.25
2208	A1151	60k	lt green & slate	.75	.25
2209	A1151	1r	lt ultra & gray	1.75	.45
			Nos. 2204-2209 (6)	3.80	1.70

N. Y. Coliseum and Spasski Tower — A1152

1959, June 25 **Litho.** ***Perf. 12***

2210	A1152	20k	multicolored	.30	.25
2211	A1152	40k	multicolored	.70	.25
a.			Souv. sheet of 1, imperf.	5.00	.50

Soviet Exhibition of Science, Technology and Culture, New York, June 20-Aug. 10. No. 2211a issued July 20.

Animal Types of 1957

No. 2213, Hare. No. 2214, Siberian horse. No. 2215, Tiger. No. 2216, Red squirrel. No. 2217, Pine marten. No. 2218, Hazel hen. No. 2219, Mute swan.

1959-60 **Litho.** ***Perf. 12***
Center in Natural Colors

2213	A1023	20k	vio blue ('60)	.60	.25
2214	A1023	25k	blue black	.60	.25
2215	A1023	25k	brown	.60	.25
2216	A1023	40k	deep green	.80	.25
2217	A1023	40k	dark green	.80	.25
2218	A1024	60k	dark green	1.25	.40
2219	A1023	1r	bright blue	1.75	.85
			Nos. 2213-2219 (7)	6.40	2.50

Louis Braille — A1153

1959, July 16
2220 A1153 60k blue grn, bis & brn .75 .35

150th anniversary of the birth of Louis Braille, French educator of the blind.

Musa Djalil — A1154

1959, July 16 **Photo.**
2221 A1154 40k violet & black 1.75 .35

Musa Djalil, Tatar poet.

Sturgeon A1155

1959, July 16

2222	A1155	40k	shown	.75	.25
2223	A1155	60k	Chum salmon	1.25	.25

See Nos. 2375-2377.

Gymnast A1156

Athletes Holding Spartacist Games emblem — A1157

Designs: 25k, Runner. 60k, Water polo.

1959, Aug. 7

2224	A1156	15k	lilac rose & gray	.30	.25
2225	A1156	25k	yel green & red brn	.60	.25
2226	A1157	30k	brt red & gray	.75	.25
2227	A1156	60k	blue & org yel	1.25	.25
			Nos. 2224-2227 (4)	2.90	1.00

2nd National Spartacist Games.

Globe and Hands — A1158

1959, Aug. 12 **Litho.**
2228 A1158 40k yel, blue & red .75 .35

2nd Intl. Conf. of Public Employees Unions.

Cathedral and Modern Building A1159

1959, Aug. 21 **Unwmk.** ***Perf. 12***
2229 A1159 40k blue, ol, yel & red 1.00 .25

1100th anniv. of the city of Novgorod.

Schoolboys in Workshop — A1160

Design: 1r, Workers in night school.

1959, Aug. 27 **Photo.**

2230	A1160	40k	dark purple	.25	.25
2231	A1160	1r	dark blue	.50	.25

Strengthening the connection between school and life.

Glacier Survey — A1161

Rocket and Observatory A1162

Designs: 25k, Oceanographic ship "Vityaz" and map. 40k, Plane over Antarctica, camp and emperor penguin.

1959

2232	A1161	10k	blue green	.25	.25
2233	A1161	25k	brt blue & red	.30	.25
2234	A1161	40k	ultra & red	.50	.25
2235	A1162	1r	ultra & buff	1.50	.30
			Nos. 2232-2235 (4)	2.55	1.05

Intl. Geophysical Year. 1st Russian rocket to reach the moon, Sept. 14, 1959 (#2235).

Workers and Farmers Holding Atom Symbol — A1163

1959, Sept. 23 **Litho.**
2236 A1163 40k red org & bister .75 .35

All-Union Economic Exhibition, Moscow.

Russian and Chinese Students A1164

40k, Russian miner and Chinese steel worker.

1959, Sept. 25 **Litho.** ***Perf. 12***
2237 A1164 20k multicolored .80 .30
2238 A1164 40k multicolored 1.20 .45

People's Republic of China, 10th anniv.

Letter Carrier A1165

1959, Sept.
2239 A1165 40k dk car rose & black .40 .25
2240 A1165 60k blue & black .60 .25

Intl. Letter Writing Week, Oct. 4-10.

Makhtumkuli A1166

1959, Sept. 30 **Photo.**
2241 A1166 40k brown 1.00 .25

225th anniversary of the birth of Makhtumkuli, Turkmen writer.

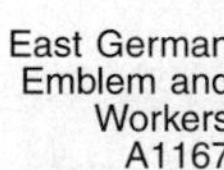

East German Emblem and Workers A1167

City Hall, East Berlin — A1168

1959, Oct. 6 **Litho.**
2242 A1167 40k multicolored .35 .25

Photo.

2243 A1168 60k dp claret & buff .45 .25

German Democratic Republic, 10th anniv.

Steel Production — A1169

7-Year Production Plan (Industries): No. 2244, Chemicals. No. 2245, Spasski Tower, hammer and sickle. No. 2246, Home building. No. 2247, Meat production, woman with farm animals. No. 2248, Man working machinery. No. 2249, Grain production, woman tractor driver. No. 2250, Oil. No. 2251, Textiles. No. 2252, Steel. No. 2253, Coal. No. 2254, Iron. No. 2255, Electric power.

1959-60 **Litho.**
2244 A1169 10k vio, grnsh blue & maroon .50 .25
2245 A1169 10k orange & dk car .50 .25
2246 A1169 15k brn, yel & red .50 .25
2247 A1169 15k brn, grn & mar .50 .25
2248 A1169 20k bl grn, yel & red .50 .25
2249 A1169 20k green, yel & red .50 .25
2250 A1169 30k lilac, sal & red .50 .25
2251 A1169 30k gldn brn, lil, red & green ('60) .50 .25
2252 A1169 40k vio bl, yel & org .50 .25
2253 A1169 40k dk blue, pink & dp rose .50 .25
2254 A1169 60k org red, yel, bl & maroon .50 .25
2255 A1169 60k ultra, buff & red .50 .25
Nos. 2244-2255 (12) 6.00 3.00

Arms of Tadzhikistan A1170

1959, Oct. 13
2258 A1170 40k red, emer, ocher & black .75 .35

Tadzhikistan statehood, 30th anniversary.

Path of Luna 3 and Electronics Laboratory A1171

1959, Oct. 12
2259 A1171 40k violet 1.50 .50

Flight of Luna 3 around the moon, Oct. 4, 1959.

Red Square, Moscow A1172

1959, Oct. 26 **Engr.**
2260 A1172 40k dark red 1.00 .50

42nd anniversary of October Revolution.

US Capitol, Globe and Kremlin — A1173

1959, Oct. 27 **Photo.**
2261 A1173 60k blue & yellow 1.00 .50

Visit of Premier Nikita Khrushchev to the US, Sept., 1959.

Helicopter — A1174

25k, Diver. 40k, Motorcyclist. 60k, Parachutist.

1959, Oct. 28
2262 A1174 10k vio blue & mar .25 .25
2263 A1174 25k blue & brown .60 .25
2264 A1174 40k red brn & indigo 1.00 .25
2265 A1174 60k blue & ol bister 1.25 .25
Nos. 2262-2265 (4) 3.10 1.00

Honoring voluntary aides of the army.

Moon, Earth and Path of Rocket A1175

No. 2267, Kremlin and diagram showing rocket and positions of moon and earth.

1959, Nov. 1 **Litho.**
2266 A1175 40k bl, dk bl, red & bis 1.50 .25
2267 A1175 40k gray, pink & red 1.50 .25

Landing of the Soviet rocket on the moon, Sept. 14, 1959.

Sandor Petöfi A1176

Victory Statue and View of Budapest — A1177

1959, Nov. 9 ***Perf. 12x12½, 12½x12***
2268 A1176 20k gray & ol bister .50 .25
2269 A1177 40k multicolored 1.50 .50

Soviet-Hungarian friendship.
For overprint see No. 2308.

Manolis Glezos and Acropolis A1178

1959, Nov. 12 **Photo.** ***Perf. 12x12½***
2270 A1178 40k ultra & brown 9.00 3.00

Manolis Glezos, Greek communist.

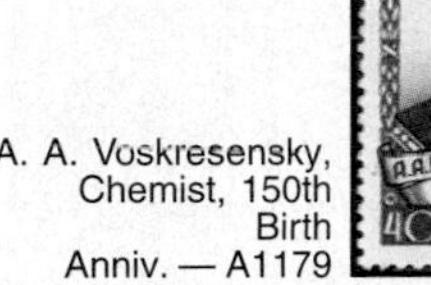

A. A. Voskresensky, Chemist, 150th Birth Anniv. — A1179

1959, Dec. 7 ***Perf. 12½x12***
2271 A1179 40k ultra & brown .75 .35

Chusovaya River, Ural — A1180

No. 2273, Lake Ritza, Caucasus. No. 2274, Lena River, Siberia. No. 2275, Seashore, Far East. No. 2276, Lake Iskander, Central Asia. No. 2277, Lake Baikal, Siberia. No. 2278, Belukha Mountain, Altai range. No. 2279, Khibiny Mountains. No. 2280, Gursuf region, Crimea.

1959, Dec. **Engr.** ***Perf. 12½***
2272 A1180 10k purple .25 .25
2273 A1180 10k rose carmine .25 .25
2274 A1180 25k dark blue .65 .25
2275 A1180 25k olive .65 .25
2276 A1180 25k dark red .65 .25
2277 A1180 40k claret 1.50 .25
2278 A1180 60k Prus blue 2.25 .35
2279 A1180 1r olive green 4.50 .75
2280 A1180 1r deep orange 4.50 .75
Nos. 2272-2280 (9) 15.20 3.35

"Trumpeters of 1st Cavalry" by M. Grekov — A1181

1959, Dec. 30 **Litho.** ***Perf. 12½x12***
2283 A1181 40k multicolored 2.00 1.00

40th anniversary of the 1st Cavalry.

Farm Woman — A1182

Designs: 25k, Architect. 60k, Steel worker.

1958-60 **Engr.** ***Perf. 12½***
2286 A1182 20k slate grn ('59) 7.00 3.75
2287 A1182 25k sepia ('59) 3.25 1.60
2288 A1182 60k carmine 9.25 4.25

Perf. 12x12½

Litho.

2290 A1182 20k green ('60) .25 .25
2291 A1182 25k sepia ('60) .75 .25
2292 A1182 60k vermilion ('59) .25 .25
2293 A1182 60k blue ('60) 1.50 .25
Nos. 2286-2293 (7) 22.25 10.60

Mikhail V. Frunze (1885-1925), Revolutionary A1183

1960, Jan. 25 Photo. *Perf. 12½*

2295 A1183 40k dark red brown 1.00 .35

G.N. Gabrichevski, Microbiologist, Birth Cent. — A1184

Perf. 12½x12

1960, Jan. 30 Unwmk.

2296 A1184 40k brt vio & brn 1.00 .35

Anton Chekhov and Moscow Home A1185

40k, Chekhov in later years, Yalta home.

1960, Jan. 20 Litho. *Perf. 12x12½*

2297 A1185 20k red, gray & vio bl .40 .25

2298 A1185 40k dk blue, buff & brn .70 .25

Anton P. Chekhov (1860-1904), playwright.

Vera Komissarzhevskaya (1864-1910), Actress — A1186

1960, Feb. 5 Photo. *Perf. 12½x12*

2299 A1186 40k chocolate 1.00 .50

8th Olympic Winter Games, Squaw Valley, Calif., Feb. 18-29 A1187

Sports: 10k, Ice hockey. 25k, Speed skating. 40k, Skier. 60k, Woman figure skater. 1r, Ski jumper.

1960, Feb. 18 Litho. *Perf. 11½*

2300 A1187 10k ocher & vio blue .25 .25

2301 A1187 25k multicolored .50 .25

2302 A1187 40k org, rose lil & vio blue .75 .25

2303 A1187 60k vio, grn & buff 1.25 .25

2304 A1187 1r bl, grn & brn 2.25 .35

Nos. 2300-2304 (5) 5.00 1.35

Sword into Plowshare Statue, UN, NY — A1188

1960 *Perf. 12x12½*

2305 A1188 40k grnsh bl, yel & brown 1.00 .50

a. Souvenir sheet, imperf. 2.00 .50

No. 2305a for Premier Nikita Khrushchev's visit to the 15th General Assembly of the UN in NYC.

Women of Various Races A1189

1960, Mar. 8

2306 A1189 40k multicolored 1.00 .35

50 years of Intl. Woman's Day, Mar. 8.

Planes in Combat and Timur Frunze A1190

1960, Feb. 23 *Perf. 12½x12*

2307 A1190 40k multicolored 2.00 1.50

Lieut. Timur Frunze, World War II hero.

No. 2269 Overprinted in Red

1960, Apr. 4

2308 A1177 40k multicolored 4.50 2.50

15th anniversary of Hungary's liberation from the Nazis.

Lunik 3 Photographing Far Side of Moon — A1191

Design: 60k, Far side of the moon.

1960 Photo. *Perf. 12x12½*

2309 A1191 40k pale bl, dk bl & yel 1.75 .30

Litho.

2310 A1191 60k lt bl, dk bl & citron 2.25 .30

Photographing of the far side of the moon, Oct. 7, 1959.

Lenin as Child A1192

Various Lenin Portraits and: 20k, Lenin with children and Christmas tree. 30k, Flag, workers and ship. 40k, Kremlin, banners and marchers. 60k, Map of Russia, buildings and ship. 1r, Peace proclamation and globe.

1960, Apr. 10 Litho. *Perf. 12½x12*

2311 A1192 10k multicolored .25 .25

2312 A1192 20k red, green & blk .30 .25

2313 A1192 30k multicolored .50 .25

2314 A1192 40k multicolored .75 .25

2315 A1192 60k multicolored 1.00 .30

2316 A1192 1r red, vio bl & brn 2.00 .45

Nos. 2311-2316 (6) 4.80 1.75

90th anniversary of the birth of Lenin.

Steelworker A1193

1960, Apr. 30 Photo.

2317 A1193 40k brown & red 1.00 .50

Industrial overproduction by 50,000,000r during the 1st year of the 7-year plan.

Government House, Baku A1194

1960, Apr. Litho. *Perf. 12x12½*

2318 A1194 40k bister & brown 1.00 .30

Azerbaijan, 40th anniv.

For surcharge see #2898.

Brotherhood Monument, Prague — A1195

Design: 60k, Charles Bridge, Prague.

1960, Apr. 29 Photo. *Perf. 12½x12*

2319 A1195 40k brt blue & blk .25 .25

2320 A1195 60k blk brn & yel .75 .30

Czechoslovak Republic, 15th anniv.

Radio Tower and Popov Central Museum of Communications, Leningrad — A1196

1960, May 6 Litho.

2321 A1196 40k blue, ocher & brn 1.00 .50

Radio Day.

Gen. I. D. Tcherniakovski and Soldiers — A1197

1960, May 4

2322 A1197 1r multicolored 1.00 .50

Gen. I. D. Tcherniakovski, World War II hero and his military school.

Robert Schumann (1810-56), German Composer A1198

1960, May 20 Photo. *Perf. 12x12½*

2323 A1198 40k ultra & black 1.00 .50

Yakov M. Sverdlov (1885-1919), 1st USSR Pres. — A1199

1960, May 24 *Perf. 12½x12*

2324 A1199 40k dk brn & org brn 1.00 .50

Stamp of 1957 Under Magnifying Glass A1200

1960, May 28 Litho. *Perf. 11½*

2325 A1200 60k multicolored 1.00 .50

Stamp Day.

Karl Marx Avenue, Petrozavodsk, Karelian Autonomous Republic — A1201

No. 2327

No. 2329

No. 2330

No. 2332

No. 2333

No. 2339

No. 2341

No. 2342

Capitals, Soviet Autonomous Republics: No. 2327, Lenin street, Batum, Adzhar. No. 2328, Cultural Palace, Izhevsk, Udmurt. No. 2329, August street, Grozny, Chechen-Ingush. No. 2330, Soviet House, Cheboksary, Chuvash. No. 2331, Buinak Street, Makhachkala, Dagestan. No. 2332, Soviet street, Ioshkar Ola, Mari. No. 2333, Chkalov street, Dzaudzhikau, North Ossetia. No. 2334, October street, Yakutsk, Yakut. No. 2335, House of Ministers, Nukus, Kara-Kalpak.

1960 Engr. *Perf. 12½*

2326 A1201 40k Prus green 1.10 .50
2327 A1201 40k violet blue 1.10 .50
2328 A1201 40k green 1.10 .50
2329 A1201 40k maroon 1.10 .50
2330 A1201 40k dull red 1.10 .50
2331 A1201 40k carmine .90 .30
2332 A1201 40k dark brown .90 .30
2333 A1201 40k orange brown .90 .30
2334 A1201 40k dark blue .90 .30
2335 A1201 40k brown .90 .30
Nos. 2326-2335 (10) 10.00 4.00

See Nos. 2338-2344C. For overprints see Nos. 2336-2337.

No. 2326 Overprinted in Red

1960, June 4

2336 A1201 40k Prus green 5.00 3.00

Karelian Autonomous Rep., 40th anniv.

No. 2328 Overprinted in Red

1960, Nov. 4

2337 A1201 40k green 5.00 3.00

Udmurt Autonomous Rep., 40th anniv.

1961-62 *Perf. 12½, 12½x12*

Capitals, Soviet Autonomous Republics: No. 2338, Rustaveli Street, Sukhumi, Abkhazia. No. 2339, House of Soviets, Nalchik, Kabardino-Balkar. No. 2340, Lenin Street, Ulan-Ude, Buriat. No. 2341, Soviet Street, Syktyvkar, Komi. No. 2342, Lenin Street, Nakhichevan, Nakhichevan. No. 2343, Elista, Kalmyk. No. 2344, Ufa, Bashkir. No. 2344A, Lobachevsky Square, Kazan, Tartar. No. 2344B, Kizil, Tuvinia. No. 2344C, Saransk, Mordovia.

2338 A1201 4k orange ver .30 .25
2339 A1201 4k dark violet .30 .25
2340 A1201 4k dark blue .30 .25
2341 A1201 4k gray .30 .25
2342 A1201 4k dk car rose .30 .25
2343 A1201 4k olive green .30 .25
2344 A1201 4k dull purple .30 .25
2344A A1201 4k grnsh blk ('62) .40 .25
2344B A1201 4k claret ('62) .40 .25
2344C A1201 4k deep grn ('62) .40 .25
Nos. 2338-2344C (10) 3.30 2.50

Denominations of Nos. 2338-2344C are in the revalued currency.

Children's Friendship A1202

Drawings by Children: 20k, Collective farm, vert. 25k, Winter joys. 40k, "In the Zoo."

Perf. 12x12½, 12½x12

1960, June 1 Litho.

2345 A1202 10k multicolored .50 .25
2346 A1202 20k multicolored .50 .25
2347 A1202 25k multicolored .50 .25
2348 A1202 40k multicolored .50 .25
Nos. 2345-2348 (4) 2.00 1.00

Lomonosov University and Congress Emblem — A1203

1960, June 17 Photo. *Perf. 12½x12*

2349 A1203 60k yel & dk brn 1.25 .40

1st congress of the International Federation for Automation Control, Moscow.

Sputnik 4 and Globe — A1204

1960, June 17 *Perf. 12x12½*

2350 A1204 40k vio blue & dp org 3.00 .55

Launching on May 15, 1960, of Sputnik 4, which orbited the earth with a dummy cosmonaut.

Kosta Hetagurov (1859-1906), Ossetian Poet — A1205

1960, June 20 Litho. *Perf. 12½*

2351 A1205 40k gray blue & brn 1.00 .50

Flag and Tallinn, Estonia A1206

Soviet Republics, 20th Annivs.: No. 2353, Flag and Riga, Latvia. No. 2354, Flag and Vilnius, Lithuania.

Perf. 12x12½, 12½ (#2353)

1960 Photo.

2352 A1206 40k red & ultra .65 .25

Typo.

2353 A1206 40k blue, gray & red .65 .25

Litho.

2354 A1206 40k blue, red & grn .65 .25
Nos. 2352-2354 (3) 1.95 .75

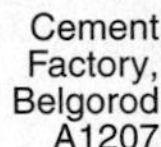

Cement Factory, Belgorod A1207

Design: 40k, Factory, Novy Krivoi.

1960, June 28 *Perf. 12½x12*

2355 A1207 25k ultra & black .40 .25
2356 A1207 40k rose brn & blk .60 .25

"New buildings of the 1st year of the 7-year plan."

Automatic Production Line and Roller Bearing A1208

No. 2358, Automatic production line and gear.

1960, June 13 *Perf. 11½*

2357 A1208 40k rose violet .50 .25
2358 A1208 40k Prus green .50 .25

Publicizing mechanization and automation of factories.

Running A1209

Sports: 10k, Wrestling. 15k, Basketball. 20k, Weight lifting. 25k, Boxing. No. 2364, Fencing. No. 2365, Diving. No. 2366, Women's gymnastics. 60k, Canoeing. 1r, Steeplechase.

1960, Aug. 1 Litho. *Perf. 11½*

2359 A1209 5k multicolored .25 .25
2360 A1209 10k brn, blue & yel .25 .25
2361 A1209 15k multicolored .25 .25
2362 A1209 20k blk, crim & sal .30 .25
2363 A1209 25k lake, sl & rose .30 .25
2364 A1209 40k vio bl, bl & bis .40 .25
2365 A1209 40k vio, gray & pink .40 .25
2366 A1209 40k multicolored .50 .25
2367 A1209 60k multicolored .60 .25
2368 A1209 1r brn, lil & pale grn .90 .45
Nos. 2359-2368 (10) 4.15 2.70

17th Olympic Games, Rome, 8/25-9/11.

No. 2365 Overprinted in Red

1960, Aug. 23

2369 A1209 40k vio, gray & pink 10.00 7.50

12th San Marino-Riccione Stamp Fair.

Kishinev, Moldavian Republic A1210

1960, Aug. 2 *Perf. 12x12½*

2370 A1210 40k multicolored 1.00 .50

20th anniversary of Moldavian Republic.

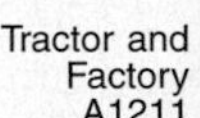

Tractor and Factory A1211

Book Museum, Hanoi — A1212

Perf. 12x12½, 12½x12

1960, Aug. 25

2371 A1211 40k green, ocher & blk .60 .25
2372 A1212 60k blue, lilac & brn .90 .25

15th anniversary of North Viet Nam.

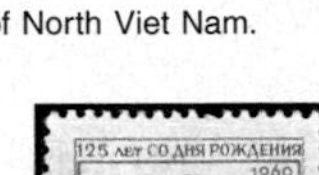

Gregory N. Minkh, Microbiologist, 125th Birth Anniv. — A1213

1960, Aug. 25 Photo. *Perf. 12½x12*

2373 A1213 60k bister brn & dk brn 1.00 .50

"March," by I. I. Levitan A1214

1960, Aug. 29

2374 A1214 40k ol bister & black .75 .30

I. I. Levitan, painter, birth cent.

Fish Type of 1959

Designs: 20k, Pikeperch. 25k, Fur seals. 40k, Ludogan whitefish.

1960, Sept. 3 *Perf. 12½*

2375 A1155 20k blue & black .40 .25
2376 A1155 25k vio gray & red brn .40 .25
2377 A1155 40k rose lil & pur .75 .25
Nos. 2375-2377 (3) 1.55 .75

Forest by I. I. Shishkin — A1215

1960, Aug. 29 Engr.

2378 A1215 1r red brown 2.00 .50

5th World Forestry Congress, Seattle, Wash., Aug. 29-Sept. 10.

Globe with USSR and Letter A1216

1960, Sept. 10 Litho. *Perf. 12x12½*

2379 A1216 40k multicolored .40 .25
2380 A1216 60k multicolored .50 .30

Intl. Letter Writing Week, Oct. 3-9.

Farmer, Worker, Scientist A1217

1960, Oct. 4 Typo. *Perf. 12½*

2381 A1217 40k multicolored .60 .25

Kazakh SSR, 40th anniv.

Globes and Olive Branch — A1218

1960, Sept. 29 Litho. *Perf. 12½x12*

2382 A1218 60k pale vio, bl & gray .70 .25

World Federation of Trade Unions, 15th anniv.

Kremlin, Sputnik 5 and Dogs Belka and Strelka A1219

1960, Sept. 29 Photo.

2383 A1219 40k brt pur & yellow .75 .30
2384 A1219 1r blue & salmon 2.25 .40

Flight of Sputnik 5, Aug. 19-20, 1960.

Passenger Ship "Karl Marx" A1220

Ships: 40k, Turbo-electric ship "Lenin." 60k, Speedboat "Raketa" (Rocket).

1960, Oct. 24 Litho. *Perf. 12x12½*

2385 A1220 25k bl, blk, red & yel .40 .25
2386 A1220 40k blue, black & red .60 .25
2387 A1220 60k blue, blk & rose 1.00 .35
Nos. 2385-2387 (3) 2.00 .85

A. N. Voronikhin and Kasansky Cathedral, Leningrad A1221

1960, Oct. 24 Photo.

2388 A1221 40k gray & brn black 1.00 .50

Voronikhin, architect, 200th birth anniv.

J. S. Gogebashvili A1222

1960, Oct. 29

2389 A1222 40k dk gray & mag 1.00 .50

120th anniversary of the birth of J. S. Gogebashvili, Georgian teacher and publicist.

Red Flag, Electric Power Station and Factory — A1223

1960, Oct. 29 Litho.

2390 A1223 40k red, yel & brown .70 .25

43rd anniversary of October Revolution.

Leo Tolstoy A1224

Designs: 40k, Tolstoy in Yasnaya Polyana. 60k, Portrait, vert.

Perf. 12x12½, 12½x12

1960, Nov. 14

2391 A1224 20k violet & brown .30 .25
2392 A1224 40k blue & lt brown .70 .25
2393 A1224 60k dp clar & sep 1.00 .35
Nos. 2391-2393 (3) 2.00 .85

50th anniversary of the death of Count Leo Tolstoy, writer.

Yerevan, Armenian Republic A1225

1960, Nov. 14 *Perf. 12x12½*

2394 A1225 40k bl, red, buff & brn 1.00 .50

Armenian Soviet Rep., 40th anniv.

Friedrich Engels, 140th Birth Anniv. — A1226

1960, Nov. 25 Engr. *Perf. 12½*

2395 A1226 60k slate 1.00 .50

Badge of Youth Federation A1227

1960, Nov. 2 Litho.

2396 A1227 60k brt pink, blk & yel .50 .25

Intl. Youth Federation, 15th anniv.

40-ton Truck MAL-530 A1228

Automotive Industry: 40k, "Volga" car. 60k, "Moskvitch 407" car. 1r, "Tourist LAS-697" Bus.

1960, Oct. 29 Photo. *Perf. 12x12½*

2397 A1228 25k ultra & gray .40 .25
2398 A1228 40k ol bister & ultra .60 .25
2399 A1228 60k Prus green & dp car .90 .25

Litho.

2400 A1228 1r multicolored 1.40 .35
Nos. 2397-2400 (4) 3.30 1.10

N. I. Pirogov — A1229

1960, Dec. 13 Photo. *Perf. 12½x12*

2401 A1229 40k grn & brn blk 1.00 .50

Pirogov, surgeon, 125th birth anniv.

Friendship University and Students A1230

1960, Nov. *Perf. 12x12½*

2402 A1230 40k brown carmine 1.00 .50

Completion of Friendship of Nations University in Moscow.
For surcharge see No. 2462.

Mark Twain A1231

1960, Nov. 30 Photo. *Perf. 12½x12*

2403 A1231 40k dp org & brown 2.00 .90

Mark Twain, 125th birth anniv.

Dove and Globe — A1232

1960, Oct. 29 Photo.

2404 A1232 60k maroon & gray 1.00 .50

Intl. Democratic Women's Fed, 15th anniv.

Akaki Tsereteli — A1233

1960, Dec. 27

2405 A1233 40k vio & blk brn 1.00 .30

Tsereteli, Georgian poet, 120th birth anniv.

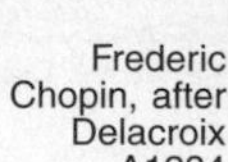

Frederic Chopin, after Delacroix A1234

1960, Dec. 24 *Perf. 12x11½*

2406 A1234 40k bister & brown 1.10 .25

Chopin, Polish composer, 150th birth anniv.

North Korean Flag and Flying Horse — A1235

1960, Dec. 24 Litho. *Perf. 12½x12*

2407 A1235 40k multicolored 1.00 .50

15th anniversary of "the liberation of the Korean people by the Soviet army."

Crocus — A1236

Asiatic Flowers: No. 2409, Tulip. No. 2410, Trollius. No. 2411, Tulip. No. 2412, Ginseng. No. 2413, Iris. No. 2414, Hypericum. 1r, Dog rose.

1960 *Perf. 12x12½*

Flowers in Natural Colors

2408 A1236 20k green & violet .30 .25
2409 A1236 20k vio blue & black .30 .25
2410 A1236 25k gray .35 .25
2411 A1236 40k ol bister & black .40 .25
2412 A1236 40k grn & blk, wmkd. .40 .25
2413 A1236 60k yel, green & red .75 .25
2414 A1236 60k bluish grn & blk .75 .25
2415 A1236 1r slate grn & blk 1.25 .25
Nos. 2408-2415 (8) 4.50 2.00

The watermark on No. 2412 consists of vertical rows of chevrons.

Lithuanian Costumes A1237

Regional Costumes: 60k, Uzbek.

Perf. 12½ (10k), 11½ (60k)

1960, Dec. 24 Typo. Unwmk.

2416 A1237 10k multicolored .25 .25
2417 A1237 60k multicolored 1.00 .40

Currency Revalued

1961-62 Litho. *Perf. 11½*

Regional Costumes: No. 2418, Moldavia. No. 2419, Georgia. No. 2420, Ukrainia. No. 2421, White Russia. No. 2422, Kazakhstan. No. 2422A, Latvia. 4k, Koryak. 6k, Russia. 10k, Armenia. 12k, Estonia.

2418 A1237 2k buff, brn & ver .25 .25
2419 A1237 2k red, brn, ocher & black .25 .25
2420 A1237 3k ultra, buff, red & brown .30 .25
2421 A1237 3k red org, ocher & black .30 .25
2422 A1237 3k buff, brn, grn & red .30 .25
2422A A1237 3k org red, gray ol & blk ('62) .30 .25
2423 A1237 4k multicolored .50 .25

2424 A1237 6k multicolored .60 .30
2425 A1237 10k brn, ol bis & vermilion .90 .35
2426 A1237 12k red, ultra & black 1.25 .45
Nos. 2418-2426 (10) 4.95 2.85

See Nos. 2723-2726.

Lenin and Map Showing Electrification — A1238

1961 ***Perf. 12½x12***
2427 A1238 4k blue, buff & brown .50 .25
2428 A1238 10k red org & blue blk 1.00 .35

State Electrification Plan, 40th anniv. (in 1960).

Animal Types of 1957

1961, Jan. 7 ***Perf. 12½***
2429 A1024 1k Brown bear .75 .25
2430 A1023 6k Beaver 2.25 .70
2431 A1023 10k Roe deer 3.00 .95
Nos. 2429-2431 (3) 6.00 1.90

Georgian Flag and Views A1239

1961, Feb. 15 ***Perf. 12½x12***
2432 A1239 4k multicolored .40 .25

40th anniv. of Georgian SSR.

Nikolai D. Zelinski, Chemist, Birth Cent. A1240

1961, Feb. 6 **Photo.** ***Perf. 12x12½***
2433 A1240 4k rose violet .50 .25

Nikolai A. Dobrolyubov (1836-61), Journalist and Critic — A1241

1961, Feb. 5 ***Perf. 11½x12***
2434 A1241 4k brt blue & brown .55 .25

A1242

Designs: 3k, Cattle. 4k, Tractor in cornfield. 6k, Mechanization of Grain Harvest. 10k, Women picking apples.

1961 ***Perf. 12x12½, 12x11½***
2435 A1242 3k blue & magenta .30 .25
2436 A1242 4k green & dk gray .30 .25
2437 A1242 6k vio blue & brn .70 .25
2438 A1242 10k maroon & ol grn 1.00 .40
Nos. 2435-2438 (4) 2.30 1.15

Agricultural development.

A1243

Designs: 1k, "Labor" Holding Peace Flag. 2k, Harvester and silo. 3k, Space rockets. 4k, Arms and flag of USSR. 6k, Kremlin tower. 10k, Workers' monument. 12k, Minin and Pozharsky Monument and Spasski tower. 16k, Plane over power station and dam.

Perf. 12x12½; 12x11½ (Nos. 2439A, 2442 & 12k)

1961-65 **Engr.** **Unwmk.**
2439 A1243 1k olive bister 1.00 .25

Litho.

2439A A1243 1k olive bister 1.00 .25
2440 A1243 2k green .35 .30
2441 A1243 3k dk violet 2.50 .25

Engr.

2442 A1243 3k dk violet 5.25 2.50

Litho.

2443 A1243 4k red .75 .25
2443A A1243 4k org brn ('65) 13.00 9.00
2444 A1243 6k vermilion 6.00 .90
2445 A1243 6k dk car rose 2.00 .25
2446 A1243 10k orange 3.75 .25

Photo.

2447 A1243 12k brt magenta 3.50 .30

Litho.

2448 A1243 16k ultra 4.50 .80
Nos. 2439-2448 (12) 43.60 15.30

V. P. Miroshnitchenko — A1244

1961, Feb. 23 **Photo.** ***Perf. 12½x12***
2449 A1244 4k violet brn & slate .75 .40

Soldier hero of World War II.
See Nos. 2570-2571.

Taras G. Shevchenko and Birthplace — A1245

Shevchenko Statue, Kharkov — A1246

6k, Book, torch and Shevchenko with beard.

Perf. 12½, 11½x12

1961, Mar. **Litho.; Photo. (4k)**
2450 A1245 3k brown & violet .50 .25
2451 A1246 4k red org & gray .40 .25
2452 A1245 6k blk, grn & red brn .85 .30
Nos. 2450-2452 (3) 1.75 .80

Shevchenko, Ukrainian poet, death cent.
No. 2452 was printed with alternating green and black label, containing a quotation.
See No. 2852.

Andrei Rubljov — A1247

1961, Mar. 13 **Litho.** ***Perf. 12½x12***
2453 A1247 4k ultra, bister & brn 1.00 .50

Rubljov, painter, 600th birth anniv.

N. V. Sklifosovsky A1248

1961, Mar. 26 **Photo.** ***Perf. 11½x12***
2454 A1248 4k ultra & black 1.00 .35

Sklifosovsky, surgeon, 125th birth anniv.

Robert Koch — A1249

1961, Mar. 26
2455 A1249 6k dark brown 2.00 .50

Koch, German microbiologist, 59th death anniv.

Globe and Sputnik 8 — A1250

10k, Venera 1 space probe and its path to Venus.

1961, Apr. **Litho.** ***Perf. 11½***
2456 A1250 6k dk & lt blue & org .65 .25

Photo.

2457 A1250 10k vio blue & yel .90 .35

Launching of the Venera 1 space probe, 2/12/61.

Open Book and Globe A1251

1961, Apr. 7 **Litho.** ***Perf. 12½x12***
2458 A1251 6k ultra & sepia .75 .25

Centenary of the magazine "Around the World."

Musician, Dancers and Singers A1252

1961, Apr. 7 **Unwmk.**
2459 A1252 4k yel, red & black .50 .25

Russian National Choir, 50th anniv.

African Breaking Chains and Map — A1253

6k, Globe, torch & black & white handshake.

1961, Apr. 15 ***Perf. 12½***
2460 A1253 4k multicolored .60 .25
2461 A1253 6k blue, pur & org .60 .25

Africa Day and 3rd Conference of Independent African States, Cairo, Mar. 25-31.

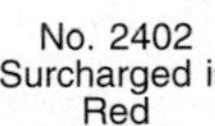

No. 2402 Surcharged in Red

1961, Apr. 15 **Photo.** ***Perf. 12x12½***
2462 A1230 4k on 40k brn car 1.00 .40

Naming of Friendship University, Moscow, in memory of Patrice Lumumba, Premier of Congo.

Maj. Yuri A. Gagarin A1254

6k, Kremlin, rockets and radar equipment. 10k, Rocket, Gagarin with helmet and Kremlin.

1961, Apr. ***Perf. 11½ (3k), 12½x12***
2463 A1254 3k Prus blue .35 .25

Litho.

2464 A1254 6k blue, vio & red .70 .25
2465 A1254 10k red, blue grn & brn 1.20 .25
Nos. 2463-2465 (3) 2.25 .75

1st man in space, Yuri A. Gagarin, Apr. 12, 1961. No. 2464 printed with alternating light blue and red label.
Nos. 2463-2465 exist imperf. Value $5.

Lenin — A1255

1961, Apr. 22 Litho. *Perf. 12x12½*
2466 A1255 4k dp car, sal & blk .75 .25

91st anniversary of Lenin's birth.

Rabindranath Tagore — A1256

1961, May 8 Engr. *Perf. 11½x12*
2467 A1256 6k bis, maroon & blk 1.00 .25

Tagore, Indian poet, birth cent.

The Hunchbacked Horse — A1257

Fairy Tales: 1k, The Geese and the Swans. 3k, Fox, Hare and Cock. 6k, The Peasant and the Bear. 10k, Ruslan and Ludmilla.

1961 Litho. *Perf. 12½*

2468	A1257	1k multicolored	.25	.25
2469	A1257	3k multicolored	.75	.35
2470	A1257	4k multicolored	.50	.25
2471	A1257	6k multicolored	.90	.40
2472	A1257	10k multicolored	1.10	.45
		Nos. 2468-2472 (5)	3.50	1.70

"Man Conquering Space" A1258

Design: 6k, Giuseppe Garibaldi.

1961, May 24 Photo.
2481 A1258 4k orange brown .40 .30
2482 A1258 6k lilac & salmon .60 .30

International Labor Exposition, Turin.

Lenin — A1259

Various portraits of Lenin.

1961 Photo. *Perf. 12½x12*
Olive Bister Frame

2483	A1259	20k dark green	1.75	1.00
2484	A1259	30k dark blue	2.75	2.00
2485	A1259	50k rose red	8.00	6.00
		Nos. 2483-2485 (3)	12.50	9.00

Patrice Lumumba — A1260

1961, May 29 Litho.
2486 A1260 2k yellow & brown .50 .25

Lumumba (1925-61), premier of Congo.

Kindergarten — A1261

Children's Day: 3k, Young Pioneers in camp. 4k, Young Pioneers, vert.

Perf. 12½x12, 12x12½
1961, May 31 Photo.

2487	A1261	2k orange & ultra	.25	.25
2488	A1261	3k ol bister & purple	.60	.30
2489	A1261	4k red & gray	1.00	.25
		Nos. 2487-2489 (3)	1.85	.80

Dog Zvezdochka and Sputnik 10 — A1263

Sputniks 9 and 10: 4k, Dog Chernushka and Sputnik 9, vert.

1961, June 8 Litho. *Perf. 12½, 11½*
2491 A1263 2k vio, Prus blue & blk 5.00 2.50

Photo.
2492 A1263 4k Prus blue & brt grn 5.00 2.50

Vissarion G. Belinski, Author, 150th Birth. Anniv. — A1265

Engraved and Photogravure
1961, June 13 *Perf. 11½x12*
2493 A1265 4k carmine & black .75 .35

Lt. Gen. D.M. Karbishev A1266

1961, June 22 Litho. *Perf. 12½*
2494 A1266 4k black, red & yel .35 .25

Karbishev was tortured to death in the Nazi prison camp at Mauthausen, Austria.

Hydro-meteorological Map and Instruments — A1267

1961, June 21 *Perf. 12x12½*
2495 A1267 6k ultra & green .50 .35

40th anniversary of hydro-meteorological service in Russia.

Gliders A1268

6k, Motorboat race. 10k, Motorcycle race.

1961, July 5 Photo. *Perf. 12½*
2497 A1268 4k dk slate grn & crim .30 .25

Litho.

2498	A1268	6k slate & vermilion	.45	.25
2499	A1268	10k slate & vermilion	1.40	.35
		Nos. 2497-2499 (3)	2.15	.85

USSR Technical Sports Spartakiad.

Javelin Thrower A1269

1961, Aug. 8 Photo. *Perf. 12½x12*
2500 A1269 6k dp car & pink .50 .25

7th Trade Union Spartacist Games.

S. I. Vavilov — A1270

1961, July 25
2501 A1270 4k lt green & sepia .60 .25

Vavilov, president of Academy of Science.

Vazha Pshavela — A1271

1961 Photo. *Perf. 11½x12*
2502 A1271 4k dk brn & cream .75 .35

Pshavela, Georgian poet, birth cent.

Scientists at Control Panel for Rocket — A1272

Globe and Youth Activities A1273

Design: 2k, Men pushing tank into river.

1961 Unwmk. *Perf. 11½*

2503	A1273	2k orange & sepia	.25	.25
2504	A1272	4k lilac & dk green	.60	.40
2505	A1273	6k ultra & citron	1.00	.60
		Nos. 2503-2505 (3)	1.85	1.25

International Youth Forum, Moscow.

Arms of Mongolian Republic and Sukhe Bator Statue A1274

1961, July 25 Litho. *Perf. 12½x12*
2506 A1274 4k multicolored 1.00 .50

Mongol national revolution, 40th anniv.

Knight Kalevipoeg A1275

1961, July 31
2507 A1275 4k black, blue & yel .75 .35

1st publication of "Kalevipoeg," Estonian national saga, recorded by R. K. Kreutzwald, Estonian writer, cent.

Symbols of Biochemistry A1276

1961, July 31
2508 A1276 6k multicolored .75 .35

5th Intl. Biochemistry Congress, Moscow.

Major Titov and Vostok 2 — A1277

4k, Globe with orbit and cosmonaut.

1961, Aug. Photo. *Perf. 11½*
2509 A1277 4k vio blue & dp plum .35 .25
2510 A1277 6k brown, grn & org .65 .25

1st manned space flight around the world, Maj. Gherman S. Titov, Aug. 6-7, 1961. Nos. 2509-2510 exist imperf. Value, set $10.

A. D. Zacharov and Admiralty Building, Leningrad A1278

1961, Aug. 8 *Perf. 12x11½*

2511 A1278 4k blue, dk brn & buff .50 .25

Zacharov (1761-1811), architect.

Defense of Brest, 1941 A1279

Designs: No. 2512, Defense of Moscow. No. 2514, Defense of Odessa. No. 2514A, Defense of Sevastopol. No. 2514B, Defense of Leningrad. No. 2514C, Defense of Kiev. No. 2514D, Battle of the Volga (Stalingrad).

1961-63 **Photo.** *Perf. 12½x12*

2512 A1279 4k blk & red brn (Moscow) .50 .25

Litho.

2513 A1279 4k (Brest) .50 .25
2514 A1279 4k (Odessa) .50 .25
2514A A1279 4k (Sevastopol; '62) .50 .25
2514B A1279 4k brn, dl bl & bis (Leningrad; '63) .50 .25
2514C A1279 4k blk & multi (Kiev; '63) .50 .25
2514D A1279 4k dl org & multi (Volga; '63) .50 .25
Nos. 2512-2514D (7) 3.50 1.75

"War of Liberation," 1941-1945.
See Nos. 2757-2758.

Students' Union Emblem A1280

1961, Aug. 8 **Litho.** *Perf. 12½*

2515 A1280 6k ultra & red .75 .35

15th anniversary of the founding of the International Students' Union.

Soviet Stamps A1281

Stamps and background different on each denomination.

1961, Aug. *Perf. 12½x12*

2516 A1281 2k multicolored .40 .25
2517 A1281 4k multicolored .75 .30
2518 A1281 6k multicolored 1.25 .35
2519 A1281 10k multicolored 2.00 .50
Nos. 2516-2519 (4) 4.40 1.40

40 years of Soviet postage stamps.

Nikolai A. Schors Statue, Kiev — A1282

Statue: 4k, Gregori I. Kotovski, Kishinev.

1961 **Photo.** *Perf. 11½x12*

2520 A1282 2k lt ultra & sepia .50 .25
2521 A1282 4k rose vio & sepia .50 .25

Letters and Means of Transportation — A1283

1961, Sept. 15 *Perf. 11½*

2522 A1283 4k dk car & black .50 .25

International Letter Writing Week.

Angara River Bridge, Irkutsk A1284

1961, Sept. 15 **Litho.** *Perf. 12½x12*

2523 A1284 4k ol bis, lil & blk 2.00 .50

300th anniversary of Irkutsk.

Lenin, Marx, Engels and Marchers — A1285

3k, Obelisk commemorating conquest of space and Moscow University. #2526, Harvester combine. #2527, Industrial control center. #2528, Worker pointing to globe.

1961 **Litho.**

2524 A1285 2k ver, yel & brown .40 .25
2525 A1285 3k org & deep blue 2.25 .40
2526 A1285 4k mar, bis & red brown .75 .40
2527 A1285 4k car rose, brn, org & blue .75 .40
2528 A1285 4k red & dk brown .75 .40
Nos. 2524-2528 (5) 4.90 1.85

22nd Congress of the Communist Party of the USSR, Oct. 17-31.

Soviet Soldier Monument, Berlin — A1286

1961, Sept. 28 **Photo.** *Perf. 12x12½*

2529 A1286 4k red & gray violet .75 .30

10th anniversary of the International Federation of Resistance, FIR.

Workers Studying Mathematics — A1287

Designs: 2k, Communist labor team. 4k, Workers around piano.

1961, Sept. 28 **Litho.** *Perf. 12½x12*

2530 A1287 2k plum & red, *cream* .50 .35
2531 A1287 3k brn & red, *yellow* 1.00 .50
2532 A1287 4k vio blue & red, *cr* 1.50 .65
Nos. 2530-2532 (3) 3.00 1.50

Publicizing Communist labor teams in their efforts for labor, education and relaxation.

Rocket and Stars — A1288

Engraved on Aluminum Foil

1961, Oct. 17 *Perf. 12½*

2533 A1288 1r black & red 25.00 25.00

Soviet scientific and technical achievements in exploring outer space.

Overprinted in Red

1961, Oct. 23

2534 A1288 1r black & red 27.50 27.50

Communist Party of the USSR, 22nd cong.

Amangaldi Imanov — A1289

1961, Oct. 25 **Photo.** *Perf. 11½x12*

2535 A1289 4k green, buff & brn .75 .25

Amangaldi Imanov (1873-1919), champion of Soviet power in Kazakhstan.

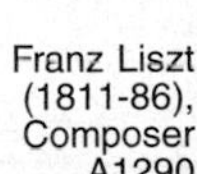

Franz Liszt (1811-86), Composer A1290

1961, Oct. 31 *Perf. 12x11½*

2536 A1290 4k mar, dk brn & ocher 5.00 2.00

Flags and Slogans A1291

1961, Nov. 4 *Perf. 11½*

2537 A1291 4k red, yel & dark red .75 .35

44th anniversary of October Revolution.

Hand Holding Hammer — A1292

Congress Emblem A1293

Designs: Nos. 2538, 2542, Congress emblem. Nos. 2539, 2543, African breaking chains. No. 2541, Three hands holding globe.

1961, Nov. *Perf. 12, 12½, 11½*

2538 A1293 2k scarlet & bister .25 .25
2539 A1293 2k dk purple & gray .25 .25
2540 A1292 4k plum, org & blue .60 .25
2541 A1292 4k blk, lt blue & pink .75 .25
2542 A1293 6k grn, bister & red .75 .25
2543 A1293 6k ind, dull yel & red .75 .25
Nos. 2538-2543 (6) 3.35 1.50

Fifth World Congress of Trade Unions, Moscow, Dec. 4-16.

Lomonosov Statue — A1294

Designs: 6k, Lomonosov at desk. 10k, Lomonosov, his birthplace and Leningrad Academy of Science, horiz.

Perf. 11½x12, 12x11½

1961, Nov. 19 **Photo. & Engr.**

2544 A1294 4k Prus blue, yel grn & brown .60 .25
2545 A1294 6k grn, yel & blk 1.00 .35
2546 A1294 10k mar, slate & brn 1.25 .60
Nos. 2544-2546 (3) 2.85 1.20

250th anniversary of the birth of M. V. Lomonosov, scientist and poet.

Hands Holding Hammer and Sickle — A1295

1961, Nov. 27 **Litho.** *Perf. 12x12½*

2547 A1295 4k red & yellow .60 .30

USSR constitution, 25th anniv.

Romeo and Juliet Ballet — A1296

Ballets: 2k, Red Flower. 3k, Paris Flame. 10k, Swan Lake.

1961-62 *Perf. 12x12½*

2548 A1296 2k brn, car & lt green ('62) .25 .25
2549 A1296 3k multi ('62) .45 .25
2550 A1296 6k dk brn, bis & vio .65 .25

2551 A1296 10k blue, pink & dk brn 1.00 .30
Nos. 2548-2551 (4) 2.35 1.05

Honoring the Russian Ballet.

Linemen A1297

1961 ***Perf. 12½***

2552 A1297 3k shown .75 .25
2553 A1297 4k Welders .75 .25
2554 A1297 6k Surveyor 1.50 .35
Nos. 2552-2554 (3) 3.00 .85

Honoring self-sacrificing work of youth in the 7-year plan.

Andrejs Pumpurs (1841-1902), Latvian Poet and Satirist A1298

1961, Dec. 20 ***Perf. 12x11½***

2555 A1298 4k gray & claret 2.00 .50

Bulgarian Couple, Flag, Emblem and Building A1299

1961, Dec. 28 ***Perf. 12½x12***

2556 A1299 4k multicolored 1.00 .50

Bulgarian People's Republic, 15th anniv.

Fridtjof Nansen A1300

1961, Dec. 30 **Photo.** ***Perf. 11½***

2557 A1300 6k dk blue & brown 2.00 .60

Centenary of the birth of Fridtjof Nansen, Norwegian Polar explorer.

Mihael Ocipovich Dolivo-Dobrovolsky — A1301

1962, Jan. 25 ***Perf. 12x11½***

2558 A1301 4k bister & dark blue .50 .25

Dolivo-Dobrovolsky, scientist and electrical engineer, birth cent.

Woman and Various Activities A1302

1962, Jan. 26 ***Perf. 11½***

2559 A1302 4k bister, blk & dp org .60 .25

Honoring Soviet Women.

Aleksander S. Pushkin, 125th Death Anniv. — A1303

1962, Jan. 26 **Litho.** ***Perf. 12½x12***

2560 A1303 4k buff, dk brn & ver .50 .25

Dancers A1304

1962, Feb. 6 ***Perf. 12x12½***

2561 A1304 4k bister & ver .60 .25

State ensemble of folk dancers, 25th anniv.

Speed Skating, Luzhniki Stadium A1305

Perf. 11½

1962, Feb. 17 **Unwmk.** **Photo.**

2562 A1305 4k orange & ultra .60 .25

Intl. Winter Sports Championships, Moscow.

No. 2562 Overprinted

1962, Mar. 3

2563 A1305 4k orange & ultra 2.40 1.50

Victories of I. Voronina and V. Kosichkin, world speed skating champions, 1962.

Ski Jump A1305a

10k, Woman long distance skier, vert.

1962, May 31 ***Perf. 11½***

2564 A1305a 2k ultra, brn & red .30 .25
2565 A1305a 10k org, ultra & black .70 .25

Intl. Winter Sports Championships, Zakopane.

Hero Type of 1961

4k, V. S. Shalandin. 6k, Magomet Gadgiev.

1962, Feb. 22 ***Perf. 12½x12***

2570 A1244 4k dk blue & brown 1.60 .80
2571 A1244 6k brn & slate grn 1.60 .80

Soldier heroes of World War II.

Skier A1306

1962, Mar. 3 ***Perf. 11½***

2572 A1306 4k shown .40 .25
2573 A1306 6k Ice hockey .50 .25
2574 A1306 10k Ice skating 1.00 .40
Nos. 2572-2574 (3) 1.90 .90

First People's Winter Games, Sverdlovsk. For overprints see Nos. 2717, 3612.

Aleksandr Ivanovich Herzen (1812-70), Political Writer A1307

1962, Mar. 28 **Litho.** ***Perf. 12x12½***

2575 A1307 4k ultra, black & buff .50 .25

Lenin — A1308

Design: 6k, Lenin, horiz.

1962, Mar. 28 ***Perf. 12x12½, 12½x12***

2576 A1308 4k brown, red & yel .80 .25
2577 A1308 6k blue, org & brn 1.20 .25

14th congress of the Young Communist League (Komsomol).

Vostok 1 — A1309

1962, Apr. **Unwmk.** ***Perf. 11x11½***

2578 A1309 10k multicolored 1.00 .60

1st anniv. of Yuri A. Gagarin's flight into space.

No. 2578 was printed in sheets of 20 stamps alternating with 20 labels.

No. 2578 was also issued imperf. Value $2.

Bust of Tchaikovsky A1310

1962, Apr. 19 **Photo.** ***Perf. 11½x12***

2579 A1310 4k blue, blk & bis 1.00 .30

Second International Tchaikovsky Competition in Moscow.

Youths of 3 Races, Broken Chain, Globe A1311

1962, Apr. 19 ***Perf. 11½***

2580 A1311 6k black, brn & yel .50 .25

International Day of Solidarity of Youth against Colonialism.

Ulyanov (Lenin) Family Portrait A1312

Lenin A1313

1962, Apr. 21 ***Perf. 12x11½***

2581 A1312 4k gray, red & dk brn .40 .25

Typographed and Embossed

Perf. 12½

2582 A1313 10k dk red, gray & blk .90 .35
a. Souv. sheet of 2, perf. 12 5.00 3.00

92nd anniversary of the birth of Lenin.

No. 2582a for 94th anniv. of the birth of Lenin. Issued Nov. 6, 1964.

Cosmos 3 Satellite — A1314

1962, Apr. 26 **Litho.** ***Perf. 12½x12***

2586 A1314 6k blk, lt blue & vio .50 .25

Cosmos 3 earth satellite launching, Apr. 24.

Charles Dickens — A1315

No. 2589, Jean Jacques Rousseau.

1962, Apr. 29

2588 A1315 6k blue, brn & pur .50 .25

Perf. 11½x12

Photo.

2589 A1315 6k gray, lilac & brn .50 .25

Charles Dickens, English writer, 150th birth anniv., and Jean Jacques Rousseau, French writer, 250th birth anniv.

Karl Marx Monument, Moscow — A1316

1962, Apr. 29 ***Perf. 12x12½***
2590 A1316 4k deep ultra & gray .50 .25

Pravda, Lenin, Revolutionists A1317

Lenin Reading Pravda — A1318

No. 2592, Pravda, Lenin and rocket.

1962, May 4 **Litho.**
2591 A1317 4k blk, bis & red .65 .25
2592 A1317 4k red, blk & ocher .65 .25

Perf. 11½

Photo.

2593 A1318 4k ocher, dp clar & red .65 .25
Nos. 2591-2593 (3) 1.95 .75

50th anniversary of Pravda, Russian newspaper founded by Lenin.

Malaria Eradication Emblem and Mosquito A1319

1962
2594 A1319 4k Prus blue, red & blk .50 .25
2595 A1319 6k ol grn, red & blk .50 .35

WHO drive to eradicate malaria.
Issue dates: 4k, May 6; 6k, June 23.
No. 2595 exists imperf. Value $1.

Pioneers Taking Oath before Lenin and Emblem A1320

Designs (Emblem and): 3k, Lenja Golikov and Valja Kotik. No. 2598, Pioneers building rocket model. No. 2599, Red Cross, Red Crescent and nurse giving health instruction. 6k, Pioneers of many races and globe.

1962, May 19 **Litho.** ***Perf. 12½x12***
2596 A1320 2k green, red & brn .30 .25
2597 A1320 3k multicolored .30 .25
2598 A1320 4k multicolored .50 .25
2599 A1320 4k multicolored .50 .25
2600 A1320 6k multicolored .80 .25
Nos. 2596-2600 (5) 2.40 1.25

All-Union Lenin Pioneers, 40th anniv.

Mesrob — A1321

1962, May 27 **Photo.** ***Perf. 12½x12***
2601 A1321 4k yel & dk brn 1.00 .25

"1600th" anniversary of the birth of Bishop Mesrob (350?-439), credited as author of the Armenian and Georgian alphabets.

Ivan A. Goncharov A1322

1962, June 18
2602 A1322 4k gray & brown .75 .35

Ivan Aleksandrovich Goncharov (1812-91), novelist, 150th birth anniv.

Volleyball — A1323

2k, Bicyclists, horiz. 10k, Eight-man shell. 12k, Goalkeeper, soccer, horiz. 16k, Steeplechase.

1962, June 27 ***Perf. 11½***
2603 A1323 2k lt brn, blk & ver .25 .25
2604 A1323 4k brn org, black & buff .30 .25
2605 A1323 10k ultra, black & yel .85 .25
2606 A1323 12k lt blue, brn & yel .95 .35
2607 A1323 16k lt green, blk & red 1.10 .45
Nos. 2603-2607 (5) 3.45 1.55

Intl. Summer Sports Championships, 1962.

Louis Pasteur — A1324

1962, June 30 ***Perf. 12½x12***
2608 A1324 6k blk & brn org .60 .25

Invention of the sterilization process by Louis Pasteur, French chemist, cent.

Library, 1862 A1325

Design: No. 2610, New Lenin Library.

1962, June 30 **Photo.**
2609 A1325 4k slate & black .40 .25
2610 A1325 4k slate & black .40 .25
a. Pair, #2609-2610 2.00 .75

Centenary of the Lenin Library, Moscow.

Auction Building and Ermine — A1326

1962, June 30 **Litho.**
2611 A1326 6k multicolored 1.00 .25

International Fur Auction, Leningrad.

Young Couple, Lenin, Kremlin — A1327

Workers of Three Races and Dove — A1328

1962, June 30 ***Perf. 12x12½***
2612 A1327 2k multicolored .40 .30
2613 A1328 4k multicolored .60 .30

Program of the Communist Party of the Soviet Union for the Peace and Friendship among all people.

Hands Breaking Bomb A1329

1962, July 7 ***Perf. 11½***
2614 A1329 6k blue, blk & olive .50 .35

World Congress for Peace and Disarmament, Moscow, July 9-14.

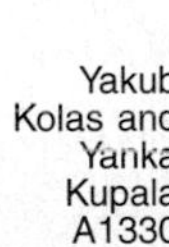

Yakub Kolas and Yanka Kupala A1330

1962, July 7 **Photo.** ***Perf. 12½x12***
2615 A1330 4k henna brn & buff .50 .35

Byelorussian poets. Kolas (1882-1956), and Kupala (1882-1942).

Alekper Sabir (1862-1911), Azerbaijani Poet, Satirist — A1331

1962, July 16 ***Perf. 11½***
2616 A1331 4k buff, dk brn & blue .70 .35

Examples inscribed "Azerbajanyn" were withdrawn before release. Value, $250.

Cancer Congress Emblem A1332

1962, July 16 **Litho.** ***Perf. 12½***
2617 A1332 6k grnsh blue, blk & red .50 .35

8th Anti-Cancer Cong., Moscow, July 1962.

N. N. Zinin, Chemist, 150th Birth Anniv. A1333

1962, July 16 **Photo.** ***Perf. 12x11½***
2618 A1333 4k violet & dk brown .45 .25

I. M. Kramskoy, Painter — A1334

I. D. Shadr, Sculptor A1335

M. V. Nesterov, Painter A1336

1962, July 28 ***Perf. 11½x12, 12x12½***
2619 A1334 4k gray, mar & dk brn .50 .30
2620 A1335 4k blk & red brn .50 .30
2621 A1336 4k multicolored .50 .30
Nos. 2619-2621 (3) 1.50 .90

Vostok 2 Going into Space — A1337

Perf. 11½

1962, Aug. 7 **Unwmk.** **Photo.**
2622 A1337 10k blk, lilac & blue .65 .25
2623 A1337 10k blk, org & blue .65 .25

1st anniv. of Gherman Titov's space flight. Issued imperf. on Aug. 6. Value, set $4.50.

Friendship House, Moscow
A1338

1962, Aug. 15 *Perf. 12x12½*
2624 A1338 6k ultra & gray .50 .25

Moscow State University and Atom Symbol — A1339

Design: 6k, Map of Russia, atom symbol and "Peace" in 10 languages.

1962, Aug. 15 Litho. *Perf. 12½x12*
2625 A1339 4k multicolored .50 .25
2626 A1339 6k multicolored .50 .25

Use of atomic energy for peace.

Andrian G. Nikolayev
A1340

Cosmonauts in Space Helments — A1341

"To Space" Monument by G. Postnikov — A1342

Design: No. 2628, Pavel R. Popovich, with inscription at left and dated "12-15-VIII, 1962." 1r, Monument and portraits of Gagarin, Titov, Nikolayev and Popovich.

1962 Photo. *Perf. 11½*
2627 A1340 4k blue, brn & red .40 .25
2628 A1340 4k blue, brn & red .40 .25

Perf. 12½x12

Litho.

2629 A1341 6k dk bl, lt bl, org & yellow 1.00 .30

Perf. 11½

Photo.

2630 A1342 6k brt blue & multi 1.00 .25
2631 A1342 10k violet & multi 1.40 .35
Nos. 2627-2631 (5) 4.20 1.40

Souvenir Sheet

1962, Nov. 27 Litho. *Perf. 12½*
2631A A1342 1r brt bl, blk & sil 35.00 5.00

Nos. 2627-2631A honor the four Russian "conquerors of space," with Nos. 2627-2629 for the 1st group space flight, by Vostoks 3 and 4, Aug. 11-15, 1962. Also issued imperf. Value, set $6, souvenir sheet $50.
For overprint see No. 2662.

Carp and Bream — A1343

Design: 6k, Freshwater salmon.

1962, Aug. 28 Photo. *Perf. 11½x12*
2632 A1343 4k blue & orange .45 .25
2633 A1343 6k blue & orange .60 .30

Fish preservation in USSR.

Feliks E. Dzerzhinski — A1344

1962, Sept. 6 Litho. *Perf. 12½x12*
2634 A1344 4k ol grn & dk blue .70 .50

Dzerzhinski (1877-1926), organizer of Soviet secret police, 85th birth anniv.

O. Henry and New York Skyline
A1345

1962, Sept. 10 Photo. *Perf. 12x11½*
2635 A1345 6k yel, red brn & black .55 .35

O. Henry (William Sidney Porter, 1862-1910), American writer.

Barclay de Tolly, Mikhail I. Kutuzov, Petr I. Bagration
A1346

4k, Denis Davidov leading partisans. 6k, Battle of Borodino. 10k, Wasilisa Kozhina and partisans.

1962, Sept. 25 *Perf. 12½x12*
2636 A1346 3k orange brown .30 .25
2637 A1346 4k ultra .30 .25
2638 A1346 6k blue gray .65 .25
2639 A1346 10k violet .75 .25
Nos. 2636-2639 (4) 2.00 1.00

War of 1812 against the French, 150th anniv.

Street in Vinnitsa
A1347

1962, Sept. 25 **Photo.**
2640 A1347 4k yel bister & black .50 .25

Town of Vinnitsa, Ukraine, 600th anniv.

"Mail and Transportation" — A1348

1962, Sept. 25 *Perf. 11½*
2641 A1348 4k blue grn, blk & lil .50 .25

Intl. Letter Writing Week, Oct. 7-13.

Cedar — A1349

4k, Canna. 6k, Arbutus. 10k, Chrysanthemum.

1962, Sept. 27 Engr. & Photo.
2642 A1349 3k ver, black & grn .75 .25
2643 A1349 4k multicolored .75 .25
2644 A1349 6k multicolored 1.25 .25
2645 A1349 10k multicolored 2.25 .25
Nos. 2642-2645 (4) 5.00 1.00

Nikitsky Botanical Gardens, 150th anniv.

Construction Worker — A1350

Designs: No. 2647, Hiker. No. 2648, Surgeon. No. 2649, Worker and lathe. No. 2650, Agricultural worker. No. 2651, Textile worker. No. 2652, Modern home.

1962, Sept. 29 Litho. *Perf. 12x12½*
2646 A1350 4k org, gray & vio blue .30 .25
2647 A1350 4k yel, gray, grn & blue .30 .25
2648 A1350 4k grn, gray & lilac rose .30 .25
2649 A1350 4k ver, gray & lilac .30 .25
2650 A1350 4k bl, gray & emer .30 .25
2651 A1350 4k brt pink, gray & vio .30 .25
2652 A1350 4k yel, gray, dp vio, red & brown .30 .25
Nos. 2646-2652 (7) 2.10 1.75

Sputnik and Stars
A1351

1962, Oct. 4 *Perf. 12½x12*
2653 A1351 10k multicolored 1.00 .30

5th anniversary, launching of Sputnik 1.

M. F. Ahundov, Azerbaijan Poet and Philosopher, 150th Birth Anniv. — A1352

1962, Oct. 2 **Photo.**
2654 A1352 4k lt grn & dk brn .50 .25

Farm and Young Couple with Banner
A1353

Designs: No. 2656, Tractors, map and surveyor. No. 2657, Farmer, harvester and map.

1962, Oct. 18 Litho. *Perf. 12½x12*
2655 A1353 4k multicolored 1.00 .45
2656 A1353 4k multicolored 1.00 .45
2657 A1353 4k brown, yel & red 1.00 .45
Nos. 2655-2657 (3) 3.00 1.35

Honoring pioneer developers of virgin soil.

N. N. Burdenko
A1354

V. P. Filatov
A1355

1962, Oct. 20 *Perf. 12½x12*
2658 A1354 4k red brn, lt brn & blk .50 .25
2659 A1355 4k multicolored .50 .25

Scientists and academicians.

Lenin Mausoleum, Red Square — A1356

1962, Oct. 26 **Litho.**
2660 A1356 4k multicolored .60 .25

92nd anniversary of Lenin's birth.

Worker, Flag and Factories
A1357

1962, Oct. 29 *Perf. 12x12½*
2661 A1357 4k multicolored .50 .25

45th anniv. of the October Revolution.

No. 2631 Overprinted in Dark Violet

1962, Nov. 3 Photo. *Perf. 11½*
2662 A1342 10k violet & multi 3.00 2.50

Launching of a rocket to Mars.

Togolok Moldo (1860-1942), Kirghiz Poet A1358

Sajat Nova (1712-1795), Armenian Poet A1359

1962, Nov. 17 *Perf. 12x12½*

2663 A1358 4k brn red & black .50 .25
2664 A1359 4k ultra & black .50 .25

Arms, Hammer & Sickle and Map of USSR A1360

1962, Nov. 17 *Perf. 11½*

2665 A1360 4k red, org & dk red .50 .25

USSR founding, 40th anniv.

Space Rocket, Earth and Mars — A1361

1962, Nov. 17 *Perf. 12½x12*
Size: 73x27mm

2666 A1361 10k purple & org red 1.00 .40

Launching of a space rocket to Mars, Nov. 1, 1962.

Electric Power Industry — A1362

Designs: No. 2668, Machines. No. 2669, Chemicals and oil. No. 2670, Factory construction. No. 2671, Transportation. No. 2672, Telecommunications and space. No. 2673, Metals. No. 2674, Grain farming. No. 2675, Dairy, poultry and meat.

1962 **Litho.** *Perf 12½x12*

2667 A1362 4k ultra, red, blk & gray .60 .25
2668 A1362 4k ultra, gray, yel & cl .60 .25
2669 A1362 4k yel, pink, blk, gray & brown .60 .25
2670 A1362 4k yel, blue, red brn & gray .45 .25
2671 A1362 4k mar, yel, red & blue .45 .25
2672 A1362 4k brt yel, blue & brn .45 .25
2673 A1362 4k lil, org, yel & dk brn .45 .25
2674 A1362 4k vio, bis, org red & dk brown .45 .25
2675 A1362 4k emer, dk brn, brn & gray .45 .25
Nos. 2667-2675 (9) 4.50 2.25

"Great decisions of the 22nd Communist Party Congress" and Russian people at work. Issued: #2667-2669, 11/19; others, 12/28.

Queen, Rook and Knight — A1363

Perf. 12½

1962, Nov. 24 **Unwmk.** **Photo.**

2676 A1363 4k org yel & blk .60 .40

30th Russian Chess Championships.

Gen. Vasili Blucher A1364

1962, Nov. 27 *Perf. 11½*

2677 A1364 4k multicolored 3.00 .25

General Vasili Konstantinovich Blucher (1889-1938).

V. N. Podbelski (1887-1920), Minister of Posts — A1365

1962, Nov. 27 *Perf. 12½x12*

2678 A1365 4k red brn, gray & blk .60 .25

Makarenko A1366

Gaidar A1367

1962, Nov. 30 *Perf. 11½x12*

2679 A1366 4k multicolored .50 .45
2680 A1367 4k multicolored .50 .45

A. S. Makharenko (1888-1939) and Arkadi Gaidar (1904-1941), writers.

Dove and Globe — A1368

1962, Dec. 22 **Litho.** *Perf. 12½x12*

2681 A1368 4k multicolored .60 .50

New Year 1963. Has alternating label inscribed "Happy New Year!" Issued imperf. on Dec. 20. Value $1.25.

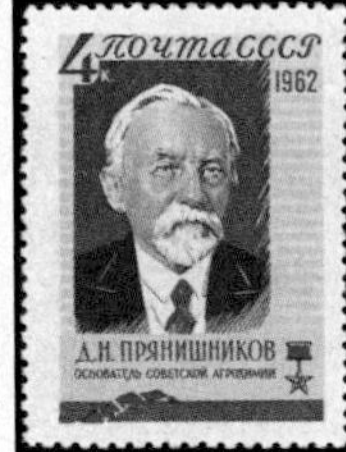

D. N. Prjanishnikov A1369

1962, Dec. 22 *Perf. 12x12½*

2682 A1369 4k multicolored .50 .25

Prjanishnikov, founder of Russian agricultural chemistry.

Rose-colored Starlings — A1370

4k, Red-breasted geese. 6k, Snow geese. 10k, White storks. 16k, Greater flamingos.

1962, Dec. 26 **Photo.** *Perf. 11½*

2683 A1370 3k grn, blk & pink .35 .25
2684 A1370 4k brn, blk & dp org .50 .25
2685 A1370 6k gray, blk & red .60 .25
2686 A1370 10k blue, blk & red .90 .30
2687 A1370 16k lt bl, rose & blk 1.50 .50
Nos. 2683-2687 (5) 3.85 1.55

FIR Emblem A1371

1962, Dec. 26 *Perf. 12x12½*

2688 A1371 4k violet & red .35 .25
2689 A1371 6k grnsh blue & red .35 .25

4th Cong. of the Intl. Federation of Resistance.

Map of Russia, Bank Book and Number of Savings Banks A1372

Design: 6k, as 4k, but with depositors.

1962, Dec. 30 **Litho.** *Perf. 12½x12*

2690 A1372 4k multicolored .75 .25
2691 A1372 6k multicolored 1.25 .30

40th anniv. of Russian savings banks.

Rustavsky Fertilizer Plant — A1373

Hydroelectric Power Stations: No. 2693, Bratskaya. No. 2964, Volzhskaya.

1962, Dec. 30 **Photo.** *Perf. 12½*

2692 A1373 4k ultra, lt blue & black .40 .25
2693 A1373 4k yel grn, bl grn & blk .40 .25
2694 A1373 4k gray bl, brt bl & blk .40 .25
Nos. 2692-2694 (3) 1.20 .75

Stanislavski A1374

Perf. 12½

1963, Jan. 15 **Unwmk.** **Engr.**

2695 A1374 4k slate green .50 .25

Stanislavski (professional name of Konstantin Sergeevich Alekseev, 1863-1938), actor, producer and founder of the Moscow Art Theater.

A. S. Serafimovich (1863-1949), Writer — A1375

1963, Jan. 19 **Photo.** *Perf. 11½*

2696 A1375 4k mag, dk brn & gray .50 .25

Children in Nursery A1376

Designs: No. 2698, Kindergarten. No. 2699, Pioneers marching and camping. No. 2700, Young people studying and working.

1963, Jan. 31

2697 A1376 4k brn org, org red & black .50 .25
2698 A1376 4k blue, mag & org .50 .25
2699 A1376 4k brt grn, red & brn .50 .25
2700 A1376 4k multicolored .50 .25
Nos. 2697-2700 (4) 2.00 1.00

Wooden Dolls and Toys, Russia — A1377

National Handicrafts: 6k, Pottery, Ukraine. 10k, Bookbinding, Estonia. 12k, Metalware, Dagestan.

1963, Jan. 31 **Litho.** *Perf. 12x12½*

2701 A1377 4k multicolored .45 .25
2702 A1377 6k multicolored .60 .25
2703 A1377 10k multicolored .90 .35
2704 A1377 12k ultra, org & black 1.00 .40
Nos. 2701-2704 (4) 2.95 1.25

Gen. Mikhail N. Tukhachevski — A1378

Designs: No. 2706, U. M. Avetisian. No. 2707, A. M. Matrosov. No. 2708, J. V. Panfilov. No. 2709, Y. F. Fabrisciuss.

Perf. 12½x12

1963, Feb. Photo. Unwmk.

2705 A1378 4k blue grn & slate grn	.60	.25
2706 A1378 4k org brown & blk	.60	.25
2707 A1378 4k ultra & dk brown	.60	.25
2708 A1378 4k dp rose & black	.60	.25
2709 A1378 4k rose lil & vio bl	.60	.25
Nos. 2705-2709 (5)	3.00	1.25

45th anniv. of the Soviet Army and honoring its heroes. No. 2705 for Gen. Mikhail Nikolaevich Tukhachevski (1893-1937).

M. A. Pavlov — A1379

E. O. Paton and Dnieper Bridge, Kiev — A1379a

Portraits: No. 2711, I. V. Kurchatov. No. 2712, V. I. Vernadski. No. 2713, Aleksei N. Krylov. No. 2714, V. A. Obrutchev, geologist.

1963 *Perf. 11½x12*

Size: 21x32mm

2710 A1379 4k gray, buff & dk bl	.50	.25
2711 A1379 4k slate & brown	.50	.25

Perf. 12

2712 A1379 4k lil gray & lt brn	.50	.25

Perf. 11½

Size: 23x34½mm

2713 A1379 4k dk blue, sep & red	.50	.25
2714 A1379 4k brn ol, gray & red	.50	.25
2715 A1379a 4k grnsh bl, blk & red	.50	.25
Nos. 2710-2715 (6)	3.00	1.50

Members of the Russian Academy of Science. No. 2715 for Eugene Oskarovich Paton (1870-1953), bridge building engineer.

Winter Sports A1380

1963, Feb. 28 *Perf. 11½*

2716 A1380 4k brt blue, org & blk	.50	.25

5th Trade Union Spartacist Games. Printed in sheets of 50 (5x10) with every other row inverted.

No. 2573 Overprinted

1963, Mar. 20

2717 A1306 6k Prus blue & plum	3.00	1.00

Victory of the Soviet ice hockey team in the World Championships, Stockholm. For overprint see No. 3612.

Victor Kingisepp A1381

1963, Mar. 24 *Perf. 12x12½*

2718 A1381 4k blue gray & choc	.50	.25

75th anniversary of the birth of Victor Kingisepp, communist party leader. Exists imperf.

Rudolfs Blaumanis (1863-1908), Latvian Writer — A1382

1963, Mar. 24 *Perf. 12½x12*

2719 A1382 4k ultra & dk red brn	.50	.25

Flower and Globe — A1383

Designs: 6k, Atom diagram and power line. 10k, Rocket in space.

1963, Mar. 26 *Perf. 11½*

2720 A1383 4k red, ultra & grn	.50	.25
2721 A1383 6k red, grn & lilac	1.00	.35
2722 A1383 10k red, vio & lt blue	1.50	.45
Nos. 2720-2722 (3)	3.00	1.05

"World without Arms and Wars."

The 10k exists imperf. Value: $2 mint; $1 used.

For overprint see No. 2754.

Costume Type of 1960-62

Regional Costumes: 3k, Tadzhik. No. 2724, Kirghiz. No. 2725, Azerbaijan. No. 2726, Turkmen.

1963, Mar. 31 Litho. *Perf. 11½*

2723 A1237 3k blk, red, ocher & org	1.25	.30
2724 A1237 4k brown, ver, ocher & ultra	1.25	.30
2725 A1237 4k blk, ocher, red & grn	1.25	.30
2726 A1237 4k red, lil, ocher & blk	1.25	.30
Nos. 2723-2726 (4)	5.00	1.20

Lenin A1384

1963, Mar. 30 Engr. *Perf. 12*

2727 A1384 4k red & brown	4.75	1.00

93rd anniversary of the birth of Lenin.

Luna 4 Approaching Moon — A1385

1963, Apr. 2 **Photo.**

2728 A1385 6k black, lt blue & red	1.00	.25

Soviet rocket to the moon, Apr. 2, 1963. Exists imperforate. Value, $3.

For overprint see No. 3160.

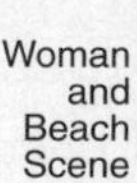

Woman and Beach Scene A1386

Designs: 4k, Young man's head and factory. 10k, Child's head and kindergarden.

1963, Apr. 7 Litho. *Perf. 12½x12*

2729 A1386 2k multicolored	.35	.25
2730 A1386 4k multicolored	.40	.30
2731 A1386 10k multicolored	.50	.40
Nos. 2729-2731 (3)	1.25	.95

15th anniversary of World Health Day.

A1387

No. 2732: a, d, Sputnik & Earth. b, e, Vostok 1, earth & moon. c, f, Rocket & Sun.

1963, Apr. 12

2732 Block of 6	6.50	2.10
a. A1387 10k "10k" blk, blue & lil rose	1.00	.35
b. A1387 10k "10k" lil rose, blue & blk	1.00	.35
c. A1387 10k "10k" black, red & yel	1.00	.35
d. A1387 10k "10k" blue	1.00	.35
e. A1387 10k "10k" lilac rose	1.00	.35
f. A1387 10k "10k" yellow	1.00	.35

Cosmonauts' Day.

Demian Bednii (1883-1945), Poet — A1388

1963, Apr. 13 **Photo.**

2735 A1388 4k brown & black	.50	.25

Soldiers on Horseback and Cuban Flag — A1389

Soviet-Cuban friendship: 6k, Cuban flag, hands with gun and book. 10k, Cuban and USSR flags and crane lifting tractor.

1963, Apr. 25 *Perf. 11½*

2736 A1389 4k blk, red & ultra	.30	.25
2737 A1389 6k blk, red & ultra	.35	.25
2738 A1389 10k red, ultra & blk	.65	.35
Nos. 2736-2738 (3)	1.30	.85

Karl Marx — A1390

1963, May 9 *Perf. 12x12½*

2739 A1390 4k dk red brn & blk	.50	.25

145th anniversary of the birth of Marx.

Hasek — A1391

1963, Apr. 29 *Perf. 11½x12*

2740 A1391 4k black	.75	.25

Jaroslav Hasek (1883-1923), Czech writer.

Moscow P.O. for Foreign Mail A1392

1963, May 9 *Perf. 11½*

2741 A1392 6k brt vio & red brn	.55	.25

5th Conference of Communications Ministers of Socialist countries, Budapest.

King and Pawn A1393

6k, Queen, bishop. 16k, Rook, knight.

1963, May 22 **Photo.**

2742 A1393 4k multicolored	.60	.25
2743 A1393 6k ultra, brt pink & grnsh blue	1.00	.30
2744 A1393 16k brt plum, brt pink & black	2.40	.55
Nos. 2742-2744 (3)	4.00	1.10

25th Championship Chess Match, Moscow. Exists imperf., issued May 18. Value $6.

Richard Wagner — A1394

Design: No. 2745A, Giuseppe Verdi.

1963 Unwmk. *Perf. 11½x12*

2745 A1394 4k black & red	.80	.30
2745A A1394 4k red & violet brn	.80	.30

150th annivs. of the births of Wagner and Verdi, German and Italian composers.

15th European Boxing Championships, Moscow A1395

4k, Boxers. 6k, Referee proclaiming victor.

1963, May 29 Litho. *Perf. 12½*

2746 A1395 4k multicolored	.60	.25
2747 A1395 6k multicolored	.90	.35

A1396

Valentina Tereshkova — A1397

Designs: No. 2748, Valeri Bykovski. No. 2749, Valentina Tereshkova. No. 2751, Bykovski. No. 2752, Symbolic man and woman fliers. No. 2753, Valentina Tereshkova, vert.

Litho. (A1396); Photo. (A1397)

1963 ***Perf. 12½x12, 12x12½***

2748 4k multicolored .90 .25
2749 4k multicolored .90 .25
a. A1396 Pair #2748-2749 1.80 .80
2750 A1397 6k grn & dk car rose .75 .25
2751 A1397 6k purple & brown .75 .25
2752 A1397 10k blue & red 1.50 .40
2753 A1396 10k multicolored 2.10 .50
Nos. 2748-2753 (6) 6.90 1.90

Space flights of Valeri Bykovski, June 14-19, and Valentina Tereshkova, 1st woman cosmonaut, June 16-19, 1963, in Vostoks 5 and 6.

No. 2749a has continuous design.

Nos. 2750-2753 exist imperf. Value $9.

No. 2720 Overprinted in Red

1963, June 24 **Photo.** ***Perf. 11½***

2754 A1383 4k red, ultra & green .75 .35

Intl. Women's Cong., Moscow, June 24-29.

Globe, Camera and Film A1398

1963, July 7 **Photo.** ***Perf. 11½***

2755 A1398 4k gray & ultra .75 .35

3rd International Film Festival, Moscow.

Vladimir V. Mayakovsky, Poet, 70th Birth Anniv. — A1399

1963, July 19 **Engr.** ***Perf. 12½***

2756 A1399 4k red brown .60 .25

Tanks and Map A1400

Design: 6k, Soldier, tanks and flag.

1963, July **Litho.** ***Perf. 12½x12***

2757 A1400 4k sepia & orange .60 .25
2758 A1400 6k org, slate green & blk .80 .35

20th anniversary of the Battle of Kursk in the "War of Liberation," 1941-1945.

Bicyclist — A1401

Sports: 4k, Long jump. 6k, Women divers, horiz. 12k, Basketball. 16k, Soccer.

1963, July 27 ***Perf. 12½x12, 12x12½***

2759 A1401 3k multicolored .25 .25
2760 A1401 4k multicolored .25 .25
2761 A1401 6k multicolored .40 .25
2762 A1401 12k multicolored .85 .25
2763 A1401 16k multicolored 1.25 .30
a. Souvenir sheet of 4, imperf. 10.00 2.00
Nos. 2759-2763 (5) 3.00 1.30

3rd Spartacist Games.

Exist imperf. Value $5.

No. 2763a contains stamps similar to the 3k, 4k, 12k and 16k, with colors changed. Issued Dec. 22.

Ice Hockey — A1402

1963, July 27 **Photo.**

2764 A1402 6k red & gray blue .75 .30

World Ice Hockey Championship, Stockholm.

For overprint see No. 3012.

Lenin — A1403

1963, July 29

2765 A1403 4k red & black .50 .25

60th anniversary of the 2nd Congress of the Social Democratic Labor Party.

Freighter and Relief Shipment — A1404

Design: 12k, Centenary emblem.

1963, Aug. 8 ***Perf. 12½***

2766 A1404 6k Prus green & red .50 .25
2767 A1404 12k dark blue & red 1.10 .40

Centenary of International Red Cross.

Lapp Reindeer Race A1405

Designs: 4k, Pamir polo, vert. 6k, Burjat archery. 10k, Armenian wrestling, vert.

1963, Aug. 8 ***Perf. 11½***

2768 A1405 3k lt vio bl, brn & red .45 .25
2769 A1405 4k bis brn, red & blk .60 .25
2770 A1405 6k yel, black & red .75 .25
2771 A1405 10k sepia, blk & dk red 1.25 .35
Nos. 2768-2771 (4) 3.05 1.10

A. F. Mozhaisky (1825-1890), Pioneer Airplane Builder — A1406

Aviation Pioneers: 10k, P. N. Nesterov (1887-1914), pioneer stunt flyer. 16k, N. E. Zhukovski (1847-1921), aerodynamics pioneer, and pressurized air tunnel.

1963, Aug. 18 **Engr. & Photo.**

2772 A1406 6k black & brt blue .30 .35
2773 A1406 10k black & brt blue .60 .35
2774 A1406 16k black & brt blue 1.00 .35
Nos. 2772-2774 (3) 1.90 1.05

Alexander S. Dargomyzhski and Scene from "Rusalka" — A1408

S. S. Gulak-Artemovsky and Scene from "Cossacks on the Danube" — A1409

No. 2777, Georgi O. Eristavi and theater.

Perf. 11½x12, 12x12½

1963, Sept. 10 **Photo.**

2776 A1408 4k violet & black .50 .25
2777 A1408 4k gray violet & brn .60 .25
2778 A1409 4k red & black .50 .25
Nos. 2776-2778 (3) 1.60 .75

Dargomyzhski, Ukrainian composer; Eristavi, Georgian writer, and Gulak-Artemovsky, Ukrainian composer, 150th birth annivs.

Map of Antarctica, Penguins, Research Ship and Southern Lights — A1410

Designs: 4k, Map, southern lights and snocats (trucks). 6k, Globe, camp and various planes. 12k, Whaler and whales.

1963, Sept. 16 **Litho.** ***Perf. 12½x12***

2779 A1410 3k multicolored .40 .25
2780 A1410 4k multicolored .60 .30
2781 A1410 6k vio, blue & red 1.00 .40
2782 A1410 12k multicolored 2.00 .50
Nos. 2779-2782 (4) 4.00 1.45

"The Antarctic - Continent of Peace."

Letters, Globe, Plane, Train and Ship A1411

1963, Sept. 20 **Photo.** ***Perf. 11½***

2783 A1411 4k violet, black & org .75 .25

International Letter Writing Week.

Denis Diderot — A1412

1963, Oct. 10 **Unwmk.** ***Perf. 11½***

2784 A1412 4k dk blue, brn & yel bister .75 .25

Denis Diderot (1713-84), French philosopher and encyclopedist.

Gleb Uspenski — A1414

Portraits: No. 2787, N. P. Ogarev. No. 2788, V. Brusov. No. 2789, F. Gladkov.

1963, Oct. 10

2786 A1414 4k buff, red brn & dk brown .75 .25
2787 A1414 4k blk & pale grn .75 .25
2788 A1414 4k car, brown & gray .75 .25
2789 A1414 4k car, ol brn & gray .75 .25
Nos. 2786-2789 (4) 3.00 1.00

Gleb Ivanovich Uspenski (1843-1902), historian and writer; Ogarev, politician, 150th birth anniv.; Brusov, poet, 90th birth anniv., Fyodor Gladkov (1883-1958), writer.

"Peace" Worker, Student, Astronaut and Lenin — A1415

Designs: No. 2794, "Labor," automatic controls. No. 2795, "Liberty," painter, lecturer, woman reading newspaper. No. 2796, "Equality," elections, regional costumes. No. 2797, "Brotherhood," Recognition of achievement. No. 2798, "Happiness," Family.

1963, Oct. 15 **Litho.** ***Perf. 12½x12***

2793 A1415 4k dk red, red & blk .55 .35
2794 A1415 4k red, dk red & blk .55 .35
2795 A1415 4k dk red, red & blk .55 .35
2796 A1415 4k dk red, red & blk .55 .35
2797 A1415 4k dk red, red & blk .55 .35
2798 A1415 4k dk red, red & blk .55 .35
a. Strip of 6, #2793-2798 4.00 3.00

Proclaiming Peace, Labor, Liberty, Equality, Brotherhood and Happiness.

Kirghiz Academy and Moscow State University A1416

1963, Oct. 22 ***Perf. 12x12½***

2799 A1416 4k red, yel & vio blue .50 .25

Russia's annexation of Kirghizia, cent.

Lenin and Young Workers A1417

Design: No. 2801, Lenin and Palace of Congresses, the Kremlin.

1963, Oct. 24 **Photo.** ***Perf. 11½***

2800 A1417 4k crimson & black .50 .25
2801 A1417 4k carmine & black .50 .25

13th Congr. of Soviet Trade Unions, Moscow.

Olga Kobylyanskaya, Ukrainian Novelist, Birth Cent. — A1418

1963, Oct. 24 ***Perf. 11½x12***

2802 A1418 4k tan & dk car rose .60 .30

Ilya Mechnikov A1419

6k, Louis Pasteur. 12k, Albert Calmette.

1963, Oct. 28 ***Perf. 12***

2803 A1419 4k green & bister .50 .35
2804 A1419 6k purple & bister .70 .35
2805 A1419 12k blue & bister 1.40 .35
Nos. 2803-2805 (3) 2.60 1.05

Pasteur Institute, Paris, 75th anniv; 12k for Albert Calmette (1863-1933), bacteriologist.

Cruiser Aurora and Rockets A1420

1963, Nov. 1

2806 A1420 4k mar, blk, gray & red orange .45 .25
2807 A1420 4k mar, blk, gray & brt rose red .55 .30

Development of the Armed Forces, and 46th anniv. of the October Revolution. The bright rose red ink of No. 2807 is fluorescent.

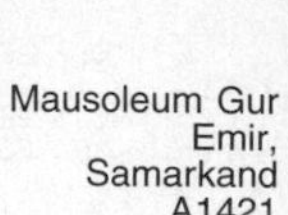

Mausoleum Gur Emir, Samarkand A1421

Architecture in Samarkand, Uzbekistan: #2809, Shakhi-Zinda Necropolis. 6k, Registan Square.

1963, Nov. 14 **Litho.** ***Perf. 12***

Size: 27½x27½mm

2808 A1421 4k bl, yel & red brn .50 .25
2809 A1421 4k bl, yel & red brn .50 .25

Size: 55x27½mm

2810 A1421 6k bl, yel & red brn 1.00 .40
Nos. 2808-2810 (3) 2.00 .90

Proclamation, Spasski Tower and Globe A1422

1963, Nov. 15 **Photo.** ***Perf. 12x11½***

2811 A1422 6k purple & lt blue .60 .25

Signing of the Nuclear Test Ban Treaty between the US and the USSR.

Pushkin Monument, Kiev — A1423

M. S. Shchepkin A1424

Portrait: No. 2814, V. L. Durov (1863-1934), circus clown.

1963 **Engr.** ***Perf. 12x12½***

2812 A1423 4k dark brown 1.50 .25
2813 A1424 4k brown 1.50 .25
2814 A1424 4k brown black 2.00 .25
Nos. 2812-2814 (3) 5.00 .75

No. 2813 for M. S. Shchepkin, actor, 75th birth anniv.

Yuri M. Steklov, 1st Editor of Izvestia, 90th Birth Anniv. A1425

1963, Nov. 17 **Photo.** ***Perf. 11½***

2815 A1425 4k black & lilac rose .60 .25

Vladimir G. Shuhov and Moscow Radio Tower — A1426

1963, Nov. 17 ***Perf. 12½x12***

2816 A1426 4k green & black .50 .30

Shuhov, scientist, 110th birth anniv.

USSR and Czech Flags, Kremlin and Hradcany A1427

1963, Nov. 25 ***Perf. 11½***

2817 A1427 6k red, ultra & brown .50 .25

Russo-Czechoslovakian Treaty, 20th anniv.

Fyodor A. Poletaev — A1428

1963, Nov. 25 **Litho.** ***Perf. 12½x12***

2818 A1428 4k multicolored .50 .30

F. A. Poletaev, Hero of the Soviet Union, National Hero of Italy, and holder of the Order of Garibaldi.

Julian Grimau and Worker Holding Flag — A1429

1963, Nov. 29 **Photo.** ***Perf. 11½***

Flag and Name Panel Embossed

2819 A1429 6k vio black, red & buff 1.00 .25

Spanish anti-fascist fighter Julian Grimau.

Rockets, Sky and Tree — A1430

1963, Dec. 12 **Litho.** ***Perf. 12x12½***

2820 A1430 6k multicolored 1.00 .25

"Happy New Year!" — A1431

Photogravure and Embossed

1963, Dec. 20 ***Perf. 11½***

2821 A1431 4k grn, dk blue & red .50 .25
2822 A1431 6k grn, dk bl & fluor. rose red .60 .30

Nos. 2820-2822 issued for New Year 1964.

Mikas J. Petrauskas, Lithuanian Composer, 90th Birth Anniv. A1432

1963, Dec. 20 **Photo.** ***Perf. 11½x12***

2823 A1432 4k brt grn & brn .75 .35

Topaz — A1433

Precious stones of the Urals: 4k, Jasper. 6k, Amethyst. 10k, Emerald. 12k, Rhodonite. 16k, Malachite.

1963, Dec. 26 **Litho.** ***Perf. 12***

2824 A1433 2k brn, yel & blue .40 .25
2825 A1433 4k multicolored .80 .25
2826 A1433 6k red & purple 1.00 .25
2827 A1433 10k multicolored 1.75 .25
2828 A1433 12k multicolored 2.25 .25
2829 A1433 16k multicolored 2.75 .25
Nos. 2824-2829 (6) 8.95 1.50

Coat of Arms and Sputnik A1434

Rockets: No. 2831, Luna I. No. 2832, Rocket around the moon. No. 2833, Vostok I, first man in space. No. 2834, Vostok III & IV. No. 2835, Vostok VI, first woman astronaut.

1963, Dec. 27 **Litho. & Embossed**

2830 A1434 10k red, gold & gray .80 .30
2831 A1434 10k red, gold & gray .80 .30
2832 A1434 10k red, gold & gray .80 .30
2833 A1434 10k red, gold & gray .80 .30
2834 A1434 10k red, gold & gray .80 .30
2835 A1434 10k red, gold & gray .80 .30
a. Vert. strip of 6, #2830-2835 5.50 2.50

Soviet achievements in space.

Dyushambe, Tadzhikistan — A1435

1963, Dec. 30 **Engr.**

2836 A1435 4k dull blue .60 .30

No. 2836 was issued after Stalinabad was renamed Dyushambe.
For overprint see No. 2943.

Flame, Broken Chain and Rainbow A1436

1963, Dec. 30 **Litho.**
2837 A1436 6k multicolored .60 .30

15th anniversary of the Universal Declaration of Human Rights.

F. A. Sergeev A1437

1963, Dec. 30 **Photo.** ***Perf. 12x12½***
2838 A1437 4k gray & red .50 .25

80th anniversary of the birth of the revolutionist Artjem (F. A. Sergeev).

Sun and Radar A1438

6k, Sun, Earth, vert. 10k, Earth, Sun.

1964, Jan. 1 **Photo.** ***Perf. 11½***
2839 A1438 4k brt mag, org & blk .45 .35
2840 A1438 6k org yel, red & bl .60 .35
2841 A1438 10k blue, vio & org .90 .35
Nos. 2839-2841 (3) 1.95 1.05

International Quiet Sun Year, 1964-65.

Christian Donalitius A1439

1964, Jan. 1 **Unwmk.** ***Perf. 12***
2842 A1439 4k green & black .60 .25

Lithuanian poet Christian Donalitius (Donelaitis), 250th birth anniv.

Women's Speed Skating A1440

Designs: 4k, Women's cross country skiing. 6k, 1964 Olympic emblem and torch. 10k, Biathlon. 12k, Figure skating pair.

1964, Feb. 4 ***Perf. 11½, Imperf.***
2843 A1440 2k ultra, blk & lil rose .25 .25
2844 A1440 4k lil rose, blk & ultra .40 .25
2845 A1440 6k dk bl, red & blk .50 .25
2846 A1440 10k grn, lil & blk .90 .30
2847 A1440 12k lil, blk & grn .90 .35
Nos. 2843-2847 (5) 2.95 1.40

9th Winter Olympic Games, Innsbruck Jan. 29-Feb. 9, 1964. See Nos. 2865, 2867-2870.

Anna S. Golubkina (1864-1927), Sculptor — A1441

1964, Feb. 4 **Photo.**
2848 A1441 4k gray, brn & buff .50 .25

No. 2450 Overprinted

and

Taras G. Shevchenko A1443

Designs: 4k, Shevchenko statue, Kiev. 10k, Shevchenko by Ilya Repin. (Portrait on 6k by I. Kramskoi.)

1964 **Litho.** ***Perf. 12***
2852 A1245 3k brown & violet 3.00 2.00

Engr.

2853 A1443 4k magenta .30 .25
2854 A1443 4k deep green .30 .25
2855 A1443 6k red brown .40 .25
2856 A1443 6k indigo .40 .25

Photo.

2857 A1443 10k bister & brown .50 .25
2858 A1443 10k buff & dull violet .50 .25
Nos. 2852-2858 (7) 5.40 3.50

Shevchenko, Ukrainian poet, 150th birth anniv.
Issued: #2852, 2857-2858, 2/22; Others, 3/1.

K. S. Zaslonov A1444

Soviet Heroes: No. 2860, N. A. Vilkov. No. 2861, J. V. Smirnov. No. 2862, V. Z. Khorujaia (heroine). No. 2862A, I. M. Sivko. No. 2862B, I. S. Polbin.

1964-65 **Photo.**
2859 A1444 4k hn brn & brn blk .50 .35
2860 A1444 4k Prus bl & vio blk .50 .35
2861 A1444 4k brn red & ind .50 .35
2862 A1444 4k bluish gray & dk brown .50 .35
2862A A1444 4k lil & blk ('65) .50 .35
2862B A1444 4k blue & dk brn ('65) .50 .35
Nos. 2859-2862B (6) 3.00 2.10

Printer Inking Form, 16th Century A1445

6k, Statue of Ivan Fedorov, 1st Russian printer.

1964, Mar. 1 **Litho.** **Unwmk.**
2863 A1445 4k multicolored .60 .25
2864 A1445 6k multicolored .80 .30

400th anniv. of book printing in Russia.

Nos. 2843-2847 Overprinted

and

Ice Hockey A1446

Olympic Gold Medal, "11 Gold, 8 Silver, 6 Bronze" A1447

Design: 3k, Ice hockey.

1964, Mar. 9 **Photo.** ***Perf. 11½***
2865 A1440 2k ultra, blk & lilac rose .25 .25
2866 A1446 3k blk, bl grn & red .30 .25
2867 A1440 4k lil rose, blk & ultra .35 .25
2868 A1440 6k dk bl, red & blk .75 .25
2869 A1440 10k grn, lil & blk .85 .30
2870 A1440 12k lilac, blk & grn .95 .35

Perf. 12

2871 A1447 16k org red & gldn brown 1.40 .40
Nos. 2865-2871 (7) 4.85 2.05

Soviet victories at the 9th Winter Olympic Games.
On Nos. 2865, 2867-2870 the black overprints commemorate victories in various events and are variously arranged in 3 to 6 lines, with "Innsbruck" in Russian added below "1964" on 2k, 4k, 10k and 12k.

Rubber Industry — A1448

Designs: No. 2873, Textile industry. No. 2874, Cotton, wheat, corn and helicopter spraying land.

1964 **Litho.** ***Perf. 12x12½***
2872 A1448 4k org, lilac, ultra & blk .65 .25
2873 A1448 4k org, blk, grn & ultra .65 .25
2874 A1448 4k dull yel, ol, red & bl .65 .25
Nos. 2872-2874 (3) 1.95 .75

Importance of the chemical industry to the Soviet economy.
Issued: #2872, 2/10; #2873-2874, 3/27.

Regular and Volunteer Militiamen A1449

1964, Mar. 27 **Photo.** ***Perf. 12***
2875 A1449 4k red & deep ultra .75 .35

Day of the Militia.

Sailor and Odessa Lighthouse — A1450

Liberation Monument, Minsk — A1451

No. 2877, Lenin statue and Leningrad.

1964 **Litho.** ***Perf. 12½x12***
2876 A1450 4k red, lt grn, ultra & black .80 .35
2877 A1450 4k red, yel, grn, brn & black .80 .35
2878 A1451 4k bl, gray, red & emer .80 .35
Nos. 2876-2878 (3) 2.40 1.05

Liberation of Odessa (#2876), Leningrad (#2877), Byelorussia (#2878), 20th anniv.
Issued: #2876, 4/10; #2877, 5/9; #2878, 6/30.

First Soviet Sputniks A1452

F. A. Tsander — A1453

Designs: 6k, Mars 1 spacecraft. No. 2886, Konstantin E. Tsiolkovsky. No. 2887, N. I. Kibaltchitch. No. 2888, Statue honoring 3 balloonists killed in 1934 accident. 12k, Gagarin and satellite.

Perf. 11½, Imperf.

1964, Apr. **Photo.**
2883 A1452 4k red org, blk & blue green .40 .25
2884 A1452 6k dk bl & org red .65 .25
2885 A1453 10k grn, blk & fluor. pink .80 .30
2886 A1453 10k dk bl grn, blk & fluor. pink .80 .30
2887 A1450 10k lilac, blk & lt grn .80 .30
2888 A1453 10k blue & black .80 .30
2889 A1452 12k blue grn, org brn & black 1.25 .40
Nos. 2883-2889 (7) 5.50 2.10

Leaders in rocket theory and technique.

Lenin, 94th Birth Anniv. A1454

Engraved and Photogravure

1964-65 ***Perf. 12x11½***

2890 A1454 4k blk, buff & lilac rose 5.00 5.00
a. Re-engraved ('65) 3.50 2.00

On No. 2890a, the portrait shading is much heavier. Lines on collar are straight and unbroken, rather than dotted.

For souvenir sheet see No. 2582a.

William Shakespeare, 400th Birth Anniv. — A1455

1964, Apr. 23 ***Perf. 11½***

2891 A1455 10k gray & red brn 1.75 .50

See Nos. 2985-2986.

"Irrigation" — A1456

1964, May 12 Litho. ***Perf. 12x12½***

2892 A1456 4k multicolored .50 .25

A1457

Perf. 12½x11½

1964, May 12 **Photo.**

2893 A1457 4k blue & gray brn .50 .25

Y. B. Gamarnik, army commander, 70th birth anniv.

D. I. Gulia A1458

Portraits: No. 2895, Hamza Hakim-Zade Nijazi. No. 2896, Saken Seifullin. No. 2896A, M. M. Kotsyubinsky. No. 2896B, Stepanos Nazaryan. No. 2896C, Toktogil Satyiganov.

Engraved and Photogravure

1964 Unwmk. ***Perf. 12x11½***

2894 A1458 4k grn, buff & blk .80 .35
2895 A1458 4k red, buff & blk .80 .35
2896 A1458 4k brn, ocher, buff & black .80 .35
2896A A1458 4k brn lake, blk & buff .80 .35
2896B A1458 4k blue, pale bl, blk & buff .80 .35
2896C A1458 4k red brn & blk .80 .35
Nos. 2894-2896C (6) 4.80 2.10

Abkhazian poet Gulia, 90th birth anniv.; Uzbekian writer and composer Nijazi, 75th birth anniv.; Kazakian poet Seifullin, 70th birth anniv.; Ukrainian writer Kotsyubinsky (1864-1913); Armenian writer Nazaryan (1814-1879); Kirghiz poet Satylganov (1864-1933).

Arkadi Gaidar (1904-41) A1459

Writers: No. 2897A, Nikolai Ostrovsky (1904-36) and battle scene (portrait at left).

1964 Photo. ***Perf. 12***

2897 A1459 4k red orange & gray .70 .30

Engr.

2897A A1459 4k brn lake & blk .70 .30

No. 2318 Surcharged

1964, May 27 Litho. ***Perf. 12***

2898 A1194 4k on 40k bis & brn 3.75 2.00

Azerbaijan's joining Russia, 150th anniv.

"Romania" A1460

No. 2900, "Poland," (map, Polish eagle, industrial and agricultural symbols). No. 2901, "Bulgaria" (flag, rose, industrial and agricultural symbols). No. 2902, Soviet and Yugoslav soldiers and embattled Belgrade. No. 2903, "Czechoslovakia" (view of Prague, arms, Russian soldier and woman). No. 2903A, Map and flag of Hungary, Liberty statue. No. 2903B, Statue of Russian Soldier and Belvedere Palace, Vienna. No. 2904, Buildings under construction, Warsaw; Polish flag and medal.

1964-65 Litho. ***Perf. 12***

2899 A1460 6k gray & multi .60 .25
2900 A1460 6k ocher, red & brn .60 .25
2901 A1460 6k tan, grn & red .60 .25
2902 A1460 6k gray, blk, dl bl, ol & red .60 .25
2903 A1460 6k ultra, black & red ('65) .60 .25
2903A A1460 6k brn, red & green ('65) .60 .25
2903B A1460 6k dp org, gray bl & black ('65) .60 .25
2904 A1460 6k blue, red, yel & bister ('65) .60 .25
Nos. 2899-2904 (8) 4.80 2.00

20th anniversaries of liberation from German occupation of Romania, Poland, Bulgaria, Belgrade, Czechoslovakia, Hungary, Vienna and Warsaw.

Elephant A1461

Designs: 2k, Giant panda, horiz. 4k, Polar bear. 6k, European elk. 10k, Pelican. 12k, Tiger. 16k, Lammergeier.

Perf. 12x12½, 12½x12, Imperf.

1964 **Photo.**

Size: 25x36mm, 36x25mm

2905 A1461 1k red & black .25 .25
2906 A1461 2k tan & black .25 .25

Perf. 12

Size: 26x28mm

2907 A1461 4k grnsh gray, black & tan .25 .25

Perf. 12x12½

Size: 25x36mm

2908 A1461 6k ol, dk brn & tan .60 .25

Perf. 12

Size: 26x28mm

2909 A1461 10k ver, gray & blk .90 .40

Perf. 12½x12, 12x12½

Size: 36x25mm, 25x36mm

2910 A1461 12k brn, ocher & blk 1.25 .40
2911 A1461 16k ultra, blk, bis & yellow 1.60 .60
Nos. 2905-2911 (7) 5.10 2.40

100th anniv. of the Moscow zoo.
Issue dates: Perf., June 18. Imperf., May.

Leningrad Post Office A1462

1964, June 30 Litho. ***Perf. 12***

2912 A1462 4k citron, blk & red .75 .25

Leningrad postal service, 250th anniv.

Corn — A1463

1964 Photo. ***Perf. 11½, Imperf.***

2913 A1463 2k shown .25 .25
2914 A1463 3k Wheat .35 .25
2915 A1463 4k Potatoes .35 .25
2916 A1463 6k Beans .55 .25
2917 A1463 10k Beets .90 .25
2918 A1463 12k Cotton 1.10 .30
2919 A1463 16k Flax 1.50 .35
Nos. 2913-2919 (7) 5.00 1.90

Issue dates: Perf., July 10. Imperf., June 25.

Thorez — A1464

1964, July 31

2920 A1464 4k black & red .80 .40

Maurice Thorez, chairman of the French Communist party.

Equestrian and Russian Olympic Emblem A1465

Designs: 4k, Weight lifter. 6k, High jump. 10k, Canoeing. 12k, Girl gymnast. 16k, Fencing.

1964, July ***Perf. 11½, Imperf.***

2921 A1465 3k lt yel grn, red, brn & black .25 .25
2922 A1465 4k yel, black & red .25 .25
2923 A1465 6k lt blue, blk & red .35 .25
2924 A1465 10k bl grn, red & blk .50 .25
2925 A1465 12k gray, blk & red .70 .25
2926 A1465 16k lt ultra, blk & red .90 .25
Nos. 2921-2926 (6) 2.95 1.50

18th Olympic Games, Tokyo, 10/10-25/64.

Two 1r imperf. souvenir sheets exist, showing emblem, woman gymnast and stadium. Size: 91x71mm.

Value, red sheet, $6 unused, $3 canceled; green sheet, $175 unused, $225 canceled.

Three Races — A1466

1964, Aug. 8 Photo. ***Perf. 12***

2929 A1466 6k orange & black .50 .40

International Congress of Anthropologists and Ethnographers, Moscow.

Indian Prime Minister Jawaharlal Nehru (1889-1964) A1467

1964, Aug. 20 ***Perf. 11½***

2930 A1467 4k brown & black .75 .25

Souvenir Sheet

Conquest of Space

1964, Aug. 20 ***Perf. 11½x12***

2930A Sheet of 6 4.25 2.50
b. On glossy paper 12.50 7.50

Marx and Engels — A1468

Designs: No. 2932 Lenin and title page of "CPSS Program." No. 2933, Worker breaking chains around the globe. No. 2934, Title pages of "Communist Manifesto" in German and Russian. No. 2935, Globe and banner inscribed "Workers of the World Unite."

1964, Aug. 27 Photo. ***Perf. 11½x12***

2931 A1468 4k red, dk red & brown .60 .25
2932 A1468 4k red, brn & slate .60 .25
2933 A1468 4k blue, fluor. brt rose & black .60 .25

Perf. 12½x12

Litho.

2934 A1468 4k ol blk, blk & red .60 .25
2935 A1468 4k bl, red & ol bis .60 .25
Nos. 2931-2935 (5) 3.00 1.25

Centenary of First Socialist International.

A. V. Vishnevsky A1469

Portraits: No. 2937, N. A. Semashko. No. 2938, D. Ivanovsky.

Size: 23½x35mm

1964 Photo. *Perf. 11½*
2936 A1469 4k gray & brown .65 .30
2937 A1469 4k buff, sepia & red .65 .30

Litho.

Size: 22x32½mm

2938 A1469 4k tan, gray & brown .65 .30
Nos. 2936-2938 (3) 1.95 .90

90th birth annivs. Vishnevsky, surgeon, and Semashko, founder of the Russian Public Health Service; Ivanovsky (1864-1920), biologist.

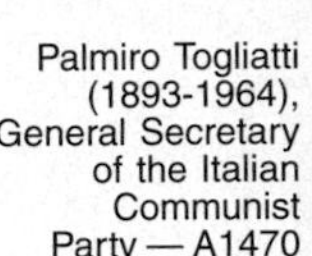

Palmiro Togliatti (1893-1964), General Secretary of the Italian Communist Party — A1470

1964, Sept. 15 *Perf. 12½x12*
2939 A1470 4k black & red .50 .25

Letter, Aerogram and Globe A1471

1964, Sept. 20 Litho.
2940 A1471 4k tan, lil rose & ultra .50 .25

Intl. Letter Writing Week, Oct. 5-11.

Arms of German Democratic Republic, Factories, Ship and Train — A1472

1964, Oct. 7 *Perf. 12*
2942 A1472 6k blk, yel, red & bis .50 .25

German Democratic Republic, 15th anniv.

No. 2836 Overprinted in Red

1964, Oct. 7 Engr.
2943 A1435 4k dull blue 5.00 5.00

40th anniversary of Tadzhik Republic.

Woman Holding Bowl of Grain and Fruit A1473

Uzbek Farm Couple and Arms — A1474

Turkmen Woman Holding Arms — A1475

1964, Oct. Litho.
2944 A1473 4k red, green & brn 1.00 .30
2945 A1474 4k red yel & claret 1.00 .30
2946 A1475 4k red, black & red brn 1.00 .30
Nos. 2944-2946 (3) 3.00 .90

40th anniv. of the Moldavian, Uzbek and Turkmen Socialist Republics.
Issue dates: #2944, Oct. 7; others, Oct. 26.

Soldier and Flags A1476

1964, Oct. 14
2947 A1476 4k red, bis, dk brn & bl .75 .25

Liberation of the Ukraine, 20th anniv.

Mikhail Y. Lermontov (1814-41), Poet — A1477

Designs: 4k, Birthplace of Tarchany. 10k, Lermontov and Vissarion G. Belinski.

1964, Oct. 14 Engr.; Litho. (10k)
2948 A1477 4k violet black .40 .25
2949 A1477 6k black .50 .25
2950 A1477 10k dk red brn & buff 1.10 .30
Nos. 2948-2950 (3) 2.00 .80

Hammer and Sickle A1478

1964, Oct. 14 Litho.
2951 A1478 4k dk blue, red, ocher & yellow .50 .25

47th anniversary of October Revolution.

Col. Vladimir M. Komarov A1479

Komarov, Feoktistov and Yegorov — A1480

Designs: No. 2953, Boris B. Yegorov, M.D. No. 2954, Konstantin Feoktistov, scientist. 10k, Spacecraft Voskhod I and cosmonauts. 50k, Red flag with portraits of Komarov, Feoktistov and Yegorov, and trajectory around earth.

Perf. 11½ (A1479), 12½x12

1964 Photo.
2952 A1479 4k bl grn, blk & org .45 .25
2953 A1479 4k bl grn, blk & org .45 .25
2954 A1479 4k bl grn, blk & org .45 .25

Size: 73x23mm

2955 A1480 6k vio & dk brn .80 .25
2956 A1480 10k dp ultra & pur 1.25 .25

Imperf

Litho.

Size: 90x45½mm

2957 A1480 50k vio, red & gray 6.00 3.00
Nos. 2952-2957 (6) 9.40 4.25

3-men space flight of Komarov, Yegorov and Feoktistov, Oct. 12-13. Issued: #2952-2954, 10/19; #2955, 10/17; #2956, 10/13; #2957, 11/20.

A. I. Yelizarova-Ulyanova — A1482

Portrait: No. 2961, Nadezhda K. Krupskaya.

1964, Nov. 6 Photo. *Perf. 11½*
2960 A1482 4k brn, org & indigo .50 .25
2961 A1482 4k indigo, red & brn .50 .25

Yelizarova-Ulyanova, Lenin's sister, birth cent. & Krupskaya, Lenin's wife, 95th birth anniv.

Farm Woman, Sheep, Flag of Mongolia A1483

1964, Nov. 20 Litho. *Perf. 12*
2962 A1483 6k multicolored .50 .25

Mongolian People's Republic, 40th anniv.

Mushrooms A1484

Designs: Various mushrooms.

1964, Nov. 25 Litho. *Perf. 12*
2963 A1484 2k ol grn, red brn & yellow .25 .25
2964 A1484 4k green & yellow .50 .25
2965 A1484 6k bluish grn, brn & yellow .75 .25
2966 A1484 10k grn, org red & brn 1.20 .40
2967 A1484 12k ultra, yel & grn 2.25 .50
Nos. 2963-2967 (5) 4.95 1.65

Nos. 2963-2967 exist varnished, printed in sheets of 25 with 10 labels in outside vertical rows. Issued Nov. 30. Value, set: mint $5; used $3.

A. P. Dovzhenko — A1485

Design: 6k, Scene from "Chapayev" (man and boy with guns).

1964, Nov. 30 Photo. *Perf. 12*
2968 A1485 4k gray & dp ultra 1.00 .35
2968A A1485 6k pale olive & blk 1.00 .35

Dovzhenko (1894-1956), film producer, and 30th anniv. of the production of the film "Chapayev."

"Happy New Year" — A1486

Photogravure and Engraved

1964, Nov. 30 *Perf. 11½*
2969 A1486 4k multicolored 1.00 .50

New Year 1965. The bright rose ink is fluorescent.

V. J. Struve — A1487

Portraits: No. 2971, N. P. Kravkov. No. 2971A, P. K. Sternberg. No. 2971B, Ch. Valikhanov. No. 2971C, V. A. Kistjakovski.

1964-65 Photo. *Perf. 12½x11½*
2970 A1487 4k sl bl & dk brn .55 .25

Litho.

2971 A1487 4k brn, red & blk .55 .25

Photo.

Perf. 11½

2971A A1487 4k dk bl & dk brn .55 .25

Perf. 12

2971B A1487 4k rose vio & blk .55 .25

Litho.

2971C A1487 4k brn vio, blk & cit .55 .25
Nos. 2970-2971C (5) 2.75 1.25

Astronomer Struve (1793-1864), founder of Pulkov Observatory; Kravkov (1865-1924), pharmacologist; Sternberg (1865-1920), astronomer; Valikhanov (1835-1865), Kazakh scientist; Kistjakovski (1865-1952), chemist.
Issued: #2970, 11/30; #2971, 1/31/65; #2971A-2971B, 9/21/65; #2971C, 12/24.

S. V. Ivanov and Skiers A1488

1964, Dec. 22 Engr. *Perf. 12½*
2972 A1488 4k black & brown .75 .35

S. V. Ivanov (1864-1910), painter.

Chemical Industry: Fertilizers and Pest Control — A1489

Importance of the chemical industry for the national economy: 6k, Synthetics factory.

1964, Dec. 25 Photo. *Perf. 12*
2973 A1489 4k olive & lilac rose .50 .25
2974 A1489 6k dp ultra & black .50 .25

European Cranberries A1490

Wild Berries: 3k, Huckleberries. 4k, Mountain ash. 10k, Blackberries. 16k, Cranberries.

1964, Dec. 25 ***Perf. 11½x12***
2975 A1490 1k pale grn & car .25 .25
2976 A1490 3k gray, vio bl & grn .30 .25
2977 A1490 4k gray, org red & brown .30 .25
2978 A1490 10k lt grn, dk vio blue & claret .90 .25
2979 A1490 16k gray, brt green & car rose 1.25 .25
Nos. 2975-2979 (5) 3.00 1.25

Academy of Science Library A1491

1964, Dec. 25 **Typo.** ***Perf. 12x12½***
2980 A1491 4k blk, pale grn & red .75 .35

250th anniv. of the founding of the Academy of Science Library, Leningrad.

Congress Palace, Kremlin — A1492

1964, Dec. 25
2981 A1492 1r dark blue 4.50 1.00

Khan Tengri — A1493

Mountains: 6k, Kazbek, horiz. 12k, Twin peaks of Ushba.

1964, Dec. 29 **Photo.** ***Perf. 11½***
2982 A1493 4k grnsh bl, vio bl & buff .70 .35
2983 A1493 6k yel, dk brn & ol .75 .35
2984 A1493 12k lt yel, grn & pur 1.50 .35
Nos. 2982-2984 (3) 2.95 1.05

Development of mountaineering in Russia.

Portrait Type of 1964

Design: 6k, Michelangelo. 12k, Galileo.

Engraved and Photogravure

1964, Dec. 30 ***Perf. 11½***
2985 A1455 6k sep, red brn & org .75 .25
2986 A1455 12k dk brn & green 2.25 .30

Michelangelo Buonarotti, artist, 400th death anniv. and Galileo Galilei, astronomer and physicist, 400th birth anniv.

Helmet A1494

Treasures from Kremlin Treasury: 6k, Quiver. 10k, Jeweled fur crown. 12k, Gold ladle. 16k, Bowl.

1964, Dec. 30 **Litho.**
2987 A1494 4k multicolored .25 .25
2988 A1494 6k multicolored .35 .25
2989 A1494 10k multicolored .50 .25
2990 A1494 12k multicolored 1.25 .25
2991 A1494 16k multicolored 1.40 .25
Nos. 2987-2991 (5) 3.75 1.25

Dante Alighieri (1265-1321), Italian Poet — A1495

1965, Jan. 29 **Photo.** ***Perf. 11½***
2995 A1495 4k dk red brn & ol bis .50 .25

Blood Donor — A1496

Honoring blood donors: No. 2997, Hand holding carnation, and donors' emblem.

1965, Jan. 31 **Litho.** ***Perf. 12***
2996 A1496 4k dk car, red, vio bl & bl .60 .25
2997 A1496 4k brt grn, red & dk grn .60 .25

Bandy — A1497

6k, Figure skaters and Moscow Sports Palace.

1965, Feb. **Photo.** ***Perf. 11½x12***
2998 A1497 4k blue, red & yellow .50 .25
2999 A1497 6k green, blk & red .50 .25

4k issued Feb. 21, for the victory of the Soviet team in the World Bandy Championship, Moscow, Feb. 21-27; 6k issued Feb. 12, for the European Figure Skating Championship. For overprint see No. 3017.

Police Dog — A1498

Dogs: 1k, Russian hound. 2k, Irish setter. No. 3003, Pointer. No. 3004, Fox terrier. No. 3005, Sheepdog. No. 3006, Borzoi. 10k, Collie. 12k, Husky. 16k, Caucasian sheepdog. (1k, 2k, 4k, 12k and No. 3006 horiz.)

Perf. 12x11½, 11½x12 (Photo. stamps); 12x12½, 12½x12 (Litho.)
Photo., Litho. (1k, 10k, 12k, 16k)

1965, Feb. 26
3000 A1498 1k blk, yel & mar .25 .25
3001 A1498 2k ultra, blk & red brown .45 .25
3002 A1498 3k blk, ocher & org red .45 .25
3003 A1498 4k org, yel grn & blk .70 .25
3004 A1498 4k brn, blk & lt grn .70 .25
3005 A1498 6k chalky blue, sep & red 1.20 .25
3006 A1498 6k chalky bl, org brn & black 1.20 .25
3007 A1498 10k yel green, ocher & red 1.90 .35
3008 A1498 12k gray, blk & ocher 2.10 .45
3009 A1498 16k multicolored 2.75 .60
Nos. 3000-3009 (10) 11.70 3.15

Richard Sorge (1895-1944), Soviet spy and Hero of the Soviet Union — A1499

1965, Mar. 6 **Photo.** ***Perf. 12x12½***
3010 A1499 4k hn brn & blk 3.00 1.00

Communications Symbols — A1500

1965, Mar. 6 ***Perf. 12½x12***
3011 A1500 6k grnsh blue, vio & brt purple .60 .30

Intl. Telecommunication Union, cent.

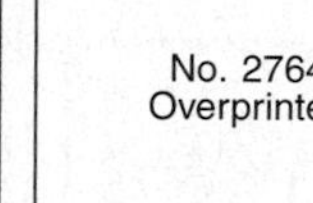

No. 2764 Overprinted

1965, Mar. 20 **Photo.** ***Perf. 12***
3012 A1402 6k red & gray blue 3.00 .75

Soviet victory in the European and World Ice Hockey Championships.

Lt. Col. Alexei Leonov Taking Movies in Space — A1501

1r, Leonov walking in space and Voskhod 2.

1965, Mar. 23 **Photo.** ***Perf. 12***
Size: 73x23mm
3015 A1501 10k brt ultra, org & gray .90 .35

First man walking in space, Lt. Col. Alexei Leonov, Mar. 17, 1965 ("18 March" on stamp). Exists imperf. Value $1.50.

Souvenir Sheet

1965, Apr. 12 **Litho.**
3016 A1501 1r multicolored 6.50 2.00

Space flight of Voskhod 2. No. 3016 contains one 81x27mm stamp.

No. 2999 Overprinted

1965, Mar. 26 ***Perf. 11½x12***
3017 A1497 6k green, black & red 3.00 1.00

Soviet victory in the World Figure Skating Championships.

Flags of USSR and Poland A1502

1965, Apr. 12 **Photo.** ***Perf. 12***
3018 A1502 6k bister & red .60 .25

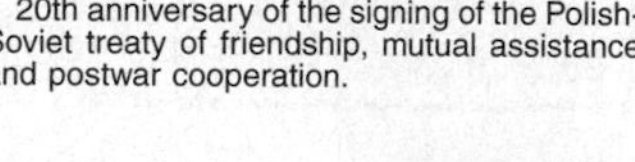

20th anniversary of the signing of the Polish-Soviet treaty of friendship, mutual assistance and postwar cooperation.

Tsiolkovsky Monument, Kaluga; Globe and Rockets — A1503

Rockets, Radio Telescope, TV Antenna A1504

Designs: 12k, Space monument, Moscow. 16k, Cosmonauts' monument, Moscow. No. 3023, Globe with trajectories, satellite and astronauts.

1965, Apr. 12 ***Perf. 11½***
3019 A1503 4k pale grn, black & brt rose .25 .25
3020 A1503 12k vio, pur & brt rose .55 .25
3021 A1503 16k multicolored .85 .25

Lithographed on Aluminum Foil

Perf. 12½x12
3022 A1504 20k black & red 5.50 4.50
3023 A1504 20k blk, blue & red 5.50 4.50
Nos. 3019-3023 (5) 12.65 9.75

National Cosmonauts' Day. On Nos. 3019-3021 the bright rose is fluorescent.

Lenin — A1505

1965, Apr. 16 **Engr.** ***Perf. 12***
3024 A1505 10k tan & indigo .75 .25

95th anniversary of the birth of Lenin.

Poppies — A1506

Flowers: 3k, Daisies. 4k, Peony. 6k, Carnation. 10k, Tulips.

1965, Apr. 23 Photo. *Perf. 11*

3025	A1506	1k mar, red & grn	.25	.25
3026	A1506	3k dk brn, yel & grn	.50	.25
3027	A1506	4k blk, grn & lilac	.90	.25
3028	A1506	6k dk sl grn, grn & red	1.25	.25
3029	A1506	10k dk plum, yel & grn	2.00	.25
		Nos. 3025-3029 (5)	4.90	1.25

Soviet Flag, Broken Swastikas, Fighting in Berlin A1507

Designs: 2k, "Fatherland Calling!" (woman with proclamation) by I. Toidze. 3k, "Attack on Moscow" by V. Bogatkin. No. 3033, "Rest after the Battle" by Y. Neprintsev. No. 3034, "Mother of Partisan" by S. Gerasimov. 6k, "Our Flag — Symbol of Victory" (soldiers with banner) by V. Ivanov. 10k, "Tribute to the Hero" (mourners at bier) by F. Bogorodsky. 12k, "Invincible Nation and Army" (worker and soldier holding shell) by V. Koretsky. 16k, "Victory celebration on Red Square" by K. Yuan. 20k, Soldier and symbols of war.

1965 *Perf. 11½*

3030	A1507	1k red, blk & gold	.25	.25
3031	A1507	2k crim, blk & gold	.25	.25
3032	A1507	3k ultra & gold	.40	.25
3033	A1507	4k green & gold	.45	.25
3034	A1507	4k violet & gold	.45	.25
3035	A1507	6k dp claret & gold	.75	.25
3036	A1507	10k plum & gold	1.10	.25
3037	A1507	12k blk, red & gold	1.40	.35
3038	A1507	16k lilac rose & gold	1.90	.40
3039	A1507	20k red, blk & gold	2.25	.50
		Nos. 3030-3039 (10)	9.20	3.00

20th anniv. of the end of World War II. Issued Apr. 25-May 1.

Souvenir Sheet

From Popov's Radio to Space Telecommunications — A1508

1965, May 7 Litho. *Perf. 11½*

3040	A1508	1r blue & multi	5.00	1.00

70th anniv. of Aleksandr S. Popov's radio pioneer work. No. 3040 contains 6 labels without denominations or country name.

Marx, Lenin and Crowd with Flags — A1509

1965, May 9 Photo. *Perf. 12x12½*

3041	A1509	6k red & black	.50	.25

6th conference of Postal Ministers of Communist Countries, Peking, June 21-July 15.

Bolshoi Theater, Moscow — A1510

1965, May 20 *Perf. 11x11½*

3042	A1510	6k grnsh blue, bis & blk	1.00	.25

International Theater Day.

Col. Pavel Belyayev A1511

Design: No. 3044, Lt. Col. Alexei Leonov.

1965, May 23 *Perf. 12x11½*

3043	A1511	6k magenta & silver	.60	.25
3044	A1511	6k purple & silver	.60	.25

Space flight of Voskhod 2, Mar. 18-19, 1965, and the 1st man walking in space, Lt. Col. Alexei Leonov.

Sverdlov — A1512

Portrait: No. 3046, Juldash Akhunbabaev.

Photogravure and Engraved

1965, May 30 *Perf. 11½x12*

3045	A1512	4k orange brn & blk	1.50	.35
3046	A1512	4k lt violet & blk	1.50	.35

Yakov M. Sverdlov, 1885-1919, 1st pres. of USSR, and J. Akhunbabaev, 1885-1943, pres. of Uzbek Republic.

Grotewohl — A1513

1965, June 12 Photo. *Perf. 12*

3051	A1513	4k black & magenta	.50	.25

Otto Grotewohl, prime minister of the German Democratic Republic (1894-1964).

Maurice Thorez — A1514

1965, June 12

3052	A1514	6k brown & red	.50	.25

Maurice Thorez (1900-1964), chairman of the French Communist party.

Communication by Satellite — A1515

Designs: No. 3054, Pouring ladle, steel mill and map of India. No. 3055, Stars, satellites and names of international organizations.

1965, June 15 Litho.

3053	A1515	3k olive, blk & gold	.50	.30
3054	A1515	6k emer, dk grn & gold	.50	.30
3055	A1515	6k vio blue, gold & blk	.50	.30
		Nos. 3053-3055 (3)	1.50	.90

Emphasizing international cooperation through communication, economic cooperation and international organizations.

Symbols of Chemistry A1516

1965, June 15 Photo. *Perf. 11½*

3056	A1516	4k blk, brt rose & brt bl	.60	.25

20th Cong. of the Intl. Union of Pure and Applied Chemistry (IUPAC), Moscow. The bright rose ink is fluorescent.

V. A. Serov A1517

Design: 6k, Full-length portrait of Feodor Chaliapin, the singer, by Serov.

1965, June 25 Typo. *Perf. 12½*

3057	A1517	4k red brn, buff & blk	.50	.25
3058	A1517	6k ol bis & blk	.50	.25

Serov (1865-1911), historical painter.

Abay Kunanbaev, Kazakh Poet — A1518

Designs (writers and poets): No. 3060, Vsevolod Ivanov (1895-1963). No. 3060A, Eduard Vilde, Estonian writer. No. 3061, Mark Kropivnitsky, Ukrainian playwright. No. 3062, Manuk Apeghyan, Armenian writer and critic. No. 3063, Musa Djalil, Tartar poet. No. 3064, Hagop Hagopian, Armenian poet. No. 3064A, Djalil Mamedkulizade, Azerbaijan writer.

1965-66 Photo. *Perf. 12½x12*

3059	A1518	4k lt violet & blk	.55	.30
3060	A1518	4k rose lilac & blk	.55	.30
3060A	A1518	4k gray & black	.55	.30
3061	A1518	4k black & org brn	.55	.30

Perf. 12½

Typo.

3062	A1518	4k crim, blue grn & blk	.55	.30

Perf. 11½

Photogravure and Engraved

3063	A1518	4k black & org brn ('66)	.55	.30
3064	A1518	4k grn & blk ('66)	.55	.30

Photo.

3064A	A1518	4k Prus green & blk ('66)	.55	.30
		Nos. 3059-3064A (8)	4.40	2.40

Sizes: Nos. 3059-3062, 38x25mm. Nos. 3063-3064A, 35x23mm.

Jan Rainis A1518a

1965, Sept. 8 Photo. *Perf. 12½x12*

3064B	A1518a	4k dl blue & blk	.50	.25

Rainis (1865-1929), Latvian playwright. "Rainis" was pseudonym of Jan Plieksans.

Film, Screen, Globe and Star A1519

1965, July 5 Litho. *Perf. 12*

3065	A1519	6k brt blue, gold & blk	.50	.25

4th Intl. Film Festival, Moscow: "For Humanism in Cinema Art, for Peace and Friendship among Nations."

Concert Bowl, Tallinn A1520

"Lithuania" A1521

"Latvia" A1522

1965, July *Perf. 12x11½, 11½x12*
3066 A1520 4k ultra, blk, red & ocher 1.00 .25
3067 A1521 4k red & brown 1.00 .25
3068 A1522 4k yel, red & blue 1.00 .25
Nos. 3066-3068 (3) 3.00 .75

25th anniversaries of Estonia, Lithuania and Latvia as Soviet Republics. Issued: #3066, 7/7; #3067, 7/14; #3068, 7/16.

"Keep Peace" — A1523

1965, July 10 **Photo.** *Perf. 11x11½*
3069 A1523 6k yel, blk & blue .55 .25

Protesting Women and Czarist Eagle A1524

Designs: No. 3071, Soldier attacking distributor of handbills. No. 3072, Fighters on barricades with red flag. No. 3073, Monument for sailors of Battleship "Potemkin," Odessa.

1965, July 20 **Litho.** *Perf. 11½*
3070 A1524 4k blk, red & ol grn .50 .25
3071 A1524 4k red, ol grn & blk .50 .25
3072 A1524 4k red, black & brn .50 .25
3073 A1524 4k red & violet blue .50 .25
Nos. 3070-3073 (4) 2.00 1.00

60th anniversary of the 1905 revolution.

Gheorghe Gheorghiu-Dej (1901-1965), President of Romanian State Council (1961-1965) A1525

1965, July 26 **Photo.** *Perf. 12*
3074 A1525 4k black & red .45 .25

Relay Race A1526

Sport: No. 3076, Bicycle race. No. 3077, Gymnast on vaulting horse.

1965, Aug. 5 **Litho.** *Perf. 12½x12*
3075 A1526 4k vio blue, bis brn & red brown 1.00 .25
3076 A1526 4k buff, red brn, gray & maroon 1.00 .25
3077 A1526 4k bl, mar, buff & lt brn 1.00 .25
Nos. 3075-3077 (3) 3.00 .75

8th Trade Union Spartacist Games.

Electric Power A1527

Designs: 2k, Metals in modern industry. 3k, Modern chemistry serving the people. 4k, Mechanization, automation and electronics. 6k, New materials for building industry. 10k, Mechanization and electrification of agriculture. 12k, Technological progress in transportation. 16k, Application of scientific discoveries to industry.

1965, Aug. 5 **Photo.** *Perf. 12x11½*
3078 A1527 1k olive, bl & blk .25 .25
3079 A1527 2k org, blk & yel .25 .25
3080 A1527 3k yel, vio & bister .25 .25
3081 A1527 4k ultra, ind & red .25 .25
3082 A1527 6k ultra & bister .45 .25
3083 A1527 10k yel, org & red brn .85 .25
3084 A1527 12k Prus blue & red .90 .30
3085 A1527 16k rose lilac, blk & violet blue 1.20 .35
Nos. 3078-3085 (8) 4.40 2.15

Creation of the material and technical basis of communism.

Gymnast — A1528

Design: 6k, Bicycling.

1965, Aug. 12 *Perf. 11½*
3086 A1528 4k multi & red 1.00 .25
3087 A1528 6k grnsh bl, red & brn 1.00 .25

9th Spartacist Games for school children.

Javelin and Running — A1529

Designs: 6k, High jump and shot put. 10k, Hammer throwing and hurdling.

1965, Aug. 27
3088 A1529 4k brn, lilac & red .50 .25
3089 A1529 6k brn, yel green & red .50 .25
3090 A1529 10k brn, chlky bl & red 1.00 .25
Nos. 3088-3090 (3) 2.00 .75

US-Russian Track and Field Meet, Kiev.

Worker and Globe — A1530

Designs: No 3092, Heads of three races and torch. No. 3093, Woman with dove.

1965, Sept. 1
3091 A1530 6k dk purple & tan .35 .25
3092 A1530 6k brt bl, brn & red org .35 .25
3093 A1530 6k Prus green & tan .35 .25
Nos. 3091-3093 (3) 1.05 .75

Intl. Fed. of Trade Unions (#3091), Fed. of Democratic Youth (#3092), Democratic Women's Fed. (#3093), 20th annivs.

Flag of North Viet Nam, Factory and Palm — A1531

1965, Sept. 1 **Litho.** *Perf. 12*
3094 A1531 6k red, yel, brn & gray .35 .25

Republic of North Viet Nam, 20th anniv.

Scene from Film "Potemkin" A1532

Film Scenes: 6k, "Young Guard." 12k, "Ballad of a Soldier."

1965, Sept. 29 **Litho.** *Perf. 12½x12*
3095 A1532 4k blue, blk & red 1.50 .35
3096 A1532 6k multicolored 1.50 .35
3097 A1532 12k multicolored 2.50 .35
Nos. 3095-3097 (3) 5.50 1.05

Post Rider, 16th Century — A1533

History of the Post: No. 3099, Mail coach, 17th-18th centuries. 2k, Train, 19th century. 4k, Mail truck, 1920. 6k, Train, ship and plane. 12k, New Moscow post office, helicopter, automatic sorting and canceling machines. 16k, Lenin, airport and map of USSR.

1965 **Photo.** **Unwmk.** *Perf. 11½x12*
3098 A1533 1k org brn, dk gray & dk green .45 .30
3099 A1533 1k gray, ocher & dk brown .45 .30
3100 A1533 2k dl lil, brt bl & brn .25 .25
3101 A1533 4k bis, rose lake & blk .55 .25
3102 A1533 6k pale brn, Prus grn & black .55 .25
3103 A1533 12k lt ultra, lt brn & blk 1.40 .40
3104 A1533 16k gray, rose red & vio black 1.40 .55
Nos. 3098-3104 (7) 5.05 2.30

For overprint see No. 3175.

Scientific Conquests of the Arctic and Antarctic — A1534

No. 3106, Icebreakers "Taimir" and "Vaigitch". No. 3107, Atomic Icebreaker "Lenin." 6k, Dickson Settlement. 10k, Sailing ships "Vostok" and "Mirni," Bellinghausen-Lazarev expedition & icebergs. 16k, Vostok South Pole station.

1965, Oct. 23 **Litho.** *Perf. 12*
Size: 37x25mm
3106 4k bl, blk & org .45 .25
3107 4k bl, blk & org .45 .25
a. A1534 Pair #3106-3107 1.00 .50
3108 A1534 6k sepia & dk vio 1.10 .25
Size: 33x33mm
3109 A1534 10k red, black & buff 1.40 .25
Size: 37x25mm
3110 A1534 16k vio blk & red brn 1.60 .50
Nos. 3106-3110 (5) 5.00 1.50

Souvenir Sheet

Basketball, Map of Europe and Flags — A1535

1965, Oct. 29 **Litho.** *Imperf.*
3111 A1535 1r multicolored 6.00 1.50

14th European Basketball Championship, Moscow.

Timiryazev Agriculture Academy, Moscow — A1536

1965, Oct. 30 **Photo.** *Perf. 11*
3112 A1536 4k brt car, gray & vio bl .50 .25

Agriculture Academy, Moscow, cent.

Souvenir Sheet

Lenin — A1537

Lithographed and Engraved
1965, Oct. 30 *Imperf.*
3113 A1537 10k sil, blk & dp org 10.00 1.25

48th anniv. of the October Revolution.

Nicolas Poussin (1594-1665), French Painter — A1538

1965, Nov. 16 Photo. *Perf. 11½*

3114 A1538 4k gray blue, dk bl & dk brown .50 .25

Kremlin A1539

1965, Nov. 16 *Perf. 12x11½*

3115 A1539 4k black, ver & silver 1.00 .25

New Year 1966.

Mikhail Ivanovich Kalinin (1875-1946), USSR President (1923-1946) A1540

1965, Nov. 19 *Perf. 12½*

3116 A1540 4k dp claret & red .50 .25

Klyuchevskaya Sopka — A1541

Kamchatka Volcanoes: 12k, Karumski erupting, vert. 16k, Koryakski snowcovered.

1965, Nov. 30 Litho. *Perf. 12*

3117	A1541	4k	multicolored	.60	.25
3118	A1541	12k	multicolored	1.60	.30
3119	A1541	16k	multicolored	2.75	.45
			Nos. 3117-3119 (3)	4.95	1.00

October Subway Station, Moscow — A1542

Subway Stations: No. 3121, Lenin Avenue, Moscow. No. 3122, Moscow Gate, Leningrad. No. 3123, Bolshevik Factory, Kiev.

1965, Nov. 30 Engr.

3120	A1542	6k	indigo	.75	.30
3121	A1542	6k	brown	.75	.30
3122	A1542	6k	gray brown	.75	.30
3123	A1542	6k	slate green	.75	.30
			Nos. 3120-3123 (4)	3.00	1.20

Buzzard — A1543

Birds: 2k, Kestrel. 3k, Tawny eagle. 4k, Red kite. 10k, Peregrine falcon. 12k, Golden eagle, horiz. 14k, Lammergeier, horiz. 16k, Gyrfalcon.

1965 Photo. *Perf. 11½x12*

3124	A1543	1k	gray grn & black	.25	.25
3125	A1543	2k	pale brn & blk	.25	.25
3126	A1543	3k	lt ol grn & black	.25	.25
3127	A1543	4k	lt gray brn & blk	.35	.25
3128	A1543	10k	lt vio brn & blk	.75	.25
3129	A1543	12k	blue & black	1.50	.35
3130	A1543	14k	bluish gray & blk	2.00	.45
3131	A1543	16k	dl red brn & blk	2.00	.50
			Nos. 3124-3131 (8)	7.35	2.55

Issued: 4k, 10k, Nov.; 1k, 2k, 12k, 14k, 12/24; 3k, 16k, 12/29.

Red Star Medal, War Scene and View of Kiev A1544

Red Star Medal, War Scene and view of: No. 3133, Leningrad. No. 3134, Odessa. No. 3135, Moscow. No. 3136, Brest Litovsk. No. 3137, Volgograd (Stalingrad). No. 3138, Sevastopol.

1965, Dec. *Perf. 11½*

Red, Gold and

3132	A1544	10k	brown	.50	.25
3133	A1544	10k	dark blue	.50	.25
3134	A1544	10k	Prussian blue	.50	.25
3135	A1544	10k	dark violet	.50	.25
3136	A1544	10k	dark brown	.50	.25
3137	A1544	10k	black	.50	.25
3138	A1544	10k	gray	.50	.25
			Nos. 3132-3138 (7)	3.50	1.75

Honoring the heroism of various cities during World War II.

Issued: #3136-3138, 12/30; others, 12/20.

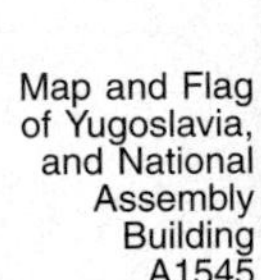

Map and Flag of Yugoslavia, and National Assembly Building A1545

1965, Dec. 30 Litho. *Perf. 12*

3139 A1545 6k vio blue, red & bis .70 .25

Republic of Yugoslavia, 20th anniv.

Collective Farm Watchman by S.V. Gerasimov A1547

Painting: 16k, "Major's Courtship" by Pavel Andreievitch Fedotov, horiz.

1965, Dec. 31 Engr.

3145	A1547	12k	red & sepia	1.50	.35
3146	A1547	16k	red & dark blue	2.50	.65

Painters: Gerasimov, 80th birth anniv; Pavel A. Fedotov (1815-52).

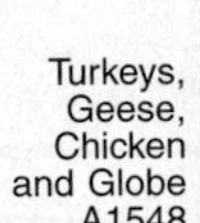

Turkeys, Geese, Chicken and Globe A1548

Congress Emblems: No. 3147, Microscope and Moscow University. No. 3149, Crystals. No. 3150, Oceanographic instruments and ship. No. 3151, Mathematical symbols.

1966 Photo. *Perf. 11½*

3147	A1548	6k	dull bl, blk & red	.60	.25
3148	A1548	6k	gray, pur & black	.60	.25
3149	A1548	6k	ol bis, blk & bl	.60	.25
3150	A1548	6k	grnsh blue & blk	.60	.25
3151	A1548	6k	dull yel, red brn & blk	.60	.25
			Nos. 3147-3151 (5)	3.00	1.25

Intl. congresses to be held in Moscow: 9th Cong. of Microbiology (#3147); 13th Cong. on Poultry Raising (#3148); 7th Cong. on Crystallography (#3150); 2nd Intl. Cong. of Oceanography (#3149); Intl. Cong. of Mathematicians (#3151).

See Nos. 3309-3310.

Mailman and Milkmaid, 19th Century Figurines — A1549

1966, Jan. 28 Litho.

3152	A1549	6k	shown	.40	.25
3153	A1549	10k	Tea set	.60	.25

Bicentenary of Dimitrov Porcelain Works.

Romain Rolland (1866-1944), French Writer — A1550

Portrait: No. 3155, Eugène Pottier (1816-1887), French poet and author of the "International."

1966 Photo. & Engr. *Perf. 11½*

3154	A1550	4k	dk blue & brn org	.75	.25
3155	A1550	4k	sl, red & dk red brn	.75	.25

Horseback Rider, and Flags of Mongolia and USSR — A1551

1966, Jan. 31 Litho. *Perf. 12½x12*

3159 A1551 4k red, ultra & vio brn .50 .25

20th anniversary of the signing of the Mongolian-Soviet treaty of friendship and mutual assistance.

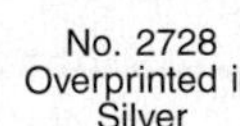

No. 2728 Overprinted in Silver

1966, Feb. 5 Photo. *Perf. 12*

3160 A1385 6k blk, lt blue & red 5.50 5.00

1st soft landing on the moon by Luna 9, Feb. 3, 1966.

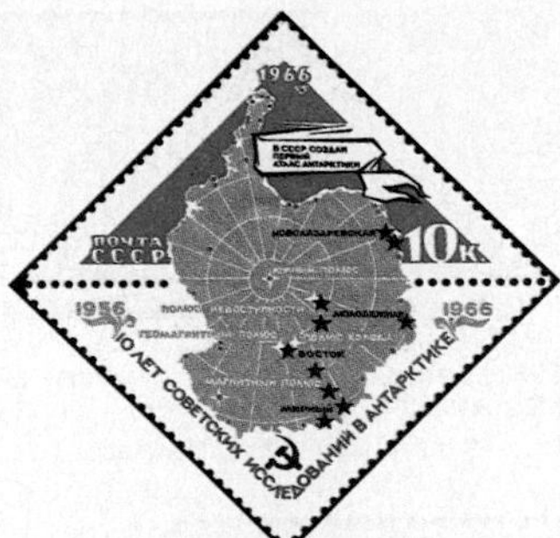

Map of Antarctica With Soviet Stations — A1552

Diesel Ship "Ob" and Emperor Penguins — A1553

No. 3164, Snocat tractors and aurora australis.

1966, Feb. 14 Photo. *Perf. 11*

3162	A1552	10k	sky bl, sil & dk car	1.50	1.00
3163	A1553	10k	silver & dk car	1.50	1.00
3164	A1553	10k	dk car, sil & sky bl	1.50	1.00
a.			Strip of 3, #3162-3164	5.00	5.00

10 years of Soviet explorations in Antarctica. No. 3162 has horizontal rows of perforation extending from either mid-side up to the map.

Lenin A1554

1966, Feb. 22 Photo. *Perf. 12x11½*

3165	A1554	10k	grnsh black & gold	1.00	.50
3166	A1554	10k	dk red & silver	1.00	.25

96th anniversary of the birth of Lenin.

N.Y. Iljin, Guardsman A1555

Soviet Heroes: #3168, Lt. Gen. G. P. Kravchenko. #3169, Pvt. Anatoli Uglovsky.

1966 *Perf. 11½x12*

3167	A1555	4k	dp org & vio black	.65	.25
3168	A1555	4k	grnsh bl & dk pur	.65	.25
3169	A1555	4k	green & brown	.65	.25
			Nos. 3167-3169 (3)	1.95	.75

Kremlin Congress Hall — A1556

1966, Feb. 28 Typo. *Perf. 12*
3172 A1556 4k gold, red & lt ultra .50 .25

23rd Communist Party Congress.

Hamlet and Queen from Film "Hamlet" A1557

Film Scene: 4k, Two soldiers from "The Quick and the Dead."

1966, Feb. 28 Litho.
3173 A1557 4k red, blk & ol .55 .25
3174 A1557 10k ultra & black .55 .25

No. 3104 Overprinted

1966, Mar. 10 Photo. *Perf. 11½x12*
3175 A1533 16k multicolored 5.00 2.50

Constituent assembly of the All-Union Society of Philatelists, 1966.

Emblem and Skater — A1558

Designs: 6k, Emblem and ice hockey. 10k, Emblem and slalom skier.

1966, Mar. 11 *Perf. 11*
3176 A1558 4k ol, brt ultra & red .35 .25
3177 A1558 6k bluish lilac, red & dk brown .60 .25
3178 A1558 10k lt bl, red & dk brn .95 .25
Nos. 3176-3178 (3) 1.90 .75

Second Winter Spartacist Games, Sverdlovsk. The label-like upper halves of Nos. 3176-3178 are separated from the lower halves by a row of perforations.

Electric Locomotive — A1559

Designs: 6k, Map of the Lenin Volga-Baltic Waterway, Admiralty, Leningrad, and Kremlin. 10k, Ship passing through lock in waterway, vert. 12k, M.S. Aleksander Pushkin. 16k, Passenger liner and globe.

1966 Litho. *Perf. 12½x12, 12x12½*
3179 A1559 4k multicolored .65 .25
3180 A1559 6k gray, ultra, red & black .65 .25
3181 A1559 10k Prus bl, gray brn & black .90 .25
3182 A1559 12k blue, ver & blk 1.25 .25
3183 A1559 16k blue & multi 1.25 .25
Nos. 3179-3183 (5) 4.70 1.25

Modern transportation.
Issued: #3179-3181, 8/6; #3182-3183, 3/25.

Supreme Soviet Building, Frunze — A1560

1966, Mar. 25 Photo. *Perf. 12*
3184 A1560 4k deep red .50 .25

40th anniv. of the Kirghiz Republic.

Sergei M. Kirov — A1561

Portraits: No. 3186, Grigori Ordzhonikidze. No. 3187, Ion Yakir.

1966 Engr. *Perf. 12*
3185 A1561 4k dk red brown 1.00 .30
3186 A1561 4k slate green 1.00 .30
3187 A1561 4k dark gray violet 1.00 .30
Nos. 3185-3187 (3) 3.00 .90

Kirov (1886-1934), revolutionist and Secretary of the Communist Party Central Committee; Ordzhonikidze (1886-1937), a political leader of the Red Army and government official; Yakir, military leader in October Revolution, 70th birth anniv.
Issued: #3185, 3/27; #3186, 6/22; #3187, 7/30.

Souvenir Sheet

Lenin — A1563

Embossed and Typographed
1966, Mar. 29 *Imperf.*
3188 A1563 50k red & silver 5.00 1.00

23rd Communist Party Congress.

Aleksandr E. Fersman (1883-1945), Mineralogist A1564

Soviet Scientists: No. 3190, D. K. Zabolotny (1866-1929), microbiologist. No. 3191, M. A. Shatelen (1866-1957), physicist. No. 3191A, Otto Yulievich Schmidt (1891-1956), scientist and arctic explorer.

1966, Mar. 30 Litho. *Perf. 12½x12*
3189 A1564 4k vio blue & multi .75 .30
3190 A1564 4k red brn & multi .75 .30
3191 A1564 4k lilac & multi .75 .30
3191A A1564 4k Prus bl & brn .75 .30
Nos. 3189-3191A (4) 3.00 1.20

Overprinted in Red

1966, Apr. 3 Typo. *Imperf.*
3192 A1565 10k gold, blk, brt bl & brt rose 2.00 1.50

Launching of the 1st artificial moon satellite, Luna 10. The bright rose ink is fluorescent on Nos. 3192-3194.

Luna 10 Automatic Moon Station — A1565

Design: 12k, Station on moon.

1966, Apr. 12 *Perf. 12*
3193 A1565 10k multicolored .80 .30
3194 A1565 12k multicolored 1.20 .30

Day of Space Research, Apr. 12, 1966.

Molniya 1 and Television Screens A1566

1966, Apr. 12 Litho. *Perf. 12½*
3195 A1566 10k gold, blk, brt bl & red 1.00 .30

Launching of the communications satellite "Lightning 1," Apr. 23, 1965.

Ernst Thälmann — A1567

Portraits: No. 3197, Wilhelm Pieck. No. 3198, Sun Yat-sen. No. 3199, Sen Katayama.

1966-67 Engr. *Perf. 12½x12*
3196 A1567 6k rose claret 1.25 .25
3197 A1567 6k blue violet 1.25 .25
3198 A1567 6k reddish brown 1.25 .25

Photo.
3199 A1567 6k gray green ('67) 1.25 .25
Nos. 3196-3199 (4) 5.00 1.00

Thälmann (1886-1944), German Communist leader; Pieck (1876-1960), German Dem. Rep. Pres.; Sun Yat-sen (1866-1925), leader of the Chinese revolution; Katayama (1859-1933), founder of Social Democratic Party in Japan in 1901.
Issued: No. 3196, 4/16; No. 3197-3198, 6/22; No. 3199, 11/2/67.

Soldier, 1917, and Astronaut A1568

1966, Apr. 30 Litho. *Perf. 11½*
3200 A1568 4k brt rose & black .50 .25

15th Congress of the Young Communist League (Komsomol).

Ice Hockey Player — A1569

1966, Apr. 30
3201 A1569 10k red, ultra, gold & black .50 .25

Soviet victory in the World Ice Hockey Championships. For souvenir sheet see No. 3232. For overprint see No. 3315.

Nicolai Kuznetsov A1570

Heroes of Guerrilla Warfare during WWII (Gold Star of Hero of the Soviet Union and): No. 3203, Imant Sudmalis. No. 3204, Anya Morozova. No. 3205, Filipp Strelets. No. 3206, Tikhon Bumazhkov.

1966, May 9 Photo. *Perf. 12x12½*
3202 A1570 4k green & black .60 .25
3203 A1570 4k ocher & black .60 .25
3204 A1570 4k blue & black .60 .25
3205 A1570 4k brt rose & black .60 .25
3206 A1570 4k violet & black .60 .25
Nos. 3202-3206 (5) 3.00 1.25

Peter I. Tchaikovsky A1571

4k, Moscow State Conservatory, Tchaikovsky monument. 16k, Tchaikovsky House, Klin.

1966, May 26 Typo. *Perf. 12½*

3207	A1571	4k red, yel & black	1.00	.25
3208	A1571	6k yel, red & black	1.25	.30
3209	A1571	16k red, bluish gray & black	3.00	.35
		Nos. 3207-3209 (3)	5.25	.90

Third International Tchaikovsky Contest, Moscow, May 30-June 29.

Runners — A1572

Designs: 6k, Weight lifters. 12k, Wrestlers.

1966, May 26 Photo. *Perf. 11x11½*

3210	A1572	4k emer, olive & brn	.50	.25
3211	A1572	6k org, blk & lt brn	.75	.25
3212	A1572	12k grnsh bl, brn ol & black	1.00	.25
		Nos. 3210-3212 (3)	2.25	.75

No. 3210, Znamensky Brothers Intl. Track Competitions; No. 3211, Intl. Weightlifting Competitions; No. 3212, Intl. Wrestling Competitions for Ivan Poddubny Prize.

Jules Rimet World Soccer Cup, Ball and Laurel — A1573

Chessboard, Gold Medal, Pawn and King A1574

Designs: No. 3214, Soccer. 12k, Fencers. 16k, Fencer, mask, foil and laurel branch.

1966, May 31 Litho. *Perf. 11½*

3213	A1573	4k rose red, gold & blk	.30	.25
3214	A1573	6k emer, tan, blk & red	.45	.25
3215	A1574	6k brn, gold, blk & white	1.75	.75
3216	A1573	12k brt bl, ol & blk	1.10	.25
3217	A1573	16k multicolored	1.40	.30
		Nos. 3213-3217 (5)	5.00	1.80

Nos. 3213-3214 for World Cup Soccer Championship, Wembley, England, July 11-30; No. 3215 the World Chess Title Match between Tigran Petrosian and Boris Spassky; Nos. 3216-3217 the World Fencing Championships. For souvenir sheet see No. 3232.

Sable and Lake Baikal, Map of Barguzin Game Reserve — A1575

Design: 6k, Map of Lake Baikal region and Game Reserve, brown bear on lake shore.

1966, June 25 Photo. *Perf. 12*

3218	A1575	4k steel blue & black	1.50	.25
3219	A1575	6k rose lake & black	1.50	.25

Barguzin Game Reserve, 50th anniv.

Pink Lotus — A1576

6k, Palms and cypresses. 12k, Victoria cruziana.

1966, June 30 *Perf. 11½*

3220	A1576	3k grn, pink & yel	.25	.25
3221	A1576	6k grnsh bl, ol brn & dk brn	1.00	.25
3222	A1576	12k multicolored	1.75	.25
		Nos. 3220-3222 (3)	3.00	.75

Sukhum Botanical Garden, 125th anniv.

Dogs Ugolek and Veterok after Space Flight A1577

Designs: No. 3224, Diagram of Solar System, globe and medal of Venera 3 flight. No. 3225, Luna 10, earth and moon.

1966, July 15 *Perf. 12x11½*

3223	A1577	6k ocher, ind & org brn	1.00	.25
3224	A1577	6k crim, blk & silver	1.00	.25

Perf. 12x12½

3225	A1577	6k dk blue & bis brn	1.00	.25
		Nos. 3223-3225 (3)	3.00	.75

Soviet achievements in space.

Itkol Hotel, Mount Cheget and Map of USSR A1578

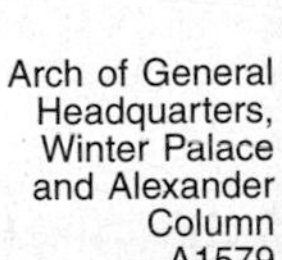

Arch of General Headquarters, Winter Palace and Alexander Column A1579

Resort Areas: 4k, Ship on Volga River and Zhigul Mountain. 10k, Castle, Kislovodsk. 12k, Ismail Samani Mausoleum, Bukhara, Uzbek. 16k, Hotel Caucasus, Sochi.

1966 Litho. *Perf. 12½x12, 12½ (6k)*

3226	A1578	1k multicolored	.25	.25
3227	A1578	4k multicolored	.35	.25
3228	A1579	6k multicolored	.40	.25
3229	A1578	10k multicolored	.65	.25
3230	A1578	12k multicolored	.90	.25
3231	A1578	16k multicolored	1.40	.30
		Nos. 3226-3231 (6)	3.95	1.55

Issue dates: 10k, Sept. 14; others, July 20.

Souvenir Sheet

A1580

1966, July 26 Litho. *Perf. 11½*

3232	A1580	Sheet of 4	10.00	2.00
a.		10k Fencers	2.00	.40
b.		10k Chess	2.00	.40
c.		10k Soccer cup	2.00	.40
d.		10k Ice hockey	2.00	.40

World fencing, chess, soccer and ice hockey championships.

See Nos. 3201, 3213-3217.

Congress Emblem, Congress Palace and Kremlin Tower — A1581

1966, Aug. 6 Photo. *Perf. 11½x12*

3233	A1581	4k brown & yellow	.35	.25

Consumers' Cooperative Societies, 7th Cong.

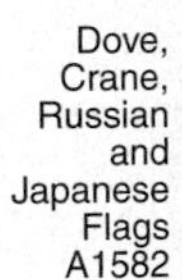

Dove, Crane, Russian and Japanese Flags A1582

1966, Aug. 9 *Perf. 12½x11½*

3234	A1582	6k gray & red	1..00	.25

Soviet-Japanese friendship, and 2nd meeting of Russian and Japanese delegates at Khabarovsk.

"Knight Fighting with Tiger" by Rustaveli A1583

Designs: 4k, Shota Rustaveli, bas-relief. 6k, "Avtandil at a Mountain Spring." 50k, Shota Rustaveli Monument and design of 3k stamp.

1966, Aug. 31 Engr. *Perf. 11½x12½*

3235	A1583	3k blk, *olive green*	.75	.25
3236	A1583	4k brown, *yellow*	.90	.25
3237	A1583	6k bluish black, *lt ultra*	1.40	.25
		Nos. 3235-3237 (3)	3.05	.75

Souvenir Sheet

Imperf

Engraved and Photogravure

3238	A1583	50k slate grn & bis	4.00	1.25

800th anniv. of the birth of Shota Rustaveli, Georgian poet, author of "The Knight in the Tiger's Skin." No. 3238 contains one 32x49mm stamp; dark green margin with design of 6k stamp.

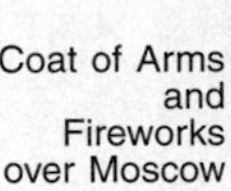

Coat of Arms and Fireworks over Moscow A1584

Lithographed (Lacquered)

1966, Sept. 14 *Perf. 11½*

3239	A1584	4k multicolored	.50	.25

49th anniversary of October Revolution.

Grayling A1585

Designs (Fish and part of design of 6k stamp): 4k, Sturgeon. 6k, Trawler, net and map of Lake Baikal, vert. 10k, Two Baikal cisco. 12k, Two Baikal whitefish.

1966, Sept. 25 Photo. & Engr.

3240	A1585	2k multicolored	.25	.25
3241	A1585	4k multicolored	.25	.25
3242	A1585	6k multicolored	.35	.25
3243	A1585	10k multicolored	.50	.25
3244	A1585	12k gray, dk grn & red brown	.75	.25
		Nos. 3240-3244 (5)	2.10	1.25

Fish resources of Lake Baikal.

Map of USSR and Symbols of Transportation and Communication — A1586

Designs (map of USSR and): No. 3246, Technological education. No. 3247, Agriculture and mining. No. 3248, Increased productivity through five-year plan. No. 3249, Technology and inventions.

1966, Sept. 29 Photo. *Perf. 11½x12*

3245	A1586	4k ultra & silver	.60	.25
3246	A1586	4k car & silver	.60	.25
3247	A1586	4k red brn & silver	.60	.25
3248	A1586	4k red & silver	.60	.25
3249	A1586	4k dp green & silver	.60	.25
		Nos. 3245-3249 (5)	3.00	1.25

23rd Communist Party Congress decisions.

Government House, Kishinev, and Moldavian Flag — A1587

1966, Oct. 8 Litho. *Perf. 12½x12*

3250	A1587	4k multicolored	.50	.50

500th anniversary of Kishinev.

Symbolic Water Cycle A1588

1966, Oct. 12 ***Perf. 11½***

3251 A1588 6k multicolored 1.00 .25

Hydrological Decade (UNESCO), 1965-1974.

Nikitin Monument in Kalinin, Ship's Prow and Map — A1589

1966, Oct. 12 **Photo.**

3252 A1589 4k multicolored .50 .25

Afanasii Nikitin's trip to India, 500th anniv.

Scene from Opera "Nargiz" by M. Magomayev — A1590

No. 3254, Scene from opera "Kerogli" by Y. Gadjubekov (knight on horseback and armed men).

1966, Oct. 12

3253 A1590 4k black & ocher .75 .25

3254 A1590 4k blk & blue green .75 .25

a. Pair, #3253-3254 2.00 .50

Azerbaijan opera. Printed in checkerboard arrangement.

Fighters A1591

1966, Oct. 26

3255 A1591 6k red, blk & ol bister .50 .25

30th anniversary of Spanish Civil War.

National Militia — A1592

1966, Oct. 26 **Litho.** ***Perf. 12x12½***

3256 A1592 4k red & dark brown .50 .25

25th anniv. of the National Militia.

Protest Rally — A1592a

1966, Oct. 26 ***Perf. 12***

3256A A1592a 6k yel, black & red .50 .30

"Hands off Viet Nam!"

Soft Landing on Moon, Luna 9 — A1593

Symbols of Agriculture and Chemistry A1594

Designs: 1k, Congress Palace, Moscow, and map of Russia. 3k, Boy, girl and Lenin banner. 4k, Flag. 6k, Plane and Ostankino Television Tower. 10k, Soldier and Soviet star. 12k, Steel worker. 16k, "Peace," woman with dove. 20k, Demonstrators in Red Square, flags, carnation and globe. 50k, Newspaper, plane, train and Communications Ministry. 1r, Lenin and industrial symbols.

Inscribed "1966"

1966 **Litho.** ***Perf. 12***

3257 A1593 1k dk red brown .25 .25

3258 A1593 2k violet .25 .25

3259 A1593 3k red lilac .25 .25

3260 A1593 4k bright red .25 .25

3261 A1593 6k ultra .25 .25

3262 A1593 10k olive .40 .25

3263 A1593 12k red brown 1.10 .25

3264 A1593 16k violet blue 1.40 .25

Perf. 11½

Photo.

3265 A1594 20k bis, red & dk bl 2.00 .25

3266 A1594 30k dp grn & green 2.50 .30

3267 A1594 50k blue & violet bl 4.50 .35

3268 A1594 1r black & red 6.50 .55

Nos. 3257-3268 (12) 19.65 3.45

No. 3260 was issued on fluorescent paper in 1969.

See Nos. 3470-3481.

Ostankino Television Tower, Molniya 1 Satellite and Kremlin A1595

1966, Nov. 19 **Litho.** ***Perf. 12***

3273 A1595 4k multicolored 1.00 .25

New Year, 1967, the 50th anniversary of the October Revolution.

Diagram of Luna 9 Flight — A1596

Arms of Russia and Pennant Sent to Moon — A1597

No. 3276, Luna 9 & photograph of moonscape.

1966, Nov. 25 **Typo.** ***Perf. 12***

3274 A1596 10k black & silver .75 .25

3275 A1597 10k red & silver .75 .25

3276 A1596 10k black & silver .75 .25

a. Strip of 3, #3274-3276 3.00 3.00

Soft landing on the moon by Luna 9, Jan. 31, 1966, and the television program of moon pictures on Feb. 2.

Battle of Moscow, 1941 — A1598

Details from "Defense of Moscow" Medal and Golden Star Medal A1599

25th anniv. of Battle of Moscow: 10k, Sun rising over Kremlin. Ostankino Tower, chemical plant and rockets.

Perf. 12, 11½ (A1599)

1966, Dec. 1 **Photo.**

3277 A1598 4k red brown .25 .25

3278 A1599 6k bister & brown 1.00 .25

3279 A1598 10k dp bister & yel 1.75 .25

Nos. 3277-3279 (3) 3.00 .75

Cervantes and Don Quixote A1600

1966, Dec. 15 **Photo.** ***Perf. 11½***

3280 A1600 6k gray & brown .50 .25

Miguel Cervantes Saavedra (1547-1616), Spanish writer.

Bering's Ship and Map of Voyage to Commander Islands — A1601

Far Eastern Territories: 2k, Medny Island and map. 4k, Petropavlosk-Kamchatski Harbor. 6k, Geyser, Kamchatka, vert. 10k, Avachinskaya Bay, Kamchatka. 12k, Fur seals, Bering Island. 16k, Guillemots in bird sanctuary, Kuril Islands.

1966, Dec. 25 **Litho.** ***Perf. 12***

3281 A1601 1k bister & multi .45 .25

3282 A1601 2k bister & multi .50 .25

3283 A1601 4k dp blue & multi .60 .25

3284 A1601 6k multicolored .75 .25

3285 A1601 10k dp blue & multi 1.00 .25

3286 A1601 12k olive & multi 1.00 .40

3287 A1601 16k lt blue & multi 1.25 .75

Nos. 3281-3287 (7) 5.55 2.40

Communications Satellite, Molniya 1 — A1602

Design: No. 3289, Luna 11 moon probe, moon, earth and Soviet emblem.

1966, Dec. 29 **Photo.** ***Perf. 12x11½***

3288 A1602 6k blk, vio bl & brt rose 1.00 .30

3289 A1602 6k black & brt rose 1.00 .30

Space explorations. The bright rose is fluorescent.

Golden Stag, Scythia, 6th Century B.C. — A1603

Treasures from the Hermitage, Leningrad: 6k, Silver jug, Persia, 5th Century A.D. 10k, Statue of Voltaire by Jean Antoine Houdon. 12k, Malachite vase, Ural, 1840. 16k, "The Lute Player," by Michelangelo de Caravaggio. (6k, 10k, 12k are vertical).

1966, Dec. 29 **Engr.** ***Perf. 12***

3290 A1603 4k yellow & black .45 .25

3291 A1603 6k gray & black .60 .25

3292 A1603 10k dull vio & black .90 .25

3293 A1603 12k emer & black 1.25 .30

3294 A1603 16k ocher & black 1.75 .35

Nos. 3290-3294 (5) 4.95 1.40

Sea Water Converter and Pavilion at EXPO '67 A1604

Pavilion and: 6k, Splitting atom, vert. 10k, "Proton" space station. 30k, Soviet pavilion.

1967, Jan. 25 **Litho.** ***Perf. 12***

3295 A1604 4k multicolored .75 .25

3296 A1604 6k multicolored .75 .25

3297 A1604 10k multicolored 1.50 .25

Nos. 3295-3297 (3) 3.00 .75

Souvenir Sheet

3298 A1604 30k multicolored 4.00 1.25

EXPO '67, Intl. Exhib., Montreal, 4/28-10/27.

1st Lieut. B. I. Sizov A1605

Design: No. 3300, Sailor V. V. Khodyrev.

1967, Feb. 16 **Photo.** ***Perf. 12x11½***

3299 A1605 4k dull yel & ocher .50 .25

3300 A1605 4k gray & dk gray .50 .25

Heroes of World War II.

Woman's Head and Pavlov Shawl — A1606

1967, Feb. 16 *Perf. 11*

3301 A1606 4k vio, red & grn .40 .25

International Woman's Day, Mar. 8.

Movie Camera and Film — A1607

1967, Feb. 16 Photo. *Perf. 11½*

3302 A1607 6k multicolored .50 .25

5th Intl. Film Festival, Moscow, July 5-20.

Trawler Fish Factory and Fish — A1608

Designs: No. 3304, Refrigerationship. No. 3305, Crab canning ship. No. 3306, Fishing trawler. No. 3307, Black Sea seiner.

1967, Feb. 28 Litho. *Perf. 12x11½*

Ships in Black and Red

3303 A1608 6k blue & gray .60 .25
3304 A1608 6k blue & gray .60 .25
3305 A1608 6k blue & gray .60 .25
3306 A1608 6k blue & gray .60 .25
3307 A1608 6k blue & gray .60 .25
a. Vert. strip of 5, #3303-3307 3.25 1.50

Soviet fishing industry.

Newspaper Forming Hammer and Sickle, Red Flag — A1609

1967, Mar. 13 Litho. *Perf. 12x12½*

3308 A1609 4k cl brn, red, yel & brn .40 .25

50th anniversary of newspaper Izvestia.

Congress Type of 1966

Congress Emblems and: No. 3309, Moscow State University, construction site and star. No. 3310, Pile driver, mining excavator, crossed hammers, globe and "V."

1967, Mar. 10 Photo. *Perf. 11½*

3309 A1548 6k ultra, brt blue & blk .50 .25
3310 A1548 6k blk, org red & blue .50 .25

Intl. congresses to be held in Moscow: 7th General Assembly Session of the Intl. Standards Association (#3309); 5th Intl. Mining Cong. (#3310).

International Tourist Year Emblem and Travel Symbols — A1610

1967, Mar. 10 *Perf. 11*

3314 A1610 4k blk, sky bl & sil .40 .25

International Tourist Year, 1967.

No. 3201 Overprinted

1967, Mar. 29 Litho. *Perf. 11½*

3315 A1569 10k multicolored 2.00 1.00

Victory of the Soviet team in the Ice Hockey Championships, Vienna, Mar. 18-29. Overprint reads: "Vienna-1967."

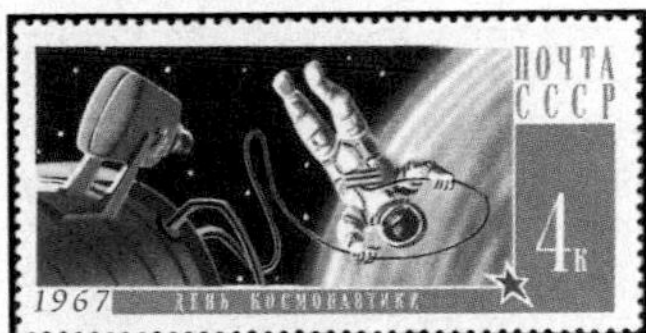

Space Walk — A1611

Designs: 10k, Rocket launching from satellite. 16k, Spaceship over moon, and earth.

1967, Mar. 30 Litho. *Perf. 12*

3316 A1611 4k bister & multi .50 .25
3317 A1611 10k black & multi 1.00 .25
3318 A1611 16k lilac & multi 1.50 .30
Nos. 3316-3318 (3) 3.00 .80

National Cosmonauts' Day.

Lenin as Student, by V. Tsigal A1612

Sculptures of Lenin: 3k, Monument at Ulyanovsk by M. Manizer. 4k, Lenin in Razliv, by V. Pinchuk, horiz. 6k, Head, by G. Neroda. 10k, Lenin as Leader, statue, by N. Andreyev.

1967 Photo. *Perf. 12x11½, 11½x12*

3319 A1612 2k ol grn, sepia & buff .30 .25
3320 A1612 3k maroon & brn .30 .25
3321 A1612 4k ol black & gold .45 .25
3322 A1612 6k dk bl, sil & blk .60 .25
3323 A1612 10k sil, gray bl & blk 1.10 .25
3323A A1612 10k gold, gray & black 1.10 .25
Nos. 3319-3323A (6) 3.85 1.50

97th anniversary of the birth of Lenin. Issued: #3323A, Oct. 25; others, Apr. 22.

Lt. M. S. Kharchenko and Battle Scenes — A1613

Designs: No. 3325, Maj. Gen. S. V. Rudnev. No. 3326, M. Shmyrev.

1967, Apr. 24 *Perf. 12x11½*

3324 A1613 4k brt pur & ol bis .50 .25
3325 A1613 4k ultra & ol bister .50 .25
3326 A1613 4k org brn & ol bister .50 .25
Nos. 3324-3326 (3) 1.50 .75

Partisan heroes of WWII.

Marshal S. S. Biryuzov, Hero of the Soviet Union — A1614

1967, May 9 Photo. *Perf. 12*

3327 A1614 4k ocher & sl grn .50 .40

Driver Crossing Lake Ladoga A1615

1967, May 9 *Perf. 11½*

3328 A1615 4k plum & blue gray .40 .25

25th anniversary of siege of Leningrad.

Views of Old and New Minsk A1616

1967, May 9

3329 A1616 4k sl grn & blk .40 .25

900th anniversary of Minsk.

Red Cross and Tulip — A1617

1967, May 15 *Perf. 12*

3330 A1617 4k yel brn & red .50 .25

Centenary of the Russian Red Cross.

Stamps of 1918 and 1967 — A1618

1967 Photo. *Perf. 11½*

3331 A1618 20k blue & black 1.00 .30
a. Souv. sheet of 2, imperf. 2.00 1.25

All-Union Philatelic Exhibition "50 Years of the Great October," Moscow, Oct. 1-10. Se-tenant with label showing exhibition emblem. Issue dates: 20k, May 25. Sheet, Oct. 1.

No. 3331 was re-issued Oct. 3 with "Oct. 1-10" printed in blue on the label. Value $2.

Komsomolsk-on-Amur and Map of Amur River — A1619

1967, June 12 *Perf. 12x12½*

3332 A1619 4k red & brown .60 .25

35th anniv. of the Soviet youth town, Komsomolsk-on-Amur. Printed with label showing boy and girl of Young Communist League and tents.

Souvenir Sheet

Sputnik Orbiting Earth — A1620

1967, June 24 Litho. *Perf. 13x12*

3333 A1620 30k black & multi 7.50 6.00

10th anniv. of the launching of Sputnik 1, the 1st artificial satellite, Oct. 4, 1957.

Motorcyclist A1621

Photogravure and Engraved

1967, June 24 *Perf. 12x11½*

3334 A1621 10k multicolored .35 .25

Intl. Motor Rally, Moscow, July 19.

G. D. Gai (1887-1937), Corps Commander of the First Cavalry, 1920 — A1622

1967, June 30 Photo. *Perf. 12*

3335 A1622 4k red & black .40 .25

Children's Games Emblem and Trophy
A1623

1967, July 8 ***Perf. 11½***
3336 A1623 4k silver, red & black .40 .25

10th National Athletic Games of School Children, Leningrad, July, 1967.

Games Emblem and Trophy
A1624

No. 3338, Cup and gymnast. No. 3339, Cup and bicyclists. No. 3340, Cup and diver.

1967, July 20
3337 A1624 4k silver, red & black .25 .25
3338 A1624 4k silver, red & black .25 .25
a. Pair, #3337-3338 1.00 .35
3339 A1624 4k silver, red & black .25 .25
3340 A1624 4k silver, red & black .25 .25
a. Pair, #3339-3340 1.00 .35

4th Natl. Spartacist Games, & USSR 50th anniv.
Se-tenant in checkerboard arrangement.

V. G. Klochkov (1911-41), Hero of the Soviet Union — A1625

1967, July 20 ***Perf. 12½x12***
3341 A1625 4k red & black .75 .30

Alternating label shows citation.

Soviet Flag, Arms and Moscow Views
A1626

Arms of USSR and Laurel — A1627

АРМЯНСКАЯ ССР
ՀԱՅԿԱԿԱՆ ՍՍՀ

No. 3343

АЗЕРБАЙДЖАНСКАЯ ССР
АЗӘРБАЈҸАН ССР

No. 3344

БЕЛОРУССКАЯ ССР
БЕЛАРУСКАЯ ССР

No. 3345

ГРУЗИНСКАЯ ССР
საქართველოს სსრ

No. 3347

КИРГИЗСКАЯ ССР
КЫРГЫЗ ССР

No. 3349

МОЛДАВСКАЯ ССР
РСС МОЛДОВЕНЯСКЭ

No. 3352

ТАДЖИКСКАЯ ССР
РСС ТОҶИКИСТОН

No. 3353

ТУРКМЕНСКАЯ ССР
ТУРКМЕНИСТАН ССР

No. 3354

УКРАИНСКАЯ ССР
УКРАЇНСЬКА РСР

No. 3355

УЗБЕКСКАЯ ССР
ЎЗБЕКИСТОН ССР

No. 3356

Flag, Crest and Capital of Republic.

1967, Aug. 4 **Litho.** ***Perf. 12½x12***
3342 A1626 4k shown .60 .25
3343 A1626 4k Armenia .60 .25
3344 A1626 4k Azerbaijan .60 .25
3345 A1626 4k Byelorussia .60 .25
3346 A1626 4k Estonia .60 .25
3347 A1626 4k Georgia .60 .25
3348 A1626 4k Kazakhstan .60 .25
3349 A1626 4k Kirghizia .60 .25
3350 A1626 4k Latvia .60 .25
3351 A1626 4k Lithuania .60 .25
3352 A1626 4k Moldavia .60 .25
3353 A1626 4k Tadzhikistan .60 .25
3354 A1626 4k Turkmenistan .60 .25
3355 A1626 4k Ukraine .60 .25
3356 A1626 4k Uzbekistan .60 .25
3357 A1627 4k red, gold & black .60 .25
Nos. 3342-3357 (16) 9.60 4.00

50th anniversary of October Revolution.

Communication Symbols — A1628

1967, Aug. 16 **Photo.** ***Perf. 12***
3358 A1628 4k crimson & silver 1.00 .50

Development of communications in USSR.

Flying Crane, Dove and Anniversary Emblem — A1629

1967, Aug. 20 ***Perf. 12½x12***
3359 A1629 16k silver, red & blk 1.00 .30

Russo-Japanese Friendship Meeting, held at Khabarovsk. Emblem is for 50th anniv. of October Revolution.

Karl Marx and Title Page of "Das Kapital" — A1630

1967, Aug. 22 **Engr.** ***Perf. 12½x12***
3360 A1630 4k sepia & dk red 3.00 .30

Centenary of the publication of "Das Kapital" by Karl Marx.

Russian Checkers Players
A1631

Design: 6k, Woman gymnast.

Photogravure and Engraved

1967, Sept. 9 ***Perf. 12x11½***
3361 A1631 1k lt brn, dp brn & sl .50 .25
3362 A1631 6k ol bister & maroon .50 .25

World Championship of Russian Checkers (Shashki) at Moscow, and World Championship of Rhythmic Gymnastics.

Javelin
A1632

1967, Sept. 9 **Engr.** ***Perf. 12x12½***
3363 A1632 2k shown .65 .25
3364 A1632 3k Running .65 .25
3365 A1632 4k Jumping .65 .25
Nos. 3363-3365 (3) 1.95 .75

Europa Cup Championships, Kiev, Sept. 15-17.

Ice Skating and Olympic Emblem
A1633

Designs: 3k, Ski jump. 4k, Emblem of Winter Olympics, vert. 10k, Ice hockey. 12k, Long-distance skiing.

Photogravure and Engraved

1967, Sept. 20 ***Perf. 11½***
3366 A1633 2k gray, blk & bl .25 .25
3367 A1633 3k bis, ocher, blk & green .25 .25
3368 A1633 4k gray, bl, red & blk .25 .25
3369 A1633 10k bis, brn, bl & blk .75 .25
3370 A1633 12k gray, blk, lil & grn 1.50 .25
Nos. 3366-3370 (5) 3.00 1.25

10th Winter Olympic Games, Grenoble, France, Feb. 6-18, 1968.

Arctic Blue Fox
A1634

Fur-bearing Animals: 4k, Silver Fox. 6k, Red fox, horiz. 10k, Muskrat, horiz. 12k, Ermine. 16k, Sable. 20k, Mink, horiz.

1967, Sept. 20 **Photo.**
3371 A1634 2k brn, blk & gray blue .25 .25
3372 A1634 4k tan, dk brn & gray blue .30 .25
3373 A1634 6k gray grn, ocher & black .45 .25
3374 A1634 10k yel grn, dk brn & ocher .65 .25
3375 A1634 12k lilac, blk & bis .75 .25
3376 A1634 16k org, brn & black .80 .25
3377 A1634 20k gray blue, blk & dk brown 1.00 .30
Nos. 3371-3377 (7) 4.20 1.80

International Fur Auctions in Leningrad.

Young Guards Memorial — A1635

1967, Sept. 23
3378 A1635 4k magenta, org & blk .50 .25

25th anniv. of the fight of the Young Guards at Krasnodon against the Germans.

Map of Cedar Valley Reservation and Snow Leopard — A1636

1967, Oct. 14 ***Perf. 12***
3379 A1636 10k ol bister & black 1.00 .25

Far Eastern Cedar Valley Reservation.

Planes and Emblem
A1637

1967, Oct. 14 ***Perf. 11½***
3380 A1637 6k dp blue, red & gold .50 .25

French Normandy-Neman aviators, who fought on the Russian Front, 25th anniv.

Militiaman and Soviet Emblem
A1638

1967, Oct. 14 ***Perf. 12½x12***
3381 A1638 4k ver & ultra .40 .25

50th anniversary of the Soviet Militia.

Space Station Orbiting Moon — A1639

Science Fiction: 6k, Explorers on the moon, horiz. 10k, Rocket flying to the stars. 12k, Landscape on Red Planet, horiz. 16k, Satellites from outer space.

1967 **Litho.** ***Perf. 12x12½, 12½x12***
3382 A1639 4k multicolored .25 .25
3383 A1639 6k multicolored .35 .25
3384 A1639 10k multicolored .45 .25
3385 A1639 12k multicolored .60 .25
3386 A1639 16k multicolored .65 .25
Nos. 3382-3386 (5) 2.30 1.25

Emblem of USSR and Red Star — A1640

Lenin Addressing 2nd Congress of Soviets, by V. A. Serov — A1641

Builders of Communism, by L. M. Merpert and Y. N. Skripkov — A1641a

Paintings: No. 3389, Lenin pointing to Map, by L. A. Schmatjko, 1957. No. 3390, The First Cavalry Army, by M. B. Grekov, 1924. No. 3391, Working Students on the March, by B. V. Yoganson, 1928. No. 3392, Russian Friendship for the World, by S. M. Karpov, 1924. No. 3393, Five-Year Plan Morning, by Y. D. Romas, 1934. No. 3394, Farmers' Holiday, by S. V. Gerasimov, 1937. No. 3395, Victory in the Great Patriotic War, by Y. K. Korolev, 1965.

Lithographed and Embossed

1967, Oct. 25 ***Perf. 11½***

3387	A1640	4k gold, yel, red & dk brown	.50	.25
3388	A1641	4k gold & multi	.50	.25
3389	A1641	4k gold & multi	.50	.25
3390	A1641	4k gold & multi	.50	.25
3391	A1641	4k gold & multi	.50	.25
3392	A1641	4k gold & multi	.50	.25
3393	A1641	4k gold & multi	.50	.25
3394	A1641	4k gold & multi	.50	.25
3395	A1641	4k gold & multi	.50	.25
3396	A1641a	4k gold & multi	.50	.25
a.		Souvenir sheet of 2	4.25	1.00
		Nos. 3387-3396 (10)	5.00	2.50

50th anniversary of October Revolution. No. 3396a contains two 40k imperf. stamps similar to Nos. 3388 and 3396. Issued Nov. 5.

Souvenir Sheet

Hammer, Sickle and Sputnik — A1642

1967, Nov. 5 **Engr.** ***Perf. 12½x12***

3397	A1642	1r lake	5.00	2.00

50th anniv. of the October Revolution. Margin contains "50" as a watermark.

Ostankino Television Tower — A1643

1967, Nov. 5 **Litho.** ***Perf. 11½***

3398	A1643	16k gray, org & black	.35	.25

Jurmala Resort and Hepatica A1644

Health Resorts of the Baltic Region: 6k, Narva-Joesuu and Labrador tea. 10k, Druskininkai and cranberry blossoms. 12k, Zelenogradsk and Scotch heather, vert. 16k, Svetlogorsk and club moss, vert.

Perf. 12½x12, 12x12½

1967, Nov. 30 **Litho.**

Flowers in Natural Colors

3399	A1644	4k blue & black	.25	.25
3400	A1644	6k ocher & black	.35	.25
3401	A1644	10k green & black	.60	.25
3402	A1644	12k gray olive & blk	.75	.25
3403	A1644	16k brown & black	1.10	.25
		Nos. 3399-3403 (5)	3.05	1.25

Emergency Commission Emblem — A1645

1967, Dec. 11 **Photo.** ***Perf. 11½***

3404	A1645	4k ultra & red	.75	.25

All-Russia Emergency Commission (later the State Security Commission), 50th anniv.

Hotel Russia and Kremlin A1646

1967, Dec. 14

3405	A1646	4k silver, dk brn & brt pink	1.00	.25

New Year 1968. The pink is fluorescent.

Soldiers, Sailors, Congress Building, Kharkov, and Monument to the Men of Arsenal — A1647

Designs: 6k, Hammer and sickle and scenes from industry and agriculture. 10k, Ukrainians offering bread and salt, monument of the Unknown Soldier, Kiev, and Lenin monument in Zaporozhye.

1967, Dec. 20 **Litho.** ***Perf. 12½***

3406	A1647	4k multicolored	.30	.25
3407	A1647	6k multicolored	.65	.25
3408	A1647	10k multicolored	.80	.25
		Nos. 3406-3408 (3)	1.75	.75

50th anniv. of the Ukrainian SSR.

Three Kremlin Towers A1648

Kremlin: 6k, Cathedral of the Annunciation, horiz. 10k, Konstantin and Elena, Nabatnaya and Spasski towers. 12k, Ivan the Great bell tower. 16k, Kutafya and Troitskaya towers.

Engraved and Photogravure

1967, Dec. 25 ***Perf. 12x11½, 11½x12***

3409	A1648	4k dk brn & claret	.25	.25
3410	A1648	6k dk brn, yel & grn	.35	.25
3411	A1648	10k maroon & slate	.65	.25
3412	A1648	12k sl grn, yel & vio	.90	.25
3413	A1648	16k brn, pink & red	1.00	.25
		Nos. 3409-3413 (5)	3.15	1.25

Coat of Arms, Lenin's Tomb and Rockets A1649

Designs: No. 3415, Agricultural Progress: Wheat, reapers and silo. No. 3416, Industrial Progress: Computer tape, atom symbol, cogwheel and factories. No. 3417, Scientific Progress: Radar, microscope, university buildings. No. 3418, Communications progress: Ostankino TV tower, railroad bridge, steamer and Aeroflot emblem, vert.

1967, Dec. 25 **Engr.** ***Perf. 12½***

3414	A1649	4k maroon	.30	.25
3415	A1649	4k green	.30	.25
3416	A1649	4k red brown	.30	.25
3417	A1649	4k violet blue	.30	.25
3418	A1649	4k dark blue	.30	.25
		Nos. 3414-3418 (5)	1.50	1.25

Material and technical basis of Russian Communism.

Monument to the Unknown Soldier, Moscow — A1650

1967, Dec. 25

3419	A1650	4k carmine	.60	.40

Dedication of the Monument of the Unknown Soldier of WWII in the Kremlin Wall.

Seascape by Ivan Aivazovsky — A1651

Paintings: 3k, Interrogation of Communists by B. V. Yoganson, 1933. No. 3422, The Lacemaker, by V. A. Tropinin, 1823, vert. No. 3423, Bread-makers, by T. M. Yablonskaya, 1949. No. 3424, Alexander Nevsky, by P. D. Korin, 1942-43, vert. No. 3425, The Boyar Morozov Going into Exile by V. I. Surikov, 1887. No. 3426, The Swan Maiden, by M. A. Vrubel, 1900, vert. No. 3427, The Arrest of a Propagandist by Ilya E. Repin, 1878. 16k, Moscow Suburb in February by G. G. Nissky, 1957.

Perf. 12½x12, 12x12½, 12, 11½

1967, Dec. 29 **Litho.**

Size: 47x33mm, 33x47mm

3420	A1651	3k multicolored	.25	.25
3421	A1651	4k multicolored	.30	.25
3422	A1651	4k multicolored	.30	.25

Size: 60x35mm, 35x60mm

3423	A1651	6k multicolored	.40	.25
3424	A1651	6k multicolored	.40	.25
3425	A1651	6k multicolored	.40	.25

Size: 47x33mm, 33x47mm

3426	A1651	10k multicolored	.70	.25
3427	A1651	10k multicolored	.70	.25
3428	A1651	16k multicolored	1.10	.40
		Nos. 3420-3428 (9)	4.55	2.40

Tretiakov Art Gallery, Moscow.

Globe, Wheel and Workers of the World — A1652

1968, Jan. 18 **Photo.** ***Perf. 12***

3429	A1652	6k ver & green	.50	.25

14th Trade Union Congress.

Lt. S. Baikov and Velikaya River Bridge A1653

Heroes of WWII (War Memorial and): No. 3431. Lt. A. Pokalchuk. No. 3432, P. Gutchenko.

1968, Jan. 20 ***Perf. 12½x12***

3430	A1653	4k blue gray & black	.35	.25
3431	A1653	4k rose & black	.35	.25
3432	A1653	4k gray green & black	.35	.25
		Nos. 3430-3432 (3)	1.05	.75

Thoroughbred and Horse Race — A1654

Horses: 6k, Arab mare and dressage, vert. 10k, Orlovski trotters. 12k, Altekin horse performing, vert. 16k, Donskay race horse.

1968, Jan. 23 ***Perf. 11½***

3433	A1654	4k ultra, blk & red lil	.40	.25
3434	A1654	6k crim, blk & ultra	.65	.25
3435	A1654	10k grnsh blue, blk & orange	.95	.40
3436	A1654	12k org brn, black & apple green	1.25	.50
3437	A1654	16k ol grn, blk & red	1.75	.70
		Nos. 3433-3437 (5)	5.00	2.10

Horse breeding.

Maria I. Ulyanova (1878-1937), Lenin's Sister — A1655

1968, Jan. 30 ***Perf. 12x12½***

3438 A1655 4k indigo & pale green .50 .25

Soviet Star and Flags of Army, Air Force and Navy A1656

Lenin Addressing Troops in 1919 — A1657

No. 3441, Dneprostroi Dam & sculpture "On Guard." No. 3442, 1918 poster & marching volunteers. No. 3443, Red Army entering Vladivostok, 1922, & soldiers' monument in Primorie. No. 3444, Poster "Red Army as Liberator," Western Ukraine. No. 3445, Poster "Westward," defeat of German army. No. 3446, "Battle of Stalingrad" monument & German prisoners of war. No. 3447, Victory parade on Red Square, May 24, 1945, & Russian War Memorial, Berlin. Nos. 3448-3449, Modern weapons and Russian flag.

1968, Feb. 20 **Typo.** ***Perf. 12x12½***

3439 A1656 4k gold & multi .30 .25

Photo.

Perf. 11½x12

3440 A1657 4k blk, red, pink & silver .30 .25
3441 A1657 4k gold, black & red .30 .25

Litho.

Perf. 12½x12

3442 A1657 4k yel grn, blk, red & buff .30 .25
3443 A1657 4k grn, dk brn, red & bis .30 .25
3444 A1657 4k green & multi .30 .25
3445 A1657 4k yel green & multi .30 .25

Perf. 11½x12, 12x11½

Photo.

3446 A1657 4k blk, silver & red .30 .25
3447 A1657 4k gold, blk, pink & red .30 .25
3448 A1656 4k blk, red & silver .30 .25
Nos. 3439-3448 (10) 3.00 2.50

Souvenir Sheet

1968, Feb. 23 **Litho.** ***Imperf.***

3449 A1656 1r blk, silver & red 4.50 1.50

50th anniv. of the Armed Forces of the USSR. No. 3449 contains one 25x37½mm stamp with simulated perforations.

Maxim Gorki (1868-1936), Writer — A1658

1968, Feb. 29 **Photo.** ***Perf. 12***

3450 A1658 4k gray ol & dk brown .50 .25

Fireman, Fire Truck and Boat — A1659

1968, Mar. 30 **Photo.** ***Perf. 12x12½***

3451 A1659 4k red & black .60 .25

50th anniversary of Soviet Fire Guards.

Link-up of Cosmos 186 and 188 Satellites — A1660

1968, Mar. 30 ***Perf. 11½***

3452 A1660 6k blk, dp lilac rose & gold .50 .25

First link-up in space of two satellites, Cosmos 186 and Cosmos 188, Oct. 30, 1967.

N. N. Popudrenko — A1661

Design: No. 3454, P. P. Vershigora.

1968, Mar. 30 ***Perf. 12½x12***

3453 A1661 4k gray green & black .30 .25
3454 A1661 4k lt purple & black .30 .25

Partisan heroes of World War II.

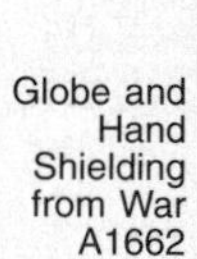

Globe and Hand Shielding from War A1662

1968, Apr. 11 ***Perf. 11½***

3455 A1662 6k sil, mar, ver & black .60 .35

Emergency session of the World Federation of Trade Unions and expressing solidarity with the people of Vietnam.

Space Walk A1663

6k, Docking operation of Kosmos 186 & Kosmos 188. 10k, Exploration of Venus.

1968, Apr. 12 **Litho.**

3456 A1663 4k multicolored .50 .25
3457 A1663 6k multicolored .50 .25
3458 A1663 10k multicolored 1.00 .25
a. Block of 3, #3456-3458 + 3 labels 3.50 .50

National Astronauts' Day.

Lenin, 1919 A1664

Lenin Portraits: No. 3460, Addressing crowd on Red Square, Nov. 7, 1918. No. 3461, Full-face portrait, taken in Petrograd, Jan. 1918.

Engraved and Photogravure

1968, Apr. 16 ***Perf. 12x11½***

3459 A1664 4k gold, brown & red 1.00 .25
3460 A1664 4k gold, red & black 1.00 .25
3461 A1664 4k gold, brn, buff & red 1.00 .25
Nos. 3459-3461 (3) 3.00 .75

98th anniversary of the birth of Lenin.

Alisher Navoi, Uzbek Poet, 525th Birth Anniv. — A1665

1968, Apr. 29 **Photo.** ***Perf. 12x12½***

3462 A1665 4k deep brown .50 .25

Karl Marx (1818-83) A1666

1968, May 5 **Engr.** ***Perf. 11½x12***

3463 A1666 4k black & red .50 .25

Frontier Guard — A1667

Jubilee Badge — A1668

1968, May 22 **Photo.** ***Perf. 11½***

3464 A1667 4k sl grn, ocher & red 1.00 .25
3465 A1668 6k sl grn, blk & red brn 1.00 .25

Russian Frontier Guards, 50th anniv.

Crystal and Congress Emblem A1669

Congress Emblems and: No. 3467, Power lines and factories. No. 3468, Ground beetle. No. 3469, Roses and carbon rings.

1968, May 30

3466 A1669 6k blue, dk blue & grn .45 .25
3467 A1669 6k org, gold & dk brn .45 .25
3468 A1669 6k red brn, gold & blk .45 .25
3469 A1669 6k lil rose, org & blk .45 .25
Nos. 3466-3469 (4) 1.80 1.00

Intl. congresses, Leningrad: 8th Cong. for Mineral Research; 7th World Power Conf.; 13th Entomological Cong.; 4th Cong. for the Study of Volatile Oils.

Types of 1966

Designs as before.

1968, June 20 **Engr.** ***Perf. 12***

3470 A1593 1k dk red brown .45 .25
3471 A1593 2k deep violet .45 .25
3472 A1593 3k plum .55 .25
3473 A1593 4k bright red .60 .25
3474 A1593 6k blue .80 .30
3475 A1593 10k olive 1.00 .40
3476 A1593 12k red brown 1.10 .45
3477 A1593 16k violet blue 1.40 .60

Perf. 12½

3478 A1594 20k red 1.60 .75
3479 A1594 30k bright green 2.75 .90
3480 A1594 50k violet blue 5.75 1.10

Perf. 12x12½

3481 A1594 1r gray, red brn & black 8.50 2.75
Nos. 3470-3481 (12) 24.95 8.25

Sadriddin Aini A1670

1968, June 30 **Photo.** ***Perf. 12½x12***

3482 A1670 4k olive bister & mar .50 .25

Aini (1878-1954), Tadzhik poet.

Post Rider and C.C.E.P. Emblem A1671

#3484, Modern means of communications (train, ship, planes and C.C.E.P. emblem).

1968, June 30

3483 A1671 6k gray & red brown .50 .25
3484 A1671 6k org brn & bis .50 .25

Annual session of the Council of the Consultative Commission on Postal Investigation of the UPU (C.C.E.P.), Moscow, 9/20-10/5.

Bolshevik Uprising, Kiev — A1672

1968, July 5 *Perf. 11½*

3485 A1672 4k gold, red & plum .50 .25

Ukrainian Communist Party, 50th anniv.

Athletes A1673

1968, July 9

3486 A1673 4k yel, dp car & bis .50 .25

1st Youth Summer Sports Games for 50th anniv. of the Leninist Young Communists League.

Field Ball — A1674

Table Tennis A1675

Designs: 6k, 20th Baltic Regatta. 10k, Soccer player and cup. 12k, Scuba divers.

Perf. 12x12½, 12½x12

1968, July 18 **Litho.**

3487 A1674 2k red & multi .25 .25
3488 A1675 4k purple & multi .30 .25
3489 A1674 6k blue & multi .60 .25
3490 A1674 10k multicolored .90 .25
3491 A1675 12k green & multi 1.00 .25
Nos. 3487-3491 (5) 3.05 1.25

European youth sports competitions.

Rhythmic Gymnast A1676

6k, Weight lifting. 10k, Rowing. 12k, Women's hurdling. 16k, Fencing. 40k, Running.

1968, July 31 **Photo.** *Perf. 11½*

Gold Background

3492 A1676 4k blue & green .30 .25
3493 A1676 6k dp rose & pur .45 .25
3494 A1676 10k yel grn & grn .60 .25
3495 A1676 12k org & red brn .75 .25
3496 A1676 16k ultra & pink 1.00 .25
Nos. 3492-3496 (5) 3.10 1.25

Souvenir Sheet

Perf. 12½x12

Lithographed and Photogravure

3497 A1676 40k gold, grn, org & gray 3.00 1.00

19th Olympic Games, Mexico City, 10/12-27.

Gediminas Tower, Vilnius — A1677

1968, Aug. 14 **Photo.** *Perf. 11½*

3498 A1677 4k mag, tan & red .50 .25

Soviet power in Lithuania, 50th anniv.

Tbilisi State University A1678

1968, Aug. 14 *Perf. 12*

3499 A1678 4k slate grn & lt brn .50 .25

Tbilisi State University, Georgia, 50th anniv.

Laocoon — A1679

1968, Aug. 16 *Perf. 11½*

3500 A1679 6k sepia, blk & mar 3.50 .50

"Promote solidarity with Greek democrats."

Red Army Man, Cavalry Charge and Order of the Red Banner of Battle — A1680

Designs: 3k, Young man and woman, Dneprostroi Dam and Order of the Red Banner of Labor. 4k, Soldier, storming of the Reichstag, Berlin, and Order of Lenin. 6k, "Restoration of National Economy" (workers), and Order of Lenin. 10k, Young man and woman cultivating virgin land and Order of Lenin. 50k, like 2k.

1968, Aug. 25 **Litho.** *Perf. 12½x12*

3501 A1680 2k gray, red & ocher .25 .25
3502 A1680 3k multicolored .50 .25
3503 A1680 4k org, ocher & rose car .50 .25
3504 A1680 6k multicolored .75 .25
3505 A1680 10k olive & multi 1.25 .25
Nos. 3501-3505 (5) 3.25 1.25

Souvenir Sheet

Imperf

3506 A1680 50k ultra, red & bister 2.00 .50

50th anniv. of the Lenin Young Communist League, Komsomol.

Chemistry Institute and Dimeric Molecule A1681

1968, Sept. 3 **Photo.** *Perf. 11½*

3507 A1681 4k vio bl, dp lil rose & black .50 .25

50th anniversary of Kurnakov Institute for General and Inorganic Chemistry.

Letter, Compass Rose, Ship and Plane A1682

Compass Rose and Stamps of 1921 and 1965 A1683

1968, Sept. 16 **Photo.** *Perf. 11½*

3508 A1682 4k dk car rose, brn & brt red .50 .25
3509 A1683 4k dk blue, blk & bister .50 .25

No. 3508 for Letter Writing Week, Oct. 7-13, and No. 3509 for Stamp Day and the Day of the Collector.

The 26 Baku Commissars, Sculpture by Merkurov — A1684

1968, Sept. 20

3510 A1684 4k multicolored .50 .25

50th anniversary of the shooting of the 26 Commissars, Baku, Sept. 20, 1918.

Toyvo Antikaynen (1898-1941), Finnish Workers' Organizer — A1685

1968, Sept. 30 *Perf. 12*

3511 A1685 6k gray & sepia .60 .25

Russian Merchant Marine Emblem A1686

1968, Sept. 30 *Perf. 12x11½*

3512 A1686 6k blue, red & indigo .50 .25

Russian Merchant Marine.

Order of the October Revolution — A1687

Typographed and Embossed

1968, Sept. 30 *Perf. 12x12½*

3513 A1687 4k gold & multi .50 .25

51st anniv. of the October Revolution. Printed with alternating label.

Pavel P. Postyshev — A1688

Designs: No. 3515, Stepan G. Shaumyan (1878-1918). No. 3516, Akmal Ikramov (1898-1938). No. 3516A, N. G. Markin (1893-1918). No. 3516B, P. E. Dybenko (1889-1938). No. 3516C, S. V. Kosior (1889-1939). No. 3516D, Vasili Kikvidze (1895-1919).

Size: 21½x32½mm

1968-70 **Engr.** *Perf. 12½x12*

3514 A1688 4k bluish black .65 .25
3515 A1688 4k bluish black .65 .25
3516 A1688 4k gray black .65 .25
3516A A1688 4k black .65 .25
3516B A1688 4k dark car ('69) .65 .25
3516C A1688 4k indigo ('69) .65 .25
3516D A1688 4k dk brown ('70) .65 .25
Nos. 3514-3516D (7) 4.55 1.75

Honoring outstanding workers for the Communist Party and the Soviet State.

Issued: #3514-3516, 9/30/68; #3516A, 12/31/68; #3516D, 9/24/70; others, 5/15/69.

See #3782.

American Bison and Zebra A1689

Designs: No. 3518, Purple gallinule and lotus. No. 3519, Great white egrets, vert. No. 3520, Ostrich and golden pheasant, vert. No. 3521, Eland and guanaco. No. 3522, European spoonbill and glossy ibis.

Perf. 12½x12, 12x12½

1968, Oct. 16 **Litho.**

3517 A1689 4k ocher, brn & blk .65 .30
3518 A1689 4k ocher & multi .65 .30
3519 A1689 6k olive & black .75 .30
3520 A1689 6k gray & multi .75 .30
3521 A1689 10k dp grn & multi 1.10 .40
3522 A1689 10k emerald & multi 1.10 .40
Nos. 3517-3522 (6) 5.00 2.00

Askania Nova and Astrakhan state reservations.

Ivan S. Turgenev (1818-83), Writer — A1690

1968, Oct. 10 **Engr.** *Perf. 12x12½*

3523 A1690 4k green 4.50 .50

Warrior, 1880 B.C. and Mt. Ararat — A1691

Design: 12k, David Sasountsi monument, Yerevan, and Mt. Ararat.

Engraved and Photogravure

1968, Oct. 18 *Perf. 11½*

3524	A1691	4k blk & dk blue, *gray*	.35	.25
3525	A1691	12k dk brn & choc, *bis*	.45	.25

Yerevan, capital of Armenia, 2,750th anniv.

First Radio Tube Generator and Laboratory A1692

1968, Oct. 26 **Photo.** *Perf. 11½*

3526	A1692	4k dk bl, dp bis & blk	.50	.25

50th anniversary of Russia's first radio laboratory at Gorki (Nizhni Novgorod).

Prospecting Geologist and Crystals A1693

6k, Prospecting for metals: seismographic test apparatus with shock wave diagram, plane, truck. 10k, Oil derrick in the desert.

1968, Oct. 31 **Litho.** *Perf. 11½*

3527	A1693	4k blue & multi	.50	.25
3528	A1693	6k multicolored	.30	.25
3529	A1693	10k multicolored	.70	.25
		Nos. 3527-3529 (3)	1.50	.75

Geology Day. Printed with alternating label.

Borovoe, Kazakhstan — A1694

Landscapes: No. 3531, Djety-Oguz, Kirghizia, vert. No. 3532, Issyk-kul Lake, Kirghizia. No. 3533, Borovoe, Kazakhstan, vert.

Perf. 12½x12, 12x12½

1968, Nov. 20 **Typo.**

3530	A1694	4k dk red brn & multi	.35	.25
3531	A1694	4k gray & multi	.35	.25
3532	A1694	6k dk red brn & multi	.35	.25
3533	A1694	6k black & multi	.35	.25
		Nos. 3530-3533 (4)	1.40	1.00

Recreational areas in the Kazakh and Kirghiz Republics.

Medals and Cup, Riccione, 1952, 1961 and 1965 — A1695

4k, Medals, Eiffel Tower and Arc de Triomphe, Paris, 1964. 6k, Porcelain plaque, gold medal and Brandenburg Gate, Debria, Berlin, 1950, 1959. 12k, Medal and prize-winning stamp #2888, Buenos Aires. 16k, Cups and medals, Rome, 1952, 1954. 20k, Medals, awards and views, Vienna, 1961, 1965. 30k, Trophies, Prague, 1950, 1955, 1962.

1968, Nov. 27 **Photo.** *Perf. 11½x12*

3534	A1695	4k dp cl, sil & blk	.25	.25
3535	A1695	6k dl bl, gold & blk	.25	.25
3536	A1695	10k lt ultra, gold & blk	.30	.35
3537	A1695	12k blue, sil & blk	.35	.25
3538	A1695	16k red, gold & blk	.55	.25
3539	A1695	20k brt blue, gold & blk	.60	.25
3540	A1695	30k org brn, gold & blk	.90	.30
		Nos. 3534-3540 (7)	3.20	1.90

Awards to Soviet post office at foreign stamp exhibitions.

Worker with Banner — A1696

1968, Nov. 29 *Perf. 12x12½*

3541	A1696	4k red & black	.50	.35

Estonian Workers' Commune, 50th anniv.

V. K. Lebedinsky and Radio Tower — A1697

1968, Nov. 29 *Perf. 11½x12*

3542	A1697	4k gray grn, blk & gray	.50	.25

V. K. Lebedinsky (1868-1937), scientist.

Souvenir Sheet

Communication via Satellite — A1698

1968, Nov. 29 **Litho.** *Perf. 12*

3543	A1698	Sheet of 3	3.00	.75
a.		16k Molniya I	.70	.25
b.		16k Map of Russia	.70	.25
c.		16k Ground Station "Orbite"	.70	.25

Television transmission throughout USSR with the aid of the earth satellite Molniya I.

Sprig, Spasski Tower, Ministry of Foreign Affairs and Library A1699

1968, Dec. 1 *Perf. 11½*

3544	A1699	4k ultra, sil, grn & red	.60	.30

New Year 1969.

Maj. Gen. Georgy Beregovoi A1700

1968, Dec. 14 **Photo.** *Perf. 11½*

3545	A1700	10k Prus blue, blk & red	.60	.25

Flight of Soyuz 3, Oct. 26-30.

Rail-laying and Casting Machines A1701

Soviet railroad transportation: 4k, Railroad map of the Soviet Union and Train.

1968, Dec. 14 *Perf. 12½x12*

3546	A1701	4k rose mag & org	.60	.25
3547	A1701	10k brown & emerald	.60	.25

Newspaper Banner and Monument A1702

1968, Dec. 23 *Perf. 11½*

3548	A1702	4k tan, red & dk brn	.50	.25

Byelorussian communist party, 50th anniv.

The Reapers, by A. Venetzianov A1703

Knight at the Crossroads, by Viktor M. Vasnetsov — A1704

Paintings: 2k, The Last Day of Pompeii, by Karl P. Bryullov. 4k, Capture of a Town in Winter, by Vasili I. Surikov. 6k, On the Lake, by I.I. Levitan. 10k, Alarm, 1919 (family), by K. Petrov-Vodkin. 16k, Defense of Sevastopol, 1942, by A. Deineka. 20k, Sculptor with a Bust of Homer, by G. Korzhev. 30k, Celebration on Uritsky Square, 1920, by G. Koustodiev. 50k, Duel between Peresvet and Chelubey, by Avilov.

Perf. 12x12½, 12½

1968, Dec. 25 **Litho.**

3549	A1703	1k multicolored	.25	.25
3550	A1704	2k multicolored	.25	.25
3551	A1704	3k multicolored	.25	.25
3552	A1704	4k multicolored	.25	.25
3553	A1704	6k multicolored	.40	.25
3554	A1703	10k multicolored	.70	.25
3555	A1704	16k multicolored	1.10	.25
3556	A1703	20k multicolored	1.25	.25
3557	A1704	30k multicolored	2.00	.40
3558	A1704	50k multicolored	3.50	.80
		Nos. 3549-3558 (10)	9.95	3.20

Russian State Museum, Leningrad.

House, Zaoneje, 1876 — A1705

Russian Architecture: 4k, Carved doors, Gorki Oblast, 1848. 6k, Church, Kizhi Pogost, 1714. 10k, Fortress wall, Rostov-Yaroslav, 16th-17th centuries. 12k, Gate, Tsaritsino, 1785. 16k, Architect Rossi Street, Leningrad.

1968, Dec. 27 **Engr.** *Perf. 12x12½*

3559	A1705	3k dp brown, *ocher*	.35	.25
3560	A1705	4k green, *yellow*	.35	.25
3561	A1705	6k vio, *gray violet*	.60	.25
3562	A1705	10k dl bl, *grnsh gray*	.95	.30
3563	A1705	12k car, *gray*	1.20	.40
3564	A1705	16k black, *yellowish*	1.50	.50
		Nos. 3559-3564 (6)	4.95	1.95

Banners of Young Communist League, October Revolution Medal — A1707

1968, Dec. 31 **Litho.** *Perf. 12*

3566	A1707	12k red, yel & black	.60	.30

Award of Order of October Revolution to the Young Communist League on its 50th anniversary.

Soldiers on Guard — A1708

1969, Jan. 1 *Perf. 12x12½*

3567	A1708	4k orange & claret	.40	.25

Latvian Soviet Republic, 50th anniv.

Revolutionaries and Monument — A1709

Designs: 4k, Partisans and sword. 6k, Workers and Lenin Medals.

1969, Jan. **Photo.** ***Perf. 11½***

3568 A1709 2k ocher & rose clar .25 .25
3569 A1709 4k ocher & red .25 .25
3570 A1709 6k dk ol, mag & red .25 .25
Nos. 3568-3570 (3) .75 .75

Byelorussian Soviet Republic, 50th anniv.

Souvenir Sheet

Vladimir Shatalov, Boris Volynov, Alexei S. Elisseyev, Evgeny Khrunov — A1710

1969, Jan. 22 ***Imperf.***

3571 A1710 50k dp bis & dk brn 2.00 .75

1st team flights of Soyuz 4 and 5, 1/16/69.

Leningrad University A1711

1969, Jan. 23 **Photo.** ***Perf. 12½x12***

3572 A1711 10k black & maroon .40 .25

University of Leningrad, 150th anniv.

Ivan A. Krylov (1769?-1844), Fable Writer — A1712

1969, Feb. 13 **Litho.** ***Perf. 12x12½***

3573 A1712 4k black & multi .50 .30

Nikolai Filchenkov A1713

Designs: No. 3575, Alexander Kosmodemiansky. No. 3575A, Otakar Yarosh, member of Czechoslovak Svoboda Battalion.

1969 **Photo.**

3574 A1713 4k dl rose & blk .25 .25
3575 A1713 4k emer & dk brn .25 .25
3575A A1713 4k blue & black .25 .25
Nos. 3574-3575A (3) .75 .75

Heroes of World War II. Issued: #3575A, May 9; others, Feb. 23.

"Shoulder to the Wheel," Parliament, Budapest A1714

Design: "Shoulder to the Wheel" is a sculpture by Zigmond Kisfaludi-Strobl.

1969, Mar. 21 **Typo.** ***Perf. 11½***

3576 A1714 6k black, ver & lt grn .50 .25

Hungarian Soviet Republic, 50th anniv.

Oil Refinery and Salavat Tualeyev Monument — A1715

1969, Mar. 22 **Litho.** ***Perf. 12***

3577 A1715 4k multicolored .40 .25

50th anniv. of the Bashkir Autonomous Socialist Republic.

Sergei P. Korolev, Sputnik 1, Space Monument, Moscow — A1716

Vostok on Launching Pad — A1717

Natl. Cosmonauts' Day: No. 3579, Zond 2 orbiting moon, and photograph of earth made by Zond 5. 80k, Spaceship Soyuz 3.

Perf. 12½x12, 12x12½

1969, Apr. 12 **Litho.**

3578 A1716 10k black, vio & grn .65 .25
3579 A1716 10k dk brn, yel & brn red .65 .25
3580 A1717 10k multicolored .65 .25
Nos. 3578-3580 (3) 1.95 .75

Souvenir Sheet

Perf. 12

3581 A1716 80k vio, green & red 2.00 .75

No. 3581 contains one 37x24mm stamp.

Lenin University, Kazan, and Kremlin A1718

Lenin House, Kuibyshev A1718a

Lenin House, Pskov A1718b

Lenin House, Shushensko — A1718c

Smolny Institute, Leningrad A1718d

Places Connected with Lenin: #3586, Straw Hut, Razliv. #3587, Lenin Museum, Gorki. #3589, Lenin's room, Kremlin. #3590, Lenin Museum, Ulyanovsk. #3591, Lenin House, Ulyanovsk.

1969 **Photo.** ***Perf. 11½***

3582 A1718 4k pale rose & multi .35 .25
3583 A1718a 4k beige & multi .35 .25
3584 A1718b 4k bis brn & multi .35 .25
3585 A1718c 4k gray vio & multi .35 .25
3586 A1718 4k violet & multi .35 .25
3587 A1718 4k blue & multi .35 .25
3588 A1718d 4k brick red & multi .35 .25
3589 A1718 4k rose red & multi .35 .25
3590 A1718 4k lt red brn & multi .35 .25
3591 A1718 4k dull grn & multi .35 .25
Nos. 3582-3591 (10) 3.50 2.50

99th anniv. of the birth of Lenin.

Telephone, Transistor Radio and Trademark — A1719

1969, Apr. 25 ***Perf. 12½x12***

3592 A1719 10k sepia & dp org .50 .25

50th anniversary of VEF Electrical Co.

ILO Emblem and Globe — A1720

1969, May 9 ***Perf. 11***

3593 A1720 6k car rose & gold .40 .25

50th anniversary of the ILO.

Suleiman Stalsky A1721

1969, May 15 **Photo.** ***Perf. 12½x12***

3595 A1721 4k tan & ol green .40 .25

Stalsky (1869-1937), Dagestan poet.

Yasnaya Polyana Rose A1722

4k, "Stroynaya" lily. 10k, Cattleya orchid. 12k, "Listopad" dahlia. 14k, "Ural Girl" gladioli.

1969, May 15 **Litho.** ***Perf. 11½***

3596 A1722 2k multicolored .25 .25
3597 A1722 4k multicolored .45 .25
3598 A1722 10k multicolored 1.10 .25
3599 A1722 12k multicolored 1.40 .25
3600 A1722 14k multicolored 1.50 .25
Nos. 3596-3600 (5) 4.70 1.25

Work of the Botanical Gardens of the Academy of Sciences.

Ukrainian Academy of Sciences A1723

1969, May 22 **Photo.** ***Perf. 12½x12***

3601 A1723 4k brown & yellow .50 .25

Ukrainian Academy of Sciences, 50th anniv.

Film, Camera and Medal A1724

Ballet Dancers A1725

1969, June 3 **Litho.** ***Perf. 12x12½***

3602 A1724 6k rose car, blk & gold .30 .25
3603 A1725 6k dk brown & multi .30 .25

Intl. Film Festival in Moscow, and 1st Intl. Young Ballet Artists' Competitions.

Congress Emblem and Cell Division — A1726

1969, June 10 **Photo.** ***Perf. 11½***

3605 A1726 6k dp clar, lt bl & yel .50 .30

Protozoologists, 3rd Intl. Cong., Leningrad.

Estonian Singer and Festival Emblem — A1727

1969, June 14 ***Perf. 12x12½***
3606 A1727 4k ver & bister .90 .25

Centenary of the Estonian Song Festival.

Mendeleev and Formula with Author's Corrections — A1728

30k, Dmitri Ivanovich Mendeleev, vert.

Engraved and Lithographed

1969, June 20 ***Perf. 12***
3607 A1728 6k brown & rose .90 .30

Souvenir Sheet

3608 A1728 30k carmine rose 5.00 1.25

Cent. of the Periodic Law (classification of elements), formulated by Dimitri I. Mendeleev (1834-1907). No. 3608 contains one engraved 29x37mm stamp.

Hand Holding Peace Banner and World Landmarks A1729

1969, June 20 **Photo.** ***Perf. 11½***
3609 A1729 10k bl, dk brn & gold .40 .25

20th anniversary of the Peace Movement.

Laser Beam Guiding Moon Rocket — A1730

1969, June 20
3610 A1730 4k silver, black & red .50 .25

Soviet scientific inventions, 50th anniv.

Ivan Kotlyarevski (1769-1838), Ukrainian Writer — A1731

Typographed and Photogravure

1969, June 25 ***Perf. 12½x12***
3611 A1731 4k blk, olive & lt brn .50 .25

No. 2717 Overprinted in Vermilion

1969, June 25 **Photo.** ***Perf. 11½***
3612 A1306 6k Prus blue & plum 4.00 1.50

Soviet victory in the Ice Hockey World Championships, Stockholm, 1969.

"Hill of Glory" Monument and Minsk Battle Map A1732

1969, July 3 **Litho.** ***Perf. 12x12½***
3613 A1732 4k red & olive .40 .25

25th anniv. of the liberation of Byelorussia from the Germans.

Eagle, Flag and Map of Poland A1733

No. 3615, Hands holding torch, flags of Bulgaria, USSR, Bulgarian coat of arms.

1969, July 10 **Photo.** ***Perf. 12***
3614 A1733 6k red & bister .60 .25

Litho.

3615 A1733 6k bis, red, grn & blk .60 .25

25th anniv. of the Polish Republic; liberation of Bulgaria from the Germans.

Monument to 68 Heroes — A1734

1969, July 15 **Photo.** ***Perf. 12***
3616 A1734 4k red & maroon .50 .30

25th anniversary of the liberation of Nikolayev from the Germans.

Old Samarkand A1735

Design: 6k, Intourist Hotel, Samarkand.

1969, July 15 **Typo.**
3617 A1735 4k multicolored .35 .25
3618 A1735 6k multicolored .35 .25

2500th anniversary of Samarkand.

Volleyball — A1736

Design: 6k, Kayak race.

Photogravure and Engraved

1969, July 20 ***Perf. 11½***
3619 A1736 4k dp org & red brn .35 .25
3620 A1736 6k multicolored .35 .25

Championships: European Junior Volleyball; European Rowing.

Munkascy & "Woman Churning Butter" — A1737

1969, July 20 **Photo.**
3621 A1737 6k dk brn, blk & org .40 .25

Mihaly von Munkascy (1844-1900), Hungarian painter.

Miners' Monument A1738

1969, July 30
3622 A1738 4k silver & magenta .40 .25

Centenary of the founding of the city of Donetsk, in the Donets coal basin.

Machine Gun Cart, by Mitrofan Grekov — A1739

1969, July 30 **Engr.** ***Perf. 12½x12***
3623 A1739 4k red brn & brn red 1.00 .25

First Mounted Army, 50th anniv.

Barge Pullers Along the Volga, by Repin — A1740

Ilya E. Repin (1844-1930), Self-portrait A1741

Repin Paintings: 6k, "Not Expected." 12k, Confession. 16k, Dnieper Cossacks.

Perf. 12½x12, 12x12½

1969, Aug. 5 **Litho.**
3624 A1740 4k multicolored .75 .25
3625 A1740 6k multicolored .75 .25
3626 A1741 10k bis, red brn & blk 1.00 .25
3627 A1740 12k multicolored 1.50 .25
3628 A1740 16k multicolored 2.00 .25
Nos. 3624-3628 (5) 6.00 1.25

Runner — A1742

Design: 10k, Athlete on rings.

1969, Aug. 9 ***Perf. 12x12½***
3629 A1742 4k red, green & blk .30 .25
3630 A1742 10k grn, lt bl & blk .30 .25

Souvenir Sheet

Imperf

3631 A1742 20k red, bister & blk 2.50 .60

9th Trade Union Spartakiad, Moscow.

Komarov — A1743

1969, Aug. 22 **Photo.** ***Perf. 12x11½***
3632 A1743 4k olive & brown .40 .25

V. L. Komarov (1869-1945), botanist.

Hovannes Tumanian, Armenian Landscape — A1744

1969, Sept. 1 **Typo.** ***Perf. 12½x12***
3633 A1744 10k blk & peacock blue 1.50 .25

Tumanian (1869-1923), Armenian poet.

Turkmenian Wine Horn, 2nd Century — A1745

Designs: 6k, Persian Simurg vessel (giant anthropomorphic bird), 13th century. 12k, Head of goddess Kannon, Korea, 8th century. 16k, Bodhisattva, Tibet, 7th century. 20k, Statue of Ebisu and fish (tai), Japan, 17th century.

1969, Sept. 3 Litho. *Perf. 12x12½*

3634	A1745	4k blue & multi	.25	.25
3635	A1745	6k lilac & multi	.25	.25
3636	A1745	12k red & multi	.40	.25
3637	A1745	16k blue vio & multi	.55	.25
3638	A1745	20k pale grn & multi	.70	.30
		Nos. 3634-3638 (5)	2.15	1.30

Treasures from the State Museum of Oriental Art.

Mahatma Gandhi (1869-1948) A1746

1969, Sept. 10 Engr.

3639	A1746	6k deep brown	.90	.35

Black Stork Feeding Young A1747

Belovezhskaya Forest reservation: 6k, Doe and fawn (red deer). 10k, Fighting bison. 12k, Lynx and cubs. 16k, Wild pig and piglets.

1969, Sept. 10 Photo. *Perf. 12*

Size: 75x23mm, 10k; 35x23mm, others

3640	A1747	4k blk, yel grn & red	.50	.25
3641	A1747	6k blue grn, dk brn & ocher	.75	.25
3642	A1747	10k dk brn, dull org & dp org	1.50	.25
3643	A1747	12k dk & yel green, brn & gray	1.50	.25
3644	A1747	16k gray, yel grn & dk brown	2.00	.25
		Nos. 3640-3644 (5)	6.25	1.25

Komitas A1748

1969, Sept. 18 Typo. *Perf. 12½x12*

3645	A1748	6k blk, gray & sal	.50	.30

Komitas (S. N. Sogomonian, 1869-1935), Armenian composer.

Lisa Chaikina A1749

A. Cheponis, J. Aleksonis and G. Borisa A1750

#3647, Major S. I. Gritsevets & fighter planes.

1969, Sept. 20 Photo. *Perf. 12½x12*

3646	A1749	4k olive & brt green	.35	.25
3647	A1749	4k gray & black	.35	.25

Perf. 11½

3648	A1750	4k hn brn, brn & buff	.35	.25
		Nos. 3646-3648 (3)	1.05	.75

Heroes of the Soviet Union.

Ivan Petrovich Pavlov (1849-1936), Physiologist A1751

1969, Sept. 26

3649	A1751	4k multicolored	.50	.25

East German Arms, TV Tower and Brandenburg Gate — A1752

1969, Oct. 7 Litho. *Perf. 12*

3650	A1752	6k red, black & yel	.60	.25

German Democratic Republic, 20th anniv.

Aleksei Vasilievich Koltsov (1809-42), Poet — A1753

1969, Oct. 14 Photo. *Perf. 12x12½*

3652	A1753	4k lt blue & brown	.50	.25

National Emblem A1754

1969, Oct. 14 *Perf. 12x11½*

3653	A1754	4k gold & red	.50	.30

25th anniversary of the liberation of the Ukraine from the Nazis.

Stars, Hammer and Sickle A1755

1969, Oct. 21 Typo. *Perf. 11½*

3654	A1755	4k vio blue, gold, yel & red	.50	.25

52nd anniversary of October Revolution.

Georgy Shonin and Valery Kubasov A1756

Designs: No. 3656, Anatoly Filipchenko, Vladislav Volkov and Viktor Gorbatko. No. 3657, Vladimir Shatalov and Alexey Elisyev.

1969, Oct. 22 Photo. *Perf. 12½x12*

3655	A1756	10k black & gold	.65	.25
3656	A1756	10k black & gold	.65	.25
3657	A1756	10k black & gold	.65	.25
a.		Strip of 3, #3655-3657	2.00	.60

Group flight of the space ships Soyuz 6, Soyuz 7 and Soyuz 8, Oct. 11-13.

Lenin as a Youth A1757

1969, Oct. 25 Engr. *Perf. 11½*

3658	A1757	4k dark red, *pink*	.50	.25

1st Soviet Youth Philatelic Exhibition, Kiev, dedicated to Lenin's 100th birthday.

Emblem of Communications Unit of Army — A1758

1969, Oct. 30 Photo.

3659	A1758	4k dk red, red & bister	.50	.25

50th anniversary of the Communications Troops of Soviet Army.

Souvenir Sheet

Lenin and Quotation — A1759

Lithographed and Embossed

1969, Nov. 6 *Imperf.*

3660	A1759	50k red, gold & pink	3.00	.75

52nd anniv. of the October Revolution.

Cover of "Rules of the Kolkhoz" and Farm Woman's Monument — A1760

1969, Nov. 18 Photo. *Perf. 12½x12*

3661	A1760	4k brown & gold	.50	.25

3rd All Union Collective Farmers' Congress, Moscow, Nov.-Dec.

Vasilissa, the Beauty, by Ivan Y. Bilibin A1761

Designs (Book Illustrations by Ivan Y. Bilibin): 10k, Marya Morevna. 16k, Finist, the Fine Fellow, horiz. 20k, Tale of the Golden Cockerel. 50k, The Tale of Tsar Sultan. The inscriptions on the 16k and 20k are transposed. 4k, 10k, 16k are fairy tales; 20k and 50k are tales by Pushkin.

1969, Nov. 20 Litho. *Perf. 12*

3662	A1761	4k gray & multi	.25	.25
3663	A1761	10k gray & multi	.60	.50
3664	A1761	16k gray & multi	.75	.75
3665	A1761	20k gray & multi	.85	.85
3666	A1761	50k gray & multi	3.00	1.40
a.		Strip of 5, #3662-3666	6.50	5.50

Illustrator and artist Ivan Y. Bilibin.

USSR Emblems Dropped on Venus, Radar Installation and Orbits A1762

6k, Interplanetary station, space capsule, orbits.

1969, Nov. 25 Photo. *Perf. 12x11½*

3667	A1762	4k bis, blk & red	.35	.25
3668	A1762	6k gray, lil rose & blk	.35	.25

Completion of the fights of the space stations Venera 5 and Venera 6.

Flags of USSR and Afghanistan — A1763

1969, Nov. 30 Photo. *Perf. 11½*

3669	A1763	6k red, blk & grn	.50	.25

50th anniversary of diplomatic relations between Russia and Afghanistan.

Russian State Emblem and Star — A1764

Coil Stamp

1969, Nov. 13 *Perf. 11x11½*

3670	A1764	4k red	2.00	.30

MiG Jet and First MiG Fighter Plane — A1765

1969, Dec. 12 *Perf. 11½x12*

3671 A1765 6k red, black & gray .60 .25

Soviet aircraft builders.

Lenin and Flag A1766

Typographed and Lithographed

1969, Dec. 25 *Perf. 11½*

3672 A1766 4k gold, blue, red & blk .40 .25

Happy New Year 1970, birth cent. of Lenin.

Antonov 2 — A1767

Aircraft: 3k, PO-2. 4k, ANT-9. 6k, TsAGI 1-EA. 10k, ANT-20 "Maxim Gorki." 12k, Tupolev-104. 16k, Mi-10 helicopter. 20k, Ilyushin-62. 50k, Tupolev-144.

Photogravure and Engraved

1969 *Perf. 11½x12*

3673 A1767 2k bister & multi .25 .25
3674 A1767 3k multicolored .25 .25
3675 A1767 4k multicolored .25 .25
3676 A1767 6k multicolored .30 .25
3677 A1767 10k lt vio & multi .50 .25
3678 A1767 12k multicolored .70 .25
3679 A1767 16k multicolored .85 .25
3680 A1767 20k multicolored .90 .25
Nos. 3673-3680 (8) 4.00 2.00

Souvenir Sheet
Imperf

3681 A1767 50k blue & multi 3.00 1.00

History of national aeronautics and aviation. No. 3681 margin contains signs of the zodiac, partly overlapping the stamp.

Issued: #3679, 3681, 12/31; others 12/25.

Photograph of Earth by Zond 7 — A1768

Designs: No. 3683a, same as 10k. No. 3683b, Photograph of moon.

1969, Dec. 26 **Photo.** *Perf. 12x11½*

3682 A1768 10k black & multi .40 .30

Souvenir Sheet

Litho. *Imperf.*

3683 Sheet of 2 4.00 1.50
a. A1768 50k indigo & multi 1.65 .90
b. A1768 50k dark brown & multi 1.65 .90

Space explorations of the automatic stations Zond 6, Nov. 10-17, 1968, and Zond 7, Aug. 8-14, 1969. No. 3683 contains 27x40mm stamps with simulated perforations.

Model Aircraft — A1769

Technical Sports: 4k, Motorboats. 6k, Parachute jumping.

1969, Dec. 26 **Engr.** *Perf. 12½x12*

3684 A1769 3k bright magenta .45 .25
3685 A1769 4k dull blue green .45 .25
3686 A1769 6k red orange .45 .25
Nos. 3684-3686 (3) 1.35 .75

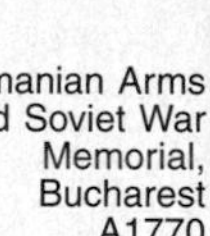

Romanian Arms and Soviet War Memorial, Bucharest A1770

1969, Dec. 31 **Photo.** *Perf. 11½*

3687 A1770 6k rose red & brown .60 .35

25th anniversary of Romania's liberation from fascist rule.

Ostankino Television Tower, Moscow A1771

1969, Dec. 31 **Typo.** *Perf. 12*

3688 A1771 10k multicolored 1.00 .35

Conversation with Lenin, by A. Shirokov (in front of red table) — A1772

Paintings: No. 3689, Lenin, by N. Andreyev. No. 3690, Lenin at Marxist Meeting, St. Petersburg, by A. Moravov (behind table). No. 3691, Lenin at Second Party Congress, by Y. Vinogradov (next to table). No. 3692, First Day of Soviet Power, by N. Babasyuk (leading crowd). No. 3694, Farmers' Delegation Meeting Lenin, by F. Modorov (seated at desk). No. 3695, With Lenin, by V. A. Serov (with cap, in background). No. 3696, Lenin on May 1, 1920, by I. Brodsky (with cap, in foreground). No. 3697, Builder of Communism, by a group of painters (in red). No. 3698, Mastery of Space, by A. Deyneka (rockets).

1970, Jan. 1 **Litho.** *Perf. 12*

3689 A1772 4k multicolored .35 .25
3690 A1772 4k multicolored .35 .25
3691 A1772 4k multicolored .35 .25
3692 A1772 4k multicolored .35 .25
3693 A1772 4k multicolored .35 .25
3694 A1772 4k multicolored .35 .25
3695 A1772 4k multicolored .35 .25
3696 A1772 4k multicolored .35 .25
3697 A1772 4k multicolored .35 .25
3698 A1772 4k multicolored .35 .25
Nos. 3689-3698 (10) 3.50 2.50

Centenary of birth of Lenin (1870-1924).

Map of Antarctic, "Mirny" and "Vostok" A1773

Design: 16k, Camp and map of the Antarctic with Soviet Antarctic bases.

1970, Jan. 27 **Photo.** *Perf. 11½*

3699 A1773 4k multicolored .30 .25
3700 A1773 16k multicolored 1.50 .25

150th anniversary of the Bellingshausen-Lazarev Antarctic expedition.

F. W. Sychkov and "Tobogganing" — A1774

1970, Jan. 27 *Perf. 12½x12*

3701 A1774 4k sepia & vio blue .50 .25

F. W. Sychkov (1870-1958), painter.

Col. V. B. Borsoyev A1775

Design: No. 3703, Sgt. V. Peshekhonov.

1970, Feb. 10 *Perf. 12x12½*

3702 A1775 4k brown olive & brn .30 .25
3703 A1775 4k dark gray & plum .30 .25

Heroes of the Soviet Union.

Geographical Society Emblem and Globes — A1776

1970, Feb. 26 **Photo.** *Perf. 11½*

3704 A1776 6k bis, Prus bl & dk brn .50 .30

Russian Geographical Society, 125th anniv.

Torch of Peace — A1777

1970, Mar. 3 **Litho.** *Perf. 12*

3705 A1777 6k blue green & tan .50 .25

Intl. Women's Solidarity Day, Mar. 8.

Symbols of Russian Arts and Crafts — A1778

Lenin — A1779

Designs: 6k, Russian EXPO '70 pavilion. 10k, Boy holding model ship.

1970, Mar. 10 **Photo.** *Perf. 11½*

3706 A1778 4k dk blue grn, red & black .25 .25
3707 A1778 6k blk, silver & red .25 .25
3708 A1778 10k vio bl, sil & red .25 .25
Nos. 3706-3708 (3) .75 .75

Souvenir Sheet
Engr. & Litho.
Perf. 12x12½

3709 A1779 50k dark red 2.00 1.00

EXPO '70 Intl. Exhibition, Osaka, Japan, 3/15-4/13.

Lenin — A1780

1970, Mar. 14 **Photo.** *Perf. 11½*

3710 A1780 4k red, blk & gold .50 .30

Souvenir Sheet
Photogravure and Embossed
Imperf

3711 A1780 20k red, blk & gold 5.00 2.00

USSR Philatelic Exhibition dedicated to the centenary of the birth of Lenin.

Friendship Tree, Sochi — A1781

1970, Mar. 18 Litho. *Perf. 11½*

3712 A1781 10k multicolored .50 .30

Friendship among people. Printed with alternating label.

National Emblem, Hammer and Sickle, Oil Derricks A1782

1970, Mar. 18 Photo. *Perf. 11½*

3713 A1782 4k dk car rose & gold .75 .25

Azerbaijan Republic, 50th anniversary.

Ice Hockey Players A1783

1970, Mar. 18

3714 A1783 6k blue & slate green .35 .25

World Ice Hockey Championships, Sweden.

Overprinted in Red

1970, Apr. 1 Photo. *Perf. 11½*

3715 A1783 6k blue & slate green 1.00 .25

Soviet hockey players as the tenfold world champions.

D. N. Medvedev A1784

Portrait: No. 3717, K. P. Orlovsky.

1970, Mar. 26 Engr. *Perf. 12x12½*

3716 A1784 4k chocolate .30 .25
3717 A1784 4k dk redsh brown .30 .25

Heroes of the Soviet Union.

Worker, Books, Globes and UNESCO Symbol A1785

1970, Mar. 26 Photo. *Perf. 12½x12*

3718 A1785 6k car lake & ocher .50 .25

UNESCO-sponsored Lenin Symposium, Tampere, Finland, Apr. 6-10.

Hungarian Arms, Budapest Landmarks A1786

1970, Apr. 4 Typo. *Perf. 11½*

3719 A1786 6k multicolored .50 .25

Liberation of Hungary, 25th anniv. See No. 3738.

Cosmonauts' Emblem A1787

1970, Apr. 12 Litho. *Perf. 11½*

3720 A1787 6k buff & multi .50 .25

Cosmonauts' Day.

Lenin, 1891 — A1788

Designs: Various portraits of Lenin.

Lithographed and Typographed

1970, Apr. 15 *Perf. 12x12½*

3721 A1788 2k green & gold .25 .25
3722 A1788 2k ol gray & gold .25 .25
3723 A1788 4k vio blue & gold .25 .25
3724 A1788 4k lake & gold .25 .25
3725 A1788 6k red brn & gold .25 .25
3726 A1788 6k lake & gold .25 .25
3727 A1788 10k dk brn & gold .25 .25
3728 A1788 10k dk rose brn & gold .35 .25
3729 A1788 12k blk, sil & gold .45 .25

Photo.

3730 A1788 12k red & gold .45 .25
Nos. 3721-3730 (10) 3.00 2.50

Souvenir Sheet

1970, Apr. 22 Litho. & Typo.

3731 A1788 20k blk, silver & gold 2.00 .70

Cent. of the birth of Lenin. Issued in sheets of 8 stamps surrounded by 16 labels showing Lenin-connected buildings, books, coats of arms and medals. No. 3731 contains one stamp in same design as No. 3729.

Order of Victory — A1789

Designs: 2k, Monument to the Unknown Soldier, Moscow. 3k, Victory Monument, Berlin-Treptow. 4k, Order of the Great Patriotic War. 10k, Gold Star of the Order of Hero of the Soviet Union and Medal of Socialist Labor. 30k, Like 1k.

1970, May 8 Photo. *Perf. 11½*

3732 A1789 1k red lil, gold & gray .25 .25
3733 A1789 2k dark brn, gold & red .25 .25
3734 A1789 3k dark brn, gold & red .40 .25
3735 A1789 4k dark brn, gold & red .70 .25
3736 A1789 10k red lil, gold & red 1.40 .25
Nos. 3732-3736 (5) 3.00 1.25

Souvenir Sheet

Imperf

3737 A1789 30k dk red, gold & gray 2.00 .60

25th anniv. of victory in WWII. No. 3737 has simulated perforations.

Arms-Landmark Type of 1970

Czechoslovakia arms and view of Prague.

1970, May 8 Typo. *Perf. 12½*

3738 A1786 6k dk brown & multi .50 .25

25th anniversary of the liberation of Czechoslovakia from the Germans.

Young Fighters, and Youth Federation Emblem A1791

1970, May 20 Litho. *Perf. 12*

3739 A1791 6k blue & black .50 .25

25th anniversary of the World Federation of Democratic Youth.

Lenin A1792

1970, May 20 Photo. *Perf. 11½*

3740 A1792 6k red .50 .25

Intl. Youth Meeting dedicated to the cent. of the birth of Lenin, UN, NY, June 1970.

Komsomol Emblem with Lenin — A1793

1970, May 20 Litho. *Perf. 12*

3741 A1793 4k red, yel & purple .50 .25

16th Congress of the Young Communist League, May 26-30.

Hammer and Sickle Emblem and Building of Supreme Soviet in Kazan A1794

No. 3744

No. 3744B

No. 3744C

Designs (Hammer-Sickle Emblem and Supreme Soviet Building in): No. 3743, Petrozavodsk. No. 3744, Cheboksary. No. 3744A, Elista. No. 3744B, Izhevsk. No. 3744C, Yoshkar-Ola.

1970 Engr. *Perf. 12x12½*

3742 A1794 4k violet blue .50 .25
3743 A1794 4k green .50 .25
3744 A1794 4k dark carmine .50 .25
3744A A1794 4k red .50 .25
3744B A1794 4k dark green .50 .25
3744C A1794 4k dark carmine .50 .25
Nos. 3742-3744C (6) 3.00 1.50

50th annivs. of the Tatar (#3742), Karelian (#3743), Chuvash (#3744), Kalmyk (#3744A), Udmurt (#3744B) and Mari (#3744C) autonomous SSRs.

Issued: #3742, 5/27; #3743, 6/5; #3744, 6/24; #3744A-3744B, 10/22; #3744C, 11/4.

See Nos. 3814-3823, 4286, 4806.

9th World Soccer Championships for the Jules Rimet Cup, Mexico City, May 29-June 21 — A1795

10k, Woman athlete on balancing bar.

1970, May 31 Photo. *Perf. 11½*

3745 A1795 10k lt gray & brt rose .40 .25
3746 A1795 16k dk grn & org brn .65 .25

17th World Gymnastics Championships, Ljubljana, Oct. 22-27 (#3745).

Sword into Plowshare Statue, UN, NY — A1796

1970, June 1 Litho. *Perf. 12x12½*

3747 A1796 12k gray & lake .50 .25

25th anniversary of the United Nations.

Soyuz 9, Andrian Nikolayev, Vitaly Sevastyanov A1797

1970, June 7 Photo. *Perf. 12x11½*

3748 A1797 10k multicolored .50 .25

424 hour space flight of Soyuz 9, June 1-19.

Friedrich Engels A1798

1970, June 16 Engr. *Perf. 12x12½*

3749 A1798 4k chocolate & ver .50 .25

Friedrich Engels (1820-1895), German socialist, collaborator with Karl Marx.

Armenian Woman and Symbols of Agriculture and Industry
A1799

Design: No. 3751, Kazakh woman and symbols of agriculture and industry.

1970, June 16 Photo. *Perf. 11½*

3750 A1799 4k red brn & silver .30 .30
3751 A1799 4k brt rose lilac & gold .30 .30

50th anniv. of the Armenian & Kazakh Soviet Socialist Republics.

Missile Cruiser "Grozny" — A1800

Soviet Warships: 3k, Cruiser "Aurora." 10k, Cruiser "October Revolution." 12k, Missile cruiser "Varyag." 20k, Atomic submarine "Leninsky Komsomol."

1970, July 26 Photo. *Perf. 11½x12*

3752 A1800 3k lilac, pink & blk .25 .25
3753 A1800 4k yellow & black .25 .25
3754 A1800 10k rose & black .45 .25
3755 A1800 12k buff & dk brown .45 .25
3756 A1800 20k blue grn, dk brn & vio blue .90 .25
Nos. 3752-3756 (5) 2.30 1.25

Navy Day.

Soviet and Polish Workers and Flags — A1801

1970, July 26 *Perf. 12*

3757 A1801 6k red & slate .40 .25

25th anniversary of the Treaty of Friendship, Collaboration and Mutual Assistance between USSR and Poland.

"History," Petroglyphs, Sputnik and Emblem — A1802

1970, Aug. 16 *Perf. 11½*

3758 A1802 4k red brn, buff & blue .50 .25

13th International Congress of Historical Sciences in Moscow.

Mandarin Ducks
A1803

Animals from the Sikhote-Alin Reserve: 6k, Pine marten. 10k, Asiatic black bear, vert. 16k, Red deer. 20k, Ussurian tiger.

Perf. 12½x12, 12x12½

1970, Aug. 19 Litho.

3759 A1803 4k multicolored .55 .25
3760 A1803 6k multicolored .65 .25
3761 A1803 10k multicolored .80 .30
3762 A1803 16k ultra & multi 1.25 .45
3763 A1803 20k gray & multi 1.75 .60
Nos. 3759-3763 (5) 5.00 1.85

Magnifying Glass over Stamp, and Covers — A1804

1970, Aug. 31 Photo. *Perf. 12x12½*

3764 A1804 4k red & silver .50 .25

2nd All-Union Philatelists' Cong., Moscow.

Pioneers' Badge — A1805

Soviet general education: 2k, Lenin and Children, monument. 4k, Star and scenes from play "Zarnitsa."

1970, Sept. 24 Photo. *Perf. 11½*

3765 A1805 1k gray, red & gold .25 .25
3766 A1805 2k brn red & slate grn .25 .25
3767 A1805 4k lt ol, car & gold .25 .25
Nos. 3765-3767 (3) .75 .75

Yerevan University
A1806

1970, Sept. 24 Photo. *Perf. 12½x12*

3768 A1806 4k ultra & salmon pink .50 .25

Yerevan State University, 50th anniv.

Library Bookplate, Vilnius University
A1807

1970, Oct. Typo. *Perf. 12x12½*

3772 A1807 4k silver, gray & blk .50 .25

Vilnius University Library, 400th anniv.

Woman Holding Flowers — A1808

1970, Oct. 30 Photo.

3773 A1808 6k blue & lt brown .50 .25

25th anniversary of the International Democratic Federation of Women.

Farm Woman, Cattle Farm — A1809

Designs: No. 3775, Farmer and mechanical farm equipment. No. 3776, Farmer, fertilization equipment and plane.

1970, Oct. 30 *Perf. 11½x12*

3774 A1809 4k olive, yellow & red .25 .25
3775 A1809 4k ocher, yellow & red .25 .25
3776 A1809 4k lt vio, yellow & red .25 .25
Nos. 3774-3776 (3) .75 .75

Aims of the new agricultural 5-year plan.

Lenin — A1810

Lithographed and Embossed

1970, Nov. 3 *Perf. 12½x12*

3777 A1810 4k red & gold .50 .25

Souvenir Sheet

3778 A1810 30k red & gold 2.00 .75

53rd anniv. of the October Revolution.

No. 3389 Overprinted in Gold

1970, Nov. 3 *Perf. 11½*

3779 A1641 4k gold & multi 1.00 .50

50th anniversary of the GOELRO Plan for the electrification of Russia.

Spasski Tower and Fir Branch — A1811

1970, Nov. 23 Litho. *Perf. 12x12½*

3780 A1811 6k multicolored .50 .25

New Year, 1971.

A. A. Baykov — A1812

1970, Nov. 25 Photo. *Perf. 12½x12*

3781 A1812 4k sepia & golden brn .50 .25

Baykov (1870-1946), metallurgist and academician.

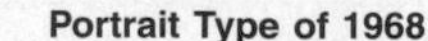

Portrait Type of 1968

Portrait: No. 3782, A. D. Tsyurupa.

1970, Nov. 25 Photo. *Perf. 12x12½*

3782 A1688 4k brown & salmon .50 .25

Tsyurupa (1870-1928), First Vice Chairman of the Soviet of People's Commissars.

Vasily Blazhenny Church, Red Square
A1813

Tourist publicity: 6k, Performance of Swan Lake. 10k, Two deer. 12k, Folk art. 14k, Sword into Plowshare statue, by E. Vouchetich, and museums. 16k, Automobiles and woman photographer.

Photogravure and Engraved

1970, Nov. 29 *Perf. 12x11½*

Frame in Brown Orange

3783 A1813 4k multicolored .25 .25
3784 A1813 6k multicolored .25 .25
3785 A1813 10k brn org & sl green .35 .25
3786 A1813 12k multicolored .45 .25
3787 A1813 14k multicolored .50 .25
3788 A1813 16k multicolored .65 .25
Nos. 3783-3788 (6) 2.45 1.50

Daisy — A1814

1970, Nov. 29 Litho. *Perf. 11½*

3789 A1814 4k shown .25 .25
3790 A1814 6k Dahlia .25 .25
3791 A1814 10k Phlox .40 .25
3792 A1814 12k Aster .50 .25
3793 A1814 16k Clementis .85 .25
Nos. 3789-3793 (5) 2.25 1.25

UN Emblem, African Mother and Child, Broken Chain — A1815

1970, Dec. 10 Photo. *Perf. 12x12½*

3794 A1815 10k blue & dk brown .50 .25

United Nations Declaration on Colonial Independence, 10th anniversary.

Ludwig van Beethoven (1770-1827), Composer — A1816

1970, Dec. 16 Engr. *Perf. 12½x12*

3795 A1816 10k deep claret, *pink* .50 .30

Skating — A1817

Design: 10k, Skiing.

1970, Dec. 18 Photo. *Perf. 11½*

3796 A1817 4k lt gray, ultra & dk red .35 .25
3797 A1817 10k lt gray, brt grn & brn .65 .25

1971 Trade Union Winter Games.

Luna 16 — A1818

Designs: No. 3799, 3801b, Luna 16 leaving moon. No. 3800, 3801c, Capsule landing on earth. No. 3801a, like No. 3798.

1970, Dec. Photo. *Perf. 11½*

3798 A1818 10k gray blue .40 .25
3799 A1818 10k dk purple .40 .25
3800 A1818 10k gray blue .40 .25
Nos. 3798-3800 (3) 1.20 .75

Souvenir Sheet

3801 Sheet of 3 4.00 1.00
a. A1818 20k blue 1.00 .25
b. A1818 20k dark purple 1.00 .25
c. A1818 20k blue 1.00 .25

Luna 16 unmanned, automatic moon mission, Sept. 12-24, 1970.

Nos. 3801a-3801c have attached labels (no perf. between vignette and label). Issue dates: No. 3801. Dec. 18; Nos. 3798-3800, Dec. 28.

The Conestabile Madonna, by Raphael A1819

Paintings: 4k, Apostles Peter and Paul, by El Greco. 10k, Perseus and Andromeda, by Rubens, horiz. 12k, The Prodigal Son, by Rembrandt. 16k, Family Portrait, by van Dyck. 20k, The Actress Jeanne Samary, by Renoir. 30k, Woman with Fruit, by Gauguin. 50k, The Little Madonna, by da Vinci. All paintings from the Hermitage in Leningrad, except 20k from Pushkin Museum, Moscow.

Perf. 12x12½, 12½x12

1970, Dec. 23 Litho.

3802 A1819 3k gray & multi .25 .25
3803 A1819 4k gray & multi .25 .25
3804 A1819 10k gray & multi .60 .25
3805 A1819 12k gray & multi .60 .25
3806 A1819 16k gray & multi .70 .25
3807 A1819 20k gray & multi .85 .25
3808 A1819 30k gray & multi 1.75 .25
Nos. 3802-3808 (7) 5.00 1.75

Souvenir Sheet

Imperf

3809 A1819 50k gold & multi 3.00 .90

Harry Pollitt and Shipyard A1820

1970, Dec. 31 Photo. *Perf. 12*

3810 A1820 10k maroon & brown .40 .30

Pollitt (1890-1960), British labor leader.

International Cooperative Alliance A1821

1970, Dec. 31 *Perf. 11½x12*

3811 A1821 12k yel green & red .50 .30

Intl. Cooperative Alliance, 75th anniv.

Lenin — A1822

1971, Jan. 1 *Perf. 12*

3812 A1822 4k red & gold .50 .25

Year of the 24th Congress of the Communist Party of the Soviet Union.

Georgian Republic Flag A1823

1971, Jan. 12 Litho. *Perf. 11½*

3813 A1823 4k ol bister & multi .50 .25

Georgian SSR, 50th anniversary.

Republic Anniversaries Type of 1970

No. 3816

No. 3818

Designs (Hammer-Sickle Emblem and): No. 3814, Supreme Soviet Building, Makhachkala. No. 3815, Fruit, ship, mountain, conveyor. No. 3816, Grapes, refinery, ship. No. 3817, Supreme Soviet Building, Nalchik. No. 3818, Supreme Soviet Building, Syktyvkar, and lumber industry. No. 3819, Natural resources, dam, mining. No. 3820, Industrial installations and natural products. No. 3821, Ship, "industry." No. 3822, Grapes, pylons and mountains. No. 3823, Kazbek Mountain, industrial installations, produce.

Engraved; Litho. (#3815, 3823)

1971-74 *Perf. 12x12½*

3814 A1794 4k dk blue green .30 .25
3815 A1794 4k rose red .30 .25
3816 A1794 4k red .30 .25
3817 A1794 4k blue .30 .25
3818 A1794 4k green .30 .25
3819 A1794 4k brt bl ('72) .30 .25
3820 A1794 4k car rose ('72) .30 .25
3821 A1794 4k brt ultra ('73) .30 .25
3822 A1794 4k golden brn ('74) .30 .25
3823 A1794 4k dark red ('74) .30 .25
Nos. 3814-3823 (10) 3.00 2.50

50th annivers. of Dagestan (No. 3814), Abkazian (No. 3815), Adzhar (No. 3816), Kabardino-Balkarian (No. 3817), Komi (No. 3818), Yakut (No. 3819), Checheno-Ingush (No. 3820), Buryat (No. 3821), Nakhichevan (No. 3822), and North Ossetian (No. 3823) autonomous SSRs.

No. 3823 also for bicentenary of Ossetia's union with Russia.

Issued: No. 3814, 1/20; No. 3815, 3/3; No. 3816, 6/16; Nos. 3817-3818, 8/17; No. 3819, 4/20; No. 3820, 11/22; No. 3821, 5/24; No. 3822, 2/6; No. 3823, 7/7.

Tower of Genoa, Cranes, Hammer and Sickle A1824

1971, Jan. 28 Typo. *Perf. 12*

3824 A1824 10k dk red, gray & yel .50 .25

Founding of Feodosiya, Crimea, 2500th anniv.

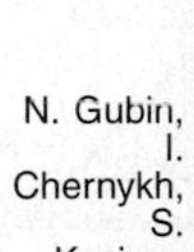

Palace of Culture, Kiev — A1825

1971, Feb. 16 Photo. *Perf. 11½*

3825 A1825 4k red, bister & blue .50 .25

Ukrainian Communist Party, 24th cong.

N. Gubin, I. Chernykh, S. Kosinov A1826

1971, Feb. 16 *Perf. 12½x12*

3826 A1826 4k slate grn & vio brn .50 .25

Heroes of the Soviet Union.

"Industry and Agriculture" A1827

1971, Feb. 16 *Perf. 12x12½*

3827 A1827 6k olive bister & red .50 .25

State Planning Organization, 50th anniv.

Lesya Ukrayinka (1871-1913), Ukrainian Poet — A1828

1971, Feb. 25

3828 A1828 4k orange red & bister .50 .25

"Summer" Dance — A1829

Dancers of Russian Folk Dance Ensemble: No. 3830, "On the Skating Rink." No. 3831, Ukrainian dance "Hopak." No. 3832, Adzharian dance. No. 3833, Gypsy dance.

1971, Feb. 25 Litho. *Perf. 12½x12*

3829 A1829 10k bister & multi .40 .25
3830 A1829 10k olive & multi .40 .25
3831 A1829 10k olive bis & multi .40 .25
3832 A1829 10k gray & multi .40 .25
3833 A1829 10k grnsh gray & multi .40 .25
Nos. 3829-3833 (5) 2.00 1.25

Luna 17 on Moon A1830

Designs: No. 3835, Ground control. No. 3836, Separation of Lunokhod 1 and carrier. 16k, Lunokhod 1 in operation.

1971, Mar. 16 Photo. *Perf. 11½*

3834 A1830 10k dp vio & sepia .35 .25
3835 A1830 12k dk blue & sepia .50 .25
3836 A1830 12k dk blue & sepia .50 .25
3837 A1830 16k dp vio & sepia .65 .25
a. Souv. sheet of 4 2.50 1.00
Nos. 3834-3837 (4) 2.00 1.00

Luna 17 unmanned, automated moon mission, Nov. 10-17, 1970.

No. 3837a contains Nos. 3834-3837, size 32x21mm each.

Paris Commune, Cent. — A1831

1971, Mar. 18 Litho. *Perf. 12*

3838 A1831 6k red & black .50 .25

Industry, Science, Culture A1832

1971, Mar. 29 *Perf. 11½*

3839 A1832 6k bister, brn & red .50 .25

24th Communist Party Cong., 3/30-4/3.

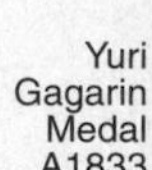

Yuri Gagarin Medal A1833

1971, Mar. 30 Photo. *Perf. 11½*
3840 A1833 10k brown & lemon .50 .25

10th anniv. of man's first flight into space.

Space Research A1834

1971, Mar. 30
3841 A1834 12k slate bl & vio brn .50 .25

Cosmonauts' Day, Apr. 12.

E. Birznieks-Upitis (1871-1960), Latvian Writer — A1835

1971, Apr. 1 *Perf. 12x12½*
3842 A1835 4k red brown & gray .30 .25

Bee and Blossom — A1836

1971, Apr. 1 *Perf. 11½*
3843 A1836 6k olive & multi .90 .25

23rd International Beekeeping Congress, Moscow, Aug. 22-Sept. 2.

Souvenir Sheet

Cosmonauts and Spacecraft — A1837

Designs: 10k, Vostok. No. 3844b, Yuri Gagarin. No. 3844c, First man walking in space. 16k, First orbital station.

1971, Apr. 12 Litho. *Perf. 12*
3844 A1837 Sheet of 4 3.00 1.00
a. 10k violet brown .45 .25
b.-c. 12k Prussian green .45 .25
d. 16k violet brown .50 .25

10th anniv. of man's 1st flight into space. Size of stamps: 26x19mm.

Lenin Memorial, Ulyanovsk — A1838

1971, Apr. 16 Photo. *Perf. 12*
3845 A1838 4k cop red & ol bister .50 .25

Lenin's birthday. Memorial was built for centenary celebration of his birth.

Lt. Col. Nikolai I. Vlasov — A1839

1971, May 9 Photo. *Perf. 12x12½*
3846 A1839 4k gray olive & brn .50 .25

Hero of the Soviet Union.

Khafiz Shirazi, Tadzhik-Persian Poet, 650th Birth Anniv. — A1840

1971, May 9 Litho.
3847 A1840 4k olive, brn & black .50 .25

GAZ-66 — A1841

Soviet Cars: 3k, BelAZ-540 truck. No. 3850, Moskvich-412. No. 3851, ZAZ-968. 10k, Volga.

1971, May 12 Photo. *Perf. 11x11½*
3848 A1841 2k yellow & multi .25 .25
3849 A1841 3k lt blue & multi .25 .25
3850 A1841 4k lt lilac & multi .25 .25
3851 A1841 4k lt gray & multi .25 .25
3852 A1841 10k lt lilac & multi .25 .25
Nos. 3848-3852 (5) 1.25 1.25

Bogomolets A1842

1971, May 24 Photo. *Perf. 12*
3853 A1842 4k orange & black .50 .25

A. A. Bogomolets, physician, 90th birth anniv.

Satellite — A1843

1971, June 9 *Perf. 11½*
3854 A1843 6k blue & multi .50 .25

15th General Assembly of the International Union of Geodesics and Geophysics.

Symbols of Science and History A1844

1971, June 9 *Perf. 12*
3855 A1844 6k green & gray .50 .25

13th Congress of Science History.

Oil Derrick & Symbols A1845

1971, June 9 *Perf. 11½*
3856 A1845 6k multicolored .50 .25

8th World Oil Congress.

Sukhe Bator Monument — A1846

1971, June 16 Typo. *Perf. 12*
3857 A1846 6k red, gold & black .50 .25

50th anniversary of Mongolian revolution.

Monument of Defenders of Liepaja A1847

1971, June 21 Photo.
3858 A1847 4k gray, black & brn .50 .25

30th anniversary of the defense of Liepaja (Libau) against invading Germans.

Map of Antarctica and Station — A1848

Engraved and Photogravure

1971, June 21 *Perf. 11½*
3859 A1848 6k black, grn & ultra .50 .30

Antarctic Treaty pledging peaceful uses of & scientific co-operation in Antarctica, 10th anniv.

Weather Map, Plane, Ship and Satellite — A1849

1971, June 21
3860 A1849 10k black, red & ultra .50 .30

50th anniversary of Soviet Hydrometeorological service.

FIR Emblem, "Homeland" by E. Vouchetich A1850

1971, June 21 Photo. *Perf. 12x12½*
3861 A1850 6k dk red & slate .50 .25

International Federation of Resistance Fighters (FIR), 20th anniversary.

Discus and Running A1851

Designs: 4k, Archery (women). 6k, Dressage. 10k, Basketball. 12k, Wrestling.

Lithographed and Engraved

1971, June 24 *Perf. 11½*
3862 A1851 3k vio blue, *rose* .25 .25
3863 A1851 4k slate grn, *pale pink* .25 .25
3864 A1851 6k red brn, *apple grn* .30 .25
3865 A1851 10k dk pur, *gray blue* .40 .25
3866 A1851 12k red brn, *yellow* .50 .25
Nos. 3862-3866 (5) 1.70 1.25

5th Summer Spartakiad.

Benois Madonna, by da Vinci A1852

Paintings: 4k, Mary Magdalene, by Titian. 10k, The Washerwoman, by Jean Simeon Chardin, horiz. 12k, Portrait of a Young Man, by Frans Hals. 14k, Tancred and Arminia, by Nicolas Poussin, horiz. 16k, Girl with Fruit, by Murillo. 20k, Girl with Ball, by Picasso.

Perf. 12x12½, 12½x12

1971, July 7 Litho.
3867 A1852 2k bister & multi .25 .25
3868 A1852 4k bister & multi .25 .25
3869 A1852 10k bister & multi .40 .25
3870 A1852 12k bister & multi .45 .25
3871 A1852 14k bister & multi .55 .25
3872 A1852 16k bister & multi .65 .25
3873 A1852 20k bister & multi .75 .25
Nos. 3867-3873 (7) 3.30 1.75

Foreign master works in Russian museums.

Kazakhstan Flag, Lenin Badge — A1853

1971, July 7 Photo. *Perf. 11½*

3874 A1853 4k blue, red & brown .50 .25

50th anniversary of the Kazakh Communist Youth League.

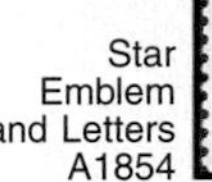

Star Emblem and Letters A1854

1971, July 14

3875 A1854 4k oliver, blue & black .50 .25

International Letter Writing Week.

Nikolai A. Nekrasov, by Ivan N. Kramskoi A1855

Portraits: No. 3877, Aleksandr Spendiarov, by M. S. Saryan. 10k, Fedor M. Dostoevski, by Vassili G. Perov.

1971, July 14 Litho. *Perf. 12x12½*

3876 A1855 4k citron & multi .25 .25
3877 A1855 4k gray blue & multi .25 .25
3878 A1855 10k multicolored .40 .25
Nos. 3876-3878 (3) .90 .75

Nikolai Alekseevitch Nekrasov (1821-1877), poet, Fedor Mikhailovich Dostoevski (1821-1881), novelist, Spendiarov (1871-1928), Armenian composer.
See Nos. 4056-4057.

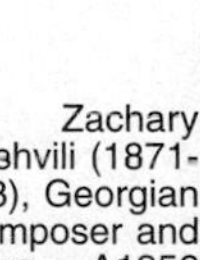

Zachary Paliashvili (1871-1933), Georgian Composer and Score — A1856

1971, Aug. 3 Photo. *Perf. 12x12½*

3879 A1856 4k brown .50 .25

Gorki Kremlin, Stag and Hydrofoil A1857

1971, Aug. 3 Litho. *Perf. 12*

3880 A1857 16k multicolored .60 .25

Gorki (formerly Nizhni Novgorod), 750th anniv. See Nos. 3889, 3910-3914.

Federation Emblem and Students A1858

1971, Aug. 3 Photo. *Perf. 11½*

3881 A1858 6k ultra & multi .50 .25

Intl. Students Federation, 25th anniv.

Common Dolphins A1859

Sea Mammals: 6k, Sea otter. 10k, Narwhals. 12k, Walrus. 14k, Ribbon seals.

Photogravure and Engraved

1971, Aug. 12 *Perf. 11½*

3882 A1859 4k silver & multi .40 .25
3883 A1859 6k silver & multi .40 .25
3884 A1859 10k silver & multi .60 .25
3885 A1859 12k silver & multi .70 .25
3886 A1859 14k silver & multi .90 .25
Nos. 3882-3886 (5) 3.00 1.25

Miner's Star of Valor — A1860

1971, Aug. 17 Photo. *Perf. 11½*

3887 A1860 4k bister, black & red .50 .25

250th anniversary of the discovery of coal in the Donets Basin.

Ernest Rutherford and Diagram of Movement of Atomic Particles A1861

1971, Aug. 24 Photo. *Perf. 12*

3888 A1861 6k magenta & dk ol .75 .25

Rutherford (1871-1937), British physicist.

Gorki and Gorki Statue — A1862

1971, Sept. 14 *Perf. 11½*

3889 A1862 4k steel blue & multi .50 .25

Gorki (see No. 3880).

Troika and Spasski Tower A1863

1971, Sept. 14

3890 A1863 10k black, red & gold .50 .25

New Year 1972.

Automatic Production Center — A1864

#3892, Agricultural development. #3893, Family in shopping center. #3894, Hydro-generators, thermoelectric station. #3895, Marchers, flags, books inscribed Marx and Lenin.

1971, Sept. 29 Photo. *Perf. 12x11½*

3891 A1864 4k purple, red & blk .40 .25
3892 A1864 4k ocher, red & brn .40 .25
3893 A1864 4k yel, olive & red .40 .25
3894 A1864 4k bister, red & brn .40 .25
3895 A1864 4k ultra, red & slate .40 .25
Nos. 3891-3895 (5) 2.00 1.25

Resolutions of 24th Soviet Union Communist Party Congress.

The Meeting, by Vladimir Y. Makovsky A1865

Ivan N. Kramskoi, Self-portrait — A1866

Paintings: 4k, Woman Student, by Nikolai A. Yaroshenko. 6k, Woman Miner, by Nikolai A. Kasatkin. 10k, Harvest, by G. G. Myasoyedov, horiz. 16k, Country Road, by A. K. Savrasov. 20k, Pine Forest, by I. I. Shishkin, horiz.

Perf. 12x12½, 12½x12

1971, Oct. 14 Litho.

Frame in Light Gray

3896 A1865 2k multicolored .25 .25
3897 A1865 4k multicolored .25 .25
3898 A1865 6k multicolored .25 .25
3899 A1865 10k multicolored .50 .25
3900 A1865 16k multicolored .55 .25
3901 A1865 20k multicolored 1.10 .25
Nos. 3896-3901 (6) 2.90 1.50

Souvenir Sheet

Lithographed and Gold Embossed

3902 A1866 50k dk green & multi 2.00 .60

History of Russian painting.

V. V. Vorovsky, Bolshevik Party Leader and Diplomat, Birth Cent. — A1867

1971, Oct. 14 Engr. *Perf. 12*

3903 A1867 4k red brown .50 .25

Cosmonauts Dobrovolsky, Volkov and Patsayev — A1868

1971, Oct. 20 Photo. *Perf. 11½x12*

3904 A1868 4k black, lilac & org .50 .25

In memory of cosmonauts Lt. Col. Georgi T. Dobrovolsky, Vladislav N. Volkov and Viktor I. Patsayev, who died during the Soyuz 11 space mission, June 6-30, 1971.

Order of October Revolution — A1869

1971, Oct. 20 Litho. *Perf. 12*

3905 A1869 4k red, yel & black .50 .25

54th anniversary of October Revolution.

E. Vakhtangov and "Princess Turandot" A1870

Designs: No. 3907, Boris Shchukin and scene from "Man with Rifle (Lenin)," horiz. No. 3908, Ruben Simonov and scene from "Cyrano de Bergerac," horiz.

Perf. 12x12½, 12½x12

1971, Oct. 26 Photo.

3906 A1870 10k mar & red brn .35 .25
3907 A1870 10k brown & dull yel .35 .25
3908 A1870 10k rod brn & ocher .35 .25
Nos. 3906-3908 (3) 1.05 .75

Vakhtangov Theater, Moscow, 50th anniv.

Dzhambul Dzhabayev(1846-1945), Kazakh Poet — A1871

1971, Nov. 16 *Perf. 12x12½*

3909 A1871 4k orange & brown .50 .25

Gorki Kremlin Type, 1971

Designs: 3k, Pskov Kremlin and Velikaya River. 4k, Novgorod Kremlin and eternal flame memorial. 6k, Smolensk Fortress and liberation monument. 10k, Kolomna Kremlin and buses. 50k, Moscow Kremlin.

1971, Nov. 16 Litho. *Perf. 12*

3910 A1857 3k multicolored .75 .25
3911 A1857 4k multicolored .75 .25
3912 A1857 6k gray & multi .75 .25
3913 A1857 10k olive & multi .75 .25
Nos. 3910-3913 (4) 3.00 1.00

Souvenir Sheet
Engraved and Lithographed
Perf. 11½

3914 A1857 50k yellow & multi 2.00 1.00

Historic buildings. No. 3914 contains one 21½x32mm stamp.

William Foster, View of New York A1872

1971 Litho. *Perf. 12*

3915 A1872 10k brn & blk ("-1961") 1.00 .25
a. "-1964" 20.00 7.25

William Foster (1881-1961), chairman of Communist Party of US.

No. 3915a was issued Nov. 16 with incorrect death date (1964). No. 3915, with corrected date (1961), was issued Dec. 8.

Aleksandr Fadeyev and Cavalrymen — A1873

1971, Nov. 25 Photo. *Perf. 12½x12*

3916 A1873 4k slate & orange .50 .25

Aleksandr Fadeyev (1901-1956), writer.

Amethyst and Diamond Brooch A1874

Precious Jewels: No. 3918, Engraved Shakh diamond, India, 16th cent. No. 3919, Diamond daffodils, 18th cent. No. 3920, Amethyst & diamond pendant. No. 3921, Diamond rose made for centenary of Lenin's birth. No. 3922, Diamond & pearl pendant.

1971, Dec. 8 Litho. *Perf. 11½*

3917	A1874 10k brt blue & multi		.35	.25
3918	A1874 10k dk red & multi		.35	.25
3919	A1874 10k grnsh black & multi		.35	.25
3920	A1874 20k grnsh black & multi		.70	.30
3921	A1874 20k rose red & multi		.70	.30
3922	A1874 30k black & multi		1.00	.45
	Nos. 3917-3922 (6)		3.45	1.80

Souvenir Sheet

Workers with Banners, Congress Hall and Spasski Tower — A1875

1971, Dec. 15 Photo. *Perf. 11x11½*

3923 A1875 20k red, pale grn & brn 2.00 1.00

See note after No. 3895. No. 3923 contains one partially perforated stamp.

Vanda Orchid — A1876

Flowers: No. 3924, No. 3929b, shown. No. 3925, Anthurium. No. 3926, No. 3929c, Flowering crab cactus. No. 3927, No. 3929a, Amaryllis. No. 3928, No. 3929d, Medinilla magnifica.

1971, Dec. 15 Litho. *Perf. 12x12½*

3924	A1876 1k olive & multi	.25	.25
3925	A1876 2k green & multi	.25	.25
3926	A1876 4k blue & multi	.40	.25
3927	A1876 12k multicolored	.50	.25
3928	A1876 14k multicolored	.65	.25
	Nos. 3924-3928 (5)	2.05	1.25

Miniature Sheet
Perf. 12

3929 Sheet of 4 1.50 .75
a.-d. A1876 10k any single .40 .25

Nos. 3929a-3929d have white background, black frame line and inscription. Size of stamps 19x57mm.

Issued: Nos. 3924-3928, 12/15; No. 3929, 12/30.

Peter I Reviewing Fleet, 1723 — A1877

History of Russian Fleet: 4k, Oriol, first ship built in Eddinovo, 1668, vert. 10k, Battleship Poltava, 1712, vert. 12k, Armed ship Ingermanland, 1715, vert. 16k, Frigate Vladimir, 1848.

Perf. 11½x12, 12x11½

1971, Dec. 15 Engr. & Photo.

3930	A1877 1k multicolored	.30	.25
3931	A1877 4k brown & multi	.45	.30
3932	A1877 10k multicolored	1.20	.75
3933	A1877 12k multicolored	1.40	.75
3934	A1877 16k lt green & multi	1.90	1.00
	Nos. 3930-3934 (5)	5.25	3.05

Ice Hockey A1878

1971, Dec. 15 Litho. *Perf. 12½*

3935 A1878 6k multicolored .50 .25

25th anniversary of Soviet ice hockey.

A1879

Oil rigs and causeway in Caspian Sea.

1971, Dec. 30 *Perf. 11½*

3936 A1879 4k dp blue, org & blk .50 .25

Baku oil industry.

A1880

1972, Jan. 5 Engr. *Perf. 12*

3937 A1880 4k yellow brown .50 .25

G. M. Krzhizhanovsky (1872-1959), scientist and co-worker with Lenin.

Alexander Scriabin (1872-1915), Composer A1881

1972, Jan. 6 Photo. *Perf. 12x12½*

3938 A1881 4k indigo & olive .50 .25

Bering's Cormorant A1882

Birds: 6k, Ross' gull, horiz. 10k, Barnacle geese. 12k, Spectacled eiders, horiz. 16k, Mediterranean gull.

1972, Jan. 12 *Perf. 11½*

3939	A1882 4k dk grn, blk & yel	.30	.25
3940	A1882 6k ind, pink & blk	.50	.25
3941	A1882 10k grnsh blue, blk & brown	.80	.35
3942	A1882 12k multicolored	.95	.45
3943	A1882 16k ultra, gray & red	1.25	.60
	Nos. 3939-3943 (5)	3.80	1.90

Waterfowl of the USSR.

11th Winter Olympic Games, Sapporo, Japan, Feb. 3-13 — A1883

Designs (Olympic Rings and): 4k, Speed skating. 6k, Women's figure skating. 10k, Ice hockey. 12k, Ski jump. 16k, Long-distance skiing. 50k, Sapporo '72 emblem.

1972, Jan. 20 Litho. *Perf. 12x12½*

3944	A1883 4k bl grn, red & brn	.25	.25
3945	A1883 6k yel grn, blue & dp orange	.25	.25
3946	A1883 10k vio, bl & dp org	.40	.25
3947	A1883 12k light blue, blue & brick red	.50	.25
3948	A1883 16k gray, bl & brt rose	.60	.25
	Nos. 3944-3948 (5)	2.00	1.25

Souvenir Sheet

3949 A1883 50k multicolored 2.00 .75

For overprint see No. 3961.

Heart, Globe and Exercising Family — A1884

1972, Feb. 9 Photo.

3950 A1884 4k brt grn & rose red .50 .25

Heart Month sponsored by the WHO.

Leipzig Fair Emblem and Soviet Pavilion — A1885

1972, Feb. 22 *Perf. 11½*

3951 A1885 16k red & gold .75 .25

50th anniversary of the participation of the USSR in the Leipzig Trade Fair.

Hammer, Sickle and Cogwheel Emblem — A1886

1972, Feb. 29 *Perf. 12x12½*

3952 A1886 4k rose red & lt brn .50 .25

15th USSR Trade Union Congress, Moscow, March 1972.

Aloe — A1887

Medicinal Plants: 2k, Horn poppy. 4k, Groundsel. 6k, Orthosiphon stamineus. 10k, Nightshade.

1972, Mar. 14 Litho. *Perf. 12x12½*

Flowers in Natural Colors

3953	A1887 1k olive bister	.80	.25
3954	A1887 2k slate green	.80	.25
3955	A1887 4k brt purple	.80	.25
3956	A1887 6k violet blue	.80	.25
3957	A1887 10k dk brown	.80	.25
	Nos. 3953-3957 (5)	4.00	1.25

Aleksandra Kollontai — A1888

No. 3959, Georgy Chicherin. No. 3960, Kamo (pseudonym of S.A. Ter-Petrosyan).

1972, Mar. 20 Engr. *Perf. 12½x12*

3958 A1888 4k red brown .35 .25
3959 A1888 4k claret .35 .25
3960 A1888 4k olive bister .35 .25
Nos. 3958-3960 (3) 1.05 .75

Outstanding workers of the Communist Party of the Soviet Union and for the State.

No. 3949 Overprinted
Souvenir Sheet

1972, Mar. 20 Litho. *Perf. 12x12½*

3961 A1883 50k multicolored 4.00 2.00

Victories of Soviet athletes in the 11th Winter Olympic Games (8 gold, 5 silver, 3 bronze medals).

For similar overprints see Nos. 4028, 4416.

Orbital Station Salyut and Spaceship Soyuz Docking Above Earth — A1889

Designs: No. 3963, Mars 2 approaching Mars, and emblem dropped on Mars. 16k, Mars 3, which landed on Mars, Dec. 2, 1971.

1972, Apr. 5 Photo. *Perf. 11½x12*

3962 A1889 6k vio, blue & silver .40 .25
3963 A1889 6k pur, ocher & sil .40 .25
3964 A1889 16k pur, blue & sil 1.20 .25
Nos. 3962-3964 (3) 2.00 .75

Cosmonauts' Day.

Shield and Products of Izhory Factory A1890

1972, Apr. 20 *Perf. 12½x12*

3965 A1890 4k purple & silver .50 .25

250th anniversary of Izhory Factory, founded by Peter the Great.

Leonid Sobinov in "Eugene Onegin," by Tchaikovsky — A1891

1972, Apr. 20

3966 A1891 10k dp brown & buff .50 .25

Sobinov (1872-1934), opera singer.

Book, Torch, Children and Globe A1892

1972, May 5 *Perf. 11½*

3967 A1892 6k brn, grnsh bl & buff .35 .25

International Book Year 1972.

Girl in Laboratory and Pioneers A1893

Designs: 1k, Pavlik Morosov (Pioneer hero), Pioneers saluting and banner. 3k, Pioneers with wheelbarrow, Chukchi boy, and Chukotka Pioneer House. 4k, Pioneer Honor Guard and Parade. 30k, Pioneer Honor Guard, vert.

1972, May 10

3968 A1893 1k red & multi .50 .25
3969 A1893 2k multicolored .50 .25
3970 A1893 3k multicolored .50 .25
3971 A1893 4k gray & multi .50 .25
Nos. 3968-3971 (4) 2.00 1.00

Souvenir Sheet
Perf. 12x12½

3972 A1893 30k multicolored 2.00 .75

50th anniversary of the Lenin Pioneer Organization of the USSR.

Pioneer Bugler A1894

1972, May 27 Photo. *Perf. 11½*

3973 A1894 4k red, ocher & plum .50 .25

2nd Youth Philatelic Exhibition, Minsk, and 50th anniv. of Lenin Pioneer Org.

M. S. Ordubady (1872-1950), Azerbaijan Writer and Social Worker — A1895

1972, May 25 *Perf. 12x12½*

3974 A1895 4k orange & rose brn .50 .25

Globe A1896

1972, May 25 *Perf. 11½*

3975 A1896 6k multicolored .60 .30

European Safety and Cooperation Conference, Brussels.

Cossack Leader, by Ivan Nikitin A1897

Paintings: 4k, Fedor G. Volkov (actor), by Anton Losenko. 6k, V. Majkov (poet), by Fedor Rokotov. 10k, Nikolai I. Novikov (writer), by Dimitri Levitsky. 12k, Gavriil R. Derzhavin (poet, civil servant), by Vladimir Borovikovsky. 16k, Peasants' Supper, by Mikhail Shibanov, horiz. 20k, View of Moscow, by Fedor Alexeyev, horiz.

Perf. 12x12½, 12½x12

1972, June 7 Litho.

3976 A1897 2k gray & multi .25 .25
3977 A1897 4k gray & multi .25 .25
3978 A1897 6k gray & multi .25 .25
3979 A1897 10k gray & multi .30 .25
3980 A1897 12k gray & multi .30 .25
3981 A1897 16k gray & multi .45 .25
3982 A1897 20k gray & multi .60 .25
Nos. 3976-3982 (7) 2.40 1.75

History of Russian painting. See Nos. 4036-4042, 4074-4080, 4103-4109.

George Dimitrov (1882-1949), Bulgarian Communist Party Leader — A1898

1972, June 15 Photo. *Perf. 12½x12*

3983 A1898 6k brown & ol bister .50 .25

20th Olympic Games, Munich, 8/26-9/11 A1899

Olympic Rings and: 4k, Fencing. 6k, Women's gymnastics. 10k, Canoeing. 14k, Boxing. 16k, Running. 50k, Weight lifting.

1972, July 1 *Perf. 12x11½*

3984 A1899 4k brt mag & gold .25 .25
3985 A1899 6k dp green & gold .25 .25
3986 A1899 10k brt blue & gold .55 .25
3987 A1899 14k Prus bl & gold .60 .25
3988 A1899 16k red & gold .85 .25
Nos. 3984-3988 (5) 2.50 1.25

Souvenir Sheet
Perf. 11½

3989 A1899 50k gold & multi 1.50 .60

No. 3989 contains one 25x35mm stamp.

For overprint see No. 4028.

Congress Palace, Kiev A1900

1972, July 1 Photo. & Engr.

3990 A1900 6k Prus blue & bister .50 .25

9th World Gerontology Cong., Kiev, 7/2-7.

Roald Amundsen, "Norway," Northern Lights A1901

1972, July 13 Photo. *Perf. 11½*

3991 A1901 6k vio blue & dp bister .65 .25

Roald Amundsen (1872-1928), Norwegian polar explorer.

17th Century House, Chernigov A1902

Designs: 4k, Market Square, Lvov, vert. 10k, Kovnirov Building, Kiev. 16k, Fortress, Kamenets-Podolski, vert.

Perf. 12x12½, 12½x12

1972, July 18 Litho.

3992 A1902 4k citron & multi .25 .25
3993 A1902 6k gray & multi .25 .25
3994 A1902 10k ocher & multi .60 .25
3995 A1902 16k salmon & multi .80 .25
Nos. 3992-3995 (4) 1.90 1.00

Historic and architectural treasures of the Ukraine.

Asoka Pillar, Indian Flag, Red Fort, New Delhi A1903

1972, July 27 Photo. *Perf. 11½*

3996 A1903 6k dk blue, emer & red .50 .25

25th anniversary of India's independence.

Miners' Emblem A1904

1972, Aug. 10

3997 A1904 4k violet gray & red .50 .25

25th Miners' Day.

Far East Fighters' Monument A1905

Designs: 4k, Monument for Far East Civil War heroes, industrial view. 6k, Vladivostok rostral column, Pacific fleet ships.

1972, Aug. 10

3998 A1905 3k red org, car & black .50 .25
3999 A1905 4k yel, sepia & blk .50 .25
4000 A1905 6k pink, dk car & black .50 .25
Nos. 3998-4000 (3) 1.50 .75

50th anniversary of the liberation of the Far Eastern provinces.

Boy with Dog, by Murillo
A1906

Paintings from the Hermitage, Leningrad: 4k, Breakfast, Velazquez. 6k, Milkmaid's Family, Louis Le Nain. 16k, Sad Woman, Watteau. 20k, Moroccan Saddling Steed, Delacroix. 50k, Self-portrait, Van Dyck. 4k, 6k horiz.

Perf. 12½x12, 12x12½

1972, Aug. 15 **Litho.**

4001	A1906	4k	multicolored	.25	.25
4002	A1906	6k	multicolored	.25	.25
4003	A1906	10k	multicolored	.40	.25
4004	A1906	16k	multicolored	.60	.25
4005	A1906	20k	multicolored	.90	.25
	Nos. 4001-4005 (5)			2.40	1.25

Souvenir Sheet

Perf. 12

4006 A1906 50k multicolored 2.50 1.00

Sputnik 1 — A1907

No. 4008, Launching of Vostok 2. No. 4009, Lenov floating in space. No. 4010, Lunokhod on moon. No. 4011, Venera 7 descending to Venus. No. 4012, Mars & descending to Mars.

1972, Sept. 14 **Litho.** ***Perf. 12x11½***

4007	A1907	6k	shown	.35	.25
4008	A1907	6k	multicolored	.35	.25
4009	A1907	6k	multicolored	.35	.25
4010	A1907	6k	multicolored	.35	.25
4011	A1907	6k	multicolored	.35	.25
4012	A1907	6k	multicolored	.35	.25
	Nos. 4007-4012 (6)			2.10	1.50

15 years of space era. Sheets of 6.

Konstantin Aleksandrovich Mardzhanishvili (1872-1933), Theatrical Producer
A1908

1972, Sept. 20 **Engr.** ***Perf. 12x12½***
4013 A1908 4k slate green .50 .25

Museum Emblem, Communications Symbols — A1909

1972, Sept. 20 **Photo.** ***Perf. 11½***
4014 A1909 4k slate green & multi .50 .25

Centenary of the A. S. Popov Central Museum of Communications.

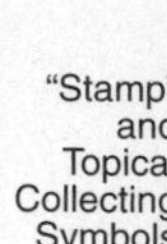

"Stamp" and Topical Collecting Symbols
A1910

Engraved and Lithographed

1972, Oct. 4 ***Perf. 12***
4015 A1910 4k yel, black & red .50 .25

Philatelic Exhibition in honor of 50th anniversary of the USSR.

Lenin
A1911

1972, Oct. 12 **Photo.** ***Perf. 11½***
4016 A1911 4k gold & red .50 .25

55th anniversary of October Revolution.

Militia Badge — A1912

1972, Oct. 12
4017 A1912 4k gold, red & dk brn .30 .25

55th anniv. of the Militia of the USSR.

Arms of USSR
A1913

USSR, 50th anniv.: No. 4019, Arms and industrial scene. No. 4020, Arms, Supreme Soviet, Kremlin. No. 4021, Lenin. No. 4022, Arms, worker, book (Constitution).
30k, Coat of arms and Spasski Tower, horiz.

1972, Oct. 28 ***Perf. 12x11½***

4018	A1913	4k	multicolored	.30	.25
4019	A1913	4k	multicolored	.30	.25
4020	A1913	4k	multicolored	.30	.25
4021	A1913	4k	multicolored	.30	.25
4022	A1913	4k	multicolored	.30	.25
	Nos. 4018-4022 (5)			1.50	1.25

Souvenir Sheet

Lithographed; Embossed

Perf. 12

4023 A1913 30k red & gold 1.50 .40

Kremlin and Snowflake
A1914

Engraved and Photogravure

1972, Nov. 15 ***Perf. 11½***
4024 A1914 6k multicolored 1.00 .25

New Year 1973.

Savings Bank Book — A1915

1972, Nov. 15 **Photo.** ***Perf. 12x12½***
4025 A1915 4k lilac & slate .50 .25

50th anniv. of savings banks in the USSR.

Soviet Olympic Emblem and Laurel
A1916

Design: 30k, Soviet Olympic emblem and obverse of gold, silver and bronze medals.

1972, Nov. 15 ***Perf. 11½***

4026	A1916	20k	brn ol, red & gold	.50	.40
4027	A1916	30k	dp car, gold & brn	1.00	.60

No. 3989 Overprinted in Red

Souvenir Sheet

1972, Nov. 15
4028 A1899 50k gold & multi 2.50 1.25

Soviet medalists at 20th Olympic Games.

Battleship Peter the Great, 1872 — A1917

History of Russian Fleet: 3k, Cruiser Varyag, 1899. 4k, Battleship Potemkin, 1900. 6k, Cruiser Ochakov, 1902. 10k, Mine layer Amur, 1907.

Engraved and Photogravure

1972, Nov. 22 ***Perf. 11½x12***

4029	A1917	2k	multicolored	.35	.25
4030	A1917	3k	multicolored	.35	.25
4031	A1917	4k	multicolored	.45	.25
4032	A1917	6k	multicolored	.70	.25
4033	A1917	10k	multicolored	1.10	.25
	Nos. 4029-4033 (5)			2.95	1.25

Grigory S. Skovoroda (1722-1794), Ukrainian Philosopher and Humanist
A1918

1972, Dec. 7 **Engr.** ***Perf. 12***
4034 A1918 4k dk violet blue .50 .25

Child Reading Traffic Rules — A1919

1972, Dec. 7 **Photo.** ***Perf. 11½***
4035 A1919 4k Prus blue, blk & red .50 .25

Traffic safety campaign.

Russian Painting Type of 1972

2k, Meeting of Village Party Members, by E. M. Cheptsov, horiz. 4k, Pioneer Girl, by Nicolai A. Kasatkin. 6k, Woman Delegate, by G. G. Ryazhsky. 10k, Winter's End, by K. F. Yuon, horiz. 16k, The Partisan A. G. Lunev, by N. I. Strunnikov. 20k, Igor E. Grabar, self-portrait. 50k, Blue Space (seascape with flying geese), by Arcadi A. Rylov, horiz.

Perf. 12x12½, 12½x12

1972, Dec. 7 **Litho.**

4036	A1897	2k	olive & multi	.25	.25
4037	A1897	4k	olive & multi	.25	.25
4038	A1897	6k	olive & multi	.25	.25
4039	A1897	10k	olive & multi	.35	.25
4040	A1897	16k	olive & multi	.55	.25
4041	A1897	20k	olive & multi	.65	.25
	Nos. 4036-4041 (6)			2.30	1.50

Souvenir Sheet

Perf. 12

4042 A1897 50k multicolored 1.75 1.25

History of Russian painting.

Symbolic of Theory and Practice — A1920

Engraved and Photogravure

1972, Dec. 7 ***Perf. 11½***
4043 A1920 4k sl grn, yel & red brn .50 .25

Centenary of Polytechnic Museum, Moscow.

Venera 8 and Parachute
A1921

1972, Dec. 28 **Photo.** ***Perf. 11½***
4044 A1921 6k dl claret, bl & blk .50 .25

Souvenir Sheet

Imperf

4045		Sheet of 2	7.00	2.00
a.	A1921	50k Venera 8	3.00	.90
b.	A1921	50k Mars 3	3.00	.90

Soviet space research. No. 4045 contains 2 40x20mm stamps with simulated perforations.

Globe, Torch and Palm — A1922

1973, Jan. 5 *Perf. 11x11½*

4046 A1922 10k tan, vio blue & red .50 .30

15th anniversary of Afro-Asian Peoples' Solidarity Organization (AAPSO).

I. V. Babushkin — A1923

1973, Jan. 10 **Engr.** *Perf. 12*

4047 A1923 4k greenish black .50 .25

Babushkin (1873-1906), revolutionary.

"30," Map and Admiralty Tower, Leningrad A1924

1973, Jan. 10 **Photo.** *Perf. 11½*

4048 A1924 4k pale brn, ocher & blk .50 .25

30th anniversary of the breaking of the Nazi blockade of Leningrad.

TU-154 Turbojet Passenger Plane — A1925

1973, Jan. 10 **Litho.** *Perf. 12*

4049 A1925 6k multicolored .75 .25

50th anniversary of Soviet Civil Aviation.

Gediminas Tower, Flag, Modern Vilnius A1926

1973, Jan. 10 **Photo.** *Perf. 11½*

4050 A1926 10k gray, red & green .50 .30

650th anniversary of Vilnius.

Heroes' Memorial, Stalingrad — A1927

Designs (Details from Monument): 3k, Man with rifle and "Mother Russia," vert. 10k, Mourning mother and child. 12k, Arm with torch, vert. No. 4055a, Red star, hammer and sickle emblem and statuary like 3k. No. 4055b, "Mother Russia," vert.

1973, Feb. 1 **Litho.** *Perf. 11½*

4051 A1927 3k dp org & blk 1.25 .25
4052 A1927 4k dp yel & blk 1.25 .25
4053 A1927 10k olive & multi 1.25 .25
4054 A1927 12k dp car & black 1.25 .25
Nos. 4051-4054 (4) 5.00 1.00

Souvenir Sheet

Perf. 12x12½, 12½x12

4055 Sheet of 2 3.00 1.00
a.-b. A1927 20k any single .75 .25

30th anniv. of the victory over the Germans at Stalingrad. #4055 contains 2 40x18mm stamps.

Large Portrait Type of 1971

Designs: 4k, Mikhail Prishvin (1873-1954), author. 10k, Fedor Chaliapin (1873-1938), opera singer, by K. Korovin.

1973 **Litho.** *Perf. 11½x12*

4056 A1855 4k pink & multi .50 .25
4057 A1855 10k lt blue & multi .50 .25

Issue dates: 4k, Feb. 1; 10k, Feb. 8.

"Mayakovsky Theater" — A1928 "Mossovet Theater" — A1929

1973, Feb. 1 **Photo.** *Perf. 11½*

4058 A1928 10k red, gray & indigo .50 .25
4059 A1929 10k red, mag & gray .50 .25

50th anniversary of the Mayakovsky and Mossovet Theaters in Moscow.

Copernicus and Solar System A1930

1973, Feb. 8 **Engr. & Photo.**

4060 A1930 10k ultra & sepia .75 .25

500th anniversary of the birth of Nicolaus Copernicus (1473-1543), Polish astronomer.

Ice Hockey A1931

Design: 50k, Two players, vert.

1973, Mar. 14 **Photo.** *Perf. 11½*

4061 A1931 10k gold, blue & sep .50 .25

Souvenir Sheet

4062 A1931 50k bl grn, gold & sep 2.00 1.00

European and World Ice Hockey Championships, Moscow.

See No. 4082.

Athletes and Banners of Air, Land and Naval Forces — A1932

1973, Mar. 14

4063 A1932 4k bright blue & multi .50 .25

Sports Society of Soviet Army, 50th anniv.

Tank, Red Star and Map of Battle of Kursk — A1933

1973, Mar. 14

4064 A1933 4k gray, black & red .50 .25

30th anniversary of Soviet victory in the Battle of Kursk during World War II.

Nikolai E. Bauman (1873-1905), Bolshevist Revolutionary A1934

1973, Mar. 20 **Engr.** *Perf. 12½x12*

4065 A1934 4k brown .50 .25

Red Cross and Red Crescent — A1935

6k, Theater curtain & mask. 16k, Youth Festival emblem & young people.

1973, Mar. 20 **Photo.** *Perf. 11*

4066 A1935 4k gray grn & red .45 .25
4067 A1935 6k violet blue & red .45 .25
4068 A1935 16k multicolored 1.10 .25
Nos. 4066-4068 (3) 2.00 .75

Union of Red Cross and Red Crescent Societies of the USSR, 50th annivs.; 15th Cong. of the Intl. Theater Institute; 10th World Festival of Youth and Students, Berlin.

Aleksandr N. Ostrovsky, by V. Perov A1936

1973, Apr. 5 **Litho.** *Perf. 12x12½*

4069 A1936 4k tan & multi .50 .25

Ostrovsky (1823-1886), dramatist.

Earth Satellite "Interkosmos" A1937 Lunokhod 2 on Moon and Lenin Moon Plaque A1938

1973, Apr. 12 **Photo.** *Perf. 11½*

4070 A1937 6k brn ol & dull cl .25 .25
4071 A1938 6k vio blue & multi .25 .25

Souvenir Sheets

Perf. 12x11½

4072 Sheet of 3, purple & multi 1.50 .75
a. A1938 20k Lenin plaque .40 .25
b. A1938 20k Lunokhod 2 .40 .25
c. A1938 20k Telecommunications .40 .25
4073 Sheet of 3, slate grn & multi 1.50 .75
a. A1938 20k Lenin plaque .40 .25
b. A1938 20k Lunokhod 2 .40 .25
c. A1938 20k Telecommunications .40 .25

Cosmonauts' Day. No. 4070 for cooperation in space research by European communist countries.

Souvenir sheets contain 3 50x21mm stamps.

Russian Painting Type of 1972

Paintings: 2k, Guitarist, V. A. Tropinin. 4k, Young Widow, by P. A. Fedotov. 6k, Self-portrait, by O. A. Kiprensky. 10k, Woman with Grapes ("An Afternoon in Italy") by K. P. Bryullov. 12k, Boy with Dog ("That was my Father's Dinner"), by A. Venetsianov. 16k, "Lower Gallery of Albano," by A. A. Ivanov. 20k, Soldiers ("Conquest of Siberia"), by V. I. Surikov, horiz.

Perf. 12x12½, 12½x12

1973, Apr. 18 **Litho.**

4074 A1897 2k gray & multi .25 .25
4075 A1897 4k gray & multi .25 .25
4076 A1897 6k gray & multi .25 .25
4077 A1897 10k gray & multi .45 .25
4078 A1897 12k gray & multi .60 .25
4079 A1897 16k gray & multi .65 .25
4080 A1897 20k gray & multi .80 .35
Nos. 4074-4080 (7) 3.25 1.85

Athlete, Ribbon of Lenin Order — A1939

1973, Apr. 18 **Photo.** *Perf. 11½*

4081 A1939 4k blue, red & ocher .50 .25

50th anniversary of Dynamo Sports Society.

No. 4062 with Blue Green Inscription and Ornaments Added in Margin

Souvenir Sheet

1973, Apr. 26 **Photo.** *Perf. 11½*

4082 A1931 50k multicolored 5.00 2.00

Soviet victory in European and World Ice Hockey Championships, Moscow.

"Mikhail Lermontov," Route Leningrad to New York — A1940

1973, May 20 **Photo.** *Perf. 11½*

4083 A1940 16k multicolored .60 .25

Inauguration of transatlantic service Leningrad to New York.

Ernest E. T. Krenkel, Polar Stations and Ship Chelyuskin A1941

1973, May 20 **Litho. & Engr.**

4084 A1941 4k dull blue & olive .50 .30

Krenkel (1903-1971), polar explorer.

Emblem and Sports — A1942

1973, May 20 Litho. *Perf. 12x12½*
4085 A1942 4k multicolored .50 .25

Sports Association for Labor and Defense.

Latvian Song Festival, Cent. — A1943

1973, May 24
4086 A1943 10k Singers .50 .25

Throwing the Hammer — A1944

Designs: 3k, Athlete on rings. 4k, Woman diver. 16k, Fencing. 50k, Javelin.

1973, June 14 Litho. *Perf. 11½*
4087 A1944 2k lemon & multi .25 .25
4088 A1944 3k blue & multi .25 .25
4089 A1944 4k citron & multi .25 .25
4090 A1944 16k lilac & multi .35 .25
Nos. 4087-4090 (4) 1.10 1.00

Souvenir Sheet

4091 A1944 50k gold & multi 1.75 1.25

Universiad, Moscow, 1973.

Souvenir Sheet

Valentina Nikolayeva-Tereshkova — A1945

1973, June 14 Photo. *Perf. 12x11½*
4092 A1945 Sheet of 3 + label 3.00 1.25
a. 20k as cosmonaut .55 .25
b. 20k with Indian and African women .55 .25
c. 20k with daughter .55 .25

Flight of the 1st woman cosmonaut, 10th anniv.

European Bison — A1946

1973, July 26 Photo. *Perf. 11x11½*
4093 A1946 1k shown .25 .25
4094 A1946 3k Ibex .25 .25
4095 A1946 4k Caucasian snowcock .25 .25
4096 A1946 6k Beaver .35 .25
4097 A1946 10k Deer and fawns .50 .25
Nos. 4093-4097 (5) 1.60 1.25

Caucasus and Voronezh wildlife reserves.

Party Membership Card with Lenin Portrait — A1947

1973, July 26 Litho. *Perf. 11½*
4098 A1947 4k multicolored .50 .25

70th anniversary of 2nd Congress of the Russian Social Democratic Workers' Party.

Abu-al-Rayhan al-Biruni (973-1048), Arabian (Persian) Scholar and Writer — A1948

1973, Aug. 9 Engr. *Perf. 12x12½*
4099 A1948 6k red brown .50 .25

White House, Spasski Tower, Hemispheres — A1949

#4101, Eiffel Tower, Spasski Tower, globe. #4102, Schaumburg Palace, Bonn, Spasski Tower, globe. Stamps show representative buildings of Moscow, Washington, New York, Paris & Bonn.

1973, Aug. 10 Photo. *Perf. 11½x12*
4100 A1949 10k magenta & multi 1.00 .50
4101 A1949 10k brown & multi 1.00 .50
4102 A1949 10k dp car & multi 1.00 .50
a. Souv. sheet of 3 + 3 labels 4.50 2.50
Nos. 4100-4102 (3) 3.00 1.50

Visit of General Secretary Leonid I. Brezhnev to Washington, Paris and Bonn. Nos. 4100-4102 each printed with se-tenant label with different statements by Brezhnev in Russian and English, French and German, respectively.

No. 4102a contains 4k stamps similar to Nos. 4100-4102 in changed colors. Issued Nov. 26.

See Nos. 4161-4162.

Russian Painting Type of 1972

2k, S. T. Konenkov, sculptor, by P. D. Korin. 4k, Tractor Operators at Supper, by A. A. Plastov. 6k, Letter from the Front, by A. I. Laktionov. 10k, Mountains, by M. S. Saryan. 16k, Wedding on a Future Street, by Y. I. Pimenov. 20k, Ice Hockey, mosaic by A. A. Deineka. 50k, Lenin at 3rd Congress of Young Communist League, by B. V. Yoganson.

1973, Aug. 22 Litho. *Perf. 12x12½*
Frame in Light Gray
4103 A1897 2k multicolored .25 .25
4104 A1897 4k multicolored .25 .25
4105 A1897 6k multicolored .25 .25
4106 A1897 10k multicolored .25 .25
4107 A1897 16k multicolored .45 .25
4108 A1897 20k multicolored .55 .25
Nos. 4103-4108 (6) 2.00 1.50

Souvenir Sheet
Perf. 12

4109 A1897 50k multicolored 3.00 1.50

History of Russian Painting.

Museum, Tashkent A1950

1973, Aug. 23 Photo. *Perf. 12x12½*
4110 A1950 4k multicolored .50 .25

Lenin Central Museum, Tashkent branch.

Y. M. Steklov — A1951

1973, Aug. 27 Photo. *Perf. 11½x12*
4111 A1951 4k multicolored .50 .25

Steklov (1873-1941), party worker, historian, writer.

Book, Pen and Torch — A1952

1973, Aug. 31 *Perf. 11½*
4112 A1952 6k multicolored .50 .25

Conf. of Writers of Asia & Africa, Alma-Ata.

Echinopanax Elatum — A1953

Medicinal Plants: 2k, Ginseng. 4k, Orchis maculatus. 10k, Arnica montana. 12k, Lily of the valley.

1973, Sept. 5 Litho. *Perf. 12x12½*
4113 A1953 1k yellow & multi .25 .25
4114 A1953 2k lt blue & multi .25 .25
4115 A1953 4k gray & multi .25 .25
4116 A1953 10k sepia & multi .30 .25
4117 A1953 12k green & multi .55 .25
Nos. 4113-4117 (5) 1.60 1.25

Imadeddin Nasimi, Azerbaijani Poet, 600th Birth Anniv. — A1954

1973, Sept. 5 Engr.
4118 A1954 4k sepia .50 .25

Cruiser Kirov — A1955

Soviet Warships: 4k, Battleship October Revolution. 6k, Submarine Krasnogvardeyets. 10k, Torpedo boat Soobrazitelny. 16k, Cruiser Red Caucasus.

Engraved and Photogravure
1973, Sept. 12 *Perf. 11½x12*
4119 A1955 3k violet & multi .25 .25
4120 A1955 4k green & multi .25 .25
4121 A1955 6k multicolored .25 .25
4122 A1955 10k blue grn & multi .30 .25
4123 A1955 16k multicolored .50 .25
Nos. 4119-4123 (5) 1.55 1.25

Globe and Red Flag Emblem — A1956

1973, Sept. 25 Photo. *Perf. 11½*
4124 A1956 6k gold, buff & red .50 .25

15th anniversary of the international communist review "Problems of Peace and Socialism," published in Prague.

Emelyan I. Pugachev and Peasant Army — A1957

Engraved and Photogravure
1973, Sept. 25 *Perf. 11½x12*
4125 A1957 4k brn, bister & red .75 .25

Bicentenary of peasant revolt of 1773-75 led by Emelyn Ivanovich Pugachev.

Crystal, Institute Emblem and Building A1958

1973, Oct. 5 *Perf. 11½*
4126 A1958 4k black & multi .50 .25

Leningrad Mining Institute, 150th anniv.

Palm, Globe, Flower — A1959

1973, Oct. 5 **Photo.**
4127 A1959 6k red, gray & dk blue .50 .25

World Cong. of Peace-loving Forces, Moscow.

Elena Stasova — A1960

1973, Oct. 5 ***Perf. 11½x12***
4128 A1960 4k deep claret .50 .25

Elena Dmitriyevna Stasova (1873-1966), communist party worker.
See Nos. 4228-4229.

Order of Friendship — A1961

1973, Oct. 5 **Litho.** ***Perf. 12***
4129 A1961 4k red & multi .75 .25

56th anniv. of the October Revolution. Printed se-tenant with coupon showing Arms of USSR and proclamation establishing Order of Friendship of People, in 1972, on the 50th anniv. of the USSR.

Marshal Malinovsky A1962

1973, Oct. 5 **Engr.**
4130 A1962 4k slate .50 .25

Rodion Y. Malinovsky (1898-1967).
See Nos. 4203-4205.

Ural Man, Red Guard, Worker — A1963

1973, Oct. 17 **Photo.** ***Perf. 11½***
4131 A1963 4k red, gold & black .50 .25

250th anniversary of the city of Sverdlovsk.

Dimitri Cantemir (1673-1723), Prince of Moldavia, Writer — A1964

1973, Oct. 17 **Engr.** ***Perf. 12x12½***
4132 A1964 4k rose claret .50 .25

Salvador Allende (1908-73), Pres. of Chile A1965

1973, Nov. 26 **Photo.** ***Perf. 11½***
4133 A1965 6k rose brn & black .50 .25

Spasski Tower, Kremlin — A1966

1973, Nov. 30 **Litho.** ***Perf. 12x12½***
4134 A1966 6k brt blue & multi 1.00 .25

New Year 1974.

Nariman Narimanov A1967

1973, Nov. 30 **Engr.** ***Perf. 12***
4135 A1967 4k slate green .50 .25

Nariman Narimanov (1870-1925), Chairman of Executive Committee of USSR.

Russo-Balt, 1909 — A1968

Designs: 3k, AMO-F15 truck, 1924. 4k, Spartak, NAMI-1 car, 1927. 12k, Ya-6 autobus, 1929. 16k, GAZ-A car, 1932.

1973, Nov. 30 **Photo.** ***Perf. 12x11½***
4136 A1968 2k purple & multi .25 .25
4137 A1968 3k olive & multi .25 .25
4138 A1968 4k ocher & multi .25 .25
4139 A1968 12k vio blue & multi .45 .25
4140 A1968 16k red & multi .75 .25
Nos. 4136-4140 (5) 1.95 1.25

Development of Russian automotive industry. See Nos. 4216-4220, 4325-4329, 4440-4444.

Still Life, by Frans Snyders — A1969

Paintings: 6k, Woman Trying on Earrings, by Rembrandt, vert. 10k, Sick Woman and Physician, by Jan Steen, vert. 12k, Still Life with Sculpture, by Jean-Baptiste Chardin. 14k, Lady in Garden, by Claude Monet. 16k, Young Love, by Jules Bastien-Lepage, vert. 20k Girl with Fan, by Auguste Renoir, vert. 50k, Flora, by Rembrandt, vert.

Perf. 12x11½, 11½x12
1973, Dec. 12 **Litho.**
4141 A1969 4k bister & multi .25 .25
4142 A1969 6k bister & multi .25 .25
4143 A1969 10k bister & multi .40 .25
4144 A1969 12k bister & multi .45 .25
4145 A1969 14k bister & multi .50 .25
4146 A1969 16k bister & multi .55 .25
4147 A1969 20k bister & multi .70 .25
Nos. 4141-4147 (7) 3.10 1.75

Souvenir Sheet
Perf. 12
4148 A1969 50k multicolored 6.00 1.00

Foreign paintings in Russian museums.

Pablo Picasso (1881-1973), Painter A1970

1973, Dec. 20 **Photo.** ***Perf. 12x11½***
4149 A1970 6k gold, slate grn & red .75 .25

Organ Pipes and Dome, Riga — A1971

No. 4151, Small Trakai Castle, Lithuania. No. 4152, Great Sea Gate, Tallinn, Estonia. 10k, Town Hall and "Old Thomas" weather vane, Tallinn.

1973, Dec. 20 **Engr.** ***Perf. 12x12½***
4150 A1971 4k blk, red & slate grn .25 .25
4151 A1971 4k gray, red & buff .25 .25
4152 A1971 4k black, red & grn .25 .25
4153 A1971 10k sep, grn, red & blk .25 .25
Nos. 4150-4153 (4) 1.00 1.00

Architecture of the Baltic area.

I. G. Petrovsky A1972

L. A. Artsimovich A1973

No. 4154, I. G. Petrovsky (1901-73), mathematician, rector of Moscow State University. No. 4155, L. A. Artsimovich (1909-73), physicist, academician. No. 4156, K. D. Ushinsky (1824-71), teacher. No. 4157, M. D. Millionschikov (1913-73), vice president of Academy of Sciences.

1973-74 **Photo.** ***Perf. 11½***
4154 A1972 4k orange & multi .50 .25
4155 A1973 4k blk brn & olive .50 .25

Engr.
Perf. 12½x12
4156 A1973 4k multicolored .50 .25

Litho.
Perf. 12
4157 A1973 4k multicolored .50 .25
Nos. 4154-4157 (4) 2.00 1.00

Issued: #4154, 12/28/73; others, 2/6/74.

Flags of India and USSR, Red Fort, Taj Mahal and Kremlin — A1974

Design: No. 4162, Flags of Cuba and USSR, José Marti Monument, Moncada Barracks and Kremlin.

1973-74 **Litho.** ***Perf. 12***
4161 A1974 4k lt ultra & multi 1.00 .25
4162 A1974 4k lt grn & multi ('74) 1.00 .25

Visit of General Secretary Leonid I. Brezhnev to India and Cuba. Nos. 4161-4162 each printed with se-tenant label with different statements by Brezhnev in Russian and Hindi, and Russian and Spanish respectively.

Red Star, Soldier, Newspaper A1975

1974, Jan. 1 **Photo.** ***Perf. 11x11½***
4166 A1975 4k gold, red & black .50 .25

50th anniversary of the Red Star newspaper.

Victory Monument, Peter-Paul Fortress, Statue of Peter I — A1976

1974, Jan. 16 **Litho.** ***Perf. 11½***
4167 A1976 4k multicolored 1.00 .25

30th anniversary of the victory over the Germans near Leningrad.

Oil Workers, Refinery — A1977

1974, Jan. 16 **Photo.** ***Perf. 11½***
4168 A1977 4k dull blue, red & blk .50 .25

10th anniversary of the Tyumen oilfields.

Comecon Building — A1978

1974, Jan. 16 Photo. *Perf. 11½*
4169 A1978 16k red brn, ol & red .50 .25

25th anniversary of the Council for Mutual Economic Assistance.

Skaters and Rink, Medeo A1979

1974, Jan. 28
4170 A1979 6k slate, brn red & bl .50 .25

European Women's Skating Championships, Medeo, Alma-Ata.

Art Palace, Leningrad, Academy, Moscow A1980

1974, Jan. 30 Photo. & Engr.
4171 A1980 10k multicolored .50 .25

25th anniversary of the Academy of Sciences of the USSR.

3rd Winter Spartiakad Emblem — A1981

1974, Mar. 20 Photo. *Perf. 11½*
4172 A1981 10k gold & multi .50 .25

Third Winter Spartiakad.

Young People and Emblem — A1982

1974, Mar. 20 Photo. & Engr.
4173 A1982 4k multicolored .50 .25

Youth scientific-technical work.

Azerbaijan Theater — A1983

1974, Mar. 20 Photo. *Perf. 11½*
4174 A1983 6k org, red brn & brn .50 .25

Centenary of Azerbaijan Theater.

Meteorological Satellite "Meteor" — A1984

Cosmonauts V. G. Lazarev and O. G. Makarov and Soyuz 12 — A1985

Design: No. 4177, Cosmonauts P. I. Klimuk and V. V. Lebedev, and Soyuz 13.

1974, Mar. 27 *Perf. 11½*
4175 A1984 6k violet & multi .60 .25

Perf. 12x11½

4176 A1985 10k grnsh bl & multi .70 .25
4177 A1985 10k dull yel & multi .70 .25
Nos. 4175-4177 (3) 2.00 .75

Cosmonauts' Day.

Odessa by Moonlight, by Aivazovski — A1986

Seascapes by Aivazovski: 4k, Battle of Chesma, 1848, vert. 6k, St. George's Monastery. 10k, Stormy Sea. 12k, Rainbow (shipwreck). 16k, Shipwreck. 50k, Portrait of Aivazovski, by Kramskoy, vert.

Perf. 12x11½, 11½x12

1974, Mar. 30 Litho.

4178 A1986 2k gray & multi .25 .25
4179 A1986 4k gray & multi .25 .25
4180 A1986 6k gray & multi .35 .25
4181 A1986 10k gray & multi .50 .25
4182 A1986 12k gray & multi .55 .25
4183 A1986 16k gray & multi .85 .25
Nos. 4178-4183 (6) 2.75 1.50

Souvenir Sheet

4184 A1986 50k gray & multi 1.50 .90

Ivan Konstantinovich Aivazovski (1817-1900), marine painter. Sheets of Nos. 4178-4183 each contain 2 labels with commemorative inscriptions.

See Nos. 4230-4234.

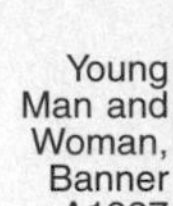

Young Man and Woman, Banner A1987

1974, Mar. 30 Litho. *Perf. 12½x12*
4185 A1987 4k red, yel & brown .50 .25

17th Cong. of the Young Communist League.

Lenin, by V. E. Tsigal A1988

1974, Mar. 30
4186 A1988 4k yel, red & brown .50 .25

50th anniversary of naming the Komsomol (Young Communist League) after Lenin.

Souvenir Sheet

Lenin at the Telegraph, by Igor E. Grabar — A1989

1974, Apr. 16 Litho. *Perf. 12*
4187 A1989 50k multicolored 2.00 .90

104th anniv. of the birth of Lenin.

Rainbow, Swallow over Clouds — A1990

6k, Fish in water. 10k, Crystal. 16k, Rose. 20k, Fawn. 50k, Infant.

1974, Apr. 24 Photo. *Perf. 11½*
4188 A1990 4k lilac & multi .25 .25
4189 A1990 6k multicolored .25 .25
4190 A1990 10k multicolored .35 .25
4191 A1990 16k blue & multi .55 .25
4192 A1990 20k citron & multi .60 .25
Nos. 4188-4192 (5) 2.00 1.25

Souvenir Sheet

Litho.

Perf. 12x12½

4193 A1990 50k blue & multi 2.00 .80

EXPO '74 World's Fair, theme "Preserve the Environment," Spokane, WA, May 4-Nov. 4.

Congress Emblem and Clover — A1991

1974, May 7 Photo. *Perf. 11½*
4194 A1991 4k green & multi .50 .25

12th International Congress on Meadow Cultivation, Moscow, 1974.

"Cobblestones, Weapons of the Proletariat," by I. D. Shadr — A1992

1974, May 7
4195 A1992 4k gold, red & olive .50 .25

50th anniversary of the Lenin Central Revolutionary Museum of the USSR.

Saiga — A1993

Fauna of USSR: 3k, Koulan (wild ass). 4k, Desman. 6k, Sea lion. 10k, Greenland whale.

1974, May 22 Litho. *Perf. 11½*
4196 A1993 1k olive & multi .40 .25
4197 A1993 3k green & multi .80 .35
4198 A1993 4k multicolored .80 .35
4199 A1993 6k multicolored 1.10 .50
4200 A1993 10k multicolored 1.90 .60
Nos. 4196-4200 (5) 5.00 2.05

Peter Ilich Tchaikovsky — A1994

1974, May 22 Photo. *Perf. 11½*
4201 A1994 6k multicolored .50 .25

5th International Tchaikovsky Competition, Moscow.

Souvenir Sheet

Aleksander S. Pushkin, by O. A. Kiprensky — A1995

1974, June 4 Litho. *Imperf.*
4202 A1995 50k multicolored 2.00 .80

Aleksander S. Pushkin (1799-1837).

Marshal Type of 1973

Designs: No. 4203, Marshal F. I. Tolbukhin (1894-1949); No. 4204, Admiral I. S. Isakov (1894-1967); No. 4205, Marshal S. M. Budenny (1883-1973).

1974 Engr. *Perf. 12*
4203 A1962 4k olive green .50 .25
4204 A1962 4k indigo .50 .25
4205 A1962 4k slate green .50 .25
Nos. 4203-4205 (3) 1.50 .75

Issued: #4203, 6/5; #4204, 7/18; #4205, 8/20.

Stanislavski and Nemirovich-Danchenko — A1996

1974, June 12 Litho. *Perf. 12*

4211 A1996 10k yel, black & dk red .50 .25

75th anniv. of the Moscow Arts Theater.

Runner, Track, Open Book A1997

1974, June 12 Photo. *Perf. 11½*

4212 A1997 4k multicolored .50 .25

13th Natl. School Spartakiad, Alma-Ata.

Railroad Car A1998

1974, June 12

4213 A1998 4k multicolored 1.00 .25

Egorov Railroad Car Factory, cent.

Victory Monument, Minsk — A1999

No. 4215, Monument & Government House, Kiev.

1974, June 20

4214 A1999 4k violet, black & yel .50 .25
4215 A1999 4k blue, black & yel .50 .25

30th anniversary of liberation of Byelorussia (No. 4214), and of Ukraine (No. 4215).
Issued: #4214, June 20; #4215, July 18.

Automotive Type of 1973

Designs: 2k, GAZ AA truck, 1932. 3k, GAZ 03-30 bus, 1933. 4k, Zis 5 truck, 1933. 14k, Zis 8 bus, 1934. 16k, Zis 101 car, 1936.

1974, June 20 *Perf. 12x11½*

4216 A1968 2k brown & multi .25 .25
4217 A1968 3k multicolored .25 .25
4218 A1968 4k orange & multi .25 .25
4219 A1968 14k multicolored .50 .25
4220 A1968 16k multicolored .60 .25
Nos. 4216-4220 (5) 1.85 1.25

Soviet automotive industry.

Liberation Monument, Poltava — A2000

1974, July 7 *Perf. 11½*

4221 A2000 4k dull red & sepia .50 .25

800th anniversary of city of Poltava.

Nike Monument, Warsaw and Polish Flag — A2001

1974, July 7 Litho. *Perf. 12½x12*

4222 A2001 6k olive & red .50 .25

Polish People's Republic, 30th anniversary.

Mine Layer — A2002

Soviet Warships: 4k, Landing craft. 6k, Anti-submarine destroyer and helicopter. 16k, Anti-submarine cruiser.

Engraved and Photogravure

1974, July 25 *Perf. 11½x12*

4223 A2002 3k multicolored .25 .25
4224 A2002 4k multicolored .70 .25
4225 A2002 6k multicolored 1.00 .25
4226 A2002 16k multicolored 2.00 .25
Nos. 4223-4226 (4) 3.95 1.00

Pentathlon A2003

1974, Aug. 7 Photo. *Perf. 11½*

4227 A2003 16k gold, blue & brown .50 .25

World Pentathlon Championships, Moscow.

Portrait Type of 1973

No. 4228, Dimitri Ulyanov (1874-1943). Soviet official and Lenin's brother. No. 4229, V. Menzhinsky (1874-1934), Soviet official.

1974, Aug. 7 Engr. *Perf. 12½x12*

4228 A1960 4k slate green .50 .25

Litho.

Perf. 12x11½

4229 A1960 4k rose lake .50 .25

Painting Type of 1974

Russian paintings: 4k, Lilac, by W. Kontchalovski. 6k, "Towards the Wind" (sailboats), by E. Kalnins. 10k, "Spring" (girl and landscape), by O. Zardarjan. 16k, Northern Harbor, G. Nissky. 20k, Kirghiz Girl, by S. Chuikov, vert.

Perf. 12x11½, 11½x12

1974, Aug. 20 Litho.

4230 A1986 4k gray & multi .25 .25
4231 A1986 6k gray & multi .25 .25
4232 A1986 10k gray & multi .55 .25
4233 A1986 16k gray & multi .80 .25
4234 A1986 20k gray & multi 1.10 .25
Nos. 4230-4234 (5) 2.95 1.25

Printed in sheets of 18 stamps and 2 labels.

Page of First Russian Primer — A2004

1974, Aug. 20 Photo. *Perf. 11½*

4235 A2004 4k black, red & gold .50 .25

1st printed Russian primer, 400th anniv.

Monument, Russian and Romanian Flags — A2005

1974, Aug. 23

4236 A2005 6k dk blue, red & yel .50 .25

Romania's liberation from Fascist rule, 30th anniversary.

Vitebsk A2006

1974, Sept. 4 Litho. *Perf. 12*

4237 A2006 4k dk car & olive .50 .25

Millennium of city of Vitebsk.

Kirghiz Republic A2007

50th Anniv. of Founding of Republics (Flags, industrial and agricultural themes): No. 4239, Moldavia. No. 4240, Turkmen. No. 4241, Uzbek. No. 4242, Tadzhik.

1974, Sept. 4 *Perf. 11½x11*

4238 A2007 4k vio blue & multi 1.00 .25
4239 A2007 4k maroon & multi 1.00 .25
4240 A2007 4k yellow & multi 1.00 .25
4241 A2007 4k green & multi 1.00 .25
4242 A2007 4k lt blue & multi 1.00 .25
Nos. 4238-4242 (5) 5.00 1.25

Arms and Flag of Bulgaria — A2008

Photogravure and Engraved

1974, Sept. 4 *Perf. 11½*

4243 A2008 6k gold & multi .50 .25

30th anniv. of the Bulgarian revolution.

Arms of DDR and Soviet War Memorial, Treptow A2009

1974, Sept. 4 Photo.

4244 A2009 6k multicolored .50 .25

German Democratic Republic, 25th anniv.

Souvenir Sheet

Soviet Stamps and Exhibition Poster — A2010

1974, Sept. 4 Litho. *Perf. 12x12½*

4245 A2010 50k multicolored *7.50 3.00*

3rd Cong. of the Phil. Soc. of the USSR.

Maly State Theater — A2011

1974, Oct. 3 Photo. *Perf. 11x11½*

4246 A2011 4k red, black & gold .50 .25

150th anniversary of the Lenin Academic Maly State Theater, Moscow.

"Guests from Overseas," by N. K. Roerich — A2012

1974, Oct. 3 Litho. *Perf. 12*

4247 A2012 6k multicolored .50 .25

Nicholas Konstantin Roerich (1874-1947), painter and sponsor of Roerich Pact and Banner of Peace.

UPU Monument, Bern, and Arms of USSR A2013

Development of Postal Service — A2014

UPU Cent.: No. 4248, Ukrainian coat of arms, letters, UPU emblem and headquarters, Bern. No. 4249, Arms of Byelorussia, UPU emblem, letters, stagecoach and rocket.

Photogravure and Engraved

1974, Oct. 9 *Perf. 12x11½*

4248 A2013 10k red & multi .35 .25
4249 A2013 10k red & multi .35 .25
4250 A2013 10k red & multi .35 .25
Nos. 4248-4250 (3) 1.05 .75

Souvenir Sheet
Typo.
Perf. 11½x12

4251 A2014 Sheet of 3 5.00 2.50
a. 30k Jet and UPU emblem 1.25 .75
b. 30k Mail coach, UPU emblem 1.25 .75
c. 40k UPU emblem 1.25 .75

Order of Labor, 1st, 2nd and 3rd Grade A2015

KAMAZ Truck Leaving Kama Plant — A2016

Design: No. 4254, Nurek Hydroelectric Plant.

1974, Oct. 16 Litho. *Perf. 12½x12*
4252 A2015 4k multicolored .65 .25
4253 A2016 4k multicolored .65 .25
4254 A2016 4k multicolored .65 .25
Nos. 4252-4254 (3) 1.95 .75

Space Stations Mars 4-7 over Mars A2017

P. R. Popovitch, Y. P. Artyukhin and Soyuz 14 — A2018

Design: No. 4257, Cosmonauts G. V. Sarafanov and L. S. Demin, Soyuz 15, horiz.

Perf. 12x11½, 11½
1974, Oct. 28 Photo.
4255 A2017 6k multicolored .25 .25
4256 A2018 10k multicolored .40 .25
4257 A2018 10k multicolored .40 .25
Nos. 4255-4257 (3) 1.05 .75

Russian explorations of Mars (6k); flight of Soyuz 14 (No. 4256) and of Soyuz 15, Aug. 26-28 (No. 4257).

Mongolian Flag and Arms A2019

1974, Nov. 14 Photo. *Perf. 11½*
4258 A2019 6k gold & multi .50 .25

Mongolian People's Republic, 50th anniv.

Guards' Ribbon, Estonian Government Building, Tower — A2020

1974, Nov. 14
4259 A2020 4k multicolored .50 .25

Liberation of Estonia, 30th anniversary.

Tanker, Passenger and Cargo Ships — A2021

1974, Nov. 14 Typo. *Perf. 12½x12*
4260 A2021 4k multicolored .50 .25

USSR Merchant Marine, 50th anniversary.

Spasski Tower Clock — A2022

1974, Nov. 14 Litho. *Perf. 12*
4261 A2022 4k multicolored .50 .25

New Year 1975.

The Fishmonger, by Pieters A2023

Paintings: 4k, The Marketplace, by Beuckelaer, 1564, horiz. 10k, A Drink of Lemonade, by Gerard Terborch. 14k, Girl at Work, by Gabriel Metsu. 16k, Saying Grace, by Jean Chardin. 20k, The Spoiled Child, by Jean Greuze. 50k, Self-portrait, by Jacques Louis David.

Perf. 12x12½, 12½x12
1974, Nov. 20 Litho.
4262 A2023 4k bister & multi .25 .25
4263 A2023 6k bister & multi .25 .25
4264 A2023 10k bister & multi .35 .25
4265 A2023 14k bister & multi .50 .25
4266 A2023 16k bister & multi .55 .25
4267 A2023 20k bister & multi .75 .30
Nos. 4262-4267 (6) 2.65 1.55

Souvenir Sheet
Perf. 12
4268 A2023 50k multicolored 2.00 .75

Foreign paintings in Russian museums. Printed in sheets of 16 stamps and 4 labels.

Morning Glory — A2024

Designs: Flora of the USSR.

1974, Nov. 20 *Perf. 12x12½*
4269 A2024 1k red brn & multi .25 .25
4270 A2024 2k green & multi .25 .25
4271 A2024 4k multicolored .25 .25
4272 A2024 10k brown & multi .50 .25
4273 A2024 12k dk blue & multi .55 .25
Nos. 4269-4273 (5) 1.80 1.25

Ivan S. Nikitin (1824-1861), Poet — A2025

1974, Dec. 11 Photo. *Perf. 11½*
4274 A2025 4k gray grn, grn & blk .50 .25

Leningrad Mint — A2026

Photogravure and Engraved
1974, Dec. 11 *Perf. 11*
4275 A2026 6k silver & multi .50 .25

250th anniversary of the Leningrad Mint.

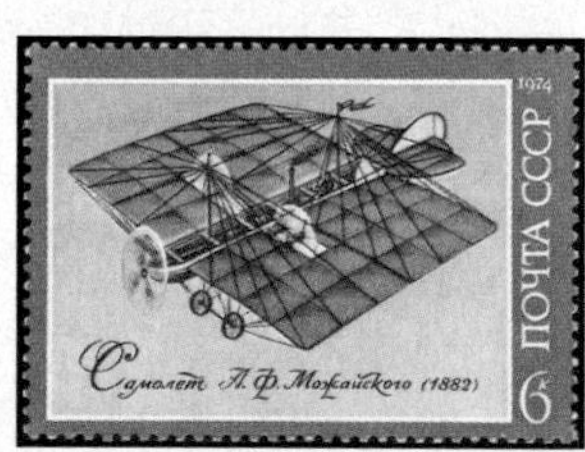

Mozhajsky Plane, 1882 — A2027

Early Russian Aircraft: No. 4277, Grizidubov-N biplane, 1910. No. 4278, Russia-A, 1910. No. 4279, Russian Vityaz (Sikorsky), 1913. No. 4280, Grigorovich flying boat, 1914.

1974, Dec. 25 Photo. *Perf. 11½x12*
4276 A2027 6k olive & multi .60 .25
4277 A2027 6k ultra & multi .60 .25
4278 A2027 6k magenta & multi .60 .25
4279 A2027 6k red & multi .60 .25
4280 A2027 6k brown & multi .60 .25
Nos. 4276-4280 (5) 3.00 1.25

Russian aircraft history, 1882-1914.

Souvenir Sheet

Sports and Sport Buildings, Moscow — A2028

1974, Dec. 25 *Perf. 11½*
4281 A2028 Sheet of 4 1.00 .50
a. 10k Woman gymnast .25 .25
b. 10k Running .25 .25
c. 10k Soccer .25 .25
d. 10k Canoeing .25 .25

Moscow preparing for Summer Olympic Games, 1980.

Rotary Press, Masthead A2029

1975, Jan. 20
4282 A2029 4k multicolored .50 .25

Komsomolskaya Pravda newspaper, 50th anniv.

Masthead and Pioneer Emblems — A2030

1975, Jan. 20
4283 A2030 4k red, blk & silver .50 .25

Pioneers' Pravda newspaper, 50th anniv.

Spartakiad Emblem and Skiers — A2031

1975, Jan. 20
4284 A2031 4k blue & multi .50 .25

8th Winter Spartakiad of USSR Trade Unions.

Games' Emblem, Hockey Player and Skier A2032

1975, Jan. 20
4285 A2032 16k multicolored .50 .25

5th Winter Spartakiad of Friendly Armies, Feb. 23-Mar. 1.

Republic Anniversaries Type of 1970

Design (Hammer-Sickle Emblem and): No. 4286, Landscape and produce.

1975, Jan. 24 Engr. ***Perf. 12x12½***
4286 A1794 4k green .50 .25

50th anniversary of Karakalpak Autonomous Soviet Socialist Republic.

David, by Michelangelo — A2033

Michelangelo, Self-portrait — A2034

Works by Michelangelo: 6k, Squatting Boy. 10k, Rebellious Slave. 14k, The Creation of Adam. 20k, Staircase, Laurentian Library, Florence. 30k, The Last Judgment.

Lithographed and Engraved

1975, Feb. 27 ***Perf. 12½x12***
4296 A2033 4k slate grn & grn .25 .25
4297 A2033 6k red brn & bister .25 .25
4298 A2033 10k slate grn & grn .40 .25
a. Min. sheet, 2 ea #4296-4298 5.00 5.00
4299 A2033 14k red brn & bister .60 .25
4300 A2033 20k slate grn & grn .85 .40
4301 A2033 30k red brn & bister 1.00 .60
a. Min. sheet, 2 ea #4299-4301 4.25 2.00
Nos. 4296-4301 (6) 3.35 2.00

Souvenir Sheet

Perf. 12x11½
4302 A2034 50k gold & multi 4.00 .80

Michelangelo Buonarroti (1475-1564), Italian sculptor, painter and architect. Issued only in the min. sheets of 6.

Mozhajski, Early Plane and Supersonic Jet TU-144 — A2035

1975, Feb. 27 Photo. ***Perf. 12x11½***
4303 A2035 6k violet blue & ocher .50 .25

A. F. Mozhajski (1825-1890), pioneer aircraft designer, birth sesquicentennial.

"Metric System" A2036

1975, Mar. 14 ***Perf. 11½***
4304 A2036 6k blk, vio blue & org .50 .25

Intl. Meter Convention, Paris, 1875, cent.

Spartakiad Emblem and Sports A2037

1975, Mar. 14
4305 A2037 6k red, silver & black .50 .25

6th Summer Spartakiad.

Liberation Monument, Parliament, Arms — A2038

Charles Bridge Towers, Arms and Flags — A2039

1975, Mar. 14
4306 A2038 6k gold & multi .25 .25
4307 A2039 6k gold & multi .25 .25

30th anniv. of liberation from fascism, Hungary (#4306) & Czechoslovakia (#4307).

Flags of France and USSR — A2040

1975, Mar. 25 Litho. ***Perf. 12***
4308 A2040 6k lilac & multi .50 .25

50th anniv. of the establishment of diplomatic relations between France and USSR, 1st foreign recognition of Soviet State.

Yuri A. Gagarin, by L. Kerbel — A2041

A. V. Filipchenko, N.N. Rukavishnikov, Russo-American Space Emblem, Soyuz 16 — A2042

Cosmonauts' Day: 10k, A. A. Gubarev, G. M. Grechko aboard Soyuz 17 & orbital station Salyut 4.

Perf. 11½x12, 12x11½

1975, Mar. 28 Photo.
4309 A2041 6k blue, sil & red .25 .25
4310 A2042 10k blk, blue & red .50 .25
4311 A2042 16k multicolored .75 .25
Nos. 4309-4311 (3) 1.50 .75

Warsaw Treaty Members' Flags — A2043

1975, Apr. 16 Litho. ***Perf. 12***
4312 A2043 6k multicolored .50 .25

Signing of the Warsaw Treaty (Bulgaria, Czechoslovakia, German Democratic Rep., Hungary, Poland, Romania, USSR), 20th anniv.

Lenin on Steps of Winter Palace, by V. G. Zyplakow A2044

1975, Apr. 22 ***Perf. 12x12½***
4313 A2044 4k multicolored .60 .25

105th anniversary of the birth of Lenin.

Communications Emblem and Exhibition Pavilion — A2045

1975, Apr. 22 ***Perf. 11½***
4314 A2045 6k ultra, red & silver .50 .25

International Communications Exhibition, Sokolniki Park, Moscow, May 1975.

Lenin and Red Flag — A2046

Order of Victory — A2047

No. 4316, Eternal Flame and guard. No. 4317, Woman munitions worker. No. 4318, Partisans. No. 4319, Soldier destroying swastika. No. 4320, Soldier with gun and banner.

1975, Apr. 22 Typo. ***Perf. 12***
4315 A2046 4k shown .25 .25
4316 A2046 4k multicolored .25 .25
4317 A2046 4k multicolored .25 .25
4318 A2046 4k multicolored .25 .25
4319 A2046 4k multicolored .25 .25
4320 A2046 4k multicolored .25 .25
Nos. 4315-4320 (6) 1.50 1.50

Souvenir Sheet

Litho., Typo. & Photo.

Imperf
4321 A2047 50k multicolored 2.00 1.00

World War II victory, 30th anniversary.

War Memorial, Berlin-Treptow A2048

1975, Apr. 25 Litho. ***Perf. 12x12½***
4322 A2048 6k buff & multi .50 .25

Souvenir Sheet

4323 A2048 50k dull blue & multi 2.00 .60

Socfilex 75 Intl. Phil. Exhib. honoring 30th anniv. of WWII victory, Moscow, May 8-18.

Soyuz-Apollo Docking Emblem and Painting by Cosmonaut A. A. Leonov — A2049

1975, May 23 Photo. ***Perf. 12x11½***
4324 A2049 20k multicolored .70 .35

Russo-American space cooperation.

Automobile Type of 1973

2k, GAZ-M-l car, 1936. 3k, 5-ton truck, YAG-6, 1936. 4k, ZIZ-16, autobus, 1938. 12k, KIM-10 car, 1940. 16k, GAZ-67B jeep, 1943.

1975, May 23 Photo. ***Perf. 12x11½***
4325 A1968 2k dp org & multi .25 .25
4326 A1968 3k green & multi .25 .25
4327 A1968 4k dk green & multi .25 .25
4328 A1968 12k maroon & multi .30 .25
4329 A1968 16k olive & multi .45 .25
Nos. 4325-4329 (5) 1.50 1.25

Canal, Emblem, Produce — A2050

1975, May 23 ***Perf. 11½***
4330 A2050 6k multicolored .50 .25

9th Intl. Congress on Irrigation and Drainage, Moscow, and International Commission on Irrigation and Drainage, 25th anniv..

Flags and Arms of Poland and USSR, Factories A2051

1975, May 23
4331 A2051 6k multicolored .50 .25

Treaty of Friendship, Cooperation and Mutual Assistance between Poland & USSR, 30th anniv.

Man in Space and Earth A2052

1975, May 23
4332 A2052 6k multicolored .50 .25

First man walking in space, Lt. Col. Alexei Leonov, 10th anniversary.

Yakov M. Sverdlov (1885-1919), Organizer and Early Member of Communist Party — A2053

1975, June 4

4333 A2053 4k multicolored .50 .25

Congress, Emblem, Forest and Field A2054

1975, June 4

4334 A2054 6k multicolored .50 .25

8th International Congress for Conservation of Plants, Moscow.

Symbolic Flower with Plants and Emblem A2055

1975, June 20 Litho. *Perf. 11½*

4335 A2055 6k multicolored .50 .25

12th International Botanical Congress.

Souvenir Sheet

UN Emblem — A2056

1975, June 20 Photo. *Perf. 11½x12*

4336 A2056 50k gold & blue 2.00 1.00

30th anniversary of United Nations.

Globe and Film A2057

1975, June 20 Photo. *Perf. 11½*

4337 A2057 6k multicolored .50 .25

9th Intl. Film Festival, Moscow, 1975.

Soviet and American Astronauts and Flags — A2058

Apollo and Soyuz After Link-up and Earth — A2059

Soyuz Launch A2060

Designs: No. 4340, Spacecraft before link-up, earth and project emblem. 50k, Soviet Mission Control Center.

1975, July 15 Litho. *Perf. 11½*

4338 A2058 10k multicolored .35 .25
4339 A2059 12k multicolored .45 .25
4340 A2059 12k multicolored .45 .25
a. Vert. pair, #4339-4340 1.50 .50
4341 A2060 16k multicolored .75 .40
Nos. 4338-4341 (4) 2.00 1.15

Souvenir Sheet

Photo.

Perf. 12x11½

4342 A2058 50k multicolored 3.00 1.25

Apollo-Soyuz space test project (Russo-American space cooperation), launching, July 15; link-up July 17.

No. 4342 contains one 50x21mm stamp.

See US Nos. 1569-1570.

Sturgeon, Caspian Sea, Oceanexpo 75 Emblem — A2061

Designs (Oceanexpo 75 Emblem and): 4k, Salt-water shell, Black Sea. 6k, Eel, Baltic Sea. 10k, Sea duck, Arctic Sea. 16k, Crab, Far Eastern waters. 20k, Chrisipther (fish), Pacific Ocean.

1975, July 22 Photo. *Perf. 11*

4343 A2061 3k multicolored .25 .25
4344 A2061 4k multicolored .25 .25
4345 A2061 6k green & multi .25 .25
4346 A2061 10k dk blue & multi .65 .30
4347 A2061 16k purple & multi 1.25 .30
4348 A2061 20k multicolored 2.25 .65
Nos. 4343-4348 (6) 4.90 2.00

Souvenir Sheet

Perf. 12x11½

4349 Sheet of 2 2.00 .90
a. A2061 30k Dolphin rising .75 .30
b. A2061 30k Dolphin diving .75 .30

Oceanexpo 75, 1st Intl. Oceanographic Exhib., Okinawa, July 20, 1975-Jan. 1976. No. 4349 contains 55x25mm stamps.

Parade, Red Square, 1941, by K. F. Yuon — A2062

Paintings: 2k, Morning of Industrial Moscow, by Yuon. 6k, Soldiers Inspecting Captured Artillery, by Lansere. 10k, Excavating Metro Tunnel, by Lansere. 16k, Pushkin and His Wife at Court Ball, by Ulyanov, vert. 20k, De Lauriston at Kutuzov's Headquarters, by Ulyanov.

1975, July 22 Litho. *Perf. 12½x11½*

4350 A2062 1k gray & multi .25 .25
4351 A2062 2k gray & multi .25 .25
4352 A2062 6k gray & multi .25 .25
4353 A2062 10k gray & multi .45 .25
4354 A2062 16k gray & multi .85 .25
4355 A2062 20k gray & multi .95 .30
Nos. 4350-4355 (6) 3.00 1.55

Konstantin F. Yuon (1875-1958), Yevgeni Y. Lansere (1875-1946), Nikolai P. Ulyanov (1875-1949).

Nos. 4350-4355 issued in sheets of 16 plus 4 labels.

Finlandia Hall, Map of Europe, Laurel — A2063

1975, Aug. 18 Photo. *Perf. 11½*

4356 A2063 6k brt blue, gold & blk .50 .25

European Security and Cooperation Conference, Helsinki, July 30-Aug. 1. Printed se-tenant with label with quotation by Leonid I. Brezhnev, first secretary of Communist party.

Ciurlionis, Waves and Lighthouse A2064

1975, Aug. 20 Photo. & Engr.

4357 A2064 4k grn, indigo & gold .50 .25

M. K. Ciurlionis, Lithuanian composer, birth centenary.

Avetik Isaakyan, by Martiros Saryan A2065

1975, Aug. 20 Litho. *Perf. 12x12½*

4358 A2065 4k multicolored .50 .25

Isaakyan (1875-1957), Armenian poet.

Jacques Duclos — A2066

1975, Aug. 20 Photo. *Perf. 11½x12*

4359 A2066 6k maroon & silver .50 .25

Duclos (1896-1975), French labor leader.

al-Farabi — A2067

1975, Aug. 20 *Perf. 11½*

4360 A2067 6k grnsh blue, brn & bis .50 .25

Nasr al-Farabi (870?-950), Arab philosopher.

Male Ruffs A2068

1975, Aug. 25 Litho. *Perf. 12½x12*

4361 A2068 1k shown .25 .25
4362 A2068 4k Altai roebuck .25 .25
4363 A2068 6k Siberian marten .25 .25
4364 A2068 10k Old squaw (duck) .40 .25
4365 A2068 16k Badger .55 .25
Nos. 4361-4365 (5) 1.70 1.25

Berezina River and Stolby wildlife reservations, 50th anniversary.

A2069

A2070

Designs: No. 4366, Flags of USSR, North Korea, arms of N. K., Liberation monument, Pyongyang. No. 4367, Flags of USSR, North Viet Nam, arms of N.V., industrial development.

1975, Aug. 28 *Perf. 12*

4366 A2069 6k multicolored .30 .25
4367 A2070 6k multicolored .30 .25

Liberation of North Korea from Japanese occupation (#4366); and establishment of Democratic Republic of Viet Nam (#4367), 30th annivs.

P. Klimuk and V. Sevastyanov, Soyuz 18 and Salyut 4 Docking — A2071

1975, Sept. 12 Photo. *Perf. 12x11½*

4368 A2071 10k ultra, blk & dp org .50 .25

Docking of space ship Soyuz 18 and space station Salyut 4.

S. A. Esenin and Birches A2072

Photogravure and Engraved

1975, Sept. 12 *Perf. 11½*

4369 A2072 6k brown & ocher .50 .25

Sergei A. Esenin (1895-1925), poet.

Standardization Symbols — A2073

1975, Sept. 12 Photo. *Perf. 11½*

4370 A2073 4k red & multi .50 .25

USSR Committee for Standardization of Communications Ministry, 50th anniversary.

Karakul Lamb A2074

1975, Sept. 22 Photo. *Perf. 11½*

4371 A2074 6k black, yel & grn .50 .25

3rd International Symposium on astrakhan production, Samarkand, Sept. 22-27.

Dr. M. P. Konchalovsky A2075

1975, Sept. 30 *Perf. 11½x12*

4372 A2075 4k brown & red .50 .25

Konchalovsky (1875-1942), physician.

Exhibition Emblem — A2076

1975, Sept. 30 *Perf. 11½*

4373 A2076 4k deep blue & red .50 .25

3rd All-Union Youth Phil. Exhib., Yerevan.

IWY Emblem and Rose — A2077

1975, Sept. 30 Litho. *Perf. 12x11½*

4374 A2077 6k multicolored .50 .25

International Women's Year 1975.

Yugoslavian Flag and Parliament A2078

1975, Sept. 30 Photo. *Perf. 11½*

4375 A2078 6k gold, red & blue .50 .25

Republic of Yugoslavia, 30th anniv.

Illustration from 1938 Edition, by V. A. Favorsky — A2079

1975, Oct. 20 Typo. *Perf. 12*

4376 A2079 4k buff, red & black .50 .25

175th anniversary of the 1st edition of the old Russian saga "Slovo o polku Igoreve."

Mikhail Ivanovich Kalinin — A2080

No. 4378, Anatoli Vasilievich Lunacharski.

1975, Oct. 20 Engr. *Perf. 12*

4377 A2080 4k sepia .25 .25
4378 A2080 4k sepia .25 .25

Kalinin (1875-1946), chairman of Central Executive Committee and Presidium of Supreme Soviet; Lunacharski (1875-1933), writer, commissar for education.

Hand Holding Torch and Lenin Quotation — A2081

1975, Oct. 20 **Engr.**

4379 A2081 4k red & olive .50 .25

First Russian Revolution (1905), 70th anniv.

Building Baikal-Amur Railroad — A2082

Novolipetsk Metallurgical Plant — A2083

Nevynomyssk Chemical Plant, Fertilizer Formula — A2084

1975, Oct. 30 Photo. *Perf. 11½*

4380 A2082 4k gold & multi .50 .25
4381 A2083 4k red, gray & sl grn .50 .25
4382 A2084 4k red, blue & silver .50 .25
Nos. 4380-4382 (3) 1.50 .75

58th anniversary of October Revolution.

Bas-relief of Decembrists and "Decembrists at the Senate Square," by D. N. Kardovsky — A2085

1975, Nov. 12 Litho. & Engr.

4383 A2085 4k gray & multi .50 .25

Sesquicentennial of Decembrist rising.

Star and "1976" — A2086

1975, Nov. 12 Litho. *Perf. 12x12½*

4384 A2086 4k green & multi .50 .25

New Year 1976.

Village Street, by F. A. Vasilev A2087

Paintings by Vasilev: 4k, Road in Birch Forest. 6k, After the Thunderstorm. 10k, Swamp, horiz. 12k, In the Crimean Mountains. 16k, Meadow, horiz. 50k, Portrait, by Kramskoi.

Perf. 12x12½, 12½x12

1975, Nov. 25

4385 A2087 2k gray & multi .25 .25
4386 A2087 4k gray & multi .25 .25
4387 A2087 6k gray & multi .25 .25
4388 A2087 10k gray & multi .30 .25
4389 A2087 12k gray & multi .55 .25
4390 A2087 16k gray & multi .60 .25
Nos. 4385-4390 (6) 2.20 1.50

Souvenir Sheet

Perf. 12

4391 A2087 50k gray & multi 2.00 .90

Fedor Aleksandrovich Vasilev (1850-1873), landscape painter. Nos. 4385-4390 printed in sheets of 7 stamps and one label.

Landing Capsule, Venus Surface, Lenin Banner A2088

1975, Dec. 8 Photo. *Perf. 11½*

4392 A2088 10k multicolored .50 .25

Flights of Soviet interplanetary stations Venera 9 and Venera 10.

Gabriel Sundoukian — A2089

1975, Dec. 8 Litho. *Perf. 12*

4393 A2089 4k multicolored .50 .30

Sundoukian (1825-1912), Armenian playright.

Polar Poppies, Taiga A2090

Regional Flowers: 6k, Globeflowers, tundra. 10k, Buttercups, oak forest. 12k, Wood anemones, steppe. 16k, Eminium Lehmannii, desert.

Photogravure and Engraved

1975, Dec. 25 *Perf. 12x11½*

4394 A2090 4k black & multi .25 .25
4395 A2090 6k black & multi .50 .25
4396 A2090 10k black & multi .60 .25
4397 A2090 12k black & multi 1.20 .25
4398 A2090 16k black & multi 1.75 .25
Nos. 4394-4398 (5) 4.30 1.25

A. L. Mints (1895-1974), Academician A2091

1975, Dec. 31 Photo. *Perf. 11½x12*

4399 A2091 4k dp brown & gold .50 .25

Demon, by A. Kochupalov A2092

Paintings: 6k, Vasilisa the Beautiful, by I. Vakurov. 10k, Snow Maiden, by T. Zubkova. 16k, Summer, by K. Kukulieva. 20k, The Fisherman and the Goldfish, by I. Vakurov, horiz.

1975, Dec. 31 Litho. *Perf. 12*

4400 A2092 4k bister & multi .25 .25
4401 A2092 6k bister & multi .35 .25
4402 A2092 10k bister & multi .60 .25
4403 A2092 16k bister & multi .75 .25
4404 A2092 20k bister & multi 1.00 .25
a. Strip of 5, #4400-4404 5.00 1.25

Palekh Art State Museum, Ivanov Region.

Wilhelm Pieck (1876-1960), Pres. of German Democratic Republic — A2093

1976, Jan. 3 Engr. *Perf. 12½x12*

4405 A2093 6k greenish black .50 .25

M. E. Saltykov-Shchedrin, by I.N. Kramskoi — A2094

1976, Jan. 14 Litho. *Perf. 12x12½*

4406 A2094 4k multicolored .50 .25

Mikhail Evgrafovich Saltykov-Shchedrin (1826-1889), writer and revolutionist.

Congress Emblem — A2095

1976, Feb. 2 Photo. *Perf. 11½*

4407 A2095 4k red, gold & mar .50 .25

Souvenir Sheet

Perf. 11½x12

4408 A2095 50k red, gold & mar 1.75 .65

25th Congress of the Communist Party of the Soviet Union.

Lenin Statue, Kiev — A2096

1976, Feb. 2 *Perf. 11½*

4409 A2096 4k red, black & blue .50 .25

Ukrainian Communist Party, 25th Congress.

Ice Hockey, Games' Emblem A2097

Designs (Winter Olympic Games' Emblem and): 4k, Cross-country skiing. 6k, Figure skating, pairs. 10k, Speed skating. 20k, Luge. 50k, Winter Olympic Games' emblem, vert.

1976, Feb. 4 Litho. *Perf. 12½x12*

4410 A2097 2k multicolored .25 .25
4411 A2097 4k multicolored .25 .25
4412 A2097 6k multicolored .25 .25
4413 A2097 10k multicolored .35 .25
4414 A2097 20k multicolored .90 .30
Nos. 4410-4414 (5) 2.00 1.30

Souvenir Sheet

Perf. 12x12½

4415 A2097 50k vio bl, org & red 2.00 1.00

12th Winter Olympic Games, Innsbruck, Austria, Feb. 4-15. No. 4415 contains one stamp; silver and violet blue margin showing designs of Nos. 4410-4414. Size: 90x80mm.

No. 4415 Overprinted in Red

Souvenir Sheet

1976, Mar. 24

4416 A2097 50k multicolored 3.00 2.00

Success of Soviet athletes in 12th Winter Olympic Games. Translation of overprint: "Glory to Soviet Sport! The athletes of the USSR have won 13 gold, 6 silver and 8 bronze medals."

K.E. Voroshilov A2098

1976, Feb. 4 Engr. *Perf. 12*

4417 A2098 4k slate green .50 .25

Kliment Efremovich Voroshilov (1881-1969), pres. of revolutionary military council, commander of Leningrad front, USSR pres. 1953-60. See Nos. 4487-4488, 4545-4548.

Flag over Kremlin Palace of Congresses, Troitskaya Tower A2099

Photogravure on Gold Foil

1976, Feb. 24 *Perf. 12x11½*

4418 A2099 20k gold, grn & red 2.00 1.00

25th Congress of the Communist Party of the Soviet Union (CPSU).

Lenin on Red Square, by P. Vasiliev — A2100

1976, Mar. 10 Litho. *Perf. 12½x12*

4419 A2100 4k yellow & multi .50 .25

106th anniversary of the birth of Lenin.

Atom Symbol and Dubna Institute — A2101

1976, Mar. 10 Photo. *Perf. 11½*

4420 A2101 6k vio bl, red & silver .50 .25

Joint Institute of Nuclear Research, Dubna, 20th anniversary.

Bolshoi Theater — A2102

1976, Mar. 24 Litho. *Perf. 11x11½*

4421 A2102 10k yel, blue & dk brn .50 .25

Bicentenary of Bolshoi Theater.

Back from the Fair, by Konchalovsky — A2103

Paintings by P. P. Konchalovsky: 2k, The Green Glass. 6k, Peaches. 16k, Meat, Game and Vegetables. 20k, Self-portrait, 1943, vert.

1976, Apr. 6 *Perf. 12½x12, 12x12½*

4422 A2103 1k yellow & multi .25 .25
4423 A2103 2k yellow & multi .25 .25
4424 A2103 6k yellow & multi .30 .25
4425 A2103 16k yellow & multi .60 .25
4426 A2103 20k yellow & multi .75 .30
Nos. 4422-4426 (5) 2.15 1.30

Birth centenary of P. P. Konchalovsky.

Vostok, Salyut-Soyuz Link-up — A2104

Yuri A. Gagarin — A2105

Designs: 6k, Meteor and Molniya Satellites, Orbita Ground Communications Center. 10k, Cosmonauts on board Salyut space station and Mars planetary station. 12k, Interkosmos station and Apollo-Soyuz linking.

Lithographed and Engraved

1976, Apr. 12 *Perf. 11½*

4427 A2104 4k multicolored .25 .25
4428 A2104 6k multicolored .35 .25
4429 A2104 10k multicolored .50 .25
4430 A2104 12k multicolored .90 .25
Nos. 4427-4430 (4) 2.00 1.00

Souvenir Sheet

Engr. *Perf. 12*

4431 A2105 50k black 10.00 2.00

1st manned flight in space, 15th anniv.

I. A. Dzhavakhishvili A2106

1976, Apr. 20 Photo. *Perf. 11½x12*

4432 A2106 4k multicolored .50 .25

Dzhavakhishvili (1876-1940), scientist.

Samed Vurgun and Derrick — A2107

1976, Apr. 20 ***Perf. 11½***

4433 A2107 4k multicolored .50 .25

Vurgun (1906-56), natl. poet of Azerbaijan.

1st All-Union Festival of Amateur Artists — A2108

USSR Flag, Worker and Farmer Monument.

1976, May 12 Litho. ***Perf. 11½x12***

4434 A2108 4k multicolored .50 .25

Intl. Federation of Philately, 50th Anniv. — A2109

1976, May 12 Photo. ***Perf. 11½***

4435 A2109 6k FIP Emblem .50 .25

Souvenir Sheet

V. A. Tropinin, Self-portrait — A2110

1976, May 12 Litho. ***Perf. 12***

4436 A2110 50k multicolored 1.50 1.00

Vasily Andreevich Tropinin (1776-1857), painter.

Emblem, Dnieper Bridge — A2111

1976, May 20 Photo. ***Perf. 11½***

4437 A2111 4k Prus blue, gold & blk .50 .25

Bicentenary of Dnepropetrovsk.

Dr. N. N. Burdenko — A2112

1976, May 20 ***Perf. 11½x12***

4438 A2112 4k deep brown & red .50 .25

Burdenko (1876-1946), neurosurgeon.

K. A. Trenev (1876-1945), Playwright A2113

1976, May 20 ***Perf. 11½***

4439 A2113 4k black & multi .50 .25

Automobile Type of 1973

2k, ZIS-110 passenger car. 3k, GAZ-51 Gorky truck. 4k, GAZ-M-20 Pobeda passenger car. 12k, ZIS-150 Moscow Motor Works truck. 16k, ZIS-154 Moscow Motor Works bus.

1976, June 15 Photo. ***Perf. 12x11½***

4440 A1968 2k grnsh bl & multi .25 .25
4441 A1968 3k bister & multi .25 .25
4442 A1968 4k dk blue & multi .25 .25
4443 A1968 12k brown & multi .55 .25
4444 A1968 16k deep car & multi .70 .25
Nos. 4440-4444 (5) 2.00 1.25

Canoeing A2114

USSR National Olympic Committee Emblem and: 6k, Basketball, vert. 10k, Greco-Roman wrestling. 14k, Women's discus, vert. 16k, Target shooting. 50k, Olympic medal, obverse and reverse.

Perf. 12½x12, 12x12½

1976, June 23 Litho.

4445 A2114 4k red & multi .25 .25
4446 A2114 6k red & multi .25 .25
4447 A2114 10k red & multi .35 .25
4448 A2114 14k red & multi .45 .25
4449 A2114 16k red & multi .55 .25
Nos. 4445-4449 (5) 1.85 1.25

Souvenir Sheet

4450 A2114 50k red & multi 3.00 .75

21st Olympic Games, Montreal, Canada, July 17-Aug. 1.

For overprint see No. 4472.

Electric Trains, Overpass A2115

1976, June 23 Photo. ***Perf. 11½***

4451 A2115 4k multicolored 1.00 .25

Electrification of USSR railroads, 50th anniversary.

L. Emilio Recabarren — A2116

1976, July 6

4452 A2116 6k gold, red & blk .50 .25

Luis Emilio Recabarren (1876-1924), founder of Chilean Communist Party.

Ljudmilla Mikhajlovna Pavlichenko (1916-1974), WWII Heroine — A2117

1976, July 6

4453 A2117 4k dp brn, silver & yel .50 .25

Pavel Andreevich Fedotov (1815-1852), Painter A2118

Paintings: 2k, New Partner, by P. A. Fedotov. 4k, The Fastidious Fiancée, horiz. 6k, Aristocrat's Breakfast. 10k, Gamblers, horiz. 16k, The Outing. 50k, Self-portrait.

Perf. 12x12½, 12½x12

1976, July 15 Litho.

4454 A2118 2k black & multi .25 .25
4455 A2118 4k black & multi .25 .25
4456 A2118 6k black & multi .25 .25
4457 A2118 10k black & multi .50 .25
4458 A2118 16k black & multi .75 .25
Nos. 4454-4458 (5) 2.00 1.25

Souvenir Sheet

Perf. 12

4459 A2118 50k multicolored 1.50 .75

Nos. 4454-4458 each printed in sheets of 20 stamps and center label with black commemorative inscription.

S. S. Nametkin — A2119

1976, July 20 Photo. ***Perf. 11½x12***

4460 A2119 4k blue, black & buff .50 .25

Sergei Semenovich Nametkin (1876-1950), organic chemist.

Squacco Heron — A2120

Waterfowl: 3k, Arctic loon. 4k, European coot. 6k, Atlantic puffin. 10k, Slender-billed gull.

1976, Aug. 18 Litho. ***Perf. 12x12½***

4465 A2120 1k dk green & multi .25 .25
4466 A2120 3k ol green & multi .50 .50
4467 A2120 4k orange & multi .80 .80
4468 A2120 6k purple & multi 1.10 1.10
4469 A2120 10k brt blue & multi 2.40 2.40
Nos. 4465-4469 (5) 5.05 5.05

Nature protection.

Peace Dove A2121

1976, Aug. 25 Photo. ***Perf. 11½***

4470 A2121 4k salmon, gold & blue .50 .25

2nd Stockholm appeal and movement to stop arms race.

Resistance Movement Emblem A2122

1976, Aug. 25

4471 A2122 6k dk bl, blk & gold .50 .25

Intl. Resistance Movement Fed., 25th anniv.

No. 4450 Overprinted in Gold

Souvenir Sheet

1976, Aug. 25 Litho. ***Perf. 12½x12***

4472 A2114 50k red & multi 3.00 .75

Victories of Soviet athletes in 21st Olympic Games (47 gold, 43 silver and 35 bronze medals).

Flags of India and USSR — A2123

1976, Sept. 8 ***Perf. 12***

4473 A2123 4k multicolored .50 .25

Friendship and cooperation between USSR and India.

UN, UNESCO Emblems, Open Book — A2124

1976, Sept. 8 Engr. *Perf. 12x12½*

4474 A2124 16k multicolored .50 .30

UNESCO, 30th anniv.

B. V. Volynov, V. M. Zholobov, Star Circling Globe — A2125

1976, Sept. 8 Photo. *Perf. 12x11½*

4475 A2125 10k brn, blue & black .50 .35

Exploits of Soyuz 21 and Salyut space station.

"Industry" — A2126

1976, Sept. 17

4476	A2126	4k shown	.40	.25
4477	A2126	4k Farm industry	.40	.25
4478	A2126	4k Science	.40	.25
4479	A2126	4k Transport & communications	.40	.25
4480	A2126	4k Intl. cooperation	.40	.25
		Nos. 4476-4480 (5)	2.00	1.25

25th Congress of the Communist Party of the Soviet Union.

Victory, by I. I. Vakurov A2127

Paintings: 2k, Plower, by I. I. Golikov, horiz. 4k, Au (woman), by I. V. Markichev. 12k, Firebird, by A. V. Kotuhin, horiz. 14k, Festival, by A. I. Vatagin.

Perf. 12½x12, 12x12½

1976, Sept. 22 Litho.

4481	A2127	2k black & multi	.25	.25
4482	A2127	4k black & multi	.25	.25
4483	A2127	12k black & multi	1.25	.25
4484	A2127	14k black & multi	1.40	.25
4485	A2127	20k black & multi	1.75	.35
		Nos. 4481-4485 (5)	4.90	1.35

Palekh Art State Museum, Ivanov Region.

Shostakovich, Score from 7th Symphony, Leningrad — A2128

1976, Sept. 25 Engr. *Perf. 12½x12*

4486 A2128 6k dk vio blue .50 .25

Dimitri Dimitrievich Shostakovich (1906-1975), composer.

Voroshilov Type of 1976

No. 4487, Zhukov. No. 4488, Rokossovsky.

1976, Oct. 7 Engr. *Perf. 12*

4487	A2098	4k slate green	.25	.25
4488	A2098	4k brown	.25	.25

Marshal Georgi Konstantinovich Zhukov (1896-1974), commander at Stalingrad and Leningrad and Deputy of Supreme Soviet; Marshal Konstantin K. Rokossovsky (1896-1968), commander at Stalingrad.

Intercosmos-14 A2129

10k, India's satellite Arryabata. 12k, Soyuz-19 and Apollo before docking. 16k, French satellite Aureole and Northern Lights. 20k, Docking of Soyuz-Apollo, Intercosmos-14 and Aureole.

1976, Oct. 15 Photo. *Perf. 11½*

4489	A2129	6k black & multi	.25	.25
4490	A2129	10k black & multi	.30	.25
4491	A2129	12k black & multi	.40	.25
4492	A2129	16k black & multi	.45	.25
4493	A2129	20k black & multi	.60	.25
		Nos. 4489-4493 (5)	2.00	1.25

Interkosmos Program for Scientific and Experimental Research.

Vladimir I. Dahl A2130

Photogravure and Engraved

1976, Oct. 15 *Perf. 11½*

4494 A2130 4k green & dk grn .50 .25

Vladimir I. Dahl (1801-1872), physician, writer, compiled Russian Dictionary.

Electric Power Industry A2131

No. 4496, Balashovo textile mill. No. 4497, Laying of drainage pipes and grain elevator.

1976, Oct. 20 Photo. *Perf. 11½*

4495	A2131	4k dk blue & multi	.25	.25
4496	A2131	4k rose brn & multi	.25	.25
4497	A2131	4k slate grn & multi	.25	.25
		Nos. 4495-4497 (3)	.75	.75

59th anniversary of the October Revolution.

Petrov Tumor Research Institute A2132

M. A. Novinski — A2133

1976, Oct. 28

4498 A2132 4k vio blue & gold .50 .25

Perf. 11½x12

4499 A2133 4k dk brn, buff & blue .50 .25

Petrov Tumor Research Institute, 50th anniversary, and 135th birth anniversary of M. A. Novinski, cancer research pioneer.

Aviation Emblem, Gakkel VII, 1911 A2134

Russian Aircraft (Russian Aviation Emblem and): 6k, Gakkel IX, 1912. 12k, I. Steglau No. 2, 1912. 14k, Dybovski's Dolphin, 1913. 16k, Iliya Muromets, 1914.

Lithographed and Engraved

1976, Nov. 4 *Perf. 12x12½*

4500	A2134	3k multicolored	.25	.25
4501	A2134	6k multicolored	.25	.25
4502	A2134	12k multicolored	.50	.35
4503	A2134	14k multicolored	.55	.35
4504	A2134	16k multicolored	.60	.50
		Nos. 4500-4504 (5)	2.15	1.70

See Nos. C109-C120.

Saffron A2135

Flowers of the Caucasus: 2k, Pasqueflowers. 3k, Gentian. 4k, Columbine. 6k, Checkered lily.

1976, Nov. 17 *Perf. 12x11½*

4505	A2135	1k multicolored	.40	.40
4506	A2135	2k multicolored	.40	.40
4507	A2135	3k multicolored	.40	.40
4508	A2135	4k multicolored	.40	.40
4509	A2135	6k multicolored	.40	.40
		Nos. 4505-4509 (5)	2.00	2.00

Spasski Tower Clock, Greeting Card A2136

1976, Nov. 25 Litho. *Perf. 12½x12*

4510 A2136 4k multicolored .50 .25

New Year 1977.

Parable of the Workers in the Vineyard, by Rembrandt — A2137

Rembrandt Paintings in Russian Museums: 6k, Danae. 10k, David and Jonathan, vert. 14k, Holy Family, vert. 20k, Rembrandt's brother Adrian, 1654, vert. 50k, Artaxerxes, Esther and Haman.

Perf. 12½x12, 12x12½

1976, Nov. 25 Photo.

4511	A2137	4k multicolored	.25	.25
4512	A2137	6k multicolored	.25	.25
4513	A2137	10k multicolored	.50	.25
4514	A2137	14k multicolored	.75	.25
4515	A2137	20k multicolored	1.00	.30
		Nos. 4511-4515 (5)	2.75	1.30

Souvenir Sheet

4516 A2137 50k multicolored 6.50 2.00

Rembrandt van Rijn (1606-69). Nos. 4511 and 4515 printed in sheets of 7 stamps and decorative label.

Armed Forces Order A2138

Worker and Farmer, by V. I. Muhina A2139

Marx and Lenin, by Fridman and Belostotsky A2140

Council for Mutual Economic Aid Building A2141

Lenin, 1920 Photograph A2142

Globe and Sputnik Orbits A2143

Designs: 2k, Golden Star and Hammer and Sickle medals. 4k, Coat of arms and "CCCP." 6k, TU-154 plane, globe and airmail envelope. 10k, Order of Labor. 12k, Space exploration medal with Gagarin portrait. 16k, Lenin Prize medal.

1976 Engr. *Perf. 12x12½*

No.	Type	Value	Color	Unused	Used
4517	A2138	1k	greenish black	.25	.25
4518	A2138	2k	brt magenta	.25	.25
4519	A2139	3k	red	.25	.25
4520	A2138	4k	brick red	.25	.25
4521	A2139	6k	Prus blue	.25	.25
4522	A2138	10k	olive green	.45	.25
4523	A2139	12k	violet blue	.50	.25
4524	A2139	16k	deep green	.60	.25
			Perf. 12½x12		
4525	A2140	20k	brown red	.80	.25
4526	A2141	30k	brick red	1.10	.25
4527	A2142	50k	brown	1.90	.25
4528	A2143	1r	dark blue	4.00	.25
			Nos. 4517-4528 (12)	10.60	3.00

Issued: Nos. 4517-4524, 12/17; Nos. 4525-4528, 8/10.

See Nos. 4596-4607. For overprint see No. 5720.

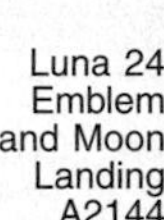

Luna 24 Emblem and Moon Landing A2144

1976, Dec. 17 Photo. *Perf. 11½*

No.	Type	Value	Color	Unused	Used
4531	A2144	10k	multicolored	.50	.25

Moon exploration of automatic station Luna 24.

Icebreaker "Pilot" — A2145

Icebreakers: 6k, Ermak, vert. 10k, Fedor Litke. 16k, Vladimir Ilich, vert. 20k, Krassin.

Perf. 12x11½, 11½x12

1976, Dec. 22 Litho. & Engr.

No.	Type	Value	Color	Unused	Used
4532	A2145	4k	multicolored	.25	.25
4533	A2145	6k	multicolored	.35	.25
4534	A2145	10k	multicolored	.55	.25
4535	A2145	16k	multicolored	.75	.25
4536	A2145	20k	multicolored	1.10	.30
			Nos. 4532-4536 (5)	3.00	1.30

See Nos. 4579-4585.

Soyuz 22 Emblem, Cosmonauts V. F. Bykovsky and V. V. Aksenov — A2146

1976, Dec. 28 Photo. *Perf. 12x11½*

No.	Type	Value	Color	Unused	Used
4537	A2146	10k	multicolored	.50	.25

Soyuz 22 space flight, Sept. 15-23.

Society Emblem — A2147

1977, Jan. 1 *Perf. 11½*

No.	Type	Value	Color	Unused	Used
4538	A2147	4k	multicolored	.50	.25

Red Banner Voluntary Soc., supporting Red Army, Navy & Air Force, 50th anniv.

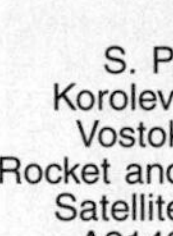

S. P. Korolev, Vostok Rocket and Satellite A2148

1977, Jan. 12

No.	Type	Value	Color	Unused	Used
4539	A2148	4k	multicolored	.50	.25

Sergei Pavlovich Korolev (1907-1966), creator of first Soviet rocket space system.

Globe and Palm A2149

1977, Jan. 12

No.	Type	Value	Color	Unused	Used
4540	A2149	4k	multicolored	.50	.25

World Congress of Peace Loving Forces, Moscow, Jan. 1977.

Sedov and "St. Foka" A2150

1977, Jan. 25 Photo. *Perf. 11½*

No.	Type	Value	Color	Unused	Used
4541	A2150	4k	multicolored	.50	.25

G.Y. Sedov (1877-1914), polar explorer and hydrographer.

Worker and Farmer Monument and Izvestia Front Page — A2151

1977, Jan. 25

No.	Type	Value	Color	Unused	Used
4542	A2151	4k	silver, black & red	.50	.25

60th anniversary of newspaper Izvestia.

Ship Sailing Across the Oceans — A2152

1977, Jan. 25

No.	Type	Value	Color	Unused	Used
4543	A2152	6k	deep blue & gold	.50	.25

24th Intl. Navigation Cong., Leningrad.

Congress Hall and Troitskaya Tower, Kremlin — A2153

1977, Feb. 9 Photo. *Perf. 11½*

No.	Type	Value	Color	Unused	Used
4544	A2153	4k	red, gold & black	.50	.25

16th Congress of USSR Trade Unions.

Voroshilov Type of 1976

Marshals of the Soviet Union: No. 4545, Leonid A. Govorov (1897-1955). No. 4546, Ivan S. Koniev. No. 4547, K. A. Merezhkov. No. 4548, W. D. Sokolovsky.

1977 Engr. *Perf. 12*

No.	Type	Value	Color	Unused	Used
4545	A2098	4k	brown	.40	.25
4546	A2098	4k	slate green	.40	.25
4547	A2098	4k	brown	.40	.25
4548	A2098	4k	black	.40	.25
			Nos. 4545-4548 (4)	1.60	1.00

Issue dates: #4545, Feb. 9; others, June 7.

Academy, Crest, Anchor and Ribbons A2155

Photogravure and Engraved

1977, Feb. 9 *Perf. 11½*

No.	Type	Value	Color	Unused	Used
4549	A2155	6k	multicolored	.50	.25

A. A. Grechko Naval Academy, Leningrad, sesquicentennial.

Jeanne Labourbe — A2156

1977, Feb. 25 Photo. *Perf. 11½*

No.	Type	Value	Color	Unused	Used
4550	A2156	4k	multicolored	.50	.25

Jeanne Labourbe (1877-1919), leader of French communists in Moscow.

Queen and Knights — A2157

1977, Feb. 25

No.	Type	Value	Color	Unused	Used
4551	A2157	6k	multicolored	.50	.25

4th European Chess Championships.

Cosmonauts V. D. Zudov and V. I. Rozhdestvensky — A2158

1977, Feb. 25 *Perf. 12x11½*

No.	Type	Value	Color	Unused	Used
4552	A2158	10k	multicolored	.50	.25

Soyuz 23 space flight, Oct. 14-16, 1976.

A. S. Novikov-Priboy (1877-1944), Writer — A2159

1977, Mar. 16 Photo. *Perf. 11½*

No.	Type	Value	Color	Unused	Used
4553	A2159	4k	multicolored	.50	.25

Welcome, by M. N. Soloninkin A2160

Folk Tale Paintings from Fedoskino Artists' Colony: 6k, Along the Street, by V. D. Antonov, horiz. 10k, Northern Song, by J. V. Karapaev. 12k, Tale of Tsar Saltan, by A. I. Kozlov. 14k, Summer Troika, by V. A. Nalimov, horiz. 16k, Red Flower, by V. D. Lipitsky.

Perf. 12x12½, 12½x12

1977, Mar. 16 Litho.

No.	Type	Value	Color	Unused	Used
4554	A2160	4k	black & multi	.45	.25
4555	A2160	6k	black & multi	.45	.25
4556	A2160	10k	black & multi	.65	.25
4557	A2160	12k	black & multi	.95	.25
4558	A2160	14k	black & multi	1.10	.25
4559	A2160	16k	black & multi	1.40	.30
			Nos. 4554-4559 (6)	5.00	1.55

Lenin on Red Square, by K.V. Filatov — A2161

1977, Apr. 12 *Perf. 12½x11½*

No.	Type	Value	Color	Unused	Used
4560	A2161	4k	multicolored	.50	.25

107th anniversary of the birth of Lenin.

Electricity Congress Emblem A2162

1977, Apr. 12 Photo. *Perf. 11½*

No.	Type	Value	Color	Unused	Used
4561	A2162	6k	blue, red & gray	.50	.25

World Electricity Congress, Moscow 1977.

Yuri Gagarin, Sputnik, Soyuz and Salyut — A2163

1977, Apr. 12 *Perf. 12x11½*

No.	Type	Value	Color	Unused	Used
4562	A2163	6k	multicolored	.50	.25

Cosmonauts' Day.

N. I. Vavilov — A2164

1977, Apr. 26 Photo. *Perf. 11½*

No.	Type	Value	Color	Unused	Used
4563	A2164	4k	multicolored	.50	.25

Vavilov (1887-1943), agricultural geneticist.

Feliks E. Dzerzhinski A2165

1977, May 12 Engr. *Perf. 12½x12*
4564 A2165 4k black .50 .25

Feliks E. Dzerzhinski (1877-1926), organizer and head of secret police (OGPU).

Saxifraga Sibirica — A2166

Siberian Flowers: 3k, Dianthus repena. 4k, Novosieversia glactalis. 6k, Cerasticum maxinicem. 16k, Golden rhododendron.

1977, May 12 Litho. *Perf. 12x12½*
4565 A2166 2k multicolored .25 .25
4566 A2166 3k multicolored .25 .25
4567 A2166 4k multicolored .25 .25
4568 A2166 6k multicolored .35 .25
4569 A2166 16k multicolored .90 .25
Nos. 4565-4569 (5) 2.00 1.25

V. V. Gorbatko, Y. N. Glazkov, Soyuz 24 Rocket A2167

1977, May 16 Photo. *Perf. 12x11½*
4570 A2167 10k multicolored .50 .25

Space explorations of cosmonauts on Salyut 5 orbital station, launched with Soyuz 24 rocket.

Film and Globe — A2168

1977, June 21 Photo. *Perf. 11½*
4571 A2168 6k multicolored .50 .25

10th Intl. Film Festival, Moscow 1977.

Lion Hunt, by Rubens — A2169

Rubens Paintings, Hermitage, Leningrad: 4k, Lady in Waiting, vert. 10k, Workers in Quarry. 12k, Alliance of Water and Earth, vert. 20k, Landscape with Rainbow. 50k, Self-portrait.

Perf. 12x12½, 12½x12
1977, June 24 Litho.
4572 A2169 4k yellow & multi .30 .25
4573 A2169 6k yellow & multi .30 .25
4574 A2169 10k yellow & multi .60 .25
4575 A2169 12k yellow & multi .75 .25
4576 A2169 20k yellow & multi 1.00 .30
Nos. 4572-4576 (5) 2.95 1.30

Souvenir Sheet

4577 A2169 50k yellow & multi 2.00 .60

Peter Paul Rubens (1577-1640), painter. Sheets of No. 4575 contain 2 labels with commemorative inscriptions and Atlas statue from Hermitage entrance.

Souvenir Sheet

Judith, by Giorgione — A2170

1977, July 15 Litho. *Perf. 12x12½*
4578 A2170 50k multicolored 2.00 1.00

Il Giorgione (1478-1511), Venetian painter.

Icebreaker Type of 1976

Icebreakers: 4k, Aleksandr Sibiryakov. 6k, Georgi Sedov. 10k, Sadko. 12k, Dezhnev. 14k, Siberia. 16k, Lena. 20k, Amguyema.

Lithographed and Engraved
1977, July 27 *Perf. 12x11½*
4579 A2145 4k multicolored .25 .25
4580 A2145 6k multicolored .40 .25
4581 A2145 10k multicolored .75 .25
4582 A2145 12k multicolored 1.00 .25
4583 A2145 14k multicolored 1.25 .25
4584 A2145 16k multicolored 1.50 .35
4585 A2145 20k multicolored 1.75 .45
Nos. 4579-4585 (7) 6.90 2.05

Souvenir Sheet

Icebreaker Arctica — A2171

Lithographed and Engraved
1977, Sept. 15 *Perf. 12½x12*
4586 A2171 50k multicolored 5.00 3.00

Arctica, first ship to travel from Murmansk to North Pole, Aug. 9-17.

View and Arms of Stavropol — A2172

1977, Aug. 16 Photo. *Perf. 11½*
4587 A2172 6k multicolored .50 .25

200th anniversary of Stavropol.

Stamps and Exhibition Emblem — A2173

1977, Aug. 16
4588 A2173 4k multicolored .50 .25

October Revolution Anniversary Philatelic Exhibition, Moscow.

Yuri A. Gagarin and Spacecraft — A2174

No. 4590, Alexei Leonov floating in space. No. 4591, Orbiting space station, cosmonauts at control panel.

Nos. 4592-4594, Various spacecraft: No. 4592, International cooperation for space research. No. 4593, Interplanetary flights. No. 4594, Exploring earth's atmosphere.

50k, "XX," laurel, symbolic Sputnik with Red Star.

1977, Oct. 4 Photo. *Perf. 11½x12*
4589 A2174 10k sepia & multi .25 .25
4590 A2174 10k gray & multi .25 .25
4591 A2174 10k gray green & multi .25 .25
4592 A2174 20k green & multi .45 .35
4593 A2174 20k vio bl & multi .45 .35
4594 A2174 20k bister & multi .45 .35
Nos. 4589-4594 (6) 2.10 1.80

Souvenir Sheet

4595 A2174 50k claret & gold *5.00 5.00*

20th anniv. of space research. No. 4595 contains one stamp, size: 22x32mm.

Types of 1976

Designs: 15k, Communications emblem and globes; others as before.

1977-78 Litho. *Perf. 12x12½*
4596 A2138 1k olive green .25 .25
4597 A2138 2k lilac rose .25 .25
4598 A2139 3k brick red .25 .25
4599 A2138 4k vermilion .25 .25
4600 A2139 6k Prus blue .30 .25
4601 A2138 10k gray green .50 .25
4602 A2139 12k vio blue .65 .25
4602A A2139 15k blue ('78) 5.00 .25
4603 A2139 16k slate green .80 .25

Perf. 12½x12
4604 A2140 20k brown red .80 .25
4605 A2141 30k dull brick red 1.10 .25
4606 A2142 50k brown 1.25 .25
4607 A2143 1r dark blue 3.75 .25
Nos. 4596-4607 (13) 15.15 3.25

Nos. 4596-4602A, 4604-4607 were printed on dull and shiny paper.

For overprint see No. 5720. For surcharges see Uzbekistan Nos. 16-17, 23, 27-29, 61A.

Souvenir Sheet

Bas-relief, 12th Century, Cathedral of St. Dimitri, Vladimir — A2175

6k, Necklace, Ryazan excavations, 12th cent. 10k, Mask, Cathedral of the Nativity, Suzdal, 13th cent. 12k, Archangel Michael, 15th cent. icon. 16k, Chalice by Ivan Fomin, 1449. 20k, St. Basil's Cathedral, Moscow, 16th cent.

1977, Oct. 12 Litho. *Perf. 12*
4608 Sheet of 6 3.00 1.25
a. A2175 4k gold & black .20
b. A2175 6k gold & multi .20
c. A2175 10k gold & multi .35
d. A2175 12k gold & multi .45
e. A2175 16k gold & multi .50
f. A2175 20k gold & multi .60

Masterpieces of old Russian culture.

Fir, Snowflake, Molniya Satellite — A2176

1977, Oct. 12 *Perf. 12x12½*
4609 A2176 4k multicolored 1.00 .25

New Year 1978.

Cruiser Aurora and Torch A2177

60th Anniversary of Revolution Medal — A2178

60th Anniv. of October Revolution: No. 4611, Lenin speaking at Finland Station (monument), 1917. No. 4612, 1917 Peace Decree, Brezhnev's book about Lenin. No. 4613, Kremlin tower with star and fireworks.

1977, Oct. 26 Photo. *Perf. 12x11½*
4610 A2177 4k gold, red & blk .25 .25
4611 A2177 4k gold, red & blk .25 .25
4612 A2177 4k gold, red & blk .25 .25
4613 A2177 4k gold, red & blk .25 .25
Nos. 4610-4613 (4) 1.00 1.00

Souvenir Sheet
Perf. 11½
4614 A2178 30k gold, red & blk 1.50 .60

Flag of USSR, Constitution (Book) with Coat of Arms — A2179

Designs: No. 4616, Red banner, people and cover of constitution. 50k, Constitution, Kremlin and olive branch.

1977, Oct. 31 Litho. *Perf. 12½x12*
4615 A2179 4k red, black & yel .25 .25
4616 A2179 4k red, black & yel .25 .25

Souvenir Sheet
Perf. 11½x12½
Lithographed and Embossed

4617 A2179 50k red, gold & yel 2.00 1.00

Adoption of new constitution. No. 4617 contains one 70x50mm stamp.

Souvenir Sheet

Leonid Brezhnev — A2180

Lithographed and Embossed

1977, Nov. 2 ***Perf. 11½x12***
4618 A2180 50k gold & multi 4.00 1.00

Adoption of new constitution, General Secretary Brezhnev, chairman of Constitution Commission.

Postal Official and Postal Code — A2181

Mail Processing (Woman Postal Official and): No. 4620, Mail collection and Moskvich 430 car. No. 4621, Automatic letter sorting machine. No. 4622, Mail transport by truck, train, ship and planes. No. 4623, Mail delivery in city and country.

Lithographed and Engraved

1977, Nov. 16 ***Perf. 12½x12***
4619 A2181 4k multicolored .35 .25
4620 A2181 4k multicolored .35 .25
4621 A2181 4k multicolored .35 .25
4622 A2181 4k multicolored .35 .25
4623 A2181 4k multicolored .35 .25
Nos. 4619-4623 (5) 1.75 1.25

Capital, Asoka Pillar, Red Fort — A2182

1977, Dec. 14 **Photo.** ***Perf. 11½***
4624 A2182 6k maroon, gold & red .60 .25

30th anniversary of India's independence.

Proclamation Monument, Charkov A2183

1977, Dec. 14 **Litho.** ***Perf. 12x12½***
4625 A2183 6k multicolored .50 .25

60th anniv. of Soviet power in the Ukraine.

Lebetina Viper — A2184

Protected Fauna: 1k to 12k, Venomous snakes, useful for medicinal purposes. 16k, Polar bear and cub. 20k, Walrus and calf. 30k, Tiger and cub.

Photogravure and Engraved

1977, Dec. 16 ***Perf. 11½x12***
4626 A2184 1k black & multi .25 .25
4627 A2184 4k black & multi .25 .25
4628 A2184 6k black & multi .25 .25
4629 A2184 10k black & multi .35 .25
4630 A2184 12k black & multi .45 .25
4631 A2184 16k black & multi .55 .25
4632 A2184 20k black & multi .75 .25
4633 A2184 30k black & multi 1.00 .35
Nos. 4626-4633 (8) 3.85 2.10

Wheat, Combine, Silos — A2185

1978, Jan. 27 **Photo.** ***Perf. 11½***
4634 A2185 4k multicolored .50 .25

Gigant collective grain farm, Rostov Region, 50th anniversary.

Congress Palace, Spasski Tower — A2186

1978, Jan. 27 **Litho.** ***Perf. 12x12½***
4635 A2186 4k multicolored .50 .25

Young Communist League, Lenin's Komsomol, 60th anniv. and its 25th Cong.

Liberation Obelisk, Emblem, Dove — A2187

1978, Jan. 27 **Photo.** ***Perf. 11½***
4636 A2187 6k multicolored .50 .25

8th Congress of International Federation of Resistance Fighters, Minsk, Belorussia.

Soldiers Leaving for the Front — A2188

Designs: No. 4638, Defenders of Moscow Monument, Lenin banner. No. 4639, Soldier as defender of the people.

1978, Feb. 21 **Litho.** ***Perf. 12½x12***
4637 A2188 4k red & multi .50 .25
4638 A2188 4k red & multi .50 .25
4639 A2188 4k red & multi .50 .25
Nos. 4637-4639 (3) 1.50 .75

60th anniversary of USSR Military forces.

Celebration in Village — A2189

Kustodiev Paintings: 6k, Shrovetide (winter landscape). 10k, Morning, by Kustodiev. 12k, Merchant's Wife Drinking Tea. 20k, Bolshevik. 50k, Self-portrait, vert.

1978, Mar. 3 ***Perf. 11½***
Size: 70x33mm
4640 A2189 4k lilac & multi .25 .25
4641 A2189 6k lilac & multi .30 .25

Size: 47x32mm
Perf. 12½x12
4642 A2189 10k lilac & multi .50 .25
4643 A2189 12k lilac & multi .65 .25
4644 A2189 20k lilac & multi .85 .25
Nos. 4640-4644 (5) 2.55 1.25

Souvenir Sheet
Perf. 11½x12½
4644A A2189 50k lilac & multi 2.00 .75

Boris Mikhailovich Kustodiev (1878-1927), painter. Nos. 4640-4644 have se-tenant label showing museum where painting is kept. No. 4644A has label giving short biography.

Docking in Space, Intercosmos Emblem A2190

Designs: 6k, Rocket, Soviet Cosmonaut Aleksei Gubarev and Czechoslovak Capt. Vladimir Remek on launching pad. 32k, Parachute, helicopter, Intercosmos emblem, USSR and Czechoslovakian flags.

1978, Mar. 10 **Litho.** ***Perf. 12x12½***
4645 A2190 6k multicolored .25 .25
4646 A2190 15k multicolored .60 .25
4647 A2190 32k multicolored 1.20 .40
Nos. 4645-4647 (3) 2.05 .90

Intercosmos, Soviet-Czechoslovak cooperative space program.

Festival Emblem — A2191

1978, Mar. 17 **Litho.** ***Perf. 12x12½***
4648 A2191 4k blue & multi .50 .25

11th Youth & Students' Cong., Havana.

Tulip, Bolshoi Theater A2192

Moscow Flowers: 2k, Rose "Moscow morning" and Lomonosov University. 4k, Dahlia "Red Star" and Spasski Tower. 10k, Gladiolus "Moscovite" and VDNH Building. 12k, Ilich anniversary iris and Lenin Central Museum.

1978, Mar. 17 ***Perf. 12½x12***
4649 A2192 1k multicolored .40 .25
4650 A2192 2k multicolored .40 .25
4651 A2192 4k multicolored .40 .25
4652 A2192 10k multicolored .40 .25
4653 A2192 12k multicolored .40 .25
Nos. 4649-4653 (5) 2.00 1.25

IMCO Emblem and Waves — A2193

1978, Mar. 17 **Litho.** ***Perf. 12x12½***
4654 A2193 6k multicolored .50 .25

Intergovernmental Maritime Consultative Org., 20th anniv., and World Maritime Day.

Spaceship, Orbits of Salyut 5, Soyuz 26 and 27 — A2194

1978, Apr. 12 **Photo.** ***Perf. 12***
4655 A2194 6k blue, dk blue & gold .50 .25

Cosmonauts' Day, Apr. 12.

World Federation of Trade Unions Emblem — A2195

1978, Apr. 16 ***Perf. 12***
4656 A2195 6k multicolored .50 .25

9th World Trade Union Congress, Prague.

2-2-0 Locomotive, 1845, Petersburg and Moscow Stations — A2196

Locomotives: 1k, 1st Russian model by E. A. and M. W. Cherepanov, vert. 2k, 1-3-0 freight, 1845. 16k, Aleksandrov 0-3-0, 1863. 20k, 2-2-0 passenger and Sergievsk Pustyn platform, 1863.

1978, Apr. 20 **Litho.** ***Perf. 11½***
4657 A2196 1k orange & multi .25 .25
4658 A2196 2k ultra & multi .25 .25
4659 A2196 3k yellow & multi .30 .25

4660 A2196 16k green & multi 1.20 .25
4661 A2196 20k rose & multi 1.00 .25
Nos. 4657-4661 (5) 3.00 1.25

Souvenir Sheet

Lenin, by V. A. Serov — A2197

1978, Apr. 22 ***Perf. 12x12½***
4662 A2197 50k multicolored 2.25 .75

108th anniversary of the birth of Lenin.

A2198

No. 4663, Soyuz and Salyut 6 docking in space. No. 4664, Y. V. Romanenko and G. M. Grechko.

1978, June 15 ***Perf. 12***
4663 15k multicolored .40 .25
4664 15k multicolored .40 .25
a. A2198 Pair, #4663-4664 1.00 .40

Photographic survey and telescopic observations of stars by crews of Soyuz 26, Soyuz 27 and Soyuz 28, Dec. 10, 1977-Mar. 16, 1978. Nos. 4663-4664 printed se-tenant with label showing schematic pictures of various experiments.

Space Meteorology, Rockets, Spaceship, Earth — A2200

No. 4665, Natural resources of earth and Soyuz. No. 4667, Space communications, "Orbita" Station and Molnyia satellite. No. 4668, Man, earth and Vostok. 50k, Study of magnetosphere, Prognoz over earth.

1978, June 23 ***Perf. 12x12½***
4665 A2200 10k green & multi .50 .25
4666 A2200 10k blue & multi .50 .25
4667 A2200 10k violet & multi .50 .25
4668 A2200 10k rose lil & multi .50 .25
Nos. 4665-4668 (4) 2.00 1.00

Souvenir Sheet

Perf. 11½x12½

4669 A2200 50k multicolored 2.00 .75

Space explorations of the Intercosmos program. #4669 contains one 36x51mm stamp.

Soyuz Rocket on Carrier — A2201

Designs (Flags of USSR and Poland, Intercosmos Emblem): 15k, Crystal, spaceship (Sirena, experimental crystallogenesis in space). 32k, Research ship "Cosmonaut Vladimir Komarov," spaceship, world map and paths of Salyut 6, Soyuz 29-30.

1978, **Litho.** ***Perf. 12½x12***
4670 A2201 6k multicolored .25 .25
4671 A2201 15k multicolored .40 .25
4672 A2201 32k multicolored .80 .40
Nos. 4670-4672 (3) 1.45 .90

Intercosmos, Soviet-Polish cooperative space program. Issued: 6k, 6/28; 15k, 6/30; 32k, 7/5.

Lenin, Awards Received by Komsomol A2202

Kamaz Car, Train, Bridge, Hammer and Sickle — A2203

1978, July 5 ***Perf. 12x12½***
4673 A2202 4k multicolored .25 .25
4674 A2203 4k multicolored .25 .25

Leninist Young Communist League (Komsomol), 60th anniv. (#4673); Komsomol's participation in 5-year plan (#4674).

For overprint see No. 4703.

M. V. Zaharov (1898-1972), Marshal of the Soviet Union — A2204

1978, July 5 **Engr.** ***Perf. 12***
4675 A2204 4k sepia .50 .25

Torch, Flags of Participants A2205

1978, July 25 **Litho.** ***Perf. 12x12½***
4676 A2205 4k multicolored .50 .25

Construction of Soyuz gas-pipeline (Friendship Line), Orenburg. Flags of participating countries shown: Bulgaria, Hungary, German Democratic Republic, Poland, Romania, USSR, Czechoslovakia.

Dr. William Harvey (1578-1657), Discoverer of Blood Circulation — A2206

1978, July 25 ***Perf. 12***
4677 A2206 6k blue, blk & dp grn .50 .25

Nikolai Gavilovich Chernyshevsky (1828-1889), Revolutionary — A2207

1978, July 30 **Engr.** ***Perf. 12x12½***
4678 A2207 4k brown, *yellow* .50 .25

Whitewinged Petrel A2208

Antarctic Fauna: 1k, Crested penguin, horiz. 4k, Emperor penguin and chick. 6k, White-blooded pikes. 10k, Sea elephant, horiz.

Perf. 12x11½, 11½x12

1978, July 30 **Litho.**
4679 A2208 1k multicolored .25 .25
4680 A2208 3k multicolored .30 .25
4681 A2208 4k multicolored .75 .25
4682 A2208 6k multicolored .75 .25
4683 A2208 10k multicolored 1.50 .25
Nos. 4679-4683 (5) 3.55 1.25

The Red Horse, by Petrov-Votkin — A2209

Paintings by Petrov-Votkin: 6k, Mother and Child, Petrograd, 1918. 10k, Death of the Commissar. 12k, Still-life with Fruit. 16k, Still-life with Teapot and Flowers. 50k, Self-portrait, 1918, vert.

1978, Aug. 16 **Litho.** ***Perf. 12½x12***
4684 A2209 4k silver & multi .25 .25
4685 A2209 6k silver & multi .35 .25
4686 A2209 10k silver & multi .55 .25
4687 A2209 12k silver & multi .85 .25
4688 A2209 16k silver & multi 1.00 .25
Nos. 4684-4688 (5) 3.00 1.25

Souvenir Sheet

Perf. 11½x12

4689 A2209 50k silver & multi 1.50 .75

Kozma Sergeevich Petrov-Votkin (1878-1939), painter. Nos. 4684-4688 have se-tenant labels. No. 4689 has label the size of stamp.

Soyuz 31 in Shop, Intercosmos Emblem, USSR and DDR Flags A2210

Designs (Intercosmos Emblem, USSR and German Democratic Republic Flags and): 15k, Pamir Mountains photographed from space; Salyut 6, Soyuz 29 and 31 complex and spectrum. 32k, Soyuz 31 docking, photographed from Salyut 6.

1978 **Litho.** ***Perf. 12x12½***
4690 A2210 6k multicolored .25 .25
4691 A2210 15k multicolored .40 .25
4692 A2210 32k multicolored 1.00 .45
Nos. 4690-4692 (3) 1.65 .95

Intercosmos, Soviet-East German cooperative space program.

Issued: 6k, 8/27; 15k, 8/31; 32k, 9/3.

PRAGA '78 Emblem, Plane, Radar, Spaceship A2211

Photogravure and Engraved

1978, Aug. 29 ***Perf. 11½***
4693 A2211 6k multicolored .50 .25

PRAGA '78 International Philatelic Exhibition, Prague, Sept. 8-17.

Leo Tolstoi (1828-1910), Novelist and Philosopher A2212

1978, Sept. 7 **Engr.** ***Perf. 12x12½***
4694 A2212 4k slate green 1.40 .90

Stag, Conference Emblem — A2213

1978 **Photo.** ***Perf. 11½***
4695 A2213 4k multicolored .50 .25

14th General Assembly of the Society for Wildlife Preservation, Ashkhabad.

Bronze Figure, Erebuni, 8th Century A2214

Armenian Architecture: 6k, Etchmiadzin Cathedral, 4th century. 10k, Stone crosses, Dzaghkatzor, 13th century. 12k, Library, Erevan, horiz. 16k, Lenin statue, Lenin Square, Erevan, horiz.

1978 Litho. *Perf. 12x12½, 12½x12*

4696	A2214	4k multicolored	.25	.25
4697	A2214	6k multicolored	.25	.25
4698	A2214	10k multicolored	.30	.25
4699	A2214	12k multicolored	.40	.25
4700	A2214	16k multicolored	.50	.25
		Nos. 4696-4700 (5)	1.70	1.25

Issued: 4k, 10k, 16k, 9/12; others, 10/14.

Memorial, Messina, Russian Warships A2215

1978, Sept. 12 Photo. *Perf. 11½*
4701 A2215 6k multicolored .50 .25

70th anniversary of aid given by Russian sailors during Messina earthquake.

Communications Emblem, Ostankino TV Tower — A2216

1978, Sept. 20 Photo. *Perf. 11½*
4702 A2216 4k multicolored .50 .25

Organization for Communication Cooperation of Socialist Countries, 20th anniv.

No. 4673 Overprinted

1978, Sept. 20 Litho. *Perf. 12x12½*
4703 A2202 4k multicolored 2.00 .70

Philatelic Exhibition for the Leninist Young Communist League.

Souvenir Sheet

Diana, by Paolo Veronese — A2217

1978, Sept. 28 Litho. *Perf. 12x11½*
4704 A2217 50k multicolored 2.00 1.00

Veronese (1528-88), Italian painter.

Souvenir Sheet

Kremlin, Moscow — A2218

Lithographed and Embossed
1978, Oct. 7 *Perf. 11½x12*
4705 A2218 30k gold & multi 2.00 .65

Russian Constitution, 1st anniversary.

Stepan Georgevich Shaumyan (1878-1918), Communist Party Functionary A2219

1978, Oct. 11 Engr. *Perf. 12½x12*
4706 A2219 4k slate green .50 .25

Ferry, Russian and Bulgarian Colors — A2220

1978, Oct. 14 Photo. *Perf. 11½*
4707 A2220 6k multicolored .50 .25

Opening of Ilychovsk-Varna Ferry.

Hammer and Sickle, Flags — A2221

1978, Oct. 26 Photo. *Perf. 11½*
4708 A2221 4k gold & multi .50 .25

61st anniversary of October Revolution.

Silver Gilt Cup, Novgorod, 12th Century — A2222

Old Russian Art: 10k, Pokrowna Nerli Church, 12th century, vert. 12k, St. George Slaying the Dragon, icon, Novgorod, 15th century, vert. 16k, The Czar, cannon, 1586.

Perf. 12½x12, 12x12½
1978, Nov. 28 Litho.

4709	A2222	6k multicolored	.25	.25
4710	A2222	10k multicolored	.45	.25
4711	A2222	12k multicolored	.50	.25
4712	A2222	16k multicolored	.75	.25
		Nos. 4709-4712 (4)	1.95	1.00

Oncology Institute, Emblem — A2223

1978, Dec. 1 Photo. *Perf. 11½*
4713 A2223 4k multicolored .50 .25

P.A. Herzen Tumor Institute, 75th anniv.

Savior Tower, Kremlin — A2224

1978, Dec. 20 Litho. *Perf. 12x12½*
4714 A2224 4k silver, blue & red .50 .25

New Year 1979.

Nestor Pechersky, Chronicler, c. 885 — A2225

History of Postal Service: 6k, Birch bark letter and stylus. 10k, Messenger with trumpet and staff, from 14th century Psalm book. 12k, Winter traffic, from 16th century book by Sigizmund Gerberstein. 16k, Prikaz post office, from 17th century icon.

Lithographed and Engraved
1978, Dec. 20 *Perf. 12½x12*

4715	A2225	4k multicolored	.25	.25
4716	A2225	6k multicolored	.25	.25
4717	A2225	10k multicolored	.50	.25
4718	A2225	12k multicolored	.55	.25
4719	A2225	16k multicolored	.65	.25
		Nos. 4715-4719 (5)	2.20	1.25

Kovalenok and Ivanchenkov, Salyut 6-Soyuz — A2226

1978, Dec. 20 Photo. *Perf. 11½x12*
4720 A2226 10k multicolored .50 .25

Cosmonauts V. V. Kovalenok and A. S. Ivanchenkov spent 140 days in space, June 15-Nov. 2, 1978.

Vasilii Pronchishchev — A2227

Icebreakers: 6k, Captain Belousov, 1954, vert. 10k, Moscow. 12k, Admiral Makarov, 1974. 16k, Lenin, 1959, vert. 20k, Nuclear-powered Arctica.

Perf. 11½x12, 12x11½
1978, Dec. 20 Photo. & Engr.

4721	A2227	4k multicolored	.25	.25
4722	A2227	6k multicolored	.35	.25
4723	A2227	10k multicolored	.45	.25
4724	A2227	12k multicolored	.60	.25
4725	A2227	16k multicolored	.70	.25
4726	A2227	20k multicolored	.80	.25
		Nos. 4721-4726 (6)	3.15	1.50

Souvenir Sheet

Mastheads and Globe with Russia — A2228

1978, Dec. 28 Litho. *Perf. 12*
4727 A2228 30k multicolored 1.50 .35

Distribution of periodicals through the Post and Telegraph Department, 60th anniversary.

Cuban Flags Forming Star — A2229

1979, Jan. 1 Photo. *Perf. 11½*
4728 A2229 6k multicolored .50 .25

Cuban Revolution, 20th anniversary.

Russian and Byelorussian Flags, Government Building, Minsk — A2230

1979, Jan. 1
4729 A2230 4k multicolored .50 .25

Byelorussian SSR and Byelorussian Communist Party, 60th annivs.

Ukrainian and Russian Flags, Reunion Monument A2231

1979, Jan. 16
4730 A2231 4k multicolored .50 .25

Reunion of Ukraine & Russia, 325th anniv.

Old and New Vilnius University Buildings A2232

1979, Jan. 16 **Photo. & Engr.**
4731 A2232 4k black & salmon .50 .25

400th anniversary of University of Vilnius.

Bulgaria No. 1 and Exhibition Hall A2233

1979, Jan. 25 **Litho.** ***Perf. 12½x12***
4732 A2233 15k multicolored .50 .25

Filaserdica '79 Philatelic Exhibition, Sofia, for centenary of Bulgarian postal service.

Sputniks, Soviet Radio Hams Emblem — A2234

1979, Feb. 23 **Photo.** ***Perf. 11½***
4733 A2234 4k multicolored .50 .25

Sputnik satellites Radio 1 and Radio 2, launched, Oct. 1978.

1-3-0 Locomotive, 1878 — A2235

Locomotives: 3k, 1-4-0, 1912. 4k, 2-3-1, 1915. 6k, 1-3-1, 1925. 15k, 1-5-0, 1947.

1979, Feb. 23 **Litho.** ***Perf. 11½***
4734 A2235 2k multicolored .25 .25
4735 A2235 3k multicolored .25 .25
4736 A2235 4k multicolored .25 .25
4737 A2235 6k multicolored .40 .25
4738 A2235 15k multicolored 1.00 .25
Nos. 4734-4738 (5) 2.15 1.25

Souvenir Sheet

Medal for Land Development — A2236

1979, Mar. 14 ***Perf. 11½x12½***
4739 A2236 50k multicolored 2.00 .75

25th anniv. of drive to develop virgin lands.

Venera 11 and 12 over Venus — A2237

1979, Mar. 16 **Photo.** ***Perf. 11½***
4740 A2237 10k multicolored .50 .25

Interplanetary flights of Venera 11 and Venera 12, December 1978.

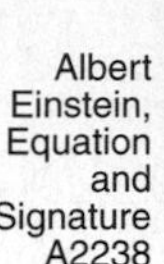

Albert Einstein, Equation and Signature A2238

1979, Mar. 16
4741 A2238 6k multicolored .50 .25

Einstein (1879-1955), theoretical physicist.

Congress Emblem A2239

1979, Mar. 16
4742 A2239 6k multicolored .50 .25

21st World Veterinary Congress, Moscow.

"To Arms," by Robert Berény (1887-1953) — A2240

1979, Mar. 21
4743 A2240 4k multicolored .50 .25

Soviet Republic of Hungary, 60th anniv.

Salyut 6, Soyuz, Research Ship, Letters — A2241

1979, Apr. 12 **Litho.** ***Perf. 11½x12***
4744 A2241 15k multicolored .50 .25

Cosmonauts' Day.

Souvenir Sheet

Ice Hockey — A2242

1979, Apr. 14 **Photo.** ***Perf. 12x11½***
4745 A2242 50k multicolored 2.00 .75

World and European Ice Hockey Championships, Moscow, Apr. 14-27.
For overprint see No. 4751.

Souvenir Sheet

Lenin — A2243

1979, Apr. 18
4746 A2243 50k red, gold & brn 1.50 .75

109th anniversary of the birth of Lenin.

Astronauts' Training Center A2244

Design: 32k, Astronauts, landing capsule, radar, helicopter and emblem.

1979, Apr. 12 **Litho.** ***Perf. 11½***
4747 A2244 6k multicolored .30 .25
4748 A2244 32k multicolored .70 .40

Joint Soviet-Bulgarian space flight.

Exhibition Emblem — A2245

1979, Apr. 18 **Photo.** ***Perf. 11½***
4749 A2245 15k sil, red & vio blue 1.00 .25

National USSR Exhibition in the United Kingdom. Se-tenant label with commemorative inscription.

Blast Furnace, Pushkin Theater, "Tent" Sculpture — A2246

1979, May 24 **Photo.** ***Perf. 11½***
4750 A2246 4k multicolored .50 .25

50th anniversary of Magnitogorsk City.

No. 4745 Overprinted in Red

1979, May 24 ***Perf. 12x11½***
4751 A2242 50k multicolored 2.00 .80

Victory of Soviet team in World and European Ice Hockey Championships.

Infant, Flowers, IYC Emblem — A2247

1979, June 1 **Litho.** ***Perf. 12x12½***
4752 A2247 4k multicolored .50 .25

International Year of the Child.

Horn Player and Bears Playing Balalaika, Bogorodsk Wood Carvings — A2248

Folk Art: 3k, Decorated wooden bowls, Khokhloma. 4k, Tray decorated with flowers, Zhestovo. 6k, Carved bone boxes, Kholmogory. 15k, Lace, Vologda.

1979, June 14 **Litho.** ***Perf. 12½x12***
4753 A2248 2k multicolored .25 .25
4754 A2248 3k multicolored .25 .25
4755 A2248 4k multicolored .25 .25
4756 A2248 6k multicolored .25 .25
4757 A2248 15k multicolored .25 .25
Nos. 4753-4757 (5) 1.25 1.25

Nos. 4753-4757 printed in sheets of 7 stamps and decorative label.

V. A. Djanibekov, O. G. Makarov, Spacecraft A2249

1979, June *Perf. 12x11½*
4758 A2249 4k multicolored .50 .25

Flights of Soyuz 26-27 and work on board of orbital complex Salyut 6.

COMECON Building, Members' Flags — A2250

1979, June 26 *Perf. 12*
4759 A2250 16k multicolored .50 .25

Council for Mutual Economic Aid of Socialist Countries, 30th anniversary.

Scene from "Potemkin" and Festival Emblem — A2251

Photogravure and Engraved

1979, July *Perf. 11½*
4760 A2251 15k multicolored .50 .25

11th International Film Festival, Moscow, and 60th anniversary of Soviet film industry.

Lenin Square Station, Tashkent A2252

1979, July Litho. *Perf. 12*
4761 A2252 4k multicolored .50 .25

Tashkent subway.

Souvenir Sheets

Atom Symbol, Factories, Dam — A2253

1979, July 23 Photo. *Perf. 11½x12*
4762 A2253 30k multicolored 2.00 .45

50th anniversary of 1st Five-Year Plan.

USSR Philatelic Society Emblem — A2254

1979, July 25 Litho. *Perf. 12x12½*
4763 A2254 50k gray grn & red 2.00 .70

4th Cong. of USSR Phil. Soc., Moscow.

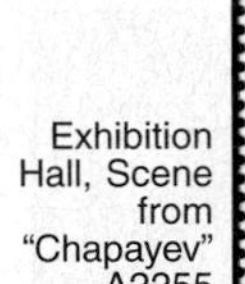

Exhibition Hall, Scene from "Chapayev" A2255

1979, Aug. 8 Photo. *Perf. 11½*
4764 A2255 4k multicolored .50 .25

60th anniversary of Soviet Film and Exhibition of History of Soviet Film.

Roses, by P. P. Konchalovsky, 1955 — A2256

Russian Flower Paintings: 1k, Flowers and Fruit, by I. F. Khrutsky, 1830. 2k, Phlox, by I. N. Kramskoi, 1884. 3k, Lilac, by K. A. Korovin, 1915. 15k, Bluebells, by S. V. Gerasimov, 1944. 2k, 3k, 15k, vert.

Perf. 12½x12, 12x12½

1979, Aug. 16 **Litho.**
4765 A2256 1k multicolored .25 .25
4766 A2256 2k multicolored .25 .25
4767 A2256 3k multicolored .25 .25
4768 A2256 15k multicolored .30 .25
4769 A2256 32k multicolored .45 .30
Nos. 4765-4769 (5) 1.50 1.30

John Maclean — A2257

1979, Aug. 29 Litho. *Perf. 11½*
4770 A2257 4k red & black .50 .25

John Maclean (1879-1923), Scottish Communist labor leader.

Soviet Circus Emblem — A2258

1979, Sept.
4771 A2258 4k multicolored .50 .25

Soviet Circus, 60th anniversary.

Friendship — A2259

Children's Drawings: 3k, Children and Horses. 4k, Dances. 15k, The Excursion.

1979, Sept. 10 *Perf. 12½x12*
4772 A2259 2k multicolored .50 .25
4773 A2259 3k multicolored .50 .25
4774 A2259 4k multicolored .50 .25
4775 A2259 15k multicolored .50 .25
Nos. 4772-4775 (4) 2.00 1.00

International Year of the Child.
Exist imperf. Value, $50 each.

Oriolus oriolus — A2260

Birds: 3k, Dendrocopus minor. 4k, Parus cristatus. 10k, Tyto alba. 15k, Caprimulgus europaeus.

1979, Sept. 18
4776 A2260 2k multicolored .25 .25
4777 A2260 3k multicolored .25 .25
4778 A2260 4k multicolored .45 .25
4779 A2260 10k multicolored .90 .25
4780 A2260 15k multicolored 1.40 .25
Nos. 4776-4780 (5) 3.25 1.25

German Arms, Marx, Engels, Lenin, Berlin A2261

1979, Oct. 7 Photo. *Perf. 11½*
4781 A2261 6k multicolored .50 .25

German Democratic Republic, 30th anniv.

Valery Ryumin, Vladimir Lyakhov, Salyut 6 — A2262

Design: No. 4783, Spacecraft.

1979, Oct. 10 *Perf. 12x11½*
4782 A2262 15k multicolored .50 .25
4783 A2262 15k multicolored .50 .25
a. Pair, #4782-4783 1.25 .75

175 days in space, Feb. 25-Aug. 19. No. 4783a has continuous design.

Star — A2264

1979, Oct. 18 *Perf. 11½*
4784 A2264 4k multicolored .50 .25

USSR Signal Troops, 60th anniversary.

Hammer and Sickle — A2265

1979, Oct. 18
4785 A2265 4k multicolored .50 .25

October Revolution, 62nd anniversary.

Katherina, by T. G. Shevchenko A2266

Ukrainian Paintings: 3k, Working Girl, by K.K. Kostandi. 4k, Lenin's Return to Petrograd, by A.M. Lopuhov. 10k, Soldier's Return, by N.V. Kostetsky. 15k, Going to Work, by M.G. Belsky.

1979, Nov. 18 Litho. *Perf. 12x12½*
4786 A2266 2k multicolored .25 .25
4787 A2266 3k multicolored .25 .25
4788 A2266 4k multicolored .25 .25
4789 A2266 10k multicolored .50 .25
4790 A2266 15k multicolored .75 .25
Nos. 4786-4790 (5) 2.00 1.25

Shabolovka Radio Tower, Moscow — A2267

1979, Nov. 28 Photo. *Perf. 12*
4791 A2267 32k multicolored .50 .35

Radio Moscow, 50th anniversary.

Mischa Holding Stamp — A2268

1979, Nov. 28 *Perf. 12x12½*

4792	A2268	4k	multicolored	.90	.25

New Year 1980.

Hand Holding Peace Message A2269

Peace Program in Action: No. 4794, Hands holding cultural symbols. No. 4795, Hammer and sickle, flag.

1979, Dec. 5 **Litho.** *Perf. 12*

4793	A2269	4k	multicolored	.65	.25
4794	A2269	4k	multicolored	.65	.25
4795	A2269	4k	multicolored	.65	.25
			Nos. 4793-4795 (3)	1.95	.75

Policeman, Patrol Car, Helicopter A2270

Traffic Safety: 4k, Car, girl and ball. 6k, Speeding cars.

1979, Dec. 20 *Perf. 12x12½*

4796	A2270	3k	multicolored	.50	.25
4797	A2270	4k	multicolored	.50	.25
4798	A2270	6k	multicolored	.50	.25
			Nos. 4796-4798 (3)	1.50	.75

Vulkanolog — A2271

Research Ships and Portraits: 2k, Professor Bogorov. 4k, Ernst Krenkel. 6k, Vladislav Volkov. 10k, Cosmonaut Yuri Gagarin. 15k, Academician E.B. Kurchatov.

Lithographed and Engraved

1979, Dec. 25 *Perf. 12x11½*

4799	A2271	1k	multicolored	.25	.25
4800	A2271	2k	multicolored	.25	.25
4801	A2271	4k	multicolored	.25	.25
4802	A2271	6k	multicolored	.30	.25
4803	A2271	10k	multicolored	.35	.25
4804	A2271	15k	multicolored	.60	.25
			Nos. 4799-4804 (6)	2.00	1.50

See Nos. 4881-4886.

Souvenir Sheet

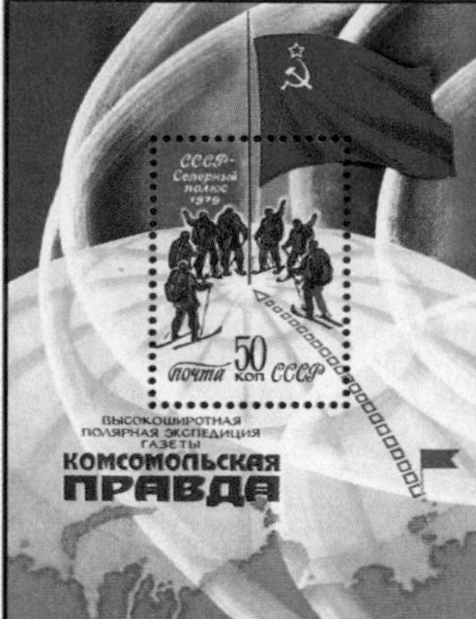
Explorers Raising Red Flag at North Pole — A2272

1979, Dec. 25 **Photo.** *Perf. 11½x12*

4805	A2272	50k	multicolored	2.00	.75

Komsomolskaya Pravda North Pole expedition.

Type of 1970

4k, Coat of arms, power line, factories.

1980, Jan. 10 **Litho.** *Perf. 12x12½*

4806	A1794	4k	carmine	.50	.25

Mordovian Autonomous SSR, 50th anniv.

Freestyle Skating A2273

1980, Jan. 22 *Perf. 12x12½, 12½x12*

4807	A2273	4k	Speed skating, vert.	.25	.25
4808	A2273	6k	shown	.25	.25
4809	A2273	10k	Ice hockey	.25	.25
4810	A2273	15k	Downhill skiing	.35	.25
4811	A2273	20k	Luge, vert.	.50	.35
			Nos. 4807-4811 (5)	1.60	1.35

Souvenir Sheet

4812	A2273	50k	Cross-country skiing, vert.	2.00	1.00

13th Winter Olympic Games, Lake Placid, NY, Feb. 12-24.

Nos. 4808, 4809 exist imperf. Value, $50 for both.

Nikolai Ilyitch Podvoiski (1880-1948), Revolutionary A2274

1980, Feb. 16 **Engr.** *Perf. 12½x12*

4813	A2274	4k	claret brown	1.00	.25

Rainbow, by A.K. Savrasov — A2275

No. 4815, Summer Harvest, by A.G. Venetsianov, vert. No. 4816, Old Erevan, by M.S. Saryan.

1980, Mar. 4 **Litho.** *Perf. 11½*

4814	A2275	6k	multicolored	.35	.25
4815	A2275	6k	multicolored	.35	.25
4816	A2275	6k	multicolored	.35	.25
			Nos. 4814-4816 (3)	1.05	.75

Souvenir Sheet

Cosmonaut Alexei Leonov — A2276

1980, Mar. 18 **Litho.** *Perf. 12½x12*

4817	A2276	50k	multicolored	1.50	.75

Man's first walk in space (Voskhod 2, Mar. 18-19, 1965).

Georg Ots, Estonian Artist — A2277

1980, Mar. 21 **Engr.**

4818	A2277	4k	slate blue	.50	.25

Lenin Order, 50th Anniversary A2278

1980, Apr. 6 **Photo.** *Perf. 11½*

4819	A2278	4k	multicolored	.50	.25

Souvenir Sheet

Cosmonauts, Salyut 6 and Soyuz — A2279

1980, Apr. 12 **Litho.** *Perf. 12*

4820	A2279	50k	multicolored	1.50	1.00

Intercosmos cooperative space program.

Flags and Arms of Azerbaijan, Government House — A2280

1980, Apr. 22 **Photo.**

4821	A2280	4k	multicolored	.50	.25

Azerbaijan Soviet Socialist Republic, Communist Party of Azerbaijan, 60th anniv.

Souvenir Sheet

Lenin, 110th Birth Anniversary — A2281

1980, Apr. 22 *Perf. 12x11½*

4822	A2281	30k	multicolored	1.50	.75

"Mother Russia," Fireworks over Moscow — A2282

No. 4824, Soviet War Memorial, Berlin, raising of Red flag. No. 4825, Parade, Red Square, Moscow.

1980, Apr. 25 **Litho.**

4823	A2282	4k	multicolored	.35	.25
4824	A2282	4k	multicolored	.35	.25
4825	A2282	4k	multicolored	.35	.25
			Nos. 4823-4825 (3)	1.05	.75

35th anniv. of victory in World War II.

Nos. 4823, 4824 exist imperf. Value, $25 for both.

Workers' Monument A2283

1980, May 12 **Litho.** *Perf. 12*

4826	A2283	4k	multicolored	.50	.25

Workers' Delegates in Ivanovo-Voznesensk, 75th anniversary.

"XXV" — A2284

1980, May 14 **Photo.** *Perf. 11½*

4827	A2284	32k	multicolored	.50	.35

Signing of Warsaw Pact (Bulgaria, Czechoslovakia, German Democratic Rep., Hungary, Poland, Romania, USSR), 25th anniv.

YaK-24 Helicopter, 1953 — A2285

1980, May 15 Litho. *Perf. 12½x12*

4828	A2285	1k	shown	.25	.25
4829	A2285	2k	MI-8, 1962	.25	.25
4830	A2285	3k	KA-26, 1965	.25	.25
4831	A2285	6k	MI-6, 1957	.25	.25
4832	A2285	15k	MI-10	.35	.25
4833	A2285	32k	V-12	.65	.40
			Nos. 4828-4833 (6)	2.00	1.65

Nos 4832-4833 exist imperf. Value, $50 for both.

David Anhaght, Illuminated Manuscript A2286

1980, May 16 *Perf. 12*

4834	A2286	4k	multicolored	.50	.25

David Anacht, Armenian philosopher, 1500th birth anniversary.

Emblem, Training Lab — A2287

15k, Cosmonauts meeting. 32k, Press conference.

1980, June 4

4835	A2287	6k	shown	.25	.25
4836	A2287	15k	multicolored	.40	.25
4837	A2287	32k	multicolored	.85	.55
			Nos. 4835-4837 (3)	1.50	1.05

Intercosmos cooperative space program (USSR-Hungary).

Polar Fox A2288

2k, Dark silver fox,vert. 6k, Mink. 10k, Azerbaijan nutria, vert. 15k, Black sable.

1980, June 25 Litho. *Perf. 12x12½*

4838	A2288	2k	multicolored	.25	.25
4839	A2288	4k	shown	.25	.25
4840	A2288	6k	multicolored	.25	.25
4841	A2288	10k	multicolored	.25	.25
4842	A2288	15k	multicolored	.25	.25
			Nos. 4838-4842 (5)	1.25	1.25

Factory, Buildings, Arms of Tatar A.S.S.R. A2289

1980, June 25 *Perf. 12*

4843	A2289	4k	multicolored	.50	.25

Tatar Autonomous SSR, 60th anniv.

College — A2290

1980, July 1 Photo. *Perf. 11½*

4844	A2290	4k	multicolored	.50	.25

Bauman Technological College, Moscow, 150th anniversary.

Ho Chi Minh — A2291

1980, July 7

4845	A2291	6k	multicolored	.50	.25

Red Flag, Lithuanian Arms, Flag, Red Guards Monument A2292

1980, July 12 Litho. *Perf. 12*

4846	A2292	4k	multicolored	.50	.25

Lithuanian SSR, 40th anniv.

Russian Flag and Arms, Latvian Flag, Monument, Buildings A2293

Design: No. 4848, Russian flag and arms, Estonian flag, monument, buildings.

1980, July 21 Litho. *Perf. 12*

4847	A2293	4k	multicolored	.35	.25
4848	A2293	4k	multicolored	.35	.25

Restoration of Soviet power.

Cosmonauts Boarding Soyuz A2294

1980, July 24 *Perf. 12x12½*

4849	A2294	6k	shown	.25	.25
4850	A2294	15k	Working aboard spacecraft	.45	.25
4851	A2294	32k	Return flight	.80	.55
			Nos. 4849-4851 (3)	1.50	1.05

Center for Cosmonaut Training, 20th anniv.

Avicenna (980-1037), Philosopher and Physician — A2295

Photogravure and Engraved

1980, Aug. 16 *Perf. 11½*

4852	A2295	4k	multicolored	.50	.25

Soviet Racing Car KHADI-7 — A2296

1980, Aug. 25 Litho. *Perf. 12*

4853	A2296	2k	shown	.25	.25
4854	A2296	6k	KHADI-10	.25	.25
4855	A2296	15k	KHADI-113	.25	.25
4856	A2296	32k	KHADI-133	.25	.25
			Nos. 4853-4856 (4)	1.00	1.00

No. 4856 exists imperf. Value, $50.

Kazakhstan Republic, 60th Anniversary A2297

1980, Aug. 26

4857	A2297	4k	multicolored	.50	.25

Ingres, Self-portrait, and Nymph A2298

1980, Aug. 29 *Perf. 12x12½*

4858	A2298	32k	multicolored	.50	.35

Jean Auguste Dominique Ingres (1780-1867), French painter.
Exists imperf. Value, $25.

Morning on the Field of Kulikovo, by A. Bubnov — A2299

1980, Sept. 6 Litho. *Perf. 12*

4859	A2299	4k	multicolored	.50	.25

Battle of Kulikovo, 600th anniversary.

Town Hall, Tartu — A2300

1980, Sept. 15 Photo. *Perf. 11½*

4860	A2300	4k	multicolored	.50	.25

Tartu, 950th anniversary.

Y.V. Malyshev, V.V. Aksenov A2301

1980, Sept. 15 Litho. *Perf. 12x12½*

4861	A2301	10k	multicolored	.50	.25

Soyuz T-2 space flight.

Flight Training, Yuri Gagarin — A2302

1980, Sept. 15 Photo. *Perf. 11½x12*

4862	A2302	6k	shown	.25	.25
4863	A2302	15k	Space walk	.40	.25
4864	A2302	32k	Endurance test	.85	.45
			Nos. 4862-4864 (3)	1.50	.95

Gagarin Cosmonaut Training Center, 20th anniversary.

Intercosmos A2303

6k, Intercosmos Emblem, Flags of USSR and Cuba, and Cosmonauts training. 15k, Inside weightless cabin. 32k, Landing.

1980, Sept. 15 Litho. *Perf. 12x12½*

4865	A2303	6k	multicolored	.25	.25
4866	A2303	15k	multicolored	.40	.25
4867	A2303	32k	multicolored	.85	.45
			Nos. 4865-4867 (3)	1.50	.95

Intercosmos cooperative space program (USSR-Cuba).

October Revolution, 63rd Anniversary
A2304

1980, Sept. 20 Photo. ***Perf. 11½***
4868 A2304 6k multicolored .50 .25

David Guramishvili (1705-1792), Poet — A2305

1980, Sept. 20
4869 A2305 6k multicolored .50 .25

Family with Serfs, by N.V. Nevrev (1830-1904) — A2305a

Design: No. 4869B, Countess Tarakanova, by K.D. Flavitsky (1830-1866), vert.

1980, Sept. 25 Litho. ***Perf. 11½***
4869A A2305a 6k multicolored .50 .25
4869B A2305a 6k multicolored .50 .25

A.F. Ioffe (1880-1960), Physicist — A2306

1980, Sept. 29
4870 A2306 4k multicolored .50 .25

Siberian Pine
A2307

1980, Sept. 29 Litho. ***Perf. 12½x12***
4871 A2307 2k shown .25 .25
4872 A2307 4k Oak .25 .25
4873 A2307 6k Lime tree, vert. .25 .25
4874 A2307 10k Sea bucthorn .50 .25
4875 A2307 15k European ash .75 .25
Nos. 4871-4875 (5) 2.00 1.25

A.M. Vasilevsky (1895-1977), Soviet Marshal — A2308

1980, Sept. 30 Engr. ***Perf. 12***
4876 A2308 4k dark green .50 .25

Souvenir Sheet

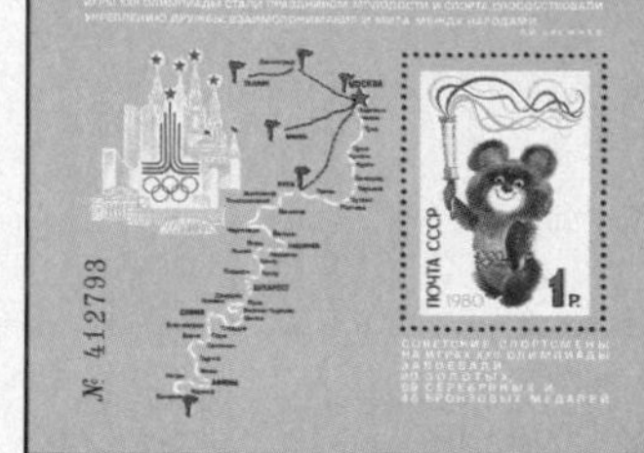
Mischa Holding Olympic Torch — A2309

1980, Nov. 24 ***Perf. 12x12½***
4877 A2309 1r multicolored 5.00 1.75

Completion of 22nd Summer Olympic Games, Moscow, July 19-Aug. 3.

A.V. Suvorov (1730-1800), General and Military Theorist
A2310

1980, Nov. 24 Engr.
4878 A2310 4k slate .50 .25

A2311

1980, Nov. 24 Litho. ***Perf. 12***
4879 A2311 4k multicolored .50 .25

Armenian SSR & Armenian Communist Party, 60th annivs.

Aleksandr Blok (1880-1921), Poet — A2312

1980, Nov. 24
4880 A2312 4k multicolored .50 .25

Research Ship Type of 1979
Lithographed and Engraved

1980, Nov. 24 ***Perf. 12x11½***
4881 A2271 2k Aju Dag, Fleet arms .25 .25
4882 A2271 3k Valerian Urywaev .25 .25
4883 A2271 4k Mikhail Somov .25 .25
4884 A2271 6k Sergei Korolev .30 .25
4885 A2271 10k Otto Schmidt .60 .25
4886 A2271 15k Mstislav Keldysh .75 .25
Nos. 4881-4886 (6) 2.40 1.50

For overprint see No. 5499.

Russian Flag — A2313

1980, Dec. 1 Engr. ***Perf. 12x12½***
4887 A2313 3k orange red 2.00 .25

Soviet Medical College, 50th Anniversary
A2314

1980, Dec. 1 Photo. ***Perf. 11½***
4888 A2314 4k multicolored .50 .25

New Year 1981
A2315

1980, Dec. 1 Litho. ***Perf. 12***
4889 A2315 4k multicolored .50 .25

Lenin, Electrical Plant
A2316

1980, Dec. 18
4890 A2316 4k multicolored .50 .25

60th anniversary of GOELRO (Lenin's electro-economic plan).

A.N. Nesmeyanov (1899-1980), Chemist — A2317

1980, Dec. 19 ***Perf. 12½x12***
4891 A2317 4k multicolored .50 .25

Nagatinski Bridge, Moscow — A2318

Photogravure and Engraved

1980, Dec. 23 ***Perf. 11½x12***
4892 A2318 4k shown .25 .25
4893 A2318 6k Luzhniki Bridge .30 .25
4894 A2318 15k Kalininski Bridge .60 .25
Nos. 4892-4894 (3) 1.15 .75

S.K. Timoshenko (1895-1970), Soviet Marshal — A2319

1980, Dec. 25 Engr. ***Perf. 12***
4895 A2319 4k rose lake .50 .25

Flags of India and USSR, Government House, New Delhi
A2320

1980, Dec. 30 Litho. ***Perf. 12x12½***
4896 A2320 4k multicolored .50 .35

Visit of Pres. Brezhnev to India. Printed se-tenant with inscribed label.

Mirny Base — A2321

6k, Earth station, rocket. 15k, Map, supply ship.

1981, Jan. 5 ***Perf. 12***
4897 A2321 4k shown .25 .25
4898 A2321 6k multicolored .35 .25
4899 A2321 15k multicolored .90 .25
Nos. 4897-4899 (3) 1.50 .75

Soviet Antarctic research, 25th anniv.

Dagestan Soviet Socialist Republic, 60th Anniversary
A2322

1981, Jan. 20
4900 A2322 4k multicolored .50 .25

Bandy World Championship, Khabarovsk — A2323

1981, Jan. 20
4901 A2323 6k multicolored .50 .25

26th Congress of Ukrainian Communist Party
A2324

1981, Jan. 23 Photo. ***Perf. 11½***
4902 A2324 4k multicolored .50 .25

Lenin, "XXVI"
A2325

1981 Photo. ***Perf. 11½***
4903 A2325 4k multicolored .50 .25

Lenin and Congress Building — A2326

Banner and Kremlin — A2327

Photogravure and Embossed

1982 ***Perf. 11½x12***
4904 A2326 20k multicolored 1.50 .75

Souvenir Sheet

Litho.

Perf. 12x12½
4905 A2327 50k multicolored 1.50 .75

26th Communist Party Congress. Issue dates: 4k, 20k, Jan. 22; 50k, Feb. 16.

Mstislav V. Keldysh — A2328

Photogravure and Engraved

1981, Feb. 10 ***Perf. 11½x12***
4906 A2328 4k multicolored .50 .25

Mstislav Vsevolodovich Keldysh (1911-1978), mathematician.

Freighter, Flags of USSR and India — A2329

1981, Feb. 10 **Litho.** ***Perf. 12***
4907 A2329 15k multicolored .50 .30

Soviet-Indian Shipping Line, 25th anniv.

Baikal-Amur Railroad and Map — A2330

10th Five-Year Plan Projects (1976-1980): No. 4909, Gas plant, Urengoi (spherical tanks). No. 4910, Enisei River power station (dam). No. 4911, Atomic power plant. No. 4912, Paper mill. No. 4913, Coal mining, Ekibstyi.

1981, Feb. 18 ***Perf. 12½x12***
4908 A2330 4k multicolored .25 .25
4909 A2330 4k multicolored .25 .25
4910 A2330 4k multicolored .25 .25
4911 A2330 4k multicolored .25 .25
4912 A2330 4k multicolored .25 .25
4913 A2330 4k multicolored .25 .25
Nos. 4908-4913 (6) 1.50 1.50

Georgian Soviet Socialist Republic, 60th Anniv. A2331

1981, Feb. 25 ***Perf. 12***
4914 A2331 4k multicolored .50 .25

Abkhazian Autonomous Soviet Socialist Republic, 60th Anniv. — A2332

1981, Mar. 4
4915 A2332 4k multicolored .50 .25

Exists imperf.

Communications Institute — A2333

1981, Mar. 12 **Photo.** ***Perf. 11½***
4916 A2333 4k multicolored .50 .25

Moscow Electrotechnical Institute of Communications, 60th anniv.

Satellite, Radio Operator — A2334

1981, Mar. 12
4917 A2334 4k multicolored .50 .25

30th All-Union Amateur Radio Designers Exhibition.

Cosmonauts L.I. Popov and V.V. Ryumin A2335

1981, Mar. 20 **Litho.** ***Perf. 12***
4918 A2335 15k shown .25 .25
4919 A2335 15k Spacecraft complex .35 .25
a. Pair, #4918-4919 + label 1.00 .50

185-day flight of Cosmos 35-Salyut 6-Cosmos 37 complex, Apr. 9-Oct. 11, 1980. No. 4919a has a continuous design.

Cosmonauts O. Makarov, L. Kizim and G. Strekalov — A2336

1981, Mar. 20 ***Perf. 12½x12***
4920 A2336 10k multicolored .50 .25

Soyuz T-3 flight, Nov. 27-Dec. 10, 1980.

Lift-Off, Baikonur Base — A2337

15k, Mongolians watching flight on TV. 32k, Re-entry.

1981, Mar. 23
4921 A2337 6k shown .25 .25
4922 A2337 15k multicolored .40 .25
4923 A2337 32k multicolored .85 .50
Nos. 4921-4923 (3) 1.50 1.00

Intercosmos cooperative space program (USSR-Mongolia).

Vitus Bering A2338

1981, Mar. 25 **Engr.** ***Perf. 12x12½***
4924 A2338 4k dark blue .50 .25

Bering (1680-1741), Danish navigator.

Yuri Gagarin and Earth — A2339

Yuri Gagarin — A2340

1981, Apr. 12 **Photo.** ***Perf. 11½x12***
4925 A2339 6k shown .25 .25
4926 A2339 15k S.P. Korolev (craft designer) .45 .25
4927 A2339 32k Monument .90 .50
Nos. 4925-4927 (3) 1.60 1.00

Souvenir Sheet
4928 A2340 50k shown 5.00 1.00

Soviet space flights, 20th anniv. Nos. 4925-4927 each se-tenant with label.

Salyut Orbital Station, 10th Anniv. of Flight A2341

1981, Apr. 19 **Litho.** ***Perf. 12x12½***
4929 A2341 32k multicolored .50 .35

Souvenir Sheet

111th Birth Anniv. of Lenin — A2342

1981, Apr. 22 ***Perf. 11½x12½***
4930 A2342 50k multicolored 1.50 .60

Sergei Prokofiev (1891-1953), Composer A2343

1981, Apr. 23 **Engr.** ***Perf. 12***
4931 A2343 4k dark purple .50 .25

New Hofburg Palace, Vienna — A2344

1981, May 5 **Litho.**
4932 A2344 15k multicolored .50 .25

WIPA 1981 Phil. Exhib., Vienna, May 22-31.

Adzhar Autonomous Soviet Socialist Republic, 60th Anniv. — A2345

1981, May 7
4933 A2345 4k multicolored .50 .25

Centenary of Welding (Invented by N.N. Benardos) A2346

Lithographed and Engraved
1981, May 12 ***Perf. 11½***
4934 A2346 6k multicolored .50 .25

Intl. Architects Union, 14th Congress, Warsaw — A2347

1981, May 12 **Photo.**
4935 A2347 15k multicolored .50 .25

Albanian Girl, by A.A. Ivanov A2348

No. 4937, Horseman, by F.A. Roubeau. No. 4938, The Demon, by M.A. Vrubel, horiz. No. 4939, Sunset over the Sea, by N.N. Ge, horiz.

1981, May 15 **Litho.** ***Perf. 12x12½***
4936 A2348 10k multicolored .50 .25
4937 A2348 10k multicolored .50 .25
4938 A2348 10k multicolored .50 .25
4939 A2348 10k multicolored .50 .25
Nos. 4936-4939 (4) 2.00 1.00

Cosmonauts in Training A2349

1981, May 15
4940 A2349 6k shown .25 .25
4941 A2349 15k In space .40 .25
4942 A2349 32k Return .85 .50
Nos. 4940-4942 (3) 1.50 1.00

Intercosmos cooperative space program (USSR-Romania).

Dwarf Primrose — A2350

Flowers of the Carpathian Mountains: 6k, Great carline thistle. 10k, Mountain parageum. 15k, Alpine bluebell. 32k, Rhododendron kotschyi.

1981, May 20 ***Perf. 12***
4943 A2350 4k multicolored .25 .25
4944 A2350 6k multicolored .25 .25
4945 A2350 10k multicolored .25 .25
4946 A2350 15k multicolored .40 .25
4947 A2350 32k multicolored .85 .50
Nos. 4943-4947 (5) 2.00 1.50

Luigi Longo, Italian Labor Leader, 1st Death Anniv. — A2351

1981, May 24 **Photo.** ***Perf. 11½***
4948 A2351 6k multicolored .50 .25

Nizami Gjanshevi (1141-1209), Azerbaijan Poet — A2352

1981, May 25 **Photo. & Engr.**
4949 A2352 4k multicolored .50 .25

A2353

1981, June 18 **Litho.** ***Perf. 12***
4950 A2353 4k Running .25 .25
4951 A2353 6k Soccer .25 .25
4952 A2353 10k Discus throwing .25 .25
4953 A2353 15k Boxing .30 .25
4954 A2353 32k Diving .60 .35
Nos. 4950-4954 (5) 1.65 1.35

Mongolian Revolution, 60th anniv. — A2354

1981, July 6
4955 A2354 6k multicolored 1.50 .25

12th Intl. Film Festival, Moscow — A2355

1981, July 6 **Photo.** ***Perf. 11½***
4956 A2355 15k multicolored .60 .30

River Tour Boat Lenin A2356

6k, Cosmonaut Gagarin. 15k, Valerian Kuibyshev. 32k, Freighter Baltijski.

1981, July 9 **Litho.** ***Perf. 12½***
4957 A2356 4k shown .25 .25
4958 A2356 6k multicolored .25 .25
4959 A2356 15k multicolored .35 .25
4960 A2356 32k multicolored .65 .45
Nos. 4957-4960 (4) 1.50 1.20

Icebreaker Maligin — A2357

Photogravure and Engraved
1981, July 9 ***Perf. 11½x12***
4961 A2357 15k multicolored .60 .30

26th Party Congress Resolutions (Intl. Cooperation) — A2358

1981, July 15 **Photo.** ***Perf. 12x11½***
4962 A2358 4k shown .25 .25
4963 A2358 4k Industry .25 .25
4964 A2358 4k Energy .25 .25
4965 A2358 4k Agriculture .25 .25
4966 A2358 4k Communications .25 .25
4967 A2358 4k Arts .25 .25
Nos. 4962-4967 (6) 1.50 1.50

I.N. Ulyanov (Lenin's Father), 150th Anniv. of Birth — A2359

1981, July 25 **Engr.** ***Perf. 11½***
4968 A2359 4k multicolored .50 .25

Leningrad Theater, 225th Anniv. — A2360

1981, Aug. 12 **Photo.** ***Perf. 11½***
4969 A2360 6k multicolored .50 .25

A.M. Gerasimov, Artist, Birth Centenary A2361

1981, Aug. 12 **Litho.** ***Perf. 12***
4970 A2361 4k multicolored .50 .25

Physical Chemistry Institute, Moscow Academy of Science, 50th Anniv. A2362

1981, Aug. 12 **Photo.** ***Perf. 11½***
4971 A2362 4k multicolored .50 .25

Siberian Tit A2363

Song birds — 10k, Tersiphone paradisi, vert. 15k, Emberiza jankovski. 20k, Sutora webbiana, vert. 32k, Saxicola torquata, vert.

Perf. 12½x12, 12x12½ **Litho.**
1981, Aug. 20
4972 A2363 6k shown .25 .25
4973 A2363 10k multicolored .30 .25
4974 A2363 15k multicolored .40 .25
4975 A2363 20k multicolored .45 .30
4976 A2363 32k multicolored .60 .35
Nos. 4972-4976 (5) 2.00 1.40

60th Anniv. of Komi Autonomous Soviet Socialist Republic — A2364

1981, Aug. 22 ***Perf. 12***
4977 A2364 4k multicolored .50 .25

Svyaz-'81 Intl. Communications Exhibition — A2365

Photogravure and Engraved
1981, Aug. 22 ***Perf. 11½***
4978 A2365 4k multicolored .50 .25

60th Anniv. of Kabardino-Balkar Autonomous Soviet Socialist Republic — A2366

1981, Sept. 1 Litho. *Perf. 12*

4979 A2366 4k multicolored .50 .25

War Veterans' Committee, 25th Anniv. — A2367

1981, Sept. 1 Photo. *Perf. 11½*

4980 A2367 4k multicolored .50 .25

Schooner Kodor — A2368

Training ships — 4k, 4-masted bark Tovarich I. 6k, Barkentine Vega I. 15k, 3-masted bark Tovarich. 20k, 4-masted bark Kruzenstern. 32k, 4-masted bark Sedov.

4k, 6k, 15k, 20k, horiz.

Perf. 12½x12, 12x12½

1981, Sept. 18 Litho.

4981	A2368	4k multicolored	.25	.25
4982	A2368	6k multicolored	.25	.25
4983	A2368	10k shown	.25	.25
4984	A2368	15k multicolored	.30	.25
4985	A2368	20k multicolored	.45	.25
4986	A2368	32k multicolored	.60	.30
		Nos. 4981-4986 (6)	2.10	1.55

A2369

1981, Oct. 10 *Perf. 12*

4987 A2369 4k multicolored .50 .25

Kazakhstan's Union with Russia, 250th Anniv.

A2370

1981, Oct. 10 Photo. *Perf. 11½*

4988 A2370 4k multicolored .50 .25

Mikhail Alekseevich Lavrentiev (1900-80), mathematician. Exists imperf.

64th Anniv. of October Revolution — A2371

1981, Oct. 15 Litho.

4989 A2371 4k multicolored .50 .25

Ekran Satellite TV Broadcasting System — A2372

1981, Oct. 15 *Perf. 12*

4990 A2372 4k multicolored .50 .25

Salyut 6-Soyuz flight of V.V. Kovalionok and V.P. Savinykh A2373

1981, Oct. 15

4991		10k Text	.40	.25
4992		10k Cosmonauts	.40	.25
a.	A2373	Pair, #4991-4992	1.00	.30

Souvenir Sheet

Birth Centenary of Pablo Picasso — A2375

1981, Oct. 25 *Perf. 12x12½*

4993 A2375 50k multicolored 2.00 .75

A2376

Photogravure and Engraved

1981, Nov. 5 *Perf. 11½*

4994 A2376 4k multicolored .50 .25

Sergei Dmitrievich Merkurov (1881-1952), artist.

Autumn, by Niko Piromanashvili, 1913 — A2377

Paintings: 6k, Gurian Woman, by S.G. Kikodze, 1921. 10k, Fellow Travelers, by U.M. Dzhaparidze, 1936, horiz. 15k, Shota Rustaveli, by S.S. Kobuladze, 1938. 32k, Collecting Tea, by V.D. Gudiashvili, 1964, horiz.

Perf. 12x12½, 12½x12

1981, Nov. 5 Litho.

4995	A2377	4k multicolored	.25	.25
4996	A2377	6k multicolored	.25	.25
4997	A2377	10k multicolored	.30	.25
4998	A2377	15k multicolored	.40	.25
4999	A2377	32k multicolored	1.00	.40
		Nos. 4995-4999 (5)	2.20	1.40

New Year 1982 — A2378

1981, Dec. 2 Litho. *Perf. 12*

5000 A2378 4k multicolored 1.00 .25

Public Transportation 19th-20th Cent. — A2379

Photogravure and Engraved

1981, Dec. 10 *Perf. 11½x12*

5001	A2379	4k Sled	.25	.25
5002	A2379	6k Horse-drawn trolley	.25	.25
5003	A2379	10k Coach	.25	.25
5004	A2379	15k Taxi, 1926	.25	.25
5005	A2379	20k Bus, 1926	.35	.30
5006	A2379	32k Trolley, 1912	.50	.40
		Nos. 5001-5006 (6)	1.85	1.70

Souvenir Sheet

Kremlin and New Delhi Parliament — A2380

1981, Dec. 17 Photo.

5007 A2380 50k multicolored 1.50 .75

1st direct telephone link with India.

A2381

A2382

1982, Jan. 11 Litho. *Perf. 12*

5008	A2381	4k multicolored	.50	.25
5009	A2382	4k multicolored	.50	.25

60th anniv. of Checheno-Ingush Autonomous SSR and of Yakutsk Autonomous SSR.

1500th Anniv. of Kiev — A2383

1982, Jan. 12 Photo. *Perf. 11½x12*

5010 A2383 10k multicolored .50 .25

S.P. Korolev (1907-66), Rocket Designer — A2384

1982, Jan. 12 *Perf. 11½*

5011 A2384 4k multicolored .50 .25

Nazym Khikmet (1902-1963), Turkish Poet — A2385

1982, Jan. 20 Litho. *Perf. 12*

5012 A2385 6k multicolored .50 .25

10th World Trade Union Congress, Havana — A2386

1982, Feb. 1 Photo. *Perf. 11½*

5013 A2386 15k multicolored .50 .25

17th Soviet Trade Union Congress A2387

1982, Feb. 10 **Litho.**

5014 A2387 4k multicolored .50 .25

Edouard Manet (1832-1883) A2388

1982, Feb. 10 ***Perf. 12x12½***

5015 A2388 32k multicolored 1.00 .45

Equestrian Sports A2389

1982, Feb. 16 **Photo.** ***Perf. 11½***

5016	A2389	4k Hurdles	.25	.25
5017	A2389	6k Riding	.30	.25
5018	A2389	15k Racing	.45	.25
		Nos. 5016-5018 (3)	1.00	.75

No. 5016 exists imperf. Value, $25.

2nd Death Anniv. of Marshal Tito of Yugoslavia A2390

1982, Feb. 25 **Litho.** ***Perf. 12***

5019 A2390 6k olive black .50 .25

350th Anniv. of State University of Tartu A2392

1982, Mar. 4 **Photo.** ***Perf. 11½***

5020 A2392 4k multicolored .50 .25

9th Intl. Cardiologists Congress, Moscow — A2393

1982, Mar. 4

5021 A2393 15k multicolored .50 .25

Souvenir Sheet

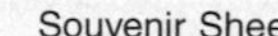

Biathlon, Speed Skating — A2394

1982, Mar. 6 **Litho.** ***Perf. 12½x12***

5022 A2394 50k multicolored 1.50 .70

5th Natl. Athletic Meet.

Blueberry Bush — A2395

4k, Cloudberries. 10k, Brambles. 15k, Cornelian cherries. 32k, Wild strawberries.

1982, Mar. 10 **Litho.** ***Perf. 12x12½***

5023	A2395	4k multicolored	.25	.25
5024	A2395	6k shown	.25	.25
5025	A2395	10k multicolored	.25	.25
5026	A2395	15k multicolored	.25	.25
5027	A2395	32k multicolored	.50	.25
		Nos. 5023-5027 (5)	1.50	1.25

Venera 13 and Venera 14 Flights — A2396

1982, Mar. 10 **Photo.** ***Perf. 11½***

5028 A2396 10k multicolored .50 .25

Marriage Ceremony, by V.V. Pukirev (1832-1890) A2397

Paintings: No. 5030, M.I. Lopukhina, by V. L. Borovikovsky (1757-1825). No. 5031, E.V. Davidov, by O.A. Kiprensky (1782-1836). No. 5032, Oak Trees, by I.I. Shishkin (1832-1898).

1982, Mar. 18 ***Perf. 12***

5029	A2397	6k multicolored	.25	.25
5030	A2397	6k multicolored	.25	.25
5031	A2397	6k multicolored	.25	.25
5032	A2397	6k multicolored	.25	.25
		Nos. 5029-5032 (4)	1.00	1.00

K.I. Chukovsky (1882-1969), Writer — A2398

1982, Mar. 31 **Engr.**

5033 A2398 4k gray & black .50 .25

Cosmonauts' Day — A2399

1982, Apr. 12 **Photo.** ***Perf. 12x11½***

5034 A2399 6k multicolored .50 .25

Souvenir Sheet

112th Birth Anniv. of Lenin — A2400

1982, Apr. 22 **Photo.** ***Perf. 11½x12***

5035 A2400 50k multicolored 1.50 .70

V.P. Soloviev-Sedoi (1907-79), Composer A2401

1982, Apr. 25 **Engr.** ***Perf. 12***

5036 A2401 4k brown .50 .25

G. Dimitrov (1882-1949), 1st Bulgarian Prime Minister — A2402

1982, Apr. 25

5037 A2402 6k green .50 .25

Kremlin Tower, Moscow — A2403

1982 **Litho.** ***Perf. 12½x12***

5038 A2403 45k brown 1.00 .65

a. Engraved 1.00 .65

Issued: #5038, Apr. 25. #5038a, Oct. 12.

70th Anniv. of Pravda Newspaper A2404

1982, May 5 **Photo.** ***Perf. 12x11½***

5039 A2404 4k multicolored .50 .25

UN Conf. on Human Environment, 10th anniv. — A2405

1982, May 10 ***Perf. 11½***

5040 A2405 6k multicolored .50 .25

Pioneers' Org., 60th anniv. — A2406

1982, May 19

5041 A2406 4k multicolored .50 .25

Communist Youth Org., 19th Cong. — A2407

1982, May 19

5042 A2407 4k multicolored .50 .25

ITU Delegates Conf., Nairobi — A2408

1982, May 19

5043 A2408 15k multicolored .50 .25

TUL-80 Electric Locomotive — A2409

1982, May 20 ***Perf. 12x11½***

5044	A2409	4k shown	.25	.25
5045	A2409	6k TEP-75 diesel	.25	.25
5046	A2409	10k TEP-7 diesel	.30	.25
5047	A2409	15k WL-82m electric	.45	.30
5048	A2409	32k EP-200 electric	.95	.45
		Nos. 5044-5048 (5)	2.20	1.50

1982 World Cup — A2410

1982, June 4 ***Perf. 11½x12***

5049 A2410 20k olive & purple .50 .30

Rare Birds — A2411

18th Ornithological Cong., Moscow — 2k, Grus Monacha. 4k, Haliaeetus pelagicus. 6k, Eurynorhynchus. 10k, Eulabeia indica. 15k, Chettusia gregaria. 32k, Ciconia boyciana.

1982, June 10 **Litho.** ***Perf. 12x12½***

5050	A2411	2k multicolored	.25	.25
5051	A2411	4k multicolored	.25	.25
5052	A2411	6k multicolored	.25	.25
5053	A2411	10k multicolored	.25	.25
5054	A2411	15k multicolored	.30	.25
5055	A2411	32k multicolored	.70	.35
		Nos. 5050-5055 (6)	2.00	1.60

Komomolsk-on-Amur City, 50th Anniv. — A2412

Photogravure and Engraved

1982, June 10 ***Perf. 11½***

5056 A2412 4k multicolored .50 .25

Tatchanka, by M.B. Grekov (1882-1934) — A2413

1982, June 15 **Litho.** ***Perf. 12½x12***

5057 A2413 6k multicolored .50 .25

2nd UN Conference on Peaceful Uses of Outer Space, Vienna, Aug. 9-21 — A2414

1982, June 15 **Photo.** ***Perf. 11½***

5058 A2414 15k multicolored .50 .25

Intercosmos Cooperative Space Program (USSR-France) — A2415

1982 **Litho.** ***Perf. 12½x12***

5059	A2415	6k Cosmonauts	.25	.25
5060	A2415	20k Rocket, globe	.35	.25
5061	A2415	45k Satellites	.80	.40
a.		Miniature sheet of 8	70.00	
		Nos. 5059-5061 (3)	1.40	.90

Souvenir Sheet

5062 A2415 50k Emblem, satellite 1.50 .75

No. 5062 contains one 41x29mm stamp. Issue dates: 6k, 50k, June 24. 20k, 45k, July 2.

The Tale of the Golden Cockerel, by P. Sosin, 1968 — A2416

Lacquerware Paintings, Ustera: 10k, Minin's Appeal to Count Posharski, by J. Fomichev, 1953. 15k, Two Peasants, by A. Klykov, 1933. 20k, The Fisherman, by N. Klykov, 1933, 32k, The Arrest of the Propagandists, by N. Shishakov, 1968.

1982, July 6 **Litho.** ***Perf. 12½x12***

5063	A2416	6k multicolored	.25	.25
5064	A2416	10k multicolored	.25	.25
5065	A2416	15k multicolored	.30	.25
5066	A2416	20k multicolored	.50	.25
5067	A2416	32k multicolored	.75	.30
		Nos. 5063-5067 (5)	2.05	1.30

Telephone Centenary A2417

1982, July 13 ***Perf. 12***

5068 A2417 4k Phone, 1882 .50 .25

P. Schilling's Electro-magnetic Telegraph Sesquicentennial — A2418

Photogravure and Engraved

1982, July 16 ***Perf. 11½***

5069 A2418 6k Voltaic cells .50 .25

Intervision Gymnastics Contest A2419

1982, Aug. 10 **Photo.**

5070 A2419 15k multicolored .50 .30

Gliders A2420

4k, Mastjahart Glider, 1923. 6k, Red Star, 1930. 10k, ZAGI-2, 1934.

20k, Stakhanovets, 1939. 32k, Troop carrier GR-29, 1941.

1982, Aug. 20 **Litho.** ***Perf. 12½x12***

5071	A2420	4k multicolored	.25	.25
5072	A2420	6k multicolored	.25	.25
5073	A2420	10k multicolored	.30	.25

Size: 60x28mm

Perf. 11½x12

5074	A2420	20k multicolored	.60	.25
5075	A2420	32k multicolored	.75	.35
		Nos. 5071-5075 (5)	2.15	1.35

See Nos. 5118-5122.

Garibaldi (1807-1882) A2421

1982, Aug. 25 **Photo.** ***Perf. 11½***

5076 A2421 6k multicolored .50 .25

Exists imperf. Value, $25.

Intl. Atomic Energy Authority, 25th Anniv. — A2422

1982, Aug. 30

5077 A2422 20k multicolored .50 .25

Marshal B.M. Shaposhnikov (1882-1945) A2423

1982, Sept. 10 **Engr.** ***Perf. 12***

5078 A2423 4k red brown .50 .25

World Chess Championship A2424

1982, Sept. 10 **Photo.** ***Perf. 11½***

5079	A2424	6k King	.50	.25
5080	A2424	6k Queen	.50	.25

See #5084.

African Natl. Congress, 70th Anniv. — A2425

1982, Sept. 10

5081 A2425 6k multicolored .50 .25

S.P. Botkin (1832-89), Physician — A2426

1982, Sept. 17 **Engr.** ***Perf. 12½x12***

5082 A2426 4k green .50 .25

Souvenir Sheet

25th Anniv. of Sputnik — A2427

1982, Sept. 17 **Litho.** ***Perf. 12x12½***

5083 A2427 50k multicolored 2.00 .65

No. 5079 Overprinted in Gold for Karpov's Victory

1982, Sept. 22 **Photo.** ***Perf. 11½***

5084 A2424 6k multicolored 1.00 .30

World War II Warships — A2428

4k, Submarine S-56. 6k, Minelayer Gremjashtsky. 15k, Mine sweeper T-205. 20k, Cruiser Red Crimea. 45k, Sebastopol.

Photogravure and Engraved

1982, Sept. 22 ***Perf. 11½x12***

5085	A2428	4k multicolored	.25	.25
5086	A2428	6k multicolored	.25	.25
5087	A2428	15k multicolored	.30	.25
5088	A2428	20k multicolored	.40	.25
5089	A2428	45k multicolored	.80	.45
		Nos. 5085-5089 (5)	2.00	1.45

65th Anniv. of October Revolution A2429

1982, Oct. 12 **Litho.** ***Perf. 12***

5090 A2429 4k multicolored .50 .25

House of the Soviets, Moscow — A2430

60th Anniv. of USSR: No. 5092, Dnieper Dam, Komosomol Monument, Statue of worker. No. 5093, Soviet War Memorial, resistance poster. No. 5094, Worker at podium, decree text. No. 5095, Workers' Monument, Moscow, Rocket, jet. No. 5096, Arms, Kremlin.

1982, Oct. 25 Photo. *Perf. 11½x12*

5091	A2430	10k	multicolored	.50	.25
5092	A2430	10k	multicolored	.50	.25
5093	A2430	10k	multicolored	.50	.25
5094	A2430	10k	multicolored	.50	.25
5095	A2430	10k	multicolored	.50	.25
5096	A2430	10k	multicolored	.50	.25
	Nos. 5091-5096 (6)			3.00	1.50

No. 5095 Overprinted in Red for All-Union Philatelic Exhibition, 1984

1982, Nov. 10

5097 A2430 10k multicolored 1.00 .25

Portrait of an Actor, by Domenico Fetti A2431

Paintings from the Hermitage: 10k, St. Sebastian, by Perugino. 20k, Danae, by Titian, horiz. 45k, Portrait of a Woman, by Correggio. No. 5102, Self-portrait, by Capriolo. No. 5103a, Portrait of a Young Woman, by Melzi.

Perf. 12x12½

1982, Nov. 25 Litho. Wmk. 383

5098	A2431	4k	multicolored	.25	.25
5099	A2431	10k	multicolored	.25	.25
5100	A2431	20k	multicolored	.30	.25
5101	A2431	45k	multicolored	.50	.40
5102	A2431	50k	multicolored	.75	.55
	Nos. 5098-5102 (5)			2.05	1.70

Souvenir Sheet

5103	Sheet of 2	2.50	1.65
a.	A2431 50k multicolored	1.00	.65

Printed in sheets of 24 stamps + label and 15 stamps + label.

See Nos. 5129-5134, 5199-5204, 5233-5238, 5310-5315, 5335-5340.

New Year 1983 — A2432

1982, Dec. 1 Unwmk.

5104 A2432 4k multicolored .50 .25

Exists imperf. Value, $50.

Souvenir Sheet

60th Anniv. of USSR — A2433

1982, Dec. 3 *Perf. 12½x12*

5105 A2433 50k multicolored 2.00 .90

Souvenir Sheet

Mountain Climbers Scaling Mt. Everest — A2434

1982, Dec. 20 Photo. *Perf. 11½x12*

5106 A2434 50k multicolored 2.00 .90

Lighthouses A2435

1982, Dec. 29 Litho. *Perf. 12*

5107	A2435	6k	green & multi	.50	.25
5108	A2435	6k	lilac & multi	.50	.25
5109	A2435	6k	salmon & multi	.50	.25
5110	A2435	6k	lt gldn brn & multi	.50	.25
5111	A2435	6k	lt brown & multi	.50	.25
	Nos. 5107-5111 (5)			2.50	1.25

No. 5111 exists imperf. Value, $25.

See Nos. 5179-5183, 5265-5269.

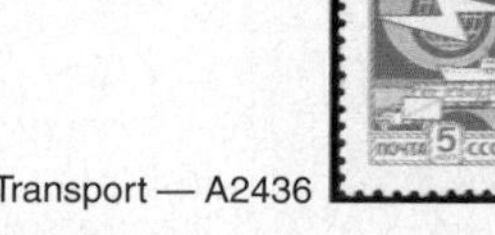

Mail Transport — A2436

1982, Dec. 22 *Perf. 12*

5112 A2436 5k greenish blue 5.00 1.00

1983, May 20 Litho. *Perf. 12*

5113 A2436 5k blue 5.00 .35

For surcharge see Uzbekistan #61E.

Iskra Newspaper Masthead A2438

1983, Jan. 5 Litho. *Perf. 12x12½*

5114 A2438 4k multicolored .50 .25

80th anniv. of 2nd Congress of Social-Democratic Workers' Party.

Fedor P. Tolstoi (1783-1873), Painter — A2439

1983, Jan. 5 Photo. *Perf. 11½*

5115 A2439 4k multicolored .50 .25

65th Anniv. of Armed Forces — A2440

1983, Jan. 25 Litho. *Perf. 12*

5116 A2440 4k multicolored .50 .25

Exists imperf. Value, $25.

Souvenir Sheet

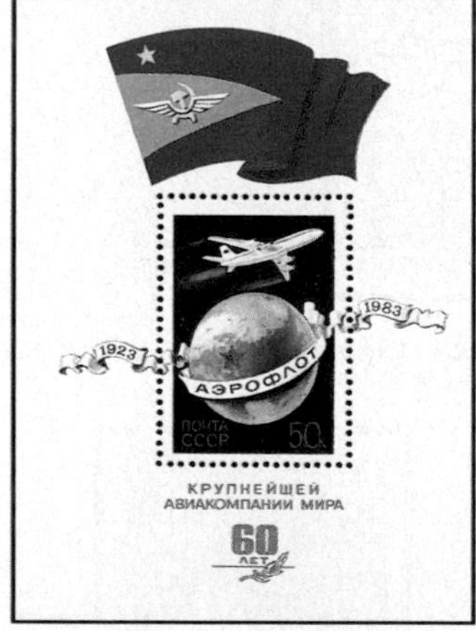

60th Anniv. of Aeroflot Airlines — A2441

1983, Feb. 9 *Perf. 12x12½*

5117 A2441 50k multicolored 1.50 1.00

Glider Type of 1982

1983, Feb. 10 *Perf. 12½x12*

5118	A2420	2k	A-9, 1948	.25	.25
5119	A2420	4k	KAJ-12, 1957	.25	.25
5120	A2420	6k	A-15, 1960	.25	.25
5121	A2420	20k	SA-7, 1970	.40	.25
5122	A2420	45k	LAJ-12, 1979	.75	.60
	Nos. 5118-5122 (5)			1.90	1.60

Tashkent Bimillennium — A2442

1983, Feb. 17 *Perf. 12½x12*

5123 A2442 4k View .50 .25

B.N. Petrov (1913-1980), Scientist — A2443

1983, Feb. 17

5124 A2443 4k multicolored .50 .25

Holy Family, by Raphael A2444

1983, Feb. 17 *Perf. 12x12½*

5125 A2444 50k multicolored .50 .25

Soyuz T-7-Salyut 7-Soyuz T-5 Flight A2445

10k, L. Popov, A. Serebrov, S. Savitskaya.

1983, Mar. 10 *Perf. 12x12½*

5126 A2445 10k multicolored .50 .25

Souvenir Sheet

World Communications Year — A2446

1983, Mar. 10 Photo. *Perf. 11½*
5127 A2446 50k multicolored 2.00 1.25

A.W. Aleksandrov, Natl. Anthem Composer — A2447

1983, Mar. 22 Litho. *Perf. 12*
5128 A2447 4k multicolored .50 .25

Exists imperf. Value, $50.

Hermitage Type of 1982

Rembrandt Paintings, Hermitage, Leningrad: 4k, Portrait of an Old Woman. 10k, Portrait of a Learned Man. 20k, Old Warrior. 45k, Portrait of Mrs. B. Martens Doomer. No. 5133, Sacrifice of Abraham. No. 5134a, Portrait of an Old Man in a Red Garment.

Perf. 12x12½

1983, Mar. 25 Wmk. 383
5129 A2431 4k multicolored .25 .25
5130 A2431 10k multicolored .25 .25
5131 A2431 20k multicolored .35 .35
5132 A2431 45k multicolored .70 .70
5133 A2431 50k multicolored .75 .75
Nos. 5129-5133 (5) 2.30 2.30

Souvenir Sheet

Lithographed and Embossed

5134 Sheet of 2 + label 2.00 1.50
a. A2431 50k multicolored .75 .75

Souvenir Sheet

Cosmonauts' Day — A2449

Perf. 12½x12

1983, Apr. 12 Litho. Unwmk.
5135 A2449 50k Soyuz T *2.00* 2.00

Souvenir Sheet

113th Birth Anniv. of Lenin — A2450

Photogravure and Engraved

1983, Apr. 22 *Perf. 11½x12*
5136 A2450 50k multicolored 1.50 .80

A. Berezovoy, V. Lebedev — A2451

Salyut 7-Soyuz T Spacecraft — A2452

1983, Apr. 25 Litho. *Perf. 12½x12*
5137 A2451 10k multicolored .50 .25
5138 A2452 10k multicolored .50 .25
a. Pair, #5137-5138 1.00 .50

Salyut 7-Soyuz T 211-Day Flight. Exists se-tenant with label.

Karl Marx (1818-1883) A2453

1983, May 5 *Perf. 12x12½*
5139 A2453 4k multicolored .50 .25

View of Rostov-on-Don — A2454

1983, May 5 Photo. *Perf. 11½*
5140 A2454 4k multicolored .50 .25

Exists imperf. Value, $50.

Buriat Autonomous Soviet Socialist Republic, 60th Anniv. — A2455

1983, May 12 Litho. *Perf. 12*
5141 A2455 4k multicolored .50 .25

Kirov Opera and Ballet Theater, Leningrad, 200th Anniv. — A2456

Photogravure and Engraved

1983, May 12 *Perf. 11½x12*
5142 A2456 4k multicolored .50 .25

Emblem of Motorcycling, Auto Racing, Shooting, Motorboating, Parachuting Organization — A2457

1983, May 20 Litho. *Perf. 11½*
5143 A2457 6k multicolored .50 .25

A.I. Khachaturian (1903-1978), Composer — A2458

1983, May 25 Engr. *Perf. 12½x12*
5144 A2458 4k violet brown 1.00 .30

Chelyabinsk Tractor Plant, 50th Anniv. — A2459

1983, June 1 Photo. *Perf. 11½*
5145 A2459 4k multicolored .50 .25

Simon Bolivar Bicentenary A2460

Photogravure and Engraved

1983, June 10 *Perf. 12*
5146 A2460 6k brown & dk brown .50 .25

City of Sevastopol, 200th Anniv. — A2461

1983, June 14 Photo. *Perf. 11½x12*
5147 A2461 5k multicolored .50 .25

Spring Flowers — A2462

1983, June 14 Litho. *Perf. 12x12½*
5148 A2462 4k multicolored .25 .25
5149 A2462 6k multicolored .25 .25
5150 A2462 10k multicolored .30 .25
5151 A2462 15k multicolored .50 .30
5152 A2462 20k multicolored .70 .35
Nos. 5148-5152 (5) 2.00 1.40

Valentina Tereshkova's Spaceflight, 20th Anniv. — A2463

1983, June 16 Litho. *Perf. 12*
5153 A2463 10k multicolored .50 .25
a. Miniature sheet of 8 200.00

P.N. Pospelov (1898-1979), Academician A2464

Photogravure and Engraved

1983, June 20 *Perf. 11½*
5154 A2464 4k multicolored .50 .25

10th European Cong. of Rheumatologists A2465

1983, June 21 Photo. *Perf. 11½*
5155 A2465 4k multicolored .50 .25

13th International Film Festival, Moscow — A2466

1983, July 7 Litho. *Perf. 12*
5156 A2466 20k multicolored .50 .25

Ships of the Soviet Fishing Fleet — A2467

4k, Two trawlers. 6k, Refrigerated trawler. 10k, Large trawler. 15k, Large refrigerated ship. 20k, Base ship.

Photogravure and Engraved
1983, July 20 *Perf. 12x11½*
5157 A2467 4k multicolored .25 .25
5158 A2467 6k multicolored .25 .25
5159 A2467 10k multicolored .35 .25
5160 A2467 15k multicolored .50 .25
5161 A2467 20k multicolored .65 .25
Nos. 5157-5161 (5) 2.00 1.25

E.B. Vakhtangov (1883-1922), Actor and Producer — A2468

1983, July 20 Photo. *Perf. 11½*
5162 A2468 5k multicolored .50 .25

"USSR-1" Stratospheric Flight, 50th Anniv. — A2469

1983, July 25 Photo. *Perf. 12*
5163 A2469 20k multicolored .50 .40
a. Miniature sheet of 8 125.00

Food Fish A2470

4k, Oncorhynchus nerka. 6k, Perciformes. 15k, Anarhichas minor. 20k, Neogobius fluviatilis, 45k, Platichthys stellatus.

1983, Aug. 5 Litho. *Perf. 12½x12*
5164 A2470 4k multicolored .25 .25
5165 A2470 6k multicolored .25 .25
5166 A2470 15k multicolored .25 .25
5167 A2470 20k multicolored .30 .30
5168 A2470 45k multicolored .50 .60
Nos. 5164-5168 (5) 1.55 1.65

A2471

SOZPHILEX '83 Philatelic Exhibition — A2472

1983, Aug. 18 Photo. *Perf. 11½*
5169 A2471 6k multicolored .50 .25

Souvenir Sheet
5170 A2472 50k Moscow Skyline 2.00 .80

Miniature Sheet

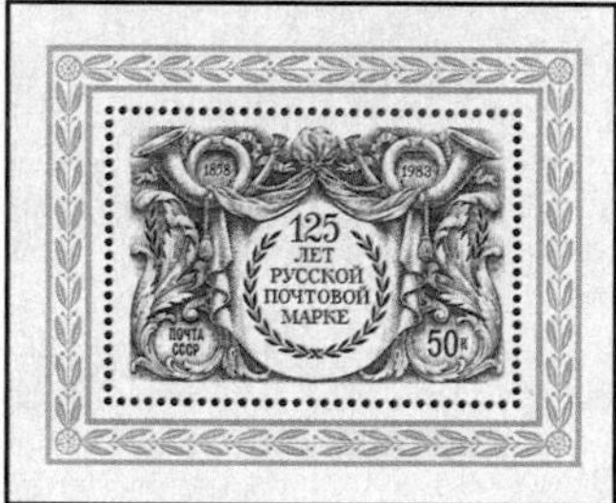

First Russian Postage Stamp, 125th Anniv. — A2473

Photogravure and Engraved
1983, Aug. 25 *Perf. 11½x12*
5171 A2473 50k pale yel & black 2.00 .70

No. 5171 Ovptd. in Red for the 5th Philatelic Society Congress

1984, Oct. 1
5171A A2473 50k pale yel & blk 4.00 3.50

Namibia Day — A2474

1983, Aug. 26 Photo. *Perf. 11½*
5172 A2474 5k multicolored .50 .25

Palestinian Solidarity — A2475

1983, Aug. 29 Photo. *Perf. 11½*
5173 A2475 5k multicolored .50 .25

1st European Championship of Radio-Telegraphy, Moscow — A2476

1983, Sept. 1 Photo. *Perf. 11½*
5174 A2476 6k multicolored .50 .25

Exists imperf. Value, $50.

4th UNESCO Council on Communications Development — A2477

1983, Sept. 2 Photo. *Perf. 12x11½*
5175 A2477 10k multicolored .50 .25

Muhammad Al-Khorezmi, Uzbek Mathematician, 1200th Birth Anniv. — A2478

Photogravure and Engraved
1983, Sept. 6 *Perf. 11½*
5176 A2478 4k multicolored .50 .25

Marshal A.I. Egorov (1883-1939) A2479

1983, Sept. 8 Engr. *Perf. 12*
5177 A2479 4k brown violet .50 .25

Union of Georgia and Russia, 200th Anniv. — A2480

1983, Sept. 8 Photo. *Perf. 11½*
5178 A2480 6k multicolored .50 .25

Lighthouse Type of 1982

Baltic Sea lighthouses.

1983, Sept. 19 Litho. *Perf. 12*
5179 A2435 1k Kipu .25 .25
5180 A2435 5k Keri .25 .25
5181 A2435 10k Stirsudden .30 .25
5182 A2435 12k Tahkun .50 .25
5183 A2435 20k Tallinn .70 .30
Nos. 5179-5183 (5) 2.00 1.30

Early Spring, by V.K. Bialynicki-Birula, 1912 — A2481

Belorussian Paintings: 4k, Portrait of the Artist's Wife with Fruit and Flowers, by J.F. Khrutzky, 1838. 15k, Young Partisan, by E.A. Zaitsev, 1943. 20k, Partisan Madonna, by M.A. Savitsky, 1967. 45k, Harvest, by V.K. Tsvirko, 1972. 15k, 20k, vert.

Perf. 12½x12, 12x12½
1983, Sept. 28
5184 A2481 4k multicolored .25 .25
5185 A2481 6k multicolored .25 .25
5186 A2481 15k multicolored .25 .25
5187 A2481 20k multicolored .30 .25
5188 A2481 45k multicolored .40 .25
Nos. 5184-5188 (5) 1.45 1.25

Hammer and Sickle Steel Mill, Moscow, Centenary A2482

1983, Oct. 1 Photo. *Perf. 11½*
5189 A2482 4k multicolored .50 .25

Natl. Food Program A2483

1983, Oct. 10
5190 A2483 5k Wheat production .50 .25
5191 A2483 5k Cattle, dairy products .50 .25
5192 A2483 5k Produce .50 .25
Nos. 5190-5192 (3) 1.50 .75

October Revolution, 66th anniv. — A2484

1983, Oct. 12 Litho. *Perf. 12*
5193 A2484 4k multicolored .50 .25

Ivan Fedorov — A2485

1983, Oct. 12 Engr. *Perf. 12x12½*

5194 A2485 4k dark brown .50 .25

Ivan Fedorov, first Russian printer (Book of the Apostles), 400th death anniv.

Urengoy-Uzgorod Transcontinental Gas Pipeline Completion — A2486

1983, Oct. 12 Photo. *Perf. 12x11½*

5195 A2486 5k multicolored .50 .25

A.W. Sidorenko (1917-82), Geologist — A2487

1983, Oct. 19 Litho. *Perf. 12*

5196 A2487 4k multicolored .50 .25

Campaign Against Nuclear Weapons — A2488

1983, Oct. 19 Photo. *Perf. 11½*

5197 A2488 5k Demonstration .50 .25

Exists imperf. Value $50.

Maktumkuli, Turkmenistan Poet, 250th Birth Anniv. — A2489

1983, Oct. 27

5198 A2489 5k multicolored .50 .25

Hermitage Painting Type of 1982

Paintings by Germans: 4k, Madonna and Child with Apple Tree, by Lucas Cranach the Elder. 10k, Self-portrait, by Anton R. Mengs. 20k, Self-portrait, by Jüurgen Ovens. 45k, Sailboat, by Caspar David Friedrich. No. 5203, Rape of the Sabines, by Johann Schoenfeld, horiz. No. 5204a, Portrait of a Young Man, by Ambrosius Holbein.

Perf. 12x12½, 12½x12

1983, Nov. 10 Litho. Wmk. 383

5199 A2431 4k multicolored .25 .25
5200 A2431 10k multicolored .25 .25
5201 A2431 20k multicolored .30 .25
5202 A2431 45k multicolored .60 .40
5203 A2431 50k multicolored .70 .50
Nos. 5199-5203 (5) 2.10 1.65

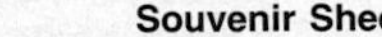

Souvenir Sheet

5204 Sheet of 2 + label 3.00 1.50
a. A2431 50k multicolored 1.50 .50

Nos. 5199-5203 with labels, value $5.
Printed in sheets of 24+label and 15+label. Value, each $75.

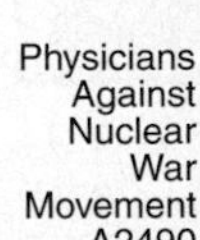

Physicians Against Nuclear War Movement A2490

Perf. 11½

1983, Nov. 17 Photo. Unwmk.

5205 A2490 5k Baby, dove, sun .50 .25

Sukhe Bator (1893-1923), Mongolian People's Rep. Founder — A2491

1983, Nov. 17

5206 A2491 5k Portrait .50 .25

New Year 1984 A2492

1983, Dec. 1

5207 A2492 5k Star, snowflakes .25 .25

Exists imperf; Value, $50.
Printed in sheets of 50. Also exist in miniature sheets of 16. Value, $150.

Newly Completed Buildings, Moscow — A2493

3k, Children's Musical Theater. 4k, Tourist Hotel, vert. 6k, Council of Ministers. 20k, Ismaelovo Hotel. 45k, Novosti Press Agency.

Perf. 12½x12, 12x12½

1983, Dec. 15 Engr.

5208 A2493 3k multicolored .25 .25
5209 A2493 4k multicolored .25 .25
5210 A2493 6k multicolored .25 .25
5211 A2493 20k multicolored .50 .35
5212 A2493 45k multicolored 1.40 .70
Nos. 5208-5212 (5) 2.65 1.80

Souvenir Sheet

Environmental Protection Campaign — A2494

1983, Dec. 20 Photo. *Perf. 11½*

5213 A2494 50k multicolored 1.50 1.50

Moscow Local Broadcasting Network, 50th anniv. — A2495

1984, Jan. 1

5214 A2495 4k multicolored .50 .25

European Women's Skating Championships — A2496

1984, Jan. 1 *Perf. 12x11½*

5215 A2496 5k multicolored .50 .25

Exists imperf. Value, $50.

Cuban Revolution, 25th Anniv. A2497

1984, Jan. 1 *Perf. 11½*

5216 A2497 5k Flag, "25" .50 .25

Exists imperf. Value, $50.

World War II Tanks — A2498

1984, Jan. 25 Litho. *Perf. 12½x12*

5217 A2498 10k KW .60 .25
5218 A2498 10k IS-2 .60 .25
5219 A2498 10k T-34 .60 .25
5220 A2498 10k ISU-152 .60 .25
5221 A2498 10k SU-100 .60 .25
Nos. 5217-5221 (5) 3.00 1.25

No. 5220 exists imperf. Value, $50.

1984 Winter Olympics — A2499

1984, Feb. 8 Photo. *Perf. 11½x12*

5222 A2499 5k Biathlon .25 .25
a. Miniature sheet of 8 45.00
5223 A2499 10k Speed skating .25 .25
a. Miniature sheet of 8 45.00
5224 A2499 20k Hockey .25 .25
a. Miniature sheet of 8 45.00
5225 A2499 45k Figure skating .25 .25
a. Miniature sheet of 8 45.00
Nos. 5222-5225 (4) 1.00 1.00

Exist imperf. Value, each $50.

Moscow Zoo, 120th Anniv. — A2500

1984, Feb. 16 Litho. *Perf. 12½x12*

5226 A2500 2k Mandrill .25 .25
5227 A2500 3k Gazelle .25 .25
5228 A2500 4k Snow leopard .25 .25
5229 A2500 5k Crowned crane .25 .25
5230 A2500 20k Macaw .25 .25
Nos. 5226-5230 (5) 1.25 1.25

Yuri Gagarin (1934-68) — A2501

1984, Mar. 9 Engr. *Perf. 12½x12*

5231 A2501 15k Portrait, Vostok .50 .25
a. Miniature sheet of 8 200.00

Souvenir Sheet

Mass Development of Virgin and Unused Land, 30th Anniv. — A2502

1984, Mar. 14 Photo. *Perf. 11½x12*

5232 A2502 50k multicolored 1.50 .75

Hermitage Painting Type of 1982

Paintings by English Artists: 4k, E.K. Vorontsova, by George Hayter. 10k, Portrait of Mrs. Greer, by George Romney. 20k, Before a Thunderstorm, by George Morland, horiz. 45k, Portrait of an Unknown Man, by Marcus Gheeraerts Jr. No. 5237, Cupid and Venus, by Joshua Reynolds. No. 5238a, Portrait of a Lady in Blue, by Thomas Gainsborough.

Perf. 12x12½, 12½x12

1984, Mar. 20 Litho. Wmk. 383

5233 A2431 4k multicolored .25 .25
5234 A2431 10k multicolored .25 .25
5235 A2431 20k multicolored .30 .25
5236 A2431 45k multicolored .70 .40
5237 A2431 50k multicolored .80 .45
Nos. 5233-5237 (5) 2.30 1.60

Souvenir Sheet

5238 Sheet of 2 2.00 1.00
a. A2431 50k multicolored .50 .40

Nos. 5233-5237 each se-tenant with label showing text and embossed emblem.

S.V. Ilyushin — A2503

Perf. 11½

1984, Mar. 23 Photo. Unwmk.

5239 A2503 5k Aircraft designer, (1894-1977) .50 .25

Andrei S. Bubnov — A2504

1984, Apr. 3 ***Perf. 11½x12***

5240 A2504 5k Statesman, (1884-1940) .50 .25

Intercosmos Cooperative Space Program (USSR-India) A2505

Designs: 5k, Weather Station M-100 launch. 20k, Geodesy (satellites, observatory). 45k, Rocket, satellites, dish antenna. 50k, Flags, cosmonauts.

1984 ***Perf. 12x11½***

5241 A2505 5k multicolored .25 .25
5242 A2505 20k multicolored .35 .25
5243 A2505 45k multicolored .40 .25
Nos. 5241-5243 (3) 1.00 .75

Souvenir Sheet

5244 A2505 50k multicolored 1.50 .75

No. 5244 contains one 25x36mm stamp. Issue dates: 50k, Apr. 5; others, Apr. 3.

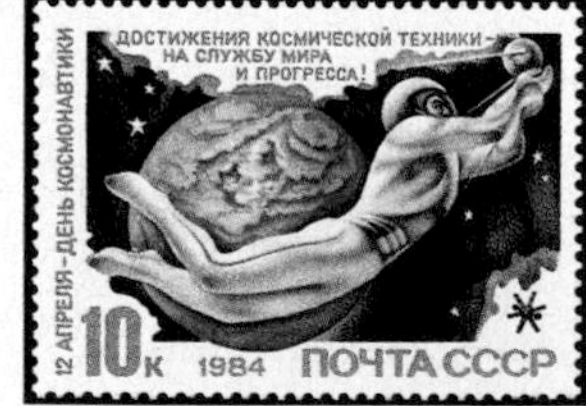

Cosmonauts' Day — A2506

1984, Apr. 12 ***Perf. 11½x12***

5245 A2506 10k Futuristic spaceman .50 .30

Tchelyuskin Arctic Expedition, 50th Anniv. — A2507

Photogravure and Engraved

1984, Apr. 13 ***Perf. 11½x12***

5246 A2507 6k Ship .25 .25
a. Miniature sheet of 8 *40.00*

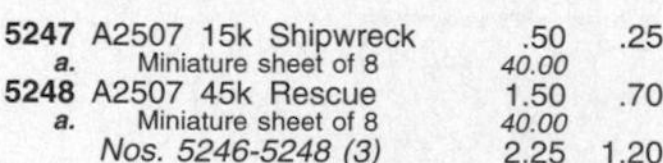

5247 A2507 15k Shipwreck .50 .25
a. Miniature sheet of 8 *40.00*
5248 A2507 45k Rescue 1.50 .70
a. Miniature sheet of 8 *40.00*
Nos. 5246-5248 (3) 2.25 1.20

Souvenir Sheet

Photo.

5249 A2507 50k Hero of Soviet Union medal 1.50 .70

First HSU medal awarded to rescue crew. No. 5249 contains one 27x39mm stamp.

Souvenir Sheet

114th Birth Anniv. of Lenin — A2508

1984, Apr. 22 Litho. ***Perf. 11½x12½***

5250 A2508 50k Portrait 1.50 .70

Aquatic Plants — A2509

1k, Lotus. 2k, Euriola. 3k, Water lilies, horiz. 10k, White nymphaea, horiz. 20k, Marshflowers, horiz.

1984, May 5 ***Perf. 12x12½, 12½x12***

5251 A2509 1k multicolored .25 .25
5252 A2509 2k multicolored .25 .25
5253 A2509 3k multicolored .25 .25
5254 A2509 10k multicolored .25 .25
a. Miniature sheet of 8 30.00
5255 A2509 20k multicolored .45 .25
Nos. 5251-5255 (5) 1.45 1.25

Soviet Peace Policy — A2510

No. 5256, Marchers, banners (at left). No. 5257, Text. No. 5258, Marchers, banners (at right).

1984, May 8 Photo. ***Perf. 11½***

5256 A2510 5k multicolored .35 .25
5257 A2510 5k multicolored .35 .25
5258 A2510 5k multicolored .35 .25
a. Strip of 3, #5256-5258 2.00 .50

A2511

1984, May 15 Photo. ***Perf. 11½***

5259 A2511 10k multicolored .50 .25

E.O. Paton Institute of Electric Welding, 50th anniv.

A2512

1984, May 21

5260 A2512 10k multicolored .50 .30

25th Conf. for Electric and Postal Communications Cooperation.

A2513

1984, May 29

5261 A2513 5k violet brown .50 .25

Maurice Bishop, Grenada Prime Minister (1944-83).

A2514

1984, May 31

5262 A2514 5k multicolored 1.00 .25

V.I. Lenin Central Museum, 60th anniv.

City of Archangelsk, 400th Anniv. — A2515

1984, June 1 Photo. & Engr.

5263 A2515 5k multicolored .50 .25

European Youth Soccer Championship — A2516

1984, June 1 Photo. ***Perf. 12x11½***

5264 A2516 15k multicolored .50 .30

Lighthouse Type of 1982

Far Eastern seas lighthouses.

1984, June 14 Litho. ***Perf. 12***

5265 A2435 1k Petropavlovsk .40 .25
5266 A2435 2k Tokarev .40 .25
5267 A2435 4k Basargin .40 .25

5268 A2435 5k Kronitsky .40 .25
5269 A2435 10k Marekan .40 .25

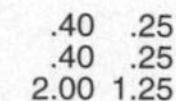

Nos. 5265-5269 (5) 2.00 1.25

Salyut 7-Soyuz T-9 150-Day Flight — A2517

1984, June 27 Litho. ***Perf. 12***

5270 A2517 15k multicolored .50 .25

A2518

Photogravure and Engraved

1984, July 1 ***Perf. 11½***

5271 A2518 10k multicolored .50 .25

Morflot, Merchant & Transport Fleet, 60th anniv.

60th Anniv. of Awarding V.I. Lenin Name to Youth Communist League — A2519

1984, July 1 Photo. ***Perf. 11½x12***

5272 A2519 5k multicolored .50 .25

Liberation of Byelorussia, 40th Anniv. A2520

1984, July 3 Photo. ***Perf. 12x11½***

5273 A2520 5k multicolored .50 .25

CMEA Conference, Moscow — A2521

1984, June 12 Photo. ***Perf. 11½***

5274 A2521 5k CMEA Building & Kremlin .50 .25

A2522

1984, July 20 Photo. *Perf. 11½*

5275 A2522 5k Convention seal .50 .25

27th Intl. Geological Cong., Moscow.

A2523

1984, July 22 Photo. *Perf. 11½*

5276 A2523 5k Arms, draped flag .50 .25

People's Republic of Poland, 40th anniv.

B. V. Asafiev (1884-1949), Composer — A2524

1984, July 25 Engr. *Perf. 12½x12*

5277 A2524 5k greenish black .50 .25

Relations with Mexico, 60th Anniv. A2525

1984, Aug. 4 Litho. *Perf. 12*

5278 A2525 5k USSR, Mexican flags .50 .25

Miniature Sheet

Russian Folk Tales A2526

Designs: a, 3 archers. b, Prince and frog. c, Old man and prince. d, Crowd and swans. e, Wolf and men. f, Bird and youth. g, Youth on white horse. h, Couple with Tsar. i, Village scene. j, Man on black horse. k, Old man. l, Young woman.

1984, Aug. 10 Litho. *Perf. 12x12½*

5279 Sheet of 12 5.00 2.00
a.-l. A2526 5k, any single .30 .25

Friendship '84 Games A2527

1984, Aug. 15 Photo. *Perf. 11½*

5280 A2527 1k Basketball .25 .25
5281 A2527 5k Gymnastics, vert. .25 .25
5282 A2527 10k Weightlifting .25 .25
5283 A2527 15k Wrestling .25 .25
5284 A2527 20k High jump .25 .25
Nos. 5280-5284 (5) 1.25 1.25

A2528

1984, Aug. 23 Litho. *Perf. 12*

5285 A2528 5k Flag, monument .50 .25

Liberation of Romania, 40th anniv.

A2529

Designs: 35k, Sable. 2r, Ship, arctic map. 3r, Child and globe. 5r, Palm frond and globe.

Subjects: 35k, 3r, Environmental protection. 2r, Arctic development. 5r, World peace.

1984, Sept. 5 Litho. *Perf. 12½x12*

5286 A2529 35k multicolored .65 .35
5287 A2529 2r multicolored .80 .45

Engr.

5288 A2529 3r multicolored 4.00 1.10
5289 A2529 5r multicolored 5.00 1.90
Nos. 5286-5289 (4) 10.45 3.80

Nos. 5286 and 5287 were issued in 1984 on chalky paper, which fluoresces under UV light. Reprints on ordinary paper were made in 1988 and 1991, respectively. Values above are for the later printings. The 1984 printings are valued, mint or used, at 90c for No. 5286, and $3 for No. 5287.

See Nos. 6016B-6017A.

World Chess Championships A2530

No. 5290, Motherland statue, Volgograd. No. 5291, Spasski Tower, Moscow.

1984, Sept. 7 Photo. *Perf. 11½*

5290 A2530 15k multicolored .50 .30
5291 A2530 15k multicolored .50 .30

Bulgarian Revolution, 40th Anniv. — A2531

1984, Sept. 9 Photo. *Perf. 11½*

5292 A2531 5k Bulgarian arms .50 .25

Ethiopian Revolution, 10th Anniv. A2532

1984, Sept. 12 Litho. *Perf. 12*

5293 A2532 5k Ethiopian flag, seal .50 .25

Novokramatorsk Machinery Plant, 50th Anniv. — A2533

Photogravure and Engraved

1984, Sept. 20 *Perf. 11½*

5294 A2533 5k Excavator .50 .25

Nakhichevan ASSR, 60th Anniv. — A2534

1984, Sept. 20 Litho. *Perf. 12*

5295 A2534 5k Arms .50 .25

Television from Space, 25th Anniv. A2535

1984, Oct. 4 Photo. *Perf. 11½*

5296 A2535 5k Luna 3 .25 .25
5297 A2535 20k Venera 9 .35 .25
5298 A2535 45k Meteor satellite .40 .25
Nos. 5296-5298 (3) 1.00 .75

Souvenir Sheet

Perf. 11½x12

5299 A2535 50k Camera, space walker, vert. 1.50 .75

No. 5299 contains one 26x37mm stamp.

German Democratic Republic, 35th Anniv. A2536

1984, Oct. 7 Photo. *Perf. 11½*

5300 A2536 5k Flag, arms .50 .25

Ukrainian Liberation, 40th Anniv. A2537

1984, Oct. 8 Photo. *Perf. 12x11½*

5301 A2537 5k Motherland statue, Kiev .50 .25

Soviet Republics and Parties, 60th Anniv. A2538

SSR Flags & Arms: No. 5302, Moldavian. No. 5303, Kirgiz. No. 5304, Tadzhik. No. 5305, Uzbek. No. 5306, Turkmen.

1984 Litho. *Perf. 12*

5302 A2538 5k multicolored .25 .25
5303 A2538 5k multicolored .25 .25
5304 A2538 5k multicolored .25 .25
5305 A2538 5k multicolored .25 .25
5306 A2538 5k multicolored .25 .25
Nos. 5302-5306 (5) 1.25 1.25

Issued: No. 5302, 10/12; Nos. 5303-5304, 10/14; Nos. 5305-5306, 10/27.

Kremlin, 1917 Flag — A2539

1984, Oct. 23 Photo. *Perf. 11½*

5307 A2539 5k multicolored .50 .25

October Revolution, 67th anniv.

Aircraft, Spacecraft A2540

1984, Nov. 6 Photo. *Perf. 11½*

5308 A2540 5k multicolored .50 .25

M. Frunze Inst. of Aviation & Cosmonautics.

Baikal — Amur Railway Completion A2541

5k, Workers, map, engine.

1984, Nov. 7 Photo. *Perf. 11½*

5309 A2541 5k multicolored .50 .25

Hermitage Type of 1982

Paintings by French Artists: 4k, Girl in a Hat, by Jean Louis Voille. 10k, A Stolen Kiss, by Jean-Honore Fragonard. 20k, Woman Combing her Hair, by Edgar Degas. 45k, Pigmalion and Galatea, by Francois Boucher. 50k, Landscape with Polyphenus, by Nicholas Poussin. No. 5315a, Child with a Whip, by Pierre-Auguste Renoir.

Perf. 12x12½, 12½x12

1984, Nov. 20 Litho. Wmk. 383

5310 A2431 4k multicolored .25 .25
5311 A2431 10k multi, horiz. .35 .25
5312 A2431 20k multicolored .55 .45
5313 A2431 45k multi, horiz. .85 .55
5314 A2431 50k multi, horiz. 1.00 .65
Nos. 5310-5314 (5) 3.00 2.15

Souvenir Sheet

5315 Sheet of 2 2.00 1.50
a. A2431 50k multicolored .75 .50

Mongolian Peoples' Republic, 60th Anniv. — A2542

5k, Mongolian flag, arms.

Perf. 11½

1984, Nov. 26 Photo. Unwmk.

5316 A2542 5k multicolored .50 .25

New Year 1985 — A2543

5k, Kremlin, snowflakes.

1984, Dec. 4 Litho. *Perf. 11½*

5317 A2543 5k multicolored .50 .25
a. Miniature sheet of 8 110.00

Souvenir Sheet

Environmental Protection — A2544

50k, Leaf, pollution sources.

1984, Dec. 4 Litho. *Perf. 12½x12*

5318 A2544 50k multicolored 2.00 .75

Russian Fire Vehicles — A2545

3k, Crew wagon, 19th cent. 5k, Pumper, 19th cent. 10k, Ladder truck, 1904. 15k, Pumper, 1904. 20k, Ladder truck, 1913.

Photogravure and Engraved

1984, Dec. 12 *Perf. 12x11½*

5319 A2545 3k multicolored .25 .25
5320 A2545 5k multicolored .25 .25
5321 A2545 10k multicolored .55 .25
5322 A2545 15k multicolored .75 .25
5323 A2545 20k multicolored 1.20 .25
Nos. 5319-5323 (5) 3.00 1.25

See Nos. 5410-5414.

Intl. Venus-Halley's Comet Project — A2546

15k, Satellite, flight path.

1984, Dec. 15 Photo. *Perf. 12x11½*

5324 A2546 15k multicolored .50 .25
a. Miniature sheet of 8 *40.00*

Indira Gandhi (1917-1984), Indian Prime Minister — A2547

1984, Dec. 28 Litho. *Perf. 12*

5325 A2547 5k Portrait .75 .50

1905 Revolution A2548

5k, Flag, Moscow memorial.

1985, Jan. 22 Photo. *Perf. 11½*

5326 A2548 5k multicolored .50 .25

A2549

1985, Jan. 24

5327 A2549 5k multicolored .40 .25

Patrice Lumumba Peoples' Friendship University, 25th Anniv.

Mikhail Vasilievich Frunze (1885-1925), Party Leader — A2550

1985, Feb. 2

5328 A2550 5k bluish, blk & ocher .40 .25

Karakalpak ASSR, 60th Anniv. A2551

1985, Feb. 16 *Perf. 12*

5329 A2551 5k Republic arms .40 .25

10th Winter Spartakiad of Friendly Armies — A2552

1985, Feb. 23 *Perf. 11½*

5330 A2552 5k Hockey player, emblem .50 .25

Kalevala, 150th Anniv. A2553

1985, Feb. 25 Litho. *Perf. 12*

5331 A2553 5k Rune singer, frontispiece .50 .25

Finnish Kalevala, collection of Karelian epic poetry compiled by Elias Lonrot.

Yakov M. Sverdlov (1885-1919), Party Leader — A2554

1985, Mar. 3 Engr. *Perf. 12½x12*

5332 A2554 5k rose lake .40 .25

Yakov M. Sverdlov (1885-1919), party leader.

Pioneer Badge, Awards — A2555

1985, Mar. 6 Photo. *Perf. 11½*

5333 A2555 5k multicolored .40 .25

Pionerskaya Pravda, All-Union children's newspaper, 60th Anniv.

Maria Alexandrovna Ulyanova (1835-1916), Lenin's Mother — A2556

1985, Mar. 6 Engr. *Perf. 12½x12*

5334 A2556 5k black .40 .25

Hermitage Type of 1982

Paintings by Spanish artists: 4k, The Young Virgin Praying, vert., by Francisco de Zurbaran (1598-1664). 10k, Still-life, by Antonio Pereda (c. 1608-1678). 20k, The Immaculate Conception, vert., by Murillo (1617-1682). 45k, The Grinder, by Antonio Puga. No. 5339, Count Olivares, vert., by Diego Velazques (1599-1660). No. 5340a, Portrait of the actress Antonia Zarate, vert., by Goya (1746-1828).

Perf. 12x12½, 12½x12

1985, Mar. 14 Litho. Wmk. 383

5335 A2431 4k multicolored .25 .25
5336 A2431 10k multicolored .30 .25
5337 A2431 20k multicolored .50 .40
5338 A2431 45k multicolored 1.25 .90
5339 A2431 50k multicolored 1.40 .95
Nos. 5335-5339 (5) 3.70 2.75

Souvenir Sheet

Lithographed and Embossed

5340 Sheet of 2 + label 10.00 2.00
a. A2431 50k multicolored 1.10 .75

EXPO '85, Tsukuba, Japan A2557

Soviet exhibition, Expo '85 emblems and: 5k, Cosmonauts in space. 10k, Communications satellite. 20k, Alternative energy sources development. 45k, Future housing systems. 50k, Soviet exhibition emblem, globe.

Perf. 12x11½

1985, Mar. 17 Photo. Unwmk.

5341 A2557 5k multicolored .25 .25
5342 A2557 10k multicolored .25 .25
5343 A2557 20k multicolored .50 .35
5344 A2557 45k multicolored 1.00 .70
Nos. 5341-5344 (4) 2.00 1.55

Souvenir Sheet

5345 A2557 50k multicolored 1.50 .90

Nos. 5341-5344 issued in sheets of 8.

Souvenir Sheet

Johann Sebastian Bach (1685-1750), Composer — A2558

Photogravure and Engraved

1985, Mar. 21 *Perf. 12x11½*

5346 A2558 50k black 1.50 1.00

Natl. Crest, Budapest Memorial — A2559

1985, Apr. 4 Litho. *Perf. 12*

5347 A2559 5k multi .50 .25

Hungary liberated from German occupation, 40th Anniv.

Emblem — A2560

1985, Apr. 5 Photo. *Perf. 11½*

5348 A2560 15k multi .50 .30

Society for Cultural Relations with Foreign Countries, 60th anniv.

Victory over Fascism, 40th Anniv. A2561

#5349, Battle of Moscow, soldier, Kremlin, portrait of Lenin. #5350, Soldier, armed forces. #5351, Armaments production, worker. #5352, Partisan movement, cavalry. #5353, Berlin-Treptow war memorial, German Democratic Republic. #5354, Order of the Patriotic War, second class.

1985, Apr. 20 ***Perf. 12x11½***

5349 A2561 5k multicolored .25 .25
5350 A2561 5k multicolored .25 .25
5351 A2561 5k multicolored .25 .25
5352 A2561 5k multicolored .25 .25
5353 A2561 5k multicolored .25 .25
Nos. 5349-5353 (5) 1.25 1.25

Souvenir Sheet

Perf. 11½

5354 A2561 50k multicolored 1.50 .50

No. 5354 contains one 28x40mm stamp. Issued in sheets of 8.

No. 5353 Ovptd. in Red for 40th Year Since World War II Victory All-Union Philatelic Exhibition

1985, Apr. 29 **Photo.** ***Perf. 12x11½***

5354A A2561 5k brn lake, gold & vermilion 2.00 .50

Yuri Gagarin Center for Training Cosmonauts, 25th Anniv. — A2562

Cosmonauts day: Portrait, cosmonauts, Soyuz-T spaceship.

1985, Apr. 12 **Photo.** ***Perf. 11½x12***

5355 A2562 15k multicolored .50 .25
a. Miniature sheet of 8 *125.00*

12th World Youth Festival, Moscow A2563

1985, Apr. 15 **Litho.** ***Perf. 12x12½***

5356 A2563 1k Three youths .25 .25
5357 A2563 3k African girl .25 .25
5358 A2563 5k Girl, rainbow .25 .25
5359 A2563 20k Asian youth, camera .35 .35
5360 A2563 45k Emblem 1.50 .60
Nos. 5356-5360 (5) 2.60 1.70

No. 5358 issued in sheets of 8.

Souvenir Sheet

1985, July 4

5361 A2563 30k Emblem 1.50 1.00

115th Birth Anniv. of Lenin — A2564

Portrait and: No. 5362, Lenin Museum, Tampere, Finland. No. 5363, Memorial apartment, Paris, France.

1985, Apr. 22 **Photo.** ***Perf. 11½x12***

5362 A2564 5k multicolored .25 .25
5363 A2564 5k multicolored .25 .25

Souvenir Sheet

Litho.

Perf. 12x12½

5364 A2564 30k Portrait 1.50 1.00

No. 5364 contains one 30x42mm stamp.

Order of Victory — A2565

Photogravure and Engraved

1985, May 9 ***Perf. 11½***

5365 A2565 20k sil, royal bl, dk red & gold .60 .35

Allied World War II victory over Germany and Japan, 40th anniv.

Arms — A2566

1985, May 9 **Litho.** ***Perf. 12½x12***

5366 A2566 5k multicolored .50 .25

Liberation of Czechoslovakia from German occupation, 40th Anniv.

Flags of Member Nations — A2567

1985, May 14 **Photo.** ***Perf. 11½***

5367 A2567 5k multicolored .50 .25

Warsaw Treaty Org., 30th anniv.

Mikhail Alexandrovich Sholokhov (1905-1984), Novelist & Nobel Laureate — A2568

Portraits and book covers: No. 5368, Tales from the Don, Quiet Flows the Don, A Human Tragedy. No. 5369, The Quiet Don, Virgin Lands Under the Plow, Thus They Have Fought for Their Homeland. No. 5370, Portrait.

1985, May 24 **Litho.** ***Perf. 12½x12***

5368 A2568 5k Portrait at left .35 .25
5369 A2568 5k Portrait at right .35 .25

Photo.

Perf. 12x11½

Size: 37x52mm

5370 A2568 5k brn, gold & black .35 .25
Nos. 5368-5370 (3) 1.05 .75

INTERCOSMOS Project Halley-Venus — A2570

15k, Spacecraft, satellites, Venus.

1985, June 11 **Litho.** ***Perf. 12***

5372 A2570 15k multicolored .50 .25
a. Miniature sheet of 8 *150.00*

Artek Pioneer Camp, 60th Anniv. A2571

4k, Camp, badges, Lenin Pioneers emblem.

1985, June 14 **Photo.** ***Perf. 11½***

5373 A2571 4k multicolored .50 .25

Mutiny on the Battleship Potemkin, 80th Anniv. — A2572

Photogravure and Engraved

1985, June 16 ***Perf. 11½x12***

5374 A2572 5k dk red, gold & black .50 .25

Miniature Sheet

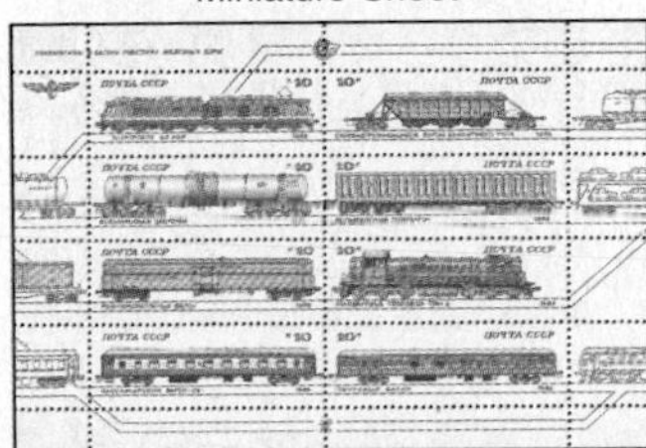

Soviet Railways Rolling Stock — A2573

Designs: a, Electric locomotive WL 80-R (grn). b, Tanker car (bl). c, Refrigerator car (bl). d, Sleeper car (brn). e, Tipper car (brn). f, Box car (brn). g, Shunting diesel locomotive (bl). h, Mail car (grn).

1985, June 15 **Engr.** ***Perf. 12½x12***

5375 A2573 Sheet of 8 3.00 1.65
a.-h. 10k any single .35 .25

Cosmonauts L. Kizim, V. Soloviov, O. Atkov and Salyut-7 Spacecraft — A2574

1985, June 25 **Litho.**

5376 A2574 15k multicolored .50 .25
a. Miniature sheet of 8 *50.00*

Soyuz T 10, Salyut-7 and Soyuz T-11 flights, Feb. 8-Oct. 2, 1984.

Beating Sword into Plowshares, Sculpture Donated to UN Hdqtrs. by USSR — A2575

Photogravure and Engraved

1985, June 26 ***Perf. 11½***

5377 A2575 45k multicolored .50 .35

UN 40th anniv.

Intl. Youth Year A2576

1985, June 26 **Photo.** ***Perf. 12***

5378 A2576 10k multicolored .50 .25

Medicinal Plants from Siberia — A2577

2k, O. dictiocarpum. 3k, Thermopsis lanceolata. 5k, Rosa acicularis lindi. 20k, Rhaponticum carthamoides. 45k, Bergenia crassifolia fritsch.

1985, July 10 **Litho.** ***Perf. 12½x12***

5379 A2577 2k multicolored .25 .25
5380 A2577 3k multicolored .25 .25
5381 A2577 5k multicolored .25 .25
5382 A2577 20k multicolored .50 .35
a. Miniature sheet of 8 *35.00*
5383 A2577 45k multicolored .75 .50
Nos. 5379-5383 (5) 2.00 1.60

Cosmonauts V. A. Dzhanibekov, S. E. Savistskaya, and I. P. Volk, Soyuz T-12 Mission, July 17-29, 1984 — A2578

1985, July 17

5384 A2578 10k multicolored .50 .25
a. Miniature sheet of 8 *100.00*

1st woman's free flight in space.

A2579

Caecilienhof Palace, Potsdam, Flags of UK, USSR, & US.

1985, July 17
5385 A2579 15k multicolored .50 .25

Potsdam Conference, 40th anniv.

Finlandia Hall, Helsinki — A2580

1985, July 25 Photo. *Perf. 11½*
5386 A2580 20k multicolored .50 .30
a. Miniature sheet of 8 100.00

Helsinki Conference on European security and cooperation, 10th anniv.

Flags of USSR, North Korea, Liberation Monument in Pyongyang A2581

1985, Aug. 1
5387 A2581 5k multicolored .50 .25

Socialist Rep. of North Korea, 40th anniv.

Endangered Wildlife — A2582

Designs: 2k, Sorex bucharensis, vert. 3k, Cardiocranius paradoxus. 5k, Selevinia betpakdalensis, vert. 20k, Felis caracal. 45k, Gazella subgutturosa. 50k, Panthera pardus.

Perf. 12x12½, 12½x12

1985, Aug. 15 Litho.
5388 A2582 2k multicolored .25 .25
5389 A2582 3k multicolored .25 .25
5390 A2582 5k multicolored .25 .25

Size: 47x32mm

5391 A2582 20k multicolored .60 .30
a. Miniature sheet of 8 75.00
5392 A2582 45k multicolored 1.20 .60
Nos. 5388-5392 (5) 2.55 1.65

Souvenir Sheet

5393 A2582 50k multicolored 2.50 .75

Youth World Soccer Cup Championships, Moscow — A2583

1985, Aug. 24 *Perf. 12*
5394 A2583 5k multicolored .50 .25

Alexander G. Stakhanov, Coal Miner & Labor Leader A2584

1985, Aug. 30 Photo. *Perf. 11½*
5395 A2584 5k multicolored .50 .25

Stakhanovite Movement for high labor productivity, 50th anniv.

Bryansk Victory Memorial, Buildings, Arms A2585

1985, Sept. 1
5396 A2585 5k multicolored .50 .25

Millennium of Bryansk.

Socialist Republic of Vietnam, 40th Anniv. — A2586

1985, Sept. 2 Litho. *Perf. 12½x12*
5397 A2586 5k Arms .50 .25

A2587

1985, Sept. 2 Photo. *Perf. 11½*
5398 A2587 10k multicolored .50 .25

1985 World Chess Championship match, A. Karpov Vs. G. Kasparov, Moscow.

Lutsk City, Ukrainian SSR, 900th Anniv. — A2588

1985, Sept. 14
5399 A2588 5k Lutsk Castle .50 .25

Open Book, the Weeping Jaroslavna and Prince Igor's Army — A2589

Photogravure and Engraved

1985, Sept. 14 *Perf. 11½x12*
5400 A2589 10k multicolored .50 .25

The Song of Igor's Campaign, epic poem, 800th anniv.

Sergei Vasilievich Gerasimov (1885-1964), Painter A2590

1985, Sept. 26 *Perf. 12x11½*
5401 A2590 5k Portrait .50 .25

October Revolution, 68th Anniv. — A2591

1985, Oct. 10 Photo. *Perf. 11½*
5402 A2591 5k multicolored .50 .25

UN 40th Anniv. — A2592

1985, Oct. 24
5403 A2592 15k multicolored .50 .25

Krisjanis Barons (1835-1923), Latvian Folklorist — A2593

Lithographed and Engraved

1985, Oct. 31
5404 A2593 5k beige & black .50 .25

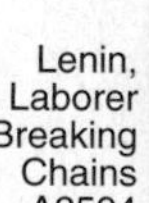

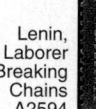

Lenin, Laborer Breaking Chains A2594

1985, Nov. 20 Photo.
5405 A2594 5k multicolored .50 .25

Petersburg Union struggle for liberation of the working classes, founded by Lenin, 90th anniv.

Largest Soviet Telescope, 10th Anniv. — A2595

1985, Nov. 20 Engr. *Perf. 12½x12*
5406 A2595 10k dark blue .50 .25

Soviet Observatory inauguration.

A2596

1985, Nov. 25 Photo.
5407 A2596 5k multicolored .50 .25

Angolan Independence, 10th anniv.

A2597

1985, Nov. 29 *Perf. 11½*
5408 A2597 5k multicolored .50 .25

Socialist Federal Republic of Yugoslavia, 40th anniv.

New Year — A2598

1985, Dec. 3 Litho. *Perf. 12*
5409 A2598 5k multicolored 1.00 .25
a. Miniature sheet of 8 25.00

Vehicle Type of 1984

1985, Dec. 18 Photo. *Perf. 12x11½*
5410 A2545 3k AMO-F15, 1926 .25 .25
5411 A2545 5k PMZ-1, 1933 .25 .25
5412 A2545 10k AC-40, 1977 .35 .25
5413 A2545 20k AL-30, 1970 .55 .35
5414 A2545 45k AA-60, 1978 1.10 .70
Nos. 5410-5414 (5) 2.50 1.80

Samantha Smith — A2599

1985, Dec. 25 *Perf. 12*
5415 A2599 5k vio blue, choc & ver .50 .25

American student invited to meet with Soviet leaders in 1984.

A2600

1985, Dec. 30 **Litho.**
5416 A2600 5k multicolored .50 .25

N.M. Emanuel (1915-1984), chemist.

A2601

1985, Dec. 30
5417 A2601 5k Sightseeing .50 .25
5418 A2601 5k Sports .50 .25

Family leisure activities.

Intl. Peace Year — A2602

1986, Jan. 2 **Photo.** ***Perf. 11½***
5419 A2602 20k brt blue, bluish grn & silver .50 .30

Flags, Congress Palace, Carnation A2603

Lenin, Spasskaya Tower, Congress Palace A2604

Lenin — A2605

1986, Jan. 3
5420 A2603 5k multicolored .25 .25

Photogravure and Engraved
Perf. 12x11½
5421 A2604 20k multicolored 1.00 .30

Souvenir Sheet
Photo.
Perf. 11½
5422 A2605 50k multicolored 2.50 .70

27th Communist Party Congress.

A2606

1986, Jan. 10 ***Perf. 11½x12***
5423 A2606 15k multicolored .50 .25

Modern Olympic Games, 90th anniv.

A2607

Flora of Russian Steppes, different.

Perf. 12½x12, 12x12½
1986, Jan. 15 **Litho.**
5424 A2607 4k multicolored .25 .25
5425 A2607 5k multi, horiz. .25 .25
5426 A2607 10k multicolored .35 .25
5427 A2607 15k multicolored .50 .30
5428 A2607 20k multicolored .60 .35
a. Miniature sheet of 8 *32.50*
Nos. 5424-5428 (5) 1.95 1.40

A2608

Vodovzvodnaya Tower, Grand Kremlin Palace.

1986, Jan. 20 ***Perf. 12½x12***
5429 A2608 50k grayish green 1.50 .70

A2609

1986, Feb. 20 ***Perf. 11½***
5430 A2609 5k multicolored .50 .25

Voronezh City, 400th anniv.

A2610

1986, Feb. 20 **Engr.** ***Perf. 12***
5431 A2610 10k bluish black .50 .25

Bela Kun (1886-1939), Hungarian party leader.

A2611

1986, Feb. 28 ***Perf. 12½x12***
5432 A2611 5k grayish black .50 .25

Karolis Pozhela (1896-1926), Lithuanian party founder.

Intercosmos Project Halley, Final Stage — A2612

15k, Vega probe, comet. 50k, Vega I, comet.

1986, Mar. 6 **Litho.** ***Perf. 12***
5433 A2612 15k multi .50 .25
a. Miniature sheet of 8 *150.00*

Souvenir Sheet
Perf. 12½x12
5434 A2612 50k multi 5.00 .75

No. 5434 contains one 42x30mm stamp.

Butterflies A2613

4k, Utetheisa pulchella. 5k, Allancastria caucasica. 10k, Zegris eupheme. 15k, Catocala sponsa. 20k, Satyrus bischoffi.

1986, Mar. 18 ***Perf. 12x12½***
5435 A2613 4k multicolored .25 .25
5436 A2613 5k multicolored .25 .25
5437 A2613 10k multicolored .40 .25
5438 A2613 15k multicolored .50 .50
5439 A2613 20k multicolored .65 .55
a. Miniature sheet of 8 *60.00*
Nos. 5435-5439 (5) 2.05 1.80

EXPO '86, Vancouver A2614

1986, Mar. 25 **Photo.** ***Perf. 12x11½***
5440 A2614 20k Globe, space station .50 .30
a. Miniature sheet of 8 *35.00*

S.M. Kirov (1886-1934), Party Leader — A2615

1986, Mar. 27 **Engr.** ***Perf. 12½x12***
5441 A2615 5k black .50 .25

Cosmonauts' Day — A2616

Designs: 5k, Konstantin E. Tsiolkovsky (1857-1935), aerodynamics innovator, and futuristic space station. 10k, Sergei P. Korolev (1906-1966), rocket scientist, and Vostok spaceship, vert. 15k, Yuri Gagarin, 1st cosmonaut, Sputnik I and Vega probe.

Perf. 12½x12, 12x12½
1986, Apr. 12 **Litho.**
5442 A2616 5k multicolored .50 .25
a. Miniature sheet of 8 25.00
5443 A2616 10k multicolored .50 .25
a. Miniature sheet of 8 25.00
5444 A2616 15k multicolored 1.00 .25
a. Miniature sheet of 7 + label 25.00
Nos. 5441-5444 (4) 2.50 1.00

No. 5444 printed se-tenant with label picturing Vostok and inscribed for the 25th anniv. of first space flight.

1986 World Ice Hockey Championships, Moscow — A2617

1986, Apr. 12 **Photo.** ***Perf. 11½***
5445 A2617 15k multicolored .50 .25

Ernst Thalmann (1886-1944), German Communist Leader — A2618

1986, Apr. 16 **Engr.** ***Perf. 12½x12***
5446 A2618 10k dark brown .35 .25
5447 A2618 10k reddish brown .35 .25

Lenin, 116th Birth Anniv. — A2619

Portraits and architecture: No. 5448, Social-ist-Democratic People's House, Prague. No. 5449, Lenin Museum, Leipzig. No. 5450, Lenin Museum, Poronino, Poland.

1986, Apr. 22 **Photo.** ***Perf. 11½x12***
5448 A2619 5k multicolored .35 .25
5449 A2619 5k multicolored .35 .25
5450 A2619 5k multicolored .35 .25
Nos. 5448-5450 (3) 1.05 .75

Tambov City, 350th Anniv. A2620

1986, Apr. 27 *Perf. 11½*

5451 A2620 5k Buildings, city arms .50 .25

Soviet Peace Fund, 25th Anniv. A2621

1986, Apr. 27

5452 A2621 10k lt chalky bl, gold & brt ultra .50 .25

29th World Cycle Race, May 6-22 — A2622

1986, May 6

5453 A2622 10k multicolored .50 .25

Toadstools A2623

No. 5454, Amanita phalloides. No. 5455, Amanita muscaria. No. 5456, Amanita pantherina. No. 5457, Tylopilus felleus. No. 5458, Hypholoma fasciculare.

1986, May 15 **Litho.** *Perf. 12*

5454 A2623 4k multi .25 .25
5455 A2623 5k multi .25 .25
5456 A2623 10k multi .45 .25
5457 A2623 15k multi .50 .30
5458 A2623 20k multi .65 .35
Nos. 5454-5458 (5) 2.10 1.40

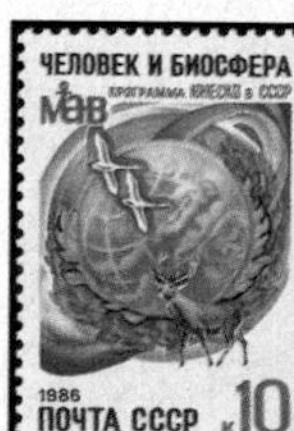

A2624

1986, May 19 **Photo.** *Perf. 11½*

5459 A2624 10k multicolored .50 .25

UNESCO Campaign, Man and Biosphere.

A2625

1986, May 20

5460 A2625 10k multicolored .50 .25

9th Soviet Spartakiad.

A2626

Design: Lenin's House, Eternal Glory and V. I. Chapaiev monuments, Gorky State Academic Drama Theater.

1986, May 24

5461 A2626 5k multicolored .50 .25

City of Kuibyshev, 400th anniv.

A2627

1986, May 25

5462 A2627 5k multicolored .50 .25

"COMMUNICATION '86, Moscow."

1986 World Cup Soccer Championships, Mexico — A2628

5k, 10k, Various soccer plays. 15k, World Cup on FIFA commemorative gold medal.

1986, May 31

5463 A2628 5k multicolored .25 .25
a. Miniature sheet of 8 15.00
5464 A2628 10k multicolored .30 .25
a. Miniature sheet of 8 15.00
5465 A2628 15k multicolored .45 .25
a. Miniature sheet of 8 15.00
Nos. 5463-5465 (3) 1.00 .75

Paintings in the Tretyakov Gallery, Moscow — A2629

Designs: 4k, Lane in Albano, 1837, by M.I. Lebedev, vert. 5k, View of the Kremlin in Foul Weather, 1851, by A.K. Savrasov. 10k, Sunlit Pine Trees, 1896, by I.I. Shishkin, vert. 15k, Return, 1896, by A.E. Arkhipov. 45k, Wedding Procession in Moscow, the 17th Century, 1901, by A.P. Ryabushkin.

Perf. 12x12½, 12½x12

1986, June 11 **Litho.**

5466 A2629 4k multicolored .25 .25
a. Miniature sheet of 8 10.00
5467 A2629 5k multicolored .25 .25
a. Miniature sheet of 8 10.00
5468 A2629 10k multicolored .35 .25
a. Miniature sheet of 8 10.00

Size: 74x37mm

Perf. 11½

5469 A2629 15k multicolored .40 .30
a. Miniature sheet of 8 10.00
5470 A2629 45k multicolored 1.10 .75
a. Miniature sheet of 8 10.00
Nos. 5466-5470 (5) 2.35 1.80

Irkutsk City, 300th Anniv. — A2630

1986, June 28 **Photo.** *Perf. 11½*

5471 A2630 5k multicolored .50 .25

Goodwill Games, Moscow, July 5-20 A2631

1986, July 4 **Photo.** *Perf. 11½*

5472 A2631 10k Prus bl, gold & blk .50 .25
5473 A2631 10k brt blue, gold & blk .50 .25

UNESCO Projects in Russia — A2632

Designs: 5k, Information sciences. 10k, Geological correlation. 15k, Inter-governmental oceanographic commission. 35k, Intl. hydrologic program.

1986, July 15

5474 A2632 5k multicolored .25 .25
5475 A2632 10k multicolored .40 .25
5476 A2632 15k multicolored .50 .30
5477 A2632 35k multicolored .95 .55
Nos. 5474-5477 (4) 2.10 1.35

Tyumen, 400th Anniv. A2633

1986, July 27

5478 A2633 5k multicolored .50 .25

A2634

1986, Aug. 1 **Photo.** *Perf. 11½*

5479 A2634 10k multicolored .50 .25

Olof Palme (1927-86), Prime Minister of Sweden.

A2635

1986, Aug. 8

5480 A2635 15k multicolored .50 .25

10th World Women's Basketball Championships, Moscow, Aug. 15-17.

Natl. Sports Committee Intl. Alpinist Camps — A2636

4k, Mt. Lenin. 5k, Mt. E. Korzhenevskaya. 10k, Mt. Belukha. 15k, Mt. Communism. 30k, Mt. Elbrus.

1986, Sept. 5 **Litho.** *Perf. 12*

5481 A2636 4k multi .25 .25
5482 A2636 5k multi .25 .25
a. Miniature sheet of 8 *35.00*
5483 A2636 10k multi .35 .25
5484 A2636 15k multi .40 .25
5485 A2636 30k multi .70 .30
Nos. 5481-5485 (5) 1.95 1.30

See Nos. 5532-5535.

Souvenir Sheet

Red Book, Rainbow, Earth — A2637

1986, Sept. 10 *Perf. 11½*

5486 A2637 50k multicolored 2.00 .75

Nature preservation.

A2638

1986, Sept. 13 **Photo.**

5487 A2638 5k multicolored .50 .25

Chelyabinsk, 250th anniv.

A2639

1986, Sept. 23

5488 A2639 15k multicolored .50 .25

Mukran, DDR to Klaipeda, Lithuania, Train Ferry, inauguration.

A2640

1986, Sept. 26

5489 A2640 5k multicolored .50 .25

Siauliai, Lithuanian SSR, 750th anniv.

Trucks — A2641

No. 5490, Ural-375D, 1964. No. 5491, GAZ-53A, 1965. No. 5492, KrAZ-256B, 1966. No. 5493, MAZ-515B, 1974. No. 5494, ZIL-133GY, 1979.

1986, Oct. 15 *Perf. 11½x12*

5490	A2641 4k multicolored	.25	.25
5491	A2641 5k multicolored	.25	.25
5492	A2641 10k multicolored	.60	.25
a.	Miniature sheet of 8	25.00	
5493	A2641 15k multicolored	.75	.30
5494	A2641 20k multicolored	1.25	.35
	Nos. 5490-5494 (5)	3.10	1.40

October Revolution, 69th anniv. — A2642

Design: Lenin Monument in October Square, Kremlin, Moscow.

1986, Oct. 1 **Litho.** *Perf. 12*

5495 A2642 5k multicolored .50 .25

A2643

5k, Icebreaker, helicopters. 10k, Mikhail Somov port side.

1986, Oct. 10 **Photo.** *Perf. 11½*

5496	5k multicolored	.40	.25
5497	10k multicolored	.40	.25
a.	A2643 Pair, #5496-5497	1.00	.25
b.	Miniature sheet of 8, 4 each	75.00	

Souvenir Sheet

Perf. 12½x11½

5498 A2643 50k Trapped in ice 3.00 .65

Mikhail Somov trapped in the Antarctic. No. 5497a has a continuous design. No. 5498 contains one 51½x36½mm stamp.

No. 4883 Ovptd. in Black for Rescue of the Mikhail Somov

Lithographed & Engraved

1986, Oct. 10 *Perf. 12x11½*

5499 A2271 4k multicolored 1.00 .25

Locomotives — A2644

4k, EU 684-37, 1929. 5k, FD 21-3000, 1941. 10k, OV-5109, 1907. 20k, C017-1613, 1944. 30k, FDP 20-578, 1941.

1986, Oct. 15 **Litho.** *Perf. 12*

5500	A2644 4k multi	.25	.25
5501	A2644 5k multi	.25	.25
5502	A2644 10k multi	.55	.25
a.	Miniature sheet of 8	25.00	
5503	A2644 20k multi	.85	.40
5504	A2644 30k multi	1.10	.65
	Nos. 5500-5504 (5)	3.00	1.80

Grigori Konstantinovich Ordzhonikidze (1886-1937), Communist Party Leader — A2645

1986, Oct. 18 **Engr.** *Perf. 12½x12*

5505 A2645 5k dark blue green .50 .25

A.G. Novikov (1896-1984), Composer — A2646

1986, Oct. 30

5506 A2646 5k dark brown 1.00 .25

A2647

1986, Nov. 4 **Photo.** *Perf. 11½*

5507 A2647 10k blue & silver .50 .25

UNSECO, 40th anniv.

A2648

1986, Nov. 12

5508 A2648 5k lt grnsh gray & blk .50 .25

Sun Yat-sen (1866-1925), Chinese statesman.

Mikhail Vasilyevich Lomonosov, Scientist A2649

1986, Nov. 19 **Engr.** *Perf. 12x12½*

5509 A2649 5k dk violet brown .50 .25

Aircraft by A.S. Yakovlev — A2650

1986, Nov. 25 **Photo.** *Perf. 11½x12*

5510	A2650 4k 1927	.25	.25
5511	A2650 5k 1935	.25	.25
a.	Miniature sheet of 8	40.00	
5512	A2650 10k 1946	.40	.25
5513	A2650 20k 1972	.65	.35
5514	A2650 30k 1981	.95	.50
	Nos. 5510-5514 (5)	2.50	1.60

New Year 1987 A2651

1986, Dec. 4 **Litho.** *Perf. 11½*

5515 A2651 5k Kremlin towers .50 .25

a. Miniature sheet of 8 25.00

27th Communist Party Cong., 2/25-3/6 — A2652

Red banner and: No. 5516, Computers. No. 5517, Engineer, computer, dish receivers. No. 5518, Aerial view of city. No. 5519, Council for Mutual Economic Assistance building, workers. No. 5520, Spasski Tower, Kremlin Palace.

1986, Dec. 12 **Photo.** *Perf. 11½x12*

5516	A2652 5k multicolored	.25	.25
5517	A2652 5k multicolored	.25	.25
5518	A2652 5k multicolored	.25	.25
5519	A2652 5k multicolored	.25	.25
5520	A2652 5k multicolored	.25	.25
	Nos. 5516-5520 (5)	1.25	1.25

A2653

1986, Dec. 24 **Engr.** *Perf. 12½x12*

5521 A2653 5k black .50 .25

Alexander Yakovlevich Parkhomenko (1886-1921), revolution hero.

A2654

1986, Dec. 25 **Photo.** *Perf. 11½*

5522 A2654 5k brown & buff .50 .25

Samora Moises Machel (1933-1986) Pres. of Mozambique.

Miniature Sheet

Palace Museums in Leningrad — A2655

1986, Dec. 25 **Engr.** *Perf. 12*

5523	A2655 Sheet of 5 + label	3.00	1.40
a.	5k State Museum, 1898	.25	.25
b.	10k The Hermitage, 1764	.35	.25
c.	15k Petrodvorets, 1728	.45	.30
d.	20k Yekaterininsky, 1757	.55	.35
e.	50k Pavlovsk, restored c. 1945	1.25	.75

18th Soviet Trade Unions Congress, Feb. 24-28 — A2656

1987, Jan. 7 Photo. *Perf. 11½*

5524 A2656 5k multicolored .50 .25

Butterflies A2657

4k, Atrophaneura alcinous. 5k, Papilio machaon. 10k, Papilio alexanor. 15k, Papilio maackii. 30k, Iphiclides podalirius.

1987, Jan. 15 Litho. *Perf. 12x12½*

5525 A2657 4k multicolored .25 .25
5526 A2657 5k multicolored .25 .25
5527 A2657 10k multicolored .30 .25
5528 A2657 15k multicolored .40 .30
5529 A2657 30k multicolored .80 .50
Nos. 5525-5529 (5) 2.00 1.55

A2658

1987, Jan. 31 *Perf. 12½x12*

5530 A2658 5k multicolored .50 .25

Karlis Miyesniyek (1887-1977), Artist.

A2659

1987, Feb. 4 *Perf. 12*

5531 A2659 5k buff & lake .50 .25

Stasis Shimkus (1887-1943), composer.

Alpinist Camps Type of 1986

4k, Chimbulak Gorge. 10k, Shavla Gorge. 20k, Mts. Donguz-orun, Nakra-tau. 35k, Mt. Kazbek.

1987, Feb. 4

5532 A2636 4k multicolored .25 .25
5533 A2636 10k multicolored .30 .25
5534 A2636 20k multicolored .50 .35
5535 A2636 35k multicolored .75 .55
Nos. 5532-5535 (4) 1.80 1.40

Vasily Ivanovich Chapayev (1887-1919), Revolution Hero — A2660

1987, Feb. 9 Engr.

5536 A2660 5k dark red brown .50 .25

Heino Eller (1887-1970), Estonian Composer — A2661

1987, Mar. 7 Litho. *Perf. 12*

5537 A2661 5k buff & brown .50 .25

A2662

1987, Mar. 8 Photo. *Perf. 11½*

5538 A2662 5k multicolored .40 .25

Souvenir Sheet

Perf. 11½x12

5539 A2662 50k "XX," and colored bands 2.00 .75

All-Union Leninist Young Communist League 20th Congress, Moscow. No. 5539 contains one 26x37mm stamp.

A2663

Photogravure and Engraved

1987, Mar. 20 *Perf. 11½*

5540 A2663 5k buff & sepia .50 .25

Iosif Abgarovich Orbeli (1887-1961), first president of the Armenian Academy of Sciences.

World Wildlife Fund — A2664

Polar bears.

1987, Mar. 25 Photo. *Perf. 11½x12*

5541 A2664 5k multicolored .45 .25
a. Miniature sheet of 8 250.00
5542 A2664 10k multicolored .65 .25
a. Miniature sheet of 8 250.00
5543 A2664 20k multicolored 1.40 .40
a. Miniature sheet of 8 250.00
5544 A2664 35k multicolored 2.25 .75
a. Miniature sheet of 8 250.00
Nos. 5541-5544 (4) 4.75 1.65

Cosmonauts' Day — A2665

1987, Apr. 12 *Perf. 11½*

5545 A2665 10k Sputnik, 1957 .35 .25
5546 A2665 10k Vostok 3 and 4, 1962 .35 .25
5547 A2665 10k Mars 1, 1962 .35 .25
a. Miniature sheet of 8 50.00
Nos. 5545-5547 (3) 1.05 .75

UN Emblem, ESCAP Headquarters, Bangkok — A2666

1987, Apr. 21

5548 A2666 10k multicolored .50 .25

UN Economic and Social Commission for Asia and the Pacific, 40th anniv.

Lenin, 117th Birth Anniv. — A2667

Paintings: No. 5549, Lenin's Birthday, by N.A. Sysoyev. No. 5550, Lenin with Delegates at the 3rd Congress of the Soviet Young Communist League, by P.O. Belousov. No. 5551a, Lenin's Underground Activity (Lenin, lamp), by D.A. Nalbandyan. No. 5551b, Before the Assault (Lenin standing at table), by S.P. Viktorov. No. 5551c, We'll Show the Earth the New Way (Lenin, soldiers, flags), by A.G. Lysenko. No. 5551d, Lenin in Smolny, October 1917 (Lenin seated), by M.G. Sokolov. No. 5551e, Lenin, by N.A. Andreyev.

1987, Apr. 22 Litho. *Perf. 12½x12*

5549 A2667 5k multicolored .50 .25
5550 A2667 5k multicolored .50 .25

Souvenir Sheet

Perf. 12

5551 Sheet of 5 2.00 .75
a.-e. A2667 10k any single .30 .25

Sizes: Nos. 5551a-5551d, 40x28mm; No. 5551e, 40x56mm.

A2668

1987, May 5 Photo. *Perf. 11½*

5552 A2668 10k multicolored .50 .25

European Gymnastics Championships, Moscow, May 18-26.

Bicycle Race — A2669

1987, May 6

5553 A2669 10k multicolored .50 .25

40th Peace Bicycle Race, Poland-Czechoslovakia-German Democratic Republic, May.

Fauna — A2670

5k, Menzbira marmot. 10k, Bald badger, horiz. 15k, Snow leopard.

Perf. 12½x12 (#5554), 12x12½

1987, May 15 Litho.

5554 A2670 5k multicolored .50 .25
a. Miniature sheet of 8 *35.00*
5555 A2670 10k multicolored .60 .25

Size: 32x47mm

5556 A2670 15k multicolored .90 .25
Nos. 5554-5556 (3) 2.00 .75

Passenger Ships — A2671

5k, Maxim Gorki. 10k, Alexander Pushkin. 30k, The Soviet Union.

1987, May 20 Photo. *Perf. 12x11½*

5557 A2671 5k multicolored .25 .25
5558 A2671 10k multicolored .50 .25
a. Miniature sheet of 8 *125.00*
5559 A2671 30k multicolored 1.25 .45
Nos. 5557-5559 (3) 2.00 .95

Paintings by Foreign Artists in the Hermitage Museum A2672

4k, Portrait of a Woman, by Lucas Cranach Sr. (1472-1553). 5k, St. Sebastian, by Titian. 10k, Justice, by Durer. 30k, Adoration of the Magi, by Pieter Brueghel the Younger (c. 1564-1638). 50k, Ceres, by Rubens.

Perf. 12x12½, 12½x12

1987, June 5 Litho.

5560 A2672 4k multicolored .25 .25
5561 A2672 5k multicolored .25 .25
a. Miniature sheet of 8 *275.00*
5562 A2672 10k multicolored .25 .25
a. Miniature sheet of 8 *275.00*
5563 A2672 30k multicolored .60 .40
5564 A2672 50k multicolored .75 .50
Nos. 5560-5564 (5) 2.10 1.65

Tolyatti City, 250th Anniv. — A2673

Design: Zhiguli car, Volga Motors factory, Lenin Hydroelectric plant.

1987, June 6 Photo. *Perf. 11½*

5565 A2673 5k multicolored .50 .25

Intl. Letter-Writing Week — A2749

1988, Aug. 25 Photo. *Perf. 11½*
5701 A2749 5k blue grn & dark blue green .50 .25

Earth, Mir space station and Soyuz-TM A2750

1988, Aug. 29
5702 A2750 15k multicolored .50 .30

Soviet-Afghan joint space flight.

A2751

1988, Sept. 1 Photo. *Perf. 11½*
5703 A2751 10k multicolored .50 .25

Problems of Peace and Socialism magazine, 30th anniv.

Party Leader Type of 1988

1988, Sept. 13 Engr. *Perf. 12*
5704 A2712 5k black .50 .25

Emmanuil Ionovich Kviring (1888-1937).

A2753

A2753a

A2753b

A2753c

A2753d

Designs: No. 5705, *Ilya Muromets,* Russian lore. No. 5706, *Ballad of the Cossack Golota,* Ukrainian lore. No. 5707, *Musician-Magician,* a Byelorussian fairy tale. No. 5708, *Koblandy-batyr,* a poem from Kazakh. No. 5709, *Alpamysh,* a fairy tale from Uzbek.

Perf. 12x12½, 12½x12

1988, Sept. 22 Litho.

5705	A2753	10k multicolored	.25	.25
5706	A2753a	10k multicolored	.25	.25
5707	A2753b	10k multicolored	.25	.25
5708	A2753c	10k multicolored	.25	.25
5709	A2753d	10k multicolored	.25	.25
		Nos. 5705-5709 (5)	1.25	1.25

Nos. 5705-5709 each printed se-tenant with inscribed labels. See design A2795.

Appeal of the Leader, 1947, by I.M. Toidze A2754

1988, Oct. 5 *Perf. 12x12½*
5710 A2754 5k multicolored .40 .25

October Revolution, 71st anniv.

A2755

1988, Oct. 18 Engr. *Perf. 12*
5711 A2755 10k black .50 .25

Andrei Timofeyevich Bolotov (1738-1833), agricultural scientist, publisher.

A2756

1988, Oct. 18
5712 A2756 10k steel blue .50 .25

Andrei Nikolayevich Tupolev (1888-1972), aeronautical engineer.

A2757

20k, Map of expedition route, atomic ice-breaker *Sibirj* & expedition members.

1988, Oct. 25 Litho.
5713 A2757 20k multicolored .50 .35

North Pole expedition (in 1987).
Exists imperf. Value, $35.

A2758

1988, Oct. 30 Engr.
5714 A2758 5k brown black .40 .25

Dmitry F. Ustinov (1908-84), minister of defense.

Soviet-Vietnamese Treaty, 10th Anniv. — A2759

1988, Nov. 3 Photo. *Perf. 11½*
5715 A2759 10k multicolored .50 .25

State Broadcasting and Sound Recording Institute, 50th Anniv. — A2760

1988, Nov. 3
5716 A2760 10k multicolored .50 .25

UN Declaration of Human Rights, 40th Anniv. A2761

1988, Nov. 21
5717 A2761 10k multicolored .50 .25

New Year 1989 — A2762

Design: Preobrazhensky Regiment body-guard riding to announce Peter the Great's decree to celebrate new year's eve as of January 1, 1700.

1988, Nov. 24 Litho. *Perf. 12x11½*
5718 A2762 5k multicolored .50 .25

Soviet-French Joint Space Flight — A2763

1988, Nov. 26 Photo. *Perf. 11½*
5719 A2763 15k Space walkers .50 .30

No. 4607 Overprinted in Red

1988, Dec. 16 Litho. *Perf. 12½x12*
5720 A2143 1r dark blue 5.00 2.25

Space mail.

Party Leader Type of 1988

1988, Dec. 16 Engr.
5721 A2712 5k slate green .50 .25

Martyn Ivanovich Latsis (1888-1938).

No. 5685 Overprinted in Bright Blue

Souvenir Sheet

1988, Dec. 20 Litho. *Perf. 12*
5722 A2742 50k multicolored 2.00 1.00

Victory of Soviet athletes at the 1988 Summer Olympics, Seoul. Overprint on margin of No. 5722 specifies that Soviet athletes won 55 gold, 31 silver and 46 bronze medals.

Post Rider — A2765

Designs: 3k, Cruiser *Aurora.* 4k, Spasski Tower, Lenin Mausoleum. 5k, Natl. flag, crest. 10k, *The Worker and the Collective Farmer,* 1935, sculpture by V.I. Mukhina. 15k, Satellite dish. 20k, Lyre, art tools, quill pen, parchment (arts and literature). 25k, *Discobolus,* 5th cent. sculpture by Myron (c. 480-440 B.C.). 30k, Map of the Antarctic, penguins. 35k, *Mercury,* sculpture by Giambologna (1529-1608). 50k, White cranes (nature conservation). 1r, UPU emblem.

1988, Dec. 22 Engr. *Perf. 12x11½*

5723	A2765	1k dark brown	.25	.25
5724	A2765	3k dark blue green	.25	.25
5725	A2765	4k indigo	.25	.25
5726	A2765	5k red	.25	.25
5727	A2765	10k claret	.25	.25
5728	A2765	15k deep blue	.30	.25
5729	A2765	20k olive gray	.35	.30
5730	A2765	25k dark green	.40	.35
5731	A2765	30k dark blue	.50	.40
5732	A2765	35k dark red brown	.60	.50
5733	A2765	50k sapphire	.80	.50

Perf. 12x12½

5734	A2765	1r blue gray	1.60	1.25
		Nos. 5723-5734 (12)	5.80	4.80

See Nos. 5838-5849, 5984-5987. For surcharges see Uzbekistan #15, 22, 25-26, 61B, 61D, 61F.

Fountains of Petrodvorets
A2766

Designs: 5k, Samson Fountain, 1723, and Great Cascade. 10k, Adam Fountain, 1722, and sculptures, 1718, by D. Bonazza. 15k, Golden Mountain Cascade, by N. Miketti (1721-1723) and M.G. Zemtsov. 30k, Roman Fountains, 1763. 50k, Oak Tree Fountain, 1735.

1988, Dec. 25 Engr. *Perf. 11½x12*

5735 A2766	5k myrtle green		.25	.25
5736 A2766	10k myrtle green		.25	.25
5737 A2766	15k myrtle green		.30	.25
5738 A2766	30k myrtle green		.60	.40
5739 A2766	50k myrtle green		1.00	.70
a.	Pane of 5, #5735-5739		2.25	1.50

Panes have photogravure margin. Panes are printed bilaterally and separated in the center by perforations so that stamps in the 2nd pane are arranged in reverse order from the 1st pane.

19th Communist Party Congress — A2767

1988, Dec. 30 Photo. *Perf. 12x11½*
Multicolored and

5740 A2767	5k deep car (power)	.50	.25
5741 A2767	5k dp bl vio (industry)	.50	.25
5742 A2767	5k green (land)	.50	.25
	Nos. 5740-5742 (3)	1.50	.75

Souvenir Sheet

Inaugural Flight of the *Buran* Space Shuttle, Nov. 15 — A2768

1988, Dec. 30 *Perf. 11½x12*
5743 A2768 50k multicolored 2.00 .75

Luna 1, 30th Anniv. — A2769

1989, Jan. 2 Photo. *Perf. 11½*
5744 A2769 15k multicolored .50 .30

Jalmari Virtanen (1889-1939), Karelian Poet — A2770

1989, Jan. 8
5745 A2770 5k olive brown .50 .25

Council for Mutual Economic Assistance, 40th Anniv.
A2771

1989, Jan. 8
5746 A2771 10k multicolored .50 .25

Environmental Protection — A2772

1989, Jan. 18 Litho. *Perf. 12½x12*

5747 A2772	5k Forest	.30	.25
5748 A2772	10k Arctic deer	.50	.25
5749 A2772	15k Stop desert encroachment	.70	.30
	Nos. 5747-5749 (3)	1.50	.80

Nos. 5747-5749 printed se-tenant with inscribed labels picturing maps.

Samovars
A2773

Samovars in the State Museum, Leningrad: 5k, Pear-shaped urn, late 18th cent. 10k, Barrel-shaped urn by Ivan Listisin, early 19th cent. 20k, "Kabachok" urn by the Sokolov Bros., Tula, c. 1830. 30k, Vase-shaped urn by the Nikolari Malikov Studio, Tula, c. 1840.

1989, Feb. 8 Photo. *Perf. 11½*

5750 A2773	5k multicolored	.25	.25
5751 A2773	10k multicolored	.30	.25
5752 A2773	20k multicolored	.60	.30
5753 A2773	30k multicolored	.85	.45
	Nos. 5750-5753 (4)	2.00	1.25

Modest Petrovich Mussorgsky (1839-1881), Composer — A2774

1989, Feb. 15 Litho. *Perf. 12½x12*
5754 A2774 10k dull vio & vio brn 1.00 .25

P.E. Dybenko (1889-1938), Military Commander
A2775

1989, Feb. 28 Engr. *Perf. 12*
5755 A2775 5k black .50 .25

T.G. Shevchenko (1814-1861), Poet
A2776

1989, Mar. 6 Litho. *Perf. 11½*
5756 A2776 5k pale grn, blk & brn .50 .25

Exists imperf. Value, $25.

Cultivated Lilies — A2777

1989, Mar. 15 *Perf. 12½x12*

5757 A2777	5k Lilium speciosum	.25	.25
5758 A2777	10k African queen	.25	.25
5759 A2777	15k Eclat du soir	.30	.25
5760 A2777	30k White tiger	.80	.55
	Nos. 5757-5760 (4)	1.60	1.30

Souvenir Sheet

Labor Day, Cent. — A2778

1989, Mar. 25 *Perf. 11½x12*
5761 A2778 30k multicolored 2.00 .60

Victory Banner, by P. Loginov and V. Pamfilov
A2779

1989, Apr. 5 Litho. *Perf. 12x12½*
5762 A2779 5k multicolored .50 .25

World War II Victory Day.

Cosmonauts' Day — A2780

1989, Apr. 12 Photo. *Perf. 11x11½*
5763 A2780 15k Mir space station .50 .30

A2781

1989, Apr. 14 *Perf. 11½*
5764 A2781 10k multicolored .75 .25

Bering Bridge Soviet-American Expedition, Anadyr and Kotzebue.

Type of 1988

Portraits and branches of the Lenin Central Museum: No. 5765, Kazan. No. 5766, Kuibyshev. No. 5767, Frunze.

1989, Apr. 14 Litho. *Perf. 12*

5765 A2727	5k rose brown & multi	.25	.25
5766 A2727	5k olive gray & multi	.25	.25
5767 A2727	5k deep brown & multi	.25	.25
	Nos. 5765-5767 (3)	.75	.75

Lenin's 119th Birth Anniv.

Souvenir Sheet

Launch of Interplanetary Probe *Phobos* — A2783

1989, Apr. 24 *Perf. 11½x12*
5768 A2783 50k multicolored 1.75 .85

A2784

1989, May 5 Photo. *Perf. 11½*
5769 A2784 5k multicolored .50 .25

Hungarian Soviet Republic, 70th anniv.

A2785

1989, May 5 Photo. & Engr.
5770 A2785 5k multicolored .40 .25

Volgograd, 400th anniv.

Honeybees
A2786

No. 5771, Drone. No. 5772, Workers, flowers, man-made hive. No. 5773, Worker collecting pollen. No. 5774, Queen, drones, honeycomb.

1989, May 18 Litho. *Perf. 12*

5771 A2786 5k multi .25 .25
5772 A2786 10k multi .25 .25
5773 A2786 20k multi .50 .25
5774 A2786 35k multi .90 .50
Nos. 5771-5774 (4) 1.90 1.25

No. 5771 exists imperf. Value, $30.

Photography, 150th Anniv. — A2787

1989, May 24 Photo. *Perf. 11½*

5775 A2787 5k multicolored .50 .25

I.A. Kuratov (1839-1875), Author — A2788

1989, June 26 Litho. *Perf. 12½x12*

5776 A2788 5k dk golden brn .40 .25

Jean Racine (1639-1699), French Dramatist A2789

Photo. & Engr.

1989, June 16 *Perf. 12x11½*

5777 A2789 15k multicolored .50 .25

Europe, Our Common Home — A2790

Designs: 5k, Map of Europe, stylized bird. 10k, Crane, two men completing a bridge, globe. 15k, Stork's nest, globe.

1989, June 20 Photo. *Perf. 11½*

5778 A2790 5k multicolored .25 .25
5779 A2790 10k multicolored .30 .25
5780 A2790 15k multicolored .50 .35
Nos. 5778-5780 (3) 1.05 .85

Mukhina, by Nesterov A2791

1989, June 25 Litho. *Perf. 12x12½*

5781 A2791 5k chalky blue .50 .25

Vera I. Mukhina (1889-1953), sculptor.

13th World Youth and Student Festival, Pyongyang A2792

1989, July 1 Litho. *Perf. 12*

5782 A2792 10k multicolored .40 .25

Ducks A2793

No. 5783, Tadorna tadorna. No. 5784, Anas crecca. No. 5785, Tadorna ferruginea.

1989, July 1

5783 A2793 5k multicolored .25 .25
5784 A2793 15k multicolored .35 .25
5785 A2793 20k multicolored .40 .30
a. Min. sheet, 2 5k, 4 15k, 3 20k 5.00 3.00
Nos. 5783-5785 (3) 1.00 .80

French Revolution, Bicent. A2794

Designs: 5k, PHILEXFRANCE '89 emblem and Storming of the Bastille. 15k, Marat, Danton, Robespierre. 20k, "La Marseillaise," from the Arc de Triomphe carved by Francois Rude (1784-1855).

Photo. & Engr., Photo. (15k)

1989, July 7 *Perf. 11½*

5786 A2794 5k multicolored .25 .25
5787 A2794 15k multicolored .35 .25
5788 A2794 20k multicolored .40 .30
a. Miniature sheet of 8 9.00
Nos. 5786-5788 (3) 1.00 .80

A2795

A2795a

A2795b

A2795c

Folklore and Legends A2795d

Designs: No. 5789, *Amiraniani,* Georgian lore. No. 5790, *Koroglu,* Azerbaijan lore. No. 5791, *Fir, Queen of the Grass-snakes,* Lithuanian lore. No. 5792, *Miorilsa,* Moldavian lore. No. 5793, *Lachplesis,* Latvian lore.

1989, July 12 Litho. *Perf. 12x12½*

5789 A2795 10k multicolored .40 .25
5790 A2795a 10k multicolored .40 .25
5791 A2795b 10k multicolored .40 .25
5792 A2795c 10k multicolored .40 .25
5793 A2795d 10k multicolored .40 .25
Nos. 5789-5793 (5) 2.00 1.25

Each printed with a se-tenant label. See types A2753-A2753d & #5890-5894.

Tallinn Zoo, 50th Anniv. — A2796

1989, July 20 Photo. *Perf. 11½*

5794 A2796 10k Lynx .50 .25

Intl. Letter Writing Week — A2797

1989, July 20 Litho. *Perf. 12*

5795 A2797 5k multicolored .40 .25

Exists imperf. Value, $35.

Pulkovskaya Observatory, 150th Anniv. — A2798

Photo. & Engr.

1989, July 20 *Perf. 11½*

5796 A2798 10k multicolored .50 .25

Souvenir Sheet

Peter the Great and Battle Scene — A2799

1989, July 27 Photo. *Perf. 11½x12*

5797 A2799 50k dk bl & dk brn 1.50 1.00

Battle of Hango, 275th anniv.

City of Nikolaev, Bicent. A2800

1989, Aug. 3 Photo. *Perf. 11½*

5798 A2800 5k multicolored .50 .25

80th Birth Anniv. of Kwame Nkrumah, 1st Pres. of Ghana — A2801

1989, Aug. 9

5799 A2801 10k multicolored .40 .25

6th Congress of the All-Union Philatelic Soc., Moscow A2802

1989, Aug. 9 *Perf. 12*

5800 A2802 10k bl, blk & pink .50 .25

Printed se-tenant with label picturing simulated stamps and congress emblem.

James Fenimore Cooper (1789-1851), American Novelist A2803

Photo. & Engr.

1989, Aug. 19 *Perf. 12x11½*

5801 A2803 15k multicolored .50 .35

A2804

Soviet Circus Performers — A2805

Performers and scenes from their acts: 1k, V.L. Durov, clown and trainer. 3k, M.N. Rumyantsev, clown. 4k, V.I. Filatov, bear trainer. 5k, E.T. Kio, magician. 10k, V.E. Lazarenko, acrobat and clown. 30k, Moscow Circus, Tsvetnoi Boulevard.

1989, Aug. 22 Litho. *Perf. 12*

5802 A2804 1k multicolored .40 .25
5803 A2804 3k multicolored .40 .25
5804 A2804 4k multicolored .40 .25
5805 A2804 5k multicolored .40 .25
5806 A2804 10k multicolored .40 .25
Nos. 5802-5806 (5) 2.00 1.25

Souvenir Sheet

Perf. 12x12½

5807 A2805 30k multicolored 2.00 .70

Nos. 5802-5806 exist imperf. Value, $30 each.

5th World Boxing Championships, Moscow — A2806

1989, Aug. 25 Photo. *Perf. 11½*

5808 A2806 15k multicolored .50 .35

Aleksandr Popov (1859-1905), Inventor of Radio in Russia — A2807

Design: *Demonstration of the First Radio Receiver,* 1895, by N. Sysoev.

1989, Oct. 5 Litho. *Perf. 12x12½*

5809 A2807 10k multicolored .50 .25

A2808

1989, Oct. 7 Photo. *Perf. 11½*

5810 A2808 5k multicolored .40 .25

German Democratic Republic, 40th anniv.

Polish People's Republic, 45th Anniv. A2809

1989, Oct. 7

5811 A2809 5k multicolored .50 .25

Party Leader Type of 1988

1989, Oct. 10 Engr. *Perf. 12*

5812 A2712 5k black .40 .25

S.V. Kosior (1889-1939).

A2811

1989, Oct. 10

5813 A2811 15k dark red brown .60 .25

Jawaharlal Nehru, 1st prime minister of independent India.

Guardsmen of October, by M.M. Chepik — A2812

1989, Oct. 14 Litho. *Perf. 12½x12*

5814 A2812 5k multicolored .40 .25

October Revolution, 72nd anniv. Exists imperf. Value, $30.

Kosta Khetagurov (1859-1906), Ossetic Poet — A2813

1989, Oct. 14

5815 A2813 5k dark red brown .40 .25

Exists imperf.

A2814

1989, Oct. 14 Photo. *Perf. 11½*

5816 A2814 5k buff, sepia & black .50 .25

Li Dazhao (1889-1927), communist party leader of China.

A2815

1989, Oct. 20 Engr. *Perf. 12*

5817 A2815 5k black .40 .25

Jan Karlovich Berzin (1889-1938), army intelligence leader.

Russian — A2816

Musical Instruments: No. 5819, Byelorussian. No. 5820, Ukrainian. No. 5821, Uzbek.

Photo. & Engr.

1989, Oct. 20 *Perf. 12x11½*

Denomination Color

5818 A2816 10k blue .25 .25
5819 A2816 10k brown .25 .25
5820 A2816 10k lemon .25 .25
5821 A2816 10k blue green .25 .25
Nos. 5818-5821 (4) 1.00 1.00

See Nos. 5929-5932, 6047-6049.

Scenes from Novels by James Fenimore Cooper A2817

Designs: No. 5822, *The Hunter,* (settlers, canoe). No. 5823, *Last of the Mohicans* (Indians, settlers). No. 5824, *The Pathfinder,* (couple near cliff). No. 5825, *The Pioneers* (women, wild animals). No. 5826, *The Prairie* (injured Indians, horse).

1989, Nov. 17 Litho. *Perf. 12x12½*

5822 A2817 20k multicolored .60 .40
5823 A2817 20k multicolored .60 .40
5824 A2817 20k multicolored .60 .40
5825 A2817 20k multicolored .60 .40
5826 A2817 20k multicolored .60 .40
a. Strip of 5, #5822-5826 3.00 2.00

Printed in a continuous design.

Monuments A2818

No. 5827, Pokrovsky Cathedral, St. Basil's, statue of K. Minin and D. Pozharsky, Moscow. No. 5828, Petropavlovsky Cathedral, statue of Peter the Great, Leningrad. No. 5829, Sofiisky Cathedral, Bogdan Chmielnicki monument, Kiev. No. 5830, Khodzha Akhmed Yasavi Mausoleum, Turkestan. No. 5831, Khazret-Khyzr Mosque, Samarkand.

1989, Nov. 20 *Perf. 11½*

Color of "Sky"

5827 A2818 15k tan .40 .30
5828 A2818 15k gray green .40 .30
5829 A2818 15k blue green .40 .30
5830 A2818 15k violet blue .40 .30
5831 A2818 15k bright blue .40 .30
Nos. 5827-5831 (5) 2.00 1.50

New Year 1990 A2819

1989, Nov. 22 *Perf. 12*

5832 A2819 5k multicolored .50 .25

Space Achievements A2820

Designs: Nos. 5833, 5837a, Unmanned Soviet probe on the Moon. Nos. 5834, 5837b, American astronaut on Moon, 1969. Nos. 5835, 5837c, Soviet cosmonaut and American astronaut on Mars. Nos. 5836, 5837d, Mars, planetary body, diff.

1989, Nov. 24

5833 A2820 25k multicolored .75 .55
5834 A2820 25k multicolored .75 .55
5835 A2820 25k multicolored .75 .55
5836 A2820 25k multicolored .75 .55
a. Block of 4, #5833-5836 3.00 2.20

Souvenir Sheet

Imperf

5837 Sheet of 4 3.00 2.20
a.-d. A2820 25k any single .75 .55

World Stamp Expo '89, Washington DC, Nov. 17-Dec. 3; 20th UPU Cong. See US No. C126.

Type of 1988

Dated 1988

1989, Dec. 25 Litho. *Perf. 12x12½*

5838 A2765 1k dark brown .25 .25
5839 A2765 3k dark blue green .25 .25
5840 A2765 4k indigo .25 .25
5841 A2765 5k red .25 .25
5842 A2765 10k claret .30 .25
5843 A2765 15k deep blue .45 .30
5844 A2765 20k olive gray .60 .40
5845 A2765 25k dark green .75 .50
5846 A2765 30k dark blue .90 .60
5847 A2765 35k dark red brown 1.00 .70
5848 A2765 50k sapphire 1.50 1.00
5849 A2765 1r blue gray 3.50 2.00
Nos. 5838-5849 (12) 10.00 6.75

For surcharges see Uzbekistan #15, 22, 25-26, 61B, 61D, 61F.

Admirals Type of 1987

Miniature Sheet

Admirals & battle scenes: 5k, V.A. Kornilov (1806-54). 10k, V.I. Istomin (1809-55). 15k, G.I. Nevelskoi (1813-76). 20k, G.I. Butakov (1820-82). 30k, A.A. Popov (1821-98). 35k, Stepan O. Makarov (1849-1904).

1989, Dec. 28 Engr. *Perf. 12½x12*

5850 Sheet of 6 3.00 2.00
a. A2705 5k brown & Prus blue .25 .25
b. A2705 10k brown & Prus blue .25 .25
c. A2705 15k dark blue & Prus blue .40 .25
d. A2705 20k dark blue & Prus blue .50 .35
e. A2705 30k brown & Prus blue .75 .50
f. A2705 35k brown & Prus blue .85 .60

Global Ecology — A2821

10k, Flower dying, industrial waste entering the environment. 15k, Bird caught in industrial waste, Earth. 20k, Sea of chopped trees.

1990, Jan. 5 Photo. *Perf. 11½*

5851 A2821 10k multicolored .35 .25
5852 A2821 15k multicolored .50 .35
5853 A2821 20k multicolored .65 .45
Nos. 5851-5853 (3) 1.50 1.05

Capitals of the Republics

A2822

A2822a

A2822b

A2822c

A2822d

A2822e

A2822f

A2822g

A2822h

A2822i

A2822j

A2822k

A2822l

A2822m

A2822n

1990, Jan. 18 Litho. *Perf. 12x12½*

5854	A2822	5k	Moscow	.30	.25
5855	A2822a	5k	Tallinn	.30	.25
5856	A2822b	5k	Riga	.30	.25
5857	A2822c	5k	Vilnius	.30	.25
5858	A2822d	5k	Minsk	.30	.25
5859	A2822e	5k	Kiev	.30	.25
5860	A2822f	5k	Kishinev	.30	.25
5861	A2822g	5k	Tbilisi	.30	.25
5862	A2822h	5k	Yerevan	.30	.25
5863	A2822i	5k	Baku	.30	.25
5864	A2822j	5k	Alma-Ata	.30	.25
5865	A2822k	5k	Tashkent	.30	.25
5866	A2822l	5k	Frunze	.30	.25
5867	A2822m	5k	Ashkhabad	.30	.25
5868	A2822n	5k	Dushanbe	.30	.25
			Nos. 5854-5868 (15)	4.50	3.75

A2823

1990, Feb. 3 *Perf. 11½*

5869	A2823	10k	black & brown	.50	.25

Ho Chi Minh (1890-1969).

A2824

1990, Feb. 3 Photo.

5870	A2824	5k	multicolored	.50	.25

Vietnamese Communist Party, 60th anniv.

Owls A2825

Perf. 12x12½, 12½x12

1990, Feb. 8 Litho.

5871	A2825	10k	Nyctea scandiaca	.30	.25
5872	A2825	20k	Bubo bubo, vert.	.60	.40
5873	A2825	35k	Aslo otus	1.60	1.00
			Nos. 5871-5873 (3)	2.50	1.65

Penny Black, 150th Anniv. A2826

Emblems and various Penny Blacks: No. 5875, Position TP. No. 5876, Position TF. No. 5877, Position AH. No. 5878, Position VK. No. 5879, Position AE.

1990, Feb. 15 Photo. *Perf. 11½*

5874	A2826	10k	shown	.35	.25
5875	A2826	20k	gold & black	.65	.45
5876	A2826	20k	gold & black	.65	.45
5877	A2826	35k	multicolored	1.10	.75
5878	A2826	35k	multicolored	1.10	.75
			Nos. 5874-5878 (5)	3.85	2.65

Souvenir Sheet

Perf. 12x11½

5879	A2826	1r	dk green & blk	4.00	2.00

Stamp World London '90 (35k).
No. 5879 contains one 37x26mm stamp.

ITU, 125th Anniv. A2827

1990, Feb. 20 Photo. *Perf. 11½*

5880	A2827	20k	multicolored	.50	.35

Labor Day A2828

1990, Mar. 28 Photo. *Perf. 11½*

5881	A2828	5k	multicolored	.40	.25

Victory, 1945, by A. Lysenko A2829

1990, Mar. 28 Litho. *Perf. 12x12½*

5882	A2829	5k	multicolored	.50	.25

End of World War II, 45th anniv.

Mir Space Station, Cosmonaut A2830

1990, Apr. 12

5883	A2830	20k	multicolored	.50	.35

Cosmonauts' Day.

Lenin, 120th Birth Anniv. — A2831

1990, Apr. 14 Engr. *Perf. 11½*

5884	A2831	5k	red brown	.40	.25

LENINIANA '90 all-union philatelic exhibition.

Lenin Birthday Type of 1988

Portrait of Lenin and: No. 5885, Lenin Memorial (birthplace), Ulyanovsk. No. 5886, Branch of the Central Lenin Museum, Baku. No. 5887, Branch of the Central Lenin Museum, Tashkent.

1990, Apr. 14 Litho. *Perf. 12*

5885	A2727	5k	dark car & multi	.30	.25
5886	A2727	5k	rose vio & multi	.30	.25
5887	A2727	5k	dark grn & multi	.30	.25
			Nos. 5885-5887 (3)	.90	.75

Lenin, 120th Birth Anniv.

Tchaikovsky, Scene from *Iolanta* — A2832

1990, Apr. 25 Engr. *Perf. 12½x12*

5888	A2832	15k	black	1.00	.35

Tchaikovsky (1840-1893), composer.

Kalmyk Legend *Dzhangar*, 550th Anniv. — A2833

1990, May 22 Litho. *Perf. 12x12½*

5889	A2833	10k	blk & blk brn	.50	.25

Folklore Type of 1989

Designs: No. 5890, *Manas*, Kirghiz legend (Warrior with saber leading battle). No. 5891, *Guraguli*, Tadzhik legend (Armored warriors and elephant). No. 5892, *David Sasunsky*, Armenian legend (Men, arches), vert. No. 5893, *Gerogly*, Turkmen legend (Sleeping woman, man with lute), vert. No. 5894, *Kalevipoeg*, Estonian legend (Man with boards), vert. Nos. 5890-5894 printed se-tenant with descriptive label.

1990, May 22 *Perf. 12½x12, 12x12½*

5890	A2795	10k	multicolored	.40	.25
5891	A2795	10k	multicolored	.40	.25
5892	A2795	10k	multicolored	.30	.25
5893	A2795	10k	multicolored	.40	.25
5894	A2795	10k	multicolored	.40	.25
			Nos. 5890-5894 (5)	1.90	1.25

World Cup Soccer Championships, Italy 1990 — A2834

Various soccer players.

1990, May 25 *Perf. 12x12½*

5895	A2834	5k	multicolored	.25	.25
5896	A2834	10k	multicolored	.30	.25
5897	A2834	15k	multicolored	.40	.30
5898	A2834	25k	multicolored	.70	.55
5899	A2834	35k	multicolored	.90	.75
a.			Strip of 5, #5895-5899	3.00	2.00

A2835

1990, June 5 Litho. *Perf. 11½*

5900	A2835	15k	multicolored	.50	.30

Final agreement, European Conference on Security and Cooperation, 15th anniv.

45th World Shooting Championships, Moscow — A2836

1990, June 5 Photo.

5901	A2836	15k	multicolored	.50	.30

Cooperation in Antarctic Research A2837

1990, June 13 Litho. *Perf. 12x12½*

5902	A2837	5k	Scientists on ice	.35	.25
5903	A2837	50k	Krill	1.60	1.00
a.			Souv. sheet of 2, #5902-5903	2.00	

See Australia Nos. 1182-1183.

Goodwill Games A2838

1990, June 14 Litho. *Perf. 11½*

5904	A2838	10k	multicolored	.50	.25

Souvenir Sheet

Battle of the Neva River, 750th Anniv. — A2839

1990, June 20 Litho. *Perf. 12½x12*

5905	A2839 50k multicolored		2.00	1.25

Duck Conservation — A2840

5k, Anas platyrhychos. 15k, Bucephala clangula. 20k, Netta rufina.

1990, July 1 Litho. *Perf. 12*

5906	A2840 5k multicolored	.25	.25
5907	A2840 15k multicolored	.30	.25
5908	A2840 20k multicolored	.45	.25
	Nos. 5906-5908 (3)	1.00	.75

Poultry A2841

5k, Obroshinsky geese. 10k, Adler rooster & hen. 15k, North Caucasian turkeys.

1990, July 1 *Perf. 12x12½*

5909	A2841 5k multicolored	.25	.25
5910	A2841 10k multicolored	.45	.25
5911	A2841 15k multicolored	.75	.35
	Nos. 5909-5911 (3)	1.45	.85

Spaso-Efrosinievsky Monastery, Polotsk — A2842

Statue of Nicholas Baratashvili and Pantheon, Mtasminda A2843

Palace of Shirvanshahs, Baku A2844

Statue of Stefan III the Great, Kishinev — A2845

St. Nshan's Church, Akhpat — A2846

Historic Architecture: No. 5915, Cathedral, Vilnius. No. 5917, St. Peter's Church, Riga. No. 5919, Niguliste Church, Tallinn.

1990, Aug. 1 Litho. *Perf. 11½*

5912	A2842 15k multicolored	.40	.25
5913	A2843 15k multicolored	.40	.25
5914	A2844 15k multicolored	.40	.25
5915	A2842 15k multicolored	.40	.25
5916	A2845 15k multicolored	.40	.25
5917	A2842 15k multicolored	.40	.25
5918	A2846 15k multicolored	.40	.25
5919	A2842 15k multicolored	.40	.25
	Nos. 5912-5919 (8)	3.20	2.00

See Nos. 5968-5970.

Prehistoric Animals — A2847

1990, Aug. 15

5920	A2847 1k Sordes	.25	.25
5921	A2847 3k Chalicotherium	.25	.25
5922	A2847 5k Indricotherium	.25	.25
5923	A2847 10k Saurolophus	.25	.25
5924	A2847 20k Thyestes	.50	.35
	Nos. 5920-5924 (5)	1.50	1.35

Nos. 5921-5923 vert.

Indian Child's Drawing of the Kremlin A2848

No. 5926, Russian child's drawing of India.

1990, Aug. 15 *Perf. 12*

5925	A2848 10k multicolored	.40	.25
5926	A2848 10k multicolored	.40	.25
a.	Pair, #5925-5926	1.00	.50

See India Nos. 1318-1319.

Letter Writing Week — A2849

1990, Sept. 12 Engr. *Perf. 12x11½*

5927	A2849 5k blue	.50	.25

Traffic Safety — A2850

1990, Sept. 12 Litho. *Perf. 11½*

5928	A2850 5k multicolored	.50	.25

Musical Instruments Type of 1989

#5929, Kazakh. #5930, Georgian. #5931, Azerbaijanian. #5932, Lithuanian.

Photo. & Engr.

1990, Sept. 20 *Perf. 12x11½*

Denomination Color

5929	A2816 10k brown	.35	.25
5930	A2816 10k green	.35	.25
5931	A2816 10k orange	.35	.25
5932	A2816 10k blue	.35	.25
	Nos. 5929-5932 (4)	1.40	1.00

Killer Whales A2855

Northern Sea Lions A2856

Sea Otter A2857

Common Dolphin A2858

1990, Oct. 3 Litho. *Perf. 12x11½*

5933	A2855 25k multicolored	.45	.30
5934	A2856 25k multicolored	.45	.30
5935	A2857 25k multicolored	.45	.30
5936	A2858 25k multicolored	.45	.30
a.	Block of 4, #5933-5936	2.00	1.50

See US Nos. 2508-2511.

October Revolution, 73rd Anniv. — A2859

Design: Lenin Among the Delegates to the 2nd Congress of Soviets, by S.V. Gerasimov.

1990, Oct. 10 Litho. *Perf. 12x12½*

5937	A2859 5k multicolored	.50	.25

Nobel Laureates in Literature — A2860

#5938, Ivan A. Bunin (1870-1953). #5939, Boris Pasternak (1890-1960). #5940, Mikhail A. Sholokov (1905-1984).

1990, Oct. 22 *Perf. 12*

5938	A2860 15k brown olive	.50	.25
5939	A2860 15k bluish black	.50	.25
5940	A2860 15k black	.50	.25
	Nos. 5938-5940 (3)	1.50	.75

Submarines — A2861

1990, Nov. 14 Litho. *Perf. 12*

5941	A2861 5k Sever-2	.25	.25
5942	A2861 10k Tinro-2	.25	.25
5943	A2861 15k Argus	.25	.25
5944	A2861 25k Paisis	.70	.55
5945	A2861 35k Mir	.90	.75
	Nos. 5941-5945 (5)	2.35	2.05

A2862

Armenia-Mother Monument by E. Kochar.

1990, Nov. 27 Litho. *Perf. 11½*

5946	A2862 10k multicolored	.50	.25

Armenia '90 Philatelic Exhibition.

A2863

Soviet Agents: #5947, Rudolf I. Abel (1903-71). #5948, Kim Philby (1912-88). #5949, Konon T. Molody (1922-70). #5950, S.A. Vaupshasov (1899-1976). #5951, I.D. Kudrya (1912-42).

1990, Nov. 29 Photo. *Perf. 11½*

5947	A2863 5k black & brown	.40	.25
5948	A2863 5k black & bluish blk	.40	.25
5949	A2863 5k black & yel brown	.40	.25
5950	A2863 5k black & yel green	.40	.25
5951	A2863 5k black & brown	.40	.25
	Nos. 5947-5951 (5)	2.00	1.25

Joint Soviet-Japanese Space Flight — A2864

1990, Dec. 2 Litho. *Perf. 12*

5952	A2864 20k multicolored	.75	.50

Happy New Year — A2865

1990, Dec. 3 *Perf. 11½*

5953	A2865 5k multicolored	.50	.25
b.	Miniature sheet of 8	4.00	

Charter for a New Europe — A2865a

1990, Dec. 31 Litho. *Perf. 11½*

5953A A2865a 30k Globe, Eiffel Tower .75 .50

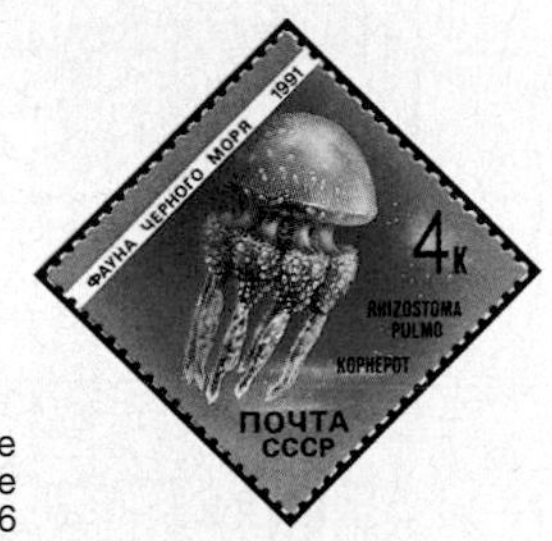

Marine Life A2866

4k, Rhizostoma pulmo. 5k, Anemonia sulcata. 10k, Squalus acanthias. 15k, Engraulis encrasicolus. 20k, Tursiops truncatus.

1991, Jan. 4 Litho. *Perf. 12*

5954	A2866	4k multicolored	.25	.25
5955	A2866	5k multicolored	.25	.25
5956	A2866	10k multicolored	.35	.25
5957	A2866	15k multicolored	.50	.35
5958	A2866	20k multicolored	.65	.45
		Nos. 5954-5958 (5)	2.00	1.55

Chernobyl Nuclear Disaster, 5th Anniv. A2867

1991, Jan. 22 *Perf. 11½*

5959 A2867 15k multicolored .50 .25

Sorrento Coast with View of Capri, 1826, by S.F. Shchedrin (1791-1830) — A2868

Evening in the Ukraine, 1878, by A.I. Kuindzhi (1841-1910) — A2869

Paintings: No. 5961, New Rome, St. Angel's Castle, 1823, by Shchedrin. No. 5963, Birch Grove, 1879, by Kuindzhi.

1991, Jan. 25 *Perf. 12½x12*

5960	A2868	10k multicolored	.35	.25
5961	A2868	10k multicolored	.35	.25
a.		Pair, #5960-5961+label	.70	.50
5962	A2869	10k multicolored	.35	.25
5963	A2869	10k multicolored	.35	.25
a.		Pair, #5962-5963+label	.70	.50
		Nos. 5960-5963 (4)	1.40	1.00

Paul Keres (1916-1975), Chess Grandmaster — A2870

1991, Jan. 7 Litho. *Perf. 11½*

5964 A2870 15k dark brown .50 .35

Environmental Protection — A2871

Designs: 10k, Bell tower near Kaliazin, Volga River region. 15k, Lake Baikal. 20k, Desert zone of former Aral Sea.

1991, Feb. 5 Litho. *Perf. 11½*

5965	A2871	10k multicolored	.35	.25
5966	A2871	15k multicolored	.50	.35
5967	A2871	20k multicolored	.65	.45
		Nos. 5965-5967 (3)	1.50	1.05

Moslem Tower, Uzgen, Kirghizia A2872

Mukhammed Bashar Mausoleum, Tadzhikstan A2873

Talkhatan-baba Mosque, Turkmenistan A2874

1991, Mar. 5

5968	A2872	15k multicolored	.30	.25
5969	A2873	15k multicolored	.30	.25
5970	A2874	15k multicolored	.30	.25
		Nos. 5968-5970 (3)	.90	.75

See Nos. 5912-5919.

Russian Settlements in America — A2875

Designs: 20k, G. I. Shelekhov (1747-1795), Alaska colonizer. 30k, A. A. Baranov, (1746-1819), first governor of Russian America. 50k, I. A. Kuskov, founder of Fort Ross, California.

1991, Mar. 14 *Perf. 12x11½*

5971	A2875	20k brt blue & black	.35	.25
5972	A2875	30k olive brn & blk	.65	.45
5973	A2875	50k red brn & black	1.10	.60
		Nos. 5971-5973 (3)	2.10	1.30

Yuri A. Gagarin A2876

Inscription, Nos. 5977c, 5977e

1991, Apr. 6 *Perf. 11½x12*

5974	A2876	25k Pilot	.75	.50
5975	A2876	25k Cosmonaut	.75	.50
5976	A2876	25k Pilot, wearing hat	.75	.50
5977	A2876	25k As civilian	.75	.50
a.		Block of 4, #5974-5977	3.00	2.50
b.		Sheet of 4, #5974-5977, imperf.	4.00	2.80
c.		As "b," inscribed	10.00	5.00
d.		Sheet, 2 each, #5974-5977, Perf. 12x11½	10.00	6.00
e.		As "d," inscribed	10.00	6.00

Nos. 5977b-5977c have simulated perforations.

May 1945 by A. and S. Tkachev A2877

1991, Apr. 10 *Perf. 12*

5978 A2877 5k multicolored .50 .25

World War II Victory Day.

Asia and Pacific Transport Network, 10th Anniv. — A2878

1991, Apr. 15 *Perf. 11½*

5979 A2878 10k multicolored .50 .25

Type of 1988
Dated 1991

Designs: 2k, Early ship, train, and carriage. 7k, Airplane, helicopter, ocean liner, cable car, van. 12k, Space shuttle. 13k, Space station.

1991, Apr. 15 Litho. *Perf. 12x12½*

5984	A2765	2k orange brown	.50	.25
a.		Imperf	.50	.25
5985	A2765	7k bright blue	.50	.25
a.		Perf. 12x11½, photo.	.50	.25
5986	A2765	12k dk lilac rose	.90	.30
5987	A2765	13k deep violet	1.00	.35
		Nos. 5984-5987 (4)	2.90	1.15

Nos. 5984-5987 were also issued on chalky paper. Vaue, $4.

For surcharges see Tadjikistan #10-11, Uzbekistan #18, 61C.

Lenin, 121st Birth Anniv. A2879

Painting: Lenin working on "Materialism and Empirical Criticism" by P.P. Belousov.

1991, Apr. 22 Litho. *Perf. 12*

5992 A2879 5k multicolored .50 .25

Sergei Prokofiev (1891-1953), Composer — A2880

1991, Apr. 23 *Perf. 12½x12*

5993 A2880 15k brown .60 .40

Orchids — A2881

3k, Cypripedium calceolus. 5k, Orchis purpurea. 10k, Ophrys apifera. 20k, Calypso bulbosa. 25k, Epipactis palustris.

1991, May 7 *Perf. 12*

5994	A2881	3k multicolored	.25	.25
5995	A2881	5k multicolored	.25	.25
5996	A2881	10k multicolored	.25	.25
5997	A2881	20k multicolored	.45	.35
5998	A2881	25k multicolored	.60	.40
		Nos. 5994-5998 (5)	1.80	1.50

A2882

Nobel Prize Winners: No. 5999, Ivan P. Pavlov (1849-1936), 1904, Physiology. No. 6000, Elie Metchnikoff (1845-1916), 1908, Physiology. No. 6001, Andrei D. Sakharov, (1921-89), 1975, Peace.

1991, May 14

5999	A2882	15k black	.50	.30
6000	A2882	15k black	.50	.30
6001	A2882	15k blue black	.50	.30
		Nos. 5999-6001 (3)	1.50	.90

William Saroyan (1908-1981), American Writer — A2883

1991, May 22 *Perf. 11½*

6002 A2883 1r multicolored 3.00 2.25

See United States No. 2538.

Russia-Great Britain Joint Space Mission — A2884

1991, May 18 Litho. *Perf. 12*

6003 A2884 20k multicolored .75 .50

Cultural Heritage A2885

Designs: 10k, Miniature from "Ostomirov Gospel," by Sts. Cyril & Methodius, 1056-1057. 15k, "Russian Truth," manuscript, 11th-13th century by Jaroslav Mudrin. 20k, Sergei Radonezhski by Troitse Sergeiev Lavra, 1424. 25k, Trinity, icon by Andrei Rublev, c. 1411. 30k, Illustration from "Book of the Apostles," by Ivan Feodorov and Petr Mstislavetz, 1564.

1991, June 20 Litho. *Perf. 12x12½*

6004 A2885 10k multicolored .35 .25
6005 A2885 15k multicolored .55 .35
6006 A2885 20k multicolored .70 .50
6007 A2885 25k multicolored .90 .60
6008 A2885 30k multicolored 1.00 .80
a. Strip of #6004-6008 5.00 3.00

Ducks A2886

Designs: 5k, Anas acuta. 15k, Aythya marila. 20k, Oxyura leucocephala.

1991, July 1 *Perf. 12*

6009 A2886 5k multicolored .25 .25
6010 A2886 15k multicolored .35 .35
6011 A2886 20k multicolored .45 .45
a. Min. sheet of 9, 2 #6009, 4 #6010, 3 #6011 4.25 3.25
Nos. 6009-6011 (3) 1.05 1.05

Airships A2887

Designs: 1k, Albatross, 1910, vert. 3k, GA-42, 1987, vert. 4k, Norge, 1923. 5k, Victory, 1944. 20k, Graf Zeppelin, 1928.

1991, July 18

6012 A2887 1k multicolored .40 .25
6013 A2887 3k multicolored .40 .25
6014 A2887 4k multicolored .40 .25
6015 A2887 5k multicolored .40 .25
6016 A2887 20k multicolored .40 .25
a. Miniature sheet of 8 4.00
Nos. 6012-6016 (5) 2.00 1.25

Types of 1984

2r, Ship, Arctic map. 3r, Child & globe. 5r, Palm frond and globe.

1991-92 Litho. *Perf. 12½x12*

6016B A2529 2r multicolored .50 .25
c. Imperf 1.00 .50
6017 A2529 3r multicolored 5.00 2.50
6017A A2529 5r multicolored 4.00 1.50
Nos. 6016B-6017A (3) 9.50 4.25

Issued: 3r, 6/25; 5r, 11/10; No. 6016B, 8/22/91; No. 6016Bc, 4/20/92.

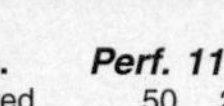

Conf. on Security and Cooperation in Europe — A2888

1991, July 1 Photo. *Perf. 11½*

6018 A2888 10k multicolored .50 .25

Bering & Chirikov's Voyage to Alaska, 250th Anniv. — A2889

Design: No. 6020, Sailing ship, map.

1991, July 27 *Perf. 12x11½*

6019 A2889 30k multicolored .50 .25
6020 A2889 30k multicolored .50 .25

A2890

1991, Aug. 1 *Perf. 12*

6021 A2890 30k multicolored .50 .25

Ukrainian declaration of sovereignty.

A2891

1991, Aug. 1 *Perf. 12x11½*

6022 A2891 7k brown 1.00 .25

Letter Writing Week.

1992 Summer Olympic Games, Barcelona A2892

1991, Sept. 4 Litho. *Perf. 12x12½*

6023 A2892 10k Canoeing .25 .25
a. Miniature sheet of 8 3.50
6024 A2892 20k Running .25 .25
a. Miniature sheet of 8 3.50
6025 A2892 30k Soccer .40 .25
a. Miniature sheet of 8 3.50
Nos. 6023-6025 (3) .90 .75

Victims of Aug. 1991 Failed Coup — A2893

Citizens Protecting Russian "White House" — A2893a

No. 6026, Vladimir Usov, b. 1954. No. 6027, Illya Krichevsky, b. 1963. No. 6028, Dmitry Komar, b. 1968.

1991, Oct. 11 Litho. *Perf. 11½*

6026 A2893 7k multicolored .30 .25
6027 A2893 7k multicolored .30 .25
6028 A2893 7k multicolored .30 .25
Nos. 6026-6028 (3) .90 .75

Souvenir Sheet

6029 A2893a 50k multicolored 2.00 .50

USSR-Austria Joint Space Mission — A2894

1991, Oct. 2 Litho. *Perf. 11½*

6030 A2894 20k multicolored .50 .25

Folk Holidays

Ascension, Armenia A2895

New Year, Azerbaijan A2895a

Ivan Kupala Day, Byelorussia A2895b

New Year, Estonia A2895c

Berikaoba, Georgia A2895d

Kazakhstan — A2895e

Kys Kumai, Kirgizia — A2895f

Ivan Kupala Day, Latvia — A2895g

Palm Sunday, Lithuania A2895h

Plugushorul, Moldavia A2895i

Shrovetide, Russia — A2895j

New Year, Tadzhikistan A2895k

Harvest, Turkmenistan — A2895l

Christmas, Ukraine — A2895m

Spring Tulips, Uzbekistan A2895n

Perf. 12x12½, 12½x12

1991, Oct. 4 **Litho.**

6031	A2895	15k multicolored	.25	.25
6032	A2895a	15k multicolored	.25	.25
6033	A2895b	15k multicolored	.25	.25
6034	A2895c	15k multicolored	.25	.25
6035	A2895d	15k multicolored	.25	.25
6036	A2895e	15k multicolored	.25	.25
6037	A2895f	15k multicolored	.25	.25
6038	A2895g	15k multicolored	.25	.25
6039	A2895h	15k multicolored	.25	.25
6040	A2895i	15k multicolored	.25	.25
6041	A2895j	15k multicolored	.25	.25
6042	A2895k	15k multicolored	.25	.25
6043	A2895l	15k multicolored	.25	.25
6044	A2895m	15k multicolored	.25	.25
6045	A2895n	15k multicolored	.25	.25
a.		Min. sheet, 2 each #6031-6045	10.00	
		Nos. 6031-6045 (15)	3.75	3.75

A2896

1991, Oct. 29 **Litho.** ***Perf. 11½***

6046	A2896	7k multicolored	.50	.25

Election of Boris Yeltsin, 1st president of Russian Republic, June 12, 1991.

Musical Instruments Type of 1989

Musical Instruments: No. 6047, Moldavia. No. 6048, Latvia. No. 6049, Kirgiz.

Photo. & Engr.

1991, Nov. 19 ***Perf. 12x11½***

Denomination Color

6047	A2816	10k red	.50	.25
6048	A2816	10k brt greenish bl	.50	.25
6049	A2816	10k red lilac	.50	.25
		Nos. 6047-6049 (3)	1.50	.75

New Year 1992 A2897

1991, Dec. 8 **Litho.** ***Perf. 12x12½***

6050	A2897	7k multicolored	.50	.25

A2899

Russian Historians: No. 6052, V. N. Tatischev (1686-1750). No. 6053, N. M. Karamzin (1766-1826). No. 6054, S. M. Soloviev (1820-79). No. 6055, Vasili O. Klyuchevsky (1841-1911).

1991, Dec. 12 **Photo. & Engr.**

6052	A2899	10k multicolored	.50	.25
6053	A2899	10k multicolored	.50	.25
6054	A2899	10k multicolored	.50	.25
6055	A2899	10k multicolored	.50	.25
		Nos. 6052-6055 (4)	2.00	1.00

With the breakup of the Soviet Union on Dec. 26, 1991, eleven former Soviet republics established the Commonwealth of Independent States. Stamps inscribed "Rossija" are issued by the Russian Republic.

1992 Winter Olympics, Albertville — A2900

14k, Cross-country skiing, ski jumping. 1r, Freestyle skiing. 2r, Bobsleds.

1992, Jan. 10 **Litho.** ***Perf. 11½x12***

6056	A2900	14k multicolored	.45	.25
a.		Miniature sheet of 8	2.75	
6057	A2900	1r multicolored	.50	.25
a.		Miniature sheet of 8	3.25	
6058	A2900	2r multicolored	1.00	.25
a.		Miniature sheet of 8	5.00	
		Nos. 6056-6058 (3)	1.95	.75

Souvenir Sheet

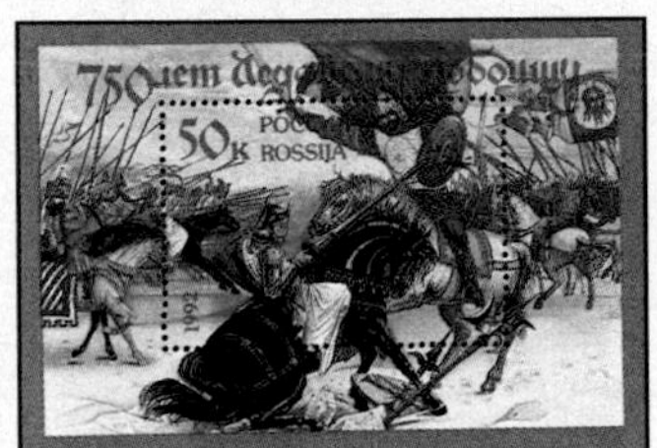

Battle on the Ice, 750th Anniv. — A2901

1992, Feb. 20 **Litho.** ***Perf. 12½x12***

6059	A2901	50k multicolored	1.00	.65

A2902

Designs: 10k, Golden Portal, Vladimir. 15k, Kremlin, Pskov. 20k, 50k, St. George Slaying the Dragon. 25k, 55k, Triumph Gate, Moscow. 30k, 80k, "Millennium of Russia," by M.O. Mikeshin, Novgorod. 60k, Minin-Posharsky Monument, Moscow. 1r, Church, Kizhi. 1.50r, Monument to Peter the Great, St. Petersburg. 2r, St. Basil's Cathedral, Moscow. 3r, Tretyakov Gallery, Moscow. 5r, Morosov House, Moscow. 10r, St. Isaac's Cathedral, St. Petersburg. 25r, Monument to Yuri Dolgoruky, Moscow. 100r, Kremlin, Moscow.

Perf. 12½x12, 11½x12 (15k, 25k, 3r)

1992 **Litho.**

6060	A2902	10k salmon	.45	.25
6060A	A2902	15k dark brn	.45	.25
6061	A2902	20k red	.45	.25
6062	A2902	25k red brown	.45	.25
6063	A2902	30k black	.45	.25
6064	A2902	50k dark blue	.45	.25
6065	A2902	55k dark bl grn	.45	.25
6066	A2902	60k blue green	.45	.25
6066A	A2902	80k lake	.45	.25
6067	A2902	1r yel brown	.45	.25
6067A	A2902	1.50r olive	.50	.25
6068	A2902	2r blue	.45	.25
6068A	A2902	3r red	.45	.25
6069	A2902	5r dark brn	.75	.25
6070	A2902	10r bright blue	.80	.25
6071	A2902	25r dark red	3.00	.50
6071A	A2902	100r brt olive	4.50	1.00
		Nos. 6060-6071A (17)	14.95	5.25

Issued: 20k, 30k, 2/26; 10k, 60k, 2r, 4/20; 25r, 5/25; 10r, 100r, May; 1r, 1.50r, 5r, 6/25; 55k, 8/11; 50k, 80k, 8/18; 15k, 25k, 3r, 9/10.

Nos. 6060-6071A were also issued on chalky paper. Value, same.

See Nos. 6109-6124.

Victory by N. N. Baskakov A2903

1992, Mar. 5 ***Perf. 12x12½***

6072	A2903	5k multicolored	.50	.25

End of World War II, 47th anniv.

Prioksko-Terrasny Nature Reserve — A2904

1992, Mar. 12 ***Perf. 12***

6073	A2904	50k multicolored	.25	.25

Russia-Germany Joint Space Mission — A2905

1992, Mar. 17

6074	A2905	5r multicolored	1.00	.30

Souvenir Sheet

Discovery of America, 500th Anniv. — A2906

1992, Mar. 18 ***Perf. 12x11½***

6075	A2906	3r Ship, Columbus	1.00	.80

Characters from Children's Books A2907

1992, Apr. 22 **Litho.** ***Perf. 12***

6076	A2907	25k Pinocchio	.50	.25
6077	A2907	30k Cipollino	.50	.25
6078	A2907	35k Dunno	.50	.25
6079	A2907	50k Karlson	.50	.25
		Nos. 6076-6079 (4)	2.00	1.00

Space Accomplishments A2908

Designs: No. 6081, Astronaut, Russian space station and space shuttle. No. 6082, Sputnik, Vostok, Apollo Command and Lunar modules. No. 6083, Soyuz, Mercury and Gemini spacecraft.

1992, May 29 **Litho.** ***Perf. 11½x12***

6080	A2908	25r multicolored	.85	.40
6081	A2908	25r multicolored	.85	.40
6082	A2908	25r multicolored	.85	.40
6083	A2908	25r multicolored	.85	.40
a.		Block of 4, #6080-6083	4.00	1.60

See US Nos. 2631-2634.

1992 Summer Olympics, Barcelona A2909

Perf. 11½x12, 12x11½

1992, June 5 **Photo.**

6084	A2909	1r Team handball, vert.	.25	.25
a.		Miniature sheet of 8	1.00	1.00
6085	A2909	2r Fencing	.30	.25
a.		Miniature sheet of 8	2.40	2.00
6086	A2909	3r Judo	.50	.25
a.		Miniature sheet of 8	4.00	2.00
		Nos. 6084-6086 (3)	1.05	.75

Explorers — A2910

Designs: 55r, L. A. Zagoskin, Alaska-Yukon. 70r, N. N. Miklucho-Maklai, New Guinea. 1r, G. I. Langsdorf, Brazil.

1992, June 23 **Litho.** ***Perf. 12x11½***

6087	A2910	55k multicolored	.30	.25
6088	A2910	70k multicolored	.30	.25
6089	A2910	1r multicolored	.30	.25
		Nos. 6087-6089 (3)	.90	.75

Ducks A2911

1992, July 1 ***Perf. 12***

6090	A2911	1r Anas querquedula	.30	.25
6091	A2911	2r Aythya ferina	.30	.25
6092	A2911	3r Anas falcata	.30	.25
a.		Min. sheet of 9, 3 #6090, 4 #6091, 2 #6092	3.00	2.10
		Nos. 6090-6092 (3)	.90	.75

The Saviour, by Andrei Rublev A2912

1992, July 3 *Perf. 12x12½*

6093 A2912 1r multicolored .50 .25
a. Miniature sheet of 8 3.00 1.60

The Taj Mahal Mausoleum in Agra, by Vasili Vereshchagin (1842-1904) — A2913

Design: No. 6095, Let Me Approach (detail), by Vereshchagin.

1992, July 3 *Perf. 12½x12*

6094 A2913 1.50r multicolored .30 .25
6095 A2913 1.50r multicolored .30 .25
a. Pair, #6094-6095 + label .75 .30

Cathedral of the Assumption, Moscow A2914

Cathedral of the Annunciation, Moscow A2915

No. 6098, Archangel Cathedral, Moscow.

1992, Sept. 3 Litho. *Perf. 11½*

6096 A2914 1r multicolored .30 .25
a. Miniature sheet of 9 3.00
6097 A2915 1r multicolored .30 .25
a. Miniature sheet of 9 3.00
6098 A2915 1r multicolored .30 .25
a. Miniature sheet of 9 3.00
Nos. 6096-6098 (3) .90 .75

The Nutcracker, by Tchaikovsky, Cent. — A2916

Designs: No. 6099, Nutcrackers, one holding rifle. No. 6100, Nutcrackers, diff. No. 6101, Pas de deux before Christmas tree. No. 6102, Ballet scene.

1992, Nov. 4 Litho. *Perf. 12½x12*

6099 A2916 10r multicolored .50 .25
6100 A2916 10r multicolored .50 .25
6101 A2916 25r multicolored 1.00 .50
6102 A2916 25r multicolored 1.00 .50
a. Block of 4, #6099-6102 4.00 2.00

A2917

A2918

A2919 Icons — A2920

Christmas: No. 6103, Joachim and Anna, 16th cent. No. 6104, Madonna and Child, 14th cent. No. 6105, Archangel Gabriel, 12th cent. No. 6106, St. Nicholas, 16th cent.

1992, Nov. 27 *Perf. 11½*

6103 A2917 10r multicolored .45 .35
6104 A2918 10r multicolored .45 .35
6105 A2919 10r multicolored .45 .35
6106 A2920 10r multicolored .45 .35
a. Block of 4, #6103-6106 3.00 2.00

See Sweden Nos. 1979-1982.

New Year 1993 A2921

1992, Dec. 2 Litho. *Perf. 12x12½*

6107 A2921 50k multicolored .30 .25
a. Miniature sheet of 9 3.00

Discovery of America, 500th Anniv. — A2922

1992, Dec. 29 *Perf. 11½x12*

6108 A2922 15r Flags, sculpture .50 .35

Monuments Type of 1992

Designs: 4r, Church, Kizhi. 6r, Monument to Peter the Great, St. Petersburg. 15r, 45r, The Horsebreaker, St. Petersburg. 50r, Kremlin, Rostov. 75r, Monument to Yuri Dolgoruky, Moscow. 150r, Golden Gate of Vladimir. 250r, Church, Bogolyubovo. 300r, Monument of Minin and Pozharsky. 500r, Lomonosov University, Moscow. 750r, State Library, Moscow. 1000r, Fortress of St. Peter and St. Paul, St. Petersburg. 1500r, Pushkin Museum, Moscow. 2500r, Admiralty, St. Petersburg. 5000r, Bolshoi Theater, Moscow.

Litho., Photo. (50r, 250r, 500r)
Perf. 12½x12, 12x11½ (1000r)

1992-95

6109	A2902	4r red brown	.25	.25
6110	A2902	6r gray blue	.25	.25
6111	A2902	15r brown	.30	.25
a.		Photo.	.30	.25
6112	A2902	45r slate	1.40	.45
6113	A2902	50r purple	.40	.25
6114	A2902	75r red brown	2.75	.70
6115	A2902	150r blue	.35	.25
6116	A2902	250r green	4.00	.30
6117	A2902	300r red brown	.70	.45
6118	A2902	500r violet	8.00	.60
6119	A2902	750r olive grn	.60	.35
6120	A2902	1000r slate	.70	.50
6121	A2902	1500r green	1.10	.60
6122	A2902	2500r olive brn	1.75	1.00
6123	A2902	5000r blue grn	3.50	2.00
		Nos. 6109-6123 (15)	26.05	8.20

Issued: #6111a, 6113, 6116, 6118, 12/25/92; #6109-6110, 6/4/93; #6112, 6114, 1/25/93; 150r, 300r, 12/30/93; 1000r, 1/27/95; 750r, 1500r, 2500r, 5000r, 2/21/95.

For surcharge see #6529.

Marius Petipa (1818-1910), Choreographer — A2923

Ballets: No. 6126, Paquita (1847). No. 6127, Sleeping Beauty (1890). No. 6128, Swan Lake (1895). No. 6129, Raymonda (1898).

1993, Jan. 14 Litho. *Perf. 12½x12*

6126 A2923 25r multicolored .75 .25
6127 A2923 25r multicolored .75 .25
6128 A2923 25r multicolored .75 .25
6129 A2923 25r multicolored .75 .25
a. Block of 4, #6126-6129 4.00 2.00

A2924

Characters from Children's Books: a, 2r, Scrub and Rub. b, 3r, Big Cockroach. c, 10r, The Buzzer Fly. d, 15r, Doctor Doolittle. e, 25r, Barmalei.

1993, Feb. 25 Litho. *Perf. 12½x12*

6130 A2924 Strip of 5, #a.-e. 1.00 .75

No. 6130 printed in continuous design.

A2925

1993, Mar. 18 Photo. *Perf. 11½x12*

6131 A2925 10r Vyborg Castle .50 .25

City of Vyborg, 700th anniv.

Battle of Kursk, 50th Anniv. A2926

1993, Mar. 25 *Perf. 12x12½*

6132 A2926 10r multicolored .50 .25

Victory Day.

Flowers — A2927

10r, Saintpaulia ionantha. 15r, Hibiscus rosa-sinensis. 25r, Cyclamen persicum. 50r, Fuchsia hybrida. 100r, Begonia semperflorens.

1993, Mar. 25 *Perf. 12½x12*

6133 A2927 10r multicolored .25 .25
6134 A2927 15r multicolored .25 .25
6135 A2927 25r multicolored .25 .25
6136 A2927 50r multicolored .40 .30
6137 A2927 100r multicolored .85 .60
Nos. 6133-6137 (5) 2.00 1.65

See Nos. 6196-6200.

Communications Satellites — A2928

1993, Apr. 12 Photo. *Perf. 11½*

6138 A2928 25r Molniya-3 .25 .25
6139 A2928 45r Ekran-M .30 .25
6140 A2928 50r Gorizont .30 .25
6141 A2928 75r Luch .50 .35
6142 A2928 100r Express .65 .50
Nos. 6138-6142 (5) 2.00 1.60

Souvenir Sheet

Perf. 12x11½

6143 A2928 250r Ground station, horiz. 2.00 1.40

No. 6143 contains one 37x26mm stamp.

Antique Silver A2929

15r, Snuff box, 1820, mug, 1849. 25r, Tea pot, 1896-1908. 45r, Vase, 1896-1908. 75r, Tray, candlestick holder, 1896-1908. 100r, Coffee pot, cream and sugar set, 1852. 250r, Sweet dish, 1896-1908, biscuit dish, 1844.

1993, May 5 Litho. *Perf. 11½*

6144 A2929 15r multicolored .25 .25
6145 A2929 25r multicolored .25 .25
6146 A2929 45r multicolored .30 .25
6147 A2929 75r multicolored .50 .35
6148 A2929 100r multicolored .70 .45
Nos. 6144-6148 (5) 2.00 1.55

Souvenir Sheet

Perf. 12½x12

6149 A2929 250r multicolored 2.50 1.25

No. 6149 contains one 52x37mm stamp.

A2930

Novgorod Kremlin A2931

Designs: No. 6150, Kremlin towers, 14th-17th cent. No. 6151, St. Sofia's Temple, 11th cent. No. 6152, Belfry of St. Sophia's, 15th-18th cent. 250r, Icon, "Sign of the Virgin," 12th cent.

1993, June 4 Litho. *Perf. 12*

6150 A2930 25r multicolored .50 .25
6151 A2931 25r multicolored .50 .25
6152 A2931 25r multicolored .50 .25
a. Sheet, 3 each #6150-6152 5.00 3.00
Nos. 6150-6152 (3) 1.50 .75

Souvenir Sheet

Perf. 12½x12

6153 A2930 250r multicolored 3.00 1.75

No. 6153 contains one 42x30mm stamp.

Russian-Danish Relations, 500th Anniv. — A2932

1993, June 17 *Perf. 11½*

6154 A2932 90r grn & light grn 1.50 .75

See Denmark No. 985.

Ducks A2933

90r, Somateria stelleri. 100r, Somateria mollissima. 250r, Somateria spectabilis.

1993, July 1 **Litho.** *Perf. 12*

6155 A2933 90r multicolored .50 .25
6156 A2933 100r multicolored .50 .25
6157 A2933 250r multicolored 1.00 .30
a. Min. sheet, 4 each #6155-6156, 1 #6157 8.00
Nos. 6155-6157 (3) 2.00 .80

Sea Life A2934

50r, Pusa hispida. 60r, Paralithodes brevipes. 90r, Todarodes pacificus. 100fr, Oncorhynchus masu. 250r, Fulmarus glacialis.

1993, July 6

6158 A2934 50r multicolored .25 .25
6159 A2934 60r multicolored .25 .25
6160 A2934 90r multicolored .40 .25
6161 A2934 100r multicolored .40 .25
6162 A2934 250r multicolored 1.10 .75
a. Sheet, #6162, 2 each #6158-6161 5.50 5.50
Nos. 6158-6162 (5) 2.40 1.75

Natl. Museum of Applied Arts and Folk Crafts, Moscow — A2935

Designs: No. 6163, Skopino earthenware candlestick. No. 6164, Painted tray, horiz. No. 6165, Painted box, distaff. No. 6166, Enamel icon of St. Dmitry of Solun. 250r, Fedoskino lacquer miniature Easter egg depicting the Resurrection.

Perf. 12x12½, 12½x12

1993, Aug. 11 **Litho.**

6163 A2935 50r multicolored .25 .25
6164 A2935 50r multicolored .25 .25
6165 A2935 100r multicolored .35 .25
6166 A2935 100r multicolored .35 .25
6167 A2935 250r multicolored .75 .45
Nos. 6163-6167 (5) 1.95 1.45

Goznak (Bank Note Printer and Mint), 175th Anniv. A2936

1993, Sept. 2 **Litho.** *Perf. 12*

6168 A2936 100r multicolored 1.00 .25

Shipbuilders — A2937

No. 6169, Peter the Great (1672-1725), Goto Predestinatsia. No. 6170, K.A. Shilder (1786-1854), first all-metal submarine. No. 6171, I.A. Amosov (1800-78), screw steamship Archimedes. No. 6172, I.G. Bubnov (1872-1919), submarine Bars. No. 6173, B.M. Malinin (1889-1949), submarine Dekabrist. No. 6174, A.I. Maslov (1894-1968), cruiser Kirov.

1993, Sept. 7

6169 A2937 100r multicolored .50 .25
6170 A2937 100r multicolored .50 .25
6171 A2937 100r multicolored .50 .25
6172 A2937 100r multicolored .50 .25
6173 A2937 100r multicolored .50 .25
6174 A2937 100r multicolored .50 .25
a. Block of 6, #6169-6174 3.50 1.25

A2938

Moscow Kremlin A2939

No. 6175, Granovitaya Chamber (1487-91). No. 6176, Church of Rizpolozheniye (1484-88). No. 6177, Teremnoi Palace (1635-36).

1993, Oct. 28 **Litho.** *Perf. 12*

6175 A2938 100r multicolored .60 .25
6176 A2939 100r multicolored .60 .25
6177 A2939 100r multicolored .60 .25
Nos. 6175-6177 (3) 1.80 .75

Panthera Tigris A2940

Designs: 100r, Adult in woods. 250r, Two cubs. 500r, Adult in snow.

1993, Nov. 25 **Litho.** *Perf. 12½x12*

6178 A2940 50r multicolored .35 .25
6179 A2940 100r multicolored .35 .25
6180 A2940 250r multicolored .50 .25
6181 A2940 500r multicolored 1.25 .60
a. Block of 4, #6178-6181 3.00 1.75
b. Miniature sheet, 2 #6181a 6.00

World Wildlife Fund.

New Year 1994 — A2941

1993, Dec. 2 **Photo.** *Perf. 11½*

6182 A2941 25r multicolored 1.00 .25
a. Sheet of 8 50.00

A2942

1993, Nov. 25 **Photo.** *Perf. 11½x12*

6183 A2942 90r gray, blk & red .75 .25

Prevention of AIDS.

Wildlife — A2943

No. 6184, Phascolarctos cinereus. No. 6185, Monachus schauinslandi. No. 6186, Haliaeetus leucocephalus. No. 6187, Elephas maximus. No. 6188, Grus vipio. No. 6189, Ailuropoda melanoleuca. No. 6190, Phocoenoides dalli. No. 6191, Eschrichtius robustus.

1993, Dec. 30 **Litho.** *Perf. 12½x12*

6184 A2943 250r multicolored .50 .25
6185 A2943 250r multicolored .50 .25
6186 A2943 250r multicolored .50 .25
6187 A2943 250r multicolored .50 .25
6188 A2943 250r multicolored .50 .25
6189 A2943 250r multicolored .50 .25
6190 A2943 250r multicolored .50 .25
6191 A2943 250r multicolored .50 .25
a. Min. sheet of 8, #6184-6191 7.50
Nos. 6184-6191 (8) 4.00 2.00

Nikolai Rimsky-Korsakov (1844-1908), Scene from "Sadko" — A2944

Scenes from operas: No. 6193, "Golden Cockerel," 1907. No. 6194, "The Czar's Bride," 1898. No. 6195, "The Snow Maiden," 1881.

1994, Jan. 20 **Litho.** *Perf. 12½x12*

6192 A2944 250r multicolored 1.25 .50
6193 A2944 250r multicolored 1.25 .50
6194 A2944 250r multicolored 1.25 .50
6195 A2944 250r multicolored 1.25 .50
a. Block of 4, #6192-6195 5.00 2.00

Flower Type of 1993

Designs: 50r, Epiphyllum peacockii. No. 6197, Mammillaria swinglei. No. 6198, Lophophora williamsii. No. 6199, Opuntia basilaris. No. 6200, Selenicereus grandiflorus.

1994, Feb. 25 **Litho.** *Perf. 12½x12*

6196 A2927 50r multicolored .25 .25
6197 A2927 100r multicolored .35 .25
a. Min. sheet of 8 7.50 4.00
6198 A2927 100r multicolored .35 .25
a. Min. sheet of 8 7.50 4.00
6199 A2927 250r multicolored .50 .25
6200 A2927 250r multicolored .50 .25
Nos. 6196-6200 (5) 1.95 1.25

Cathedral of St. Peter, York, Great Britain — A2945

Metropolis Church, Athens — A2946

Gothic Church, Roskilde, Denmark A2947

Notre Dame Cathedral, Paris — A2948

St. Peter's Basilica, Vatican City — A2949

Cologne Cathedral, Germany A2950

St. Basil's Cathedral, Moscow — A2951

Seville Cathedral, Spain — A2952

No. 6207, St. Patrick's Cathedral, NYC, US.

1994, Mar. 24 Litho. *Perf. 12x12½*

6201 A2945 150r multicolored .25 .25
6202 A2946 150r multicolored .25 .25
6203 A2947 150r multicolored .25 .25
6204 A2948 150r multicolored .25 .25
6205 A2949 150r multicolored .25 .25
6206 A2950 150r multicolored .25 .25
6207 A2950 150r multicolored .25 .25
6208 A2951 150r multicolored .25 .25
a. Min. sheet of 9 *6.00 6.00*
6209 A2952 150r multicolored .25 .25
a. Min. sheet of 9, #6201-6209 *6.00 6.00*
Nos. 6201-6209 (9) 2.25 2.25

Space Research A2953

Designs: 100r, TS-18 Centrifuge, Soyuz landing module during re-entry. 250r, Soyuz spacecraft docked at Mir space station. 500r, Training in hydrolaboratory, cosmonaut during space walk.

1994, Apr. 12 Litho. *Perf. 12x11½*

6210 A2953 100r multicolored .25 .25
6211 A2953 250r multicolored .30 .25
6212 A2953 500r multicolored .45 .25
Nos. 6210-6212 (3) 1.00 .75

Liberation of Soviet Areas, 50th Anniv. A2954

Battle maps and: a, Katyusha rockets, liberation of Russia. b, Fighter planes, liberation of Ukraine. c, Combined offensive, liberation of Belarus.

1994, Apr. 26 *Perf. 12*

6213 A2954 100r Block of 3, #a.-c., + label 2.00 .45

See Belarus No. 78, Ukraine No. 195.

Russian Architecture A2955

Structure, architect: 50r, Krasniye Vorota, Moscow, Prince D.V. Ukhtomsky (1719-74). 100r, Academy of Science, St. Petersburg, Giacomo Quarenghi (1744-1817). 150r, Trinity Cathedral, St. Petersburg, V.P. Stasov (1769-1848). 300r, Church of Christ the Saviour, Moscow, K.A. Ton (1794-1881).

1994, May 25 Litho. *Perf. 12½x12*

6214 A2955 50r lt brown & blk .50 .25
6215 A2955 100r red brn & blk .50 .25
6216 A2955 150r olive grn & blk .50 .25
6217 A2955 300r gray vio & blk .50 .25
Nos. 6214-6217 (4) 2.00 1.00

Painting Type of 1992

Paintings by V. D. Polenov (1844-1927): No. 6218, Christ and the Adultress, 1886-87. No. 6219, Golden Autumn, 1893.

1994, June 1 Litho. *Perf. 12½x12*

6218 A2913 150r multicolored .25 .25
6219 A2913 150r multicolored .25 .25
a. Pair, #6218-6219 + label .45 .35

Ducks A2956

1994, July 1 *Perf. 12*

6220 A2956 150r Anas penelope .35 .25
6221 A2956 250r Aythya fuligula .50 .25
6222 A2956 300r Anas formosa 1.40 .25
a. Min. sheet, 3 #6220, 4 #6221, 2 #6222 *5.00* 2.00
b. As "a," overprinted *10.00* 2.00
Nos. 6220-6222 (3) 2.25 .75

No. 6222b is overprinted in sheet margin: "World Philatelic Exhibition Moscow-97" in Cyrillic and Latin with four exhibition emblems.

A2957

1994, July 5 Photo. *Perf. 11½x12*

6223 A2957 100r multicolored 1.00 .25

1994 Goodwill Games, St. Petersburg.

A2958

Nobel Prize Winners in Physics: No. 6224, P.L. Kapitsa (1894-1984). No. 6225, P.A. Cherenkov (1904-90).

1994, July 5 Litho. *Perf. 12*

6224 A2958 150r sepia .50 .25
6225 A2958 150r sepia .50 .25

Intl. Olympic Committee, Cent. A2959

1994, July 5

6226 A2959 250r multicolored 1.00 .25

Russian Postal Day — A2960

1994, July 8 *Perf. 11½x12*

6227 A2960 125r multicolored 1.00 .25

Porcelain A2961

Designs: 50r, Snuff box, 1752. 100r, Candlestick, 1750-1760. 150r, Statue of watercarrier, 1818. 250r, Vase, 19th cent. 300r, Statue of lady with mask, 1910. 500r, Monogramed dinner service, 1848.

1994, Aug. 10 Litho. *Perf. 11½*

6228 A2961 50r multicolored .40 .25
a. Min. sheet of 9 5.00 2.50
b. As "a," overprinted 5.00 3.00
6229 A2961 100r multicolored .40 .25
6230 A2961 150r multicolored .40 .25
6231 A2961 250r multicolored .40 .25
6232 A2961 300r multicolored .40 .25
Nos. 6228-6232 (5) 2.00 1.25

Souvenir Sheet

6233 A2961 500r multicolored 3.00 1.00

No. 6228b is overprinted in sheet margin: "World Philatelic Exhibition Moscow 97" in Cyrillic and Latin with four exhibition logos.

Integration of Tuva into Russia, 50th Anniv. — A2962

1994, Oct. 13 Photo. *Perf. 11½x12*

6234 A2962 125r multicolored 1.00 .25

Russian Voyages of Exploration — A2963

Sailing ships and: No. 6235, V.M. Golovnin, Kurile Islands expedition, 1811. No. 6236, I.F. Kruzenstern, trans-global expedition, 1803-06. No. 6237, F.P. Wrangel, North American expedition, 1829-35. No. 6238, F.P. Litke, Novaya Zemlya expedition, 1821-24.

Photo. & Engr.

1994, Nov. 22 *Perf. 12x11½*

6235 A2963 250r multicolored .50 .25
6236 A2963 250r multicolored .50 .25
a. Miniature sheet of 8 5.00 1.10
6237 A2963 250r multicolored .50 .25
6238 A2963 250r multicolored .50 .25
Nos. 6235-6238 (4) 2.00 1.00

Russian Fleet, 300th anniv. (#6236a).

New Year 1995 — A2964

1994, Dec. 6 Photo. *Perf. 12x11½*

6239 A2964 125r multicolored 1.00 .25
a. Min. sheet of 8 10.00 2.00

Alexander Griboedov (1795-1829), Poet, Diplomat A2965

1995, Jan. 5 Litho. *Perf. 11½*

6240 A2965 250r sepia & black .75 .25

No. 6240 printed se-tenant with label.

A2966

Mikhail Fokine (1880-1942), Choreographer — A2967

Scenes from ballets: No. 6241, Scheherazade. No. 6242, The Fire Bird. No. 6243, Petrouchka.

1995, Jan. 18 Litho. *Perf. 12½x12*

6241 A2966 500r multicolored .50 .25
6242 A2967 500r multicolored .50 .25
6243 A2967 500r multicolored .50 .25
a. Block of 3 + label 5.00 1.00

Mikhail Kutuzov (1745-1813), Field Marshal — A2968

1995, Jan. 20

6244 A2968 300r multicolored .50 .25
a. Miniature sheet of 8 4.00 3.00

16th-17th Cent. Architecture, Moscow A2969

Designs: 125r, English Yard, Varvarka St. 250r, Averki Kirillov's house, Bersenevskaya Embankment. 300r, Volkov's house, Kharitonievsky Lane.

1995, Feb. 15 Litho. *Perf. 12x12½*

6245 A2969 125r multicolored 1.00 .25
6246 A2969 250r multicolored 1.00 .25
6247 A2969 300r multicolored 1.00 .25
a. Min. sheet, 2 #6245, 4 #6246, 3 #6247 *15.00 15.00*
b. Min. sheet, as "a," diff. margin *60.00 60.00*
Nos. 6245-6247 (3) 3.00 .75

Sheet margin on No. 6247b has emblems and inscriptions in Cyrillic and Latin for "World Philatelic Exhibition Moscow '97."

UN Fight Against Drug Abuse — A2970

1995, Mar. 1 *Perf. 12½x12*

6248	A2970 150r multicolored		.60	.25

Endangered Species — A2971

a, Shoreline. b, Pusa hispida. c, Lynx. d, River, trees.

1995, Mar. 1 *Perf. 12x12½*

6249	A2971 250r Block of 4, #a.-d.	1.50	.75

Nos. 6249a-6249b, 6249c-6249d are continuous designs. See Finland No. 960.

End of World War II, 50th Anniv. A2972

#6250, Churchill, Roosevelt, Stalin at Yalta. #6251, Ruins of Reichstag, Berlin. #6252, Monument to concentration camp victims. #6253, Tomb of the Unknown Soldier, Moscow, vert. #6254, Potsdam Conference, map of divided Germany, vert. #6255, Russian planes over Manchuria. #6256, Victory parade, Moscow, vert.

1995, Apr. 7 *Perf. 12x12½, 12½x12*

6250	A2972 250r multicolored	.35	.25
6251	A2972 250r multicolored	.35	.25
6252	A2972 250r multicolored	.35	.25
6253	A2972 250r multicolored	.35	.25
6254	A2972 250r multicolored	.35	.25
6255	A2972 250r multicolored	.35	.25

Size: 37x52mm

6256	A2972 500r multicolored	.35	.25
a.	Souv. sheet of 1, perf 11½x12	2.00	1.50
	Nos. 6250-6256 (7)	2.45	1.75

MIR-Space Shuttle Docking, Apollo-Soyuz Link-Up — A2973

a, Space shuttle Atlantis. b, MIR space station. c, Apollo command module. d, Soyuz spacecraft.

1995, June 29 **Litho.** *Perf. 12x12½*

6257	A2973 1500r Block of 4, #a.-d.	5.00	3.00

No. 6257 is a continuous design.

Radio, Cent. A2974

Design: 250r, Alexander Popov (1859-1905), radio-telegraph.

1995, May 3 **Litho.** *Perf. 11½*

6258	A2974 250r multicolored	.50	.25

Flowers — A2975

No. 6259, Campanula patula. No. 6260, Leucanthemum vulgare. No. 6261, Trifolium pratense. No. 6262, Centaurea jacea. 500r, Geranium pratense.

1995, May 18 **Litho.** *Perf. 12½x12*

6259	A2975 250r multicolored	.60	.25
6260	A2975 250r multicolored	.60	.25
6261	A2975 300r multicolored	.60	.25
a.	Min. sheet of 8	5.00	
b.	As "a," different margin	4.00	
6262	A2975 300r multicolored	.60	.25
6263	A2975 500r multicolored	.60	.25
	Nos. 6259-6263 (5)	3.00	1.25

No. 6261b has emblems and inscriptions in Cyrillic and Latin for "World Philatelic Exhibition Moscow '97."

Songbirds — A2976

No. 6264, Alauda arvensis. No. 6265, Turdus philomelos. No. 6266, Carduelis carduelis. No. 6267, Cyanosylvia svecica. No. 6268, Luscinia luscinia.

1995, June 15 **Litho.** *Perf. 12½x12*

6264	A2976 250r multicolored	.40	.25
6265	A2976 250r multicolored	.40	.25
6266	A2976 500r multicolored	.40	.25
6267	A2976 500r multicolored	.40	.25
6268	A2976 750r multicolored	.40	.25
a.	Min. sheet, 2 each #6264-6265, 1 #6268 + label	5.00	1.10
b.	Min. sheet, 2 each #6266-6267, 1 #6268 + label	5.00	1.50
	Nos. 6264-6268 (5)	2.00	1.25

St. Trinity, Jerusalem A2977

Sts. Peter & Paul, Karlovy Vary — A2978

St. Nicholas, Vienna — A2979

St. Nicholas, New York — A2980

Russian Orthodox Churches abroad: 750r, St. Alexei, Leipzig.

1995, July 5 **Litho.** *Perf. 12x12½*

6269	A2977 300r multicolored	.35	.25
6270	A2978 300r multicolored	.35	.25
6271	A2979 500r multicolored	.35	.25
6272	A2980 500r multicolored	.35	.25
6273	A2980 750r multicolored	.35	.25
a.	Min. sheet, 2 ea #6269-6273	4.00	4.00
	Nos. 6269-6273 (5)	1.75	1.25

Principality of Ryazan, 900th Anniv. — A2981

1995, July 20 **Photo.** *Perf. 11½*

6274	A2981 250r Kremlin Cathedral	.50	.25

Fabergé Jewelry in Kremlin Museums A2982

Designs: 150r, Easter egg, 1909, St. Petersburg. 250r, Goblet, 1899-1908, Moscow. 300r, Cross, 1899-1908, St. Petersburg. 600r, Ladle, 1890, Moscow. 750r, Easter egg, 1910, St. Petersburg.

1500r, Easter egg, 1904-06, St. Petersburg.

1995, Aug. 15 **Litho.** *Perf. 11½*

6275	A2982 150r multicolored	.40	.25
6276	A2982 250r multicolored	.40	.25
6277	A2982 300r multicolored	.40	.25
6278	A2982 500r multicolored	.40	.25
6279	A2982 750r multicolored	.40	.30
	Nos. 6275-6279 (5)	2.00	1.30

Souvenir Sheet

6280	A2982 1500r multicolored	1.00	1.00

No. 6280 contains one 37x51mm stamp.

Souvenir Sheet

Singapore '95 — A2983

1995, Sept. 1 *Perf. 12½x12*

6281	A2983 2500r multicolored	2.00	1.75

Ducks A2984

Designs: 500r, Histrionicus histrionicus. 750r, Aythya baeri. 1000r, Mergus merganser.

1995, Sept. 1 *Perf. 12*

6284	A2984 500r multicolored	.40	.25
6285	A2984 750r multicolored	.60	.25
6286	A2984 1000r multicolored	1.00	.40
a.	Miniature sheet, 2 #6284, 4 #6285, 3 #6286	4.00	4.00
	Nos. 6284-6286 (3)	2.00	.90

Russian Fleet, 300th Anniv. — A2985

Paintings: 250r, Battle of Grengam, 1720. 300r, Bay of Cesme, 1770. 500r, Battle of Revel Roadstead, 1790. 750r, Kronstadt Roadstead, 1840.

1995, Sept. 14 **Litho.** *Perf. 12*

6287	A2985 250r multicolored	.25	.25
6288	A2985 300r multicolored	.25	.25
6289	A2985 500r multicolored	.30	.25
6290	A2985 750r multicolored	.40	.25
	Nos. 6287-6290 (4)	1.20	1.00

Arms & Flag of the Russian Federation — A2986

1995, Oct. 4 **Litho.** *Perf. 12x12½*

6291	A2986 500r multicolored	.50	.25

No. 6291 is printed with se-tenant label.

UN, 50th Anniv. — A2987

1995, Oct. 4

6292	A2987 500r multicolored	.50	.30

Peace and Freedom — A2988

Europa: No. 6293, Storks in nest, countryside. No. 6294, Stork in flight.

1995, Nov. 15 **Litho.** *Perf. 12x12½*

6293	1500r multicolored	1.00	.75
6294	1500r multicolored	1.00	.75
a.	A2988 Pair, Nos. 6293-6294	2.25	1.75

No. 6294a is a continuous design.

Christmas A2989

1995, Dec. 1 *Perf. 12*
6295 A2989 500r multicolored .50 .25

A2990

A2990a

A2990b

Early Russian Dukes — A2990c

Designs: No. 6296, Yuri Dolgorouki (1090-1157), Duke of Souzdal, Grand Duke of Kiev, founder of Moscow. No. 6297, Alexander Nevski (1220-63), Duke of Novgorod, Grand Duke of Vladimir. No. 6298, Michael Alexandrovitsch (1333-39), Prince of Tver. No. 6299, Dimitri Donskoi (1350-89), Duke of Moscow, Vladimir. No. 6300, Ivan III (1440-1505), Grand Duke of Moscow.

Litho. & Engr.

1995, Dec. 21 *Perf. 12*
6296 A2990 1000r multicolored .60 .40
6297 A2990a 1000r multicolored .60 .40
6298 A2990b 1000r multicolored .60 .40
6299 A2990c 1000r multicolored .60 .40
6300 A2990c 1000r multicolored .60 .40
Nos. 6296-6300 (5) 3.00 2.00

See #6359-6362.

A2991

1996, Jan. 31 **Litho.** *Perf. 12*
6301 A2991 750r dull olive black .50 .25

Nikolai N. Semenov (1896-1986), chemist.

A2992

Flowers: 500r, Viola wittrockiana. No. 6303, Dianthus barbatus. No. 6304, Lathyrus odoratus. No. 6305, Fritillaria imperialis. No. 6306, Antirrhinum majus.

1996, Feb. 22 **Litho.** *Perf. 12*
6302 A2992 500r multicolored .35 .25
6303 A2992 750r multicolored .60 .25
6304 A2992 750r multicolored .60 .25
6305 A2992 1000r multicolored .25 .30
6306 A2992 1000r multicolored .25 .30
a. Min. sheet of 20, 4 each #6302-6306 + 4 labels 12.00 12.00
Nos. 6302-6306 (5) 2.05 1.35

Domestic Cats A2993

Designs: No. 6307, European tiger. No. 6308, Russian blue. No. 6309, Persian white. No. 6310, Siamese. No. 6311, Siberian.

1996, Mar. 21

Color of Background

6307 A2993 1000r orange .60 .30
6308 A2993 1000r brown .60 .30
6309 A2993 1000r red .60 .30
6310 A2993 1000r blue violet .60 .30
6311 A2993 1000r green .60 .30
a. Sheet, 2 each #6307-6311 7.00 7.00
Nos. 6307-6311 (5) 3.00 1.50

Souvenir Sheet

Modern Olympic Games, Cent. — A2994

1996, Mar. 27
6312 A2994 5000r multicolored 3.00 2.00

Victory Day — A2995

Design: Painting, "Plunged Down Banners," by A. S. Mikhailov.

1996, Apr. 19 **Litho.** *Perf. 12*
6313 A2995 1000r multicolored 2.00 .30
a. Sheet of 8 + label 6.00

Tula, 850th Anniv. A2996

1996, May 14 *Perf. 12½x12*
6314 A2996 1500r Tula Kremlin .75 .40

Russian Trams A2997

Designs: 500r, Putilovsky plant. No. 6316, Sormovo, 1912. No. 6317, "X" series, 1928. No. 6318, "KM" series, 1931. No. 6319, LM-57, 1957. 2500r, Model 71-608 K, 1993.

1996, May 16 **Photo.** *Perf. 11½*
6315 A2997 500r multicolored .25 .25
6316 A2997 750r multicolored .30 .25
6317 A2997 750r multicolored .30 .25
6318 A2997 1000r multicolored .45 .30
6319 A2997 1000r multicolored .45 .30
6320 A2997 2500r multicolored 1.25 .90
a. Souvenir sheet 2.00 2.00
b. Sheet of 6 5.00 5.00
Nos. 6315-6320 (6) 3.00 2.25

A2998

Europa (Famous Women): No. 6321, E.R. Daschkova (1744-1810), scientist. No. 6322, S.V. Kovalevskaya (1850-91), mathematician.

1996, May 20 **Litho.** *Perf. 12x12½*
6321 A2998 1500r green & black 1.00 .75
6322 A2998 1500r lilac & black 1.00 .75

A2999

1996, June 1 **Litho.** *Perf. 12½x12*
6323 A2999 1000r multicolored .50 .35

UNICEF, 50th anniv.

Summer, by P.P. Sokolov A3000

Post Troika, by P.N. Gruzinsky A3001

Design: No. 6326, Winter, by Sokolov.

1996, June 14
6324 A3000 1500r multicolored .65 .50
6325 A3001 1500r multicolored .65 .50
6326 A3000 1500r multicolored .65 .50
Nos. 6324-6326 (3) 1.95 1.50

Moscow, 850th Anniv. — A3002

Paintings of urban views: No. 6327, Yauza River, 1790's. No. 6328, Kremlin Palace, 1797. No. 6329, Kamenny Bridge, 1811. No. 6330, Volkhonka Steet, 1830's. No. 6331, Vorvarka St. 1830-40's. No. 6332, Petrovsky Park, troikas.

1996, June 20 **Litho.** *Perf. 12*
6327 A3002 500r multicolored .25 .25
6328 A3002 500r multicolored .25 .25
6329 A3002 750r multicolored .35 .25
6330 A3002 750r multicolored .35 .25
6331 A3002 1000r multicolored .40 .25
a. Sheet, 2 ea #6327, 6330-6331 5.00
6332 A3002 1000r multicolored .40 .25
a. Sheet, 2 ea #6328-6329, 6332 5.00
b. Sheet of 6, #6327-6332 5.00
Nos. 6327-6332 (6) 2.00 1.50

No. 6332b has emblems and inscriptions in Cyrillic and Latin for "World Philatelic Exhibition Moscow '97."

Traffic Police, 60th Anniv. A3003

a, Pedestrian crossing guard. b, Children receiving traffic safety education. c, Officer writing citation.

1996, July 3 **Litho.** *Perf. 12x12½*
6333 A3003 1500r Sheet of 3, #a.-c. 3.00 1.50

1996 Summer Olympic Games, Atlanta — A3004

1996, July 10 *Perf. 12*
6334 A3004 500r Basketball .25 .25
6335 A3004 1000r Boxing .35 .25
6336 A3004 1000r Swimming .35 .25
6337 A3004 1500r Women's gymnastics .60 .30
6338 A3004 1500r Hurdles .60 .30
a. Sheet of 8 5.00
Nos. 6334-6338 (5) 2.15 1.35

A3005

Russian Navy, 300th Anniv. A3006

Ships: 750r, Yevstafy, 1762. No. 6340, Petropavlovsk, 1894. No. 6341, Novik, 1913. Nos. 6342, 6346a, Galera, 1696. Nos. 6343, 6346d, Aircraft carrier Admiral Kuznetzov, 1985. No. 6344, Tashkent, 1937. No. 6345, Submarine C-13, 1939.

No. 6346: b, Atomic submarine, 1981. c, Sailing ship Azov, 1826.

Litho. & Engr.

1996, July 26 *Perf. 12*

6339	A3005	750r multicolored	.50	.25
6340	A3005	1000r multicolored	.80	.25
6341	A3005	1000r multicolored	.80	.25
6342	A3006	1000r multicolored	.80	.25
6343	A3006	1000r multicolored	.80	.25
a.		Sheet, 3 each #6342-6343	10.00	10.00
6344	A3005	1500r multicolored	.65	.40
6345	A3005	1500r multicolored	.65	.40
		Nos. 6339-6345 (7)	5.00	2.05

Souvenir Sheet

6346	A3006	1000r Sheet of 4, #a.-d. + label	2.00	1.25

No. 6346 has blue background.

Aleksandr Gorsky (1871-1924), Choreographer — A3006a

a, 750r, Portrait, scenes from "The Daughter of Gudule," "Salambo." b, 1500r, Don Quixote. c, 1500r, Giselle. d, 750r, La Bayadere.

1996, Aug. 7 **Litho.** *Perf. 12½x12*

6347	A3006a	Block of 4, #a.-d.	2.00	1.00
e.		Sheet of 6, #6347b	3.50	1.75

Treaty Between Russia and Belarus A3006b

1996, Aug. 27 *Perf. 12x12½*

6348	A3006b	1500r Natl. flags	.50	.30

17th-20th Cent. Enamelwork — A3007

Designs: No. 6349, Chalice, 1679. No. 6350, Aromatic bottle, 17th cent. No. 6351, Ink pot, ink set, 17th-18th cent. No. 6352, Coffee pot, 1750-1760. No. 6353, Perfume bottle, 19th-20th cent.

5000r, Icon, Our Lady of Kazan, 1894.

1996, Sept. 10 *Perf. 11½*

6349	A3007	1000r multicolored	.50	.25
6350	A3007	1000r multicolored	.50	.25
a.		Sheet of 9	4.50	
6351	A3007	1000r multicolored	.50	.25
6352	A3007	1500r multicolored	.50	.30
6353	A3007	1500r multicolored	.50	.30
a.		Sheet of 9	4.50	
		Nos. 6349-6353 (5)	2.50	1.35

Souvenir Sheet

6354	A3007	5000r multicolored	2.00	1.00

No. 6353a inscribed in sheet margin for Moscow '97.

No. 6354 contains one 35x50mm stamp.

UNESCO, 50th Anniv. A3008

1996, Oct. 15 *Perf. 12x12½*

6355	A3008	1000r multicolored	.50	.25

No. 6355 issued in sheets of 8.

Icons, Religious Landmarks A3009

Designs: a, Icon of Our Lady of Iverone, Moscow. b, Holy Monastery of Stavrovouni, Cyprus. c, Icon of St. Nicholas, Cyprus. d, Resurrection (Iverone), Gate, Moscow.

1996, Nov. 13 *Perf. 11½*

6356	A3009	1500r Block of 4, #a.-d.	3.25	1.60

See Cyprus Nos. 893-896.

New Year 1997 — A3010

Design: Chiming Clock of Moscow, Kremlin.

1996, Dec. 5

6357	A3010	1000r multicolored	.50	.25
a.		Sheet of 8	4.25	2.10

Natl. Ice Hockey Team, 50th Anniv. A3011

Action scenes: a, Two players. b, Three players. c, Three players, referee.

1996, Dec. 5 *Perf. 12*

6358	A3011	1500r Strip of 3, #a.-c.	3.00	1.10

Basil III — A3012

Ivan IV (the Terrible) — A3013

Feodor Ivanovich — A3014

Boris Godunov — A3015

Litho. & Engr.

1996, Dec. 20 *Perf. 12*

6359	A3012	1500r multicolored	.75	.35
6360	A3013	1500r multicolored	.75	.35
6361	A3014	1500r multicolored	.75	.35
6362	A3015	1500r multicolored	.75	.35
		Nos. 6359-6362 (4)	3.00	1.40

See #6296-6300.

Flowers — A3016

Designs: No. 6363, Chaenomeles japonica. No. 6364, Amygdalus triloba. No. 6365, Cytisus scoparius. No. 6366, Rosa pimpinellifolia. No. 6367, Philadelphus coronarius.

1997, Jan. 21 **Litho.** *Perf. 12½x12*

6363	A3016	500r multicolored	.75	.25
6364	A3016	500r multicolored	.75	.25
6365	A3016	1000r multicolored	1.25	.55
6366	A3016	1000r multicolored	1.25	.55
6367	A3016	1000r multicolored	1.25	.55
		Nos. 6363-6367 (5)	5.25	2.15

Souvenir Sheet

Moscow, 850th Anniv. — A3017

1997, Feb. 20 *Perf. 12x12½*

6368	A3017	3000r Coat of arms	2.00	1.00

Shostakovich Intl. Music Festival — A3018

Dmitri D. Shostakovich (1906-75), composer.

1997, Feb. 26 *Perf. 12*

6369	A3018	1000r multicolored	.50	.25

Souvenir Sheet

Coat of Arms of Russia, 500th Anniv. — A3019

1997, Mar. 20

6370	A3019	3000r multicolored	2.00	.70

Post Emblem — A3020

Designs: 100r, Agriculture. 150r, Oil rig. 250r, Cranes (birds). 300r, Radio/TV tower. 500r, Russian Post emblem. 750r, St. George slaying dragon. 1000r, Natl. flag, arms. 1500r, Electric power. 2000r, Train. 2500r, Moscow Kremlin. 3000r, Satellite. 5000r, Fine arts.

1997 **Chalky Paper** *Perf. 12x12½*

6371	A3020	100r blk & yel brn	.25	.25
6372	A3020	150r blk & red lilac	.25	.25
6373	A3020	250r blk & olive	.35	.25
6374	A3020	300r blk & dk grn	.65	.25
6375	A3020	500r blk & dk bl	.55	.25
6376	A3020	750r blk & brown	1.10	.25
6377	A3020	1000r blue & red	1.10	.25
6378	A3020	1500r blk & grn bl	1.60	.30
6379	A3020	2000r blk & green	1.25	.40
6380	A3020	2500r blk & red	2.25	.45
6381	A3020	3000r blk & purple	2.25	.60
6382	A3020	5000r blk & brown	3.25	1.00
		Nos. 6371-6382 (12)	14.85	4.50

Nos. 6371-6382 exist on normal (glossy) paper. Values, same.

Issued: 500r, 750r, 1000r, 1500r, 2500r, 3/31; 100r, 150r, 250r, 300r, 2000r, 3000r, 5000r, 4/30.

See Nos. 6423-6433, 6550-6560, 6617-6620.

A3021

1997, Mar. 31 **Litho.** *Perf. 12*

6383	A3021	1000r multicolored	*10.00*	.25

City of Vologda, 850th anniv.

A3022

Europa (Stories and Legends): Legend of Volga.

1997, May 5 **Litho.** *Perf. 12x12½*

6384	A3022	1500r multicolored	3.50	.80

Moscow, 850th Anniv. — A3023

Historic buildings: a, Cathedral of Christ the Savior. b, Turrets and roofs of the Kremlin. c, Grand Palace of the Kremlin, cathedral plaza. d, St. Basil's Cathedral. e, Icon, St. George slaying the Dragon. f, Text of first chronicled record of Moscow, 1147. g, Prince Aleksandr Nevski, Danilov Monastery. h, 16th cent. miniature of Moscow Kremlin. i, Miniature of coronation of Czar Ivan IV. j, 16th cent. map of Moscow.

1997, May 22

6385 A3023 1000r Sheet of 10, #a.-j. 4.50 4.50

Nos. 6385c, 6385h are 42x42mm.

Helicopters — A3024

1997, May 28 Litho. *Perf. 12½x12*

6386 A3024 500r Mi-14 *1.00* .25
6387 A3024 1000r Mi-24 *2.00* .25
6388 A3024 1500r Mi-26 *2.50* .55
6389 A3024 2000r Mi-28 *4.50* .40
a. Sheet of 6 *35.00*
6390 A3024 2500r Mi-34 *5.00* .55
Nos. 6386-6390 (5) *15.00* 2.00

Fairy Tales by Aleksander S. Pushkin — A3025

Designs: 500r, Man holding rope beside lake, devil running, from "The Tale of the Priest and his Workman Balda." 1000r, Two women, two men, from "The Tale of Tsar Saltan." 1500r, Man fishing, fish, man, castle, from "The Tale of the Fisherman and the Fish." 2000r, Princess on steps, old woman holding apple, from "The Tale of the Dead Princess." 3000r, Woman, King bowing while holding scepter, rooster up in air, from "The Tale of the Golden Cockerel."

Photo. & Engr.

1997, June 6 *Perf. 12x12½*

6391 A3025 500r multicolored *.60* .25
6392 A3025 1000r multicolored *1.25* .25
6393 A3025 1500r multicolored *1.75* .30
6394 A3025 2000r multicolored *2.50* .40
6395 A3025 3000r multicolored *3.50* .60
a. Strip of 5, #6391-6395 *8.00* 1.90
b. Sheet of 2 #6395a 11.50

Diplomatic Relations Between Russia and Thailand A3026

Design: St. Petersburg, Russian flag, Bangkok, Thailand flag.

1997, June 20 Litho. *Perf. 12½x12*

6396 A3026 1500r multicolored 1.00 .30

Wildlife A3027

Designs: a, 500r, Pteromys volans. b, 750r, Felix lynx. c, 1000r, Tetrao urogallus. d, 2000r, Lutra lutra. e, 3000r, Numenius arguata.

1997, July 10 *Perf. 12*

6397 A3027 Block of 5. #a.-e., + label 3.00 1.50

Russian Regions A3028

No. 6398, Winter scene, Archangel Oblast. No. 6399, Ocean, beach, Kaliningrad Oblast, vert. No. 6400, Ship, Krasnodarsky Krai. No. 6401, Mountains, Yakutia, vert. No. 6402, Mountain, sailing ship monument, Kamchatka Oblast.

1997, July 15 *Perf. 12½x12, 12x12½*

6398 A3028 1500r multicolored .55 .30
6399 A3028 1500r multicolored .55 .30
6400 A3028 1500r multicolored .55 .30
6401 A3028 1500r multicolored .55 .30
6402 A3028 1500r multicolored .55 .30
Nos. 6398-6402 (5) 2.75 1.50

Cartoon Character Kljopa A3029

Kljpoa and: 500r, Rainbow, balloons. 1000r, Hang glider. 1500r, Troika.

1997, July 25 *Perf. 11½*

6403 A3029 500r multicolored .50 .25
6404 A3029 1000r multicolored 1.00 .25

Size: 45x33mm

Perf. 12

6405 A3029 1500r multicolored 1.50 .40
Nos. 6403-6405 (3) 3.00 .90

World Philatelic Exhibition, Moscow 97 — A3030

Designs: a, No. 1, No. 35. b, No. 6061.

1997, Aug. 5 *Perf. 11½*

6406 A3030 1500r Pair, #a.-b. 1.00 .50
c. Sheet of 6 stamps 8.00 8.00

A3031

History of Russia, Peter I: No. 6407, Planning new capital. No. 6408, Reforming the military. No. 6409, In Baltic Sea naval battle. No. 6410, Ordering administrative reform. No. 6411, Advocating cultural education.
5000r, Peter I (1672-1725).

1997, Aug. 15 *Perf. 12x12½*

6407 A3031 2000r multicolored 1.10 .50
6408 A3031 2000r multicolored 1.10 .50
6409 A3031 2000r multicolored 1.10 .50
6410 A3031 2000r multicolored 1.10 .50
6411 A3031 2000r multicolored 1.10 .50
Nos. 6407-6411 (5) 5.50 2.50

Souvenir Sheet

Litho. & Engr.

6411A A3031 5000r multicolored 3.50 1.50

Indian Independence, 50th Anniv. — A3032

1997, Aug. 15 *Perf. 12*

6412 A3032 500r multicolored .50 .25

Russian Pentathlon, 50th Anniv. — A3033

1997, Sept. 1 *Perf. 12½x12*

6413 A3033 1000r multicolored .50 .25

Russian Soccer, Cent. A3034

1997, Sept. 4

6414 A3034 2000r multicolored .75 .35

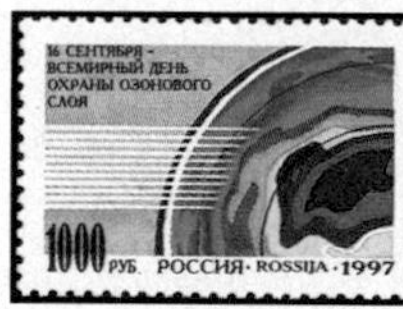

World Ozone Layer Day A3035

1997, Sept. 16 *Perf. 12x12½*

6415 A3035 1000r multioclored .50 .25

A3036

1997, Oct. 1

6416 A3036 1000r multicolored 1.00 .50

Russia's admission to European Council. No. 6416 printed with se-tenant label.

Souvenir Sheet

Pushkin's "Eugene Onegin," Translated by Abraham Shlonsky — A3038

1997, Nov. 19 Litho. *Perf. 12*

6418 A3038 3000r multicolored 2.00 1.60

See Israel No. 1319.

Russian State Museum, St. Petersburg, Cent. — A3039

500r, Boris and Gleb, 14th cent. icon. 1000r, "The Volga Boatmen," by I. Repin. 1500r, "A Promenade," by Marc Chagall. 2000r, "A Merchant's Wife Having Tea," by Kustodiyev.

1997, Nov. 12 Litho. *Perf. 12*

6419 A3039 500r multi, vert. .25 .25
6420 A3039 1000r multi, vert. .40 .25
6421 A3039 1500r multi .60 .30
6422 A3039 2000r multi, vert. .80 .40
Nos. 6419-6422 (4) 2.05 1.20

Nos. 6419-6422 were each issued in sheets of 8 + label.
See Nos. 6446-6450.

Post Emblem Type of 1997

1998, Jan. 1 Litho. *Perf. 12x12½*

6423 A3020 10k like #6371 .25 .25
6424 A3020 15k like #6372 .25 .25
6425 A3020 25k like #6373 .25 .25
6426 A3020 30k like #6374 .25 .25
6427 A3020 50k like #6375 .30 .25
6428 A3020 1r like #6377 .60 .30
6429 A3020 1.50r like #6378 .90 .45
6430 A3020 2r like #6379 1.25 .60
6431 A3020 2.50r like #6380 1.40 .70
6432 A3020 3r like #6381 1.75 .90
6433 A3020 5r like #6382 3.00 1.40
Nos. 6423-6433 (11) 10.20 5.60

Nos. 6423-6433 were printed on chalky paper and normal (glossy) paper. Values, same.

Vasily Surikov (1848-1916), V. Vasnetsov (1848-1926), Painters — A3040

Entire paintings or details by Surikov: No. 6434, Menshikov in Berezovo, 1887. No. 6435, Boyarynya Morozova, 1887.
By Vasnetsov, vert.: No. 6436, The Struggle of Slavs with the Nomads, 1881. No. 6437, Ivan Tsarevitch on a Wolf, 1889.

1998, Jan. 24 *Perf. 12*

6434 A3040 1.50r multicolored .90 .45
6435 A3040 1.50r multicolored .90 .45
a. Pair, #6434-6435 + label 3.00 .90
6436 A3040 1.50r multicolored .90 .45
6437 A3040 1.50r multicolored .90 .45
a. Pair, #6436-6437 + label 3.00 .90

1998 Winter Olympic Games, Nagano — A3041

50k, Cross country skiing. 1r, Pairs figure skating. 1.50r, Biathlon.

1998, Jan. 27 Litho. *Perf. 12*

6438	A3041	50k multicolored	.40	.25
6439	A3041	1r multicolored	1.00	.30
6440	A3041	1.50r multicolored	1.60	.45
a.		Sheet, 2 each #6438-6440	10.00	3.00
		Nos. 6438-6440 (3)	3.00	1.00

Aquarium Fish A3042

Designs: No. 6441, Hyphessobrycon callistus. No. 6442, Epalzeorhynchus bicolor. 1r, Synodontis galinae. No. 6444, Botia kristinae. No. 6445, Cichlasoma labiatum.

1998, Feb. 25 Litho. *Perf. 12½x12*

6441	A3042	50k multicolored	.35	.25
6442	A3042	50k multicolored	.35	.25
6443	A3042	1r multicolored	.60	.25
a.		Sheet of 6	*22.50*	*10.00*
6444	A3042	1.50r multicolored	.90	.30
6445	A3042	1.50r multicolored	.90	.30
		Nos. 6441-6445 (5)	3.10	1.35

Russian State Museum, St. Petersburg, Cent., Type of 1997

Designs: No. 6446, The Last Day of Pompeii, by K.P. Bryullov, 1833. No. 6447, Our Lady of Malevolent Hearts Tenderness, by K.S. Petrov-Vodkin, 1914-15. No. 6448, Mast Pine Grove, by I.I. Shishkin, 1898. No. 6449, The Ninth Wave, by I.K. Aivazovsky, 1850.

3r, The Mihailovksy Palace (detail), by K.P. Beggrov, 1832.

1998, Mar. 17 *Perf. 12x12½*

6446	A3039	1.50r multicolored	1.20	.30
6447	A3039	1.50r multicolored	1.20	.30
6448	A3039	1.50r multicolored	1.20	.30
6449	A3039	1.50r multicolored	1.20	.30
a.		Sheet, 2 each #6446-6449 + label	9.50	4.50
		Nos. 6446-6449 (4)	4.80	1.20

Souvenir Sheet

6450	A3039	3r multicolored	2.00	1.00

Souvenir Sheet

Expo '98, Lisbon — A3043

1998, Apr. 15 *Perf. 12½x12*

6451	A3043	3r Emblem, dolphins	2.00	.75

Theater of Arts, Moscow, Cent. — A3044

1998, Apr. 24 *Perf. 12*

6452	A3044	1.50r multicolored	2.00	.40

No. 6452 was printed se-tenant with label.

Shrove-tide Natl. Festival — A3045

1998, May 5 Litho. *Perf. 12½x12*

6453	A3045	1.50r multicolored	1.00	.50

Europa.

A3046

A3046a

A3046b

Aleksander S. Pushkin (1799-1837), Poet — A3046c

Pushkin's drawings: No. 6454, Lyceum where Puskin studied 1811-17. No. 6455, A. N. Wolf, contemporary of Pushkin's. No. 6456, Tatyana, heroine of novel, "Eugene Onegin." No. 6457, Cover of 1830 manuscript. No. 6458, Self-portrait.

Litho. & Engr.

1998, May 28 *Perf. 12x12½*

6454	A3046	1.50r multicolored	.60	.30
6455	A3046a	1.50r multicolored	.60	.30
6456	A3046b	1.50r multicolored	.60	.30
6457	A3046c	1.50r multicolored	.60	.30
6458	A3046c	1.50r multicolored	.60	.30
a.		Sheet, 2 each #6454-6458	20.00	5.00
		Nos. 6454-6458 (5)	3.00	1.50

City of Ulyanovsk (Simbirsk), 350th Anniv. — A3047

1998, May 28 Litho. *Perf. 12½x12*

6459	A3047	1r multicolored	3.00	.30

Czar Nicholas II (1868-1918) — A3048

1998, June 30 Litho. *Perf. 11½*

6460	A3048	3r multicolored	1.00	.60

Printed se-tenant with label.

City of Taganrog, 300th Anniv. — A3049

1998, June 10 Litho. *Perf. 12½x12*

6461	A3049	1r multicolored	.50	.25

Souvenir Sheet

1998 World Youth Games, Moscow — A3049a

1998, June 25 Litho. *Perf. 12½x12*

6461A	A3049a	3r multicolored	1.25	.75

A3050

Wild Berries: 50k, Vitis amurensis. 75k, Rubus idaeus. 1r, Schisandra chinensis. 1.50r, Vaccinium vitis-idaea. 2r, Rubus arcticus.

1998, July 10

6462	A3050	50k multicolored	.25	.25
6463	A3050	75k multicolored	.40	.25
6464	A3050	1r multicolored	.50	.25
6465	A3050	1.50r multicolored	.75	.30
6466	A3050	2r multicolored	1.00	.40
		Nos. 6462-6466 (5)	2.90	1.45

A3051

1998, July 15

6467	A3051	1r multicolored	1.00	.25

Ekaterinburg, 275th anniv.

Soviet Intelligence Agents — A3052

No. 6468, L. R. Kvasnikov (1905-93). No. 6469, Morris Cohen (1910-95). No. 6470, Leontina Cohen (1913-92). No. 6471, A.A. Yatskov (1913-93).

1998, Aug. 10 Litho. *Perf. 12*

6468	A3052	1r green & black	.75	.25
6469	A3052	1r brn, bister & blk	.75	.25
6470	A3052	1r slate & black	.75	.25
6471	A3052	1r claret & black	.75	.25
		Nos. 6468-6471 (4)	3.00	1.00

Orders of Russia — A3053

1r, St. Andrey Pervozvanny. 1.50r St. Catherine. 2r, St. Alexander Nevsky. 2.50r, St. George.

1998, Aug. 20 Litho. *Perf. 12x12½*

6472	A3053	1r multi	.35	.25
6472A	A3053	1.50r multi	.55	.25
6472B	A3053	2r multi	.70	.35
6472C	A3053	2.50r multi	.90	.45
d.		Block of 4, #6472-6472C	3.50	1.75
e.		Souvenir sheet of 4, #6472-6472C + label	25.00	10.00

See #6496-6500.

Murmansk Oblast A3054

Khabarovsk Krai — A3055

Karelia Republic — A3056

Buryat Republic — A3057

1998, Sept. 15 Litho. *Perf. 12*

6473	A3054	1.50r multicolored	.60	.30
6474	A3055	1.50r multicolored	.60	.30
6475	A3056	1.50r multicolored	.60	.30
6476	A3057	1.50r multicolored	.60	.30
6477	A3054	1.50r Primorski Krai	.60	.30
		Nos. 6473-6477 (5)	3.00	1.50

World Stamp Day
A3058

1998, Oct. 9 **Litho.** ***Perf. 12***
6478 A3058 1r multicolored .50 .25

Universal Declaration of Human Rights, 50th Anniv. — A3059

1998, Oct. 15
6479 A3059 1.50r multicolored .50 .30

No. 6479 released with se-tenant label.

Menatep Bank, 10th Anniv. — A3060

1998, Oct. 29
6480 A3060 2r multicolored 1.00 .40

A sheet of eight was withdrawn from sale because the Menatep Bank went bankrupt. Value, $50.

20th Cent. Achievements — A3061

1998, Nov. 12
6481 A3061 1r Aviation .50 .25
6482 A3061 1r Space .50 .25
6483 A3061 1r Television .50 .25
6484 A3061 1r Genetics .50 .25
6485 A3061 1r Nuclear power .50 .25
6486 A3061 1r Computers .50 .25
Nos. 6481-6486 (6) 3.00 1.50

M.I. Koshkin (1898-1940), Tank Designer — A3062

1998, Nov. 20
6487 A3062 1r multicolored 1.00 .25

New Year — A3063

1998, Dec. 1 **Litho.** ***Perf. 11½***
6488 A3063 1r multicolored .50 .25
a. Sheet of 9 12.00 5.00

Moscow-St. Petersburg Telephone Line, Cent. — A3064

1999, Jan. 13
6489 A3064 1r multicolored .50 .25

Hunting
A3065

1999, Jan. 29 **Litho.** ***Perf. 11¼***
6490 A3065 1r Wild turkey .25 .25
6491 A3065 1.50r Ducks .45 .25
6492 A3065 2r Releasing raptor .55 .25
6493 A3065 2.50r Wolves .75 .30
6494 A3065 3r Bear .90 .35
Nos. 6490-6494 (5) 2.90 1.40

Souvenir Sheet

Mediterranean Cruise of Feodor F. Ushakov, Bicent. — A3066

1999, Feb. 19 ***Perf. 12½x12***
6495 A3066 5r multicolored 2.00 .55

Order of Russia Type of 1998

1r, St. Vladimir, 1782. 1.50r, St. Anne, 1797. 2r, St. John of Jerusalem, 1798. 2.50r, White Eagles, 1815. 3r, St. Stanislas, 1815.

1999, Feb. 25 **Litho.** ***Perf. 12x12¼***
6496 A3053 1r multicolored .35 .25
6497 A3053 1.50r multicolored .45 .25
6498 A3053 2r multicolored .60 .25
6499 A3053 2.50r multicolored .75 .30
6500 A3053 3r multicolored .90 .40
a. Sheet of 5, #6496-6500 10.00 5.00

Children's Paintings — A3067

Designs: No. 6501, Family picnic. No. 6502, City, bridge, boats on water, helicopter. No. 6503, Stylized city, vert.

1999, Mar. 24 **Litho.** ***Perf. 12¼x12***
6501 A3067 1.20r multicolored .65 .25
6502 A3067 1.20r multicolored .65 .25
6503 A3067 1.20r multicolored .65 .25
Nos. 6501-6503 (3) 1.95 .75

Souvenir Sheet

Russian Navy's Use of Flag with St. Andrew's Cross, 300th Anniv. — A3068

1999, Mar. 24 **Litho.** ***Perf. 12½x12***
6504 A3068 7r multicolored 2.00 1.00

Souvenir Sheet

Intl. Space Station — A3069

1999, Apr. 12 ***Perf. 11½x12½***
6505 A3069 7r multicolored 5.00 .60

IBRA '99 World Philatelic Exhibition, Nuremberg — A3070

1999, Apr. 27 ***Perf. 12½x12***
6506 A3070 3r multicolored .50 .25

Fishermen and Fishing Gear — A3071

1999, Apr. 30 ***Perf. 11¾***
6507 A3071 1r Raft .25 .25
6508 A3071 2r Three fishermen .30 .25
6509 A3071 2r Fisherman, boat .30 .25
6510 A3071 3r Spear fishing .45 .25
6511 A3071 3r Ice fishermen .45 .25
Nos. 6507-6511 (5) 1.75 1.25

Council of Europe, 50th Anniv.
A3072

1999, May 5 ***Perf. 12x12¼***
6512 A3072 3r multicolored .50 .25

Europa
A3073

1999, May 5 ***Perf. 12½x12***
6513 A3073 5r Bison, Oka Natl. Nature Reserve 1.50 .60

Red Deer — A3074

Designs: a, Bucks. b, Does.

1999, May 18 ***Perf. 12½x12***
6514 A3074 2.50r Pair, #a.-b. 3.00 .35
Complete booklet #6514 3.00

See People's Republic of China #2958-2959.

Aleksander Pushkin (1799-1837), Poet
A3075

Paintings of Pushkin by: 1r, S. G. Chirikov, 1815. 3r, J. E. Vivien, 1826. 5r, Karl P. Bryulov, 1836.
7r, Vasily A. Tropinin, 1827

Litho. & Engr.

1999, May 27 ***Perf. 12***
6515 A3075 1r multicolored .35 .25
6516 A3075 3r multicolored .55 .25
6517 A3075 5r multicolored 1.10 .35
a. Min. sheet, 2 ea #6515-6517 9.00 3.75
Nos. 6515-6517 (3) 2.00 .85

Souvenir Sheet

Perf. 12x12½

6518 A3075 7r multicolored 1.25 .60

No. 6518 contains one 30x41mm stamp.

North Ossetia Republic
A3076

Stavropol Kray
A3077

Evenki Autonomous Okrug — A3078

Bashkir Republic — A3079

1999, June 2 **Litho.** ***Perf. 12***
6519 A3076 2r multicolored .30 .25
6520 A3077 2r multicolored .30 .25
6521 A3078 2r multicolored .30 .25
6522 A3079 2r multicolored .30 .25
6523 A3076 2r Kirov Oblast .30 .25
Nos. 6519-6523 (5) 1.50 1.25

Roses — A3080

1999, June 10 ***Perf. 12¼x11¾***

Color of Rose

6524 A3080 1.20r pink .25 .25
6525 A3080 1.20r yellow .25 .25
6526 A3080 2r red & yellow .30 .25
6527 A3080 3r white .45 .25
6528 A3080 4r red .60 .30
a. Min. sheet of 5, #6524-6528 10.00 4.50
b. Strip of 5, #6524-6528 5.00 2.50
Nos. 6524-6528 (5) 1.85 1.30

No. 6123 Surcharged

1999, June 22 Litho. ***Perf. 12½x12***
6529 A2902 1.20r on 5000r 1.00 .30

Rostov-on-Don, 250th Anniv. — A3081

1999, July 8 Litho. ***Perf. 11¾x12¼***
6530 A3081 1.20r multi *2.50* .25

UPU, 125th Anniv. — A3082

1999, Aug. 23 ***Perf. 11¾***
6531 A3082 3r multi .55 .30

Paintings of Karl P. Bryullov (1799-1852) — A3083

Paintings: a, Horsewoman, 1832. b, Portrait of Y. P. Samoilova and Amacillia Paccini.

1999, Aug. 25 Litho. ***Perf. 11¾x12***
6532 A3083 2.50r Pair, #a-b, + central label 2.00 .35

Motorcycles — A3084

Designs: a, 1r, IZ-1, 1929. b, 1.50r, L-300, 1930. c, 2r, M-72, 1941. d, 2.50r, M-1A, 1945. e, 5r, IZ Planet 5, 1987.

1999, Sept. 9 Litho. ***Perf. 11¾***
6533 A3084 Block of 5, #a.-e., + label 3.00 .85
Booklet #6533 5.50

The booklet also contains an unfranked cacheted envelope with First Day Cancel.

Field Marshal Aleksandr Suvorov's Alpine Campaign, Bicent. A3085

Designs: No. 6534, Suvorov and soldiers, monument at Schöllenen Gorge. No. 6535, Suvorov's vanguard at Lake Klöntal.

1999, Sept. 24 Litho. ***Perf. 12x11½***
6534 A3085 2.50r multi *3.00 1.50*
6535 A3085 2.50r multi *3.00 1.50*

See Switzerland Nos. 1056-1057.

Native Sports — A3086

#6536, Kalmyk wrestling. #6537, Horse racing. #6538, Stick tossing. #6539, Reindeer racing. #6540, Weight lifting.

Perf. 11¾x11½, 11½x11¾

1999, Sept. 30 **Litho.**
6536 A3086 2r multi .30 .25
6537 A3086 2r multi .30 .25
6538 A3086 2r multi .30 .25
6539 A3086 2r multi .30 .25
6540 A3086 2r multi, vert. .30 .25
Nos. 6536-6540 (5) 1.50 1.25

Popular Singers A3087

Designs: No. 6542, Leonid Utesov (1895-1982). No. 6543, Mark Bernes (1911-69). No. 6544, Claudia Shulzhenko (1906-84). No. 6545, Lidia Ruslanova (1900-73). No. 6546, Bulat Okudzhava (1924-97). No. 6547, Vladimir Vysotsky (1938-80). No. 6548, Viktor Tsoi (1962-90). No. 6549, Igor Talkov (1956-91).

1999, Oct. 6 Litho. ***Perf. 12x12¼***
6542 A3087 2r multi .40 .25
6543 A3087 2r multi .40 .25
6544 A3087 2r multi .40 .25
6545 A3087 2r multi .40 .25
6546 A3087 2r multi .40 .25
6547 A3087 2r multi .40 .25
6548 A3087 2r multi .40 .25
6549 A3087 2r multi .40 .25
a. Miniature sheet, #6542-6549 10.00
Nos. 6542-6549 (8) 3.20 2.00

Types of 1997 Redrawn with Microprinting Replacing Vertical Lines

1999, Oct. 26 Litho. ***Perf. 12x12¼***

Granite Paper

6550 A3020 10k Like #6371 .50 .25
6551 A3020 15k Like #6372 .50 .25
6552 A3020 25k Like #6373 .50 .25
6553 A3020 30k Like #6374 .50 .25
6554 A3020 50k Like #6375 .50 .25
6555 A3020 1r Like #6377 .50 .25
6556 A3020 1.50r Like #6378 .50 .25
6557 A3020 2r Like #6379 .50 .25
6558 A3020 2.50r Like #6380 .50 .25
6559 A3020 3r Like #6381 .50 .30
6560 A3020 5r Like #6382 .50 .40
Nos. 6550-6560 (11) 5.50 2.95

Dated 1998.

Spartak, Russian Soccer Champions A3088

1999, Nov. 27 ***Perf. 12x12¼***
6561 A3088 2r multi .60 .25

New Year 2000 — A3089

Designs: a, Grandfather Frost, planets. b, Tree, earth in shell.

1999, Dec. 1 ***Perf. 11½x11¾***
6562 A3089 1.20r Pair, #a-b 2.25 .25
c. Sheet of 6 #6562a *20.00*
d. Sheet of 6 #6562b *27.50*

No. 6562 printed in sheets of 30 stamps.

Christianity, 2000th Anniv. — A3090

Paintings: No. 6563, The Raising of the Daughter of Jairus, by Vassili D. Polenov, 1871. No. 6564, Christ in the Wilderness, by Ivan N. Kramskoy, 1872. No. 6565, Christ in the House of Mary and Martha, by G. I. Semiradsky, 1886. No. 6566, What is Truth?, by Nikolai N. Gay, 1890, vert.

7r, Appearance of the Risen Christ, by Alexander A. Ivanov, 1837-57.

2000, Jan. 1 Litho. ***Perf. 12***
6563 A3090 3r multi .50 .25
6564 A3090 3r multi .50 .25
6565 A3090 3r multi .50 .25
6566 A3090 3r multi .50 .25
Nos. 6563-6566 (4) 2.00 1.00

Souvenir Sheet

Perf. 12¼x12
6567 A3090 7r multi 2.00 1.00

No. 6567 contains one 52x37mm stamp.

Souvenir Sheet

Christianity, 2000th Anniv. — A3091

a, Mother of God mosaic, St. Sofia Cathedral, Kiev, 11th cent. b, Christ Pantocrator fresco, Church of the Savior's Transfiguration, Polotsk, Belarus, 12th cent. c, Volodymyr Madonna, Tretiakov Gallery, Moscow, 12th cent.

2000, Jan. 5 ***Perf. 12x12¼***
6568 A3091 3r Sheet of 3, #a-c 3.00 1.25

See Belarus No. 330, Ukraine No. 370.

Nikolai D. Psurtsev (1900-80), Communications Minister — A3092

Litho. & Engr.

2000, Feb. 1 ***Perf. 12x12¼***
6569 A3092 2.50r multi .50 .25

Souvenir Sheet

Christianity, 2000th Anniv. — A3093

2000, Feb. 10 Litho. ***Perf. 12¼***
6570 A3093 10r Kremlin Cathedrals 5.00 .70

No. 6570 contains two 37x52mm labels.

Polar Explorers — A3094

Designs: No. 6571, R. L. Samoilovich (1881-1940). No. 6572, V. Y. Vize (1886-1954). No. 6573, Mikhail M. Somov (1908-73). No. 6574, P. A. Gordienko (1913-82). No. 6575, A. F. Treshnikov (1914-91).

2000, Feb. 24 ***Perf. 11¾***
6571 A3094 2r multi .80 .25
6572 A3094 2r multi .80 .25
6573 A3094 2r multi .80 .25
6574 A3094 2r multi .80 .25
6575 A3094 2r multi .80 .25
a. Miniature sheet of 5, #6571-6575, + label *60.00 60.00*
Nos. 6571-6575 (5) 4.00 1.25

National Sporting Milestones of the 20th Century — A3095

a, 25k, N. A. Panin-Kolomenkin, 1st Olympic champion, 1908. b, 30k, Stockholm Olympics, 1912. c, 50k, All-Russian Olympiad, 1913-14. d, 1r, All-Union Spartacist Games, 1928. e, 1.35r, Sports Association for Labor & Defense, 1931. f, 1.50r, Honored Master of Sport award, 1934. g, 2r, Helsinki Olympics, 1952. h, 2.50r, Vladimir P. Kuts, gold medalist at Melbourne Olympics, 1956. i, 3r, Gold medalist soccer team at Melbourne, 1956. j, 4r Mikhail M. Botvinnik, chess champion. k, 5r, Hockey series between Canada and Soviet Union, 1972. l, 6r, Moscow Olympics, 1980.

2000, Mar. 15 ***Perf. 12¼x12***
6576 A3095 Sheet of 12, #a-l 7.50 2.50

Souvenir Sheet

World Meteorological Organization, 50th Anniv. — A3096

2000, Mar. 20
6577 A3096 7r multi 2.00 .45

A3097 A3098

End of World War II, 55th Anniv. — A3099

War effort posters: No. 6581, Soldier holding child.
5r, Soldier and medal.

2000, Apr. 10

6578 A3097 1.50r multi .50 .25
6579 A3098 1.50r multi .50 .25
6580 A3099 1.50r multi .50 .25
6581 A3099 1.50r multi .50 .25
Nos. 6578-6581 (4) 2.00 1.00

Souvenir Sheet

6582 A3099 5r multi 3.00 .75
a. Miniature sheet, #6578-6581, 2 #6582 20.00 10.00

International Space Cooperation A3100

2r, Apollo-Soyuz mission. 3r, Intl. Space Station. 5r, Sea-based launching station.

2000, Apr. 12 ***Perf. 12***

6583 A3100 2r multi, vert. .65 .25
a. Miniature sheet of 6 15.00 6.00
6584 A3100 3r multi .75 .25
6585 A3100 5r multi, vert. 1.60 .25
Nos. 6583-6585 (3) 3.00 .75

Traffic Safety Week — A3101

2000, Apr. 20 Litho. ***Perf. 12x12½***

6586 A3101 1.75r multi .50 .25

Holocaust A3102

2000, May 5 ***Perf. 12***

6587 A3102 2r multi 7.50 2.50

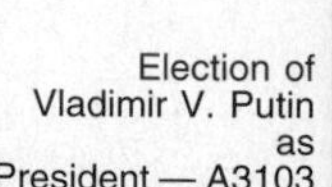

Election of Vladimir V. Putin as President — A3103

2000, May 7 Litho. ***Perf. 12***

6588 A3103 1.75r multi 2.00 .35

Europa, 2000

Common Design Type

2000, May 9 Litho. ***Perf. 12½x12***

6589 CD17 7r multi 2.00 .85
Booklet, #6589 *10.00*

Souvenir Sheet

Expo 2000, Hanover — A3104

2000, May 17 Litho. ***Perf. 12½x12***

6590 A3104 10r multi 3.00 .60

Yamalo-Nenets Autonomous Okrug — A3105

Kalmykia Republic — A3106

Mari El Republic — A3107

Tatarstan Republic — A3108

2000, May 25 ***Perf. 12***

6591 A3105 3r shown .60 .25
6592 A3105 3r Chuvash Republic .60 .25
6593 A3106 3r shown .60 .25
6594 A3107 3r shown .60 .25
6595 A3108 3r shown .60 .25
6596 A3108 3r Udmurtia Republic .60 .25
Nos. 6591-6596 (6) 3.60 1.50

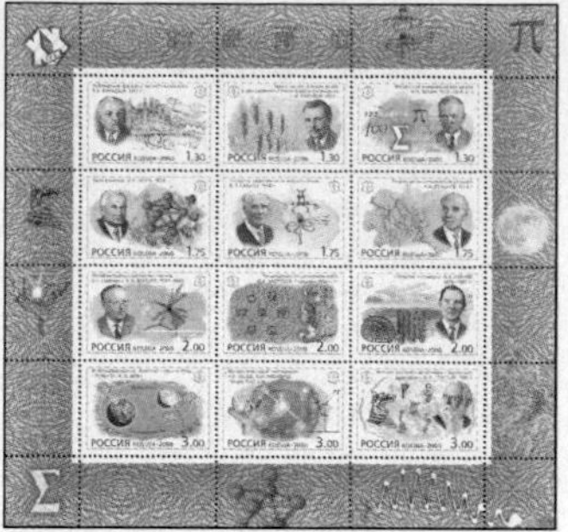

National Scientific Milestones in the 20th Century — A3109

No. 6597: a, 1.30r, Observation of ferromagnetic resonance by V. K. Arkadjev, 1913. b, 1.30r, Botanical diversity studies by N. I. Vavilov, 1920. c, 1.30r, Moscow Mathematical School, N. N. Luzin, 1920-30. d, 1.75r, Theories on light wave emissions by I. Y. Tamm, 1929. e, 1.75r, Discovery of superfluidity of liquid helium, by P. L. Kapitsa, 1938. f, 1.75r, Research in chemical chain reactions by N. N. Semenov, 1934. g, 2r, Phase stability in particle accelerators, by V. I. Veksler, 1944-45. h, 2r, Translation of Mayan texts by Y. V. Knorozov, 1950s. i, 2r, Research into pogonophorans by A. V. Ivanov. j, 3r, Photographing of the dark side of the moon by Luna 3, 1959. k, 3r, Research in quantum electronics by N. G. Basov and A. M. Prokhorov, 1960s. l, 3r, Slavic ethnolinguistic dictionary by N. I. Tolstoi, 1995.

2000, June 20 ***Perf. 12½x12***

6597 A3109 Sheet of 12, #a-l 10.00 3.50

Dogs — A3110

2000, July 20 ***Perf. 12x11¾***

6598 Horiz. strip of 5 3.00 1.00
a. A3110 1r Chihuahua .45 .25
b. A3110 1.50r Toy terrier .45 .25
c. A3110 2r Miniature poodle .45 .25
d. A3110 2.50r French bulldog .50 .25
e. A3110 3r Japanese chin .60 .25
f. Souvenir sheet, #6598e, 2 each #6598a-6598d, perf. 11¾ 14.00 14.00

2000 Summer Olympics, Sydney — A3111

Designs: 2r, Fencing. 3r, Synchronized swimming. 5r, Volleyball.

2000, Aug. 15 Litho. ***Perf. 12***

6599-6601 A3111 Set of 3 1.50 .65

Geological Service, 300th Anniv. — A3112

Minerals: 1r, Charoite. 2r, Hematite. 3r, Rock crystals. 4r, Gold.

2000, Aug. 22 ***Perf. 11¾***

6602-6605 A3112 Set of 4 1.50 .60

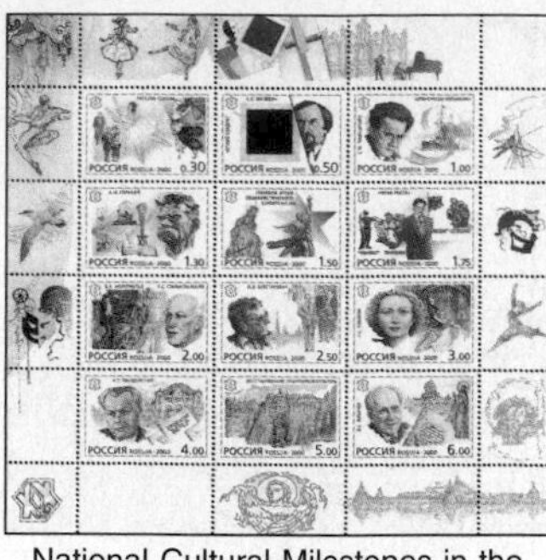

National Cultural Milestones in the 20th Century — A3113

No. 6606: a, 30k, Tours of Russian ballet and opera companies, 1908-14. b, 50k, Black Square on White, by Kazimir S. Malevich, 1913. c, 1r, Battleship Potemkin, movie by Sergein Eisenstein, 1925. d, 1.30r, Maxim Gorki, writer. e, 1.50r, Symbols of socialism. f, 1.75r, Vladimir V. Mayakovsky, poet, and propaganda posters. g, 2r, Vsevolod V. Meyerhold, Konstantin S. Stanislavsky, actors. h, 2.50r, Dmitry D. Shostakovich, composer. i, 3r, Galina S. Ulanova, ballet dancer. j, 4r, A. T. Tvardovsky, poet. k, 5r, Restoration of historical monuments and buildings. l, 6r, D. S. Likhachev, literary critic.

2000, Sept. 20 Litho. ***Perf. 12½x12***

6606 A3113 Sheet of 12, #a-l 6.00 2.00

Fish in Lake Peipus — A3114

No. 6607: a, Stizostedion lucioperka, Coregonus lauaretus manaenoides. b, Osmerus eperlanus spirinchus, Coregonus albula.

2000, Oct. 25 ***Perf. 12x12¼***

6607 A3114 Horiz. pair + central label 1.25 .50
a.-b. 2.50r Any single .40 .25
Booklet, #6607 1.50

See Estonia No. 403.

National Technological Milestones in the 20th Century — A3115

No. 6608: a, 1.50r, Medicine. b, 1.50r, Construction. c, 1.50r, Motor transport. d, 2r, Power generation. e, 2r, Communications. f, 2r, Space technology. g, 3r, Aviation. h, 3r, Rail transport. i, 3r, Sea transport. j, 4r, Metallurgy. k, 4r, Oil refining. l, 4r, Mineral extraction.

2000, Nov. 28 ***Perf. 12½x12***

6608 A3115 Sheet of 12, #a-l 5.00 2.50

Happy New Millennium — A3116

2000, Dec. 1 ***Perf. 12***

6609 A3116 2r multi 1.00 .35
a. Sheet of 6 6.00 2.50

Foreign Intelligence Service, 80th Anniv. — A3117

2000, Dec. 14 Litho. *Perf. 12x12½*

6610	A3117 2.50r multi	.40	.25

Kabardino-Balkaria Republic — A3118

Dagestan Republic A3119

Samara Oblast A3120

2001, Jan. 10 *Perf. 12*

6611	A3118 3r shown	.60	.25
6612	A3119 3r shown	.60	.25
6613	A3120 3r shown	.60	.25
6614	A3118 3r Chita Oblast	.60	.25
6615	A3118 3r Komi Republic, vert.	.60	.25
	Nos. 6611-6615 (5)	3.00	1.25

Souvenir Sheet

Naval Education in Russia, 300th Anniv. — A3121

No. 6616: a, 1.50r, Mathematics and Navigation School, Moscow. b, 2r, Geographical expeditions. c, 8r, St. Petersburg Naval Institute.

2001, Jan. 10 *Perf. 12x12¼*

6616	A3121 Sheet of 3, #a-c	2.00	1.00

Type of 1997 With Lines of Microprinting for Vertical Lines

Designs: 10r, Ballerina. 25r, Rhythmic gymnast. 50r, Earth and computer. 100r, UPU emblem.

2001, Jan. 24 Litho. *Perf. 11¾x12¼*

6617	A3020 10r multi	.75	.45
6618	A3020 25r blk & yel brn	3.00	1.10
6619	A3020 50r blk & blue	5.00	2.00
6620	A3020 100r blk & claret	9.00	3.50
	Nos. 6617-6620 (4)	17.75	7.05

A3122

A3123

A3124

A3124a

Tulips — A3125

2001, Feb. 2 Litho. *Perf. 12¼x12*

6625	Horiz. strip of 5	3.00	.75
a.	A3122 2r Happy Birthday	.40	.25
b.	A3123 2r Be Happy	.40	.25
c.	A3124 2r Congratulations	.40	.25
d.	A3124a 2r Good luck	.40	.25
e.	A3125 2r With Love	.40	.25
f.	Sheet, #6625a-6625e + label	10.00	2.00

Paintings — A3126

No. 6626, 3r (brown background): a, Portrait of P. A. Bulakhov, by Vasily Andreevich Tropinin, 1823. b, Portrait of E. I. Karzinkina, by Tropinin, 1838.

No. 6627, 3r (tan and white background): a, Portrait of I. A. Galitsin, by A. M. Matveev, 1728 . b, Portrait of A. P. Galitsina, by Matveev, 1728.

2001, Feb. 15 Litho. *Perf. 12*

Pairs, #a-b, + Central Label

6626-6627	A3126 Set of 2	3.00	.60

St. Petersburg, 300th Anniv. — A3127

Paintings: 1r, Senate Square and Peter the Great Monumnet, by B. Patersen, 1799. 2r, English Embankment Near senate, by Patersen, 1801. 3r, View of Mikhailovsky Castle From Fontanka Embankment, by Patersen, 1801. 4r, View of the River Moika Near the Stable Department Building, by A. E. Martynov, 1809. 5r, View of the Neva River From the Peter and Paul Fortress, by K. P. Beggrov, 19th cent.

2001, Mar. 15 *Perf. 12x11¾*

6628-6632	A3127 Set of 5	1.50	.80
6632a	Sheet, #6628-6632, + label	7.50	3.00

Dragonflies — A3128

No. 6633: a, 1r, Pyrrhosoma nymphula. b, 1.50r, Epitheca bimaculata. c, 2r, Aeschna grandis. d, 3r, Libellula depressa. e, 5r, Coenagrion hastulatum.

2001, Apr. 5 *Perf. 12x12¼*

6633	A3128 Block of 5, #a-e, + label	3.00	.75

First Manned Space Flight, 40th Anniv. — A3129

No. 6634: a, Cosmonaut Yuri Gagarin and rocket designer Sergei Korolev. b, Gagarin saluting.

2001, Apr. 12 Litho. *Perf. 12½x12*

6634	A3129 3r Horiz. pair, #a-b	2.00	.60
c.	Sheet, 3 #6634	6.00	2.75

Europa — A3130

2001, May 9 Litho. *Perf. 11¾*

6635	A3130 8r multi	1.00	.50
a.	Sheet of 6	10.00	5.00

Intl. Federation of Philately, 75th Anniv. — A3131

2001, May 17 *Perf. 11½*

6636	A3131 2.50r multi	.50	.25

Declaration of State Sovereignty Day — A3132

Litho. & Embossed

2001, June 5 *Perf. 13¼*

6637	A3132 5r multi	3.00	1.00

Russian Emblems A3133

Designs: No. 6638a, Flag. No. 6638b, National anthem. Nos. 6638c, 6639a, Arms.

Litho. & Embossed

2001, June 5 *Perf. 13¼*

6638	Horiz. strip of 3	2.00	.75
a.-b.	A3133 2.50r Any single	.30	.25
c.	A3133 5r multi	.60	.30
d.	Booklet pane of 1, #6638a	—	—
e.	Booklet pane of 1, #6638b	—	—

Souvenir Sheet

6639	Sheet of 3, #6638a-6638b, 6639a	35.00	15.00
a.	A3133 100r multi	30.00	8.00
b.	Booklet pane of 1, #6639a	*100.00*	—
	Booklet, #6638d, 6638e, 6639b	*100.00*	

A souvenir booklet, produced in a quantity of 3,000, exists. It comprises a pane of No. 6639 and panes of 4 each of Nos. 6638a, 6638b and 6639a. Booklets were issued with red, blue or white borders. Value, each $650.

A3134

Houses of Worship — A3135

Designs: No. 6640, Cathedral, Vladimir, 1189. No. 6641, Cathedral, Zvenigorod, 1405. No. 6642, Cathedral, Moscow, 1792. No. 6643, Cathedral, Rostov-on-Don, 1792. No. 6644, Mosque, Ufa, 1830. No. 6645, Church, St. Petersburg, 1838. No. 6646, Mosque, Kazan, 1849. No. 6647, Synagogue, Moscow, 1891. No. 6648, Synagogue, St. Petersburg, 1893. No. 6649, Cathedral, Moscow, 1911. No. 6650, Temple, Ulan-Ude, 1976. No. 6651, Church, Bryansk, 1996. No. 6652, Church, Ryazan, 1996. No. 6653, Church, Lesosibirsk, 1999.

2001, July 12 Litho. *Perf. 11½*

6640	A3134 2.50r multi	.35	.25
6641	A3134 2.50r multi	.35	.25
6642	A3134 2.50r shown	.35	.25
6643	A3134 2.50r multi	.35	.25
6644	A3134 2.50r multi	.35	.25
6645	A3134 2.50r multi	.35	.25
6646	A3134 2.50r multi	.35	.25
6647	A3134 2.50r multi	.35	.25
6648	A3134 2.50r multi	.35	.25
6649	A3134 2.50r multi	.35	.25
6650	A3134 2.50r multi	.35	.25
6651	A3135 2.50r shown	.35	.25
6652	A3135 2.50r multi	.35	.25
6653	A3134 2.50r multi	.35	.25
	Nos. 6640-6653 (14)	4.90	3.50

Souvenir Sheet

First Russian Railroad, 150th Anniv. — A3136

2001, July 25 *Perf. 12*

6654	A3136 12r multi	2.00	.50

Flight of Gherman Titov on Vostok 2, 40th Anniv. A3137

2001, Aug. 6 Litho. ***Perf. 12¼x12***

6655 A3137 3r multi 1.00 .25
a. Sheet of 6 6.00 3.00

Film Stars A3138

Designs: No. 6656, 2.50r, Mikhail Zharov (1899-1981). No. 6657, 2.50r, Faina Ranevskaya (1896-1984). No. 6658, 2.50r, Nikolai Kryuchkov (1910-94). No. 6659, 2.50r, Nikolai Rybnikov (1930-90). No. 6660, 2.50r, Lubov Orlova (1902-75). No. 6661, 2.50r, Yuri Nikulin (1921-97). No. 6662, 2.50r, Evgeny Leonov (1926-94). No. 6663, 2.50r, Anatoly Papanov (1922-87). No. 6664, 2.50r, Andrei Mironov (1941-87).

2001, Sept. 20 ***Perf. 12***

6656-6664 A3138 Set of 9 2.00 1.25
6664a Sheet, #6656-6664 10.00 5.00

Ivan Lazarev (1735-1801) and Institute of Eastern Languages — A3139

2001, Sept. 26 ***Perf. 11¾***

6665 A3139 2.50r multi .50 .35

See Armenia No. 635.

Arkady Raikin (1911-87), Comedian — A3140

2001, Oct. 9 ***Perf. 12***

6666 A3140 2r gray & black .25 .25

Year of Dialogue Among Civilizations A3141

2001, Oct. 9

6667 A3141 5r multi .50 .35

Souvenir Sheet

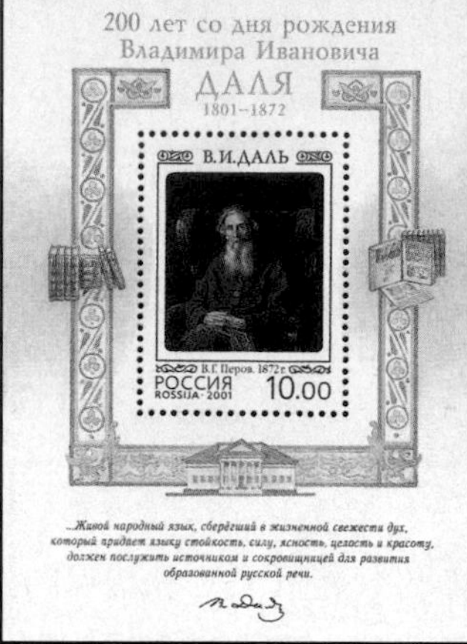

Vladimir Dal (1801-72), Author — A3142

2001, Oct. 16 ***Perf. 12x12½***

6668 A3142 10r multi 2.00 .75

Constitutional Court, 10th Anniv. A3143

2001, Nov. 1 ***Perf. 11¾x12***

6669 A3143 3r multi .25 .25

Savings Bank of Russia, 160th Anniv. — A3144

2001, Nov. 2 ***Perf. 12x11¾***

6670 A3144 2.20r multi .25 .25

Souvenir Sheet

Defense of Moscow, 60th Anniv. — A3145

2001, Nov. 15 ***Perf. 12x12½***

6671 A3145 10r multi 2.00 .60

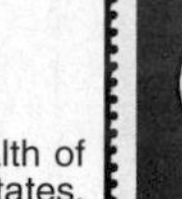

Commonwealth of Independent States, 10th Anniv. — A3146

2001, Nov. 28 ***Perf. 12***

6672 A3146 2r multi 2.00 .75

Happy New Year — A3147

2001, Dec. 4 ***Perf. 12x12¼***

6673 A3147 2.50r multi .25 .25
a. Sheet of 6 10.00 5.00

Amur Oblast A3148

Khakassia Republic A3149

Karachay-Cherkessia Republic — A3150

Sakhalin Oblast A3151

Altai Republic — A3152

2002, Jan. 2 ***Perf. 12x12¼, 12¼x12***

6674 A3148 3r multi .45 .25
6675 A3149 3r multi .45 .25
6676 A3150 3r multi .45 .25
6677 A3151 3r multi .45 .25
6678 A3152 3r multi .45 .25
Nos. 6674-6678 (5) 2.25 1.25

2002 Winter Olympics, Salt Lake City A3153

Designs: 3r, Skier. 4r, Figure skater. 5r, Ski jumper.

2002, Jan. 24 ***Perf. 12x12¼***

6679-6681 A3153 Set of 3 1.50 .75

World Unity Against Terrorism A3154

2002, Jan. 30

6682 A3154 5r multi .50 .35

Souvenir Sheet

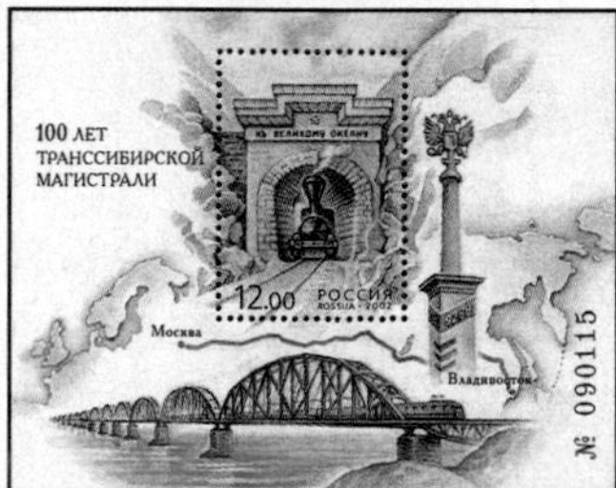

Trans-Siberian Railway, Cent. — A3155

2002, Jan. 30 ***Perf. 12¼x12***

6683 A3155 12r multi 3.00 .60

New Hermitage, 150th Anniv. A3156

Designs: No. 6684, Ecce Homo, by Peter Paul Rubens, before 1612. No. 6685, Courtesan, by Hendrik Goltzius, 1606. No. 6686, Helmet, by Philippo Negroli, 1530s. No. 6687, Gonzaga Cameo, 3rd Cent. B.C.

15r, New Hermitage, 1861, by Luigi Premazzi.

Litho. & Embossed

2002, Feb. 15 ***Perf. 13¼***

6684 A3156 2.50r multi .75 .30
a. Booklet pane of 1 *20.00* —
6685 A3156 2.50r multi .75 .30
a. Booklet pane of 1 *20.00* —
6686 A3156 5r multi 1.50 .60
a. Booklet pane of 1 *40.00* —
6687 A3156 5r multi 1.50 .60
a. Booklet pane of 1 *40.00* —
Nos. 6684-6687 (4) 4.50 1.80

Souvenir Sheet

6688 A3156 15r multi 2.00 1.00
a. Booklet pane of 1 *125.00* —
Booklet, #6684a-6688a *350.00*

Lilies

A3157 A3158

Flower color: No. 6690, White. No. 6692, White with red spots. No. 6693, Red and white with red spots.

Perf. 12¼x11¾

2002, Feb. 20 **Litho.**

6689 A3157 2.50r multi .50 .25
6690 A3157 2.50r multi .50 .25
6691 A3158 2.50r multi .50 .25
6692 A3157 2.50r multi .50 .25
6693 A3157 2.50r multi .50 .25
b. Miniature sheet, #6689-6693 + label 5.00 2.00
Nos. 6689-6693 (5) 2.50 1.25

Dogs — A3159

2002, Mar. 15 ***Perf. 11¾***

6694 Horiz. strip of 5 4.00 2.00
a. A3159 1r Cane Corso .60 .25
b. A3159 2r Shar-pei .60 .25
c. A3159 3r Bull mastiff .60 .25
d. A3159 4r Fila Brasileiro .60 .25
e. A3159 5r Neapolitan mastiff .60 .25
f. Miniature sheet of 9, #6694c, 6694d, 6694e, 2 # 6694a, 4 #6694b 5.00 2.00

St. Petersburg, 300th Anniv. (In 2003) — A3160

Designs: No. 6695, Kazan Cathedral (semi-circular colonnade), monument to Marshal Barclay de Tolly. No. 6696, St. Isaac's Cathedral and sculpture. No. 6697, Cathedral of the Resurrection, bridge, griffin. No. 6698, St. Peter and Paul Cathedral, angel and cross steeple, vert. No. 6699, Admiralty and ship steeple, vert.

Litho. & Embossed

2002, Apr. 25 ***Perf. 13¼***

6695 A3160 5r multi 5.00 1.50
a. Booklet pane of 1 *20.00* —
6696 A3160 5r multi 5.00 1.50
a. Booklet pane of 1 *20.00* —
6697 A3160 25r multi 20.00 6.50
a. Booklet pane of 1 *52.50* —
6698 A3160 25r multi 20.00 6.50
a. Booklet pane of 1 *52.50* —
6699 A3160 25r multi 20.00 6.50
a. Booklet pane of 1 *52.50* —
Booklet, #6695a-6699a *200.00*
Nos. 6695-6699 (5) 70.00 22.50

The embossed portions of the designs of the 25r values bear 22k gold applications.

Security Services, 80th Anniv. — A3161

No. 6700: a, A. K. Artuzov (1891-1937). b, N. I. Demidenko (1896-1934). c, J. K. Olsky (1898-1937). d, S. V. Puzitsky (1895-1937). e, V. A. Styrne (1897-1937). f, G. S. Syroezhkin (1900-37).

2002, Apr. 30 **Litho.** ***Perf. 12x12¼***

6700 A3161 2r Sheet of 6, #a-f 5.00 1.75

Europa A3162

2002, May 9 ***Perf. 12½x12***

6701 A3162 8r multi *1.00* *.50*
a. Miniature sheet of 6 *6.00* *3.00*

Admiral P. S. Nakhimov (1802-55) — A3163

2002, May 24 ***Perf. 12x11¾***

6702 A3163 2r multi .25 .25
a. Miniature sheet of 8 5.00 2.00

European Organization of Supreme Audit Institutions, 5th Congress — A3164

2002, May 24 ***Perf. 12x12¼***

6703 A3164 2r multi .50 .25

Kamchatka Peninsula Volcanos — A3165

No. 6704: a, 1r, Steaming geysers. b, 2r, Mud hole. c, 3r, Karymski Volcano. d, 5r, Crater lake.

2002, June 20 **Litho.** ***Perf. 12***

6704 A3165 Block of 4, #a-d 1.00 .60

Carriages A3166

Designs: No. 6705a, Russian carriage, 1640s. No. 6705b, Closed sleigh, 1732. Nos. 6705c, 6706a, Coupe carriage, 1746. Nos. 6705d, 6706b, 25r, English calash, 1770s. Nos. 6705e, 6706c, Berline carriage, 1769.

Litho. & Embossed

2002, July 25 ***Perf. 13x13¼***

6705 Block of 5 + label 3.00 .95
a.-b. A3166 2.50r Any single .25 .25
c.-e. A3166 5r Any single .40 .40
f. Booklet pane, #6705a *27.50*
g. Booklet pane, #6705b *27.50*
h. Booklet pane, #6705c *57.50*
i. Booklet pane, #6705d *57.50*
j. Booklet pane, #6705e *57.50*
Booklet, #6705f-6705j *250.00*

Souvenir Sheet

6706 A3166 25r Sheet of 3, #a-c 6.00 6.00

Kamov Helicopters — A3167

2002, Aug. 8 **Litho.** ***Perf. 12½x12***

6707 Block of 5 + label 3.00 1.00
a. A3167 1r KA-10 .45 .25
b. A3167 1.50r KA-22 .45 .25
c. A3167 2r KA-26 .45 .25
d. A3167 2.50r KA-27 .45 .25
e. A3167 5r KA-50 .45 .25

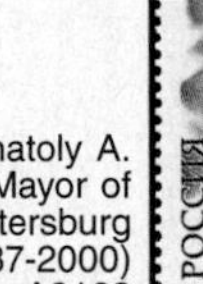

Anatoly A. Sobchak, Mayor of St. Petersburg (1937-2000) A3168

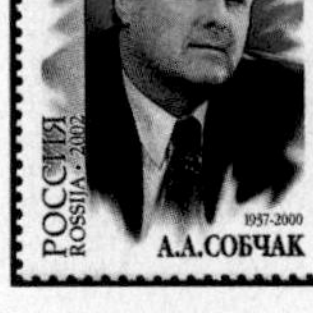

2002, Aug. 10 ***Perf. 12x12½***

6708 A3168 3.25r multi *5.00* .35

Birds — A3169

No. 6709: a, Anthropoides virgo. b, Larus ichthyactus.

2002, Aug. 29 ***Perf. 12¼x12***

6709 A3169 2.50r Horiz. pair, #a-b .50 .50

See Kazakhstan No. 385.

Kostroma, 850th Anniv. A3170

2002, Sept. 2 **Litho.** ***Perf. 12x12¼***

6710 A3170 2r multi .25 .25

Government Ministries, 200th Anniv. — A3171

Arms and/or Russian flag and ministry buildings or symbols: No. 6711, 3r, Defense (light green background, dark green frame). No. 6712, 3r, Foreign Affairs (light blue background, dark green frame). No. 6713, 3r, Internal Affairs (light blue background, dark blue frame). No. 6714, 3r, Education (pink background, red frame). No. 6715, 3r, Finance (lilac background, dark blue frame). No. 6716, 3r, Justice (light yellow background, gray blue frame).

2002, Sept. 2 ***Perf. 12***

6711-6716 A3171 Set of 6 2.00 .85

Russian State, 1140th Anniv. — A3172

2002, Sept. 17 ***Perf. 11½x11¾***

6717 A3172 3r multi .90 .25

2002 Census — A3173

Litho. & Embossed

2002, Sept. 17 ***Perf. 13¼x13***

Stamp + label

6718 A3173 4r shown 5.00 .75
a. Booklet pane of 4, no labels *550.00*
Complete booklet, #6718a *550.00*

Litho.

Self-Adhesive

Serpentine Die Cut 10¾x11

6719 A3173 3r Emblem, people 4.50 .50
a. Booklet pane of 8, no labels *45.00*
Complete booklet, #6719a *45.00*

Customs Service — A3174

No. 6720: a, 2r, Customs house, Arkhangelsk, 18th cent. b, 3r, Customs officers, St. Petersburg, 1830s. c, 5r, Kalanchovsky customs warehouse, Moscow, 19th cent.

2002, Sept. 25 **Litho.** ***Perf. 12x12¼***

6720 A3174 Sheet of 3, #a-c 3.00 .70

Souvenir Sheet

Battle of Stalingrad, 60th Anniv. — A3175

2002, Oct. 4

6721 A3175 10r multi 1.00 .70

Eyes Displaying Interest A3176

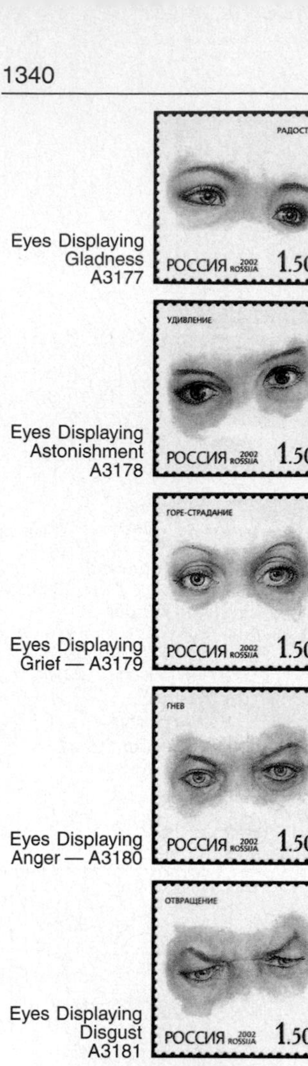

Eyes Displaying Gladness A3177

Eyes Displaying Astonishment A3178

Eyes Displaying Grief — A3179

Eyes Displaying Anger — A3180

Eyes Displaying Disgust A3181

Eyes Displaying Shame — A3182

Eyes Displaying Contempt A3183

Eyes Displaying Guilt — A3184

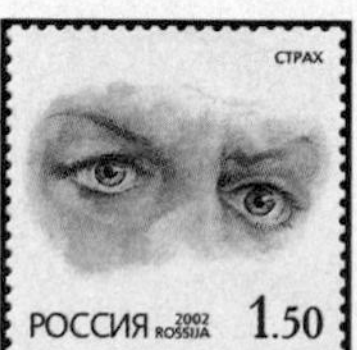

Eyes Displaying Fear — A3185

2002, Oct. 17 ***Perf. 12x11¾***

6722	Sheet of 10	5.00	2.50
a.	A3176 1.50r multi	.40	.25
b.	A3177 1.50r multi	.40	.25
c.	A3178 1.50r multi	.40	.25
d.	A3179 1.50r multi	.40	.25
e.	A3180 1.50r multi	.40	.25
f.	A3181 1.50r multi	.40	.25
g.	A3182 1.50r multi	.40	.25
h.	A3183 1.50r multi	.40	.25
i.	A3184 1.50r multi	.40	.25
j.	A3185 1.50r multi	.40	.25

Emperor Alexander I (1777-1825) A3186

Alexander I: No. 6723, 4r, And Manifesto of March 12, 1801 (blue frame). No. 6724, 4r, Taking over codification of laws from his secretary Mikhail M. Speransky, Oct. 1809 (green frame). No. 6725, 7r, Receiving historian N. M. Karamzin (red frame). No. 6726, 7r, Entering Paris with troops, Mar. 1814 (brown frame).

10r, Portrait of Alexander I, by Francois Gérard.

Litho. & Engr.

2002, Nov. 12 ***Perf. 12x12½***

6723-6726	A3186	Set of 4	8.00	1.50

Souvenir Sheet

6727	A3186	10r multi	6.00	1.60

Russian Orthodox Monasteries — A3187

Designs: No. 6728, 5r, Monastery of St. Daniel, 1282. No. 6729, 5r, Sergii Lavra, 1337. No. 6730, 5r, Valaam Monastery, 14th cent. No. 6731, 5r, Monastery of Reverend Savva, 1398. No. 6732, 5r, Pskov Cave Monastery, 1470.

Litho. & Embossed

2002, Nov. 26 ***Perf. 12½***

6728-6732	A3187	Set of 5	10.00	3.50
6732a		Souvenir sheet, #6728-6732 + label	8.00	4.00

Nos. 6728-6732 each were issued in sheets of 9 stamps + label. The labels on these sheets differ from the label on No. 6732a. Value, set of 5 sheets $100.

See Nos. 6756-6761, 6818-6822.

A limited edition booklet exists containing booklet panes of one of each of Nos. 6728-6732 and 6756-6761. Value, *$400.*

Happy New Year — A3188

2002, Dec. 2 Litho. ***Perf. 12¼x11¾***

6733	A3188	3.50r multi	.25	.25
a.		Sheet of 6	7.00	3.50

Sculpture and Buildings A3189

Designs: 2r, Sculpture "Artemis with Deer," Palace, Arkhangelskoye. 2.50r, Sculpture "Omphala," Chinese Palace, Oranienbaum. 3r, Sculpture of griffin, mansion, Marfino. 4r, Sculpture "Erminia," Grand Palace, Pavlovsk. 5r, Allegorical sculpture of Scamander River, Palace, Kuskovo.

Town name Panels with Colored Backgrounds

Denomination Color

Serpentine Die Cut 11

2002, Dec. 16 **Self-Adhesive**

6734	A3189	2r brown	.50	.25
6735	A3189	2.50r blue	.75	.25
6736	A3189	3r indigo	1.00	.25
6737	A3189	4r violet	1.25	.60
6738	A3189	5r purple	1.50	.60
		Nos. 6734-6738 (5)	5.00	1.95

See also Nos. 6802-6805, 6823-6827.

Nuclear Physicists A3190

Reactor diagrams and: No. 6739, 2.50r, Anatoly P. Alexandrov (1903-94). No. 6740, 2.50r, Igor V. Kurchatov (1903-60).

2003, Jan. 8 ***Perf. 12½x12***

6739-6740	A3190	Set of 2	2.00	.25

Souvenir Sheet

Antarctic Research — A3191

No. 6741: a, Ice borings, map. b, Vostok research station.

2003, Jan. 8 ***Perf. 11½x12¼***

6741	A3191	5r Sheet of 2, #a-b	3.00	1.10

Kemerovo Oblast A3192

Kurgan Oblast A3193

Magadan Oblast A3194

Perm Oblast A3195

Ulyanovsk Oblast A3196

Astrakhan Oblast — A3197

2003, Jan. 10 ***Perf. 12x12¼, 12¼x12***

6742	A3192	3r multi	.35	.25
6743	A3193	3r multi	.35	.25
6744	A3194	3r multi	.35	.25
6745	A3195	3r multi	.35	.25
6746	A3196	3r multi	.35	.25
6747	A3197	3r multi	.35	.25
		Nos. 6742-6747 (6)	2.10	1.50

Commonwealth of Independent States Intergovernmental Communications by Courier, 10th Anniv. — A3198

2003, Jan. 16 ***Perf. 12x12½***

6748	A3198	3r multi	.50	.25

Victory at 2002 Davis Cup Tennis Championships — A3199

Designs: 4r, Fans with signs and Russian flags. 8r, Ball and net, fans with Russian flags. 50r, Davis Cup.

2003, Feb. 19 **Litho.** ***Perf. 13¼***

6749-6750	A3199	Set of 2	1.50	.45

Souvenir Sheet

Litho. with Foil Application & Embossed

Perf. 13¼x13

6751	A3199	50r silver & multi	8.00	2.10

No. 6751 contains one 51x39mm stamp.

Yaroslav Mudry (the Wise) (978-1054), Grand Prince of Kiev — A3200

Vladimir II Monomakh (1053-1125), Grand Prince of Kiev — A3201

Daniel Aleksandrovich Moscowsky (1261-1303), Grand Prince of Moscow — A3202

Ivan II Ivanovich Krasny (the Red) (1320-1359), Grand Prince of Moscow — A3203

Litho. & Engr.

2003, Mar. 4 *Perf. 11¾*

6752	A3200 8r multi	1.00	.40
6753	A3201 8r multi	1.00	.40
6754	A3202 8r multi	1.00	.40
6755	A3203 8r multi	1.00	.40
	Nos. 6752-6755 (4)	4.00	1.60

Monasteries Type of 2002

Designs: No. 6756, 5r, Yuriev Monastery, Novgorod, 1030. No. 6757, 5r, Tolgsky Nunnery, 1314. No. 6758, 5r, Kozelsk Optina Pustyn Monastery, 14th-15th cent. No. 6759, 5r, Solovetsky Zosima and Savvatii Monastery, 15th cent. No. 6760, 5r, Novodevichy Nunnery, 1524. No. 6761, 5r, Seraphim Nunnery, Diveyevo, 1780.

Litho. & Embossed

2003, Mar. 26 *Perf. 12½*

6756-6761	A3187 Set of 6	5.00	1.10
6761a	Souvenir sheet, #6756-6761	10.00	2.00

Nos. 6756-6761 each were issued in sheets of 9 stamps + label. A limited edtion booklet exists containing booklet panes of one of each of Nos. 6728-6732 and 6756-6761. Value, *$450.*

Petrozavodsk, 300th Anniv. — A3204

Perf. 12¼x11¾

2003, Mar. 26 **Litho.**

6762	A3204 3r multi	.50	.25

Novosibirsk, Cent. A3205

2003, Apr. 15 *Perf. 11¾x12¼*

6763	A3205 3r multi	.50	.25

Souvenir Sheet

Baltic Fleet, 300th Anniv. — A3206

2003, Apr. 15 *Perf. 12¼x11¾*

6764	A3206 12r multi	4.00	2.00

Aram Khatchaturian (1903-78), Composer — A3207

2003, Apr. 23 *Perf. 12*

6765	A3207 2.50r multi	1.00	.35

Europa — A3208

2003, May 5 *Perf. 12¼x11¾*

6766	A3208 8r multi	1.50	.75
a.	Sheet of 6	9.50	4.75

Carillons — A3209

No. 6767: a, St. Rombout's Cathedral, Mechelen, Belgium, and bells (denomination at left). b, Sts. Peter and Paul Cathedral, St. Petersburg, and bells (denomination at right).

Litho. & Engr.

2003, May 15 *Perf. 12*

6767	A3209 5r Horiz. pair, #a-b	1.50	.75
c.	Sheet, 3 #6767	5.00	2.00

See Belgium No. 1956.

Anichkov Bridge — A3210

Neva River Drawbridge — A3211

Vasilievsky Island — A3212

Palace Square — A3213

Winter Palace — A3214

Summer Garden — A3215

Peter I Monument — A3216

Designs: 75r, 100r, Peter I Monument.

Litho. & Embossed

2003, May 15 *Perf. 13x13¼*

6768	A3210 5r multi	2.50	.80
6769	A3211 5r multi	2.50	.80
6770	A3212 5r multi	2.50	.80
6771	A3213 5r multi	2.50	.80
6772	A3214 5r multi	2.50	.80
6773	A3215 5r multi	2.50	.80
	Nos. 6768-6773 (6)	15.00	4.80

Souvenir Sheet

Perf. 13¼

6774	A3216 50r multi	12.50	3.50
6775	A3216 75p multi	12.00	3.25
6776	A3216 100p multi	15.00	4.25

St. Petersburg, 300th anniv.

Nos. 6775 and 6776 contain one 37x51mm stamp.

A booklet exists containing one pane of Nos. 6768-6773 and one pane of No. 6774 with an extended margin. Value, *$750.*

Space Flight of Valentina Tereshkova, 40th Anniv. — A3217

2003, May 20 **Litho.** *Perf. 12¼x11¾*

6777	A3217 3r multi	.50	.25
a.	Sheet of 6	7.00	1.50

Second World Anti-Narcotics Congress A3218

2003, May 25 **Litho.** *Perf. 12x12½*

6778	A3218 3r multi	.45	.25

Pskov, 1100th Anniv. A3219

2003, June 3 *Perf. 11¾x12¼*

6779	A3219 3r multi	.50	.25

Krasnoyarsk, 375th Anniv. A3220

2003, June 10

6780	A3220 4r multi	.50	.25

Symbols of Industry, 5 Ruble Coin A3221

2003, June 10 *Perf. 12½x12*

6781	A3221 5r multi	.50	.25

Promotion of "Transparent Economy."

Souvenir Sheet

Battle of Kursk, 60th Anniv. — A3222

2003, June 10 *Perf. 12x12½*

6782	A3222 10r multi	3.00	1.25

Komi Republic Forests — A3223

No. 6783: a, 2r, Stone pillars, Man-Pupuner Mountain. b, 3r, Kozhim River. c, 5r, Upper Pechora River.

2003, June 25 *Perf. 12x12¼*

6783	A3223 Block of 3, #a-c, + label	5.00	.50

Souvenir Sheet

St. Petersburg Postal Service, 300th Anniv. — A3224

2003, June 29 *Perf. 12¼x12*

6784	A3224 12r multi	3.00	.60

Beetles A3225

No. 6785: a, Lucanus cervus. b, Calosoma sycophanta. c, Carabus lopatini. d, Carabus constricticollis. e, Carabus caucasicus.

2003, July 22 *Perf. 12*

6785	Horiz. strip of 5	3.00	.85
a.	A3225 1r multi	.40	.25
b.	A3225 2r multi	.40	.25
c.	A3225 3r multi	.50	.25
d.	A3225 4r multi	.65	.25
e.	A3225 5r multi	.85	.25
f.	Sheet, #6785a-6785e, + label	5.00	1.75

Intl. Association of Academies of Science, 10th Anniv. A3226

2003, July 30 ***Perf. 11¼***
6786 A3226 2.50r multi .50 .25

Chita, 350th Anniv. A3227

2003, Aug. 14 ***Perf. 12x12¼***
6787 A3227 3r multi .50 .25

World Conference on Climate Fluctuations, Moscow — A3228

2003, Aug. 14 ***Perf. 11¾***
6788 A3228 4r multi 1.25 .45

Mushrooms A3229

Various mushrooms.

2003, July 22 ***Perf. 11¾***
6789 Horiz. strip of 5 3.00 .85
a. A3229 2r multi .40 .25
b. A3229 2.50r multi .40 .25
c. A3229 3r multi .50 .25
d. A3229 4r multi .70 .25
e. A3229 5r multi .90 .25
f. Sheet, #6789a-6789e, + label 7.00 3.00

Fruit A3230

Designs: No. 6790, 5r, Melon. No. 6791, 5r, Apples. No. 6792, 5r, Pear. No. 6793, 5r, Pineapple. No. 6794, 5r, Strawberries.

2003, Aug. 27 ***Perf. 13½***
6790-6794 A3230 Set of 5 3.50 2.50

Nos. 6790-6794 are impregnated with fruit scents. Values are for stamps with surrounding selvage.

Caspian Sea Fauna — A3231

No. 6795: a, Phoca caspica. b, Huso huso.

2003, Sept. 9 ***Perf. 12½x12***
6795 A3231 2.50r Horiz. pair, #a-b 1.25 .45
c. Sheet, 3 each #6795a-6795b 35.00 10.00

See Iran No. 2873.

Souvenir Sheet

Russian Journalism, 300th Anniv. — A3232

2003, Sept. 12 ***Perf. 12x12¼***
6796 A3232 10r multi 3.00 .35

Automobiles — A3233

Designs: a, 3r, 1911 Russo-Balt K 12/20. b, 4r, 1929 NAMI-1. c, 4r, 1939 GAZ-M1. d, 5r, 1946 GAZ-67b. e, 5r, 1954 GAZ-M20 Pobeda.

2003, Sept. 17 ***Perf. 11¾x11½***
6797 A3233 Block of 5, #a-e, + label 6.00 1.25

Constitution, 10th Anniv. — A3234

2003, Oct. 15 ***Perf. 12½x12***
6798 A3234 3r multi .50 .25

E. T. Krenkel (1903-71), Polar Explorer — A3235

2003, Oct. 15 ***Perf. 12x12½***
6799 A3235 4r multi .60 .30

Souvenir Sheet

Battle of Sinop, 150th Anniv. — A3236

2003, Nov. 5 ***Perf. 12¼x12***
6800 A3236 12r multi 3.00 .55

Happy New Year — A3237

2003, Dec. 1 ***Perf. 12½***
Flocked Paper
6801 A3237 7r multi 1.40 .70

Sculpture and Buildings Type of 2002

Designs: 1r, Ostankino Palace. 1.50r, Gatchinsky Palace. 6r, Grand Palace, Petrodvorets. 10r, Empress Catherine's Palace, Tsarskoye Selo.

2003, Dec. 5 ***Serpentine Die Cut 11***
Self-Adhesive
6802 A3189 1r multi .75 .25
6803 A3189 1.50r multi .75 .25
6804 A3189 6r multi 1.25 .25
6805 A3189 10r multi 2.25 .35
Nos. 6802-6805 (4) 5.00 1.10

Legislative Bodies, 10th Anniv. A3238

No. 6806: a, Federation Council (denomination at right). b, State Duma (denomination at left).

2003, Dec. 10 ***Perf. 12¼x12***
6806 Horiz. pair + central label .40 .25
a.-b. A3238 2.50r Either single .25 .25

Belgorod Oblast A3239

Ivanovo Oblast A3240

Lipetsk Oblast A3241

Moscow Oblast A3242

Nenetsky Okrug A3243

Nizhny Novgorod Oblast A3244

2004, Jan. 6 ***Perf. 12x12¼***
6807 A3239 5r multi .55 .25
6808 A3240 5r multi .55 .25
6809 A3241 5r multi .55 .25
6810 A3242 5r multi .55 .25
6811 A3243 5r multi .55 .25
6812 A3244 5r multi .55 .25
Nos. 6807-6812 (6) 3.30 1.50

Souvenir Sheet

World War II Offensives of 1944, 60th Anniv. — A3245

2004, Jan. 16 **Litho.** ***Perf. 12x12¼***
6813 A3245 10r multi 3.00 .75

V. P. Chkalov (1904-38), Test Pilot — A3246

2004, Jan. 23 ***Perf. 11¾x12***
6814 A3246 3r multi .50 .25

Tales by P. P. Bazhov (1879-1950) — A3247

No. 6815: a, 2r, The Stone Flower. b, 4r, The Malachite Box. c, 6r, The Golden Hair.

2004, Jan. 27 ***Perf. 12x11¾***
6815 A3247 Horiz. strip of 3, #a-c 1.50 .60
d. Miniature sheet, 2 #6815 7.50 2.75

Yuly B. Khariton (1904-66), Physicist — A3248

2004, Feb. 12 **Litho.** ***Perf. 12¼x12***
6816 A3248 3r multi .50 .25

Yuri Gagarin (1934-68), First Man in Space — A3249

2004, Feb. 20 ***Perf. 12***

6817 A3249 3r multi 1.00 .50

Monasteries Type of 2002

Designs: No. 6818, 8r, St. Panteleimon Monastery, Mt. Athos, Greece, 11th cent. No. 6819, 8r, Holy Assumption Kiev-Pecherskaya Lavra, Ukraine, 1051. No. 6820, 8r, Convent of the Savior and Efrosinia, Polotsk, Belarus, 1128. No. 6821, 8r, Gorney Convent, Israel, 1886. No. 6822, 8r, Pyukhtitsky Convent of the Assumption, Estonia.

Litho. & Embossed

2004, Mar. 16 ***Perf. 12½***

6818-6822 A3187 Set of 5 6.00 2.25
6822a Miniature sheet, #6818-6822 + label 8.00 3.00

A limited edition booklet exists containing booklet panes of one of each of Nos. 6818-6822. Value, *$300.*

Sculptures and Buildings Type of 2002 Redrawn

Designs as before.

Town Name Panels At Bottom With White Background

Denomination Color

2004 Litho. ***Serpentine Die Cut 11***

Self-Adhesive

6823 A3189 2r brown .50 .25
6824 A3189 2.50r blue .50 .25
6825 A3189 3r indigo .50 .25
6826 A3189 4r violet .70 .25
6827 A3189 5r purple .80 .25
Nos. 6823-6827 (5) 3.00 1.25

Issued: 2r, 4r, 4/5; 2.50r, 5r, 4/12; 3r, 4/15.
Nos. 6823-6827 have a crest with stronger lines and vignettes in slightly different shades than Nos. 6734-6738. The background of the town name panels on Nos. 6734-6738 have dots of color, which on some stamps are faint, but are easily seen under magnification.

Kronshtadt, 300th Anniv. — A3250

2004, Apr. 15 ***Perf. 12½x12***

6828 A3250 4r multi .50 .25

Zodiac Signs A3251

No. 6829: a, Aries. b. Leo. c, Sagittarius.
No. 6830: a, Gemini. b, Aquarius. c, Libra.
No. 6831: a, Capricorn. b, Taurus. c, Virgo.
No. 6832: a, Pisces. b, Cancer. c, Scorpio.

Litho. & Embossed

2004, Apr. 21 ***Perf. 13¼x13***

6829 Horiz. strip of 3 2.50 .65
a.-c. A3251 5r Any single .50 .25
6830 Horiz. strip of 3 2.50 .65
a.-c. A3251 5r Any single .50 .25
6831 Horiz. strip of 3 2.50 .65
a.-c. A3251 5r Any single .50 .25
6832 Horiz. strip of 3 2.50 .65
a.-c. A3251 5r Any single .50 .25
d. Miniature sheet, #6829a-6829c, 6830a-6830c, 6831a-6831c, 6832a-6832c 14.00 5.00

Empress Catherine II (1729-96) A3252

Catherine the Great: 6r, Watching scientific presentation of Mikhail Lomonosov. 7r, Giving money to support education, vert. 8r, At legislative commission meeting, vert. 9r, Viewing ships at Inkerman Palace, Crimea.
15r, Portrait.

Perf. 12½x12, 12x12½

2004, Apr. 27 **Litho. & Engr.**

6833-6836 A3252 Set of 4 3.50 1.60

Souvenir Sheet

Perf. 11¾x12¼

6837 A3252 15r multi 3.50 1.00

No. 6837 contains one 33x47mm stamp.

Europa A3253

2004, May 5 **Litho.** ***Perf. 11¾x12¼***

6838 A3253 8r multi *2.00 .75*
a. Miniature sheet of 8 *15.00 6.00*

Souvenir Sheet

Defense of Port Arthur (Lüshun, China) in Russo-Japanese War, Cent. — A3254

2004, May 12 ***Perf. 11¼***

6839 A3254 10r multi 2.50 1.00

Mikhail I. Glinka (1804-57), Composer — A3255

No. 6840: a, Portrait. b, Scene from opera "Life for the Tsar," 1836. c, Scene from opera "Ruslan and Ludmila," 1842.

2004, May 20 ***Perf. 12***

6840 A3255 4r Block of 3, #a-c, + label 1.50 .60

Russian Crown — A3256

Carved Head — A3257

Treasures from the Amber Room, State Museum, St. Petersburg: No. 6842, Cameo depicting Moses and Pharaoh, vert.
25r, Touch and Smell, Florentine mosaic.

Litho. & Embossed

2004, May 25 ***Perf. 13¼***

6841 A3256 5r multi 1.00 .50
6842 A3256 5r multi 1.00 .50
6843 A3257 5r multi 1.00 .50
Nos. 6841-6843 (3) 3.00 1.50

Souvenir Sheet

Perf. 13

6844 A3257 25r multi 6.00 3.50

A limited edition booklet exists containing booklet panes of one of each of Nos. 6841-6844. Value, *$350.*

German - Russian Youth Meeting A3258

2004, June 3 **Litho.** ***Perf. 11¼***

6845 A3258 8r multi 1.25 .65

See Germany No. 2287.

Vladimir K. Kokkinaki (1904-85), Test Pilot — A3259

2004, June 8 ***Perf. 12***

6846 A3259 3r multi .50 .25

Victory — A3260

Who Comes With the Sword Will Die by the Sword — A3261

Patriotic paintings by S. Prisekin: No. 6848, Marshal Zhukov. No. 6850, And the Oath of Allegiance We Have Honored, Smolensk, 1812.

2004, June 8 ***Perf. 11¾x11½***

6847 A3260 5r shown .50 .25
6848 A3260 5r multi .50 .25

Perf. 11¾

6849 A3261 5r shown .50 .25
6850 A3261 5r multi .50 .25
Nos. 6847-6850 (4) 2.00 1.00

Women's Riding Habits — A3262

Designs: No. 6851, 4r, Three women, horse. No. 6852, 4r, Three women, horse, dog. No. 6853, 4r, Two women, horse, two dogs.

2004, July 15 ***Perf. 12x11¾***

6851-6853 A3262 Set of 3 2.50 .75
6853a Miniature sheet, 2 each #6851-6853 8.00 4.00

2004 Summer Olympics, Athens — A3267

2004, July 20 ***Perf. 12***

6854 A3267 Horiz. pair with central label 1.00 .50
a. 3r Running .25 .25
b. 8r Wrestling .75 .35

Souvenir Sheet

Admiralty Shipyard, 300th Anniv. — A3268

2004, July 22 ***Perf. 12x12¼***

6855 A3268 12r multi 3.00 .60

Miniature Sheet

Children and Road Safety — A3269

No. 6856: a, Ducks crossing street at pedestrian crossing. b, Boy and turtle crossing street with green light. c, Driver near fenced garden. d, Girl playing in street. e, Accident showing eggs flying out of car.

2004, Aug. 5 *Perf. 12*

6856 A3269 4r Sheet of 5, #a-e, + label 3.00 1.00

Worldwide Fund for Nature (WWF) — A3270

Gulo gulo: a, With pine branches. b, With dead bird. c, On tree branch. d, With young.

2004, Aug. 12 *Perf. 11¼*

6857	A3270 Block of 4	3.00	1.10
a.-d.	8r Any single	.75	.25
e.	Miniature sheet, #6857a, 2 each #6857b-6857c, 3 #6857d + label	7.50	2.50

Tomsk, 400th Anniv. — A3271

2004, Aug. 20 *Perf. 12¼x12*

6858 A3271 4r multi .50 .25

ITAR-TASS News Agency, Cent. — A3272

2004, Aug. 20 *Perf. 12*

6859 A3272 4r multi .75 .35

Famous Men — A3273

Designs: No. 6860, 5r, B. G. Muzrukov (1904-79), organizer of defense industry. No. 6861, 5r, N. L. Dukhov (1904-64), rocket designer.

2004, Sept. 8

6860-6861 A3273 Set of 2 .90 .45

Tsar Paul I (1754-1801) A3274

Designs: No. 6862, 10r, Seated. No. 6863, 10r, Standing.
20p, Wearing hat.

Litho. & Engr.

2004, Sept. 10 *Perf. 12*

6862-6863 A3274 Set of 2 3.00 .75

Souvenir Sheet

6864 A3274 20r multi 3.00 1.00

S. N. Rerikh (1904-93), Painter — A3275

Perf. 11¾x11½

2004, Sept. 16 **Litho.**

6865 A3275 4r multi 1.00 .25

Vsevolod III (1154-1212), Grand Prince of Novgorod — A3276

Litho. & Engr.

2004, Oct. 7 *Perf. 11¾*

6866 A3276 12r multi 2.00 .55

Kazan State University, 200th Anniv. — A3277

2004, Oct. 20 **Litho.** *Perf. 12x11¾*

6867 A3277 5r multi 1.00 .25

Silver Containers — A3278

Designs: No. 6868, 4.70r, Bowl, c. 1880-1890. No. 6869, 4.70r, Milk container, 1900. No. 6870, 4.70r, Ladle, 1910. No. 6871, 4.70r, Vase, c. 1900-08, vert.

Litho. & Embossed

2004, Oct. 26 *Perf. 13¼*

6868-6871 A3278 Set of 4 4.00 1.00

Happy New Year — A3279

Serpentine Die Cut

2004, Nov. 12 **Litho.**

Self-Adhesive

6872 A3279 5r multi 10.00 5.00

Altai Republic Landscapes — A3280

No. 6873: a, 2r, Belukha Mountain. b, 3r, Katun River. c, 5r, Teletskoye Lake.

2004, Nov. 18 *Perf. 12*

6873 A3280 Block of 3, #a-c, + label 2.00 .50

Baikonur Cosmodrome, 50th Anniv. — A3281

2004, Dec. 1

6874	Horiz. strip of 4	3.00	1.00
a.	A3281 2.50r R-7 missile	.35	.25
b.	A3281 3.50r Proton rocket	.40	.25
c.	A3281 4r Soyuz rocket	.50	.25
d.	A3281 6r Zenit rocket	.75	.30
e.	Miniature sheet, 2 #6874	7.50	3.00

Mordovian Republic A3282

Smolensk Oblast A3283

Tver Oblast A3284

Chukotsky Autonomous Okrug — A3285

Koryak Autonomous Okrug — A3286

Taimyr Autonomous Okrug — A3287

2005, Jan. 10

6875	A3282 5r multi	1.00	.40
6876	A3283 5r multi	1.00	.40
6877	A3284 5r multi	1.00	.40
6878	A3285 5r multi	1.00	.40
6879	A3286 5r multi	1.00	.40
6880	A3287 5r multi	1.00	.40
	Nos. 6875-6880 (6)	6.00	2.40

Moscow M. V. Lomonosov State University, 250th Anniv. — A3288

2005, Jan. 12

6881 A3288 5r multi 1.00 .25

Souvenir Sheet

Expo 2005, Aichi, Japan — A3289

2005, Feb. 21 **Litho.** *Perf. 12½x12*

6882 A3289 15r multi 5.50 2.75

Archaeological Treasures of Sarmatia — A3290

Designs: No. 6883, 5r, Silver bowl with bull design (shown). No. 6884, 5r, Gold and wood bowl with bear design. No. 6885, 7r, Gold ornament with camel design. No. 6886, 7r, Gold ornament with deer design, vert.

Litho. & Embossed

2005, Feb. 25 *Perf. 13¼*

6883-6886 A3290 Set of 4 8.00 4.00

Submarine Force, Cent. A3291

Submarines: 2r, Type M, VI-bis series. 3r, Type S, IX-bis series. 5r, Type Sch, X-bis series. 8r, Type K.

2005, Mar. 3 Litho. ***Perf. 12x12¼***
6887-6890 A3291 Set of 4 25.00 12.50

Kazan, 1000th Anniv. A3292

Designs: No. 6891, 5r, Suyumbike Tower (shown). No. 6892, 5r, Kul Sharif Mosque. 7r, Cathedral of the Annunciation.

2005, Mar. 10 ***Perf. 11¾x12***
6891-6893 A3292 Set of 3 2.50 .60
6893a Souvenir sheet, #6891-6893 15.00 5.00

Emperor Alexander II (1818-81) A3293

Alexander II and: No. 6894, 10r, Educator Vasily Zhukovsky, pillar (blue frame). No. 6895, 10r, Coronation (red frame). No. 6896, 10r, At desk (green frame). No. 6897, 10r, On horse (brown frame).
25r, Portrait.

Litho. & Engr.

2005, Mar. 28 ***Perf. 12x12½***
6894-6897 A3293 Set of 4 5.00 2.00

Souvenir Sheet

6898 A3293 25r multi 3.50 1.25

Victory in World War II, 60th Anniv. — A3294

Designs: No. 6899, 2r, Soldier at column with grafitti. No. 6900, 2r, Soldiers and tank. No. 6901, 3r, Soldier watching pigeons eat. No. 6902, 3r, Jubilant soldiers return to Moscow. 5r, Soldiers and captured Nazi banners.
10r, Soldiers saluting Soviet flag over Reichstag building.

2005, Apr. 5 Litho. ***Perf. 12***
6899-6903 A3294 Set of 5 2.00 .55
6899a Sheet of 9 + label 15.00 6.00
6903a Souvenir sheet, #6899-6903, + label 5.00 2.50

Souvenir Sheet

Perf. 12x12¼

6904 A3294 10r multi 3.00 1.50

Liberation of Vienna by Soviet Troops, 60th Anniv. A3295

2005, Apr. 13 Litho. ***Perf. 12***
6905 A3295 6r multi 1.00 .30

Souvenir Sheet

Fauna — A3296

No. 6906: a, Aquila danga (eagle). b, Catocala sponsa (butterflies). c, Castor fiber (beaver). d, Meles meles (badger).

2005, Apr. 15
6906 A3296 5r Sheet of 4, #a-d, + label 3.00 1.00

See Belarus No. 554.

Souvenir Sheet

Opening of First Line of Moscow Metro, 70th Anniv. — A3297

No. 6907: a, 5r, Old train, stations, map of first line. b, 10r, Modern train, modern Metro map.

2005, Apr. 25 ***Perf. 11½x12¼***
6907 A3297 Sheet of 2, #a-b 2.50 .75

Bid of Moscow to Host 2012 Summer Olympics A3298

2005, May 5 ***Perf. 12***
6908 A3298 4r multi 1.00 .25

Europa — A3299

2005, May 5 ***Perf. 12¼x12***
6909 A3299 8r multi *1.50 .75*
a. Sheet of 6 *9.50 4.75*

Mikhail A. Sholokhov (1905-84), 1965 Nobel Laureate in Literature A3300

2005, May 20 ***Perf. 11¾***
6910 A3300 5r multi 1.00 .25

Fauna A3301

No. 6911: a, Martes zibellina. b, Panthera tigris altaica.

2005, June 1 ***Perf. 12***
6911 Horiz. pair, #a-b, + central label 2.50 .75
a.-b. A3301 8r Either single 1.00 .35

See North Korea Nos. 4436-4437.

Bees A3302

2005, June 15 ***Perf. 11¼***
6912 Horiz. strip of 5 3.50 1.25
a. A3302 3r Bombus armeniacus .40 .25
b. A3302 4r Bombus fragrans .60 .25
c. A3302 5r Bombus anachoreta .75 .30
d. A3302 6r Bombus unicus .60 .30
e. A3302 7r Bombus czerskii .80 .35
f. Souvenir sheet, #6912a-6912e, + label 5.00 2.50

Kaliningrad, 750th Anniv. — A3303

2005, June 23 ***Perf. 12¼x12***
6913 A3303 5r multi 1.00 .45

N. E. Bauman Moscow State Technical University, 175th Anniv. — A3304

2005, July 1 ***Perf. 12***
6914 A3304 5r multi .70 .35

Lighthouses — A3305

Map and: 5r, Mudyugsky Lighthouse. 6r, Solovetsky Lighthouse. 8r, Svyatonossky Lighthouse.

2005, July 4 **Litho.**
6915-6917 A3305 Set of 3 2.00 1.00

MiG Fighters A3306

Designs: No. 6918, 5r, MiG-3. No. 6919, 5r, MiG-15. No. 6920, 5r, MiG-21. No. 6921, 5r, MiG-25. No. 6922, 5r, MiG-29.

2005, July 6
6918-6922 A3306 Set of 5 2.50 1.25
6922a Souvenir sheet, #6918-6922, + label 6.50 3.25

Souvenir Sheet

Battle of Kulikovo, 625th Anniv. — A3307

2005, Aug. 2 ***Perf. 12½x12***
6923 A3307 15r multi 2.50 .75

Souvenir Sheet

Water — A3308

No. 6924: a, 3r, Hands in water. b, 3.50r, Ocean wave. c, 4r, Iceberg. d, 4.50r, Waterfall. e, 5r, Water droplets on leaf.

2005, Aug. 16 ***Perf. 12***
6924 A3308 Sheet of 5, #a-e, + label 3.50 1.00

Field Marshal Aleksandr V. Suvorov (1729-1800) — A3309

2005, Sept. 15 Litho. ***Perf. 12x11¾***
6925 A3309 4r multi .90 .25
a. Miniature sheet of 8 9.50 3.25

Sea Infantry, 300th Anniv. — A3310

No. 6926 — Sea infantrymen from: a, 2r, 18th cent. b, 3r, 19th cent. c, 4r, 20th cent. d, 5r, 21st cent.

2005, Oct. 19 Litho. ***Perf. 11¾***
6926 A3310 Block of 4, #a-d 2.50 .75

Santa Claus (Ded Moroz) A3311

2005, Oct. 26 ***Perf. 12***
6927 A3311 5r multi .75 .25

Printed in sheets of 8.

UNESCO, 60th Anniv. A3312

2005, Nov. 1 *Perf. 11¼*

6928 A3312 5.60r multi 1.00 .30

Christmas and New Year's Day A3313

2005, Dec. 1

6929 A3313 5.60r multi .80 .30
a. Sheet of 9 7.50 3.00

Antonov Airplanes A3314

Designs: No. 6930, 5.60r, An-3T. No. 6931, 5.60r, An-12. No. 6932, 5.60r, An-24. No. 6933, 5.60r, An-74. No. 6934, 5.60r, An-124.

2006, Jan. 12 **Litho.** *Perf. 12*

6930-6934 A3314 Set of 5 3.50 1.50
6934a Sheet, #6930-6934, + label 4.00 2.00

2006 Winter Olympics, Turin A3315

Designs: No. 6935, 4r, Luge. No. 6936, 4r, Speed skating. No. 6937, 4r, Snowboarding.

2006, Jan. 18

6935-6937 A3315 Set of 3 1.50 .70

Armenia Day in Russia — A3316

2006, Jan. 22 *Perf. 11¼*

6938 A3316 10r multi 1.25 .60

See Armenia No. 723.

Antarctic Research, 50th Anniv. A3317

Designs: No. 6939, 7r, Underwater researcher, transport vehicle. No. 6940, 7r, Scientific ship, airplane. No. 6941, 7r, Ice-breaker, penguins.

2006, Jan. 26 *Perf. 12*

6939-6941 A3317 Set of 3 2.50 1.25
6941a Sheet of 6 #6941 6.50 3.25

Peter I Interrogating Tsarevich Aleksei, by N. N. Ge (1831-94) — A3318

Design: No. 6943, 5.60r, Portrait of N. N. Ge, by I. E. Repin, vert.

2006, Feb. 16

6942-6943 A3318 Set of 2 1.40 .55

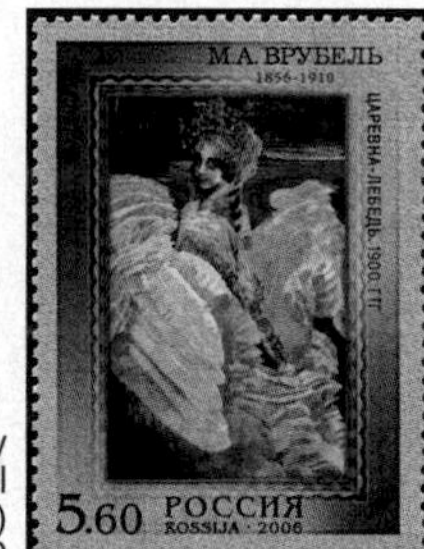

Paintings by M. A. Vrubel (1856-1910) A3319

Designs: No. 6944, 5.60r, Tsarevna-Swan (shown). No. 6945, 5.60r, Self-portrait.

2006, Feb. 27 **Litho.** *Perf. 12*

6944-6945 A3319 Set of 2 1.40 .55

Russian Submarine Fleet, Cent. A3320

Submarine: 3r, 667A. 4r, 671. 6r, 941. 7r, 949A.

2006, Feb. 28 *Perf. 12*

6946-6949 A3320 Set of 4 6.50 3.25

Moscow Kremlin Museums, Bicent. A3321

Designs: No. 6950, 5r, No. 6954b, 20r, Throne of Ivan IV. No. 6951, 5r, No. 6954c, 20r, Orb of Tsar Michael. No. 6952, 5r, No. 6954d, 20r, Helmet of Tsar Michael. No. 6953, 5r, No. 6954e, 20r, State sword and shield. No. 6954a, 20r, No. 6955, 15r, Monomakh's cap.

Litho., Litho. & Embossed (#6954)

2006, Mar. 6 *Perf. 11¾x12*

6950-6953 A3321 Set of 4 2.50 1.00
6954 Horiz. strip of 5 *45.00 45.00*
a.-e. A3321 20r Any single *8.25 8.25*

Souvenir Sheet

Perf. 11¾x12¼

6955 A3321 15r multi 1.50 .75

Airplanes Designed by Aleksandr S. Yakovlev (1906-89) A3322

Designs: No. 6956, 5r, AIR-1. No. 6957, 5r, Yak-42. No. 6958, 5r, Yak-54. No. 6959, 5r, Yak-130. No. 6960, 5r, Yak-141.

2006, Mar. 20 **Litho.** *Perf. 12¼x12*

6956-6960 A3322 Set of 5 3.25 1.25
6960a Souvenir sheet, #6956-6960 4.00 2.00

Souvenir Sheet

Duma, Cent. — A3323

2006, Apr. 8 *Perf. 12½x12*

6961 A3323 15p multi 1.75 .75

Arms A3324

Flag A3325

2006, Apr. 20 *Perf. 14*

6962 A3324 5.60r multi 2.00 .75
Booklet, 10 #6962 20.00
Booklet, 15 #6962 30.00
Booklet, 20 #6962 40.00
6963 A3325 5.60r multi 2.00 .75
Booklet, 10 #6963 20.00
Booklet, 15 #6963 30.00
Booklet, 20 #6963 40.00

Paintings In Tretyakov Gallery, Moscow A3326

Tretyakov Gallery and Statue of Pavel M. Tretyakov — A3327

Designs: No. 6964, 5.60r, Trinity, by Anrrej Roubljov, c. 1420. No. 6965, 5.60r, Girl with Peaches, by V. A. Serov, 1887. No. 6966, 5.60r, Beyond the Eternal Calm, by I. I. Levitan, 1894, horiz. No. 6967, 5.60r, Three Heroes, by V. M. Vasnetsov, 1898, horiz.

Perf. 11¾x12, 12x11¾

2006, Apr. 26 **Litho.**

6964-6967 A3326 Set of 4 2.75 1.25

Souvenir Sheet

Perf. 12½x12

6968 A3327 15r multi 1.90 .85

Emperor Alexander III (1845-94) A3328

Designs: No. 6970, 10r, Alexander III and map. No. 6971, 10r, Alexander III, flag and ship.
25r, Alexander III.

Litho. & Engr.

2006, May 4 *Perf. 12x12½*

6970-6971 A3328 Set of 2 2.00 1.00

Souvenir Sheet

Perf. 12x12¼

6972 A3328 25r multi 2.75 1.25

Blagoveschensk, 150th Anniv. — A3329

2006, May 11 **Litho.** *Perf. 12x12¼*

6973 A3329 5r multi .80 .25

Souvenir Sheet

Baltic Shipyards, 150th Anniv. — A3330

2006, May 22 *Perf. 12x12½*

6974 A3330 12p multi 1.40 .60

Luzhniki Olympic Stadium, 50th Anniv. A3331

2006, May 29 *Perf. 12*

6975 A3331 6r multi .75 .35

Flowers — A3332

No. 6976: a, Spring flowers (denomination at UL). b, Summer flowers (denomination at UR). c, Fall flowers (denomination at LL). d, Winter flowers (denomination at LR).

2006, June 6 ***Perf. 11½***
6976 A3332 7r Block of 4, #a-d 3.00 1.40

Altai Territories as Part of Russia, 250th Anniv. — A3333

Litho. & Embossed

2006, June 15 ***Perf. 11¼***
6977 A3333 5r multi .80 .25

Adygeya Republic — A3334

Vladimir Oblast — A3335

Ryazan Oblast A3336

Kostroma Oblast A3337

Pskov Oblast A3338

Tula Oblast A3339

2006, June 20 **Litho.** ***Perf. 12***

6978	A3334 6r multi		.75	.35
6979	A3335 6r multi		.75	.35
6980	A3336 6r multi		.75	.35
6981	A3337 6r multi		.75	.35
6982	A3338 6r multi		.75	.35
6983	A3339 6r multi		.75	.35
	Nos. 6978-6983 (6)		4.50	2.10

Circumnavigation by the Kruzenshtern, 2005-06 — A3340

2006, June 29
6984 A3340 4r multi 1.00 .50

Arcticcoal, 75th Anniv. A3341

2006, July 12 ***Perf. 11¼***
6985 A3341 4r multi .70 .35

Souvenir Sheet

Bolshoi Tsarskoselski Palace, 250th Anniv. — A3342

No. 6986: a, 5r, Left portion. b, 6r, Central portion. c, 7r, Right portion.

2006, July 17 ***Perf. 12x11¾***
6986 A3342 Sheet of 3, #a-c 2.25 .85

Branch, by A. A. Ivanov (1806-58) — A3343

Design: No. 6988, 6r, Portrait of A. A. Ivanov, by S. P. Postnikov, vert.

2006, July 17 ***Perf. 12***
6987-6988 A3343 Set of 2 1.25 .60

Novodevichy Monastery, by A. M. Vasnetsov (1856-1933) — A3344

Design: No. 6990, 6r, Portrait of A. M. Vasnetsov, by N.D. Kuznetsov, vert.

2006, July 24
6989-6990 A3344 Set of 2 1.25 .60

Barents Sea Lighthouses — A3345

Designs: 5r, Kaninsky Lighthouse. 6r, Kildinsky North Lighthouse. 8r, Vaidagubsky Lighthouse, vert.

2006, Aug. 10
6991-6993 A3345 Set of 3 2.00 1.00

Souvenir Sheet

Russian State Theater, 250th Anniv. — A3346

2006, Aug. 16 ***Perf. 12¼x12***
6994 A3346 15r multi 1.75 .75

Fauna of Sakha Republic A3347

Designs: 3r, Rhodostethia rosea. 4r, Grus leucogeranus. 5r, Ursus maritimus. 6r, Equus caballus. 7r, Rangifer tarandus.

2006, Aug. 29 ***Perf. 11½x11¼***
6995-6999 A3347 Set of 5 2.75 1.40
6999a Souvenir sheet, #6995-6999, + label 3.75 1.90

Russian Language Development International Youth Project — A3348

2006, Sept. 5 **Litho.** ***Perf. 11¼***
7000 A3348 7r multi 1.50 .75

D. S. Likhachev (1906-99), Literary Critic — A3349

2006, Sept. 19 ***Perf. 12***
7001 A3349 5r multi .60 .35
a. Sheet of 6 + 2 labels 3.75 2.00

Nature of the Caucausus Region — A3350

No. 7002: a, 6r, Mountain. b, 7r, Stream. c, 8r, Bison.

2006, Sept. 22 ***Perf. 12***
7002 A3350 Block of 3, #a-c, + label 2.50 1.00

Television Broadcasting In Russia, 75th Anniv. A3351

2006, Oct. 5 ***Perf. 11¼***
7003 A3351 7r multi .95 .35

Mobile Telephone Communications in Russia, 15th Anniv. — A3352

2006, Oct. 12 ***Perf. 12***
7004 A3352 7r multi .80 .35

Admission to European Council, 10th Anniv. — A3353

2006, Oct. 18 ***Perf. 12x12¼***
7005 A3353 8r multi .95 .45

Savings Banks, 165th Anniv. — A3354

Designs: 7r, N. A. Kristofari (1802-81), bank founder, and bank building. 15r, Kristofari, vert.

2006, Oct. 18 ***Perf. 12***
7006 A3354 7r multi 1.00 .50

Souvenir Sheet
Perf. 12x12½

7007 A3354 15r multi 1.75 .85

No. 7007 contains one 30x42mm stamp.

Regional Communications Commonwealth, 15th Anniv. — A3355

2006, Nov. 9 ***Perf. 12¼x12***
7008 A3355 5r multi .70 .30

Ded Moroz (Russian Santa Claus) — A3356

2006, Nov. 29 ***Perf. 11¾***
7009 A3356 7r multi .95 .35

Printed in sheets of 6.

Russian National Atlas — A3357

2006, Dec. 7 ***Perf. 12x11¾***
7010 A3357 6r multi .95 .30

New Year 2007 A3358

2006, Dec. 12 ***Perf. 12***
7011 A3358 7r multi .95 .35
a. Souvenir sheet of 6 6.00 3.00

Vladimir M. Bekhterev (1857-1927), Psychoneurologist — A3359

2007, Jan. 15 **Litho.** ***Perf. 12***
7012 A3359 5r multi .70 .30

Ivan I. Shishkin (1832-98), Painter A3360

Designs: No. 7013, 7r, Portrait of Shishkin, by I. N. Kramskoy (shown). No. 7014, 7r, In the North Wild, by Shishkin

2007, Jan. 25
7013-7014 A3360 Set of 2 1.75 .85

Order of St. George, 200th Anniv. A3361

2007, Feb. 7 **Litho.**
7015 A3361 10r multi 1.25 .60

Souvenir Sheet
Litho. & Embossed

7016 A3361 50r multi 6.00 3.00

No. 7015 was printed in sheets of 8 + label. No. 7016 contains one diamond-shaped 57x57mm stamp.

Russian G. V. Plekhanov Economic Academy, Cent. — A3362

2007, Feb. 9 **Litho.** ***Perf. 13¾x13½***
7017 A3362 5r multi .70 .30

Orest A. Kiprensky (1782-1836), Painter A3363

Paintings by Kiprensky: No. 7018, 7r, Self-portrait (shown). No. 7019, 7r, Poor Eliza.

Perf. 12, 13½x13¾ (#7019)
2007, Mar. 2
7018-7019 A3363 Set of 2 1.75 .85

Russian Post Emblem — A3364

2007, Mar. 12 ***Perf. 12¼x12***
7020 A3364 6.50r blue 1.00 .50
Complete booklet, 10 #7020 15.00
Complete booklet, 20 #7020 30.00

Compare with type A3827.

Souvenir Sheet

Intl. Polar Year — A3365

No. 7021: a, 6r, Icebreaker, scientific station. b, 7r, Glacier. c, 8r, Wildlife and cultural heritage.

2007, Mar. 21 ***Perf. 12***
7021 A3365 Sheet of 3, #a-c 2.50 1.25

Souvenir Sheet

Famous Men — A3366

No. 7022: a, Arkady Tarkovsky (1907-89), poet. b, Andrei Tarkovsky (1932-86), film director.

2007, Apr. 4 ***Perf. 12¼x12***
7022 A3366 8r Sheet of 2, #a-b 2.00 1.00

Souvenir Sheet

Space Exploration, 50th Anniv. — A3367

No. 7023: a, 10r, Sputnik 1. b, 20r, Sergei P. Korolev (1907-66), aeronautical engineer. c, 20r, Konstantin E. Tsiolkovsky (1857-1935), scientist.

2007, Apr. 12 ***Perf. 11¾***
7023 A3367 Sheet of 3, #a-c 6.00 3.00

Bashkiria as Part of Russia, 450th Anniv. — A3368

2007, Apr. 24 ***Perf. 11¼***
7024 A3368 6.50r multi .80 .35

Pavel P. Chistyakov (1832-1919), Painter A3369

Paintings of Chistyakov by: No. 7025, 7r, I. E. Repin (shown). No. 7026, 7r, V. A. Serov.

2007, May 11 ***Perf. 12***
7025-7026 A3369 Set of 2 1.50 .85

Vladimir L. Borovikovsky (1757-1825), Painter A3370

Designs: No. 7027, 7r, Portrait of Borovikovsky, by I. V. Bugaevsky-Blagodatny (shown). No. 7028, 7r, Portrait of Sisters Anna and Barbara Gavrilovna.

2007, May 15
7027-7028 A3370 Set of 2 1.50 .85

Souvenir Sheet

First Russian Postage Stamps, 150th Anniv. — A3371

2007, May 24 ***Perf. 12¼x12***
7029 A3371 10r multi 1.25 .60

Telephones in Russia, 125th Anniv. — A3372

2007, June 14 ***Perf. 14***
7030 A3372 5r multi .70 .30

Souvenir Sheet

Russian Academy of Arts, 250th Anniv. — A3373

Litho. & Engr.

2007, June 15 *Perf. 12¼x12*
7031 A3373 25r multi 3.00 1.50

Emblem of 2007 St. Petersburg World Stamp Exhibition A3374

2007, June 19 Litho. *Perf. 12x12½*
7032 A3374 5r multi .70 .30
a. Perf. 12 1.00 .50

No. 7032a was printed in sheets of 8 + central label.

Souvenir Sheet

Plesetsk Cosmodrome, 50th Anniv. — A3375

2007, July 2 *Perf. 12¼x12*
7033 A3375 12r multi 1.50 .75

Khakassia as Part of Russia, 300th Anniv. — A3376

2007, July 12 Litho. *Perf. 11¼*
7034 A3376 6.50r multi .70 .45

N. A. Lunin (1907-70), Submariner — A3377

M. I. Gadzhiev (1907-42), Submariner — A3378

2007, July 25 *Perf. 12x12¼*
7035 Horiz. pair + central label 1.50 .85
a. A3377 7r multi .75 .40
b. A3378 7r multi .75 .40

S. P. Botkin (1832-89), Physician A3379

2007, Aug. 14 *Perf. 12x12½*
7036 A3379 5r blue & black .65 .30

Irkutsk Oblast A3380

Orel Oblast A3381

Altai Kray A3382

Vologda Oblast A3383

Rostov Oblast A3384

Novosibirsk Oblast — A3385

2007, Aug. 21 *Perf. 12x12¼*
7037 A3380 7r multi .85 .40
7038 A3381 7r multi .85 .40
7039 A3382 7r multi .85 .40
7040 A3383 7r multi .85 .40
7041 A3384 7r multi .85 .40
7042 A3385 7r multi .85 .40
Nos. 7037-7042 (6) 5.10 2.40

Souvenir Sheet

Biblio-Globus Bookstore, 50th Anniv. — A3386

2007, Aug. 24
7043 A3386 12r multi 1.40 .70

Souvenir Sheet

Russian Language Year — A3387

2007, Sept. 14 *Perf. 12¼x12*
7044 A3387 12r multi 1.40 .70

Souvenir Sheet

Flowers — A3388

No. 7045: a, Gladiolus gandavensis. b, Iris ensata. c, Rosa hybrida. d, Nelumbo nucifera.

2007, Sept. 26 Litho.
7045 A3388 6r Sheet of 4, #a-d 3.00 1.50

See North Korea No. 4689.

Worldwide Fund for Nature (WWF) — A3389

Designs: 5r, Ciconia boyciana. 6r, Uncia uncia. 7r, Bison bonasus.

2007, Oct. 1 *Perf. 11¼*
7046-7048 A3389 Set of 3 2.25 1.10
7048a Miniature sheet of 8, 2 #7048, 3 each #7046-7047, + label 5.75 2.75

Trucks — A3390

No. 7049: a, 1924 AMO-F-15. b, 1932 GAZ-AA (MM). c, 1942 ZIS-5V.

2007, Oct. 25 *Perf. 11¾x11½*
7049 A3390 Horiz. strip of 3 3.00 1.50
a.-c. 8r Any single 1.00 .50
d. Miniature sheet of 8, 2 #7049a, 3 each #7049b-7049c, + label 7.75 3.75

Russian House of Science and Culture, Berlin A3391

2007, Oct. 29 *Perf. 12*
7050 A3391 8r multi .90 .45

Russian Language Year.

Horses — A3392

Horse's head and: 6r, Vladimir horse pulling wagon. No. 7052, 7r, Orlov Trotter pulling sulky. No. 7053, 7r, Don horse with rider. 8r, Vyatsky horse jumping.

2007, Nov. 7 *Perf. 11¾*
7051-7054 A3392 Set of 4 3.25 1.60
7054a Souvenir sheet, #7051-7054 3.25 1.60

Arctic Deep Sea Exploration A3393

No. 7055: a, Mir-1 bathyscaphe. b, Russian flag on North Pole on map.

2007, Dec. 7 Litho. *Perf. 12*
7055 A3393 8r Vert. pair, #a-b, + label 1.75 1.00

New Year's Day — A3394

2007, Dec. 7 *Perf. 11¾x11½*
7056 A3394 8r multi .85 .45
a. Miniature sheet of 6 6.00 3.00

First Russian Postage Stamps, 150th Anniv. — A3395

2008, Jan. 10 ***Perf. 12x11¼***
7057 A3395 8r No. 1 .90 .45

Count Alexei N. Tolstoy (1883-1945), Writer — A3396

2008, Jan. 10 ***Perf. 12***
7058 A3396 6r multi .70 .30

Nobel Laureates in Physics A3397

Designs: No. 7059, 6r, Ilya M. Frank (1908-90), 1958 laureate. No. 7060, 6r, Lev D. Landau (1908-68), 1962 laureate.

2008, Jan. 22 ***Perf. 11¾***
7059-7060 A3397 Set of 2 1.25 .70

Agustín de Betancourt (1758-1824), Engineer — A3398

2008, Feb. 1 Litho. ***Perf. 12½x12***
7061 A3398 9r multi 1.00 .50

See note under No. 7097.

Astrakhan, 450th Anniv. — A3399

2008, Feb. 22 ***Perf. 11¾***
7062 A3399 9r multi 1.00 .50

Valentin P. Glushko (1908-89), Spacecraft Designer — A3400

2008, Mar. 17 ***Perf. 12¼x12***
7063 A3400 8r multi .90 .45

Miniature Sheet

Archaeology — A3401

No. 3401 — Metal plates featuring: a, Mythological beast, 2nd cent. B.C.- 1st cent. A. D. b, Two oxen, 2nd cent. B.C.- 1st cent. A.D. c, Deer, 4th-3rd cents. B.C.

Litho. & Embossed

2008, Mar. 25 ***Perf. 12½x12***
7064 A3401 12r Sheet of 3, #a-c 4.00 2.00

2008 Summer Olympics, Beijing — A3402

No. 7065 — Various athletes with stripe at upper right corner in: a, Gray. b, Blue. c, Black.

2008, Apr. 15 Litho. ***Perf. 11¾***
7065 A3402 8r Horiz. strip of 3, #a-c 3.50 1.75
d. Souvenir sheet, #7065 4.50 2.25

Souvenir Sheet

Black Sea Naval Fleet, 225th Anniv. — A3403

2008, Apr. 29 ***Perf. 12x12¼***
7066 A3403 15r multi 2.00 1.00

Europa A3404

2008, May 5 ***Perf. 12¼x12***
7067 A3404 8r multi .70 .35
a. Miniature sheet of 6 4.25 2.10

Election of Pres. Dmitry Medvedev A3405

2008, May 7 ***Perf. 12x12¼***
7068 A3405 7r multi .75 .35

Krasnoyarsk Kray — A3406

Sverdlovsk Oblast — A3407

Penza Oblast A3408

Volgograd Oblast A3409

Yaroslavl Oblast A3410

2008, May 20 ***Perf. 12¼x12, 12x12¼***
7069 A3406 8r multi .75 .35
7070 A3407 8r multi .75 .35
7071 A3408 8r multi .75 .35
7072 A3409 8r multi .75 .35
7073 A3410 8r multi .75 .35
Nos. 7069-7073 (5) 3.75 1.75

Cathedrals — A3411

No. 7074: a, St. Demetrius's Cathedral, Vladimir, Russia, 12th cent., and winged beast. b, St. George's Cathedral, Voronets Monastery, Romania, 15th cent., and chrismon.

2008, June 23 ***Perf. 11½***
7074 A3411 Horiz. pair, #a-b, + central label 2.75 1.50
a.-b. 12r Either single 1.50 .75
c. Miniature sheet, 3 #7074 11.00 5.75

See Romania Nos. 5057-5058.

Helicopter Sports in Russia, 50th Anniv. — A3412

2008, July 12 Litho. ***Perf. 11¾***
7075 A3412 5r multi .50 .25

Pokrovsk Cathedral — A3413

2008, July 25 ***Perf. 11¾x12¼***
7076 A3413 7.50r multi .80 .35
Complete booklet, 10 #7076 8.00
Complete booklet, 20 #7076 16.00

Souvenir Sheet

Northern Navy, 75th Anniv. — A3414

2008, July 26 ***Perf. 12x12½***
7077 A3414 15r multi 2.00 1.00

Udmurtia as Part of Russia, 450th Anniv. — A3415

2008, July 28 ***Perf. 11½***
7078 A3415 7.50r multi .80 .35

Souvenir Sheet

Kizhi UNESCO World Heritage Site — A3416

No. 7079: a, Church, 1714. b, Bell tower, 1862. c, Church, 1694-1764.

2008, July 31 ***Perf. 11¾x12¼***
7079 A3416 10r Sheet of 3, #a-c 3.50 1.75

Souvenir Sheet

Emperor Nicholas I (1796-1855) — A3417

Litho. & Engr.

2008, Aug. 8 *Perf. 12x12½*
7080 A3417 35r multi 4.00 2.00

Souvenir Sheet

International Polar Year — A3418

No. 7081 — Map of Northern Russia and various ships: a, 6r. b, 7r. c, 8r.

2008, Aug. 28 Litho. *Perf. 12x11½*
7081 A3418 Sheet of 3, #a-c 2.50 1.25

Wildlife — A3419

Perf. 12¼x12 Syncopated

2008, Aug. 29 Litho.

No.	Type	Value	Design	Unused	Used
7082	A3419	10k	Hare	.25	.25
7083	A3419	15k	Hare	.25	.25
7084	A3419	25k	Hare	.25	.25
7085	A3419	30k	Fox	.25	.25
7086	A3419	50k	Fox	.25	.25
7087	A3419	1r	Fox	.25	.25
7088	A3419	1.50r	Lynx	.25	.25
7089	A3419	2r	Lynx	.25	.25
7090	A3419	2.50r	Lynx	.25	.25
7091	A3419	3r	Elk	.30	.25
7092	A3419	4r	Elk	.40	.25
7093	A3419	5r	Elk	.45	.25
7094	A3419	6r	Bear	.50	.25
7095	A3419	10r	Bear	.85	.40
7096	A3419	25r	Bear	2.10	1.00
	Nos. 7082-7096 (15)			6.85	4.65

Souvenir Sheet

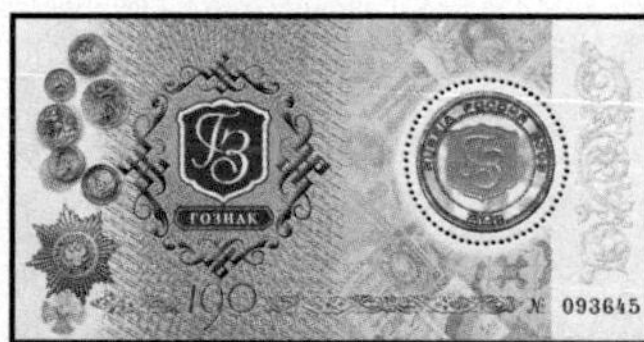

Goznak (State Currency Printers), 190th Anniv. — A3420

Litho. & Embossed With Foil Application

2008, Sept. 1 *Perf.*
7097 A3420 20r black & gold 2.25 1.10

No. 7097 contains one 33mm diameter stamp.

A booklet containing booklet panes of 1 of Nos. 7061 and 7097 exists. Value, $45.

Flora and Fauna — A3421

No. 7098: a, Woodpecker and squirrel in birch tree. b, Fawn. c, Mushrooms, evergreens and birch tree.

2008, Sept. 12 Litho. *Perf. 12x12¼*
7098 A3421 7r Block of 3, #a-c, + label 2.50 1.25

Leningrad Oblast A3422

2008, Sept. 17
7099 A3422 8r multi .80 .40

Souvenir Sheet

History of the Cossacks — A3423

No. 7100: a, Silver medal. b, Crossed swords and wreath. c, Sword hilt.

2008, Sept. 17 *Perf. 11¾x12¼*
7100 A3423 10r Sheet of 3, #a-c 3.25 1.60

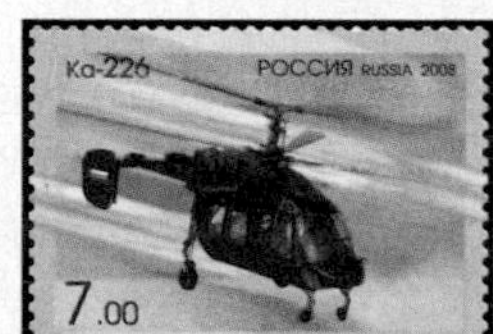

Helicopters — A3424

2008, Oct. 2 *Perf. 12¼x12*
7101 A3424 7r Ka-226 .80 .40
7102 A3424 7r Ka-32 .80 .40
a. Miniature sheet, 3 each #7101-7102 5.50 2.75

Central Sikhote-Alin UNESCO World Heritage Site — A3425

No. 7103 — Various forest views: a, 7r. b, 8r. c, 9r.

2008, Oct. 15 Litho. *Perf. 12*
7103 A3425 Block of 3, #a-c, + label 2.50 1.25

Federation Council, 15th Anniv. — A3426

State Duma, 15th Anniv. A3427

2008, Nov. 13 *Perf. 12½x12*
7104 A3426 10r multi 1.10 .50
7105 A3427 10r multi 1.10 .50

Nos. 7104-7105 each were printed in sheets of 14 + label.

Bridges — A3428

Bridges over: 6r, Moscow River, Moscow. 7r, Volga River, Kimry. 8r, Ob River, Surgut. 9r, Neva River, St. Petersburg.

2008, Nov. 28 *Perf. 12x12¼*
7106-7109 A3428 Set of 4 3.25 1.50
7109a Miniature sheet of 8, 2 each #7106-7109 6.50 3.00

Shuvalov Swimming School, Cent. A3429

2008, Dec. 5
7110 A3429 8r multi .85 .40

Russia, 2008 World Ice Hockey Champions A3430

2008, Dec. 5
7111 A3430 8r multi .85 .40

For surcharge, see No. 7375.

Bicycles — A3431

Designs: No. 7112, 7r, 1946 bicycle, derailleur. No. 7113, 7r, 1954 bicycle, front chain ring, chain guard and pedals. No. 7114, 7r, 1917 bicycle, saddle. No. 7115, 7r, 1938 bicycle, handlebars.

2008, Dec. 11 Litho. *Perf. 12x11½*
7112-7115 A3431 Set of 4 3.00 1.50
7115a Miniature sheet, 2 each # 7112-7115 5.75 2.75

Nos. 7112-7115 each were printed in sheets of 8 + central label.

A3432

A3433

A3434

Traditional Dagestan Costumes and Decorations A3435

2008, Dec. 18 *Perf. 11½x12*
7116 A3432 7.50r multi .75 .30
7117 A3433 7.50r multi .75 .30
7118 A3434 7.50r multi .75 .30
7119 A3435 7.50r multi .75 .30
a. Miniature sheet, 2 each #7116-7119 6.50 3.00
Nos. 7116-7119 (4) 3.00 1.20

Nos. 7116-7119 each were printed in sheets of 11 + label.

New Year 2009 — A3436

2008, Dec. 18 *Perf. 11¾*

7120 A3436 7.50r multi .80 .35

Voronezh Oblast A3437

Chelyabinsk Oblast — A3438

Saratov Oblast A3439

2009, Jan. 17 *Perf. 12*

7121 A3437 9r multi .90 .35

7122 A3438 9r multi .90 .35

7123 A3439 9r multi .90 .35

Nos. 7121-7123 (3) 2.70 1.05

Ernesto "Che" Guevara and Cuban Flag — A3440

2009, Jan. 19 *Perf. 12x12¼*

7124 A3440 10r multi 1.10 .75

Cuban Revolution, 50th anniv. See Cuba No. 4924A.

Naval Museum, 300th Anniv. — A3441

2009, Jan. 22 Litho. *Perf. 12x11½*

7125 A3441 7r multi .75 .30

Vasily G. Perov (1834-82), Painter A3442

Designs: No. 7126, 9r, Self-portrait, 1851. No. 7127, 9r, Drinking of Tea in Mytischi, Near Moscow, 1862, horiz.

2009, Jan. 28 *Perf. 11½x12, 12x11½*

7126-7127 A3442 Set of 2 1.75 .75

Souvenir Sheet

Dmitri Mendeleev (1834-1907), Chemist — A3443

2009, Feb. 6 *Perf. 12x12¼*

7128 A3443 15r multi 1.50 .60

G. Bakhchivandji (1909-43), Test Pilot — A3444

2009, Feb. 16 *Perf. 12¼x12*

7129 A3444 10r multi .80 .45

Yuri Gagarin (1934-68), First Cosmonaut A3445

2009, Mar. 6 *Perf. 12x12¼*

7130 A3445 10r multi .80 .45

Printed in sheets of 10 + 2 central labels.

Souvenir Sheet

Aleksandr S. Popov (1859-1905), Electrical Engineer — A3446

2009, Mar. 16 Litho. *Perf.*

7131 A3446 20r multi 2.00 .85

Scenes From Novels By Nikolai V. Gogol (1809-52) — A3447

Gogol — A3448

No. 7132 — Scenes from: a, 6r, The Inspector General. b, 7r, Dead Souls. c, 8r, The Overcoat. d, 9r, Taras Bulba.

2009, Apr. 1 *Perf. 12*

7132 A3447 Sheet of 4, #a-d 3.00 1.40

Souvenir Sheet

Perf. 12x12¼

7133 A3448 15r multi 1.75 .60

Weapons of World War II — A3449

Designs: 7r, SRT-40 and ARS-36 rifles. 8r, 1895 Nagan revolver and 1933 Tokarev pistol. 9r, PPS-43 and PPSh-41 machine guns. 10r, DP and SG-43 machine guns.

2009, Apr. 27 *Perf. 11¾*

7134-7137 A3449 Set of 4 3.00 1.50

7137a Sheet of 8, 2 each #7134-7137 6.00 3.00

A booklet containing four panes of one of Nos. 7134-7137 sold for 225r.

Europa A3450

2009, May 5 *Perf. 12*

7138 A3450 9r multi .80 .40

a. Miniature sheet of 9 7.00 3.50

Intl. Year of Astronomy.

Hydrometeorolgogical Service, 175th Anniv. — A3451

Weather map and: 8r, Weather measuring equipment, A. Y. Kupfer (1799-1865), weather scientist. 9r, Weather satellite.

2009, May 15 *Perf. 12x12¼*

7139-7140 A3451 Set of 2 1.75 .85

7140a Sheet of 8, 4 each #7139-7140 6.50 3.25

Souvenir Sheet

Empress Catherine I (1684-1727) — A3452

Litho. & Engr.

2009, May 21 *Perf. 12x12¼*

7141 A3452 35r multi 3.25 1.60

Kalmykia as Part of Russia, 400th Anniv. — A3453

2009, June 2 Litho. *Perf. 11½x11¼*

7142 A3453 7r multi .65 .30

Atomic-powered Icebreakers — A3454

Ships: 7r, Lenin. 8r, Taimyr. 9r, Yamal. 10r, 50 Let Pobedy.

2009, June 18 Litho. *Perf. 12x11½*

7143-7146 A3454 Set of 4 3.25 1.60

Nos. 7143-7146 each were printed in sheets of 8 + 2 labels.

Souvenir Sheet

Battle of Poltava, 300th Anniv. — A3455

2009, June 26 *Perf. 11¾x12¼*

7147 A3455 30r multi 2.75 1.40

Youth Year — A3456

2009, June 27 *Perf. 12¼x12*

7148 A3456 8r multi .80 .40

Ingushetia Republic A3457

Chechen Republic A3458

Tomsk Oblast A3459

2009, July 7 *Perf. 12*

7149	A3457	9r multi	.85	.40
7150	A3458	9r multi	.85	.40
7151	A3459	9r multi	.85	.40
	Nos. 7149-7151 (3)		2.55	1.20

Miniature Sheet

Helicopters Designed by M. L. Mil (1909-70) — A3460

No. 7152: a, 5r, Mi-1. b, 6r, Mi-4. c, 7r, Mi-8. d, 8r, Mi-34. e, 9r, Mi-28.

2009, July 10 *Perf. 12¼x12*

7152 A3460 Sheet of 5, #a-e, + label 3.50 1.75

Zinaida E. Serebryakova (1884-1967), Painter — A3461

Paintings by Serebryakova: No. 7153, 9r, Self-portrait in Dressing Room (shown). No. 7154, 9r, Autumn Field.

2009, July 15 *Perf. 11½x12*

7153-7154 A3461 Set of 2 1.75 .85

Andrei A. Gromyko (1909-89), Foreign Affairs Minister of Soviet Union A3462

2009, July 17 Litho. *Perf. 11½*

7155 A3462 7r multi .65 .30

Miniature Sheet

Solovetski Islands — A3463

No. 7156 — Map and: a, St. Troitsky Church, 17th cent., and horse. b, St. Serglev Church, 19th cent., and cow. c, Solovetski Monastery, 15th cent. d, Andrei Pervozvannyi Church, 18th cent.

2009, July 27 *Perf. 12*

7156 A3463 12r Sheet of 4, #a-d 4.50 2.25

Emblem of St. Petersburg A3464

Emblem of Moscow A3465

2009, Aug. 6 Litho. *Perf. 11¾x12¼*

7157	A3464	6.60r multi	.65	.30
		Complete booklet, 10 #7157	6.50	
		Complete booklet, 20 #7157	13.00	
7158	A3465	9r multi	.85	.45
		Complete booklet, 10 #7158	8.50	
		Complete booklet, 20 #7158	17.00	

Bridges — A3466

Designs: 6r, Oka River Bridge, Nizhni Novgorod. 7r, Irtysh River Bridge, Khanty-Mansiysk. 8r, Matsesta River Bridge, Sochi. 9r, Don River Bridge, Rostov-na-Donu.

2009, Aug. 12 Litho. *Perf. 12x12¼*

7159-7162	A3466	Set of 4	2.75	1.40
7162a		Miniature sheet of 8, 2 each #7159-7162	5.75	2.75

Miniature Sheet

Towns of Military Glory — A3467

No. 7163 — City names at top: a, Belgorod (8 letters in city name, tanks). b, Kursk. c, Orel (4 letters in city name, tanks and guns). d, Polyarny (8 letters in city name, ships). e, Rzhev (4 letters in city name, tanks and trucks).

Litho. With Foil Application

2009, Aug. 24 *Perf. 11¼*

7163 A3467 10r Sheet of 5, #a-e, + label 4.75 2.40

Souvenir Sheet

Great Novgorod, 1150th Anniv. — A3468

Litho. & Embossed

2009, Sept. 4 *Perf. 12½x12*

7164 A3468 50r multi 4.75 2.70

Souvenir Sheet

Famous Cossacks — A3469

No. 7165: a, Ermak Timofeevich (c. 1540-1585), explorer of Siberia (with helmet). b, Semen Ivanovich Dezhnev (c. 1605-72), explorer of Siberia (with beard). c, Count Matvei Ivanovich Platov (1757-1818), general (with mustache).

Perf. 11¾x12¼

2009, Sept. 15 **Litho.**

7165 A3469 10r Sheet of 3, #a-c 2.75 1.40

19th Century Headdresses A3470

Designs: No. 7166, 9r, Tver region man wearing hat. No. 7167, 9r, Moscow region woman wearing headdress with blue ribbon (blue background). No. 7168, 9r, Nizhny Novgorod region woman wearing veiled headdress (red background). No. 7169, 9r, Yaroslavl region woman wearing veiled headdress (blue green background).

2009, Sept. 23 *Perf. 11¼x12*

7166-7169	A3470	Set of 4	3.50	1.75
7169a		Miniature sheet of 8, 2 each #7166-7169	7.00	3.50

Nos, 7166-7169 each were printed in sheets of 11 + label.

Kremlins A3471

Kremlins in: 1r, Astrakhan. 1.50r, Zaraisk. 2r, Kazan. 2.50r, Kolomna. 3r, Rostov. 4r, Nizhny Novgorod. 5r, Novgorod. 6r, Pskov. 10r, Moscow. 25r, Ryazan. 50r, Tobolsk. 100r, Tula.

2009, Oct. 1 ***Serpentine Die Cut 11***

Self-Adhesive

7170	A3471	1r multi	.30	.25
7171	A3471	1.50r multi	.30	.25
7172	A3471	2r multi	.30	.25
7173	A3471	2.50r multi	.30	.25
7174	A3471	3r multi	.30	.25
7175	A3471	4r multi	.35	.25
7176	A3471	5r multi	.50	.25
7177	A3471	6r multi	.55	.25
7178	A3471	10r multi	.90	.45
7179	A3471	25r multi	2.50	1.25
a.		Sheet of 10, #7170-7179	3.50	
7180	A3471	50r multi	5.00	2.50
7181	A3471	100r multi	9.50	4.75
a.		Miniature sheet of 12, #7170-7181	21.00	
	Nos. 7170-7181 (12)		20.80	10.95

Issued: No. 7179a, 1/24/14.

World Food Program — A3472

2009, Oct. 7 *Perf. 11¾*

7182 A3472 10r multi 1.00 .50

Admiral Vladimir Ivanovich Istomin (1809-55) — A3473

2009, Oct. 14 *Perf. 12x11½*

7183 A3473 10r multi 1.00 .50

Traffic Safety A3474

2009, Oct. 22 *Perf. 12½x12*

7184 A3474 9r multi .90 .45

Order of the Hero of the Soviet Union, 75th Anniv. — A3475

Litho. & Embossed With Foil Application

2009, Oct. 29 ***Perf. 12x12¼***

7185 A3475 9r multi .90 .45

Souvenir Sheet

Empress Elizabeth Petrovna (1709-62) — A3476

Litho. & Engr.

2009, Nov. 6 ***Perf. 12x12¼***

7186 A3476 40r multi 4.00 2.00

Department of Transportation, 200th Anniv. — A3477

2009, Nov. 9 Litho. ***Perf. 12¼x12***

7187 A3477 9r multi .90 .45

Shchepkin Drama School, 200th Anniv. A3478

2009, Nov. 25

7188 A3478 10r multi 1.00 .50

Antarctic Treaty, 50th Anniv. A3479

2009, Nov. 30 **Litho.**

7189 A3479 15r multi 1.50 .75

New Year's Day — A3480

2009, Dec. 1 ***Die Cut***

Self-Adhesive

7190 A3480 10r multi 1.00 .50

Strategic Rocket Forces, 50th Anniv. A3481

2009, Dec. 10 ***Perf. 11¼x12***

7191 A3481 9r multi .90 .45

Fountains A3482

Fountain in: 9r, Verkhnyaya Pyshma. 10r, Nizhny Novgorod. 12r, Novy Urengoi, vert. 15r, Yaroslavl.

Serpentine Die Cut 11¼

2009, Dec. 15 **Self-Adhesive**

7192-7195 A3482 Set of 4 4.50 2.25

Anatoly K. Serov (1910-39), Pilot A3483

Valentina S. Grizodubova (1910-93), Pilot — A3484

2010, Jan. 14 Litho. ***Perf. 12½x12***

7196 A3483 10r multi 1.00 .50

7197 A3484 10r multi 1.00 .50

A3485

Anton P. Chekhov (1860-1904), Writer — A3486

No. 7198 — Characters from: a, 8r, Lady with the Dog. b, 10r, The Seagull. c, 12r, The Artist's Story (The House with the Mezzanine). 20r, Chekhov.

2010, Jan. 29 Litho. ***Perf. 11¾x12¼***

7198 A3485 Sheet of 3, #a-c 4.00 2.00

Souvenir Sheet

Perf.

7199 A3486 20r multi 3.00 1.50

Peoples' Friendship University, Moscow, 50th Anniv. — A3487

2010, Feb. 5 Litho. ***Perf. 12x11½***

7200 A3487 10r multi 1.00 .50

2010 Winter Olympics, Vancouver — A3488

Litho. & Embossed

2010, Feb. 11 ***Perf. 11½***

7201 A3488 15r multi 1.25 .60

Paintings by Fedor S. Rokotov (c. 1735-1808) A3489

Portraits of: No. 7202, 10.50r, Prince D. M. Golitsyn. No. 7203, 10.50r, Countess E. A. Musina-Pushkina.

2010, Mar. 19 Litho. ***Perf. 11¼x12***

7202-7203 A3489 Set of 2 2.00 1.00

Orenburg Oblast A3490

Tuva Republic A3491

2010, Mar. 24 ***Perf. 12x12¼***

7204 A3490 10.50r multi 1.00 .50

7205 A3491 10.50r multi 1.00 .50

Evgeny K. Fedorov (1910-81), Polar Explorer — A3492

2010, Apr. 9 ***Perf. 12x12¼***

7206 A3492 12r multi .85 .40

Miniature Sheet

Towns of Military Glory — A3493

No. 7207 — City names at top: a, Malgobek (8 letters in city name, airplanes, cannons and cavalry). b, Elnja (5 letters in city name, bazookas, cannons and tanks). c, Elets (4 letters in city name, trucks, cannons and tanks). d, Voronezh (7 letters in city name, airplanes and cannons). e, Luga (4 letters in city name, cannons and tanks).

Litho. With Foil Application

2010, Apr. 15 ***Perf. 11¼***

7207 A3493 10r Sheet of 5, #a-e, + label 3.50 1.75

World War II Tanks — A3494

Designs: 9r, BT-7M. 10r, T-70. 11r, T-34-85. 12r, IS-2.

2010, Apr. 20 Litho. ***Perf. 13½***

7208-7211 A3494 Set of 4 3.00 1.50

7211a Sheet of 8, 2 each #7208-7211 6.00 3.00

Souvenir Sheet

Soviet Union Order of Victory — A3495

Litho. & Embossed

2010, Apr. 26 *Perf. 12*

7212 A3495 50r multi 3.50 1.75

Victory in World War II, 65th anniv.

Europa — A3496

2010, May 5 Litho. *Perf. 12x12½*

7213 A3496 10.50r multi .70 .35

a. Miniature sheet of 6 4.25 2.10

Modernization of Cyrillic Alphabet, 300th Anniv. — A3497

2010, May 18 *Perf. 12x12¼*

7214 A3497 7.70r multi .50 .25

Souvenir Sheet

Ivan Fedorov (c. 1510-83), Printer — A3498

Litho. & Engr.

2010, May 18 *Perf. 12½x12*

7215 A3498 50r multi 3.25 1.60

Miniature Sheet

Watches — A3499

No. 7216 — Watch from: a, 6r, Wooden pocket watch by M. S. Bronnikov and Son. 9r, Pobeda wrist watch, 1946. 12r, Shturmanskle wrist watch, 1949. 15r, Chaika wrist watch, 1990.

2010, May 28 Litho. *Perf. 12¼*

7216 A3499 Sheet of 4, #a-d 2.75 1.40

Dmitry Levitzky (c.1735-1822), Painter — A3500

Designs: No. 7217, 10.50r, Self-portrait (detail), 1783. No. 7218, 10.50r, Portrait of G. I. Alymova, 1776.

2010, June 7 *Perf. 11½x12*

7217-7218 A3500 Set of 2 1.40 .70

Souvenir Sheet

Valaam Archipelago — A3501

2010, June 8 *Perf. 12*

7219 A3501 25r multi 1.60 .80

Souvenir Sheet

Tsarskoye Selo (Tsar's Village) UNESCO World Heritage Site, 300th Anniv. — A3502

No. 7220: a, Egyptian Gates. b, Pushkin Monument, vert. c, Alexander Palace.

Perf. 12x12¼, 12¼x12

2010, June 18

7220 A3502 15r Sheet of 3, #a-c 3.00 1.50

Icons of Russia and Serbia — A3503

No. 7221: a, Archangel Michael, by Andrei Rublev, 15th cent., Russia. b, Odigitria Virgin, Belgrade, Serbia, 14th cent.

2010, June 28 *Perf. 11½*

7221 A3503 15r Pair, #a-b 2.00 1.00

See Serbia No. 515.

Vladivostok, 150th Anniv. — A3504

2010, July 2 *Perf. 13½*

7222 A3504 15r multi 1.00 .50

Bryansk Oblast A3505

Jewish Autonomous Oblast — A3506

2010, July 14 *Perf. 12x12¼*

7223 A3505 10.50r multi .70 .35

7224 A3506 10.50r multi .70 .35

Curonian Spit UNESCO World Heritage Site — A3507

No. 7225 — Spit with denomination at: a, Left. b, Right.

2010, June 26 Litho. *Perf. 13½*

7225 Horiz. pair + central label 2.00 1.00

a.-b. A3507 15r Either single 1.00 .50

A gritty substance is affixed to the areas of the stamps and labels showing sand.

A3508

A3509

A3510

Headdresses of Tatarstan A3511

2010, July 30 Litho. *Perf. 11½x12*

7226 A3508 11r multi .75 .35

7227 A3509 11r multi .75 .35

7228 A3510 11r multi .75 .35

7229 A3511 11r multi .75 .35

a. Miniature sheet of 8, 2 each #7226-7229 6.00 3.00

Nos. 7226-7229 (4) 3.00 1.40

Nos. 7226-7229 each were printed in sheets of 11 + label.

Souvenir Sheet

Ferapontov Monastery UNESCO World Heritage Site — A3512

2010, Aug. 2 *Perf. 12½x12*

7230 A3512 30r multi 2.00 1.00

Nikolai N. Zubov (1885-1960), Arctic Explorer, and Icebreaker Sadko — A3513

2010, Aug. 12 *Perf. 12x12¼*

7231 A3513 12r multi .80 .40

Souvenir Sheet

Cossacks — A3514

No. 7232: a, Don Cossacks, brown horse. b, Kuban Cossacks, white horse. c, Terek Cossacks, black horse.

2010, Aug. 20
7232 A3514 12r Sheet of 3, #a-c 2.40 1.25

Arms of Vladivostok A3515

Arms of Yaroslavl A3516

2010, Aug. 27 ***Perf. 11¾x12¼***
7233 A3515 7.70r multi .50 .25
Complete booklet, 10 #7233 5.00
Complete booklet, 20 #7233 10.00
7234 A3516 10.50r multi .70 .35
Complete booklet, 10 #7234 7.00
Complete booklet, 20 #7234 14.00

Souvenir Sheet

Fresh Wind, Volga, by Isaac I. Levitan (1860-1900) — A3517

2010, Aug. 30 ***Perf. 12½x12***
7235 A3517 25r multi 1.75 .85

Memorial to End of World War II, Moscow A3518

2010, Sept. 2 ***Perf. 11½***
7236 A3518 15r multi 1.00 .50
End of World War II, 65th anniv.

Gherman Titov (1935-2000), Cosmonaut A3519

2010, Sept. 10 ***Perf. 13½***
7237 A3519 10.50r multi .70 .35

Souvenir Sheet

Yaroslavl, 1000th Anniv. — A3520

Serpentine Die Cut 10
2010, Sept. 10 **Self-Adhesive**
7238 A3520 50r multi 3.25 1.60

Bridges — A3521

Designs: 9r, Jubilee Bridge, Yaroslavl. 10r, Matsesta Valley Bridge, Sochi. 11r, Moscow Canal Bridge, Khlebnikovo, Moscow Oblast. 12r, Kola Bay Bridge, Murmansk.

2010, Sept. 15 ***Perf. 12x12¼***
7239-7242 A3521 Set of 4 2.75 1.40
7242a Miniature sheet of 8, 2 each #7239-7242 5.50 2.75

Miniature Sheet

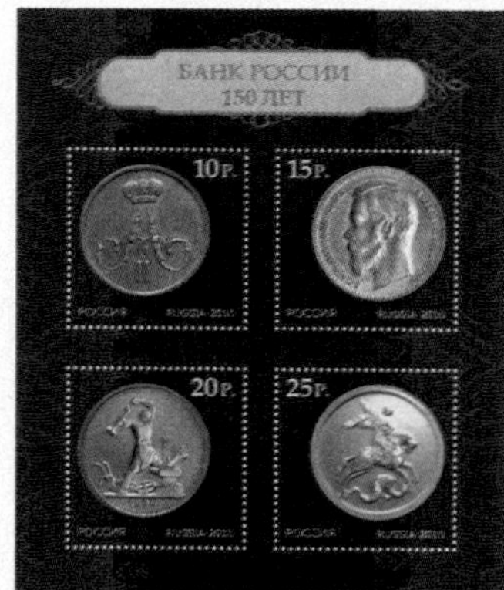

Bank of Russia, 150th Anniv. — A3522

No. 7243: a, 10r, 1855 copper half-kopeck coin. b, 15r, 1895 one-ruble coin. c, 20r, 1924 fifty-kopeck coin. d, 25r, 2006 gold fifty-ruble coin.

Litho. & Embossed
2010, Sept. 22 ***Perf. 12¼***
7243 A3522 Sheet of 4, #a-d 4.75 2.40

Teacher's Year A3523

Serpentine Die Cut 10
2010, Oct. 5 **Self-Adhesive** **Litho.**
7244 A3523 10.50r multi .70 .35

2010 Census — A3524

2010, Oct. 14 ***Serpentine Die Cut 10***
Self-Adhesive
7245 A3524 12r red & blue .80 .40

Shokan Valikhanov (1835-65), Diplomat, Ethnologist A3525

2010, Oct. 21 ***Perf. 12x12½***
7246 A3525 15r multi 1.00 .50
See Kazakhstan No. 628.

Sputnik 5 Spaceflight Carrying Dogs Belka and Strelka, 50th Anniv. — A3526

2010, Oct. 29 ***Perf. 12x12¼***
7247 A3526 10r multi .65 .35

Khanty-Mansi Autonomous Okrug — A3527

Kursk Oblast A3528

2010, Nov. 1
7248 A3527 10.50r multi .70 .35
7249 A3528 10.50r multi .70 .35

Soviet Union Victory in UEFA European Soccer Championships, 50th Anniv. — A3529

2010, Nov. 10 ***Perf. 11½***
7250 A3529 12r multi .80 .40
Printed in sheets of 8 + central label.

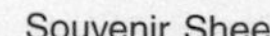

Souvenir Sheet

Nikolai I. Pirogov (1810-81), Surgeon — A3530

2010, Nov. 25 ***Perf. 12x12½***
7251 A3530 20r multi 1.40 .70

Kachino Aviation School, Cent. — A3531

2010, Nov. 29 ***Perf. 11½***
7252 A3531 15r multi 1.00 .50
Printed in sheets of 8 + central label.

New Year's Day A3532

2010, Dec. 1 **Self-Adhesive** ***Die Cut***
7253 A3532 10.50r multi .70 .35

Mstislav Keldysh (1911-78), Mathematician and Space Propulsion Pioneer — A3533

2011, Jan. 25 ***Perf. 12½x12***
7254 A3533 12r multi .85 .40

Souvenir Sheet

Princess Maria Alexandrovna (1824-80) — A3534

2011, Feb. 21 ***Perf.***
7255 A3534 40r multi 3.00 1.50
City of Mariehamn, Aland Islands, 150th anniv. See Finland (Aland Islands) No. 313.

Souvenir Sheet

Sochi, Host City of 2014 Winter Olympics — A3535

2011, Mar. 15 ***Perf. 12½x12***
7256 A3535 25r multi 1.90 .95

Novgorod Oblast — A3536

Tyumen Oblast — A3537

Tambov Oblast — A3538

2011, Mar. 30 ***Perf. 12¼x12***
7257 A3536 11.80r multi .85 .40
7258 A3537 11.80r multi .85 .40
7259 A3538 11.80r multi .85 .40
Nos. 7257-7259 (3) 2.55 1.20

Souvenir Sheet

Yuri Gagarin, First Man in Space, 50th Anniv. — A3539

2011, Apr. 12 Litho. ***Perf. 12x12¼***
7260 A3539 50r multi 3.75 1.90

Miniature Sheet

Towns of Military Glory — A3540

No. 7261 — City names at top: a, Vyborg (6 letters in city name, airplanes and tanks). b, Rostov-on-Don (city name with hyphens, cannons). c, Tuapse (6 letters in city name, airplanes, cannons and ships). d, Vladikavkaz (11 letters in name, airplanes and cannons). e, Veliki Novgorod (15 letters in city name, vehicle on skis, cannons and tanks). f, Velikiye Luki (10 letters in city name, biplanes, cannons and tanks).

Litho. With Foil Application
2011, Apr. 20 ***Perf. 11¼***
7261 A3540 12r Sheet of 6, #a-f 5.25 2.60

Russian Peace Fund, 50th Anniv. A3541

2011, Apr. 27 Litho. ***Perf. 13½***
7262 A3541 8.50r multi .60 .30

World War II Military Aircraft — A3542

Designs: 9r, Yakovlev Yak-3 fighter. 10r, Lavochkin La-5 fighter. 11r, Ilyushin Il-2 attack plane. 12r, Petlyakov Pe-2 bomber.

2011, Apr. 29
7263-7266 A3542 Set of 4 3.00 1.50
7266a Sheet of 8, 2 each #7263-7266 6.00 3.00

A booklet containing panes of one of each of the stamps was produced in limited quantities.

Europa A3543

2011, May 5 ***Perf. 11¼***
7267 A3543 15r multi 1.10 .55

Intl. Year of Forests.

Miniature Sheet

Clocks — A3544

No. 7268 — Clock at: a, 9r, Central Telegraph Office, Moscow. b, 12r, Admiralty Building, St. Petersburg. c, 15r, Moscow State University. d, 25r, Railway Station, Sochi.

2011, May 16 ***Perf. 12¼***
7268 A3544 Sheet of 4, #a-d 4.50 2.25

Kiril I. Shchelkin (1911-68), Physicist A3545

2011, May 17 ***Perf. 12x12½***
7269 A3545 12r multi .85 .45

Irkutsk Arms A3546

Komi Republic Arms A3547

2011, May 26 ***Perf. 11¾x12¼***
7270 A3546 8.50r multi .60 .30
Complete booklet, 10 #7270 6.00
Complete booklet, 20 #7270 12.00
7271 A3547 11.80r multi .85 .40
Complete booklet, 10 #7271 8.50
Complete booklet, 20 #7271 17.00

Kazansky Cathedral, St. Petersburg — A3548

Russian Diplomatic Mission, Cetinje, Montenegro — A3549

2011, May 26 ***Perf. 12½x12***
7272 Horiz. pair + central label 2.25 1.10
a. A3548 15r multi 1.10 .55
b. A3549 15r multi 1.10 .55

See Montenegro Nos. 285-286.

Famous Men — A3550

Designs: No. 7273, 12r, Valery Bryusov (1873-1924), painter. No. 7274, 12r, Hovannes Tumanian (1869-1923), poet.

2011, June 1 ***Perf. 12x12½***
7273-7274 A3550 Set of 2 1.75 .85

Nos. 7273-7274 each were printed in sheets of 14 + label. See Armenia Nos. 877-878.

Independence of Venezuela, Bicent. — A3551

2011, June 20 ***Perf. 12½x12***
7275 A3551 12r multi .85 .45

Irkutsk, 350th Anniv. — A3552

2011, June 24 ***Perf. 12x11½***
7276 A3552 15r multi 1.10 .55

Buryatia as Part of Russia, 350th Anniv. — A3553

2011, June 27 ***Perf. 11½***
7277 A3553 11.80r multi .85 .40

State Road Inspection, 75th Anniv. A3554

2011, June 27 **Litho.**
7278 A3554 15r multi 1.10 .55

Souvenir Sheet

Order of St. Andrew the Apostle — A3555

2011, July 1 ***Perf. 12x12½***

7279 A3555 50r multi 3.75 1.90

Souvenir Sheet

Pechora-Ilych Nature Reserve — A3556

2011, July 29 ***Perf. 12x12¼***

7280 A3556 25r multi 1.75 .85

Souvenir Sheet

Malye Korely Museum of Wooden Architecture — A3557

No. 7281: a, 10r, Chapel of St. Makary, 18th cent. b, 15r, Resurrection Church, 17th cent. c, 20r, Windmill, 20th cent.

2011, Aug. 1

7281 A3557 Sheet of 3, #a-c 3.25 1.60

Bridges — A3558

Designs: 9r, Pochtamtsky Bridge, St. Petersburg. 10r, Patriarshy Bridge, Moscow. 12r, Kena River Bridge, Arkhangelsk Oblast. 15r, Vezelka River Bridge, Belgorod.

2011, Aug. 15 **Litho.**

7282-7285 A3558 Set of 4 3.25 1.60

7285a Souvenir sheet of 8, 2 each #7282-7285 6.50 3.25

Souvenir Sheet

Cossacks — A3559

No. 7286: a, Amur Cossacks (woman holding pail). b, Astrakhan Cossacks (man on horse). c, Volga Cossacks (woman holding jar).

2011, Aug. 29 ***Perf. 12x12¼***

7286 A3559 15r Sheet of 3, #a-c 3.00 1.50

Recipients of the Order of St. Andrew the Apostle — A3560

Designs: No. 7287, 15r, Dmitry S. Likhachev (1906-99), Russian language and literature scholar. No. 7288, 15r, Lyudmila G. Zykina (1929-2009), singer. No. 7289, 15r, Boris V. Petrovsky (1908-2004), Health minister.

2011, Sept. 1 ***Perf. 12x11¼***

7287-7289 A3560 Set of 3 3.00 1.50

See Nos. 7369-7371, 7442, 7457, 7478, 7578.

Field Marshal Michael Barclay de Tolly (1761-1818) — A3561

2011, Sept. 9

7290 A3561 15r multi 1.00 .50

Printed in sheets of 8 + central label.

Modern Art — A3562

Designs: No. 7291, 14r, Monument to Yuri Nikulin, sculpture by A. I. Rukavishnikov, 2000. No. 7292, 14r, View of Borisoglebsky Monastery, painting by N. I. Borovskoy, 2001. No. 7293, 14r, Seascape, by A. V. Adamov, 2007. No. 7294, 14r, Gymnasts of the U.S.S.R., painting by D.D. Zhilinsky, 1964-65, vert. No. 7295, 14r, Aidan, painting by T.T. Salakhov, 1967, vert. No. 7296, 14r, Akinshino Village, painting by V. Y. Yukin, 1995 (50x50mm).

Perf. 12x11¼, 11¼x12, 12 (#7296)

2011, Sept. 12

7291-7296 A3562 Set of 6 5.50 2.75

Souvenir Sheet

Derbent Citadel UNESCO World Heritage Site — A3563

2011, Sept. 13 ***Perf. 12½x12***

7297 A3563 50r multi 3.50 1.75

A3564

A3565

A3566

Traditional 19th and 20th Century Headdresses of Northern Russia A3567

2011, Sept. 15 ***Perf. 12***

7298 A3564 12r multi .80 .40

7299 A3565 12r multi .80 .40

7300 A3566 12r multi .80 .40

7301 A3567 12r multi .80 .40

a. Souvenir sheet of 8, 2 each #7298-7301, perf. 11½x12 6.50 3.25

Nos. 7298-7301 (4) 3.20 1.60

Worldwide Fund for Nature (WWF), 50th Anniv. A3568

2011, Sept. 26 ***Perf. 11¼***

7302 A3568 15r multi .95 .50

Tourist Sites in Sochi — A3569

Designs: 15r, Krasnaya Polyana Ski Resort. 20r, Marine Terminal Building. 25r, Watchtower on Bolshoy Akhun Mountain. 30r, Volkonskiy dolmen

2011, Sept. 27 ***Perf. 12½x12***

Dated "2011"

7303 A3569 15r multi + label 1.00 .50

7304 A3569 20r multi + label 1.25 .65

7305 A3569 25r multi + label 1.60 .80

7306 A3569 30r multi + label 1.90 .95

a. Souvenir sheet of 4, #7303-7306, + 4 labels 5.75 3.00

Nos. 7303-7306 (4) 5.75 2.90

Sochi, host city of 2014 Winter Olympics. Nos. 7303-7306 each were printed in sheets of 6 + 6 labels, with each label being in one of six languages (Russian, English, Chinese, French, Spanish, German). No. 7306a was printed in six versions, with the inscriptions on the labels in the sheet all being in one of the six languages.

See Nos. 7348-7351.

Eurasian Economin Community Innovative Biotechnologies Program — A3570

2011, Sept. 30 ***Perf. 13½***

7307 A3570 9r multi .60 .30

Sports of the 2014 Winter Olympics, Sochi A3571

Designs: No. 7308, 25r, Cross-country skiing. No. 7309, 25r, Ski jumping. No. 7310, 25r, Short-track speed skating.

Litho. & Embossed

2011, Oct. 3 ***Perf. 11¼***

7308-7310 A3571 Set of 3 4.75 2.40

7308a Dated "2014" at right 1.40 .70

7309a Dated "2014" at right 1.40 .70

7310a Dated "2014" at right 1.40 .70

Nos. 7308-7310 each were printed in sheets of 8 + label.

Issued: Nos. 7308a, 7309a, 7310a, 1/24/14.

Regional Communications Commonwealth, 20th Anniv. — A3572

2011, Oct. 10 Litho. ***Perf. 12x12½***
7311 A3572 12r multi .80 .40

Arsenal Factory, 300th Anniv. A3573

2011, Oct. 14 ***Perf. 11¼***
7312 A3573 15r multi 1.00 .50

A3574

Moscow Post Office, 300th Anniv. — A3575

No. 7313: a, Afanasy L. Ordin-Naschokin (c. 1605-80), founder of Russian postal system, horse-drawn mail sleigh, sealed and rolled document . b, Russia #1, 19th cent. stage-coach. c, Russia #856, 5795, postal card, mail box, Moskvich 400-422 mail vehicle. d, Russia #7178, postal cards, Moscow Post Office, mail van.

50r, Wax seal with 300th anniversary emblem.

2011, Oct. 21 Litho. ***Perf. 12½x12***
7313 Horiz. strip of 4 3.25 1.60
a.-d. A3574 11.80r Any single .80 .40

Souvenir Sheet

Litho. & Embossed

Perf.

7314 A3575 50r multi 3.25 1.60

State Kremlin Palace (Kremlin Palace of Congresses), 50th Anniv. — A3576

2011, Oct. 24 Litho. ***Perf. 12x12¼***
7315 A3576 12r multi .80 .40

Constitutional Court, 20th Anniv. — A3577

2011, Oct. 27
7316 A3577 12r multi .80 .40

Petr G. Sobolevsky (1782-1841) and People Near Gas Streetlight — A3578

2011, Oct. 28 ***Perf. 12½x12***
7317 A3578 12r multi .80 .40

Gas use in Russia, 200th anniv.

Commonweath of Independent States, 20th Anniv. — A3579

2011, Nov. 3 ***Perf. 12x11½***
7318 A3579 11.80r multi .80 .40

Souvenir Sheet

Mikhail V. Lomonosov (1711-65), Scientist — A3580

Litho. & Engr.

2011, Nov. 17 ***Perf. 12¼x12***
7319 A3580 100r multi 6.50 3.25

Souvenir Sheet

Moskvoretsky Bridge, Painting by Konstantin A. Korovin (1861-1939) — A3581

2011, Nov. 21 Litho. ***Perf. 12x12½***
7320 A3581 45r multi 3.00 1.50

Empress Catherine II (1729-96) — A3582

2011, Nov. 25 ***Perf. 12x11½***
7321 A3582 8.50r multi .55 .30

Insurance in Russia, 225th anniv.

Russian Olympic Committee, Cent. — A3583

2011, Nov. 25 ***Perf. 12½x12***
7322 A3583 15r multi 1.00 .50

Kaluga Oblast A3584

Omsk Oblast A3585

2011 Litho. ***Perf. 12x12¼***
7323 A3584 11.80r multi .80 .40
7324 A3585 11.80r multi .75 .40

Issued: No. 7323, 11/30; No. 7324, 12/12.

New Year's Day A3586

Litho. With Foil Application

2011, Dec. 1 ***Perf. 11¼***
7325 A3586 20r multi 1.40 .70

Russian-Italian Year of Culture — A3587

2011, Dec. 10 Litho. ***Perf. 12¼x12***
7326 A3587 15r multi .95 .50

See Italy No. 3110.

Lace — A3588

Lace from: No. 7327, 15r, Belev (brown background). No. 7328, 15r, Elets (red brown background). No. 7329, 15r, Vyatka (purple background). No. 7330, 15r, Vologda (blue background).

Perf. 11¼x11½

2011, Dec. 12 Litho. & Engr.
7327-7330 A3588 Set of 4 3.75 1.90

Souvenir Sheet

Tula Small Arms Factory, 300th Anniv. — A3589

2012, Feb. 1 Litho. ***Perf. 12***
7331 A3589 50r multi 3.50 1.75

Whales — A3590

No. 7332: a, 15r, Orcinus orca. b, 20r, Megaptera novaeangliae.

2012, Feb. 8 ***Perf. 13½***
7332 A3590 Vert. pair, #a-b 2.40 1.25

Pyotr N. Nesterov (1887-1914), Aeronautical Pioneer — A3591

2012, Feb. 13 ***Perf. 12½x12***
7333 A3591 15r multi 1.10 .55

No. 7333 was printed in sheets of 10 + 2 central labels.

Souvenir Sheet

Wrangel Island — A3592

2012, Feb. 27 ***Perf. 12***

7334 A3592 45r multi 3.25 1.60

Mascots for 2014 Winter Olympics, Sochi — A3593

No. 7335: a, Snow Leopard (48x53mm). b, Zaya the Hare (28x44mm). c, Polar Bear (44x59mm).

2012, Feb. 27 ***Die Cut***

Self-Adhesive

7335 A3593 15r Sheet of 3, #a-c 3.25 1.60

Snowflake and Fire Boy, Mascots for 2014 Winter Paralympics, Sochi — A3594

2012, Feb. 27 ***Die Cut***

Self-Adhesive

7336 A3594 30r multi 2.10 1.10

Gold Star Medal A3596

Order of St. George A3597

Order of Merit for the Fatherland A3598

Litho. & Embossed

2012, Mar. 2 ***Perf. 11¾***

7337 A3596 25r multi	1.75	.85
7338 A3597 25r multi	1.75	.85
7339 A3598 25r multi	1.75	.85
Nos. 7337-7339 (3)	5.25	2.55

Nos. 7337-7339 each were printed in sheets of 7 + label.

Marina M. Raskova (1912-43), Combat Pilot — A3599

2012, Mar. 21 **Litho.** ***Perf. 12½x12***

7340 A3599 15r multi 1.00 .50

No. 7540 was pritned in sheets of 10 + central label.

Pyotr A. Stolypin (1862-1911), Prime Minister A3600

2012, Apr. 6 ***Perf. 11½***

7341 A3600 15r multi 1.00 .50

World War II Military Vehicles — A3601

Designs: 10r, GAZ-AA truck. 12r, ZIS-5B truck. 14r, GAZ-67B general personnel carrier. 15r, GAZ-M1 automobile.

2012, Apr. 16 ***Perf. 13½***

7342-7345 A3601 Set of 4 3.50 1.75

7345a Souvenir sheet of 8, 2 each #7342-7345 7.00 3.50

A booklet containing panes of one of each of Nos. 7342-7345 was produced in limited quantities.

Miniature Sheet

Towns of Military Glory — A3602

No. 7346 — City names at top: a, Pskov (5 letters in city name with last letter "B", airplanes, cannons and tanks). b, Vyazma (6 letters in city name, airplanes, cannons, artillery launchers). c, Naro-Fominsk (10 letters and hyphen in city name, airplanes, cannons and tanks). d, Tver (5 letters in city name with last letter "b", airplanes, cannons and tanks). e, Kronshtadt (9 letters in city name, cannons, airplanes and ships). f, Dmitrov (7 letters in city name, airplanes, cannons, machine guns).

Litho. With Foil Application

2012, Apr. 20 ***Perf. 11¼***

7346 A3602 15r Sheet of 6, #a-f 6.25 3.25

Emblem of Russian War Veteran's Association — A3603

2012, Apr. 26 **Litho.** ***Perf. 11½***

7347 A3603 10r multi .70 .35

Tourist Sites in Sochi Type of 2011

Designs: 15r, Sail Rock, near Gelendzhik. 20r, Sochi Railway Station. 25r, Gazebo in Botanical Gardens, Sochi. 30r, Orehovsky Waterfall, Sochi.

2012, Apr. 27 ***Perf. 12½x12***

Dated "2012"

7348 A3569 15r multi + label	1.00	.50
7349 A3569 20r multi + label	1.40	.70
7350 A3569 25r multi + label	1.75	.85
7351 A3569 30r multi + label	2.10	1.10
a. Souvenir sheet of 4, #7348-7351 + 4 labels	6.25	3.25
Nos. 7348-7351 (4)	6.25	3.15

Nos. 7348-7351 each were printed in sheets of 6 + 6 labels, with each label being in one of six languages (Russian, English, Chines, French, Spanish, German). No. 7351a was printed in six versions, with the inscriptions on the labels in the sheet all being in one of the six languages.

Third Inauguration of Pres. Vladimir Putin — A3605

2012, May 7 **Litho. & Embossed**

7353 A3605 15r multi .95 .45

Heroes A3606

Gold Star Medal and: No. 7354, 15r, V. V. Zamaryev (1959-2004). No. 7355, 15r, D. A. Razumovsky (1968-2004). No. 7356, 15r, Irina Janina (1966-99). No. 7357, 15r, A. V. Putsykin (1980-2008). No. 7358, 15r, A. B. Tsydenzhapov (1991-2010).

2012, May 7 **Litho.** ***Perf. 12½x12***

7354-7358 A3606 Set of 5 4.75 2.40

Nos. 7354-7358 each were printed in sheets of 5 + label.

Souvenir Sheet

Mikhail V. Nesterov (1862-1942), Painter — A3607

2012, May 17 ***Perf. 12x12½***

7359 A3607 30r multi 1.90 .95

Ivan N. Kramskoi (1837-87), Painter A3608

Designs: No. 7360, 15r, Self-portrait (detail), 1867. No. 7361, 15r, Portrait of an Unknown Woman, 1883, horiz.

2012, May 29 ***Perf. 11½x12, 12x11½***

7360-7361 A3608 Set of 2 1.90 .95

Europa A3604

2012, May 4 ***Perf. 11½***

7352 A3604 15r multi .95 .45

Souvenir Sheet

Ivan A. Goncharov (1812-91), Writer — A3609

2012, June 4 ***Perf.***
7362 A3609 30r multi 1.90 .95

First Non-stop Transpolar Flight, 75th Anniv. A3610

2012, June 6 ***Perf. 11½***
7363 A3610 13r multi .80 .40

No. 7363 was printed in sheets of 8 + central label.

Souvenir Sheet

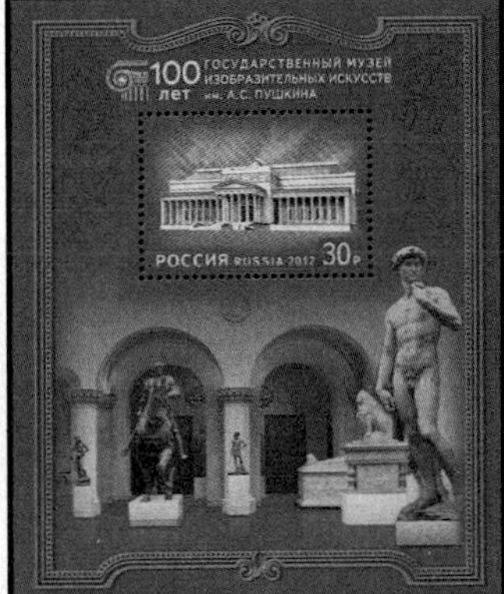

Pushkin Museum of Fine Arts, Moscow, Cent. — A3611

2012, June 6 ***Perf. 12½x12***
7364 A3611 30r multi 1.90 .95

Monument to Minin and Pozharsky, Moscow A3612

Triumphal Arch, Moscow A3613

2012, June 14 ***Perf. 11¾x12¼***
7365 A3612 9.20r multi .55 .30
Complete booklet, 10 #7365 5.50
Complete booklet, 20 #7365 11.00
7366 A3613 13r multi .80 .40
Complete booklet, 10 #7366 8.00
Complete booklet, 20 #7366 16.00

Newts — A3614

No. 7367: a, Lissotriton vulgaris. b, Triturus cristatus.

2012, June 25 ***Perf. 11¼x12***
7367 A3614 13r Pair, #a-b 1.60 .80

See Belarus Nos. 829-830.

Oleg E. Kutafin (1937-2008), Lawyer, and Order of Merit for the Fatherland — A3615

2012, June 26 ***Perf. 12½x12***
7368 A3615 15r multi .95 .45

Printed in sheets of 14 + label.

Recipients of the Order of St. Andrew Type of 2011

Order of St. Andrew and: No. 7369, 15r, Patriarch Aleksei II (1929-2008). No. 7370, 15r, Irina K. Arkhipova (1925-2010), opera singer. No. 7371, 15r, Valeri I. Shumakov (1931-2008), transplant surgery pioneer.

2012, June 29 ***Perf. 12x11½***
7369-7371 A3560 Set of 3 2.75 1.40

Nos. 7369-7371 each were printed in sheets of 11 + label.

Souvenir Sheet

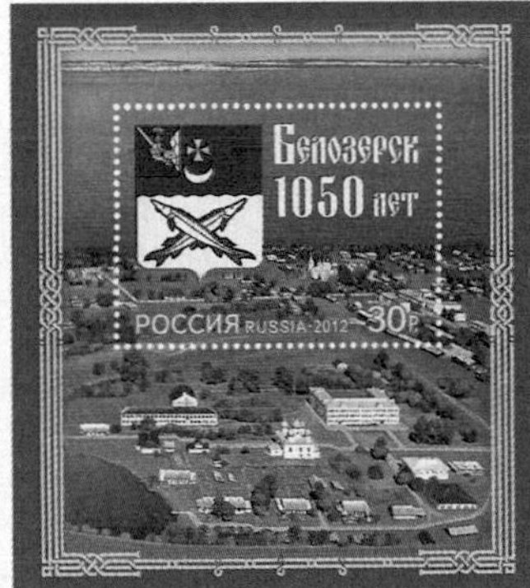

Belozersk, 1050th Anniv. — A3617

2012, July 4 ***Perf. 12***
7372 A3617 30r multi 1.90 .95

Souvenir Sheet

Izborsk, 1150th Anniv. — A3618

2012, July 4 ***Perf. 12¼x12***
7373 A3618 30r multi 1.90 .95

Record Non-stop Transpolar Flight, 75th Anniv. A3619

2012, July 6 ***Perf. 11¼***
7374 A3619 13r multi .80 .40

Printed in sheets of 8 + central label.

No. 7111 Srchd.

Method and Perf. As Before

2012, July 6
7375 A3430 12r on 8r #7111 *3.50 1.75*

Victory of Russian men's ice hockey team in 2012 World Championships.

Churches — A3620

No. 7376: a, Church of the Savior on Spilled Blood, St. Petersburg, Russia. b, Episcopal Palace, Astorga, Spain.

2012, July 17 **Litho.** ***Perf. 11¼***
7376 A3620 13r Pair, #a-b 1.75 .85

No. 7376 was printed in sheets containing 4 pairs + central label. See Spain No. 3863.

Mordovia, 1000th Anniv. — A3621

2012, July 20
7377 A3621 13r multi .85 .40

Souvenir Sheet

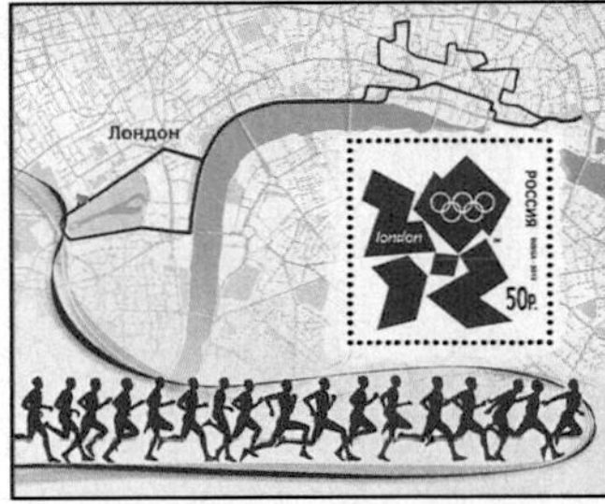

2012 Summer Olympics, London — A3622

2012, July 26 ***Perf. 11½***
7378 A3622 50r multi 3.25 1.60

A3623

A3624

Modern Art — A3625

Designs: No. 7379, Warm Day, by Georgy A. Leman, 1996. No. 7380, Cossacks' Send Off, by Sergei A. Gavrilyachenko, 1999. No. 7381, Autumn Interior, by Aleksei N. Sukhovetsky, 1992. No. 7382, Monument to F. I. Shalyapin in Kazan, by Andrei V. Balashov, 1999. No. 7383, Russian Madonna, by Vasily I. Nestorenko, 1992. No. 7384, Mammoths in Khanty-Mansiysk, by Andrei N. Kovalchuk, 2007.

2012, July 30 ***Perf. 12x11½***
7379 A3623 15r multi .95 .45
7380 A3623 15r multi .95 .45

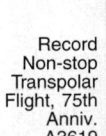

Perf. 11½x12

7381 A3624 15r multi .95 .45
7382 A3624 15r multi .95 .45

Perf. 11¼

7383 A3625 15r multi .95 .45
7384 A3625 15r multi .95 .45
Nos. 7379-7384 (6) 5.70 2.70

Gleb E. Kotelnikov (1872-1944), Inventor of Packable Parachute — A3626

2012, Aug. 2 *Perf. 12½x12*
7385 A3626 13r multi .85 .40

Friedrich A. Tsander (1887-1933), Rocketry Pioneer — A3627

2012, Aug. 9 **Litho.**
7386 A3627 9.20r multi .60 .30

Russian Air Force, Cent. — A3628

2012, Aug. 10 *Perf. 13½*
7387 A3628 15r multi .95 .45

Souvenir Sheet

Rostov, 1150th Anniv. — A3629

2012, Aug. 20 *Perf. 11¾*
7388 A3629 30r multi 1.90 .95

Souvenir Sheet

Cossacks — A3630

No. 7389: a, Enisei Cossacks (woman touching horse). b, Orenburg Cossacks (woman seated). c, Ussuriisk Cossacks (man on horse).

2012, Aug. 22 *Perf. 12x12¼*
7389 A3630 15r Sheet of 3, #a-c 3.00 1.50

Souvenir Sheet

War of 1812, Bicent. — A3631

2012, Aug. 27 *Perf. 12*
7390 A3631 50r multi 3.25 1.60

Souvenir Sheet

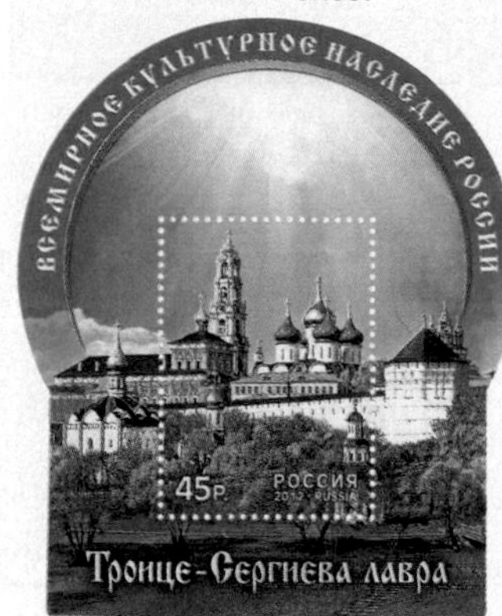

Trinity Monastery of St. Sergius — A3632

2012, Aug. 30 *Perf. 12x12¼*
7391 A3632 45r multi 3.00 1.50

Asia-Pacific Economic Cooperation Summit, Vladivostok — A3633

2012, Aug. 31 *Perf. 13½*
7392 A3633 13r multi .85 .40

A booklet containing one pane of two No. 7392 was printed in a limited edition.

Souvenir Sheet

On a Visit, Painting by Abram E. Arkhipov (1862-1930) — A3634

2012, Sept. 7 *Perf. 12x12½*
7393 A3634 50r multi 3.25 1.60

Lawyers A3635

Designs: No. 7394, 15r, Gavrila R. Derzhavin (1741-1816). No. 7395, 15r, Mikhail M. Speransky (1772-1839). No. 7396, 15r, Anatoly F. Koni (1844-1927).

2012, Sept. 7 *Perf. 11½*
7394-7396 A3635 Set of 3 3.00 1.50

Nos. 7394-7396 each were printed in sheets of 8 + label. See Nos. 7499-7500, 7588-7590, 7629, 7702-7704.

Fort Ross, Russian Outpost on California Coast, 200th Anniv. — A3636

2012, Sept. 11 *Perf. 12x12¼*
7397 A3636 13r multi .85 .40

Quick Response Code and Emblem of 2014 Winter Olympics, Sochi A3637

Serpentine Die Cut 10

2012, Sept. 18 **Self-Adhesive**
7398 A3637 25r multi 1.60 .80

Russian Statehood (Founding of Rurik Dynasty), 1150th Anniv. — A3638

2012, Sept. 19 *Perf. 12x11¼*
7399 A3638 10r multi .65 .30

Vologda Region Costumes A3639

2012, Sept. 21 *Perf. 11½x12*
7400 A3639 15r multi 1.00 .50

Souvenir Sheet

Russian Railways, 175th Anniv. — A3640

2012, Sept. 30 *Perf. 11¾*
7401 A3640 50r multi 3.25 1.60

North Shipyard, Saint Petersburg, Cent. A3641

2012, Oct. 1 *Perf. 11¼*
7402 A3641 15r multi 1.00 .50

Souvenir Sheet

Completion of Gas Pipeline Between Vyborg and Greifswald, Germany — A3642

2012, Oct. 5 *Perf. 12*
7403 A3642 40r multi 2.60 1.40

Border Guards, 500th Anniv. A3643

2012, Oct. 10 *Perf. 12¼x12*
7404 A3643 13r multi .85 .40

No. 7404 was printed in sheets of 11 + 4 labels.

Sports of the 2014 Winter Olympics, Sochi A3644

Designs: No. 7405, 25r, Freestyle skiing. No. 7406, 25r, Alpine (downhill) skiing. No. 7407, 25r, Snowboarding. No. 7408, 25r, Skeleton. No. 7409, 25r, Luge. No. 7410, 25r, Speed skating.

Litho. & Embossed

2012, Oct. 19 *Perf. 11¼*
7405-7410 A3644 Set of 6 9.50 4.75
7405a Dated "2014" at right 1.40 .70
7406a Dated "2014" at right 1.40 .70
7407a Dated "2014" at right 1.40 .70
7408a Dated "2014" at right 1.40 .70
7409a Dated "2014" at right 1.40 .70

7409b	Booklet pane of 3, #7309a, 7408a, 7409a	6.75	—
7410a	Dated "2014" at right	1.40	.70

Nos. 7405-7410 each were printed in sheets of 8 + central label.

Issued: Nos. 7405a, 7406a, 7407a, 7408a, 7409a, 7409b, 7410a, 1/24/14.

Souvenir Sheet

Restoration of National Unity After "Time of Troubles," 400th Anniv. — A3645

2012, Nov. 2 Litho. ***Perf. 12x12½***
7411 A3645 40r multi 2.60 1.40

A3646

A3647

A3648

Cast Iron Moldings From Kasli — A3649

Litho. & Thermography

2012, Nov. 15

7412	A3646	20r blk & green	1.40	.70
7413	A3647	20r blk & blue	1.40	.70
7414	A3648	20r blk & rose brn	1.40	.70
7415	A3649	20r blk & lilac	1.40	.70
		Nos. 7412-7415 (4)	5.60	2.80

Nos. 7412-7415 each were printed in sheets of 4.

Souvenir Sheets

Moscow Coat of Arms — A3650

Saint Petersburg Coat of Arms — A3651

Litho. & Embossed

2012, Nov. 30 ***Perf. 12***

7416	A3650	50r multi	3.25	1.60
7417	A3651	50r multi	3.25	1.60

Russian Animated Films — A3652

No. 7418: a, Winnie the Pooh (Winnie, Piglet with umbrella, bees). b, Mowgli (Mowgli, with wolf, bear and panther). c, A Kid and Karlson (Man, boy sitting in chair, cat and dog). d, Vovka in the Far-Away Kingdom (boy sitting, two men in polka-dot clothing).

2012, Dec. 3 Litho. ***Perf. 12x12¼***
7418 A3652 10r Block of 4, #a-d 2.60 1.40

New Year 2013 — A3653

2012, Dec. 3 ***Perf. 11¼***
7419 A3653 13r blue .85 .40

Souvenir Sheet

Konstantin Stanislavsky (1863-1938), Theater Director — A3654

2013, Jan. 17 ***Perf.***
7420 A3654 50r multi 3.50 1.75

Georgy Flyorov (1913-90), Nuclear Physicist A3655

2013, Jan. 21 ***Perf. 12¼x12***
7421 A3655 15r multi 1.00 .50

Adoption of name of Flevorium (in honor of Flyorov) for element 114.

Rams — A3656

No. 7422: a, Ovis ammon. b, Capra caucasica. c, Capra aegagrus. d, Ovis nivicola.

2013, Jan. 30 ***Perf. 11½***
7422 A3656 15r Block or strip of 4, #a-d 4.00 2.00

Miniature Sheet

Towns of Military Glory — A3657

No. 7423 — City names at top: a, Arkhangelsk (11 letters in city name, airplanes, artillery and ships). b, Bryansk (6 letters in city name, airplanes, mortars on tripods, and trucks). c, Volokolamsk (11 letters in city name, biplanes, cannons, and tanks). d, Kalach-na-Donu (hyphenated city name, airplanes and tanks). e, Kozelsk (8 letters in city name, biplanes, cannons, and armored locomotives). f, Nalchik (7 letters in city name, mortars and artillery).

Litho. With Foil Application

2013, Jan. 30
7423 A3657 15r Sheet of 6, #a-f 6.00 3.00

Penza, 350th Anniv. — A3658

2013, Feb. 8 Litho. ***Perf. 12x12¼***
7424 A3658 15r multi 1.00 .50

Russian Orders — A3659

Designs: No. 7425, 25r, Order of Suvorov (name at top on one line). No. 7426, 25r, Order of Alexander Nevsky (name at top on two lines). No. 7427, 25r, Order of St. Catherine the Great (name at top on three lines).

Litho. & Embossed

2013, Feb. 18 ***Perf. 11¾***
7425-7427 A3659 Set of 3 5.00 2.50

Nos. 7425-7427 each were printed in sheets of 7 + label.

Alexander I. Pokryshkin (1913-85), Soviet Air Force Marshal — A3660

2013, Feb. 22 Litho. ***Perf. 12½x12***
7428 A3660 15r multi 1.00 .50

No. 7428 was printed in sheets of 10 + central label.

Military Heroes A3661

Designs: No. 7429, 15r, Nikolai S. Maidanov (1956-2000). No. 7430, 15r, Valery I. Shkurny (1959-2000). No. 7431, 15r, Evgeny N. Chernyshev (1963-2010). No. 7432, 15r, Oleg G. Ilyin (1967-2004). No. 7433, 15r, Yuri A. Dmitriev (1978-2002).

2013, Feb. 22
7429-7433 A3661 Set of 5 5.00 2.50

Nos. 7429-7433 each were printed in sheets of 5 + label.

Souvenir Sheet

Uvs Nuur Basin UNESCO World Heritage Site — A3662

2013, Feb. 27
7434 A3662 45r multi 3.00 1.50

A gritty substance was applied to portions of the design.

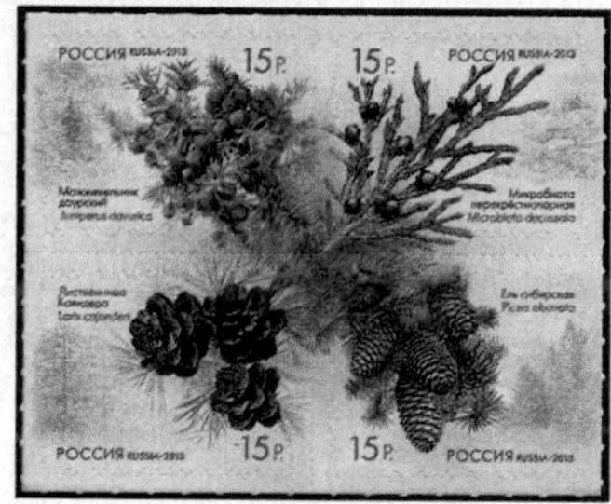

Conifers — A3663

No. 7435: a, Juniperus davurica. b, Microbiota decussata. c, Larix cajanderi. d, Picea obovata.

2013, Mar. 4 ***Serpentine Die Cut 11***
Self-Adhesive
7435 A3663 15r Block of 4, #a-d 4.00 2.00

Souvenir Sheet

General Mikhail D. Skobolev on Horse, by Nikolai D. Dmitriev-Orenburgsky — A3664

2013, Mar. 5 ***Perf. 12x12½***
7436 A3664 35r multi 2.25 1.10

Russo-Turkish War, 135th anniv. See Bulgaria No. 4626.

Viktor S. Chernomyrdin (1938-2010), Prime Minister — A3665

2013, Mar. 14 ***Perf. 12½x12***
7437 A3665 15r multi .95 .50

Printed in sheets of 14 + label.

Obukhov State Plant, St. Petersburg, 150th Anniv. A3666

2013, Mar. 26 ***Perf. 11¼***
7438 A3666 15r multi .95 .50

A booklet containing a pane containing one No. 7438 was printed in limited quantities.

Diplomatic Relations Between Russia and Algeria, 50th Anniv. — A3667

2013, Apr. 1 ***Perf. 12½x12***
7439 A3667 10r multi .65 .30

Europa — A3668

2013, Apr. 26 ***Perf. 13½***
7440 A3668 15r multi 1.00 .50

Winter Palace — A3669

Admiralty and St. Isaac's Cathedral — A3670

Old Stock Exchange, Vasilyevsky Island — A3671

2013, Apr. 26 ***Perf. 12x12¼***
7441 Horiz. strip of 3 3.00 1.50
a. A3669 10r multi .65 .30
b. A3670 15r multi .95 .50
c. A3671 20r multi 1.40 .70

Historic Center of St. Petersburg UNESCO World Heritage Site.

Recipients of Order of St. Andrew Type of 2011

Design: Order of St. Andrew and Heidar Aliyev (1923-2003), Pres. of Azerbaijan.

2013, May 6 ***Perf. 12x11¼***
7442 A3560 15r multi .95 .50

No. 7442 was printed in sheets of 11 + label. Compare with No. 7457. See Azerbaijan No. 1022.

World War II Ships — A3672

Designs: 10r, Mine sweeper "Mina." 12r, Escort ship "Metel." 15r, Armored boat "BKA-75." 20r, Gunboat "Usyskin."

2013, May 8 ***Perf. 13½***
7443-7446 A3672 Set of 4 3.75 1.90
7446a Sheet of 8, 2 each #7443-7446 7.50 4.00

A booklet containing panes of one of each of the stamps was produced in limited quantities.

Souvenir Sheet

Alexandrovskaya Sloboda, 500th Anniv. — A3673

2013, May 18 ***Perf. 12x12½***
7447 A3673 50r multi 3.25 1.60

Souvenir Sheet

Mission of Saints Cyril and Methodius to Slavic Lands, 1150th Anniv. — A3674

2013, May 24 ***Perf. 12¼x12***
7448 A3674 40r multi 2.50 1.25

Scientific Research Ship "Vyacheslav Tikhonov" — A3675

Oil Tanker "Timofey Guzhenko" — A3676

2013, June 5 ***Perf. 12x11¾***
7449 A3675 14.25r multi .90 .45
7450 A3676 14.25r multi .90 .45

Nos. 7449-7450 each were printed in sheets of 8 + label.

A3677

Modern Art — A3678

Designs: No. 7451, On the Trubezh River, by V. P. Polotnov, 2008. No. 7452, Indian Summer, by D. A. Belyukin, 2003. No. 7453, The Girl and the City, by A. A. Lubavin, 2005.

2013, June 17 ***Perf. 11¼x12***
7451 A3677 15r multi .95 .45

Perf. 11¼
7452 A3678 15r multi .95 .45
7453 A3678 15r multi .95 .45
Nos. 7451-7453 (3) 2.85 1.35

Arms of Aleksandrov A3679

Arms of Kazan A3680

2013, June 18 ***Perf. 11¾x12¼***
7454 A3679 10r multi .65 .30
Complete booklet, 10 #7454 6.50
Complete booklet, 20 #7454 13.00
7455 A3680 14.25r multi .90 .45
Complete booklet, 10 #7455 9.00
Complete booklet, 20 #7455 18.00

Souvenir Sheet

27th Summer Universiade, Kazan — A3681

2013, June 25 ***Perf. 12x12¼***
7456 A3681 25r multi 1.60 .80

A booklet containing one example of No. 7456 sold for 255r.

Order of St. Andrew and Rasul G. Gamzatov (1923-2003), Poet — A3682

2013, June 28 *Perf. 12x11½*
7457 A3682 15r multi .95 .45

No. 7457 was printed in sheets of 11 + label. Compare with No. 7442.

Sports of the 2014 Winter Olympics, Sochi A3683

Designs: No. 7458, 25r, Nordic combined skiing. No. 7459, 25r, Bobsled. No. 7460, 25r, Pairs figure skating.

Litho. & Embossed

2013, June 29 *Perf. 11¼*

7458-7460	A3683	Set of 3	4.75	2.40
7458a		Dated "2014" at right	1.40	.70
7459a		Dated "2014" at right	1.40	.70
7460a		Dated "2014" at right	1.40	.70
7460b		Booklet pane of 3, #7407a, 7410a, 7460a	6.75	—

Nos. 7458-7460 each were printed in sheets of 8 + central label.
Issued: Nos. 7458a, 7459a, 7460a, 7460b, 1/24/14.

Gull and Russia No. 2753 — A3684

2013, July 5 **Litho.** *Perf. 11¾*
7461 A3684 14.25r multi .90 .45

Space flight of Valentina Tereshkova, first woman in space, 50th anniv.

Kerchief From Karabanovo — A3685

Kerchief From Trekhgorny Factory, Moscow — A3686

Kerchief From Orenburg — A3687

Shawl From Pavlovsky Posad — A3688

2013, July 5 *Perf. 11½*

7462	A3685	15r multi	.95	.45
7463	A3686	15r multi	.95	.45
7464	A3687	15r multi	.95	.45
7465	A3688	15r multi	.95	.45
		Nos. 7462-7465 (4)	3.80	1.80

Nos. 7462-7465 each were printed in sheets of 4.

Souvenir Sheet

Christianization of Russia, by V. M. Vasnetsov — A3689

2013, July 28 **Litho.** *Perf. 12*
7466 A3689 30r multi 1.90 .95

Christianization of Russia, 1025th anniv. See Belarus No. 870, Ukraine No. 930.

Souvenir Sheet

Penza Coat of Arms — A3690

2013, Aug. 2 **Litho.** *Perf. 12x12½*
7467 A3690 50r multi 3.00 1.50

MS Princess Anastasia — A3691

2013, Aug. 5 **Litho.** *Perf. 12*
7468 A3691 14.25r multi .90 .45

See Finland (Aland Islands) No. 347.

18th Intl. Track and Field Championships, Moscow — A3692

2013, Aug. 10 **Litho.** *Perf. 12¼x12*
7469 A3692 14.25r multi .90 .45

Miniature Sheet

Aircraft Designed by Andrei N. Tupolev (1888-1972) — A3693

No. 7470: a, 10r, Tu-2. b, 13r, Tb-7. c, 15r, Tu-16. d, 17r, Tu-22M3. e, 20r, Tu-95.

2013, Aug. 13 **Litho.** *Perf. 12¼x12*
7470 A3693 Sheet of 5, #a-e, + label 4.75 2.10

Kolomna Locomotive Works, 150th Anniv. A3694

2013, Aug. 15 **Litho.** *Perf. 11¼*
7471 A3694 15r multi .95 .45

Communications Satellite, Arrows and Map of Russia — A3695

2013, Aug. 21 **Litho.** *Perf. 12¼x12*
7472 A3695 14.25r multi .90 .45

Paintings by Ivan Myasoyedov (Eugen Zotow) (1881-1953) — A3696

No. 7473: a, Voyage of the Argonauts, 1909. b, Silum, 1945.

2013, Sept. 2 **Litho.** *Perf. 12x11¼*
7473 A3696 15r Pair, #a-b 1.90 .95

Printed in sheets of 10 containing 5 each #7473a-7473b, + 2 labels. See Liechtenstein No. 1592.

Souvenir Sheet

Discovery of Severnaya Zemlya Archipelago, Cent. — A3697

No. 7474: a, Icebreaker Vaigach (ship facing left). b, Boris A. Vilkitsky (1885-1961), hydrographer and expedition leader, vert. c, Icebreaker Taimyr (ship facing right).

Perf. 12x12¼, 12¼x12 (#7474b)
2013, Sept. 4 **Litho.**
7474 A3697 15r Sheet of 3, #a-c 2.75 1.40

18th Conference of Intl. Association of Prosecutors, Moscow — A3698

2013, Sept. 6 **Litho.** *Perf. 12x12¼*
7475 A3698 15r multi .95 .45

Souvenir Sheet

Smolensk, 1150th Anniv. — A3699

2013, Sept. 21 **Litho.** *Perf. 12¼x12*
7476 A3699 50r multi 3.25 1.60

Souvenir Sheet

Olympic Flame — A3700

2013, Oct. 7 **Litho.** *Perf. 12*
7477 A3700 50r multi 3.25 1.60

2014 Winter Olympics, Sochi.

Recipients of the Order of St. Andrew Type of 2012

Design: Order of St. Andrew and Sergey V. Mikhalkov (1913-2009), writer.

2013, Oct. 9 **Litho.** *Perf. 12x11¼*
7478 A3560 15r multi .95 .45

No. 7478 was printed in sheets of 11 + label.

Souvenir Sheet

Coat of Arms of Yaroslavl — A3701

2013, Oct. 11 Litho. *Perf. 12x12½*

7479 A3701 50r multi 3.25 1.60

Souvenir Sheet

Battle of Leipzig, by Carl Rechlin — A3702

2013, Oct. 19 Litho. *Perf. 12x12½*

7480 A3702 50r multi 3.25 1.60

Battle of Leipzig, 200th anniv.

Modern Art — A3703

Designs: No. 7481, 15r, Monument to A. I. Pokryshkin, by M. V. Pereyaslavets, 2005. No. 7482, 15r, Bouquet, by V. M. Malyi, 2005. No. 7483, 15r, Kerosene, by A. L. Bobykin, 2012, horiz.

Perf. 11½x12, 12x11½

2013, Oct. 25 Litho.

7481-7483 A3703 Set of 3 2.75 1.40

Sports of the 2014 Winter Olympics, Sochi A3704

Designs: No. 7484, Biathlon. No. 7485, Curling. No. 7486, Ice hockey.

Litho. & Embossed

2013-14 *Perf. 11¼*

Dated "2013" at Right

7484 A3704 25r multi 1.50 .75
a. Dated "2014" at right 1.40 .70
b. Booklet pane of 3, #7406a, 7459a, 7484a 6.75 —

7485 A3704 25r multi 1.50 .75
a. Dated "2014" at right 1.40 .70
b. Booklet pane of 3, #7308a, 7458a, 7485a 6.75 —

7486 A3704 25r multi 1.50 .75
a. Dated "2014" at right 1.40 .70
b. Sheet of 15, #7308a, 7309a, 7310a, 7405a, 7406a, 7407a, 7408a, 7409a, 7410a, 7458a, 7459a, 7460a, 7484a, 7485a, 7486a, + label 21.50 10.50
c. Booklet pane of 3, #7310a, 7405a, 7486a 6.75 —

Complete booklet, #7409b, 7460b, 7484b, 7485b, 7486c 34.00
Nos. 7484-7486 (3) 4.50 2.25

Issued: Nos. 7484-7486, 11/1; Nos. 7484a, 7484b, 7485a, 7485b, 7486a, 7486b, 7486c, 1/24/14.

Nos. 7484-7486 were each printed in sheets of 8 + central label. Complete booklet sold for 595r.

Sambo, 75th Anniv. — A3705

2013, Nov. 1 Litho. *Perf. 12x12½*

7487 A3705 10r multi .60 .30

Police Uniforms A3706

Designs: No. 7488, 15r, Dragoon and police officer, 1718. No. 7489, 15r, Police officer and captain, 19th cent. No. 7490, 15r, Traffic policeman and militia foreman, 1934. No. 7491, 15r, Police lieutenant and major general, 2012.

2013, Nov. 8 Litho. *Perf. 11¾*

7488-7491 A3706 Set of 4 3.75 1.90
7491a Souvenir sheet of 8, 2 each #7488-7491 7.50 3.75

Miniature Sheets

A3707

Sports Legends — A3708

No. 7492: a, Yevgeny Grishin (1931-2005), speed skater. b, Lyudmila Pakhomova (1946-86), ice dancer. c, Vladimir Melanin (1933-94), biathlete. d, Alexander Ragulin (1941-2004), ice hockey player. e, Anatoly Firsov (1941-2000), ice hockey player.

No. 7493: a, Klavdiya Boyarskikh (1939-2009), cross-country skier. b, Vsevolod Bobrov (1922-79), soccer and ice hockey player. c, Tatyana Averina (1950-2001), speed skater. d, Pierre de Coubertin (1863-1937), founder of the Modern Olympic Games. e, Ludwig Guttman (1899-1980), founder of the Paralympic Games.

2013 Litho. *Perf. 11¾*

7492 A3707 15r Sheet of 5, #a-e 4.75 2.40
7493 A3708 15r Sheet of 5, #a-e 4.75 2.40

2014 Winter Olympics, Sochi. Issued: No. 7492, 11/15; No. 7493, 12/14.

New Year 2014 A3709

Mascots of the 2014 Winter Olympics, Sochi: No. 7494, 20r, Leopard. No. 7495, 20r, Hare. No. 7496, 20r, Polar Bear. No. 7497, 20r, Snowflake and Ray of Light.

Serpentine Die Cut 11

2013, Nov. 29 Litho.

Self-Adhesive

7494-7497 A3709 Set of 4 5.00 2.50
7497a Sheet of 8, 2 each #7494-7497 10.00

Miniature Sheet

Venues of the 2014 Winter Olympics and Paralympics, Sochi — A3710

No. 7498: a, Crowd outside of Fisht Olympic Stadium. b, Biathletes at Laura Biathlon and Ski Complex. c, Ski jumps at Russki Gorki Jumping Center. d, Crowds and flagpoles outside of Bolshoi Ice Dome. e, Iceberg Skating Palace at night. f, Photographer and crowd outside of Shayba Arena.

2013, Nov. 30 Litho. *Perf. 11¾*

7498 A3710 20r Sheet of 6, #a-f 7.50 3.75

Lawyers Type of 2012

Designs: No. 7499, 15r, Alexander N. Radishchev (1749-1802). No. 7500, 15r, Fedor N. Plevako (1842-1909).

2013, Dec. 3 Litho. *Perf. 11½*

7499-7500 A3635 Set of 2 1.90 .95

Nos. 7499-7500 each were printed in sheets of 8 + label.

Automobiles A3711

No. 7501: a, ZiL-111B. b, Sunbeam Alpine.

2013, Dec. 5 Litho. *Perf. 11½*

7501 A3711 15r Pair, #a-b 1.90 .95

Printed in sheets containing four each #7501a-7501b + central label. See Monaco No. 2740.

State Duma, 20th Anniv. — A3712

Federation Council, 20th Anniv. — A3713

Constitution, 20th Anniv. — A3714

2013, Dec. 12 Litho. *Perf. 11½*

7502 A3712 20r multi 1.25 .60
7503 A3713 20r multi 1.25 .60

Souvenir Sheet

Perf. 12

7504 A3714 50r multi 3.25 1.60

Vladimir A. Steklov (1864-1926), Mathematician — A3715

2014, Jan. 9 Litho. *Perf. 12½x12*

7505 A3715 15r multi .85 .45

Order of Zhukov A3716

Order of Kutuzov A3717

Order of Ushakov A3718

Litho. & Embossed

2014, Jan. 31 *Perf. 11¾*

7506 A3716 25r multi 1.40 .70
7507 A3717 25r multi 1.40 .70
7508 A3718 25r multi 1.40 .70
Nos. 7506-7508 (3) 4.20 2.10

Nos. 7506-7508 each were printed in sheets of 7 + label.

Souvenir Sheet

Medals of the 2014 Winter Olympics, Sochi — A3719

No. 7509: a, 25r, Bronze medal. b, 50r, Silver medal. c, 75r, Gold medal, vert.

Perf. 12x12¼, 12¼x12 (75r)

2014, Feb. 7 Litho. & Embossed

7509 A3719 Sheet of 3, #a-c 8.50 4.25
d. As #7509, overprinted with Cyrillic text in red in sheet margin 8.50 4.25

Issued: No. 7509d, 4/25. Overprint on No. 7509d gives medal count of Russian team (13 gold, 11 silver, 9 bronze) at 2014 Winter Olympics.

Souvenir Sheet

Moscow Zoo, 150th Anniv. — A3720

2014, Feb. 13 Litho. *Perf. 12*

7510 A3720 40r multi 2.25 1.10

Military Heroes A3721

Designs: No. 7511, 15r, Aleksandr V. Perov (1975-2004) (shown). No. 7512, 15r, Andrei A. Turkin (1975-2004). No. 7513, 15r, Andrei N. Rozhkov (1961-98). No. 7514, 15r, Viktor S. Chechviy (1960-99). No. 7515, 15r, Mikhail Y. Malofeev (1956-2000).

2014, Feb. 21 Litho. *Perf. 12½x12*

7511-7515 A3721 Set of 5 4.25 2.10

Nos. 7511-7515 were each printed in sheets of 5 + label.

Souvenir Sheet

Medals of the 2014 Winter Paralympics, Sochi — A3722

No. 7516: a, 25r, Bronze medal. b, 50r, Silver medal. c, 75r, Gold medal, vert.

Perf. 12x12¼, 12¼x12 (75r)

2014 Litho. & Embossed

7516 A3722 Sheet of 3, #a-c 8.50 4.25
d. As #7516, overprinted with Cyrillic text in red in sheet margin 8.50 4.25

Issued: No. 7516, 3/7; No. 7516d, 4/25. Overprint on No. 7516d gives medal count of Russian team (30 gold, 28 silver, 22 bronze) at 2014 Winter Paralympics.

Souvenir Sheet

Summer Garden, by Aleksei Mikhailovich Gritsai (1914-98) — A3723

2014, Mar. 7 Litho. *Perf. 12x12¼*

7517 A3723 50r multi 3.00 1.50

Flowers — A3724

No. 7518: a, Chamaenerion angustifolium. b, Lupinus polyphyllus. c, Cichorium intybus. d, Matricaria recutita.

2014, Mar. 14 Litho. *Perf. 11¼*

7518 A3724 15r Block of 4, #a-d 3.50 1.75

Mark L. Gallai (1914-98), Test Pilot, and M-3 Bomber A3725

2014, Mar. 28 Litho. *Perf. 12½x12*

7519 A3725 15r multi .85 .40

No. 7519 was printed in sheets of 10 + central label.

Souvenir Sheet

Liberation of Russia, Belarus and Ukraine From Nazi Occupation, 70th Anniv. — A3726

2014, Apr. 18 Litho. *Perf. 12x12¼*

7520 A3726 50r multi 3.00 1.50

See Belarus No. 898.

Ekaterina I. Zelenko (1916-41), World War II Pilot — A3727

Boris I. Kovzan (1922-85), World War II Pilot — A3728

Alexei S. Khlobystov (1918-43), World War II Pilot — A3729

Petr V. Eremeyev (1911-41), World War II Pilot — A3730

2014, Apr. 18 Litho. *Perf. 13½*

7521 A3727 15r multi .85 .40
7522 A3728 15r multi .85 .40
7523 A3729 15r multi .85 .40
7524 A3730 15r multi .85 .40
a. Sheet of 8, 2 each #7521-7524 7.00 3.50
Nos. 7521-7524 (4) 3.40 1.60

Nos. 7521-7524 were each printed in sheets of 7 + label.

World War II Artillery — A3731

Designs: 12r, 53-K 45-mm anti-tank gun. 15r, ZIS-3 76-mm divisional gun. 18r, 52-K 85-mm anti-aircraft gun. 20r, M-30 122-mm howitzer.

2014, Apr. 25 Litho. *Perf. 13½*

7525-7528 A3731 Set of 4 3.75 1.90
7528a Sheet of 8, 2 each #7525-7528 7.50 4.00

Musicians Playing Balalaika and Accordion A3732

2014, Apr. 30 Litho. *Perf. 12*

7529 A3732 18r multi 1.00 .50

Europa.

Yakov B. Zeldovich (1914-87), Physicist A3733

2014, May 5 Litho. *Perf. 12¼x12*

7530 A3733 15r multi .85 .45

Clock Towers and Clocks — A3734

No. 7531: a, 15r, Zytglogge, Bern, Switzerland. b, 20r, Kazansky Tower, Moscow.

2014, May 21 Litho. *Perf. 11¼*

7531 A3734 Pair, #a-b 2.00 1.00

No. 7531 was printed in sheets of 8 (4 of each stamp) + central label. See Switzerland Nos. 1528-1529.

Concord Tower, Magas — A3735

2014, June 4 Litho. *Perf. 11¼*

7532 A3735 15r multi .90 .45

Souvenir Sheet

St. Petersburg Post Office, 300th Anniv. — A3736

2014, June 10 **Litho.** ***Perf.***
7533 A3736 50r multi 3.00 1.50

Crimean Republic A3737

Sevastopol A3738

2014 **Litho.** ***Perf. 12x12¼***
7534 A3737 15r multi .90 .45
Perf. 12¼x12
7535 A3738 15r multi .90 .45

Issued: No. 7534, 6/19; No. 7535, 6/20.

Souvenir Sheet

Hermitage Museum, 250th Anniv. — A3739

2014, June 20 **Litho.** ***Perf. 11¾***
7536 A3739 50r multi 3.00 1.50

Arms of Sergiev Posad — A3740

Perf. 11¾x12¼
2014, June 24 **Litho.**
7537 A3740 10.50r multi .65 .30
Complete booklet, 10 #7537 6.50
Complete booklet, 20 #7537 13.00

Topol-M Missile Launcher and Barricades Manufacturing Plant — A3741

2014, June 26 **Litho.** ***Perf. 11¼***
7538 A3741 15r multi .90 .45

Barricades Manufacturing Plant, Volgograd, cent.

Vladimir N. Chelomey (1914-84). Missile Engineer A3742

2014, June 27 **Litho.** ***Perf. 12¼x12***
7539 A3742 15r multi .90 .45

Tuva as Part of Russia, Cent. — A3743

2014, June 27 **Litho.** ***Perf. 11¼***
7540 A3743 15r multi .90 .45

Souvenir Sheet

Approval of Construction of Baikal-Amur Mainline Railway, 40th Anniv. — A3744

2014, July 2 **Litho.** ***Perf. 12***
7541 A3744 40r multi 2.40 1.25

Diplomatic Relations Between Russia and Bulgaria, 135th Anniv. A3745

2014, July 7 **Litho.** ***Perf. 12¼x12***
7542 A3745 15r multi .85 .40

See Bulgaria No. 4684.

Hero of Labor of the Russian Federation Medal — A3746

Medal for the Defense of Leningrad A3747

Medal for the Defense of Sevastopol A3748

Medal for the Defense of Stalingrad A3749

Medal for the Defense of Moscow A3750

Litho. & Embossed

2014, July 7 ***Perf. 11¾***

7543	A3746	25r multi	1.40	.70
7544	A3747	25r multi	1.40	.70
7545	A3748	25r multi	1.40	.70
7546	A3749	25r multi	1.40	.70
7547	A3750	25r multi	1.40	.70
		Nos. 7543-7547 (5)	7.00	3.50

Nos. 7543-7547 were each printed in sheets of 7 + label.

Hugo Chávez (1954-2013), President of Venezuela A3751

2014, July 28 **Litho.** ***Perf. 12x12¼***
7548 A3751 15r multi .85 .40

World War I, Cent. — A3752

Designs: No. 7549, 20r, Soldiers charging with rifles with bayonets, map of battle for Osovets Fortress. No. 7550, 20r, Soldiers and cannon, map of battle for Erzum Fortress. No. 7551, 20r, General Aleksei A. Brusilov (seated) and his officers, map of Brusilov Offensive. No. 7552, 20r, Russian Expeditionary Corps in France (with flag), map of Europe and Asia.

2014, July 31 **Litho.** ***Perf. 12***
7549-7552 A3752 Set of 4 4.50 2.25

Nos. 7549-7552 were each printed in sheets of 11 + label. A booklet containing panes of one of each of the stamps was produced in limited quantities.

Souvenir Sheet

Battle of Gangut, 300th Anniv. — A3753

2014, Aug. 1 **Litho.** ***Perf. 11¾***
7553 A3753 50r multi 2.75 1.40

Wild Cats — A3754

No. 7554: a, 15r, Otocolobus manul. b, 16r, Felis silvestris. c, 17r, Prionailurus bengalensis euptilurus. d, 18r, Felis chaus.

2014, Aug. 1 **Litho.** ***Perf. 13½***
7554 A3754 Block or vert. strip of 4, #a-d 3.75 1.90

See No. 7581.

Medal for the Defense of the Caucasus A3755

Medal for the Defense of Kiev — A3756

Medal for the Defense of Odessa A3757

Medal for the Defense of the Arctic — A3758

Litho. & Embossed

2014, Aug. 8 *Perf. 11¾*

7555 A3755 25r multi	1.40	.70
7556 A3756 25r multi	1.40	.70
7557 A3757 25r multi	1.40	.70
7558 A3758 25r multi	1.40	.70
Nos. 7555-7558 (4)	5.60	2.80

Nos. 7555-7558 were each printed in sheets of 7 + label.

Kyzyl, Cent. A3759

2014, Aug. 23 Litho. *Perf. 12½x12*

7559 A3759 15r multi .80 .40

Icebreaker Vitus Bering — A3760

Tugboat Sadko — A3761

2014, Aug. 26 Litho. *Perf. 12*

7560 A3760 15r multi .80 .40
7561 A3761 15r multi .80 .40

Battles of Khakhin Gol, 75th Anniv. — A3762

2014, Aug. 28 Litho. *Perf. 11½*

7562 A3762 15r multi .80 .40

See Mongolia No. 2816.

Miniature Sheet

Towns of Military Glory — A3763

No. 7563 — City names at top: a, Anapa (5 letters in city name, airplanes, guns and ships). b, Vladivostok (11 letters in city name, airplanes, trucks and ships). c, Kovrov (6 letters in city name, guns and tanks). d, Kolpino (7 letters in city name, airplanes and tanks). e, Stary Oscol (2 words in city name, airplanes, guns and tanks). f, Tikhvin (6 letters in city name, airplanes and tanks).

Litho. With Foil Application

2014, Aug. 28 *Perf. 11½*

7563 A3763 20r Sheet of 6, #a-f 6.50 3.25

Uniforms of Postal and Communications Workers — A3764

Designs: No. 7564, 15r, Clerk and postman of Yamskoi Post Office, 1671. No. 7565, 15r, Postman and official from Yamskoi Post Office, 1767. No. 7566, 15r, Official and telegraph operator, 1870. No. 7567, 15r, Postman and operator, 1950.

2014, Sept. 1 Litho. *Perf. 13½*

7564-7567 A3764 Set of 4 3.25 1.60
7567a Souvenir sheet of 8, 2 each #7564-7567 6.50 3.25

Printing in Russia, 450th Anniv. — A3765

2014, Sept. 3 Litho. *Perf. 12x11¼*

7568 A3765 15r multi .75 .40

Souvenir Sheet

Kolomenskoye Church of the Ascenscion UNESCO World Heritage Site — A3766

2014, Sept. 5 Litho. *Perf. 12x12½*

7569 A3766 45r multi 2.25 1.10

Souvenir Sheet

St. Sergius of Radonezh (1314-92), Monk — A3767

Litho. & Silk-Screened

2014, Sept. 16 *Perf. 12*

7570 A3767 70r multi 3.50 1.75

Special Communications Center and Vehicles — A3768

2014, Sept. 18 Litho. *Perf. 12½x12*

7571 A3768 18r multi .95 .45

Souvenir Sheet

Coat of Arms of City of Krasnodar — A3769

2014, Sept. 25 Litho. *Perf. 12x12½*

7572 A3769 50r multi 2.50 1.25

Ice Hockey — A3770

2014, Oct. 7 Litho. *Perf. 13½*

7573 A3770 20r multi .85 .45

Formula 1 Race Cars — A3771

2014, Oct. 12 Litho. *Perf. 13½*

7574 A3771 15r multi .65 .30

2014 Sochi Grand Prix.

Birds — A3772

2014, Oct. 12 Litho. *Perf. 12½x12*

7575 A3772 Horiz. pair 1.50 .70
a. 15r Accipiter nisus .65 .30
b. 18r Pandion haliaetus .80 .40

See North Korea No.

Souvenir Sheet

Mikhail Lermontov (1814-41), Writer — A3773

2014, Oct. 15 Litho. *Perf. 12½x12*

7576 A3773 50r multi 2.25 1.10

Arms of Sochi — A3774

2014, Oct. 21 Litho. *Perf. 11¾x12¼*
7577 A3774 15r multi .65 .30
Complete booklet, 10 #7577 6.50
Complete booklet, 20 #7577 13.00

Recipients of the Order of St. Andrew Type of 2011

Design: Order of St. Andrew and General Mikhail Kalashnikov (1919-2013), arms designer.

2014, Oct. 24 Litho. *Perf. 12x11¼*
7578 A3560 15r multi .65 .30

No. 7578 was printed in sheets of 11 + label.

Galina Vishnevskaya (1926-2012), Opera Singer — A3775

2014, Oct. 24 Litho. *Perf. 12½x12*
7579 A3775 15r multi .65 .30

No. 7579 was printed in sheets of 14 + label.

Souvenir Sheet

Imperial Orthodox Palestine Society — A3776

No. 7580: a, Grand Duchess Elizabeth (1864-1918), holy martyr of Russian Orthodox Church. b, Society emblem. c, Sergei Imperial Hospice, Russian Compound, Jerusalem.

2014, Oct. 29 Litho. *Perf. 12x12¼*
7580 A3776 20r Sheet of 3, #a-c 2.60 1.40

Wild Cats Type of 2014

No. 7581: a, 15r, Uncia uncia. b, 18r, Panthera pardus orientalis. c, 20r, Panthera tigris altaica.

2014, Nov. 7 Litho. *Perf. 11¾*
7581 A3754 Horiz. strip of 3, #a-c 2.40 1.25

Georgi N. Babakin (1914-71), Designer of Spacecraft A3777

2014, Nov. 13 Litho. *Perf. 12½x12*
7582 A3777 15r multi .55 .30

Souvenir Sheet

2014 World Cup Soccer Championships, Brazil — A3778

2014, Nov. 25 Litho. *Perf.*
7583 A3778 50r multi 1.90 .95

Kerzhensky Nature Reserve — A3779

2014, Nov. 25 Litho. *Perf. 12x12¼*
7584 A3779 15r multi .55 .30

Carved Wooden Door Trim From Nizhny Novgorod — A3780

Carved Wooden Door Trim From Pskov — A3781

Nos. 7585 and 7586: a, Denomination at left. b, Denomination at right.

2014, Nov. 28 Litho. *Perf. 11½*
7585 A3780 20r Horiz. pair, #a-b 1.50 .75
7586 A3781 20r Horiz. pair, #a-b 1.50 .75

A varnish applied to parts of the vignette has a rough feel.

Souvenir Sheet

Coat of Arms of City of Tver — A3782

2014, Dec. 2 Litho. *Perf. 12x12½*
7587 A3782 50r multi 1.90 .95

Lawyers Type of 2012

Designs: No. 7588, 15r, Count Pavel I. Yaguzhinsky (1683-1736). No. 7589, 15r, Fedor F. Martens (1845-1909). No. 7590, 15r, Sergei A. Muromtsev (1850-1910).

2014, Dec. 3 Litho. *Perf. 11½*
7588-7590 A3635 Set of 3 1.60 .80

Nos. 7588-7590 were each printed in sheets of 8 + label.

Modern Art — A3783

Designs: No. 7591, 15r, Peresvet's Victory, by Pavel V. Ryzhenko, 2005. No. 7592, 15r, Lilacs, by Polina V. Mineeva, 2010. No. 7593, 15r, Pskov Kremlin, by Sergei N. Troshin, 2011. No. 7594, 15r, Spring in Kolomenskoe, by Ivan Krivshinko, 2002 (50x38mm). No. 7595, 15r, River Vorya Near Radonezh, by Aleksandr K. Sytov, 2005 (50x38mm). No. 7596, 15r, Statue of Alexander Nevsky, by Alexei I. Ignatov, 2013 (33x65mm).

Perf. 11¼, 12x11½ (#7594-7595), 13½ (#7596)

2014, Dec. 12 Litho.
7591-7596 A3783 Set of 6 3.25 1.60

New Year 2015 — A3784

2014, Dec. 12 Litho. *Perf. 12x11½*
7597 A3784 15r multi .55 .25

Europa A3785

2015, Jan. 16 Litho. *Perf. 11½x12*
7598 A3785 23r multi .70 .35

Souvenir Sheet

October, Domotkanovo, by Valentin A. Serov (1865-1911) — A3786

2015, Jan. 22 Litho. *Perf. 12½x12*
7599 A3786 50r multi 1.50 .75

Postcrossing A3787

Serpentine Die Cut 10

2015, Jan. 27 Litho.

Self-Adhesive

7600 A3787 23r multi .70 .35

Souvenir Sheet

Lena Pillars Nature Park UNESCO World Heritage Site — A3788

2015, Feb. 10 Litho. *Perf. 12½x12*
7601 A3788 50r multi 1.60 .80

Sergei P. Kapitsa (1928-2012), Physicist and Host of Television Science Shows A3789

2015, Feb. 12 Litho. *Perf. 11½x12*
7602 A3789 15r multi .50 .25

Miniature Sheet

Towns of Military Glory — A3790

No. 7603 — City names at top: a, Lomonosov (9 letters in city name, trucks, tanks, ships). b, Maloyaroslavets (13 letters in city name, artillery). c, Mozhaisk (7 letters in city name, airplanes, cannons, barricades). d, Petropavlovsk-Kamchatsky (23 letters in city name, airplanes, guns, submarines). e, Taganrog (8 letters in city name, airplanes, tanks, submarines). f, Khabarovsk (9 letters in city name, airplanes, trucks, ships).

Litho. With Foil Application

2015, Feb. 15 *Perf. 11½*
7603 A3790 20r Sheet of 6, #a-f 4.00 2.00

Order of Nakhimov A3791

Order of Courage A3792

Order of Friendship A3793

Litho. & Embossed

2015, Feb. 19 *Perf. 11¾*

7604 A3791 25r multi .80 .40
7605 A3792 25r multi .80 .40
7606 A3793 25r multi .80 .40
Nos. 7604-7606 (3) 2.40 1.20

Nos. 7604-7606 were each printed in sheets of 7 + label.

Spies A3794

Designs: No. 7607, 16r, Alexander I. Galushkin (1903-42). No. 7608, 16r, Pavel M. Silaev (1916-42).

2015, Mar. 18 **Litho.** *Perf. 11½*

7607-7608 A3794 Set of 2 1.25 .60

Nos. 7607-7608 were each printed in sheets of 8 + label.

Submariners — A3795

No. 7609: a, Captain Evgeni Y. Osipov (1913-43), denomination at LR. b, Captain Alexander I. Marinesco (1913-63), denomination at LL.

2015, Mar. 19 **Litho.** *Perf. 12*

7609 Horiz. pair + central label 1.25 .60
a.-b. A3795 16r Either single .60 .30

Felix Dzerzhinsky Independent Operational Purpose Division — A3796

2015, Mar. 21 **Litho.** *Perf. 13½*

7610 A3796 17r multi .65 .30

Zemstvo Post, 150th Anniv. A3797

2015, Mar. 26 **Litho.** *Perf. 12½x12*

7611 A3797 20r multi .75 .35

Liberation of Warsaw Medal — A3798

Liberation of Prague Medal — A3799

Liberation of Belgrade Medal — A3800

Litho. & Embossed

2015, Apr. 2 *Perf. 11¾*

7612 A3798 30r multi 1.10 .55
7613 A3799 30r multi 1.10 .55
7614 A3800 30r multi 1.10 .55
Nos. 7612-7614 (3) 3.30 1.65

Nos. 7612-7614 were each printed in sheets of 7 + label.

First Spacewalk, 50th Anniv. — A3801

2015, Apr. 10 **Litho.** *Perf. 12x12½*

7615 A3801 17r multi .70 .35

Blood Donation Program — A3802

2015, Apr. 16 **Litho.** *Perf. 12x12½*

7616 A3802 17r multi .70 .35

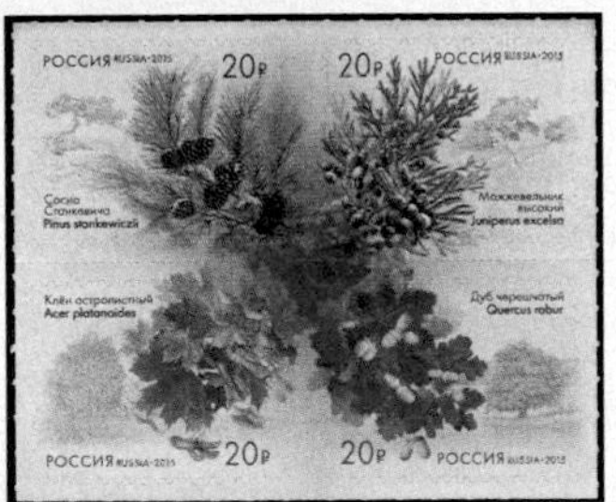

Trees — A3803

No. 7617: a, Pinus stankewiczii. b, Juniperus excelsa. c, Acer platanoides. d, Quercus robur.

Serpentine Die Cut 11

2015, Apr. 16 **Litho.**

Self-Adhesive

7617 A3803 20r Block of 4, #a-d 3.25 1.60

Russian Federation Accounting Bureau — A3804

2015, Apr. 17 **Litho.** *Perf. 12x11½*

7618 A3804 20r multi .80 .40

Penny Black, 175th Anniv. — A3805

2015, Apr. 23 **Litho.** *Perf. 12x11½*

7619 A3805 26.50r multi 1.10 .55

World War II Armored Trains — A3806

Train named: 12r, Moscow Metro. 17r, Fighter of the German Invaders. 19r, Moskvich. 27r, Kozma Minin.

2015, Apr. 30 **Litho.** *Perf. 13½*

7620-7623 A3806 Set of 4 3.00 1.50
7623a Souvenir sheet of 8, 2 each #7620-7623 6.00 3.00

A booklet containing panes of one of each of the stamps was produced in limited quantities.

Souvenir Sheet

Victory in Europe in World War II, 70th Anniv. — A3807

2015, May 5 **Litho.** *Perf. 11¾*

7624 A3807 70r multi 3.00 1.50

Liberation of Konigsberg Medal — A3808

Liberation of Vienna Medal — A3809

Liberation of Berlin Medal — A3810

Liberation of Budapest Medal — A3811

Litho. & Embossed

2015, May 5 ***Perf. 11¾***

7625 A3808 30r multi 1.25 .60
7626 A3809 30r multi 1.25 .60
7627 A3810 30r multi 1.25 .60
7628 A3811 30r multi 1.25 .60
Nos. 7625-7628 (4) 5.00 2.40

Nos. 7625-7628 were each printed in sheets of 7 + label.

Lawyers Type of 2012

Design: 17r, Roman A. Rudenko (1907-81).

2015, May 6 Litho. ***Perf. 11½***

7629 A3635 17r multicolored .70 .35

No. 7629 was printed in sheets of 8 + label.

International Telecommunication Union, 150th Anniv. — A3812

2015, May 7 Litho. ***Perf. 12½x12***

7630 A3812 17r dull blue .65 .30

Sviaz-Expocomm 2015 Intl. Telecommunications Exhibition, Moscow — A3813

2015, May 12 Litho. ***Perf. 13½***

7631 A3813 19r multi .75 .35

Eurasian Economic Union — A3814

2015, May 21 Litho. ***Perf. 12x11½***

7632 A3814 17r multi .65 .30

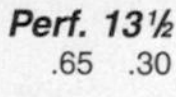

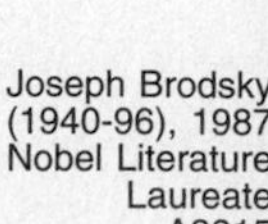

Joseph Brodsky (1940-96), 1987 Nobel Literature Laureate A3815

2015, May 22 Litho. ***Perf. 13½***

7633 A3815 17r multi .65 .30

Dogs — A3816

No. 7634: a, 16r, South Russian shepherds. b, 18r, Caucasian shepherds. c, 20r, Central Asian shepherds. d, 26.50r, Black Russian terriers.

2015, May 28 Litho. ***Perf. 13½***

7634 A3816 Block or vert. strip of 4, #a-d 3.00 1.50

Souvenir Sheet

Pyotr Ilyich Tchaikovsky (1840-93), Composer — A3817

Litho. & Engr.

2015, May 28 ***Perf. 12***

7635 A3817 150r multi 5.75 3.00

Norilsk Nickel Mining Company, 80th Anniv. — A3818

Litho. & Embossed

2015, June 2 ***Perf. 13½***

7636 A3818 26.50r multi 1.00 .50

Souvenir Sheet

Bank of Russia, 155th Anniv. — A3819

No. 7637: a, Evgeny I. Lamansky (1825-1902), bank governor. b, Russian coins. c, Bank building, Moscow.

Litho., Litho. & Embossed (#7637b)

2015, June 4 ***Perf. 12***

7637 A3819 40r Sheet of 3, #a-c 4.25 2.10

Artek International Children's Center, 90th Anniv. — A3820

2015, June 16 Litho. ***Perf. 11¼***

7638 A3820 26.50r multi .95 .45

Arms of Derbent A3821

Arms of Nizhny Novgorod A3822

Perf. 11¾x12¼

2015, June 16 Litho.

7639 A3821 12r multi .45 .25
Complete booklet, 10 #7639 4.50
Complete booklet, 20 #7639 9.00
7640 A3822 17r multi .60 .30
Complete booklet, 10 #7640 6.00
Complete booklet, 20 #7640 12.00

Paintings by Pavel A. Fedotov (1815-52) — A3823

Designs: No. 7641, 25r, Encore! Encore! No. 7642, 25r, Portrait of N. P. Zhdanovich at the Harpsichord, vert.

Perf. 12x11½, 11½x12

2015, June 23 Litho.

7641-7642 A3823 Set of 2 1.75 .90

Silhouettes of Alexander Pushkin, Nikolai Gogol and Anna Akhmatova A3824

2015, June 25 Litho. ***Perf. 11¼***

7643 A3824 17r multi .60 .30

Literature Year in Russia.

International Summits in Ufa — A3825

2015, July 7 Litho. ***Perf. 12x12½***

7644 A3825 19r multi .60 .30

Prince Pyotr Bagration (1765-1812), General — A3826

2015, July 10 Litho. ***Perf. 12x11½***

7645 A3826 21r multi .70 .35

No. 7645 was printed in sheets of 8 + central label.

Russian Post Emblem A3827

Emblem of the Russian Geographical Society A3828

Serpentine Die Cut 14½x15

2015, July 23 Litho.

Self-Adhesive

7646 A3827 17r multi .55 .25
7647 A3828 35r multi 1.10 .55

Compare type A3827 to type A3364.

2015 Intl. Swimming Federation World Championships, Kazan — A3829

2015, July 24 Litho. ***Perf. 13½***

7648 A3829 17r multi .55 .25

World War I Heroes A3830

Designs: No. 7649, 21r, Konstantin I. Nedorubov (1889-1978). No. 7650, 21r, Ivan V. Tyulenev (1892-1978). No. 7651, 21r, Nikolai I. Ulanov (1881-1948). No. 7652, 21r, Ivan L. Khizhnyak (1893-1980).

2015, Aug. 3 Litho. ***Perf. 11½x12***

7649-7652 A3830 Set of 4 2.75 1.40

Nos. 7649-7652 were each printed in sheets of 11 + label.

19th-20th Cent. Porcelain Tile From Moscow — A3831

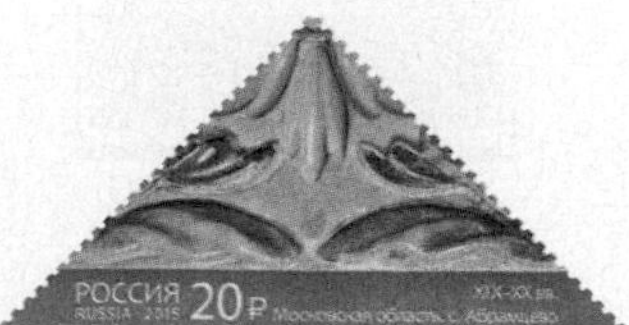

19th-20th Cent. Porcelain Tile From Abramtsevo — A3832

19th-20th Cent. Porcelain Tile From Turygino — A3833

17th-18th Cent. Porcelain Tile From Yaroslavl — A3834

2015, Aug. 4 Litho. *Perf. 11½*

7653 A3831 20r multi .60 .30
7654 A3832 20r multi .60 .30
7655 A3833 20r multi .60 .30
7656 A3834 20r multi .60 .30
Nos. 7653-7656 (4) 2.40 1.20

Uniforms of Railway Employees A3835

Uniforms of: No. 7657, 17r, General and Conductor of Officer of Lines of Communications, 1843. No. 7658, 17r, Head of Depot and second-class driver, 1952. No. 7659, 17r, Head of Railways and conductor, 1979. No. 7660, 17r, Trainmaster and conductor, 2015.

2015, Aug. 11 Litho. *Perf. 13½*

7657-7660 A3835 Set of 4 2.00 1.00
7660a Souvenir sheet of 8, 2 each #7657-7660 4.00 2.00

Admiral Gennady Nevelskoy Monument, Nikolayevsk-on-Amur — A3836

2015, Aug. 14 Litho. *Perf. 12x12½*

7661 A3836 17r multi .50 .25

Leningrad Zoo, St. Petersburg, 150th Anniv. — A3837

2015, Aug. 14 Litho. *Perf. 13½*

7662 A3837 19r multi .60 .30

Vysokopetrovsky Monastery, 700th Anniv. — A3838

St. Laurentius Monastery, 500th Anniv. — A3839

2015, Aug. 23 Litho. *Perf. 13½*

7663 A3838 19r multi .60 .30
7664 A3839 19r multi .60 .30

Nos. 7663-7664 were each printed in sheets of 9 + label.

Boris F. Safonov (1915-42), Military Pilot A3840

2015, Aug. 26 Litho. *Perf. 12½x12*

7665 A3840 12r multi .35 .25

No. 7665 was printed in sheets of 10 + central label.

Arch of Triumph, Pyongyang A3841

2015, Aug. 28 Litho. *Perf. 11¼*

7666 A3841 19r multi .60 .30

Liberation of Korea, 70th anniv. See North Korea No.

Souvenir Sheet

Kazan Coat of Arms — A3842

2015, Aug. 28 Litho. *Perf. 12x12½*

7667 A3842 50r gold & multi 1.50 .75

End of World War II, 70th Anniv. — A3843

2015, Sept. 2 Litho. *Perf. 13½*

7668 A3843 17r multi .50 .25

Souvenir Sheet

Nizhny Novgorod Stone Kremlin, 500th Anniv. — A3844

2015, Sept. 9 Litho. *Perf. 11¾*

7669 A3844 35r multi 1.10 .55

World War I Military Equipment — A3845

Designs: No. 7670, 21r, Mosin-Nagant 7.62mm rifle. No. 7671, 21r, 76.2mm rapid firing gun. No. 7672, 21r, Destroyer "Novik." No. 7673, 21r, Sikorsky S-22 Ilya Muroments bomber.

2015, Sept. 10 Litho. *Perf. 12*

7670-7673 A3845 Set of 4 2.60 1.40

Nos. 7670-7673 were each printed in sheets of 11 + label.

United Nations, 70th Anniv. A3846

Serpentine Die Cut 10

2015, Sept. 15 Litho.

Self-Adhesive

7674 A3846 26.50r multi .85 .40

Souvenir Sheet

World Cup Trophy — A3847

2015, Sept. 18 Litho. *Perf. 12*

7675 A3847 100r multi 3.25 1.60

2018 World Cup Soccer Championships, Russia.

Federal Anti-Monopoly Service, 25th Anniv. — A3848

2015, Sept. 21 Litho. *Perf. 12x11½*

7676 A3848 21r multi .65 .30

Architecture A3849

No. 7677: a, Kremlin, Moscow (denomination at LR). b, Maiden's Tower, Baku, Azerbaijan (denomination at LL).

2015, Sept. 22 Litho. *Perf. 11½*

7677 Pair 1.25 .60
a.-b. A3849 19r Either single .60 .30

Printed in sheets containing 4 pairs + central label. See Azerbaijan No. 1092.

Arctic Oil Production — A3850

No. 7678: a, Prirazlomnaya Oil Platform (denomination at LL). b, Mikhail Ulyanov tanker (denomination at LR).

2015, Sept. 23 Litho. *Perf. 11½*

7678 A3850 19r Horiz. pair, #a-b 1.25 .60

Russian Nuclear Industry, 70th Anniv. A3851

2015, Sept. 24 Litho. *Perf. 11½*

7679 A3851 17r multi .55 .25

St. Vladimir the Great (c. 958-1015), Christianizer of Klevan Rus' — A3852

2015, Sept. 25 Litho. *Perf. 13½*

7680 A3852 21r multi .65 .30

Miniature Sheet

Russian Stamps Commemorating the World Cup Soccer Championships — A3853

No. 7681: a, Russia #2073 (green panel). b, Russia #2606 (orange panel). c, Russia #3214 (purple panel). d, Russia #3746 (dark blue panel). e, Russia #5049 (Prussian blue panel). f, Russia #5463 (red panel).

2015, Oct. 1 Litho. *Perf. 11¼*
7681 A3853 26.50r Sheet of 6, #a-f 5.00 2.50

Victor Vasnetsov House Museum, Moscow A3854

2015, Oct. 2 Litho. *Perf. 12½x12*
7682 A3854 19r multi .60 .30

Souvenir Sheet

Derbent, 2000th Anniv. — A3855

2015, Oct. 2 Litho. *Perf. 12*
7683 A3855 35r multi 1.10 .55

All-Russian Society for Protection of Monuments of History and Culture, 50th Anniv. — A3856

2015, Oct. 14 Litho. *Perf. 12½x12*
7684 A3856 26.50r multi .85 .40

Diplomatic Relations Between Russia and Mexico, 125th Anniv. — A3857

No. 7685: a, Saints Peter and Paul Cathedral, St. Petersburg. b, Chapultepec Castle, Mexico City.

2015, Oct. 19 Litho. *Perf. 11½*
7685 A3857 19r Pair, #a-b 1.25 .60

Printed in sheets containing 4 pairs + central label. See Mexico Nos. 2955-2956.

Souvenir Sheet

Ancient City of Tauric Chersonese and its Chora UNESCO World Hereitage Site — A3858

2015, Oct. 23 Litho. *Perf. 12*
7686 A3858 35r multi 1.10 .55

Disaster Risk Reduction A3859

Serpentine Die Cut 11
2015, Oct. 28 Litho.
Self-Adhesive
7687 A3859 19r multi .60 .30

Sobibor Monument, by Mieczyslaw Welter — A3860

2015, Oct. 30 Litho. *Perf. 12x12½*
7688 A3860 21r multi .65 .30

Uprising at Sobibor Death Camp, 72nd anniv.

St. Tikhon of Moscow (1865-1925), 11th Patriarch of Moscow A3861

2015, Nov. 5 Litho. *Perf. 11½x12*
7689 A3861 19r multi .60 .30

Souvenir Sheet

Kostroma Coat of Arms — A3862

2015, Nov. 5 Litho. *Perf. 12x12½*
7690 A3862 50r multi 1.50 .75

Ashot L. Badalov (1915-2011), Founder of State Commission for Radio Frequencies — A3863

2015, Nov. 10 Litho. *Perf. 12½x12*
7691 A3863 19r multi .60 .30

Heroes of the Russian Federation A3864

Designs: No. 7692, 17r, Vladimir V. Maksimchuk (1947-94). No. 7693, 17r, Valery A. Tinkov (1957-95). No. 7694, 17r, Ivan Y. Shelohvostov (1978-2003). No. 7695, 17r, Sergey A. Solnechnikov (1980-2012). No. 7696, 17r, Vitaly V. Maiboroda (1981-2013).

2015, Nov. 10 Litho. *Perf. 12½x12*
7692-7696 A3864 Set of 5 2.60 1.40

Nos. 7692-7696 were each printed in sheets of 5 + label.

Cathedral of the Intercession of the Holy Virgin, Bogolyubovo A3865

Pha That Luang, Vientiane, Laos A3866

Serpentine Die Cut 10
2015, Nov. 11 Litho.
Self-Adhesive

7697	Pair	1.25	.60
a.	A3865 21r multi	.60	.30
b.	A3866 21r multi	.60	.30

Printed in sheets containing 4 pairs + central label. See Laos No.

Zlatoust Arms Factory, 200th Anniv. A3867

2015, Nov. 17 Litho. *Perf. 11½*
7698 A3867 17r multi .55 .25

Stadiums for 2018 World Cup Soccer Championships — A3868

No. 7699: a, Luzhniki Stadium, Moscow (blue panel). b, Fisht Stadium, Sochi (orange panel). c, Kazan Arena, Kazan (red panel). d, Spartak Stadium, Moscow (green panel).

2015, Nov. 17 Litho. *Perf. 13½*
7699 A3868 21r Block or vert. strip of 4, #a-d 2.50 1.25

Ministry for Civil Defense, Emergencies and Natural Disasters, 25th Anniv. — A3869

2015, Nov. 27 Litho. *Perf. 12x11½*
7700 A3869 21r multi .65 .30

Timiryazev State Agrarian University, 150th Anniv. A3870

Serpentine Die Cut 10
2015, Dec. 3 Litho.
Self-Adhesive
7701 A3870 17r multi .50 .25

Lawyers Type of 2012

Designs: No. 7702, 17r, Nikolai V. Muraviev (1850-1908). No. 7703, 17r, Konstantin P. Pobedonostsev (1827-1907). No. 7704, 17r, Nikolai S. Tagantsev (1843-1923).

2015, Dec. 3 Litho. *Perf. 11½*
7702-7704 A3635 Set of 3 1.40 .70

Nos. 7702-7704 were each printed in sheets of 8 + label.

Miniature Sheet

Russian Soccer Players — A3871

No. 7705: a, Gavriil D. Kachalin (1911-95). b, Valentin B. Bubukin (1933-2008). c, Yuriy M. Voynov (1931-2003). d, Valentin K. Ivanov (1934-2011). e, Sergei S. Salnikov (1925-84). f, Eduard A. Streltsov (1937-90). g, Lev I. Yashin (1929-90).

2015, Dec. 9 Litho. *Perf. 12½x12*
7705 A3871 26.50r Sheet of 7, #a-g, + 9 labels 5.25 2.60

2018 World Cup Soccer Championships, Russia.

New Year 2016 — A3872

2015, Dec. 10 Litho. *Perf. 13½*
7706 A3872 35r multi .95 .50

Russian Cuisine A3873

2016, Jan. 13 Litho. *Perf. 11½x12*

7707 A3873 21r multi .55 .25

Souvenir Sheet

Night on the Dnieper River, by Arkhip Kuindzhi (1841-1910) — A3874

2016, Jan. 27 Litho. *Perf. 12x12½*

7708 A3874 50r multi 1.25 .65

Historians — A3875

No. 7709 — History books and: a, Nikolai M. Karamzin (1766-1826). b, Vasily O. Klyuchevsky (1841-1911).

2016, Jan. 28 Litho. *Perf. 12x12½*

7709 Horiz. pair + central label 1.25 .60

a.-b. A3875 25r Either single .60 .30

Ice Hockey Players and Gagarin Cup — A3877

2016, Feb. 20 Litho. *Perf. 11½*

7711 A3877 19r multi .55 .25

Miniature Sheet

Russian Medals and Orders — A3878

No. 7712: a, Gold Star Medal (like #7337). b, Hero of Labor of the Russian Federation Medal (like #7543). c, Order of St. Andrew (double-headed eagle with crucifix at top). d, Order of St. George (like #7338). e, Order of Merit for the Fatherland (like #7339). f, Order of St. Catherine the Great (like #7427). g, Order of Alexander Nevsky (like #7426). h, Order of Suvorov (like #7425). i, Order of Ushakov (like #7508). j, Order of Zhukov (like #7506). k, Order of Kutuzov (like #7507). l, Order of Nakhimov (like #7604). m, Order of Courage (like #7605). n, Order of Military Merit (blue ribbon with central red stripe). o, Order of Naval Merit (white ribbon with three blue stripes), p, Order of Honor (blue ribbon with one white stripe). q, Order of Friendship (like #7606). r, Order of Parental Glory (white ribbon with two blue stripes).

Litho. & Embossed

2016, Feb. 20 *Perf. 12¼x12*

Dated "2016" Above "Russia"

7712 A3878 25r Sheet of 18, #a-r 12.50 6.25

Russian Membership in Council of Europe, 20th Anniv. — A3879

2016, Feb. 26 Litho. *Perf. 12x12¼*

7713 A3879 21r multi .60 .30

Regional Communications Commonwealth, 25th Anniv. — A3880

2016, Mar. 3 Litho. *Perf. 12½x12*

7714 A3880 17r multi .50 .25

POSTAL-FISCAL STAMPS

During 1918-22, Postal Savings stamps and Control stamps were authorized for postal use. Because of hyper-inflation during 1920-22, Russian Arms stamps and these postal-fiscal stamps were sold and used at different rates at different times: 1918-20, sold at face value; from March, 1920, sold at 100 times face value; from Aug. 15, 1921, sold at 250r each, regardless of face value; from April, 1922, sold at 10,000r per 1k or 1r. In Oct. 1922, these issues were superseded by gold currency stamps.

Postal Savings Stamps

PF1

Perf. 14½x14¾

1918, Jan. 12 Wmk. 171 Typo.

AR1	PF1	1k	dp red, *buff*	.60	*1.00*
AR2	PF1	5k	green, *buff*	.60	*1.00*
AR3	PF1	10k	chocolate, *buff*	1.20	*1.00*
			Nos. AR1-AR3 (3)	2.40	*3.00*

Nos. AR1-AR14 have a faint burelé background, which is noted as the paper color in these listings.

For surcharges of Nos. AR1-AR3, see Armenia Nos. 250-253, Far Eastern Republic Nos. 35 and 36, South Russia Nos. 47-49 and numerous Ukraine issues beginning with Nos. 45e-47e.

Postal Savings Stamps

PF2

PF3

1918, June 5 Litho. *Perf. 13*

AR4	PF2	25k	black, *rose*	11.00	*37.50*
AR5	PF2	50k	brn, *pale brn*	24.00	*50.00*
AR6	PF3	50k	brn, *pale brn*	35.00	*62.50*
			Nos. AR4-AR6 (3)	70.00	*150.00*

Control Stamps

PF4

PF5

PF6

PF7

PF8

1918, June 5 Litho. *Perf. 13*

AR7	PF4	25k	blk, *pale brn*	24.00	*32.50*
AR8	PF4	50k	brn, *buff*	17.50	*50.00*
AR9	PF5	1r	org, *buff*	1.50	*3.50*
AR10	PF5	3r	grn, *buff*	1.50	*3.50*
AR11	PF5	5r	dp blue, *buff*	1.50	*3.75*
AR12	PF6	10r	dp red, *buff*	1.50	*3.75*
AR13	PF7	25r	dp brn, *buff*	5.00	*15.00*
AR14	PF8	100r	blk, *blue & car*	3.75	*6.25*
			Nos. AR7-AR14 (8)	56.25	*118.25*

General Revenue Stamps

PF9

1918 Litho. *Perf. 12x12½*

AR15	PF9	5k	lil brn, *buff*	1.50	—
AR16	PF9	10k	ol brn, *lt blue*	1.50	—
AR17	PF9	15k	dp blue, *pink*	1.50	—
AR18	PF9	20k	reddish brn, *buff*	1.50	—
AR19	PF9	50k	org red, *gray*	1.50	—
AR20	PF9	75k	ol grn, *buff*	3.25	—
AR21	PF9	1r	red, *pale blue*	6.25	—
AR22	PF9	1.25r	dk brn, *redsh brn*	30.00	—
AR23	PF9	2r	vio, *dk grn*	30.00	—
AR24	PF9	3r	dp vio blue, *rose lil*	3.50	—
AR25	PF9	5r	dp blue grn, *lt grn*	6.50	—
			Nos. AR15-AR25 (11)	87.00	

Nos, AR15-AR25 exist in tête-bêche vertical pairs and in tête-bêche vertical gutter pairs.

SEMI-POSTAL STAMPS

Empire

Admiral Kornilov Monument, Sevastopol SP1

Pozharski and Minin Monument, Moscow SP2

Statue of Peter the Great, Leningrad SP3

Alexander II Memorial and Kremlin, Moscow SP4

1905 Typo. Unwmk. *Perf. 12x12½*

B1	SP1	3k	red, brn & grn	24.00	5.25
			Never hinged	72.50	
B2	SP2	5k	lil, vio & straw	5.00	3.50
			Never hinged	10.00	
B3	SP3	7k	lt bl, dk bl & pink	5.00	3.50
			Never hinged	10.00	
B4	SP4	10k	lt blue, dk bl & yel	7.50	.50
			Never hinged	15.00	
			Nos. B1-B4 (4)	41.50	12.75

These stamps were sold for 3 kopecks over face value. The surtax was donated to a fund for the orphans of soldiers killed in the Russo-Japanese war.

Ilya Muromets Legendary Russian Hero — SP5

Designs: 3k, Don Cossack Bidding Farewell to His Sweetheart. 7k, Symbolical of Charity. 10k, St. George Slaying the Dragon.

1914 Colored Papers *Perf. 11½*

No.	Type	Description	Unused	Used
B5	SP5	1k red brn & dk grn, *straw*	2.00	2.00
B6	SP5	3k mar & gray grn, *pink*	3.00	3.00
B7	SP5	7k dk brn & dk grn, *buff*	3.50	2.00
B8	SP5	10k dk bl & brn, *blue*	12.00	4.50
		Nos. B5-B8 (4)	20.50	11.50

Perf. 12½

No.	Type	Description	Unused	Used
B5a	SP5	1k red brn & dk grn, *straw*	3.75	3.25
B6a	SP5	3k mar & gray grn, *pink*	4.25	3.25
B7a	SP5	7k dk brn & dk grn, *buff*	9.50	7.50
B8a	SP5	10k dk bl & brn, *blue*	21.00	7.50
		Nos. B5a-B8a (4)	38.50	21.50

Perf. 13¼

No.	Type	Description	Unused	Used
B5b	SP5	1k red brn & dk grn, *straw*	8.50	2.00
B6b	SP5	3k mar & gray grn, *pink*	225.00	45.00
B7b	SP5	7k dk brn & dk grn, *buff*	3.75	3.75
B8b	SP5	10k dk bl & brn, *blue*	24.00	5.50

For expanded listings, see the *Scott Classic Specialized Catalogue of Stamps and Covers 1840-1940.*

1915 White Paper *Perf. 11½*

No.	Type	Description	Unused	Used
B9	SP5	1k org brn & gray	2.25	2.00
B10	SP5	3k car & gray blk	2.25	2.00
B11	SP5	7k dk brn & dk grn	12.00	
B12	SP5	10k dk bl & dk brn	4.25	2.25
		Nos. B9-B12 (3)	8.75	
d.		Horiz. pair, imperf. between	175.00	

These stamps were sold for 1 kopeck over face value. The surtax was donated to charities connected with the war of 1914-17.

No. B11 not regularly issued. It exists only perf 11½ (with Specimen overprint) and 12½.

For surcharges of Nos. B5-B13, see Armenia Nos. 255-265 and Siberia No. 64.

Russian Soviet Federated Socialist Republic
Volga Famine Relief Issue

Relief Work on Volga River — SP9

Administering Aid to Famine Victim — SP10

1921 Litho. *Imperf.*

No.	Type	Description	Unused	Used
B14	SP9	2250r green	3.75	6.00
a.		Pelure paper	165.00	125.00
B15	SP9	2250r deep red	2.00	11.00
a.		Pelure paper	19.00	15.00
B16	SP9	2250r brown	3.75	11.00
B17	SP10	2250r dark blue	9.50	30.00
a.		2250r dark blue	20.00	—
		Nos. B14-B17 (4)	19.00	58.00

Forged cancels and counterfeits of Nos. B14-B17 are plentiful.

Stamps of type A33 with this overprint were not charity stamps nor did they pay postage in any form.

They represent taxes paid on stamps exported from or imported into Russia. In 1925 the semi-postal stamps of 1914-15 were surcharged for the same purpose. Stamps of the regular issues 1918 and 1921 have also been surcharged with inscriptions and new values, to pay the importation and exportation taxes.

Nos. 149-150 Surcharged in Black, Red, Blue or Orange

1922, Feb. *Perf. 13½*

No.	Type	Description	Unused	Used
B18	A33	100r + 100r on 70k	1.60	1.25
a.		"100 p. + p. 100"	225.00	290.00
B19	A33	100r + 100r on 70k (R)	1.60	1.25
B20	A33	100r + 100r on 70k (Bl)	1.00	1.25
B21	A33	250r + 250r on 35k	.50	.75
B22	A33	250r + 250r on 35k (R)	1.00	2.00
B23	A33	250r + 250r on 35k (O)	1.60	5.00
		Nos. B18-B23 (6)	7.30	11.50

Surcharge Inverted

No.	Type	Description	Unused	Used
B18a	A33	100r + 100r on 70k	160.00	1.00
B19a	A33	100r + 100r on 70k (R)	140.00	60.00
B20a	A33	100r + 100r on 70k (Bl)	70.00	45.00
B21a	A33	250r + 250r on 35k	70.00	—
B22a	A33	250r + 250r on 35k (R)	200.00	45.00
B23a	A33	250r + 250r on 35k (O)	225.00	100.00

Surcharge Double

No.	Type	Description	Unused	Used
B18b	A33	100r + 100r on 70k	*200.00*	—
B19b	A33	100r + 100r on 70k (R)	*200.00*	—
B21b	A33	250r + 250r on 35k	*200.00*	—
B22b	A33	250r + 250r on 35k (R)	*200.00*	—

Issued to raise funds for Volga famine relief.

Regular Issues of 1909-18 Overprinted

1922, Aug. 19 *Perf. 14*

No.	Type	Description	Unused	Used
B24	A14	1k orange	550.00	425.00
B25	A14	2k green	22.50	*22.50*
B26	A14	3k red	22.50	*22.50*
B27	A14	5k claret	22.50	*22.50*
B28	A15	10k dark blue	22.50	*22.50*

Imperf

No.	Type	Description	Unused	Used
B29	A14	1k orange	425.00	375.00
		Nos. B24-B29 (6)	1,065.	890.00

Overprint Inverted (Reading Up)

No.	Type	Description	Unused	Used
B24a	A14	1k orange	825.00	
B25a	A14	2k green	325.00	
B26a	A14	3k red	825.00	
		Never hinged	1,750.	
B27a	A14	5k claret	825.00	
		Never hinged	1,750.	
B28a	A15	10k dark blue	825.00	
		Never hinged	1,900.	
B29a	A14	1k orange	825.00	
		Never hinged	1,750.	

Double Overprint

No.	Type	Description	Unused	Used
B25b	A14	2k green	600.00	900.00
B26b	A14	3k red	1,450.	
B27b	A14	5k claret	725.00	
B28b	A15	10k dark blue	1,200.	
B29b	A14	1k orange	2,400.	

The overprint means "Philately for the Children". The stamps were sold at five million times their face values and 80% of the amount was devoted to child welfare. The stamps were sold only at Moscow and for one day.

Nos. B24-B26 were reprinted ("second issue"). Values are for the second issue. The 1k from the first issue are worth about 3 times the values shown. Expertization is recommended to distinguish the two printings.

Worker and Peasant (Industry and Agriculture) — SP11

Allegory: Agriculture Will Help End Distress SP12

Star of Hope, Wheat and Worker-Peasant Handclasp — SP13

Sower — SP14

1922 Litho. *Imperf.*

Without Gum

No.	Type	Description	Unused	Used
B30	SP11	2t (2000r) green	15.00	*250.00*
B31	SP12	2t (2000r) rose	29.00	*125.00*
B32	SP13	4t (4000r) rose	42.50	*125.00*
B33	SP14	6t (6000r) green	22.50	*125.00*
		Nos. B30-B33 (4)	109.00	625.00

Double Impression

No.	Type	Description	Unused	Used
B30a	SP11	(2000r) green	*475.00*	
B31a	SP12	(2000r) rose	*650.00*	
B32a	SP13	(4000r) rose	*725.00*	
B33a	SP14	(6000r) green	*575.00*	

Triple Impression

No.	Type	Description	Unused	Used
B30b	SP11	(2000r) green	*450.00*	
B31b	SP12	(2000r) rose	*600.00*	
B32b	SP13	(4000r) rose	*675.00*	
B33b	SP14	(6000r) green	*500.00*	

Nos. B30-B33 exist with double impression.

Counterfeits of Nos. B30-B33 exist; beware also of forged cancellations.

Miniature examples of Nos. B30-B33 exist, taken from the 1933 Soviet catalogue.

Automobile SP15

Steamship SP16

Railroad Train SP17

Airplane SP18

1922 *Imperf.*

No.	Type	Description	Unused	Used
B34	SP15	(20r+5r) light violet	.40	.75
B35	SP16	(20r+5r) violet	.50	.75
B36	SP17	(20r+5r) gray blue	.40	.75
B37	SP18	(20r+5r) blue gray	2.25	*4.25*
		Nos. B34-B37 (4)	3.55	*6.50*

Inscribed "For the Hungry." Each stamp was sold for 200,000r postage and 50,000r charity.

Counterfeits of Nos. B34-B37 exist.

Nos. 212, 183, 202 Surcharged in Bronze, Gold or Silver

1923 *Imperf.*

No.	Type	Description	Unused	Used
B38	A48	1r +1r on 10r	400.00	400.00
a.		Inverted surcharge	1,250.	1,000.
B39	A48	1r +1r on 10r (G)	40.00	25.00
a.		Inverted surcharge	325.00	225.00
B40	A43	2r +2r on 250r	40.00	25.00
a.		Pelure paper	40.00	25.00
b.		Inverted surcharge	325.00	200.00
c.		Double surcharge	—	

Wmk. 171

No.	Type	Description	Unused	Used
B41	A46	4r +4r on 5000r	40.00	25.00
a.		Date spaced "1 923"	425.00	375.00
b.		Inverted surcharge	1,150.	1,150.
B42	A46	4r +4r on 5000r (S)	1,100.	850.00
a.		Inverted surcharge	4,750.	2,500.
b.		Date spaced "1 923"	2,500.	1,850.
c.		As "b," inverted surch.	*22,500.*	8,000.
		Nos. B38-B42 (5)	1,620.	1,325.

The inscriptions mean "Philately's Contribution to Labor." The stamps were on sale only at Moscow and for one day. The surtax was for charitable purposes.

Counterfeits of No. B42 exist.

Leningrad Flood Issue

Nos. 181-182, 184-186 Surcharged

1924 Unwmk. *Imperf.*

No.	Type	Description	Unused	Used
B43	A40	3k + 10k on 100r	3.50	1.50
a.		Pelure paper	2.50	4.00
b.		Inverted surcharge	250.00	—
B44	A40	7k + 20k on 200r	3.75	1.50
a.		Inverted surcharge	300.00	—
B45	A40	14k + 30k on 300r	3.75	2.25
a.		Pelure paper	625.00	—

Similar Surcharge in Red or Black

No.	Type	Description	Unused	Used
B46	A41	12k + 40k on 500r (R)	3.75	1.75
a.		Double surcharge	1,600.	—
b.		Inverted surcharge	1,550.	—
B47	A41	20k + 50k on 1000r	3.00	1.25
a.		Thick paper	20.00	25.00
b.		Pelure paper	10.00	10.00
c.		Chalk surface paper	60.00	25.00
		Nos. B43-B47 (5)	17.75	8.25

The surcharge on Nos. B43 to B45 reads: "S.S.S.R. For the sufferers by the inundation at Leningrad." That on Nos. B46 and B47 reads: "S.S.S.R. For the Leningrad Proletariat, 23, IX, 1924."

No. B46 is surcharged vertically, reading down, with the value as the top line.

Orphans
SP19

Lenin as a Child
SP20

1926 Typo. *Perf. 13½*

B48 SP19 10k brown *14.50 8.75*
B49 SP20 20k deep blue *60.00 16.00*

Wmk. 170

B50 SP19 10k brown 3.00 1.50
B51 SP20 20k deep blue 7.50 3.50
Nos. B48-B51 (4) 85.00 29.75

Two kopecks of the price of each of these stamps was donated to organizations for the care of indigent children.

Types of 1926 Issue

1927

B52 SP19 8k + 2k yel green 1.75 .50
B53 SP20 18k + 2k deep rose 15.00 5.00

Surtax was for child welfare.

Industrial Training
SP21

Agricultural Training
SP22

Perf. 10, 10½, 12½

1929-30 Photo. Unwmk.

B54 SP21 10k +2k ol brn & org brn 14.50 *3.00*
a. Perf. 10½ 200.00 *25.00*
B55 SP21 10k +2k ol grn ('30) 6.00 *1.50*
B56 SP22 20k +2k blk brn & bl, perf. 10½ 200.00 25.00
a. Perf. 12½ 125.00 37.50
b. Perf. 10 20.00 7.50
B57 SP22 20k +2k bl grn ('30) 8.50 *2.25*
Nos. B54-B57 (4) 229.00 31.75

Surtax was for child welfare.

Catalogue values for unused stamps in this section, from this point to the end of the section, are for Never Hinged items.

"Montreal Passing Torch to Moscow" — SP23

Moscow '80 Olympic Games Emblem — SP24

22nd Olympic Games, Moscow, 1980: 16k+6k, like 10k+5k. 60k+30k, Aerial view of Kremlin and Moscow '80 emblem.

1976, Dec. 28 Litho. *Perf. 12x12½*

B58 SP23 4k + 2k multi .25 .25
B59 SP24 10k + 5k multi .35 .35
B60 SP24 16k + 6k multi .40 .40
Nos. B58-B60 (3) 1.00 1.00

Souvenir Sheet

Photo.

Perf. 11½

B61 SP23 60k + 30k multi 2.25 1.65

Greco-Roman Wrestling — SP25

Moscow '80 Emblem and: 6k+3k, Free-style wrestling. 10k+5k, Judo. 16k+6k, Boxing. 20k+10k, Weight lifting.

1977, June 21 Litho. *Perf. 12½x12*

B62 SP25 4k + 2k multi .25 .25
B63 SP25 6k + 3k multi .25 .25
B64 SP25 10k + 5k multi .25 .30
B65 SP25 16k + 6k multi .40 .35
B66 SP25 20k + 10k multi .60 .45
Nos. B62-B66 (5) 1.75 1.60

Perf. 12½x12, 12x12½

1977, Sept. 22

Designs: 4k+2k, Bicyclist. 6k+3k, Woman archer, vert. 10k+5k, Sharpshooting. 16k+6k, Equestrian. 20k+10k, Fencer. 50k+25k, Equestrian and fencer.

B67 SP25 4k + 2k multi .25 .25
B68 SP25 6k + 3k multi .25 .25
B69 SP25 10k + 5k multi .40 .30
B70 SP25 16k + 6k multi .55 .35
B71 SP25 20k + 10k multi .70 .45
Nos. B67-B71 (5) 2.15 1.60

Souvenir Sheet

Perf. 12½x12

B72 SP25 50k + 25k multi 2.00 1.65

1978, Mar. 24 *Perf. 12½x12*

Designs: 4k+2k, Swimmer at start. 6k+3k, Woman diver, vert. 10k+5k, Water polo. 16k+6k, Canoeing. 20k+10k, Canadian single. 50k+25k, Start of double scull race.

B73 SP25 4k + 2k multi .25 .25
B74 SP25 6k + 3k multi .25 .25
B75 SP25 10k + 5k multi .30 .25
B76 SP25 16k + 6k multi .60 .30
B77 SP25 20k + 10k multi .60 .45
Nos. B73-B77 (5) 1.80 1.50

Souvenir Sheet

B78 SP25 50k + 25k grn & blk 2.00 2.00

Star-class Yacht — SP26

Keel Yachts and Moscow '80 Emblem: 6k+3k, Soling class. 10k+5k, Centerboarder 470. 16k+6k, Finn class. 20k+10k, Flying Dutchman class. 50k+25k, Catamaran Tornado, horiz.

1978, Oct. 26 Litho. *Perf. 12x12½*

B79 SP26 4k + 2k multi .25 .25
B80 SP26 6k + 3k multi .25 .25
B81 SP26 10k + 5k multi .30 .25
B82 SP26 16k + 6k multi .40 .30
B83 SP26 20k + 10k multi .60 .40
Nos. B79-B83 (5) 1.80 1.45

Souvenir Sheet

Perf. 12½x12

B84 SP26 50k + 25k multi 2.00 1.40

Women's Gymnastics
SP27

Designs: 6k+3k, Man on parallel bars. 10k+5k, Man on horizontal bar. 16k+6k, Woman on balance beam. 20k+10k, Woman on uneven bars. 50k+25k, Man on rings.

1979, Mar. 21 Litho. *Perf. 12x12½*

B85 SP27 4k + 2k multi .25 .25
B86 SP27 6k + 3k multi .25 .25
B87 SP27 10k + 5k multi .30 .25
B88 SP27 16k + 6k multi .40 .30
B89 SP27 20k + 10k multi .60 .40
Nos. B85-B89 (5) 1.80 1.45

Souvenir Sheet

Perf. 12½x12

B90 SP25 50k + 25k multi 2.00 1.40

1979, June *Perf. 12½x12, 12x12½*

Designs: 4k+2k, Soccer. 6k+3k, Basketball. 10k+5k, Women's volleyball. 16k+6k, Handball. 20k+10k, Field hockey.

B91 SP25 4k + 2k multi .25 .25
B92 SP27 6k + 3k multi .25 .25
B93 SP27 10k + 5k multi .30 .25
B94 SP25 16k + 6k multi .40 .30
B95 SP25 20k + 10k multi .60 .40
Nos. B91-B95 (5) 1.80 1.45

22nd Olympic Games, Moscow, July 19-Aug. 3, 1980.

Running, Moscow '80 Emblem
SP27a

No. B97, Pole vault. No. B98, Discus. No. B99, Hurdles. No. B100, Javelin. No. B101, Walking, vert. No. B102, Hammer throw. No. B103, High jump. No. B104, Shot put. No. B105, Long jump.

No. B106, Relay race.

1980 Litho. *Perf. 12½x12, 12x12½*

B96 SP27a 4k + 2k shown .25 .25
B97 SP27a 4k + 2k multi .25 .25
B98 SP27a 6k + 3k multi .25 .25
B99 SP27a 6k + 3k multi .25 .25
B100 SP27a 10k + 5k multi .40 .25
B101 SP27a 10k + 5k multi .40 .25
B102 SP27a 16k + 6k multi .70 .30
B103 SP27a 16k + 6k multi .70 .30
B104 SP27a 20k + 10k multi .90 .40
B105 SP27a 20k + 10k multi .90 .40
Nos. B96-B105 (10) 5.00 2.90

Souvenir Sheet

B106 SP27a 50k + 25k multi 2.00 1.00

22nd Olympic Games, Moscow, July 19-Aug. 3. Issued: Nos. B96, B99, B101, B103, B105, Feb. 6; others, Mar. 12.

Moscow '80 Emblem, Relief from St. Dimitri's Cathedral, Arms of Vladimir — SP28

Moscow '80 Emblem and: No. B108, Bridge over Klyazma River and Vladimir Hotel. No. B109, Relief from Nativity Cathedral and coat of arms (falcon), Suzdal. No. B110, Tourist complex and Pozharski Monument, Suzdal. No. B111, Frunze Monument, Ivanovo, torch and spindle. No. B112, Museum of First Soviets, Fighters of the Revolution Monument, Ivanovo.

Photogravure and Engraved

1977, Dec. 30 *Perf. 11½x12*

B107 SP28 1r + 50k multi 1.40 1.00
B108 SP28 1r + 50k multi 1.40 1.00
B109 SP28 1r + 50k multi 1.40 1.00
B110 SP28 1r + 50k multi 1.40 1.00
B111 SP28 1r + 50k multi 1.40 1.00
B112 SP28 1r + 50k multi 1.40 1.00
Nos. B107-B112 (6) 8.40 6.00

"Tourism around the Golden Ring."

Fortifications and Arms of Zagorsk
SP29

Moscow '80 Emblem and (Coat of Arms design): No. B114, Gagarin Palace of Culture and new arms of Zagorsk (building & horse). No. B115, Rostov Kremlin with St. John the Divine Church and No. B116, View of Rostov from Nero Lake (deer). No. B117, Alexander Nevski and WWII soldiers' monuments, Pereslav-Zalesski and No. B118, Peter the Great monument, Pereslav-Zalesski (lion & fish). No. B119, Tower and wall of Monastery of the Transfiguration, Yaroslavl and No. B120, Dock and monument for Soviet heroes, Yaroslava (bear).

1978 *Perf. 12x11½*

Multicolored and

B113 SP29 1r + 50k gold 2.00 1.00
B114 SP29 1r + 50k silver 2.00 1.00
B115 SP29 1r + 50k silver 2.00 1.00
B116 SP29 1r + 50k gold 2.00 1.00
B117 SP29 1r + 50k gold 2.00 1.00
B118 SP29 1r + 50k silver 2.00 1.00
B119 SP29 1r + 50k gold 2.00 1.00
B120 SP29 1r + 50k silver 2.00 1.00
Nos. B113-B120 (8) 16.00 8.00

Issued: #B113-B116, 10/16; #B117-B120, 12/25.

1979 *Perf. 12x11½*

Moscow '80 Emblem and: No. B121, Narikaly Fortress, Tbilisi, 4th century. No. B122, Georgia Philharmonic Concert Hall, "Muse" sculpture, Tbilisi. No. B123, Chir-Dor Mosque, 17th century, Samarkand. No. B124, Peoples Friendship Museum, "Courage" monument, Tashkent. No. B125, Landscape, Erevan. B126, Armenian State Opera and Ballet Theater, Erevan.

Multicolored and

B121 SP29 1r+50k sil, bl circle 1.75 1.25
B122 SP29 1r+50k gold, yel circle 1.75 1.25
B123 SP29 1r+50k sil, bl 8-point star 1.75 1.25
B124 SP29 1r+50k gold, red 8-point star 1.75 1.25
B125 SP29 1r+50k sil, bl diamond 1.75 1.25
B126 SP29 1r+50k gold, red diamond 1.75 1.25
Nos. B121-B126 (6) 10.50 7.50

Issued: #B121-B124, 9/5; #B125-B126, Oct.

Kremlin
SP29a

Kalinin Prospect, Moscow
SP29b

Admiralteistvo, St. Isaak Cathedral, Leningrad — SP29c

World War II Defense Monument, Leningrad
SP29d

Bogdan Khmelnitisky Monument, St. Sophia's Monastery Kiev
SP29e

Metro Bridge, Dnieper River, Kiev — SP29f

Palace of Sports, Obelisk, Minsk
SP29g

Republican House of Cinematography, Minsk — SP29h

Vyshgorodsky Castle, Town Hall, Tallinn
SP29i

Viru Hotel, Tallinn
SP29j

Moscow '80 Emblem, Coat of Arms.

1980 ***Perf. 12x11½***

B127	SP29a	1r + 50k multi		2.50	1.75
B128	SP29b	1r + 50k multi		2.50	1.75
B129	SP29c	1r + 50k multi		2.50	1.75
B130	SP29d	1r + 50k multi		2.50	1.75
B131	SP29e	1r + 50k multi		2.50	1.75
B132	SP29f	1r + 50k multi		2.50	1.75
B133	SP29g	1r + 50k multi		2.50	1.75
B134	SP29h	1r + 50k multi		2.50	1.75
B135	SP29i	1r + 50k multi		2.50	1.75
B136	SP29j	1r + 50k multi		2.50	1.75
	Nos. B127-B136 (10)			25.00	17.50

Tourism. Issue dates: #B127-B128, Feb. 29. #B129-B130, Mar. 25; #B131-B136, Apr. 30.

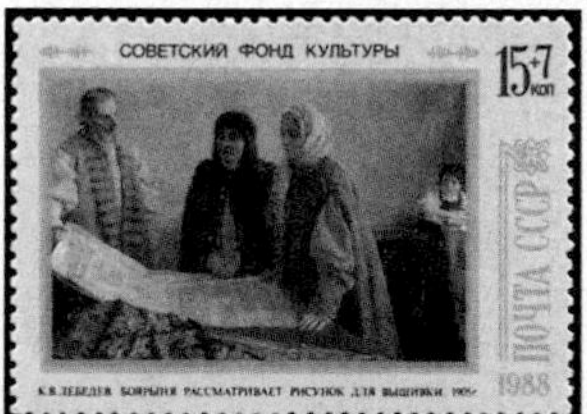

Soviet Culture Fund — SP30

Art treasures: No. B137, *O.K. Lansere,* 1910, by Z.E. Serebriakova, vert. No. B138, *Boyar's Wife Examining an Embroidery Design,* 1905, by K.V. Lebedev. No. B139, *Talent,* 1910, by N.P. Bogdanov-Belsky, vert. No. B140, *Trinity,* 15th-16th cent., Novgorod School, vert.

Perf. 12x12½, 12½x12

1988, Aug. 22 **Litho.**

B137	SP30	10k +5k multi	.35	.25
B138	SP30	15k +7k multi	.45	.35
B139	SP30	30k +15k multi	1.25	.75
	Nos. B137-B139 (3)		2.05	1.35

Souvenir Sheet

B140	SP30	1r +50k multi	2.00	1.00

SP31

1988, Oct. 20 **Litho.** ***Perf. 12***

B141	SP31	10k +5k Bear	.25	.25
B142	SP31	10k +5k Wolf	.25	.25
B143	SP31	20k +10k Fox	.40	.35
B144	SP31	20k +10k Boar	.40	.35
B145	SP31	20k +10k Lynx	.40	.35
a.		Block of 5+label, #B141-B145	2.00	1.60

Zoo Relief Fund. See #B152-B156, B166-B168.

Lenin Children's Fund
SP32

Children's drawings and fund emblem: No. B146, Skating Rink. No. B147, Rooster. No. B148, May (girl and flowers).

1988, Dec. 12 **Litho.** ***Perf. 12***

B146	SP32	5k +2k multi	.25	.25
B147	SP32	5k +2k multi	.25	.25
B148	SP32	5k +2k multi	.25	.25
a.		Block of 3+label, #B146-B148	.75	.45

See Nos. B169-B171.

SP33

#B149, Tigranes I (c. 140-55 B.C.), king of Armenia, gold coin. #B150, St. Ripsime Temple, c. 618. #B151, *Virgin and Child,* fresco (detail) by Ovnat Ovnatanyan, 18th cent., Echmiadzin Cathedral.

1988, Dec. 27 ***Perf. 12½x12***

B149	SP33	20k +10k multi	.40	.25
B150	SP33	30k +15k multi	.50	.30
B151	SP33	50k +25k multi	1.00	.50
a.		Block of 3+label, #B149-B151	2.00	1.00

Armenian earthquake relief. For surcharges see Nos. B173-B175.

Zoo Relief Type of 1988

Nos. B152-B156 are horiz. stamps.

1989, Mar. 20 **Litho.** ***Perf. 12***

B152	SP31	10k+5k Marten	.40	.30
B153	SP31	10k+5k Squirrel	.40	.30
B154	SP31	20k+10k Hare	.75	.50
B155	SP31	20k+10k Hedgehog	.75	.50
B156	SP31	20k+10k Badger	.75	.50
a.		Block of 5+label, #B152-B156	3.00	2.00

Lenin Children's Fund Type of 1988

Fund emblem and children's drawings: No. B157, Rabbit. No. B158, Cat. No. B159, Doctor. Nos. B157-B159 vert.

1989, June 14 **Litho.** ***Perf. 12***

B157	SP32	5k +2k multi	.50	.25
B158	SP32	5k +2k multi	.50	.25
B159	SP32	5k +2k multi	.50	.25
a.		Block of 3+label, #B157-B159	2.00	.75

Surtax for the fund.

Soviet Culture Fund
SP34

Paintings and porcelain: No. B160, *Village Market,* by A. Makovsky. No. B161, *Lady Wearing a Hat,* by E. Zelenin. No. B162, *Portrait of the Actress Bazhenova,* by A. Sofronova. No. B163, *Two Women,* by H. Shaiber. No. B164, Popov porcelain coffee pot and plates, 19th cent.

1989 **Litho.** ***Perf. 12x12½***

B160	SP34	4k +2k multi	.25	.25
B161	SP34	5k +2k multi	.25	.25
B162	SP34	10k +5k multi	.30	.25
B163	SP34	20k +10k multi	.50	.30
B164	SP34	30k +15k multi	.85	.50
	Nos. B160-B164 (5)		2.15	1.55

Souvenir Sheet

Nature Conservation — SP35

1989, Dec. 14 **Photo.** ***Perf. 11½***

B165	SP35	20k + 10k Swallow	5.00	5.00

Surtax for the Soviet Union of Philatelists.

Zoo Relief Type of 1988

No. B166, Aquila chrysaetos. No. B167, Falco cherrug. No. B168,

1990, May 4 **Litho.** ***Perf. 12***

B166	SP31	10k +5k multi	.45	.30
B167	SP31	20k +10k multi	1.00	.65
B168	SP31	20k +10k multi	1.00	.65
a.		Block of 3 + label, #B166-B168	3.00	1.65

Nos. B166-B168 horiz.

Lenin's Children Fund Type of 1988

No. B169, Clown. No. B170, Group of women. No. B171, Group of children. No. B169-B171, vert.

1990, July 3 **Litho.** ***Perf. 12***

B169	SP32	5k +2k multi	.65	.25
B170	SP32	5k +2k multi	.65	.25
B171	SP32	5k +2k multi	.65	.25
a.		Block of 3, #B169-B171 + label	2.00	.45

Nature Conservation — SP36

1990, Sept. 12 Litho. *Perf. 12*
B172 SP36 20k +10k multi 1.10 1.10

Surtax for Soviet Union of Philatelists.

Nos. B149-B151 Overprinted

No. B173

Nos. B174-B175

1990, Nov. 24 Litho. *Perf. 12x12½*
B173 SP33 20k +10k multi .90 .65
B174 SP33 30k +15k multi 1.40 .90
B175 SP33 50k +25k multi 2.25 1.50
a. Block of 3+label, #B173-B175 4.00 3.00

Armenia '90 Philatelic Exhibition.

Soviet Culture Fund — SP37

Paintings by N. K. Roerich: 10k+5k, Unkrada, 1909. 20k+10k, Pskovo-Pechorsky Monastery, 1907.

1990, Dec. 20 Litho. *Perf. 12½x12*
B176 SP37 10k +5k multi .40 .25
B177 SP37 20k +10k multi .60 .35

Souvenir Sheet

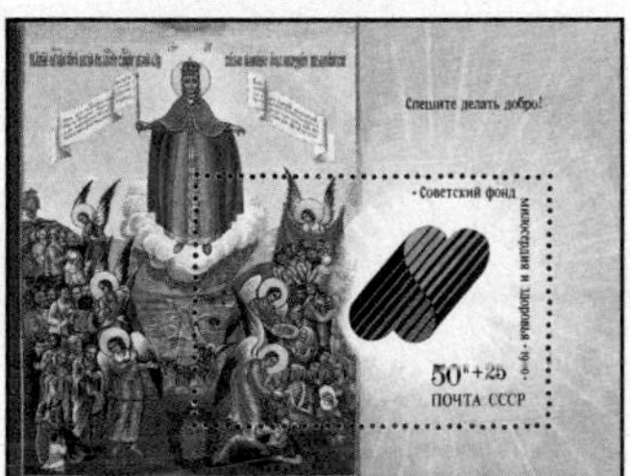

Joys of All Those Grieving, 18th Cent. — SP38

1990, Dec. 23 *Perf. 12½x12*
B178 SP38 50k +25k multi 2.00 1.00

Surtax for Charity and Health Fund.

Ciconia Ciconia SP39

1991, Feb. 4 Litho. *Perf. 12*
B179 SP39 10k +5k multi .55 .35

Surtax for the Zoo Relief Fund.

Souvenir Sheet

USSR Philatelic Society, 25th Anniv. — SP40

1991, Feb. 15 *Perf. 12x12½*
B180 SP40 20k +10k multi 1.10 1.10

The Universe by V. Lukianets SP41

No. B182, Another Planet by V. Lukianets.

1991, June 1 Litho. *Perf. 12½x12*
B181 SP41 10k +5k multi .50 .25
B182 SP41 10k +5k multi .50 .25

Lenin's Children's Fund.

SP42

1991, July 10 *Perf. 12x12½*
B183 SP42 20k +10k multi .50 .25

Surtax for Soviet Culture Fund.

SP43

1991, July 10 *Perf. 12*
B184 SP43 20k +10k multi .50 .25

Surtax for Soviet Charity & Health Fund

Souvenir Sheet

SP44

1992, Jan. 22 Litho. *Perf. 12½x12*
B185 SP44 3r +50k multi 1.00 .70

Surtax for Nature Preservation.

AIR POST STAMPS

AP1

Plane Overprint in Red

1922 Unwmk. *Imperf.*
C1 AP1 45r green & black 12.50 —
a. Translucent paper 85.00 —

5th anniversary of October Revolution.
No. C1 was on sale only at the Moscow General Post Office. Counterfeits exist.

Fokker F-111 — AP2

1923 Photo.
C2 AP2 1r red brown 14.50
C3 AP2 3r deep blue 14.50
C4 AP2 5r green 4.75
a. Wide "5" *40,000.*
C5 AP2 10r carmine 4.75
Nos. C2-C5 (4) 38.50

Nos. C2-C5 were not placed in use.

Nos. C2-C5 Surcharged

1924
C6 AP2 5k on 3r dp blue 8.25 3.75
C7 AP2 10k on 5r green 3.75 1.25
a. Wide "5" *1,250.* *700.00*
b. Inverted surcharge *2,750.* —
C8 AP2 15k on 1r red brown 15.00 4.00
a. Inverted surcharge *1,400.* *500.00*
C9 AP2 20k on 10r car 3.75 1.00
a. Inverted surcharge *4,000.* *2,500.*
Nos. C6-C9 (4) 30.75 10.00

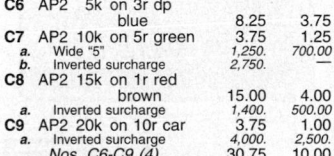

Airplane over Map of World AP3

1927, Sept. 1 Litho. *Perf. 13x12*
C10 AP3 10k dk bl & yel brn 18.00 *7.50*
C11 AP3 15k dp red & ol grn 30.00 *10.00*

1st Intl. Air Post Cong. at The Hague, initiated by the USSR.

Graf Zeppelin and "Call to Complete 5-Year Plan in 4 Years" — AP4

1930 Photo. Wmk. 226 *Perf. 12½*
C12 AP4 40k dark blue 60.00 24.00
a. Perf. 10½ 72.50 24.00
b. Imperf. *1,650.* *1,325.*
C13 AP4 80k carmine 60.00 24.00
a. Perf. 10½ 72.50 24.00
b. Imperf. *1,650.* *1,325.*

Flight of the Graf Zeppelin from Friedrichshafen to Moscow and return.

Symbolical of Airship Communication from the Tundra to the Steppes — AP5

Airship over Dneprostroi Dam — AP6

Airship over Lenin Mausoleum — AP7

Airship Exploring Arctic Regions — AP8

Constructing an Airship AP9

1931-32 Wmk. 170 Photo. *Imperf.*
C15 AP5 10k dark violet 40.00 30.00

Litho.
C16 AP6 15k gray blue 40.00 30.00

Typo.
C17 AP7 20k dk carmine 40.00 30.00

Photo.
C18 AP8 50k black brown 40.00 30.00
a. 50k gray blue (error) *85,000.*
C19 AP9 1r dark green 40.00 32.50
Nos. C15-C19 (5) 200.00 152.50

Perf. 12x12¼, 12¼x12½x12 (#C21, C23)
C20 AP5 10k dark violet 3.00 1.75

Litho.
C21 AP6 15k gray blue 120.00 19.00

Typo.
C22 AP7 20k dk carmine 3.00 1.75
a. 20k light red 3.00 —

Photo.
C23 AP8 50k black brown 14.50 4.00
a. 50k gray blue (error) 500.00 300.00
C24 AP9 1r dark green 15.00 2.50

Perf. 12½

Unwmk. **Engr.**

C25	AP6 15k gray blk ('32)	6.00	1.25
a.	Perf. 10½	*2,000.*	*135.00*
b.	Perf. 14	17.50	*22.50*
c.	Imperf.	—	*3,250.*
	Nos. C20-C25 (6)	161.50	30.25

The 11½ perforation on Nos. C20-C25 is of private origin; beware also of bogus perforation "errors."

North Pole Issue

Graf Zeppelin and Icebreaker "Malygin" Transferring Mail — AP10

1931 **Wmk. 170** ***Imperf.***

C26	AP10 30k dark violet	35.00	*17.50*
C27	AP10 35k dark green	7.25	*4.25*
C28	AP10 1r gray black	48.00	*17.50*
C29	AP10 2r deep ultra	24.00	17.50
	Nos. C26-C29 (4)	114.25	56.75

Perf. 12x12¼

C30	AP10 30k dark violet	45.00	*15.00*
C31	AP10 35k dark green	60.00	*12.50*
C32	AP10 1r gray black	105.00	*35.00*
C33	AP10 2r deep ultra	45.00	*15.00*
	Nos. C30-C33 (4)	255.00	*77.50*

Perf. 12¼

C30a	AP10 30k dark violet	40.00	17.50
C31a	AP10 35k dark green	37.50	25.00
C32a	AP10 1r gray black	60.00	60.00
C33a	AP10 2r deep ultra	45.00	20.00

Map of Polar Region, Airplane and Icebreaker "Sibiryakov" — AP11

Perf. 12, 10½

1932, Aug. 26 **Wmk. 170**

C34	AP11 50k car rose	75.00	12.50
a.	Perf. 10½	*30,000.*	*14,000.*
b.	Perf. 10½x12		*20,000.*
C35	AP11 1r green	37.50	22.50
a.	Perf. 12	75.00	*37.50*

2nd International Polar Year in connection with proposed flight from Franz-Josef Land to Archangel which, being impossible, actually went from Archangel to Moscow to destinations.

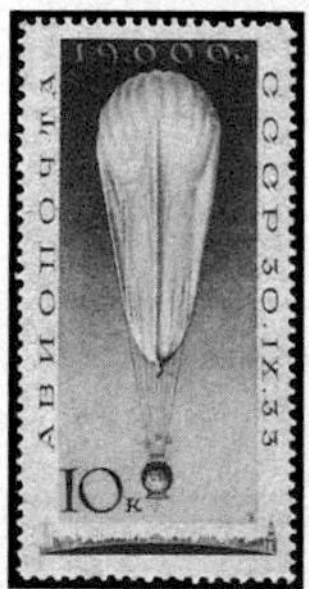

Stratostat "U.S.S.R." — AP12

1933 **Photo.** ***Perf. 14***

C37	AP12 5k ultra	125.00	10.00
C38	AP12 10k carmine	27.50	10.00
C39	AP12 20k violet	11.50	9.50
	Nos. C37-C39 (3)	164.00	29.50

Pairs, Imperf. Between

C37a	Vert. pair, imperf. between	*11,250.*	—

Ascent into the stratosphere by Soviet aeronauts, Sept. 30th, 1933.

Furnaces of Kuznetsk AP13

Designs: 10k, Oil wells. 20k, Collective farm. 50k, Map of Moscow-Volga Canal project. 80k, Arctic cargo ship.

1934, Feb. **Wmk. 170** ***Perf. 14***

C40	AP13 5k ultra	27.50	6.00
C41	AP13 10k green	27.50	6.75
C42	AP13 20k carmine	60.00	7.50
C43	AP13 50k dull blue	175.00	35.00
C44	AP13 80k purple	60.00	9.00
	Nos. C40-C44 (5)	350.00	64.25

Unwmk.

C45	AP13 5k ultra	22.50	*4.00*
C46	AP13 10k green	22.50	*3.75*
a.	Horiz. pair, imperf. btwn.	2,000.	*1,250.*
C47	AP13 20k carmine	30.00	*6.00*
C48	AP13 50k dull blue	160.00	*28.50*
C49	AP13 80k purple	18.00	*6.00*
	Nos. C45-C49 (5)	253.00	*48.25*

10th anniversary of Soviet civil aviation and airmail service. Counterfeits exist, perf 11½.

I. D. Usyskin AP18

10k, A. B. Vasenko. 20k, P. F. Fedosenko.

1934 **Wmk. 170** ***Perf. 11***

C50	AP18 5k vio brown	17.50	6.00
C51	AP18 10k brown	115.00	6.00
C52	AP18 20k ultra	27.50	8.25
	Nos. C50-C52 (3)	160.00	20.25

Perf. 13¾

C50a	AP18 5k	135.	
C51a	AP18 10k	—	*4,500.*
C52a	AP18 20k	10,000.	
	Nos. C50a-C52a (3)	10,135.	*4,500.*

Honoring victims of the stratosphere disaster. See Nos. C77-C79.

Beware of examples of Nos. C50-C52 reperforated to resemble Nos. C50a-C52a.

Airship "Pravda" — AP19

Airship Landing — AP20

Airship "Voroshilov" — AP21

Sideview of Airship — AP22

Airship "Lenin" — AP23

1934 ***Perf. 14***

C53	AP19 5k red orange	25.00	*2.40*
C54	AP20 10k claret	27.50	*3.75*
C55	AP21 15k brown	75.00	*10.00*
C56	AP22 20k black	15.00	*7.50*
C57	AP23 30k ultra	375.00	*55.00*
	Nos. C53-C57 (5)	517.50	78.65

Capt. V. Voronin and "Chelyuskin" — AP24

Prof. Otto Y. Schmidt — AP25

A. V. Lapidevsky AP26

S. A. Levanevsky AP27

"Schmidt Camp" — AP28

Designs: 15k, M. G. Slepnev. 20k, I. V. Doronin. 25k, M. V. Vodopianov. 30k, V. S. Molokov. 40k, N. P. Kamanin.

1935 ***Perf. 14***

C58	AP24	1k red orange	12.50	2.25
C59	AP25	3k rose car	12.50	2.25
C60	AP26	5k emerald	7.50	2.25
C61	AP27	10k dark brown	17.50	2.25
C62	AP27	15k black	17.50	3.75
C63	AP27	20k deep claret	22.50	3.75
C64	AP27	25k indigo	120.00	17.50
C65	AP27	30k dull green	750.00	50.00
C66	AP27	40k purple	22.00	12.00
C67	AP28	50k dark ultra	50.00	30.00
		Nos. C58-C67 (10)	1,032.	126.00

Aerial rescue of ice-breaker Chelyuskin crew and scientific expedition.

No. C61 Surcharged in Red

1935, Aug.

C68	AP27 1r on 10k dk brn	725.00	525.00
a.	Inverted surcharge	*90,000.*	
b.	Lower case Cyrillic "F"	1,500.	1,450.
c.	As "b," inverted surcharge	*600,000.*	

Moscow-San Francisco flight. Counterfeits exist.

Single-Engined Monoplane — AP34

Five-Engined Transport — AP35

20k, Twin-engined cabin plane. 30k, 4r-motored transport. 40k, Single-engined amphibian. 50k, Twin-motored transport. 80k, 8-motored transport.

1937 **Unwmk.** ***Perf. 12***

C69	AP34 10k yel brn & blk	3.00	1.00
a.	Imperf.		—
C70	AP34 20k gray grn & blk	3.00	1.00
C71	AP34 30k red brn & blk	3.00	1.00
C72	AP34 40k vio brn & blk	5.25	1.00
C73	AP34 50k dk vio & blk	16.50	2.00
C74	AP35 80k bl vio & brn	16.50	6.00
C75	AP35 1r blk, brn & buff	45.00	8.50
a.	Sheet of 4, imperf.	175.00	*215.00*

Vertical Pairs, Imperf. Between

C69b	AP34 10k yel brn & blk	—	*62.50*
C70a	AP34 20k gray grn & blk	*3,250.*	*3,250.*
	Nos. C69-C75 (7)	92.25	20.50
	Set, never hinged	168.00	

Jubilee Aviation Exhib., Moscow, Nov. 15-20.

Vertical pairs, imperf. between, exist for No. C71, value $4,000; No. C72, value $5,750; No. C73, value $2,300.

Types of 1938 Regular Issue Overprinted in Various Colors

1939 **Typo.**

C76	A282	10k red (C)	4.00	1.00
C76A	A285	30k blue (R)	6.75	1.00
C76B	A286	40k dl grn (Br)	8.25	1.20
C76C	A287	50k dl vio (R)	6.75	2.00
C76D	A289	1r brown (Bl)	12.50	2.50
a.		Double overprint		1,500.
		Nos. C76-C76D (5)	38.25	7.70
		Set, never hinged	100.00	

Soviet Aviation Day, Aug. 18, 1939.

Types of 1934 with "30.1.1944" Added at Lower Left

Designs: No. C77, P. F. Fedosenko. No. C78, I. D. Usyskin. No. C79, A. B. Vasenko.

1944 **Photo.** ***Perf. 12***
C77 AP18 1r deep blue 5.00 .75
C78 AP18 1r slate green 5.00 .75
C79 AP18 1r brt yellow green 5.00 .75
Nos. C77-C79 (3) 15.00 2.25
Set, never hinged 30.00

1934 stratosphere disaster, 10th anniv.

Nos. 860A and 861A Surcharged in Red

1944, May 25
C80 A431 1r on 30k Prus green .50 .25
C81 A432 1r on 30k deep ultra .50 .25
Set, never hinged 2.00

Catalogue values for unused stamps in this section, from this point to the end of the section, are for Never Hinged items.

Planes and Soviet Air Force Flag — AP42

1948, Dec. 10 **Litho.** ***Perf. 12½***
C82 AP42 1r dark blue 10.00 1.00

Air Force Day.

Plane over Zages, Caucasus — AP43

Plane over Farm Scene AP44

Map of Russian Air Routes and Transport Planes — AP45

No. C85, Sochi, Northern Caucasus. No. C86, Far East. No. C87, Leningrad. 2r, Moscow. 3r, Arctic.

Perf. 12x12½
1949, Nov. 9 **Photo.** **Unwmk.**
C83 AP43 50k red brn, *lemon* 4.50 .80
C84 AP44 60k sepia, *pale buff* 8.50 1.00
C85 AP44 1r org brn, *yelsh* 8.50 1.40
C86 AP43 1r blue, *bluish* 8.50 1.40
C87 AP43 1r red brn, *pale fawn* 8.50 1.40
C88 AP45 1r blk, ultra & red, *gray* 17.50 4.00
C89 AP43 2r org brn, *bluish* 26.00 11.00
C90 AP43 3r dk green, *bluish* 42.50 4.00
Nos. C83-C90 (8) 124.50 25.00

Plane and Mountain Stream — AP46

Design: 1r, Like No. C86.

1955 **Litho.** ***Perf. 12½x12***
C91 AP46 1r multicolored 5.00 .50
C92 AP46 2r black & yel grn 10.00 .50

For overprints see Nos. C95-C96.

Globe and Plane — AP47

1955, May 31 **Photo.**
C93 AP47 2r chocolate 1.25 .25
C94 AP47 2r deep blue 1.25 .25

Nos. C91 and C92 Overprinted in Red

Perf. 12x12½
1955, Nov. 22 **Litho.** **Unwmk.**
C95 AP46 1r multicolored 8.00 2.00
C96 AP46 2r black & yel grn 12.00 3.00

Issued for use at the scientific drifting stations North Pole-4 and North Pole-5. The inscription reads "North Pole-Moscow, 1955." Counterfeits exist.

Arctic Camp AP48

1956, June 8 ***Perf. 12½x12***
C97 AP48 1r blue, grn, brn, yel & red 1.50 .50

Opening of scientific drifting station North Pole-6.

Helicopter over Kremlin — AP49

1960, Mar. 5 **Photo.** ***Perf. 12***
C98 AP49 60k ultra 1.00 .25

Surcharged with New Value, Bars and "1961"

1961, Dec. 20
C99 AP49 6k on 60k ultra .50 .25

Air Force Emblem and Arms of Normandy — AP50

1962, Dec. 30 **Unwmk.** ***Perf. 11½***
C100 AP50 6k blue grn, ocher & car .35 .25

French Normandy-Neman Escadrille, which fought on the Russian front, 20th anniv.

Jet over Map Showing Airlines in USSR AP51

Designs: 12k, Aeroflot emblem and globe. 16k, Jet over map showing Russian international airlines.

1963, Feb.
C101 AP51 10k red, blk & tan .75 .25
C102 AP51 12k blue, red, tan & blk 1.00 .25
C103 AP51 16k blue, blk & red 1.25 .25
Nos. C101-C103 (3) 3.00 .75

Aeroflot, the civil air fleet, 40th anniv.

Tupolev 134 at Sheremetyevo Airport, Moscow — AP52

Civil Aviation: 10k, An-24 (Antonov) and Vnukovo Airport, Moscow. 12k, Mi-10 (Mil helicopter) and Central Airport, Moscow. 16k, Be-10 (Beriev) and Chinki Riverport, Moscow. 20k, Antei airliner and Domodedovo Airport, Moscow.

1965, Dec. 31
C104 AP52 6k org, red & vio .30 .25
C105 AP52 10k lt grn, org red & gray .50 .25
C106 AP52 12k lil, dk sep & lt grn .50 .25
C107 AP52 16k lil, lt brn, red & grn .75 .25
C108 AP52 20k org red, pur & gray .95 .25
Nos. C104-C108 (5) 3.00 1.25

Aviation Type of 1976

Aviation 1917-1930 (Aviation Emblem and): 4k, P-4 BIS biplane, 1917. 6k, AK-1 monoplane, 1924. 10k, R-3 (ANT-3) biplane, 1925. 12k, TB-1 (ANT-4) monoplane, 1925. 16k, R-5 biplane, 1929. 20k, Shcha-2 amphibian, 1930.

Lithographed and Engraved

1977, Aug. 16 ***Perf. 12x11½***
C109 A2134 4k multicolored .25 .25
C110 A2134 6k multicolored .25 .25
C111 A2134 10k multicolored .25 .25
C112 A2134 12k multicolored .35 .25
C113 A2134 16k multicolored .45 .25
C114 A2134 20k multicolored .60 .25
Nos. C109-C114 (6) 2.15 1.50

1978, Aug. 10

4k, PO-2 biplane, 1928. 6k, K-5 passenger plane, 1929. 10k, TB-3, cantilever monoplane, 1930. 12k, Stal-2, 1931. 16k, MBR-2 hydroplane, 1932. 20k, I-16 fighter plane, 1934.

C115 A2134 4k multicolored .25 .25
C116 A2134 6k multicolored .25 .25
C117 A2134 10k multicolored .30 .25
C118 A2134 12k multicolored .30 .25
C119 A2134 16k multicolored .40 .25
C120 A2134 20k multicolored .50 .30
Nos. C115-C120 (6) 2.00 1.55

Aviation 1928-1934.

Jet and Compass Rose — AP53

1978, Aug. 4 **Litho.** ***Perf. 12***
C121 AP53 32k dark blue 3.00 .35

Aeroflot Plane AH-28 — AP54

Designs: Various Aeroflot planes.

Photogravure and Engraved

1979 ***Perf. 11½x12***
C122 AP54 2k shown .25 .25
C123 AP54 3k YAK-42 .25 .25
C124 AP54 10k T4-154 .30 .25
C125 AP54 15k IL76 transport .45 .25
C126 AP54 32k IL86 jet liner .85 .45
Nos. C122-C126 (5) 2.10 1.45

AIR POST OFFICIAL STAMPS

Used on mail from Russian embassy in Berlin to Moscow. Surcharged on Consular Fee stamps. Currency: the German mark.

OA1

Surcharge in Carmine Bicolored Burelage

1922, July **Litho.** ***Perf. 13½***
CO1 OA1 12m on 2.25r 105.00 —
a. Inverted surcharge 7,500.
CO2 OA1 24m on 3r 130.00 —
CO3 OA1 120m on 2.25r 195.00 —
CO4 OA1 600m on 3r 260.00 —
CO5 OA1 1200m on 10k 725.00 —
CO6 OA1 1200m on 50k *37,500.* —
CO7 OA1 1200m on 2.25r 1,300. —
CO8 OA1 1200m on 3r 2,250. —

Three types of each denomination, distinguished by shape of "C" in surcharge and length of second line of surcharge. Used stamps have pen or crayon cancel. Forgeries exist.

SPECIAL DELIVERY STAMPS

Motorcycle Courier — SD1

Express Truck — SD2

Design: 80k, Locomotive.

Perf. 12½x12, 12x12½

1932 Photo. Wmk. 170

E1 SD1	5k dull brown	7.25	3.00
E2 SD2	10k violet brown	28.50	10.00
E3 SD2	80k dull green	60.00	8.50
	Nos. E1-E3 (3)	95.75	21.50
	Set, never hinged	150.00	

Used values are for c-t-o.

POSTAGE DUE STAMPS

Regular Issue of 1918 Surcharged in Red or Carmine

1924-25 Unwmk. *Perf. 13½*

J1 A33	1k on 35k blue	2.00	*.50*
J2 A33	3k on 35k blue	2.00	*.50*
J3 A33	5k on 35k blue	2.00	*.50*
a.	Imperf.	*450.00*	
J4 A33	8k on 35k blue ('25)	2.00	*.50*
a.	Imperf.	*450.00*	
J5 A33	10k on 35k blue	2.00	*.50*
a.	Pair, one without surcharge	*550.00*	
J6 A33	12k on 70k brown	2.00	*.50*
J7 A33	14k on 35k blue ('25)	2.00	*.50*
a.	Imperf.	*450.00*	
J8 A33	32k on 35k blue	2.50	*.50*
J9 A33	40k on 35k blue	2.50	*.50*
a.	Imperf.	*450.00*	
c.	Pair, one without surcharge	*675.00*	
	Nos. J1-J9 (9)	19.00	*4.50*

Inverted Surcharge

J1b A33	1k on 35k blue	*150.00*	—
J2b A33	3k on 35k blue	*150.00*	—

Regular Issue of 1921 Surcharged in Violet

1924 *Imperf.*

J10 A40	1k on 100r orange	6.75	*8.00*
a.	1k on 100r yellow	8.75	*8.00*
b.	Pelure paper	6.75	*8.00*
c.	Inverted surcharge	*225.00*	

D1

Lithographed or Typographed

1925 *Perf. 12*

J11 D1	1k red	2.00	.75
J12 D1	2k violet	2.00	.75
J13 D1	3k light blue	2.00	.75
J14 D1	7k orange	2.00	.75
J15 D1	8k green	2.00	.75
J16 D1	10k dark blue	2.00	.75
J17 D1	14k brown	2.00	.75
	Nos. J11-J17 (7)	14.00	5.25

Perf. 14½x14

J13a D1	3k	12.50	1.00
J14a D1	7k	20.00	1.00
J16a D1	10k	—	—
J17a D1	14k	5.00	1.00
	Nos. J13a-J17a (4)	37.50	3.00

Value of No. J16a unused is based on 2012 auction realization.

1925 Wmk. 170 Typo. *Perf. 12*

J18 D1	1k red	1.60	.40
J19 D1	2k violet	1.75	.40
J20 D1	3k light blue	1.75	.40
J21 D1	7k orange	1.75	.40
J22 D1	8k green	1.75	.40
J23 D1	10k dark blue	1.75	.40
J24 D1	14k brown	1.75	.40
	Nos. J18-J24 (7)	12.10	2.80

For surcharges see Nos. 359-372.

WENDEN (LIVONIA)

A former district of Livonia, a province of the Russian Empire, which became part of Latvia, under the name of Vidzeme.

Used values for Nos. L2-L12 are for pen-canceled stamps. Postmarked examples sell for considerably more.

A1

1862 Unwmk. *Imperf.*

L1 A1	(2k) blue	30.00	
a.	Tête bêche pair	*350.00*	

No. L1 may have been used for a short period of time but withdrawn because of small size. Some consider it an essay.

A2

A3

1863

L2 A2	(2k) rose & black	240.00	240.00
a.	Background inverted	600.00	600.00
L3 A3	(4k) blue grn & blk	175.00	250.00
a.	(4k) yellow green & black	300.00	300.00
b.	Half used as 2k on cover		*2,500.*
c.	Background inverted	950.00	500.00
d.	As "a," background inverted	650.00	400.00

The official imitations of Nos. L2 and L3 have a single instead of a double hyphen after "WENDEN." Value, each $20.

Coat of Arms

A4 A5 A6

1863-71

L4 A4	(2k) rose & green	90.00	90.00
a.	Yellowish paper		
b.	Green frame around central oval	95.00	60.00
c.	Tête bêche pair	*2,500.*	
L5 A5	(2k) rose & grn ('64)	100.00	75.00
L6 A6	(2k) rose & green	75.00	75.00
	Nos. L4-L6 (3)	265.00	240.00

Official imitations of Nos. L4b and L5 have a rose instead of a green line around the central oval. The first official imitation of No. L6 has the central oval 5½mm instead of 6¼mm wide; the second imitation is less clearly printed than the original and the top of the "f" of "Briefmarke" is too much hooked. Value, each $20.

Coat of Arms

A7 A8

1872-75 *Perf. 12½*

L7 A7	(2k) red & green	75.00	*75.00*
L8 A8	2k yel grn & red ('75)	8.50	*11.00*
a.	Numeral in upper right corner resembles an inverted "3"	30.00	*30.00*

Reprints of No. L8 have no horizontal lines in the background. Those of No. L8a have the impression blurred and only traces of the horizontal lines.

A9

1878-80

L9 A9	2k green & red	8.50	*10.00*
a.	Imperf.		
L10 A9	2k blk, grn & red ('80)	10.00	10.00
a.	Imperf., pair	35.00	

No. L9 has been reprinted in blue green and yellow green with perforation 11½ and in gray green with perforation 12½ or imperforate.

1884 *Perf. 11½*

L11 A9	2k black, green & red	10.00	3.00
a.	Green arm omitted	21.00	
b.	Arm inverted	21.00	
c.	Arm double	27.50	
d.	Imperf., pair	150.00	

Wenden Castle — A10

1901 Litho.

L12 A10	2k dk green & brown	12.00	10.00
a.	Tête bêche pair	45.00	
b.	Imperf., pair	120.00	

OCCUPATION STAMPS

ISSUED UNDER GERMAN OCCUPATION

German Stamps Overprinted in Black

On Stamps of 1905-17

1916-17 Wmk. 125 *Perf. 14, 14½*

N1	A22	2½pf gray	.65	*1.00*
N2	A16	3pf brown	.25	.25
N3	A16	5pf green	.65	*1.00*
N4	A22	7½pf orange	.65	*1.00*
N5	A16	10pf carmine	.65	*1.00*
N6	A22	15pf yel brn	3.00	2.00
N7	A22	15pf dk vio ('17)	.65	*1.00*
N8	A16	20pf ultra	1.00	1.00
N9	A16	25pf org & blk, *yel*	.50	*.50*
N10	A16	40pf lake & blk	1.00	*3.75*
N11	A16	50pf vio & blk, *buff*	1.00	*1.50*
N12	A17	1m car rose	12.00	3.50
		Nos. 1N1-1N12 (12)	22.00	*17.50*
		Set, never hinged	40.00	

These stamps were used in the former Russian provinces of Suvalki, Vilnius, Kaunas, Kurland, Estland and Lifland.

ISSUED UNDER FINNISH OCCUPATION

Finnish Stamps of 1917-18 Overprinted

1919 Unwmk. *Perf. 14*

N13 A19	5p green	12.50	15.00
N14 A19	10p rose	12.50	15.00
N15 A19	20p buff	12.50	15.00
N16 A19	40p red violet	12.50	15.00
N17 A19	50p orange brn	150.00	150.00
N18 A19	1m dl rose & blk	140.00	140.00
N19 A19	5m violet & blk	425.00	425.00
N20 A19	10m brown & blk	725.00	725.00
	Nos. N13-N20 (8)	1,490.	1,500.
	Set, never hinged	3,000.	

"Aunus" is the Finnish name for Olonets, a town of Russia.

Counterfeits overprints exist.

Catalogue values for unused stamps in this section, from this point to the end of the section, are for Never Hinged items.

Issued under German Occupation

Germany Nos. 506 to 523 Overprinted in Black

1941-43 Unwmk. Typo. *Perf. 14*

N21 A115	1pf gray black	.25	.25
N22 A115	3pf light brown	.25	.25
N23 A115	4pf slate	.25	.25
N24 A115	5pf dp yellow green	.25	.25
N25 A115	6pf purple	.25	.25
N26 A115	8pf red	.25	.25
N27 A115	10pf dk brown ('43)	.65	*3.25*
N28 A115	12pf carmine ('43)	.65	*2.75*

Engr.

N29 A115	10pf dark brown	1.25	*1.40*
N30 A115	12pf brt carmine	1.25	*1.40*
N31 A115	15pf brown lake	.25	.25
N32 A115	16pf peacock grn	.25	.25
N33 A115	20pf blue	.25	.25
N34 A115	24pf orange brown	.25	.25
N35 A115	25pf brt ultra	.25	.25
N36 A115	30pf olive green	.25	.25
N37 A115	40pf brt red violet	.25	.25
N38 A115	50pf myrtle green	.25	.25
N39 A115	60pf dk red brown	.25	.25
N40 A115	80pf indigo	.25	*.65*
	Nos. N21-N40 (20)	7.80	*13.20*

Issued for use in Estonia, Latvia and Lithuania.

Same Overprinted in Black

Typo.

N41 A115	1pf gray black	.25	.25
N42 A115	3pf lt brown	.25	.25
N43 A115	4pf slate	.25	.25
N44 A115	5pf dp yel green	.25	.25
N45 A115	6pf purple	.25	.25
N46 A115	8pf red	.25	.25
N47 A115	10pf dk brown ('43)	.55	*2.40*
N48 A115	12pf carmine ('43)	.55	*2.40*

Engr.

N49 A115	10pf dk brown	1.00	*1.60*
N50 A115	12pf brt carmine	1.00	*1.60*
N51 A115	15pf brown lake	.25	.25
N52 A115	16pf peacock green	.25	.25
N53 A115	20pf blue	.25	.25
N54 A115	24pf orange brown	.25	.25
N55 A115	25pf bright ultra	.25	.25
N56 A115	30pf olive green	.25	.25
N57 A115	40pf brt red violet	.25	.25
N58 A115	50pf myrtle green	.25	.25
N59 A115	60pf dk red brown	.25	.25
N60 A115	80pf indigo	.25	.25
	Nos. N42-N60 (20)	7.10	*12.00*

ARMY OF THE NORTHWEST

(Gen. Nicolai N. Yudenich)

Russian Stamps of 1909-18 Overprinted in Black or Red

On Stamps of 1909-12

Perf. 14 to 15 and Compound

1919, Aug. 1

1	A14	2k green	5.00	*10.00*
2	A14	5k claret	5.00	*10.00*
3	A15	10k dk blue (R)	10.00	*15.00*
4	A11	15k red brn & bl	5.00	*8.00*
5	A8	20k blue & car	8.00	*15.00*
6	A11	25k grn & gray vio	15.00	*20.00*
7	A8	50k brn vio & grn	10.00	*15.00*

Perf. 13½

8	A9	1r pale brn, dk brn & org	25.00	*50.00*
9	A13	10r scar, yel & gray	75.00	*125.00*

On Stamps of 1917

Imperf

10	A14	3k red	5.00	*10.00*
11	A12	3.50r mar & lt grn	17.50	*35.00*
12	A13	5r dk blue, grn & pale bl	17.50	*30.00*

13 A12 7r dk grn & pink 150.00 *200.00*

No. 2 Surcharged

Perf. 14, 14½x15

14 A14 10k on 5k claret 12.00 *24.00*
Nos. 1-14 (14) 360.00 *567.00*

Nos. 1-14 exist with inverted overprint or surcharge. The 1, 3½, 5, 7 and 10 rubles with red overprint are trial printings (value $150 each). The 20k on 14k, perforated, and the 1, 2, 5, 15, 70k and 1r imperforate were overprinted but never placed in use. Value: $300, $30, $45, $45, $45, $45 and $65.

These stamps were in use from Aug. 1 to Oct. 15, 1919.

Counterfeits of Nos. 1-14 abound.

ARMY OF THE NORTH

A1

A2

A3

A4

A5

1919, Sept. Typo. *Imperf.*

1 A1 5k brown violet .60 *1.00*
2 A2 10k blue .60 *1.00*
3 A3 15k yellow .60 *1.00*
4 A4 20k rose .60 *1.00*
5 A5 50k green .60 *1.00*
Nos. 1-5 (5) 3.00 *5.00*

The letters OKCA are the initials of Russian words meaning "Special Corps, Army of the North." The stamps were in use from about the end of September to the end of December, 1919.

Used values are for c-t-o stamps.

(General Miller)

A set of seven stamps of this design was prepared in 1919, but not issued. Value, set $35. Counterfeits exist.

RUSSIA OFFICES ABROAD

For various reasons the Russian Empire maintained Post Offices to handle its correspondence in several foreign countries. These were similar to the Post Offices in foreign countries maintained by other world powers.

OFFICES IN CHINA

100 Kopecks = 1 Ruble
100 Cents = 1 Dollar (1917)

Russian Stamps Overprinted in Blue or Red

On Issues of 1889-92
Horizontally Laid Paper

1899-1904 Wmk. 168 *Perf. 14½x15*

1 A10 1k orange (Bl) .75 *1.00*
2 A10 2k yel green (R) .75 *1.00*
3 A10 3k carmine (Bl) .75 *1.00*
4 A10 5k red violet (Bl) .75 *1.00*
5 A10 7k dk blue (R) 1.50 *2.50*
a. Inverted overprint *500.00*
6 A8 10k dk blue (R) 1.50 *2.50*
7 A8 50k vio & grn (Bl) ('04) 12.00 *8.50*

Perf. 13½

8 A9 1r lt brn, brn & org (Bl) ('04) 150.00 150.00
Nos. 1-8 (8) 168.00 167.50

On Issues of 1902-05
Overprinted in Black, Red or Blue
Perf. 14½ to 15 and Compound

1904-08 Vertically Laid Paper

9 A8 4k rose red (Bl) 6.00 *3.50*
10 A10 7k dk blue (R) 15.00 15.00
11 A8 10k dk blue (R) 1,500. 1,300.
a. Groundwork inverted *14,500.*
12 A11 14k bl & rose (R) 10.00 10.00
13 A11 15k brn vio & blue (Bl) ('08) 35.00 *30.00*
14 A8 20k blue & car (Bl) 5.00 5.00
15 A11 25k dull grn & lil (R) ('08) 50.00 50.00
16 A11 35k dk vio & grn (R) 10.00 10.00
17 A8 50k vio & grn (Bl) 100.00 125.00
18 A11 70k brn & org (Bl) 15.00 13.00

Perf. 13½

19 A9 1r lt brn, brn & org (Bl) 25.00 25.00
20 A12 3.50r blk & gray (R) 5.00 *5.00*
21 A13 5r dk bl, grn & pale bl (R) ('07) 8.50 *12.00*
a. Inverted overprint *2,500.*
22 A12 7r blk & yel (Bl) 25.00 12.00
23 A13 10r scar, yel & gray (Bl) ('07) 100.00 *100.00*
Nos. 9-10,12-23 (14) 409.50 415.50

On Issues of 1909-12
Wove Paper
Lozenges of Varnish on Face

1910-16 Unwmk. *Perf. 14x14½*

24 A14 1k orange yel (Bl) .50 .50
25 A14 1k org yel (Bl Bk) 6.00 5.00
26 A14 2k green (Bk) 1.00 1.00
27 A14 2k green (Bl) 7.50 *15.00*
a. Double ovpt. (Bk and Bl)
28 A14 3k rose red (Bl) 2.00 *5.00*
29 A14 3k rose red (Bk) 12.00 12.00
30 A15 4k carmine (Bl) 1.00 2.00
31 A15 4k carmine (Bk) 10.00 10.00
32 A14 7k lt blue (Bk) 1.00 *1.00*
33 A15 10k blue (Bk) 1.00 1.00
34 A11 14k blue & rose (Bk) 10.00 5.00
35 A11 14k blue & rose (Bl)
36 A11 15k dl vio & bl (Bk) 1.00 *1.25*
37 A8 20k blue & car (Bk) *5.00* *7.00*
38 A11 25k green & vio (Bl) 3.50 *6.00*
39 A11 25k grn & vio (Bk) 1.00 *1.60*
40 A11 35k vio & grn (Bk) 1.00 1.00
42 A8 50k vio & grn (Bl) 2.00 *2.00*
43 A8 50k brn vio & grn (Bk) 18.00 *20.00*
44 A11 70k lt brn & org (Bl) 1.00 *2.00*

Perf. 13½

45 A9 1r pale brn, brn & org (Bl) 1.25 *2.40*
47 A13 5r dk bl, grn & pale bl (R) 25.00 15.00
Nos. 24-34,36-47 (21) 110.75 115.75

The existence of #35 is questioned.

Russian Stamps of 1902-12 Surcharged

a

b

c

On Stamps of 1909-12

1917 *Perf. 11½, 13½, 14, 14½x15*

50 A14(a) 1c on 1k dl org yel .60 *5.50*
51 A14(a) 2c on 2k dull grn .60 *5.50*
a. Inverted surcharge 100.00
52 A14(a) 3c on 3k car .60 *5.50*
a. Inverted surcharge 100.00
b. Double surcharge 150.00
53 A15(a) 4c on 4k car 1.25 *4.25*
54 A14(a) 5c on 5k claret 1.25 *15.00*
55 A15(b) 10c on 10k dk blue 1.25 *15.00*
a. Inverted surcharge 100.00 100.00
b. Double surcharge 115.00
56 A11(b) 14c on 14k dk blue & car 1.25 *10.00*
a. Imperf. 6.00
b. Inverted surcharge 100.00
57 A11(a) 15c on 15k brn lil & dp blue 1.25 *15.00*
a. Inverted surcharge 50.00
58 A8(b) 20c on 20k bl & car 1.25 *15.00*
59 A11(a) 25c on 25k grn & vio 1.25 *15.00*
60 A11(a) 35c on 35k brn vio & grn 1.50 *15.00*
a. Inverted surcharge 50.00
61 A8(a) 50c on 50k brn vio & grn 1.25 *15.00*
62 A11(a) 70c on 70k brn & red org 1.25 *15.00*
63 A9(c) $1 on 1r pale brn, brn & org 1.25 *15.00*
Nos. 50-63 (14) 15.80

On Stamps of 1902-05
Vertically Laid Paper
Perf. 11½, 13, 13½, 13½x11½
Wmk. Wavy Lines (168)

64 A12 $3.50 on 3.50r blk & gray 20.00 *40.00*
65 A13 $5 on 5r dk bl, grn & pale blue 20.00 *40.00*
66 A12 $7 on 7r blk & yel 10.00 *32.50*

On Stamps of 1915
Wove Paper

Unwmk. *Perf. 13½*

68 A13 $5 on 5r ind, grn & lt blue 25.00 *50.00*
a. Inverted surcharge 500.00
70 A13 $10 on 10r car lake, yel & gray 50.00 *100.00*
Nos. 64-70 (5) 125.00 262.50

The surcharge on Nos. 64-70 is in larger type than on the $1.

Russian Stamps of 1909-18 Surcharged in Black or Red

On Stamps of 1909-12

1920 *Perf. 14, 14½x15*

72 A14 1c on 1k dull org yel 175.00 *275.00*
73 A14 2c on 2k dull grn (R) 16.00 *27.50*
74 A14 3c on 3k car 16.00 *37.50*
75 A15 4c on 4k car 18.00 22.50
a. Inverted surcharge 130.00 150.00
76 A14 5c on 5k claret 60.00 90.00
77 A15 10c on 10k dk bl (R) 150.00 225.00
78 A14 10c on 10k on 7k blue (R) 125.00 190.00

On Stamps of 1917-18

Imperf

79 A14 1c on 1k orange 42.50 37.50
a. Inverted surcharge 125.00 *150.00*
80 A14 5c on 5k claret 35.00 55.00
a. Inverted surcharge 150.00
b. Double surcharge 250.00
c. Surcharged "Cent" only 95.00
Nos. 72-80 (9) 637.50 960.00

OFFICES IN THE TURKISH EMPIRE

Various powers maintained post offices in the Turkish Empire before World War I by authority of treaties which ended with the signing of the Treaty of Lausanne in 1923. The foreign post offices were closed Oct. 27, 1923.

100 Kopecks = 1 Ruble
40 Paras = 1 Piaster (1900)

Coat of Arms
A1

1863 Unwmk. Typo. *Imperf.*

1 A1 6k blue 375.00 *1,000.*
a. 6k light blue, thin paper 350.00 *1,350.*
b. 6k light blue, medium paper 350.00 *1,350.*
c. 6k dark blue, chalky paper 200.00

Forgeries exist.

A2

A3

1865 Litho.

2 A2 (2k) brown & blue 800.00 750.00
3 A3 (20k) blue & red 900.00 850.00

Twenty-eight varieties of each.

A4

A5

1866 Horizontal Network

4 A4 (2k) rose & pale bl 25.00 *30.00*
5 A5 (20k) deep blue & rose 40.00 *50.00*

1867 Vertical Network

6 A4 (2k) rose & pale bl 75.00 *100.00*
7 A5 (20k) dp blue & rose 200.00 *100.00*

The initials inscribed on Nos. 2 to 7 are those of the Russian Company of Navigation and Trade.

The official imitations of Nos. 2 to 7 are on yellowish white paper. The colors are usually paler than those of the originals and there are minor differences in the designs.

A6

Horizontally Laid Paper

1868 Typo. Wmk. 168 *Perf. 11½*

8 A6 1k brown 50.00 20.00
9 A6 3k green 60.00 25.00
10 A6 5k blue 60.00 25.00
11 A6 10k car & green 75.00 25.00
Nos. 8-11 (4) 245.00 95.00

Colors of Nos. 8-11 dissolve in water.

1872-90 *Perf. 14½x15*

12 A6 1k brown 10.00 2.00
13 A6 3k green 25.00 3.00
14 A6 5k blue 5.00 1.00

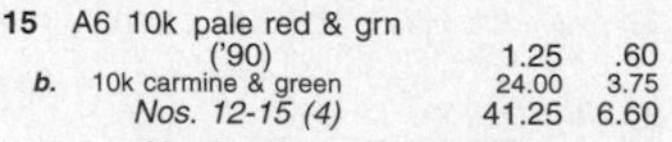

15 A6 10k pale red & grn ('90) 1.25 .60
b. 10k carmine & green 24.00 3.75
Nos. 12-15 (4) 41.25 6.60

Vertically Laid Paper

12a A6 1k 75.00 18.00
13a A6 3k 75.00 18.00
14a A6 5k 75.00 18.00
15a A6 10k 190.00 47.50
Nos. 12a-15a (4) 415.00 101.50

Nos. 12-15 exist imperf.

No. 15 Surcharged in Black or Blue

a

b

c

1876

16 A6(a) 8k on 10k (Bk) 75.00 45.00
a. Vertically laid *2,750.*
b. Inverted surcharge 400.00
17 A6(a) 8k on 10k (Bl) 90.00 75.00
a. Vertically laid
b. Inverted surcharge

1879

18 A6(b) 7k on 10k (Bk) 80.00 65.00
a. Vertically laid 750.00 750.00
b. Inverted surcharge
19 A6(b) 7k on 10k (Bl) 125.00 85.00
a. Vertically laid 1,750. 1,750.
b. Inverted surcharge 500.00
19C A6(c) 7k on 10k (Bl) 1,250. 1,250.
19D A6(c) 7k on 10k (Bk) 1,250. 1,250.

Nos. 16-19D have been extensively counterfeited.

1879 *Perf. 14½x15*

20 A6 1k black & yellow 3.00 1.00
a. Vertically laid 10.00 5.00
21 A6 2k black & rose 5.00 3.00
a. Vertically laid 10.00 5.00
22 A6 7k carmine & gray 9.00 1.00
a. Vertically laid 42.50 15.00
Nos. 20-22 (3) 17.00 5.00

1884

23 A6 1k orange .75 .50
24 A6 2k green 1.00 .75
25 A6 5k pale red violet 4.00 2.00
26 A6 7k blue 2.00 1.50
Nos. 23-26 (4) 7.75 4.75

Nos. 23-26 imperforate are believed to be proofs.

No. 23 surcharged "40 PARAS" is bogus, though some examples were postally used.

Russian Company of Navigation and Trade

This overprint, in two sizes, was privately applied in various colors to Russian Offices in the Turkish Empire stamps of 1900-1910.

A7

A8

Surcharged in Blue, Black or Red

1900 Horizontally Laid Paper

27 A7 4pa on 1k orange (Bl) 1.25 1.25
a. Inverted surcharge 30.00 30.00
28 A7 4pa on 1k orange (Bk) 1.25 1.25
a. Inverted surcharge 30.00 30.00
29 A7 10pa on 2k green .25 .25
a. Inverted surcharge
30 A8 1pi on 10k dk blue .50 .60
a. Inverted surcharge
Nos. 27-30 (4) 3.25 3.35

A9

A10

A11

1903-05 Vertically Laid Paper

31 A7 10pa on 2k yel green .60 *.40*
a. Inverted surcharge 75.00
32 A8 20pa on 4k rose red (Bl) .60 *.40*
a. Inverted surcharge 95.00
33 A8 1pi on 10k dk blue .60 *.40*
a. Groundwork inverted 50.00 *15.00*
34 A8 2pi on 20k blue & car (Bk) 1.40 *.75*
35 A8 5pi on 50k brn vio & grn 3.50 *1.25*
36 A9 7pi on 70k brn & org (Bl) 4.00 *2.00*

Perf. 13½

37 A10 10pi on 1r lt brn, brn & org (Bl) 6.50 *4.00*
38 A11 35pi on 3.50r blk & gray 20.00 *10.00*
39 A11 70pi on 7r blk & yel 24.00 *12.50*
Nos. 31-39 (9) 61.20 31.70

A12

A13

A14

Wove Paper
Lozenges of Varnish on Face

1909 Unwmk. *Perf. 14½x15*

40 A12 5pa on 1k orange .30 *.40*
41 A12 10pa on 2k green .35 *.65*
a. Inverted surcharge 30.00 *30.00*
42 A12 20pa on 4k carmine .70 *1.00*
43 A12 1pi on 10k blue .75 *1.20*
44 A12 5pi on 50k vio & grn 1.40 *1.60*
45 A12 7pi on 70k brn & org 2.00 *2.75*

Perf. 13½

46 A13 10pi on 1r brn & org 3.00 *5.00*
47 A14 35pi on 3.50r mar & lt grn 12.00 *14.00*
48 A14 70pi on 7r dk grn & pink 20.00 *25.00*
Nos. 40-48 (9) 40.50 *51.60*

50th anniv. of the establishing of the Russian Post Offices in the Levant.

Nos. 40-48 Overprinted with Names of Various Cities Overprinted "Constantinople" in Black

1909-10 *Perf. 14½x15*

61 A12 5pa on 1k .40 *.40*
c. Inverted overprint 50.00
62 A12 10pa on 2k .40 *.40*
c. Inverted overprint 30.00
63 A12 20pa on 4k .75 *.75*
c. Inverted overprint 30.00
64 A12 1pi on 10k .75 *.75*
65 A12 5pi on 50k 1.50 *1.50*
66 A12 7pi on 70k 3.00 *3.00*

Perf. 13½

67 A13 10pi on 1r 15.00 *15.00*
a. "Constanttnople" 100.00 100.00
68 A14 35pi on 3.50r 50.00 *30.00*
c. "Constautinople" 100.00 100.00
d. "Constantjnople" 100.00 100.00
69 A14 70pi on 7r 45.00 *42.50*
c. "Constautinople" 100.00 100.00
d. "Constantjnople" 100.00 100.00

Blue Overprint
Perf. 14½x15

70 A12 5pa on 1k 8.00 *8.00*
Nos. 61-70 (10) 124.80 *102.30*

"Consnantinople"

61a A12 5pa on 1k 10.00
62a A12 10pa on 2k 10.00
63a A12 20pa on 4k 10.00
64a A12 1pi on 10k 10.00
65a A12 5pi on 50k 10.00
66a A12 7pi on 70k 12.00
68a A14 35pi on 3.50r 50.00
69a A14 70pi on 7r 90.00
70a A12 5pa on 1k 10.00
Nos. 61a-70a (9) 212.00

"Constantinopie"

61b A12 5pa on 1k 25.00
d. Inverted overprint 50.00
62b A12 10pa on 2k 25.00
d. Inverted overprint 50.00
63b A12 20pa on 4k 30.00
d. Inverted overprint 60.00
64b A12 1pi on 10k 30.00
65b A12 5pi on 50k 30.00
66b A12 7pi on 70k 30.00
68b A14 35pi on 3.50r 60.00
69b A14 70pi on 7r 90.00
Nos. 61b-69b (8) 320.00

Overprinted "Jaffa"
Black Overprint

71 A12 5pa on 1k 2.10 *3.75*
a. Inverted overprint 75.00
72 A12 10pa on 2k 2.50 *4.00*
a. Inverted overprint 50.00
73 A12 20pa on 4k 3.00 *5.25*
a. Inverted overprint 60.00
74 A12 1pi on 10k 3.75 *5.25*
a. Double overprint 95.00
75 A12 5pi on 50k 9.00 *10.50*
76 A12 7pi on 70k 11.00 *14.00*

Perf. 13½

77 A13 10pi on 1r 50.00 50.00
78 A14 35pi on 3.50r 100.00 100.00
79 A14 70pi on 7r 125.00 *150.00*

Blue Overprint
Perf. 14½x15

80 A12 5pa on 1k 12.00 12.00
Nos. 71-80 (10) 318.35 *354.75*

Overprinted "Ierusalem" in Black
Black Overprint

81 A12 5pa on 1k 2.10 *2.75*
a. Inverted overprint 60.00
b. "erusalem" 25.00
c. As "b," overprint inverted 50.00
82 A12 10pa on 2k 2.75 *4.25*
a. Inverted overprint 30.00
b. "erusalem" 25.00
c. As "b," overprint inverted 50.00
83 A12 20pa on 4k 4.25 *5.50*
a. Inverted overprint 30.00
b. "erusalem" 25.00
c. As "b," overprint inverted 50.00
84 A12 1pi on 10k 4.25 *5.50*
a. "erusalem" 30.00
85 A12 5pi on 50k 7.25 *11.00*
a. "erusalem" 35.00
86 A12 7pi on 70k 14.00 *17.50*
a. "erusalem" 35.00

Perf. 13½

87 A13 10pi on 1r 50.00 *50.00*
88 A14 35pi on 3.50r 125.00 125.00
89 A14 70pi on 7r 125.00 *150.00*

Blue Overprint
Perf. 14½x15

90 A12 5pa on 1k 15.00 25.00
Nos. 81-90 (10) 349.60 *396.50*

Overprinted "Kerassunde"
Black Overprint

91 A12 5pa on 1k .60 *.80*
a. Inverted overprint 50.00
92 A12 10pa on 2k .60 *.80*
a. Inverted overprint 50.00
93 A12 20pa on 4k 1.00 *1.10*
a. Inverted overprint 50.00
94 A12 1pi on 10k 1.25 *1.25*
95 A12 5pi on 50k 2.25 *2.50*
96 A12 7pi on 70k 3.50 *4.00*

Perf. 13½

97 A13 10pi on 1r 13.00 *15.00*
98 A14 35pi on 3.50r 42.50 *42.50*
99 A14 70pi on 7r 65.00 *52.50*

Blue Overprint
Perf. 14½x15

100 A12 5pa on 1k 15.00 *15.00*
Nos. 91-100 (10) 144.70 *135.45*

Overprinted "Mont Athos"
Black Overprint

101 A12 5pa on 1k 1.00 *1.50*
b. Inverted overprint 50.00

102 A12 10pa on 2k 1.00 *1.50*
b. Inverted overprint 50.00
103 A12 20pa on 4k 1.50 *3.00*
b. Inverted overprint 50.00
104 A12 1pi on 10k 2.00 *4.00*
b. Double overprint 60.00
105 A12 5pi on 50k 6.50 *7.00*
106 A12 7pi on 70k 8.00 *8.00*
b. Pair, one without "Mont Athos" 60.00

Perf. 13½

107 A13 10pi on 1r 30.00 *35.00*
108 A14 35pi on 3.50r 70.00 *80.00*
109 A14 70pi on 7r 130.00 *145.00*

Blue Overprint

Perf. 14½x15

110 A12 5pa on 1k 10.00 *15.00*
Nos. 101-110 (10) 260.00 *300.00*

"Mont Atho"

101a A12 5pa on 1k 25.00
102a A12 10pa on 2k 25.00
103a A12 20pa on 4k 25.00
c. Inverted overprint 100.00
104a A12 1pi on 10k 25.00
c. As "a," double overprint 125.00
105a A12 5pi on 50k 25.00
106a A12 7pi on 70k 25.00
110a A12 5pa on 1k 35.00

"M nt Athos"

101d A12 5pa on 1k 25.00
102d A12 10pa on 2k 25.00
103d A12 20pa on 4k 25.00
105d A12 5pi on 50k 50.00
106d A12 7pi on 70k 75.00

Overprinted 

111 A12 5pa on 1k 1.50 *2.00*
a. Pair, one without overprint 50.00
112 A12 10pa on 2k 1.50 *2.00*
a. Pair, one without overprint 65.00
113 A12 20pa on 4k 2.50 *3.50*
a. Pair, one without overprint 65.00
114 A12 1pi on 10k 4.50 *6.00*
a. Pair, one without overprint 75.00
115 A12 5pi on 50k 7.00 *9.50*
a. Pair, one without overprint 100.00
116 A12 7pi on 70k 13.00 *17.50*
a. Pair, one without overprint 125.00

Perf. 13½

117 A13 10pi on 1r 80.00 *80.00*
Nos. 111-117 (7) 110.00 *120.50*

The overprint is larger on No. 117.

Overprinted "Salonique"
Black Overprint
Perf. 14½x15

131 A12 5pa on 1k 1.50 *2.00*
a. Inverted overprint 55.00
b. Pair, one without overprint 60.00
132 A12 10pa on 2k 2.00 *4.00*
a. Inverted overprint 55.00
b. Pair, one without overprint 60.00
133 A12 20pa on 4k 2.50 *5.00*
a. Inverted overprint 55.00
b. Pair, one without overprint 60.00
134 A12 1pi on 10k 3.00 *6.00*
a. Pair, one without overprint 75.00
135 A12 5pi on 50k 3.50 *8.00*
136 A12 7pi on 70k 5.00 *10.00*

Perf. 13½

137 A13 10pi on 1r 32.50 40.00
138 A14 35pi on 3.50r 80.00 *85.00*
139 A14 70pi on 7r 100.00 115.00

Blue Overprint

Perf. 14½x15

140 A12 5pa on 1k 15.00 *15.00*
Nos. 131-140 (10) 245.00 *290.00*

Overprinted "Smyrne"
Black Overprint

141 A12 5pa on 1k .65 *1.25*
a. Double overprint
b. Inverted overprint 10.00
142 A12 10pa on 2k .65 *1.25*
a. Inverted overprint 25.00
143 A12 20pa on 4k 1.40 *1.60*
a. Inverted overprint 17.50
144 A12 1pi on 10k 1.40 *1.75*
145 A12 5pi on 50k 3.00 *3.00*
146 A12 7pi on 70k 4.50 *6.00*

Perf. 13½

147 A13 10pi on 1r 18.00 *22.50*
148 A14 35pi on 3.50r 37.50 *40.00*
149 A14 70pi on 7r 55.00 *62.50*

Blue Overprint

Perf. 14½x15

150 A12 5pa on 1k 11.00 *11.00*
Nos. 141-150 (10) 133.10 150.85

"Smyrn"

141c A12 5pa on 1k 18.00 *20.00*
142b A12 10pa on 2k 18.00 *20.00*
143b A12 20pa on 4k 18.00 *20.00*
144a A12 1pi on 10k 20.00 *25.00*
145a A12 5pi on 50k 20.00 *25.00*
146a A12 7pi on 70k 20.00 25.00
Nos. 141c-146a (6) 114.00 135.00

Overprinted "Trebizonde"
Black Overprint

151 A12 5pa on 1k .80 *1.00*
a. Inverted overprint 25.00
b. Pair, one without overprint 60.00
152 A12 10pa on 2k .80 *1.00*
a. Inverted overprint 25.00
b. Pair, one without "Trebizonde" 60.00
153 A12 20pa on 4k .95 .95
a. Inverted overprint 25.00
b. Pair, one without overprint 100.00
154 A12 1pi on 10k .95 *1.50*
a. Pair, one without "Trebizonde" 35.00
155 A12 5pi on 50k 2.10 *2.50*
156 A12 7pi on 70k 4.25 *5.50*

Perf. 13½

157 A13 10pi on 1r 19.00 *20.00*
158 A14 35pi on 3.50r 37.50 *37.50*
159 A14 70pi on 7r 52.50 *55.00*

Blue Overprint

Perf. 14½x15

160 A12 5pa on 1k 6.25 *7.50*
Nos. 151-160 (10) 125.10 *132.45*

On Nos. 158 and 159 the overprint is spelled "Trebisonde".

Overprinted "Beyrouth"
Black Overprint

1910

161 A12 5pa on 1k .50 *.85*
162 A12 10pa on 2k .50 *.85*
a. Inverted overprint 25.00
163 A12 20pa on 4k .80 *1.10*
164 A12 1pi on 10k .80 *1.40*
165 A12 5pi on 50k 1.90 *2.75*
166 A12 7pi on 70k 4.00 *5.50*

Perf. 13½

167 A13 10pi on 1r 19.00 *21.00*
168 A14 35pi on 3.50r 40.00 *42.50*
169 A14 70pi on 7r 55.00 *60.00*
Nos. 161-169 (9) 122.50 135.95

Overprinted "Dardanelles"

Perf. 14½x15

171 A12 5pa on 1k 1.25 *2.50*
a. Pair, one without overprint 60.00
172 A12 10pa on 2k 1.25 *2.50*
a. Pair, one without overprint 60.00
173 A12 20pa on 4k 3.25 3.25
a. Inverted overprint 25.00
174 A12 1pi on 10k 3.50 *3.50*
175 A12 5pi on 50k 6.50 *7.50*
176 A12 7pi on 70k 14.00 14.00

Perf. 13½

177 A13 10pi on 1r 21.00 *21.00*
178 A14 35pi on 3.50r 37.50 *40.00*
a. Center and ovpt. inverted *5,000.* *2,750.*
179 A14 70pi on 7r 60.00 *65.00*
Nos. 171-179 (9) 148.25 159.25

Overprinted "Metelin"

Perf. 14½x15

181 A12 5pa on 1k 1.00 *2.00*
a. Inverted overprint 50.00
182 A12 10pa on 2k 1.00 *2.00*
a. Inverted overprint 50.00
183 A12 20pa on 4k 2.00 *5.00*
a. Inverted overprint 50.00
184 A12 1pi on 10k 3.00 *6.00*
185 A12 5pi on 50k 5.00 *8.00*
186 A12 7pi on 70k 8.00 *10.00*

Perf. 13½

187 A13 10pi on 1r 20.00 *30.00*
188 A14 35pi on 3.50r 70.00 70.00
189 A14 70pi on 7r 80.00 *85.00*

Blue Overprint

Perf. 14½x15

190 A12 5pa on 1k 10.00 *15.00*
Nos. 181-190 (10) 200.00 *233.00*

Overprinted "Rizeh"

Perf. 14½x15

191 A12 5pa on 1k .65 *1.00*
a. Inverted overprint 30.00
192 A12 10pa on 2k .65 *1.00*
a. Inverted overprint 30.00
193 A12 20pa on 4k 1.10 *1.40*
a. Inverted overprint 30.00
194 A12 1pi on 10k 1.10 *1.40*
195 A12 5pi on 50k 1.75 *3.75*
196 A12 7pi on 70k 3.25 *6.00*

Perf. 13½

197 A13 10pi on 1r 17.50 *21.00*
198 A14 35pi on 3.50r 27.50 *35.00*
199 A14 70pi on 7r 44.00 *52.50*
Nos. 191-199 (9) 97.50 123.05

Nos. 61-199 for the establishing of Russian Post Offices in the Levant, 50th anniv.

A15

Vertically Laid Paper

1910 Wmk. 168 Perf. 14½x15

200 A15 20pa on 5k red violet (Bl) .60 .60

A16

A17

Wove Paper
Vertical Lozenges of Varnish on Face

1910 Unwmk. Perf. 14x14½

201 A16 5pa on 1k org yel (Bl) .40 *.50*
202 A16 10pa on 2k green (R) .40 *.50*
a. Inverted overprint 25.00
203 A17 20pa on 4k car rose (Bl) .40 *.50*
204 A17 1pi on 10k blue (R) .40 *.50*
a. Inverted overprint 25.00
205 A8 5pi on 50k vio & grn (Bl) .75 *1.20*
206 A9 7pi on 70k lt brn & org (Bl) 1.00 *1.25*

Perf. 13½

207 A10 10pi on 1r pale brn, brn & org (Bl) 1.40 *1.50*
Nos. 201-207 (7) 4.75 *5.95*

Russian Stamps of 1909-12 Surcharged in Black

No. 208

Nos. 209-212

1912 Perf. 14x14½

208 A14 20pa on 5k claret .80 .60
209 A11 1½pi on 15k dl vio & blue .80 .75
210 A8 2pi on 20k bl & car .80 .90
211 A11 2½pi on 25k grn & vio 1.00 1.25
a. Double surcharge 150.00 150.00
212 A11 3½pi on 35k vio & grn 1.60 1.60
Nos. 208-212 (5) 5.00 5.10

Russia Nos. 88-91, 93, 95-104 Surcharged

c

d

e

f

g

1913 Perf. 13½

213 A16(c) 5pa on 1k .25 .25
214 A17(d) 10pa on 2k .25 .25
215 A18(c) 15pa on 3k .25 .25
216 A19(c) 20pa on 4k .25 .25
217 A21(e) 1pi on 10k .25 .25
218 A23(f) 1½pi on 15k .50 *.50*
219 A24(f) 2pi on 20k .50 *.50*
220 A25(f) 2½pi on 25k .75 *.75*
221 A26(f) 3½pi on 35k 1.60 1.60
222 A27(e) 5pi on 50k 2.00 2.00
223 A28(f) 7pi on 70k 8.00 15.00
224 A29(e) 10pi on 1r 9.00 15.00
225 A30(e) 20pi on 2r 1.60 8.00
226 A31(g) 30pi on 3r 2.75 250.00
227 A32(e) 50pi on 5r 150.00 500.00
Nos. 213-227 (15) 177.95 794.60

Romanov dynasty tercentenary.
Forgeries exist of overprint on No. 227.

Russia Nos. 75, 71, 72 Surcharged

h

i

Perf. 14x14½
Wove Paper

228 A14(h) 15pa on 3k .25 .25

Perf. 13, 13½

230 A13(i) 50pi on 5r 3.00 *10.00*

Vertically Laid Paper
Wmk. Wavy Lines (168)

231 A13(i) 100pi on 10r 7.00 *20.00*
a. Double surcharge 750.00 —
Nos. 228-231 (3) 10.25 30.25

No. 228 has lozenges of varnish on face but No. 230 has not.

Wrangel Issues

For the Posts of Gen. Peter Wrangel's army and civilian refugees from South Russia, interned in Turkey, Serbia, etc.

Very few of the Wrangel overprints were actually sold to the public, and many of the covers were made up later with the original cancels. Reprints abound. Values probably are based on sales of reprints in most cases.

Russian Stamps of 1902-18 Surcharged in Blue, Red or Black

On Russia Nos. 69-70
Vertically Laid Paper

1921 Wmk. 168 Perf. 13½

232 A12 10,000r on 3.50r 250.00 250.00
233 A12 10,000r on 7r 250.00 250.00
234 A12 20,000r on 3.50r 250.00 250.00
235 A12 20,000r on 7r 250.00 250.00
Nos. 232-235 (4) 1,000. 1,000.

On Russia Nos. 71-86, 87a, 117-118, 137-138
Wove Paper
Perf. 14x14½, 13½
Unwmk.

236 A14 1000r on 1k 3.25 3.25
237 A14 1000r on 2k (R) 3.25 3.25
237A A14 1000r on 2k (Bk) 47.50 47.50
238 A14 1000r on 3k 1.10 1.10
a. Inverted surcharge 10.00 10.00
239 A15 1000r on 4k 1.10 1.10
a. Inverted surcharge 10.00 10.00
240 A14 1000r on 5k 1.10 1.10
a. Inverted surcharge 10.00 10.00
241 A14 1000r on 7k 1.10 1.10
a. Inverted surcharge 10.00 10.00
242 A15 1000r on 10k 1.10 1.10
a. Inverted surcharge 10.00 10.00
243 A14 1000r on 10k on 7k 1.10 1.10
244 A14 5000r on 3k 1.10 1.10
245 A11 5000r on 14k 10.00 10.00
246 A11 5000r on 15k 1.10 1.10
a. "PYCCKIN" 12.00 12.00
247 A8 5000r on 20k 3.50 3.50
a. "PYCCKIN" 12.00 12.00
248 A11 5000r on 20k on 14k 3.50 3.50

249 A11 5000r on 25k 1.10 1.10
250 A11 5000r on 35k 1.10 1.10
a. Inverted surcharge 10.00 10.00
b. New value omitted 10.00 10.00
251 A8 5000r on 50k 1.10 1.10
a. Inverted surcharge 10.00 10.00
252 A11 5000r on 70k 1.10 1.10
a. Inverted surcharge 10.00 10.00
253 A9 10,000r on 1r (Bl) 1.10 1.10
254 A9 10,000r on 1r (Bk) 8.25 8.25
255 A12 10,000r on 3.50r 3.50 3.50
256 A13 10,000r on 5r 45.00 45.00
257 A13 10,000r on 10r 4.25 4.25
258 A9 20,000r on 1r 2.50 2.50
259 A12 20,000r on 3.50r 2.50 2.50
a. Inverted surcharge 10.00 10.00
b. New value omitted 20.00 20.00
260 A12 20,000r on 7r 92.50 92.50
261 A13 20,000r on 10r 2.50 2.50
Nos. 236-261 (27) 246.30 246.30

On Russia No. 104

261A A32 20,000r on 5r 950.00

On Russia Nos. 119-123, 125-135

Imperf

262 A14 1000r on 1k 1.20 1.20
263 A14 1000r on 2k (R) 1.20 1.20
263A A14 1000r on 2k (Bk) 1.50 1.50
264 A14 1000r on 3k 1.20 1.20
265 A15 1000r on 4k 40.00 40.00
266 A14 1000r on 5k 1.50 1.50
267 A14 5000r on 3k 1.20 1.20
268 A11 5000r on 15k 1.50 1.50
268A A8 5000r on 20k 60.00
268B A11 5000r on 25k 60.00
269 A11 5000r on 35k 3.00 3.00
270 A8 5000r on 50k 3.00 3.00
271 A11 5000r on 70k 1.20 1.20
272 A9 10,000r on 1r (Bl) 1.20 1.20
a. Inverted surcharge 10.00 10.00
273 A9 10,000r on 1r (Bk) 1.20 1.20
274 A12 10,000r on 3.50r 1.20 1.20
275 A13 10,000r on 5r 10.00 10.00
276 A12 10,000r on 7r 60.00 60.00
276A A13 10,000r on 10r *200.00*
277 A9 20,000r on 1r (Bl) 1.20 1.20
a. Inverted surcharge 10.00 10.00
278 A9 20,000r on 1r (Bk) 1.20 1.20
279 A12 20,000r on 3.50r 10.00 10.00
280 A13 20,000r on 5r 1.20 1.20
281 A12 20,000r on 7r 47.50 47.50
281A A13 20,000r on 10r *275.00*
Nos. 262-268,269-276,277-281 (21) 191.20 191.20

A18 A19

On Russia AR1-AR3

Perf. 14½x15

Wmk. 171

282 A18 10,000r on 1k red, *buff* 6.50 6.50
283 A19 10,000r on 5k grn, *buff* 6.50 6.50
a. Inverted surcharge 10.00
284 A19 10,000r on 10k brn, *buff* 6.50 6.50
a. Inverted surcharge 10.00
Nos. 282-284 (3) 19.50 19.50

On Stamps of Russian Offices in Turkey On No. 38-39

Vertically Laid Paper

Wmk. Wavy Lines (168)

284B A11 20,000r on 35pi on 3.50r 300.00
284C A11 20,000r on 70pi on 7r 400.00

On Nos. 200-207

Vertically Laid Paper

284D A15 1000r on 20pa on 5k 5.00 5.00

Wove Paper
Unwmk.

285 A16 1000r on 5pa on 1k 2.50 2.50
286 A16 1000r on 10pa on 2k 2.50 2.50
287 A17 1000r on 20pa on 4k 2.50 2.50
288 A17 1000r on 1pi on 10k 2.50 2.50
289 A8 5000r on 5pi on 50k 2.50 2.50
290 A9 5000r on 7pi on 70k 2.50 2.50
291 A10 10,000r on 10pi on 1r 12.50 12.50
a. Inverted surcharge 25.00 25.00
b. Pair, one without surcharge 20.00 20.00
292 A10 20,000r on 10pi on 1r 2.50 2.50
a. Inverted surcharge 25.00 25.00
b. Pair, one without surcharge 25.00 25.00
Nos. 284D-292 (9) 35.00 35.00

On Nos. 208-212

293 A14 1000r on 20pa on 5k 2.50 2.50
294 A11 5000r on 1½pi on 15k 2.50 2.50
295 A8 5000r on 2pi on 20k 2.50 2.50
296 A11 5000r on 2½pi on 25k 2.50 2.50
297 A11 5000r on 3½pi on 35k 2.50 2.50
Nos. 293-297 (5) 12.50 12.50

On Nos. 228, 230-231

298 A14 1000r on 15pa on 3k 1.00 1.00
299 A13 10,000r on 50pi on 5r 65.00 65.00
300 A13 10,000r on 100pi on 10r 92.50 92.50
301 A13 20,000r on 50pi on 5r 1.00 1.00
302 A13 20,000r on 100pi on 10r 92.50 92.50
Nos. 298-302 (5) 252.00 252.00

On Stamps of South Russia Denikin Issue

Imperf

303 A5 5000r on 5k org 1.00 1.00
a. Inverted surcharge 10.00
304 A5 5000r on 10k green 1.00 1.00
305 A5 5000r on 15k red 1.00 1.00
306 A5 5000r on 35k lt bl 1.00 1.00
307 A5 5000r on 70k dk blue 1.00 1.00
307A A5 10,000r on 70k dk blue 50.00 50.00
308 A6 10,000r on 1r brn & red 1.00 1.00
309 A6 10,000r on 2r gray vio & yel 1.00 1.00
a. Inverted surcharge 30.00 30.00
310 A6 10,000r on 3r dull rose & grn 3.50 3.50
311 A6 10,000r on 5r slate & vio 2.50 2.50
312 A6 10,000r on 7r gray grn & rose 100.00 100.00
313 A6 10,000r on 10r red & gray 2.00 2.00
314 A6 20,000r on 1r brn & red 1.00 1.00
315 A6 20,000r on 2r gray vio & yel (Bl) 35.00 35.00
a. Inverted surcharge 30.00 30.00
315B A6 20,000r on 2r gray vio & yel (Bk) 1.00 1.00
316 A6 20,000r on 3r dull rose & grn (Bl) 50.00 50.00
316A A6 20,000r on 3r dull rose & grn (Bk) 30.00 30.00
317 A6 20,000r on 5r slate & vio 1.00 1.00
318 A6 20,000r on 7r gray grn & rose 60.00 60.00
319 A6 20,000r on 10r red & gray 1.00 1.00
Nos. 303-319 (20) 344.00 344.00

Trident Stamps of Ukraine Surcharged in Blue, Red, Black or Brown

1921 ***Perf. 14, 14½x15***

320 A14 10,000r on 1k org .45 .45
321 A14 10,000r on 2k grn 5.00 5.00
322 A14 10,000r on 3k red .45 .45
a. Inverted surcharge 10.00 10.00
323 A15 10,000r on 4k car .45 .45
324 A14 10,000r on 5k cl .45 .45
325 A14 10,000r on 7k lt bl .45 .45
a. Inverted surcharge 10.00 10.00
326 A15 10,000r on 10k dk bl .45 .45
a. Inverted surcharge 10.00 10.00
327 A14 10,000r on 10k on 7k lt bl .45 .45
a. Inverted surcharge 10.00 10.00
328 A8 20,000r on 20k bl & car (Br) .45 .45
a. Inverted surcharge 10.00 10.00
329 A8 20,000r on 20k bl & car (Bk) .45 .45
a. Inverted surcharge 35.00 35.00
330 A11 20,000r on 20k on 14k bl & rose .45 .45
331 A11 20,000r on 35k red brn & grn 75.00 75.00
332 A8 20,000r on 50k brn vio & grn .45 .45
a. Inverted surcharge 10.00 10.00
Nos. 320-332 (13) 84.95 84.95

Imperf

333 A14 10,000r on 1k org .75 .75
a. Inverted surcharge 10.00
334 A14 10,000r on 2k grn 2.00 2.00
335 A14 10,000r on 3k red .75 .75
336 A8 20,000r on 20k bl & car .75 .75
337 A11 20,000r on 35k red brn & grn 40.00 40.00
338 A8 20,000r on 50k brn vio & grn 2.00 2.00
Nos. 333-338 (6) 46.25 46.25

There are several varieties of the trident surcharge on Nos. 320 to 338.

Same Surcharge on Russian Stamps

On Stamps of 1909-18

Perf. 14x14½

338A A14 10,000r on 1k dl org yel 2.50 2.50
339 A14 10,000r on 2k dl grn 2.50 2.50
340 A14 10,000r on 3k car .50 .50
341 A15 10,000r on 4k car .50 .50
342 A14 10,000r on 5k dk cl .50 .50
343 A14 10,000r on 7k blue .50 .50
344 A15 10,000r on 10k dk bl 2.50 2.50
344A A14 10,000r on 10k on 7k bl 3.75 3.75
344B A11 20,000r on 14k dk bl & car 35.00 35.00
345 A11 20,000r on 15k red brn & dp bl .50 .50
346 A8 20,000r on 20k dl bl & dk car .50 .50
347 A11 20,000r on 20k on 14k dk bl & car 3.50 3.50
348 A11 20,000r on 35k red brn & grn 2.00 2.00
349 A8 20,000r on 50k brn vio & grn .50 .50
349A A11 20,000r on 70k brn & red org 2.50 2.50
Nos. 338A-349A (15) 57.75 57.75

On Stamps of 1917-18

Imperf

350 A14 10,000r on 1k org .75 .75
351 A14 10,000r on 2k gray grn .75 .75
352 A14 10,000r on 3k red .75 .75
353 A15 10,000r on 4k car 40.00 40.00
354 A14 10,000r on 5k claret .75 .75
355 A11 20,000r on 15k red brn & dp bl .75 .75
356 A8 20,000r on 50k brn vio & grn 2.00 2.00
357 A11 20,000r on 70k brn & org .75 .75
Nos. 350-357 (8) 46.50 46.50

Same Surcharge on Stamps of Russian Offices in Turkey

On Nos. 40-45

Perf. 14½x15

358 A12 10,000r on 5pa on 1k 5.00 5.00
359 A12 10,000r on 10pa on 2k 5.00 5.00
360 A12 10,000r on 20pa on 4k 5.00 5.00
361 A12 10,000r on 1pi on 10k 5.00 5.00
362 A12 20,000r on 5pi on 50k 5.00 5.00
363 A12 20,000r on 7pi on 70k 5.00 5.00
Nos. 358-363 (6) 30.00 30.00

On Nos. 201-206

364 A16 10,000r on 5pa on 1k 6.00 6.00
365 A16 10,000r on 10pa on 2k 6.00 6.00
366 A17 10,000r on 20pa on 4k 6.00 6.00
367 A17 10,000r on 1pi on 10k 6.00 6.00
368 A8 20,000r on 5pi on 50k 6.00 6.00
369 A9 20,000r on 7pi on 70k 6.00 6.00
Nos. 364-369 (6) 36.00 36.00

On Nos. 228, 208-212, Stamps of 1912-13

370 A14 10,000r on 15pa on 3k 5.00 5.00
371 A14 10,000r on 20pa on 5k 5.00 5.00
372 A11 20,000r on 1½pi on 15k 5.00 5.00
373 A8 20,000r on 2pi on 20k 5.00
374 A11 20,000r on 2½pi on 25k 5.00
375 A11 20,000r on 3½pi on 35k 5.00

Same Surcharge on Stamp of South Russia, Crimea Issue

376 A8 20,000r on 5r on 20k bl & car 750.00
Nos. 370-376 (7) 780.00 15.00

RWANDA

ru-ˈän-də

(Rwandaise Republic)

LOCATION — Central Africa, adjoining the ex-Belgian Congo, Tanganyika, Uganda and Burundi
GOVT. — Republic
AREA — 10,169 sq. mi.
POP. — 8,154,933(?) (1999 est.)
CAPITAL — Kigali

Rwanda was established as an independent republic on July 1, 1962. With Burundi, it had been a UN trusteeship territory administered by Belgium.

See Ruanda-Urundi.

100 Centimes = 1 Franc

Catalogue values for all unused stamps in this country are for Never Hinged items.

Watermark

Wmk. 368 — JEZ Multiple

Gregoire Kayibanda and Map of Africa — A1

Design: 40c, 1.50fr, 6.50fr, 20fr, Rwanda map spotlighted, "R" omitted.

Perf. 11½

1962, July 1 Unwmk. Photo.

No.	Type	Description	Unused	Used
1	A1	10c brown & gray grn	.25	.25
2	A1	40c brown & rose lil	.25	.25
3	A1	1fr brown & blue	.75	.40
4	A1	1.50fr brown & lt brn	.25	.25
5	A1	3.50fr brown & dp org	.25	.25
6	A1	6.50fr brown & lt vio bl	.25	.25
7	A1	10fr brown & citron	.35	.25
8	A1	20fr brown & rose	.50	.40
		Nos. 1-8 (8)	2.85	2.30

Map of Africa and Symbolic Honeycomb A2

Ruanda-Urundi Nos. 151-152 Overprinted with Metallic Frame Obliterating Previous Inscription and Denomination. Black Commemorative Inscription and "REPUBLIQUE RWANDAISE." Surcharged with New Value.

1963, Jan. 28 Unwmk. *Perf. 11½*

No.	Type	Description	Unused	Used
9	A2	3.50fr sil, blk, ultra & red	.25	.25
10	A2	6.50fr brnz, blk, ultra & red	1.25	1.00
11	A2	10fr stl bl, blk, ultra & red	.30	.25
12	A2	20fr sil, blk, ultra & red	.75	.50
		Nos. 9-12 (4)	2.55	2.00

Rwanda's admission to UN, Sept. 18, 1962.

Ruanda-Urundi Stamps of 1953 Overprinted in Metallic and Black

Designs as before.

1963, Mar. 21 Unwmk. *Perf. 11½*

Flowers in Natural Colors

No.	Type	Description	Unused	Used
13	A27	25c dk grn & dl org	.40	.25
14	A27	40c green & salmon	.40	.25
15	A27	60c bl grn & pink	.40	.25
16	A27	1.25fr dk green & blue	1.60	1.25
17	A27	1.50fr vio & apple grn	1.40	1.00
18	A27	2fr on 1.50fr vio & ap grn	2.50	1.25
19	A27	4fr on 1.50fr vio & ap grn	3.00	1.25
20	A27	5fr dp plum & lt bl grn	3.00	1.50
21	A27	7fr dk green & fawn	3.00	1.50
22	A27	10fr dp plum & pale ol	4.50	2.00
		Nos. 13-22 (10)	20.20	10.50

The overprint consists of silver panels with black lettering. The panels on No. 19 are bluish gray.

Imperforates exist of practically every issue, starting with Nos. 1-8, except Nos. 9-12, 13-22, 36 and 55-69.

Wheat Emblem, Bow, Arrow, Hoe and Billhook — A4

1963, June 25 Photo. *Perf. 13½*

No.	Type	Description	Unused	Used
23	A4	2fr brown & green	.25	.25
24	A4	4fr magenta & ultra	.25	.25
25	A4	7fr red & gray	.25	.25
26	A4	10fr olive grn & yel	.70	.40
		Nos. 23-26 (4)	1.45	1.15

FAO "Freedom from Hunger" campaign.

The 20fr leopard and 50fr lion stamps of Ruanda-Urundi, Nos. 149-150, overprinted "Republique Rwandaise" at top and "Contre la Faim" at bottom, were intended to be issued Mar. 21, 1963, but were not placed in use. Value, set $200.

Coffee A5

Designs: 10c, 40c, 4fr, Coffee. 20c, 1fr, 7fr, Bananas. 30c, 2fr, 10fr, Tea.

1963, July 1 *Perf. 11½*

No.	Type	Description	Unused	Used
27	A5	10c violet bl & brn	.25	.25
28	A5	20c slate & yellow	.25	.25
29	A5	30c vermilion & grn	.25	.25
30	A5	40c dp green & brown	.25	.25
31	A5	1fr maroon & yellow	.25	.25
32	A5	2fr dk blue & green	1.00	.50
33	A5	4fr red & brown	.25	.25
34	A5	7fr yellow grn & yellow	.25	.25
35	A5	10fr violet & green	.25	.25
		Nos. 27-35 (9)	3.00	2.50

First anniversary of independence.

Common Design Types pictured following the introduction.

African Postal Union Issue

Common Design Type

1963, Sept. 8 Unwmk. *Perf. 12½*

No.	Type	Description	Unused	Used
36	CD114	14fr black, ocher & red	.90	.55

Post Horn and Pigeon — A6

1963, Oct. 25 Photo. *Perf. 11½*

No.	Type	Description	Unused	Used
37	A6	50c ultra & rose	.25	.25
38	A6	1.50fr brown & blue	.75	.50
39	A6	3fr dp plum & gray	.25	.25
40	A6	20fr green & yellow	.45	.25
		Nos. 37-40 (4)	1.70	1.25

Rwanda's admission to the UPU, Apr. 6.

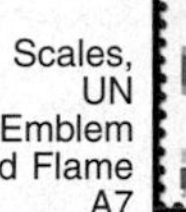

Scales, UN Emblem and Flame A7

1963, Dec. 10 Unwmk. *Perf. 11½*

No.	Type	Description	Unused	Used
41	A7	5fr crimson	.25	.25
42	A7	6fr brt purple	.70	.35
43	A7	10fr brt blue	.30	.25
		Nos. 41-43 (3)	1.25	.85

15th anniversary of the Universal Declaration of Human Rights.

Children's Clinic — A8

Designs: 20c, 7fr, Laboratory examination, horiz. 30c, 10fr, Physician examining infant. 40c, 20fr, Litter bearers, horiz.

1963, Dec. 30 Photo.

No.	Type	Description	Unused	Used
44	A8	10c yel org, red & brn blk	.25	.25
45	A8	20c grn, red & brn blk	.25	.25
46	A8	30c bl, red & brn blk	.25	.25
47	A8	40c red lil, red & brn	.25	.25
48	A8	2fr bl grn, red brn & blk	.90	.50
49	A8	7fr ultra, red & blk	.25	.25
50	A8	10fr red brn, red & brn blk	.30	.25
51	A8	20fr dp org, red & brn	.60	.25
		Nos. 44-51 (8)	3.05	2.25

Centenary of the International Red Cross.

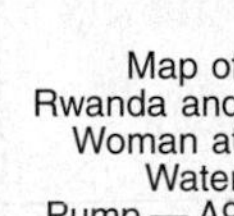

Map of Rwanda and Woman at Water Pump — A9

1964, May 4 Unwmk. *Perf. 11½*

No.	Type	Description	Unused	Used
52	A9	3fr lt grn, dk brn & ultra	.25	.25
53	A9	7fr pink, dk brn & ultra	.35	.25
54	A9	10fr yel, dk brn & ultra	.50	.30
		Nos. 52-54 (3)	1.10	.80

Souvenir Sheet

Imperf

No.	Type	Description	Unused	Used
54A	A9	25fr lilac, bl, brn & blk	9.00	9.00

UN 4th World Meteorological Day, Mar. 23.

Overprinted & Surcharged in Silver and Black

Ruanda-Urundi Nos. 138, 142

Ruanda-Urundi Nos. 139, 141, 143, 149-150

Ruanda-Urundi Nos. 140, 144-148

Ruanda-Urundi No. 153

Designs: 10c, 20c, 30c, Buffaloes. 40c, 2fr, Black-and-white colobus (monkey). 50c, 7.50fr, Impalas. 1fr, Mountain gorilla. 3fr, 4fr, 8fr, African elephants. 5fr, 10fr, Eland and zebras. 20fr, Leopard. 50fr, Lions. 40c, 1fr and 2fr are vertical.

1964, June 29 Photo. *Perf. 11½*

Size: 33x23mm, 23x33mm

No.	Type	Description	Unused	Used
55	A30	10c on 20c gray, ap grn & blk	.25	.25
56	A30	20c blk, gray & ap grn	.25	.25
57	A30	30c on 1.50fr blk, gray & org	.25	.25
58	A29	40c mag, blk & gray grn	.25	.25
59	A30	50c grn, org yel & brn	.25	.25
60	A29	1fr ultra, blk & brn	.30	.25
61	A29	2fr grnsh bl, ind & brn	.30	.25
62	A30	3fr brn, dp car & blk	.40	.25
63	A30	4fr on 3.50fr on 3fr brn, dp car & blk	.50	.25
64	A30	5fr brn, dl yel, grn & blk	.50	.25
65	A30	7.50fr on 6.50fr red, org yel & brn	.90	.25
66	A30	8fr blue, mag & blk	8.00	3.25
67	A30	10fr brn, dl yel, brt pink & blk	1.75	.25

Size: 45x26½mm

No.	Type	Description	Unused	Used
68	A30	20fr hn brn, ocher & blk	2.75	.75
69	A30	50fr dp blue & brown	4.25	2.00
		Nos. 55-69 (15)	20.90	9.00

Inverted overprints/surcharges exist. Value, each $10.

Boy with Crutch and Gatagara Home — A11

Designs: 40c, 8fr, Girls with sewing machines, horiz. 4fr, 10fr, Girl on crutches, map of Rwanda and Gatagara Home.

1964, Nov. 10 Photo. *Perf. 11½*

No.	Type	Description	Unused	Used
70	A11	10c lilac blk brn	.25	.25
71	A11	40c blue & blk brn	.25	.25
72	A11	4fr org red & blk brn	.30	.25
73	A11	7.50fr yel grn & blk brn	.50	.25
74	A11	8fr bister & blk brn	1.60	.70
75	A11	10fr magenta & blk brn	.75	.35
		Nos. 70-75 (6)	3.65	2.05

Gatagara Home for handicapped children.

Basketball — A12

Sport: 10c, 4fr, Runner, horiz. 30c, 20fr, High jump, horiz. 40c, 50fr, Soccer.

Size: 26x38mm

1964, Dec. 8 Litho. *Perf. 13½*

76 A12 10c gray, sl & dk grn .25 .25
77 A12 20c pink, sl & rose red .25 .25
78 A12 30c lt grn, sl & grn .25 .25
79 A12 40c buff, sl & brn .25 .25
80 A12 4fr vio gray, sl & vio .25 .25
81 A12 5fr pale grn, sl & yel grn 1.60 1.25
82 A12 20fr pale lil, sl & red lil .45 .35
83 A12 50fr gray, sl & dk gray 1.10 .75
a. Souvenir sheet of 4 7.25 7.25
Nos. 76-83 (8) 4.40 3.60

18th Olympic Games, Tokyo, Oct. 10-25. No. 83a contains 4 stamps (10fr, soccer; 20fr, basketball; 30fr, high jump; 40fr, runner). Size of stamps: 28x38mm.

Quill, Books, Radical and Retort — A13

Medical School and Student with Microscope — A14

30c, 10fr, Scales, hand, staff of Mercury and globe. 40c, 12fr, View of University.

1965, Feb. 22 Engr. *Perf. 11½*

84 A13 10c multicolored .25 .25
85 A14 20c multicolored .25 .25
86 A13 30c multicolored .25 .25
87 A14 40c multicolored .25 .25
88 A13 5fr multicolored .25 .25
89 A14 7fr multicolored .25 .25
90 A13 10fr multicolored 1.10 .90
91 A14 12fr multicolored .40 .25
Nos. 84-91 (8) 3.00 2.65

National University of Rwanda at Butare.

Abraham Lincoln, Death Cent. A15

1965, Apr. 15 Photo. *Perf. 13½*

92 A15 10c emerald & dk red .25 .25
93 A15 20c red brn & dk bl .25 .25
94 A15 30c brt violet & red .25 .25
95 A15 40c brt grnsh bl & red .25 .25
96 A15 9fr orange brn & pur .25 .25
97 A15 40fr black & brt grn 2.25 .80
Nos. 92-97 (6) 3.50 2.05

Souvenir Sheet

98 A15 50fr red lilac & red 3.75 3.75

Nos. 92-96 exist without figure of value.

Marabous — A16

Zebras A17

30c, Impalas. 40c, Crowned cranes, hippopotami & cattle egrets. 1fr, Cape buffalos. 3fr, Cape hunting dogs. 5fr, Yellow baboons. 10fr, Elephant & map of Rwanda with location of park. 40fr, Anhinga, great & reed cormorants. 100fr, Lions.

1965, Apr. 28 Photo. *Perf. 11½*

Size: 32x23mm

99 A16 10c multicolored .25 .25
100 A17 20c multicolored .25 .25
101 A16 30c multicolored .25 .25
102 A17 40c multicolored .25 .25
103 A16 1fr multicolored .60 .35
104 A17 3fr multicolored .60 .35
105 A16 5fr multicolored 8.50 2.50
106 A17 10fr multicolored .75 .35

Size: 45x26mm

107 A17 40fr multicolored 2.50 .50
108 A17 100fr multicolored 4.50 .50
Nos. 99-108 (10) 18.45 5.55

Kagera National Park publicity.

Telstar and ITU Emblem A18

Designs: 40c, 50fr, Syncom satellite. 60fr, old and new communications equipment.

1965 Unwmk. *Perf. 13½*

109 A18 10c red brn, ultra & car .25 .25
110 A18 40c violet, emer & yel .25 .25
111 A18 4.50fr blk, car & dk bl 1.75 .50
112 A18 50fr dk brn, yel grn & brt grn 1.60 .30
Nos. 109-112 (4) 3.85 1.30

Souvenir Sheet

113 A18 60fr blk brn, org brn & bl 4.25 4.25

ITU, cent. Issued: #113, 7/19; others, 5/17.

Papilio Bromius Chrapkowskii Suffert — A19

Various butterflies and moths in natural colors.

1965-66 Photo. *Perf. 12½*

114 A19 10c black & yellow .25 .25
115 A19 15c blk & dp org ('66) .25 .25
116 A19 20c black & lilac .25 .25
117 A19 30c black & red lil .25 .25
118 A19 35c dk brn & dk bl ('66) .25 .25
119 A19 40c black & Prus bl .35 .25
120 A19 1.50fr black & grn ('66) .50 .25
121 A19 3fr dk brn & ol grn ('66) 5.00 1.50
122 A19 4fr black & red brn 4.00 2.00
123 A19 10fr black & pur ('66) 1.00 .30
124 A19 50fr black & brown 3.50 1.75
125 A19 100fr dk brn & bl ('66) 5.25 1.50
Nos. 114-125 (12) 20.85 8.80

The 15c, 20c, 40c, 1.50fr, 10fr and 50fr are horizontal.

Cattle, ICY Emblem and Map of Africa — A20

Map of Africa and: 40c, Tree & lake. 4.50fr, Gazelle under tree. 45fr, Mount Ruwenzori.

1965, Oct. 25 Unwmk. *Perf. 12*

126 A20 10c olive bis & bl grn .25 .25
127 A20 40c lt ultra, red brn & grn .25 .25
128 A20 4.50fr brt grn, yel & brn 1.25 .45
129 A20 45fr rose claret 1.00 .30
Nos. 126-129 (4) 2.75 1.25

John F. Kennedy (1917-1963) — A21

1965, Nov. 22 Photo. *Perf. 11½*

130 A21 10c brt grn & dk brn .25 .25
131 A21 40c brt pink & dk brn .25 .25
132 A21 50c dk blue & dk brn .25 .25
133 A21 1fr gray ol & dk brn .25 .25
134 A21 8fr violet & dk brn 2.25 1.25
135 A21 50fr gray & dk brn 1.75 1.00
Nos. 130-135 (6) 5.00 3.25

Souvenir Sheet

136 Sheet of 2 11.00 11.00
a. A21 40fr org & dark brown 4.50 4.50
b. A21 60fr ultra & dark brown 5.00 5.00

Madonna — A22

1965, Dec. 20

137 A22 10c gold & dk green .25 .25
138 A22 40c gold & dk brn red .25 .25
139 A22 50c gold & dk blue .25 .25
140 A22 4fr gold & slate .90 .55
141 A22 6fr gold & violet .30 .25
142 A22 30fr gold & dk brown .75 .50
Nos. 137-142 (6) 2.70 2.05

Christmas.

Father Joseph Damien and Lepers — A23

Designs: 40c, 45fr, Dr. Albert Schweitzer and Hospital, Lambarene.

1966, Jan. 31 *Perf. 11½*

143 A23 10c ultra & red brn .25 .25
144 A23 40c dk red & vio bl .25 .25
145 A23 4.50fr slate & brt grn .25 .25
146 A23 45fr brn & hn brn 2.00 1.10
Nos. 143-146 (4) 2.75 1.85

Issued for World Leprosy Day.

Pope Paul VI, St. Peter's, UN Headquarters and Statue of Liberty — A24

Design: 40c, 50fr, Pope Paul VI, Papal arms and UN emblem.

1966, Feb. 28 Photo. *Perf. 12*

147 A24 10c henna brn & slate .25 .25
148 A24 40c brt blue & slate .25 .25
149 A24 4.50fr lilac & slate 1.75 1.00
150 A24 50fr brt green & slate 1.25 .45
Nos. 147-150 (4) 3.50 1.95

Visit of Pope Paul VI to the UN, New York City, Oct. 4, 1965.

Globe Thistle — A25

Flowers: 20c, Blood lily. 30c, Everlasting. 40c, Natal plum. 1fr, Tulip tree. 3fr, Rendle orchid. 5fr, Aloe. 10fr, Ammocharis tinneana. 40fr, Coral tree. 100fr, Caper. (20c, 40c, 1fr, 3fr, 5fr, 10fr are vertical).

1966, Mar. 14 *Perf. 11½*

Granite Paper

151 A25 10c lt blue & multi .25 .25
152 A25 20c orange & multi .25 .25
153 A25 30c car rose & multi .25 .25
154 A25 40c green & multi .25 .25
155 A25 1fr multicolored .25 .25
156 A25 3fr indigo & multi .25 .25
157 A25 5fr multicolored 7.00 2.25
158 A25 10fr blue grn & multi .35 .25
159 A25 40fr brown & multi 1.75 .50
160 A25 100fr dk bl grn & multi 3.50 1.50
a. Miniature sheet 9.00 9.00
Nos. 151-160 (10) 14.10 6.00

No. 160a contains one 100fr stamp in changed color, bright blue and multicolored.

Opening of WHO Headquarters, Geneva — A26

1966, May 1 Litho. *Perf. 12½x12*

161 A26 2fr lt olive green .25 .25
162 A26 3fr vermilion .25 .25
163 A26 5fr violet blue .25 .25
Nos. 161-163 (3) .75 .75

Soccer — A27

20c, 9fr, Basketball. 30c, 50fr, Volleyball.

1966, May 30 Photo. *Perf. 15x14*

164 A27 10c dl grn, ultra & blk .25 .25
165 A27 20c crimson, grn & blk .25 .25
166 A27 30c bl, brt rose lil & blk .25 .25
167 A27 40c yel bis, grn & blk .25 .25
168 A27 9fr gray, red lil & blk .25 .25

169	A27	50fr rose lil, Prus bl & blk	.90	.70
		Nos. 164-169 (6)	2.15	1.95

National Youth Sports Program.

Mother and Child, Planes Dropping Bombs — A28

1966, June 29 *Perf. 13½*

Design and Inscription Black and Red

170	A28	20c rose lilac	.25	.25
171	A28	30c yellow green	.25	.25
172	A28	50c lt ultra	.25	.25
173	A28	6fr yellow	.25	.25
174	A28	15fr blue green	.85	.40
175	A28	18fr lilac	.85	.40
		Nos. 170-175 (6)	2.70	1.80

Campaign against nuclear weapons.

A29

Global soccer ball.

1966, July *Perf. 11½*

176	A29	20c org & indigo	.25	.25
177	A29	30c lilac & indigo	.25	.25
178	A29	50c brt grn & indigo	.25	.25
179	A29	6fr brt rose & indigo	.90	.35
180	A29	12fr lt vio brn & ind	2.50	.50
181	A29	25fr ultra & indigo	3.00	1.00
		Nos. 176-181 (6)	7.15	2.60

World Soccer Cup Championship, Wembley, England, July 11-30.

A30

Designs: 10c, Mikeno Volcano and crested shrike, horiz. 40c, Nyamilanga Falls. 4.50fr, Gahinga and Muhabura volcanoes and lobelias, horiz. 55fr, Rusumu Falls.

1966, Oct. 24 **Engr.** *Perf. 14*

182	A30	10c green	.25	.25
183	A30	40c brown carmine	.30	.25
184	A30	4.50fr violet blue	.50	.30
185	A30	55fr red lilac	.80	.45
		Nos. 182-185 (4)	1.85	1.25

UNESCO Emblem, African Artifacts and Musical Clef — A31

UNESCO 20th Anniv.: 30c, 10fr, Hands holding primer showing giraffe and zebra. 50c, 15fr, Atom symbol and power drill. 1fr, 50fr, Submerged sphinxes and sailboat.

1966, Nov. 4 **Photo.** *Perf. 12*

186	A31	20c brt rose & dk bl	.25	.25
187	A31	30c grnsh blue & blk	.25	.25
188	A31	50c ocher & blk	.25	.25
189	A31	1fr violet & blk	.25	.25
190	A31	5fr yellow grn & blk	.25	.25
191	A31	10fr brown & blk	.25	.25
192	A31	15fr red lilac & dk bl	.40	.30
193	A31	50fr dull bl & blk	.50	.40
		Nos. 186-193 (8)	2.40	2.20

Rock Python — A32

Snakes: 20c, 20fr, Jameson's mamba. 30c, 3fr, Rock python. 50c, Gaboon viper. 1fr, Black-lipped spitting cobra. 5fr, African sand snake. 70fr, Egg-eating snake. (20c, 50c, 3fr and 20fr are horizontal.)

1967, Jan. 30 **Photo.** *Perf. 11½*

194	A32	20c red & black	.25	.25
195	A32	30c bl, dk brn & yel	.25	.25
196	A32	50c yel grn & multi	.25	.25
197	A32	1fr lt lil, blk & bis	.25	.25
198	A32	3fr lt vio, dk brn & yel	.40	.25
199	A32	5fr yellow & multi	.60	.25
200	A32	20fr pale pink & multi	2.25	1.00
201	A32	70fr pale vio, brn & blk	3.00	1.25
		Nos. 194-201 (8)	7.25	3.75

Ntaruka Hydroelectric Station and Tea Flowers — A33

Designs: 30c, 25fr, Transformer and chrysanthemums (pyrethrum). 50c, 50fr, Sluice and coffee.

1967, Mar. 6 **Photo.** *Perf. 13½*

202	A33	20c maroon & dp bl	.25	.25
203	A33	30c black & red brn	.25	.25
204	A33	50c brown & violet	.25	.25
205	A33	4fr dk grn & dp plum	.25	.25
206	A33	25fr violet & sl grn	.50	.30
207	A33	50fr dk blue & brn	1.10	.65
		Nos. 202-207 (6)	2.60	1.95

Ntaruka Hydroelectric Station.

Souvenir Sheets

Cogwheels — A34

1967, Apr. 15 **Engr.** *Perf. 11½*

208	A34	100fr dk red brown	4.50	4.50
209	A34	100fr brt rose lilac	4.50	4.50

7th "Europa" Phil. Exhib. and the Philatelic Salon of African States, Naples, Apr. 8-16.

Souvenir Sheet

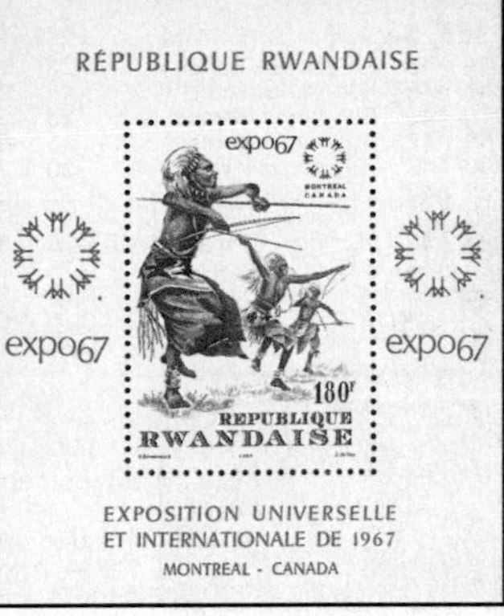

African Dancers and EXPO '67 Emblem — A35

1967, Apr. 28 *Perf. 11½*

210	A35	180fr dark purple	4.75	4.75

EXPO '67, Intl. Exhib., Montreal, Apr. 28-Oct. 27.

A similar imperf. sheet has the stamp in violet brown.

St. Martin, by Van Dyck and Caritas Emblem A36

Paintings: 40c, 15fr, Rebecca at the Well, by Murillo, horiz. 60c, 18fr, St. Christopher, by Dierick Bouts. 80c, 26fr, Job and his Friends, by Il Calabrese (Mattia Preti), horiz.

Perf. 13x11, 11x13

1967, May 8 **Photo.**

Black Inscription on Gold Panel

211	A36	20c dark purple	.25	.25
212	A36	40c blue green	.25	.25
213	A36	60c rose carmine	.25	.25
214	A36	80c deep blue	.25	.25
215	A36	9fr redsh brown	.85	.45
216	A36	15fr orange ver	.30	.25
217	A36	18fr dk olive grn	.35	.25
218	A36	26fr dk carmine rose	.40	.35
		Nos. 211-218 (8)	2.90	2.30

Issued to publicize the work of Caritas-Rwanda, Catholic welfare organization.

Round Table Emblem and Zebra — A37

Round Table Emblem and: 40c, Elephant. 60c, Cape buffalo. 80c, Antelope. 18fr, Wheat. 100fr, Palm tree.

1967, July 31 **Photo.** *Perf. 14*

219	A37	20c gold & multi	.25	.25
220	A37	40c gold & multi	.25	.25
221	A37	60c gold & multi	.25	.25
222	A37	80c gold & multi	.25	.25
223	A37	18fr gold & multi	.40	.25
224	A37	100fr gold & multi	2.00	1.00
		Nos. 219-224 (6)	3.40	2.25

Rwanda Table No. 9 of Kigali, a member of the Intl. Round Tables Assoc.

EXPO '67 Emblem, Africa Place and Dancers and Drummers — A38

EXPO '67 Emblem, Africa Place and: 30c, 3fr, Drum and vessels. 50c, 40fr, Two dancers. 1fr, 34fr, Spears, shields and bow.

1967, Aug. 10 **Photo.** *Perf. 12*

225	A38	20c brt blue & sepia	.25	.25
226	A38	30c brt rose lil & sepia	.25	.25
227	A38	50c orange & sepia	.25	.25
228	A38	1fr green & sepia	.25	.25
229	A38	3fr violet & sepia	.25	.25
230	A38	15fr emerald & sepia	.25	.25
231	A38	34fr rose red & sepia	.50	.35
232	A38	40fr grnsh bl & sepia	.70	.45
		Nos. 225-232 (8)	2.70	2.30

Lions Emblem, Globe and Zebra — A39

1967, Oct. 16 **Photo.** *Perf. 13½*

233	A39	20c lilac, bl & blk	.25	.25
234	A39	80c lt grn, bl & blk	.25	.25
235	A39	1fr rose car, bl & blk	.25	.25
236	A39	8fr bister, bl & blk	.30	.25
237	A39	10fr ultra, bl & blk	.40	.25
238	A39	50fr yel grn, bl & blk	1.75	1.00
		Nos. 233-238 (6)	3.20	2.25

50th anniversary of Lions International.

Woodland Kingfisher — A40

Birds: 20c, Red bishop, vert. 60c, Red-billed quelea, vert. 80c, Double-toothed barbet. 2fr, Pin-tailed whydah, vert. 3fr, Solitary cuckoo. 18fr, Green wood hoopoe, vert. 25fr, Blue-collared bee-eater. 80fr, Regal sunbird, vert. 100fr, Red-shouldered widowbird.

1967, Dec. 18 *Perf. 11½*

239	A40	20c multicolored	.25	.25
240	A40	40c multicolored	.25	.25
241	A40	60c multicolored	.25	.25
242	A40	80c multicolored	.25	.25
243	A40	2fr multicolored	.35	.30
244	A40	3fr multicolored	.40	.30
245	A40	18fr multicolored	1.25	.75
246	A40	25fr multicolored	1.75	1.00
247	A40	80fr multicolored	4.00	3.25
248	A40	100fr multicolored	5.75	4.75
		Nos. 239-248 (10)	14.50	11.35

Souvenir Sheet

Ski Jump, Speed Skating — A41

1968, Feb. 12 **Photo.** *Perf. 11½*

249	A41	Sheet of 2	11.00	11.00
	a.	50fr bl, blk & grn (skier)	3.50	3.50
	b.	50fr grn, blk & bl (skater)	3.50	3.50
	c.	Souv. sheet of 2, #249a at right	11.00	11.00

10th Winter Olympic Games, Grenoble, France, Feb. 6-18.

Runner, Mexican Sculpture and Architecture — A42

Sport and Mexican Art: 40c, Hammer throw, pyramid and animal head. 60c, Hurdler and sculptures. 80c, Javelin and sculptures.

1968, May 27 Photo. *Perf. 11½*

250	A42	20c ultra & multi	.35	.25
251	A42	40c multicolored	.35	.25
252	A42	60c lilac & multi	.35	.25
253	A42	80c orange & multi	.35	.25
		Nos. 250-253 (4)	1.40	1.00

19th Olympic Games, Mexico City, 10/12-27.

Souvenir Sheet

19th Olympic Games, Mexico City — A43

a, 8fr, Soccer. b, 10fr, Mexican horseman, cactus. c, 12fr, Field hockey. d, 18fr, Cathedral, Mexico City. e, 20fr, Boxing. f, 30fr, Modern buildings, musical instruments, vase.

1968, May 27 Photo. *Perf. 11½*

Granite Paper

254	A43	Sheet of 6, #a.-f.	11.00	11.00

Three sets of circular gold "medal" overprints with black inscriptions were applied to the six stamps of No. 254 to honor 18 Olympic winners. Issued Dec. 12, 1968. Value $70.

Souvenir Sheet

Martin Luther King, Jr. — A44

1968, July 29 Engr. *Perf. 13½*

255	A44	100fr sepia	3.00	1.75

Rev. Dr. Martin Luther King, Jr. (1929-68), American civil rights leader. See No. 406.

Diaphant Orchid — A45

Flowers: 40c, Pharaoh's scepter. 60c, Flower of traveler's-tree. 80c, Costus afer. 2fr, Banana tree flower. 3fr, Flower and fruit of papaw tree. 18fr, Clerodendron. 25fr, Sweet potato flowers. 80fr, Baobab tree flower. 100fr, Passion flower.

1968, Sept. 9 Litho. *Perf. 13*

256	A45	20c lilac & multi	.25	.25
257	A45	40c multicolored	.25	.25
258	A45	60c bl grn & multi	.25	.25
259	A45	80c multicolored	.25	.25
260	A45	2fr brt yellow & multi	.25	.25
261	A45	3fr multicolored	.25	.25
262	A45	18fr multicolored	.40	.25
263	A45	25fr gray & multi	.70	.30
264	A45	80fr multicolored	2.75	.75
265	A45	100fr multicolored	3.00	1.25
		Nos. 256-265 (10)	8.35	4.05

Equestrian and "Mexico 1968" A46

Designs: 40c, Judo and "Tokyo 1964." 60c, Fencing and "Rome 1960." 80c, High jump and "Berlin 1936." 38fr, Women's diving and "London 1908 and 1948." 60fr, Weight lifting and "Paris 1900 and 1924."

1968, Oct. 24 Litho. *Perf. 14x13*

266	A46	20c orange & sepia	.25	.25
267	A46	40c grnsh bl & sepia	.25	.25
268	A46	60c car rose & sepia	.25	.25
269	A46	80c ultra & sepia	.25	.25
270	A46	38fr red & sepia	.55	.25
271	A46	60fr emerald & sepia	1.30	.50
		Nos. 266-271 (6)	2.85	1.75

19th Olympic Games, Mexico City, 10/12-27.

Tuareg, Algeria — A47

African National Costumes: 40c, Musicians, Upper Volta. 60c, Senegalese women. 70c, Girls of Rwanda going to market. 8fr, Young married couple from Morocco. 20fr, Nigerian officials in state dress. 40fr, Man and women from Zambia. 50fr, Man and woman from Kenya.

1968, Nov. 4 Litho. *Perf. 13*

272	A47	30c multicolored	.25	.25
273	A47	40c multicolored	.25	.25
274	A47	60c multicolored	.25	.25
275	A47	70c multicolored	.25	.25
276	A47	8fr multicolored	.25	.25
277	A47	20fr multicolored	.75	.25
278	A47	40fr multicolored	1.40	.35
279	A47	50fr multicolored	1.60	.55
		Nos. 272-279 (8)	5.00	2.40

Souvenir Sheet

Nativity, by Giorgione — A48

1968, Dec. 16 Engr. *Perf. 11½*

280	A48	100fr green	7.00	7.00

Christmas.

See Nos. 309, 389, 422, 494, 564, 611, 713, 787, 848, 894.

Singing Boy, by Frans Hals — A49

Paintings and Music: 20c, Angels' Concert, by van Eyck. 40c, Angels' Concert, by Matthias Grunewald. 60c, No. 283a, Singing Boy, by Frans Hals. 80c, Lute Player, by Gerard Terborch. 2fr, The Fifer, by Manet. 6fr, No. 286a, Young Girls at the Piano, by Renoir.

1969, Mar. 31 Photo. *Perf. 13*

281	A49	20c gold & multi	.25	.25
282	A49	40c gold & multi	.25	.25
283	A49	60c gold & multi	.25	.25
	a.	Souvenir sheet, 75fr	3.50	3.50
284	A49	80c gold & multi	.25	.25
285	A49	2fr gold & multi	.25	.25
286	A49	6fr gold & multi	.25	.25
	a.	Souvenir sheet, 75fr	3.50	3.50
		Nos. 281-286,C6-C7 (8)	6.50	5.25

Tuareg Men — A50

African Headdresses: 40c, Ovambo woman, South West Africa. 60c, Guinean man and Congolese woman. 80c, Dagger dancer, Guinean forest area. 8fr, Mohammedan Nigerians. 20fr, Luba dancer, Kabondo, Congo. 40fr, Senegalese and Gambian women. 80fr, Rwanda dancer.

1969, May 29 Litho. *Perf. 13*

287	A50	20c multicolored	.25	.25
288	A50	40c multicolored	.25	.25
289	A50	60c multicolored	.25	.25
290	A50	80c multicolored	.25	.25
291	A50	8fr multicolored	.40	.25
292	A50	20fr multicolored	.75	.25
293	A50	40fr multicolored	1.75	.45
294	A50	80fr multicolored	4.00	.85
		Nos. 287-294 (8)	7.90	2.80

See #398-405. For overprints see #550-557.

The Moneylender and his Wife, by Quentin Massys — A51

Design: 70fr, The Moneylender and his Wife, by Marinus van Reymerswaele.

1969, Sept. 10 Photo. *Perf. 13*

295	A51	30fr silver & multi	1.00	.75
296	A51	70fr gold & multi	2.50	1.50

5th anniv. of the African Development Bank. Printed in sheets of 20 stamps and 20 labels with commemorative inscription.

For overprints see Nos. 612-613.

Souvenir Sheet

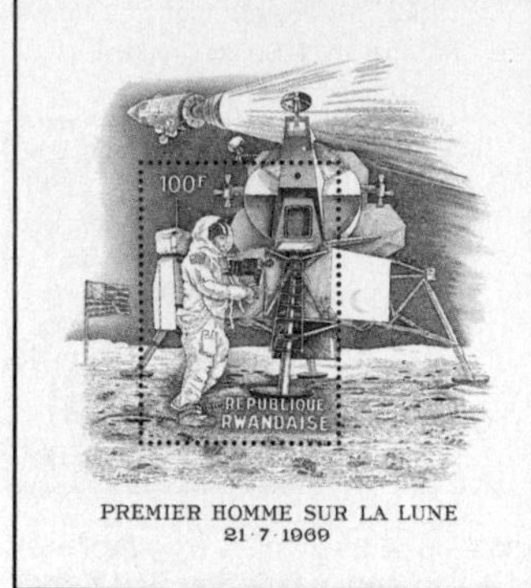

First Man on the Moon — A52

1969, Oct. 9 Engr. *Perf. 11½*

297	A52	100fr blue gray	4.25	4.25

See note after Mali No. C80. See No. 407.

Camomile and Health Emblem — A53

Medicinal Plants and Health Emblem: 40c, Aloe. 60c, Cola. 80c, Coca. 3fr, Hagenia abissinica. 75fr, Cassia. 80fr, Cinchona. 100fr, Tephrosia.

1969, Nov. 24 Photo. *Perf. 13*

Flowers in Natural Colors

298	A53	20c gold, blue & blk	.25	.25
299	A53	40c gold, yel grn & blk	.25	.25
300	A53	60c gold, pink & blk	.25	.25
301	A53	80c gold, green & blk	.25	.25
302	A53	3fr gold, org & blk	.25	.25
303	A53	75fr gold, yel & blk	2.75	1.25
304	A53	80fr gold, lilac & blk	3.25	1.40
305	A53	100fr gold, dl yel & blk	3.75	1.75
		Nos. 298-305 (8)	11.00	5.65

For overprints & surcharge see #534-539, B1.

Worker with Pickaxe and Flag — A54

1969, Nov. Photo. *Perf. 11½*

306	A54	6fr brt pink & multi	.40	.25
307	A54	18fr ultra & multi	.85	.45
308	A54	40fr brown & multi	1.50	.90
		Nos. 306-308 (3)	2.75	1.60

10th anniversary of independence.

For overprints see Nos. 608-610.

Christmas Type of 1968

Souvenir Sheet

Design: "Holy Night" (detail), by Correggio.

1969, Dec. 15 Engr. *Perf. 11½*

309	A48	100fr ultra	4.50	4.50

The Cook, by Pierre Aertsen — A55

Paintings: 20c, Quarry Worker, by Oscar Bonnevalle, horiz. 40c, The Plower, by Peter Brueghel, horiz 60c, Fisherman, by Constantin Meunier. 80c, Slipway, Ostende, by Jean van Noten, horiz. 10fr, The Forge of Vulcan, by Velasquez, horiz. 50fr, "Hiercheuse" (woman shoveling coal), by Meunier. 70fr, Miner, by Pierre Paulus.

1969, Dec. 22 Photo. *Perf. 13½*

310	A55	20c	gold & multi	.25	.25
311	A55	40c	gold & multi	.25	.25
312	A55	60c	gold & multi	.25	.25
313	A55	80c	gold & multi	.25	.25
314	A55	8fr	gold & multi	.25	.25
315	A55	10fr	gold & multi	.25	.25
316	A55	50fr	gold & multi	1.40	.45
317	A55	70fr	gold & multi	1.90	.70
			Nos. 310-317 (8)	4.80	2.65

ILO, 50th anniversary.

Napoleon Crossing St. Bernard, by Jacques L. David — A56

Paintings of Napoleon Bonaparte (1769-1821): 40c, Decorating Soldier before Tilsit, by Jean Baptiste Debret. 60c, Addressing Troops at Augsburg, by Claude Gautherot. 80c, First Consul, by Jean Auguste Ingres. 8fr, Battle of Marengo, by Jacques Auguste Pajou. 20fr, Napoleon Meeting Emperor Francis II, by Antoine Jean Gros. 40fr, Gen. Bonaparte at Arcole, by Gros. 80fr Coronation, by David.

1969, Dec. 29

318	A56	20c	gold & multi	.25	.25
319	A56	40c	gold & multi	.25	.25
320	A56	60c	gold & multi	.25	.25
321	A56	80c	gold & multi	.25	.25
322	A56	8fr	gold & multi	.30	.25
323	A56	20fr	gold & multi	.85	.40
324	A56	40fr	gold & multi	1.75	.85
325	A56	80fr	gold & multi	3.25	1.40
			Nos. 318-325 (8)	7.15	3.90

Epsom Derby, by Gericault — A57

Paintings of Horses: 40c, Horses Emerging from the Sea, by Delacroix. 60c, Charles V at Muhlberg, by Titian, vert. 80c, Amateur Jockeys, by Edgar Degas, 8fr, Horsemen at Rest, by Philips Wouwerman. 20fr, Imperial Guards Officer, by Géricault, vert. 40fr, Friends of the Desert, by Oscar Bonnevalle. 80fr, Two Horses (detail from the Prodigal Son), by Rubens.

1970, Mar. 31 Photo. *Perf. 13½*

326	A57	20c	gold & multi	.25	.25
327	A57	40c	gold & multi	.25	.25
328	A57	60c	gold & multi	.25	.25
329	A57	80c	gold & multi	.25	.25
330	A57	8fr	gold & multi	.25	.25
331	A57	20fr	gold & multi	1.25	.25
332	A57	40fr	gold & multi	2.00	.45
333	A57	80fr	gold & multi	3.25	.80
			Nos. 326-333 (8)	7.75	2.75

Souvenir Sheet

Fleet in Bay of Naples, by Peter Brueghel, the Elder — A58

1970, May 2 Engr. *Perf. 11½*

334	A58	100fr	brt rose lilac	12.50	12.50

10th Europa Phil. Exhib., Naples, Italy, May 2-10.

Examples of No. 334 were trimmed to 68x58mm and overprinted in silver or gold "NAPLES 1973" on the stamp, and "Salon Philatelique des Etats Africains / Exposition du Timbre-Poste Europa" in October, 1973.

Soccer and Mexican Decorations A59

Designs: Various scenes from soccer game and pre-Columbian decorations.

1970, June 15 Photo. *Perf. 13*

335	A59	20c	gold & multi	.25	.25
336	A59	30c	gold & multi	.25	.25
337	A59	50c	gold & multi	.25	.25
338	A59	1fr	gold & multi	.25	.25
339	A59	6fr	gold & multi	.25	.25
340	A59	18fr	gold & multi	.85	.25
341	A59	30fr	gold & multi	1.10	.45
342	A59	90fr	gold & multi	2.25	.85
			Nos. 335-342 (8)	5.45	2.80

9th World Soccer Championships for the Jules Rimet Cup, Mexico City, 5/30-6/21.

Tharaka Meru Woman, East Africa — A60

African National Costumes: 30c, Musician with wooden flute, Niger. 50c, Woman water carrier, Tunisia. 1fr, Ceremonial costumes, North Nigeria. 3fr, Strolling troubadour "Griot," Mali. 5fr, Quipongos women, Angola. 50fr, Man at prayer, Mauritania. 90fr, Sinehatiali dance costumes, Ivory Coast.

1970, June 1 Litho.

343	A60	20c	multi	.25	.25
344	A60	30c	multi	.25	.25
345	A60	50c	multi	.25	.25
346	A60	1fr	multi	.25	.25
347	A60	3fr	multi	.25	.25
348	A60	5fr	multi	.30	.25
349	A60	50fr	multi	2.00	.45
350	A60	90fr	multi	3.25	.80
			Nos. 343-350 (8)	6.80	2.75

For overprints and surcharges see Nos. 693-698, B2-B3.

Flower Arrangement, Peacock, EXPO '70 Emblem — A61

EXPO Emblem and: 30c, Torii and Camellias, by Yukihiko Yasuda. 50c, Kabuki character and Woman Playing Samisen, by Nampu Katayama. 1fr, Tower of the Sun, and Warrior Riding into Water. 3fr, Pavilion and Buddhist deity. 5fr, Pagoda and modern painting by Shuho Yamakawa. 20fr, Japanese inscription "Omatsuri" and Osaka Castle. 70fr, EXPO '70 emblem and Warrior on Horseback.

1970, Aug. 24 Photo. *Perf. 13*

351	A61	20c	gold & multi	.25	.25
352	A61	30c	gold & multi	.25	.25
353	A61	50c	gold & multi	.25	.25
354	A61	1fr	gold & multi	.25	.25
355	A61	3fr	gold & multi	.25	.25
356	A61	5fr	gold & multi	.30	.25
357	A61	20fr	gold & multi	.70	.35
358	A61	70fr	gold & multi	2.00	.70
			Nos. 351-358 (8)	4.25	2.55

EXPO '70 International Exhibition, Osaka, Japan, Mar. 15-Sept. 13.

Young Mountain Gorillas — A62

Various Gorillas. 40c, 80c, 2fr, 100fr are vert.

1970, Sept. 7

359	A62	20c	olive & blk	.25	.25
360	A62	40c	brt rose lil & blk	.25	.25
361	A62	60c	blue, brn & blk	.25	.25
362	A62	80c	org brn & blk	.30	.25
363	A62	1fr	dp car & blk	.85	.25
364	A62	2fr	black & multi	1.25	.45
365	A62	15fr	sepia & blk	2.75	1.25
366	A62	100fr	brt bl & blk	6.50	2.75
			Nos. 359-366 (8)	12.40	5.70

Pierre J. Pelletier and Joseph B. Caventou A63

Designs: 20c, Cinchona flower and bark. 80c, Quinine powder and pharmacological vessels. 1fr, Anopheles mosquito. 3fr, Malaria patient and nurse. 25fr, "Malaria" (mosquito).

1970, Oct. 27 Photo. *Perf. 13*

367	A63	20c	silver & multi	.25	.25
368	A63	80c	silver & multi	.25	.25
369	A63	1fr	silver & multi	.25	.25
370	A63	3fr	silver & multi	.25	.25
371	A63	25fr	silver & multi	.75	.25
372	A63	70fr	silver & multi	1.75	.30
			Nos. 367-372 (6)	3.50	1.55

150th anniv. of the discovery of quinine by Pierre Joseph Pelletier (1788-1842) and Joseph Bienaimé Caventou (1795-1877), French pharmacologists.

Apollo Spaceship A64

Apollo Spaceship: 30c, Second stage separation. 50c, Spaceship over moon surface. 1fr, Landing module and astronauts on moon. 3fr, Take-off from moon. 5fr, Return to earth. 10fr, Final separation of nose cone. 80fr, Splashdown.

1970, Nov. 23 Photo. *Perf. 13*

373	A64	20c	silver & multi	.25	.25
374	A64	30c	silver & multi	.25	.25
375	A64	50c	silver & multi	.25	.25
376	A64	1fr	silver & multi	.25	.25
377	A64	3fr	silver & multi	.25	.25
378	A64	5fr	silver & multi	.25	.25
379	A64	10fr	silver & multi	.75	.30
380	A64	80fr	silver & multi	3.00	1.00
			Nos. 373-380 (8)	5.25	2.80

Conquest of space.

Franklin D. Roosevelt and Brassocattleya Olympia Alba — A65

Portraits of Roosevelt and various orchids.

1970, Dec. 21 Photo. *Perf. 13*

381	A65	20c	blue, blk & brn	.25	.25
382	A65	30c	car rose, blk & brn	.25	.25
383	A65	50c	dp org, blk & brn	.25	.25
384	A65	1fr	green, blk & brn	.30	.25
385	A65	2fr	maroon, blk & grn	.35	.25
386	A65	6fr	lilac & multi	.40	.25
387	A65	30fr	bl, blk & sl grn	1.25	.30
388	A65	60fr	lil rose, blk & sl grn	2.50	.65
			Nos. 381-388 (8)	5.55	2.45

Pres. Roosevelt, 25th death anniv.

Christmas Type of 1968

Souvenir Sheet

Design: 100fr, Adoration of the Shepherds, by José de Ribera, vert.

1970, Dec. 24 Engr. *Perf. 11½*

389	A48	100fr	Prus blue	4.50	4.50

Pope Paul VI — A66

Popes: 20c, John XXIII, 1958-1963. 30c, Pius XII, 1939-1958. 40c, Pius XI, 1922-39. 1fr, Benedict XV, 1914-22. 18fr, St. Pius X, 1903-14. 20fr, Leo XIII, 1878-1903. 60fr, Pius IX, 1846-78.

1970, Dec. 31 Photo. *Perf. 13*

390	A66	10c	gold & dk brn	.25	.25
391	A66	20c	gold & dk grn	.25	.25
392	A66	30c	gold & dp claret	.25	.25
393	A66	40c	gold & indigo	.30	.25
394	A66	1fr	gold & dk pur	.35	.25
395	A66	18fr	gold & purple	.80	.25
396	A66	20fr	gold & org brn	1.10	.35
397	A66	60fr	gold & blk brn	2.50	.80
			Nos. 390-397 (8)	5.80	2.65

Centenary of Vatican I, Ecumenical Council of the Roman Catholic Church, 1869-70.

For overprints, see Nos. 644-651.

Headdress Type of 1969

African Headdresses: 20c, Rendille woman. 30c, Young Toubou woman, Chad. 50c, Peul man, Niger. 1fr, Young Masai man, Kenya. 5fr, Young Peul girl, Niger. 18fr, Rwanda woman. 25fr, Man, Mauritania. 50fr, Rwanda women with pearl necklaces.

1971, Feb. 15 Litho. *Perf. 13*

398	A50	20c	multi	.25	.25
399	A50	30c	multi	.25	.25
400	A50	50c	multi	.25	.25
401	A50	1fr	multi	.25	.25
402	A50	5fr	multi	.30	.25
403	A50	18fr	multi	.75	.25
404	A50	25fr	multi	1.75	.30
405	A50	50fr	multi	3.25	.50
			Nos. 398-405 (8)	7.05	2.30

For overprints see Nos. 550-557.

M. L. King Type of 1968
Souvenir Sheet

Design: 100fr, Charles de Gaulle (1890-1970), President of France.

1971, Mar. 15 Engr. *Perf. 13½*

406	A44	100fr ultra	4.25	4.25

Astronaut Type of 1969 Inscribed in Dark Violet with Emblem and: "APOLLO / 14 / SHEPARD / ROOSA / MITCHELL"

1971, Apr. 15 Engr. *Perf. 11½*

Souvenir Sheet

407	A52	100fr brown orange	12.00	12.00

Apollo 14 US moon landing, Jan. 31-Feb. 9.

Beethoven, by Christian Horneman A67

Beethoven Portraits: 30c, Joseph Stieler. 50c, by Ferdinand Schimon. 3fr, by H. Best. 6fr, by W. Fassbender. 90fr, Beethoven's Funeral Procession, by Leopold Stöber.

1971, July 5 Photo. *Perf. 13*

408	A67	20c gold & multi	.25	.25
409	A67	30c gold & multi	.25	.25
410	A67	50c gold & multi	.25	.25
411	A67	3fr gold & multi	.25	.25
412	A67	6fr gold & multi	.50	.25
413	A67	90fr gold & multi	2.75	1.75
		Nos. 408-413 (6)	4.25	3.00

Ludwig van Beethoven (1770-1827), composer.

Equestrian — A68

Olympic Sports: 30c, Runner at start. 50c, Basketball. 1fr, High jump. 8fr, Boxing. 10fr, Pole vault. 20fr, Wrestling. 60fr, Gymnastics (rings).

1971, Oct. 25 Photo. *Perf. 13*

414	A68	20c gold & black	.25	.25
415	A68	30c gold & dp rose lil	.25	.25
416	A68	50c gold & vio bl	.25	.25
417	A68	1fr gold & dp grn	.25	.25
418	A68	8fr gold & henna brn	.25	.25
419	A68	10fr gold & purple	.30	.25
420	A68	20fr gold & dp brn	.50	.25
421	A68	60fr gold & Prus bl	1.50	.50
		Nos. 414-421 (8)	3.55	2.25

20th Summer Olympic Games, Munich, Aug. 26-Sept. 10, 1972.

Christmas Type of 1968
Souvenir Sheet

100fr, Nativity, by Anthony van Dyck, vert.

1971, Dec. 20 Engr. *Perf. 11½*

422	A48	100fr indigo	5.75	5.75

Adam by Dürer — A69

Paintings by Albrecht Dürer (1471-1528), German painter and engraver: 30c, Eve. 50c, Hieronymus Holzschuher, Portrait. 1fr, Lamentation of Christ. 3fr, Madonna with the Pear. 5fr, St. Eustace. 20fr, Sts. Paul and Mark. 70fr, Self-portrait, 1500.

1971, Dec. 31 Photo. *Perf. 13*

423	A69	20c gold & multi	.25	.25
424	A69	30c gold & multi	.25	.25
425	A69	50c gold & multi	.25	.25
426	A69	1fr gold & multi	.25	.25
427	A69	3fr gold & multi	.25	.25
428	A69	5fr gold & multi	.35	.25
429	A69	20fr gold & multi	.70	.25
430	A69	70fr gold & multi	1.50	1.25
		Nos. 423-430 (8)	3.80	3.00

A 600fr stamp on gold foil honoring Apollo 15 was issued Jan. 15, 1972. Value $160.

Guardsmen Exercising — A70

National Guard Emblem and: 6fr, Loading supplies. 15fr, Helicopter ambulance. 25fr, Health Service for civilians. 50fr, Guardsman and map of Rwanda, vert.

1972, Feb. 7 *Perf. 13½x14, 14x13½*

431	A70	4fr dp org & multi	.25	.25
432	A70	6fr yellow & multi	.25	.25
433	A70	15fr lt blue & multi	.35	.25
434	A70	25fr red & multi	.90	.40
435	A70	50fr multicolored	2.00	1.00
		Nos. 431-435 (5)	3.75	2.15

"The National Guard serving the nation." For overprints see Nos. 559-563.

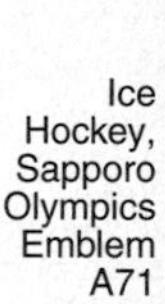

Ice Hockey, Sapporo Olympics Emblem A71

1972, Feb. 12 *Perf. 13x13½*

436	A71	20c shown	.25	.25
437	A71	30c Speed skating	.25	.25
438	A71	50c Ski jump	.25	.25
439	A71	1fr Men's figure skating	.25	.25
440	A71	6fr Cross-country skiing	.25	.25
441	A71	12fr Slalom	.25	.25
442	A71	20fr Bobsledding	.40	.25
443	A71	60fr Downhill skiing	1.30	1.00
		Nos. 436-443 (8)	3.20	2.75

11th Winter Olympic Games, Sapporo, Japan, Feb. 3-13.

Antelopes and Cercopithecus — A72

1972, Mar. 20 Photo. *Perf. 13*

444	A72	20c shown	.25	.25
445	A72	30c Buffaloes	.25	.25
446	A72	50c Zebras	.30	.25
447	A72	1fr Rhinoceroses	.35	.30
448	A72	2fr Wart hogs	.45	.35
449	A72	6fr Hippopotami	.60	.45
450	A72	18fr Hyenas	1.10	.60
451	A72	32fr Guinea fowl	2.00	.85
452	A72	60fr Antelopes	2.75	1.40
453	A72	80fr Lions	4.00	2.25
		Nos. 444-453 (10)	12.05	6.95

Akagera National Park.

A73

Family raising flag of Rwanda.

1972, Apr. 4 *Perf. 13x12½*

454	A73	6fr dk red & multi	.25	.25
455	A73	18fr green & multi	.45	.25
456	A73	60fr brown & multi	1.40	.80
		Nos. 454-456 (3)	2.10	1.30

10th anniversary of the Referendum establishing Republic of Rwanda.

A74

Birds: 20c, Common Waxbills and Hibiscus. 30c, Collared sunbird. 50c, Variable sunbird. 1fr, Greater double-collared sunbird. 4fr, Ruwenzori puff-back flycatcher. 6fr, Red-billed fire finch. 10fr, Scarlet-chested sunbird. 18fr, Red-headed quelea. 60fr, Black-headed gonolek. 100fr, African golden oriole.

1972, May 17 Photo. *Perf. 13*

457	A74	20c dl grn & multi	.25	.25
458	A74	30c buff & multi	.25	.25
459	A74	50c yellow & multi	.25	.25
460	A74	1fr lt blue & multi	.25	.25
461	A74	4fr dl rose & multi	.30	.25
462	A74	6fr lilac rose & multi	.35	.25
463	A74	10fr pink & multi	.40	.25
464	A74	18fr gray & multi	1.00	.30
465	A74	60fr multicolored	3.25	1.10
466	A74	100fr violet & multi	4.75	2.50
		Nos. 457-466 (10)	11.05	5.65

Belgica '72 Emblem, King Baudouin, Queen Fabiola, Pres. and Mrs. Kayibanda — A75

1972, June 24 Photo. *Perf. 13*

Size: 37x34mm

467	A75	18fr Rwanda landscape	1.00	.35
468	A75	22fr Old houses, Bruges	1.25	.35

Size: 50x34mm

469	A75	40fr shown	2.50	.50
a.		Strip of 3, #467-469	6.50	6.50

Belgica '72 Intl. Phil. Exhib., Brussels, June 24-July 9.

Pres. Kayibanda Addressing Meeting — A76

Pres. Grégoire Kayibanda: 30c, promoting officers of National Guard. 50c, with wife and children. 6fr, casting vote. 10fr, with wife and dignitaries at Feast of Justice. 15fr, with Cabinet and members of Assembly. 18fr, taking oath of office. 50fr, Portrait, vert.

1972, July 4

470	A76	20c gold & slate grn	.25	.25
471	A76	30c gold & dk pur	.25	.25
472	A76	50c gold & choc	.25	.25
473	A76	6fr gold & Prus bl	.25	.25
474	A76	10fr gold & dk pur	.25	.25
475	A76	15fr gold & dk bl	.35	.25
476	A76	18fr gold & brn	.45	.30
477	A76	50fr gold & Prus bl	1.10	.70
		Nos. 470-477 (8)	3.15	2.50

10th anniversary of independence.

Equestrian, Olympic Emblems A77

Stadium, TV Tower and: 30c, Hockey. 50c, Soccer. 1fr, Broad jump. 6fr, Bicycling. 18fr, Yachting. 30fr, Hurdles. 44fr, Gymnastics, women's.

1972, Aug. 16 Photo. *Perf. 14*

478	A77	20c dk brn & gold	.25	.25
479	A77	30c vio bl & gold	.25	.25
480	A77	50c dk green & gold	.25	.25
481	A77	1fr dp claret & gold	.25	.25
482	A77	6fr black & gold	.25	.25
483	A77	18fr brown & gold	.40	.25
484	A77	30fr dk vio & gold	.75	.40
485	A77	44fr Prus bl & gold	1.25	.70
		Nos. 478-485 (8)	3.65	2.60

20th Olympic Games, Munich, 8/26-9/11.

Relay (Sport) and UN Emblem A78

1972, Oct. 23 Photo. *Perf. 13*

486	A78	20c shown	.25	.25
487	A78	30c Musicians	.25	.25
488	A78	50c Dancers	.25	.25
489	A78	1fr Operating room	.25	.25
490	A78	6fr Weaver & painter	.25	.25
491	A78	18fr Classroom	.35	.25
492	A78	24fr Laboratory	.55	.30
493	A78	50fr Hands of 4 races reaching for equality	1.10	.70
		Nos. 486-493 (8)	3.25	2.50

Fight against racism.

Christmas Type of 1968
Souvenir Sheet

Design: 100fr, Adoration of the Shepherds, by Jacob Jordaens, vert.

1972, Dec. 11 *Perf. 11½*

494	A48	100fr red brown	4.50	4.50

Phymateus Brunneri — A79

Various insects. 30c, 1fr, 6fr, 22fr, 100fr, vert.

1973, Jan. 31 Photo. *Perf. 13*

495 A79 20c multi .25 .25
496 A79 30c multi .25 .25
497 A79 50c multi .25 .25
498 A79 1fr multi .25 .25
499 A79 2fr multi .25 .25
500 A79 6fr multi .40 .25
501 A79 18fr multi .80 .40
502 A79 22fr multi 1.25 .70
503 A79 70fr multi 3.50 2.25
504 A79 100fr multi 5.00 3.50
Nos. 495-504 (10) 12.20 8.35

Souvenir Sheet

Perf. 14

505 A79 80fr like 20c 10.00 10.00

No. 505 contains one stamp 43½x33½mm.

Emile Zola, by Edouard Manet — A80

Paintings Connected with Reading, and Book Year Emblem: 30c, Rembrandt's Mother. 50c, St. Jerome Removing Thorn from Lion's Paw, by Colantonio. 1fr, Apostles Peter and Paul, by El Greco. 2fr, Virgin and Child with Book, by Roger van der Weyden. 6fr, St. Jerome in his Cell, by Antonella de Messina. 40fr, St. Barbara, by Master of Flemalle. No. 513, Don Quixote, by Oscar Vonnevalle. No. 514, Pres. Kayibanda reading book.

1973, Mar. 12 Photo. *Perf. 13*

506 A80 20c gold & multi .25 .25
507 A80 30c gold & multi .25 .25
508 A80 50c gold & multi .25 .25
509 A80 1fr gold & multi .25 .25
510 A80 2fr gold & multi .25 .25
511 A80 6fr gold & multi .25 .25
512 A80 40fr gold & multi 1.00 .60
513 A80 100fr gold & multi 2.50 1.90
Nos. 506-513 (8) 5.00 4.00

Souvenir Sheet

Perf. 14

514 A80 100fr gold, bl & ind 4.00 4.00

International Book Year.

Longombe A81

Musical instruments of Central & West Africa.

1973, Apr. 9 Photo. *Perf. 13½*

515 A81 20c shown .25 .25
516 A81 30c Horn .25 .25
517 A81 50c Xylophone .25 .25
518 A81 1fr Harp .25 .25
519 A81 4fr Alur horns .25 .25
520 A81 6fr Drum, bells and horn .25 .25
521 A81 18fr Large drums (Ngoma) .50 .25
522 A81 90fr Toba 2.50 1.25
Nos. 515-522 (8) 4.50 3.00

Rubens and Isabella Brandt, by Rubens — A82

Paintings from Old Pinakothek, Munich (IBRA Emblem and): 30c, Young Man, by Cranach. 50c, Woman Peeling Turnips, by Chardin. 1fr, The Abduction of Leucippa's Daughters, by Rubens. 2fr, Virgin and Child, by Filippo Lippi. 6fr, Boys Eating Fruit, by Murillo. 40fr, The Lovesick Woman, by Jan Steen. No. 530, Jesus Stripped of His Garments, by El Greco. No. 531, Oswolt Krel, by Dürer.

1973, May 11

523 A82 20c gold & multi .25 .25
524 A82 30c gold & multi .25 .25
525 A82 50c gold & multi .25 .25
526 A82 1fr gold & multi .25 .25
527 A82 2fr gold & multi .25 .25
528 A82 6fr gold & multi .25 .25
529 A82 40fr gold & multi 1.00 .75
530 A82 100fr gold & multi 2.75 1.75
Nos. 523-530 (8) 5.25 4.00

Souvenir Sheet

531 A82 100fr gold & multi 4.00 4.00

IBRA München 1973 Intl. Phil. Exhib., Munich, May 11-20. #531 contains one 40x56mm stamp.

Map of Africa and Peace Doves A83

Design: 94fr, Map of Africa and hands.

1973, July 23 Photo. *Perf. 13½*

532 A83 6fr gold & multi .30 .25
533 A83 94fr gold & multi 2.75 2.50

Org. for African Unity, 10th anniv.
For overprints see Nos. 895-896.

Nos. 298-303 Overprinted in Blue, Black, Green or Brown: "SECHERESSE / SOLIDARITE AFRICAINE"

1973, Aug. 23 Photo. *Perf. 13*

534 A53 20c multi (Bl) .25 .25
535 A53 40c multi (Bk) .25 .25
536 A53 60c multi (Bl) .25 .25
537 A53 80c multi (G) .25 .25
538 A53 3fr multi (G) .45 .25
539 A53 75fr multi (Br) 3.00 1.00
Nos. 534-539,B1 (7) 10.45 8.25

African solidarity in drought emergency.

African Postal Union Issue

Common Design Type

1973, Sept. 12 Engr. *Perf. 13*

540 CD137 100fr dp brn, bl & brn 3.75 2.00

Six-lined Distichodus — A84

African Fish: 30c, Little triggerfish. 50c, Spotted upside-down catfish. 1fr, Nile mouthbreeder. 2fr, African lungfish. 6fr, Pareutropius mandevillei. 40fr, Congo characin. 100fr, Like 20c. 150fr, Julidochromis ornatus.

1973, Sept. 3 Photo. *Perf. 13*

541 A84 20c gold & multi .25 .25
542 A84 30c gold & multi .25 .25
543 A84 50c gold & multi .25 .25
544 A84 1fr gold & multi .25 .25
545 A84 2fr gold & multi .25 .25
546 A84 6fr gold & multi .35 .25
547 A84 40fr gold & multi 1.50 .75
548 A84 150fr gold & multi 5.50 3.25
Nos. 541-548 (8) 8.60 5.50

Souvenir Sheet

549 A84 100fr gold & multi 6.00 6.00

No. 549 contains one stamp 48x29mm.

Nos. 398-405 Overprinted in Black, Silver, Green or Blue

1973, Sept. 15 Litho.

550 A50 20c multi (Bk) .25 .25
551 A50 30c multi (S) .25 .25
552 A50 50c multi (Bk) .25 .25
553 A50 1fr multi (G) .25 .25
554 A50 5fr multi (S) .25 .25
555 A50 18fr multi (Bk) .75 .25
556 A50 25fr multi (Bk) 1.50 .50
557 A50 50fr multi (Bl) 3.00 1.00
Nos. 550-557 (8) 6.50 3.00

Africa Weeks, Brussels, Sept. 15-30, 1973. On the 30c, 1fr and 25fr the text of the overprint is horizontal.

Nos. 431-435 Overprinted in Gold

Perf. 13½x14, 14x13½

1973, Oct. 31 Photo.

559 A70 4fr dp org & multi .25 .25
560 A70 6fr yellow & multi .25 .25
561 A70 15fr lt blue & multi .50 .30
562 A70 25fr red & multi .90 .40
563 A70 50fr multicolored 1.75 .90
Nos. 559-563 (5) 3.65 2.10

25th anniv. of the Universal Declaration of Human Rights.

Christmas Type of 1968

Souvenir Sheet

Adoration of the Shepherds, by Guido Reni.

1973, Dec. 15 Engr. *Perf. 11½*

564 A48 100fr brt violet 4.50 4.50

Copernicus and Astrolabe A85

Designs: 30c, 18fr, 100fr, Portrait. 50c, 80fr, Copernicus and heliocentric system. 1fr, like 20c.

1973, Dec. 26 Photo. *Perf. 13*

565 A85 20c silver & multi .25 .25
566 A85 30c silver & multi .25 .25
567 A85 50c silver & multi .25 .25
568 A85 1fr gold & multi .25 .25
569 A85 18fr gold & multi .80 .50
570 A85 80fr gold & multi 2.75 2.25
Nos. 565-570 (6) 4.55 3.75

Souvenir Sheet

571 A85 100fr gold & multi 5.50 5.50

Nicolaus Copernicus (1473-1543).

Pres. Juvénal Habyarimana — A86

1974, Apr. 8 Photo. *Perf. 11½*

Black Inscriptions

572 A86 1fr bister & sepia .25 .25
573 A86 2fr ultra & sepia .25 .25
574 A86 5fr rose red & sep .25 .25
575 A86 6fr grnsh bl & sep .25 .25
576 A86 26fr lilac & sepia .55 .30
577 A86 60fr ol grn & sepia 1.50 1.00
Nos. 572-577 (6) 3.05 2.30

Souvenir Sheet

Christ Between the Thieves (Detail), by Rubens — A87

1974, Apr. 12 Engr. *Perf. 11½*

578 A87 100fr sepia 14.00 14.00

Easter.

Yugoslavia-Zaire Soccer Game — A88

Games' emblem and soccer games.

1974, July 6 Photo. *Perf. 13½*

579 A88 20c shown .25 .25
580 A88 40c Netherlands-Sweden .25 .25
581 A88 60c Germany (Fed.)-Australia .25 .25
582 A88 80c Haiti-Argentina .25 .25
583 A88 2fr Brazil-Scotland .25 .25
584 A88 6fr Bulgaria-Uruguay .30 .25
585 A88 40fr Italy-Poland 1.25 .50
586 A88 50fr Chile-Germany (DDR) 1.75 .85
Nos. 579-586 (8) 4.55 2.85

World Cup Soccer Championship, Munich, June 13-July 7.

Marconi's Laboratory Yacht "Elletra" — A89

Designs: 30c, Marconi and steamer "Carlo Alberto." 50c, Marconi's wireless apparatus and telecommunications satellites. 4fr, Marconi and globes connected by communications waves. 35fr, Marconi's radio, and radar. 60fr, Marconi and transmitter at Poldhu, Cornwall. 50fr, like 20c.

1974, Aug. 19 Photo. *Perf. 13½*

587 A89 20c violet, blk & grn .25 .25
588 A89 30c green, blk & vio .25 .25
589 A89 50c yellow, blk & lil .25 .25
590 A89 4fr salmon, blk & bl .25 .25
591 A89 35fr lilac, blk & yel .80 .50
592 A89 60fr blue, blk & brnz 1.50 1.00
Nos. 587-592 (6) 3.30 2.50

Souvenir Sheet

593 A89 50fr gold, blk & lt bl 3.00 3.00

Guglielmo Marconi (1874-1937), Italian electrical engineer and inventor.

The Flute Player, by J. Leyster — A90

Paintings: 20c, Diane de Poitiers, Fontainebleau School. 50c, Virgin and Child, by David. 1fr, Triumph of Venus, by Boucher. 10fr, Seated Harlequin, by Picasso. 18fr, Virgin and Child, 15th century. 20fr, Beheading of St. John, by Hans Fries. 50fr, Daughter of Andersdotter, by J. F. Höckert.

1974, Sept. 23 Photo. *Perf. 14x13*

594	A90	20c gold & multi	.25	.25
595	A90	30c gold & multi	.25	.25
596	A90	50c gold & multi	.25	.25
597	A90	1fr gold & multi	.25	.25
598	A90	10fr gold & multi	.25	.25
599	A90	18fr gold & multi	.50	.30
600	A90	20fr gold & multi	.50	.40
601	A90	50fr gold & multi	1.50	1.10
		Nos. 594-601 (8)	3.75	3.05

INTERNABA 74 Intl. Phil. Exhib., Basel, June 7-10, and Stockholmia 74, Intl. Phil. Exhib., Stockholm, Sept. 21-29.

Six multicolored souvenir sheets exist containing two 15fr stamps each in various combinations of designs of Nos. 594-601. One souvenir sheet of four 25fr stamps exists with designs of Nos. 595, 597, 599 and 601.

Messenger Monk — A91

UPU Emblem and Messengers: 30c, Inca. 50c, Morocco. 1fr, India. 18fr, Polynesia. 80fr, Rwanda.

1974, Oct. 9 *Perf. 14*

602	A91	20c gold & multi	.25	.25
603	A91	30c gold & multi	.25	.25
604	A91	50c gold & multi	.25	.25
605	A91	1fr gold & multi	.25	.25
606	A91	18fr gold & multi	.60	.35
607	A91	80fr gold & multi	2.25	1.50
		Nos. 602-607 (6)	3.85	2.85

Centenary of Universal Postal Union.

Nos. 306-308 Overprinted

1974, Dec. 16 Photo. *Perf. 11½*

608	A54	6fr brt pink & multi	5.50	3.75
609	A54	18fr ultra & multi	5.50	3.75
610	A54	40fr brn & multi	5.50	3.75
		Nos. 608-610 (3)	16.50	11.25

15th anniversary of independence.

Christmas Type of 1968

Souvenir Sheet

Adoration of the Kings, by Joos van Cleve.

1974, Dec. 23 Engr. *Perf. 11½*

611	A48	100fr slate green	17.00	17.00

Nos. 295-296 Overprinted: "1974 / 10e Anniversaire"

1974, Dec. 30 Photo. *Perf. 13*

612	A51	30fr sil & multi	1.25	.85
613	A51	70fr gold & multi	2.25	1.60

African Development Bank, 10th anniversary.

Uganda Kob — A92

Antelopes: 30c, Bongos, horiz. 50c, Rwanda antelopes. 1fr, Young sitatungas, horiz. 4fr, Greater kudus. 10fr, Impalas, horiz. 34fr, Waterbuck. 40fr, Impalas. 60fr, Greater kudu. 100fr, Derby's elands, horiz.

1975, Mar. 17 Photo. *Perf. 13*

614	A92	20c multi	.25	.25
615	A92	30c multi	.30	.25
616	A92	50c multi	.45	.25
617	A92	1fr multi	.75	.25
618	A92	4fr multi	.90	.30
619	A92	10fr multi	1.75	.55
620	A92	34fr multi	3.75	1.00
621	A92	100fr multi	7.50	3.00
		Nos. 614-621 (8)	15.65	5.85

Miniature Sheets

622	A92	40fr multi	25.00	25.00
623	A92	60fr multi	25.00	25.00

Miniature Sheets

Pietá, by Cranach the Elder — A93

20fr, The Burial of Jesus, by Raphael. 50fr, By van der Weyden. 100fr, By Bellini.

1975, Apr. 1 Photo. *Perf. 13x14*

624	A93	20fr multicolored	3.00	3.00
625	A93	30fr shown	3.00	3.00
626	A93	50fr multicolored	3.00	3.00
627	A93	100fr multicolored	3.00	3.00
		Nos. 624-627 (4)	12.00	12.00

Easter. Size of stamps: 40x52mm. See Nos. 681-684.

Souvenir Sheets

Prince Balthazar Charles, by Velazquez — A94

Paintings: 30fr, Infanta Margaret of Austria, by Velazquez. 50fr, The Divine Shepherd, by Murillo. 100fr, Francisco Goya, by V. Lopez y Portana.

1975, Apr. 4 Photo. *Perf. 13*

628	A94	20fr multi	4.00	4.00
629	A94	30fr multi	4.00	4.00
630	A94	50fr multi	4.00	4.00
631	A94	100fr multi	4.00	4.00
		Nos. 628-631 (4)	16.00	16.00

Espana 75 Intl. Phil. Exhib., Madrid, Apr. 4-13. Size of stamps: 38x48mm. See Nos. 642-643. For overprints see Nos. 844-847.

Pyrethrum (Insect Powder) — A95

1975, Apr. 14 *Perf. 13*

632	A95	20c shown	.25	.25
633	A95	30c Tea	.25	.25
634	A95	50c Coffee (beans and pan)	.25	.25
635	A95	4fr Bananas	.25	.25
636	A95	10fr Corn	.25	.25
637	A95	12fr Sorghum	.30	.25
638	A95	26fr Rice	.75	.35
639	A95	47fr Coffee (workers and beans)	1.50	.75
		Nos. 632-639 (8)	3.80	2.60

Souvenir Sheets

Perf. 13½

640	A95	25fr like 50c	1.75	1.75
641	A95	75fr like 47fr	3.50	3.50

Year of Agriculture and 10th anniversary of Office for Industrialized Cultivation.

Painting Type of 1975

Souvenir Sheets

75fr, Louis XIV, by Hyacinthe Rigaud. 125fr, Cavalry Officer, by Jean Gericault.

1975, June 6 Photo. *Perf. 13*

642	A94	75fr multi	6.00	6.00
643	A94	125fr multi	8.00	8.00

ARPHILA 75, Intl. Philatelic Exhibition, Paris, June 6-16. Size of stamps: 38x48mm.

Nos. 390-397 Overprinted: "1975 / ANNEE / SAINTE"

1975, June 23 Photo. *Perf. 13*

644	A66	10c gold & dk brn	.25	.25
645	A66	20c gold & dk grn	.25	.25
646	A66	30c gold & dp claret	.25	.25
647	A66	40c gold & indigo	.25	.25
648	A66	1fr gold & dk pur	.25	.25
649	A66	18fr gold & purple	.45	.35
650	A66	20fr gold & org brn	.75	.60
651	A66	60fr gold & blk brn	2.25	1.90
		Nos. 644-651 (8)	4.70	4.10

Holy Year 1975.

White Pelicans — A96

African birds — 30c, Malachite kingfisher. 50c, Goliath herons. 1fr, Saddle-billed storks. 4fr, African jacana. 10fr, African anhingas. 34fr, Sacred ibis. 80fr, Hartlaub ducks.

40fr, Flamingoes. 60fr, Crowned cranes.

1975, June 20

652	A96	20c shown	.25	.25
653	A96	30c multicolored	.25	.25
654	A96	50c multicolored	.25	.25
655	A96	1fr multicolored	.25	.25
656	A96	4fr multicolored	.40	.25
657	A96	10fr multicolored	.75	.25
658	A96	34fr multicolored	2.25	1.00
659	A96	80fr multicolored	5.50	2.00
		Nos. 652-659 (8)	9.90	4.50

Miniature Sheets

660	A96	40fr multicolored	17.50	17.50
661	A96	60fr multicolored	22.50	22.50

Globe Representing Races and WPY Emblem — A97

World Population Year: 26fr, Population graph and emblem. 34fr, Globe with open door and emblem.

1975, Sept. 1 Photo. *Perf. 13½x13*

662	A97	20fr dp bl & multi	.60	.30
663	A97	26fr dl red brn & multi	.70	.40
664	A97	34fr yel & multi	1.00	.80
		Nos. 662-664 (3)	2.30	1.50

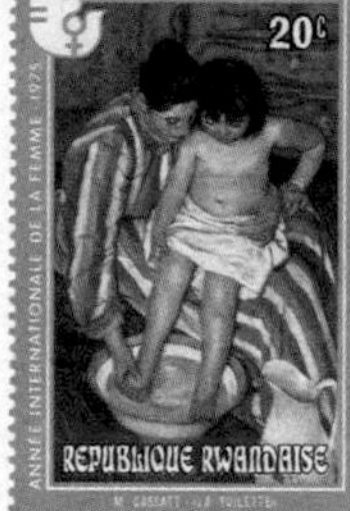

The Bath, by Mary Cassatt and IWY Emblem — A98

IWY Emblem and: 30c, Mother and Infant Son, by Julius Gari Melchers. 50c, Woman with Milk Jug, by Jan Vermeer. 1fr, Water Carrier, by Goya. 8fr, Rwanda woman cotton picker. 12fr, Scientist with microscope. 18fr, Mother and child. 25fr, Empress Josephine, by Pierre-Paul Prud'hon. 40fr, Madame Vigee-Lebrun and Daughter, self-portrait. 60fr, Woman carrying child on back and water jug on head.

1975, Sept. 15 *Perf. 13*

665	A98	20c gold & multi	.25	.25
666	A98	30c gold & multi	.25	.25
667	A98	50c gold & multi	.25	.25
668	A98	1fr gold & multi	.25	.25
669	A98	8fr gold & multi	.25	.25
670	A98	12fr gold & multi	.30	.25
671	A98	18fr gold & multi	.65	.30
672	A98	60fr gold & multi	2.40	1.25
		Nos. 665-672 (8)	4.60	3.05

Souvenir Sheets

Perf. 13½

673	A98	25fr multi	90.00	90.00
674	A98	40fr multi	90.00	90.00

International Women's Year. Nos. 673-674 each contain one stamp 37x49mm.

Owl, Quill and Book — A99

30c, Hygiene emblem. 1.50fr, Kneeling woman holding scales of Justice. 18fr, Chemist in laboratory. 26fr, Symbol of commerce & chart. 34fr, University Building.

1975, Sept. 29 *Perf. 13*

675	A99	20c pur & multi	.25	.25
676	A99	30c ultra & multi	.25	.25
677	A99	1.50fr lilac & multi	.25	.25
678	A99	18fr blue & multi	.35	.25
679	A99	26fr olive & multi	.55	.30
680	A99	34fr blue & multi	1.00	.70
		Nos. 675-680 (6)	2.65	2.00

National Univ. of Rwanda, 10th anniv.

Painting Type of 1975

Souvenir Sheets

Paintings by Jan Vermeer (1632-1675): 20fr, Man and Woman Drinking Wine. 30fr, Woman in Blue Reading Letter. 50fr, Painter in his Studio. 100fr, Young Woman Playing Virginal.

1975, Oct. 13 Photo. *Perf. 13x14*

681	A93	20fr multi	3.25	3.25
682	A93	30fr multi	3.25	3.25
683	A93	50fr multi	3.25	3.25
684	A93	100fr multi	3.25	3.25
		Nos. 681-684 (4)	13.00	13.00

Size of stamps: 40x52mm.

Waterhole and Impatiens Stuhlmannii — A100

Designs: 30c, Antelopes, zebras, candelabra cactus. 50c, Brush fire, and tapinanthus prunifolius. 5fr, Bulera Lake and Egyptian white lotus. 8fr, Erosion prevention and protea madiensis. 10fr, Marsh and melanthera brownei. 26fr, Landscape, lobelias and senecons. 100fr, Sabyinyo Volcano and polystachya kermesina.

1975, Oct. 25 *Perf. 13*

685	A100	20c blk & multi	.25	.25
686	A100	30c blk & multi	.25	.25
687	A100	50c blk & multi	.25	.25
688	A100	5fr blk & multi	.25	.25
689	A100	8fr blk & multi	.25	.25
690	A100	10fr blk & multi	.25	.25
691	A100	26fr blk & multi	1.00	.75
692	A100	100fr blk & multi	3.00	2.25
		Nos. 685-692 (8)	5.50	4.50

Nature protection.
For overprints see Nos. 801-808.

Nos. 343-348 Overprinted

1975, Nov. 10 Litho. *Perf. 13*

693	A60	20c multi	.25	.25
694	A60	30c multi	.25	.25
695	A60	50c multi	.25	.25
696	A60	1fr multi	.25	.25
697	A60	3fr multi	.25	.25
698	A60	5fr multi	.25	.25
		Nos. 693-698,B2-B3 (8)	6.75	6.00

African solidarity in drought emergency.

Fork-lift Truck on Airfield A101

Designs: 30c, Coffee packing plant. 50c, Engineering plant. 10fr, Farmer with hoe, vert. 35fr, Coffee pickers, vert. 54fr, Mechanized harvester.

Wmk. JEZ Multiple (368)

1975, Dec. 1 Photo. *Perf. 14x13½*

699	A101	20c gold & multi	.25	.25
700	A101	30c gold & multi	.25	.25
701	A101	50c gold & multi	.25	.25
702	A101	10fr gold & multi	.25	.25
703	A101	35fr gold & multi	.65	.45
704	A101	54fr gold & multi	1.30	.85
		Nos. 699-704 (6)	2.95	2.30

Basket Carrier and Themabelga Emblem — A102

Themabelga Emblem and: 30c, Warrior with shield and spear. 50c, Woman with beads. 1fr, Indian woman. 5fr, Male dancer with painted body. 7fr, Woman carrying child on back. 35fr, Male dancer with spear. 51fr, Female dancers.

1975, Dec. 8 Unwmk. *Perf. 13½*

705	A102	20c blk & multi	.25	.25
706	A102	30c blk & multi	.25	.25
707	A102	50c blk & multi	.25	.25
708	A102	1fr blk & multi	.25	.25
709	A102	5fr blk & multi	.25	.25
710	A102	7fr blk & multi	.35	.25
711	A102	35fr blk & multi	.90	.45
712	A102	51fr blk & multi	1.75	1.10
		Nos. 705-712 (8)	4.25	3.05

THEMABELGA Intl. Topical Philatelic Exhibition, Brussels, Dec. 13-21.

Christmas Type of 1968

Adoration of the Kings, by Peter Paul Rubens.

1975, Dec. 22 Engr. *Perf. 11½*

713	A48	100fr brt rose lil	10.00	10.00

Dr. Schweitzer, Keyboard, Score — A103

Albert Schweitzer and: 30c, 5fr, Lambaréné Hospital. 50c, 10fr, Organ pipes from Strassbourg organ, and score. 1fr, 80fr, Dr. Schweitzer's house, Lambaréné. 3fr, like 20c.

1976, Jan. 30 Photo. *Perf. 13½*

714	A103	20c maroon & pur	.25	.25
715	A103	30c grn & pur	.25	.25
716	A103	50c brn org & pur	.25	.25
717	A103	1fr red lil & pur	.25	.25
718	A103	3fr vio bl & pur	.25	.25
719	A103	5fr brn & pur	.25	.25
720	A103	10fr bl & pur	.30	.25
721	A103	80fr ver & pur	2.10	1.25
		Nos. 714-721 (8)	3.90	3.00

World Leprosy Day.
For overprints see Nos. 788-795.

Surrender at Yorktown A104

American Bicentennial (Paintings): 30c, Instruction at Valley Forge. 50c, Presentation of Captured Colors at Yorktown. 1fr, Washington at Fort Lee. 18fr, Washington Boarding British Warship. 26fr, Washington Studying Battle Plans at Night. 34fr, Washington Firing Cannon. 40fr, Washington Crossing the Delaware. 100fr, Sailing Ship "Bonhomme Richard," vert.

1976, Mar. 22 Photo. *Perf. 13x13½*

722	A104	20c gold & multi	.25	.25
723	A104	30c gold & multi	.25	.25
724	A104	50c gold & multi	.25	.25
725	A104	1fr gold & multi	.25	.25
726	A104	18fr gold & multi	.55	.25
727	A104	26fr gold & multi	.60	.30
728	A104	34fr gold & multi	.90	.55
729	A104	40fr gold & multi	1.25	1.00
		Nos. 722-729 (8)	4.30	3.10

Souvenir Sheet

Perf. 13½

730	A104	100fr gold & multi	5.00	5.00

See Nos. 754-761.

Sister Yohana, First Nun — A105

30c, Abdon Sabakati, one of first converts. 50c, Father Alphonse Brard, first Superior of Save Mission. 4fr, Abbot Balthazar Gafuku, one of first priests. 10fr, Msgr. Bigirumwami, first bishop. 25fr, Save Church, horiz. 60fr, Kabgayi Cathedral, horiz.

Perf. 13x13½, 13½x13

1976, Apr. 26 Photo.

731	A105	20c multi	.25	.25
732	A105	30c multi	.25	.25
733	A105	50c multi	.25	.25
734	A105	4fr multi	.25	.25
735	A105	10fr multi	.25	.25
736	A105	25fr multi	.50	.30
737	A105	60fr multi	1.25	.45
		Nos. 731-737 (7)	3.00	2.00

50th anniv. of the Roman Catholic Church of Rwanda.

Yachting — A106

Montreal Games Emblem and: 30c, Steeplechase. 50c, Long jump. 1fr, Hockey. 10fr, Swimming. 18fr, Soccer. 29fr, Boxing. 51fr, Vaulting.

1976, May 24 Photo. *Perf. 13x13½*

738	A106	20c gray & dk car	.25	.25
739	A106	30c gray & Prus bl	.25	.25
740	A106	50c gray & blk	.25	.25
741	A106	1fr gray & pur	.25	.25
742	A106	10fr gray & ultra	.30	.25
743	A106	18fr gray & dk brn	.40	.25
744	A106	29fr gray & blk	.70	.35
745	A106	51fr gray & slate grn	1.10	.75
		Nos. 738-745 (8)	3.50	2.60

21st Olympic Games, Montreal, Canada, July 17-Aug. 1.

First Message, Manual Switchboard — A107

Designs: 30c, Telephone, 1876 and interested crowd. 50c, Telephone c. 1900, and woman making a call. 1fr, Business telephone exchange, c. 1905. 4fr, "Candlestick" phone, globe and A. G. Bell. 8fr, Dial phone and Rwandan man making call. 26fr, Telephone, 1976, satellite and radar. 60fr, Push-button telephone, Rwandan international switchboard operator.

1976, June 21 Photo. *Perf. 14*

746	A107	20c dl red & indigo	.25	.25
747	A107	30c grnsh bl & indigo	.25	.25
748	A107	50c brn & indigo	.25	.25
749	A107	1fr org & indigo	.25	.25
750	A107	4fr lilac & indigo	.25	.25
751	A107	8fr grn & indigo	.30	.25
752	A107	26fr dl red & indigo	.75	.35
753	A107	60fr vio & indigo	1.60	.85
		Nos. 746-753 (8)	3.90	2.70

Centenary of first telephone call by Alexander Graham Bell, Mar. 10, 1876.

Type of 1976 Overprinted in Silver with Bicentennial Emblem and "Independence Day"

Designs as before.

1976, July 4 *Perf. 13x13½*

754	A104	20c silver & multi	.25	.25
755	A104	30c silver & multi	.25	.25
756	A104	50c silver & multi	.25	.25
757	A104	1fr silver & multi	.25	.25
758	A104	18fr silver & multi	.60	.30
759	A104	26fr silver & multi	.80	.35
760	A104	34fr silver & multi	.90	.55
761	A104	40fr silver & multi	1.10	.80
		Nos. 754-761 (8)	4.40	3.00

Independence Day.

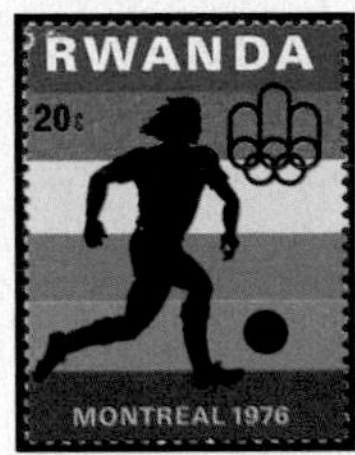

Soccer, Montreal Olympic Emblem — A108

30c, Shooting. 50c, Woman canoeing. 1fr, Gymnast. 10fr, Weight lifting. 12fr, Diving. 26fr, Equestrian. 50fr, Shot put.

1976, Aug. 1 Photo. *Perf. 13½x13*

762	A108	20c multi	.25	.25
763	A108	30c multi	.25	.25
764	A108	50c multi	.25	.25
765	A108	1fr multi	.25	.25
766	A108	10fr multi	.25	.25
767	A108	12fr multi	.25	.25
768	A108	26fr multi	.75	.50
769	A108	50fr multi	1.75	1.00
		Nos. 762-769 (8)	4.00	3.00

Souvenir Sheet

Various phases of hurdles race, horiz.

770		Sheet of 4	5.50	5.50
a.	A108	20fr Start	.55	.55
b.	A108	30fr Sprint	.90	.90
c.	A108	40fr Hurdle	1.10	1.10
d.	A108	60fr Finish	1.75	1.75

21st Olympic Games, Montreal, Canada, July 17-Aug. 1.

Apollo and Soyuz Take-offs, Project Emblem A109

Designs: 30c, Soyuz in space. 50c, Apollo in space. 1fr, Apollo. 2fr, Spacecraft before docking. 12fr, Spacecraft after docking. 30fr, Astronauts visiting in docked spacecraft. 54fr, Apollo splashdown.

1976, Oct. 29 Photo. *Perf. 13½x14*

771	A109	20c multi	.25	.25
772	A109	30c multi	.25	.25
773	A109	50c multi	.25	.25
774	A109	1fr multi	.25	.25
775	A109	2fr multi	.25	.25
776	A109	12fr multi	.75	.35
777	A109	30fr multi	2.50	1.00
778	A109	54fr multi	3.50	1.75
		Nos. 771-778 (8)	8.00	4.35

Apollo Soyuz space test program (Russo-American cooperation), July 1975.
For overprints see Nos. 836-843.

Eulophia Cucullata — A110

Orchids: 30c, Eulophia streptopetala. 50c, Disa Stairsii. 1fr, Aerangis kotschyana. 10fr, Eulophia abyssinica. 12fr, Bonatea steudneri. 26fr, Ansellia gigantea. 50fr, Eulophia angolensis.

1976, Nov. 22 Photo. *Perf. 14x13½*

779	A110	20c multi	.25	.25
780	A110	30c multi	.25	.25
781	A110	50c multi	.25	.25
782	A110	1fr multi	.25	.25
783	A110	10fr multi	.45	.25
784	A110	12fr multi	.70	.30

785 A110 26fr multi 1.75 .60
786 A110 50fr multi 3.50 1.10
Nos. 779-786 (8) 7.40 3.25

Christmas Type of 1968

Souvenir Sheet

Design: Nativity, by Francois Boucher.

1976, Dec. 20 Engr. *Perf. 11½*
787 A48 100fr brt ultra 8.00 8.00

Nos. 714-721 Overprinted: "JOURNEE / MONDIALE / 1977"

1977, Jan. 29 Photo. *Perf. 13½*
788 A103 20c mar & pur .25 .25
789 A103 30c grn & pur .25 .25
790 A103 50c brn org & pur .25 .25
791 A103 1fr red lil & pur .25 .25
792 A103 3fr vio bl & pur .25 .25
793 A103 5fr brn & pur .25 .25
794 A103 10fr bl & pur .35 .25
795 A103 80fr ver & pur 2.50 1.00
Nos. 788-795 (8) 4.35 2.75

World Leprosy Day.

Hands and Symbols of Learning — A111

Designs: 26fr, Hands and symbols of science. 64fr, Hands and symbols of industry.

1977, Feb. 7 Litho. *Perf. 12½*
796 A111 10fr multi .25 .25
797 A111 26fr multi .70 .45
798 A111 64fr multi 1.40 .85
Nos. 796-798 (3) 2.35 1.55

10th Summit Conference of the African and Malagasy Union, Kigali, 1976.

Souvenir Sheets

Descent from the Cross, by Rubens — A112

Easter: 25fr, Crucifixion, by Rubens.

1977, Apr. 27 Photo. *Perf. 13*
799 A112 25fr multi 9.00 9.00
800 A112 75fr multi 11.00 11.00

Size of stamp: 40x40mm.

Nos. 685-692 Overprinted

1977, May 2
801 A100 20c blk & multi .25 .25
802 A100 30c blk & multi .25 .25
803 A100 50c blk & multi .25 .25
804 A100 5fr blk & multi .25 .25
805 A100 8fr blk & multi .40 .30
806 A100 10fr blk & multi .50 .40
807 A100 26fr blk & multi 1.75 1.00
808 A100 100fr blk & multi 6.50 3.50
Nos. 801-808 (8) 10.15 6.20

World Water Conference.

Roman Fire Tower, African Tom-tom A113

ITU Emblem and: 30c, Chappe's optical telegraph and postilion. 50c, Morse telegraph and code. 1fr, Tug Goliath laying cable in English Channel. 4fr, Telephone, radio, television. 18fr, Kingsport (US space exploration ship) and Marots communications satellite. 26fr, Satellite tracking station and O.T.S. satellite. 50fr, Mariner II, Venus probe.

1977, May 23 Litho. *Perf. 12½*
809 A113 20c multi .25 .25
810 A113 30c multi .25 .25
811 A113 50c multi .25 .25
812 A113 1fr multi .25 .25
813 A113 4fr multi .25 .25
814 A113 18fr multi .50 .25
815 A113 26fr multi .75 .50
816 A113 50fr multi 1.50 1.00
Nos. 809-816 (8) 4.00 3.00

World Telecommunications Day.

Souvenir Sheets

Amsterdam Harbor, by Willem van de Velde, the Younger — A114

40fr, The Night Watch, by Rembrandt.

1977, May 26 Photo. *Perf. 13½*
817 A114 40fr multi 7.00 7.00
818 A114 60fr multi 7.00 7.00

AMPHILEX '77 Intl. Philatelic Exhibition, Amsterdam, May 27-June 5. Size of stamp: 38x49mm.

Road to Calvary, by Rubens — A115

Paintings by Peter Paul Rubens (1577-1640): 30c, Judgment of Paris, horiz. 50c, Marie de Medicis. 1fr, Heads of Black Men, horiz. 4fr, 26fr, Details from St. Ildefonso triptych. 8fr, Helene Fourment and her Children, horiz. 60fr, Helene Fourment.

1977, June 13 *Perf. 14*
819 A115 20c gold & multi .25 .25
820 A115 30c gold & multi .25 .25
821 A115 50c gold & multi .35 .25
822 A115 1fr gold & multi .40 .25
823 A115 4fr gold & multi .45 .25
824 A115 8fr gold & multi .50 .30
825 A115 26fr gold & multi 1.10 .75
826 A115 60fr gold & multi 1.75 1.50
Nos. 819-826 (8) 5.05 3.80

Souvenir Sheet

Viking on Mars — A116

1977, June 27 Photo. *Perf. 13*
827 A116 100fr multi 60.00 60.00

US Viking landing on Mars, first anniv.

Crested Eagle — A117

Birds of Prey: 30c, Snake eagle. 50c, Fish eagle. 1fr, Monk vulture. 3fr, Red-tailed buzzard. 5fr, Yellow-beaked kite. 20fr, Swallow-tailed kite. 100fr, Bateleur.

1977, Sept. 12 Litho. *Perf. 14*
828 A117 20c multi .25 .25
829 A117 30c multi .25 .25
830 A117 50c multi .25 .25
831 A117 1fr multi .25 .25
832 A117 3fr multi .25 .25
833 A117 5fr multi .30 .25
834 A117 20fr multi 2.25 .90
835 A117 100fr multi 6.75 3.25
Nos. 828-835 (8) 10.55 5.65

Nos. 771-778 Overprinted: "in memoriam / WERNHER VON BRAUN / 1912-1977"

1977, Sept. 19 Photo. *Perf. 13½x14*
836 A109 20c multi .25 .25
837 A109 30c multi .25 .25
838 A109 50c multi .25 .25
839 A109 1fr multi .25 .25
840 A109 2fr multi .25 .25
841 A109 12fr multi .30 .25
842 A109 30fr multi 2.25 1.40
843 A109 54fr multi 4.25 2.25
Nos. 836-843 (8) 8.05 5.15

Wernher von Braun (1912-1977), space and rocket expert.

Nos. 628-631 Gold Embossed "ESPAMER '77" and ESPAMER Emblem

Souvenir Sheets

1977, Oct. 3 Photo. *Perf. 13*
844 A94 20fr multi 6.25 6.25
845 A94 30fr multi 6.25 6.25
846 A94 50fr multi 6.25 6.25
847 A94 100fr multi 6.25 6.25
Nos. 844-847 (4) 25.00 25.00

ESPAMER '77, International Philatelic Exhibition, Barcelona, Oct. 7-13.

Christmas Type of 1968

Souvenir Sheet

100fr, Nativity, by Peter Paul Rubens.

1977, Dec. 12 Engr. *Perf. 13½*
848 A48 100fr violet blue 5.75 5.75

Marginal inscription typographed in red.

Boy Scout Playing Flute — A118

Designs: 30c, Campfire. 50c, Bridge building. 1fr, Scouts with unit flag. 10fr, Map reading. 18fr, Boating. 26fr, Cooking. 44fr, Lord Baden-Powell.

1978, Feb. 20 Litho. *Perf. 12½*
849 A118 20c yel grn & multi .25 .25
850 A118 30c blue & multi .25 .25
851 A118 50c lilac & multi .25 .25
852 A118 1fr blue & multi .25 .25
853 A118 10fr pink & multi .40 .25
854 A118 18fr lt grn & multi .90 .35
855 A118 26fr orange & multi 1.50 .60
856 A118 44fr salmon & multi 2.25 1.25
Nos. 849-856 (8) 6.05 3.45

10th anniversary of Rwanda Boy Scouts.

Chimpanzees A119

Designs: 30c, Gorilla. 50c, Colobus monkey. 3fr, Galago. 10fr, Cercopithecus monkey (mone). 26fr, Potto. 60fr, Cercopithecus monkey (griuet). 150fr, Baboon.

1978, Mar. 20 Photo. *Perf. 13½x13*
857 A119 20c multi .25 .25
858 A119 30c multi .25 .25
859 A119 50c multi .25 .25
860 A119 3fr multi .25 .25
861 A119 10fr multi .65 .50
862 A119 26fr multi 1.50 1.25
863 A119 60fr multi 4.00 3.00
864 A119 150fr multi 8.00 8.00
Nos. 857-864 (8) 15.15 13.75

Euporus Strangulatus — A120

Coleoptera: 30c, Rhina afzelii, vert. 50c, Pentalobus palini. 3fr, Corynodes dejeani, vert. 10fr, Mecynorhina torquata. 15fr, Mecocerus rhombeus, vert. 20fr, Macrotoma serripes. 25fr, Neptunides stanleyi, vert. 26fr, Petrognatha gigas. 100fr, Eudicella gralli, vert.

1978, May 22 Litho. *Perf. 14*
865 A120 20c multi .25 .25
866 A120 30c multi .25 .25
867 A120 50c multi .25 .25
868 A120 3fr multi .30 .25
869 A120 10fr multi .40 .25
870 A120 15fr multi .60 .30
871 A120 20fr multi .85 .35
872 A120 25fr multi 1.10 .50
873 A120 26fr multi 1.40 .55
874 A120 100fr multi 4.00 2.25
Nos. 865-874 (10) 9.40 5.20

Crossing "River of Poverty" A121

Emblem and: 10fr, 60fr, Men poling boat, facing right. 26fr, like 4fr.

1978, May 29 *Perf. 12½*
875 A121 4fr multi .25 .25
876 A121 10fr multi .25 .25
877 A121 26fr multi .60 .35
878 A121 60fr multi 1.25 .80
Nos. 875-878 (4) 2.35 1.65

Natl. Revolutionary Development Movement (M.R.N.D.).

Soccer, Rimet Cup, Flags of Netherlands and Peru — A122

11th World cup, Argentina, June 1-25, (Various Soccer Scenes and Flags of): 30c, Sweden & Spain. 50c, Scotland & Iran. 2fr, Germany & Tunisia. 3fr, Italy & Hungary. 10fr, Brazil and Austria. 34fr, Poland & Mexico. 100fr, Argentina & France.

1978, June 19 *Perf. 13*

879	A122	20c multi	.25	.25
879A	A122	30c multi	.25	.25
879B	A122	50c multi	.25	.25
880	A122	2fr multi	.25	.25
881	A122	3fr multi	.25	.25
882	A122	10fr multi	.35	.25
883	A122	34fr multi	1.25	.70
884	A122	100fr multi	2.75	2.00
		Nos. 879-884 (8)	5.60	4.20

Wright Brothers, Flyer I — A123

History of Aviation: 30c, Santos Dumont and Canard 14, 1906. 50c, Henry Farman and Voisin No. 1, 1908. 1fr, Jan Olieslaegers and Bleriot, 1910. 3fr, Marshal Balbo and Savoia S-17, 1919. 10fr, Charles Lindbergh and Spirit of St. Louis, 1927. 55fr, Hugo Junkers and Junkers JU52/3, 1932. 60fr, Igor Sikorsky and Sikorsky VS 300, 1939. 130fr, Concorde over New York.

1978, Oct. 30 **Litho.** *Perf. 13½x14*

885	A123	20c multi	.25	.25
886	A123	30c multi	.25	.25
887	A123	50c multi	.25	.25
888	A123	1fr multi	.25	.25
889	A123	3fr multi	.25	.25
890	A123	10fr multi	.35	.25
891	A123	55fr multi	1.40	.75
892	A123	60fr multi	1.75	.85
		Nos. 885-892 (8)	4.75	3.10

Souvenir Sheet

Perf. 13x13½

893	A123	130fr multi	6.50	6.50

No. 893 contains one stamp 47x35mm.

Christmas Type of 1968

Souvenir Sheet

Design: 200fr, Adoration of the Kings, by Albrecht Dürer, vert.

1978, Dec. 11 **Engr.** *Perf. 11½*

894	A48	200fr brown	8.00	8.00

Nos. 532-533, Overprinted "1963 1978" in Black or Blue

1978, Dec. 18 **Photo.** *Perf. 13½*

895	A83	6fr multi (Bk)	.25	.25
896	A83	94fr multi (Bl)	2.50	2.00

Org. for African Unity, 15th anniv.

Goats A124

20c, Ducks, vert. 50c, Cock and chickens, vert. 4fr, Rabbits. 5fr, Pigs, vert. 15fr, Turkey. 50fr, Sheep and cattle, vert. 75fr, Bull.

1978, Dec. 28 **Litho.** *Perf. 14*

897	A124	20c multi	.25	.25
898	A124	30c multi	.25	.25
899	A124	50c multi	.25	.25
900	A124	4fr multi	.30	.25
901	A124	5fr multi	.30	.25
902	A124	15fr multi	.70	.35
903	A124	50fr multi	2.25	.95
904	A124	75fr multi	4.00	1.60
		Nos. 897-904 (8)	8.30	4.15

Husbandry Year.

Papilio Demodocus A125

Butterflies: 30c, Precis octavia. 50c, Charaxes smaragdalis. 4fr, Charaxes guderiana. 15fr, Colotis evippe. 30fr, Danaus limniace. 50fr, Byblia acheloia. 150fr, Utetheisa pulchella.

1979, Feb. 19 **Photo.** *Perf. 14½*

905	A125	20c multi	.25	.25
906	A125	30c multi	.30	.25
907	A125	50c multi	.35	.25
908	A125	4fr multi	.50	.25
909	A125	15fr multi	.90	.30
910	A125	30fr multi	2.25	.45
911	A125	50fr multi	3.00	.90
912	A125	150fr multi	7.50	2.50
		Nos. 905-912 (8)	15.05	5.15

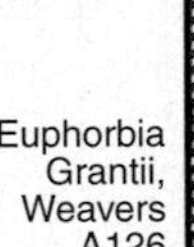

Euphorbia Grantii, Weavers A126

Design: 60fr, Drummers and Intelsat IV-A.

1979, June 8 **Photo.** *Perf. 13*

913	A126	40fr multi	1.25	1.00
914	A126	60fr multi	2.50	1.50

Philexafrique II, Libreville, Gabon, June 8-17.

Entandrophragma Excelsum — A127

Trees and Shrubs: 20c, Polyscias fulva. 50c, Ilex mitis. 4fr, Kigelia Africana. 15fr, Ficus thonningi. 20fr, Acacia Senegal. 50fr, Symphonia globulifera. 110fr, Acacia sieberana. 20c, 50c, 15fr, 50fr, vertical.

1979, Aug. 27 *Perf. 14*

915	A127	20c multi	.25	.25
916	A127	30c multi	.25	.25
917	A127	50c multi	.25	.25
918	A127	4 fr multi	.30	.25
919	A127	15fr multi	.45	.25
920	A127	20fr multi	.65	.40
921	A127	50fr multi	1.50	.80
922	A127	110fr multi	3.25	2.25
		Nos. 915-922 (8)	6.90	4.70

Black and White Boys, IYC Emblem A128

26fr, 100fr, Children of various races, diff., vert.

Perf. 13½x13, 13x13½

1979, Nov. 19 **Photo.**

923	A128	Block of 8	10.00	10.00
a.		26fr, any single	.90	.45
924	A128	42fr multi	1.50	.90

Souvenir Sheet

925	A128	100fr multi	6.00	6.00

Intl. Year of the Child. No. 923 printed in sheets of 16 (4x4).

Basket Weaving A129

Perf. 12½x13, 13x12½

1979, Dec. 3 **Litho.**

926	A129	50c shown	.25	.25
927	A129	1.50fr Wood carving, vert.	.25	.25
928	A129	2fr Metal working	.25	.25
929	A129	10fr Jewelry, vert.	.25	.25
930	A129	20fr Straw plaiting	.30	.25
931	A129	26fr Wall painting, vert.	.65	.45
932	A129	40fr Pottery	1.50	1.00
933	A129	100fr Smelting, vert.	3.25	1.50
		Nos. 926-933 (8)	6.70	4.20

Souvenir Sheet

Children of Different Races, Christmas Tree — A130

1979, Dec. 24 **Engr.** *Perf. 12*

934	A130	200fr ultra & dp mag	10.00	10.00

Christmas; Intl. Year of the Child.

German East Africa #N5, Hill A131

Sir Rowland Hill (1795-1879), originator of penny postage, and Stamps of Ruanda-Urundi or: 30c, German East Africa #N23. 50c, German East Africa #NB9. 3fr, #25. 10fr, #42. 26fr, #123. 100fr, #B28.

1979, Dec. 31 **Litho.** *Perf. 14*

935	A131	20c multi	.25	.25
936	A131	30c multi	.25	.25
937	A131	50c multi	.25	.25
938	A131	3fr multi	.25	.25
939	A131	10fr multi	.25	.25
940	A131	26fr multi	.65	.35
941	A131	60fr multi	1.75	.80
942	A131	100fr multi	3.00	1.25
		Nos. 935-942 (8)	6.65	3.65

Sarothrura Pulchra A132

Birds of the Nyungwe Forest: 20c Ploceus alienus, vert. 30c, Regal sunbird, vert. 3fr, Tockus alboterminatus. 10fr, Pygmy owl, vert. 26fr, Emerald cuckoo. 60fr, Finch, vert. 100fr, Stepanoaetus coronatus, vert.

Perf. 13½x13, 13x13½

1980, Jan. 7 **Photo.**

943	A132	20c multi	.25	.25
944	A132	30c multi	.25	.25
945	A132	50c multi	.25	.25
946	A132	3fr multi	.25	.25
947	A132	10fr multi	.60	.30
948	A132	26fr multi	1.50	.70
949	A132	60fr multi	3.75	1.50
950	A132	100fr multi	5.50	3.00
		Nos. 943-950 (8)	12.35	6.50

First Footstep on Moon, Spacecraft A133

Spacecraft and Moon Exploration: 1.50fr, Descent onto lunar surface. 8fr, American flag. 30fr, Solar panels. 50fr, Gathering soil samples. 60fr, Adjusting sun screen. 200fr, Landing craft.

1980, Jan. 31 **Photo.** *Perf. 13x13½*

951	A133	50c multi	.25	.25
952	A133	1.50fr multi	.25	.25
953	A133	8fr multi	.25	.25
954	A133	30fr multi	1.00	.50
955	A133	50fr multi	1.75	.90
956	A133	60fr multi	2.25	1.00
		Nos. 951-956 (6)	5.75	3.15

Souvenir Sheet

957	A133	200fr multi	8.00	8.00

Apollo 11 moon landing, 10th anniv. (1979).

Globe, Butare and 1905 Chicago Club Emblems A134

Rotary Intl., 75th Anniv. (Globe, Emblems of Butare or Kigali Clubs and): 30c, San Francisco, 1908. 50c, Chicago, 1910. 4fr, Buffalo, 1911. 15fr, London, 1911. 20fr, Glasgow, 1912. 50fr, Bristol, 1917. 60fr, Rotary Intl., 1980.

1980, Feb. 23 **Litho.** *Perf. 13*

958	A134	20c multi	.25	.25
959	A134	30c multi	.25	.25
960	A134	50c multi	.25	.25
961	A134	4fr multi	.25	.25
962	A134	15fr multi	.35	.25
963	A134	20fr multi	.50	.25
964	A134	50fr multi	.90	.40
965	A134	60fr multi	1.50	.65
		Nos. 958-965 (8)	4.25	2.55

Gymnast, Moscow '80 Emblem A135

1980, Mar. 10 *Perf. 12½*

966	A135	20c shown	.25	.25
967	A135	30c Basketball	.25	.25
968	A135	50c Bicycling	.25	.25
969	A135	3fr Boxing	.25	.25
970	A135	20fr Archery	.55	.25
971	A135	26fr Weight lifting	.75	.30
972	A135	50fr Javelin	1.50	.65
973	A135	100fr Fencing	2.75	1.25
		Nos. 966-973 (8)	6.55	3.45

22nd Summer Olympic Games, Moscow, July 19-Aug. 3.

Souvenir Sheet

Amalfi Coast, by Giacinto Gigante — A136

1980, Apr. 28 Photo. *Perf. 13½*

974 A136 200fr multi 7.50 7.50

20th Intl. Philatelic Exhibition, Europa '80, Naples, Apr. 26-May 4.

Geaster Mushroom A137

30c, Lentinus atrobrunneus. 50c, Gomphus stereoides. 4fr, Cantharellus cibarius. 10fr, Stilbothamnium dybowskii. 15fr, Xeromphalina tenuipes. 70fr, Podoscypha elegans. 100fr, Mycena.

1980, July 21 Photo. *Perf. 13½*

975 A137 20c shown .30 .25
976 A137 30c multicolored .45 .25
977 A137 50c multicolored .55 .25
978 A137 4fr multicolored .90 .25
979 A137 10fr multicolored 1.50 .30
980 A137 15fr multicolored 3.25 .75
981 A137 70fr multicolored 9.00 2.00
982 A137 100fr multicolored 15.00 4.00
Nos. 975-982 (8) 30.95 8.05

Still Life, by Renoir — A138

Impressionist Painters: 30c, 26fr, At the Theater, by Toulouse-Lautrec, vert. 50c, 10fr, Seaside Garden, by Monet. 4fr, Mother and Child, by Mary Cassatt, vert. 5fr, Starry Night, by Van Gogh. 10fr, Dancers at their Toilet, by Degas, vert. 50fr, The Card Players, by Cezanne. 70fr, Tahitian Women, by Gauguin, vert. 75fr, like 20c. 100fr, In the Park, by Seurat.

1980, Aug. 4 Litho. *Perf. 14*

983 A138 20c multi .25 .25
984 A138 30c multi .25 .25
985 A138 50c multi .25 .25
986 A138 4fr multi .25 .25
a. Sheet of 2, 4fr, 26fr 3.00 3.00
987 A138 5fr multi .30 .25
a. Sheet of 2, 5fr, 75fr 3.00 3.00
988 A138 10fr multi .40 .25
a. Sheet of 2, 10fr, 70fr 3.00 3.00
989 A138 50fr multi 1.50 .55
a. Sheet of 2, 50fr, 10fr 3.00 3.00
990 A138 70fr multi 2.25 .85
991 A138 100fr multi 3.50 1.25
Nos. 983-991 (9) 8.95 4.15

Souvenir Sheet

Virgin of the Harpies, by Andrea Del Sarto — A139

Photogravure and Engraved

1980, Dec. 22 *Perf. 11½*

992 A139 200fr multi 8.00 8.00

Christmas.

Belgian War of Independence, Engraving — A140

Belgian Independence Sesquicentennial: Engravings of War of Independence.

1980, Dec. 29 Litho. *Perf. 12½*

993 A140 20c pale grn & brn .25 .25
994 A140 30c brn org & brn .25 .25
995 A140 50c lt bl & brn .25 .25
996 A140 9fr yel & brn .25 .25
997 A140 10fr brt lil & brn .25 .25
998 A140 20fr ap grn & brn .45 .25
999 A140 70fr pink & brn 1.90 .75
1000 A140 90fr lem & brn 2.75 1.00
Nos. 993-1000 (8) 6.35 3.25

Swamp Drainage A141

1980, Dec. 31 Photo. *Perf. 13½*

1001 A141 20c shown .25 .25
1002 A141 30c Fertilizer shed .25 .25
1003 A141 1.50fr Rice fields .25 .25
1004 A141 8fr Tree planting .30 .25
1005 A141 10fr Terrace planting .40 .25
1006 A141 40fr Farm buildings 1.25 .60
1007 A141 90fr Bean cultivation 2.50 1.10
1008 A141 100fr Tea cultivation 2.75 1.40
Nos. 1001-1008 (8) 7.95 4.35

Soil Conservation Year.

Pavetta Rwandensis — A142

30c, Cyrtorchis praetermissa. 50c, Pavonia urens. 4fr, Cynorkis kassnerana. 5fr, Gardenia ternifolia. 10fr, Leptactina platyphylla. 20fr, Lobelia petiolata. 40fr, Tapinanthus brunneus. 70fr, Impatiens niamniamensis. 150fr, Dissotis rwandensis.

1981, Apr. 6 Photo. *Perf. 13x13½*

1009 A142 20c shown .25 .25
1010 A142 30c multicolored .25 .25
1011 A142 50c multicolored .25 .25
1012 A142 4fr multicolored .25 .25
1013 A142 5fr multicolored .25 .25
1014 A142 10fr multicolored .35 .25
1015 A142 20fr multicolored .60 .30
1016 A142 40fr multicolored 1.50 .75
1017 A142 70fr multicolored 2.75 1.25
1018 A142 150fr multicolored 5.50 2.50
Nos. 1009-1018 (10) 11.95 6.30

Girl Knitting — A143

SOS Children's Village: Various children.

1981, Apr. 27 *Perf. 13*

1019 A143 20c multi .25 .25
1020 A143 30c multi .25 .25
1021 A143 50c multi .25 .25
1022 A143 1fr multi .25 .25
1023 A143 8fr multi .25 .25
1024 A143 10fr multi .30 .25
1025 A143 70fr multi 1.75 .75
1026 A143 150fr multi 4.25 1.50
Nos. 1019-1026 (8) 7.55 3.75

Carolers, by Norman Rockwell A144

Designs: Saturday Evening Post covers by Norman Rockwell.

1981, May 11 Litho. *Perf. 13½x14*

1027 A144 20c multi .25 .25
1028 A144 30c multi .25 .25
1029 A144 50c multi .25 .25
1030 A144 1fr multi .25 .25
1031 A144 8fr multi .40 .25
1032 A144 20fr multi .80 .25
1033 A144 50fr multi 2.00 .75
1034 A144 70fr multi 2.75 1.10
Nos. 1027-1034 (8) 6.95 3.35

Cerval A145

Meat-eating animals — 30c, Jackals. 2fr, Genet. 2.50fr, Banded mongoose. 10fr, Zorille. 15fr, White-cheeked otter. 70fr, Golden wild cat. 200fr, Hunting dog, vert.

1981, June 29 Photo. *Perf. 13½x14*

1035 A145 20c shown .25 .25
1036 A145 30c multicolored .25 .25
1037 A145 2fr multicolored .30 .25
1038 A145 2.50fr multicolored .35 .25
1039 A145 10fr multicolored .60 .30
1040 A145 15fr multicolored 1.25 .65
1041 A145 70fr multicolored 4.25 2.25
1042 A145 200fr multicolored 7.50 5.00
Nos. 1035-1042 (8) 14.75 9.20

Drummer Sending Message — A146

30c, Map, communication waves. 2fr, Jet, radar screen. 2.50fr, Satellite, teletape. 10fr, Dish antenna. 15fr, Ship, navigation devices. 70fr, Helicopter. 200fr, Satellite with solar panels.

1981, Sept. 1 Litho. *Perf. 13*

1043 A146 20c shown .25 .25
1044 A146 30c multicolored .25 .25
1045 A146 2fr multicolored .25 .25
1046 A146 2.50fr multicolored .25 .25
1047 A146 10fr multicolored .30 .25
1048 A146 15fr multicolored .40 .25
1049 A146 70fr multicolored 2.00 1.25
1050 A146 200fr multicolored 6.25 3.50
Nos. 1043-1050 (8) 9.95 6.25

1500th Birth Anniv. of St. Benedict A147

Paintings and Frescoes of St. Benedict: 20c, Leaving his Parents, Mt. Oliveto Monastery, Maggiore. 30c, Oldest portrait, 10th cent., St. Chrisogone Church, Rome, vert. 50c, Portrait, Virgin of the Misericord polyptich, Borgo San Sepolcro. 4fr, Giving the Rules of the order to his Monks, Mt. Oliveto Monastery. 5fr, Monks at their Meal, Mt. Oliveto Monastery. 20fr, Portrait, 13th cent., Lower Church of the Holy Spirit, Subiaco, vert. 70fr, Our Lady in Glory with Sts. Gregory and Benedict, San Gimigniao, vert. 100fr, Priest Carrying Easter Meal to St. Benedict, by Jan van Coninxloo, 16th cent.

Perf. 13½x13, 13x13½

1981, Nov. 30 Photo.

1051 A147 20c multi .25 .25
1052 A147 30c multi .25 .25
1053 A147 50c multi .30 .25
1054 A147 4fr multi .30 .25
1055 A147 5fr multi .40 .25
1056 A147 20fr multi 1.00 .50
1057 A147 70fr multi 2.25 1.25
1058 A147 100fr multi 3.25 2.50
Nos. 1051-1058 (8) 8.00 5.50

Intl. Year of the Disabled A148

1981, Dec. 7 Litho. *Perf. 13*

1059 A148 20c Painting .25 .25
1060 A148 30c Soccer .25 .25
1061 A148 4.50fr Crocheting .25 .25
1062 A148 5fr Painting vase .25 .25
1063 A148 10fr Sawing .30 .25
1064 A148 60fr Sign language 1.40 .60
1065 A148 70fr Doing puzzle 1.90 .70
1066 A148 100fr Juggling 2.75 1.25
Nos. 1059-1066 (8) 7.35 3.80

Souvenir Sheet

Christmas — A149

200fr, Adoration of the Kings, by van der Goes.

Photo. & Engr.

1981, Dec. 21 *Perf. 13½*

No.	Type	Description	Unused	Used
1067	A149	200fr multicolored	8.00	8.00

Natl. Rural Water Supply Year A150

20c, Deer drinking. 30c, Women carrying water, vert. 50c, Pipeline. 10fr, Filing pan, vert. 19fr, Drinking. 70fr, Mother, child, vert. 100fr, Lake pumping station, vert.

1981, Dec. 28 **Litho.** *Perf. 12½*

No.	Type	Description	Unused	Used
1068	A150	20c multicolored	.25	.25
1069	A150	30c multicolored	.25	.25
1070	A150	50c multicolored	.25	.25
1071	A150	10fr multicolored	.25	.25
1072	A150	19fr multicolored	.55	.30
1073	A150	70fr multicolored	1.75	.80
1074	A150	100fr multicolored	2.75	1.25
		Nos. 1068-1074 (7)	6.05	3.35

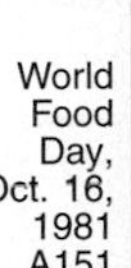

World Food Day, Oct. 16, 1981 A151

1982, Jan. 25 **Litho.** *Perf. 13*

No.	Type	Description	Unused	Used
1075	A151	20c Cattle	.25	.25
1076	A151	30c Bee	.25	.25
1077	A151	50c Fish	.25	.25
1078	A151	1fr Avocados	.25	.25
1079	A151	8fr Boy eating bananas	.25	.25
1080	A151	20fr Sorghum	.60	.30
1081	A151	70fr Vegetables	2.00	.85
1082	A151	100fr Balanced diet	3.25	1.25
		Nos. 1075-1082 (8)	7.10	3.65

Hibiscus Berberidifolius — A152

No. 1084, Hypericum lanceolatum, vert. No. 1085, Canarina eminii. No. 1086, Polygala ruwenxoriensis. No. 1087, Kniphofia grantii, vert. No. 1088, Euphorbia candelabrum, vert. No. 1089, Disa erubescens, vert. No. 1090, Gloriosa simplex.

1982, June 14 **Litho.** *Perf. 13*

No.	Type	Description	Unused	Used
1083	A152	20c multi	.25	.25
1084	A152	30c multi	.25	.25
1085	A152	50c multi	.25	.25
1086	A152	4fr multi	.30	.25
1087	A152	10fr multi	.45	.25
1088	A152	35fr multi	1.40	.50
1089	A152	70fr multi	2.50	.90
1090	A152	80fr multi	3.00	1.50
		Nos. 1083-1090 (8)	8.40	4.15

20th Anniv. of Independence — A153

1982, June 28

No.	Type	Description	Unused	Used
1091	A153	10fr Flags	.25	.25
1092	A153	20fr Hands releasing doves	.40	.25
1093	A153	30fr Flag, handshake	.70	.40
1094	A153	50fr Govt. buildings	1.50	.65
		Nos. 1091-1094 (4)	2.85	1.55

1982 World Cup — A154

Designs: Various soccer players.

1982, July 6 *Perf. 14x14½*

No.	Type	Description	Unused	Used
1095	A154	20c multi	.25	.25
1096	A154	30c multi	.25	.25
1097	A154	1.50fr multi	.25	.25
1098	A154	8fr multi	.25	.25
1099	A154	10fr multi	.25	.25
1100	A154	20fr multi	.65	.40
1101	A154	70fr multi	2.25	.80
1102	A154	90fr multi	3.00	1.25
		Nos. 1095-1102 (8)	7.15	3.70

TB Bacillus Centenary — A155

1982, Nov. 22 **Litho.** *Perf. 14½*

No.	Type	Description	Unused	Used
1103	A155	10fr Microscope, slide	.25	.25
1104	A155	20fr Serum, slide	.55	.25
1105	A155	70fr Lungs, slide	2.75	1.00
1106	A155	100fr Koch	3.25	1.75
		Nos. 1103-1106 (4)	6.80	3.25

Souvenir Sheets

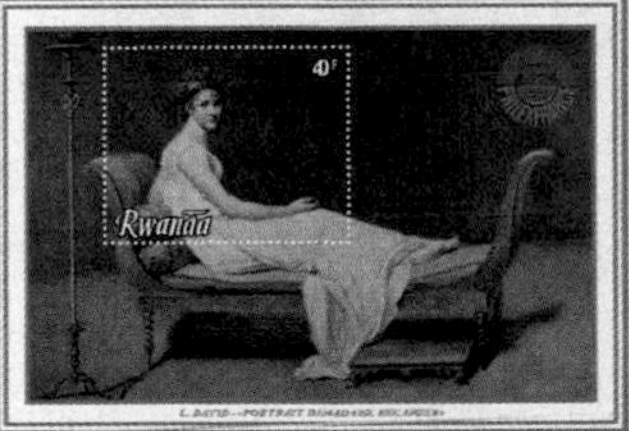

Madam Recamier, by David — A156

PHILEXFRANCE '82 Intl. Stamp Exhibition, Paris, June 11-21: No. 1108, St. Anne and Virgin and Child with Franciscan Monk, by H. van der Goes. No. 1109, Liberty Guiding the People, by Delacroix. No. 1110, Pygmalion, by P. Delvaux.

1982, Dec. 11 *Perf. 13½*

No.	Type	Description	Unused	Used
1107	A156	40fr multi	3.00	3.00
1108	A156	40fr multi	3.00	3.00
1109	A156	60fr multi	3.00	3.00
1110	A156	60fr multi	3.00	3.00
		Nos. 1107-1110 (4)	12.00	12.00

Souvenir Sheet

Rest During the Flight to Egypt, by Murillo — A157

1982, Dec. 20 **Photo. & Engr.**

No.	Type	Description	Unused	Used
1111	A157	200fr carmine rose	8.50	8.50

Christmas.

10th Anniv. of UN Conference on Human Environment — A158

1982, Dec. 27 **Litho.** *Perf. 14*

No.	Type	Description	Unused	Used
1112	A158	20c Elephants	.25	.25
1113	A158	30c Lion	.25	.25
1114	A158	50c Flower	.25	.25
1115	A158	4fr Bull	.25	.25
1116	A158	5fr Deer	.25	.25
1117	A158	10fr Flower, diff.	.30	.25
1118	A158	20fr Zebras	.60	.30
1119	A158	40fr Crowned cranes	1.25	.65
1120	A158	50fr Bird	1.75	.85
1121	A158	70fr Woman pouring coffee beans	2.60	1.10
		Nos. 1112-1121 (10)	7.75	4.40

Scouting Year A159

20c, Animal first aid. 30c, Camp. 1.50fr, Campfire. 8fr, Scout giving sign. 10fr, Knot. 20fr, Camp, diff. 70fr, Chopping wood. 90fr, Sign, map.

Perf. 13½x14½

1983, Jan. 17 **Photo.**

No.	Type	Description	Unused	Used
1122	A159	20c multicolored	.25	.25
1123	A159	30c multicolored	.25	.25
1124	A159	1.50fr multicolored	.25	.25
1125	A159	8fr multicolored	.50	.25
1126	A159	10fr multicolored	.60	.30
1127	A159	20fr multicolored	1.40	.65
1128	A159	70fr multicolored	4.75	2.00
1129	A159	90fr multicolored	7.00	2.25
		Nos. 1122-1129 (8)	15.00	6.20

For overprints see Nos. 1234-1241.

Nectar-sucking Birds — A160

20c, Angola nectar bird. 30c, Royal nectar birds. 50c, Johnston's nectar bird. 4fr, Bronze nectar birds. 5fr, Collared souimangas. 10fr, Blue-headed nectar bird. 20fr, Purple-bellied nectar bird. 40fr, Copper nectar birds. 50fr, Olive-bellied nectar birds. 70fr, Red-breasted nectar bird.

Perf. 14x14½, 14½x14

1983, Jan. 31 **Litho.**

No.	Type	Description	Unused	Used
1130	A160	20c multicolored	.25	.25
1131	A160	30c multicolored	.25	.25
1132	A160	50c multicolored	.25	.25
1133	A160	4fr multicolored	.30	.25
1134	A160	5fr multicolored	.40	.25
1135	A160	10fr multicolored	.85	.35
1136	A160	20fr multicolored	1.50	.50
1137	A160	40fr multicolored	2.75	.85
1138	A160	50fr multicolored	3.50	1.25
1139	A160	70fr multicolored	5.50	2.00
		Nos. 1130-1139 (10)	15.55	6.20

30c, 4fr, 10fr, 40fr, 70fr horiz. Inscribed 1982.

Soil Erosion Prevention A161

20c, Driving cattle. 30c, Pineapple field. 50c, Interrupted ditching. 9fr, Hedges, ditches. 10fr, Reafforestation. 20fr, Anti-erosion barriers. 30fr, Contour planting. 50fr, Terracing. 60fr, Protection of river banks. 70fr, Fallow, planted strips.

1983, Feb. 14 *Perf. 14½*

No.	Type	Description	Unused	Used
1140	A161	20c multicolored	.25	.25
1141	A161	30c multicolored	.25	.25
1142	A161	50c multicolored	.25	.25
1143	A161	9fr multicolored	.30	.25
1144	A161	10fr multicolored	.35	.30
1145	A161	20fr multicolored	.50	.35
1146	A161	30fr multicolored	.80	.60
1147	A161	50fr multicolored	1.75	1.00
1148	A161	60fr multicolored	2.00	1.10
1149	A161	70fr multicolored	3.00	1.25
		Nos. 1140-1149 (10)	9.45	5.60

For overprints & surcharges see Nos. 1247-1255.

Cardinal Cardijn (1882-1967) A162

Young Catholic Workers Movement Activities. Inscribed 1982.

1983, Feb. 22 *Perf. 12½x13*

No.	Type	Description	Unused	Used
1150	A162	20c Feeding ducks	.25	.25
1151	A162	30c Harvesting bananas	.25	.25
1152	A162	50c Carrying melons	.25	.25
1153	A162	10fr Teacher	.30	.25
1154	A162	19fr Shoemakers	.40	.25
1155	A162	20fr Growing millet	.50	.25
1156	A162	70fr Embroidering	2.00	.75
1157	A162	80fr shown	2.25	1.00
		Nos. 1150-1157 (8)	6.20	3.25

Gorilla — A163

Various gorillas. Nos. 1158-1163 horiz.

1983, Mar. 14 *Perf. 14*

No.	Type	Description	Unused	Used
1158	A163	20c multi	.25	.25
1159	A163	30c multi	.25	.25
1160	A163	9.50fr multi	.35	.25
1161	A163	10fr multi	.45	.35
1162	A163	20fr multi	1.25	.65
1163	A163	30fr multi	1.75	.85
1164	A163	60fr multi	3.00	1.50
1165	A163	70fr multi	3.25	2.00
		Nos. 1158-1165 (8)	10.55	6.10

Souvenir Sheet

The Granduca Madonna, by Raphael — A164

Typo. & Engr.

1983, Dec. 19 *Perf. 11½*

1166	A164	200fr multi	8.00	8.00

Christmas.

Local Trees — A165

No. 1167, Hagenia abyssinica. No. 1168, Dracaena steudneri. No. 1169, Phoenix reclinata. No. 1170, Podocarpus milanjianus. No. 1171, Entada abyssinica. No. 1172, Parinari excelsa. No. 1173, Newtonia buchananii. No. 1174, Acacia gerrardi, vert.

1984, Jan. 15 Litho. *Perf. 13½x13*

1167	A165	20c multicolored	.25	.25
1168	A165	30c multicolored	.25	.25
1169	A165	50c multicolored	.25	.25
1170	A165	10fr multicolored	.30	.25
1171	A165	19fr multicolored	.75	.30
1172	A165	70fr multicolored	2.25	.90
1173	A165	100fr multicolored	3.50	1.10
1174	A165	200fr multicolored	6.00	2.25
		Nos. 1167-1174 (8)	13.55	5.55

World Communications Year — A166

1984, May 21 Litho. *Perf. 12½*

1175	A166	20c Train	.25	.25
1176	A166	30c Ship	.25	.25
1177	A166	4.50fr Radio	.25	.25
1178	A166	10fr Telephone	.30	.25
1179	A166	15fr Mail	.40	.25
1180	A166	50fr Jet	1.50	.50
1181	A166	70fr Satellite, TV screen	2.00	.75
1182	A166	100fr Satellite	3.25	1.00
		Nos. 1175-1182 (8)	8.20	3.50

1st Manned Flight Bicent. — A167

Historic flights: 20c, Le Martial, Sept. 19, 1783. 30c, La Montgolfiere, Nov. 21, 1783. 50c, Charles and Robert, Dec. 1, 1783, and Blanchard, Mar. 2, 1784. 9fr, Jean-Pierre Blanchard and wife in balloon. 10fr, Blanchard and Jeffries, 1785. 50fr, E. Demuyter, 1937. 80fr, Propane gas balloons. 200fr, Abruzzo, Anderson and Newman, 1978.

1984, June 4 Litho. *Perf. 13*

1183	A167	20c multi	.25	.25
1184	A167	30c multi	.25	.25
1185	A167	50c multi	.25	.25
1186	A167	9fr multi	.30	.25
1187	A167	10fr multi	.35	.25
1188	A167	50fr multi	1.75	.75
1189	A167	80fr multi	2.50	1.00
1190	A167	200fr multi	7.50	3.50
		Nos. 1183-1190 (8)	13.15	6.50

1984 Summer Olympics — A168

1984, July 16 *Perf. 14*

1191	A168	20c Equestrian	.25	.25
1192	A168	30c Wind surfing	.25	.25
1193	A168	50c Soccer	.30	.25
1194	A168	9fr Swimming	.70	.35
1195	A168	10fr Field hockey	.80	.40
1196	A168	40fr Fencing	2.50	1.50
1197	A168	80fr Running	3.50	2.50
1198	A168	200fr Boxing	8.50	4.75
		Nos. 1191-1198 (8)	16.80	10.25

Zebras and Buffaloes — A169

20c, Zebra with colt. 30c, Buffalo with calf, vert. 50c, Two zebras, vert. 9fr, Zebras fighting. 10fr, Buffalo, vert. 80fr, Zebra herd. 100fr, Zebra, vert. 200fr, Buffalo.

1984, Nov. 26 Litho. *Perf. 13*

1199	A169	20c multicolored	.25	.25
1200	A169	30c multicolored	.25	.25
1201	A169	50c multicolored	.25	.25
1202	A169	9fr multicolored	.60	.25
1203	A169	10fr multicolored	.70	.30
1204	A169	80fr multicolored	3.00	1.50
1205	A169	100fr multicolored	4.00	2.25
1206	A169	200fr multicolored	8.50	4.00
		Nos. 1199-1206 (8)	17.55	9.05

Souvenir Sheet

Christmas 1984 — A170

Design: Virgin and Child, by Correggio.

1984, Dec. 24 **Typo. & Engr.**

1207	A170	200fr multicolored	8.00	8.00

Gorilla Gorilla Beringei — A171

10fr, Adults and young. 15fr, Adults. 25fr, Female holding young. 30fr, Three adults. 200fr, Baby climbing branch, vert.

1985, Mar. 25 Litho. *Perf. 13*

1208	A171	10fr multi	*3.00*	*1.50*
1209	A171	15fr multi	*5.00*	*2.50*
1210	A171	25fr multi	*10.00*	*4.50*
1211	A171	30fr multi	*12.00*	*5.00*
		Nos. 1208-1211 (4)	*30.00*	13.50

Souvenir Sheet

Perf. 11½x12

1212	A171	200fr multi	*15.00*	*15.00*

No. 1212 contains one 37x52mm stamp.

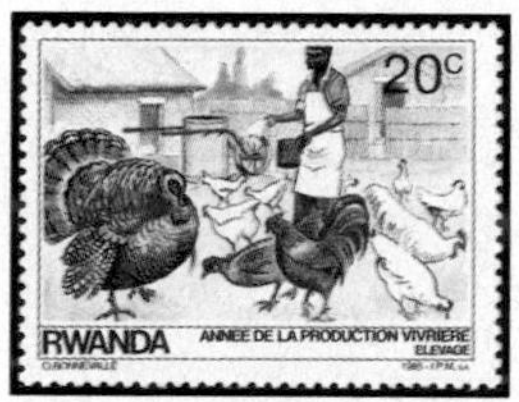

Self-Sufficiency in Food Production — A172

Designs: 20c, Raising chickens and turkeys. 30c, Pineapple harvest. 50c, Animal husbandry. 9fr, Grain products. 10fr, Education. 50fr, Sowing grain. 80fr, Food reserves. 100fr, Banana harvest.

1985, Mar. 30

1213	A172	20c multi	.25	.25
1214	A172	30c multi	.25	.25
1215	A172	50c multi	.25	.25
1216	A172	9fr multi	.25	.25
1217	A172	10fr multi	.30	.25
1218	A172	50fr multi	1.10	.55
1219	A172	80fr multi	1.75	.85
1220	A172	100fr multi	2.50	2.00
		Nos. 1213-1220 (8)	6.65	4.65

Natl. Redevelopment Movement, 10th Anniv. — A173

1985, July 5

1221	A173	10fr multi	.25	.25
1222	A173	30fr multi	1.00	.25
1223	A173	70fr multi	2.00	1.00
		Nos. 1221-1223 (3)	3.25	1.50

UN, 40th Anniv. A174

1985, July 25

1224	A174	50fr multi	1.75	1.50
1225	A174	100fr multi	3.50	2.50

Audubon Birth Bicent. — A175

Illustrations of North American bird species by John J. Audubon — 10fr, Barn owl. 20fr, White-faced owl. 40fr, Red-breasted hummingbird. 80fr, Warbler.

1985, Sept. 18

1226	A175	10fr multicolored	*2.50*	*1.00*
1227	A175	20fr multicolored	*3.00*	*2.00*
1228	A175	40fr multicolored	*6.00*	*4.00*
1229	A175	80fr multicolored	*10.00*	*7.00*
		Nos. 1226-1229 (4)	*21.50*	*14.00*

Intl. Youth Year A176

1985, Oct. 14

1230	A176	7fr Education and agriculture	.25	.25
1231	A176	9fr Bicycling	.25	.25
1232	A176	44fr Construction	1.25	.60
1233	A176	80fr Schoolroom	2.25	.90
		Nos. 1230-1233 (4)	4.00	2.00

Nos. 1122-1129 Ovptd. in Green or Rose Violet with the Girl Scout Trefoil and "1910/1985"

1985, Nov. 25 *Perf. 13½x14½*

1234	A159	20c multi	.25	.25
1235	A159	30c multi (RV)	.25	.25
1236	A159	1.50fr multi	*.50*	.25
1237	A159	8fr multi (RV)	*1.00*	.25
1238	A159	10fr multi	*1.50*	*.75*
1239	A159	20fr multi	*3.00*	*1.25*
1240	A159	70fr multi (RV)	*8.00*	*2.50*
1241	A159	90fr multi	*12.00*	*5.00*
		Nos. 1234-1241 (8)	*26.50*	*10.50*

Natl. Girl Scout Movement, 75th anniv.

Souvenir Sheet

Adoration of the Magi, by Titian — A177

Photo. & Engr.

1985, Dec. 24 *Perf. 11½*

1242	A177	200fr violet	8.50	8.50

Christmas.

Transportation and Communication — A178

1986, Jan. 27 Litho. *Perf. 13*

1243 A178 10fr Articulated truck .30 .25
1244 A178 30fr Hand-canceling letters 1.00 .50
1245 A178 40fr Kigali Satellite Station 1.50 .90

Size: 52x34mm

1246 A178 80fr Kayibanda Airport, Kigali 2.50 1.75
Nos. 1243-1246 (4) 5.30 3.40

Nos. 1141-1149 Surcharged or Ovptd. with Silver Bar and "ANNEE 1986 / INTENSIFICATION AGRICOLE"

1986, May 5 Litho. *Perf. 14½*

1247 A161 9fr #1143 *1.25* *.50*
1248 A161 10fr on 30c #1141 *1.25* *.50*
1249 A161 10fr on 50c #1142 *1.50* *.50*
1250 A161 10fr #1144 *1.50* *.50*
1251 A161 20fr #1145 *2.50* *1.00*
1252 A161 30fr #1146 *3.75* *1.50*
1253 A161 50fr #1147 *5.00* *2.25*
1254 A161 60fr #1148 *7.00* *3.50*
1255 A161 70fr #1149 *8.00* *4.50*
Nos. 1247-1255 (9) *31.75* *14.75*

1986 World Cup Soccer Championships, Mexico — A179

Various soccer plays, natl. flags.

1986, June 16 *Perf. 13*

1256 A179 2fr Morocco, England .50 .25
1257 A179 4fr Paraguay, Iraq .75 .25
1258 A179 5fr Brazil, Spain 1.00 .50
1259 A179 10fr Italy, Argentina 1.75 .75
1260 A179 40fr Mexico, Belgium 6.00 1.75
1261 A179 45fr France, USSR 8.00 2.50
Nos. 1256-1261 (6) 18.00 6.00

For overprints see Nos. 1360-1365.

Akagera Natl. Park — A180

1986, Dec. 15 Litho. *Perf. 13*

1262 A180 4fr Antelopes .75 .25
1263 A180 7fr Shoebills .75 .30
1264 A180 9fr Cape elands 1.00 .30
1265 A180 10fr Giraffe 1.00 .30
1266 A180 80fr Elephants 6.00 3.00
1267 A180 90fr Crocodiles 7.00 3.00

Size: 48x34mm

1268 A180 100fr Weaver birds 7.00 5.00
1269 A180 100fr Pelican, zebras 7.00 5.00
a. Pair, #1268-1269 + label 22.50 22.50
Nos. 1262-1269 (8) 30.50 17.15

No. 1269a has continuous design.
A souvenir sheet containing five No. 1269a exists. Value $200.

Christmas, Intl. Peace Year — A181

1986, Dec. 24 Litho. *Perf. 13*

1270 A181 10fr shown .25 .25
1271 A181 15fr Dove, Earth .75 .50
1272 A181 30fr like 10fr 1.00 .80
1273 A181 70fr like 15fr 2.25 2.25
Nos. 1270-1273 (4) 4.25 3.80

UN Child Survival Campaign A182

1987, Feb. 13

1274 A182 4fr Breast feeding .25 .25
1275 A182 6fr Rehydration therapy .30 .25
1276 A182 10fr Immunization .50 .30
1277 A182 70fr Growth monitoring 3.25 1.75
Nos. 1274-1277 (4) 4.30 2.55

Year of Natl. Self-sufficiency in Food Production — A183

1987, June 15 Litho. *Perf. 13*

1278 A183 5fr Farm .25 .25
1279 A183 7fr Storing produce .25 .25
1280 A183 40fr Boy carrying basket of fish, produce 1.50 .80
1281 A183 60fr Tropical fruit 2.00 1.25
Nos. 1278-1281 (4) 4.00 2.55

Nos. 1279-1281 vert.

Natl. Independence, 25th Anniv. — A184

10fr, Pres. Habyarimana, soldiers, farmers. 40fr, Pres. officiating government session. 70fr, Pres., Pope John Paul II. 100fr, Pres.

1987, July 1

1283 A184 10fr multi .50 .30
1284 A184 40fr multi 1.60 1.25
1285 A184 70fr multi 2.75 2.25
1286 A184 100fr multi, vert. 3.75 3.25
Nos. 1283-1286 (4) 8.60 7.05

A 5fr value exists but was not officially issued. Value $100.

Fruit A185

1987, Sept. 28

1287 A185 10fr Bananas, vert. .45 .25
1288 A185 40fr Pineapples 1.40 1.00
1289 A185 80fr Papayas 3.00 2.25
1290 A185 90fr Avocados 3.50 2.50
1291 A185 100fr Strawberries, vert. 4.75 3.00
Nos. 1287-1291 (5) 13.10 9.00

Leopards — A186

No. 1292, Female, cub. No. 1293, Three cubs playing. No. 1294, Adult attacking gazelle. No. 1295, In tree. No. 1296, Leaping from tree.

1987, Nov. 18 Litho. *Perf. 13*

1292 A186 50fr multi 6.00 2.75
1293 A186 50fr multi 6.00 2.75
1294 A186 50fr multi 6.00 2.75
1295 A186 50fr multi 6.00 2.75
1296 A186 50fr multi 6.00 2.75
a. Strip of 5, Nos. 1292-1296 40.00 40.00
Nos. 1292-1296 (5) 30.00 13.75

A souvenir sheet containing five No. 1296a exists. Value $200.

Intl. Year of the Volunteer — A187

5fr, Constructing village water system. 12fr, Education, vert. 20fr, Modern housing, vert. 60fr, Animal husbandry, vert.

1987, Dec. 12

1297 A187 5fr multicolored .25 .25
1298 A187 12fr multicolored .50 .25
1299 A187 20fr multicolored 1.00 .50
1300 A187 60fr multicolored 2.75 2.00
Nos. 1297-1300 (4) 4.50 3.00

Souvenir Sheet

Virgin and Child, by Fra Angelico (c. 1387-1455) — A188

1987, Dec. 24 Engr. *Perf. 11½*

1301 A188 200fr deep mag & dull blue 9.50 9.50

Christmas.

Maintenance of the Rural Economy Year — A189

1988, June 13 Litho. *Perf. 13*

1302 A189 10fr Furniture store .35 .25
1303 A189 40fr Dairy farm 1.00 1.00
1304 A189 60fr Produce market 1.75 1.25
1305 A189 80fr Fruit market 2.50 2.00
Nos. 1302-1305 (4) 5.60 4.50

Primates, Nyungwe Forest — A190

2fr, Chimpanzee. 3fr, Black and white colobus. 10fr, Pygmy galago. 90fr, Cercopithecidae ascagne.

1988, Sept. 15 Litho. *Perf. 13*

1306 A190 2fr multicolored .50 .25
1307 A190 3fr multicolored .70 1.25
1308 A190 10fr multicolored 2.00 .75
1309 A190 90fr multicolored 11.00 4.50
Nos. 1306-1309 (4) 14.20 6.75

1988 Summer Olympics, Seoul — A191

1988, Sept. 19

1310 A191 5fr Boxing .35 .25
1311 A191 7fr Relay .40 .25
1312 A191 8fr Table tennis .50 .25
1313 A191 10fr Women's running 1.50 .50
1314 A191 90fr Hurdles 5.75 2.25
Nos. 1310-1314 (5) 8.50 3.50

Organization of African Unity, 25th Anniv. — A192

1988, Nov. 30 Litho. *Perf. 13*

1315 A192 5fr shown .25 .25
1316 A192 7fr Handskake, map .25 .25
1317 A192 8fr "OAU" in brick, map .25 .25
1318 A192 90fr Slogan 3.00 2.25
Nos. 1315-1318 (4) 3.75 3.00

Souvenir Sheet

Detail of The Virgin and the Soup, by Paolo Veronese — A193

1988, Dec. 23 Engr. *Perf. 13½*

1319 A193 200fr multicolored 7.00 7.00

Christmas. Margin is typographed.

Intl. Red Cross and Red Crescent Organizations, 125th Annivs. — A194

1988, Dec. 30 Litho. *Perf. 13*

1320 A194	10fr Refugees	.40	.25
1321 A194	30fr First aid	1.10	.75
1322 A194	40fr Elderly	1.50	1.00
1323 A194	100fr Travelling doctor	3.50	2.50
	Nos. 1320-1323 (4)	6.50	4.50

Nos. 1322-1323 vert.

Medicinal Plants — A195

5fr, Plectranthus barbatus. 10fr, Tetradenia riparia. 20fr, Hygrophila auriculata. 40fr, Datura stramonium. 50fr, Pavetta ternifolia.

1989, Feb. 15 Litho. *Perf. 13*

1324 A195	5fr multicolored	*1.00*	*.50*
1325 A195	10fr multicolored	*2.00*	*1.00*
1326 A195	20fr multicolored	*4.00*	*2.00*
1327 A195	40fr multicolored	*8.00*	*4.00*
1328 A195	50fr multicolored	*14.00*	*7.00*
	Nos. 1324-1328 (5)	*29.00*	*14.50*

Interparliamentary Union, Cent. — A196

1989, Oct. 20 Litho. *Perf. 13*

1329 A196	10fr shown	.35	.25
1330 A196	30fr Hills, lake	1.00	.75
1331 A196	70fr Hills, stream	2.25	2.00
1332 A196	90fr Sun rays, hills	2.75	2.25
	Nos. 1329-1332 (4)	6.35	5.25

Souvenir Sheet

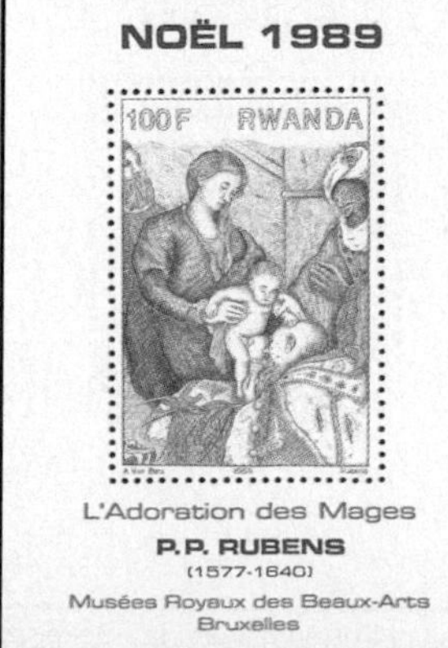

Christmas — A197

Adoration of the Magi by Rubens.

1989, Dec. 29 Engr. *Perf. 11½*

1333 A197 100fr blk, red & grn 9.00 9.00

Rural Organization Year — A198

Designs: 10fr, Making pottery. 70fr, Carrying produce to market. 90fr, Firing clay pots. 100fr, Clearing land.

1989, Dec. 29 Litho. *Perf. 13½x13*

1334 A198	10fr multi	.50	.25
1335 A198	70fr multi, vert.	2.00	1.50
1336 A198	90fr multi	2.50	2.00
1337 A198	200fr multi	6.00	4.50
	Nos. 1334-1337 (4)	11.00	8.25

Revolution, 30th Anniv. (in 1989) — A199

Designs: 10fr, Improved living conditions. 60fr, Couple, farm tools. 70fr, Modernization. 100fr, Flag, map, native.

1990, Jan. 22 *Perf. 13*

1338 A199	10fr multi	.40	.40
1339 A199	60fr multi, vert.	2.00	1.25
1340 A199	70fr multi	2.25	1.75
1341 A199	100fr multi	4.00	2.25
	Nos. 1338-1341 (4)	8.65	5.65

Inscribed 1989.

French Revolution, Bicent. (in 1989) — A200

Paintings of the Revolution: 10fr, Triumph of Marat by Boilly. 60fr, Rouget de Lisle singing La Marseillaise by Pils. 70fr, Oath of the Tennis Court by David. 100fr, Trial of Louis XVI by Court.

1990, Jan. 22

1342 A200	10fr multicolored	.40	.40
1343 A200	60fr multicolored	2.00	2.00
1344 A200	70fr multicolored	2.25	2.25
1345 A200	100fr multicolored	4.00	4.00
	Nos. 1342-1345 (4)	8.65	8.65

Inscribed 1989.

African Development Bank, 25th Anniv. (in 1989) — A201

1990, Feb. 22 *Perf. 13½x13*

1346 A201	10fr Building construction	.45	.25
1347 A201	20fr Harvesting	.75	.75
1348 A201	40fr Cultivation	1.25	1.00
1349 A201	90fr Building, truck, harvesters	3.00	2.50
	Nos. 1346-1349 (4)	5.45	4.50

Belgica '90, Intl. Philatelic Exhibition — A202

No. 1350, Great Britain #1. No. 1351, Belgium #B1011. No. 1352, Rwanda #516.

1990, May 21 Litho. *Imperf.*

1350 A202	100fr multi	4.25	4.25
1351 A202	100fr multi	4.25	4.25
1352 A202	100fr multi	4.25	4.25
	Nos. 1350-1352 (3)	12.75	12.75

Visit of Pope John Paul II — A203

1990, Aug. 27 Litho. *Perf. 13½x13*

1353 A203	10fr shown	3.00	3.00
1354 A203	70fr Holding crucifix	17.00	17.00

Souvenir Sheet

Perf. 11½

1355 A203 100fr Hands together 20.00 20.00

No. 1355 contains one 36x51mm stamp.

Intl. Literacy Year — A204

Designs: 10fr, Teacher at blackboard. 20fr, Teacher seated at desk. 50fr, Small outdoor class. 90fr, Large outdoor class.

1991, Jan. 25 Litho. *Perf. 13½x13*

1356 A204	10fr multicolored	.50	.25
1357 A204	20fr multicolored	.75	.40
1358 A204	50fr multicolored	1.75	1.25
1359 A204	90fr multicolored	3.25	1.75
	Nos. 1356-1359 (4)	6.25	3.65

Nos. 1256-1261 Ovptd. in Black on Silver

1990, May 25 Litho. *Perf. 13*

1360 A179	2fr on No. 1256	3.00	3.00
1361 A179	4fr on No. 1257	4.00	4.00
1362 A179	5fr on No. 1258	5.00	5.00
1363 A179	10fr on No. 1259	9.00	9.00
1364 A179	40fr on No. 1260	25.00	25.00
1365 A179	45fr on No. 1261	30.00	30.00
	Nos. 1360-1365 (6)	76.00	76.00

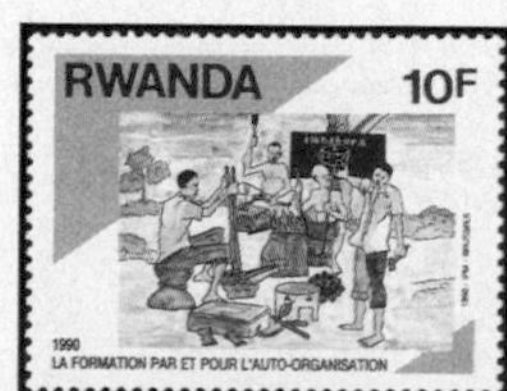

Self-help Organizations — A205

No. 1366, Tool making. No. 1367, Animal husbandry. No. 1368, Textile manufacturing. No. 1369, Road construction.

1991, Jan. 25 Litho. *Perf. 13½x13*

1366 A205	10fr multicolored	.60	.30
1367 A205	20fr multicolored	1.25	.60
1368 A205	50fr multicolored	2.00	1.25
1369 A205	90fr multicolored	4.00	2.50
	Nos. 1366-1369 (4)	7.85	4.65

Dated 1990.

Cardinal Lavigerie, Founder of the Order of White Fathers and Sisters, Death Cent. A206

5fr, Statue of Madonna. 15fr, One of the Order's nuns. 70fr, Group photo, vert. 110fr, Cardinal Lavigerie.

1992, Oct. 1 Litho. *Perf. 14*

1370 A206	5fr multi, vert.	2.00	2.00
1371 A206	15fr multi, vert.	7.00	7.00
1372 A206	70fr multi	22.50	22.50
1373 A206	110fr multi, vert.	40.00	40.00
	Nos. 1370-1373 (4)	71.50	71.50

1992 Summer Olympic Games, Barcelona — A207

Designs: a, 20fr, Runners. b, 30fr, Swimmer. c, 90fr, Soccer players.

1993, Feb. 1

1374 A207 Sheet of 3, #a.-c. 40.00 40.00

Protection of Vegetable Crops A208

Designs: 10fr, Removing parasites and weeds. 15fr, Spraying pesticides. 70fr, Zonocerus elegans on plants. 110fr, Phenacoccus manihoti.

1993, June 15 Litho. *Perf. 14*

1375 A208	10fr multicolored	4.50	4.50
1376 A208	15fr multicolored	7.50	7.50
1377 A208	70fr multicolored	32.50	32.50
1378 A208	110fr multicolored	55.00	55.00
	Nos. 1375-1378 (4)	99.50	99.50

World Conference on Nutrition, Rome — A209

Designs: 15fr, Man fishing. 50fr, People at fruit market. 100fr, Man milking cow. 500fr, Mother breastfeeding.

1992, Dec. Litho. *Perf. 14*

1381	A209	15fr multicolored	1.00	1.00
1382	A209	50fr multicolored	3.25	3.25
1383	A209	100fr multicolored	5.50	5.50
1384	A209	500fr multicolored	32.50	32.50
		Nos. 1381-1384 (4)	42.25	42.25

Wildlife A210

1998 Litho. *Perf. 14*

1385	A210	15fr Toad	3.00	3.00
1386	A210	100fr Snail	5.00	5.00
1387	A210	150fr Porcupine	6.00	6.00
1388	A210	300fr Chameleon	8.00	8.00
a.		Souvenir sheet, #1385-1388, Imperf.	24.00	24.00
		Nos. 1385-1388 (4)	22.00	22.00

Plants A211

15fr, Opuntia. 100fr, Gloriosa superba. 150fr, Markhamia lutea. 300fr, Hagenia abyssinica.

1998 Litho. *Perf. 14*

1389	A211	15fr multi, vert.	3.00	3.00
1390	A211	100fr multi, vert.	5.00	5.00
1391	A211	150fr multi, vert.	6.00	6.00
1392	A211	300fr multi	8.00	8.00
a.		Souvenir sheet, #1389-1392, imperf.	24.00	24.00
		Nos. 1389-1392 (4)	22.00	22.00

Remembrance of Genocide Victims — A212

20fr, Map, coffins, horiz. 30fr, Orphans, horiz. 400fr, People protesting.

1999 (?) Litho. *Perf. 14*

1392B	A212	20fr multi	*1.50*	*1.50*
1392C	A212	30fr multi	*2.50*	*2.50*
1393	A212	200fr multi	*11.50*	*11.50*
1394	A212	400fr multi	*20.00*	*20.00*

Rwandan postal officials have declared "illegal" sets depicting: Millennium (eleven sheets of 9 with various subjects), Pornography (two sheets of 9), Chess (sheet of 9 unoverprinted, and also overprinted in Russian), Double-decker buses (sheet of 9), Butterflies (sheet of 9), Hot air balloons (sheet of 9), Old automobiles (sheet of 9), Motorcycle racing (sheet of 9), Trains (sheet of 9), Fungi (sheet of 6), Cats (sheet of 6), Roses (sheet of 6).

Sheet of six stamps of various values depicting Wildlife Trusts (Snakes).

Souvenir sheet of two 500fr stamps depicting Mother Teresa.

Souvenir sheet of one 500fr stamp depicting Wildlife Trusts (Snakes).

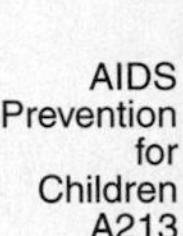
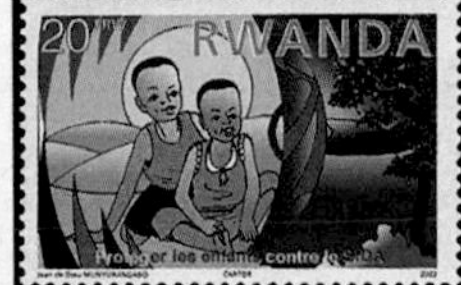

AIDS Prevention for Children A213

AIDS Prevention for Children — A214

Designs: 20fr, Children, red ribbon, tree. 30fr, Red ribbon, hands, children, vert. 200fr, Children, hand, red ribbon.

Perf. 13½x13¾, 13¾x13½

2003, Jan. 1 Litho.

1395	A213	20fr multi	*1.00*	*1.00*
1396	A213	30fr multi	*1.50*	*1.50*
1397	A214	200fr multi	*19.00*	*19.00*
1398	A214	500fr multi	*37.50*	*37.50*

Art and Culture — A215

Designs: 34fr, Two dancers. 300fr, People dancing. 500fr, Basket weaving. 600fr, Face looking through torn fabric. 1000fr, Containers, horiz.

Perf. 13¾x13¼, 13¼x13¾

2010, Nov. 15 Litho.

1399	A215	34fr multi	*1.00*	*1.00*
1400	A215	300fr multi	*2.00*	*2.00*
1401	A215	500fr multi	*4.00*	*4.00*
1402	A215	600fr multi	*5.00*	*5.00*
1403	A215	1000fr multi	*9.00*	*9.00*

Mountain Gorilla — A216

Design: 30fr, Gorilla and foliage. 40fr, Adults and juveniles. 2000fr, Side view of gorilla. 5000fr, Gorilla sitting in front of trees.

Perf. 13¼x13¾

2010, Nov. 15 Litho.

1404	A216	30fr multi	*1.00*	*1.00*
1405	A216	40fr multi	*1.25*	*1.25*
1406	A216	2000fr multi	*17.50*	*17.50*
1407	A216	5000fr multi	*35.00*	*35.00*

SEMI-POSTAL STAMPS

No. 305 Srchd. in Black and Ovptd. in Brown: "SECHERESSE/SOLIDARITE AFRICAINE"

1973, Aug. 23 Photo. *Perf. 13*

B1	A53	100fr + 50fr multi	6.00	6.00

African solidarity in drought emergency.

Nos. 349-350 Srchd. and Ovptd. Like Nos. 693-698

1975, Nov. 10 Litho. *Perf. 13*

B2	A60	50fr + 25fr multi	2.25	2.00
B3	A60	90fr + 25fr multi	3.00	2.50

African solidarity in drought emergency.

AIR POST STAMPS

African Postal Union Issue, 1967
Common Design Type

1967, Sept. 18 Engr. *Perf. 13*

C1	CD124	6fr brn, rose cl & gray	.30	.25
C2	CD124	18fr brt lil, ol brn & plum	.60	.35
C3	CD124	30fr grn, dp bl & red	1.40	.65
		Nos. C1-C3 (3)	2.30	1.25

PHILEXAFRIQUE Issue

Alexandre Lenoir, by Jacques L. David AP1

1968, Dec. 30 Photo. *Perf. 12½*

C4	AP1	100fr emerald & multi	3.25	1.75

Issued to publicize PHILEXAFRIQUE, Philatelic exhibition in Abidjan, Feb. 14-23, 1969. Printed with alternating emerald label.

2nd PHILEXAFRIQUE Issue

Ruanda-Urundi No. 123, Cowherd and Lake Victoria — AP2

1969, Feb. 14 Litho. *Perf. 14*

C5	AP2	50fr multicolored	1.75	1.25

Opening of PHILEXAFRIQUE, Abidjan, 2/14.

Painting Type of Regular Issue

Paintings and Music: 50fr, The Music Lesson, by Fragonard. 100fr, Angels' Concert, by Memling, horiz.

1969, Mar. 31 Photo. *Perf. 13*

C6	A49	50fr gold & multi	1.75	1.25
C7	A49	100fr gold & multi	3.25	2.50

African Postal Union Issue, 1971
Common Design Type

Design: Woman and child of Rwanda and UAMPT Building, Brazzaville, Congo.

1971, Nov. 13 *Perf. 13x13½*

C8	CD135	100fr blue & multi	2.75	2.25

No. C8 Overprinted in Red

a

b

1973, Sept. 17 Photo. *Perf. 13x13½*

C9	CD135(a)	100fr multi	4.50	4.50
C10	CD135(b)	100fr multi	4.50	4.50
a.		Pair, #C9-C10	11.00	11.00

3rd Conference of French-speaking countries, Liège, Sept. 15-Oct. 14. Overprints alternate checkerwise in same sheet.

Sassenage Castle, Grenoble — AP3

1977, June 20 Litho. *Perf. 12½*

C11	AP3	50fr multi	2.00	1.25

Intl. French Language Council, 10th anniv.

Philexafrique II-Essen Issue
Common Design Types

Designs: No. C12, Okapi, Rwanda #239. No. C13, Woodpecker, Oldenburg #4.

1978, Nov. 1 Litho. *Perf. 12½*

C12	CD138	30fr multi	1.50	1.50
C13	CD139	30fr multi	1.50	1.50
a.		Pair, #C12-C13	4.00	4.00

SAAR

'sär

LOCATION — On the Franco-German border southeast of Luxembourg
POP. — 1,400,000 (1959)
AREA — 991 sq. mi.
CAPITAL — Saarbrücken

A former German territory, the Saar was administered by the League of Nations 1920-35. After a January 12, 1935, plebiscite, it returned to Germany, and the use of German stamps was resumed. After World War II, France occupied the Saar and later established a protectorate. The provisional semi-independent State of Saar was established Jan. 1, 1951. France returned the Saar to the German Federal Republic Jan. 1, 1957.

Saar stamps were discontinued in 1959 and replaced by stamps of the German Federal Republic.

100 Pfennig = 1 Mark
100 Centimes = 1 Franc (1921)

Catalogue values for unused stamps in this country are for Never Hinged items, beginning with Scott 221 in the regular postage section, and Scott B85 in the semi-postal section.

Watermark

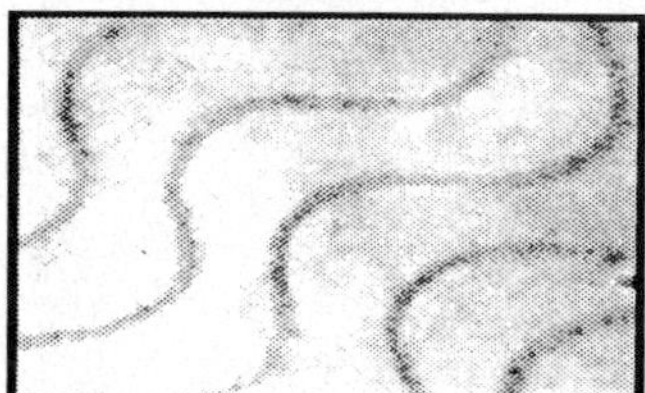

Wmk. 285 — Marbleized Pattern

German Stamps of 1906-19 Overprinted

Perf. 14, 14½

1920, Jan. 30 — Wmk. 125

No.			Unused	Used
1	A22	2pf gray	1.60	*4.50*
c.		Inverted overprint	325.00	*550.00*
d.		Double overprint	2,000.	*2,600.*
1A	A16	2pf blue gray (ovptd. on Germany #80)	*8,500.*	
2	A22	2½pf gray	9.50	*27.50*
c.		Inverted overprint	350.00	*650.00*
3	A16	3pf brown	1.00	*2.75*
c.		Inverted overprint	325.00	*550.00*
4	A16	5pf deep green	.50	*1.00*
c.		Inverted overprint	600.00	—
f.		Double overprint	800.00	*1,450.*
5	A22	7½pf orange	.65	*1.75*
c.		Inverted overprint	—	800.00
6	A16	10pf carmine	.55	*1.25*
c.		Inverted overprint	550.00	*1,050.*
d.		Double overprint	725.00	*1,200.*
7	A22	15pf dk violet	.50	*1.00*
c.		Double overprint	800.00	*1,450.*
8	A16	20pf blue violet	.50	*1.00*
c.		Double overprint	600.00	*950.00*
9	A16	25pf red org & blk, *yellow*	9.50	20.00
c.		Inverted overprint	800.00	*2,400.*
10	A16	30pf org & blk, *yel buff*	17.50	*35.00*
11	A22	35pf red brown	.55	*1.25*
c.		Inverted overprint	475.00	*1,050.*
12	A16	40pf dp lake & blk	.55	*1.25*
c.		Inverted overprint	475.00	*1,050.*
13	A16	50pf pur & blk, *yel buff*	.55	*1.60*
c.		Inverted overprint	400.00	*725.00*
14	A16	60pf dp gray lilac	.55	*1.25*
15	A16	75pf green & blk	.55	*1.25*
c.		Inverted overprint	240.00	*400.00*
16	A16	80pf lake & blk, *rose*	190.00	*275.00*

Overprinted

Type I

No.			Unused	Used
17	A17	1m carmine rose	27.50	*40.00*
a.		Inverted overprint	725.00	*1,450.*
b.		Double overprint	800.00	*1,450.*

Type II

No.			Unused	Used
17f	A17	1m carmine rose	40.00	*80.00*
		Nos. 1-17 (17)	262.05	417.35

Three types of overprint exist on Nos. 1-5, 12, 13; two types on Nos. 6-11, 14-16. For detailed listings, see the *Scott Classic Specialized Catalogue.*

The 3m type A19 exists overprinted like No. 17, but was not issued. Values: unused $16,000; never hinged $33,000.

Overprint forgeries exist.

Bavarian Stamps of 1914-16 Overprinted

Perf. 14x14½

1920, Mar. 1 — Wmk. 95

No.			Unused	Used
19	A10	2pf gray	*900.00*	*4,750.*
20	A10	3pf brown	80.00	*650.00*
21	A10	5pf yellow grn	.75	*1.60*
a.		Double overprint	800.00	
22	A10	7½pf green	32.50	*275.00*
23	A10	10pf carmine rose	.75	*1.60*
a.		Double overprint	325.00	*650.00*
24	A10	15pf vermilion	.95	*1.90*
a.		Double overprint	400.00	*800.00*
25	A10	15pf carmine	7.25	*16.00*
26	A10	20pf blue	.65	*1.60*
a.		Double overprint	325.00	*650.00*
27	A10	25pf gray	11.00	*16.00*
28	A10	30pf orange	6.50	*11.00*
30	A10	40pf olive green	10.50	*16.00*
31	A10	50pf red brown	2.00	*4.50*
a.		Double overprint	350.00	*650.00*
32	A10	60pf dark green	3.25	*8.00*

Overprinted

Perf. 11½

No.			Unused	Used
35	A11	1m brown	24.00	*35.00*
a.		1m dark brown	16.00	*32.50*
36	A11	2m dk gray violet	60.00	*140.00*
37	A11	3m scarlet	120.00	*160.00*
		Nos. 35-37 (3)	204.00	*335.00*

Overprinted

No.			Unused	Used
38	A12	5m deep blue	800.00	*875.00*
39	A12	10m yellow green	140.00	*250.00*

Nos. 19, 20 and 22 were not officially issued, but were available for postage. Examples are known legitimately used on cover. The 20m type A12 was also overprinted in small quantity. Values: unused $125,000; never hinged $200,000.

No. 21a is valued without gum.

Overprint forgeries exist.

German Stamps of 1906-20 Overprinted

Perf. 14, 14½

1920, Mar. 26 — Wmk. 125

No.			Unused	Used
41	A16	5pf green	.25	*.50*
a.		Inverted overprint	16.00	*160.00*
42	A16	5pf red brown	.50	.80
43	A16	10pf carmine	.25	*.50*
a.		Inverted overprint	47.50	*325.00*
44	A16	10pf orange	.45	.50
a.		Inverted overprint	16.00	
45	A22	15pf dk violet	.25	*.50*
a.		Inverted overprint	27.50	*240.00*
46	A16	20pf blue violet	.25	*.50*
a.		Inverted overprint	35.00	—
47	A16	20pf green	.95	.50
a.		Double overprint, never hinged	80.00	
48	A16	30pf org & blk, *buff*	.40	*.50*
a.		Double overprint	65.00	
b.		Inverted overprint	—	
49	A16	30pf dull blue	.55	*.75*
50	A16	40pf lake & blk	.30	*.50*
51	A16	40pf car rose	1.00	*.75*
52	A16	50pf pur & blk, *buff*	.55	*.50*
a.		Double overprint	65.00	*400.00*
53	A16	60pf red violet	.65	.50
a.		Inverted overprint	80.00	*325.00*
54	A16	75pf green & blk	.75	.50
a.		Double overprint	110.00	*400.00*
b.		Inverted overprint	110.00	
55	A17	1.25m green	2.75	1.25
a.		Inverted overprint	95.00	
56	A17	1.50m yellow brn	2.00	1.25
a.		Inverted overprint	95.00	800.00
57	A21	2.50m lilac red	4.75	*13.50*
58	A16	4m black & rose	8.75	*22.50*
a.		Double overprint	110.00	
		Nos. 41-58 (18)	25.35	*46.30*

On No. 57 the overprint is placed vertically at each side of the stamp.

No. 58a is valued never hinged.

Counterfeit overprints exist.

Germany No. 90 Surcharged in Black

1921, Feb.

No.			Unused	Used
65	A16	20pf on 75pf grn & blk	.40	*1.25*
a.		Inverted surcharge	24.00	*72.50*
b.		Double surcharge	55.00	*125.00*

Germany No. 120 Surcharged

No.			Unused	Used
66	A22	5m on 15pf vio brn	5.50	*16.00*
67	A22	10m on 15pf vio brn	6.00	*19.00*
		Nos. 65-67 (3)	11.90	*36.25*

Forgeries exist of Nos. 66-67.

Old Mill near Mettlach — A3

Miner at Work — A4

Entrance to Reden Mine — A5

Saar River Traffic — A6

Saar River near Mettlach — A7

Slag Pile at Völklingen — A8

Signal Bridge, Saarbrücken — A9

Church at Mettlach — A10

"Old Bridge," Saarbrücken A11

Cable Railway at Ferne — A12

Colliery Shafthead — A13

Saarbrücken City Hall — A14

Pottery at Mettlach — A15

St. Ludwig's Cathedral — A16

Presidential Residence, Saarbrücken A17

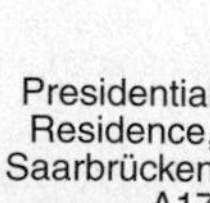

Burbach Steelworks, Dillingen A18

1921 Unwmk. Typo. *Perf. 12½*

No.			Unused	Used
68	A3	5pf ol grn & vio	.35	*.50*
a.		Tête bêche pair	3.50	*20.00*
c.		Center inverted	100.00	*340.00*
69	A4	10pf org & ultra	.35	*.50*
70	A5	20pf grn & slate	.35	*1.00*
a.		Tête bêche pair	6.50	*40.00*
c.		Perf. 10½	22.50	*225.00*
d.		As "c," tête bêche pair	140.00	*675.00*
71	A6	25pf brn & dk bl	.40	*.80*
a.		Tête bêche pair	7.25	*40.00*

No.	Type	Description	Unused	Used
72	A7	30pf gray grn & brn	.40	.75
a.		Tête bêche pair	12.00	60.00
c.		30pf ol grn & blk	2.40	22.50
d.		As "c," tête bêche pair	12.50	72.50
e.		As "c," imperf., pair	120.00	
73	A8	40pf vermilion	.40	.50
a.		Tête bêche pair	19.00	80.00
74	A9	50pf gray & blk	.95	4.00
75	A10	60pf red & dk brn	1.60	3.50
76	A11	80pf deep blue	.75	1.00
a.		Tête bêche pair	21.00	110.00
77	A12	1m lt red & blk	.80	1.60
a.		1m grn & blk	450.00	
78	A13	1.25m lt brn & dk grn	.95	2.00
79	A14	2m red & blk	2.40	4.00
80	A15	3m brn & dk ol	3.25	9.50
a.		Center inverted	125.00	
81	A16	5m yel & vio	12.00	24.00
82	A17	10m grn & red brn	12.00	24.00
83	A18	25m ultra, red & blk	32.50	80.00
		Nos. 68-83 (16)	69.45	157.65

Values for tête bêche pairs are for vertical pairs. Horizontal pairs sell for about twice as much.

The ultramarine ink on No. 69 appears to be brown where it overlays the orange.

Exist imperf but were not regularly issued. Value $1,400. (hinged).

Nos. 70-83 Surcharged in Red, Blue or Black

a

b

c

1921, May 1

No.	Type	Description	Unused	Used
85	A5(a)	3c on 20pf (R)	.40	.50
a.		Tête bêche pair	4.75	32.50
b.		Inverted surcharge	95.00	
d.		Perf. 10½	4.75	160.00
e.		As "d," tête bêche pair	21.00	—
86	A6(a)	5c on 25pf (R)	.40	.50
a.		Tête bêche pair	95.00	400.00
87	A7(a)	10c on 30pf (Bl)	.40	.50
a.		Tête bêche pair	4.75	25.00
b.		Inverted surcharge	95.00	450.00
c.		Double surcharge	95.00	475.00
88	A8(a)	15c on 40pf (Bk)	.50	.50
a.		Tête bêche pair	95.00	400.00
b.		Inverted surcharge	95.00	450.00
89	A9(a)	20c on 50pf (R)	.40	.50
90	A10(a)	25c on 60pf (Bl)	.50	.50
91	A11(a)	30c on 80pf (Bk)	1.60	1.00
a.		Tête bêche pair	12.50	60.00
c.		Inverted surcharge	140.00	600.00
d.		Double surcharge	140.00	600.00
92	A12(a)	40c on 1m (Bl)	2.00	.50
a.		Inverted surcharge	110.00	450.00
b.		Double surcharge	140.00	600.00
93	A13(a)	50c on 1.25m (Bk)	3.25	1.00
a.		Double surcharge	275.00	950.00
b.		Perf. 10½	72.50	140.00
94	A14(a)	75c on 2m (Bl)	4.75	2.00
a.		Inverted surcharge	110.00	
95	A15(b)	1fr on 3m (Bl)	4.50	2.40
96	A16(b)	2fr on 5m (Bl)	12.00	6.50
97	A17(b)	3fr on 10m (Bk)	17.50	25.00
b.		Double surcharge	200.00	800.00

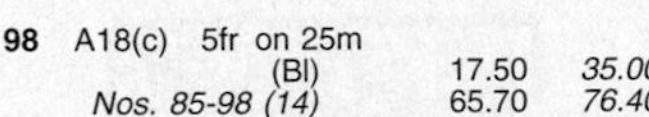

No.	Type	Description	Unused	Used
98	A18(c)	5fr on 25m (Bl)	17.50	35.00
		Nos. 85-98 (14)	65.70	76.40

In these surcharges the period is occasionally missing and there are various wrong font and defective letters.

Values for tête bêche pairs are for vertical pairs. Horizontal pairs sell for about twice as much.

Nos. 85-89, 91, 93, 97-98 exist imperforate but were not regularly issued.

Cable Railway, Ferne — A19

Miner at Work — A20

"Old Bridge," Saarbrücken A21

Saarbrücken City Hall — A22

Slag Pile at Völklingen A23

Pottery at Mettlach — A24

Saar River Traffic — A25

St. Ludwig's Cathedral A26

Colliery Shafthead A27

Mettlach Church — A28

Burbach Steelworks, Dillingen A29

Perf. 12½x13½, 13½x12½

1922-23 **Typo.**

No.	Type	Description	Unused	Used
99	A19	3c ol grn & straw	.40	.65
100	A20	5c orange & blk	.40	.40
101	A21	10c blue green	.40	.40
102	A19	15c deep brown	1.25	.40
103	A19	15c orange ('23)	2.40	.40
104	A22	20c dk bl & lem	13.50	.40
105	A22	20c brt bl & straw ('23)	4.00	.40
106	A22	25c red & yellow	6.50	2.25
107	A22	25c mag & straw ('23)	2.40	.40
108	A23	30c carmine & yel	2.00	2.10
109	A24	40c brown & yel	1.60	.40
110	A25	50c dk bl & straw	.95	.40
111	A24	75c dp grn & straw	13.50	24.00
112	A24	75c blk & straw ('23)	32.50	3.25
113	A26	1fr brown red	2.40	.80
114	A27	2fr deep violet	6.50	3.25
115	A28	3fr org & dk grn	24.00	6.50
116	A29	5fr brn & red brn	24.00	45.00
		Nos. 99-116 (18)	138.70	91.40

Nos. 99-116 exist imperforate but were not regularly issued.

For overprints see Nos. O1-O15.

Madonna of Blieskastel — A30

1925, Apr. 9 **Photo.** ***Perf. 13½x12½***

Size: 23x27mm

No.	Type	Description	Unused	Used
118	A30	45c lake brown	2.75	5.25

Size: 31½x36mm

Perf. 12

No.	Type	Description	Unused	Used
119	A30	10fr black brown	16.00	24.00

Nos. 118-119 exist imperforate but were not regularly issued.

For overprint see No. 154.

Market Fountain, St. Johann — A31

View of Saar Valley A32

Colliery Shafthead A35

Burbach Steelworks A36

Designs: 15c, 75c, View of Saar Valley. 20c, 40c, 90c, Scene from Saarlouis fortifications. 25c, 50c, Tholey Abbey.

1927-32 ***Perf. 13½***

No.	Type	Description	Unused	Used
120	A31	10c deep brown	.75	.50
121	A32	15c olive black	.40	1.10
122	A32	20c brown org	.40	.50
123	A32	25c bluish slate	.75	.50
124	A31	30c olive green	.95	.50
125	A32	40c olive brown	.75	.50
126	A32	50c magenta	.95	.50
127	A35	60c red org ('30)	4.00	.55
128	A32	75c brown violet	.75	.50
129	A35	80c red orange	2.40	8.75
130	A32	90c dp red ('32)	12.00	17.50
131	A35	1fr violet	2.40	.50
132	A36	1.50fr sapphire	6.50	.50
133	A36	2fr brown red	6.50	.50
134	A36	3fr dk olive grn	14.50	1.25
135	A36	5fr deep brown	14.50	7.25
		Nos. 120-135 (16)	68.50	41.40

For surcharges and overprints see Nos. 136-153, O16-O26.

Nos. 126 and 129 Surcharged

1930-34

No.	Type	Description	Unused	Used
136	A32	40c on 50c mag ('34)	1.60	1.60
137	A35	60c on 80c red orange	2.00	2.40

Plebiscite Issue

Stamps of 1925-32 Ovptd. in Various Colors

Perf. 13½, 13½x13, 13x13½

1934, Nov. 1

No.	Type	Description	Unused	Used
139	A31	10c brown (Br)	.40	.55
140	A32	15c black grn (G)	.40	.55
141	A32	20c brn org (O)	.65	1.40
142	A32	25c bluish sl (Bl)	.65	1.40
143	A31	30c olive grn (G)	.40	.55
144	A32	40c olive brn (Br)	.40	.75
145	A32	50c magenta (R)	.75	1.40
146	A35	60c red orge (O)	.65	.55
147	A32	75c brown vio (V)	.75	1.25
148	A32	90c deep red (R)	.75	1.40
149	A35	1fr violet (V)	.75	1.60
150	A36	1.50fr sapphire (Bl)	1.25	3.25
151	A36	2fr brn red (R)	2.00	4.75
152	A36	3fr dk ol grn (G)	4.75	9.50
153	A36	5fr dp brn (Br)	20.00	32.50

Size: 31½x36mm

Perf. 12

No.	Type	Description	Unused	Used
154	A30	10fr blk brn (Br)	24.00	60.00
		Nos. 139-154 (16)	58.55	121.40

French Administration

Miner A37

Steel Workers A38

Harvesting Sugar Beets — A39

Mettlach Abbey — A40

Marshal Ney — A41

Saar River near Mettlach A42

1947 Unwmk. Photo. *Perf. 14*

155	A37	2pf gray	.25	*.40*
156	A37	3pf orange	.25	*.50*
157	A37	6pf dk Prus grn	.25	*.40*
158	A37	8pf scarlet	.25	*.35*
159	A37	10pf rose violet	.25	*.40*
160	A38	15pf brown	.25	*6.50*
161	A38	16pf ultra	.25	*.40*
162	A38	20pf brown rose	.25	*.40*
163	A38	24pf dp brown org	.25	*.40*
164	A39	25pf cerise	.25	*22.50*
165	A39	30pf lt olive grn	.25	*.80*
166	A39	40pf orange brn	.25	*1.20*
167	A39	50pf blue violet	.25	*22.50*
168	A40	60pf violet	.25	*22.50*
169	A40	80pf dp orange	.25	*.40*
170	A41	84pf brown	.25	*.40*
171	A42	1m gray green	.25	*.50*
		Nos. 155-171 (17)	4.25	*80.55*
		Set, never hinged	5.50	

Nos. 155-162, 164-171 exist imperf.

Types of 1947

1947 Wmk. 285

172	A37	12pf olive green	.25	*.40*
173	A39	45pf crimson	.25	*16.00*
174	A40	75pf brt blue	.25	*.40*
		Nos. 172-174 (3)	.75	*16.80*
		Set, never hinged	1.00	

Nos. 172-174 exist imperf.

Types of 1947 Surcharged in Black or Red

Printing II

1947, Nov. 27 Unwmk.

175	A37	10c on 2pf gray	.25	*.55*
176	A37	60c on 3pf org	.25	*1.10*
177	A37	1fr on 10pf rose vio	.25	*.55*
178	A37	2fr on 12pf ol grn, wmk. 285	.25	*1.50*
179	A38	3fr on 15pf brn	.25	*1.50*
180	A38	4fr on 16pf ultra	.25	*8.00*
181	A38	5fr on 20pf brn rose	.25	*1.10*
182	A38	6fr on 24pf dp brn org	.25	*.65*
183	A39	9fr on 30pf lt ol grn	.25	*13.50*
184	A39	10fr on 50pf bl vio (R)	.25	*20.00*
185	A40	14fr on 60pf vio	.25	*13.50*
186	A41	20fr on 84pf brn	.35	*21.00*
187	A42	50fr on 1m gray grn	.50	*21.00*
		Nos. 175-187 (13)	3.60	*103.95*
		Set, never hinged	5.50	

Printing I

175a	A37	10c on 2pf gray	35.00	*360.00*
176a	A37	60c on 3pf org	29.00	*800.00*
177a	A37	1fr on 10pf rose vio	2.40	*16.00*
178a	A37	2fr on 12pf ol grn, wmk. 285	.75	*4.00*
179a	A38	3fr on 15pf brn	350.00	*2,400.*
180a	A38	4fr on 16pf ultra	7.25	*110.00*
181a	A38	5fr on 20pf brn rose	80.00	*4,750.*
182a	A38	6fr on 24pf dp brn org	.25	*4.75*
183a	A39	9fr on 30pf lt ol grn	45.00	*800.00*
184a	A39	10fr on 50pf bl vio (R)	550.00	*4,750.*
185a	A40	14fr on 60pf violet	87.50	*950.00*
186a	A41	20fr on 84pf brn	2.00	*8.00*

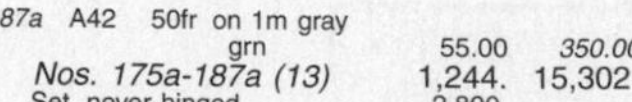

187a	A42	50fr on 1m gray grn	55.00	*350.00*
		Nos. 175a-187a (13)	1,244.	15,302.
		Set, never hinged	2,800.	

Printing I was surcharged on Nos. 155-171, which was printed on yellowish paper with brownish gum. The crossbar of the A's in SAAR is high on the 10c, 60c, 1fr, 2fr, 9fr and 10fr; numeral "1" has no base serif on the 3fr and 4fr, 5fr, 6fr; 14fr, 14fr, wide space between vignette and SAAR panel; 1m inscribed "1M."

Printing II was surcharged on a special printing of the basic stamps, on white paper with white gum, and with details of design that differ on each denomination. The "A" crossbar is low on 10c, 60c, 1fr, 2fr, 9fr, 10fr; numeral "1" has base serif on 3fr, 4fr, 5fr, 6fr; 14fr, narrow space between vignette and SAAR panel; 20fr, minor retouches; 1m inscribed "1SM."

Inverted surcharges exist on Nos. 175-187 and 175a-187a.

French Protectorate

Clasped Hands — A43

Colliery Shafthead — A44

2fr, 3fr, Worker. 4fr, 5fr, Girl gathering wheat. 6fr, 9fr, Miner. 14fr, Smelting. 20fr, Reconstruction. 50fr, Mettlach Abbey portal.

Perf. 14x13, 13

1948, Apr. 1 Engr. Unwmk.

188	A43	10c henna brn	.35	*2.00*
189	A43	60c dk Prus grn	.35	*2.00*
190	A43	1fr brown blk	.25	*.30*
191	A43	2fr rose car	.25	*.30*
192	A43	3fr black brn	.25	*.30*
193	A43	4fr red	.25	*.30*
194	A43	5fr red violet	.25	*.30*
195	A43	6fr henna brown	.35	.30
196	A43	9fr dk Prus grn	2.00	.50
197	A44	10fr dark blue	1.25	.80
198	A44	14fr dk vio brn	1.60	1.10
199	A44	20fr henna brn	3.25	1.10
200	A44	50fr blue blk	6.50	2.75
		Nos. 188-200 (13)	16.90	12.05
		Set, never hinged	35.00	

Map of the Saar A45

1948, Dec. 15 Photo. *Perf. 13½x13*

201	A45	10fr dark red	.75	*4.00*
202	A45	25fr deep blue	1.25	*8.00*
		Set, never hinged	4.75	

French Protectorate establishment, 1st anniv.

Caduceus, Microscope, Bunsen Burner and Book — A46

1949, Apr. 2 *Perf. 13x13½*

203	A46	15fr carmine	2.75	.50
		Never hinged	7.25	

Issued to honor Saar University.

Ludwig van Beethoven A47

Laborer Using Spade A51

Saarbrücken — A52

Designs: 10c, Building trades. 1fr, 3fr, Gears, factories. 5fr, Dumping mine waste. 6fr, 15fr, Coal mine interior. 8fr, Communications symbols. 10fr, Emblem of printing. 12fr, 18fr, Pottery. 25fr, Blast furnace worker. 45fr, Rock formation "Great Boot." 60fr, Reden Colliery, Landsweiler. 100fr, View of Weibelskirchen.

1949-51 Unwmk. *Perf. 13x13½*

204	A47	10c violet brn	.25	*2.00*
205	A47	60c gray ('51)	.25	*2.00*
206	A47	1fr carmine lake	.50	.35
207	A47	3fr brown ('51)	3.25	.40
208	A47	5fr dp violet ('50)	.80	.35
209	A47	6fr Prus grn ('51)	4.75	.40
210	A47	8fr olive grn ('51)	.50	.65
211	A47	10fr orange ('50)	2.00	.35
212	A47	12fr dk green	6.50	.35
213	A47	15fr red ('50)	2.75	.35
214	A47	18fr brn car ('51)	1.25	*5.25*

Perf. 13½

215	A51	20fr gray ('50)	.80	.35
216	A51	25fr violet blue	9.50	.35
217	A52	30fr red brown ('51)	6.50	.50
218	A52	45fr rose lake ('51)	1.60	.55
219	A51	60fr deep grn ('51)	3.25	2.00
220	A51	100fr brown	4.75	2.40
		Nos. 204-220 (17)	49.20	*18.60*
		Set, never hinged	125.00	

Catalogue values for unused stamps in this section, from this point to the end of the section, are for Never Hinged items.

Peter Wust — A54

1950, Apr. 3

221	A54	15fr carmine rose	12.50	7.25

Wust (1884-1940), Catholic philosopher.

St. Peter — A55

1950, June 29 Engr. *Perf. 13*

222	A55	12fr deep green	3.25	*10.00*
223	A55	15fr red brown	4.75	*9.50*
224	A55	25fr blue	8.00	*21.00*
		Nos. 222-224 (3)	16.00	*40.50*

Holy Year, 1950.

Street in Ottweiler — A56

1950, July 10 Photo. *Perf. 13x13½*

225	A56	10fr orange brown	6.00	*8.00*

Founding of Ottweiler, 400th anniv.

Symbols of the Council of Europe A57

1950, Aug. 8 *Perf. 13½*

226	A57	25fr deep blue	35.00	12.00

Issued to commemorate the Saar's admission to the Council of Europe. See No. C12.

Post Rider and Guard — A62

1951, Apr. 29 Engr. *Perf. 13*

227	A62	15fr dk violet brn	8.75	*19.00*

Issued to publicize Stamp Day, 1951.

"Agriculture and Industry" and Fair Emblem — A63

1951, May 12 Photo. *Perf. 13x13½*

228	A63	15fr dk gray grn	2.75	*6.50*

1951 Fair at Saarbrücken.

Tower of Mittelbexbach and Flowers — A67

1951, June 9 Engr. *Perf. 13*

229	A67	15fr dark green	2.75	1.75

Exhibition of Gardens & Flowers, Bexbach, 1951.

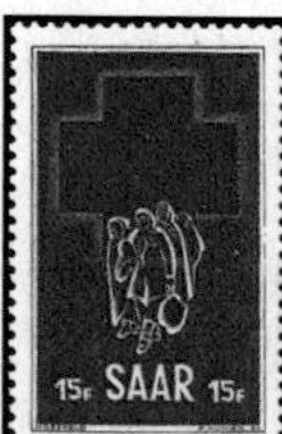

Refugees — A68

1952, May 2 Unwmk. *Perf. 13*

230	A68	15fr bright red	3.50	1.40

Issued to honor the Red Cross.

Globe & Stylized Fair Building — A69

1952, Apr. 26

231	A69	15fr red brown	2.50	1.40

1952 Fair at Saarbrücken.

Mine Shafts A70

Ludwig's Gymnasium A71

General Post Office A72

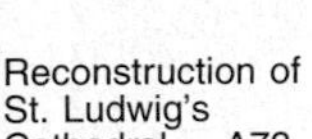

Reconstruction of St. Ludwig's Cathedral — A73

3fr, 18fr, Bridge building. 6fr, Transporter bridge, Mettlach. 30fr, Saar University Library.

1952-55 **Engr.**

232	A70	1fr dk bl grn ('53)	.25	.25
233	A71	2fr purple ('53)	.25	.25
234	A72	3fr dk car rose ('53)	.25	.25
235	A72	5fr dk grn (no inscription)	4.75	.25
236	A72	5fr dk grn ("Hauptpostamt Saarbrücken") ('54)	.25	.25
237	A72	6fr vio brn ('53)	.40	.25
238	A71	10fr brn ol ('53)	.40	.25
239	A72	12fr green ('53)	.75	.25
240	A70	15fr blk brn (no inscription)	8.00	.25
241	A70	15fr blk brn ("Industrie-Landschaft") ('53)	3.50	.25
242	A70	15fr dp car ('55)	.35	.25
243	A72	18fr dk rose brn ('55)	2.75	*4.75*
244	A72	30fr ultra ('53)	.95	*.95*
245	A73	500fr brn car ('53)	16.00	*65.00*
		Nos. 232-245 (14)	38.85	*73.45*

For overprints see Nos. 257-259.

"SM" Monogram — A74

1953, Mar. 23

246	A74	15fr dark ultra	2.10	1.60

1953 Fair at Saarbrücken.

Bavarian and Prussian Postilions A75

1953, May 3

247	A75	15fr deep blue	6.75	*13.00*

Stamp Day.

Fountain and Fair Buildings — A76

1954, Apr. 10

248	A76	15fr deep green	2.10	.95

1954 International Fair at Saarbrücken.

Post Coach and Post Bus of 1920 — A77

1954, May 9 **Engr.**

249	A77	15fr red	9.50	*13.50*

Stamp Day, May 9, 1954.

Madonna and Child, Holbein A78

Designs: 10fr, Sistine Madonna, Raphael. 15fr, Madonna and Child with pear, Durer.

1954, Aug. 14

250	A78	5fr deep carmine	2.40	*3.25*
251	A78	10fr dark green	2.40	*3.25*
252	A78	15fr dp violet bl	3.25	*5.50*
		Nos. 250-252 (3)	8.05	*12.00*

Centenary of the promulgation of the Dogma of the Immaculate Conception.

Cyclist and Flag — A79

1955, Feb. 28 **Photo.** ***Perf. 13x13½***

253	A79	15fr multicolored	.40	*.75*

World championship cross country bicycle race.

Symbols of Industry and Rotary Emblem — A80

1955, Feb. 28

254	A80	15fr orange brown	.40	*.95*

Rotary International, 50th anniversary.

Flags of Participating Nations — A81

1955, Apr. 18 **Photo.** ***Perf. 13x13½***

255	A81	15fr multicolored	.40	*.75*

1955 International Fair at Saarbrücken.

Postman at Illingen A82

Unwmk.

1955, May 8 **Engr.** ***Perf. 13***

256	A82	15fr deep claret	2.00	*2.40*

Issued to publicize Stamp Day, 1955.

Nos. 242-244 Overprinted "VOLKSBEFRAGUNG 1955"

1955, Oct. 22

257	A70	15fr deep carmine	.45	*.70*
258	A72	18fr dk rose brn	.45	*.55*
259	A72	30fr ultra	.65	*.70*
		Nos. 257-259 (3)	1.55	*1.95*

Plebiscite, Oct. 23, 1955.

Symbols of Industry and the Fair — A83

1956, Apr. 14 **Photo.** ***Perf. 11½***

260	A83	15fr dk brn red & yel grn	.40	*.95*

Intl. Fair at Saarbrücken, Apr. 14-29, 1956.

Radio Tower, Saarbrücken — A84

1956, May 6 **Granite Paper**

261	A84	15fr grn & grnsh bl	.40	*.95*

Stamp Day.

German Administration

Arms of Saar — A85

Perf. 13x13½

1957, Jan. 1 **Litho.** **Wmk. 304**

262	A85	15fr brick red & blue	.25	*.40*

Return of the Saar to Germany.

Pres. Theodor Heuss — A86

1957 **Typo.** ***Perf. 14***

Size: 18x22mm

263	A86	1(fr) brt green	.25	.25
264	A86	2(fr) brt violet	.25	.25
265	A86	3(fr) bister brown	.25	.25
266	A86	4(fr) red violet	.35	*.80*
267	A86	5(fr) lt olive green	.25	.25
268	A86	6(fr) vermilion	.25	*.50*
269	A86	10(fr) gray	.25	*.35*
270	A86	12(fr) deep orange	.25	.25
271	A86	15(fr) lt blue green	.25	.25
272	A86	18(fr) carmine rose	.65	*2.40*
273	A86	25(fr) brt lilac	.45	*.80*

Engr.

274	A86	30(fr) pale purple	.45	*.80*
275	A86	45(fr) gray olive	1.10	*2.75*
276	A86	50(fr) violet brn	1.10	*1.25*
277	A86	60(fr) dull rose	1.60	*3.25*
278	A86	70(fr) red orange	2.90	*4.75*
279	A86	80(fr) olive green	.95	*3.75*
280	A86	90(fr) dark gray	2.75	*6.50*

Size: 24x29mm

281	A86	100(fr) dk carmine	2.40	*8.00*
282	A86	200(fr) violet	6.50	*25.00*
		Nos. 263-282 (20)	23.20	*62.40*

See Nos. 289-308.

Steel Industry — A87

Perf. 13x13½

1957, Apr. 20 Litho. Wmk. 304

284 A87 15fr gray & magenta .25 *.40*

The 1957 Fair at Saarbrücken.

Merzig Arms and St. Peter's Church — A88

1957, May 25 ***Perf. 14***

285 A88 15fr blue .25 *.40*

Centenary of the town of Merzig.

"United Europe" — A89

Lithographed; Tree Embossed

Perf. 14x13½

1957, Sept. 16 Unwmk.

286 A89	20fr orange & yel	.40	*1.00*
287 A89	35fr violet & pink	.95	*1.20*

Europa, publicizing a united Europe for peace and prosperity.

Carrier Pigeons — A90

Wmk. 304

1957, Oct. 5 Litho. ***Perf. 14***

288 A90 15fr dp carmine & blk .25 .40

Intl. Letter Writing Week, Oct. 6-12.

Redrawn Type of 1957; "F" added after denomination

1957 Wmk. 304 Litho. ***Perf. 14***

Size: 18x22mm

289 A86	1fr gray green	.25	.25
290 A86	3fr blue	.25	.25
291 A86	5fr olive	.25	.25
292 A86	6fr lt brown	.25	*.50*
293 A86	10fr violet	.25	.25
294 A86	12fr brown org	.25	.25
295 A86	15fr dull green	.40	.25
296 A86	18fr gray	2.00	*4.75*
297 A86	20fr lt olive grn	1.25	*3.25*
298 A86	25fr orange brn	.40	.40
299 A86	30fr rose lilac	.95	.40
300 A86	35fr brown	2.40	*3.25*
301 A86	45fr lt blue grn	2.00	*4.00*
302 A86	50fr dk red brown	.95	*2.00*
303 A86	70fr brt green	4.75	*5.50*
304 A86	80fr chalky blue	2.40	*5.25*
305 A86	90fr rose carmine	5.50	*6.50*

Engr.

Size: 24x29mm

306 A86	100fr orange	5.50	*7.25*
307 A86	200fr brt green	8.75	*25.00*
308 A86	300fr blue	9.50	*29.00*
	Nos. 289-308 (20)	48.25	*98.55*

"Max and Moritz" — A91

Design: 15fr, Wilhelm Busch.

Perf. 13½x13

1958, Jan. 9 Litho. Wmk. 304

309 A91	12fr lt ol grn & blk	.25	*.25*
310 A91	15fr red & black	.25	*.40*

Death of Wilhelm Busch, humorist, 50th anniv.

"Prevent Forest Fires" — A92

1958, Mar. 5 ***Perf. 14***

311 A92 15fr brt red & blk .25 *.40*

Issued to aid in the prevention of forest fires.

Rudolf Diesel A93

1958, Mar. 18 Engr.

312 A93 12fr dk blue grn .25 *.40*

Centenary of the birth of Rudolf Diesel, inventor.

Fair Emblem and City Hall, Saarbrücken A94

1958, Apr. 10 Litho. ***Perf. 14***

313 A94 15fr dull rose .25 *.40*

1958 Fair at Saarbrücken.

View of Homburg A95

1958, June 14 Engr. Wmk. 304

314 A95 15fr gray green .25 *.40*

400th anniversary of Homburg.

Turner Emblem — A96

1958, July 21 Litho. ***Perf. 13½x14***

315 A96 12fr gray, blk & dl grn .25 *.40*

150 years of German Gymnastics and the 1958 Gynastic Festival.

Herman Schulze-Delitzsch A97

1958, Aug. 29 Engr. Wmk. 304

316 A97 12fr yellow green .25 *.40*

150th anniv. of the birth of Schultze-Delitzsch, founder of German trade organizations.

Common Design Types pictured following the introduction.

Europa Issue, 1958

Common Design Type

1958, Sept. 13 Litho.

Size: 24½x30mm

317 CD1	12fr yellow grn & bl	.45	*.80*
318 CD1	30fr lt blue & red	.60	*1.50*

Issued to show the European Postal Union at the service of European integration.

Jakob Fugger — A98

Perf. 13x13½

1959, Mar. 6 Wmk. 304

319 A98 15fr dk red & blk .25 *.40*

500th anniv. of the birth of Jakob Fugger the Rich, businessman and banker.

Old and New City Hall and Burbach Mill — A99

1959, Apr. 1 Engr. ***Perf. 14x13½***

320 A99 15fr light blue .25 *.40*

Greater Saarbrucken, 50th anniversary.

Hands Holding Merchandise A100

1959, Apr. 1 Litho.

321 A100 15fr deep rose .25 *.40*

1959 Fair at Saarbrucken.

Alexander von Humboldt — A101

1959, May 6 Engr. ***Perf. 13½x14***

322 A101 15fr blue .40 *.50*

Cent. of the death of Alexander von Humboldt, naturalist and geographer.

SEMI-POSTAL STAMPS

Red Cross Dog Leading Blind Man — SP1

Maternity Nurse with Child — SP4

Designs: No. B2, Nurse and invalid. No. B3, Children getting drink at spring.

Perf. 13½

1926, Oct. 25 Photo. Unwmk.

B1	SP1	20c + 20c dk ol grn	8.00	*20.00*
B2	SP1	40c + 40c dk brn	8.00	*20.00*
B3	SP1	50c + 50c red org	8.00	*20.00*
B4	SP4	1.50fr + 1.50fr brt bl	19.00	*47.50*
		Nos. B1-B4 (4)	43.00	*107.50*

Nos. B1-B4 Overprinted

1927, Oct. 1

B5	SP1	20c + 20c dk ol grn	12.50	*35.00*
B6	SP1	40c + 40c dk brn	12.50	*35.00*
B7	SP1	50c + 50c red org	11.00	*32.50*
B8	SP4	1.50fr + 1.50fr brt bl	17.50	*72.50*
		Nos. B5-B8 (4)	53.50	*175.00*

"The Blind Beggar" by Dyckmans SP5

"Almsgiving" by Schiestl SP6

"Charity" by Raphael — SP7

1928, Dec. 23 Photo.

B9	SP5	40c (+40c) blk brn	12.00	*72.50*
B10	SP5	50c (+50c) brn rose	12.00	*72.50*
B11	SP5	1fr (+1fr) dl vio	12.00	*72.50*
B12	SP6	1.50fr (+1.50fr) cob bl	12.00	*72.50*
B13	SP6	2fr (+2fr) red brn	14.00	*100.00*
B14	SP6	3fr (+3fr) dk ol grn	14.00	*135.00*
B15	SP7	10fr (+10fr) dk brn	360.00	*4,000.*
		Nos. B9-B15 (7)	436.00	4,525.

"Orphaned" by Kaulbach SP8

"St. Ottilia" by Feuerstein SP9

"Madonna" by Ferruzzio — SP10

1929, Dec. 22

B16	SP8	40c (+15c) ol grn	2.00	*5.50*
B17	SP8	50c (+20c) cop red	4.00	*9.50*
B18	SP8	1fr (+50c) vio brn	4.00	*11.00*
B19	SP9	1.50fr (+75c) Prus bl	4.00	*11.00*
B20	SP9	2fr (+1fr) brn car	4.00	*11.00*
B21	SP9	3fr (+2fr) sl grn	8.00	*25.00*
B22	SP10	10fr (+8fr) blk brn	47.50	*135.00*
		Nos. B16-B22 (7)	73.50	*208.00*

"The Safety-Man" SP11

"The Good Samaritan" SP12

"In the Window" — SP13

1931, Jan. 20

B23	SP11	40c (+15c)	8.00	*24.00*
B24	SP11	60c (+20c)	8.00	*24.00*
B25	SP12	1fr (+50c)	8.00	*47.50*
B26	SP11	1.50fr (+75c)	8.00	*47.50*
B27	SP12	2fr (+1fr)	8.00	*47.50*
B28	SP12	3fr (+2fr)	20.00	*47.50*
B29	SP13	10fr (+10fr)	95.00	*290.00*
		Nos. B23-B29 (7)	155.00	*528.00*

St. Martin of Tours — SP14

Nos. B33-B35, Charity. No. B36, The Widow's Mite.

1931, Dec. 23

B30	SP14	40c (+15c)	12.50	*35.00*
B31	SP14	60c (+20c)	12.50	*35.00*
B32	SP14	1fr (+50c)	16.00	*55.00*
B33	SP14	1.50fr (+75c)	19.00	*55.00*
B34	SP14	2fr (+1fr)	22.50	*55.00*
B35	SP14	3fr (+2fr)	27.50	*95.00*
B36	SP14	5fr (+5fr)	95.00	*325.00*
		Nos. B30-B36 (7)	205.00	*655.00*

Ruins at Kirkel — SP17

Illingen Castle, Kerpen SP23

Designs: 60c, Church at Blie. 1fr, Castle Ottweiler. 1.50fr, Church of St. Michael, Saarbrucken. 2fr, Statue of St. Wendel. 3fr, Church of St. John, Saarbrucken.

1932, Dec. 20

B37	SP17	40c (+15c)	9.50	*22.50*
B38	SP17	60c (+20c)	9.50	*22.50*
B39	SP17	1fr (+50c)	14.00	*40.00*
B40	SP17	1.50fr (+75c)	20.00	*47.50*
B41	SP17	2fr (+1fr)	20.00	*55.00*
B42	SP17	3fr (+2fr)	55.00	*175.00*
B43	SP23	5fr (+5fr)	125.00	*290.00*
		Nos. B37-B43 (7)	253.00	*652.50*

Scene of Neunkirchen Disaster — SP24

1933, June 1

B44	SP24	60c (+ 60c) org red	16.00	20.00
B45	SP24	3fr (+ 3fr) ol grn	35.00	*72.50*
B46	SP24	5fr (+ 5fr) org brn	35.00	*72.50*
		Nos. B44-B46 (3)	86.00	*165.00*

The surtax was for the aid of victims of the explosion at Neunkirchen, Feb. 10.

"Love" — SP25

Designs: 60c, "Anxiety." 1fr, "Peace." 1.50fr, "Solace." 2fr, "Welfare." 3fr, "Truth." 5fr, Figure on Tomb of Duchess Elizabeth of Lorraine

1934, Mar. 15 **Photo.**

B47	SP25	40c (+15c) blk brn	5.50	*16.00*
B48	SP25	60c (+20c) red org	5.50	*16.00*
B49	SP25	1fr (+50c) dl vio	7.25	*20.00*
B50	SP25	1.50fr (+75c) blue	14.00	*35.00*
B51	SP25	2fr (+1fr) car rose	12.50	*35.00*
B52	SP25	3fr (+2fr) ol grn	14.00	*35.00*
B53	SP25	5fr (+5fr) red brn	32.50	*87.50*
		Nos. B47-B53 (7)	91.25	*244.50*

Nos. B47-B53 Overprinted like Nos. 139-154 in Various Colors Reading up

1934, Dec. 1 ***Perf. 13x13½***

B54	SP25	40c (+15c) (Br)	3.50	*14.00*
B55	SP25	60c (+20c) (R)	3.50	*14.00*
B56	SP25	1fr (+50c) (V)	11.00	*25.00*
B57	SP25	1.50fr (+75c) (Bl)	7.25	*25.00*
B58	SP25	2fr (+1fr) (R)	11.00	*35.00*
B59	SP25	3fr (+2fr) (G)	10.00	*32.50*
B60	SP25	5fr (+5fr) (Br)	15.00	*40.00*
		Nos. B54-B60 (7)	61.25	*185.50*

French Protectorate

SP32

Various Flood Scenes — SP33

Inscribed "Hochwasser-Hilfe 1947-48"

Perf. 13½x13, 13x13½

1948, Oct. 12 **Photo.**

B61	SP32	5fr + 5fr dl grn	2.25	*35.00*
B62	SP33	6fr + 4fr dk vio	2.25	*32.50*
B63	SP32	12fr + 8fr red	3.00	*47.50*
B64	SP33	18fr + 12fr bl	4.00	*47.50*
a.		Souv. sheet of 4, #B61-B64, imperf.	325.00	*2,750.*
		Nos. B61-B64,CB1 (5)	22.50	*402.50*
		Set, never hinged	47.50	

The surtax was for flood relief.

Hikers and Ludweiler Hostel SP34

No. B66, Hikers approaching Weisskirchen Hostel.

1949, Jan. 11 ***Perf. 13½x13***

B65	SP34	8fr + 5fr dk brn	1.00	*105.00*
B66	SP34	10fr + 7fr dk grn	1.40	*105.00*
		Set, never hinged	8.00	

The surtax aided youth hostels.

Mare and Foal SP35

Design: No. B68, Jumpers.

1949, Sept. 25 ***Perf. 13½***

B67	SP35	15fr + 5fr brn red	5.50	*32.50*
B68	SP35	25fr + 15fr blue	6.75	*35.00*
		Set, never hinged	27.50	

Day of the Horse, Sept. 25, 1949.

Detail from "Moses Striking the Rock" — SP36

No. B70, "Christ at the Pool of Bethesda." No. B71, "The Sick Child." No. B72, "St. Thomas of Villeneuve." No. B73, Madonna of Blieskastel.

1949, Dec. 20 **Engr.** ***Perf. 13***

B69	SP36	8fr + 2fr indigo	3.50	*40.00*
B70	SP36	12fr + 3fr dk grn	4.00	*47.50*
B71	SP36	15fr + 5fr brn lake	6.00	*80.00*
B72	SP36	25fr + 10fr dp ultra	10.00	*125.00*
B73	SP36	50fr + 20fr choc	15.00	*225.00*
		Nos. B69-B73 (5)	38.50	*517.50*
		Set, never hinged	87.50	

Adolph Kolping — SP37

1950, Apr. 3 **Photo.** ***Perf. 13x13½***

B74	SP37	15fr + 5fr car rose	13.00	*80.00*
		Never hinged	25.00	

Relief for the Hungry — SP38

Engraved and Typographed

1950, Apr. 28 ***Perf. 13***

B75	SP38	25fr + 10fr dk brn car & red	12.50	*65.00*
		Never hinged	27.50	

Stagecoach — SP39

1950, Apr. 22 **Engr.**

B76	SP39	15fr + 5fr brn red & dk brn	30.00	*110.00*
		Never hinged	67.50	

Stamp Day, Apr. 27, 1950. Sold at the exhibition and to advance subscribers.

Lutwinus Seeking Admission to Abbey SP40

Designs: 12fr+3fr, Lutwinus Building Mettlach Abbey. 15fr+5fr, Lutwinus as Abbot. 25fr+10fr, Bishop Lutwinus at Rheims. 50fr+20fr, Aid to the poor and sick.

1950, Nov. 10 **Unwmk.** ***Perf. 13***

B77	SP40	8fr + 2fr dk brn	4.00	*32.50*
B78	SP40	12fr + 3fr dk grn	4.00	*32.50*
B79	SP40	15fr + 5fr red brn	4.25	*52.50*
B80	SP40	25fr + 10fr blue	6.50	*72.50*
B81	SP40	50fr + 20fr brn car	9.00	*125.00*
		Nos. B77-B81 (5)	27.75	*315.00*
		Set, never hinged	60.00	

The surtax was for public assistance.

Mother and Child — SP41

1951, Apr. 28

B82	SP41	25fr + 10fr dk grn & car	10.00	*65.00*
		Never hinged	19.00	

The surtax was for the Red Cross.

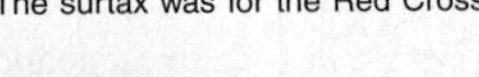

John Calvin and Martin Luther — SP42

1951, Oct. 31

B83	SP42	15fr + 5fr blk brn	1.60	*7.25*
		Never hinged	3.50	

Reformation in Saar, 375th anniv.

"Mother" — SP43

15fr+5fr, "Before the Theater." 18fr+7fr, "Sisters of Charity." 30fr+10fr, "The Good Samaritan." 50fr+ 20fr, "St. Martin and Beggar."

1951, Nov. 3

B84	SP43	12fr + 3fr dk grn	3.00	*19.00*
B85	SP43	15fr + 5fr pur	3.00	*19.00*
B86	SP43	18fr + 7fr dk red	3.25	*19.00*
B87	SP43	30fr + 10fr dp bl	5.25	*35.00*
B88	SP43	50fr + 20fr blk brn	10.50	*72.50*
		Nos. B84-B88 (5)	25.00	*164.50*
		Set, never hinged	52.50	

Catalogue values for unused stamps in this section, from this point to the end of the section, are for Never Hinged items.

Runner with Torch — SP44

30fr+5fr, Hand with olive branch, and globe.

1952, Mar. 29 Unwmk. *Perf. 13*

B89	SP44	15fr + 5fr dp grn	6.00	*12.00*
B90	SP44	30fr + 5fr dp bl	6.00	*13.50*

XV Olympic Games, Helsinki, 1952.

Postrider Delivering Mail SP45

1952, Mar. 30

B91	SP45	30fr + 10fr dark blue	12.00	*27.50*

Stamp Day, Mar. 29, 1952.

Count Stroganoff as a Boy — SP46

Portraits: 18fr+7fr, The Holy Shepherd by Murillo. 30fr+10fr, Portrait of a Boy by Georg Melchior Kraus.

1952, Nov. 3

B92	SP46	15fr + 5fr dk brn	3.25	*11.00*
B93	SP46	18fr + 7fr brn lake	4.75	*14.00*
B94	SP46	30fr + 10fr dp bl	6.50	*16.00*
		Nos. B92-B94 (3)	14.50	*41.00*

The surtax was for child welfare.

Henri Dunant — SP47

1953, May 3 Cross in Red

B95	SP47	15fr + 5fr blk brn	2.75	*7.25*

Clarice Strozzi by Titian — SP48

Children of Rubens SP49

Portrait: 30fr+10fr, Rubens' son.

1953, Nov. 16

B96	SP48	15fr + 5fr purple	3.25	*5.50*
B97	SP49	18fr + 7fr dp claret	3.50	*6.00*
B98	SP48	30fr + 10fr dp ol grn	4.75	*9.50*
		Nos. B96-B98 (3)	11.50	*21.00*

The surtax was for child welfare.

St. Benedict Blessing St. Maurus — SP50

1953, Dec. 18 Litho.

B99	SP50	30fr + 10fr black	2.50	*8.00*

The surtax was for the abbey at Tholey.

Child and Cross — SP51

1954, May 10 Engr.

B100	SP51	15fr + 5fr chocolate	3.25	*7.25*

The surtax was for the Red Cross.

Street Urchin with Melon, Murillo — SP52

Paintings: 10fr+5fr, Maria de Medici, Bronzino. 15fr+7fr, Baron Emil von Maucler, Dietrich.

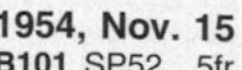

1954, Nov. 15

B101	SP52	5fr + 3fr red	.95	*1.40*
B102	SP52	10fr + 5fr dk grn	.95	*1.40*
B103	SP52	15fr + 7fr purple	.95	*2.00*
		Nos. B101-B103 (3)	2.85	*4.80*

The surtax was for child welfare.

Nurse Holding Baby — SP53

Perf. 13x13½

1955, May 5 Photo. Unwmk.

B104	SP53	15fr + 5fr blk & red	.55	*1.00*

The surtax was for the Red Cross.

Dürer's Mother, Age 63 — SP54

Etchings by Dürer: 10fr+5fr, Praying hands. 15fr+7fr, Old man of Antwerp.

1955, Dec. 10 Engr. *Perf. 13*

B105	SP54	5fr + 3fr dk grn	.50	*1.25*
B106	SP54	10fr + 5fr ol grn	.80	*1.60*
B107	SP54	15fr + 7fr ol bis	1.10	*1.90*
		Nos. B105-B107 (3)	2.40	*4.75*

The surtax was for public assistance.

First Aid Station, Saarbrücken, 1870 — SP55

1956, May 7

B108	SP55	15fr + 5fr dk brn	.40	*.95*

The surtax was for the Red Cross.

"Victor of Benevent" — SP56

1956, July 25 Unwmk. *Perf. 13*

B109	SP56	12fr + 3fr dk yel grn & bl grn	.55	*.75*
B110	SP56	15fr + 5fr brn vio & brn	.55	*.75*

Melbourne Olympics, 11/22-12/8/56.

Winterberg Monument — SP57

1956, Oct. 29

B111	SP57	5fr + 2fr green	.30	*.50*
B112	SP57	12fr + 3fr red lilac	.30	*.50*
B113	SP57	15fr + 5fr brown	.30	*.65*
		Nos. B111-B113 (3)	.90	*1.65*

The surtax was for the rebuilding of monuments.

"La Belle Ferronnière" by da Vinci — SP58

Designs: 10fr + 5fr, "Saskia" by Rembrandt. 15fr+7fr, "Family van Berchem," by Frans Floris. (Detail: Woman playing Spinet.)

1956, Dec. 10

B114	SP58	5fr + 3fr deep blue	.30	*.30*
B115	SP58	10fr + 5fr deep claret	.30	*.50*
B116	SP58	15fr + 7fr dark green	.30	*.80*
		Nos. B114-B116 (3)	.90	*1.60*

The surtax was for charitable works.

German Administration

Miner with Drill — SP59

6fr+4fr, Miner. 15fr+7fr, Miner and conveyor. 30fr+10fr, Miner and coal elevator.

Wmk. 304

1957, Oct. 1 Litho. *Perf. 14*

B117	SP59	6fr + 4fr bis brn & blk	.25	*.25*
B118	SP59	12fr + 6fr blk & yel grn	.25	*.35*
B119	SP59	15fr + 7fr blk & red	.35	*.40*
B120	SP59	30fr + 10fr blk & bl	.40	*.75*
		Nos. B117-B120 (4)	1.25	*1.75*

The surtax was to finance young peoples' study trip to Berlin.

"The Fox who Stole the Goose" — SP60

15fr+7fr, "A Hunter from the Palatinate."

1958, Apr. 1 Wmk. 304 *Perf. 14*

B121	SP60	12fr + 6fr brn red, grn & blk	.25	*.30*
B122	SP60	15fr + 7fr grn, red, blk & gray	.25	*.40*

The surtax was to finance young peoples' study trip to Berlin.

Friedrich Wilhelm Raiffeisen SP61

Dairy Maid SP62

Designs: 15fr+7fr, Girl picking grapes. 30fr+10fr, Farmer with pitchfork.

1958, Oct. 1 Wmk. 304 *Perf. 14*

B123	SP61	6fr + 4fr gldn brn & dk brn	.25	.25
B124	SP62	12fr + 6fr grn, red & yel	.25	*.25*

B125 SP62 15fr + 7fr red, yel & bl .50 *.50*
B126 SP62 30fr + 10fr bl & ocher .65 *.75*
Nos. B123-B126 (4) 1.65 *1.75*

AIR POST STAMPS

Airplane over Saarbrücken — AP1

Perf. 13½

1928, Sept. 19 Unwmk. Photo.

C1 AP1 50c brown red 4.00 4.00
C2 AP1 1fr dark violet 6.50 4.75

For overprints see Nos. C5, C7.

Saarbrücken Airport and Church of St. Arnual — AP2

1932, Apr. 30

C3 AP2 60c orange red 6.50 4.75
C4 AP2 5fr dark brown 45.00 *95.00*

For overprints see Nos. C6, C8.

Nos. C1-C4 Overprinted like Nos. 139-154 in Various Colors

1934, Nov. 1 ***Perf. 13½, 13½x13***

C5 AP1 50c brn red (R) 4.00 *7.25*
C6 AP2 60c org red (O) 3.25 *2.75*
C7 AP1 1fr dk vio (V) 7.25 *9.50*
C8 AP2 5fr dk brn (Br) 9.50 *14.00*
Nos. C5-C8 (4) 24.00 *33.50*

French Protectorate

Shadow of Plane over Saar River AP3

Unwmk.

1948, Apr. 1 Engr. *Perf. 13*

C9 AP3 25fr red 2.00 3.25
C10 AP3 50fr dk Prus grn 1.25 2.40
C11 AP3 200fr rose car 12.00 *35.00*
Nos. C9-C11 (3) 15.25 *40.65*
Set, never hinged 35.00

Symbols of the Council of Europe AP4

1950, Aug. 8 Photo. *Perf. 13½*

C12 AP4 200fr red brown 65.00 *210.00*
Never hinged 140.00

Saar's admission to the Council of Europe.

AIR POST SEMI-POSTAL STAMP

French Protectorate

Flood Scene SPAP1

Perf. 13½x13

1948, Oct. 12 Photo. Unwmk.

CB1 SPAP1 25fr + 25fr sep 11.00 *240.00*
Never hinged 24.00
a. Souvenir sheet of 1 325.00 *2,700.*
Never hinged 800.00

The surtax was for flood relief.

OFFICIAL STAMPS

Regular Issue of 1922-1923 Ovptd. Diagonally in Red or Blue

Perf. 12½x13½, 13½x12½

1922-23 Unwmk.

O1 A19 3c ol grn & straw (R) .95 *35.00*
O2 A20 5c org & blk (R) .40 *.40*
a. Pair, one without overprint 275.00
O3 A21 10c bl grn (R) .40 .35
a. Inverted overprint 32.50
O4 A19 15c dp brn (Bl) .40 .35
a. Pair, one without overprint 290.00
b. Double overprint 65.00
O5 A19 15c org (Bl) ('23) 2.40 .50
O6 A22 20c dk bl & lem (R) .40 .35
a. Inverted overprint 32.50
b. Double overprint 65.00
O7 A22 20c brt bl & straw (R) ('23) 2.40 .50
O8 A22 25c red & yel (Bl) 4.00 1.20
O9 A22 25c mag & straw (Bl) ('23) 2.40 .50
O10 A23 30c car & yel (Bl) .40 .35
a. Inverted overprint 52.50
O11 A24 40c brn & yel (Bl) .55 .35
O12 A25 50c dk bl & straw (R) .55 .35
a. Inverted overprint 32.50
O13 A24 75c dp grn & straw (R) 24.00 27.50
O14 A24 75c blk & straw (R) ('23) 4.75 2.40
O15c A26 1fr brn red (Bl) 12.00 2.40
Nos. O1-O15 (15) 56.00 *72.50*

The set (Type I) exists imperf. Value, hinged $1850. No. O15c (Type II) exists imperf. Value, hinged $325.

Regular Issue of 1927-30 Overprinted in Various Colors

1927-34 ***Perf. 13½***

O16 A31 10c dp brn (Bl) ('34) 2.00 2.40
O17 A32 15c ol blk (Bl) ('34) 2.00 *6.50*
O18 A32 20c brn org (Bk) ('31) 2.00 1.60
O19 A32 25c bluish sl (Bl) 2.40 *6.50*
O20a A31 30c ol grn (Org red) 2.00 .50
O21b A32 40c olive brn (C) 2.00 .35
O22b A32 50c mag (Bl) 4.00 .40
O23 A35 60c red org (Bk) ('30) 1.20 .35
O24b A32 75c brn vio (C) 2.40 .80
O25b A35 1fr vio (RO) 2.40 .40
O26b A26 2fr brn red (Bl) 2.40 .40
Nos. O16-O26 (11) 24.80 *20.20*

The overprint exists in two types: at a 32 degree angle, applied to O20-O22, O24-O26 in 1927; and at a 23-25 degree angle, applied to all values 1929/1934. The less expensive varieties are listed. For detailed listings, see the *Scott Classic Specialized Catalogue.*

The overprint on Nos. O16 and O20 is known only inverted. Nos. O21-O26 exist with double overprint.

French Protectorate

Arms — O1

1949, Oct. 1 Engr. *Perf. 14x13*

O27 O1 10c deep carmine .25 *19.00*
O28 O1 30c blue black .25 *22.50*
O29 O1 1fr Prus green .25 1.00
O30 O1 2fr orange red .55 1.20
O31 O1 5fr blue .75 1.00
O32 O1 10fr black .35 1.00
O33 O1 12fr red violet 3.25 *11.00*
O34 O1 15fr indigo .35 1.00
O35 O1 20fr green .75 1.20
O36 O1 30fr violet rose 3.25 *4.75*
O37 O1 50fr purple .75 *4.00*
O38 O1 100fr red brown 32.50 *300.00*
Nos. O27-O38 (12) 43.25 *367.65*
Set, never hinged 120.00

ST. CHRISTOPHER

sānt 'kris-tə-fər

LOCATION — Island in the West Indies, southeast of Puerto Rico
GOVT. — A Presidency of the former Leeward Islands Colony
AREA — 68 sq. mi.
POP. — 18,578 (estimated)
CAPITAL — Basseterre

Stamps of St. Christopher were discontinued in 1890 and replaced by those of Leeward Islands. For later issues, inscribed "St. Kitts-Nevis" or "St. Christopher-Nevis-Anguilla," see St. Kitts-Nevis.

12 Pence = 1 Shilling

Queen Victoria — A1

Wmk. Crown and C C (1)

1870, Apr. 1 Typo. *Perf. 12½*

1 A1 1p dull rose 95.00 52.50
2 A1 1p lilac rose 82.50 35.00
3 A1 6p green ('71) 140.00 8.75
Nos. 1-3 (3) 317.50 96.25

1875-79 ***Perf. 14***

4 A1 1p lilac rose 80.00 8.00
b. Half used as ½p on cover (2½p rate) *2,500.*
5 A1 2½p red brown ('79) 200.00 *275.00*
6 A1 4p blue ('79) 225.00 16.00
7 A1 6p green 60.00 6.00
a. Horiz. pair, imperf. vert. —
Nos. 4-7 (4) 565.00 305.00

For surcharges see Nos. 18-20.

1882-90 Wmk. Crown and C A (2)

8 A1 ½p green 6.25 3.75
9 A1 1p rose 3.50 2.25
a. Half used as ½p on cover —
10 A1 1p lilac rose 600.00 77.50
a. Diagonal half used as ½p on cover —
11 A1 2½p red brown 200.00 67.50
a. 2½p deep red brown 210.00 72.50
12 A1 2½p ultra ('84) 5.25 2.00
13 A1 4p blue 550.00 27.50
14 A1 4p gray ('84) 1.75 1.10
15 A1 6p olive brn ('90) 95.00 *425.00*
16 A1 1sh violet ('87) 105.00 75.00
a. 1sh bright mauve ('90) 95.00 180.00
Nos. 8-16 (9) 1,566. 681.60

For surcharges see Nos. 17, 21-23.

No. 9 Bisected and Handstamp Surcharged in Black

1885, Mar.

17 A1 ½p on half of 1p 29.00 *45.00*
b. Inverted surcharge 250.00 125.00
c. Unsevered pair 140.00 *140.00*
d. As "c," one surcharge inverted *450.00* *325.00*
e. Double surcharge —

No. 7 Surcharged in Black

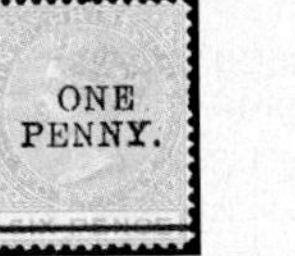

No. 18

No. 19

No. 20

1884-86 Wmk. 1

18 A1 1p on 6p grn ('86) 22.50 *50.00*
a. Inverted surcharge 10,000.
b. Double surcharge 1,650.
19 A1 4p on 6p green 75.00 57.50
a. Period after "PENCE" 75.00 57.50
b. Double surcharge — 3,000.
20 A1 4p on 6p grn ('86) 60.00 105.00
a. Without period after "d" 250.00 325.00
b. Double surcharge *2,750.* *3,000.*
Nos. 18-20 (3) 157.50 212.50

The line through original value on Nos. 18 and 20 was added by hand. Value for No. 18b is for stamp with pen cancellation or with violet handstamp (revenue cancels).

Nos. 8 and 12 Surcharged in Black Like No. 18 or

No. 21

ONE PENNY.

No. 22

1887-88 Wmk. 2

21 A1 1p on ½p green 50.00 *60.00*
22 A1 1p on 2½p ('88) 72.50 72.50
a. Inverted surcharge *27,500.* *11,000.*
23 A1 1p on 2½p, no line over original value ('88) *22,000.* *15,000.*

Nos. 18 and 21 have the same type of One Penny surcharge. The line through the original value on Nos. 21 and 22 were added by hand. No. 23 probably is a sheet that was meant to be No. 22 but was missed when the bars were added.

Antigua No. 18 was used in St. Christopher in 1890. It is canceled "A12" instead of "A02." Values: used $140, on cover $850.

POSTAL FISCAL ISSUES

Nevis Nos. 22 and 28 Overprinted "REVENUE" Horizontally and "Saint Christopher" Diagonally

1883

AR1 A5 1p violet 425.00
AR2 A5 6p green 130.00 *170.00*

Stamps of St. Christopher Ovptd. "SAINT KITTS / NEVIS / REVENUE" in 3 Lines

1885

AR3 A1 1p rose 3.00 *19.00*
AR4 A1 3p violet 17.50 *72.50*
AR5 A1 6p orange brown 20.00 *55.00*
AR6 A1 1sh olive 3.75 *47.50*

Other values exist with the above overprints but were not available for postal purposes.

ST. HELENA

sānt 'he-lə-nə

LOCATION — Island in the Atlantic Ocean, 1,200 miles west of Angola
GOVT. — British Crown Colony
AREA — 47 sq. mi.
POP. — 7,145 (?) (1999 est.)
CAPITAL — Jamestown

12 Pence = 1 Shilling
20 Shillings = 1 Pound
100 Pence = 1 Pound (1971)

Catalogue values for unused stamps in this country are for Never Hinged items, beginning with Scott 128 in the regular postage section, Scott B1 in the semi-postal section and Scott J1 in the postage due section.

Values for unused stamps are for examples with original gum as defined in the catalogue introduction. Very fine examples of Nos. 2-7, 11-39a and 47-47b will have perforations touching the design on one or more sides due to the narrow spacing of the stamps on the plates. Stamps with perfs clear of the design on all four sides are scarce and will command higher prices.

Watermark

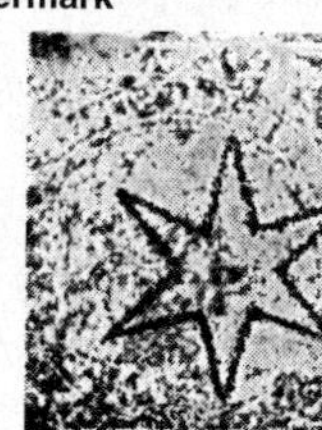

Wmk. 6 — Star

Queen Victoria — A1

1856, Jan. Wmk. 6 Engr. *Imperf.*
1 A1 6p blue 600.00 225.00

For types surcharged see Nos. 8-39, 47.

1861 *Clean-Cut Perf. 14 to 15½*
2 A1 6p blue 2,100. 325.00

1863 *Rough Perf. 14 to 15½*
2B A1 6p blue 525.00 160.00

1871-74 Wmk. 1 *Perf. 12½*
3 A1 6p dull blue 900.00 125.00
4 A1 6p ultra ('73) 500.00 97.50

1879 *Perf. 14x12½*
5 A1 6p gray blue 475.00 60.00

1889 *Perf. 14*
6 A1 6p gray blue 550.00 60.00

1889 Wmk. Crown and C A (2)
7 A1 6p gray 42.50 6.00

Type of 1856 Surcharged

a

b

Long Bar, 16, 17, 18 or 19mm

1863 Wmk. 1 *Imperf.*
8 A1(a) 1p on 6p brn red (srch. 17mm) 150.00 *250.00*
a. Double surcharge 6,750. 4,250.
b. Surcharge omitted *23,000.*
9 A1(a) 1p on 6p brn red (srch. 19mm) 150.00 *275.00*
10 A1(b) 4p on 6p car 600.00 300.00
b. Double surcharge *16,000. 10,000.*

1864-73 *Perf. 12½*
11 A1(a) 1p on 6p brn red 70.00 35.00
a. Double surcharge *12,000.*
12 A1(b) 1p on 6p brn red ('71) 140.00 21.00
a. Blue black surcharge *1,200. 675.00*
13 A1(b) 2p on 6p yel ('73) 160.00 50.00
a. Blue black surcharge *4,800. 2,700.*
14 A1(b) 3p on 6p dk vio ('73) 140.00 72.50
15 A1(b) 4p on 6p car 175.00 60.00
a. Double surcharge *6,750.*
16 A1(b) 1sh on 6p grn (bar 16 to 17mm) 450.00 35.00
a. Double surcharge *24,000.*
17 A1(b) 1sh on 6p dp grn (bar 18mm) ('73) 750.00 20.00
a. Blue black surcharge —

1868 Short Bar, 14 or 15mm
18 A1(a) 1p on 6p brn red 225.00 67.50
a. Imperf., pair *6,000.*
b. Double surcharge —
19 A1(b) 2p on 6p yel 200.00 72.50
a. Imperf 12,000.
20 A1(b) 3p on 6p dk vio 120.00 60.00
a. Double surcharge 7,250.
b. Imperf., pair *2,000.*
c. 3p on 6p pale purple 3,300. 900.00
21 A1(b) 4p on 6p car (words 18mm) 140.00 72.50
a. Double surcharge *6,000.*
b. Imperf, single 14,500.
22 A1(b) 4p on 6p car (words 19mm) 325.00 150.00
a. Words double, 18mm and 19mm *26,000. 11,000.*
b. Imperf. —
c. Surcharge omitted *6,000.*
23 A1(a) 1sh on 6p yel grn 750.00 160.00
a. Double surcharge *19,500.*
b. Pair, one without surcharge *19,500.*
c. Imperf *17,000.*
24 A1(a) 5sh on 6p org 67.50 77.50

1882 *Perf. 14x12½*
25 A1(a) 1p on 6p brown red 90.00 18.00
26 A1(b) 2p on 6p yellow 140.00 60.00
27 A1(b) 3p on 6p violet 350.00 85.00
28 A1(b) 4p on 6p carmine (words 16½mm) 170.00 72.50

1883 *Perf. 14*
29 A1(a) 1p on 6p brown red 120.00 22.50
30 A1(b) 2p on 6p yellow 150.00 37.50
31 A1(a) 1sh on 6p yel grn 25.00 15.00

Long Bar, 18mm

1882 *Perf. 14x12½*
32 A1(b) 1sh on 6p dp grn 900.00 30.00

Short Bar, 14 or 14½mm

1884-94 Wmk. 2 *Perf. 14*
33 A1(b) ½p on 6p grn (words 17mm) 12.00 20.00
a. ½p on 6p emer, blurred print (words 17mm) ('84) 16.00 23.00
b. Double surcharge 1,450. 1,575.
34 A1(b) ½p on 6p grn (words 15mm) ('94) 3.25 3.50
35 A1(a) 1p on 6p red ('87) 5.75 4.50
36 A1(b) 2p on 6p yel ('94) 3.25 9.50
37 A1(b) 3p on 6p dp vio ('87) 9.00 13.50
a. 3p on 6p red violet 6.00 6.00
b. Double surcharge,#37a *11,500. 7,250.*
c. Double surcharge, #37 *11,000.*
38 A1(b) 4p on 6p pale brn (words 16½mm; '90) 37.50 *35.00*
a. 4p on 6p dk brn (words 17mm; '94) 30.00 21.00
b. With thin bar below thick one 850.00

1894 Long Bar, 18mm
39 A1(b) 1sh on 6p yel grn 65.00 30.00
a. Double surcharge *5,750.*

See note after No. 47.

Queen Victoria — A3

1890-97 Typo. *Perf. 14*
40 A3 ½p green ('97) 3.25 7.75
41 A3 1p rose ('96) 20.00 2.40
42 A3 1½p red brn & grn 5.50 12.00
43 A3 2p yellow ('96) 6.00 14.50
44 A3 2½p ultra ('96) 18.00 14.50
45 A3 5p violet ('96) 13.50 37.50
46 A3 10p brown ('96) 29.00 *72.50*
Nos. 40-46 (7) 95.25 *161.15*

Type of 1856 Surcharged

1893 Engr. Wmk. 2
47 A1 2½p on 6p blue 3.75 6.75
a. Double surcharge *24,000.*
b. Double impression *11,500.*

In 1905 remainders of Nos. 34-47 were sold by the postal officials. They are canceled with bars, arranged in the shape of diamonds, in purple ink. No such cancellation was ever used on the island and the stamps so canceled are of slight value. With this cancellation removed, these remainders are sometimes offered as unused. Some have been recanceled with a false dated postmark.

King Edward VII — A5

1902 Typo. Wmk. 2
48 A5 ½p green 2.00 *3.00*
49 A5 1p carmine rose 13.00 .85

Government House — A6

"The Wharf" — A7

1903, June Wmk. 1
50 A6 ½p gray grn & brn 2.40 4.00
51 A7 1p carmine & blk 1.90 .50
52 A6 2p ol grn & blk 12.00 1.50
53 A7 8p brown & blk 26.50 *37.50*
54 A6 1sh org buff & brn 27.50 *47.50*
55 A7 2sh violet & blk 65.00 *100.00*
Nos. 50-55 (6) 135.30 *191.00*

A8

1908, May Wmk. 3
56 A8 2½p ultra 2.00 *1.90*
57 A8 4p black & red, *yel* 7.00 *21.00*
58 A8 6p dull violet 7.75 *17.00*
Nos. 56-58 (3) 16.75 *39.90*

Wmk. 2
60 A8 10sh grn & red, *grn* 275.00 *325.00*

Nos. 57 and 58 exist on both ordinary and chalky paper; No. 56 on ordinary and No. 60 on chalky paper.

Government House — A9

"The Wharf" — A10

1912-16 Ordinary Paper Wmk. 3
61 A9 ½p green & blk 3.25 12.00
62 A10 1p carmine & blk 5.75 2.00
a. 1p scarlet & black ('16) 14.50 *24.00*
63 A10 1½p orange & blk 4.25 9.00
64 A9 2p gray & black 6.75 2.00
65 A10 2½p ultra & blk 4.25 7.25
66 A9 3p vio & blk, *yel* 4.25 6.00
67 A10 8p dull vio & blk 10.00 60.00
68 A9 1sh black, *green* 11.00 42.50
69 A10 2sh ultra & blk, *bl* 50.00 *100.00*
70 A10 3sh violet & blk 75.00 *160.00*
Nos. 61-70 (10) 174.50 *400.75*

See Nos. 75-77.

King Edward VII — A11

Die I

For description of dies I and II see "Dies of British Colonial Stamps" in the front of the catalogue.

1912 Chalky Paper
71 A11 4p black & red, *yel* 15.00 *30.00*
72 A11 6p dull vio & red vio 4.75 *6.00*

A12

1913 Ordinary Paper
73 A12 4p black & red, *yel* 10.00 3.25
74 A12 6p dull vio & red vio 16.00 *35.00*

1922 Wmk. 4
75 A10 1p green 3.25 *55.00*
76 A10 1½p rose red 12.00 *47.50*
77 A9 3p ultra 25.00 *95.00*
Nos. 75-77 (3) 40.25 *197.50*

Badge of the Colony — A13

1922-27 Chalky Paper Wmk. 4
79 A13 ½p blk & gray 4.00 4.00
80 A13 1p grn & blk 3.25 2.00
81 A13 1½p rose red 3.25 *15.00*
82 A13 2p pale gray & gray 4.50 2.40
83 A13 3p ultra 2.40 *4.75*

84 A13 5p red & grn, *emer* 5.00 *6.75*
85 A13 6p red vio & blk 5.50 *9.75*
86 A13 8p vio & blk 4.50 *8.50*
87 A13 1sh dk brn & blk 7.75 *11.00*
88 A13 1sh6p grn & blk, *emer* 18.00 *60.00*
89 A13 2sh ultra & vio, *bl* 22.50 *55.00*
90 A13 2sh6p car & blk, *yel* 17.00 *77.50*
91 A13 5sh grn & blk, *yel* 45.00 *90.00*
92 A13 7sh6p org & blk 140.00 *200.00*
93 A13 10sh ol grn & blk 170.00 *250.00*
94 A13 15sh vio & blk, *bl* 1,100. *2,750.*
Nos. 79-93 (15) 452.65 *796.65*

Nos. 88, 90, and 91 are on ordinary paper.

Wmk. 3

Chalky Paper

95 A13 4p black, *yel* 15.00 *7.25*
96 A13 1sh6p bl grn & blk, *grn* 26.50 *72.50*
97 A13 2sh6p car & blk, *yel* 30.00 *77.50*
98 A13 5sh grn & blk, *yel* 50.00 *120.00*
99 A13 £1 red vio & blk, *red* 475.00 *650.00*
Nos. 95-99 (5) 596.50 *927.25*

Issue dates: ½p, 1½p, 2p, 3p, 4p, 8p, February, 1923; 5p, Nos. 88-91, 1927; others, June 1922.

Centenary Issue

Lot and Lot's Wife — A14

Plantation; Queen Victoria and Kings William IV, Edward VII, George V A15

Map of the Colony A16

Quay, Jamestown A17

View of James Valley — A18

View of Jamestown A19

View of Mundens A20

St. Helena — A21

View of High Knoll — A22

Badge of the Colony A23

Perf. 12

1934, Apr. 23 Engr. Wmk. 4

101 A14 ½p dk vio & blk 1.25 *1.00*
102 A15 1p green & blk .80 *1.00*
103 A16 1½p red & blk 3.00 *4.00*
104 A17 2p orange & blk 3.75 *1.50*
105 A18 3p blue & blk 1.75 *5.50*
106 A19 6p lt blue & blk 4.00 *3.75*
107 A20 1sh dk brn & blk 8.00 *22.50*
108 A21 2sh6p car & blk 50.00 *60.00*
109 A22 5sh choc & blk 100.00 *100.00*
110 A23 10sh red vio & blk 300.00 *350.00*
Nos. 101-110 (10) 472.55 *549.25*
Set, never hinged 725.00

Common Design Types pictured front of this volume.

Silver Jubilee Issue

Common Design Type

1935, May 6 ***Perf. 13½x14***

111 CD301 1½p car & dk blue 1.25 *6.75*
112 CD301 2p gray blk & ultra 2.40 1.25
113 CD301 6p indigo & grn 8.50 4.25
114 CD301 1sh brt vio & ind 19.00 *21.00*
Nos. 111-114 (4) 31.15 *33.25*
Set, never hinged 52.50

Coronation Issue

Common Design Type

1937, May 19

115 CD302 1p deep green .45 *.90*
116 CD302 2p deep orange .40 *.55*
117 CD302 3p bright ultra .60 .60
Nos. 115-117 (3) 1.45 2.05
Set, never hinged 2.00

Badge of the Colony — A24

1938-40 ***Perf. 12½***

118 A24 ½p purple .25 .75
119 A24 1p dp green 7.00 2.40
119A A24 1p org yel ('40) .25 .30
120 A24 1½p carmine .30 .40
121 A24 2p orange .25 .25
122 A24 3p ultra 55.00 18.00
122A A24 3p gray ('40) .35 .30
122B A24 4p ultra ('40) 1.10 .85
123 A24 6p gray blue 1.10 1.40
123A A24 8p olive ('40) 1.75 1.00
124 A24 1sh sepia 1.10 .35
125 A24 2sh6p deep claret 11.00 6.75
126 A24 5sh brown 11.00 12.50
127 A24 10sh violet 11.00 *18.00*
Nos. 118-127 (14) 101.45 63.25
Set, never hinged 160.00

Issue dates: May 12, 1938, July 8, 1940.

See Nos. 136-138.

Catalogue values for unused stamps in this section, from this point to the end of the section, are for Never Hinged items.

Peace Issue

Common Design Type

Perf. 13½x14

1946, Oct. 21 Wmk. 4 Engr.

128 CD303 2p deep orange .30 .40
129 CD303 4p deep blue .35 .30

Silver Wedding Issue

Common Design Types

1948, Oct. 20 Photo. ***Perf. 14x14½***

130 CD304 3p black .30 .30

Perf. 11½x11

Engr.; Name Typo.

131 CD305 10sh blue violet 32.50 *42.50*

UPU Issue

Common Design Types

Engr.; Name Typo. on 4p, 6p

1949, Oct. 10 ***Perf. 13½, 11x11½***

132 CD306 3p rose carmine .30 1.00
133 CD307 4p indigo 3.50 1.60
134 CD308 6p olive .65 *3.25*
135 CD309 1sh slate .40 *1.25*
Nos. 132-135 (4) 4.85 7.10

George VI Type of 1938

1949, Nov. 1 Engr. ***Perf. 12½***

Center in Black

136 A24 1p blue green 1.35 1.60
137 A24 1½p carmine rose 1.35 1.60
138 A24 2p carmine 1.35 1.60
Nos. 136-138 (3) 4.05 4.80

Coronation Issue

Common Design Type

1953, June 2 ***Perf. 13½x13***

139 CD312 3p purple & black 1.25 1.25

Badge of the Colony A25

A26

Designs: 1p, Flax plantation. 1½p, Heart-shaped waterfall. 2p, Lace making. 2½p, Drying flax. 3p, Wire bird. 4p, Flagstaff and barn. 6p, Donkeys carrying flax. 7p, Map. 1sh, Entrance, government offices. 2sh 6p, Cutting flax. 5sh, Jamestown. 10sh, Longwood house.

1953, Aug. 4 ***Perf. 13½x14, 14x13½***

Center and Denomination in Black

140 A25 ½p emerald .45 .40
141 A25 1p dark green .25 .25
142 A26 1½p red violet 3.00 1.50
143 A25 2p rose lake .75 .40
144 A25 2½p red .60 .40
145 A25 3p brown 4.25 .40
146 A25 4p deep blue .60 1.00
147 A25 6p purple .60 .45
148 A25 7p gray .95 1.75
149 A25 1sh dk car rose .60 .95
150 A25 2sh 6p violet 17.00 8.00
151 A25 5sh chocolate 21.00 13.50
152 A25 10sh orange 42.50 30.00
Nos. 140-152 (13) 92.55 59.00

A27

Perf. 11½

1956, Jan. 3 Wmk. 4 Engr.

153 A27 3p dk car rose & blue .25 .25
154 A27 4p redsh brown & blue .25 .25
155 A27 6p purple & blue .30 .30
Nos. 153-155 (3) .80 .80

Cent. of the 1st St. Helena postage stamp.

Arms of East India Company A28

Designs: 6p, Dutton's ship "London" off James Bay. 1sh, Memorial stone from fort built by Governor Dutton.

Perf. 12½x13

1959, May 5 Wmk. 314

156 A28 3p rose & black .25 .25
157 A28 6p gray & yellow green .35 .65
158 A28 1sh orange & black .40 .65
Nos. 156-158 (3) 1.00 1.55

300th anniv. of the landing of Capt. John Dutton on St. Helena and of the 1st settlement.

Cape Canary A29

Elizabeth II A30

Queen and Prince Andrew A31

Designs: 1p, Cunning fish, horiz. 2p, Brittle starfish, horiz. 4½p, Redwood flower. 6p, Red fody (Madagascar weaver). 7p, Trumpetfish, horiz. 10p, Keeled feather starfish, horiz. 1sh, Gumwood flowers. 1sh6p, Fairy tern. 2sh6p, Orange starfish, horiz. 5sh, Night-blooming cereus. 10sh, Deepwater bull's-eye, horiz.

Perf. 11½x12, 12x11½

1961, Dec. 12 Photo. Wmk. 314

159 A29 1p multicolored .40 .25
160 A29 1½p multicolored .50 .25
161 A29 2p gray & red .25 .25
162 A30 3p dk blue, rose & grnsh blue .50 .40
163 A29 4½p slate, brn & grn .65 .60
164 A29 6p cit, brn & dp car 4.00 .75
165 A29 7p vio, blk & red brn .50 .75
166 A29 10p blue & dp cl .90 .75
167 A29 1sh red brn, grn & yel .90 *1.25*
168 A29 1sh6p gray bl & blk 10.00 5.00
169 A29 2sh6p grnsh bl, yel & red 5.00 2.75
170 A29 5sh grn, brn & yel 12.00 4.50
171 A29 10sh gray bl, blk & sal 15.00 10.50

Perf. 14x14½

172 A31 £1 turq blue & choc 22.50 *22.50*
Nos. 159-172 (14) 73.10 50.50

For overprints see Nos. 176-179.

Freedom from Hunger Issue

Common Design Type

1963, Apr. 4 ***Perf. 14x14½***

173 CD314 1sh6p ultra 2.25 1.10

Red Cross Centenary Issue
Common Design Type
Wmk. 314

1963, Sept. 2 Litho. *Perf. 13*
174 CD315 3p black & red .30 .30
175 CD315 1sh6p ultra & red 1.40 2.00

Nos. 159, 162, 164 and 168 Overprinted: "FIRST LOCAL POST / 4th JANUARY 1965"
Perf. 11½x12, 12x11½

1965, Jan. 4 Photo. Wmk. 314
176 A29 1p multicolored .25 .25
177 A30 3p dk bl, rose & grnsh bl .25 .25
178 A29 6p cit, brn & dp car .25 .30
179 A29 1sh6p gray blue & blk .60 .35
Nos. 176-179 (4) 1.35 1.15

Establishment of the 1st internal postal service on the island.

ITU Issue
Common Design Type
Perf. 11x11½

1965, May 17 Litho. Wmk. 314
180 CD317 3p ultra & gray .30 .30
181 CD317 6p red lil & blue grn .50 .30

Intl. Cooperation Year Issue
Common Design Type

1965, Oct. 25 Litho. *Perf. 14½*
182 CD318 1p blue grn & claret .25 .25
183 CD318 6p lt violet & green .70 .25

Churchill Memorial Issue
Common Design Type

1966, Jan. 24 Photo. *Perf. 14*
Design in Black, Gold and Carmine Rose
184 CD319 1p bright blue .25 .25
185 CD319 3p green .35 .35
186 CD319 6p brown .50 .50
187 CD319 1sh6p violet .75 .85
Nos. 184-187 (4) 1.85 1.95

World Cup Soccer Issue
Common Design Type

1966, July 1 Litho. *Perf. 14*
188 CD321 3p multicolored .35 .30
189 CD321 6p multicolored .90 .30

WHO Headquarters Issue
Common Design Type

1966, Sept. 20 Litho. *Perf. 14*
190 CD322 3p multicolored 1.00 .25
191 CD322 1sh6p multicolored 2.50 1.25

UNESCO Anniversary Issue
Common Design Type

1966, Dec. 1 Litho. *Perf. 14*
192 CD323 3p "Education" .75 .50
193 CD323 6p "Science" 1.25 .90
194 CD323 1sh6p "Culture" 3.25 2.25
Nos. 192-194 (3) 5.25 3.65

Badge of St. Helena — A32

Perf. 14½x14

1967, May 5 Photo. Wmk. 314
195 A32 1sh dk grn & multi .25 .25
196 A32 2sh6p blue & multi .40 .40
a. Carmine omitted 1,100.

St. Helena's New Constitution.

The Great Fire of London A33

3p, Three-master Charles. 6p, Boats bringing new settlers to shore. 1sh6p, Settlers at work.

Perf. 13½x13

1967, Sept. 4 Engr. Wmk. 314
197 A33 1p black & carmine .25 .25
198 A33 3p black & vio blue .25 .25
199 A33 6p black & dull violet .25 .25
200 A33 1sh6p black & ol green .25 .25
Nos. 197-200 (4) 1.00 1.00

Tercentenary of the arrival of settlers from London after the Great Fire of Sept. 2-4, 1666.

Maps of Tristan da Cunha and St. Helena A34

Designs: 8p, 2sh3p, Maps of St. Helena and Tristan da Cunha.

Perf. 14x14½

1968, June 4 Photo. Wmk. 314
Maps in Sepia
201 A34 4p dp red lilac .25 .25
202 A34 8p olive .25 .30
203 A34 1sh9p deep ultra .25 *.40*
204 A34 2sh3p Prus blue .25 *.40*
Nos. 201-204 (4) 1.00 1.35

30th anniv. of Tristan da Cunha as a Dependency of St. Helena.

Sir Hudson Lowe A35

1sh6p, 2sh6p, Sir George Bingham.

Perf. 13½x13

1968, Sept. 4 Litho. Wmk. 314
205 A35 3p multicolored .25 .25
206 A35 9p multicolored .25 .25
207 A35 1sh6p multicolored .25 .30
208 A35 2sh6p multicolored .25 .45
Nos. 205-208 (4) 1.00 1.25

Abolition of slavery in St. Helena, 150th anniv.

Road Construction — A36

Designs: 1p, Electricity development. 1½p, Dentist. 2p, Pest control. 3p, Apartment houses in Jamestown. 4p, Pasture and livestock improvement. 6p, School children listening to broadcast. 8p, Country cottages. 10p, New school buildings. 1sh, Reforestation. 1sh6p, Heavy lift crane. 2sh6p, Playing children in Lady Field Children's Home. 5sh, Agricultural training. 10sh, Ward in New General Hospital. £1, Lifeboat "John Dutton."

Wmk. 314

1968, Nov. 4 Litho. *Perf. 13½*
209 A36 ½p multicolored .25 .25
210 A36 1p multicolored .25 .25
211 A36 1½p multicolored .25 .25
212 A36 2p multicolored .25 .25
213 A36 3p multicolored .30 .25
214 A36 4p multicolored .25 .25
215 A36 6p multicolored .30 .25
216 A36 8p multicolored .30 .30
217 A36 10p multicolored .30 .50
218 A36 1sh multicolored .30 .70
219 A36 1sh6p multicolored .60 *3.00*
220 A36 2sh6p multicolored .75 *3.50*
221 A36 5sh multicolored 1.30 *3.50*
222 A36 10sh multicolored 2.75 *5.25*
223 A36 £1 multicolored 7.50 *14.00*
Nos. 209-223 (15) 15.65 32.50

See Nos. 244-256.

Brig Perseverance, 1819 — A37

Ships: 8p, M.S. Dane, 1857. 1sh9p, S.S. Llandovery Castle, 1925. 2sh3p, M.S. Good Hope Castle, 1969.

1969, Apr. 19 Litho. *Perf. 13½*
224 A37 4p violet & multi .25 .25
225 A37 8p ocher & multi .30 .45
226 A37 1sh9p ver & multi .40 .60
227 A37 2sh3p dk blue & multi .45 .75
Nos. 224-227 (4) 1.40 2.05

Issued in recognition of St. Helena's dependence on sea mail.

Surgeon and Officer (Light Company) 20th Foot, 1816 — A38

British Uniforms: 6p, Warrant Officer and Drummer, 53rd Foot, 1815. 1sh8p, Drum Major, 66th Foot, 1816, and Royal Artillery Officer, 1820. 2sh6p, Private 91st Foot and 2nd Corporal, Royal Sappers and Miners, 1832.

Perf. 14x14½

1969, Sept. 3 Litho. Wmk. 314
228 A38 6p red & multi .35 .35
229 A38 8p blue & multi .45 .45
230 A38 1sh8p green & multi .45 .45
231 A38 2sh6p gray & multi .45 .55
Nos. 228-231 (4) 1.70 1.80

Charles Dickens, "The Pickwick Papers" A39

Dickens and: 8p, "Oliver Twist." 1sh6p, "Martin Chuzzlewit." 2sh6p, "Bleak House."

Perf. 13½x13

1970, June 9 Litho. Wmk. 314
232 A39 4p dk brown & multi .35 .25
233 A39 8p slate & multi .45 .25
234 A39 1sh6p multicolored .70 .25
235 A39 2sh6p multicolored 1.50 .35
Nos. 232-235 (4) 3.00 1.10

Charles Dickens (1812-70), English novelist.

Mouth to Mouth Resuscitation — A40

Centenary of British Red Cross Society: 9p, Girl in wheelchair and nurse. 1sh9p, First aid. 2sh3p, British Red Cross Society emblem.

1970, Sept. 15 *Perf. 14½*
236 A40 6p bister, red & blk .25 .25
237 A40 9p lt blue grn, red & blk .25 .25
238 A40 1sh9p gray, red & blk .25 .30
239 A40 2sh3p pale vio, red & blk .30 .45
Nos. 236-239 (4) 1.05 1.25

A41

Regimental Emblems: 4p, Officer's Shako Plate, 20th Foot, 1812-16. 9p, Officer's breast plate, 66th Foot, before 1818. 1sh3p, Officer's full dress shako, 91st Foot, 1816. 2sh11p, Ensign's shako, 53rd Foot, 1815.

Wmk. 314

1970, Nov. 2 Litho. *Perf. 14½*
240 A41 4p multicolored .25 .25
241 A41 9p red & multi .30 .30
242 A41 1sh3p dk gray & multi .50 .50
243 A41 2sh11p dk gray grn & multi .80 .80
Nos. 240-243 (4) 1.85 1.85

See Nos. 263-270, 273-276.

Type of 1968
"P" instead of "d"

1971, Feb. 15 Litho. *Perf. 13½*
244 A36 ½p like #210 .25 .25
245 A36 1p like #211 .25 .25
246 A36 1½p like #212 .25 .25
247 A36 2p like #213 2.00 1.00
a. Perf. 14½ ('75) 1.25 7.50
248 A36 2½p like #214 .30 .30
249 A36 3½p like #215 .45 .35
250 A36 4½p like #216 .45 .45
251 A36 5p like #217 .55 .55
252 A36 7½p like #218 .70 .70
253 A36 10p like #219 .80 .80
254 A36 12½p like #220 1.00 1.00
255 A36 25p like #221 1.60 1.60
256 A36 50p like #222 2.00 2.00
Nos. 244-256 (13) 10.60 9.50

The paper of Nos. 244-256 is thinner than the paper of Nos. 209-223 and No. 223 (£1) has been reprinted in slightly different colors. Value $16.

A42

St. Helena, from Italian Miniature, 1460

Perf. 14x14½

1971, Apr. 5 Litho. Wmk. 314
257 A42 2p violet blue & multi .25 .25
258 A42 5p multicolored .25 .25
259 A42 7½p multicolored .25 .25
260 A42 12½p olive & multi .25 .25
Nos. 257-260 (4) 1.00 1.00

Easter 1971.

Napoleon, after J. L. David, and Tomb in St. Helena A43

34p, Napoleon, by Hippolyte Paul Delaroche.

1971, May 5 *Perf. 13½*
261 A43 2p multicolored .25 .25
262 A43 34p multicolored 1.75 1.25

Sesquicentennial of the death of Napoleon Bonaparte (1769-1821).

Military Type of 1970

1½p, Sword Hilt, Artillery Private, 1815. 4p, Baker rifle, socket bayonet, c. 1816. 6p, Infantry officer's sword hilt, 1822. 22½p, Baker rifle, light sword bayonet, c. 1823.

1971, Nov. 10 ***Perf. 14½***

263 A41 1½p green & multi .50 .25
264 A41 4p gray & multi .75 .35
265 A41 6p purple & multi .75 .45
266 A41 22½p multicolored 1.25 1.25
Nos. 263-266 (4) 3.25 2.30

1972, June 19

Designs: 2p, Royal Sappers and Miners breastplate, 1823. 5p, Infantry sergeant's pike, 1830. 7½p, Royal Artillery officer's breastplate, 1830. 12½p, English military pistol, 1800.

267 A41 2p multicolored .40 .25
268 A41 5p plum & black .55 .45
269 A41 7½p dp blue & multi .75 .55
270 A41 12½p olive & multi .75 1.00
Nos. 267-270 (4) 2.45 2.25

Silver Wedding Issue, 1972

Common Design Type

Design: Queen Elizabeth II, Prince Philip, St. Helena plover and white fairy tern.

1972, Nov. 20 Photo. ***Perf. 14x14½***

271 CD324 2p sl grn & multi .25 *.35*
272 CD324 16p rose brn & multi .45 *.85*

Military Type of 1970

Designs: 2p, Shako, 53rd Foot, 1815. 5p, Band and Drums sword hilt, 1830. 7½p, Royal Sappers and Miners officers' hat, 1830. 12½p, General's sword hilt, 1831.

1973, Sept. 20 Litho. ***Perf. 14½***

273 A41 2p dull brown & multi .50 .55
274 A41 5p multicolored .60 1.00
275 A41 7½p olive grn & multi .85 1.25
276 A41 12½p lilac & multi 1.05 1.50
Nos. 273-276 (4) 3.00 4.30

Princess Anne's Wedding Issue

Common Design Type

1973, Nov. 14 Wmk. 314 ***Perf. 14***

277 CD325 2p multicolored .25 .25
278 CD325 18p multicolored .25 .25

Westminster and Claudine Beached During Storm, 1849 — A45

Designs: 4p, East Indiaman True Briton, 1790. 6p, General Goddard in action off St. Helena, 1795. 22½p, East Indiaman Kent burning in Bay of Biscay, 1825.

Perf. 14½x14

1973, Dec. 17 Litho. Wmk. 314

279 A45 1½p multicolored .25 *.55*
280 A45 4p multicolored .45 *.80*
281 A45 6p multicolored .45 *.80*
282 A45 22½p multicolored 1.75 *2.25*
Nos. 279-282 (4) 2.90 4.40

Tercentenary of the East India Company Charter.

UPU Emblem, Ships A46

Design: 25p, UPU emblem and letters.

1974, Oct. 15 ***Perf. 14½x14***

283 A46 5p blue & multi .25 .25
284 A46 25p red & multi .50 .50
a. Souvenir sheet of 2, #283-284 1.05 *1.50*

Centenary of Universal Postal Union.

Churchill and Blenheim Palace — A47

25p, Churchill, Tower Bridge & Thames.

1974, Nov. 30 Wmk. 373 ***Perf. 14½***

285 A47 5p black & multi .25 .25
286 A47 25p black & multi .50 .60
a. Souvenir sheet of 2, #285-286 1.20 *2.00*

Sir Winston Churchill (1874-1965).

Capt. Cook and Jamestown — A48

5p, Capt. Cook and "Resolution," vert.

Perf. 14x13½, 13½x14

1975, July 14 Litho.

287 A48 5p multicolored .50 .35
288 A48 25p multicolored .90 *1.50*

Return of Capt. James Cook to St. Helena, bicent.

Mellissia Begonifolia — A49

Designs: 5p, Mellissius adumbratus (insect). 12p, Aegialitis St. Helena (bird), horiz. 25p, Scorpaenia mellissii (fish), horiz.

1975, Oct. 20 Wmk. 373 ***Perf. 13***

289 A49 2p gray & multi .25 .25
290 A49 5p gray & multi .25 .25
291 A49 12p gray & multi .60 .75
292 A49 25p gray & multi .65 .90
Nos. 289-292 (4) 1.75 2.15

Centenary of the publication of "St. Helena," by John Charles Melliss.

Pound Note A50

Design: 33p, 5-pound note.

1976, Apr. 15 Wmk. 314 ***Perf. 13½***

293 A50 8p claret & multi .30 .30
294 A50 33p multicolored .80 .80

First issue of St. Helena bank notes.

St. Helena No. 8 — A51

Designs: 8p, St. Helena No. 80, vert. 25p, Freighter Good Hope Castle.

Perf. 13½x14, 14x13½

1976, May 4 Litho. Wmk. 373

295 A51 5p buff, brown & blk .25 .25
296 A51 8p lt grn, grn & blk .25 .25
297 A51 25p multicolored .40 .60
Nos. 295-297 (3) .90 1.10

Festival of stamps 1976. See Tristan da Cunha #208a for souvenir sheet that contains one each of Ascension #214, St. Helena #297 and Tristan da Cunha #208.

High Knoll, by Capt. Barnett A52

Views on St. Helena, lithographs: 3p, Friar Rock, by G. H. Bellasis, 1815. 5p, Column Lot, by Bellasis. 6p, Sandy Bay Valley, by H. Salt, 1809. 8p, View from Castle terrace, by Bellasis. 9p, The Briars, 1815. 10p, Plantation House, by J. Wathen, 1821. 15p, Longwood House, by Wathen, 1821. 18p, St. Paul's Church, by Vincent Brooks. 26p, St. James's Valley, by Capt. Hastings, 1815. 40p, St. Matthew's Church, Longwood, by Brooks. £1, St. Helena and sailing ship, by Bellasis. £2, Sugar Loaf Hill, by Wathen, 1821.

Wmk. 373

1976, Nov. 28 Litho. ***Perf. 14***

No Date Imprint Below Design

Size: 38½x25mm

298 A52 1p multicolored .30 *1.15*
a. Inscribed "1982" .30 *1.15*
299 A52 3p multicolored .35 *1.15*
300 A52 5p multicolored .30 *1.15*
301 A52 6p multicolored .30 *1.15*
302 A52 8p multicolored .30 *1.15*
303 A52 9p multicolored .30 *1.15*
304 A52 10p multicolored .50 *.60*
a. Inscribed "1982" .50 *.60*
305 A52 15p multicolored .45 *.55*
306 A52 18p multicolored .45 *1.50*
307 A52 26p multicolored .65 *1.50*
308 A52 40p multicolored .85 *1.75*

Size: 47½x35mm

Perf. 13½

309 A52 £1 multicolored 2.00 4.00
310 A52 £2 multicolored 3.00 5.50
a. Inscribed "1982" 4.00 *5.50*
Nos. 298-310 (13) 9.75 22.30

Issue dates: 1p, 3p, 5p, 8p, 10p, 18p, 26p, 40p, £1, Sept. 28; others Nov. 23. Nos. 298a, 304a, 310a, 5/10/82.

For overprints see Nos. 376-377.

Royal Party Leaving St. Helena, 1947 — A53

15p, Queen's scepter, dove. 26p, Prince Philip paying homage to the Queen.

1977, Feb. 7 Wmk. 373 ***Perf. 13***

311 A53 8p multicolored .25 .25
312 A53 15p multicolored .25 *.30*
313 A53 26p multicolored .25 *.40*
Nos. 311-313 (3) .75 .95

25th anniv. of the reign of Elizabeth II.

Halley's Comet, from Bayeux Tapestry A54

8p, 17th cent. sextant. 27p, Edmund Halley and Halley's Mount, St. Helena.

1977, Aug. 23 Litho. ***Perf. 14***

314 A54 5p multicolored .45 .45
315 A54 8p multicolored .60 .45
316 A54 27p multicolored 1.25 1.25
Nos. 314-316 (3) 2.30 2.15

Edmund Halley's visit to St. Helena, 300th anniv.

Elizabeth II Coronation Anniversary Issue

Common Design Types

Souvenir Sheet

Unwmk.

1978, June 2 Litho. ***Perf. 15***

317 Sheet of 6 1.75 1.75
a. CD326 25p Black dragon of Ulster .30 .30
b. CD327 25p Elizabeth II .30 .30
c. CD328 25p Sea Lion .30 .30

No. 317 contains 2 se-tenant strips of Nos. 317a-317c, separated by horizontal gutter.

St. Helena, 17th Century Engraving — A55

Designs: 5p, 9p, 15p, Various Chinese porcelain and other utensils salvaged from wreck. 8p, Bronze cannon. 20p, Dutch East Indiaman.

Wmk. 373

1978, Aug. 14 Litho. ***Perf. 14½***

318 A55 3p multicolored .25 .25
319 A55 5p multicolored .25 .25
320 A55 8p multicolored .25 .30
321 A55 9p multicolored .30 .35
322 A55 15p multicolored .40 .50
323 A55 20p multicolored .55 .65
Nos. 318-323 (6) 2.00 2.30

Wreck of the Witte Leeuw, 1613.

"Discovery" A56

Capt. Cook's voyages: 8p, Cook's portable observatory. 12p, Pharnaceum acidum (plant), after sketch by Joseph Banks. 25p, Capt. Cook, after Flaxman/Wedgwood medallion.

1979, Feb. 19 Litho. ***Perf. 11***

324 A56 3p multicolored .25 .25
325 A56 8p multicolored .25 .25
326 A56 12p multicolored .40 .35

Litho.; Embossed

327 A56 25p multicolored .75 .90
Nos. 324-327 (4) 1.65 1.75

St. Helena No. 176 A57

5p, Rowland Hill and his signature. 20p, St. Helena No. 8. 32p, St. Helena No. 49.

1979, Aug. 20 Litho. ***Perf. 14***

328 A57 5p multi, vert. .25 .25
329 A57 8p multi .25 .25
330 A57 20p multi .25 .25
331 A57 32p multi .25 .25
Nos. 328-331 (4) 1.00 1.00

Sir Rowland Hill (1795-1879), originator of penny postage.

Seale's Chart, 1823 — A58

8p, Jamestown & Inclined Plane, 1829. 50p, Inclined Plane (stairs), 1979.

1979, Dec. 10 **Litho.** *Perf. 14*
332 A58 5p multi .25 .25
333 A58 8p multi .25 .25
334 A58 50p multi, vert. .40 .70
Nos. 332-334 (3) .90 1.20

Inclined Plane, 150th anniversary.

Tomb of Napoleon I, 1848 — A59

Empress Eugenie: 8p, Landing at St. Helena. 62p, Visiting Napoleon's tomb.

1980, Feb. 23 **Litho.** *Perf. 14½*
335 A59 5p multicolored .25 .25
336 A59 8p multicolored .25 .25
337 A59 62p multicolored .75 .75
a. Souvenir sheet of 3, #335-337 1.10 1.10
Nos. 335-337 (3) 1.25 1.25

Visit of Empress Eugenie (widow of Napoleon III) to St. Helena, centenary.

East Indiaman, London 1980 Emblem — A60

8p, "Dolphin" postal stone. 47p, Jamestown castle postal stone.

1980, May 6 **Litho.** *Perf. 14½*
338 A60 5p shown .25 .25
339 A60 8p multicolored .25 .25
340 A60 47p multicolored .50 .50
a. Souvenir sheet of 3, #338-340 1.00 1.00
Nos. 338-340 (3) 1.00 1.00

London 1980 Intl. Stamp Exhib., May 6-14.

Queen Mother Elizabeth Birthday Issue
Common Design Type

1980, Aug. 18 **Litho.** *Perf. 14*
341 CD330 24p multicolored .50 .50

The Briars, 1815 A61

30p, Wellington, by Goya, vert.

1980, Nov. 17 **Litho.** *Perf. 14*
342 A61 9p shown .25 .25
343 A61 30p multicolored .45 .45

Duke of Wellington's visit to St. Helena, 175th anniv. Nos. 342-343 issued in sheets of 10 with gutter giving historical background.

Redwood Flower A62

8p, Old father-live-forever. 15p, Gumwood. 27p, Black cabbage.

1981, Jan. 5 *Perf. 13½*
344 A62 5p shown .25 .25
345 A62 8p multicolored .25 .25
346 A62 15p multicolored .25 .25
347 A62 27p multicolored .35 .35
Nos. 344-347 (4) 1.10 1.10

John Thornton's Map of St. Helena, 1700 — A63

5p, Reinel Portolan Chart, 1530. 20p, St. Helena, 1815. 30p, St. Helena, 1817.
24p, Gastaldi's map of Africa, 16th cent.

1981, May 22 **Litho.** *Perf. 14½*
348 A63 5p multicolored .25 .25
349 A63 8p shown .25 .25
350 A63 20p multicolored .30 .30
351 A63 30p multicolored .50 .50
Nos. 348-351 (4) 1.30 1.30

Souvenir Sheet

352 A63 24p multicolored .70 .70

Royal Wedding Issue
Common Design Type
Wmk. 373

1981, July 22 **Litho.** *Perf. 14*
353 CD331 14p Bouquet .25 .25
354 CD331 29p Charles .30 .30
355 CD331 32p Couple .30 .30
Nos. 353-355 (3) .85 .85

Charonia Variegata — A64

1981, Sept. 10 **Litho.** *Perf. 14*
356 A64 7p shown .25 .25
357 A64 10p Cypraea spurca sanctahelenae .25 .25
358 A64 25p Janthina janthina .75 .75
359 A64 53p Pinna rudis 1.25 1.25
Nos. 356-359 (4) 2.50 2.50

Traffic Guards Taking Oath — A65

1981, Nov. 5
360 A65 7p shown .25 .25
361 A65 11p Posting signs .25 .25
362 A65 25p Animal care .40 .40
363 A65 50p Duke of Edinburgh .70 .70
Nos. 360-363 (4) 1.60 1.60

Duke of Edinburgh's Awards, 25th anniv.

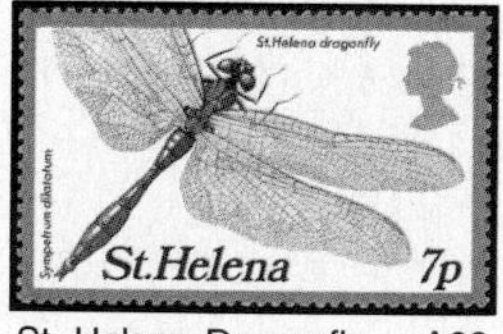

St. Helena Dragonfly — A66

1982, Jan. 4 **Litho.** *Perf. 14½*
364 A66 7p shown .25 .25
365 A66 10p Burchell's beetle .25 .25
366 A66 25p Cockroach wasp .50 .50
367 A66 32p Earwig .65 .65
Nos. 364-367 (4) 1.65 1.65

See Nos. 386-389.

Sesquicentennial of Charles Darwin's Visit — A67

7p, Portrait. 14p, Flagstaff Hill, hammer. 25p, Ring-necked pheasants. 29p, Beagle.

1982, Apr. 19 **Litho.** *Perf. 14*
368 A67 7p multicolored .25 .25
369 A67 14p multicolored .35 .35
370 A67 25p multicolored .60 .60
371 A67 29p multicolored .75 .75
Nos. 368-371 (4) 1.95 1.95

Princess Diana Issue
Common Design Type

1982, July 1 **Litho.** *Perf. 14*
372 CD333 7p Arms .25 .25
373 CD333 11p Honeymoon .50 .50
374 CD333 29p Diana .80 .80
375 CD333 55p Portrait 1.40 1.40
Nos. 372-375 (4) 2.95 2.95

Nos. 305, 307 Overprinted "1st PARTICIPATION / COMMONWEALTH GAMES 1982"

1982, Oct. 25 **Litho.** *Perf. 14*
376 A52 15p multicolored .30 .30
377 A52 26p multicolored .40 .40

Scouting Year A68

1982, Nov. 29
378 A68 3p Baden-Powell, vert. .25 .25
379 A68 11p Campfire .25 .25
380 A68 29p Canon Walcott, vert. .50 .50
381 A68 59p Thompsons Wood camp 1.00 1.00
Nos. 378-381 (4) 2.00 2.00

Coastline from Jamestown — A69

1983, Jan.
382 A69 7p King and Queen Rocks, vert. .25 .25
383 A69 11p Turk's Cap, vert. .25 .25
384 A69 29p shown .50 .50
385 A69 59p Munden's Point 1.00 1.00
Nos. 382-385 (4) 2.00 2.00

Insect Type of 1982

1983, Apr. 22 **Litho.** *Perf. 14½*
386 A66 11p Death's-head hawk-moth .25 .25
387 A66 15p Saldid-shore bug .30 .30
388 A66 29p Click beetle .45 .45
389 A66 59p Weevil 1.00 1.00
Nos. 386-389 (4) 2.00 2.00

Local Fungi A70

11p, Coriolus versicolor, vert. 15p, Pluteus brunneisucus, vert. 29p, Polyporus induratus. 59p, Coprinus angulatus, vert.

Wmk. 373

1983, June 16 **Litho.** *Perf. 14*
390 A70 11p multicolored .40 .40
391 A70 15p multicolored .45 .45
392 A70 29p multicolored .75 .75
393 A70 59p multicolored 1.20 1.20
Nos. 390-393 (4) 2.80 2.80

Local Birds — A71

1983, Sept. 12 **Litho.** *Perf. 14x14½*
394 A71 7p Padda oryzivora .30 .25
395 A71 15p Foudia madagascariensis .60 .50
396 A71 33p Estrilda astrild 1.25 1.00
397 A71 59p Serinus flaviventris 2.00 1.75
Nos. 394-397 (4) 4.15 3.50

Souvenir Sheet

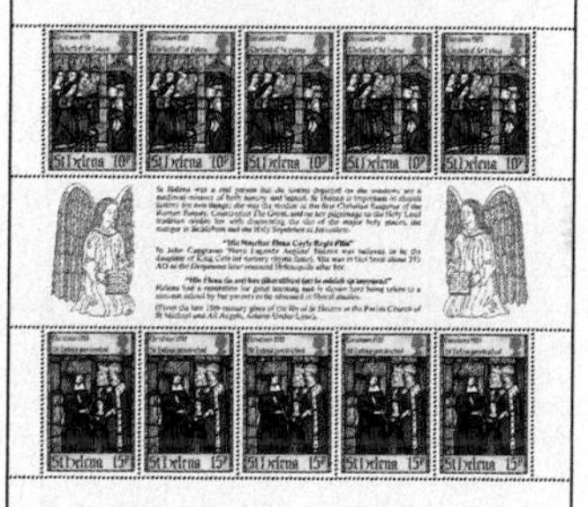

Christmas 1983 — A72

Stained Glass, Parish Church of St. Michael.

1983, Oct. 17 **Litho.** *Perf. 14x13½*
398 A72 Sheet of 10 4.00 3.00
a. 10p multicolored .25 .25
b. 15p multicolored .45 .35

Sheet contains strips of 5 of 10p and 15p with center margin telling St. Helena story.

See Nos. 424-427, 442-445.

150th Anniv. of the Colony — A73

1984, Jan. 3 **Litho.** *Perf. 14*
399 A73 1p No. 101 .25 .25
400 A73 3p No. 102 .25 .25
401 A73 6p No. 103 .25 .25
402 A73 7p No. 104 .25 .25
403 A73 11p No. 105 .25 .25
404 A73 15p No. 106 .30 .30
405 A73 29p No. 107 .50 .50
406 A73 33p No. 109 .55 .55
407 A73 59p No. 110 .85 .85
408 A73 £1 No. 108 1.60 1.60
409 A73 £2 New coat of arms 3.25 3.25
Nos. 399-409 (11) 8.30 8.30

Visit of Prince Andrew A74

1984, Apr. 4 **Litho.** *Perf. 14*
410 A74 11p Andrew, Invincible .25 .25
411 A74 60p Andrew, Herald 1.15 1.15

Lloyd's List Issue
Common Design Type

1984, May *Perf. 14½x14*
412 CD335 10p St. Helena, 1814 .25 .25
413 CD335 18p Solomon's facade .40 .40
414 CD335 25p Lloyd's Coffee House .55 .55
415 CD335 50p Papanui, 1898 1.20 1.20
Nos. 412-415 (4) 2.40 2.40

New Coin Issue A75

1984, July *Perf. 14*
416 A75 10p 2p, Donkey .25 .25
417 A75 15p 5p, Wire bird .35 .35
418 A75 29p 1p, Yellowfin tuna .70 .70
419 A75 50p 10p, Arum lily 1.20 1.20
Nos. 416-419 (4) 2.50 2.50

Centenary of Salvation Army in St. Helena — A76

7p, Secretary Rebecca Fuller, vert. 11p, Meals on Wheels service. 25p, Jamestown SA Hall. 60p, Hymn playing, clock tower, vert.

1984, Sept. **Litho.** **Wmk. 373**
420 A76 7p multicolored .25 .25
421 A76 11p multicolored .25 .25
422 A76 25p multicolored .50 .50
423 A76 60p multicolored 1.25 1.25
Nos. 420-423 (4) 2.25 2.25

Stained Glass Windows Type of 1983

6p, St. Helena visits prisoners. 10p, Betrothal of St. Helena. 15p, Marriage of St. Helena & Constantius. 33p, Birth of Constantine.

1984, Nov. 9
424 A72 6p multicolored .25 .25
425 A72 10p multicolored .30 .30
426 A72 15p multicolored .40 .40
427 A72 33p multicolored .90 .90
Nos. 424-427 (4) 1.85 1.85

Queen Mother 85th Birthday Issue
Common Design Type

11p, Portrait, age 2. 15p, Queen Mother, Elizabeth II. 29p, Attending ballet, Covent Garden. 55p, Holding Prince Henry.

70p, Queen Mother and Ford V8 Pilot.

Perf. 14½x14
1985, June 7 **Litho.** **Wmk. 384**
428 CD336 11p multicolored .25 .25
429 CD336 15p multicolored .30 .30
430 CD336 29p multicolored .60 .60
431 CD336 55p multicolored 1.10 1.10
Nos. 428-431 (4) 2.25 2.25

Souvenir Sheet
432 CD336 70p multicolored 3.00 3.00

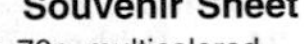

Marine Life — A78

Perf. 13x13½
1985, July 12 **Litho.** **Wmk. 373**
433 A78 7p Rock bullseye .25 .25
434 A78 11p Mackerel .25 .25
435 A78 15p Skipjack tuna .40 .40
436 A78 33p Yellowfin tuna 1.00 1.00
437 A78 50p Stump 1.50 1.50
Nos. 433-437 (5) 3.40 3.40

Audubon Birth Bicent. A79

Portrait of naturalist and his illustrations of American bird species.

1985, Sept. 2 *Perf. 14*
438 A79 11p John Audubon, vert. .30 .30
439 A79 15p Common gallinule .40 .40
440 A79 25p Tropic bird .70 .70
441 A79 60p Noddy tern 1.75 1.75
Nos. 438-441 (4) 3.15 3.15

Stained Glass Windows Type of 1983

Christmas: 7p, St. Helena journeys to the Holy Land. 10p, Zambres slays the bull. 15p, The bull restored to life, conversion of St. Helena. 60p, Resurrection of the corpse, the true cross identified.

1985, Oct. 14
442 A72 7p multicolored .30 .30
443 A72 10p multicolored .35 .35
444 A72 15p multicolored .40 .40
445 A72 60p multicolored 1.50 1.50
Nos. 442-445 (4) 2.55 2.55

Society Banners A80

Designs: 10p, Church Provident Society for Women. 11p, Working Men's Christian Assoc. 25p, Church Benefit Society for Children. 29p, Mechanics & Friendly Benefit Society. 33p, Ancient Order of Foresters.

Perf. 13x13½
1986, Jan. 7 **Wmk. 384**
446 A80 10p multicolored .25 .25
447 A80 11p multicolored .25 .25
448 A80 25p multicolored .60 .60
449 A80 29p multicolored .70 .70
450 A80 33p multicolored .80 .80
Nos. 446-450 (5) 2.60 2.60

Queen Elizabeth II 60th Birthday
Common Design Type

Designs: 10p, Making 21st birthday broadcast, royal tour of South Africa, 1947. 15p, In robes of state, Throne Room, Buckingham Palace, Silver Jubilee, 1977. 20p, Onboard HMS Implacable, en route to South Africa, 1947. 50p, State visit to US, 1976. 65p, Visiting Crown Agents' offices, 1983.

1986, Apr. 21 *Perf. 14½*
451 CD337 10p scarlet, blk & sil .25 .25
452 CD337 15p ultra & multi .30 .30
453 CD337 20p green, blk & sil .35 .35
454 CD337 50p violet & multi .95 .95
455 CD337 65p rose vio & multi 1.20 1.20
Nos. 451-455 (5) 3.05 3.05

For overprints see Nos. 488-492.

Halley's Comet — A81

Designs: 9p, Site of Halley's observatory on St. Helena. 12p, Edmond Halley, astronomer. 20p, Halley's planisphere of the southern stars. 65p, Voyage to St. Helena on the Unity.

1986, May 15 **Wmk. 373** *Perf. 14½*
456 A81 9p multicolored .55 .55
457 A81 12p multicolored .65 .65
458 A81 20p multicolored .90 .90
459 A81 65p multicolored 2.00 2.00
Nos. 456-459 (4) 4.10 4.10

Royal Wedding Issue, 1986
Common Design Type

Designs: 10p, Informal portrait. 40p, Andrew in dress uniform at parade.

Wmk. 384
1986, July 23 **Litho.** *Perf. 14*
460 CD338 10p multicolored .25 .25
461 CD338 40p multicolored .80 .80

Explorers and Ships — A82

Designs: 1p, James Ross (1800-62), Erebus. 3p, Robert FitzRoy (1805-65), Beagle. 5p, Adam Johann von Krusenstern (1770-1846), Nadezhda, Russia. 9p, William Bligh (1754-1817), Resolution. 10p, Otto von Kotzebue (1786-1846), Rurik, Germany. 12p, Philip Carteret (1639-82), Swallow. 15p, Thomas Cavendish (c.1560-92), Desire. 20p, Louis-Antoine de Bougainville (1729-1811), La Boudeuse, France. 25p, Fyodor Petrovitch Litke (1797-1882), Seniavin, Russia. 40p, Louis Isidore Duperrey (1786-1865), La Coquille, France. 60p, John Byron (1723-86), Dolphin. £1, James Cook, Endeavour. £2, Jules Dumont d'Urville (1790-1842), L'Astrolabe, France.

Wmk. 384
1986, Sept. 22 **Litho.** *Perf. 14½*
462 A82 1p red brown .40 1.50
463 A82 3p bright ultra .40 1.50
464 A82 5p olive green .40 1.50
465 A82 9p deep claret .50 1.50
466 A82 10p sepia .55 1.50
467 A82 12p brt blue green .55 1.50
468 A82 15p brown lake .65 1.50
469 A82 20p sapphire .85 1.50
470 A82 25p red brown .90 1.50
471 A82 40p myrtle green 1.40 2.00
472 A82 60p brown 1.75 2.75
473 A82 £1 Prussian blue 2.75 4.50
474 A82 £2 bright violet 5.50 8.00
Nos. 462-474 (13) 16.60 30.75

Ships of Royal Visitors A83

Portraits and vessels: 9p, Prince Edward, HMS Repulse, 1925. 13p, King George VI, HMS Vanguard, 1947. 38p, Prince Philip, HMY Britannia, 1957. 45p, Prince Andrew, HMS Herald, 1984.

1987, Feb. 16 **Wmk. 373** *Perf. 14*
475 A83 9p multicolored 1.50 1.25
476 A83 13p multicolored 2.25 1.50
477 A83 38p multicolored 3.50 3.50
478 A83 45p multicolored 4.00 4.00
Nos. 475-478 (4) 11.25 10.25

Rare Plants — A84

1987, Aug. 3 *Perf. 14½x14*
479 A84 9p St. Helena tea plant .70 .70
480 A84 13p Baby's toes 1.10 1.10
481 A84 38p Salad plant 2.10 2.10
482 A84 45p Scrubwood 2.60 2.60
Nos. 479-482 (4) 6.50 6.50

Marine Mammals A85

Wmk. 384
1987, Oct. 24 **Litho.** *Perf. 14*
483 A85 9p Lesser rorqual 1.50 1.50
484 A85 13p Risso's dolphin 1.60 1.60
485 A85 45p Sperm whale 4.00 4.00
486 A85 60p Euphrosyne dolphin 5.75 5.75
Nos. 483-486 (4) 12.85 12.85

Souvenir Sheet
487 A85 75p Humpback whale 10.50 10.50

Nos. 451-455 Ovptd. "40TH WEDDING ANNIVERSARY" in Silver

Wmk. 384
1987, Dec. 9 **Litho.** *Perf. 14½*
488 CD337 10p scarlet, blk & sil .25 .25
489 CD337 15p ultra & multi .25 .25
490 CD337 20p green, blk & sil .40 .40
491 CD337 50p violet & multi .85 .85
492 CD337 65p rose vio & multi 1.10 1.10
Nos. 488-492 (5) 2.85 2.85

Australia Bicentennial A86

Ships and signatures: 9p, HMS Defence, 1691, and William Dampier. 13p, HMS Resolution, 1775, and James Cook. 45p, HMS Providence, 1792, and William Bligh. 60p, HMS Beagle, 1836, and Charles Darwin.

Wmk. 384
1988, Mar. 1 **Litho.** *Perf. 14½*
493 A86 9p multicolored 2.25 2.00
494 A86 13p multicolored 3.00 3.00
495 A86 45p multicolored 4.75 4.75
496 A86 60p multicolored 6.25 6.25
Nos. 493-496 (4) 16.25 16.00

Christmas — A87

Religious paintings by unknown artists: 5p, The Holy Family with Child. 20p, Madonna. 38p, The Holy Family with St. John. 60p, The Holy Virgin with the Child.

Wmk. 373
1988, Oct. 11 **Litho.** *Perf. 14*
497 A87 5p multicolored .25 .25
498 A87 20p multicolored .65 .65
499 A87 38p multicolored 1.20 1.20
500 A87 60p multicolored 1.75 1.75
Nos. 497-500 (4) 3.85 3.85

Lloyds of London, 300th Anniv.
Common Design Type

Designs: 9p, Underwriting room, 1886. 20p, Edinburgh Castle. 45p, Bosun Bird. 60p, Spangereid on fire off St. Helena, 1920.

Wmk. 384
1988, Nov. 1 **Litho.** *Perf. 14*
501 CD341 9p multi .45 .40
502 CD341 20p multi, horiz. 2.00 1.25
503 CD341 45p multi, horiz. 2.75 2.50
504 CD341 60p multi 3.50 3.00
Nos. 501-504 (4) 8.70 7.15

Rare Plants — A88

1989, Jan. 6 *Perf. 14*
505 A88 9p Ebony .45 .45
506 A88 20p St. Helena lobelia 1.10 1.10
507 A88 45p Large bellflower 2.00 2.00
508 A88 60p She cabbage tree 2.60 2.60
Nos. 505-508 (4) 6.15 6.15

Souvenir Sheet

Napoleonic Sites on St. Helena — A176

No. 947: a, 90p, Longwood House in 1821. b, £1, Napoleon's tomb. c, £1.25, Longwood House in 2008.

Perf. 13¼x13¾

2008, May 7 Litho. Wmk. 373

947 A176 Sheet of 3, #a-c 15.00 15.00

Bird Type of 2007 Without BirdLife International Emblem

Designs: 15p, Brown boobies. 35p, Brown noddies. 40p, Fairy terns. £1.25, Red-billed tropicbirds.

2008, July 17 ***Perf. 12½x13***

948-951 A172 Set of 4 10.00 10.00

Fish A177

Designs: 5p, Deepwater bullseye. 10p, Five finger. 15p, Deepwater greenfish. 20p, Hardback soldier. 25p, Deepwater gurnard. 35p, Red mullet. 40p, Softback soldier. 50p, Rock bullseye. 80p, Gurnard. £1, Cunningfish. £2, Hogfish. £5, Marmalade razorfish.

2008, Aug. 19 ***Perf. 13¾***

952	A177	5p multi	.30	.30
953	A177	10p multi	.45	.45
954	A177	15p multi	.65	.65
955	A177	20p multi	.90	.90
956	A177	25p multi	1.05	1.05
957	A177	35p multi	1.60	1.60
958	A177	40p multi	1.75	1.75
959	A177	50p multi	2.10	2.10
960	A177	80p multi	3.50	3.50
961	A177	£1 multi	4.50	4.50
962	A177	£2 multi	8.50	8.50
963	A177	£5 multi	21.00	21.00
a.		Sheet of 12, #952-963	47.50	47.50
		Nos. 952-963 (12)	46.30	46.30

Flag — A178

2008, Aug. 19 Unwmk. ***Die Cut***

Booklet Stamp

Self-Adhesive

964 A178 35p multi 2.00 2.00

a. Booklet pane of 12 24.00

Christmas A179

Flowers: 15p, African lily. 25p, Christmas cactus. 35p, Honeysuckle. 40p, St. John's lily. £1, Crucifix orchid.

Perf. 13x12½

2008, Sept. 1 Litho. Wmk. 373

965-969 A179 Set of 5 8.25 8.25

End of World War I, 90th Anniv. — A180

Poetry about World War I: 10p, "The Soldier," by Rupert Brooke. 15p, "Aftermath," by Siegfried Sassoon. 25p, "Anthem for Doomed Youth," by Wilfred Owen. 35p, "For the Fallen," by Laurence Binyon. 40p, "In Flanders Fields," by John McCrae. 50p, "In Memoriam," by Edward Thomas.

£2, Cenotaph, St. Helena.

2008, Sept. 16 Wmk. 406 ***Perf. 14***

970-975 A180 Set of 6 7.50 7.50

Souvenir Sheet

976 A180 £2 multi 8.50 8.50

Miniature Sheet

Ascension to Throne of King Henry VIII (1491-1547), 500th Anniv. — A181

No. 977: a, Henry VIII holding scroll. b, Catherine of Aragon (1485-1536), first wife. c, Anne Boleyn (c. 1507-36), second wife. d, Jane Seymour (c. 1509-37), third wife. e, Henry VIII, diff. f, Ship Mary Rose. g, Anne of Cleves (1515-57), fourth wife. h, Catherine Howard (c. 1520-42), fifth wife. i, Catherine Parr (1512-48), sixth wife. j, Hampton Court.

Wmk. 373

2009, Jan. 5 Litho. ***Perf. 14***

977 A181 50p Sheet of 10, #a-j 17.50 17.50

Naval Aviation, Cent. A182

Designs: 15p, Westland Sea King helicopter and Royal Navy ship. 35p, Fairey Swordfish and Royal Navy ships. 40p, BAe Harrier. 50p, Blackburn Buccaneer and Royal Navy ship.

£1.50, Lieutenant E. L. Gerrard in airplane at Central Flying School, 1913.

Wmk. 406

2009, Apr. 17 Litho. ***Perf. 14***

978-981 A182 Set of 4 7.25 7.25

Souvenir Sheet

982 A182 £1.50 multi 7.50 7.50

Nos. 978-981 each were printed in sheets of 8 + central label.

Souvenir Sheet

Donation of the Briars Pavilion, 50th Anniv. — A183

No. 983: a, 90p, Briars Pavilion, c. 1857. b, £1, Napoleon Bonaparte and Betsy Balcombe. c, £1.25, Briars Pavilion, 2008.

2009, May 26 Litho. ***Perf. 13¼x13¾***

983 A183 Sheet of 3, #a-c 13.00 13.00

Space Exploration A184

Designs: 15p, Deep Space Tracking Station, Ascension Island. 35p, Early rocketry experiment by Dr. Robert Goddard. 40p, Launch of Apollo 11. 90p, Space Shuttle Discovery landing. No. 988, £1.20, Astronauts working on International Space Station.

No. 989, £1.20, Astronauts on Moon, painting by Capt. Alan Bean, vert.

Wmk. 406

2009, July 20 Litho. ***Perf. 13¼***

984-988 A184 Set of 5 11.50 11.50

Souvenir Sheet

Perf. 13x13½

989 A184 £1.20 multi 5.00 5.00

First man on the Moon, 40th anniv. No. 989 contains one 40x60mm stamp.

Christmas — A185

Designs: 15p, Christmas parade. 25p, Christmas pageant in church. 40p, Church at night. £1, Christmas lights on buildings.

Wmk. 406

2009, Sept. 1 Litho. ***Perf. 14***

990-993 A185 Set of 4 7.00 7.00

Anglican Diocese of St. Helena, 150th Anniv. — A186

Designs: 15p, St. Paul's Cathedral. 35p, St. Matthew's Church. 40p, St. James' Church. £1, Piers Calveley Claughton (1814-84), first bishop of St. Helena.

2009, Oct. 1

994-997 A186 Set of 4 7.00 7.00

Miniature Sheet

History of 17th Century England — A187

No. 998: a, King Charles I (1600-49). b, King Charles II (1630-85). c, Prince Rupert (1619-82). d, Oliver Cromwell (1599-1658). e, Richard Cromwell (1626-1712). f, King Charles I arrests members of Parliament. g, New Model Army. h, Execution of King Charles I. i, Dissolution of Parliament. j, Coronation of King Charles II.

Wmk. 406

2010, Jan. 29 Litho. ***Perf. 14***

998 A187 50p Sheet of 10, #a-j 19.00 19.00

Battle of Britain, 70th Anniv. — A188

Designs: 15p, Children in bunker. 25p, Fire fighters. 35p, Milkman delivering through rubble. 40p, Bus in bomb crater. 90p, Contrails. £1, Lookout.

£1.50, Sir Douglas Bader (1910-82), flying ace.

Wmk. 406

2010, Mar. 18 Litho. ***Perf. 13***

999-1004 A188 Set of 6 12.00 12.00

Souvenir Sheet

1005 A188 £1.50 black & gray 6.00 6.00

Nos. 999-1004 each were printed in sheets of 6.

Souvenir Sheet

Great Britain No. 154 — A189

Wmk. 406

2010, May 8 Litho. *Perf. 14*
1006 A189 £1.50 multi 6.00 6.00

Reign of King George V, cent. London 2010 Festival of Stamps.

World of Soccer — A190

Designs: No. 1007, 40p, Soccer player and ball. No. 1008, 40p, Map of Africa and St. Helena. No. 1009, 40p, Two soccer players and ball.

2010, May 14 *Perf. 14x14¾*
1007-1009 A190 Set of 3 5.00 5.00
1009a Souvenir sheet of 3, #1007-1009 5.00 5.00

Girl Guides, Cent. A191

Designs: 15p, Rainbows. 25p, Brownies. 40p, Girl Guides. 90p, Lord Robert Baden-Powell and wife, Olave.

2010, Aug. 23 *Perf. 14*
1010-1013 A191 Set of 4 7.00 7.00

Christmas A192

Sites and flowers: 15p, Jacob's Ladder, Crucifix orchid. 25p, Diana's Peak, St. John's lily. 40p, High Knoll Fort, Agapanthus. £1, Heart-shaped Waterfall, Honeysuckle.

2010, Oct. 25 *Perf. 13¾*
1014-1017 A192 Set of 4 7.50 7.50

RMS St. Helena, 20th Anniv. — A193

Designs: 15p, Ship in 2010. 35p, Arrival on maiden voyage in St. Helena. 40p, Launch of ship, 1990. 90p, Captain's table.

2010, Nov. 19 *Perf. 14x14¾*
1018-1021 A193 Set of 4 7.50 7.50

Service of Queen Elizabeth II and Prince Philip — A194

Designs: 15p, Queen Elizabeth II. 25p, Queen and Prince Philip. 35p, Queen and Prince Philip, diff. No. 1025, 40p, Queen and Prince Philip, Queen wearing yellow dress. No. 1026, 40p, Queen and Prince Philip, Queen wearing blue hat. 90p, Prince Philip. £1.50, Queen and Prince Philip, diff.

Perf. 13¼

2011, Mar. 1 Litho. Unwmk.
1022-1027 A194 Set of 6 9.50 9.50
1027a Sheet of 6, #1022-1027, + 3 labels 9.50 9.50

Souvenir Sheet

1028 A194 £1.50 multi 6.00 6.00

Souvenir Sheet

Wedding of Prince William and Catherine Middleton — A195

Perf. 14¾x14¼

2011, Apr. 29 Litho. Wmk. 406
1029 A195 £3 multi 11.50 11.50

Photographs of Wedding of Prince William and Catherine Middleton — A196

Designs: 15p, Bride and her sister, Pippa. 35p, Couple in coach waving. 40p, Couple standing, holding hands, vert. 60p, Couple standing and waving, vert. £1, Couple kissing, vert.

2011, Sept. 1 *Perf. 14¼x14, 14x14¼*
1030-1034 A196 Set of 5 9.00 9.00

Worldwide Fund for Nature (WWF) — A197

Island hogfish: 35p, Male. 40p, Juvenile. 50p, Immature female. £1.20, £1.50, Male near rocks.

2011, Oct. 31 *Perf. 14¼x14*
1035-1038 A197 Set of 4 8.00 8.00
1038a Sheet of 16, 4 each #1035-1038 32.00 32.00

Souvenir Sheet

1039 A197 £1.50 multi 5.00 5.00

Christmas A198

Royal Fleet auxiliary ships: 35p, RFA Gold Rover. 50p, RFA Black Rover. 60p, RFA Lyme Bay. £1.20, RFA Darkdale.

2011, Nov. 14 *Perf. 13¾*
1040-1043 A198 Set of 4 8.50 8.50

Commonwealth Parliamentary Association, Cent. — A199

Centenary emblem and: No. 1044, 50p, Court House, Jamestown. No. 1045, 50p, Royal Charter. No. 1046, 50p, Commonwealth Parliamentary Association Headquarters, London.

2011, Nov. 28 *Perf. 13¾x13¼*
1044-1046 A199 Set of 3 4.75 4.75
1046a Souvenir sheet of 3, #1044-1046 4.75 4.75

Reign of Queen Elizabeth II, 60th Anniv. — A200

Various photographs of Queen Elizabeth II: 20p, 35p, 40p, 50p, 60p, £1.
£1.50, Queen Elizabeth II wearing tiara.

2012, Feb. 6 *Perf. 13½*
1047-1052 A200 Set of 6 9.75 9.75
1052a Souvenir sheet, #1047-1052 + 3 labels 9.75 9.75

Souvenir Sheet

1053 A200 £1.50 multi 4.75 4.75

Children's Art — A201

Various children's drawings commemorating the 60th anniversary of the reign of Queen Elizabeth II: 20p, 35p, 50p, £1.

2012, June 12 Wmk. 406 *Perf. 14*
1054-1057 A201 Set of 4 6.50 6.50

Falkland Islands War, 30th Anniv. A202

1982 photographs of RMS St Helena: 20p, Crew. 35p, At Grytviken. 40p, At Ascension Island. 50p, At Grytviken, diff. £1, Under escort.

2012, June 26
1058-1062 A202 Set of 5 7.75 7.75

Christmas A203

Titles of Chirstmas hymns: 20p, O Little Town of Bethlehem. 35p, While Shepherds Watched. 50p, Away in a Manger. £1, Silent Night, Holy Night.

Perf. 13¼x13¾

2012, Nov. 5 Wmk. 406
1063-1066 A203 Set of 4 6.75 6.75

Items Commemorating British Coronations — A204

Coronation of Queen Elizabeth, 60th Anniv. — A205

Various items commemorating the coronation of: 20p, Queen Victoria. 35p, King Edward VII. 40p, King George V. 50p, King George VI. £1, Queen Elizabeth II.

2013, Feb. 6 *Perf. 14*
1067-1071 A204 Set of 5 7.50 7.50

Souvenir Sheet

Perf. 14¾x14

1072 A205 £2 multi 6.00 6.00

Lady Margaret Thatcher (1925-2013), British Prime Minister A206

Various photographs: 40p, 50p, 60p, £1.

2013, Aug. 8 *Perf. 13¾*
1073-1076 A206 Set of 4 8.00 8.00
1076a Souvenir sheet of 4, #1073-1076 8.00 8.00

Birth of Prince George of Cambridge A207

Designs: 25p, Duke of Cambridge holding Prince George. 40p, Duchess of Cambridge holding Prince George. 60p, Prince George. £1, Duke and Duchess of Cambridge, Prince George.

Perf. 13½x13¼

2013, Nov. 6 Litho. Wmk. 406
1077-1080 A207 Set of 4 7.25 7.25

Airport Project A208

Designs: 25p, NP Glory 4 docked at Rupert's. 40p, Haul Road. 50p, Bradley's Camp. 60p, Dry Gut.
£2, Plant machinery.

Wmk. 406

2014, June 27 Litho. *Perf. 14*
1081-1084 A208 Set of 4 6.00 6.00

Souvenir Sheet

1085 A208 £2 multi 7.00 7.00

Miniature Sheet

Brownies, Cent. — A209

No. 1086: a, 25p, Emblem (48x54mm). b, 40p, Jamestown Brownies, 1970 (48x27mm). c, 60p, Pat Benjamin presenting bouquet to Princess Margaret (24x54mm). d, 70p, Brownie pack, 1960 (24x54mm). e, £1, Brownie pack Thinking Day, 2014 (48x27mm).

Perf. 14x14¾

2014, Oct. 15 Litho. Wmk. 406

1086 A209	Sheet of 5, #a-e	9.50	9.50

Christmas A210

Designs: 25p, Whale shark. 30p, Sea slug. 40p, St. Helena Gregory. 50p, Cunning fish. 60p, Silver eel. £1, Orange cup coral.

Wmk. 406

2014, Oct. 15 Litho. *Perf. 14*

1087-1092 A210	Set of 6	9.75	9.75

St. Helena's Participation in the Commonwealth Games — A211

Designs: 30p, Team members at Brisbane Commonwealth Games, 1982. 50p, RMS St. Helena crew holding Queen's baton, 2014. 60p, St. Helena National Amateur Sports Association, 2014. £1, Team members at Glasgow Commonwealth Games, 2014.

Wmk. 406

2014, Oct. 20 Litho. *Perf. 14*

1093-1096 A211	Set of 4	7.75	7.75

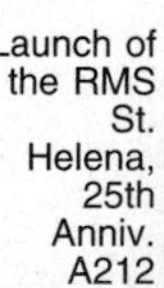

Launch of the RMS St. Helena, 25th Anniv. A212

Designs: 25p, Laying of the keel. 30p, Hull construction. 50p, Hull on launch day. 60p, Sea trials.

Wmk. 406

2014, Oct. 31 Litho. *Perf. 14*

1097-1099 A212	Set of 3	3.50	3.50

Souvenir Sheet

1100 A212	60p multi	1.90	1.90

Paintings of Jamestown Main Street Buildings, by Andy Crowe A213

Various buildings. 50p, 80p are 20x36mm.

Wmk. 406

2015, May 21 Litho. *Perf. 13¼*

1101	Horiz. strip of 4	7.25	7.25
a.	A213 40p multi	1.25	1.25
b.	A213 50p multi	1.60	1.60
c.	A213 60p multi	1.90	1.90
d.	A213 80p multi	2.50	2.50

Christmas — A214

Santa Claus: 25p, In sleigh. 40p, Holding Christmas tree and bag of gifts. 50p, By Christmas tree. 60p, On chimney. £1, Holding Christmas pudding.

Wmk. 406

2015, Nov. 21 Litho. *Perf. 14*

1102-1106 A214	Set of 5	8.25	8.25

Airport Project A215

Designs: 25p, Students burying time capsule. 40p, Final rock blast. 50p, Permanent wharf, Rupert's. 60p, Control tower construction.
£2, Runway construction.

Wmk. 406

2016, Jan. 1 Litho. *Perf. 14*

1107-1110 A215	Set of 4	5.25	5.25

Souvenir Sheet

1111 A215	£2 multi	6.00	6.00

SEMI-POSTAL STAMPS

Catalogue values for unused stamps in this section are for Never Hinged items.

Tristan da Cunha Nos. 46, 49-51 Ovptd. "ST. HELENA / Tristan Relief" and Srchd. with New Value and "+"

Perf. 12½x13

1961, Oct. 12 Wmk. 314 Engr.

B1 A3	2½c + 3p	*1,500.*	*600.00*
B2 A3	5c + 6p	*1,600.*	*650.00*
B3 A3	7½c + 9p	*2,250.*	*900.00*
B4 A3	10c + 1sh	*2,250.*	*1,100.*
	Nos. B1-B4 (4)	*7,600.*	*3,250.*

Withdrawn from sale Oct. 19.

POSTAGE DUE STAMPS

Catalogue values for unused stamps in this section are for Never Hinged items.

Map — D1

Perf. 15x14

1986, June 9 Litho. Wmk. 384

Background Color

J1 D1	1p tan	.25	.45
J2 D1	2p orange	.25	.45
J3 D1	5p vermilion	.25	.45
J4 D1	7p violet	.25	.45
J5 D1	10p chalky blue	.25	.55
J6 D1	25p dull yellow grn	.70	1.50
	Nos. J1-J6 (6)	1.95	3.85

WAR TAX STAMPS

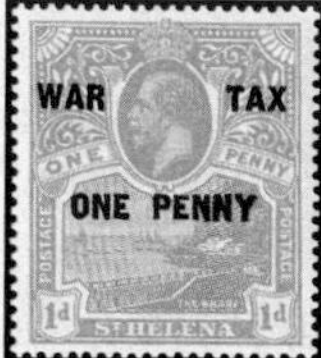

No. 62a Surcharged

1916 Wmk. 3 *Perf. 14*

MR1 A10	1p + 1p scar & blk	3.00	4.00
a.	Double surcharge		*20,000.*

No. 62 Surcharged

1919

MR2 A10	1p + 1p car & blk	2.10	5.50

ST. KITTS

sānt 'kits

LOCATION — West Indies southeast of Puerto Rico
GOVT. — With Nevis, Associated State in British Commonwealth
AREA — 65 sq. mi.
POP. — 31,824 (1991)
CAPITAL — Basseterre

See St. Christopher for stamps used in St. Kitts until 1890. From 1890 until 1903, stamps of the Leeward Islands were used. From 1903 until 1956, stamps of St. Kitts-Nevis and Leeward Islands were used concurrently. See St. Kitts-Nevis for stamps used through June 22, 1980, after which St. Kitts and Nevis pursued separate postal administrations.

100 Cents = 1 Dollar

Catalogue values for all unused stamps in this country are for Never Hinged items.

Watermark

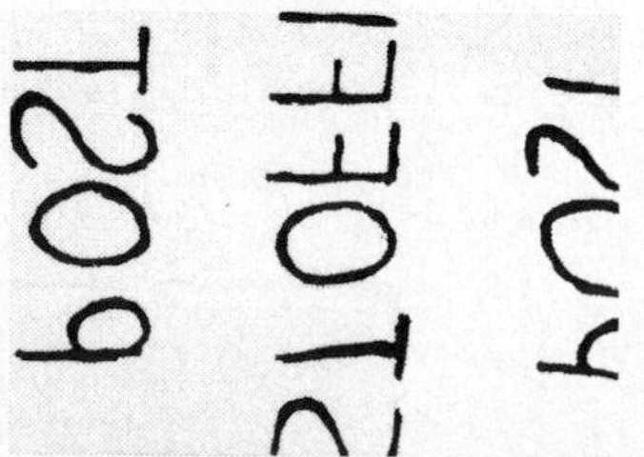

Wmk. 380 — "POST OFFICE"

St. Kitts-Nevis Nos. 357-369 Ovptd.

Perf. 14½x14

1980, June 23 Litho. Wmk. 373

25 A61	5c multicolored	.25	.25
26 A61	10c multicolored	.25	.25
27 A61	12c multicolored	.35	.50
28 A61	15c multicolored	.25	.25
29 A61	25c multicolored	.25	.25
30 A61	30c multicolored	.25	.25
31 A61	40c multicolored	.25	.25
32 A61	45c multicolored	.50	.25
33 A61	50c multicolored	.25	.25
34 A61	55c multicolored	.25	.25
35 A61	$1 multicolored	.25	.25
36 A61	$5 multicolored	.30	.90
37 A61	$10 multicolored	.45	1.75
	Nos. 25-37 (13)	3.85	5.65

All but 12c, 45c, 50c, exist unwatermarked. About the same values.

Ships A2

4c, HMS Vanguard, 1762. 10c, HMS Boreas, 1787. 30c, HMS Druid, 1827. 55c, HMS Winchester, 1831. $1.50, Philosopher, 1857. $2, S.S. Contractor, 1930.

1980, Aug. 8 *Perf. 13½*

38 A2	4c multicolored	.25	.25
39 A2	10c multicolored	.25	.25
40 A2	30c multicolored	.25	.25
41 A2	55c multicolored	.25	.25
42 A2	$1.50 multicolored	.30	.30
43 A2	$2 multicolored	.35	.40
	Nos. 38-43 (6)	1.65	1.70

Nos. 38-43 not issued without overprint. The 4c, and possibly others, exist without the overprint.

Queen Mother, 80th Birthday — A3

1980, Sept. 4 *Perf. 14*

44 A3	$2 multicolored	.40	.40

Christmas — A4

1980, Nov. 10 *Perf. 14½*

45 A4	5c Magi following star	.25	.25
46 A4	15c Shepherds, star	.25	.25
47 A4	30c Bethlehem, star	.25	.25
48 A4	$4 Adoration of the Magi	.60	.60
	Nos. 45-48 (4)	1.35	1.35

Birds — A5

1c, Frigatebird. 4c, Rusty-tailed flycatcher. 5c, Purple-throated carib. 6c, Burrowing owl. 8c, Purple martin. 10c, Yellow-crowned night heron. 15c, Bananaquit. 20c, Scaly-breasted thrasher. 25c, Grey kingbird. 30c, Green-throated carib. 40c, Ruddy turnstone. 45c, Black-faced grassquit. 50c, Cattle egret. 55c, Brown pelican. $1, Lesser Antillean bullfinch. $2.50, Zenaida dove. $5, Sparrow hawk. $10, Antillean crested hummingbird.

No Date Imprint Below Design

1981 Wmk. 373 *Perf. 13½x14*

49 A5	1c multicolored	.25	.25
50 A5	4c multicolored	.25	.25
51 A5	5c multicolored	.25	.25
52 A5	6c multicolored	.25	.25

53 A5 8c multicolored .25 .25
54 A5 10c multicolored .25 .25

Perf. 14

Size: 38x25mm

55 A5 15c multicolored .25 .25
56 A5 20c multicolored .25 .25
57 A5 25c multicolored .25 .25
58 A5 30c multicolored .25 .25
59 A5 40c multicolored .30 .30
60 A5 45c multicolored .40 .40
61 A5 50c multicolored .40 .40
62 A5 55c multicolored .40 .40
63 A5 $1 multicolored .75 .75
64 A5 $2.50 multicolored 1.50 1.50
65 A5 $5 multicolored 3.00 3.00
66 A5 $10 multicolored 5.00 5.00
Nos. 49-66 (18) 14.25 14.25

Issued: Nos. 51, 54-66, Feb. 5; others, May 30.

"1982" Imprint Below Design

1982, June 8

49a A5 1c multicolored .50 .35
50a A5 4c multicolored .50 .30
51a A5 5c multicolored .60 .30
52a A5 6c multicolored .65 .40
53a A5 8c multicolored .70 .30
54a A5 10c multicolored .70 .30

Perf. 14

Size: 38x25mm

55a A5 15c multicolored .75 .30
56a A5 20c multicolored .80 .30
57a A5 25c multicolored .80 .30
58a A5 30c multicolored .80 .35
59a A5 40c multicolored 1.00 .40
60a A5 45c multicolored 1.25 .45
61a A5 50c multicolored 1.50 .50
62a A5 55c multicolored 1.75 .75
63a A5 $1 multicolored 2.75 1.00
64a A5 $2.50 multicolored 4.50 3.00
65a A5 $5 multicolored 7.00 6.50
66a A5 $10 multicolored 11.50 10.00
Nos. 49a-66a (18) 38.05 25.80

"1983" Imprint Below Design

1983

55b A5 15c multicolored 2.00 .50
56b A5 20c multicolored 2.00 .50
57b A5 25c multicolored 2.00 .50
58b A5 30c multicolored 2.00 .50
59b A5 40c multicolored 3.00 .60
60b A5 45c multicolored 3.50 1.25
63b A5 $1 multicolored 7.50 2.50
64b A5 $2.50 multicolored 12.50 5.00
Nos. 55b-64b (8) 34.50 11.35

For overprints see Nos. 112-122.

Military Uniforms — A6

Foot Regiments: 5c, Battalion Company sergeant, 3rd Regiment, c. 1801. 15c, Light Company private, 15th Regiment, c. 1814. No. 69, Battalion Company officer, 45th Regiment, 1796-7. No. 70, Officer, 15th Regiment, c. 1780. No. 71, Officer, 9th Regiment, 1790. No. 72, Light Company officer, 5th Regiment, c. 1822. No. 73, Grenadier, 38th Regiment, 1751. No. 74, Battalion Company officer, 11th Regiment, c. 1804.

1981-83 *Perf. 14½*

67 A6 5c multi .25 .25
68 A6 15c multi ('83) .25 .25
69 A6 30c multi .25 .25
70 A6 30c multi ('83) .25 .25
71 A6 55c multi .25 .25
72 A6 55c multi ('83) .35 .35
73 A6 $2.50 multi .55 .55
74 A6 $2.50 multi ('83) .80 .80
Nos. 67-74 (8) 2.95 2.95

Issued: 3/5/81; 5/25/83.

Prince Charles, Lady Diana, Royal Yacht Charlotte A6a

Prince Charles and Lady Diana — A6b

1981, June 23 *Perf. 14*

75 A6a 55c Saudadoes .25 .25
76 A6b 55c Couple .25 .25
a. Bklt. pane of 4, perf. 12½x12, unwmkd. .90
77 A6a $2.50 The Royal George .40 .40
78 A6b $2.50 like 55c .75 .75
a. Bklt. pane of 2, perf. 12½x12, unwmkd. 1.75 1.75
79 A6a $4 HMY Britannia 1.00 1.00
80 A6b $4 like 55c 1.25 1.25
Nos. 75-80 (6) 3.90 3.90

Souvenir Sheet

1981, Dec. 14 *Perf. 12½x12*

81 A6b $5 like 55c 2.00 2.00

Wedding of Prince Charles and Lady Diana Spencer. Nos. 76a, 78a issued Nov. 19, 1981.

Natl. Girl Guide Movement, 50th Anniv. — A7

Designs: 5c, Miriam Pickard, 1st Guide commissioner. 30c, Lady Baden-Powell's visit, 1964. 55c, Visit of Princess Alice, 1960. $2, Thinking-Day Parade, 1980s.

1981, Sept. 21

82 A7 5c multicolored .25 .25
83 A7 30c multicolored .25 .25
84 A7 55c multicolored .25 .25
85 A7 $2 multicolored .40 .40
Nos. 82-85 (4) 1.15 1.15

Christmas — A8

Stained-glass windows — 5c, Annunciation. 30c, Nativity, baptism. 55c, Last supper, crucifixion. $3, Appearance before Apostles, ascension to heaven.

1981, Nov. 30

86 A8 5c multicolored .25 .25
87 A8 30c multicolored .25 .25
88 A8 55c multicolored .25 .25
89 A8 $3 multicolored .50 .50
Nos. 86-89 (4) 1.25 1.25

Brimstone Hill Siege, Bicent. — A9

1982, Mar. 15

90 A9 15c Adm. Samuel Hood .25 .25
91 A9 55c Marquis de Bouille .25 .25

Souvenir Sheet

92 A9 $5 Battle scene 1.40 1.40

No. 92 has multicolored margin picturing battle scene. Size: 96x71mm.

21st Birthday of Princess Diana, July 1 — A10

15c, Alexandra of Denmark, Princess of Wales, 1863. 55c, Paternal arms of Alexandra. $6, Diana.

1982, June 22 *Perf. 13½x14*

93 A10 15c multicolored .25 .25
94 A10 55c multicolored .25 .25
95 A10 $6 multicolored .50 .50
Nos. 93-95 (3) 1.00 1.00

Nos. 93-95 Ovptd.

1982, July 12

96 A10 15c multicolored .25 .25
97 A10 55c multicolored .25 .25
98 A10 $6 multicolored .45 .45
Nos. 96-98 (3) .95 .95

Birth of Prince William of Wales.

Scouting, 75th Anniv. — A11

Merit badges.

1982, Aug. 18 *Perf. 14x13½*

99 A11 5c Nature .25 .25
100 A11 55c Rescue .35 .35
101 A11 $2 First aid 1.10 1.10
Nos. 99-101 (3) 1.70 1.70

Christmas — A12

Children's drawings.

1982, Oct. 20

102 A12 5c shown .25 .25
103 A12 55c Nativity .25 .25
104 A12 $1.10 Three Kings .25 .25
105 A12 $3 Annunciation .30 .30
Nos. 102-105 (4) 1.05 1.05

A13

Commonwealth Day: 55c, Cruise ship Stella Oceanis docked. $2, RMS Queen Elizabeth 2 anchored in harbor off St. Kitts.

1983, Mar. 14 *Perf. 14*

106 A13 55c multicolored .25 .25
107 A13 $2 multicolored .40 .40

Boys' Brigade, Cent. — A14

Designs: 10c, Sir William Smith, founder. 45c, Brigade members outside Sandy Point Methodist Church. 50c, Drummers. $3, Badge.

1983, July 27

108 A14 10c multicolored .30 .30
109 A14 45c multicolored .40 .40
110 A14 50c multicolored .40 .40
111 A14 $3 multicolored .70 .70
Nos. 108-111 (4) 1.80 1.80

Nos. 51//66 Overprinted

a

b

Without Date Imprint Below Design

1983, Sept. 19

112 A5(a) 5c multicolored .25 .25
c. Local overprint 10.00 10.00
113c A5(b) 15c multicolored 7.00 1.25
116c A5(b) 30c multicolored 27.50 27.50
118c A5(b) 55c multicolored .65 .65
119c A5(b) $1 multicolored 11.00 11.00
120 A5(b) $2.50 multicolored 2.75 2.75
121c A5(b) $5 multicolored 4.75 4.75
122c A5(b) $10 multicolored 6.50 6.50
Nos. 112-122c (8) 60.40 54.65

No. 112c has serifed letters and reads down. Exists reading up. Value $25.

Nos. 51a//65a Overprinted "1982" Imprint Below Design

1983, Sept. 19

112a A5(a) 5c multicolored .45 .25
d. Local overprint 2.25 2.25
113a A5(b) 15c multicolored 2.00 2.00
115a A5(b) 25c multicolored 2.00 2.00
116a A5(b) 30c multicolored 2.00 2.00
121a A5(b) $5 multicolored 5.50 5.50
Nos. 112a-121a (5) 11.95 11.75

No. 112a exists with inverted overprint. Value $32.50. No. 113a exists with double overprint. Value $8.50. No. 115a exists with inverted overprint. Value $14.

No. 112d has serifed letters and reads down. Exists reading up. Value $7.50.

Nos. 52b//66b Overprinted "1983" Imprint Below Design

113 A5(b) 15c multicolored .35 .25
114 A5(b) 20c multicolored .35 .25
115 A5(b) 25c multicolored .55 .25
116 A5(b) 30c multicolored .55 .25
117 A5(b) 40c multicolored .60 .25
118 A5(b) 55c multicolored .65 .30
119 A5(b) $1 multicolored 1.25 .60
120b A5(b) $2.50 multicolored 2.50 2.50

121 A5(b) $5 multicolored 3.75 *4.50*
122 A5(b) $10 multicolored 4.50 4.50
Nos. 113-122 (10) 15.05 13.65

No. 118 exists with inverted overprint. Value $10.

Manned Flight Bicent. — A15

Designs: 10c, *Montgolfiere,* 1783, vert. 45c, Sikorsky *Russian Knight,* 1913. 50c, Lockheed TriStar. $2.50, Bell XS-1, 1947.

1983, Sept. 28 **Wmk. 380**
123 A15 10c multicolored .25 .25
124 A15 45c multicolored .25 .25
125 A15 50c multicolored .25 .25
126 A15 $2.50 multicolored .75 .75
a. Souvenir sheet of 4, #123-126 1.50 1.50
Nos. 123-126 (4) 1.50 1.50

1st Flight of a 4-engine aircraft, May 1913 (45c); 1st manned supersonic aircraft, 1947 ($2.50).

Christmas — A16

1983, Nov. 7
127 A16 15c shown .25 .25
128 A16 30c Shepherds .25 .25
129 A16 55c Mary, Joseph .25 .25
130 A16 $2.50 Nativity .30 .30
a. Souvenir sheet of 4, #127-130 1.00 1.00
Nos. 127-130 (4) 1.05 1.05

Batik Art A17

1984-85
131 A17 15c Country bus .25 .25
132 A17 40c Donkey cart .30 .25
133 A17 45c Parrot, vert. .25 .25
134 A17 50c Man under palm tree, vert. .25 .25
135 A17 60c Rum shop, cyclist .60 .25
136 A17 $1.50 Fruit seller, vert. .45 *.65*
137 A17 $3 Butterflies, vert. .70 *1.25*
138 A17 $3 S.V. Polynesia 1.25 *1.75*
Nos. 131-138 (8) 4.05 4.90

Issued: 15c, 40c, 60c, No. 138, 2/6/85; others, 1/30/84.

Marine Life A18

5c, Cushion star. 10c, Rough file shell. 15c, Red-lined cleaning shrimp. 20c, Bristleworm. 25c, Flamingo tongue. 30c, Christmas tree worm. 40c, Pink-tipped anemone. 50c, Small-mouth grunt. 60c, Glasseye snapper. 75c, Reef squirrelfish. $1, Sea fans, flamefish. $2.50, Reef butter-flyfish. $5, Black soldierfish. $10, Cocoa damselfish.

1984, July 4
139 A18 5c multicolored .25 .25
140 A18 10c multicolored .25 .25
a. Wmk. 384 "1986" 1.50 1.00
b. As "a," "1988" imprint 1.25 1.00
141 A18 15c multicolored .25 .25
142 A18 20c multicolored .25 .25
143 A18 25c multicolored .25 .25
144 A18 30c multicolored .40 .35
145 A18 40c multicolored .55 .40
146 A18 50c multicolored .60 .40
147 A18 60c multicolored 1.10 1.10
a. Wmk. 384 ('88) 1.25 1.40
148 A18 75c multicolored 2.50 .75
149 A18 $1 multicolored 1.00 1.00
150 A18 $2.50 multicolored 3.00 3.75
151 A18 $5 multicolored 7.00 15.00
a. Wmk. 384 ('88) 9.00 *11.00*
152 A18 $10 multicolored 11.00 *15.00*
a. Wmk. 384 ('88) 14.00 *15.00*
Nos. 139-152 (14) 28.40 39.00

Nos. 149-152 vert.
Nos. 147a, 151a, 152a have "1988" imprint.

4-H in St. Kitts, 25th Anniv. A19

1984, Aug. 15
153 A19 30c Agriculture .25 .25
154 A19 55c Animal husbandry .30 .30
155 A19 $1.10 Pledge, flag, youths .50 .50
156 A19 $3 Parade 1.00 1.00
Nos. 153-156 (4) 2.05 2.05

1st Anniv. of Independence — A20

15c, Construction of Royal St. Kitts Hotel. 30c, Folk dancers. $1.10, O Land of Beauty, vert. $3, Sea, palm trees, map, vert.

1984, Sept. 18
157 A20 15c multicolored .25 .25
158 A20 30c multicolored .30 .30
159 A20 $1.10 multicolored .50 .50
160 A20 $3 multicolored 1.00 1.00
Nos. 157-160 (4) 2.05 2.05

Christmas — A21

1984, Nov. 1
161 A21 15c Opening gifts .25 .25
162 A21 60c Caroling .55 .55
163 A21 $1 Nativity .75 .75
164 A21 $2 Leaving church 1.40 1.40
Nos. 161-164 (4) 2.95 2.95

Ships A22

1985, Mar. 27 ***Perf. 13½x14***
165 A22 40c Tropic Jade 1.00 1.00
166 A22 $1.20 Atlantic Clipper 2.00 2.00
167 A22 $2 M.V. Cunard Countess 3.00 3.00
168 A22 $2 Mandalay 3.50 3.50
Nos. 165-168 (4) 9.50 9.50

Mt. Olive Masonic Lodge, 150th Anniv. — A23

Designs: 15c, James Derrick Cardin (1871-1954). 75c, Lodge banner. $1.20, Compass, Bible, square, horiz. $3, Charter, 1835.

1985, Nov. 9 ***Perf. 15***
169 A23 15c multicolored .65 .40
170 A23 75c multicolored 1.40 1.40
171 A23 $1.20 multicolored 1.40 1.40
172 A23 $3 multicolored 1.75 1.75
Nos. 169-172 (4) 5.20 4.95

Christmas — A24

1985, Nov. 27 **Unwmk.**
173 A24 10c Map of St. Kitts .30 .25
174 A24 40c Golden Hind .60 .40
175 A24 60c Sir Francis Drake .60 .50
176 A24 $3 Drake's shield of arms .80 *3.00*
Nos. 173-176 (4) 2.30 4.15

Visit of Sir Francis Drake to St. Kitts, 400th anniv.

Queen Elizabeth II, 60th Birthday — A25

Designs: 10c, With Prince Philip. 20c, Walking with government officials. 40c, Riding horse in parade. $3, Portrait.

1986, July 9 ***Perf. 14***
177 A25 10c multicolored .25 .25
178 A25 20c multicolored .35 .25
179 A25 40c multicolored .60 .45
180 A25 $3 multicolored 2.40 2.40
Nos. 177-180 (4) 3.60 3.35

For overprints see Nos. 185-188.

Common Design Types pictured following the introduction.

Royal Wedding Issue, 1986
Common Design Type

Designs: 15c, Prince Andrew and Sarah Ferguson, formal engagement announcement. $2.50, Prince Andrew in military dress uniform.

Perf. 14½x14
1986, July 23 **Wmk. 384**
181 CD338 15c multicolored .25 .25
182 CD338 $2.50 multicolored 1.25 1.25

Agriculture Exhibition — A26

Children's drawings: 15c, Family farm, by Kevin Tatem, age 14. $1.20, Striving for growth, by Alister Williams, age 19.

1986, Sept. 18 ***Perf. 13½x14***
183 A26 15c multicolored .25 .25
184 A26 $1.20 multicolored 1.25 1.25

Nos. 177-180 Ovptd. "40th ANNIVERSARY / U.N. WEEK 19-26 OCT." in Gold

1986, Oct. 22 **Unwmk.** ***Perf. 14***
185 A25 10c multicolored .25 .25
186 A25 20c multicolored .25 .25
187 A25 40c multicolored .40 .40
188 A25 $3 multicolored 1.90 1.90
Nos. 185-188 (4) 2.80 2.80

World Wildlife Fund — A27

Various green monkeys, Cercopithecus aethiops sabaeus.

1986, Dec. 1
189 A27 15c multi *5.00* *.75*
190 A27 20c multi, diff. *5.50* *.75*
191 A27 60c multi, diff. *8.50* *3.75*
192 A27 $1 multi, diff. *11.50* *6.00*
Nos. 189-192 (4) *30.50* *11.25*

Auguste Bartholdi — A28

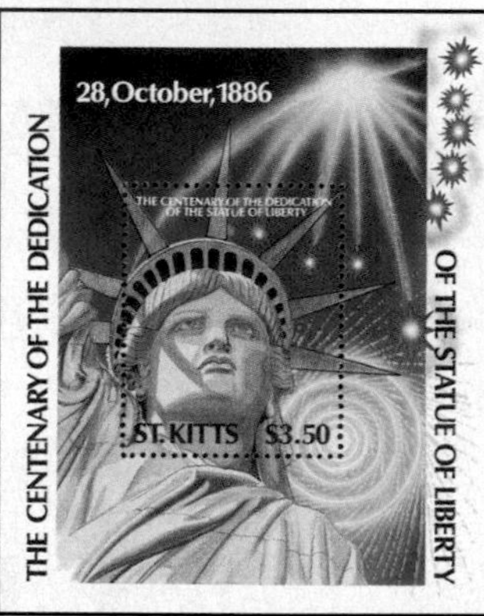

Statue of Liberty, Cent. — A29

60c, Torch, head, 1876-78. $1.50, Warship Isere, France. $3, Delivering statue, 1884. $3.50, Head.

1986, Dec. 17 ***Perf. 14x14½, 14½x14***
193 A28 40c shown .30 .30
194 A28 60c multicolored .40 *.50*
195 A28 $1.50 multicolored 1.10 *1.40*
196 A28 $3 multicolored 1.25 *2.50*
Nos. 193-196 (4) 3.05 *4.70*

Souvenir Sheet

197 A29 $3.50 multicolored 2.50 2.50

Nos. 194-195 horiz.

British and French Uniforms — A30

Designs: No. 198, Officer, East Norfolk Regiment, 1792. No. 199, Officer, De Neustrie Regiment, 1779. No. 200, Sergeant, Third Foot the Buffs, 1801. No. 201, Artillery officer, 1812. No. 202, Private, Light Company, 5th Foot Regiment, 1778. No. 203, Grenadier, Line Infantry, 1796.

1987, Feb. 25 ***Perf. 14½***
198 A30 15c multicolored .45 .30
199 A30 15c multicolored .45 .30
200 A30 40c multicolored .75 .55
201 A30 40c multicolored .75 .55
202 A30 $2 multicolored 1.75 *2.75*

203 A30 $2 multicolored 1.75 *2.75*
a. Souvenir sheet of 6, #198-203 9.00 9.00
Nos. 198-203 (6) 5.90 *7.20*

Sugar Cane Industry — A31

No. 204: a, Warehouse. b, Barns. c, Steam emitted by processing plant. d, Processing plant. e, Field hands.
No. 205a, Locomotive. b, Locomotive and tender. c, Open cars. d, Empty and loaded cars, tractor. e, Loading sugar cane.

1987, Apr. 15 ***Perf. 14***
204 Strip of 5 1.00 1.00
a.-e. A31 15c any single .25 .25
205 Strip of 5 2.00 2.00
a.-e. A31 75c any single .30 .30

Visiting Aircraft A32

40c, L-1011-500 Tri-Star. 60c, BAe Super 748. $1.20, DHC-6 Twin Otter. $3, Aerospatiale ATR-42.

Perf. 14x14½
1987, June 24 **Wmk. 373**
206 A32 40c multicolored .70 .50
207 A32 60c multicolored 1.00 1.00
208 A32 $1.20 multicolored 1.60 1.60
209 A32 $3 multicolored 3.75 3.75
Nos. 206-209 (4) 7.05 6.85

Fungi — A33

15c, Hygrocybe occidentalis. 40c, Marasmius haemato-cephalus. $1.20, Psilocybe cubensis. $2, Hygrocybe acutoconica. $3, Boletellus cubensis.

1987, Aug. 26 **Wmk. 384** ***Perf. 14***
210 A33 15c multicolored 1.00 .30
211 A33 40c multicolored 1.75 .40
212 A33 $1.20 multicolored 3.50 3.50
213 A33 $2 multicolored 4.50 4.50
214 A33 $3 multicolored 5.50 5.50
Nos. 210-214 (5) 16.25 14.20

Carnival Clowns — A34

1987, Oct. 28 ***Perf. 14½***
215 A34 15c multi .25 .25
216 A34 40c multi, diff. .60 .60
217 A34 $1 multi, diff. 1.50 1.50
218 A34 $3 multi, diff. 3.25 3.25
Nos. 215-218 (4) 5.60 5.60

Christmas 1987. See Nos. 235-238.

Flowers — A35

1988, Jan. 20
219 A35 15c Ixora .25 .25
220 A35 40c Shrimp plant .50 .50
221 A35 $1 Poinsettia 1.10 1.10
222 A35 $3 Honolulu rose 3.75 3.75
Nos. 219-222 (4) 5.60 5.60

Tourism A36

No. 223, Ft. Thomas Hotel. No. 224, Fairview Inn. No. 225, Frigate Bay Beach Hotel. No. 226, Ocean Terrace Inn. No. 227, The Golden Lemon. No. 228, Royal St. Kitts Casino and Jack Tar Village. No. 229, Rawlins Plantation Hotel and Restaurant.

1988, Apr. 20 **Wmk. 373**
223 A36 60c multicolored .95 .95
224 A36 60c multicolored .95 .95
225 A36 60c multicolored .95 .95
226 A36 60c multicolored .95 .95
227 A36 $3 multicolored 2.60 2.60
228 A36 $3 multicolored 2.60 2.60
229 A36 $3 multicolored 2.60 2.60
Nos. 223-229 (7) 11.60 11.60

See Nos. 239-244.

Leeward Islands Cricket Tournament, 75th Anniv. — A37

Designs: 40c, Leeward Islands Cricket Assoc. emblem, ball and wicket. $3, Cricket match at Warner Park.

1988, July 13 ***Perf. 13x13½***
230 A37 40c multicolored 2.00 .30
231 A37 $3 multicolored 4.25 4.25

Independence, 5th Anniv. — A38

Designs: 15c, Natl. flag. 60c, Natl. coat of arms. $5, Princess Margaret presenting the Nevis Constitution Order to Prime Minister Simmonds, Sept. 19, 1983.

1988, Sept. 19 **Wmk. 384** ***Perf. 14½***
232 A38 15c shown 1.25 .45
233 A38 60c multicolored 1.60 1.00

Souvenir Sheet

234 A38 $5 multicolored 5.50 5.50

Christmas Type of 1987

Carnival clowns.

1988, Nov. 2 **Wmk. 373**
235 A34 15c multi .25 .25
236 A34 40c multi, diff. .25 .25
237 A34 80c multi, diff. .40 .40
238 A34 $3 multi, diff. 1.60 1.60
Nos. 235-238 (4) 2.50 2.50

Tourism Type of 1988
Wmk. 384

1989, Jan. 25 **Litho.** ***Perf. 14***
239 A36 20c Old Colonial House .25 .25
240 A36 20c Georgian House .25 .25
241 A36 $1 Romney Manor .65 .65
242 A36 $1 Lavington Great House .65 .65
243 A36 $2 Treasury Building 1.00 *1.50*
244 A36 $2 Government House 1.00 *1.50*
Nos. 239-244 (6) 3.80 *4.80*

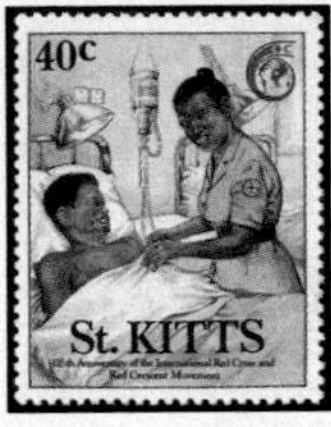

Intl. Red Cross and Red Crescent Organizations, 125th Annivs. (in 1988) — A39

Perf. 14x14½
1989, May 8 **Litho.** **Wmk. 384**
245 A39 40c shown .30 .30
246 A39 $1 Ambulance .80 .80
247 A39 $3 Anniv. emblem 2.50 2.50
Nos. 245-247 (3) 3.60 3.60

Moon Landing, 20th Anniv.
Common Design Type

Apollo 13: 10c, Lunar rover at Taurus-Littrow landing site. 20c, Fred W. Haise Jr., John L. Swigert Jr., and James A. Lovell Jr. $1, Mission emblem. $2, Splashdown in the South Pacific. $5, Buzz Aldrin disembarking from the lunar module, Apollo 11 mission.

1989, July 20 ***Perf. 14***
Size of Nos. 249-250: 29x29mm
248 CD342 10c multicolored .25 .25
249 CD342 20c multicolored .25 .25
250 CD342 $1 multicolored .75 .75
251 CD342 $2 multicolored 1.25 1.25
Nos. 248-251 (4) 2.50 2.50

Souvenir Sheet

252 CD342 $5 multicolored 5.50 5.50

Souvenir Sheet

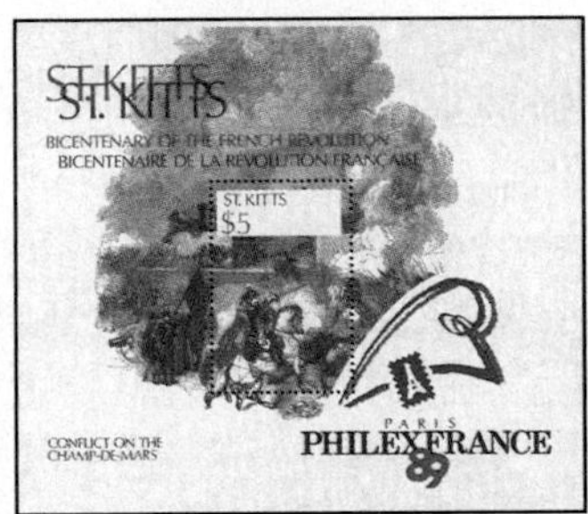

Conflict on the Champ-de-Mars — A40

1989, July 7
253 A40 $5 multicolored 5.25 5.25

PHILEXFRANCE '89, French revolution bicent.

Outline Map of St. Kitts — A41

1989 ***Perf. 15x14***
255 A41 10c purple & blk .25 .25
256 A41 15c red & blk .25 .25
257 A41 20c org brn & blk .25 .25
259 A41 40c bister & blk .60 .25
261 A41 60c blue & blk .80 .50
265 A41 $1 green & blk 1.40 .90
Nos. 255-265 (6) 3.55 2.40

Discovery of America, 500th Anniv. (in 1992) A42

Designs: 15c, Galleon passing St. Kitts during Columbus's 2nd voyage, 1493. 80c, Coat of arms and map of 4th voyage. $1, Navigational instruments, c. 1500. $5, Exploration of Cuba and Hispaniola during Columbus's 2nd voyage, 1493-1496.

1989, Nov. 8 **Wmk. 384** ***Perf. 14***
269 A42 15c multicolored 2.25 .30
270 A42 80c multicolored 4.00 2.00
271 A42 $1 multicolored 4.50 2.00
272 A42 $5 multicolored 13.00 *14.00*
Nos. 269-272 (4) 23.75 18.30

World Stamp Expo '89 A43

Exhibition emblem, flags and: 15c, Poinciana tree. 40c, Ft. George Citadel, Brimstone Hill. $1, Light Company private, 5th Foot Regiment, 1778. $3, St. George's Anglican Church.

1989, Nov. 17 **Wmk. 373**
273 A43 15c multicolored .50 .25
274 A43 40c multicolored .90 .40
275 A43 $1 multicolored 2.25 1.75
276 A43 $3 multicolored 3.75 *5.00*
Nos. 273-276 (4) 7.40 7.40

Butterflies A45

15c, Junonia evarete. 40c, Anartia jatrophae. 60c, Heliconius charitonius. $3, Biblis hyperia.

Wmk. 373
1990, June 6 **Litho.** ***Perf. 13½***
277 A45 15c multicolored 1.25 .75
278 A45 40c multicolored 2.25 1.25
279 A45 60c multicolored 2.25 1.25
280 A45 $3 multicolored 6.50 6.50
Nos. 277-280 (4) 12.25 9.75

Nos. 277-280 with EXPO '90 Emblem Added to Design

1990, June 6
281 A45 15c multicolored 1.50 .75
282 A45 40c multicolored 2.50 .75
283 A45 60c multicolored 2.50 1.25
284 A45 $3 multicolored 7.00 7.00
Nos. 281-284 (4) 13.50 9.75

Expo '90, International Garden and Greenery Exposition, Osaka, Japan.

Cannon on Brimstone Hill, 300th Anniv. — A46

15c, 40c, View of Brimstone Hill. 60c, Fort Charles under bombardment. $3, Men firing cannon.

1990 June 30 **Wmk. 384** ***Perf. 14***
285 A46 15c multicolored .35 .25
286 A46 40c multicolored .65 .35
287 A46 60c multicolored 1.25 1.00
288 Pair 7.00 7.00
a. A46 60c multicolored 1.25 1.00
b. A46 $3 multicolored 3.50 3.50
Nos. 285-288 (4) 9.25 8.60

No. 288 has a continuous design.

Souvenir Sheet

Battle of Britain, 50th Anniv. — A47

1990, Sept. 15

289 A47 Sheet of 2 25.00 25.00
a.-b. $3 any single 10.00 10.00

Ships A48

1990, Oct. 10 **Wmk. 373**

294 A48 10c Romney .75 .50
a. Wmk. 384 .75 .60
295 A48 15c Baralt .75 .30
296 A48 20c Wear 1.00 .35
297 A48 25c Sunmount 1.00 .35
298 A48 40c Inanda 1.00 .35
299 A48 50c Alcoa Partner 1.00 .35
300 A48 60c Dominica 1.40 .35
301 A48 80c CGM Provence 1.50 .50
302 A48 $1 Director 1.50 .90
303 A48 $1.20 Typical barque, 1860-1880 2.00 1.50
304 A48 $2 Chignecto 2.50 2.50
305 A48 $3 Berbice 3.50 *4.00*
a. Souvenir sheet of 1 3.00 3.00
306 A48 $5 Vamos 6.00 6.00
307 A48 $10 Federal Maple 9.50 *11.00*
Nos. 294-307 (14) 33.40 28.95

No. 305a issued 2/3/97 for Hong Kong '97.

Christmas — A49

Traditional games.

1990, Nov. 14 ***Perf. 14***

308 A49 10c Single fork .25 .25
309 A49 15c Boulder breaking .25 .25
310 A49 40c Double fork .40 .40
311 A49 $3 Run up 2.50 2.50
Nos. 308-311 (4) 3.40 3.40

Flowers — A50

10c, White periwinkle, horiz. 40c, Pink oleander, horiz. 60c, Pink periwinkle. $2, White oleander.

Perf. 14x13½, 13½x14

1991, May 8 **Litho.** **Wmk. 373**

312 A50 10c multicolored .75 .30
313 A50 40c multicolored 1.50 .45
314 A50 60c multicolored 2.00 .90
315 A50 $2 multicolored 3.50 3.50
Nos. 312-315 (4) 7.75 5.15

Natl. Census — A51

1991, May 13 **Wmk. 384** ***Perf. 14***

316 A51 15c multicolored .25 .25
317 A51 $2.40 multicolored 3.50 3.50

Elizabeth & Philip, Birthdays

Common Design Types

Wmk. 384

1991, June 17 **Litho.** ***Perf. 14½***

318 CD346 $1.20 multicolored 1.00 1.00
319 CD345 $1.80 multicolored 1.50 1.50
a. Pair, #318-319 + label 3.00 3.00

Fish A52

1991, Aug. 28 **Wmk. 373** ***Perf. 14***

320 A52 10c Nassau grouper .75 .35
321 A52 60c Hogfish 1.50 .75
322 A52 $1 Red hind 2.50 2.50
323 A52 $3 Porkfish 4.25 4.25
Nos. 320-323 (4) 9.00 7.85

University of the West Indies A53

Designs: 15c, Chancellor Sir Shridath Ramphal, School of Continuing Studies, St. Kitts. 50c, Administration Bldg., Cave Hill Campus, Barbados. $1, Engineering Bldg., St. Augustine Campus, Trinidad & Tobago. $3, Ramphal, Mona Campus, Jamaica.

1991, Sept. 25 **Wmk. 384**

324 A53 15c multicolored .40 .35
325 A53 50c multicolored .80 .80
326 A53 $1 multicolored 1.60 1.40
327 A53 $3 multicolored 4.50 4.50
Nos. 324-327 (4) 7.30 7.05

Christmas — A54

Various scenes of traditional play, "The Bull."

1991, Nov. 6 **Wmk. 373**

328 A54 10c multicolored .40 .40
329 A54 15c multicolored .40 .40
330 A54 60c multicolored 1.25 1.25
331 A54 $3 multicolored 4.75 4.75
Nos. 328-331 (4) 6.80 6.80

Queen Elizabeth II's Accession to the Throne, 40th Anniv.

Common Design Type

1992, Feb. 6 **Wmk. 384**

332 CD349 10c multicolored .30 .25
333 CD349 40c multicolored 1.25 .55
334 CD349 60c multicolored .80 .45
335 CD349 $1 multicolored 1.25 1.25

Wmk. 373

336 CD349 $3 multicolored 3.00 3.00
Nos. 332-336 (5) 6.60 5.50

St. Kitts and Nevis Red Cross Society, 50th Anniv. A55

10c, Map of St. Kitts & Nevis. 20c, St. Kitts & Nevis flag. 50c, Red Cross House, St. Kitts. $2.40, Jean-Henri Dunant, founder of Red Cross.

Perf. 13½x14

1992, May 8 **Litho.** **Wmk. 373**

337 A55 10c multicolored 1.50 .75
338 A55 20c multicolored 2.25 .60
339 A55 50c multicolored 2.00 1.00
340 A55 $2.40 multicolored 4.50 4.50
Nos. 337-340 (4) 10.25 6.85

Discovery of America, 500th Anniv. — A56

1992, July 6 ***Perf. 13***

341 A56 $1 Coming ashore 2.00 1.25
342 A56 $2 Natives, ships 4.00 4.00

Organization of East Caribbean States.

A57

Designs: 25c, Fountain, Independence Square. 50c, Berkeley Memorial drinking fountain and clock. 80c, Sir Thomas Warner's tomb. $2, War Memorial.

1992, Aug. 19 ***Perf. 12½x13***

343 A57 25c multicolored .25 .25
344 A57 50c multicolored .45 .45
345 A57 80c multicolored .75 .75
346 A57 $2 multicolored 1.75 1.75
Nos. 343-346 (4) 3.20 3.20

Christmas — A58

Stained glass windows: 20c, Mary and Joseph. 25c, Shepherds. 80c, Three Wise Men. $3, Mary, Joseph and Christ Child.

1992, Oct. 28 **Wmk. 384** ***Perf. 14½***

347 A58 20c multicolored .30 .25
348 A58 25c multicolored .30 .25
349 A58 80c multicolored .70 .70
350 A58 $3 multicolored 3.00 3.00
Nos. 347-350 (4) 4.30 4.20

Royal Air Force, 75th Anniv.

Common Design Type

Designs: 25c, Short Singapore III. 50c, Bristol Beaufort. 80c, Westland Whirlwind. $1.60, English Electric Canberra.

No. 355a, Handley Page 0/400. b, Fairey Long Range Monoplane. c, Vickers Wellesley. d, Sepecat Jaguar.

Wmk. 373

1993, Apr. 1 **Litho.** ***Perf. 14***

351 CD350 25c multicolored .85 .85
352 CD350 50c multicolored 1.60 1.60
353 CD350 80c multicolored 2.25 3.25
354 CD350 $1.60 multicolored 4.75 3.25
Nos. 351-354 (4) 9.45 8.95

Miniature Sheet

355 CD350 $2 Sheet of 4, #a.-d. 15.00 15.00

Diocese of the Northeastern Caribbean and Aruba, 150th Anniv. — A59

Designs: 25c, Diocesan Conference, Basseterre, horiz. 50c, Cathedral of St. John the Divine. 80c, Diocesan coat of arms and motto, horiz. $2, First Bishop, Right Reverend Daniel G. Davis.

Perf. 13½x14, 14x13½

1993, May 21 **Litho.** **Wmk. 384**

356 A59 25c multicolored .30 .30
357 A59 50c multicolored .50 .50
358 A59 80c multicolored 1.00 1.00
359 A59 $2 multicolored 2.25 3.25
Nos. 356-359 (4) 4.05 5.05

Coronation of Queen Elizabeth II, 40th Anniv. — A60

Royal regalia and stamps of St. Kitts-Nevis: 10c, Eagle-shaped ampulla, #119. 25c, Anointing spoon, #334. 80c, Tassels, #333. $2, Staff of Scepter with the Cross, #354a-354c.

1993, June 2 ***Perf. 14½x14***

360 A60 10c multicolored .50 .50
361 A60 25c multicolored .70 .70
362 A60 80c multicolored 1.25 1.25
363 A60 $2 multicolored 2.50 2.50
Nos. 360-363 (4) 4.95 4.95

Girls' Brigade Intl., Cent. — A61

1993, July 1 ***Perf. 13½x14***

364 A61 80c Flags 2.50 1.00
365 A61 $3 Badge, coat of arms 4.25 4.25

Independence, 10th Anniv. — A62

Designs: 20c, Flag, map of St. Kitts and Nevis, plane, ship and island scenes. 80c, Natl. arms, independence emblem. $3, Natl. arms, map.

Wmk. 373

1993, Sept. 10 **Litho.** ***Perf. 14***

366 A62 20c multicolored 1.00 .25
367 A62 80c multicolored 1.25 .80
368 A62 $3 multicolored 3.75 3.75
Nos. 366-368 (3) 6.00 4.80

Christmas — A63

Perf. 13½x14

1993, Nov. 16 Litho. Wmk. 373

369 A63 25c Roselle .50 .50
370 A63 50c Poinsettia .75 .75
371 A63 $1.60 Snow on the Mountain 2.50 2.50
Nos. 369-371 (3) 3.75 3.75

Prehistoric Aquatic Reptiles — A64

Designs: a, Mesosaurus. b, Placodus. c, Liopleurodon. d, Hydrotherosaurus. e, Caretta.

Wmk. 384

1994, Feb. 18 Litho. *Perf. 14*

372 A64 $1.20 Strip of 5, #a.-e. 9.75 9.75
373 A64 $1.20 #372 ovptd. with Hong Kong '94 emblem 9.75 9.75

Souvenir Sheet

Treasury Building, Cent. — A65

Wmk. 373

1994, Mar. 21 Litho. *Perf. 13½*

374 A65 $10 multicolored 11.00 11.00

Order of the Caribbean Community — A66

First award recipients: Nos. 375a, 376a, Sir Shridath Ramphal, statesman, Guyana. Nos. 375b, 376b, Emblem of the Order. Nos. 375c, 376c, Derek Walcott, writer, St. Lucia. Nos. 375d, 376d, William Demas, economist, Trinidad and Tobago.

Wmk. 373

1994, July 13 Litho. *Perf. 14*

375 A66 10c Strip of 5, #a, b, c, b, d 1.25 1.25
376 A66 $1 Strip of 5, #a, b, c, b, d 7.00 7.00

CARICOM, 20th anniv. (Nos. 375b, 376b).

Christmas — A67

1994, Oct. 31

377 A67 25c Carol singing .25 .25
378 A67 25c Opening presents .25 .25
379 A67 80c Carnival .75 .75
380 A67 $2.50 Nativity 2.75 2.75
Nos. 377-380 (4) 4.00 4.00

Intl. Year of the Family.

Green Turtle A68

Wmk. 373

1995, Feb. 27 Litho. *Perf. 14*

381 A68 10c shown .75 .75
382 A68 40c On beach .90 .90
383 A68 50c Laying eggs 1.25 1.25
384 A68 $1 Hatchlings 1.75 1.75
a. Strip of 4, #381-384 6.00 6.00

World Wildlife Fund.
No. 384a issued in sheets of 16 stamps.

First St. Kitts Postage Stamp, 125th Anniv. A69

St. Christopher #1 at left and: 25c, St. Christopher #1. 80c, St. Kitts-Nevis #72. $2.50, St. Kitts-Nevis #91. $3, St. Kitts-Nevis #119.

Wmk. 373

1995, Apr. 10 Litho. *Perf. 13½*

385 A69 25c multicolored .25 .25
386 A69 80c multicolored .60 .50
387 A69 $2.50 multicolored 2.50 2.50
388 A69 $3 multicolored 3.00 3.00
Nos. 385-388 (4) 6.35 6.25

End of World War II, 50th Anniv.

Common Design Types

Designs: 20c, Caribbean Regiment, North Africa. 50c, TBM Avengers on anti-submarine patrol. $2, Spitfire MkVb. $8, US destroyer escort on anti-submarine duty.
$3, Reverse of War Madal 1939-45.

Wmk. 373

1995, May 8 Litho. *Perf. 13½*

389 CD351 20c multicolored .25 .25
390 CD351 50c multicolored .60 .60
391 CD351 $2 multicolored 2.25 2.25
392 CD351 $8 multicolored 7.00 7.00
Nos. 389-392 (4) 10.10 10.10

Souvenir Sheet

Perf. 14

393 CD352 $3 multicolored 3.50 3.50

SKANTEL, 10th Anniv. — A70

Designs: 10c, Satellite transmission. 25c, Telephones, computer. $2, Transmission tower, satellite dish. $3, Satellite dish silhouetted against sun.

1995, Sept. 27 *Perf. 13½x14*

394 A70 10c multicolored .25 .25
395 A70 25c multicolored .35 .35
396 A70 $2 multicolored 2.50 2.50
397 A70 $3 multicolored 3.75 3.75
Nos. 394-397 (4) 6.85 6.85

UN, 50th Anniv.

Common Design Type

Designs: 40c, Energy, clean environment. 50c, Coastal, ocean resources. $1.60, Solid waste management. $2.50, Forestry reserves.

1995, Oct. 24 *Perf. 13½x13*

398 CD353 40c multicolored .50 .50
399 CD353 50c multicolored .65 .65
400 CD353 $1.60 multicolored 2.00 2.00
401 CD353 $2.50 multicolored 3.00 3.00
Nos. 398-401 (4) 6.15 6.15

FAO, 50th Anniv. A71

Designs: 25c, Vegetables. 50c, Glazed carrots, West Indian peas & rice. 80c, Tania, Cassava plants. $1.50, Waterfall, Green Hill Mountain.

1995, Nov. 13 *Perf. 13½*

402 A71 25c multicolored .25 .25
403 A71 50c multicolored .50 .50
404 A71 80c multicolored .85 .85
405 A71 $1.50 multicolored 1.75 1.75
Nos. 402-405 (4) 3.35 3.35

Sea Shells — A72

a, Flame helmet. b, Triton's trumpet. c, King helmet. d, True tulip. e, Queen conch.

Wmk. 373

1996, Jan. 10 Litho. *Perf. 13*

406 A72 $1.50 Strip of 5, #a.-e. 7.50 7.50

CAPEX '96 — A73

Leeward Islands LMS Jubilee Class 4-6-0 Locomotives: 10c, No. 45614. $10, No. 5614.

Perf. 13½x14

1996, June 8 Litho. Wmk. 373

407 A73 10c multicolored .80 .80

Souvenir Sheet

Perf. 14x15

408 A73 $10 multicolored 9.00 9.00

No. 408 is 48x31mm.

A74

Modern Olympic Games, Cent.: 10c, Runner, St. Kitts & Nevis flag. 25c, High jumper, US flag. 80c, Runner, Olympic flag. $3, Athens Games poster, 1896.
$6, Olympic torch.

Wmk. 384

1996, June 30 Litho. *Perf. 14*

409 A74 10c multicolored .25 .25
410 A74 25c multicolored .25 .25
411 A74 80c multicolored .75 .75
412 A74 $3 multicolored 2.50 2.50
Nos. 409-412 (4) 3.75 3.75

Souvenir Sheet

413 A74 $6 multicolored 5.25 5.25

Olymphilex '96 (#413).

A75

Defense Force, Cent.: 10c, Volunteer rifleman, 1896. 50c, Mounted infantry, 1911. $2, Bandsman, 1940-60. $2.50, Modern uniform, 1996.

1996, Nov. 1 Wmk. 373

414 A75 10c multicolored .25 .25
415 A75 50c multicolored .45 .45
416 A75 $2 multicolored 1.75 1.75
417 A75 $2.50 multicolored 2.00 2.00
Nos. 414-417 (4) 4.45 4.45

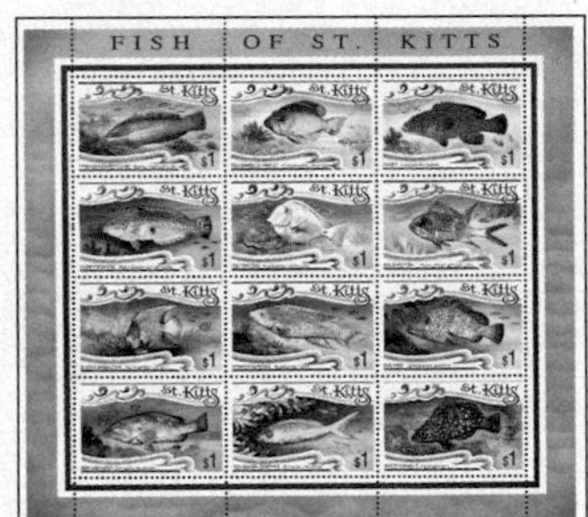

Christmas — A76

Paintings: 15c, Holy Virgin and Child, by Anais Colin, 1844. 25c, Holy Family, After Rubens. 50c, Madonna with the Goldfinch, by Krause on porcelain after Raphael, 1507. 80c, Madonna on Throne with Angels, by unknown Spanish, 17th cent.

1996, Dec. 9

418 A76 15c multicolored .25 .25
419 A76 25c multicolored .35 .25
420 A76 50c multicolored .80 .65
421 A76 80c multicolored 1.00 1.00
Nos. 418-421 (4) 2.40 2.15

Fish — A77

a, Princess parrot fish. b, Yellowbelly hamlet. c, Coney. d, Clown wrasse. e, Doctor fish. f, Squirrelfish. g, Queen angelfish. h, Spanish hogfish. i, Red hind. j, Red grouper. k, Yellowtail snapper. l, Mutton hamlet.

1997, Apr. 24 *Perf. 13½*

422 A77 $1 Sheet of 12, #a.-l. 13.00 13.00

Queen Elizabeth II and Prince Philip, 50th Wedding Anniv. — A78

Designs: No. 423, Queen. No. 424, Prince riding with Royal Guard. No. 425, Queen riding in carriage. No. 426, Prince Philip. No. 427, Early photo of Queen, Prince. No. 428, Prince riding horse.
Queen, Prince riding in open carriage, horiz.

Wmk. 373

1997, July 10 Litho. *Perf. 13½*

423		10c multicolored	.55	.55
424		10c multicolored	.55	.55
a.	A78	Pair, #423-424	1.50	1.50
425		25c multicolored	.85	.85
426		25c multicolored	.85	.85
a.	A78	Pair, #425-426	2.00	2.00
427		$3 multicolored	2.50	2.50
428		$3 multicolored	2.50	2.50
a.	A78	Pair, #427-428	6.75	6.75
		Nos. 423-428 (6)	7.80	7.80

Souvenir Sheet

Perf. 14x14½

429	A78	$6 multicolored	8.00	8.00

Christmas — A79

Churches: No. 430, Zion Moravian. No. 431, Wesley Methodist. $1.50, St. Georges Anglican. $15, Co-Cathedral of the Immaculate Conception.

Perf. 13½x14

1997, Oct. 31 Litho. Wmk. 384

430	A79	10c multi	.25	.25
431	A79	10c multi	.25	.25
432	A79	$1.50 multi, vert.	1.40	1.40
433	A79	$15 multi, vert.	12.00	12.00
		Nos. 430-433 (4)	13.90	13.90

Natl. Heroes' Day — A80

No. 434, Robert L. Bradshaw (1916-78), 1st premier of St. Kitts, Nevis, & Anguilla. No. 435, Joseph N. France, trade unionist. No. 436, C.A. Paul Southwell (1913-79), 1st chief minister of St. Kitts, Nevis, & Anguilla. $3, France, Bradshaw, & Southwell.

1997, Sept. 16 *Perf. 13½*

434	A80	25c multi, vert.	.25	.25
435	A80	25c multi, vert.	.25	.25
436	A80	25c multi, vert.	.25	.25
437	A80	$3 multi	2.25	2.25
		Nos. 434-437 (4)	3.00	3.00

Diana, Princess of Wales (1961-97)

Common Design Type

No. 438: a, like No. 437A. b, Wearing red jacket. c, Wearing white dress. d, Holding flowers.

Perf. 14½x14

1998, Mar. 31 Litho. Wmk. 373

437A	CD355	30c Wearing white hat	.40	.40

Sheet of 4

438	CD355	$1.60 Sheet of 4, #a.-d.	4.75	4.75

No. 438 sold for $6.40 + 90c, with surtax from international sales being donated to Princess Diana Memorial Fund and surtax from national sales being donated to designated local charity.

Butterflies A81

Designs: 10c, Common long-tail skipper. 15c, White peacock. 25c, Caribbean buckeye. 30c, Red rim. 40c, Cassius blue. 50c, Flambeau. 60c, Lucas's blue. 90c, Cloudless sulphur. $1, Monarch. $1.20, Fiery skipper. $1.60, Zebra. $3, Southern dagger tail. $5, Polydamus swallowtail. $10, Tropical checkered skipper.

Perf. 14¼x14½

1997, Dec. 29 Litho. Wmk. 373

439	A81	10c multicolored	.25	.25
a.		"S" in "Proteus" to left of mid-line of leaf above	.45	.45
440	A81	15c multicolored	.30	.30
441	A81	25c multicolored	.40	.40
442	A81	30c multicolored	.40	.40
443	A81	40c multicolored	.40	.40
444	A81	50c multicolored	.60	.60
445	A81	60c multicolored	.70	.70
446	A81	90c multicolored	1.10	1.10
447	A81	$1 multicolored	1.10	1.10
448	A81	$1.20 multicolored	1.40	1.40
449	A81	$1.60 multicolored	1.75	1.75
450	A81	$3 multicolored	2.75	2.75
a.		"S" in "$" same size as numeral	4.00	4.00
451	A81	$5 multicolored	4.00	4.00
a.		Inscribed "Polydamas"	6.00	6.00
452	A81	$10 multicolored	7.00	7.00
a.		"S" in "$" same size as numeral	10.00	10.00
		Nos. 439-452 (14)	22.15	22.15

Nos. 439a, 450a, 451a and 452a have other minor design differences.

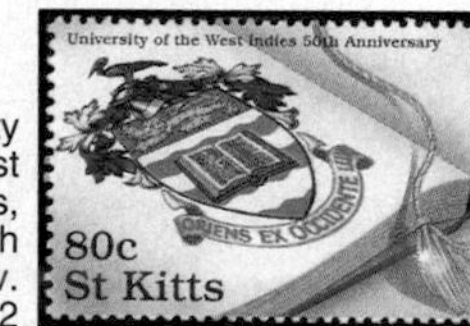

University of West Indies, 50th Anniv. A82

Perf. 13½x13

1998, July 20 Litho. Wmk. 373

453	A82	80c shown	.65	.65
454	A82	$2 Arms, mortarboard	1.75	1.75

Carnival Santa A83

Wmk. 373

1998, Oct. 30 Litho. *Perf. 14*

455	A83	80c shown	.65	.65
456	A83	$1.20 With two dancers	1.00	1.00

UPU, 125th Anniv. — A84

Wmk. 373

1999, Mar. 5 Litho. *Perf. 14*

457	A84	30c shown	.40	.40
458	A84	90c Map of St. Kitts	1.00	1.00

Birds of the Eastern Caribbean A85

Designs: a, Caribbean martin. b, Spotted sandpiper. c, Sooty tern. d, Red-tailed hawk. e, Trembler. f, Belted kingfisher. g, Black-billed duck. h, Yellow warbler. i, Blue-headed hummingbird. j, Antillean euphonia. k, Fulvous whistling duck. l, Mangrove cuckoo. m, Carib grackle. n, Caribbean elaenia. o, Common ground dove. p, Forest thrush.

Wmk. 373

1999, Apr. 27 Litho. *Perf. 14*

459	A85	80c Sheet of 16, #a.-p.	13.00	13.00

IBRA '99.

1st Manned Moon Landing, 30th Anniv.

Common Design Type

Designs: 80c, Lift-off. 90c, In lunar orbit. $1, Aldrin deploying scientific equipment. $1.20, Heat shield burns on re-entry.

$10, Earth as seen from moon.

Perf. 14x13¾

1999, July 20 Litho. Wmk. 384

460	CD357	80c multicolored	.75	.75
461	CD357	90c multicolored	.90	.90
462	CD357	$1 multicolored	1.00	1.00
463	CD357	$1.20 multicolored	1.10	1.10
		Nos. 460-463 (4)	3.75	3.75

Souvenir Sheet

Perf. 14

464	CD357	$10 multicolored	8.25	8.25

No. 464 contains one 40mm circular stamp.

Christmas — A86

Wmk. 373

1999, Oct. 29 Litho. *Perf. 13¾*

465	A86	10c shown	.25	.25
466	A86	30c 3 musicians	.25	.25
467	A86	80c 6 musicians	.70	.70
468	A86	$2 4 musicians, diff.	1.90	1.90
		Nos. 465-468 (4)	3.10	3.10

Children's Drawings Celebrating the Millennium — A87

1999, Dec. 29 Litho. *Perf. 14*

469	A87	10c by Adom Taylor	.35	.35
470	A87	30c by Travis Liburd	.35	.35
471	A87	50c by Darren Moses	.90	.90
472	A87	$1 by Pierre Liburd	1.60	1.60
		Nos. 469-472 (4)	3.20	3.20

Carifesta VII — A88

Designs: 30c, Festival participants. 90c, Emblem. $1.20, Dancer, vert.

Wmk. 373

2000, Aug. 30 Litho. *Perf. 14*

473	A88	30c multi	.25	.25
474	A88	90c multi	.75	.75
475	A88	$1.20 multi	1.15	1.15
		Nos. 473-475 (3)	2.15	2.15

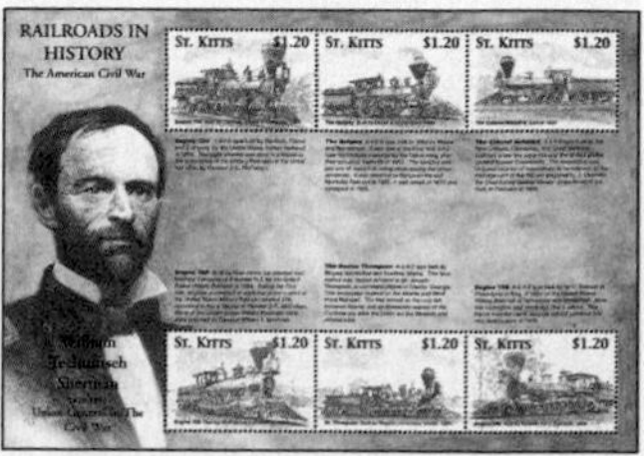

Railroads in American Civil War — A89

No. 476, $1.20, horiz.: a, Engine 133. b, Quigley. c, Colonel Holobird. d, Engine 150. e, Doctor Thompson. f, Engine 156.

No. 477, $1.20, horiz.: a, Governor Nye. b, Engine 31. c, C. A. Henry. d, Engine 152. e, Engine 116. f, Job Terry.

No. 478, $1.60, horiz.: a, Dover. b, Scout. c, Baltimore & Ohio Railroad locomotive. d, John M. Forbes. e, Edward Kidder. f, William W. Wright.

No. 479, $1.60, horiz.: a, Engine 83. b, General. c, Engine 38. d, Texas. e, Engine 162. f, Christopher Adams, Jr.

No. 480, $5, Ulysses S. Grant. No. 481, $5, George B. McClellan. No. 482, $5, Herman Haupt. No. 483, $5, Robert E. Lee.

Unwmk.

2001, Feb. 19 Litho. *Perf. 14*

Sheets of 6, #a-f

476-479	A89	Set of 4	*35.00*	*35.00*

Souvenir Sheets

480-483	A89	Set of 4	*35.00*	*35.00*

Flora & Fauna — A90

No. 484, $1.20 — Flowers: a, Heliconia. b, Anthurium. c, Oncidium splendidum. d, Trumpet creeper. e, Bird of paradise. f, Hibiscus.

No. 485, $1.20: a, Bananaquit. b, Anthurium (hills and clouds in background). c, Common dolphin. d, Horse mushroom. e, Green anole. f, Monarch butterfly.

No. 486, $1.60 — Birds: a, Laughing gull. b, Sooty tern. c, White-tailed tropicbird. d, Painted bunting. e, Belted kingfisher. f, Yellow-bellied sapsucker.

No. 487, $1.60 — Butterflies: a, Figure-of-eight. b, Banded king shoemaker. c, Orange theope. d, Grecian shoemaker. e, Clorinde. f, Small lace-wing.

No. 488, $1.60, horiz.: a, Beaugregory. b, Banded butterflyfish. c, Cherubfish. d, Rock beauty. e, Red snapper. f, Leatherback turtle.

No. 489, $5, Leochilus carinatus. No. 489, $5, Iguana, horiz. No. 490, $5, Ruby-throated hummingbird, horiz. No. 491, $5, Common morpho, horiz.

No. 493, $5, Redband parrotfish, horiz.

2001, Mar. 12 *Perf. 14*

Sheets of 6, #a-f

484-488	A90	Set of 5	*40.00*	*40.00*

Souvenir Sheets

489-493	A90	Set of 5	*27.50*	*27.50*

Compare No. 490 with No. 520.

2001 Census — A91

Designs: 30c, People in house. $3, People, barn, silos.

2001, Apr. 18 Litho. *Perf. 14½x14¼*

494-495	A91	Set of 2	3.75	3.75

Queen Victoria (1819-1901) — A92

No. 496: a, At coronation. b, In wedding gown. c, With Prince Albert visiting wounded Crimean War veterans. d, With Prince Albert, 1854.
$5, Wearing crown.

2001, Apr. 26 ***Perf. 14***
496 A92 $2 Sheet of 4, #a-d 9.00 9.00

Souvenir Sheet

497 A92 $5 black 6.00 6.00

No. 496 contains four 28x42mm stamps.

Monet Paintings — A93

No. 498, horiz.: a, On the Coast of Trouville. b, Vétheuil in Summer. c, Field of Yellow Iris Near Giverny. d, Coastguard's Cottage at Varengeville.
$5, Poplars on the Banks of the Epte, Seen From the Marshes.

2001, July 16 ***Perf. 13¾***
498 A93 $2 Sheet of 4, #a-d 11.50 11.50

Souvenir Sheet

499 A93 $5 multi 5.75 5.75

Giuseppe Verdi (1813-1901), Opera Composer — A94

No. 500 — Scenes from the Sicilian Vespers: a, French soldiers in Palermo (all standing). b, French soldiers in Palermo (some seated). c, Costume design. d, Sicilian people and French soldiers
$5, Montserrat Caballé.

2001, July 16 ***Perf. 14***
500 A94 $2 Sheet of 4, #a-d 8.50 8.50

Souvenir Sheet

501 A94 $5 multi 5.75 5.75

Royal Navy Submarines, Cent. — A95

No. 502, horiz.: a, A Class submarine. b, HMS Dreadnaught battleship. c, HMS Amethyst. d, HMS Barnham. e, HMS Exeter. f, HMS Eagle.
$5, HMS Dreadnaught submarine.

2001, July 16 ***Perf. 14***
502 A95 $1.40 Sheet of 6, #a-f *19.00 19.00*

Souvenir Sheet

503 A95 $5 multi *10.00 10.00*

No. 502 contains six 42x28mm stamps.

Queen Elizabeth II, 75th Birthday — A96

No. 504: a, In blue hat, holding flowers. b, In flowered hat, looking right. c, In blue hat and coat. d, In flowered hat, looking left.
$5, On horse.

2001, July 16
504 A96 $2 Sheet of 4, #a-d 8.50 8.50

Souvenir Sheet

505 A96 $5 multi 5.25 5.25

Phila Nippon '01, Japan — A97

Woodcuts: 50c, Hatsufunedayu as a Tatebina, by Shigenobu. Yamagawa 80c, Samurai Kodenji as Tsuyu No Mae, by Kiyonobu I. $1, Senya Nakamura as Tokonatsu, by Kiyomasu I. $1.60, Sumida River, by Shunsho. $2, Wrestler, Kuemon Yoba, by Shun-ei. $3, Two Actors in Roles, by Kiyonobu Torii I.
$5, Full Length Actor Protraits, by Shun-ei.

2001, July 16 ***Perf. 12x12¼***
506-511 A97 Set of 6 9.25 9.25

Souvenir Sheet

512 A97 $5 multi 6.25 6.25

Mao Zedong (1893-1976) — A98

No. 514: a, In 1926. b, In 1945 (green background). c, In 1945 (lilac background).
$3, Undated picture.

2001, July 16 **Litho.** ***Perf. 13¾***
513 A98 $2 Sheet of 3, #a-c 9.00 9.00

Souvenir Sheet

514 A98 $3 multi 4.50 4.50

Flora & Fauna — A99

No. 515, $1.20 — Birds: a, Trembler. b, White-tailed tropicbird. c, Red-footed booby. d, Red-legged thrush. e, Painted bunting. f, Bananaquit.
No. 516, $1.20 — Orchids: a, Maxillaria cucullata. b, Cattleya dowiana. c, Rossioglossum grande. d, Aspasia epidendroides. e, Lycaste skinneri. f, Cattleya percivaliana.
No. 517, $1.60 — Butterflies: a, Orange-barred sulphur. b, Giant swallowtail. c, Orange theope. d, Blue night. e, Grecian shoemaker. f, Cramer's mesene.
No. 518, $1.60 — Mushrooms: a, Pholiota spectabilis. b, Flammula penetrans. c, Ungulina marginata. d, Collybia iocephala. e, Amanita muscaria. f, Corinus comatus.
No. 519, $1.60, horiz. — Whales: a, Killer.whale b, Cuvier's beaked whale. c, Humpback whale. d, Sperm whale. e, Blue whale. f, Whale shark.
No. 520, $5, Ruby-throated hummingbird. No. 521, $5, Psychilis atropurpurea. No. 522, $5, Figure-of-eight butterfly. No. 523, $5, Lepiota procera. No. 524, $5, Sei whale, horiz.

2001, Sept. 18 ***Perf. 14***

Sheets of 6, #a-f

515-519 A99 Set of 5 35.00 35.00

Souvenir Sheets

520-524 A99 Set of 5 25.00 25.00

Compare No. 520 with No. 490.

Christmas and Carnival — A100

Designs: 10c, Angel, Christmas tree. 30c, Fireworks. 80c, Wreath, dove, bells, candy cane. $2, Steel drums.

2001, Nov. 26
525-528 A100 Set of 4 4.00 4.00

Reign of Queen Elizabeth II, 50th Anniv. — A101

No. 529: a, Ceremonial coach. b, Prince Philip. c, Queen and Queen Mother. d, Queen wearing tiara.
$5, Queen and Prince Philip.

2002, Feb. 6 ***Perf. 14¼***
529 A101 $2 Sheet of 4, #a-d 8.00 8.00

Souvenir Sheet

530 A101 $5 multi 5.50 5.50

United We Stand — A102

Perf. 13½x13¼

2002, June 17 **Litho.**
531 A102 80c multi 1.90 1.90

Printed in sheets of 4.

2002 Winter Olympics, Salt Lake City A103

Designs: No. 532, $3, Cross-country skiing. No. 533, $3, Alpine skiing.

2002, June 17 ***Perf. 13¼x13½***
532-533 A103 Set of 2 5.75 5.75
533a Souvenir sheet, #532-533 5.75 5.75

Souvenir Sheet

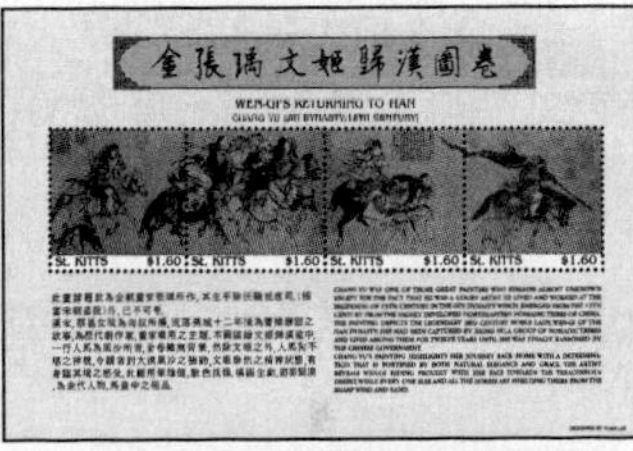

New Year 2002 (Year of the Horse) — A104

Details of Wen-Gi's Returning to Han, by Chang Yu: a, Horse and rider, dog. b, Group of horses and riders. c, Horse and rider, two attendants. d, Standard bearer on horse.

2002, June 17 ***Perf. 12½***
534 A104 $1.60 Sheet of 4, #a-d 5.75 5.75

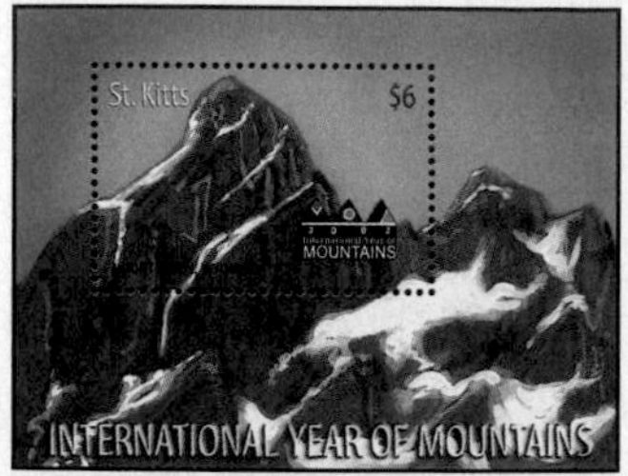

Intl. Year of Mountains — A105

No. 535: a, Mt. Sakura, Japan. b, Mount Assiniboine, Canada. c, Mt. Asgard, Canada. d, Bugaboo Spire, Canada.
$6, Mt. Owen, Wyoming.

2002, June 17 ***Perf. 13¼x13½***
535 A105 $2 Sheet of 4, #a-d 7.00 7.00

Souvenir Sheet

536 A105 $6 multi 6.00 6.00

2002 World Cup Soccer Championships, Japan and Korea — A106

No. 537 — World Cup trophy and: a, $1.65, 1982 World Cup poster. b, $1.65, Just Fontaine, French flag. c, $1.65, U.S. player and flag. d, $1.65, Swedish player and flag. e, $6, Daegu Sports Complex, Korea (55x41mm).
$6, Roger Milla.

2002, June 17 ***Perf. 13½x13¼***
537 A106 Sheet of 5, #a-e 10.50 10.50

Souvenir Sheet

538 A106 $6 multi 6.00 6.00

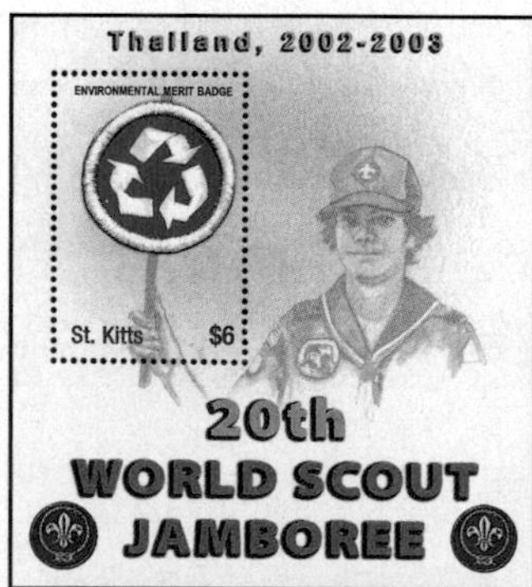

20th World Scout Jamboree, Thailand — A107

No. 539, horiz.: a, Scout sign. b, Silver Award 2. c, Council patch. d, Scout with sword.
$6, Environmental Studies merit badge.

2002, June 17 ***Perf. 13¼x13½***
539 A107 $2 Sheet of 4, #a-d 7.50 7.50

Souvenir Sheet

Perf. 13½x13¼

540 A107 $6 multi 6.00 6.00

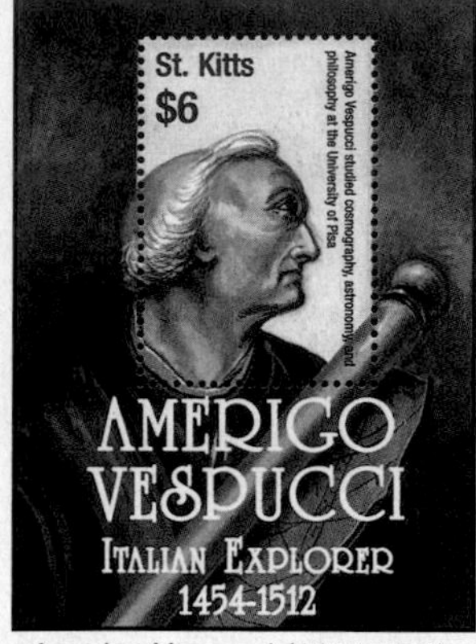

Amerigo Vespucci (1454-1512), Explorer — A108

No. 541, horiz.: a, Vespucci with feathered hat. b, 1507 World map by Martin Waldseemüller. c, Vespucci with beard.
$6, Vespucci with bald head.

2002, June 17 ***Perf. 13¼x13½***
541 A108 $3 Sheet of 3, #a-c 8.00 8.00

Souvenir Sheet

Perf. 13½x13¼

542 A108 $6 multi 5.75 5.75

Kim Collins, Sprinter — A109

Collins: 30c, Running. 90c, Wearing 2001 IAAF bronze medal.

2002, July 2 ***Perf. 14***
543-544 A109 Set of 2 2.50 2.50

Christmas — A110

Fruits: 10c, Soursop. 80c, Passion fruit. $1, Sugar apple. $2, Custard apple.

2002, Oct. 14 **Litho.**
545-548 A110 Set of 4 6.00 6.00

Queen Mother Elizabeth (1900-2002) — A111

No. 549: a, Wearing green dress. b, Wearing yellow dress and hat.

2002, Nov. 18 **Litho.** ***Perf. 14***
549 A111 $2 Pair, #a-b 8.00 8.00

No. 549 printed in sheets containing 2 pairs.

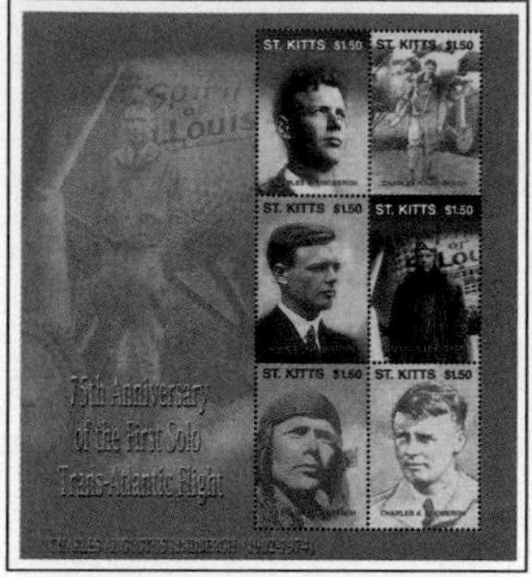

First Non-stop Solo Transatlantic Flight, 75th Anniv. — A112

Charles Lindbergh: a, In suit, denomination in white. b, And Spirit of St. Louis, denomination in blue violet. c, In suit, looking right, denomination in blue violet. d, And Spirit of St. Louis, denomination in white. e, Wearing pilot's headgear. f, Wearing overcoat.

2002, Nov. 18
550 A112 $1.50 Sheet of 6, #a-f 11.00 11.00

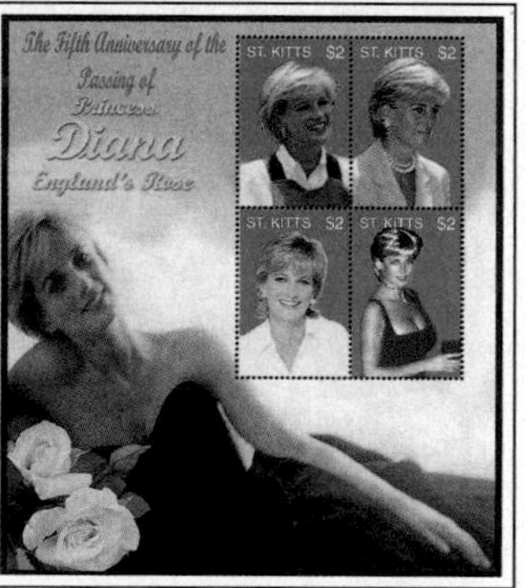

Princess Diana (1961-97) — A113

No. 551, $2: a, Wearing bulletproof vest. b, Wearing gray suit with pearls. c, Wearing yellow blouse. d, Wearing red dress and necklace.
No. 552, $2: a, Wearing white coat with purple piping. b, With hands clasped. c, Wearing red dress without necklace. d, Wearing white dress.

2002, Nov. 18 **Litho.**

Sheets of 4, #a-d

551-552 A113 Set of 2 15.00 15.00

Pres. John F. Kennedy (1917-63) — A114

No. 553, $2: a, With sailors, Solomon Islands, 1942. b, On PT109, 1942. c, As Navy Ensign, 1941. d, Receiving medal for gallantry, 1944.
No. 554, $2: a, Peace Corps. b, Space program. c, Civil rights. d, Nuclear disarmament.

2002, Nov. 18 ***Perf. 14***

Sheets of 4, #a-d

553-554 A114 Set of 2 13.00 13.00

New Year 2003 (Year of the Ram) — A115

No. 555: a, Piebald ram. b, Ram with long coat. c, Ram sculpture, looking right.

2003, Jan. 27 ***Perf. 14¼x13¾***
555 A115 $1 Vert. strip of 3, #a-c 4.50 4.50

No. 555 printed in sheets containing 2 strips.

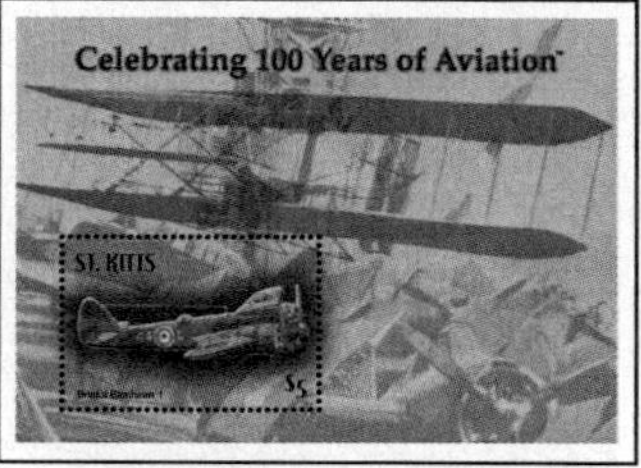

Powered Flight, Cent. — A116

No. 556: a, Voisin LA5. b, Gotha G.V. c, Polikarpov I-16. d, Bell YFM-1.
$5, Bristol Blenheim 1.

2003, June 17 **Litho.** ***Perf. 14***
556 A116 $2 Sheet of 4, #a-d 7.50 7.50

Souvenir Sheet

557 A116 $5 multi 4.00 4.00

Tour de France Bicycle Race, Cent. — A117

No. 558: a, Miguel Indurain, 1994. b, Indurain, 1995. c, Bjarne Riis, 1996. d, Jan Ullrich, 1997.
$5, Indurain, 1991-95.

2003, June 17 ***Perf. 13½x13¼***
558 A117 $2 Sheet of 4, #a-d 7.00 7.00

Souvenir Sheet

559 A117 $5 multi 4.00 4.00

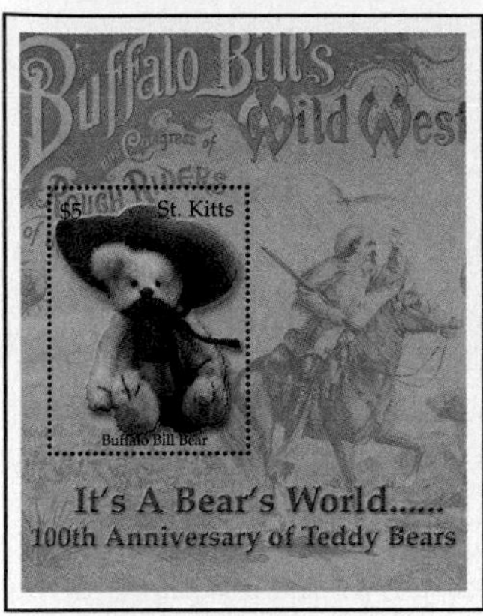

Teddy Bears, Cent. — A118

No. 560: a, Queen Victoria Bear. b, Teddy Roosevelt Bear. c, George Washington Bear. d, General Patton Bear.
$5, Buffalo Bill Bear.

2003, June 17 ***Perf. 13¾***
560 A118 $2 Sheet of 4, #a-d 7.50 7.50

Souvenir Sheet

561 A118 $5 multi 4.50 4.50

Coronation of Queen Elizabeth II, 50th Anniv. — A119

No. 562: a, Wearing tiara as young woman. b, Wearing tiara and red sash. c, Wearing tiara and blue sash.
$5, Queen waving.

2003, June 17 **Litho.** ***Perf. 14***
562 A119 $3 Sheet of 3, #a-c 7.00 7.00

Souvenir Sheet

563 A119 $5 multi 4.00 4.00

Caribbean Community, 30th Anniv. — A120

2003, June 23
564 A120 30c multi 1.25 1.25

Prince William, 21st Birthday — A121

No. 565: a, As toddler, in jacket. b, As young boy, in striped shirt. c, Wearing sports shirt.
$5, As child, waving.

2003, July 1
565 A121 $3 Sheet of 3, #a-c 7.00 7.00

Souvenir Sheet

566 A121 $5 multi 4.00 4.00

Norman Rockwell Paintings of Boy Scouts from Boy Scout Calendars — A122

No. 567: a, Scout and Sailors, 1937. b, Scouts with Camping Gear, 1937. c, Boy and Dog at Window, 1968. d, Scout at Attention, 1932.
$5, Boy Scout and Cub Scout, 1950.

2003, Aug. 18 ***Perf. 14***
567 A122 $2 Sheet of 4, #a-d 6.50 6.50

Souvenir Sheet

568 A122 $5 multi 4.00 4.00

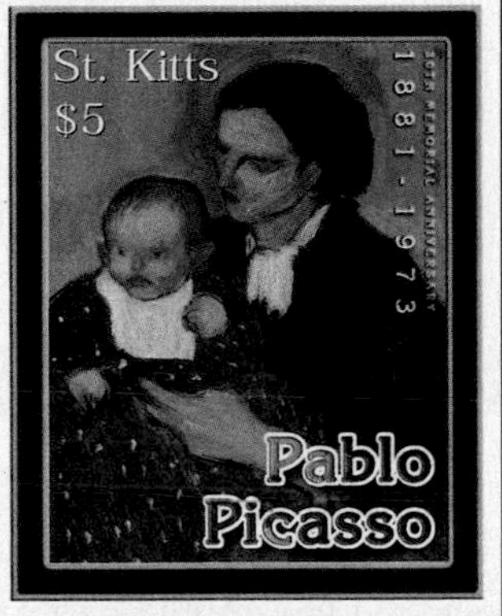

Painting by Pablo Picasso — A123

No. 569: a, Child with Wooden Horse. b, Child with a Ball. c, The Butterfly Catcher. d, Boy with a Lobster. e, Baby Wearing Polka Dot Dress. f, El Bobo, After Murillo.
$5, Untitled painting.

2003, Aug. 18 ***Perf. 14***
569 A123 $1.60 Sheet of 4, #a-d 7.50 7.50

Souvenir Sheet

Imperf

570 A123 $5 multi 4.00 4.00

No. 569 contains six 28x42mm stamps.

Rembrandt Paintings A124

Designs: 50c, A Family Group. $1, Portrait of Cornelis Claesz Anslo and Aetje Gerritsor Schouten, horiz. $1.60, Portrait of a Young Woman. $3, Man in Military Costume.
No. 575: a, An Old Woman Reading. b, Hendrickje Stoffels. c, Rembrandt's Mother. d, Saskia.
$5, Judas Returning the Thirty Pieces of Silver.

2003, Aug. 18 ***Perf. 14¼***
571-574 A124 Set of 4 4.75 4.75
575 A124 $2 Sheet of 4, #a-d 6.00 6.00

Souvenir Sheet

576 A124 $5 multi 3.75 3.75

Japanese Art — A125

Designs: 90c, Tokiwa Gozen with Her Son in the Snow, by Hokumei Shunkyokusai. $1, Courtesan and Asahina, attributed to Choki Eishosai. $1.50, Parody of Sugawara No Michizane Seated on an Ox, by Toyokuni Utagawa. $3, Visiting a Flower Garden, by Kunisada Utagawa.
No. 581 — Akugenta Yoshihira, by Kunisada Utagawa: a, Man with bow. b, Man with sword at waist. c, Man holding scarf. d, Man with sword on shoulder.
$6, The Courtesan Katachino Under a Cherry Tree, by Toyoharu Utagawa.

2003, Aug. 18
577-580 A125 Set of 4 5.50 5.50
581 A125 $2 Sheet of 4, #a-d 6.75 6.75

Souvenir Sheet

582 A125 $6 multi 5.00 5.00

White Gibbon, by Giuseppe Castiglione A126

2004, Jan. 15 ***Perf. 13¾x13½***
583 A126 $1.60 shown 2.00 2.00

Souvenir Sheet

Perf. 13¼

584 A126 $3 Painting detail 3.25 3.25

New Year 2004 (Year of the Monkey). No. 583 printed in sheets of 4. No. 584 contains one 30x37mm stamp.

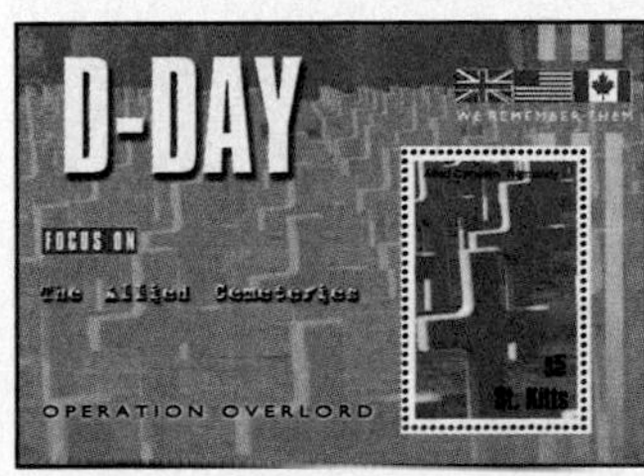

D-Day, 60th Anniv. — A127

No. 585, horiz.: a, 12th Panzer Division moves into position. b, German heavy tank. c, British and Germans clash (soldiers). d, British and Germans clash (soldiers, tank).
$5, Allied cemetery, Normandy.

2004, Sept. 21 **Litho.** ***Perf. 14***
585 A127 $2 Sheet of 4, #a-d 6.75 6.75

Souvenir Sheet

586 A127 $5 multi 4.50 4.50

2004 Summer Olympics, Athens A128

Designs: 50c, Jiri Guth Jarkovsky, member of first International Olympic Committee. 90c, Poster for 1972 Munich Olympics. $1, Poster for 1900 Paris Olympics. $3, Sculpture of wrestlers.

2004, Sept. 21 ***Perf. 14¼***
587-590 A128 Set of 4 4.00 4.00

Souvenir Sheet

Deng Xiaoping (1904-97), Chinese Leader — A129

2004, Sept. 21 **Litho.** ***Perf. 14***
591 A129 $5 multi 4.00 4.00

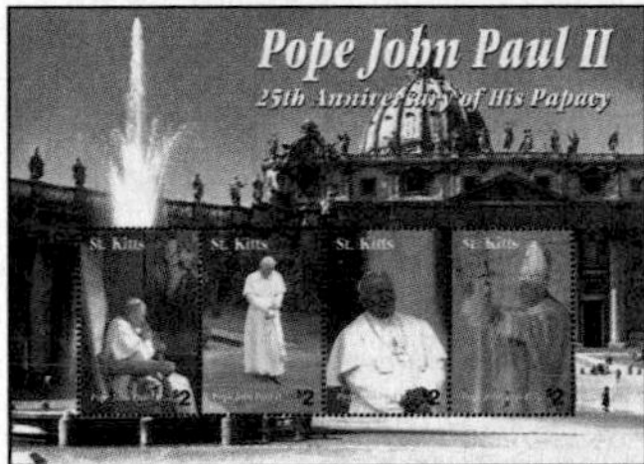

Election of Pope John Paul II, 25th Anniv. (in 2003) — A130

No. 592: a, Seated. b, Walking in garden. c, With arms clasped. d, Holding crucifix.

2004, Sept. 21
592 A130 $2 Sheet of 4, #a-d 8.00 8.00

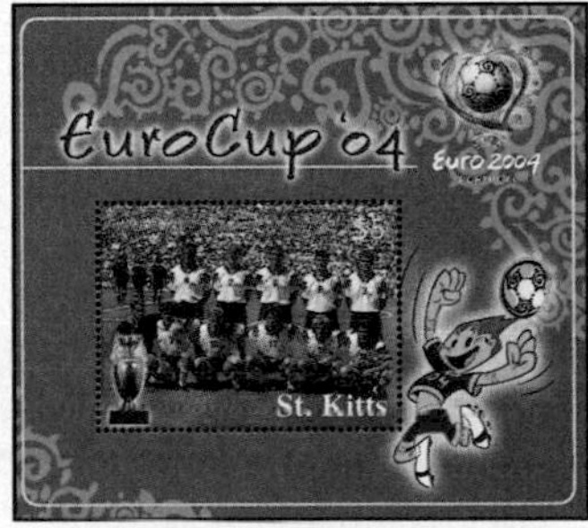

2004 European Soccer Championships, Portugal — A131

No. 593, vert.: a, Berti Vogts. b, Patrik Berger. c, Oliver Bierhoff. d, Empire Stadium.
$5, 1996 German team.

2004, Sept. 21 ***Perf. 14¼***
593 A131 $2 Sheet of 4, #a-d 6.50 6.50

Souvenir Sheet

594 A131 $5 multi 4.00 4.00

No. 593 contains four 28x42mm stamps.

Locomotives, 200th Anniv. — A132

No. 595, $2: a, Italian State Railways Class 685 2-8-2. b, Swiss Federal Railways 4-6-0. c, BESA Class 4-6-0. d, Great Western City Class 4-4-0.

No. 596, $2: a, Northumbrian 0-2-2. b, Prince Class 2-2-2. c, Adler 2-2-2. d, L&NWR Webb Compound 2-4-0.

No. 597, $2: a, American Standard 4-4-0. b, New South Wales Government Class 79 4-4-0. c, Johnson Midland Single 4-2-2. d, Union Pacific FEF-3 Class 4-8-4.

No. 598, $5, Crampton Type 4-2-0. No. 599, $5, CN Class U-2 4-8-4. No. 600, $5, Baldwin 2-8-2, vert.

Perf. 13¼x13½, 13½x13¼

2004, Sept. 21

Sheets of 4, #a-d

595-597 A132 Set of 3 20.00 20.00

Souvenir Sheets

598-600 A132 Set of 3 12.50 12.50

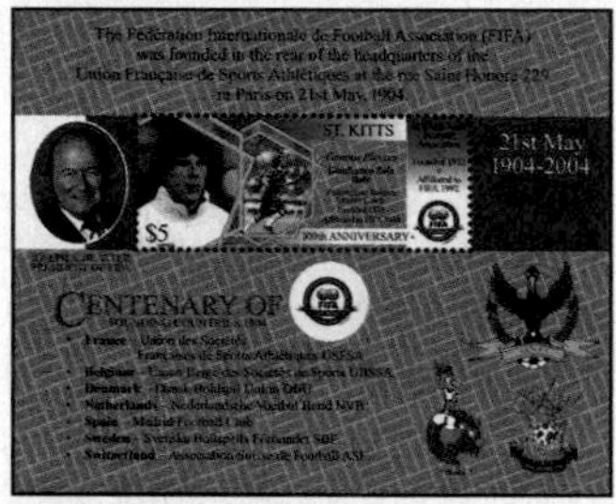

FIFA (Fédération Internationale de Football Association), Cent. — A133

No. 601: a, Demetrio Albertini. b, Romario. c, Gerd Muller. d, Danny Blanchflower.

$5, Gianfranco Zola.

2004, Nov. 8 ***Perf. 12¾x12½***

601 A133 $2 Sheet of 4, #a-d 6.00 6.00

Souvenir Sheet

602 A133 $5 multi 3.75 3.75

World AIDS Day — A134

Posters by: 30c, Ngozi Nicholls. 80c, Travis Liburd. 90c, Darren Kelly, horiz. $1, Shane Berry.

2004, Dec. 1 ***Perf. 14***

603-606 A134 Set of 4 4.25 4.25

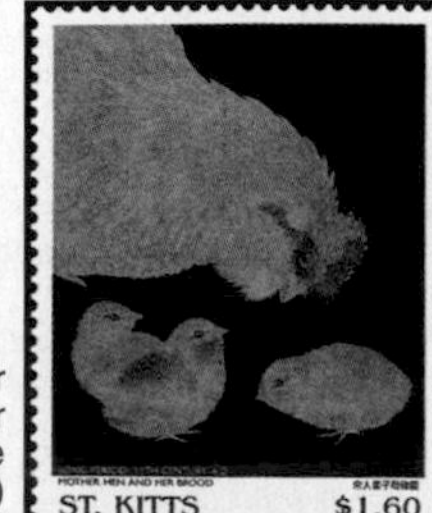

New Year 2005 (Year of the Rooster) A135

Mother Hen and Her Brood, by unknown artist: $1.60, Detail. $5, Entire painting.

2005, Feb. 7 ***Perf. 12***

607 A135 $1.60 multi 1.50 1.50

Souvenir Sheet

608 A135 $5 multi 5.75 5.75

Wildcats — A136

No. 609, vert.: a, Ocelot. b, Bengal leopard. c, Tiger. d, Leopard.

$5, Sumatran tiger.

2005, Feb. 7 ***Perf. 12¾***

609 A136 $2 Sheet of 4, #a-d 7.00 7.00

Souvenir Sheet

610 A136 $5 multi 5.50 5.50

Prehistoric Animals — A137

No. 611, horiz.: a, Triceratops. b, Deinonychus. c, Apatosaurus.

No. 612, horiz.: a, Dimetrodon. b, Homalocephale. c, Stegosaurus.

No. 613, horiz.: a, Sabre-toothed tiger. b, Edmontosaurus. c, Tyrannosaurus rex.

No. 614: $5, Brontosaurus. No. 615, $5, Woolly mammoth. No. 616, $5, Andrewsarchus, horiz.

2005, Feb. 7

611 A137 $3 Sheet of 3, #a-c 7.00 7.00
612 A137 $3 Sheet of 3, #a-c 7.00 7.00
613 A137 $3 Sheet of 3, #a-c 7.00 7.00

Souvenir Sheet

614 A137 $5 multi 4.00 4.00
615 A137 $5 multi 4.00 4.00
616 A137 $5 multi 4.00 4.00

Parrots — A138

No. 617, vert.: a, Australian king parrot. b, Rose-breasted cockatoo. c, Pale-headed rosella. d, Eastern rosella.

$5, Rainbow lorikeets.

2005, Feb. 7 **Litho.** ***Perf. 12¾***

617 A138 $2 Sheet of 4, #a-d 6.75 6.75

Souvenir Sheet

618 A138 $5 multi 5.00 5.00

Insects and Butterflies — A139

No. 619, vert.: a, Papilio demoleus. b, Ephemeroptera. c, Hamadryas februa. d, Aphylla caraiba.

$5, Small blue butterfly.

2005, Feb. 7

619 A139 $2 Sheet of 4, #a-d 7.50 7.50

Souvenir Sheet

620 A139 $5 multi 4.50 4.50

Ducks A140

Designs: 25c, White-cheeked pintails. $1, Fulvous whistling ducks. $2, White-faced whistling duck. $3, Black-bellied whistling ducks.

2005, Feb. 7

621-624 A140 Set of 4 5.50 5.50

Souvenir Sheet

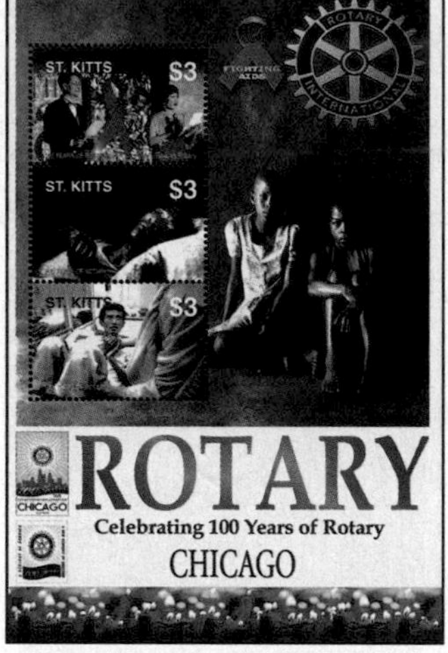

Rotary International, Cent. — A141

No. 625: a, Beijing Rotary meeting. b, Sick man. c, Sick man and visitor.

2005, May 11

625 A141 $3 Sheet of 3, #a-c 7.50 7.50

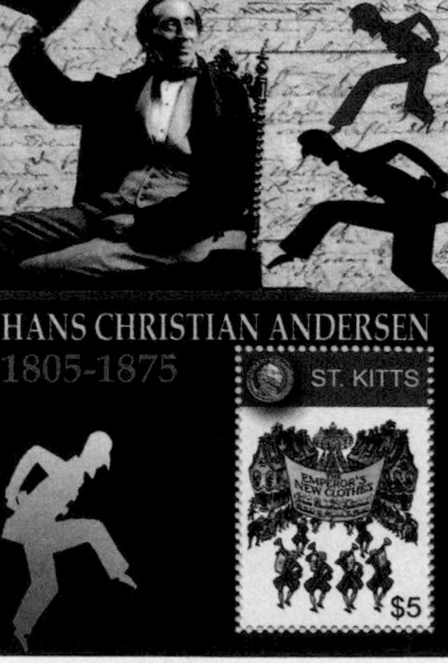

Hans Christian Andersen (1805-75), Author — A142

No. 626 — Book covers: a, Hans Christian Andersen's Fairy Tales. b, The Emperor's New Clothes. c, The Nutcracker.

$5, The Emperor's New Clothes, diff.

2005, May 11

626 A142 $3 Sheet of 3, #a-c 7.00 7.00

Souvenir Sheet

627 A142 $5 multi 4.00 4.00

Jules Verne (1828-1905), Writer — A143

No. 628, vert.: a, Verne. b, Sea monster attack. c, Rouquayrol. d, Modern Aqualung.

$5, Atomic submarine.

2005, May 11

628 A143 $3 Sheet of 4, #a-d 6.75 6.75

Souvenir Sheet

629 A143 $5 multi 4.00 4.00

End of World War II, 60th Anniv. — A144

No. 630, $2: a, US Navy Hudson PDB-1 patrol bombers. b, World War II combat. c, Gen. Dwight D. Eisenhower. d, Transporting German prisoners of war. e, Newspaper announcing Nazi surrender.

No. 631, $2: a, USS Arizona under attack. b, USS Arizona Captain Franklin Van Valkenburgh. c, Hiroshima atomic blast. d, Historic marker of first atomic bomb loading pit, Tinian Island. e, Memorial Cenotaph, Hiroshima Peace Park.

2005, May 11 **Litho.**

Sheets of 5, #a-e

630-631 A144 Set of 2 18.00 18.00

Battle of Trafalgar, Bicent. — A145

Ships: 50c, Montagne. 90c, San Jose. $2, Imperieuse. $3, San Nicolas.

$5, British Navy gun crew on HMS Victory.

2005, May 11 ***Perf. 12¾***

632-635 A145 Set of 4 5.75 5.75

Souvenir Sheet

636 A145 $5 multi 4.75 4.75

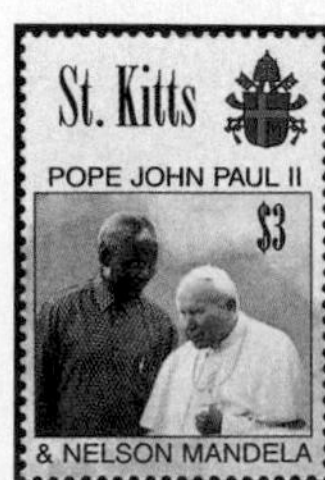

Pope John Paul II (1920-2005) and Nelson Mandela — A146

2005, July 19 ***Perf. 13½***

637 A146 $3 multi 2.50 2.50

Printed in sheets of 4.

Souvenir Sheet

Taipei 2005 Stamp Exhibition — A147

No. 638 — Various Chinese junks with denominations in: a, Red. b, Blue. c, Gray. d, Yellow orange.

2005, Aug. 19 *Perf. 14*
638 A147 $2 Sheet of 4, #a-d 6.75 6.75

Christmas — A148

Paintings: 30c, Virgin and Child, by Gerard David. 50c, Virgin and Child, by David, diff. 90c, Virgin and Child, by David, diff. $2, Virgin and Child, by Bartolomeo Suardi Bramentine.
$5, Nativity, by Martin Schongauer.

2005, Dec. 6 Litho. *Perf. 13¾x13½*
639-642 A148 Set of 4 3.00 3.00

Souvenir Sheet

643 A148 $5 multi 4.00 4.00

Treaty of Basseterre, 25th Anniv. — A149

Designs: 30c, Eastern Caribbean Central Bank. 90c, 25th anniversary emblem of Organization of Eastern Caribbean States.
$2.50, Heads of government of Organization of Eastern Caribbean States, vert.

2006, Sept. 11 Litho. *Perf. 12¾*
644-645 A149 Set of 2 1.00 1.00

Souvenir Sheet

Perf. 12

646 Sheet of 2 #646a 4.00 4.00
a. A149 $2.50 multi 1.75 1.75

Rembrandt (1606-69), Painter A150

Paintings or painting details: 50c, Bathsheba with King David's Letter. 80c, Isaac and Rebecca (Rebecca). 90c, Isaac and Rebecca (Isaac). $1, Samson Threatening His Father-in-Law (father-in-law). $1.60, Samson Threatening His Father-in-Law (Samson). $2, Equestrian Portrait.
$6, Landscape with a Stone Bridge, horiz.

2006, Nov. 15 *Perf. 12*
647-652 A150 Set of 6 5.50 5.50

Imperf

Size: 101x70mm

653 A150 $6 multi 4.75 4.75

Christmas — A151

Paintings or painting details by Peter Paul Rubens: 25c, Mary In Adoration Before the Sleeping Infant. 60c, The Holy Family Under the Apple Tree (Madonna and Child). $1, The Holy Family Under the Apple Tree (cherub). $1.20, St. Francis of Assisi Receives the Infant Jesus from Mary.
No. 658: a, Like 25c. b, Like 60c. c, Like $1. d, Like $1.20.

2006, Dec. 27 *Perf. 13½*
654-657 A151 Set of 4 2.50 2.50

Souvenir Sheet

658 A151 $2 Sheet of 4, #a-d 6.50 6.50

Souvenir Sheet

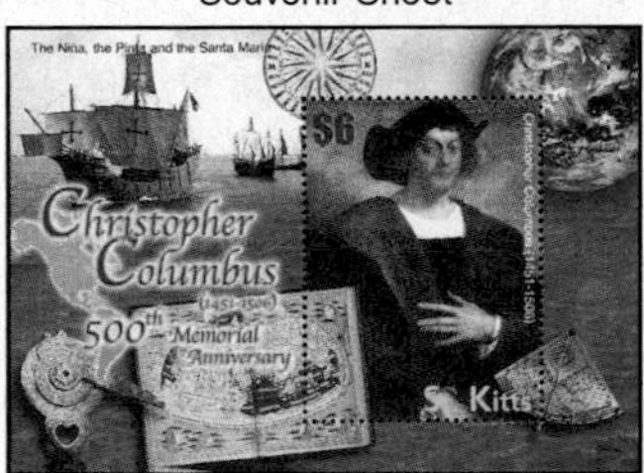

Christopher Columbus (1451-1506), Explorer — A152

2007, Jan. 3 *Perf. 13¼*
659 A152 $6 multi 4.75 4.75

Queen Elizabeth II, 80th Birthday (in 2006) — A153

No. 660: a, Wearing beige and brown hat. b, Wearing tiara. c, Wearing light blue hat. d, Wearing crown.
$5, Seated at desk.

2007, Jan. 3
660 A153 $2 Sheet of 4, #a-d 6.00 6.00

Souvenir Sheet

661 A153 $5 multi 3.75 3.75

Betty Boop — A154

No. 662 — Betty Boop in spotlight with background color of: a, Red. b, Green. c, White. d, Purple. e, Blue. f, Yellow.
No. 663 — Betty Boop in: a, Green heart. b, Purple heart.

2007, Jan. 3
662 A154 $1.60 Sheet of 6, #a-f 7.75 7.75

Souvenir Sheet

663 A154 $3 Sheet of 2, #a-b 4.75 4.75

Scouting, Cent. A155

Dove with flags, Scouting emblem, text and: $3, Years "1907" and "2007." $5, No years, horiz.

2007, Jan. 3
664 A155 $3 multi 2.50 2.50

Souvenir Sheet

665 A155 $5 multi 3.75 3.75

No. 664 was printed in sheets of 4.

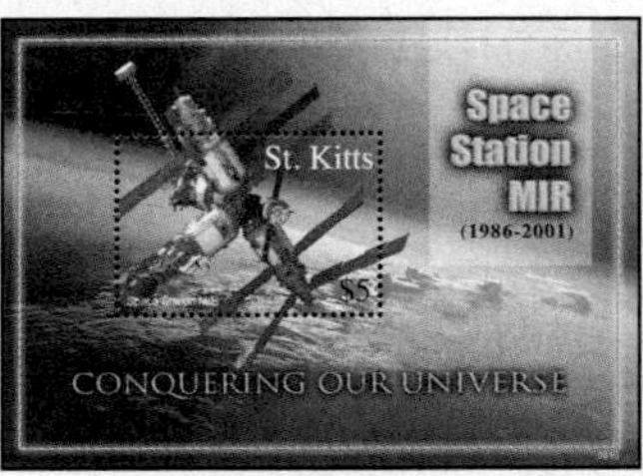

Space Achievements — A156

No. 666 — Giotto Comet Probe: a, Prelaunch test at Kourou launch site. b, Halley's Comet (black sky). c, Halley's Comet above cloud. d, Giotto Comet Probe. e, Giotto spacecraft mounted on Ariane rocket. f, Halley's Comet (blue sky).
No. 667, vert. — Launching of Luna 9: a, Molniya launch vehicle. b, Luna 9 flight apparatus. c, Luna 9 soft lander. d, Photograph of Ocean of Storms taken by Luna 9.
$5, Space Station Mir.

2007, Jan. 3 Litho. *Perf. 13¼*
666 A156 $1.60 Sheet of 6, #a-f 7.25 7.25
667 A156 $2 Sheet of 4, #a-d 6.00 6.00

Souvenir Sheet

668 A156 $5 multi 3.75 3.75

Miniature Sheets

Pres. John F. Kennedy (1917-63) — A157

No. 669, $2: a, Kennedy and map of Central America. b, Kennedy, woman and child, map of Caribbean. c, Kennedy addressing group, map of Western South America. d, Kennedy shaking hands with man, map of Eastern South America.
No. 670, $2: a, Kennedy greeting Peace Corps volunteers (inscription in black). b, Peace Corps volunteer Ida Shoatz and Peruvians. c, R. Sargent Shriver, Peace Corps Director. d, Kennedy greeting Peace Corps volunteers, diff. (inscription in white).

2007, Jan. 3 **Litho.**

Sheets of 4, #a-d

669-670 A157 Set of 2 12.00 12.00

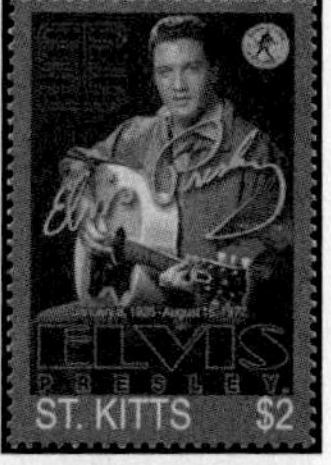

A158

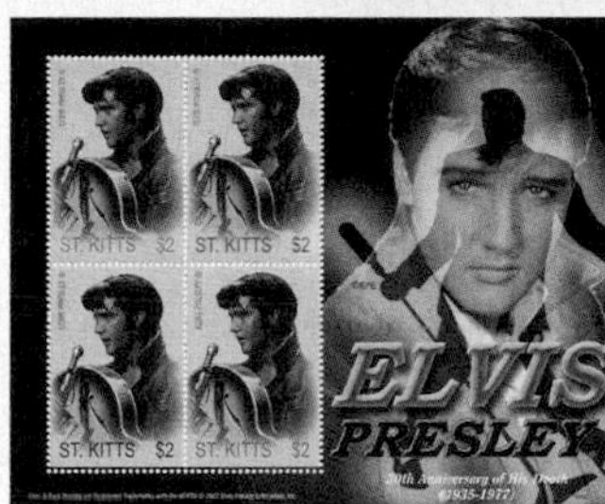

Elvis Presley (1935-77) — A159

No. 672 — Denomination color: a, Blue. b, Red. c, Black. d, Lilac.

2007, Feb. 15 *Perf. 14*
671 A158 $2 multi 2.00 2.00
672 A159 $2 Sheet of 4, #a-d 7.50 7.50

No. 671 was printed in sheets of 4.

Miniature Sheet

Marilyn Monroe (1926-62), Actress — A160

No. 673 — Monroe with: a, Pinkie in mouth. b, Glasses. c, Strapless gown. d, Hand on cheek.

2007, Feb. 15 *Perf. 13½*
673 A160 $2 Sheet of 4, #a-d 6.50 6.50

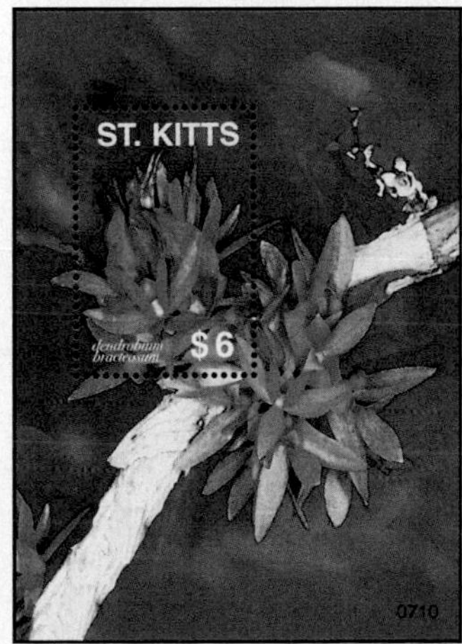

Orchids — A161

No. 674: a, Rhynchostele cervantesii. b, Oerstedella wallisii. c, Disa uniflora. d, Pleione formosana.
$6, Dendrobium bracteosum.

2007, June 18 *Perf. 12¾*
674 A161 $2 Sheet of 4, #a-d 7.00 7.00

Souvenir Sheet

675 A161 $6 multi 5.00 5.00

Birds — A162

No. 676, horiz.: a, Brown noddy. b, Royal albatross. c, Masked booby. d, Cormorant.
$6, Rock cormorant.

2007, June 18 ***Perf. 12¾***

676 A162 $2 Sheet of 4, #a-d 7.00 7.00

Souvenir Sheet

677 A162 $6 multi 5.00 5.00

Worldwide Fund for Nature (WWF) — A163

Tiger sharks: a, Three sharks. b, Two sharks. c, Two sharks and sunlight. d, One shark.

2007, June 18

678 Strip or block of 4 4.00 4.00
a.-d. A163 $1.20 Any single .90 .90
e. Sheet, 2 each #a-d 8.50 8.50

Souvenir Sheets

National Basketball Association Players and Team Emblems — A164

No. 679, $8: a, Steve Nash. b, Phoenix Suns emblem.
No. 680, $8: a, Shaquille O'Neal. b, Miami Heat emblem, denomination in black.
No. 681, $8: a, Dwayne Wade. b, Miami Heat emblem, denomination in orange.
No. 682, $8: a, Yao Ming. b, Houston Rockets emblem.

Litho. (Margin Embossed)

2007, Aug. 16 ***Imperf.***

Without Gum

Sheets of 2, #a-b

679-682 A164 Set of 4 50.00 50.00

Fruit — A165

2007, Oct. 16 Litho. ***Perf. 13¼x12½***

683 A165 10c Cherries .25 .25
684 A165 15c Coconuts .25 .25
685 A165 30c Watermelons .25 .25
686 A165 40c Pineapples .30 .30
687 A165 50c Guava .40 .40
688 A165 60c Sugar apples .45 .45
689 A165 80c Passion fruit .60 .60
690 A165 90c Starfruit .70 .70
691 A165 $1 Tangerines .75 .75
692 A165 $5 Noni fruit 3.75 3.75
693 A165 $10 Papayas 7.50 7.50
Nos. 683-693 (11) 15.20 15.20

Miniature Sheet

Elvis Presley (1935-77) — A166

No. 694 — Presley wearing: a, White shirt. b, Jacket with bird design. c, Black shirt. d, Blue jacket. e, Red and white shirt. f, White jacket and red shirt, holding microphone.

2007, Oct. 26 ***Perf. 13¼***

694 A166 $1.60 Sheet of 6, #a-f 7.50 7.50

Pope Benedict XVI — A167

2007, Nov. 26

695 A167 $1.10 multi 1.25 1.25

Wedding of Queen Elizabeth II and Prince Philip, 60th Anniv. A168

No. 696: a, Queen Elizabeth II. b, Couple on wedding day.
$6, Couple waving.

2007, Nov. 26

696 A168 $1.60 Pair, #a-b 2.50 2.50

Souvenir Sheet

697 A168 $6 multi 5.00 5.00

No. 696 printed in sheets containing three of each stamp.

Concorde A169

No. 698, $1.60: a, Concorde flying left. b, Concorde flying right.
No. 699, $1.60: a, Concorde over Singapore. b, Concorde at Melbourne, Australia airport.

2007, Nov. 26 Pairs, #a-b Litho.

698-699 A169 Set of 2 5.00 5.00

Nos. 698-699 each printed in sheets containing three of each stamp in pairs.

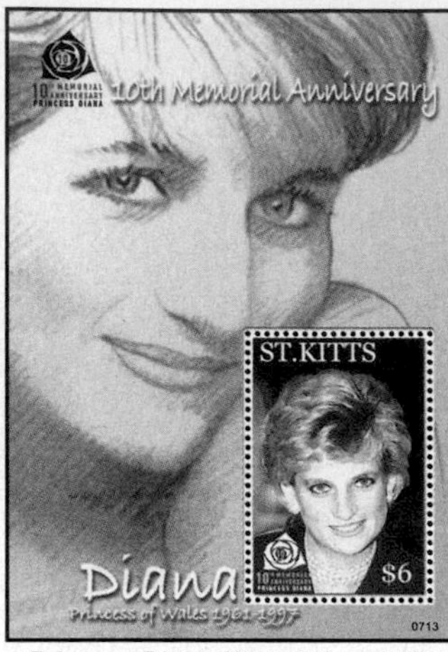

Princess Diana (1961-97) — A170

No. 700 — Various depictions of Princess Diana: a, Country name in black, "Princess Diana" at right. b, Country name in white, "Princess Diana" at left. c, Country name in white, "Princess Diana" at right. d, Country name in black, "Princess Diana" at left.
$6, Like #700c, gray background.

2007, Nov. 26 ***Perf. 13¼***

700 A170 $2 Sheet of 4, #a-d 6.00 6.00

Souvenir Sheet

701 A170 $6 multi 4.50 4.50

Christmas A171

Various ribboned wreaths: 10c, 30c, 60c, $1.

2007, Dec. 3 ***Perf. 12½***

702-705 A171 Set of 4 1.75 1.75

Miniature Sheet

2008 Summer Olympics, Beijing — A172

No. 706 — 2008 Summer Olympics emblem and: a, Paris World's Fair, 1900. b, 1900 Olympics poster. c, Charlotte Cooper. d, Alvin Kraenzlein.

2008, June 18 Litho. ***Perf. 12¾***

706 A172 $1.40 Sheet of 4, #a-d 5.50 5.50

Robert L. Bradshaw (1916-78), Chief Minister — A173

Perf. 11¼x11½

2008, Sept. 19 Litho.

707 A173 10c multi .40 .40

St. Kitts Labor Party, 75th anniv.

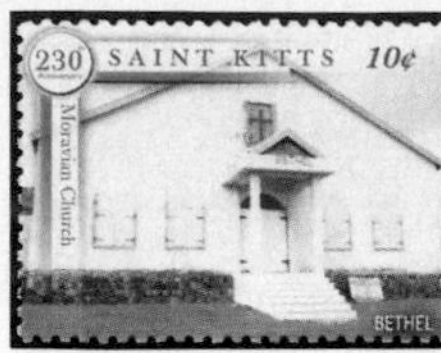

Moravian Churches A174

Designs: 10c, Bethel Church. $3, Zion Church. $10, Bethesda Church, vert.

Perf. 11½x11¼, 11¼x11½

2008, Sept. 19

708-710 A174 Set of 3 12.00 12.00

Moravian Church in St. Kitts, 230th anniv.

University of the West Indies, 60th Anniv. A175

Designs: 30c, University Center, St. Kitts. 90c, 60th anniv. emblem. $5, 60th anniv. emblem, horiz.

2008, Sept. 19

711-713 A175 Set of 3 6.00 6.00

Independence, 25th Anniv. — A176

Designs: 30c, Stars, lines and "25." $1, Agriculture. $5, Sailing Towards Our Future, vert.

2008, Sept. 19

714-716 A176 Set of 3 4.75 4.75

Miniature Sheet

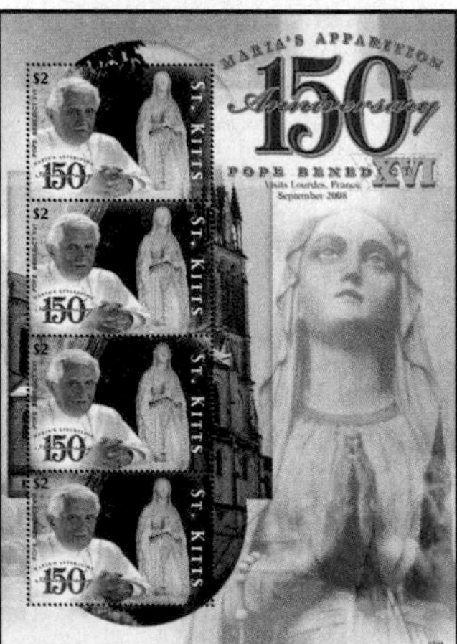

Visit to Lourdes of Pope Benedict XVI — A177

No. 717 — Pope Benedict, statue of St. Bernadette with: a, Leaves at top. b, Cathedral spires at UR. c, Cathedral roof and side of spire at UR. d, Gray triangle at LR.

2008, Sept. 26 ***Perf. 13¼***

717 A177 $2 Sheet of 4, #a-d 8.50 8.50

Miniature Sheet

Elvis Presley (1935-77) — A178

No. 718 — Presley wearing: a, Brown shirt. b, Leather jacket. c, Red shirt and black vest. d, Blue shirt. e, Olive green shirt. f, White shirt.

2008, Sept. 26
718 A178 $1.60 Sheet of 6, #a-f 8.50 8.50

Christmas A179

Designs: 10c, Palm trees with Christmas ornaments. 50c, Palm trees and beach house. 60c, Star and palm trees. $1, Christmas ornaments and palm fronds.

2008, Dec. 29 Litho. *Perf. 14x14¾*
719-722 A179 Set of 4 1.75 1.75

Inauguration of U.S. Pres. Barack Obama — A180

Obama with: $3, Blue gray tie. $10, Red tie.

Perf. 12½x11¾
2009, Feb. 24 Litho.
723 A180 $3 multi *3.50 3.50*

Souvenir Sheet
Perf.
724 A180 $10 multi *10.00 10.00*

No. 723 was printed in sheets of 4. No. 724 contains one 38mm diameter stamp.

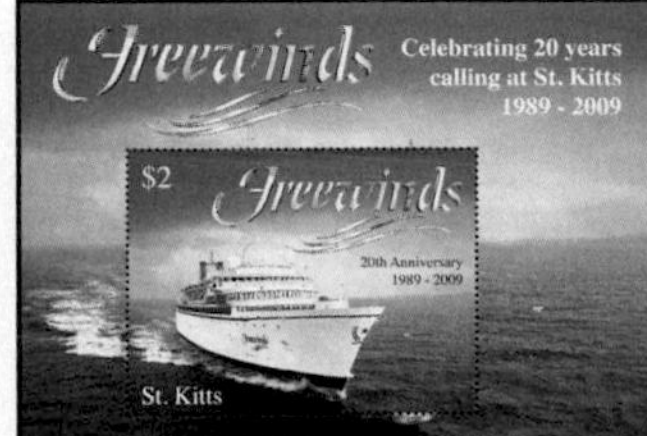

Freewinds Docking at St. Kitts, 20th Anniv. — A181

No. 725: a, 30c, Freewinds at night (42x28mm). b, 90c, Freewinds and yacht near harbor (42x28mm). c, $3, Bow of Freewinds, vert. (42x57mm).

2009, July 20 Litho. *Perf. 13¼*
725 A181 Sheet of 3, #a-c 3.25 3.25

Souvenir Sheet
Perf. 11½x12
726 A181 $2 shown 1.50 1.50

Miniature Sheet

Princess Diana (1961-97) — A182

No. 727 — Color of gown: a, Red. b, Purple. c, White. d, Blue.

2009, Sept. 7 *Perf. 13½x13¼*
727 A182 $2 Sheet of 4, #a-d 6.50 6.50

Brimstone Hill as UNESCO World Heritage Site, 10th Anniv. A183

2009, Dec. 7 Litho. *Perf. 13½*
728 A183 90c multi .70 .70

Miniature Sheet

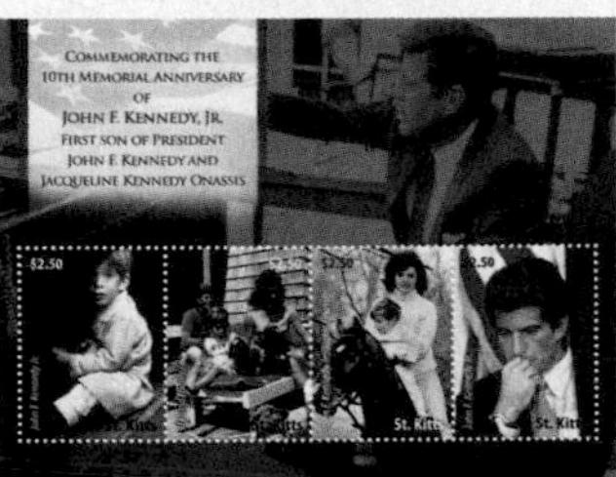

John F. Kennedy, Jr. (1960-99), Magazine Publisher — A184

No. 729: a, As child, sitting under father's desk. b, As child with father, mother and dogs. c, As child, with mother on horse. d, As adult.

2009, Dec. 15 *Perf. 11½*
729 A184 $2.50 Sheet of 4, #a-d 8.00 8.00

Miniature Sheets

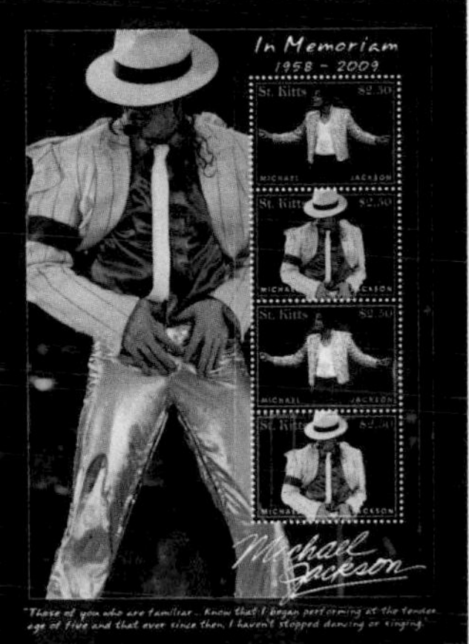

A185

Michael Jackson (1958-2009), Singer — A186

No. 730: a, With arms extended, denomination in green. b, Wearing hat, denomination in green. c, With arms extended, denomination in blue. d, Wearing hat, denomination in blue.

No. 731: a, Wearing red jacket, without yellow spot in background at left center. b, With snake, yellow spot in background at left center. c, Wearing red jacket, yellow spot in background at left center. d, With snake, without yellow spot in background at left center.

2009, Dec. 15
730 A185 $2.50 Sheet of 4, #a-d 8.00 8.00
731 A186 $2.50 Sheet of 4, #a-d 8.00 8.00

First Man on the Moon, 40th Anniv. — A187

No. 732: a, Saturn V rocket. b, Bootprint on Moon. c, Pres. John F. Kennedy, eagle, Moon and Earth. d, Apollo 11 command module.
$6, Command module, diff.

2009, Dec. 30 *Perf. 11½x12*
732 A187 $2.50 Sheet of 4, #a-d 8.00 8.00

Souvenir Sheet
733 A187 $6 multi 5.00 5.00

Christmas A188

Designs: 10c, "Merry Christmas" on flag of St. Kitts & Nevis. 30c, Candy canes. $1.20, Christmas trees on map of St. Kitts. $3, Christmas tree and candles on box showing flag.

2009, Dec. 30 *Perf. 14¾x14*
734-737 A188 Set of 4 3.50 3.50

Miniature Sheet

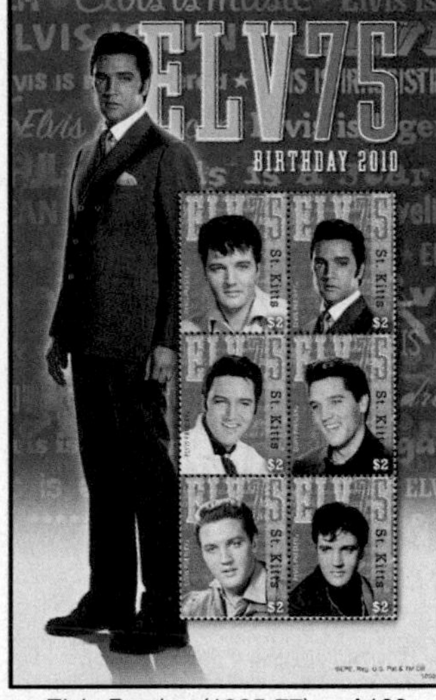

Elvis Presley (1935-77) — A189

No. 738 — Presley wearing: a, Shirt with open collar. b, Suit and tie. c, Shirt with neckerchief. d, Black jacket. e, Shirt with open collar and jacket. f, Black shirt, guitar strap over shoulder.

2010, Jan. 8 *Perf. 11½*
738 A189 $2 Sheet of 6, #a-f 9.25 9.25

Butterflies A190

Designs: 30c, Scarlet peacock. 90c, Gulf fritillary. No. 741, $3, White peacock. $5, Painted lady.

No. 743: a, Ruddy daggerwing. b, Danaid eggfly. c, Mangrove buckeye. d, Black swallowtail.

No. 744, $3: a, Owl butterfly. b, Giant swallowtail.

2010, Mar. 15 Litho. *Perf. 12*
739-742 A190 Set of 4 7.00 7.00
743 A190 $2.50 Sheet of 4, #a-d 7.50 7.50

Souvenir Sheet
744 A190 $3 Sheet of 2, #a-b 5.00 5.00

Birds A191

Designs: 30c, Solitary sandpiper. 90c, Piping plover. No. 747, $3, Prairie warbler. $5, Western sandpiper.

No. 749, vert.: a, Masked booby. b, Sooty tern. c, Brown booby. d, Black noddy.

No. 750, $3: a, Long-billed dowitcher. b, Willet.

2010, Mar. 22
745-748 A191 Set of 4 7.00 7.00
749 A191 $2.50 Sheet of 4, #a-d 7.50 7.50

Souvenir Sheet
750 A191 $3 Sheet of 2, #a-b 5.00 5.00

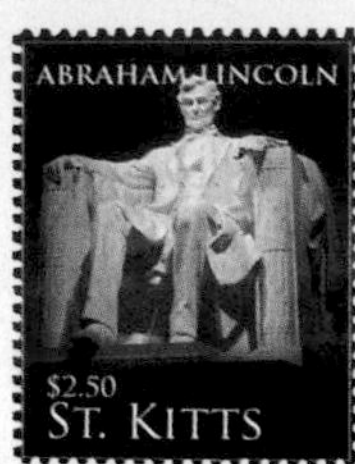

Pres. Abraham Lincoln (1809-65)
A192

2010, May 11

751 A192 $2.50 black 1.90 1.90

Printed in sheets of 4.

Fish
A193

Designs: 30c, Red lionfish. 90c, Stoplight parrotfish. $3, Black jack. $5, Bermuda blue angelfish.

No. 756: a, Banggai cardinalfish. b, Barrier reef anemonefish. c, Crevelle jack. d, Lookdown.

No. 757, $3: a, Red Sea clownfish. b, Saddleback clownfish.

2010, June 7 Litho. ***Perf. 14¾x14¼***

752-755 A193 Set of 4 7.00 7.00
756 A193 $2.50 Sheet of 4, #a-d 7.50 7.50

Souvenir Sheet

757 A193 $3 Sheet of 2, #a-b 5.00 5.00

A194

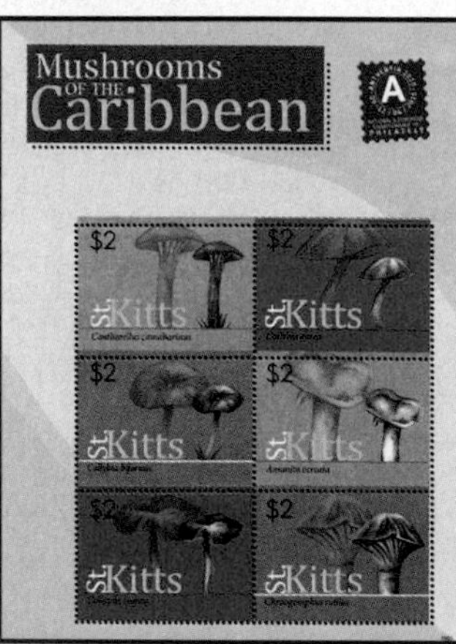

Mushrooms — A195

Designs: 25c, Alboleptonia stylophora. 80c, Cantharellus cibarius. $1, Armillaria puiggarii. $5, Battarrea phalloides.

No. 762: a, Cantharellus cinnabarinus. b, Collybia aurea. c, Collybia biformis. d, Amanita ocreata. e, Calocybe cyanea. f, Chroogomphus rutilus.

2010, June 7 ***Perf. 14¼x14¾***

758-761 A194 Set of 4 5.25 5.25

Perf. 14¾x14¼

762 A195 $2 Sheet of 6, #a-f 9.00 9.00

Antverpia 2010 National and European Championship of Philately, Antwerp (#762).

Miniature Sheets

Boy Scouts of America, Cent. — A196

No. 763, $2.50: a, Cub Scouting. b, Boy Scouting. c, Varsity Scouting. d, Venturing.

No. 764, $2.50: a, Eagle Scout emblem. b, Order of the Arrow. c, Alpha Phi Omega. d, National Eagle Scout Association.

2010, June 30 ***Perf. 13¼***

Sheets of 4, #a-d

763-764 A196 Set of 2 15.00 15.00

Arctic Animals — A197

No. 765: a, Ermine. b, Arctic fox. c, Harp seal. d, Arctic wolf. e, Arctic hare. f, Snowy owl.

$6, Polar bear.

2010, Aug. 4 ***Perf. 11½***

765 A197 $2 Sheet of 6, #a-f 9.00 9.00

Souvenir Sheet

766 A197 $6 multi 4.50 4.50

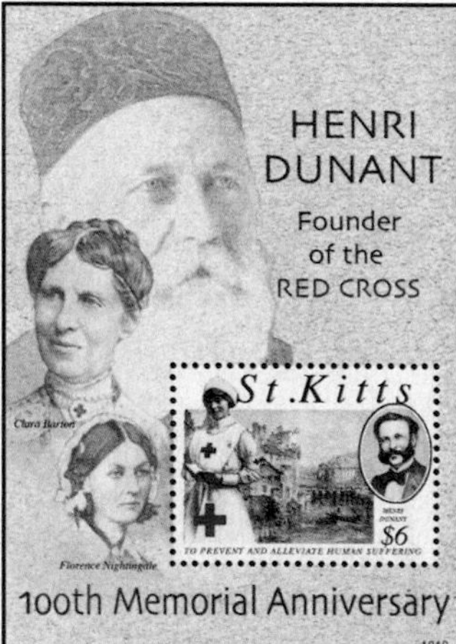

Henri Dunant (1828-1910), Founder of the Red Cross — A198

No. 767 — Dunant, Red Cross and: a, Czar Nicholas II of Russia. b, Henri Dufour. c, Frédéric Passy. d, Victor Hugo.

$6, Red Cross nurse.

2010, Sept. 1 ***Perf. 11½x12***

767 A198 $2.50 Sheet of 4, #a-d 7.50 7.50

Souvenir Sheet

Perf. 11½

768 A198 $6 multi 4.50 4.50

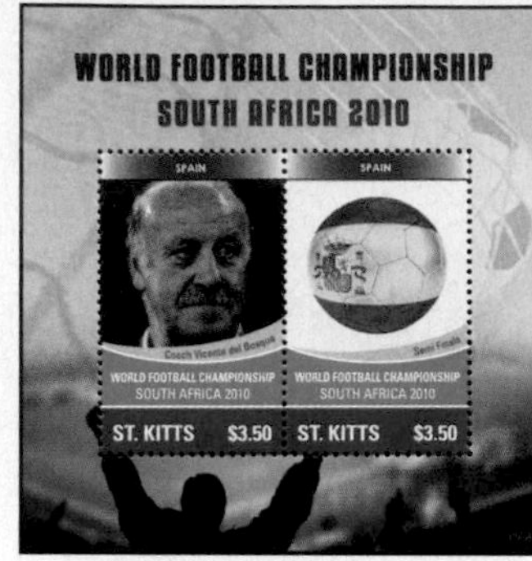

2010 World Cup Soccer Championships, South Africa — A199

No. 769: a, Pedro. b, Miroslav Klose. c, Xavi. d, Piotr Trochowski. e, Carlos Puyol. f, Philipp Lahm.

No. 770, $3.50: a, Spain Coach Vicente del Bosque. b, Soccer ball with Spanish flag.

No. 771, $3.50: Germany Coach Joachim Loew. b, Soccer ball with German flag.

2010, Oct. 6 ***Perf. 12***

769 A199 $1.50 Sheet of 6, #a-f 6.75 6.75

Souvenir Sheets of 2, #a-b

770-771 A199 Set of 2 10.50 10.50

Souvenir Sheets

A200

A201

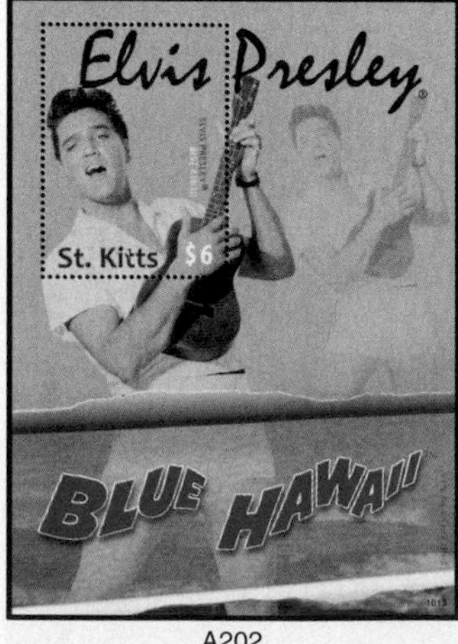

A202

Elvis Presley (1935-77) — A203

2010, Oct. 6 ***Perf. 13½***

772	A200 $6 multi		4.50	4.50
773	A201 $6 multi		4.50	4.50
774	A202 $6 multi		4.50	4.50
775	A203 $6 multi		4.50	4.50
	Nos. 772-775 (4)		18.00	18.00

A204

Princess Diana (1961-97) — A205

No. 776 — Princess Diana wearing: a, Beige hat. b, Rose lilac and white hat.

No. 777: a, Princess Diana wearing red hat, area below line shaded. b, Princess Diana wearing strapless gown, area below line shaded. c, Princess Diana wearing tiara, entire dress below line. d, As "c," strap of dress above line above denomination. e, As "a," area below line not shaded. f, As "b," area below line not shaded.

2010, Dec. 8 ***Perf. 12***

776 A204 $2.75 Pair, #a-b 4.25 4.25
777 A205 $2 Sheet of 6, #a-f 9.00 9.00

No. 776 was printed in sheets containing two pairs.

Christmas
2010 — A206

Paintings: 10c, Journey of the Magi, by Fra Angelico. 25c, Madonna Worshipping the Child and an Angel, by Biagio d'Antonio. 30c, The Nativity, by Master of Vyssi Brod. 90c, The Journey of the Magi, by James Tissot. $1.80, Worship of the Shepherds, by Agnolo di Cosimo. $3, Madonna with Child, by Carlo Crivelli.

Perf. 11½ (10c, 25c), 12¾x13 Syncopated

2011, Feb. 21 **Litho.**

778-783 A206 Set of 6 4.75 4.75

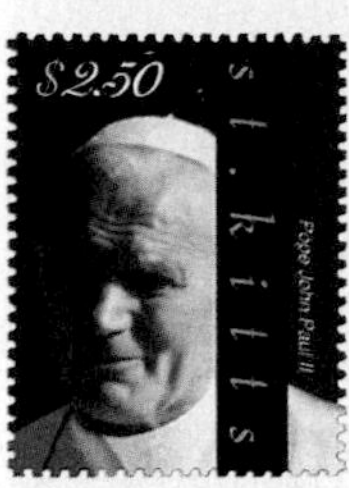

Pope John Paul II (1920-2005) A207

Pope John Paul II wearing: No. 784, $2.50, Zucchetto. No. 785, $2.50, Miter.

2011, Feb. 21 ***Perf. 12***

784-785 A207 Set of 2 3.75 3.75

Nos. 784-785 each were printed in sheets of 4.

Visit of Pope Benedict XVI to Portugal A208

Designs: No. 786, Pope Benedict XVI and buildings. No. 787 — Arms of Portugal, Pope Benedict XVI and background color of: a, Red. b, Green.

2011, Feb. 21 ***Perf. 12***

786 A208 $2.75 multi 2.10 2.10

Perf. 13 Syncopated

787 A208 $2.75 Sheet of 4, #787a, 3 #787b 8.25 8.25

No. 786 was printed in sheets of 4.

Paintings by Sandro Botticelli (1445-1510) — A209

No. 788: a, Giovanna Albizi with Venus and the Graces. b, Lemmi Fresco. c, Portrait of a Young Woman. d, St. Sebastian.

$6, The Last Communion of St. Jerome, horiz.

2011, Feb. 21 ***Perf. 12***

788 A209 $2.50 Sheet of 4, #a-d 7.50 7.50

Souvenir Sheet

Perf. 13 Syncopated

789 A209 $6 multi 4.50 4.50

Miniature Sheets

A210

Pres. Barack Obama — A211

Nos. 790 and 791 — Pres. Obama and one-quarter of Presidential seal at: a, LR. b, LL. c, UR. d, UL.

2011, Feb. 21 ***Perf. 12***

790 A210 $2.50 Sheet of 4, #a-d 7.50 7.50

791 A211 $2.50 Sheet of 4, #a-d 7.50 7.50

Dolphins — A212

No. 792: a, Pantropical spotted dolphin. b, Killer whale. c, Tucuxi. d, Clymene dolphin.

No. 793, $6, Rough-toothed dolphin. No. 794, $6, Bottlenose dolphin.

2011, Feb. 21 ***Perf. 13 Syncopated***

792 A212 $2.50 Sheet of 4, #a-d 7.50 7.50

Souvenir Sheets

Perf. 12

793-794 A212 Set of 2 9.00 9.00

Engagement of Prince William and Catherine Middleton — A213

No. 795, $2.50 — Red background: a, Couple, Middleton standing in front of door. b, Prince William. c, Middleton. d, Couple, diff.

No. 796, $2.50 — Blue background: a, Couple, Middleton wearing hat. b, Prince William. c, Middleton. d, Couple, diff.

No. 797, $6, Couple, red background, vert. No. 798, $6, Couple, blue background, vert.

2011, Feb. 21 ***Perf. 12***

Sheets of 4, #a-d

795-796 A213 Set of 2 15.00 15.00

Souvenir Sheets

Perf. 13 Syncopated

797-798 A213 Set of 2 9.00 9.00

Miniature Sheet

Cricket World Cup, India, Sri Lanka and Bangladesh — A214

No. 799 — Cricket players: a, Ricky Ponting, Australia. b, Shakib Al Hasan (incorrectly identified as Shahid Afridi), Bangladesh. c, Ashish Bagai, Canada. d, Mahendra Singh Dhoni, India. e, Andrew Strauss (incorrectly identified as Ricky Ponting), England. f, William Portorfield, Ireland. g, Maurice Ouma, Kenya. h, Daniel Vettori, New Zealand. i, Shahid Afridi, Pakistan. j, Graeme Smith, South Africa. k, Kumar Sangakkara, Sri Lanka. l, Peter Borren, Netherlands. m, Elton Chigumbura, Zimbabwe. n, Darren Sammy, West Indies.

2011, Apr. 2 **Litho.** ***Perf.***

799 A214 $1.90 Sheet of 14, #a-n 20.00 20.00

No. 799 exists with inscriptions corrected. Values, same.

Souvenir Sheets

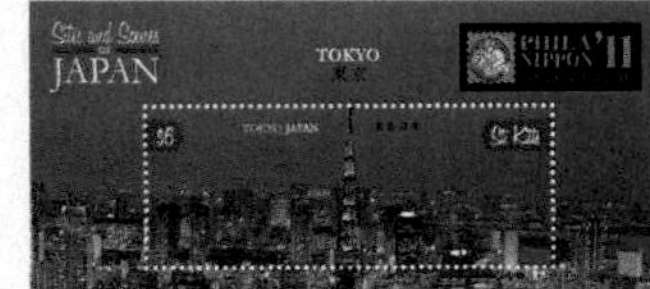

PhilaNippon '11, Yokohama, Japan — A215

Designs: No. 800, $6, Tokyo. No. 801, $6, Okinawa. No. 802, $6, Mt. Fuji.

2011, May 18 ***Perf. 11½x11¼***

800-802 A215 Set of 3 13.50 13.50

St. Kitts-Nevis-Anguilla National Bank, 40th Anniv. — A216

Designs: 10c, Bank building. $3, Anniversary emblem and olive branch, vert.

Perf. 14¾x14¼, 14¼x14¾

2011, June 27

803-804 A216 Set of 2 2.40 2.40

Miniature Sheets

Mother Teresa (1910-97, Humanitarian — A217

No. 805, $2.75 — Stamps with purple and maroon panels: a, Mother Teresa with Ronald and Nancy Reagan. b, Mother Teresa with Sister of Charity at doorway. c, Mother Tersa holding child. d, Mother Teresa and Paris Mayor Jacques Chirac.

No. 806, $2.75 — Stamps with blue and olive green panels and flower: a, Mother Tereesa. b, Mother Teresa and Prince Charles. c, Mother Teresa holding baby. d, Mother Teresa touching baby held by Sister of Charity.

2011, July 5 ***Perf. 13 Syncopated***

Sheets of 4, #a-d

805-806 A217 Set of 2 16.50 16.50

Miniature Sheets

A218

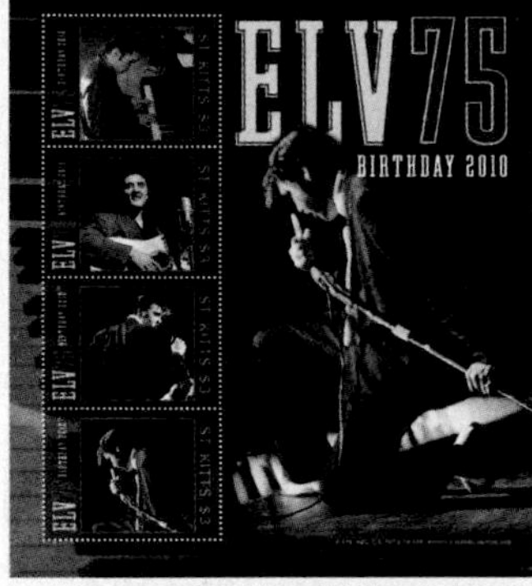

Elvis Presley (1935-77) — A219

No. 807: a, Presley in decorated jacket, seen from back. b, Presley with blue face. c, Presley with pink face. d, Presley with arms raised.

No. 808: a, Presley at piano. b, Presley splaying guitar. c, Prelsy holding microphone, facing right. d, Presley holding microphone, facing left.

2011, July 14 ***Perf. 12½x12¾***

807 A218 $3 Sheet of 4, #a-d 9.00 9.00

Perf. 12¾x12½

808 A219 $3 Sheet of 4, #a-d 9.00 9.00

Princess Diana (1961-97) — A220

No. 809 — Princess Diana: a, Greeting crowd. b, Holding baby. c, Wearing red and white dress. d, Wearing checked overcoat.

$6, Princess Diana wearing white sweater, horiz.

2011, July 14 ***Perf. 13 Syncopated***

809 A220 $2.75 Sheet of 4, #a-d 8.25 8.25

Souvenir Sheet

Perf. 12½

810 A220 $6 multi 4.50 4.50

No. 810 contains one 51x38mm stamp.

A221

Wedding of Prince William and Catherine Middleton — A222

No. 811: a, $2, Bride facing right (40x30mm). b, $2, Groom facing left (40x30mm). c, $2, Couple facing right (40x30mm). d, $2, Couple facing left (40x30mm). e, $4, Bride facing left (40x60mm).

No. 812: a, Couple facing right, wall in background. b, Couple facing forward, wall in background. c, As "b," horse in background. d, As "a," horse in background.

$6, Couple facing right.

2011, July 14 ***Perf. 11½***

811 A221 Sheet of 5, #a-e 9.00 9.00

Perf. 12½x12

812 A222 $2.75 Sheet of 4, #a-d 8.25 8.25

Souvenir Sheet

Perf. 13½x13¼

813 A221 $6 multi 4.50 4.50

No. 813 contains one 51x38mm stamp.

Miniature Sheets

U.S. Civil War, 150th Anniv. — A223

No. 814, $2.50 — Eagle, shield, Union and Confederate flags, General Robert E. Lee and General George G. Meade from Battle of Gettysburg, July 1-3, 1863, and: a, Union positions near Cemetery Ridge (image in green). b, Union artillery, Haziltt's Battery in action. c, Union positions near Cemetery Ridge (images in brown). d, Union artillery, Cemetery hill in the distance.

No. 815, $2.50 — Eagle, shield, Union and Confederate flags, Lieutenant General James Longstreet and Major General Oliver O. Howard from Battle of Gettysburg, July 1-3, 1863, and: a, Behind the breastworks on Culp's Hill. b, Jubal Early's attack on East Cemetery Hill. c, Confederate Army's 2nd Maryland Infantry at Culp's Hill. d, Confederate pickets on Culp's Hill.

No. 816, $2.50 — Eagle, shield, Union and Confederate flags, Lieutenant General Richard S. Ewell and Brigadier General George S. Greene from Battle of Gettysburg, July 1-3, 1863, and: a, Cavalry engagement. b, Battle of Gettysburg. c, Hand to hand combat. d, Battery A, 1st Rhode Island, at Cemetery Ridge.

2011, July 14 ***Perf. 13 Syncopated***

Sheets of 4, #a-d

814-816 A223 Set of 3 22.50 22.50

Flowers — A224

No. 817, horiz.: a, Bird of paradise. b, Gardenia. c, Dutch amaryllis. d, Ginger flower. e, Lobster claw. f, Bleeding heart.

No. 818: a, Cockscomb. b, Passion flower. c, Prairie Blue Eyes day lily. d, Blue water lily.

No. 819, $6, Painted feather. No. 820, $6, Cuban lily, horiz.

2011, July 14 ***Perf. 12***

817 A224 $2 Sheet of 6, #a-f 9.00 9.00

818 A224 $2.75 Sheet of 4, #a-d 8.25 8.25

Souvenir Sheets

819-820 A224 Set of 2 9.00 9.00

No. 817 contains six 64x32mm triangular stamps.

Miniature Sheet

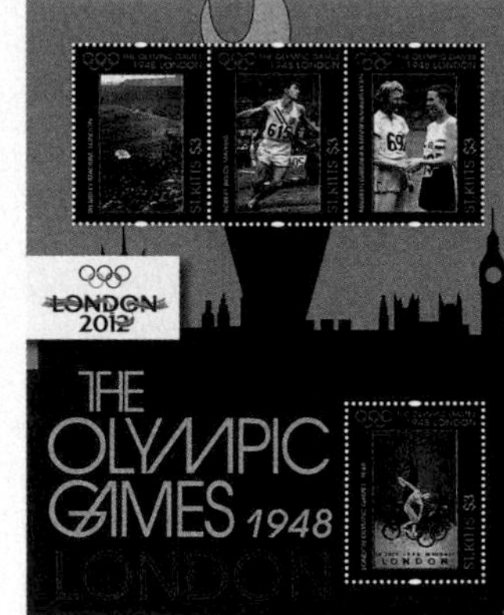

2012 Summer Olympics, London — A225

No. 821 — Scenes from 1948 Summer Olympics, London: a, Crowd at Wembley Stadium. b, Robert Mathias. c, Maureen Gardner and Fanny Blankers-Koen. d, Poster for 1948 Summer Olympics.

2011, Nov. 14 ***Perf. 13 Syncopated***

821 A225 $3 Sheet of 4, #a-d 9.00 9.00

Commonwealth Games Federation General Assembly, St. Kitts & Nevis — A226

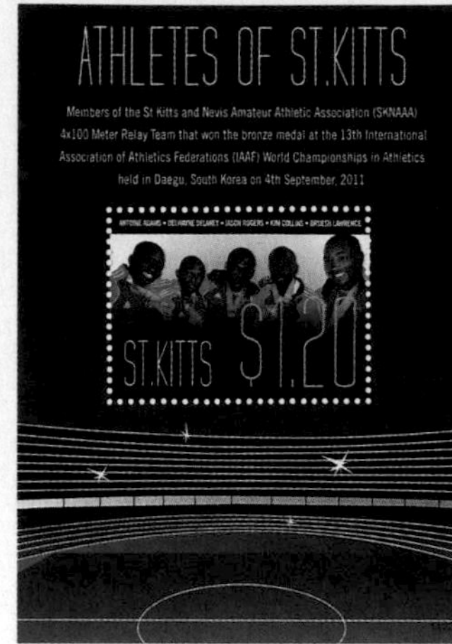

Members of St. Kitts & Nevis Men's 4x100 Meter Relay Team — A227

2011, Dec. 8 ***Perf. 14***

822 A226 25c multi .25 .25

Souvenir Sheet

Perf. 12

823 A227 $1.20 multi .90 .90

Princess Diana (1961-97) A228

Princess Diana: $3, Wearing tiara. $9, Without tiara.

2012, Oct. 1 ***Perf. 13¾***

824 A228 $3 multi 2.25 2.25

Souvenir Sheet

825 A228 $9 multi 6.75 6.75

No. 824 was printed in sheets of 4. No. 825 contains one 49x49mm diamond-shaped stamp.

A229

A230

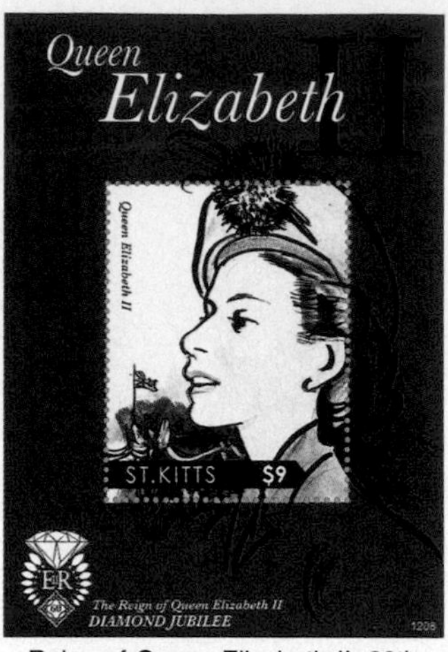

Reign of Queen Elizabeth II, 60th Anniv. — A231

Children's drawings: No. 826, 10c, Child's drawing for £2 stamp. No. 827, 10c, Diamond, crown, arrow, flags of St. Christopher, Nevis and Anguilla and St. Kitts and Nevis. 25c, Crown. 30c, Wreath of flags and "60." $1.20, Flags of St. Kitts and Nevis and Great Britain, "60" clock towers, handshake.

No. 831 — Queen Elizabeth II: a, Wearing hat. b, Without head covering. c, Wearing crown. d, Wearing tiara.

$9, Sketch of Queen Elizabeth II.

2012, Oct. 1 ***Perf. 14***

826-830 A229 Set of 5 1.50 1.50

Perf. 13¾

831 A230 $3.50 Sheet of 4, #a-d 10.50 10.50

Souvenir Sheet

Perf. 12¾

832 A231 $9 multi 6.75 6.75

Pres. Abraham Lincoln (1809-65) — A233

No. 833 — Photographs of Lincoln: a, Blue field of flag across top in background. b, Blue field of flag at UL. c, Red stripe of flag across top, Lincoln's arms visible to country name. d, Red stripe of flag across top, Lincoln's arms not visible.

$6, Sculpture of Lincoln in Lincoln Memorial.

2012, Oct. 1 ***Perf. 14***

833 A233 $2.75 Sheet of 4, #a-d 8.25 8.25

Souvenir Sheet

834 A233 $6 multi 4.50 4.50

A234

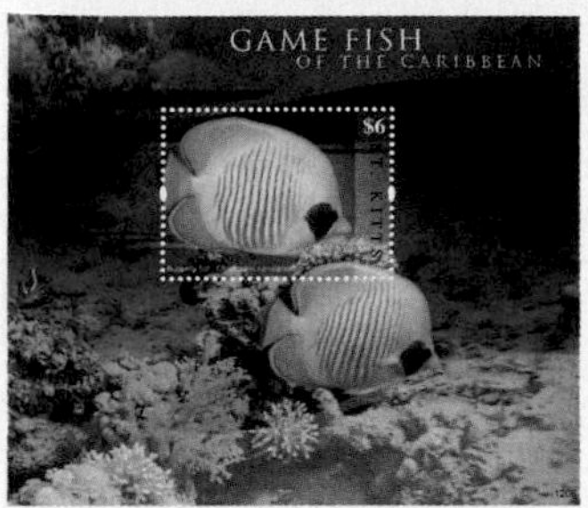

Fish — A235

No. 835: a, French angelfish. b, Barracuda. c, Spotted trunkfish. d, Trumpetfish. e, Orange-lined triggerfish. f, Eagle ray.
$6, Butterflyfish.

2012, Oct. 1 ***Perf. 13 Syncopated***
835 A234 $2.50 Sheet of 6, #a-f 11.00 11.00

Souvenir Sheet

836 A235 $6 multi 4.50 4.50

Parrots — A236

No. 837: a, Green-winged macaw. b, St. Vincent Amazon. c, Yellow-headed Amazon. d, Orange-winged Amazon.
$6, Blue and gold macaw, horiz.

2012, Oct. 1 ***Perf. 14***
837 A236 $2.75 Sheet of 4, #a-d 8.25 8.25

Souvenir Sheet
Perf. 12¾

838 A236 $6 multi 4.50 4.50

No. 838 contains one 51x38mm stamp.

Shells — A237

No. 839: a, Turbo petholatus. b, Mitra stictica. c, Muricanthus radix. d, Murex bicolor.
$6, Haliotis asinina, vert.

2012, Oct. 1 ***Perf.***
839 A237 $2.75 Sheet of 4, #a-d 8.25 8.25

Souvenir Sheet
Perf. 12

840 A237 $6 multi 4.50 4.50

No. 840 contains one 30x80mm rectangular stamp.

Souvenir Sheets

A238

A239

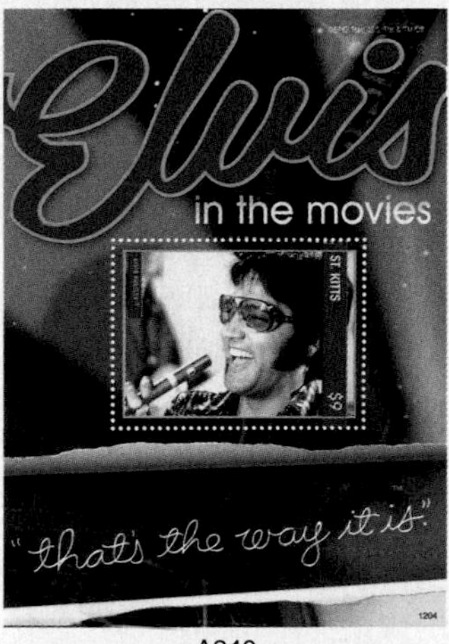

A240

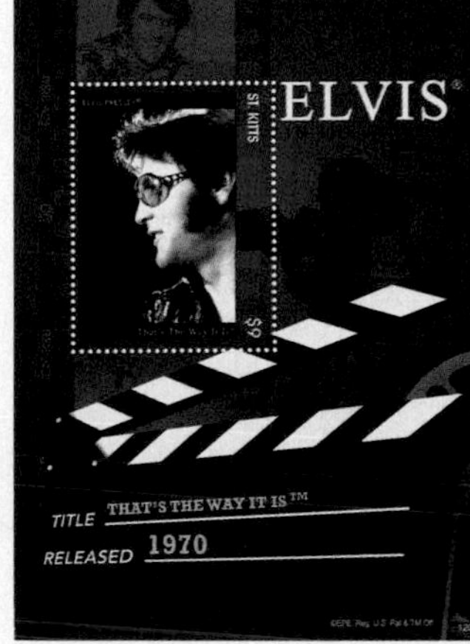

Elvis Presley (1935-77) — A241

2012, Oct. 1 ***Perf. 12¾***

841 A238 $9 multi	6.75	6.75
842 A239 $9 multi	6.75	6.75
843 A240 $9 multi	6.75	6.75
844 A241 $9 multi	6.75	6.75
Nos. 841-844 (4)	27.00	27.00

Antioch Baptist Church, 50th Anniv. — A242

Designs: 10c, Reverend Dr. William Manasseh Connor. 30c, Church building.

2013, June 3 ***Perf. 13¼x12½***
845-846 A242 Set of 2 .30 .30

Election of Pope Francis — A243

No. 847 — Pope Francis: a, Carrying censer. b, Waving from window. c, Holding crucifix. d, Kneeling in prayer.
$9, Pope Francis waving from window, diff.

2013, Aug. 7 **Litho.** ***Perf. 14***
847 A243 $3.25 Sheet of 4, #a-d 9.75 9.75

Souvenir Sheet
Perf. 12½

848 A243 $9 multi 6.75 6.75

No. 848 contains one 38x51mm stamp.

Miniature Sheet

Butterflies — A244

No. 849: a, Bates olivewing butterfly. b, Orange-barred sulphur butterfly. c, Blue satyr butterfly. d, Red flasher butterfly. e, Nymphalid butterfly. f, Hypolereia ocalea. g, Isamia carpenteri. h, Blue morpho butterfly. i, Variable cattleheart butterfly. j, Heliconius aoede.

2013, Aug. 12 **Litho.** ***Perf. 14***
849 A244 $1.60 Sheet of 10, #a-j 12.00 12.00

Miniature Sheet

Moths — A245

No. 850: a, Athis clitarcha. b, Oryba kadeni. c, Copaxa denda. d, Citheronia azteca.

2013, Aug. 12 **Litho.** ***Perf. 12***
850 A245 $3 Sheet of 4, #a-d 9.00 9.00

Souvenir Sheets

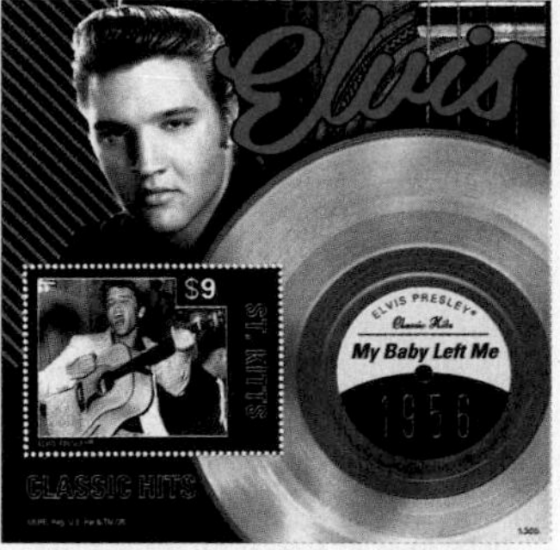

Elvis Presley (1935-77) — A246

Various photographs of Presley with frame color of: No. 851, $9, Black. No. 852, $9, Gray. No. 853, $9, Red (color photograph of Presley). No. 854, $9, Purple. No. 855, $9, Red (black-and-white photograph of Presley).

2013, Aug. 12 **Litho.** ***Perf. 13¼***
851-855 A246 Set of 5 34.00 34.00

Orchids — A247

No. 856: a, Bletilla striata. b, Phaius hybrid. c, Cymbidium "Showgirl." d, Dendrobium nobile. e, Zygopetalum crinitum.
$9, Cuitlauzina pendula.

2013, Aug. 26 **Litho.** ***Perf. 14***
856 A247 $2.75 Sheet of 5, #a-e 10.50 10.50

Souvenir Sheet
Perf. 12½

857 A247 $9 multi 6.75 6.75

No. 857 contains one 38x51mm stamp.

Birth of Prince George of Cambridge — A248

No. 858: a, Duchess of Cambridge holding Prince George. b, Duke of Cambridge holding Prince George. c, Duke and Duchess of Cambridge, Prince George. d, Prince George.
$9, Duke and Duchess of Cambridge, horiz.

2013, Sept. 10 **Litho.** ***Perf. 13¾***
858 A248 $3.25 Sheet of 4, #a-d 9.75 9.75

Souvenir Sheet
Perf. 12½

859 A248 $9 multi 6.75 6.75

No. 859 contains one 51x38mm stamp.

A249

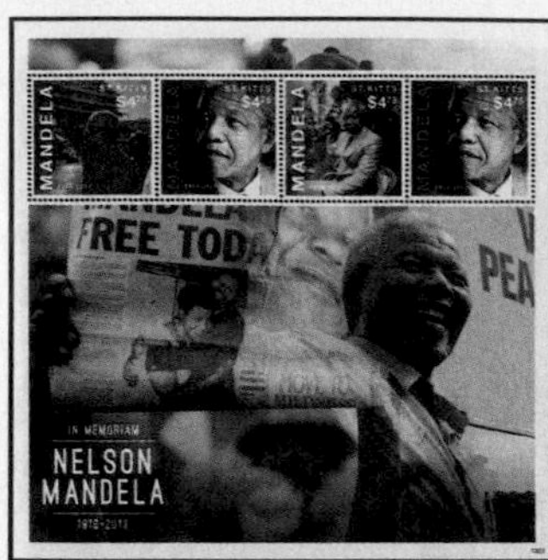

Nelson Mandela (1918-2013), President of South Africa — A250

No. 860: a, People holding signs with pictures of Mandela. b, Black-and-white photograph of Mandela, "Mandela" at left in orange.
No. 861: a, Mandela in red shirt, waving. b, Mandela in suit, seated. c, Like #860b, "Mandela" at left in red.

2013-14 Litho. *Perf. 13¾*

860 A249 $4.75 Horiz. pair, #a-b 7.00 7.00
861 A250 $4.75 Sheet of 4, #861a, 861b, 2 #861c 14.00 14.00

Issued: No. 860, 2/19/14; No. 861, 12/19. No. 860 was printed in sheets containing two pairs.

Miniature Sheet

Hummingbirds — A251

No. 862: a, Lophornis regulus. b, Lophornis delattrei. c, Calothorax fanny. d, Lophornis ornatus. e, Lophornis helenae. f, Selaphorus platycerus.

2014, Feb. 19 Litho. *Perf. 13¾*

862 A251 $2.50 Sheet of 6, #a-f 11.00 11.00

Reptiles — A252

No. 863: a, Anolis carolinensis. b, Anolis cristatellus. c, Hemidactylus mabouia. d, Iguana iguana.
$9, Sphaerodactylus sabanus, vert.

2014, Feb. 19 Litho. *Perf. 13¾*

863 A252 $3.25 Sheet of 4, #a-d 9.75 9.75

Souvenir Sheet

Perf. 12¾

864 A252 $9 multi 6.75 6.75

No. 864 contains one 38x51mm stamp.

Marine Mammals — A253

No. 865: a, Pygmy killer whale. b, Short-finned pilot whale. c, Dwarf sperm whale. d, Humpback whale.
$9, West Indian manatee.

2014, Feb. 19 Litho. *Perf. 14*

865 A253 $3.50 Sheet of 4, #a-d 10.50 10.50

Souvenir Sheet

Perf. 12

866 A253 $9 multi 6.75 6.75

Pres. John F. Kennedy (1917-63) — A254

No. 867 — Various photos of Pres. Kennedy at lectern, with denomination at: a, UL. b, UR. c, LL, d, LR.
No. 868, $9, Black-and-white photograph of Pres. Kennedy. No. 869, $9, Color photograph of Pres. Kennedy at White House.

Perf. 13 Syncopated

2014, Feb. 19 Litho.

867 A254 $3 Sheet of 4, #a-d 9.00 9.00

Souvenir Sheets

868-869 A254 Set of 2 13.50 13.50

Miniature Sheets

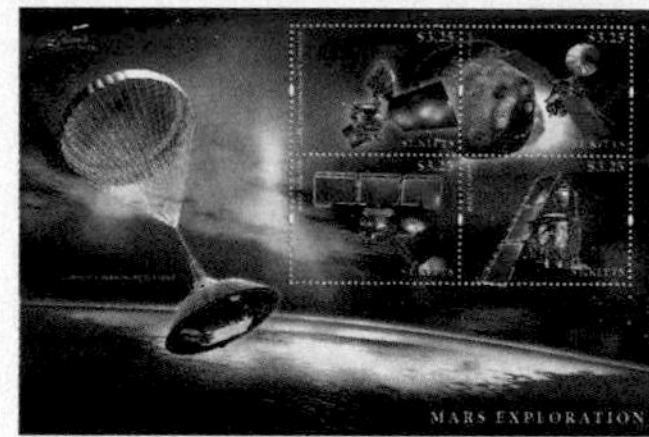

A255

Exploration of Mars — A256

No. 870 — Inscriptions: a, Mars Reconnaissance Orbiter. b, Phobos. c, Mars Orbiter. d, Mars Climate.
No. 871 — Inscriptions: a, Mars Reconnaissance Orbiter, diff. b, Mariner 7. c, Mars Rover. d, Viking.

Perf. 13 Syncopated

2014, Feb. 19 Litho.

870 A255 $3.25 Sheet of 4, #a-d 9.75 9.75
871 A256 $3.25 Sheet of 4, #a-d 9.75 9.75

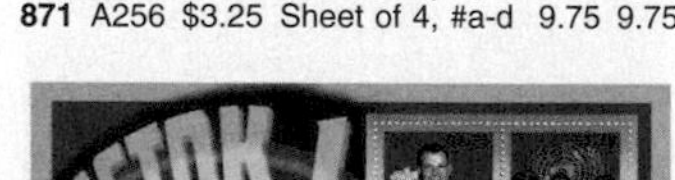

Yuri Gagarin (1934-68), First Man in Space — A257

No. 872 — Gagarin with: a, His daughters. b, Cosmonaut Valentina Tereshkova and United Nations Secretary General U Thant. c, Indian Prime Minister Jawaharlal Nehru. d, Rocket designer Sergei Korolev.
$9, Gagarin and Vostok 1.

2014, Feb. 19 Litho. *Perf. 12*

872 A257 $2.75 Sheet of 4, #a-d 8.25 8.25

Souvenir Sheet

873 A257 $9 multi 6.75 6.75

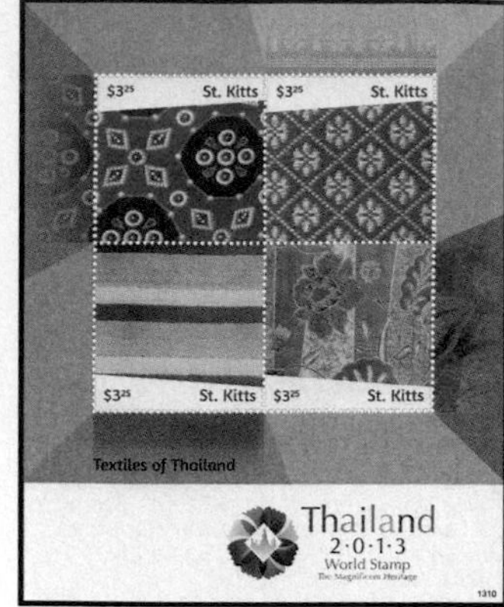

Thailand 2013 World Stamp Exhibition, Bangkok — A258

No. 874 — Textile designs: a, Circles and diamonds in red and pink. b, White geometric in diamond with blue background. c, Stripes. d, Flowers.
$9, Blue flower.

2014, Feb. 19 Litho. *Perf. 13¾*

874 A258 $3.25 Sheet of 4, #a-d 9.75 9.75

Souvenir Sheet

875 A258 $9 multi 6.75 6.75

Children's Art — A259

Winning art in Human Rights Sensitization Project for Persons with Disabilities stamp design contest by: 10c, Xouria Jefferson. 15c, Nijaunte David. 30c, Nyiel Mayen. $50, Shernel Evans.

2014, Aug. 18 Litho. *Perf. 13¼*

876-879 A259 Set of 4 37.50 37.50

Cactus Flowers — A260

No. 880: a, Echinocactus quehlianus. b, Cereus chalybaeus. c, Cereus rhodoleucanthus. d, Cereus hankeanus. e, Phyllocactus gordonianus. f, Cereus peruvianus.
$9, Echinocactus damsii.

2014, Sept. 4 Litho. *Perf. 14*

880 A260 $2.25 Sheet of 6, #a-f 10.00 10.00

Souvenir Sheet

Perf.

881 A260 $9 multi 6.75 6.75

No. 881 contains one 38mm diameter stamp.

World War I, Cent. — A261

No. 882, $3.25: a, Dove with olive branch. b, Jigsaw puzzle pieces. c, Helmet on rifle. d, Highway bridge.
No. 883, $3.25, horiz.: a, U.S. M1917 tank. b, German Stürmpanzerwagen A7V-U tank. c, British Mark A Whippet tank. d, French Renault FT-17 tank.
No. 884, $5, horiz. — U.S. President Woodrow Wilson: a, With handkerchief in pocket of suit. b, Without handkerchief in pocket of suit.
No. 885, $5: a, British Mark IV tank. b, German A7V tank.

2014, Sept. 4 Litho. *Perf. 14*
Sheets of 4, #a-d

882-883 A261 Set of 2 19.50 19.50

Souvenir Sheets of 2, #a-b

884-885 A261 Set of 2 15.00 15.00

No. 884 contains two 51x38mm stamps. No. 885 contains two 38x51mm stamps.

Christmas A262

Paintings by Raphael: $2.20, Reading Madonna and Child. $2.25, The Sistine Madonna. $3.50, Madonna Del Granduca. $5, The Virgin and Child.

2014, Dec. 15 Litho. *Perf. 12¾*

886-889 A262 Set of 4 9.75 9,75

Trains — A263

No. 890: a, Light rail. b, Monorail. c, Steam engine train. d, Diesel train.
No. 891: a, Electric train. b, Maglev train.

Perf. 13 Syncopated
2014, Dec. 31 Litho.

890 A263 $3.25 Sheet of 4, #a-d 9.75 9.75

Souvenir Sheet

891 A263 $5 Sheet of 2, #a-b 7.50 7.50

A264

A265

A266

Sunflowers — A267

Various sunflowers, as shown.

2014, Dec. 31 Litho. *Perf. 13¾*

892 A264 $3.25 Sheet of 4, #a-d 9.75 9.75
893 A265 $3.25 Sheet of 4, #a-d 9.75 9.75

Souvenir Sheets
Perf.

894 A266 $10 multi 7.50 7.50
895 A267 $10 multi 7.50 7.50

Seagulls — A268

No. 896, $3.25: a, Black-tailed gull. b, California gull. c, Gray-headed gull. d, European herring gull.
No. 897, $3.25: a, Yellow-legged gull. b, Common gull. c, Audouin's gull. d, Iceland gull.
No. 898, $10, Caspian gull. No. 899, $10, Dolphin gull.

2014, Dec. 31 Litho. *Perf. 14*
Sheets of 4, #a-d

896-897 A268 Set of 2 19.50 19.50

Souvenir Sheets

898-899 A268 Set of 2 15.00 15.00

Tropical Fish — A269

No. 900, $3.25: a, French angelfish. b, Queen parrotfish. c, Rock beauty. d, Spotted drum.
No. 901, $3.25: a, Fairy basslet. b, Four-eyed butterflyfish. c, Glasseye snapper. d, Spotted eagle ray.
No. 902, $10, Queen angelfish. No. 903, $10, Smooth trunkfish, vert.

2014, Dec. 31 Litho. *Perf. 14*
Sheets of 4, #a-d

900-901 A269 Set of 2 19.50 19.50

Souvenir Sheets
Perf. 12

902-903 A269 Set of 2 15.00 15.00

Marine Life of Taiwan — A271

No. 906: a, Warty frogfish. b, White-margin sea slug. c, Blue-ringed angelfish. d, Maroon clownfish. e, Huang Ze gray crab. f, Hawksbill sea turtle.
No. 907: a, Head of Peacock mantis shrimp. b, Body of Peacock mantis shrimp.

2015, Mar. 24 Litho. *Perf. 14*

906 A271 $3.15 Sheet of 6, #a-f 14.00 14.00

Souvenir Sheet
Perf. 12

907 A271 $5 Sheet of 2, #a-b 7.50 7.50

World War I Posters — A272

No. 908, $3.15 — Posters from United States depicting: a, Old woman and flag. b, Soldier with bugle, flag. c, Marines attacking, flag in background. d, Soldiers landing on shore, ships in background. e, Bald eagle attacking black eagle, airplanes in background. f, Statue of Liberty pointing.
No. 909, $3.15 — Posters from Great Britain depicting: a, Picture of soldier on pendant. b, Airplane and soldiers. c, Soldier with pipe in mouth marching. d, Crowd watching soldiers marching past British flag. e, Soldier pulling on airplane propeller. f, Woman holding British flag.
No. 910, $10, Uncle Sam pointing. No. 911, $10, British Army hat.

2015, Mar. 24 Litho. *Perf. 12½*
Sheets of 6, #a-f

908-909 A272 Set of 2 28.00 28.00

Souvenir Sheets

910-911 A272 Set of 2 15.00 15.00

Palm Trees — A273

No. 912: a, Coconut palm, denomination in pink. b, Petticoat palm. c, Coconut palm, denomination in pale yellow. d, Royal palm, denomination in light blue. e, Royal palm, denomination in pink. f, Palmetto palm.
$10, Cococnut palm, horiz.

2015, Apr. 1 Litho. *Perf. 13¼x13*

912 A273 $3.15 Sheet of 6, #a-f 14.00 14.00

Souvenir Sheet
Perf. 13¼

913 A273 $10 multi 7.50 7.50

No. 913 contains one 51x38mm stamp.

Green-throated Carib Hummingbird and Other Birds — A274

Design: $10, Green-throated Carib hummingbird.

2015, June 1 Litho. *Perf. 14*

914 A274 $1 multi .75 .75

Souvenir Sheet
Perf. 12¾

915 A274 $10 multi 7.50 7.50

No. 915 contains one 51x38mm stamp.

Singapore 2015 World Stamp Exhibition — A275

No. 916 — Tourist attractions in Singapore: a, Sentosa Island. b, Singapore Flyer. c, Tiger Sky Tower. d, Kusu Island.
$10, Flower at Botanic Gardens, vert.

2015, Aug. 3 Litho. *Perf. 12*
916 A275 $3.25 Sheet of 4, #a-d 9.75 9.75

Souvenir Sheet

917 A275 $10 multi 7.50 7.50

Cats — A276

No. 918: a, Birman. b, Devon Rex. c, Selkirk Rex. d, American Curl. e, Scottish Fold. f, Exotic shorthair.
$10, Bengal cat, vert.

2015, Aug. 3 Litho. *Perf. 14*
918 A276 $3.15 Sheet of 6, #a-f 14.00 14.00

Souvenir Sheet
Perf. 12

919 A276 $10 multi 7.50 7.50

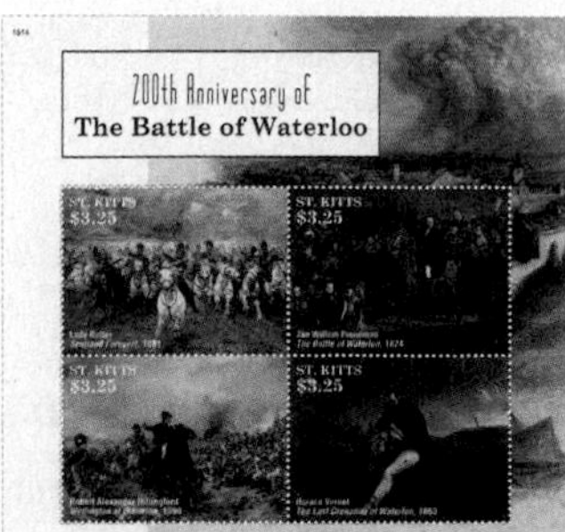

Battle of Waterloo, 200th Anniv. — A277

No. 920 — Paintings: a, Scotland Forever!, by Lady Butler. b, The Battle of Waterloo, by Jan Willem Pieneman. c, Wellington at Waterloo, by Robert Alexander Hillingford. d, The Last Grenadier at Waterloo, by Horace Vernet.
$10, The Battle of Waterloo, by William Sadler.

2015, Aug. 3 Litho. *Perf. 12½*
920 A277 $3.25 Sheet of 4, #a-d 9.75 9.75

Souvenir Sheet
Perf. 12

921 A277 $10 multi 7.50 7.50

No. 921 contains one 80x30mm stamp.

Birth of Princess Charlotte of Cambridge — A278

No. 922: a, Duke and Duchess of Cambridge, Duchess carrying Princess Charlotte. b, Duke and Duchess of Cambridge, Duke holding Princess Charlotte's baby carrier. c, Duke of Cambridge putting baby carrier in automobile. d, Duke of Cambridge and Prince George.
$10, Duchess of Cambridge and Princess Charlotte, vert.

2015, Aug. 10 Litho. *Perf. 12*
922 A278 $3.25 Sheet of 4, #a-d 9.75 9.75

Souvenir Sheet

923 A278 $10 multi 7.50 7.50

Owls — A279

No. 924, $3.25 — Owl and feather, white background: a, Barn owl. b, Burrowing owl. c, Central American pygmy owl. d, Great horned owl.
No. 925, $3.25 — Owl, black frame: a, Barred owl. b, Burrowing owl. c, Bare-legged owls. d, Barn owl.
No. 926, $10, Ashy-faced owl. No. 927, $10, Short-eared owl.

2015, Sept. 8 Litho. *Perf. 12*
Sheets of 4, #a-d

924-925 A279 Set of 2 19.50 19.50

Souvenir Sheets

926-927 A279 Set of 2 15.00 15.00

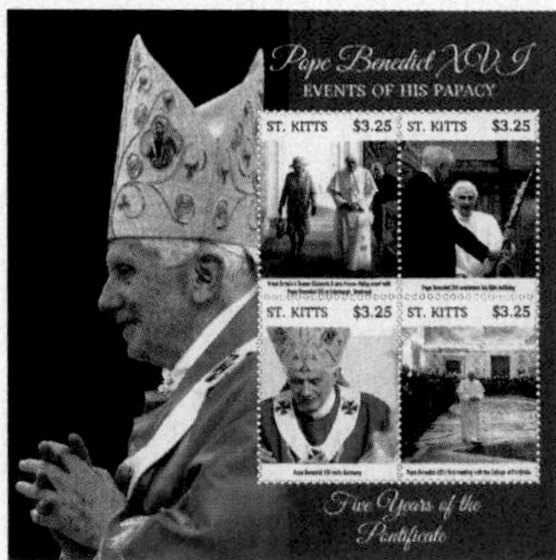

Events of Reign of Pope Benedict XVI — A280

No. 928 — Pope Benedict XVI: a, Meeting Queen Elizabeth II and Prince Philip. b, Celebrating 85th birthday. c, Visiting Germany. d, At first meeting with College of Cardinals.
$10, Pope Benedict XVI giving *Urbi et Orbi* Easter blessing, horiz.

2015, Sept. 8 Litho. *Perf. 12x12½*
928 A280 $3.25 Sheet of 4, #a-d 9.75 9.75

Souvenir Sheet
Perf. 12

929 A280 $10 multi 7.50 7.50

No. 929 contains one 50x30mm stamp.

Christmas A281

Paintings by Raphael: 30c, Small Cowper Madonna. $2.25, The Tempi Madonna. $3.50, Madonna with Beardless Saint Joseph. $5, Sistine Madonna.

2015, Nov. 2 Litho. *Perf. 13½*
930-933 A281 Set of 4 8.25 8.25

OFFICIAL STAMPS

Nos. 28-37 Ovptd. "OFFICIAL"
Perf. 14½x14

1980, June 23 Litho. Wmk. 373

O1	A61	15c multicolored	.25	.25
O2	A61	25c multicolored	.25	.25
O3	A61	30c multicolored	.25	.25
O4	A61	40c multicolored	.25	.25
O5	A61	45c multicolored	.25	.25
O6	A61	50c multicolored	.25	.25
O7	A61	55c multicolored	.25	.25
O8	A61	$1 multicolored	.30	.30
O9	A61	$5 multicolored	1.00	*1.50*
O10	A61	$10 multicolored	1.50	*2.75*
		Nos. O1-O10 (10)	4.55	6.30

No. O7 exists with inverted overprint. Value $22. No. O10 exists with inverted overprint. Value $110.

Unwmk.

O2a	A61	25c	.30	.25
O3a	A61	30c	.60	.40
O4a	A61	40c	11.50	12.50
O7a	A61	55c	.85	.65
O8a	A61	$1	1.40	1.00
O9a	A61	$5	3.25	4.50
O10a	A61	$10	4.25	6.50
		Nos. O2a-O10a (7)	22.15	25.80

Nos. 55-66 Ovptd. "OFFICIAL"

1981, Feb. 5 *Perf. 14*

O11	A5	15c multicolored	.25	.25
O12	A5	20c multicolored	.25	.25
O13	A5	25c multicolored	.25	.25
O14	A5	30c multicolored	.25	.25
O15	A5	40c multicolored	.40	.25
O16	A5	45c multicolored	.45	.25
O17	A5	50c multicolored	.45	.25
O18	A5	55c multicolored	.55	.30
O19	A5	$1 multicolored	.90	.70
O20	A5	$2.50 multicolored	1.75	1.25
O21	A5	$5 multicolored	3.00	2.50
O22	A5	$10 multicolored	5.00	4.50
		Nos. O11-O22 (12)	13.50	11.00

Nos. 75-80 Ovptd. or Surcharged "OFFICIAL" in Ultra or Black

1983, Feb. 2

O23	A6a	45c on $2.50 No. 77 (U)	.25	.25
a.		Black surcharge		
O24	A6b	45c on $2.50 No. 78 (U)	.30	.30
a.		Black surcharge		
O25	A6a	55c No. 75	.25	.25
O26	A6b	55c No. 76	.40	.40
O27	A6a	$1.10 on $4 No. 79 (B)	.40	*.40*
a.		Ultra surcharge	3.00	
O28	A6b	$1.10 on $4 No. 80 (B)	.75	.75
a.		Ultra surcharge	25.00	
		Nos. O23-O28 (6)	2.35	2.35

No. O23 exists with double surcharge and inverted surcharge. Values, $16 and $3, respectively. No. O24 exists with double surcharge and inverted surcharge. Values, $60 and $20, respectively. No. O25 exists with double surcharge and inverted surcharge. Values, $18 and $6, respectively. No. O26 exists with double surcharge and inverted surcharge. Values, $60 and $19, respectively. No. O27 exists with double surcharge. Value $15. No. O28 exists with double surcharge. Value $45. Nos. O27a and O28a exist with inverted surcharge.

Nos. 141-152 Ovptd. "OFFICIAL"

1984, July 4 Wmk. 380

O29	A18	15c multicolored	.70	1.50
O30	A18	20c multicolored	.80	1.50
O31	A18	25c multicolored	.80	1.50
O32	A18	30c multicolored	.90	1.50
O33	A18	40c multicolored	1.00	1.50
O34	A18	50c multicolored	1.00	1.50
O35	A18	60c multicolored	1.25	2.00
O36	A18	75c multicolored	1.60	2.00
O37	A18	$1 multicolored	2.50	2.50
O38	A18	$2.50 multicolored	4.50	4.50
O39	A18	$5 multicolored	8.00	3.00
O40	A18	$10 multicolored	14.50	6.00
		Nos. O29-O40 (12)	37.55	29.00

ST. KITTS-NEVIS

sānt 'kits-'nē-vəs

(St. Christopher-Nevis-Anguilla)

LOCATION — West Indies southeast of Puerto Rico
GOVT. — Associated State in British Commonwealth
AREA — 153 sq. mi.
POP. — 43,309, excluding Anguilla (1991)
CAPITAL — Basseterre, St. Kitts

St. Kitts-Nevis was one of the presidencies of the former Leeward Islands colony until it became a colony itself in 1956. In 1967 Britain granted internal self-government.

See "St. Christopher" for stamps used in St. Kitts before 1890. From 1890 until 1903, stamps of the Leeward Islands were used. From 1903 until 1956, stamps of St. Kitts-Nevis and Leeward Islands were used concurrently.

Starting in 1967, issues of Anguilla are listed under that heading. Starting in 1980 stamps inscribed St. Kitts or Nevis are listed under those headings.

12 Pence = 1 Shilling
20 Shillings = 1 Pound
100 Cents = 1 Dollar (1951)

Catalogue values for unused stamps in this country are for Never Hinged items, beginning with Scott 91 in the regular postage section and Scott O1 in the officials section.

Columbus Looking for Land — A1

Medicinal Spring — A2

Wmk. Crown and C A (2)

1903 Typo. *Perf. 14*

1	A1	½p grn & vio	2.00	.80
2	A2	1p car & black	5.25	.25
3	A1	2p brn & vio	3.00	*12.00*
4	A1	2½p ultra & black	20.00	4.75
5	A2	3p org & green	22.50	*32.50*
6	A1	6p red vio & blk	8.00	*47.50*
7	A1	1sh org & grn	7.75	*12.00*
8	A2	2sh blk & grn	13.50	*22.50*
9	A1	2sh6p violet & blk	20.00	*50.00*
10	A2	5sh ol grn & gray vio	70.00	*62.50*
		Nos. 1-10 (10)	172.00	*244.80*

1905-18 Wmk. 3

11	A1	½p green & violet	15.00	*7.50*
12a	A1	½p dl blue grn ('16)	.70	3.25
13	A2	1p carmine & blk	8.00	.30
14a	A2	1p scarlet ('16)	1.00	.25
15	A1	2p brn & vio, ordinary paper	11.00	9.00
16	A1	2½p ultra & blk	35.00	4.75
17	A1	2½p ultra	4.00	.60
18	A2	3p org & grn, chalky paper	3.25	3.00
19	A1	6p red violet & gray blk ('16)	10.00	*35.00*
a.		6p purple & gray, chalky paper ('08)	24.00	*32.50*
20	A1	1sh org & grn, chalky paper ('09)	4.00	*35.00*

21 A2 5sh ol grn & gray vio ('18) 42.50 *120.00*
Nos. 11-21 (11) 134.45 *218.65*

Nos. 13, 19a and 21 are on chalky paper only and Nos. 15, 18 and 20 are on both ordinary and chalky paper.

For stamp and type overprinted see #MR1-MR2.

King George V — A3

A4

1920-22 Ordinary Paper

24 A3 ½p green 4.25 *6.00*
25 A4 1p carmine 3.50 *6.75*
26 A3 1½p orange 1.40 2.00
27 A4 2p gray 3.25 *5.00*
28 A3 2½p ultramarine 7.50 *10.00*
a. "A" missing from watermark 600.00

Chalky Paper

29 A4 3p vio & dull vio, *yel* 2.00 *12.00*
30 A3 6p red vio & dull vio 4.00 *12.00*
31 A4 1sh blk, *gray grn* 4.00 *4.50*
32 A3 2sh ultra & dull vio, *bl* 25.00 *50.00*
33 A4 2sh 6p red & blk, *bl* 5.50 *40.00*
34 A3 5sh red & grn, *yel* 5.50 *45.00*
35 A4 10sh red & grn, *grn* 14.50 *52.50*
36 A3 £1 blk & vio, *red* ('22) 300.00 *375.00*
Nos. 24-36 (13) 380.40 *620.75*

1921-29 Ordinary Paper Wmk. 4

37 A3 ½p yel green 2.50 1.50
38 A4 1p rose red 1.25 .25
39 A4 1p dp violet ('22) 7.50 1.10
40 A3 1½p rose red ('25) 6.00 2.00
41 A3 1½p fawn ('28) 1.50 .35
42 A4 2p gray 1.00 .65
44 A3 2½p brown ('22) 4.00 *10.00*

Chalky Paper

43a A3 2½p ultra ('27) 1.75 *2.00*
45 A4 3p ultra ('22) 1.25 *4.75*
46 A4 3p vio & dl vio, *yel* 1.50 *3.00*
47 A3 6p red vio & dl vio ('24) 1.50 *6.75*
48 A4 1sh blk, *grn* ('29) 5.50 *5.00*
49 A3 2sh ultra & vio, *bl* ('22) 13.00 *35.00*
50 A4 2sh6p red & blk, *bl* ('27) 22.50 *29.00*
51 A3 5sh red & grn, *yel* ('29) 55.00 *100.00*
Nos. 37-51 (15) 125.75 *201.35*
Set, ovptd. "SPEICMEN" 450.00

No. 43 exists on ordinary and chalky paper.

Caravel in Old Road Bay — A5

1923 Wmk. 4

52 A5 ½p green & blk 2.50 *8.25*
53 A5 1p violet & blk 5.00 1.75
54 A5 1½p car & blk 5.00 *11.00*
55 A5 2p dk gray & blk 4.25 1.75
56 A5 2½p brown & blk 6.50 *35.00*
57 A5 3p ultra & blk 5.00 *16.00*
58 A5 6p red vio & blk 10.50 *35.00*
59 A5 1sh ol grn & blk 15.00 *35.00*
60 A5 2sh ultra & blk, *bl* 52.50 *85.00*
61 A5 2sh6p red & blk, *blue* 55.00 *100.00*
62 A5 10sh red & blk, *emer* 325.00 *600.00*

Wmk. 3

63 A5 5sh red & blk, *yel* 92.50 *225.00*
64 A5 £1 vio & blk, *red* 825.00 *1,775.*
Nos. 52-63 (12) 578.75 *1,153.*

Tercentenary of the founding of the colony of St. Kitts (or St. Christopher).

Common Design Types pictured following the introduction.

Silver Jubilee Issue

Common Design Type

Inscribed "St. Christopher and Nevis"

Perf. 11x12

1935, May 6 Engr. Wmk. 4

72 CD301 1p car & dk blue 1.10 *.75*
73 CD301 1½p gray blk & ultra .85 .85
74 CD301 2½p ultra & brown 1.10 .90
75 CD301 1sh brn vio & ind 8.50 *16.00*
Nos. 72-75 (4) 11.55 *18.50*
Set, never hinged 19.50

Coronation Issue

Common Design Type

Inscribed "St. Christopher and Nevis"

1937, May 12 *Perf. 13½x14*

76 CD302 1p carmine .25 .30
77 CD302 1½p brown .30 .25
78 CD302 2½p bright ultra .40 1.50
Nos. 76-78 (3) .95 2.05
Set, never hinged 1.25

George VI A6

Medicinal Spring A7

Columbus Looking for Land — A8

Map Showing Anguilla A9

Perf. 13½x14 (A6, A9), 14 (A7, A8)

1938-48 Typo.

79 A6 ½p green .25 .25
80 A6 1p carmine 1.00 .55
81 A6 1½p orange .25 .30
82 A7 2p gray & car .90 1.40
83 A6 2½p ultra .50 .35
84 A7 3p car & pale lilac 2.75 5.50
85 A8 6p rose lil & dl grn 5.00 1.60
86 A7 1sh green & gray blk 3.00 1.00
87 A7 2sh6p car & gray blk 8.50 4.50
88 A8 5sh car & dull grn 17.50 13.00

Typo., Center Litho.

Chalky Paper

89 A9 10sh brt ultra & blk 9.50 *21.00*
90 A9 £1 brown & blk 9.50 *25.00*
Nos. 79-90 (12) 58.65 *74.45*
Set, never hinged 85.00

Issued: ½, 1, 1½, 2½p, 8/15/38; 2p, 1941; 3, 6p, 2sh6p, 5sh, 1942; 1sh, 1943; 10sh, £1, 9/1/48.

For types overprinted see Nos. 99-104.

1938, Aug. 15 *Perf. 13x11½*

82a A7 2p 18.00 3.00
84a A7 3p 16.00 7.50
85a A8 6p 6.50 3.00
86a A7 1sh 8.50 1.50
87a A7 2sh6p 22.50 10.00
88a A8 5sh 47.50 23.00
Nos. 82a-88a (6) 119.00 48.00

Catalogue values for unused stamps in this section, from this point to the end of the section, are for Never Hinged items.

Peace Issue

Common Design Type

Inscribed "St. Kitts-Nevis"

1946, Nov. 1 Engr. *Perf. 13½x14*

91 CD303 1½p deep orange .25 .25
92 CD303 3p carmine .25 .25

Silver Wedding Issue

Common Design Types

Inscribed: "St. Kitts-Nevis"

1949, Jan. 3 Photo. *Perf. 14x14½*

93 CD304 2½p bright ultra .25 .50

Perf. 11½x11

Engraved; Name Typographed

94 CD305 5sh rose carmine 11.00 *6.75*

UPU Issue

Common Design Types

Inscribed: "St. Kitt's-Nevis"

Engr.; Name Typo. on 3p, 6p

1949, Oct. 10 *Perf. 13½, 11x11½*

95 CD306 2½p ultra .25 *.35*
96 CD307 3p deep carmine 2.50 *2.50*
97 CD308 6p red lilac .25 *1.40*
98 CD309 1sh blue green .35 *.45*
Nos. 95-98 (4) 3.35 4.70

Types of 1938 Overprinted in Black or Carmine

On A6

On A7-A8

Perf. 13½x14, 13x12½

1950, Nov. 10 Wmk. 4

99 A6 1p carmine .25 .25
100 A6 1½p orange .25 *.55*
a. Wmk. 4a (error) 3,000.
101 A6 2½p ultra .25 .25
102 A7 3p car & pale lilac .80 *.85*
103 A8 6p rose lil & dl grn .45 .25
104 A7 1sh grn & gray blk (C) 1.50 .40
Nos. 99-104 (6) 3.50 2.55

300th anniv. of the settlement of Anguilla.

University Issue

Common Design Types

Inscribed: "St. Kitts-Nevis"

Perf. 14x14½

1951, Feb. 16 Engr. Wmk. 4

105 CD310 3c org yel & gray blk .45 .25
106 CD311 12c red violet & aqua .45 1.25

St. Christopher-Nevis-Anguilla

Bath House and Spa, Nevis — A10

Map — A11

Designs: 2c, Warner Park, St. Kitts. 4c, Brimstone Hill, St. Kitts. 5c, Nevis. 6c, Pinney's Beach, Nevis. 12c, Sir Thomas Warner's Tomb. 24c, Old Road Bay, St. Kitts. 48c, Picking Cotton. 60c, Treasury, St. Kitts. $1.20, Salt Pond, Anguilla. $4.80, Sugar Mill, St. Kitts.

1952, June 14 *Perf. 12½*

107 A10 1c ocher & dp grn .25 *1.75*
108 A10 2c emerald 1.00 1.00
109 A11 3c purple & red .40 *1.25*
110 A10 4c red .25 .25
111 A10 5c gray & ultra .40 .25
112 A10 6c deep ultra .40 .25
113 A11 12c redsh brn & dp blue 1.25 .25
114 A10 24c car & gray blk .40 .25
115 A10 48c vio brn & ol bis 3.00 *4.75*
116 A10 60c dp grn & och 2.25 *4.50*
117 A10 $1.20 dp ultra & dp green 8.00 4.75
118 A10 $4.80 car & emer 15.00 *20.00*
Nos. 107-118 (12) 32.60 39.25

Coronation Issue

Common Design Type

1953, June 2 *Perf. 13½x13*

119 CD312 2c brt green & blk .35 .25

Types of 1952 with Portrait of Queen Elizabeth II

½c, Salt Pond, Anguilla. 8c, Sombrero Lighthouse. $2.40, Map of Anguilla & Dependencies.

1954-57 Engr. *Perf. 12½*

120 A10 ½c gray olive ('56) .40 .25
121 A10 1c ocher & dp grn .25 .25
a. Horiz. pair, imperf. vert.
122 A10 2c emerald 1.00 .25
123 A11 3c purple & red .80 .25
124 A10 4c red .25 .25
125 A10 5c gray & ultra .25 .25
126 A10 6c deep ultra 1.50 .25
127 A11 8c dark gray ('57) 3.00 .30
128 A11 12c redsh brn & dp blue .25 .25
129 A10 24c carmine & blk .25 .25
130 A10 48c brn & ol bister 1.50 .65
131 A10 60c dp grn & ocher 5.75 *7.50*
132 A10 $1.20 dp ultra & dp green 20.00 3.00
133 A10 $2.40 red org & blk ('57) 18.00 13.00
134 A10 $4.80 car & emer 22.50 11.00
Nos. 120-134 (15) 75.70 37.70

Issued: 24c-$1.20, $4.80, 12/1/54; ½c, 7/3/56; 8c, $2.40, 2/1/57; others, 3/1/54.

Alexander Hamilton and Nevis Scene A12

1957, Jan. 11 *Perf. 12½*

135 A12 24c dp ultra & yel grn .40 .25

Bicent. of the birth of Alexander Hamilton.

West Indies Federation

Common Design Type

Perf. 11½x11

1958, Apr. 22 Engr. Wmk. 314

136 CD313 3c green .75 .35
137 CD313 6c blue 1.00 1.00
138 CD313 12c carmine rose 1.25 .50
Nos. 136-138 (3) 3.00 1.85

Federation of the West Indies, Apr. 22, 1958.

Stamp of Nevis, 1861 A13

Designs (Stamps of Nevis, 1861 issue): 8c, 4p stamp. 12c, 6p stamp. 24c, 1sh stamp.

1961, July 15 *Perf. 14*

139 A13 2c green & brown .25 .25
140 A13 8c blue & pale brown .30 .25
141 A13 12c carmine & gray .35 .25
142 A13 24c orange & green .55 .50
Nos. 139-142 (4) 1.45 1.25

Centenary of the first stamps of Nevis.

Red Cross Centenary Issue

Common Design Type

1963, Sept. 2 Litho. *Perf. 13*

143 CD315 3c black & red .25 .25
144 CD315 12c ultra & red .65 .65

New Lighthouse, Sombrero — A14

Loading Sugar Cane, St. Kitts
A15

Designs: 2c, Pall Mall Square, Basseterre. 3c, Gateway, Brimstone Hill Fort, St. Kitts. 4c, Nelson's Spring, Nevis. 5c, Grammar School, St. Kitts. 6c, Mt. Misery Crater, St. Kitts. 10c, Hibiscus. 15c, Sea Island cotton, Nevis. 20c, Boat building, Anguilla. 25c, White-crowned pigeon. 50c, St. George's Church tower, Basseterre. 60c, Alexander Hamilton. $1, Map of St. Kitts-Nevis. $2.50, Map of Anguilla. $5, Arms of St. Christopher-Nevis-Anguilla.

1963, Nov. 20 Photo. *Perf. 14*

145 A14 ½c blue & dk brn .25 .25
146 A15 1c multicolored .25 .25
147 A14 2c multicolored .25 .25
a. Yellow omitted 300.00
148 A14 3c multicolored .25 .25
149 A15 4c multicolored .25 .25
150 A15 5c multicolored 3.50 .25
151 A15 6c multicolored .25 .25
152 A15 10c multicolored .25 .25
153 A14 15c multicolored .70 .25
154 A15 20c multicolored .30 .25
155 A14 25c multicolored 2.50 .25
156 A15 50c multicolored .60 .35
157 A14 60c multicolored 1.25 .40
158 A14 $1 multicolored 3.00 .55
159 A15 $2.50 multicolored 3.25 3.25
160 A14 $5 multicolored 8.00 8.00
Nos. 145-160 (16) 24.85 15.30

For overprints see Nos. 161-162.

1967-69 Wmk. 314 Sideways

145a A14 ½c ('69) .25 *2.00*
147b A14 2c 1.75 .25
148a A14 3c ('68) .35 .25
153a A14 15c ('68) .90 .45
155a A14 25c ('68) 2.50 .25
158a A14 $1 ('68) 6.00 4.00
Nos. 145a-158a (6) 11.75 7.20

Nos. 148 and 155 Overprinted: "ARTS / FESTIVAL / ST. KITTS / 1964"

1964, Sept. 14

161 A14 3c multicolored .25 .25
162 A14 25c multicolored .25 .25

ITU Issue

Common Design Type

Perf. 11x11½

1965, May 17 Litho. Wmk. 314

163 CD317 2c bister & rose red .25 .25
164 CD317 50c grnsh blue & ol .35 .35

Intl. Cooperation Year Issue

Common Design Type

1965, Oct. 25 *Perf. 14½*

165 CD318 2c blue grn & claret .25 .30
166 CD318 25c lt violet & green .45 .30

Churchill Memorial Issue

Common Design Type

1966, Jan. 24 Photo. *Perf. 14*

Design in Black, Gold and Carmine Rose

167 CD319 ½c bright blue .25 *.85*
a. Denomination omitted 450.00
168 CD319 3c green .25 .25
169 CD319 15c brown .40 .30
170 CD319 25c violet .80 .30
Nos. 167-170 (4) 1.70 1.70

Royal Visit Issue

Common Design Type

1966, Feb. 14 Litho. *Perf. 11x12*

171 CD320 3c violet blue .25 *.35*
172 CD320 25c dk carmine rose .55 .40

World Cup Soccer Issue

Common Design Type

1966, July 1 Litho. *Perf. 14*

173 CD321 6c multicolored .35 .40
174 CD321 25c multicolored .50 .40

Festival Emblem With Dolphins — A16

Unwmk.

1966, Aug. 15 Photo. *Perf. 14*

175 A16 3c gold, grn, yel & blk .25 .25
176 A16 25c silver, grn, yel & blk .30 .30

Arts Festival of 1966.

WHO Headquarters Issue

Common Design Type

1966, Sept. 20 Litho. *Perf. 14*

177 CD322 3c multicolored .25 .25
178 CD322 40c multicolored .40 .40

UNESCO Anniversary Issue

Common Design Type

1966, Dec. 1 Litho. *Perf. 14*

179 CD323 3c "Education" .25 .25
180 CD323 6c "Science" .25 .25
181 CD323 40c "Culture" .40 .40
Nos. 179-181 (3) .90 .90

Independent State

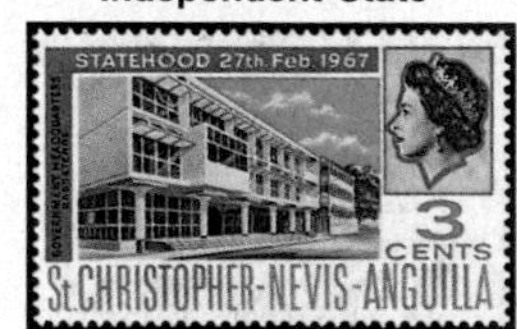

Government Headquarters, Basseterre — A17

Designs: 10c, Flag and map of Anguilla, St. Christopher and Nevis. 25c, Coat of Arms.

Wmk. 314

1967, July 1 Photo. *Perf. 14½*

182 A17 3c multicolored .25 .25
183 A17 10c multicolored .25 .25
184 A17 25c multicolored .25 .25
Nos. 182-184 (3) .75 .75

Achievement of independence, Feb. 27, 1967.

Charles Wesley, Cross and Palm — A18

3c, John Wesley. 40c, Thomas Coke.

1967, Dec. 1 Litho. *Perf. 13x13½*

185 A18 3c dp lilac, dp car & blk .25 .25
186 A18 25c ultra, grnsh blue & blk .25 .25
187 A18 40c ocher, yellow & blk .25 .25
Nos. 185-187 (3) .75 .75

Attainment of autonomy by the Methodist Church in the Caribbean and the Americas, and for the opening of headquarters near St. John's, Antigua, May 1967.

Cargo Ship and Plane
A19

Perf. 13½x13

1968, July 30 Litho. Wmk. 314

188 A19 25c multicolored .25 .25
189 A19 50c brt blue & multi .45 .45

Issued to publicize the organization of the Caribbean Free Trade Area, CARIFTA.

Martin Luther King, Jr. — A20

Perf. 12x12½

1968, Sept. 30 Litho. Wmk. 314

190 A20 50c multicolored .40 .35

Dr. Martin Luther King, Jr. (1929-68), American civil rights leader.

Mystical Nativity, by Botticelli — A21

Christmas (Paintings): 25c, 50c, The Adoration of the Magi, by Rubens.

Perf. 14½x14

1968, Nov. 27 Photo. Wmk. 314

191 A21 12c brt violet & multi .25 .25
192 A21 25c multicolored .25 .25
193 A21 40c gray & multi .25 .25
194 A21 50c crimson & multi .25 .25
Nos. 191-194 (4) 1.00 1.00

Snook
A22

Fish: 12c, Needlefish (gar). 40c, Horse-eye jack. 50c, Red snapper. The 6c is misinscribed "tarpon."

Perf. 14x14½

1969, Feb. 25 Photo. Wmk. 314

195 A22 6c brt green & multi .25 .25
196 A22 12c blue & multi .30 .25
197 A22 40c gray blue & multi .30 .25
198 A22 50c multicolored .40 .30
Nos. 195-198 (4) 1.25 1.05

Arms of Sir Thomas Warner and Map of Islands — A23

Designs: 25c, Warner's tomb in St. Kitts. 40c, Warner's commission from Charles I.

1969, Sept. 1 Litho. *Perf. 13½*

199 A23 20c multicolored .25 .25
200 A23 25c multicolored .25 .25
201 A23 40c multicolored .25 .25
Nos. 199-201 (3) .75 .75

Issued in memory of Sir Thomas Warner, first Governor of St. Kitts-Nevis, Barbados and Montserrat.

Adoration of the Kings, by Jan Mostaert — A24

Christmas (Painting): 40c, 50c, Adoration of the Kings, by Geertgen tot Sint Jans.

1969, Nov. 17 *Perf. 13½*

202 A24 10c olive & multi .25 .25
203 A24 25c violet & multi .25 .25
204 A24 40c yellow grn & multi .25 .25
205 A24 50c maroon & multi .25 .25
Nos. 202-205 (4) 1.00 1.00

Pirates Burying Treasure, Frigate Bay — A25

Caravels, 16th Century
A26

Designs: 1c, English two-decker, 1650. 2c, Flags of England, Spain, France, Holland and Portugal. 3c, Hilt of 17th cent. rapier. 5c, Henry Morgan and fire boats. 6c, The pirate L'Ollonois and a carrack (pirate vessel). 10c, Smugglers' ship. 15c, Spanish 17th cent. piece of eight and map of Caribbean. 20c, Garrison and ship cannon and map of Spanish Main. 25c, Humphrey Cole's astrolabe, 1574. 50c, Flintlock pistol and map of Spanish Main. 60c, Dutch Flute (ship). $1, Capt. Bartholomew Roberts and document with death sentence for his crew. $2.50, Railing piece (small cannon), 17th cent. and map of Spanish Main. $5, Francis Drake, John Hawkins and ships. $10, Edward Teach (Blackbeard) and his capture.

Wmk. 314 Upright (A25), Sideways (A26)

1970, Feb. 1 Litho. *Perf. 14*

206 A25 ½c multicolored .25 .25
207 A25 1c multicolored .40 .25
208 A25 2c multicolored .25 .25
209 A25 3c multicolored .25 .25
210 A26 4c multicolored .25 .25
211 A26 5c multicolored .40 .25
212 A26 6c multicolored .40 .25
213 A26 10c multicolored .40 .25
214 A25 15c Hispanianum 2.50 .50
215 A25 15c Hispaniarum 5.00 .25
216 A26 20c multicolored .45 .25
217 A25 25c multicolored .40 .25
218 A26 50c multicolored .85 .90
219 A25 60c multicolored 1.75 .80
220 A25 $1 multicolored 1.75 .80
221 A26 $2.50 multicolored 1.75 *4.50*
222 A26 $5 multicolored 3.00 *5.00*
Nos. 206-222 (17) 20.05 15.25

Coin inscription was misspelled on No. 214, corrected on No. 215 (issued Sept. 8).

Wmk. 314 Sideways (A25), Upright (A26)

1973-74

206a A25 ½c multicolored .25 *1.25*
208a A25 2c multicolored .25 *1.25*
209a A25 3c multicolored .25 *1.25*
211a A26 5c multicolored .35 *1.25*
212a A26 6c multicolored .40 *.80*
213a A26 10c multicolored .50 *.80*
215a A25 15c multicolored .85 *1.00*
216a A26 20c multicolored 1.00 *1.25*
217a A25 25c multicolored 1.25 *1.75*
218a A26 50c multicolored 1.75 *1.75*
220a A25 $1 multicolored 3.25 *3.75*
222A A26 $10 multi ('74) 21.00 *13.00*
Nos. 206a-220a,222A (12) 31.10 29.10

Issue dates: $10, Nov. 16; others, Sept. 12.

1975-77 Wmk. 373

207b A25 1c multi ('77) .40 .25
209b A25 3c multi ('76) .25 .25
210b A26 4c multi ('76) .25 .25
211b A26 5c multicolored .30 .35

212b A26 6c multicolored 1.00 .25
213b A26 10c multi ('76) .45 .25
215b A25 15c multi ('76) .55 .25
216b A26 20c multicolored 9.50 *7.50*
219b A25 60c multi ('76) 12.00 *7.50*
220b A25 $1 multi ('77) 8.00 *2.00*
Nos. 207b-220b (10) 32.70 18.85

Pip Meeting Convict, from "Great Expectations" — A27

Designs: 20c, Miss Havisham from "Great Expectations." 25c, Dickens' birthplace, Portsmouth, vert. 40c, Charles Dickens, vert.

Perf. 13x13½, 13½x13

1970, May 1 Litho. Wmk. 314

223 A27 4c gold, Prus blue & brn .25 *.30*
224 A27 20c gold, claret & brn .25 .25
225 A27 25c gold, olive & brn .25 .25
226 A27 40c dk blue, gold & brn .25 *.35*
Nos. 223-226 (4) 1.00 1.15

Charles Dickens (1812-70), English novelist.

Local Steel Band A28

25c, Local string band. 40c, "A Midsummer Night's Dream," 1963 performance.

1970, Aug. 1 ***Perf. 13½***

227 A28 20c multicolored .25 .25
228 A28 25c multicolored .25 .25
229 A28 40c multicolored .25 .25
Nos. 227-229 (3) .75 .75

Issued to publicize the 1970 Arts Festival.

St. Christopher No. 1 and St. Kitts Post Office, 1970 — A29

Designs: 20c, 25c, St. Christopher Nos. 1 and 3. 50c, St. Christopher No. 3 and St. Kitts postmark, Sept. 2, 1871.

Wmk. 314

1970, Sept. 14 Litho. ***Perf. 14½***

230 A29 ½c green & rose .25 .25
231 A29 20c vio bl, rose & grn .25 .25
232 A29 25c brown, rose & grn .25 .25
233 A29 50c black, grn & dk red .30 *.45*
Nos. 230-233 (4) 1.05 1.20

Centenary of stamps of St. Christopher.

Holy Family, by Anthony van Dyck — A30

Christmas: 3c, 40c, Adoration of the Shepherds, by Frans Floris.

1970, Nov. 16 ***Perf. 14***

234 A30 3c multicolored .25 .25
235 A30 20c ocher & multi .25 .25
236 A30 25c dull red & multi .25 .25
237 A30 40c green & multi .25 .25
Nos. 234-237 (4) 1.00 1.00

Monkey Fiddle A31

Flowers: 20c, Mountain violets. 30c, Morning glory. 50c, Fringed epidendrum.

1971, Mar. 1 Litho. ***Perf. 14***

238 A31 ½c multicolored .25 .25
239 A31 20c multicolored .25 .25
240 A31 30c multicolored .25 .25
241 A31 50c multicolored .35 *.75*
Nos. 238-241 (4) 1.10 1.50

Chateau de Poincy, St. Kitts — A32

Designs: 20c, Royal poinciana. 50c, De Poincy's coat of arms, vert.

1971, June 1 Litho. Wmk. 314

242 A32 20c green & multi .25 .25
243 A32 30c dull yellow & multi .25 .25
244 A32 50c brown & multi .25 .25
Nos. 242-244 (3) .75 .75

Philippe de Longvilliers de Poincy became first governor of French possessions in the Antilles in 1639.

East Yorks A33

Designs: 20c, Royal Artillery. 30c, French Infantry. 50c, Royal Scots.

1971, Sept. 1 ***Perf. 14***

245 A33 ½c black & multi .25 .25
246 A33 20c black & multi .30 .25
247 A33 30c black & multi .35 .25
248 A33 50c black & multi .45 .25
Nos. 245-248 (4) 1.35 1.00

Siege of Brimstone Hill, 1782.

Crucifixion, by Quentin Massys — A34

Perf. 14x13½

1972, Apr. 1 Litho. Wmk. 314

249 A34 4c brick red & multi .25 .25
250 A34 20c gray green & multi .25 .25
251 A34 30c dull blue & multi .25 .25
252 A34 40c lt brown & multi .25 .25
Nos. 249-252 (4) 1.00 1.00

Easter 1972.

Madonna and Child, by Bergognone A35

Paintings: 20c, Adoration of the Kings, by Jacopo da Bassano, horiz. 25c, Adoration of the Shepherds, by Il Domenichino. 40c, Madonna and Child, by Fiorenzo di Lorenzo.

1972, Oct. 2 ***Perf. 13½x14, 14x13½***

253 A35 3c gray green & multi .25 .25
254 A35 20c deep plum & multi .25 .25
255 A35 25c sepia & multi .25 .25
256 A35 40c red & multi .25 .25
Nos. 253-256 (4) 1.00 1.00

Christmas 1972.

Silver Wedding Issue, 1972

Common Design Type

Queen Elizabeth II, Prince Philip, pelicans.

1972, Nov. 20 Photo. ***Perf. 14x14½***

257 CD324 20c car rose & multi .30 .25
258 CD324 25c ultra & multi .35 .25

Warner Landing at St. Kitts — A36

Designs: 25c, Settlers growing tobacco. 40c, Building fort at "Old Road." $2.50, Warner's ship off St. Kitts, Jan. 28, 1623.

1973, Jan. 28 Litho. ***Perf. 14x13½***

259 A36 4c pink & multi .25 .25
260 A36 25c brown & multi .25 .25
261 A36 40c blue & multi .25 .25
262 A36 $2.50 multicolored .85 *1.00*
Nos. 259-262 (4) 1.60 1.75

350th anniversary of the landing of Sir Thomas Warner at St. Kitts.

For overprints see Nos. 266-269.

The Last Supper, by Juan de Juanes — A37

Easter (The Last Supper, by): 4c, Titian, vert. 25c, ascribed to Roberti, vert.

Perf. 14x13½, 13½x14

1973, Apr. 16 Photo. Wmk. 314

263 A37 4c blue black & multi .25 .25
264 A37 25c multicolored .25 .25
265 A37 $2.50 purple & multi .80 .60
Nos. 263-265 (3) 1.30 1.10

Nos. 259-262 Overprinted

1973, May 31 Litho. ***Perf. 14x13½***

266 A36 4c pink & multi .25 .25
267 A36 25c brown & multi .25 .25
268 A36 40c blue & multi .25 .25
269 A36 $2.50 multicolored .30 .30
Nos. 266-269 (4) 1.05 1.05

Visit of Prince Charles, May 1973.

Harbor Scene and St. Kitts-Nevis No. 3 — A38

25c, Sugar mill and #2. 40c, Unloading of boat and #1. $2.50, Rock carvings and #5.

1973, Oct. 1 Litho. ***Perf. 13½x14***

270 A38 4c salmon & multi .25 .25
271 A38 25c lt blue & multi .40 .30
272 A38 40c multicolored .60 .50
273 A38 $2.50 multicolored 1.50 1.00
a. Souvenir sheet of 4, #270-273 2.75 2.75
Nos. 270-273 (4) 2.75 2.05

70th anniv. of 1st St. Kitts-Nevis stamps.

Princess Anne's Wedding Issue

Common Design Type

1973, Nov. 14 ***Perf. 14***

274 CD325 25c brt green & multi .25 .25
275 CD325 40c citron & multi .25 .25

Virgin and Child, by Murillo — A39

Christmas (Paintings): 40c, Holy Family, by Anton Raphael Mengs. 60c, Holy Family, by Sassoferrato. $1, Holy Family, by Filippino Lippi, horiz.

1973, Dec. 1 Litho. ***Perf. 14x13½***

276 A39 4c brt blue & multi .25 .25
277 A39 40c orange & multi .25 .25
278 A39 60c multicolored .25 .25
279 A39 $1 multicolored .35 .35
Nos. 276-279 (4) 1.10 1.10

Christ Carrying Cross, by Sebastiano del Piombo — A40

Easter: 25c, Crucifixion, by Goya. 40c, Trinity, by Diego Ribera. $2.50, Burial of Christ, by Fra Bartolomeo, horiz.

1974, Apr. 8 ***Perf. 13***

280 A40 4c olive & multi .25 .25
281 A40 25c lt blue & multi .25 .25
282 A40 40c purple & multi .25 .25
283 A40 $2.50 gray & multi .90 .90
Nos. 280-283 (4) 1.65 1.65

University Center, St. Kitts, Chancellor Hugh Wooding — A41

1974, June 1 *Perf. 13½*

284	A41	10c blue & multi	.25	.25
285	A41	$1 pink & multi	.25	.25
a.		Souvenir sheet of 2, #284-285	.50	.50

University of the West Indies, 25th anniv.

Nurse Explaining Family Planning — A42

Designs: 4c, Globe and hands reaching up, vert. 40c, Family, vert. $2.50, WPY emblem and scale balancing embryo and world.

Wmk. 314

1974, Aug. 5 **Litho.** *Perf. 14*

286	A42	4c blk, blue & brn	.25	.25
287	A42	25c multicolored	.25	.25
288	A42	40c multicolored	.25	.25
289	A42	$2.50 lilac & multi	.30	.30
		Nos. 286-289 (4)	1.05	1.05

Family planning and World Population Week, Aug. 4-10.

Churchill as Lieutenant, 21st Lancers — A43

Knight of the Garter — A44

Designs: 25c, Churchill as Prime Minister. 60c, Churchill Statue, Parliament Square, London.

1974, Nov. 30

290	A43	4c dull violet & multi	.25	.25
291	A43	25c yellow & multi	.25	.25
292	A44	40c lt blue & multi	.25	.25
293	A44	60c lt blue & multi	.25	.25
a.		Souvenir sheet of 4, #290-293	.90	.90
		Nos. 290-293 (4)	1.00	1.00

Sir Winston Churchill (1874-1965).

Souvenir Sheets

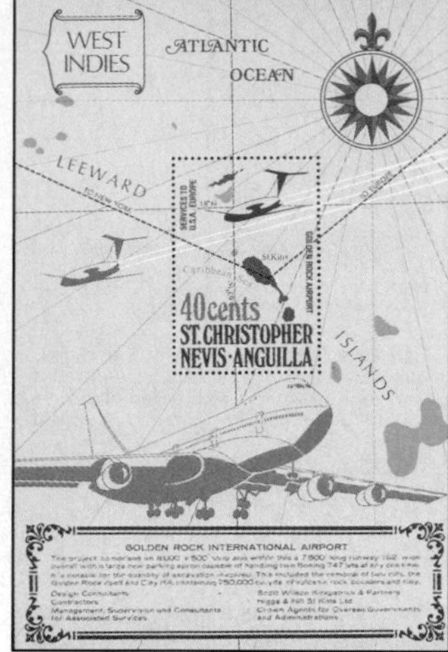

Boeing 747 over St. Kitts-Nevis — A45

1974, Dec. 16 *Perf. 14x13½*

294	A45	40c multicolored	.90	.90
295	A45	45c multicolored	1.00	1.00

Opening of Golden Rock Intl. Airport.

The Last Supper, by Doré — A46

Easter: 25c, Jesus mocked. 40c, Jesus falling beneath the Cross. $1, Raising the Cross. Designs based on Bible illustrations by Paul Gustave Doré (1833-1883).

1975, Mar. 24 *Perf. 14½*

296	A46	4c ultra & multi	.25	.25
297	A46	25c lt blue & multi	.25	.25
298	A46	40c bister & multi	.25	.25
299	A46	$1 salmon pink & multi	.25	.25
		Nos. 296-299 (4)	1.00	1.00

ECCA Headquarters, Basseterre, and Map of St. Kitts — A47

Designs: 25c, Specimen of $1 note, issued by ECCA. 40c, St. Kitts half dollar, 1801, and $4 coin, 1875. 45c, Nevis "9 dogs" coin, 1801, and 2c, 5c, coins, 1975.

Perf. 13½x14

1975, June 2 **Wmk. 373**

300	A47	12c orange & multi	.25	.25
301	A47	25c olive & multi	.25	.25
302	A47	40c vermilion & multi	.25	.25
303	A47	45c brt blue & multi	.25	.25
		Nos. 300-303 (4)	1.00	1.00

East Caribbean Currency Authority Headquarters, Basseterre, opening.

Evangeline Booth, Salvation Army — A48

Designs (IWY Emblem and): 25c, Sylvia Pankhurst, suffragette. 40c, Marie Curie, scientist. $2.50, Lady Annie Allen, teacher.

Perf. 14x14½

1975, Sept. 15 **Litho.** **Wmk. 314**

304	A48	4c orange brn & blk	.40	.25
305	A48	25c lilac pur & blk	.50	.25
306	A48	40c blue, vio bl & blk	2.75	.80
307	A48	$2.50 yellow brn & blk	1.75	*4.25*
		Nos. 304-307 (4)	5.40	5.55

International Women's Year 1975.

Golfer Swinging Club — A49

1975, Nov. 1 *Perf. 14*

308	A49	4c rose red & blk	.90	.25
309	A49	25c yellow & blk	1.25	.25
310	A49	40c emerald & blk	1.50	.40
311	A49	$1 blue & blk	2.25	2.25
		Nos. 308-311 (4)	5.90	3.15

Opening of Frigate Bay Golf Course.

St. Paul, by Sacchi Pier Francesco A50

Christmas (Paintings, details): 40c, St. James, by Bonifazio di Pitati. 45c, St. John, by Pier Francesco Mola. $1, Virgin Mary, by Raphael.

Wmk. 373

1975, Dec. 1 **Litho.** *Perf. 14*

312	A50	25c ultra & multi	.35	.25
313	A50	40c multicolored	.50	.40
314	A50	45c red brown & multi	.55	.45
315	A50	$1 gold & multi	1.40	*2.00*
		Nos. 312-315 (4)	2.80	3.10

The Crucifixion — A51

The Last Supper — A52

Stained Glass Windows: No. 316, Virgin Mary. No. 317, Christ on the Cross. No. 318, St. John. 40c, The Last Supper (different). $1, Baptism of Christ.

Perf. 14x13½

1976, Apr. 14 **Litho.** **Wmk. 373**

316		4c black & multi	.25	.25
317		4c black & multi	.25	.25
318		4c black & multi	.25	.25
a.	A51	Triptych, #316-318	1.25	1.25

Perf. 14½

319	A52	25c black & multi	.35	.30
320	A52	40c black & multi	.40	.30
321	A52	$1 black & multi	.75	.75
		Nos. 319-321 (3)	1.50	1.35

Easter 1976. No. 318a has continuous design.

Map of West Indies, Bats, Wicket and Ball A52a

Prudential Cup — A52b

Unwmk.

1976, July 8 **Litho.** *Perf. 14*

322	A52a	12c lt blue & multi	.40	.35
323	A52b	40c lilac rose & blk	1.40	.75
a.		Souvenir sheet of 2, #322-323	6.00	6.00

World Cricket Cup, won by West Indies Team, 1975.

Crispus Attucks and Boston Massacre — A53

Designs: 40c, Alexander Hamilton and Battle of Yorktown. 45c, Thomas Jefferson and Declaration of Independence. $1, George Washington and Crossing of the Delaware.

1976, July 26 **Litho.** **Wmk. 373**

324	A53	20c gray & multi	.25	.25
325	A53	40c gray & multi	.30	.25
326	A53	45c gray & multi	.30	.25
327	A53	$1 gray & multi	.65	.65
		Nos. 324-327 (4)	1.50	1.40

American Bicentennial.

Nativity, Sforza Book of Hours — A54

Christmas (Paintings): 40c, Virgin and Child, by Bernardino Pintoricchio. 45c, Our Lady of Good Children, by Ford Maddox Brown. $1, Christ Child, by Margaret W. Tarrant.

1976, Nov. 1 *Perf. 14*

328	A54	20c purple & multi	.25	.25
329	A54	40c dk blue & multi	.25	.25
330	A54	45c multicolored	.25	.25
331	A54	$1 multicolored	.30	.30
		Nos. 328-331 (4)	1.05	1.05

Queen Planting Tree, 1966 Visit — A55

Designs: 55c, The scepter. $1.50, Bishops paying homage to the Queen.

1977, Feb. 7 Litho. *Perf. 14x13½*

332 A55 50c multicolored .25 .25
333 A55 55c multicolored .25 .25
334 A55 $1.50 multicolored .30 .30
Nos. 332-334 (3) .80 .80

25th anniv. of the reign of Elizabeth II.

Christ on the Cross, by Niccolo di Liberatore — A56

Easter: 30c, Resurrection (Imitator of Mantegna). 50c, Resurrection, by Ugolino, horiz. $1, Christ Rising from Tomb, by Gaudenzio.

Wmk. 373

1977, Apr. 1 Litho. *Perf. 14*

335 A56 25c yellow & multi .25 .25
336 A56 30c deep blue & multi .25 .25
337 A56 50c olive green & multi .25 .25
338 A56 $1 red & multi .25 .25
Nos. 335-338 (4) 1.00 1.00

Estridge Mission A57

20c, Mission emblem. 40c, Basseterre Mission.

1977, June 27 Litho. *Perf. 12½*

339 A57 4c blue & black .25 .25
340 A57 20c multicolored .25 .25
341 A57 40c orange yel & blk .25 .25
Nos. 339-341 (3) .75 .75

Bicentenary of Moravian Mission.

Microscope, Flask, Syringe — A58

12c, Blood, fat, nerve cells. 20c, Symbol of community participation. $1, Inoculation.

1977, Oct. 11 Litho. *Perf. 14*

342 A58 3c multicolored .25 .25
343 A58 12c multicolored .40 *.60*
344 A58 20c multicolored .45 .25
345 A58 $1 multicolored 1.10 1.10
Nos. 342-345 (4) 2.20 2.20

Pan American Health Organization, 75th anniversary (PAHO).

Nativity, West Window — A59

Christmas, Stained-glass Windows, Chartres Cathedral: 6c, Three Kings. 40c, Virgin and Child. $1, Virgin and Child, Rose Window.

1977, Nov. 15 Wmk. 373

346 A59 4c multicolored .25 .25
347 A59 6c multicolored .25 .25
348 A59 40c multicolored .35 .25
349 A59 $1 multicolored .65 .45
Nos. 346-349 (4) 1.50 1.20

Green Monkey and Young — A60

Green Monkeys: 5c, $1.50, Mother and young sitting on branch. 55c, like 4c.

Wmk. 373

1978, Apr. 15 Litho. *Perf. 14½*

350 A60 4c multicolored .25 .25
351 A60 5c multicolored .25 .25
352 A60 55c multicolored .75 .30
353 A60 $1.50 multicolored 1.75 1.50
Nos. 350-353 (4) 3.00 2.30

Elizabeth II Coronation Anniversary Issue

Common Design Types

Souvenir Sheet

Unwmk.

1978, Apr. 21 Litho. *Perf. 15*

354 Sheet of 6 1.00 1.00
a. CD326 $1 Falcon of Edward III .25 .25
b. CD327 $1 Elizabeth II .25 .25
c. CD328 $1 Pelican .25 .25

No. 354 contains 2 se-tenant strips of Nos. 354a-354c, separated by horizontal gutter with commemorative and descriptive inscriptions and showing central part of coronation procession with coach.

Tomatoes A61

Designs: 2c, Defense Force band. 5c, Radio and TV station. 10c, Technical College. 12c, TV assembly plant. 15c, Sugar cane harvest. 25c, Craft Center. 30c, Cruise ship. 40c, Sea crab and lobster. 45c, Royal St. Kitts Hotel and golf course. 50c, Pinneys Beach, Nevis. 55c, New Runway at Golden Rock. $1, Cotton pickers. $5, Brewery. $10, Pineapples and peanuts.

Perf. 14½x14

1978, Sept. 8 Wmk. 373

355 A61 1c multicolored .25 .25
356 A61 2c multicolored .25 .25
357 A61 5c multicolored .25 .25
358 A61 10c multicolored .25 .25
359 A61 12c multicolored .25 .75
360 A61 15c multicolored .25 .25
361 A61 25c multicolored .25 .25
362 A61 30c multicolored 1.50 1.50
363 A61 40c multicolored .45 .25
364 A61 45c multicolored 2.75 1.25
365 A61 50c multicolored .35 .25
366 A61 55c multicolored 1.25 .25
367 A61 $1 multicolored .40 .40
368 A61 $5 multicolored .75 *1.25*
369 A61 $10 multicolored 1.25 *1.75*
Nos. 355-369 (15) 10.45 9.15

For overprints see Nevis #100-112, O1-O10.

Investiture — A62

Designs: 10c, Map reading. 25c, Pitching tent. 40c, Cooking. 50c, First aid. 55c, Rev. W. A. Beckett, founder of Scouting in St. Kitts.

Wmk. 373

1978, Oct. 9 Litho. *Perf. 13½*

370 A62 5c multicolored .25 .25
371 A62 10c multicolored .25 .25
372 A62 25c multicolored .35 .35
373 A62 40c multicolored .45 .45
374 A62 50c multicolored .50 .55
375 A62 55c multicolored .60 .55
Nos. 370-375 (6) 2.40 2.40

50th anniversary of St. Kitts-Nevis Scouting.

King Bringing Gift — A63

Christmas: 15c, 30c, King bringing gift, diff. $2.25, Three Kings paying homage to Infant Jesus.

1978, Dec. 1 *Perf. 14x13½*

376 A63 5c multicolored .25 .25
377 A63 15c multicolored .25 .25
378 A63 30c multicolored .25 .25
379 A63 $2.25 multicolored .25 .25
Nos. 376-379 (4) 1.00 1.00

Canna Coccinea — A64

Flowers: 30c, Heliconia bihai. 55c, Ruellia tuberosa. $1.50, Gesneria ventricosa.

1979, Mar. 19 *Perf. 14*

380 A64 5c multicolored .25 .25
381 A64 30c multicolored .40 .40
382 A64 55c multicolored .50 .50
383 A64 $1.50 multicolored .85 *1.25*
Nos. 380-383 (4) 2.00 2.40

See Nos. 393-396.

Rowland Hill and St. Christopher No. 1 — A65

Rowland Hill and: 15c, St. Kitts-Nevis #233. 50c, Great Britain #4. $2.50, St. Kitts-Nevis #64.

Wmk. 373

1979, July 2 Litho. *Perf. 14½*

384 A65 5c multicolored .25 .25
385 A65 15c multicolored .25 .25
386 A65 50c multicolored .30 .30
387 A65 $2.50 multicolored .65 .65
Nos. 384-387 (4) 1.45 1.45

Sir Rowland Hill (1795-1879), originator of penny postage.

The Woodman's Daughter, by Millais — A66

Paintings by John Everett Millais and IYC Emblem: 25c, Cherry Ripe. 30c, The Rescue, horiz. 55c, Bubbles. $1, Christ in the House of His Parents.

1979, Nov. 12 Litho. *Perf. 14*

388 A66 5c multicolored .25 .25
389 A66 25c multicolored .30 .30
390 A66 30c multicolored .30 .30
391 A66 55c multicolored .40 .40
Nos. 388-391 (4) 1.25 1.25

Souvenir Sheet

392 A66 $1 multicolored 1.25 1.25

Christmas 1979; Intl. Year of the Child.

Flower Type of 1979

Flowers: 4c, Clerodendrum aculeatum. 55c, Inga laurina. $1.50, Epidendrum difforme. $2, Salvia serontina.

1980, Feb. 4 Litho. *Perf. 14*

393 A64 4c multicolored .40 .25
394 A64 55c multicolored .50 .30
395 A64 $1.50 multicolored 1.75 1.75
396 A64 $2 multicolored .90 *2.00*
Nos. 393-396 (4) 3.55 4.30

Nevis Lagoon, London 1980 Emblem — A67

30c, Fig Tree Church, vert. 55c, Nisbet Plantation. $3, Lord Nelson, by Fuger, vert. 75c, Nelson Falling, by D. Dighton.

1980, May 6 Litho. *Perf. 13½*

397 A67 5c shown .25 .25
398 A67 30c multicolored .30 .30
399 A67 55c multicolored .50 .50
400 A67 $3 multicolored 2.50 2.50
Nos. 397-400 (4) 3.55 3.55

Souvenir Sheet

401 A67 75c multicolored 2.50 2.00

London 80 Intl. Phil. Exhib., May 6-14; Lord Nelson, (1758-1805).

WAR TAX STAMPS

No. 12 Overprinted

1916 Wmk. 3 *Perf. 14*

MR1 A1 ½p deep green 1.10 .55

Type of 1905-18 Issue Overprinted

1918

MR2	A1	1½p orange	1.75	1.00

OFFICIAL STAMPS

Catalogue values for unused stamps in this section are for Never Hinged items.

Nos. 359, 361, 363-369 Overprinted: OFFICIAL

Perf. 14½x14

1980 Litho. Wmk. 373

O1	A61	12c multicolored	.80	*1.25*
O2	A61	25c multicolored	.25	.25
O3	A61	40c multicolored	.55	.50
O4	A61	45c multicolored	3.50	2.00
O5	A61	50c multicolored	.40	.45
O6	A61	55c multicolored	1.45	.40
O7	A61	$1 multicolored	.75	*2.25*
O8	A61	$5 multicolored	.85	*2.50*
O9	A61	$10 multicolored	1.50	*3.50*
		Nos. O1-O9 (9)	10.05	13.10

ST. LUCIA

sānt ˈlü-shə

LOCATION — Island in the West Indies, one of the Windward group

GOVT. — Independent state in British Commonwealth

AREA — 240 sq. mi.

POP. — 154,020 (1999 est.)

CAPITAL — Castries

The British colony of St. Lucia became an associated state March 1, 1967, and independent in 1979.

12 Pence = 1 Shilling

100 Cents = 1 Dollar (1949)

Catalogue values for unused stamps in this country are for Never Hinged items, beginning with Scott 127 in the regular postage section, Scott C1 in the air post section, Scott J3 in the postage due section, and Scott O1 in the officials section.

Watermarks

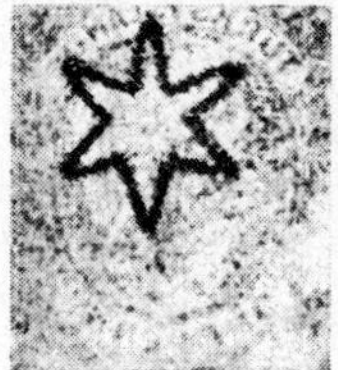

Wmk. 5 — Small Star

Wmk. 380 — "POST OFFICE"

Values for unused stamps are for examples with original gum as defined in the catalogue introduction. Very fine examples of Nos. 1-26 will have perforations touching the design on at least one side due to the narrow spacing of the stamps on the plates. Stamps with perfs clear of the framelines on all four sides are very scarce and will command higher prices.

Queen Victoria — A1

Perf. 14 to 16

1860, Dec. 18 Engr. Wmk. 5

1	A1	(1p) rose red	110.00	75.00
a.		Double impression	*2,500.*	
b.		Horiz. pair, imperf vert.	—	
2	A1	(4p) blue	250.00	175.00
a.		Horiz. pair, imperf vert.	—	
3	A1	(6p) green	325.00	225.00
a.		Horiz. pair, imperf vert.	—	
		Nos. 1-3 (3)	685.00	475.00

For types overprinted see Nos. 15, 17, 19-26.

1863 Wmk. 1 *Perf. 12½*

4	A1	(1p) lake	95.00	*110.00*
5	A1	(4p) slate blue	140.00	150.00
6	A1	(6p) emerald	225.00	225.00
		Nos. 4-6 (3)	460.00	485.00

Nos. 4-6 exist imperforate on stamp paper, from proof sheets.

1864

7	A1	(1p) black	30.00	14.00
8	A1	(4p) yellow	190.00	50.00
a.		(4p) olive yellow	425.00	100.00
b.		(4p) lemon yellow	*1,750.*	
9	A1	(6p) violet	140.00	42.50
a.		(6p) lilac	210.00	32.50
b.		(6p) deep lilac	160.00	42.50
10	A1	(1sh) red orange	250.00	32.50
a.		(1sh) orange	275.00	32.50
c.		Horiz. pair, imperf between	—	
		Nos. 7-10 (4)	610.00	139.00

Nos. 7-10 exist imperforate on stamp paper, from proof sheets.

Perf. 14

11	A1	(1p) deep black	50.00	22.00
a.		Horiz. pair, imperf between	—	
12	A1	(4p) yellow	130.00	24.00
a.		(4p) olive yellow	325.00	105.00
13	A1	(6p) pale lilac	125.00	24.00
a.		(6p) deep lilac	125.00	45.00
b.		(6p) violet	275.00	77.50
14	A1	(1sh) deep orange	175.00	19.00
a.		(1sh) orange	250.00	25.00
		Nos. 11-14 (4)	480.00	89.00

Type of 1860 Surcharged in Black or Red

a

b

1881

15	A1(a)	½p green	85.00	*120.00*
17	A1(b)	2½p scarlet	60.00	27.50

1883-84 Wmk. Crown and CA (2)

19	A1(a)	½p green	32.50	*47.50*
20	A1(a)	1p black (R)	47.50	16.00
a.		Half used as ½p on cover		—
21	A1(a)	4p yellow	325.00	24.00
22	A1(a)	6p violet	50.00	50.00
23	A1(a)	1sh orange	310.00	190.00
		Nos. 19-23 (5)	765.00	327.50

1884 *Perf. 12*

24	A1(a)	4p yellow	300.00	32.50

Nos. 5 & 6 Surcharged

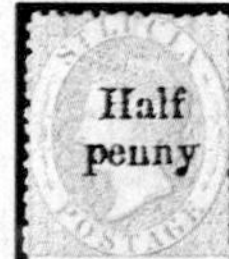

1885 Wmk. 1 *Perf. 12½*

25	A1	½p emerald	77.50	
26	A1	6p slate blue	1,500.	

Nos. 25 and 26 were prepared for use but not issued.

A5

For explanation of dies A and B see "Dies of British Colonial Stamps..." in the catalogue Table of Contents.

1883-98 Typo. Wmk. 2 *Perf. 14*

27	A5	½p green ('91)	4.00	1.25
a.		Die A ('83)	17.50	10.00
28	A5	1p rose	55.00	19.00
29	A5	1p lilac ('91)	7.00	.35
a.		Die A ('86)	15.00	7.25
b.		Imperf., pair	900.00	
30	A5	2p ultra & brn org ('98)	6.00	1.25
31	A5	2½p ultra ('91)	12.50	1.25
a.		Die A ('83)	75.00	3.00
32	A5	3p lilac & grn ('91)	9.00	6.50
a.		Die A ('86)	150.00	20.00
33	A5	4p brown ('93)	8.00	3.00
a.		Die A ('85)	50.00	1.50
b.		Imperf., pair	*1,050.*	
34	A5	6p violet ('86)	300.00	240.00
a.		Imperf., pair	*2,000.*	
35	A5	6p lilac & blue ('87)	7.00	*18.00*
a.		Die A ('91)	40.00	29.00
36	A5	1sh brn org ('85)	450.00	175.00
37	A5	1sh lil & red ('91)	14.00	6.00
a.		Die A ('87)	150.00	37.50
38	A5	5sh lil & org ('91)	60.00	*175.00*
39	A5	10sh lil & blk ('91)	110.00	*175.00*
		Nos. 27-39 (13)	1,042.	821.60

Nos. 32, 32a, 35a and 33a Surcharged in Black

No. 40 No. 41 No. 42

1892

40	A5	½p on 3p lil & grn	95.00	30.00
b.		Double surcharge	1,000.	800.00
c.		Inverted surcharge	2,450.	800.00
d.		Triple surcharge, one on back	*1,350.*	*1,500.*
41	A5	½p on half of 6p lilac & blue	32.50	4.00
a.		Slanting serif	240.00	150.00
c.		Without the bar of "½"	325.00	160.00
d.		"2" of "½" omitted	575.00	600.00
e.		Surcharged sideways	1,700.	
f.		Double surcharge	725.00	725.00
g.		Triple surcharge	*1,450.*	
42	A5	1p on 4p brown	9.00	*4.75*
b.		Double surcharge	275.00	
c.		Inverted surcharge	1,100.	950.00
d.		Thick diagonal stroke in first "N"	30.00	24.00
e.		Thick diagonal stroke in second "N"	30.00	24.00
		Nos. 40-42 (3)	136.50	38.75

No. 40 is found with wide or narrow "O" in "ONE," and large or small "A" in "HALF." For more detailed listings, see the *Scott Classic Specialized Catalogue of Stamps and Covers.*

Edward VII — A9

Numerals of 3p, 6p, 1sh and 5sh of type A9 are in color on plain tablet.

1902-03 Typo.

43	A9	½p violet & green	4.50	1.90
44	A9	1p violet & car rose	6.50	.90
46	A9	2½p violet & ultra	40.00	8.00
47	A9	3p violet & yellow	9.50	*10.00*
48	A9	1sh green & black	17.00	*50.00*
		Nos. 43-48 (5)	77.50	*70.80*

The Pitons — A10

Wmk. 1 sideways

1902, Dec. 16 Engr.

49	A10	2p brown & green	16.00	2.50

Fourth centenary of the discovery of the island by Columbus.

1904-05 Typo. Wmk. 3

50	A9	½p violet & green	10.00	.65
a.		Chalky paper	13.00	1.40
51	A9	1p violet & car rose	9.00	1.40
a.		Chalky paper	12.00	1.40
52	A9	2½p violet & ultra	40.00	2.75
a.		Chalky paper	18.00	5.00
53	A9	3p violet & yellow	13.00	3.25
54	A9	6p vio & dp vio ('05)	27.50	*35.00*
a.		Chalky paper	21.00	47.50
55	A9	1sh green & blk ('05)	50.00	32.50
56	A9	5sh green & car ('05)	85.00	*200.00*
		Nos. 50-56 (7)	234.50	*275.55*

No. 55 is on chalky paper only.

BUYING, SELLING, EXPERTIZATIONS, ST. LUCIA, BRITISH W.I. & WORLD CLASSICS
HELPING COLLECTORS AVOID THE MINEFIELDS!
Send Your Stamps & Covers with Confidence.
PHOTOGRAPHIC CERTIFICATES OF AUTHENTICITY
Reliable and Fast • Recognized • Competitively Priced • Contact Us for Terms and Prices
LIANE & SERGIO SISMONDO • PO Box 10035 • Syracuse, NY 13290-3301
T. 315-422-2331 • F. 315-422-2956 • EMAIL: sismondo@dreamscape.com

ASDA • PTS • CNEP • CSDA • FCFI
VISIT US ONLINE AT WWW.SISMONDOSTAMPS.COM

1907-10

No.	Type	Description	Unused	Used
57	A9	½p green	2.00	1.10
58	A9	1p carmine	4.75	.35
59	A9	2½p ultra	4.25	2.00

Chalky Paper

No.	Type	Description	Unused	Used
60	A9	3p violet, *yel* ('09)	3.25	*19.00*
61	A9	6p violet & red vio	9.25	*40.00*
a.		6p violet & dull vio ('10)	75.00	*90.00*
62	A9	1sh black, *grn* ('09)	5.25	*8.75*
63	A9	5sh grn & red, *yel*	67.50	*77.50*
		Nos. 57-63 (7)	96.25	*148.70*

King George V
A11 A12

Numerals of 3p, 6p, 1sh and 5sh of type A11 are in color on plain tablet.

For description of dies I and II see "Dies of British Colonial Stamps" in Table of Contents.

Die I

1912-19 Ordinary Paper

No.	Type	Description	Unused	Used
64	A11	½p deep green	.75	.50
65	A11	1p scarlet	8.00	.25
a.		1p carmine	2.00	.25
66	A12	2p gray ('13)	1.60	*4.50*
67	A11	2½p bright blue	4.50	3.00

Chalky Paper

Numeral on White Tablet

No.	Type	Description	Unused	Used
68	A11	3p violet, *yel*	1.40	*2.50*
a.		Die II	30.00	*60.00*
69	A11	6p vio & red vio	2.25	*21.00*
70	A11	1sh black, *green*	7.00	*5.50*
a.		1sh black, *bl grn, ol back*	17.50	*19.00*
71	A11	1sh fawn	20.00	*50.00*
72	A11	5sh grn & red, *yel*	26.50	*85.00*
		Nos. 64-72 (9)	72.00	*172.25*

A13

A14

1913-14 Chalky Paper

No.	Type	Description	Unused	Used
73	A13	4p scar & blk, *yel*	1.00	*2.25*
74	A14	2sh6p blk & red, *bl*	25.00	*50.00*

Surface-colored Paper

No.	Type	Description	Unused	Used
75	A13	4p scarlet & blk, *yel*	.75	*1.60*

Die II

1921-24 Wmk. 4 Ordinary Paper

No.	Type	Description	Unused	Used
76	A11	½p green	1.25	.55
77	A11	1p carmine	14.50	*20.00*
78	A11	1p dk brn ('22)	1.60	.25
79	A13	1½p rose red ('22)	.85	*2.75*
80	A12	2p gray	.85	.25
81	A11	2½p ultra	7.50	*3.00*
82	A11	2½p orange ('24)	16.00	*60.00*
83	A11	3p dull blue ('24)	7.00	*12.00*

Chalky Paper

No.	Type	Description	Unused	Used
84	A11	3p violet, *yel*	3.75	*13.50*
85	A13	4p scar & blk, *yel* ('24)	1.40	*2.75*
86	A11	6p vio & red vio	2.25	*5.25*
87	A11	1sh fawn	6.00	*3.50*
88	A14	2sh6p blk & red, *bl* ('24)	20.00	*30.00*
89	A11	5sh grn & red, *yel*	60.00	*95.00*
		Nos. 76-89 (14)	142.95	*248.80*

Common Design Types pictured following the introduction.

Silver Jubilee Issue

Common Design Type

1935, May 6 Engr. *Perf. 13½x14*

No.	Type	Description	Unused	Used
91	CD301	½p green & blk	.30	2.00
92	CD301	2p gray blk & ultra	.95	1.40
93	CD301	2½p blue & brn	1.25	1.40
94	CD301	1sh brt vio & ind	13.50	*16.00*
		Nos. 91-94 (4)	16.00	*20.80*
		Set, never hinged	26.00	

Port Castries
A15

Columbus Square, Castries
A16

Ventine Falls
A17

Soldiers' Monument
A19

Fort Rodney, Pigeon Island
A18

Government House
A20

Seal of the Colony
A21

Center in Black

1936, Mar. 1 *Perf. 14*

No.	Type	Description	Unused	Used
95	A15	½p light green	.35	.55
a.		Perf. 13x12	5.50	*26.00*
96	A16	1p dark brown	.45	.25
a.		Perf. 13x12	10.00	4.25
97	A17	1½p carmine	.70	.35
a.		Perf. 12x13	17.50	2.50
98	A15	2p gray	.60	.25
99	A16	2½p blue	.60	.25
100	A17	3p dull green	1.50	.75
101	A15	4p brown	2.00	*1.25*
102	A16	6p orange	2.00	1.25
103	A18	1sh lt bl, perf. 13x12	3.50	2.50
104	A19	2sh6p ultra	15.00	14.00
105	A20	5sh violet	19.00	*25.00*
106	A21	10sh car rose, perf. 13x12	60.00	*100.00*
		Nos. 95-106 (12)	105.70	*146.40*
		Set, never hinged	225.00	

Nos. 95a, 96a and 97a are coils.
Issue date: Nos. 95a, 96a, Apr. 8.

Coronation Issue

Common Design Type

1937, May 12 *Perf. 11x11½*

No.	Type	Description	Unused	Used
107	CD302	1p dark purple	.25	.40
108	CD302	1½p dark carmine	.40	.25
109	CD302	2½p deep ultra	.40	1.40
		Nos. 107-109 (3)	1.05	2.05
		Set, never hinged	1.75	

King George VI — A22

Columbus Square, Castries
A23

Government House
A24

The Pitons
A25

Loading Bananas
A26

Arms of the Colony — A27

Perf. 12½ (#110-111, 1½p-3½p, 8p, 3sh, 5sh, £1), 12 (6p, 1sh, 2sh, 10sh)

1938-48

No.	Type	Description	Unused	Used
110	A22	½p green ('43)	.25	.25
a.		Perf. 14½x14	1.40	.25
111	A22	1p deep violet	.25	.25
a.		Perf. 14½x14	2.00	.85
112	A22	1p red, Perf. 14½x14 ('47)	.25	.25
a.		Perf. 12½	.65	.25
113	A22	1½p carmine ('43)	1.00	1.40
a.		Perf. 14½x14	1.40	.50
114	A22	2p gray ('43)	.25	.25
a.		Perf. 14½x14	2.25	*1.75*
115	A22	2½p ultra ('43)	.25	.25
a.		Perf. 14½x14	3.00	.25
116	A22	2½p violet ('47)	.85	.25
117	A22	3p red org ('43)	.25	.25
a.		Perf. 14½x14	1.00	.25
118	A22	3½p brt ultra ('47)	.85	.25
119	A23	6p magenta ('48)	6.50	1.75
a.		Perf. 13½	2.00	.50
120	A22	8p choc ('46)	2.75	.40
121	A24	1sh lt brn ('48)	.75	.40
a.		Perf. 13½	1.10	.40
122	A25	2sh red vio & sl bl	3.50	1.50
123	A22	3sh brt red vio ('46)	6.75	2.00
124	A26	5sh rose vio & blk	10.00	11.00
125	A27	10sh black, *yel*	7.50	*9.00*
126	A22	£1 sepia ('46)	9.00	8.00
		Nos. 110-126 (17)	50.95	37.45
		Set, never hinged	75.00	

See Nos. 135-148.

Catalogue values for unused stamps in this section, from this point to the end of the section, are for Never Hinged items.

Peace Issue

Common Design Type

Perf. 13½x14

1946, Oct. 8 Wmk. 4 Engr.

No.	Type	Description	Unused	Used
127	CD303	1p lilac	.25	.30
128	CD303	3½p deep blue	.25	.30

Silver Wedding Issue

Common Design Types

1948, Nov. 26 Photo. *Perf. 14x14½*

No.	Type	Description	Unused	Used
129	CD304	1p scarlet	.25	.25

Perf. 11½x11

Engraved; Name Typographed

No.	Type	Description	Unused	Used
130	CD305	£1 violet brown	22.00	*45.00*

UPU Issue

Common Design Types

Engr.; Name Typo. on 6c, 12c.

Perf. 13½, 11x11½

1949, Oct. 10 Wmk. 4

No.	Type	Description	Unused	Used
131	CD306	5c violet	.25	*.85*
132	CD307	6c deep orange	1.60	*2.50*
133	CD308	12c red lilac	.30	.25
134	CD309	24c blue green	.40	.25
		Nos. 131-134 (4)	2.55	*3.85*

Types of 1938

Values in Cents and Dollars

1949, Oct. 1 Engr. *Perf. 12½*

No.	Type	Description	Unused	Used
135	A22	1c green	.35	.25
a.		Perf. 14	3.25	.50
136	A22	2c rose lilac	1.25	.25
a.		Perf. 14½x14	4.50	1.25
137	A22	3c red	1.60	*2.50*
138	A22	4c gray	.95	.25
a.		Perf. 14½x14		*17,000.*
139	A22	5c violet	1.75	.25
140	A22	6c red orange	1.25	*3.50*
141	A22	7c ultra	4.00	3.00
142	A22	12c rose lake	6.75	4.00
a.		Perf. 14½x14 ('50)	750.00	550.00
143	A22	16c brown	5.75	.65

Perf. 11½

No.	Type	Description	Unused	Used
144	A27	24c Prus blue	.75	.25
145	A27	48c olive green	1.75	1.60
146	A27	$1.20 purple	2.75	*10.00*
147	A27	$2.40 blue green	4.50	*20.00*
148	A27	$4.80 dk car rose	11.50	*21.00*
		Nos. 135-148 (14)	44.90	*67.50*

Nos. 144 to 148 are of a type similar to A27, but with the denomination in the top corners and "St. Lucia" at the bottom.

For overprints see Nos. 152-155.

University Issue

Common Design Types

Perf. 14x14½

1951, Feb. 16 Wmk. 4

No.	Type	Description	Unused	Used
149	CD310	3c red & gray black	.55	.75
150	CD311	12c brn car & blk	.85	.75

Phoenix Rising from Burning Buildings — A28

Engr. & Typo.

1951, June 19 *Perf. 13½x13*

No.	Type	Description	Unused	Used
151	A28	12c dp blue & car	.50	1.10

Reconstruction of Castries.

Nos. 136, 138, 139 and 142 Overprinted in Black

1951, Sept. 25 *Perf. 12½*

No.	Type	Description	Unused	Used
152	A22	2c rose lilac	.25	.85
153	A22	4c gray	.25	.60
154	A22	5c violet	.25	.85
155	A22	12c rose lilac	.45	.60
		Nos. 152-155 (4)	1.20	2.90

Adoption of a new constitution for the Windward Islands, 1951.

Coronation Issue

Common Design Type

1953, June 2 Engr. *Perf. 13½x13*

No.	Type	Description	Unused	Used
156	CD312	3c carmine & black	.70	.35

Queen Elizabeth II
A29

Arms of St. Lucia
A30

1953-54 Engr. *Perf. 14½x14*

No.	Type	Description	Unused	Used
157	A29	1c green	.25	.25
158	A29	2c rose lilac	.25	.25
159	A29	3c red	.25	.25
160	A29	4c gray	.25	.25
161	A29	5c violet	.25	.25
162	A29	6c orange	.25	.25
163	A29	8c rose lake	.55	.25
164	A29	10c ultra	.25	.25
165	A29	15c brown	.50	.25

Perf. 11x11½

166 A30 25c Prus blue .55 .25
167 A30 50c brown olive 5.50 .50
168 A30 $1 blue green 5.25 2.50
169 A30 $2.50 dark car rose 6.75 4.75
Nos. 157-169 (13) 20.85 10.25

Issued: 2c, 10/28; 4c, 1/7/54; 1c, 5c, 4/1/54; others, 9/2/54.

West Indies Federation
Common Design Type

Perf. 11½x11

1958, Apr. 22 **Wmk. 314**
170 CD313 3c green .40 .25
171 CD313 6c blue .65 *1.75*
172 CD313 12c carmine rose 1.00 .80
Nos. 170-172 (3) 2.05 2.80

16th Century Ship and Pitons — A31

1960, Jan. 1 *Perf. 12½x13*
173 A31 8c carmine rose .40 .40
174 A31 10c orange .50 .50
175 A31 25c dark blue .60 .60
Nos. 173-175 (3) 1.50 1.50

Granting of new constitution.

St. Lucia Stamp of 1860 — A32

1960, Dec. 18 **Engr.** *Perf. 13½*
176 A32 5c ultra & red brown .25 .25
177 A32 16c yel grn & blue blk .30 *.75*
178 A32 25c carmine & green .30 .25
Nos. 176-178 (3) .85 1.25

Centenary of St. Lucia's first postage stamps.

Freedom from Hunger Issue
Common Design Type

1963, June 4 **Photo.** *Perf. 14x14½*
179 CD314 25c green .40 .40

Red Cross Centenary Issue
Common Design Type

Wmk. 314

1963, Sept. 2 **Litho.** *Perf. 13*
180 CD315 4c black & red .25 .25
181 CD315 25c ultra & red 1.00 1.00

A33

A34

Fishing Boats, Soufrière Bay — A35

Designs: 15c, Pigeon Island. 25c, Reduit Beach. 35c, Castries Harbor. 50c, The Pitons. $1, Vigie Beach, vert. $2.50, Queen Elizabeth II, close-up.

Wmk. 314

1964, Mar. 1 **Photo.** *Perf. 14½*
182 A33 1c dark car rose .30 .25
183 A33 2c violet .50 .60
184 A33 4c brt blue green 1.30 .35
185 A33 5c slate blue .40 .25
186 A33 6c brown 1.30 *2.00*
187 A34 8c lt blue & multi .30 .25
188 A34 10c multicolored .60 .25
189 A35 12c multicolored .70 *1.25*
190 A35 15c blue & ocher .30 .25
a. Wmkd. sideways ('68) .30 .25
191 A35 25c multicolored .50 .25
192 A35 35c dk blue & buff 1.75 .25
193 A35 50c brt blue, blk & yel 2.10 .25
194 A35 $1 multicolored 2.75 2.00
195 A34 $2.50 multicolored 4.25 2.25
Nos. 182-195 (14) 17.05 10.45

For overprints see Nos. 215-225.

Shakespeare Issue
Common Design Type

1964, Apr. 23 *Perf. 14x14½*
196 CD316 10c bright green .45 .25

ITU Issue
Common Design Type

Perf. 11x11½

1965, May 17 **Litho.** **Wmk. 314**
197 CD317 2c red lil & brt pink .25 .25
198 CD317 50c lilac & yel grn 1.00 1.00

Intl. Cooperation Year Issue
Common Design Type

1965, Oct. 25 **Wmk. 314** *Perf. 14½*
199 CD318 1c blue grn & claret .25 .25
200 CD318 25c lt violet & grn .30 .30

Churchill Memorial Issue
Common Design Type

1966, Jan. 24 **Photo.** *Perf. 14*
Design in Black, Gold and Carmine Rose
201 CD319 4c bright blue .25 .25
202 CD319 6c green .25 .25
203 CD319 25c brown .40 .40
204 CD319 35c violet .60 .60
Nos. 201-204 (4) 1.50 1.50

Royal Visit Issue
Common Design Type

1966, Feb. 4 **Litho.** *Perf. 11x12*
205 CD320 4c violet blue .40 .35
206 CD320 25c dk carmine rose 1.10 1.00

World Cup Soccer Issue
Common Design Type

1966, July 1 **Litho.** *Perf. 14*
207 CD321 4c multicolored .30 .25
208 CD321 25c multicolored .85 .65

WHO Headquarters Issue
Common Design Type

1966, Sept. 20 **Litho.** *Perf. 14*
209 CD322 4c multicolored .25 .25
210 CD322 25c multicolored .55 .55

UNESCO Anniversary Issue
Common Design Type

1966, Dec. 1 **Litho.** *Perf. 14*
211 CD323 4c "Education" .25 .25
212 CD323 12c "Science" .35 .35
213 CD323 25c "Culture" .55 .55
Nos. 211-213 (3) 1.15 1.15

Associated State

Nos. 183, 185-194 Overprinted in Red: "STATEHOOD / 1st MARCH 1967"

Wmk. 314

1967, Mar. 1 **Photo.** *Perf. 14½*
215 A33 2c violet .35 .35
216 A33 5c slate blue .25 .25
217 A33 6c brown .25 .25
218 A34 8c lt blue & multi .35 .25
219 A34 10c multicolored .50 .25
220 A35 12c multicolored 1.10 .30
221 A35 15c blue & ocher 1.40 1.40
222 A35 25c multicolored 1.40 1.10
223 A35 35c dk blue & buff 1.40 *1.60*
224 A35 50c multicolored 1.40 *1.75*
225 A35 $1 multicolored 1.40 *2.00*
Nos. 215-225 (11) 9.80 9.50

The 1c and $2.50, similarly overprinted, were not sold to the public at the post office but were acknowledged belatedly (May 10) by the government and declared valid. Values for both stamps: unused $6; used $9.

The 1c, 6c and $2.50 overprints exist in black as well as red. No. 213 also exists with this overprint in blue and in black.

Madonna and Child with St. John, by Raphael — A36

1967, Oct. 16 **Wmk. 314** *Perf. 14½*
227 A36 4c black, gold & multi .25 .25
228 A36 25c multicolored .25 .25

Christmas 1967.

Cricket Batsman and Gov. Frederick Clarke — A37

Perf. 14½x14

1968, Mar. 8 **Photo.** **Wmk. 314**
229 A37 10c multicolored .25 .25
230 A37 35c multicolored .40 .40

Visit of the Marylebone Cricket Club to the West Indies, Jan.-Feb. 1968.

"Noli me Tangere," by Titian — A38

Easter: 10c, 25c, The Crucifixion, by Raphael.

1968, Mar. 25 *Perf. 14½*
231 A38 10c multicolored .25 .25
232 A38 15c multicolored .25 .25
233 A38 25c multicolored .25 .25
234 A38 35c multicolored .25 .25
Nos. 231-234 (4) 1.00 1.00

Martin Luther King, Jr. — A39

Perf. 13½x14

1968, July 4 **Photo.** **Wmk. 314**
235 A39 25c dp blue, blk & brn .25 .25
236 A39 35c violet, blk & brn .25 .25

Dr. Martin Luther King, Jr. (1929-68), American civil rights leader.

Virgin and Child in Glory, by Murillo — A40

Christmas: 10c, 35c, Virgin and Child, by Bartolomé E. Murillo.

Perf. 14½x14

1968, Oct. 17 **Photo.** **Wmk. 314**
237 A40 5c dark blue & multi .25 .25
238 A40 10c multicolored .25 .25
239 A40 25c red brown & multi .25 .25
240 A40 35c deep blue & multi .25 .25
Nos. 237-240 (4) 1.00 1.00

Purple-throated Carib — A41

Birds: 15c, 35c, St. Lucia parrot.

1969, Jan. 10 **Litho.** *Perf. 14½*
241 A41 10c multicolored .70 .70
242 A41 15c multicolored .90 .90
243 A41 25c multicolored 1.10 1.10
244 A41 35c multicolored 1.25 1.25
Nos. 241-244 (4) 3.95 3.95

Ecce Homo, by Guido Reni — A42

Painting: 15c, 35c, The Resurrection, by Il Sodoma (Giovanni Antonio de Bazzi).

Perf. 14½x14

1969, Mar. 20 **Photo.** **Wmk. 314**
245 A42 10c purple & multi .25 .25
246 A42 15c green & multi .25 .25
247 A42 25c black & multi .25 .25
248 A42 35c ocher & multi .25 .25
Nos. 245-248 (4) 1.00 1.00

Easter 1969.

Map of Caribbean — A43

Design: 25c, 35c, Clasped hands and arrows with names of CARIFTA members.

1969, May 29 **Wmk. 314** *Perf. 14*
249 A43 5c violet blue & multi .25 .25
250 A43 10c deep plum & multi .25 .25
251 A43 25c ultra & multi .25 .25
252 A43 35c green & multi .25 .25
Nos. 249-252 (4) 1.00 1.00

First anniversary of CARIFTA (Caribbean Free Trade Area).

Silhouettes of Napoleon and Josephine — A44

Perf. 14½x13

1969, Sept. 22 **Photo.** **Unwmk.**
Gold Inscription; Gray and Brown Medallions
253 A44 15c dull blue .25 .25
254 A44 25c deep claret .25 .25
255 A44 35c deep green .25 .25
256 A44 50c yellow brown .25 *.55*
Nos. 253-256 (4) 1.00 1.30

Napoleon Bonaparte, 200th birth anniv.

Madonna and Child, by Paul Delaroche — A45

Christmas: 10c, 35c, Holy Family, by Rubens.

Perf. 14½x14

1969, Oct. 27 Photo. Wmk. 314

Center Multicolored

257 A45 5c dp rose lil & gold .25 .25
258 A45 10c Prus blue & gold .25 .25
259 A45 25c maroon & gold .25 .25
260 A45 35c dp yel grn & gold .25 .25
Nos. 257-260 (4) 1.00 1.00

House of Assembly — A46

Queen Elizabeth II, by A. C. Davidson-Houston A47

2c, Roman Catholic Cathedral. 4c, Castries Boulevard. 5c, Castries Harbor. 6c, Sulphur springs. 10c, Vigie Airport. 12c, Reduit beach. 15c, Pigeon Island. 25c, The Pitons & sailboat. 35c, Marigot Bay. 50c, Diamond Waterfall. $1, St. Lucia flag & motto. $2.50, Coat of arms. $10, Map of St. Lucia.

Wmk. 314 Sideways, Upright (#271-274)

1970-73 Litho. *Perf. 14½*

261 A46 1c multicolored .25 .25
262 A46 2c multicolored .25 .25
a. Wmk. upright .90 .90
263 A46 4c multicolored 1.25 .25
a. Wmk. upright 1.75 1.75
264 A46 5c multicolored 1.90 .25
265 A46 6c multicolored .25 .25
266 A46 10c multicolored 2.10 .25
267 A46 12c multicolored .30 .25
268 A46 15c multicolored .40 .25
269 A46 25c multicolored 1.00 .25
270 A46 35c multicolored .50 .25
271 A47 50c multicolored .85 .80
272 A47 $1 multicolored .50 *.70*
273 A47 $2.50 multicolored .75 *1.75*
274 A47 $5 multicolored 1.50 *4.00*
274A A47 $10 multicolored 6.00 *9.00*
Nos. 261-274A (15) 17.80 18.75

Issued: #261-274, Feb. 1, 1970; #274A, Dec. 3, 1973; #262a, 263a, Mar. 15, 1974.

1975, July 28 Wmk. 373

263b A46 4c multicolored 1.10 2.10
264a A46 5c multicolored 1.40 1.00
266a A46 10c multicolored 2.00 1.75
268a A46 15c multicolored 3.00 2.25
Nos. 263b-268a (4) 7.50 7.10

The Three Marys at the Tomb, by Hogarth — A48

35c, The Sealing of the Tomb. $1, The Ascension. The designs are from the altarpiece painted by William Hogarth for the Church of St. Mary Redcliffe in Bristol, 1755-56.

Roulette 8½xPerf. 12½

1970, Mar. 7 Litho. Wmk. 314

Size: 27x54mm

275 A48 25c dark brown & multi .25 .25
276 A48 35c dark brown & multi .25 .25

Size: 38x54mm

277 A48 $1 dark brown & multi .40 .40
a. Triptych (#275-277) 1.20 1.20

Easter 1970.

Nos. 275-277 printed se-tenant in sheets of 30 (10 triptychs) with the center $1 stamp 10mm raised compared to the flanking 25c and 35c stamps.

Charles Dickens and Characters from his Works — A49

1970, June 8 Wmk. 314 *Perf. 14*

278 A49 1c brown & multi .25 .25
279 A49 25c Prus blue & multi .30 .25
280 A49 35c brown red & multi .35 .30
281 A49 50c red lilac & multi .40 *1.00*
Nos. 278-281 (4) 1.30 1.80

Charles Dickens (1812-70), English novelist.

Nurse Holding Red Cross Emblem A50

15c, 35c, British, St. Lucia & Red Cross flags.

Perf. 14½x14

1970, Aug. 18 Litho. Wmk. 314

282 A50 10c multicolored .25 .25
283 A50 15c multicolored .25 .25
284 A50 25c buff & multi .35 .40
285 A50 35c multicolored .45 .40
Nos. 282-285 (4) 1.30 1.30

Centenary of British Red Cross Society.

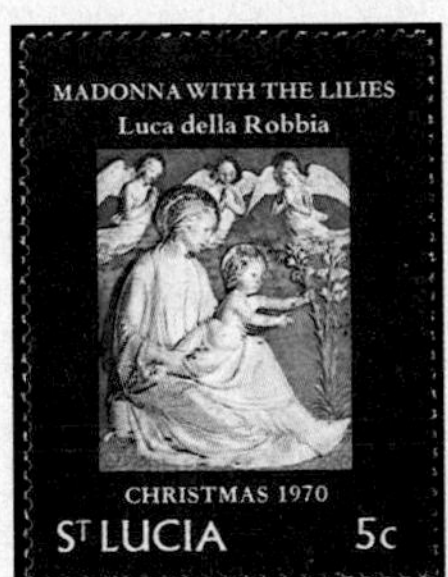

Madonna with the Lilies, by Luca della Robbia A51

Lithographed and Embossed

1970, Nov. 16 Unwmk. *Perf. 11*

286 A51 5c dark blue & multi .25 .25
287 A51 10c violet blue & multi .25 .25
288 A51 35c car lake & multi .30 .25
289 A51 40c deep green & multi .30 .30
Nos. 286-289 (4) 1.10 1.05

Christmas 1970.

Christ on the Cross, by Rubens — A52

Easter: 15c, 40c, Descent from the Cross, by Peter Paul Rubens.

Perf. 14x13½

1971, Mar. 29 Litho. Wmk. 314

290 A52 10c dull green & multi .25 .25
291 A52 15c dull red & multi .25 .25
292 A52 35c brt blue & multi .30 .25
293 A52 40c multicolored .30 .40
Nos. 290-293 (4) 1.10 1.15

Moule à Chique Lighthouse — A53

Design: 25c, Beane Field Airport.

1971, Apr. 30 *Perf. 14½x14*

294 A53 5c olive & multi .35 .25
295 A53 25c bister & multi .55 .25

Opening of Beane Field Airport.

View of Morne Fortune (Old Days) — A54

The "a" stamp shows an old print (as shown) and the "b" stamp a contemporary photograph of the same view (plain frame). 10c, Castries City. 25c, Pigeon Island. 50c, View from Government House.

Perf. 13½x14

1971, Aug. 10 Litho. Wmk. 314

296 A54 5c Pair, #a.-b. .40 .40
297 A54 10c Pair, #a.-b. .50 .50
298 A54 25c Pair, #a.-b. .60 .60
299 A54 50c Pair, #a.-b. 1.10 1.10
Nos. 296-299 (4) 2.60 2.60

Virgin and Child, by Verrocchio — A55

Virgin and Child painted by: 10c, Paolo Moranda. 35c, Giovanni Battista Cima. 40c, Andrea del Verrocchio.

1971, Oct. 15 *Perf. 14*

304 A55 5c green & multi .25 .25
305 A55 10c brown & multi .25 .25
306 A55 35c ultra & multi .25 .25
307 A55 40c red & multi .25 .25
Nos. 304-307 (4) 1.00 1.00

Christmas 1971.

St. Lucia, School of Dolci, and Arms — A56

1971, Dec. 13 *Perf. 14x14½*

308 A56 5c gray & multi .25 .25
309 A56 10c lt green & multi .25 .25
310 A56 25c tan & multi .35 .25
311 A56 50c lt blue & multi .75 .75
Nos. 308-311 (4) 1.60 1.50

National Day.

Lamentation, by Carracci A57

Easter: 25c, 50c, Angels Weeping over Body of Jesus, by Guercino.

1972, Feb. 15 Wmk. 314

312 A57 10c lt violet & multi .25 .25
313 A57 25c ocher & multi .25 .25
314 A57 35c ultra & multi .35 .25
315 A57 50c lt green & multi .45 .45
Nos. 312-315 (4) 1.30 1.20

Teachers' College and Science Building — A58

15c, University Center and coat of arms. 25c, Secondary School. 35c, Technical College.

1972, Apr. 18 Litho. *Perf. 14*

316 A58 5c multicolored .25 .25
317 A58 15c multicolored .25 .25
318 A58 25c multicolored .25 .25
319 A58 35c multicolored .25 .25
Nos. 316-319 (4) 1.00 1.00

Opening of Morne Educational Complex.

Steam Conveyance Co. Stamp and Map of St. Lucia — A59

Designs: 10c, Castries Harbor and 3c stamp. 35c, Soufriere Volcano and 1c stamp. 50c, One cent, 3c, 6c stamps.

1972, June 22 *Perf. 14½*

320 A59 5c yellow & multi .25 .25
321 A59 10c violet blue & multi .25 .25
322 A59 35c car rose & multi .65 .25
323 A59 50c emerald & multi 1.10 1.25
Nos. 320-323 (4) 2.25 2.00

Centenary of St. Lucia Steam Conveyance Co. Ltd. postal service.

Holy Family, by Sebastiano Ricci — A60

1972, Oct. 18 *Perf. 14½x14*

324 A60 5c dk brown & multi .25 .25
325 A60 10c green & multi .25 .25
326 A60 35c carmine & multi .25 .25
327 A60 40c dk blue & multi .30 .25
Nos. 324-327 (4) 1.05 1.00

Christmas 1972.

Silver Wedding Issue

Common Design Type

Design: Queen Elizabeth II, Prince Philip, St. Lucia coat of arms and St. Lucia parrot.

1972, Nov. Photo. *Perf. 14x14½*

328 CD324 15c car rose & multi .30 .30
329 CD324 35c olive & multi .45 .45

Weekday Headdress A61

Women's Headdresses: 10c, For church wear. 25c, Unmarried girl. 50c, Formal occasions.

1973, Feb. 1 Wmk. 314 *Perf. 13*

330 A61 5c multicolored .25 .25
331 A61 10c dark gray & multi .25 .25
332 A61 25c multicolored .25 .25
333 A61 50c slate blue & multi .25 *.85*
Nos. 330-333 (4) 1.00 1.60

Arms of St. Lucia — A62

Coil Stamps

1973, Apr. 19 Litho. *Perf. 14½x14*

334 A62 5c gray olive .35 *.70*
a. Watermark sideways ('76) .80 *2.00*
335 A62 10c blue .35 *.70*
a. Watermark sideways ('76) .80 *2.00*
336 A62 25c claret .35 *.70*
a. Watermark sideways ('76) 14.00
Nos. 334-336 (3) 1.05 *2.10*

H.M.S. St. Lucia A63

Designs: Old Sailing ships.

1973, May 24 Litho. *Perf. 13½x14*

337 A63 15c shown .25 .25
338 A63 35c "Prince of Wales" .40 .40
339 A63 50c "Oliph Blossom" .60 .60
340 A63 $1 "Rose" 1.25 1.25
a. Souv. sheet of 4, #337-340, perf. 15 3.00 3.00
Nos. 337-340 (4) 2.50 2.50

Banana Plantation and Flower — A64

Designs: 15c, Aerial spraying. 35c, Washing and packing bananas. 50c, Loading.

1973, July 26 Litho. *Perf. 14*

341 A64 5c multicolored .25 .25
342 A64 15c multicolored .25 .25
343 A64 35c multicolored .25 .25
344 A64 50c multicolored .65 .65
Nos. 341-344 (4) 1.40 1.40

Banana industry.

Madonna and Child, by Carlo Maratta — A65

Christmas (Paintings): 15c, Virgin in the Meadow, by Raphael. 35c, Holy Family, by Angelo Bronzino. 50c, Madonna of the Pear, by Durer.

1973, Oct. 17 Litho. *Perf. 14x13½*

345 A65 5c citron & multi .25 .25
346 A65 15c ultra & multi .25 .25
347 A65 35c dp green & multi .25 .25
348 A65 50c red & multi .25 .25
Nos. 345-348 (4) 1.00 1.00

Princess Anne's Wedding Issue
Common Design Type

1973, Nov. 14 Wmk. 314 *Perf. 14*

349 CD325 40c gray green & multi .25 .25
350 CD325 50c lilac & multi .25 .25

The Betrayal of Christ, by Ugolino — A66

Easter (Paintings by Ugolino, 14th Cent.): 35c, The Way to Calvary. 80c, Descent from the Cross. $1, Resurrection.

1974, Apr. 1 *Perf. 13½x13*

351 A66 5c ocher & multi .25 .25
352 A66 35c ocher & multi .25 .25
353 A66 80c ocher & multi .25 .25
354 A66 $1 ocher & multi .25 .30
a. Souvenir sheet of 4, #351-354 1.75 1.75
Nos. 351-354 (4) 1.00 1.05

3 Escalins, 1798 — A67

Pieces of Eight: 35c, 6 escalins, 1798. 40c, 2 livres 5 sols, 1813. $1, 6 livres 15 sols, 1813.

1974, May 20 *Perf. 13½*

355 A67 15c lt olive & multi .25 .25
356 A67 35c multicolored .25 .25
357 A67 40c green & multi .35 .35
358 A67 $1 brown & multi .65 .65
a. Souvenir sheet of 4, #355-358 2.00 2.00
Nos. 355-358 (4) 1.50 1.50

Coins of Old St. Lucia.

Baron de Laborie, 1784 — A68

Portraits: 35c, Sir John Moore, Lieutenant Governor, 1796-97. 80c, Major General Sir Dudley St. Leger Hill, 1834-37. $1, Sir Frederick Joseph Clarke, 1967-71.

Wmk. 314

1974, Aug. 29 Litho. *Perf. 14½*

359 A68 5c ocher & multi .25 .25
360 A68 35c brt blue & multi .25 .25
361 A68 80c violet & multi .25 .25
362 A68 $1 multicolored .25 .25
a. Souvenir sheet of 4, #359-362 1.00 1.00
Nos. 359-362 (4) 1.00 1.00

Past Governors of St. Lucia.

Virgin and Child, by Verrocchio — A69

Christmas (Virgin and Child): 35c, by Andrea della Robbia. 80c, by Luca della Robbia. $1, by Antonio Rossellino.

1974, Nov. 13 Wmk. 314 *Perf. 13½*

363 A69 5c gray & multi .25 .25
364 A69 35c pink & multi .25 .25
365 A69 80c brown & multi .25 .25
366 A69 $1 olive & multi .25 .25
a. Souvenir sheet of 4, #363-366 1.25 *2.25*
Nos. 363-366 (4) 1.00 1.00

Churchill and Gen. Montgomery — A70

Design: $1, Churchill and Pres. Truman.

1974, Nov. 30 *Perf. 14*

367 A70 5c multicolored .25 .25
368 A70 $1 multicolored .30 .35

Sir Winston Churchill (1874-1965).

Crucifixion, by Van der Weyden — A71

Easter: 35c, "Noli me Tangere," by Julio Romano. 80c, Crucifixion, by Fernando Gallego. $1, "Noli me Tangere," by Correggio.

Perf. 14x13½

1975, Mar. 27 Wmk. 314

369 A71 5c brown & multi .25 .25
370 A71 35c ultra & multi .25 .25
371 A71 80c red brown & multi .25 .25
372 A71 $1 green & multi .25 .35
Nos. 369-372 (4) 1.00 1.10

Nativity — A72 Adoration of the Kings — A73

No. 375, Virgin & Child. No. 376, Adoration of the Shepherds. 40c, Nativity. $1, Virgin & Child with Sts. Catherine of Alexandria and Siena.

Wmk. 314

1975, Dec. Litho. *Perf. 14½*

373 A72 5c lilac rose & multi .25 .25
374 A73 10c yellow & multi .25 .25
375 A73 10c yellow & multi .25 .25
376 A73 10c yellow & multi .25 .25
a. Strip of 3, #374-376 .40 .40
377 A72 40c yellow & multi .30 .30
378 A72 $1 blue & multi .70 .70
a. Souv. sheet of 3, #373, 377-378 1.10 *1.25*
Nos. 373-378 (6) 2.00 2.00

Christmas 1975.

"Hanna," First US Warship — A74

Revolutionary Era Ships: 1c, "Prince of Orange," British packet. 2c, "Edward," British sloop. 5c, "Millern," British merchantman. 15c, "Surprise," Continental Navy lugger. 35c, "Serapis," British warship. 50c, "Randolph," first Continental Navy frigate. $1, Frigate "Alliance."

Perf. 14½

1976, Jan. 26 Litho. Unwmk.

379-386 A74 Set of 8 4.00 4.00
386a Souv. sheet, #383-386, perf. 13 4.00 4.00

American Bicentennial.

Laughing Gull — A75

Birds: 2c, Little blue heron. 4c, Belted kingfisher. 5c, St. Lucia parrot. 6c, St. Lucia oriole. 8c, Brown trembler. 10c, American kestrel. 12c, Red-billed tropic bird. 15c, Common gallinule. 25c, Brown noddy. 35c, Sooty tern. 50c, Osprey. $1, White-breasted thrasher. $2.50, St. Lucia black finch. $5, Rednecked pigeon. $10, Caribbean elaenia.

Wmk. 314 (1c); 373 (others)

1976, May 7 Litho. *Perf. 14½*

387 A75 1c gray & multi .30 *1.40*
388 A75 2c gray & multi .30 *1.40*
389 A75 4c gray & multi .35 *1.40*
390 A75 5c gray & multi 1.60 1.10
391 A75 6c gray & multi 1.10 1.10
392 A75 8c gray & multi 1.25 *2.25*
393 A75 10c gray & multi 1.10 .40
394 A75 12c gray & multi 1.75 *2.50*
395 A75 15c gray & multi 1.10 .25
396 A75 25c gray & multi 1.60 1.00
397 A75 35c gray & multi 2.75 1.40
398 A75 50c gray & multi 5.25 3.75
399 A75 $1 gray & multi 3.25 3.75
400 A75 $2.50 gray & multi 6.00 6.75
401 A75 $5 gray & multi 6.50 4.75
402 A75 $10 gray & multi 6.00 *8.00*
Nos. 387-402 (16) 40.20 41.20

Map of West Indies, Bats, Wicket and Ball A75a

Prudential Cup — A75b

1976, July 19 Unwmk. *Perf. 14*

403 A75a 50c lt blue & multi .90 .90
404 A75b $1 lilac rose & black 1.75 1.75
a. Souvenir sheet of 2, #403-404 5.00 *5.50*

World Cricket Cup, won by West Indies Team, 1975.

Arms of H.M.S. Ceres — A76

Coats of Arms of Royal Naval Ships: 20c, Pelican. 40c, Ganges. $2, Ariadne.

1976, Sept. 6 Wmk. 373 *Perf. 14½*

405 A76 10c gold & multi .35 .30
406 A76 20c gold & multi .65 .60
407 A76 40c gold & multi .95 .85
408 A76 $2 gold & multi 2.40 2.40
Nos. 405-408 (4) 4.35 4.15

Madonna and Child, by Murillo — A77

Paintings: 20c, Virgin and Child, by Lorenzo Costa. 50c, Madonna and Child, by Adriaea Isenbrandt. $2, Madonna and Child with St. John, by Murillo. $2.50, Like 10c.

1976, Nov. 15 Litho. *Perf. 14½*

409 A77 10c multicolored .25 .25
410 A77 20c multicolored .25 .25
411 A77 50c multicolored .25 .25
412 A77 $2 multicolored .70 .70
Nos. 409-412 (4) 1.45 1.45

Souvenir Sheet

413 A77 $2.50 multicolored 1.40 1.40

Christmas.

Elizabeth II, "Palms and Water" — A78

Wmk. 373

1977, Feb. 7 Litho. *Perf. 14½*

414 A78 10c multicolored .25 .25
415 A78 20c multicolored .25 .25
416 A78 40c multicolored .25 .25
417 A78 $2 multicolored .25 .25
Nos. 414-417 (4) 1.00 1.00

Souvenir Sheet

418 A78 $2.50 multicolored .75 *1.00*

25th anniv. of the reign of Elizabeth II.

Scouts of Tapion School — A79

1c, Sea Scouts, St. Mary's College. 2c, Scout giving oath. 10c, Tapion School Cub Scouts. 20c, Venture Scout, Soufrière. 50c, Scout from Gros Islet Division. $1, $2.50, Boat drill, St. Mary's College.

1977, Oct. 17 Unwmk. *Perf. 15*

419 A79 ½c multicolored .25 .25
420 A79 1c multicolored .25 .25
421 A79 2c multicolored .25 .25
422 A79 10c multicolored .25 .25
423 A79 20c multicolored .25 .25
424 A79 50c multicolored .40 .40
425 A79 $1 multicolored .90 .90
Nos. 419-425 (7) 2.55 2.55

Souvenir Sheet

426 A79 $2.50 multicolored 2.00 2.00

6th Caribbean Boy Scout Jamboree, Kingston, Jamaica, Aug. 5-14.

Nativity, by Giotto — A80

Christmas (Virgin and Child by): 1c, Fra Angelico. 2c, El Greco. 20c, Caravaggio. 50c, Velazquez. $1, Tiepolo. $2.50, Adoration of the Kings, by Tiepolo.

1977, Oct. 31 Litho. *Perf. 14*

427-433 A80 Set of 7 2.75 2.75

Suzanne Fourment in Velvet Hat, by Rubens — A81

Rubens Paintings: 35c, Rape of the Sabine Women (detail). 50c, Ludovicus Nonnius, portrait. $2.50, Minerva Protecting Pax from Mars (detail).

Perf. 14x14½

1977, Nov. 28 Litho. Wmk. 373

434 A81 10c multicolored .25 .25
435 A81 35c multicolored .25 .25
436 A81 50c multicolored .30 .30
437 A81 $2.50 multicolored 1.60 1.60
a. Souv. sheet, #434-437, perf. 15 3.00 3.00
Nos. 434-437 (4) 2.40 2.40

Peter Paul Rubens (1577-1640).

Yeoman of the Guard and Life Guard A82

Dress Uniforms: 20c, Groom and postilion. 50c, Footman and coachman. $3, State trumpeter and herald. $5, Master of the Queen's House and Gentleman at Arms.

Unwmk.

1978, June 2 Litho. *Perf. 14*

438 A82 15c multicolored .25 .25
439 A82 20c multicolored .25 .25
440 A82 50c multicolored .30 .30
441 A82 $3 multicolored .50 .50
Nos. 438-441 (4) 1.30 1.30

Souvenir Sheet

442 A82 $5 multicolored .90 .90

25th anniv. of coronation of Elizabeth II.

Nos. 438-441 exist in miniature sheets of 3 plus label, perf. 12.

Queen Angelfish A83

Tropical Fish: 20c, Four-eyed butterflyfish. 50c, French angelfish. $2, Yellowtail damselfish. $2.50, Rock beauty.

1978, June 19 Litho. *Perf. 14½*

443 A83 10c multicolored .35 .25
444 A83 20c multicolored .55 .25
445 A83 50c multicolored .80 .70
446 A83 $2 multicolored 2.40 2.40
Nos. 443-446 (4) 4.10 3.60

Souvenir Sheet

447 A83 $2.50 multicolored 4.00 4.00

French Grenadier, Map of Battle — A84

30c, British Grenadier & Bellin map of St. Lucia, 1762. 50c, British fleet opposing French landing & map of coast from Gros Islet to Cul-de-Sac. $2.50, Light infantrymen & Gen. James Grant.

1978, Nov. 15 Litho. *Perf. 14*

448 A84 10c multicolored .50 .25
449 A84 30c multicolored .75 .35
450 A84 50c multicolored 1.00 .60
451 A84 $2.50 multicolored 2.50 2.50
Nos. 448-451 (4) 4.75 3.70

Bicent. of Battle of St. Lucia (Cul-de-Sac).

Annunciation A85

Christmas: 55c, 80c, Adoration of the Kings.

Perf. 14x14½

1978, Dec. 4 Wmk. 373

452 A85 30c multicolored .25 .25
453 A85 50c multicolored .25 .25
454 A85 55c multicolored .30 .30
455 A85 80c multicolored .40 .40
Nos. 452-455 (4) 1.20 1.20

Independent State

Hewanorra Airport A86

Independence: 30c, New coat of arms. 50c, Government house and Allen Lewis, first Governor General. $2, Map of St. Lucia, French, St. Lucia and British flags.

1979, Feb. 22 Litho. *Perf. 14*

456 A86 10c multicolored .25 .25
457 A86 30c multicolored .25 .25
458 A86 50c multicolored .25 .25
459 A86 $2 multicolored .50 .50
a. Souvenir sheet of 4, #456-459 1.50 1.50
Nos. 456-459 (4) 1.25 1.25

Paul VI and John Paul I A87

Pope Paul VI and: 30c, Pres. Anwar Sadat of Egypt. 50c, Secretary General U Thant and UN emblem. 55c, Prime Minister Golda Meir of Israel. $2, Martin Luther King, Jr.

1979, May 7 Litho. *Perf. 14*

460 A87 10c multicolored .25 .25
461 A87 30c multicolored .30 .25
462 A87 50c multicolored .40 .40
463 A87 55c multicolored .50 .45
464 A87 $2 multicolored 1.50 1.50
Nos. 460-464 (5) 2.95 2.85

In memory of Popes Paul VI and John Paul I.

Jersey Cows A88

Agricultural Diversification: 35c, Fruits and vegetables. 50c, Waterfall (water conservation). $3, Coconuts, copra industry.

1979, July 2 Litho. *Perf. 14*

465 A88 10c multicolored .25 .25
466 A88 35c multicolored .25 .25
467 A88 50c multicolored .25 .25
468 A88 $3 multicolored .60 .60
Nos. 465-468 (4) 1.35 1.35

Lindbergh's Route over St. Lucia, Puerto Rico-Paramaribo — A89

1979, Nov. Litho. *Perf. 14*

469 A89 10c Lindbergh, hydroplane .40 .25
470 A89 30c shown .45 .25
471 A89 50c Landing at La Toc .60 .40
472 A89 $2 Flight covers 1.65 1.65
Nos. 469-472 (4) 3.10 2.55

Lindbergh's inaugural airmail flight (US-Guyana) via St. Lucia, 50th anniversary.

Prince of Saxony, by Cranach the Elder — A90

IYC (Emblem and): 50c, Infanta Margarita, by Velazquez. $2, Girl Playing Badminton, by Jean Baptiste Chardin. $2.50, Mary and Francis Wilcox, by Stock. $5, Two Children, by Pablo Picasso.

1979, Dec. 17 Litho. *Perf. 14*

473 A90 10c multicolored .25 .25
474 A90 50c multicolored .25 .25
475 A90 $2 multicolored .50 .50
476 A90 $2.50 multicolored .50 .50
Nos. 473-476 (4) 1.50 1.50

Souvenir Sheet

477 A90 $5 multicolored 2.00 2.00

A91

Maltese Cross Cancels and: 10c, Penny Post notice, 1839. 50c, Hill's original stamp design. $2, St. Lucia #1. $2.50, Penny Black. $5, Hill portrait.

1979, Dec. 27

478 A91 10c multicolored .25 .25
479 A91 50c multicolored .25 .25
480 A91 $2 multicolored .25 *.50*
481 A91 $2.50 multicolored .40 *.60*
Nos. 478-481 (4) 1.15 1.60

Souvenir Sheet

482 A91 $5 multicolored 1.25 1.25

Sir Rowland Hill (1793-1879), originator of penny postage.

Nos. 478-481 also issued in sheets of 5 plus label, perf. 12x12½.

A92

IYC Emblem, Virgin and Child Paintings by: 10c, Virgin and Child, by Bernardino Fungi, IYC emblem. 50c, Carlo Dolci. $2, Titian. $2.50, Giovanni Bellini.

1980, Jan. 14
483 A92 10c multicolored .25 .25
484 A92 50c multicolored .25 .25
485 A92 $2 multicolored .75 .75
486 A92 $2.50 multicolored 1.00 1.00
a. Souvenir sheet of 4, #483-486 3.00 3.00
Nos. 483-486 (4) 2.25 2.25

Christmas 1979; Intl. Year of the Child.

St. Lucia Conveyance Co. Ltd. Stamp, 1873 A92a

London 1980 Emblem and Covers: 30c, "Assistance" 1p postmark, 1879. 50c, Postage due handstamp, 1929. $2, Postmarks on 1844 cover.

Wmk. 373
1980, May 6 Litho. *Perf. 14*
487 A92a 10c multicolored .25 .25
488 A92a 30c multicolored .25 .25
489 A92a 50c multicolored .25 .25
490 A92a $2 multicolored .25 .25
a. Souvenir sheet of 4, #487-490 .80 .80
Nos. 487-490 (4) 1.00 1.00

London 1980 Intl. Stamp Exhib., May 6-14.

Intl. Year of the Child — A93

½c, Mickey on rocket. 1c, Donald Duck spacewalking. 2c, Minnie Mouse on moon. 3c, Goofy hitch hiking. 4c, Goofy on moon. 5c, Pluto digging on moon. 10c, Donald Duck, space creature. $2, Donald Duck paddling satellite. $2.50, Mickey Mouse in lunar rover.
$5, Goofy on moon.
Space scenes. 1c, 4c, 5c, 10c, $2, $2.50 horiz.

1980, May 29 Litho. *Perf. 11*
491 A93 ½c multicolored .25 .25
492 A93 1c multicolored .25 .25
493 A93 2c multicolored .25 .25
494 A93 3c multicolored .25 .25
495 A93 4c multicolored .25 .25
496 A93 5c multicolored .25 .25
497 A93 10c multicolored .25 .25
498 A93 $2 multicolored 2.25 2.25
499 A93 $2.50 multicolored 2.25 2.25
Nos. 491-499 (9) 6.25 6.25

Souvenir Sheet
500 A93 $5 multicolored 5.50 5.50

Queen Mother Elizabeth, 80th Birthday A94

1980, Aug. 4 Litho. *Perf. 14*
501 A94 10c multicolored .25 .25
502 A94 $2.50 multicolored .40 *1.00*

Souvenir Sheet
Perf. 12½x12
503 A94 $3 multicolored .80 .80

HS-748 on Runway, St. Lucia Airport, Hewanorra — A95

10c, DC-10, St. Lucia Airport. 15c, Bus, Castries. 20c, Refrigerator ship. 25c, Islander plane. 30c, Pilot boat. 50c, Boeing 727. 75c, Cruise ship. $1, Lockheed Tristar, Piton Mountains. $2, Cargo ship. $5, Boeing 707. $10, Queen Elizabeth 2.

Wmk. 373
1980, Aug. 11 Litho. *Perf. 14½*
504 A95 5c shown .30 .30
505 A95 10c multicolored .50 .30
506 A95 15c multicolored .35 .40
507 A95 20c multicolored .35 .40
508 A95 25c multicolored .50 .40
509 A95 30c multicolored .40 .45
510 A95 50c multicolored .75 .75
511 A95 75c multicolored .60 *1.75*
512 A95 $1 multicolored .75 *1.50*
513 A95 $2 multicolored 1.40 *2.40*
514 A95 $5 multicolored 3.50 *6.00*
515 A95 $10 multicolored 6.75 *10.00*
Nos. 504-515 (12) 16.15 24.65

For surcharges see Nos. 531-533.

1984, May 15 Wmk. 380
507a A95 20c 2.50 2.50
508a A95 25c 3.25 3.25
509a A95 30c 3.25 3.25
512a A95 $1 6.50 6.50
513a A95 $2 7.50 7.50
515a A95 $10 15.00 15.00
Nos. 507a-515a (6) 38.00 38.00

Shot Put, Moscow '80 Emblem — A96

1980, Sept. 22 Litho. *Perf. 14*
516 A96 10c shown .25 .25
517 A96 50c Swimming .25 .25
518 A96 $2 Gymnastics .90 .90
519 A96 $2.50 Weight lifting 1.10 1.10
Nos. 516-519 (4) 2.50 2.50

Souvenir Sheet
520 A96 $5 Passing the torch 2.00 2.00

22nd Summer Olympic Games, Moscow, July 19-Aug. 3.

A97

1980, Sept. 30 *Perf. 14*
521 A97 10c Palms, coast at dusk .25 .25
522 A97 50c Rocky shore .25 .25
523 A97 $2 Sand beach .40 .40
524 A97 $2.50 Pitons at sunset .50 .50
Nos. 521-524 (4) 1.40 1.40

Souvenir Sheet
525 A97 $5 Two-master 1.75 1.75

Rotary International, 75th Anniversary.

A98

Nobel Prize Winners: 10c, Sir Arthur Lewis, Economics. 50c, Martin Luther King, Jr., peace, 1964. $2, Ralph Bunche, peace, 1950. $2.50, Albert Schweitzer, peace, 1952. $5, Albert Einstein, physics, 1921.

1980, Oct. 23 Litho. *Perf. 14*
526 A98 10c multicolored .25 .25
527 A98 50c multicolored .25 .25
528 A98 $2 multicolored .60 .60
529 A98 $2.50 multicolored 1.00 1.00
Nos. 526-529 (4) 2.10 2.10

Souvenir Sheet
530 A98 $5 multicolored 2.75 2.75

Nos. 506-507, 510 Surcharged

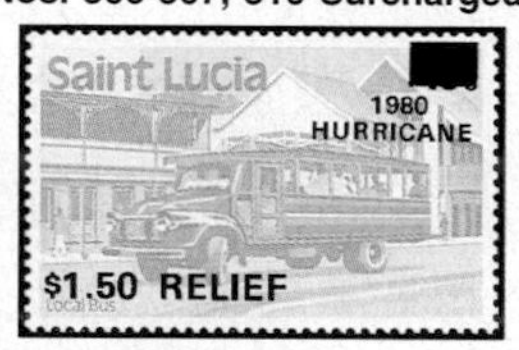

1980, Nov. 3 Litho. *Perf. 14½*
531 A95 $1.50 on 15c multi .35 .35
532 A95 $1.50 on 20c multi .35 .35
533 A95 $1.50 on 50c multi .35 .35
Nos. 531-533 (3) 1.05 1.05

Nativity, by Battista — A99

Angel and Citizens of St. Lucia — A100

Christmas: 30c, Adoration of the Kings, by Bruegel the Elder. $2, Adoration of the Shepherds, by Murillo.

1980, Dec. 1 *Perf. 14*
534 A99 10c multicolored .25 .25
535 A99 30c multicolored .25 .25
536 A99 $2 multicolored .45 .45
Nos. 534-536 (3) .95 .95

Souvenir Sheet
537 A100 Sheet of 3 1.00 1.00
a. $1 any single .30 .30

Agouti — A101

1981, Jan. 19 Litho. *Perf. 14*
538 A101 10c shown .25 .25
539 A101 50c St. Lucia parrot 1.00 .40
540 A101 $2 Purple-throated carib 2.75 1.50
541 A101 $2.50 Fiddler crab 2.25 1.90
Nos. 538-541 (4) 6.25 4.05

Souvenir Sheet
542 A101 $5 Monarch butterfly 4.75 4.75

Royal Wedding Issue
Common Design Type

1981, June 16 Litho. *Perf. 14*
543 CD331a 25c Couple .25 .25
544 CD331a 50c Clarence House .25 .25
545 CD331a $4 Charles .30 .30
Nos. 543-545 (3) .80 .80

Nos. 543-545 also printed in sheets of 5 plus label, perf. 12, in changed colors.

Souvenir Sheet
546 CD331 $5 Glass coach .70 .70
549 CD331 Booklet 7.00 7.00
a. Pane of 1, $5, Couple 2.50 2.50
b. Pane of 6 (3x50c, Diana, 3x$2, Charles) 4.50 4.50

A102

Picasso Birth Centenary: 30c, The Cock. 50c, Man with Ice Cream. 55c, Woman Dressing her Hair. $3, Seated Woman. $5, Night Fishing at Antibes.

1981, May Litho. *Perf. 14*
550 A102 30c multicolored .25 .25
551 A102 50c multicolored .30 .30
552 A102 55c multicolored .35 .35
553 A102 $3 multicolored 1.75 1.75
Nos. 550-553 (4) 2.65 2.65

Souvenir Sheet
554 A102 $5 multicolored 3.50 3.50

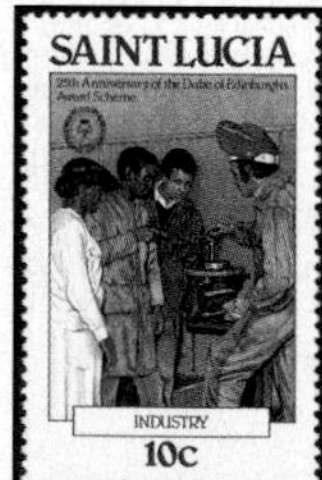

A103

10c, Industry. 35c, Community service. 50c, Hikers. $2.50, Duke of Edinburgh.

Wmk. 373
1981, Sept. 28 Litho. *Perf. 14½*
555 A103 10c multicolored .25 .25
556 A103 35c multicolored .25 .25
557 A103 50c multicolored .25 .25
558 A103 $2.50 multicolored .30 .30
Nos. 555-558 (4) 1.05 1.05

Duke of Edinburgh's Awards, 25th anniv.

Intl. Year of the Disabled A104

1981, Oct. 30 Litho. *Perf. 14*

559 A104 10c Louis Braille .25 .25
560 A104 50c Sarah Bernhardt .25 .25
561 A104 $2 Joseph Pulitzer .70 .70
562 A104 $2.50 Henri de Toulouse-Lautrec 1.10 1.10
Nos. 559-562 (4) 2.30 2.30

Souvenir Sheet

563 A104 $5 Franklin D. Roosevelt 1.75 1.75

A105

Christmas: Adoration of the King Paintings.

1981, Dec. 15

564 A105 10c Sfoza .25 .25
565 A105 30c Orcanga .25 .25
566 A105 $1.50 Gerard .60 .60
567 A105 $2.50 Foppa 1.25 1.25
Nos. 564-567 (4) 2.35 2.35

A106

1981, Dec. 29 Unwmk.

568 A106 10c No. 1 .25 .25
569 A106 30c No. 251 .30 .30
570 A106 50c No. 459 .45 .45
571 A106 $2 UPU, St. Lucia flags 1.50 1.50
Nos. 568-571 (4) 2.50 2.50

Souvenir Sheets

572 A106 $5 GPO, Castries 2.50 2.50

First anniv. of UPU membership.

A107

1980s Decade for Women (Paintings of Women by Women): 10c, Fanny Travis Cochran, by Cecilia Beaux. 50c, Women with Dove, by Marie Laurencin. $2, Portrait of a Young Pupil of David. $2.50, Self-portrait, by Rosalba Carriera. $5, Self-portrait, by Elisabeth Vigee-Le Brun.

Unwmk.

1981, Dec. 11 Litho. *Perf. 14*

573 A107 10c multicolored .25 .25
574 A107 50c multicolored .30 .25
575 A107 $2 multicolored .90 .75
576 A107 $2.50 multicolored 1.25 1.25
Nos. 573-576 (4) 2.70 2.50

Souvenir Sheet

577 A107 $5 multicolored 1.75 1.75

1982 World Cup Soccer A108

Designs: Various soccer players.

1982, Feb. 15 Litho. *Perf. 14½*

578 A108 10c multicolored .55 .55
579 A108 50c multicolored 1.75 1.75
580 A108 $2 multicolored 2.10 2.10
581 A108 $2.50 multicolored 2.50 2.50
Nos. 578-581 (4) 6.90 6.90

Souvenir Sheet

582 A108 $5 multicolored 4.00 4.00

Battle of the Saints Bicentenary — A109

10c, Pigeon Island 35c, Battle. 50c, Admirals Rodney, DeGrasse. $2.50, Map.

Wmk. 373

1982, Apr. 13 Litho. *Perf. 14*

583 A109 10c multicolored .40 .40
584 A109 35c multicolored .80 .80
585 A109 50c multicolored 1.20 1.20
586 A109 $2.50 multicolored 4.25 4.25
a. Souvenir sheet of 4, #583-586 9.50 9.50
Nos. 583-586 (4) 6.65 6.65

Scouting Year — A110

1982, Aug. 4 Litho. *Perf. 14*

587 A110 10c Map reading .25 .25
588 A110 50c First aid .45 .45
589 A110 $1.50 Camping 1.40 1.40
590 A110 $2.50 Campfire sing 2.40 2.40
Nos. 587-590 (4) 4.50 4.50

Princess Diana Issue

Common Design Type

Perf. 14½x14

1982, Sept. 1 Unwmk.

591 CD332 50c Leeds Castle .40 .40
592 CD332 $2 Diana 1.75 1.75
593 CD332 $4 Wedding 2.75 2.75
Nos. 591-593 (3) 4.90 4.90

Souvenir Sheet

594 CD332 $5 Diana, diff. 5.00 5.00

Christmas 1982 — A111

Paintings: 10c, Adoration of the Kings, by Brueghel the Elder. 30c, Nativity, by Lorenzo Costa. 50c, Virgin and Child, Fra Filippo Lippi. 80c, Adoration of the Shepherds, by Nicolas Poussin.

Wmk. 373

1982, Nov. 10 Litho. *Perf. 14*

595 A111 10c multicolored .25 .25
596 A111 30c multicolored .35 .35
597 A111 50c multicolored .50 .50
598 A111 80c multicolored .85 .85
Nos. 595-598 (4) 1.95 1.95

A111a

1983, Mar. 14 Litho.

599 A111a 10c Twin Peaks .30 .30
600 A111a 30c Beach .40 .40
601 A111a 50c Banana harvester .30 .30
602 A111a $2 Flag 1.75 1.75
Nos. 599-602 (4) 2.75 2.75

Commonwealth day.

Crown Agents Sesquicentennial A112

Wmk. 373

1983, Apr. 1 Litho. *Perf. 14½*

603 A112 10c Headquarters, London .25 .25
604 A112 15c Road construction .25 .25
605 A112 50c Map .25 .25
606 A112 $2 First stamp 1.25 1.25
Nos. 603-606 (4) 2.00 2.00

World Communications Year — A113

10c, Shipboard intercommunication. 50c, Air-to-air. $1.50, Satellite. $2.50, Computer communications.
$5, Weather satellite.

Unwmk.

1983, July 12 Litho. *Perf. 15*

607 A113 10c multicolored .25 .25
608 A113 50c multicolored .55 .55
609 A113 $1.50 multicolored 1.25 1.25
610 A113 $2.50 multicolored 2.00 2.00
Nos. 607-610 (4) 4.05 4.05

Souvenir Sheet

611 A113 $5 multicolored 4.00 4.00

Coral Reef Fish A114

10c, Longspine squirrelfish. 50c, Banded butter-flyfish. $1.50, Blackbar soldierfish. $2.50, Yellowtail snappers.
$5, Red hind.

1983, Aug. 23

612 A114 10c multicolored .30 .30
613 A114 50c multicolored .30 .30
614 A114 $1.50 multicolored 1.10 1.10
615 A114 $2.50 multicolored 1.75 1.75
Nos. 612-615 (4) 3.45 3.45

Souvenir Sheet

616 A114 $5 multicolored 5.25 5.25

For overprint see No. 800.

Locomotives — A115

No. 617, Princess Coronation. No. 618, Duke of Sutherland. No. 619, Leeds United. No. 620, Lord Nelson. No. 621, Bodmin. No. 622, Eton. No. 623, Flying Scotsman. No. 624, Stephenson's Rocket.

Perf. 12½

1983, Oct. 13 Litho. Unwmk.

Se-tenant Pairs, #a.-b.

a. — Side and front views.

b. — Action scene.

617 A115 35c multicolored .25 .25
618 A115 35c multicolored .25 .25
619 A115 50c multicolored .35 *.65*
620 A115 50c multicolored .35 *.65*
621 A115 $1 multicolored .75 *1.10*
622 A115 $1 multicolored .75 *1.10*
623 A115 $2 multicolored 1.50 *2.10*
624 A115 $2 multicolored 1.50 *2.10*
Nos. 617-624 (8) 5.70 *8.20*

See Nos. 674-679, 711-718, 774-777, 807-814.

Virgin and Child Paintings by Raphael — A115a

10c, Niccolini-Cowper Madonna. 30c, Holy Family with a Palm Tree. 50c, Sistine Madonna. $5, Alba Madonna

Wmk. 373

1983, Oct. 24 Litho. *Perf. 14*

629 A115a 10c multicolored .25 .25
630 A115a 30c multicolored .25 .25
631 A115a 50c multicolored .25 .25
632 A115a $5 multicolored 1.60 1.60
Nos. 629-632 (4) 2.35 2.35

Christmas.

Battle of Waterloo, King George III — A116

Nos. 633a, 633b, shown. No. 634a, George III, diff. No. 634b, Kew Palace. No. 635a, Arms of Elizabeth I. No. 635b, Elizabeth I. No. 636a, Arms of George III. No. 636b, George III, diff. No. 637a, Elizabeth I, diff. No. 637b, Hatfield Palace. No. 638a, Spanish Armada. No. 638b, Elizabeth, I, diff.

Perf. 12½

1984, Mar. 13 Litho. Unwmk.

633 A116 5c Pair, #a.-b. .25 *.35*
634 A116 10c Pair, #a.-b. .25 *.35*
635 A116 35c Pair, #a.-b. .25 *.50*
636 A116 60c Pair, #a.-b. .40 *.90*

637 A116 $1 Pair, #a.-b. .60 *1.25*
638 A116 $2.50 Pair, #a.-b. 1.75 *3.50*
Nos. 633-638 (6) 3.50 *6.85*

Unissued 30c, 50c, $1, $2.50 and $5 values became available with the liquidation of the printer.

Colonial Building, Late 19th Cent. — A118

Local Architecture. 10c, Buildings, mid-19th cent., vert. 65c, Wooden chattel, early 20th cent. $2.50, Treasury, 1906.

Perf. 14x13½, 13½x14

1984, Apr. 6 Wmk. 380

645 A118 10c multicolored .25 .25
646 A118 45c shown .40 .35
647 A118 65c multicolored .55 .45
648 A118 $2.50 multicolored 2.00 1.75
Nos. 645-648 (4) 3.20 2.80

For overprints see Nos. 796, 801.

Logwood Tree and Blossom — A118a

Perf. 13½x14, 14x13½

1984, June 12 Wmk. 380

649 A118a 10c shown .25 .25
650 A118a 45c Calabash .30 .30
651 A118a 65c Gommier, vert. .40 .40
652 A118a $2.50 Rain tree 1.50 1.50
Nos. 649-652 (4) 2.45 2.45

For overprint see No. 802.

Automobiles — A119

5c, Bugatti 57SC, 1939. 10c, Chevrolet Bel Air, 1957. $1, Alfa Romeo, 1930. $2.50, Duesenberg, 1932.

Perf. 12½

1984, June 25 Litho. Unwmk.
Se-tenant Pairs, #a.-b.
a. — Side and front views.
b. — Action scene.

653 A119 5c multicolored .25 .25
654 A119 10c multicolored .25 .25
655 A119 $1 multicolored .40 *1.25*
656 A119 $2.50 multicolored .75 *3.00*
Nos. 653-656 (4) 1.65 4.75

See Nos. 686-693, 739-742, 850-855.

Endangered Reptiles — A120

Wmk. 380

1984, Aug. 8 Litho. *Perf. 14*

661 A120 10c Pygmy gecko .25 .25
662 A120 45c Maria Isld. ground lizard .45 .45
663 A120 65c Green iguana .60 .60
664 A120 $2.50 Couresse snake 1.25 1.25
Nos. 661-664 (4) 2.55 2.55

For overprint see No. 797.

Leaders of the World, 1984 Olympics — A121

#665a, Volleyball. #665b, Volleyball, diff.. #666a, Women's hurdles. #666b, Men's hurdles. #667a, Showjumping. #667b, Dressage. #668a, Women's gymnastics. #668b, Men's gymnastics.

Perf. 12½

1984, Sept. 21 Litho. Unwmk.

665 A121 5c Pair, #a.-b. .25 .25
666 A121 10c Pair, #a.-b. .25 .25
667 A121 65c Pair, #a.-b. .35 *.60*
668 A121 $2.50 Pair, #a.-b. 1.25 *2.00*
Nos. 665-668 (4) 2.10 3.10

Locomotive Type of 1983

1c, TAW 2-6-2T, 1897. 15c, Crocodile 1-C.C.-1, 1920. 50c, The Countess 0.6.0T, 1903. 75c, Class GE6/6C.C., 1921. $1, Class P8, 4.6.0, 1906. $2, Der Alder 2.2.2., 1835.

1984, Sept. 21 Litho. *Perf. 12½*
Se-tenant Pairs, #a.-b.
a. — Side and front views.
b. — Action scene.

674 A115 1c multicolored .25 .25
675 A115 15c multicolored .25 *.40*
676 A115 50c multicolored .35 *.55*
677 A115 75c multicolored .35 *.85*
678 A115 $1 multicolored .45 *.60*
679 A115 $2 multicolored .55 *.80*
Nos. 674-679 (6) 2.20 *3.45*

Automobile Type of 1983

10c, Panhard and Levassor, 1889. 30c, N.S.U. R0-80 Saloon, 1968. 55c, Abarth, Balbero, 1958. 65c, TVR Vixen 2500M, 1972. 75c, Ford Mustang Convertible, 1965. $1, Ford Model T, 1914. $2, Aston Martin DB3S, 1954. $3, Chrysler Imperial CG, 1931.

1984, Dec. 19 Litho. *Perf. 12½*
Se-tenant Pairs, #a.-b.
a. — Side and front views.
b. — Action scene.

686 A119 10c multicolored .25 .25
687 A119 30c multicolored .30 *.35*
688 A119 55c multicolored .30 *.65*
689 A119 65c multicolored .30 *.75*
690 A119 75c multicolored .30 *.90*
691 A119 $1 multicolored .40 *1.25*
692 A119 $2 multicolored 1.10 *2.50*
693 A119 $3 multicolored 1.25 *3.50*
Nos. 686-693 (8) 4.20 *10.15*

Christmas — A122

Wmk. 380

1984, Oct. 31 Litho. *Perf. 14*

702 A122 10c Wine glass .25 .25
703 A122 35c Altar .25 .25
704 A122 65c Creche .25 *.25*
705 A122 $3 Holy family, abstract .35 *1.00*
a. Souvenir sheet of 4, #702-705 2.60 2.60
Nos. 702-705 (4) 1.10 *1.75*

Abolition of Slavery, 150th Anniv. — A123

Engraving details, Natl. Archives, Castries: 10c, Preparing manioc. 35c, Working with cassava flour. 55c, Cooking, twisting and drying tobacco. $5, Tobacco production, diff.

1984, Dec. 12 Litho. *Perf. 14*

706 A123 10c bright buff & blk .25 .25
707 A123 35c bright buff & blk .25 .25
708 A123 55c bright buff & blk .25 .25
709 A123 $5 bright buff & blk .75 *2.50*
Nos. 706-709 (4) 1.50 3.25

Souvenir Sheet

710 Sheet of 4 2.75 2.75
a. A123 10c like No. 706 .25 .25
b. A123 35c like No. 707 .25 .25
c. A123 55c like No. 708 .25 .25
d. A123 $5 like No. 709 .70 .70

#710a-710d se-tenant in continuous design.

Locomotive Type of 1983

5c, J.N.R. Class C-53, 1928, Japan. 15c, Heavy L, 1885, India. 35c, QGR Class B18¼, 1926, Australia. 60c, Owain Glyndwr, 1923, U.K. 75c, Lion, 1838, U.K. $1, Coal Engine, 1873, U.K. $2, No. 2238 Class Q6, 1921, U.K. $2.50, Class H, 1920, U.K.

1985, Feb. 4 Unwmk. *Perf. 12½*
Se-tenant Pairs, #a.-b.
a. — Side and front views.
b. — Action scene.

711 A115 5c multicolored .25 .25
712 A115 15c multicolored .25 .25
713 A115 35c multicolored .40 *.60*
714 A115 60c multicolored .40 *.60*
715 A115 75c multicolored .25 *.75*
716 A115 $1 multicolored .40 *.80*
717 A115 $2 multicolored .60 *1.20*
718 A115 $2.50 multicolored .80 *1.50*
Nos. 711-718 (8) 3.35 *5.95*

Girl Guides, 75th Anniv. — A124

1985, Feb. 21 Wmk. 380 *Perf. 14*

727 A124 10c multicolored .40 .25
728 A124 35c multicolored 1.00 .25
729 A124 65c multicolored 2.25 .75
730 A124 $3 multicolored 4.25 *5.50*
Nos. 727-730 (4) 7.90 6.75

For overprint see No. 795.

Butterflies — A125

No. 731a, Clossiana selene. No. 731b, Inachis io. No. 732a, Philaethria werneckei. No. 732b, Catagramma sorana. No. 733a, Kallima inachus. No. 733b, Hypanartia paullus. No. 734a, Morpho rhetenor helena. No. 734b, Ornithoptera meridionalis.

1985, Feb. 28 Unwmk. *Perf. 12½*

731 A125 15c Pair, #a.-b. .25 .25
732 A125 40c Pair, #a.-b. .40 .40
733 A125 60c Pair, #a.-b. .40 .40
734 A125 $2.25 Pair, #a.-b. 2.25 2.25
Nos. 731-734 (4) 3.30 3.30

Automobile Type of 1983

15c, 1940 Hudson Eight, US. 50c, 1937 KdF, Germany. $1, 1925 Kissel Goldbug, US. $1.50, 1973 Ferrari 246GTS, Italy.

1985, Mar. 29 Se-tenant Pairs

739 A119 15c multicolored .25 *.25*
740 A119 50c multicolored .50 *.60*
741 A119 $1 multicolored .50 *.60*
742 A119 $1.50 multicolored 1.00 *1.50*
Nos. 739-742 (4) 2.25 *2.95*

Military Uniforms — A126

Designs: 5c, Grenadier, 70th Foot Reg., c. 1775. 10c, Grenadier Co. Officer, 14th Foot Reg., 1780. 20c, Battalion Co. Officer, 46th Foot Reg., 1781. 25c, Officer, Royal Artillery Reg., c. 1782. 30c, Officer, Royal Engineers Corps., 1782. 35c, Battalion Co. Officer, 54th Foot Reg., 1782. 45c, Grenadier Co. Private, 14th Foot Reg., 1782. 50c, Gunner, Royal Artillery Reg., 1796. 65c, Battalion Co. Private, 85th Foot Reg., c. 1796. 75c, Battalion Co. Private, 76th Foot Reg., 1796. 90c, Battalion Co. Private, 81st Foot Reg., c. 1796. $1, Sergeant, 74th (Highland) Foot Reg., 1796. $2.50, Private, Light Co., 93rd Foot Reg., 1803. $5, Battalion Co. Private, 1st West India Reg., 1803. $15, Officer, Royal Artillery Reg., 1850.

1985, May 7 Wmk. 380 *Perf. 15*
"1984" Imprint Below Design

747 A126 5c multicolored .35 *.65*
748 A126 10c multicolored .45 .25
749 A126 20c multicolored .50 .35
a. "1986" Imprint .65 .65
750 A126 25c multicolored .65 .25
a. "1986" Imprint .65 .65
751 A126 30c multicolored .80 .35
752 A126 35c multicolored .75 .25
753 A126 45c multicolored .85 *.50*
754 A126 50c multicolored 1.00 *.50*
755 A126 65c multicolored 1.10 *.65*
756 A126 75c multicolored 1.25 *1.00*
757 A126 90c multicolored 1.50 1.00
758 A126 $1 multicolored 1.60 1.00
759 A126 $2.50 multicolored 4.00 *6.50*
760 A126 $5 multicolored 6.25 13.00
761 A126 $15 multicolored 17.00 *26.00*
Nos. 747-761 (15) 38.05 *52.25*

See Nos. 876-879.

1987 Unwmk.
1986 Imprint Below Design

747a A126 5c .40 .75
748a A126 10c .60 .40
751a A126 30c .85 .65
753a A126 45c .95 .75
754a A126 50c 1.00 .90
759a A126 $2.50 5.00 *6.00*
760a A126 $5 6.50 *11.00*
Nos. 747a-760a (7) 15.30 20.45

Issued: No. 747a-748a, 2/24; No. 751a-760a, 3/16.

1989 Wmk. 384

747b A126 5c "1988" Imprint .85 1.25
748b A126 10c "1989" Imprint 1.10 .65
749a A126 20c "1989" Imprint 1.50 1.25
750b A126 25c "1988" imprint 1.00 1.25
750c A126 25c "1989" Imprint 1.00 1.25

No. 750b issued 9/88.

World War II Aircraft A127

5c, Messerschmitt 109-E. 55c, Avro 683 Lancaster Mark I Bomber. 60c, North American P.51-D Mustang. $2, Supermarine Spitfire Mark II.

1985, May 30 Unwmk. *Perf. 12½*

Se-tenant Pairs, #a.-b.

a. — Action scene.

b. — Bottom, front and side views.

762 A127 5c multicolored .25 *.40*
763 A127 55c multicolored .60 *.90*
764 A127 60c multicolored .60 *.90*
765 A127 $2 multicolored .80 *1.60*
Nos. 762-765 (4) 2.25 *3.80*

Nature Reserves A128

Birds in habitats: 10c, Frigate bird, Frigate Island Sanctuary. 35c, Mangrove cuckoo, Savannes Bay, Scorpion Island. 65c, Yellow sandpiper, Maria Island. $3, Audubon's shearwater, Lapins Island.

1985, June 20 Wmk. 380 *Perf. 15*

770 A128 10c multicolored .35 .25
771 A128 35c multicolored .65 .40
772 A128 65c multicolored .75 .75
773 A128 $3 multicolored 2.40 2.40
Nos. 770-773 (4) 4.15 3.80

Locomotive Type of 1983

10c, No. 28 Tender engine, 1897, U.K. 30c, No. 1621 Class M, 1893, U.K. 75c, Class Dunalastair, 1896, U.K. $2.50, Big Bertha No. 2290, 1919, U.K.

1985, June 26 Unwmk. *Perf. 12½*

Se-tenant Pairs, #a.-b.

a. — Side and front views.

b. — Action scene.

774 A115 10c multicolored .25 .25
775 A115 30c multicolored .40 .40
776 A115 75c multicolored .40 *.60*
777 A115 $2.50 multicolored 1.00 *1.60*
Nos. 774-777 (4) 2.05 2.85

Queen Mother, 85th Birthday — A129

Nos. 782a, 787a, Facing right. Nos. 782b, 787b, Facing left. No. 783a, Facing right. No. 783b, Facing left. Nos. 784a, 788a, Facing right. Nos. 784b, 788b, Facing front. No. 785a, Facing front. No. 785b, Facing left. No. 786a, Facing right. No. 786b, Facing left.

1985, Aug. 16

782 A129 40c Pair, #a.-b. .25 *.50*
783 A129 75c Pair, #a.-b. .40 *.60*
784 A129 $1.10 Pair, #a.-b. .40 *1.00*
785 A129 $1.75 Pair, #a.-b. .50 *1.50*
Nos. 782-785 (4) 1.55 *3.60*

Souvenir Sheets of 2

786 A129 $2 #a.-b. 1.00 1.00
787 A129 $3 #a.-b. 2.50 2.50
788 A129 $6 #a.-b. 3.50 3.50

For overprints see No. 799.

Intl. Youth Year — A130

Abstracts, by Lyndon Samuel — A131

Illustrations by local artists: 10c, Youth playing banjo, by Wayne Whitfield. 45c, Riding tricycle, by Mark D. Maragh. 75c, Youth against landscape, by Bartholemew Eugene. $3.50, Abstract, by Lyndon Samuel.

1985, Sept. 5 Wmk. 380 *Perf. 15*

791 A130 10c multicolored .25 .25
792 A130 45c multicolored .50 .25
793 A130 75c multicolored .50 .50
794 A130 $3.50 multicolored 1.10 *3.00*
Nos. 791-794 (4) 2.35 *4.00*

Souvenir Sheet

795 A131 $5 multicolored 2.25 2.25

Intl. Youth Year.

Stamps of 1983-85 Ovptd. "CARIBBEAN ROYAL VISIT 1985" in Two or Three Lines

Perfs. as Before

1985, Nov. Wmk. as Before

796 A124 35c #728 3.75 3.00
797 A118 65c #647 2.00 *2.75*
798 A120 65c #663 4.00 4.00
799 A129 $1.10 #784a-784b 14.00 *17.50*
800 A114 $2.50 #615 8.00 8.00
801 A118 $2.50 #648 7.00 7.00
802 A119 $2.50 #652 7.00 7.00
Nos. 796-802 (7) 45.75 49.25

Masquerade Figures — A132

Madonna and Child, by Dunstan St. Omer — A133

Unwmk.

1985, Dec. 23 Litho. *Perf. 15*

803 A132 10c Papa Jab .25 .25
804 A132 45c Paille Bananne .25 .25
805 A132 65c Cheval Bois .30 .30
Nos. 803-805 (3) .80 .80

Miniature Sheet

806 A133 $4 multi 1.75 1.75

Christmas 1985.

Locomotive Type of 1983

5c, 1983 MWCR Rack Loco Tip Top, US. 15c, 1975 BR Class 87 Stephenson Bo-Bo, UK. 30c, 1901 Class D No. 737, UK. 60c, 1922 No. 13 2-Co-2, UK. 75c, 1954 BR Class EM2 Electra Co-Co, UK. $1, 1922 City of Newcastle, UK. $2.25, 1930 DRG Von Kruckenberg, Propeller-driven Rail Car, Germany. $3, 1893 JNR No. 860, Japan.

1986, Jan. 17 *Perf. 12½x13*

Se-tenant Pairs, #a.-b.

a. — Side and front views.

b. — Action scene.

807 A115 5c multicolored .25 *.40*
808 A115 15c multicolored .25 .25
809 A115 30c multicolored .40 *.60*
810 A115 60c multicolored .50 *.80*
811 A115 75c multicolored .60 *1.00*
812 A115 $1 multicolored .80 *1.20*
813 A115 $2.25 multicolored 1.20 *1.60*
814 A115 $3 multicolored 1.20 *1.60*
Nos. 807-814 (8) 5.20 7.45

Miniature Sheets

Cook-out — A134

Designs: No. 823b, Scout sign. No. 824a, Wicker basket, weavings. No. 824b, Lady Olave Baden-Powell, Girl Guides founder.

1986, Mar. 3 Litho. *Perf. 13x12½*

823 A134 Sheet of 2 2.50 3.50
a.-b. $4 any single 1.25 *1.75*
824 A134 Sheet of 2 4.00 4.00
a.-b. $6 any single 2.00 2.00

Scouting anniv., Girl Guides 75th anniv. Values are for sheets with plain border. Exist with decorative border. Value, set, $8.50.

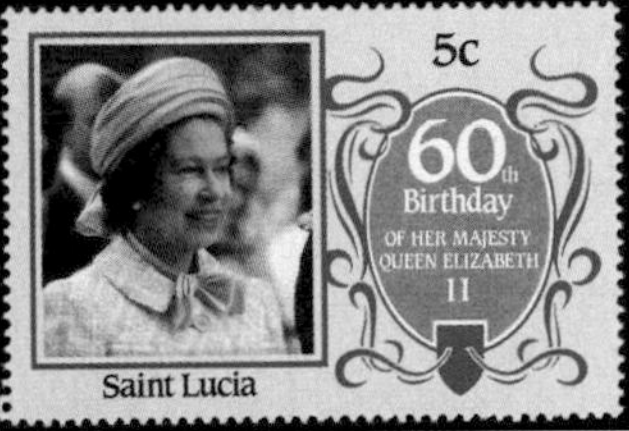

A135

Queen Elizabeth II, 60th Birthday — A136

Various photographs: 5c, Pink hat. 10c, Visiting Marian Home. 45c, Mindoo Phillip Park speech. 50c, Opening Leon Hess School. $1, Princess Elizabeth. $3.50, Blue hat. $5, Government House. $6, Canberra, 1982, vert.

$7, HMY Britannia, Castries Harbor. $8, Straw hat.

Perf. 13x12½, 12½x13, 14x15 (A136)

1986

825 A135 5c multicolored .25 .25
826 A136 10c multicolored .25 .25
827 A136 45c multicolored .30 .30
828 A136 50c multicolored .35 .35
829 A135 $1 multicolored .25 *.30*
830 A135 $3.50 multicolored .50 1.25
831 A136 $5 multicolored 3.25 3.25
832 A135 $6 multicolored .60 1.75
Nos. 825-832 (8) 5.75 7.70

Souvenir Sheets

833 A136 $7 multicolored 5.00 5.00
834 A135 $8 multicolored 4.00 *5.50*

Issue dates: Nos. 825, 829-830, 832, Apr. 21; Nos. 826-828, 831, 833, June 14.

State Visit of Pope John Paul II A137

55c, Kissing the ground. 60c, St. Joseph's Convent. 80c, Cathedral, Castries. $6, Pope.

1986, July 7 *Perf. 14x15, 15x14*

835 A137 55c multicolored 1.50 1.00
836 A137 60c multicolored 1.60 1.00
837 A137 80c multicolored 2.00 2.00
Nos. 835-837 (3) 5.10 4.00

Souvenir Sheet

838 A137 $6 multicolored 12.00 12.00

Nos. 837-838 vert.

Wedding of Prince Andrew and Sarah Ferguson — A138

No. 839a, Sarah. No. 839b, Prince Andrew. No. 840a, Couple, horiz. No. 840b, Prince Andrew, Nancy Reagan, horiz.

1986, July 23 *Perf. 12½*

839 A138 80c Pair, #a.-b. 1.00 1.00
840 A138 $2 Pair, #a.-b. 2.50 2.50

#840a-840b show Westminster Abbey in LR.

US Peace Corps in St. Lucia, 25th Anniv. A139

80c, Technical instruction. $2, Pres. Kennedy, vert. $3.50, Natl. crests, corps emblem.

1986, Sept. 25 Litho. *Perf. 14*

843 A139 80c multicolored .40 *.50*
844 A139 $2 multicolored 1.10 *1.50*
845 A139 $3.50 multicolored 1.75 *2.60*
Nos. 843-845 (3) 3.25 *4.60*

Wedding of Prince Andrew and Sarah Ferguson — A140

1986, Oct. 15 *Perf. 15*

846 A140 50c Andrew .40 .40
847 A140 80c Sarah .60 .60
848 A140 $1 At altar .75 .75
849 A140 $3 In open carriage 1.50 1.50
Nos. 846-849 (4) 3.25 3.25

Souvenir Sheet

849A A140 $7 Andrew, Sarah 5.50 5.50

Automobile Type of 1983

20c, 1969 AMC AMX, US. 50c, 1912 Russo-Baltique, Russia. 60c, 1932 Lincoln KB, US. $1, 1933 Rolls Royce Phantom II Continental, UK. $1.50, 1939 Buick Century, US. $3, 1957 Chrysler 300 C, US.

1986, Oct. 23 Litho. *Perf. 12½x13*

Se-tenant Pairs, #a.-b.

a. — Side and front views.

b. — Action scene.

No.	Type	Description	Unused	Used
850	A119	20c multicolored	.30	*.35*
851	A119	50c multicolored	.30	*.60*
852	A119	60c multicolored	.30	*.60*
853	A119	$1 multicolored	.50	*1.25*
854	A119	$1.50 multicolored	.70	*1.75*
855	A119	$3 multicolored	1.40	*3.50*
		Nos. 850-855 (6)	3.50	*8.05*

Chak-Chak Band — A141

1986, Nov. 7 *Perf. 15*

No.	Type	Description	Unused	Used
862	A141	15c shown	.25	.25
863	A141	45c Folk dancing	.35	.25
864	A141	80c Steel band	.60	.60
865	A141	$5 Limbo dancer	1.00	*3.00*
		Nos. 862-865 (4)	2.20	*4.10*

Souvenir Sheet

No.	Type	Description	Unused	Used
866	A141	$10 Gros Islet	5.25	5.25

Christmas A142

Churches: 10c, St. Ann Catholic, Mon Repos. 40c, St. Joseph the Worker Catholic, Gros Islet. 80c, Holy Trinity Anglican, Castries. $4, Our Lady of the Assumption Catholic, Soufriere, vert. $7, St. Lucy Catholic, Micoud.

1986, Nov.

No.	Type	Description	Unused	Used
867	A142	10c multicolored	.25	.25
868	A142	40c multicolored	.25	.25
869	A142	80c multicolored	.50	.50
870	A142	$4 multicolored	.80	*2.75*
		Nos. 867-870 (4)	1.80	*3.75*

Souvenir Sheet

No.	Type	Description	Unused	Used
871	A142	$7 multicolored	3.50	3.50

Map of St. Lucia — A143

Perf. 14x14½

1987, Feb. 24 Litho. Wmk. 373

No Date Imprint Below Design

No.	Type	Description	Unused	Used
872	A143	5c beige & blk	.25	.25
a.		Imprint "1988"	.25	.25
b.		Wmk. 384, "1989" imprint	.25	.25
873	A143	10c pale yel grn & blk	.25	.25
a.		Imprint "1988"	.25	.25
b.		Wmk. 384, "1989" imprint	.25	.25
874	A143	45c orange & blk	.60	.60
a.		Imprint "1992"	.60	.60
875	A143	50c pale violet & blk	.60	.60
a.		Imprint "1989"	.60	.60
		Nos. 872-875 (4)	1.70	1.70

Issued: #872a, 873a, 9/88; #875a, 3/17/89; #872b, 873b, 4/12/89.

See #937.

Uniforms Type of 1985

Designs: 15c, Battalion company private, 2nd West India Regiment, 1803. 60c, Battalion company officer, 5th Regiment of Foot, 1778. 80c, Battalion company officer, 27th (or Inniskilling) Regiment of Foot, c. 1780. $20, Grenadier company private, 46th Regiment of Foot, 1778.

1987, Mar. 16 Unwmk. *Perf. 15*

"1986" Imprint Date Below Design

No.	Type	Description	Unused	Used
876	A126	15c multicolored	.45	.25
877	A126	60c multicolored	1.00	.75
878	A126	80c multicolored	1.50	1.00
879	A126	$20 multicolored	17.50	*25.00*
b.		Imprint "1987"	—	—
		Nos. 876-879 (4)	20.45	*27.00*

Dated 1986.

1988 Wmk. 384

Imprint Date Below Design As Noted

No.	Type	Description	Unused	Used
876a	A126	15c "1988"	1.25	.90
b.		Imprint "1989"	1.25	.90
877a	A126	60c "1988"	2.50	2.00
878a	A126	80c "1988"	2.75	2.25
879a	A126	$20 "1989"	24.50	35.00
		Nos. 876a-879a (4)	31.00	40.15

A144

Statue of Liberty, Cent. — A145

1987, Apr. 29 Wmk. 373 *Perf. 14½*

No.	Type	Description	Unused	Used
880	A144	15c Statue, flags	.45	.45
881	A144	80c Statue, ship	.95	.95
882	A144	$1 Statue, Concorde jet	1.50	1.50
883	A144	$5 Statue, flying boat	5.00	5.00
		Nos. 880-883 (4)	7.90	7.90

Souvenir Sheet

No.	Type	Description	Unused	Used
884	A145	$6 Statue, New York City	5.25	5.25

Maps, Surveying Instruments A147

Wmk. 384

1987, Aug. 31 Litho. *Perf. 14*

No.	Type	Description	Unused	Used
888	A147	15c 1775	.65	.65
889	A147	60c 1814	1.50	1.50
890	A147	$1 1888	2.25	2.25
891	A147	$2.50 1987	4.75	4.75
		Nos. 888-891 (4)	9.15	9.15

First cadastral survey of St. Lucia.

Victoria Hospital, Cent. — A148

No. 894a, Ambulance, nurse, 1987. No. 894b, Nurse, hammock, 1913. No. 895a, Hospital, 1987. No. 895b, Hospital, 1887.

Wmk. 384

1987, Nov. 4 Litho. *Perf. 14½*

No.	Type	Description	Unused	Used
894	A148	$1 Pair, #a.-b.	5.00	5.00
895	A148	$2 Pair, #a.-b.	9.00	9.00

Souvenir Sheet

No.	Type	Description	Unused	Used
896	A148	$4.50 Main gate, 1987	11.50	11.50

Christmas A149

Paintings (details) by unidentified artists — 15c, The Holy Family. 50c, Adoration of the Shepherds. 60c, Adoration of the Magi. 90c, Madonna and Child.

$6, Holy Family.

1987, Nov. 30

No.	Type	Description	Unused	Used
897	A149	15c multicolored	.40	.40
898	A149	50c multicolored	.85	.85
899	A149	60c multicolored	1.10	1.10
900	A149	90c multicolored	1.30	1.30
		Nos. 897-900 (4)	3.65	3.65

Souvenir Sheet

No.	Type	Description	Unused	Used
901	A149	$6 multicolored	6.25	6.25

World Wildlife Fund — A150

Amazonian parrots, Amazona versicolor.

Wmk. 384

1987, Dec. 18 Litho. *Perf. 14*

No.	Type	Description	Unused	Used
902	A150	15c multi	3.00	3.00
903	A150	35c multi, diff.	4.00	4.00
904	A150	50c multi, diff.	5.50	5.50
905	A150	$1 multi, diff.	8.50	8.50
		Nos. 902-905 (4)	21.00	21.00

American Indian Artifacts — A151

25c, Carib clay zemi. 30c, Troumassee cylinder. 80c, Three-pointer stone. $3.50, Dauphine petroglyph.

Wmk. 384

1988, Feb. 12 Litho. *Perf. 14½*

No.	Type	Description	Unused	Used
906	A151	25c multicolored	.25	.25
907	A151	30c multicolored	.35	.35
908	A151	80c multicolored	.75	.75
909	A151	$3.50 multicolored	3.25	3.25
		Nos. 906-909 (4)	4.60	4.60

St. Lucia Cooperative Bank, 50th Anniv. — A152

Perf. 15x14

1988, Apr. 29 Litho. Wmk. 373

No.	Type	Description	Unused	Used
910	A152	10c Coins, banknotes	.55	.55
911	A152	45c Branch in Castries	1.00	1.00
912	A152	60c like 45c	1.10	1.10
913	A152	80c Branch in Vieux Fort	1.60	1.60
		Nos. 910-913 (4)	4.25	4.25

Cable and Wireless in St. Lucia, 50th Anniv. A153

Designs: 15c, Rural telephone exchange. 25c, Antique and modern telephones. 80c, St. Lucia Teleport (satellite dish). $2.50, Map of Eastern Caribbean microwave communications system.

Wmk. 384

1988, June 10 Litho. *Perf. 14*

No.	Type	Description	Unused	Used
914	A153	15c multicolored	.40	.40
915	A153	25c multicolored	.40	.40
916	A153	80c multicolored	.95	.95
917	A153	$2.50 multicolored	3.75	3.75
		Nos. 914-917 (4)	5.50	5.50

Cent. of the Methodist Church in St. Lucia — A154

Wmk. 384

1988, Aug. 15 Litho. *Perf. 14½*

No.	Type	Description	Unused	Used
918	A154	15c Altar, window	.25	.25
919	A154	80c Chancel	.60	.60
920	A154	$3.50 Exterior	2.25	2.25
		Nos. 918-920 (3)	3.10	3.10

Tourism — A155

Lagoon and: 10c, Tourists, gourmet meal. 30c, Beverage, tourists. 80c, Tropical fruit. $2.50, Fish and chef. $5.50, Market.

Perf. 14x13½

1988, Sept. 15 Litho. Wmk. 384

No.	Type	Description	Unused	Used
921	A155	Strip of 4	7.50	7.50
a.		10c multicolored	.60	.60
b.		30c multicolored	.60	.60
c.		80c multicolored	1.60	1.60
d.		$2.50 multicolored	4.50	4.50

Souvenir Sheet

No.	Type	Description	Unused	Used
922	A155	$5.50 multicolored	5.00	5.00

Lloyds of London, 300th Anniv.

Common Design Type

Designs: 10c, San Francisco earthquake, 1906. 60c, Castries Harbor, horiz. 80c, *Lady Nelson*, sunk off Castries Harbor, 1942, horiz. $2.50, Castries on fire, 1948.

Wmk. 373

1988, Oct. 17 Litho. *Perf. 14*

No.	Type	Description	Unused	Used
923	CD341	10c multicolored	.65	.65
924	CD341	60c multicolored	1.75	1.75
925	CD341	80c multicolored	2.25	2.25
926	CD341	$2.50 multicolored	4.75	4.75
		Nos. 923-926 (4)	9.40	9.40

A156

Christmas: Flowers — 15c, Snow on the mountain. 45c, Christmas candle. 60c, Balisier. 80c, Poinsettia.

$5.50, Flower arrangement.

Perf. 14½x14

1988, Nov. 22 Litho. Wmk. 384

No.	Type	Description	Unused	Used
927	A156	15c multicolored	.50	.50
928	A156	45c multicolored	.85	.85
929	A156	60c multicolored	1.10	1.10
930	A156	80c multicolored	1.30	1.30
		Nos. 927-930 (4)	3.75	3.75

Souvenir Sheet

No.	Type	Description	Unused	Used
931	A156	$5.50 multicolored	4.00	4.00

A157

Natl. Independence, 10th Anniv.: 15c, Princess Alexandra presenting constitution to Prime Minister Compton. 80c, Sulfur springs geothermal well. $1, Sir Arthur Lewis Community College. $2.50, Pointe Seraphine tax-free shopping center. $5, Emblem.

Perf. 13½x13

1989, Feb. 22 Wmk. 373

932 A157 15c Nationhood .30 .30
933 A157 80c Development .80 .80
934 A157 $1 Education 1.10 1.10
935 A157 $2.50 Progress 2.25 2.25
Nos. 932-935 (4) 4.45 4.45

Souvenir Sheet

936 A157 $5 With Confidence We Progress 4.00 4.00

Map Type of 1987

Perf. 14x14½

1989, Mar. 17 Litho. Wmk. 373

937 A143 $1 scarlet & black 1.25 1.25

Indigenous Mushrooms A158

15c, Gerronema citrinum. 25c, Lepiota spiculata. 50c, Calocybe cyanocephala. $5, Russula puiggarii.

Perf. 14½x14

1989, May 22 Litho. Wmk. 384

938 A158 15c multicolored 1.25 1.00
939 A158 25c multicolored 1.75 1.25
940 A158 50c multicolored 2.75 1.75
941 A158 $5 multicolored 14.00 14.00
Nos. 938-941 (4) 19.75 18.00

PHILEXFRANCE '89, French Revolution Bicent. — A159

Views of St. Lucia and text: 10c, Independence day announcement, vert. 60c, French revolutionary flag at Morne Fortune, 1791. $1, "Men are born and live free and equal in rights," vert. $3.50, Captain La Crosse's arrival at Gros Islet, 1792.

Wmk. 373

1989, July 14 Litho. *Perf. 14*

942 A159 10c multicolored .75 .65
943 A159 60c multicolored 3.25 1.75
944 A159 $1 multicolored 3.50 2.50
945 A159 $3.50 multicolored 11.50 8.00
Nos. 942-945 (4) 19.00 12.90

Intl. Red Cross, 125th Anniv. A160

50c, Natl. headquarters. 80c, Seminar in Castries, 1987. $1, Ambulance.

1989, Oct. 10 Wmk. 384 *Perf. 14½*

946 A160 50c multicolored 1.90 1.90
947 A160 80c multicolored 2.50 2.50
948 A160 $1 multicolored 3.50 3.50
Nos. 946-948 (3) 7.90 7.90

Christmas Lanterns Shaped Like Buildings A161

1989, Nov. 17 *Perf. 14x14½*

949 A161 10c multi .35 .35
950 A161 50c multi, diff. .75 .75
951 A161 90c multi, diff. 1.45 1.45
952 A161 $1 multi, diff. 1.60 1.60
Nos. 949-952 (4) 4.15 4.15

Trees In Danger of Extinction — A162

10c, Chinna. 15c,

"1990" Imprint Date Below Design

1990 Wmk. 384 *Perf. 14*

953 A162 10c multi .60 .60
954 A162 15c Latanier .60 .25
955 A162 20c Gwi gwi .60 .60
956 A162 25c L'encens .30 .25
957 A162 50c Bois lele .45 .45
958 A162 80c Bois d'amande 1.15 .50
959 A162 95c Mahot piman grand bois 2.10 1.15
960 A162 $1 Balata 1.40 1.40
961 A162 $1.50 Pencil cedar 2.50 2.50
962 A162 $2.50 Bois cendre 5.00 5.00
963 A162 $5 Lowye canelle 7.50 7.50
964 A162 $25 Chalantier grand bois 19.50 *22.00*
Nos. 953-964 (12) 41.70 42.20

Issued: 20c, 25c, 50c, $25, 2/21; 10c, 15c, 80c, $1.50, 4/12; 95c, $1, $2.50, $5, 6/25.

For overprints see Nos. 971, O28-O39.

Year Imprint Dates as Noted

1992-95 Wmk. 373 *Perf. 14*

953a A162 10c "1992" 2.00 2.00
b. "1993" 2.00 2.00
c. "1994" 2.00 2.00
954a A162 15c "1992" 2.00 2.00
b. "1994" 2.00 2.00
955a A162 20c "1995" 2.00 2.00
956a A162 25c "1994" 2.00 2.00
957a A162 50c "1992" 4.00 4.00
b. "1993" 4.00 4.00
c. "1994" 4.00 4.00
Nos. 953a-957a (5) 12.00 12.00

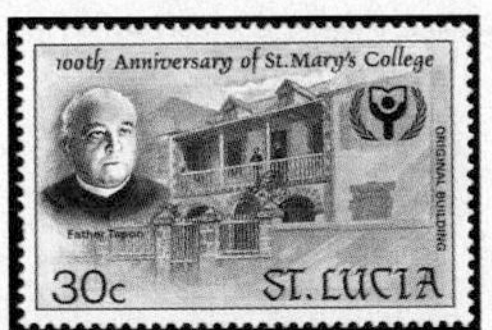

Centenary of St. Mary's College, Intl. Literacy Year — A163

Designs: 30c, Father Tapon, original building. 45c, Rev. Brother Collins, current building. 75c, Students in literacy class. $2, Door to knowledge, children.

1990, June 6 Wmk. 373

965 A163 30c multicolored .35 .35
966 A163 45c multicolored .55 .55
967 A163 75c multicolored .85 .85
968 A163 $2 multicolored 2.25 2.25
Nos. 965-968 (4) 4.00 4.00

Queen Mother, 90th Birthday

Common Design Types

1990, Aug. 3 Wmk. 384 *Perf. 14x15*

969 CD343 50c Coronation, 1937 .75 .75

Perf. 14½

970 CD344 $5 Arriving at theater, 1949 4.50 4.50

No. 963 Overprinted

1990, Aug. 13 *Perf. 14*

971 A162 $5 multicolored 4.75 4.75

Intl. Garden and Greenery Exposition, Osaka, Japan.

Christmas — A164

Paintings: 10c, Adoration of the Magi by Rubens. 30c, Adoration of the Shepherds by Murillo. 80c, Adoration of the Magi by Rubens, diff. $5, Adoration of the Shepherds by Champaigne.

1990, Dec. 3 *Perf. 14*

972 A164 10c multicolored .65 .65
973 A164 30c multicolored 1.30 1.30
974 A164 80c multicolored 2.00 2.00
975 A164 $5 multicolored 9.00 9.00
Nos. 972-975 (4) 12.95 12.95

Boats A165

Various boats.

1991, Mar. 27 Wmk. 373 *Perf. 14½*

976 A165 50c multicolored 2.50 2.50
977 A165 80c multicolored 3.00 3.00
978 A165 $1 multicolored 3.50 3.50
979 A165 $2.50 multicolored 7.75 7.75
Nos. 976-979 (4) 16.75 16.75

Souvenir Sheet

980 A165 $5 multicolored 12.50 12.50

Butterflies — A166

60c, Polydamas swallowtail. 80c, St. Christopher's hairstreak. $1, St. Lucia mestra. $2.50, Godman's hairstreak.

Wmk. 373

1991, Aug. 15 Litho. *Perf. 14*

981 A166 60c multicolored 3.00 3.00
982 A166 80c multicolored 3.25 3.25
983 A166 $1 multicolored 3.50 3.50
984 A166 $2.50 multicolored 7.25 *8.25*
Nos. 981-984 (4) 17.00 *18.00*

Christmas A167

10c, Jacmel Church. 15c, Red Madonna, vert. 80c, Monchy Church. $5, Blue Madonna, vert.

Perf. 14x14½

1991, Nov. 20 Litho. Wmk. 384

985 A167 10c multicolored .50 .25
986 A167 15c multicolored .70 .25
987 A167 80c multicolored 2.75 2.75
988 A167 $5 multicolored 6.00 6.00
Nos. 985-988 (4) 9.95 9.25

Atlantic Rally for Cruisers A168

Designs: 60c, Cruisers crossing Atlantic, map. 80c, Cruisers tacking.

1991, Dec. 10 Wmk. 384 *Perf. 14*

989 A168 60c multicolored 2.50 2.50
990 A168 80c multicolored 3.25 3.25

Discovery of America, 500th Anniv. — A169

Wmk. 373

1992, July 6 Litho. *Perf. 13*

991 A169 $1 Coming ashore 2.50 2.50
992 A169 $2 Natives, ships 4.75 4.75

Organization of East Caribbean States.

Contact with New World A170

15c, Amerindians. 40c, Juan de la Cosa, 1499. 50c, Columbus, 1502. $5, Gimle, Dec. 13th.

1992, Aug. 4 *Perf. 13½*

993 A170 15c multicolored .50 .25
994 A170 40c multicolored 2.25 .50
995 A170 50c multicolored 3.00 .75
996 A170 $5 multicolored 9.00 9.00
Nos. 993-996 (4) 14.75 10.50

Christmas A171

Paintings: 10c, Virgin and Child, by Delaroche. 15c, The Holy Family, by Rubens. 60c, Virgin and Child, by Luini. 80c, Virgin and Child, by Sassoferrato.

Wmk. 373

1992, Nov. 9 Litho. *Perf. 14½*

997 A171 10c multicolored .70 .25
998 A171 15c multicolored .70 .40
999 A171 60c multicolored 2.75 1.75
1000 A171 80c multicolored 2.75 2.25
Nos. 997-1000 (4) 6.90 4.65

Anti-Drugs Campaign — A172

Perf. 13½x14

1993, Feb. 1 Litho. Wmk. 373

1001 A172 $5 multicolored 9.00 9.00

Gros Piton from Delcer, Choiseul, by Dunstan St. Omer A173

Paintings: 75c, Reduit Bay, by Derek Walcott. $5, Woman and Child at River, by Nancy Cole Auguste.

1993, Nov. 1 Wmk. 373 *Perf. 13*

1002 A173 20c multicolored .35 .25
1003 A173 75c multicolored 1.25 1.00
1004 A173 $5 multicolored 6.25 *7.00*
Nos. 1002-1004 (3) 7.85 *8.25*

Christmas A174

Details of paintings: 15c, The Madonna of the Rosary, by Murillo. 60c, The Madonna and Child, by Van Dyck. 95c, The Annunciation, by Champaigne.

1993, Dec. 6 *Perf. 14*

1005 A174 15c multicolored .25 .25
1006 A174 60c multicolored 1.00 .60
1007 A174 95c multicolored 1.75 1.75
Nos. 1005-1007 (3) 3.00 2.60

A175

1994, July 25 *Perf. 13*

1008 A175 20c multicolored 1.10 .75

Souvenir Sheet

1009 A175 $5 multicolored 7.75 7.75

Abolition of Slavery on St. Lucia, bicent.

A176

Christmas (Flowers): 20c, Euphorbia pulcherrima. 75c, Heliconia rostrata. 95c, Alpinia purpurata. $5.50, Anthurium andreanum.

1994, Dec. 9 *Perf. 12½x13*

1010 A176 20c multicolored .25 .25
1011 A176 75c multicolored 1.00 1.00
1012 A176 95c multicolored 1.40 1.40
1013 A176 $5.50 multicolored 5.75 5.75
Nos. 1010-1013 (4) 8.40 8.40

Battle of Rabot, Bicent. A177

1995, Apr. 28 *Perf. 13½*

1014 A177 20c Map of island .45 .25
1015 A177 75c Rebelling slaves 1.10 1.10
1016 A177 95c Battle scene 1.60 1.60
Nos. 1014-1016 (3) 3.15 2.95

Souvenir Sheet

Perf. 13

1017 A177 $5.50 Battle map 6.50 6.50

End of World War II, 50th Anniv.

Common Design Types

Designs: 20c, ATS women in Britain. 75c, German U-boat off St. Lucia. 95c, Caribbean regiment, North Africa. $1.10, Presentation Spitfire Mk V.

$5.50, Reverse of War Medal 1939-45.

Wmk. 373

1995, May 8 Litho. *Perf. 13½*

1018 CD351 20c multi .60 .25
1019 CD351 75c multi 2.00 1.00
1020 CD351 95c multi 2.40 1.40
1021 CD351 $1.10 multi 2.75 2.00
Nos. 1018-1021 (4) 7.75 4.65

Souvenir Sheet

Perf. 14

1022 CD352 $5.50 multi 6.50 6.50

UN, 50th Anniv.

Common Design Type

10c, Puma helicopter. 65c, Renault truck. $1.35, Transall C160. $5, Douglas DC3.

Wmk. 373

1995, Oct. 24 Litho. *Perf. 14*

1023 CD353 10c multi .25 .25
1024 CD353 65c multi .75 .50
1025 CD353 $1.35 multi 1.50 1.50
1026 CD353 $5 multi 5.00 5.00
Nos. 1023-1026 (4) 7.50 7.25

Christmas — A178

Flowers: 15c, Eranthemum nervosum. 70c, Bougainvillea. $1.10, Allamanda cathartica. $3, Hibiscus rosa sinensis.

Wmk. 373

1995, Nov. 20 Litho. *Perf. 13*

1027 A178 15c multicolored .25 .25
1028 A178 70c multicolored .60 .50
1029 A178 $1.10 multicolored .95 .95
1030 A178 $3 multicolored 2.40 2.40
Nos. 1027-1030 (4) 4.20 4.10

Carnival — A179

Wmk. 384

1996, Feb. 16 Litho. *Perf. 14*

1031 A179 20c Calypso king .85 .85
1032 A179 65c Carnival band 2.00 2.00
1033 A179 95c King of the band 2.75 2.75
1034 A179 $3 Carnival queen 5.25 5.25
Nos. 1031-1034 (4) 10.85 10.85

Water — A180

1996, Mar. 5 Wmk. 373

1035 A180 20c Muddy stream .25 .25
1036 A180 65c Clear stream .75 .50
1037 A180 $5 Modern dam 5.00 5.00
Nos. 1035-1037 (3) 6.00 5.75

Tourism A181

Designs: 65c, Market. 75c, Riding horses on beach. 95c, Outdoor wedding ceremony. $5, Annual Intl. Jazz Festival.

Wmk. 373

1996, May 13 Litho. *Perf. 14*

1038-1041 A181 Set of 4 7.00 7.00

Modern Olympic Games, Cent. — A182

No. 1042a, Early runner. No. 1042b, Modern runner. No. 1043a, Two sailboats. No. 1043b, Four sailboats.

Wmk. 373

1996, July 19 Litho. *Perf. 14*

1042 A182 15c Pair, #a.-b. 1.60 1.60
1043 A182 75c Pair, #a.-b. 4.75 4.75

Nos. 1042-1043 have continuous designs.

Flags & Ships A183

Flag, ship: 10c, Spanish Royal banner, 1502, Spanish caravel. 15c, Skull & cross-bones, 1550, pirate carrack. 20c, Royal Netherlands, 1660, Dutch 80-gun ship. 25c, Union flag, 1739, Royal Navy 64-gun ship. 40c, French Imperial, 1750, French 74-gun ship. 50c, Martinique & St. Lucia, 1766, French brig. 55c, British White Ensign, 1782, Royal Navy Frigate Squadron. 65c, British Red Ensign, 1782, Battle of the Saints. 75c, British Blue Ensign, 1782, RN brig. 95c, Fench Tri-color, 1792, French 38-gun frigate. $1. British Union, 1801, West Indies Grand Fleet. $2.50, Confederate, 1861, CSA steam/sail armed cruiser. $5, Canada, 1915-19, Canadian V & W class destroyer. $10, US, 1942-48, Fletcher class destroyer. $25, National, cruise ship.

Perf. 14x15

1996-97 Litho. Wmk. 384

"1996" Date Imprint Below Design

1046 A183 10c multi 1.10 .30
b. Imprint "2000" .40 .40
1047 A183 15c multi 1.90 .30
b. Imprint "2000" .40 .40
1048 A183 20c multi .80 .25
b. Imprint "2000" .40 .40
1049 A183 25c multi .85 .30
b. Imprint "2000" .40 .40
1050 A183 40c multi 2.25 .50
1051 A183 50c multi 1.10 .50
1052 A183 55c multi 1.10 .50
1053 A183 65c multi 1.10 .55
1054 A183 75c multi 1.40 .65
1055 A183 95c multi 1.40 .65
1056 A183 $1 multi 1.40 .80
1057 A183 $2.50 multi 3.00 2.50
1058 A183 $5 multi 4.50 4.50
1059 A183 $10 multi 8.00 *9.00*
1060 A183 $25 multi 16.00 16.00
Nos. 1046-1060 (15) 45.90 37.30

Issued: 10c, 15c, 20c, 25c, 40c, 9/16/96; 50c, 55c, 65c, 75c, 95c, 11/18/96; $1, $2.50, $5, $10, $25, 1/8/97.

1998-2004 Wmk. 373

Date Imprint Below Design as Noted

1046a A183 10c multi, "1998" .75 .40
1047a A183 15c multi, "1998" .75 .40
1048a A183 20c multi, "1998" .75 .40
c. Imprint "2001" .40 .40
d. Imprint "2002" .75 .30
e. Imprint "2003" .40 .40
f. Imprint "2004" .40 .40
1049a A183 25c multi, "2002" .40 .40
1051a A183 50c multi, "1998" 1.00 .50
1053a A183 65c multi, "2001" .70 .55
1054a A183 75c multi, "2003" 1.00 1.00
1056a A183 $1 multi, "2001" 1.40 1.40
1059a A183 $10 multi, "2001" 10.00 *11.00*
Nos. 1046a-1059a (9) 16.75 16.05

#1046a, 1047a, 1048a, 1051a, 7/12/98; #1053a, 1056a, 1059a, 4/2001. #1049a, 2002. No. 1054a, May 2003.

Christmas — A184

Flowers: 20c, Cordia sebestena. 75c, Cryptostegia grandiflora. 95c, Hibiscus elatus. $5, Caularthron bicornutum.

Wmk. 384

1996, Dec. 1 Litho. *Perf. 14*

1061-1064 A184 Set of 4 7.50 7.50

Queen Elizabeth II and Prince Philip, 50th Wedding Anniv. — A185

No. 1068a, Queen. No. 1068b, Prince with horses. No. 1069a, Prince. No. 1069b, Queen riding in carriage. No. 1070a, Queen, Prince. No. 1070b, Princess Anne riding horse.

$5, Queen, Prince riding in open carriage, horiz.

Perf. 14½x14

1997, July 10 Litho. Wmk. 384

1068 A185 75c Pair, #a.-b. 2.50 2.50
1069 A185 95c Pair, #a.-b. 2.75 2.75
1070 A185 $1 Pair, #a.-b. 3.00 3.00
Nos. 1068-1070 (3) 8.25 8.25

Souvenir Sheet

Perf. 14x14½

1071 A185 $5 multicolored 7.00 7.00

Disasters — A186

20c, MV St. George capsizes, 1935. 55c, SS Belle of Bath founders. $1, SS Ethelgonda runs aground, 1897. $2.50, Hurricane devastation, 1817.

1997, July 14 *Perf. 14x15*
1072-1075 A186 Set of 4 11.50 11.50

Events of 1797 — A187

Designs: 20c, Taking of Praslin. 55c, Battle of Dennery. 70c, Peace. $3, Brigands join 1st West India Regiment.

Wmk. 373
1997, Aug. 15 **Litho.** *Perf. 14*
1076-1079 A187 Set of 4 10.50 10.50

Christmas — A188

Church art: 20c, Roseau Church. 60c, Altar piece, Regional Seminary, Trinidad. 95c, Our Lady of the Presentation, Trinidad. $5, The Four Days of Creation.

Perf. 14x15
1997, Dec. 1 **Litho.** **Wmk. 384**
1080-1083 A188 Set of 4 7.00 7.00

Diana, Princess of Wales (1961-97) — A189

1998, Jan. 19 **Litho.** *Perf. 14*
1084 A189 $1 multicolored .90 .90

No. 1084 was issued in sheets of 9.

CARICOM, 25th Anniv. — A190

20c, Errol Barrow, Forbes Burnham, Dr. Eric Williams, Michael Manley signing CARICOM Treaty, 1973. 75c, CARICOM flag, St. Lucia Natl. flag.

Wmk. 373
1998, July 1 **Litho.** *Perf. 13½*
1085 A190 20c multicolored .25 .25
1086 A190 75c multicolored 1.25 1.25

Birds — A191

Designs: 70c, St. Lucia oriole. 75c, Lesser Antillean pewee. 95c, Bridled quail dove. $1.10, Semper's warbler.

1998, Oct. 23 **Wmk. 373** *Perf. 14*
1087-1090 A191 70c Set of 4 9.50 9.50

Universal Declaration of Human Rights, 50th Anniv. — A192

Various butterflies, chains or rope.

1998, Oct. 28
1091 A192 20c multicolored .90 .30
1092 A192 65c multicolored 1.75 .75
1093 A192 70c multicolored 1.90 .75
1094 A192 $5 multicolored 6.50 6.50
Nos. 1091-1094 (4) 11.05 8.30

Christmas — A193

Flowers: 20c, Tabebuia serratifolia. 50c, Hibiscus sabdariffa. 95c, Euphorbia leucocephala. $2.50, Calliandra slaneae.

Wmk. 373
1998, Nov. 27 **Litho.** *Perf. 14*
1095-1098 A193 20c Set of 4 6.25 6.25

University of West Indies, 50th Anniv. A194

15c, The Black Prometheus. 75c, Sir Arthur Lewis, Sir Arthur Lewis College. $5, The Pitons.

1998, Nov. 30
1099 A194 15c multicolored .25 .25
1100 A194 75c multicolored 1.00 .50
1101 A194 $5 multicolored 5.25 5.25
Nos. 1099-1101 (3) 6.50 6.00

Wildlife A195

Designs: 20c, Saint Lucia tree lizard. 75c, Boa constrictor. 95c, Leatherback turtle. $5, Saint Lucia whiptail.

Wmk. 373
1999, July 15 **Litho.** *Perf. 13½*
1102-1105 A195 Set of 4 8.25 8.25

UPU, 125th Anniv. A196

20c, Mail steamer "Tees". 65c, Sikorsky S.38. 95c, Mail ship "Lady Drake". $3, DC-10. $5, Heinrich von Stephan.

Wmk. 373
1999, Oct. 9 **Litho.** *Perf. 14*
1106 A196 20c multicolored .70 .30
1107 A196 65c multicolored 1.40 .55
1108 A196 95c multicolored 1.60 .65
1109 A196 $3 multicolored 4.00 4.00
Nos. 1106-1109 (4) 7.70 5.50

Souvenir Sheet
Perf. 14¼
1110 A196 $5 multicolored 6.25 6.25

Stamp inscription on No. 1107 is misspelled. No. 1110 contains one 30x38mm stamp.

Christmas and Millennium — A197

Designs: 20c, Nativity. $1, Cathedral of the Immaculate Conception.

Perf. 13¾x14
1999, Dec. 14 **Litho.** **Wmk. 373**
1111 A197 20c multi .25 .25
1112 A197 $1 multi 1.60 1.60

Independence, 21st Anniv. — A198

20c, Vintage badge of the colony. 75c, 1939 badge. 95c, 1967 arms. $1, 1979 arms.

Perf. 14x13¾
2000, Feb. 29 **Litho.** **Wmk. 373**
1113 A198 20c multi .30 .30
1114 A198 75c multi .75 .60
1115 A198 95c multi .95 .85
1116 A198 $1 multi 1.25 1.00
Nos. 1113-1116 (4) 3.25 2.75

Historical Views A199

Designs: 20c, Fort sugar factory, 1886-1941. 60c, Coaling at Port Castries, 1885-1940. $1, Fort Rodney, Pigeon Island, 1780-1861. $5, Military hospital ruins, Pigeon Island, 1824-1861.

Wmk. 373
2000, Sept. 4 **Litho.** *Perf. 14*
1117-1120 A199 Set of 4 6.50 6.50

First Municipality of Castries, 150th Anniv. — A200

Designs: 20c, Old Castries Market. 75c, Central Library. 95c, Port Castries. $5, Mayors Henry H. Breen, Joseph Desir.

Perf. 13¼x13½
2000, Oct. 9 **Litho.** **Wmk. 373**
1121-1124 A200 Set of 4 8.00 8.00

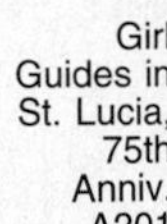

Girl Guides in St. Lucia, 75th Anniv. A201

Guides: 70c, Marching in brown uniforms. $1, Marching in blue uniforms. $2.50, At campground.

2000, Oct. 16
1125-1127 A201 Set of 3 6.00 6.00

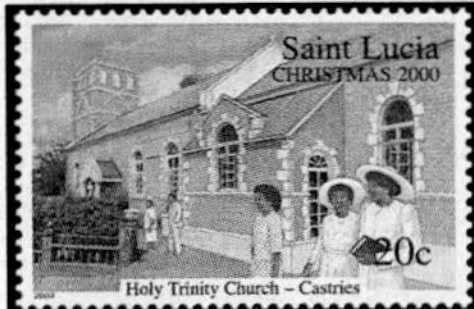

Christmas — A202

Churches: 20c, Holy Trinity, Castries. 50c, St. Paul's, Vieux-Fort. 95c, Christ, Soufriere. $2.50, Grace, River D'Oree.

2000, Nov. 22 *Perf. 14*
1128-1131 A202 Set of 4 6.00 6.00

Worldwide Fund for Nature (WWF) — A203

Birds: No. 1132, 20c, White breasted thrasher. No. 1133, 20c, St. Lucia black finch. No. 1134, 95c, St. Lucia oriole. No. 1135, 95c, Forest thrush.

Wmk. 373
2001, Jan. 2 **Litho.** *Perf. 14*
1132-1135 A203 Set of 4 6.50 6.50
1135a Strip of 4, #1132-1135 7.50 7.50

Jazz Festival, 10th Anniv. — A204

Designs: 20c, Crowd, stage. $1, Crowd, stage, ocean. $5, Musicians.

Perf. 13¾x14
2001, May 3 **Litho.** **Wmk. 373**
1136-1138 A204 Set of 3 8.25 8.25

Civil Administration, Bicent. — A205

Designs: 20c, British flag, island, ship. 65c, French flag, Napoleon Bonaparte, signing of the Treaty of Amiens. $1.10, British flag, King George III, ships. $3, Island map, King George IV.

Perf. 14x13¾
2001, Sept. 24 **Litho.** **Unwmk.**
1139-1142 A205 Set of 4 6.25 6.25

Christmas — A206

Various stained glass windows: 20c, 95c, $2.50.

2001, Dec. 7 Wmk. 373 *Perf. 13½*
1143-1145 A206 Set of 3 5.25 5.25

Reign Of Queen Elizabeth II, 50th Anniv. Issue

Common Design Type

Designs: Nos. 1146, 1150a, 25c, Princess Elizabeth, 1927. Nos. 1147, 1150b, 65c, Wearing hat. Nos. 1148, 1150c, 75c, In 1947. Nos. 1149, 1150d, 95c, In 1996. No. 1150e, $5, 1955 portrait by Annigoni (38x50mm).

Perf. 14¼x14½, 13¾ (#1150e)
2002, Feb. 6 Litho. Wmk. 373
With Gold Frames

1146 CD360 25c multicolored .50 .50
1147 CD360 65c multicolored 1.25 1.25
1148 CD360 75c multicolored 1.45 1.45
1149 CD360 95c multicolored 1.80 1.80
Nos. 1146-1149 (4) 5.00 5.00

Souvenir Sheet
Without Gold Frames

1150 CD360 Sheet of 5, #a-e 7.25 7.25

Royal Navy Ships A207

Designs: 15c, HMS St. Lucia, 1803. 75c, HMS Thetis, 1781. $1, HMS Berwick, 1903. $5, HMS Victory, 1805.

Wmk. 373
2002, May 22 Litho. *Perf. 14*
1151-1154 A207 Set of 4 11.00 11.00

Queen Mother Elizabeth (1900-2002)

Common Design Type

Designs: 50c, Holding baby (black and white photograph). 65c, Wearing red hat. 95c, Wearing hat (black and white photograph). $1, Wearing blue hat.

No. 1159: a, $2, Wearing tiara. b, $2, Wearing blue hat, diff.

Perf. 13¾x14¼
2002, Aug. 5 Litho. Wmk. 373
With Purple Frames

1155 CD361 50c multicolored .80 .80
1156 CD361 65c multicolored 1.10 1.10
1157 CD361 95c multicolored 1.50 1.50
1158 CD361 $1 multicolored 1.60 1.60
Nos. 1155-1158 (4) 5.00 5.00

Souvenir Sheet
Without Purple Frames
Perf. 14½x14¼

1159 CD361 Sheet of 2, #a-b 8.00 8.00

Awarding of Nobel Literature Prize to Derek Walcott, 10th Anniv. — A208

Designs: 20c, Walcott. 65c, Men and children, horiz. 70c, Women. $5, People in boat.

Wmk. 373
2002, Oct. 11 Litho. *Perf. 13¾*
1160-1163 A208 Set of 4 8.75 8.75

Salvation Army in St. Lucia, Cent. A209

Designs: 20c, William and Catherine Booth, Salvation Army workers. $1, Early Salvation Army officers in parade. $2.50, Salvation Army shield, "Blood and Fire" crest.

Wmk. 373
2002, Nov. 27 Litho. *Perf. 14*
1164-1166 A209 Set of 3 8.50 8.50

Christmas — A210

Paintings: 20c, Adoration of the Shepherds, by Bernardino. 50c, Adoration of the Kings, by Girolamo, vert. 75c, Adoration of the Kings, by Foppa, vert. $5, Adoration of the Shepherds, by the Le Nain Brothers.

2002, Dec. 4 *Perf. 14x14¾, 14¾x14*
1167-1170 A210 Set of 4 9.00 9.00

Coronation of Queen Elizabeth II, 50th Anniv.

Common Design Type

Designs: Nos. 1171, 20c, 1173b, Queen with crown. Nos. 1172, 75c, 1173a, Queen's carriage.

Perf. 14¼x14½
2003, June 2 Litho. Wmk. 373
Vignettes Framed, Red Background

1171 CD363 20c multicolored .50 .50
1172 CD363 75c multicolored 1.75 1.75

Souvenir Sheet
Vignettes Without Frame, Purple Panel

1173 CD363 $2.50 Sheet of 2, #a-b 6.50 6.50

200 Years of Continuous Mail Service — A211

Designs: 20c, Letters from 1803 and 1844, 1822 fleuron postmark. 25c, St. Lucia #1-3. 65c, Map, mail ship Hewanorra. 75c, Post offices of 1900 and present time.

Wmk. 373
2003, July 14 Litho. *Perf. 14¼*
1174-1177 A211 Set of 4 3.75 3.75

Powered Flight, Cent. — A212

Designs: 20c, Sikorsky S-38. 70c, Consolidated PBY-5A Catalina. $1, Lockheed Lodestar. $5, Spitfire Mk V "St. Lucia."

Perf. 13¼x13¾
2003, Nov. 28 Litho. Wmk. 373
Stamps + Labels

1178-1181 A212 Set of 4 9.75 9.75

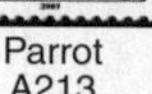

Parrot A213

Island A214

Perf. 14x14¼
2003, Nov. Coil Stamps

1182 A213 10c multicolored .25 .25
1183 A214 25c multicolored .40 .30

Christmas A215

Madonna and Child and: 20c, Sorrel flowers, ginger root. 75c, Sorrel drink, ginger ale. 95c, Masqueraders. $1, Christmas lanterns.

2003, Dec. 2 *Perf. 14*
1184-1187 A215 Set of 4 5.25 5.25

Independence, 25th Anniv. — A216

Designs: 20c, Flag raising ceremony, vert. 95c, People, book, airplane, ships, banana plant, vert. $1.10, "25" and leaves. $5, Harbor.

2004, Feb. 20 *Perf. 13¾*
1188-1191 A216 Set of 4 7.50 7.50

Caribbean Bird Festival — A217

No. 1192: a, Antillean crested hummingbird. b, St. Lucia pewee. c, Purple-throated carib. d, Gray trembler. e, Rufous-throated solitaire. f, St. Lucia warbler. g, Antillean euphonia. h, Semper's warbler.

Perf. 13¼x13
2004, June 30 Litho. Wmk. 373
1192 A217 Block of 8 11.00 11.00
a.-h. $1 Any single 1.25 1.25

Tourism A218

Designs: 45c, Sailing. 65c, Horse riding. 70c, Scuba diving. $1, Walking.

2004, Sept. 6 *Perf. 13¼*
1193-1196 A218 Set of 4 5.00 5.00

World AIDS Day A219

Designs: No. 1197, 30c, Condoms, syringe, couple. No. 1198, 30c, Children, woman.

Wmk. 373
2004, Dec. 1 Litho. *Perf. 14*
1197-1198 A219 Set of 2 2.50 2.50

Christmas — A220

Painting details: 30c, Adoration of the Kings, by Dosso Dossi. 75c, Adoration of the Shepherds, by Nicolas Poussin, vert. 95c, Adoration of the Kings, by Joos van Wassenhove, vert. $1, Adoration of the Shepherds, by Carel Fabritius.

2004, Dec. 14 *Perf. 14x14¾, 14¾x14*
1199-1202 A220 Set of 4 3.50 3.50

St. Joseph's Convent, 150th Anniv. A221

Nun and: 30c, Women. 95c, Convent and steps. $2.50, Building and street.

Wmk. 373
2005, Mar. 14 Litho. *Perf. 13¾*
1203-1205 A221 Set of 3 5.50 5.50

Battle of Trafalgar, Bicent. — A222

Designs: 30c, HMS Thunderer off St. Lucia. 75c, HMS Britannia in action against the Bucentaure. 95c, Admiral Horatio Nelson, vert. $5, HMS Victory.

$10, HMS Thunderer (44x44mm).

Wmk. 373, Unwmkd. ($5)
2005, June 13 Litho. *Perf. 13¼*
1206-1209 A222 Set of 4 8.75 8.75

Souvenir Sheet
Perf. 13¾

1210 A222 $10 multi 11.00 11.00

No. 1209 has particles of wood from the HMS Victory embedded in the areas covered by a thermographic process that produces a shiny, raised effect.

Pope John Paul II (1920-2005) A223

2005, Aug. 29 Wmk. 373 *Perf. 14*
1211 A223 $2 multi 3.00 3.00

Christmas — A224

Designs: 30c, Church of the Purification of the Blessed Virgin, Castries. $5, Minor Basilica of the Immaculate Conception, Castries.

Wmk. 373

2005, Nov. 28 Litho. *Perf. 14*

1212-1213 A224 Set of 2 5.00 5.00

Fruits and Nuts A225

Designs: 15c, Blighia sapida. 20c, Solanum melongena. 25c, Mangifera indica. 30c, Coccoloba uvifera. 50c, Carica papaya. 55c, Spondias mombin. 65c, Chrysobalanus icaco. 70c, Artocarpus altilis. 75c, Annona reticulata. 95c, Psidium guajava. $1, Musa sp. $2.50, Manilkara achras. $5, Anacardium occidentale. $25, Mammea americana.

2005, Dec. 5 *Perf. 14*

1214	A225	15c multi	.30	.30
1215	A225	20c multi	.30	.30
1216	A225	25c multi	.30	.30
1217	A225	30c multi	.30	.30
a.		Wmk. 406, dated "2010"	.30	.30
b.		Wmk. 406, dated "2013"	.25	.25
1218	A225	50c multi	.40	.40
1219	A225	55c multi	.45	.45
1220	A225	65c multi	.50	.50
1221	A225	70c multi	.55	.55
1222	A225	75c multi	.60	.60
1223	A225	95c multi	.80	.80
1224	A225	$1 multi	.85	.85
1225	A225	$2.50 multi	2.10	2.10
1226	A225	$5 multi	4.25	4.25
1227	A225	$25 multi	20.00	20.00
		Nos. 1214-1227 (14)	31.70	31.70

Issued: No. 1217a, 4/7/10.

Art by Llewellyn Xavier — A226

Designs: 20c, Axe Head. 30c, Turtle. $2.50, Pre-Columbian Vase. $5, Pre-Columbian Zemi.

Wmk. 373

2006, Mar. 15 Litho. *Perf. 12¾*

1228-1231 A226 Set of 4 6.00 6.00

2006 World Cup Soccer Championships, Germany — A227

Various soccer players: 95c, $2.

Wmk. 373

2006, June 9 Litho. *Perf. 14*

1232-1233 A227 Set of 2 2.25 2.25

1233a Souvenir sheet, #1232-1233 2.25 2.25

Leeward Islands Air Transport, 50th Anniv. A228

LIAT airplane: 30c, In flight. 75c, On ground.

Perf. 12½x13

2006, Oct. 16 Litho. Wmk. 373

1234-1235 A228 Set of 2 .80 .80

Christmas A229

Designs: 95c, Choir and director. $2, Sesenne Descartes, folk singer, and musicians.

2006, Nov. 16

1236-1237 A229 Set of 2 2.25 2.25

Cricket — A230

Designs: 30c, Mindoo Phillip. 75c, Map and flag of St. Lucia. 95c, Beausejour Cricket Grounds, horiz.

$5, Beausejour Cricket Grounds, horiz. diff.

Perf. 13x12½, 12½x13

2007, Feb. 28 Litho.

1238-1240 A230 Set of 3 1.50 1.50

Souvenir Sheet

1241 A230 $5 multi 3.75 3.75

No. 1241 contains one 56x42mm stamp.

Scouting, Cent. A231

Designs: 30c, Inspection of St. Lucia Scouts, 1954 Queen's Birthday Parade, hands and trumpet. $5, St. Lucia Cub Scout laying wreath, 2005 Remembrance Day Parade, poppies.

No. 1244, vert.: a, St. Lucia Scout Association emblem. b, Lord Robert Baden-Powell and Chief Joe Big Plume.

Wmk. 373

2007, Aug. 20 Litho. *Perf. 13¾*

1242-1243 A231 Set of 2 4.00 4.00

Souvenir Sheet

1244 A231 $2.50 Sheet of 2, #a-b 3.75 3.75

Christmas A232

Designs: 30c, Lantern Parade. $10, Nativity scene.

Perf. 12½x13

2007, Dec. 10 Litho. Wmk. 373

1245-1246 A232 Set of 2 7.75 7.75

2008 Summer Olympics, Beijing A233

Designs: 75c, Bamboo, diving. 95c, Dragon, running. $1, Lanterns, running. $2.50, Fish, high jump.

Wmk. 373

2008, Apr. 30 Litho. *Perf. 13¼*

1247-1250 A233 Set of 4 4.00 4.00

Worldwide Fund For Nature (WWF) — A234

Saint Lucia whiptail: 75c, On leaves. $2.50, On grass and rocks. $5, Two whiptails facing left. $10, Two whiptails facing left and right.

Wmk. 373

2008, Nov. 4 Litho. *Perf. 14*

1251-1254 A234 Set of 4 14.00 14.00

1254a Miniature sheet of 16, 4 each #1251-1254 56.00 56.00

University of the West Indies, 60th Anniv. A235

Wmk. 373

2008, Nov. 14 Litho. *Perf. 13*

1255 A235 $5 multi 4.00 4.00

Christmas A236

Designs: 95c, Wreath, bell, ornaments, gift, rose. $5, Star, candle, Holy Family, holly.

2008, Nov. 25 *Perf. 13¼*

1256-1257 A236 Set of 2 4.75 4.75

Independence, 30th Anniv. — A237

Designs: 30c, Castries waterfront. $2.50, Roseau Dam. $5, Rodney Bay Marina. $10, Sir John G. M. Compton (1925-2007), prime minister, and flag.

Perf. 12½x13

2009, Feb. 20 Litho. Wmk. 406

1258-1261 A237 Set of 4 13.50 13.50

Intl. Year of Biodiversity — A238

Designs: 30c, Lobelia. 75c, Iguana. 95c, Hercules beetle. $2.50, White-breasted thrasher.

Perf. 13x12¾

2010, June 11 Litho. Wmk. 406

1262-1265 A238 Set of 4 3.50 3.50

Gros-Islets Township, 25th Anniv. — A239

Perf. 14x15

2010, Aug. 27 Litho. Wmk. 406

1266 A239 95c multi .70 .70

Service of Queen Elizabeth II and Prince Philip — A240

Designs: No. 1267, $1.50, Prince Philip. No. 1268, $1.50, Queen Elizabeth II and Prince Philip. No. 1269, $2, Queen and Prince Philip, color photograph, diff. No. 1270, $2, Queen and Prince Philip, black-and-white photograph. No. 1271, $2.50, Queen and Prince Philip, black-and-white photograph, diff. No. 1272, $2.50, Queen.

$6, Queen and Prince Philip, diff.

Perf. 13¼

2011, Mar. 1 Litho. Unwmk.

1267-1272 A240 Set of 6 9.00 9.00

1272a Sheet of 6, #1267-1272, + 3 labels 9.00 9.00

Souvenir Sheet

1273 A240 $6 multi 4.50 4.50

Campaign Against HIV and AIDS, 30th Anniv. — A241

Perf. 12¾x13

2011, Sept. 1 Litho. Wmk. 406

1274 A241 30c multicolored .25 .25

Bishop Charles Gachet (1911-84) and Church, Soufriere — A242

2011, Dec. 1 *Perf. 14*
1275 A242 30c multicolored .25 .25

Christmas.

Reign of Queen Elizabeth II, 60th Anniv. — A243

Queen Elizabeth II: No. 1276, $1.50, Wearing blue green dress. No. 1277, $1.50, Wearing crown. No. 1278, $2, Without tiara. No. 1279, $2, Wearing tiara. No. 1280, $2.50, Without hat. No. 1281, $2.50, Wearing hat. $6, Wearing tiara.

2012, Feb. 6 **Unwmk.** *Perf. 13½*
1276-1281 A243 Set of 6 9.00 9.00
1281a Souvenir sheet, #1276-1281 + 3 labels 9.00 9.00

Souvenir Sheet

1282 A243 $6 multi 4.50 4.50

Paintings by Llewellyn Xavier A244

Designs: $5, Pitons. $10, The Spirit of Freedom, vert.

Perf. 13¼x13½, 13½x13¼

2013, Apr. 8 **Litho.** **Unwmk.**
1283-1284 A244 Set of 2 11.50 11.50

Dragonflies — A245

Designs: 5c, Antillean skimmer. 20c, Spot-tailed dasher. 30c, Vermillion saddlebags. 50c, Tawny pennant. 75c, Great pondhawk. $1, Band-winged dragonlet. $1.50, Wandering glider. $2, Rambur's forktail.

2013, Apr. 8 **Litho.** *Perf. 13½*
1285 A245 5c multi .25 .25
1286 A245 20c multi .25 .25
1287 A245 30c multi .25 .25
1288 A245 50c multi .35 .35
1289 A245 75c multi .55 .55
1290 A245 $1 multi .75 .75
1291 A245 $1.50 multi 1.10 1.10
1292 A245 $2 multi 1.50 1.50
Nos. 1285-1292 (8) 5.00 5.00

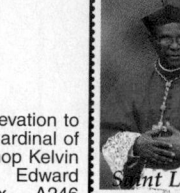

Elevation to Cardinal of Archbishop Kelvin Edward Felix — A246

Designs: $3, Cardinal Felix. $5, Pope Francis and Cardinal Felix, horiz.

Perf. 13¾x13½, 13½x13¾

2014, Dec. 12 **Litho.**
1293-1294 A246 Set of 2 6.00 6.00

AIR POST STAMP

Catalogue values for unused stamps in this section are for Never Hinged items.

Map of St. Lucia — AP1

Perf. 14½x14

1967, Mar. 1 **Photo.** **Unwmk.**
C1 AP1 15c blue .50 .50

St. Lucia's independence.
Exists imperf. and also in souvenir sheet. Values: single, $15; souvenir sheet $50.

POSTAGE DUE STAMPS

D1

Type I — "No." 3mm wide (shown).
Type II — "No." 4mm wide.

Rough Perf. 12

1931 **Unwmk.** **Typeset**
J1 D1 1p blk, *gray bl,* type I 10.00 *20.00*
a. Type II 24.00 *47.50*
J2 D1 2p blk, *yel,* type I 22.00 *47.50*
a. Type II 45.00 *105.00*
b. Vertical pair, imperf. btwn. *7,500.*

The serial numbers are handstamped. Type II has round "o" and period. Type I has tall "o" and square period.

Catalogue values for unused stamps in this section, from this point to the end of the section, are for Never Hinged items.

D2

1933-47 **Typo.** **Wmk. 4** *Perf. 14*

Chalky Paper

J3 D2 1p black 15.00 *8.00*
J4 D2 2p black 40.00 *10.00*
J5 D2 4p black ('47) 11.00 *50.00*
J6 D2 8p black ('47) 11.00 *60.00*
Nos. J3-J6 (4) 77.00 *128.00*

Issue date: June 28, 1947.

Chalky Paper

1952, Nov. 27 **Values in Cents**
J7 D2 2c black .25 *9.50*
a. Ordinary paper ('49) 1.90 30.00
J8 D2 4c black .60 *14.00*
a. Ordinary paper ('49) 3.75 24.00
J9 D2 8c black 3.50 *50.00*
a. Ordinary paper ('49) 3.50 30.00
J10 D2 16c black 5.00 *65.00*
a. Ordinary paper ('49) 16.00 75.00
Nos. J7-J10 (4) 9.35 *138.50*

Nos. J7a-J10a issued 10/1/1949.

Wmk. 4a (error)

J7a D2 2c 40.00
J8a D2 4c 55.00
J9a D2 8c 350.00
J10a D2 16c 475.00
Nos. J7a-J10a (4) 920.00

1965, Mar. 9 **Wmk. 314**
J11 D2 2c black .75 *10.00*
J12 D2 4c black 1.00 *11.00*

In the 2c center the "c" is heavier and the period bigger.
Nos. J9-J12 exist with overprint "Statehood/1st Mar. '67" in red. Values: unused $190; used $160.

Arms of St. Lucia — D3

1981, Aug. 4 **Litho.** **Wmk. 373**
J13 D3 5c red brown .25 *.65*
J14 D3 15c green .25 *.50*
J15 D3 25c deep orange .25 *.50*
J16 D3 $1 dark blue .45 *1.25*
Nos. J13-J16 (4) 1.20 2.90

1990 **Wmk. 384** *Perf. 15x14*
J17 D3 5c red brown .25 .25
J18 D3 15c green .25 .25
J19 D3 25c deep orange .25 .25
J20 D3 $1 dark blue .75 *1.00*
Nos. J17-J20 (4) 1.50 1.75

WAR TAX STAMPS

No. 65 Overprinted

1916 **Wmk. 3** *Perf. 14*
MR1 A11 1p scarlet 13.00 *19.00*
a. Double overprint 550.00 *650.00*
b. 1p carmine 67.50 55.00

Overprinted

MR2 A11 1p scarlet 1.40 .35

OFFICIAL STAMPS

Catalogue values for unused stamps in this section are for Never Hinged items.

Nos. 504-515 Overprinted

Wmk. 373

1983, Oct. 13 **Litho.** *Perf. 14½*
O1 A95 5c multicolored .30 .25
O2 A95 10c multicolored .30 .25
O3 A95 15c multicolored .30 .25
O4 A95 20c multicolored .35 .25
O5 A95 25c multicolored .50 .45
O6 A95 30c multicolored .70 .45
O7 A95 50c multicolored .80 .45
O8 A95 75c multicolored 1.10 .80
O9 A95 $1 multicolored 1.50 1.00
O10 A95 $2 multicolored 2.00 *2.25*
O11 A95 $5 multicolored 4.00 *4.25*
O12 A95 $10 multicolored 8.50 *10.00*
Nos. O1-O12 (12) 20.35 20.65

Nos. 747-761 Overprinted

1985, May 7 **Litho.** *Perf. 15*
O13 A126 5c multicolored .65 *1.00*
O14 A126 10c multicolored .65 *1.00*
O15 A126 20c multicolored .75 *1.00*
O16 A126 25c multicolored .75 .75
O17 A126 30c multicolored .90 .90
O18 A126 35c multicolored 1.00 1.00
O19 A126 45c multicolored 1.10 1.10
O20 A126 50c multicolored 1.25 1.25
O21 A126 65c multicolored 1.40 *1.50*
O22 A126 75c multicolored 1.40 *2.00*
O23 A126 90c multicolored 1.50 *2.10*
O24 A126 $1 multicolored 2.00 2.25
O25 A126 $2.50 multicolored 3.25 *4.00*
O26 A126 $5 multicolored 5.00 *5.50*
O27 A126 $15 multicolored 10.50 *12.00*
Nos. O13-O27 (15) 32.10 *37.35*

Nos. 953-964 Overprinted

1990, Feb. 21 **Wmk. 384** *Perf. 14*
O28 A162 10c multicolored .40 *1.00*
O29 A162 15c multicolored .40 *1.00*
O30 A162 20c multicolored .50 .50
O31 A162 25c multicolored .50 .50
O32 A162 50c multicolored .65 .65
O33 A162 80c multicolored .75 .75
O34 A162 95c multicolored 1.25 1.25
O35 A162 $1 multicolored 1.40 1.40
O36 A162 $1.50 multicolored 2.00 *2.50*
O37 A162 $2.50 multicolored 3.25 *3.75*
O38 A162 $5 multicolored 6.00 *6.50*
O39 A162 $25 multicolored 16.00 *18.00*
Nos. O28-O39 (12) 33.10 37.80

Issued: 20c, 25c, 50c, $25, 2/21; 10c, 15c, 80c, $1.50, 4/12; 95c, $1, $2.50, $5, 6/25.

STE. MARIE DE MADAGASCAR

sānt-mə-rē-də-ˌmad-ə-ˈgas-kər

LOCATION — An island off the east coast of Madagascar
GOVT. — French Possession
AREA — 64 sq. mi.
POP. — 8,000 (approx.)

In 1896 Ste.-Marie de Madagascar was attached to the colony of Madagascar for administrative purposes.

100 Centimes = 1 Franc

Navigation and Commerce — A1

1894 Unwmk. Typo. *Perf. 14x13½*
Name of Colony in Blue or Carmine

No.	Type	Description	Unused	Used
1	A1	1c black, *lil bl*	1.75	1.75
2	A1	2c brown, *buff*	2.75	2.75
3	A1	4c claret, *lavender*	5.00	5.00
4	A1	5c green, *grnsh*	12.00	11.00
5	A1	10c black, *lavender*	13.50	10.50
6	A1	15c blue	40.00	36.00
7	A1	20c red, *green*	30.00	28.00
8	A1	25c black, *rose*	25.00	22.00
9	A1	30c brown, *bister*	17.50	16.00
10	A1	40c red, *straw*	17.50	16.00
11	A1	50c carmine, *rose*	52.50	52.50
12	A1	75c violet, *org*	100.00	72.50
13	A1	1fr brnz grn, *straw*	52.50	47.50
		Nos. 1-13 (13)	370.00	321.50

Perf. 13½x14 stamps are counterfeits.

These stamps were replaced by those of Madagascar.

ST. MARTIN

sānt ˌmär-tən

LOCATION — The southern part of the island of St. Martin in the Caribbean Sea.
AREA — 13 sq. mi.
POP. — 33,119 (2007)
CAPITAL — Philipsburg

On Oct. 10, 2010, St. Martin, formerly part of Netherlands Antilles, became a constituent state within the Kingdom of the Netherlands.

100 Cents = 1 Gulden

Catalogue values for all unused stamps in this country are for Never Hinged items.

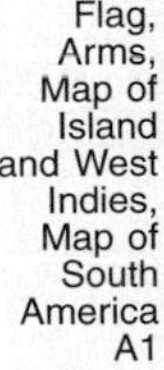

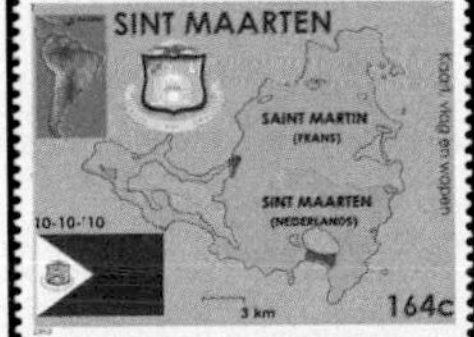

Flag, Arms, Map of Island and West Indies, Map of South America A1

Perf. 13¾
2010, Oct. 10 Litho. Unwmk.

No.	Type	Description	Unused	Used
1	A1	164c multi	1.90	1.90

25th Paper Money Fair, Maastricht, Nedtherlands — A2

No. 2: a, 80c, 50 koruna banknote, Slovakia, 1999. b, 112c, 100 franc banknote, New Hebrides, 1977. c, 145c, 20 pula banknote, Botswana, 1982. d, 195c, 50 dalasi banknote, Gambia, 1989. e, 240c, 10 rupee banknote, Sri Lanka, 1979. f, 285c, 10 riyal banknote, Qatar, 2003.

2011, Apr. 6 *Perf. 14*

No.	Type	Description	Unused	Used
2	A2	Block of 6, #a-f	12.00	12.00

Miniature Sheet

Peonies — A3

No. 3: a, Pink peony. b, Two white peonies and bud. c, White peony. d, Red peony and bud.
350c, Blue peonies.

2011, Apr. 28

No.	Type	Description	Unused	Used
3	A3	110c Sheet of 4, #a-d	5.00	5.00

Souvenir Sheet

No.	Type	Description	Unused	Used
4	A3	350c multi	4.00	4.00

Butterflies — A4

No. 5: a, 50c, Ornithoptera chimaera. b, 70c, Morpho cypris. c, 120c, Paralaxita lacoon. d, 145c, Eurytides iphitas. e, 166c, Dercas lycorias. f, 210c, Ancyluris jurgensenii.

2011, June 1 Litho. *Perf. 14*

No.	Type	Description	Unused	Used
5	A4	Block of 6, #a-f	8.50	8.50

Flowers — A5

No. 6: a, 21c, Camellia "Yuletide." b, 25c, Cornus kousa. c, 30c, Magnolia "Vulcan." d, 34c, Bidens laevis. e, 40c, Syringa vulgaris. f, 60c, Rosa "Charmian." g, 80c, Philadelphus. h, 170c, Rhododendron arboreum. i, 190c, Hydrangea macrophylla. j, 220c, Magnolia grandiflora. k, 295c, Buddleja davidii. l, 335c, Ribes sanguineum.

2011, Aug. 24

No.	Type	Description	Unused	Used
6	A5	Block of 12, #a-l	17.00	17.00

Maps — A6

No. 7: a, 111c, Map of St. Martin. b, 145c, Map of Caribbean Sea with St. Martin highlighted, vert. c, 350c, Map of South America with St. Martin highlighted, vert.

2011, Oct. 5

No.	Type	Description	Unused	Used
7	A6	Vert. strip of 3, #a-c	7.00	7.00

A7

A8

Designs of stamps inscribed "A": No. 8, Clock. No. 9, Agraulis vanillae. No. 10, Salt pickers. No. 11, Mangos. No. 12, Coconuts.
Designs of denominated stamps: 115c, Princess Juliana International Airport. 145c, Ocean Liner *Allure of the Seas.* 195c, Flamboyant tree. 205c, Danaus plexippus. 240c, Winair airplane. 285c, Pelican. 405c, Aerial view of Philipsburg.
No. 20: a, Beach. b, Maho Beach Airport. c, Harbor.

2011 Litho. *Perf. 14*
Stamps Inscribed "A"

No.	Type	Description	Unused	Used
8	A7	(115c) multi	1.40	1.40
9	A7	(204c) multi	2.25	2.25
10	A7	(205c) multi	2.40	2.40
11	A7	(285c) multi	3.25	3.25
12	A7	(380c) multi	4.25	4.25
		Nos. 8-12 (5)	13.55	13.55

Stamps With Denominations

No.	Type	Description	Unused	Used
13	A8	115c multi	1.40	1.40
14	A8	145c multi	1.75	1.75
15	A8	195c multi	2.25	2.25
16	A8	205c multi	2.40	2.40
17	A8	240c multi	2.75	2.75
18	A8	285c multi	3.25	3.25
19	A8	405c multi	4.50	4.50
		Nos. 13-19 (7)	18.30	18.30

Size: 19x15mm
Perf. 13¾x13¼

No.	Type	Description	Unused	Used
20		Strip of 3, #a-c	5.75	5.75
a.-c.	A8	170c Any single	1.90	1.90

Issued: Nos. 8-12, 14-15, 17-19, 10/6; Nos. 13, 16, 11/15; No. 20, 11/11. See Nos. 26-27.

Ships — A9

No. 21: a, 50c, Skuldelev Knorr, c. 1030. b, 60c, Mataro, 1450. c, 80c, St. Micahel, 1669. d, 380c, Herring buss, 1700. e, 405c, Wendur, 1884. f, 525c, Pearling dhow, c. 1900.

2011, Nov. 30 *Perf. 14*

No.	Type	Description	Unused	Used
21	A9	Block of 6, #a-f	17.00	17.00

Butterflies — A10

No. 22: a, 25c, Boloria selene. b, 50c, Hesperia comma. c, 75c, Lysandra bellargus. d, 100c, Limenitis camilla. e, 150c, Erebia aethiops. f, 200c, Minois dryas. g, 250c, Vanessa atalanta. h, 300c, Zerynthia polyxena. i, 305c, Parnassius phoebus smintheus. j, 310c, Clossiana dia. k, 335c, Pieris rapae. l, 400c, Brenthis daphne.

2012, Feb. 29

No.	Type	Description	Unused	Used
22	A10	Block of 12, #a-l	28.00	28.00

Flowers — A11

No. 23: a, 10c, Anemone hupehensis. b, 25c, Caltha palustris. c, 50c, Helleborus thibetanus. d, 125c, Lobelia cardinalis. e, 125c, Osteospermum jucundum. f, 175c, Narcissus. g, 225c, Hemerocallis. h, 355c, Doronicum orientale. i, 455c, Catharanthus roseus. j, 500c, Alstromeria.

2012, Apr. 4

23 A11 Block of 10, #a-j 23.00 23.00

Women's Carnival Costumes — A12

No. 24 — Various costumes: a, 115c. b, 250c. c, 275c. d, 375c.

2012, May 2

24 A12 Horiz. strip of 4, #a-d 11.50 11.50

Historical Sites — A13

No. 25: a, 170c, Border Monument with two dates at Fort St. Louis. b, 200c, Border Monument with one date. c, 300c, Courthouse.

2012, May 30

25 A13 Horiz. strip of 3, #a-c 7.50 7.50

Type of 2011

Designs: 10c, Flamboyant tree in bloom. 175c, Princess Juliana International Airport.

2012, June 13 ***Perf. 14***

26 A8 10c multi .25 .25
27 A8 175c multi 2.00 2.00

A14

Indonesia 2012 Intl. Stamp Exhibition, Jakarta — A15

No. 28: a, 120c, Prambanan Hindu Temple. b, 300c, Varanus komodoensis. c, 400c, Borobudur Buddhist Temple.

No. 29 — Rafflesia arnoldii flower with denomination at: a, 50c, LL. b, 100c, LR. c, 250c, UL. d, 400c, UR.

2012, June 13

28 A14 Vert. strip of 3, #a-c 9.25 9.25

Souvenir Sheet

29 A15 Sheet of 4, #a-d 9.00 9.00

2012 Summer Olympics, London — A16

No. 30: a, 25c, Handball. b, 50c, Running. c, 75c, Field hockey. d, 90c, Judo. e, 100c, Tennis. f, 120c, Soccer. g, 170c, Kayaking. h, 200c, Cycling. i, 220c, Gymnastics. j, 250c, Basketball. k, 300c, Beach volleyball. l, 400c, Triple jump.

No. 31: a, 125c, Archery. b, 225c, Diving. c, 350c, Weight lifting.

2012, July 18

30 A16 Block of 12, #a-l 22.50 22.50

Souvenir Sheet

31 A16 Sheet of 3, #a-c 8.00 8.00

Dutch Royalty — A17

No. 32: a, 100c, Queen Beatrix. b, 125c, Queen Beatrix at ship's wheel. c, 200c, Queen Beatrix holding infant. d, 275c, Prince Willem-Alexander. e, 325c, Princess Margriet. f, 475c, Princess Máxima.

2012, Sept. 12

32 A17 Block of 6, #a-f 17.00 17.00

Miniature Sheet

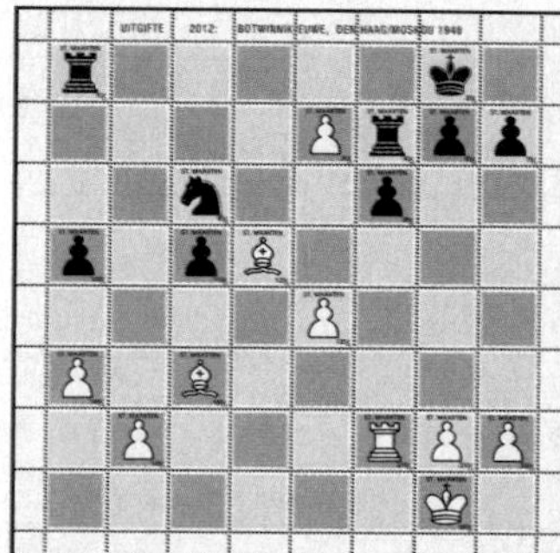

Final Position of 1948 Chess Match Between Mikhail Botvinnik and Max Euwe — A18

No. 33: a, 10c, Black rook. b, 20c, Black king. c, 30c, White pawn. d, 40c, Black rook. e, 55c, Black pawn. f, 75c, Black pawn. g, 85c, Black knight. h, 95c, Black pawn. i, 100c, Black pawn. j, 110c, Black pawn. k, 120c, White bishop. l, 135c, White pawn. m, 165c, White pawn. n, 185c, White bishop. o, 195c, White pawn. p, 210c, White rook. q, 230c, White pawn. r, 260c, White pawn. s, 380c, White king.

2012, Oct. 17

33 A18 Sheet of 19, #a-s, + 45 labels 28.00 28.00

Local Scenes — A19

No. 34: a, 115c, Fort Amsterdam. b, 200c, Hoofdstraat. c, 250c, View of beach. d, 350c, Airplane on final approach over Maho Beach.

2012, Nov. 14

34 A19 Block of 4, #a-d 10.50 10.50

Birds — A20

No. 35: a, 10c, Amazilia leucogaster. b, 30c, Aulacorhynchus derbianus. c, 50c, Bubo virginianus. d, 75c, Jacamerops aurea. e, 100c, Pteroglossus aracari. f, 150c, Discosura longicauda. g, 175c, Accipiter bicolor. h, 200c, Gampsonyx swainsonii. i, 240c, Leptodon cayanensis. j, 300c, Topaza pella. k, 350c, Trogon violaceus. l, 400c, Cotinga cayana.

2012, Dec. 12

35 A20 Block of 12, #a-l 24.00 24.00

Churches — A21

No. 36: a, 110c, Cole Bay Seventh Day Adventist Church. b, 150c, Simpson Bay Catholic Church. c, 200c, Philipsburg Methodist Church, vert. d, 350c, South Reward Catholic Church, vert.

2013, Jan. 2 **Litho.** ***Perf. 14***

36 A21 Block of 4, #a-d 9.25 9.25

Miniature Sheet

Birds — A22

No. 37: a, 25c, Columba plumbea. b, 50c, Chlorostilbon mellisugus. c, 75c, Cyanocorax cyanomelas. d, 100c, Eucometis penicillata. e, 150c, Mionectes oleagineus. f, 200c, Hemithraupis flavicollis. g, 225c, Myrmotherula guttata. h, 250c, Piaya cayana. i, 300c, Piaya melanogaster. j, 350c, Piaya minuta. k, 400c, Pygiptila stellaris. l, 475c, Turdus fumigatus.

2013, Feb. 6 **Litho.** ***Perf. 14***

37 A22 Sheet of 12, #a-l, + 3 labels 29.00 29.00

Politicians — A23

No. 38: a, 250c, Dr. Albert Claudius Wathey (1926-98). b, 300c, Vance James, Jr. (1949-2008).

2013, Mar. 6 Litho. *Perf. 14*
38 A23 Horiz. pair, #a-b 6.25 6.25

Cruise Ships A24

Designs: No. 39, 180c, Allure of the Seas. No. 40, 180c, Oasis of the Seas. No. 41, 180c, Ruby Princess. No. 42, 180c, Queen Victoria. No. 43, 180c, Carnival Dream. No. 44, 180c, Disney Fantasy.

2013 Litho. *Perf. 13¾*
39-44 A24 Set of 6 12.00 12.00

Issued: Nos. 39-40, 3/6; Nos. 41-42, 4/3; Nos. 43-44, 6/5.
Compare with type A43.

Local Scenes — A25

No. 45: a, 75c, A. C. Wathey Cruise Pier. b, 100c, Dr. A. C. Wathery Port Complex. c, 215c, Grote Bay. d, 325c, KLM airplane landing.

2013, Apr. 3 Litho. *Perf. 14*
45 A25 Block of 4, #a-d 8.00 8.00

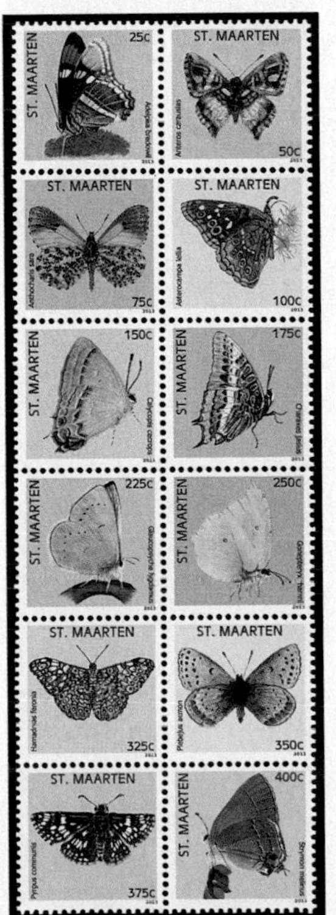

Butterflies — A26

No. 46: a, 25c, Adelpha bredowii. b, 50c, Anteros carausias. c, 75c, Anthocharis sara. d, 100c, Asterocampa leilia. e, 150c, Calycopis cecrops. f, 175c, Charaxes jasius. g, 225c, Glaucopsyche lygdamus. h, 250c, Gonepteryx rhamni. i, 325c, Hamadryas feronia. j, 350c, Plebejus acmon. k, 375c, Pyrgus communis. l, 400c, Strymon melinus.

2013, May 2 Litho. *Perf. 14*
46 A26 Block of 12, #a-l 28.00 28.00

Miniature Sheet

Scouting — A27

No. 47: a, 175c, Scout holding St. Martin troop sign. b, 200c, Four Scouts. c, 250c, Two Scouts in kayaks, horiz. d, 350c, Four Scouts, horiz.

2013, June 5 Litho. *Perf. 14*
47 A27 Sheet of 4, #a-d 11.00 11.00

Dutch Royalty — A28

No. 48: a, 100c, King William I. b, 200c, King William II. c, 300c, King William III. d, 400c, Queen Wilhelmina. e, 450c, Queen Juliana. f, 550c, Queen Beatrix.

No. 49: a, 300c, Queen Máxima. b, 550c, King Willem-Alexander.

2013, July 10 Litho. *Perf. 14*
48 A28 Sheet of 6, #a-f, + 3 labels 22.50 22.50

Souvenir Sheet

49 A28 Sheet of 2, #a-b 9.50 9.50

Ships — A29

No. 50: a, 125c, Savannah, 1819. b, 200c, Steam trawler, 1877. c, 275c, Alice M. Colburn, 1896. d, 325c, Muirneag, 1903. e, 350c, S.T.S. Lord Nelson, 1985. f, 350c, S.T.S. Young Endeavour, 1987.

2013, Sept. 4 Litho. *Perf. 14*
50 A29 Block of 6, #a-f 18.50 18.50

United States Lighthouses — A30

No. 51: a, 150c, Cape Hatteras Lighthouse, North Carolina. b, Portland Breakwater Lighthouse, Maine. c, 250c, Cape St. George Lighthouse, Florida. d, 300c, Molokai Lighthouse, Hawaii. e, 400c, Pensacola Lighthouse, Florida. f, 450c, Rock of Ages Lighthouse, Michigan.

2013, Oct. 2 Litho. *Perf. 14*
51 A30 Block or vert. strip of 6, #a-f 19.50 19.50

Miniature Sheet

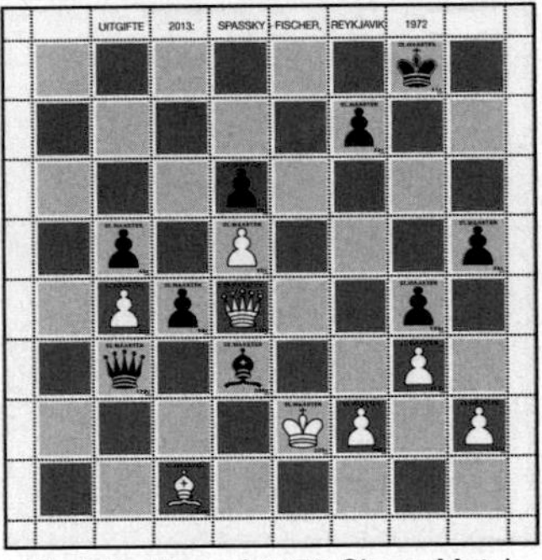

Final Position of 1972 Chess Match Between Boris Spassky and Bobby Fischer — A31

No. 52: a, 11c, Black king. b, 22c, Black pawn. c, 33c, Black pawn. d, 44c, Black pawn. e, 60c, White pawn. f, 70c, Black pawn. g, 80c, White pawn. h, 90c, Black pawn. i, 125c, White queen. j, 150c, Black pawn. k, 175c, Black queen. l, 200c, Black bishop. m, 215c, White pawn. n, 225c, White king. o, 300c, White pawn. p, 350c, White pawn. q, 350c, White bishop.

2013, Nov. 6 Litho. *Perf. 14*
52 A31 Sheet of 17, #a-q, + 47 labels 28.00 28.00

Miniature Sheet

Paintings by Johannes Vermeer — A32

No. 53: a, 100c, Girl with a Red Hat. b, 250c, The Milkmaid. c, 350c, Girl with a Pearl Earring. d, 500c, Woman in Blue Reading a Letter.

2013, Dec. 4 Litho. *Perf. 14*
53 A32 Sheet of 4, #a-d, + 2 labels 13.50 13.50

Miniature Sheet

Flowers — A33

No. 54: a, 10c, Costus speciosus. b, 20c, Cynara cardunculus. c, 50c, Dendrobium macrophyllum. d, 70c, Disa diores. e, 90c, Hibiscus rosa-sinensis. f, 100c, Kniphofia. g, 150c, Leontopodium alpinum. h, 210c, Phalaenopsis chibae. i, 300c, Phalaenopsis schilleriana. j, 350c, Rhynchostylis coelestis. k, 400c, Tillandsia cyanea. l, 650c, Vanda coerulea.

2014, Apr. 9 Litho. *Perf. 14*
54 A33 Sheet of 12, #a-l 27.00 27.00

Miniature Sheet

Paintings by Frans Hals (c. 1582-1666) — A34

No. 55: a, 150c, De Vrolijke Drinker (The Merry Drinker). b, 250c, Het Zigeunemeisje (Gypsy Girl). c, 450c, Malle Babbe. d, 550c, De Luitspeler (Jester with a Lute).

2014, May 14 Litho. *Perf. 14*
55 A34 Sheet of 4, #a-d, + 2 labels 16.00 16.00

Miniature Sheet

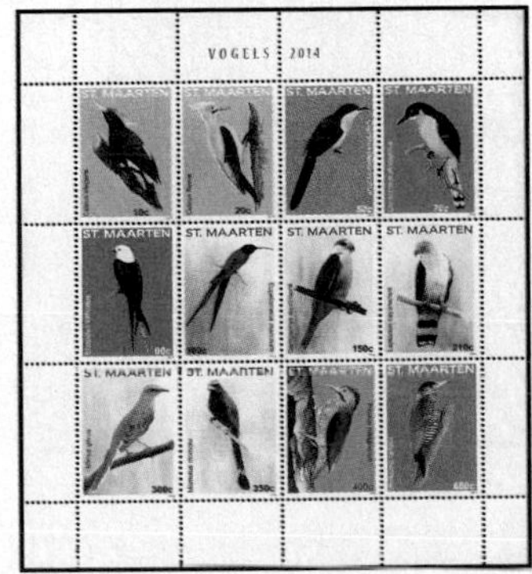

Birds — A35

No. 56: a, 10c, Celeus elegans. b, 20c, Celeus flavus. c, 50c, Coccyzus melacoryphus. d, 70c, Donacobius atricapillus. e, 90c, Elanoides forficatus. f, 100c, Eupetomena macroura. g, 150c, Gampsonyx swainsonii. h, 210c, Leptodon cayanensis. i, 300c, Mimus gilvus. j, 350c, Momotus momota. k, 400c, Piculus rubiginosus. l, 650c, Venilornis cassini.

2014, June 18 Litho. *Perf. 14*
56 A35 Sheet of 12, #a-l 27.00 27.00

Miniature Sheet

Fruits — A36

No. 57: a, 75c, Fragaria ananassa. b, 125c, Malus domestica. c, 275c, Nephelium lappaceum. d, 325c, Prunus armeniaca. e, 475c, Prunus persica. f, 525c, Pyrus.

2014, Aug. 20 Litho. *Perf. 14*
57 A36 Sheet of 6, #a-f 20.00 20.00

Miniature Sheet

Soccer — A37

No. 58 — Soccer ball and: a, 150c, Two players chasing ball. b, 250c, Goalie diving for ball. c, 450c, Player dribbling ball. d, 550c, Player ready to kick ball.

2014, Sept. 17 Litho. *Perf. 14*
58 A37 Sheet of 4, #a-d, + 2 labels 16.00 16.00

Miniature Sheet

Netherlands Stamps — A38

No. 59 — Canceled examples of stamps with incorrect perforations: a, 175c, Netherlands #47. b, 325c, Netherlands #154. c, 575c, Netherlands #5. d, 725c, Netherlands #70.

2014, Oct. 15 Litho. *Perf. 14*
59 A38 Sheet of 4, #a-d 20.00 20.00

Miniature Sheet

Traditional Women's Dresses — A39

No. 60 — Various dresses: a, 150c. b, 250c. c, 450c. d, 550c.

2014, Nov. 19 Litho. *Perf. 14*
60 A39 Sheet of 4, #a-d 16.00 16.00

Butterflies — A40

No. 61: a, 10c, Colias cesonia. b, 20c, Historis acheronta. c, 50c, Historis acheronta, diff. d, 70c, Issoria lathonia. e, 90c, Marpesia chiron. f, 100c, Ornithoptera paradisea. g, 150c, Papilio zelicaon. h, 210c, Polygonia interrogationis. i, 300c, Precis orithya. j, 350c, Speyeria diana. k, 400c, Speyeria idalia. l, 650c, Troides aeacus.

2014, Dec. 10 Litho. *Perf. 14*
61 A40 Block of 12, #a-l 27.00 27.00

Birds — A41

No. 62: a, 10c, Micrastur semitorquatus. b, 30c, Brachygalba lugubris. c, 60c, Camprimulgus rufus. d, 90c, Camprimulgus nigrescens. e, 110c, Chondrohierax uncinatus. f, 150c, Colaptes campestris. g, 200c, Chordeiles acutipennis. h, 250c, Hydropsalis climacocerca. i, 300c, Otus atricapillus. j, 325c, Galbula dea. k, 475c, Zebrilus undulates. l, 500c, Eurypyga helias.

2015, Jan. 14 Litho. *Perf. 14*
62 A41 Block of 12, #a-l 28.00 28.00

Miniature Sheet

Shells — A42

No. 63: a, 90c, Buccinum politum. b, 110c, Bulla striata. c, 270c, Cypraecassis testiculus. d, 330c, Neptunea contraria. e, 500c, Phos senticosus. f, 600c, Trigonostoma pellucida.

2015, Feb. 11 Litho. *Perf. 14*
63 A42 Sheet of 6, #a-f 21.50 21.50

Allure of the Seas — A43

2015, Mar. 2 Litho. *Perf. 14*
64 A43 180c multi 2.00 2.00

Compare with type A24.

Banknotes — A44

No. 65: a, 90c, Gabon 5000-franc note. b, 110c, Sri Lanka 2-rupee note. c, 270c, Oman 1-rial note. d, 330c, Zambia 50-kwacha note. e, 500c, Gambia 25-dalasi note. f, 600c, Tanzania 5000-shilling note.

2015, Mar. 18 Litho. *Perf. 14*
65 A44 Block of 6, #a-f 21.50 21.50

Souvenir Sheet

Queen Wilhelmina (1880-1962) — A45

No. 66 — Various depictions of Queen Wilhelmina: a, 500c. b, 700c.

2015, Apr. 15 Litho. *Perf. 14*
66 A45 Sheet of 2, #a-b 13.50 13.50

Cruise Ships — A46

No. 67: a, Norwegian Getaway. b, Jewel of the Seas. c, Freedom of the Seas. d, Royal Princess.

2015, June 17 Litho. *Perf. 14*
67 Horiz. strip of 4 18.00 18.00
a. A46 275c multi 3.25 3.25
b. A46 325c multi 3.75 3.75
c. A46 475c multi 5.25 5.25
d. A46 525c multi 5.75 5.75

Miniature Sheets

A47

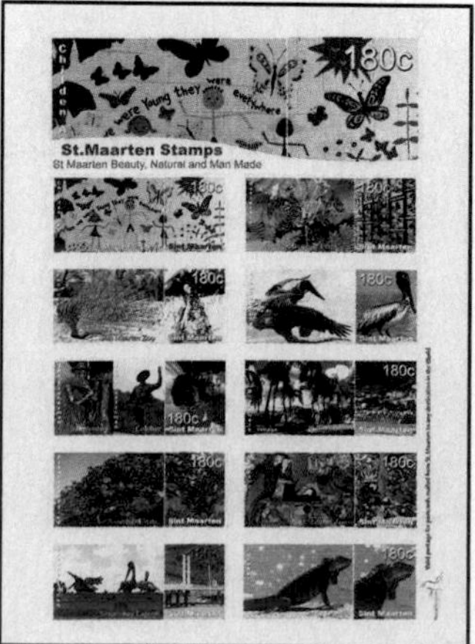

Tourism — A48

No. 68: a, Bottles on Guavaberry Emporium table and shelves. b, Exterior of Guavaberry Emporium. c. Macaws in St. Martin Zoo. d, Peacock in St. Martin Zoo. e, Flamboyant tree on Saunders Estate. f, Boardwalk Village, Philipsburg.

No. 69: a, Children's art on wall, Madam Estate Zoo. b, Mounted butterflies. c, Brown pelican. d, Sculpture. e, Bridge, Simpson Bay Lagoon. f, Iguana.

Serpentine Die Cut 14¼

2015, July 1 Self-Adhesive Litho.

68	A47	Sheet of 6 + 6 labels	12.00	
a.-f.		180c Any single	2.00	2.00
69	A48	Sheet of 10, #68c-68f, 69a-69f + 10 labels	20.00	
a.-f.		180c Any single	2.00	2.00

Flowers — A49

No. 70: a, 25c, Antigonon leptopus. b, 50c, Fritillaria imperialis, c, 75c, Callistemom lanceolatus. d, 100c, Hibiscus schizopetalus. e, 150c, Canna generalis. f, 250c, Lilium pumilum. g, 350c, Hymenocallis caribaea. h, 400c, Narcissus tazetta. i, 500c, Pyrostegia venusta. j, 600c, Ricinus communis.

2015, Aug. 19 Litho. *Perf. 14*

70 A49 Block of 10, #a-j 28.00 28.00

Miniature Sheets

Butterflies — A50

No. 71: a, 25c, Hypolimnas misippus. b, 50c, Papilio krishna. c, 75c, Euphydryas chalcedona. d, 100c, Feniseca tarquinius. e, 150c, Papilio demodocus.

No. 72: a, 250c, Brephidium exile. b, 350c, Pseudotergumia fidia. c, 400c, Satyrium titus. d, 500c, Papilio arcturus. e, 600c, Thessalia theona.

2015, Sept. 16 Litho. *Perf. 14*

71 A50 Sheet of 5, #a-e 4.50 4.50
72 A50 Sheet of 5, #a-e 23.50 23.50

Fish — A51

No. 73: a, 25c, Acanthodoras spinosissimus. b, 50c, Acaronia nassa, c, 75c, Acestrorhynchus falcatus. d, 100c, Amphilophus citrinellus. e, 150c, Brochis splendens. f, 250c, Erythrinus erythrinus. g, 350c, Copeina arnoldi. h, 400c, Charax gibbosus. i, 500c, Symphysodon aequifasciatus. j, 600c, Phractocephalus hemioliopterus.

2015, Oct. 14 Litho. *Perf. 14*

73 A51 Block of 10, #a-j 28.00 28.00

Primates — A52

No. 74: a, 75c, Cebus capucinus. b, 125c, Ateles geoffroyi. c, 275c, Presbytis obscura. d, 325c, Ateles paniscus. e, 475c, Cebus apella. f, 525c, Callicebus torquatus.

2015, Nov. 18 Litho. *Perf. 14*

74 A52 Block of 6, #a-f 20.00 20.00

Pilioko Paintings — A53

No. 75 — Various paintings with frame color at bottom of: a, 275c, Lilac. b, 325c, Light blue. c, 475c, Dark blue. d, 525c, Ultramarine.

2015, Dec. 9 Litho. *Perf. 14*

75 A53 Vert. strip of 4, #a-d 18.00 18.00

ST. PIERRE & MIQUELON

sānt-ˈpi̧ə̧r and ˈmik-ə-ˌlän

LOCATION — Two small groups of islands off the southern coast of Newfoundland

GOVT. — Formerly a French colony, now a Department of France

AREA — 93 sq. mi.

POP. — 6,966 (1999 est.)

CAPITAL — St. Pierre

The territory of St. Pierre and Miquelon became a Department of France in July 1976.

100 Centimes = 1 Franc
100 Cents = 1 Euro (2002)

Catalogue values for unused stamps in this country are for Never Hinged items, beginning with Scott 300 in the regular postage section, Scott B13 in the semi-postal section, Scott C1 in the airpost section, and Scott J68 in the postage due section.

Stamps of French Colonies Handstamp Surcharged in Black

1885 Unwmk. *Imperf.*

1	A8	05c on 40c ver, *straw*	150.00	60.00
2	A8	10c on 40c ver, *straw*	45.00	35.00
a.		"M" inverted	375.00	350.00
3	A8	15c on 40c ver, *straw*	45.00	35.00
		Nos. 1-3 (3)	240.00	130.00

Nos. 2 and 3 exist with "SPM" 17mm wide instead of 15½mm.

Nos. 1-3 exist with surcharge inverted and with it doubled.

Handstamp Surcharged in Black

b

c

d

1885

4	A8 (b)	05c on 35c blk, *yel*	160.00	110.00
5	A8 (b)	05c on 75c car, *rose*	375.00	300.00
6	A8 (b)	05c on 1fr brnz grn, *straw*	40.00	32.50
7	A8 (c)	25c on 1fr brnz grn, *straw*	*14,000.*	*2,800.*
8	A8 (d)	25c on 1fr brnz grn, *straw*	*2,700.*	*1,925.*

Nos. 7 and 8 exist with surcharge inverted, and with it vertical. No. 7 exists with "S P M" above "25" (the handstamping was done in two steps). See the *Scott Specialized Catalogue of Stamps and Covers* for detailed listings.

1885 *Perf. 14x13½*

9	A9 (c)	5c on 2c brn, *buff*	*7,250.*	*2,700.*
10	A9 (d)	5c on 4c cl, *lav*	550.00	350.00
11	A9 (b)	05c on 20c red, *grn*	47.50	47.50

No. 9 surcharge is normally inverted. Nos. 10 and 11 exist with a variety of overprint errors. See the *Scott Specialized Catalogue of Stamps and Covers* for detailed listings.

A15

1886, Feb. Typo. *Imperf.*
Without Gum

12	A15	5c black	1,500.
13	A15	10c black	1,600.
14	A15	15c black	1,400.
		Nos. 12-14 (3)	4,500.

"P D" are the initials for "Payé a destination." Excellent forgeries exist.

Stamps of French Colonies Surcharged in Black

e

f

1891 *Perf. 14x13½*

15	A9 (e)	15c on 30c brn, *bis*	52.50	40.00
a.		Inverted surcharge	*310.00*	*260.00*
16	A9 (e)	15c on 35c blk, *org*	725.00	575.00
a.		Inverted surcharge	*875.00*	*700.00*
17	A9 (f)	15c on 35c blk, *org*	2,000.	1,650.
a.		Inverted surcharge		*2,100.*
18	A9 (e)	15c on 40c red, *straw*	125.00	95.00
a.		Inverted surcharge	*300.00*	*250.00*

Stamps of French Colonies Overprinted in Black or Red

1891, Oct. 15

19	A9	1c blk, *lil bl*	17.00	13.50
a.		Inverted overprint	40.00	40.00
20	A9	1c blk, *lil bl* (R)	17.00	15.00
a.		Inverted overprint	40.00	40.00
21	A9	2c brn, *buff*	17.00	13.50
a.		Inverted overprint	40.00	40.00
b.		"S" omitted in "ST"	110.00	110.00
22	A9	2c brn, *buff* (R)	32.50	30.00
a.		Inverted overprint	82.50	82.50
23	A9	4c claret, *lav*	17.00	13.50
a.		Inverted overprint	40.00	40.00
24	A9	4c claret, *lav* (R)	32.50	30.00
a.		Inverted overprint	65.00	65.00
25	A9	5c grn, *grnsh*	27.50	19.00
a.		Double surcharge	260.00	
26	A9	10c blk, *lav*	47.50	40.00
a.		Inverted overprint	95.00	*95.00*
b.		"S" omitted in "ST"	160.00	160.00
27	A9	10c blk, *lav* (R)	32.50	30.00
a.		Inverted overprint	65.00	*65.00*
28	A9	15c blue	45.00	32.50
29	A9	20c red, *grn*	110.00	100.00
30	A9	25c blk, *rose*	40.00	27.50
31	A9	30c brn, *bis*	150.00	125.00
32	A9	35c vio, *org*	525.00	400.00
33	A9	40c red, *straw*	100.00	80.00
a.		Double surcharge	500.00	
34	A9	75c car, *rose*	140.00	130.00
a.		Inverted overprint	240.00	225.00
35	A9	1fr brnz grn, *straw*	120.00	105.00
a.		Inverted overprint	220.00	220.00
		Nos. 19-35 (17)	1,470.	1,204.

Numerous varieties of mislettering occur in the preceding overprint: "ST," "P," "M," "ON," or "-" missing; "-" instead of "ON"; "=" instead of "-" These varieties command values double or triple those of normal stamps.

Surcharged in Black

1891-92

36	A9	1c on 5c grn, *grnsh*	16.00	16.00
37	A9	1c on 10c blk, *lav*	18.00	16.50
38	A9	1c on 25c blk, *rose* ('92)	12.50	12.00
39	A9	2c on 10c blk, *lav*	16.00	16.00
a.		Double surcharge	170.00	170.00
b.		Triple surcharge	350.00	350.00
40	A9	2c on 15c bl	18.00	16.50
41	A9	2c on 25c blk, *rose* ('92)	12.50	12.00
42	A9	4c on 20c red, *grn*	16.00	16.00
43	A9	4c on 25c blk, *rose* ('92)	12.50	12.00
a.		Double surcharge	160.00	160.00
44	A9	4c on 30c brn, *bis*	32.50	26.00
45	A9	4c on 40c red, *straw*	32.50	26.00
		Nos. 36-45 (10)	186.50	169.00

See note after No. 35.

French Colonies 1881-86 Stamps Surcharged in Black

j

k

1892, Nov. 4

46 A9 (j) 1c on 5c grn, *grnsh* 16.00 14.00
47 A9 (j) 2c on 5c grn, *grnsh* 16.00 14.00
48 A9 (j) 4c on 5c grn, *grnsh* 16.00 14.00
49 A9 (k) 1c on 25c blk, *rose* 12.50 12.00
50 A9 (k) 2c on 25c blk, *rose* 12.50 12.00
51 A9 (k) 4c on 25c blk, *rose* 12.50 12.00
Nos. 46-51 (6) 85.50 78.00

See note after No. 35.

Postage Due Stamps of French Colonies Overprinted in Red

1892, Dec. 1 ***Imperf.***

52 D1 10c black 60.00 40.00
53 D1 20c black 40.00 35.00
54 D1 30c black 37.50 37.50
55 D1 40c black 32.50 32.50
56 D1 60c black 140.00 140.00

Black Overprint

57 D1 1fr brown 190.00 190.00
58 D1 2fr brown 325.00 325.00
59 D1 5fr brown 500.00 475.00
Nos. 52-59 (8) 1,325. 1,275.

See note after No. 35. "T P" stands for "Timbre Poste."

Navigation and Commerce — A16

1892-1908 Typo. ***Perf. 14x13½***

60 A16 1c blk, *lil bl* 1.90 1.90
61 A16 2c brown, *buff* 1.90 1.90
62 A16 4c claret, *lav* 3.00 3.00
63 A16 5c green, *grnsh* 4.50 3.75
64 A16 5c yel grn ('08) 6.00 3.75
65 A16 10c black, *lav* 8.25 6.75
66 A16 10c red ('00) 6.00 3.75
67 A16 15c bl, quadrille paper 19.00 6.00
68 A16 15c gray, *lt gray* ('00) 100.00 65.00
69 A16 20c red, *grn* 30.00 24.00
70 A16 25c black, *rose* 13.50 3.75
71 A16 25c blue ('00) 25.00 15.00
72 A16 30c brown, *bis* 13.50 9.00
73 A16 35c blk, *yel* ('06) 8.00 7.25
74 A16 40c red, *straw* 9.75 9.00
75 A16 50c car, *rose* 52.50 42.50
76 A16 50c brown, *az* ('00) 40.00 37.50
77 A16 75c violet, *org* 35.00 30.00
78 A16 1fr brnz grn, *straw* 35.00 26.00
Nos. 60-78 (19) 412.80 299.80

Perf. 13½x14 stamps are counterfeits.

For surcharges and overprints see Nos. 110-120, Q1-Q2.

Fisherman A17

Fulmar Petrel A18

Fishing Schooner A19

1909-30

79 A17 1c org red & ol .40 *.50*
80 A17 2c olive & dp bl .40 *.50*
81 A17 4c violet & ol .55 *.75*
a. Perf 11 160.00
82 A17 5c bl grn & ol grn 1.20 .75
83 A17 5c blue & blk ('22) .55 *.75*
84 A17 10c car rose & red 1.20 1.10
85 A17 10c bl grn & ol grn ('22) .75 .75
86 A17 10c bis & mag ('25) .55 *.75*
86A A17 15c dl vio & rose ('17) .80 .75
87 A17 20c bis brn & vio brn 1.25 1.10
88 A18 25c dp blue & blue 4.50 3.00
89 A18 25c ol brn & bl grn ('22) 1.25 *1.50*
90 A18 30c org & vio brn 2.60 2.60
91 A18 30c rose & dull red ('22) 1.75 *2.25*
92 A18 30c red brn & bl ('25) 1.00 1.00
93 A18 30c gray grn & bl grn ('26) 1.50 *2.25*
94 A18 35c ol grn & vio brn .80 .80
95 A18 40c vio brn & ol grn 4.00 3.00
96 A18 45c vio & ol grn 1.10 *1.50*
97 A18 50c ol & ol grn 2.25 2.25
98 A18 50c bl & pale bl ('22) 1.75 *2.25*
99 A18 50c yel brn & mag ('25) 1.60 *2.25*
100 A18 60c dk bl & ver ('25) 1.40 *1.90*
101 A18 65c vio & org brn ('28) 2.50 *3.00*
102 A18 75c brn & ol 1.90 *2.25*
103 A18 90c brn red & org red ('30) 35.00 *37.50*
104 A19 1fr ol grn & dp bl 5.00 3.75
105 A19 1.10fr bl grn & org red ('28) 5.50 *7.50*
106 A19 1.50fr bl & dp bl ('30) 15.00 15.00
107 A19 2fr violet & brn 6.00 4.50
108 A19 3fr red vio ('30) 18.00 *22.50*
109 A19 5fr vio brn & ol grn 13.50 12.50
Nos. 79-109 (32) 135.55 142.75

For overprints and surcharges see Nos. 121-131, 206C-206D, B1-B2, Q3-Q5.

Stamps of 1892-1906 Surcharged in Carmine or Black

n

o

1912

110 A16 5c on 2c brn, *buff* 3.75 *4.00*
111 A16 5c on 4c claret, *lav* (C) 1.10 *1.50*
112 A16 5c on 15c blue (C) 1.10 *1.50*
113 A16 5c on 20c red, *grn* .90 *1.10*
114 A16 5c on 25c blk, *rose* (C) .90 *1.10*
115 A16 5c on 30c brn, *bis* (C) 1.10 *1.50*
116 A16 5c on 35c blk, *yel* (C) 1.90 *2.25*
117 A16 10c on 40c red, *straw* 1.50 *1.90*
118 A16 10c on 50c car, *rose* 1.50 *1.90*
119 A16 10c on 75c dp vio, *org* 3.75 *4.50*
120 A16 10c on 1fr brnz grn, *straw* 5.25 *6.25*
Nos. 110-120 (11) 22.75 *27.50*

Two spacings between the surcharged numerals are found on Nos. 110 to 120. For detailed listings, see the *Scott Classic Specialized Catalogue of Stamps and Covers.*

Stamps and Types of 1909-17 Surcharged in Black, Blue (Bl) or Red

1924-27

121 A17 25c on 15c dl vio & rose ('25) .55 *.75*
a. Double surcharge 190.00
b. Triple surcharge 210.00
122 A19 25c on 2fr vio & lt brn (Bl) .80 *1.10*
123 A19 25c on 5fr brn & ol grn (Bl) .90 *1.10*
a. Triple surcharge 210.00
124 A18 65c on 45c vio & ol grn ('25) 2.25 *3.00*
125 A18 85c on 75c brn & ol ('25) 2.25 *3.00*
126 A18 90c on 75c brn red & dp org ('27) 3.00 *3.75*
127 A19 1.25fr on 1fr dk bl & ultra (R) ('26) 3.00 *3.75*
128 A19 1.50fr on 1fr ultra & dk bl ('27) 4.00 *4.50*
129 A19 3fr on 5fr ol brn & red vio ('27) 5.25 *6.00*
130 A19 10fr on 5fr ver & ol grn ('27) 25.00 *29.00*
131 A19 20fr on 5fr vio & ver ('27) 32.50 *40.00*
Nos. 121-131 (11) 79.50 95.95

Common Design Types pictured following the introduction.

Colonial Exposition Issue
Common Design Types

1931, Apr. 13 Engr. ***Perf. 12½***

Name of Country in Black

132 CD70 40c deep green 6.00 6.00
133 CD71 50c violet 6.00 *6.00*
134 CD72 90c red orange 6.00 *6.00*
135 CD73 1.50fr dull blue 6.00 *6.00*
Nos. 132-135 (4) 24.00 24.00

Map and Fishermen — A20

Lighthouse and Fish — A21

Fishing Steamer and Sea Gulls A22

Perf. 13½x14, 14x13½

1932-33 Typo.

136 A20 1c red brn & ultra .25 *.35*
137 A21 2c blk & dk grn .40 *.50*
138 A22 4c mag & ol brn .40 *.60*
139 A22 5c vio & dk brn .80 *1.10*
140 A21 10c red brn & blk .80 *1.10*
141 A21 15c dk blue & vio 1.60 *2.25*
142 A20 20c blk & red org 1.90 *2.25*
143 A20 25c lt vio & lt grn 1.90 *2.25*
144 A22 30c ol grn & bl grn 1.90 *2.25*
145 A22 40c dp bl & dk brn 1.90 *2.25*
146 A21 45c ver & dp grn 1.90 2.25
147 A21 50c dk brn & dk grn 2.25 *2.60*
148 A22 65c ol brn & org 2.60 *3.00*
149 A20 75c grn & red org 2.25 *2.60*
150 A20 90c dull red & red 2.75 *3.75*
151 A22 1fr org brn & org red 2.60 *3.00*
152 A20 1.25fr dp bl & lake ('33) 2.60 *3.00*
153 A20 1.50fr dp blue & blue 2.60 *3.00*
154 A22 1.75fr blk & dk brn ('33) 3.25 *3.75*
155 A22 2fr bl blk & Prus bl 12.00 *13.50*
156 A21 3fr dp grn & dk brn 15.00 *19.00*
157 A21 5fr brn red & dk brn 32.50 *37.50*
158 A22 10fr dk grn & vio 75.00 *82.50*
159 A20 20fr ver & dp grn 85.00 *92.50*
Nos. 136-159 (24) 254.15 286.85

For overprints and surcharges see Nos. 160-164, 207-221.

Nos. 147, 149, 153-154, 157 Overprinted in Black, Red or Blue

p

q

1934, Oct. 18

160 A21(p) 50c (Bk) 6.50 *7.50*
161 A20(q) 75c (Bk) 9.50 *10.50*
162 A20(q) 1.50fr (Bk) 9.50 *10.50*
163 A22(p) 1.75fr (R) 10.00 *12.50*
164 A21(p) 5fr (Bl) 45.00 *47.50*
Nos. 160-164 (5) 80.50 88.50

400th anniv. of the landing of Jacques Cartier.

Paris International Exposition Issue
Common Design Types

1937 ***Perf. 13***

165 CD74 20c deep violet 2.40 *2.75*
166 CD75 30c dark green 2.40 *2.75*
167 CD76 40c carmine rose 2.40 *2.75*
168 CD77 50c dk brn & bl 2.40 *2.75*
169 CD78 90c red 2.50 *2.75*
170 CD79 1.50fr ultra 2.50 *2.75*
Nos. 165-170 (6) 14.60 16.50

Colonial Arts Exhibition Issue
Souvenir Sheet
Common Design Type

1937 ***Imperf.***

171 CD78 3fr dark ultra 35.00 *47.50*

Dog Team A23

Port St. Pierre A24

Tortue Lighthouse A25

Soldiers' Bay at Langlade A26

1938-40 Photo. *Perf. 13½x13*

172 A23 2c dk bl grn .25 *.35*
a. Value omitted 425.00
173 A23 3c brown violet .25 *.35*
174 A23 4c dk red violet .30 *.40*
175 A23 5c carmine lake .30 *.40*
176 A23 10c bister brown .30 *.40*
177 A23 15c red violet .65 *.80*
178 A23 20c blue violet .90 *1.10*
179 A23 25c Prus blue 2.50 *3.00*
180 A24 30c dk red violet .65 *.80*
181 A24 35c deep green .90 *1.10*
182 A24 40c slate blue ('40) .25 *.35*
183 A24 45c dp grn ('40) .50 *.60*
a. Value omitted 110.00
184 A24 50c carmine rose .90 *1.10*
185 A24 55c Prus blue 4.25 *4.50*
186 A24 60c violet ('39) .65 *.90*
187 A24 65c brown 6.50 *6.75*
188 A24 70c org yel ('39) .75 *1.00*
189 A25 80c violet 1.60 *1.90*
190 A25 90c ultra ('39) 1.00 *1.25*
191 A25 1fr brt pink 13.00 *14.00*
192 A25 1fr pale ol grn ('40) 1.00 *1.25*
193 A25 1.25fr brt rose ('39) 2.40 *2.75*
194 A25 1.40fr dk brn ('40) 1.25 *1.50*
195 A25 1.50fr blue green 1.25 *1.50*
196 A25 1.60fr rose vio ('40) 1.25 *1.50*
197 A25 1.75fr deep blue 3.50 *4.50*
198 A26 2fr rose violet .90 *1.10*
199 A26 2.25fr brt blue ('39) 1.25 *1.60*
200 A26 2.50fr org yel ('40) 1.25 *1.50*
201 A26 3fr gray brown 1.10 *1.50*
202 A26 5fr henna brown 1.25 *1.50*
203 A26 10fr dk bl, *bluish* 1.90 *2.25*
204 A26 20fr slate green 2.50 *3.00*
Nos. 172-204 (33) 57.20 66.50

For overprints and surcharges see Nos. 222-255, 260-299, B9-B10.

New York World's Fair Issue
Common Design Type

1939, May 10 Engr. *Perf. 12½x12*

205 CD82 1.25fr carmine lake 2.40 *3.00*
206 CD82 2.25fr ultra 2.40 *3.00*

For overprints and surcharges see Nos. 256-259.

Lighthouse on Cliff — A27

1941 Engr. *Perf. 12½x12*

206A A27 1fr dull lilac 2.00
206B A27 2.50fr blue 2.00

Nos. 206A-206B were issued by the Vichy government in France, but were not placed on sale in St. Pierre & Miquelon.

For surcharges, see B11-B12.

> Free French Administration
>
> The circumstances surrounding the overprinting and distribution of these stamps were most unusual. Practically all of the stamps issued in small quantities, with the exception of Nos. 260-299, were obtained by speculators within a few days after issue. At a later date, the remainders were taken over by the Free French Agency in Ottawa, Canada, by whom they were sold at a premium for the benefit of the Syndicat des Oeuvres Sociales. Large quantities appeared on the market in 1991, including many "errors." More may exist.
>
> Excellent counterfeits of these surcharges and overprints are known.

Nos. 86 & 92 Ovptd. in Black — a

1942 Unwmk. *Perf. 14x13½*

206C A17 10c 1,600. *1,700.*
206D A18 30c 1,600. *1,700.*

The letters "F. N. F. L." are the initials of "Forces Navales Francaises Libres" or "Free French Naval Forces."

Ovptd. in Black on Nos. 137-139, 145-148, 151, 154-155, 157

207 A21 2c 275.00 *300.00*
208 A22 4c 67.50 *80.00*
208A A22 5c 1,000. *1,200.*
209 A22 40c 17.50 *21.00*
210 A21 45c 210.00 *250.00*
211 A21 50c 17.50 *21.00*
212 A22 65c 60.00 *67.50*
213 A22 1fr 450.00 *500.00*
214 A22 1.75fr 17.50 *21.00*
215 A22 2fr 24.00 *27.50*
216 A22 5fr 425.00 *475.00*

Nos. 142, 149, 152-153 Overprinted in Black

Perf. 13½x14

216A A20 20c 500.00 *575.00*
217 A20 75c 45.00 *55.00*
218 A20 1.25fr 40.00 *47.50*
218A A20 1.50fr 600.00 *675.00*

On Nos. 152, 149 Surcharged with New Value and Bars

219 A20 10fr on 1.25fr 65.00 *72.50*
220 A20 20fr on 75c 65.00 *72.50*

No. 154 Srchd. in Red

Perf. 14x13½

221 A22 5fr on 1.75fr 22.50 *27.50*

Stamps of 1938-40 Ovptd.

Perf. 13½x13

222 A23 2c dk bl grn 575.00 *650.00*
223 A23 3c brn vio 225.00 *250.00*
224 A23 4c dk red vio 110.00 *140.00*
225 A23 5c car lake 1,000. *1,200.*
226 A23 10c bis brn 17.00 *18.00*
227 A23 15c red vio 1,900. *2,100.*
228 A23 20c blue vio 210.00 *210.00*
229 A23 25c Prus blue 17.00 *18.00*
230 A24 35c dp grn 1,000. *1,100.*
231 A24 40c slate blue 21.00 *25.00*
232 A24 45c dp grn 21.00 *25.00*
233 A24 55c Prus blue 11,000. *12,500.*
234 A24 60c violet 675.00 *775.00*
235 A24 65c brown 25.00 *30.00*
236 A24 70c org yel 47.50 *55.00*
237 A25 80c violet 500.00 *575.00*
238 A25 90c ultra 21.00 *25.00*
239 A25 1fr pale ol grn 26.00 *30.00*
240 A25 1.25fr brt rose 22.50 *26.00*
241 A25 1.40fr dk brn 21.00 *25.00*
242 A25 1.50fr bl grn 950.00 *1,100.*
243 A25 1.60fr rose vio 21.00 *25.00*
244 A26 2fr rose vio 87.50 *110.00*
245 A26 2.25fr brt blue 21.00 *25.00*
246 A26 2.50fr org yel 26.00 *30.00*
247 A26 3fr gray brn 12,500. *13,000.*
248 A26 5fr hen brn 2,500. *2,750.*
248A A26 20fr sl grn 1,200. *1,300.*

Nos. 176, 190 Srchd. in Black

249 A23 20c on 10c 14.50 *17.00*
250 A23 30c on 10c 12.00 *13.50*
251 A25 60c on 90c 13.50 *16.00*
252 A25 1.50fr on 90c 17.50 *20.00*
253 A23 2.50fr on 10c 22.50 *25.00*
254 A23 10fr on 10c 67.50 *80.00*
255 A25 20fr on 90c 75.00 *87.50*
Nos. 249-255 (7) 222.50 *259.00*

New York World's Fair Issue Overprinted type "a" in Black

Perf. 12½x12

256 CD82 1.25fr car lake 22.50 *25.00*
257 CD82 2.25fr ultra 21.00 *24.00*

Nos. 205-206 Surcharged

258 CD82 2.50fr on 1.25fr 22.50 25.00
259 CD82 3fr on 2.25fr 22.50 25.00

Stamps of 1938-40 Ovptd. in Carmine

1941 *Perf. 13½x13*

260 A23 10c bister brn 47.50 55.00
261 A23 20c blue violet 47.50 55.00
262 A23 25c Prus blue 47.50 55.00
263 A24 40c slate blue 47.50 55.00
264 A24 45c dp grn 52.50 60.00
265 A24 65c brown 52.50 60.00
266 A24 70c org yel 52.50 *60.00*
267 A25 80c violet 52.50 *60.00*
268 A25 90c ultra 52.50 *60.00*
269 A25 1fr pale ol grn 52.50 *60.00*
270 A25 1.25fr brt rose 52.50 *60.00*
271 A25 1.40fr dk brown 52.50 *60.00*
272 A25 1.60fr rose violet 52.50 *60.00*
273 A25 1.75fr brt blue 52.50 *60.00*
274 A26 2fr rose violet 52.50 *60.00*
275 A26 2.25fr brt blue 52.50 *60.00*
276 A26 2.50fr org yel 52.50 *60.00*
277 A26 3fr gray brn 52.50 *60.00*

Same Surcharged in Carmine with New Values

278 A23 10fr on 10c bis brn 125.00 *140.00*
279 A25 20fr on 90c ultra 125.00 *140.00*
Nos. 260-279 (20) 1,175. *1,340.*

Stamps of 1938-40 Overprinted in Black

280 A23 10c bister brn 72.50 *87.50*
281 A23 20c blue violet 72.50 *87.50*
282 A23 25c Prus blue 72.50 *87.50*
283 A24 40c slate blue 72.50 *87.50*
284 A24 45c dp grn 72.50 *87.50*
285 A24 65c brown 72.50 *87.50*
286 A24 70c orange yel 72.50 *87.50*
287 A25 80c violet 72.50 *87.50*
288 A25 90c ultra 72.50 *87.50*
289 A25 1fr pale ol grn 72.50 *87.50*
290 A25 1.25fr brt rose 72.50 *87.50*
291 A25 1.40fr dk brown 72.50 *87.50*
292 A25 1.60fr rose violet 72.50 *87.50*
293 A25 1.75fr brt blue 950.00 1,100.
294 A26 2fr rose vio 72.50 87.50
295 A26 2.25fr brt blue 72.50 87.50
296 A26 2.50fr orange yel 72.50 87.50
297 A26 3fr gray brn 72.50 87.50

Same Surcharged in Black with New Values

298 A23 10fr on 10c bis brn 175.00 *200.00*
299 A25 20fr on 90c ultra 190.00 225.00
Nos. 280-299 (20) 2,547. *3,012.*

Christmas Day plebiscite ordered by Vice Admiral Emile Henri Muselier, commander of the Free French naval forces (Nos. 260-299).

Types of 1938-40 Without RF

1942 Photo. *Perf. 13½*

299A A23 4c dk red vio .55
299B A23 15c red violet 1.40
299C A23 20c blue violet 1.40
299D A26 10fr dk blue 2.10
299E A26 20fr olive 2.50
Nos. 299A-299E (5) 7.95

Nos. 299A-299E were issued by the Vichy government in France, but were not placed on sale in St. Pierre & Miquelon.

> **Catalogue values for unused stamps in this section, from this point to the end of the section, are for Never Hinged items.**

St. Malo Fishing Schooner A28

1942 Photo. *Perf. 14x14½*

300 A28 5c dark blue .55 .30
301 A28 10c dull pink .50 .30
302 A28 25c brt green .50 .30
303 A28 30c slate black .50 .30
304 A28 40c brt grnsh blue .50 .30
305 A28 60c brown red .55 .40
306 A28 1fr dark violet .80 .65
307 A28 1.50fr brt red 1.75 1.40
308 A28 2fr brown 1.10 .80
309 A28 2.50fr brt ultra 1.75 1.40
310 A28 4fr dk orange 1.40 1.00
311 A28 5fr dp plum 1.50 1.10
312 A28 10fr lt ultra 2.10 1.75
313 A28 20fr dark green 2.40 1.90
Nos. 300-313 (14) 15.90 11.90

Nos. 300, 302, 309 Surcharged in Carmine or Black

1945

314 A28 50c on 5c (C) .50 .30
315 A28 70c on 5c (C) .50 .30
316 A28 80c on 5c (C) .55 .40
317 A28 1.20fr on 5c (C) .70 .55
318 A28 2.40fr on 25c .70 .55
319 A28 3fr on 25c .95 .80
320 A28 4.50fr on 25c 1.60 1.25
321 A28 15fr on 2.50fr (C) 2.00 1.75
Nos. 314-321 (8) 7.50 5.90

Eboue Issue
Common Design Type

1945 Engr. *Perf. 13*

322 CD91 2fr black 1.40 .95
323 CD91 25fr Prussian green 3.00 2.50

Nos. 322 and 323 exist imperforate. Value, set $47.50.

Soldiers' Bay — A29

Fishing Industry Symbols A30

Fishermen A31

Weighing the Catch A32

Fishing Boat and Dinghy A33

Storm-swept Coast — A34

1947, Oct. 6 Engr. *Perf. 12½*

324 A29 10c chocolate .55 .40
325 A29 30c violet .55 .40
326 A29 40c rose lilac .55 .40
327 A29 50c intense blue .55 .40
328 A30 60c carmine 1.25 .95
329 A30 80c brt ultra 1.25 .95
330 A30 1fr dk green 1.25 .95
331 A31 1.20fr blue grn 1.25 .95
332 A31 1.50fr black 1.25 .95
333 A31 2fr red brown 1.25 .95
334 A32 3fr rose violet 3.50 3.00
335 A32 3.60fr dp brown org 2.50 2.10
336 A32 4fr sepia 3.25 2.25
337 A33 5fr orange 3.50 2.50
338 A33 6fr blue 3.25 2.50
339 A33 10fr Prus green 4.50 3.25
340 A34 15fr dk slate grn 6.00 4.50
341 A34 20fr vermilion 8.50 6.50
342 A34 25fr dark blue 10.50 7.50
Nos. 324-342 (19) 55.20 41.40

Imperforates

Most stamps of St. Pierre and Miquelon from 1947 onward exist imperforate in issued and trial colors, and also in small presentation sheets in issued colors.

Silver Fox — A35

1952, Oct. 10 Unwmk. *Perf. 13*

343 A35 8fr dk brown 6.00 2.40
344 A35 17fr blue 7.50 3.25

Military Medal Issue
Common Design Type

1952, Dec. 15 Engr. & Typo.

345 CD101 8fr multicolored 17.00 13.00

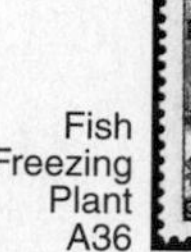

Fish Freezing Plant A36

1955-56 Engr.

346 A36 30c ultra & dk blue .95 .80
347 A36 50c gray, blk & sepia .95 .80
348 A36 3fr purple 1.60 1.10
349 A36 40fr Prussian blue 4.00 2.75
Nos. 346-349 (4) 7.50 5.45

Issued: 40fr, July 4; others, Oct. 22, 1956.

FIDES Issue

Fish Freezer "Le Galantry" A37

Perf. 13x12½

1956, Mar. 15 Unwmk.

350 A37 15fr blk brn & chestnut 6.50 3.50

See note in Common Design section after CD103.

Codfish A38

4fr, 10fr, Lighthouse and fishing fleet.

1957, Nov. 4 *Perf. 13*

351 A38 40c dk brn & grnsh bl .55 .35
352 A38 1fr brown & green .90 .55
353 A38 2fr indigo & dull blue 1.10 .90
354 A38 4fr maroon, car & pur 2.10 1.75
355 A38 10fr grnsh bl, dk bl & brn 3.00 2.50
Nos. 351-355 (5) 7.65 6.05

Human Rights Issue
Common Design Type

1958, Dec. 10 Engr. *Perf. 13*

356 CD105 20fr red brn & dk blue 3.50 2.50

Flower Issue
Common Design Type

1959, Jan. 28 Photo. *Perf. 12½x12*

357 CD104 5fr Spruce 4.50 2.40

Ice Hockey A39

1959, Oct. 7 Engr. *Perf. 13*

358 A39 20fr multicolored 3.75 2.00

Mink A40

1959, Oct. 7 Engr. *Perf. 13*

359 A40 25fr ind, yel grn & brn 5.25 2.40

Cypripedium Acaule — A41

Flower: 50fr, Calopogon pulchellus.

1962, Apr. 24 Unwmk. *Perf. 13*

360 A41 25fr grn, org & car rose 5.25 2.75
361 A41 50fr green & car lake 7.50 4.50
Nos. 360-361,C24 (3) 25.75 12.50

Eider Ducks — A42

Birds: 1fr, Rock ptarmigan. 2fr, Ringed plovers. 6fr, Blue-winged teal.

1963, Mar. 4 *Perf. 13*

362 A42 50c blk, ultra & ocher .95 .80
363 A42 1fr red brn, ultra & rose 1.40 .80
364 A42 2fr blk, dk bl & bis 1.75 1.25
365 A42 6fr multicolored 3.50 2.00
Nos. 362-365 (4) 7.60 4.85

Albert Calmette A43

1963, Aug. 5 Engr.

366 A43 30fr dk brn & dk blue 10.00 6.75

Albert Calmette, bacteriologist, birth cent.

Red Cross Centenary Issue
Common Design Type

1963, Sept. 2 Unwmk. *Perf. 13*

367 CD113 25fr ultra, gray & car 12.00 6.75

Human Rights Issue
Common Design Type

1963, Dec. 10 Unwmk. *Perf. 13*

368 CD117 20fr org, bl & dk brn 6.50 3.50

Philatec Issue
Common Design Type

1964, Apr. 4 Engr.

369 CD118 60fr choc, grn & dk bl 11.00 8.00

Rabbits A44

1964, Sept. 28 *Perf. 13*

370 A44 3fr shown 2.00 1.40
371 A44 4fr Fox 2.40 1.90
372 A44 5fr Roe deer 4.50 2.75
373 A44 34fr Charolais bull 14.00 7.50
Nos. 370-373 (4) 22.90 13.55

Airport and Map of St. Pierre and Miquelon A45

40fr, Television tube and tower, map. 48fr, Map of new harbor of St. Pierre.

1967 Engr. *Perf. 13*

374 A45 30fr ind, bl & dk red 8.00 4.50
375 A45 40fr sl grn, ol & dk red 8.00 4.50
376 A45 48fr dk red, brn & sl bl 12.00 5.25
Nos. 374-376 (3) 28.00 14.25

Issued: 30fr, 10/23; 40fr, 11/20; 48fr, 9/25.

WHO Anniversary Issue
Common Design Type

1968, May 4 Engr. *Perf. 13*

377 CD126 10fr multicolored 12.00 8.00

René de Chateaubriand and Map of Islands — A46

Designs: 4fr, J. D. Cassini and map. 15fr, Prince de Joinville, Francois F. d'Orleans (1818-1900), ships and map. 25fr, Admiral Gauchet, World War I warship and map.

1968, May 20 Photo. *Perf. 12½x13*

378 A46 4fr multicolored 5.50 3.50
379 A46 6fr multicolored 6.50 4.50
380 A46 15fr multicolored 10.00 5.25
381 A46 25fr multicolored 13.50 6.00
Nos. 378-381 (4) 35.50 19.25

Human Rights Year Issue
Common Design Type

1968, Aug. 10 Engr. *Perf. 13*

382 CD127 20fr bl, ver & org yel 10.00 5.50

Belle Rivière, Langlade A47

Design: 15fr, Debon Brook, Langlade.

1969, Apr. 30 Engr. *Perf. 13*
Size: 36x22mm

383 A47 5fr bl, slate grn & brn 4.00 2.75
384 A47 15fr brn, bl & dl grn 5.50 4.00
Nos. 383-384,C41-C42 (4) 50.00 27.75

Treasury A48

Designs: 25fr, Scientific and Technical Institute of Maritime Fishing. 30fr, Monument to seamen lost at sea. 60fr, St. Christopher College.

1969, May 30 Engr. *Perf. 13*

385 A48 10fr brt bl, cl & blk 5.25 2.75
386 A48 25fr dk bl, brt bl & brn red 9.25 4.50
387 A48 30fr blue, grn & gray 10.00 5.50
388 A48 60fr brt bl, brn red & blk 17.00 9.50
Nos. 385-388 (4) 41.50 22.25

Ringed Seals A49

Designs: 3fr, Sperm whales. 4fr, Pilot whales. 6fr, Common dolphins.

1969, Oct. 6 Engr. *Perf. 13*

389 A49 1fr lil, vio brn & red brn 2.75 2.40
390 A49 3fr bl grn, ind & red 2.75 2.40
391 A49 4fr ol, gray grn & mar 5.25 3.50
392 A49 6fr brt grn, pur & red 6.75 3.50
Nos. 389-392 (4) 17.50 11.80

L'Estoile and Granville, France A50

40fr, "La Jolie" & St. Jean de Luz, France, 1750. 48fr, "Le Juste" & La Rochelle, France, 1860.

1969, Oct. 13 Engr. *Perf. 13*
393 A50 34fr grn, mar & slate grn 17.00 9.50
394 A50 40fr brn red, lem & sl grn 26.00 9.50
395 A50 48fr multicolored 35.00 12.00
Nos. 393-395 (3) 78.00 31.00

Historic ships connecting St. Pierre and Miquelon with France.

ILO Issue
Common Design Type

1969, Nov. 24
396 CD131 20fr org, gray & ocher 10.00 5.50

UPU Headquarters Issue
Common Design Type

1970, May 20 Engr. *Perf. 13*
397 CD133 25fr dk car, brt bl & brn 14.00 8.00
398 CD133 34fr maroon, brn & gray 20.00 9.50

Rowers and Globe A51

1970, Oct. 13 Photo. *Perf. 12½x12*
399 A51 20fr lt grnsh bl & brn 18.00 8.00

World Rowing Championships, St. Catherine.

Blackberries A52

1970, Oct. 20 Engr. *Perf. 13*
400 A52 3fr shown 2.00 1.40
401 A52 4fr Strawberries 2.00 1.60
402 A52 5fr Raspberries 2.75 1.75
403 A52 6fr Blueberries 5.25 2.50
Nos. 400-403 (4) 12.00 7.25

Ewe and Lamb A53

30fr, Animal quarantine station. 34fr, Charolais bull. 48fr, Refrigeration ship slaughterhouse.

1970 Engr. *Perf. 13*
404 A53 15fr plum, grn & olive 12.00 4.50
405 A53 30fr sl, bis brn & ap grn 16.00 6.75
406 A53 34fr red lil, org brn & emer 26.00 8.75
407 A53 48fr multicolored 21.00 8.00
Nos. 404-407 (4) 75.00 28.00

Issue dates: 48fr, Nov. 10; others, Dec. 8.

Saint François d'Assise 1900 A54

Ships: 35fr, Sainte Jehanne, 1920. 40fr, L'Aventure, 1950. 80fr, Commandant Bourdais, 1970.

1971, Aug. 25
408 A54 30fr Prus bl & hn brn 32.50 14.50
409 A54 35fr Prus bl, lt grn & ol brn 45.00 14.50
410 A54 40fr sl grn, bl & dk brn 55.00 15.00
411 A54 80fr dp grn, bl & blk 65.00 20.00
Nos. 408-411 (4) 197.50 64.00

Deep-sea fishing fleet.

"Aconit" and Map of Islands — A55

1971, Sept. 27 Engr. *Perf. 13*
412 A55 22fr shown 32.50 13.00
413 A55 25fr Alysse 37.50 13.50
414 A55 50fr Mimosa 45.00 20.00
Nos. 412-414 (3) 115.00 46.50

Rallying of the Free French forces, 30th anniv.

Ship's Bell — A56

St. Pierre Museum: 45fr, Old chart and sextants, horiz.

1971, Oct. 25 Photo. *Perf. 12½x13*
415 A56 20fr gray & multi 21.00 8.50
416 A56 45fr red brn & multi 37.50 15.00

De Gaulle Issue
Common Design Type

Designs: 35fr, Gen. de Gaulle, 1940. Pres. de Gaulle, 1970.

1971, Nov. 9 Engr. *Perf. 13*
417 CD134 35fr vermilion & blk 22.50 12.00
418 CD134 45fr vermilion & blk 35.00 18.00

Haddock A57

Fish: 3fr, Hippoglossoides platessoides. 5fr, Sebastes mentella. 10fr, Codfish.

1972, Mar. 7
419 A57 2fr vio bl, ind & pink 5.25 2.50
420 A57 3fr grn & gray olive 6.75 3.75
421 A57 5fr Prus bl & brick red 6.75 3.50
422 A57 10fr grn & slate grn 13.00 6.00
Nos. 419-422 (4) 31.75 15.75

Oldsquaws — A58

Birds: 10c, 70c, Puffins. 20c, 90c, Snow owl. 40c, like 6c. Identification of birds on oldsquaw and puffin stamps transposed.

1973, Jan. 1 Engr. *Perf. 13*
423 A58 6c Prus bl, pur & brn 2.25 1.25
424 A58 10c Prus bl, blk & org 3.25 1.90
425 A58 20c ultra, bis & dk vio 3.50 2.50
426 A58 40c pur, sl grn & brn 6.00 3.00
427 A58 70c brt grn, blk & org 10.00 4.00
428 A58 90c Prus bl, bis & pur 13.00 6.00
Nos. 423-428 (6) 38.00 18.65

Indoor Swimming Pool — A59

Design: 1fr, Cultural Center of St. Pierre.

1973, Sept. 25 Engr. *Perf. 13*
429 A59 60c brn, brt bl & dk car 5.50 3.50
430 A59 1fr bl grn, ocher & choc 8.00 4.75

Opening of Cultural Center of St. Pierre.

Map of Islands, Weather Balloon and Ship, WMO Emblem A60

1974, Mar. 23 Engr. *Perf. 13*
431 A60 1.60fr multicolored 13.00 6.50

World Meteorological Day.

Gannet Holding Letter — A61

1974, Oct. 9 Engr. *Perf. 13*
432 A61 70c blue & multi 6.00 2.75
433 A61 90c red & multi 7.50 4.50

Centenary of Universal Postal Union.

Clasped Hands over Red Cross — A62

1974, Oct. 15 Photo. *Perf. 12½x13*
434 A62 1.50fr multicolored 12.00 5.50

Honoring blood donors.

Hands Putting Money into Fish-shaped Bank — A63

1974, Nov. 15 Engr. *Perf. 13*
435 A63 50c ocher & vio bl 6.75 4.00

St. Pierre Savings Bank centenary.

Church of St. Pierre and Seagulls A64

Designs: 10c, Church of Miquelon and fish. 20c, Church of Our Lady of the Sailors, and fishermen.

1974, Dec. 9 Engr. *Perf. 13*
436 A64 6c multicolored 2.50 1.75
437 A64 10c multicolored 4.50 2.00
438 A64 20c multicolored 6.50 2.75
Nos. 436-438 (3) 13.50 6.50

Danaus Plexippus A65

Design: 1fr, Vanessa atalanta, vert.

1975, July 17 Litho. *Perf. 12½*
439 A65 1fr blue & multi 12.00 5.00
440 A65 1.20fr green & multi 17.50 5.50

Pottery — A66

Mother and Child, Wood Carving — A67

1975, Oct. 2 Engr. *Perf. 13*
441 A66 50c ol, brn & choc 4.50 3.50
442 A67 60c blue & dull yel 6.50 3.50

Local handicrafts.

Pointe Plate Lighthouse and Murres A68

10c, Galantry lighthouse and Atlantic puffins. 20c, Cap Blanc lighthouse, whale and squid.

1975, Oct. 21
443 A68 6c vio bl, blk & lt grn 3.25 2.25
444 A68 10c lil rose, blk & dk ol 5.50 3.50
445 A68 20c blue, indigo & brn 8.25 6.75
Nos. 443-445 (3) 17.00 12.50

Georges Pompidou (1911-74), Pres. of France — A68a

1976, Feb. 17 Engr. *Perf. 13*
446 A68a 1.10fr brown & slate 7.25 4.00

Georges Pompidou (1911-1974), President of France.

Washington and Lafayette, American Flag — A69

1976, July 12 Photo. *Perf. 13*
447 A69 1fr multicolored 7.00 3.50

American Bicentennial.

Woman Swimmer and Maple Leaf — A70

70c, Basketball and maple leaf, vert.

1976, Aug. 10 Engr. *Perf. 13*

448	A70	70c multicolored	6.00	4.00
449	A70	2.50fr multicolored	12.50	5.00

21st Olympic Games, Montreal, Canada, July 17-Aug. 1.

Vigie Dam — A71

1976, Sept. 7 Engr. *Perf. 13*

450	A71	2.20fr multicolored	9.50	5.00

Croix de Lorraine — A72

Fishing Vessels: 1.40fr, Goelette.

1976, Oct. 5 Photo. *Perf. 13*

451	A72	1.20fr multicolored	10.00	4.50
452	A72	1.40fr multicolored	12.00	6.75

France Nos. 1783-1784, 1786-1789, 1794, 1882, 1799, 1885, 1802, 1889, 1803-1804 and 1891 Ovptd. "SAINT PIERRE / ET / MIQUELON"

1986, Feb. 4 Engr. *Perf. 13*

453	A915	5c dark green	.50	.50
454	A915	10c dull red	.30	.30
455	A915	20c brt green	.30	.30
456	A915	30c orange	.30	.30
457	A915	40c brown	.30	.30
458	A915	50c lilac	.30	.30
459	A915	1fr olive green	.50	.50
460	A915	1.80fr emerald	.90	.70
461	A915	2fr brt yellow grn	.90	.75
462	A915	2.20fr red	1.00	.70
463	A915	3fr chocolate brn	1.25	1.00
464	A915	3.20fr sapphire	1.60	1.00
465	A915	4fr brt carmine	1.75	1.40
466	A915	5fr gray blue	2.25	1.75
467	A915	10fr purple	4.50	2.75
		Nos. 453-467 (15)	16.65	12.55

Discovery of St. Pierre & Miquelon by Jacques Cartier, 450th Anniv. — A73

1986, June 11 Engr. *Perf. 13*

476	A73	2.20fr sep, sage grn & redsh brn	1.50	.90

Statue of Liberty, Cent. — A74

1986, July 4

477	A74	2.50fr Statue, St. Pierre Harbor	1.75	1.25

Fishery Resources — A75

1986-89 Engr. *Perf. 13*

478	A75	1fr bright red	.75	.40
479	A75	1.10fr brt orange	.65	.45
480	A75	1.30fr dark red	.75	.50
481	A75	1.40fr violet	1.00	.55
482	A75	1.40fr dark red	.75	.50
483	A75	1.50fr brt ultra	.90	.55
484	A75	1.60fr emerald grn	.90	.60
485	A75	1.70fr green	.95	.55
		Nos. 478-485 (8)	6.65	4.10

Issued: 1fr, #481, 10/22; 1.10fr, 1.50fr, 10/14/87; 1.30fr, 1.60fr, 8/7/88; #482, 1.70fr, 7/14/89.

Holy Family, Stained Glass by J. Balmet — A76

1986, Dec. 10 Litho. *Perf. 13*

486	A76	2.20fr multicolored	1.50	1.00

Christmas.

Hygrophorus Pratensis — A77

No. 488, Russula paludosa britz. No. 489, Tricholoma virgatum. No. 490, Hydnum repandum.

1987-90 Engr. *Perf. 12½*

487	A77	2.50fr multicolored	1.75	1.00
488	A77	2.50fr multicolored	1.40	.90
489	A77	2.50fr multicolored	1.00	.90
490	A77	2.50fr multicolored	1.00	.90
		Nos. 487-490 (4)	5.15	3.70

Issued: #487, Feb. 14; #488, Jan. 29, 1988; #489, Jan. 28, 1989; #490, Jan. 17, 1990.

Dr. François Dunan (1884-1961), Clinic — A78

1987, Apr. 29 Engr. *Perf. 13*

491	A78	2.20fr brt bl, blk & dk red brn	1.25	.90

Transat Yacht Race, Lorient to St. Pierre to Lorient A79

1987, May 16

492	A79	5fr dp ultra, dk rose brn & brt bl	2.50	1.40

Visit of Pres. Mitterand A80

1987, May 29 Litho. *Perf. 12½x13*

493	A80	2.20fr dull ultra, gold & scar	2.00	1.00

Marine Slip, Cent. A81

1987, June 20 Litho. *Perf. 13*

494	A81	2.50fr pale sal & dk red brn	1.75	1.10

Stern Trawler La Normande — A82

1987-91 Photo.

495	A82	3fr shown	3.00	1.75
496	A82	3fr Le Marmouset	1.50	1.10
497	A82	3fr Tugboat Le Malabar	1.25	.80
498	A82	3fr St. Denis, St. Pierre	1.25	.90
499	A82	3fr Cryos	1.25	.90
		Nos. 495-499 (5)	8.25	5.45

Issued: #495, 10/14; #496, 9/28/88; #497, 10/11/89; #498, 10/24/90; #499, 11/6/91.

St. Christopher and the Christ Child, Stained Glass Window and Scout Emblem — A83

1987, Dec. 9 Litho. *Perf. 13*

503	A83	2.20fr multicolored	1.50	1.00

Christmas, Scout movement in St. Pierre & Miquelon, 50th anniv.

The Great Barachoise Nature Reserve — A84

1987, Dec. 16 Engr. *Perf. 13x12½*

504	3fr Horses, waterfowl	2.00	1.25
505	3fr Waterfowl, seals	2.00	1.25
a.	A84 Pair, #504-505 + label	4.50	3.25

No. 505a is in continous design.

1988, Nov. 2

506	A84	2.20fr Ross Cove	1.50	.75
507	A84	13.70fr Cap Perce	5.50	4.75
a.		Pair, #506-507 + label	8.50	8.50

No. 507a is in continous design.

1988 Winter Olympics, Calgary A86

1988, Mar. 5 Engr. *Perf. 13*

508	A86	5fr brt ultra & dark red	2.25	1.60

Louis Thomas (1887-1976), Photographer — A87

1988, May 4 Engr. *Perf. 13*

509	A87	2.20fr blk, dk ol bis & Prus bl	1.10	.70

France No. 2105 Overprinted "ST-PIERRE ET MIQUELON"

1988, July 25 Engr. *Perf. 13*

510	A1107	2.20fr ver, blk & violet blue	1.75	.90

Seizure of Schooner Nellie J. Banks, 50th Anniv. A88

1988, Aug. 7

511	A88	2.50fr brn, vio blue & brt blue	1.75	1.10

The Nellie J. Banks was seized by Canada for carrying prohibited alcohol in 1938.

Christmas — A89

1988, Dec. 17 Litho. *Perf. 13*

512	A89	2.20fr multicolored	1.10	.90

Judo Competitions in St. Pierre & Miquelon, 25th Anniv. — A90

1989, Mar. 4 Engr. *Perf. 13*

513 A90 5fr brn org, blk & yel grn 2.25 1.40

French Revolution Bicent.; 40th Anniv. of the UN Declaration of Human Rights (in 1988) — A91

1989 Engr. *Perf. 12½x13*

514	A91	2.20fr Liberty	1.00	.75
515	A91	2.20fr Equality	1.00	.75
516	A91	2.20fr Fraternity	1.00	.75
		Nos. 514-516 (3)	3.00	2.25

Issued: #514, 3/22; #515, 5/3; #516, 6/17.

Souvenir Sheet

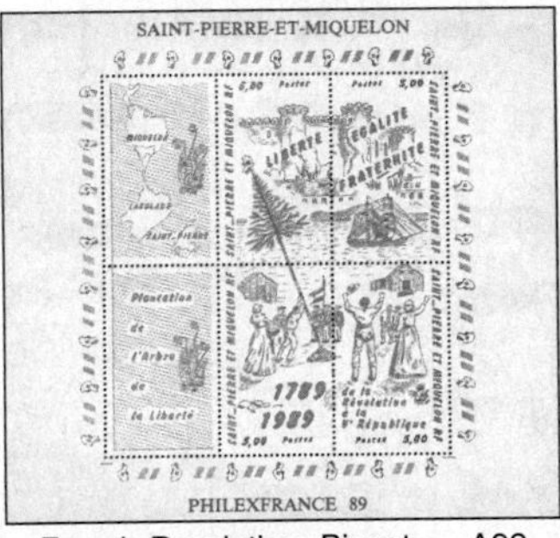

French Revolution, Bicent. — A92

Designs: a, Bastille, liberty tree. b, Bastille, ship. c, Building, revolutionaries raising flag and liberty tree. d, Revolutionaries, building with open doors.

1989, July 14 Engr. *Perf. 13*

517 A92 Sheet of 4 + 2 labels 9.50 9.50
a.-d. 5fr any single 2.25 2.25

Heritage of Ile aux Marins — A93

Designs: 2.20fr, Coastline, ships in harbor, girl in boat, fish. 13.70fr, Coastline, ships in harbor, boy flying kite from boat, map of Ile aux Marins.

1989, Sept. 9 Engr. *Perf. 13x12½*

518		2.20fr multi	1.75	.70
519		13.70fr multi	5.75	4.25
a.	A93	Pair, #518-519 + label	8.50	8.50

Nos. 519a is in continuous design.

Christmas — A96

1989, Dec. 2 Litho. *Perf. 13*

521 A96 2.20fr multicolored 1.10 .75

France Nos. 2179-2182, 2182A-2186, 2188-2189, 2191-2194, 2204B, 2331, 2333-2334, 2336-2339, 2342 Ovptd.

1990-96 Engr. *Perf. 13*

522	A1161	10c brn blk	.25	.25
523	A1161	20c light grn	.25	.25
524	A1161	50c bright vio	.25	.25
525	A1161	1fr orange	.50	.35
526	A1161	2fr apple grn	.90	.70
527	A1161	2fr blue	1.00	.75
528	A1161	2.10fr green	.95	.75
529	A1161	2.20fr green	1.10	.80
530	A1161	2.30fr red	1.10	.30
531	A1161	2.40fr emerald	1.25	.50
532	A1161	2.50fr red	1.25	.25
533	A1161	2.70fr emerald	1.25	1.10
534	A1161	3.20fr bright bl	1.75	1.10
535	A1161	3.40fr blue	1.75	.95
536	A1161	3.50fr apple grn	1.75	.75
537	A1161	3.80fr brt pink	2.00	.75
538	A1161	3.80fr blue	1.75	.75
539	A1161	4fr brt lil rose	2.25	.75
540	A1161	4.20fr rose lilac	2.25	.95
541	A1161	4.40fr blue	2.10	1.00
542	A1161	4.50fr magenta	2.40	1.90
543	A1161	5fr dull blue	2.00	1.00
544	A1161	10fr violet	4.00	1.00
544A	A1161	(2.50fr) red	1.50	.50
		Nos. 522-544A (24)	35.55	17.65

Booklet Stamps

Self-Adhesive

Die Cut

545	A1161	2.50fr red	1.60	1.00
a.		Booklet pane of 10	16.00	
545B	A1161	(2.80fr) red	1.75	1.10
a.		Booklet pane of 10	17.50	

Issued: 2.30fr, 1/2/90; 2.10fr, 2/5/90; 10c, 20c, 50c, 3.20fr, #537, 4/17/90; 1fr, 5fr, #526, 10fr, 7/16/90; #532, 2.20fr, 12/21/91; 3.40fr, 4fr, 1/8/92; #545, 2/8/92; 4.20fr, 1/13/93; #544A, 7/5/93; 2.40fr, 3.50fr, 4.40fr, #545B, 10/6/93; #527, 8/17/94; #538, 4/10/96; 2.70fr, 4.50fr, 6/12/96.

Gen. Charles de Gaulle's Call for French Resistance, 50th Anniv. — A97

1990, June 18 *Perf. 13*

546 A97 2.30fr red, claret & blue 1.10 .70

Charles de Gaulle (1890-1970) A98

Design: 1.70fr, De Gaulle as General. 2.30fr, De Gaulle as President of France.

1990, Nov. 22

547	A98	1.70fr red, claret & blue	.75	.55
548	A98	2.30fr red, claret & blue	1.25	.80
a.		Pair, #547-548 + central label	2.25	2.25

25 Kilometer Race of Miquelon A99

1990, June 23

549 A99 5fr Runner, map 2.10 1.10

Micmac Canoe, 1875 A100

1990, Aug. 15 Engr. *Perf. 13x13½*

550 A100 2.50fr multicolored 1.25 .70

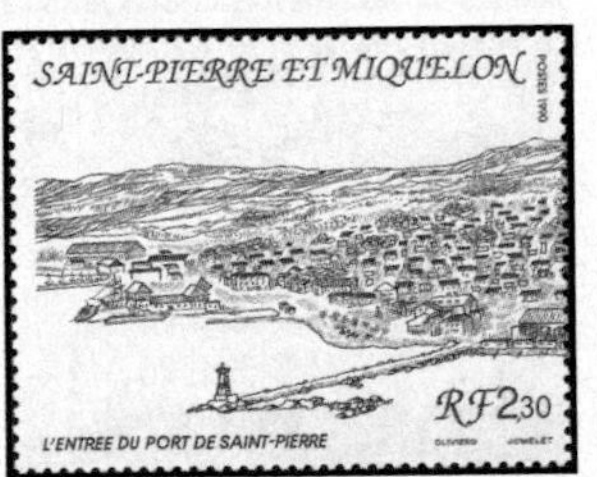

Views of St. Pierre — A101

Harbor scene.

1990, Oct. 24 Engr. *Perf. 13x12½*

551	A101	2.30fr bl, grn & brn	1.00	.50
552	A101	14.50fr bl, grn & brn	6.50	3.50
a.		Pair, #551-552 + label	9.00	9.00

No. 552a is in continous design.

Christmas — A103

1990, Dec. 15 Litho.

553 A103 2.30fr multicolored 1.25 .65

Papilio Brevicaudata A104

3.60fr, Aeshna Eremita, Nuphar Variegatum.

1991-92 Litho. *Perf. 13*

554 A104 2.50fr multicolored 1.25 .95

Perf. 12

555 A104 3.60fr multicolored 1.60 1.00

Issued: 2.50fr, Jan. 16; 3.60fr, Mar. 4, 1992.

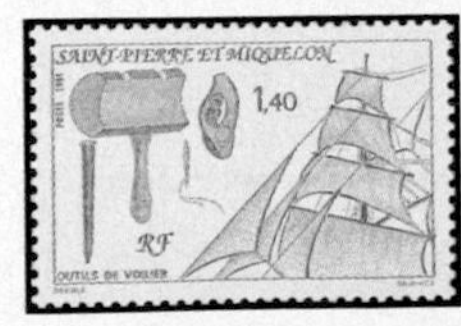

Marine Tools, Sailing Ship A105

Litho. & Engr.

1991, Mar. 6 *Perf. 13*

559	A105	1.40fr yellow & green	.75	.50
560	A105	1.70fr yellow & red	.90	.55

Scenic Views A106

Designs: Nos. 548, 552, Saint Pierre. Nos. 549, 553, Ile aux Marins. Nos. 550, 554, Langlade. Nos. 551, 555, Miquelon.

1991, Apr. 17 Engr. *Perf. 13*

561	A106	1.70fr blue	.80	.65
562	A106	1.70fr blue	.80	.65
563	A106	1.70fr blue	.80	.65
564	A106	1.70fr blue	.80	.65
a.		Strip of 4, #561-564	3.25	3.25
565	A106	2.50fr red	1.25	.95
566	A106	2.50fr red	1.25	.95
567	A106	2.50fr red	1.25	.95
568	A106	2.50fr red	1.25	.95
a.		Strip of 4, #565-568	5.00	5.00
		Nos. 561-568 (8)	8.20	6.40

Lyre Music Society, Cent. — A107

1991, June 21 Engr. *Perf. 13*

569 A107 2.50fr multicolored 1.10 .70

Newfoundland Crossing by Rowboat "Los Gringos" — A108

1991, Aug. 3 Engr. *Perf. 13x12½*

570 A108 2.50fr multicolored 1.10 .70

Basque Sports A109

1991, Aug. 24 *Perf. 13*

571 A109 5fr red & green 2.10 1.40

Natural Heritage — A110

2.50fr, Fishermen. 14.50fr, Shoreline, birds.

1991, Oct. 18 Engr. *Perf. 13x12½*

572	A110	2.50fr multicolored	1.50	.90
573	A110	14.50fr multicolored	6.50	5.00
a.		Pair, #572-573 + label	8.50	8.50

No. 573a is in continuous design.

George Landry and Bank Emblem A95

1989, Nov. 8 Engr. *Perf. 13*

520 A95 2.20fr bl & golden brn 1.10 .75

Bank of the Islands, cent.

Central Economic Cooperation Bank, 50th Anniv. — A111

1991, Dec. 2 Engr. *Perf. 13x12½*
574 A111 2.50fr 1941 100fr note 1.10 .70

Christmas A112

1991, Dec. 21 Litho. *Perf. 13*
575 A112 2.50fr multicolored 1.10 .75

Christmas Day Plebiscite, 50th anniv.

Vice Admiral Emile Henri Muselier (1882-1965), Commander of Free French Naval Forces — A113

1992, Jan. 8 Litho. *Perf. 13*
576 A113 2.50fr multicolored 1.50 .75

1992 Winter Olympics, Albertville A114

1992, Feb. 8 Engr. *Perf. 13*
577 A114 5fr vio bl, blue & mag 2.10 1.25

Caulking Tools, Bow of Ship A115

Litho. & Engr.

1992, Apr. 1 *Perf. 13x12½*
578 A115 1.50fr pale bl gray & brn .75 .45
579 A115 1.80fr pale bl gray & bl .90 .45

Lighthouses — A116

Designs: a, Galantry. b, Feu Rouge. c, Pointe-Plate. d, Ile Aux Marins.

1992, July 8 Litho. *Perf. 13*
580 A116 2.50fr Strip of 4, #a.-d. 5.50 3.50

Natural Heritage — A117

1992, Sept. 9 Engr. *Perf. 13x12½*
581 A117 2.50fr Langlade 1.50 .75
582 A117 15.10fr Doulisie Valley 7.50 3.75
a. Pair, #581-582 + label 9.00 9.00

No. 582a is in continuous design.
See Nos. 593-594, 605-606.

Discovery of America, 500th Anniv. — A118

Photo. & Engr.

1992, Oct. 12 *Perf. 13x12½*
583 A118 5.10fr multicolored 2.25 1.25

Le Baron de L'Esperance — A119

1992, Nov. 18 Engr. *Perf. 13*
584 A119 2.50fr claret, brn & bl 1.25 .75

Christmas — A120

1992, Dec. 9 Litho. *Perf. 13*
585 A120 2.50fr multicolored 1.25 .80

Commander R. Birot (1906-1942) — A121

1993, Jan. 13
586 A121 2.50fr multicolored 1.50 .90

Deep Sea Diving A122

1993, Feb. 10 Engr. *Perf. 12*
587 A122 5fr multicolored 2.50 1.25

A123

Monochamus Scutellatus, Cichorium Intybus.

1993, Mar. 10 Litho. *Perf. 13½x13*
588 A123 3.60fr multicolored 1.50 .80

See No. 599.

A124

Slicing cod.

1993, Apr. 7 Litho. *Perf. 13½x13*
589 A124 1.50fr green & multi .75 .50
590 A124 1.80fr red & multi .90 .55

Move to the Magdalen Islands, Quebec, by Miquelon Residents, Bicent. — A125

1993, June 9 Engr. *Perf. 13*
591 A125 5.10fr brn, bl & grn 2.10 1.25

Fish A126

Designs: a, Capelin. b, Ray. c, Halibut (fletan). d, Toad fish (crapaud).

1993, July 30 Photo. *Perf. 13*
592 A126 2.80fr Strip of 4, #a.-d. 6.00 6.00

Natl. Heritage Type of 1992

1993, Aug. 18 Engr. *Perf. 13x12½*
593 A117 2.80fr Miquelon 1.50 1.00
594 A117 16fr Otter pool 6.50 5.75
a. Pair, #593-594 + label 9.00 9.00

No. 594a is a continuous design.

Commissioner's Residence — A127

1993, Oct. 6 Engr. *Perf. 13*
595 A127 3.70fr multicolored 1.60 .90

Christmas A128

1993, Dec. 13 Litho. *Perf. 13*
596 A128 2.80fr multicolored 1.50 .80

Commander Louis Blaison (1906-1942), Submarine Surcouf — A129

1994, Jan. 12 Litho. *Perf. 13*
597 A129 2.80fr multicolored 1.60 .80

Petanque World Championships — A130

1994, Feb. 9 Engr. *Perf. 12½x12*
598 A130 5.10fr multicolored 2.25 1.75

Insect and Flower Type of 1993

Cristalis tenax, taraxacum officinale, horiz.

1994, Mar. 9 Litho. *Perf. 13x13½*
599 A123 3.70fr multicolored 2.00 1.25

Drying Codfish, 1905 A131

1994 Litho. *Perf. 13*
600 A131 1.50fr blk & bl grn .75 .55
601 A131 1.80fr multicolored 1.00 .65

Issued: 1.50fr, 5/4/94; 1.80fr, 4/6/94.

Women's Right to Vote, 50th Anniv. A132

1994, Apr. 21
602 A132 2.80fr multicolored 1.50 .80

Hospital Ship St. Pierre, Cent. A133

1994, July 2
603 A133 2.80fr multicolored 1.50 .80

Souvenir Sheet

Ships — A134

Designs: a, Miquelon. b, Isle of St. Pierre. c, St. George XII. d, St. Eugene IV.

1994, July 6 ***Perf. 12***

604 A134 Sheet of 4 8.50 8.50
a.-b. 2.80fr any single 1.50 1.25
c.-d. 3.70fr any single 2.00 1.75

See No. 628.

Natl. Heritage Type of 1992

1994, Aug. 17 **Engr.** ***Perf. 13***

605 A117 2.80fr Woods 2.00 .90
606 A117 16fr "The Hat" 7.50 4.00
a. Pair, #605-606 + label 10.50 10.00

Parochial School A135

1994, Oct. 5 **Engr.** ***Perf. 13***

607 A135 3.70fr multicolored 1.50 .95

Stamp Show A136

1994, Oct. 15

608 A136 3.70fr grn, yel & bl 1.75 1.10

Christmas A137

1994, Nov. 23 **Litho.** ***Perf. 13***

609 A137 2.80fr multicolored 1.50 .80

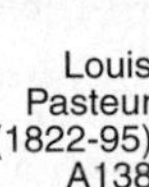

Louis Pasteur (1822-95) A138

1995, Jan. 11 **Litho.** ***Perf. 13***

610 A138 2.80fr multicolored 1.50 .80

Triathlon A139

1995, Feb. 8 **Engr.** ***Perf. 12***

611 A139 5.10fr multicolored 2.25 1.25

A140

Dicranum Scoparium & Cladonia Cristatella.

1995, Mar. 8 **Litho.** ***Perf. 13***

612 A140 3.70fr multicolored 1.60 1.10

See Nos. 625, 635.

A141

Cooper and his tools.

1995, Apr. 5 **Litho.** ***Perf. 13½x13***

613 A141 1.50fr black & multi .75 .50
614 A141 1.80fr red & multi .90 .55

Shellfish A142

a, Snail. b, Crab. c, Scallop. d, Lobster.

1995, July 5 **Litho.** ***Perf. 13***

616 Strip of 4 6.00 6.00
a.-d. A142 2.80fr any single 1.40 1.00

Geological Mission — A143

Designs: 2.80fr, Rugged terrain along shoreline, diagram of mineral location, zircon. 16fr, Geological map, terrain.

1995, Aug. 16 **Engr.** ***Perf. 13x12½***

617 A143 2.80fr multicolored 2.00 1.00
618 A143 16fr multicolored 7.00 5.00
a. Pair, #617-618 + label 9.50 9.50

Sister Cesarine (1845-1922), St. Joseph de Cluny — A144

1995, Sept. 6 **Litho.** ***Perf. 13***

619 A144 1.80fr multicolored 1.00 .75

The Francoforum Public Building — A145

1995, Oct. 4 **Engr.**

620 A145 3.70fr multicolored 1.75 1.00

Christmas — A146

Design: 2.80fr, Toys in store window.

1995, Nov. 22 **Litho.** ***Perf. 13***

621 A146 2.80fr multicolored 1.50 .90

Charles de Gaulle (1890-1970) A147

1995, Nov. 9 **Litho.** ***Perf. 13x13½***

622 A147 14fr multicolored 5.75 3.50

Commandant Jean Levasseur (1909-47) — A148

1996, Jan. 10 ***Perf. 13***

623 A148 2.80fr multicolored 1.50 .80

Boxing A149

1996, Feb. 7 **Engr.** ***Perf. 12x12½***

624 A149 5.10fr multicolored 2.50 1.25

Plant Type of 1995

Design: Cladonia verticillata and polytrichum juniperinum.

1996, Mar. 13 **Litho.** ***Perf. 13***

625 A140 3.70fr multicolored 1.75 1.10

Blacksmiths and Their Tools A150

1996, Apr. 10

626 A150 1.50fr black & multi .75 .35
627 A150 1.80fr red & multi .85 .50

Ship Type of 1994

Designs: a, Radar II. b, SPM Roro. c, Pinta. d, Pascal Anne.

1996, July 10 **Litho.** ***Perf. 13***

628 Sheet of 4 7.00 7.00
a.-d. A134 3fr Any single 1.50 1.00

Aerial View of Miquelon — A151

Designs: 3fr, "Le Cap," mountains, buildings. 15.50fr, "Le Village," buildings.

1996, Aug. 14 **Engr.** ***Perf. 13x12½***

629 3fr multicolored 1.25 1.25
630 15.50fr multicolored 6.00 6.00
a. A151 Pair, #629-630 + label 7.75 7.75

Customs House, Cent. A152

1996, Oct. 9 **Engr.** ***Perf. 12½x13***

631 A152 3.80fr blue & black 1.50 .90

Fall Stamp Show — A153

1996, Nov. 6 **Litho.** ***Perf. 13***

632 A153 1fr multicolored .60 .45

Christmas — A154

1996, Nov. 20 **Litho.** ***Perf. 13***

633 A154 3fr multicolored 1.50 .90

Constant Colmay (1903-65) A155

1997, Jan. 8 **Litho.** ***Perf. 13***

634 A155 3fr multicolored 1.50 .90

Plant Type of 1995

Design: Phalacrocorax carbo, sedum rosea.

1997, Mar. 12 Litho. *Perf. 13*

635 A140 3.80fr multicolored 1.50 .90

Maritime Heritage A156

Designs: 1.70fr, Man in doorway of salt house. 2fr, Boat, naval architect's drawing.

1997, Apr. 9 Litho. *Perf. 13*

636 A156 1.70fr multicolored .75 .50

637 A156 2fr multicolored .90 .60

Volleyball A157

Litho. & Engr.

1997, Apr. 9 *Perf. 12*

638 A157 5.20fr multicolored 2.10 1.10

Fish — A158

a, Shark. b, Salmon. c, Poule d'eau. d, Mackerel.

1997, July 9 Litho. *Perf. 13*

639 A158 3fr Strip of 4, #a.-d. 6.50 4.50

Bay, Headlands — A159

3fr, Basque Cape. 15.50fr, Diamant.

1997, Aug. 13 *Perf. 13x12*

640 A159 3fr multicolored 1.50 1.00

641 A159 15.50fr multicolored 5.50 3.50

a. Pair #640-641 + label 7.00 6.25

France Nos. 2589-2603 Ovptd. "ST. PIERRE / ET / MIQUELON"

1997-98 Engr. *Perf. 13*

642 A1409 10c brown .25 .25

643 A1409 20c brt blue grn .25 .25

644 A1409 50c purple .30 .30

645 A1409 1fr bright org .35 .25

646 A1409 2fr bright blue .80 .30

647 A1409 2.70fr bright green 1.10 .30

648 A1409 (3fr) red 1.40 .30

649 A1409 3.50fr apple green 1.50 .55

650 A1409 3.80fr blue 1.40 .65

651 A1409 4.20fr dark orange 1.60 .65

652 A1409 4.40fr blue 1.75 .65

653 A1409 4.50fr bright pink 1.75 .75

654 A1409 5fr brt grn bl 1.90 .80

655 A1409 6.70fr dark green 2.75 1.25

656 A1409 10fr violet 3.75 1.40

Nos. 642-656 (15) 20.85 8.65

Issued: 2.70fr, (3fr), 3.80fr, 8/13/97; 10c, 20c, 50c, 3.50fr, 4.40fr, 10fr, 10/8/97; 1fr, 2fr, 4.20fr, 4.50fr, 5fr, 6.70fr, 1/7/98.

See No. 664 for self-adhesive (3fr).

Post Office Building A160

1997, Oct. 8 Engr. *Perf. 13*

657 A160 3.80fr multicolored 1.50 .90

Christmas — A161

1997, Nov. 19 Litho. *Perf. 13*

658 A161 3fr multicolored 1.50 .80

Alain Savary (1918-88), Governor, Territorial Deputy A162

1998, Jan. 7 Litho. *Perf. 13*

659 A162 3fr multicolored 1.40 .70

1998 Winter Olympic Games, Nagano A163

1998, Feb. 11 Engr. *Perf. 12*

660 A163 5.20fr Curling 2.25 1.10

Flora and Fauna A164

1998, Mar. 11 Photo. *Perf. 13*

661 A164 3.80fr multicolored 1.75 .95

Ice Workers A165

1998, Apr. 8 Litho.

662 A165 1.70fr shown .75 .65

663 A165 2fr Cutting ice from lake .90 .65

France Nos. 2604, 2620 Ovptd. "ST. PIERRE / ET / MIQUELON"

Die Cut x Serpentine Die Cut

1998, Apr. 8 Engr.

Self-Adhesive

664 A1409 (3fr) red 1.25 .60

a. Booklet pane of 10 15.00

No. 664a is a complete booklet. The peelable backing serves as a booklet cover.

1998, May 13 *Perf. 13*

665 A1424 3fr red & blue 1.25 .60

Houses — A166

a, Gray. b, Yellow, red roof. c, Pink. d, White, red roof.

1998, July 8 Litho. *Perf. 13*

666 A166 3fr Strip of 4, #a.-d. 5.00 2.50

French in North America — A167

1998, Sept. 30 Engr. *Perf. 13x12½*

670 A167 3fr multicolored 1.25 .60

Cape Blue Natl. Park — A168

Designs: 3fr, Point Plate Lighthouse, shoreline. 15.50fr, Cape Blue.

1998, Sept. 30 *Perf. 13x12*

671 A168 3fr multicolored 1.25 .95

672 A168 15.50fr multicolored 6.50 3.50

a. Pair, #671-672 + label 8.75 8.75

France, 1998 World Cup Soccer Champions A169

1998, Oct. 21 Litho. *Perf. 13*

673 A169 3fr multicolored 1.40 .60

Memorial to War Dead — A170

1998, Nov. 11 Engr.

674 A170 3.80fr multicolored 1.60 .75

Christmas — A171

1998, Nov. 18 Litho.

675 A171 3fr multicolored 1.25 .60

Emile Letournel (1927-94), Orthopedic Surgeon, Traumatologist — A172

1999, Jan. 6 Engr. *Perf. 13*

676 A172 3fr multicolored 1.25 .60

Painting, "The Beach at Fisherman Island," by Patrick Guillaume — A173

1999, Feb. 10 Litho.

677 A173 5.20fr multicolored 2.00 .95

See No. 692.

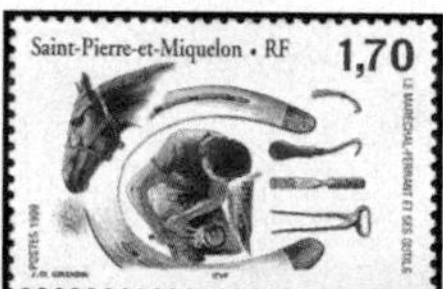

La Plate-Bière A174

3.80fr, Rubus chamaemorus.

1999, Mar. 10 Litho. *Perf. 13*

678 A174 3.80fr multicolored 1.60 .75

See No. 693, 705, 736.

Horseshoeing — A175

1.70fr, Horse, blacksmith and his tools. 2fr, Applying horseshoes in blacksmith's shop.

1999, Apr. 7 Litho. *Perf. 13*

679 A175 1.70fr multicolored .75 .50

680 A175 2fr multicolored .85 .50

France No. 2691 Ovptd. "ST. PIERRE / ET / MIQUELON"

1999, Apr. 7 Engr.

681 A1470 3fr red & blue 1.25 .60

Value is shown in both francs and euros on No. 681.

France No. 2691A Overprinted "ST. PIERRE / ET / MIQUELON"

Die Cux x Serpentine Die Cut 7

1999, Apr. 5 Engr.

Self-Adhesive

681A A1470 3fr red & blue 2.00 1.00

b. Booklet of 10 20.00

First Stamps of France, 150th Anniv. A176

a, France #3, St. Pierre & Miquelon #9, 79. b, #145, 270. c, #C21, C36. d, #476, 676.

1999, June 23 Litho. *Perf. 13*
682 A176 3fr Sheet of 4, #a.-d. 7.00 7.00

PhilexFrance '99, World Philatelic Exhibition.

Ships — A177

a, Bearn. b, Pro Patria. c, Erminie. d, Colombier.

1999, July 7 Litho. *Perf. 13x13½*
683 A177 3fr Sheet of 4, #a.-d. 6.00 6.00

General de Gaulle Place — A178

1999, Aug. 11 Engr. *Perf. 13x12¼*
684 3fr Cars, yield sign 1.00 1.00
685 15.50fr Docked boats 5.50 5.50
a. A178 Pair, #684-685 + label 6.50 6.50

Visit of Pres. Jacques Chirac, Sept. 1999 — A179

1999, Sept. 7 Litho. *Perf. 13¼x13*
686 A179 3fr multicolored 1.25 .60

Archives A180

1999, Oct. 6 Engr. *Perf. 13x12¾*
687 A180 5.40fr deep rose lilac 2.00 1.00

Christmas A181

1999, Nov. 17 Litho. *Perf. 13*
688 A181 3fr multi 1.50 .75

Year 2000 — A182

2000, Jan. 12 Litho. *Perf. 13¼x13*
689 A182 3fr multi 1.50 .75

Whales A183

Designs: 3fr, Megaptera novaeangliae. 5.70fr, Balaenoptera physalus.

2000, Jan. 26 Engr. *Perf. 13x12¾*
690 A183 3fr blk & Prus bl 1.25 .60
691 A183 5.70fr Prus grn & blk 2.75 1.10

See also Nos. 702-703.

Painting Type of 1999

2000, Feb. 9 Litho. *Perf. 13*
692 A173 5.20fr Les Graves 2.00 1.00

Plant Type of 1999

2000, Mar. 8
693 A174 3.80fr Vaccinium vitis-idaea 1.50 .70

Wood Gatherer A184

Vignette colors: 1.70fr, Blue. 2fr, Brown.

2000, Apr. 5 Engr.
694-695 A184 Set of 2 2.00 1.00

Millennium A185

No. 696: a, Lobstermen on Newfoundland coast, 1904. b, Women on shore, 1905. c, World War I conscripts on ship Chicago, 1915. d, Soldiers in action at Souain Hill, 1915. e, Men walking on ice, 1923. f, Unloading cases of champagne to be smuggled to US, 1925. g, St. Pierre & Miquelon Pavilion at Colonial Expostion in Paris, 1931. h, Alcohol smugglers, 1933. i, Adm. Emile Muselier inspecting troops on ship Mimosa, 1942. j, World War II soldiers crossing bridge, 1945.

No. 697: a, Fishery employees, 1951. b, Fishing trawler, 1960. c, Visit of Gen. Charles de Gaulle, 1967. d, First television images, 1967. e, Port facilities, 1970. f, New high school, 1977. g, Resumption of stamp issuing, 1986. h, Voyage fo Eric Tabarly, 1987. i, Exclusive Economic Zone, 1992. j, New airport, 1999.

2000 Litho. *Perf. 13x13¼*
696 Sheet of 10 16.00 13.00
a.-j. A185 3fr Any single 1.40 .75
697 Sheet of 10 14.00 11.00
a.-j. A185 2fr Any single 1.25 .75

Issue: No. 696, 6/21; No. 697, 12/6.

The Inger — A186

2000, Oct. 4 Engr. *Perf. 13x13¼*
698 A186 5.40fr green 3.00 1.40

Boathouses in November — A187

2000, Oct. 4 *Perf. 13x12¼*
699 Pair + central label 9.50 8.50
a. A187 3fr Hill 1.50 1.00
b. A187 15.50fr Church 7.50 5.00

Christmas — A188

2000, Nov. 15 Litho. *Perf. 13¼x13*
700 A188 3fr multi 1.50 .80

New Year 2001 — A189

2001, Jan. 3 Litho. *Perf. 13x12¾*
701 A189 3fr multi 3.00 1.75

Whale Type of 2000

Designs: 3fr, Orcinus orca. 5.70fr, Globicephala melaena.

2001, Jan. 24 Engr. *Perf. 13x12¾*
702-703 A183 Set of 2 4.00 2.40

Landscape A190

2001, Feb. 21 Litho. *Perf. 13*
704 A190 5.20fr multi 2.50 1.10

Plant Type of 1999

2001, Mar. 21 Litho. *Perf. 13*
705 A174 3.80fr Vaccinium oxycoccos 1.75 .80

Hay Gatherers A191

Denomination colors: 1.70fr, Red brown. 2fr, Lilac.

2001, Apr. 18
706-707 A191 Set of 2 2.00 .95

Seasons A192

Designs: No. 708, 3fr, Autumn. No. 709, 3fr, Winter.

2001, June 20
708-709 A192 Set of 2 3.00 1.50

See Nos. 714-715.

Vestibules — A193

No. 710: a, Guillou House. b, Jugan House. c, Ile-aux-Marins town hall. d, Vogé House.

2001, July 25
710 A193 Horiz. strip of 4 5.75 5.00
a.-d. 3fr Any single 1.50 1.00

Anse du Gouvernement — A194

Houses and: a, Boat. b, Rocks near shore.

2001, Sept. 12 Engr. *Perf. 13x12¼*
711 A194 Horiz. pair, #a-b, + central label 10.00 8.50
a.-b. 10fr Any single 4.75 3.25

Saint Pierre Pointe Blanche — A195

2001, Sept. 26 Litho. *Perf. 13*
712 A195 5fr multi 2.40 1.40

The Marie-Thérèse — A196

2001, Sept. 26 Engr. *Perf. 13x13¼*
713 A196 5.40fr green 2.60 1.40

Seasons Type of 2001

Designs: No. 714, 3fr, Spring. No. 715, 3fr, Summer

2001, Oct. 17 Litho. *Perf. 13*
714-715 A192 Set of 2 3.00 1.60

Commander Jacques Pepin Lehalleur (1911-2000) A197

2001, Nov. 14
716 A197 3fr multi 1.80 .80

Christmas — A198

2001, Nov. 28
717 A198 3fr multi 1.50 .80

100 Cents = 1 Euro (€)

France Nos. 2849-2863 Overprinted

2002, Jan. 1		**Engr.**	***Perf. 13***	
718 A1583	1c	yellow	.25	.25
719 A1583	2c	brown	.25	.25
720 A1583	5c	brt bl grn	.25	.25
721 A1583	10c	purple	.30	.25
722 A1583	20c	brt org	.60	.50
723 A1583	41c	brt green	1.40	1.00
724 A1583	50c	dk blue	1.60	1.25
725 A1583	53c	apple grn	1.75	1.25
726 A1583	58c	blue	1.90	1.40
727 A1583	64c	dark org	2.00	1.50
728 A1583	67c	brt blue	2.10	1.60
729 A1583	69c	brt pink	2.10	1.60
730 A1583	€1	Prus blue	3.00	2.40
731 A1583	€1.02	dk green	3.25	2.50
732 A1583	€2	violet	6.25	4.75
Nos. 718-732 (15)			27.00	20.75

Introduction of the Euro A199

2002, Jan. 30 Litho. *Perf. 13*
733 A199 €1 multi 3.00 1.50

Pinnipeds A200

Designs: 46c, Phoca vitulina. 87c, Halichoerus grypus.

2002, Mar. 7 Engr. *Perf. 13¼*
734-735 A200 Set of 2 4.00 2.00

See Nos. 748-749.

Plant Type of 1999

2002, Mar. 20 Litho. *Perf. 13*
736 A174 58c Pomme de pré 1.75 .90

Laranaga Farm, c. 1900 — A201

2002, Mar. 20 Engr. *Perf. 13x12¾*
737 A201 79c green 2.50 1.25

See also Nos. 751, 772.

Net Mender A202

Colors: 26c, Orange brown. 30c, Blue.

2002, Apr. 15 Engr. *Perf. 13x13¼*
738-739 A202 Set of 2 1.75 .90

West Point — A204

2002, June 24 Litho. *Perf. 13*
741 A204 75c multi 2.40 1.10

Tiaude de Morue, Local Cod Dish — A205

2002, July 10
742 A205 50c multi 1.60 .80

France No. 2835 Overprinted "ST. PIERRE / ET / MIQUELON"

2002, Sept. 11 Engr. *Perf. 13*
743 A1409 (46c) red 1.50 .75

Arctic Hare A206

2002, Sept. 11 Litho. *Perf. 13*
744 A206 46c multi 1.50 .75

The Troutpool — A207

2002, Oct. 11 Engr. *Perf. 13x13¼*
745 A207 84c green 2.75 1.40

Henry Cove — A208

No. 208: a, Gull and islands. b, Aerial view of St. Pierre.

2002, Nov. 6 Engr. *Perf. 13x12¼*
746 A208 Horiz. pair + central label 13.50 11.00
a.-b. €2 Either single 6.25 3.25

Christmas A209

2002, Nov. 27 Litho. *Perf. 13*
747 A209 46c multi 1.50 .75

Pinnipeds Type of 2002

Designs: 46c, Phoca groenlandica. 87c, Cystophora cristata.

2003, Jan. 5 Engr. *Perf. 13¼*
748-749 A200 Set of 2 4.25 2.25

Msgr. François Maurer (1922-2000) A210

2003, Jan. 8 Litho. *Perf. 13*
750 A210 46c multi 1.50 .75

Farm Type of 2002

2003, Mar. 12 Engr. *Perf. 13x13¼*
751 A201 79c Capandeguy Farm, c. 1910 2.50 1.25

France Nos. 2835A, 2921, and 2952-2957 Overprinted Like No. 718

2003		**Engr.**	***Perf. 13***	
752 A1409	(41c)	brt green	1.40	.70
753 A1583	58c	apple grn	1.90	.95
754 A1583	70c	yellow grn	2.25	1.10
755 A1583	75c	bright blue	2.40	1.25
756 A1583	90c	dark blue	3.00	1.50
757 A1583	€1.11	red lilac	3.50	1.75
758 A1583	€1.90	vio brn	6.00	3.00
Nos. 752-758 (7)			20.45	10.25

Booklet Stamp
Self-Adhesive
Serpentine Die Cut 6¾ Vert.

758A A1409 (46c) red 1.50 .75
b. Booklet pane of 10 15.00

Issued: (46c), 3/12. (41c), 4/23. 58c, 70c, 75c, 90c, €1.11, €1.90, 9/24.

Blueberries — A211

2003, Apr. 23 Litho. *Perf. 13*
759 A211 75c multi 2.40 1.25

Pulley Repairer A212

2003, May 14 Engr.
760 A212 30c blue gray 1.00 .70

Intl. Congress on Traditional Architecture — A213

No. 761: a, Patrice, Jézéquel and Jugan houses. b, Notre-Dame des Marins Church, Borotra house.

2003, May 22 *Perf. 13x12¼*
761 A213 Horiz. pair + central label 13.50 11.00
a.-b. €2 Either single 6.25 4.00

ASSP Soccer Team, Cent. A214

2003, Aug. 7 Litho. *Perf. 13*
762 A214 50c multi 1.60 .80

Buck A215

2003, Sept. 10
763 A215 50c multi 1.75 1.75

Lions Club in St. Pierre & Miquelon, 50th Anniv. A216

2003, Oct. 29 Litho. *Perf. 13x13¼*
764 A216 50c multi 1.75 1.75

Langlade Strawberry Preserves — A217

2003, Oct. 29 *Perf. 13*
765 A217 50c multi 1.75 1.75

The Afrique — A218

2003, Nov. 6 Engr. *Perf. 13x12½*
766 A218 90c blue green 3.25 3.25

Christmas — A219

2003, Dec. 3 Litho. *Perf. 13*
767 A219 50c multi 1.75 1.75

Joseph Lehuenen (d. 2001), Historian, Mayor — A220

2004, Feb. 25 Engr. ***Perf. 13x13¼***
768 A220 50c brown 1.75 1.75

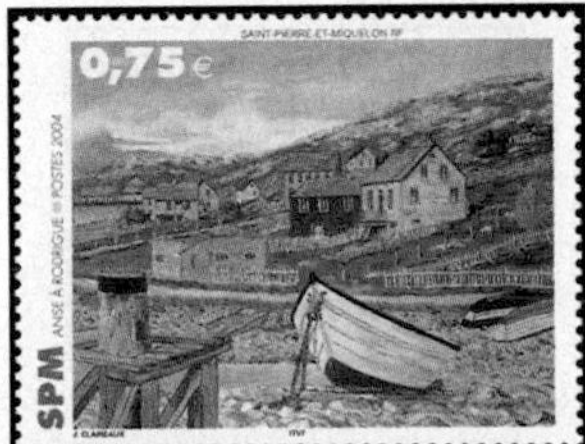

Rodrigue Cove — A221

2004, Mar. 10 Litho. ***Perf. 13***
769 A221 75c multi 3.00 3.00

Marine Mammals A222

Designs: 50c, Lagenorhynchus acutus. €1.08, Phocoena phocoena.

2004, Mar. 24 Engr. ***Perf. 13¼***
770-771 A222 Set of 2 6.00 6.00

See also Nos. 806-807.

Farm Type of 2002

2004, Apr. 7 Engr. ***Perf. 13x12½***
772 A201 90c Ollivier Farm, c. 1920 3.00 3.00

Fishermen in Boat A223

2004, May 12 Litho. ***Perf. 13***
773 A223 30c multi 1.10 1.10

Port of St. Pierre — A224

No. 774: a, Ships, denomination at right. b, Ships and dock, denomination at left.

2004, June 26 Engr. ***Perf. 13x12¼***
774 A224 Horiz. pair + central label 13.50 13.50
a.-b. €2 Either single 6.25 6.25

Micmac Indians of Miquelon — A225

2004, July 17 Litho. ***Perf. 13***
775 A225 50c multi 1.75 1.75

No. 775 Overprinted

2004, Aug. 14
776 A225 50c multi 3.25 3.25

Red Fox A226

2004, Sept. 13
777 A226 50c multi 1.75 1.75

Dinner Table — A227

2004, Sept. 13
778 A227 90c multi 3.50 3.50

The Fulwood — A228

2004, Nov. 5 Engr. ***Perf. 13x13¼***
779 A228 75c dark purple 2.75 2.75

Souvenir Sheet

Ships — A229

No. 780: a, Cap Blanc. b, Lisabeth-C. c, Shamrock. d, Aldona.

2004, Nov. 17 Litho. ***Perf. 13***
780 A229 50c Sheet of 4, #a-d 8.00 8.00

SIAA Soccer Team, 50th Anniv. (in 2003) A230

2004, Nov. 24
781 A230 44c multi 1.60 1.60

Christmas — A231

2004, Dec. 8
782 A231 50c multi 1.75 1.75

France Nos. 3066, 3068-3070, 3072, 3074-3075, 3077-3079, 3081 and 3083 Overprinted

2005		**Engr.**		***Perf. 13***
783	A1713	1c yellow	.25	.25
784	A1713	5c brown black	.25	.25
785	A1713	10c violet	.30	.30
786	A1713	(45c) green	1.40	1.40
787	A1713	(50c) red	1.60	1.60
788	A1713	55c dark blue	1.75	1.75
789	A1713	58c olive green	1.90	1.90
790	A1713	64c dark green	2.00	2.00
791	A1713	70c dark green	2.25	2.25
792	A1713	75c light blue	2.40	2.40
793	A1713	82c fawn	2.60	2.60
794	A1713	90c dark blue	3.00	3.00
795	A1713	€1 orange	3.25	3.25
796	A1713	€1.11 red violet	3.50	3.50
797	A1713	€1.22 red violet	3.75	3.75
798	A1713	€1.90 chocolate	6.00	6.00
799	A1713	€1.98 chocolate	6.25	6.25
		Nos. 783-799 (17)	42.45	42.45

Booklet Stamp
Self-Adhesive
Serpentine Die Cut 6¾ Vert.

800 A1713 (50c) red 1.60 1.60
a. Booklet pane of 10 (on France #3083a) 16.00

Issued: Nos. 1c, 10c, (45c), (50c), 58c, 70c, 75c, 90c, €1, €1.11, €1.90, 1/12. 5c, 55c, 64c, 82c, €1.22, €1.98, 3/23. Face values shown for Nos. 786, 787 and 800 are those the stamps sold for on the day of issue.

Henri Claireaux (1911-2001), Senator — A232

2005, Jan. 25 Engr. ***Perf. 13x13¼***
804 A232 50c lilac 1.75 1.75

Allumette Cove — A233

2005, Feb. 16 Litho. ***Perf. 13***
805 A233 75c multi 2.75 2.75

Marine Mammals Type of 2004

Designs: 53c, Delphinus delphis. €1.15, Lagenorhynchus albirostris.

2005, Mar. 9 Engr. ***Perf. 13¼***
806-807 A222 Set of 2 6.50 6.50

Horse Point Farm — A234

2005, Apr. 20 ***Perf. 13x13¼***
808 A234 90c olive green 3.50 3.50

Fog, Clouds and Houses A235

2005, May 11 Litho. ***Perf. 13***
809 A235 30c multi 1.10 1.10

Seven Ponds Valley — A236

No. 810: a, Bird at left. b, Rabbit at right.

2005, June 14 Engr. ***Perf. 13x12¼***
810 A236 Horiz. pair + central label 15.00 15.00
a.-b. €2 Either single 6.25 6.25

Variable Hare A237

2005, Sept. 7 Litho. ***Perf. 13***
811 A237 53c multi 2.00 2.00

Local Expression "Ben Vous Savez Madame" — A238

2005, Sept. 29
812 A238 90c multi 3.50 3.50

The Transpacific — A239

2005, Oct. 12 Engr. ***Perf. 13x13¼***
813 A239 75c blue 2.75 2.75

Status as Territorial Collectivity, 20th Anniv. — A240

2005, Oct. 27 Litho. *Perf. 13*
814 A240 53c multi 2.00 2.00

Christmas A241

2005, Dec. 7
815 A241 53c multi 2.00 1.50

Snow on Trees — A242

2006, Jan. 25
816 A242 53c multi 2.00 1.50

Sailors' Festival — A243

2006, Feb. 8
817 A243 53c multi 2.00 1.75

Albert Pen (1935-2003), President of General Council — A244

2006, Mar. 1 Engr.
818 A244 53c henna brn 2.00 1.75

Whales A245

Designs: 53c, Little rorqual. €1.15, Physeter catodon.

2006, Apr. 12 Engr. *Perf. 13¼*
819-820 A245 Set of 2 7.00 7.00

Houses on Clear Day A246

2006, June 7 Litho. *Perf. 13*
821 A246 30c multi 1.10 1.10

Sénat Archipelago — A247

2006, June 20
822 A247 53c multi 2.00 1.75

Prohibition, by Jean-Claude Girardin — A248

2006, July 19 Litho. *Perf. 13*
823 A248 75c multi 2.75 2.75

Le Petit-Barachois — A249

No. 824: a, Houses. b, Houses and boats.

2006, July 26 Engr. *Perf. 13x12¾*
824 A249 Horiz. pair with central label 13.50 13.50
a.-b. €2 Either single 6.25 6.25

Zazpiak Bat Pelota Fronton, Cent. — A250

2006, Aug. 23 Litho. *Perf. 13*
825 A250 53c multi 1.60 1.60

Orchids — A251

No. 826: a, Spiranthe de Romanzoff. b, Arethusa. c, Habenaire papillon. d, Habenaire lacérée.

2006, Sept. 6 Engr. *Perf. 13x13¼*
826 Horiz. strip of 4 7.00 7.00
a.-d. A251 53c Any single 1.60 1.60

Dugue Farm — A252

2006, Sept. 20 Engr. *Perf. 13x12½*
827 A252 95c black 3.00 3.00

The Penny Fair — A253

2006, Oct. 4 Engr. *Perf. 13x12½*
828 A253 95c black 3.00 3.00

Souvenir Sheet

Passenger Boats — A254

No. 829: a, Anahitra. b, Maria Galanta. c, Saint-Eugène V. d, Atlantic Jet.

2006, Nov. 15 Litho. *Perf. 13*
829 A254 54c Sheet of 4, #a-d 8.00 8.00

Christmas A255

2006, Dec. 6
830 A255 54c multi 1.75 1.75

Sister Hilarion (1913-2003) A256

2007, Jan. 10 Engr. *Perf. 13*
831 A256 54c multi 1.75 1.75

Horses — A257

2007, Feb. 21 Litho. *Perf. 13*
832 A257 €1.01 multi 3.00 3.00

Plactopecten Magellanicus — A258

2007, Mar. 10 Engr. *Perf. 13¼*
833 A258 €1 multi 3.50 3.50

Audit Office, Bicent. A259

2007, Mar. 19
834 A259 54c multi 1.75 1.75

France Nos. 3247-3251 Overprinted Like No. 783

2007, Mar. 28 Engr. *Perf. 13*
835 A1713 10c gray .25 .25
836 A1713 60c dark blue 1.60 1.60
837 A1713 70c yel green 1.90 1.90
838 A1713 85c purple 2.25 2.25
839 A1713 86c fawn 2.40 2.40
Nos. 835-839 (5) 8.40 8.40

Yellow-beaked Warbler — A260

2007, Apr. 14 Litho. *Perf. 13*
840 A260 44c multi 1.50 1.50

The Mi'kmaqs on Miquelon, by Jean-Claude Roy — A261

2007, May 26
841 A261 80c multi 2.75 2.75

Fog and House A262

2007, June 9
842 A262 30c multi 1.00 1.00

France Nos. 3252-3254 Overprinted Like No. 783

2007, June 20 Engr. *Perf. 13*

843	A1713	€1.15 blue	3.75	3.75
844	A1713	€1.30 red violet	4.00	4.00
845	A1713	€2.11 chocolate	6.75	6.75
		Nos. 843-845 (3)	14.50	14.50

Entrance to the Port of St. Pierre — A263

No. 846: a, Seagull and buoy. b, Ship and lighthouses.

2007, June 30 Engr. *Perf. 13x12¼*

846	Horiz. pair + central label	15.00	15.00
a.-b.	A263 €2.40 Either single	6.50	6.50

Delamaire Farm — A264

2007, Sept. 8 Engr. *Perf. 13x12½*

847 A264 €1.06 black 3.00 3.00

Carnivorous Plants — A265

No. 848: a, Sundew (Rossolis intermédiaire). b, Bladderwort (Utriculaire cornue). c, Butterwort (Grassette vulgaire). d, Pitcher plant (Sarracénie pourpre).

Litho. & Engr.

2007, Sept. 29 *Perf. 13x13¼*

848	Horiz. strip of 4	7.00	7.00
a.-d.	A265 54c Any single	1.60	1.60

Deer Hunting — A266

2007, Oct. 20 Litho. *Perf. 13*

849 A266 €1.65 multi 5.25 5.25

Miniature Sheet

Passenger Boats — A267

No. 850: a, Petit Miquelon. b, Marguerite II. c, Ile-aux-Marins. d, Mousse.

2007, Nov. 10

850 A267 54c Sheet of 4, #a-d 7.00 7.00

Christmas — A268

2007, Dec. 1 Litho. *Perf. 13*

851 A268 54c multi 1.75 1.75

René Autin (1921-60), Soldier — A269

2008, Jan. 19 Engr. *Perf. 13*

852 A269 54c blk & henna brn 1.75 1.75

Window — A270

2008, Feb. 23 Litho. *Perf. 13*

853 A270 €1.01 multi 3.25 3.25

Cod Pens A271

2008, Mar. 8 Engr. *Perf. 13¼*

854 A271 €1 multi 3.25 3.25

Langlade Dune — A272

No. 855: a, Birds and butterfly. b, Bird.

2008, Mar. 29 *Perf. 13x12¼*

855	A272	Horiz. pair + central label	15.00	15.00
a.-b.		€2.40 Either single	7.50	7.50

Black-throated Warbler — A273

2008, May 3 Litho. *Perf. 13*

856 A273 47c multi 1.50 1.50

Local Artisan Crafts A274

2008, May 17 Engr.

857 A274 33c black & olive 1.10 1.10

France Nos. 3383-3388 Overprinted Like No. 783

2008, May 28 Engr. *Perf. 13*

858	A1713	(65c) dark blue	2.10	2.10
859	A1713	72c yel green	2.25	2.25
860	A1713	88c fawn	2.75	2.75
861	A1713	€1.25 blue	4.00	4.00
862	A1713	€1.33 red violet	4.25	4.25
863	A1713	€2.18 chocolate	7.00	7.00
		Nos. 858-863 (6)	22.35	22.35

Return of the Fishermen, by Michelle Foliot — A275

2008, June 7 Litho. *Perf. 13*

864 A275 80c multi 2.50 2.50

Waves, Music and Guitar — A276

2008, July 12

865 A276 55c multi 1.75 1.75

Rowboat On Shore — A277

2008, Aug. 10 Litho. *Perf. 13*

866 A277 55c multi 1.60 1.60

Taekwondo A278

2008, Oct. 4 Litho. & Engr. *Perf. 13*

867 A278 55c multi 1.50 1.50

Miniature Sheet

Ice Block Cutting — A279

No. 868: a, Workers pushing ice block up ramp onto sled. b, Workers pulling up ice blocks with tongs. c, Sleds awaiting ice blocks. d, Ice cutters with saws.

2008, Oct. 22 Litho.

868 A279 €1 Sheet of 4, #a-d 10.50 10.50

France Nos. 3453-3465 Overprinted

2008-09 Engr. *Perf. 13*

869	A1912	1c yellow	.25	.25
870	A1912	5c gray brown	.25	.25
871	A1912	10c gray	.25	.25
872	A1912	(50c) green	1.25	1.25
873	A1912	(55c) red	1.40	1.40
874	A1912	(65c) dark blue	1.75	1.75
875	A1912	72c olive green	1.90	1.90
876	A1912	85c purple	2.25	2.25
877	A1912	88c fawn	2.25	2.25
878	A1912	€1 orange	2.75	2.75
879	A1912	€1.25 blue	3.50	3.50
880	A1912	€1.33 red violet	3.50	3.50
881	A1912	€2.18 chocolate	5.75	5.75
		Nos. 869-881 (13)	27.05	27.05

Issued: Nos. 869-873, 11/1, Nos. 874-877, 2/28/09; Nos. 878-881, 4/22/09.

Hare Hunting — A280

2008, Nov. 8 Litho. *Perf. 13*

882 A280 €1.65 multi 4.25 4.25

Christmas A281

2008, Nov. 26 Litho. *Perf. 13*

883 A281 55c multi 1.40 1.40

Fox Sparrow — A282

2009, Jan. 14

884 A282 47c multi 1.25 1.25

Colors of Winter — A283

2009, Feb. 14
885 A283 €1 multi 2.60 2.60

Henri Morazé (1903-86), Alcohol Merchant — A284

2009, Mar. 14 **Engr.**
886 A284 56c blk & org brown 1.40 1.40

ATR 42 Airplane — A285

Litho. & Engr.

2009, Mar. 28 ***Perf. 13x13¼***
887 A285 80c blue & black 2.25 2.25

Local Artisan Crafts A286

2009, Apr. 8 **Engr.** ***Perf. 13***
888 A286 33c dp bl & bl grn .90 .90

The Blue Bench, by Raphaele Goineau — A287

2009, May 13 **Litho.** ***Perf. 13***
889 A287 56c multi 1.60 1.60

Place Monsigneur François Maurer — A288

No. 890: a, Buildings. b, Buildings and parking lot with two lampposts.

Perf. 13x12¼x13x13

2009, May 27 **Engr.**
890 A288 Horiz. pair + central label 14.00 14.00
a.-b. €2.50 Either single 7.00 7.00

No. 890b is upside-down in relation to No. 890a.

Tennis A289

2009, June 10 **Engr.** ***Perf. 12¼***
891 A289 €1.05 multi 3.00 3.00

Pictorial Stamps of 1909, Cent. A290

2009, June 27 **Engr.** ***Perf. 13¼***
892 A290 €1 multi 3.00 3.00

France No. 3471 Overprinted "SPM" Like No. 869

Serpentine Die Cut 6¾ Vert.

2009, Sept. 15 **Engr.**

Booklet Stamp

Self-Adhesive

893 A1912 (56c) red 1.75 1.75
a. Booklet pane of 12 21.00

Duck Hunting — A291

2009, Sept. 26 **Litho.** ***Perf. 13***
894 A291 €1.50 multi 4.50 4.50

Past and Present Radio Station Buildings A292

2009, Oct. 10 ***Perf. 13x13¼***
895 A292 56c multi 1.75 1.75

Man at Window — A293

2009, Oct. 24 ***Perf. 13***
896 A293 80c multi 2.40 2.40

Miniature Sheet

Winter Scenes of Port of St. Pierre — A294

No. 897: a, Men standing on ice in harbor, boats in background. b, Bull on ice near ship. c, Pointe-aux-Canons Lighthouse. d, Fishing boats in ice.

2009, Nov. 4 **Litho.** ***Perf. 13***
897 A294 56c Sheet of 4, #a-d 6.75 6.75

Christmas — A295

2009, Nov. 25
898 A295 56c multi 1.75 1.75

Richard Bartlett (1913-81), Member of French Resistance — A296

2010, Jan. 16 **Engr.** ***Perf. 13***
899 A296 56c blk & org brn 1.60 1.60

France Nos. 3612-3616 Overprinted "SPM" Like No. 869

2010	**Engr.**	***Perf. 13***	
900 A1912	73c olive green	2.10	2.10
901 A1912	90c fawn	2.50	2.50
902 A1912	€1.30 blue	3.75	3.75
903 A1912	€1.35 red violet	3.75	3.75
904 A1912	€2.22 chocolate	6.00	6.00
	Nos. 900-904 (5)	18.10	18.10

Issued: Nos. 900-902, 1/27, Nos. 903-904, 2/24.

Black and White Warbler — A297

2010, Feb. 10 **Litho.** ***Perf. 13***
905 A297 47c multi 1.25 1.25

Crabber and Crab Pot — A298

2010, Mar. 13 **Litho.** ***Perf. 13***
906 A298 €1 multi 2.75 2.75

Miquelon Cape — A299

No. 907: a, Birds in flight. b, Cape, buoy.

2010, Apr. 10 **Engr.** ***Perf. 13x12¼***
907 A299 Horiz. pair + central label 13.50 13.50
a.-b. €2.50 Either single 6.75 6.75

Helicopter Carrier Jeanne d'Arc — A300

Litho. & Engr.

2010, Apr. 24 ***Perf. 13***
908 A300 €1 multi 2.75 2.75

Children's Art — A301

No. 909: a, Lighthouse, boat and bird, by Eric Coste. b, Ship, whale and houses, by Laura Caspar.

2010, Apr. 24 **Litho.**
909 A301 €1 Horiz. pair, #a-b 5.50 5.50

Reims F406 — A302

2010, May 15 **Engr.** ***Perf. 13x12½***
910 A302 80c multi 2.00 2.00

Telegraph Office and Morse Code A303

2010, June 19 **Litho.** ***Perf. 13x13¼***
911 A303 56c multi 1.40 1.40

Local Artisan Crafts A304

2010, June 26 **Engr.**
912 A304 33c multi .85 .85

Swimming A305

2010, July 10 ***Perf. 12¼***
913 A305 €1.05 multi 2.75 2.75

Hunt for 1927 Oiseau Blanc Transatlantic Flight — A306

Litho. & Engr.

2010, Sept. 1 *Perf. 13*

914 A306 €1.10 multi 3.00 3.00

Duck Hunting — A307

2010, Sept. 22 **Litho.**

915 A307 €1.65 multi 4.50 4.50

Children Sledding Past Side of Building — A308

2010, Oct. 20

916 A308 58c multi 1.75 1.75

Christmas A309

2010, Dec. 1 *Perf. 13x13¼*

917 A309 58c multi 1.60 1.60

Miniature Sheet

Festivals and Parades — A310

No. 918: a, Departing of the Fleet Festival. b, Assumption Day (August 15) Parade. c, Holy Child (Sainte-Enfance) Festival. d, Corpus Christi (Fête-Dieu) Parade.

2010, Nov. 6 **Litho.** *Perf. 13*

918	A310	Sheet of 4	9.00	9.00
a.-b.		58c Either single	1.60	1.60
c.		€1 multi	2.75	2.75
d.		€1.05 multi	3.00	3.00

Cape May Warbler — A311

2011, Jan. 15

919 A311 47c multi 1.25 1.25

France Nos. 3871-3876 Overprinted "SPM" Like No. 869

2011 **Engr.** *Perf. 13*

920	A1912	75c olive green	2.10	2.10
921	A1912	87c purple	2.50	2.50
922	A1912	95c fawn	2.60	2.60
923	A1912	€1.35 blue	3.75	3.75
924	A1912	€1.40 red violet	4.00	4.00
925	A1912	€2.30 chocolate	6.25	6.25
		Nos. 920-925 (6)	21.20	21.20

Issued: 75c, 95c, €2.30, 1/29. 87c, €1.35, €1.40, 2/26.

Larch Cones — A312

2011, Feb. 12 **Litho.**

926 A312 €1.05 multi 3.00 3.00

Henriette Bonin (1899-1985), School Teacher — A313

2011, Mar. 12 **Engr.**

927 A313 58c blk & org brn 1.75 1.75

Notre Dame des Marins Church, Ile Aux Marins — A314

2011, Apr. 9 **Litho.** *Perf. 13¼x13*

928 A314 58c multi 1.75 1.75

St. Pierre & Miquelon Literary Prize A315

2011, Apr. 9 *Perf. 13x13¼*

929 A315 58c multi 1.75 1.75

Miniature Sheet

A316

No. 930 — Old photographs of Ile aux Chiens (Ile aux Marins): a, Fishing boats on shore, houses close in background. b, Ile aux Chiens Festival. c, Procession of fishermen outside church. d, Fishermen preparing boats at harbor, houses in distance.

2011, Apr. 20 *Perf. 13*

930 A316 58c Sheet of 4, #a-d 6.75 6.75

Local Artisan Crafts A317

2011, May 14 **Engr.** *Perf. 13¼x13*

931 A317 33c multi .95 .95

St. Pierre & Miquelon 2011 Philatelic Exhibition — A318

2011, June 4 **Litho.** *Perf. 13*

932 A318 85c multi 2.50 2.50

Man and Boy Throwing Rocks at Cans — A319

2011, June 25

933 A319 58c multi 1.75 1.75

Sailing A320

2011, July 10 **Engr.** *Perf. 12¼*

934 A320 €1.05 multi 3.00 3.00

L'Anse à Bertrand — A321

No. 935: a, White house with red trim. b, Red house with white trim.

2011, Sept. 7 *Perf. 13x12¼*

935	A321	Horiz. pair + central label	14.00	14.00
a.-b.		€2.50 Either single	7.00	7.00

Miniature Sheet

Rescue Boats — A322

No. 936: a, P'tit Saint-Pierre. b, Jaro II. c, Radar IV. d, Fulmar.

2011, Sept. 28 **Litho.** *Perf. 13*

936 A322 60c Sheet of 4, #a-d 6.75 6.75

A323

A324

A325

A326

A327

Details From "Sous le Vol du Goéland, " Painting by Jean-Jacques Oliviéro A328

2011, Oct. 19 *Perf. 13x13½, 13½x13*

937	Sheet of 6	10.50	10.50
a.	A323 60c multi	1.75	1.75
b.	A324 60c multi	1.75	1.75
c.	A325 60c multi	1.75	1.75
d.	A326 60c multi	1.75	1.75
e.	A327 60c multi	1.75	1.75
f.	A328 60c multi	1.75	1.75

Souvenir Sheet

Squadron Escort Forbin — A329

Litho. & Engr.

2011, Nov. 8 *Perf. 13½x13*

938 A329 €1.10 multi 3.00 3.00

See French Southern & Antarctic Territories No. 449.

Christmas A330

2011, Nov. 30 **Litho.** *Perf. 13*

939 A330 60c multi 1.60 1.60

Birds and Birdhouse — A331

2012, Jan. 7 **Litho.** *Perf. 13*

940 A331 47c multi 1.25 1.25

France Nos. 4050-4056 Overprinted "SPM" Like No. 869

Methods and Perfs As Before

2012

941	A2178	(55c)	gray	.95	.95
942	A2179	(60c)	red	1.60	1.60
943	A2180	(€1.07)	dark blue	3.00	3.00
944	A2181	(€1.07)	purple	3.00	3.00
945	A2182	(€1.25)	fawn	3.25	3.25
946	A2183	(€1.95)	red violet	5.25	5.25
947	A2184	(€3.65)	chocolate	9.75	9.75
	Nos. 941-947 (7)			26.80	26.80

Issued: Nos. 941, 942, 943, 946, 1/21; others, 2/11.

Trawler Le Ravenel — A332

2012, Feb. 4 **Litho.** *Perf. 13*

948 A332 60c multi 1.60 1.60

Church, Langlade — A333

2012, Mar. 10

949 A333 87c multi 2.25 2.25

Marine Life A334

No. 950: a, Leptasterias polaris. b, Urticina felina. c, Pagurus acadianus. d, Cynea capilata.

2012, Mar. 24 *Perf. 13x13¼*

950 Horiz. strip of 4 6.50 6.50

a.-d. A334 60c Any single 1.60 1.60

France Nos. 4079-4082 Overprinted "SPM" Like No. 869

Methods and Perfs As Before

2012, Apr. 14

951	A2191	(33c)	green	.90	.90
952	A2192	(47c)	yellow green	1.25	1.25
953	A2193	(58c)	blue green	1.60	1.60
954	A2194	(85c)	dk bl green	2.25	2.25
	Nos. 951-954 (4)			6.00	6.00

A335

A336

A337

A338

A339

Details From "Le Travail des Graves," by Gaston Roullet A340

Perf. 13¼x13, 13x13¼ (horiz. stamps)

2012, May 16 **Photo.**

955	Sheet of 6	9.00	9.00
a.	A335 60c multi	1.50	1.50
b.	A336 60c multi	1.50	1.50
c.	A337 60c multi	1.50	1.50
d.	A338 60c multi	1.50	1.50
e.	A339 60c multi	1.50	1.50
f.	A340 60c multi	1.50	1.50

Archipélitude Museum, 25th Anniv. — A341

Litho. & Engr.

2012, June 16 *Perf. 13x13¼*

956 A341 60c multi 1.50 1.50

André Paturel (1942-87), Designer of Local St. Pierre & Miquelon Flag — A342

2012, July 16 **Engr.** *Perf. 13*

957 A342 33c org brn & blk .85 .85

2012 Summer Olympics, London A343

2012, July 28 *Perf. 12¼*

958 A343 €1.07 multi 2.75 2.75

Children's Art, Lighthouse, Swans and Puffins — A344

Litho. & Engr.

2012, Sept. 15 *Perf. 13x13¼*

959 A344 €1.15 multi 3.00 3.00

Child at Play — A345

2012, Sept. 29 **Litho.** *Perf. 13*

960 A345 60c multi 1.60 1.60

Paintings of Boats — A346

No. 961: a, Le Béothuk, by Dirk Verdoorn. b, Esprit du Barachois, by François Bellec.

2012, Oct. 13

961 A346 60c Horiz. pair, #a-b 3.25 3.25

Chapeau de Miquelon — A347

No. 962: a, Seals on rocks. b, Chapeau de Miquelon and seal in water.

2012, Oct. 27 **Engr.** *Perf. 13x12¼*

962 A347 Horiz. pair + central label 13.00 13.00

a.-b. €2.50 Either single 6.50 6.50

Christmas — A348

2012, Dec. 1 **Litho.** *Perf. 13*

963 A348 60c multi 1.60 1.60

Blue Jay — A349

2013, Jan. 12

964 A349 47c multi 1.25 1.25

Rock Formation — A350

2013, Jan. 26

965 A350 90c multi 2.50 2.50

Bulot, the Carnival King A351

2013, Feb. 16 **Engr.** *Perf. 13¼*

966 A351 €1.13 multi 3.00 3.00

Maison Chartier A352

2013, Feb. 27 **Litho.** *Perf. 13x13¼*

967 A352 63c multi 1.75 1.75

Miniature Sheet

Fishing — A353

No. 968: a, Workers processing cod on table. b, Fishermen in boats. c, Workers and stack of dried cod. d, Fishermen in water pulling in net.

2013, Mar. 13 ***Perf. 13***
968 A353 63c Sheet of 4, #a-d 6.50 6.50

Trawler "Le Finlande" — A354

2013, Mar. 27 Engr. ***Perf. 13x13¼***
969 A354 €1.30 multi 3.50 3.50

Ship's Rigging A355

2013, Apr. 24 Litho. & Engr.
970 A355 €1.25 multi 3.25 3.25

Rugby A356

2013, May 15 Engr. ***Perf. 12x12¼***
971 A356 €1.13 multi 3.00 3.00

Miniature Sheet

Church of Miquelon Frescoes, by Yvette Detcheverry — A357

No. 972: a, Le sacrifice d'Abraham (The Sacrifice of Abraham). b, Le jugement de Salomon (The Judgment of Solomon). c, Présenation des tables de la loi (Moses Receiving the Law). d, Moise sur le mont Sinai (Moses on Mount Sinai). e, La nativité (Nativity). f, Le baptême du Christ (Baptism of Christ). g, La peche miraculeuse (The Miraculous Catch).

2013, June 1 Photo. ***Perf. 13¼x13***
972 A357 Sheet of 7 12.50 12.50
a.-g. 63c Any single 1.75 1.75

No. 972 has rows of rouletting between stamps.

Brother Sénier (1885-1978) A358

2013, June 15 Engr. ***Perf. 13***
973 A358 (33c) org brn & blk .90 .90

Boys Playing Marbles — A359

2013, June 29 Litho. ***Perf. 13***
974 A359 63c multi 1.75 1.75

Miniature Sheet

Fire Trucks — A360

No. 975: a, 1961 Ford F600 (Le plateau). b, 2003 Freightliner FL80 4X4 (Le premier secours). c, 1992 Ford F350 4X4 (La garderobe). d, 1972 Ford F600 (Le camion dévidoir).

2013, July 13 Litho. ***Perf. 13***
975 A360 63c Sheet of 4, #a-d 6.75 6.75

Old and New Hospital Buildings A361

2013, Sept. 21 Litho. ***Perf. 13x13¼***
976 A361 63c multi 1.75 1.75

France Nos. 4411-4421 Overprinted

2013-14 Engr. ***Perf. 13***

977	A2320	1c	yellow	.25	.25
978	A2320	5c	dk brown	.25	.25
979	A2320	10c	brown	.30	.30
980	A2321	(56c)	dk gray	1.50	1.50
981	A2322	(63c)	red	1.75	1.75
982	A2320	€1	orange	2.75	2.75
983	A2323	(€1.13)	blue	3.00	3.00
984	A2324	(€1.13)	purple	3.00	3.00
985	A2322	(€1.30)	fawn	3.50	3.50
986	A2322	(€2.15)	red violet	6.00	6.00
987	A2322	(€3.90)	chocolate	11.00	11.00

Issued: Nos. 986-987, 3/15/14.

Nos. 977-987 (11) 33.30 33.30

Issued: Nos. 977, 983-985, 10/26; Nos. 978-982, 10/5; Nos. 986-987, 3/15/14.

Doyen Lions Club, 60th Anniv. A362

Litho. & Engr.

2013, Oct. 19 ***Perf. 13x13¼***
988 A362 (47c) multi 1.25 1.25

Anse à Ravenel — A363

No. 989: a, Horse-drawn carts on beach, houses. b, Shoreline and birds.

2013, Nov. 8 Engr. ***Perf. 13x12¼***
989 A363 Horiz. pair + central label 13.50 13.50
a.-b. €2.50 Either single 6.75 6.75

Christmas — A364

2013, Dec. 7 Litho. ***Perf. 13***
990 A364 63c multi 1.75 1.75

Treaty of Utrecht, 300th Anniv. A365

2013, Dec. 18 Engr. ***Perf. 12¾***
991 A365 90c multi 2.50 2.50

Values are for stamps with surrounding selvage.

Bombycilla Garrulus — A366

2014, Jan. 16 Litho. ***Perf. 13***
992 A366 47c multi 1.25 1.25

Girl Blowing Bubbles — A367

2014, Feb. 1 Litho. ***Perf. 13***
993 A367 93c black 2.50 2.50

Trawler Shamrock III — A368

2014, Feb. 16 Engr. ***Perf. 13***
994 A368 €1.16 multi 3.25 3.25

Albert Briand (1909-66), Politician — A369

2014, Mar. 29 Engr. ***Perf. 13***
995 A369 33c org brn & blk .90 .90

Ship's Rigging
A370

Litho. & Engr.

2014, Feb. 26 *Perf. 13x13¼*
996 A370 €1.25 multi 3.50 3.50

Miniature Sheet

Working Dogs — A371

No. 997: a, Two dogs pulling sled carrying sticks. b, Two children with dog pulling four-wheeled wagon. c, One dog pulling sled carrying sticks. d, Dog pulling two-wheeled cart carrying tree.

2014, Apr. 19 Litho. *Perf. 13*
997 A371 66c Sheet of 4, #a-d 7.50 7.50

Lebailly Forge — A372

2014, May 3 Engr. *Perf. 13¼*
998 A372 66c multi 1.90 1.90

Les Voiles Blanches — A373

No. 999: a, 60c, House on Les Voiles Blanches (38x40mm). b, €1.40, Les Voiles Blanches, painting by Jean-Clause Girardin (62x40mm).

2014, May 24 Photo. *Perf. 13*
999 A373 Horiz. pair, #a-b 5.50 5.50

Old and New Photographs of Court House — A374

2014, June 21 Litho. *Perf. 13x13¼*
1000 A374 €1.35 multi 3.75 3.75

Miniature Sheet

Old Automobiles — A375

No. 1001: a, Three people in Ford Model T. b, Eugene Folquet standing next to automobile. c, Family of four in automobiles. d, Red Ford Model A.

2014, July 5 Litho. *Perf. 13*
1001 A375 66c Sheet of 4, #a-d 7.25 7.25

Stamp Exhibitions — A376

No. 1002: a, 33c, Emblems of St. Pierre & Miquelon International Stamp Exhibition and Inter-American Federation of Philately (38x40mm). b, 66c, Emblems of Thailand 2013 World Stamp Exhibition and International Philatelic Federation, surcharged stamps of St. Pierre & Miquelon (62x40mm).

2014, Sept. 27 Photo. *Perf. 13*
1002 A376 Horiz. pair, #a-b 2.50 2.50

Leatherback Turtle — A377

Litho. & Engr.

2014, Oct. 18 *Perf. 13*
1003 A377 69c multi 1.75 1.75

Savoyard Pond — A378

No. 1004: a, Runner, man flying kite. b, Fisherman, sailboats on pond, rider on horse.

2014, Nov. 8 Engr. *Perf. 13x12¼*
1004 Horiz. pair + central label 12.50 12.50
a.-b. A378 €2.50 Either single 6.25 6.25

Departure of the Jeannette, Cent. — A379

Litho. & Engr.

2014, Nov. 15 *Perf. 13*
1005 A379 €1 multi 2.50 2.50

World War I, cent.

Christmas — A380

2014, Nov. 22 Litho. *Perf. 13*
1006 A380 66c multi 1.75 1.75

Visit of French President François Hollande to St. Pierre & Miquelon — A381

2014, Dec. 27 Litho. *Perf. 13*
1007 A381 76c multi 1.90 1.90

American Redstart — A382

2015, Jan. 17 Engr. *Perf. 13*
1008 A382 38c multi .90 .90

Painting of Blueberry Fields by Claude L'Espagnol — A383

2015, Feb. 6 Engr. *Perf. 13*
1009 A383 76c multi 1.75 1.75

Francis Leroux (1908-82), Tourist Bureau President — A384

2015, Mar. 28 Engr. *Perf. 13*
1010 A384 38c blk & org brn .85 .85

Fishing Trawler Victor Pleven — A385

2015, Mar. 28 Engr. *Perf. 13*
1011 A385 €1.05 dark blue & grn 2.40 2.40

Miniature Sheet

Animals at Work — A386

No. 1012: a, Map of St. Pierre & Miquelon, horse-drawn ice sled. b, Line of horse-drawn ice sleds. c, Horse-drawn ice sleds on ice with ice cutters. d, Ox-drawn cart.

2015, Apr. 18 Litho. *Perf. 13*
1012 A386 76c Sheet of 4, #a-d 7.00 7.00

Renovation of Theater to Renaissance Fire Station — A387

2015, Apr. 28 Litho. *Perf. 13x13¼*
1013 A387 €1.50 multi 3.50 3.50

Miniature Sheet

Automobiles of the 1950s — A388

No. 1014: a, 1958 Studebaker President. b, 1955 Mercury Custom. c, 1957 Citroen ID 19 Luxe. d, 1955 Renault 4 CV.

2015, June 6 Litho. *Perf. 13*
1014 A388 76c Sheet of 4, #a-d 6.75 6.75

Souvenir Sheet

First Voyage of Reproduction of the Hermione — A389

No. 1015: a, €1.05, Marquis de Lafayette (1757-1834). b, €1.38, Lafayette's ship, Hermione, horiz.

Engr. (#1015a), Litho.

2015, July 22 *Perf. 13*
1015 A389 Sheet of 2, #a-b 5.50 5.50

The Laundrette of the Mountain A390

2015, Sept. 9 Engr. *Perf. 13¼*
1016 A390 76c multi 1.75 1.75

Pointe aux Canons Lighthouse — A391

Litho. & Engr.

2015, Sept. 23 *Perf. 13*
1017 A391 76c multi 1.75 1.75

Lithobates Clamitans and Nuphar Variegata — A392

2015, Oct. 7 Litho. & Engr. ***Perf. 13***
1018 A392 76c multi 1.75 1.75

Miniature Sheet

Gendarmerie — A393

No. 1019 — Various emblems, map of St. Pierre & Miquelon and: a, 38c, Gendarme. b, 76c, Snowplow. c, €1.05, Boat. d, €1.38, Two officers.

Litho. & Embossed
2015, Nov. 5 ***Perf. 13***
1019 A393 Sheet of 4, #a-d 7.75 7.75

Admiral Dominque Gauchet (1857-1931) — A394

2015, Nov. 11 Engr. ***Perf. 13x13¼***
1020 A394 €1 blk & dk bl 2.10 2.10

Christmas — A395

2015, Nov. 28 Litho. ***Perf. 13***
1021 A395 80c multi 1.75 1.75

Carpodacus Purpureus — A396

2016, Jan. 29 Litho. ***Perf. 13***
1022 A396 40c multi .90 .90

Overturned Fishing Boat and Other Fishing Boat Equipment A397

2016, Feb. 19 Litho. ***Perf. 13x13¼***
1023 A397 80c multi 1.75 1.75

Fishing Trawler La Grande Hermine — A398

2016, Mar. 18 Engr. ***Perf. 13x13¼***
1024 A398 €1.10 multi 2.50 2.50

SEMI-POSTAL STAMPS

Regular Issue of 1909-17 Surcharged in Red

1915-17 Unwmk. ***Perf. 14x13½***
B1 A17 10c + 5c car rose & red 3.00 *3.75*
B2 A17 15c + 5c dl vio & rose ('17) 3.00 *3.75*

Curie Issue
Common Design Type

1938, Oct. 24 Engr. ***Perf. 13***
B3 CD80 1.75fr + 50c brt ultra 21.00 *22.50*

French Revolution Issue
Common Design Type

1939, July 5 Photo.
Name and Value Typo. in Black

B4	CD83	45c + 25c green	13.50	*14.50*
B5	CD83	70c + 30c brown	13.50	*14.50*
B6	CD83	90c + 35c red org	13.50	*14.50*
B7	CD83	1.25fr + 1fr rose pink	13.50	*14.50*
B8	CD83	2.25fr + 2fr blue	13.50	*14.50*
		Nos. B4-B8 (5)	67.50	72.50

Common Design Type and

Sailor of Landing Force — SP1

Dispatch Boat "Ville d'Ys" SP2

1941 Photo. ***Perf. 13½***

B8A	SP1	1fr + 1fr red	3.75
B8B	CD86	1.50fr + 3fr maroon	3.75
B8C	SP2	2.50fr + 1fr blue	3.75
		Nos. B8A-B8C (3)	11.25

Nos. B8A-B8C were issued by the Vichy government, and were not placed on sale in the colony.

Nos. 239, 246 Srchd. in Carmine

1942 Unwmk. ***Perf. 13½x13***
B9 A25 1fr + 50c 65.00 *75.00*
B10 A26 2.50fr + 1fr 65.00 *75.00*

Petain Type of 1941 Srchd. in Black or Red

1944 Engr. ***Perf. 12½x12***
B11 50c + 1.50fr on 2.50fr dp bl (R) 1.60
B12 + 2.50fr on 1fr vio 1.60

Colonial Development Fund.

Nos. B11-B12 were issued by the Vichy government in France, but were not placed on sale in St. Pierre & Miquelon.

Catalogue values for unused stamps in this section, from this point to the end of the section, are for Never Hinged items.

Red Cross Issue
Common Design Type

1944 ***Perf. 14½x14***
B13 CD90 5fr + 20fr dp ultra 2.75 2.40

Surtax for the French Red Cross and national relief.

Tropical Medicine Issue
Common Design Type

1950, May 15 Engr. ***Perf. 13***
B14 CD100 10fr + 2fr red brn & red 17.00 13.00

The surtax was for charitable work.

Art School Telethon — SP3

2007, Nov. 24 Litho. ***Perf. 13¼x13***
B15 SP3 54c +16c multi 2.50 2.50

AIR POST STAMPS

Catalogue values for unused stamps in this section are for Never Hinged items.

Common Design Type
Perf. 14½x14

1942, Aug. 17 Photo. Unwmk.

C1	CD87	1fr dark orange	.80	.65
C2	CD87	1.50fr bright red	.85	.70
C3	CD87	5fr brown red	1.10	.95
C4	CD87	10fr black	1.60	1.25
C5	CD87	25fr ultra	1.75	1.25
C6	CD87	50fr dark green	2.50	2.10
C7	CD87	100fr plum	3.00	2.50
		Nos. C1-C7 (7)	11.60	9.40

Victory Issue
Common Design Type

1946, May 8 Engr. ***Perf. 12½***
C8 CD92 8fr deep claret 2.10 1.75

Chad to Rhine Issue
Common Design Types

1946, June 6

C9	CD93	5fr brown red	1.90	1.40
C10	CD94	10fr lilac rose	1.90	1.40
C11	CD95	15fr gray blk	2.75	2.40
C12	CD96	20fr violet	3.00	2.40
C13	CD97	25fr chocolate	3.75	3.25
C14	CD98	50fr grnsh blk	4.00	3.50
		Nos. C9-C14 (6)	17.30	14.35

Plane, Sailing Vessel and Coast — AP2

AP3

AP4

1947, Oct. 6

C15	AP2	50fr yel grn & rose	9.25	4.50
C16	AP3	100fr dk blue grn	13.50	6.00
C17	AP4	200fr bluish blk & brt rose	21.00	8.75
		Nos. C15-C17 (3)	43.75	19.25

UPU Issue
Common Design Type

1949, Oct. 1 Engr. ***Perf. 13***
C18 CD99 25fr multicolored 20.00 12.00

Liberation Issue
Common Design Type

1954, June 8
C19 CD102 15fr sepia & red 18.00 12.00

10th anniversary of the liberation of France.

Plane over St. Pierre Harbor — AP6

1956, Oct. 22
C20 AP6 500fr ultra & indigo 62.50 25.00

Dog and Village — AP7

Design: 100fr, Caravelle over archipelago.

1957, Nov. 4 Unwmk. ***Perf. 13***
C21 AP7 50fr gray, brn blk & bl 55.00 24.00
C22 AP7 100fr black & gray 24.00 12.00

Anchors and Torches — AP8

1959, Sept. 14 Engr. ***Perf. 13***
C23 AP8 200fr dk pur, grn & cl 21.00 8.75

Approval of the constitution and the vote which confirmed the attachment of the islands to France.

Pitcher Plant — AP9

1962, Apr. 24 **Unwmk.** ***Perf. 13***

C24 AP9 100fr green, org & car 13.00 5.25

Gulf of St. Lawrence and Submarine "Surcouf" — AP10

Perf. 13½x12½

1962, July 24 **Photo.**

C25 AP10 500fr dk red & bl 130.00 100.00

20th anniv. of St. Pierre & Miquelon's joining the Free French.

Telstar Issue

Common Design Type

1962, Nov. 22 **Engr.** ***Perf. 13***

C26 CD111 50fr Prus grn & bis 7.25 5.50

Arrival of Governor Dangeac, 1763 — AP11

1963, Aug. 5 **Unwmk.** ***Perf. 13***

C27 AP11 200fr dk bl, sl grn & brn 26.00 12.50

Bicentenary of the arrival of the first French governor.

Jet Plane and Map of Maritime Provinces and New England — AP12

1964, Sept. 28 **Engr.** ***Perf. 13***

C28 AP12 100fr choc & Prus bl 15.00 8.75

Inauguration of direct airmail service between St. Pierre and New York City.

ITU Issue

Common Design Type

1965, May 17

C29 CD120 40fr org brn, dk bl & lil rose 24.00 11.00

French Satellite A-1 Issue

Common Design Type

Designs: 25fr, Diamant rocket and launching installations. 30fr, A-1 satellite.

1966, Jan. 24 **Engr.** ***Perf. 13***

C30 CD121 25fr dk brn, dk bl & rose cl 6.50 4.00

C31 CD121 30fr dk bl, rose cl & dk brn 8.00 5.50

a. Strip of 2, #C30-C31 + label 15.00 15.00

French Satellite D-1 Issue

Common Design Type

1966, May 23 **Engr.** ***Perf. 13***

C32 CD122 48fr brt grn, ultra & rose claret 10.50 6.50

Arrival of Settlers — AP13

1966, June 22 **Photo.** ***Perf. 13***

C33 AP13 100fr multicolored 15.00 6.75

150th anniv. of the return of the islands of St. Pierre and Miquelon to France.

Front Page of Official Journal and Printing Presses — AP14

1966, Oct. 20 **Engr.** ***Perf. 13***

C34 AP14 60fr dk bl, lake & dk pur 13.50 6.75

Centenary of the Government Printers and the Official Journal.

Map of Islands, Old and New Fishing Vessels — AP15

Design: 100fr, Cruiser Colbert, maps of Brest, St. Pierre and Miquelon.

1967, July 20 **Engr.** ***Perf. 13***

C35 AP15 25fr dk bl, gray & crim 24.00 16.00

C36 AP15 100fr multicolored 45.00 30.00

Visit of President Charles de Gaulle.

Speed Skater and Olympic Emblem — AP16

60fr, Ice hockey goalkeeper.

1968, Apr. 22 **Photo.** ***Perf. 13***

C37 AP16 50fr ultra & multi 10.50 4.50

C38 AP16 60fr green & multi 12.00 6.00

10th Winter Olympic Games, Grenoble, France, Feb. 6-18.

War Memorial, St. Pierre — AP17

1968, Nov. 11 **Photo.** ***Perf. 12½***

C39 AP17 500fr multicolored 27.50 20.00

World War I armistice, 50th anniv.

Concorde Issue

Common Design Type

1969, Apr. 17 **Engr.** ***Perf. 13***

C40 CD129 34fr dk brn & olive 32.50 12.00

Scenic Type of Regular Issue, 1969

Designs: 50fr, Grazing horses, Miquelon. 100fr, Gathering driftwood on Mirande Beach, Miquelon.

1969, Apr. 30 **Engr.** ***Perf. 13***

Size: 47½x27mm

C41 A47 50fr ultra, brn & ol 14.50 7.00

C42 A47 100fr dk brn, bl & sl 26.00 14.00

L'Esperance Leaving Saint-Malo, 1600 — AP18

1969, June 16 **Engr.** ***Perf. 13***

C43 AP18 200fr blk, grn & dk red 52.50 22.50

Pierre Loti and Sailboats — AP19

1969, June 23

C44 AP19 300fr lemon, choc & Prus bl 60.00 27.50

Loti (1850-1923), French novelist and naval officer.

EXPO Emblem and "Mountains" by Yokoyama Taikan — AP20

34fr, Geisha, rocket and EXPO emblem, vert.

1970, Sept. 8 **Engr.** ***Perf. 13***

C45 AP20 34fr dp cl, ol & ind 24.00 8.75

C46 AP20 85fr org, ind & car 40.00 17.50

EXPO '70 Intl. Exposition, Osaka, Japan, Mar. 15-Sept. 13.

Etienne François Duke of Choiseul and his Ships — AP21

Designs: 50fr, Jacques Cartier, ship and landing party. 60fr, Sebastien Le Gonrad de Sourdeval, ships and map of islands.

1970, Nov. 25 **Portrait in Lake**

C47 AP21 25fr lilac & Prus bl 25.00 10.00

C48 AP21 50fr sl grn & red lil 32.50 12.00

C49 AP21 60fr red lil & sl grn 40.00 17.00

Nos. C47-C49 (3) 97.50 39.00

De Gaulle, Cross of Lorraine, Sailor, Soldier, Coast Guard — AP22

1972, June 18 **Engr.** ***Perf. 13***

C50 AP22 100fr lil, brn & grn 30.00 14.00

Charles de Gaulle (1890-1970), French pres.

Louis Joseph de Montcalm — AP23

Designs: 2fr, Louis de Buade Frontenac, vert. 4fr, Robert de La Salle.

1973, Jan. 1

C51 AP23 1.60fr multicolored 10.00 4.00

C52 AP23 2fr multicolored 12.50 6.25

C53 AP23 4fr multicolored 22.50 11.00

Nos. C51-C53 (3) 45.00 21.25

Transall C 160 over St. Pierre — AP24

1973, Oct. 16 **Engr.** ***Perf. 13***

C54 AP24 10fr multicolored 50.00 22.50

Arms and Map of Islands, Fish and Bird — AP25

1974, Nov. 5 **Photo.** ***Perf. 13***

C55 AP25 2fr gold & multi 16.00 6.50

Copernicus, Kepler, Newton and Einstein — AP26

1974, Nov. 26 **Engr.**

C56 AP26 4fr multicolored 18.50 9.00

Nicolaus Copernicus (1473-1543), Polish astronomer.

Type of 1909, Cod and ARPHILA Emblem AP27

1975, Aug. 5 Engr. *Perf. 13*
C57 AP27 4fr ultra, red & indigo 21.00 9.50

ARPHILA 75, International Philatelic Exhibition, Paris, June 6-16.

Judo, Maple Leaf, Olympic Rings AP28

1975, Nov. 18 Engr. *Perf. 13*
C58 AP28 1.90fr red, blue & vio 10.50 5.25

Pre-Olympic Year.

Concorde — AP29

1976, Jan. 21 Engr. *Perf. 13*
C59 AP29 10fr red, blk & slate 32.50 16.00

1st commercial flight of supersonic jet Concorde from Paris to Rio, Jan. 21.

A. G. Bell, Telephone and Satellite AP30

1976, June 22 Litho. *Perf. 12½*
C60 AP30 5fr vio bl, org & red 10.00 5.50

Centenary of first telephone call by Alexander Graham Bell, Mar. 10, 1876.

Aircraft — AP31

5fr, Hawker-Siddeley H. S. 748, 1987. 10fr, Latecoere 522, 1939.

1987, June 30 Engr. *Perf. 13*
C61 AP31 5fr multicolored 2.75 1.40
C62 AP31 10fr multicolored 5.25 2.75

Hindenburg — AP32

10fr, Douglas DC3, 1948-1988. 20fr, Piper Aztec.

1988-89 Engr. *Perf. 13*
C63 AP32 5fr multicolored 2.50 1.25
C64 AP32 10fr multicolored 5.00 2.75
C65 AP32 20fr multicolored 7.50 4.00
Nos. C63-C65 (3) 15.00 8.00

Issued: 20fr, May 31, 1989; others, June 22.

Flying Flea, Bird — AP33

1990, May 16 Engr.
C66 AP33 5fr multicolored 2.50 1.50

Piper Tomahawk — AP34

1991, May 29 Engr. *Perf. 13*
C67 AP34 10fr multicolored 4.00 2.50

Radio-controlled Model Airplanes — AP35

1992, May 6
C68 AP35 20fr brown, red & org 8.00 4.25

Migratory Birds — AP36

1993-97 *Perf. 13x12½*
C69 AP36 5fr Shearwater (Puffin) 2.00 1.40
C70 AP36 10fr Golden plover 4.00 2.25

Perf. 13x13½
C71 AP36 10fr Arctic Tern 4.25 2.25

Perf. 13
C72 AP36 15fr Courlis 6.25 3.50
C73 AP36 5fr Peregrine falcon, vert. 2.50 1.50
Nos. C69-C73 (5) 19.00 10.90

Issued: #C69-C70, 5/12; #C71, 5/10/95; #C72, 5/15/96; #C73, 5/28/97.

Disappearance of the Flight of Nungesser and Coli, 70th Anniv. — AP37

1997, June 11
C74 AP37 14fr blk, grn bl & brn 6.00 3.50

Bald Eagle — AP38

1998-2001 Engr. *Perf. 13*
C74A AP38 5fr Buzzard 2.25 1.25
C75 AP38 10fr shown 4.75 3.00
C75A AP38 15fr Heron 5.25 3.00
C76 AP38 20fr Wild duck 7.25 5.00

Issued: 5fr, 12/13/00; 10fr, 5/6; 15fr, 5/23/01; 20fr, 5/5/99.

Puffin — AP39

2002, Apr. 22
C77 AP39 €2.50 multi 8.75 4.50

Solan Goose — AP40

2003, June 18 Engr. *Perf. 13x12½*
C78 AP40 €2.50 multi 8.75 5.75

Bustard — AP41

2004, July 7 Engr. *Perf. 13x13¼*
C79 AP41 €2.50 multi 8.75 6.25

Piping Plover — AP42

2005, June 22 *Perf. 13x12½*
C80 AP42 €2.50 multi 8.75 6.00

Atlantic Sea Gull — AP43

2006, June 14 Engr. *Perf. 13x12½*
C81 AP43 €2.53 multi 8.75 7.75

Eider — AP44

2007, May 5 Engr. *Perf. 13x12½*
C82 AP44 €1.50 multi 4.00 4.00

Harlequin Ducks — AP45

2008, June 28 Engr. *Perf. 13x12¾*
C83 AP45 €1.50 multi 4.75 4.75

AIR POST SEMI-POSTAL STAMPS

Bringing Children to Hospital — SPAP1

Perf. 13½x12½
1942, June 22 Unwmk. Photo.
CB1 SPAP1 1.50fr + 3.50fr green 4.50
CB2 SPAP1 2fr + 6fr brown 4.50

Native children's welfare fund.

Nos. CB1-CB2 were issued by the Vichy government in France, but were not placed on sale in St. Pierre & Miquelon.

Colonial Education Fund
Common Design Type

1942, June 22
CB3 CD86a 1.20fr + 1.80fr blue & red 5.25

No. CB3 was issued by the Vichy government in France, but was not placed on sale in St. Pierre & Miquelon.

POSTAGE DUE STAMPS

Postage Due Stamps of French Colonies Overprinted in Red

1892 Unwmk. *Imperf.*

J1	D1	5c black	85.00	85.00
J2	D1	10c black	26.00	26.00
J3	D1	15c black	26.00	26.00
J4	D1	20c black	26.00	26.00
J5	D1	30c black	26.00	26.00
J6	D1	40c black	26.00	26.00
J7	D1	60c black	82.50	90.00

Black Overprint

J8	D1	1fr brown	200.00	200.00
J9	D1	2fr brown	200.00	200.00
		Nos. J1-J9 (9)	697.50	705.00

These stamps exist with and without hyphen. See note after No. 59.

Postage Due Stamps of France, 1893-1924, Overprinted

1925-27 *Perf. 14x13½*

J10	D2	5c blue	.75	*1.10*
J11	D2	10c dark brown	.75	*1.10*
J12	D2	20c olive green	.80	*1.10*
J13	D2	25c rose	1.10	*1.50*
J14	D2	30c red	1.90	*2.25*
J15	D2	45c blue green	1.90	*2.25*
J16	D2	50c brown vio	2.60	*3.75*
J17	D2	1fr red brn, *straw*	3.50	*4.00*
J18	D2	3fr magenta ('27)	12.00	*15.00*

Surcharged

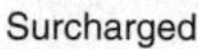

J19	D2	60c on 50c buff	2.75	*3.75*
J20	D2	2fr on 1fr red	4.50	*5.50*
		Nos. J10-J20 (11)	32.55	41.30

Newfoundland Dog — D3

1932, Dec. 5 **Typo.**

J21	D3	5c dk blue & blk	1.50	*1.90*
J22	D3	10c green & blk	1.50	*1.90*
J23	D3	20c red & blk	1.75	*2.25*
J24	D3	25c red vio & blk	1.75	*2.25*
J25	D3	30c orange & blk	3.50	*4.50*
J26	D3	45c lt blue & blk	5.50	*6.75*
J27	D3	50c blue grn & blk	8.50	*10.50*
J28	D3	60c brt rose & blk	12.00	*15.00*
J29	D3	1fr yellow brn & blk	22.50	*30.00*
J30	D3	2fr dp violet & blk	32.50	*37.50*
J31	D3	3fr dk brown & blk	45.00	*55.00*
		Nos. J21-J31 (11)	136.00	167.55

For overprints and surcharge see Nos. J42-J46.

Codfish — D4

1938, Nov. 17 **Photo.** *Perf. 13*

J32	D4	5c gray black	.40	*.50*
J33	D4	10c dk red violet	.40	*.50*
J34	D4	15c slate green	.50	*.75*
J35	D4	20c deep blue	.55	*.75*
J36	D4	30c rose carmine	.55	*.75*
J37	D4	50c dk blue green	.70	*.80*
J38	D4	60c dk blue	.95	*1.10*
J39	D4	1fr henna brown	1.90	*2.25*
J40	D4	2fr gray brown	4.50	*5.25*
J41	D4	3fr dull violet	4.75	*6.00*
		Nos. J32-J41 (10)	15.20	18.65

For overprints see Nos. J48-J67.

Postage Due Stamps of 1932 Overprinted in Black

1942 **Unwmk.** *Perf. 14x13½*

J42	D3	25c red vio & blk	425.00	425.00
J43	D3	30c orange & blk	425.00	425.00
J44	D3	50c blue grn & blk	1,400.	1,400.
J45	D3	2fr dp vio & bl blk	60.00	60.00

Same Surcharged in Black

No. J46

No. J46a

J46	D3	3fr on 2fr dp vio & blk, "F.N.F.L." omitted	24.00	24.00
a.		With "F.N.F.L."	40.00	40.00
		Nos. J42-J46 (5)	2,334.	2,334.

Postage Due Stamps of 1938 Overprinted in Black

1942 *Perf. 13*

J48	D4	5c gray black	24.00	*27.50*
J49	D4	10c dk red violet	24.00	*27.50*
J50	D4	15c slate green	24.00	*27.50*
J51	D4	20c deep blue	24.00	*27.50*
J52	D4	30c rose carmine	24.00	*27.50*
J53	D4	50c dk blue green	47.50	*52.50*
J54	D4	60c dark blue	100.00	*110.00*
J55	D4	1fr henna brown	110.00	*125.00*
J56	D4	2fr gray brown	125.00	*140.00*
J57	D4	3fr dull violet	140.00	*160.00*
		Nos. J48-J57 (10)	642.50	*725.00*

Christmas Day plebiscite ordered by Vice Admiral Emile Henri Muselier, commander of the Free French naval forces.

Postage Due Stamps of 1938 Overprinted in Black

1942

J58	D4	5c gray black	52.50	*60.00*
J59	D4	10c dk red violet	11.00	*12.00*
J60	D4	15c slate green	11.00	*12.00*
J61	D4	20c deep blue	11.00	*12.00*
J62	D4	30c rose carmine	11.00	*12.00*
J63	D4	50c dk blue green	11.00	*12.00*
J64	D4	60c dark blue	11.00	*12.00*
J65	D4	1fr henna brown	27.50	*32.50*
J66	D4	2fr gray brown	32.50	*35.00*
J67	D4	3fr dull violet	575.00	*625.00*
		Nos. J58-J67 (10)	753.50	*824.50*

Catalogue values for unused stamps in this section, from this point to the end of the section, are for Never Hinged items.

Arms and Fishing Schooner — D5

1947, Oct. 6 **Engr.** *Perf. 13*

J68	D5	10c deep orange	.40	.30
J69	D5	30c deep ultra	.40	.30
J70	D5	50c dk blue green	.65	.50
J71	D5	1fr deep carmine	.80	.65
J72	D5	2fr dk green	1.25	.80
J73	D5	3fr violet	2.25	1.75
J74	D5	4fr chocolate	2.25	1.75
J75	D5	5fr yellow green	2.50	1.90
J76	D5	10fr black brown	3.00	2.40
J77	D5	20fr orange red	4.00	3.25
		Nos. J68-J77 (10)	17.50	13.60

Newfoundland Dog — D6

1973, Jan. 1 **Engr.** *Perf. 13*

J78	D6	2c brown & blk	1.00	1.00
J79	D6	10c purple & blk	1.40	1.40
J80	D6	20c grnsh bl & blk	2.25	2.25
J81	D6	30c dk car & blk	4.50	4.50
J82	D6	1fr blue & blk	11.00	11.00
		Nos. J78-J82 (5)	20.15	20.15

France Nos. J106-J115 Overprinted "ST - PIERRE ET MIQUELON" Reading Up in Red

1986, Sept. 15 **Engr.** *Perf. 13*

J83	D8	10c multicolored	.25	.25
J84	D8	20c multicolored	.25	.25
J85	D8	30c multicolored	.25	.25
J86	D8	40c multicolored	.25	.25
J87	D8	50c multicolored	.40	.40
J88	D8	1fr multicolored	.50	.50
J89	D8	2fr multicolored	.95	.95
J90	D8	3fr multicolored	1.40	1.40
J91	D8	4fr multicolored	1.75	1.75
J92	D8	5fr multicolored	2.50	2.50
		Nos. J83-J92 (10)	8.50	8.50

PARCEL POST STAMPS

No. 65 Overprinted

1901 **Unwmk.** *Perf. 14x13½*

Q1	A16	10c blk, *lav*	140.00	140.00
a.		Inverted overprint	1,250.	1,250.

No. 66 Overprinted

Q2	A16	10c red	30.00	*32.50*

Nos. 84 and 87 Overprinted

1917-25

Q3	A17	10c car rose & red	4.50	*6.00*
a.		Double overprint	300.00	
Q4	A17	20c bis brn & vio brn ('25)	3.75	*5.25*
a.		Double overprint	190.00	

No. Q4 with Additional Overprint in Black

1942

Q5	A17	20c bis brn & vio brn	1,100.	*1,200.*

ST. THOMAS & PRINCE ISLANDS

sānt-ˈtäm-əs and ˈprin͏ₜs ˈī-lənd

Democratic Republic of Sao Tome and Principe

LOCATION — Two islands in the Gulf of Guinea, 125 miles off the west coast of Africa
GOVT. — Republic
AREA — 387 sq. mi.
POP. — 154,878 (1999 est.)
CAPITAL — Sao Tome

This colony of Portugal became a province, later an overseas territory, and achieved independence on July 12, 1975.

1000 Reis = 1 Milreis
100 Centavos = 1 Escudo (1913)
100 Cents = 1 Dobra (1977)

Catalogue values for unused stamps in this country are for Never Hinged items, beginning with Scott 353 in the regular postage section, Scott J52 in the postage due section, and Scott RA4 in the postal tax section.

Portuguese Crown — A1

5, 25, 50 REIS:
Type I — "5" is upright.
Type II — "5" is slanting.

10 REIS:
Type I — "1" has short serif at top.
Type II — "1" has long serif at top.

40 REIS:
Type I — "4" is broad.
Type II — "4" is narrow.

Perf. 12½, 13½

1869-75 **Unwmk.** **Typo.**

1	A1	5r black, I	3.00	1.90
a.		Type II	3.00	1.90
2	A1	10r yellow, I	14.00	8.50
a.		Type II	17.50	10.50
3	A1	20r bister	3.50	2.75
4	A1	25r rose, I	1.25	1.10
a.		25r red	4.50	1.50
5	A1	40r blue ('75), I	5.00	3.50
a.		Type II	5.50	4.50
6	A1	50r gray grn, II	9.00	7.00
a.		Type I	15.00	14.00
7	A1	100r gray lilac	6.00	5.50
8	A1	200r red orange ('75)	9.00	6.25
9	A1	300r chocolate ('75)	9.00	7.00
		Nos. 1-9 (9)	59.75	43.50

1881-85

10	A1	10r gray grn, I	8.00	6.75
a.		Type II	9.50	6.00
b.		Perf. 13½, I	11.00	8.00
11	A1	20r car rose ('85)	4.00	3.00
12	A1	25r vio ('85), II	2.25	1.75
13	A1	40r yel buff, II	5.00	4.00
a.		Perf. 13½	6.00	4.50
14	A1	50r dk blue, I	3.00	2.25
a.		Type II	3.00	2.25
		Nos. 10-14 (5)	22.25	17.75

For surcharges and overprints see Nos. 63-64, 129-129B, 154.

Nos. 1-14 have been reprinted on stout white paper, ungummed, with rough perforation 13½, also on ordinary paper with shiny white gum and clean-cut perforation 13½ with large holes.

King Luiz — A2

Typo., Head Embossed

1887 *Perf. 12½, 13½*

15	A2	5r black	4.00	2.50
16	A2	10r green	4.50	2.50
17	A2	20r brt rose	4.50	3.00
a.		Perf. 12½	55.00	55.00
18	A2	25r violet	4.50	1.60
19	A2	40r brown	4.50	2.25
20	A2	50r blue	4.50	2.50
21	A2	100r yellow brn	4.50	2.00
22	A2	200r gray lilac	15.00	10.50
23	A2	300r orange	15.00	10.50
		Nos. 15-23 (9)	61.00	37.35

For surcharges and overprints see Nos. 24-26, 62, 65-72, 130-131, 155-158, 234-237.

Nos. 15, 16, 19, 21, 22, and 23 have been reprinted in paler colors than the originals, with white gum and cleancut perforation 13½. Value $1.50 each.

Nos. 16-17, 19 Surcharged

a

b

c

1889-91 Without Gum

24 A2(a) 5r on 10r 35.00 20.00
25 A2(b) 5r on 20r 25.00 20.00
26 A2(c) 50r on 40r ('91) 240.00 50.00
Nos. 24-26 (3) 300.00 90.00

Varieties of Nos. 24-26, including inverted and double surcharges, "5" inverted, "Cinoc" and "Cinco," were deliberately made and unofficially issued.

King Carlos — A6

1895 Typo. *Perf. 11½, 12½*

27 A6 5r yellow 1.00 .60
28 A6 10r red lilac 1.50 1.00
29 A6 15r red brown 1.50 1.10
30 A6 20r lavender 2.00 1.10
31 A6 25r green 2.00 .75
32 A6 50r light blue 2.00 .70
a. Perf. 13½ 3.00 1.50
33 A6 75r rose 8.00 3.25
34 A6 80r yellow grn 8.00 6.25
35 A6 100r brn, *yel* 4.00 3.00
36 A6 150r car, *rose* 6.00 5.00
37 A6 200r dk bl, *bl* 7.75 6.50
38 A6 300r dk bl, *sal* 8.50 7.75
Nos. 27-38 (12) 52.25 37.00

For surcharges and overprints see Nos. 73-84, 132-137, 159-165, 238-243, 262-264, 268-274.

King Carlos — A7

1898-1903 *Perf. 11½*
Name and Value in Black except 500r

39 A7 2½r gray .30 .25
40 A7 5r orange .30 .25
41 A7 10r lt green .40 .30
42 A7 15r brown 2.00 1.75
43 A7 15r gray grn ('03) 1.10 1.10
44 A7 20r gray violet .90 .50
45 A7 25r sea green .70 .25
46 A7 25r carmine ('03) 1.10 .30
47 A7 50r blue 1.00 .50
48 A7 50r brown ('03) 4.50 4.50
49 A7 65r dull blue ('03) 22.50 9.00
50 A7 75r rose 10.00 6.50
51 A7 75r red lilac ('03) 2.50 1.40
52 A7 80r brt violet 5.00 5.00
53 A7 100r dk blue, *bl* 3.00 2.00
54 A7 115r org brn, *pink* ('03) 10.00 8.00
55 A7 130r brn, *straw* ('03) 10.00 6.00
56 A7 150r brn, *buff* 5.00 2.25
57 A7 200r red lil, *pnksh* 6.00 2.75
58 A7 300r dk blue, *rose* 8.00 5.00
59 A7 400r dull bl, *straw* ('03) 15.00 8.50
60 A7 500r blk & red, *bl* ('01) 12.00 5.00
61 A7 700r vio, *yelsh* ('01) 20.00 12.00
Nos. 39-61 (23) 141.30 83.10

For overprints and surcharges see Nos. 86-105, 116-128, 138-153, 167-169, 244-249, 255-261, 265-267.

Stamps of 1869-95 Surcharged in Red or Black

1902 On Stamp of 1887

62 A2 130r on 5r blk (R) 6.00 5.00
a. Perf. 13½ 32.50 32.50

On Stamps of 1869

63 A1 115r on 50r grn 10.00 7.50
64 A1 400r on 10r yel 25.00 12.00
a. Double surcharge 75.00 50.00

On Stamps of 1887

65 A2 65r on 20r rose 6.25 4.50
a. Perf. 13½ 8.50 7.00
66 A2 65r on 25r violet 5.00 4.00
a. Inverted surcharge 35.00 25.00
67 A2 65r on 100r yel brn 5.00 4.75
68 A2 115r on 10r blue grn 5.00 4.00
69 A2 115r on 300r orange 5.00 4.00
70 A2 130r on 200r gray lil 6.00 5.00
71 A2 400r on 40r brown 8.00 7.00
72 A2 400r on 50r blue 14.00 12.00
a. Perf. 13½ 110.00 90.00

On Stamps of 1895

73 A6 65r on 5r yellow 6.00 3.00
74 A6 65r on 10r red vio 6.00 3.00
75 A6 65r on 15r choc 6.00 3.00
76 A6 65r on 20r lav 6.00 3.00
77 A6 115r on 25r grn 6.00 3.00
78 A6 115r on 150r car, *rose* 6.00 3.00
79 A6 115r on 200r bl, *bl* 6.00 3.00
80 A6 130r on 75r rose 6.00 3.00
81 A6 130r on 100r brn, *yel* 6.00 3.50
a. Double surcharge 30.00 20.00
82 A6 130r on 300r bl, *sal* 6.00 3.00
83 A6 400r on 50r lt blue 1.10 .95
a. Perf. 13½ 2.00 1.60
84 A6 400r on 80r yel grn 2.00 1.50

On Newspaper Stamp No. P12

85 N3 400r on 2½r brown 1.10 .95
a. Double surcharge
Nos. 62-85 (24) 159.45 103.65

Reprints of Nos. 63, 64, 67, 71, and 72 have shiny white gum and clean-cut perf. 13½.

Stamps of 1898 Overprinted

1902

86 A7 15r brown 2.00 1.50
87 A7 25r sea green 2.00 1.25
88 A7 50r blue 2.25 1.25
89 A7 75r rose 5.00 3.50
Nos. 86-89 (4) 11.25 7.50

No. 49 Surcharged in Black

1905

90 A7 50r on 65r dull blue 5.00 2.75

Stamps of 1898-1903 Overprinted in Carmine or Green

1911

91 A7 2½r gray .25 .25
a. Inverted overprint 15.00 11.00
92 A7 5r orange .25 .25
93 A7 10r lt green .25 .25
a. Inverted overprint 15.00 12.00
94 A7 15r gray green .25 .25
95 A7 20r gray violet .25 .25
96 A7 25r carmine (G) .60 .25
97 A7 50r brown .30 .25
a. Inverted overprint 15.00 12.00
98 A7 75r red lilac .40 .25
99 A7 100r dk bl, *bl* .75 .50
a. Inverted overprint 17.50 14.00
100 A7 115r org brn, *pink* 1.50 .95
101 A7 130r brown, *straw* 1.50 .95
102 A7 200r red lil, *pnksh* 6.00 4.25
103 A7 400r dull blue, *straw* 2.00 1.00
104 A7 500r blk & red, *bl* 2.00 1.00
105 A7 700r violet, *yelsh* 2.00 1.00
Nos. 91-105 (15) 18.30 11.65

King Manuel II — A8

Overprinted in Carmine or Green

1912 *Perf. 11½, 12*

106 A8 2½r violet .25 .25
a. Double overprint 16.00 16.00
b. Double overprint, one inverted 25.00
107 A8 5r black .25 .25
108 A8 10r gray green .25 .25
a. Double overprint 14.00 14.00
109 A8 20r carmine (G) 1.00 .75
110 A8 25r violet brn .60 .45
111 A8 50r dk blue .60 .55
112 A8 75r bister brn .90 .55
113 A8 100r brn, *lt grn* 1.10 .50
114 A8 200r dk grn, *sal* 2.00 1.40
115 A8 300r black, *azure* 2.00 2.00
Nos. 106-115 (10) 8.95 6.95

Stamps of 1898-1905 Overprinted in Black

1913 On Stamps of 1898-1903

116 A7 2½r gray 3.00 1.00
a. Inverted overprint 15.00 15.00
b. Double overprint 12.00 12.00
117 A7 5r orange 2.00 1.00
118 A7 15r gray green 25.00 17.50
a. Inverted overprint 75.00
119 A7 20r gray violet 6.00 1.50
a. Inverted overprint 15.00
120 A7 25r carmine 9.00 4.50
a. Inverted overprint 30.00
b. Double overprint 30.00
121 A7 75r red lilac 7.00 5.00
122 A7 100r bl, *bluish* 10.00 7.50
123 A7 115r org brn, *pink* 37.50 35.00
a. Double overprint 75.00 60.00
124 A7 130r brn, *straw* 13.00 13.00
125 A7 200r red lil, *pnksh* 20.00 13.00
126 A7 400r dl bl, *straw* 14.00 12.50
127 A7 500r blk & red, *gray* 40.00 42.50
128 A7 700r vio, *yelsh* 50.00 40.00
Nos. 116-128 (13) 236.50 194.00

On Provisional Issue of 1902

129 A1 115r on 50r grn 125.00 85.00
a. Inverted overprint
129B A1 400r on 10r yel 700.00 500.00
130 A2 115r on 10r blue grn 3.00 2.50
a. Inverted overprint 25.00
131 A2 400r on 50r blue 80.00 75.00
132 A6 115r on 25r grn 2.00 1.75
a. Inverted overprint 20.00
133 A6 115r on 150r car, *rose* 60.00 40.00
a. Inverted overprint 20.00
134 A6 115r on 200r bl, *bl* 3.00 2.00
135 A6 130r on 75r rose 3.00 2.00
a. Inverted overprint 25.00
136 A6 400r on 50r lt bl 4.00 4.00
a. Perf. 13½ 20.00 10.00
137 A6 400r on 80r yel grn 5.00 4.25

Same Overprint on Nos. 86, 88, 90

138 A7 15r brown 3.00 1.75
139 A7 50r blue 3.00 2.00
140 A7 50r on 65r dl bl 16.00 12.00
Nos. 138-140 (3) 22.00 15.75

No. 123-125, 130-131 and 137 were issued without gum.

Stamps of 1898-1905 Overprinted in Black

On Stamps of 1898-1903

141 A7 2½r gray .60 .50
a. Inverted overprint 9.00
b. Double overprint 11.00 11.00
c. Double overprint inverted 30.00
142 A7 5r orange 30.00 22.50
143 A7 15r gray green 2.00 1.50
a. Inverted overprint 25.00
144 A7 20r gray violet 450.00 200.00
a. Inverted overprint 600.00
145 A7 25r carmine 50.00 27.50
a. Inverted overprint 75.00
146 A7 75r red lilac 5.00 2.25
a. Inverted overprint 5.00
147 A7 100r blue, *bl* 3.00 1.75
148 A7 115r org brn, *pink* 10.00 8.00
a. Inverted overprint 25.00
149 A7 130r brown, *straw* 8.00 7.00
a. Inverted overprint 25.00
150 A7 200r red lil, *pnksh* 4.00 1.75
a. Inverted overprint 10.00
151 A7 400r dull bl, *straw* 10.00 8.00
152 A7 500r blk & red, *gray* 9.00 8.50
153 A7 700r violet, *yelsh* 9.00 8.50

On Provisional Issue of 1902

154 A1 115r on 50r green 200.00 150.00
155 A2 115r on 10r bl grn 2.50 2.25
156 A2 115r on 300r org 250.00 125.00
157 A2 130r on 5r black 300.00 125.00
158 A2 400r on 50r blue 200.00 90.00
159 A6 115r on 25r green 3.00 1.75
160 A6 115r on 150r car, *rose* 3.00 2.25
a. "REPUBLICA" inverted 20.00
161 A6 115r on 200r bl, *bl* 3.00 2.25
162 A6 130r on 75r rose 3.00 2.00
a. Inverted surcharge 20.00
163 A6 130r on 100r brn, *yel* 900.00 500.00
164 A6 400r on 50r lt bl 3.50 3.00
a. Perf. 13½ 17.50 6.00
165 A6 400r on 80r yel grn 3.00 2.25
166 N3 400r on 2½r brn 2.00 1.75

Same Overprint on Nos. 86, 88, 90

167 A7 15r brown 1.50 1.25
a. Inverted overprint 20.00
168 A7 50r blue 1.50 1.25
a. Inverted overprint 20.00
169 A7 50r on 65r dull bl 2.25 1.50
Nos. 167-169 (3) 5.25 4.00

Most of Nos. 141-169 were issued without gum.

Common Design Types pictured following the introduction.

Vasco da Gama Issue of Various Portuguese Colonies Surcharged

On Stamps of Macao

170 CD20 ¼c on ½a bl grn 1.60 1.40
171 CD21 ½c on 1a red 1.60 1.40
172 CD22 1c on 2a red vio 1.60 1.40
173 CD23 2½c on 4a yel grn 1.60 1.40
174 CD24 5c on 8a dk bl 1.90 1.60
175 CD25 7½c on 12a vio brn 3.00 3.00
176 CD26 10c on 16a bis brn 1.90 1.60
177 CD27 15c on 24a bister 1.90 1.60
Nos. 170-177 (8) 15.10 13.40

On Stamps of Portuguese Africa

178 CD20 ¼c on 2½r bl grn 1.25 1.00
179 CD21 ½c on 5r red 1.25 1.00
180 CD22 1c on 10r red vio 1.25 1.00
181 CD23 2½c on 25r yel grn 1.25 1.00
182 CD24 5c on 50r dk bl 1.25 1.00
183 CD25 7½c on 75r vio brn 2.10 2.00
184 CD26 10c on 100r bis brn 1.25 1.00
185 CD27 15c on 150r bister 1.40 1.00
Nos. 178-185 (8) 11.00 9.00

On Stamps of Timor

186 CD20 ¼c on ½a bl grn 1.40 1.25
187 CD21 ½c on 1a red 1.40 1.25
188 CD22 1c on 2a red vio 1.40 1.25
a. Double surcharge 30.00
189 CD23 2½c on 4a yel grn 1.40 1.25
190 CD24 5c on 8a dk bl 1.75 1.60
191 CD25 7½c on 12a vio brn 2.50 2.50
192 CD26 10c on 16a bis brn 1.40 1.40
193 CD27 15c on 24a bister 1.40 1.40
Nos. 186-193 (8) 12.65 11.90
Nos. 170-193 (24) 38.75 34.30

Ceres — A9

Name and Value in Black
Chalky Paper

1914 Typo. *Perf. 15x14*

194 A9 ¼c olive brown .40 .40
195 A9 ½c black .40 .40
196 A9 1c blue green .50 .40
197 A9 1½c lilac brn .30 .25
198 A9 2c carmine .40 .40
199 A9 2½c lt violet .40 .40
200 A9 5c deep blue .45 .35
201 A9 7½c yellow brn .65 .50

202 A9 8c slate .65 .50
203 A9 10c orange brn .65 .50
204 A9 15c plum 2.00 1.25
205 A9 20c yellow green 1.25 .75
206 A9 30c brown, *grn* 2.00 1.40
207 A9 40c brown, *pink* 1.75 1.40
208 A9 50c orange, *sal* 4.00 3.00
209 A9 1e green, *blue* 4.00 3.00
Nos. 194-209 (16) 19.80 14.90

For surcharges see Nos. 250-253, 281-282.

1920

Ordinary Paper

210 A9 ¼c olive brown .25 .25
211 A9 1½c lilac brn .75 .75
212 A9 7½c yellow brn 1.25 1.25
213 A9 10c orange brn 1.50 1.25
Nos. 210-213 (4) 3.75 3.50

1922-26 ***Perf. 12x11½***

214 A9 ¼c olive brown .25 .25
215 A9 ½c black .25 .25
216 A9 1c yellow grn ('22) .25 .25
217 A9 1½c lilac brn .30 .25
218 A9 2c carmine .25 .25
219 A9 2c gray ('26) .25 .25
220 A9 2½c lt violet .25 .25
221 A9 3c orange ('22) .25 .25
222 A9 4c rose ('22) .25 .25
223 A9 4½c gray ('22) .25 .25
224 A9 5c brt blue ('22) .25 .25
225 A9 6c lilac ('22) .25 .25
226 A9 7c ultra ('22) .25 .25
227 A9 7½c yellow brn .25 .25
228 A9 8c slate .25 .25
229 A9 10c orange brn .30 .25
230 A9 12c blue green ('22) .40 .40
231 A9 15c brn rose ('22) .25 .25
232 A9 20c yellow green .45 .45
233 A9 24c ultra ('26) 3.00 2.00
233A A9 25c choc ('26) 3.00 2.00
233B A9 30c gray grn ('22) .40 .30
233C A9 40c turq bl ('22) .40 .30
233D A9 50c lt violet ('26) .40 .30
233E A9 60c dk blue ('22) 2.00 .75
233F A9 60c rose ('26) 3.00 .75
233G A9 80c brt rose ('22) 3.00 .50

Glazed Paper

233H A9 1e pale rose ('22) 3.00 1.40
233I A9 1e blue ('26) 3.00 1.00
233J A9 2e dk violet ('22) 3.00 1.50
233K A9 5e buff ('26) 18.00 7.50
233L A9 10e pink ('26) 30.00 14.00
233M A9 20e pale turq ('26) 80.00 40.00
Nos. 214-233M (33) 157.40 77.40

Preceding Issues Overprinted in Bt. Red

1915

On Provisional Issue of 1902

234 A2 115r on 10r green 1.75 1.60
235 A2 115r on 300r org 1.75 1.75
236 A2 130r on 5r black 4.00 2.75
237 A2 130r on 200r gray lil 1.40 1.25
238 A6 115r on 25r green .60 .40
239 A6 115r on 150r car, *rose* .60 .40
240 A6 115r on 200r bl, *bl* .60 .40
241 A6 130r on 75r rose .60 .40
242 A6 130r on 100r brn, *yel* 1.10 1.25
243 A6 130r on 300r bl, *sal* 1.00 .75

Same Overprint on Nos. 88 and 90

244 A7 50r blue .70 .55
245 A7 50r on 65r dull bl .70 .55
Nos. 234-245 (12) 14.80 12.05

No. 86 Overprinted in Blue and Surcharged in Black

1919

246 A7 2½c on 15r brown .60 .55

No. 91 Surcharged in Black

247 A7 ½c on 2½r gray 3.00 2.75
248 A7 1c on 2½r gray 2.25 2.00
249 A7 2½c on 2½r gray 1.10 .65

No. 194 Surcharged in Black

250 A9 ½c on ¼c ol brn 2.00 1.75
251 A9 2c on ¼c ol brn 2.25 1.90
252 A9 2½c on ¼c ol brn 6.00 5.00

No. 199 Surcharged in Black

253 A9 4c on 2½c lt vio .90 .75
Nos. 246-253 (8) 18.10 15.35

Nos. 246-253 were issued without gum.

Stamps of 1898-1905 Overprinted in Green or Red

1920 **On Stamps of 1898-1903**

255 A7 75r red lilac (G) .55 .50
256 A7 100r blue, *blue* (R) .80 .75
257 A7 115r org brn, *pink* (G) 2.00 1.40
258 A7 130r brn, *straw* (G) 100.00 50.00
259 A7 200r red lil, *pnksh* (G) 2.00 1.00
260 A7 500r blk, & red, *gray* (G) 1.50 1.00
261 A7 700r vio, *yelsh* (G) 2.00 1.25

On Stamps of 1902

262 A6 115r on 25r grn (R) 1.00 .60
263 A6 115r on 200r bl, *bl* (R) 1.50 1.00
264 A6 130r on 75r rose (G) 2.00 1.50

On Nos. 88-89

265 A7 50r blue (R) 1.50 1.10
266 A7 75r rose (G) 25.00 7.00

On No. 90

267 A7 50r on 65r dl bl (R) 25.00 7.00
Nos. 255-257,259-267 (12) 64.85 24.10

Nos. 238-243 Surcharged in Blue or Red

1923 **Without Gum**

268 A6 10c on 115r on 25r (Bl) .70 .50
269 A6 10c on 115r on 150r (Bl) .70 .50
270 A6 10c on 115r on 200r (R) .70 .50
271 A6 10c on 130r on 75r (Bl) .70 .50
272 A6 10c on 130r on 100r (Bl) .70 .50
273 A6 10c on 130r on 300r (R) .70 .50
Nos. 268-273 (6) 4.20 3.00

Nos. 268-273 are usually stained and discolored.

Nos. 84-85 Surcharged

1925

274 A6 40c on 400r on 80r yel grn .90 .45
275 N3 40c on 400r on 2½r brn .90 .45

Nos. 233H and 233J Surcharged

1931

281 A9 70c on 1e pale rose 2.50 1.25
282 A9 1.40e on 2e dk vio 3.00 2.50

Ceres — A11

Perf. 12x11½

1934 **Typo.** **Wmk. 232**

283 A11 1c bister .25 .25
284 A11 5c olive brown .25 .25
285 A11 10c violet .25 .25
286 A11 15c black .25 .25
287 A11 20c gray .25 .25
288 A11 30c dk green .25 .25
289 A11 40c red orange .25 .25
290 A11 45c brt blue .50 .50
291 A11 50c brown .25 .25
292 A11 60c olive grn .50 .50
293 A11 70c brown org .50 .50
294 A11 80c emerald .50 .50
295 A11 85c deep rose 2.25 1.60
296 A11 1e maroon .95 .65
297 A11 1.40e dk blue 2.50 2.10
298 A11 2e dk violet 2.50 1.75
299 A11 5e apple green 10.00 3.75
300 A11 10e olive bister 20.00 6.00
301 A11 20e orange 50.00 18.00
Nos. 283-301 (19) 92.20 37.85

Common Design Types

Inscribed "S. Tomé"

1938 **Unwmk.** ***Perf. 13½x13***

Name and Value in Black

302 CD34 1c gray green .25 .25
303 CD34 5c orange brown .25 .25
304 CD34 10c dk carmine .25 .25
305 CD34 15c dk violet brn .25 .25
306 CD34 20c slate .25 .25
307 CD35 30c rose violet .25 .25
308 CD35 35c brt green .25 .25
309 CD35 40c brown .25 .25
310 CD35 50c brt red vio .25 .25
311 CD36 60c gray black .25 .25
312 CD36 70c brown violet .25 .25
313 CD36 80c orange .45 .25
314 CD36 1e red 2.25 1.10
315 CD37 1.75e blue 2.00 1.50
316 CD37 2e brown car 15.00 5.00
317 CD37 5e olive green 15.00 5.50
318 CD38 10e blue violet 17.00 7.50
319 CD38 20e red brown 30.00 9.50
Nos. 302-319 (18) 84.45 33.10

Marble Column and Portuguese Arms with Cross — A12

1938 ***Perf. 12½***

320 A12 80c blue green 2.75 1.40
321 A12 1.75e deep blue 10.50 4.00
322 A12 20e brown 40.00 17.50
Nos. 320-322 (3) 53.25 22.90

Visit of the President of Portugal in 1938.

Common Design Types

Inscribed "S. Tomé e Principe"

1939 ***Perf. 13½x13***

Name and Value in Black

323 CD34 1c gray grn .25 .25
324 CD34 5c orange brn .25 .25
325 CD34 10c dk carmine .25 .25
326 CD34 15c dk vio brn .25 .25
327 CD34 20c slate .45 .25
328 CD35 30c rose violet .25 .25
329 CD35 35c brt green .25 .25
330 CD35 40c brown .45 .25
331 CD35 50c brt red vio .45 .25
332 CD36 60c gray black .45 .25
333 CD36 70c brown violet .45 .25
334 CD36 80c orange .45 .25
335 CD36 1e red .90 .60
336 CD37 1.75e blue 1.50 .60
337 CD37 2e brown car 2.40 1.50
338 CD37 5e olive green 6.25 2.75
339 CD38 10e blue violet 9.00 4.00
340 CD38 20e red brown 15.00 5.50
Nos. 323-340 (18) 39.25 17.95

Cola Nuts — A13

Designs: 5c, Cola Nuts. 10c, Breadfruit. 30c, Annona. 50c, Cacao pods. 1e, Coffee. 1.75e, Dendem. 2e, Avocado. 5e, Pineapple. 10e, Mango. 20e, Coconuts.

1948 **Litho.** ***Perf. 14½***

341 A13 5c black & yellow .30 .30
342 A13 10c black & buff .40 .30
343 A13 30c indigo & gray 1.50 1.25
344 A13 50c brown & yellow 1.50 1.25
345 A13 1e red & rose 3.00 1.75
346 A13 1.75e blue & gray 4.00 3.25
347 A13 2e black & grn 3.00 1.50
348 A13 5e brown & lil rose 9.00 4.00
349 A13 10e black & pink 12.00 7.50
350 A13 20e black & gray 35.00 20.00
a. Sheet of 10, #341-350 125.00 125.00
Nos. 341-350 (10) 69.70 41.10

No. 350a sold for 42.50 escudos.

Lady of Fatima Issue

Common Design Type

1948, Dec. **Unwmk.**

351 CD40 50c purple 7.25 6.50

Catalogue values for unused stamps in this section, from this point to the end of the section, are for Never Hinged items.

UPU Symbols — A14

1949 **Unwmk.** ***Perf. 14***

352 A14 3.50e black & gray 9.00 6.50

UPU, 75th anniv.

Holy Year Issue

Common Design Types

1950 ***Perf. 13x13½***

353 CD41 2.50e blue 3.00 1.90
354 CD42 4e orange 4.50 2.50

Holy Year Extension Issue

Common Design Type

1951 ***Perf. 14***

355 CD43 4e indigo & bl gray + label 2.50 2.00

Stamp without label attached sells for less.

Medical Congress Issue

Common Design Type

1952 ***Perf. 13½***

356 CD44 10c Clinic .30 .30

Joao de Santarem — A15

Portraits: 30c, Pero Escobar. 50c, Fernao de Po 1e, Alvaro Esteves. 2e, Lopo Goncalves. 3.50e, Martim Fernandes.

1952 Unwmk. Litho. *Perf. 14*
Centers Multicolored

357 A15 10c cream & choc .25 .25
358 A15 30c pale grn & dk grn .25 .25
359 A15 50c gray & dk gray .25 .25
360 A15 1e gray bl & dk bl .85 .25
361 A15 2e lil gray & vio brn .55 .25
362 A15 3.50e buff & choc .85 .25
Nos. 357-362 (6) 3.00 1.50

For overprints and surcharges see Nos. 423, 425, 428-429, 432, 450-457, 474-481.

Jeronymos Convent A16

1953 *Perf. 13x13½*

363 A16 10c dk brown & gray .25 .25
364 A16 50c brn org & org .50 .40
365 A16 3e blue blk & gray blk 2.00 .80
Nos. 363-365 (3) 2.75 1.45

Exhib. of Sacred Missionary Art, Lisbon, 1951.

Stamp Centenary Issue

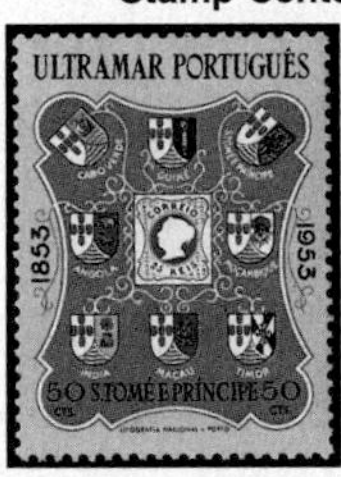

Stamp of Portugal and Arms of Colonies — A17

1953 Photo. *Perf. 13*

366 A17 50c multicolored 1.25 .85

Centenary of Portugal's first postage stamps.

Presidential Visit Issue

Map and Plane — A18

1954 Typo. & Litho. *Perf. 13½*

367 A18 15c blk, bl, red & grn .25 .25
368 A18 5e brown, green & red 1.10 .80

Visit of Pres. Francisco H. C. Lopes.

Sao Paulo Issue
Common Design Type

1954 Litho.

369 CD46 2.50e bl, gray bl & blk .80 .60

Fair Emblem, Globe and Arms — A19

1958 Unwmk. *Perf. 12x11½*

370 A19 2.50e multicolored .70 .60

World's Fair at Brussels.

Tropical Medicine Congress Issue
Common Design Type

Design: Cassia occidentalis.

1958 *Perf. 13½*

371 CD47 5e pale grn, brn, yel, grn & red 2.75 2.25

Compass Rose — A20

1960 Litho. *Perf. 13½*

372 A20 10e gray & multi 1.25 .65

500th death anniv. of Prince Henry the Navigator.

Going to Church — A21

1960 *Perf. 14½*

373 A21 1.50e multicolored .55 .45

10th anniv. of the Commission for Technical Co-operation in Africa South of the Sahara (C.C.T.A.).

Sports Issue
Common Design Type

Sports: 50c, Angling. 1e, Gymnast on rings. 1.50e, Handball. 2e, Sailing. 2.50e, Sprinting. 20e, Skin diving.

1962, Jan. 18 Litho. *Perf. 13½*
Multicolored Design

374 CD48 50c gray green .25 .25
a. "$50 CORREIOS" omitted 50.00
375 CD48 1e lt lilac .65 .25
376 CD48 1.50e salmon .70 .25
377 CD48 2e blue .80 .35
378 CD48 2.50e gray green 1.10 .50
379 CD48 20e dark blue 3.25 1.60
Nos. 374-379 (6) 6.75 3.20

On No. 374a, the blue impression, including imprint, is missing.
For overprint see No. 449.

Anti-Malaria Issue
Common Design Type

Design: Anopheles gambiae.

1962 Unwmk. *Perf. 13½*

380 CD49 2.50e multicolored 2.00 1.50

Airline Anniversary Issue
Common Design Type

1963 Unwmk. *Perf. 14½*

381 CD50 1.50e pale blue & multi .70 .60

National Overseas Bank Issue
Common Design Type

Design: Francisco de Oliveira Chamico.

1964, May 16 *Perf. 13½*

382 CD51 2.50e multicolored .70 .50

ITU Issue
Common Design Type

1965, May 17 Litho. *Perf. 14½*

383 CD52 2.50e tan & multi 1.50 1.00

Infantry Officer, 1788 — A22

35c, Sergeant with lance, 1788. 40c, Corporal with pike, 1788. 1e, Private with musket, 1788. 2.50e, Artillery officer, 1806. 5e, Private, 1811. 7.50e, Private, 1833. 10e, Lancer officer, 1834.

1965, Aug. 24 Litho. *Perf. 13½*

384 A22 20c multicolored .25 .25
385 A22 35c multicolored .25 .25
386 A22 40c multicolored .35 .25
387 A22 1e multicolored 1.25 .60
388 A22 2.50e multicolored 1.25 .60
389 A22 5e multicolored 2.00 1.50
390 A22 7.50e multicolored 2.75 2.25
391 A22 10e multicolored 3.50 2.40
Nos. 384-391 (8) 11.60 8.10

For overprints and surcharges see Nos. 424, 426-427, 435, 458-463, 482-485, 489-490.

National Revolution Issue
Common Design Type

Design: 4e, Arts and Crafts School and Anti-Tuberculosis Dispensary.

1966, May 28 Litho. *Perf. 11½*

392 CD53 4e multicolored .75 .50

Navy Club Issue
Common Design Type

Designs: 1.50e, Capt. Campos Rodrigues and ironclad corvette Vasco da Gama. 2.50e, Dr. Aires Kopke, microscope and tsetse fly.

1967, Jan. 31 Litho. *Perf. 13*

393 CD54 1.50e multicolored 1.30 .50
394 CD54 2.50e multicolored 1.90 .75

Valinhos Shrine, Children and Apparition — A23

1967, May 13 Litho. *Perf. 12½x13*

395 A23 2.50e multicolored .30 .25

50th anniv. of the apparition of the Virgin Mary to 3 shepherd children, Lucia dos Santos, Francisco and Jacinta Marto, at Fatima.

Cabral Medal, from St. Jerome's Convent — A24

1968, Apr. 22 Litho. *Perf. 14*

396 A24 1.50e blue & multi .70 .50

500th birth anniv. of Pedro Alvares Cabral, navigator who took possession of Brazil for Portugal.

Admiral Coutinho Issue
Common Design Type

Design: 2e, Adm. Coutinho, Cago Coutinho Island and monument, vert.

1969, Feb. 17 Litho. *Perf. 14*

397 CD55 2e multicolored .50 .35

Vasco da Gama's Fleet — A25

1969, Aug. 29 Litho. *Perf. 14*

398 A25 2.50e multicolored .60 .60

Vasco da Gama (1469-1524), navigator.

Administration Reform Issue
Common Design Type

1969, Sept. 25 Litho. *Perf. 14*

399 CD56 2.50e multicolored .45 .45

For overprint see No. 430.

Manuel Portal of Guarda Episcopal See — A26

1969, Dec. 1 Litho. *Perf. 14*

400 A26 4e multicolored .50 .35

500th birth anniv. of King Manuel I.

Pero Escobar, Joao de Santarem and Map of Islands — A27

1970, Jan. 25 Litho. *Perf. 14*

401 A27 2.50e lt blue & multi .35 .30

500th anniv. of the discovery of St. Thomas and Prince Islands.

Pres. Américo Rodrigues Thomaz — A28

1970 Litho. *Perf. 12½*

402 A28 2.50e multicolored .45 .40

Visit of Pres. Américo Rodrigues Thomaz of Portugal.

Marshal Carmona Issue
Common Design Type

Antonio Oscar Carmona in dress uniform.

1970, Nov. 15 Litho. *Perf. 14*

403 CD57 5e multicolored .75 .45

Coffee Plant and Stamps — A29

Designs: 1.50e, Postal Administration Building and stamp No. 1, horiz. 2.50e, Cathedral of St. Thomas and stamp No. 2.

1970, Dec. *Perf. 13½*

404 A29 1e multicolored .25 .25
405 A29 1.50e multicolored .35 .25
406 A29 2.50e multicolored .60 .25
Nos. 404-406 (3) 1.20 .75

Centenary of St. Thomas and Prince Islands postage stamps.

Descent from the Cross — A30

1972, May 25 Litho. *Perf. 13*

407 A30 20e lilac & multi 2.50 1.90

4th centenary of publication of The Lusiads by Luiz Camoens.

Olympic Games Issue
Common Design Type

Track and javelin, Olympic emblem.

1972, June 20 ***Perf. 14x13½***
408 CD59 1.50e multicolored .35 .25

Lisbon-Rio de Janeiro Flight Issue
Common Design Type

Design: 2.50e, "Lusitania" flying over warship at St. Peter Rocks.

1972, Sept. 20 Litho. ***Perf. 13½***
409 CD60 2.50e multicolored .35 .25

WMO Centenary Issue
Common Design Type

1973, Dec. 15 Litho. ***Perf. 13***
410 CD61 5e dull grn & multi .60 .50

For overprint see No. 434.

Republic

Flags of Portugal and St. Thomas & Prince A31

1975, July 12 Litho. ***Perf. 13½***
411 A31 3e gray & multi .25 .25
412 A31 10e yellow & multi .90 .45
413 A31 20e lt blue & multi 1.60 .90
414 A31 50e salmon & multi 3.75 1.75
Nos. 411-414 (4) 6.50 3.35

Argel Agreement, granting independence, Argel, Sept. 26, 1974.
For overprints see Nos. 675-678.

Man and Woman with St. Thomas & Prince Flag A32

1975, Dec. 21
415 A32 1.50e pink & multi .25 .25
416 A32 4e multicolored .45 .40
417 A32 7.50e org & multi .95 .60
418 A32 20e blue & multi 1.25 1.40
419 A32 50e ocher & multi 3.00 2.40
Nos. 415-419 (5) 5.90 5.05

Proclamation of Independence, 12/7/75.

Chart and Hand — A33

1975, Dec. 21 Litho. ***Perf. 13½***
420 A33 1e ocher & multi .25 .25
421 A33 1.50e multicolored .25 .25
422 A33 2.50e orange & multi .30 .25
Nos. 420-422 (3) .80 .75

National Reconstruction Fund.

Stamps of 1952-1973 Overprinted

1977 Litho. ***Perf. 13½, 14, 13***
423 A15 10c multi (#357) .25 .25
424 A22 20c multi (#384) .25 .25
425 A15 30c multi (#358) .25 .25
426 A22 35c multi (#385) .25 .25
427 A22 40c multi (#386) .25 .25
428 A15 50c multi (#359) .25 .25
429 A15 1e multi (#360) .55 .45
430 CD56 2.50e multi (#399) .40 .30
431 A27 2.50e multi (#401) .40 .30
432 A15 3.50e multi (#362) 1.30 1.10
433 A26 4e multi (#400) .80 .60
434 CD61 5e multi (#410) 1.00 .80
435 A22 7.50e multi (#390) 1.60 1.30
436 A20 10e multi (#372) 2.40 2.00
Nos. 423-436 (14) 9.95 8.35

The 10c, 30c, 50c, 1e, 3.50e, 10e issued with glassine interleaving stuck to back.

Pres. Manuel Pinto da Costa and Flag A34

Designs: 3.50e, 4.50e, Portuguese Governor handing over power. 12.50e, like 2e.

1977, Jan. ***Perf. 13½***
437 A34 2e yellow & multi .25 .25
438 A34 3.50e blue & multi .40 .25
439 A34 4.50e red & multi .55 .25
440 A34 12.50e multicolored .90 .40
Nos. 437-440 (4) 2.10 1.15

1st anniversary of independence.

Some of the sets that follow may not have been issued by the government.

Peter Paul Rubens (1577-1640), Painter — A35

Details from or entire paintings: 1e (60x44mm), Diana and Calixto, horiz. 5e (60x36mm), The Judgement of Paris, horiz. 10e (60x28mm), Diana and her Nymphs Surprised by Fauns, horiz. 15e (40x64mm), Andromeda and Perseus. 20e (40x64mm), The Banquet of Tereo. 50e (32x64mm) Fortuna.

No. 447a, 20e, (30x40mm) like #445. No. 447b, 75e, (40x30mm) The Banquet of Tereo, diff.

1977, June 28 Litho. ***Perf. 13½***
441 A35 1e multicolored .25 .25
442 A35 5e multicolored .25 .25
443 A35 10e multicolored .40 .30
444 A35 15e multicolored 2.00 1.60
445 A35 20e multicolored 3.00 2.50
446 A35 50e multicolored 5.50 4.75
Nos. 441-446 (6) 11.40 9.65

Souvenir Sheet
Perf. 14

447 A35 Sheet of 2, #a.-b. 13.00 13.00

See type A40 for Rubens stamps without "$" in denomination.

Ludwig van Beethoven — A36

Designs: a, 20e, Miniature, 1802, by C. Hornemann. b, 30e, Life mask, 1812, by F. Klein. c, 50e, Portrait, 1818, by Ferdinand Schimon.

1977, June 28 ***Perf. 13½***
448 A36 Strip of 3, #a.-c. 11.00 9.50

For overprint see No. 617.

No. 379 Ovptd. "Rep. Democr. / 12-7-77"

1977, July 12
449 CD48 20e multicolored *100.00*

Pairs of Nos. 358-359, 357, 362, 384-386 Overprinted Alternately in Black

a

b

1977, Oct. 19 Litho. ***Perf. 14, 13½***
450 A15(a) 3e on 30c multi 1.75 1.25
451 A15(b) 3e on 30c multi 1.75 1.25
452 A15(a) 5e on 50c multi .50 .30
453 A15(b) 5e on 50c multi .50 .30
454 A15(a) 10e on 10c multi .90 .60
455 A15(b) 10e on 10c multi .90 .60
456 A15(a) 15e on 3.50e multi 2.25 1.00
457 A15(b) 15e on 3.50e multi 2.25 1.00
458 A22(a) 20e on 20c multi 2.75 1.40
459 A22(b) 20e on 20c multi 2.75 1.40
460 A22(a) 35e on 35c multi 4.00 1.90
461 A22(b) 35e on 35c multi 4.00 1.90
462 A22(a) 40e on 40c multi 4.50 3.25
463 A22(b) 40e on 40c multi 4.50 3.25
Nos. 450-463 (14) 33.30 19.40

Centenary of membership in UPU. Overprints "a" and "b" alternate in sheets. Nos. 450-457 issued with glassine interleaving stuck to back.

These overprints exist in red on Nos. 452-453, 458-463 and on 1e on 10c, 3.50e and 30e on 30c. Value, set $125.

Mao Tse-tung (1893-1976), Chairman, People's Republic of China — A37

1977, Dec. Litho. ***Perf. 13½x14***
464 A37 50d multicolored 9.00
a. Souvenir sheet 9.00

For overprint see No. 597.

Lenin — A38

Russian Supersonic Plane — A39

Designs: 40d, Rowing crew. 50d, Cosmonaut Yuri A. Gagarin.

1977, Dec. ***Perf. 13½x14, 14x13½***
465 A38 15d multicolored 2.00 1.20
466 A39 30d multicolored 4.00 2.10
467 A39 40d multicolored 5.25 3.25
468 A38 50d red & black 6.50 3.50
a. Sheet of 4, #465-468 27.50 27.50
Nos. 465-468 (4) 17.75 10.05

60th anniv. of Russian October Revolution.
For overprints see Nos. 592-595.

Paintings by Rubens — A40

Designs: 5d, 70d, Madonna and Standing Child. 10d, Holy Family. 25d, Holy Family, diff. 50d, Madonna and Child.

1977, Dec. ***Perf. 13½, 13½x14 (50d)***
Size: 31x47mm (50d)

469 A40 5d multicolored 2.00 1.00
470 A40 10d multicolored 3.50 1.75
471 A40 25d multicolored 7.25 4.00
472 A40 50d multicolored 8.00 4.50
473 A40 70d multicolored 15.00 7.50
a. Sheet of 4, #469-471, #473 40.00 40.00
Nos. 469-473 (5) 35.75 18.75

No. 472 exists in souvenir sheets of 1, perf. and imperf.

Pairs of Nos. 357-359, 362, 384-385 Surcharged

c

#475

#477

#479

#481

#483, 485

1978, May 25 ***Perf. 14½, 13½***

474	A15 (c)	3d on 30c #358	.40	.40
475	A15	3d on 30c #358	.40	.40
a.		Pair, #474-475	1.00	1.00
476	A15 (c)	5d on 50c #359	.60	.60
477	A15	5d on 50c #359	.60	.60
a.		Pair, #476-477	1.20	1.20
478	A15 (c)	10d on 10c #357	1.25	1.25
479	A15	10d on 10c #357	1.25	1.25
a.		Pair, #478-479	2.60	2.60
480	A15 (c)	15d on 3.50e #362	1.60	1.60
481	A15	15d on 3.50e #362	1.60	1.60
a.		Pair, #480-481	3.25	3.25
482	A22 (c)	20d on 20c #384	2.50	2.50
483	A22	20d on 20c #384	2.50	2.50
a.		Pair, #482-483	5.25	5.25
484	A22 (c)	35d on 35c #385	4.50	4.50
485	A22	35d on 35c #385	4.50	4.50
a.		Pair, #484-485	10.00	10.00
		Nos. 474-485 (12)	21.70	21.70
		Nos. 475a-485a (6)	23.30	23.30

Overprints for each denomination alternate on sheet. Nos. 474-481 issued with glassine interleaving stuck to back.

Flag of St. Thomas and Prince Islands — A41

Designs: Nos. 487, 487a, Map of Islands, vert. No. 488, Coat of arms, vert.

1978, July 12 ***Perf. 14x13½, 13½x14***

486	A41	5d multi	1.10	1.10
487	A41	5d multi	1.10	1.10
a.		Souvenir sheet, 50d	26.00	26.00
488	A41	5d multi	1.10	1.10
a.		Strip of 3, #486-488	3.75	3.75

Third anniversary of independence. Printed in sheets of 9. No. 487a contains one imperf. stamp.

No. 386 Surcharged

1978, Sept. 3 **Litho.** ***Perf. 13½***

489	A22	40d on 40e #386	3.00	3.00
490	A22	40d on 40e #386	3.00	3.00
a.		Pair, #489-490	6.75	6.75

Membership in United Nations, 3rd anniv.

Miniature Sheets

Intl. Philatelic Exhibition, 1978 — A42

#491: a, Tahitian Women with Fan, by Paul Gauguin. b, Still Life, by Matisse. c, Barbaric Tales, by Gauguin. d, Portrait of Armand Roulin, by Van Gogh. e, Abstract, by Georges Braque.

#492: a, 20d, like #491c. b, 30d, Horsemen on the Beach, by Gauguin.

1978, Nov. 1 ***Perf. 14***

491	A42	10d Sheet of 9, #e., 2 each #a.-d.	20.00

Imperf

492	A42	Sheet of 3, #491a, 492a-492b	10.00

Intl. Philatelic Exhibition, Essen.

No. 492 has simulated perfs and exists with green margin and without simulated perfs and stamps in different order.

Miniature Sheet of 12

UPU, Centennial A43

Designs: Nos. 493a, Emblem, yellow & black. b, Emblem, green & black. c, Emblem, blue & black. d, Emblem, red & black. e, Concorde, balloon. f, Sailing ship, satellite. g, Monorail, stagecoach. h, Dirigible, steam locomotive. 50d, like #487g.

1978, Nov. 1 ***Perf. 14***

493	A43	#a.-d., 2 ea, #e.-h.	45.00
a.-d.		5d any single	2.00
e.-h.		15d any single	4.50

Souvenir Sheet

494	A43	50d multicolored	27.50

For overprint see No. 706.

Miniature Sheets

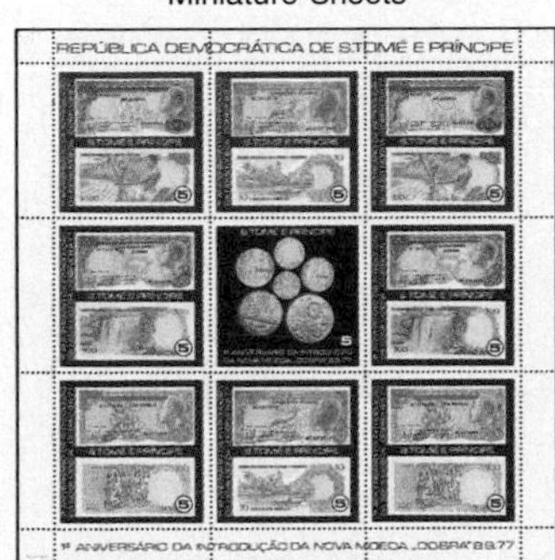

New Currency, 1st Anniv. — A44

Obverse and reverse of bank notes: #a, 1000d. b, 50d. c, 500d. d, 100d. e, Obverse of 50c, 1d, 2d, 5d, 10d, 20d coins.

1978, Dec. 15 ***Perf. 13½***

Sheets of 9

495	A44	5d #e., 2 each #a.-d.	7.00
496	A44	8d #e., 2 each #a.-d.	9.00

World Cup Soccer Championships, Argentina — A45

Various soccer plays: No. 497a, Two players in yellow shirts, one in blue. b, Two players in blue shirts, one in white. c, Six players, referee. d, Two players. No. 498a, Seven players. b, Two players at goal. c, Six players.

1978, Dec. 15 ***Perf. 14***

497	A45	3d Block of 4, #a.-d.	*5.50*
498	A45	25d Strip of 3, #a.-c.	*22.50*

Souvenir sheets of one exist, also exist imperf.

Overprinted with Names of Winning Countries

No. 499b, ITALIA, 1934/38. c, BRASIL, 1958/62/70. d, ALEMANIA 1954/74. No. 500a, INGLATERRA, 1966. b, Vencedores 1978 / 1o ARGENTINA / 2o HOLANDA / 3o BRASIL. c, ARGENTINA 1978.

1979, June 1 **Litho.** ***Perf. 14***

499	A45	3d Block of 4, #a.-d.	2.00
500	A45	25d Strip of 3, #a.-c.	9.00

Souvenir sheets of one exist.

Flowers — A47

Butterflies — A46

Designs: 50c, Charaxes odysseus. 1d, Crinum giganteum. No. 503a, Quisqualis indicia. b, Tecoma stans. c, Nerium oleander. d, Pyrostegia venusta. 10d, Hypolimnas salmacis thomensis. No. 505a, Charaxes monteiri, male. b, Charaxes monteiri, female. c, Papillio leonidas thomasius. d, Crenis boisduvali insularis. 25d, Asystasia gangetica. No. 507, Charaxes varanes defulvata. Nos. 508, Hibiscus mutabilis.

Perf. 15, 15x14½ (#503), 14½x15 (#505)

1979, June 8

501	A46	50c multicolored	.80	.80
502	A47	1d multicolored	.60	.60
503	A47	8d Block of 4, #a.-d.	6.50	6.50
504	A46	10d multicolored	1.75	1.75
505	A46	11d Block of 4, #a.-d.	7.00	7.00
506	A47	25d multicolored	3.75	3.75
		Nos. 501-506 (6)	20.40	20.40

Souvenir Sheets

Perf. 15

507	A46	50d multicolored	13.50	13.50

Imperf

508	A47	50d multicolored	10.50	10.50

No. 508 contains one 30x46mm stamp with simulated perforations.

Intl. Communications Day — A48

1979, July 6 ***Perf. 13***

509	A48	1d shown	.25	.25
510	A48	11d CCIR emblem	1.75	1.75
a.		Pair, #509-510 + label	2.10	2.10
511	A48	14d Syncom, 1963	2.10	2.10
512	A48	17d Symphony, 1975	2.75	2.75
a.		Pair, #511-512 + label	5.00	5.00
		Nos. 509-512 (4)	6.85	6.85

Intl. Advisory Council on Radio Commmunications (CCIR), 50th anniv. (#510).

Intl. Year of the Child A49

Designs: 1d, Child's painting of bird. 7d, Young Pioneers. 14d, Children coloring on paper. 17d, Children eating fruit. 50d, Children from different countries joining hands.

1979, July 6

513	A49	1d multicolored	.30	.30
514	A49	7d multicolored	1.80	1.80
515	A49	14d multicolored	2.25	2.25
516	A49	17d multicolored	3.25	3.25

Size: 100x100mm

Imperf

517	A49	50d multicolored	22.50	22.50
		Nos. 513-517 (5)	30.10	30.10

Souvenir Sheets

Sir Rowland Hill, 1795-1879 — A50

1979, Sept. 15 ***Perf. 15***

518	A50	25d DC-3 Dakota	*27.50*

Perf. 14

519	A50	25d Graf Zeppelin, vert.	*22.50*

1st Air Mail Flight, Lisbon to St. Thomas & Prince, 30th anniv. (#518), Brasiliana '79 Intl. Philatelic Exhibition and 18th UPU Congress (#519).

See Nos. 528-533 for other stamps inscribed "Historia da Aviancao."

For overprint see No. 700.

Albrecht Durer, 450th Death Anniv. — A51

Portraits: No. 520, Willibald Pirckheimer. No. 521, Portrait of a Negro. 1d, Portrait of a Young Man, facing right. 7d, Adolescent boy. 8d, The Negress Catherine. No. 525, Girl with Braided Hair. No. 526, Self-portrait as a Boy. No. 527, Feast of the Holy Family.

1979 Background Color *Perf. 14*

520	A51	50c blue green	.25	.25
521	A51	50c orange	.25	.25
522	A51	1d blue	.40	.40
523	A51	7d brown	2.00	2.00
524	A51	8d red	2.00	2.00
525	A51	25d lilac	7.25	7.25
		Nos. 520-525 (6)	12.15	12.15

Souvenir Sheets

Perf. 13½

526 A51 25d lil, buff & blk 20.00 20.00

Perf. 13½x14

527 A51 25d blk, lil & buff 20.00 20.00

Christmas, Intl. Year of the Child (#527). No. 527 contains one 35x50mm stamp.

Issued: #520-526, Nov. 29; #527, Dec. 25.

For overprint see No. 591.

History of Aviation A52

1979, Dec. 21 *Perf. 15*

528	A52	50c Wright Flyer I	.25	.25
529	A52	1d Sikorsky VS 300	.30	.30
530	A52	5d Spirit of St. Louis	1.40	1.40
531	A52	7d Dornier DO X	1.90	1.90
532	A52	8d Santa Cruz Fairey III D	2.00	2.00
533	A52	17d Space Shuttle	4.75	4.75
		Nos. 528-533 (6)	10.60	10.60

See No. 518 for souvenir sheet inscribed "Historia da Aviancao."

History of Navigation A53

50c, Caravel, 1460. 1d, Portuguese galleon, 1560. 3d, Sao Gabriel, 1497. 5d, Caravelao Navio Dos. 8d, Caravel Redonda, 1512. No. 539, Galley Fusta, 1540. No. 540, Map of St. Thomas & Prince, 1602.

1979, Dec. 21

534	A53	50c multicolored	.25	.25
535	A53	1d multicolored	.30	.30
536	A53	3d multicolored	.70	.70
537	A53	5d multicolored	1.25	1.25
538	A53	8d multicolored	1.75	1.75
539	A53	25d multicolored	5.50	5.50
		Nos. 534-539 (6)	9.75	9.75

Size: 129x98mm

Imperf

540 A53 25d multicolored 10.00 10.00

Birds — A54

No. 541, Serinus rufobrunneus. No. 542, Euplectes aureus. No. 543, Alcedo leucogaster nais. No. 544, Dreptes thomensis. No. 545, Textor grandis. No. 546, Speirops lugubris.

No. 547, Treron S. thomae.

1979, Dec. 21 *Perf. 14*

541	A54	50c multicolored	.25	.25
542	A54	50c multicolored	.25	.25
543	A54	1d multicolored	.25	.25
544	A54	7d multicolored	1.60	1.60
545	A54	8d multicolored	2.00	2.00
546	A54	100d multicolored	16.00	16.00
		Nos. 541-546 (6)	20.35	20.35

Souvenir Sheet

Perf. 14½

547 A54 25d multicolored 13.50 13.50

No. 546 is airmail.

Fish A55

50c, Cypselurus lineatus. 1d, Canthidermis maculatus. 5d, Diodon hystrix. 7d, Ostracion tricornis. 8d, Rhinecanthus aculeatus. 50d, Chaetodon striatus. 25d, Holocentrus axensionis.

1979, Dec. 28 *Perf. 14*

548	A55	50c multicolored	.25	.25
549	A55	1d multicolored	.25	.25
550	A55	5d multicolored	.30	.30
551	A55	7d multicolored	1.90	1.90
552	A55	8d multicolored	2.25	2.25
553	A55	50d multicolored	11.00	11.00
		Nos. 548-553 (6)	15.95	15.95

Souvenir Sheet

Perf. 14½

554 A55 25d multicolored 14.00 14.00

No. 553 is airmail.

Balloons — A56

Designs: 50c, Blanchard, 1784. 1d, Lunardi II, 1785. 3d, Von Lutgendorf, 1786. 7d, John Wise "Atlantic," 1859. 8d, Salomon Anree "The Eagle," 1896. No. 560, Stratospheric balloon of Prof. Piccard, 1931. No. 560A, Indoor demonstration of hot air balloon, 1709, horiz.

1979, Dec. 28 *Perf. 15*

555	A56	50c multicolored	.25	.25
556	A56	1d multicolored	.25	.25
557	A56	3d multicolored	.60	.60
558	A56	7d multicolored	1.40	1.40
559	A56	8d multicolored	1.50	1.50
560	A56	25d multicolored	5.25	5.25
		Nos. 555-560 (6)	9.25	9.25

Souvenir Sheet

Perf. 14

560A A56 25d multicolored 10.00 10.00

No. 560A contains one 50x38mm stamp.

Dirigibles A57

Designs: 50c, Dupuy de Lome, 1872. 1d, Paul Hanlein, 1872. 3d, Gaston brothers, 1882. 7d, Willows II, 1909. 8d, Ville de Lucerne, 1910. 17d, Mayfly, 1910.

1979, Dec. 28 *Perf. 15*

561	A57	50c multicolored	.25	.25
562	A57	1d multicolored	.25	.25
563	A57	3d multicolored	.90	.90
564	A57	7d multicolored	1.75	1.75
565	A57	8d multicolored	2.00	2.00
566	A57	17d multicolored	4.50	4.50
		Nos. 561-566 (6)	9.65	9.65

1980 Olympics, Lake Placid & Moscow A58

Olympic Venues: 50c, Lake Placid, 1980. Nos. 568, 572a, Mexico City, 1968. Nos. 569, 572b, Munich, 1972. Nos. 570, 572c, Montreal, 1976. Nos. 571, 572d, Moscow, 1980.

1980, June 13 Litho. *Perf. 15*

567	A58	50c multicolored	.50	.50
568	A58	11d multicolored	2.50	2.50
569	A58	11d multicolored	2.50	2.50
570	A58	11d multicolored	2.50	2.50
571	A58	11d multicolored	2.50	2.50
		Nos. 567-571 (5)	10.50	10.50

Souvenir Sheet

572 A58 7d Sheet of 4, #a.-d. 9.00 9.00

Proclamation Type of 1975 and

Sir Rowland Hill (1795-1879) — A59

Sir Rowland Hill and: 50c, #1. 1d, #415. 8d, #411. No. 576, #449. No. 577, #418.

1980, June 1 *Perf. 15*

573	A59	50c multicolored	.25	.25
574	A59	1d multicolored	.30	.30
575	A59	8d multicolored	2.25	2.25
576	A59	20d multicolored	6.00	6.00
		Nos. 573-576 (4)	8.80	8.80

Souvenir Sheet

Imperf

577 A32 20d multicolored 11.00 11.00

No. 577 contains one 38x32mm stamp with simulated perforations.

Moon Landing, 10th Anniv. (in 1979) A60

50c, Launch of Apollo 11, vert. 1d, Astronaut on lunar module ladder, vert. 14d, Setting up research experiments. 17d, Astronauts, experiment. 25d, Command module during reentry.

1980, June 13 *Perf. 15*

578	A60	50c multicolored	.40	.40
579	A60	1d multicolored	.55	.55
580	A60	14d multicolored	6.00	6.00
581	A60	17d multicolored	7.00	7.00
		Nos. 578-581 (4)	13.95	13.95

Souvenir Sheet

582 A60 25d multicolored 10.00 10.00

Miniature Sheet

Independence, 5th Anniv. — A61

#583: a, US #1283B. b, Venezuela #C942. c, Russia #3710. d, India #676. e, T. E. Lawrence (1888-1935). f, Ghana #106. g, Russia #2486. h, Algeria #624. i, Cuba #1318. j, Cape Verde #366. k, Mozambique #617. l, Angola #601. 25d, King Amador.

1980, July 12 *Perf. 13*

583 A61 5d Sheet of 12, #a.-l. + 13 labels 13.50 13.50

Souvenir Sheet

Perf. 14

584 A61 25d multicolored 10.00 10.00

No. 584 contains one 35x50mm stamp. For overprint see No. 596.

No. 527 Ovptd. "1980" on Stamp and Intl. Year of the Child emblem in Sheet Margin

1980, Dec. 25 *Perf. 14*

591 A51 25d on No. 527 20.00 20.00

Christmas.

Nos. 465-468a Overprinted in Black or Silver

1981, Feb. 2 *Perf. 13½x14, 14x13½*

592	A38	15d on #465 (S)	*2.75*	*2.75*
593	A39	30d on #466 (S)	*3.75*	*3.75*
594	A39	40d on #467	*7.25*	*7.25*
595	A38	50d on #468	*9.00*	*9.00*
a.		on No. 468a	*50.00*	
		Nos. 592-595 (4)	*22.75*	*22.75*

No. 584 Ovptd. with UN and Intl. Year of the Child emblems and Three Inscriptions

1981, Feb. 2 *Perf. 14*

596 A61 25d on No. 584 *29.00 29.00*

Nos. 464-464a Ovptd. in Silver and Black "UNIAO / SOVIETICA / VENCEDORA / 1980" with Olympic emblem and "JOGOS OLIMPICOS DE MOSCOVO 1980"

1981, May 15 *Perf. 13½x14*

597	A37	50d on #464	*9.00*	*9.00*
a.		on #464a	*9.00*	*9.00*

Mammals — A65

No. 598, Crocidura thomensis. No. 599, Mustela nivalis. 1d, Viverra civetta. 7d, Hipposioleros fuliginosus. 8d, Rattus norvegicus. 14d, Eidolon helvum.
25d, Cercopithecus mona.

1981, May 22 *Perf. 14*

598 A65 50c multicolored *.25 .25*
599 A65 50c multicolored *.25 .25*
600 A65 1d multicolored *.45 .40*
601 A65 7d multicolored *2.50 2.10*
602 A65 8d multicolored *3.00 2.50*
603 A65 14d multicolored *5.25 4.50*
Nos. 598-603 (6) 11.70 10.00

Souvenir Sheet

Perf. 14½

604 A65 25d multicolored *21.00 21.00*

Shells — A66

No. 605, Haxaplex hoplites. No. 606, Bolinus cornutus. 1d, Cassis tessellata. 1.50d, Harpa doris. 11d, Strombus latus. 17d, Cymbium glans.
No. 611: a, 10d, Bolinus cornutus, diff. b, 15d, Conus genuanus.

1981, May 22 *Perf. 14*

605 A66 50c multicolored .25 .25
606 A66 50c multicolored .25 .25
607 A66 1d multicolored .45 .40
608 A66 1.50d multicolored .75 .60
609 A66 11d multicolored 3.50 3.00
610 A66 17d multicolored 6.00 4.75
Nos. 605-610 (6) 11.20 9.25

Souvenir Sheet

Perf. 14½

611 A66 Sheet of 2, #a.-b. 20.00 20.00

For surcharges, see Nos. 1987, 1990, 1993, 2014, 2017, 2020, 2041, 2044, 2047, 2068, 2071, 2074.

Johann Wolfgang von Goethe (1749-1832), Poet — A67

Design: 75d, Goethe in the Roman Campagna, by Johann Heinrich W. Tischbein.

1981, Nov. 14 *Perf. 14*

612 A67 25d multicolored 2.75 2.00

Souvenir Sheet

613 A67 75d multicolored 7.25 7.25

PHILATELIA '81, Frankfurt/Main, Germany.

Tito — A68

1981, Nov. 14 *Perf. 12½x13*

614 A68 17d Wearing glasses 1.20 1.20
615 A68 17d shown 1.20 1.20
a. Sheet of 2, #614-615 6.75 6.75

Souvenir Sheet

Perf. 14x13½

616 A68 75d In uniform *6.75*

Nos. 614-615 issued in sheets of 4 each plus label. For overprints see Nos. 644-646.

No. 448 Overprinted in White

1981, Nov. 28 *Perf. 13½*

617 A36 Strip of 3, #a.-c. *20.00*

Wedding of Prince Charles and Lady Diana.
On No. 617 the white overprint was applied by a thermographic process producing a shiny, raised effect.
Overprint exists in gold, $35 value.

World Chess Championships — A69

Chess pieces: No. 618, Egyptian. No. 619, Two Chinese, green. No. 620, Two Chinese, red. No. 621, English. No. 622, Indian. No. 623, Scandinavian. 75d, Khmer.
No. 624: a, Anatoly Karpov. b, Victor Korchnoi.

1981, Nov. 28 Litho. *Perf. 14*

618 A69 1.50d multicolored *.30 .30*
619 A69 1.50d multicolored *.30 .30*
620 A69 1.50d multicolored *.30 .30*
621 A69 1.50d multicolored *.30 .30*
622 A69 30d multicolored *3.50 3.50*
623 A69 30d multicolored *3.50 3.50*
624 A69 30d Pair, #a.-b. *3.50 3.50*
Nos. 618-624 (7) 11.70 11.70

Souvenir Sheet

625 A69 75d multicolored *21.00 21.00*

Nos. 618-623 exist in souvenir sheets of one. No. 624 exists in souvenir sheet with simulated perfs. Nos. 618-625 exist imperf.

No. 624 Ovptd. in red "ANATOLIJ KARPOV / Campeao Mundial / de Xadrez 1981"

1981, Dec. 10 *Perf. 14*

627 A69 30d Pair, #a.-b. *14.00 14.00*

Exists in souvenir sheet with simulated perfs or imperf.

Pablo Picasso — A70

Paintings: 14d, The Old and the New Year.
No. 629: a, Young Woman. b, Child with Dove. c, Paul as Pierrot with Flowers. d, Francoise, Claude, and Paloma.
No. 630: a, Girl. b, Girl with Doll. 75d, Father, Mother and Child.

1981, Dec. 10 *Perf. 14x13½*

628 A70 14d multicolored *1.40 1.40*
629 A70 17d Strip of 4, #a.-d. *6.50 6.50*
630 A70 20d Pair, #a.-b. *6.50 6.50*
Nos. 628-630 (3) 14.40 14.40

Souvenir Sheet

Perf. 13½

631 A70 75d multicolored *15.00 15.00*

Intl. Year of the Child. Christmas (#628, 631). No. 630 is airmail.
Nos. 628, 629a-629d, 630a-630b exist in souvenir sheets of one. No. 631 contains one 50x60mm stamp.
See Nos. 683-685.

Intl. Year of the Child — A71

Paintings, No. 632, 1.50d: a, Girl with Dog, by Thomas Gainsborough. b, Miss Bowles, by Sir Joshua Reynolds. c, Sympathy, by Riviere. d, Master Simpson, by Devis. e. Two Boys with Dogs, by Gainsborough.
No. 633, 1.50d: a, Girl feeding cat. b, Girl wearing cat mask. c, White cat. d, Cat wearing red bonnet. e, Girl teaching cat to read.
No. 634, 50d: a, Boy and Dog, by Picasso. b, Clipper, by Picasso.
No. 635, 50d: a, Two white cats. b, Himalayan cat.

1981, Dec. 30 *Perf. 14*

632 A71 Strip of 5, #a.-e. *1.25 1.25*
633 A71 Strip of 5, #a.-e. *1.25 1.25*
634 A71 Pair, #a.-b. *9.50 9.50*
635 A71 Pair, #a.-b. + label *9.50 9.50*
Nos. 632-635 (4) 21.50 21.50

Souvenir Sheets

Perf. 13½

636 A71 75d Girl with dog *9.00 9.00*
637 A71 75d Girl with cat *9.00 9.00*

Nos. 636-637 contain one 30x40mm stamp.

2nd Central Africa Games, Luanda, Angola — A73

No. 638: a, Shot put. b, Discus. c, High jump. d, Javelin.
50d, Team handball. 75d, Runner.

1981, Dec. 30 *Perf. 13½x14*

638 A73 17d Strip of 4, #a.-d. 6.50 6.50
639 A73 50d multicolored 4.50 4.50

Souvenir Sheet

640 A73 75d multicolored 8.50 8.50

World Food Day — A74

No. 641: a, Ananas sativus. b, Colocasia esculenta. c, Artocarbus altilis.
No. 642: a, Mangifera indica. b, Theobroma cacao. c, Coffea arabica.
75d, Musa sapientum (Bananas).

1981, Dec. 30

641 A74 11d Strip of 3, #a.-c. *3.25 3.25*
642 A74 30d Strip of 3, #a.-c. *8.25 8.25*

Souvenir Sheet

643 A74 75d multicolored *8.00 8.00*

No. 643 also exist imperf.

Nos. 614-616 Ovptd. in Black

1982, May 25 *Perf. 12½x13*

644 A68 17d on #614 *2.75 2.75*
645 A68 17d on #615 *2.75 2.75*
a. On #615a *8.00 8.00*

Souvenir Sheet

Perf. 14

646 A68 75d on #616 *15.00 15.00*

World Cup Soccer Championships, Spain — A75

Emblem and: No. 647: a, Goalie in blue shirt jumping to catch ball. b, Two players, yellow, red shirts. c, Two players, black shirts. d, Goalie in green shirtcatching ball.
No. 648: a, Player dribbling. b, Goalie facing opponent.
No. 649, Goalie catching ball from emblem in front of goal. No. 650, Like #649 with continuous design.

1982, June 21 *Perf. 13½x14*

647 A75 15d Strip of 4, #a.-d. *6.00 6.00*
648 A75 25d Pair, #a.-b. *5.75 5.75*

Souvenir Sheets

649 A75 75d multicolored — —
650 A75 75d multicolored 9.00 9.00

Nos. 648a-648b are airmail. Nos. 647a-647d, 648a-648b exist in souvenir sheets of one.

A76

Transportation: No. 651, Steam locomotive, TGV train. No. 652, Propeller plane and Concorde.

1982, June 21 *Perf. 12½x13*

651 A76 15d multicolored 6.00 2.00
652 A76 15d multicolored 6.00 2.00
a. Souv. sheet of 2, #651-652 15.00 15.00

PHILEXFRANCE '82.

A77

1982, July 31

653 A77 25d multicolored *6.00 4.00*

Robert Koch, discovery of tuberculosis bacillus, cent.

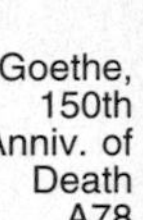

Goethe, 150th Anniv. of Death A78

1982, July 31 ***Perf. 13x12½***

654 A78 50d multicolored *7.25 6.50*

Souvenir Sheet

655 A78 10d like #654 12.50 12.50

A79

1982, July 31 ***Perf. 12½x13***

656 A79 75d multicolored *6.75 6.75*

Souvenir Sheet

657 A79 10d Sheet of 1 *6.00*
657A A79 10d Sheet of 2, purple & multi *10.00*

Princess Diana, 21st birthday. No. 657A exists with red violet inscriptions and different central flower.

A80

Boy Scouts, 75th Anniv.: 15d, Cape of Good Hope #178-179. 30d, Lord Baden-Powell, founder of Boy Scouts.

1982, July 31

658 A80 15d multicolored 1.60 1.20
659 A80 30d multicolored 3.25 2.75
a. Souv. sheet, #658-659 + label *13.50*

Nos. 658-659 exits in sheets of 4 each plus label.

A81

Caricatures by Picasso — #660: a, Musicians. b, Stravinsky.

1982, July 31

660 A81 30d Pair, #a.-b. *5.00 5.00*

Souvenir Sheet

661 A81 5d like #660b *13.50 13.50*

Igor Stravinsky (1882-1971), composer.

A82

George Washington, 250th Anniv. of Birth: Nos. 662, 663b, Washington, by Gilbert Stuart. Nos. 663, 663c, Washington, by Roy Lichtenstein.

1982, July 31

662 A82 30d multicolored *2.40 2.40*
663 A82 30d blk & pink *2.40 2.40*

Souvenir Sheet

663A A82 5d Sheet of 2, #b.-c. 10.00 10.00

Dinosaurs — A83

No. 664, Parasaurolophus. No. 665, Stegosaurus. No. 666, Triceratops. No. 667, Brontosaurus. No. 668, Tyrannosaurus rex. No. 669, Dimetrodon.
No. 670: a, 25d, Pteranodon. b, 50d, Stenopterygius.

1982, Nov. 30 ***Perf. 14x13½***

664 A83 6d multicolored *.95 .70*
665 A83 16d multicolored *2.50 2.00*
666 A83 16d multicolored *2.50 2.00*
667 A83 16d multicolored *2.50 2.00*
668 A83 16d multicolored *2.50 2.00*
669 A83 50d multicolored *8.00 6.00*
Nos. 664-669 (6) 18.95 14.70

Souvenir Sheet

670 A83 Sheet of 2, #a.-b. *15.00 15.00*

Charles Darwin, cent. of death (#670).

Explorers A84

Departure of Marco Polo from Venice — A85

Explorers and their ships: 50c, Thor Heyerdahl, Kon-tiki.
No. 672: a, Magellan, Carrack. b, Drake, Golden Hind. c, Columbus, Santa Maria. d, Leif Eriksson, Viking longship.
50d, Capt. Cook, Endeavour.

1982, Dec. 21 **Litho.**

671 A84 50c multicolored *.25 .25*
672 A84 18d Strip of 4, #a.-d. *7.00 7.00*
673 A84 50d multicolored *5.25 5.25*
Nos. 671-673 (3) 12.50 12.50

Souvenir Sheet

674 A85 75d multicolored *15.00 15.00*

Nos. 411-414 Ovptd. with Assembly Emblem and "2o ANIVERSARIO DA 1a ASSEMBLEIA DA J.M.L.S.T.P." in Silver

1982, Dec. 24 ***Perf. 13½x14***

675 A31 3d on #411 *.45 .30*
676 A31 10d on #412 *1.10 1.10*
677 A31 20d on #413 *3.00 3.00*
678 A31 50d on #414 *5.50 5.50*
Nos. 675-678 (4) 10.05 9.90

MLSTP 3rd Assembly A86

1982, Dec. 24 ***Perf. 13½x14***

679 A86 8d bl & multi *.70 .70*
680 A86 12d grn & multi *1.05 1.05*
681 A86 16d brn org & multi *1.50 1.50*
682 A86 30d red lilac & multi *2.75 2.75*
Nos. 679-682 (4) 6.00 6.00

Picasso Painting Type of 1981

Designs: No. 683a, Lola. b, Aunt Pepa. c, Mother. d, Lola with Mantilla.
No. 684: a, Corina Romeu. b, The Aperitif.
75d, Holy Family in Egypt, horiz.

1982, Dec. 24

683 A70 18d Strip of 4, #a.-d. *7.75 7.75*
684 A70 25d Pair, #a.-b. *5.00 5.00*

Souvenir Sheet

Perf. 14x13½

685 A70 75d multicolored *30.00 30.00*

Intl. Women's Year (#683-684), Christmas (#685).

Locomotives — A87

9d, Class 231K, France, 1941.
No. 687: a, 1st steam locomotive, Great Britain, 1825. b, Class 59, Africa, 1947. c, William Mason, US, 1850. d, Mallard, Great Britain, 1938.
50d, Henschel, Portugal, 1929. 75d, Locomotive barn, Swindon, Great Britain.

1982, Dec. 31 ***Perf. 14x13½***

686 A87 9d multicolored *.65 .50*
687 A87 16d Strip of 4, #a.-d. *6.50 6.50*
688 A87 50d multicolored *4.75 4.75*
Nos. 686-688 (3) 11.90 11.75

Souvenir Sheet

689 A87 75d multicolored 9.00 9.00

Easter — A88

Paintings: No. 690: a, St. Catherine, by Raphael. b, St. Margaret, by Raphael.
No. 691: a, Young Man with a Pointed Beard, by Rembrandt. b, Portrait of a Young Woman, by Rembrandt.
No. 692: a, Rondo (Dance of the Italian Peasants), by Rubens, horiz. b, The Garden of Love, by Rubens, horiz.
No. 693, Samson and Delilah, by Rubens. No. 694, Descent from the Cross, by Rubens.
No. 695: a, Elevation of the Cross, by Rembrandt. b, Descent from the Cross, by Rembrandt.
Nos. 696a, 697, The Crucifixion, by Raphael. Nos. 696b, 698, The Transfiguration, by Raphael.

1983, May 9 ***Perf. 13½x14, 14x13½***

690 A88 16d Pair, #a.-b. *3.50 3.50*
691 A88 16d Pair, #a.-b. *3.50 3.50*
692 A88 16d Pair, #a.-b. *3.50 3.50*
693 A88 18d multicolored *2.25 2.25*
694 A88 18d multicolored *2.25 2.25*
695 A88 18d Pair, #a.-b. *4.50 4.50*
696 A88 18d Pair, #a.-b. *4.50 4.50*
Nos. 690-696 (7) 24.00 24.00

Souvenir Sheets

697 A88 18d vio & multi *10.00*
698 A88 18d multicolored *10.00*

Souvenir sheets containing Nos. 690a-690b, 691a-691b, 692a-692b, 693, 694, 695a-695b exist.

BRASILIANA '83, Rio de Janeiro — A89

Santos-Dumont dirigibles: No. 699a, #5. b, #14 with airplane.

1983, July 29 **Litho.** ***Perf. 13½***

699 A89 25d Pair, #a.-b. 4.75 4.00

First manned flight, bicent.

No. 519 Overprinted with Various Designs

1983, July 29 **Litho.** ***Perf. 14***

Souvenir Sheet

700 A50 25d multicolored 50.00

BRASILIANA '83.

First Manned Flight, Bicent. — A90

No. 701: a, Wright Flyer No. 1, 1903. b, Alcock & Brown Vickers Vimy, 1919.
No. 702: a, Bleriot monoplane, 1909. b, Boeing 747, 1983.
No. 703: a, Graf Zeppelin, 1929. b, Montgolfiere brother's balloon, 1783. No. 704, Pierre Tetu-Brissy. 60d, Flight of Vincent Lunardi's second balloon, vert.

1983, Sept. 16 ***Perf. 14x13½***

701 A90 18d Pair, #a.-b. 4.00 4.00
702 A90 18d Pair, #a.-b. 4.00 4.00
703 A90 20d Pair, #a.-b. 4.75 4.75
704 A90 20d multicolored 2.40 2.40
Nos. 701-704 (4) 15.15 15.15

Souvenir Sheet

Perf. 13½x14

705 A90 60d multicolored 7.50 7.50

Individual stamps from Nos. 701-704 exist in souvenir sheets of 1. Value of 4 $50.

Nos. 493e, 493a, 493e (#706a) and 493g, 493c, 493g (#706b) Ovptd. in Gold with UPU and Philatelic Salon Emblems and:
"SALON DER PHILATELIE ZUM / XIX WELTPOSTKONGRESS / HAMBURG 1984" Across Strips of Three Stamps
Nos. 493f, 493b, 493f (#706c) 493h, 493d, 493h (#706d) Ovptd. in Gold with UPU and Philatelic Salon Emblems and:
"19TH CONGRESSO DA / UNIAO POSTAL UNIVERSAL / HAMBURGO 1984" Across Strips of Three Stamps

1983, Dec. 24 ***Perf. 14***

706 A43 Sheet of 12, #a.-d. 32.50

Overprint is 91x30mm. Exists imperf with silver overprint.

Christmas — A91

Paintings: No. 707, Madonna of the Promenade, 1518, by Raphael. No. 708, Virgin of Guadalupe, 1959, by Salavador Dali.

1983, Dec. 24 ***Perf. 12½x13***

707 A91 30d multicolored 3.00 3.00
708 A91 30d multicolored 3.00 3.00

Nos. 707-708 exist in souvenir sheets of 1.

Automobiles — A92

No. 709: a, Renault, 1912. b, Rover Phaeton, 1907.
No. 710: a, Morris, 1913. b, Delage, 1910.
No. 711: a, Mercedes Benz, 1927. b, Mercedes Coupe, 1936.
No. 712: a, Mercedes Cabriolet, 1924. b, Mercedes Simplex, 1902.
75d, Peugeot Daimler, 1894.

1983, Dec. 28 ***Perf. 14x13½***

709 A92 12d Pair, #a.-b. 2.40 2.40
710 A92 12d Pair, #a.-b. 2.40 2.40
711 A92 20d Pair, #a.-b. 4.00 4.00
712 A92 20d Pair, #a.-b. 4.00 4.00
Nos. 709-712 (4) 12.80 12.80

Souvenir Sheet

713 A92 75d multicolored 10.00 10.00

Nos. 709-712 exist as souvenir sheets. No. 713 contains one 50x41mm stamp.

Medicinal Plants — A93

50c, Cymbopogon citratus. 1d, Adenoplus breviflorus. 5.50d, Bryophillum pinatum. 15.50d, Buchholzia coriacea. 16d, Hiliotropium indicum. 20d, Mimosa pigra. 46d, Piperonia pallucila. 50d, Achyranthes aspera.

1983, Dec. 28 ***Perf. 13½***

714 A93 50c multi .25 .25
715 A93 1d multi .25 .25
716 A93 5.50d multi .45 .45
717 A93 15.50d multi 1.60 1.60
718 A93 16d multi 1.60 1.60
719 A93 20d multi 2.00 2.00
720 A93 46d multi 4.75 4.75
721 A93 50d multi 5.50 5.50
Nos. 714-721 (8) 16.40 16.40

For surcharges, see Nos. 1984, 1991, 1992, 2011, 2018, 2019, 2038, 2045, 2046, 2065, 2072, 2073.

1984 Olympics, Sarajevo and Los Angeles A94

No. 722, Pairs' figure skating.
No. 723: a, Downhill skiing. b, Speed skating. c, Ski jumping.
No. 724, Equestrian.
No. 725: a, Cycling. b, Rowing. c, Hurdling.
No. 726: a, Bobsled. b, Women's archery.

1983, Dec. 29 ***Perf. 13½x14***

722 A94 16d multicolored 1.60 1.60
723 A94 16d Strip of 3, #a.-c. 4.75 4.75
724 A94 18d multicolored 1.90 1.90
725 A94 18d Strip of 3, #a.-c. 5.75 5.75
Nos. 722-725 (4) 14.00 14.00

Souvenir Sheet

726 A94 30d Sheet of 2, #a.-b. 7.50 7.50

Souvenir sheets of 2 exist containing Nos. 722 and 723b, 723a and 723c, 724 and 725b, 725a and 725c.

Birds — A95

50c, Spermestes cucullatus. 1d, Xanthophilus princeps. 1.50d, Thomasophantes sanctithomae. 2d, Quelea erythrops. 3d, Textor velatus peixotoi. 4d, Anabathmis hartlaubii. 5.50d, Serinus mozambicus santhome. 7d, Estrilda astrild angolensis. 10d,Horizorhinus dohrni. 11d, Zosterops ficedulinus. 12d, Prinia molleri. 14d, Chrysococcyx cupreus insularum. 15.50d, Halcyon malimhicus dryas. 16d, Turdus olivaceofuscus. 17d, Oriolus crassirostris. 18.50d, Dicrurus modestus. 20d, Columba thomensis. 25d, Stigmatopelia senegalensis thome. 30d, Chaetura thomensis. 42d, Onychognatus fulgidus. 46d, Lamprotornis ornatus. 100d, Tyto alba thomenis.

1983, Dec. 30 ***Perf. 13½***

727 A95 50c multi .25 .25
728 A95 1d multi .25 .25
729 A95 1.50d multi .25 .25
730 A95 2d multi .25 .25
731 A95 3d multi .25 .25
732 A95 4d multi .45 .45
733 A95 5.50d multi .45 .45
734 A95 7d multi .80 .80
735 A95 10d multi 1.05 1.05

Size: 30x43mm

736 A95 11d multi 1.30 1.30
737 A95 12d multi 1.30 1.30
738 A95 14d multi 1.45 1.45
739 A95 15.50d multi 1.60 1.60
740 A95 16d multi 1.75 1.75
741 A95 17d multi 1.75 1.75
742 A95 18.50d multi 1.90 1.90
743 A95 20d multi 2.00 2.00
744 A95 25d multi 2.75 2.75

Size: 31x47mm

Perf. 13½x14

745 A95 30d multi 3.25 3.25
746 A95 42d multi 4.50 4.50
747 A95 46d multi 5.25 5.25
748 A95 100d multi 10.00 10.00
Nos. 727-748 (22) 42.80 42.80

For surcharges see Nos. 1296-1300, 1361-1363, 1372-1373, 1988, 1994, 2015, 2042, 2069, 2092, C21.

Souvenir Sheet

ESPANA '84, Madrid — A96

Paintings: a, 15.50d, Paulo Riding Donkey, by Picasso. b, 16d, Abstract, by Miro. c, 18.50d, My Wife in the Nude, by Dali.

1984, Apr. 27 ***Perf. 13½x14***

749 A96 Sheet of 3, #a.-c. 7.00 7.00

LUBRAPEX '84, Lisbon — A97

Children's drawings: 16d, Children watching play. 30d, Adults.

1984, May 9 ***Perf. 13½***

750 A97 16d multicolored 1.75 1.75
751 A97 30d multicolored 3.00 3.00

Intl. Maritime Organization, 25th Anniv. — A98

Ships: Nos. 752a, 753a, Phoenix, 1869. 752b, 753b, Hamburg, 1893. 752c, 753c, Prince Heinrich, 1900.
No. 754: a, Leopold, 1840. b, Stadt Schaffhausen, 1851. c, Crown Prince, 1890. d, St. Gallen, 1905.
No. 755: a, Elise, 1816. b, De Zeeuw, 1824. c, Friedrich Wilhelm, 1827. d, Packet Hansa.
No. 756: a, Savannah, 1818. b, Chaperone, 1884. c, Alida, 1847. d, City of Worcester, 1881.
No. 757, Ferry, Lombard Bridge, Hamburg, c. 1900. No. 758, Train, coaches on bridge, c. 1880, vert. No. 759, Windmill, bridge, vert. No. 760, Queen of the West. No. 761, Bremen. No. 762, Union.

1984, June 19 Litho. ***Perf. 14x13½***

752 A98 50c Strip of 3, #a.-c. 3.75 3.75
753 A98 50c Strip of 3, #a.-c. 3.75 3.75
754 A98 7d Piece of 4, #a.-d. 4.75 4.75
e. Souv. sheet of 2, #754a-754b
f. Souv. sheet of 2, #754c-754d
755 A98 8d Piece of 4, #a.-d. 4.75 4.75
e. Souv. sheet of 2, #755a-755b
f. Souv. sheet of 2, #755c-755d
756 A98 15.50d Piece of 4, #a.-d. 8.25 8.25
e. Souv. sheet of 2, #756a, 756d
f. Souv. sheet of 2, #756b-756c
Nos. 752-756 (5) 25.25 25.25
Nos. 754e-754f, 755e-755f, 756e-756f (6) 80.00

Souvenir Sheets

Perf. 14x13½, 13½x14

757 A98 10d multicolored 9.50 9.50
758 A98 10d multicolored 9.50 9.50
759 A98 10d multicolored 9.50 9.50

Perf. 13½

760 A98 15d multicolored 13.50 13.50
761 A98 15d multicolored 13.50 13.50
762 A98 15d multicolored 13.50 13.50
Nos. 757-762 (6) 69.00 69.00

Nos. 757-759 exist imperf in different colors. Nos. 760-762 contain one 60x33mm stamp each. Nos. 753a-753c have UPU and Hamburg Philatelic Salon emblems and are additionally inscribed "PARTICIPACAO DE S. TOME E PRINCIPE / NO CONGRESSO DA U.P.U. EM HAMBURGO."
Sheets containing Nos. 754-756 contain one label.

Natl. Campaign Against Malaria A99

1984, Sept. 30 ***Perf. 13½***

764 A99 8d Malaria victim 1.30 1.30
765 A99 16d Mosquito, DDT, vert. 2.25 2.25
766 A99 30d Exterminator, vert. 4.00 4.00
Nos. 764-766 (3) 7.55 7.55

A100

World Food Day: 8d, Emblem, animals, produce. 16d, Silhouette, animals. 46d, Plowed field, produce. 30d, Tractor, field, produce, horiz.

1984, Oct. 16

767 A100 8d multicolored 1.05 1.05
768 A100 16d multicolored 1.60 1.60
769 A100 46d multicolored 3.25 3.25
Nos. 767-769 (3) 5.90 5.90

Souvenir Sheet

770 A100 30d multicolored 3.75 3.75

A101

Mushrooms: 10d, Coprinus micaceus. 20d, Amanita rubescens. 30d, Armillariella mellea. 50d, Hygrophorus chrysodon, horiz.

1984, Nov. 5

771 A101 10d multicolored 3.25 3.25
772 A101 20d multicolored 6.00 6.00
773 A101 30d multicolored 9.00 9.00
Nos. 771-773 (3) 18.25 18.25

Souvenir Sheet

774 A101 50d multicolored 17.50 17.50

Christmas A102

Designs: 30d, Candles, offering, stable. 50d, Stable, Holy Family, Kings.

1984, Dec. 25

775 A102 30d multicolored *3.00 3.00*

Souvenir Sheet

776 A102 50d multicolored 5.25 5.25

No. 776 contains one 60x40mm stamp.

Conference of Portuguese Territories in Africa A103

1985, Feb. 14

777 A103 25d multicolored *2.75 2.75*

Reinstatement of Flights from Lisbon to St. Thomas, 1st Anniv. — A104

Designs: 25d, Douglas DC-3, map of northwest Africa. 30d, Air Portugal Douglas DC-8. 50d, Fokker Friendship.

1985, Dec. 6 Litho. *Perf. 13½*

778 A104 25d multicolored *2.40 2.40*
779 A104 30d multicolored *2.75 2.75*

Souvenir Sheet

779A A104 50d multicolored 9.00 9.00

Flowers — A105

1985, Dec. 30 *Perf. 11½x12*

780 A105 16d Flowering cactus *1.20 1.20*
781 A105 20d Sunflower *1.90 1.90*
782 A105 30d Porcelain rose *2.10 2.10*
Nos. 780-782 (3) 5.20 5.20

Mushrooms A106

6d, Fistulina hepatica. 25d, Collybia butyracea. 30d, Entoloma clypeatum.
75d, Cogumelos II.

1986, Sept. 18 *Perf. 13½*

783 A106 6d multicolored *.65 .65*
784 A106 25d multicolored *2.40 2.40*
785 A106 30d multicolored *2.50 2.50*
Nos. 783-785 (3) 5.55 5.55

Souvenir Sheet

786 A106 75d multicolored *10.00 8.00*

No. 786 exists with margins trimmed on four sides removing the control number.

Miniature Sheet

World Cup Soccer, Mexico A107

No. 787: a, Top of trophy. b, Bottom of trophy. c, Interior of stadium. d, Exterior of stadium.

1986, Oct. 1

787 A107 25d Sheet of 4, #a.-d. 11.50 11.50

For overprints see Nos. 818-818A.

Miniature Sheet

1988 Summer Olympics, Seoul — A108

Seoul Olympic Games emblem, and: No. 788a, Map of North Korea. b, Torch. c, Olympic flag, map of South Korea. d, Text.

1986, Oct. 2

788 A108 25d Sheet of 4, #a.-d. *16.00 16.00*

Halley's Comet — A109

Designs: No. 789a, 5d, Challenger space shuttle, 1st launch. b, 6d, Vega probe. c, 10d, Giotto probe. d, 16d, Comet over Nuremberg, A.D. 684.
90d, Comet, Giotto probe, horiz.

1986, Oct. 27

789 A109 Sheet of 4, #a.-d. + 5 labels *10.00 7.00*

Souvenir Sheet

790 A109 90d multicolored 10.00 10.00

Automobiles — A110

Designs: No. 791a, 50c, Columbus Monument, Barcelona. b, 6d, Fire engine ladder truck, c. 1900. c, 16d, Fire engine, c. 1900. d, 30d, Fiat 18 BL Red Cross ambulance, c. 1916.

1986, Nov. 1

791 A110 Sheet of 4, #a.-d. + 5 labels *10.00 8.00*

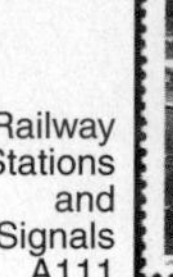

Railway Stations and Signals A111

Designs: 50c, London Bridge Station, 1900. 6d, 100-300 meter warning signs. 20d, Signal lamp. 50d, St. Thomas & Prince Station.

1986, Nov. 2 *Perf. 13½*

792 A111 50c multicolored *.45 .45*
793 A111 6d multicolored *1.20 1.20*
794 A111 20d multicolored *4.00 4.00*
Nos. 792-794 (3) 5.65 5.65

Souvenir Sheet

795 A111 50d multicolored 7.00 7.00

LUBRAPEX '86, Brazil — A112

Exhibition emblem and: No. 796a, 1d, Line fisherman on shore. b, 1d, Line fisherman in boat. c, 2d, Net fisherman. d, 46d, Couple trap fishing, lobster.

1987, Jan. 15

796 A112 Sheet of 4, #a.-d. + 2 labels *5.00 4.25*

Intl. Peace Year A113

Designs: 8d, Mahatma Gandhi. 10d, Martin Luther King, Jr. 16d, Red Cross, Intl. Peace Year, UN, UNESCO, Olympic emblems and Nobel Peace Prize medal. 20d, Albert Luthuli. 75d, Peace Dove, by Picasso.

1987, Jan. 15

797 A113 8d bl, blk & pur *1.05 1.05*
798 A113 10d bl, blk & grn *1.30 1.30*
799 A113 16d multicolored *2.25 2.25*
800 A113 20d multicolored *2.75 2.75*
Nos. 797-800 (4) 7.35 7.35

Souvenir Sheet

801 A113 75d multicolored *7.00* 7.00

Christmas 1986 — A114

Paintings by Albrecht Durer: No. 802a, 50c, Virgin and Child. b, 1d, Madonna of the Carnation. c, 16d, Virgin and Child, diff. d, 20d, The Nativity. 75d, Madonna of the Goldfinch.

1987, Jan. 15

802 A114 Strip of 4, #a.-d. 6.00 4.00

Souvenir Sheet

803 A114 75d multicolored 8.00 8.00

Fauna and Flora — A115

Birds: a, 1d, Agapornis fischeri. b, 2d, Psittacula krameri. c, 10d, Psittacus erithacus. d, 20d, Agapornis personata psittacidae.
Flowers: e, 1d, Passiflora caerulea. f, 2d, Oncidium nubigenum. g, 10d, Helicontia wagneriana. h, 20d, Guzmania liguiata.
Butterflies: i, 1d, Aglais urticae. j, 2d, Pieris brassicae. k, 10d, Fabriciana niobe. l, 20d, Zerynthia polyxena.
Dogs: m, 1d, Sanshu. n, 2d, Hamiltonstovare. o, 10d, Gran spitz. p, 20d, Chowchow.

1987, Oct. 15 *Perf. 14x13½*

804 A115 Sheet of 16, #a.-p. *20.00* 20.00

Sports Institute, 10th Anniv. — A116

No. 805: a, 50c, Three athletes. b, 20d, Map of St. Thomas and Prince, torchbearers. c, 30d, Volleyball, soccer, team handball and basketball players.
50d, Bjorn Borg.

1987, Oct. 30

805 A116 Strip of 3, #a.-c. *4.50 4.50*

Souvenir Sheet

Perf. 13½x14

806 A116 50d Sheet of 1 + label 5.75 5.75

Miniature Sheet

Discovery of America, 500th Anniv. (in 1992) — A117

Emblem and: No. 807: a, 15d, Columbus with globe, map and arms. b, 20d, Battle between Spanish galleon and pirate ship. c, 20d, Columbus landing in New World. 100d, Model ship, horiz.

1987, Nov. 3 *Perf. 13½x14*

807 A117 Sheet of 3, #a.-c. + 3 labels *9.00 9.00*

Souvenir Sheet

Perf. 14x13½

808 A117 100d multicolored *10.00 10.00*

Mushrooms — A118

Designs: No. 809a, 6d, Calocybe ionides. b, 25d, Hygrophorus coccineus. c, 30d, Boletus versipellis. 35d, Morchella vulgaris, vert.

1987, Nov. 10 *Perf. 14x13½*

809 A118 Strip of 3, #a.-c. 5.75 5.75

Souvenir Sheet

Perf. 13½x14

810 A118 35d multicolored *5.25 5.25*

Locomotives — A119

No. 811: a, 5d, Jung, Germany. b, 10d, Mikado 2413. c, 20d, Baldwin, 1920. 50d, Pamplona Railroad Station, 1900.

1987, Dec. 1 Litho. *Perf. 14x13½*

811 A119 Strip of 3, #a.-c. 6.75 6.75

Souvenir Sheet

812 A119 50d multicolored 5.50 5.50

Miniature Sheet

Christmas — A120

Paintings of Virgin and Child by: No. 813a, 1d, Botticelli. b, 5d, Murillo. c, 15d, Raphael. d, 20d, Memling.

50d, Unkmown artist, horiz.

1987, Dec. 20 *Perf. 13½x14*

813 A120 Sheet of 4, #a.-d. *4.00 4.00*

Souvenir Sheet

Perf. 14x13½

814 A120 50d multicolored *5.75 5.75*

World Boy Scout Jamboree, Australia, 1987-88 — A121

1987, Dec. 30 *Perf. 14x13½*

815 A121 50c multicolored 3.00 .80

Russian October Revolution, 70th Anniv. A122

1988 Litho. *Perf. 12*

816 A122 25d Lenin addressing revolutionaries 2.25 2.25

Souvenir Sheet

Lubrapex '88 — A123

1988, May *Perf. 14x13½*

817 A123 80d Trolley 5.50 5.50

Nos. 787a-787d Ovptd. "CAMPEONATO MUNDIAL / DE FUTEBOL MEXICO '86 / ALEMANHA / SUBCAMPIAO" in Silver (#818) or Same with "ARGENTINA / CAMPIAO" Instead in Gold (#818A) Across Four Stamps

1988, Aug. 15 *Perf. 13½*

818 A107 25d Block of 4 (S) 25.00 25.00

818A A107 25d Block of 4 (G) 25.00 25.00

Medicinal Plants — A123a

Mushrooms — A123b

Medicinal plants: No. 819a, 5d, Datura metel. b, 5d, Salaconta. c, 5d, Cassia occidentalis. d, 10d, Solanum ovigerum. e, 20d, Leonotis nepetifolia.

Mushrooms: No. 820a, 10d, Rhodopaxillus nudus. b, 10d, Volvaria volvacea. c, 10d, Psalliota bispora. d, 10d, Pleurotus ostreatus. e, 20d, Clitocybe geotropa.

1988, Oct. 26 *Perf. 13½x14*

819 A123a Strip of 5, #a.-e. 6.75 6.75

820 A123b Strip of 5, #a.-e. 8.00 8.00

Souvenir Sheets

821 A123a 35d Hiersas durero *6.25 6.25*

822 A123b 35d Mushroom on wood *6.25 6.25*

Miniature Sheets of 4

Passenger Trains — A123c

No. 823: a, Swiss Federal Class RE 6/6, left. b, Class RE 6/6, right.

No. 824: a, Japan Natl. Class EF 81, left. b, Class EF 81, right.

No. 825: a, German Electric E 18, 1930, left. b, E 18, 1930, right.

60d, Japan Natl. Class 381 Electric.

1988, Nov. 4 *Perf. 14x13½*

823 A123c 10d 2 ea #a.-b. + 2 labels *5.50 5.50*

824 A123c 10d 2 ea #a.-b. + 2 labels *5.50 5.50*

825 A123c 10d 2 ea #a.-b. + 2 labels *5.50 5.50*

Nos. 823-825 (3) 16.50 16.50

Souvenir Sheet

826 A123c 60d multicolored *8.00* 8.00

Butterflies — A123d

Various flowers and: No. 827a, White and brown spotted butterfly. b, Dark brown and white butterfly, flower stigma pointing down. c, Brown and white butterfly, flower stigma pointing down.

50d, Brown, white and orange butterly.

1988, Nov. 25 *Perf. 13½x14*

827 A123d 10d Strip of 3, #a.-c. *4.50 4.00*

Souvenir Sheet

828 A123d 50d multicolored *9.00 9.00*

Ferdinand von Zeppelin (1838-1917) A123e

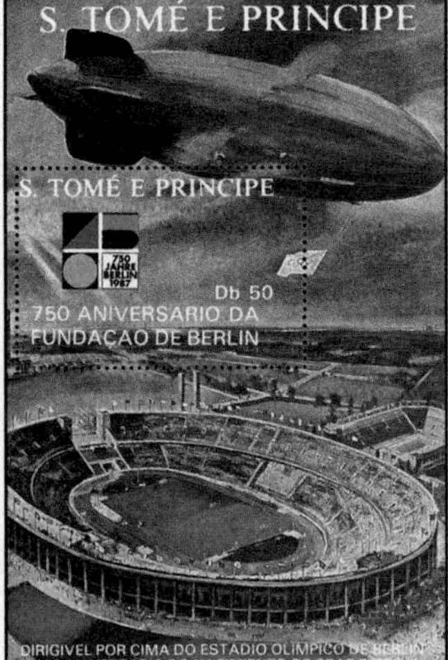

Berlin, 750th Anniv. — A123f

No. 829: a, Sailing ship, dirigible L23. b, Dirigibles flying over British merchant ships. c, Rendezvous of zeppelin with Russian ice breaker Malygin.

No. 830: a, Airship Le Jeune at mooring pad, Paris, 1903, vert. b, von Zeppelin, vert.

Perf. 14x13½, 13½x14

1988, Nov. 25

829 A123e 10d Strip of 3, #a.-c. *8.50 8.50*

830 A123e 10d Pair, #a.-b. *5.75 5.75*

Souvenir Sheet

831 A123f 50d multicolored 8.00 8.00

Natl. Arms — A123g

Automatic Telephone Exchange Linking the Islands, 1st Anniv. — A123h

1988, Dec. 15 *Perf. 13½*

832 A123g 10d multicolored *1.50 1.50*

833 A123h 25d multicolored *3.25 3.25*

Olympics Games, Seoul, Barcelona and Albertville — A123i

World Cup Soccer Championships, Italy, 1990 — A123j

No. 834, View of Barcelona, Cobi. No. 835, Barcelona Games emblem. No. 836, Gold medal from 1988 Seoul games. No. 837, Emblems of 1988 & 1992 games. No. 838, Bear on skis, Albertville, 1992. No. 839, Soccer ball. No. 840, Italy '90 Championships emblem. No. 841, World Cup Trophy. No. 842, Transfer of Olympic flag during Seoul closing ceremony. No. 843, Olympic pins. No. 844, like No. 838. No. 845, Soccer balls as hemispheres of globe.

1988, Dec. 15 *Perf. 14x13½, 13½x14*

834 A123i 5d multi *1.60 1.60*

835 A123i 5d multi, vert. *1.60 1.60*

836 A123i 5d multi, vert. *1.60 1.60*

837 A123i 5d multi *1.60 1.60*

838 A123i 5d grn & multi *1.60 1.60*

839 A123j 5d multi *1.60 1.60*

840 A123j 5d multi, vert. *1.60 1.60*

841 A123j 5d multi, vert. *1.60 1.60*

Nos. 834-841 (8) 12.80 12.80

Souvenir Sheets

Perf. 14x13½

842 A123i 50d multi *10.00 10.00*

843 A123i 50d multi *10.00 10.00*

844 A123i 50d blue & multi *10.00 10.00*

845 A123j 50d multi *10.00 10.00*

No. 842 exists with Olympic emblems in gold or silver. No. 845 exists with marginal inscriptions in gold or silver. See Nos. 876-877 for souvenir sheets similar in design to No. 840.

Intl. Boy Scout Jamboree, Australia, 1987-88 — A123k

No. 846: a, Campfire. b, Scout emblem, pitched tents, flag. c, Scout emblem, tent flaps, flag, axe.
110d, Trefoil center point, horiz.

1988, Dec. 15 ***Perf. 13½x14***
846 A123k 10d Strip of 3, #a.-c. 6.75 6.75

Souvenir Sheet
Perf. 14x13½
847 A123k 110d multicolored 25.00 25.00

Intl. Red Cross, 125th Anniv. — A123m

No. 848: a, 50c, Patient in hospital. b, 5d, Transporting victims. c, 20d, Instructing workers. 50d, Early mail train, horiz.

1988, Dec. 15 ***Perf. 13½x14***
848 A123m Strip of 3, #a.-c. *8.00 8.00*

Souvenir Sheet
Perf. 14x13½
849 A123m 50d multicolored *10.50 10.50*

No. 848c is airmail.

Miniature Sheet

Christmas — A123n

No. 850: a, 10d, Madonna and Child with St. Anthony Abbot and the Infant Baptism, by Titian. b, 10d, Madonna and Child with St. Catherine and a Rabbit, by Titian. c, 10d, Nativity Scene, by Rubens. d, 30d, Adoration of the Magi, by Rubens.
50d, The Annunciation (detail), by Titian, vert.

1988, Dec. 23 ***Perf. 14x13½***
850 A123n Sheet of 4, #a.-d. 8.00 8.00

Souvenir Sheet
Perf. 13½x14
851 A123n 50d multicolored 6.75 6.75

Titian, 500th anniv. of birth. Country name does not appear on No. 850d.

French Revolution, Bicent. — A123o

Designs: No. 852, Eiffel Tower, Concorde, stylized doves, flag. No. 853 Eiffel Tower, flag, stylized doves. No. 854, Eiffel Tower, flag, stylized doves, TGV train, vert. 50d, TGV train.

Perf. 14x13½, 13½x14
1989, July 14 **Litho.**
852 A123o 10d multicolored *1.40 1.40*
853 A123o 10d multicolored *1.40 1.40*
854 A123o 10d multicolored *1.40 1.40*
Nos. 852-854 (3) 4.20 4.20

Souvenir Sheet
855 A123o 50d multicolored *6.25 6.25*

Fruit — A123p

1989, Sept. 15 ***Perf. 13½x14***
856 A123p 50c Chapu-chapu *.25 .25*
857 A123p 1d Guava *.25 .25*
858 A123p 5d Mango *.25 .25*
859 A123p 10d Carambola *.25 .25*
860 A123p 25d Nona *.45 .45*
861 A123p 50d Avacado *.90 .90*
862 A123p 50d Cajamanga *.90 .90*

Perf. 14x13½
863 A123p 60d Jackfruit *.95 .95*
864 A123p 100d Cacao *1.60 1.60*
865 A123p 250d Bananas *4.50 4.50*
866 A123p 500d Papaya *9.75 9.75*
Nos. 856-866 (11) 20.05 20.05

For surcharges see Nos. 1170B, 1170E, 1295-1295A.

Souvenir Sheet
Perf. 13½x14
867 A123p 1000d Pomegranate *20.00 20.00*

Nos. 863-866 are horiz.

Orchids A123q

Designs: No. 868, Dendrobium phalaenopsis. No. 869, Catteleya granulosa. 50d, Diothonea imbricata and maxillaria eburnea.

1989, Oct. 15 ***Perf. 13½x14***
868 A123q 20d multicolored *1.75 1.75*
869 A123q 20d multicolored *1.75 1.75*

Souvenir Sheet
870 A123q 50d multicolored 4.75 4.75

Hummingbirds — A124

Designs: No. 871, Topaza bella, Sappho sparganura, vert. No. 872, Petasophores anais. No. 873, Lophornis adorabilis, Chalcostigma herrani, vert. 50d, Oreotrochilus chimborazo.

1989, Oct. 15 ***Perf. 13½x14, 14x13½***
871 A124 20d multicolored 1.75 1.75
872 A124 20d multicolored 1.75 1.75
873 A124 20d multicolored 1.75 1.75
Nos. 871-873 (3) 5.25 5.25

Souvenir Sheet
Perf. 14x13½
874 A124 50d multicolored 5.25 5.25

Miniature Sheet

1990 World Cup Soccer Championships, Italy — A125

Program covers: No. 875: a, 10d, Globe and soccer ball, 1962. b, 10d, Foot kicking ball, 1950. c, 10d, Abstract design, 1982. d, 20d, Player kicking ball, 1934.
No. 876: a, Character emblem, horiz. b, USA 94, horiz. 50d, like #876a, horiz.

1989, Oct. 24 ***Perf. 13½x14***
875 A125 Block of 4, #a.-d. *7.50 7.50*

Souvenir Sheets
Perf. 14x13½
876 A125 25d Sheet of 2, #a.-b. *6.50 6.50*
877 A125 50d blue & multi *6.50 6.50*

1992 Summer Olympics, Barcelona — A126

1989, Oct. 24 ***Perf. 13½x14, 14x13½***
878 A126 5d Tennis, vert. *.90 .90*
879 A126 5d Basketball, vert. *.90 .90*
880 A126 5d Running *.90 .90*
881 A126 35d Baseball, vert. *7.25 7.25*
Nos. 878-881 (4) 9.95 9.95

Souvenir Sheet
Perf. 14x13½
882 A126 50d Sailing *8.00 8.00*
883 A126 50d Mosaic *8.00 8.00*

Nos. 878-881 exist in souvenir sheets of one. Value for 4 sheets, $22.50. The country name on souvenir sheet of one of No. 878 appears in the margin, rather than on the stamp itself.

Locomotives — A127

1989, Oct. 27 ***Perf. 14x13½, 13½x14***
884 A127 20d Japan 2.50 2.50
885 A127 20d Philippines 2.50 2.50
886 A127 20d Spain, vert. 2.50 2.50
887 A127 20d India 2.50 2.50
888 A127 20d Asia 2.50 2.50
Nos. 884-888 (5) 12.50 12.50

Souvenir Sheets
889 A127 50d Garratt, Africa *8.00 8.00*
890 A127 50d Trans-Gabon, vert. *8.00 8.00*

Nos. 884-888 exist in souvenir sheets of one.

Ships A128

#891, Merchant ships at sea, 16th cent. #892, Caravels, merchant ships in harbor, 16th cent. #893, 3 merchant ships at sea, 18th cent. #894, War ships, 18th cent. #895, 4 merchant ships, 18th cent. #896, Passenger liner, Port of Hamburg. #897, German sailing ship, 17th cent.

1989, Oct. 27 ***Perf. 14x13½***
891 A128 20d multicolored *2.00 2.00*
892 A128 20d multicolored *2.00 2.00*
893 A128 20d multicolored *2.00 2.00*
894 A128 20d multicolored *2.00 2.00*
895 A128 20d multicolored *2.00 2.00*
Nos. 891-895 (5) 10.00 10.00

Souvenir Sheets
896 A128 50d multicolored 6.00 6.00

Perf. 13½x14
897 A128 50d multi, vert. 6.00 6.00

Discovery of America, 500th anniv., in 1992 (#891-895) and Hamburg, 800th anniv. (#891-897).

Nos. 891-895 exist in souvenir sheets of one. Value for 5 sheets, $15.

Butterflies A129

1989, Dec. 20 ***Perf. 13½x14***
898 A129 20d Tree bark *2.25 2.25*
899 A129 20d Leaves *2.25 2.25*
900 A129 20d Flowers *2.25 2.25*
901 A129 20d Bird *2.25 2.25*
902 A129 20d Blades of grass *2.25 2.25*
Nos. 898-902 (5) 11.25 11.25

Souvenir Sheet
903 A129 100d yel, brn & multi *10.50 10.50*

Nos. 898-902 exist in souvenir sheets of one. Value for 5 sheets, $30.

African Development Bank, 25th Anniv. — A130

1989, Dec. 20 ***Perf. 13½x14***
904 A130 25d blk, lt bl & grn *3.25 3.25*

World Telecommunications Day — A131

1989, Dec. 20 ***Perf. 14x13½***
905 A131 60d multicolored *5.00*

Souvenir Sheet

Perf. 13½x14

906 A131 100d Early Bird satellite, vert. 9.00 8.00

Christmas A132

Paintings: No. 907, Adoration of the Magi (detail), by Durer. No. 908, Young Virgin Mary, by Titian. No. 909, Adoration of the King, by Rubens. No. 910, Sistine Madonna, by Raphael. 100d, Madonna and Child Surrounded by Garland and Boy Angels, by Rubens.

1989, Dec. 23 *Perf. 13½x14*

907 A132 25d multicolored *2.50 2.50*
908 A132 25d multicolored *2.50 2.50*
909 A132 25d multicolored *2.50 2.50*
910 A132 25d multicolored *2.50 2.50*
Nos. 907-910 (4) 10.00 10.00

Souvenir Sheet

911 A132 100d multicolored *10.50 10.50*

Nos. 907-910 exist in souvenir sheets of one. Value for 4 sheets, $13.50.

Expedition of Sir Arthur Eddington to St. Thomas and Prince, 70th Anniv. A133

Designs: No. 912, Albert Einstein with Eddington. No. 913, Locomotive on Prince Island. No. 914, Roca Sundy railway station.

1990 **Litho.** *Perf. 13½*

912 A133 60d multicolored 5.25 5.25
913 A133 60d multicolored 5.25 5.25
914 A133 60d multicoloed 5.25 5.25
a. Souvenir sheet of 3, #912-914 20.00 16.00
Nos. 912-914 (3) 15.75 15.75

For surcharge see No. 1295D.

Souvenir Sheet

Independence, 15th Anniv. — A134

Designs: a, Map, arms. b, Map, birds carrying envelope. c, Flag.

1990, July 12 *Perf. 13½*

916 A134 50d Sheet of 3, #a.-c. *14.00 14.00*

Orchids — A135

No. 917, Eulophia guineensis. No. 918, Ancistrochilus. No. 919, Oeceoclades maculata. No. 920, Vanilla imperialis. No. 921, Ansellia africana.

No. 922, Angraecum distichum, horiz. No. 923, Polystachya affinis, horiz.

1990, Sept. 15 **Litho.** *Perf. 13½*

917 A135 20d multicolored 1.75 1.75
918 A135 20d multicolored 1.75 1.75
919 A135 20d multicolored 1.75 1.75
920 A135 20d multicolored 1.75 1.75
921 A135 20d multicolored 1.75 1.75
Nos. 917-921 (5) 8.75 8.75

Souvenir Sheets

Perf. 14x13½

922 A135 50d multicolored 4.50 4.50
923 A135 50d multicolored 4.50 4.50

Expo '90, Intl. Garden and Greenery Exposition, Osaka.

Locomotives — A136

5d, Bohemia, 1923-41. 20d, W. Germany, 1951-56. No. 926, Mallet, 1896-1903. No. 927, Russia, 1927-30. No. 928, England, 1927-30.
No. 929, Camden-Amboy, 1834-38. No. 930, Stockton-Darlington, 1825.

1990, Sept. 28 *Perf. 14x13½*

924 A136 5d multicolored *.45 .45*
925 A136 20d multicolored *1.75 1.75*
926 A136 25d multicolored *2.25 2.25*
927 A136 25d multicolored *2.25 2.25*
928 A136 25d multicolored *2.25 2.25*
Nos. 924-928 (5) 8.95 8.95

Souvenir Sheets

929 A136 50d multicolored 6.00 6.00
930 A136 50d multicolored 6.00 6.00

Souvenir Sheet

Iberoamericana '90 Philatelic Exposition — A137

1990, Oct. 7

931 A137 300d Armas Castle 17.50 12.00

1990 World Cup Soccer Championships, Italy — A138

No. 932, German team with World Cup Trophy. No. 933, 2 players with ball. No. 934, 3 players with ball. No. 935, Italian player. No. 936, US Soccer Federation emblem and team members. No. 937, World Cup Trophy.

1990, Oct. 15 *Perf. 13½*

932 A138 25d multicolored 2.25 2.25
933 A138 25d multicolored 2.25 2.25
934 A138 25d multicolored 2.25 2.25
935 A138 25d multicolored 2.25 2.25
Nos. 932-935 (4) 9.00 9.00

Souvenir Sheets

Perf. 14x13½

936 A138 50d multi, horiz. 4.50 4.50
937 A138 50d multi, horiz. 4.50 4.50

Mushrooms A139

No. 938, Boletus aereus. No. 939, Coprinus micaceus. No. 940, Pholiota spectabilis. No. 941, Krombholzia aurantiaca. No. 942, Stropharia aeruginosa.
No. 943, Hypholoma capnoides. No. 944, Pleurotus ostreatus.

1990, Nov. 2 *Perf. 13½x14*

938 A139 20d multicolored *1.75 1.75*
939 A139 20d multicolored *1.75 1.75*
940 A139 20d multicolored *1.75 1.75*
941 A139 20d multicolored *1.75 1.75*
942 A139 20d multicolored *1.75 1.75*
Nos. 938-942 (5) 8.75 8.75

Souvenir Sheets

Perf. 14x13½

943 A139 50d multicolored *5.75 5.75*
944 A139 50d multicolored *5.75 5.75*

Nos. 943-944 horiz. See Nos. 1014-1020.

Butterflies — A140

No. 945, Megistanis baeotus. No. 946, Ascia vamillae. No. 947, Danaus chrysippus. No. 948, Morpho menelaus. No. 949, Papilio rutulus, vert. No. 950, Papilio paradiesa.
No. 951, Parnassius clodius, vert. No. 952, Papilio macmaon, vert.

1990, Nov. 2 *Perf. 14x13½, 13½x14*

945 A140 15d multicolored *1.30 1.30*
946 A140 15d multicolored *1.30 1.30*
947 A140 15d multicolored *1.30 1.30*
948 A140 15d multicolored *1.30 1.30*
949 A140 15d multicolored *1.30 1.30*
950 A140 25d multicolored *2.10 2.10*
Nos. 945-950 (6) 8.60 8.60

Souvenir Sheets

951 A140 50d multicolored 8.00 8.00
952 A140 50d multicolored 8.00 8.00

Presenting Gifts to the Newborn King — A141

Christmas: No. 954, Nativity scene. No. 955, Adoration of the Magi. No. 956, Flight into Egypt. No. 957, Adoration of the Magi, diff. No. 958, Portrait of Artist's Daughter Clara (detail), by Rubens, horiz.

1990, Nov. 30 *Perf. 13½x14*

953 A141 25d multicolored *2.25 2.25*
954 A141 25d multicolored *2.25 2.25*
955 A141 25d multicolored *2.25 2.25*
956 A141 25d multicolored *2.25 2.25*
Nos. 953-956 (4) 9.00 9.00

Souvenir Sheets

957 A141 50d multicolored *4.50 4.50*

Perf. 14x13½

958 A141 50d multicolored *4.50 4.50*

Death of Rubens, 350th anniv. (#958).

Anniversaries and Events A142

No. 960, Oath of Confederation. No. 961, Pointed roof. No. 962, William Tell statue, vert. No. 963, Brandenburg Gate. No. 964, Penny Black, vert. No. 965, 100d bank note.

1990, Dec. 15 *Perf. 13½x14*

959 A142 20d multicolored 1.75 1.75

Souvenir Sheets

Perf. 14x13½, 13½x14 (#962, 964)

960 A142 50d multicolored 4.50 4.50
961 A142 50d multicolored 4.50 4.50
962 A142 50d multicolored 4.50 4.50
963 A142 50d multicolored 4.50 4.50
964 A142 50d multicolored 4.50 4.50
965 A142 50d multicolored 4.50 4.50

Swiss Confederation, 700th anniv. (#959-962). Brandenburg Gate, 200th anniv. (#963). First postage stamp, 150th anniv. (#964). Independence of St. Thomas and Prince, 15th anniv. (#965).

Paintings — A143

No. 966, The Bathers, by Renoir. No. 967, Girl Holding Mirror for Nude, by Picasso. No. 968, Nude, by Rubens. No. 969, Descent from the Cross (detail), by Rubens. No. 970, Nude, by Titian. No. 971, Landscape, by Durer. No. 972, Rowboats, by Van Gogh. No. 973, Nymphs, by Titian. No. 974, Bather, by Titian. No. 975, Postman Joseph Roulin (detail), by Van Gogh. No. 976, The Abduction of the Daughters of Leucippus, by Rubens. No. 977, Nude, by Titian, diff.

1990, Dec. 15 *Perf. 14x13½, 13½x14*

966 A143 10d multi *1.05 1.05*
967 A143 10d multi, vert. *1.05 1.05*
968 A143 10d multi, vert. *1.05 1.05*
969 A143 10d multi, vert. *1.05 1.05*
970 A143 10d multi, vert. *1.05 1.05*
971 A143 20d multi *2.10 2.10*
972 A143 20d multi *2.10 2.10*
973 A143 25d multi *2.40 2.40*
974 A143 25d multi, vert. *2.40 2.40*
Nos. 966-974 (9) 14.25 14.25

Souvenir Sheets

Perf. 13½x14

975 A143 50d multi, vert. *8.00 8.00*
976 A143 50d multi, vert. *8.00 8.00*
977 A143 50d multi, vert. *8.00 8.00*

Rubens, 350th anniv. of death (Nos. 968-969, 976). Titian, 500th anniv. of death (Nos. 970, 973-974, 977). Van Gogh, centennial of death (Nos. 972, 975).
See No. 958 for other souvenir sheet for Rubens death anniv.

Flora and Fauna — A144

Designs: 1d, Gecko. 5d, Cobra. 10d, No. 980, Sea turtle. No. 981, Fresh water turtle. No. 982, Civet. 70d, Civet in tree. No. 984, Civet with young. No. 985, Civet in den.
Psittacus erithacus: 80d, In tree, vert. 100d, On branch with wings spread, vert. 250d, Feeding young, vert. No. 989, Three in flight, vert.

1991, Feb. 2 *Perf. 14x13½*

978 A144 1d multicolored *.25 .25*
979 A144 5d multicolored *.25 .25*
980 A144 10d multicolored *.25 .25*
981 A144 50d multicolored *.70 .70*
982 A144 50d multicolored *.70 .70*
983 A144 70d multicolored *1.20 1.20*
984 A144 75d multicolored *1.20 1.20*
985 A144 75d multicolored *1.20 1.20*

Perf. 13½x14

986 A144 80d multicolored *1.30 1.30*
987 A144 100d multicolored *1.50 1.50*
988 A144 250d multicolored *4.00 4.00*
989 A144 500d multicolored *8.00 8.00*
Nos. 978-989 (12) 20.55 20.55

Souvenir Sheets

990 A144 500d Orchid, vert. 9.00 9.00
991 A144 500d Rose, vert. 9.00 9.00

See Nos. 1054I-1054M. For surcharges see Nos. 1170F, 1170I-1170J.

Locomotives — A145

1991, May 7 *Perf. 14x13½, 13½x14*

992 A145 75d shown *.90 .90*
993 A145 75d North America, vert. *.90 .90*
994 A145 75d Germany, vert. *.90 .90*
995 A145 75d New Delhi, vert. *.90 .90*
996 A145 75d Brazil, vert. *.90 .90*
997 A145 200d Two leaving terminal *2.40 2.40*
Nos. 992-997 (6) 6.90 6.90

Souvenir Sheets

998 A145 500d Engine 120, vert. 6.00 6.00
999 A145 500d Engine 151-001 6.00 6.00

Birds — A146

No. 1000, Psittacula kuhlii. No. 1001, Plydolophus rosaceus. No. 1002, Falco tinnunculus. No. 1003, Platycercus palliceps. No. 1004, Marcrocercus aracanga.

No. 1005, Ramphastos culmenatus. No. 1006, Strix nyctea.

1991, July 8 *Perf. 13½x14*

1000 A146 75d multicolored *1.20 1.20*
1001 A146 75d multicolored *1.20 1.20*
1002 A146 75d multicolored *1.20 1.20*
1003 A146 75d multicolored *1.20 1.20*
1004 A146 200d multicolored *3.25 3.25*
Nos. 1000-1004 (5) 8.05 8.05

Souvenir Sheets

1005 A146 500d multicolored *14.00 9.25*
1006 A146 500d multicolored 9.25 9.25

Paintings A147

50d, Venus and Cupid, by Titian. #1008, Horse's Head (detail), by Rubens. #1009, Child's face (detail), by Rubens. 100d, Spanish Woman, by Picasso. 200d, Man with Christian Flag, by Titian. #1012, Study of a Negro, by Rubens. #1013, Madonna and Child, by Raphael.

1991, July 31

1007 A147 50d multicolored *.70 .70*
1008 A147 75d multicolored *1.05 1.05*
1009 A147 75d multicolored *1.05 1.05*
1010 A147 100d multicolored *1.60 1.60*
1011 A147 200d multicolored *3.25 3.25*
Nos. 1007-1011 (5) 7.65 7.65

Souvenir Sheets

1012 A147 500d multicolored *7.75 7.75*
1013 A147 500d multicolored *7.75 7.75*

Mushroom Type of 1990

No. 1014, Clitocybe geotropa. No. 1015, Lepiota procera. 75d, Boletus granulatus. 125d, Coprinus comatus. 200d, Amanita rubescens.

No. 1019, Armillariella mellea. No. 1020, Nictalis parasitica, horiz.

1991, Aug. 30

1014 A139 50d multicolored *.70 .70*
1015 A139 50d multicolored *.70 .70*
1016 A139 75d multicolored *1.05 1.05*
1017 A139 125d multicolored *1.75 1.75*
1018 A139 200d multicolored *3.25 3.25*
Nos. 1014-1018 (5) 7.45 7.45

Souvenir Sheets

1019 A139 500d multicolored *7.75 7.75*

Perf. 14x13½

1020 A139 500d multicolored *7.75 7.75*

Flowers A148

No. 1022, Zan tedeschia elliotiana. No. 1023, Cyrtanthes pohliana. No. 1024, Phalaenopsis lueddemanniana. No. 1025, Haemanthus katharinae. 500d, Arundina graminifolia.

1991, Sept. 9 *Perf. 13½x14*

1021 A148 50d shown *.70 .70*
1022 A148 50d multicolored *.70 .70*
1023 A148 100d multicolored *1.50 1.50*
1024 A148 100d multicolored *1.50 1.50*
1025 A148 200d multicolored *3.25 3.25*
Nos. 1021-1025 (5) 7.65 7.65

Souvenir Sheet

1026 A148 500d multicolored 7.50 7.50

Souvenir Sheet

Iberoamericano '92 Intl. Philatelic Exhibition — A149

1991, Oct. 11 **Litho.** *Perf. 14x13½*

1027 A149 800d multicolored *7.00 7.00*

Discovery of America, 500th Anniv. (in 1992) — A150

No. 1028, Columbus. No. 1029, Sailing ship. No. 1030, Sailing ship, diff. No. 1031, Landing in New World. No. 1032, Pointing the way.

No. 1033, Columbus' fleet, horiz.

1991, Oct. 12 *Perf. 13½x14*

1028 A150 50d multicolored
1029 A150 50d multicolored
1030 A150 75d multicolored
1031 A150 125d multicolored
1032 A150 200d multicolored
Nos. 1028-1032 (5) 10.00

Souvenir Sheet

Perf. 14x13½

1033 A150 500d multicolored *10.00*

Butterflies — A151

1991, Oct. 16 *Perf. 14x13½*

1034 A151 125d Limentis popul 3.25 3.25
1035 A151 125d Pavon inachis io 3.25 3.25

Souvenir Sheet

Perf. 13½x14

1036 A151 500d Zerynthia polyxena *6.75 6.75*

Phila Nippon '91.

1991, Nov. 15 *Perf. 14x13½*

1037 A151 125d Macaon papilio machaon *1.75 1.75*
1038 A151 125d Gran pavon *1.75 1.75*
1039 A151 125d Pavon inachis io, diff. *1.75 1.75*
1040 A151 125d Artia caja *1.75 1.75*
Nos. 1037-1040 (4) 7.00 7.00

Souvenir Sheet

Perf. 13½x14

1041 A151 500d Unnamed butterfly, vert. *7.00 7.00*

Christmas.

Landmarks — A152

Landmarks of France: No. 1042, Ile de France, vert. No. 1043, Chenonceau Castle. No. 1044, Azay-le-Rideau Castle. No. 1045, Chambord Castle. No. 1046, Chaumont Castle. No. 1047, Fountainebleau Palace.

Perf. 13½x14, 14x13½

1991, Nov. 15

1042-1047 A152 25d Set of 6 *2.50 2.50*

Souvenir Sheet

1048 A152 500d Paris map, 1615 *7.50 7.50*

French National Exposition.

Souvenir Sheet

Fauna — A153

Animals and birds: a, Weasel, monkey. b, Civet, rats. c, Goat, cow. d, Rabbits, wildcat. e, Parrot, black bird. f, White bird, multicolored bird.

1991, Nov. 15 *Perf. 14x13½*

1049 A153 25d Sheet of 6, #a.-f. *8.00 8.00*

French National Exposition.

Express Mail Service from St. Thomas and Prince — A154

1991 **Litho.** *Perf. 14*

1050 A154 3000d multicolored *16.00 16.00*

Souvenir Sheets

1991 Intl. Olympic Committee Session, Birmingham — A154a

Designs: No. 1050A, IOC emblem, Birmingham Session. No. 1050B, 1998 Winter Olympics emblem, Nagano. No. 1050C, 1998 Winter Olympics mascot.

1992 **Litho.** *Perf. 14*

1050A A154a 800d multi *10.00 10.00*
1050B A154a 800d multi *10.00 10.00*
1050C A154a 800d multi *10.00 10.00*
Nos. 1050A-1050C (3) 30.00 30.00

Souvenir Sheet

IBEREX '91 — A154b

1992

1050D A154b 800d multi 10.00 10.00

Souvenir Sheets

1992 Winter Olympics, Albertville — A154c

Olympic medals.

1992 **Set of 4, a.-d.**
1050E A154c 50d multi 40.00 25.00

No. 1050E exists as four souvenir sheets with pictures of different medalists in sheet margins: a., Blanca Fernandez, Spain; b., Alberto Tomba, Italy; c., Mark Kirchner, Germany; d., Torgny Mogren, Norway.

1992 Summer Olympics, Barcelona A154d

View of earth from space with: No. 1050F, High jumper. No. 1050G, Roller hockey player. No. 1050H, Equestrian. No. 1050I, Kayaker. No. 1050J, Weight lifter. No. 1050K, Archer. No. 1050L, Michael Jordan, horiz.

1992
1050F-1050K A154d 50d Set of 6 *8.00 8.00*

Souvenir Sheet

1050L A154d 50d multicolored *8.00 8.00*

Whales — A155

Designs: No. 1051, Orcinus orca. No. 1052, Orcinus orca, four on surface of water. No. 1053, Pseudoraca crassidens. No. 1054, Pseudoraca crassidens, three under water.

1992 **Litho.** ***Perf. 14***
1051-1054 A155 450d Set of 4 16.00 3.50

World Wildlife Fund.

Visit of Pope John Paul II — A155a

c, Flags, Pope. d, Church with two steeples. e, Church, diff.
f, Pope, vert. g, Church, blue sky, vert. h, Church, closer view, vert.

1992, Apr. 19 **Litho.** ***Perf. 14***

Sheets of 4

1054A A155a 200d #d.-e., 2 #c 10.00 10.00
1054B A155a 200d #g.-h., 2 #f 10.00 10.00

Miniature Sheets

Pope John Paul II and Flower — A155c

Pope John Paul II and Bird — A155d

No. 1054C — Flower and Pope looking: t, Straight ahead. u, To right, three-quarters. v, Slightly to left. w, To right, profile.
No. 1054D — Bird and Pope looking: x, Straight ahead. y, To right, three-quarters. z, Slightly to left. aa, To right, profile.
No. 1054E — Flower, diff. and Pope looking: ab, Straight ahead. ac, To right, three-quarters. ad, Slightly to left. ae, To right, profile.
No. 1054F — Bird, diff. and Pope looking: af, Straight ahead. ag, To right, three-quarters. ah, Slightly to left. ai, To right, profile.
No. 1054G — Flower, diff. and Pope looking: aj, Straight ahead. ak, To right, three-quarters. al, Slightly to left. am, To right, profile.
No. 1054H — Bird, diff. and Pope looking: an, Straight ahead. ao, To right, three-quarters. ap, Slightly to left. aq, To right, profile.

1992, Apr. 19 ***Perf. 13¾x14***
1054C A155c 120d Sheet of 4, #t-w — —
1054D A155d 120d Sheet of 4, #x-aa — —
1054E A155c 150d Sheet of 4, #ab-ae — —
1054F A155d 150d Sheet of 4, #af-ai — —
1054G A155c 180d Sheet of 4, #aj-am — —
1054H A155d 250d Sheet of 4, #an-aq — —
Set of 6 sheets 85.00

Flora and Fauna Type of 1991

Designs: No. 1054I, 1000d, Brown & white bird, vert. No. 1054J, 1500d, Yellow flower, vert. No. 1054K, 2000d, Red flower, vert. No. 1054L, 2500d, Black bird, vert.
No. 1054M, 800d, Sea turtle.

1992, Apr. 19
1054I-1054L A144 Set of 4 35.00 35.00

Souvenir Sheet

1054M A144 800d multi — —

An additional souvenir sheet was issued in this set. The editors would like to examine any example of it.

UN Conference on Environmental Development, Rio — A155b

Designs: 65d, Rain forest. 110d, Walruses. 150d, Raptor. 200d, Tiger. 275d, Elephants.
Each 800d: No. 1054T, Panda, horiz. No. 1054U, Zebras, horiz.

1992, June 6 **Litho.** ***Perf. 14***
1054O-1054S A155b Set of 5 15.00

Souvenir Sheets

1054T-1054U A155b Set of 2 30.00

Souvenir Sheet

Olymphilex '92 — A156

Olympic athletes: a, Women's running. b, Women's gymnastics. c, Earvin "Magic" Johnson.

1992, July 29
1055 A156 300d Sheet of 3, #a.-c. 11.50 11.50

Mushrooms A157

75d, Leccinum ocabrum. 100d, Amanita spissa, horiz. 125d, Strugilomyces floccopus. 200d, Suillus luteus. 500d, Agaricus siluaticus. #1061, Amanita pantherma, horiz. #1062, Agaricus campestre.

1992, Sept. 5 ***Perf. 14***
1056 A157 75d multicolored .70 .70
1057 A157 100d multicolored .90 .90
1058 A157 125d multicolored 1.05 1.05
1059 A157 200d multicolored 1.75 1.75
1060 A157 500d multicolored 4.50 4.50
Nos. 1056-1060 (5) 8.90 8.90

Souvenir Sheets

Perf. 14x13½, 13½x14

1061 A157 1000d multicolored 10.00 10.00
1062 A157 1000d multicolored 10.00 10.00

Birds — A158

Designs: 75d, Paradisea regie, pipra rupicole. 100d, Trogon pavonis. 125d, Paradisea apoda. 200d, Pavocriotctus. 500d, Ramphatos maximus. No. 1068, Woodpecker. No. 1069, Picus major.

1992, Sept. 15 ***Perf. 14***
1063 A158 75d multicolored .55 .55
1064 A158 100d multicolored .80 .80
1065 A158 125d multicolored .95 .95
1066 A158 200d multicolored 1.50 1.50
1067 A158 500d multicolored 3.75 3.75
Nos. 1063-1067 (5) 7.55 7.55

Souvenir Sheets

Perf. 13½x14

1068 A158 1000d multicolored 9.00 9.00
1069 A158 1000d multicolored 9.00 9.00

Marcelo da Veiga (1892-1976), Writer — A159

Designs: a, 10d. b, 40d. c, 50d. d, 100d.

1992, Oct. 3 ***Perf. 13½***
1070 A159 Sheet of 4, #a.-d. 4.00 4.00

Locomotives — A160

Designs: 75d, 100d, 125d, 200d, 500d, Various locomotives. No. 1076, Steam train arriving at station. No. 1077, Engineer, stoker in locomotive cab.

1992, Oct. 3 ***Perf. 14x13½***
1071 A160 75d black .65 .65
1072 A160 100d black .80 .80
1073 A160 125d black 1.05 1.05
1074 A160 200d black 1.60 1.60
1075 A160 500d black 4.00 4.00
Nos. 1071-1075 (5) 8.10 8.10

Souvenir Sheets

1076 A160 1000d black 8.00 8.00
1077 A160 1000d black 8.00 8.00

Butterflies and Moths — A161

75d, Chelonia purpurea. 100d, Hoetera philocteles. 125d, Attacus pavonia major. 200d, Ornithoptera urvilliana. 500d, Acherontia atropos. No. 1083, Peridromia amphinome, vert. No. 1084, Uramia riphacus, vert.

1992, Oct. 18 ***Perf. 14x13½***
1078 A161 75d multicolored *.55 .55*
1079 A161 100d multicolored *.80 .80*
1080 A161 125d multicolored *.95 .95*

1081 A161 200d multicolored *1.50 1.50*
1082 A161 500d multicolored *3.75 3.75*
Nos. 1078-1082 (5) 7.55 7.55

Souvenir Sheets

Perf. 13½x14

1083 A161 1000d multicolored *8.00 8.00*
1084 A161 1000d multicolored *8.00 8.00*

1992, 1996 Summer Olympics, Barcelona and Atlanta — A162

50d, Wind surfing. No. 1086, Wrestling. No. 1087, Women's 4x100 meters relay. No. 1088, Swimming. No. 1089, Equestrian, vert. No. 1090, Field hockey. No. 1091, Men's 4x100 meters relay, vert. No. 1092, Mascots for Barcelona and Atlanta. No. 1093, Opening ceremony, Barcelona.

No. 1094, Atlanta '96 Emblem, vert. No. 1095, Archer lighting Olympic Flame with flaming arrow, vert. No. 1096, Transfer of Olympic Flag, closing ceremony, vert. No. 1097, Gymnastics. No. 1098, Tennis players.

1992, Oct. 1 Litho. *Perf. 14*

1085 A162 50d multicolored .65 .65
1086 A162 300d multicolored 2.25 2.25
1087 A162 300d multicolored 2.25 2.25
1088 A162 300d multicolored 2.25 2.25
1089 A162 300d multicolored 2.25 2.25
1090 A162 300d multicolored 2.25 2.25
1091 A162 300d multicolored 2.25 2.25
1092 A162 300d multicolored 2.25 2.25
1093 A162 300d multicolored 2.25 2.25
Nos. 1085-1093 (9) 18.65 18.65

Souvenir Sheets

1094 A162 800d multicolored 9.00 9.00
1095 A162 1000d multicolored 7.00 7.00
1096 A162 1000d multicolored 7.00 7.00

Perf. 13½

1097 A162 1000d multicolored 7.25 7.25

Perf. 14

1098 A162 1000d multicolored 7.25 7.25

Butterflies A163

Designs: No. 1099, White butterfly. No. 1100, Black and orange butterfly. No. 1101, Pink flower, black, white, red and blue butterfly. No. 1102, Black and white butterfly on right side of flower stem. No. 1103, Yellow and black butterfly. 2000d, Iris flower, black butterfly wing, horiz.

1993, May 26 Litho. *Perf. 14*

1099-1103 A163 500d Set of 5 *22.50 22.50*

Souvenir Sheet

1104 A163 2000d multi *18.00 18.00*

Flowers A164

No. 1105, Fucinho de porco. No. 1106, Heliconia. No. 1107, Gravo nacional. No. 1108, Tremessura. No. 1109, Anturius.
No. 1110, Girassol.

1993, June 18

1105 A164 500d multicolored *3.25 3.25*
1106 A164 500d multicolored *3.25 3.25*
1107 A164 500d multicolored *3.25 3.25*
1108 A164 500d multicolored *3.25 3.25*
1109 A164 500d multicolored *3.25 3.25*
Nos. 1105-1109 (5) 16.25 16.25

Souvenir Sheet

1110 A164 2000d multicolored 14.00 12.00

Miniature Sheet

Union of Portuguese Speaking Capitals — A165

Designs: a, 100d, Emblem. b, 150d, Grotto. c, 200d, Statue of Christ the Redeemer, Rio de Janeiro. d, 250d, Skyscraper. e, 250d, Monument. f, 300d, Building with pointed domed roof. g, 350d, Municipal building. h, 400d, Square tower. i, 500d, Residence, flag, truck.

1993, July 30

1111 A165 Sheet of 9, #a.-i. 18.00 18.00

Brasiliana '93.

Birds — A166

Designs: No. 1112, Cecia. No. 1113, Suisui. No. 1114, Falcon. No. 1115, Parrot. No. 1116, Heron.
No. 1117, Macaw, toucan, horiz.

1993, June 15 Litho. *Perf. 14*

1112-1116 A166 500d Set of 5 *18.50 18.50*

Souvenir Sheet

1117 A166 1000d multi *9.00 9.00*

Dinosaurs — A167

No. 1118, Lystrosaurus. No. 1119, Patagosaurus. No. 1120, Shonisaurus icti-osaurios, vert. No. 1121, Dilophosaurus, vert. No. 1122, Dicraeosaurus, vert. No. 1123, Tyrannosaurus rex, vert.

1993, July 21

1118-1123 A167 500d Set of 6 19.00 19.00

Souvenir Sheets

1124 A167 1000d Protoavis 9.00 9.00
1125 A167 1000d Brachiosaurus 9.00 9.00

Mushrooms A168

No. 1126, Agrocybe aegerita. No. 1127, Psalliota arvensis. No. 1128, Coprinus comatus. No. 1129, Hygrophorus psittacinus. No. 1130, Amanita caesarea.

No. 1131, Ramaria aurea. No. 1132, Pluteus murinus, horiz.

1993, May 25 Litho. *Perf. 14*

1126-1130 A168 800d Set of 5 *20.00 20.00*

Souvenir Sheets

1131-1132 A168 2000d Set of 2 *20.00 20.00*

Locomotives — A169

Nos. 1133-1137, Various views of small diesel locomotive.

Nos. 1138-1139, Various steam locomotives, vert.

1993, June 16

1133-1137 A169 800d Set of 5 24.00 24.00

Souvenir Sheets

1138-1139 A169 2000d Set of 2 *24.00 24.00*

1994 World Cup Soccer Championships, U.S. — A170

Designs: No. 1140, Team photo. No. 1141, Players in white uniforms. No. 1142, Two players in yellow uniforms, player in red, white and blue uniform. No. 1143, Players with yellow shirts and green shorts celebrating. No. 1144, Two players in red and white uniforms, one player in red, white and blue uniform. No. 1145, Player in yellow and blue uniform, player in red, white and blue uniform. No. 1146, Two players and official. No. 1147, Two players, vert.

No. 1148, Fans, faces painted as flags. No. 1149, Stylized player.

1993, July 6

1140-1147 A170 800d Set of 8 25.00 25.00

Souvenir Sheets

1148-1149 A170 2000d Set of 2 15.00 15.00

UPU Congress — A171

1993, Aug. 16

1150 A171 1000d shown 6.00 4.50

Souvenir Sheet

1151 A171 2000d Ship 10.00 10.00

1996 Summer Olympics, Atlanta — A172

Each 800d: No. 1152, Fencing. No. 1153, Women's running. No. 1154, Water polo. No. 1155, Soccer. No. 1156, Men's running. No. 1157, Boxing. No. 1158, Wrestling. No. 1159, High jump.

Each 2000d: No. 1160, Shooting, vert. No. 1161, Sailing, vert. No. 1162, Equestrian, vert. No. 1163, Kayak, vert.

1993, Oct. 19 Litho. *Perf. 13½x14*

1152-1159 A172 Set of 8 *40.00 40.00*

Souvenir Sheets

1160-1163 A172 Set of 4 *40.00 40.00*

1994 World Cup Soccer Championships, U.S. — A173

1994, Jan. 12 *Perf. 14*

1164 A173 500d blk, bl & red 3.00 3.00

Issued in miniature sheets of 4.

Movie Stars — A174

Each 10d: No. 1165a, James Dean. b, Bette Davis. c, Elvis Presley. d, Humphrey Bogart. e, John Lennon. f, Marilyn Monroe. g, Birthday cake. h, Audrey Hepburn.

Each 10d: No. 1166a-1166i, Various portraits of Elvis Presley.

Each 10d: No. 1167a-1167i, Various portraits of Marilyn Monroe.

Each 50d: No. 1168, James Dean, diff. No. 1169, Elvis Presley, diff.

No. 1169A: Marilyn Monroe.

1994, Feb. 15

1165 A174 Sheet of 8, #a.-h. 8.00 8.00

Sheets of 9, #a-i

1166-1167 A174 Set of 2 8.00 8.00

Souvenir Sheets

1168-1169 A174 Set of 2 8.00 8.00
1169A A174 2000d multi 15.00 15.00

Souvenir Sheet

Sydney 2000 — A175

1994, June 8
1170 A175 3000d multicolored 15.00 15.00

Signing of Argel Accord, 20th Anniv. A175a

1994 Litho. *Perf. 14*
1170A A175a 250d multi 4.00 4.00

Nos. 860, 979 Surcharged

d

Nos. 856, 978-979 Surcharged

e

Methods and Perfs as Before

1995, Mar. 2

1170B	A123p(d)	100d on 25d #860	7.50	.50
1170E	A123p(e)	350d on 50c #856	7.50	1.00
1170F	A144(e)	350d on 1d #978	7.50	1.00
1170I	A144(d)	400d on 5d #979	7.50	1.00
1170J	A144(e)	400d on 5d #979	7.50	1.00

Numbers have been reserved for additional surcharges. The editors would like to examine any examples.

Butterflies A176

No. 1171, Timeleoa maqulata-formosana. No. 1172, Morfho cypris. No. 1173, Thais polixena. No. 1174, Argema moenas. No. 1175, Leptocircus megus-ennius.

2000d, Armandia lidderdalei.

1995, May 10 Litho. *Perf. 14*
1171-1175 A176 1200d Set of 5 12.50 12.50

Souvenir Sheet

1176 A176 2000d multi 8.00 8.00

Flowering Fruits, Orchids A177

Flowering fruits: No. 1177, 350d, Pessego. No. 1178, 370d, Untue. No. 1179, 380d, Pitanga. No. 1180, 800d, Morango. No. 1181, 1000d, Izaquente.
Orchids, each 2000d: No. 1182, Max. houtteana. No. 1183, Max. marginata.

1995, June 6
1177-1181 A177 Set of 5 16.00 4.00

Souvenir Sheets

1182-1183 A177 Set of 2 17.50 *17.50*

Mushrooms A179

Designs, each 1000d: No. 1185, Lactarius deliciosus. No. 1186, Marasmius oreades. No. 1187, Boletus edulis. No. 1188, Boletus aurantiacus. No. 1189, Lepiota procera. No. 1190, Cortinarius praestans.
Each 2000d: No. 1191, Chantharellus cibarius. No. 1192, Lycoperdon pyriforme, horiz.

1995, Nov. 2 Litho. *Perf. 14*
1185-1190 A179 Set of 6 14.00 14.00

Souvenir Sheets

1191-1192 A179 Set of 2 14.00 14.00

UN, 50th Anniv. — A180

Traditional handicrafts made from palm leaves: No. 1193, 350d, Baskets. No. 1194, 350d, Brooms. No. 1195, 400d, Lamp shades. No. 1196, 500d, Klissakli, mussuá. No. 1197, 500d, Pávu. No. 1198, 1000d, Vámplêgá.

1995, June 20 Litho. *Perf. 13½x14*
1193-1198 A180 Set of 6 8.00 7.50

Trains — A181

Locomotives, each 1000d: No. 1199, Steam, "#100." No. 1200, Steam, "#778." No. 1201, G. Thommen steam. No. 1202, Steam "#119," vert. No. 1203, Mt. Washington cog railway. No. 1204, Electric.
Each 2000d: No. 1205, Electric train on snow-covered mountain, vert. No. 1206, Electric train car with door open, vert.

1995, July 24 *Perf. 14x13½, 13½x14*
1199-1204 A181 Set of 6 22.50 22.50

Souvenir Sheets

1205-1206 A181 Set of 2 19.00 19.00

See Nos. 1280-1286.

Dogs & Cats — A182

No. 1207, each 1000d: Various dogs. b, d, f, h, vert.
No. 1208, each 1000d: Various cats. b, d, f, h, vert.
Each 2000d: No. 1209, St. Bernard, German shepherd. No. 1210, Beagle, vert. No. 1211, Cat, kittens. No. 1212, Kitten on top of mother, vert.

1995, Aug. 12 *Perf. 14*
Sheets of 9, #a-i
1207-1208 A182 Set of 2 45.00 45.00

Souvenir Sheets

1209-1212 A182 Set of 5 37.50 37.50

New Year 1996 (Year of the Rat) A183

Various species of rats, mice, each 100d.

1995, Oct. 28
1213 A183 Sheet of 9, #a.-i. 6.00 6.00

Motion Pictures, Cent. — A184

Movie posters, each 1000d: No. 1214: a, Gone with the Wind. b, Stagecoach. c, Tarzan and His Mate. d, Oregon Trail. e, The Oklahoma Kid. f, King Kong. g, A Lady Fights Back. h, Steamboat Around the Bend. i, Wee Willie Winkie.
Each 2000d: No. 1215, Bring 'Em Back Alive. No. 1216 Indian chief.

1995, May 10 Litho. *Perf. 14*
1214 A184 Sheet of 9, #a.-i. 15.00 15.00

Souvenir Sheets

1215-1216 A184 Set of 2 15.00 15.00

Horses — A185

Designs: No. 1217, Various horses, each 1000d.
Each 2000d: No. 1218, Painting of Indian on horse, wild horses, horiz. No. 1219, City scene, horses, carriage, horiz.

1995, May 16
1217 A185 Sheet of 9, #a.-i. 15.00 15.00

Souvenir Sheets

1218-1219 A185 Set of 2 15.00 15.00

Nos. 1218-1219 each contain one 50x35mm stamp.

Souvenir Sheet

Euro '96, European Soccer Championships, Great Britain — A186

1995, July 2 *Perf. 13½x14*
1220 A186 2000d multicolored 8.00 8.00

Souvenir Sheet

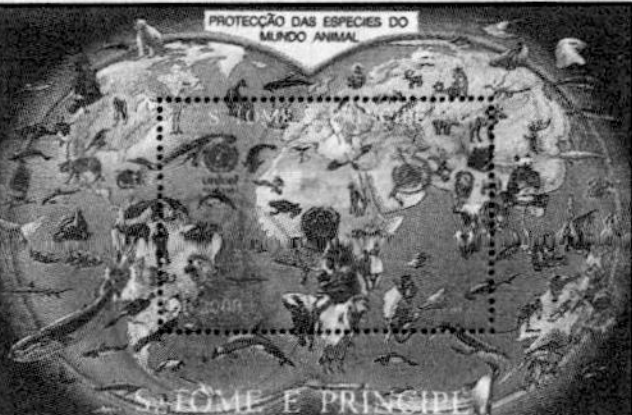

Protection of World's Endangered Species — A187

1995, July 6 *Perf. 14*
1221 A187 2000d multicolored 8.00 8.00

Mushrooms — A188

Designs, each 1000d: No. 1222a, Xerocomus rubellus. b, Rozites caperata. c, Cortinarius violaceus. d, Pholiota flammans. e, Lactarius volemus. f, Cortinarius (yellow). g, Cartinarius (blue). h, Higroforo. i, Boletus chrysenteron.
Each 2000d: No. 1223, Amanita muscaria, vert. No. 1224, Russula cyanoxantha, vert.

1995, Nov. 2
1222 A188 Sheet of 9, #a.-i. 16.00 16.00

Souvenir Sheets
1223-1224 A188 Set of 2 14.00 14.00

Details or Entire Paintings — A189

No. 1225, each 1000d: a, Aurora and Cefalo. b, Madonna and Child with St. John as a Boy. c, Romulus and Remus. d, Lamentation over the Dead Christ. e, Vison of All Saints Day. f, Perseus and Andromeda. g. The Scent. h, The Encounter in Lyon. i, The Art School of Rubens-Bildern.
Each 2000d: No. 1226, Statue of Ceres. No. 1227, Flight into Egypt, horiz.
All but #1225g (Jan Brueghel the Elder) and 1225i are by Rubens.

1995, Sept. 27 Litho. *Perf. 14*
1225 A189 Sheet of 9, #a.-i. 20.00 20.00

Souvenir Sheets
1226-1227 A189 Set of 2 20.00 20.00

Greenpeace, 25th Anniv. — A190

Designs: No. 1237, Potto. No. 1238, Iguana. No. 1239, Tiger. No. 1240, Lion.
50d, Elephant, horiz.

1996, Aug. 5 Litho. *Perf. 14*
1237-1240 A190 50d Set of 4 15.00 10.00

Souvenir Sheet
1241 A190 50d multicolored 4.25 4.25

Dogs & Cats — A191

Dogs — A191a

Nos. 1242a-1242i: Various pictures of dogs with cats, kittens.
Nos. 1243a-1243i: Various close-up pictures of different breeds of dogs.
No. 1244, Labrador retriever. No. 1245, Bird, woman's eye, vert. No. 1246, Two kittens. No. 1247, Collie, vert. No. 1248, Poodle, vert. No. 1249, Pit bull terrier, vert. No. 1250, Brown and white terrier, vert.

1995, Aug. 12 Litho. *Perf. 14*
Sheets of 9, #a-i
1242 A191 1000d multi 22.50 22.50
1243 A191a 1000d multi 22.50 22.50

Souvenir Sheets
1244 A191 2000d multi 6.50 6.50
1245 A191a 2000d multi 6.50 6.50
1246 A191 2000d multi 6.50 6.50
1247 A191a 2000d multi 6.50 6.50
1248 A191a 2000d multi 6.50 6.50
1249 A191a 2000d multi 6.50 6.50
1250 A191a 2000d multi 6.50 6.50

Orchids A192

No. 1251, each 1000d: a, Findlayanum. b, Stan. c, Cruentum. d, Trpla suavis. e, Lowianum. f, Gratiosissimum. g, Cyrtorchis monteirae. h, Sarcanthus birmanicus. i, Loddigesii.
Each 2000d: No. 1252, Barkeria Skinneri. No. 1253, Dendrobium nobile.

1995, Sept. 12
1251 A192 Sheet of 9, #a.-i. 19.00 19.00

Souvenir Sheets
1252-1253 A192 Set of 2 16.00 16.00

Paintings, Drawings by Durer, Rubens — A193

Designs, each 750d: No. 1254, Soldier on Horseback, by Durer, vert. No. 1255, Archangel St. Michael Slaying Satan, by Rubens, vert. No. 1256, Nursing Madonna in Half Length, by Durer, vert. No. 1257, Head of a Deer, by Durer, vert. No. 1258, View of Innsbruck from the North, by Durer. No. 1259, Madonna Nursing on a Grassy Bench, by Durer, vert. No. 1260, Helene Fourment and Her Children, by Rubens, vert. No. 1261, Adam and Eve, by Durer, vert.
Each 2000d: No. 1262, A Young Hare, by Durer, vert. No. 1263, Mills on a River Bank, by Durer. No. 1264, Holy Family with a Basket, by Rubens, vert. No. 1265, The Annunciation, by Rubens, vert.

1995, Dec. 16 Litho. *Perf. 14*
1254-1261 A193 Set of 8 16.00 16.00

Souvenir Sheets
1262-1265 A193 Set of 4 35.00 35.00
Christmas.

Independence, 20th Anniv. — A194

1995, July 12 Litho. *Perf. 13½*
1266 A194 350d multicolored 5.00 1.90

1996 Summer Olympic Games, Atlanta — A195

Various shells, Nos. 1267-1271 each 1000d.

1996, Jan. 10 Litho. *Perf. 14*
1267-1271 A195 Set of 5 16.00 16.00

Souvenir Sheet
1272 A195 2000d multicolored 9.00 9.00

Anniversaries and Events — A196

1996, Aug. 2 *Perf. 14x13½*
1273 A196 500d multicolored 6.00 2.00

UNICEF, 50th anniv., Alfred Nobel, 150th anniv. of birth, Phila-Seoul 96, KOREA 2002, 1996 Summer Olympic Games, Atlanta.

UNESCO A197

Butterflies, each 1000d: No. 1274, Papilio weiskei. No. 1275, Heliconius melpomene. No. 1276, Papilio arcas-mylotes. No. 1277, Mesomenia cresus. No. 1278, Catagramma iyca-satrana.
No. 1279, Lemonius sudias.

1996, Sept. 10 *Perf. 13½x14*
1274-1278 A197 Set of 5 15.00 15.00

Souvenir Sheet
1279 A197 2000d multicolored 6.00 6.00

Train Type of 1995

Each 1000d: No. 1280, SNCF. No. 1281, CN. No. 1282, White locomotive. No. 1283, Green locomotive. No. 1284, Train in city.
Each 2000d: No. 1285, Modern train. No. 1286, Old train.

1996, Oct. 7 *Perf. 14*
1280-1284 A181 Set of 5 16.00 16.00

Souvenir Sheets
1285-1286 A181 Set of 2 10.00 10.00

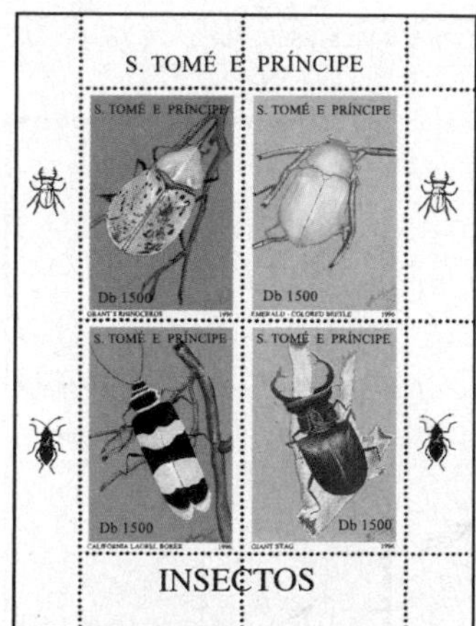

Beetles — A198

No. 1287, each 1500d: a, Grant's rhinoceros. b, Emerald-colored. c, California laurel borer. d, Giant stag.
Each 2000d: No. 1288, Maple borer. No. 1289, Arizona june.

1996, Nov. 7 *Perf. 13½x14*
1287 A198 Sheet of 4, #a.-d. 16.00 16.00

Souvenir Sheets
1288-1289 A198 Set of 2 15.00 15.00

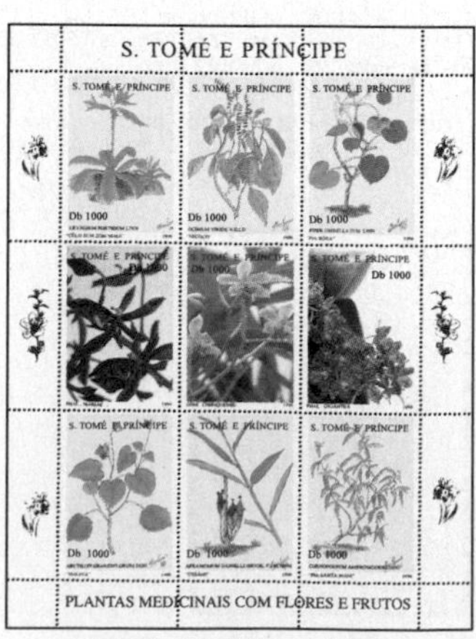

Plants, Orchids — A199

Each 1000d: No. 1290: a, Eryngium fortidum. b, Ocimum viride. c, Piper umbellatum.

d, Phal. mariae. e, Odm. chiriquense. f, Phal. gigantea. g, Abutilon grandiflorum. h, Aframomium danielli. i, Chemopodium ambrosiodes.

Each 2000d: No. 1291, Crinum jacus. No. 1292, Oncoba apinosa forsk. No. 1293, Z. mackai. No. 1294, Aspasia principissa.

1996, Oct. 14

1290 A199 Sheet of 9, #a.-i. 25.00 25.00

Souvenir Sheets

1291-1294 A199 Set of 4 40.00 40.00

Nos. 729, 736-737, 744, 746, 748, 857-858 Surcharged in Blue or Black

No. 1295

No. 1296

No. 1298B

Perfs. & Printing Methods as Before

1996?

1295	A123p	350d on 1d #857		
1295A	A123p	400d on 5d #858		
1295D	A133	500d on 60d #914	4.50	4.50
1296	A95	1000d on 11d #736 (Bl)	—	—
1297	A95	1000d on 12d #737 (Bl)	—	—
1298	A95	1000d on 42d #746	2.75	2.75
1298B	A95	2500d on 1.50d #729 (Bl)	6.75	6.75
1299	A95	2500d on 25d #744 (Bl)	6.75	6.75
1300	A95	2500d on 100d #748 (Bl)	6.75	6.75

Numerous additional surcharges exist in this set. The editors would like to examine any examples.

Musicians, Musical Instruments A200

"The Beatles" — No. 1301, each 1500d: a, John Lennon. b, Paul McCartney. c, George Harrison. d, Ringo Starr.

Traditional instruments — No. 1302, each 1500d: a, Animal horn. b, Flutes. c, Tambourine, drum, sticks. d, Canza.

Each 2000d: No. 1303, Guitar, Elvis Presley (in sheet margin). No. 1304, Maraca, Antonio Machin.

1996, Nov. 19 Litho. *Perf. 13½x14*

Sheets of 4, #a-d

1301-1302 A200 Set of 2 40.00 40.00

Souvenir Sheets

1303-1304 A200 Set of 2 20.00 20.00

Fish — A201

No. 1305, each 1500d: a, Sailfish. b, Barracuda. c, Cod. d, Atlantic mackerel.

Each 2000d: No. 1306, Bluefin tuna. No. 1307, Squirrelfish.

1996, Dec. 10 ***Perf. 14x13½***

1305 A201 Sheet of 4, #a.-d. 18.00 18.00

Souvenir Sheets

1306-1307 A201 Set of 2 20.00 20.00

No. 988 Surcharged in Dark Blue

Methods and Perfs as Before

1997, Apr. 16

1307A A144 1000d on 250d multi *26.00* *8.00*

Diana, Princess of Wales (1961-97) — A202

No. 1308: Various portraits, vert.

100d, Diana talking with her sons (in sheet margin), vert. 500d, Portrait. 2000d, Diana, Mother Teresa (in sheet margin), vert.

1997 Litho. *Perf. 14*

1308 A202 10d Sheet of 9, #a.-i. 25.00 25.00

Souvenir Sheets

Perf. 13½x14, 14x13½

1309 A202 100d multicolored 12.00 12.00
1310 A202 500d gold & multi 12.00 12.00
1311 A202 2000d gold & multi 10.00 10.00

Issued: No. 1308, 100d, 500d, 10/15/97; 2000d, 10/20/97.

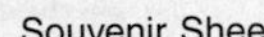

Souvenir Sheet

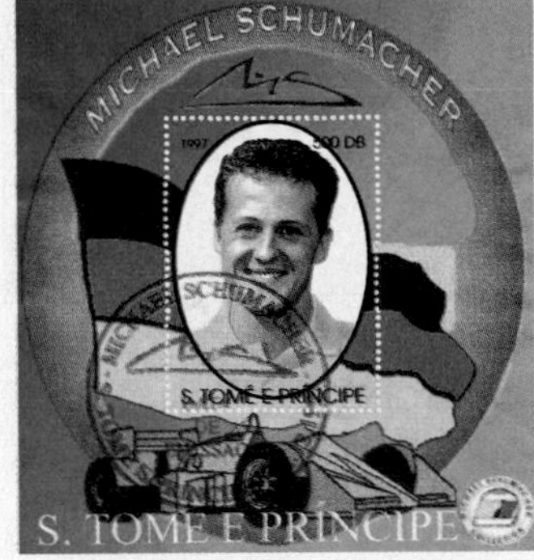

Michael Schumacher, World Champion Formula I Driver — A203

1997, Dec. 12 ***Perf. 14***

1312 A203 500d multicolored 8.00 8.00

Titanic — A205

No. 1317, 1000d — Titanic, White Star Line flag and inset image of: a, Captain Edward J. Smith. b, Titanic approaching icebergs. c, Titanic shooting flares. d, Distress codes. e, Titanic cruising in daylight. f, Titanic with icebergs at left. g, Lifeboats near sinking Titanic. h, Sinking Titanic. i, Map showing location of sinking.

No. 1318, 1000d: a, Construction of Titanic. b, Titanic leaving dock. c, Titanic and seagulls. d, Titanic shooting flares. e, Lifeboats near sinking Titanic. f, Sinking Titanic. g, Titanic, lifeboat, ship's officer. h, Bow of sunken Titanic. i, Stern of sunken Titanic.

No. 1319, 2000d, Captain and Titanic (multicolored). No. 1320, 2000d, Captain and Titanic (black).

1998, July 1 Litho. *Perf. 14x13¾*

Sheets of 9, #a-i

1317-1318 A205 Set of 2 — —

Souvenir Sheets

1319-1320 A205 Set of 2 15.00 15.00

Expo '98, Lisbon — A206

Sea around the islands, each 3500d: No. 1326, Man fishing from shore. No. 1327, Man in small sailboat, sharks in water below. No. 1328, Flying fish. No. 1329, Diver connecting line on sea bottom. No. 1330, Man paddling boat, turtle, fish below.

8000d, Map of St. Thomas & Prince, vert.

1998 Litho. *Perf. 14*

1326-1330 A206 Set of 5 16.00 13.50

Souvenir Sheet

1331 A206 8000d multicolored 20.00 8.00

2nd AICEP Philatelic Exhibition — A207

Traditional food, each 3500d: No. 1332, Feijao de coco, coconuts. No. 1333, Cooked bananas, fruit, wine. No. 1334, Molho no fogo, fish, fruit, wine. No. 1335, Calulu, fruits, vegetables, wine. No. 1336, Izaquente de acucar, sugar beet.

7000d, Pot cooking over open fire, vert.

1998, Aug. 1

1332-1336 A207 Set of 5 16.00 7.00

Souvenir Sheet

1337 A207 7000d multicolored 8.00 8.00

Souvenir Sheet

Portugal 98 Stamp Exhibition — A210

1998, Sept. 4 Litho. *Perf. 14x13¾*

1342 A210 7000d Ship on map 19.00 8.00

Five stamps were issued with the souvenir sheet. The editors would like to examine them.

Nos. 856-858 Surcharged

Methods and Perfs. As Before

1999

1358 A123p 3000d on 50c #856 *15.00* *5.00*
1359 A123p 3000d on 1d #857 *15.00* *5.00*
1360 A123p 3000d on 5d #858 *15.00* *5.00*

Nos. 1358 and 1360 have various obliterators. No. 1359 has no obliterator.

Nos. 728, 735, 739 Surcharged

Methods and Perfs as Before

1999, Nov.

1361	A95	5000d on 15.50d #739	*10.00*	*10.00*
1362	A95	7000d on 10d #735	*15.00*	*15.00*
1363	A95	10,000d on 1d #728	*20.00*	*20.00*
		Nos. 1361-1363 (3)	*45.00*	*45.00*

Christmas — A211

Designs: Nos. 1364, 1367, 5000d, Adoration of the Shepherds. Nos. 1365, 1368, 6000d, Presentation of Jesus in the Temple. Nos. 1366, 1369, 10,000d, Flight Into Egypt.

1999, Dec. 23 Litho. *Perf. 12¾x13*
1364-1366 A211 Set of 3 *9.00 9.00*

Souvenir Sheets

1367-1369 A211 Set of 3 *10.00 10.00*

Stamps on Nos. 1367-1369 have continuous designs.

Souvenir Sheet

Independence, 25th Anniv. — A213

No. 1371: a, 5000d, Mountain, bird. b, 6000d, Stylized mountains, birds, flag. c, 7000d, Mountains, "25," flag. d, 10,000d, Mountain, bird, diff.

2000, July 12 Litho. *Perf. 12¾*
1371 A213 Sheet of 4, #a-d 14.00 14.00

Nos. 746, 748 Surcharged

Methods & Perfs as Before

2000, Aug. 7
1372 A95 5000d on 42d multi 3.00 2.50
1373 A95 5000d on 100d multi 3.00 2.50

2000 Summer Olympics, Sydney — A214

Olympic rings and: 5000d, Runner, stadium, kangaroos, bird. 7000d, Runner, Sydney Opera House, kangaroos, emu.
15,000d, Sydney Harbour Bridge, Opera House, kangaroo, horiz.

2000, Sept. 14 Litho. *Perf. 12¾*
1374-1375 A214 Set of 2 6.00 6.00

Souvenir Sheet
Perf. 13

1376 A214 15,000d multi 7.50 7.50

Souvenir Sheet

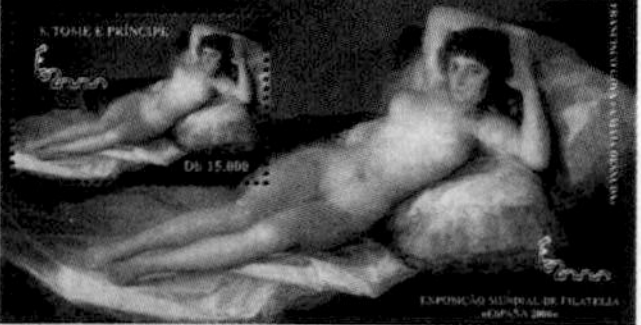

España 2000 Intl. Philatelic Exhibition — A215

2000, Oct. 6 *Perf. 12¾*
1377 A215 15,000d multi 7.50 7.50

Holy Year 2000 — A216

Designs: No. 1381a, 3000d, God, the Father. No. 1381b, 5000d, St. Anne, Virgin Mary, infant Jesus. Nos. 1378, 1381c, 6000d, St. Thomas. No. 1381d, 6000d, Processional cross. Nos. 1379, 1381e, 7000d, Altarpiece. Nos. 1380, 1381f, 8000d, Cathedral.

2000, Dec. 21 *Perf. 12¾*
With "Natal 2000" Inscription
1378-1380 A216 Set of 3 10.00 10.00
Without "Natal 2000" Inscription
1381 A216 Sheet of 6, #a-f 17.00 17.00
g. Souvenir sheet, #1381a-1381b, 1381d-1381e, perf. 12 10.00 10.00

Rosa de Porcellana A218

Flower in: Nos. 1391, 5000d, 1393a, 7000d, Pink. Nos. 1392, 5000d, 1393b, 8000d, Red.

2001, Apr. 12 Litho. *Perf. 13¾x14*
1391-1392 A218 Set of 2 5.00 5.00

Souvenir Sheet

1393 A218 Sheet of 2, #a-b 7.50 7.50

Butterflies A219

Designs: No. 1394, 3500d, Graphium leonidas (brown frame). No. 1395, 5000d, Acraea newtoni (bright red frame). No. 1396, 6000d, Papilio bromius (bright red frame). No. 1397, 7500d, Papilio dardanos (brown frame).
No. 1398: a, 3500d, Graphium leonidas (orange frame). b, 5000d, Acraea newtoni (dark red frame). c, 6000d, Papilio bromius (dark red frame). d, 7500d, Papilio dardanos (orange frame).
15,000d, Euchloron megaera serrei.

2001, July 15 *Perf. 13¼x13½*
1394-1397 A219 Set of 4 11.00 11.00

Souvenir Sheets

1398 A219 Sheet of 4, #a-d 11.00 11.00
1399 A219 15,000d multi 7.50 7.50

Worldwide Fund for Nature (WWF) A220

Lepidochelys olivacea: 3500d, One swimming. 5000d, Two swimming. 6000d, Three leaving water. 7500d, Three hatchlings in sand.

2001, Oct.
1400-1403 A220 Set of 4 8.00 7.00

Nos. 1400-1403 were each issued in sheets of four. The margin of each of the four stamps on the sheets differs.
See No. 1431. For surcharges, see Nos. 2199-2201.

Souvenir Sheets

Famous Men — A221

Designs: No. 1404, 15,000d, Charlie Chaplin (1889-1977), comedian. No. 1405, 15,000d, Louis Armstrong (1900-71), musician. No. 1406, 15,000d, Walt Disney (1901-66), film producer, vert. No. 1407, 15,000d, Giuseppe Verdi (1813-1901), composer, vert.

2002 Litho. *Perf. 13¼*
1404-1407 A221 Set of 4 30.00 30.00

Issued: No. 1404, 3/11; No. 1405, 3/12; No. 1406, 3/13; No. 1407, 3/14.

Insects A222

Designs: No. 1408, 5000d, Euchroea clementi. No. 1409, 5000d, Dicranorrhina derbyana. No. 1410, 5000d, Stephanorrhirna guttata. 8000d, Polybothris sumptuosa gemma.

2002, Mar. 15 *Perf. 13¼x13½*
1408-1411 A222 Set of 4 12.50 12.50

Souvenir Sheet

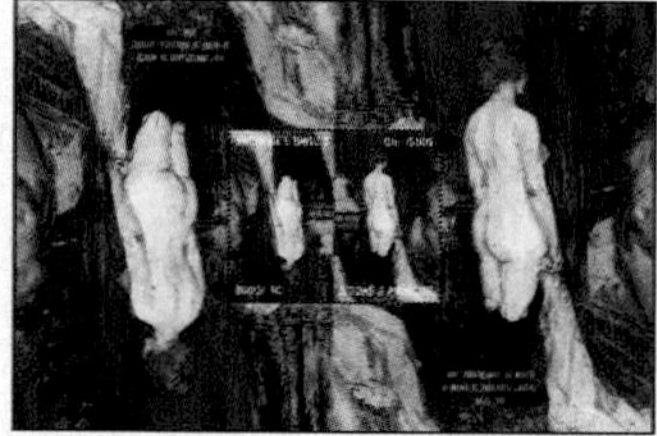

Henri de Toulouse-Lautrec (1865-1901), Painter — A223

Perf. 13¼x13¼x13¼x Rouletted
2002, Mar. 16
1412 A223 15,000d Sheet of 2 14.00 14.00

Stamps in No. 1412 are tete-beche. The rouletting continues through the selvage allowing the sheet to be broken up into two half-sheets.

Souvenir Sheets

Chinese Zodiac Animals — A224

No. 1413, 15,000d: a, Rat. b, Tiger. c, Ox. d, Rabbit.
No. 1414, 15,000d: a, Dragon. b, Horse. c, Snake. d, Goat.
No. 1415, 15,000d: a, Monkey. b, Dog. c, Cock. d, Pig.

2002 *Perf.*
1413-1415 A224 Set of 3 75.00 75.00

Each sheet was rouletted into quadrants.

In Remembrance of Sept. 11, 2001 Terrorist Attacks — A225

2002, May 27 *Perf. 13½x13¼*
With White Frame
1416 A225 5000d multi 2.75 2.75

Souvenir Sheet
Without White Frame

1417 A225 15,000d multi 8.00 8.00

No. 1417 contains one 40x51mm stamp.

Souvenir Sheet

Barcelona Architecture of Antonio Gaudí — A226

No. 1418: a, 7000d, Casa Battló (dark brown building, 27x41mm). b, 7000d, Casa Mila (light building, 27x41mm). c, 20,000d, Church of Sagrada Familia (29x47mm).

Perf. 13½x13¼, 13¼ (#1418c)
2002, Sept. 28
1418 A226 Sheet, #a-c 12.00 12.00

A column of rouletting separates the sheet into two halves, one containing Nos. 1418a-1418b, and the other containing No. 1418c. An additional column of rouletting is found at the left side of the half sheet containing No. 1418c.

Orchids — A227

Designs: 2000d, Phaius mannii. 6000d, Cyrtorchis arcuata. 9000d, Calanthe sylvatica. 10,000d, Bulbophyllum lizae.
20,000d, Bulbophyllum saltatorium.

Perf. 13½x13¼
2002, Nov. 19 Litho.
1419-1422 A227 Set of 4 14.00 14.00

Souvenir Sheet

1424 A227 20,000d multi 10.00 10.00

A number has been reserved for an additional item in this set.

Birds — A228

Designs: 1000d, Nectarinia newtonii. 7000d, Prinior molleri. 9000d, Neospiza concolor. 10,000d, Lanius newtoni.
20,000d, Otus hartlaubi.

Perf. 13½x13¼

2002, Nov. 20 Litho.

1425-1428	A228	Set of 4	14.00	14.00
1428a		Souvenir sheet, #1425-1428	14.00	14.00

Souvenir Sheet

1429	A228	20,000d multi	10.00	10.00

Miniature Sheet

Circus Animals — A229

No. 1430: a, 2000d, Horses (30x40mm). b, 6000d, Chimpanzees (30x40mm). c, 9000d, Seals (30x40mm). d, 10,000d, Tigers (30x40mm). e, 20,000d, Elephants (60x80mm).

2002, Nov. 22 *Perf. 13¼x13*

1430	A229	Sheet of 5, #a-e	14.00	14.00

A column of rouletting separates the sheet into two halves, one containing Nos. 1430a-1430d and the other containing No. 1430e.

Worldwide Fund for Nature Type of 2001

Souvenir Sheet

No. 1431 — Lepidochelys olivacea: a, 6000d, Two swimming. b, 6000d, Three hatchlings in sand. c, 7000d, One swimming. d, 7000d, Three leaving water.

2002, Dec. 31 *Perf. 13¼x13½*

1431	A220	Sheet of 4, #a-d	14.00	14.00

Space Travelers A230

Designs: 6000d, Laika. 7000d, Yuri Gagarin. 8000d, Dennis Tito.

2003, Feb. 20 *Perf. 13x13¼*

1432-1434	A230	Set of 3	10.00	10.00
1434a		Souvenir sheet, #1432-1434, perf. 12½x12¾	10.00	10.00

Souvenir Sheet

The Last Supper, by Leonardo da Vinci — A231

2003, Apr. 17 *Perf. 13½x13¼*

1435	A231	25,000d multi	12.00	12.00

Easter.

Crustaceans — A232

Designs: Nos. 1436, 1440a, 3500d, Coenobita perlatus. Nos. 1437, 1440b, 7000d, Carcinus maenas. Nos. 1438, 1440c, 8000d, Uca tetragonon. Nos. 1439, 1440d, 9000d, Ovalipes ocellatus.
20,000d, Panulirus pencillatus.

2003, Apr. 24 *Perf. 13¼x13½*

With White Frames

1436-1439	A232	Set of 4	12.50	12.50

Without White Frames

1440	A232	Sheet of 4, #a-d	12.50	12.50

Souvenir Sheet

1441	A232	20,000d multi	9.00	9.00

Vincent van Gogh (1853-90), Painter — A233

Paintings: No. 1442, 6000d, Young Peasant Woman with Straw Hat Sitting in the Wheat, 1890. No. 1443, 6000d, Head of a Peasant Woman with White Cap, 1885. No. 1444, 7000d, Patience Escalier. No. 1445, 7000d, Charles-Elzéard Trabuc.

No. 1446 — Self-portraits from: a, 6000d, 1886 (head at left). b, 6000d, 1886 (head at right). c, 7000d, 1888. d, 7000d, 1889.

2003, May 30 Litho. *Perf. 13½x13*

1442-1445	A233	Set of 4	12.00	12.00

Souvenir Sheet

1446	A233	Sheet of 4, #a-d	12.00	12.00

Skull With Burning Cigarette, by Vincent van Gogh — A234

2003, May 31

1447	A234	7000d multi	3.25	3.25

WHO anti-smoking campaign.

A235

A236

Famous People — A237

No. 1448: a, Lord Robert Baden-Powell, dogs. b, Pres. George W. Bush, rescue workers. c, Pope John Paul II, Copernicus. d, Astronaut Neil Armstrong, Russian cosmonaut. e, Vincent van Gogh self-portrait, and painting. f, Louis Pasteur, cat. g, Sir Alexander Fleming, mushrooms. h, Elvis Presley on motorcylce, automobile. i, Walt Disney, dog.

No. 1449: a, Pope John Paul II, Pres. George W. Bush. b, Male chess player. c, Nelson Mandela, mineral. d, Charles Darwin, dinosaur. e, Tiger Woods, Rotary emblem. f, Dr. Albert Schweitzer, bird. g, Hector Berlioz. h, Pablo Picasso and painting. i, Pope John Paul II and Mother Teresa.

No. 1450: a, Pope John Paul II and UN Secretary General Kofi Annan. b, Formula I race car driver and car. c, Lady Olave Baden-Powell, cat. d, Female chess player. e, Sir Rowland Hill, train. f, Rotary emblem, Lions emblem and founders. g, Henri Dunant, Princess Diana. h, Paul Gauguin and painting. i, Pope John Paul II, Princess Diana.

2003 Litho. *Perf. 12¾x13¼*

1448	A235	5000d Sheet of 9, #a-i	10.00	10.00
1449	A236	5000d Sheet of 9, #a-i	10.00	10.00
1450	A237	5000d Sheet of 9, #a-i	10.00	10.00
		Nos. 1448-1450 (3)	30.00	30.00

Each stamp exists in a souvenir sheet of 1.

A238

A239

A240

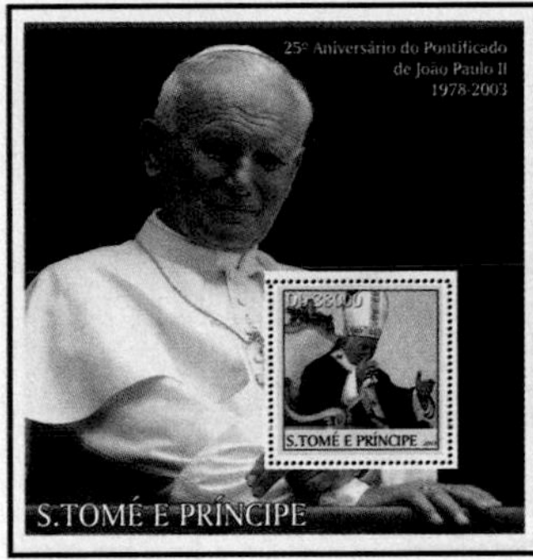

Reign of Pope John Paul II, 25th Anniv. — A241

Various photographs of Pope John Paul II.

2003

1451	A238	5000d Sheet of 9, #a-i	10.00	10.00
1452	A239	5000d Sheet of 9, #a-i	10.00	10.00

Souvenir Sheets

1453	A240	38,000d multi	8.50	8.50
1454	A241	38,000d multi	8.50	8.50

A242

A243

A244

Marilyn Monroe (1926-62), Actress — A245

Various Marilyn Monroe photographs and magazine covers.

2003

1455	A242	5000d Sheet of 9, #a-i	10.00	10.00
1456	A243	5000d Sheet of 9, #a-i	10.00	10.00

Souvenir Sheets

1457	A244	38,000d multi	8.50	8.50
1458	A245	38,000d multi	8.50	8.50

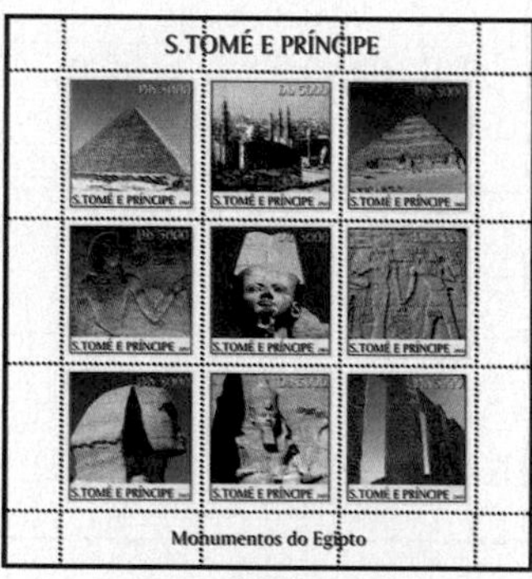

A246

A247

A248

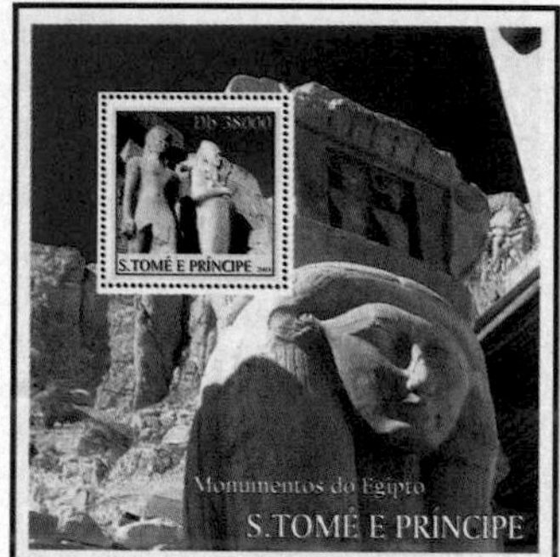

Ancient Egyptian Monuments — A249

Various photographs.

2003

1459	A246	5000d Sheet of 9, #a-i	10.00	10.00
1460	A247	5000d Sheet of 9, #a-i	10.00	10.00

Souvenir Sheets

1461	A248	38,000d multi	8.50	8.50
1462	A249	38,000d multi	8.50	8.50

A250

A251

A252

A253

A254

St. Petersburg, Russia, 300th Anniv. — A255

Various unnamed paintings or buildings.

2003

1463	A250	5000d Sheet of 9, #a-i	10.00	10.00
1464	A251	5000d Sheet of 9, #a-i	10.00	10.00
1465	A252	5000d Sheet of 9, #a-i	10.00	10.00
		Nos. 1463-1465 (3)	30.00	30.00

Souvenir Sheets

1466	A253	38,000d multi	8.50	8.50
1467	A254	38,000d multi	8.50	8.50
1468	A255	38,000d multi	8.50	8.50

A256

Volcanoes, Minerals and Firefighters — A257

A258

Fire Vehicles — A259

Nos. 1469 — Various pictures of volcanoes and minerals: a, 1000d, With firefighter. b, 2000d, Without firefighter. c, 3000d, With firefighter. d, 5000d, Without firefighter. e, 6000d, With firefighter. f, 15,000d, Without firefighter.

Nos. 1470 — Various pictures of volcanoes and minerals: a, 1000d, Without firefighter. b, 2000d, With firefighter. c, 3000d, Without firefighter. d, 5000d, With firefighter. e, 6000d, Without firefighter. f, 15,000d, With firefighter.

Nos. 1471 and 1472 — Various fire vehicles: a, 1000d. b, 2000d, c, 3000d. d, 5000d. e, 6000d. f, 15,000d.

No. 1473, Like #1469e. No. 1474, Like #1470d. No. 1475, Like #1471c. No. 1476, Like #1472f.

Perf. 12¾x13¼, 13¼x12¾ (#1474)

2003

1469	A256	Sheet of 6, #a-f	9.00	9.00
1470	A257	Sheet of 6, #a-f	9.00	9.00
1471	A258	Sheet of 6, #a-f	9.00	9.00
1472	A259	Sheet of 6, #a-f	9.00	9.00
		Nos. 1469-1472 (4)	36.00	36.00

Souvenir Sheets

1473	A256	38,000d multi	8.50	8.50
1474	A257	38,000d multi	8.50	8.50
1475	A258	38,000d multi	8.50	8.50
1476	A259	38,000d multi	8.50	8.50

A260

Red Cross Emblem and Dogs — A261

No. 1477 — Red Cross emblem and various dogs: a, 1000d. b, 2000d, c, 3000d. d, 5000d. e, 6000d. f, 15,000d.

Perf. 12¾x13¼, 13¼x12¾ (#1478)

2003

1477 A260 Sheet of 6, #a-f 9.00 9.00

Souvenir Sheet

1478 A261 38,000d multi 8.50 8.50

Pope John Paul II and Orchids — A262

No. 1479 — Pope and orchids: a, 1000d, Phalaenopsis bellina. b, 2000d, Rhynchostylis monachica. c, 3000d, Vanda bensonii. d, 5000d, Paphiopedilum hirsutissimum. e, 6000d, Liparis latifolia. f, 15,000d, Trichoglottis seidenfadenii.
38,000d, Like #1479a.

2003 ***Perf. 12¾x13¼***

1479 A262 Sheet of 6, #a-f 9.00 9.00

Souvenir Sheet

1480 A262 38,000d multi 8.50 8.50

Marilyn Monroe and Orchids — A263

No. 1481 — Monroe and orchids: a, 1000d, Phalaenopsis amabilis. b, 2000d, Rhynchostylis retusa. c, 3000d, Phalaenopsis stuartiana. d, 5000d, Rhynchostylis gigantea. e, 6000d, Vanda coerulea. f, 15,000d, Trichoglottis brachiata.
38,000d, Like #1481b.

2003

1481 A263 Sheet of 6, #a-f 9.00 9.00

Souvenir Sheet

1482 A263 38,000d multi 8.50 8.50

Birds and Concorde — A264

No. 1483 — Concorde and penguins: a, 1000d. b, 2000d. c, 3000d. d, 5000d. e, 6000d. f, 15,000d.
No. 1484 — Birds: a, 1000d, Lybius torquatus, and Concorde. b, 2000d, Prinia subflava. c, 3000d, Tockus erythrorhynchus, and Concorde. d, 5000d, Poicephalus meyeri. e, 6000d, Uraeginthus angolensis, and Concorde. f, 15,000d, Laniarius atrococcineus.
No. 1485, 38,000d, Like #1483e. No. 1486, 38,000d, Like #1484c.

2003 **Sheets of 6, #a-f**

1483-1484 A264 Set of 2 18.00 18.00

Souvenir Sheets

1485-1486 A264 Set of 2 17.00 17.00

Birds — A265

No. 1487 — Various pheasants: a, 1000d. b, 2000d. c, 3000d. d, 5000d. e, 6000d. f, 15,000d.
No. 1488 — Birds and orchids: a, Polytelis alexandrae, Dendrochilum wenzelii. b, Neophena splendida, Dendrobium sulcatum. c, Pyrrhura calliptera, Dendrobium nobile. d, Aratinga jandaya, Cymbidium lowianum. e, Melopsittacus undulatus, Dendrobium bulleniianum. f, Psittacula himalayana, Chiloschista parishii.
No. 1489, 38,000d, Like #1487a, with Bangkok 2003 Jamboree emblem added. No. 1490, 38,000d, Like #1488b, with Bangkok 2003 Jamboree emblem added. See illustration A266 for stamps showing Bangkok 2003 Jamboree emblem.

2003

1487 A265 Sheet of 6, #a.-f. 9.00 9.00

1488 A265 10,000d Sheet of 6, #a-f 13.50 13.50

Souvenir Sheets

1489-1490 A265 Set of 2 17.00 17.00

For surcharges, see Nos. 2000-2002, 2007-2009, 2027-2029, 2034-2036, 2054-2056, 2061-2063, 2081-2083, 2088-2090.

Bangkok 2003 Scout Jamboree Emblem and Birds, Orchids, Mushrooms, Insects or Butterflies — A266

No. 1491 — Emblem and various fighting roosters: a, 1000d. b, 2000d. c, 3000d. d, 5000d. e, 6000d. f, 15,000d.
No. 1492 — Emblem and unnamed water birds or orchids: a, 1000d, Bird in flight. b, 2000d, Aerides odorata. c, 3000d, Two birds at nest. d, 5000d, Aerides roaea. e, 6000d, Two birds. f, 15,000d, Aerides quinquevulnera.
No. 1493 — Emblem and mushrooms and orchids: a, 1000d, Xerocomus cubtomentosus, Aerides quinquevulnera. b, 2000d, Suillus placidus, Bulbophyllum wendlandianum. c, 3000d, Boletus edulis, Coelogyne mooreana. d, 5000d, Suillus variegatus, Dendrobium bullenianum. e, 6000d, Tylopilus felleus, Dendrobium crumenatum. f, 15,000d, Aureoboletus gentilis, Ascocentrum garayi.
No. 1494 — Emblem, wasp and mushrooms: a, 1000d, Boletus edulis f. betulicola. b, 2000d, Boletus edulis f. pinicola. c, 3000d, Boletus appendiculatus. d, 5000d, Boletus fechtneri. e, 6000d, Boletus luirdus. f, 15,000d, Boletus impolitus.
No. 1495 — Emblem, mushroom and butterfly: a, 1000d, Russula nigricans, Papilio demoleus. b, 2000d, Lactarius volemus, Libythea geoffroyi. c, 3000d, Russula cyanoxantha, Catonephele numili. d, 5000d, Gomphidius roseus, Doxocopa cherubina. e, 6000d, Russula integra, Dione juno. f, 15,000d, Agaricus bisporus, Philaethria.
No. 1496, 38,000d, Like #1491a. No. 1497, 38,000d, Like #1493c. No. 1498, 38,000d, Like #1494a. No. 1499, 38,000d, Like #1495f.

2003 **Sheets of 6, #a-f**

1491-1495 A266 Set of 5 45.00 45.00

Souvenir Sheets

1496-1499 A266 Set of 4 35.00 35.00

See Nos. 1489-1490 for additional souvenir sheets with Jamboree emblem.

Lord Robert Baden-Powell and Songbirds — A267

Lord Robert Baden-Powell and Cats, Dogs, Butterflies or Owls — A268

No. 1500 — Lord Baden-Powell and unnamed songbirds: a, 1000d. b, 2000d. c, 3000d. d, 5000d. e, 6000d. f, 15,000d.
No. 1501 — Lord Baden-Powell and unnamed cats or dogs: a, 1000d, Cat. b, 2000d, Cat, diff. c, 3000d, Cat, diff. d, 5000d, Dog. e, 6000d, Dog, diff. f, 15,000d, Dog, diff.
No. 1502 — Lord Baden-Powell and butterflies: a, 1000d, Lycaena dispar. b, 2000d, Papilio macheon. c, 3000d, Cethosia biblis. d, 5000d, Netrocoryne repanda. e, 6000d, Eupackardia calleta. f, 15,000d, Gangara thyrsis.
No. 1503 — Lord Baden-Powell and owls: a, 1000d, Bbubo lacteus. b, 2000d, Asio capensis. c, 3000d, Strix woodfordii. d, 5000d, Strix butleri. e, 6000d, Otus insularis. f, 15,000d, Glaucidium perlatum.
No. 1504, 38,000d, Like #1500c. No. 1505, 38,000d, Like #1501e. No. 1506, 38,000d, Like #1502c. No. 1507, 38,000d, Like #1503a.

2003

1500 A267 Sheet of 6, #a-f 9.00 9.00

1501 A268 Sheet of 6, #a-f 9.00 9.00

1502 A268 Sheet of 6, #a-f 9.00 9.00

1503 A268 Sheet of 6, #a-f 9.00 9.00

Nos. 1500-1503 (4) 36.00 36.00

Souvenir Sheets

1504 A267 38,000d multi 8.50 8.50

1505 A268 38,000d multi 8.50 8.50

1506 A268 38,000d multi 8.50 8.50

1507 A268 38,000d multi 8.50 8.50

A269

Lady Olave Baden-Powell and Pandas — A270

No. 1508 — Lady Baden-Powell and various pandas: a, 1000d. b, 2000d. c, 3000d. d, 5000d. e, 6000d. f, 15,000d.

2003

1508 A269 Sheet of 6, #a-f 9.00 9.00

Souvenir Sheet

1509 A270 38,000d multi 8.50 8.50

Scouting Emblem and Cats or Prehistoric Animals and Minerals — A271

No. 1510 — Scouting emblem and various cats: a, 1000d. b, 2000d. c, 3000d. d, 5000d. e, 6000d. f, 15,000d.
No. 1511 — Scouting emblem, unnamed minerals and prehistoric animals: a, 1000d, Corythosaurus causarius. b, 2000d, Compsognathus. c, 3000d, Edaphosaurus. d, 5000d, Monoclonius. e, 6000d, Rhamphorhynchus. f, 15,000d, Stegosaurus.
38,000d, Like #1511a.

2003

1510 A271 Sheet of 6, #a-f 9.00 9.00

1511 A271 Sheet of 6, #a-f 9.00 9.00

Souvenir Sheet

1512 A271 38,000d multi 8.50 8.50

See No. 1522.

Rotary Emblem and Roses — A272

No. 1513 — Rotary emblem and various roses: a, 1000d. b, 2000d. c, 3000d. d, 5000d. e, 6000d. f, 15,000d.
38,000d, Like #1513e.

2003

1513 A272 Sheet of 6, #a-f 9.00 9.00

Souvenir Sheet

1514 A272 38,000d multi 8.50 8.50

Rotary or Lions Emblems and Pinnipeds or Birds — A273

No. 1515 — Various pinnipeds and: a, 1000d, Rotary emblem. b, 2000d, Lions emblem. c, 3000d, Rotary emblem. d, 5000d, Lions emblem. e, 6000d, Rotary emblem. f, 15,000d, Lions emblem.

No. 1516: a, 1000d, Rotary emblem, Polemaetus bellicosus. b, 2000d, Lions emblem, Aquila verreauxi. c, 3000d, Rotary emblem, Circus aeruginosus. d, 5000d, Lions emblem, Aquila nipalensis. e, 6000d, Rotary emblem, Hieraetus fasciatus. f, 15,000d, Lions emblem, Aquila pomarina.

No. 1517, 38,000d, Like #1515a. No. 1518, 38,000d, Like #1516b.

2003 **Sheets of 6, #a-f**

1515-1516 A273 Set of 2 18.00 18.00

Souvenir Sheets

1517-1518 A273 Set of 2 17.00 17.00

A274

A275

A276

Dogs and Cats — A277

No. 1519: a, 1000d, Dog. b, 2000d, Cat. c, 3000d, Dogs. d, 5000d, Cat, diff. e, 6000d, Dog, diff. f, 15,000d, Cat, diff.

No. 1520: a, 1000d, Dog, diff. b, 2000d, Cat, diff. c, 3000d, Dogs, diff. d, 5000d, Cat, diff. e, 6000d, Dog, diff. f, 15,000d, Cat, diff.

No. 1523, Like #1520e.

2003

1519 A274 Sheet of 6, #a-f 9.00 9.00
1520 A275 Sheet of 6, #a-f 9.00 9.00

Souvenir Sheets

1521 A276 38,000d multi 8.50 8.50
1522 A277 38,000d multi 8.50 8.50
1523 A275 38,000d multi 8.50 8.50

Sled Dogs — A278

No. 1524 — Various sled dogs: a, 1000d. b, 2000d. c, 3000d. d, 5000d. e, 6000d. f, 15,000d.

38,000d, Like #1524b.

2003

1524 A278 Sheet of 6, #a-f 9.00 9.00

Souvenir Sheet

1525 A278 38,000d multi 8.50 8.50

Dolphins — A279

No. 1526 — Various dolphins: a, 1000d. b, 2000d. c, 3000d. d, 5000d. e, 6000d. f, 15,000d.

2003

1526 A279 Sheet of 6, #a-f 8.00 8.00

Rams — A280

Various rams.

2003

1527 A280 7000d Sheet of 6, #a-f 8.00 8.00

For surcharges, see Nos. 1995, 1996, 2004, 2006, 2022, 2023, 2031-2033, 2049, 2050, 2058-2060, 2076, 2077, 2085, 2087.

Hot Air Balloons and Zeppelins — A281

No. 1528: a, 1000d, Balloon. b, 2000d, Zeppelin. c, 3000d, Balloon, diff. d, 5000d, Moored Zeppelin. e, 6000d, Balloons. f, 15,000d, Zeppelin cockpit.

38,000d, Like #1528e.

2003

1528 A281 Sheet of 6, #a-f 8.00 8.00

Souvenir Sheet

1529 A281 38,000d multi 7.50 7.50

Aviation, Cent. — A282

No. 1530 — Various military aircraft: a, 1000d, Helicopter. b, 2000d, Airplane. c, 3000d, Helicopter, diff. d, 5000d, Airplanes. e, 6000d, Helicopter, diff. f, 15,000d, Airplane.

38,000d, Like #1530c.

2003

1530 A282 Sheet of 6, #a-f 9.00 9.00

Souvenir Sheet

1531 A282 38,000d multi 8.50 8.50

Apollo 11 — A283

Space — A284

Concorde and Spacecraft — A285

Deceased Crew of Space Shuttle Columbia — A286

No. 1532: a, 1000d, Astronaut Edwin Aldrin. b, 2000d, Lift-off. c, 3000d, Crew in capsule. d, 5000d, Retrieval of crew at sea. e, 6000d, Astronauts Neil Armstrong, Michael Collins and Aldrin. f, 15,000d, Astronaut on Moon.

No. 1533: a, 1000d, Lift-off of Space Shuttle. b, 2000d, Astronaut, vehicle and structures on planet. c, 3000d, Intl. Space Station. d, 5000d, Astronauts working in outer space. e, 6000d, Untethered astronaut. f, 15,000d, Lift-off of rocket.

No. 1534: a, 1000d, Concorde. b, 2000d, Lift-off of Space Shuttle, diff. c, 3000d, Concorde, diff. d, 5000d, Intl. Space Station. e, 6000d, Concorde on runway. f, 15,000d, Space Shuttle in outer space.

No. 1535, Like #1532e. No. 1536, Like #1533c. No. 1537, Like #1534b.

2003

1532 A283 Sheet of 6, #a-f 9.00 9.00
1533 A284 Sheet of 6, #a-f 9.00 9.00
1534 A285 Sheet of 6, #a-f 9.00 9.00
Nos. 1532-1534 (3) 27.00 27.00

Souvenir Sheets

1535 A283 38,000d multi 8.50 8.50
1536 A284 38,000d multi 8.50 8.50
1537 A285 38,000d multi 8.50 8.50
1538 A286 38,000d multi 8.50 8.50

Tandem Bicycles — A287

No. 1539 — Various tandem bicycles and riders: a, 1000d. b, 2000d. c, 3000d. d, 5000d. e, 6000d. f, 15,000d.

38,000d, Like #1539a.

2003

1539 A287 Sheet of 6, #a-f 9.00 9.00

Souvenir Sheet

1540 A287 38,000d multi 8.50 8.50

Tractor Trailer Trucks — A288

No. 1541 — Trucks with cabs in: a, 1000d, Red. b, 2000d, Blue. c, 3000d, Red, diff. d, 5000d, White. e, 6000d, Black. f, 15,000d, Purple.

38,000d, Like #1542a.

2003

1541 A288 Sheet of 6, #a-f 9.00 9.00

Souvenir Sheet

1542 A288 38,000d multi 8.50 8.50

Volkswagen Beetles — A289

Mercedes-Benz Automobiles — A290

No. 1543: a, 1000d. b, 2000d. c, 3000d. d, 5000d. e, 6000d. f, 15,000d.

No. 1544: a, 1000d. b, 2000d. c, 3000d. d, 5000d. e, 6000d. f, 15,000d.

No. 1545, Like #1543d. No. 1546, Like #1544d.

2003

1543	A289	Sheet of 6, #a-f	9.00	9.00
1544	A290	Sheet of 6, #a-f	9.00	9.00

Souvenir Sheets

1545	A289	38,000d multi	8.50	8.50
1546	A290	38,000d multi	8.50	8.50

Auto Racing — A291

Formula 1 Racing — A292

Formula 1 Racing — A293

Motorcycle Racing — A294

No. 1547: a, 1000d, Car 4x. b, 2000d, Cars 12 and 21. c, 3000d, Cars 46, 54 and 42. d, 5000d, Cars 11, 37 and 4. e, 6000d, South-side Fina car. f, 15,000d, Car 16.

No. 1548: a, 1000d, Two cars. b, 2000d, Two drivers holding trophies. c, 3000d, Car. d, 5000d, Two drivers with champagne bottles. e, 6000d, Car, diff. f, 15,000d, Three drivers.

No. 1549: a, 1000d, Red car with Marlboro wing. b, 2000d, Yellow car with Benson & Hedges wing. c, 3000d, Red car, driver with arms raised. d, 5000d, Black, red and white car. e, 6000d, Blue and yellow car. f, 15,000d, Black, red and white car, diff.

No. 1550: a, Yellow motorcycle without number. b, Green motorcycle #1. c, Motorcycle #26. d, White motorcycle #1. e, Motorcycle #9. f, Motorcycle #21.

No. 1551, Like #1548a. No. 1552, Like #1549c.

2003

1547	A291	Sheet of 6, #a-f	9.00	9.00
1548	A292	Sheet of 6, #a-f	9.00	9.00
1549	A293	Sheet of 6, #a-f	9.00	9.00
1550	A294	10,000d Sheet of 6, #a-f	13.50	13.50
		Nos. 1547-1550 (4)	40.50	40.50

Souvenir Sheets

1551	A292	38,000d multi	8.50	8.50
1552	A293	38,000d multi	8.50	8.50

For surcharges, see Nos. 2003, 2010, 2030, 2037, 2057, 2064, 2084, 2091.

A295

A296

A297

A298

A299

A300

A301

A302

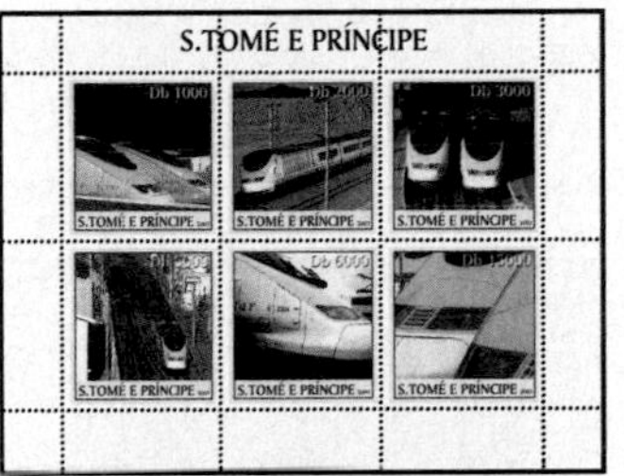

A303

Trains — A304

Nos. 1553-1562 — Various trains: a, 1000d. b, 2000d. c, 3000d. d, 5000d. e, 6000d. f, 15,000d.

No. 1563, Like #1553d. No. 1564, Like #1554c. No. 1565, Like #1555f. No. 1566, Like #1556d. No. 1567, Like #1557a. No. 1568, Like #1558e. No. 1569, Like #1559f. No. 1570, Like #1560b. No. 1571, Like #1561c. No. 1572, Like #1562d.

2003

1553	A295	Sheet of 6, #a-f	9.00	9.00
1554	A296	Sheet of 6, #a-f	9.00	9.00
1555	A297	Sheet of 6, #a-f	9.00	9.00
1556	A298	Sheet of 6, #a-f	9.00	9.00
1557	A299	Sheet of 6, #a-f	9.00	9.00
1558	A300	Sheet of 6, #a-f	9.00	9.00
1559	A301	Sheet of 6, #a-f	9.00	9.00
1560	A302	Sheet of 6, #a-f	9.00	9.00
1561	A303	Sheet of 6, #a-f	9.00	9.00
1562	A304	Sheet of 6, #a-f	9.00	9.00
		Nos. 1553-1562 (10)	90.00	90.00

Souvenir Sheets

1563	A295	38,000d multi	8.50	8.50
1564	A296	38,000d multi	8.50	8.50
1565	A297	38,000d multi	8.50	8.50
1566	A298	38,000d multi	8.50	8.50
1567	A299	38,000d multi	8.50	8.50
1568	A300	38,000d multi	8.50	8.50
1569	A301	38,000d multi	8.50	8.50
1570	A302	38,000d multi	8.50	8.50
1571	A303	38,000d multi	8.50	8.50
1572	A304	38,000d multi	8.50	8.50

Ships — A305

Paintings of various ships by Richard C. Moore: a, *Constitution* and *Guerriere*; b, Privateer *Rattlesnake*; c, H.M.S. *Victory*; d, H.M.S. *Victory* at Trafalgar; e, Clipper Ship *Comet*; f, U.S.S. *Constitution*.

2003

1573	A305	7000d Sheet of 6, #a-f	9.50	9.50

For surcharges, see Nos. 1997-1999, 2024-2026, 2051-2053, 2078-2080.

2004 Summer Olympics, Athens — A306

No. 1574 — Various rowing teams: a, 1000d. b, 2000d. c, 3000d. d, 5000d. e, 6000d. f, 15,000d.

38,000d, Like #1574b.

2003

1574	A306	Sheet of 6, #a-f	6.75	6.75

Souvenir Sheet

1575	A306	38,000d multi	7.00	7.00

The editors believe that stamps dated "2004" were not put on sale in St. Thomas and Prince Islands. St. Thomas and Prince postal officials have declared that any stamps dated "2005" are illegal stamps, as well as a sheet of nine 7000d stamps depicting Marilyn Monroe, dated "2006", and a sheet of nine 7000d stamps 2006 World Cup Soccer, dated "2006."

A307

No. 1576 — Sphinx and: a, 7000d, Pyramid stones on ships. b, 9000d, Construction of Pyramid. c, 10,000d, Egyptians and balance scale. d, 14,000d, Egyptians preparing dead man for burial.

No. 1577 — Wolfgang Amadeus Mozart (1756-91), composer: a, 7000d, Wearing black jacket. b, 9000d, Wearing red jacket, at piano. c, 10,000d, Wearing red jacket. d, 14,000d, Wearing gray jacket.

No. 1578 — Gold medalists at 2004 Summer Olympics, Athens: a, 7000d, Keiji Suzuki, judo. b, 9000d, Hicham El Guerrouj, running.

c, 10,000d, Seung Min Ryu, table tennis. d, 14,000d, Michael Phelps, swimming.

No. 1579 — Participants at 2006 Winter Olympics, Turin: a, 7000d, Tanith Belbin and Benjamin Agosto, ice dancing. b, 9000d, Carolina Kostner, figure skating. c, 10,000d, Shizuka Arakawa, figure skating. d, 14,000d, Maxim Marinin and Tatiana Totmianina, figure skating.

No. 1580 — European soccer players: a, 7000d, Zinedine Zidane. b, 9000d, Raul Gonzalez. c, 10,000d, David Beckham. d, 14,000d, Pavel Nedved.

No. 1581 — African soccer players: a, 7000d, Nwankwo Kanu. b, 9000d, Patrick Vieira. c, 10,000d, Claude Makelele. d, 14,000d, Aiyegbeni Yakubu.

No. 1582 — Marilyn Monroe (1926-62), actress: a, 7000d, With umbrella. b, 9000d, Wearing red hat and shorts. c, 10,000d, Wearing bikini. d, 14,000d, Wearing dress.

No. 1583 — Spanish painters and their paintings: a, 7000d, El Greco (1541-1614). b, 9000d, Joaquin Sorolla (1863-1923). c, 10,000d, Diego Velazquez (1599-1660). d, 14,000d, Francisco Goya (1746-1828).

No. 1584 — Various views of the Concorde above clouds: a, 7000d. b, 9000d. c, 10,000d. d, 14,000d.

No. 1585, 40,000d, Sphinx. No. 1586, 40,000d, Mozart. No. 1587, 40,000d, Virgilijus Alekna, discus. No. 1588, 40,000d, Seth Wescott, snowboarding. No. 1589, 40,000d, John Terry. No. 1590, 40,000d, Samuel Eto'o. No. 1591, 40,000d, White House and American flag. No. 1592, 40,000d, Pablo Picasso (1881-1973). No. 1593, 40,000d, Concorde.

2006, Apr. 4 Litho. *Perf. 12¾x13¼*

Sheets of 4, #a-d

1576-1584 A307 Set of 9 105.00 105.00

Souvenir Sheets

Perf. 13¼ Syncopated

1585-1593 A307 Set of 9 105.00 105.00

Europa Stamps, 50th Anniv. — A308

No. 1594 — Emblems and: a, Charles de Gaulle (1890-1970), French President. b, Wolfgang Amadeus Mozart (1756-91), composer. c, Pope John Paul II (1920-2005). d, Concorde.

40,000d, Emblems and map of Europe.

2006, Apr. 4 *Perf. 12¾x13¼*

1594 A308 14,000d Sheet of 4, #a-d 16.00 16.00

Souvenir Sheet

Perf. 13¼ Syncopated

1595 A308 40,000d multi 11.50 11.50

A309

No. 1596 — Turtles: a, 7000d, Testudo graeca. b, 9000d, Pseudemys scripta. c, 10,000d, Clemmys insculpta. d, 14,000d, Trionyx spiniferus.

No. 1597 — Predators: a, 7000d, Crocodylus porosus. b, 9000d, Ursus maritimus. c, 10,000d, Carcharodon carcharias. d, 14,000d, Varanus komodoensis.

No. 1598 — Endangered animals: a, 7000d, Tyto alba. b, 9000d, Phascolarctos cinearus. c, 10,000d, Panthera tigris. d, 14,000d, Balaenoptera musculus.

No. 1599 — Illustrations from book *After Man: A Zoology of the Future* by Dougal Dixon : a, 7000d, Alesimia lapsus. b, 9000d, Aquator adepsicautus. c, 10,000d, Tetraceras africanus. d, 14,000d, Harundopes virgatus.

No. 1600 — Dogs and cats: a, 7000d, Golden retriever, British shorthair cat. b, 9000d, Portuguese Podengo hound, Black smoke Persian cat. c, 10,000d, Greyhound, Norwegian forest cat. d, 14,000d, Black Labrador retriever, Tiffanie cat.

No. 1601 — Owls and mushrooms: a, 7000d, Pseudoscops grammicus, Cortinarius triumphans. b, 9000d, Strix woodfordi, Cortinarius subfulgens. c, 10,000d, Athene noctua, Agaricus augustus. d, 14,000d, Strix nebulosa, Leucocortinarius bulbiger.

No. 1602 — Butterflies and orchids: a, 7000d, Mosaic gynandromorph, Phalaenopsis. b, 9000d, Nymphalidae, Coral Cymbidium. c, 10,000d, Papilio polymnestor, Pleione praecox. d, 14,000d, Charaxes bohemani, Rhyncholaelia glauca.

No. 1603 — Butterflies and bees: a, 7000d, Heliconius nattereri, Apis mellifera scutella. b, 9000d, Nymphalidae, Bombus hypnorum. c, 10,000d, Eterusia, repleta, Bombus terrestris. d, 14,000d, Lasaia mocros, Apis mellifera.

No. 1604 — Dinosaurs and minerals: a, 7000d, Pachycephalosaurus, Spodumene and kunzite. b, 9000d, Psittacosaurus, Opal. c, 10,000d, Troodon, Calcite and limestone. d, 14,000d, Struthiomimus, Barite and calcite.

No. 1605 — Dolphins and Swedish lighthouses: a, 7000d, Lagenorhynchus obliquidens, Berlin Lighthouse. b, 9000d, Delphinus delphis, Brämskär Lighthouse. c, 10,000d, Tursiops truncatus, Hättan Lighthouse. d, 14,000d, Lagenorhynchus acutus, Ursholmen Lighthouse.

No. 1606, 40,000d, Malacochersus tornieri. No. 1607, 40,000d, Carcharodon carcharias, diff. No. 1608, 40,000d, Felis lynx. No. 1609, 40,000d, Reteostium cortepellium, Cornophilius ophicaudatus. No. 1610, 40,000d, Chow chow, Turkish angora cat. No. 1611, 40,000d, Phodilus badius, mushrooms. No. 1612, 40,000d, Athletes steindachneri moth, Angulocaste orchid. No. 1613, 40,000d, Heliconiinae hermatena, Apidae. No. 1614, 40,000d, Stegosaurus, Topaz. No. 1615, 40,000d, Delphinus delphis, Lista Lighthouse, Norway.

2006, May 25 *Perf. 12¾x13¼*

Sheets of 4, #a-d, + 4 Labels

1596-1605 A309 Set of 10 120.00 120.00

Souvenir Sheets

Perf. 13¼ Syncopated

1606-1615 A309 Set of 10 120.00 120.00

Paintings — A310

No. 1616 — Paintings by Michelangelo: a, 7000d, Martyrdom of St. Peter. b, 9000d, The Doni Tondo. c, 10,000d, Ezekiel. d, 14,000d, Last Judgment.

No. 1617 — Paintings by Peter Paul Rubens: a, 7000d, The Union of Earth and Water. b, 9000d, Daniel in the Lion's Den. c, 10,000d, The Judgment of Paris. d, 14,000d, Bacchus.

No. 1618 — Paintings by Rembrandt: a, 7000d, Tobit and Anna. b, 9000d, The Apostle Paul in Prison. c, 10,000d, The Militia Company of Captain Frans Banning Cocq. d, 14,000d, The Return of the Prodigal Son.

No. 1619 — Paintings by Gustave Courbet: a, 7000d, The Woman in the Waves. b, 9000d, Still Life: Fruit. c, 10,000d, The Stormy Sea. d, 14,000d, Sleep.

No. 1620 — Paintings by Auguste Renoir: a, 7000d, Bather Arranging Her Hair. b, 9000d, Blonde Nude. c, 10,000d, The Nymphs. d, 14,000d, The Bathers.

No. 1621 — Paintings by Vincent van Gogh: a, 7000d, The Starry Night. b, 9000d, The Church at Auvers-sur-Oise. c, 10,000d, First Steps. d, 14,000d, Midday Siesta.

No. 1622 — Paintings by Henri de Toulouse-Lautrec: a, 7000d, La Goulue Arriving with Two Women. b, 9000d, Yvette Guilbert. c, 10,000d, The Two Girlfriends. d, 14,000d, Rue des Moulins: The Medical Inspection.

No. 1623 — Various unnamed Japanese paintings by: a, 7000d, Utagawa Kuniyoshi. b, 9000d, Toshi Yoshida. c, 10,000d, Tsukioka Yoshitoshi. d, 14,000d, Utagawa Hiroshige II.

No. 1624 — American impressionist paintings: a, 7000d, Mother and Child, by Mary Cassatt. b, 9000d, Rock Garden in Giverny, by Leslie Breck. c, 10,000d, Oyster Gatherers of Cancale, by John Singer Sargent. d, 14,000d, Two Sisters, by William Merritt Chase.

No. 1625 — Paintings by Spanish-speaking artists: a, 7000d, Slave Market with the Disappearing Bust of Voltaire, by Salvador Dali. b, 9000d, The Flower Carrier, by Diego Rivera. c, 10,000d, Self-portrait, by Frida Kahlo. d, 14,000d, Dutch Interior I, by Joan Miró.

No. 1626, 40,000d, The Flood, by Michelangelo. No. 1627, 40,000d, Simon and Pero, by Rubens. No. 1628, 40,000d, Bathsheba at her Bath, by Rembrandt. No. 1629, 40,000d, The Bathers, by Courbet. No. 1630, 40,000d, Nude in the Sunlight, by Renoir. No. 1631, 40,000d, The Night Café, by van Gogh. No. 1632, 40,000d, Ball at the Moulin de la Galette (incorrectly inscribed "The Bathers"), by Toulouse-Lautrec. No. 1633, 40,000d, Painting by Narita Morikane. No. 1634, 40,000d, Sleep, by Frederick Carl Freiseke. No. 1635, 40,000d, A Couple, by Fernando Botero.

2006, Aug. 25 *Perf. 12¾x13¼*

Sheets of 4, #a-d

1616-1625 A310 Set of 10 120.00 120.00

Souvenir Sheets

Perf. 13¼ Syncopated

1626-1635 A310 Set of 10 120.00 120.00

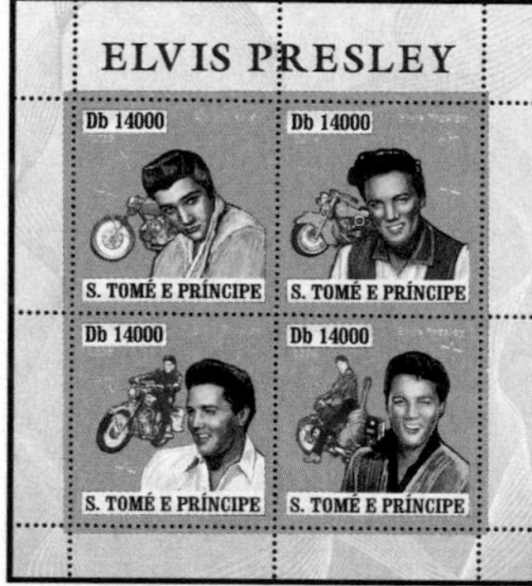

A311

Nos. 1636 and 1646, 14,000d — Motorcyle and Elvis Presley (1935-77) wearing: a, Lilac shirt (motorcycle rider not visible). b, Red and white shirt. c, White shirt. b, Black and purple shirt.

Nos. 1637 and 1647, 14,000d — Marilyn Monroe (1926-62) and: a, Flash camera. b, Film cans. c, Film reel. b, Director's clapboard.

Nos. 1638 and 1648, 14,000d — Sports and games: a, Garry Kasparov, chess player. b, Won Hee Lee, judo. c, Wang Liqin, table tennis. b, Tiger Woods, golf.

Nos. 1639 and 1649, 14,000d — Lord Robert Baden-Powell (1847-1941), founder of Scouting movement and: a, Mushrooms, opal. b, Flower, owl. c, Mineral, mushrooms. b, Owl, orchid.

Nos. 1640 and 1650, 14,000d — Humanists: a, Pope John Paul II. b, Abraham Lincoln. c, Dr. Albert Schweitzer. b, Mahatma Gandhi.

Nos. 1641 and 1651, 14,000d — The Beatles: a, George Harrison. b, John Lennon. c, Ringo Starr. b, Paul McCartney.

Nos. 1642 and 1652, 14,000d — The Rolling Stones: a, Keith Richards. b, Mick Jagger. c, Charlie Watts. b, Ron Wood.

Nos. 1643 and 1653, 14,000d — Fire vehicles: a, Mercedes-Benz Metz. b, MAN 415 H-LF. c, Mercedes-Benz LF 16. b, Magirus KW 16.

Nos. 1644 and 1654, 14,000d — High-speed trains: a, Shinkansen JR 500. b, Eurostar. c, AGV. b, TGV.

Nos. 1645 and 1655, 14,000d — Scouting emblem, mushrooms and owls: a, Bubo zeylonensis. b, Nyctea ulula. c, Phodilus badius. b, Asio otus.

Nos. 1656 and 1666, 56,000d, Presley with guitar. Nos. 1657 and 1667, 56,000d, Monroe with film reel. Nos. 1658 and 1668, 56,000d, Kim Clijsters, tennis. Nos. 1659 and 1669, 56,000d, Baden-Powell and orchid. Nos. 1660 and 1670, 56,000d, Mother Teresa. Nos. 1661 and 1671, 56,000d, The Beatles. Nos. 1662 and 1672, 56,000d, Jagger. Nos. 1663 and 1673, 56,000d, Fischer fire vehicle. Nos. 1664 and 1674, 56,000d, Swiss Metro. Nos. 1665 and 1675, 56,000d, Strix cinereots.

Litho. & Embossed With Foil Application

2006, Dec. 15 *Perf. 12¾x13¼*

Without Gum

Sheets of 4 #a-d

Silver Background

1636-1645 A311 Set of 10 165.00 165.00

Gold Background

1646-1655 A311 Set of 10 165.00 165.00

Souvenir Sheets

Silver Background

1656-1665 A311 Set of 10 165.00 165.00

Gold Background

1666-1675 A311 Set of 10 165.00 165.00

Miniature Sheets

A312

No. 1676 — Princess Diana (image at left): a, 7000d, Holding papers. b, 9000d, Walking with Mother Teresa. c, 10,000d, Talking with girl. d, 14,000d, Riding in coach with Prince Charles.

No. 1677 — Steve Irwin (1962-2006), conservationist, with: a, 7000d, Pterois volitans. b, 9000d, Crotalus viridis. c, 10,000d, Crocodylus porosus. d, 14,000d, Myliobatis australis and Phascolarctos cinereus.

No. 1678 — Popes and their arms: a, 7000d, Pope Paul VI. b, 9000d, Pope John Paul I. c, 10,000d, Pope Benedict XVI. d, 14,000d, Pope John Paul II.

No. 1679 — Mushrooms: a, 7000d, Boletus badius and Sir Alexander Fleming (1881-1955), pharmacologist. b, 9000d, Boletus edulis and Leccinum quercinum. c, 10,000d, Amanita pantherina and Russula vesca. d, 14,000d, Amanita muscaria and Fleming.

No. 1680 — Neanerthals and minerals: a, 7000d, Celestine. b, 9000d, Sulfur. c, 10,000d, Pyrargyrite. d, 14,000d, Orthoclase and adularia.

No. 1681 — Minerals: a, 7000d, Barite, calcite and smoky quartz. b, 9000d, Malachite, beryl and emerald. c, 10,000d, Elbaite, rubellite tourmaline, microcline and amazonite. d, 14,000d, Quartz, amethyst and topaz.

No. 1682 — International Polar Year: a, 7000d, Admiral Robert Peary (1856-1920), polar explorer, and expedition members. b, 9000d, Eudyptes chrysolophus. c, 10,000d, Aptenodytes patagonicus. d, 14,000d, Fridtjof Nansen (1861-1930), polar explorer and Ursus maritimus.

No. 1683 — Owls and their prey: a, 7000d, Tyto alba, Ochotona collaris. b, 9000d, Nyctea scandiaca, Lepus arcticus. c, 10,000d, Scotopelia peli, Thunnus albacares. d, 14,000d, Ninox novaeseelandiae, Platacanthomyinae.

No. 1684 — Satellites: a, 7000d, Sputnik 1. b, 9000d, Sputnik 1, diff. c, 10,000d, Sputnik 2. d, 14,000d, Sputnik 2, diff.

No. 1685 — Martian probes: a, 7000d, Mars Odyssey. b, 9000d, Mars Rover. c, 10,000d, Mars Rover, diff. d, 14,000d, Mars Odyssey, diff.

2007, Feb. 2 Litho. *Perf. 12¾x13¼*

Sheets of 4, #a-d

1676-1685 A312 Set of 10 120.00 120.00

Souvenir Sheets

U.S. Presidents — A313

No. 1686, 40,000d, George Washington (1732-99). No. 1687, 40,000d, Thomas Jefferson (1743-1826). No. 1688, 40,000d, Abraham Lincoln (1809-65). No. 1689, 40,000d, Franklin D. Roosevelt (1882-1945). No. 1690, 40,000d, Dwight D. Eisenhower (1890-1969). No. 1691, 40,000d, John F. Kennedy (1917-63). No. 1692, 40,000d, Lyndon B. Johnson (1908-73). No. 1693, 40,000d, Ronald Reagan (1911-2004). No. 1694, 40,000d, George H. W. Bush. No. 1695, 40,000d, William J. Clinton.

2007, Feb. 2 *Perf. 13¼ Syncopated*

1686-1695 A313 Set of 10 120.00 120.00

A314

No. 1696 — Bears: a, 7000d, Three bears. b, 9000d, Three bears in tree. c, 10,000d, Four bears and anthills. d, 14,000d, Three bears, diff.

No. 1697 — Wolves: a, 7000d, Two wolves upright. b, 9000d, Wolf on ground, wolf upright. c, 10,000d, Wolf's head, howling wolf. d, 14,000d, Two woves on ground.

No. 1698 — Birds: a, 7000d, Couroucou oranga. b, 9000d, Couroucou rosalba. c, 10,000d, Ramphocele scarlatte. d, 14,000d, Cotinga ouette.

No. 1699 — Birds: a, 7000d, Tangara passe-ver. b, 9000d, Carouge iamacaii. c, 10,000d, Cassique huppe. d, 14,000d, Psittacule caica-barraband.

No. 1700 — Insects and lizards preying on butterflies and moths: a, 7000d, Pseudocreabotra wahlbergi and butterfly. b, 9000d, Spodoptera exigua and lizard. c, 10,000d, Cmenidophorus lemniscatus and moth. d, 14,000d, Asilus crabroniformis and butterfly.

No. 1701 — Animals preying on butterflies: a, 7000d, Frog and Euclidia glyphica. b, 9000d, Aegotheles cristata and butterfies. c, 10,000d, Leiothrix lutea, flowers and butterfly. d, 14,000d, Araneidae, Oxyopidae, and butterflies.

No. 1702 — Fish: a, 7000d, Chaetodon lineolatus, Osphronemidae. b, 9000d, Gymnarchus niloticus, Polyodon spathula. c, 10,000d, Climatius, Dunkleosteus. d, 14,000d, Latimeria chalumnae, Chlorostigma.

No. 1703 — Snakes: a, 7000d, And nest. b, 9000d, And unhatched eggs. c, 10,000d, And hatching eggs. d, 14,000d, With heads raised.

No. 1704 — Dinosaurs: a, 7000d, Velociraptor, Protoceratops. b, 9000d, Deinonychus, Sinosauropteryx. c, 10,000d, Oviraptor, Beipaiosaurus. d, 14,000d, Oviraptors.

No. 1705 — Mushrooms: a, 7000d, Pleurotus salignus, Catathelasma, Suillis luteus. b, 9000d, Lactarius torminosus, Tricholoma portentosum. c, 10,000d, Pleurotus ostreatus, Lactarius necator. d, 14,000d, Pleurotus eryngii, Tricholomopsis rutilans.

No. 1706, 40,000d, Ursus maritimus. No. 1707, 40,000d, Canidae. No. 1708, 40,000d, Fringille daroare. No. 1709, 40,000d, Euphonea diademe. No. 1710, 40,000d, Cyanositta cristata and butterfly. No. 1711, 40,000d, Gerrhonotus multicarinatus and butterflies. No. 1712, 40,000d, Siniperca chuatsi. No. 1713, 40,000d, Snake. No. 1714, 40,000d, Carcharodontosaurus. No. 1715, 40,000d, Entoloma sinuatum, Calocybe gambosa.

2007, Mar. 15 ***Perf. 12¾x13¼***

Sheets of 4, #a-d, + 2 labels

1696-1705 A314 Set of 10 120.00 120.00

Souvenir Sheets

1706-1715 A314 Set of 10 120.00 120.00

Scouting, cent.

Independence of India, 60th Anniv. — A315

No. 1716: a, 9000d, Mahatma Gandhi (1869-1948), Independence leader. b, 10,000d, Indira Gandhi (1917-84), Prime Minister. c, 14,000d, Jawaharlal Nehru (1889-1964), Prime Minister.

40,000d, Vasco da Gama (1469-1524), explorer.

2007, Nov. 5 ***Perf. 12¾x13¼***

1716 A315 Sheet of 3, #a-c, + label 4.75 4.75

Souvenir Sheet

Perf. 13¼ Syncopated

1717 A315 40,000d multi 5.75 5.75

Souvenir sheets of 1 of Nos. 1716a-1716c with colored frames exist.

Cruise Liners — A316

No. 1718: a, 7000d, Queen Mary 2. b, 9000d, Freedom of the Seas. c, 10,000d, Crystal Symphony. d, 14,000d, Star Princess. 40,000d, Titanic.

2007, Nov. 5 ***Perf. 12¾x13¼***

1718 A316 Sheet of 4, #a-d 5.75 5.75

Souvenir Sheet

Perf. 13¼ Syncopated

1719 A316 40,000d multi 5.75 5.75

Souvenir sheets of 1 of Nos. 1718a, 1718b, and 1718d with colored frames exist.

A317

No. 1720 — Chess: a, 7000d, Chess player looking at board, knight. b, 9000d, Queen and pawn, hand moving piece. c, 10,000d, Player, rook and pawns. d, 14,000d, Queen, pieces on board.

No. 1721 — Race cars and Colin McRae (1968-2007), race car driver: a, 7000d, Wearing blue uniform. b, 9000d, Holding bottle of champagne. c, 10,000d, Holding trophy. d, 14,000d, Wearing earphones.

No. 1722 — Luciano Pavarotti (1935-2007), opera singer, and: a, 7000d, Princess Diana. b, 9000d, Spice Girls. c, 10,000d, Placido Domingoa and José Carreras. d, 14,000d, Bono.

No. 1723 — Photographs by Anton Corbijn of: a, 7000d, Miles Davis. b, 9000d, Clint Eastwood. c, 10,000d, Depeche Mode. d, 14,000d, Bono.

No. 1724 — Minerals: a, 7000d, Gypsum. b, 9000d, Rhodonite. c, 10,000d, Cerussite. d, 14,000d, Malachite.

No. 1725 — Lighthouses: a, 7000d, Alexandria Lighthouse. b, 9000d, Tower of Hercules. c, 10,000d, Yokohama Marine Tower. d, 14,000d, Cordouan Lighthouse, France.

No. 1726 — Tangula Express Train, China: a, 7000d, Train, tunnel, bridge. b, 9000d, Train on bridge. c, 10,000d, Train, lake. d, 14,000d, Train, train on bridge.

No. 1727, 40,000d, King, queen, chess players. No. 1728, 40,000d, McRae and race car. No. 1729, 40,000d, Pavarotti. No. 1730, 40,000d, Photograph of Dave Gahan by Corbijn. No. 1731, 40,000d, Fluorite, barite. No. 1732, 40,000d, Statue of Liberty.

2007, Nov. 5 ***Perf. 12¾x13¼***

Sheets of 4, #a-d

1720-1726 A317 Set of 7 40.00 40.00

Souvenir Sheets

Perf. 13¼ Syncopated

1727-1732 A317 Set of 6 35.00 35.00

Souvenir sheets of 1 of Nos. 1725a, 1725c, and 1725d exist.

Paintings in Prado Museum by Spanish Artists — A318

No. 1733 — Various paintings by El Greco (1541-1614): a, 7000d. b, 9000d. c, 10,000d. d, 14,000d.

No. 1734 — Various paintings by Diego Velázquez (1541-1614): a, 7000d. b, 9000d. c, 10,000d. d, 14,000d.

No. 1735 — Various paintings by Francisco Goya (1746-1828): a, 7000d. b, 9000d. c, 10,000d. d, 14,000d.

No. 1736 — Various paintings by Joaquín Sorolla (1863-1923): a, 7000d. b, 9000d. c, 10,000d. d, 14,000d.

No. 1737 — Various paintings by Pablo Picasso (1881-1973): a, 7000d. b, 9000d. c, 10,000d. d, 14,000d.

No. 1738, 40,000d, Painting by El Greco, diff. No. 1739, 40,000d, Painting by Velázquez, diff. No. 1740, 40,000d, Painting by Goya, diff. No. 1741, 40,000d, Painting by Sorolla, diff. No. 1742, 40,000d, Painting by Picasso, diff.

2007, Nov. 5 ***Perf. 12¾x13¼***

Sheets of 4, #a-d

1733-1737 A318 Set of 5 29.00 29.00

Souvenir Sheets

Perf. 13¼ Syncopated

1738-1742 A318 Set of 5 29.00 29.00

Souvenir sheets of 1 of Nos. 1733a, 1734b, 1735b, 1736b and 1737d exist.

Marine Science — A319

No. 1743: a, 7000d, Diver and Stenella alymene. b, 9000d, Diver and Natator depressus. c, 10,000d, Jacques Cousteau (1910-97), marine researcher, and submarine. d, 14,000d, Cousteau and research ship.

40,000d, Cousteau, research ship, diff.

2007, Nov. 5 ***Perf. 12¾x13¼***

1743 A319 Sheet of 4, #a-d, + 4 labels 5.75 5.75

Souvenir Sheet

Perf. 13¼ Syncopated

1744 A319 40,000d multi 5.75 5.75

Miniature Sheets

A320

No. 1745, 7000d — Early locomotives: a, Trevithick. b, Marc Seguin. c, Blenkinsop. d, Puffing Billy. e, Rocket. f, Liverpool.

No. 1746, 7000d — Red Cross flag and: a, Airplane. b, Red fire truck with plow attachment. c, Yellow fire truck. d, Ship. e, Helicopter. f, Motorcycle.

No. 1747, 7000d — Divers and marine life: a, Montastrea cavernosa. b, Pisaster ochraceus. c, Gymnothorax javanicus. d, Carassius auratus. e, Octopus vulgaris. f, Lepidochelys olivacea.

No. 1748, 7000d — Extreme sports: a, Skateboarders. b, Motorcyclists. c, Rock climbers. d, Hang gliders. e, Surfer. f, Parachutist.

No. 1749, 7000d — Track and field athletes at 2007 World Championships, Osaka: a, Stefan Holm, high jump. b, Liu Xiang, hurdles. c, Irving Saladino, long jump. d, Steffi Nerius, javelin. e, Agustin Felix, pole vault. f, Liu Xiang running.

No. 1750, 7000d — Rugby players: a, Jonny Wilkinson. b, Felipe Contepomi. c, Chris Paterson. d, Percy Montgomery. e, Jean-Baptiste Elissalde. f, Nick Evans.

No. 1751, 40,000d, Red Cross flag and 1926 Kingsbury motor-driven pumper. No. 1752, 40,000d, Divers and Pomacanthus arcuataus. No. 1753, 40,000d, Monster truck. No. 1754, 40,000d, Alfred Kirwa Yego.

2007, Nov. 5 ***Perf. 12¾x13¼***

Sheets of 6, #a-f

1745-1750 A320 Set of 6 36.00 36.00

Souvenir Sheets

Perf. 13¼ Syncopated

1751-1754 A320 Set of 4 23.00 23.00

Souvenir sheets of 1 of Nos. 1745a-1745f, 1746a, 1746c and 1746d with colored frames exist.

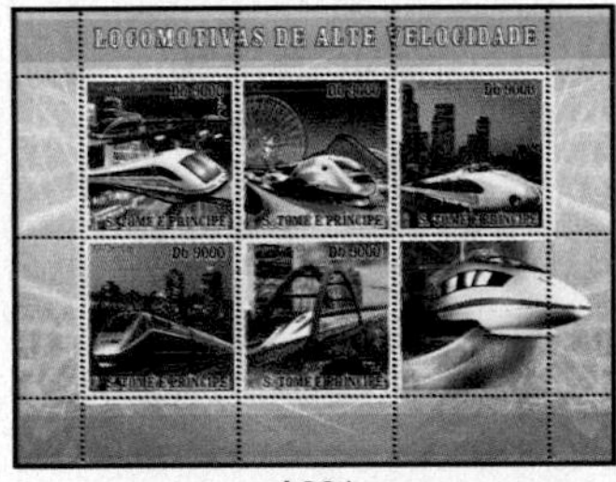

A321

No. 1755, 9000d — High-speed trains: a, Transrapid 08. b, TGV. c, Shinkansen. d, TGV Duplex. e, Maglev MLX-01.

No. 1756, 9000d — Paintings by Antoine Wiertz (1806-65): a, The Reader of Novels. b, The Young Witch. c, Beautiful Rosine. d, The Outrage of Belgian Women. e, Esmerelda.

No. 1757, 9000d — Fire engines: a, 1965 Ford Crown. b, 1881 Merryweather. c, 1894 Merryweather 2. d, 1933 Delahaye. e, 1933 Dennis.

No. 1758, 9000d — Automobiles and automotive pioneers: a, Gottlieb Daimler (1834-1900). b, Karl Benz (1844-1929). c, Enzo Ferrari (1898-1988). d, Henry Ford (1863-1947). e, Ferdinand Porsche (1875-1951).

No. 1759, 40,000d, M Set train. No. 1760, 40,000d, Christ in the Tomb, by Wiertz. No. 1761, 40,000d, Fire truck. No. 1762, 40,000d, Juan Manuel Fangio (1911-95), race car driver.

2007, Nov. 5 ***Perf. 12¾x13¼***

Sheets of 5, #a-e, + Label

1755-1758 A321 Set of 4 26.00 26.00

Souvenir Sheets

Perf. 13¼ Syncopated

1759-1762 A321 Set of 4 23.00 23.00

Souvenir sheets of 1 of Nos. 1757a-1757e, 1758a-1758e with colored frames exist.

A322

No. 1763 — Various Scouts and dogs: a, 7000d. b, 9000d. c, 10,000d. d, 14,000d.

No. 1764 — Inventors: a, 7000d, Dmitri Mendeleev (1834-1907). b, 9000d, Auguste (1862-1954) and Louis Lumière (1864-1948). c, 10,000d, Joseph Michel (1740-1810) and Jacques Etienne Montgolfier (1745-99). d, Samuel F. B. Morse (1791-1872).

No. 1765 — Orchids and famous Blacks: a, Malcolm X (1925-65). b, Albert Luthuli (1898-1967). c, Dr. Martin Luther King, Jr. (1929-68). d, Steve Biko (1946-77).

No. 1766, 40,000d, Scout and dog, diff. No. 1767, 40,000d, John Logie Baird (1888-1946), inventor. No. 1768, 40,000d, Nelson Mandela.

2007, Dec. 31 ***Perf. 12¾x13¼***

Sheets of 4, #a-d

1763-1765 A322 Set of 3 17.00 17.00

Souvenir Sheets

1766-1768 A322 Set of 3 17.00 17.00

Souvenir sheets of 1 of Nos. 1765a-1765d with colored frames exist.

Miniature Sheets

Flora and Fauna — A323

No. 1769 — Rabbits: a, 5000d, Lepus saxatilis. b, 5000d, Pronolagus crassicaudatus. c, 10,000d, Bunolagus monticularis. d, 15,000d, Lepus stracki.

No. 1770 — Hogs: a, 5000d, Phacochoerus africanus. b, 5000d, Potamochoerus porcus. c, 10,000d, Sus scrofa. d, 15,000d, Potamochoerus larvatus.

No. 1771 — Hippopotami: a, 5000d, Hippopotamus amphibius. b, 5000d, Hexaprotodon liberiensis. c, 10,000d, Hexaprotodon liberiensis, diff. d, 15,000d, Hippopotamus amphibius, diff.

No. 1772 — Hyenas: a, 5000d, Lycaon pictus. b, 5000d, Crocuta crocuta. c, 10,000d, Hyaena brunnea. d, 15,000d, Hyaena hyaena.

No. 1773 — Bats: a, 5000d, Mops condylurus. b, 5000d, Cardioderma cor. c, 10,000d, Taphozous mauritianus. d, 15,000d, Hypsignatus monstrosus.

No. 1774 — Cats: a, 5000d, Felis caracal. b, 5000d, Felis serval. c, 10,000d, Felis chaus. d, 15,000d, Felis sylvestris.

No. 1775 — Butterflies: a, 5000d, Charaxes monteiri female. b, 5000d, Papilio leonidas thomasius. c, 10,000d, Hypolimas salmacis thomensis. d, 10,000d, Charaxes monteiri male. e, 15,000d, Charaxes odysseus.

No. 1776 — Fish: a, 5000d, Ostracion tricornis. b, 5000d, Holocentrus axensionis "Caqui". c, 10,000d, Canthidermis maculatus. d, 10,000d, Rhinecanthus aculeatus. e, 15,000d, Diodon hystrix.

No. 1777 — Medicinal plants: a, 5000d, Buchholzia coriacea. b, 5000d, Piperonia pallucila. c, 5000d, Achyranthes aspera. d, 10,000d, Adenoplus breviflorus. e, 10,000d, Hiliotropium indicum. f, 10,000d, Mimosa pigra. g, 15,000d, Cymbopogon citratus. h, 15,000d, Bryophilllum pinatum.

No. 1778 — Birds: a, 5000d, Alcedo leucogaster nais. b, 5000d, Prinia molleri. c, 5000d, Spermestes cucullatus. d, 5000d, Treron S. thomae. e, 5000d, Euplectes aureus. f, 10,000d, Speirops lugubris. g, 10,000d, Textor grandis. h, 10,000d, Alcedo leucogaster nais, diff. i, 10,000d, Anabathmis hartlaubii. j, 10,000d, Xanthophilus princeps. k, 15,000d, Serinus rufobrunneus. l, 15,000d, Cheatura thomensis. m, 15,000d, Tyto alba thomensis. n, 15,000d, Estrilda astrild.

2007, Dec. 31 Litho. ***Perf. 13x13¼***

Sheets of 4, #a-d

1769-1774 A323 Set of 6 30.00 30.00

Sheets of 5, #a-e

1775-1776 A323 Set of 2 13.00 13.00

Perf. 13¼x13

1777 A323 Sheet of 8, #a-h 11.00 11.00
1778 A323 Sheet of 14, #a-n 19.00 19.00

Dated 2008.

A324

A325

No. 1779 — Napoleon Bonaparte (1769-1821), French emperor, and: a, 5000d, Painting of Napoleon on horseback at right. b, 5000d, Military medal at left. c, 5000d, Military medal at right. d, 70,000d, Painting of Napoleon on horseback at left.

No. 1780 — United States ambulances: a, 5000d, Ambulance and helicopter. b, 5000d, Specialized transport team ambulance. c, 5000d, Ambulance with blue and red stripes. d, 70,000d, Ambulance with blue stripes.

No. 1781 — Japanese ambulances: a, 5000d, Ambulance at hospital ambulance bay, red cross at right. b, 5000d, Ambulance at hospital, red cross at UL c, 5000d, Ambulance at hospital, red cross at UR. d, 70,000d, Ambulance and rear view mirror, red cross at UL.

No. 1782 — European ambulances: a, 5000d, Italian ambulance and Leaning Tower of Pisa. b, 5000d, German ambulance and Cologne Cathedral. c, 5000d, British ambulance and Big Ben. d, 70,000d, French ambulance and Eiffel Tower.

No. 1783 — African ambulances: a, 5000d, Ambulance, people, red cross at LL. b, 5000d, Tractor ambulance, red cross at UL. c, 5000d, Ambulance and Red Cross workers. d, 70,000d, Ambulance with red diagonal stripes.

No. 1784 — Henry Ford (1863-1947), automobile manufacturer, 1908 Model T, and : a, 5000d, Drawing of automobile. b, 5000d, Ford poster, Red Cross flag above Model T ambulance. c, 5000d, Ford advertisement in Spanish. d, 70,000d, Horn.

No. 1785 — Harley-Davidson motorcycles, 105th anniv.: a, 5000d, FLHTCU Ultra Classic Electra Glide. b, 5000d, XL-1200C Sportster 1200 Custom. c, 5000d, FLSTC Heritage Softail Classic. d, 70,000d, FXDC Dyna Super Glide Custom.

No. 1786 — Franz Schubert (1797-1828), composer, and: a, 5000d, Schubert reading book. b, 5000d, Men and women. c, 5000d, Buildings. d, 70,000d, Piano and bench.

No. 1787 — Giacomo Puccini (1858-1924), composer, and: a, 5000d, Puccini and piano. b, 5000d, Costumed man in chair. c, 5000d, Room. d, 70,000d, Man and woman from Puccini opera.

No. 1788 — Nikolai Rimsky-Korsakov (1844-1908), composer, and: a, 5000d, Frog Tsarevna, painting by Viktor Vasnetzov. b, 5000d, Scene from opera "Mlada." c, 5000d, Scene from opera "The Tsar's Bride." d, 70,000d, Scene from opera "Boris Godunov."

No. 1789 — Bee Gees rock band and: a, 5000d, Bee Gees Greatest Hits album cover. b, 5000d, Guitar at left. c, 5000d, Microphone at LR. d, 70,000d, Record of "More Than an Woman" at LL.

No. 1790 — Vivian Ernest Fuchs (1908-99), Polar explorer, and: a, 5000d, Canis lupus familiaris. b, 5000d, Pygoscelis papua. c, 5000d, Stercorarius pomarinus. d, 70,000d, Ursus maritimus.

No. 1791 — Discovery of Halley's comet, 250th anniv: a, 5000d, Edmond Halley and sextant. b, 5000d, Halley and globe. c, 5000d, Halley and compass, people viewing comet. d, 70,000d, People viewing comet.

No. 1792 — NASA, 50th anniv.: a, 5000d, Pres. John F. Kennedy, space shuttle on launch pad. b, 5000d, Astronaut David R. Scott, Gemini 7. c, 5000d, Astronaut Neil A. Armstrong, Viking lander. d, 70,000d, Crew of Apollo 17 and Lunar Rover.

No. 1793 — Snakes: a, 5000d, Macroprotodon cucullatus. b, 5000d, Python regius. c, 5000d, Bitis arietans and Bitis nasicornis. d, 70,000d, Green mamba.

No. 1794 — Crocodilians: a, 5000d, Caiman crocodilus. b, 5000d, Crocodylus acutus. c, 5000d, Crocodylus niloticus. d, 70,000d, Caiman latirostris.

No. 1795 — Various frogs with background color of: a, 5000d, Blue green. b, 5000d, Yellow orange. c, 5000d, Red orange. d, 70,000d, Blue.

No. 1796 — Butterflies: a, 5000d, Delias aglaia. b, 5000d, Junonia almana. c, 5000d, Junonia coenia. d, 70,000d, Cethosia biblis.

No. 1797 — Naturalists, flora and fauna: a, 5000d, Aristoteles (384 B.C.-322 B.C.), Phalacrocorax. b, 5000d, Theophrastus (372 B.C.-288 B.C.), Arum maculatum. c, 5000d, Pedanius Dioscorides (40-90), illustrations from Dioscorides Neapolitanus. d, 70,000d, Pliny the Elder (23-79), manuscript illustration.

No. 1798 — Frank Sinatra (1915-98), singer, and: a, 5000d, Pres. John F. Kennedy, U.S. flag. b, 5000d, Pres. Ronald Reagan. c, 5000d, Elvis Presley. d, 70,000d, Marilyn Monroe.

No. 1799 — Shells and lighthouses: a, 5000d, Aporrhais pespelecani, Cape Hatteras Lighthouse, U.S., Kéréon Lighthouse, France. b, 5000d, Boroetrophon fraseri, La Laterna Lighthouse, Italy, St. Mary's Lighthouse, United Kingdom. c, 5000d, Conus guanche, Cabo de Palos Lighthouse, Spain, La Martrre Lighthouse, Canada. d, 70,000d, Marginella senegalensis, Kap Arkona Lighthouse, Germany, New Brighton Lighthouse, United Kingdom.

No. 1800 — Billy Karam, race car driver and Porsches: a, 7000d. b, 9000d. c, 10,000d. d, 14,000d.

No. 1801 — Naturalists: a, 15,000d, Andrea Cesalpino (c. 1519-1603), flower illustration, books. b, 15,000d, Conrad Gessner (1516-65), Quadrupedibus illustrations. c, 15,000d, Leonard Fuchs (1501-66), illustration of asparagus. d, 40,000d, Ulisse Aldrovandi (1522-1605), illustrations of mythical beasts.

No. 1802 — Elvis Presley (1935-77) in army uniform: a, 5000d, Wearing cap in foreground and background. b, 10,000d, Wearing cap in background photograph. c, 10,000d, Wearing helmet with goggles in foreground. d, 15,000d, Wearing cap in foreground photograph. e, 15,000d, Guitar in background. f, 30,000d, Reading mail.

No. 1803 — Bridges: a, 5000d, Humber Bridge, United Kingdom, and ship. b, 10,000d, Chain Bridge, Hungary, and police car. c, 10,000d, Erasmus Bridge, Netherlands, and ship. d, 15,000d, Sydney Harbour Bridge, Australia, and rescue boat. e, 15,000d, Brooklyn Bridge, U.S., and airplane. f, 30,000d, Oresund Bridge, Denmark, and hydroplane ambulance.

No. 1804 — Submarines: a, 5000d, Type XXI U-boat, Germany. b, 10,000d, K-21, Soviet Union. c, 10,000d, U-boat 530, Germany, Boat I-52, Japan. d, 15,000d, Royal Navy "S" Class, United Kingdom. e, 15,000d, USS Tang. f, 30,000d, Delta-17, Soviet Union.

No. 1805 — Medicinal plants: a, 5000d, Sophora denudata. b, 10,000d, Mussaenda landia. c, 10,000d, Agarista salicifolia. d, 15,000d, Dodonea viscosa. e, 15,000d, Jumellea fragrans. f, 30,000d, Centella asiatica.

No. 1806, 10,000d, — Mushrooms and orchids: a, Strobilomyces floccopus, Cymbidium. b, Entoloma clypeatum, Calypso bulbosa. c, Gymnopilus spectabilis, Coeloglossum viride. d, Leccinum scabrum, Arachnis annamensis. e, Cortinarius praestans, Galanthus nivalis. f, Cortinarius traganus, Arundina graminifolia. g, Inocybe fastigiata, Aspasia epidendroides. h, Pholiota destruens, Orchis papilionacea. i, Hebeloma radicosum, Dendrophylax lindenii.

No. 1807, 95,000d, Napoleon Bonaparte, diff. No. 1808, 95,000d, Ambulances and airplane. No. 1809, 95,000d, Japanese ambulance and fire station. No. 1810, 95,000d, Ambulance and word "Ambulance" painted on vehicle roof. No. 1811, 95,000d, Animal-drawn ambulance wagon. No. 1812, 95,000d, Ford and Model T. No. 1813, 95,000d, Harley-Davidson FXDWC Dyna Wide Glide motorcycle. No. 1814, 95,000d, Schubert at piano. No. 1815, 95,000d, Puccini, poster for "La Boheme." No. 1816, 95,000d, Rimsky-Korsakov, scene from opera "Sadko." No. 1817, 95,000d, Bee Gees. No. 1818, 95,000d, Vivian Fuchs and Ursus maritimus, diff. No. 1819, 95,000d, Halley and Halley's Comet. No. 1820, 95,000d, Astronauts, Explorer I spacecraft. No. 1821, 95,000d, Osteolaemus. No. 1822, 95,000d, Hyla gratiosa, Pseudis paradoxa. No. 1823, 95,000d, Caligo memnon. No. 1824, 95,000d, Nicolas Steno (1638-86), naturalist, and drawing of shark's head. No. 1825, 95,000d, John Ray (1627-1705), naturalist, drawings of dodo and turkey. No. 1826, 95,000d, Sinatra. No. 1827, 95,000d, Presley. No. 1828, 95,000d, Tower Bridge, United Kingdom, and tugboat. No. 1829, 95,000d, Type XXI U-boat, Germany, diff. No. 1830, 95,000d, Psiloxylon mauritanum. No. 1831, 95,000d, Arundina graminifola, Suillus aeruginascens.

2008, Feb. 4 Litho. ***Perf. 12¾x13¼***

Sheets of 4, #a-d

1779-1795 A324 Set of 17 200.00 200.00
1796-1801 A325 Set of 6 65.00 65.00

Sheets of 6, #a-f

1802-1803 A324 Set of 2 24.00 24.00
1804-1805 A325 Set of 2 24.00 24.00

Miniature Sheet

1806 A325 10,000d Sheet of 9, #a-i 12.50 12.50

Souvenir Sheets

Perf. 13¼ Syncopated

1807-1831 A324 Set of 25 330.00 330.00

2008 Summer Olympics, Beijing — A326

Olympic Stamps — A327

No. 1832: a, Tennis. b, Pole vault. c, Weight lifting. d, Rowing.

No. 1833: a, 5000d, Angola #614. b, 5000d, St. Thomas & Prince Islands #838. c, 5000d, Guinea-Bissau #369E. d, 70,000d, Guinea-Bissau #370.

No. 1834: a, 5000d, Cape Verde #826. b, 5000d, Guinea-Bissau #776. c, 5000d, Mozambique #626. d, 70,000d, Mozambique #861.

No. 1835: a, 5000d, Mozambique #945. b, 5000d, St. Thomas & Prince Islands #568. c, 5000d, Guinea-Bissau #936. d, 70,000d, Mozambique #898.

No. 1836: a, 5000d, Guinea-Bissau #612. b, 5000d, St. Thomas & Prince Islands #1170. c, 5000d, St. Thomas & Prince Islands #569. d, 70,000d, Guinea-Bissau #C20.

No. 1837: a, 5000d, St. Thomas & Prince Islands #805c. b, 5000d, Guinea-Bissau #402B. c, 5000d, Guinea-Bissau #369D. d, 70,000d, St. Thomas & Prince Islands #1094.

No. 1838: a, 5000d, Mozambique #1156. b, 5000d, Guinea-Bissau #C18. c, 5000d, Cape Verde #828. d, 70,000d, St. Thomas & Prince Islands #1050C.

No. 1839: a, 5000d, Cape Verde #406. b, 5000d, Angola #843. c, 5000d, Guinea-Bissau #775. d, 70,000d, Angola #1268.

2008, Mar. 10 ***Perf. 12¾x13¼***

1832 A326 5000d Sheet of 4, #a-d 2.75 2.75

Sheets of 4, #a-d

1833-1839 A327 Set of 7 82.50 82.50

Nos. 1834a, 1834c, 1838a, 1839b each exist in a souvenir sheet of 1.

A328

A329

No. 1840 — People holding Chinese porcelain, with background color of: a, 5000d, Dull green. b, 5000d, Lilac. c, 5000d, Light blue. d, 70,000d, Light lilac.

No. 1841 — Castles: a, 5000d, Bran Castle, Romania. b, 5000d, Windsor Castle, Great Britain. c, 5000d, Neuschwanstein Castle, Germany. d, 70,000d, Carcassonne, France.

No. 1842 — Herbert von Karajan (1908-89), conductor, with inset photograph of: a, 5000d, Karajan and woman. b, 5000d, Karajan and machine. c, 5000d, Karajan conducting. d, 70,000d, Outer space scene.

No. 1843 — Lord Robert Baden-Powell (1857-1941), founder of Boy Scouts, and: a, 5000d, *The Scout* magazine cover, orchids. b, 5000d, Owl with wings spread, butterfly on flower. c, 5000d, Owl, butterfly, flower. d, 70,000d, *Scouting for Boys* book cover.

No. 1844 — Table tennis players: a, 5000d, Wang Liqin. b, 5000d, Wang Hao. c, 5000d, Werner Schlager. d, 70,000d, Kong Linghui.

No. 1845 — Table tennis players: a, 5000d, Guo Yue. b, 5000d, Zhang Yining. c, 5000d, Wang Nan. d, 70,000d, Deng Yaping.

No. 1846 — Apparition at Lourdes, 150th anniv.: a, 5000d, Lourdes Basilica, photograph and arms of Pope Benedict XVI. b, 5000d, Lourdes Basilica, apparition. c, 5000d, Statue of Virgin Mary, Bernadette Soubirous. d, 70,000d, St. Peter's Basilica, photograph and arms of Pope John Paul II.

No. 1847 — Pandas, Scouting emblem, and: a, 5000d, Tree with foliage. b, 5000d, Snowflakes. c, 5000d, Stars and tree stump. d, 70,000d, Tree, baby panda.

No. 1848 — Loxodonta africana at LR and: a, 5000d, Hippotigris. b, 5000d, Second elephant. c, 5000d, Second elephant and antelope. d, 70,000d, Giraffa camelopardalis.

No. 1849 — Horse racing: a, 5000d, Horse and jockey, denomination over orange red area. b, 5000d, Horse and jockey, denomination over blue area. c, 5000d, Horse and sulky. d, 70,000d, Horse and sulky, diff.

No. 1850 — Waterfalls and wildlife: a, 5000d, Jog Falls, India, Panthera tigris bengalensis. b, 5000d, Gocta Falls, Peru, Vultur gryphus. c, 5000d, Ouzoud Falls, Morocco, Camelus dromedarius. d, 70,000d, Huangguoshu Falls, People's Republic of China, Ailurus fulgens.

No. 1851 — Inventors: a, 5000d, Muhammad al-Khwarizmi, inventor of algebra. b, 10,000d, Alexander Graham Bell, inventor of telephone. c, 10,000d, Christiaan Huygens, inventor of pendulum clock. d, 15,000d, Guglielmo Marconi, inventor of radiotelegraph. e, 15,000d, James Watt, inventor of steam engine. f, 30,000d, Thomas Edison, inventor of long-lasting light bulb.

No. 1852 — Inventors: a, 5000d, Samuel F. B. Morse, inventor of Morse code. b, 10,000d, Blaise Pascal, inventor of mechanical calculator. c, 10,000d, Nicolas Cugnot, inventor of first automobile. d, 15,000d, Emile Berliner, inventor of disc record gramophone. e, 15,000d, Rudolf Diesel, inventor of Diesel engine. f, 30,000d, Ivan Kulibin, inventor of elevator.

No. 1853 — Airbus airplanes: a, 5000d, Airbus 380, Claude Lelaie, test pilot. b, 10,000d, Airbus Beluga. c, 10,000d, Airbus 380, Jacques Rosay, test pilot. d, 15,000d, Airbus 380, cockpit instruments. e, 15,000d, Airbus Beluga, Rosay. f, 30,000d, Airbus 380, passenger cabin.

2008, Mar. 28 ***Perf. 12¾x13¼***

Sheets of 4, #a-d, + 2 labels

1840-1841 A328 Set of 2 24.00 24.00

Sheets of 4, #a-d

1842-1850 A329 Set of 9 110.00 110.00

Sheets of 6, #a-f

1851-1853 A329 Set of 3 35.00 35.00

A330

No. 1854 — Fire trucks: a, 15,000d, 1906 Shand Mason & Co., Aztec god of fire. b, 25,000d, 1928 Stoughton, Ctesibius, Greek inventor. c, 30,000d, 1939 Scammell, Xiuhtechutli, Aztec lord of volcanoes. d, 30,000d, 1931 Leyland, Mexican god of fire.

No. 1855 — Churches: a, 15,000d, Santa Maria del Fiore Basilica, Florence, Italy, crucifix. b, 25,000d, Basilica of Our Lady of Lichen, Poland, Pope John Paul II. c, 30,000d, Cologne Cathedral, Germany, Pope Benedict XVI. d, 30,000d, Notre Dame Cathedral, Paris, France, dragon gargoyle.

No. 1856 — Agriculture: a, 20,000d, Grapes and vineyard. b, 20,000d, Bee on flower, beekeeper and hive. c, 20,000d, Wheat stalks and harvested field. d, 40,000d, Tulips and windmill.

No. 1857 — Rotary International emblem and chess champions: a, 20,000d, Bobby Fischer. b, 20,000d, Anatoly Karpov. c, 20,000d, Garry Kasparov. d, 40,000d, Vladimir Kramnik.

No. 1858 — Pre-historic rock art: a, 25,000d, Buffalos, hunters. b, 25,000d, Horned animals, pre-historic man. c, 25,000d, Animal, pre-historic man with spear. d, 25,000d, Animals, stick figures of men.

No. 1859 — Jewelry made with: a, 25,000d, Silver (prata). b, 25,000d, Platinum (platina). c, 25,000d, Pearls (carbonato de cálcio. d, 25,000d, Diamond (diamante).

No. 1860 — European urban transportation: a, 5,000d, Electric train, Budapest. b, 10,000d, Subway train, Barcelona. c, 15,000d, Double-decker bus, London. d, 20,000d, Trolley bus, Milan. e, 20,000d, Taxi, Berlin. f, 30,000d, Subway train, Paris.

No. 1861 — Nobel Peace laureates: a, 5,000d, Henri Dunant, 1901. b, 10,000d, Lech Walesa, 1983. c, 15,000d, Albert Schweitzer, 1953. d, 20,000d, Mikhail Gorbachev, 1990. e, 20,000d, F. W. de Klerk, 1993. f, 30,000d, Dalai Lama Tenzin Gyatso, 1989.

No. 1862 — Albatrosses: a, 5,000d, Phoebastria nigripes. b, 10,000d, Diomedea exulans. c, 15,000d, Phoebetria. d, 20,000d, Thalassarche melanophrys, bird in flight at left. e, 20,000d, Thalassarche melanophrys, bird in water at right. f, 30,000d, Phoebastria immutabilis.

No. 1863 — World War II: a, 5,000d, Sir Winston Churchill, Hawker Tempest airplane. b, 10,000d, Soviet T34/85 tanks. c, 15,000d, Gen. Charles de Gaulle, Bloch MB 210 airplanes. d, 20,000d, Douglas TBD Devastator airplane, HMS Hood. e, 20,000d, Messerscmitt Bf-109E-3 and Bf-109E7/Trop airplanes. f, 30,000d, USS Sawfish.

No. 1864 — Scientists: a, 5,000d, Haroun Tazieff, vulcanologist. b, 10,000d, John Gould, ornithologist. c, 15,000d, Norman L. Bowen, geologist. d, 20,000d, Johann Wolfgang von Goethe, poet and morphologist. e, 20,000d, Ivan Pavlov, physiologist. f, 30,000d, Charles Darwin, naturalist.

No. 1865 — Famous people and dogs: a, 5,000d, Pres. Bill Clinton, Labrador retriever. b, 10,000d, Tony Parker, basketball player, Eva Longoria, actress, Maltese. c, 15,000d, Knud Rasmussen, polar explorer, Husky. d, 20,000d, Madonna, singer, Chihuahua. e, 20,000d, Steve Irwin, conservationist, Staffordshire bull terrier. f, 30,000d, Dorothy Gladys "Dodie" Smith, author, Dalmatian.

No. 1866, 95,000d, St. Peter's Basilica, Vatican City, Pope Benedict XVI. No. 1867, 95,000d, St. Bernard and German shepherd. No. 1868, 100,000d, 1927 Dandy fire engine, fire helmet. No. 1869, 100,000d, Diomedea (albatrosses). No. 1870, 100,000d, Gold nugget and ring.

2008, May 19 ***Perf. 12¾x13¼***

1854 A330 Sheet of 4, #a-d 14.00 14.00

Sheets of 4, #a-d, + 2 labels

1855-1859 A330 Set of 5 70.00 70.00

Sheets of 6, #a-f

1860-1865 A330 Set of 6 84.00 84.00

Souvenir Sheets

Perf. 13¼ Syncopated

1866-1870 A330 Set of 5 67.50 67.50

Nos. 1866-1870 each contain one 50x39mm stamp.

A331

No. 1871 — Animals on bank notes of the world: a, 15,000d, Snake, Aruba 25-florin note. b, 25,000d, Owl, Surinam 25,000-gulden note. c, 30,000d, Moose, Belarus 25-ruble note. d, 30,000d, Buffalo, Tanzania 500-shilling note.

No. 1872 — Dogs: a, 15,000d, Alaskan malamute. b, 25,000d, Siberian husky. c, 30,000d, Greenland dog. d, 30,000d, Samoyed.

No. 1873 — Various nudes by Pierre-Auguste Renoir (1841-1919) with Renoir at: a, 20,000d, Left, without hat. b, 20,000d, Right, wearing hat. c, 20,000d, Left, wearing hat. d, 30,000d, Right, wearing hat, diff.

No. 1874 — Various nudes by George-Pierre Seurat (1859-91) with Seurat at: a, 20,000d, Left, facing forward. b, 20,000d, Right, facing left. c, 20,000d, Left, facing right. d, 30,000d, Right, facing forward.

No. 1875 — Various paintings by Utagawa Kunisada (1786-1865) with Japanese flag at: a, 20,000d, UL, gray panel at right. b, 20,000d, LL, gray panel at left. c, 20,000d, LL, gray panel at right. d, 30,000d, UL, gray panel at left.

No. 1876 — Orchids and butterflies: a, 25,000d, Cypripedium kentuckiense, Papilio laglaizei. b, 25,000d, Phalaenopsis lindenii toapei, Prepona xenagoras. c, 25,000d, Paphiopedilum, Danaus sita. d, 25,000d, Phragmipedium sedenii, Ornithoptera priamus urvilianus.

No. 1877 — German lighthouses: a, 25,000d, Amrum Lighthouse. b, 25,000d, Neuland Lighthouse. c, 25,000d, Eckernförde Lighthouse. d, 25,000d, List Ost Lighthouse.

No. 1878 — Israel, 60th anniv.: a, 25,000d, Theodor Herzl, arms of Israel. b, 25,000d, David Ben-Gurion, arms of Jerusalem. c, 25,000d, Golda Meir, star of David. d, 25,000d, Dome of the Rock, Jerusalem, menorah.

No. 1879, 100,000d, Paintings by Utagawa Kunisada. No. 1880, 100,000d, Cattleya intermedia, Ornithoptera paradisea.

2008, July 17 ***Perf. 12¾x13¼***

Sheets of 4, #a-d

1871-1878 A331 Set of 8 110.00 110.00

Souvenir Sheets

Perf. 13¼ Syncopated

1879-1880 A331 Set of 2 28.00 28.00

Nos. 1879-1880 each contain one 50x39mm stamp.

A332

No. 1881 — Various trolley cars with background color of: a, 15,000d, Pink. b, 25,000d, Yellow. c, 30,000d, Green. d, 30,000d, Blue.

No. 1882 — Fishermen and fish: a, 15,000d, Sphyraena sphyraena. b, 25,000d, Thunnus alalunga. c, 30,000d, Salmo trutta. d, 30,000d, Lutjanus gibbus.

No. 1883 — Zeppelins: a, 20,000d, LZ-127 Graf Zeppelin over Alps. b, 20,000d, LZ-2 over Friedrichshafen, Germany. c, 20,000d, L-9 over Würzburg, Germany. d, 40,000d, LZ-130 Graf Zeppelin II over Rothenburg, Germany.

No. 1884 — Ancient Egyptian artifacts: a, 20,000d, Bust of Queen Nefertiti, Ankh. b, 20,000d, Sarcophagus, Queen Cleopatra VII. c, 20,000d, Funerary mask of King Tutankhamun, scarab beetle. d, 40,000d, Horus depicted as falcon, King Ramses II.

No. 1885 — Golfers: a, 25,000d, Tiger Woods. b, 25,000d, Todd Hamilton. c, 25,000d, Ernie Els. d, 25,000d, Ben Curtis.

No. 1886 — Circus performers: a, 25,000d, Billy Smart Circus, British flag. b, 25,000d, Moscow State Circus, Russian flag. c, 25,000d, Herman Renz Circus, Netherlands flag. d, 25,000d, Chinese State Circus, flag of People's Republic of China.

No. 1887 — Campaign against AIDS: a, 25,000d, Pres. Bill Clinton, doctor treating child. b, 25,000d, Test tubes in laboratory, woman being treated, AIDS ribbon. c, 25,000d, Doctor getting blood sample from finger, doctor examining infant, AIDS ribbon. d, 25,000d, Hilary Koprowski, immunologist, vials of polio vaccine.

No. 1888, 95,000d, Salmo salar and fisherman. No. 1889, 95,000d, LZ-129 Hindenburg over Lake Constance. No. 1890, 95,000d, Eye of Ra, Anubis attending the mummy of Sennedjem. No. 1891, 95,000d, Woods, diff. No. 1892, 95,000d, Cirque du Soleil performers. No. 1893, 95,000d, Dr. Albert Schweitzer and staff at Lambaréné, Gabon hospital.

2008, July 17 ***Perf. 12¾x13¼***

Sheets of 4, #a-d

1881-1887 A332 Set of 7 97.50 97.50

Souvenir Sheets

Perf. 13¼ Syncopated

1888-1893 A332 Set of 6 80.00 80.00

Nos. 1888-1893 each contain one 50x39mm stamp.

Archaeology — A333

No. 1894 — Archaeologists and items from: a, 20,000d, Paleolithic Era. b, 20,000d, Neolithic Era. c, 20,000d, Bronze Age. d, 40,000d, Iron Age.

100,000d, Archaeologist and items from Persian Period.

2008, Sept. 14 ***Perf. 12¾x13¼***

1894 A333 Sheet of 4, #a-d 14.00 14.00

Souvenir Sheet

Perf. 13¼ Syncopated

1895 A333 100,000d multi 14.00 14.00

No. 1895 contains one 38x39mm stamp.

A334

No. 1896 — Various nudes of Paul Gauguin (1848-1903), with Gauguin at: a, 15,000d, Left. b, 25,000d, Right. c, 30,000d, Left, diff. d, 30,000d, Right, diff.

No. 1897 — Various nudes of Pablo Picasso (1881-1973), with Picasso at: a, 15,000d, Left. b, 25,000d, Right. c, 30,000d, Left, diff. d, 30,000d, Right, diff.

No. 1898 — Various nudes of Peter Paul Rubens (1577-1640), with Rubens at: a, 20,000d, Left, in sepia. b, 20,000d, Right. c, 20,000d, Left, in color. d, 40,000d, Right, diff.

No. 1899 — Various nudes of Gustave Moreau (1826-98), with Moreau at: a, 20,000d, Left, in black. b, 20,000d, Right. c, 20,000d, Left, in brown. d, 40,000d, Right, diff.

No. 1900 — Costumes of: a, 20,000d, Ancient Greece. b, 20,000d, France, 18th cent. c, 20,000d, Russia, 17th cent. d, 40,000d, Japan, 19th cent.

No. 1901 — Divers, starfish, and dolphins: a, 20,000d, Delphinus delphis. b, 20,000d, Grampus griseus. c, 20,000d, Platanista gangetica. d, 40,000d, Cephalorhynchus commersonii.

No. 1902 — Dogs: a, 20,000d, Fox terriers. b, 20,000d, Whippets. c, 20,000d, Rhodesian ridgebacks. d, 40,000d, Basset hounds.

No. 1903 — Rescue dogs: a, 20,000d, St. Bernards. b, 20,000d, Labrador retrievers. c, 20,000d, Border collies. d, 40,000d, German shepherds (one with Red Cross identification).

No. 1904 — Domesticated animals: a, 25,000d, Cattle. b, 25,000d, Dogs. c, 25,000d, Cats. d, 25,000d, Horses.
No. 1905 — Horses: a, 25,000d, Cowboy riding chestnut horse (Alazao). b, 25,000d, Friesians. c, 25,000d, Clydesdales. d, 25,000d, Icelandic horses.
No. 1906 — Cat breeds: a, 25,000d, Persian. b, 25,000d, Russian Blue. c, 25,000d, Devon Rex. d, 25,000d, Siamese.
No. 1907 — Sir Peter Markham Scott (1909-89), conservationist and: a, 25,000d, Phascolarctos cinereus. b, 25,000d, Gorilla. c, 25,000d, Ailurus fulgens. d, 25,000d, Ailuropoda melanoleuca.
No. 1908 — Masonic emblem and: a, 25,000d, Alexander Pushkin, writer. b, 25,000d, Louis Armstrong, musician. c, 25,000d, Oscar Wilde, writer. d, 25,000d, Wolfgang Amadeus Mozart, composer.
No. 1909, 100,000d, Tursiops truncatus, starfish and diver, horiz. No. 1910, 100,000d, Two cats, horiz.

2008, Sept. 14 ***Perf. 12¾x13¼***

Sheets of 4, #a-d

1896-1908 A334 Set of 13 180.00 180.00

Souvenir Sheets

Perf. 13¼ Syncopated

1909-1910 A334 Set of 2 28.00 28.00

Nos. 1909-1910 each contain one 50x39mm stamp.

A335

No. 1911 — Illustrations of women by Alphonse Mucha (1860-1939) with woman at right with: a, 5000d, Hands in hair. b, 5000d, Hands folded below chin. c, 5000d, Hands on chin. d, 70,000d, Hand at top of chest.
No. 1912 — Charlton Heston (1923-2008), actor, and scenes from: a, 15,000d, *The Ten Commandments,* 1956. b, 25,000d, *Planet of the Apes,* 1968. c, 30,000d, *The Agony and the Ecstasy,* 1965. d, 30,000d, *Ben-Hur,* 1959.
No. 1913 — Shells: a, 20,000d, Cypraea algoensis, Adamussium colbecki. b, 20,000d, Lunatia grossularia, Trophon geversianus. c, 20,000d, Buccinum undatum, Angaria vicdani. d, 40,000d, Mytilus edulis, Haliotis iris.
No. 1914, 95,000d, The Times of the Day Series, by Mucha. No. 1915, 100,000d, Heston and wife, Lydia Clarke. No. 1916, 100,000d, Cardium edule, Architectonica perspectiva.

2008, Nov. 3 ***Perf. 12¾x13¼***

Sheets of 4, #a-d

1911-1913 A335 Set of 3 40.00 40.00

Souvenir Sheets

Perf. 13¼ Syncopated

1914-1916 A335 Set of 3 41.00 41.00

Nos. 1914-1916 each contain one 50x39mm stamp.

A336

No. 1917 — Various nudes of Gustave Courbet (1819-77), with Courbet at: a, 15,000d, Left. b, 25,000d, Right. c, 30,000d, Left, diff. d, 30,000d, Right, diff.
No. 1918 — Various nudes of Edouard Manet (1832-83), with Manet at: a, 15,000d, Left. b, 25,000d, Right. c, 30,000d, Left, diff. d, 30,000d, Right, diff.
No. 1919 — Various nudes of Paul Cézanne (1839-1906), with Cézannne at: a, 15,000d, Left. b, 25,000d, Right. c, 30,000d, Left, diff. d, 30,000d, Right, diff.
No. 1920 — Various nudes of Pierre Bonnard (1867-1947), with Bonnard at: a, 15,000d, Left. b, 25,000d, Right. c, 30,000d, Left, diff. d, 30,000d, Right, diff.

No. 1921 — Jules Verne (1828-1905), and illustrations from his books depicting: a, 15,000d, Spaceship. b, 25,000d, Spaceship, diff. c, 30,000d, Men, hat in air. d, 30,000d, Octopus.
No. 1922 — Dogs: a, 15,000d, Dingos. b, 25,000d, Pharaoh hounds. c, 30,000d, Mexican hairless dogs. d, 30,000d, Basenjis.
No. 1923 — Dogs: a, 20,000d, Groenendael Belgian shepherds. b, 20,000d, Caucasian shepherds. c, 20,000d, Central Asian shepherds. d, 40,000d, German shepherds.
No. 1924 — Red Cross flag and seaplanes: a, 20,000d, Sikorsky S-43. b, 20,000d, Canadair CL-215. c, 20,000d, Shin Meiwa US-1A. d, 40,000d, Grumman HU-16E Albatross.
No. 1925 — Helicopters, cent.: a, 20,000d, Paul Cornu, aircraft engineer. b, 20,000d, Cornu helicopter. c, 20,000d, VS-300A helicopter. d, 40,000d, Igor Sikorsky, helicopter designer, and helicopter.
No. 1926 — Moai of Easter Island and sailing ships: a, 20,000d, Grande Hermine. b, 20,000d, Sparrow. c, 20,000d, Victoria. d, 40,000d, Concorde.
No. 1927 — Animals and dams: a, 25,000d, Lynx lynx, Nurek Dam, Tajikistan. b, 25,000d, Capra ibex nubiana, Aswan High Dam, Egypt. c, 25,000d, Ailurus fulgens, Three Gorges Dam, People's Republic of China. d, 25,000d, Sciurus carolinensis, Fort Peck Dam, U.S.
No. 1928 — Various paintings of Edgar Degas (1834-1917), with Degas at: a, 25,000d, Left, wearing hat. b, 25,000d, Right, without hat. c, 25,000d, Left, without hat. d, 25,000d, Right, holding hat.

2008, Nov. 3 ***Perf. 12¾x13¼***

Sheets of 4, #a-d

1917-1928 A336 Set of 12 170.00 170.00

Election of Pres. Barack Obama — A337

No. 1929 — Pres. Obama, U.S. flag, and: a, 13,000d, White House. b, 13,000d, American Indians. c, 39,000d, Slave in chains, group of slaves. d, 39,000d, Statue of Liberty.
100,000d, Pres. Obama, Confederate soldiers.

2008, Dec. 4 ***Perf. 12¾x13¼***

1929 A337 Sheet of 4, #a-d 14.50 14.50

Souvenir Sheet

Perf. 13¼ Syncopated

1930 A337 100,000d multi 14.00 14.00

No. 1930 contains one 50x39mm stamp.

Miniature Sheets

Fruits — A338

No. 1931 — Fruit from Republic of China: a, 1000d, Guavas. b, 1500d, Carambolas. c, 2000d, Jujubes. d, 2500d, Wax apples. e, 3000d, Papayas.
No. 1932 — Fruit from St. Thomas & Prince Islands: a, 1000d, Avocados (abacate). b, 1500d, Jackfruit (jaca), horiz. c, 2000d, Soursops (sap-sap). d, 2500d, Cherimoyas (anona). e, 3000d, Mangos (manga).

2008 **Litho.** ***Perf. 12½***

Sheets of 5, #a-e, + 4 labels

1931-1932 A338 Set of 2 2.75 2.75

Cooperation between Republic of China and St. Thomas & Prince Islands, 9th anniv. Dated. 2006.

Worldwide Fund for Nature (WWF) A339

Psittacus eritahcus: No. 1933, 25,000d, One bird on branch. No. 1934, 25,000d, Two birds on branch. No. 1935, 25,000d, Chicks in nest. No. 1936, 25,000d, Bird in flight.

2009, Jan. 31 ***Perf. 13x13¼***

1933-1936 A339 Set of 4 14.00 14.00
1936a Souvenir sheet of 8, 2 each #1933-1936 28.00 28.00

A340

No. 1937 — Japanese film and music stars: a, 13,000d, Ken Watanabe. b, 13,000d, Miyavi. c, 39,000d, Chiaki Kuriyama. d, 39,000d, Utada Hikaru.
No. 1938 — Cats: a, 13,000d, Somali cat, Mogadishu, Somalia. b, 13,000d, Singapura cat, Singapore. c, 39,000d, Egyptian Mau cat, Giza Pyramids. d, 39,000d, Russian Blue cat, Red Square, Moscow.
No. 1939 — Polistes fuscatus and flowers: a, 13,000d, Malva sylvestris. b, 13,000d, Helianthus annuus. c, 39,000d, Lantana camara. d, 39,000d, Hebe x franciscana.
No. 1940 — High-speed trains: a, 13,000d, Eurostar. b, 13,000d, JR-Maglev. c, 39,000d, Shinkansen. d, 39,000d, Korea Train Express.
No. 1941 — Chess champions: a, 13,000d, Garry Kasparov. b, 13,000d, Anatoly Karpov. c, 39,000d, Vladimir Kremnik. d, 39,000d, Bobby Fischer.
No. 1942 — Shells: a, 13,000d, Thatcheria mirabilis. b, 13,000d, Amplustrum amplustre. c, 39,000d, Cryptospira elegans. d, 39,000d, Mercenaria mercenaria.
No. 1943 — Liverpool, 2008 European City of Culture: a, 13,000d, SuperLamBanana sculpture, Philharmonic Hall. b, 13,000d, King John, Metropolitan Cathedral. c, 39,000d, The Beatles, Yellow Submarine replica. d, 39,000d, Statue of Emlyn Hughes, Albert Docks.
No. 1944 — Paintings by Lucian Freud (1922-2011): a, 13,000d, Girl with a White Dog. b, 13,000d, Naked Portrait. c, 39,000d, Naked Portrait, diff. d, 39,000d, Naked Girl Asleep II.
No. 1945 — 90th birthday of Nelson Mandela, 1993 Nobel Peace laureate, and butterflies: a, 13,000d, Papilio dardanus. b, 13,000d, Zeuxidia aurelius. c, 39,000d, Speyeria cybele. d, 39,000d, Taenaris horsfieldii birchi.
No. 1946 — Crabs and lighthouses: a, 15,000d, Corystes cassivelaunus, Redonda Island Lighthouse, Sri Lanka. b, 25,000d, Macrocheira kaempferi, Cape Reinga Lighthouse, New Zealand. c, 30,000d, Callinectes sapidus, Hook Head Lighthouse, Ireland. d, 30,000d, Pseudocarcinus gigas, Vieille Lighthouse, France.
No. 1947 — Children, with child at left: a, 25,000d, Touching eye. b, 25,000d, With wound below eye. c, 25,000d, Wearing necklace. d, 25,000d, With flowers in hair.
No. 1948 — Nudes by Paul Delvaux (1897-1994), with inscription: a, 25,000d, O Elogio da Melancolla. b, 25,000d, Pompei. c, 25,000d, O despertar da Floresta. d, 25,000d, As Mulhares diante do Mar.
No. 1949 — Paintings by Tsukioka Yoshitoshi (1839-92), with inscriptions: a, 25,000d, Ichikawa Kodanji IV, Bando Hikosaburo V. b, 25,000d, 28 Assassinatos Famosas, Komagine Hachibyoe. c, 25,000d, Façanhasdo Shogunato Tokugawa, Hideyoshi. d, 25,000d, Apariçao da Princesa Aranha, Marshall Takamori.
No. 1950 — Paul Newman (1925-2008), actor, and: a, 25,000d, Scene from *The Life and Times of Judge Roy Bean,* 1972. b, 25,000d, Scene from *Empire Falls,* 2005. c, 25,000d, Wife, Joanne Woodward. d, 25,000d, Scene from *The Color of Money,* 1986.
No. 1951 — Indian film and music stars: a, 25,000d, Aamir Khan. b, 25,000d, Alka Yagnik. c, 25,000d, Lata Mangeshkar. d, 25,000d, Amitabh Bachchan.
No. 1952, 100,000d, Takeshi Kitano. No. 1953, 100,000d, Angora cats, Sultan Ahmed Mosque, Istanbul, Turkey. No. 1954, 100,000d, Painting of nudes by Delvaux, diff. No. 1955, 100,000d, Paintings by Yoshitoshi, diff. No. 1956, 100,000d, Newman and race car. No. 1957, 100,000d, Asha Bhosle.

2009, Jan. 31 ***Perf. 12¾x13¼***

Sheets of 4, #a-d

1937-1951 A340 Set of 15 215.00 215.00

Souvenir Sheets

Perf. 13¼ Syncopated

1952-1957 A340 Set of 6 85.00 85.00

Nos. 1952-1957 each contain one 50x39mm stamp.

A341

No. 1958 — Local dishes: a, 25,000d, Molho no Fogo, map of Prince Island. b, 30,000d, Calúlú, Map of St. Thomas Island.
No. 1959 — Sister Emmanuelle (1908-2008), and: a, 13,000d, Pope John Paul II. b, 13,000d, Child amidst ruins. c, 39,000d, Children. d, 39,000d, Pope Benedict XVI.
No. 1960 — Sharks and jellyfish: a, 15,000d, Isurus oxyrinchus, Carukia barnesi. b, 25,000d, Sphyrna lewini, Aurelia aurita. c, 30,000d, Carcharhinus brevipinna, Phacellophora camtschatica. d, 30,000d, Pristiophorus nudipinnis, Pelagia noctiluca.
No. 1961 — Butterflies and caterpillars: a, 15,000d, Alcides agatnyrsus, Papilio machaon caterpillar. b, 25,000d, Danaus sita, Brahmaea wallichi caterpillar. c, 30,000d, Troides aeacus, Danaus chrysippus caterpillar. d, 30,000d, Atrophaneura horishanus, Apatele alni caterpillar.
No. 1962 — Pres. Abraham Lincoln (1809-65), and: a, 25,000d, Son, Tad, head of Lincoln at Mount Rushmore. b, 25,000d, General Winfield Scott. c, 25,000d, Crowd at second inauguration, bust of Lincoln. d, 25,000d, Lincoln in chair, crowd at second inauguration.
No. 1963 — Indian Space Program: a, 25,000d, Abdul Kalam, Endusat satellite. b, 25,000d, Vikram Sarabhai, Aryabhata 1 satellite. c, 25,000d, Mahatma Gandhi, Chandrayaan 1 satellite. d, 25,000d, Astronaut Rakesh Sharma, launch of Chandrayaan 1.
No. 1964 — Joseph Haydn (1732-1809), composer, and: a, 25,000d, Musicians. b, 25,000d, Theater stage and orchestra. c, 25,000d, Hanover Square, London, 1791. d, 25,000d, Harpsichord and chair.
No. 1965 — Felix Mendelssohn (1809-47), composer, and: a, 25,000d, Building. b, 25,000d, Woman on piano bench, musical score. c, 25,000d, Woman and man listening to pianist. d, 25,000d, Mendelssohn's sister, Fanny.
No. 1966 — Louis Braille (1809-52), inventor of Braille writing, and: a, 25,000d, Building, Braille at left. b, 25,000d, Building, Braille at right. c, 25,000d, hand touching Braille text, Braille at left. d, 25,000d, Blind woman writing in Braille, Braille at right.
No. 1967 — Edgar Allan Poe (1809-49), writer, and: a, 25,000d, Poe's home, Bronx, New York. b, 25,000d, Illustration for poem, "The Raven." c, 25,000d, Books and room. d, 25,000d, Poe writing.
No. 1968 — Paintings by Shi Tao (1642-1707): a, 25,000d, Eight Scenic Spots in Huangshan, Shi Tao. b, 25,000d, An Old Man on a Boat. c, 25,000d, Mingxianquan and Hutouyan. d, 25,000d, Spring River.
No. 1969 — Various paintings by Toshusai Sharaku (1770-1825) with white line separating paintings below letters: a, 25,000d, "os" in "Toshusai." b, 25,000d, "us" in "Toshusai." c, 25,000d, "sh" in "Toshusai." d, 25,000d, "To" in "Toshusai."
No. 1970 — Two Strigops habroptilus in trees with animal name at: a, 25,000d, LL. b, 25,000d, UR. c, 25,000d, UL, below date. d, 25,000d, UL, below tree branch.
No. 1971 — New Zealand parrots: a, 25,000d, Strigops habroptilus, orange background. b, 25,000d, Nestor notabilis. c,

25,000d, Heterolocha acutirostris. d, 25,000d, Philesturnus carunculatus.

No. 1972 — Intl. Reconciliation Year: a, 25,000d, Mother Teresa. b, 25,000d, Pope John Paul II. c, 25,000d, Dalai Lama. d, 25,000d, Mohandas Gandhi.

No. 1973 — Primates and fruits: a, 25,000d, Saimiri sciureus, Anacardium occidentale. b, 25,000d, Saguinus oedipus, Passiflora edulis. c, 25,000d, Callithrix jacchus, Mangifera indica. d, 25,000d, Leontopithecus chrysomelas, Feijoa sellowiana.

No. 1974, 100,000d, Isurus paucus, Carukia barnesi. No. 1975, 100,000d, Euplagia quadripunctaria and caterpillar. No. 1976, 100,000d, Lincoln and U.S. flag. No. 1977, 100,000d, Krishnaswamy Kasturirangan, Insat-3c satellite. No. 1978, 100,000d, Perodictus potto, Tarsius spectrum. No. 1979, 100,000d, Panthera leo. No. 1980, 100,000d, Acinonyx jubatus. No. 1981, 100,000d, Felis chaus. No. 1982, 100,000d, Apis mellifica. No. 1983, 100,000d, Jackie Chan, film actor.

2009, Mar. 31 *Perf. 12¾x13¼*

1958 A341 Sheet of 2, #a-b, + 2 labels 6.75 6.75

Sheets of 4, #a-d

1959-1973 A341 Set of 15 185.00 185.00

Souvenir Sheets

Perf. 13¼ Syncopated

1974-1983 A341 Set of 10 125.00 125.00

No. 1958 is dated 2008. Nos. 1974-1983 each contain one 50x39mm stamp.

Nos. 608-610, 714, 717-718, 735, 742, 747, 1488c, 1488e, 1527b, 1527e, 1550b & 1573e Srchd. in Black, Silver, Red and Gold

Methods and Perfs As Before

2009, Apr. 15

1984 A93 (8000d) on 50c #714 *1.00 1.00*
1987 A66 (8000d) on 1.50d #608 (S) *1.00 1.00*
1988 A95 (8000d) on 10d #735 *1.00 1.00*
1990 A66 (8000d) on 11d #609 (S) *1.00 1.00*
1991 A93 (8000d) on 15.50d #717 *1.00 1.00*
1992 A93 (8000d) on 16d #718 *1.00 1.00*
1993 A66 (8000d) on 17d #610 (S) *1.00 1.00*
1994 A95 (8000d) on 18.50d #742 (R) *1.00 1.00*
1995 A280 (8000d) on 7000d #1527b (S) *1.00 1.00*
1996 A280 (8000d) on 7000d #1527e (S) *1.00 1.00*
1997 A305 (8000d) on 7000d #1573e *1.00 1.00*
1998 A305 (8000d) on 7000d #1573e (R) *1.00 1.00*
1999 A305 (8000d) on 7000d #1573e (G) *1.00 1.00*
2000 A265 (8000d) on 10,000d #1488c (S) *1.00 1.00*
2001 A265 (8000d) on 10,000d #1488e *1.00 1.00*
2002 A265 (8000d) on 10,000d #1488e (S) *1.00 1.00*
2003 A294 (8000d) on 10,000d #1550b *1.00 1.00*

Dated 2009

2004 A280 (8000d) on 7000d #1527b (R) *1.00 1.00*
2006 A280 (8000d) on 7000d #1527e (R) *1.00 1.00*
2007 A265 (8000d) on 10,000d #1488c (R) *1.00 1.00*
2008 A265 (8000d) on 10,000d #1488e (R) *1.00 1.00*
2009 A265 (8000d) on 10,000d #1488e (G) *1.00 1.00*
2010 A294 (8000d) on 10,000d #1550b (R) *1.00 1.00*

2011 A93 (14,000d) on 50c #714 *1.75 1.75*
2014 A66 (14,000d) on 1.50d #608 (S) *1.75 1.75*
2015 A95 (14,000d) on 10d #735 *1.75 1.75*
2017 A66 (14,000d) on 11d #609 (S) *1.75 1.75*
2018 A93 (14,000d) on 15.50d #717 *1.75 1.75*
2019 A93 (14,000d) on 16d #718 *1.75 1.75*
2020 A66 (14,000d) on 17d #610 (S) *1.75 1.75*
2022 A280 (14,000d) on 7000d #1527b (S) *1.75 1.75*
2023 A280 (14,000d) on 7000d #1527e (S) *1.75 1.75*
2024 A305 (14,000d) on 7000d #1573e *1.75 1.75*
2025 A305 (14,000d) on 7000d #1573e (R) *1.75 1.75*
2026 A305 (14,000d) on 7000d #1573e (G) *1.75 1.75*
2027 A265 (14,000d) on 10,000d #1488c (S) *1.75 1.75*
2028 A265 (14,000d) on 10,000d #1488e *1.75 1.75*
2029 A265 (14,000d) on 10,000d #1488e (S) *1.75 1.75*
2030 A294 (14,000d) on 10,000d #1550b *1.75 1.75*

Dated 2009

2031 A280 (14,000d) on 7000d #1527b (R) *1.75 1.75*
2032 A280 (14,000d) on 7000d #1527b (G) *1.75 1.75*
2033 A280 (14,000d) on 7000d #1527e (R) *1.75 1.75*
2034 A265 (14,000d) on 10,000d #1488c (R) *1.75 1.75*
2035 A265 (14,000d) on 10,000d #1488e (R) *1.75 1.75*
2036 A265 (14,000d) on 10,000d #1488e (G) *1.75 1.75*
2037 A294 (14,000d) on 10,000d #1550b (R) *1.75 1.75*

2038 A93 (14,000d) on 50c #714 *1.75 1.75*
2041 A66 (14,000d) on 1.50d #608 (S) *1.75 1.75*
2042 A95 (14,000d) on 10d #735 *1.75 1.75*
2044 A66 (14,000d) on 11d #609 (S) *1.75 1.75*
2045 A93 (14,000d) on 15.50d #717 *1.75 1.75*
2046 A93 (14,000d) on 16d #718 *1.75 1.75*
2047 A66 (14,000d) on 17d #610 (S) *1.75 1.75*
2049 A280 (14,000d) on 7000d #1527b (S) *1.75 1.75*
2050 A280 (14,000d) on 7000d #1527e (S) *1.75 1.75*
2051 A305 (14,000d) on 7000d #1573e *1.75 1.75*
2052 A305 (14,000d) on 7000d #1573e (R) *1.75 1.75*
2053 A305 (14,000d) on 7000d #1573e (G) *1.75 1.75*
2054 A265 (14,000d) on 10,000d #1488c (S) *1.75 1.75*
2055 A265 (14,000d) on 10,000d #1488e *1.75 1.75*
2056 A265 (14,000d) on 10,000d #1488e (S) *1.75 1.75*
2057 A294 (14,000d) on 10,000d #1550b *1.75 1.75*

Dated 2009

2058 A280 (14,000d) on 7000d #1527b (R) *1.75 1.75*
2059 A280 (14,000d) on 7000d #1527b (G) *1.75 1.75*
2060 A280 (14,000d) on 7000d #1527e (R) *1.75 1.75*
2061 A265 (14,000d) on 10,000d #1488c (R) *1.75 1.75*
2062 A265 (14,000d) on 10,000d #1488e (R) *1.75 1.75*
2063 A265 (14,000d) on 10,000d #1488e (G) *1.75 1.75*
2064 A294 (14,000d) on 10,000d #1550b (R) *1.75 1.75*

2065 A93 (14,000d) on 50c #714 *1.75 1.75*
2068 A66 (14,000d) on 1.50d #608 (S) *1.75 1.75*
2069 A95 (14,000d) on 10d #735 *1.75 1.75*
2071 A66 (14,000d) on 11d #609 (S) *1.75 1.75*
2072 A93 (14,000d) on 15.50d #717 *1.75 1.75*
2073 A93 (14,000d) on 16d #718 *1.75 1.75*
2074 A66 (14,000d) on 17d #610 (S) *1.75 1.75*
2076 A280 (14,000d) on 7000d #1527b (S) *1.75 1.75*
2077 A280 (14,000d) on 7000d #1527e (S) *1.75 1.75*
2078 A305 (14,000d) on 7000d #1573e *1.75 1.75*
2079 A305 (14,000d) on 7000d #1573e (R) *1.75 1.75*
2080 A305 (14,000d) on 7000d #1573e (G) *1.75 1.75*
2081 A265 (14,000d) on 10,000d #1488c (S) *1.75 1.75*
2082 A265 (14,000d) on 10,000d #1488e *1.75 1.75*
2083 A265 (14,000d) on 10,000d #1488e (S) *1.75 1.75*
2084 A294 (14,000d) on 10,000d #1550b *1.75 1.75*

Dated 2009

2085 A280 (14,000d) on 7000d #1527b (R) *1.75 1.75*
2087 A280 (14,000d) on 7000d #1527e (R) *1.75 1.75*
2088 A265 (14,000d) on 10,000d #1488c (R) *1.75 1.75*
2089 A265 (14,000d) on 10,000d #1488e (R) *1.75 1.75*
2090 A265 (14,000d) on 10,000d #1488e (G) *1.75 1.75*
2091 A294 (14,000d) on 10,000d #1550b (R) *1.75 1.75*

2092 A95 (40,950d) on 46d #747 *5.00 5.00*
Nos. 1984-2092 (91) *145.25 145.25*

Twenty-one additional stamps were issued in this set. The editors would like to examine any examples.

A342

A343

A344

No. 2097 — Rocket launches: a, 13,000d, Delta II. b, 13,000d, Ariane 5. c, 39,000d, CZ-4C. d, 39,000d, Atlas 5.

No. 2098 — Airships: a, 13,000d, U.S. Navy C-7 over Swiss Alps. b, 13,000d, U.S. Navy ZRS-5 Macon over Friedrichshafen, Germany. c, 39,000d, Italian M.1 airship over Rothenburg, Germany. d, 39,000d, LZ-127 Graf Zeppelin, Ferdinand von Zeppelin.

No. 2099 — Native Americans and wildlife: a, 13,000d, Canis lupus. b, 13,000d, Haliaeetus leucocephalus. c, 39,000d, Haliaeetus leucocephalus, diff. d, 39,000d, Aquila chrysaetos.

No. 2100 — Intl. Year of Science: a, 13,000d, Equus grevyi, Serengeti National Park, Tanzania. b, 13,000d, Haroun Tazieff, vulcanologist. c, 39,000d, Dmitri Mendeleev, chemist. d, 39,000d, Dr. Albert Schweitzer and hospital operating room.

No. 2101 — Fishermen and fish: a, 13,000d, Latimeria chalumnae. b, 13,000d, Anabas testudineus. c, 39,000d, Argyropelecus affinis. d, 39,000d, Pantodon buchholzi.

No. 2102 — Movies starring Charlie Chaplin (1889-1977): a, 13,000d, Modern Times, 1936. b, 13,000d, A Dog's Life, 1918. c, 39,000d, City Lights, 1931. d, 39,000d, The Gold Rush, 1925.

No. 2103 — Submarines: a, 15,000d, 1834 Russian submarine made by K. A. Schilder. b, 25,000d, 1866 Russian submarine made by I. F. Alexander. c, 35,000d, 1881 Russian submarine made by S. K. Drzewiecki. d, 35,000d, 1775 Turtle submarine.

No. 2104 — Intl. Year of Science: a, 20,000d, Carl Linnaeus, taxonomist, taxonomic tree. b, 25,000d, Charles Darwin, naturalist, skulls and depiction of evolution of man. c, 25,000d, Albert Einstein, atoms. d, 40,000d, Richard Feynman, energy sources.

No. 2105 — Cyclists: a, 20,000d, Grégory Baugé, French flag. b, 30,000d, Victoria Pendleton, British flag. c, 30,000d, Simona Krupeckaite, Lithuanian flag. d, 30,000d, Cameron Meyer, Australian flag.

No. 2106 — Shells and pre-historic creatures: a, 20,000d, Tylosaurus. b, 30,000d, Hybodus. c, 35,000d, Ichthyosaurus. d, 35,000d, Eurhinosaurus.

No. 2107 — Nude paintings of mythological or religious figures: a, 20,000d, Birth of Venus, by Amaury Duval. b, 30,000d, Susanna and the Elders, by Alessandro Allori. c, 35,000d, Phyllis and Demophon, by Agnolo di Cosimo. d, 35,000d, Birth of Venus, by William-Adolphe Bouguereau.

No. 2108 — High-speed trains: a, 20,000d, V150. b, 30,000d, Maglev. c, 35,000d, Maglev, diff. d, 35,000d, TGV.

No. 2109 — Intl. Year of Science: a, 25,000d, Wangari Maathai, 2004 Nobel Peace laureate, tropical rain forest. b, 25,000d, Jacques Cousteau, marine conservationist, Tursiops truncatus. c, 25,000d, Nicolaus Copernicus, heliocentric solar system. d, 25,000d, Al Gore, climate change activist, globe.

No. 2110 — North Atlantic Treaty Organization, 60th anniv.: a, 25,000d, B-2 Spirit airplane and dove. b, 30,000d, HMS Bulwark. c, 30,000d, Soldier, child in hospital bed, Red Cross, helicopter and humanitarian supplies. d, 30,000d, Leclerc tanks.

No. 2111 — Pre-historic animals and minerals.: a, 25,000d, Triceratops, Siderite, sphalerite and calcite. b, 30,000d, Batrachognathus, Pyromorphite. c, 30,000d, Caudipteryx, Dioptase. d, 30,000d, Compsognathus, Vanadinite and hollandite.

No. 2112 — Butterflies and moths: a, 25,000d, Attacus atlas. b, 30,000d, Ornithoptera alexandrae. c, 30,000d, Attacus atlas, diff. d, 35,000d, Ornithoptera alexandrae, diff.

No. 2113 — Expedition of Sir Arthur Stanley Eddington to Prince Island, 90th anniv.: a, 13,000d, Forest. b, 13,000d, Mountain. c, 39,000d, Building. d, 39,000d, Beach.

No. 2114 — Dragonflies: a, 15,000d, Libellula depressa. b, 25,000d, Libellula quadrimaculata. c, 30,000d, Enallagma cyathigerum. d, 30,000d, Cordulegaster boltoni.

No. 2115 — Mushrooms, vert.: a, 20,000d, Chanterelle (girolle). b, 20,000d, Hydne. c, 20,000d, Psalliote. d, 40,000d, Xerocomus rubellus.

No. 2116 — Map of Africa, child, handprints, and Postal Union of the Americas, Spain and Portugal (UPAEP) emblem at: a, 25,000d, LR. b, 25,000d, UL. c, 25,000d, Center. d, 25,000d, LL.

No. 2117, 95,000d, Ophiophagus hannah.

No. 2118, 100,000d, Concordes in flight. No. 2119, 100,000d, Eddington, 1919 solar eclipse. No. 2120, 100,000d, Astronaut Rakesh Sharma, GSAT-3 satellite. No. 2121, LZ-129 Hindenburg, Ferdinand von Zeppelin. No. 2122, 100,000d, Native Americans around fire, moccasins and pipe. No. 2123, 100,000d, Caranx hippos and fishermen. No. 2124, Chaplin, Ben Turpin, scene from His New Job, 1915. No. 2125, 100,000d, 1904 Russian submarine Delfin. No. 2126, 100,000d, Anomalocaris and shell. No. 2127, 100,000d, Gen. Hastings Lionel Ismay, NATO conference room. No. 2128, 104,000d, Cyclists Michael Morkov, and Alex Rasmussen, Danish flag. No. 2129, 110,000d, Maglev tain, diff. No. 2130, 110,000d, Platecarpus, Vanadinite. No. 2131, 110,000d, Brephidium exilis.No. 2132, 115,000d, The Bath of Venus, by François Boucher.

No. 2133, 100,000d, Signing of 1974 Argel Accords. No. 2134, 100,000d, Man, woman, AIDS ribbon.

Perf. 12¾x13¼, 13¼x12¾ (#2115)

2009, May 29 — Sheets of 4, #a-d

2097-2112	A342	Set of 16	230.00	230.00
2113-2116	A343	Set of 4	52.50	52.50

Souvenir Sheets

Perf. 13¼ Syncopated

2117	A342 95,000d multi		12.50	12.50
2118-2132	A343	Set of 15	200.00	200.00

Perf. 13¼x12¾

2133-2134	A344	Set of 2	26.00	26.00

Nos. 2118-2132 each contain one 50x39mm stamp. Nos. 2114, 2115, 2117, 2118 are dated 2008.

A345

No. 2135 — Pigeons in military service and : a, 10,000d, Soldier lifting pigeon. b, 20,000d, Soldier with helmet, tanks. c, 40,00d, Soldier with hat with pigeon on finger, tank. d, 50,000d, Pigeon in flight, pilot.

No. 2136 — Table tennis players: a, 13,000d, Werner Schlager, Austrian flag. b, 13,000d, Wang Liqin, flag of People's Republic of China. c, 39,000d, Jörgen Persson, Swedish flag. d, 39,000d, Jan-Ove Waldner, Swedish flag.

No. 2137 — Scouts and mushrooms: a, 13,000d, Clitocybe odora. b, 13,000d, Gomphidius roseus. c, 39,000d, Xerocomus porosporus. d, 39,000d, Russula olivacea.

No. 2138 — Lunar satellites and vehicles: a, 13,000d, LRO. b, 13,000d, LCROSS. c, 39,000d, Lunokhod 1. d, 45,000d, Apollo 15 Lunar Rover.

No. 2139 — Dinosaurs: a, 13,000d, Pterodaustro and Alfred Russel Wallace, naturalist. b, 13,000d, Pelorosaurus and Wallace. c, 39,000d, Xiaosaurus and Wallace. d, 45,000d, Utahraptor.

No. 2140 — Israeli history: a, 13,000d, Golda Meir, prime minister, Báb Shrine, Haifa. b, 23,000d, Pres. Chaim Weizmann, Jerusalem skyline. c, 30,000d, Ron Huldai, mayor of Tel Aviv, arms and skyline of Tel Aviv. d, 49,000d, Theodor Herzl, promulgator of Zionism.

No. 2141 — Malaria prevention: a, 13,000d, Anopheles annulipes, blood test. b, 23,000d, Malaria plasmodium, doctor examining infant. c, 30,000d, Malaria plasmodia, nurse treating child. d, 49,000d, Malaria plasmodium, mother holding child for medical examination.

No. 2142 — 2008 Chess Olympiad champions: a, 13,000d, Gabriel Sargissian, Armenian flag. b, 23,000d, Joanna Majdan, Polish flag. c, 30,000d, Maia Chiburdanidze, Georgian flag. d, 49,000d, Peter Leko, Hungarian flag.

No. 2143 — Jewish Nobel laureates: a, 15,000d, Yitzhak Rabin, Peace, 1994. b, 25,000d, Andrew Fire, Physiology or Medicine, 2006. c, 35,000d, Martin Chalfie, Chemistry, 2008. d, 35,000d, Robert Aumann, Economics, 2005.

No. 2144 — Michael Jackson (1958-2009) singer, wearing: a, 25,000d, Black hat at left, white and red hat at right. b, 25,000d, White shirt with straps at left. c, 25,000d, White shirt and pants at left. d, 25,000d, Black hat and pink shirt at left.

No. 2145 — Natural disasters: a, 25,000d, Tornado. b, 25,000d, Earthquake. c, 25,000d, Flood. d, 25,000d, Tsunami.

No. 2146 — Brigitte Bardot, actress, wearing: a, 26,000d, Red brown dress at right. b, 26,000d, Blue dress at right. c, 26,000d, Striped blouse at right. d, 26,000d, Hat at right.

No. 2147 — Paintings by Amadeo Modigliani (1884-1920): a, 30,000d, Cypress Trees and Houses, 1919. b, 30,000d, Seated Nude, 1918. c, 30,000d, Red-headed Girl in Evening Dress, 1918. d, 30,000d, Self-portrait, 1919.

No. 2148, 100,000d, Table tennis player Wang hao, flag of People's Republic of China. No. 2149, 100,000d, Scouts and Clitocybe gibba. No. 2150, 100,000d, Albert Einstein, 1921 Nobel Physics laureate. No. 2151, 100,000d, Jackson, diff. No. 2152, 100,000d, Forest fire. No. 2153, 100,000d, Bardot, diff. No. 2154, 104,000d, Pigeons in military service, diff. No. 2155, 104,000d, Atlas rocket, LCROSS. No. 2156, 104,000d, Tropeognathus and Charles Darwin. No. 2157, 104,000d, Shimon Peres, Israeli president. No. 2158, 104,000d, Malaria plasmodia, nurse treating infant. No. 2159, 104,000d, Chess player Vladimir Kramnik.No. 2160, 110,000d, Jeanne Hébuterne in Front of a Door, by Modigliani.

2009, July 1 — *Perf. 12¾x13¼*

Sheets of 4, #a-d

2135-2147	A345	Set of 13	185.00	185.00

Souvenir Sheets

Perf. 13¼ Syncopated

2148-2160	A345	Set of 13	175.00	175.00

A346

A347

No. 2161 — Marilyn Monroe (1926-62), actress, wearing: a, 25,000d, Green plaid blouse at left. b, 25,000d, Pink bathing suit at right. c, 25,000d, Red dress at right. d, 25,000d, Pink dress at left (hands above head).

No. 2162 — Paul Morphy (1837-84), chess player, and chess pieces: a, 25,000d, Black rook and white pawn. b, 25,000d, White knight and black king. c, 25,000d, White pawn and black knight. d, 29,000d, Black queen and white pawn.

No. 2163 — Mushrooms and orchids: a, 25,000d, Russula paludosa, Stanhopea tigrina. b, 25,000d, Tricholomopsis rutilans, Angraecum sesquipedale. c, 25,000d, Boletus reticulatus, Cattleya intermedia. d, 35,000d, Lentinus tigrinus, Scuticaria steelii.

No. 2164 — African animals and steam locomotives: a, 30,000d, Crocodylus niloticus, 4-8-2. b, 30,000d, Equus quagga, 2-8-4. c, 30,000d, Loxodonta africana, Mallett 0-4-4-0. d, 30,000d, Panthera leo, 4-4-0.

No. 2165 — Buddhist temples: a, 10,000d, Puning Temple, People's Republic of China. b, 10,000d, Todai-ji Temple, Japan. c, 30,000d, Jogyesa Temple, South Korea. d, 30,000d, Akshardham Temple, India. e, 30,000d, Horyu-ji Temple, Japan.

No. 2166 — Foods and flags: a, 10,000d, Tacos, Mexican flag. b, 10,000d, Pelmeni, Russian flag. c, 30,000d, Lutefisk, Norwegian flag. d, 30,000d, Kimchi, South Korean flag. e, 30,000d, Pot-au-feu, French flag.

No. 2167 — Asian military aircraft: a, 15,000d, Kawasaki Ki-61-I, Japan. b, 25,000d, T-50 Golden Eagle, South Korea. c, 25,000d, Shijiazhuang Y-5B, People's Republic of China. d, 25,000d, Mitsubishi F-15J Eagle, Japan. e, 25,000d, Chengdu J-10, People's Republic of China.

No. 2168 — Taekwondo gold medalists at 2008 Summer Olympics, Beijing: a, 15,000d, Sujeong Lim, South Korea. b, 25,000d, Kyungseon Hwang, South Korea. c, 25,000d, Jingyu Wu, People's Republic of China. d, 25,000d, Hadi Saei, Japan. e, 25,000d, Guillermo Perez, Mexico.

No. 2169 — Sea birds and lighthouses: a, 15,000d, Rissa tridactyla, Split Point Lighthouse, Australia. b, 25,000d, Neophron percnopterus, Europa Point Lighthouse, Gibraltar. c, 25,000d, Calonectris diomedea, Cabo Espichel Lighthouse, Portugal. d, 25,000d, Larus ridibundus, Pigeon Point Lighthouse, U.S. e, 30,000d, Fulmarus glacialis, Gumundo Lighthouse, South Korea.

No. 2170 — Asian astronauts and spacecraft: a, 15,000d, Yang Liwei, People's Republic of China, Shenzhou 5. b, 25,000d, Koichi Wakata. Japan, Space Shuttle Discovery. c, 25,000d, Fei Junlong, People's Republic of China, Shenzhou 6. d, 25,000d, Soichi Noguchi, Japan, Space Shuttle Discovery. e, 30,000d, Yi So-Yeon, South Korea, Soyuz TMA-9.

No. 2171, 100,000d, Monroe, diff. No. 2172, 100,000d, Morphy, white king, black rook. No. 2173, 100,000d, Omphalotus olearius, Ophrys holoserica. No. 2174, 100,000d, Giraffa camelopardalis, 4-4-0 steam locomotive. No. 2175, 100,000d, Lama Temple, People's Republic of China. No. 2176, 100,000d, Ackee and saltfish, Jamaican flag. No. 2177, 104,000d, KAI KT-1 Woong-Bee airplane, South Korea. No. 2178, 104,000d, Taekwondo gold medalist Maria del Rosario Espinoza, Mexico. No. 2179, 104,000d, Astronaut Chiaki Mukai, Japan, Space Shuttle Discovery. No. 2180, 115,000d, Fratercula arctica, Sunderland Lighthouse, United Kingdom.

2009, July 30 — *Perf. 12¾x13¼*

Sheets of 4, #a-d

2161-2164	A346	Set of 4	57.50	57.50

Sheets of 5, #a-e

2165-2170	A347	Set of 6	90.00	90.00

Souvenir Sheets

2171-2180	A346	Set of 10	135.00	135.00

Souvenir sheets of 1 of Nos. 2165c, 2166d, 2167b, 2168b, 2169e, and 2170e with English and Portuguese text exist.

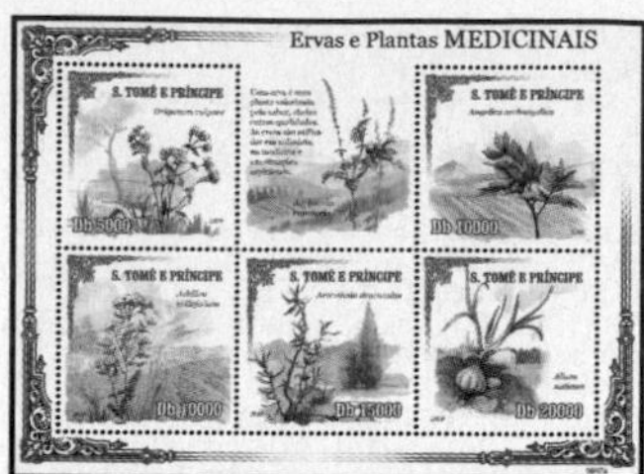

A348

No. 2181 — Medicinal plants: a, 5,000d, Origanum vulgare. b, 10,000d, Angelica archangelica. c, 10,000d, Achillea millefolium. d, 15,000d, Artemissia dracumulus. e, 20,000d, Allium sativum.

No. 2182 — Cetaceans: a, 10,000d, Tursiops truncatus, Balaena mysticetus. b, 10,000d, Unnamed cetaceans. c, 10,000d, Globicephala melas, Physeter catodon. d, 20,000d, Stenella pernettyi, Lithofaga lithofaga. e, 20,000d, Grampus griseus, Megaptera novaeangliae.

No. 2183 — Famous people and their cats: a, 10,000d, Freddie Mercury, rock star, and cats, Oscar and Tiffany. b, 10,000d, Gustav Klimt, painter, and cat, Katze. c, 15,000d, Pres. Ronald Reagan, wife, Nancy, and cats Cleo and Sara. d, 20,000d, John Lennon and Yoko Ono, rock stars, and cat, Pepper. e, 25,000d, Frank Zappa, rock star, and cat, Marshmoff.

No. 2184 — Automobiles: a, 10,000d, 1930 Walter 6B Sodomka. b, 15,000d, 1923-27 Tatra T11. c, 20,000d, 1935 Walter Junior SS. d, 25,000d, 1931 Aero 662. e, 30,000d, 1932 Wikov 40.

No. 2185 — Dogs in military service: a, 10,000d, Dog and soldier with machine gun. b, 15,000d, Dog and paratrooper in dive. c, 25,000d, Dog with soldier with rifle, airplane in sky. d, 25,000d, Soldier holding dog's leash, boxes at right. e, 25,000d, Soldier with dog, tank at right.

No. 2186 — Birds: a, 10,000d, Falco subbuteo. b, 15,000d, Sarcoramphus papa. c, 25,000d, Bubo virginianus. d, 25,000d, Haliaeetus leucocephalus. e, 35,000d, Ninox strenua.

No. 2187 — Charles Lindbergh (1902-74), pilot, and Spirit of St. Louis: a, 10,000d. b, 15,000d. c, 25,000d, Airplane name below airplane. d, 25,000d, Airplane name above airplane. e, 35,000d.

No. 2188 — Paintings by Paul Cézanne (1839-1906) and Pablo Picasso (1881-1973): a, 10,000d, Still Life, by Cézanne, 1892. b, 15,000d, Jacqueline, by Picasso, 1960. c, 25,000d, Nude Woman, by Cézanne, 1898-99. d, 30,000d, The Bathers, by Cézanne, 1890. e, 35,000d, Gardanne, by Cézanne, 1886.

No. 2189 — Paintings by Pablo Picasso (1881-1973): a, 10,000d, Still Life, 1901. b, 20,000d, Nude on a Divan, 1960. c, 25,000d, Study for "Le Dejeuner sur l'Herbe," 1960. d, 25,000d, Les Demoiselles d'Avignon, 1907. e, 35,000d, The Artist and His Model, 1963.

No. 2190 — Farrah Fawcett (1947-2009), actress: a, 20,000d, Holding drink at left. b, 20,000d, With bicycle at right. c, 20,000d, On skateboard at right. d, 20,000d, In black dress at right, 1890. e, 20,000d, Holding handbag at right.

No. 2191, 60,000d, Artemisia vulgaris. No. 2192, 70,000d, Phocoena phocoena. No. 2193, 80,000d, David Bowie, rock star, and cat, Purrie. No. 2194, 100,000d, Fawcett, diff. No. 2195, 104,000d, 1933 Tatra 52 automobile. No. 2196, 110,000d, Sergeant Stubby, military dog. No. 2197, 110,000d, Five Bathers, by Cézanne, 1877-78. No. 2198, 110,000d, Nude Under a Pine Tree, by Picasso, 1959.

2009, Oct. 20 — *Perf. 12¾x13¼*

Sheets of 5, #a-e

2181-2190	A348	Set of 10	125.00	125.00

Souvenir Sheets

Perf. 13¼ Syncopated

2191-2198	A348	Set of 8	95.00	95.00

Nos. 1400, 1401, 1403 Surcharged in Red

Methods and Perfs As Before

2009, Oct. 25

2199 A220 (8000d) on 3500d #1400 *1.00 1.00*
2200 A220 (8000d) on 5000d #1401 *1.00 1.00*
2201 A220 (8000d) on 7500d #1403 *1.00 1.00*
Nos. 2199-2201 (3) 3.00 3.00

No. 1402 exists with this surcharge but was not issued.

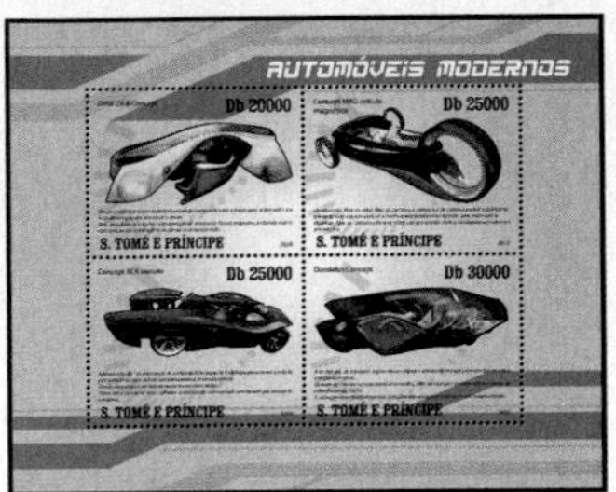

A349

A350

No. 2202 — Futuristic automobile concepts: a, 20,000d, BMW ZC-6 concept vehicle. b, 25,000d, Magnetic concept vehicle. c, 25,000d, RCA concept vehicle. d, 30,000d, Daedalus concept vehicle.

No. 2203 — Princess Diana (1961-97), with: a, 25,000d, Mother Teresa. b, 25,000d, Sons, William and Harry. c, 25,000d, Prince Charles. d, 25,000d, Child.

No. 2204 — Elvis Presley (1935-77) and Presley: a, 20,000d, In boxing trunks. b, 25,000d, Holding microphone stand. c, 25,000d, Dancing with woman. d, 34,000d, With woman, playing ukulele.

No. 2205 — Various Camargue horses: a, 20,000d. b, 25,000d. c, 30,000d. d, 35,0000d.

No. 2206 — Eiffel Tower and Concorde: a, 25,000d, G-BOAC. b, 25,000d, F-BTSD. c, 30,000d, G-BOAC, diff. d, 30,000d, G-BOAF.

No. 2207 — Dinosaurs: a, 25,000d, Quetzalcoatlus, Psittacosaurus. b, 30,000d, Dsungaripterus, Troodon. c, 30,000d, Pteranodon ingens, Stegosaurus. d, 35,000d, Pteranodon, Euoplocephalus.

No. 2208 — Papal visit to Africa: a, 25,000d, Pope Benedict XVI holding crucifix, meeting cardinals. b, 30,000d, Pope Benedict XVI walking with African leader. c, 30,000d, Pope Benedict XVI greeting nuns. d, 35,000d, Pope Benedict XVI on airplane steps.

No. 2209 — Writers and poets: a, 20,000d, Johann Wolfgang von Goethe (1749-1832). b, 20,000d, William Shakespeare (1564-1616). c, 20,000d, George Gordon Byron (Lord Byron) (1788-1824). d, 20,000d, Charles Dickens (1812-70). e, 20,000d, Friedrich von Schiller (1759-1805).

No. 2210 — Humanists: a, 10,000d, Pope John Paul II (1920-2005). b, 15,000d, Tenzin Gyatso, 14th Dalai Lama. c, 25,000d, Mother Teresa (1910-97). d, 30,000d, Mahatma Gandhi (1869-1948). e, 30,000d, Pope Benedict XVI.

No. 2211 — World War II airplanes: a, 10,000d, I 16 Type 18 and I-16 Type 24, Soviet Union. b, 15,000d, Bf 109E-4 and Bf 109F-2, Germany. c, 25,000d, Bf 109E-3 and Me 262, Germany. d, 30,000d, Bf 109F-4Z/Trop, Germany, and Mustang P-51D-15, United States. e, 35,000d, TU-25 and SB-2M-100A, Soviet Union.

No. 2212 — Expensive paintings: a, 15,000d, Rideau, Cruchon et Compotier, by Paul Cézanne. b, 15,000d, Portrait of Dr. Gachet, by Vincent van Gogh. c, 30,000d, Garçon à la Pipe, by Pablo Picasso. d, 30,000d, Massacre of the Innocents, by Peter Paul Rubens. e, 30,000d, Dance at Le Moulin de la Galette, by Pierre-Auguste Renoir.

No. 2213 — Chinese film personalities: a, 5000d, Feng Zhe (1921-69). b, 7000d, Wang Xingang. c, 10,000d, Jiang Wen. d, 13,000d, Shangguan Yunzhu (1920-68). e, 25,000d, Qin Yi. f, 40,000d, Liu Xiaoqing.

No. 2214 — Race car, checkered flag, and Ayrton Senna (1960-94), race car driver, wearing : a, 10,000d, Red racing suit (red and white car). b, 15,000d, White suit, holding helmet (red and white car). c, 15,000d, Red suit (black car). d, 20,000d, Red suit (black car). e, 20,000d, Red suit and black cap (red and white car). f, 20,000d, Black shirt (yellow car).

No. 2215 — Pre-historic crocodilians: a, 10,000d, Guarinisuchus munizi, Metriorhynchus. b, 10,000d, Two Metriorhynchus. c, 15,000d, Steneosaurus. d, 20,000d, Two Metriorhynchus, diff. e, 25,000d, Kaprosuchus saharicus. f, 35,000d, Steneosaurus, Guarinisuchus munizi.

No. 2216 — Cats and dogs: a, 10,000d, Chinese crested dogs. b, 15,000d, Cesky terriers. c, 20,000d, Sphinx cats. d, 20,000d, Oriental shorthair cats. e, 25,000d, Devon Rex cats. f, 25,000d, Italian greyhounds.

No. 2217 — Peter Paul Rubens (1577-1640), painter: a, 10,000d, Cimon and Iphegenia. b, 15,000d, Rubens. c, 20,000d, Pan and Syrinx. c, 20,000d, Jupiter and Calisto. d, 25,000d, Rubens Museum Antwerp, Belgium. e, 30,000d, The Judgement of Paris.

No. 2218, 80,000d, Audi O concept vehicle. No. 2219, 90,000d, Presley and two women. No. 2220, 100,000d, Camargue horses, diff. No. 2221, 100,000d, Senna wearing racing helmet. No. 2222, 104,000d, Princess Diana and Tower Bridge. No. 2223, 104,000d, Shar Peis. No. 2224, 104,000d, Pope Benedict XVI kissing infant. No. 2225, 115,000d, The Four Continents, by Rubens.

No. 2226, 100,000d, Oscar Wilde (1854-1900), writer. No. 2227, 104,000d, Bf 109F-4 and B-71 airplanes, Germany. No. 2228, 110,000d, Nelson Mandela, Tockus erythrorhynchus, Tsavorite. No. 2229, 110,000d, Portrait of Adele Bloch-Bauer I, by Gustav Klimt. No. 2230, 110,000d, Metriorhynchus. No. 2231, 110,000d, Zhang Yimou, film director. No. 2232, 115,000d, Eiffel Tower and Concorde G-BOAC, diff. No. 2233, 115,000d, Euoplocephalus and other dinosaurs.

2010, Jan. 25 Litho. ***Perf. 12¾x13¼***

Sheets of 4, #a-d

2202-2208 A349 Set of 7 100.00 100.00

Sheets of 5, #a-e

2209-2212 A350 Set of 4 57.50 57.50

Sheets of 6, #a-f

2213-2217 A350 Set of 5 72.50 72.50

Souvenir Sheets

Perf. 13¼ Syncopated

2218-2225 A349 Set of 8 105.00 105.00
2226-2233 A350 Set of 8 115.00 115.00

Antverpia 2010 National & European Championship of Philately, Antwerp, Belgium (#2217, 2225).

African Mammals — A351

No. 2234 — Primates: a, 10,000d, Cercopithecus neglectus. b, 15,000d, Mandrillus sphinx. c, 20,000d, Pan paniscus. d, 25,000d, Lophocebus albigena. e, 30,000d, Pan troglodytes.

No. 2235 — Elephants (Loxodonta africana): a, 10,000d, Adult and juvenile. b, 15,000d, Adult and juvenile, diff. c, 20,000d, Juvenile and two adults. d, 25,000d, Two adults facing each other. e, 34,000d, Two adults walking.

No. 2236 — Whales: a, 10,000d, Megaptera novaeangliae. b, 15,000d, Physeter catodon. c, 25,000d, Feresa attenuata. d, 30,000d, Orcinus orca. e, 30,000d, Kogia breviceps.

No. 2237 — Lions (Panthera leo): a, 22,000d, Female and cubs. b, 22,000d, Female attacking antelope. c, 22,000d, Male, tail at left. d, 22,000d, Two females attacking buffalo. e, 22,000d, Male, tail at center.

No. 2238 — Bats: a, 10,000d, Chalinolobus gouldii, Tadarida aegyptiaca. b, 15,000d, Taphozous mauritianus, Rousettus aegyptiacus. c, 25,000d, Epomophorus wahlbergi. d, 30,000d, Megaloglossus woermanni. e, 35,000d, Miniopterus schreibersii.

No. 2239, 80,000d, Papio hamadryas, horiz. No. 2240, 80,000d, Loxodonta cyclotis, horiz. No. 2241, 80,000d, Orcinus orca, horiz. No. 2242, 80,000d, Panthera leo, horiz. No. 2243, 80,000d, Plecotus austriacus, Hypsignathus monstrosus, horiz.

2010, Mar. 29 ***Perf. 12¾x13¼***

Sheets of 5, #a-e

2234-2238 A351 Set of 5 60.00 60.00

Souvenir Sheets

Perf. 13¼ Syncopated

2239-2243 A351 Set of 5 45.00 45.00

Nos. 2239-2243 each contain one 50x39mm stamp.

A352

No. 2244 — Albert Camus (1913-60), writer: a, 20,000d, Three book covers. b, 20,000d, Smoking cigarette. c, 20,000d, Standing with arms crossed. d, 20,000d, Book covers and Eiffel Tower. e, 20,000d, Monument to Camus, Villeblevin, France, and gravestone.

No. 2245 — Remembrance of Holocaust victims: a, 20,000d, Cupped hands and spiral. b, 20,000d, Menorah. c, 20,000d, Star of David. d, 20,000d, Symbol with crying eye. e, 20,000d, Heart and barbed wire.

No. 2246 — Paintings by Michelangelo Merisia da Caravaggio (1571-1610): a, 10,000d, Self-portrait as Bacchus, 1593-94. b, 15,000d, Narcissus, 1596. c, 20,000d, The Musicians, 1595. d, 30,000d, Supper at Emmaus, 1601. e, Saint Jerome Writing, 1605.

No. 2247 — Steam locomotives: a, 10,000d, Train facing left. b, 15,000d, Wheels. c, 20,000d, Locomotive on bridge. d, 30,000d, Train facing right, telegraph poles. e, 35,000d, Train and African boys.

No. 2248 — Diego Maradona, soccer player, 50th birthday: a, 10,000d, Maradona and World Cup. b, 15,000d, Maradona and flag of Argentina. c, 20,000d, Maradona cheering. d, 30,000d, Face fo Maradona. e, 35,000d, Maradona dribbling ball.

No. 2249 — Moto GP motorcycles and riders: a, 10,000d, Geoff Duke, Gilera motorcycle. b, 15,000d, Valentino Rossi, Yamaha motorcycle. c, 25,000d, Jarno Saarinen, Yamaha motorcycle. d, 30,000d, Daijiro Kato, Honda motorcycle. e, 35,000d, Dani Pedrosa, Honda motorcycle.

No. 2250 — 2010 Winter Olympics gold medalists: a, 10,000d, Simon Ammann, ski jumping, Switzerland. b, 15,000d, Evan Lysacek, figure skating, United States. c, 25,000d, Wang Meng, speed skating, People's Republic of China. d, 30,000d, Jason Lamy-Chappuis, ski jumping, France. e, 35,000d, Andrea Fischbacher, Alpine skiing, Austria.

No. 2251 — Japanese Military Aviation in World War II: a, 10,000d, Japanese airplane. b, 15,000d, Admiral Isoroku Yamamoto (1884-1943). c, 25,000d, Japanese pilots. d, 30,000d, Damaged ships at Pearl Harbor. e, 35,000d, Japanese airplanes.

No. 2252 — Boy Scouts of America, cent.: a, 10,000d, Emblem, Scouts on obstacle course. b, 15,000d, Binoculars, Scouts on rope. c, 25,000d, Emblem, Scouts playing horns. d, 30,000d, Scouts, tents and compass. e, 35,000d, Scout and canteen.

No. 2253 — Firefighting: a, 15,000d, Airplane dropping water on fire. b, 15,000d, Five firefighters. c, 25,000d, Firefighter and truck. d, 30,000d, Helmet and firefighting tools. e, 35,000d, Two firefighters.

No. 2254 — Lighthouses: a, 24,000d, Eddystone Lighthouse, Great Britain. b, 24,000d, Lighthouse and Robert Stevenson (1772-1850), lighthouse builder and civil engineer. c, 24,000d, Ukrainian lighthouse designed by Vladimir G. Shukhov. d, 24,000d, Cockspur Island Lighthouse, United States, Gelochelidon nilotica. e, 24,000d, Kopu Lighthouse, Estonia.

No. 2255, 80,000d, Camus and aerial view of Paris, horiz. No. 2256, 80,000d, The Card Players, by Caravaggio, horiz. No. 2257, 100,000d, Star of David and clouds, horiz. No. 2258, 100,000d, Steam locomotive, horiz. No. 2259, 100,000d, Fire truck, horiz. No. 2260, 100,000d, Casey Stoner, Ducati motorcycle, horiz. No. 2261, 104,000d, Maradona playing soccer and flag of Argentina, horiz. No. 2262, 104,000d, Magdalena Neuner, cross-country skiing, Germany, horiz. No. 2263, 104,000d, Mitsubishi AM-6 Zero, horiz. No. 2264, 110,000d, Boy Scout, tents, emblem, horiz. No. 2265, 110,000d, Pigeon Point Lighthouse, United States, horiz.

2010, Mar. 29 ***Perf. 12¾x13¼***

Sheets of 5, #a-e

2244-2254 A352 Set of 11 140.00 140.00

Souvenir Sheets

Perf. 13¼ Syncopated

2255-2265 A352 Set of 11 125.00 125.00

Nos. 2255-2265 each contain one 50x39mm stamp.

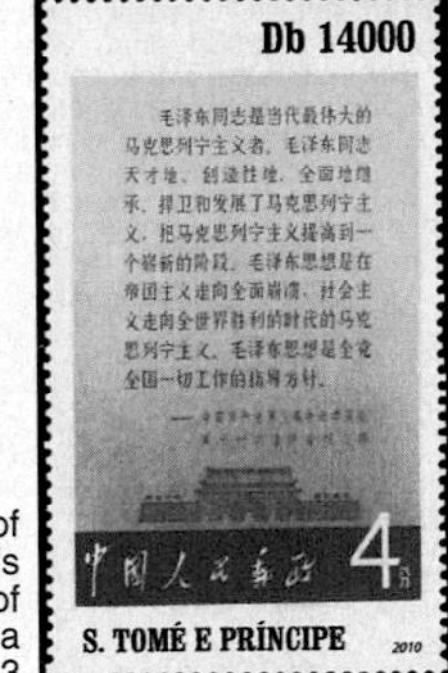

Stamps of the People's Republic of China
A353

Designs: No. 2266, 14,000d, #949 (4f Chinese text). No. 2267, 14,000d, #950 (8f Mao Zedong and text). No. 2268, 14,000d, #951 (8f Mao Zedong waving in crowd). No. 2269, 14,000d, #952, (8f Mao Zedong above crowd). No. 2270, 14,000d, #953 (8f Mao Zedong waving). No. 2271, 14,000d, #954 (8f Mao Zedong leaning on rail, Lin Piao in background). No. 2272, 14,000d, #955 (8f Mao Zedong with arm on rail), horiz. No. 2273, 14,000d, #956 (10f Lin Piao and Mao Zedong reviewing document), horiz. No. 2274, 14,000d, #991 (8f Mao Zedong waving, Chinese text), horiz. No. 2275, 14,000d, #998 (8f Mao Zedong Going to An Yuan).

140,000d, #628 ($3 Mei Lan-fang in opera scene).

Perf. 12¾x13¼, 13¼x12¾

2010, May 5

2266-2275 A353 Set of 10 15.50 15.50

Size: 98x147mm

Imperf

2276 A353 140,000d multi 15.50 15.50

A354

A355

No. 2277 — Clark Gable (1901-60), actor, in scenes from: a, 15,000d, Gone With the Wind, 1939. b, 15,000d, Manhattan Melodrama, 1934. c, 20,000d, Mogambo, 1953. d, 20,000d, Command Decision, 1948. e, 20,000d, It Started in Naples, 1960. f, 25,000d, San Francisco, 1936.

No. 2278 — Year of the Tiger with diagonal lines at: a, 15,000d, UL. b, 15,000d, LL. c, 20,000d, UR. d, 20,000d, LR. e, 20,000d, UL, diff. f, 25,000d, UR, diff.

No. 2279 — Henri Fabre (1882-1984), aviator: a, 15,000d, Beriev A-40 Albatross hydroplane. b, 15,000d, Fabre's 1910 hydroplane. c, 20,000d, Fabre and plane's propeller. d, 20,000d, Fabre and Notre Dame de la Garde, Marseille. e, 25,000d, Fabre's 1910 hydroplane, diff. f, 25,000d, Cessna TU206D hydroplane.

No. 2280 — Buildings at Expo 2010, Shanghai: a, 15,000d, Canadian Pavilion. b,

15,000d, Israeli Pavilion. c, 20,000d, United Africa Pavilion. d, 20,000d, Hong Kong Pavilion. e, 25,000d, Malaysian Pavilion. f, 30,000d, Swedish Pavilion.

No. 2281 — Count Leo Tolstoy (1828-1910), writer and: a, 15,000d, Tales of Sebastopol, 1855. b, 15,000d, The Cossacks, 1863. c, 20,000d, Wife, Sophia. d, 20,000d, Wife, Sophia, and daughter, Alexandra. e, 20,000d, The Death of Ivan Ilyich, 1886, and stack of books. f, 37,000d, Anna Karenina, 1878.

No. 2282 — Track and field athletes: a, 15,000d, Bryan Clay, decathlete. b, 15,000d, Reese Hoffa, shot putter. c, 20,000d, Meseret Defar, long-distance runner. d, 20,000d, Dwain Chambers, sprinter. e, 25,000d, Dayron Robles, hurdler. f, 32,000d, Veronica Campbell-Brown, sprinter.

No. 2283 — Dinosaurs: a, 15,000d, Alectrosaurus. b, 15,000d, Caudipteryx. c, 20,000d, Gorgosaurus. d, 20,000d, Spinosaurus. e, 25,000d, Plesiosaurus. f, 35,000d, Tapejara.

No. 2284 — Mother Teresa (1910-97): a, 15,000d, Mother Teresa holding child. b, 15,000d, Head of Mother Teresa. c, 20,000d, Mother Teresa holding child, diff. d, 20,000d, Mother Teresa and two angels. e, 25,000d, Mother Teresa and Pope John Paul II. f, 35,000d, Mother Teresa and three putti.

No. 2285 — Brephidium exilis butterfly under magnifying glass with handle at: a, 15,000d, UL. b, 15,000d, Top. c, 20,000d, UR. d, 20,000d, LL. e, 25,000d, Bottom. f, 35,000d, Right.

No. 2286 — Hubble Space Telescope, 20th anniv.: a, 15,000d, Hubble Space Telescope and Lyman Spitzer (1914-97), astronomer. b, 15,000d, Launch of Space Shuttle STS-31. c, 20,000d, Hubble Space Telescope, red violet background. d, 20,000d, Hubble Space Telescope, Eagle Nebula, blue green background. e, 25,000d, Hubble Space Telescope above Earth. f, 35,000d, Hubble Space Telescope and Earth.

No. 2287 — Paintings by Sandro Botticelli (1445-1510): a, 15,000d, The Lamentation Over the Dead Christ. b, 20,000d, The Birth of Venus. c, 20,000d, Madonna and Child and Two Angels. d, 20,000d, Cestello Annunciation. e, 25,000d, Allegory of Spring (Primavera). f, 35,000d, Madonna and Child with Six Saints.

No. 2288 — Lech Kaczynski (1949-2010), President of Poland, and: a, 15,000d, Tupolev TU-154M airplane. b, 15,000d, Flag of Poland. c, 20,000d, Wife, Maria, aerial view and arms of Warsaw. d, 25,000d, Flag of Poland, diff. e, 25,000d, Map and arms of Poland. f, 35,000d, Wife, Maria, and Pope Benedict XVI.

No. 2289, 100,000d, Fabre. No. 2290, 104,000d, Hubble Space Telescope and V838 Monocerotis. No. 2291, 110,000d, Gable and Marilyn Monroe. No. 2292, 110,000d, Tiger, diff. No. 2293, 110,000d, Equatorial Guinea Pavilion. Expo 2010, Shanghai. No. 2294, 110,000d, War and Peace, by Tolstoy. No. 2295, 110,000d, Nodosaur. No. 2296, 115,000d, Ivan Ukhov, high jumper. No. 2297, 120,000d, Mother Teresa holding infant. No. 2298, 120,000d, Self-portrait, by Botticelli. No. 2299, 125,000d, Woman and Ornithoptera goliath. No. 2300, 125,000d, Kaczynski, Pope John Paul II, flag of Poland.

2010, May 5 ***Perf. 13¼x12¾***

Sheets of 6, #a-f

2277-2288 A354 Set of 12 170.00 170.00

Souvenir Sheets

Perf. 13¼ Syncopated, 13¼x12¾ (#2300)

2289-2300 A355 Set of 12 155.00 155.00

A356

A357

No. 2301 — World War II military commanders: a, 15,000d, Field Marshal Erwin Rommel (1891-1944), Germany. b, 15,000d, Gen. Dwight D. Eisenhower (1890-1969), United States. c, 20,000d, Marshal Georgy K. Zhukov (1896-1974), Soviet Union. d, 25,000d, Field Marshal Bernard Montgomery (1887-1976), Great Britain. e, 35,000d, Field Marshal Friedrich Paulus (1890-1957), Germany.

No. 2302 — Cats: a, 24,000d, Two brown and white tabby cats. b, 24,000d, Brown and white tabby cat, Siamese cat. c, 24,000d, Gray and white cat. d, 24,000d, Three Siamese cats. e, 24,000d, Brown and white tabby cat.

No. 2303 — Butterflies and caterpillars: a, 15,000d, Cethosia cyane. b, 20,000d, Danaus plexippus. c, 25,000d, Papilio polyxenes. d, 30,000d, Siproeta epaphus. e, 35,000d, Antheraea polyphemus.

No. 2304 — Pope John Paul II (1920-2005): a, 15,000d, With hand raised. b, 20,000d, With Pope Benedict XVI. c, 25,000d, Holding crucifix. d, 30,000d, With arms of Vatican City. e, 35,000d, Holding young girl.

No. 2305 — Locomotives: a, 20,000d, Canadian Pacific S3 Diesel-electric. b, 20,000d, Class 53 Diesel, Great Britain. c, 25,000d, DB Class V 200. d, 30,000d, Bombardier AGC B 81500, France. e, 35,000d, CN Diesel, Canada.

No. 2306 — Pin-up art of Paul Butvila, with woman: a, 5000d, With life preserver. b, 5000d, With red cross. c, 5000d, With airplane. d, 10,000d, With mirror having image showing hand holding bra. e, 10,000d, In black dress in spotlight. f, 10,000d, With playing cards and poker chips. g, 15,000d, Wearing necklace, as seen from back. h, 15,000d, With binoculars. i, 15,000d, Reclining, with legs above head.

No. 2307, 110,000d, Tabby cat. No. 2308, 115,000d, World War II soldiers. No. 2309, 115,000d, Heliconius charithonia. No. 2310, 115,000d, Rudolf Diesel (1858-1913), inventor, and EMD FT Diesel-electric locomotive.

No. 2311, 90,000d, Tenzin Gyatso, 14th Dalai Lama and Potala Palace, Lhasa, Tibet. No. 2312, 90,000d, Mahatma Gandhi and Sabarnati Ashram. No. 2313, 90,000d, Reclining Nude from the Back, by Amedeo Modigliani.

2010, July 11 ***Perf. 12¾x13¼***

Sheets of 5, #a-e

2301-2305 A356 Set of 5 65.00 65.00
2306 A356 Sheet of 9, #a-i 9.75 9.75

Souvenir Sheets

Perf. 13¼ Syncopated

2307-2310 A356 Set of 4 50.00 50.00

Perf. 13¼x12¾

2311-2313 A357 Set of 3 29.00 29.00

A358

No. 2314 — Crustaceans: a, 10,000d, Anonyx nugax, Aristas timidus. b, 15,000d, Leander tenuicornis, Dyastylis glabra. c, 20,000d, Lophozozymus incisus. d, 20,000d, Lybia tessellata, Petrolisthes donadio. e, 25,000d, Leander tenuicornis.

No. 2315 — Intl. Year of Biodiversity: a, 22,000d, Falco punctatus. b, 22,000d, Planting of seedlings. c, 22,000d, Panthera tigris. d, 22,000d, Ursus maritimus. e, 22,000d, Daubentonia madagascariensis.

No. 2316 — Dogs: a, 15,000d, Chinese crested dogs. b, 20,000d, Great Danes (Dogue alemao). c, 20,000d, Samoyeds. d, 25,000d, Australian kelpies. e, 35,000d, Whippets.

No. 2317 — Worldwide Fund for Nature (WWF) stamps of other countries: a, 15,000d, Bulgaria #3401. b, 20,000d, Jamaica #594. c, 20,000d, Maldive Islands #1187. d, 25,000d, Gambia #516. e, 35,000d, South Georgia and South Sandwich Islands #165.

No. 2318 — Robert Schumann (1810-56), composer, and: a, 15,000d, Cover of score for "Papillons." b, 20,000d, Grave monument, Bonn. c, 25,000d, Wife, Clara. d, 25,000d, His house, Germany. e, 35,000d, Wife at piano.

No. 2319 — Oil spills: a, 15,000d, Grounding of the Exxon Valdez, 1989. b, 20,000d, Ixtoc I blowout, 1979. c, 25,000d, Nowruz Field Platform fire, 1983. d, 25,000d, Gulf War well fires, 1991. e, 35,000d, Collision of Atlantic Princess and Aegean Captain, 1979.

No. 2320 — Juliette Gordon Low (1860-1927), founder of Girl Scouts of America, Scouting trefoil, and: a, 20,000d, Dog. b, 20,000d, Three Girl Scout leaders. c, 20,000d, Girl Scouts around campfire. d, 25,000d, Birthplace in Savannah, Georgia. e, 35,000d, Girl Scouts and leaders.

No. 2321 — Korean War, 60th anniv.: a, 20,000d, Zhang Taofang, Chinese sniper. b, 20,000d, Mao Zedong and son, Anying. c, 25,000d, General Douglas MacArthur and officers. d, 25,000d, Chinese Commander Peng Dehuai and North Korean leader Kim Il Sung. e, 35,000d, Negotiators at Panmunjom peace talks.

No. 2322 — Various rabbits and Chinese character (Year of the Rabbit): a, 15,000d. b, 20,000d. c, 25,000d, Rabbit at right. d, 25,000d, Rabbit at left. e, 35,000d.

No. 2323, 80,000d, Cardisoma guanhumi. No. 2324, 100,000d, Ailuropoda melanoleuca. No. 2325, 104,000d, France #2713c and flag of France. No. 2326, 110,000d, Beagles. No. 2327, 110,000d, Zil Elwannyen Sesel #108. No. 2328, 110,000d, Robert Schumann and hands playing piano. No. 2329, 110,000d, Low and Girl Scouts. No. 2330, 115,000d, Deepwater Horizon oil platform explosion, 2010. No. 2331, 120,000d, Wang Hai, Chinese pilot in Korean War. No. 2332, 120,000d, Rabbit and Chinese character, diff.

2010, Sept. 2 ***Perf. 12¾x13¼***

Sheets of 5, #a-e

2314-2322 A358 Set of 9 110.00 110.00

Souvenir Sheets

2323-2332 A358 Set of 10 115.00 115.00

Stamp Collectors and Stamps of Portugal — A359

No. 2333 — Collector and Portugal: a, #1716 (wildcat). b, #2155 (mouse). c, #1503 (dog). d, #1512 (train). e, #2343f (astronaut). f, #1519 (fire truck).

120,000d, Collector and Portugal #1539, 1540.

2010, Sept. 2 ***Perf. 12¾x13¼***

2333 A359 20,000d Sheet of 6, #a-f 12.50 12.50

Souvenir Sheet

2334 A359 120,000d multi 12.50 12.50

No. 2334 contains one 50x39mm stamp.

Miniature Sheets

Chinese Zodiac Animals — A360

No. 2335: a, 10,000d, Rat. b, 10,000d, Ox. c, 15,000d, Tiger. d, 20,000d, Rabbit. e, 24,000d, Dragon. f, 25,000, Snake.

No. 2336: a, 10,000d, Horse. b, 10,000d, Goat. c, 15,000d, Monkey. d, 20,000d, Rooster. e, 24,000d, Dog. f, 25,000d, Pig.

2010, Sept. 2 ***Perf. 12¾x13¼***

Sheets of 6, #a-f

2335-2336 A360 Set of 2 22.00 22.00

Independence, 35th Anniv. — A361

No. 2337 — Statues of Discoverers and Colonizers of St. Thomas & Prince Islands: a, 10,000d, Joao de Paiva, colonizer. b, 15,000d, Pero Escobar, discoverer. c, 25,000d, Joao de Santarém, discoverer.

No. 2338 — Symbols and maps: a, 10,000d, Map of St. Thomas & Prince Islands. b, 15,000d, Torch, national flag. c, 15,000d, Map of Africa with St. Thomas & Prince Islands circled, building. d, 25,000d, National flag, maps of St. Thomas & Prince Islands, Africa.

No. 2339 — Obverse and reverse of banknotes: a, 10,000d, 5000 dobra note. b, 15,000d, 50,000 dobra note. c, 20,000d, 20,000 dobra note. d, 25,000d, 10,000 dobra note.

No. 2340 — National heroes: a, 10,000d, King of Angolares, orange background. b, 15,000d, King Amador, green background. c, 20,000d, King Amador, yellow background. d, King of Angolares, rose background.

No. 2341, horiz. — Slaves and slave warehouses: a, 10,000d, Slave working on produce drying racks. b, 15,000d, Warehouse. c, 20,000d, Train and buildings. e, 25,000d, Slaves with baskets.

No. 2342, horiz. — Various traditional homes: a, 10,000d, House with painting of dancers. b, 15,000d, Gray house on stilts. c, 20,000d, Curtain in window. d, 25,000d, Blue house on stilts.

No. 2343, horiz. — Beaches: a, 10,000d, Micoló Beach, St. Thomas Island. b, 15,000d, Banana Beach, Prince Island. c, 20,000d, Boats on Café Beach, Ilhêu das Rolas. d, 25,000d, Lagoa Azul Beach, St. Thomas Island.

No. 2344 — Flowers: a, 15,000d, Red flower with stem at bottom. b, 15,000d, Red flower and bud. c, 15,000d, Red and yellow flowers. d, 15,000d, Pink and red five-petaled flowers. e, 15,000d, Red flower, no stem visible. f, 15,000d, Yellow flowers.

No. 2345 — Cuisine of St. Thomas & Prince Islands: a, 10,000d, Plantains. b, 10,000d, Okra. c, 15,000d, Breadfruit. d, 15,000d, Eggplant. e, 25,000d, Calulu de Peixe (fish stew). f, 25,000d, Bananas, diff.

No. 2346, horiz. — Colonial houses: a, 10,000d, House with balcony. b, 10,000d, House with flag. c, 15,000d, House with balcony, sepia-tone photograph. d, 15,000d, House with balcony, colkor photograph. e, 25,000d, House with balcony, diff. f, 25,000d, Road leading to large house.

No. 2347 — Coins: a, 10,000d, 50 centimo coin. b, 15,000d, 1 dobra coin. c, 15,000d, 2 dobra coin. d, 20,000d, 50 dobra coin. e, 20,000d, 100 dobra coin. f, 25,000d, 250 dobra coin.

No. 2348 — Coins: a, 10,000d, 5 dobra coin. b, 15,000d, 10 dobra coin. c, 15,000d, 20 dobra coin. d, 20,000d, 500 dobra coin. e, 20,000d, 1000 dorba coin. f, 25,000d, 2000 dobra coin.

No. 2349 — Agricultural products: a, 10,000d, Yellow cacao pod. b, 15,000d, Green cacao pods on tree. c, 15,000d, Sugar cane. d, 20,000d, Coffee berries. e, 20,000d, Cacao pods approaching ripeness on tree. f, 25,000d, Sugar cane, diff.

No. 2350 — Drawings of people in colonial era dress: a, 10,000d, Woman. b, 15,000d, Man, artist's name at UL. c, 15,000d, Man, diff., artist's name at LL. d, 20,000d, Two women, artist's name at LL. e, 20,000d, Two men, artist's name at UL. f, 25,000d, Man, diff.

No. 2351 — Wood carvings: a, 10,000d, Head and map of St. Thomas & Prince Islands. b, 15,000d, People in rowboats. c, 15,000d, Stylized Africans. d, 20,000d, People and house. e, 20,000d, Statue of woman holding basket. f, 25,000d, Man climbing tree.

No. 2352 — Waterfalls, mountains and rivers: a, 10,000d, Milagrosa Waterfall. b, 10,000d, St. Nicolau Waterfall. c, 15,000d, St. Nicolau Waterfall, diff. d, 15,000d, Vilela Waterfall. e, 20,000d, Foliage near Pico Maria Fernanda. f, 20,000d, Pico Maria Fernanda shrouded in clouds. g, 25,000d, Rio Manuel Jorge. h, 25,000d, Pico Cao Grande.

No. 2353 — Birds and butterflies: a, 10,000d, Speirops lugubris. b, 10,000d, Unidentified bird. c, 15,000d, Ploceus grandis facing right. d, 15,000d, Parrot facing left (incorrectly identified as Ploceus grandis). e, 15,000d, Monarch butterfly. f, 20,000d, Treron sanctithomae. g, 20,000d, Oriolus crassirostris. h, 20,000d, Piombode mato. i, 25,000d, Thomasophantes sanctithomae. j, 25,000d, Prima molleri.

No. 2354, 100,000d, Head of person waving flag of St. Thomas & Prince Islands. No. 2355, 100,000d, Obverse and reverse of 100,000 dobra banknote. No. 2356, 100,000d, First Baron de Agua-Izé Sousa e Almeda, yellow and orange cacao pods. No. 2357, 100,000d, Like #2356, with green cacao pods. No. 2358, 100,000d, Bananas. No. 2359, 100,000d, Okra. No. 2360, 100,000d, Flowers held by gloved hands of woman. No. 2361, 100,000d, Hands of Tchiloli. No. 2362, 100,000d, Wood carving of people and house, basket weaving. No. 2363, 100,000d, Woman in traditional dress. No. 2364, 100,000d, Yellow flower. No. 2365, 100,000d, Bowl of nuts, coconut shells, horiz. No. 2366, 100,000d, National Museum, flag of St. Thomas & Prince Islands, horiz. No. 2367, 100,000d, National Museum, arms of St. Thomas & Prince Islands, horiz.

Perf. 13¼x12¾, 13¼, 12¾x13¼

2010, Dec. 1

2337 A361 Sheet of 3, #a-c 5.50 5.50

Sheets of 4, #a-d

2338-2343 A361 Set of 6 45.00 45.00

Sheets of 6, #a-f

2344-2351 A361 Set of 8 90.00 90.00
2352 A361 Sheet of 8, #a-h 15.50 15.50
2353 A361 Sheet of 10, #a-j 19.00 19.00

Souvenir Sheets

2354-2367 A361 Set of 14 150.00 150.00

Wedding of Prince William and Catherine Middleton — A362

No. 2368: a, Couple skiing. b, Prince William and Princess Diana. c, Princes William, Charles and Harry. d, Middleton with Princes William and Harry.

104,000d, Couple, coat of arms and castle.

Perf. 12¾x13¼

2011, Feb. 14 **Litho.**

2368 A362 27,500d Sheet of 4, #a-d 12.50 12.50

Souvenir Sheet

Perf. 13¼ Syncopated

2369 A362 104,000d multi 12.00 12.00

No. 2369 contains one 50x39mm stamp.

Internazionale Milan, 2010 Winner of FIFA Club World Cup — A363

No. 2370: a, 1964 team. b, 2010 team, Italian Series A champions, player in foreground running. c, Team members, player in foreground holding 2010 European Champions League trophy. d, Players celebrating 2010 Italian Cup championship, player in foreground smiling. e, 2010 team, Italia Supercup champions, player in foreground kicking ball. f, 2010 team celebratin Club World Cup victory.

150,000d, Javier Zanetti holding Club World Cup.

Perf. 12¾x13¼

2011, Feb. 14 **Litho.**

2370 A363 25,000d Sheet of 6, #a-f 17.00 17.00

Souvenir Sheet

Perf. 13¼ Syncopated

2371 A363 150,000d multi 17.00 17.00

Marilyn Monroe (1926-62), Actress — A364

No. 2372 — Monroe and: a, Men from *Gentlemen Prefer Blondes.* b, Yves Montand and cat from *Let's Make Love.* c, Laurence Olivier from *The Prnce and the Showgirl.* d, Scene from *The Misfits.*

110,000d, Monroe, diff.

Perf. 13¼x12¾

2011, Feb. 25 **Litho.**

2372 A364 25,000d Sheet of 4, #a-d 11.50 11.50

Souvenir Sheet

Perf. 13¼ Syncopated

2373 A364 110,000d multi 12.50 12.50

Miniature Sheets

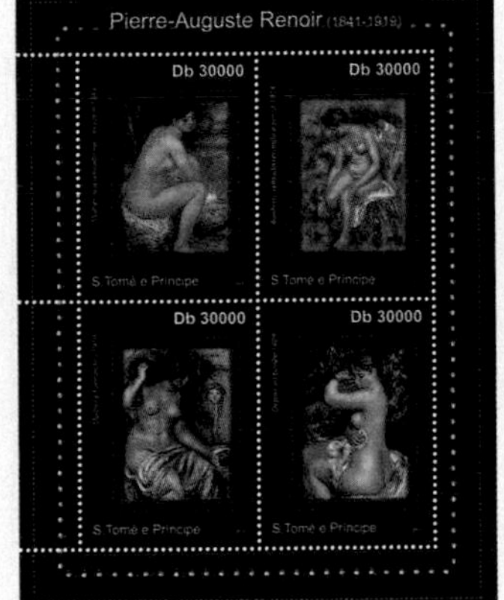

Nudes — A365

No. 2374, 30,000d — Paintings by Pierre-Auguste Renoir: a, Nude in a Landscape, 1883. b, Seated Bather Drying Her Leg, 1914. c, Woman at the Fountain, 1910. d, After the Bath, 1888.

No. 2375, 31,750d — Paintings by Eugène Delacroix: a, Female Nude Reclining on a Divan, 1825-26. b, Mlle. Rose, 1817-20. c, Reclining Odalisque, 1827. d, The Death of Sardanapalus, 1827.

No. 2376, 32,500d — Paintings by Titian: a, Sacred and Profane Love, 1514. b, Venus with a Mirror, 1555. c, Tarquin and Lucretia, 1508-71. d, Venus Anadyomene, 1520.

No. 2377 — Paintings by Peter Paul Rubens: a, 31,250d, Perseus Liberating Andromeda, 1639-40. b, 31,250d, Diana and Her Nymphs Surprised by the Fauns, 1638-40. c, 31,250d, Venus and Adonis, 1635. d, 312,500d, The Three Graces, 1639.

Perf. 13¼x12¾

2011, Feb. 25 **Litho.**

Sheets of 4, #a-d

2374-2377 A365 Set of 4 87.50 87.50

Miniature Sheets

A366

No. 2378, 31,250d — Protected animals on Christmas Island: a, Sula sula. b, Pipistrellus murrayi. c, Birgus latro. d, Phaethon lepturus.

No. 2379, 31,250d — Dolphins: a, Lagenorhynchus obscurus. b, Stenella attenuata. c, Cephalorhynchus commersonii. d, Tursiops truncatus.

No. 2380, 31,250d — Peonies: a, Paeonia mascula, subspecies russi, Paeonia officinalis. b, Paeonia daurica, Paeonia wittmanniana. c, Paeonia peregrina, Paeonia cambessedesii. d, Paeonia russi var. reverchoni, Paeonia clusii.

No. 2381, 31,250d, vert. — Birds of prey: a, Buteo lagopus lagopus. b, Falco subbuteo subbuteo. c, Aquila chrysaetos chrysaetos. d, Hieraaetus fasciatus fasciatus.

No. 2382, 31,250d, vert. — Pope John Paul II holding crucifix: a, Wearing zucchetto, facing left. b, Wearing miter, facing right. c, Wearing miter, facing forward with hand raised. d, Wearing miter and red stole, hand raised.

No. 2383, 31,750d — Solar-powered items: a, Meguru electric vehicle. b, NanoSail-D2 satellite. c, Solar panels. d, Solar-powered bus.

No. 2384, 31,750d — Cats: a, Acinonyx jubatus raineyii. b, Acinonyx jubatus hecki. c, Panthera leo bleyenberghi. d, Panthera pardus pardus.

No. 2385, 31,750d, vert. — Cats: a, Felis margarita. b, Felis nigripes. c, Prionailurus rubiginosus. d, Felis chaus.

No. 2386, 32,500d — African animals: a, Mellivora capensis. b, Kobus ellipsiprymnus. c, Phacochoerus aethiopicus. d, Orycteropus afer.

No. 2387, 32,500d — Fish: a, Ostracion tricornis. b, Rhinecanthus aculaetus. c, Holocentrus axensionis. d, Diodon hystrix.

No. 2388, 32,500d — Dinosaurs: a, Xiphactinus, Liopleurodon. b, Tyrannosaurus rex, Archaeopteryx. c, Rahonavis ostromi, Ankylosaurus. d, Stegosaurus, Velociraptor.

No. 2389, 32,500d — Service organizations: a, Paul P. Harris, founder of Rotary International, Rotary International emblem and New Orleans skyline. b, Cattleya rex, Rotary Intenational emblem. c, Map of Africa, African child, Lions International emblem. d, Melvin Jones, Lions International founder, Lions International emblem, New Orleans skyline.

No. 2390, 32,500d — Princess Diana (1961-97): a, With sons, William and Harry. b, Dancing with Prince Charles. c, Wearing sailor's hat, holding African child. d, Holding Prince William, holding flowers.

No. 2391, 32,500d, vert. — Owls: a, Tyto soumagnei. b, Bubo lacteus. c, Bubo leucostictus. d, Scotopelia ussheri.

No. 2392, 33,750d — Indian luxury trains: a, Palace on Wheels (Palacio Sobre Carris). b, Deccan Odyssey. c, Golden Chariot (Bigo Dourada). d, Royal Rajasthan.

No. 2393, 33,750d, vert. — Butterflies: a, Urania sloanus. b, Anaea electra. c, Alcides aurora. d, Chrysiridia ripheus.

Perf. 12¾x13¼, 13¼x12¾

2011, Feb. 25 **Litho.**

Sheets of 4, #a-d

2378-2393 A366 Set of 16 230.00 230.00

Souvenir Sheets

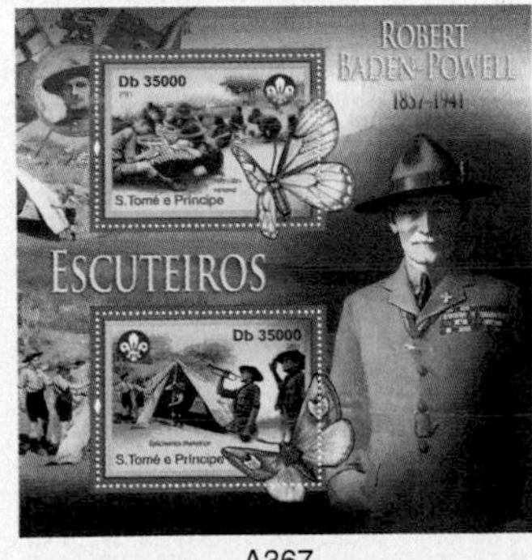

A367

No. 2394, 35,000d — Scouts, scouting emblem and butterflies: a, Hibrildes venosa. b, Epicimelia theresidae.

No. 2395, 35,000d — Ships: a, Adler von Lübeck, 1566. b, Gorch Fock, 1958.

No. 2396, 35,000d — Fire fighters and fire trucks from: a, Wagga Wagga, Australia. b, Sapporo, Japan.

No. 2397, 35,000d — Motorcycles: a, Kiwi Indian Retro 30. b, 2009 Harley-Davidson FLHRC Road King Classic.

No. 2398, 35,000d, vert. — Mushrooms: a, Boletus junquilleus. b, Xerocomus badius.

No. 2399, 40,000d — Lighthouses and birds: a, Onychoprion fuscata. b, Diomedea exulans.

No. 2400, 40,000d — Protected species in the Galapagos Islands: a, Conolophus subcristatus. b, Chelonoidis nigra.

No. 2401, 40,000d — Flying dinosaurs: a, Pterodactylus, Anurognathus. b, Pterodactylus, Pterosaur.

No. 2402, 40,000d — Mohandas K. Gandhi (1869-1948), Indian nationalist: a, Waving, with men. b, In bed, young girl sitting on bed.

No. 2403, 40,000d — Maia Chiburdanidze, chess player: a, Playing opponent at right. b, Holding large pawn at left.

No. 2404, 45,000d — Cats: a, Stewie, world's longest cat. b, Scarlett's Magic, world's tallest cat..

No. 2405, 45,000d — Dogs: a, Beagles. b, Airedale terriers.

No. 2406, 45,000d — Minerals: a, Quartz. b, Beryl aquamarine with muscovite.

No. 2407, 45,000d — High-speed trains: a, V150 TGV, France. b, CHR380, China.

No. 2408, 50,000d — World War II aircraft: a, Mitsubishi A5M4 and A5M2, Japan. b, Messerschmitt Me-262A-1a, Focke-Wulf FW-190-A7, Germany.

No. 2409, 50,000d — Yuri Gagarin (1934-68), first man in space, and: a, Vostok 1. b, Floating cosmonaut.

No. 2410, 50,000d — Princess Diana (1961-97): a, Campaigning for land mines elimination in Angola. b, With Zimbabwean Red Cross worker.

No. 2411, 50,000d, vert. — Dogs: a, Alaskan malamute. b, Greenlandic dog.

No. 2412, 50,000d, vert. — Marilyn Monroe (1926-62), actress: a, Leaning backward. b, Leaning forward.

No. 2413, 52,000d — Whales: a, Megaptera novaeangliae. b, Eubalaena glacialis.

No. 2414, 52,000d — Turtles: a, Megalochelis gigantea. b, Chrysemys concinna.

No. 2415, 52,000d, vert. — Butterflies: a, Ornithoptera alexandrae. b, Brephidium exilis.

No. 2416, 52,000d, vert. — Orchids: a, Ansellia africana, Habenaria radiata. b, Calanthe sieboldii, Dracula vampira.

No. 2417, 55,000d — Scouting trefoil and Scouts: a, Hiking. b, Forming human chain.

No. 2418, 55,000d — Ailuropoda melanoleuca: a, Sleeping. b, Eating.

No. 2419, 55,000d — Frogs: a, Gastrotheca cornuta. b, Rhinoderma darwinii.

No. 2420, 55,000d, vert. — Owls: a, Glaucidium californicum. b, Otus asio.

No. 2421, 55,000d, vert. — Mushrooms: a, Amanita muscaria. b, Macrolepiota procera.

No. 2422, 57,500d — Dinosaurs: a, Einiosaurus. b, Medusaceratops.

No. 2423, 57,500d — Red Cross: a, Worker with child, disaster workers, helicopter. b, Worker with child, Worker carrying sack, ambulance.

No. 2424, 57,500d — Wedding of Prince William and Catherine Middleton: a, Prince William at right. b, Middleton at right.

No. 2425, 57,500d, vert. — Fish: a, Regalecus glesne, Lampris guttatus. b, Silurus glanis, Zeus faber.

Perf. 13¼ Syncopated

2011, Mar. 30 **Litho.**

Sheets of 2, #a-b

2394-2425 A367 Set of 32 355.00 355.00

A368

No. 2426, 25,000d — Two images of Babe Ruth (1895-1948), baseball player: a, Ruth holding brown bat in image at left. b, Ruth holding two bats in image at right. c, Glove and oversized baseball in batter's box at LR. d, Ruth holding brown bat in image at right.

No. 2427, 25,000d — Bobby Fischer (1943-2008), chess champion: a, Wearing red suit. b, Wearing headband and blue suit. c, Wearing no suit. d, Wearing gray suit.

No. 2428, 25,000d — Sebastian Vettel, Formula 1 race car driver, and: a, Race car at LL. b, Race car above Vettel's arm. c, Vettel kissing trophy. d, Vettel wearing racing helmet at left.

No. 2429, 25,000d — 2014 Winter Olympics, Sochi, Russia: a, Ski jumping. b, Ice hockey. c, Speed skating. d, Snowboarding.

No. 2430, 25,000d — Mohandas K. Gandhi (1869-1948), Indian nationalist: a, Gandhi sitting, Indian flag. b, Kanyakumari Temple. c, Dove, head of Gandhi. d, Gandhi facing left.

No. 2431, 25,000d — Pres. John F. Kennedy (1917-63), and: a, Fidel Castro and Minuteman missiles. b, Wife, Jacquline, and Marilyn Monroe. c, Buzz Aldrin on Moon. d, Berlin Wall.

No. 2432, 25,000d — Queen Elizabeth II: a, Wearing crown at left. b, With Australia #259. c, As young child at right. d, With Prince Philip at left.

No. 2433, 25,000d — London Underground, 150th anniv.: a, 1996 train in Notting Hill Gate Station. b, S8 train, Piccadilly Station entrance sign, buildings. c, Docklands Light Rail train in tunnel. d, D78 train in Paddington Station.

No. 2434, 25,000d — Ferdinand von Zeppelin (1838-1917), founder of Zeppelin Airship Company: a, With wife, Isabella. b, Graf Zeppelin in air. c, Hindenburg near ground. d, Hindenburg and hangars.

No. 2435, 25,000d — Space flight of Valentina Tereshkova, first woman in space, 50th anniv.: a, Tereshkova wearing helmet. b, Tereshkova feeding infant, emblem of Vostok 5 and 6. c, Tereshkova and Vostok 6. d, Tereshkova and flight technicians.

No. 2436, 25,000d — Rudolf Nureyev (1938-93), ballet dancer: a, Without hat. b, Wearing ski cap at right. c, Wearing ski cap at left. d, Wearing beret at right.

No. 2437, 25,000d — Louis de Funès (1914-83), actor: a, With thumb touching forefinger. b, With finger touching tongue. c, Wearing costume with neck frill. d, Wearing military uniform.

No. 2438, 25,000d — Richard Wagner (1813-83), composer: a, Playing piano at production of *Tristan and Isolde*. b, And Temple of the Grail from 1882 production of *Parsifal*. c, And Wagner Monument, Berlin. d, And Bayreuth Festival Theater.

No. 2439, 25,000d — Giuseppe Verdi (1813-1901), composer: a, Portrait of Verdi by Francesco Paolo Michetti, musical score. b, Verdi, piano keyboard. c, Caricature of Verdi by Théobald Chartran. d, Verdi in Venice, Verdi's signature.

No. 2440, 25,000d — Jim Morrison (1943-71), rock musician: a, Holding microphone stand, belt visible. b, Two images of Morrison, holding microphone above head at right. c, Two images of Morrison, holding microphone stand at right. d, Holding microphone stand, belt not visible.

No. 2441, 25,000d — Nude paintings by Lucas Cranach the Elder (1472-1553): a, *Lucretia*, 1538. b, *The Three Graces*, 1535. c, *The Silver Age*, 1516. d, *The Suicide of Lucretia*, 1538.

No. 2442, 25,000d — Paintings by Eugène Delacroix (1798-1863): a, *Fanatics of Tangier*, 1838. b, *The Barque of Dante*, 1822. c, *The Natchez*, 1835. d, *Cleopatra and the Peasant*, 1838.

No. 2443, 25,000d — Paintings by Pablo Picasso (1881-1973): a, *Self-portrait*, 1901. b, *Les Demoiselles d'Avignon*, 1907. c, *Three Musicians*, 1921. d, *Still Life with Bull's Head*, 1939.

No. 2444, 25,000d — International Year of Water Cooperation: a, Child carrying water bucket on head. b, Child at faucet. c, Child getting splashed with water. d, Child drinking from bowl.

No. 2445, 25,000d — Year of the Snake: a, Denomination at UL, snake head at LR. b, Denomination at UL, snake head at LL. c, Denomination at UR, snake head at right. d, Denomination and snake head at UL.

No. 2446, 96,000d, Ruth, diff. No. 2447, 96,000d, Fischer, diff. No. 2448, 96,000d, Vettel and race car, diff. No. 2449, 96,000d, Downhill skiing. No. 2450, 96,000d, Gandhi and crowd. No. 2451, 96,000d, Pres. Kennedy and U-2 spy plane. No. 2452, 96,000d, Queen Elizabeth II and scene from her coronation. No. 2453, 96,000d, 1986 train in Canary Wharf London Underground station. No. 2454, 96,000d, Ferdinand von Zeppelin and Zeppelin LZ-11. No. 2455, 96,000d, Tereshkova and Vostok 6, diff. No. 2456, 96,000d, Nurevey and Margot Fonteyn. No. 2457, 96,000d, De Funès and flowers. No. 2458, 96,000d, Wagner, diff. No. 2459, 96,000d, Portrait of Verdi, by Michetti and G clef. No. 2460, 96,000d, Morrison, diff. No. 2461, 96,000d, *Nymph of the Spring*, by Cranach, the Elder. No. 2462, 96,000d, *The Massacre at Chios*, by Delacroix. No. 2463, 96,000d, *The Weeping Woman*, by Picasso. No. 2464, 96,000d, Child drinking, diff. No. 2465, 96,000d, Snake, diff.

2013, Mar. 29 Litho. *Perf. 13¼*

Sheets of 4, #a-d

2426-2445 A368 Set of 20 210.00 210.00

Souvenir Sheets

2446-2465 A368 Set of 20 200.00 200.00

Animals and Prehistoric Animals — A369

No. 2466, 25,000d — Rhinoceroses: a, Diceros bicornis facing right. b, Diceros bicornis facing left. c, Adult and juvenile Ceratotherium simum. d, Adult Ceratotherium simum.

No. 2467, 25,000d — Antelopes: a, Gazella cuvieri. b, Gazella spekei. c, Gazella rufifrons. d, Gazella leptoceros.

No. 2468, 25,000d — Cercopithecus mona and fruit: a, Carica papaya. b, Artocarpus rigidus. c, Psidium guajava. d, Annona glabra.

No. 2469, 25,000d — Primates: a, Cercopithecus neglectus, Cercopithecus diana. b, Procolobus badius. c, Two Papio anubis. d, Cercopithecus roloway, Colobus guereza.

No. 2470, 25,000d — Bats: a, Rousettus aegyptiacus. b, Tadarida pumila. c, Taphozous mauritianus. d, Hipposideros ruber.

No. 2471, 25,000d — Cats: a, Leptailurus serval. b, Panthera pardus pardus. c, Acinonyx jubatus and prey. d, Panthera leo and prey.

No. 2472, 25,000d — Loxodonta africana: a, Adult and juvenile. b, Adult and two juveniles. c, Elephants stampeding. d, Two adults.

No. 2473, 25,000d — Dolphins: a, Grampus griseus. b, Steno bredanensis. c, Delphinus delphis. d, Tursiops truncatus.

No. 2474, 25,000d — Whales: a, Feresa attenuata. b, Balaenoptera edeni. c, Kogia breviceps. d, Mesoplodon densirostris.

No. 2475, 25,000d — Birds: a, Sula leucogaster. b, Morus capensis. c, Head of Sula leucogaster and bird in flight. d, Head of Morus capensis. and bird in flight.

No. 2476, 25,000d — Birds: a, Sarkidiornis melanotos. b, Phoenicopterus minor. c, Phoenicopterus roseus. d, Dendrocygne bicolor.

No. 2477, 25,000d — Two Alcedo thomensis: a, Birds sharing prey, denomination at UR. b, Perched bird with fish, bird in flight, denomination at UL. c, Bird on ground at left, bird in flight at right with fish, denomination at UR. d, Two birds on ground, denomination at UL.

No. 2478, 25,000d — Owls: a, Tyto alba. b, Otus senegalensis. c, Otus senegalensis, Tyto alba. d, Tyto alba, Otus hartlaubi.

No. 2479, 25,000d — Apis mellifera: a, Two bees at flowers on branch, denomination in white. b, Two bees on red flower. c, One bee on flower. d, Bee on flower and bee flying near flower.

No. 2480, 25,000d — Butterflies: a, Pseudacraea lucretia. b, Mycalesis sciathis, Myrina marciana. c, Papilio hippocoon, Melantis leda. d, Acraea zetes.

No. 2481, 25,000d — Butterflies: a, Bicyclus dorothea, Hypolimnas salmacis. b, Sevenia boisduvali, Hypolimnas salmacis. c, Graphium angolanus baronis, Leptotes pirithous. d, Precis sinuata, Deudorix lorisona.

No. 2482, 25,000d — Fish: a, Coryphaena hippurus. b, Dactylopterus volitans. c, Histrio histrio. d, Bodianus pulchellus.

No. 2483, 25,000d — Crocodiles: a, Crocodylus cataphractus. b, Crocodylus niloticus. c, Crocodylus suchus. d, Osteolaemus tetraspis.

No. 2484, 25,000d — Turtles: a, Geochelone gigantea. b, Geochelone pardalis. c, Caretta caretta. d, Geochelone sulcata.

No. 2485, 25,000d — Dinosaurs: a, Gorgosaurus. b, Daspletosaurus. c, Dryosaurus. d, Yutyrannus.

No. 2486, 96,000d, Diceros bicornis, diff. No. 2487, 96,000d, Gazella dorcas. No. 2488, 96,000d, Cercopithecus mona and Lycium ferocissimum. No. 2489, 96,000d, Papio anubis. No. 2490, 96,000d, Eidolon helvum. No. 2491, 96,000d, Caracal caracal. No. 2492, 96,000d,Two Loxodonta africana, diff. No. 2493, 96,000d, Stenella frontalis. No. 2494, 96,000d, Megaptera novaeangliae. No. 2495, 96,000d, Morus capensis, diff. No. 2496, 96,000d, Phoenicopterus roseus, diff. No. 2497, 96,000d, Two Alcedo thomensis, diff. No. 2498, 96,000d, Otus senegalensis, Tyto alba, diff. No. 2499, 96,000d, Apis mellifera on honeycomb. No. 2500, 96,000d, Libythea labdaca, Graphium leonidas. No. 2501, 96,000d, Iolaus iulus, Charaxes jasius. No. 2502, 96,000d, Anthias anthias. No. 2503, 96,000d, Crocodylus niloticus and Pluvianus aegyptius. No. 2504, 96,000d, Pelomedusa subrufa. No. 2505, 96,000d, Tyrannosaurus, Edmontosaurus.

2013, May 10 Litho. *Perf. 13¼*

Sheets of 4, #a-d

2466-2485 A369 Set of 20 220.00 220.00

Souvenir Sheets

2486-2505 A369 Set of 20 210.00 210.00

Birth of Prince George of Cambridge — A370

No. 2506: a, Duke and Duchess of Cambridge with Prince George, blue banner at bottom. b, Princess Diana holding Prince William, Duke of Cambridge holding Prince George. c, Duke and Duchess of Cambridge with Prince George, blue banner at top. d, Duchess of Cambridge holding Prince George.

96,000d, Duke and Duchess of Cambridge with Prince George, diff.

2013, Aug. 2 Litho. *Perf. 13¼*

2506 A370 25,000d Sheet of 4, #a-d 11.00 11.00

Souvenir Sheet

2507 A370 96,000d multi 10.50 10.50

A371

No. 2508, 25,000d — Elvis Presley (1935-77): a, With guitar, holding microphone. b, Holding microphone, no guitar. c, With guitar, no microphone. d, Without guitar of microphone.

No. 2509, 25,000d — Marilyn Monroe (1926-62), actress: a, Wearing blue dress. b, Wearing red dress, with Academy Award. c, Wearing potato sack, standing against pillar. d, Wearing blue dress, with Hollywood Walk of Fame star.

No. 2510, 25,000d — Scouts and minerals: a, Scout reading map, Uraninite. b, Scout lifting rock, Orpiment. c, Scouts examining rocks, Emerald. d, Two Scouts, Carbonate.

No. 2511, 25,000d — Scouting trefoil, cats and dogs: a, American Shorthair cat. b, Great Dane. c, Boxer. d, Persian cat.

No. 2512, 25,000d — Rotary International emblem and orchids: a, Cattleya acklandiae. b, Sobralia macrantha. c, Cypripedium lowii. d, Cattleya labiata.

No. 2513, 25,000d — International Red Cross, 150th anniv.: a, Red Cross workers on battlefield. b, Nurse tending to patient with arm in sling. c, Nurse reading newspaper to man in bed. d, Nurse and children.

No. 2514, 25,000d — Pope Benedict XVI and: a, Tiger Woods lily. b, Easter lily with red and white petals. c, Red ginger lily. d, White Easter lily.

No. 2515, 25,000d — Pope Francis and orchids: a, Cattleya walkeriana. b, Vanda tricolor. c, Odontoglossum nevadense. d, Pescatoria lehmanni.

No. 2516, 25,000d — Mushrooms: a, Hygrocybe punicea. b, Amanita phalloides. c, Suillus grevillei. d, Agaricus campester.

No. 2517, 25,000d — High-speed trains: a, Bombardier TWINDEXX Express, Switzerland. b, Talgo 350, Spain. c, Proposed California bullet train. d, West Japan Railways Series 500.

No. 2518, 25,000d — Fire trucks: a, Scania 93. b, Pierce 105-foot truck with rear mount ladder. c, Scania G82M. d, New South Wales Category 11 truck, Australia.

No. 2519, 25,000d — Rescue vehicles: a, Harley-Davidson Ultra Classic fire motorcycle. b, Severn Class lifeboat. c, Christophorus 12 air ambulance. d, Medic 8 ambulance.

No. 2520, 25,000d — Ships and lighthouses: a, Sailing School Vessel Robert C. Seamans. b, Gulden Leeuw, Bremerhaven Lighthouse, Germany. c, Vittoria Lighthouse, Italy. d, Alexander von Humboldt II, Hellevoetsluis Lighthouse, Netherlands.

No. 2521, 25,000d — French people and items: a, Napoleon Bonaparte (1769-1821), emperor. b, Concorde. c, Charles de Gaulle (1890-1970), president. d, TGV Atlantique.

No. 2522, 25,000d — Paintings in Rijksmuseum, Amsterdam: a, *The Milkmaid*, by Johannes Vermeer, 1658-60. b, *Self-portrait with Felt Hat*, by Vincent van Gogh, 1887. c, *The Square Man*, by Karel Appel, 1951. d, *The Merry Drinker*, by Frans Hals, 1628-30.

No. 2523, 25,000d — Paintings by Paul Cézanne (1839-1906): a, *Nude Woman Standing*, 1899. b, *The Blue Vase*, 1887. c, *Self-portrait*, 1882. d, *Bather*, 1887.

No. 2524, 25,000d — Paintings of nudes: a, *Two Nudes*, by Pablo Picasso, 1906. b, *Nude Woman on Green Cushions*, by Pierre-Auguste Renoir, 1909. c, *Seated Female Nude*, by Amadeo Modigliani, 1916. d, *Adam and Eve*, by Tamara de Lempicka, 1932.

No. 2525, 25,000d — 50th birthday of Garry Kasparov, chess player: a, Viewing chessboard with arms folded. b, Wearing red tie. c, Viewing chessboard with hands on head. d, Standing over chessboard.

No. 2526, 25,000d — Guan Tianlang, golfer: a, Crouching, holding putter. b, Swinging golf club. c, Wearing plaid pants. d, Holding golf ball.

No. 2527, 25,000d — Russian postage stamps, 155th anniv.: a, Russia #2. b, Picture post card depicting Yuri Gagarin wearing helmet. c, Russia Nos. 2, 3, 4, 5, 5a, 6, 7 and 11. d, Russia #5266.

No. 2528, 96,000d, Presley with guitar, diff. No. 2529, 96,000d, Monroe and Academy Award, diff. No. 2530, 96,000d, Lord Robert Baden-Powell in Scouting uniform. No. 2531, 96,000d, Scouting trefoil, Italian greyhound, American Shorthair cat. No. 2532, 96,000d, Rotary International emblem and Dendrobium albosanguineum. No. 2533, 96,000d, Red Cross nurse assisting man with crutches. No. 2534, 96,000d, Pope Benedict XVI and lily, diff. No. 2535, 96,000d, Pope Francis and Cymbidium Valley Regent Reggae. No. 2536, 96,000d, Boletus calopus. No. 2537, 96,000d, Italo high-speed train, Italy. No. 2538, 96,000d, Dennis Sabre fire engine, Kent, England. No. 2539, 96,000d, Tanker 910 fire plane. No. 2540, 96,000d, Split Rock Lighthouse, Minnesota. No. 2541, 96,000d, Concorde, diff. No. 2542, 96,000d, *The Night Watch*, by Rembrandt, 1642. No. 2543, 96,000d, *Self-portrait with Palette*, by Cézanne. No. 2544, 96,000d, *Morning Toilette*, by Lotte Laserstein, 1930. No. 2545, 96,000d, Kasparov, diff. No. 2546, 96,000d, Guan Tianlang, diff. No. 2547, 96,000d, Russia #104, 4589, 4779.

2013, Aug. 15 Litho. *Perf. 13¼*

Sheets of 4, a-d

2508-2527 A371 Set of 20 220.00 220.00

Souvenir Sheets

2528-2547 A371 Set of 20 210.00 210.00

China International Collection Expo, Beijing (Nos. 2526, 2546); Rossica 2013 International Philatelic Exhibition, Moscow (Nos. 2527, 2547).

A372

No. 2548, 25,000d — Wang Yaping, Chinese astronaut: a, Standing in front of capsule wearing space suit. b, At control panel. c, Wearing space suit, waving, parachute in background. d, Waving.

No. 2549, 25,000d — Haroun Tazieff (1914-98), geologist: a, Tazieff and Skutterudite. b, Tungurahua Volcano, Ecuador, andTyrannosaurus rex. c, Karymsky Volcano, Russia, and Pterodactylus. d, Tazieff and Labradorite.

No. 2550, 25,000d — Lions International emblem and: a, Panthera leo, Manis crassicaudata. b, Panthera leo with prey in mouth. c, Panthera leo male, female and cub. d, Male Panthera leo.

No. 2551, 25,000d — Endangered animals: a, Pongo abelii. b, Campephilus principalis. c, Loxodonta africana. d, Lepilemur septentrionalis.

No. 2552, 25,000d — Dolphins: a, Stenella attenuata. b, Lipotes vexillifer. c, Orcaella brevirostris. d, Delphinus delphis.

No. 2553, 25,000d — Birds of prey: a, Pandion haliaetus. b, Strix varia. c, Falco peregrinus. d, Buteo jamaicensis.

No. 2554, 25,000d — Scouting trefoil and parrots: a, Eclectus roratus. b, Ara ararauna. c, Amazona viridigenalis. d, Cacatua alba.

No. 2555, 25,000d — Butterflies and flowers: a, Argynnis paphia, Tulipa gesneriana. b, Danaus plexippus, Hemerocallis. c, Callithea philotima, Alcea setosa. d, Diaethria clymena, Helianthus annuus.

No. 2556, 25,000d — Pope John Paul II: a, Wearing white vestments, St. Peter's Basilica in background. b, Wearing white vestments, doves flying overhead. c, Wearing miter and red robe, doves flying overhead. d, Wearing red robe, St. Peter's Basilica in background.

No. 2557, 25,000d — Nelson Mandela (1918-2013), President of South Africa, and: a, Whitney Houston (1963-2012), singer. b, Princess Diana (1961-97). c, Margaret Thatcher (1925-2013), British Prime Minister. d, Queen Elizabeth II.

No. 2558, 25,000d — Nobel Peace Prize winners: a, Aung San Suu Kyi, 1991. b, Wangari Maathai, 2004. c, Henri Dunant, 1901, and Red Cross flag. d, Dr. Albert Schweitzer, 1952, and Red Cross flag.

No. 2559, 25,000d — James Gandolfini (1961-2013), actor and scenes from: a, *The Sopranos* (with cigar). b, *The Last Castle* (wearing Army uniform). c, *Lonely Hearts* (wearing hat). d, *Cinema Verite* (with beard).

No. 2560, 25,000d — Magnus Carlsen, chess player: a, With knight. b, At chessboard, with hands clasped. c, With knight and queen. d, With Boris Becker, tennis player.

No. 2561, 25,000d — Brasiliana 2013 Intl. Philatelic Exhibition emblem and soccer players: a, David Luiz, Brazil, and Mario Balotelli, Italy. b, Thiago Silva, Brazil, and Shinji Okazaki, Japan. c, Fred, Brazil, and Walter Gargano, Uruguay. d, Marcelo, Brazil, and Giovani Dos Santos, Mexico.

No. 2562, 25,000d — Paintings by Leonardo da Vinci (1452-1519): a, *Lady with an Ermine,* 1489-90. b, *Madonna Litta,* c.1490. c, *Virgin and Child with St. Anne,* 1508. d, *La Belle Ferronière,* 1490-96.

No. 2563, 25,000d — Nude paintings by Peter Paul Rubens (1577-1640): a, *Andromeda,* 1638. b, *Venus at Her Toilet,* 1608. c, *Bathsheba at the Fountain,* 1635. d, *Hélène Fourment,* 1638.

No. 2564, 25,000d — Paintingsby Vincent van Gogh (1853-90): a, *La Mousmé, Sitting,* 1888. b, *Paul Gauguin's Armchair,* 1888. c, *Still Life: Vase with Fifteen Sunflowers,*1889. d, *Café Terrace on the Place du Forum, Arles, at Night,* 1888.

No. 2565, 25,000d — Steam trains: a, Canadian International Limited, Central 4-4-0. b, London, Midlands and Scotland Railway Jubilee locomotive, Somerset & Dorset Railway 4-4-0. c, Indian Railroad 2-8-2, Royal Scot locomotive. d, Paris-Reims Express, South African Railway 4-8-2.

No. 2566, 25,000d — Year of the Horse: a, Horse with front leg lifted. b, Horse bucking. c, Horse in circle of flowers. d, Horse walking to right.

No. 2567, 96,000d, Wang Yaping, diff. No. 2568, 96,000d, Tazieff, Colima Volcano, Mexico. No. 2569, 96,000d, Lions International emblem, Panthera leo chasing prey. No. 2570, 96,000d, Panthera pardus orientalis. No. 2571, 96,000d, Platanista gangetica. No. 2572, 96,000d, Strix varia, diff. No. 2573, 96,000d, Scouting trefoil and Calyptorhynchus lathami. No. 2574, 96,000d, Agrias hewitsonius, Paeonia officinalis. No. 2575, 96,000d, Pope John Paul II and dove. No. 2576, 96,000d, Mandela and Queen Elizabeth II, diff. No. 2577, 96,000d, Dalai Lama, 1989 winner of Nobel Peace Prize. No. 2578, 96,000d, Gandolfini in *The Sopranos,* diff. No. 2579, 96,000d, Carlsen and knight, diff. No. 2580, 96,000d, Brasiliana 2013 emblem, Hulk, Brazil, and Sergio Ramos, Spain. No. 2581, 96,000d, *Mona Lisa,* by Leonardo. No. 2582, 96,000d, *Venus, Cupid, Bacchus and Ceres,* by Rubens. No. 2583, 96,000d, *The Church at Auvers,* by van Gogh. No. 2584, 96,000d, Highland Chief 4-4-2, Flying Scotsman locomotives. No. 2585, 96,000d, Three horses in circle.

2013, Sept. 10 Litho. *Perf. 13¼*

Sheets of 4, #a-d

2548-2566	A372	Set of 19	210.00	210.00

Souvenir Sheets

2567-2585	A372	Set of 19	200.00	200.00

Sports — A373

No. 2586, 19,000d — Cricket players: a, Hashim Amla. b, Michael John Clarke. c, Alastair Cook. d, Sachin Tendulkar.

No. 2587, 19,000d — Table tennis players: a, Timo Boll. b, Ma Long. c, Xu Xin. d, Liu Shiwen.

No. 2588, 75,000d, Cricket ball. No. 2589, 75,000d, Table tennis ball and paddles.

2013, Dec. 10 Litho. *Perf.*

Sheets of 4, #a-d

2586-2587	A373	Set of 2	17.00	17.00

Souvenir Sheets

2588-2589	A373	Set of 2	17.00	17.00

A374

No. 2590, 20,000d — Ursus maritimus: a, Adult walking. b, Adult and juvenile. c, Two adults fighting. d, Adult resting.

No. 2591, 20,000d — Gorillas: a, Adult and juvenile Gorilla gorilla gorilla. b, Adult Gorilla gorilla. c, Adult Gorilla gorilla sitting on rock. d, Adult and juvenile Gorilla beringei beringei.

No. 2592, 20,000d — Marine life: a, Megaptera novaeangliae. b, Makaira nigricans. c, Aluterus scriptus. d, Tursiops truncatus.

No. 2593, 20,000d — Tropical fish: a, Pseudanthias pleurotaenia. b, Ctenochaetus hawaiiensis. c, Ostracion cubicus. d, Symphysodon discus.

No. 2594, 20,000d — Extinct and endangered birds: a, Columba versicolor. b, Rhipidura rufifrons. c, Pyrocephalus rubinus. d, Porphyrio coerulescens.

No. 2595, 20,000d — Mao Zedong (1893-1976), Chinese communist leader: a, With soldiers and peasants, flag at right. b, With young girl. c, Clapping. d, Waving, flag in background.

No. 2596, 20,000d — African trains: a, Blue Train, South Africa. b, Pride of Africa. c, Class 25NC 4-8-4, South Africa. d, Class 19E, South Africa.

No. 2597, 20,000d — Christmas paintings: a, *Adoration of the Shepherds,* by Charles Le Brun. b, *Nativity,* by Piero della Francesca. c, *Nativity,* by Giotto. d, *Nativity,* by Lorenzo Lotto.

No. 2598, 25,000d — 2013 International Track and Field Championships, Moscow: a, Valerie Adams, shot putter, flag of New Zealand. b, LaShawn Merritt, sprinter, flag of U.S. c, Aleksandr Menkov, long jumper, flag of Russia. d, Pawel Fajdek, hammer thrower, flag of Poland.

No. 2599, 25,000d — Owls: a, Tyto capensis. b, Bubo lacteus. c, Otus ireneae. d, Ninox superciliaris.

No. 2600, 25,000d — Scouting trefoil and turtles: a, Batagur trivittata. b, Pseudemys peninsularis. c, Indotestudo elongata. d, Pseudemys rubriventris.

No. 2601, 25,000d — Paintings by Pierre-Auguste Renoir (1841-1919): a, *Gabrielle with Open Blouse,* 1907. b, *Algiers Landscape,* 1895. c, *Anemones,* 1909. d, *After the Bath,* 1888.

No. 2602, 25,000d — Impressionist paintings: a, *Paris Street, Rainy Day,* by Gustave Caillebotte, 1877. b, *Woman with Umbrella,* by Claude Monet, 1875. c, *A Bar at the Folies-Bergère,* by Edouard Manet, 1881-82. d, *The Dance Class,* by Edgar Degas, 1874.

No. 2603, 25,000d — Composers: a, Johann Sebastian Bach (1685-1750). b, Franz Liszt (1811-86). c, Franz Schubert (1797-1828). d, Johannes Brahms (1833-97).

No. 2604, 25,000d — Japanese high-speed trains: a, E5 Series Shinkansen. b, E6 Series Shinkansen. c, 500 Series Shinkansen. d, N700-7000 Series Sakura Shinkansen.

No. 2605, 25,000d — Yuri Gagarin (1934-68), first man in space: a, At left, wearing space helmet. b, Waving. c, Laughing, rocket launch in background. d, At right, wearing space helmet.

No. 2606, 25,000d — Future space flight: a, Space plane with foldable wings. b, Martian lander. c, Asteroid redirection mission. d, Satellite with solar panels at sides.

No. 2607, 79,000d, Ursus maritimus, diff. No. 2608, 79,000d, Gorilla beringei graueri. No. 2609, 79,000d, Sphyrna lewini. No. 2610, 79,000d, Chaetodon capistratus. No. 2611, 79,000d, Vanellus macropterus. No. 2612, 79,000d, Mao Zedong, mountains. No. 2613, 79,000d, Shosholoza Meyl train, South Africa. No. 2614, 79,000d, *Holy Family,* by El Greco. No. 2615, 96,000d, Svetlana Shkolina, high jumper, flag of Russia. No. 2616, 96,000d, Bubo ascalaphus. No. 2617, 96,000d, Scouting trefoil and Leucocephalon yuwonoi. No. 2618, 96,000d, *Self-portrait,* by Renoir, 1876. No. 2619, 96,000d, *Little Italian Street Singer,* by Jean Frédéric Bazille. No. 2620, 96,000d, Joseph Haydn (1732-1809), composer. No. 2621, 96,000d, Series E6 Shinkansen, diff. No. 2622, 96,000d, Gagarin with Valentina Tereshkova, cosmonaut. No. 2623, 96,000d, Mars rocket.

2013, Dec. 10 Litho. *Perf. 13¼*

Sheets of 4, #a-d

2590-2606	A374	Set of 17	175.00	175.00

Souvenir Sheets

2607-2623	A374	Set of 17	170.00	170.00

A375

A376

Personalizable Stamps — A377

2013, Dec. 10 Litho. *Perf. 13¼*

2624	A375	25,000d multi	3.00	3.00

Perf. 12¾

2625	A376	50,000d multi	5.75	5.75

Perf. 13¼x13

2626	A377	150,000d multi	17.00	17.00
		Nos. 2624-2626 (3)	25.75	25.75

Nos. 2624-2626 could be personalized. The stamps exist with a St. Thomas & Prince Islands flag printed in the vignette portion.

Nelson Mandela (1918-2013), President of South Africa — A378

No. 2627 — Mandela wearing: a, Gray suit and tie, b, Yellow and black shirt. c, Dark blue jacket. d, Sports jersey.

96,000d, Black suit jacket with sash.

2014, Jan. 30 Litho. *Perf. 13¼*

2627	A378	25,000d Sheet of 4, #a-d	11.00	11.00

Souvenir Sheet

2628	A378	96,000d multi	10.50	10.50

A379

No. 2629, 25,000d — USS Nautilus: a, With crew on top of submarine, flag painted on bow. b, Aerial view. c, Nuclear reactor. d, Submarine leaving wake.

No. 2630, 25,000d — Charles A. Lindbergh (1902-74), aviator: a, Medal of Honor. b, Spirit of St. Louis in flight. c, Bourguet Airport Statue, U.S. #C10. d, Wearing helmet, Spirit of St. Louis in flight.

No. 2631, 25,000d — Adolphe Sax (1814-94), inventor of saxophone, wearing: a, Blue jacket. b, Green jacket. c, Red vest. d, Purple jacket.

No. 2632, 25,000d — Louis Lumière (1864-1948), first filmmaker: a, With brother, Auguste. b, Operating projector at Eden Theater. c, Inspecting film. d, With Walt Disney.

No. 2633, 25,000d — Charlie Chaplin (1889-1977), film actor: a, In *City Lights,* 1931. b, Behind camera. c, In *One A.M.,* 1916. d, In *The Great Dictator,* 1940.

No. 2634, 25,000d — Dorothy Lamour (1914-96), actress: a, In *Road to Rio,* 1947. b, In front of P-51D Mustang. c, With U.S. flag. d, In *Typhoon,* 1940.

No. 2635, 25,000d — Jawaharlal Nehru (1889-1964), Prime Minister of India, and: a, Queen Elizabeth II. b, Mahatma Gandhi. c, Mother Teresa. d, Albert Einstein.

No. 2636, 25,000d — Ayrton Senna (1960-94), race car driver: a, Wearing cap. b, Wearing racing suit, cars in background. c, Sitting next to helmet. d, Wearing balaclava.

No. 2637, 25,000d — Louis Renault (1877-1944), automobile manufacturer, and: a, Renault Nervastella. b, Renault Type A. c, Renault Type KZ. d, Renault Reinastella.

No. 2638, 25,000d — Eusebio da Silva Ferreira (1942-2014), Brazilian soccer player: a, Preparing to head ball. b, Sitting with ball. c, With Pelé. d, Preparing to kick ball.

No. 2639, 25,000d — 2014 World Cup Soccer Championships, Brazil: a, Purple player. b, Sepia player. c, Green player. d, Blue player.

No. 2640, 25,000d — Opening of Forth Road Bridge, Scotland, 50th anniv: a, Bridge, Sterna paradisaea. b,Queen Elizabeth II, opening of bridge. c, Construction of bridge. d, Bridge under construction, Sterna sandvicensis.

No. 2641, 25,000d — World War I, cent.: a, Bristol F.2b fighter, HMS Caesar, Great Britain. b, Aviatik (Berg) D.I. fighter, SMS Radetzky, Austria-Hungary. c, Sikorsky S-16 fighter, Frunze, Russia. d, Halberstadt CL.IV airplane, SMS Helgoland, Germany.

No. 2642, 25,000d — Paintings by Lavinia Fontana (1552-1614): a, Christ with the Symbols of Passion, 1581. b, Portrait of Constanza Alidosi, 1594. c, Portrait of a Lady with Lap Dog, 1590. d, Holy Family with Saints, 1578.

No. 2643, 25,000d — Paintings by Paul Cézanne (1839-1906): a, Still Life with Apples, 1893-94. b, Self-portrait, 1878-80. c, Pierrot and Harlequin, 1888. d, Fruit and Jug on a Table, 1894.

No. 2644, 25,000d — Paintings by Henri de Toulouse-Lautrec (1864-1901): a, Horsemen Riding in the Bois de Boulogne, 1888. b, Reine de Joie, 1892. c, The Passenger in Cabin 54, 1896. d, Fashionable People at Les Ambassadeurs, 1893.

No. 2645, 25,000d — Paintings by Wassily Kandinsky (1866-1944): a, Cemetery and Vicarage in Kochel, 1909. b, The Singer, 1903. c, Points, 1920. d, Colorful Ensemble, 1938.

No. 2646, 25,000d — Paintings by Henri Matisse (1869-1954): a, Portrait of Madame Matisse, 1905. b, Open Window, Collioure, 1905. c, A Glimpse of Notre Dame in the Late Afternoon, 1902. d, Self-portrait, 1906.

No. 2647, 25,000d — Paintings by Salvador Dalí (1904-89): a, Millet's Architectonic Angelus, 1933. b, Galatea of the Spheres, 1952. c, The Ship, 1943. d, Apparition of Face and Fruit Dish on a Beach, 1938.

No. 2648, 25,000d — Red List of Threatened Species, 50th anniv.: a, Strix uralensis. b, Cyanoramphus unicolor. c, Leontopithecus rosalia. d, Panthera uncia.

No. 2649, 96,000d, USS Nautilus, Adm. Hyman G. Rickover. No. 2650, 96,000d, Lindbergh, route of transatlantic flight. No. 2651, 96,000d, Adolphe Sax and saxophones. No. 2652, 96,000d, Lumiere holding film strip. No. 2653, 96,000d, Chaplin as the Little Tramp. No. 2654, 96,000d, Lamour and Jon Hall in *The Hurricane,* 1937. No. 2655, 96,000d, Nehru and Gandhi, diff. No. 2656, 96,000d, Senna, diff. No. 2657, 96,000d, Renault Type B. No. 2658, 96,000d, Eusebio holding Golden Boot award. No. 2659, 96,000d, Soccer ball, brown player. No. 2660, 96,0000d, Forth Road Bridge, Morus bassanus. No. 2661, 96,000d, Thomas-Morse S-4 airplane, U.S., HIJMS Aki, Japan. No. 2662, 96,000d, Holy Family with St. Catherine of Alexandria, by Fontana, 1581. No. 2663, 96,000d, Madame Cézanne in a Red Armchair, by Cézanne, 1877. No. 2664, 96,000d, Chau U Kao, Chinese Clown, Seated, by Toulouse-Lautrec, 1896. No. 2665, 96,000d, Orange, by Kandinsky, 1923. No. 2666, 96,000d, Woman with a Hat, by Matisse, 1905. No. 2667, 96,000d, The Hallucinogenic Toreador, by Dalí, 1968-70. No. 2668, 96,000d, Tarsius sangirensis.

2014, Mar. 25 Litho. *Perf. 13¼*

Sheets of 4, #a-d

2629-2648 A379 Set of 20 225.00 225.00

Souvenir Sheets

2649-2668 A379 Set of 20 215.00 215.00

Worldwide Fund for Nature (WWF) A380

No. 2669 — Halcyon malimbica: a, Head. b, On horizontal branch, c, On rock. d, In flight.

96,000d, Halcyon malimbica looking over right wing.

2014, Aug. 8 Litho. *Perf. 13x13¼*

2669	Horiz. strip of 4	11.00	11.00
a.-d.	A380 25,000d Any single	2.75	2.75
e.	Souvenir sheet of 4, #2669a-2669d	11.00	11.00
f.	Souvenir sheet of 8, 2 each #2669a-2669d, + central label	22.00	22.00

Souvenir Sheet

Perf. 12¾x13¼

2670 A380 96,000d multi 10.50 10.50

No. 2670 contains one 50x39mm stamp.

2014 World Cup Soccer Championships, Brazil — A381

No. 2671: a, Player kicking ball into net, names of four countries in white. b, Soccer ball, names of four countries in white. c, As "b," names of four countries in blue. d, As "a," names of four countries in blue.

96,000d, World Cup trophy, flags of four countries.

Litho. With Foil Application, Litho. (#2671b, 2671c)

2014, Aug. 8 *Perf. 13¼*

2671 A381 25,000d Sheet of 4, #a-d 11.00 11.00

Souvenir Sheet

2672 A381 96,000d multi 10.50 10.50

A382

No. 2673, 25,000d — Giant Pandas: a, Ailuropoda melanoleuca, bamboo at right. b, Ailuropoda melanoleuca hanging from branch. c, Two Ailuropoda melanoleuca. d, Ailuropoda melanoleuca qinlingensis.

No. 2674, 25,000d — Dolphins: a, Cephalorhynchus hectori. b, Inia geoffrensis. c, Delphinus delphis. d, Platanista gangetica.

No. 2675, 25,000d — Owls: a, Strix nebulosa. b, Bubo scandiacus. c, Bubo bubo. d, Tyto alba.

No. 2676, 25,000d — Eagles: a, Harpia harpyja. b, Haliaeetus leucocephalus. c, Haliaeetus vocifer. d, Pithecophaga jefferyi.

No. 2677, 25,000d — Butterflies: a, Polyommatus icarus. b, Pieris brassicae. c, Delias eucharis. d, Vanessa atalanta, Polyradicion lindenii.

No. 2678, 25,000d — Turtles: a, Clemmys guttata. b, Macroclemys temminckii. c, Trionyx spiniferus. d, Geochelone sulcata.

No. 2679, 25,000d — Dinosaurs: a, Thyreophora. b, Allosaurus. c, Triceratops. d, Pachycephalosaurus.

No. 2680, 25,000d — Orchids: a, Cattleya hardyana. b, Angraecum sesquipedale. c, Burrageara Stefan Isler. d, Dendrobium chrysotoxum.

No. 2681, 25,000d — Mushrooms: a, Pleurotus eryngii. b, Boletus edulis. c, Cantharellus cibarius. d, Flammulina velutipes.

No. 2682, 25,000d — Minerals: a, Stibnite (estibina). b, Rhodochrosite (rodocrosita). c, Hutchinsonite. d, Torbernite.

No. 2683, 25,000d — Deng Xiaoping (1904-97), leader of People's Republic of China: a, Reading, flag in background. b, With Mao Zedong, train and city skyline in background. c, With Mao Zedong and other Chinese officials, flag across table. d, With Pres. Jimmy Carter, map in background.

No. 2684, 25,000d — Canonized popes: a, Pope John Paul II, wearing miter. b, Pope John XXIII, wearing red and white cap. c, Pope John Paul II, wearing zucchetto. d, Pope John XXIII, wearing zucchetto.

No. 2685, 25,000d — Fire engines: a, 1917 Glendale. b, Dennis 4 FJH 324. c, HME 34C. d, Pierce.

No. 2686, 25,000d — Airships: a, NS Airships NS11. b, N-Class ZPG-2. c, Goodyear ZPG-3W (N Class). d, MZ-3A.

No. 2687, 25,000d — Chinese high-speed trains: a, CRH3. b, CRH1, facing left. c, CRH1, facing right. d, CRH2.

No. 2688, 25,000d — Lighthouses: a, Longstone Lighthouse, Great Britain. b, Alexandria Lighthouse, Egypt. c, Portland Head Lighthouse, U.S. d, Bonaire Lighthouse, Caribbean Netherlands.

No. 2689, 25,000d — Worldwide Fund for Nature postage stamps: a, Viet Nam #3392, Cook Islands #1412. b, Hungary #2798, Liechtenstein, #1525h. c, Russia ##5543, Indonesia #1911. d, Russia #6178, Benin #1086c without denomination.

No. 2690, 25,000d — 2014 Winter Olympics, Sochi, Russia: a, Alpine skiing. b, Snowboarding. c, Ice hockey. d, Figure skating.

No. 2691, 96,000d, Ailuropoda melanoleuca rolling with foot up to mouth. No. 2692, 96,000d, Tursiops truncatus. No. 2693, 96,000d, Strix varia. No. 2694, 96,000d, Haliaeetus pelagicus. No. 2695, 96,000d, Aglais urticae. No. 2696, 96,000d, Eretmochelys imbricata. No. 2697, 96,000d, Tyrannosaurus rex. No. 2698, 96,000d, Cattleya aurea statteriana. No. 2699, 96,000d, Leccinum aurantiacum. No. 2700, 96,000d, Galena. No. 2701, 96,000d, Deng Xiaoping, train. No. 2702, 96,000d, Pope John Paul II, wearing miter, diff. No. 2703, 96,000d, Fire truck, diff. No. 2704, 96,000d, Zeppelin NT. No. 2705, 96,000d, CRH2, diff. No. 2706, 96,000d, Tourlitis Lighthouse, Greece. No. 2707, 96,000d, British Guiana #13. No. 2708, 96,000d, Biathlon.

2014, Aug. 8 Litho. *Perf. 13¼*

Sheets of 4, #a-d

2673-2690 A382 Set of 18 195.00 195.00

Souvenir Sheets

2691-2708 A382 Set of 18 185.00 185.00

Nos. 2677, 2680, 2695 and 2698 are impregnated with a floral scent

AIR POST STAMPS

Common Design Type

Inscribed "S. Tomé"

1938 *Perf. 13½x13*

Name and Value in Black

C1	CD39	10c	red orange	62.50	45.00
C2	CD39	20c	purple	30.00	22.50
C3	CD39	50c	orange	3.00	2.50
C4	CD39	1e	ultra	5.25	4.00
C5	CD39	2e	lilac brown	7.75	6.25
C6	CD39	3e	dark green	12.00	8.00
C7	CD39	5e	red brown	15.00	13.00
C8	CD39	9e	rose carmine	17.50	13.00
C9	CD39	10e	magenta	19.00	13.00
			Nos. C1-C9 (9)	172.00	127.25

Common Design Type

Inscribed "S. Tomé e Principe"

1939 Engr. Unwmk.

Name and Value Typo. in Black

C10	CD39	10c	scarlet	.60	.30
C11	CD39	20c	purple	.60	.30
C12	CD39	50c	orange	.60	.30
C13	CD39	1e	deep ultra	.60	.30
C14	CD39	2e	lilac brown	1.75	1.25
C15	CD39	3e	dark green	2.40	1.50
C16	CD39	5e	red brown	3.50	2.10
C17	CD39	9e	rose carmine	6.25	3.00
C18	CD39	10e	magenta	7.25	3.00
			Nos. C10-C18 (9)	23.55	12.05

No. C16 exists with overprint "Exposicao International de Nova York, 1939-1940" and Trylon and Perisphere.

No. 742 Surcharged in Red

Method and Perf As Before

2009, Apr. 15

C21 A95 (45,000d) on 18.50d #742 *5.50 5.50*

Two additional stamps were issued in this set. The editors would like to examine any examples.

POSTAGE DUE STAMPS

"S. Thomé" — D1

1904 Unwmk. Typo. *Perf. 12*

J1	D1	5r	yellow green	.55	.55
J2	D1	10r	slate	.65	.65
J3	D1	20r	yellow brown	.65	.65
J4	D1	30r	orange	1.00	.65
J5	D1	50r	gray brown	1.75	1.40
J6	D1	60r	red brown	2.50	1.60
J7	D1	100r	red lilac	3.00	1.75
J8	D1	130r	dull blue	4.00	3.25
J9	D1	200r	carmine	4.50	3.50
J10	D1	500r	gray violet	8.00	5.00
			Nos. J1-J10 (10)	26.60	19.00

Overprinted in Carmine or Green

1911

J11	D1	5r	yellow green	.30	.30
J12	D1	10r	slate	.30	.30
J13	D1	20r	yellow brown	.30	.30
J14	D1	30r	orange	.30	.30
J15	D1	50r	gray brown	.30	.30
J16	D1	60r	red brown	.65	.65
J17	D1	100r	red lilac	.80	.80
J18	D1	130r	dull blue	.80	.80
J19	D1	200r	carmine (G)	.80	.80
J20	D1	500r	gray violet	1.25	1.25
			Nos. J11-J20 (10)	5.80	5.80

Nos. J1-J10 Overprinted in Black

1913 Without Gum

J21	D1	5r	yellow green	5.00	3.75
J22	D1	10r	slate	6.00	4.50
J23	D1	20r	yellow brown	4.00	2.50

J24 D1 30r orange 4.00 2.50
J25 D1 50r gray brown 4.00 2.50
J26 D1 60r red brown 5.00 3.00
J27 D1 100r red lilac 5.00 4.00
J28 D1 130r dull blue 35.00 35.00
a. Inverted overprint 70.00 70.00
J29 D1 200r carmine 50.00 50.00
J30 D1 500r gray violet 75.00 40.00
Nos. J21-J30 (10) 193.00 147.75

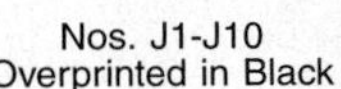
Nos. J1-J10 Overprinted in Black

1913 Without Gum
J31 D1 5r yellow green 5.00 3.00
a. Inverted overprint 50.00 40.00
J32 D1 10r slate 6.00 4.00
J33 D1 20r yellow brown 5.00 3.00
J34 D1 30r orange 5.00 3.00
a. Inverted overprint 55.00
J35 D1 50r gray brown 5.00 3.00
J36 D1 60r red brown 6.00 4.00
J37 D1 100r red lilac 6.00 4.00
J38 D1 130r dull blue 6.00 4.00
J39 D1 200r carmine 7.00 6.00
J40 D1 500r gray violet 17.00 15.00
Nos. J31-J40 (10) 68.00 49.00

No. J5 Overprinted "Republica" in Italic Capitals like Regular Issue in Green

1920 Without Gum
J41 D1 50r gray brn 40.00 35.00

"S. Tomé" — D2

1921 Typo. *Perf. 11½*
J42 D2 ½c yellow green .25 .25
J43 D2 1c slate .25 .25
J44 D2 2c orange brown .25 .25
J45 D2 3c orange .25 .25
J46 D2 5c gray brown .25 .25
J47 D2 6c lt brown .25 .25
J48 D2 10c red violet .25 .25
J49 D2 13c dull blue .25 .25
J50 D2 20c carmine .25 .25
J51 D2 50c gray .35 .40
Nos. J42-J51 (10) 2.60 2.65

In each sheet one stamp is inscribed "S. Thomé" instead of "S. Tomé." Value, set of 10, $60.

Catalogue values for unused stamps in this section, from this point to the end of the section, are for Never Hinged items.

Common Design Type
Photo. & Typo.
1952 Unwmk. *Perf. 14*
Numeral in Red, Frame Multicolored
J52 CD45 10c chocolate .30 .30
J53 CD45 30c red brown .30 .30
J54 CD45 50c dark blue .30 .30
J55 CD45 1e dark blue .50 .50
J56 CD45 2e olive green .75 .75
J57 CD45 5e black brown 2.00 2.00
Nos. J52-J57 (6) 4.15 4.15

NEWSPAPER STAMPS

N1

N2

Perf. 11½, 12½ and 13½
1892 Without Gum Unwmk.
Black Surcharge
P1 N1 2½r on 10r green 95.00 55.00
P2 N1 2½r on 20r rose 125.00 57.50
P3 N2 2½r on 10r green 125.00 57.50
P4 N2 2½r on 20r rose 125.00 57.50
Nos. P1-P4 (4) 470.00 227.50

Green Surcharge
P5 N1 2½r on 5r black 67.50 30.00
P6 N1 2½r on 20r rose 125.00 57.50
P8 N2 2½r on 5r black 125.00 60.00
P9 N2 2½r on 10r green 125.00 62.50
P10 N2 2½r on 20r rose 125.00 77.50
Nos. P5-P10 (5) 567.50 287.50

Both surcharges exist on No. 18 in green.

N3

1893 Typo. *Perf. 11½, 13½*
P12 N3 2½r brown .45 .40

For surcharges and overprints see Nos. 85, 166, 275, P13.

No. P12 Overprinted Type "d" in Blue

1899 Without Gum
P13 N3 2½r brown 30.00 16.00

POSTAL TAX STAMPS

Pombal Issue
Common Design Types
1925 Unwmk. *Perf. 12½*
RA1 CD28 15c orange & black .45 .45
RA2 CD29 15c orange & black .45 .45
RA3 CD30 15c orange & black .45 .45
Nos. RA1-RA3 (3) 1.35 1.35

Certain revenue stamps (5e, 6e, 7e, 8e and other denominations) were surcharged in 1946 "Assistencia," 2 bars and new values (1e or 1.50e) and used as postal tax stamps.

Catalogue values for unused stamps in this section, from this point to the end of the section, are for Never Hinged items.

PT1

1948-58 Typo. *Perf. 12x11½*
Denomination in Black
RA4 PT1 50c yellow grn 4.00 1.10
RA5 PT1 1e carmine rose 4.25 1.50
RA6 PT1 1e emerald ('58) 1.75 .75
RA7 PT1 1.50e bister brown 2.50 1.90
Nos. RA4-RA7 (4) 12.50 5.25

Denominations of 2e and up were used only for revenue purposes. No. RA6 lacks "Colonia de" below coat of arms.

Type of 1958 Surcharged

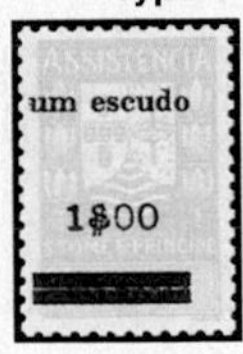
m

n

1964-65 Typo. *Perf. 12x11½*
RA8 PT1(m) 1e on 5e org yel 12.00 12.00
RA9 PT1(n) 1e on 5e org yel ('65) 4.50 4.50

The basic 5e orange yellow does not carry the words "Colonia de."

No. RA6 Surcharged: "Um escudo"
1965
RA10 PT1 1e emerald 2.00 2.00

Type of 1948 Surcharged

1965 Typo. *Perf. 12x11½*
RA11 PT1 1e emerald .75 .75

POSTAL TAX DUE STAMPS

Pombal Issue
Common Design Types
1925 Unwmk. *Perf. 12½*
RAJ1 CD28 30c orange & black .75 .75
RAJ2 CD29 30c orange & black .75 .75
RAJ3 CD30 30c orange & black .75 .75
Nos. RAJ1-RAJ3 (3) 2.25 2.25

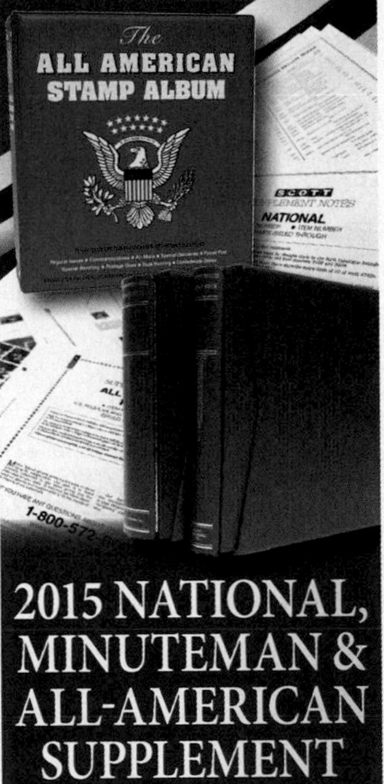

2015 NATIONAL, MINUTEMAN & ALL-AMERICAN SUPPLEMENT

Make sure to get your collection up-to-date with the 2015 Scott National, Minuteman or Minkus All-American Supplement. Don't forget to pick-up one of our classic, durable binders and slipcase.

Retail AA*

SCOTT NATIONAL SUPPLEMENT
United States National 2015 (13 Pages) #83
Item #100S015 $16.99 $13.99

SCOTT MINUTEMAN SUPPLEMENT
United States Minuteman 2015 (14 Pages) #47
Item #180S015 $16.99 $13.99

MINKUS ALL-AMERICAN SUPPLEMENT
2015 Part 1 Reg. & Commems. (14 Pages)
Item #MAA115 $15.99 $12.99

SCOTT SPECIALTY BINDERS & CASES
Large Green 3-RING Binder (Metal Hinge)
Item #ACBR03D $41.99 $34.99
Large Green 3-RING Slipcase
Item #ACSR03 $37.50 $26.99
Large Green 2-SQUARE POST Binder
Item #ACBS03 $54.99 $46.99
Large Green 2-POST Slipcase
Item #ACSS03 $37.50 $26.99
Small Green 3-RING Binder (Metal Hinge)
Item #ACBR01D $41.99 $34.99
Small Green 3-RING Slipcase
Item #ACSR01 $37.50 $26.99

MINKUS BINDER
2.25" Red All-American Binder
Item #MUSAAB $34.99 $19.99

Visit
AmosAdvantage.com
Call
1-800-572-6885
Outside U.S. & Canada 937-498-0800
P.O. Box 4129, Sidney OH 45365

*AA prices apply to paid subscribers of Amos Media publications, or orders placed online. Prices, terms and product availability subject to change. Shipping and handling charges will apply. Taxes will apply in CA, OH & IL.

AMOS ADVANTAGE

ST. VINCENT

sānt 'vin,t,-sənt

LOCATION — Island in the West Indies
GOVT. — Independent state in the British Commonwealth
AREA — 150 sq. mi.
POP. — 120,519 (1999 est.)
CAPITAL — Kingstown

The British colony of St. Vincent became an associated state in 1969 and independent in 1979.

12 Pence = 1 Shilling
20 Shillings = 1 Pound
100 Cents = 1 Dollar (1949)

Catalogue values for unused stamps in this country are for Never Hinged items, beginning with Scott 152 in the regular postage section, Scott B1 in the semi-postal section, and Scott O1 in the officials section.

Values for unused stamps are for examples with original gum as defined in the catalogue introduction. Early stamps were spaced extremely narrowly on the plates, and the perforations were applied irregularly.

Therefore, very fine examples of Nos. 1-28, 30-39 will have perforations that cut into the design slightly on one or more sides. Also, very fine examples of Nos. 40-53, 55-60 will have perforations touching the design on at least one side. These stamps with perfs clear of the design on all four sides, especially Nos. 1-28, 30-39, are extremely scarce and command substantially higher prices.

Watermarks

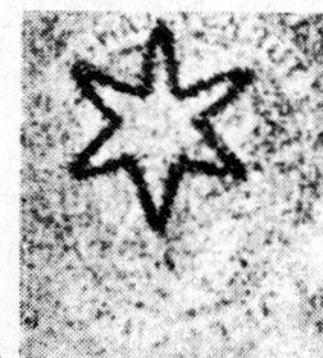

Wmk. 5 — Small Star

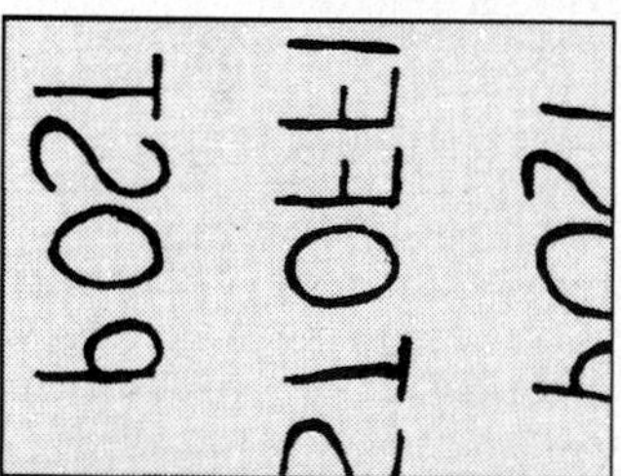

Wmk. 380 — "POST OFFICE"

Queen Victoria — A1

1861 Engr. Unwmk. *Perf. 14 to 16*

1 A1 1p rose *62.50* 20.00
 a. Imperf., pair 300.00
 c. Horiz. pair, imperf. vert. *400.00*
1B A1 6p yellow green *8,250.* 250.00

Perfs on Nos. 1-1B are not clean cut. See Nos. 2-3 for rough perfs.

1862-66 *Rough Perf. 14 to 16*

2 A1 1p rose 55.00 15.50
 a. Horiz. pair, imperf. vert. 400.00
3 A1 6p dark green 65.00 21.00
 a. Imperf., pair 1,250.
 b. Horiz. pair, imperf. between *14,500.* *15,500.*
4 A1 1sh slate ('66) 425.00 160.00
 Nos. 2-4 (3) 545.00 196.50

1863-69 *Perf. 11 to 13*

5 A1 1p rose 45.00 22.50
6 A1 4p blue ('66) 300.00 125.00
 a. Horiz. pair, imperf. vert.
7 A1 4p orange ('69) 400.00 175.00
8 A1 6p deep green 250.00 82.50
8A A1 1sh slate ('66) *2,750.* 1,000.
9 A1 1sh indigo ('69) 425.00 100.00
10 A1 1sh brown ('69) 550.00 175.00

Perf. 11 to 13x14 to 16

11 A1 1p rose *6,500.* 1,250.
12 A1 1sh slate 300.00 140.00

Rough Perf. 14 to 16

1871-78 Wmk. 5

13 A1 1p black 65.00 15.50
 a. Vert. pair, imperf. btwn. *20,000.*
14 A1 6p dk blue green 350.00 77.50
 a. Watermark sideways 100.00

Clean-Cut Perf. 14 to 16

14A A1 1p black 65.00 15.50
14B A1 6p dp bl grn 1,650. 55.00
 c. 6p dull blue green 2,250. 55.00
15 A1 6p pale yel green ('78) 800.00 32.50
15A A1 1sh vermilion ('77) *50,000.*

For surcharge see No. 30.

Perf. 11 to 13

16 A1 4p dk bl ('77) 600.00 110.00
17 A1 1sh dp rose ('72) 825.00 160.00
18 A1 1sh claret ('75) 675.00 300.00

Perf. 11 to 13x14 to 16

20 A1 1p black 95.00 16.50
 a. Horiz. pair, imperf. btwn. *25,000.*
21 A1 6p pale yel grn ('77) 725.00 55.00
22 A1 1sh lilac rose ('72) *6,250.* 400.00
23 A1 1sh vermilion ('77) 1,100. 100.00
 a. Horiz. pair, imperf. vert. —

See Nos. 25-28A, 36-39, 42-53. For surcharges see Nos. 30, 32-33, 40, 55-60.

Victoria A2

Seal of Colony A3

1880-81 *Perf. 11 to 13*

24 A2 ½p org ('81) 8.00 8.75
25 A1 1p gray green 190.00 5.50
26 A1 1p drab ('81) 800.00 15.50
27 A1 4p ultra ('81) 1,350. 130.00
 a. Horiz. pair, imperf. btwn.
28 A1 6p yel grn 550.00 77.50
28A A1 1sh vermilion 900.00 65.00
29 A3 5sh rose 1,275. *1,650.*

No. 29 is valued well centered with design well clear of the perfs.

See Nos. 35, 41, 54, 598. For surcharges see Nos. 31-33.

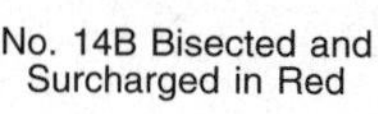

No. 14B Bisected and Surcharged in Red

1880, May *Perf. 14 to 16*

30 A1 1p on half of 6p 600.00 425.00
 a. Unsevered pair *2,250.* *1,350.*

No. 28 Bisected and Surcharged in Red

1881, Sept. 1

31 A1 ½p on half of 6p yel grn ('81) 150. 190.
 a. Unsevered pair 525. 550.
 b. "1" with straight top 1,100.
 c. Without fraction bar, pair, #31, 31c 4,750. *5,500.*

Nos. 28 and 28A Surcharged in Black

c

d

1881, Nov. *Perf. 11 to 13*

32 A1(c) 1p on 6p yel grn 500. 400.
33 A1(d) 4p on 1sh ver 1,850. 925.
 a. 3 mm spacing between "4d" and bar *3,500.* *2,500.*

1883-84 Wmk. 2 *Perf. 12*

35 A2 ½p green ('84) 110.00 40.00
36 A1 4p ultra 825.00 55.00
37 A1 4p dull blue ('84) 2,500. 275.00
38 A1 6p yellow grn 175.00 350.00
39 A1 1sh orange ver 175.00 65.00
 a. Imperf., pair

The ½p orange, 1p rose red, 1p milky blue and 5sh carmine lake were never placed in use. Some authorities believe them to be color trials.

Nos. 35-60 may be found watermarked with single straight line. This is from the frame which encloses each group of 60 watermark designs.

Type of A1 Surcharged in Black — e

1883 *Perf. 14*

40 A1(e) 2½p on 1p lake 27.50 1.75

1883-97

41 A2 ½p green ('85) 1.10 .65
42 A1 1p drab 80.00 3.50
43 A1 1p rose red ('85) 3.00 1.00
44 A1 1p pink ('86) 6.75 1.90
45 A1 2½p brt blue ('97) 10.00 2.25
46 A1 4p ultra 725.00 85.00
47 A1 4p red brn ('85) 1,100. 25.00
48 A1 4p lake brn ('86) 100.00 1.60
49 A1 4p yellow ('93) 2.00 *15.00*
 a. 4p olive yellow *350.00* *350.00*
50 A1 5p gray brn ('97) 8.75 *32.50*
51 A1 6p violet ('88) 225.00 *225.00*
52 A1 6p red violet ('91) 3.00 *25.00*
53 A1 1sh org ver ('91) 6.00 17.50
54 A3 5sh car lake ('88) 32.50 *60.00*
 a. 5sh brown lake 35.00 *60.00*

Grading footnote after No. 29 applies equally to Nos. 54-54a.

For other shades, see the *Scott Classic Catalogue.*

No. 40 Resurcharged in Black

1885, Mar.

55 A1 1p on 2½p on 1p lake 37.50 27.50

Examples with 3-bar cancel are proofs.

Stamps of Type A1 Surcharged in Black or Violet

g

h

j

1890-91

56 A1(e) 2½p on 1p brt blue 2.00 .40
 a. 2½p on 1p milky blue 27.50 9.50
 b. 2½p on 1p gray blue 27.50 .75
57 A1(g) 2½p on 4p vio brn ('90) 90.00 *130.00*
 a. Without fraction bar 475.00 *575.00*

1892-93

58 A1(h) 5p on 4p lake brn (V) 40.00 *55.00*
59 A1(j) 5p on 6p dp lake ('93) *2.00* *1.90*
 a. 5p on 6p carmine lake 22.50 *32.50*
 b. Double surcharge *7,750.* *4,500.*

1897

60 A1(j) 3p on 1p lilac 6.00 *26.50*

Victoria — A13

Numerals of 1sh and 5sh, type A13, and of 2p, 1sh, 5sh and £1, type A14, are in color on plain tablet.

1898 Typo. *Perf. 14*

62 A13 ½p lilac & grn 3.00 3.00
63 A13 1p lil & car rose 5.00 1.70
64 A13 2½p lilac & ultra 6.50 2.25
65 A13 3p lilac & ol grn 4.50 *21.00*
66 A13 4p lilac & org 7.25 *25.00*
67 A13 5p lilac & blk 8.25 *21.00*
68 A13 6p lilac & brn 14.50 *55.00*
69 A13 1sh grn & car rose 18.50 *60.00*
70 A13 5sh green & ultra 100.00 *175.00*
 Nos. 62-70 (9) 167.50 *363.95*

Edward VII — A14

1902

71 A14 ½p violet & green 4.75 .75
72 A14 1p vio & car rose 4.75 .35
73 A14 2p violet & black 6.50 6.00
74 A14 2½p violet & ultra 5.50 4.00
75 A14 3p violet & ol grn 5.50 7.25
76 A14 6p violet & brn 12.00 *45.00*
77 A14 1sh grn & car rose 28.00 *70.00*
78 A14 2sh green & violet 27.50 *65.00*
79 A14 5sh green & ultra 82.50 *140.00*
 Nos. 71-79 (9) 177.00 *338.35*

1904-11 Wmk. 3 Chalky Paper

82 A14 ½p vio & grn 1.50 1.50
83 A14 1p vio & car rose 26.00 1.75
84 A14 2½p vio & ultra 19.00 *52.50*
85 A14 6p vio & brn 19.00 *55.00*
86 A14 1sh grn & car rose 15.50 *17.50*
87 A14 2sh vio & bl, *bl* 25.00 *52.50*
88 A14 5sh grn & red, *yel* 19.00 *55.00*
89 A14 £1 vio & blk, *red* 300.00 *400.00*
 Nos. 82-88 (7) 125.00 *235.75*

#82, 83 and 86 also exist on ordinary paper.

Issued: 1p, 1904, ½p, 6p, 1905; 2½p, 1906; 1sh, 1908; 2sh, 5sh, 1909; £1, July 22, 1911.

"Peace and Justice" — A15

1907 Engr. Ordinary Paper

90 A15 ½p yellow green 4.00 2.75
91 A15 1p carmine 4.25 .25
92 A15 2p orange 1.75 *7.75*
93 A15 2½p ultra 45.00 10.00
94 A15 3p dark violet 9.50 *18.00*
 Nos. 90-94 (5) 64.50 *38.75*

"Peace and Justice" — A16

1909 Without Dot under "d"

95 A16 1p carmine 1.50 .35
96 A16 6p red violet 8.75 *50.00*
97 A16 1sh black, *green* 5.00 *11.00*
Nos. 95-97 (3) 15.25 *61.35*

1909-11 With Dot under "d"

98 A16 ½p yel grn ('10) 2.50 .70
99 A16 1p carmine 4.00 .25
100 A16 2p gray ('11) 6.50 12.00
101 A16 2½p ultra 9.50 4.50
102 A16 3p violet, *yel* 3.00 *14.50*
103 A16 6p red violet 20.00 11.00
Nos. 98-103 (6) 45.50 *42.95*

King George V — A17

1913-17 ***Perf. 14***

104 A17 ½p gray green .45 .25
105 A17 1p carmine 1.00 .90
106 A17 2p slate 3.50 *42.50*
107 A17 2½p ultra .60 .90
108 A17 3p violet, *yellow* 1.00 *7.50*
109 A17 4p red, *yellow* 1.00 *2.40*
110 A17 5p olive green 2.50 *17.00*
111 A17 6p claret 2.50 *5.00*
112 A17 1sh black, *green* 1.75 *4.25*
113 A17 1sh bister ('14) 4.75 *35.00*
114 A16 2sh vio & ultra 5.75 *40.00*
115 A16 5sh dk grn & car 15.00 *60.00*
116 A16 £1 black & vio 110.00 *200.00*
Nos. 104-116 (13) 149.80 *415.70*

Issued: 5p, 11/7; #113, 5/1/14; others, 1/1/13.

For overprints see Nos. MR1-MR2.

No. 112 Surcharged in Carmine

1915

117 A17 1p on 1sh blk, *grn* 11.00 *45.00*
a. "PENNY" & bar double 750.00 725.00
b. Without period 15.00
c. "ONE" omitted 1,550. 1,350.
d. "ONE" double 750.00
e. "PENNY" & bar omitted 1,450.

Space between surcharge lines varies from 8 to 10mm.

1921-32 Wmk. 4

118 A17 ½p green 2.10 .35
119 A17 1p carmine ('21) 1.15 1.00
120 A17 1½p yel brn ('32) 4.00 .25
121 A17 2p gray 3.00 1.00
122 A17 2½p ultra ('26) 1.50 1.75
123 A17 3p ultra 1.15 *7.25*
124 A17 3p vio, *yel* ('27) 1.15 *1.75*
125 A17 4p red, *yel* ('30) 2.10 *7.25*
126 A17 5p olive green 1.15 *7.75*
127 A17 6p claret ('27) 1.75 *4.25*
128 A17 1sh ocher ('27) 4.00 *20.00*
129 A16 2sh brn vio & ultra 9.00 *15.00*
130 A16 5sh dk grn & car 21.00 *37.50*
131 A16 £1 blk & vio ('28) 110.00 *150.00*
Nos. 118-131 (14) 163.05 *255.10*

Common Design Types pictured following the introduction.

Silver Jubilee Issue
Common Design Type

1935, May 6 ***Perf. 11x12***

134 CD301 1p car & dk bl .55 *4.75*
135 CD301 1½p gray blk & ultra 1.40 *4.50*
136 CD301 2½p ultra & brn 2.50 *5.00*
137 CD301 1sh brn vio & ind 5.00 *7.00*
Nos. 134-137 (4) 9.45 *21.25*
Set, never hinged 16.00

Coronation Issue
Common Design Type

1937, May 12 ***Perf. 11x11½***

138 CD302 1p dark purple .25 *1.25*
139 CD302 1½p dark carmine .25 *1.25*
140 CD302 2½p deep ultra .30 *2.25*
Nos. 138-140 (3) .80 *4.75*
Set, never hinged 1.50

Seal of the Colony — A18

Young's Island and Fort Duvernette — A19

Kingstown and Fort Charlotte — A20

Villa Beach — A21

Victoria Park, Kingstown — A22

1938-47 Wmk. 4 ***Perf. 12***

141 A18 ½p grn & brt bl .25 .25
142 A19 1p claret & blue .25 .25
143 A20 1½p scar & lt grn .25 .25
144 A18 2p black & green .30 .25
145 A21 2½p pck bl & ind .25 .25
145A A22 2½p choc & grn ('47) .25 .25
146 A18 3p dk vio & org .25 .25
146A A21 3½p dp bl grn & ind ('47) .40 *2.25*
147 A18 6p claret & blk .70 .40
148 A22 1sh green & vio .70 .75
149 A18 2sh dk vio & brt blue 5.25 1.00
149A A18 2sh6p dp bl & org brn ('47) .95 *4.25*
150 A18 5sh dk grn & car 8.75 3.00
150A A18 10sh choc & dp vio ('47) 7.50 *10.00*
151 A18 £1 black & vio 22.50 *18.00*
Nos. 141-151 (15) 48.55 *41.40*
Set, never hinged 55.00

Issue date: Mar. 11, 1938.

See Nos. 156-169, 180-184.

Catalogue values for unused stamps in this section, from this point to the end of the section, are for Never Hinged items.

Peace Issue
Common Design Type

1946, Oct. 15 Engr. ***Perf. 13½x14***

152 CD303 1½p carmine .25 .25
153 CD303 3½p deep blue .25 .25

Silver Wedding Issue
Common Design Types

1948, Nov. 30 Photo. ***Perf. 14x14½***

154 CD304 1½p scarlet .25 .25

Engraved; Name Typographed
Perf. 11½x11

155 CD305 £1 red violet 27.50 *30.00*

Types of 1938

1949, Mar. 26 Engr. ***Perf. 12***

156 A18 1c grn & brt bl .25 *1.75*
157 A19 2c claret & bl .25 *.50*
158 A20 3c scar & lt grn .55 *1.00*
159 A18 4c gray blk & grn .40 .25
160 A22 5c choc & grn .25 .25
161 A18 6c dk vio & org .55 *1.25*
162 A21 7c pck blue & ind 5.50 1.50
163 A18 12c claret & blk .50 .25
164 A22 24c green & vio .50 .55
165 A18 48c dk vio & brt bl 4.50 *6.00*
166 A18 60c dp bl & org brn 2.00 *5.50*
167 A18 $1.20 dk grn & car 4.75 4.75
168 A18 $2.40 choc & dp vio 6.75 *10.00*
169 A18 $4.80 gray blk & vio 13.00 *20.00*
Nos. 156-169 (14) 39.75 *53.55*

For overprints see Nos. 176-179.

UPU Issue
Common Design Types
Engr.; Name Typo. on 6c, 12c
Perf. 13½, 11x11½

1949, Oct. 10 Wmk. 4

170 CD306 5c blue .25 .25
171 CD307 6c dp rose violet .55 2.00
172 CD308 12c red lilac .30 2.00
173 CD309 24c blue green 1.10 .80
Nos. 170-173 (4) 2.20 *5.05*

University Issue
Common Design Types

1951, Feb. 16 Engr. ***Perf. 14x14½***

174 CD310 3c red & blue green .50 .65
175 CD311 12c rose lilac & blk .50 *1.50*

Nos. 158-160 and 163 Overprinted in Black

1951, Sept. 21 ***Perf. 12***

176 A20 3c scarlet & lt grn .30 *1.60*
177 A18 4c gray blk & grn .30 .60
178 A22 5c chocolate & grn .30 .60
179 A18 12c claret & blk .95 *1.25*
Nos. 176-179 (4) 1.85 *4.05*

Adoption of a new constitution for the Windward Islands, 1951.

Type of 1938-47

1952

180 A18 1c gray black & green .30 *2.25*
181 A18 3c dk violet & orange .30 *2.25*
182 A18 4c green & brt blue .30 .25
183 A20 6c scarlet & dp green .30 *2.00*
184 A21 10c peacock blue & ind .45 .35
Nos. 180-184 (5) 1.65 *7.10*

Coronation Issue
Common Design Type

1953, June 2 ***Perf. 13½x13***

185 CD312 4c dk green & blk .50 .30

Elizabeth II — A23

Seal of Colony — A24

Perf. 13x14

1955, Sept. 16 Wmk. 4 Engr.

186 A23 1c orange .25 .25
187 A23 2c violet blue .25 .25
188 A23 3c gray .25 .25
189 A23 4c dk red brown .25 .25
190 A23 5c scarlet .25 .25
191 A23 10c purple .45 .25
192 A23 15c deep blue .70 1.00
193 A23 20c green .85 .25
194 A23 25c brown black 1.50 .25

Perf. 14

195 A24 50c chocolate 9.25 3.25
196 A24 $1 dull green 15.00 2.10
197 A24 $2.50 deep blue 15.00 15.00
Nos. 186-197 (12) 44.00 23.35

See Nos. 205-213.

West Indies Federation
Common Design Type
Perf. 11½x11

1958, Apr. 22 Wmk. 314

198 CD313 3c green .30 .25
199 CD313 6c blue .40 1.00
200 CD313 12c carmine rose .80 .50
Nos. 198-200 (3) 1.50 1.75

Freedom from Hunger Issue
Common Design Type

1963, June 4 Photo. ***Perf. 14x14½***

201 CD314 8c lilac .90 .50

Red Cross Centenary Issue
Common Design Type

1963, Sept. 2 Litho. ***Perf. 13***

202 CD315 4c black & red .25 .25
203 CD315 8c ultra & red .65 .65

Types of 1955
Perf. 13x14

1964-65 Wmk. 314 Engr.

205 A23 1c orange .25 .25
206 A23 2c violet blue .25 .25
207 A23 3c gray .55 *.60*
208 A23 5c scarlet .30 .30
209 A23 10c purple .45 .45
a. Perf. 12½ .25 .25
210 A23 15c deep blue 1.00 .80
a. Perf. 12½ .45 .30
211 A23 20c green .70 *.75*
a. Perf. 12½ 5.00 2.00
212 A23 25c brown black 1.25 *1.35*
a. Perf. 12½ .80 1.25

Perf. 14

213 A24 50c chocolate ('65) 5.75 5.50
a. Perf. 12½ 5.00 7.00
Nos. 205-213 (9) 10.50 10.25

Scout Emblem and Merit Badges — A25

1964, Nov. 23 Litho. ***Perf. 14***

216 A25 1c dk brn & brt yel grn .25 .25
217 A25 4c dk red brn & brt bl .25 .25
218 A25 20c dk vio & org .30 .25
219 A25 50c green & red .45 .60
Nos. 216-219 (4) 1.25 1.35

Boy Scouts of St. Vincent, 50th anniv.

Breadfruit and Capt. Bligh's Ship "Providence" — A26

Designs: 1c, Tropical fruit. 25c, Doric temple and pond, vert. 40c, Blooming talipot palm and Doric temple, vert.

Perf. 14½x13½, 13½x14½

1965, Mar. 23 Photo. Wmk. 314

220 A26 1c dk green & multi .25 .25
221 A26 4c lt & dk brn grn & yel .25 .25
222 A26 25c blue, grn & bister .25 .25
223 A26 40c dk blue & multi .30 1.10
Nos. 220-223 (4) 1.05 1.85

Bicentenary of the Botanic Gardens.

ITU Issue
Common Design Type

1965, May 17 Litho. ***Perf. 11x11½***

224 CD317 4c blue & yel grn .25 .25
225 CD317 48c yellow & orange .55 .65

Boat Building, Bequia A27

Woman Carrying Bananas — A28

Designs: 2c, Friendship Beach, Bequia. 3c, Terminal building. 5c, Crater Lake. 6c, Rock carvings, Carib Stone. 8c, Arrowroot. 10c, Owia saltpond. 12c, Ship at deep water wharf. 20c, Sea Island cotton. 25c, Map of St. Vincent and neighboring islands. 50c, Breadfruit. $1, Baleine Falls. $2.50, St. Vincent parrot. $5, Coat of arms.

Perf. 14x13½, 13½x14

1965-67 Photo. Wmk. 314

226	A27	1c	(BEQUIA)	.25	.75
226A	A27	1c	(BEQUIA)	.60	.35
227	A27	2c	lt ultra, grn, yel & red	.25	.25
228	A27	3c	red, yel & brn	.40	.25
229	A28	4c	brn, ultra & yel	.75	.35
a.			Wmkd. sideways	.50	.25
230	A27	5c	pur, bl, yel & grn	.25	.25
231	A28	6c	sl grn, yel & gray	.25	.30
232	A28	8c	pur, yel & grn	.40	.25
233	A27	10c	org brn, yel & bluish grn	.40	.25
234	A27	12c	grnsh bl, yel & pink	.65	.25
235	A28	20c	brt yel, grn, pur & brn	.40	.25
236	A28	25c	ultra, grn & vio blue	.45	.25
237	A28	50c	grn, yel & bl	.45	.35
238	A28	$1	vio bl, lt grn & dk sl grn	4.00	.45
239	A28	$2.50	pale lilac & multi	19.00	8.50
240	A28	$5	dull vio blue & multi	4.25	10.50
			Nos. 226-240 (16)	32.75	23.55

Issued: No. 226A, 8/8/67; others, 8/16/65.
For overprint see No. 270.

Churchill Memorial Issue
Common Design Type

1966, Jan. 24 ***Perf. 14***

Design in Black, Gold and Carmine Rose

241	CD319	1c	bright blue	.25	.25
242	CD319	4c	green	.25	.25
243	CD319	20c	brown	.35	.35
244	CD319	40c	violet	.65	.90
			Nos. 241-244 (4)	1.50	1.75

Royal Visit Issue
Common Design Type

1966, Feb. 4 Litho. ***Perf. 11x12***

Portrait in Black

245	CD320	4c	violet blue	.50	.25
246	CD320	25c	dk carmine rose	2.25	1.10

WHO Headquarters Issue
Common Design Type

1966, Sept. 20 Litho. ***Perf. 14***

247	CD322	4c	multicolored	.25	.25
248	CD322	25c	multicolored	.90	.80

UNESCO Anniversary Issue
Common Design Type

1966, Dec. 1 Litho. ***Perf. 14***

249	CD323	4c	"Education"	.25	.25
250	CD323	8c	"Science"	.45	.25
251	CD323	25c	"Culture"	1.60	.85
			Nos. 249-251 (3)	2.30	1.35

View of Mt. Coke Area
A29

Designs: 8c, Kingstown Methodist Church. 25c, First license to perform marriage, May 15, 1867. 35c, Arms of Conference of the Methodist Church in the Caribbean and the Americas.

Perf. 14x14½

1967, Dec. 1 Photo. Wmk. 314

252	A29	2c	multicolored	.25	.25
253	A29	8c	multicolored	.25	.25
254	A29	25c	multicolored	.25	.25
255	A29	35c	multicolored	.25	.25
			Nos. 252-255 (4)	1.00	1.00

Attainment of autonomy by the Methodist Church in the Caribbean and the Americas, and opening of headquarters near St. John's, Antigua, May 1967.
For overprints see Nos. 268-269, 271.

Caribbean Meteorological Institute, Barbados — A30

Perf. 14x14½

1968, June 28 Photo. Wmk. 314

256	A30	4c	cerise & multi	.25	.25
257	A30	25c	vermilion & multi	.25	.25
258	A30	35c	violet blue & multi	.25	.25
			Nos. 256-258 (3)	.75	.75

Issued for World Meteorological Day.

Martin Luther King, Jr. and Cotton Pickers
A31

Perf. 13½x13

1968, Aug. 28 Litho. Wmk. 314

259	A31	5c	violet & multi	.25	.25
260	A31	25c	gray & multi	.25	.25
261	A31	35c	brown red & multi	.25	.25
			Nos. 259-261 (3)	.75	.75

Dr. Martin Luther King, Jr. (1929-68), American civil rights leader.

Scales of Justice and Human Rights Flame — A32

3c, Speaker addressing demonstrators, horiz.

Perf. 13x14, 14x13

1968, Nov. 1 Photo. Unwmk.

262	A32	3c	orange & multi	.25	.25
263	A32	35c	grnsh blue & vio blue	.25	.25

International Human Rights Year.

"Strength in Unity" — A34

Carnival Costume — A33

5c, Sketch of a steel bandsman. 8c, Revelers, horiz. 25c, Queen of Bands & attendants.

1969, Feb. 17 Litho. ***Perf. 14½***

264	A33	1c	multicolored	.25	.25
265	A33	5c	red & dark brown	.25	.25
266	A33	8c	multicolored	.25	.25
267	A33	25c	multicolored	.25	.25
			Nos. 264-267 (4)	1.00	1.00

St. Vincent Carnival celebration, Feb. 17.

Nos. 252-253, 236 and 255 Overprinted: "METHODIST / CONFERENCE / MAY / 1969"

Perf. 14x14½, 13½x14

1969, May 14 Photo. Wmk. 314

268	A29	2c	multicolored	.25	.25
269	A29	8c	multicolored	.25	.25
270	A28	25c	multicolored	.25	.25
271	A29	35c	multicolored	1.00	*2.00*
			Nos. 268-271 (4)	1.75	2.75

1st Caribbean Methodist Conf. held outside Antigua.

5c, 25c, Map of the Caribbean, vert.

Perf. 13½x13, 13x13½

1969, July 1 Litho.

272	A34	2c	orange, yel & blk	.25	.25
273	A34	5c	lilac & multi	.25	.25
274	A34	8c	emerald, yel & blk	.25	.25
275	A34	25c	blue & multi	.25	.25
			Nos. 272-275 (4)	1.00	1.00

1st anniv. of CARIFTA (Caribbean Free Trade Area.)

Flag and Arms of St. Vincent — A35

Designs: 10c, Uprising of 1795. 50c, Government House.

Perf. 14x14½

1969, Oct. 27 Photo. Wmk. 314

276	A35	4c	deep ultra & multi	.25	.25
277	A35	10c	olive & multi	.25	.25
278	A35	50c	orange, gray & blk	.75	.50
			Nos. 276-278 (3)	1.25	1.00

Green Heron
A36

Birds: ½c, House wren, vert. 2c, Bullfinches. 3c, St. Vincent parrots. 4c, St. Vincent solitaire, vert. 5c, Scalynecked pigeon, vert. 6c, Bananaquits. 8c, Purple-throated Carib. 10c, Mangrove cuckoo, vert. 12c, Black hawk, vert. 20c, Bare-eyed thrush. 25c, Hooded tanager. 50c, Blue-hooded euphonia. $1, Barn owl, vert. $2.50, Yellow-bellied elaenia, vert. $5, Ruddy quail-dove.

Wmk. 314 Upright on ½c, 4c, 5c, 10c, 12c, 50c, $5, Sideways on Others

1970, Jan. 12 Photo. ***Perf. 14***

279	A36	½c	multicolored	.25	.25
280	A36	1c	multicolored	.25	.25
281	A36	2c	multicolored	.25	.25
282	A36	3c	multicolored	.25	.25
283	A36	4c	multicolored	.25	.25
284	A36	5c	multicolored	1.25	.65
285	A36	6c	multicolored	.40	.35
286	A36	8c	multicolored	.40	.25
287	A36	10c	multicolored	.45	.35
288	A36	12c	multicolored	.60	.40
289	A36	20c	multicolored	.80	.50
290	A36	25c	multicolored	.80	.50
291	A36	50c	multicolored	1.25	.75
292	A36	$1	multicolored	3.00	1.50
293	A36	$2.50	multicolored	6.00	4.00
294	A36	$5	multicolored	14.00	10.00
			Nos. 279-294 (16)	30.20	20.50

See Nos. 379-381. For surcharges see Nos. 364-366, 3239, 3242, 3265.

Wmk. 314 Upright on 2c, 3c, 6c, 20c, Sideways on Others

1973

281a	A36	2c	multicolored	.35	*.45*
282a	A36	3c	multicolored	.35	*.45*
283a	A36	4c	multicolored	.35	.40
284a	A36	5c	multicolored	.35	.30
285a	A36	6c	multicolored	.50	*.65*
287a	A36	10c	multicolored	.50	.30
288a	A36	12c	multicolored	.75	.65
289a	A36	20c	multicolored	.85	.40
			Nos. 281a-289a (8)	4.00	3.60

DHC6 Twin Otter
A37

20th anniv. of regular air services: 8c, Grumman Goose amphibian. 10c, Hawker Siddeley 748. 25c, Douglas DC-3.

Perf. 14x13

1970, Mar. 13 Litho. Wmk. 314

295	A37	5c	lt blue & multi	.25	.25
296	A37	8c	lt green & multi	.25	.25
297	A37	10c	pink & multi	.35	.25
298	A37	25c	yellow & multi	.75	.65
			Nos. 295-298 (4)	1.60	1.40

Nurse and Children
A38

Red Cross and: 5c, First aid. 12c, Volunteers. 25c, Blood transfusion.

1970, June 1 Photo. ***Perf. 14***

299	A38	3c	blue & multi	.25	.25
300	A38	5c	yellow & multi	.25	.25
301	A38	12c	lt green & multi	.35	.25
302	A38	25c	pale salmon & multi	.65	.55
			Nos. 299-302 (4)	1.50	1.30

Centenary of British Red Cross Society.

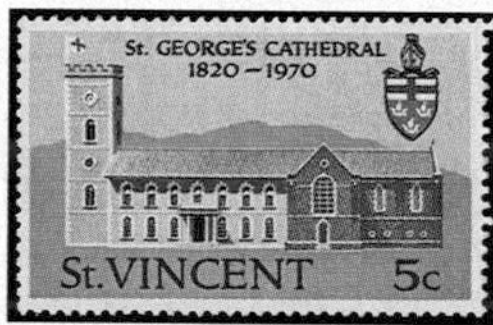

St. George's Cathedral — A39

Designs: ½c, 50c, Angel and Two Marys at the Tomb, stained glass window, vert. 25c, St. George's Cathedral, front view, vert. 35c, Interior with altar.

Perf. 14x14½, 14½x14

1970, Sept. 7 Litho. Wmk. 314

303	A39	½c	multicolored	.25	.25
304	A39	5c	multicolored	.25	.25
305	A39	25c	multicolored	.25	.25
306	A39	35c	multicolored	.25	.25
307	A39	50c	multicolored	.25	.30
			Nos. 303-307 (5)	1.25	1.30

St. George's Anglican Cathedral, 150th anniv.

Virgin and Child, by Giovanni Bellini — A40

Christmas: 25c, 50c, Adoration of the Shepherds, by Louis Le Nain, horiz.

1970, Nov. 23 Litho. Wmk. 314

308	A40	8c	brt violet & multi	.25	.25
309	A40	25c	crimson & multi	.25	.25
310	A40	35c	yellow grn & multi	.25	.25
311	A40	50c	sapphire & multi	.25	.25
			Nos. 308-311 (4)	1.00	1.00

Post Office and St. Vincent No. 1B
A41

New Post Office and: 4c, $1, St. Vincent No. 1. 25c, as 2c.

1971, Mar. 29 ***Perf. 14½x14***

312	A41	2c	violet & multi	.25	.25
313	A41	4c	olive & multi	.25	.25
314	A41	25c	brown org & multi	.25	.25
315	A41	$1	lt green & multi	.25	.45
			Nos. 312-315 (4)	1.00	1.20

110th anniv. of 1st stamps of St. Vincent.

National Trust Emblem, Fish and Birds — A42

Designs: 30c, 45c, Cannon at Ft. Charlotte.

Perf. 13½x14

1971, Aug. 4 Litho. Wmk. 314

316 A42 12c emerald & multi	.25	.80
317 A42 30c lt blue & multi	.35	.35
318 A42 40c brt pink & multi	.50	.40
319 A42 45c black & multi	.70	1.00
Nos. 316-319 (4)	1.80	2.55

Publicity for the National Trust (for conservation of wild life and historic buildings).

Holy Family with Angels (detail), by Pietro da Cortona A43

Christmas: 5c, 25c, Madonna Appearing to St. Anthony, by Domenico Tiepolo, vert.

1971, Oct. 6 *Perf. 14x14½, 14½x14*

320 A43 5c rose & multi	.25	.25
321 A43 10c lt green & multi	.25	.25
322 A43 25c lt blue & multi	.25	.25
323 A43 $1 yellow & multi	.25	.45
Nos. 320-323 (4)	1.00	1.20

Careening A44

Designs: 5c, 20c, Seine fishermen. 6c, 50c, Map of Grenadines. 15c, as 1c.

1971, Nov. 25 *Perf. 14x13½*

324 A44 1c dp ver & multi	.25	.25
325 A44 5c blue & multi	.25	.25
326 A44 6c yel grn & multi	.25	.25
327 A44 15c org brn & multi	.25	.25
328 A44 20c yellow & multi	.25	.30
329 A44 50c blue, blk & plum	.50	1.00
a. Souvenir sheet of 6, #324-329	11.00	11.00
Nos. 324-329 (6)	1.75	2.30

The Grenadines of St. Vincent tourist issue.

Grenadier Company Private, 1764 — A45

Designs: 30c, Battalion Company officer, 1772. 50c, Grenadier Company private, 1772.

1972, Feb. 14 *Perf. 14x13½*

330 A45 12c gray violet & multi	.30	.30
331 A45 30c gray blue & multi	.80	.50
332 A45 50c dark gray & multi	1.40	1.25
Nos. 330-332 (3)	2.50	2.05

Breadnut — A46

1972, May 16 Litho. *Perf. 14x13½*

333 A46 3c shown	.25	.35
334 A46 5c Papaya	.25	.25
335 A46 12c Rose apples	.30	.40
336 A46 25c Mangoes	.80	.75
Nos. 333-336 (4)	1.60	1.75

Flowers of St. Vincent — A47

1972, July 31 Litho. *Perf. 13½x13*

337 A47 1c Candlestick Cassia	.25	.25
338 A47 30c Lobster claw	.30	.30
339 A47 40c White trumpet	.35	.35
340 A47 $1 Flowers, Soufriere tree	.90	1.10
Nos. 337-340 (4)	1.80	2.00

For surcharge see No. 3266.

Sir Charles Brisbane, Family Arms — A48

Designs: 30c, Sailing ship "Arethusa." $1, Sailing ship "Blake."

1972, Sept. 29 Wmk. 314 *Perf. 13½*

341 A48 20c yel, brn & gold	.30	.30
342 A48 30c lilac & multi	.30	.30
343 A48 $1 multicolored	1.15	1.25
a. Souvenir sheet of 3, #341-343	6.50	6.50
Nos. 341-343 (3)	1.75	1.85

Bicentenary of the birth of Sir Charles Brisbane, naval hero, governor of St. Vincent.

Silver Wedding Issue, 1972
Common Design Type

Design: Queen Elizabeth II, Prince Philip, arrowroot plant, breadfruit foliage and fruit.

1972, Nov. 20 Photo. *Perf. 14x14½*

344 CD324 30c rose brn & multi	.25	.25
345 CD324 $1 multicolored	.30	.30

Columbus Sighting St. Vincent — A49

12c, Caribs watching Columbus' ships. 30c, Christopher Columbus. 50c, Santa Maria.

1973, Jan. 18 Litho. *Perf. 13*

346 A49 5c multicolored	.25	.30
347 A49 12c multicolored	.25	.45
348 A49 30c multicolored	.70	.75
349 A49 50c multicolored	1.40	2.25
Nos. 346-349 (4)	2.60	3.75

475th anniversary of Columbus's Third Voyage to the West Indies.

The Last Supper — A50

Perf. 14x13½

1973, Apr. 19 Litho. Wmk. 314

350 15c red & multi	.25	.25
351 60c red & multi	.25	.25
352 $1 red & multi	.30	.30
a. A50 Strip of 3, #350-352	.80	.80

Easter.

William Wilberforce and Slave Auction Poster — A51

40c, Slaves working on sugar plantation. 50c, Wilberforce & medal commemorating 1st anniversary of abolition of slavery.

1973, July 11 *Perf. 14x13½*

353 A51 30c multicolored	.25	.25
354 A51 40c multicolored	.25	.25
355 A51 50c multicolored	.30	.30
Nos. 353-355 (3)	.80	.80

140th anniv. of the death of William Wilberforce (1759-1833), member of British Parliament who fought for abolition of slavery.

Families — A52

Design: 40c, Families and "IPPF."

1973, Oct. 3 *Perf. 14½*

356 A52 12c multicolored	.25	.25
357 A52 40c multicolored	.25	.25

Intl. Planned Parenthood Assoc., 21st anniv.

Princess Anne's Wedding Issue
Common Design Type

1973, Nov. 14 *Perf. 14*

358 CD325 50c slate & multi	.25	.25
359 CD325 70c gray green & multi	.25	.25

Administration Buildings, Mona University — A53

Designs: 10c, University Center, Kingstown. 30c, Mona University, aerial view. $1, Coat of arms of University of West Indies.

1973, Dec. 13 *Perf. 14½x14, 14x14½*

360 A53 5c multicolored	.25	.25
361 A53 10c multicolored	.25	.25
362 A53 30c multicolored	.25	.25
363 A53 $1 multicolored	.25	.50
Nos. 360-363 (4)	1.00	1.25

University of the West Indies, 25th anniv.

Nos. 291, 286 and 292 Surcharged

1973, Dec. 15 Photo. *Perf. 14*

364 A36 30c on 50c multi	.25	1.00
365 A36 40c on 8c multi	.35	.35
366 A36 $10 on $1 multi	8.50	8.50
Nos. 364-366 (3)	9.10	9.85

The position of the surcharge and shape of obliterating bars differs on each denomination.

Descent from the Cross — A54

Easter: 30c, Descent from the Cross. 40c, Pietà. $1, Resurrection. Designs are from sculptures in Victoria and Albert Museum, London, and Provincial Museum, Valladolid (40c).

1974, Apr. 10 Litho. *Perf. 13½x13*

367 A54 5c multicolored	.25	.25
368 A54 30c multicolored	.25	.25
369 A54 40c multicolored	.25	.25
370 A54 $1 multicolored	.25	.25
Nos. 367-370 (4)	1.00	1.00

"Istra" A55

1974, June 28 *Perf. 14½*

371 A55 15c shown	.25	.25
372 A55 20c "Oceanic"	.25	.25
373 A55 30c "Alexander Pushkin"	.30	.25
374 A55 $1 "Europa"	.80	1.10
a. Souvenir sheet of 4, #371-374	1.75	1.75
Nos. 371-374 (4)	1.60	1.85

Cruise ships visiting Kingstown.

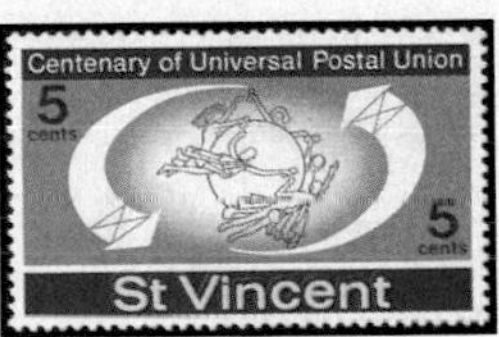

Arrows Circling UPU Emblem A56

UPU, cent.: 12c, Post horn and globe. 60c, Target over map of islands, hand canceler. 90c, Goode's map projection.

1974, July 25 *Perf. 14½*

375 A56 5c violet & multi	.25	.25
376 A56 12c ocher, green & blue	.25	.25
377 A56 60c blue green & multi	.25	.25
378 A56 90c red & multi	.25	.30
Nos. 375-378 (4)	1.00	1.05

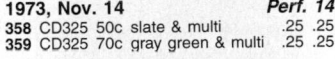

Bird Type of 1970

Birds: 30c, Royal tern. 40c, Brown pelican, vert. $10, Magnificent frigate bird, vert.

Wmk. 314 Sideways on 40c, $10, Upright on 30c

1974, Aug. 29 Litho. *Perf. 14½*

379 A36 30c multicolored 2.00 .75
380 A36 40c multicolored 2.00 .75
381 A36 $10 multicolored 13.00 10.00
Nos. 379-381 (3) 17.00 11.50

Scout Emblem and Badges — A57

Perf. 13½x14

1974, Oct. 9 Wmk. 314

385 A57 10c lilac & multi .25 .25
386 A57 25c bister & multi .25 .25
387 A57 45c gray & multi .35 .30
388 A57 $1 multicolored .65 1.10
Nos. 385-388 (4) 1.50 1.90

St. Vincent Boy Scouts, 60th anniversary.

Churchill as Prime Minister — A58

Designs (Churchill as): 35c, Lord Warden of the Cinque Ports. 45c, First Lord of the Admiralty. $1, Royal Air Force officer.

1974, Nov. 28 *Perf. 14½x14*

389 A58 25c multicolored .25 .25
390 A58 35c multicolored .25 .25
391 A58 45c multicolored .25 .25
392 A58 $1 multicolored .25 .45
Nos. 389-392 (4) 1.00 1.20

Sir Winston Churchill (1874-1965), birth centenary. Sheets of 30 in 2 panes of 15 with inscribed gutter between.

A59 A60

1974, Dec. 5 *Perf. 12x12½*

393 A59 3c like 8c .25 .25
394 A59 3c like 35c .25 .25
395 A60 3c like 45c .25 .25
396 A60 3c like $1 .25 .25
a. Strip of 4, #393-396 .25 .25
397 A59 8c Shepherds .25 .25
398 A59 35c Virgin, Child and Star .25 .25
399 A60 45c St. Joseph, Ass & Ox .25 .25
400 A60 $1 Three Kings .25 .40
Nos. 393-400 (8) 2.00 2.15

Christmas. Nos. 396a, 397-400 have continuous picture.

Giant Mask and Dancers — A61

Designs: 15c, Pineapple dancers. 25c, Giant bouquet. 35c, Girl dancers. 45c, Butterfly dancers. $1.25, Sun and moon dancers and float.

Wmk. 314

1975, Feb. 7 Litho. *Perf. 14*

401 A61 1c multicolored .25 .25
a. Bklt. pane of 2 + label .30
b. Bklt. pane of 3, #401, 403, 405 .75
402 A61 15c multicolored .25 .25
a. Bklt. pane of 3, #402, 404, 406 1.75
403 A61 25c multicolored .25 .25
404 A61 35c multicolored .25 .25
405 A61 45c multicolored .25 .25
406 A61 $1.25 multicolored .25 .45
a. Souvenir sheet of 6, #401-406 1.75 1.75
Nos. 401-406 (6) 1.50 1.70

Kingstown carnival 1975.

French Angelfish — A62

Type I

Type II

Two types of $2.50:
I — Line to fish's mouth.
II — Line removed (1976).

Fish and whales — 2c, Spotfin butter-flyfish. 3c, Horse-eyed jack. 4c, Mackerel. 5c, French grunts. 6c, Spotted goatfish. 8c, Ballyhoos. 10c, Sperm whale. 12c, Humpback whale. 15c, Cowfish. 20c, Queen angelfish. 25c, Princess parrotfish. 35c, Red hind. 45c, Atlantic flying fish. 50c, Porkfish. $1, Queen triggerfish. $2.50, Sailfish. $5, Dolphinfish. $10, Blue marlin.

Wmk. 373

1975, Apr. 10 Litho. *Perf. 14*

407 A62 1c shown .25 .50
408 A62 2c multicolored .25 .75
409 A62 3c multicolored .25 .45
410 A62 4c multicolored .25 .25
411 A62 5c multicolored .25 .35
412 A62 6c multicolored .25 .75
413 A62 8c multicolored .25 2.00
414 A62 10c multicolored .50 .25
415 A62 12c multicolored .50 1.75
416 A62 15c multicolored 1.25 1.75
417 A62 20c multicolored .30 .25
418 A62 25c multicolored .35 .25
419 A62 35c multicolored .60 2.00
420 A62 45c multicolored .60 .90
421 A62 50c multicolored .70 2.25
422 A62 $1 multicolored 1.50 .90
423 A62 $2.50 Type I 3.25 2.25
a. Type II 3.00 1.25
424 A62 $5 multicolored 7.00 4.00
425 A62 $10 multicolored 12.00 8.50
Nos. 407-425 (19) 30.30 30.10

The 4c, 10c, 20c, $1, were reissued with "1976" below design; 1c, 2c, 3c, 5c, 6c, 8c, 12c, 50c, $10, with "1977" below design; 10c with "1978" below design.

No. 423a issued 7/12/76.

See Nos. 472-474. For surcharges and overprints see Nos. 463-464, 499-500, 502-503, 572-581, 584-586.

Cutting Bananas — A63

Banana industry: 35c, La Croix packing station. 45c, Women cleaning and packing bananas. 70c, Freighter loading bananas.

1975, June 26 Wmk. 314 *Perf. 14*

426 A63 25c blue & multi .25 .25
427 A63 35c blue & multi .25 .25
428 A63 45c carmine & multi .25 .25
429 A63 70c carmine & multi .30 .30
Nos. 426-429 (4) 1.05 1.05

Snorkel Diving — A64

Designs: 20c, Aquaduct Golf Course. 35c, Steel band at Mariner's Inn. 45c, Sunbathing at Young Island. $1.25, Yachting marina.

Wmk. 373

1975, July 31 Litho. *Perf. 13½*

430 A64 15c multicolored .30 .25
431 A64 20c multicolored .65 .65
432 A64 35c multicolored .95 .40
433 A64 45c multicolored .95 .40
434 A64 $1.25 multicolored 2.25 2.00
Nos. 430-434 (5) 5.10 3.70

Tourist publicity.
For surcharge see No. 3302.

Presidents Washington, John Adams, Jefferson and Madison — A65

U.S. Presidents: 1c, Monroe, John Quincy Adams, Jackson, Van Buren. 1½c, Wm. Harrison, Tyler, Polk, Taylor. 5c, Fillmore, Pierce, Buchanan, Lincoln. 10c, Johnson, Grant, Hayes, Garfield. 25c, Arthur, Cleveland, Benjamin Harrison, McKinley. 35c, Theodore Roosevelt, Taft, Wilson, Harding. 45c, Coolidge, Hoover, Franklin D. Roosevelt, Truman. $1, Eisenhower, Kennedy, Lyndon B. Johnson, Nixon. $2, Ford and White House.

1975, Sept. 11 Unwmk. *Perf. 14½*

435 A65 ½c violet & blk .25 .25
436 A65 1c green & black .25 .25
437 A65 1½c rose lilac & blk .25 .25
438 A65 5c yellow grn & blk .25 .25
439 A65 10c ultra & blk .25 .25
440 A65 25c ocher & blk .25 .25
441 A65 35c brt blue & blk .25 .25
442 A65 45c carmine & blk .25 .25
443 A65 $1 orange & blk .25 .35
444 A65 $2 lt olive & blk .25 .65
a. Souvenir sheet of 10, #435-444 + 2 labels 2.75 2.75
Nos. 435-444 (10) 2.50 3.00

Bicentenary of American Independence. Each issued in sheets of 10 stamps and 2 labels picturing the White House, Capitol, Mt. Vernon, etc.

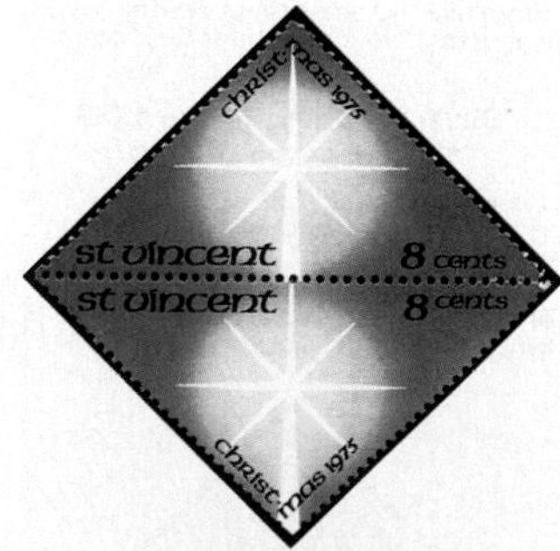

Nativity — A66

No. 445a, 8c, Star of Bethlehem. No. 445b, 45c, Shepherds. No. 445c, $1, Kings. No. 445d, 35c, Nativity.

Se-tenant Pairs, #a.-b.

a. — Top stamp.

b. — Bottom stamp.

Wmk. 314

1975, Dec. 4 Litho. *Perf. 14*

445 A66 3c Triangular block of 4, #a.-d. .55 .45
446 A66 8c Pair, #a.-b. .25 .25
447 A66 35c Pair, #a.-b. .45 .25
448 A66 45c Pair, #a.-b. .45 .30
449 A66 $1 Pair, #a.-b. .75 .60
Nos. 445-449 (5) 2.45 1.85

Christmas. No. 445 has continuous design.

Carnival Costumes — A68

Designs: 2c, Humpty-Dumpty people. 5c, Smiling faces (masks). 35c, Dragon worshippers. 45c, Duck costume. $1.25, Bumble bee dance.

Perf. 13x13½

1976, Feb. 19 Litho. Wmk. 373

457 A68 1c carmine & multi .25 .25
a. Bklt pane of 2, #457-458 + label .25
458 A68 2c black & multi .25 .25
a. Bklt. pane of 3, #458-460 .60
459 A68 5c lt blue & multi .25 .25
460 A68 35c lt blue & multi .25 .25
a. Bklt. pane of 3, #460-462 2.00
461 A68 45c black & multi .25 .25
462 A68 $1.25 carmine & multi .30 .30
Nos. 457-462 (6) 1.55 1.55

Kingstown carnival 1976.

Nos. 409 and 421 Surcharged with New Value and Bar

1976, Apr. 8 Wmk. 314 *Perf. 14*

463 A62 70c on 3c multi .65 *1.00*
464 A62 90c on 50c multi .65 *1.25*

Yellow Hibiscus and Blue-headed Hummingbird A69

Designs: 10c, Single pink hibiscus and crested hummingbird. 35c, Single white hibiscus and purple-throated carib. 45c, Common red hibiscus and blue-headed hummingbird. $1.25, Single peach hibiscus and green-throated carib.

1976, May 20 Litho. Wmk. 373

465 A69 5c multicolored .25 .25
466 A69 10c multicolored .35 .30
467 A69 35c multicolored 1.15 1.00
468 A69 45c multicolored 1.75 1.50
469 A69 $1.25 multicolored 5.50 4.00
Nos. 465-469 (5) 9.00 7.05

Map of West Indies, Bats, Wicket and Ball A69a

Prudential Cup — A69b

1976, Sept. 16 Unwmk. *Perf. 14*

470 A69a 15c lt blue & multi .60 .30
471 A69b 45c lilac rose & blk 1.40 1.00

World Cricket Cup, won by West Indies Team, 1975.

Fish Type of 1975

1976, Oct. 14 Wmk. 373 *Perf. 14*

472 A62 15c Skipjack 3.50 2.50
473 A62 70c Albacore 6.50 3.25
474 A62 90c Pompano 6.50 .70
Nos. 472-474 (3) 16.50 6.45

The 15c exists dated "1977."
For overprints see Nos. 501, 582-583.

St. Mary's R.C. Church, Kingstown — A70

Christmas: 45c, Anglican Church, Georgetown. 50c, Methodist Church, Georgetown. $1.25, St. George's Anglican Cathedral, Kingstown.

1976, Nov. 18 Litho. *Perf. 14*

475 A70 35c multicolored .25 .25
476 A70 45c multicolored .25 .25
477 A70 50c multicolored .25 .25
478 A70 $1.25 multicolored .30 .55
Nos. 475-478 (4) 1.05 1.30

For surcharge see No. 3303.

Barrancoid Pot-stand, c. 450 A.D. — A71

Designs (National Trust Emblem and): 45c, National Museum. 70c, Carib stone head, c. 1510. $1, Ciboney petroglyph, c. 4000 B.C.

1976, Dec. 16 *Perf. 13½*

479 A71 5c multicolored .25 .25
480 A71 45c multicolored .25 .25
481 A71 70c multicolored .25 .25
482 A71 $1 multicolored .25 .45
Nos. 479-482 (4) 1.00 1.20

Carib Indian art and establishment of National Museum in Botanical Gardens, Kingstown.
For surcharges see Nos. 3256, 3290.

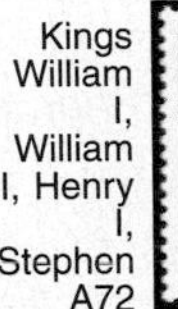

Kings William I, William II, Henry I, Stephen A72

Kings and Queens of England: 1c, Henry II, Richard I, John, Henry III. 1½c, Edward I, II, III, Richard II. 2c, Henry IV, V, VI, Edward IV. 5c, Edward V, Richard III, Henry VII, VIII. 10c, Edward VI, Lady Jane Grey, Mary I, Elizabeth I. 25c, James I, Charles I, II, James II. 35c, William III, Mary II, Anne, George I. 45c, George II, III, IV. 75c, William IV, Victoria, Edward VII. $1, George V, Edward VIII, George VI. $2, Elizabeth II, coronation.

Wmk. 373

1977, Feb. 7 Litho. *Perf. 13½*

483 A72 ½c multicolored .25 .25
a. Bklt. pane of 4, #483-486 3.00
484 A72 1c multicolored .25 .25
485 A72 1½c multicolored .25 .25
486 A72 2c multicolored .25 .25
487 A72 5c multicolored .25 .25
a. Bklt. pane of 4, #487-490 3.00
488 A72 10c multicolored .25 .25
489 A72 25c multicolored .25 .25
490 A72 35c multicolored .25 .25
491 A72 45c multicolored .25 .25
a. Bklt. pane of 4, #491-494 3.00
492 A72 75c multicolored .25 .25
493 A72 $1 multicolored .25 .35
494 A72 $2 multicolored .25 .50
a. Souv. sheet of 12, #483-494, perf. 14½x14 2.25 3.00
Nos. 483-494 (12) 3.00 3.35

25th anniv. of the reign of Elizabeth II.
Nos. 483a, 487a and 491a are unwmkd.
See No. 508.

Bishop Alfred P. Berkeley, Bishop's Miters — A73

15c, Grant of Arms to Bishopric, 1951, & names of former Bishops. 45c, Coat of arms & map of Diocese. $1.25, Interior of St. George's Anglican Cathedral & Bishop G. C. M. Woodroffe.

Wmk. 373

1977, May 12 Litho. *Perf. 13½*

495 A73 15c multicolored .25 .25
496 A73 35c multicolored .25 .25
497 A73 45c multicolored .25 .25
498 A73 $1.25 multicolored .25 .50
Nos. 495-498 (4) 1.00 1.25

Diocese of the Windward Islands, centenary.
For surcharge see No. 3304.

Nos. 411, 414, 472, 417, 422 Overprinted in Black or Red: "CARNIVAL 1977/ JUNE 25TH - JULY 5TH"

1977, June 2 Litho. *Perf. 14*

499 A62 5c multi .25 .25
500 A62 10c multi (R) .25 .25
501 A62 15c multi (R) .25 .25
502 A62 20c multi (R) .25 .25
503 A62 $1 multi .50 .50
Nos. 499-503 (5) 1.50 1.50

St. Vincent Carnival, June 25-July 5.
5c, 15c dated "1977," 10c, 20c, $1 "1976."

Girl Guide and Emblem — A74

Designs: 15c, Early Guide's uniform, Ranger, Brownie and Guide. 20c, Guide uniforms, 1917 and 1977. $2, Lady Baden-Powell, World Chief Guide, 1930-1977.

Wmk. 373

1977, Sept. 1 Litho. *Perf. 13½*

504 A74 5c multicolored .25 .25
505 A74 15c multicolored .25 .25
506 A74 20c multicolored .25 .25
507 A74 $2 multicolored .30 .75
Nos. 504-507 (4) 1.05 1.50

St. Vincent Girl Guides, 50th anniversary.

No. 494 with Additional Inscription: "CARIBBEAN / VISIT 1977"

1977, Oct. 27

508 A72 $2 multicolored .50 .50

Caribbean visit of Queen Elizabeth II.

"While Shepherds Watched" A75

Christmas: 10c, "Fear not" said He. 15c, David's Town. 25c, The Heavenly Babe. 50c, Thus Spake and Seraph. $1.25, All Glory be to God.

1977, Nov. Litho. *Perf. 13x11*

509 A75 5c buff & multi .25 .25
510 A75 10c buff & multi .25 .25
511 A75 15c buff & multi .25 .25
512 A75 25c buff & multi .25 .25
513 A75 50c buff & multi .25 .25
514 A75 $1.25 buff & multi .25 *.60*
a. Souv. sheet, #509-514, perf. 13½ 1.50 *1.60*
Nos. 509-514 (6) 1.50 1.85

Map of St. Vincent — A76

Perf. 14½x14

1977-78 Litho. Wmk. 373

515 A76 20c dk bl & lt bl ('78) .25 .25
516 A76 40c salmon & black .30 .30
517 A76 40c car, sal & ocher ('78) .25 .25
Nos. 515-517 (3) .80 .80

Issued: #516, 11/30; #515, 517, 1/31.
For types surcharged see Nos. B1-B4, AR1-AR3.

Painted Lady and Bougainvillea — A77

Butterflies and Bougainvillea: 25c, Silver spot. 40c, Red anartia. 50c, Mimic. $1.25, Giant hairstreak.

1978, Apr. 6 Litho. *Perf. 14*

523 A77 5c multicolored .25 .25
524 A77 25c multicolored .50 .25
525 A77 40c multicolored .65 .25
526 A77 50c multicolored .70 .25
527 A77 $1.25 multicolored 1.40 .85
Nos. 523-527 (5) 3.50 1.85

For surcharges see Nos. 3259, 3306-3308.

Westminster Abbey — A78

Cathedral: 50c, Gloucester. $1.25, Durham. $2.50, Exeter.

Perf. 13x13½

1978, June 2 Litho. Wmk. 373

528 A78 40c multicolored .25 .25
529 A78 50c multicolored .25 .25
530 A78 $1.25 multicolored .25 .25
531 A78 $2.50 multicolored .25 .25
a. Souv. sheet, #528-531, perf. 13½x14 .75 *1.00*
Nos. 528-531 (4) 1.00 1.00

25th anniv. of coronation of Queen Elizabeth II. Nos. 528-531 issued in sheets of 10.
Nos. 528-531 also exist in booklet panes of two.

Rotary Emblem A79

Emblems: 50c, Lions Intl. $1, Jaycees.

Wmk. 373

1978, July 13 Litho. *Perf. 14½*

532 A79 40c brown & multi .25 .25
533 A79 50c dark green & multi .25 .25
534 A79 $1 crimson & multi .35 .45
Nos. 532-534 (3) .85 .95

Service clubs aiding in development of St. Vincent.
For surcharge see No. 3296.

Flags of Ontario and St. Vincent, Teacher A80

Design: 40c, Flags of St. Vincent and Ontario, teacher pointing to board, vert.

1978, Sept. 7 Litho. *Perf. 14*

535 A80 40c multicolored .25 .25
536 A80 $2 multicolored .40 *.60*

School to School Project between children of Ontario, Canada, and St. Vincent, 10th anniversary.

Arnos Vale Airport A81

40c, Wilbur Wright landing Flyer I. 50c, Flyer I airborne. $1.25, Orville Wright and Flyer I.

1978, Oct. 19 *Perf. 14½*

537 A81 10c multicolored .25 .25
538 A81 40c multicolored .25 .25
539 A81 50c multicolored .25 .25
540 A81 $1.25 multicolored .30 .70
Nos. 537-540 (4) 1.05 1.45

75th anniversary of 1st powered flight.
For overprint see No. 568.

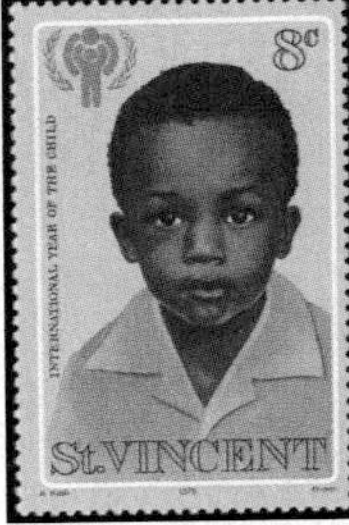

Vincentian Boy, IYC Emblem — A82

Children and IYC Emblem: 20c, Girl. 50c, Boy. $2, Girl and boy.

1979, Feb. 14 Litho. *Perf. 14x13½*

541 A82 8c multicolored .25 .25
542 A82 20c multicolored .25 .25
543 A82 50c multicolored .25 .30
544 A82 $2 multicolored .25 .50
Nos. 541-544 (4) 1.00 1.30

International Year of the Child.
For surcharge see No. 3262.

Rowland Hill A83

50c, Great Britain #1-2. $3, St. Vincent #1-1B.

1979, May 31 Litho. *Perf. 14*

545 A83 40c multicolored .25 .25
546 A83 50c multicolored .25 .25
547 A83 $3 multicolored .40 .90
a. Souvenir sheet of 6 1.50 2.25
Nos. 545-547 (3) .90 1.40

Sir Rowland Hill (1795-1879), originator of penny postage.
No. 547a contains Nos. 545-547 and Nos. 560, 561 and 565.

Buccament Cancellations, Map of St. Vincent — A84

Cancellations and location of village.

1979, Sept. 1 Litho. *Perf. 14*

548	A84	1c shown	.25	.25
549	A84	2c Sion Hill	.25	.25
550	A84	3c Cumberland	.25	.40
551	A84	4c Questelles	.25	.30
552	A84	5c Layou	.25	.25
553	A84	6c New Ground	.25	.25
554	A84	8c Mesopotamia	.25	.25
555	A84	10c Troumaca	.25	.25
556	A84	12c Arnos Vale	.25	.30
557	A84	15c Stubbs	.25	.30
558	A84	20c Orange Hill	.25	.30
559	A84	25c Calliaqua	.25	.25
560	A84	40c Edinboro	.25	.25
561	A84	50c Colonarie	.25	.25
562	A84	80c Babou St. Vincent	.40	.35
563	A84	$1 Chateaubelair	.40	.50
564	A84	$2 Kingstown	.50	*.80*
565	A84	$3 Barrouallie	.55	*1.25*
566	A84	$5 Georgetown	.75	*2.00*
567	A84	$10 Kingstown	1.75	*4.00*
		Nos. 548-567 (20)	7.85	12.75

See No. 547a.

The 5c, 10c, 25c reissued inscribed 1982. Singles of #562-564 from #601a are inscribed 1980.

No. 537 Overprinted in Red: "ST. VINCENT AND THE GRENADINES AIR SERVICE 1979"

1979, Aug. 6 Litho. *Perf. 14½*

568	A81	10c multicolored	.40	.40

St. Vincent and Grenadines air service inauguration.

Independent State

St. Vincent Flag, Ixora Coccinea A85

Designs: 50c, House of Assembly, ixora stricta. 80c, Prime Minister R. Milton Cato.

1979, Oct. 27 *Perf. 12½x12*

569	A85	20c multi + label	.25	.25
570	A85	50c multi + label	.25	.25
571	A85	80c multi + label	.40	.25
		Nos. 569-571 (3)	.90	.75

Independence of St. Vincent.

Nos. 407, 410-416, 418, 421, 473-474, 422-423, 425 Overprinted in Black: "INDEPENDENCE 1979"

1979, Oct. 27 Litho. *Perf. 14½*

572	A62	1c multicolored	.25	.25
573	A62	4c multicolored	.25	.25
574	A62	5c multicolored	.25	.25
575	A62	6c multicolored	.25	.25
576	A62	8c multicolored	.25	.25
577	A62	10c multicolored	.25	.25
578	A62	12c multicolored	.25	.25
579	A62	15c multicolored	.25	.25
580	A62	25c multicolored	.25	.25
581	A62	50c multicolored	.40	.30
582	A62	70c multicolored	.70	.35
583	A62	90c multicolored	.70	.40
584	A62	$1 multicolored	.70	.40
585	A62	$2.50 multicolored	.90	1.00
586	A62	$10 multicolored	2.00	*4.75*
		Nos. 572-586 (15)	7.65	9.45

Silent Night Text, Virgin and Child A86

Silent Night Text and: 20c, Infant Jesus and angels. 25c, Shepherds. 40c, Angel. 50c, Angels holding Jesus. $2, Nativity.

1979, Nov. 1 *Perf. 13½x14*

587	A86	10c multicolored	.25	.25
588	A86	20c multicolored	.25	.25
589	A86	25c multicolored	.25	.25
590	A86	40c multicolored	.25	.25
591	A86	50c multicolored	.25	.25
592	A86	$2 multicolored	.25	.40
a.		Souvenir sheet of 6, #587-592	1.10	*1.25*
		Nos. 587-592 (6)	1.50	1.65

Christmas.

Oleander and Wasp — A87

Oleander and Insects: 10c, Beetle. 25c, Praying mantis. 50c, Green guava beetle. $2, Citrus weevil.

1979, Dec. 13 Litho. *Perf. 14*

593	A87	5c multicolored	.25	.25
594	A87	10c multicolored	.25	.25
595	A87	25c multicolored	.25	.25
596	A87	50c multicolored	.25	.25
597	A87	$2 multicolored	.50	.50
		Nos. 593-597 (5)	1.50	1.50

Type of 1880
Souvenir Sheet

1980, Feb. 28 Litho. *Perf. 14x13½*

598		Sheet of 3	1.00	1.00
a.		A3 50c brown	.25	.25
b.		A3 $1 dark green	.25	.25
c.		A3 $2 dark blue	.50	.50

Coat of arms stamps centenary; London 1980 Intl. Stamp Exhibition, May 6-14.

London '80 Intl. Stamp Exhibition, May 6-14 — A88

Wmk. 373

1980, Apr. 24 Litho. *Perf. 14*

599	A88	80c Queen Elizabeth II	.25	.25
600	A88	$1 GB #297, SV #190	.25	.25
601	A88	$2 Unissued stamp, 1971	.50	.60
a.		Souv. sheet, #562-564, 599-601	1.00	*1.75*
		Nos. 599-601 (3)	1.00	1.10

Steel Band A89

a, shown. b, Drummers, dancers.

1980, June 12 Litho. *Perf. 14*

602	A89	20c Pair, #a.-b.	.35	*.75*

Kingstown Carnival, July 7-8.

Soccer, Olympic Rings — A90

1980, Aug. 7 *Perf. 13½*

604	A90	10c shown	.25	.25
605	A90	60c Bicycling	.25	.25
606	A90	80c Women's basketball	.30	.40
607	A90	$2.50 Boxing	.30	*1.10*
		Nos. 604-607 (4)	1.10	2.00

Sport for all.

For surcharges see Nos. 3264, 3278, B5-B8.

Agouti A91

1980, Oct. 2 Litho. *Perf. 14x14½*

608	A91	25c shown	.25	.25
609	A91	50c Giant toad	.25	.25
610	A91	$2 Mongoose	.50	.60
		Nos. 608-610 (3)	1.00	1.10

Map of North Atlantic showing St. Vincent — A92

Maps showing St. Vincent: 10c, World. $1, Caribbean. $2, St. Vincent, sail boats, plane.

1980, Dec. 4 Litho. *Perf. 13½x14*

611	A92	10c multicolored	.25	.25
612	A92	50c multicolored	.25	.25
613	A92	$1 multicolored	.25	.25
614	A92	$2 multicolored	.50	.30
a.		Souv. sheet of 1, perf. 14	.90	.90
		Nos. 611-614 (4)	1.25	1.05

Ville de Paris in Battle of the Saints, 1782 — A93

60c, Ramillies lost in storm, 1782. $1.50, Providence, 1793. $2, Mail Packet Dee, 1840.

Wmk. 373

1981, Feb. 19 Litho. *Perf. 14*

615	A93	50c shown	.35	.25
616	A93	60c multicolored	.45	.40
617	A93	$1.50 multicolored	1.25	1.25
618	A93	$2 multicolored	1.50	1.50
		Nos. 615-618 (4)	3.55	3.40

For surcharges see Nos. 3262A, 3279, 3318.

A94

No. 619a, Arrowroot processing. No. 619b, Arrowroot Cultivation. No. 620a, Banana packing plant. No. 620b, Banana cultivation. No. 621a, Copra drying frames. No. 621b, Coconut plantation. No. 622a, Cocoa beans. No. 622b, Cocoa cultivation.

Wmk. 373

1981, May 21 Litho. *Perf. 14*

619	A94	25c Pair, #a.-b.	.25	.40
620	A94	50c Pair, #a.-b.	.35	.60
621	A94	60c Pair, #a.-b.	.35	.60
622	A94	$1 Pair, #a.-b.	.55	1.00
		Nos. 619-622 (4)	1.50	2.60

For surcharge see No. 3297.

Prince Charles, Lady Diana, Royal Yacht Charlotte — A94a

Prince Charles and Lady Diana — A94b

Wmk. 380

1981, July 13 Litho. *Perf. 14*

627	A94a	60c Couple, Isabella	.25	.25
a.		Bklt. pane of 4, perf. 12	.60	
628	A94b	60c Couple	.25	.25
629	A94a	$2.50 Alberta	.60	.60
630	A94b	$2.50 like #628	.70	.70
a.		Bklt. pane of 2, perf. 12	1.00	
631	A94a	$4 Britannia	1.25	1.25
632	A94b	$4 like #628	1.50	1.50
		Nos. 627-632 (6)	4.55	4.55

Royal wedding. Each denomination issued in sheets of 7 (6 type A94a, 1 type A94b).

For surcharges and overprints see Nos. 891-892, O1-O6.

Souvenir Sheet

1981 Litho. *Perf. 12*

632A	A95b	$5 Couple	1.25	1.25

Kingstown General Post Office — A95

Wmk. 373

1981, Sept. 1 Litho. *Perf. 14*

633	A95	$2 Pair, #a.-b.	1.25	*1.90*

UPU membership centenary.

First Anniv. of UN Membership A96

Wmk. 373

1981, Sept. 1 Litho. *Perf. 14*

634A	A96	$1.50 Flags	.30	.30
634B	A96	$2.50 Prime Minister Cato	.50	.55

"The People that Walked in Darkness . . ." — A97

1981, Nov. 19 Litho. *Perf. 12*

635 A97 50c shown .25 .25
636 A97 60c Angel .25 .25
637 A97 $1 "My soul . . ." .25 .25
638 A97 $2 Flight into Egypt .35 .35
a. Souvenir sheet of 4, #635-638 1.25 *1.50*
Nos. 635-638 (4) 1.10 1.10

Christmas. For surcharges see Nos. 674, 3280, 3298, 3320-3321.

Re-introduction of Sugar Industry, First Anniv. — A98

1982, Apr. 5 Litho. *Perf. 14*

639 A98 50c Boilers .25 .25
640 A98 60c Drying plant .25 .25
641 A98 $1.50 Gearwheels .45 .65
642 A98 $2 Loading sugar cane .80 1.00
Nos. 639-642 (4) 1.75 2.15

For surcharges see Nos. 3251, 3260, 3263, 3281, 3322.

50th Anniv. of Airmail Service A99

50c, DH Moth, 1932. 60c, Grumman Goose, 1952. $1.50, Hawker-Siddeley 748, 1968. $2, Britten-Norman Islander, 1982.

1982, July 29 Litho. *Perf. 14*

643 A99 50c multicolored .60 .45
644 A99 60c multicolored .75 .50
645 A99 $1.50 multicolored 1.75 *1.90*
646 A99 $2 multicolored 2.40 *2.50*
Nos. 643-646 (4) 5.50 *5.35*

For surcharges see Nos. 3260A, 3309.

21st Birthday of Princess Diana, July 1 — A99a

Wmk. 380

1982, June Litho. *Perf. 14*

647 A99a 50c Augusta of Saxe, 1736 .30 .30
648 A99a 60c Saxe arms .35 .35
649 A99a $6 Diana 1.60 1.60
Nos. 647-649 (3) 2.25 2.25

For overprints see Nos. 652-654.

Scouting Year — A100

1982, July 15 Wmk. 373

650 A100 $1.50 Emblem .75 *1.00*
651 A100 $2.50 "75" 1.10 *1.75*

For overprints see Nos. 890, 893.

Nos. 647-649 Overprinted: "ROYAL BABY"

1982, July Wmk. 380

652 A99a 50c multicolored .25 .30
653 A99a 60c multicolored .25 .30
654 A99a $6 multicolored .75 *1.40*
Nos. 652-654 (3) 1.25 2.00

Birth of Prince William of Wales, June 21.

Carnival A101

50c, Butterfly float. 60c, Angel dancer, vert. $1.50, Winged dancer, vert. $2, Eagle float.

1982, June 10 Litho. *Perf. 13½*

655 A101 50c multicolored .25 .25
656 A101 60c multicolored .35 .35
657 A101 $1.50 multicolored .70 .80
658 A101 $2 multicolored .90 1.25
Nos. 655-658 (4) 2.20 2.65

Cruise Ships A103

Wmk. 373

1982, Dec. 29 Litho. *Perf. 14*

662 A103 45c Geestport .35 .35
663 A103 60c Stella Oceanis .45 .45
664 A103 $1.50 Victoria 1.10 1.40
665 A103 $2 QE 2 1.30 1.90
Nos. 662-665 (4) 3.20 4.10

For surcharges see Nos. 3310, 3324-3325.

Pseudocorynactis Caribbeorum — A104

Sea Horses and Anemones — 60c, Actinoporus elegans. $1.50, Arachnanthus nocturnus. $2, Hippocampus reidi.
60c, $1.50, $2 vert.

1983, Jan. 12 Wmk. 373 *Perf. 12*

666 A104 50c shown .90 .90
667 A104 60c multicolored 1.10 1.10
668 A104 $1.50 multicolored 1.90 2.10
669 A104 $2 multicolored 2.10 2.25
Nos. 666-669 (4) 6.00 6.35

For overprint see No. 886. For surcharges see Nos. 3282, 3311, 3326.

Commonwealth Day — A104a

45c, Map. 60c, Flag. $1.50, Prime Minister Cato. $2, Banana industry.

Wmk. 373

1983, Mar. 14 Litho. *Perf. 14*

670 A104a 45c multi .35 .25
671 A104a 60c multi .35 .35
672 A104a $1.50 multi .55 .65
673 A104a $2 multi .80 .90
Nos. 670-673 (4) 2.05 2.15

For surcharge see No. 3252.

No. 635 Surcharged

Wmk. 373

1983, Apr. 26 Litho. *Perf. 12*

674 A97 45c on 50c multi .45 .35

A104b

Wmk. 373

1983, July 6 Litho. *Perf. 12*

675 A104b 45c Handshake .25 *.30*
676 A104b 60c Emblem .25 *.35*
677 A104b $1.50 Map .50 *1.10*
678 A104b $2 Flags .90 *1.40*
Nos. 675-678 (4) 1.90 *3.15*

10th anniv. of Chaguaramas (Caribbean Free Trade Assoc.)
For surcharges see Nos. 3233, 3283, 3313, 3327.

A105

45c, Founder William A. Smith. 60c, Boy, officer. $1.50, Emblem. $2, Community service.

Perf. 12x11½

1983, Oct. 6 Litho. Wmk. 373

679 A105 45c multicolored .25 .25
680 A105 60c multicolored .35 .35
681 A105 $1.50 multicolored .80 *1.25*
682 A105 $2 multicolored 1.10 *1.40*
Nos. 679-682 (4) 2.50 *3.25*

Boys' Brigade, cent. For overprint see #887. For surcharges see Nos. 3261, 3275, 3284, 3314, 3328.

Christmas — A106

10c, Shepherds at Watch. 50c, The Angel of the Lord. $1.50, A Glorious Light. $2.40, At the Manger.

1983, Nov. 15 Litho. *Perf. 12*

683 A106 10c multicolored .25 .25
684 A106 50c multicolored .30 .30
685 A106 $1.50 multicolored .80 1.10
686 A106 $2.40 multicolored 1.50 1.75
a. Souvenir sheet of 4, #683-686 2.75 2.75
Nos. 683-686 (4) 2.85 3.40

For surcharge, see No. 3263A.

Classic Cars A107

No. 687, Ford Model T. No. 688, Supercharged Cord. No. 689, Mercedes-Benz. No. 690, Citroen Open Tourer. No. 691, Ferrari Boxer. No. 692, Rolls-Royce Phantom.

Se-tenant Pairs, #a.-b.
a. — Side and front views.
b. — Action scene.

1983, Nov. 9 Litho. *Perf. 12½*

687 A107 10c multicolored .25 .25
688 A107 60c multicolored .25 .25
689 A107 $1.50 multicolored .35 .35
690 A107 $1.50 multicolored .35 .35
691 A107 $2 multicolored .35 .35
692 A107 $2 multicolored .35 .35
Nos. 687-692 (6) 1.90 1.90

See Nos. 773-777, 815-822, 906-911.

Locomotives Type of 1985

No. 699, King Henry VIII. No. 700, Royal Scots Greys. No. 701, Hagley Hall. No. 702, Sir Lancelot. No. 703, B12 Class. No. 704, #1000 Deeley Compound. No. 705, Cheshire. No. 706, Bulleid Austerity.

Se-tenant Pairs, #a.-b.
a. — Side and front views.
b. — Action scene.

1983, Dec. 8 Litho. *Perf. 12½x13*

699 A120 10c multicolored .25 .25
700 A120 10c multicolored .25 .25
701 A120 25c multicolored .25 .25
702 A120 50c multicolored .40 .40
703 A120 60c multicolored .40 .40
704 A120 75c multicolored .40 .40
705 A120 $2.50 multicolored .50 .50
706 A120 $3 multicolored .55 .55
Nos. 699-706 (8) 3.00 3.00

Fort Duvernette A108

Perf. 14x14½

1984, Feb. 13 Litho. Wmk. 380

715 A108 35c View .25 .25
716 A108 45c Wall, flag .30 .30
717 A108 $1 Canon .60 .60
718 A108 $3 Map 1.75 1.75
Nos. 715-718 (4) 2.90 2.90

For surcharge see No. 3334.

Flowering Trees — A109

Perf. 13½x14

1984, Apr. 2 Litho. Wmk. 373

719 A109 5c White frangipani .25 .25
720 A109 10c Genip .25 .25
721 A109 15c Immortelle .25 .25
722 A109 20c Pink poui .25 .25
723 A109 25c Buttercup .25 .25
724 A109 35c Sandbox .30 .30
725 A109 45c Locust .40 .40
726 A109 60c Colville's glory .75 .60
727 A109 75c Lignum vitae .75 .70
728 A109 $1 Golden shower .80 1.40

729	A109	$5 Angelin	3.00	*8.00*
730	A109	$10 Roucou	6.00	*13.00*
		Nos. 719-730 (12)	13.25	25.65

For surcharges see Nos. 3247, 3258, 3285-3288.

World War I Battle Scene, King George V — A110

No. 732a, Battle of Bannockburn. No. 732b, Edward II. No. 733a, George V. No. 733b, York Cottage, Sandringham. No. 734a, Edward II. No. 734b, Berkeley Castle. No. 735a, Arms of Edward II. No. 735b, Edward II. No. 736a, Arms of George V. No. 736b, George V.

1984, Apr. 25 Litho. *Perf. 13x12½*

731	A110	1c Pair, #a.-b.	.25	.25
732	A110	5c Pair, #a.-b.	.25	.25
733	A110	60c Pair, #a.-b.	.30	.30
734	A110	75c Pair, #a.-b.	.30	.30
735	A110	$1 Pair, #a.-b.	.30	.30
736	A110	$4 Pair, #a.-b.	.60	.60
		Nos. 731-736 (6)	2.00	2.00

Carnival A112

Wmk. 380

1984, June 25 Litho. *Perf. 14*

743	A112	35c Musical fantasy	.25	.25
744	A112	45c African woman	.25	.25
745	A112	$1 Market woman	.65	.65
746	A112	$3 Carib hieroglyph	1.75	1.75
		Nos. 743-746 (4)	2.90	2.90

For surcharges see Nos. 3243, 3276.

Locomotives Type of 1985

1c, Liberation Class 141R, 1945. 2c, Dreadnought Class 50, 1967. 3c, No. 242A1, 1946. 50c, Dean Goods, 1883. 75c, Hetton Colliery, 1822. $1, Penydarren, 1804. $2, Novelty, 1829. $3, Class 44, 1925.

Se-tenant Pairs, #a.-b.

a. — Side and front views.

b. — Action scene.

1984, July 27 Litho. *Perf. 12½*

747	A120	1c multicolored	.25	.25
748	A120	2c multicolored	.25	.25
749	A120	3c multicolored	.25	.25
750	A120	50c multicolored	.50	.50
751	A120	75c multicolored	.50	.50
752	A120	$1 multicolored	.50	.50
753	A120	$2 multicolored	.70	.70
754	A120	$3 multicolored	.70	.70
		Nos. 747-754 (8)	3.65	3.65

Slavery Abolition Sesquicentennial — A113

35c, Hoeing. 45c, Gathering sugar cane. $1, Cutting sugar cane. $3, Abolitionist William Wilberforce.

1984, Aug. 1 Litho. *Perf. 14*

761	A113	35c multicolored	.25	.25
762	A113	45c multicolored	.25	.25
763	A113	$1 multicolored	.65	.65
764	A113	$3 multicolored	1.75	2.40
		Nos. 761-764 (4)	2.90	3.55

For surcharges see Nos. 3273, 3337.

1984 Summer Olympics — A114

No. 765a, Judo. No. 765b, Weight lifting. No. 766a, Bicycling (facing left). No. 766b, Bicycling (facing right). No. 767a, Swimming (back stroke). No. 767b, Breast stroke. No. 768a, Running (start). No. 768b, Running (finish).

1984, Aug. 30 Unwmk. *Perf. 12½*

765	A114	1c Pair, #a.-b.	.25	.25
766	A114	3c Pair, #a.-b.	.25	.25
767	A114	60c Pair, #a.-b.	.50	.50
768	A114	$3 Pair, #a.-b.	2.00	2.00
		Nos. 765-768 (4)	3.00	3.00

Car Type of 1983

5c, Austin-Healey Sprite, 1958. 20c, Maserati, 1971. 55c, Pontiac GTO, 1964. $1.50, Jaguar, 1957. $2.50, Ferrari, 1970.

Se-tenant Pairs, #a.-b.

a. — Side and front views.

b. — Action scene.

1984, Oct. 22 Litho. *Perf. 12½*

773	A107	5c multicolored	.25	.25
774	A107	20c multicolored	.25	.25
775	A107	55c multicolored	.35	.35
776	A107	$1.50 multicolored	.45	.45
777	A107	$2.50 multicolored	.60	.60
		Nos. 773-777 (5)	1.90	1.90

Military Uniforms — A115

1984, Nov. 12 Wmk. 380 *Perf. 14*

783	A115	45c Grenadier, 1773	.35	.35
784	A115	60c Grenadier, 1775	.55	.55
785	A115	$1.50 Grenadier, 1768	1.10	1.10
786	A115	$2 Battalion Co. Officer, 1780	1.60	1.60
		Nos. 783-786 (4)	3.60	3.60

For surcharges see Nos. 3289, 3315, 3329.

Locomotives Type of 1985

5c, 1954 R.R. Class 20, Zimbabwe. 40c, 1928 Southern Maid, U.K. 75c, 1911 Prince of Wales, U.K. $2.50, 1935 D.R.G. Class 05, Germany.

Se-tenant Pairs, #a.-b.

a. — Side and front views.

b. — Action scene.

1984, Nov. 21 Litho. *Perf. 12½x13*

787	A120	5c multicolored	.25	.25
788	A120	40c multicolored	.30	.30
789	A120	75c multicolored	.30	.30
790	A120	$2.50 multicolored	1.00	1.00
		Nos. 787-790 (4)	1.85	1.85

Cricket Players — A116

5c, N.S. Taylor, portrait. 35c, T.W. Graveney with bat. 50c, R.G.D. Willis at wicket. $3, S.D. Fletcher at wicket.

Se-tenant Pairs, #a.-b.

a. — Side and front views.

b. — Action scene.

1985, Jan. 7 Litho. *Perf. 12½*

795	A116	5c multicolored	.25	.25
796	A116	35c multicolored	.40	.40
797	A116	50c multicolored	.60	.60
798	A116	$3 multicolored	2.00	3.00
		Nos. 795-798 (4)	3.25	4.25

Orchids — A117

35c, Epidendrum ciliare. 45c, Ionopsis utricularioides. $1, Epidendrum secundum. $3, Oncidium altissimum.

1985, Jan. 31 Litho. *Perf. 14*

803	A117	35c multicolored	.30	.30
804	A117	45c multicolored	.35	.35
805	A117	$1 multicolored	.70	.70
806	A117	$3 multicolored	1.50	1.50
		Nos. 803-806 (4)	2.85	2.85

For surcharge see No. 3338.

Audubon Birth Bicent. — A118

Illustrations of North American bird species by artist/naturalist John J. Audubon: #807a, Brown pelican. #807b, Green heron. #808a, Pileated woodpecker. #808b, Common flicker. #809a, Painted bunting. #809b, White-winged crossbill. #810a, Red-shouldered hawk. #810b, Crested caracara.

1985, Feb. 7 Litho. *Perf. 12½*

807	A118	15c Pair, #a.-b.	.25	.25
808	A118	40c Pair, #a.-b.	.45	.45
809	A118	60c Pair, #a.-b.	.45	.45
810	A118	$2.25 Pair, #a.-b.	.90	.90
		Nos. 807-810 (4)	2.05	2.05

Car Type of 1983

1c, 1937 Lancia Aprilia, Italy. 25c, 1922 Essex Coach, US. 55c, 1973 Pontiac Firebird Trans Am, US. 60c, 1950 Nash Rambler, US. $1, 1961 Ferrari Tipo 156, Italy. $1.50, 1967 Eagle-Weslake Type 58, US. $2, 1953 Cunningham C-5R, US.

Se-tenant Pairs, #a.-b.

a. — Side and front views.

b. — Action scene.

1985

815-821	A107	Set of 7 pairs	2.00	2.00

Souvenir Sheet of 4

822	A107	#a.-d.	2.25	2.25

No. 822 contains a pair of $4 stamps like No. 820 (#a.-b.), and a pair of $5 stamps like No. 819 (#c.-d.).

Issued: 1c, 55c, $2, 3/11; others, 6/7.

Herbs and Spices — A119

1985, Apr. 22 *Perf. 14*

829	A119	25c Pepper	.25	.25
830	A119	35c Sweet marjoram	.25	.25
831	A119	$1 Nutmeg	.50	.50
832	A119	$3 Ginger	1.00	1.00
		Nos. 829-832 (4)	2.00	2.00

For surcharge see No. 3339.

Locomotives of the United Kingdom — A120

1c, 1913 Glen Douglas. 10c, 1872 Fenchurch Terrier. 40c, 1870 No. 1 Stirling Single. 60c, 1866 No. 158A. $1, 1893 No. 103 Class Jones Goods. $2.50, 1908 Great Bear.

Se-tenant Pairs, #a.-b.

a. — Side and front views.

b. — Action scene.

1985, Apr. 26 *Perf. 12½*

833	A120	1c multicolored	.25	.25
834	A120	10c multicolored	.25	.25
835	A120	40c multicolored	.30	.30
836	A120	60c multicolored	.30	.30
837	A120	$1 multicolored	.50	.50
838	A120	$2.50 multicolored	.80	.80
		Nos. 833-838 (6)	2.40	2.40

See Nos. 699-706, 747-754, 787-790, 849-854, 961-964.

Traditional Instruments — A121

25c, Bamboo flute. 35c, Quatro. $1, Bamboo base, vert. $2, Goat-skin drum, vert.

1985, May 16 *Perf. 15*

845	A121	25c multicolored	.25	.25
846	A121	35c multicolored	.25	.25
847	A121	$1 multicolored	.50	.50
848	A121	$2 multicolored	1.00	1.00
a.		Sheet of 4, #845-848	2.00	2.00
		Nos. 845-848 (4)	2.00	2.00

For surcharge see No. 3299.

Locomotives Type of 1985

5c, 1874 Loch, U.K. 30c, 1919 Class 47XX, U.K. 60c, 1876 P.L.M. Class 121, France. 75c, 1927 D.R.G. Class 24, Germany. $1, 1889 No. 1008, U.K. $2.50, 1926 S.R. Class PS-4, US.

Se-tenant Pairs, #a.-b.

a. — Side and front views.

b. — Action scene.

1985, June 27 *Perf. 12½*

849	A120	5c multicolored	.25	.25
850	A120	30c multicolored	.30	.30
851	A120	60c multicolored	.40	.40
852	A120	75c multicolored	.40	.40
853	A120	$1 multicolored	.50	.50
854	A120	$2.50 multicolored	.60	.60
		Nos. 849-854 (6)	2.45	2.45

Queen Mother, 85th Birthday — A122

Nos. 861a, 867a, Facing right. Nos. 861b, 867b, Facing left. Nos. 862a, 866a, Facing right. Nos. 862b, 866b, Facing left. No. 863a, Facing right. No. 863b, Facing left. No. 864a, Facing front. No. 864b, Facing left. No. 865a, Facing right. No. 865b, Facing front.

1985

861	A122	35c	Pair, #a.-b.	.25	.25
862	A122	85c	Pair, #a.-b.	.25	.25
863	A122	$1.20	Pair, #a.-b.	.35	.35
864	A122	$1.60	Pair, #a.-b.	.35	.35
			Nos. 861-864 (4)	1.20	1.20

Souvenir Sheets of 2

865	A122	$2.10	#a.-b.	.75	.75
866	A122	$3.50	#a.-b.	3.25	3.25
867	A122	$6	#a.-b.	5.50	5.50
			Nos. 865-867 (3)	9.50	9.50

Issued: #861-865, 8/9; #866-867, 12/19.

For overprints see No. 888.

Elvis Presley (1935-77), American Entertainer — A123

Nos. 874a, 878a, In concert. Nos. 874b, 878b, Facing front. Nos. 875a, 879a, In concert. Nos. 875b, 879b, Facing left. Nos. 876a, 880a, In concert. Nos. 876b, 880b, Facing front. Nos. 877a, 881a, Wearing leather jacket. Nos. 877b, 881b, Facing left.

1985, Aug. 16

874	A123	10c	Pair, #a.-b.	.55	.55
875	A123	60c	Pair, #a.-b.	.80	.80
876	A123	$1	Pair, #a.-b.	.80	.80
877	A123	$5	Pair, #a.-b.	1.10	1.10
			Nos. 874-877 (4)	3.25	3.25

Souvenir Sheets of 4

878	A123	30c	#a.-b.	.90	.90
879	A123	50c	#a.-b.	1.50	1.50
880	A123	$1.50	#a.-b.	4.25	4.25
881	A123	$4.50	#a.-b.	12.00	12.00
			Nos. 878-881 (4)	18.65	18.65

Nos. 878-881 contain two of each stamp.
Two $4 "stamps" were not issued.

For other Presley souvenir sheet see No. 1567. For overprints see Nos. 1009-1016.

Flour Milling A124

1985, Oct. 17 Wmk. 373 *Perf. 15*

882	A124	20c	Conveyor from elevators	.25	.25
883	A124	30c	Roller mills	.25	.25
884	A124	75c	Office	.50	.50
885	A124	$3	Bran finishers	2.00	2.00
			Nos. 882-885 (4)	3.00	3.00

Nos. 667, 680, 862, 650, 631-632, 651 Ovptd. "CARIBBEAN / ROYAL VISIT / -1985-" or Srchd. with 3 Black Bars and New Value in Black

1985, Oct. 27 *Perfs. as Before*

886	A104	60c	multi	*1.90*	*1.90*
887	A105	60c	multi	*1.90*	*1.90*
888	A122	85c	Pair, #a.-b.	*6.00*	*6.00*
890	A100	$1.50	multi	*5.25*	*5.25*
891	A94a	$1.60	on $4	*5.50*	*5.50*
892	A94b	$1.60	on $4	*5.50*	*5.50*
893	A100	$2.50	multi	*8.50*	*8.50*
			Nos. 886-893 (7)	*34.55*	*34.55*

Michael Jackson (b. 1960), American Entertainer — A125

No. 894a, Portrait. No. 894b, On stage. No. 895a, Singing. No. 895b, Portrait. No. 896a, Black jacket. No. 896b, Red jacket. No. 897a, Portrait. No. 897b, Wearing white glove.

1985, Dec. 2 *Perf. 12½*

894	A125	60c	Pair, #a.-b.	.45	.45
895	A125	$1	Pair, #a.-b.	.75	.75
896	A125	$2	Pair, #a.-b.	1.50	1.50
897	A125	$5	Pair, #a.-b.	4.00	4.00
			Nos. 894-897 (4)	6.70	6.70

Souvenir Sheets of 4
Perf. 13x12½

898	A125	45c	#a.-b.	.70	.70
899	A125	90c	#a.-b.	1.40	1.40
900	A125	$1.50	#a.-b.	2.25	2.25
901	A125	$4	#a.-b.	6.25	6.25

#898-901 contain two of each stamp.

Christmas A126

Children's drawings: 25c, Serenade, 75c, Poinsettia. $2.50, Jesus, Our Master.

1985, Dec. 9 Wmk. 373 *Perf. 14*

903	A126	25c	multicolored	.25	.25
904	A126	75c	multicolored	.50	.50
905	A126	$2.50	multicolored	1.75	1.75
			Nos. 903-905 (3)	2.50	2.50

For surcharges see Nos. 3268, 3333.

Car Type of 1983

30c, 1916 Cadillac Type 53, US. 45c, 1939 Triumph Dolomite, UK. 60c, 1972 Panther J-72, UK. 90c, 1967 Ferrari 275 GTB/4, Italy. $1.50, 1953 Packard Caribbean, US. $2.50, 1931 Bugatti Type 41 Royale, France.

Se-tenant Pairs, #a.-b.
a. — Side and front views.
b. — Action scene.

1986, Jan. 27 *Perf. 12½*

906-911	A107	Set of 6 pairs	7.00	7.00

Halley's Comet A127

Wmk. 380

1986, Apr. 14 Litho. *Perf. 15*

918	A127	45c	shown	.35	.35
919	A127	60c	Edmond Halley	.45	.45
920	A127	75c	Newton's reflector telescope	.55	.55
921	A127	$3	Local astronomer	2.10	2.10
a.			Souvenir sheet of 4, #918-921	3.50	3.50
			Nos. 918-921 (4)	3.45	3.45

Souvenir Sheets of 2

Scouting Movement, 75th Anniv. — A127a

American flag & Girl Guides or Boy Scouts emblem and: No. 922b, Scout sign, handshake. No. 922c, Paintbrushes, pallet. No. 922Ad, Knots. No. 922Ae, Lord Baden-Powell.

1986, Feb. 25 Litho. *Perf. 13x12½*

922	A127a	$5	#b.-c.	4.00	4.00
922A	A127a	$6	#d.-e.	5.00	5.00

"Capex '87" overprints on this issue were not authorized.

Nos. 922-922A exist with decorative selvage. Value, set, $11.50.

Elizabeth II Wearing Crown Jewels — A128

Various portraits.

1986, Apr. 21 Wmk. 373 *Perf. 12½*

923	A128	10c	multicolored	.25	.25
924	A128	90c	multicolored	.50	.50
925	A128	$2.50	multicolored	1.25	1.25
926	A128	$8	multi, vert.	4.50	4.50
			Nos. 923-926 (4)	6.50	6.50

Souvenir Sheet

927	A128	$10	multicolored	5.50	5.50

Elizabeth II at Victoria Park A129

Designs: No. 929, with Prime Minister Mitchell. No. 930, Arriving at Port Elizabeth. No. 931, at Independence Day Parade.

Perf. 15x14

1986, June 14 Wmk. 373

928	A129	45c	multicolored	.40	.40
929	A129	60c	multicolored	.55	.55
930	A129	75c	multicolored	.70	.70
931	A129	$2.50	multicolored	2.25	2.25
			Nos. 928-931 (4)	3.90	3.90

Souvenir Sheet

932	A129	$3	multicolored	3.75	3.75

Queen Elizabeth II, 60th birthday.

Discovery of America, 500th Anniv. (1992) — A130

No. 936a, Fleet. No. 936b, Columbus. No. 937a, At Spanish Court. No. 937b, Ferdinand, Isabella. No. 938a, Fruit, Santa Maria. No. 938b, Fruit.

1986, Jan. 23 Litho. *Perf. 12½*

936	A130	60c	Pair, #a.-b.	.90	.90
937	A130	$1.50	Pair, #a.-b.	2.25	2.25
938	A130	$2.75	Pair, #a.-b.	4.00	4.00
			Nos. 936-938 (3)	7.15	7.15

Souvenir Sheet

939	A130	$6	Columbus, diff.	4.50	4.50

1986 World Cup Soccer Championships, Mexico — A131

No. 940, Emblem. No. 941, Mexico. No. 942, Mexico, diff. No. 943, Hungary vs. Scotland. No. 944, Spain vs. Scotland. No. 945, England vs. USSR. No. 946, Spain vs. France. No. 947, England vs. Italy.

No. 948, Mexico. No. 949, Scotland. No. 950, Spain. No. 951, England.

1986, May 7 Litho. *Perf. 15*

940	A131	1c	multicolored	.25	.25
941	A131	2c	multicolored	.25	.25
942	A131	5c	multicolored	.25	.25
943	A131	5c	multicolored	.25	.25
944	A131	10c	multicolored	.25	.25
945	A131	30c	multicolored	.25	.25
946	A131	45c	multicolored	.30	.30
947	A131	$1	multicolored	.60	.60

Perf. 13½
Size: 56x36mm

948	A131	75c	multicolored	.40	.40
949	A131	$2	multicolored	1.10	1.10
950	A131	$4	multicolored	2.25	2.25
951	A131	$5	multicolored	2.75	2.75
			Nos. 940-951 (12)	8.90	8.90

1986, July 7 Souvenir Sheets

952	A131	$1.50	like #950	.95	.95
953	A131	$1.50	like #941	.95	.95
954	A131	$2.25	like #949	1.40	1.40
955	A131	$2.50	like #948	1.40	1.40
956	A131	$3	like #946	1.50	1.50
957	A131	$5.50	like #951	3.25	3.25
			Nos. 952-957 (6)	9.45	9.45

Nos. 941-944, 946-947, vert.

Wedding of Prince Andrew and Sarah Ferguson — A132

A132a

No. 958a, Andrew. No. 958b, Sarah. No. 959a, Andrew, horiz. No. 959b, Andrew, Nancy Reagan, horiz.

1986 Litho. *Perf. 12½x13, 13x12½*

958	A132	60c	Pair, #a.-b.	.65	.65
959	A132	$2	Pair, #a.-b.	2.25	2.25
960	A132a	$10	In coach	5.50	5.50
			Nos. 958-960 (3)	8.40	8.40

Issued: $10, Nov.; others, July 23.

For overprints see Nos. 976-977.

A number of unissued items, imperfs., part perfs., missing color varieties, etc., were made available when the Format International inventory was liquidated.

Locomotives Type of 1985

Designs: 30c, 1926 JNR ABT Rack & Adhesion Class ED41 BZZB, Japan. 50c, 1883 Chicago RR Exposition, The Judge, 1A Type, US. $1, 1973 BM & LPRR E60C Co-Co, US. $3, 1972 GM (EMD) SD40-2 Co-Co, US.

a. — Side and front views.
b. — Action scene.

1986, July *Perf. 12½x13*

961 A120 30c Pair, #a.-b. .30 .30
962 A120 50c Pair, #a.-b. .40 .40
963 A120 $1 Pair, #a.-b. .55 .55
964 A120 $3 Pair, #a.-b. .90 .90
Nos. 961-964 (4) 2.15 2.15

Trees — A133

10c, Acrocomia aculeata. 60c, Pithecellobium saman. 75c, Tabebuia pallida. $3, Andira inermis.

1986, Sept. *Perf. 14*

968 A133 10c multicolored .35 .35
969 A133 60c multicolored .90 .90
970 A133 75c multicolored 1.10 1.10
971 A133 $3 multicolored 4.25 4.25
Nos. 968-971 (4) 6.60 6.60

Anniversaries — A134

45c, Cadet Force emblem, vert. 60c, Grimble Building, GHS. $1.50, GHS class. $2, Cadets in formation.

1986, Sept. 30

972 A134 45c multicolored .40 .40
973 A134 60c multicolored .50 .50
974 A134 $1.50 multicolored 1.10 1.10
975 A134 $2 multicolored 1.50 1.50
Nos. 972-975 (4) 3.50 3.50

St. Vincent Cadet Force, 50th anniv., and Girls' High School, 75th anniv.

For surcharges see Nos. 3316, 3330-3331.

Nos. 958-959 Ovptd. "Congratulations to T.R.H. The Duke & Duchess of York" in Silver

Perf. 12½x13, 13x12½

1986, Oct. **Litho.**

976 A132 60c Pair, #a.-b. .75 .75
977 A132 $2 Pair, #a.-b. 2.75 2.75

Stamps of the same denomination also exist printed tete-beche.

The Legend of King Arthur — A134a

30c, King Arthur. 45c, Merlin raises Arthur. 60c, Arthur pulls Excalibur from stone. 75c, Camelot. $1, Lady of the Lake. $1.50, Knights of the Round Table. $2, Holy Grail. $5, Sir Lancelot.

1986, Nov. 3 *Perf. 14*

979 A134a 30c multi .30 .30
979A A134a 45c multi .45 .45
979B A134a 60c multi .50 .50
979C A134a 75c multi .65 .65
979D A134a $1 multi .80 .80
979E A134a $1.50 multi 1.10 1.10
979F A134a $2 multi 1.60 1.60
979G A134a $5 multi 4.25 4.25
Nos. 979-979G (8) 9.65 9.65

A134b

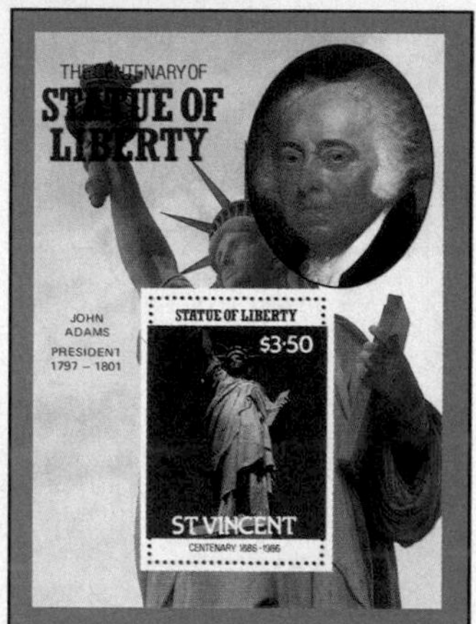

Statue of Liberty, Cent. — A135

Various views of the statue.

1986, Nov. 26 **Litho.** *Perf. 14*

980 A134b 15c multicolored .25 .25
980A A134b 25c multicolored .25 .25
980B A134b 40c multicolored .25 .25
980C A134b 55c multicolored .35 .35
980D A134b 75c multicolored .50 .50
980E A134b 90c multicolored .60 .60
980F A134b $1.75 multicolored 1.10 1.10
980G A134b $2 multicolored 1.25 1.25
980H A134b $2.50 multicolored 1.65 1.65
980I A134b $3 multicolored 1.90 1.90
Nos. 980-980I (10) 8.10 8.10

Souvenir Sheets

981 A135 $3.50 multicolored 2.00 2.00
982 A135 $4 multicolored 2.25 2.25
983 A135 $5 multicolored 2.75 2.75

Fresh-water Fishing — A136

No. 984a, Tri tri fishing. No. 984b, Tri tri. No. 985a, Crayfishing. No. 985b, Crayfish.

1986, Dec. 10 *Perf. 15*

984 A136 75c Pair, #a.-b. 1.10 1.10
985 A136 $1.50 Pair, #a.-b. 2.25 2.25

For surcharges see Nos. 3292-3293, 3317.

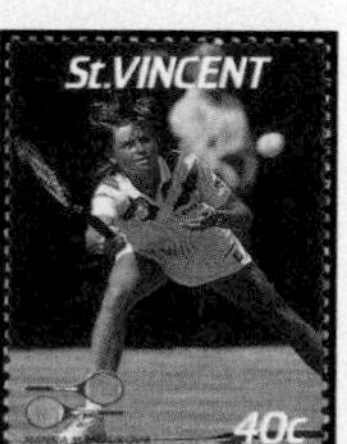

1987 Wimbledon Tennis Championships A137

1987, June 22 *Perf. 13x12½*

988 A137 40c Hana Mandlikova .25 .25
989 A137 60c Yannick Noah .30 .30
990 A137 80c Ivan Lendl .40 .40
991 A137 $1 Chris Evert Lloyd .50 .50
992 A137 $1.25 Steffi Graf .65 .65
993 A137 $1.50 John McEnroe .85 .85
994 A137 $1.75 Martina Navratilova .95 .95
995 A137 $2 Boris Becker 1.10 1.10
Nos. 988-995 (8) 5.00 5.00

Souvenir Sheet

996 Sheet of 2 3.00 3.00
a. A137 $2.25 like $2 1.50 1.50
b. A137 $2.25 like $1.75 1.50 1.50

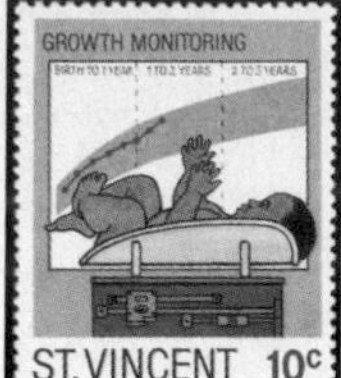

Natl. Child Survival Campaign A138

10c, Growth monitoring. 50c, Oral rehydration therapy. 75c, Breast-feeding. $1, Universal immunization.

1987, June 10 *Perf. 14x14½*

997 A138 10c multicolored .25 .25
998 A138 50c multicolored .40 .40
999 A138 75c multicolored .60 .60
1000 A138 $1 multicolored .75 .75
Nos. 997-1000 (4) 2.00 2.00

For overprints see Nos. 1040-1043. For surcharge see No. 3294.

Carnival, 10th Anniv. A139

Designs: 20c, Queen of the Bands, Miss Prima Donna 1986. 45c, Donna Young, Miss Carnival 1985. 55c, M. Haydock, Miss. St. Vincent and the Grenadines 1986. $3.70, Spirit of Hope Year 1986.

1987, June 29 *Perf. 12½x13*

1001 A139 20c multicolored .25 .25
1002 A139 45c multicolored .35 .35
1003 A139 55c multicolored .40 .40
1004 A139 $3.70 multicolored 2.50 2.50
Nos. 1001-1004 (4) 3.50 3.50

For surcharges see Nos. 3342-3343.

Nos. 874-881 Overprinted "THE KING OF ROCK AND ROLL LIVES FOREVER . AUGUST 16TH" and "1977-1987" (Nos. 1009-1012) or "TENTH ANNIVERSARY" (Nos. 1013-1016)

1987, Aug. 26 **Litho.** *Perf. 12½*

1009 A123 10c Pair, #a.-b. .25 .25
1010 A123 60c Pair, #a.-b. .70 .70
1011 A123 $1 Pair, #a.-b. 1.10 1.10
1012 A123 $5 Pair, #a.-b. 6.00 6.00
Nos. 1009-1012 (4) 8.05 8.05

Souvenir Sheets

1013 A123 30c Sheet of 4, 2 each #a.-b. .75 .75
1014 A123 50c Sheet of 4, 2 each #a.-b. 1.25 1.25
1015 A123 $1.50 Sheet of 4, 2 each #a.-b. 3.75 3.75
1016 A123 $4.50 Sheet of 4, 2 each #a.-b. 11.00 11.00

Portrait of Queen Victoria, 1841, by R. Thorburn A140

Portraits and photographs: 75c, Elizabeth and Charles, 1948. $1, Coronation, 1953. $2.50, Duke of Edinburgh, 1948. $5, Elizabeth, c. 1980. $6, Elizabeth and Charles, 1948, diff.

1987, Nov. 20 **Litho.** *Perf. 12½x13*

1017 A140 15c multicolored .25 .25
1018 A140 75c multicolored .45 .45
1019 A140 $1 multicolored .55 .55
1020 A140 $2.50 multicolored 1.25 1.25
1021 A140 $5 multicolored 2.50 2.50
Nos. 1017-1021 (5) 5.00 5.00

Souvenir Sheet

1022 A140 $6 multicolored 4.00 4.00

Sesquicentennial of Queen Victoria's accession to the throne, wedding of Queen Elizabeth II and Prince Philip, 40th anniv.

Nos. 997-1000 Ovptd. "WORLD POPULATION / 5 BILLION / 11TH JULY 1987"

1987, July 11 **Litho.** *Perf. 14x14½*

1040 A138 10c on No. 997 .40 .40
1041 A138 50c on No. 998 .80 .80
1042 A138 75c on No. 999 1.25 1.25
1043 A138 $1 on No. 1000 1.50 1.50
Nos. 1040-1043 (4) 3.95 3.95

Automobile Centenary — A143

Automotive pioneers and vehicles: $1, $3, Carl Benz (1844-1929) and the Velocipede, patented 1886. $2, No. 1049, Enzo Ferrari (b. 1898) and 1966 Ferrari Dino 206SP. $4, $6, Charles Rolls (1877-1910), Sir Henry Royce (1863-1933) and 1907 Rolls Royce Silver Ghost. No. 1047, $5, $8, Henry Ford (1863-1947) and Model T Ford.

1987, Dec. 4 *Perf. 13x12½*

1044 A143 $1 multicolored .65 .65
1045 A143 $2 multicolored 1.00 1.00
1046 A143 $4 multicolored 2.10 2.10
1047 A143 $5 multicolored 2.50 2.50
Nos. 1044-1047 (4) 6.25 6.25

Souvenir Sheets

1048 A143 $3 like No. 1044 2.00 2.00
1049 A143 $5 like No. 1045 3.25 3.25
1050 A143 $6 like No. 1046 4.00 4.00
1051 A143 $8 like No. 1047 5.50 5.50
Nos. 1048-1051 (4) 14.75 14.75

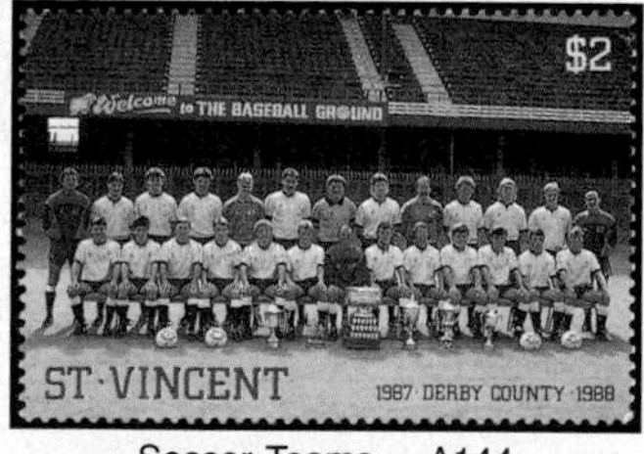

Soccer Teams — A144

1987, Dec. 4

1052 A144 $2 Derby County 1.40 1.40
1053 A144 $2 Leeds United 1.40 1.40
1054 A144 $2 Tottenham Hotspur 1.40 1.40
1055 A144 $2 Manchester United 1.40 1.40
1056 A144 $2 Everton 1.40 1.40
1057 A144 $2 Liverpool 1.40 1.40
1058 A144 $2 Portsmouth 1.40 1.40
1059 A144 $2 Arsenal 1.40 1.40
Nos. 1052-1059 (8) 11.20 11.20

A145

A Christmas Carol, by Charles Dickens (1812-1870) — A147

6c, Mr. Fezziwig's Ball. 25c, Ghost of Christmases to Come. 50c, The Cratchits. 75c, Carolers.
$5, Reading book to children.
Portrait of Dickens as left page of book (Nos. 1061a-1064a) and various scenes from novels as right page of book (Nos. 1061b-1064b).

1987, Dec. 17 ***Perf. 14x14½***

Horiz. Pairs, #a.-b.

1061	A145	6c	multicolored	.35	.35
1062	A145	25c	multicolored	.70	.70
1063	A145	50c	multicolored	1.25	1.25
1064	A145	75c	multicolored	1.90	1.90
	Nos. 1061-1064 (4)			4.20	4.20

Souvenir Sheet

1065	A147	$5	multicolored	3.75	3.75

For surcharge see No. 3267.

Eastern Caribbean Currency — A148

Various Eastern Caribbean coins (Nos. 1069-1081) and banknotes (Nos. 1082-1086) in denominations equaling that of the stamp on which they are pictured.

1987-89 **Litho.** ***Perf. 15***

1069	A148	5c	multicolored	.25	.25
1070	A148	6c	multicolored	.25	.25
1071	A148	10c	multicolored	.25	.25
1072	A148	12c	multicolored	.25	.25
1073	A148	15c	multicolored	.25	.25
1074	A148	20c	multicolored	.25	.25
1075	A148	25c	multicolored	.25	.25
1076	A148	30c	multicolored	.25	.25
1077	A148	35c	multicolored	.30	.30
1078	A148	45c	multicolored	.35	.35
1079	A148	50c	multicolored	.40	.40
1080	A148	65c	multicolored	.50	.50
1081	A148	75c	multicolored	.60	.60
1082	A148	$1	multi, horiz.	.75	.75
1083	A148	$2	multi, horiz.	1.50	1.50
1084	A148	$3	multi, horiz.	2.25	2.25
1085	A148	$5	multi, horiz.	3.75	3.75
1086	A148	$10	multi, horiz.	7.50	7.50

Perf. 14

1086A	A148	$20	multi, horiz.	15.00	15.00
	Nos. 1069-1086A (19)			34.90	34.90

Issued: $20, Nov. 7, 1989; others, Dec. 11.
For surcharges see Nos. 3240-3241, 3246, 3249, 3295.

1991 ***Perf. 12***

1071a	A148	10c	.20
1073a	A148	15c	.20
1074a	A148	20c	.20
1075a	A148	25c	.20
1078a	A148	45c	.30
1079a	A148	50c	.35
1080a	A148	65c	.45
1081a	A148	75c	.55
1082a	A148	$1	.70
1083a	A148	$2	1.40
1085a	A148	$5	3.50
	Nos. 1071a-1085a (11)		8.05

This perf may not have been issued in St. Vincent.

1991 ***Perf. 14***

1071b	A148	10c	.25	.25
1073b	A148	15c	.25	.25
1074b	A148	20c	.25	.25
1075b	A148	25c	.25	.25
1078b	A148	45c	.30	.30
1079b	A148	50c	.35	.35
1080b	A148	65c	.45	.45
1081b	A148	75c	.55	.55
1082b	A148	$1	.70	.70
1083b	A148	$2	1.40	1.40
1085b	A148	$5	3.50	3.50
	Nos. 1071b-1085b (11)		8.25	8.25

For surcharges see Nos. 3242, 3244, 3248, 3249a, 3254-3255, 3257-3257A.

US Constitution Bicentennial A149

Christopher Columbus's fleet: 15c, Santa Maria. 75c, Nina and Pinta. $1, Hour glass, compass. $1.50, Columbus planting flag of Spain on American soil. $3, Arawak natives. $4, Parrot, hummingbird, corn, pineapple, eggs. $5, $6, Columbus, Columbus'l coat of arms and caravel.

1988, Jan. 11 ***Perf. 14½x14***

1087	A149	15c	multicolored	.25	.25
1088	A149	75c	multicolored	.60	.60
1089	A149	$1	multicolored	.75	.75
1090	A149	$1.50	multicolored	1.25	1.25
1091	A149	$3	multicolored	2.25	2.25
1092	A149	$4	multicolored	3.00	3.00
	Nos. 1087-1092 (6)			8.10	8.10

Souvenir Sheets

Perf. 14x14½, 14½x14

1093	A149	$5	multicolored	3.50	3.50
1093A	A149	$6	multicolored	4.25	4.25

US Constitution, bicent.; 500th anniv. of the discovery of America (in 1992).

Brown Pelican — A150

1988, Feb. 15 ***Perf. 14***

1094	A150	45c	multicolored	.75	.75

See No. 1298.

A151

Tourism — A152

10c, Windsurfing, diff., vert. 45c, Scuba diving, vert. $5, Chartered ship.

1988, Feb. 22 **Litho.** ***Perf. 15***

1095	A151	10c	multicolored	.25	.25
1096	A151	45c	multicolored	.30	.30
1097	A151	65c	shown	.45	.45
1098	A151	$5	multicolored	3.25	3.25
	Nos. 1095-1098 (4)			4.25	4.25

Souvenir Sheet

Perf. 13x12½

1099	A152	$10	shown	6.75	6.75

For surcharges see Nos. 3250, 3277.

A153

Destruction of the Spanish Armada by the English, 400th Anniv. — A154

16th cent. ships and artifacts: 15c, Nuestra Senora del Rosario, Spanish Chivalric Cross. 75c, Ark Royal, Armada medal. $1.50, English fleet, 16th cent. navigational instrument. $2, Dismasted galleon, cannon balls. $3.50, English fireships among the Armada, firebomb. $5, Revenge, Drake's drum. $8, Shoreline sentries awaiting the outcome of the battle.

1988, July 29 **Litho.** ***Perf. 12½***

1100	A153	15c	multicolored	.25	.25
1101	A153	75c	multicolored	.40	.40
1102	A153	$1.50	multicolored	.90	.90
1103	A153	$2	multicolored	1.10	1.10
1104	A153	$3.50	multicolored	1.90	1.90
1105	A153	$5	multicolored	2.75	2.75
	Nos. 1100-1105 (6)			7.30	7.30

Souvenir Sheet

1106	A154	$8	multicolored	4.75	4.75

Cricket Players A156

15c, D.K. Lillee. 50c, G.A. Gooch. 75c, R.N. Kapil Dev. $1, S.M. Gavaskar. $1.50, M.W. Gatting. $2.50, Imran Khan. $3, I.T. Botham. $4, I.V.A. Richards.

1988, July 29 **Litho.** ***Perf. 14½x14***

1108	A156	15c	multicolored	.25	.25
1109	A156	50c	multicolored	.35	.35
1110	A156	75c	multicolored	.55	.55
1111	A156	$1	multicolored	.70	.70
1112	A156	$1.50	multicolored	1.00	1.00
1113	A156	$2.50	multicolored	1.75	1.75
1114	A156	$3	multicolored	2.00	2.00
1115	A156	$4	multicolored	2.75	2.75
	Nos. 1108-1115 (8)			9.35	9.35

A souvenir sheet containing a $2 stamp like No. 1115 and a $3.50 stamp like No. 1114 was not issued by the post office.

1988 Summer Olympics, Seoul A158

1988, Dec. 7 **Litho.** ***Perf. 14***

1116	A158	10c	Running	.25	.25
1117	A158	50c	Long jump, vert.	.35	.35
1118	A158	$1	Triple jump	.65	.65
1119	A158	$5	Boxing, vert.	3.50	3.50
	Nos. 1116-1119 (4)			4.75	4.75

Souvenir Sheet

1120	A158	$10	Torch	6.25	6.25

1st Participation of St. Vincent athletes in the Olympics.
For overprints see Nos. 1346-1351.

Christmas — A159

Walt Disney characters: 1c, Minnie Mouse in freight car. 2c, Morty and Ferdy in open rail car. 3c, Chip 'n Dale in open boxcar. 4c, Huey, Dewey, Louie and reindeer. 5c, Donald and Daisy Duck aboard dining car. 10c, Gramma Duck conducting chorus including Scrooge McDuck, Goofy and Clarabelle Cow. $5, No. 1127, Mickey Mouse in locomotive. $6, Santa Claus in caboose.
No. 1129, $5, Mickey, Minnie Mouse and nephews in train station, vert. No. 1130, $5, Characters riding carousel, vert.

Perf. 14x13½, 13½x14

1988, Dec. 23 **Litho.**

1121-1128	A159	Set of 8	10.50	10.50

Souvenir Sheets

1129-1130	A159	Set of 2	10.50	10.50

Babe Ruth (1895-1948), American Baseball Star — A160

1988, Dec. 7 **Litho.** ***Perf. 14***

1131	A160	$2	multicolored	2.00	2.00

India '89, Jan. 20-29, New Delhi — A161

Exhibition emblem and Walt Disney characters: 1c, Mickey Mouse as snake charmer, Minnie Mouse as dancer. 2c, Goofy tossing rings at a chowsingha antelope. 3c, Mickey, Minnie, blue peacock. 5c, Goofy and Mickey as miners, Briolette diamond. 10c, Goofy as count presenting Orloff Diamond to Catherine the Great of Russia (Clarabelle Cow). 25c, Regent Diamond and Donald Duck as Napoleon (portrait) in the Louvre. $4, Minnie as Queen Victoria, Mickey as King Albert, crown bearing the Kohinoor Diamond. $5, Mickey and Goofy on safari.
No. 1140, $6, Mickey as Nehru, riding an elephant. No. 1141, $6, Mickey as postman delivering Hope Diamond to the Smithsonian Institute.

1989, Feb. 7 **Litho.** ***Perf. 14***

1132-1139	A161	Set of 8	11.50	11.50

Souvenir Sheets

1140-1141	A161	Set of 2	12.00	12.00

Entertainers of the Jazz and Big Band Eras — A162

Designs: 10c, Harry James (1916-83). 15c, Sidney Bechet (1897-1959). 25c, Benny Goodman (1909-86). 35c, Django Reinhardt (1910-50). 50c, Lester Young (1909-59). 90c, Gene Krupa (1909-73). $3, Louis Armstrong (1900-71). $4, Duke Ellington (1899-1974).
No. 1150, $5, Charlie Parker, Jr. (1920-55). No. 1151, $5, Billie Holiday (1915-59).

1989, Apr. 3 **Litho.** ***Perf. 14***

1142-1149	A162	Set of 8	10.00	10.00

Souvenir Sheets

1150-1151	A162	Set of 2	11.00	11.00

Holiday misspelled "Holliday" on No. 1151.
For surcharge see No. 3274.

Miniature Sheet

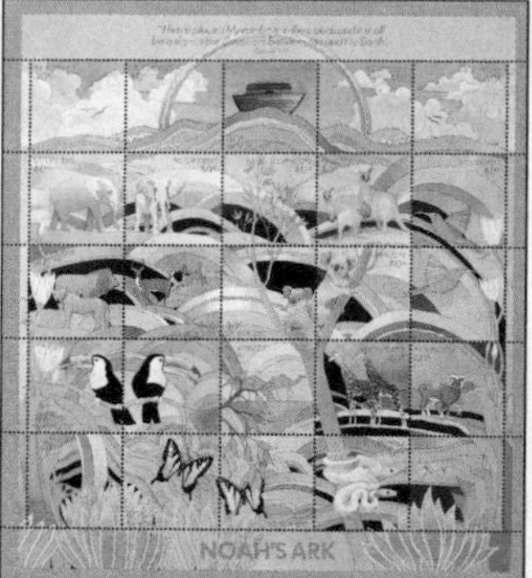

Noah's Ark — A163

Designs: a, Clouds, 2 birds at right. b, Rainbow, 4 clouds. c, Ark. d, Rainbow, 3 clouds. e, Clouds, 2 birds at left. f, African elephant facing right. g, Elephant facing forward. h, Leaves on tree branch. i, Kangaroos. j, Hummingbird facing left, flower. k, Lions. l, White-tailed deer. m, Koala at right. n, Koala at left. o, Hummingbird facing right, flower. p, Flower, toucan facing left. q, Toucan facing right. r, Camels. s, Giraffes. t, Sheep. u, Ladybugs. v, Butterfly (UR). w, Butterfly (LL). x, Snakes. y, Dragonflies.

1989, Apr. 10 ***Perf. 14***

1152	A163	Sheet of 25	14.50	14.50
a.-y.		40c any single	.30	.30

Easter A164

Paintings by Titian: 5c, Baptism of Christ. 30c, Temptation of Christ. 45c, Ecce Homo. 65c, Noli Me Tangere. 75c, Christ Carrying the Cross. $1, Christ Crowned with Thorns. $4, Lamentation Over Christ. $5, The Entombment.

No. 1161, $6, Pieta. No. 1162, $6, The Deposition.

1989, Apr. 17 ***Perf. 13½x14***

1153-1160	A164	Set of 8	12.50	12.50

Souvenir Sheets

1161-1162	A164	Set of 2	11.50	11.50

Telstar II and Cooperation in Space — A165

Designs: 15c, Recovery of astronaut L. Gordon Cooper, Mercury 9/Faith 7 mission. 35c, Satellite transmission of Martin Luther King's civil rights march address, 1963. 40c, US shuttle STS-7, 1st use of Canadarm, deployment & recovery of a W. German free-flying experiment platform. 50c, Satellite transmission of the 1964 Olympics, Innsbruck (speed skater). 60c, Vladimir Remek of Czechoslovakia, 1st non-Soviet cosmonaut, 1978. $1, CNES Hermes space plane, France, ESA emblem, Columbus space station. $3, Satellite transmission of Pope John XXIII (1881-1963) blessing crowd at the Vatican. $4, Ulf Merbold, W. Germany, 1st non-American astronaut, 1983.

No. 1171, $5, Launch of Telstar II, 5/7/63. No. 1172, $5, 1975 Apollo-Soyuz mission members shaking hands.

1989, Apr. 26 **Litho.** ***Perf. 14***

1163-1170	A165	Set of 8	10.00	10.00

Souvenir Sheets

1171-1172	A165	Set of 2	9.00	9.00

Famous Ocean Liners A166

1989, Apr. 21 **Litho.** ***Perf. 14***

1173	A166	10c Ile de France	.35	.35
1174	A166	40c Liberte	.50	.50
1175	A166	50c Mauretania	.70	.70
1176	A166	75c France	.95	.95
1177	A166	$1 Aquitania	1.25	1.25
1178	A166	$2 United States	2.50	2.50
1179	A166	$3 Olympic	3.50	3.50
1180	A166	$4 Queen Elizabeth	4.75	4.75
		Nos. 1173-1180 (8)	14.50	14.50

Souvenir Sheets

1181	A166	$6 Queen Mary	7.25	7.25
1182	A166	$6 QE 2	7.25	7.25

Nos. 1181-1182 contain 84x28mm stamps.

For overprints see Nos. 1352-1361.

Souvenir Sheet

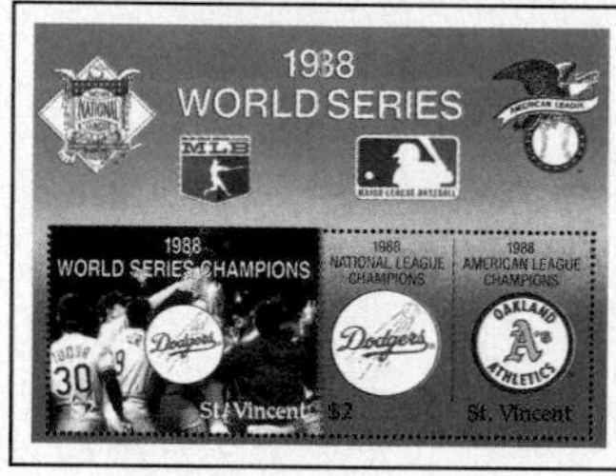

1988 World Series — A167

No. 1183: a, Dodgers emblem and players celebrating victory. b, Emblems of the Dodgers and the Oakland Athletics.

1989, May 3 **Litho.** ***Perf. 14x13½***

1183	A167	Sheet of 2	6.25	6.25
a.-b.		$2 any single	1.60	1.60

World Wildlife Fund, St. Vincent Parrots A168

Indigenous Birds — A169

10c, Parrot's head. 20c, Parrot's wing span. 25c, Mistletoe bird. 40c, Parrot feeding, vert. 70c, Parrot on rock, vert. 75c, Crab hawk. $2, Coucou. $3, Prince bird.

No. 1192, Doctor bird. No. 1193, Soufrieres, vert.

1989, Apr. 5 ***Perf. 14***

1184	A168	10c multicolored	.70	.55
1185	A168	20c multicolored	1.25	.55
1186	A169	25c multicolored	.55	.55
1187	A168	40c multicolored	2.00	2.25
1188	A168	70c multicolored	2.50	1.40
1189	A169	75c multicolored	1.75	1.75
1190	A169	$2 multicolored	2.00	2.00
1191	A169	$3 multicolored	3.00	3.00
		Nos. 1184-1191 (8)	13.75	12.05

Souvenir Sheets

1192	A169	$5 multicolored	4.25	4.25
1193	A169	$5 multicolored	4.25	4.25

Fan Paintings — A170

Paintings by Hiroshige unless otherwise stated: 10c, Autumn Flowers in Front of the Full Moon. 40c, Hibiscus. 50c, Iris. 75c, Morning Glories. $1, Dancing Swallows. $2, Sparrow and Bamboo. $3, Yellow Bird and Cotton Rose. $4, Judos Chrysanthemums in a deep ravine in China.

No. 1202, $6, Rural Cottages in Spring, by Sotatsu. No. 1203, $6, The Six Immortal Poets Portrayed as Cats, by Kuniyoshi.

1989, July 6 **Litho.** ***Perf. 14x13½***

1194-1201	A170	Set of 8	11.00	11.00

Souvenir Sheets

1202-1203	A170	Set of 2	10.00	10.00

Hirohito (1901-89) and enthronement of Akihito as emperor of Japan.

First Moon Landing, 20th Anniv. A171

Apollo 11 Mission: 35c, Columbia command module. 75c, Lunar module Eagle landing. $1, Rocket launch. No. 1207a, Buzz Aldrin conducting solar wind experiments. No. 1207b, Lunar module on plain. No. 1207c, Earthrise. No. 1207d, Neil Armstrong. No. 1208, Separation of lunar and command modules. No. 1209a, Command module. No. 1209b, Lunar module. $6, Armstrong preparing to take man's 1st step onto the Moon.

1989, Sept. 11 ***Perf. 14***

1204	A171	35c multicolored	.40	.30
1205	A171	75c multicolored	1.00	.55
1206	A171	$1 multicolored	1.10	.75
1207		Strip of 4	8.00	8.00
a.-d.		A171 $2 any single	1.40	1.40
1208	A171	$3 multicolored	3.25	3.25
		Nos. 1204-1208 (5)	13.75	12.85

Souvenir Sheets

1209		Sheet of 2	6.50	6.50
a.-b.		A171 $3 any single	2.25	2.25
1210	A171	$6 multicolored	6.50	6.50

No. 1207 has continuous design.

Players Elected to the Baseball Hall of Fame — A172

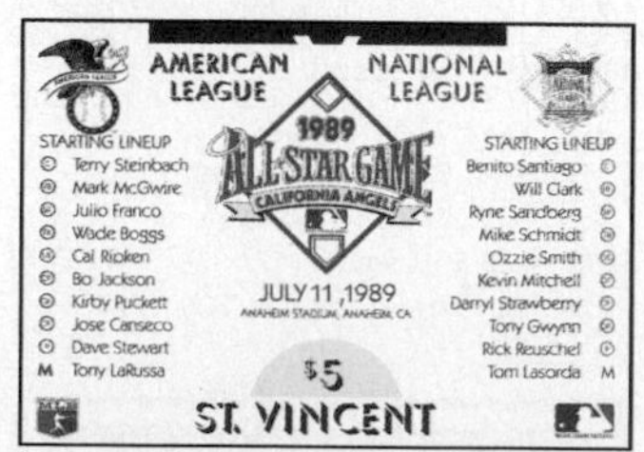

1989 All-Star Game, July 11, Anaheim, California — A173

1989, July 23 **Litho.** ***Perf. 14***

1211	A172	$2 Cobb, 1936	1.40	1.40
1212	A172	$2 Mays, 1979	1.40	1.40
1213	A172	$2 Musial, 1969	1.40	1.40
1214	A172	$2 Bench, 1989	1.40	1.40
1215	A172	$2 Banks, 1977	1.40	1.40
1216	A172	$2 Schoendienst, 1989	1.40	1.40
1217	A172	$2 Gehrig, 1939	1.40	1.40
1218	A172	$2 Robinson, 1962	1.40	1.40
1219	A172	$2 Feller, 1962	1.40	1.40
1220	A172	$2 Williams, 1966	1.40	1.40
1221	A172	$2 Yastrzemski, 1989	1.40	1.40
1222	A172	$2 Kaline, 1980	1.40	1.40
		Nos. 1211-1222 (12)	16.80	16.80

"Yastrzemski" is misspelled on No. 1221.

Size: 116x82mm

Imperf

1223	A173	$5 multicolored	5.75	5.75

Baseball Hall of Fame Members — A173a

No. 1223A, Johnny Bench. No. 1223B, Carl Yastrzemski. No. 1223C, Ernie Banks. No. 1223D, Willie Mays. No. 1223E, Al Kaline. No. 1223F, Ty Cobb. No. 1223G, Ted Williams. No. 1223H, Red Schoendienst. No. 1223I, Jackie Robinson. No. 1223J, Lou Gehrig. No. 1223K, Bob Feller. No. 1223L, Stan Musial.

1989 **Embossed** ***Perf. 13***

1223A-1223L	A173a	$20	Set of 12

Miniature Sheets

Rookies and Team Emblems — A174

Rookies of the Year, Most Valuable Players and Cy Young Award Winners A175

No. 1224: a, Dante Bichette, 1989. b, Carl Yastrzemski, 1961. c, Randy Johnson, 1989. d, Jerome Walton, 1989. e, Ramon Martinez, 1989. f, Ken Hill, 1989. g, Tom McCarthy, 1989. h, Gaylord Perry, 1963. i, John Smoltz, 1989.

No. 1225: a, Bob Milacki, 1989. b, Babe Ruth, 1915. c, Jim Abbott, 1989. d, Gary Sheffield, 1989. e, Gregg Jeffries, 1989. f, Kevin Brown, 1989. g, Cris Carpenter, 1989. h, Johnny Bench, 1968. i, Ken Griffey Jr., 1989.

No. 1226: a, Chris Sabo, 1988 Natl. League Rookie of the Year. b, Walt Weiss, 1988 American League Rookie of the Year. c, Willie Mays, 1951 Rookie of the Year. d, Kirk Gibson, 1988 Natl. League Most Valuable Player. e, Ted Williams, Most Valuable Player of 1946 and 1949. f, Jose Canseco, 1988 American League Most Valuable Player. g, Gaylord Perry, Cy Young winner for 1972 and 1978. h, Orel Hershiser, 1988 National League Cy Young winner. i, Frank Viola, 1988 American League Cy Young winner.

Perf. 13½

1224	A174	Sheet of 9	5.00	5.00
a.-i.		60c any single	.50	.50

1225 A174 Sheet of 9 5.00 5.00
a.-i. A174 60c any single .50 .50
1226 Sheet of 9 5.00 5.00
a.-i. A175 60c any single .50 .50

For surcharges see Nos. B9-B11.

French Revolution Bicent., PHILEXFRANCE '89 — A176

French governors and ships.

1989, July 7 Litho. *Perf. 13½x14*

1227 A176 30c Goelette .65 .65
1228 A176 55c Corvette 1.00 1.00
1229 A176 75c Fregate 36 1.60 1.60
1230 A176 $1 Vaisseau 74 2.00 2.00
1231 A176 $3 Ville de Paris 6.00 6.00
Nos. 1227-1231 (5) 11.25 11.25

Souvenir Sheet

1232 A176 $6 Map 6.00 6.00

Miniature Sheet

Discovery of the New World, 500th Anniv. (in 1992) — A177

No. 1233: a, Map of Florida, queen conch and West Indian purpura. b, Caribbean reef fish. c, Sperm whale. d, Columbus's fleet. e, Cuba, Isle of Pines, remora. f, The Bahamas, Turks & Caicos Isls., Columbus raising Spanish flag. g, Navigational instruments. h, Sea monster. i, Kemp's Ridley turtle, Cayman Isls. j, Jamaica, parts of Cuba and Hispaniola, magnificent frigatebird. k, Caribbean manatee, Hispaniola, Puerto Rico, Virgin Isls. l, Caribbean Monk seal, Anguilla and Caribbean isls. m, Mayan chief, galleon, dugout canoe. n, Masked boobies. o, Venezuelan village on pilings and the Netherlands Antilles. p, Atlantic wing oyster, lion's paw scallop, St. Vincent, Grenada, Trinidad & Tobago, Barbados. q, Panama, great hammerhead and mako sharks. r, Brown pelican, Colombia, Hyacinthine macaw. s, Venezuela, Indian bow and spear hunters. t, Capuchin and squirrel monkeys.

1989, Aug. 31 *Perf. 14*

1233 A177 Sheet of 20 17.00 17.00
a.-t. 50c any single .70 .70

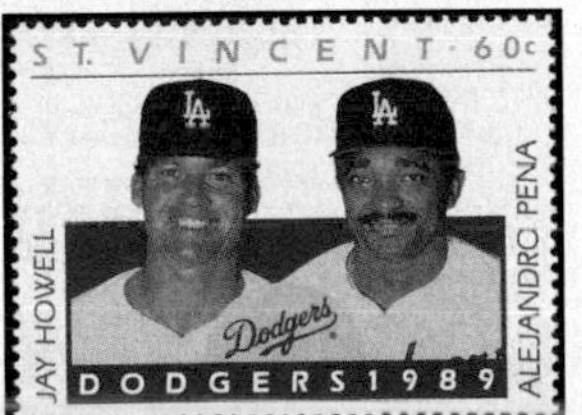

Major League Baseball: Los Angeles Dodgers — A178

No. 1234: a, Jay Howell, Alejandro Pena. b, Mike Davis, Kirk Gibson. c, Fernando Valenzuela, John Shelby. d, Jeff Hamilton, Franklin Stubbs. e, Dodger Stadium. f, Ray Searage, John Tudor. g, Mike Sharperson, Mickey Hatcher. h, Coaches Amalfitano, Cresse, Ferguson, Hines, Mota, Perranoski, Russell. i, John Wetteland, Ramon Martinez.

No. 1235: a, Tim Belcher, Tim Crews. b, Orel Hershiser, Mike Morgan. c, Mike Scioscia, Rick Dempsey. d, Dave Anderson, Alfredo Griffin. e, Team emblem. f, Kal Daniels, Mike Marshall. g, Eddie Murray, Willie Randolph. h, Manager Tom Lasorda, Jose Gonzalez. i, Lenny Harris, Chris Gwynn, Billy Bean.

1989, Sept. 23 *Perf. 12½*

1234 Sheet of 9 6.50 6.50
a.-i. A178 60c any single .55 .55
1235 Sheet of 9 6.50 6.50
a.-i. A178 60c any single .55 .55

See Nos. 1344-1345.

1990 World Cup Soccer Championships, Italy — A179

55c, Youth soccer teams. $1, Natl. team. $5, Trophy winners.

No. 1240, Youth soccer team. No. 1241, Natl. team, diff.

1989, Oct. 16 Litho. *Perf. 14*

1236 A179 10c shown .30 .30
1237 A179 55c multicolored .60 .60
1238 A179 $1 multicolored 1.10 1.10
1239 A179 $5 multicolored 5.50 5.50
Nos. 1236-1239 (4) 7.50 7.50

Souvenir Sheets

1240 A179 $6 multicolored 6.50 6.50
1241 A179 $6 multicolored 6.50 6.50

Fauna and Flora A180

1989, Nov. 1

1242 A180 65c St. Vincent parrot .90 .90
1243 A180 75c Whistling warbler 1.10 1.10
1244 A180 $5 Black snake 7.00 7.00
Nos. 1242-1244 (3) 9.00 9.00

Souvenir Sheet

1245 A180 $6 Volcano plant, vert. 6.50 6.50

Butterflies A181

1989, Oct. 16 *Perf. 14x14½, 14½x14*

1246 A181 6c Little yellow .30 .25
1247 A181 10c Orion .30 .25
1248 A181 15c American painted lady .30 .25
1249 A181 75c Cassius blue .95 .60
1250 A181 $1 Polydamus swallowtail 1.20 1.20
1251 A181 $2 Guaraguao skipper 2.40 2.40
1252 A181 $3 The Queen 3.50 3.50
1253 A181 $5 Royal blue 6.00 6.00
Nos. 1246-1253 (8) 14.95 14.45

Souvenir Sheets

1254 A181 $6 Monarch 6.50 6.50
1255 A181 $6 Barred sulphur 6.50 6.50

Exhibition Emblem, Disney Characters and US Natl. Monuments A182

Designs: 1c, Seagull Monument, UT. 2c, Lincoln Memorial, Washington, DC. 3c, Crazy Horse Memorial, SD. 4c, Uncle Sam Wilson, Troy, NY. 5c, Benjamin Franklin Natl. Memorial, Philadelphia, PA. 10c, Statue of George Washington, Federal Hall, NY. $3, John F. Kennedy's birthplace, Brookline, MA. $6, George Washington's home, Mount Vernon, VA.

No. 1264, $5, Mt. Rushmore, SD. No. 1265, $5, Stone Mountain, GA.

1989, Nov. 17 *Perf. 13½x14*

1256-1263 A182 Set of 8 12.50 12.50

Souvenir Sheets

1264-1265 A182 Set of 2 13.50 13.50

World Stamp Expo '89.

Souvenir Sheet

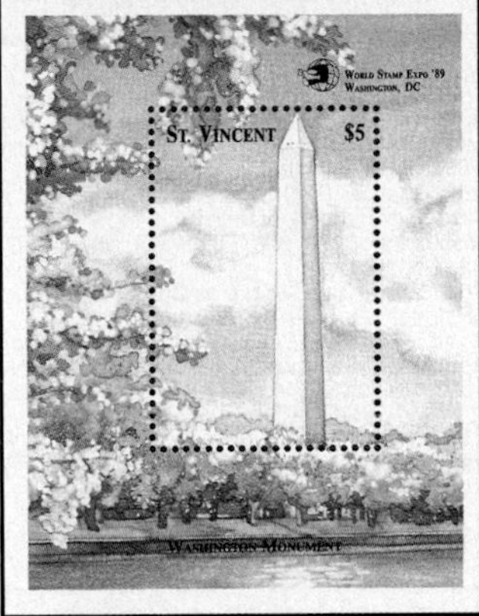

The Washington Monument, Washington, DC — A183

1989, Nov. 17 Litho. *Perf. 14*

1266 A183 $5 multicolored 4.25 4.25

World Stamp Expo '89.

Major League Baseball — A184

Players, owners and commissioner.

No. 1267, 30c: a, Early Wynn. b, Cecil Cooper. c, Joe DiMaggio. d, Kevin Mitchell. e, Tom Browning. f, Bobby Witt. g, Tim Wallach. h, Bob Gibson. i, Steve Garvey.

No. 1268, 30c: a, Rick Sutcliffe. b, A. Bartlett Giamatti, commissioner. c, Cory Snyder. d, Rollie Fingers. e, Willie Hernandez. f, Sandy Koufax. g, Carl Yastrzemski. h, Ron Darling. i, Gerald Perry.

No. 1269, 30c: a, Mike Marshall. b, Tom Seaver. c, Bob Milacki. d, Dave Smith. e, Robin Roberts. f, Kent Hrbek. g, Bill Veeck, owner. h, Carmelo Martinez. i, Rogers Hornsby.

No. 1270, 30c: a, Barry Bonds. b, Jim Palmer. c, Lou Boudreau. d, Ernie Whitt. e, Jose Canseco. f, Ken Griffey, Jr. g, Johnny Vander Meer. h, Kevin Seitzer. i, Dave Dravecky.

No. 1271, 30c: a, Glenn Davis. b, Nolan Ryan. c, Hank Greenberg. d, Richie Allen. e, Dave Righetti. f, Jim Abbott. g, Harold Reynolds. h, Dennis Martinez. i, Rod Carew.

No. 1272, 30c: a, Joe Morgan. b, Tony Fernandez. c, Ozzie Guillen. d, Mike Greenwell. e, Bobby Valentine. f, Doug DeCinces. g, Mickey Cochrane. h, Willie McGee. i, Von Hayes.

No. 1273, 30c: a, Frank White. b, Brook Jacoby. c, Boog Powell. d, Will Clark. e, Ray Kroc, owner. f, Fred McGriff. g, Willie Stargell. h, John Smoltz. i, B. J. Surhoff.

No. 1274, 30c: a, Keith Hernandez. b, Eddie Matthews. c, Tom Paciorek. d, Alan Trammell. e, Greg Maddux. f, Ruben Sierra. g, Tony Oliva. h, Chris Bosio. i, Orel Hershiser.

No. 1275, 30c: a, Casey Stengel. b, Jim Rice. c, Reggie Jackson. d, Jerome Walton. e, Bob Knepper. f, Andres Galarraga. g, Christy Mathewson. h, Willie Wilson. i, Ralph Kiner.

1989, Nov. 30 *Perf. 12½*

Sheets of 9, #a-i

1267-1275 A184 Set of 9 29.00 29.00

No. 1268d is incorrectly inscribed "Finger." Cochrane is misspelled "Cochpane" on No. 1272g.

No. 1272d was also issued in sheets of 9.

Achievements of Nolan Ryan, American Baseball Player — A185

No. 1276 — Portrait and inscriptions: a, 383 League-leading strikeouts, 1973. b, No hitter, Kansas City Royals, May 15, 1973. c, No hitter, Detroit Tigers, July 15, 1973. d, No hitter, Minnesota Twins, Sept. 28, 1974. e, No hitter, Baltimore Orioles, June 1, 1975. f, No hitter, Los Angeles Dodgers, Sept. 26, 1981. g, Won 100+ games in both leagues. h, Struck out 200+ batters in 13 seasons. i, 5000th Strikeout, Aug. 22, 1989, Arlington, Texas.

1989, Nov. 30 Litho. *Perf. 12½*

1276 Sheet of 9 12.00 12.00
a.-i. A185 $2 any single 1.30 1.30

For overprints see Nos. 1336-1337.

Coat of Arms, No. 570 — A186

1989, Dec. 20 *Perf. 14*

1278 A186 65c multicolored .90 .90

Souvenir Sheet

1279 A186 $10 multicolored 8.75 8.75

Independence, 10th anniv.

Boy Scouts and Girl Guides — A187

Lord or Lady Baden-Powell and: No. 1280, Boy's modern uniform. No. 1281, Guide, ranger and brownie. No. 1282, Boy's old uniform. No. 1283, Mrs. Jackson. No. 1284, 75th anniversary emblem. No. 1285, Mrs. Russell

No. 1286, Canoeing, merit badges, No. 1287, Flag-raising, Camp Yourumei, 1985.

1989, Dec. 20 *Perf. 14*

1280 A187 35c multi .65 .65
1281 A187 35c multi .65 .65
1282 A187 55c multi .85 .85
1283 A187 55c multi .85 .85
1284 A187 $2 multi 3.25 3.25
1285 A187 $2 multi 3.25 3.25
Nos. 1280-1285 (6) 9.50 9.50

Souvenir Sheets

1286 A187 $5 multi 6.25 6.25
1287 A187 $5 multi 6.25 6.25

Christmas — A188

Paintings by Da Vinci and Botticelli: 10c, The Adoration of the Magi (holy family), by Botticelli. 25c, The Adoration of the Magi (witnesses). 30c, The Madonna of the Magnificat, by Botticelli. 40c, The Virgin and Child with St. Anne and St. John the Baptist, by Da Vinci. 55c, The Annunciation (angel), by Da Vinci. 75c, The Annunciation (Madonna). No. 1294, $5, Madonna of the Carnation, by Da Vinci. $6, The Annunciation, by Botticelli. No. 1296, $5 The Virgin of the Rocks, by Da Vinci. No. 1297, $5, The Adoration of the Magi, by Botticelli.

1989, Dec. 20 ***Perf. 14***
1288-1295 A188 Set of 8 12.00 12.00

Souvenir Sheets

1296-1297 A188 Set of 2 8.75 8.75

Bird Type of 1988

1989, July 31 Litho. ***Perf. 15x14***
1298 A150 55c St. Vincent parrot .90 .90

Lions Intl. of St. Vincent, 25th Anniv. (in 1989) A189

Services: 10c, Scholarships for the blind, vert. 65c, Free textbooks. 75c, Health education (diabetes). $2, Blood sugar testing machines. $4, Publishing and distribution of pamphlets on drug abuse.

1990, Mar. 5 Litho. ***Perf. 14***
1303-1307 A189 Set of 5 7.75 7.75

For surcharge see No. 3345.

World War II A190

Historic events: 5c, Defeat of the Graf Spee, 12/13-17/39. 10c, Charles De Gaulle calls the French Resistance to arms, 6/18/40. 15c, The British drive the Italian army out of Egypt, 12/15/40. 25c, US destroyer Reuben James torpedoed off Iceland, 10/31/41. 30c, MacArthur becomes allied supreme commander of the southwest Pacific, 4/18/42. 40c, US forces attack Corregidor, 2/16/45. 55c, HMS King George V engages the Bismarck, 5/27/41. 75c, US fleet enters Tokyo Harbor, 8/27/45. $5, Russian takeover of Berlin completed, 5/2/45. $6, #1317, Battle of the Philippine Sea, 6/18/44. #1318, Battle of the Java Sea, 2/28/42.

1990, Apr. 2 ***Perf. 14x13½***
1308-1317 A190 Set of 10 17.00 17.00

Souvenir Sheet

1318 A190 $6 multi 7.75 7.75

Penny Black, 150th Anniv. — A191

Great Britain No. 1 (various plate positions).

1990, May 3 Litho. ***Perf. 14x15***
1319 A191 $2 "NK" 2.25 2.25
1320 A191 $4 "AB" 4.50 4.50

Souvenir Sheet

1321 A191 $6 Simulated #1, "SV" 6.75 6.75

Stamp World London '90 — A192

Walt Disney characters in British military uniforms: 5c, Donald Duck as 18th cent. Admiral. 10c, Huey as Bugler, 68th Light Infantry, 1854. 15c, Minnie Mouse as Drummer, 1st Irish Guards, 1900. 25c, Goofy as Lance Corporal, Seaforth Highlanders, 1944. $1, Mickey Mouse as officer, 58th Regiment, 1879, 1881. $2, Donald Duck as officer, Royal Engineers, 1813. $4, Mickey Mouse as Drum Major, 1914. $5, Goofy as Pipe Sergeant, 1918.

No. 1330, $6, Scrooge as Company Clerk and Goofy as King's Lifeguard of Foot. No. 1331, $6, Mickey Mouse as British Grenadier.

1990, May Litho. ***Perf. 13½x14***
1322-1329 A192 Set of 8 17.00 17.00

Souvenir Sheets

1330-1331 A192 Set of 2 13.50 13.50

A193

1990, July 5 ***Perf. 14***
1332 $2 In robes 1.75 1.75
1333 $2 Queen Mother signing book 1.75 1.75
1334 $2 In fur coat 1.75 1.75
a. A193 Strip of 3, #1332-1334 5.25 5.25
Nos. 1332-1334 (3) 5.25 5.25

Souvenir Sheet

1335 A194 $6 Like No. 1334 4.75 4.75

No. 1276 Overprinted

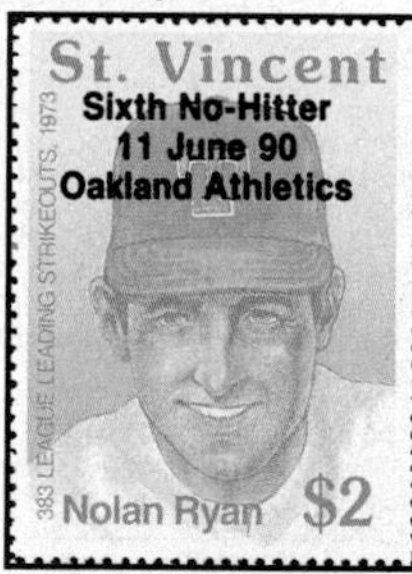

a

b

1990, July 23 Litho. ***Perf. 12½***

Miniature Sheets

1336 A185(a) $2 Sheet of 9, #a-i 12.50 12.50
1337 A185(b) $2 Sheet of 9, #a-i 12.50 12.50

World Cup Soccer Championships, Italy — A195

Players from participating countries.

1990, Sept. 24 Litho. ***Perf. 14***
1338 A195 10c Argentina .35 .25
1339 A195 75c Colombia .95 .95
1340 A195 $1 Uruguay 1.25 1.25
1341 A195 $5 Belgium 7.00 7.00
Nos. 1338-1341 (4) 9.55 9.45

Souvenir Sheets

1342 A195 $6 Brazil 5.75 5.75
1343 A195 $6 West Germany 5.75 5.75

Dodger Baseball Type of 1989

No. 1344: a, Hubie Brooks, Orel Hershiser. b, Manager Tom Lasorda, Tim Crews. c, Fernando Valenzuela, Eddie Murray. d, Kal Daniels, Jose Gonzalez. e, Dodger centennial emblem. f, Chris Gwynn, Jeff Hamilton. g, Kirk Gibson, Rick Dempsey. h, Jim Gott, Alfredo Griffin. i, Coaches, Ron Perranoski, Bill Russell, Joe Ferguson, Joe Amalfitano, Mark Cresse, Ben Hines, Manny Mota.

No. 1345: a, Mickey Hatcher, Jay Howell. b, Juan Samuel, Mike Scioscia. c, Lenny Harris, Mike Hartley. d, Ramon Martinez, Mike Morgan. e, Dodger Stadium. f, Stan Javier, Don Aase. g, Ray Searage, Mike Sharperson. h, Tim Belcher, Pat Perry. i, Dave Walsh, Jose Vizcaino, Jim Neidlinger, Jose Offerman, Carlos Hernandez.

Hyphen-hole roulette 7

1990, Sept. 21
1344 Sheet of 9 6.50 6.50
a.-i. A178 60c any single .35 .35
1345 Sheet of 9 6.50 6.50
a.-i. A178 60c any single .35 .35

Nos. 1116-1120 Overprinted

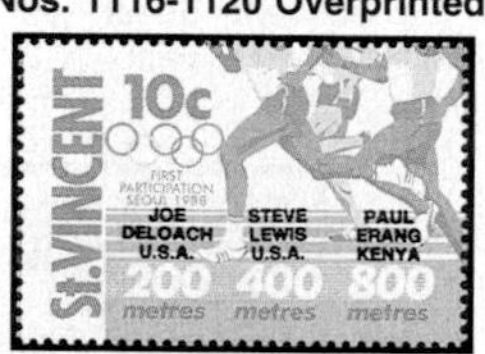

Overprints: 50c, "CARL / LEWIS / U.S.A.". $1, "HRISTO / MARKOV / BULGARIA". $5, "HENRY / MASKE / E. GERMANY".

No. 1350, USSR, US medals. No. 1351, South Korea, Spain medals.

1990, Oct. 18 ***Perf. 14***
1346 A158 10c shown .30 .30
1347 A158 50c multicolored .55 .55
1348 A158 $1 multicolored .95 .95
1349 A158 $5 multicolored 5.00 5.00
Nos. 1346-1349 (4) 6.80 6.80

Souvenir Sheets

1350 A158 $10 multicolored 6.75 6.75
1351 A158 $10 multicolored 6.75 6.75

Nos. 1173-1182 Overprinted

1990, Oct. 18 Litho. ***Perf. 14***
1352 A166 10c Ile de France .30 .30
1353 A166 40c Liberte .35 .35
1354 A166 50c Mauretania .50 .50
1355 A166 75c France .70 .70
1356 A166 $1 Aquitania 1.00 1.00
1357 A166 $2 United States 1.90 1.90
1358 A166 $3 Olympic 2.75 2.75
1359 A166 $4 Queen Elizabeth 4.00 4.00
Nos. 1352-1359 (8) 11.50 11.50

Souvenir Sheets

1360 A166 $6 Queen Mary 5.75 5.75
1361 A166 $6 QE 2 5.75 5.75

Overprint on #1360-1361 is 12mm in diameter.

Orchids — A196

Designs: 10c, Dendrophylax funalis, Dimeranda emarginata. 15c, Epidendrum elongatum. 45c, Comparettia falcata. 60c, Brassia maculata. $1, Encyclia cochleata, Encyclia cordigera. $2, Cyrtopodium punctatum. $4, Cattelya labiata. $5, Bletia purpurea.

No. 1370, $6, Ionopsis utricularioides. No. 1371, $6, Vanilla planifolia.

1990, Nov. 23
1362-1369 A196 Set of 8 20.00 20.00

Souvenir Sheets

1370-1371 A196 Set of 2 17.00 17.00

Christmas A197

Details from paintings by Rubens: 10c, Miraculous Draught of Fishes. 45c, $2, Crowning of Holy Katherine. 50c, St. Ives of Treguier. 65c, Allegory of Eternity. $1, $4, St. Bavo Receives Monastic Habit of Ghent. $5, Communion of St. Francis.

No. 1380, $6, St. Ives of Treguier (entire). No. 1381, $6, Allegory of Eternity. No. 1382, $6, St. Bavo Receives Monastic Habit of Ghent, horiz. No. 1383, $6, The Miraculous Draft of Fishes, horiz.

1990, Dec. 3 Litho. ***Perf. 14***
1372-1379 A197 Set of 8 13.00 13.00

Souvenir Sheets

1380-1383 A197 Set of 4 16.50 16.50

Intl. Literacy Year A198

Canterbury Tales: a, Geoffrey Chaucer (1342-1400), author. b, "When April with his showers sweet..." c, "When Zephyr also has,..." d. "And many little birds make melody..." e, "And palmers to go seeking out strange strands..." f, Quill pen, open book. g, Bluebird in tree. h, Trees, rider's head with white hair. i, Banner on staff. j, Town. k, Rider's head, diff. l, Blackbird in tree. m, Old monk. n, Horse, rider. o, Nun, monk carrying banner. p, Monks. q, White horse, rider. r, Black horse, rider. s, Squirrel. t, Rooster. u, Chickens. v, Rabbit. w, Butterfly. x, Mouse.

1990, Dec. 12 ***Perf. 13½***
1384 Sheet of 24 17.00 17.00
a.-x. A198 40c any single .30 .30

Vincent Van Gogh (1853-1890), Painter — A198a

Self-portraits.

1990, Dec. 17 Litho. *Perf. 13*

1385	A198a	1c	1889	.30	.30
1386	A198a	5c	1886	.30	.30
1387	A198a	10c	1888, with hat & pipe	.30	.30
1388	A198a	15c	1888, painting	.30	.30
a.			Strip of 4, #1385-1388	.50	.50
1389	A198a	20c	1887	.30	.30
1390	A198a	45c	1889, diff.	.55	.55
1391	A198a	$5	1889, with bandaged ear	5.75	5.75
1392	A198a	$6	1887, with straw hat	7.00	7.00
a.			Strip of 4, #1389-1392	14.50	14.50
			Nos. 1385-1392 (8)	14.80	14.80

Hummel Figurines — A199

10c, Photographer. 15c, Boy with ladder & rope. 40c, Pharmacist. 60c, Boy answering telephone. $1, Bootmaker. $2, Artist. $4, Waiter. $5, Mailman.

1990, Dec. 30 Litho. *Perf. 14*

1393	A199	10c	multicolored	.25	.25
1394	A199	15c	multicolored	.25	.25
1395	A199	40c	multicolored	.35	.30
1396	A199	60c	multicolored	.50	.40
1396A	A199	$1	multicolored	.85	.60
1396B	A199	$2	multicolored	1.75	1.75
1397	A199	$4	multicolored	3.75	3.75
a.			Sheet of 4, 15c, 40c, $2, $4	6.00	6.00
1398	A199	$5	multicolored	3.75	3.75
a.			Sheet of 4, 10c, 60c, $1, $5	6.00	6.00
			Nos. 1393-1398 (8)	11.45	11.05

Souvenir Sheets

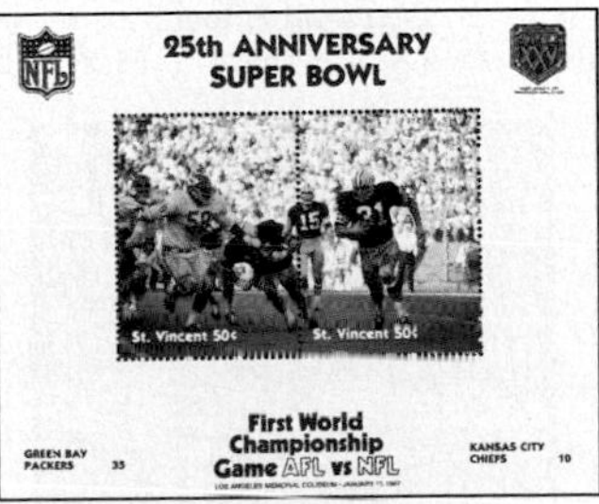

Super Bowl Highlights — A200

Designs: Nos. 1400-1424, Players in action in Super Bowl I (1967) through Super Bowl XXV (1991). Nos. 1400-1423 contain two 50c stamps printed with continuous design showing game highlights. No. 1424 contains three 50c stamps showing AFC and NFC team helmets and the Vince Lombardi Trophy.

Nos. 1425-1449, $2, picture Super Bowl Program Covers. Nos. 1443, 1449 horiz.

1991, Jan. 15 Litho. *Perf. 13½x14*

1400-1424	A200	Set of 25	32.00	32.00

Size: 99x125mm

Imperf

1425-1449	A200	$2 Set of 25	60.00	60.00

Miniature Sheets

Discovery of America, 500th Anniv. (in 1992) — A201

No. 1450: a, 1c, US #230. b, 2c, US #231. c, 3c, US #232. d, 4c, US #233. e, $10, Sailing ship, parrot. f, 5c, US #234. g, 6c, US #235. h, 8c, US #236. i, 10c, US #237.

No. 1451: a, 15c, US #238. b, 30c, US #239. c, 50c, US #240. d, $1, US #241. e, $10, Compass rose, sailing ship. f, $2, US #242. g, $3, US #243. h, $4, US #244. i, $5, US #245.

No. 1452, Bow of sailing ship. No. 1453, Ship's figurehead.

1991, Mar. 18 Litho. *Perf. 14*

1450	A201	Sheet of 9, #a-i	9.00	9.00
1451	A201	Sheet of 9, #a-i	22.50	22.50

Souvenir Sheets

1452	A201	$6 multicolored	6.75	6.75
1453	A201	$6 multicolored	6.75	6.75

Nos. 1452-1453 each contain one 38x31mm stamp.

Jetsons, The Movie — A202

Hanna-Barbera characters: 5c, Cosmo Spacely, vert. 20c, Elroy, Judy, Astro, Jane & George Jetson, vert. 45c, Judy, Apollo Blue, vert. 50c, Mr. Spacely, George, vert. 60c, George, sprocket factory. $1, Apollo Blue, Judy, Elroy and Grungees. $2, Jane and George in Grungee cavern. $4, George, Elroy, Jane and Little Grungee, vert. $5, Jetsons leaving for Earth, vert.

No. 1463, $6, Jetsons in sprocket factory. No. 1464, $6, Jetsons traveling to Orbiting Ore Asteroid.

1991, Mar. 25 Litho. *Perf. 13½*

1454-1462	A202	Set of 9	14.00	14.00

Souvenir Sheets

1463-1464	A202	Set of 2	11.00	11.00

The Flintstones Enjoy Sports — A203

1991, Mar. 25

1465	A203	10c	Boxing	.35	.25
1466	A203	15c	Soccer	.35	.20
1467	A203	45c	Rowing	.55	.35
1468	A203	55c	Dinosaur riding	.65	.40
1469	A203	$1	Basketball	1.00	.65
1470	A203	$2	Wrestling	2.25	1.75
1471	A203	$4	Tennis	4.50	4.50
1472	A203	$5	Cycling	5.75	5.75
			Nos. 1465-1472 (8)	15.40	13.90

Souvenir Sheets

1473	A203	$6	Baseball, batting	6.75	6.75
1474	A203	$6	Baseball, sliding home	6.75	6.75

Voyages of Discovery A204

Designs: 5c, Sanger 2. 10c, Magellan probe, 1990. 25c, Buran space shuttle. 75c, American space station. $1, Mars mission, 21st century. $2, Hubble space telescope, 1990. $4, Sailship to Mars. $5, Craf satellite, 2000.

No. 1483, $6, Sailing ship, island hopping. No. 1484, $6, Sailing ship returning home.

1991, May 13

1475-1482	A204	Set of 8	13.00	13.00

Souvenir Sheets

1483-1484	A204	Set of 2	13.00	13.00

Discovery of America, 500th anniv. (in 1992).

Royal Family Birthday, Anniversary Common Design Type

Designs: 20c, 25c, $1, Nos. 1492, 1494, Charles and Diana, 10th wedding anniversary. Others, Queen Elizabeth II, 65th birthday.

1991, July Litho. *Perf. 14*

1485	CD347	5c	multicolored	.25	.25
1486	CD347	20c	multicolored	.35	.25
1487	CD347	25c	multicolored	.35	.25
1488	CD347	60c	multicolored	.70	.45
1489	CD347	$1	multicolored	1.10	.70
1490	CD347	$2	multicolored	2.25	2.25
1491	CD347	$4	multicolored	4.25	4.25
1492	CD347	$5	multicolored	5.50	5.50
			Nos. 1485-1492 (8)	14.75	13.90

Souvenir Sheets

1493	CD347	$5	Elizabeth, Philip	6.00	6.00
1494	CD347	$5	Charles, Diana, sons	6.00	6.00

Japanese Trains A205

No. 1495: a, D51 steam locomotive. b, 9600 steam locomotive. c, Chrysanthemum emblem. d, Passenger coach. e, C57 steam locomotive. f, Oil tank car. g, C53 steam locomotive. h, First steam locomotive. i, C11 steam locomotive.

No. 1496: a, Class 181 electric train. b, EH-10 electric locomotive. c, Special Express emblem. d, Sendai City Class 1 trolley. e, Class 485 electric train. f, Sendai City trolley street cleaner. g, Hakari bullet train. h, ED-11 electric locomotive. i, EF-66 electric locomotive.

No. 1497, C55 steam locomotive, vert. No. 1498, Series 400 electric train. No. 1499, C62 steam locomotive, vert. No. 1500, Super Hitachi electric train, vert.

1991, Aug. 12 Litho. *Perf. 14x13½*

1495	A205	75c	Sheet of 9, #a.-i.	7.00	7.00
1496	A205	$1	Sheet of 9, #a.-i.	9.75	9.75

Souvenir Sheets

Perf. 13x13½

1497	A205	$6	multicolored	5.75	5.75
1498	A205	$6	multicolored	5.75	5.75
1499	A205	$6	multicolored	5.75	5.75
1500	A205	$6	multicolored	5.75	5.75

Phila Nippon '91. Nos. 1497-1500 each contain 27x44mm or 44x27mm stamps.

Miniature Sheets

Entertainers — A206

No. 1501: a-i, Various portraits of Madonna.

No. 1502 — Italian entertainers: a, Marcello Mastroianni. b, Sophia Loren. c, Mario Lanza (1921-59). d, Federico Fellini. e, Arturo Toscanini (1867-1957). f, Anna Magnani (1908-73). g, Giancarlo Giannini. h, Gina Lollobrigida. i, Enrico Caruso (1873-1921).

No. 1503: a-i, Various portraits of John Lennon.

1991, Aug. 22 *Perf. 13*

1501	A206	$1	Sheet of 9, #a.-i.	13.00	13.00
1502	A206	$1	Sheet of 9, #a.-i.	9.25	9.25
1503	A206	$1	+2c, Sheet of 9, #a.-i.	11.00	11.00

Souvenir Sheets

Perf. 12x13

1504	A206	$6	Madonna	11.50	11.50

Perf. 13

1505	A206	$6	Luciano Pavarotti, horiz.	9.00	9.00

No. 1503 is semi-postal with surtax going to the Spirit Foundation.

No. 1504 contains one 28x42mm stamp. Compare with No. 1566. See Nos. 1642-1643, 1729, 2055.

Intl. Literacy Year — A207

Walt Disney characters in "The Prince and the Pauper": 5c, Pauper pals. 10c, Princely boredom. 15c, The valet. 25c, Look alikes. 60c, Trading places. 75c, How to be a prince. 80c, Food for the populace. $1, Captain's plot. $2, Doomed in the dungeon. $3, Looking for a way out. $4, A Goofy jailbreak. $5, Long live the real prince.

No. 1518, $6, Crowning the wrong guy. No. 1519, $6, Mickey meets the captain of the guard. No. 1520, $6, Real prince arrives. No. 1521, $6, Seize the guard.

1991, Nov. 18 *Perf. 14x13½*

1506-1517	A207	Set of 12	16.00	16.00

Souvenir Sheets

1518-1521	A207	Set of 4	21.00	21.00

1991, Nov. 18

Walt Disney's "The Rescuers Down Under": 5c, Miss Bianca, Heroine. 10c, Bernard, Shy Hero. 15c, Maitre d'Francois. 25c, Wilbur, the Albatross. 60c, Jake, the Aussie kangaroo mouse. 75c, Bernard, Bianca and Jake in the outback. 80c, Bianca and Bernard. $1, Marahute, the magnificent rare eagle. $2, Cody and Marahute. $3, McLeach and his pet Goanna, Joanna. $4, Frank, the frill-necked lizard. $5, Endangered animals: Red Kangaroo, Krebbs Koala, and Polly Platypus.

No. 1534, $6, Cody with the rescuers. No. 1535, $6, Delegates of Intl. Rescue Aid Society. No. 1536, $6, Wilbur's painful touchdown

"down under." No. 1537, $6, Wilbur transports Miss Bianca and Bernard to Australia.

1522-1533 A207 Set of 12 14.00 14.00

Souvenir Sheets

1534-1537 A207 Set of 4 19.00 19.00

Brandenburg Gate, Bicent. — A209

Designs: 50c, Demonstrator with sign. 75c, Soldiers at Berlin Wall. 90c, German flag, shadows on wall. $1, Pres. Gorbachev and Pres. Bush shaking hands.
$4, Coat of Arms of Berlin.

1991, Nov. 18 Litho. *Perf. 14*

1538-1541 A209 Set of 4 4.00 4.00

Souvenir Sheet

1542 A209 $4 multi 4.00 4.00

Wolfgang Amadeus Mozart, Death Bicent. A210

Designs: $1, Scene from "Marriage of Figaro." $3, Scene from "The Clemency of Titus."
$4, Portrait of Mozart, vert.

1991, Nov. 18

1543 A210 $1 multicolored 1.10 1.10
1544 A210 $3 multicolored 3.25 3.25

Souvenir Sheet

1545 A210 $4 multicolored 4.00 4.00

17th World Scout Jamboree, Korea — A211

Designs: 65c, Adventure tales around camp fire, vert. $1.50, British defenses at Mafeking, 1900, Cape of Good Hope #179. $3.50, Scouts scuba diving, queen angelfish.

1991, Nov. 18 Litho. *Perf. 14*

1546 A211 65c multicolored .45 .45
1547 A211 $1.50 multicolored 1.00 1.00
1548 A211 $3.50 multicolored 2.50 2.50
Nos. 1546-1548 (3) 3.95 3.95

Souvenir Sheet

1549 A211 $5 shown 3.50 3.50

Charles de Gaulle, Birth Cent. A212

De Gaulle and: 10c, Free French Forces, 1944. 45c, Churchill, 1944. 75c, Liberation of Paris, 1944.

1991, Nov. 18 Litho. *Perf. 14*

1550 A212 10c multicolored .60 .60
1551 A212 45c multicolored 1.00 1.00
1552 A212 75c multicolored 1.60 1.60
Nos. 1550-1552 (3) 3.20 3.20

Souvenir Sheet

1553 A212 $5 Portrait 3.50 3.50

Anniversaries and Events — A213

Designs: No. 1554, Woman, flag, map. No. 1555, Steam locomotive. $1.65, Otto Lilienthal, glider in flight. No. 1557, Gottfried Wilhelm Leibniz, mathematician. No. 1558, Street warfare.

1991, Nov. 18

1554 A213 $1.50 multicolored 3.00 3.00
1555 A213 $1.50 multicolored 3.25 3.25
1556 A213 $1.65 multicolored 3.75 3.75
1557 A213 $2 multicolored 4.75 4.75
1558 A213 $2 multicolored 4.25 4.25
Nos. 1554-1558 (5) 19.00 19.00

Swiss Confedration, 700th anniv. (#1554). Trans-Siberian Railway, 100th anniv. (#1555). First glider flight, cent. (#1556). City of Hanover, 750th anniv. (#1557). Fall of Kiev, Sept. 19, 1941 (#1558).

Heroes of Pearl Harbor — A214

No. 1559 — Congressional Medal of Honor recipients: a, Myrvyn S. Bennion. b, George H. Cannon. c, John W. Finn. d, Francis C. Flaherty. e, Samuel G. Fuqua. f, Edwin J. Hill. g, Herbert C. Jones. h, Isaac C. Kidd. i, Jackson C. Pharris. j, Thomas J. Reeves. k, Donald K. Ross. l, Robert R. Scott. m, Franklin Van Valkenburgh. n, James R. Ward. o, Cassin Young.

1991, Nov. 18 *Perf. 14½x15*

1559 A214 $1 Sheet of 15, #a-o 19.00 19.00

Famous People — A215

No. 1560 — Golfers: a, Gary Player. b, Nick Faldo. c, Severiano Ballesteros. d, Ben Hogan. e, Jack Nicklaus. f, Greg Norman. g, Jose-Marie Olazabal. h, Bobby Jones.

No. 1561 — Statesmen and historical events: a, Hans-Dietrich Genscher, German Foreign Minister, winged victory symbol. b, Destruction of Berlin Wall. c, Charles de Gaulle delivering radio appeal, Winston Churchill, de Gaulle. d, Dwight D. Eisenhower, de Gaulle, Normandy invasion. e, Brandenburg Gate. f, German Chancellor Helmut Kohl, mayors of East, West Berlin. g, De Gaulle and Konrad Adenauer. h, George Washington and Lafayette, De Gaulle and John F. Kennedy.

No. 1562 — Chess masters: a, Francois Andre Danican Philidor. b, Adolph Anderssen. c, Wilhelm Steinitz. d, Alexander Alekhine. e, Boris Spassky. f, Bobby Fischer. g, Anatoly Karpov. h, Garri Kasparov.

No. 1563 — Nobel Prize winners: a, Einstein, physics. b, Roentgen, physics. c, William Shockley, physics. d, Charles Townes, physics. e, Lev Landau, physics. f, Marconi, physics. g, Willard Libby, chemistry. h, Ernest Lawrence, physics.

No. 1564 — Entertainers: a, Michael Jackson. b, Madonna. c, Elvis Presley. d, David Bowie. e, Prince. f, Frank Sinatra. g, George Michael. h, Mick Jagger.

No. 1565, Roosevelt, de Gaulle, Churchill at Morocco Conf., 1943. No. 1566, Madonna. No. 1567, Elvis Presley.

1991, Nov. 25 Litho. *Perf. 14½*

1560 A215 $1 Sheet of 8, #a.-h. 15.50 15.50
1561 A215 $1 Sheet of 8, #a.-h. 14.00 14.00
1562 A215 $1 Sheet of 8, #a.-h. 11.50 11.50
1563 A215 $1 Sheet of 8, #a.-h. 13.00 13.00
1564 A215 $2 Sheet of 8, #a.-h. 17.50 17.50

Souvenir Sheets

Perf. 14

1565 A215 $6 multicolored 7.00 7.00
1566 A215 $6 multicolored 5.50 5.50
1567 A215 $6 multicolored 5.50 5.50

Nos. 1565-1567 each contain one 27x43mm stamp.

See Nos. 1642-1643, 1729-1730 for more Elvis Presley stamps.

Walt Disney Christmas Cards A216

Designs and year of issue: 10c, Goofy, Mickey and Pluto decorating Christmas tree, 1982. 45c, Mickey, reindeer, 1980. 55c, Christmas tree ornament, 1970. 75c, Baby duck holding 1944 sign, 1943. $1.50, Characters papering globe with greetings, 1941. $2, Lady and the Tramp beside Christmas tree, 1986. $4, Donald, Goofy, Mickey and Pluto reciting "Night Before Christmas," 1977. $5, Mickey in doorway of Snow White's Castle, 1965.

No. 1576, $6, People from around the world, 1966. No. 1577, $6, Mickey in balloon basket with people of different countries, 1966.

1991, Dec. 23 *Perf. 13½x14*

1568-1575 A216 Set of 8 14.00 14.00

Souvenir Sheets

1576-1577 A216 Set of 2 14.50 14.50

Environmental Preservation — A217

1992, Jan. Litho. *Perf. 14*

1578 A217 10c Kings Hill .30 .30
1579 A217 55c Tree planting .65 .65
1580 A217 75c Botanical Gardens .95 .95
1581 A217 $2 Kings Hill Project 2.10 2.10
Nos. 1578-1581 (4) 4.00 4.00

Queen Elizabeth II's Accession to the Throne, 40th Anniv.

Common Design Type

1992, Feb. 6

1582 CD348 10c multicolored .25 .25
1583 CD348 20c multicolored .25 .25
1584 CD348 $1 multicolored .65 .65
1585 CD348 $5 multicolored 3.25 3.25
Nos. 1582-1585 (4) 4.40 4.40

Souvenir Sheets

1586 CD348 $6 Queen, beach 5.00 5.00
1587 CD348 $6 Queen, harbor 5.00 5.00

Queen Elizabeth II's Acession to the Throne, 40th Anniv. A217a

Designs: No. 1587A, Queen Elizabeth II. No. 1587B, King George VI.

1993, Mar. 2 Embossed *Perf. 12*

Without Gum

1587A A217a $5 gold
1587B A217a $5 gold

1992 Winter Olympics, Albertville — A218

10c, Women's luge, horiz. 15c, Women's figure skating. 25c, Two-man bobsled, horiz. 30c, Mogul skiing. 45c, Nordic combined, horiz. 55c, Ski jump, horiz. 75c, Giant slalom, horiz. $1.50, Women's slalom. $5, Ice hockey, horiz. $8, Biathlon.

No. 1598, Downhill skiing. No. 1599, Speed skating.

1992, Apr. 21 Litho. *Perf. 14*

1588 A218 10c multicolored .25 .25
1589 A218 15c multicolored .25 .25
1590 A218 25c multicolored .25 .25
1591 A218 30c multicolored .30 .30
1592 A218 45c multicolored .40 .40
1593 A218 55c multicolored .45 .45
1594 A218 75c multicolored .65 .65
1595 A218 $1.50 multicolored 1.10 1.10
1596 A218 $5 multicolored 4.00 4.00
1597 A218 $8 multicolored 6.00 6.00
Nos. 1588-1597 (10) 13.65 13.65

Souvenir Sheets

1598 A218 $6 multicolored 6.75 6.75
1599 A218 $6 multicolored 6.75 6.75

1992 Summer Olympics, Barcelona — A219

10c, Women's synchronized swimming duet, horiz. 15c, High jump. 25c, Small-bore rifle, horiz. 30c, 200-meter run. 45c, Judo. 55c. 200-meter freestyle swimming, horiz. 75c, Javelin. $1.50, Pursuit cycling. $5, Boxing. $8, Women's basketball. No. 1610, $15, Tennis. No. 1611, $15, Board sailing.

1992, Apr. 21

1600-1609 A219 Set of 10 16.00 16.00

Souvenir Sheets

1610-1611 A219 Set of 2 25.00 25.00

World Columbian Stamp Expo '92, Chicago — A220

Walt Disney characters visiting Chicago area landmarks: 10c, Mickey, Pluto at Picasso Sulpture. 50c, Mickey, Donald admiring Frank Lloyd Wright's Robie House. $1, Gus Gander at Calder Sculpture in Sears Tower. $5, Pluto in Buckingham Memorial Fountain.

$6, Mickey painting Minnie at Chicago Art Institute, vert.

1992, Apr. Litho. *Perf. 14x13½*

1612-1615 A220 Set of 4 7.00 7.00

Souvenir Sheet

Perf. 13½x14

1616 A220 $6 multi 6.25 6.25

Granada '92 — A221

Walt Disney characters from "The Three Little Pigs" in Spanish military uniforms: 15c, Big Bad Wolf as General of Spanish Moors. 40c, Pig as Captain of Spanish infantry. $2, Pig in Spanish armor, c. 1580. $4, Pig as Spaniard of rank, c. 1550.

$6, Little Pig resisting wolf from castle built of stone.

1992, Apr. 28 *Perf. 13½x14*

1622-1625 A221 Set of 4 7.00 7.00

Souvenir Sheet

1626 A221 $6 multi 6.25 6.25

Discovery of America, 500th Anniv. A222

5c, Nina. 10c, Pinta. 45c, Santa Maria. 55c, Leaving Palos, Spain. $4, Columbus, vert. $5, Columbus' arms, vert.

No. 1638, Map, vert. No. 1639, Sailing ship, vert.

1992, May 22 *Perf. 14*

1632 A222 5c multicolored .35 .35
1633 A222 10c multicolored .35 .35
1634 A222 45c multicolored .60 .60
1635 A222 55c multicolored .70 .70
1636 A222 $4 multicolored 5.00 5.00
1637 A222 $5 multicolored 6.00 6.00
Nos. 1632-1637 (6) 13.00 13.00

Souvenir Sheet

1638 A222 $6 multicolored 6.50 6.50
1639 A222 $6 multicolored 6.50 6.50

World Columbian Stamp Expo '92, Chicago. Nos. 1638-1639 contain one 42x57mm stamp.

Bonnie Blair, US Olympic Speed Skating Champion A223

No. 1641:a, Skating around corner. b, Portrait holding skates. c, On straightaway.

1992, May 25 *Perf. 13½*

1640 A223 $3 shown 4.00 4.00

Souvenir Sheet

1641 A223 $2 Sheet of 3, #a.-c. 6.75 6.75

World Columbian Stamp Expo '92. No. 1641b is 48x60mm.

Entertainers Type of 1991

Miniature Sheet

Various portraits of Elvis Presley.

1992, May 25 *Perf. 13½x14*

1642 A206 $1 Sheet of 9, #a.-i. 12.50 12.50

Souvenir Sheet

Perf. 14

1643 A206 $6 multicolored 9.50 9.50

No. 1643 contains one 28x43mm stamp.

See Nos. 1729-1730.

Hummingbirds A224

Hummingbirds: 5c, Rufous-breasted hermit. 15c, Hispaniolan emerald. 45c, Green-throated carib. 55c, Jamaican mango. 65c, Vervain. 75c, Purple-throated carib. 90c, Green mango. $1, Bee. $2, Cuban emerald. $3, Puerto Rican emerald. $4, Antillean mango. $5, Streamertail.

No. 1656, Antillean crested. No. 1657, Bahama woodstar. No. 1658, Blue-headed.

1992, June 15 *Perf. 14*

1644 A224 5c multi .25 .25
1645 A224 15c multi .25 .25
1646 A224 45c multi .45 .35
1647 A224 55c multi .55 .40
1648 A224 65c multi .65 .50
1649 A224 75c multi .75 .58
1650 A224 90c multi .90 .70
1651 A224 $1 multi 1.10 .80
1652 A224 $2 multi 2.00 2.00
1653 A224 $3 multi 2.50 2.50
1654 A224 $4 multi 4.00 4.00
1655 A224 $5 multi 5.00 5.00
Nos. 1644-1655 (12) 18.40 17.33

Souvenir Sheets

1656 A224 $6 multi 6.00 6.00
1657 A224 $6 multi 6.00 6.00
1658 A224 $6 multi 6.00 6.00

Genoa '92 Intl. Philatelic Exhibition.

Butterflies A225

Designs: 5c, Dull astraptes, vert. 10c, White peacock. 35c, Tropic queen, vert. 45c, Polydamas swallowtail, vert. 55c, West Indian buckeye. 65c, Long-tailed skipper, vert. 75c, Tropical checkered skipper. $1, Crimson-banded black, vert. $2, Barred sulphur, vert. $3, Cassius blue. $4, Florida duskywing. $5, Malachite, vert.

No. 1671, $6, Cloudless giant sulphur, vert. No. 1672, $6, Julia. No. 1673, $6, Zebra longwing.

1992, June 15 **Litho.** *Perf. 14*

1659-1670 A225 Set of 12 21.00 21.00

Souvenir Sheets

1671-1673 A225 Set of 3 18.00 18.00

Genoa '92.

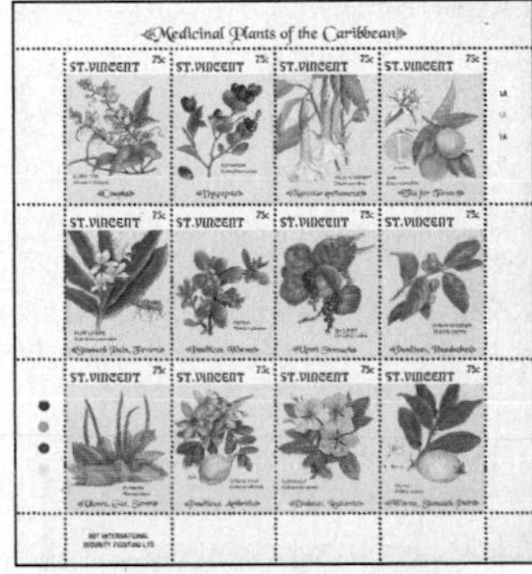

Medicinal plants — A226

No. 1674: a, Coral vine. b, Cocoplum. c, Angel's trumpet. d, Lime. e, White ginger. f, Pussley. g. Sea grape. h, Indian mulberry. i, Plantain. j, Lignum vitae. k, Periwinkle. l, Guava.

1992, July 22 **Litho.** *Perf. 14*

1674 A226 75c Sheet of 12, #a-l 14.00 14.00

Souvenir Sheets

1675 A226 $6 Aloe 5.50 5.50
1676 A226 $6 Clove tree 5.50 5.50
1677 A226 $6 Wild sage 5.50 5.50

A227

Mushrooms: 10c, Collybia subpruinosa. 15c, Gerronema citrinum. 20c, Amanita antillana. 45c, Dermoloma atrobrunneum. 50c, Inopilus maculosus. 65c, Pulveroboletus brachyspermus. 75c, Mycena violacella. $1, Xerocomus brasiliensis. $2, Amanita ingrata. $3, Leptonia caeruleocaptata. $4, Limacella myochroa. $5, Inopilus magnificus.

No. 1690, $6, Limacella guttata. No. 1691, $6, Amanita agglutinata. No. 1692, $6, Trogia buccinalis.

1992, July 2 **Litho.** *Perf. 14*

1678-1689 A227 Set of 12 18.00 18.00

Souvenir Sheets

1690-1692 A227 Set of 3 17.00 17.00

Baseball Players — A228

Designs: No. 1693, $4, Ty Cobb. No. 1694, $4, Dizzy Dean. No. 1695, $4, Bob Feller. No. 1696, $4, Whitey Ford. No. 1697, $4, Lou Gehrig. No. 1698, $4, Rogers Hornsby. No. 1699, $4, Mel Ott. No. 1700, $4, Satchel Paige. No. 1701, $4, Babe Ruth. No. 1702, $4, Casey Stengel. No. 1703, $4, Honus Wagner. No. 1704, $4, Cy Young.

Self-Adhesive

Size: 64x89mm

1992, Aug. 5 **Litho.** ***Imperf.***

1693-1704 A228 Set of 12 40.00

Nos. 1693-1704 printed on thin card and distributed in boxed sets. To affix stamps, backing containing player's statistics must be removed.

1992 Albertville Winter Olympics Gold Medalists — A229

No. 1705: a, Alberto Tomba, Italy, giant slalom. b, Fabrice Guy, France, Nordic combined. c, Patrick Ortlieb, Austria, men's downhill. d, Vegard Ulvang, Norway, cross country. e, Edgar Grospiron, France, freestyle Mogul skiing. f, Kjetil-Andre Aamodt, Norway, super giant slalom. g, Viktor Petrenko, Russia, men's figure skating.

No. 1706: a, Kristi Yamaguchi, US, women's figure skating. b, Pernilla Wiberg, Sweden, women's giant slalom. c, Lyubov Yegorova, Unified Team, women's 10-kilometer cross country. d, Josef Polig, Italy, combined Alpine skiing. e, Finn Christian-Jagge, Norway, slalom. f, Kerrin Lee-Gartner, Canada, women's downhill. g, Steffania Belmondo, Italy, women's 30-kilometer cross country.

No. 1707, Alberto Tomba, diff. No. 1708, Kristi Yamaguchi, diff.

1992, Aug. 10 **Litho.** *Perf. 14*

1705 A229 $1 Sheet of 7, #a.-g. + label 8.00 8.00
1706 A229 $1 Sheet of 7, #a.-g. + label 8.00 8.00

Souvenir Sheets

1707 A229 $6 multicolored 6.25 6.25
1708 A229 $6 multicolored 6.25 6.25

Discovery of America, 500th Anniv. — A230

1992 **Litho.** *Perf. 14½*

1709 A230 $1 Coming ashore 1.75 1.75
1710 A230 $2 Natives, ships 3.25 3.25

Organization of East Caribbean States.

Opening of Euro Disney — A231

No. 1711 — Walt Disney movies: a, Pinocchio. b, Alice in Wonderland. c, Bambi. d, Cinderella. e, Snow White and the Seven Dwarfs. f, Peter Pan.

1992 **Litho.** *Perf. 13*

1711 A231 $1 Sheet of 6, #a.-f. 10.50 10.50

Souvenir Sheet

Perf. 12½

1712 A231 $5 Mickey Mouse 8.75 8.75

Christmas A232

Details or entire paintings of The Nativity by: 10c, Hospitality Refused to the Virgin Mary and Joseph, by Jan Metsys. 40c, Albrecht Durer. 45c, The Nativity, by Geertgen Tot Sint Jans. 50c, The Nativity, by Tintoretto. 55c, Follower of Jan Joest Calcar. 65c, Workshop of Fra Angelico. 75c, Master of the Louvre Nativity. $1, Filippino Lippi. $2, Petrus Christus. $3, Edward Burne-Jones. $4, Giotto. $5, The Birth of Christ, by Domenico Ghirlandaio.

No. 1725, $6, Nativity, by Jean Fouquet. No. 1726, $6, Sandro Botticelli. No. 1727, $6, Gerard Horenbout.

1992, Nov. **Litho.** *Perf. 13½x14*

1713-1724 A232 Set of 12 16.00 16.00

Souvenir Sheets

1725-1727 A232 Set of 3 17.00 17.00

Souvenir Sheet

Jacob Javits Convention Center, NYC — A233

1992, Oct. 28 Litho. *Perf. 14*

1728 A233 $6 multicolored 10.00 10.00

Postage Stamp Mega Event '92, NYC.

Nos. 1642, 1564, 1567 Overprinted or with Additional Inscriptions

Designs: No. 1729, #1642 inscribed vertically "15th Anniversary."

No. 1729J, #1564 inscribed "15th Anniversary" and "Elvis Presley's Death / August 16, 1977."

No. 1730, #1567 overprinted in margin "15th Anniversary" and "Elvis Presley's Death / August 16, 1977."

1992, Dec. 15 *Perf. 13½x14*

1729 A206 $1 Sheet of 9, #a-i 14.00 14.00

Perf. 14½

1729J A215 $2 Sheet of 8, #k-r 20.00 20.00

Souvenir Sheet

Perf. 14

1730 A215 $6 multi 13.50 13.50

Baseball Players — A234

1992, Nov. 9 Litho. *Perf. 14*

1731 A234 $5 Howard Johnson 3.50 3.50
1732 A234 $5 Don Mattingly 3.50 3.50

1992 Summer Olympics, Barcelona.

Members of Baseball Hall Fame — A235

Player, year inducted: No. 1733, Roberto Clemente, 1973. No. 1734, Hank Aaron, 1982. No. 1735, Tom Seaver, 1992.

1992, Dec. 21

1733 A235 $2 multicolored 2.50 2.50
1734 A235 $2 multicolored 2.50 2.50
1735 A235 $2 multicolored 2.50 2.50
Nos. 1733-1735 (3) 7.50 7.50

Fishing Industry A236

1992, Nov.

1736 A236 5c Fishing with rods .25 .25
1737 A236 10c Inside fishing complex .25 .25
1738 A236 50c Landing the catch .50 .50
1739 A236 $5 Fishing with nets 4.00 4.00
Nos. 1736-1739 (4) 5.00 5.00

Uniting the Windward Islands A237

Children's paintings: 10c, Island coastline. 40c, Four people standing on islands. 45c, Four people standing on beach.

1992, Nov. Litho. *Perf. 14*

1740 A237 10c multicolored .60 .25
1741 A237 40c multicolored .85 .30
1742 A237 45c multicolored 1.00 .35
Nos. 1740-1742 (3) 2.45 .90

Miniature Sheets

US Olympic Basketball "Dream Team" — A238

No. 1744: a, Scottie Pippen. b, Earvin "Magic" Johnson. c, Larry Bird. d, Christian Laettner. e, Karl Malone. f, David Robinson.

No. 1745: a, Michael Jordan. b, Charles Barkley. c, John Stockton. d, Chris Mullin. e, Clyde Drexler. f, Patrick Ewing.

1992, Dec. 22 Litho. *Perf. 14*

1744 A238 $2 Sheet of 6, #a.-f. 8.50 8.50
1745 A238 $2 Sheet of 6, #a.-f. 8.50 8.50

1992 Summer Olympics, Barcelona.

A239

A240

A241

A242

Anniversaries and Events: 10c, Globe and UN emblem. 45c, Zeppelin Viktoria Luise over Kiel Regatta, 1912, vert. 65c, Food products. No. 1749, America's Cup Trophy and Bill Koch, skipper of America 3. No. 1750, Konrad Adenauer, German flag. No. 1751, Adenauer, diff. No. 1752, Snow leopard. $1.50, Caribbean manatee. $2, Humpback whale. No. 1755, Adenauer, John F. Kennedy. No. 1756, Lions Intl. emblem, patient having eye exam. No. 1757, Space shuttle Discovery, vert. No. 1758, Adenauer, Pope John XXIII. $5, Michael Schumacher, race car. No. 1760, Count Zeppelin's first airship over Lake Constance, 1900. No. 1761, Gondola of Graf Zeppelin. No. 1762, Formula I race car. No. 1763, Sailing ship, steam packet. No. 1764, Adenauer at podium. No. 1765, Woolly spider monkey. No. 1765A, People waving to plane during Berlin airlift.

1992-93 Litho. *Perf. 14*

1746 A239 10c multi .25 .25
1747 A239 45c multi 5.50 5.50
1748 A242 65c multi 1.50 1.50
1749 A239 75c multi 1.25 1.25
1750 A239 75c multi 8.00 8.00
1751 A239 $1 multi 8.00 8.00
1752 A239 $1 multi 7.50 7.50
1753 A239 $1.50 multi 7.50 7.50
1754 A239 $2 multi 7.50 7.50
1755 A239 $3 multi 2.25 2.25
1756 A239 $3 multi 4.50 4.50
1757 A239 $4 multi 3.00 3.00
1758 A239 $4 multi 3.00 3.00
1759 A240 $5 multi 5.50 5.50
1760 A239 $6 multi 5.50 5.50
Nos. 1746-1760 (15) 70.75 70.75

Souvenir Sheets

1761 A239 $6 multi 5.50 5.50
1762 A240 $6 multi 5.50 5.50
1763 A241 $6 multi 4.50 4.50
1764 A239 $6 multi 4.50 4.50
1765 A239 $6 multi 4.50 4.50
1765A A239 $6 multi 4.50 4.50

UN Intl. Space Year (#1746, 1757). Count Zeppelin, 75th anniv. of death (#1747, 1760-1761). Intl. Conference on Nutrition, Rome (#1748). America's Cup yacht race (#1749). Konrad Adenauer, 25th death anniv. (#1750-1751, 1755, 1758, 1764). Earth Summit, Rio de Janeiro (#1752-1754, 1765). Lions Intl., 75th anniv. (#1756). Belgian Grand Prix (#1759, 1762). Discovery of America, 500th anniv. (#1763). Konrad Adenauer, 75th death anniv. (#1765A).

Issued: #1747, 1759-1762, Dec; #1763, 10/28/92; #1746, 1749, 1750-1751, 1755-1758, 1764, Dec; #1752-1754, 1765, Dec. 15; #1765A, 6/30/93.

Care Bears Promote Conservation A243

Designs: 75c, Bear, stork. $2, Bear riding in hot air balloon, horiz.

1992, Dec. Litho. *Perf. 14*

1766 A243 75c multicolored 2.00 2.00

Souvenir Sheet

1767 A243 $2 multicolored 3.50 3.50

Elvis Presley (1935-77) — A244

No. 1767A: b, Portrait. c, With guitar. d, With microphone.

1993 Litho. *Perf. 14*

1767A A244 $1 Strip of 3, #b.-d. 2.75 2.75

Printed in sheets of 9 stamps.

Walt Disney's Beauty and the Beast — A245

Designs: 2c, Gaston. 3c, Belle and her father, Maurice. 5c, Lumiere, Mrs. Potts and Cogsworth. 10c, Philippe. 15c, Beast and Lumiere. 20c, Lumiere and Feather Duster.

No. 1774: a, Belle and Gaston. b, Maurice. c, The Beast. d, Mrs. Potts. e, Belle and the Enchanted Vase. f, Belle discovers an Enchanted Rose. g, Belle with wounded Beast. h, Belle. i, Household objects alarmed.

No. 1774J: k, Belle and Chip. l, Lumiere. m, Cogsworth. n, Armoire. o, Belle and Beast. p, Feather Duster. q, Footstool. r, Belle. All vert.

No. 1775, Belle reading, vert. No. 1776, Lumiere, diff., vert. No. 1776A, Lumiere, Mrs. Potts. No. 1776B, Belle, lake and castle, vert. No. 1776C, The Beast, vert.

Perf. 14x13½, 13½x14

1992, Dec. 15 Litho.

1768 A245 2c multicolored .25 .25
1769 A245 3c multicolored .25 .25
1770 A245 5c multicolored .25 .25
1771 A245 10c multicolored .25 .25
1772 A245 15c multicolored .25 .25
1773 A245 20c multicolored .25 .25
Nos. 1768-1773 (6) 1.50 1.50

Souvenir Sheets

1774 A245 60c Sheet of 9, #a.-i. 8.50 8.50
1774J A245 60c Sheet of 8, #k.-r. 8.50 8.50

Souvenir Sheets

1775 A245 $6 multicolored 6.50 6.50
1776 A245 $6 multicolored 6.50 6.50
1776A A245 $6 multicolored 6.50 6.50
1776B A245 $6 multicolored 6.50 6.50
1776C A245 $6 multicolored 6.50 6.50

Louvre Museum, Bicent. A246

No. 1777, $1 — Details or entire paintings by Jean-Auguste-Dominique Ingres: a, Louis-Francois Bertin. b, The Apotheosis of Homer. c, Joan of Arc. d, The Composer Cherubini with the Muse of Lyric Poetry. e, Mlle Caroline Riviere. f, Oedipus Answers the Sphinx's Riddle. g, Madame Marcotte. h, Mademoiselle Caroline Riviere.

No. 1778, $1 — Details or entire paintings by Jean Louis Andre Theodore Gericault (1791-1824): a, The Woman with Gambling Mania. b, Head of a White Horse. c, Wounded Cuirassier. d, An Officer of the Cavalry. e, The Vendean. f, The Raft of the Medusa. g-h, The Horse Market (left, right).

No. 1779, $1 — Details or entire paintings by Nicolas Poussin (1594-1665): a-b, The Arcadian Shepherds (left, right). c, Ecstasy of Paul. d-e, The Inspiration of the Poet (left, right). f-g, St. John Baptizing (left, right). h, The Miracle of St. Francis Xavier.

No. 1780, $1 — Details or entire paintings by Eustache Le Sueur (1616-1655): a-b, Melpomene, Erato & Polyhymnia (left, right). By Poussin: c, Christ and Woman Taken in Adultery. d, Spring. e, Autumn. f-h, The Plague of Ashdod (left, center, right).

No. 1781, $1: a, The Beggars, by Pieter Brueghel, the Elder (1520-1569). b, The Luncheon, by Francois Boucher (1703-1770). c, Louis Guene, Violin King, by Francois Dumont (1751-1831). d, The Virgin of Chancellor Rolin, by Jan Van Eyck. e, Conversation in the Park, by Thomas Gainsborough. f, Lady Alston, by Gainsborough. g, Mariana Waldstein, by Francisco de Goya. h, Ferdinand Guillemardet, by Goya.

No. 1782, $6, The Grand Odalisque, horiz. No. 1783, $6, The Dressing Room of Esther, by Theodore Chasseriau (1819-1856). No. 1784, $6, Liberty Guiding the People, by Eugene Delecroix (1798-1863), horiz.

1993, Apr. 19 *Perf. 12x12½*

Sheets of 8, #a-h, + Label

1777-1781 A246 Set of 5 34.00 34.00

Souvenir Sheets

Perf. 14½

1782-1784 A246 Set of 3 18.50 18.50

Nos. 1783-1784 each contain a 55x88mm or 88x55mm stamp.

Paintings on Nos. 1777d and 1777h were switched.

A247

A247a

Scenes from Disney Animated Films — A247b

No. 1787 — Symphony Hour (1942): a, Maestro Mickey. b, Goofy plays a mean horn. c, On first bass with Clara Cluck. d, Stringing along with Clarabelle. e, Donald on drums. f, Clarabelle all fiddled out. g, Donald drumming up trouble. h, Goofy's sour notes. i, Mickey's moment.

No. 1788 — Clock Cleaners (1937): a, Goofy gets in gear. b, Donald on the mainspring. c, Donald in the works. d, Mickey's fine-feathered friend. e, Stork with bundle of joy. f, Father Time. g, Goofy, Mickey leaping upward. h, Donald, Goofy, Mickey out of gear. i, Donald, Goofy, Mickey with headaches.

No. 1789 — The Art of Skiing (1941): a, The ultimate back scratcher. b, Striking a pose. c, And we're off. d, Divided he stands. e, A real twister. f, Hangin' in there. g, Over the hill. h, At the peak of his form. i, Up a tree.

No. 1790 — Orphan's Benefit (1941): a, Mickey introduces Donald. b, Donald recites "Little Boy Blue." c, Orphan mischief. d, Clara Cluck, singing sensation. e, Goofy's debut with Clarabelle. f, Encore for Clara and Mickey. g, A Bronx cheer. h, Donald blows his stack. i, Donald's final bow.

No. 1791 — Thru the Mirror (1936): a, Mickey steps thru the looking glass. b, Mickey finds a tasty treat. c, Mickey's nutty effect. d, Hats off to Mickey. e, What a card, Mickey. f, Mickey dancing with the Queen Hearts. g, A real two-faced opponent. h, Mickey with a pen mightier than a sword. i, Mickey awake at last.

No. 1791J — The Small One: k, Morning comes in Nazareth. l, Good morning, small one. m, Too old to keep. n, Heatbroken. o, Nazareth markplace. p, Auction mockery. q, Off the auction block. r, Lonely and dejected. s, Happy and useful again.

No. 1792 — The Three Little Pigs (1933): a, Fifer Pig building house of straw. b, Fiddler Pig building house of sticks. c, Practical Pig building house of bricks. d, The Big Bad Wolf. e, Wolf scaring two lazy pigs. f, Wolf blowing down staw house. g, Wolf in sheep's clothing. h, Wolf blowing down twig house. i, Wolf huffs and puffs at brick house.

No. 1792J — How to Play Football (1944): k, Cheerleaders. l, Here comes the team. m, In the huddle. n, Who's got the ball? o, Who, me coach? p, Half-time pep talk. q, Another down, and out. r, Only a little injury. s, Up and at 'em.

No. 1793 — Rescue Rangers: a, Special agents. b, Chip 'n Dale, ready for action. c, Chip 'n Dale on stakeout. d, Gadget in gear. e, Gadget and Monterey Jack rescue Zipper. f, Zipper confers with Monterey Jack. g, Zipper zaps fat cat. h, Team work. i, Innovative Gadget.

No. 1793J — Darkwing Duck: k, Darkwing Duck. l, Launchpad McQuack. m, Gosalyn. n, Honker Muddlefoot. o, Tank Muddlefoot. p, Herb & Binkie Muddlefoot. q, Drake Mallard, aka Darkwing Duck. r, Darkwing Duck logo.

No. 1794, Bird's-eye-view of Goofy. No. 1795, Mickey and Macaroni enjoying applause.

No. 1796, On the edge of Goofyness. No. 1797, Gonged-out Goofy.

No. 1798, Film poster for Art of Skiing with Goofy slaloming down mountain. No. 1799, Goofy home in bed at last.

No. 1800, Caveman ballet. No. 1801, Mickey tickles the ivories.

No. 1802, Mickey's true reflection. No. 1803, Mickey hopping home.

No. 1804, Hard Work in Nazareth. No. 1805, Finding a buyer in Nazareth.

No. 1806, Animator's sketch of little pig and brick house. No. 1807, Little pigs playing and singing at piano, vert.

No. 1807A, Goofy demonstrating how to score touchdown. No. 1807B, Goofy shouting "Hooray for the team," vert.

No. 1807C, Gadget at controls of Ranger plane, vert. No. 1807D, Dale, vert.

No. 1807E, Quarterjack. No. 1807F, Darkwing Duck and Launchpad to the rescue in Ratcatcher.

Perf. 14x13½, 13½x14

1992, Dec. 15 **Litho.**

1787	A247	60c Sheet of 9, #a.-i.	8.50	8.50
1788	A247	60c Sheet of 9, #a.-i.	8.50	8.50
1789	A247	60c Sheet of 9, #a.-i.	8.50	8.50
1790	A247	60c Sheet of 9, #a.-i.	8.50	8.50
1791	A247	60c Sheet of 9, #a.-i.	8.50	8.50
1791J	A247a	60c Sheet of 9, #k.-s.	8.50	8.50
1792	A247	60c Sheet of 9, #a.-i.	8.50	8.50
1792J	A247	60c Sheet of 9, #k.-s.	8.50	8.50
1793	A247a	60c Sheet of 9, #a.-i.	8.50	8.50
1793J	A247b	60c Sheet of 8, #k.-r.	8.50	8.50

Souvenir Sheets

1794	A247	$6 multicolored	5.50	5.50
1795	A247	$6 multicolored	5.50	5.50
1796	A247	$6 multicolored	5.50	5.50
1797	A247	$6 multicolored	5.50	5.50
1798	A247	$6 multicolored	5.50	5.50
1799	A247	$6 multicolored	5.50	5.50
1800	A247	$6 multicolored	5.50	5.50
1801	A247	$6 multicolored	5.50	5.50
1802	A247	$6 multicolored	5.50	5.50
1803	A247	$6 multicolored	5.50	5.50
1804	A247a	$6 multicolored	5.50	5.50
1805	A247a	$6 multicolored	5.50	5.50
1806	A247	$6 multicolored	5.50	5.50
1807	A247	$6 multicolored	5.50	5.50
1807A	A247	$6 multicolored	5.50	5.50
1807B	A247	$6 multicolored	5.50	5.50
1807C	A247a	$6 multicolored	5.50	5.50
1807D	A247a	$6 multicolored	5.50	5.50
1807E	A247b	$6 multicolored	5.50	5.50
1807F	A247b	$6 multicolored	5.50	5.50

See Nos. 2144-2146 for 30c & $3 stamps.

Fish A248

5c, Sergeant major. 10c, Rainbow parrotfish. 55c, Hogfish. 75c, Porkfish. $1, Spotfin butterflyfish. $2, Trunkfish. $4, Queen triggerfish. $5, Queen angelfish.

No. 1816, Bigeye, vert. No. 1817, Smallmouth grunt, vert.

1993, Apr. 1 **Litho.** ***Perf. 14***

1808	A248	5c multicolored	.30	.30
1809	A248	10c multicolored	.30	.30
1810	A248	55c multicolored	.55	.40
1811	A248	75c multicolored	.85	.60
1812	A248	$1 multicolored	1.00	.75
1813	A248	$2 multicolored	2.10	2.10
1814	A248	$4 multicolored	4.25	4.25
1815	A248	$5 multicolored	4.25	4.25
		Nos. 1808-1815 (8)	13.60	12.95

Souvenir Sheets

1816	A248	$6 multicolored	6.25	6.25
1817	A248	$6 multicolored	6.25	6.25

Birds — A249

Designs: 10c, Brown pelican. 25c, Red-necked grebe, horiz. 45c, Belted kingfisher, horiz. 55c, Yellow-bellied sapsucker. $1, Great blue heron. $2, Crab hawk, horiz. $4, Yellow warbler. $5, Northern oriole, horiz. No. 1826, White ibises, map, horiz. No. 1827, Blue-winged teal, map, horiz.

1993, Apr. 1 **Litho.** ***Perf. 14***

1818-1825	A249	Set of 8	14.50	14.50

Souvenir Sheets

1826-1827	A249	$6 Set of 2	15.00	15.00

Seashells — A250

Designs: 10c, Hexagonal murex. 15c, Caribbean vase. 30c, Measled cowrie. 45c, Dyson's keyhole limpet. 50c, Atlantic hairy triton. 65c, Orange-banded marginella. 75c, Bleeding tooth. $1, Pink conch. $2, Hawk-wing conch. $3, Music volute. $4, Alphabet cone. $5, Antillean cone.

No. 1840, $6, Flame auger, horiz. No. 1841, $6, Netted olive, horiz. No. 1842, $6, Wide-mouthed purpura, horiz.

1993, May 24 **Litho.** ***Perf. 14***

1828-1839	A250	Set of 12	20.00	20.00

Souvenir Sheets

1840-1842	A250	Set of 3	19.00	19.00

Yujiro Ishihara, Actor — A251

No. 1843 — Name in blue on 2 lines, country name on picture: a, $1, Wearing captain's hat. b, 55c, With tennis racquet. c, $1 Wearing suit. d, 55c, Holding camera. e, 55c, Wearing suit, diff. f, 55c. Wearing striped shirt, smoking. g, $1, Wearing blue shirt and vest. h, 55c, Wearing captain's hat, smoking. i, $1, Wearing pink shirt, smoking.

No. 1844 — Name in gold on one line, countrry name above picture: a, 55c Holding camera. b, $1 Wearing black suit and white tie. c, $2, Wearing white suit. d, $2, Holding guitar.

No. 1845 — Name in gold on one line, country name on picture: a, 55c Wearing captain's hat (like #1843a). b, $2, Wearing striped shirt. c, $1, Smiling. d, $2, Wearing captain's hat (like #1843h).

No. 1846 — Name in white: a, 55c, Wearing yellow suit. b, $2, Wearing yellow shirt. c, $4, Holding drink.

No. 1847 — Name in blue on 2 lines: a, 55c, Smoking, hand near face. b, $4, Smoking, wearing pink shirt. c, $4, Wearing blue shirt and vest (like #1843g).

1993, May 24 **Litho.** ***Perf. 13½x14***

1843	A251	Sheet of 9, #a.-i.	12.00	12.00

Souvenir Sheets

1844	A251	Sheet of 4, #a.-d.	6.00	6.00

Stamp Size: 32x41mm

Perf. 14½

1845	A251	Sheet of 4, #a.-d.	6.00	6.00

Stamp Size: 60x41mm

Perf. 14x14½

1846	A251	Sheet of 3, #a.-c.	7.00	7.00
1847	A251	Sheet of 3, #a.-c.	9.25	9.25

Automobiles A252

Designs: $1, 1932 Ford V8, 1915 Ford Model T, Henry Ford's 1st car. $2, Benz 540K, 1928 Benz Stuttgart, 1908 Benz Racer. $3, 1911 Blitzen Benz, 1905 Benz Tourenwagen, 1894 Benz. $4, 1935 Ford, 1903 Ford A Runabout, 1913 Ford Model T Tourer. No. 1852, $6, Karl Benz. No. 1853, $6, Henry Ford.

1993, May **Litho.** ***Perf. 14***

1848-1851	A252	Set of 4	10.00	10.00

Souvenir Sheets

1852-1853	A252	Set of 2	11.00	11.00

First Ford motor, cent. (#1848, 1851, 1853). First Benz motor car, cent. (#1849-1850, 1852).

Coronation of Queen Elizabeth II, 40th Anniv. — A253

No. 1854: a, 45c, Official coronation photograph. b, 65c, Opening Parliament, 1980s. c, $2, Coronation ceremony, 1953. d, $4, Queen with her dog, 1970s.

No. 1855, Portrait of Queen as a child.

1993, June 2 **Litho.** ***Perf. 13½x14***

1854	A253	Sheet, 2 ea #a.-d.	13.00	13.00

Souvenir Sheet

Perf. 14

1855	A253	$6 multicolored	6.25	6.25

No. 1855 contains one 28x42mm stamp.

Moths — A254

10c, Erynnyis ello. 50c, Aellopos tantalus. 65c, Erynnyis alope. 75c, Manduca rustica. $1, Xylophanes pluto. $2, Hyles lineata. $4, Pseudosphinx tetrio. $5, Protambulyx strigilis.

No. 1864, Xylophanes tersa. No. 1864A, Utetheisa ornatrix.

1993, June 14 **Litho.** ***Perf. 14***

1856	A254	10c multicolored	.25	.25
1857	A254	50c multicolored	.60	.60
1858	A254	65c multicolored	.75	.75
1859	A254	75c multicolored	.85	.85
1860	A254	$1 multicolored	1.10	1.10
1861	A254	$2 multicolored	2.25	2.25
1862	A254	$4 multicolored	4.50	4.50
1863	A254	$5 multicolored	5.75	5.75
		Nos. 1856-1863 (8)	16.05	16.05

Souvenir Sheets

1864	A254	$6 multicolored	5.75	5.75
1864A	A254	$6 multicolored	5.75	5.75

A255

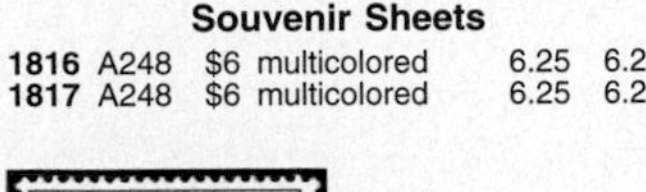

A256

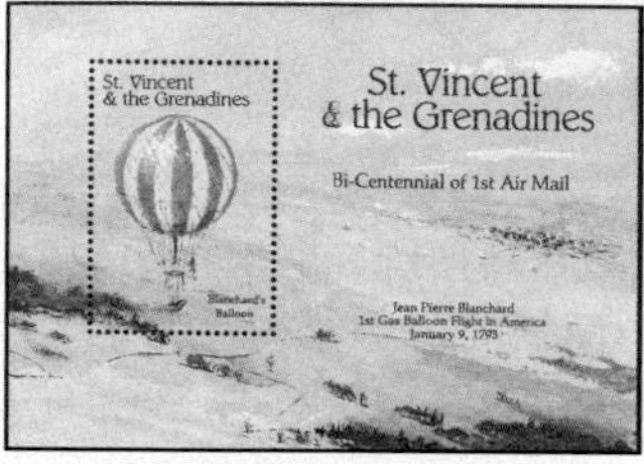

Aviation Anniversaries — A257

Designs: 50c, Supermarine Spitfire. #1866, Graf Zeppelin over Egypt, 1931, Hugo Eckener. #1867, Jean Pierre Blanchard, balloon, George Washington. #1868, De Havilland Mosquito. No. 1869, Eckener, Graf Zeppelin over New York, 1928. $3, Eckener, Graf Zeppelin over Tokyo, 1 929. $4, Philadelphia's Walnut State Prison, balloon lifting off.

No. 1872, Hawker Hurricane. No. 1873, Hugo Eckener, vert. No. 1874, Blanchard's Balloon, vert.

1993, June **Litho.** ***Perf. 14***

1865	A255	50c multi	.80	.80
1866	A256	$1 multi	1.50	1.50
1867	A257	$1 multi	1.50	1.50
1868	A255	$2 multi	3.00	3.00
1869	A256	$2 multi	3.00	3.00
1870	A256	$3 multi	4.75	4.75
1871	A257	$4 multi	6.00	6.00
		Nos. 1865-1871 (7)	20.55	20.55

Souvenir Sheets

1872	A255	$6 multi	6.50	6.50
1873	A256	$6 multi	5.00	5.00
1874	A257	$6 multi	5.00	5.00

Royal Air Force, 75th anniv. (#1865, 1868, 1872). Dr. Hugo Eckener, 125th anniv. of birth (#1866, 1869-1870, 1873). First US balloon flight, bicent. (#1867, 1871). Tokyo spelled incorrectly on No. 1870.

Two values and a souvenir sheet commemorating the Wedding of Japan's Crown Prince Naruhito and Masako Owada were printed in 1993 but not accepted by the St. Vincent post office. Set value $5.75, Souvenir Sheet $6.

1994 Winter Olympics, Lillehammer, Norway — A259

Designs: 45c, Marc Girardelli, silver medalist, giant slalom, 1992. $5, Paul Accola, downhill, 1992. $6, Thommy Moe, downhill, 1992.

1993, June 30 **Litho.** ***Perf. 14***

1878	A259	45c multicolored	.45	.45
1879	A259	$5 multicolored	4.25	4.25

Souvenir Sheet

1880	A259	$6 multicolored	5.75	5.75

Picasso (1881-1973) — A260

Paintings: 45c, Massacre in Korea, 1951. $1, Family of Saltimbanques, 1905. $4, La Joie de Vivre, 1946. $6, Woman Eating a Melon and Boy Writing, 1965, vert.

1993, June 30

1881	A260	45c multicolored	.50	.50
1882	A260	$1 multicolored	1.00	1.00
1883	A260	$4 multicolored	4.00	4.00
		Nos. 1881-1883 (3)	5.50	5.50

Souvenir Sheet

1884	A260	$6 multicolored	6.00	6.00

Willy Brandt (1913-1992), German Chancellor — A261

Designs: 45c, Brandt, Richard Nixon, 1971. $5, Brandt, Robert Kennedy, 1967. $6, Brandt at signing of "Common Declaration," 1973.

1993, June 30

1885	A261	45c multicolored	.50	.50
1886	A261	$5 multicolored	5.00	5.00

Souvenir Sheet

1887	A261	$6 multicolored	6.00	6.00

A262

Copernicus: 45c, Astronomical instrument. $4, Space shuttle lift-off. $6, Copernicus.

1993, June 30

1888	A262	45c multicolored	.60	.60
1889	A262	$4 multicolored	5.00	5.00

Souvenir Sheet

1890	A262	$6 multicolored	6.00	6.00

A263

European Royalty: 45c, Johannes, Gloria Thurn & Taxis. 65c, Thurn & Taxis family, horiz. $1, Princess Stephanie of Monaco. $2, Gloria Thurn & Taxis.

1993, June 30

1891-1894	A263	Set of 4	3.00	3.00

Inauguration of Pres. William J. Clinton — A264

Designs: $5, Bill Clinton, children. $6, Clinton wearing cowboy hat, vert.

1993, June 30

1895	A264	$5 multicolored	5.50	5.50

Souvenir Sheet

1896	A264	$6 multicolored	6.00	6.00

Polska '93 A265

No. 1897, Bogusz Church, Gozlin.

No. 1898: a, $1, Deux Tetes (Man), by S.I. Witkiewicz, 1920, vert. b, $3, Deux Tetes (Woman), vert.

No. 1899, Dancing, by Wladyslaw Roguski, vert.

1993, June 30

1897	A265	$6 multicolored	5.25	5.25
1898	A265	Pair, #a.-b.	3.50	3.50

Souvenir Sheet

1899	A265	$6 multicolored	6.00	6.00

1994 World Cup Soccer Qualifying A266

St. Vincent vs: 5c, Mexico. 10c, Honduras. 65c, Costa Rica. $5, St. Vincent goalkeeper.

1993, Sept. 2

1900-1903	A266	Set of 4	6.75	6.75

Cooperation with Japan — A267

Designs: 10c, Fish delivery van. 50c, Fish aggregation device, vert. 75c, Trawler. $5, Fish complex.

1993, Sept. 2

1904-1907	A267	Set of 4	7.00	7.00

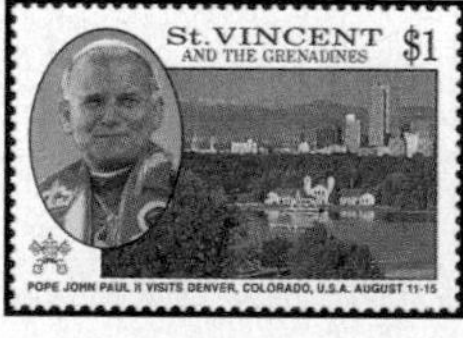

Pope John Paul II's Visit to Denver, CO A268

Design: $6, Pope, Denver skyline, diff.

1993, Aug. 13

1908	A268	$1 multicolored	1.50	1.50

Souvenir Sheet

1909	A268	$6 multicolored	7.00	7.00

No. 1908 issued in sheets of 9.

Miniature Sheet

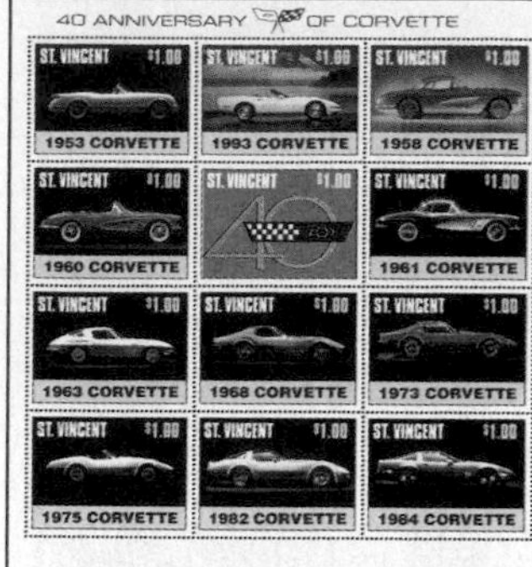

Corvette, 40th Anniv. — A269

No. 1910 — Corvettes: a, 1953. b, 1993, c, 1958, d, 1960. e, "40," Corvette emblem (no car). f, 1961. g, 1963. h, 1968, i, 1973. j, 1975. k, 1982. l, 1984.

1993, Aug. 13 ***Perf. 14x13½***

1910	A269	$1 Sheet of 12, #a.-l.	12.50	12.50

Taipei '93 — A270

Designs: 5c, Yellow Crane Mansion, Wuchang. 10c, Front gate, Chung Cheng Ceremonial Arch, Taiwan. 20c, Marble Peifang, Ming 13 Tombs, Beijing. 45c, Jinxing Den, Beijing. 55c, Forbidden City, Beijing. 75c, Tachih, the Martyrs' Shrine, Taiwan. No. 1917, Praying Hall, Xinjiang, Gaochang. No. 1918, Chih Kan Tower, Taiwan. $2, Taihu Lake, Jiangsu. $4, Chengde, Hebei, Pula Si. No. 1921, Kaohsiung, Cheng Ching Lake, Taiwan. No. 1922, Great Wall.

No. 1923 — Chinese paintings: a, Street in Macao, China, by George Chinnery. b, Pair of Birds on Cherry Branch. c, Yellow Dragon Cave, by Patrick Procktor. d, Great Wall of China, by William Simpson. e, Dutch Folly Fort Off Conton, by Chinnery. f, Forbidden City, by Procktor.

No. 1924 — Chinese silk paintings: a, Rhododendron. b, Irises and bees. c, Easter lily. d, Poinsettia. e, Peach and cherry blossoms. f, Weeping cherry and yellow bird.

No. 1925 — Chinese kites: a, Dragon and tiger fighting. b, Two immortals. c, Five boys playing round a general. d, Zheng Chenggong. e, Nezha stirs up the sea. f, Immortal maiden He.

No. 1926, Giant Buddha, Longmen Caves, Luoyang, Hunan. No. 1927, Guardian and Celestial King, Longmen Caves, Hunan, vert. No. 1928, Giant Buddha, Yungang Caves, Datong, Shanxi, vert.

1993, Aug. 16 **Litho.** ***Perf. 14x13½***

1911-1922	A270	Set of 12	15.00	15.00
1923	A270	$1.50 Sheet of 6, #a.-f.	6.75	6.75
1924	A270	$1.50 Sheet of 6, #a.-f.	6.75	6.75
1925	A270	$1.50 Sheet of 6, #a.-f.	6.75	6.75

Souvenir Sheets

1926	A270	$6 multicolored	6.00	6.00

Perf. 13½x14

1927	A270	$6 multicolored	6.00	6.00
1928	A270	$6 multicolored	6.00	6.00

No. 1925e issued missing "St." in country name. Some sheets of No. 1925 may have been withdrawn from sale after discovery of the error.

With Bangkok '93 Emblem

Designs: 5c, Phra Nakhon Khiri (Rama V's Palace), vert. 10c, Grand Palace, Bangkok. 20c, Rama IX Park, Bangkok. 45c, Phra Prang Sam Yot, Lop Buri. 55c, Dusit Maha Prasad, vert. 75c, Phimai Khmer architecture, Pak Tong Chai. No. 1935, Burmese style Chedi, Mae Hong Son. No. 1936, Antechamber, Central Prang, Prasat Hin Phimai. $2, Brick chedi on laterite base, Si Thep, vert. $4, Isan's Phanom Rung, Korat, vert. No. 1939, Phu Khao Thong, the Golden Mount, Bangkok. No. 1940, Islands, Ang Thong.

No. 1941 — Thai Buddha sculpture: a, Interior of Wat Hua Kuang Lampang, vert. b, Wat Yai Suwannaram, vert. c, Phra Buddha Sihing, City Hall Chapel, vert. d, Wat Ko Keo Suttharam, vert. e, U Thong B image, Wat Ratburana crypt, vert. f, Sri Sakyamuni Wat Suthat, vert.

No. 1942: a-f: Various details from Mural at Buddhaisawan Chapel.

No. 1943 — Thai painting: a, Untitled, by Arunothai Somsakul. b, Mural at Wat Rajapradit. c, Mural at Wat Phumin (detail). d, Serenity, by Surasit Souakong. e, Scenes of early Bangkok mural (detail). f, Ramayana.

No. 1944, Roof detail of Dusit Mahaprasad, vert. No. 1945, Standing Buddha, Hua Hin, vert. No. 1946, Masked dance.

Perf. 13½x14, 14x13½

1993, Aug. 16 **Litho.**

1929-1940 A270 5c Set of 12	14.50	14.50
1941 A270 $1.50 Sheet of 6, #a.-f.	6.50	6.50
1942 A270 $1.50 Sheet of 6, #a.-f.	6.50	6.50
1943 A270 $1.50 Sheet of 6, #a.-f.	6.50	6.50

Souvenir Sheets

1944 A270 $6 multicolored	6.00	6.00
1945 A270 $6 multicolored	6.00	6.00
1946 A270 $6 multicolored	6.00	6.00

With Indopex '93 Emblem

Indopex '93 emblem with designs: 5c, Local landmark, Gedung Sate, 1920. 10c, Masjid Jamik Mosque, Sumenep. 20c, Bromo Caldera, seen from Penanjakan. 45c, Kudus Mosque, Java. 55c, Kampung Naga. 75c, Lower level of Borobudur. No. 1953, Dieng Temple, Dieng Plateau. No. 1954, Temple 1, Gedung Songo group, Semarang. $2, Istana Bogor, 1856. $4, Taman Sari complex, Yogyakarta. No. 1957, $5, Landscape near Mt. Sumbing, Central Java. No. 1958, $5, King Adityawarman's Palace, Batusangar.

No. 1959 — Paintings: a, Female Coolies, by Djoko Pekik. b, Family Outing, by Sudjana Kerton. c, My Family, by Pekik. d, Javanese Dancers, by Arthur Melville. e, Leisure Time, by Kerton. f, In the Garden of Eden, by Agus Djaja.

No. 1960: a, Tayubon, by Pekik. b, Three Dancers, by Nyoman Gunarsa. c, Nursing Neighbor's Baby, by Hendra Gunawan. d, Imagining within a Dialogue, by Sagito. e, Three Balinese Mask Dancers, by Anton H. f, Three Prostitutes, by Gunawan.

No. 1961 — Masks: a, Hanuman. b, Subali/Sugnwa. c, Kumbakarna. d, Sangut. e, Jatayu. f, Rawana.

No. 1962, Relief of Sudamala story, Mt. Lawu. No. 1963, Plaque, 9th Cent., Banyumas, Central Java. No. 1964, Panel from Ramayana reliefs, vert.

1993, Aug. 16 **Litho.** *Perf. 14x13½*

1947-1958 A270 Set of 12	14.50	14.50
1959 A270 $1.50 Sheet of 6, #a.-f.	6.50	6.50
1960 A270 $1.50 Sheet of 6, #a.-f.	6.50	6.50
1961 A270 $1.50 Sheet of 6, #a.-f.	6.50	6.50

Souvenir Sheets

1962 A270 $6 multicolored	6.00	6.00
1963 A270 $6 multicolored	6.00	6.00

Perf. 13½x14

1964 A270 $6 multicolored	6.00	6.00

Reggie Jackson, Selection to Baseball Hall of Fame — A271

1993, Oct. 4 *Perf. 14*

1965 A271 $2 multicolored	2.00	2.00

Christmas A272

Details or entire woodcut, The Adoration of the Magi, by Durer: 10c, 35c, 40c, $5.

Details or entire paintings by Rubens: 50c, Holy Family with Saint Francis. 55c, 65c, Adoration of the Shepherds. $1, Holy Family.

No. 1974, $6, The Adoration of the Magi, by Durer, horiz. No. 1975, $6, Holy Family with St. Elizabeth & St. John, by Rubens.

Perf. 13½x14, 14x13½

1993, Nov. 18

1966-1973 A272 Set of 8	9.00	9.00

Souvenir Sheets

1974-1975 A272 Set of 2	17.50	17.50

Legends of Country Music — A273

No. 1976 — Various portraits of: a, f, l, Roy Acuff. b, g, j, Patsy Cline. c, h, i, Jim Reeves. d, e, k, Hank Williams, Sr.

1994, Jan. 17 **Litho.** *Perf. 13½x14*

1976 A273 $1 Sheet of 12, #a.-l.	12.00	12.00

Mickey's Portrait Gallery A274

Mickey Mouse as: 5c, Aviator. 10c, Foreign Legionnaire. 15c, Frontiersman. 20c, Best Pals, Mickey, Goofy, Donald. 35c, Horace, Clarabelle. 50c, Minnie, Frankie, Figuro. 75c, Donald, Pluto today. 80c, Party boy Mickey. 85c, Best Friends, Minnie, Daisy. 95c, Mickey's Girl, Minnie. $1, Cool forties Mickey. $1.50, Mickey, "Howdy!", 1950. $2, Totally Mickey. $3, Minnie, Mickey. $4, Congratulations Mickey, birthday cake. $5, Uncle Sam.

No. 1993, $6, Donald Duck, early photo of Mickey, horiz. No. 1994, $6, Minnie disco dancing, horiz. No. 1995, $6, Mickey photographing nephews, horiz. No. 1996, $6, Pluto, Mickey looking at wall of photos.

1994, May 5 **Litho.** *Perf. 13½x14*

1977-1992 A274 Set of 16	24.00	24.00

Souvenir Sheets

Perf. 14x13½

1993-1996 A274 Set of 4	28.00	28.00

Breadfruit — A275

10c, Planting. 45c, Captain Bligh, plant. 65c, Fruit sliced. $5, Fruit on branch.

1994, Jan. **Litho.** *Perf. 13½x14*

1997 A275 10c multicolored	.25	.25
1998 A275 45c multicolored	.70	.70
1999 A275 65c multicolored	.60	.60
2000 A275 $5 multicolored	5.00	5.00
Nos. 1997-2000 (4)	6.55	6.55

Intl. Year of the Family — A276

10c, Outing. 50c, Praying in church. 65c, Working in garden. 75c, Jogging. $1, Portrait. $2, Running on beach.

1994, Jan. *Perf. 14x13½, 13½x14*

2001 A276 10c multicolored	.25	.25
2002 A276 50c multicolored	.50	.50
2003 A276 65c multicolored	.65	.65
2004 A276 75c multicolored	.70	.70
2005 A276 $1 multicolored	1.05	1.05
2006 A276 $2 multicolored	2.10	2.10
Nos. 2001-2006 (6)	5.25	5.25

Nos. 2001-2004, 2006 are horiz.

Library Service, Cent. A277

1994, Jan. *Perf. 14x13½*

2007 A277 5c Mobile library	.25	.25
2008 A277 10c Old public library	.25	.25
2009 A277 $1 Family education	.85	.85
2010 A277 $1 Younger, older men	.85	.85
Nos. 2007-2010 (4)	2.20	2.20

Barbra Streisand, 1993 MGM Grand Garden Concert — A278

A278a

1994, Jan.

2011 A278 $2 multicolored	1.60	1.60

Embossed

Perf. 12

2011A A278a $20 gold	25.00	25.00

No. 2011 issued in sheets of 9.

A279

A280

A281

Hong Kong '94 — A282

No. 2012 — Stamps, 19th cent. painting of Hong Kong Harbor: a, Hong Kong #626, ship under sail. b, Ship at anchor, #1548.

No. 2013 — Porcelain ware, Qing Dynasty: a, Bowl with bamboo & sparrows. b, Bowl with flowers of four seasons. c, Bowl with lotus pool & dragon. d, Bowl with landscape. e, Shar-Pei puppies in bowl (not antiquity). f, Covered bowl with dragon & pearls.

No. 2014 — Chinese dragon boat races: a, Dragon boats. b, Tapestry of dragon races. c, Dragon race. d, Dragon boats, diff. e, Chinese crested dog. f, Dragon boats, 4 banners above boats.

No. 2015 — Chinese junks: a, Junk, Hong Kong Island. b, Junk with white sails in harbor. c, Junk with inscription on stern, Hong Kong Island. d, Junk KLN B/G. e, Chow dog, junk. f, Junk with red, white sails, Hong Kong Island.

No. 2016 — Chinese seed stitch purses: a, Vases, fruit on pink purse. b, Peonies, butterflies. c, Vase, fruit on dark blue purse. d, Vases, fruit on light blue purse. e, Fu-dog. f, Flowers.

No. 2017 — Chineses pottery: a, Plate, bird on flowering spray, Qianlong. b, Large dish, Kangxi. c, Egshell plate, cocks on rocky ground, Yongzheng. d, Gladen dish decorated with Qilin curicorn, Yuan. e, Porcelain pug dog. f, Dish with Dutch ship, Uryburg, Qianlong.

No. 2018, vert. — Ceramic figures, Qing Dynasty: a, Waterdropper. b, Two women playing chess. c, Liu-Hai. d, Laughing twins. e, Seated hound. f, Louhan (Ma Ming).

No. 2019, Dr. Sun Yat-sen. No. 2020, Chiang Kai-shek.

No. 2021 — Dinosaurs: a, Triceratops. b, Unidentified, vert. c, Apatosaurus (d). d, Stegosaurus, vert.

1994, Feb. 18 *Perf. 14*

2012 A279 40c Pair, #a.-b.	.85	.85
2013 A280 40c Sheet of 6, #a.-f.	2.25	2.25
2014 A280 40c Sheet of 6, #a.-f.	2.25	2.25
2015 A280 45c Sheet of 6, #a.-f.	2.40	2.40
2016 A280 45c Sheet of 6, #a.-f.	2.40	2.40

2017 A281 50c Sheet of 6, #a.-f. 2.75 2.75

Perf. 13

2018 A280 50c Sheet of 6, #a.-f. 4.00 4.00

Souvenir Sheets

2019 A281 $2 multicolored 1.50 1.50
2020 A281 $2 multicolored 1.50 1.50
2021 A282 $1.50 Sheet of 4, #a.-d. 4.50 4.50

No. 2012 issued in sheets of 10 stamps and has a continuous design.

Portions of the design on No. 2021 have been applied by a thermographic process producing a shiny, raised effect.

New Year 1994 (Year of the Dog) (#2013e, 2014e, 2015e, 2016e, 2017e, 2018e). Hong Kong '94 (#2018, 2021).

Miniature Sheet

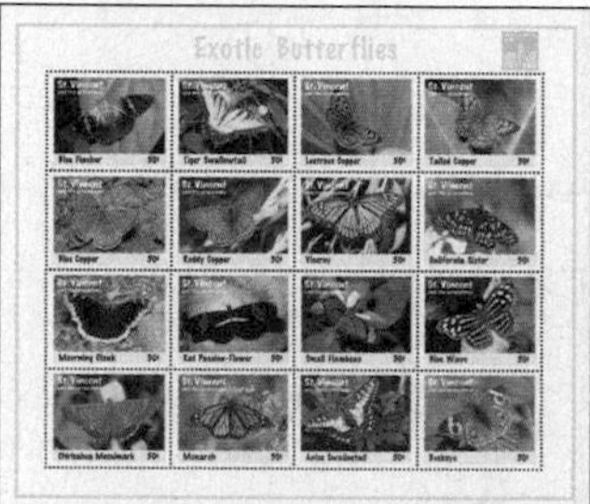

Hong Kong '94 — A283

No. 2022 — Butterflies: a, Blue flasher. b, Tiger swallowtail. c, Lustrous copper. d, Tailed copper. e, Blue copper. f, Ruddy copper. g, Viceroy. h, California sister. i, Mourning cloak. j, Red passion flower. k, Small flambeau. l, Blue wave. m, Chiricahua metalmark. n, Monarch. o, Anise swallowtail. p, Buckeye.

1994, Feb. 18 Litho. *Perf. 14½*

2022 A283 50c Sheet of 16, #a.-p. 14.50 14.50

Juventus Soccer Team — A284

Players: No. 2023, $1, Causio. No. 2024, $1, Tardelli. No. 2025, $1, Rossi. No. 2026, $1, Bettega. No. 2027, $1, Platini, Baggio. No. 2028, $1, Cabrini. No. 2029, $1, Scirea. No. 2030, $1, Furino. No. 2031, $1, Kohler. No. 2032, $1, Zoff. No. 2033, $1, Gentile.

$6, Three European Cups won by team, horiz.

1994, Mar. 22 Litho. *Perf. 14*

2023-2033 A284 Set of 11 12.00 12.00

Souvenir Sheet

2034 A284 $6 multicolored 6.00 6.00

Orchids — A285

Designs: 10c, Epidendrum ibaguense. 25c, Ionopsis utricularioides. 50c, Brassavola cucullata. 65c, Enclyclia cochleata. $1, Liparis nervosa. $2, Vanilla phaeantha. $4, Elleanthus cephalotus. $5, Isochilus linearis.

No. 2043, $6, Rodriguezia lanceolata. No. 2044, $6, Eulophia alta.

1994, Apr. 6 Litho. *Perf. 14*

2035-2042 A285 Set of 8 18.50 18.50

Souvenir Sheets

2043-2044 A285 Set of 2 16.00 16.00

A286

Dinosaurs — A287

No. 2045: a, Protoavis (e). b, Pteranodon. c, Quetzalcoatlus (b). d, Lesothosaurus (a, c, e-h). e, Hetrodontosaurus. f, Archaeopteryx (b, e). g, Cearadactylus (f). h, Anchisaurus.

No. 2046: a, Dimorphodon (e). b, Camarasaurus (e, f). c, Spinosaurus (b). d, Allosaurus (a-c, e-h). e, Rhamphorhynchus (a). f, Pteranodon (b). g, Eudimorphodon (c). h, Ornithomimus.

No. 2047, 75c: a, Dimorphodon (b). b, Pterodactylus (a). c, Rhamphorhynchus (b). d, Pteranodon. e, Gallimimus. f, Stegosaurus. g, Acanthopholis. h, Trachodon (g). i, Thecodonti (j). j, Ankylosaurus (i). k, Compsognathus. l, Protoceratops.

No. 2048, 75c: a, Hesperonis. b, Mesosaurus. c, Plesiosaurus. d, Squalicorax (a). e, Tylosaurus (d, g). f, Plesiosoar. g, Stenopterygius ichthyosaurus (j). h, Stenosaurus (f). i, Eurhinosaurus longirostris (e, f, h, l). j, Cryptocleidus oxoniensis. k, Caturus (h, i, j, l). l, Protostega (k).

No. 2049, 75c: a, Quetzalcoatlus. b, Diplodocus (a). c, Spinosaurus (f, g). d, Apatosaurus (c). e, Ornitholestes. f, Lesothosaurus (e). g, Trachodon. h, Protoavis. i, Oviraptor. j, Coelophysis (i). k, Ornitholestes (j). l, Archaeopteryx.

No. 2050, 75c, horiz: a, Albertosaurus. b, Chasmosaurus (c). c, Brachiosaurus. d, Coelophysis (e). e, Deinonychus (d). f, Anatosaurus. g, Iguanodon. h, Baryonyx. i, Steneosaurus. j, Nanotyrannus. k, Camptosaurus (j). l, Camarasaurus.

No. 2051, Tyrannosaurus rex.

No. 2052, $6, Triceratops, horiz. No. 2053, $6, Pteranodon, diplodocus carnegii, horiz. No. 2054, $6, Styracosaurus.

1994, Apr. 20 Litho. *Perf. 14*

2045 A286 75c Sheet of 8, #a.-h. 7.50 7.50
2046 A286 75c Sheet of 8, #a.-h. 7.50 7.50

Sheets of 12, #a-l

2047-2050 A287 Set of 4 37.50 37.50

Souvenir Sheets

2051 A286 $6 multi 7.00 7.00
2052-2054 A287 Set of 3 21.00 21.00

No. 2048 is horiz.

Entertainers Type of 1991

Miniature Sheet

Various portraits of Marilyn Monroe.

1994, May 16 *Perf. 13½*

2055 A206 $1 Sheet of 9, #a.-i. 10.00 10.00

1994 World Cup Soccer Championships, US — A288

Team photos: No. 2056, 50c, Colombia. No. 2057, 50c, Romania. No. 2058, 50c, Switzerland. No. 2059, 50c, US. No. 2060, 50c, Brazil. No. 2061, 50c, Cameroon. No. 2062, 50c, Russia. No. 2063, 50c, Sweden. No. 2064, 50c, Bolivia. No. 2065, 50c, Germany. No. 2066, 50c, South Korea. No. 2067, 50c, Spain. No. 2068, 50c, Argentina. No. 2069, 50c, Bulgaria. No. 2070, 50c, Greece. No. 2071, 50c, Nigeria. No. 2072, 50c, Ireland. No. 2073, 50c, Italy. No. 2074, 50c, Mexico. No. 2075, 50c, Norway. No. 2076, 50c, Belgium. No. 2077, 50c, Holland. No. 2078, 50c, Morocco. No. 2079, 50c, Saudi Arabia.

1994 *Perf. 13½*

2056-2079 A288 Set of 24 14.00 14.00

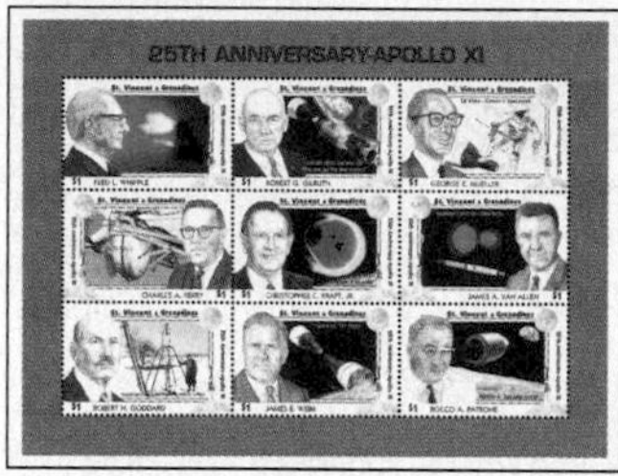

First Manned Moon Landing, 25th Anniv. — A289

No. 2080, $1 — Famous men, aviation & space scenes: a, Fred L. Whipple, Halley's Comet. b, Robert G. Gilruth, Gemini 12. c, George E. Mueller, Ed White walking in space during Gemini 4. d, Charles A. Berry, Johnsville Centrifuge. e, Christopher C. Kraft, Jr., Apollo 4 re-entry. f, James A. Van Allen, Explorer I, Van Allen Radiation Belts. g, Robert H. Goddard, Goddard Liquid Fuel Rocket, 1926. h, James E. Webb, Spirit of '76 flight. i, Rocco A. Petrone, Apollo 8 coming home.

No. 2081, $1: a, Walter R. Dornberger, missile launch, 1942. b, Alexander Lippisch, Wolfgang Spate's ME-163B. c, Kurt H. Debus, A4b Launch, 1945. d, Hermann Oberth, Oberth's Spaceship, 1923. e, Hanna Reitsch, Reichenberg (type 2) Piloted Bomb. f, Ernst Stuhlinger, Explorer I, 2nd stage ignition. g, Werner von Braun, Rocket Powered He112. h, Arthur Rudolph, Rudolph Rocket Motor, 1934. i, Willy Ley, Rocket Airplane, Greenwood Lake NY.

No. 2082, $6, Holger N. Toftoy. No. 2083, $6, Eberhard Rees.

1994, July 12 *Perf. 14*

Sheets of 9, #a-i

2080-2081 A289 Set of 2 20.00 20.00

Souvenir Sheets

2082-2083 A289 Set of 2 13.00 13.00

Nos. 2082-2083 each contain one 50x38mm stamp.

D-Day, 50th Anniv. A290

Designs: 40c, Supply armada. $5, Beached cargo ship unloads supplies.

$6, Liberty ship.

1994, July 19 Litho. *Perf. 14*

2084 A290 40c multicolored .40 .40
2085 A290 $5 multicolored 4.75 4.75

Souvenir Sheet

2086 A290 $6 multicolored 5.25 5.25

New Year 1994 (Year of the Dog) — A291

Designs: 10c, Yorkshire terrier. 25c, Yorkshire terrier, diff. 50c, Golden retriever. 65c, Bernese mountain dog. $1, Vorstehhund. $2, Tibetan terrier. $4, West highland terrier. $5, Shih tzu.

No. 2095: a, Pomeranian. b, English springer spaniel. c, Bearded collie. d, Irish wolfhound. e, Pekingese. f, Irish setter. g, Old English sheepdog. h, Basset hound. i, Cavalier King Charles spaniel. j, Kleiner munsterlander. k, Shetland sheepdog. l, Dachshund.

No. 2096, $6, Afghan hound. No. 2097, $6, German shepherd.

1994, July 21

2087-2094 A291 Set of 8 10.00 10.00
2095 A291 50c Sheet of 12, #a.-l. 4.50 4.50

Souvenir Sheets

2096-2097 A291 Set of 2 9.00 9.00

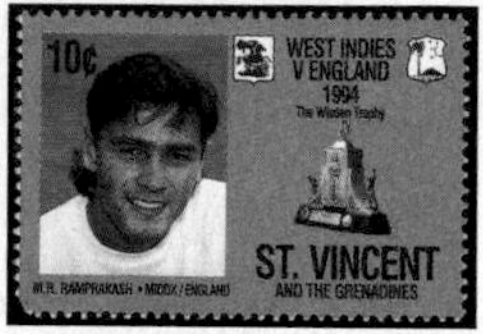

English Touring Cricket, Cent. A292

Designs: 10c, M. R. Ramprakash, England. 30c, P. V. Simmons, West Indies. $2, Sir. G. St. A. Sobers, West Indies, vert.

$3, Firsh English team, 1895.

1994, July 25

2098-2100 A292 Set of 3 3.50 3.50

Souvenir Sheet

2101 A293 $3 multicolored 3.25 3.25

A293

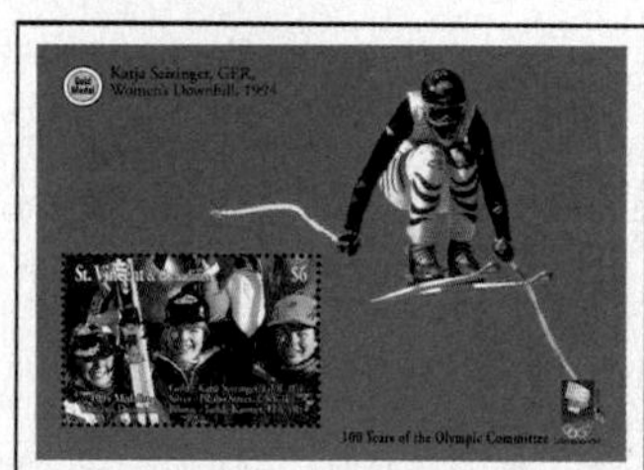

Intl. Olympic Committee, Cent. — A294

Designs: 45c, Peter Frenkel, German Democratic Republic, 20k walk, 1972. 50c, Kijung Son, Japan, marathon, 1936. 75c, Jesse Owens, US, 100-, 200-meters, 1936. $1, Greg Louganis, US, diving, 1984, 1988.

$6, Katja Seizinger, Germany, Picabo Street, US, Isolde Kastner, Italy, women's downhill, 1994.

1994, July 25

2102-2105 A293 Set of 4 3.25 3.25

Souvenir Sheet

2106 A294 $6 multicolored 6.00 6.00

A295

PHILAKOREA '94 — A296

Designs: 10c, Oryon Waterfall. 45c, Outside P'yongyang Indoor Sports Stadium, horiz. 65c, Pombong, Ch'onhwadae. 75c, Uisangdae, Naksansa. $1, Buddha of the Sokkuram Grotto, Kyangju, horiz. $2, Moksogwon, horiz.

No. 2113, 50c: a-h, Various letter pictures, eight panel screen, 18th cent. Choson Dynasty.

No. 2114, 50c — Letter pictures, 19th cent. Choson Dynasty: a, Fish. b, Birds. c-d, h, Various bookshelf pictures. e-g, Various designs from six-panel screen.

No. 2115, $4, Hunting scene, embroidery on silk, Choson Dynasty, horiz. No. 2116, $4, Chongdong Mirukbul.

1994, July 25 ***Perf. 14***

2107-2112 A295 Set of 6 8.50 8.50

Sheets of 8, #a-h

Perf. 13½

2113-2114 A296 Set of 2 13.50 13.50

Souvenir Sheets

Perf. 14

2115-2116 A295 Set of 2 7.00 7.00

Star Trek, The Next Generation, 7th Anniv. — A297

A297a

No. 2117: a, Capt. Picard. b, Cmdr. Riker. c, Lt. Cmdr. Data. d, Lt. Worf. e, Cast members. f, Dr. Crusher. g, Lt. Yar, Lt. Worf. h, Q. i, Counselor Troi.

$10, Cast members, horiz.

$20, Starship Enterprise, Capt. Picard.

1994 **Litho.** ***Perf. 14x13½***

2117 A297 $2 Sheet of 9, #a.-i. 15.00 15.00

Souvenir Sheet

Perf. 14x14½

2118 A297 $10 multicolored 9.50 9.50

Litho. & Embossed

Perf. 9

2118A A297a $20 gold & multi 25.00 25.00

Issued: Nos. 2117-2118, 6/27; No. 2118, May. No. 2117e exists in sheets of 9. No. 2118 contains one 60x40mm stamp.

Intl. Year of the Family A298

1994 ***Perf. 14***

2119 A298 75c multicolored .95 .95

Order of the Caribbean Community — A299

First award recipients: $1, Sir Shridath Ramphal, statesman, Guyana, vert. $2, Derek Walcott, writer, St. Lucia, vert. $5, William Demas, economist, Trinidad and Tobago.

1994, Sept. 1

2120-2122 A299 Set of 3 8.00 8.00

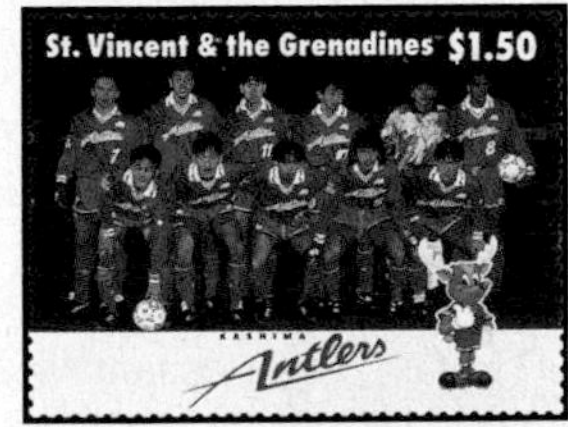

Japanese Soccer — A300

No. 2123: a, Kashima Antlers. b, JEF United. c, Red Diamonds. d, Verdy Yomiuri. e, Nissan FC Yokohama Marinos. f, AS Flugels. g, Bellmare. h, Shimizu S-pulse. i, Jubilo Iwata. j, Nagoya Grampus Eight. k, Panasonic Gamba Osaka. l, Sanfrecce Hiroshima FC.

No. 2124 — Jubilo Iwata, action scenes: a, c-d, 55c. b, e, $1.50. f, $3, Team picture.

No. 2125 — Red Diamonds, action scenes: a, c-d, 55c. b, e, $1.50. f, $3, Team pictue.

No. 2126 — Nissan FC Yokohama Marinos, action scenes: a, c-d, 55c. b, e, $1.50. f, $3, Team picture.

No. 2127 — Verdy Yomiuri, action scenes: a, c-d, 55c. b, e, $1.50. f, $3, Team picture.

No. 2128 — Nagoya Grampus eight, action scenes: a, c-d, 55c. b, e, $1.50. f, $3, Team picture.

No. 2129 — Kashima Antlers, action scenes: a, c-d, 55c. b, e, $1.50. f, $3, Team picture.

No. 2130 — JEF United, action scenes: a, c-d, 55c. b, e, $1.50. f, $3, Team picture.

No. 2131 — AS Flugels, action scenes: a, c-d, 55c. b, e, $1.50. f, $3, Team picture.

No. 2132 — Bellmare, action scenes: a, c-d, 55c. b, e, $1.50. f, $3, Team picture.

No. 2133 — Sanfrecce Hiroshima FC, action scenes: a, c-d, 55c. b, e, $1.50. f, $3, Team picture.

No. 2134 — Shimizu S-pulse, action scenes: a, c-d, 55c. b, e, $1.50. f, $3, Team picture.

No. 2135 — Panasonic Gamba Isajam, action scenes: a, c-d, 55c. b, e, $1.50. f, $3, Team picture.

No. 2136, vert. — League All-Stars: a, $1.50, League emblem. b, 55c, Shigetatsu Matsunaga. c, 55c, Masami Ihara. d, $1.50, Takumi Horiike. e, 55c, Shunzoh Ohno. f, 55c, Luiz Carlos Pereira. g, 55c, Tetsuji Hashiratani. h, 55c, Carlos Alberto Souza Dos Santos. i, $1.50, Rui Ramos. j, 55c, Yasuto Honda. k, 55c, Kazuyoshi Miura. l, $1.50, Ramon Angel Diaz.

1994, July 1 ***Perf. 14x13½***

2123 A300 $1.50 Sheet of 12, #a.-l. 11.00 11.00

Sheets of 6, #a-f

2124-2135 A300 Set of 12 70.00 70.00

Perf. 13½x14

2136 A300 Sheet of 12, #a.-l. 12.00 12.00

Christmas A301

Illustrations from Book of Hours, by Jean de Berry: 10c, The Annunciation, angel kneeling. 45c, The Visitation. 50c, The Nativity, Madonna seeing infant. 65c, The Purification of the Virgin. 75c, Presentation of Jesus in the Temple. $5, Flight into Egypt.

$6, Adoration of the Magi.

1994 **Litho.** ***Perf. 13½x14***

2137-2142 A301 Set of 6 9.50 9.50

Souvenir Sheet

2143 A301 $6 multicolored 7.50 7.50

Disney Type of 1992 Redrawn With New Denominations and Added Inscriptions

Designs: No. 2144, Like #1792. No. 2145, Like #1806. No. 2146, Like #1807.

1995, Jan. 24 ***Perf. 14x13½***

2144 A247 30c Sheet of 9, #a.-i. 6.25 6.25

Souvenir Sheets

2145 A247 $3 multi 4.25 4.25

2146 A247 $3 multi 4.25 4.25

Nos. 2144-2146 are inscribed with emblem for "New Year 1995, Year of the Pig."

ICAO, 50th Anniv. A302

Designs: 10c, Bequia Airport. 65c, Union Island. 75c, Liat 8-100, E.T. Joshua Airport. No. 2150, $1, Airplanes, ICAO emblem. No. 2151, $1, J.F. Mitchell Airport, Bequia.

1994, Dec. 1 **Litho.** ***Perf. 14***

2147-2151 A302 Set of 5 4.25 4.25

Cats A303

Parrots — A304

No. 2152 — Cats: a, Snowshoe. b, Abyssinian. c, Ocicat. d, Tiffany (e, h). e, Russian blue. f, Siamese. g, Bi-color. h, Malayan. i, Manx.

No. 2153 — Parrots: a, Mealy Amazon. b, Nanday conure. c, Black-headed caique. d, Scarlet macaw (g). e, Red-masked conure. f, Blue-headed parrot. g, Hyacinth macaw. h, Sun conure. i, Blue & yellow macaw.

No. 2154, White-eared conure. No. 2155, Birman.

1995, Apr. 25 **Litho.** ***Perf. 14***

Sheets of 9, #a-i

2152-2153 A303 $1 Set of 2 18.00 18.00

Souvenir Sheets

2154 A304 $5 multicolored 6.00 6.00

2155 A304 $6 multicolored 7.25 7.25

A305

Birds A306

No. 2156 — World Wildlife Fund, masked booby: a, One standing. b, Two birds. c, One nesting. d, One stretching wings.

No. 2157: a, Greater egret. b, Roseate spoonbill. c, Ring-billed gull. d, Ruddy quail-dove. e, Royal tern. f, Killdeer. g, Osprey. h, Frigatebird. i, Masked booby. j, Green-backed heron. k, Cormorant. l, Brown pelican.

No. 2158, Flamingo, vert. No. 2159, Purple gallinule, vert.

1995, May 2

2156 A305 75c Strip of 4, #a.-d. 4.00 4.00

2157 A306 75c Sheet of 12, #a.-l. 12.00 12.00

Souvenir Sheets

2158 A306 $5 multicolored 5.00 5.00

2159 A306 $6 multicolored 6.00 6.00

No. 2156 is a continuous design and was issued in sheets of 3.

VE Day, 50th Anniv. A307

No. 2159A: b, Douglas Devastator. c, Doolittle's B25 leads raid on Tokyo. d, Curtis Helldiver. e, USS Yorktown. f, USS Wasp. g, USS Lexington sinks.

No. 2160: a, US First Army nears the Rhine. b, Last V2 rocket fired at London, Mar. 1945. c, 8th Air Force B24 Liberators devastate industrial Germany. d, French Army advances on Strasbourg. e, Gloster Meteor, first jet aircraft to enter squadron service. f, Berlin burns from both air and ground bombardments. g, Soviet tanks on Unter Den Linden near Brandenburg Gate. h, European war is won.

No. 2161, $6, Pilot in cockpit of Allied bomber.

No. 2161A, $6, Ships in Pacific, sunset.

1995, May 8 **Litho.** ***Perf. 14***

2159A A307 $2 Sheet of 6, #b.-g. + label 11.50 11.50

2160 A307 $2 Sheet of 8, #a.-h. + label 15.50 15.50

Souvenir Sheets

2161-2161A A307 Set of 2 15.00 15.00

No. 2161 contains one 57x43mm stamp.

UN, 50th Anniv. — A308

No. 2162: a, Globe, dove. b, Lady Liberty. c, UN Headquarters.
$6, Child.

1995, May 5

2162 A308 $2 Strip of 3, #a.-c. 5.25 5.25

Souvenir Sheet

2163 A308 $6 multicolored 5.25 5.25

No. 2162 is a continuous design and was issued in miniature sheets of 3.

18th World Scout Jamboree, Netherlands A309

Designs: $1, Natl. Scout flag. $4, Lord Baden Powell. $5, Scout handshake.
No. 2167, $6, Scout sign. No. 2168, $6, Scout salute.

1995, May 5

2164-2166 A309 Set of 3 8.75 8.75

Souvenir Sheets

2167-2168 A309 Set of 2 11.50 11.50

Yalta Conference, 50th Anniv. A310

Design: $50, like #2169.

1995, May 8 Litho. *Perf. 14*

2169 A310 $1 shown 1.75 1.75

Litho. & Embossed

Perf. 9

2169A A310 $50 gold & multi *27.50 27.50*

No. 2169 was issued in sheets of 9.

New Year 1995 (Year of the Boar) — A311

No. 2170 — Stylized boars: a, blue green & multi. b, brown & multi. c, red & multi.
$2, Two boars, horiz.

1995, May 8

2170 A311 75c Strip of 3, #a.-c. 2.50 2.50

Souvenir Sheet

2171 A311 $2 multicolored 2.50 2.50

No. 2170 was issued in sheets of 3.

FAO, 50th Anniv. — A312

No. 2172: a, Girl holding plate, woman with bowl. b, Stirring pot of food. c, Working in fields of grain.
$6, Infant.

1995, May 8

2172 A312 $2 Strip of 3, #a.-c. 5.25 5.25

Souvenir Sheet

2173 A312 $6 multicolored 5.25 5.25

No. 2172 is a continuous design and was issued in sheets of 3.

Rotary Intl., 90th Anniv. A313

Designs: $5, Paul Harris, Rotary emblem.
$6, St. Vincent flag, Rotary emblem.

1995, May 8

2174 A313 $5 multicolored 4.50 4.50

Souvenir Sheet

2175 A313 $6 multicolored 5.25 5.25

Queen Mother, 95th Birthday — A314

No. 2176: a, Drawing, b, Wearing blue hat. c, Formal portrait. d, Wearing lavender outfit.
$6, Wearing crown jewels, yellow dress.

1995, May 8 *Perf. 13½x14*

2176 A314 $1.50 Block or strip of 4, #a.-d. 5.25 5.25

Souvenir Sheet

2177 A314 $6 multicolored 5.25 5.25

No. 2176 was issued in sheet of 2 blocks or strips.

In 2002, sheets of Nos. 2176 and 2177 were overprinted "In Memoriam — 1900-2002" in margin.

Miniature Sheets

Marine Life A315

No. 2178, vert: a, Humpback whale (b, d, e, f, i). b, Green turtle (c). c, Bottlenosed dolphin (f). d, Monk seal (e). e, Krill. f, Blue shark. g, Striped pork fish. h, Chaelodon sedentarius (e, g). i, Ship wreck, bottom of sea.

No. 2179: a, Pomacentrus leucostictus (b). b, Pomacanthus arcuatus (d). c, Microspathodon chrysurus (d). d, Chaetodon capistratus.

No. 2180, $6, Physalia physalis, vert. No. 2181, $6, Sea anemones, vert.

1995, May 23 *Perf. 14*

2178 A315 90c Sheet of 9, #a.-i. 7.50 7.50

2179 A315 $1 Sheet of 4, #a.-d. 5.00 5.00

Souvenir Sheets

2180-2181 A315 Set of 2 13.00 13.00

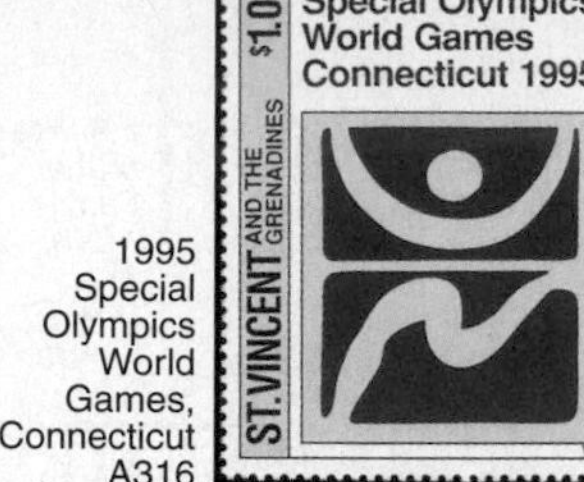

1995 Special Olympics World Games, Connecticut A316

A316a

1995, July 6

2182 A316 $1 blk, yel & bl 1.10 1.10

Embossed

Perf. 9

2182A A316a $20 gold

No. 2182 issued in sheets of 9.

1995 IAAF World Track & Field Championships, Gothenburg & 1996 Summer Olympics, Atlanta — A317

No. 2183: a, Ingrid Kristiansen, Norway. b, Trine Hattestad, Norway. c, Grete Waitz, Norway. d, Vebjorn Rodal, Norway. e, Geir Moen, Norway. f, Steinar Hoen, Norway, horiz.

1995, July 31 Litho. *Perf. 14*

2183 A317 $1 Sheet of 6, #a.-f. 4.50 4.50

A318

Designs: 15c, Breast, bowl of food, horiz. 20c, Expressing milk, cup, spoon. 90c, Drawing of mother breastfeeding child, by Picasso. $5, Mother, child, olive wreath.

1995, Aug. 4

2184-2187 A318 Set of 4 6.75 6.75

WHO, UNICEF Baby Friendly Program.

A319

Designs: 10c, Leeward Coast, horiz. 15c, Feeder roads project, horiz. 25c, Anthurium andraeanum, horiz. 50c, Coconut palm. 65c, Housing scene, Fairhall, horiz.

1995, Aug. 8

2188-2192 A319 Set of 5 1.90 1.90

Caribbean Development Bank, 25th anniv.

Fudo Myoou (God of Fire), Woodprint, by Shunichi Kadowaki — A320

1995, July 1 Litho. *Perf. 14*

2193 A320 $1.40 multicolored 1.25 1.25

A321

Nolan Ryan, Baseball Player — A322

Designs: No. 2194, Nolan Ryan Foundation emblem. No. 2195, Emblem of major league All Star Game, Arlington,TX.

No. 2196 — Portraits of Ryan: a, In NY Mets uniform. b, With western hat, dog. c, In Texas Rangers cap. d, Throwing football. e, With son. f, Laughing, without hat. g, With family. h, Wearing Houston Astros cap.

No. 2197 — Ryan in Rangers uniform: a, Blue outfit. b, "34" on front. c, Looking left. d, After pitch looking forward. e, After pitch looking left. f, With bloody lip. g, Ready to pitch ball. h, Holding up cap.

$6, Being carried by team mates.

$30, Ready to pitch (illustration reduced).

1995, Aug. 1 *Perf. 13½x14*

2194 A321 $1 multicolored .75 .75

2195 A321 $1 multicolored .75 .75

a. Pair, #2194-2195 1.50 1.50

2196 A321 $1 Sheet of 9, #a.-h. + #2194 12.00 12.00

2197 A321 $1 Sheet of 9, #a.-h. + #2195 12.00 12.00

Souvenir Sheet

2198 A321 $6 multicolored 5.25 5.25

Litho. & Embossed

Perf. 9

2199 A322 $30 gold & multi *35.00 35.00*

Nos. 2194-2195 were issued in sheets containing 5 #2194, 4 #2195.

1996 Summer Olympics, Atlanta — A323

No. 2200: a, Jean Shiley, US. b, Ruth Fuchs, Germany. c, Alessandro Andrei, Italy. d, Dorando Pietri, Italy. e, Heide Rosendahl, Germany. f, Mitsuoki Watanabe, Japan. g, Yasuhiro Yamashita, Japan. h, Dick Fosbury, US.

No. 2201: a, Long jump. b, Hurdles. c, Sprint. d, Marathon. e, Gymnastics. f, Rowing.

No. 2202, $5, Magic Johnson. No. 2203, $5, Swimmer's hand, horiz.

1995, Aug. 24 Litho. *Perf. 14*

2200	A323	$1 Sheet of 8, #a.-h.	7.00	7.00
2201	A323	$2 Sheet of 6, #a.-f.	10.50	10.50

Souvenir Sheets

2202-2203	A323	Set of 2	12.00	12.00

Miniature Sheet

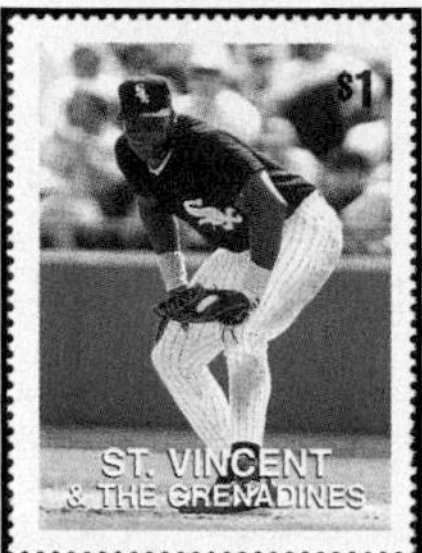

Stars of American League Baseball A324

A324a

No. 2204 — Different portraits of: a, e, i, Frank Thomas, Chicago White Sox. b, f-g, Cal Ripken, Jr., Baltimore Orioles. c-d, h, Ken Griffey, Jr., Seattle Mariners.

No. 2204J, $30, Griffey. No. 2204K, $30, Ripken. No. 2204L, $30, Thomas.

1995, Sept. 6 Litho. *Perf. 14*

2204	A324	$1 Sheet of 9, #a.-i.	8.50	8.50

Litho. & Embossed

Perf. 9

2204J-2204L	A324a	Set of 3		

Entertainers A325

Nos. 2205-2206, $1: Portraits of Elvis Presley.

No. 2207, $1: Portraits of John Lennon.

Nos. 2208-2210, $1: Portraits of Marilyn Monroe.

No. 2211, $6, Presley, diff. No. 2212, $6, Lennon, diff. No. 2213, $6, Monroe, in black. No. 2214, $6, Monroe, in red.

1995, Sept. 18 *Perf. 13½x14*

2205	A325	$1 Sheet of 6, #a.-f.	7.00	7.00

Sheets of 9, #a-i

2206-2210	A325	Set of 5	40.00	40.00

Souvenir Sheets

2211-2214	A325	Set of 4	26.00	26.00

No. 2208 has serifs in lettering. No. 2209 has pink lettering.

Entertainers — A325a

Designs: $20, Elvis Presley. $30, Marilyn Monroe.

1995 Litho. & Embossed *Perf. 9*

2214A	A325a	$20 gold & multi	*24.00*	*24.00*
2214B	A325a	$30 gold & multi	*36.00*	*36.00*

Passenger Trains — A326

No. 2215: a, German Federal Railway ET4-03, high speed four car electric. b, Tres Grande Vitesse (TGV), France. c, British Railways Class 87 electric. d, Beijing locomotive, Railways of the People's Republic of China. e, American Amtrak turbo. f, Swedish State Railways class RC4 electric.

$6, Eurostar.

1995, Oct. 3 *Perf. 14*

2215	A326	$1.50 Sheet of 6, #a.-f.	7.75	7.75

Souvenir Sheet

2216	A326	$6 multicolored	8.50	8.50

No. 2216 contains one 85x28mm stamp.

Nobel Prize Fund Established, Cent. — A327

No. 2217, $1: a, Heinrich Böll, literature, 1972. b, Walther Bothe, physics, 1954. c, Richard Kuhn, chemistry, 1938. d, Hermann Hesse, literatrue, 1946. e, Knut Hamsun, literature, 1920. f, Konrad Lorenz, medicine, 1973. g, Thomas Mann, literature, 1929. h, Fridtjof Nansen, peace, 1922. i, Fritz Pregl, chemistry, 1923. j, Christian Lange, peace, 1921. k, Otto Loewi, medicine, 1936. l, Erwin Schrodinger, physics, 1933.

No. 2218, $1: a, Giosue Carducci, literature, 1906. b, Wladyslaw Reymont, literature, 1924. c, Ivan Bunin, literature, 1933. d, Pavel Cherenkov, physics, 1958. e, Ivan Pavlov, medicine, 1904. f, Pyotr Kapitsa, physics, 1978. g, Lev Landau, physics, 1962. h, Daniel Bovet, medicine, 1957. i, Henryk Sienkiewicz, literature, 1905. j, Aleksandr Prokhorov, physics, 1964. k, Julius Wagner von Jauregg, medicine, 1927. l, Grazia Deledda, literature, 1926.

No. 2219, $1: a, Bjornstjerne Bjornson, literature, 1903. b, Frank Kellogg, peace, 1929. c, Gustav Hertz, physics, 1925. d, Har Gobind Khorana, medicine, 1968. e, Kenichi Fukui, chemistry, 1981. f, Henry Kissinger, peace, 1973. g, Martin Luther King, Jr., peace, 1964. h, Odd Hassel, chemistry, 1969. i, Polykarp Kusch, physics, 1955. j, Ragnar Frisch, economics, 1969. k, Willis E. Lamb, Jr., physics, 1955. l, Sigrid Undset, literature, 1928.

No. 2220, $1: a, Robert Barany, medicine, 1914. b, Ernest Walton, physics, 1951. c, Alfred Fried, peace, 1911. d, James Franck, physics, 1925. e, Werner Forssmann, medicine, 1956. f, Yasunari Kawabata, literature, 1968. g, Wolfgang Pauli, physics, 1945. h, Jean-Paul Sartre, literature, 1964. i, Aleksandr Solzhenitsyn, literature, 1970. j, Hermann Staudinger, chemistry, 1953. k, Igor Tamm, physics, 1958. l, Samuel Beckett, literature, 1969.

No. 2221, $6, Adolf Windaus, chemistry, 1928. No. 2222, $6, Hideki Yukawa, physics, 1949. No. 2223, $6, Bertha von Suttner, peace, 1905. No. 2224, $6, Karl Landsteiner, medicine, 1930.

1995, Oct. 2 Litho. *Perf. 14*

Sheets of 12, #a-l

2217-2220	A327	Set of 4	46.00	46.00

Souvenir Sheets

2221-2224	A327	Set of 4	26.00	26.00

Classic Cars A328

No. 2225: a, 1931 Duesenberg Model J. b, 1913 Sleeve-valve Minerva. c, 1933 Delage D.8. SS. d, 1931-32 Bugatti Royale, Coupe De Ville chassis 41111. e, 1926 Rolls Royce 7668CC Phantom 1 Landauette. f, 1927 Mercedes Benz S26/120/180 PS.

$5, Hispano-Suiza Type H6B tulipwood-bodied roadster by Neuport.

1995, Oct. 3

2225	A328	$1.50 Sheet of 6, #a.-f.	7.75	7.75

Souvenir Sheet

2226	A328	$5 multicolored	7.00	7.00

Singapore '95 (#2225). No. 2226 contains one 85x28mm stamp.

Sierra Club, Cent. — A329

No. 2227: a, Gray wolf in front of trees. b, Gray wolf pup. c, Gray wolf up close. d, Hawaiian goose. e, Two Hawaiian geese. f, Jaguar. g, Lion-tailed macaque. h, Sand cat. i, Three sand cats.

No. 2228, horiz.: a, Orangutan swinging from tree. b, Orangutan facing forward. c, Orangutan looking left. d, Jaguar on rock. e, Jaguar up close. f, Sand cats. g, Hawaiian goose. h, Three lion-tailed macaques. i, Lion-tailed macaque.

1995, Dec. 1 Litho. *Perf. 14*

2227	A329	$1 Sheet of 9, #a.-i.	9.00	9.00
2228	A329	$1 Sheet of 9, #a.-i.	9.00	9.00

Natural Wonders of the World A330

No. 2229: a, Nile River. b, Yangtze River. c, Niagara Falls. d, Victoria Falls. e, Grand Canyon, US. f, Sahara Desert, Algeria. g, Kilimanjaro, Tanzania. h, Amazon river.

No. 2230, Haleakala Crater, Hawaii.

1995, Dec. 1

2229	A330	$1.10 Sheet of 8, #a-h	9.50	9.50

Souvenir Sheet

2230	A330	$6 multicolored	6.75	6.75

Disney Christmas — A331

Antique Disney toys: 1c, Lionel Santa car. 2c, Mickey Mouse "Choo Choo." 3c, Minnie Mouse pram. 5c, Mickey Mouse circus pull toy. 10c, Mickey, Pluto wind-up cart. 25c, Mickey Mouse mechanical motorcycle. $3, Lionel's Mickey Mouse handcar. $5, Casey Jr. Disneyland Express.

No. 2239, $6, Silver Link, Mickey the Stoker. No. 2240, $6, Mickey, Streamliner Engine.

1995, Dec. 7 *Perf. 13½x14*

2231-2238	A331	Set of 8	15.50	15.50

Souvenir Sheets

2239-2240	A331	Set of 2	14.00	14.00

Crotons A331a

Codiaeum variegatum: 10c, Mons florin. 15c, Prince of Monaco. 20c, Craigii. 40c, Gloriosum. 50c, Ebureum, vert. 60c, Volutum ramshorn. 70c, Narrenii, vert. 90c, Undutatum, vert. $1, Caribbean. $1.10, Gloriosa. $1.40, Katonii. $2, Appleleaf. $5, Tapestry. $10, Cornutum. $20, Puntatum aureum.

1996, Jan. 1 Litho. *Perf. 14*

2240A	A331a	10c multi	.25	.25
2240B	A331a	15c multi	.25	.25
2240C	A331a	20c multi	.25	.25
2240D	A331a	40c multi	.30	.30
2240E	A331a	50c multi	.40	.40
2240F	A331a	60c multi	.45	.45
2240G	A331a	70c multi	.55	.55
2240H	A331a	90c multi	.70	.70
2240I	A331a	$1 multi	.75	.75
2240J	A331a	$1.10 multi	.85	.85
2240K	A331a	$1.40 multi	1.00	1.00
2240L	A331a	$2 multi	1.50	1.50
2240M	A331a	$5 multi	3.75	3.75
2240N	A331a	$10 multi	7.50	7.50
2240O	A331a	$20 multi	15.00	15.00
	Nos. 2240A-2240O (15)		33.50	33.50

New Year 1996 (Year of the Rat) — A332

Nos. 2241 and 2242 — Stylized rats, Chinese inscriptions within checkered squares: a, lilac & multi. b, orange & multi. c, pink & multi.

$2, orange, green & black.

1996, Jan. 2 Litho. *Perf. 14½*

2241	A332	75c Strip of 3, #a.-c.	2.00	2.00
2242	A332	$1 Sheet of 3, #a.-c.	2.40	2.40

Souvenir Sheet

2243	A332	$2 multicolored	1.60	1.60

No. 2241 was issued in sheets of 9 stamps.

STAR TREK
Commemorating 30 years of STAR TREK

A333

Star Trek, 30th Anniv. — A333a

No. 2244, $1: a, Spock. b, Kirk. c, Uhura. d, Sulu. e, Starship Enterprise. f, McCoy. g, Scott. h, Kirk, McCoy, Spock. i, Chekov.

No. 2245, $1: a, Spock holding up hand in Vulcan greeting. b, Kirk, Spock in "A Piece of the Action." c, Captain Kirk. d, Kirk, "The Trouble with Tribbles." e, Crew, "City on the Edge of Forever." f, Uhura, Sulu, "Mirror, Mirror." g, Romulans, "Balance of Terror." h, Building exterior. i, Khan, "Space Seed."

$6, Spock, Uhura.
$30, Spock, Kirk, McCoy, Scott, Starship Enterprise.
Illustration A333a reduced.

1996, Jan. 4 ***Perf. 13½x14***

Sheets of 9, #a-i

2244-2245 A333 $1 Set of 2 15.00 15.00

Souvenir Sheet

2246 A333 $6 multicolored 4.50 4.50

Litho. & Embossed

Perf. 9

2246A A333a $30 gold & multi 30.00 30.00

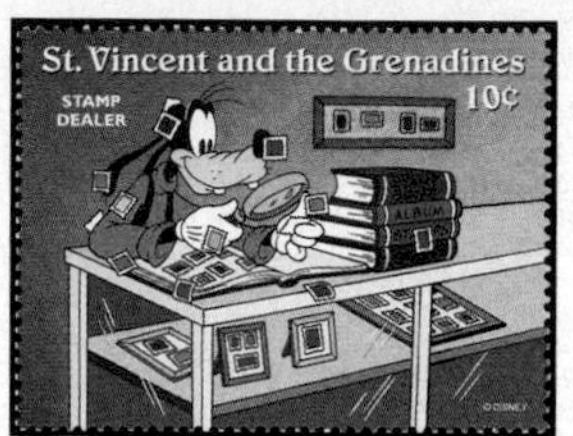

Disney Characters in Various Occupations — A334

No. 2247 — Merchants: a, Stamp dealer. b, At supermarket. c, Car salesman. d, Florist. e, Fast food carhop. f, Street vendor. g, Gift shop. h, Hobby shop owner. i, Bakery.

No. 2248 — Transport workers: a, Delivery service. b, Truck driver. c, Airplane crew. d, Railroad men. e, Bus driver. f, Tour guide. g, Messenger service. h, Trolley conductor. i, Air traffice controller.

No. 2249 — Law & order: a, Postal inspector. b, Traffic cop. c, Private detectives. d, Highway patrol. e, Justice of the peace. f, Security guard. g, Judge and lawyer. h, Sheriff. i, Court stenographer.

No. 2250 — Sports professionals: a, Basketball player. b, Referee. c, Track coach. d, Ice skater. e, Golfer and caddy. f, Sportscaster. g, Tennis champs. h, Football coach. i, Race car driver.

No. 2251 — Scientists: a, Paleontologist. b, Archaeologist. c, Inventor. d, Astronaut. e, Chemist. f, Engineer. g, Computer graphics. h, Astronomer. i, Zoologist.

No. 2252, vert. — School of education: a, Classroom teacher. b, Nursery school teacher. c, Band teacher. d, Electronic teacher. e, School psychologist. f, School principal. g, Professor. h, Graduate.

No. 2253 — Sea & shore workers: a, Ship builders. b, Fisherman. c, Pearl diver. d, Underwater photographer. e, Bait & tackle shop owner. f, Bathing suit covergirls. g, Marine life painter. h, Lifeguard. i, Lighthouse keeper.

No. 2254, $6, Donald in ice cream parlor. No. 2255, $6, Goofy as an oceanographer. No. 2256, $6, Grandma, Grandpa, Daisy Duck as jury, vert. No. 2257, $6, Donald as deep sea treasure hunter, vert. No. 2258, $6, Minnie as librarian, vert. No. 2259, $6, Mickey, ducks, as cheerleaders, vert. No. 2260, $6, Mickey as seaman, vert.

1996, Jan. 8 ***Perf. 14x13½, 13½x14***

2247 A334 10c Sheet of 9, #a.-i. 1.10 1.10
2248 A334 50c Sheet of 9, #a.-i. 5.75 5.75
2249 A334 75c Sheet of 9, #a.-i. 8.25 8.25
2250 A334 90c Sheet of 9, #a.-i. 10.00 10.00
2251 A334 95c Sheet of 9, #a.-i. 10.50 10.50
2252 A334 $1.10 Sheet of 8, #a.-h. 11.00 11.00
2253 A334 $1.20 Sheet of 9, #a.-i. 13.50 13.50

Souvenir Sheets

2254-2260 A334 Set of 7 30.00 30.00

#2248-2253 exist in sheets of 7 or 8 10c stamps + label. The label replaces the following stamps: #2248e, 2249e, 2250e, 2251e, 2252d, 2253e. The sheets had limited release on Dec. 3, 1996.

Paintings from Metropolitan Museum of Art — A335

No. 2261: a, Moses Striking Rock, by Bloemaert. b, The Last Communion, by Botticelli. c, The Musicians, by Caravaggio. d, Francesco Sassetti & Son, by Ghirlandaio. e, Pepito Costa y Bunells, by Goya. f, Saint Andrew, by Martini. g, The Nativity, by a follower of van der Weyden. h, Christ Blessing, by Solario.

No. 2262 — Art by Cézanne: a, Madame Cézanne. b, Still Life with Apples and Pears. c, Man in a Straw Hat. d, Still Life with a Ginger Jar. e, Madame Cézanne in a Red Dress. f, Still Life. g, Dominique Aubert. h, Still Life, diff. i, The Card Players.

No. 2263: a, Bullfight, by Goya. b, Portrait of a Man, by Frans Hals. c, Mother and Son, by Sully. d, Portrait of a Young Man, by Memling. e, Maltilde Stoughton de Jaudenes, by Stuart. f, Josef de Jaudenes y Nebot, by Stuart. g, Mont Sainte-Victore, by Cézanne. h, Gardanne, by Cézanne. i, The Empress Eugenie, by Winterhalter.

No. 2264: a, The Dissolute Household, by Steen. b, Portrait of Gerard de Lairesse, by Rembrandt. c, Juan de Pareja, by Velázquez. d, Curiosity, by G. Ter Borch. e, The Companions of Rinaldo, by Poussin. f, Don Gaspar de Guzman, by Velázquez. g, Merry Company on a Terrace, by Steen. h, Pilate Washing Hands, by Rembrandt. i, Portrait of a Man, by Van Dyck.

No. 2265, $6, Hagar in Wilderness, by Corot. No. 2266, $6, Young Ladies from the Village, by Courbet. No. 2267, $6, Two Young Peasant Women, by Pissaro. No. 2268, $6, Allegory of the Planets and Continents, by Tiepolo.

1996, Feb. 1 **Litho.** ***Perf. 14***

2261 A335 75c Sheet of 8, #a.-h.+label 5.00 5.00
2262 A335 90c Sheet of 9, #a.-i. 7.00 7.00
2263 A335 $1 Sheet of 9, #a.-i. 7.75 7.75
2264 A335 $1.10 Sheet of 9, #a.-i. 8.50 8.50

Souvenir Sheets

2265-2268 A335 Set of 4 20.00 20.00

Nos. 2265-2268 each contain one 81x53mm stamp.

A335a

Michael Jordan, Basketball Player, Baseball Player — A335b

Design: No. 2268E, Jordan as basketball player.

Perf. 14, Imperf. (#2268Ac)

1996, Apr. 17 **Litho.**

2268A Sheet of 17, 16 #b, 1 #c 29.00 29.00
b. A335a $2 shown 1.50 1.50
c. A335a $6 Portrait, up close 4.50 4.50

Litho. & Embossed

Perf. 9

2268D A335b $30 shown
2268E A335b $30 gold & multi

No. 2268Ac is 68x100mm and has simulated perforations.

A335c

Joe Montana, Football Player — A335d

No. 2268I: j, In red jersey. k, In white jersey.

Perf. 14, Imperf. (#2268Fh)

1996, Apr. 17 **Litho.**

2268F Sheet of 17, 16 #g, 1 #h 29.00 29.00
g. A335c $2 shown 1.50 1.50
h. A335c $6 In action 4.50 4.50

Souvenir Sheet

Litho. & Embossed

Perf. 9

2268I A335d $15 Sheet of 2, #j.-k.

No. 2268Fh is 68x100mm and has simulated perforations.

Lou Gehrig and Cal Ripken, Jr., Baseball Ironmen — A336

1995 **Litho. & Embossed** ***Perf. 9***

2269 A336 $30 gold & multi

A336a

A337

Star Wars Trilogy — A338

No. 2269: b, In Space Bar. c, Luke, Emperor. d, X-Wing Fighter. e, Star Destroyers. f, Cloud City. g, Speeders on Forest Moon.

Nos. 2270, 2273a, Darth Vader, "Star Wars," 1977. Nos. 2271, 2273c, Yoda, "Return of the Jedi," 1983. Nos. 2272, 2273b, Storm troopers, "The Empire Strikes Back," 1980.

No. 2274, $30, Darth Vader, "Star Wars," 1977. No. 2275, $30, Yoda, "Return of the Jedi," 1983. No. 2276, $30, Storm Trooper, "The Empire Strikes Back," 1980.

1996, Mar. 19 **Litho.** ***Perf. 14***

2269A A336a 35c Sheet of 6, #b.-g. 9.50 9.50

Self-Adhesive

Serpentine Die Cut 6

2270 A337 $1 sil & multi 3.00 3.00
2271 A337 $1 sil & multi 3.00 3.00
2272 A337 $1 sil & multi 3.00 3.00

Souvenir Sheet

Serpentine Die Cut 9

2273 A338 $2 Sheet of 3, #a.-c. 9.50 9.50

Litho. & Embossed

Perf. 9

2274-2276 A337 Set of 3

Nos. 2270-2272 were issued in sheets of 3 each arranged in alternating order.

Nos. 2274-2276 are gold and multi, and also exist in silver & multi.

Issued: Nos. 2274-2276, 11/18/95; others 3/19/96.

Butterflies — A339

Designs: 70c, Anteos menippe. $1, Eunica alcmena. $1.10, Doxocopa lavinia. $2, Tithorea tarricina.

No. 2281: a, Papilio lycophron. b, Prepona buckleyana. c, Parides agavus. d, Papilio cacicus. e, Euryades duponchelli. f, Diaethria dymena. g, Orimba jansoni. h, Polystichtis siaka. i, Papilio machaonides.

$5, Adelpha abia. $6, Themone pais.

1996, Apr. 15 **Litho.** ***Perf. 14***

2277-2280 A339 Set of 4 4.50 4.50
2281 A339 90c Sheet of 9, #a.-i. 7.50 7.50

Souvenir Sheets

2282 A339 $5 multicolored 4.75 4.75
2283 A339 $6 multicolored 6.00 6.00

Queen Elizabeth II, 70th Birthday — A340

No. 2284: a, Portrait. b, In robes of Order of the Garter. c, Wearing red coat, hat.

$6, Waving from balcony, horiz.

1996, June 12 **Litho.** ***Perf. 13½x14***

2284 A340 $2 Strip of 3, #a.-c. 5.25 5.25

Souvenir Sheet

Perf. 14x13½

2285 A340 $6 multicolored 5.25 5.25

No. 2284 was issued in sheets of 9 stamps.

Birds A341

Designs: 60c, Coereba flaveola, vert. $1, Myadestes genibarbis, vert. $1.10, Tangara cucullata, vert. $2, Eulampis jugularis, vert.

No. 2290: a, Progne subis. b, Buteo platypterus. c, Phaethon lepturus. d, Himantopus himantopus. e, Sterna anaethetus. f, Euphonia musica. g, Arenaria interpres. h, Sericotes holosericeus. i, Nyctanassa violacea.

$5, Dendrocygna autumnalis, vert.. $6, Amazona guildingii, vert.

1996, July 11 ***Perf. 14***

2286-2289	A341 Set of 4	4.50	4.50
2290	A341 $1 Sheet of 9, #a.-i.	8.00	8.00

Souvenir Sheets

2291	A341 $5 multi	4.25	4.25
2292	A341 $6 multi	5.25	5.25

Radio, Cent. A342

Entertainers: 90c, Walter Winchell. $1, Fred Allen. $1.10, Hedda Hopper. $2, Eve Arden. $6, Major Bowes.

1996, July 11 ***Perf. 13½x14***

2293-2296	A342 Set of 4	4.25	4.25

Souvenir Sheet

2297	A342 $6 multicolored	5.00	5.00

UNICEF, 50th Anniv. A343

Designs: $1, Boy raising arm. $1.10, Children reading. $2, Girl, microscope. $5, Boy.

1996, July 11 ***Perf. 14***

2298-2300	A343 Set of 3	3.25	3.25

Souvenir Sheet

2301	A343 $5 multicolored	3.80	3.80

Chinese Animated Films — A344

Nos. 2302, 15c, 2304, 75c, vert.: Various characters from "Uproar in Heaven."

Nos. 2303, 15c, 2305, 75c, vert.: Various characters from "Nezha Conquers the Dragon King."

1996, May 10 **Litho.** ***Perf. 12***

Strips of 5, #a-e

2302-2303	A344 15c Set of 2	3.50	3.50

Souvenir Sheets

2304-2305	A344 75c Set of 2	4.00	4.00

Nos. 2302-2303 each were issued in a sheet of 10 stamps. CHINA '96, 9th Asian Intl. Philatelic Exhibition.

Jerusalem, 3000th Anniv. — A345

Designs: $1, Knesset. $1.10, Montefiore Windmill. $2, Shrine of the Book. $5, Jerusalem of Gold.

1996, July 11 **Litho.** ***Perf. 14***

2306-2308	A345 Set of 3	4.25	4.25

Souvenir Sheet

2309	A345 $5 multicolored	4.25	4.25

The captions on Nos. 2306 and 2308 are transposed. For overprints see Nos. 2586-2589.

1996 Summer Olympic Games, Atlanta A346

Designs: 20c, Maurice King, weight lifter, vert. 70c, Eswort Coombs, 400-meter relay, vert. No. 2312, 90c, Runners, Olympia, 530BC. No. 2313, 90c, Pamenos Ballantyne, Benedict Ballantyne, runners, vert. $1, London landmarks, 1908 Olympics, Great Britain. No. 2315, $1.10, Rodney "Chang" Jack, soccer player, vert. No. 2316, $1.10, Dorando Pietri, marathon runner, London, 1908, vert. $2, Yachting.

No. 2318, $1, vert. — Past winners, event: a, Vitaly Shcherbo, gymnastics. b, Fu Mingxia, diving. c, Wilma Rudolph, track & field. d, Rafer Johnson, decathlon. e, Teofilo Stevenson, boxing. f, Babe Didrikson, track & field. g, Kyoko Iwasaki, swimming. h, Yoo Namkyu, table tennis. i, Michael Gross, swimming.

No. 2319, $1: a, Chuhei Nambu, triple jump. b, Duncan McNaughton, high jump. c, Jack Kelly, single sculls. d, Jackie Joyner-Kersee, heptathlon. e, Tyrell Biggs, boxing. f, Larisa Latynina, gymnastics. g, Bob Garrett, discus. h, Paavo Nurmi, 5000-meters. i, Eric Lemming, javelin.

No. 2320, $1: a, Yasuhiro Yamashita, judo. b, Peter Rono, 1500-meters. c, Aleksandr Kurlovich, weight lifting. d, Juha Tiainen, hammer throw. e, Sergei Bubka, pole vault. f, Q. F. Newall, women's archery. g, Nadia Comaneci, gymnastics. h, Carl Lewis, long jump. i, Bob Mathias, decathlon.

No. 2321, $1, vert. — Sporting events: a, Women's archery. b, Gymnastics. c, Basketball. d, Soccer. e, Water polo. f, Baseball. g, Kayak. h, Fencing. i, Cycling.

No. 2322, $5, Olympic Flag. No. 2323, $5, Carl Lewis, runner, vert. No. 2324, $5, Alexander Dityatin, gymnastics, 1980. No. 2325, $5, Hannes Kolehmainen, marathon runner.

1996, July 19

2310-2317	A346 Set of 8	7.00	7.00

Sheets of 9, #a-i

2318-2321	A346 Set of 4	31.00	31.00

Souvenir Sheets

2322-2325	A346 Set of 4	15.00	15.00

St. Vincent Olympic Committee (#2310-2311, 2313, 2315).

Disney's "The Hunchback of Notre Dame" A347

No. 2326: a, Quasimodo. b, Phoebus. c, Laverne, Hugo. d, Clopin. e, Frollo. f, Esmeralda. g, Victor. h, Djali.

No. 2327, $6, Esmeralda, Quasimodo, horiz. No. 2328, $6, Esmeralda, Phoebus, horiz.

1996, July 25 ***Perf. 13½x14***

2326	A347 $1 Sheet of 8, #a-h	8.00	8.00

Souvenir Sheets

Perf. 14X13½

2327-2328	A347 Set of 2	13.00	13.00

Fish A348

Designs: 70c, French angelfish. 90c, Red-spotted hawkfish. $1.10, Spiny puffer. $2, Gray triggerfish.

No. 2333, $1: a, Barred hamlet. b, Flamefish. c, Longsnout butterflyfish. d, Fairy basslet. e, Redtail parrotfish. f, Blackbar soldierfish. g, Threespot damselfish. h, Candy basslet. i, Spotfin hogfish.

No. 2334, $1: a, Equetus lanceolatus. b, Acanthurus coeruleus. c, Lutjanus analis. d, Hippocampus hudsonius. e, Serranus annularis. f, Squatina dumerili. g, Muraena miliaris. h, Bolbometopon bicolor. i, Tritonium nodiferum.

$5, Queen triggerfish. $6, Blue marlin.

1996, Aug. 10 ***Perf. 14***

2329-2332	A348 Set of 4	4.25	4.25

Sheets of 9, #a-i

2333-2334	A348 Set of 2	14.50	14.50

Souvenir Sheets

2335	A348 $5 multicolored	4.25	4.25
2336	A348 $6 multicolored	5.00	5.00

Flowers A349

Designs: 70c, Beloperone guttata. $1, Epidendrum elongatum. $1.10, Pettrea volubilis. $2, Oncidium altrissimum.

No. 2341: a, Datura candida. b, Amherstia nobilis. c, Ipomoea acuminata. d, Bougainvillea glabra. e, Cassia alata. f, Cordia sebestena. g, Opuntia dilenii. h, Cryptostegia grandiflora. i, Rodriguezia lanceolata.

No. 2342, Acalypha hispida. No. 2343, Hibiscus rosa-sinensis.

1996, Aug. 15

2337-2340	A349 Set of 4	3.50	3.50
2341	A349 90c Sheet of 9, #a.-i.	6.00	6.00

Souvenir Sheets

2342	A349 $5 multicolored	3.75	3.75

Perf. 14x13½

2343	A349 $5 multicolored	3.75	3.75

John F. Kennedy (1917-63) — A350

No. 2344, $1: a, As young boy. b, Proclamation to send man to the moon. c, With Caroline, Jackie. d, Inauguration. e, Giving speech. f, On PT 109. g, With Jackie. h, Funeral procession, portrait. i, Guard, Eternal Flame.

No. 2345, $1: a, With family on yacht. b, On yacht. c, On yacht holding sail. d, "JFK," portrait. e, Talking to astronauts in space. f, Younger picture in uniform. g, Portrait. h, Riding in motorcade. i, Giving speech, US flag.

No. 2346, $1: a, Up close picture. b, In front of house at Hyannis Port. c, Memorial plaque, picture. d, Photograph among crowd. e, Portrait, flag. f, Rocket, portrait. g, Signing document. h, Martin Luther King, John F. Kennedy, Robert F. Kennedy. i, Painting looking down toward microphones.

No. 2347, $1: a, Photograph with Jacqueline greeting people. b, Formal oval-shaped portrait. c, Photograph. d, With family. e, Space capsule, painting. f, Addressing UN. g, In rocking chair. h, Seated at desk, dignitaries. i, Holding telephone, map.

1996, Aug. ***Perf. 14x13½***

Sheets of 9, #a-i

2344-2347	A350 Set of 4	27.00	27.00

Ships A351

No. 2348, $1.10: a, SS Doric, 1923, Great Britain. b, SS Nerissa, 1926, Great Britain. c, SS Howick Hall, 1910, Great Britain. d, SS Jervis Bay, 1922, Great Britain. e, SS Vauban, 1912, Great Britain. f, MV Orinoco, 1928, Germany.

No. 2349, $1.10: a, SS Lady Rodney, 1929, Canada. b, SS Empress of Russia, 1913, Canada. c, SS Providence, 1914, France. d, SS Reina Victori-Eugenia, 1913, Spain. e, SS Balmoral Castle, 1910, Great Britain. f, SS Tivives, 1911, US.

No. 2350, $6, SS Imperator, 1913, Germany. No. 2351, $6, SS Aquitania, 1914, Great Britain.

1996, Sept. 5 ***Perf. 14***

Sheets of 6, #a-f

2348-2349	A351 Set of 2	11.00	11.00

Souvenir Sheets

2350-2351	A351 Set of 2	9.00	9.00

Elvis Presley's 1st "Hit" Year, 40th Anniv. A352

Various portraits.

1996, Sept. 8 ***Perf. 13½x14***

2352	A352 $2 Sheet of 6, #a.-f.	9.00	9.00

Richard Petty, NASCAR Driving Champion — A353

No. 2353: a, 1990 Pontiac. b, Richard Petty. c, 1972 Plymouth. d, 1974 Dodge.

$5, 1970 Plymouth Superbird. $6, 1996 STP 25th Anniversary Pontiac.

1996, Sept. 26 ***Perf. 14***

2353	A353 $2 Sheet of 4, #a.-d.	6.50	6.50

Souvenir Sheets

2354	A353 $5 multicolored	3.75	3.75
2355	A353 $6 multicolored	4.75	4.75

No. 2354 contains one 85x28mm stamp.

Sandy Koufax, Baseball Pitcher — A354

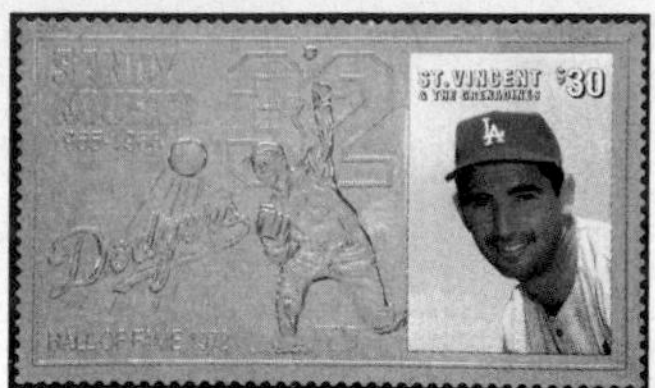

A354a

No. 2356: a.-c., Various action shots.

Perf. 14, Imperf. (#2356d)

1996, Sept. 26

2356 Sheet of 17 28.50 28.50
a.-c. A354 $2 any single 1.50 1.50
d. A354 $6 Portrait 4.50 4.50

Litho. & Embossed

Perf. 9

2356E A354a $30 gold & multi 25.00 25.00

No. 2356 contains 6 #2356a, 5 each #2356b, 2356c and 1 #2356d. No. 2356d is 70x103mm and has simulated perforations.

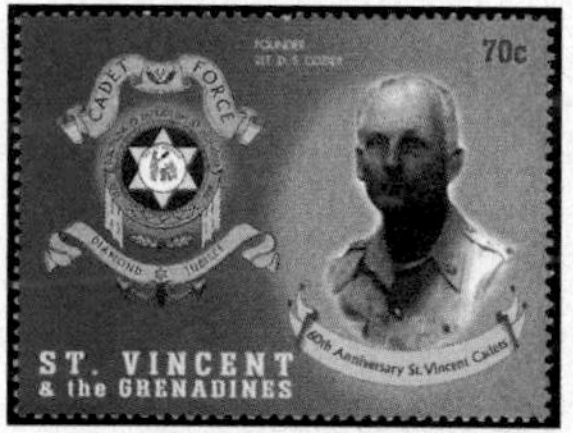

Cadet Force, 60th Anniv. — A355

Insignia and: 70c, 2nd Lt. D.S. Cozier, founder. 90c, Cozier, first 12 cadets, 1936.

1996, Oct. 23 Litho. *Perf. 14x13½*

2357 A355 70c multicolored .60 .60
2358 A355 90c multicolored .80 .80

Christmas A356

Details or entire paintings: 70c, Virgin and Child, by Memling. 90c, St. Anthony, by Memling. $1, Madonna and Child, by Bouts. $1.10, Virgin and Child, by Lorenzo Lotto. $2, St. Roch, by Lotto. $5, St. Sebastian, by Lotto.

No. 2365, $5, Virgin and Child with St. Roch and St. Sebastian, by Lotto. No. 2366, $5, Virgin and Child with St. Anthony and a Donor, by Memling.

1996, Nov. 14 *Perf. 13½x14*

2359-2364 A356 Set of 6 9.00 9.00

Souvenir Sheets

2365-2366 A356 Set of 2 8.50 8.50

Disney's "The Hunchback of Notre Dame" — A357

Designs: Various scenes from film.

No. 2370, $6, Quasimodo, Phoebus, Esmeralda. No. 2371, $6, Esmeralda, vert. No. 2372, $6, Quasimodo, citizens, vert.

1996, Dec. 12 Litho. *Perf. 13½x14*

2367 A357 10c Sheet of 6, #a.-f., vert. .90 9.00

Perf. 14x13½

2368 A357 30c Sheet of 9, #a.-i. 3.00 3.00
2369 A357 $1 Sheet of 9, #a.-i. 8.00 8.00

Souvenir Sheets

2370-2372 A357 Set of 3 19.50 19.50

Sylvester Stallone in Movie "Rocky IV" — A358

1996 Litho. *Perf. 14*

2373 A358 $2 Sheet of 3, #a.-c. 5.00 5.00

A359

New Year 1997 (Year of the Ox) — A359a

Stylized oxen, Chinese inscriptions within checkered squares: Nos. 2374a, 2375a, pale orange, pale lilac & black. Nos. 2374b, 2375b, green, violet & black. Nos. 2374c, 2375c, tan, pink & black.

1997, Jan. 2 *Perf. 14½*

2374 A359 75c Strip of 3, #a.-c. 1.70 1.70
2375 A359 $1 Sheet of 3, #a.-c. 2.25 2.25

Souvenir Sheet

2376 A359 $2 orange, yellow & blk 1.50 1.50

Litho. & Embossed

Perf. 9

2376A A359a $30 gold & multi 25.00 25.00

No. 2374 was issued in sheets of 9 stamps.

Star Trek Voyager A360

No. 2377: a, Lt. Tuvak. b, Kes. c, Lt. Paris. d, The Doctor. e, Capt. Janeway. f, Lt. Torres. g, Neelix. h, Ens. Kim. i, Cdr. Chakotay.

$6, Cast of characters.

1997, Jan. 23 Litho. *Perf. 14*

2377 A360 $2 Sheet of 9, #a.-i. 14.50 14.50

Souvenir Sheet

2378 A360 $6 multicolored 5.00 5.00

No. 2378 contains one 29x47mm stamp.

A361

A361a

Mickey Mantle (1931-95), baseball player.

Perf. 14, Imperf. (#2379b)

1997, Jan. 23

2379 Sheet of 17, 16 #2379a, 1 #2379b 28.50 28.50
a. A361 $2 shown 1.50 1.50
b. A361 $6 Portrait holding bat 4.50 4.50

Litho. & Embossed

Perf. 9

2379C A361a $30 gold & multi 25.00 25.00

No. 2379b is 70x100mm.

Black Baseball Players — A362

No. 2380: a, Frank Robinson. b, Satchel Paige. c, Billy Williams. d, Reggie Jackson. e, Roberto Clemente. f, Ernie Banks. g, Hank Aaron. h, Roy Campanella. i, Willie McCovey. j, Monte Irvin. k, Willie Stargell. l, Rod Carew. m, Ferguson Jenkins. n, Bob Gibson. o, Lou Brock. p, Joe Morgan. q, Jackie Robinson.

Perf. 14x14½, Imperf. (#2380q)

1997, Jan. 23

2380 Sheet of 17 16.50 16.50
a.-p. A362 $1 any single .75 .75
q. A362 $6 Portrait 4.50 4.50

No. 2380q is 66x100mm and has simulated perforations.

Souvenir Sheet

Chongqing Dazu Stone Carving — A363

1996, May 20 Litho. *Perf. 12*

2381 A363 $2 multicolored 1.50 1.50

China '96.

No. 2381 was not available until March 1997.

Hong Kong Changeover — A364

A364a

No. 2382 — Flags of Great Britain, Peoples' Republic of China and panoramic view of Hong Kong: a-e, In daytime. f-j, At night.

No. 2383, $2 — Market scene: a, Vendors, corner of building. b, People strolling. c, Man choosing items to purchase.

No. 2384, $2 — Buddhist religious ceremony: a, Fruit, incense pot, torch. b, Monk at fire. c, Flower.

No. 2385, $2 — Lantern ceremony: a, Boy, girl. b, Couple on bridge. c, Girls with lanterns.

Illustration A364a reduced.

1997, Feb. 12 *Perf. 14*

2382 A364 90c Sheet of 10, #a-j 7.25 7.25

Sheets of 3, #a-c

Perf. 13

2383-2385 A364 Set of 3 14.50 14.50

Litho. & Embossed

Perf. 9

2385D A364a $30 gold & multi 25.00 25.00

Hong Kong '97.

Nos. 2383-2385 each contain 3 35x26mm stamps.

UNESCO, 50th Anniv. — A365

World Heritage Sites: 70c, Lord Howe Islands, Australia, vert. 90c, Uluru-Kata Tjuta Natl. Park, Australia, vert. $1, Kakadu Natl. Park, Australia, vert. $1.10, Te Wahipounamu, New Zealand, vert. $2, $5, vert., Tongariro Natl. Park, New Zealand.

No. 2392, $1.10, vert. — Various sites in Greece: a, Monastery of Rossanou, Meteora. b, f, h, Painted ceiling, interior, Mount Athos Monastery. c, Monastery Osios Varlaam, Meteora. d, Ruins in Athens. e, Museum of the Acropolis. g, Mount Athos.

No. 2393, $1.10, vert. — Various sites in Japan: a, Himeji-Jo. b, Temple Lake, Gardens, Kyoto. c, Kyoto. d, Buddhist Temple of Ninna-Ji. e, View of city of Himeji-Jo. f, Forest, Shirakami-Sanchi. g, h, Forest, Yakushima.

No. 2394, $1.10, vert: a, City of San Gimignano, Italy. b, Cathedral of Santa Maria Asunta, Pisa, Italy. c, Cathedral of Santa Maria Fiore, Florence, Italy. d, Archaeological site, Valley of the Boyne, Ireland. e, Church of Saint-Savin-Sur-Gartempe, France. f, g, h, City of Bath, England.

No. 2395, $1.50: a, Trinidad, Valley de los Ingenios, Cuba. b, City of Zacatecas, Mexico. c, Lima, Peru. d, Ruins of Monastery, Paraguay. e, Mayan Ruins, Copan, Honduras.

No. 2396, $1.50 — Various sites in China: a, Palace, Wudang Mountains, Hubei Province. b, Cave Sanctuaries, Mogao. c, House, Desert of Taklamakan. d, e, Great Wall.

Nos. 2397, $1.50: a-e, Various sites in Quedlinberg, Germany.

No. 2398, $5, Monastery of Meteora, Greece. No. 2399, $5, Wailing Wall, Jerusalem. No. 2400, $5, Quedlinburg, Germany. No. 2401, $5, Oasis, Dunbuang, China. No. 2402, $5, Himeji-Jo, Japan. No. 2403, $5, Great Wall, China. No. 2404, $5, City of Venice, Italy.

Perf. 13½x14, 14x13½

1997, Mar. 24 Litho.

2386-2391 A365 Set of 6 8.00 8.00

Sheets of 8, #a-h, + Label

2392-2394 A365 Set of 3 20.00 20.00

Sheets of 5 + Label

2395-2397 A365 Set of 3 17.50 17.50

Souvenir Sheets

2398-2404 A365 Set of 7 25.00 25.00

Telecommunications in St. Vincent, 125th Anniv. — A366

Designs: 5c, Microwave radio relay tower, Dorsetshire Hill. 10c, Cable & wireless headquarters, Kingstown. 20c, Microwave relay tower, vert. 35c, Cable & wireless complex, Arnos Vale. 50c, Cable & wireless tower, Mt. St. Andrew. 70c, Cable ship. 90c, Eastern telecommunication network, 1872. $1.10, Telegraph map of world, 1876.

Perf. 14x14½, 14½x14

1997, Apr. 3 Litho.

2405-2412 A366 Set of 8 4.00 4.00

Birds of the World — A367

Designs: 60c, Smooth-billed ani. 70c, Belted kingfisher. 90c, Blackburnian warbler. $1.10, Blue tit. $2, Chaffinch. $5, Ruddy turnstone.

No. 2419: a, Blue grosbeak. b, Bananaquit. c, Cedar waxwing. d, Ovenbird. e, Hooded warbler. f, Flicker.

No. 2420: a, Song thrush. b, Robin. c, Blackbird. d, Great spotted woodpecker. e, Wren. f, Kingfisher.

No. 2421, $5, St. Vincent parrot. No. 2422, $5, Tawny owl.

1997, Apr. 7 ***Perf. 14***

2413-2418 A367 Set of 6 7.75 7.75
2419 A367 $1 Sheet of 6, #a.-f. 4.50 4.50
2420 A367 $2 Sheet of 6, #a.-f. 9.00 9.00

Souvenir Sheets

2421-2422 A367 Set of 2 7.50 7.50

Water Birds — A368

Designs: 70c, Mandarin duck, horiz. 90c, Green heron, horiz. $1, Drake ringed teal, horiz. $1.10, Blue-footed boobies, horiz. $2, Australian jacana. $5, Reddish egret.

No. 2429: a, Crested auklet. b, Whiskered auklet. c, Pigeon guillemot. d, Adelie penguins. e, Rockhopper penguin. f, Emperor penguin.

No. 2430, $5, Snowy egrets, horiz. No. 2431, $5, Flamingos, horiz.

1997, Apr. 7 ***Perf. 15***

2423-2428 A368 Set of 6 8.00 8.00
2429 A368 $1.10 Sheet of 6, #a.-f. 5.00 5.00

Souvenir Sheet

2430-2431 A368 Set of 2 7.50 7.50

Jackie Robinson (1919-72) A369

A369a

Serpentine Die Cut 7

1997, Jan. 23 Litho.

Self-Adhesive

2432 A369 $1 multicolored 1.00 1.00

Litho. & Embossed

Perf. 9

2432A A369a $30 gold & multi

No. 2432 was issued in sheets of 3 and was not available until June 1997.

Queen Elizabeth II, Prince Philip, 50th Wedding Anniv. A370

No. 2433: a, Queen. b, Royal arms. c, Portrait of Queen, Prince. d, Queen, Prince, crowd. e, Buckingham Palace. f, Prince.

$5, Queen seated in wedding gown, crown.

1997, June 3 Litho. ***Perf. 14***

2433 A370 $1.10 Sheet of 6, #a.-f. 5.50 5.50

Souvenir Sheet

2434 A370 $5 multicolored 4.00 4.00

Paintings by Hiroshige (1797-1858) A371

No. 2435: a, Furukawa River, Hiroo. b, Chiyogaike Pond, Meguro. c, New Fuji, Meguro. d, Moon-Viewing Point. e, Ushimachi, Takanawa. f, Original Fuji, Meguro.

No. 2436, $5, Gotenyama, Shinagawa. No. 2437, $5, Shinagawa Susaki.

1997, June 3 ***Perf. 13½x14***

2435 A371 $1.50 Sheet of 6, #a.-f. 7.00 7.00

Souvenir Sheets

2436-2437 A371 Set of 2 9.00 9.00

Paul Harris (1868-1947), Founder of Rotary Intl. — A372

Designs: $2, World Community Service, blankets from Japan donated to Thai children, Harris.

$5, Rotary Intl. Pres. Luis Vincente Giay, US Pres. Jimmy Carter, Rotary award recipient.

1997, June 3 ***Perf. 14***

2438 A372 $2 multicolored 1.75 1.75

Souvenir Sheet

2439 A372 $5 multicolored 4.00 4.00

Heinrich von Stephan (1831-97) A373

No. 2440 — Portraits of Von Stephan and: a, Bicycle postman, India, 1800's. b, UPU emblem. c, Zebu-drawn post carriage, Indochina.

$5, Post rider, Indochina.

1997, June 3

2440 A373 $2 Sheet of 3, #a.-c. 4.75 4.75

Souvenir Sheet

2441 A373 $5 gray brown 4.00 4.00

PACIFIC 97.

Chernobyl Disaster, 10th Anniv. A374

Designs: No. 2442, Chabad's Children of Chernobyl. No. 2443, UNESCO.

1997, June 3 Litho. ***Perf. 13½x14***

2442 A374 $2 multicolored 1.60 1.60
2443 A374 $2 multicolored 1.60 1.60

Grimm's Fairy Tales A375

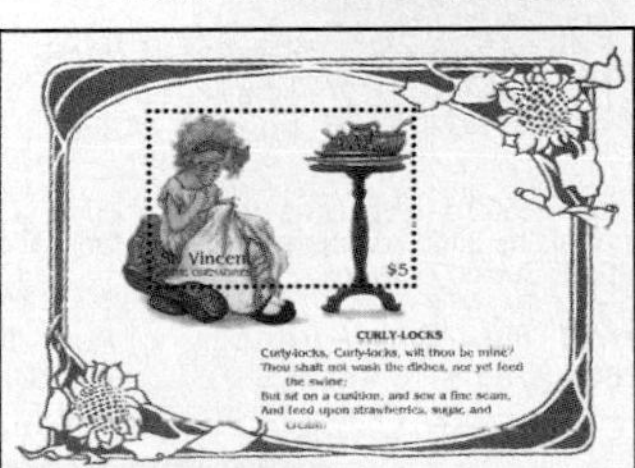

Mother Goose — A376

No. 2444, $2 — Scenes showing "Old Sultan:" a, With woman, man. b, On hillside. c, With wolf. No. 2446, Man, Old Sultan, girl.

No. 2445, $2 — Scenes from "The Cobbler and the Elves:" a, Cobbler. b, Elves. c, Cobbler holding elf.

No. 2446, $5, Elf. No. 2447, $5, Curly-Locks sewing.

1997, June 3 ***Perf. 13½x14***

Sheets of 3, #a-c

2444-2445 A375 Set of 2 9.00 9.00

Souvenir Sheets

2446-2447 A375 Set of 2 8.00 8.00

Perf. 14

2448 A376 $5 multicolored 3.75 3.75

Numbers have been reserved for two additional souvenir sheets with this set.

Inaugural Cricket Test, Arnos Vale — A377

Designs: 90c, Alphonso Theodore Roberts (1937-96), vert. $5, Arnos Vale Playing field.

Perf. 13½x14, 14x13½

1997, June 20 Litho.

2451 A377 90c multicolored .70 .70
2452 A377 $5 multicolored 3.75 3.75

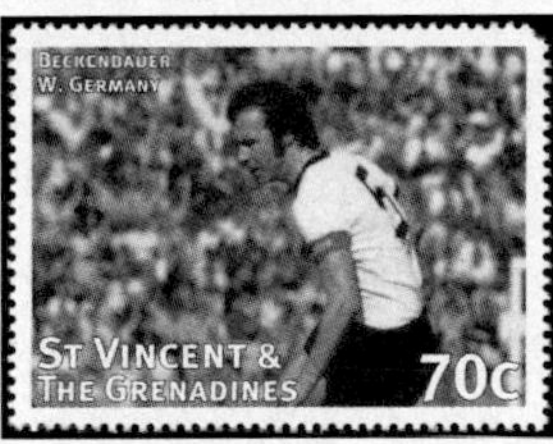

1998 World Cup Soccer Championships, France — A378

Players: 70c, Beckenbauer, W. Germany. 90c, Moore, England. $1, Lato, Poland. $1.10, Pele, Brazil. $2, Maier, W. Germany. $10, Eusebio, Portugal.

No. 2459, $1 — Scenes from England's victory, 1966: a, Stadium. b, c, d, e, f, h, Various action scenes. g, Players coming from field, holding trophy.

No. 2460, $1 — Action scenes from various finals: a, c, Argentina, W. Germany, 1986. b, e, England, W. Germany, 1966. d, Italy, W. Germany, 1982. f, g, Argentina, Holland, 1978. h, W. Germany, Holland, 1974.

No. 2461, $1, vert.: a, Bergkamp, Holland. b, Seaman, England. c, Schmeichel, Denmark. d, Ince, England. e, Futre, Portugal. f, Ravanelli, Italy. g, Keane, Ireland. h, Gascoigne, England.

No. 2462, $1, vert.: a-h, Action scenes from Argentina v. Holland, 1978.

No. 2463, $5, Ally McCoist, Scotland, vert. No. 2464, $5, Salvatori Schillaci, Italy, vert. No. 2465, $5, Mario Kempes, Argentina, vert. No. 2466, $5, Paulao, Angola.

Perf. 14x13½, 13½x14

1997, Aug. 26 Litho.

2453-2458 A378 Set of 6 6.00 6.00

Sheets of 8, #a-h, + Label

2459-2462 A378 Set of 4 32.50 32.50

Souvenir Sheets

2463-2466 A378 Set of 4 17.50 17.50

Vincy Mas Carnival, 20th Anniv. A379

Designs: 10c, Mardi Gras Band, "Cinemas." 20c, Queen of the Bands, J. Ballantyne. 50c, Queen of the Bands, vert. 70c, King of the Bands, "Conquistadore." 90c, Starlift Steel Orchestra, Panorama Champs. $2, Frankie McIntosh, musical arranger, vert.

1997, July 24 ***Perf. 14½x14, 14x14½***

2467-2472 A379 Set of 6 4.00 4.00

Sierra Club, Cent. A380

No. 2473: a, Snow leopard. b, Polar bear. c, d, Isle Royale Natl. Park. e, f, Denali Natl. Park. g, h, i, Joshua Tree Natl. Park.

No. 2474, vert: a, b, c, Mountain gorilla. d, e, Snow leopard. f, g, Polar bear. h, Denali Natl. Park. i, Isle Royale Nat. Park.

No. 2475, vert: a, b, c, Sifaka. d, e, Peregrine falcon. f, Galapagos tortoise. g, h, African Rain Forest. i, China's Yellow Mountains.

No. 2476: a, b, c, Red panda. d, Peregrine falcon. e, f, Galapagos tortoise. g, African Rain Forest. h, i, China's Yellow Mountains.

No. 2477: a, Mountain lion. b, c, Siberian tiger. d, Red wolf. e, Black bear. f, i, Wolong Natl. Reserve. g, h, Belize Rain Forest.

No. 2478, vert: a, Siberian tiger. b, c, Mountain lion. d, e, Black bear. f, g, Red wolf. h, Belize Rain Forest. i, Wolong Natl. Reserve.

No. 2479, vert: a, b, c, Indri. d, e, Gopher tortoise. f, g, Black-footed ferret. h, Haleakala Natl. Park. i, Grand Teton Natl. Park.

No. 2480: a, Black-footed ferret. b, Gopher tortoise. c, d, Grand Teton Natl. Park. e, f. Haleakala Natl. Park. g, h, i, Madagascar Rain Forest.

Scenes in Olympic Natl. Park: No. 2481, $5, Lake, trees. No. 2482, $5, Mountain summit. No. 2483, $5, Snow-topped mountains.

1997, Sept. 18 ***Perf. 14***

2473	A380	20c Sheet of 9, #a.-i.	1.40	1.40
2474	A380	40c Sheet of 9, #a.-i.	2.75	2.75
2475	A380	50c Sheet of 9, #a.-i.	3.40	3.40
2476	A380	60c Sheet of 9, #a.-i.	4.00	4.00
2477	A380	70c Sheet of 9, #a.-i.	4.75	4.75
2478	A390	90c Sheet of 9, #a.-i.	6.00	6.00
2479	A380	$1 Sheet of 9, #a.-i.	6.75	6.75
2480	A380	$1.10 Sheet of 9, #a.-i.	7.50	7.50

Souvenir Sheets

2481-2483 A380 Set of 3 13.00 13.00

Deng Xiaoping (1904-97), Chinese Leader — A381

No. 2484, $2: a-d, Various portraits in dark brown.

No. 2485, $2: a-d, Various portraits in dark blue.

No. 2486, $2: a-d, Various portraits in black.

No. 2487, Deng Xiaoping, Zhuo Lin, horiz.

1997, June 3 **Litho.** ***Perf. 14***

Sheets of 4, #a-d

2484-2486 A381 Set of 3 18.00 18.00

Souvenir Sheet

2487 A381 $5 multicolored 3.75 3.75

Montreal Protocol on Substances that Deplete Ozone Layer, 10th Anniv. — A382

1997, Sept. 16

2488 A382 90c multicolored 1.10 1.10

Orchids — A383

Designs: 90c, Rhyncholaelia digbyana. $1, Laeliocattleya. $1.10, Doritis pulcherrima. $2, Phalaenopsis.

No. 2493: a, Eulophia speciosa. b, Aerangis rhodosticta. c, Angraecum infundibularea. d, Calanthe sylvatica. e, Phalaenopsis mariae. f, Paphiopedilum insigne. g, Dendrobium nobile. h, Aerangis kotschyana. i, Cyrtorchis chailluana.

No. 2494, $5, Brassavola nodosa. No. 2495, $5, Sanguine broughtonia.

1997, Sept. 18

2489-2492 A383 Set of 4 4.75 4.75
2493 A383 $1 Sheet of 9, #a.-i. 7.75 7.75

Souvenir Sheets

2494-2495 A383 Set of 2 8.75 8.75

Nos. 2494-2495 each contain one 51x38mm stamp.

Diana, Princess of Wales (1961-97) — A384

No. 2496, $2 — Close-up portraits: a, Wearing tiara. b, Black dress. c, Blue dress. d, Denomination in black.

No. 2497, $2: a, White collar. b, Sleeveless. c, Black dress, holding flowers. d, Blue collar, flowers.

No. 2498, $6, Blue dress. No. 2499, $6, White collar.

1997 **Sheets of 4, #a-d**

2496-2497 A384 Set of 2 12.00 12.00

Souvenir Sheets

2498-2499 A384 Set of 2 9.00 9.00

Sinking of RMS Titanic, 85th Anniv. — A385

No. 2500 — Sections of the ship: a, 1st funnel. b, 2nd, 3rd funnels. c, 4th funnel. d, Upper decks. e, Stern.

1997, Nov. 5 **Litho.** ***Perf. 14***

2500 A385 $1 Sheet of 5, #a.-e. 8.00 8.00

1997 Rock & Roll Hall of Fame Inductions, Cleveland A386

Designs: $1, Exterior view of Hall of Fame. $1.50, Stylized guitar, "the house that rock built."

1997, Nov. 5

2501 A386 $1 multicolored .75 .75
2502 A386 $1.50 multicolored 1.15 1.15

Nos. 2501-2502 were each issued in sheets of 8.

"The Doors" Album Covers — A387

Designs: 90c, Morrison Hotel, 1970. 95c, Waiting for the Sun, 1968. $1, L.A. Woman, 1971. $1.10, The Soft Parade, 1969. $1.20, Strange Days, 1967. $1.50, The Doors, 1967.

1997, Nov. 5

2503-2508 A387 Set of 6 8.25 8.25

Nos. 2503-2508 were each issued in sheets of 8.

20th Cent. Artists — A388

No. 2509, $1.10 — Opera singers: a, Lily Pons (1904-76). b, Donizetti's "Lucia Di Lammermoor," Lily Pons. c, Bellini's "I Puritani," Maria Callas. d, Callas (1923-77). e, Beverly Sills (b. 1929). f, Donizetti's "Daughter of the Regiment," Sills. g, Schoenberg's "Erwartung," Jessye Norman. h, Norman (b.1945).

No. 2510, $1.10: a, Enrico Caruso (1873-1921). b, Verdi's "Rigoletto," Caruso. c, "The Seven Hills of Rome," Mario Lanza. d, Lanza (1921-59). e, Luciano Pavarotti (b. 1935). f, Donizetti's "Elixir of Love," Pavarotti. g, Puccini's "Tosca," Placido Domingo. h, Domingo (b. 1941).

No. 2511, $1.10 — Artists, sculptures: a, Constantin Brancusi (1876-1957). b, "The New Born," Brancusi, 1920. c, "Four Elements," Alexander Calder, 1962. d, Calder (1898-1976). e, Isamu Noguchi (1904-88). f, "Dodge Fountain," Noguchi, 1975. g, "The Shuttlecock," Claes Oldenburg, 1994. h, Oldenburg (b. 1929).

1997, Nov. 5 **Sheets of 8, #a-h**

2509-2511 A388 Set of 3 21.50 21.50

Size: Nos. 2509b-2509c, 2509f-2509g, 2510b-2510c, 2510f-2510g, 2511b-2511c, 2511f-2511g, 53x38mm.

Christmas A389

Paintings (entire or details), or sculptures: 60c, The Sistine Madonna, by Raphael. 70c, Angel, by Edward Burne-Jones. 90c, Cupid, by Etienne-Maurice Falconet. $1, Saint Michael, by Hubert Gerhard. $1.10, Apollo and the Horae, by Tiepolo. $2, Madonna in a Garland of Flowers, by Rubens and Bruegel the Elder.

No. 2518, $5, The Sacrifice of Isaac, by Tiepolo, horiz. No. 2519, $5, Madonna in a Garland of Flowers, by Rubens and Bruegel the Elder.

1997, Nov. 26

2512-2517 A389 Set of 6 6.25 6.25

Souvenir Sheets

2518-2519 A389 Set of 2 8.00 8.00

New Year 1998 (Year of the Tiger) — A390

No. 2520 — Stylized tigers, Chinese inscriptions within checkered squares: a, light brown & pale olive. b, tan & gray. c, pink & pale violet. $2, yellow orange & pink.

1998, Jan. 5 ***Perf. 14½***

2520 A390 $1 Sheet of 3, #a.-c. 2.25 2.25

Souvenir Sheet

2521 A390 $2 multicolored 2.00 2.00

Cooperative Foundation for Natl. Development A391

Designs: 20c, Children going to school. 90c, People working in field, Credit Union office, vert. $1.10, Industry, ship at dock.

1998, Jan. 5 **Litho.** ***Perf. 13½***

2522-2524 A391 Set of 3 2.10 2.10

Jazz Entertainers — A392

No. 2525: a, King Oliver. b, Louis Armstrong. c, Sidney Bechet. d, Nick Larocca. e, Louis Prima. f, Buddy Bolden.

1998, Feb. 2 ***Perf. 14x13½***

2525 A392 $1 Sheet of 6, #a.-f. 5.00 5.00

1998 Winter Olympic Games, Nagano
A393 A394

Designs, horiz: 70c, Ice hockey. $1.10, Bobsled. $2, Pairs figure skating. $2, Skier, vert.

No. 2530 — Medalists: a, Bjorn Daehlie. b, Gillis Grafstrom. c, Sonja Henie. d, Ingemar Stenmark. e, Christian Jagge. f, Tomas Gustafson. g, Johann Olav Koss. h, Thomas Wassberg.

No. 2531, $1.50 — Olympic rings in background: a, Downhill skier. b, Woman figure skater. c, Ski jumper. d, Speed skater. e, 4-Man bobsled team. f, Cross country country skier.

No. 2532, $1.50 — Olympic flame in background: a, Downhill skier. b, Bobsled. c, Ski jumper. d, Slalom skier. e, Luge. f, Biathlon.

No. 2533, $5, Slalom skiing. No. 2534, $5, Hockey player, horiz.

1998, Feb. 2 ***Perf. 14***

2526-2529 A393 Set of 4 5.50 5.50
2530 A394 $1.10 Sheet of 8, #a.-h. 7.50 7.50

Sheets of 6, #a-f

2531-2532 A393 Set of 2 15.00 15.00

Souvenir Sheets

2533-2534 A393 Set of 2 8.50 8.50

Butterflies A395

Designs: 20c, Amarynthis meneria. 50c, Papillo polyxenes. 70c, Emesis fatima, vert. $1, Anartia amathea.

No. 2539, vert: a, Heliconius erato. b, Danaus plexippus. c, Papillo phorcas. d, Morpho pelaides. e, Pandoriana pandora. f, Basilarchia astyanax. g, Vanessa cardui. h, Colobura dirce. i, Heraclides cresphontes.

No. 2540, $6, Colias eurytheme. No. 2541, $6, Everes comyntas.

1998, Feb, 23 ***Perf. 13½***

2535-2538 A395 Set of 4 2.50 2.50
2539 A395 $1 Sheet of 9, #a.-i. 7.50 7.50

Souvenir Sheets

2540-2541 A395 Set of 2 9.50 9.50

Endangered Fauna — A396

Designs: 50c, Anegada rock iguana. 70c, Jamaican swallowtail. 90c, Blossom bat. $1, Solenodon. $1.10, Hawksbill turtle. $2, West Indian whistling duck.

No. 2548, $1.10: a, Roseate spoonbill. b, Golden swallow. c, Short-snouted spinner dolphin. d, Queen conch. e, West Indian manatee. f, Loggerhead turtle.

No. 2549, $1.10: a, Magnificent frigatebird. b, Humpback whale. c, Southern dagger-tail. d, St. Lucia whiptail e, St. Lucia oriole. f, Green turtle.

No. 2550, $5, St. Vincent parrot. No. 2551, $5, Antiguan racer.

1998, Feb. 23 ***Perf. 13***

2542-2547 A396 Set of 6 5.25 5.25

Sheets of 6, #a-f

2548-2549 A396 Set of 2 11.50 11.50

Souvenir Sheets

2550-2551 A396 Set of 2 8.50 8.50

Mushrooms A397

Designs: 10c, Gymnopilus spectabilis. 20c, Entoloma lividium. 70c, Pholiota flammans. 90c, Panaeolus semiovatus. $1, Stropharia rugocoannulata. $1.10, Tricholoma sulphureum.

No. 2558: a, Amanita caesarea. b, Amanita muscaria. c, Aminita ovoidea. d, Amanita phalloides. e, Amanitopsis inaurata. f, Amanitopsis vaginata. g, Psalliota campestris, alfalfa butterfly. h, Psalliota arvenis. i, Coprinus comatus.

No. 2559: a, Coprinus picaceus. b, Stropharia umbonatescens. c, Hebeloma crustuliniforme, figure-of-eight butterfly. d, Cortinarius collinitus. e, Cortinarius violaceus, common dotted butterfly. f, Cortinarius armillatus. g, Tricholoma aurantium. h, Russula virescens. i, Clitocybe infundibuliformis.

No. 2560, $6, Hygrocybe conica. No. 2561, $6, Amanita caesarea.

1998, Feb. 23 Litho. ***Perf. 13½***

2552-2557 A397 Set of 6 4.00 4.00
2558 A397 $1 Sheet of 9, #a.-i. 8.25 8.25
2559 A397 $1.10 Sheet of 9, #a.-i. 9.00 9.00

Souvenir Sheets

2560-2561 A397 Set of 2 9.50 9.50

Mickey Mouse, 70th Birthday — A398

Designs: 2c, Wake up, Mickey. 3c, Morning run. 4c, Getting ready. 5c, Eating breakfast. 10c, School "daze." 65c, Time out for play. $3, Volunteer worker. $4, A date with Minnie. $5, Ready for bed.

Weekly hi-lites from "Mickey Mouse Club," vert: a, The opening march. b, Monday, fun with music day. c, Tuesday, guest star day. d, Wednesday, anything can happen day. e, Thursday, circus day. f, Friday, talent round up day.

Mickey Mouse: No. 2572, $5, Reading, vert. No. 2573, $6, Playing piano, vert. No. 2574, $6, Blowing trumpet. No. 2575, $6, On the Internet, vert.

Perf. 14x13½, 13½x14

1998, Mar. 23 Litho.

2562-2570 A398 Set of 9 10.50 10.50
2571 A398 $1.10 Sheet of 6, #a.-f. 5.00 5.00

Souvenir Sheets

2572-2575 A398 Set of 4 17.00 17.00

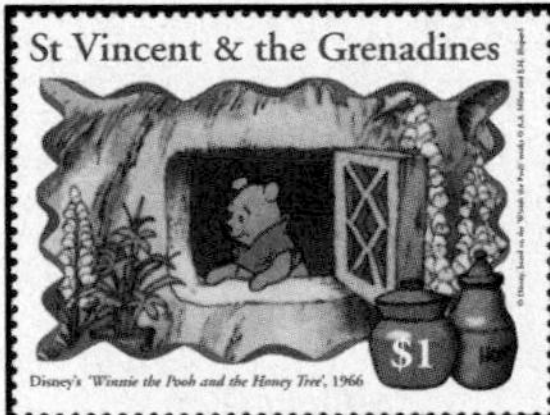

Winnie the Pooh — A399

Scenes from animated films: a, Pooh looking out open window. b, Eeyore, Kanga, Roo. c, Pooh getting honey from tree. d, Rabbit, Pooh stuck in entrance to Rabbit's house. e, Christopher Robin pulling Pooh from Rabbit's house, Owl. f, Piglet sweeping leaves. g, Pooh sleeping. h, Eeyore. i, Tigger on top of Pooh.

No. 2577, Tigger, Pooh, Piglet.

1998, Mar. 23 ***Perf. 14x13½***

2576 A399 $1 Sheet of 9, #a.-i. 8.50 8.50

Souvenir Sheet

2577 A399 $6 multicolored 7.00 7.00

Dogs — A400

Designs: 70c, Australian terrier. 90c, Bull mastiff. $1.10, Pomeranian. $2, Dandie dinmont terrier.

No. 2582, $1.10, horiz: a, Tyrolean hunting dog. b, Papillon. c, Fox terriers. d, Bernese mountain dog. e, King Charles spaniel. f, German shepherd.

No. 2583, $1.10, horiz. a, Beagle. b, German shepherd. c, Pointer. d, Vizsla. e, Bulldog. f, Shetland sheepdogs.

No. 2584, $6, Scottish terrier, wooden deck, grass. No. 2585, $6, Scottish terrier, grass, trees.

1998, Apr. 21 ***Perf. 14***

2578-2581 A400 Set of 4 4.50 4.50

Sheets of 6, #a-f

2582-2583 A400 Set of 2 12.00 12.00

Souvenir Sheets

2584-2585 A400 Set of 2 10.00 10.50

Nos. 2306-2309 Overprinted

1998, May 19 Litho. ***Perf. 14***

2586-2588 A345 Set of 3 3.75 3.75

Souvenir Sheet

2589 A345 $5 multicolored 4.25 4.25

No. 2589 contains overprint "ISRAEL 98 — WORLD STAMP EXHIBITION / TEL-AVIV 13-21 MAY 1998" in sheet margin.

Trains A401

Designs: 10c, LMS Bahamas No. 5596. 20c, Ex-Mza 1400. 50c, Mallard. 70c, Monarch 0-4-4 OT. 90c, Big Chief. $1.10, Duchess of Rutland LMS No. 6228.

No. 2596, $1.10: a, Hadrian Flyer. b, Highland Jones Goods No. 103. c, Blackmore Vale No. 34023. d, Wainwright SECR No. 27. e, Stepney Brighton Terrier. f, RENFE Freight train No. 040 2184. g, Calbourne No. 24. h, Clun Castle 1950.

No. 2597, $1.10: a, Ancient Holmes J36 060. b, Patentee 2-2-2. c, Kingfisher. d, St. Pierre No. 23. e, SAR Class 19c 4-8-2. f, SAR 6J 4-6-0. g, Evening Star No. 92220. h, Old No. 1.

No. 2598, $5, King George V No. 6000 BR. No. 2599, $5, Caledonia.

1998, June 2 Litho. ***Perf. 14***

2590-2595 A401 Set of 6 3.25 3.25

Sheets of 8, #a-h

2596-2597 A401 Set of 2 15.00 15.00

Souvenir Sheets

2598-2599 A401 Set of 2 8.25 8.25

UNESCO Intl. Year of the Ocean A402

Marine life: 70c, Beluga whale. 90c, Atlantic manta. $1.10, Forceps butterfly fish, copperband butterfly fish, moorish idol. $2, Octopus.

No. 2604, $1, vert.: a, Harlequin wrasse. b, Blue sturgeon fish. c, Spotted trunkfish. d, Regal angelfish. e, Porcupine fish. f, Clownfish, damselfish. g, Lion fish. h, Moray eel. i, French angelfish.

No. 2605, $1, vert.: a, Lemonpeel angelfish. b, Narwhal. c, Panther grouper. d, Fur seal. e, Spiny boxfish. f, Loggerhead turtle. g, Qpah. h, Clown triggerfish. i, Bighead searobin.

No. 2606, $5, Seahorse, vert. No. 2607, $5, Australian sea dragon, vert.

1998, July 1

2600-2603 A402 Set of 4 4.25 4.25

Sheets of 9, #a-i

2604-2605 A402 Set of 2 15.00 15.00

Souvenir Sheets

2606-2607 A402 Set of 2 8.25 8.25

Birds A403

Designs: 50c, Cock of the rock, vert. 60c, Quetzal, vert. 70c, Wood stork, vert. No. 2611, 90c, St. Vincent parrot, vert. No. 2612, 90c, Toucan. $1, Greater bird of paradise. $1.10, Sunbittern. $2, Green honeycreeper.

No. 2616, vert.: a, Racquet-tailed motmot. b, Red-billed quelea. c, Leadbeater's cockatoo. d, Scarlet macaw. e, Bare-throated bellbird. f, Tucaman Amazon parrot. g, Black-lored red tanager. h, Fig parrot. i, St. Vincent Amazon parrot. j, Peach-faced love birds. k, Blue fronted Amazon parrot. l, Yellow billed Amazon parrot.

No. 2617, $5, Hyacinth macaw, vert. No. 2618, $5, Blue-headed hummingbird, vert.

1998, June 16 Litho. ***Perf. 14***

2608-2615 A403 Set of 8 7.00 7.00

Sheet of 12

2616 A403 90c Sheet of 12, #a.-l. 10.00 10.00

Souvenir Sheets

2617-2618 A403 Set of 2 9.00 9.00

No. 2611 has different style of lettering.

Diana, Princess of Wales (1961-97) — A404

Designs: No. 2619, Diana in orange jacket. No. 2620, Diana in blue blouse.

Litho. & Embossed

1998, Aug. 1 ***Die Cut 7½***

2619 A404 $20 gold & multi 20.00 20.00
2620 A404 $20 gold & multi 20.00 20.00

CARICOM, 25th Anniv. — A405

1998, July 4 Litho. ***Perf. 13½***

2621 A405 $1 multicolored 1.25 1.25

Enzo Ferrari (1898-1988), Automobile Manufacturer — A406

No. 2622 — Classic Ferraris: a, 365 GTS. b, Testarossa. c, 365 GT4 BB.

$6, Dino 206 GT.

1998, Sept. 15 Litho. ***Perf. 14***

2622 A406 $2 Sheet of 3, #a.-c. 5.00 5.00

Souvenir Sheet

2623 A406 $6 multicolored 5.00 5.00

No. 2623 contains one 91x35mm stamp.

Paintings by Pablo Picasso (1881-1973) — A407

Designs: $1.10, Landscape, 1972. No. 2625, $2, The Kiss, 1969. No. 2626, $2, The Death of the Female Torero, 1933.

$5, Flute Player, 1962, vert.

1998, Sept. 15 ***Perf. 14½***

2624-2626 A407 Set of 3 4.00 4.00

Souvenir Sheet

2627 A407 $5 multicolored 4.50 4.50

Organization of American States, 50th Anniv. A408

1998, Sept. 15 Litho. *Perf. 13½*

2628 A408 $1 multicolored 1.25 1.25

Diana, Princess of Wales (1961-97) A409

1998, Sept. 15 *Perf. 14½*

2629 A409 $1.10 multicolored 1.25 1.25

Souvenir Sheet

Self-Adhesive

Serpentine Die Cut Perf. 11½

Size: 53x65mm

2630 A409 $8 Diana, buildings

No. 2629 was issued in sheets of 6. Soaking in water may affect the image of No. 2630.

Mahatma Gandhi (1869-1948) A411

Design: $5, Seated at table with officials, horiz.

1998, Sept. 15 *Perf. 14*

2631 A411 $1 shown 1.40 1.40

Souvenir Sheet

2632 A411 $5 multicolored 6.50 6.50

No. 2631 was issued in sheets of 4.

Royal Air Force, 80th Anniv. A412

No. 2633, $2: a, AEW1 AWACS. b, BAe Eurofighter EF2000. c, Sepcat Jaguar GR1A. d, BAe Hawk T1A.

No. 2634, $2: a, Two Sepcat Jaguar GR1s. b, Panavia Tornado F3. c, Three BAe Harrier GR7s. d, Panavia Tornado F3 IDV.

No. 2635, $6, Mosquito, Eurofighter. No. 2636, $6, Hawk's head, hawk, biplane. No. 2637, $6, Biplane, hawk in flight. No. 2638, $6, Vulcan B2, Eurofighter.

1998, Sept. 15 *Perf. 14*

Sheets of 4, #a-d

2633-2634 A412 Set of 2 15.00 15.00

Souvenir Sheets

2635-2638 A412 Set of 4 22.50 22.50

1998 World Scout Jamboree, Chile — A413

No. 2639: a, Astronaut John Glenn receives Silver Buffalo award, 1965. b, Herb Shriner learns knot tying at 1960 Natl. Jamboree. c, "Ready to go" Boy Scouts break camp, 1940's.

$5, Lord Robert Baden-Powell (1857-1941), vert.

1998, Sept. 15

2639 A413 $2 Sheet of 3, #a.-c. 5.00 5.00

Souvenir Sheet

2640 A413 $5 multicolored 4.25 4.25

Ancient Order of Foresters Friendly Society, Court Morning Star 2298, Cent. — A414

Designs: 10c, Bro. H.E.A. Daisley, PCR. 20c, R.N. Jack, PCR. 50c, Woman, man shaking hands, emblem. 70c, Symbol of recognition. 90c, Morning Star Court's headquarters.

1998, Oct. 29 Litho. *Perf. 13½*

2641-2645 A414 Set of 5 2.10 2.10

RMS Titanic — A415

Die Cut 7½

1998, Oct. 29 Embossed

2646 A415 $20 gold 17.50 17.50

Christmas A418

Domestic cats: 20c, Bi-color longhair. 50c, Korat. 60c, Seal-point Siamese. 70c, Red self longhair. 90c, Black longhair. $1.10, Red tabby exotic shorthair.

No. 2653, $5, Seal-point colorpoint. No. 2654, $5, Toirtoiseshell shorthair.

1998, Dec. Litho. *Perf. 14*

2647-2652 A418 Set of 6 3.00 3.00

Souvenir Sheets

2653-2654 A418 Set of 2 8.00 8.00

Hildegard von Bingen (1098?-1179) A419

No. 2655: a, Woman playing flute. b, Hildegard holding tablets. c, Woman playing violin. d, Pope Eugenius. e, Bingen, site of Hildegard's convent. f, Portrait.

$5, Portrait, diff.

1998, Dec. 15 Litho. *Perf. 14*

2655 A419 $1.10 Sheet of 6, #a.-f. 5.75 5.75

Souvenir Sheet

2656 A419 $5 multicolored 4.25 4.25

New Year 1999 (Year of the Rabbit — A420

No. 2657 — Stylized rabbits: a, Looking right. b, Looking forward. c, Looking left.

$2, Like #2657b.

1999, Jan. 4 Litho. *Perf. 14½*

2657 A420 $1 Sheet of 3, #a.-c. 2.25 2.25

Souvenir Sheet

2658 A420 $2 multicolored 1.50 1.50

Queen Elizabeth II and Prince Philip, 50th Wedding Anniv. (in 1997) — A421

Litho. & Embossed

1999, Jan. 5 *Die Cut Perf. 6*

Without Gum

2659 A421 $20 gold & multi 17.50 17.50

Disney Characters in Winter Sports A422

No. 2660, $1.10 — Wearing checkered outfits: a, Minnie. b, Mickey. c, Goofy. d, Donald. e, Mickey (goggles on head). f, Daisy.

No. 2661, $1.10 — Wearing brightly-colored outfits: a, Daisy. b, Mickey. c, Mickey, Goofy. d, Goofy. e, Minnie. f, Donald.

No. 2662, $1.10 — Wearing red, purple & yellow: a, Mickey. b, Goofy. c, Donald. d, Goofy, Mickey. e, Goofy (arms over head). f, Minnie.

No. 2663, $5, Mickey in checkered outfit. No. 2664, $5, Goofy eating ice cream cone, Mickey, horiz. No. 2665, $5, Mickey in red, purple & yellow.

1999, Jan. 21 Litho. *Perf. 13½x14*

Sheets of 6, #a-f

2660-2662 A422 Set of 3 15.00 15.00

Souvenir Sheets

2663-2665 A422 Set of 3 12.00 12.00

Mickey Mouse, 70th anniv.

World Championship Wrestling A423

No. 2666: a, Hollywood Hogan. b, Sting. c, Bret Hart. d, The Giant. e, Kevin Nash. f, Randy Savage. g, Diamond Dallas Page. h, Bill Goldberg.

1999, Jan. 25 Litho. *Perf. 13*

2666 A423 70c Sheet of 8, #a.-h. 4.25 4.25

Australia '99, World Stamp Expo A424

Prehistoric animals: 70c, Plateosaurus. 90c, Euoplacephalus. $1.10, Pachycephalosaurus. $1.40, Dilophosaurus.

No. 2671: a, Struthiomimus. b, Indricotherium. c, Giant moa. d, Deinonychus. e, Sabre tooth cat. f, Dawn horse. g, Peittacosaurus. h, Giant ground sloth. i, Wooly rhinoceros. j, Mosasaur. k, Mastodon. l, Syndoyceras.

No. 2672: a, Rhamphorhynchus. b, Pteranodon. c, Archaeopterix. d, Dimetrodon. e, Stegosaurus. f, Parasaurolophus. g, Iguanadon. h, Triceratops. i, Tyrannosaurus. j, Ichthyosaurus. k, Plesiosaurus. l, Hersperonis.

No. 2273, $5, Diplodocus. No. 2674, $5, Wooly mammoth, vert.

1999, Mar. 1 Litho. *Perf. 14*

2667-2670 A424 Set of 4 4.25 4.25

2671 A424 70c Sheet of 12, #a.-l. 6.50 6.50

m. As #2671, imperf. 6.50 6.50

2672 A424 90c Sheet of 12, #a.-l. 8.25 8.25

m. As #2672, imperf. 8.25 8.25

Souvenir Sheets

2673-2674 A424 $5 Set of 2 7.50 7.50

2673a-2674a Set of 2, imperf. 7.50 7.50

Flora and Fauna A425

Designs: 10c, Acacia tree, elephant. 20c, Green turtle, coconut palm. 25c, Mangrove tree, white ibis. 50c, Tiger swallowtail, ironweed. 70c, Eastern box turtle, jack-in-the-pulpit, vert. 90c, Praying mantis, milkweed, vert. $1.10, Zebra finch, bottle brush, vert. $1.40, Koala, gum tree, vert.

No. 2683, 70c, vert.: a, Red tailed hawk, ocitillo. b, Morning dove, organ pipe cactus. c, Paloverde tree, burrowing owl. d, Cactus wren, saguaro cactus. e, Ocitillo, puma. f, Organ pipe cactus, gray fox. g, Coyete, prickly pear cactus. h, Saguaro cactus, gila woodpecker. i, Collared lizard, barrel cactus. j, Cowblinder cactus, gila monster. k, Hedgehog cactus, roadrunner. l, Saguaro cactus, jack rabbit.

No. 2684, 70c, vert.: a, Strangler fig, basilisk lizard. b, Macaw, kapok trees. c, Cecropia tree, howler monkey. d, Cecropia tree, toucan. e, Arrrow poison frog, bromiliad. f, Rattlesnake orchid, heliconius phyllis. g, Tree fern, bat eating hawk. h, Jaguar, tillandsia. i, Margay, sierra palm. j, Lesser bird of paradise, aristolchia. k, Parides, erythrina. l, Fer-de-lance, zebra plant.

No. 2685, $5, Alligator, water lilies. No. 2686, $5, Riuolis, hummingbird.

1999, Apr. 12 Litho. *Perf. 14*

2675-2682 A425 Set of 8 3.75 3.75

Sheets of 12, #a-l

2683-2684 A425 Set of 2 13.00 13.00

Souvenir Sheets

2685-2686 A425 Set of 2 7.50 7.50

Aviation History A426

Designs: 60c, Montgolfier balloon, 1783, vert. 70c, Lilienthal glider, 1894. 90c, Zeppelin. $1, Wright brothers, 1903.

No. 2691, $1.10: a, DH-4 bomber. b, Sopwith Camel. c, Sopwith Dove. d, Jeannin Stahl Taube. e, Fokker DR-1 triplane. f, Albatros Diva. g, Sopwith Pup. h, Spad XIII Smith IV.

No. 2692, $1.10: a, M-130 Clipper. b, DC-3, 1937. c, Beech Staggerwing CVR FT C-17L. d, Hughes H-1 racer. e, Gee Bee Model R-1, 1932. f, Lockheed Sirius Tingmissartoq. g,

Fokker T-2, 1923. h, Curtiss CW-16E Floatplane.

No. 2693, $5, Bleriot XI crossing English Channel, 1914. No. 2694, $5, Le Bandy airship, 1903.

1999, Apr. 26

2687-2690 A426 Set of 4 2.50 2.50

Sheets of 8, #a-h

2691-2692 A426 Set of 2 13.50 13.50

Souvenir Sheets

2693-2694 A426 Set of 2 7.50 7.50

'N Sync, Musical Group — A427

1999, May 4 Litho. ***Perf. 12½***

2695 A427 $1 multicolored .75 .75

No. 2695 was issued in sheets of 8.

History of Space Exploration, 1609-2000 — A428

Designs: 20c, Galileo, 1609. 50c, Konstantin Tsiolkovsky, 1903. 70c, Robert H. Goddard, 1926. 90c, Sir Isaac Newton, 1668, vert.

No. 2700, $1: a, Luna 9, 1959. b, Soyuz 11, 1971. c, Mir Space Station, 1996. d, Sputnik 1, 1957. e, Apollo 4, 1967. f, Bruce McCandless, 1984. g, Sir William Herschel, telescope, 1781. h, John Glenn, 1962. i, Space Shuttle Columbia, 1981.

No. 2701, $1, vert: a, Yuri Gargarin, 1962. b, Lunar Rover, 1971. c, Mariner 10, 1974-75. d, Laika, 1957. e, Neil A. Armstrong, 1969. f, Skylab Space Station, 1973. g, German V-2 Rocket, 1942. h, Gemini 4, 1965. i, Hubble Telescope, 1990.

No. 2702, $1, vert: a, Explorer, 1958. b, Lunokhod Explorer, 1970. c, Viking Lander, 1975. d, R7 Rocket, 1957. e, Edward H. White, 1965. f, Salyut 1, 1971. g, World's oldest observatory. h, Freedom 7, 1961. i, Ariane Rocket, 1980's.

No. 2703, $5, Atlantis docking with Space Station Mir, 1995. No. 2704, $5, Saturn V, 1969, vert.

1999, May 6 ***Perf. 14***

2696-2699 A428 Set of 4 1.75 1.75

Sheets of 9, #a-i

2700-2702 A428 Set of 3 21.00 21.00

Souvenir Sheets

2703-2704 A428 Set of 2 7.50 7.50

Johann Wolfgang von Goethe (1749-1832), Poet — A430

No. 2709: a, Faust Dying in the Arms of the Lemures. b, Portraits of Goethe, Friederich von Schiller (1759-1805). c, The Immortal Spirit of Faust is Carried Aloft.

No. 2710: a, Faust and Helena with Their Son, Euphonon. b, Mephistopheles Leading the Lemures to Faust.

No. 2711, $5, The Immortal soul of Faust, vert. No. 2712, $5, Portrait of Goethe, vert.

1999, June 25 Litho. ***Perf. 14***

2709 A430 $3 Sheet of 3, #a.-c. 6.75 6.75

2710 A430 $3 Sheet of 3, #a.-b. + #2709b 6.75 6.75

Souvenir Sheets

2711-2712 A430 Set of 2 7.50 7.50

Paintings by Hokusai (1760-1849) A431

No. 2713, $1.10: a, Landscape with a Hundred Bridges (large mountain). b, Sea Life (turtle, head LL). c, Landscape with a Hundred Bridges (large bridge in center). d, A View of Aoigaoka Waterfall in Edo. e, Sea Life (crab). f, Women on the Beach at Enoshima.

No. 2714, $1.10: a, Admiring the Irises at Yatsuhashi (large tree). b, Sea Life (turtle, head UL). c, Admiring the Irises at Yatsuhashi (peak of bridge). d, Pilgrims Bathing in Roben Waterfall. e, Sea Life (turtle, head UR). f, Farmers Crossing a Suspension Bridge.

No. 2715, $5, In the Horse Washing Waterfall. No. 2716, $5, A Fisherman at Kajikazawa.

1999, June 25 ***Perf. 13¾***

Sheets of 6, #a-f

2713-2714 A431 Set of 2 10.00 10.00

Souvenir Sheet

2715-2716 A431 Set of 2 7.50 7.50

Wedding of Prince Edward and Sophie Rhys-Jones A432

No. 2717: a, Edward. b, Sophie, Edward. c, Sophie.

$6, Couple, horiz.

1999, June 19 Litho. ***Perf. 13½***

2717 A432 $3 Sheet of 3, #a-c 6.75 6.75

Souvenir Sheet

2718 A432 $6 multicolored 4.50 4.50

IBRA '99, World Philatelic Exhibition, Nuremberg — A433

Design: $1, Krauss-Maffei V-200 diesel locomotive, Germany, 1852.

1999, June 25 ***Perf. 14***

2720 A433 $1 multicolored .75 .75

A 90c value was prepared. Its status is unclear.

Souvenir Sheets

PhilexFrance '99, World Philatelic Exhibition — A434

Locomotives: No. 2721, $6, Pacific, 1930's. No. 2722, $6, Quadrt, electric hight-speed, 1940.

1999, June 25 ***Perf. 13¾***

2721-2722 A434 Set of 2 9.00 9.00

A435

No. 2723 — Children: a, Tyreek Isaacs. b, Fredique Isaacs. c, Jerome Burke III. d, Kellisha Roberts.

No. 2724: a, Girl with braided hair. b, Girl wearing hat. c, Girl holding kitten.

$5, Girl with bow in hair.

1999, June 25 ***Perf. 14***

2723 A435 90c Sheet of 4, #a.-d. 2.75 2.75

2724 A435 $3 Sheet of 3, #a.-c. 6.75 6.75

Souvenir Sheet

2725 A435 $5 multicolored 3.75 3.75

UN Convention on Rights of the Child, 10th anniv.

A436

No. 2726: a, I.M. Pei. b, Billy Graham. c, Barbara Cartland. d, Mike Wallace. e, Jeanne Moreau. f, B.B. King. g, Elie Wiesel. h, Arthur Miller. i, Colin Powell. j, Jack Palance. k, Neil Simon. l, Eartha Kitt.

No. 2727: a, Thomas M. Saunders J.P. b, Mother Sarah Baptiste, M.B.E. c, Sir Sydney Gun-Munro MD, KF, GCMG. d, Dr. Earle Kirby, JP, OBE.

1999, June 25

2726 A436 70c Sheet of 12, #a.-l. 6.25 6.25

2727 A436 $1.10 Sheet of 4, #a.-d. 3.25 3.25

Intl. Year of Older Persons.

World Teachers' Day — A437

No. 2728: a, Henry Alphaeus Robertson. b, Yvonne C. E. Francis-Gibson. c, Edna Peters. d, Christopher Wilberforce Prescod.

1999, Oct. 5 Litho. ***Perf. 14¾***

2728 A437 $2 Sheet of 4, #a.-d. 0.00 6.00

A438

Queen Mother (b. 1900) — A439

No. 2729: a, In 1909. b, With King George VI, Princess Elizabeth, 1930. c, At Badminton, 1977. d, In 1983.

$6, In 1987. $20, Close-up.

1999 Litho. ***Perf. 14***

Gold Frames

2729 A438 $2 Sheet of 4, #a.-d., + label 6.00 6.00

Souvenir Sheet

Perf. 13¾

2730 A438 $6 multicolored 4.50 4.50

Litho. & Embossed

Die Cut 9x8¾

Size: 55x93mm

2731 A439 $20 gold & multi 20.00 20.00

Issued: Nos. 2729-2730, 10/18; No. 2731, 8/4. No. 2730 contains one 38x50mm stamp.

See Nos. 3010-3011.

Christmas A440

Designs: 20c, The Resurrection, by Albrecht Dürer. 50c, Christ in Limbo, by Dürer. 70c, Christ Falling on the Way to Calvary, by Raphael. 90c, St. Ildefonso with the Madonna and Child, by Peter Paul Rubens. $5, The Crucifixion, by Raphael.

$6,The Sistine Madonna, by Raphael.

1999, Nov. 22 Litho. ***Perf. 13¾***

2732-2736 A440 Set of 5 5.50 5.50

Souvenir Sheet

2737 A440 $6 multicolored 4.50 4.50

UPU, 125th Anniv. A441

Designs: a, Mail coach. b, Intercontinental sea mail. c, Concorde.

1999, Dec. 7 ***Perf. 14***

2738 A441 $3 Sheet of 3, #a.-c. 6.75 6.75

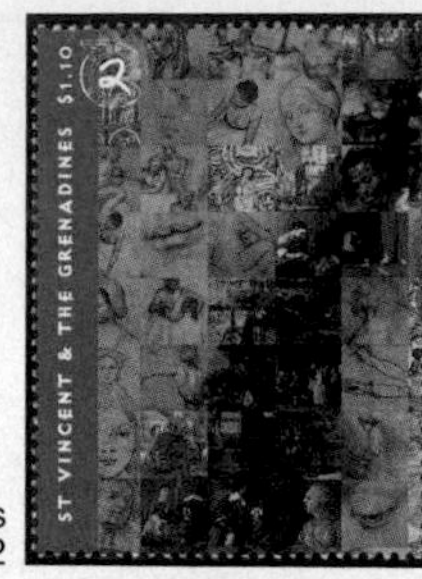

Paintings A442

Various paintings making up a photomosaic of the Mona Lisa.

1999, Dec. 7 ***Perf. 13¼***

2739 A442 $1.10 Sheet of 8, #a.-h. 6.50 6.50

See #2744, 2816.

A443

Millennium: No. 2740, Clyde Tombaugh discovers Pluto, 1930.

No. 2741 — Highlights of the 1930s: a, Mahatma Gandhi's Salt March, 1930. b, Like #2740, with colored margin. c, Empire State Building opens, 1931. d, Spain becomes a republic, 1931. e, Franklin D. Roosevelt launches New Deal, 1933. f, Reichstag burns in Germany, 1933. g, Mao Zedong leads China's revolution, 1934. h, Spanish Civil War led by Francisco Franco, 1936. i, Edward VIII abdicates, 1936. j, Diego Rivera, 50th birthday, 1936. k, Golden Gate Bridge opens, 1937. l, First atomic reaction achieved, 1939. m, World War II begins, 1939. n, Television debuts at New York World's Fair, 1939. o, Selection of Dalai Lama, 1939. p, Hindenburg explodes, 1937 (60x40mm). q, Igor Sikorsky builds first practical helicopter, 1939.

No. 2742 — Sculptures by: a, Elizabeth Murray. b, Alexander Calder. c, Charles William Moss. d, Gaston Lachaise. e, Claes Oldenburg. f, Louise Bourgeois. g, Duane Hanson. h, Brancusi. i, David Smith. j, Dan Flavin. k, Boccioni. l, George Segal. m, Lucas Samaras. n, Marcel Duchamp. o, Isamu Noguchi. p, Donald Judd (60x40mm). q, Louise Nevelson.

1999, Dec. 7 Litho. ***Perf. 13¼x13***

2740 A443 60c multicolored .45 .45

Perf. 12¾x12½

2741 A443 60c Sheet of 17, #a.-q. + label 7.50 7.50

2742 A443 60c Sheet of 17, #a.-q. + label 7.50 7.50

Inscription on No. 2742e is misspelled.
See No. 2764.

Painting Type of 1999

Various flowers making up a photomosaic of Princess Diana.

1999, Dec. 31 Litho. ***Perf. 13¾***

2744 A442 $1 Sheet of 8, #a.-h. 6.00 6.00

New Year 2000 (Year of the Dragon) — A444

No. 2745 — Background colors: a, Blue and red lilac. b, Salmon pink and olive. c, Brick red and lilac rose.

$4, Brown and dull green.

2000, Feb. 5 Litho. ***Perf. 14¾***

2745 A444 $2 Sheet of 3, #a.-c. 4.50 4.50

Souvenir Sheet

2746 A444 $4 multi 3.00 3.00

Marine Life — A445

Designs: 50c, High hat. 90c, Spotfin hogfish. $1, Royal gramma. $2, Queen angelfish.

No. 2751: a, Sergeant major. b, Hawksbill turtle, whale's tail. c, Horse-eyed jacks, rear of turtle. d, Two horse-eyed jacks, humpback whale. e, Three horse-eyed jacks, head of humpback whale. f, Black-cap gramma. g, Common dolphins. h, French grunts, with Latin inscription. i, Barracuda. j, Bottlenosed dolphin. k, Sea horse. l, Southern stingray, French grunt. m, French grunts, no Latin inscription. n, Indigo hamlet. o, Basking shark. p, Nassau grouper. q, Nurse shark, ribbonfish. r, Southern stingray. s, Southern stingray, blue shark. t, Spanish hogfish.

No. 2752, $5, Rock beauties. No. 2753, $5, Banded butterflyfish.

2000, Feb. 28 Litho. ***Perf. 14***

2747-2750 A445 Set of 4 3.25 3.25

2751 A445 50c Sheet of 20, #a.-t. 7.50 7.50

Souvenir Sheets

2752-2753 A445 Set of 2 7.50 7.50

Fish A446

Designs: 10c, Stoplight parrotfish. 20c, Spotfin hogfish. 70c, Beaugregory. 90c, Porkfish. $1, Barred hamlet. $1.40, Queen triggerfish.

No. 2760, $1.10: a, French angelfish. b, Smooth trunkfish. c, Sargassum triggerfish. d, Indigo hamlet. e, Yellowheaded jawfish. f, Peppermint bass.

No. 2761, $1.10: a, Porcupine fish. b, Blue tang. c, Bluehead wrasse. d, Juvenile queen angelfish. e, Sea horse. f, Small mouth grunt.

No. 2762, $5, Pygmy angelfish. No. 2763, $5, Four-eye butterflyfish.

2000, Feb. 28

2754-2759 A446 Set of 6 3.25 3.25

Sheets of 6, #a.-f.

2760-2761 A446 Set of 2 10.00 10.00

Souvenir Sheets

2762-2763 A446 Set of 2 7.50 7.50

Millennium Type of 1999

No. 2764 — Highlights of 1900-1950: a, Sigmund Freud publishes "Interpretation of Dreams." b, First long distance wireless transmission. c, First powered airplane flight. d, Einstein proposes theory of relativity. e, Henry Ford unveils Model T. f, Alfred Wegener develops theory of continental drift. g, World War I begins. h, 1917 Russian revolution. i, James Joyce publishes "Ulysses." j, Alexander Fleming discovers penicillin. k, Edwin Hubble determines universe is expanding. l, Mao Zedong leads "Long March." m, Alan Turing develops theory of digital computing. n, Discovery of fission. o, World War II begins. p, Allied leaders meet at Yalta. q, Mahatma Gandhi and Jawaharlal Nehru celebrate India's independence. r, Invention of the transistor.

2000, Mar. 13 ***Perf. 12½***

2764 A443 20c Sheet of 18, a.-r. + label 2.75 2.75

Date on No. 2764a is incorrect.

Paintings of Anthony Van Dyck A447

No. 2765, $1: a, Robert Rich, 2nd Earl of Warwick. b, James Stuart, Duke of Lennox and Richmond. c, Sir John Suckling. d, Sir Robert Shirley. e, Teresia, Lady Shirley. f, Thomas Wentworth, 1st Earl of Strafford.

No. 2766, $1: a, Thomas Wentworth, Earl of Strafford, in Armor. b, Lady Anne Carr, Countess of Bedford. c, Portrait of a Member of the Charles Family. d, Thomas Howard, 2nd Earl of Arundel. e, Diana Cecil, Countess of Oxford. f, The Violincellist.

No. 2767, $1: a, The Apostle Peter. b, St. Matthew. c, St. James the Greater. d, St. Bartholomew. e, The Apostle Thomas. f, The Apostle Jude (Thaddeus).

No. 2768, $1: a, The Vision of St. Anthony. b, The Mystic Marriage of St. Catherine. c, The Vision of the Blessed Herman Joseph. d, Madonna and Child Enthroned with Sts. Rosalie, Peter and Paul. e, St. Rosalie Interceding for the Plague-stricken of Palermo. f, Francesco Orero in Adoration of the Crucifixion in the Presence of Sts. Frances and Bernard.

No. 2769, $5, William Feilding, 1st Earl of Denbigh. No. 2770, $5, The Mystic Marriage of St. Catherine, diff. No. 2771, $5, St. Augustine in Ecstasy, horiz.

2000, Apr. 10 Litho. ***Perf. 13¾***

Sheets of 6, #a.-f.

2765-2768 A447 Set of 4 18.00 18.00

Souvenir Sheets

2769-2771 A447 Set of 3 11.50 11.50

Orchids A448

Designs: 70c, Brassavola nodosa. 90c, Bletia purpurea. $1.40, Brassavola cucullata.

No. 2775, $1.50, vert.: a, Oncidium urophyllum. b, Oeceoclades maculata. c, Vanilla planifolia. d, Isolhilus linearis. e, Ionopsis utricularioides. f, Nidema boothii.

No. 2776, $1.50, vert.: a, Cyrtopodium punctatum. b, Dendrophylax funalis. c, Dichaea hystricina. d, Cyrtopodium andersonii. e, Epidendrum secundum. f, Dimerandra emarginata.

No. 2777, $1.50, vert.: a, Brassavola cordata. b, Brassia caudata. c, Broughotnia sanguinea. d, Comparettia falcata. e, Clowesia rosea. f, Caularthron bicornutum.

No. 2778, $5, Neocogniauxia hexaptera, vert. No. 2779, $5, Epidendrum altissimum, vert.

2000, May 25 Litho. ***Perf. 14***

2772-2774 A448 Set of 3 2.25 2.25

Sheets of 6, #a.-f.

2775-2777 A448 Set of 3 21.00 21.00

Souvenir Sheets

2778-2779 A448 Set of 2 7.50 7.50

The Stamp Show 2000, London.

Prince William, 18th Birthday — A449

No. 2780: a, Wearing checked suit. b, Wearing scarf. c, Wearing solid suit. d, Wearing sweater.

$5, Wearing suit with boutonniere.

2000, June 21 Litho. ***Perf. 14***

2780 A449 $1.40 Sheet of 4, #a-d 4.25 4.25

Souvenir Sheet

Perf. 13¾

2781 A449 $5 multi 3.75 3.75

No. 2780 contains four 28x42mm stamps.

100th Test Match at Lord's Ground — A450

Designs: 10c, Ian Allen. 20c, T. Michael Findlay. $1.10, Winston Davis. $1.40, Nixon McLean.

$5, Lord's Ground, horiz.

2000, June 26 ***Perf. 14***

2782-2785 A450 Set of 4 2.10 2.10

Souvenir Sheet

2786 A450 $5 multi 3.75 3.75

First Zeppelin Flight, Cent. — A451

No. 2787: a, LZ-6. b, LZ-127. c, LZ-129.

$5, LZ-9.

2000, June 26

2787 A451 $3 Sheet of 3, #a-c 6.75 6.75

Souvenir Sheet

2788 A451 $5 multi 3.75 3.75

No. 2787 contains 39x24mm stamps.

Berlin Film Festival, 50th Anniv. — A452

No. 2789: a, Pane, Amore e Fantasia. b, Richard III. c, Smultronstället (Wild Strawberries). d, The Defiant Ones. e, The Living Desert. f, A Bout de Souffle.

$5, Jean-Luc Godard.

2000, June 26

2789 A452 $1.40 Sheet of 6, #a-f 6.25 6.25

Souvenir Sheet

2790 A452 $5 multi 3.75 3.75

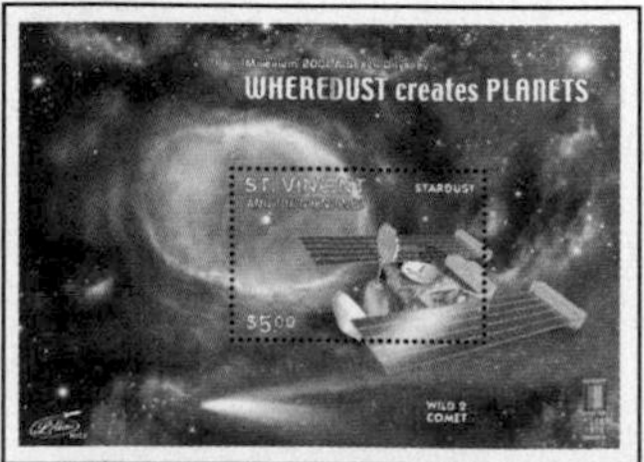

Space — A453

No. 2791, $1.50: a, Comet Hale-Bopp, Calisto. b, Galileo probe. c, Ulysses probe. d, Pioneer 11. e, Voyager 1. f, Pioneer 10.

No. 2792, $1.50: a, Voyager 2, Umbriel. b, Pluto Project. c, Voyager 1, purple background. d, Oort cloud. e, Pluto, Kuiper Express. f, Voayger 2 near Neptune.

No. 2793, $1.50: a, Cassini probe. b, Pioneer 11. c, Voyager 1, green background. d, Huygens. e, Deep Space IV Champollion. f, Voyager 2.

No. 2794, $5, Stardust. No. 2795, $5, Pluto Project, diff.

2000, June 26 **Sheets of 6, #a-f**

2791-2793 A453 Set of 3 21.00 21.00

Souvenir Sheets

2794-2795 A453 Set of 2 7.50 7.50

World Stamp Expo 2000, Anaheim.

Souvenir Sheet

2000 Summer Olympics, Sydney — A454

No. 2796: a, Mildred Didrikson. b, Pommel horse. c, Barcelona Stadium and Spanish flag. d, Ancient Greek horse racing.

2000, June 26

2796 A454 $2 Sheet of 4, #a-d 6.00 6.00

Souvenir Sheet

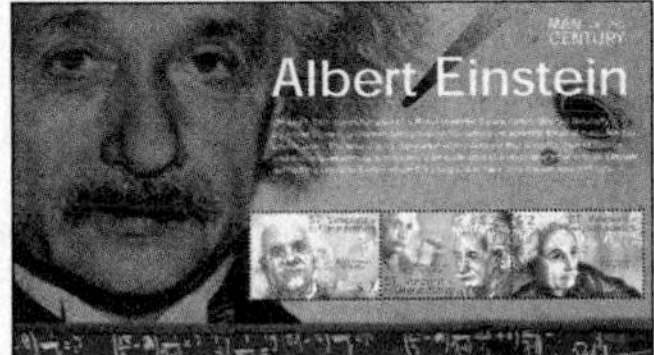

Albert Einstein (1879-1955) — A455

No. 2797: a, Wearing green sweater. b, Wearing blue sweater. c, Wearing black sweater.

2000, June 26

2797 A455 $2 Sheet of 3, #a-c 4.50 4.50

Public Railways, 175th Anniv. — A456

No. 2798: a, Locomotion No. 1, George Stephenson. b, John Bull.

2000, June 26

2798 A456 $3 Sheet of 2, #a-b 4.50 4.50

Mario Andretti, Automobile Racer — A457

No. 2799: a, In car, without helmet. b, In white racing uniform. c, With hands in front of face. d, In car, with helmet. e, In white, standing in front of car. f, With trophy. g, In red racing uniform. h, Close-up.

$5, With trophy, diff.

2000, July 6 ***Perf. 12x12¼***

2799 A457 $1.10 Sheet of 8, #a-h 6.50 6.50

Souvenir Sheet

Perf. 13¾

2800 A457 $5 multi 3.75 3.75

Souvenir Sheets

Monty Python's Flying Circus, 30th Anniv. (in 1999) — A458

No. 2801: a, Michael Palin. b, Eric Idle. c, John Cleese. d, Graham Chapman. e, Terry Gilliam. f, Terry Jones.

2000, July 6 ***Perf. 12x12¼***

2801 A458 $1.40 Sheet of 6, #a-f 6.25 6.25

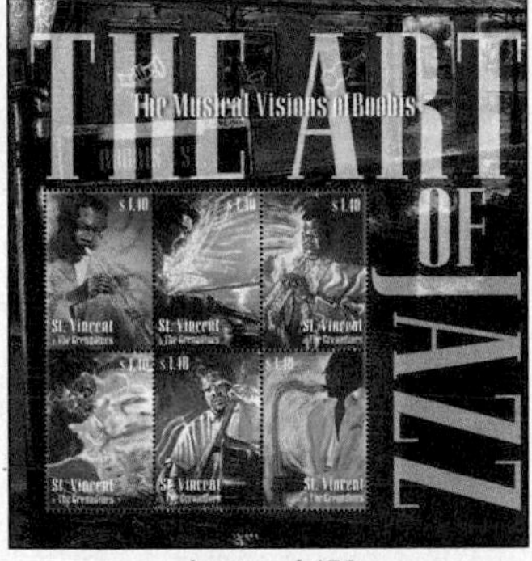

Jazz — A459

No. 2802: a, Clarinetist. b, Pianist. c, Trumpeter. d, Guitarist. e, Bassist. f, Saxophonist.

2000, July 6 ***Perf. 14***

2802 A459 $1.40 Sheet of 6, #a-f 6.25 6.25

Female Recording Groups of the 1960s — A460

No. 2803, $1.40: a-e, Portraits of the members of The Chantels (green background).

No. 2804, $1.40: a-e, Portraits of the members of The Marvelettes (blue background)

2000, July 6 **Sheets of 5, #a-e**

2803-2804 A460 Set of 2 10.50 10.50

Souvenir Sheet

Barbara Taylor Bradford, Writer — A461

2000, July 6 ***Perf. 12x12¼***

2805 A461 $5 multi 3.75 3.75

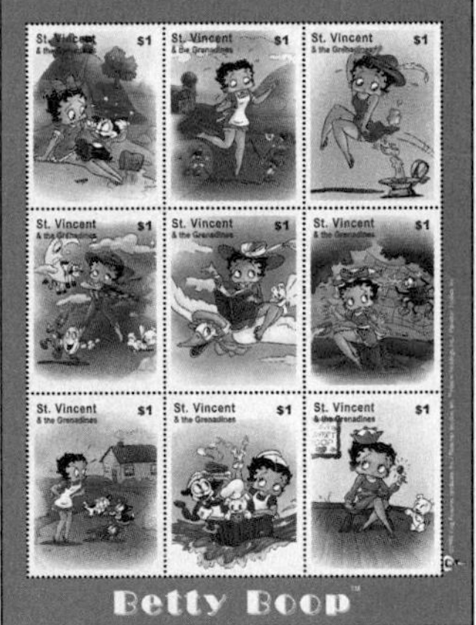

Betty Boop — A462

No. 2806: a, As Jill, with Jack. b, With three blind mice. c, Jumping over candlestick. d, As fiddler in Hey, Diddle, Diddle. e, On back of Mother Goose. f, As Little Miss Muffet. g, With three cats. h, As candlestick maker, with butcher and baker. i, As Little Jack Horner.

No. 2807, $5, As the Woman Who Lived In a Shoe. No. 2808, $5, As Little Bo Peep.

2000, July 6 ***Perf. 13¾***

2806 A462 $1 Sheet of 9, #a-i 6.75 6.75

Souvenir Sheets

2807-2808 A462 Set of 2 7.50 7.50

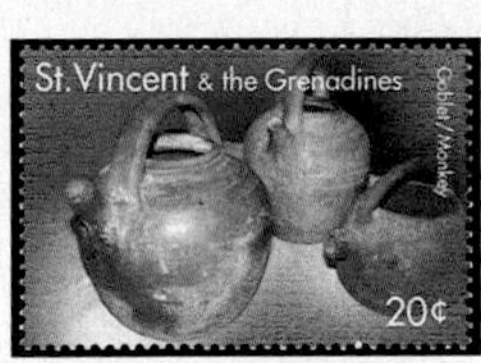

Artifacts A463

Designs: 20c, Goblet. 50c, Goose. 70c, Boley and calabash. $1, Flat iron.

2000, Aug. 21 **Litho.** ***Perf. 14***

2809-2812 A463 Set of 4 1.75 1.75

Flowers — A464

No. 2813: a, Pink ginger lily. b, Thumbergia grandiflora. c, Red ginger lily. d, Madagascar jasmine. e, Cluster palm. f, Red torch lily. g, Salvia splendens. h, Balsam apple. i, Rostrata.

No. 2814, Red flamingo. No. 2815, Balsam apple, horiz.

2000, Aug. 21

2813 A464 90c Sheet of 9, #a-i 6.00 6.00

Souvenir Sheet

2814-2815 A464 $5 Set of 2 7.50 7.50

Paintings Type of 1999

Various pictures of flowers making up a photomosaic of the Queen Mother.

2000, Sept. 5 ***Perf. 13¾***

2816 A442 $1 Sheet of 8, #a-h 6.00 6.00

i. As No. 2816, imperf. 6.00 6.00

Magician David Copperfield — A465

No. 2817: a, Head of Copperfield. b, Copperfield's body. c, Copperfield's body vanishing. d, Copperfield's body vanished.

2000, July 6 ***Perf. 14***

2817 A465 $1.40 Sheet of 4, #a-d 4.25 4.25

Local Musicians — A466

Designs: No. 2818, $1.40, Horn player with striped shirt. No. 2819, $1.40, Horn player, diff. No. 2820, $1.40, Pianist. No. 2821, $1.40, Fiddler.

2000, Oct. 16 **Litho.** ***Perf. 14***

2818-2821 A466 Set of 4 4.25 4.25

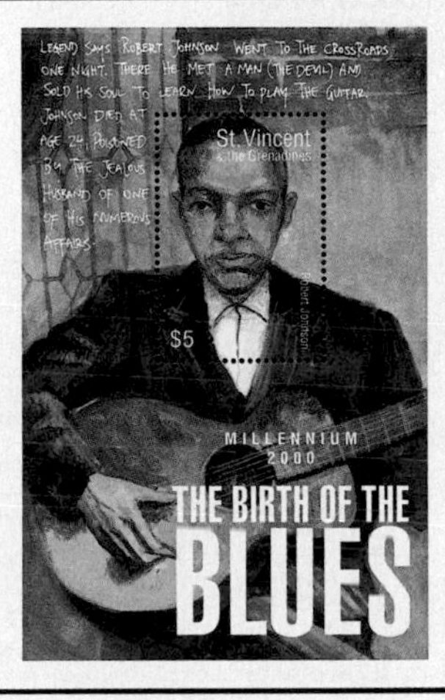

Blues Musicians — A467

No. 2822, $1.40: a, Bessie Smith. b, Willie Dixon. c, Gertrude "Ma" Rainey. d, W. C. Handy. e, Leadbelly. f, Big Bill Broonzy.

No. 2823, $1.40: a, Ida Cox. b, Lonnie Johnson. c, Muddy Waters. d, T-Bone Walker. e, Howlin' Wolf. f, Sister Rosetta Tharpe.

No. 2824, Robert Johnson. No. 2825, Billie Holiday.

2000, Oct. 16 **Sheets of 6, #a-f**
2822-2823 A467 Set of 2 12.50 12.50

Souvenir Sheets

2824-2825 A467 Set of 2 7.50 7.50

World at War — A468

No. 2826: a, USS Shaw explodes at Pearl Harbor. b, B-24s bomb Ploesti oil fields. c, Soviet T-34 tank moves towards Berlin. d, USS New Jersey off coast of North Korea. e, F-86 Sabre over North Korea. f, USS Enterprise off the Indochina coast. g, B-52 over Viet Nam. h, M-113 tank in Viet Nam.

No. 2827: a, Israeli F-4 Phantoms in action in Six-day War. b, Egyptian T-72 tank destroyed, Six-day War. c, Egyptian SAM-6 missiles, Yom Kippur War. d, Israeli M-48 tanks in desert, Yom Kippur War. e, HMS Hermes, Falkand Islands War. f, British AV-8 harriers in action, Falkland Islands War. g, Iraqi Scud missile launcher in desert, Gulf War. h, M1-A1 Abrams tanks in desert, Gulf War.

No. 2828, Israeli F-4s bomb SAM sites, Yom Kippur War. No. 2829 B-52 bomber, Pershing II missile.

2000, Oct. 16 **Sheets of 8, #a-h**
2826-2827 A468 $1 Set of 2 12.00 12.00

Souvenir Sheets

2828-2829 A468 $5 Set of 2 7.50 7.50

No. 2829 contains one 56x42mm stamp.

Independence, 21st Anniv. — A469

Designs: 10c, Government House. 15c, First session of Parliament, 1998. 50c, House of Assembly. $2, Financial Complex.

2000, Oct. 27 **Litho.** ***Perf. 14***
2830-2833 A469 Set of 4 2.00 2.00

Birds — A470

Designs: 50c, Blue and gold macaw. 90c, English fallow budgerigar. $1, Barraband parakeet. $2, Dominat pied blue.

No. 2838, $2: a, English short-faced tumbler. b, Diamond dove. c, Norwich cropper.

No. 2839, $2: a, Scarlet macaw. b, Blue-fronted Amazon. c, Buffon's macaw.

No. 2840, $2: a, Stafford canary. b, Masked lovebird. c, Parisian full canary.

No. 2841, $2, horiz.: a, Canada goose. b, Mandarin duck. c, Gouldian finch.

No. 2842, $5, Common peafowl, horiz. No. 2843, $5, Budgerigar, horiz.

2000, Nov. 15
2834-2837 A470 Set of 4 4.00 4.00

Sheets of 3, #a-c

2838-2841 A470 Set of 4 18.00 18.00

Souvenir Sheets

2842-2843 A470 Set of 2 7.50 7.50

Shirley Temple in Rebecca of Sunnybrook Farm — A471

No. 2844, horiz.: a, With man in dark suit. b, With man and woman. c, With woman wearing glasses. d, with blonde woman. e, With man in white hat. f, With three women.

No. 2845: a, At microphone, wearing checked coat and hat. b, Wearing straw hat. c, At microphone, no hat. d, With woman wearing glasses.

No. 2846, With Bill Robinson.

2000, Nov. 29 ***Perf. 13¾***
2844 A471 90c Sheet of 6, #a-f 4.00 4.00
2845 A471 $1.10 Sheet of 4, #a-d 3.25 3.25

Souvenir Sheet

2846 A471 $1.10 multi .85 .85

See also Nos. 3064-2066.

Queen Mother, 100th Birthday — A472

2000, Sept. 5 **Litho.** ***Perf. 14***
2847 A472 $1.40 multi 1.00 1.00

Printed in sheets of 6.

Christmas — A473

20c, Angel looking right. 70c, Two angels, orange background. 90c, Two angels, blue background. #2851, $5, Angel looking left.

No. 2852, Angel, yellow background.

2000, Dec. 7
2848-2851 A473 Set of 4 5.00 5.00

Souvenir Sheet

2852 A473 $5 multi 3.75 3.75

Battle of Britain, 60th Anniv. — A474

No. 2853, 90c: a, Junkers Ju87. b, Two Gloster Gladiators flying left. c, Messerschmitt BF109. d, Heinkel He111 bomber, British fighter. e, Three Hawker Hurricanes. f, Two Bristol Blenheims. g, Two Supermarine Spitfires and ground. h, Messerschmitt BF110.

No. 2854, 90c: a, Two Spitfires, flying left. b, Spitfire. c, Dornier DO217. d, Two Gladiators flying right. e, Four Hurricanes. f, Junkers Ju87 Stuka. g, Two Spitfires flying right. h, Junkers Ju88.

#2855, $5, Spitfire. #2856, $5, Hurricane.

2000, Dec. 18 ***Perf. 14¼x14½***

Sheets of 8, #a-h

2853-2854 A474 Set of 2 10.50 10.50

Souvenir Sheets

Perf. 14¼

2855-2856 A474 Set of 2 7.50 7.50

New Year 2001 (Year of the Snake) — A475

No. 2857: a, Blue and light blue background. b, Purple and pink background. c, Green and light green background.

2001, Jan. 2 **Litho.** ***Perf. 13x13¼***
2857 A475 $1 Sheet of 3, #a-c 2.25 2.25

Souvenir Sheet

2858 A475 $2 shown 1.50 1.50

Paintings of Peter Paul Rubens in the Prado A476

Designs: 10c, Three women and dog from Diana the Huntress. 90c, Adoration of the Magi. $1, Woman and two dogs from Diana the Huntress.

No. 2862, $2: a, Heraclitus, the Mournful Philosopher. b, Heraclitus, close-up. c, Anne of Austria, Queen of France, close-up. d, Anne of Austria.

No. 2863, $2: a, Prometheus Carrying Fire. b, Vulcan Forging Jupiter's Thunderbolt. c, Saturn Devouring One of His Sons. d, Polyphemus.

No. 2864, $2: a, St. Matthias. b, The Death of Seneca. c, Maria de'Medici, Queen of France. d, Achilles Discovered by Ulysses.

No. 2865, $5, The Judgment of Solomon. No. 2866, $5, The Holy Family with St. Anne.

2001, Jan. 2 ***Perf. 13¾***
2859-2861 A476 Set of 3 1.50 1.50

Sheets of 4, #a-d

2862-2864 A476 Set of 3 18.00 18.00

Souvenir Sheets

2865-2866 A476 Set of 2 7.50 7.50

Rijksmuseum, Amsterdam, Bicent. — A477

No. 2867, $1.40: a, The Spendthrift, by Cornelis Troost. b, The Art Gallery of Jan Gildermeester Jansz, by Adriaan de Lelie. c, The Rampoortje, by Wouter Johannes van Troostwijk. d, Winter Landscape, by Barend Cornelis Koekkoek. e, Man with white headdress from The Procuress, by Dirck van Baburen. f, Man and woman from The Procuress.

No. 2868, $1.40: a, A Music Party, by Rembrandt. b, Rutger Jan Schimmelpennick and Family, by Pierre Paul Prud'hon. c, Tobit and Anna With a Kid, by Rembrandt. d, The Syndics of the Amsterdam Goldsmiths' Guild, by Thomas de Keyser. e, Portrait of a Lady, by de Keyser. f, Marriage Portrait of Isaac Massa and Beatrix van der Laen, by Frans Hals.

No. 2869, $1.40: a, The Concert, by Hendrick ter Brugghen. b, Vertumnus and Pomona, by Paulus Moreelse. c, Standing couple from Dignified Couples Courting, by Willem Buytewech. d, The Sick Woman, by Jan Steen. e, Seated couple from Dignified Couples Courting. f, Don Ramón Satué, by Francisco de Goya.

No. 2870, $5, Donkey Riding on the Beach, by Isaac Lazarus Israels. No. 2871, $5, The Stone Bridge, by Rembrandt, horiz. No. 2872, $5, Child with Dead Peacocks, by Rembrandt, horiz.

2001, Jan. 15 ***Perf. 13¾***

Sheets of 6, #a-f

2867-2869 A477 Set of 3 19.00 19.00

Souvenir Sheets

2870-2872 A477 Set of 3 11.00 11.00

Birds of Prey A478

Designs: 10c, Barred owl. No. 2874, 90c, Lammergeier. $1, California condor. $2, Mississippi kite.

No. 2877, 90c: a, Crested caracara. b, Boreal owl. c, Harpy eagle. d, Oriental bay owl. e, Hawk owl. f, Laughing falcon.

No. 2878, $1.10: a, Bateleur. b, Hobby. c, Osprey. d, Goshawk. e, African fish eagle. f, Egyptian vulture.

No. 2879, $5, Great gray owl. No. 2880, $5, American kestrel.

2001, Feb. 13 ***Perf. 14***
2873-2876 A478 Set of 4 3.25 3.25

Sheets of 6, #a-f

2877-2878 A478 Set of 2 9.50 9.50

Souvenir Sheets

2879-2880 A478 Set of 2 8.00 8.00

Hong Kong 2001 Stamp Exhibition (Nos. 2877-2880).

Owls — A479

Designs: 10c, Eagle. 20c, Barn. 50c, Great gray. 70c, Long-eared. 90c, Tawny. $1, Hawk.

No. 2887, horiz.: a, Ural. b, Tengmalm's. c, Marsh. d, Brown fish. e, Little. f, Short-eared.

No. 2888, $5, Hume's. No. 2889, $5, Snowy.

2001, Feb. 13
2881-2886 A479 Set of 6 2.75 2.75
2887 A479 $1.40 Sheet of 6, #a-f 6.75 6.75

Souvenir Sheets

2888-2889 A479 Set of 2 8.00 8.00

Pokémon — A480

No. 2890: a, Kadabra. b, Spearow. c, Kakuna. d, Koffing. e, Tentacruel. f, Cloyster.

2001, Feb. 13 ***Perf. 13¾***

2890 A480 90c Sheet of 6, #a-f 4.00 4.00

Souvenir Sheet

2891 A480 $3 Meowth 2.25 2.25

UN Women's Human Rights Campaign — A481

Woman: 90c, With bird and flame. $1, With necklace.

2001, Mar. 8 ***Perf. 14***

2892-2893 A481 Set of 2 1.40 1.40

Mushrooms — A482

Designs: 20c, Amanita fulva. 90c, Hygrophorus speciosus. $1.10, Amanita phalloides. $2, Cantharellus cibarius.

No. 2898, $1.40: a, Amanita muscaria. b, Boletus zelleri. c, Coprinus picaceus. d, Stroharia aeruginosa. e, Lepista nuda. f, Hygrophorus conicus.

No. 2899, $1.40: a, Lactarius deliciosus. b, Hygrophorus psittacinus. c, Tricholomopsis rutilans. d, Hygrophorus coccineus. e, Collybia iocephala. f, Gyromitra esculenta.

No. 2900, $1.40: a, Lactarius peckii. b, Lactarius rufus. c, Cortinarius elatior. d, Boletus luridus. e, Russula cyanoxantha. f, Craterellus cornopioioles.

No. 2901, $5, Cyathus olla. No. 2902, $5, Lycoperdon pyriforme, horiz. No. 2903, $5, Pleurotus ostreatus, horiz.

Perf. 13½x13¼, 13¼x13½

2001, Mar. 15

2894-2897 A482 Set of 4 3.25 3.25

Sheets of 6, #a-f

2898-2900 A482 Set of 3 19.00 19.00

Souvenir Sheets

2901-2903 A482 Set of 3 11.00 11.00

A484

A485

Butterflies and Moths A486

Designs: No. 2904, 10c, Tiger. No. 2905, 20c, Figure-of-eight. No. 2906, 50c, Mosaic. No. 2907, 90c, Monarch. No. 2908, $1, Blue-green reflector. No. 2909, $2, Blue tharops.

No. 2910, 10c, Eunica alemena. No. 2911, 70c, Euphaedra medon. No. 2912, 90c, Prepona praeneste. No. 2913, $1, Gold-banded forester.

No. 2914, 20c, Ancycluris formosissima. No. 2915, 50c, Callicore cynosura. No. 2916, 70c, Nessaea obrinus. No. 2917, $2, Eunica alemena.

No. 2918, 90c: a, Orange theope. b, Blue night. c, Small lace-wing. d, Grecian shoemaker. e, Clorinde. f, Orange-barred sulphur.

No. 2919, $1.10: a, Atala. b, Giant swallowtail. c, Banded king shoemaker. d, White peacock. e, Cramer's mesene. f, Polydamas swallowtail.

No. 2920, 90c: a, Cepora aspasia. b, Morpho aega. c, Mazuca amoeva. d, Beautiful tiger. e, Gold-drop helicopsis. f, Esmerelda.

No. 2921, $1.10: a, Lilac nymph. b, Ruddy dagger wing. c, Tiger pierid. d, Orange forester. e, Prepona deiphile. f, Phoebus avellaneda.

No. 2922, $1: a, Calisthenia salvinii flying downward. b, Perisama vaninka. c, Malachite. d, Diaethria aurelia. e, Perisama conplandi. f, Cramer's mesene. g, Calisthenia salvinii flying upward. h, Carpella districata.

No. 2923, $1: a, Euphaedra heophron. b, Milionia grandis. c, Ruddy dagger wiry. d, Bocotus bacotus. e, Cream spot tiger moth. f, Yellow tiger moth. g, Baorisa hiroglyphica. h, Jersey tiger.

No. 2924, $5, Small flambeau. No. 2925, $5, Common morpho, vert. No. 2926, $5, Heliconius sapho. No. 2927, $5 Ornate moth. No. 2928, $5, Hewitson's blue hair streak. No. 2929, $5, Anaxita drucei.

Perf. 13¼x13½, 13½x13¼

2001, Mar. 22 **Litho.**

2904-2909 A484 Set of 6 3.50 3.50
2910-2913 A485 Set of 4 2.00 2.00
2914-2917 A486 Set of 4 2.50 2.50

Sheets of 6, #a-f

2918-2919 A484 Set of 2 9.00 9.00
2920-2921 A485 Set of 2 9.00 9.00

Sheets of 8, #a-h

2922-2923 A486 Set of 2 12.00 12.00

Souvenir Sheets

2924-2925 A484 Set of 2 7.50 7.50
2926-2927 A485 Set of 2 7.50 7.50
2928-2929 A486 Set of 2 7.50 7.50

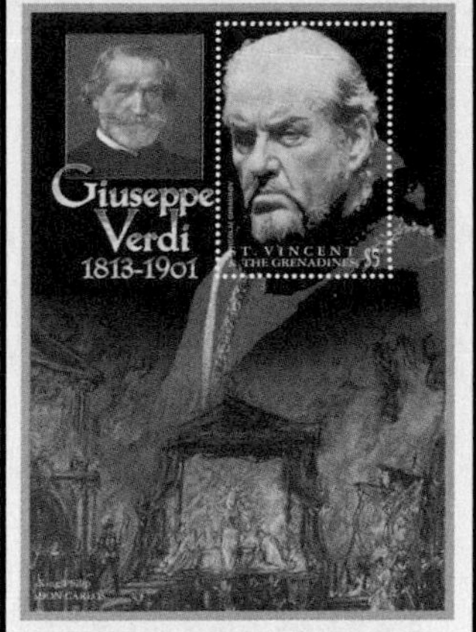

Giuseppe Verdi (1813-1901), Opera Composer — A487

No. 2930: a, Mario Del Monaco, Raina Kabaivanska in Othello. b, 1898 Costume design for Iago. c, 1898 costume design for Othello. d, Anna Tomowa-Sintow as Desdemona.

$5, Nicolai Ghiaurov in Othello.

2001, June 12 **Litho.** ***Perf. 14***

2930 A487 $2 Sheet of 4, #a-d 6.00 6.00

Souvenir Sheet

2931 A487 $5 multi 3.75 3.75

Toulouse-Lautrec Paintings — A488

No. 2932: a, Portrait of Comtesse Adèle-Zoé de Toulouse-Lautrec. b, Carmen. c, Madame Lily Grenier.

$5, Jane Avril.

2001, June 12 ***Perf. 13¾***

2932 A488 $3 Sheet of 3, #a-c 6.75 6.75

Souvenir Sheet

2933 A488 $5 multi 3.75 3.75

Mao Zedong (1893-1976) — A489

No. 2934: a, In 1924. b, In 1938. c, In 1945.

$5, Undated portrait.

2001, June 12

2934 A489 $2 Sheet of 3, #a-c 4.50 4.50

Souvenir Sheet

2935 A489 $5 multi 3.75 3.75

Queen Victoria (1819-1901) — A490

No. 2936: a, As young lady in dark blue dress. b, In white dress. c, With flowers in hair. d, Wearing crown. e, Wearing black dress, facing forward. f, With gray hair.

$5, Sky in background.

2001, June 12 ***Perf. 14***

2936 A490 $1.10 Sheet of 6, #a-f 5.00 5.00

Souvenir Sheet

Perf. 13¾

2937 A490 $5 multi 3.75 3.75

No. 2936 contains six 28x42mm stamps.

Queen Elizabeth II, 75th Birthday — A491

No. 2938: a, With gray hat. b, In gray jacket, no hat. c, In dark blue dress. d, Wearing tiara. e, With blue hat. f, With green hat.

$5, In uniform.

2001, June 12 ***Perf. 14***

2938 A491 $1.10 Sheet of 6, #a-f 5.00 5.00

Souvenir Sheet

Perf. 13¾

2939 A491 $5 multi 3.75 3.75

No. 2938 contains six 28x42mm stamps.

Monet Paintings — A492

Designs: No. 2940, $2, Venice at Dusk (shown). No. 2941, $2, Regatta at Argenteuil. No. 2942, $2, Grain Stacks, End of Summer, Evening Effect. No. 2943, $2, Impression, Sunrise.

$5, Parisians Enjoying the Parc Monceau, vert.

2001, June 12 ***Perf. 13¾***
2940-2943 A492 Set of 4 6.00 6.00

Souvenir Sheet

2944 A492 $5 multi 3.75 3.75

Phila Nippon '01, Japan
A493

Designs: 10c, The Courtesan Sunimoto of the Okanaya, by Koryusai Isoda. 15c, Oiran at Shinto Shrine-Shotenyama, by Kiyonaga. No. 2947, 20c, Two Girls on a Veranda, by Kiyonaga. No. 2948, 20c, Rooster, from A Variety of Birds, by Hoen Nishiyama, horiz. 50c, On Banks of the Sumida, by Kiyonaga. 70c, Three ducks, from A Variety of Birds, horiz. 90c, Seven ducks, from A Variety of Birds, horiz. $1, Three pigeons and other birds from A Variety of Birds, horiz. $1.10, Two birds, from A Variety of Birds, horiz. $2, Five birds, from A Variety of Birds.

No. 2955, $1.40 — Paintings by Eishi: a, Toriwagi, Geisha of Kanaya, Writing. b, Courtesan Preparing for Doll Festival. c, Two Court Ladies in a Garden. d, Lady With a Lute.

No. 2956, $1.40 — Portraits by Sharaku: a, Oniji Otani II as Edohei, a Yakko. b, Hanshiro Iwai IV. c, Kikunojo Segawa. d, Komazo Ichikawa II.

No. 2957, $1.40 — Paintings by Harunobu Suzuki: a, 6 Tama Rivers, Girls by Lespedeza Bush in Moonlight. b, Warming Sake with Maple Leaves. c, Young Samurai on Horseback. d, 6 Tamu Rivers, Ide No Tamagawa.

No. 2958, $1.40 — Paintings by Harunobu Suzuki: a, Girl on River Bank. b, Horseman Guided by Peasant Girl. c, Komachi Praying for Rain. d, Washing Clothes in the Stream.

No. 2959, $5, Peasants Ferried Across Sumida, by Hokkei. No. 2960. $5, Shadows on the Shoji, by Kikukawa. No. 2961, $5, Boy Spying on Lovers, by Suzuki. No. 2962, $5, Tayu Komurasaki and Hanamurasaki of the Kado Tamaya, by Masanobu Kitao. No. 2963, $5, Gathering Lotus Flowers, by Suzuki.

2001, June 12 **Litho.** ***Perf. 13¾***
2945-2954 A493 Set of 10 5.25 5.25

Sheets of 4, #a-d

2955-2958 A493 Set of 4 17.00 17.00

Souvenir Sheets

2959-2963 A493 Set of 5 19.00 19.00

Dale Earnhardt (1951-2001), Stock Car Racer — A494

Designs: a, Dale Earnhardt, Jr. b, Dale and Dale, Jr. with trophy. c, Dale. d, Dale with trophy. e, Dale and Dale, Jr. embracing. f, Dale Jr. with trophy.

2001, July 16
2964 A494 $2 Sheet of 6, #a-f + label 9.00 9.00

Wedding of Norwegian Prince Haakon and Mette-Marie Tjessem Hoiby — A495

2001, Aug. 1 ***Perf. 14***
2965 A495 $5 multi 3.75 3.75

Printed in sheets of 4.

Dinosaurs and Prehistoric Animals — A496

Designs: 10c, Mammoth. 20c, Pinacosaurus. No. 2968, 90c, Oviraptor. $1, Centrosaurus. No. 2970, $1.40, Protoceratops. $2, Bactrosaurus.

No. 2972, 90c: a, Saltasaurus. b, Apatosaurus. c, Brachiosaurus. d, Troodon. e, Deinonychus. f, Segnosaurus.

No. 2973, 90c: a, Iguanodon. b, Hypacrosaurus. c, Ceratosaurus. d, Hypsilophodon. e, Herrerasaurus. f, Velociraptor.

No. 2974, $1.40: a, Pteranodon. b, Archaeopteryx. c, Eudimorphodon. d, Shonisaurus. e, Elasmosaurus. f, Kronosaurus.

No. 2975, $1.40: a, Allosaurus. b, Dilophosaurus. c, Lambeosaurus. d, Coelophysis. e, Ornitholestes. f, Eustreptospondylus.

No. 2976, $5, Stegosaurus. No. 2977, $5, Triceratops. No. 2978, $5, Parasaurolophus, vert. No. 2979, $5, Tyrannosaurus, vert.

2001, Oct. 15 **Litho.** ***Perf. 14x13¾***
2966-2971 A496 Set of 6 4.25 4.25

Sheets of 6, #a-f

2972-2975 A496 Set of 4 21.00 21.00

Souvenir Sheets

Perf. 13¾

2976-2979 A496 Set of 4 15.00 15.00

Nos. 2976-2977 each contain one 50x38mm stamp; Nos. 2978-2979 each contain one 38x50mm stamp.

Photomosaic of Queen Elizabeth II — A497

2001, Nov. 12 ***Perf. 14***
2980 A497 $1 multi 1.10 1.10

Printed in sheets of 8.

2002 World Cup Soccer Championships, Japan and Korea — A498

Players and flags — No. 2981, $1.40: a, Hong Myung-Bo, Korea. b, Hidetoshi Nakata, Japan. c, Ronaldo, Brazil. d, Paolo Maidini, Italy. e, Peter Schmeichel, Denmark. f, Raul Blanco, Spain.

No. 2982, $1.40: a, Kim Bong Soo, Korea. b, Masami Ihara, Japan. c, Marcel Desailly, France. d, David Beckham, England. e, Carlos Valderrama, Colombia. f, George Popescu, Romania.

No. 2983, $5, Seoul World Cup Stadium. No. 2984, $5, International Yokohama Stadium.

2001, Nov. 29 **Sheets of 6, #a-f**
2981-2982 A498 Set of 2 12.50 12.50

Souvenir Sheets

2983-2984 A498 Set of 2 7.50 7.50

Nos. 2983-2984 each contain one 63x31mm stamp.

Attack on Pearl Harbor, 60th Anniv. — A499

No. 2985, $1.40, horiz.: a, Japanese bombing Pearl Harbor. b, Japanese pilot ties on a hachimaki. c, Emperor Hirohito. d, Japanese Adm. Isoroku Yamamoto. e, Japanese fighter planes from aircraft carrier Akagi. f, Japanese Zero plane.

No. 2986, $1.40, horiz.: a, Japanese fighter from the Kaga over Ewa Marine Base. b, Hero Dorie Miller downing four Japanese planes. c, Battleship USS Nevada sinking. d, American sailors struggle on the USS Oklahoma. e, Japanese plane takes off from the Akagi. f, Rescue during bombing.

No. 2987, $5, Dorie Miller receiving navy Cross from Adm. Chester Nimitz. No. 2988, $5, Second wave of attack at Wheeler Field, horiz.

2001, Dec. 7 **Sheets of 6, #a-f**
2985-2986 A499 Set of 2 12.50 12.50

Souvenir Sheets

2987-2988 A499 Set of 2 7.50 7.50

Pres. John F. Kennedy — A500

Pres. Kennedy — No. 2989, $1.40: a, With John, Jr. b, With Jacqueline (red dress). c, With Caroline. d, With family, 1963. e, With Jacqueline, at sea. f, With Jacqueline (white dress).

No. 2990, $1.40: a, At 1956 Democratic Convention. b, Campaigning with Jacqueline, 1959. c, At White House, 1960. d, With brother Robert. e, Announcing Cuban blockade, 1962. f, John Jr. saluting father's casket.

No. 2991, $5, Portrait with violet background. No. 2992, $5, Portrait with green background.

2001, Dec. 7 **Sheets of 6, #a-f**
2989-2990 A500 Set of 2 12.50 12.50

Souvenir Sheets

2991-2992 A500 Set of 2 7.50 7.50

Princess Diana (1961-97) — A501

Flowers and Diana: a, In gray suit. b, In pink dress. c, With tiara.

$5, With tirara and high-necked gown.

2001, Dec. 7
2993 A501 $1.40 Sheet, 2 each #a-c 6.25 6.25

Souvenir Sheet

2994 A501 $5 multi 3.75 3.75

Moths
A502

Designs: 70c, Croker's frother. 90c, Virgin tiger moth. $1, Leopard moth. $2, Fiery campylotes.

No. 2999, $1.40: a, Buff-tip. b, Elephant hawkmoth. c, Streaked sphinx. d, Cizara hawkmoth. e, Hakea moth. f, Boisduval's autumnal moth.

No. 3000, $1.40: a, Eyespot anthelid. b, Collenette's variegated browntail. c, Common epicoma moth. d, Staudinger's longtail. e, Green silver lines. f, Salt marsh moth.

No. 3001, $5, Gypsy moth. No. 3002, Orizaba silkmoth caterpillar.

2001, Dec. 10
2995-2998 A502 Set of 4 3.50 3.50

Sheets of 6, #a-f

2999-3000 A502 Set of 2 12.50 12.50

Souvenir Sheets

3001-3002 A502 Set of 2 7.50 7.50

Christmas — A503

Paintings: 10c, Madonna and Child, by Francesco Guardi. 20c, The Immaculate Conception, by Giovanni Battista Tiepolo. 70c, Adoration of the Magi, by Tiepolo. 90c, The Virgin, by Tintoretto. $1.10, The Annunciation, by Veronese. $1.40 Madonna della Quaglia, by Antonio Pisanello.

$5, Madonna and Child Appear to St. Philip Neri, by Tiepolo.

2001, Dec. 12
3003-3008 A503 Set of 6 3.25 3.25

Souvenir Sheet

3009 A503 $5 multi 3.75 3.75

Queen Mother Type of 1999 Redrawn

No. 3010: a, In 1909. b, With King George, Princess Elizabeth, 1930. c, At Badminton, 1977. d, In 1983.

$6, In 1987.

2001, Dec. 13 ***Perf. 14***
Yellow Orange Frames

3010 A438 $2 Sheet of 4, #a-d, + label 6.00 6.00

Souvenir Sheet
Perf. 13¾

3011 A438 $6 multi 4.50 4.50

Queen Mother's 101st birthday. No. 3010 contains one 38x50mm stamp with a greener background than that found on No. 2730. Sheet margins of Nos. 3010-3011 lack embossing and gold arms and frames found on Nos. 2729-2730.

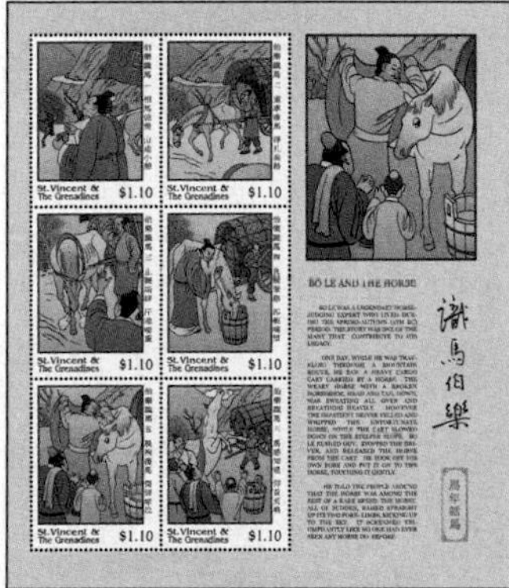

New Year 2002 (Year of the Horse) — A504

Scenes from Bo Le and the Horse: a, Man pointing at horse. b, Horse pulling cart. c, Horse snorting. d, Horse drinking. e, Man putting robe on horse. f, Horse rearing.

2001, Dec. 17 ***Perf. 13¾***
3012 A504 $1.10 Sheet of 6, #a-f 5.00 5.00

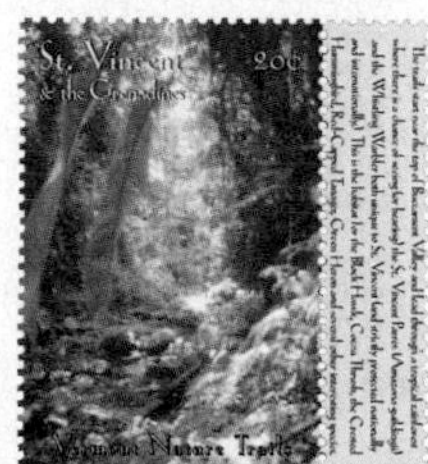

Tourism A505

Designs: 20c, Vermont Nature Trails. 70c, Tamarind Beach Hotel, horiz. 90c, Tobago Cays, horiz. $1.10, Trinity Falls.

2001, Dec. 31 ***Perf. 14***
Stamps + labels

3013-3016 A505 Set of 4 2.25 2.25

Fauna — A506

No. 3017, $1.40, vert.: a, Bumble bee. b, Green darner dragonfly. c, Small lace-wing. d, Black widow spider. e, Praying mantis. f, Firefly.

No. 3018, $1.40: a, Caspian tern. b, White-tailed tropicbird. c, Black-necked stilt. d, Black-billed plover. e, Black-winged stilt. f, Ruddy turnstone.

No. 3019, $5, Blue night butterfly. No. 3020, $5, Brown pelican, vert.

2001, Dec. 10 **Litho.** ***Perf. 14***
Sheets of 6, #a-f

3017-3018 A506 Set of 2 12.50 12.50

Souvenir Sheets

3019-3020 A506 Set of 2 7.50 7.50

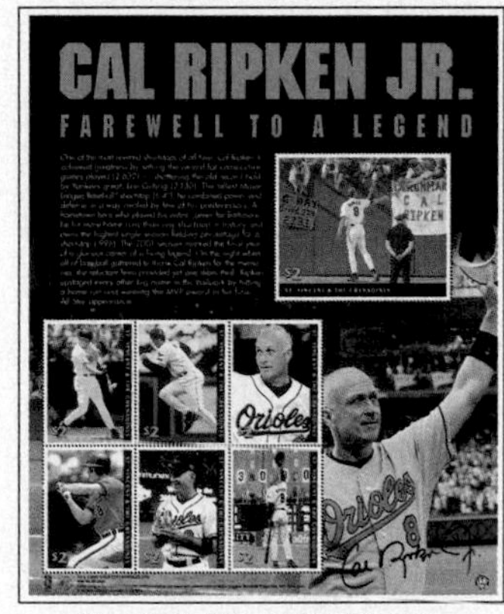

Baseball Player Cal Ripken, Jr. — A507

No. 3021: a, Hitting ball. b, Running. c, Without hat. d, Batting (orange shirt). e, Holding trophy. f, Waving hat. g, Greeting fans (68x56mm).

$6, Wearing batting helmet.

2001, Dec. 27 ***Perf. 13¼***
3021 A507 $2 Sheet of 7, #a-g 10.50 10.50

Souvenir Sheet
Perf. 13x13¼

3022 A507 $6 multi 4.50 4.50

No. 3022 contains one 36x56mm stamp.

United We Stand — A508

2001, Dec. 28 ***Perf. 14***
3023 A508 $2 multi 1.50 1.50

Reign of Queen Elizabeth II, 50th Anniv. — A509

No. 3024: a, With Prince Philip. b, With Princess Margaret. c, Wearing blue dress. d, In wedding gown.

$5, Wearing orange brown dress.

2002, Apr. 8 **Litho.** ***Perf. 14¼***
3024 A509 $2 Sheet of 4, #a-d 5.50 5.50

Souvenir Sheet

3025 A509 $5 multi 3.25 3.25

Pan-American Health Organization, Cent. — A510

Designs: 20c, Anniversary emblem, vert. 70c, Dr. Gideon Cordice, vert. 90c, Dr. Arthur Cecil Cyrus, vert. $1.10, Headquarters, Christ Church, Barbados.

2002, Apr. 8 ***Perf. 14***
3026-3029 A510 Set of 4 2.40 2.40

Vincy Mas, 25th Anniv. — A511

Designs: 10c, Section of the Bands. 20c, Cocktail, the Blue Dragon, horiz. 70c, Safari, Snake in the Grass. 90c, Bridgette Creese, 2001 Calypso Monarch. $1.10, Heat Wave, horiz. $1.40, Sion Hill Steel Orchestra, horiz.

2002, June 15 **Litho.** ***Perf. 14***
3030-3035 A511 Set of 6 3.50 3.50

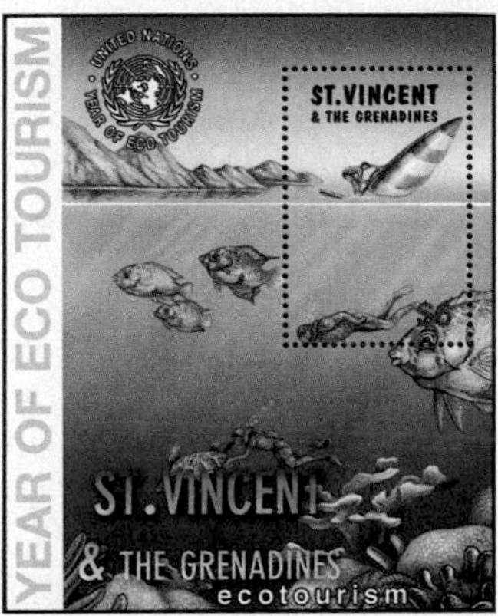

Intl. Year of Ecotourism — A512

No. 3036: a, Butterfly. b, Manatee. c, Deer. d, Plant.

$6, Windsurfer, divers and fish.

2002, July 1 ***Perf. 13½x13¼***
3036 A512 $2 Sheet of 4, #a-d 6.00 6.00

Souvenir Sheet

3037 A512 $6 multi 4.50 4.50

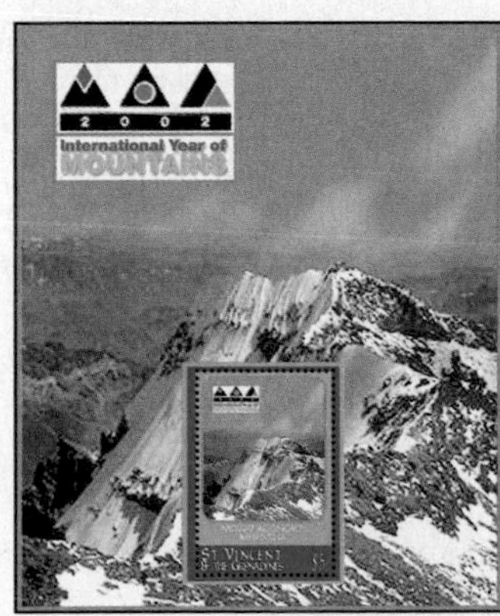

Intl. Year of Mountains — A513

No. 3038: a, Mt. Ararat, Turkey. b, Mt. Ama Dablam, Nepal. c, Mt. Cook, New Zealand. d, Mt. Kilimanjaro, Tanzania. e, Mt. Kenya, Kenya. f, Giant's Castle, South Africa.

$5, Mt. Aconcagua, Argentina.

2002, July 1
3038 A513 $1.40 Sheet of 6, #a-f 6.25 6.25

Souvenir Sheet

3039 A513 $5 multi 3.75 3.75

20th World Scout Jamboree, Thailand — A514

No. 3040, horiz.: a, Scout with kudu horn. b, Scouts breaking camp. c, Daniel Beard and Lord Robert Baden-Powell.

No. 3041, Scout.

2002, July 1 ***Perf. 13¼x13½***
3040 A514 $5 Sheet of 3, #a-c 11.50 11.50

Souvenir Sheet
Perf. 13½x13¼

3041 A514 $5 multi 3.75 3.75

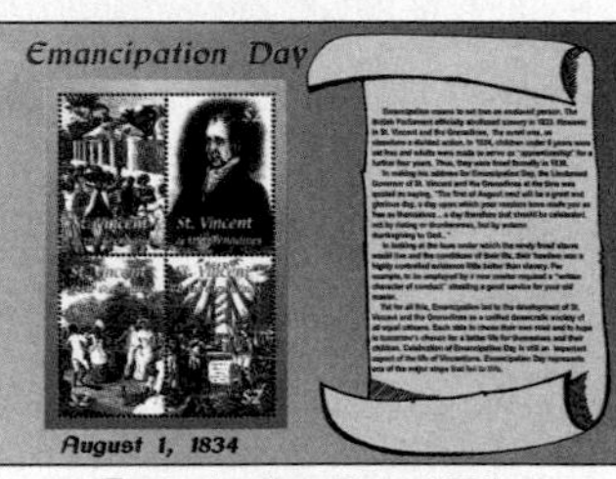

Emancipation Day, 168th Anniv. — A515

No. 3042: a, Crowd near fence. b, Lieutenant Governor of St. Vincent. c, Black couple dancing, white couple. d, Allegory of freedom.

2002, Aug. 1 ***Perf. 14***
3042 A515 $2 Sheet of 4, #a-d 6.00 6.00

2002 Winter Olympics, Salt Lake City A516

Designs: No. 3043, $3, Biathlon. No. 3044, $3, Freestyle skiing.

2002, July 1 **Litho.** ***Perf. 13¼x13½***
3043-3044 A516 Set of 2 4.50 4.50
3044a Souvenir sheet, #3043-3044 4.50 4.50

Elvis Presley (1935-77) A517

Designs: $1, With red background.

No. 3046: a, Playing guitar. b, In Army uniform. c, In suit, with guitar strap. d, With vertically striped shirt, looking left. e, In horizontally striped shirt. f, In vertically striped shirt, looking forward.

2002, Aug. 19 ***Perf. 13¾***
3045 A517 $1 multi .75 .75
3046 A517 $1.25 Sheet of 6, #a-f 5.75 5.75

No. 3045 printed in sheets of nine.

Souvenir Sheet

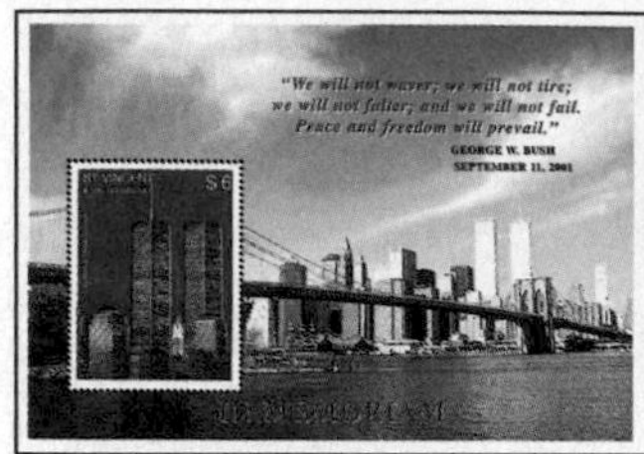

In Remembrance of Sept. 11, 2001 Terrorist Attacks — A518

2002, Sept. 11 ***Perf. 13¾***
3047 A518 $6 multi 4.50 4.50

Teddy Bears, Cent. — A519

No. 3048, $2, vert.: a, Cowboy bear. b, Fisherman bear. c, Camper bear. d, Hiker bear.
No. 3049, $2, vert.: a, Bear in kimono. b, Two bears. c, Bear with hair ribbon, baby bear. d, Bear with sunglasses.
No. 3050, vert.: a, Bear with red dress and cap. b, Bear with bonnet. c, Bear with strapless dress. d, Bear with dress with red ruffled collar. e, Bear with blue dress with ribbon.
No. 3051, $5, Four bears by Terumi Yoshikawa. No. 3052, $5, Four bears by Tomoko Suenaga.

2002, Sept. 23 ***Perf. 13¾ (#3048), 14***
Sheets of 4, #a-d
3048-3049 A519 Set of 2 12.00 12.00
3050 A519 $2 Sheet of 5, #a-e 7.50 7.50
Souvenir Sheets
3051-3052 A519 Set of 2 7.50 7.50

No. 3048 contains four 38x50mm stamps.

Souvenir Sheets

British Military Medals — A520

Designs: No. 3053, $5, Waterloo Medal. No. 3054, $5, South African War Medal. No. 3055, $5, Queen's South Africa Medal. No. 3056, $5, 1914-15 Star. No. 3057, $5, British War Medal.

2002, Oct. 7 ***Perf. 14¼***
3053-3057 A520 Set of 5 19.00 19.00

2002 World Cup Soccer Championship Semifinals, Japan and Korea — A521

No. 3058, $1.40: a, Kleberson and Emre Belozoglu. b, Cafu. c, Roberto Carlos. d, Yildiray Basturk. e, Tugay Kerimoglu and Rivaldo. f, Bulent.
No. 3059, $1.40: a, Ji Sung Park and Dietmar Hamann. b, Miroslav Klose and Tae Young Kim. c, Chong Gug Song and Christoph Metzelder. d, Tae Young Kim and Gerald Asamoah. e, Torsten Frings and Ji Sung Park. f, Oliver Neuville and Tae Young Kim.
No. 3060, $3: a, Ronaldo. b, Cafu, diff.
No. 3061, $3: a, Michael Ballack. b, Oliver Kahn.
No. 3062, $3: a, Bulent, diff. b, Yildiray Basturk, diff.
No. 3063, $3: a, Tae Young Kim. b, Du Ri Cha.

2002, Nov. 4 ***Perf. 13¼***
Sheets of 6, #a-f
3058-3059 A521 Set of 2 12.50 12.50
Souvenir Sheets of 2, #a-b
3060-3063 A521 Set of 4 18.00 18.00

Shirley Temple Movie Type of 2000

Temple in "Dimples" — No. 3046, horiz.: a, Embracing man. b, Conducting musicians. c, Seated, in blue dress. d, On stage with actors in black-face. e, Head on pillow. f, With woman, holding plate.
No. 3047: a, Standing on barrel. b, In green dress. c, Adjusting man's ascot. d, With seated woman.
$5, Dancing with man in black face.

2002, Oct. 28 ***Perf. 14¼***
3064 A471 $1.40 Sheet of 6, #a-f 6.25 6.25
3065 A471 $2 Sheet of 4, #a-d 6.00 6.00
Souvenir Sheet
3066 A471 $5 multi 3.75 3.75

Queen Mother Elizabeth (1900-2002) — A522

No. 3067: a, Wearing blue hat and dress. b, Wearing purple hat, dress and corsage. c, Wearing flowered hat.

2002, Nov. 9 **Litho.** ***Perf. 14***
3067 A522 $2 Sheet of 4, #a-b, 2 #c 6.00 6.00

Christmas — A523

Designs: 20c, Greek Madonna, by Giovanni Bellini. 90c, Kneeling Agostino Barbarigo, by Bellini. $1.10, Presentation of Jesus in the Temple, by Perugino. $1.40, Madonna and Child with the Infant St. John, by Perugino. $1.50, San Giobbe Altarpiece, by Bellini.
$5, Madonna and Child with Saints John the Baptist and Sebastian, by Perugino, horiz.

2002, Nov. 18
3068-3072 A523 Set of 5 4.00 4.00
Souvenir Sheet
3073 A523 $5 multi 3.75 3.75

Souvenir Sheets

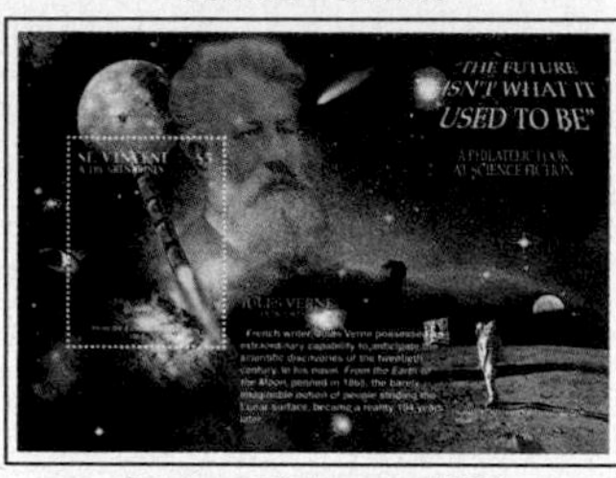

Science Fiction — A524

Designs: No. 3074, $5, From the Earth to the Moon, by Jules Verne. No. 3075, $5, The War of the Worlds, by H. G. Wells. No. 3076, $5, The Time Machine, by Wells.

2002, Dec. 2 ***Perf. 13¾***
3074-3076 A524 Set of 3 11.50 11.50

Intl. Federation of Stamp Dealers Associations, 50th Anniv. — A525

2003, Feb. 16 ***Perf. 14***
3077 A525 $2 multi 1.50 1.50

British Military Medals Type of 2002
Souvenir Sheets

Designs: No. 3078, $5, Victory Medal. No. 3079, $5, Atlantic Star. No. 3080, $5, 1939-45 Star. No. 3081, $5, Africa Star.

2003, Jan. 27 ***Perf. 13¼***
3078-3081 A520 Set of 4 15.00 15.00

New Year 2003 (Year of the Ram) — A526

No. 3082: a, Goat with gray collar. b, Goat facing left. c, Goats and kid. d, Man on goat. e, Goat facing right. f, Goat with piebald coat (flora in background).

2003, Feb. 1 ***Perf. 14¼x13¾***
3082 A526 $1 Sheet of 6, #a-f 4.50 4.50

Miniature Sheet

Reign of Queen Elizabeth II, 50th Anniv. (in 2002) — A527

Litho. & Embossed
2003, Feb. 24 ***Perf. 13¼x13***
3083 A527 $20 gold & multi 15.00 15.00

Astronauts Killed in Space Shuttle Columbia Accident — A528

No. 3084, $2 — Col. Rick D. Husband: a, Crew photo (green sky). b, Husband, interior of shuttle. c, Shuttle landing. d, Shuttle and space station.
No. 3085, $2 — Commander William C. McCool: a, Crew photo (tan sky). b, McCool in airplane cockpit. c, McCool, interior of shuttle. d, Shuttle in flight, comet.
No. 3086, $2 — Capt. David M. Brown: a, Crew photo (cloudy sky). b, Shuttle being moved to launch pad. c, Shuttle orbiting earth. d, Brown, interior of shuttle.

2003, Apr. 7 **Litho.** ***Perf. 14¼***
Sheets of 4, #a-d
3084-3086 A528 Set of 3 18.00 18.00

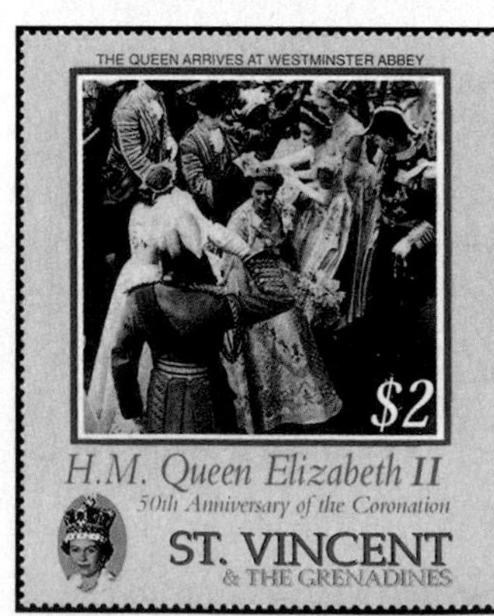

Coronation of Queen Elizabeth II, 50th Anniv. — A529

Designs: No. 3087, $2, Queen arrives at Westminster Abbey. No. 3088, $2, Queen seated in Chair of Estate. No. 3089, $2, Queen's first progress along the nave. No. 3090, $2, Queen leaving Buckingham Palace. No. 3091, $2, Queen and Duke of Edinburgh in state coach. No. 3092, $2, Gold state coach. No. 3093, $2, Westminster Abbey.
$5, Queen's portrait.

2003, Feb. 26 **Litho.** ***Perf. 13¼***
3087-3093 A529 Set of 7 10.50 10.50
Souvenir Sheet
Perf. 14¼
3094 A529 $5 multi 3.75 3.75

No. 3094 contains one 38x50mm stamp.

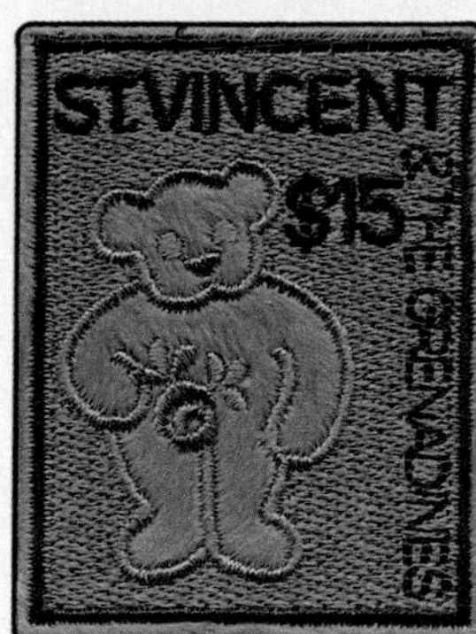
Teddy Bear A530

Self-Adhesive

2003, Apr. 30 Embroidered *Imperf.*
3095 A530 $15 multi 11.50 11.50

Issued in sheets of 4.

Japanese Art — A531

Designs: 70c, A Gathering of Sorcerers on the Tokaido Road (detail), by Kunisada Utagawa. $1.10, Kiyohime and the Moon, by Chikanobu Yoshu. $1.40, A Gathering of Sorcerers on the Tokaido Road (detail), by Kunisada Utagawa, diff. $3, A Gathering of Sorcerers on the Tokaido Road (detail), by Kunisada Utagawa, diff.

No. 3100: a, Snake Mountain, by Kuniyoshi Utagawa. b, Sadanobu and Oni, by Yoshitoshi Tsukioka. c, Shoki, by Tsukioka. d, The Nightly Weeping Rock, by Kuniyoshi Utagawa.

$5, The Ghosts of Matahachi and Kikuno, by Kunisada Utagawa.

2003, Apr. 30 Litho. *Perf. 14¼*
3096-3099 A531 Set of 4 4.75 4.75
3100 A531 $2 Sheet of 4, #a-d 6.00 6.00

Souvenir Sheet

3101 A531 $5 multi 3.75 3.75

Rembrandt Paintings A532

Designs: $1, Portrait of Jacques de Gheyn III. $1.10, Young Man in a Black Beret. $1.40, Hendrickje Stoffels. No. 3105, $2, The Polish Rider, horiz.

No. 3106, $2: a, Belthazzar Sees the Writing on the Wall. b, Portrait of a Young Man. c, Jacob Blessing the Sons of Joseph. d, King Uzzlah Stricken with Leprosy.

$5, The Stoning of St. Stephen.

2003, Apr. 30
3102-3105 A532 Set of 4 4.25 4.25
3106 A532 $2 Sheet of 4, #a-d 6.00 6.00

Souvenir Sheet

3107 A532 $5 multi 3.75 3.75

Paintings By Pablo Picasso — A533

Designs: 60c, Composition: Woman with Half-Length Hair. 70c, Sister of the Artist, vert. 90c, Maternity, vert. $1, Bearded Man's Head, vert. $1.10, Two Seated Children (Claude and Paloma), vert. $1.40, Woman with a Blue Lace Collar.

No. 3114: a, Corrida. b, Mandolin, Pitcher and Bottle. c, The Painter and Model. d, Reclining Woman Sleeping Under a Lamp.

No. 3115, Reclining Nude. No. 3116, Spanish Woman Against an Orange Background, vert.

2003, Apr. 30 *Perf. 14¼*
3108-3113 A533 Set of 6 4.25 4.25
3114 A533 $2 Sheet of 4, #a-d 6.00 6.00

Imperf

Size: 103x82mm

3115 A533 $5 multi 3.75 3.75

Size: 82x105mm

3116 A533 $5 multi 3.75 3.75

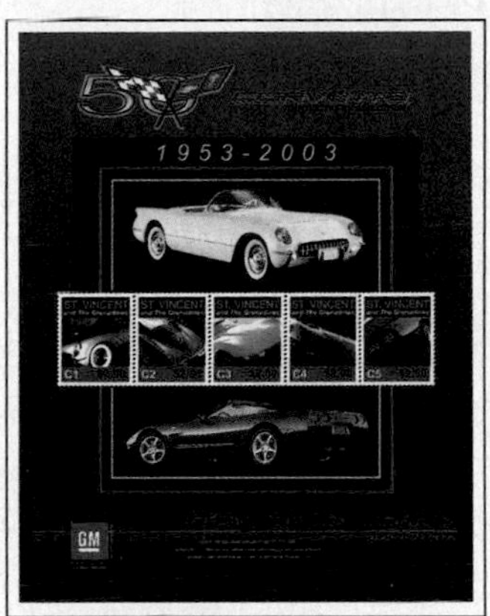
Corvette Automobiles, 50th Anniv. — A534

No. 3117: a, C1. b, C2. c, C3. d, C4. e, C5. No. 3118: a, 1953 Corvette. b, 2003 Corvette.

2003, May 5 *Perf. 13¼*
3117 A534 $2 Sheet of 5, #a-e 7.50 7.50

Perf. 14¼

3118 A534 $3 Sheet of 2, #a-b 4.50 4.50

No. 3118 contains two 50x38mm stamps.

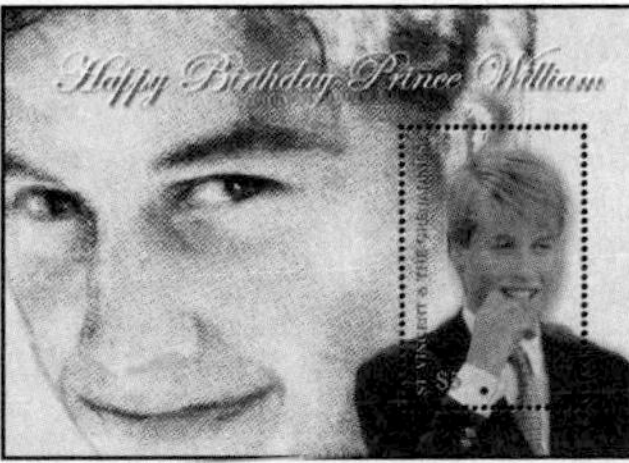
Prince William, 21st Birthday — A535

No. 3119: a, Wearing suit. b, Wearing polo jersey. c, Wearing blue shirt.

$5, Wearing suit and tie.

2003, May 13 *Perf. 14*
3119 A535 $3 Sheet of 3, #a-c 6.75 6.75

Souvenir Sheet

3120 A535 $5 multi 3.75 3.75

Princess Diana (1961-97) — A536

No. 3121, $2 (vignettes in ovals): a, As child in baby carriage. b, With Prince Charles on wedding day. c, With Princes William and Harry. d, In purple jacket.

No. 3122, $2 (white background): a, Wearing tiara. b, Wearing white gown. c, Wearing purple sweater. d, Wearing lilac dress.

2003, May 26 Sheets of 4, #a-d
3121-3122 A536 Set of 2 12.00 12.00

Cadillac Automobiles, Cent. — A537

No. 3123: a, 1953 Eldorado. b, 2002 Eldorado. c, 1967 Eldorado. d, 1962 Series 62.

$5, 1927 LaSalle.

2003, July 1 *Perf. 13¼x13¾*
3123 A537 $2 Sheet of 4, #a-d 6.00 6.00

Souvenir Sheet

3124 A537 $5 multi 3.75 3.75

Intl. Year of Fresh Water — A538

No. 3125: a, Owia Salt Pond. b, The Soufriere. c, Falls of Baleine.

$5, Trinity Falls.

2003, July 1 *Perf. 13½*
3125 A538 $3 Sheet of 3, #a-c 6.75 6.75

Souvenir Sheet

3126 A538 $5 multi 3.75 3.75

Circus — A539

No. 3127, $2: a, Linny. b, Bruce Feiler. c, Segey Provirin. d, Weezle.

No. 3128, $2: a, Mermaids. b, Robert Wolf. c, Elbrus Pilev's Group. d, Stinky.

2003, July 1 *Perf. 14*

Sheets of 4, #a-d

3127-3128 A539 Set of 2 12.00 12.00

Tour de France Bicycle Race, Cent. — A540

No. 3129: a, Antonin Magne, 1931. b, André Leducq, 1932. c, Georges Speicher, 1933. d, Magne, 1934.

No. 3130: a, Romain Maes, 1935. b, Sylvére Maes, 1936. c, Roger Lapebie, 1937. d, Gino Bartali, 1938.

No. 3131: a, Sylvére Maes, 1939. b, Jean Lazaridés, 1946. c, Jean Robic, 1947. d, Bartali, 1948.

No. 3132, $5, Magne, 1931, 1934. No. 3133, $5, Fausto Coppi, 1949. No. 3134, $5, Ferdinand Kubler, 1950.

2003, July 1 *Perf. 13¼*

Sheets of 4, #a-d

3129-3131 A540 Set of 3 18.00 18.00

Souvenir Sheets

3132-3134 A570 Set of 3 11.50 11.50

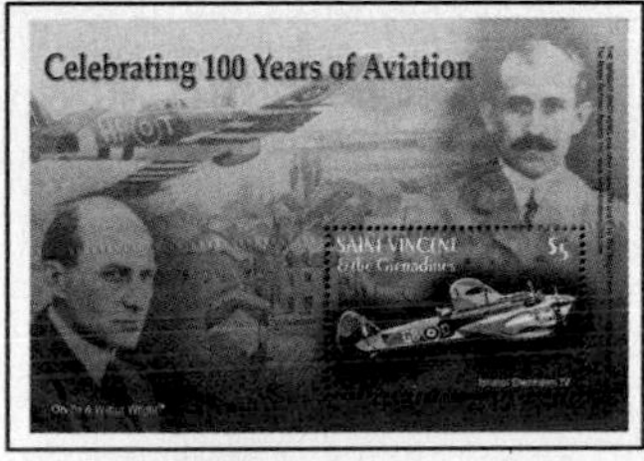
Powered Flight, Cent. — A541

No. 3135, $2: a, Handley Page Heyford. b, Heinkel He-111B. c, Gloster Gauntlet. d, Curtiss BF2C-1.

No. 3136, $2: a, Mitsubishi A6M Reisen. b, Dewoitine D520. c, Messerschmitt Bf 109E. d, Republic Thunderbolt.

No. 3137, $5, Bristol Blenheim IV. No. 3138, $5, Fairey Flycatcher.

2003, July 15 *Perf. 14*

Sheets of 4, #a-d

3135-3136 A541 Set of 2 12.00 12.00

Souvenir Sheets

3137-3138 A541 Set of 2 7.50 7.50

Salvation Army in St. Vincent, Cent. — A542

Designs: 70c, Chief musicians. 90c, District temple. $1, Christmas Kettle Appeal Fund. $1.10, Headquarters, horiz.

2003, Aug. 1

3139-3142 A542 Set of 4 2.75 2.75

Operation Iraqi Freedom — A543

No. 3143: a, Gen. Richard B. Meyers. b, Lt. Gen. David McKiernan. c, Lt. Gen. Michael Moseley. d, Vice Admiral Timothy Keating. e, Lt. Gen. Jay Garner. f, Gen. Tommy R. Franks. g, Lt. Gen. Earl B. Hailston. h, Gen. John Jumper.

No. 3144: a, Private Jessica Lynch. b, Gen. Franks. c, Spectre gunship. d, Stryker vehicle. e, USS Constellation. f, USS Kitty Hawk.

2003, Aug. 25 *Perf. 14¼*

3143 A543 $1 Sheet of 8, #a-h 6.00 6.00

3144 A543 $1.50 Sheet of 6, #a-f 6.75 6.75

A544

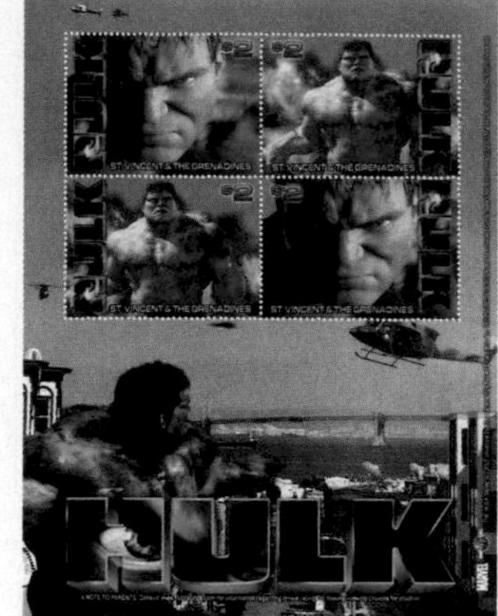

A545

Marvel Comic Book Characters — A546

No. 3145 — Spiderman: a, Shooting cable from arm. b, Grasping two cables. c, Grasping one cable. d, Climbing on building.

No. 3146, $2 — The Incredible Hulk: a, Close-up of face, denomination at UR. b, Fire in background, denomination at UL. c, Like "b," denomination at UR. d, Like "a," denomination at UL.

No. 3147, $2 — The Incredible Hulk: a, Punching ground. b, Grasping. c, Showing fists. d, Punching rocks.

No. 3148, $2 — X-Men United: a, Nightcrawler. b, Professor X. c, Iceman. d, Rogue.

No. 3149, $2 — X-Men United: a, Magneto. b, Mystique. c, Stryker. d, Lady Deathstrike.

No. 3150, $2 — X-Men United: a, Jean Grey. b, Storm. c, Wolverine. d, Cyclops.

2003, Sept. 10 *Perf. 13¼*

3145 A544 $2 Sheet of 4, #a-d 6.00 6.00

Sheets of 4, #a-d

3146-3147 A545 Set of 2 12.00 12.00

3148-3150 A546 Set of 3 18.00 18.00

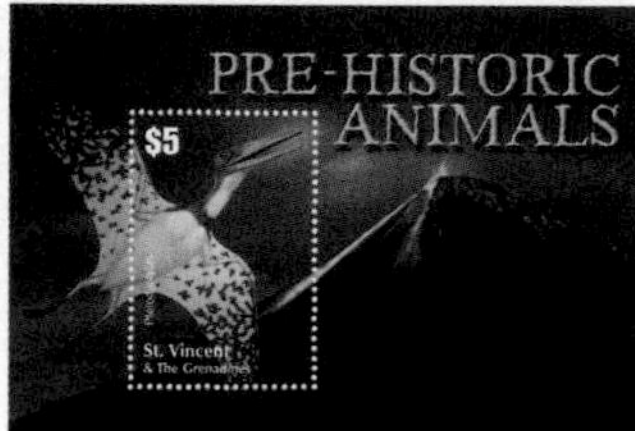

Prehistoric Animals — A547

No. 3151, $2, horiz.: a, Daspletosaurus. b, Utahraptor. c, Scutellosaurus. d, Scelidosaurus.

No. 3152, $2, horiz.: a, Syntarsus. b, Velociraptor. c, Mononikus. d, Massospondylus.

No. 3153, $5, Pterodactylus. No. 3154, $5, Giganotosaurus.

2003, Nov. 5 *Perf. 13¼x13¾*

Sheets of 4, #a-d

3151-3152 A547 Set of 2 12.00 12.00

Souvenir Sheets

Perf. 13¾x13¼

3153-3154 A547 Set of 2 7.50 7.50

Cats — A548

Designs: 50c, British Shorthair. $1, Burmese. $1.40, American Shorthair. $3, Havana Brown.

No. 3159: a, Ocicat. b, Manx. c, Somali. d, Angora.

$5, Abyssinian.

2003, Nov. 5 *Perf. 14*

3155-3158 A548 Set of 4 4.50 4.50

3159 A548 $2 Sheet of 4, #a-d 6.00 6.00

Souvenir Sheet

3160 A548 $5 multi 3.75 3.75

Dogs — A549

Designs: 10c, Chihuahua. 20c, Bulldog. 60c, Weimaraner. No. 3164, $5, Dalmatian.

No. 3165: a, Dachshund. b, Collie. c, Springer spaniel. d, Hamilton hound.

No. 3166, $5, Golden retriever.

2003, Nov. 5

3161-3164 A549 Set of 4 4.50 4.50

3165 A549 $2 Sheet of 4, #a-d 6.00 6.00

Souvenir Sheet

3166 A549 $5 multi 3.75 3.75

Orchids — A550

Designs: 40c, Laelia lobata. 90c, Miltoniopsis phalaenopsis. $1, Phalaenopsis violacea. $3, Trichopilia fragrans.

No. 3171: a, Masdevallia uniflora. b, Laelia flava. c, Barkeria lindleyana. d, Laelia tenebrosa.

$5, Cattleya lawrenceana.

2003, Nov. 5

3167-3170 A550 Set of 4 4.00 4.00

3171 A550 $2 Sheet of 4, #a-d 6.00 6.00

Souvenir Sheet

3172 A550 $5 multi 3.75 3.75

Marine Life — A551

Designs: 70c, Lutjanus kasmira. 90c, Chaetadon collare. $1.10, Istiophorus platypterus. No. 3176, $2, Pomacanthidae.

No. 3177, $2: a, Equetus lanceolatus. b, Hypoplectrus gutavarius. c, Pomacentridae. d, Cichlidae.

$5, Dolphins.

2003, Nov. 5

3173-3176 A551 Set of 4 3.50 3.50

3177 A551 $2 Sheet of 4, #a-d 6.00 6.00

Souvenir Sheet

3178 A551 $5 multi 3.75 3.75

Christmas — A552

Children's contest-winning art by: 70c, Andrew Gonsalves. 90c, Georgia Gravel. $1.10, Adam Gravel, vert.

2003, Nov. 5 *Perf. 14¼*

3179-3181 A552 Set of 3 2.00 2.00

Playboy Magazine, 50th Anniv. — A553

Magazine covers depicting: a, Marilyn Monroe. b, Playboy emblem. c, Rabbit and kisses. d, Woman with legs above head. e, Woman licking stamp. f, 50th Anniversary emblem.

2003, Dec. 1 **Litho.** *Perf. 14*

3182 A553 $1.50 Sheet of 6, #a-f 6.75 6.75

Ma Yuan (1160-1235), Painter — A554

No. 3183: a, Apricot Blossoms. b, Peach Blossoms. c, Unnamed painting, denomination at left. d, Unnamed painting, denomination at right.

$5, On a Mountain Path in Spring.

2004, Jan. 30 *Perf. 13x13½*

3183 A554 $2 Sheet of 4, #a-d 6.00 6.00

Imperf

3184 A554 $5 multi 3.75 3.75

No. 3183 contains four 40x30mm stamps.

Souvenir Sheet

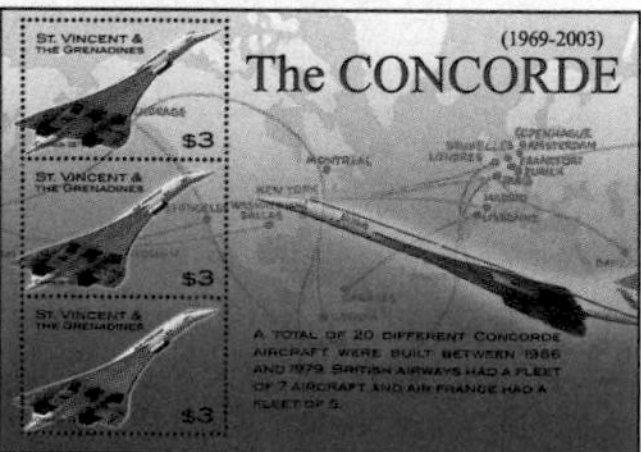

Cessation of Concorde Flights in 2003 — A555

Concorde over map showing: a, Anchorage. b, Los Angeles. c, South Pacific (no cities named).

2004, Feb. 16 *Perf. 13¼x13½*

3185 A555 $3 Sheet of 3, #a-c 6.75 6.75

New Year 2004 (Year of the Monkey) — A556

2004, Jan. 15 Litho. *Perf. 13¼x13*

3186 A556 $1.40 buff, lt brn & blk 1.10 1.10

Souvenir Sheet

3187 A556 $3 pink, brn & blk 2.25 2.25

No. 3186 printed in sheets of 4.

A557

Marilyn Monroe (1926-62), Actress — A558

No. 3188: a, Sepia-toned portrait. b, Wearing blue dress. c, Wearing white dress. d, Wearing black dress.

No. 3189: a, Wearing round white earrings. b, With hand showing. c, Wearing no earrings. d, Wearing different earrings.

2004, May 3 *Perf. 14*

3188 A557 $2 Sheet of 4, #a-d 6.00 6.00

Perf. 13½x13¼

3189 A558 $2 Sheet of 4, #a-d 6.00 6.00

European Soccer Championships, Portugal — A559

No. 3190, vert.: a, Roger Lemerre. b, Marco Delvecchio. c, David Trezeguet. d, De Kuip Stadium.

$5, 2000 French team.

2004, May 17 *Perf. 13½x13¼*

3190 A559 $2 Sheet of 4, #a-d 6.00 6.00

Souvenir Sheet

Perf. 13¼

3191 A559 $5 multi 3.75 3.75

No. 3190 contains four 28x42mm stamps.

2004 Summer Olympics, Athens A560

Designs: 70c, Pierre de Coubertin, first Intl. Olympic Committee Secretary General. $1, Pin from 1904 St. Louis Olympics. $1.40, Water Polo, 1936 Berlin Olympics, horiz. $3, Greek amphora.

2004, June 17 *Perf. 14¼*

3192-3195 A560 Set of 4 4.75 4.75

Babe Ruth (1895-1948), Baseball Player — A561

No. 3196: a, Facing right. b, Facing forward. c, Leaning on bat. d, Swinging bat.

2004, July 1 *Perf. 13½x13¼*

3196 A561 $2 Sheet of 4, #a-d 6.00 6.00

D-Day, 60th Anniv. A562

Designs: 70c, Air Chief Marshal Sir Trafford Leigh-Mallory. 90c, Lt. Col. Maureen Gara. $1, Gen. Omar Bradley. $1.10, Jean Valentine. $1.40, Jack Culshaw. $1.50, Gen. Dwight D. Eisenhower.

No. 3203, $2: a, British land on Gold Beach. b, British infantry land on Gold Beach. c, Canadians at Juno Beach. d, Canadians land at Juno Beach.

No. 3204, $2: a, Rangers take Pointe du Hoc. b, Rangers hold Pointe du Hoc. c, Invasion announced to press. d, British liberate Hermanville.

No. 3205, $5, Soldiers prepare to board assault landing craft. No. 3206, $5, Code breaking team at work.

2004, July 19 *Perf. 14*

Stamp + Label (#3197-3202)

3197-3202 A562 Set of 6 5.00 5.00

Sheets of 4, #a-d

3203-3204 A562 Set of 2 12.00 12.00

Souvenir Sheets

3205-3206 A562 Set of 2 7.50 7.50

General Employees' Cooperative Credit Union — A563

Designs: 70c, GECCU children. 90c, GECCU Building. $1.10, Calvin Nicholls, vert. $1.40, Bertrand Neehall, vert.

2004, Sept. 15 Litho.

3207-3210 A563 Set of 4 3.25 3.25

Pres. Ronald Reagan (1911-2004) A564

No. 3211: a, Portrait. b, With flag. c, At microphone.

2004, Oct. 13 *Perf. 13½x13¼*

3211 Vert. strip of 3 3.25 3.25

a.-c. A564 $1.40 Any single 1.00 1.00

Printed in sheets containing two strips.

Railroads, 200th Anniv. — A565

No. 3212, $2: a, 1911 0-6-0 Standard, Boston & Maine. b, AG locomotive. c, BA 101 Antigua locomotive. d, Aster 1449.

No. 3213, $2: a, Narrow gauge locomotive W12. b, Gambler. LNV9701 4-4-0 NG. c, No. 4 Snowdon. d, Hiawatha 3-1.

No. 3214, $2: a, CO1604-1. b, CP steam locomotive N135. c, 6042-6. d, E1 narrow gauge 0-4-0T.

No. 3215, $5, NAT2A 01-06-00. No. 3216, $5, Union Pacific 844. No. 3217, $5, Holy War-1, vert.

2004, Oct. 13 *Perf. 14*

Sheets of 4, #a-d

3212-3214 A565 Set of 3 18.00 18.00

Souvenir Sheets

3215-3217 A565 Set of 3 11.50 11.50

Independence, 25th Anniv. — A566

Designs: 10c, Halimah DeShong. 20c, Winston Davis, cricket player. No. 3220, 70c, Miss Carnival 2003. No. 3221, 70c, Flag, horiz. No. 3222, 70c, Pamenoa Ballantyne, runner, horiz. No. 3223, 90c, Carl "Blazer" Williams. No. 3224, 90c, Breadfruit, horiz. No. 3225, 90c, Rodney "Chang" Jack, soccer player, horiz. $1.10, St. Vincent parrot. No. 3227, $5, Capt. Hugh Mulzac. No. 3228, $5, George McIntosh, political leader. No. 3229, $5, E. T. Joshua, horiz. No. 3230, $10, Joseph Chatoyer, Carib chief, national hero. No. 3231, $10, Robert Milton Cato, politician.

2004, Oct. 25

3218-3231 A566 Set of 14 31.00 31.00

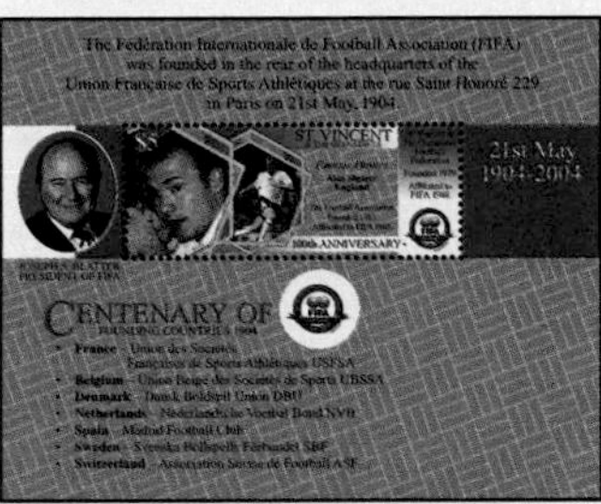

FIFA (Fédération Internationale de Football Association), Cent. — A567

No. 3232: a, David Ginola. b, Paul Scholes. c, Jurgen Kohler. d, Ian Rush.

$5, Alan Shearer.

2004, Oct. 27 *Perf. 12¾x12½*

3232 A567 $2 Sheet of 4, #a-d 6.00 6.00

Souvenir Sheet

3233 A567 $5 multi 3.75 3.75

Paintings by Norman Rockwell A568

Designs: 90c, Lion and His Keeper. $1, Weighing In. $1.40, The Young Lawyer. $2, The Bodybuilder.

$5, Triple Self-portrait.

2004, Oct. 29 *Perf. 14¼*

3234-3237 A568 Set of 4 4.00 4.00

Imperf

Size: 66x88mm

3238 A568 $5 multi 3.75 3.75

Various St. Vincent and St. Vincent Grenadines Stamps Surcharged

Surcharge Types on St. Vincent Stamps

10c on 45c No. 1078 — Type 1: "1" without bottom serif, "0" same thickness. Type 2: "1" with bottom serif, "0" thin at top and bottom.

10c on 65c No. 1080b and 10c on 75c No. 1081b — Type 1: "1" with bottom serif, "0" thin at top and bottom. Type 2: "1" without bottom serif, "0" same thickness.

20c on 60c No. 726 — Type 1: New denomiation at lower left with small "c." Type 2: New denomination at upper left, with cent sign. Type 3: New denomination below obliterator and approximately 6mm to left of it, with small "c." Type 4: New denomination below obliterator and approximately 16mm to left of it, with small "c."

20c on 75c Nos. 984a-984b horiz. pair — Type 1: Small "c." Type 2: Cent sign.

20c on $1.25 No. 527 — Type 1: New denomination to left of round obliterator, with raised "c" and serifed "2." Type 2: New denomination at lower left, round obliterator with cent sign and serifed "2". Type 3: New denomination below square obliterator, unserifed "2" and "c."

20c on $2 No. 638 — Type 1: New denomination to right and below obliterator, with serifed "2" and small "c" with ball. Type 2: New denomination to right of obliterator, with unserifed "2" and small "c" without ball.

20c on $2 No. 665 — Type 1: New denomination at left, with small "c" with ball and serifed "2." Type 2: New denomination close to obliterator at left, with small "c" without ball and unserifed "2."

20c on $2 No. 975 — Type 1: Cent sign. Type 2: Small "c."

20c on $3.70 No. 1004 — Type 1: New denomination at upper left, with serifed "2," "0" thin at top and bottom. Type 2: New denomination at upper right with unserifed "2," "0" same thickness.

Surcharge Types on St. Vincent Grenadines Stamps

20c on 75c No. 511 — Type 1: Cent sign. Type 2: Small "c."

20c on 75c No. 593 — Type 1: New denomination at lower left, below obliterator, with cent sign. Type 2: New denomination to right of obliterator, with small "c."

20c on $1.50 No. 277 — Type 1: New denomination at top center, with small "c." Type 2: New denomination at lower left, with cent sign.

20c on $2 No. 186 — Type 1: New denomination to left of obliterator, with small "c." Type 2: New denomination at upper left, with cent sign.

20c on $2.50 No. 265 — Type 1: Unserifed "2," small "c" even with base of numerals. Type 2: Serifed "2," raised small "c."

Methods, Perfs and Watermarks As Before

1994 (?)-2004

On St. Vincent Stamps

No.	Design	Surcharge	Unused	Used
3239	A36	10c on 2c #281	125.00	—
3240	A148	10c on 6c #1070	—	—
3241	A148	10c on 12c #1072	—	—
3242	A148	10c on 15c #1073b	—	—
3243	A36	10c on 25c #290	85.00	—
3244	A148	10c on 25c #1075b	—	30.00
3245	A112	10c on 35c #743	50.00	30.00
3246	A148	10c on 35c #1077		
3247	A109	10c on 45c #725	—	—
3248	A148	10c on 45c #1078b, Type 1	—	30.00
3249	A148	10c on 45c #1078, Type 2	—	75.00
a.		On #1078b (perf. 14), Type 2		
3250	A151	10c on 45c #1096	—	25.00
3251	A98	10c on 60c #640	75.00	90.00
3252	A104a	10c on 60c #671	50.00	—
3253	A104b	10c on 60c #676	25.00	10.00
3254	A148	10c on 65c #1080b, Type 1		
3255	A148	10c on 65c #1080b, Type 2		—
3256	A71	10c on 70c #481	50.00	—
3257	A148	10c on 75c #1081b, Type 1		40.00
3257A	A148	10c on 75c #1081b, Type 2		
3258	A109	10c on $1 #728	—	75.00
3259	A77	10c on $1.25 #527	95.00	—
3260	A98	10c on $1.50 #641	—	—
3260A	A99	10c on $1.50 #645		
3261	A105	10c on $1.50 #681	50.00	—
3262	A82	10c on $2 #544	50.00	—
3262A	A93	10c on $2 #618		
3263	A98	10c on $2 #642		
3263A	A106	10c on $2.40 #686		—
3264	A90	10c on $2.50 #607	25.00	25.00
3264A	A108	10c on $3 #718		
3265	A36	20c on ½c #279	15.00	20.00
3266	A47	20c on 1c #337	75.00	50.00
3267	A145	20c on 6c #1061a-1061b horiz. pair	200.00	—
3268	A126	20c on 25c #903	—	85.00
3273	A113	20c on 35c #761	—	200.00
3274	A162	20c on 35c #1145	—	175.00
3275	A105	20c on 45c #679	—	—
3276	A112	20c on 45c #744	—	—
3277	A151	20c on 45c #1096	—	—
3278	A90	20c on 60c #605	150.00	30.00
3279	A93	20c on 60c #616	—	—
3280	A97	20c on 60c #636	200.00	200.00
3281	A98	20c on 60c #640	15.00	20.00
3282	A104	20c on 60c #667	15.00	20.00
3283	A104b	20c on 60c #676	—	50.00
3284	A105	20c on 60c #680	20.00	10.00
3285	A109	20c on 60c #726, Type 1	25.00	10.00
3286	A109	20c on 60c #726, Type 2	10.00	50.00
3287	A109	20c on 60c #726, Type 3	50.00	5.00
3288	A109	20c on 60c #726, Type 4	90.00	35.00
3289	A115	20c on 60c #784	—	30.00
3290	A71	20c on 70c #481	175.00	—
3292	A136	20c on 75c #984a-984b horiz. pair, Type 1	—	150.00
3293	A136	20c on 75c #984a-984b horiz. pair, Type 2	—	—
3294	A138	20c on 75c #999	75.00	50.00
3295	A148	20c on 75c #1081	30.00	—
3296	A79	20c on $1 #534	50.00	15.00
3297	A94	20c on $1 #622a-622b pair	130.00	—
3298	A97	20c on $1 #637	50.00	50.00
3299	A121	20c on $1 #847	—	50.00
3302	A64	20c on $1.25 #434	30.00	40.00
3303	A70	20c on $1.25 #478	30.00	200.00
3304	A73	20c on $1.25 #498	—	—
3306	A77	20c on $1.25 #527, Type 1	—	110.00
3307	A77	20c on $1.25 #527, Type 2	—	—
3308	A77	20c on $1.25 #527, Type 3	85.00	125.00
3309	A99	20c on $1.50 #645	—	—
3310	A103	20c on $1.50 #664	—	100.00
3311	A104	20c on $1.50 #668	15.00	20.00
3313	A104b	20c on $1.50 #677	45.00	50.00
3314	A105	20c on $1.50 #681	—	—
3315	A115	20c on $1.50 #785	35.00	15.00
3316	A134	20c on $1.50 #974	65.00	100.00
3317	A136	20c on $1.50 #985a-985b horiz. pair	140.00	100.00
3318	A93	20c on $2 #618	40.00	100.00
3320	A97	20c on $2 #638, Type 1	40.00	50.00
3321	A97	20c on $2 #638, Type 2	100.00	60.00
3322	A98	20c on $2 #642	—	—
3324	A103	20c on $2 #665, Type 1	—	200.00
3325	A103	20c on $2 #665, Type 2	—	—
3326	A104	20c on $2 #669	40.00	50.00
3327	A104b	20c on $2 #678	15.00	25.00
3328	A105	20c on $2 #682	15.00	15.00
3329	A115	20c on $2 #786	45.00	15.00
3330	A134	20c on $2 #975, Type 1	—	—
3331	A134	20c on $2 #975, Type 2	—	—
a.		Horiz. pair, #3330-3331	—	—
3333	A126	20c on $2.50 #905	20.00	100.00
3334	A108	20c on $3 #718	—	40.00
3337	A113	20c on $3 #764	—	150.00
3338	A117	20c on $3 #806	—	—
3339	A119	20c on $3 #832	—	—
3342	A139	20c on $3.70 #1004, Type 1	80.00	40.00
3343	A139	20c on $3.70 #1004, Type 2	30.00	30.00
3345	A189	20c on $4 #1307	75.00	50.00

On St. Vincent Grenadines Stamps

No.	Design	Surcharge	Unused	Used
3346	G3	10c on 1c #33	—	—
3347	G16	10c on 1c #133		
3348	G16	10c on 6c #138	—	—
3349	G35	10c on 35c #433		
3350	G31	10c on 45c #271	—	—
3351	G33	10c on 45c #292		
3351A	G36	10c on 75c #439		
3352	G20	10c on 90c #185	—	—
3353	A90	10c on $1 #192	—	—
3354	G35	10c on $1 #435		
3355	G32	10c on $2 #278	—	—
3356	G36	10c on $3 #440		
3358	A106	20c on 20c #469	—	—
3359	G39	20c on 35c #484	—	—
3360	G31	20c on 45c #271	—	—
3361	A106	20c on 45c #470	—	—
3362	G45	20c on 45c #561	—	—
3363	G7	20c on 50c #71	—	—
3364	G31	20c on 60c #272	—	—
3366	G41	20c on 75c #511, Type 1	—	—
3367	G41	20c on 75c #511, Type 2	—	—
a.		Horiz. pair, #3366-3367	—	—
3368	G50	20c on 75c #588	—	—
3369	G51	20c on 75c #593, Type 1	—	—
3370	G51	20c on 75c #593, Type 2	—	—
a.		Double surcharge		—
3371	G20	20c on 90c #185	—	—
3372	G7	20c on $1 #72	—	—
3374	G17	20c on $1.25 #160	—	—
3375	G46	20c on $1.25 #566	—	—
3376	A97	20c on $1.50 #264	—	—
3377	G31	20c on $1.50 #273	—	—
3378	G32	20c on $1.50 #277, Type 1	—	—
3379	G32	20c on $1.50 #277, Type 2	—	—
3381	A76	20c on $2 #128	—	—
3383	G20	20c on $2 #186, Type 1	—	—
3384	G20	20c on $2 #186, Type 2	—	—
3385	G21	20c on $2 #198	—	—
3386	G27	20c on $2 #242	—	—
3387	G32	20c on $2 #278	—	—
3390	A97	20c on $2.50 #265, Type 1	—	—
3391	A97	20c on $2.50 #265, Type 2	—	—
3392	A82	20c on $3 #179	—	—
3394	G35	20c on $3 #436	—	—
3395	G37	20c on $3 #475	—	—
3396	G39	20c on $3 #487	—	—
3397	G43	20c on $3 #536	—	—
3399	G59	20c on $3 #692	—	—
3400	G50	20c on $3.50 #589	—	—
3401	G45	20c on $4 #563	—	—

These surcharges were printed from the mid-1990s to 2004, with the bulk created from 1999 to 2004. Issue dates are not certain as the stamps were available for both revenue and postal use. Numbers are reserved for stamps that printer's records indicate were surcharged. Additional stamps may also have been surcharged.

These stamps were not available through the philatelic agency, but could be bought at post offices, as well as Treasury offices and other locations throughout the country where revenue stamps were used, including retail stores.

The surcharged Grenadines issues were not necessarily sent only to the Grenadines for sale there.

Nos. 3246, 3249a, 3254, 3255, 3257A, 3263, 3347, 3349, 3351, and 3354, which are currently known only with revenue cancels, may also have been used postally.

The shape of the obliterators and the location of new denominations varies.

On No. 3240, the original denomination is obliterated with a marker. No. 3275 is known only with a double surcharge.

Nos. 3260A, 3262A, 3264A, 3351A and 3356, which are known only with revenue cancels, also may have been used postally.

The item illustrated above is a revenue stamp, though it lacks any revenue stamp inscription. 10c on 20c, 20c, 50c, $5 and $60 stamps of this design also exist. Some of these revenue stamps have been used on mail as they were available for sale to the public at the same locations as the surcharged stamps listed above. Non-governmental vendors of these stamps were lax in notifying stamp purchasers that the stamps were intended for revenue use only.

Queen Juliana of the Netherlands (1909-2004) A569

2004, Aug. 25 **Litho.** ***Perf. 13¼***

3405 A569 $2 multi 1.50 1.50

Printed in sheets of 6.

National Soccer Team — A570

2004, Oct. 27 ***Perf. 12***

3406 A570 70c multi .55 .55

Paintings in the Hermitage, St. Petersburg, Russia A571

Designs: 10c, Head of a Young Girl, by Jean-Baptiste Greuze. 20c, Two Actresses, by Jean-Baptiste Santerre. 40c, An Allegory of History, by José de Ribera. 60c, A Young Woman Trying on Earrings, by Rembrandt. $2, The Girlhood of the Virgin, by Francisco e Zurbarán. No. 3412, $5, Portrait of a Woman, by Frans Pourbus, the Elder.

No. 3413, $1.40: a, Landscape with Obelisk, by Hubert Robert. b, At the Hermit's, by Robert. c, Landscape with Ruins, by Robert. d, Landscape with Terrace and Cascade, by Robert. e, A Shepherdess, by Jan Siberecht. f, Landscape with Waterfall, by Robert.

No. 3414, $1.40: a, Count N. D. Guriev, by Jean Auguste-Domingue Ingres. b, Portrait of an Actor, by Domenico Fetti. c, Napoleon Bonaparte on the Bridge at Arcole, by Baron Antoine-Jean Gros. d, A Young Man with a Glove, by Frans Hals. e, Portrait of General Alexei Yermolov, by George Dawe. f, A Scholar, by Rembrandt.

No. 3415, The Bean King, by Jacob Jordaens, horiz. No. 3416, Three Men at a Table, by Diego Velázquez. No. 3417, Family Portrait, by Cornelis de Vos, horiz.

2004, Nov. 1 ***Perf. 14¼***
3407-3412 A571 Set of 6 6.25 6.25

Sheets of 6, #a-f
3413-3414 A571 Set of 2 13.00 13.00

Imperf

Size: 98x72mm
3415 A571 $5 multi 3.75 3.75

Size: 78x83mm
3416 A571 $5 multi 3.75 3.75

Size: 88x76mm
3417 A571 $5 multi 3.75 3.75

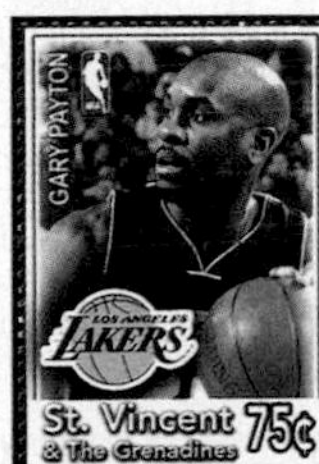

National Basketball Association Players — A572

Designs: No. 3418, 75c, Gary Payton, Los Angeles Lakers. No. 3419, 75c, Lebron James, Cleveland Cavaliers. No. 3420, 75c, Adonal Foyle, Golden State Warriors. No. 3421, 75c, Peja Stojakovic, Sacramento Kings. No. 3422, 75c, Kirk Hinrich, Chicago Bulls. $3, Steve Francis, Houston Rockets.

2004-05 ***Perf. 14***
3418-3423 A572 Set of 6 5.25 5.25

Issued: No. 3418, 11/2; Nos. 3419-3420, 11/3; No. 3421, 11/9; Nos. 3422-3423, 2/10/05.

Battle of Trafalgar, Bicent. A573

Designs: 50c, Captain Thomas Masterman Hardy. $1, Napoleon Bonaparte. $1.50, Admiral Lord Horatio Nelson. $3, Admiral Cuthbert Collingwood.

No. 3428, $5, The Nelson touch. No. 3429, $5, H.M.S. Victory.

2004, Nov. 25 ***Perf. 14¼***
3424-3427 A573 Set of 4 4.50 4.50

Souvenir Sheets
3428-3429 A573 Set of 2 7.50 7.50

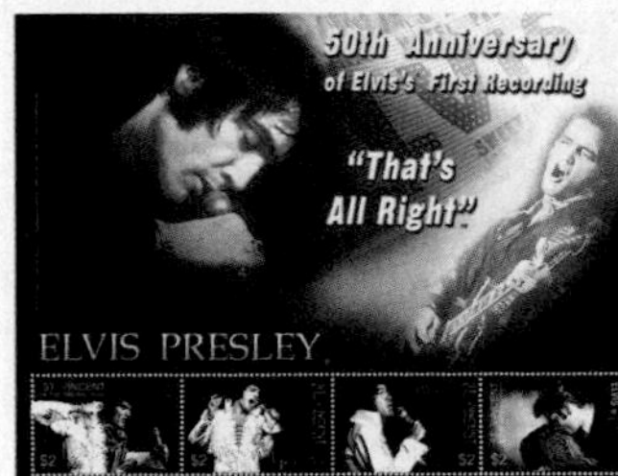

A574

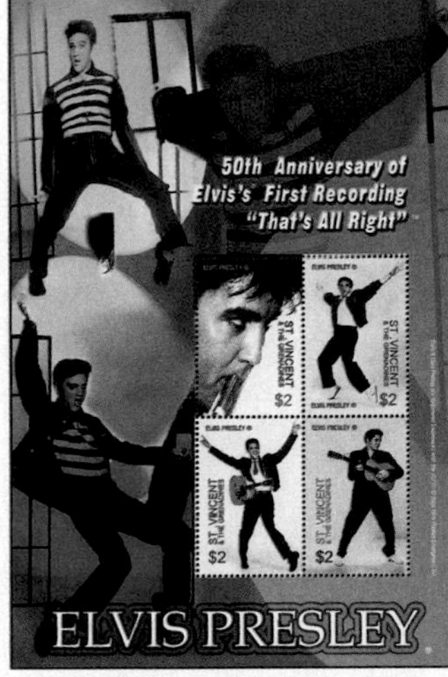

Elvis Presley (1935-77) — A575

No. 3430: a, Country name at UL reading across, denomination at LL. b, Country name at R, denomination at LL. c, Country name at R, denomination at LR. d, Country name at L reading up, denomination at LL.

No. 3431 — Denomination color: a, Green. b, Blue. c, Red. d, Purple.

2004, Nov. 25 ***Perf. 13¼x13½***
3430 A574 $2 Sheet of 4, #a-d 6.00 6.00

Perf. 13½x13¼
3431 A575 $2 Sheet of 4, #a-d 6.00 6.00

Souvenir Sheet

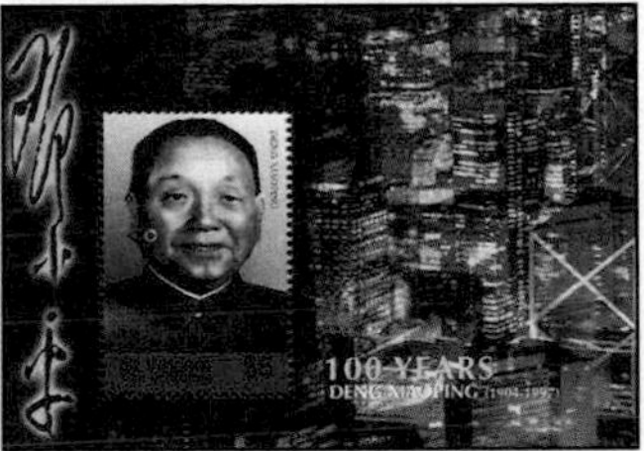

Deng Xiaoping (1904-97), Chinese Leader — A576

2004, Dec. 6 ***Perf. 14***
3432 A576 $5 multi 3.75 3.75

Subway Systems — A577

No. 3433 — New York City subway: a, 1953 subway token. b, 23rd Street IRT kiosk. c, 1935 Subway car Hi-V 3398. d, 1936 subway car R6 1208 interior. e, Construction of Harlem River Tunnel, 1904. f, Underground construction, early 1900s. g, Hoppers, above ground construction, early 1900s. h, Workers on scaffold, above ground construction early 1900s.

No. 3434, $1.40 — Subway cars from: a, Moscow Metro. b, Tokyo Metro. c, Mexico City Metro. d, Paris Metro. e, Hong Kong MTR. f, Prague Metro.

No. 3435, $1.40 — London Underground: a, Thames Tunnel, 1859. b, City & South London Railway locomotives, 1890. c, East London line. d, Picadilly line. e, Victoria line. f, Jubilee line.

No. 3436, $5, A Train, New York City. No. 3437, $5, Train in station, London Underground. No. 3438, $5, 1992 Tube, Central line, London.

2004, Dec. 13 ***Perf. 13¼x13½***
3433 A577 $1 Sheet of 8, #a-h 6.00 6.00

Sheets of 6, #a-f
3434-3435 A577 Set of 2 13.00 13.00

Souvenir Sheets
3436-3438 A577 Set of 3 11.50 11.50

Christmas A578

Paintings by Norman Rockwell: 70c, Santa's Helpers. 90c, Tiny Tim (detail). $1.10, Department Store Santa. $3, The Muggleton Stage Coach.

$5, Extra Good Boys and Girls.

2004, Dec. 13 ***Perf. 12***
3439-3442 A578 Set of 4 4.25 4.25

Imperf

Size: 64x84mm
3443 A578 $5 multi 3.75 3.75

New Year 2005 (Year of the Rooster) — A579

2005, Jan. 26 ***Perf. 12***
3444 A579 75c multi .55 .55

Issued in sheets of 3.

Miniature Sheet

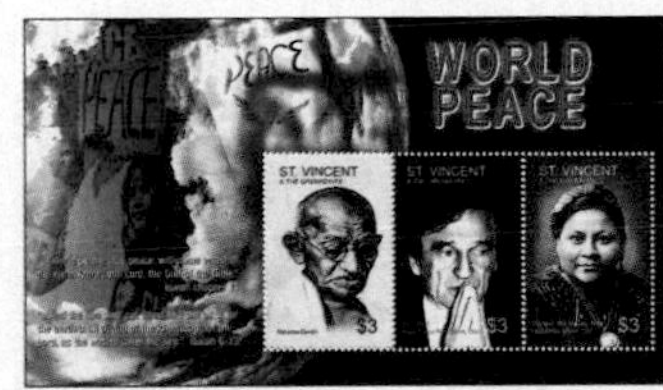

World Peace — A580

No. 3445: a, Mahatma Gandhi. b, Elie Wiesel. c, Rigoberta Menchu.

2005, Jan. 26 ***Perf. 14***
3445 A580 $3 Sheet of 3, #a-c 6.75 6.75

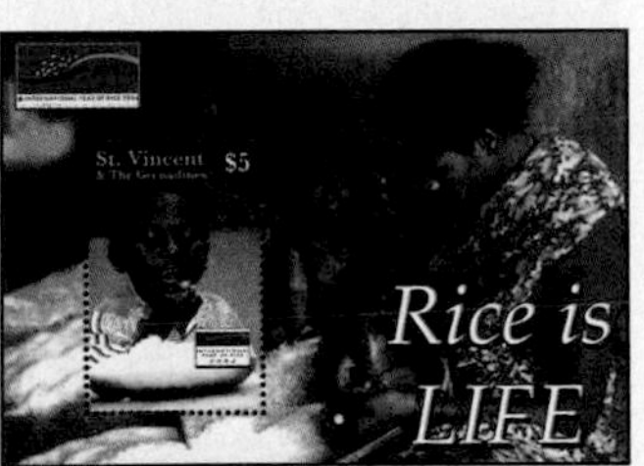

Intl. Year of Rice (in 2004) — A581

No. 3446, horiz.: a, Oxen pulling plow. b, Man and child harvesting rice. c, Man and field.

$5, Child with bowl of rice.

2005, Jan. 26
3446 A581 $3 Sheet of 3, #a-c 6.75 6.75

Souvenir Sheet
3447 A581 $5 multi 3.75 3.75

Souvenir Sheet

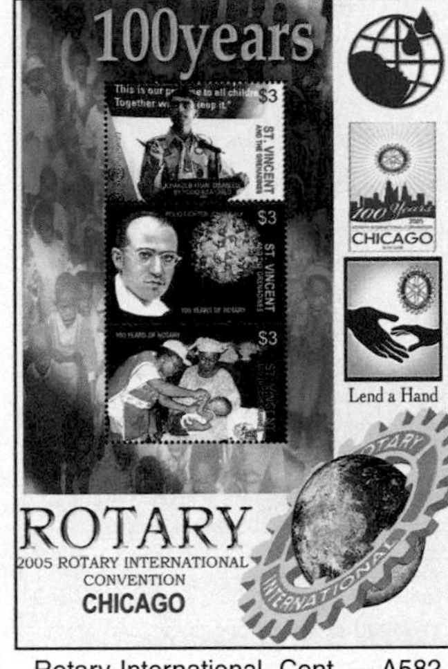

Rotary International, Cent. — A582

No. 3448: a, Jehanzeb Khan, polio victim. b, Dr. Jonas Salk. c, Child receiving polio vaccination.

2005, Apr. 4 **Litho.** ***Perf. 14***
3448 A582 $3 Sheet of 3, #a-c 6.75 6.75

Wedding of Prince Charles and Camilla Parker Bowles — A583

Various photos of couple with oval color of: No. 3449, $2, Blue. No. 3450, $2, Red violet. No. 3451, $2, Purple, horiz.

2005, Apr. 9 ***Perf. 13½***
3449-3451 A583 Set of 3 4.50 4.50

Vatican City No. 63 — A584

Pope John Paul II (1920-2005) A585

2005, June 1 ***Perf. 13x13¼***
3452 A584 70c multi .55 .55

Perf. 13½
3453 A585 $3 multi 2.25 2.25

No. 3452 issued in sheets of 12; No. 3453, in sheets of 6.

Maimonides (1135-1204), Philosopher A586

No. 3454 — Statue of Maimonides with frame in: a, Yellow. b, Yellow and black.

2005, June 7 *Perf. 12*
3454 A586 $2 Vert. pair, #a-b 3.00 3.00

Printed in sheets containing two pairs.

Souvenir Sheet

Expo 2005, Aichi, Japan — A587

No. 3455 — Woolly mammoth with country name in: a, Red. b, Black. c, White.

2005, June 7 *Perf. 12¾*
3455 A587 $3 Sheet of 3, #a-c 6.75 6.75

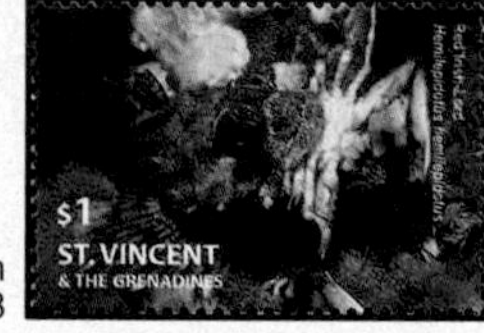

Fish A588

Designs: $1, Red Irish lord. $1.10, Deep sea anglerfish. $1.40, Viperfish. $2, Lionfish.
$5, Gulper eel.

2005, June 7
3456-3459 A588 Set of 4 4.25 4.25

Souvenir Sheet

3460 A588 $5 multi 3.75 3.75

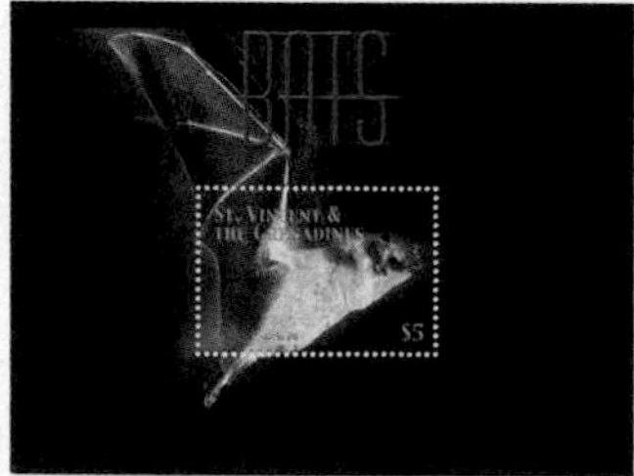

Bats — A589

No. 3461: a, Mexican long-tongued bat. b, Wahlberg's fruit bat. c, Common vampire bat. d, False vampire bat. e, Horseshoe bat. f, Spear-nosed long-tongued bat.
$5, Greater long-nosed bat.

2005, June 7
3461 A589 $1.60 Sheet of 6, #a-f 7.25 7.25

Souvenir Sheet

3462 A589 $5 multi 3.75 3.75

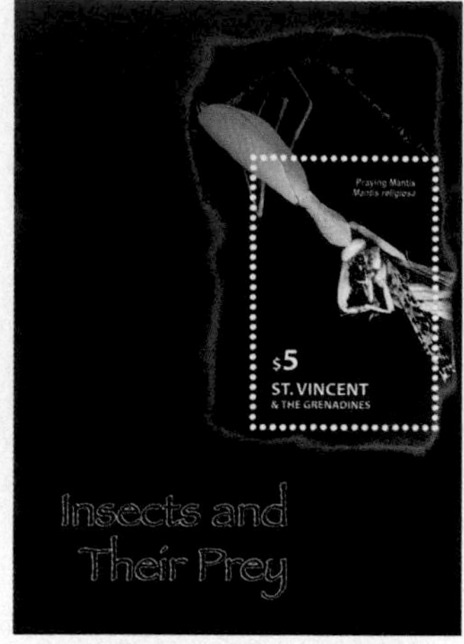

Insects and Spiders — A590

No. 3463: a, Field-digger wasp. b, Water spider. c, Yellow crab spider. d, Mantid.
$5, Praying mantis.

2005, June 7
3463 A590 $2 Sheet of 4, #a-d 6.00 6.00

Souvenir Sheet

3464 A590 $5 multi 3.75 3.75

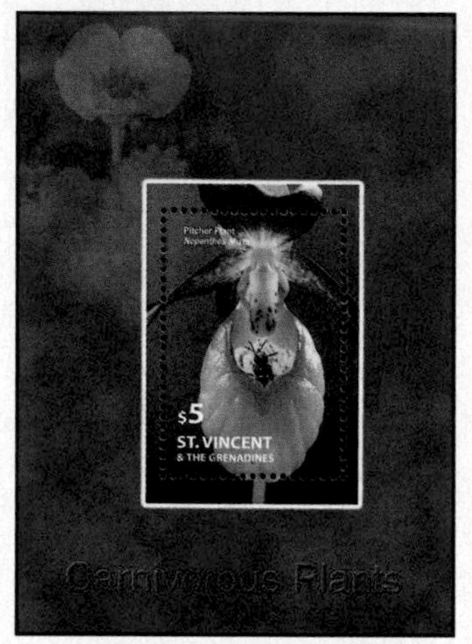

Carnivorous Plants — A591

No. 3465: a, Butterwort, denomination in black. b, Common sundew. c, Venus's flytrap. d, Butterwort, denomination in white.
$5, Pitcher plant.

2005, June 7
3465 A591 $2 Sheet of 4, #a-d 6.00 6.00

Souvenir Sheet

3466 A591 $5 multi 3.75 3.75

Friedrich von Schiller (1759-1805), Writer — A592

No. 3467 — Schiller: a, At desk. b, Facing right. c, Facing left.
$5, Facing right, diff.

2005, June 7
3467 A592 $3 Sheet of 3, #a-c 6.75 6.75

Souvenir Sheet

3468 A592 $5 multi 3.75 3.75

Hans Christian Andersen (1805-75), Author — A593

No. 3469: a, The Brave Tin Soldier. b, The Top and Ball. c, Ole-Luk-Oie, the Dream-God.
$5, The Snow Queen.

2005, June 7 *Perf. 12¾*
3469 A593 $3 Sheet of 3, #a-c 6.75 6.75

Souvenir Sheet

Perf. 12x12¼

3470 A593 $5 multi 3.75 3.75

No. 3469 contains three 43x32mm stamps.

Jules Verne (1828-1905), Writer — A594

No. 3471, $2 — Around the World in 80 Days: a, Princess Aouda. b, Characters in train windows. c, Phileas Fogg. d, Passepartout.

No. 3472, $2 — 20,000 Leagues Under the Sea: a, Mariner using sextant. b, Captain at ship's wheel. c, Sea monster at window. d, Men in diving suits.

No. 3473, $2 — Master of the World: a, Automobile. b, Ship. c, Building. d, Winged vehicle.

No. 3474, $2 — The Castle of the Carpathians: a, Man pointing at beast in sky. b, Women and men looking at woman. c, Two men, woman with arms extended. d, Man pointing.

No. 3475, $2 — From the Earth to the Moon: a, Men and dog. b, Spacecraft and moon. c, Clouds and vapor trail. d, Man on ladder on side of spacecraft.

No. 3476, $5, Hot air balloon. No. 3477, $5, Helicopter

No. 3478, $5, Atomic bomb. No. 3479, $5, Tank. No. 3480, $5, Blitzkreig of World War II.

2005, June 7 *Perf. 12¾*

Sheets of 4, #a-d

3471-3472 A594 Set of 2 12.00 12.00

Sheets of 4, #a-d

3473-3475 A594 Set of 3 18.00 18.00

Souvenir Sheets

3476-3477 A594 Set of 2 7.50 7.50
3478-3480 A594 Set of 3 11.50 11.50

End of World War II, 60th Anniv. — A595

No. 3481, $2, horiz.: a, USSR T34-85 tank. b, German Tiger tank. c, USA LVT(A)-1. d, Great Britain Cruiser tank Mk VI.

No. 3482, $2, horiz.: a, SBD-3 Dauntless. b, Mitsubishi Zero A6M5. c, USS Yorktown. d, USS Hornet.

No. 3483, $5, Winston Churchill. No. 3484, $5, Gen. Douglas MacArthur signing Japanese surrender instrument, horiz.

2005, June 7 **Sheets of 4, #a-d**
3481-3482 A595 Set of 2 12.00 12.00

Souvenir Sheets

3483-3484 A595 Set of 2 7.50 7.50

Souvenir Sheet

Taipei 2005 Stamp Exhibition — A596

No. 3485: a, Panda. b, Formosan rock monkey. c, Formosan black bear. d, Formosan sika deer.

2005, Aug. 5 *Perf. 14*
3485 A596 $2 Sheet of 4, #a-d 6.00 6.00

Souvenir Sheet

Elvis Presley (1935-77) — A597

Litho. & Embossed

2005, Nov. 21 *Imperf.*

Without Gum

3486 A597 $20 gold & multi 15.00 15.00

Christmas — A598

Designs: 70c, Small Cowper Madonna, by Raphael. 90c, Madonna of the Grand Duke, by Raphael. $1.10, Sistine Madonna, by Raphael. $3, Alba Madonna, by Raphael.
$6, Adoration of the Magi, by Rogier van der Weyden.

2005, Dec. 26 **Litho.** *Perf. 13½*
3487-3490 A598 Set of 4 4.25 4.25

Souvenir Sheet

3491 A598 $6 multi 4.50 4.50

New Year 2006 (Year of the Dog) A599

2005, Dec. 30
3492 A599 $1 multi .75 .75

Printed in sheets of 3.

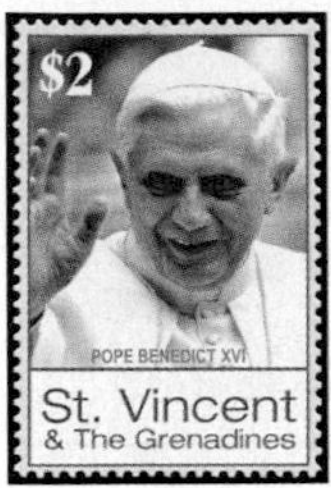

Pope Benedict XVI — A600

2005, Dec. 30
3493 A600 $2 multi 1.50 1.50

Printed in sheets of 4.

Miniature Sheet

OPEC Intl. Development Fund, 30th Anniv. (in 2006) — A601

No. 3494: a, Three parrots. b, Waterfall. c, Gazebo. d, Two parrots.

2006, Jan. 30 ***Perf. 12x11½***
3494 A601 $3 Sheet of 4, #a-d 9.00 9.00

Miniature Sheets

Children's Drawings — A602

No. 3495, $2 — Flowers: a, Flower Spot, by Tom Brier. b, Flower Vase, by Jessie Abrams. c, Green Flower Vase, by Nick Abrams. d, Red Sunflowers, by Bianca Saad.

No. 3496, $2 — Animals: a, Panda, by Lauren Van Woy. b, Giraffe, by Megal Albe. c, Orange Koala, by Holly Cramer. d, Red Monkey, by Roxanne Hanson.

No. 3497, $2 — Snails and Ladybugs: a, Snail, by Cortland Bobczynski. b, Blue Ladybug, by Jackie Wicks. c, Red Ladybug, by Emily Hawk. d, Snail Boy, by Micah Bobczynski.

2006, Jan. 30 ***Perf. 13¼***
Sheets of 4, #a-d
3495-3497 A602 Set of 3 18.00 18.00

Queen Elizabeth II, 80th Birthday — A603

Inscriptions: No. 3498, $2, The Christening of a Princess. No. 3499, $2, Princess Elizabeth and Margaret. No. 3500, $2, First Radio Broadcast to the Nation. No. 3501, $2, A Decade of War. No. 3502, $2, The Royal Wedding. No. 3503, $2, The Queen's Coronation. No. 3504, $2, The Royal Family. No. 3505, $2, The Queen Awarding the World Cup to England.

2006, Jan. 31 ***Perf. 13½***
3498-3505 A603 Set of 8 12.00 12.00

Each stamp printed in sheets of 8 + label.

Queen Angelfish A604

2006, Feb. 9 ***Perf. 11½x12***
3506 A604 20c multi .25 .25

Marilyn Monroe (1926-62), Actress — A605

2006, Mar. 31 ***Perf. 13¼***
3507 A605 $3 multi 2.25 2.25

Printed in sheets of 4.

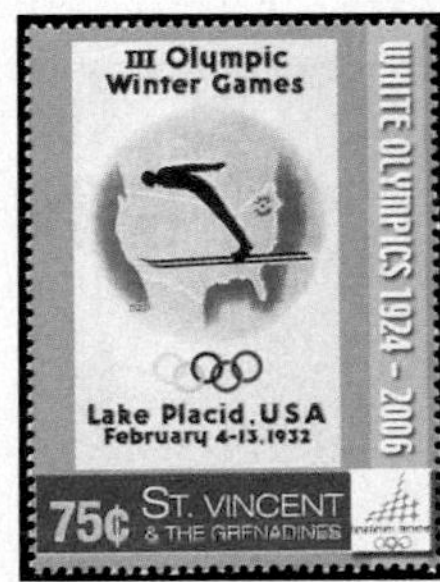

2006 Winter Olympics, Turin A606

Designs: 75c, Poster for 1932 Lake Placid Winter Olympics. 90c, US #716, horiz. $2, Poster for 1924 Chamonix Winter Olympics. $3, Cover with commemorative cancel for 1924 Chamonix Winter Olympics.

2006, May 18 ***Perf. 14¼***
3508-3511 A606 Set of 4 5.00 5.00

Nelson Mandela, 1993 Nobel Peace Prize Winner — A607

2006, May 27 ***Perf. 11½x12***
3512 A607 $3 multi 2.25 2.25

Printed in sheets of 3.

Souvenir Sheet

Airships — A608

No. 3513: a, USS Akron. b, A-170 airship. c, Altair-Z experimental airship.

2006, June 23 ***Perf. 12¾***
3513 A608 $4 Sheet of 3, #a-c 9.00 9.00

Miniature Sheet

Movie Debut of Elvis Presley, 50th Anniv. — A609

No. 3514 — Movie posters: a, King Creole. b, Love Me Tender. c, Loving You. d, Roustabout.

2006, July 12 ***Perf. 13¼***
3514 A609 $3 Sheet of 4, #a-d 9.00 9.00

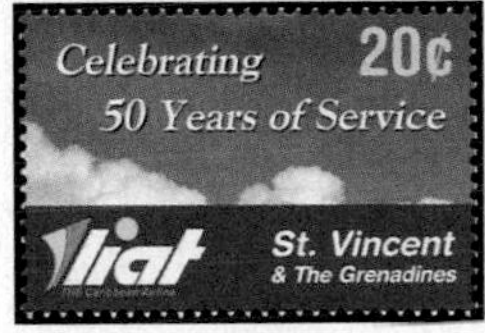

Leeward Islands Air Transport, 50th Anniv. A610

Designs: 20c, Clouds. 50c, Airplane. 70c, Airplane, diff. 90c, Airplane, diff. $5, Frank Delisle, vert.

2006, July 20 ***Perf. 12¾***
3515-3518 A610 Set of 4 1.75 1.75

Souvenir Sheet

3519 A610 $5 multi 3.75 3.75

Christopher Columbus (1451-1506), Explorer — A611

Designs: 50c, Columbus. 70c, Columbus and Queen Isabella, horiz. $2, Santa Maria. $3, Niña, Pinta and Santa Maria, horiz. $5, Pinta.

2006, July 21
3520-3523 A611 Set of 4 4.75 4.75

Souvenir Sheet

3524 A611 $5 multi 3.75 3.75

Space Achievements — A612

No. 3525 — Viking 1 and Apollo 11: a, Launch of Titan Centaur rocket. b, Viking 1. c, Viking 1 Lander. d, Apollo 11 lunar module. e, Apollo 11 command module. f, Launch of Apollo 11.

No. 3526 — Exploring our Universe: a, Mir Space Station. b, Sputnik 1. c, Soyuz. d, Luna 9.

No. 3527, $6, Conception of crew exploration vehicle for return to Moon. No. 3528, $6, Mir Space Station.

2006, Sept. 27 ***Perf. 13¼***
3525 A612 $1.50 Sheet of 6, #a-f 6.75 6.75
3526 A612 $2.50 Sheet of 4, #a-d 7.50 7.50

Souvenir Sheets

3527-3528 A612 Set of 2 9.00 9.00

Worldwide Fund for Nature (WWF) — A613

No. 3529 — Great white shark: a, Turning right. b, With fish. c, Turning left. d, With mouth open.

2006, Oct. 24 ***Perf. 14***
3529 A613 $1 Block of 4, #a-d 3.00 3.00
e. Miniature sheet, 2 #3529 6.00 6.00

No. 3529 printed in sheets of 4 blocks. Value, imperf. sheet of 4 blocks $50. No. 3259e exists imperf. Value $25.

Last Flight of the Concorde — A614

No. 3530, $1.40: a, Concorde coming to Filton. b, Concorde flying past Filton.

No. 3531, $1.40: a, Captains holding British flags. b, Concorde landing at Heathrow Airport.

2006, Dec. 6 **Pairs, #a-b**
3530-3531 A614 Set of 2 4.25 4.25

Nos. 3530-3531 each printed in sheets containing 3 pairs.

Christmas — A615

Details of Enthroned Madonna with Child Encircled by Saints, by Peter Paul Rubens: 20c, Cherub with flower. 70c, Infant Jesus. 90c, Women. $1.10, Madonna.

No. 3536: a, Like 20c. b, Like 70c. c, Like 90c. d, Like $1.10.

2006, Dec. 6
3532-3535 A615 Set of 4 2.25 2.25

Souvenir Sheet

3536 A615 $2 Sheet of 4, #a-d 6.00 6.00

Diplomatic Relations Between St. Vincent and Republic of China, 25th Anniv. — A616

Designs: 10c, St. Vincent Prime Minister Dr. Ralph Gonsalves and Taiwanese Pres. Chen Shui-bian and other dignitaries. 20c, St. Vincent woman showing dress to Gonsalves and Chen. 50c, Gonsalves and Chen shaking hands. 70c, Chen and St. Vincent honor guard. 90c, Gonsalves and Chen. $1.10, Gonsalves and Chen, diff. $1.40, Children of St. Vincent holding Taiwanese flags.

No. 3544, $5, Chen and Gonsalves seated at table. No. 3545, $5, Chen and another St. Vincent dignitary, flowers. No. 3546, $5, Presentation of gift.

2006, Dec. 12 *Perf. 13½*

3537-3543 A616 Set of 7 3.75 3.75

Souvenir Sheets

3544-3546 A616 Set of 3 11.50 11.50

Rembrandt (1606-69), Painter A617

Designs: 50c, The Jewish Physician Ephraim Bueno. 75c, Portrait of Ariantje Hollaer, Wife of Hendrick Martensz-Sorgh. $1, An Old Man in a Fur Cap. No. 3550, $2, Saskia van Uylenburgh.

No. 3551, $2 — Painting details: a, The Denial of St. Peter (woman with raised hand). b, The Raising of Lazarus (Jesus). c, The Denial of St. Peter (St. Peter). d, The Raising of Lazarus (Lazarus).

No. 3552, $2: a, Portrait of Titia van Uylenburgh. b, The Standing Syndic. c, Polish Officer. d, Seated Girl, in Profile to Left, Half Nude.

No. 3553, $5, Two Young Negroes. No. 3554, $5, Man Standing in Front of a Doorway.

2006, Dec. 22 *Perf. 13¼*

3547-3550 A617 Set of 4 3.25 3.25

Sheets of 4, #a-d

3551-3552 A617 Set of 2 12.00 12.00

Imperf

Size: 70x100mm

3553-3554 A617 Set of 2 7.50 7.50

Dutch Princesses — A618

No. 3555: a, Princess Amalia (hands showing). b, Head of Princess Amalia. c, Princess Alexia (top of head even with bottom of denomination). d, Princess Alexia (top of head even with top of denomination).

2006

3555 Vert. strip of 4 4.50 4.50
a.-d. A618 $1.50 Any single 1.10 1.10

Souvenir Sheet

Wolfgang Amadeus Mozart (1756-91), Composer — A619

2007, Jan. 15

3556 A619 $5 multi 3.75 3.75

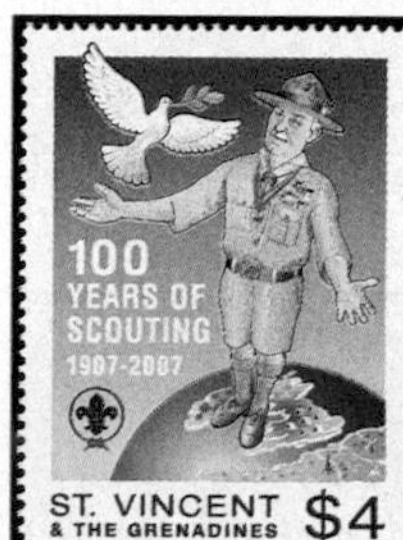

Scouting, Cent. A620

Designs: $4, Dove, Lord Robert Baden-Powell, Earth. $6, Dove, Baden-Powell, horiz.

2007, Jan. 15

3557 A620 $4 multi 3.00 3.00

Souvenir Sheet

3558 A620 $6 multi 4.50 4.50

No. 3557 printed in sheets of 3.

Mushrooms A621

Designs: 75c, Clavulinopsis sp. 90c, Cortinarius sp. $2, Cortinarius cf. $3, Conocybe spp.

$6, Galerina paludosa.

2007, Jan. 15 *Perf. 14¼*

3559-3562 A621 Set of 4 5.00 5.00

Souvenir Sheet

3563 A621 $6 multi 4.50 4.50

Pres. John F. Kennedy (1917-63) — A622

No. 3564, $3 — Kennedy as Congressman: a, Wearing pattern tie. b, At microphones. c, Wearing t-shirt. d, Wearing striped tie.

No. 3565, $3, horiz.: a, PT-109. b, PT-109 crew. c, Kennedy in boat. d, Japanese destroyer.

2007, Jan. 15 *Perf. 13¼*

Sheets of 4, #a-d

3564-3565 A622 Set of 2 17.00 17.00

New Year 2007 (Year of the Pig) A623

2007, Feb. 18 *Perf. 14*

3566 A623 $1.50 multi 1.10 1.10

Printed in sheets of 4.

Map Type of 1977-78
Inscribed "St. Vincent" at Bottom
Map of St. Vincent
Denomination at Upper Left

Perf. 14½x14¼

2007-08 Litho. Unwmk.

3566A A76 30c grn bl, lt bl & blk 100.00

Inscribed "Grenadines of St. Vincent" at Bottom
Map of Bequia

3566B A76 10c org, lt org & blk 300.00 60.00
3566C A76 30c org, lt org & blk 50.00 25.00

Map of Mayreau amd Tobago Cays
Denomination at Lower Left

3566D A76 10c org, lt org & blk 90.00 50.00

Denomination With Thick Numerals at Lower Left

3566E A76 30c org, lt org & blk 100.00 —

Denomination With Thin Numerals in Center of Stamp

3566F A76 30c org, lt org & blk 100.00

Earleist known uses: No. 3566A, 11/29; No. 3566B, 3/3; No. 3566C, 2/5/08; No. 3566D, 4/12; No. 3566E, 11/29; No. 3566F, 12/31.

No. 3566F exists with denomination shifted to the left.

Birds — A624

No. 3567: a, Bahama yellowthroat. b, Arrow-headed warbler. c, Northern jacana. d, Loggerhead kingbird.

$6, Louisiana waterthrush.

2007, Mar. 12 Litho. *Perf. 14*

3567 A624 $2 Sheet of 4, #a-d 6.50 6.50

Souvenir Sheet

3568 A624 $6 multi 4.75 4.75

Butterflies — A625

No. 3569: a, Ancyluris jurgensenii. b, Arcas cypria. c, Stalachtis phlegia. d, Xamia xami.

$5, Theritas coronata.

2007, Mar. 12

3569 A625 $2 Sheet of 4, #a-d 6.50 6.50

Souvenir Sheet

3570 A625 $5 multi 4.00 4.00

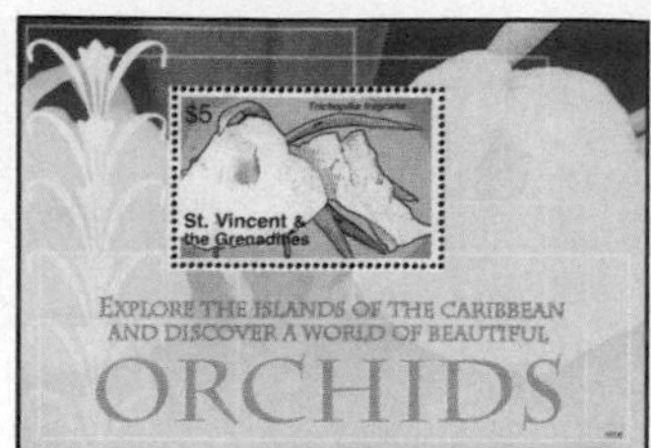

Orchids — A626

No. 3571, vert.: a, Stanhopea grandiflora. b, Psychopsis papilio. c, Vanilla planifolia. d, Tetramicra canaliculata.

$5, Trichopilia fragrans.

2007, Mar. 12

3571 A626 $2 Sheet of 4, #a-d 6.50 6.50

Souvenir Sheet

3572 A626 $5 multi 4.00 4.00

Miniature Sheet

Ferrari Automobiles, 60th Anniv. — A627

No. 3573: a, 1968 Dino 166 F2. b, 1958 246 F1. c, 1977 308 GTS. d, 1966 365 P Speciale. e, 2002 Enzo Ferrari. f, 1987 F40. g, 1993 348 Spider. h, 1951 212 Inter.

2007, May 1 *Perf. 13½*

3573 A627 $1.40 Sheet of 8, #a-h 8.50 8.50

Concorde — A628

Without Gum

Litho. & Embossed

2007, May 1 ***Die Cut Perf. 7¾***

3574 A628 $20 gold & multi 15.00 15.00

Wedding of Queen Elizabeth II and Prince Philip, 60th Anniv. A629

No. 3575: a, Couple in profile. b, Couple, queen wearing tiara.

$6, Couple, vert.

2007, May 1 Litho. *Perf. 14*
3575 A629 $1.40 Pair, #a-b 2.10 2.10

Souvenir Sheet

3576 A629 $6 multi 4.75 4.75

No. 3575 was printed in sheets containing three of each stamp.

Princess Diana (1961-97) — A630

No. 3577 — Diana wearing: a, Red dress. b, Blue pinstriped jacket. c, Black and white dress. d, White jacket.

No. 3578, $6, Diana wearing black beret. No. 3579, $6, Diana wearing hat in black and white photograph.

2007, May 1
3577 A630 $2 Sheet of 4, #a-d 6.25 6.25

Souvenir Sheets

3578-3579 A630 Set of 2 9.25 9.25

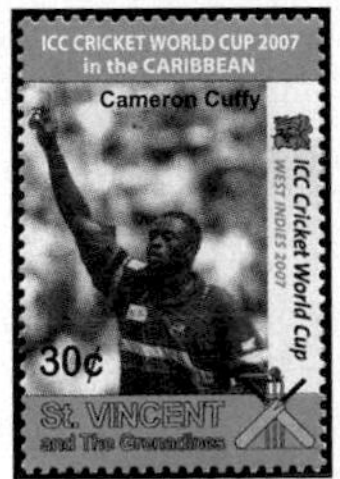

2007 ICC Cricket World Cup, West Indies — A631

Cricket players: No. 3580, 30c, Cameron Cuffy. No. 3581, 30c, Ian Allen. $1.05, Neil Williams. No. 3583, $1.35, Wilfred Slack. No. 3584, $1.35, Michael Findlay. No. 3585, $1.65, Winston Davis. No. 3586, $1.65, Nixon McLean. $2.10, Alphonso (Alfie) Roberts.

$6, Arnos Vale Stadium, horiz.

2007, May 1 *Perf. 13¼*
3580-3587 A631 Set of 8 7.50 7.50

Souvenir Sheet

3588 A631 $6 multi 4.50 4.50

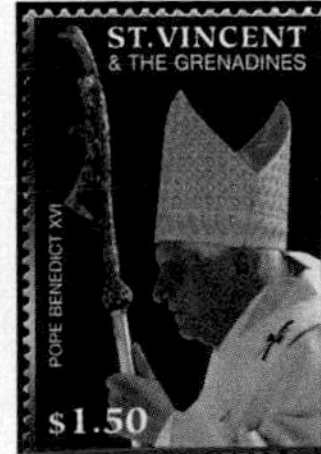

Pope Benedict XVI — A632

2007, July 5
3589 A632 $1.50 multi 1.10 1.10

Printed in sheets of 8.

Miniature Sheet

Elvis Presley (1935-77) — A633

No. 3590 — Presley: a, Wearing dark shirt, sepia photograph. b, Wearing sweater, black and white photograph. c, Wearing sweater, sepia photograph. d, Wearing striped shirt. e, Wearing suit and tie. f, Playing guitar.

2007, July 5 *Perf. 14¼*
3590 A633 $1.40 Sheet of 6, #a-f 6.00 6.00

Victoria Cross, 150th Anniv. — A634

No. 3591 — Victoria Cross, recipients and flags of home country: a, Capt. Havildar Lachhiman Gurung, Nepal. b, Ernest Alvia (Smokey) Smith, Canada. c, Nk. Yeshwant Ghadge, India. d, Lt. Col. Eric Charles Twelves Wilson, Great Britain. e, Warrant Officer Class 2 Keith Payne, Australia. f, Lance Corporal Rambahadur Limbu, Nepal.

$6, Piper James Richardson.

2007, Oct. 24 *Perf. 13¼*
3591 A634 $1.40 Sheet of 6, #a-f 6.00 6.00

Souvenir Sheet

3592 A634 $6 multi 4.75 4.75

Miniature Sheet

Intl. Holocaust Remembrance Day — A635

No. 3593 — United Nations delegates: a, Delano Bart, St. Kitts & Nevis. b, Margaret H. Ferrari, St. Vincent & the Grenadines. c, Ali'ioaiga F. Elisaia, Samoa. d, Daniele D. Bodini, San Marino. e, Pavle Jevremovic, Serbia. f, Joe R. Pemagbi, Sierra Leone. g, Peter Burian, Slovakia. h, Sanja Stiglic, Slovenia.

2007, Nov. 14
3593 A635 $1.40 Sheet of 8, #a-h 8.00 8.00

Christmas A636

Paintings: 20c, The Nativity and the Arrival of the Magi, by Giovanni di Pietro. 70c, The Annunciation, by Benozzo Gozzoli. 90c, The Nativity, by Gozzoli. $1.10, The Journey of the Magi, by Sassetta.

2007, Dec. 3 *Perf. 12*
3594-3597 A636 Set of 4 2.00 2.00

Insects A637

Designs: 5c, Bumblebee. 10c, Praying mantis. 30c, Firefly, vert. $1.35, Green darner dragonfly, vert.

2007, Dec. 4 *Perf. 13¼*
3598-3601 A637 Set of 4 1.40 1.40

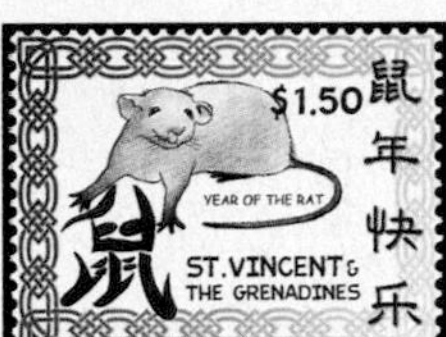

New Year 2008 (Year of the Rat) A638

2008, Jan. 8 Litho. *Perf. 12*
3602 A638 $1.50 multi 1.10 1.10

Printed in sheets of 4.

Miniature Sheet

2008 Summer Olympics, Beijing — A639

No. 3603 — 1952 Summer Olympics: a, Bob Mathias, decathlon gold medalist. b, Poster. c, Josy Barthel, 800-meter gold medalist. d, Lis Hartel, dressage silver medalist.

2008, Jan. 8 *Perf. 14*
3603 A639 $1.40 Sheet of 4, #a-d 4.00 4.00

America's Cup Yacht Races, Valencia, Spain — A640

No. 3604 — Various yachts with denomination in: a, $1.20, Red. b, $1.80, White. c, $3, Light blue. d, $5, Orange brown.

2008, Jan. 10 *Perf. 13¼*
3604 A640 Block of 4, #a-d 8.00 8.00

Hummer H3 — A641

Hummer H3 going: a, Uphill, denomination at UL. b, Over rocks. c, In water. d, Uphill, denomination at UR.

$6, Hummer H3 on level ground.

2008, Jan. 10
3605 A641 $1.50 Sheet of 4, #a-d 4.25 4.25

Souvenir Sheet

3606 A641 $6 multi 4.75 4.75

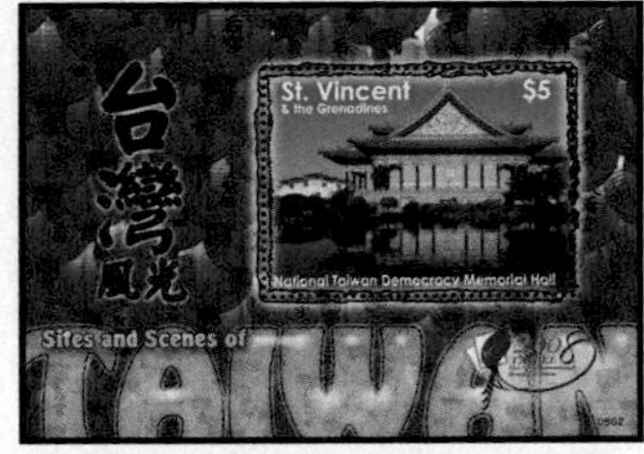

Sites and Scenes of Taiwan — A642

No. 3607, vert.: a, Taipei 101 Building. b, Pagoda. c, High speed railway. d, Lion dance.

$5, National Taiwan Democracy Memorial Hall.

2008, Feb. 8 *Perf. 11¼x11½*
3607 A642 $1.50 Sheet of 4, #a-d 4.25 4.25

Souvenir Sheet

Perf. 13¼

3608 A642 $5 multi 3.75 3.75

2008 Taipei Intl. Stamp Exhibition. No. 3607 contains four 30x40mm stamps.

Souvenir Sheet

Ocean Liners — A643

No. 3609: a, Queen Victoria. b, Queen Elizabeth 2. c, Queen Mary 2.

2008, May 1 *Perf. 13¼*
3609 A643 $3 Sheet of 3, #a-c 6.75 6.75

Miniature Sheet

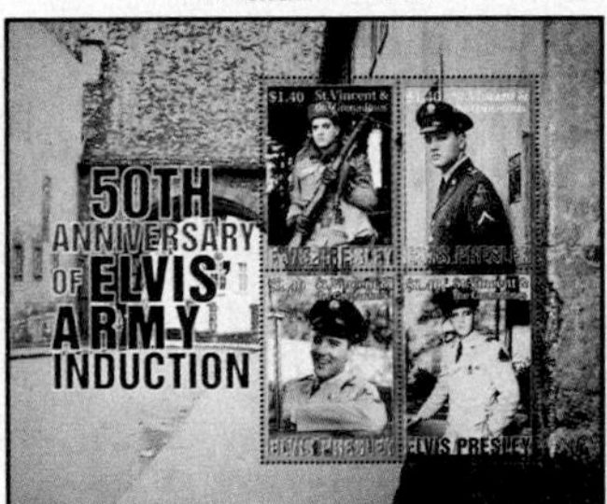

Induction of Elvis Presley into US Army, 50th Anniv. — A644

No. 3610 — Presley: a, Holding rifle. b, Standing against wall. c, In car. d, Standing next to car.

2008, May 1
3610 A644 $1.40 Sheet of 4, #a-d 4.00 4.00

Miniature Sheet

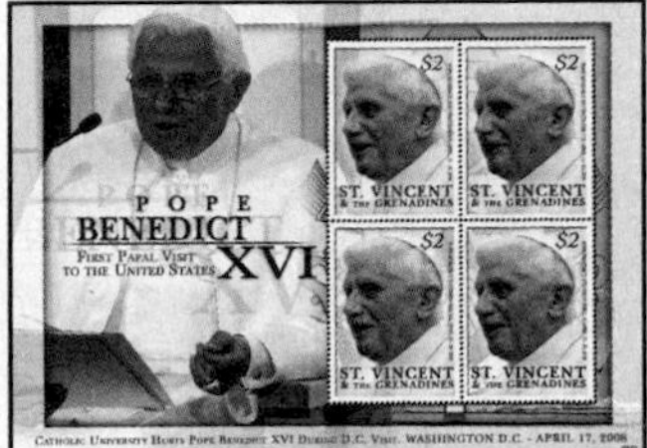

Pope Benedict XVI — A645

No. 3611 — Items in background: a, Cross at LL. b, Blue line near Pope's mouth. c, Tassel at left. d, Shell at left.

2008, May 1
3611 A645 $2 Sheet of 4, #a-d 5.50 5.50

Miniature Sheet

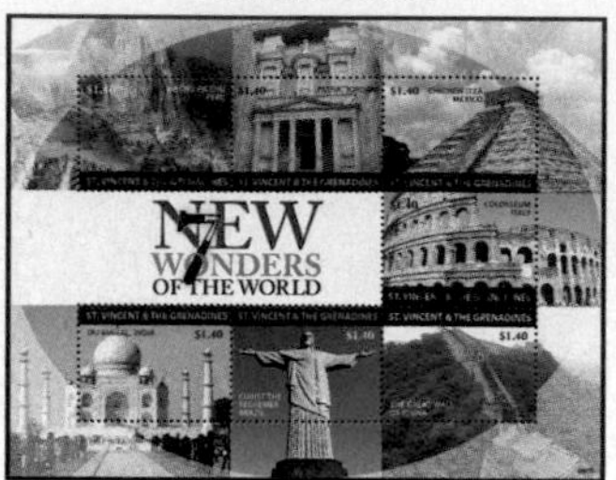

Seven New Wonders of the World — A646

No. 3612: a, Machu Picchu, Peru. b, Petra, Jordan. c, Chichén Itza, Mexico. d, Roman Colosseum, Italy. e, Taj Mahal, India. f, Christ the Redeemer Statue, Brazil. g, Great Wall of China.

2008, May 1 ***Perf. 11½***
3612 A646 $1.40 Sheet of 7, #a-g 7.50 7.50

University of the West Indies, 60th Anniv. — A647

Designs: 10c, University crest. 30c, Diploma. 90c, UWDEC Media Center, horiz. $1.05, 60th anniv. emblem.
$6, Crest, diploma, 60th anniv. emblem, horiz.

2008, June 27 ***Perf. 12¾***
3613-3616 A647 Set of 4 1.75 1.75

Souvenir Sheet

3617 A647 $6 multi 4.50 4.50

Miniature Sheets

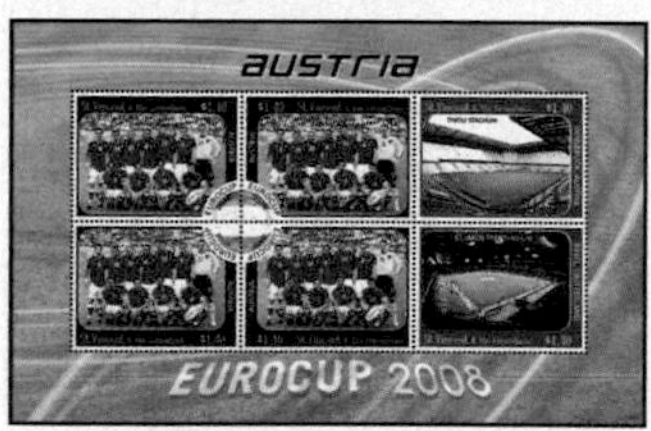

2008 European Soccer Championships — A648

No. 3618 — Teams and flags of: a, Czech Republic. b, Turkey. c, Austria. d, Croatia. e, Switzerland. f, Portugal. g, Poland. h, Germany. i, France. j, Netherlands. k, Greece. l, Sweden. m, Romania. n, Italy. o, Russia. p, Spain.
No. 3619 — Austria team with flag at: a, LR. b, LL. c, UR. d, UL. e, Tivoli Stadium. f, St. Jakob Park Stadium (stadium name at top).
No. 3620 — Croatia team with flag at: a, LR. b, LL. c, UR. d, UL. e, Stade de Geneve.
No. 3621 — Czech Republic team with flag at: a, LR. b, LL. c, UR. d, UL. e, Stade de Suisse Wankdorf.
No. 3622 — France team with flag at: a, LR. b, LL. c, UR. d, UL. e, Letzigrund Stadium.
No. 3623 — Germany team with flag at: a, LR. b, LL. c, UR. d, UL. e, Worthersee Stadium Hypo Arena.
No. 3624 — Greece team with flag at: a, LR. b, LL. c, UR. d, UL.
No. 3625 — Italy team with flag at: a, LR. b, LL. c, UR. d, UL.
No. 3626 — Netherlands team with flag at: a, LR. b, LL. c, UR. d, UL.
No. 3627 — Poland team with flag at: a, LR. b, LL. c, UR. d, UL. e, Wals-Siezenheim Stadium. f, St. Jakob Park Stadium (stadium name at bottom).
No. 3628 — Portugal team with flag at: a, LR. b, LL. c, UR. d, UL.
No. 3629 — Romania team with flag at: a, LR. b, LL. c, UR. d, UL.
No. 3630 — Russia team with flag at: a, LR. b, LL. c, UR. d, UL.
No. 3631 — Spain team with flag at: a, LR. b, LL. c, UR. d, UL. e, Ernst Happel Stadium.
No. 3632 — Sweden team with flag at: a, LR. b, LL. c, UR. d, UL.
No. 3633 — Switzerland team with flag at: a, LR. b, LL. c, UR. d, UL.
No. 3634 — Turkey team with flag at: a, LR. b, LL. c, UR. d, UL.

2008, Aug. 1 ***Perf. 13½***
3618 A648 65c Sheet of 16, #a-p 8.00 8.00
3619 A648 $1.40 Sheet of 6, #3619a-3619f 6.50 6.50
3620 A648 $1.40 Sheet of 6, #3619e, 3620a-3620e 6.50 6.50
3621 A648 $1.40 Sheet of 6, #3619e, 3621a-3621e 6.50 6.50
3622 A648 $1.40 Sheet of 6, #3619e, 3622a-3622e 6.50 6.50
3623 A648 $1.40 Sheet of 6, #3619f, 3623a-3623e 6.50 6.50
3624 A648 $1.40 Sheet of 6, #3621e, 3623e, 3624a-3624d 6.50 6.50
3625 A648 $1.40 Sheet of 6, #3620e, 3623e, 3625a-3625d 6.50 6.50
3626 A648 $1.40 Sheet of 6, #3622e, 3623e, 3626a-3626d 6.50 6.50
3627 A648 $1.40 Sheet of 6, # 3627a-3627f 6.50 6.50
3628 A648 $1.40 Sheet of 6, #3621e, 3627e, 3628a-3628d 6.50 6.50
3629 A648 $1.40 Sheet of 6, #3620e, 3627e, 3629a-3629d 6.50 6.50
3630 A648 $1.40 Sheet of 6, #3622e, 3627e, 3630a-3630d 6.50 6.50
3631 A648 $1.40 Sheet of 6, #3619f, 3631a-3631e 6.50 6.50
3632 A648 $1.40 Sheet of 6, #3621e, 3631e, 3632a-3632d 6.50 6.50
3633 A648 $1.40 Sheet of 6, #3620e, 3631e, 3633a-3633d 6.50 6.50
3634 A648 $1.40 Sheet of 6, #3622e, 3631e, 3634a-3634d 6.50 6.50
Nos. 3618-3634 (17) 112.00 112.00

Kingstown Cooperative Credit Union, 50th Anniv. — A649

Credit Union emblem and: 10c, Children. 30c, Man, vert. 90c, Woman, vert. $1.05, Man wearing sunglasses, vert.
$6, Credit Union Building.

Perf. 12½x12¾, 12¾x12½

2008, Sept. 1
3635-3638 A649 Set of 4 1.75 1.75

Souvenir Sheet

3639 A649 $6 multi 4.50 4.50

Miniature Sheets

Space Exploration, 50th Anniv. (in 2007) — A650

No. 3640, $1.40: a, Space suit of Valentina Tereshkova. b, Tereshkova wearing black suit. c, Vostok 6. d, Tereshkova in space suit and helmet. e, Statue of Tereshkova. f, Tereshkova in space suit without helmet.
No. 3641, $1.40: a, Pioneer 11. b, Pioneer 10 on Atlas Centaur 27 rocket. c, Pioneer plaque. d, Pioneer 10. e, Technical drawing of Pioneer 10 and Pioneer 11. f, Pioneer program.
No. 3642, $1.40: a, Viking 1 on Titan IIIE Centaur rocket. b, Viking 1 orbiter and lander technical drawing. c, Viking 1 lander firing retrorockets. d, Viking 1 above Mars. e, Viking 1 lander technical drawing. f, Picture from Viking 1.
No. 3643, $2: a, Freedom 7 capsule. b, Astronaut Alan Shepard. c, Vostok. d, Cosmonaut Yuri Gagarin.
No. 3644, $2: a, Luna 2. b, Luna 2 ball. c, Lift-off of Luna 2. d, Luna 2 above Moon.
No. 3645, $2: a, Mariner 4 Mars Encounter Imaging Geometry. b, Mariner 4. c, Lift-off of Mariner 4. d, Mariner 4 and Mars.

2008, Oct. 29 ***Perf. 14¼***

Sheets of 6, #a-f

3640-3642 A650 Set of 3 19.50 19.50

Sheets of 4, #a-d

3643-3645 A650 Set of 3 18.50 18.50

Christmas — A651

Crèche scenes: 75c, Adoration of the Shepherds. 90c, Angel in manger. $2, Adoration of the Shepherds, diff. $3, Holy Family.

2008, Dec. 8 ***Perf. 14***
3646-3649 A651 Set of 4 5.00 5.00

Inauguration of US Pres. Barack Obama — A652

Designs: Nos. 3650, 3652a, Pres. Obama and US flag. $2.75, Pres. Obama, US flag and statue of Abraham Lincoln (26x34mm). No. 3652b, Vice-president Joseph Biden.

Perf. 14x14¾, 12¼x11¾ (#3651)

2009, Jan. 20
3650 A652 $1.75 multi 1.40 1.40
3651 A652 $2.75 multi 2.10 2.10

Souvenir Sheet

3652 A652 $6.50 Sheet of 2, #a-b 10.00 10.00

No. 3650 was printed in sheets of 9; No. 3651, in sheets of 4.

New Year 2009 (Year of the Ox) A653

2009, Jan. 26 ***Perf. 12***
3653 A653 $2.50 multi 1.90 1.90

Printed in sheets of 4.

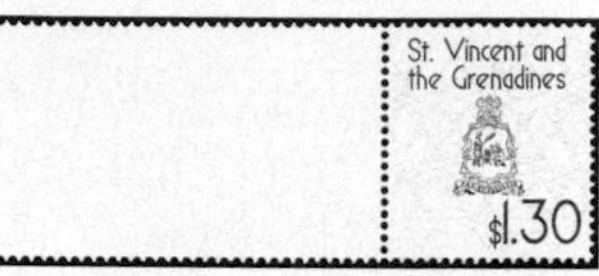

St. Vincent Coat of Arms — A654

2009, Feb. 20 ***Perf. 14x14¾***
3654 A654 $1.30 purple + label 1.00 1.00

Printed in sheets of 8 + 8 labels.The labels could be personalized.

Miniature Sheet

Juventus Soccer Team — A655

No. 3655: a, Goalie. b, Three players with gold shirts, one raising fist. c, Three players with gold shirts, one sticking out tongue. d, Four players with gold shirts. e, Fans. f, Players in striped shirts, one with fist and open mouth. g, Players in striped shirts, one with arms extended. h, Player in striped shirt kicking ball.

2009, Apr. 23 ***Perf. 13½***
3655 A655 $1.50 Sheet of 8, #a-h, + central label 9.00 9.00

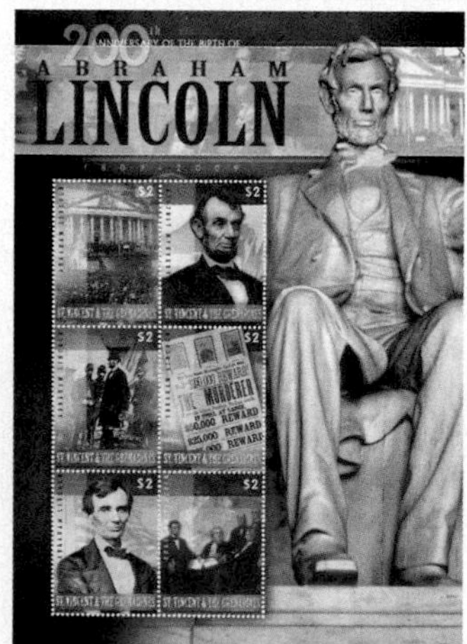

Pres. Abraham Lincoln (1809-65) — A656

No. 3656: a, Inauguration of Lincoln. b, Lincoln with beard. c, Lincoln visiting troops. d, Reward poster for Lincoln's assassin. e, Lincoln without beard. f, Lincoln and four men.
$6, Statue of Lincoln from Lincoln Memorial.

2009, Apr. 23 ***Perf. 14¼x14¾***
3656 A656 $2 Sheet of 6, #a-f 9.50 9.50

Souvenir Sheet

Perf. 14¼

3657 A656 $6 multi 4.75 4.75

No. 3657 contains one 38x50mm stamp.

Miniature Sheet

Felix Mendelssohn (1809-47), Composer — A657

No. 3658: a, A Midsummer's Night Dream, painting by David Scott. b, Portrait of Mendelssohn, by Eduard Magnus. c, Portrait of Cécile Jeanrenaud, wife of Mendelssohn, by Magnus. d, Score of "On Wings of Song." e, Gewandhausorchester. f, Church of the Holy Ghost, drawing by Mendelssohn.

2009, May 18 ***Perf. 11¼x11½***
3658 A657 $2.50 Sheet of 6, #a-f 11.50 11.50

Miniature Sheet

Pope Benedict XVI — A658

No. 3659 — Pope Benedict XVI: a, $1.50. b, $2. c, $2.50. d, $3.

2009, May 18 ***Perf. 11½***
3659 A658 Sheet of 4, #a-d 7.00 7.00

Miniature Sheet

First Man on the Moon, 40th Anniv. — A659

No. 3660: a, US 2002 Ohio state quarter. b, Apollo 11 Command Module. c, Apollo 11 patch. d, Apollo 11 Lunar Module. e, Drawing of Apollo 11 Command and Lunar Modules. f, Astronaut Neil Armstrong.

2009, May 18 ***Perf. 13¼***
3660 A659 $2 Sheet of 6, #a-f 9.50 9.50

Miniature Sheets

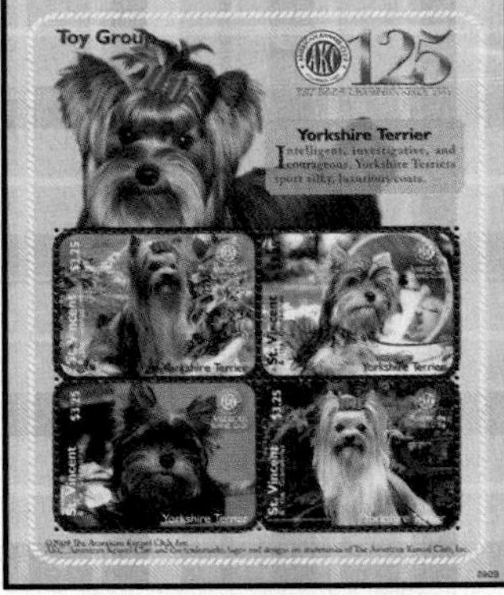

Dogs — A660

No. 3661: a, Yorkshire terrier. b, German shepherd. c, Golden retriever. d, Beagle. e, Dachshund. f, Boxer. g, Poodle. h, Shih tzu. i, Miniature schnauzer.

No. 3662 — Yorkshire terrier: a, With flowers, wearing ribbon. b, With basket at right. c, With flower at left. d, With berries at left, wearing ribbon.

2009, May 18 ***Perf. 11½***
3661 A660 $1.60 Sheet of 9, #a-i 11.00 11.00
3662 A660 $3.25 Sheet of 4, #a-d 9.00 9.00

A661

A662

Michael Jackson (1958-2009), Singer — A663

No. 3663, 45c: a, Wearing brown striped suit. b, Wearing hat.

No. 3664, 90c: a, Holding microphone. b, Wearing black sweater.

No. 3665, $1.50: a, Wearing jacket and white shirt. b, Wearing red and gold jacket.

No. 3666, $4: a, With goggles on hat. b, Wearing red and gold jacket and white glove.

No. 3667: a, $2.25, Making fist. b, $2.25, Singing. c, $2.75, As "a." d, $2.75, As "b."

No. 3668: a, With microphone in front of chin. b, Holding microphone. c, Pointing. d, With lights in background.

Horiz. Pairs, #a-b

2009 ***Perf. 14¼x14¾***
3663-3666 A661 Set of 4 10.50 10.50

Miniature Sheets

Perf. 11½
3667 A662 Sheet of 4, #a-d 7.50 7.50
3668 A663 $2.50 Sheet of 4, #a-d 7.50 7.50

Issued: Nos. 3663-3666, 7/7; Nos. 3667-3668, 7/17. Nos. 3663-3666 were each printed in sheets containing two pairs. Compare with Type A125.

Miniature Sheet

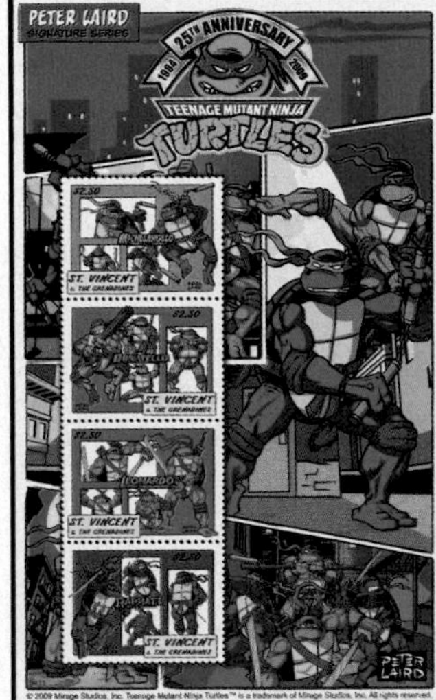

Teenage Mutant Ninja Turtles, 25th Anniv. — A664

No. 3669: a, Michelangelo. b, Donatello. c, Leonardo. d, Raphael.

2009, July 15 ***Perf. 11½x12***
3669 A664 $2.50 Sheet of 4, #a-d 7.75 7.75

A665

A666

A667

A668

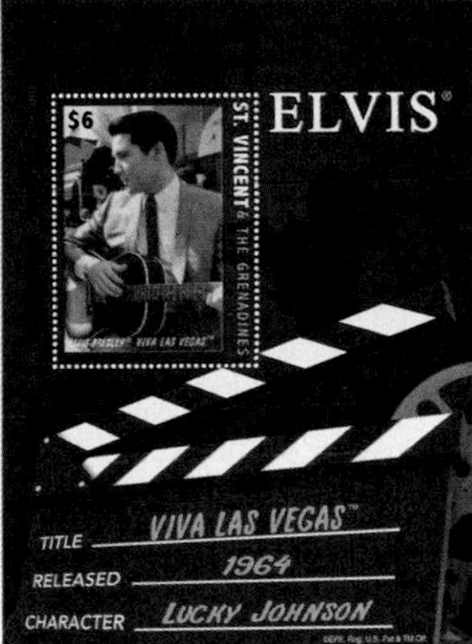

Elvis Presley (1935-77) — A669

No. 3670 — Presley and: a, "L." b, "V." c, "I." d, "S."

2009, July 15 ***Perf. 13½***
3670 A665 $2.50 Sheet of 4, #a-d 7.75 7.75

Souvenir Sheets

Perf. 14¼

3671	A666	$6 multi	4.75	4.75
3672	A667	$6 multi	4.75	4.75
3673	A668	$6 multi	4.75	4.75
3674	A669	$6 multi	4.75	4.75
		Nos. 3671-3674 (4)	19.00	19.00

Preservation of Polar Regions and Glaciers — A670

No. 3675: a, Penguin diving, two penguins swimming. b, Nine penguins. c, Three penguins, two with wings extended. d, Adult penguin feeding juvenile.
$6, Five penguins.

2009, Aug. 1 ***Perf. 13½***
3675 A670 $3 Sheet of 4, #a-d 9.00 9.00

Souvenir Sheet

3676 A670 $6 multi 4.50 4.50

No. 3676 contains one 38x51mm stamp.

Birds A671

Designs: $1.20, White-rumped sandpiper. $1.80, Tricolored heron. No. 3679, $3, Masked booby. $5, Red-footed booby, vert.

No. 3681, vert: a, Brown pelican. b, Great blue heron. c, Snowy egret. d, Pied-billed grebe.

No. 3682, vert.: a, Ring-billed gull. b, Short-billed dowitcher.

2009, Aug. 1 Litho. *Perf. 12*

3677-3680 A671 Set of 4 8.25 8.25
3681 A671 $2.50 Sheet of 4, #a-b 7.50 7.50

Souvenir Sheet

3682 A671 $3 Sheet of 2, #a-b 4.50 4.50

For overprint, see No. 3700.

Miniature Sheet

Stamp Expo 400, Albany, New York — A672

No. 3683: a, Samuel de Champlain (c. 1567-1635), explorer. b, Robert Fulton (1765-1815), steamboat builder. c, Henry Hudson (d. 1611), explorer. d, Ships, US #372.

2009, Sept. 18 *Perf. 11½*

3683 A672 $2.50 Sheet of 4, #a-d 7.50 7.50

Christmas A673

Designs: 90c, Magi on camels. $1.80, Holy Family. $2.50, Adoration of the Magi. $3, Madonna and Child.

2009, Dec. 10 *Perf. 13x13¼*

3684-3687 A673 Set of 4 6.25 6.25

Miniature Sheets

2010 World Cup Soccer Championships, South Africa — A674

No. 3688, $1.75 — Team from: a, Australia. b, Japan. c, North Korea. d, South Korea. e, Honduras. f, Mexico. g, United States. h, New Zealand.

No. 3689, $1.75 — Team from: a, South Africa. b, Brazil. c, Spain. d, Netherlands. e, Italy. f, Germany. g, Argentina. h, England.

No. 3690, $1.75 — Team from: a, Denmark. b, France. c, Greece. d, Portugal. e, Serbia. f, Slovakia. g, Slovenia. h, Switzerland.

No. 3691, $1.75 — Team from: a, Algeria. b, Cameroon. c, Ivory Coast. d, Ghana. e, Nigeria. f, Chile. g, Paraguay. h, Uruguay.

Sheets of 8, #a-h, + Central Label

2010, Jan. 20 *Perf. 14¼*

3688-3691 A674 Set of 4 45.00 45.00

Ferrari Automobiles and Parts — A675

No. 3692, $1.25: a, Engine of 1970 312 B. b, 1970 312 B.

No. 3693, $1.25: a, Engine of 1973 Dino 308 GT4. b, 1973 Dino 308 GT4.

No. 3694, $1.25: a, Shift console of 1976 400 Automatic. b, 1976 400 Automatic.

No. 3695, $1.25: a, Engine of 1981 126 CX. b, 1981 126 CX.

Vert. Pairs, #a-b

2010, Feb. 18 Litho. *Perf. 12*

3692-3695 A675 Set of 4 8.00 8.00

Miniature Sheets

Inauguration of US Pres. John F. Kennedy, 50th Anniv. — A676

No. 3696: a, White House Oval Office. b, Pres. Kennedy. c, Jacqueline Kennedy. d, Lady Bird Johnson. e, Vice-president Lyndon B. Johnson. f, Capitol Building.

No. 3697: a, Pres. Kennedy. b, John F. Kennedy Presidential Library and Museum, Boston. c, Statue of Pres. Kennedy, Regents Park, London. d, Presidential seal.

2010, Mar. 17 *Perf. 13¼*

3696 A676 $2 Sheet of 6, #a-f 9.00 9.00
3697 A676 $2.75 Sheet of 4, #a-d 8.25 8.25

Miniature Sheets

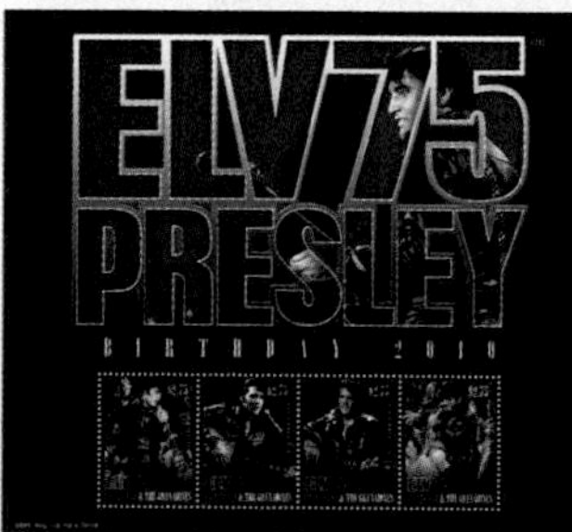

A677

Elvis Presley (1935-77) — A678

No. 3698: a, Without guitar, facing right. b, With guitar, microphone at right. c, With guitar, microphone at left. d, Without guitar, facing left.

No. 3699: a, With guitar. b, With hands near ears. c, Scratching head. d, With arms at side.

2010, Mar. 17 *Perf. 11¼x11½*

3698 A677 $2.75 Sheet of 4, #a-d 8.25 8.25
3699 A678 $2.75 Sheet of 4, #a-d 8.25 8.25

No. 3681 Overprinted With Map of Haiti and "Haiti Earthquake Relief Fund"

Method and Perf. As Before

2010, Jan. 15

3700 A671 $2.50 Sheet of 4, #a-d 7.75 7.75

A679

Flowers — A680

Designs: 25c, Huito. 80c, Tiny bladderwort. $1, Purple coral tree. $5, Apple guava. No. 3705, horiz.: a, Soufriere tree. b, Guajacum. c, Nipplefruit. d, Alpine bladderwort. e, Fetid passion flower. f, Shoreline purslane.

2010, Apr. 23 Litho. *Perf. 14x14¾*

3701-3704 A679 Set of 4 5.25 5.25

Perf. 14¾x14

3705 A680 $2 Sheet of 6, #a-f 9.00 9.00

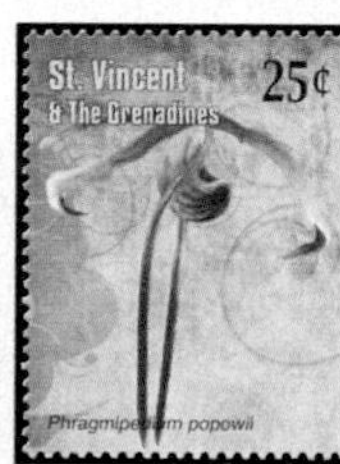

Orchids — A681

Designs: 25c, Phragmipedium popowii. 80c, Cattleya dowiana. $1, Brassavola subulifolia. $5, Brassavola acaulis. No. 3710, horiz.: a, Cattleya gaskelliana. b, Cattleya aurea. c, Cattleya mendelii. d, Cattleya schrodera. e, Cypripedium dickinsonianum. f, Phragmipedium longifolium.

2010, Apr. 23 Litho. *Perf. 13¼x13*

3706-3709 A681 Set of 4 5.25 5.25

Perf. 13x13¼

3710 A681 $2 Sheet of 6, #a-f 9.00 9.00

Marine Life A682

Designs: 25c, Leatherback turtle. 80c, Caesar grunt. $1, Atlantic tarpon. $5, Moray eel. No. 3715: a, Caribbean reef shark. b, Loggerhead sea turtle. c, Great barracuda. d, Caribbean lobster. e, Royal gramma. f, Southern stingray.

2010, Apr. 23 Litho. *Perf. 14¾x14*

3711-3714 A682 Set of 4 5.25 5.25
3715 A682 $2 Sheet of 6, #a-f 9.00 9.00

Antverpia 2010 National and European Championship of Philately, Antwerp, Belgium (No. 3715).

Girl Guides, Cent. — A683

No. 3716: a, Two Girl Guides. b, Four Girl Guides. c, Four Girl Guides and trefoil. d, Three Girl Guides.

$6, One Girl Guide, vert.

2010, June 4 *Perf. 13x13¼*

3716 A683 $2.75 Sheet of 4, #a-d 8.25 8.25

Souvenir Sheet

Perf. 13¼x13

3717 A683 $6 multi 4.50 4.50

Miniature Sheet

Accession to Throne of King George V, Cent. — A684

No. 3718: a, King William IV. b, Queen Victoria. c, King Edward VII. d, King George V on coin. e, Portrait of King George V. f, Statue of King George V.

2010, Sept. 1 *Perf. 11½*

3718 A684 $2 Sheet of 6, #a-f 9.00 9.00

Miniature Sheets

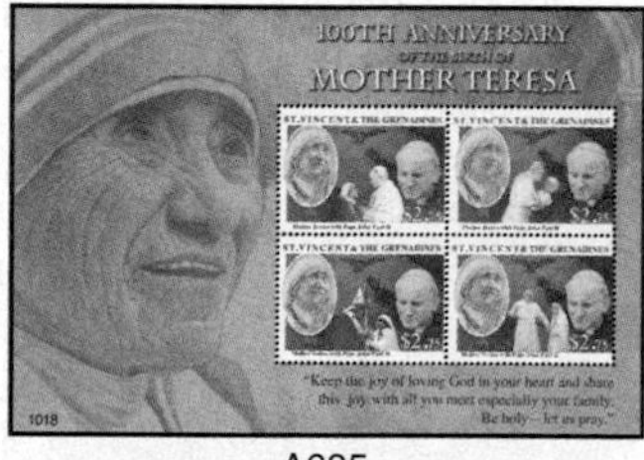

A685

Mother Teresa (1910-97), Humanitarian, and Pope John Paul II (1920-2005) — A686

No. 3719 — With dove above Mother Teresa; Pope John Paul II: a, To right of Mother Teresa. b, Touching head of Mother Teresa. c, Wearing miter. d, Holding Mother Teresa's hand.

No. 3720 — Without dove above Mother Teresa; Pope John Paul II: a, Wearing miter. b, Touching head of Mother Teresa. c, At left, holding hand of Mother Teresa. d, At right, holding hand of Mother Teresa.

2010, Sept. 1 *Perf. 13x13¼*

3719 A685 $2.75 Sheet of 4, #a-d 8.25 8.25
3720 A686 $2.75 Sheet of 4, #a-d 8.25 8.25

Miniature Sheet

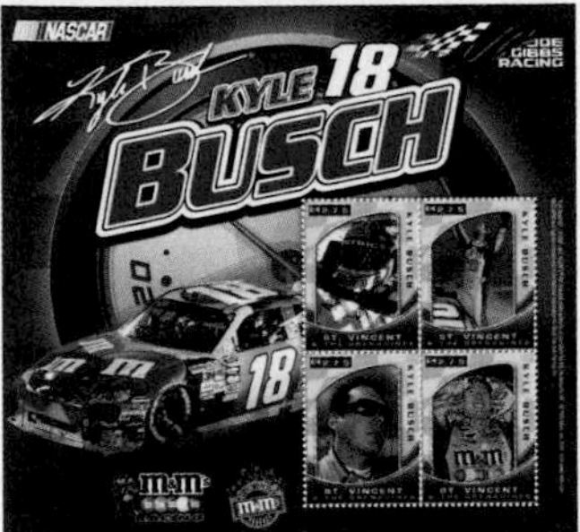

Kyle Busch, NASCAR Race Car Driver — A687

No. 3721 — Busch: a, In car wearing helmet. b, With arms raised, wearing helmet. c, Wearing sunglasses. d, Wearing cap.

2010, Oct. 5 ***Perf. 12x11½***
3721 A687 $2.75 Sheet of 4, #a-d 8.25 8.25

Paintings of Sandro Botticelli (1445-1510) — A688

No. 3722, vert.: a, The Annunciation. b, Portrait of a Young Man. c, Portrait of Simonetta Vespucci. d, Die Verstossene (The Outcast).
$6, Mystic Nativity.

2010, Oct. 5 ***Perf. 12x11½***
3722 A688 $2.50 Sheet of 4, #a-d 7.50 7.50

Souvenir Sheet

Perf. 13½

3723 A688 $6 multi 4.50 4.50

No. 3722 contains four 30x40mm stamps.

Henri Dunant (1828-1910), Founder of Red Cross — A689

No. 3724 — Nurse, soldiers and Dunant in: a, Greenish black. b, Brown. c, Violet brown. d, Blue black.
$6, Florence Nightingale, Clara Barton and Dunant.

2010, Oct. 5 ***Perf. 12***
3724 A689 $2.50 Sheet of 4, #a-d 7.50 7.50

Souvenir Sheet

3725 A689 $6 multi 4.50 4.50

Miniature Sheets

Characters in Star Trek Movies — A690

No. 3726, $2.75 — Star Trek II, The Wrath of Khan: a, Saavik. b, Spock and Dr. Leonard McCoy. c, Capt. James T. Kirk. d, Khan Noonien Singh.
No. 3727, $2.75 — Star Trek IV, The Voyage Home: a, Montgomery Scott. b, Spock. c, Kirk. d, McCoy.

Perf. 12x11½, 11½ (#3727)

2010, Oct. 5 **Sheets of 4, #a-d**
3726-3727 A690 Set of 2 16.50 16.50

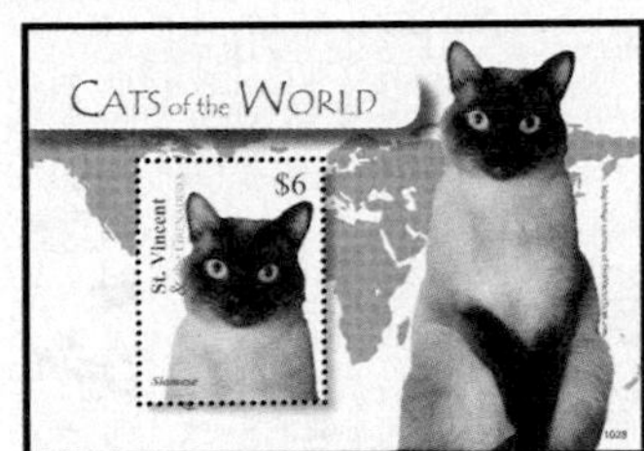

Cats — A691

No. 3728: a, Persian. b, Russian Blue. c, Chartreux. d, Bobtail. e, Selkirk Rex. f, Bengal.
$6, Siamese.

2010, Oct. 5 ***Perf. 12***
3728 A691 $2 Sheet of 6, #a-f 9.00 9.00

Souvenir Sheet

3729 A691 $6 multi 4.50 4.50

Miniature Sheets

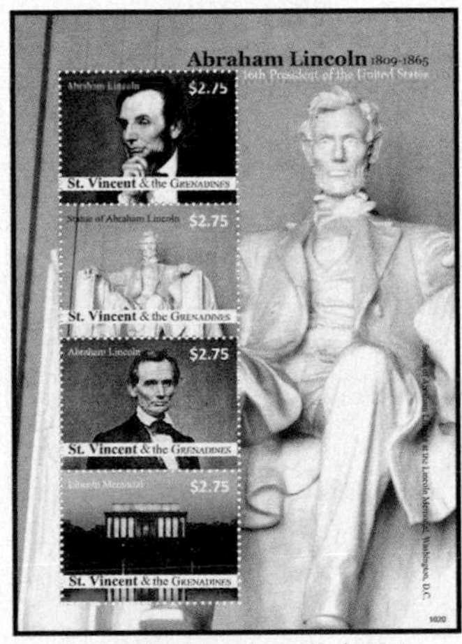

Pres. Abraham Lincoln (1809-65) — A692

No. 3730, $2.75: a, Lincoln with hand on chin. b, Statue of Lincoln in Lincoln Memorial. c, Photograph of Lincoln without beard. d, Lincoln Memorial at dusk.
No. 3731, $2.75: a, Photograph of Lincoln with beard. b, Aerial view of Lincoln Memorial. c, First Reading of the Emancipation Proclamation of President Lincoln, painting by Francis Carpenter. d, Lincoln and US No. 1282.

Sheets of 4, #a-d

2010, Oct. 5 ***Perf. 12***
3730-3731 A692 Set of 2 16.50 16.50

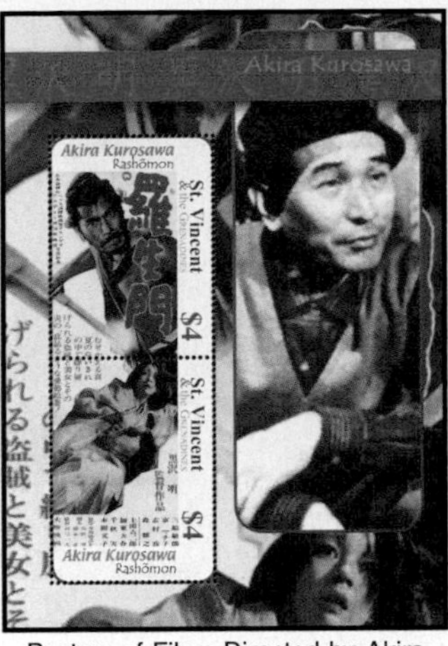

Posters of Films Directed by Akira Kurosawa (1910-98) — A693

No. 3732, $2.50: a, Shubun (Scandal). b, Subarashiki Nichiyobi (One Wonderful Sunday). c, Sugata Sanshiro (Judo Saga). d, Kakushi Toride No San Akunin (The Hidden Fortress).
No. 3733, $2.50: a, Kumonosu-jo (Throne of Blood). b, Waga Seishun Ni Kuinashi (No Regrets for Our Youth). c, Tora No o Wo Fumu Otokotachi (The Men Who Tread on the Tiger's Tail). d, Yoidore Tenshi (Drunken Angel).
No. 3734: a, Rashomon (Samurai with sword). b, Rashomon (woman with knife).

Sheets of 4, #a-d

2010, Oct. 5 ***Perf. 13¼***
3732-3733 A693 Set of 2 15.00 15.00

Souvenir Sheet

3734 A693 $4 Sheet of 2, #a-b 6.00 6.00

Miniature Sheets

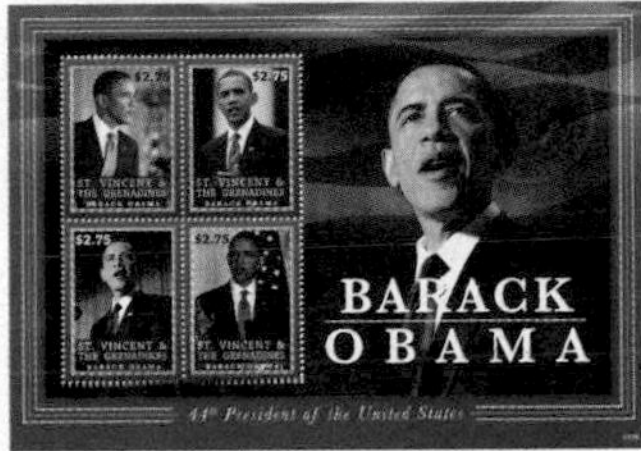

A694

Pres. Barack Obama — A695

No. 3735 — Blue frame, Pres. Obama with: a, Blue tie, microphone at right. b, Red striped tie. c, Black tie, microphone at left. d, Blue tie, flag in background.
No. 3736 — Red frame, Pres. Obama with: a, Black and white striped tie. b, Blue tie, foliage in background. c, Black and white patterned tie, red flag in background. d, Blue tie.

2010, Dec. 6 ***Perf. 12x12½***
3735 A694 $2.75 Sheet of 4, #a-d 8.25 8.25
3736 A695 $2.75 Sheet of 4, #a-d 8.25 8.25

Christmas A696

Paintings: 90c, Annunciation, by Domenico di Pace Beccafumi. $1.80, Adoration of the Shepherds, by Gerard van Honthorst. $2.50, Adoration of the Magi, by Guido Reni. $3, Nativity, by Domenico Ghirlandaio.

2010, Dec. 15 **Litho.** ***Perf. 12***
3737-3740 A696 Set of 4 6.25 6.25

British Monarchs A697

Designs: No. 3741, $2, King Henry I (c. 1068-1135). No. 3742, $2, King John (1166-1216). No. 3743, $2, King Richard II (1367-1400). No. 3744, $2, King Edward V (1470-83 ?) No. 3745, $2, King Edward VI (1537-53). nO. 3746, $2, King Charles II (1630-85). No. 3747, $2, King George III (1738-1820). No. 3748, $2, King George VI (1895-1952).

2011, Jan. 20 ***Perf. 13 Syncopated***
3741-3748 A697 Set of 8 12.00 12.00

Nos. 3741-3748 each were printed in sheets of 8 + central label.

A698

Indipex 2011 Intl. Philatelic Exhibition, New Delhi — A699

No. 3749 — Spices: a, Saffron. b, Chili peppers. c, Curry leaves. d, Turmeric. e, Peppercorns. f, Cinnamon.
No. 3750 — Animals: a, Indian peafowl. b, Indian elephant. c, Red panda. d, Blackbuck. e, King cobra. f, Indian leopard. g, Indian rhinoceros.
No. 3751— Bengal tiger with denominati at: a, LR. b, UL.

2011, Feb. 9

3749	A698	$1.85	Sheet of 6, #a-f	8.25	8.25
3750	A699	$1.85	Sheet of 7, #a-g + 2 labels	9.75	9.75

Souvenir Sheet

3751	A699	$5	Sheet of 2, #a-b	7.50	7.50

Visit to Japan of President Barack Obama — A700

No. 3752 — Pres. Obama: a, Shaking hands with Japanese Prime Minister Yukio Hatoyama. b, With Hatoyama, flags, Hatoyama waving. c, Walking with Hatoyama. d, At lectern.
$6, Pres. Obama waving.

2011, Feb. 9 ***Perf. 12***

3752	A700	$2.75	Sheet of 4, #a-d	8.25	8.25

Souvenir Sheet

Perf. 12¾

3753	A700	$6	multi	4.50	4.50

No. 3753 contains one 51x38mm stamp.

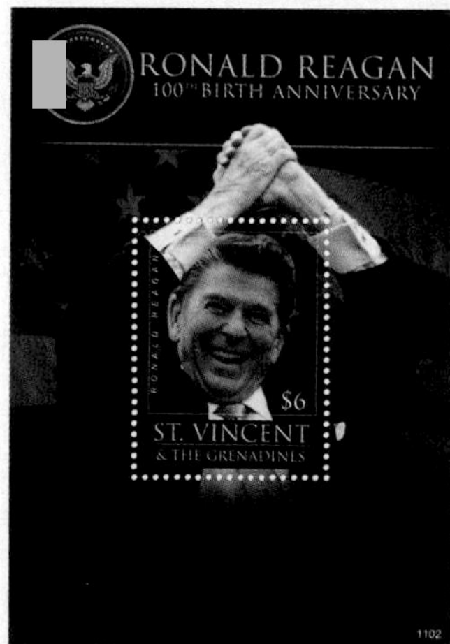

Pres. Ronald Reagan (1911-2004) — A701

No. 3754, horiz. — Pres. Reagan: a, With wife, Nancy, flag and ocean in background. b, At lectern, flag in background. c, At lectern, sign in background. c, With wife on helicopter.
$6, Pres. Reagan with arms raised.

2011, Feb. 9 ***Perf. 12***

3754	A701	$2.75	Sheet of 4, #a-d	8.25	8.25

Souvenir Sheet

3755	A701	$6	multi	4.50	4.50

Engagement of Prince William and Catherine Middleton — A702

Designs: No. 3756, Couple, maroon panels. No. 3757, Couple, diff., blue panels.
No. 3758, $6, Couple, diff. No. 3759, $6, Prince William, vert.

2011, Feb. 11 ***Perf. 12***

3756	A702	$2.50	multi	1.90	1.90

Perf. 13 Syncopated

3757	A702	$2.50	multi	1.90	1.90

Souvenir Sheets

3758-3759	A702	Set of 2	9.00	9.00

Flag of St. Vincent and the Grenadines — A703

2011, Feb. 17 ***Perf. 14¾x14¼***

3760	A703	$1	multi	.75	.75

Dolphins — A704

No. 3761: a, Stenella coeruleoalba. b, Langenodelphis hosei. c, Dephinus capensis. d, Delphinus delphis. e, Stenella longirostris. f, Stenella frontalis.
$6, Grampus griseus.

2011, Feb. 17 ***Perf. 13 Syncopated***

3761	A704	$2	Sheet of 6, #a-f	9.00	9.00

Souvenir Sheet

Perf. 12

3762	A704	$6	multi	4.50	4.50

Miniature Sheets

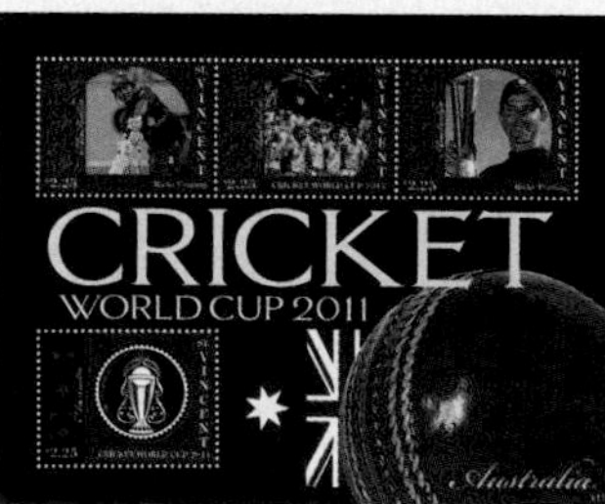

2011 World Cricket Cup, India, Bangladesh, and Sri Lanka — A705

No. 3763, $2.25 — Stamps inscribed "Australia": a, Ricky Ponting wearing helmet. b, Australia team. c, Ponting holding trophy. d, Cricket World Cup emblem.
No. 3764, $2.25 — Stamps inscribed "Bagladesh": a, Shakib Al Hasan wearing helmet. b, Al Hasan without helmet. c, Bangladesh team. d, Cricket World Cup emblem.
No. 3765, $2.25 — Stamps inscribed "England": a, Kevin Pietersen wearing helmet. b, Pietersen without helmet. c, English team. d, Cricket World Cup emblem.
No. 3766, $2.25 — Stamps inscribed "India": a, Sachin Tendulkar wearing helmet. b, Tendulkar without helmet. c, Tendulkar holding trophy. d, Cricket World Cup emblem.
No. 3767, $2.25 — Stamps inscribed "New Zealand": a, Daniel Vettori bowling. b, Vettori wearing cap. c, New Zealand team holding trophy. d, Cricket World Cup emblem.

Sheets of 4 #a-d

2011, May 2 ***Perf. 12***

3763-3767	A705	Set of 5	33.50	33.50

St. Vincent Girls' High School, Cent. A706

School crest and: 30c, 2010 steel drum orchestra. $1.05, Colette Sharlene Charles. No. 3770, $1.35, 1963 West Indian netball team, "BOA" visible on plane. No. 3770A, $1.35, 1963 West Indian netball team, "BOAC" on plane. $1.65, Beryl Baptiste, St. Vincent Director of Audit. No. 3772, $2.10, Grimble Building. No. 3773, $2.10, Betty Boyea-King, diplomat. No. 3774, $2.10, Dame Monica Dacon, deputy to Governor General.
No. 3775, $10, Mrs. Keizer and Mrs. Bowman, headmistresses of school. No. 3776, $10, Laura Smith-Moffett, headmistress. No. 3777, $10, Susan Dougan, cabinet secretary.

2011, May 16 ***Perf. 12½***

3768	A706	30c	multi	.25	.25
3769	A706	$1.05	multi	.75	.75
3770	A706	$1.35	multi	1.00	1.00
3770A	A706	$1.35	multi	1.00	1.00
3771	A706	$1.65	multi	1.25	1.25
3772	A706	$2.10	multi	1.60	1.60
3773	A706	$2.10	multi	1.60	1.60
3774	A706	$2.10	multi	1.60	1.60
	Nos. 3768-3774 (8)			9.05	9.05

Souvenir Sheets

3775-3777	A706	Set of 3	22.50	22.50

No. 3770A was printed in sheets of 4.

Sumo Wrestler — A707

Fish — A708

No. 3779: a, Pacific bluefin tuna. b, Koi. c, Porcupinefish. d, Cherry salmon.

2011, May 16 ***Perf. 12x12½***

3778	A707	$2.75	multi	2.10	2.10

Perf. 12½x12

3779	A708	$2.75	Sheet of 4, #a-d	8.25	8.25

PhilaNippon 2011 Intl. Philatelic Exhibition, Yokohama. No. 3778 was printed in sheets of 4.

Miniature Sheets

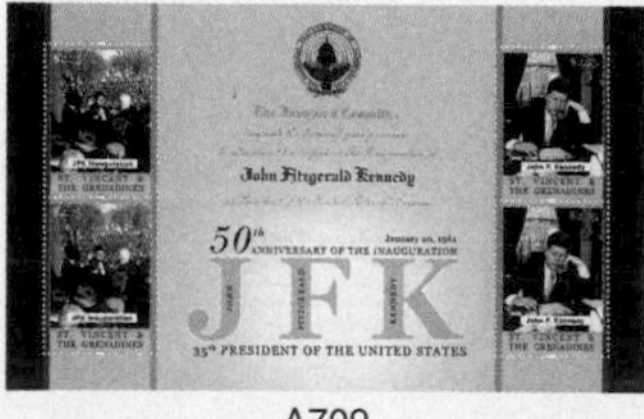

A709

Inauguration of Pres. John F. Kennedy, 50th Anniv. — A710

No. 3780: a, Kennedy taking oath. b, Kennedy on telephone.
No. 3781: a, Kennedy with wife, Jacqueline, and Vice-President Lyndon Johnson on reviewing stand. b, Kennedy at inaugural ball, flowers in background. c, Kennedy near doorway. d, Kennedy walking with wife at inaugural ball.

2011, May 16 ***Perf. 13 Syncopated***

3780	A709	$2.75	Sheet of 4, 2 each #a-b	8.25	8.25
3781	A710	$2.75	Sheet of 4, #a-d	8.25	8.25

Paintings by Michelangelo Merisi da Caravaggio (1571-1610) — A711

No. 3782: a, The Denial of Saint Peter. b, The Lute Player. c, The Fortune Teller. d, Supper at Emmaus.
$6, The Cardsharps.

2011, May 16 **Litho.**

3782	A711	$2.50	Sheet of 4, #a-d	7.50	7.50

Souvenir Sheet

3783	A711	$6	multi	4.50	4.50

Beatification of Pope John Paul II — A712

No. 3784 — Pope John Paul II with: a, Charles Eugène de Foucauld de Pontbriand (1858-1916), martyr. b, Sister Marie Simon-Pierre. c, Pope John XXIII. d, Pope Pius IX. e, Mother Teresa. f, Father Jerzy Popieluszko (1947-84), martyr.
$6, Pope John Paul II, dove, St. Peter's Basilica.

2011, May 16

3784	A712	$2	Sheet of 6, #a-f	9.00	9.00

Souvenir Sheet

3785	A712	$6	multi	4.50	4.50

Miniature Sheet

A. C. Milan Soccer Team — A713

No. 3786 — Team emblem and: a, Herbert Kilpin, team founder. b, Franco Baresi. c,

Coach Nereo Rocco and team, 1968. d, Scene from 1969 Intercontinental Cup match. e, Frank Rijkaard, Marco Van Basten, Ruud Gullit. f, Gianni Rivera. g, 1979 team. h, Van Basten. i, Scene from 1994 UEFA Champions League match.

2011, June 15 ***Perf. 13¼***

3786 A713 $1.20 Sheet of 9 #a-i 8.00 8.00

A714

Wedding of Prince William and Catherine Middleton A715

No. 3787: a, Groom. b, Bride. c, Couple.
No. 3788: a, Couple, bride waving. b, Couple, kissing.
$6, Couple in coach.

2011, June 15 ***Perf. 12***

3787	A714 $1.20	Block of 4, #3787a-3787b, 2 #3787c, + 2 labels	3.75	3.75
3788	A715 $2.75	Pair, #a-b	4.25	4.25

Souvenir Sheet

3789 A714 $6 multi 4.50 4.50

No. 3787 was printed in sheets containing 2 blocks. No. 3788 was printed in sheets containing two pairs.

Pres. Abraham Lincoln (1809-65) — A716

No. 3790, $2.75: a, Lincoln, denomination in brown at LL. b, Lincoln, denomination in white at LL. c, Soldiers, flag, at Battle of Fair Oaks, denomination at UR. d, Soldiers, flag and tree at Battle of Fair Oaks, denomination at UL.
No. 3791, $2.75: a, Lincoln, denomination in white at LR. b, Lincoln, denomination in brown at LR. c, Soldiers, horses, flag at Battle of Opequon, denomination at UR. d, Soldiers, horses, flag at Battle of Opequon, denomination at UL.

Sheets of 4, #a-d

2011, July 13 ***Perf. 13¼x13***

3790-3791 A716 Set of 2 16.50 16.50

Souvenir Sheets

A717

A718

A719

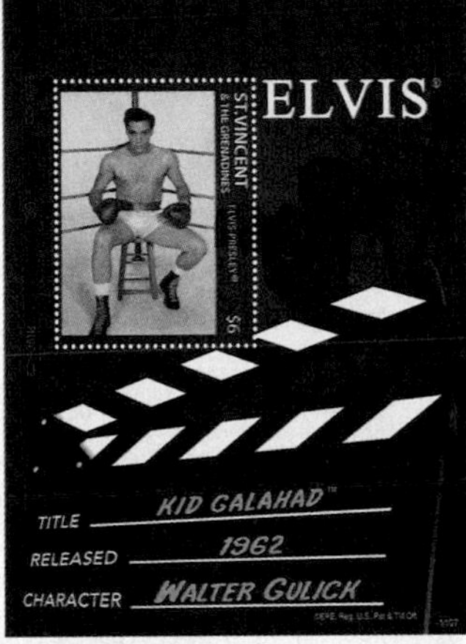

Elvis Presley (1935-77) — A720

2011, July 19 ***Perf. 12¾***

3792	A717	$6 multi	4.50	4.50
3793	A718	$6 multi	4.50	4.50
3794	A719	$6 multi	4.50	4.50
3795	A720	$6 multi	4.50	4.50
	Nos. 3792-3795 (4)		18.00	18.00

Miniature Sheets

British Royalty — A721

No. 3796, $2.75 — King George V: a, Wearing robes. b, Wearing military uniform and hat. c, Seated at desk. d, Wearing uniform and medals, without hat.
No. 3797, $2.75 — King George VI: a, With Lady Elizabeth Bowes-Lyon. b, Wearing polo shirt. c, Wearing suit and tie. d, Wearing military uniform.
No. 3798, $2.75, horiz. — Queen Elizabeth II: a, Wearing red hat. b, Wearing white blouse. c, As child, in garden. d, In automobile with Prince Philip.
No. 3799, $2.75, horiz. — Prince Philip: a, Wearing uniform, waving. b, With Queen Elizabeth II. c, In palace. d, With family, 1965.

2011, July 26 ***Perf. 13 Syncopated***

Sheets of 4, #a-d

3796-3799 A721 Set of 4 32.50 32.50

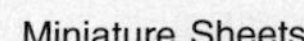

Miniature Sheets

A722

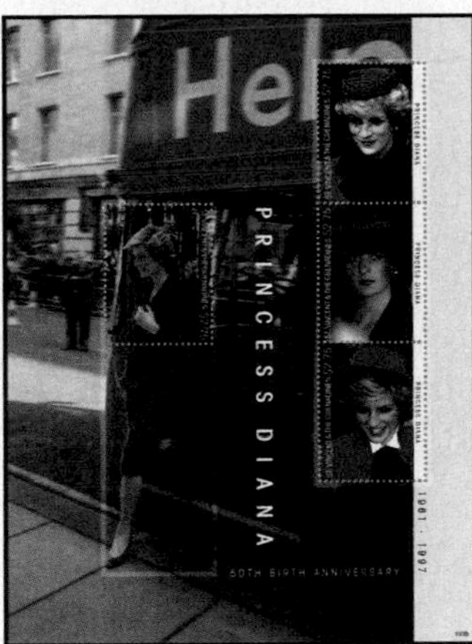

A723

No. 3800 — Princess Diana: a, Wearing striped jacket. b, Wearing dress and choker necklace. c, In vehicle. d, Wearing dark dress, no necklace.
No. 3801 — Princess Diana: a, Wearing red and black hat with veil. b, Leaving bus. c, Wearing red hat with black ribbon. d, Wearing red hat.

2011, July 28 ***Perf. 12***

3800	A722 $2.75	Sheet of 4, #a-d	8.25	8.25
3801	A723 $2.75	Sheet of 4, #a-d	8.25	8.25

Visit to Germany of Pope Benedict XVI — A724

No. 3802 — Various buildings and Pope Benedict XVI: a, Wearing white vestments, with hands together. b, Wearing miter. c, Wearing white vestments, hands not visible.
$6, Pope Benedict XVI waving, vert.

2011, Aug. 9 ***Perf. 12***

3802 A724 $3 Sheet of 3, #a-c 6.75 6.75

Souvenir Sheet

3803 A724 $6 multi 4.50 4.50

Sept. 11, 2001 Terrorist Attacks, 10th Anniv. — A725

No. 3804, horiz.: a, Candles and photograph of World Trade Center at Sept. 13, 2001 New York vigil. b, People at Sept. 13, 2001 New York vigil. c, Sept. 11 Memorial at Pentagon Building. d, Person, flag and flower at memorial in Stonycreek Township, Pennsylvania.
$6, Firemen and flags, New York.

2011, Oct. 6 ***Perf. 13x13¼***

3804 A725 $2.75 Sheet of 4, #a-d 8.25 8.25

Souvenir Sheet

Perf. 13¼x13

3805 A725 $6 multi 4.50 4.50

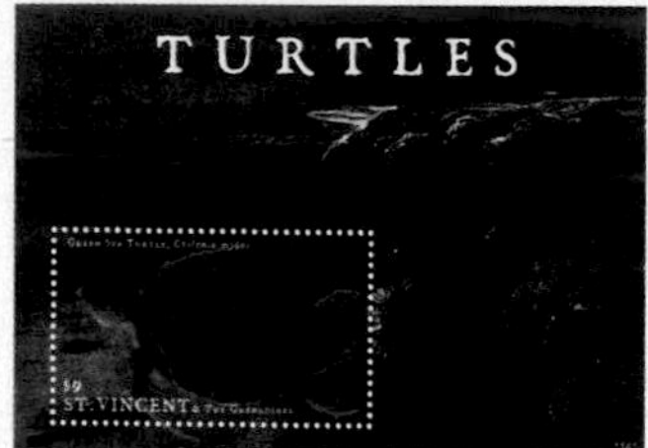

Turtles — A726

No. 3806: a, Chicken turtle. b, Diamondback terrapin. c, Red-eared slider.
$9, Green sea turtle.

2011, Oct. 26 ***Perf. 12***

3806 A726 $3 Sheet of 3, #a-c 6.75 6.75

Souvenir Sheet

3807 A726 $9 multi 6.75 6.75

Miniature Sheets

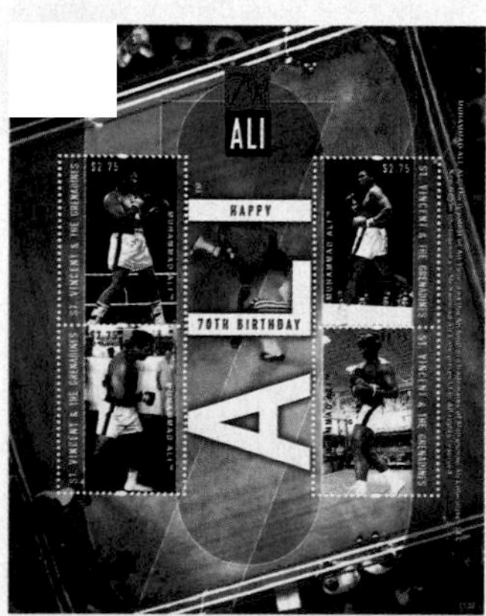

A727

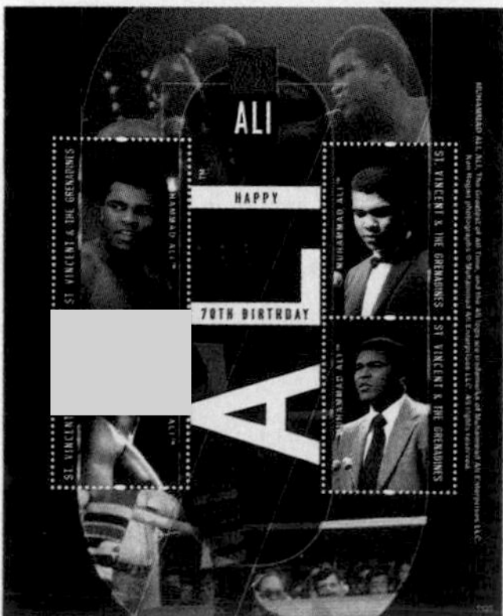

Muhammad Ali, 70th Birthday — A728

No. 3808 — Ali: a, Color photograph, wearing red gloves. b, Black-and-white photograph, during fight. c, Color photograph, wearing black gloves. d, Black-and-white photograph, in training ring wearing headgear.
No. 3809 — Ali: a, Color photograph, without shirt, facing forward. b, Black-and-white photograph, wearing bow tie. c, Color photograph, without shirt, facing right. d, Color photograph, wearing suit and tie.

2011, Nov. 2 ***Perf. 13 Syncopated***

3808 A727 $2.75 Sheet of 4, #a-d 8.25 8.25

3809 A728 $2.75 Sheet of 4, #a-d 8.25 8.25

Christmas A729

Details from paintings: 30c, Madonna and Child, by Sandro Botticelli. 90c, Madonna Enthroned, by Giotto di Bondone. $2, Madonna and Child, by Carlo Crivelli. $3, Mystic Nativity, by Botticelli.

2011, Nov. 2 ***Perf. 12***

3810-3813 A729 Set of 4 4.75 4.75

Miniature Sheet

1908 Olympic Games, London — A730

No. 3814: a, White City Stadium. b, Dorando Pietri. c, Erik Lemming. d, Poster for 1908 Olympic Games.

2011, Nov. 14 ***Perf. 13 Syncopated***

3814 A730 $2.75 Sheet of 4, #a-d 8.25 8.25

2012 Summer Olympics, London.

Anoles — A731

No. 3815: a, Barbados anole. b, Martinique's anole. c, Dominican anole. d, Leopard anole.
$9, Green anole.

2011, Nov. 14 ***Perf. 12***

3815 A731 $3.50 Sheet of 4, #a-d 10.50 10.50

Souvenir Sheet

3816 A731 $9 multi 6.75 6.75

No. 3816 contains one 30x50mm stamp.

Statue of Liberty, 125th Anniv. A732

2011, Dec. 16

3817 A732 $3 shown 2.25 2.25

Souvenir Sheet

3818 A732 $9 Statue, vert. 6.75 6.75

No. 3817 was printed in sheets of 3. No. 3818 contains one 30x50mm stamp.

Reign of Queen Elizabeth II, 60th Anniv. — A733

No. 3819 — Queen Elizabeth II: a, With Prince Philip. b, Wearing flowered hat. c, Wearing sash and tiara.
$9, Queen Elizabeth II, horiz.

2012, Jan. 1

3819 A733 $3.50 Sheet of 3, #a-c 7.75 7.75

Souvenir Sheet

3820 A733 $9 multi 6.75 6.75

No. 3820 contains one 50x30mm stamp.

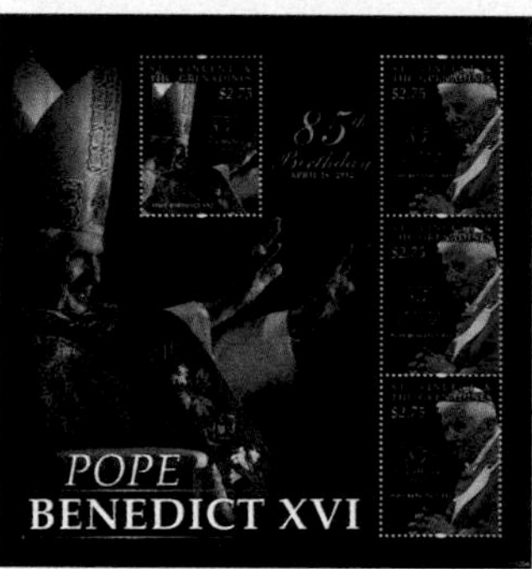

Pope Benedict XVI, 85th Birthday — A734

No. 3821: a, Facing right, waving. b, Facing left, wearing green vestments.
$6, Facing left, diff.

2012, Mar. 26 ***Perf. 13 Syncopated***

3821 A734 $2.75 Sheet of 4, #3821a, 3 #3821b 8.25 8.25

Souvenir Sheet

3822 A734 $6 multi 4.50 4.50

Miniature Sheets

A735

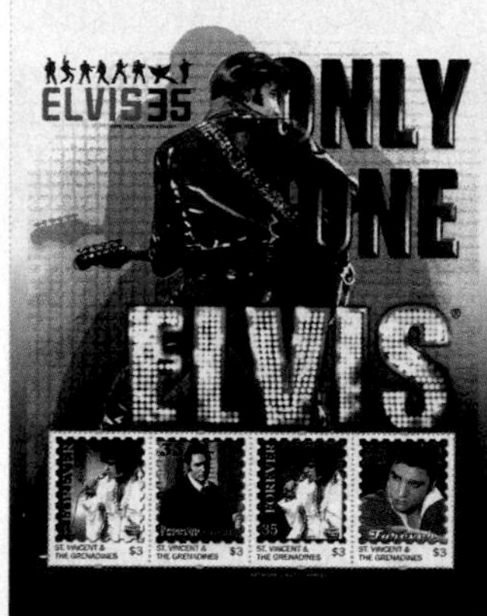

Elvis Presley (1935-77) — A736

No. 3823 — Presley: a, With guitar. b, Facing right, holding microphone. c, Wearing striped shirt. d, Facing left, holding microphone. No. 3824 — "Forever," and Presley: a, Facing right, holding microphone, "Forever" in gray. b, Wearing black jacket. c, Facing right, holding microphone, "Forever" in white. d, Wearing red jacket.

2012, Mar. 26 ***Perf. 13 Syncopated***

3823 A735 $3 Sheet of 4, #a-d 9.00 9.00

3824 A736 $3 Sheet of 4, #a-d 9.00 9.00

Miniature Sheet

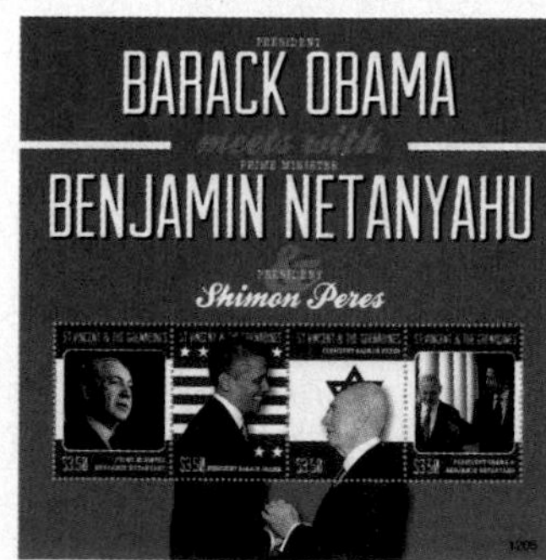

U.S. and Israeli Leaders — A737

No. 3825: a, Israeli Prime Minister Benjamin Netanyahu. b, Pres. Barack Obama. c, Israeli Pres. Shimon Peres, Israeli flag. d, Pres. Obama, Prime Minister Netanyahu.

2012, May 3 ***Perf. 13¼x13***

3825 A737 $3.50 Sheet of 4, #a-d 10.50 10.50

Miniature Sheets

French National Center for Space Studies, 50th Anniv. — A738

No. 3826, $3.50: a, SPOT satellite (denomination separated from satellite). b, SRET 2. c, Astronaut Jean-Loup Chrétien. d, JASON.
No. 3827, $3.50: a, Astronaut Claudie Haigneré. b, SPOT satellite (denomination covering part of satellite). c, Aureol 1. d, FR 1.

2012, May 3 ***Perf. 14***
Sheets of 4, #a-d
3826-3827 A738 Set of 2 21.00 21.00

Nos. 3826-3827 exist imperf. Value, set $25.

Miniature Sheets

Soft Moon Landing — A739

No. 3828, $3.50: a, Lunik 3. b, Luna 10. c, Lunik 2. d, Von Braun vehicle.
No. 3829, #3.50: a, Lunik 9. b, Russian lunar module. c, Lunar orbiter. d, Imaginative spaceship.

2012, June 27 ***Perf. 14***
Sheets of 4, #a-d
3828-3829 A739 Set of 2 21.00 21.00

Nos. 3828-3829 exist imperf. Value, set $25.

Miniature Sheet

Duke and Duchess of Cambridge, First Wedding Anniversary — A740

No. 3830: a, Duke of Cambridge. b, Duchess of Cambridge. c, Couple seated in coach. d, Couple standing.

2012, Sept. 5 ***Perf. 13¾***
3830 A740 $2.50 Sheet of 4, #a-d 7.50 7.50

Butterflies — A741

No. 3831: a, Danaus plexippus. b, Euptoieta hegesia. c, Libytheana carinenta. d, Lycorea halia.
$9, Phocides pigmalion.

2012, Sept. 5 ***Perf. 13¾***
3831 A741 $3.50 Sheet of 4, #a-d 10.50 10.50
Souvenir Sheet
3832 A741 $9 multi 6.75 6.75

Christmas A742

Paintings by Raphael: 80c, Madonna and Child with St. Johan and St. Nicholas. $1, The Holy Family with Saints Elizabeth and John. $1.70, Madonna and Child with Saints. $2.20, The Holy Family. $2.65, The Aldobrandini Madonna.
$3.40, The Visitation.

2012, Nov. 28 ***Perf. 12¾***
3833-3837 A742 Set of 5 6.25 6.25
Souvenir Sheet
3838 A742 $3.40 multi 2.50 2.50

Beetles — A743

No. 3839: a, Doryphora undata. b, Leptinotarsa lacerata. c, Chrysomela populi. d, Leptinotarsa decemlineata.
$9, Leptinotarsa puncticollis.

2013, Feb. 28 ***Perf. 12***
3839 A743 $3.50 Sheet of 4, #a-d 10.50 10.50
Souvenir Sheet
Perf. 12¾
3840 A743 $9 multi 6.75 6.75

No. 3840 contains one 38x51mm stamp.

Dogs — A744

No. 3841: a, Spanish mastiff. b, Poodle. c, Dachshund. d, Basenji.
$9, German shepherd.

2013, Feb. 28 ***Perf. 13 Syncopated***
3841 A744 $3.50 Sheet of 4, #a-d 10.50 10.50
Souvenir Sheet
3842 A744 $9 multi 6.75 6.75

Coral Reefs — A745

No. 3843: a, Hawksbill turtle. b, Sea sponges and tropical fish. c, Red cushion sea star. d, Ricordea coral.
$9, Turtle, fish, and reef, horiz.

2013, Feb. 28 ***Perf. 12***
3843 A745 $3.50 Sheet of 4, #a-d 10.50 10.50
Souvenir Sheet
3844 A745 $9 multi 6.75 6.75

No. 3844 contains one 80x30mm stamp.

Miniature Sheet

Crabs — A746

No. 3845: a, Clinging crab. b, Yellowline arrow crab. c, Redeye sponge crab. d, White-spotted hermit crab.
$9, White-spotted hermit crab, vert.

2013, Feb. 28 ***Perf. 13 Syncopated***
3845 A746 $3.50 Sheet of 4, #a-d 10.50 10.50
Souvenir Sheet
3846 A746 $9 multi 6.75 6.75

Miniature Sheet

Shells — A747

No. 3847: a, Triton's trumpet. b, Flame auger. c, Angular triton. d, Banded tulip. e, Lion's paw scallop.

Perf. 13 Syncopated
2013, Apr. 4 **Litho.**
3847 A747 $2.75 Sheet of 5, #a-e 10.50 10.50

Tel Aviv 2013 Multinational Stamp Exhibition.

Images of Celestial Objects Taken by Hubble Space Telescope — A748

No. 3848, $3.25: a, NGC 6302. b, M82. c, Orion Nebula. d, Gas clouds in the Scorpius constellation.
No. 3849, $3.25: a, Eskimo Nebula. b, Carina Nebula. c, Cat's Eye Nebula. d, Cone Nebula.
No. 3850, $9, Eagle Nebula, vert. No. 3851, $9, Saturn, horiz.

2013, Apr. 4 **Litho.** ***Perf. 13¾***
Sheets of 4, #a-d
3848-3849 A748 Set of 2 19.50 19.50
Souvenir Sheets
Perf. 12¾
3850-3851 A748 Set of 2 13.50 13.50

No. 3850 contains one 38x51mm stamp. No. 3851 contains one 51x38mm stamp.

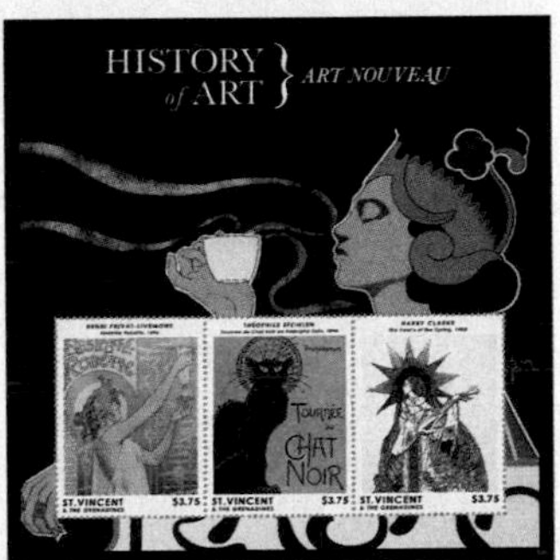

History of Art — A749

No. 3852, $3.75 — Art Nouveau: a, Absinthe Robette, by Henri Privat-Livemont. b, Tournée du Chat Noir de Rodolphe Salis, by Théophile Steinlen. c, The Year's at the Spring, by Harry Clarke.
No. 3853, $3.75 — Paintings by Gustav Klimt (1862-1918): a, The Three Ages of Woman. b, Jurisprudence. c, Judith and the Head of Holofernes.
No. 3854, $9, Ali Baba, by Aubrey Beardsley. No. 3855, $9, Job Cigarette Papers, by Alphonse Mucha, horiz.

2013, Apr. 4 **Litho.** ***Perf. 12¾***
Sheets of 3, #a-c
3852-3853 A749 Set of 2 17.00 17.00
Souvenir Sheets
3854-3855 A749 Set of 2 13.50 13.50

World Environment Day — A750

No. 3856: a, Birds. b, Leaves. c, Fish. d, Sun and clouds.
$9, Owls and leaves, vert.

2013, May 7 Litho. *Perf. 13¾*
3856 A750 $3.25 Sheet of 4, #a-d 9.75 9.75

Souvenir Sheet
Perf. 12¾

3857 A750 $9 multi 6.75 6.75

No. 3857 contains one 38x51mm stamp.

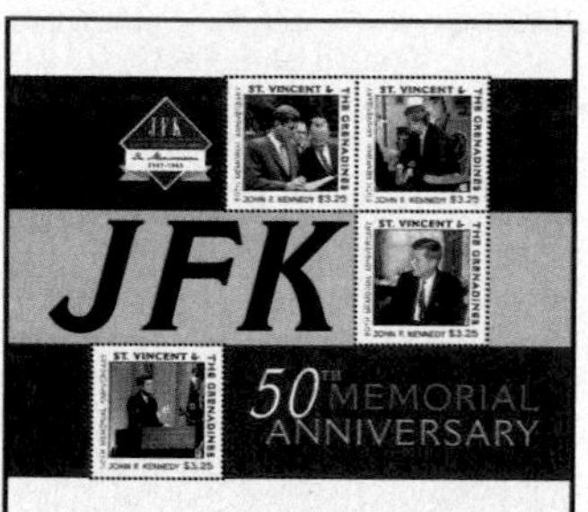

A751

Pres. John F. Kennedy (1917-63) — A752

No. 3858 — Pres. Kennedy: a, Holding paper. b, Seated in rocking chair, hands visible. c, Seated in chair, hands not visible. d, Behind lectern, pointing.
No. 3859 — Pres. Kennedy: a, With man holding medallion in box. b, Signing document. c, With Pres. Dwight D. Eisenhower. d, Standing behind lectern.
No. 3860, $9, Pres. Kennedy behind lectern, diff., denomination in blue. No. 3861, Pres. Kennedy behind lectern, diff., denomination in olive brown.

2013, May 7 Litho. *Perf. 13¾*
3858 A751 $3.25 Sheet of 4, #a-d 9.75 9.75
3859 A752 $3.25 Sheet of 4, #a-d 9.75 9.75

Souvenir Sheets

3860-3861 A752 Set of 2 13.50 13.50

Lady Margaret Thatcher (1925-2013), British Prime Minister — A753

No. 3862 — Thatcher: a, Waving. b, With hand on chin. c, With flowers. d, On telephone.
$9, Thatcher, vert.

2013, June 3 Litho. *Perf. 12*
3862 A753 $3.25 Sheet of 4, #a-d 9.75 9.75

Souvenir Sheet
Perf. 12¾

3863 A753 $9 multi 6.75 6.75

No. 3863 contains one 38x51mm stamp.

Souvenir Sheets

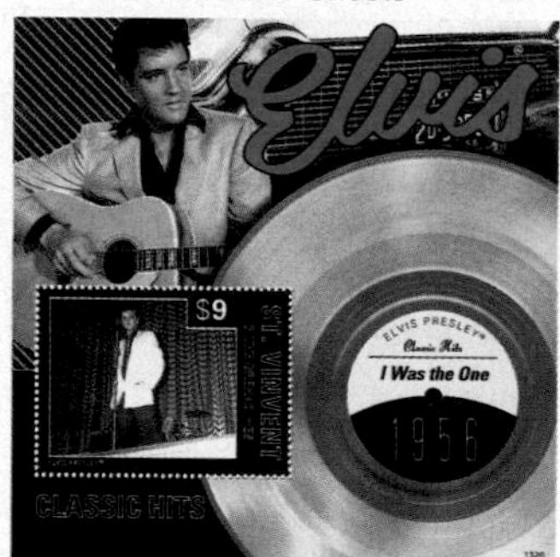

Elvis Presley (1935-77) — A754

Various photographs of Presley in: No. 3864, $9, Black-and-white, frame in black. No. 3865, $9, Color, frame in purple. No. 3866, $9, Black-and-white, frame in red. No. 3867, $9, Color, frame in red. No. 3868, $9, Color, frame in gray.

2013, June 20 Litho. *Perf. 13½*
3864-3868 A754 Set of 5 33.50 33.50

Country name is misspelled on No. 3864.

Souvenir Sheet

Elvis Presley (1935-77) — A755

Litho., Margin Embossed With Foil Application

2013, June 25 *Imperf.*
3869 A755 $25 multi 18.50 18.50

Mammals — A758

No. 3874: a, Two-toed sloth. b, Nine-banded armadillo. c, Leaf-nosed bat. d, Short-tailed shrew.
$9, West Indian manatee.

2013, Aug. 7 Litho. *Perf. 14*
3874 A758 $3.25 Sheet of 4, #a-d 9.75 9.75

Souvenir Sheet

3875 A758 $9 multi 6.75 6.75

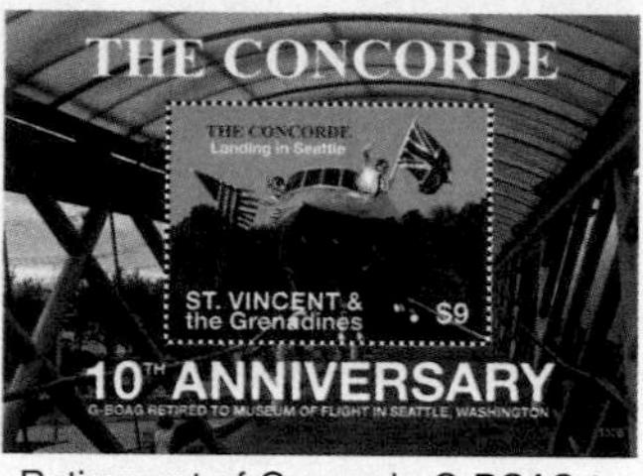

Retirement of Concorde G-BOAG to Seattle Museum of Flight, 10th Anniv. — A759

No. 3876: a, Concorde on ground in Seattle. b, Captain Bannister holding microphone. c, Crowd near Concorde. d, Concorde landing at Seattle.
$9, Nose of Concorde, crew holding flags.

2013, Aug. 26 Litho. *Perf. 12¾*
3876 A759 $3.25 Sheet of 4, #a-d 9.75 9.75

Souvenir Sheet

3877 A759 $9 multi 6.75 6.75

St. Joan of Arc (c.1412-31) A760

2013, Sept. 27 Litho. *Perf. 12*
3878 A760 $3.50 multi 2.60 2.60

No. 3878 was printed in sheets of 4.

Chess — A761

No. 3879: a, White pawn. b, White queen. c, White rook. d, Black knight. e, Black king. f, Black bishop.
$9, Wilhelm Steinitz (1836-1900), world chess champion.

2013, Sept. 30 Litho. *Perf. 13¾*
3879 A761 $2.75 Sheet of 6, #a-f 12.50 12.50

Souvenir Sheet

3880 A761 $9 multi 6.75 6.75

Coronation of Queen Elizabeth II, 60th Anniv. — A762

No. 3881 — Queen Elizabeth II: a, As child. b, Wearing crown. c, With Prince Philip. d, Wearing Girl Guide uniform.
$9, Queen Elizabeth II as young girl playing piano.

2013, Oct. 7 Litho. *Perf. 13¾*
3881 A762 $3.25 Sheet of 4, #a-d 9.75 9.75

Souvenir Sheet

3882 A762 $9 multi 6.75 6.75

Birth of Prince George of Cambridge — A763

No. 3883: a, Prince George being held by Duchess and Duke of Cambridge. b, Duchess of Cambridge holding Prince George and waving. c, Duchess handing Prince George to Duke.
$9, Prince George, Duke and Duchess of Cambridge, diff.

2013, Oct. 7 Litho. *Perf. 12¾*
3883 A763 $3.50 Sheet of 3, #a-c 7.75 7.75

Souvenir Sheet

3884 A763 $9 multi 6.75 6.75

Miniature Sheet

Hummingbirds — A764

No. 3885: a, Florisuga mellivora. b, Lampornis violicauda. c, Campylopterus obscurus. d, Thalurania furcata.

2013, Nov. 11 Litho. *Perf. 12¾*
3885 A764 $3.25 Sheet of 4, #a-d 9.75 9.75

Brasiliana 2013 Intl. Philatelic Exhibition, Rio de Janeiro.

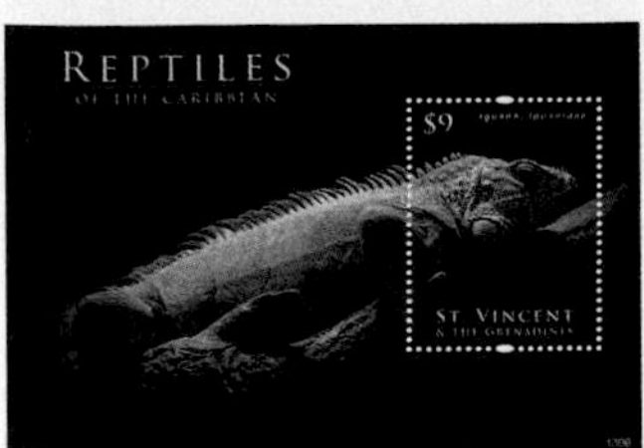

Reptiles — A765

No. 3886, horiz.: a, Dwarf gecko. b, Hawksbill turtle. c, Brown anole. d, Mona boa.
$9, Iguana.

Perf. 13 Syncopated

2013, Nov. 28 **Litho.**

3886 A765 $3.50 Sheet of 4, #a-d 10.50 10.50

Souvenir Sheet

3887 A765 $9 multi 6.75 6.75

Miniature Sheet

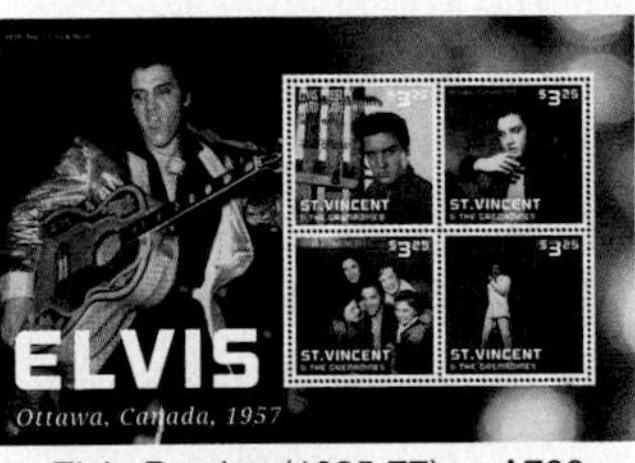

Elvis Presley (1935-77) — A766

No. 3888 — Presley: a, On album cover. b, Touching chin. c, With four women. d, Singing.

2013, Dec. 2 **Litho.** ***Perf. 13¾***

3888 A766 $3.25 Sheet of 4, #a-d 9.75 9.75

Christmas A767

Paintings: 80c, Madonna, by Don Lorenzo Monaco. $1.70, The Adoration of the Magi, by Stefano da Verona. $2, Nativity, by Giorigione. $2.20, The Annunciation, by Masolino da Panicale.
$9, Nativity, by Piero della Francesca.

2013, Dec. 2 **Litho.** ***Perf. 12¾***

3889-3892 A767 Set of 4 5.00 5.00

Souvenir Sheet

3893 A767 $9 multi 6.75 6.75

Pres. Barack Obama — A768

Designs: $3.25, Pres. Obama.
No. 3895, $9, Pres. Obama sitting. No. 3896, $9, Pres. Obama golfing with Vice President Joseph Biden.

2013, Dec. 9 **Litho.** ***Perf. 14***

3894 A768 $3.25 multi 2.40 2.40

Souvenir Sheets

Perf. 12¾

3895-3896 A768 Set of 2 13.50 13.50

No. 3894 was printed in sheets of 4. Nos. 3895-3896 each contain one 38x51mm stamp.

A769

Nelson Mandela (1918-2013), President of South Africa — A770

No. 3898 — Mandela: a, Wearing black and gray shirt. b, Standing in front of building. c, Holding microphone stand. d, With arms extended. e, Pointing. f, With raised fist.
No. 3899, $9, Mandela casting ballot, vert. No. 3900, $9, Mandela standing in front of building, diff., vert.

2013, Dec. 15 **Litho.** ***Perf. 13¾***

3897 A769 $2.50 shown 1.90 1.90

3898 A770 $2.50 Sheet of 6, #a-f 11.50 11.50

Souvenir Sheets

Perf. 12¾

3899-3900 A770 Set of 2 13.50 13.50

Nos. 3899-3900 each contain one 38x51mm stamp.

Cat Breeds — A771

No. 3901, $3.25: a, Aegean. b, Mekong Bobtail. c, Australian Mist. d, Brazilian Shorthair.
No. 3902, $3.25: a, American Shorthair. b, British Burmese. c, Ocicat. d, Oriental Shorthair.
No. 3903, $9, Cyprus Shorthair. No. 3904, $9, European Shorthair.

2013, Dec. 18 **Litho.** ***Perf. 13¾***

Sheets of 4, #a-d

3901-3902 A771 Set of 2 19.50 19.50

Souvenir Sheets

3903-3904 A771 Set of 2 13.50 13.50

Miniature Sheet

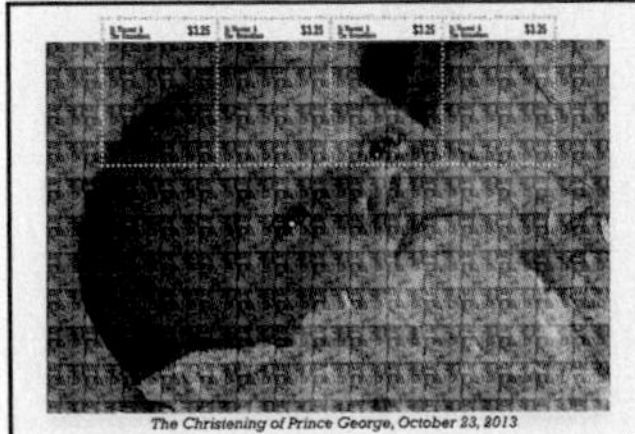

Christening of Prince George of Cambridge — A772

No. 3905: a, Top of head. b, Forehead. c, Eye. d, Upper cheek.

2013, Dec. 31 **Litho.** ***Perf. 14***

3905 A772 $3.25 Sheet of 4, #a-d 9.75 9.75

Yoesmite National Park, California — A773

No. 3906, $3.25: a, Half Dome Mountain. b, Gray wolf. c, Firefall at Horsetail Falls. d, Mountain lion.
No. 3907, $3.25: a, Merced River. b, Tenaya Lake. c, Yosemite Waterfalls. d, Yosemite Valley.
No. 3908, $9, Western mule deer, horiz. No. 3909, $9, Rock formation in Yosemite Valley, horiz.

2014, Jan. 2 **Litho.** ***Perf. 13¾***

Sheets of 4, #a-d

3906-3907 A773 Set of 2 19.50 19.50

Souvenir Sheets

Perf. 12¾

3908-3909 A773 Set of 2 13.50 13.50

Nos. 3908-3909 each contain one 51x38mm stamp.

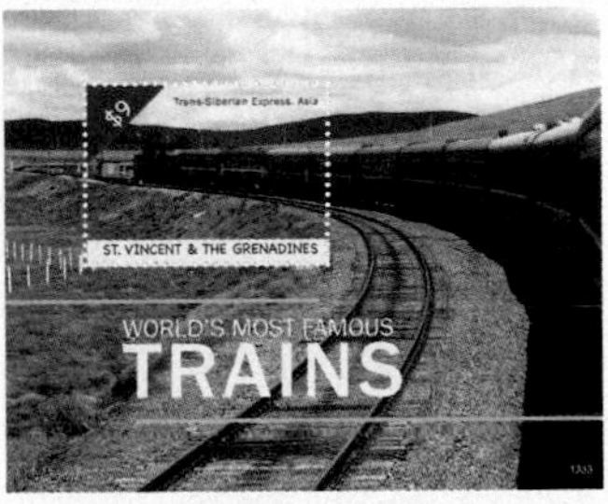

Trains — A774

No. 3910: a, TGV, France. b, Blue Train, South Africa. c, Orient Express, Europe. d, Bullet Train, Japan.
$9, Trans-Siberian Express, Asia.

2014, Jan. 14 **Litho.** ***Perf. 14***

3910 A774 $3.25 Sheet of 4, #a-d 9.75 9.75

Souvenir Sheet

Perf. 12

3911 A774 $9 multi 6.75 6.75

Garden Flowers — A775

No. 3912: a, Great bougainvillea. b, Hibiscus. c, Iris. No. 3913: a, Lily. b, Bearded iris. c, Bird of paradise.
No. 3914: a, Peony. b, Tulip. No. 3915: a, Iris, diff. b, Hyacinth.

2014, Feb. 6 **Litho.** ***Perf. 12¾***

Sheets of 3, #a.-c.

3912-3913 A775 $6.25 Set of 2 28.00 28.00

Souvenir Sheets of 2, #a.-b.

3914-3915 A775 $9.50 Set of 2 28.00 28.00

Characters From *Downton Abbey* Television Series — A776

No. 3916: a, Mr. Bates. b, Thomas Barrow. c, Mr. Carson. d, Tom Branson.
$9, William Mason and Thomas Barrow, horiz.

2014, Mar. 5 **Litho.** ***Perf. 14***

3916 A776 $3.25 Sheet of 4, #a-d 9.75 9.75

Souvenir Sheet

3917 A776 $9 multi 6.75 6.75

World War I, Cent. — A777

No. 3918, $3.25: a, Austro-Hungarian soldier with rifle. b, Austro-Hungarian soldier without weapon. c, Russian bugler. d, Russian artilleryman.
No. 3919, $3.25: a, German cavalryman, blue gray background. b, Russian cavalryman. c, German cavalryman, bucking horse, gray green background. d, British cavalryman.
No. 3920, $5 — German cavalryman with: a, Blue gray background. b, Dull green background.
No. 3921, $5, vert.: a, Russian soldier pointing pistol. b, Austro-Hungarian soldier pointing rifle.

2014, Mar. 24 **Litho.** ***Perf. 14***

Sheets of 4, #a-d

3918-3919 A777 Set of 2 19.50 19.50

Souvenir Sheets

Perf. 12¾

3920-3921 A777 Set of 2 15.00 15.00

No. 3920 contains two 51x38mm stamps. No. 3921 contains two 38x51mm stamps.

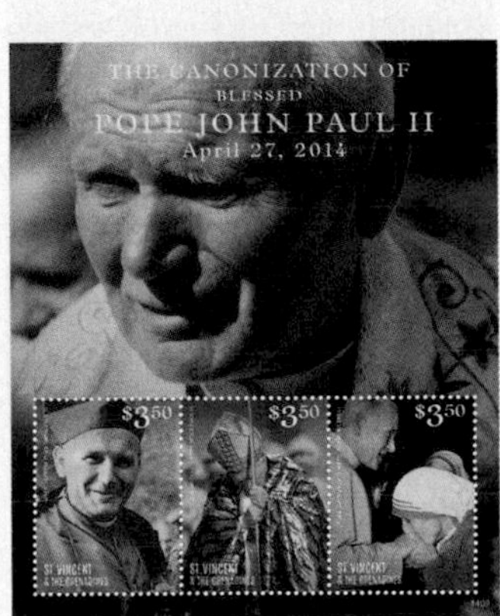

A778

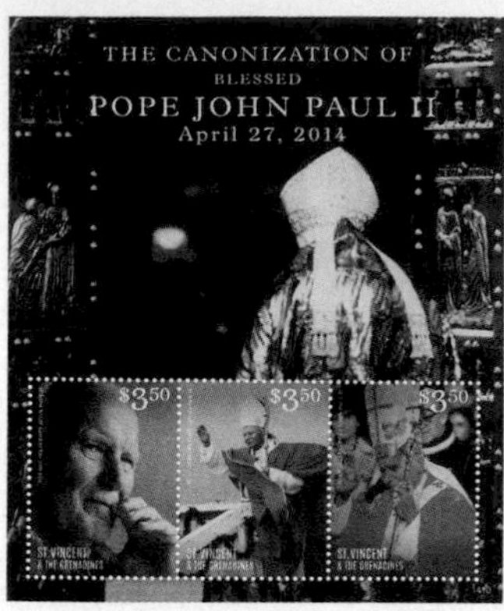

Canonization of Pope John Paul II — A779

No. 3922 — Pope John Paul II: a, As younger man, wearing biretta. b, Wearing miter and striped robe. c, With Mother Teresa.

No. 3923 — Pope John Paul II: a, With hand near mouth. b, On stairway, holding staff, wearing miter, waving. c, Wearing miter, holding staff.

No. 3924, $5, horiz. — Pope John Paul II: a, Facing crowd with arms extended. b, Holding staff, wearing miter, waving, diff.

No. 3925, $5, horiz. — Pope John Paul II: a, With Mother Teresa, diff. b, With cardinals.

2014, May 5 Litho. *Perf. 12*

3922 A778 $3.50 Sheet of 3, #a-c 7.75 7.75
3923 A779 $3.50 Sheet of 3, #a-c 7.75 7.75

Souvenir Sheets of 2, #a-b

3924-3925 A779 Set of 2 15.00 15.00

Panama Canal, Cent. — A780

No. 3926: a, Miraflores Locks, 2014. b, Miraflores Locks under construction, 1912. c, Ship in Panama Canal, 2014. d, SS Kroonland in Panama Canal, 1915.

No. 3927: a, Centennial Bridge. b, Ship in Panama Canal lock.

2014, May 12 Litho. *Perf. 14*

3926 A780 $3.25 Sheet of 4, #a-d 9.75 9.75

Souvenir Sheet

Perf. 12

3927 A780 $5 Sheet of 2, #a-b 7.50 7.50

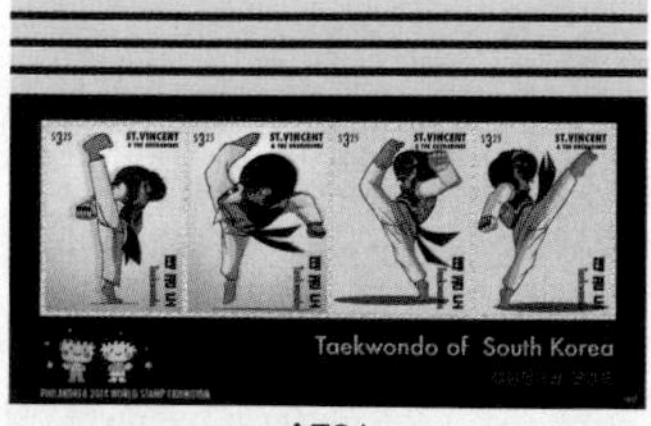

A781

A782

A783

Taekwondo — A784

Various positions, kicks and jumps, as shown.

2014, May 12 Litho. *Perf. 12¾*

3928 A781 $3.25 Sheet of 4, #a-d 9.75 9.75
3929 A782 $3.25 Sheet of 4, #a-d 9.75 9.75

Souvenir Sheets

3930 A783 $5 Sheet of 2, #a-b 7.50 7.50
3931 A784 $5 Sheet of 2, #a-b 7.50 7.50

Philakorea 2014 World Stamp Exhibition, Seoul.

Farm Animals — A785

No. 3932, $3.25: a, Anas platyrhynchos (female ducks). b, Anas platyrhynchos (male mallard ducks). c, Turkey. d, Chicken.

No. 3933, $3.25: a, Charolais cattle. b, Zebus. c, Bison. d, Pigs.

No. 3934, $5, vert.: a, Arabian horses. b, Shetland ponies.

No. 3935, $5, vert.: a, Wild goats. b, Sheep.

2014, May 19 Litho. *Perf. 14*

Sheets of 4, #a-d

3932-3933 A785 Set of 2 19.50 19.50

Souvenir Sheets of 2, #a-b

3934-3935 A785 Set of 2 15.00 15.00

A786

A787

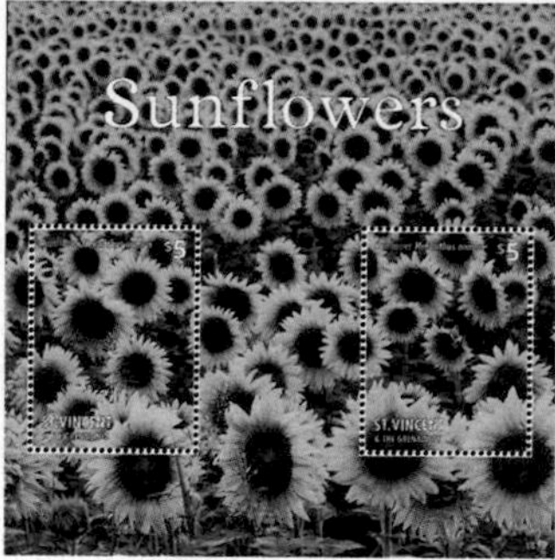

Sunflowers — A788

Various sunflowers, as shown.

2014, June 23 Litho. *Perf. 14*

3936 A786 $3.25 Sheet of 4, #a-d 9.75 9.75
3937 A787 $3.25 Sheet of 4, #a-d 9.75 9.75

Souvenir Sheets

3938 A788 $5 Sheet of 2, #a-b 7.50 7.50

Perf. 12¾

3939 A787 $10 Sunflower, horiz. 7.50 7.50

No. 3939 contains one 51x38mm stamp.

A789

A790

A791

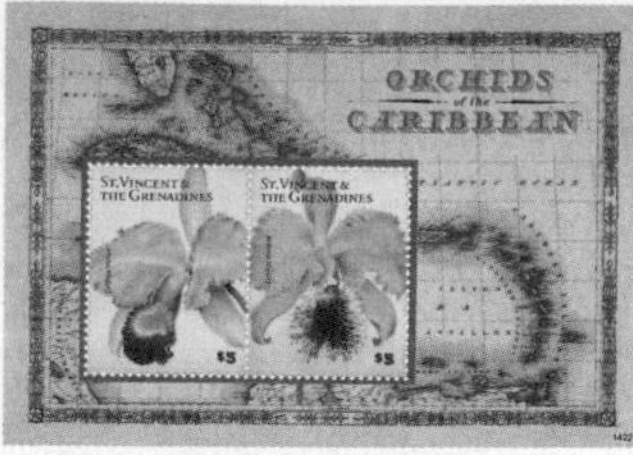

Orchids — A792

No. 3940: a, Cattleya mendelii. b, Cattleya trianae. c, Cattleya luddemanniana. d, Cattleya trianae, diff.

No. 3941: a, Cattleya mossiae. b, Cattleya trianae, diff. c, Cattleya mossiae, diff. d, Cattleya trianae, diff.

No. 3942: a, Cattleya trianae, diff. b, Cattleya trianae, diff.

No. 3943: a, Cattleya trianae, diff. b, Cattleya mossiae, diff.

2014, July 1 Litho. *Perf. 14*

3940 A789 $3.25 Sheet of 4, #a-d 9.75 9.75
3941 A790 $3.25 Sheet of 4, #a-d 9.75 9.75

Souvenir Sheets

Perf. 12

3942 A791 $5 Sheet of 2, #a-b 7.50 7.50
3943 A792 $5 Sheet of 2, #a-b 7.50 7.50

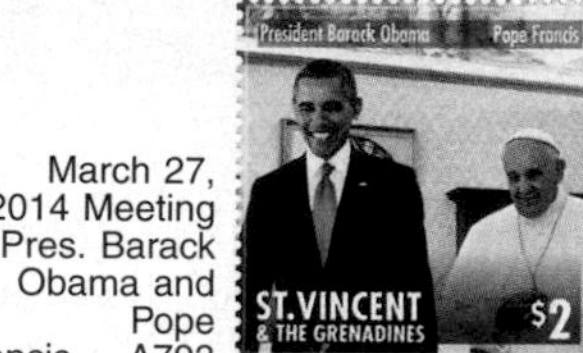

March 27, 2014 Meeting of Pres. Barack Obama and Pope Francis — A793

Designs: $2, Pres. Obama and Pope Francis.

No. 3945 — Pres. Obama and Pope Francis with: a, Painting behind head of Pope Francis. b, Window behing Pope Francis.

No. 3946, vert.: a, Pope Francis. b, Pres. Obama.

$10, Pres. Obama and Pope Francis, vert.

2014, July 21 Litho. *Perf. 13¾*

3944 A793 $2 multi 1.50 1.50
3945 A793 $2.25 Horiz. pair, #a-b 3.50 3.50

Souvenir Sheets

Perf. 12¾

3946 A793 $5 Sheet of 2, #a-b 7.50 7.50
3947 A793 $10 multi 7.50 7.50

No. 3944 was printed in sheets of 6. No. 3945 was printed in sheets of 9, containing six No. 3945a and three No. 3945b. No. 3946 contains two 38x51mm stamps. No. 3947 contains one 38x51mm stamp.

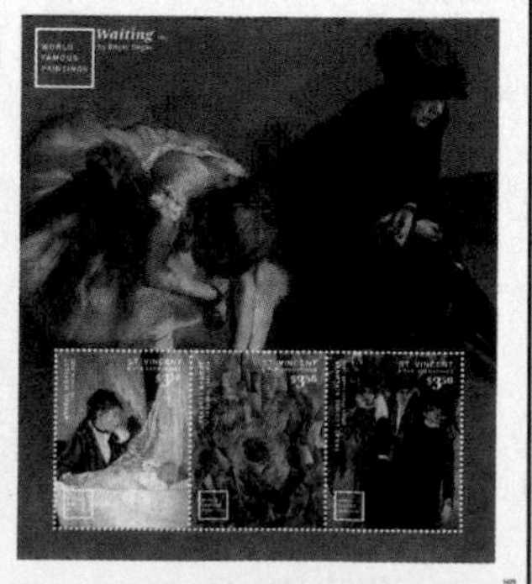

Paintings — A794

No. 3948, $3.50: a, The Cradle, by Berthe Morisot. b, Le Guitare, by Georges Braque. c, Berlin Street Scene, by Ernst Ludwig Kirchner.

No. 3949, $3.50: a, The Football Players, by Henri Rousseau. b, Boy on the Rocks, by Rousseau. c, Still Life with Cherub, by Paul Cézanne.

No. 3950, $10, Open Window, by Henri Matisse. No. 3951, $10, Shore with Red House, by Edvard Munch.

2014, Aug. 14 Litho. *Perf. 12¾*
Sheets of 3, #a-c

3948-3949 A794 Set of 2 15.50 15.50

Size: 100x100mm
Imperf

3950-3951 A794 Set of 2 15.00 15.00

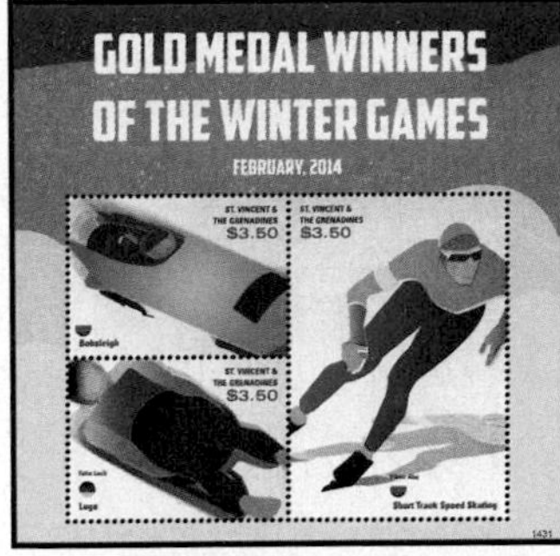

2014 Winter Olympics Gold Medalists — A796

No. 3954: a, Russian Men's two-man bobsled team (40x30mm). b, Felix Lach, luge, Germany (40x30mm). c, Viktor Ahn, short track speed skating, Russia (40x60mm).
No. 3955: a, Michael Mulder, speed skating, Netherlands (40x30mm). b, Alexander Tretiakov, skeleton, Russia (40x30mm).

2014, Sept. 15 Litho. *Perf. 14*

3954 A796 $3.50 Sheet of 3, #a-c 7.75 7.75

Souvenir Sheet

3955 A796 $5 Sheet of 2, #a-b 7.50 7.50

2014 World Cup Soccer Championships, Brazil — A797

No. 3956 — Central part of Brazilian flag and: a, Stylized soccer ball and map of Brazil. b, Soccer ball and "Brazil." c, Map of Brazil and "2014."
$10, Christ the Redeemer Statue, Rio de Janeiro.

2014, Sept. 30 Litho. *Perf. 12*

3956 A797 $3.50 Sheet of 3, #a-c 7.75 7.75

Souvenir Sheet

3957 A797 $10 multi 7.50 7.50

No. 3957 contains one 30x50mm stamp.

Rare Stamps — A798

No. 3958: a, Great Britain #1. b, Mauritius #1. c, France #3.
$10, United States #1.

2014, Sept. 30 Litho. *Perf. 14*

3958 A798 $3.50 Sheet of 3, #a-c 7.75 7.75

Souvenir Sheet

3959 A798 $10 multi 7.50 7.50

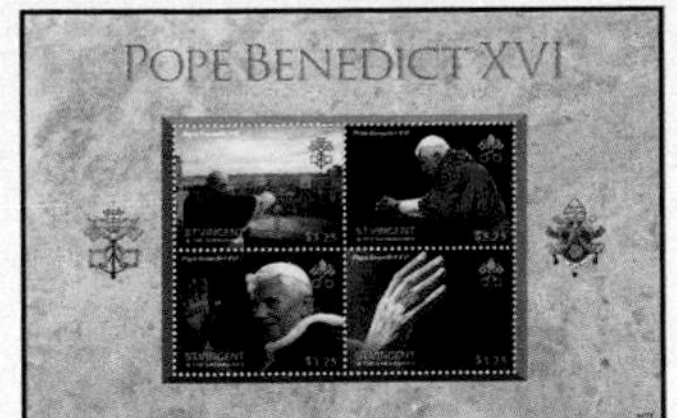

Pope Benedict XVI — A799

No. 3960: a, Pope Benedict XVI waving to crowd in St. Peter's Square. b, Pope Benedict XVI praying. c, Pope Benedict XVI waving. d, Hand of Pope Benedict XVI with papal ring.
$10, Back of head of Pope Benedict XVI.

2014, Oct. 20 Litho. *Perf. 12½x12*

3960 A799 $3.25 Sheet of 4, #a-d 9.75 9,75

Souvenir Sheet

3961 A799 $10 multi 7.50 7.50

SEMI-POSTAL STAMPS

Catalogue values for unused stamps in this section are for Never Hinged items.

Map Type of 1977-78 Overprinted: "SOUFRIERE / RELIEF / FUND 1979" and New Values, "10c+5c" etc.

Litho. and Typo.

1979 Wmk. 373 *Perf. 14½x14*

B1 A76 10c + 5c multi .25 .25
B2 A76 50c + 25c multi .25 .25
B3 A76 $1 + 50c multi .50 .50
B4 A76 $2 + $1 multi 1.00 1.00
Nos. B1-B4 (4) 2.00 2.00

The surtax was for victims of the eruption of Mt. Soufrière.

Nos. 604-607 Surcharged: "HURRICANE / RELIEF / 50c"

1980, Aug. 7 Litho. *Perf. 13½*

B5 A90 10c + 50c multi .25 .25
B6 A90 60c + 50c multi .40 .40
B7 A90 80c + 50c multi .50 .50
B8 A90 $2.50 + 50c multi 1.10 1.10
Nos. B5-B8 (4) 2.25 2.25

Surtax was for victims of Hurricane Allen.

Nos. 1224-1226 Surcharged "CALIF EARTHQUAKE RELIEF" on 1 or 2 Lines and "+10c"

1989, Nov. 17 Litho. *Perf. 13½x14*

B9 Sheet of 9 5.50 5.50
a.-i. A174 60c +10c #1224a-1224i .60 .60
B10 Sheet of 9 5.50 5.50
a.-i. A174 60c +10c #1225a-1225i .60 .60
B11 Sheet of 9 5.50 5.50
a.-i. A175 60c +10c #1226a-1226i .60 .60

WAR TAX STAMPS

No. 105 Overprinted

Type I — Words 2 to 2½mm apart.
Type II — Words 1½mm apart.
Type III — Words 3½mm apart.

1916 Wmk. 3 *Perf. 14*

MR1 A17 1p car, type III 3.25 25.00
a. Double ovpt., type III 275.00 250.00
b. 1p carmine, type I 12.50 18.50
c. Comma after "STAMP", type I 12.50 30.00
d. Double ovpt., type I 200.00 200.00
e. 1p carmine, type II 135.00 87.50
f. Double ovpt., type II 1,450.

Overprinted

MR2 A17 1p carmine 1.40 2.25

OFFICIAL STAMPS

Catalogue values for unused stamps in this section are for Never Hinged items.

Nos. 627-632 Overprinted

1982, Nov. Litho. *Perf. 14*

O1 A94a 60c Couple, Isabella .25 .25
O2 A94b 60c Couple .25 .25
O3 A94a $2.50 Couple, Alberta .45 .45
O4 A94b $2.50 Couple .65 .65
O5 A94a $4 Couple, Britannia .80 .80
O6 A94b $4 Couple .90 .90
Nos. O1-O6 (6) 3.30 3.30

POSTAL-FISCAL STAMPS

Nos. AR1-AR7 were intended primarily for fiscal use but were also authorized and commonly used for payment of postal charges.

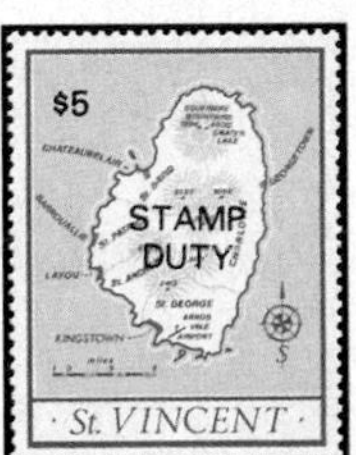

Map of St. Vincent — PF1

Perf. 14½x14

1980, Feb. Litho. Wmk. 314

AR1 PF1 $5 vio & lavender 2.50 2.50
AR2 PF1 $10 grn & apple grn 4.00 5.00
AR3 PF1 $20 red vio & pale rose lilac 7.00 12.00
Nos. AR1-AR3 (3) 13.50 19.50

State Seal — PF2

Perf. 14x13¼

1980, May 19 Engr. Wmk. 373

AR4 PF2 $5 deep blue 2.25 2.75
AR5 PF2 $10 deep green 3.75 4.75
AR6 PF2 $20 carmine rose 6.50 10.50
Nos. AR4-AR6 (3) 12.50 18.00

Nos. AR4-AR6 are dated "1980" below design.

Perf. 12¼x12

1984, May 22 Engr. Wmk. 380

AR7 PF2 $20 carmine rose 8.50 13.00

No. AR7 is dated "1984" below design.

ST. VINCENT GRENADINES

sānt 'vin(t)-sənt grə-'nā-də

LOCATION — Group of islands south of St. Vincent
CAPITAL — None

St. Vincent's portion of the Grenadines includes Bequia, Canouan, Mustique, Union and a number of smaller islands.

Catalogue values for unused stamps in this area are for Never Hinged items.

Stamps inscribed "Palm Island," "Tobago Cays," and "Young Island" are not listed as they do not meet Scott listing criteria.

The editors would like to examine any commercial covers mailed during 2000-2008 from the islands of Bequia, Canouan, Mayreau, Mustique or Union Island, which are franked only with the island's stamps.

All stamps are designs of St. Vincent unless otherwise noted or illustrated.
See St. Vincent Nos. 324-329a for six stamps and a souvenir sheet issued in 1971 inscribed "The Grenadines of St. Vincent."

Princess Anne's Wedding Issue
Common Design Type

1973, Nov. 14 Litho. *Perf. 14*

1 CD325 25c green & multi .25 .25
2 CD325 $1 org brn & multi .25 .25

Common Design Types pictured following the introduction.

Bird Type of 1970 and St. Vincent Nos. 281a-285a, 287a-289a Overprinted

a 

b 

1974 Photo. Wmk. 314 *Perf. 14*

3 A36(a) 1c multicolored .25 .25
4 A36(a) 2c multicolored .25 .25
5 A36(b) 2c multicolored .25 .35
6 A36(a) 3c multicolored .25 .25
7 A36(b) 3c multicolored .25 .35
8 A36(a) 4c multicolored .25 .25
9 A36(a) 5c multicolored .25 .25
10 A36(a) 6c multicolored .25 .25
11 A36(a) 8c multicolored .25 .25
12 A36(a) 10c multicolored .25 .25
13 A36(a) 12c multicolored .25 .25
14 A36(a) 20c multicolored .25 .25
15 A36(a) 25c multicolored .30 .25
16 A36(a) 50c multicolored .40 .35
17 A36(a) $1 multicolored .60 .70
18 A36(a) $2.50 multicolored .70 .95
19 A36(a) $5 multicolored 1.00 1.50
Nos. 3-19 (17) 6.00 6.95

Nos. 8-9, 12-13, 17-18 vert.
Issue dates: #5, 7, June 7; others, Apr. 24.

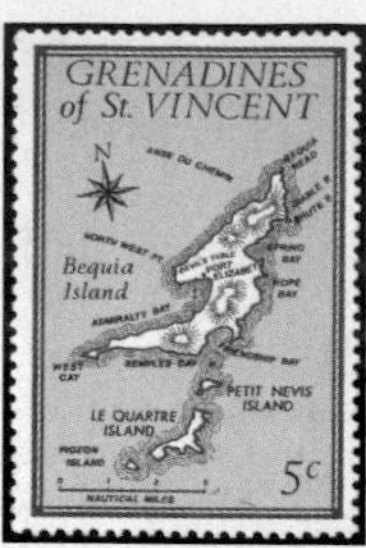

Maps of Islands — G1

Perf. 13x12½

1974, May 9 Litho. Wmk. 314

20 G1 5c Bequia .25 .25
21 G1 15c Prune .25 .25
22 G1 20c Mayreau .25 .25
23 G1 30c Mustique .25 .25
24 G1 40c Union .25 .25
24A G1 $1 Canouan .25 .25
Nos. 20-24A (6) 1.50 1.50

No. 20 has no inscription at bottom. No. 84 is dated "1976."

See Nos. 84-111.

UPU Type of 1974

2c, Arrows circling UPU emblem. 15c, Post horn, globe. 40c, Target over map of islands, hand canceler. $1, Goode's map projection.

1974, July 25 Litho. *Perf. 14½*
25-28 A56 Set of 4 .70 .60

Bequia Island G2

Designs: 5c, Boat building. 30c, Careening at Port Elizabeth. 35c, Admiralty Bay. $1, Fishing Boat Race.

1974
29-32 G2 Set of 4 .75 .70

Shells G3

Designs: 1c, Atlantic thorny oyster. 2c, Zigzag scallop. 3c, Reticulated helmet. 4c, Music volute. 5c, Amber pen shell. 6c, Angular triton. 8c, Flame helmet. 10c, Caribbean olive. 12c, Common sundial. 15c, Glory of the atlantic cone. 20c, Flame auger. 25c King venus. 35c. Long-spined star-shell. 45c, Speckled tellin. 50c, Rooster tail conch. $1, Green star-shell. $2.50, Incomparable cone. $5, Rough file clam. $10, Measled cowrie.

1974-76 Wmk. 373
33-51 G3 Set of 19 12.50 9.00

Issued: #33-50, 11/27/74; #51, 7/12/76.

#36-40, 43, 45, 47-48, exist dated "1976," #40, 42-45, 49-50 dated "1977."

For surcharge see St. Vincent No. 3346.

Churchill Type

Churchill as: 5c, Prime Minister. 40c, Lord Warden of the Cinque Ports. 50c, First Lord of the Admiralty. $1, Royal Air Force officer.

1974, Nov. 28
52-55 A58 Set of 4 .70 .70

Mustique Island G4

5c, Cotton House. 35c, Blue Waters, Endeavour. 45c, Endeavour Bay. $1, Gelliceaux Bay.

1975, Feb. 27 Wmk. 373
56 G4 5c multicolored .25 .25
57 G4 35c multicolored .25 .25
58 G4 45c multicolored .25 .25
59 G4 $1 multicolored .25 .25
Nos. 56-59 (4) 1.00 1.00

Butterflies G5

3c, Soldier martinique. 5c, Silver-spotted flambeau. 35c, Gold rim. 45c, Bright blue, Donkey's eye. $1, Biscuit.

1975, May 15 *Perf. 14*
60 G5 3c multicolored .25 .25
61 G5 5c multicolored .30 .25
62 G5 35c multicolored .55 .30
63 G5 45c multicolored .70 .30
64 G5 $1 multicolored 1.40 1.00
Nos. 60-64 (5) 3.20 2.10

Views of Petit St. Vincent G6

1975, July 24 *Perf. 14½*
65 G6 5c Resort pavilion .25 .25
66 G6 35c Harbor .25 .25
67 G6 45c Jetty .25 .25
68 G6 $1 Sailing in coral lagoon .25 .25
Nos. 65-68 (4) 1.00 1.00

Christmas — G7

Island churches: 5c, Ecumenical Church, Mustique. 25c, Catholic Church, Union. 50c, Catholic Church, Bequia. $1, Anglican Church, Bequia.

1975, Nov. 20 Wmk. 314
69-72 G7 Set of 4 .65 .65

For surcharge see St. Vincent No. 3372.

Union Island G8

5c, Sunset. 35c, Customs and post office. 45c, Anglican Church. $1, Mail boat.

1976, Feb. 26 Wmk. 373 *Perf. 13½*
73 G8 5c Sunset .25 .25
74 G8 35c multicolored .25 .25
75 G8 45c multicolored .25 .25
76 G8 $1 multicolored .25 .25
Nos. 73-76 (4) 1.00 1.00

Staghorn Coral — G9

1976, May 13 *Perf. 14½*
77 G9 5c shown .25 .25
78 G9 35c Elkhorn coral .25 .25
79 G9 45c Pillar coral .25 .25
80 G9 $1 Brain coral .40 .25
Nos. 77-80 (4) 1.15 1.00

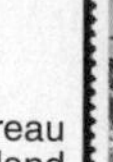

US Bicentennial Coins — G10

1976, July 15 *Perf. 13½*
81 G10 25c Washington quarter .25 .25
82 G10 50c Kennedy half dollar .25 .25
83 G10 $1 Eisenhower dollar .25 .25
Nos. 81-83 (3) .75 .75

St. Vincent Grenadines Map Type Bequia Island

1976, Sept. 23 Litho. *Perf. 14*
84 G1 5c grn, brt grn & blk .25 .25
85 G1 10c multicolored .25 .25
a. Bklt. pane of 3, 2 #84, 85 .35 .35
86 G1 35c multicolored .25 .25
a. Bklt. pane of 3, 2 #85, 86 .45 .45
87 G1 45c multicolored .25 .25
a. Bklt. pane of 3, #84, 85, 87 .50 .50
b. Bklt. pane of 3, 2 #86, 87 .70 .70
Nos. 84-87 (4) 1.00 1.00

For previous 5c see No. 20.

Canouan Island

1976, Sept. 23
88 G1 5c multicolored .25 .25
89 G1 10c multicolored .25 .25
a. Bklt. pane of 3, 2 #88, 89 .35 .35
90 G1 35c multicolored .25 .25
a. Bklt. pane of 3, 2 #89, 90 .45 .45
91 G1 45c multicolored .25 .25
a. Bklt. pane of 3, #88-89, 91 .50 .50
b. Bklt. pane of 3, 2 #90, 91 .70 .70
Nos. 88-91 (4) 1.00 1.00

Mayreau Island

1976, Sept. 23
92 G1 5c multicolored .25 .25
93 G1 10c multicolored .25 .25
a. Bklt. pane of 3, 2 #92, 93 .35 .35
94 G1 35c multicolored .25 .25
a. Bklt. pane of 3, 2 #93, 94 .45 .45
95 G1 45c multicolored .25 .25
a. Bklt. pane of 3, #92-93, 95 .50 .50
b. Bklt. pane of 3, 2 #94, 95 .70 .70
Nos. 92-95 (4) 1.00 1.00

Mustique Island

1976, Sept. 23
96 G1 5c multicolored .25 .25
97 G1 10c multicolored .25 .25
a. Bklt. pane of 3, 2 #96, 97 .35 .35
98 G1 35c multicolored .25 .25
a. Bklt. pane of 3, 2 #97, 98 .45 .45
99 G1 45c multicolored .25 .25
a. Bklt. pane of 3, #96-97, 99 .50 .50
b. Bklt. pane of 3, 2 #98, 99 .70 .70
Nos. 96-99 (4) 1.00 1.00

Petit St. Vincent

1976, Sept. 23
100 G1 5c multicolored .25 .25
101 G1 10c multicolored .25 .25
a. Bklt. pane of 3, 2 #100, 101 .35 .35
102 G1 35c multicolored .25 .25
a. Bklt. pane of 3, 2 #101, 102 .45 .45
103 G1 45c multicolored .25 .25
a. Bklt. pane of 3, #100-101, 103 .50 .50
b. Bklt. pane of 3, 2 #102, 103 .70 .70
Nos. 100-103 (4) 1.00 1.00

Prune Island

1976, Sept. 23
104 G1 5c multicolored .25 .25
105 G1 10c multicolored .25 .25
a. Bklt. pane of 3, 2 #104, 105 .35 .35
106 G1 35c multicolored .25 .25
a. Bklt. pane of 3, 2 #105, 106 .45 .45
107 G1 45c multicolored .25 .25
a. Bklt. pane of 3, #104-105, 107 .50 .50
b. Bklt. pane of 3, 2 #106, 107 .70 .70
Nos. 104-107 (4) 1.00 1.00

Union Island

1976, Sept. 23
108 G1 5c multicolored .25 .25
109 G1 10c multicolored .25 .25
a. Bklt. pane of 3, 2 #108, 109 .35 .35
110 G1 35c multicolored .25 .25
a. Bklt. pane of 3, 2 #109, 110 .45 .45
111 G1 45c multicolored .25 .25
a. Bklt. pane of 3, #108-109, 111 .50 .50
b. Bklt. pane of 3, 2 #110, 111 .70 .70
Nos. 108-111 (4) 1.00 1.00

Mayreau Island G11

Designs: 5c, Station Hill school, post office. 35c, Church at Old Wall. 45c, Cruiser at anchor, La Souciere. $1, Saline Bay.

1976, Dec. 2 *Perf. 14½*
112-115 G11 Set of 4 .75 .50

Queen Elizabeth II, Silver Jubilee — G12

Coins: 25c, Coronation Crown. 50c, Silver Wedding Crown. $1, Silver Jubilee Crown.

1977, Mar. 3
116-118 G12 Set of 3 .60 .40

Fiddler Crab G13

1977, May 19
119 G13 5c shown .25 .25
120 G13 35c Ghost crab .25 .25
121 G13 50c Blue crab .25 .25
122 G13 $1.25 Spiny lobster .50 *.90*
Nos. 119-122 (4) 1.25 1.65

Map Type of 1977 Overprinted

Perf. 14½x14

1977, Aug. 25
123 G14 5c Snorkel diving .25 .25
124 G14 35c Palm Island Resort .25 .25
125 G14 45c Casuarina Beach .25 .25
126 G14 $1 Palm Island Beach Club .25 *1.00*
Nos. 123-126 (4) 1.00 1.75

1977, Oct. 31 Wmk. 314
127 A76 40c multicolored (R) .25 .25
128 A76 $2 multicolored (B) .40 .25

For surcharge see St. Vincent No. 3381.

Prune Island G14

Canouan Island G15

5c, Clinic, Charlestown. 35c, Town jetty, Charlestown. 45c, Mailboat, Charlestown. $1, Grand Bay.

1977, Dec. 8 Wmk. 373 Perf. 14½

129 G15 5c multicolored .25 .25
130 G15 35c multicolored .25 .25
131 G15 45c multicolored .25 .25
132 G15 $1 multicolored .25 *.90*
Nos. 129-132 (4) 1.00 1.65

Birds and Eggs G16

1c, Tropical Mockingbird. 2c, Mangrove cuckoo. 3c, Osprey. 4c, Smooth bellied ani. 5c, House wren. 6c, Bananaquit. 8c, Carib grackle. 10c, Yellow bellied elaenia. 12c, Collared plover. 15c, Cattle egret. 20c, Red footed booby. 25c, Red-billed tropic bird. 40c, Royal tern. 50c, Rusty tailed flycatcher. 80c, Purple gallinule. $1, Broad winged hawk. $2, Common ground dove. $3, Laughing gull. $5, Brown noddy. $10, Grey kingbird.

1978, May 11 Perf. 13x12

133-152 G16 Set of 20 15.00 14.00

Nos. 139, 143, 149 exist imprinted "1979," Value: $1.60. Nos. 137-138, 140, 142, 144 imprinted "1980." Value: $1.50.

Nos. 147-148 imprinted "1979" are from No. 175a. Nos. 145-146, 150 imprinted "1980" are from No. 189a.

For surcharges see No. 266, St. Vincent Nos. 3347-3348.

Elizabeth II Coronation Anniv. Type

Cathedrals.

1978, June 2 Perf. 13½

153 A78 5c Worcester .25 .25
154 A78 40c Coventry .25 .25
155 A78 $1 Winchester .25 .25
156 A78 $3 Chester .25 .25
Complete booklet, 2 each #153-156 2.25
a. Souv. sheet, #153-156, perf. 14 .60 .75
Nos. 153-156 (4) 1.00 1.00

Turtles G17

1978, July 20 Perf. 14

157 G17 5c Green turtle .25 .25
158 G17 40c Hawksbill turtle .25 .25
159 G17 50c Leatherback turtle .30 .30
160 G17 $1.25 Loggerhead turtle .60 .60
Nos. 157-160 (4) 1.40 1.40

For surcharge see St. Vincent No. 3374.

Christmas G18

Christmas scenes and verses from the carol "We Three Kings of Orient Are".

1978, Nov. 2

161 G18 5c Three kings following star .25 .25
162 G18 10c Gold .25 .25
163 G18 25c Frankincense .25 .25
164 G18 50c Myrrh .25 .25
165 G18 $2 With infant Jesus .25 .25
a. Souvenir sheet of 5 + label, #161-165 .90 *1.25*
Nos. 161-165 (5) 1.25 1.25

Sailing Yachts — G19

1979

166 G19 5c multicolored .25 .25
167 G19 40c multi, diff. .25 .25
168 G19 50c multi, diff. .25 .25
169 G19 $2 multi, diff. .40 .40
Nos. 166-169 (4) 1.15 1.15

Wildlife Type of 1980

1979, Mar. 8 Perf. 14½

170 A91 20c Green iguana .25 .25
171 A91 40c Manicou .25 .25
172 A91 $2 Red-legged tortoise .70 *.90*
Nos. 170-172 (3) 1.20 1.40

Sir Rowland Hill Type of 1979

Designs: 80c, Sir Rowland Hill. $1, Great Britain Types A1 and A5 with "A10" (Kingstown, St. Vincent) cancel. $2, St. Vincent #41 & 43 with Bequia cancel.

1979, May 31 Perf. 13x12

173 A83 80c multicolored .25 .25
174 A83 $1 multicolored .25 .25
175 A83 $2 multicolored .25 *.35*
a. Souv. sheet, #173-175, 147-149 1.25 *2.00*
Nos. 173-175 (3) .75 .85

IYC Type of 1979

Children and IYC emblem: 6c, Boy. 40c, Girl. $1, Boy, diff. $3, Girl and boy.

1979, Oct. 24 Perf. 14x13½

176 A82 6c multicolored .25 .25
177 A82 40c multicolored .25 .25
178 A82 $1 multicolored .25 .25
179 A82 $3 multicolored .25 .25
Nos. 176-179 (4) 1.00 1.00

Independence Type of 1979

Designs: 5c, National flag, Ixora salici-folia. 40c, House of Assembly, Ixora odorata. $1, Prime Minister R. Milton Cato, Ixora jayanica.

1979, Oct. 27 Perf. 12½x12

180-182 A85 Set of 3 .45 .45

Printed se-tenant with label inscribed "Independence of St. Vincent and the Grenadines."

False Killer Whale G20

1979, Jan. 25 Perf. 14

183 G20 10c shown .50 .30
184 G20 50c Spinner dolphin .50 .35
185 G20 90c Bottle nosed dolphin .55 *.70*
186 G20 $2 Blackfish 1.40 *1.75*
Nos. 183-186 (4) 2.95 *3.10*

For surcharges see St. Vincent Nos. 3352, 3371, 3383-3384.

London '80 Type

1980, Apr. 24 Perf. 13x12

187 A88 40c Queen Elizabeth II .25 .25
188 A88 50c St. Vincent #227 .25 .25
189 A88 $3 #1-2 .25 *1.00*
a. Souvenir sheet of 6, #187-189, 145-146, 150 2.00 *2.25*
Nos. 187-189 (3) .75 1.50

Olympics Type of 1980

1980, Aug. 7 Perf. 13½

190 A90 25c Running .25 .25
191 A90 50c Sailing .25 .25
192 A90 $1 Long jump .25 .25
193 A90 $2 Swimming .25 .25
Nos. 190-193 (4) 1.00 1.00

For surcharge see St. Vincent No. 3353.

Christmas G21

Scenes and verse from the carol "De Borning Day."

1980, Nov. 13 Perf. 14

194 G21 5c multicolored .25 .25
195 G21 50c multicolored .25 .25
196 G21 60c multicolored .25 .25
197 G21 $1 multicolored .25 .25
198 G21 $2 multicolored .25 .25
a. Souvenir sheet of 5 + label, #194-198 .75 *1.25*
Nos. 194-198 (5) 1.25 1.25

For surcharge see St. Vincent No. 3385.

Bequia Island G22

50c, P.O., Port Elizabeth. 60c, Moonhole. $1.50, Fishing boats, Admiralty Bay. $2, Friendship Rose at jetty.

1981, Feb. 19 Perf. 14½

199 G22 50c multicolored .25 .25
200 G22 60c multicolored .25 .25
201 G22 $1.50 multicolored .25 *.45*
202 G22 $2 multicolored .25 *.50*
Nos. 199-202 (4) 1.00 *1.45*

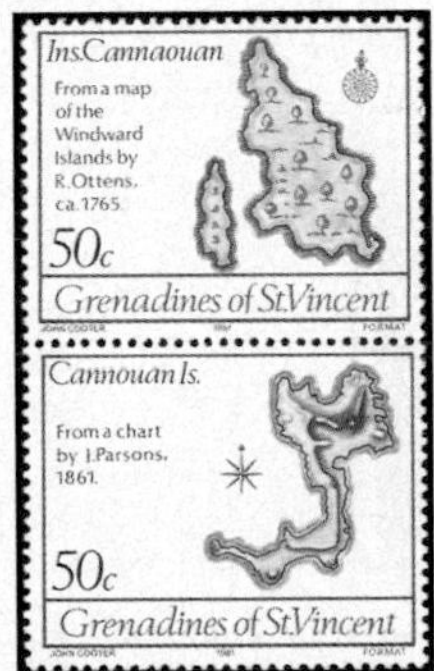

Map by R. Ottens, c. 1765 — G23

Maps: Nos. 204, 206 by J. Parsons, 1861. No. 208, by T. Jefferys, 1763.

1981, Apr. 2 Perf. 14

203 50c Ins. Cannaouan .25 .25
204 50c Cannouan Island .25 .25
a. G23 Pair, #203-204 .55 .25
205 60c Ins. Moustiques .25 .25
206 60c Mustique Island .25 .25
a. G23 Pair, #205-206 .60 .60
207 $2 Ins. Bequia .50 .65
208 $2 Bequia Island .50 .65
a. G23 Pair, #207-208 1.10 1.40
Nos. 203-208 (6) 2.00 2.30

Royal Wedding Types

No. 209, Couple, the Mary. No. 210, Couple. No. 211, Couple, the Alexandra. No. 213, Couple, the Brittania.

1981, July 17 Wmk. 380

209 A94a 50c multicolored .25 .25
a. Booklet pane of 4, perf. 12 .60 .60
210 A94b 50c multicolored .30 *.40*
211 A94a $3 multicolored .25 .25
212 A94b $3 like #210 .60 *.80*
a. Booklet pane of 2, perf. 12 2.00 2.00
213 A94a $3.50 multicolored .25 .25
214 A94b $3.50 like #210 .65 *.85*
Nos. 209-214 (6) 2.30 2.80

Each denomination issued in sheets of 7 (6 type A94a, 1 type A94b).

For surcharges see Nos. 507-508, O1-O6.

Souvenir Sheet

1981 Perf. 12

215 A94b $5 like #210 1.00 1.00

Bar Jack G25

1981, Oct. 9 Wmk. 373 Perf. 14

218 G25 10c shown .25 .25
219 G25 50c Tarpon .30 .25
220 G25 60c Cobia .40 .25
221 G25 $2 Blue marlin 1.00 .75
Nos. 218-221 (4) 1.95 1.50

Ships G26

1982, Jan. 28 Perf. 14x13½

222 G26 1c Experiment .25 .25
223 G26 3c Lady Nelson .25 .25
224 G26 5c Daisy .25 .25
225 G26 6c Carib canoe .25 .25
226 G26 10c Hairoun Star .35 .30
227 G26 15c Jupiter .45 .35
228 G26 20c Christina .45 .35
229 G26 25c Orinoco .60 .40
230 G26 30c Lively .60 .40
231 G26 50c Alabama .85 .45
232 G26 60c Denmark .95 .45
233 G26 75c Santa Maria 1.00 .50
234 G26 $1 Baffin .75 .50
235 G26 $2 QE 2 1.10 1.10
236 G26 $3 Britannia 1.10 *1.40*
237 G26 $5 Geeststar 1.10 *1.60*
238 G26 $10 Grenadines Star 1.45 *2.50*
Nos. 222-238 (17) 11.75 11.30

For overprint see No. 509.

G27

1982, Apr. 5 Perf. 14

239 G27 10c Prickly pear fruit .25 .25
240 G27 50c Flower buds .30 .30
241 G27 $1 Flower .50 .50
242 G27 $2 Cactus 1.25 1.25
Nos. 239-242 (4) 2.30 2.30

For surcharge see St. Vincent No. 3386.

Princess Diana Type of Kiribati

50c, Anne Neville. 60c, Arms of Anne Neville. $6, Diana, Princess of Wales.

1982, July 1 Wmk. 380 Perf. 14

243 A99a 50c multicolored .25 .25
244 A99a 60c multicolored .25 .25
245 A99a $6 multicolored .50 .50
Nos. 243-245 (3) 1.00 1.00

For overprints see Nos. 248-262.

G29

1982, July 1 Wmk. 373 Perf. 14½

246 G29 $1.50 Old, new uniforms .50 .50
247 G29 $2.50 Lord Baden-Powell .80 .80

75th anniversary of Boy Scouts.

Nos. 243-245 Ovptd. "ROYAL BABY / BEQUIA"

1982, July 19 Wmk. 380 *Perf. 14*

No.	Type	Value	Description	Unused	Used
248	A99a	50c	multicolored	.25	.25
249	A99a	60c	multicolored	.25	.25
250	A99a	$6	multicolored	.40	.40
			Nos. 248-250 (3)	.90	.90

Nos. 243-245 Ovptd. "ROYAL BABY / CANOUAN"

1982, July 19

No.	Type	Value	Description	Unused	Used
251	A99a	50c	multicolored	.25	.25
252	A99a	60c	multicolored	.25	.25
253	A99a	$6	multicolored	.40	.40
			Nos. 251-253 (3)	.90	.90

Nos. 243-245 Ovptd. "ROYAL BABY / MAYREAU"

1982, July 19

No.	Type	Value	Description	Unused	Used
254	A99a	50c	multicolored	.25	.25
255	A99a	60c	multicolored	.25	.25
256	A99a	$6	multicolored	.40	.40
			Nos. 254-256 (3)	.90	.90

Nos. 243-245 Ovptd. "ROYAL BABY / MUSTIQUE"

1982, July 19

No.	Type	Value	Description	Unused	Used
257	A99a	50c	multicolored	.25	.25
258	A99a	60c	multicolored	.25	.25
259	A99a	$6	multicolored	.40	.40
			Nos. 257-259 (3)	.90	.90

Nos. 243-245 Ovptd. "ROYAL BABY / UNION"

1982, July 19

No.	Type	Value	Description	Unused	Used
260	A99a	50c	multicolored	.25	.25
261	A99a	60c	multicolored	.25	.25
262	A99a	$6	multicolored	.40	.40
			Nos. 260-262 (3)	.90	.90

Christmas Type of 1981

1982, Nov. 18 *Perf. 13½*

No.	Type	Value	Description	Unused	Used
263	A97	10c	Mary and Joseph at inn	.25	.25
264	A97	$1.50	Animals of stable	.40	.40
265	A97	$2.50	Nativity	.50	.50
a.			Souvenir sheet of 3, #263-265	1.10	*1.10*
			Nos. 263-265 (3)	1.15	1.15

For surcharges see St. Vincent Nos. 3376, 3390-3391.

No. 146 Surcharged

Perf. 13x12

1983, Apr. 26 Wmk. 373

No.	Type	Description	Unused	Used
266	G16	45c on 50c multicolored	.55	.35

Union Island G30

50c, Power Station, Clifton. 60c, Sunrise, Clifton Harbor. $1.50, School, Ashton. $2, Frigate Rock, Conch Shell Beach.

1983, May 12 *Perf. 13½*

No.	Type	Value	Description	Unused	Used
267	G30	50c	multicolored	.25	.25
268	G30	60c	multicolored	.25	.25
269	G30	$1.50	multicolored	.35	.35
270	G30	$2	multicolored	.50	.50
			Nos. 267-270 (4)	1.35	1.35

Treaty of Versailles, Bicent. — G31

1983, Sept. 15 *Perf. 14½x14*

No.	Type	Value	Description	Unused	Used
271	G31	45c	British warship	.25	.25
272	G31	60c	American warship	.30	.30
273	G31	$1.50	US troops, flag	.55	.55
274	G31	$2	British troops in battle	.75	.75
			Nos. 271-274 (4)	1.85	1.85

For surcharges see St. Vincent Nos. 3350, 3360, 3364, 3377.

200 Years of Manned Flight G32

Designs: 45c, Montgolfier balloon 1783, vert. 60c, Ayres Turbo-thrush Commander. $1.50, Lebaudy "1" dirigible. $2, Space shuttle Columbia.

1983, Sept. 15 *Perf. 14*

No.	Type	Value	Description	Unused	Used
275	G32	45c	multicolored	.25	.25
276	G32	60c	multicolored	.25	.25
277	G32	$1.50	multicolored	.35	.35
278	G32	$2	multicolored	.40	.40
a.			Souvenir sheet of 4, #275-278	1.60	1.60
			Nos. 275-278 (4)	1.25	1.25

For surcharges see St. Vincent Nos. 3355, 3378-3379, 3387.

British Monarch Type of 1984

No. 279a, Arms of Henry VIII. No. 279b, Henry VIII. No. 280a, Arms of James I. No. 280b, James I. No. 281a, Henry VIII. No. 281b, Hampton Court. No. 282a, James I. No. 282b, Edinburgh Castle. No. 283a, Mary Rose. No. 283b, Henry VIII, Portsmouth harbor. No. 284a, Gunpowder Plot. No. 284b, James I & Gunpowder Plot.

1983, Oct. 25 Unwmk. *Perf. 12½*

No.	Type	Value	Description	Unused	Used
279	A110	60c	Pair, #a.-b.	.30	.30
280	A110	60c	Pair, #a.-b.	.30	.30
281	A110	75c	Pair, #a.-b.	.30	.30
282	A110	75c	Pair, #a.-b.	.30	.30
283	A110	$2.50	Pair, #a.-b.	.45	.45
284	A110	$2.50	Pair, #a.-b.	.45	.45
			Nos. 279-284 (6)	2.10	2.10

Old Coinage — G33

20c, Quarter and half dollar, 1797. 45c, Nine bitts, 1811-14. 75c, Six and twelve bitts, 1811-14. $3, Sixty six shillings, 1798.

1983, Dec. 1 Wmk. 373 *Perf. 14*

No.	Type	Value	Description	Unused	Used
291	G33	20c	multicolored	.25	.25
292	G33	45c	multicolored	.25	.25
293	G33	75c	multicolored	.25	.25
294	G33	$3	multicolored	.50	.50
			Nos. 291-294 (4)	1.25	1.25

For surcharge see St. Vincent No. 3351.

Locomotives Type of 1985

No. 295, 1948 Class C62, Japan. No. 296, 1898 P.L.M. Grosse C, France. No. 297, 1892 Class D13, US. No. 298, 1903 Class V, UK. No. 299, 1980 Class 253, UK. No. 300, 1968 Class 581, Japan. No. 301, 1874 1001 Class, UK. No. 302, 1977 Class 142, DDR. No. 303, 1899 T-9 Class, UK. No. 304, 1932 Class C12, Japan. No. 305, 1897 Class T15, Germany. No. 306, 1808 Catch-me-who-can, UK. No. 307, 1900 Claud Hamilton Class, UK. No. 308, 1948 Class E10, Japan. No. 309, 1937 Coronation Class, UK. No. 310, 1936 Class 231, Algeria. No. 311, 1927 Class 4P, UK. No. 312, 1979 Class 120, Germany. No. 313, 1941 Class J, US. No. 314, 1900 Class 13, UK. No. 315, 1913 Slieve Gullion Class S, UK. No. 316, 1929 Class A3, UK. No. 317, 1954 Class X, Australia. No. 318, 1895 Class D16, US. No. 319, 1904 J. B. Earle, UK. No. 320, 1879 Halesworth, UK. No. 321, 1930 Class V1, UK. No. 322, 1986 Class 59, UK. No. 323, 1935 Class E18, Germany. No. 324, 1923 Class D50, Japan. No. 325, 1859 Problem Class, UK. No. 326, 1958 Class 40, UK. No. 327, 1875 Class A, US. No. 328, 1907 Star Class, British. No. 329, 1898 Lyn, UK. No. 330, 1961 Western Class, UK. No. 331, 1958 Warship Class 42, UK. No. 332, 1831 Samson Type, US. No. 333, 1854 Hayes, US. No. 334, 1902 Class P-69, US. No. 335, 1865 Talyllyn, UK. No. 336, 1899 Drummond's Bug, UK. No. 337, 1913 Class 60-3 Shay, US. No. 338, 1938 Class H1-d, Canada. No. 339, 1890 Class 2120, Japan. No. 340, 1951 Clan Class, UK. No. 341, 1934 Pioneer Zephyr, US. No. 342, 1948 Blue Peter, UK. No. 343, 1874 Class Beattie Well Tank, UK. No. 344, 1906 Cardean, UK. No. 345, 1840 Fire Fly, UK. No. 346, 1884 Class 1800, Japan.

1984-87 Litho. Unwmk. *Perf. 12½*
Se-tenant Pairs, #a.-b.
a. — Side and front views.
b. — Action scene.

No.	Type	Value	Description	Unused	Used
295	A120	1c	multicolored	.25	.25
296	A120	1c	multicolored	.25	.25
297	A120	5c	multicolored	.25	.25
298	A120	5c	multicolored	.25	.25
299	A120	10c	multicolored	.25	.25
300	A120	10c	multicolored	.25	.25
301	A120	10c	multicolored	.25	.25
302	A120	10c	multicolored	.25	.25
303	A120	15c	multicolored	.25	.25
304	A120	15c	multicolored	.25	.25
305	A120	15c	multicolored	.25	.25
306	A120	20c	multicolored	.25	.25
307	A120	35c	multicolored	.25	.25
308	A120	35c	multicolored	.25	.25
309	A120	35c	multicolored	.30	.30
310	A120	40c	multicolored	.35	.35
311	A120	40c	multicolored	.45	.45
312	A120	40c	multicolored	.50	.50
313	A120	45c	multicolored	.25	.25
314	A120	45c	multicolored	.35	.35
315	A120	50c	multicolored	.40	.40
316	A120	50c	multicolored	.55	.55
317	A120	50c	multicolored	.55	.55
318	A120	60c	multicolored	.40	.40
319	A120	60c	multicolored	.40	.40
320	A120	60c	multicolored	.35	.35
321	A120	60c	multicolored	.55	.55
322	A120	60c	multicolored	.55	.55
323	A120	70c	multicolored	.40	.40
324	A120	75c	multicolored	.40	.40
325	A120	75c	multicolored	.35	.35
326	A120	75c	multicolored	.55	.55
327	A120	75c	multicolored	.60	.60
328	A120	$1	multicolored	.40	.40
329	A120	$1	multicolored	.40	.40
330	A120	$1	multicolored	.40	.40
331	A120	$1	multicolored	.60	.60
332	A120	$1	multicolored	.60	.60
333	A120	$1.20	multicolored	.50	.50
334	A120	$1.25	multicolored	.60	.60
335	A120	$1.50	multicolored	.50	.50
336	A120	$1.50	multicolored	.45	.45
337	A120	$1.50	multicolored	.70	.70
338	A120	$1.50	multicolored	.80	.80
339	A120	$2	multicolored	.50	.50
340	A120	$2	multicolored	.80	.80
341	A120	$2	multicolored	.80	.80
342	A120	$2.50	multicolored	.50	.50
343	A120	$2.50	multicolored	1.20	1.20
344	A120	$3	multicolored	.60	.60
345	A120	$3	multicolored	1.00	1.00
a.			Souvenir sheet of 4, #324, 345	3.50	3.50
346	A120	$3	multicolored	.60	.60
			Nos. 295-346 (52)	23.70	23.70

Issued: #297, 299, 303, 307, 313, 318, 328, 342, 3/15/84; #295, 298, 306, 308, 319, 329, 335, 344, 10/9/84; #296, 304, 324, 345, 1/31/85; #300, 310, 315, 343, 5/17/85; #309, 323, 333, 339, 9/16/85; #305, 314, 320, 325, 330, 336, 340, 346, 3/14/86; #301, 311, 316, 321, 326, 331, 334, 337, 5/5/87; #302, 312, 317, 322, 327, 332, 338, 341, 8/26/87.

Spotted Eagle Ray G34

Wmk. 380

1984, Apr. 26 Litho. *Perf. 14*

No.	Type	Value	Description	Unused	Used
399	G34	45c	shown	.25	.25
400	G34	60c	Queen trigger fish	.25	.25
401	G34	$1.50	White spotted file fish	.35	.35
402	G34	$2	Schoolmaster	.40	.40
			Nos. 399-402 (4)	1.25	1.25

For overprint see No. 504.

Cricket Players Type of 1985

No. 403, R. A. Woolmer, portrait. No. 404, K. S. Ranjitsinhji, portrait. No. 405, W. R. Hammond, in action. No. 406, S. F. Barnes, portrait. No. 407, D. L. Underwood, in action. No. 408, R. Peel, in action. No. 409, M. D. Moxon, in action. No. 410, W. G. Grace, portrait. No. 411, L. Potter, portrait. No. 412, E. A. E. Baptiste, portrait. No. 413, H. Larwood, in action. No. 414, A. P. E. Knott, portrait. No. 415, Yorkshire & Kent county cricket clubs. No. 416, Sir John Berry Hobbs, portrait. No. 417, L. E. G. Ames, in action.

1984-85 Unwmk. *Perf. 12½*
Pairs, #a.-b.

No.	Type	Value	Description	Unused	Used
403	A116	1c	multicolored	.25	.25
404	A116	3c	multicolored	.25	.25
405	A116	5c	multicolored	.25	.25
406	A116	5c	multicolored	.25	.25
407	A116	30c	multicolored	.55	.55
408	A116	30c	multicolored	.45	.45
409	A116	55c	multicolored	.45	.45
410	A116	60c	multicolored	.70	.70
411	A116	60c	multicolored	.45	.45
412	A116	$1	multicolored	.70	.70
413	A116	$1	multicolored	.55	.55
414	A116	$2	multicolored	.80	.80
415	A116	$2	multicolored	.70	.70
416	A116	$2.50	multicolored	.80	.80
417	A116	$3	multicolored	1.10	1.10
			Nos. 403-417 (15)	8.25	8.25

Size of stamps in No. 415: 58x38mm.

Issued: Nos. 403, 407, 410, 412, 414, 417, 8/16/84; Nos. 406, 408, 413, 416, 11/2/84; Nos. 409, 411, 415, 2/22/85.

Canouan Island G35

1984, Sept. 3 Wmk. 380

No.	Type	Value	Description	Unused	Used
433	G35	35c	Junior secondary school	.25	.25
434	G35	45c	Police station	.35	.25
435	G35	$1	Post office	.40	*.50*
436	G35	$3	Anglican church	1.00	*1.60*
			Nos. 433-436 (4)	2.00	2.60

For surcharges see St. Vincent Nos. 3349, 3354, 3394.

Night-blooming Flowers — G36

1984, Oct. 15

No.	Type	Value	Description	Unused	Used
437	G36	35c	Lady of the night	.30	.30
438	G36	45c	Four o'clock	.35	.35
439	G36	75c	Mother-in-law's tongue	.45	.45
440	G36	$3	Queen of the night	1.75	1.75
			Nos. 437-440 (4)	2.85	2.85

For surcharges see St. Vincent Nos. 3351A, 3356.

Car Type of 1983

No. 441, 1959 Facel Vega, France. No. 442, 1903 Winton, Britain. No. 443, 1914 Mercedes-Benz, Germany. No. 444, 1936 BMW, Germany. No. 445, 1954 Rolls Royce, Britain. No. 446, 1934 Frazer Nash, Britain. No. 447, 1931 Invicta, Britain. No. 448, 1974 Lamborghini, Italy. No. 449, 1959 Daimler, Britain. No. 450, 1932 Marmon, US. No. 451, 1966 Brabham Repco, Britain. No. 452, 1968 Lotus Ford. No. 453, 1949 Buick, US. No. 454, 1927 Delage, France.

1984-86 Unwmk. *Perf. 12½*
Se-tenant Pairs, #a.-b.
a. — Side and front views.
b. — Action scene.

No.	Type	Value	Description	Unused	Used
441	A107	5c	multicolored	.25	.25
442	A107	5c	multicolored	.25	.25
443	A107	15c	multicolored	.25	.25
444	A107	25c	multicolored	.25	.25
445	A107	45c	multicolored	.25	.25
446	A107	50c	multicolored	.30	.30
447	A107	60c	multicolored	.30	.30
448	A107	60c	multicolored	.25	.25
449	A107	$1	multicolored	.30	.30
450	A107	$1	multicolored	.30	.30
451	A107	$1.50	multicolored	.30	.30
452	A107	$1.75	multicolored	.30	.30
453	A107	$3	multicolored	.60	.60
454	A107	$3	multicolored	.50	.50
			Nos. 441-454 (14)	4.40	4.40

Issued: #441, 444, 446, 453, 11/28/84; #442, 447, 449, 451, 4/9/85; #443, 445, 448, 450, 452, 454, 2/20/86.

Stamps issued 2/20/86 not inscribed "Leaders of the World."

Christmas Type of 1983

20c, Three wise men, star. 45c, Journeying to Bethlehem. $3, Presenting gifts.

Wmk. 380

1984, Dec. 3 Litho. *Perf. 14½*

469 A106 20c multicolored .25 .25
470 A106 45c multicolored .25 .25
471 A106 $3 multicolored .35 *1.00*
a. Souvenir sheet of 3, #469-471 1.00 *1.50*
Nos. 469-471 (3) .85 *1.50*

For surcharges see St. Vincent Nos. 3358, 3361.

Shellfish G37

1985, Feb. 11 *Perf. 14*

472 G37 25c Caribbean king crab .25 .25
473 G37 60c Queen conch .30 .30
474 G37 $1 White sea urchin .40 *.45*
475 G37 $3 West Indian top shell .80 *1.75*
Nos. 472-475 (4) 1.75 *2.75*

For surcharge see St. Vincent No. 3395.

Flowers — G38

No. 476a, Cypripedium calceolus. No. 476b, Gentiana asclepiadea. No. 477a, Clianthus formosus. No. 477b, Celmisia coriacea. No. 478a, Erythronium americanum. No. 478b, Laelia anceps. No. 479a, Leucadendron discolor. No. 479b, Meconopsis horridula.

1985, Mar. 13 Unwmk. *Perf. 12½*

476 G38 5c Pair, #a.-b. .25 .25
477 G38 55c Pair, #a.-b. .30 .30
478 G38 60c Pair, #a.-b. .30 .30
479 G38 $2 Pair, #a.-b. .55 .55
Nos. 476-479 (4) 1.40 1.40

Water Sports G39

1985, May 9 Wmk. 380 *Perf. 14*

484 G39 35c Windsurfing .25 .25
485 G39 45c Water skiing .25 .25
486 G39 75c Scuba diving .25 .25
487 G39 $3 Deep sea fishing .40 .40
Nos. 484-487 (4) 1.15 1.15

Tourism.
For surcharge see St. Vincent No. 3396.

Fruits and Blossoms G40

1985, June 24 *Perf. 15*

488 G40 30c Passion fruit .25 .25
489 G40 75c Guava .30 .30
490 G40 $1 Sapodilla .45 .45
491 G40 $2 Mango .75 .75
a. Souvenir sheet of 4, #488-491, perf. 14½x15 2.50 2.50
Nos. 488-491 (4) 1.75 1.75

For overprint see No. 503.

Queen Mother Type of 1985

#496a, Facing right. #496b, Facing forward. #497a, Facing right. #497b, Facing left. #498a, Facing right. #498b, Facing forward. #499a, Facing right. #499b, Facing left. #500a, As girl facing forward. #500b, Facing left.

1985, July 31 Unwmk. *Perf. 12½*

496 A122 40c Pair, #a.-b. .25 .25
497 A122 75c Pair, #a.-b. .30 .30
498 A122 $1.10 Pair, #a.-b. .30 .30
499 A122 $1.75 Pair, #a.-b. .30 .30
Nos. 496-499 (4) 1.15 1.15

Souvenir Sheet of 2

500 A122 $2 Pair, #a.-b. .90 .90

Souvenir sheets containing two $4 or two $5 stamps exist.

Nos. 213-214, 236, 399, 488, and 496-497 Ovptd. or Srchd. "CARIBBEAN ROYAL VISIT 1985" in 1, 2 or 3 Lines

Perfs., Wmks. as Before

1985, Oct. 27

503 G40 30c On #488 1.00 1.00
504 G37 45c On #399 1.25 1.25
505 A122 $1.10 On #496 2.25 2.25
506 A122 $1.10 On #497 2.25 2.25
507 A94a $1.50 On $3.50, #213 2.50 2.50
508 A94b $1.50 On $3.50, #214 22.50 22.50
509 G26 $3 On #236 3.25 3.25
Nos. 503-509 (7) 35.00 35.00

Traditional Dances G41

1985, Dec. 16 Unwmk. *Perf. 15*

510 G41 45c Donkey man .25 .25
511 G41 75c Cake dance, vert. .25 .25
512 G41 $1 Bois-bois man, vert. .35 .35
513 G41 $2 Maypole dance .55 .55
Nos. 510-513 (4) 1.40 1.40

For surcharges see St. Vincent Nos. 3366-3367.

Queen Elizabeth II 60th Birthday Type

5c, Elizabeth II. $1, At Princess Anne's christening. $4, As Princess. $6, In Canberra, 1982, vert. $8, Elizabeth II with crown.

1986, Apr. 21 *Perf. 12½*

514-517 A128 Set of 4 2.00 2.00

Souvenir Sheet

518 A128 $8 multi 2.75 2.75

Handicrafts — G41a

Wmk. 380

1986, Apr. 22 Litho. *Perf. 15*

519 G41a 10c Dolls .25 .25
520 G41a 60c Basketwork .25 .25
521 G41a $1 Scrimshaw .25 .25
522 G41a $3 Model boat .55 .55
Nos. 519-522 (4) 1.30 1.30

World Cup Soccer Championship, Mexico — G42

Perf. 12½, 15 (#525-528)

1986, May 7 Unwmk.

523 G42 1c Uruguayan team .25 .25
524 G42 10c Polish team .25 .25
525 G42 45c Bulgarian player .30 .30
526 G42 75c Iraqi player .35 .35
527 G42 $1.50 S. Korean player .60 .60
528 G42 $2 N. Ireland player .70 .70
529 G42 $4 Portuguese team 1.00 1.00
530 G42 $5 Canadian team 1.10 1.10
Nos. 523-530 (8) 4.55 4.55

Souvenir Sheets

531 G42 $1 like #529 .50 .50
532 G42 $3 like #523 1.25 1.25

Size: Nos. 525-528, 25x40mm.

Fungi — G43

45c, Marasmius pallescens. 60c, Leucocoprinus fragilissimus. 75c, Hygrocybe occidentalis. $3, Xerocomus hypoxanthus.

Wmk. 380

1986, May 23 Litho. *Perf. 14*

533 G43 45c multicolored 2.50 2.50
534 G43 60c multicolored 2.75 2.75
535 G43 75c multicolored 3.00 3.00
536 G43 $3 multicolored 8.00 8.00
Nos. 533-536 (4) 16.25 16.25

For surcharge see St. Vincent No. 3397.

Royal Wedding Type of 1986

No. 539a, Sarah, Diana. No. 539b, Andrew. No. 540a, Anne, Andrew, Charles, Margaret, horiz. No. 540b, Sarah, Andrew, horiz.

1986 Unwmk. *Perf. 12½*

539 A132 60c Pair, #a.-b. .35 .35
540 A132 $2 Pair, #a.-b. 1.10 1.10

Souvenir Sheet

541 A132a $8 Andrew, Sarah, in coach 3.50 3.50

Issued: #539-540, July 18; #541, Oct. 15.

Nos. 539-540 Ovptd. in Silver "Congratulations to TRH The Duke & Duchess of York" in 3 Lines

1986, Oct. 15

542 A132 60c Pair, #a.-b. .60 .60
543 A132 $2 Pair, #a.-b. 2.00 2.00

Dragonflies — G44

45c, Brachymesia furcata. 60c, Lepthemis vesiculosa. 75c, Perithemis domitta. $2.50, Tramea abdominalis, vert.

1986, Nov. 19 *Perf. 15*

546 G44 45c multicolored .25 .25
547 G44 60c multicolored .25 .25
548 G44 75c multicolored .25 .25
549 G44 $2.50 multicolored .55 .55
Nos. 546-549 (4) 1.30 1.30

Statue of Liberty Type

Souvenir Sheets

Each stamp shows different views of Statue of Liberty and a different US president in the margin.

1986, Nov. 26 *Perf. 14*

550 A135 $1.50 multicolored .25 .25
551 A135 $1.75 multicolored .30 .30
552 A135 $2 multicolored .35 .40
553 A135 $2.50 multicolored .40 .50
554 A135 $3 multicolored .50 .50
555 A135 $3.50 multicolored .60 .60
556 A135 $5 multicolored .80 .80
557 A135 $6 multicolored .90 .90
558 A135 $8 multicolored 1.25 1.25
Nos. 550-558 (9) 5.35 5.50

Birds of Prey — G45

1986, Nov. 26 Litho.

560 G45 10c Sparrow hawk .75 .75
561 G45 45c Black hawk 1.50 1.50
562 G45 60c Duck hawk 1.75 1.75
563 G45 $4 Fish hawk 8.00 8.00
Nos. 560-563 (4) 12.00 12.00

For surcharges see St. Vincent Nos. 3362, 3401.

Christmas — G46

45c, Santa playing drums. 60c, Santa wind surfing. $1.25, Santa water skiing. $2, Santa limbo dancing.

1986, Nov. 26

564 G46 45c multicolored .25 .25
565 G46 60c multicolored .30 .30
566 G46 $1.25 multicolored .80 .80
567 G46 $2 multicolored 1.15 1.15
a. Souvenir sheet of 4, #564-567 8.50 8.50
Nos. 564-567 (4) 2.50 2.50

For surcharge see St. Vincent No. 3375.

Queen Elizabeth II, 40th Wedding Anniv. Type of 1987

15c, Elizabeth, Charles. 45c, Victoria, Albert. $1.50, Elizabeth, Philip. $3, Elizabeth, Philip, diff. $4, Elizabeth, portrait. $6, Elizabeth as Princess.

1987, Oct. 15 *Perf. 12½*

568 A140 15c multicolored .25 .25
569 A140 45c multicolored .25 .25
570 A140 $1.50 multicolored .30 .30
571 A140 $3 multicolored .35 .35
572 A140 $4 multicolored .45 .45
Nos. 568-572 (5) 1.60 1.60

Souvenir Sheet

573 A140 $6 multicolored 1.90 1.90

Victoria's accession to the throne, 150th anniv.

Marine Life G48

45c, Banded coral shrimp. 50c, Arrow crab, flamingo tongue. 65c, Cardinal fish. $5, Moray eel.
No. 578, Puffer fish.

1987, Dec. 17 *Perf. 15*

574 G48 45c multicolored .55 .55
575 G48 50c multicolored .60 .60
576 G48 65c multicolored .70 .70
577 G48 $5 multicolored 2.60 2.60
Nos. 574-577 (4) 4.45 4.45

Souvenir Sheet

578 G48 $5 multicolored 2.60 2.60

World Cup Soccer Championships, Mexico, 1986 — B5

No. 218, South Korean team . No. 219, Iraqi team. No. 220, Algerian team. No. 221, Bulgaria vs. France. No. 222, Belgium. No. 223, Danish team. No. 224, Italy vs. W. Germany. No. 225, USSR vs. England. No. 226, Italy, 1982 champions. No. 227, W. Germany. No. 228, N. Ireland. No. 229, England.

1986 July 3 *Perf. 12¼, 15 (B5)*

218 B4 1c multicolored .25 .25
219 B4 2c multicolored .25 .25
220 B4 5c multicolored .25 .25
221 B4 10c multicolored .25 .25
222 B5 45c multicolored .25 .25
223 B4 60c multicolored .25 .25
224 B4 75c multicolored .25 .25
225 B4 $1.50 multicolored .30 .30
226 B5 $1.50 multicolored .30 .30
227 B5 $2 multicolored .50 .50
228 B5 $3.50 multicolored .70 .70
229 B4 $6 multicolored 1.10 1.10
Nos. 218-229 (12) 4.65 4.65

Souvenir Sheets

230 B4 $1 like No. 219 .50 .50
231 B4 $1.75 like No. 221 .80 .80

Royal Wedding Type of 1986

No. 232, Andrew. No. 233, Andrew in helicopter. No. 234, Andrew in crowd. No. 235, Andrew, Sarah.
$8, Andrew, Sarah in coach.

1986, July 15 *Perf. 12½x13, 13x12½*

232 A132 60c multicolored .35 .35
233 A132 60c multicolored .35 .35
234 A132 $2 multicolored .85 .85
235 A132 $2 multicolored .85 .85
Nos. 232-235 (4) 2.40 2.40

Souvenir Sheet

236 A132a $8 multicolored 3.75 3.75

Nos. 234-235 horiz.

Railway Engineers and Locomotives — B6

Designs: $1, Sir Daniel Gooch, Fire Fly Class, 1840. $2.50, Sir Nigel Gresley, A4 Class, 1938. $3, Sir William Stanier, Coronation Class, 1937. $4, Oliver V. S. Bulleid, Battle of Britain Class, 1946.

1986, Sept. 30 *Perf. 13x12½*

237-240 B6 Set of 4 3.00 3.00

Nos. 232-235 Ovptd. "Congratulations to TRH The Duke & Duchess of York" in 3 Lines

1986 *Perf. 12½x13, 13x12½*

241 A132 60c on No. 232 .75 .75
242 A132 60c on No. 233 .75 .75
243 A132 $2 on No. 234 2.75 2.75
244 A132 $2 on No. 235 2.75 2.75
Nos. 241-244 (4) 7.00 7.00

Royalty Portrait Type

Portraits and photographs: 15c, Queen Victoria, 1841. 75c, Elizabeth, Charles, 1948. $1, Coronation, 1953. $2.50, Duke of Edinburgh, 1948. $5, Elizabeth c. 1980. $6, Elizabeth, Charles, 1948, diff.

1987, Oct. 15 *Perf. 12½x13*

245-249 A140 Set of 5 3.00 3.00

Souvenir Sheet

250 A140 $6 multi 3.00 3.00

Great Explorers Type of St. Vincent Grenadines

Designs: 15c, Gokstad, ship of Leif Eriksson (c. 1000). 50c, Eriksson and bearing dial. $1.75, The Mathew, ship of John Cabot. $2, Cabot, quadrant. $2.50, The Trinidad, ship of Ferdinand Magellan. $3, Arms, portrait of Christopher Columbus. $3.50, Columbus' ship Santa Maria. $4, Magellan, globe. $5, Anchor, long boat, ship.

1988, July 11 **Litho.** *Perf. 14*

251-258 G52 Set of 8 3.00 3.00

Souvenir Sheet

259 G52 $5 multi 3.25 3.25

Tennis Type of 1987

1988, July 29 *Perf. 13x13½*

260 A137 15c Anders Jarryd .30 .30
261 A137 45c Anne Hobbs .30 .30
262 A137 80c Jimmy Connors .35 .35
263 A137 $1.25 Carling Bassett .45 .45
264 A137 $1.75 Stefan Edberg, horiz. .60 .60
265 A137 $2.00 Gabriela Sabatini, horiz. .70 .70
266 A137 $2.50 Mats Wilander .90 .90
267 A137 $3.00 Pat Cash 1.10 1.10
Nos. 260-267 (8) 4.70 4.70

No. 263 inscribed "Carlene Basset" instead of "Carling Bassett."
An unissued souvenir sheet exists.

French Revolution Bicentennial B7

Designs: 1c, Grandma Duck as French peasant woman. 2c, Donald & Daisy celebrating liberty. 3c, Minnie as Marie Antoinette. 4c, Clarabelle & patriotic chair. 5c, Goofy in Republican citizen's costume. 10c, Mickey & Donald planting liberty tree. No. 274, $5, Horace taking Tennis Court Oath. $6, Grand Master Mason McDuck.
No. 276, $5, Dancing the Carmagnole. No. 277, $5, Philosophers at Cafe La Procope.

1989, July 7 *Perf. 13½x14*

268-275 B7 Set of 8 10.00 10.00

Souvenir Sheets

276-277 B7 Set of 2 6.00 6.00

Anniversaries and Events Type

$5, Otto Lililienthal, aviation pioneer.

1991, Nov. 18 **Litho.** *Perf. 14*

278 A213 $5 multicolored 5.25 5.25

Japanese Attack on Pearl Harbor, 50th Anniv. B8

Designs: 50c, Kate from second-wave over Hickam Field. $1, B17 sights Zeros in Pearl Harbor attack. $5, Firefighters rescue sailors from blazing USS Tennessee.

1991, Nov. 18

287 B8 50c multicolored .70 .70
288 B8 $1 multicolored 1.30 1.30

Souvenir Sheet

289 B8 $5 multicolored 4.25 4.25

Wolfgang Amadeus Mozart, Death Bicentennial — B9

Mozart and: 10c, Piccolo. 75c, Piano. $4, Violotta.
No. 293, $6, Mozart's last composition, Lacrimosa from the Requiem Mass. No. 294, $6, Bronze of Mozart by Adrien-Etienne Gaudez, vert. No. 295, $6, Score of opening of the "Paris" symphony, K297.

1991 **Litho.** *Perf. 14*

290-292 B9 Set of 3 5.50 5.50

Souvenir Sheets

293-295 B9 Set of 3 18.00 18.00

Nos. 293-295 each contain one 57x42mm or 42x57mm stamp.

Boy Scout Type

50c, Lord Baden-Powell, killick hitch knot. $1, Baden-Powell, clove hitch knot. $2, Drawing of Boy Scout by Baden-Powell, vert. $3, American 1st Class Scout badge, vert. $6, Baden-Powell, Lark's head knot.

1991

296-299 A211 Set of 4 8.00 8.00

Souvenir Sheet

300 A211 $6 multicolored 6.75 6.75

Diana, Princess of Wales, (1961-97) — B10

1997, Dec. 10 **Litho.** *Perf. 14*

301 B10 $1 multicolored 1.75 1.75

No. 301 was issued in sheets of 6.

Paintings Type of 1999

Various pictures of flowers making up a photomosaic of the Queen Mother.

2000, Sept. 5 *Perf. 13¾*

302 A442 $1 Sheet of 8, #a-h 6.00 6.00
i. As No. 302, imperf. 6.00 6.00

Worldwide Fund for Nature (WWF) B11

Leatherback turtle: a, Three on beach. b, One coming ashore. c, One in water. d, One digging nest.

2001, Dec. 10 **Litho.** *Perf. 14*

303 B11 $1.40 Vert or horiz. strip of 4, #a-d 5.00 5.00

Queen Elizabeth II, 50th Anniv. of Reign Type of 2002

No. 304: a, Without hat. b, Wearing tiara. c, Wearing scarf. d, With Prince Philip and baby.
$2, Wearing scarf, diff.

2002, June 17 **Litho.** *Perf. 14¼*

304 A509 80c Sheet of 4, #a-d 4.50 4.50

Souvenir Sheet

305 A509 $2 multi 4.00 4.00

United We Stand Type of 2001

2002, Nov. 4 *Perf. 14*

306 A508 $2 multi 2.00 2.00

Printed in sheets of 4.

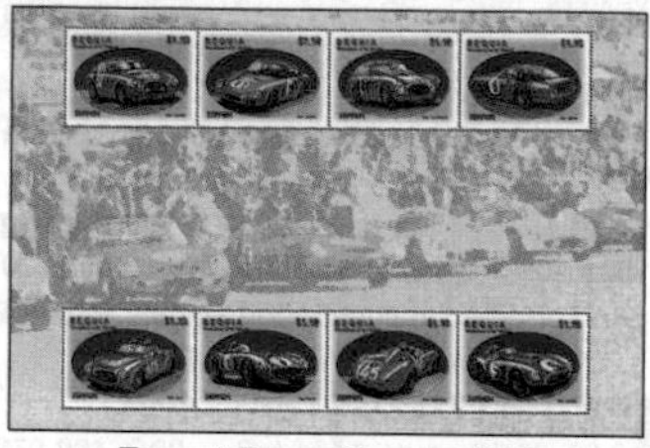

Ferrari Race Cars — B12

No. 307: a, 1953 250MM. b, 1962 330LM. c, 1952 340 Mexico. d, 1963 330LM. e, 1952 225S. f, 1956 500TR. g, 1954 750 Monza. h, 1954 375 Plus.

2002, June 10 **Litho.** *Perf. 13¾*

307 B12 $1.10 Sheet of 8, #a-h 6.75 6.75

Elvis Presley Type of 2002

2002, Aug. 19

308 A517 $1 multi 1.00 1.00

Printed in sheets of 9.

Shirley Temple Movie Type of 2000

No. 309, horiz. — Scenes from *Captain January* of Temple with: a, Man at table. b, Woman. c, Two men annd bird with bow. d, Boy and teacher. e, Two men at table. f, Three men in boat.
No. 310: a, Man with beard. b, Three men. c, Two men and doll. d, With man, dancing.
$5, With sailors.

2002, Aug. 19

309 A471 $1.40 Sheet of 6, #a-f 6.50 6.50
310 A471 $2 Sheet of 4, #a-d 6.50 6.50

Souvenir Sheet

311 A471 $5 multi 5.00 5.00

Sheet margins are dated "2003."

Queen Mother Elizabeth Type of 2002

No. 312: a, Wearing yellow dress. b, Wearing red dress.

2002, Nov. 4 *Perf. 14*

312 A522 $2 Pair, #a-b 3.00 3.00

No. 312 printed in sheets containing 2 pairs.

Year of the Horse — B13

No. 313: a, Black horse in foreground, front feet raised. b, White horse in foreground. c, Piebald horse in foreground. d, Black horse in foreground, front feet not raised.

2002, Dec. 17 *Perf. 13¼x13*

313 B13 $1.40 Sheet of 4, #a-d 5.50 5.50

Teddy Bears Type of 2002

No. 314, $2 — Bears from Germany: a, Balloon pilot bear. b, Bear in lederhosen. c, Bear in pants and ice skates. d, Bear in skirt and ice skates.
No. 315, $2 — Bears from Italy: a, Bear with feathered hat, standing in gondola. b, Bear with cap, seated on gondola. c, Bear with umbrella. d, Gondolier bear.

2003, Jan. 27 *Perf. 13½x13¼*

Sheets of 4, #a-d

314-315 A519 Set of 2 13.00 13.00

Year of the Ram Type of 2003

No. 316: a, Ram with white horns and beard, denomination at right. b, Ram with black horns, denomination at left. c, Ram with dark horns, denomination at right. d, Ram with white horns, denomination at left. e, Ram with leg raised. f, Ram with horns with lines, denomination at left.

2003, Feb. 1 *Perf. 14¼x13¾*

316 A526 $1 Sheet of 6, #a-f 5.00 5.00

Princess Diana Type of 2003

No. 317, $2: a, Wearing pink hat. b, Wearing gray dress. c, Wearing white blouse. d, Wearing checked pants.
No. 318, $2: a, Wearing black dress. b, Wearing red blouse. c, Wearing black and white hat. d, Wearing white blouse, holding flowers.

2003, May 26 Litho. *Perf. 14*
Sheets of 4, #a-d

317-318 A536 Set of 2 13.00 13.00

Corvette Type of 2003

No. 319: a, 1957 convertible. b, 1964 Sting Ray. c, 1954 convertible. d, 1989.
$5, 1988.

2003, July 1 *Perf. 13¼x13½*

319 A534 $2 Sheet of 4, #a-d 7.00 7.00

Souvenir Sheet

320 A534 $5 multi 5.00 5.00

Pres. John F. Kennedy (1917-63) — B14

No. 321: a, Denomination at UL, name at right. b, Denomination at UL, name at left. c, Denomination at UR, name at left. d, Denomination at UR, name at right.

2003, Aug. 25 *Perf. 14*

321 B14 $2 Sheet of 4, #a-d 7.50 7.50

Elvis Presley (1935-77) — B15

No. 322: a, Silhouette. b, Holding guitar.

2003, Dec. 1 *Perf. 13½*

322 B15 90c Sheet, #322a, 8 #322b 8.00 8.00

Birds — B16

Designs: 90c, Stripe-headed tanager. $1, Violaceous trogon. $1.40, Barn owl. $2, Green jay.
$5, Montezuma oropendola.

2003, Dec. 1 *Perf. 13¼*

323-326 B16 Set of 4 4.25 4.25

Souvenir Sheet

327 B16 $5 multi 4.25 4.25

New Year 2004 (Year of the Monkey) B17

Romping Monkeys, by unknown painter: $1.40, Detail. $3, Entire painting.

2004, Jan. 15 Litho. *Perf. 13¼*

328 B17 $1.40 multi 1.75 1.75

Souvenir Sheet
Perf. 13½x13¼

329 B17 $3 multi 3.00 3.00

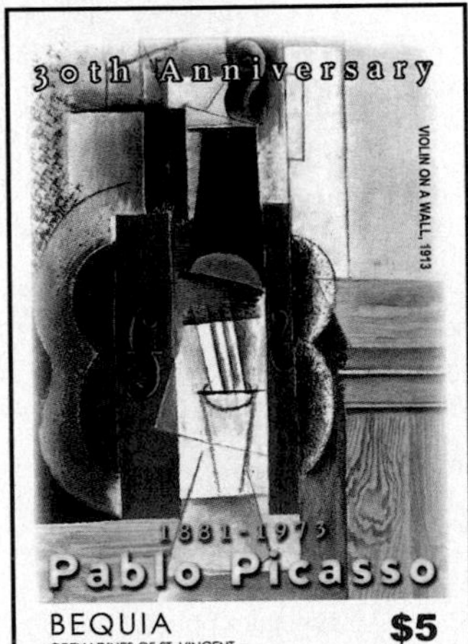

Paintings by Pablo Picasso (1881-1973) — B18

No. 330: a, Bust of a Woman with Self-Portrait. b, Jacqueline in a Turkish Jacket. c, Françoise in an Armchair. d, Still Life on a Pedestal Table.
$5, Violin on a Wall.

2004, Apr. 30 *Perf. 14¼*

330 B18 $2 Sheet of 4, #a-d 6.00 6.00

Imperf

331 B18 $5 multi 4.00 4.00

No. 330 contains four 38x51mm stamps.

Marilyn Monroe Type of 2004

2004, May 3 *Perf. 14*

332 A558 70c multi .55 .55

Printed in sheets of 12.

Babe Ruth Type of 2004

2004, July 1 *Perf. 13¼*

333 A561 70c multi .55 .55

Printed in sheets of 12.

Ancient Greece B19

Designs: 30c, Palace of Minos, Crete. 70c, Apollo's Temple, Delphi. $1, Statue of Zeus, Olympia. $1.40, Bust of Aphrodite. $2, Bust of Socrates. $3, Parthenon.
$5, Panathenaic Stadium, Athens.

2004, Aug. 16 *Perf. 14*

334-339 B19 Set of 6 7.50 7.50

Souvenir Sheet

340 B19 $5 multi 4.50 4.50

Ronald Reagan Type of 2004

No. 341, horiz.: a, Reagan with wife, Nancy. b, Reagan with George H. W. Bush.

2004, Oct. 13 *Perf. 13½*

341 Horiz. pair 2.75 2.75
a.-b. A564 $1.40 Either single 1.25 1.25

Printed in sheets containing three each #341a-341b.

Railroads Type of 2004

No. 342, $2: a, GN 2507 Class P 2-4-8-2. b, Great Northern 2507. c, Great Northern. d, GWR King Class 4-6-0.
No. 343, $2: a, LMS 2MT 2-6-2 T. b, Green Arrow. c, LMS Stainer Class 5MT 4-6-0. d, Liner Class A4 Sir Nigel Gresley.
No. 344, $2: a, Barclay 0-4-0 Saddle tank. b, Beyer Peacock. c, BR Class 4MT 2-6-0. d, Dampflok 109.
No. 345, $2: a, British Railways 2-6-4 T. b, Caledonian Railway 0-4-4 T. c, Evening Star. d, Southern Railway Carolina Special.
No. 346, $5, Pakistan Railways SPS 4-4-0. No. 347, $5, Norwegian State Railway. No. 348, $5, Russell Hunslet 2-6-2 T. No. 349, $5, North British Railway 0-6-0.

Perf. 14½x14, 14 (#344, 348)

2004, Dec. 13 Sheets of 4, #a-d

342-345 A565 Set of 4 26.00 26.00

Souvenir Sheets

346-349 A565 Set of 4 16.00 16.00

Christmas B20

Paintings: 55c, Madonna of Port Lligat, by Salvador Dali. 90c, Madonna and Child, by Barolome Esteban Murillo. $1, Madonna and Child, by Jan van Eyck. $4, Madonna of the Meadow, by Giovanni Bellini.
$6, Madonna and Child, by Caravaggio.

2004, Dec. 13 *Perf. 12*

350-353 B20 Set of 4 5.50 5.50

Souvenir Sheet

354 B20 $6 multi 4.75 4.75

End of World War II, 60th Anniv. — B21

No. 355, $2 — Sinking of the Bismarck, 1941: a, Bismarck, Map. b, Aircraft make ready for flight. c, The Bismarck getting pounded by British Navy. d, The Bismarck goes down.
No. 356, $2 — Liberation of Paris: a, Allied troops enter Paris. b, The end of German occupation. c, Allied troops help supply people of Paris. d, Victory at last.
No. 357, $5, Bismarck. No. 358, $5, General De Gaulle returns.

2005, May 9 Litho. *Perf. 13½*
Sheets of 4, #a-d

355-356 B21 Set of 2 14.00 14.00

Souvenir Sheets

357-358 B21 Set of 2 8.00 8.00

Vatican Stamp and Pope John Paul II Types of 2005

Designs: 70c, Vatican #64. $4, Pope and crowd, horiz.

2005, June 1 *Perf. 13x13¼*

359 A584 70c multi .55 .55

Perf. 13½

360 A585 $4 multi 3.25 3.25

No. 359 printed in sheets of 12; No. 360, in sheets of 4.

Moths — B22

Designs: 90c, Pericallia galactina. $1, Automeris io draudtiana. $1.40, Antherina suraka. $2, Bunaea alcinoe.
$5, Rothschildia erycina nigrescens.

2005, July 26 *Perf. 12¾*

361-364 B22 Set of 4 5.50 5.50

Souvenir Sheet

365 B22 $5 multi 4.00 4.00

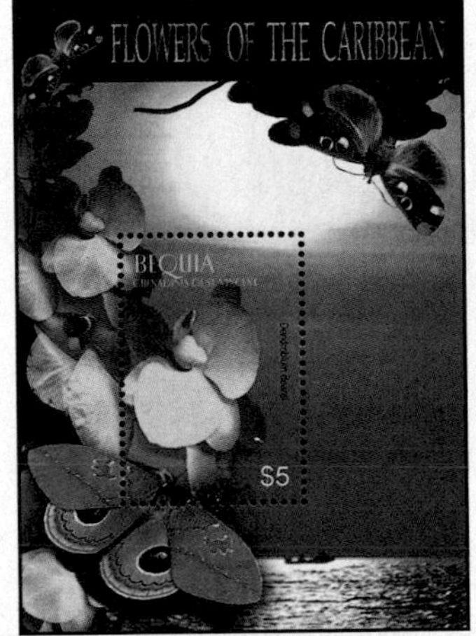

Flowers — B23

No. 366, horiz.: a, Anthurium acropolis. b, Anthurium andraeanum. c, Gloxinia avanti. d, Heliconia psittacorum choconiana.
$5, Dendrobium dearei.

2005, June 26

366 B23 $2 Sheet of 4, #a-d 6.50 6.50

Souvenir Sheet

367 B23 $5 multi 4.00 4.00

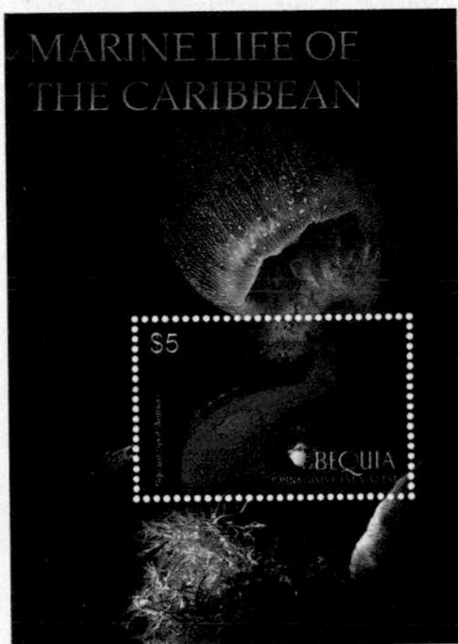

Marine Life — B24

No. 368: a, Hermissenda crassicornis. b, Chromodoris leopardus. c, Chromodoris kuniei. d, Coryphella verrucosa.
$5, Square spot anthias.

2005, June 26

368 B24 $2 Sheet of 4, #a-d 7.00 7.00

Souvenir Sheet

369 B24 $5 multi 4.00 4.00

Prehistoric Animals — B25

No. 370, $2: a, Tenontosaurus. b, Gorgosaurus. c, Psittacosaurus. d, Parasaurolophus.
No. 371, $2, horiz.: a, Brachiosaurus. b, Seismosaurus. c, Struthiomimus. d, Oviraptor.
No. 372, $2, horiz.: a, Argentinosaurus. b, Triceratops. c, Ankylosaurus. d, Stegosaurus.
No. 373, $5, Quetzalcoatlus. No. 374, $5, Mammoth. No. 375, $5, Pteranodon, horiz.

2005, Sept. 1 ***Perf. 14***

Sheets of 4, #a-d

370-372 B25 Set of 3 19.50 19.50

Souvenir Sheets

373-375 B25 Set of 3 12.00 12.00

Elvis Presley Type of 2005 and

B26

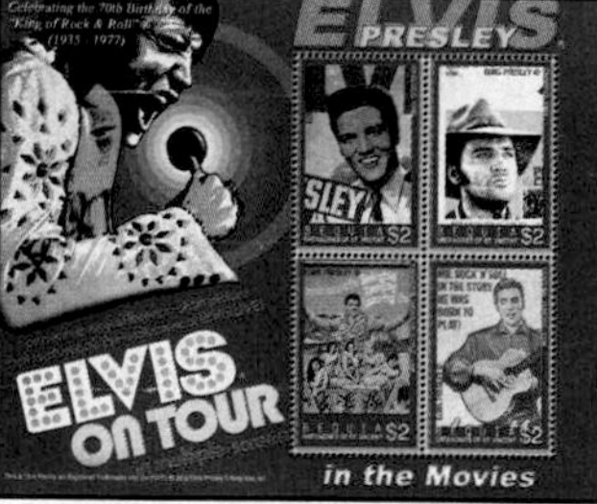

Elvis Presley (1935-77) — B27

No. 377 — Presley with: a, Tie. b, Hat. c, Lei. d, Guitar.
$20, Like #376.

Perf. 13½x13¼

2005, Nov. 21 **Litho.**

376 B26 $2 multi 1.50 1.50
377 B27 $2 Sheet of 4, #a-d 5.00 5.00

Litho. & Embossed

Without Gum

Die Cut Perf. 8

378 A597 $20 gold & multi 14.00 14.00

No. 376 was printed in sheets of 4.

Railroads Type of 2004

No. 379, $1: a, British Rail APT. b, Beyer Peacock 4-4-0. c, 1890s steam locomotive, Sao Paolo, Brazil. d, Beijing Limestone 600mm Gauge 0-8-0. e, China Railways QJ 2-10-2 Zhou De. f, Chinese SY 2-8-2 Industrial Baotou. g, Chinese SY Class Mikado 2-8-2. h, Chinese SY Class Overhaul Baotou. i, Derelict colliery, Nanpo, China.
No. 380, $1: a, Class 37 Diesel-electric. b, Indian Railways XB Class. c, Steam locomotive bringing in sugar cane, Java. d, Ji-tong Railway train on bridge, Reshui. e, Ji-tong Railway QJ at Liudigou. f, Ji-tong Railway QJ trains on Simingyi Viaduct. g, Ji-tong Railway train at Nandian. h, Ji-tong Railway QJ trains near Er-di. i, Ji-tong Railway QJ trains and banker.
No. 381, $1, vert.: a, Class 47 Diesel-electric. b, Stanier 8F, Turkey. c, Baldwin 2-8-2, Brazil. d, Sand boy, Borsing 0-8-0, Java. e, Indian Railways meter gauge 2-8-2, girl with pot. f, Locomotive graveyard, Thessaloniki, Greece. g, Greek Z Class meter gauge Peloponnese. h, Burdwan locomotive shed, West Bengal Province, India. i, SY locomotives at shed, Anshan, China.
No. 382, $5, Bridge on Asmara to Masawa line, Eritrea. No. 383, $5, Cornish Riviera Express. No. 384, $5, Zurich to Milan train.

2005, Dec. 30 ***Perf. 13½***

Sheets of 9, #a-i

379-381 A565 Set of 3 22.50 22.50

Souvenir Sheets

382-384 A565 Set of 3 12.00 12.00

Queen Elizabeth II, 80th Birthday Type

Inscriptions: No. 385, $2, The Investiture of Charles. No. 386, $2, The Queen's 50th Birthday. No. 387, $2, The Queen's Silver Jubilee. No. 388, $2, The Birth of Prince William.

2006, Jan. 31

385-388 A603 Set of 4 7.00 7.00

Each stamp printed in sheets of 8 + label.

Miniature Sheet

Marilyn Monroe (1926-62), Actress — B28

Various images.

2006, Mar. 31

389 B28 $2 Sheet of 4, #a-d 6.00 6.00

Columbus Type of 2006

Designs: 20c, Columbus and ship. 90c, Columbus, ships and crew, vert. $1.10, Niña, vert. $2, Columbus dicovers New World, 1492.
$5, Pinta, vert.

2006, July 21 ***Perf. 12¾***

390-393 A611 Set of 4 3.50 3.50

Souvenir Sheet

394 A611 $5 multi 3.75 3.75

Space Achievements Type of 2006

No. 395, $2 — Luna 9: a, Left half of Luna 9, country name at LL. b, Right half of Luna 9, country name at UR. c, Top half of Luna 9, country name and denomination at UL. d, Luna 9 in space, country name at UL, denomination at UR. e, Bottom half of Luna 9, country name at LR. f, Luna 9 on moon, country name at LR.
No. 396, $3, vert. — Mars Reconnaissance Orbiter: a, Orbiter, country name in white. b, Orbiter, coutnry name in black. c, Mission emblem. d, Exterior of rocket showing Mission and NASA emblems.
No. 397, $6, Viking 1. No. 398, $6, International Space Station.

2006, Sept. 27 ***Perf. 14¼***

395 A612 $2 Sheet of 6, #a-f 4.00 4.00
396 A612 $3 Sheet of 4, #a-d 4.00 4.00

Souvenir Sheets

397-398 A612 Set of 2 4.00 4.00

Mozart Type of 2006

Design: Painting of Mozart, by Johann Georg Edlinger.

2006, Dec. 22 **Litho.** ***Perf. 13¼***

399 A619 $6 multi 4.75 4.75

Souvenir Sheet

History of the Zeppelin — B29

No. 400: a, Ludwig Durr (1878-1956), chief engineer. b, Count Ferdinand Adolf August Heinrich von Zeppelin (1838-1917), designer. c, Dr. Hugo Eckener (1868-1954), engineer and pilot.

2006, Dec. 22

400 B29 $3 Sheet of 3, #a-c 7.00 7.00

Scouting, Cent. — B30

Designs: $4, Lord Robert Baden-Powell, Scouting emblem and doves. $6, Baden-Powell, horiz.

2007, Jan. 15

401 B30 $4 purple & blue 2.25 2.25

Souvenir Sheet

402 B30 $6 brown 4.75 4.75

No. 401 printed in sheets of 3. No. 402 contains one 51x37mm stamp.

Princess Diana Type of 2007

Miniature Sheet

No. 403 — Various photographs with panel colors of: a, Yellow. b, Red violet. c, Green. d, Blue. e, Purple. f, Black.
$6, Princess Diana and flags.

2007, May 1

403 A630 $1.40 Sheet of 6, #a-f 5.00 5.00

Souvenir Sheet

404 A630 $6 multi 4.50 4.50

Concorde Type of 2006

No. 405, $1.40 — Concorde landing at Dulles Airport: a, Side view of Concorde. b, Front view of Concorde.
No. 406, $1.40 — Concorde at Boeing Field, Seattle: a, Front view of Concorde. b, Side view of Concorde.

2007, May 1

Pairs, #a-b

405-406 A614 Set of 2 4.25 4.25

Nos. 405 and 406 were each printed in sheets containing three of each stamp.

John F. Kennedy Type of 2007

Miniature Sheets

No. 407, $2 — Kennedy: a, As Navy Ensign, 1941. b, With crew at Solomon Islands, 1942. c, Drawing in blue gray. d, At Solomon Islands, 1943.
No. 408, $2: a, Kennedy and R. Sargent Shriver. b, Kennedy giving Peace Corps speech. c, Drawing of Kennedy in claret. d, Peace Corps volunteers.

2007, July 5

Sheets of 4, #a-d

407-408 A622 Set of 2 13.00 13.00

Wedding of Queen Elizabeth II and Prince Philip, 60th Anniv. Type of 2007

No. 409: a, Couple in coach, denomination in blue. b, Couple crossing street, denomination in blue. c, Couple crossing street, denomination in light green. d, Couple in coach, denomination in light green. e, Couple in coach, denomination in lilac. f, Couple crossing street, denomination in lilac.
$6, Couple, diff.

2007, July 5

409 A629 $1.40 Sheet of 6, #a-f 7.00 7.00

Souvenir Sheet

410 A629 $6 multi 5.00 5.00

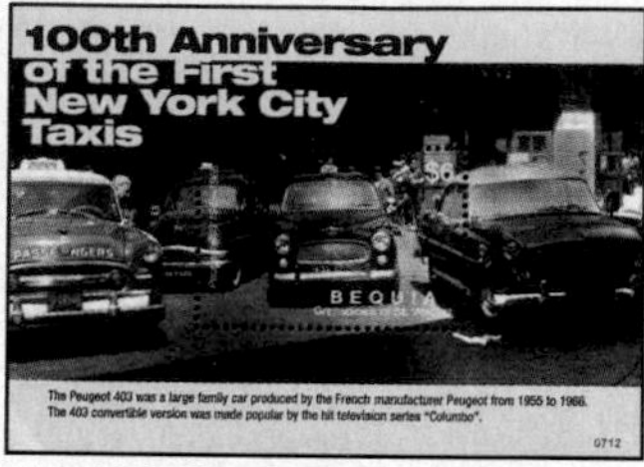

New York City Taxicabs, Cent. — B31

No. 411: a, 1909 Overland Model 31. b, 1910 Rockwell. c, 1916 Yellow Cab Model J. d, 1909 Kayton taxis. e, 1917 Yellow Cab Model K. f, 1919 Yellow Cab.
$6, 1955-66 Peugeot 403.

2007, July 5

411 B31 $1.40 Sheet of 6, #a-f 7.25 7.25

Souvenir Sheet

412 B31 $6 multi 5.00 5.00

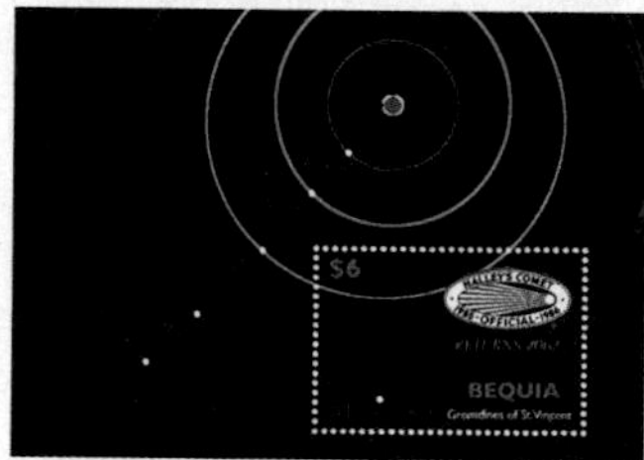

1986 Halley's Comet Merchandising Emblem — B32

No. 413 — Emblem and frame color of: a, Light blue. b, Yellow. c, Green. d, Red brown.
$6, Emblem and Halley's Comet orbit diagram.

2007, July 5

413 B32 $2 Sheet of 4, #a-d 6.50 6.50

Souvenir Sheet

414 B32 $6 multi 4.75 4.75

Elvis Presley Type of 2007

Miniature Sheets

No. 415, $2 — Silhouette of Presley and: a, Graceland and gate. b, Piano, television and table in Graceland. c, Graceland and flowers. d, Swimming pool at Graceland.
No. 416, $2.50 — Presley: a, Wearing flowered western shirt, man and woman. b, Playing guitar, with other guitarist. c, Wearing neckerchief. d, Seated.

2007 **Sheets of 4, #a-d** ***Perf. 13¼***

415-416 A633 Set of 2 13.50 13.50

Issued: No. 415, 7/5; No. 416, 7/12.

Pope Benedict XVI Type of 2007

2007, Oct. 24

417 A632 $1 multi .75 .75

Printed in sheets of 8.

Intl. Holocaust Remembrance Day Type of 2007

No. 418 — United Nations Delegates: a, Marcello Spatafora, Italy. b, Raymond Wolfe, Jamaica. c, Kenzo Oshima, Japan. d, Prince Zeid Ra'ad Zeid Al-Hussein, Jordan. e, Yerzhan Kh. Kazykhanov, Kazakhstan. f, Zachary Muburi-Muita, Kenya. g, Chi Young-jin, Republic of Korea. h, Solveiga Silkalna, Latvia.

2007, Nov. 14

418 A635 $1.40 Sheet of 8, #a-h 11.00 11.00

The editors would like to examine any commercial covers mailed during 2000-2008 from Bequia, which are franked only with the island's stamps.

CANOUAN

Diana, Princess of Wales (1961-97) — C1

1997 Litho. *Perf. 14*
1 C1 $1 multicolored 1.25 1.25

Issued in sheets of 6.
See Mustique No. 1.

Queen Mother Type of 2000 Inscribed "Canouan"

2000, Sept. 5 Litho. *Perf. 14*
2 A472 $1.40 multi 1.25 1.25

Issued in sheets of 6.

United We Stand C3

2003, Aug. 25
7 C3 $2 multi 1.75 1.75

Printed in sheets of 4.

Pres. John F. Kennedy (1917-63) — C4

No. 8: a, Peace Corps. b, Space program. c, Nuclear disarmament. d, Civil rights.

2003, Aug. 25
8 C4 $2 Sheet of 4, #a-d 6.50 6.50

Elvis Presley (1935-77) — C5

2003, Dec. 1 *Perf. 13½x13¼*
9 C5 90c multi 1.00 1.00

Printed in sheets of 9.

Butterflies C6

Designs: 90c, Atala. $1, Calico uranus. $1.40, Ceuptychia. $2, Aphrissa statira.

$5, Phoebis sennae.

2003, Dec. 1 *Perf. 13¼*
10-13 C6 Set of 4 4.00 4.00

Souvenir Sheet
14 C6 $5 multi 3.75 3.75

Pope John Paul II Type of 2005

2005, June 1 Litho. *Perf. 12½x12¾*
15 A585 $2 multi 1.75 1.75

Printed in sheets of 4.

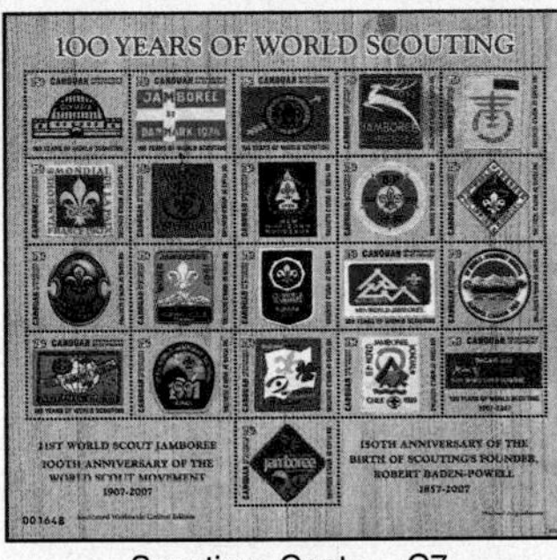

Scouting, Cent. — C7

No. 16 — Patches of International Scout Jamborees: a, Undated patch (1920), Great Britain. b, 1924, Denmark. c, 1929, Great Britain. d, 1933, Hungary. e, 1937, Netherlands. f, 1947, France. g, 1951, Austria. h, 1955, Canada. i, 1957, Great Britain. j, 1959, Philippines. k, 1963, Greece. l, 1967, United States. m, 1971, Japan. n, 1975, Norway. o, 1983, Canada. p, 1987-88, Australia. q, 1991, South Korea. r, 1995, Netherlands. s, 1999, Chile. t, 2003, Thailand. u, 2007, Great Britain.

2007, Jan. 15 Litho. *Perf. 13¼*
16 C7 75c Sheet of 21, #a-u 12.00 12.00

New York City Taxicabs, Cent. Type of 2007 of Bequia

No. 17 (51x37mm): a, 1913 Model GA. b, 1927 Yellow Cab Model 08. c, 1930 Studebaker Model 53. d, 1948 Checker Model A2. e, 1950's DeSoto. f, 1980's Checker A11.
$6, First gasoline taxi, 1907.

2007, July 5
17 B31 $1.40 Sheet of 6, #a-f 7.00 7.00

Souvenir Sheet
18 B31 $6 multi 5.00 5.00

No. 18 contains one 51x37mm stamp.

Intl. Holocaust Remembrance Day Type of 2007

No. 19 — United Nations diplomats and delegates: a, Jan Eliasson, President of 60th General Assembly. b, Julian Vila Coma, Andorra. c, Ismael A. Gaspar Martins, Angola. d, Victor Camilleri, Malta. e, César Mayoral, Argentina. f, Paulette A. Bethel, Bahamas. g, Christopher Hackett, Barbados. h, Kofi Annan, 7th United Nations Secretary General.

2007, Nov. 14
19 A635 $1.40 Sheet of 8, #a-h 8.50 8.50

Elvis Presley Type of 2007
Miniature Sheet

No. 20 — Presley: a, In olive green suit. b, Silhouette, standing, holding hand-held microphone. c, In purple shirt. d, Silhouette, with guitar. e, In blue shirt. f, Silhouette, crouching, holding hand-held microphone.

2007, Nov. 24
20 A633 $1.50 Sheet of 6, #a-f 8.00 8.00

John F. Kennedy Type of 2006
Miniature Sheet

No. 21 (26x40mm) — Kennedy: a, Facing right. b, In limousine, waving. c, Facing left in crowd. d, With arm extended.

2007, Nov. 24 *Perf. 14*
21 A622 $2 Sheet of 4, #a-d 6.50 6.50

The editors would like to examine any commercial covers mailed during 2000-2008 from Canouan, which are franked only with the island's stamps.

MAYREAU

All stamps are designs of St. Vincent ("A" illustration letter) unless otherwise illustrated.

Kennedy Type of 2007
Miniature Sheets

No. 1, $2, horiz. — John F. Kennedy and Nikita Khrushchev: a, With others, country name at LL, denomination at UR. b, With others, country name at LR, denomination at UL. c, Without others, country name and denomination at LR. d, With others, country name at LR, denomination at UR.
No. 2, $2, horiz. — Kennedy and: a, Fidel Castro, map of Cuba. b, U.S. Capitol, front page of Washington Post. c, American flag, Nikita Khrushchev, missile. d, Airplane, cameramen.

2006, Nov. 3 Litho. *Perf. 12¾*
Sheets of 4, #a-d
1-2 A622 Set of 2 13.00 13.00

Wedding of Queen Elizabeth II and Prince Philip, 60th Anniv. Type of 2007

No. 3: a, Parade in the Royal Carriage. b, Official portrait. c, Walking down the aisle (wedding attendees watching). d, Walking down the aisle (bride, groom and attendants). e, Walking down the aisle (attendants assisting bride). f, Saluting the crowd.
$6, Royal couple, vert.

2007, May 1 Litho. *Perf. 13¼*
3 A629 $1.40 Sheet of 6, #a-f 6.75 6.75

Souvenir Sheet
4 A629 $6 multi 5.00 5.00

Princess Diana Type of 2007

No. 5 — Diana: a, As child in red hooded jacket. b, As young girl in blue sweater. c, As young girl in red, orange and black sweater. d, Wearing pink jacket. e, Wearing lilac jacket. f, Wearing sleeveless dress.
$6, Wearing tiara.

2007, May 1
5 A630 $1.40 Sheet of 6, #a-f 6.75 6.75

Souvenir Sheet
6 A630 $6 multi 4.75 4.75

Pope Benedict XVI Type of 2007

2007, July 5
7 A632 $1.50 multi 1.10 1.10

Printed in sheets of 8.

The editors would like to examine any commercial covers mailed during 2000-2008 from Mayreau, which are franked only with the island's stamps.

MUSTIQUE

All stamps are designs of St. Vincent ("A" illustration letter) or Canouan ("C" illustration letter) unless otherwise illustrated.

Diana, Princess of Wales (1961-97) — M1

1997 Litho. *Perf. 14*
1 M1 $1 multicolored 1.10 1.10

Issued in sheets of 6.
See Canouan No. 1.

Paintings Type of 1999

Various pictures of flowers making up a photomosaic of the Queen Mother. Stamps inscribed "Mustique."

2000, Sept. 5 *Perf. 13¾*
2 A442 $1 Sheet of 8, #a-h 17.50 17.50
i. As No. 1017, imperf. 27.50 27.50

Coronation of Queen Elizabeth II, 50th Anniv. — M2

No. 3: a, Wearing yellow hat. b, Wearing blue dress. c, Wearing tiara.
$5, Wearing crown.

2003, Feb. 26 Litho. *Perf. 14*
3 M2 $3 Sheet of 3, #a-c 8.00 8.00

Souvenir Sheet
4 M2 $5 multi 4.50 4.50

Prince William, 21st Birthday Type of 2003

No. 5: a, Looking right. b, Wearing ski cap and goggles. c, Looking down.
$5, Wearing suit.

2003, May 13
5 A535 $3 Sheet of 3, #a-c 7.75 7.75

Souvenir Sheet
6 A535 $5 multi 4.50 4.50

Corvette Type of 2003

No. 7: a, 1960 Shark. b, 1988. c, 1956 convertible. d, 1967.
$5, 1964 Sting Ray convertible.

2003, July 1 *Perf. 13¼x13½*
7 A534 $2 Sheet of 4, #a-d 7.00 7.00

Souvenir Sheet
8 A534 $5 multi 4.50 4.50

Cadillac Type of 2003

No. 9: a, 1978 Seville. b, 1927 La Salle. c, 1953 Eldorado. d, 2002 Seville.
$5, 1961 Sedan de Ville.

2003, July 1
9 A537 $2 Sheet of 4, #a-d 7.00 7.00

Souvenir Sheet
10 A537 $5 multi 4.50 4.50

Circus Type of 2003

No. 11: a, Josaphine. b, Korolev Group (girl and monkey). c, Korolev Group (monkey). d, Zebra.

2003, July 1 *Perf. 14*
11 A539 $2 Sheet of 4, #a-d 11.00 11.00

Kennedy Type of Canouan

No. 12: a, On Solomon Islands, 1943. b, On PT 109, 1942. c, Senate campaign, 1952. d, Recieving medal for gallantry, 1944.

2003, Aug. 25
12 C4 $2 Sheet of 4, #a-d 8.00 8.00

United We Stand Type of Canouan

2003, Sept. 8
13 C5 $2 multi 1.60 1.60

Printed in sheets of 4.

Birds M3

Designs: $1, Red-billed tropicbird. $1.10, Bananaquit. $1.40, Belted kingfisher. $2, Ruby-throated hummingbird.
$5, Brown pelican, vert.

2003, Nov. 5 ***Perf. 13½x13¾***

14-17	M3	Set of 4	5.25 5.25

Souvenir Sheet

Perf. 13¾x13½

18	M3	$5 multi	4.25 4.25

Elvis Presley Type of Canouan

2003, Dec. 1 ***Perf. 13½x13¼***

19	C5	90c multi	.90 .90

Printed in sheets of 9.

Pope John Paul II Type of 2005

2005, June 1 Litho. ***Perf. 12½x12¾***

20	A585	$2 multi	1.75 1.75

Printed in sheets of 4.

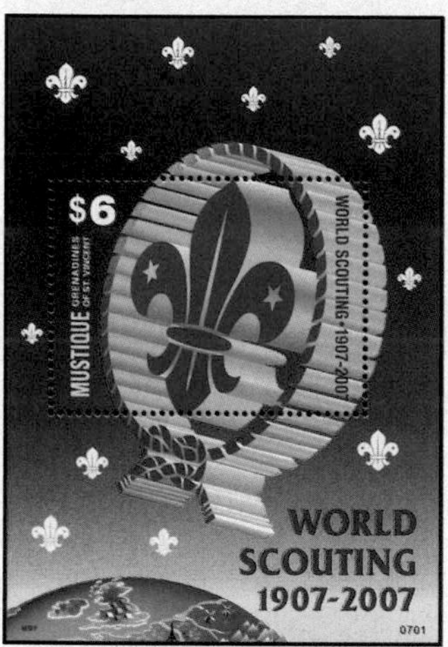

Scouting, Cent. — M4

No. 21, vert.: a, Scouting emblem over globe. b, Emblem of 21st World Scout Jamboree, doves. c, Doves. d, Various national Scouting emblems. e, Doves, map of Mustique, Scouting flag, flag of St. Vincent and the Grenadines. f, Doves, Scout handshake.
$6, Scouting emblem.

2007, July 5 Litho. ***Perf. 13¼***

21	M4	$1.50 Sheet of 6, #a-f	8.50 8.50

Souvenir Sheet

22	M4	$6 multi	4.75 4.75

Intl. Holocaust Remembrance Day Type of 2007

No. 23 — United Nations diplomats and delegates: a, Lebohand Fine Maema, Lesotho. b, Milton Nathaniel Barnes, Liberia. c, Christian Wenaweser, Liechtenstein. d, Dalius Cekuolis, Lithuania. e, Igor Dzundev, Macedonia. f, Zina Andrianarivelo-Razafy, Madagascar. g, Nebojsa Kaludjerovic, Montenegro. h, Asha-Rose Migiro, United Nations Deputy Secretary General.

2007, Nov. 14

23	A635	$1.40 Sheet of 8, #a-h	9.00 9.00

The editors would like to examine any commercial covers mailed during 2000-2008 from Mustique, which are franked only with the island's stamps.

UNION ISLAND

All stamps are types of St. Vincent ("A" illustration letter), St. Vincent Grenadines ("G" illustration letter) or Union ("U" illustration letter).

"Island" issues are listed separately beginning in 1984. See St. Vincent Grenadines Nos. 84-111, 248-262 for earlier issues.

British Monarch Type of 1984

No. 1a, Battle of Hastings. No. 1b, William the Conqueror. No. 2a, William the Conqueror. No. 2b, Abbaye Aux Dames. No. 3a, Skirmish at Dunbar. No. 3b, Charles II. No. 4a, Arms of William the Conqueror. No. 4b, William the Conqueror. No. 5a, Charles II. No. 5b, St. James Palace. No. 6a, Arms of Charles II. No. 6b, Charles II, Great Fire of London.

Perf. 12½

1984, Mar. 29 Litho. Unwmk.

1	A110	1c Pair, #a.-b.	.25 .25
2	A111	5c Pair, #a.-b.	.25 .25
3	A110	10c Pair, #a.-b.	.25 .25
4	A110	20c Pair, #a.-b.	.30 .30
5	A111	60c Pair, #a.-b.	.50 .50
6	A111	$3 Pair, #a.-b.	3.50 3.50
		Nos. 1-6 (6)	5.05 5.05

Locomotives Type of 1985

No. 13, 1813 Puffing Billy, UK. No. 14, 1911 Class 9N, UK. No. 15, 1882 Class Skye Bogie, UK. No. 16, 1912 Class G8, Germany. No. 17, 1954 Class 65.10, Germany. No. 18, 1900 Castle Class, UK. No. 19, 1887 Spinner Class 25, UK. No. 20, 1951 Fell #10100, UK. No. 21, 1942 Class 42, Germany. No. 22, 1951 Class 5MT, UK. No. 23, 1929 P.O. Rebuilt Class 3500, France. No. 24, 1886 Class 123, UK. No. 25, 1976 Class 56, UK. No. 26, 1897 Class G5, US. No. 27, 1947 9400 Class, UK. No. 28, 1888 Sir Theodore, UK. No. 29, 1929 Class Z, UK. No. 30, 1896 Atlantic City RR, US. No. 31, 1906 45xx Class, UK. No. 32, 1912 Class D15, UK. No. 33, 1938 Class U4-b, Canada. No. 34, 1812 Prince Regent, UK. No. 35, 1920 Butler Henderson, UK. No. 36, 1889 Elidir, UK. No. 37, 1934 7200 Class, UK. No. 38, 1911 Class Z, UK. No. 39, 1938 Class C, Australia. No. 40, 1879 Sir Haydn, UK. No. 41, 1850 Aberdeen No. 26, UK. No. 42, 1883 Class Y14, UK. No. 43, 1915 River Class, UK. No. 44, 1936 D51 Class, Japan. No. 45, 1837 L&B Bury, UK. No. 46, 1903 Class 900, US. No. 47, 1904 Class H-20, US. No. 48, 1905 Class L, UK. No. 49, 1952 Class 4, UK. No. 50, 1837 Campbell's 8-Wheeler, US. No. 51, 1934 Class GG1, US. No. 52, 1924 Class 01, Germany. No. 53, 1920 Gordon Highlander, UK. No. 54, 1969 Metroliner Railcar, US. No. 55, 1951 Class GP7, US. No. 56, 1873 Hardwicke Precedent Class, UK. No. 57, 1899 Highflyer Class, UK. No. 58, 1925 Class U1, UK. No. 59, 1880 Class 7100, Japan. No. 60, 1972 Gas Turbine Prototype, France.

Se-tenant Pairs, #a.-b.
a. — Side and front views.
b. — Action scene.

1984-87 ***Perf. 12½***

13	A120	5c multicolored	.25 .25
14	A120	5c multicolored	.25 .25
15	A120	5c multicolored	.25 .25
16	A120	10c multicolored	.40 .40
17	A120	15c multicolored	.40 .40
18	A120	15c multicolored	.40 .40
19	A120	15c multicolored	.40 .40
20	A120	15c multicolored	.40 .40
21	A120	20c multicolored	.40 .40
22	A120	20c multicolored	.40 .40
23	A120	25c multicolored	.40 .40
24	A120	25c multicolored	.40 .40
25	A120	30c multicolored	.40 .40
26	A120	30c multicolored	.40 .40
27	A120	40c multicolored	.50 .50
28	A120	45c multicolored	.50 .50
29	A120	45c multicolored	.50 .50
30	A120	45c multicolored	.50 .50
31	A120	50c multicolored	.60 .60
32	A120	50c multicolored	.60 .60
33	A120	50c multicolored	.60 .60
34	A120	60c multicolored	.75 .75
35	A120	60c multicolored	.75 .75
36	A120	60c multicolored	.75 .40
37	A120	60c multicolored	.75 .75
38	A120	60c multicolored	.75 .75
39	A120	75c multicolored	.90 .90
40	A120	75c multicolored	.90 .90
41	A120	75c multicolored	.90 .90
42	A120	75c multicolored	.90 .90
43	A120	75c multicolored	.90 .90
44	A120	$1 multicolored	1.25 1.25
45	A120	$1 multicolored	1.25 1.25
46	A120	$1 multicolored	1.25 1.25
47	A120	$1 multicolored	1.25 1.25
48	A120	$1 multicolored	1.25 1.25
49	A120	$1.50 multicolored	1.75 1.75
50	A120	$1.50 multicolored	1.75 1.75
51	A120	$1.50 multicolored	1.75 1.75
52	A120	$2 multicolored	2.25 2.25
53	A120	$2 multicolored	2.25 2.25
54	A120	$2 multicolored	2.25 2.25
55	A120	$2 multicolored	2.25 2.25
56	A120	$2.50 multicolored	2.75 2.75
57	A120	$2.50 multicolored	2.75 2.75
58	A120	$3 multicolored	3.50 3.50
59	A120	$3 multicolored	3.50 3.50
60	A120	$3 multicolored	3.50 3.50
		Nos. 13-60 (48)	53.70 53.35

Issued: Nos. 13, 34, 44, 52, 8/9/84; Nos. 14, 16, 21, 23, 39, 45, 56, 58, 12/18/84; Nos. 15, 31, 35, 53, 3/25/85; Nos. 17, 25, 28, 36, 40, 49, 57, 59, 1/31/86; Nos. 18, 29, 37, 41, 46, 50, 54, 60, 12/23/86; Nos. 19, 24, 27, 32, 38, 42, 47, 55, 9/87; Nos. 20, 22, 26, 308, 33, 43, 48, 51, 12/4/87.

Beginning on Jan. 31, 1986, this issue is not inscribed "Leaders of the World."

St. Vincent Grenadines Nos. 222-238 Overprinted "UNION ISLAND"

Perf. 14x13½

1984, Aug. 23 Wmk. 373

109	G26	1c on No. 222	.25 .25
110	G26	3c on No. 223	.25 .25
111	G26	5c on No. 224	.25 .25
112	G26	6c on No. 225	.25 .25
113	G26	10c on No. 226	.25 .25
114	G26	15c on No. 227	.25 .25
115	G26	20c on No. 228	.30 .30
116	G26	25c on No. 229	.30 .30
117	G26	30c on No. 230	.30 .30
118	G26	50c on No. 231	.45 .45
119	G26	60c on No. 232	.50 .50
120	G26	75c on No. 233	.60 .60
121	G26	$1 on No. 234	.90 .90
122	G26	$2 on No. 235	2.00 2.00
123	G26	$3 on No. 236	2.50 2.50
124	G26	$5 on No. 237	4.50 4.50
125	G26	$10 on No. 238	8.00 8.00
		Nos. 109-125 (17)	21.85 21.85

Cricket Players Type of 1985

1c, S. N. Hartley. 10c, G. W. Johnson. 15c, R. M. Ellison. 55c, C. S. Cowdrey. 60c, K. Sharp. 75c, M. C. Cowdrey, in action. $1.50, G. R. Dilley, in action. $3, R. Illingworth, in action.

1984, Nov. Unwmk. ***Perf. 12½***

Pairs, #a.-b.

126	A116	1c multicolored	.25 .25
127	A116	10c multicolored	.30 .30
128	A116	15c multicolored	.35 .35
129	A116	55c multicolored	.50 .50
130	A116	60c multicolored	.55 .55
131	A116	75c multicolored	.65 .65
132	A116	$1.50 multicolored	.85 .85
133	A116	$3 multicolored	1.75 1.75
		Nos. 126-133 (8)	5.20 5.20

Classic Car Type of 1983

No. 142, 1963 Lancia, Italy. No. 143, 1895 Duryea, US. No. 144, 1970 Datsun, Japan. No. 145, 1962 BRM, UK. No. 146, 1927 Amilcar, France. No. 147, 1929 Duesenberg, US. No. 148, 1913 Peugeot, France. No. 149, 1938 Lagonda, UK. No. 150, 1924 Fiat, Italy. No. 151, 1957 Alfa Romeo, Italy. No. 152, 1957 Panhard, France. No. 153, 1954 Porsche, Germany. No. 154, 1904 Darraco, France. No. 155, 1927 Daimler, UK. No. 156, 1949 Oldsmobile, US. No. 157, 1934 Chrysler, US. No. 158, 1965 MG, UK. No. 159, 1922 Fiat, Italy. No. 160, 1934 Bugatti, France. No. 161, 1963 Watson/Meyer-Drake, US. No. 162, 1917 Locomobile, US. No. 163, 1928 Ford, US.

Se-tenant Pairs, #a.-b.
a. — Side and front views.
b. — Action scene.

1985-86 ***Perf. 12½***

142	A107	1c multicolored	.25 .25
143	A107	5c multicolored	.25 .25
144	A107	10c multicolored	.25 .25
145	A107	10c multicolored	.25 .25
146	A107	50c multicolored	.30 .30
147	A107	55c multicolored	.35 .35
148	A107	60c multicolored	.40 .40
149	A107	60c multicolored	.40 .40
150	A107	60c multicolored	.40 .40
151	A107	75c multicolored	.50 .50
152	A107	75c multicolored	.50 .50
153	A107	75c multicolored	.50 .50
154	A107	90c multicolored	.55 .55
155	A107	$1 multicolored	.60 .60
156	A107	$1 multicolored	.60 .60
157	A107	$1 multicolored	.60 .60
158	A107	$1.50 multicolored	1.00 1.00
159	A107	$1.50 multicolored	1.00 1.00
160	A107	$1.50 multicolored	1.00 1.00
161	A107	$2 multicolored	1.25 1.25
162	A107	$2.50 multicolored	1.50 1.50
163	A107	$3 multicolored	1.75 1.75
		Nos. 142-163 (22)	14.20 14.20

Issued: Nos. 142, 146, 151, 162, 1/4/85; Nos. 143, 148, 155, 158, 5/20/85; Nos. 144, 147, 149, 152, 154, 156, 159, 161, 7/15/85; Nos. 145, 150, 153, 157, 160, 163, 7/30/86.

Beginning on 7/30/86, this issue is not inscribed "Leaders of the World."

Birds — U1

No. 186a, Hooded warbler. No. 186b, Carolina wren. No. 187a, Song sparrow. No. 187b, Black-headed grosbeak. No. 188a, Scarlet tanager. No. 188b, Lazuli bunting. No. 189a, Sharp-shinned hawk. No. 189b, Merlin.

1985, Feb. ***Perf. 12½***

186	U1	15c Pair, #a.-b.	.30 .30
187	U1	50c Pair, #a.-b.	.40 .40
188	U1	$1 Pair, #a.-b.	.65 .65
189	U1	$1.50 Pair, #a.-b.	1.50 1.50
		Nos. 186-189 (4)	2.85 2.85

Butterflies — U2

No. 194a, Cynthia cardui. No. 194b, Zerynthia rumina. No. 195a, Byblia ilithyia. No. 195b, Papilio machaon. No. 196a, Carterocephalus palaemon. No. 196b, Acraea anacreon. No. 197a, Anartia amathea. No. 197b, Salamis temora.

1985, Apr. 15

194	U2	15c Pair, #a.-b.	.25 .25
195	U2	25c Pair, #a.-b.	.35 .35
196	U2	75c Pair, #a.-b.	.55 .55
197	U2	$2 Pair, #a.-b.	1.75 1.75
		Nos. 194-197 (4)	2.90 2.90

Queen Mother Type of 1985

85th birthday — Hats: No. 206a, Mortarboard. No. 206b, Blue. No. 207a, Turquoise. No. 207b, Blue. Nos. 208a, 212a, Without hat. Nos. 208b, 212b, White. Nos. 209a, 211a, White hat, violet feathers. Nos. 209b, 211b, Blue. No. 210a, Crown. No. 210b, Hat.

1985, Aug. 19

206	A122	55c Pair, #a.-b.	.50 .50
207	A122	70c Pair, #a.-b.	.60 .60
208	A122	$1.05 Pair, #a.-b.	.75 .75
209	A122	$1.70 Pair, #a.-b.	1.40 1.40
		Nos. 206-209 (4)	3.25 3.25

Souvenir Sheets of 2

210	A122	$1.95 #a.-b.	2.25 2.25
211	A122	$2.25 #a.-b.	2.75 2.75
212	A122	$7 #a.-b.	7.00 7.00

Elizabeth II 60th Birthday Type of 1986

Designs: 10c, Wearing scarf. 60c, Riding clothes. $2, Wearing crown and jewels. $8, In Canberra, vert. $10, Holding flowers.

1986, Apr. 21

213-216	A128	10c Set of 4	3.25 3.25

Souvenir Sheet

217	A128	$10 multi	3.75 3.75

U3

World Cup Soccer Championships, Mexico — U4

1986, May 7 ***Perf. 12½ (U3), 15 (U4)***

218	U3	1c Moroccan team	.25 .25
219	U3	10c Argentinian team	.25 .25
220	U4	30c Algerian player	.25 .25
221	U3	75c Hungarian team	.30 .30
222	U3	$1 Russian team	.30 .30
223	U4	$2.50 Belgian player	.60 .60
224	U4	$3 French player	.65 .65
225	U4	$6 W. German player	1.25 1.25
		Nos. 218-225 (8)	3.85 3.85

Souvenir Sheets

226 U3 $1.85 like No. 222 2.00 2.00
227 U3 $2 like No. 219 2.25 2.25

Souvenir sheets contain one 60x40mm stamp.

Prince Andrew Royal Wedding Type

No. 228: a, Prince Andrew in cap. b, Prince Andrew in suit.
No. 229:a, Couple. b, Sarah Ferguson.

1986, July 15 ***Perf. 12½x13, 13x12½***
228 A132 60c Pair, #a.-b. .75 .75
229 A132 $2 Pair. #a.-b. 1.50 1.50

Nos. 228-229 Overprinted in Silver "CONGRATULATIONS TO T.R.H. THE DUKE & DUCHESS OF YORK" in 3 Lines

1986, Oct.
230 A132 60c on No. 228a-b 1.75 1.75
231 A132 $2 on No. 229a-b 5.00 5.00

Queen Elizabeth II Wedding Anniv. Type of St. Vincent Grenadines

1987, Oct. 15 ***Perf. 12½***
236 G47 15c like No. 568 .25 .25
237 G47 45c like No. 569 .35 .35
238 G47 $1.50 like No. 570 .55 .55
239 G47 $3 like No. 571 1.10 1.10
240 G47 $4 like No. 572 1.50 1.50
Nos. 236-240 (5) 3.75 3.75

U5

Disney characters in various French vehicles: No. 241, 1c, 1893 Peugeot. No. 242, 2c, 1890-91 Panhard-Levassor. No. 243, 3c, 1910 Renault. No. 244, 4c, 1919 Citroen. No. 245, 5c, 1878 La Mancelle. No. 246, 10c, 1891 De Dion Bouton Quadricycle. No. 247, $5, 1896 Leon Bollee Trike. No. 248, $6, 1911 Brasier Coupe.
No. 249, French road race, Mickey, Donald and Goofy racing. No. 250, 1769, Cugnot's artillery tractor, Mickey, Goofy and Donald dressed as soliders.

1989, July 7 ***Perf. 14x13½***
241-248 U5 Set of 8 16.00 16.00

Souvenir Sheets

249 U5 $6 multicolored 8.50 8.50
250 U5 $6 multicolored 8.50 8.50

PHILEXFRANCE '89.

Diana, Princess of Wales (1961-97) — U6

1997 **Litho.** ***Perf. 14***
251 U6 $1 multicolored 1.50 2.00

No. 251 was issued in sheets of 6.

Paintings Type of 1999

Various pictures of flowers making up a photomosaic of the Queen Mother.

2000, Sept. 5 ***Perf. 13¾***
252 A442 $1 Sheet of 8, #a-h 7.50 7.50
i. As No. 252, imperf. 15.00 *15.00*

New Year 2002 (Year of the Horse) — U7

Horse paintings by Giuseppe Castiglione: a, White horse with head down. b, Brown horse. c, Piebald horse. d, White horse with head up.

2001, Dec. 17 **Litho.** ***Perf. 12¾***
253 U7 $1.40 Sheet of 4, #a-d 5.00 5.00

Worldwide Fund for Nature (WWF) U8

Shortfin mako shark: a, View of underside. b, Side view. c, Pair of sharks. d, Shark at surface.

2002, Nov. 1 ***Perf. 14***
254 Horiz. or vert. strip 3.25 3.25
a.-d. U8 $1 Any single .80 .80
e. Souvenir sheet of 4, #a-d 27.50 27.50

United We Stand Type of 2001

2002, Nov. 4
255 A508 $1.40 multi 1.75 1.75

Printed in sheets of 4.

Queen Mother Elizabeth Type of 2002

No. 256: a, Wearing purple hat. b, Wearing green hat. c, Wearing pink hat.

2002, Nov. 4 **Litho.** ***Perf. 14***
256 A522 $2 Sheet of 4, #a-b, 2 #c 6.50 6.50

Ferrari Automobiles — U9

Designs: No. 257, $1.10, 1960 Dino 246S No. 258, $1.10, 1962 248SP. No. 259, $1.10, 1966 330GTC-GTS. No. 260, $1.10, 1967 Dino 206GT. No. 261, $1.10, 1984 Testarossa. No. 262, $1.10, 1989 348TB-TS. No. 263, $1.10, 2002 Enzo Ferrari. No. 264, $1.10, 2002 360 Challenge.

2002, Dec. 9
257-264 U9 Set of 8 9.00 9.00

Teddy Bears Type of 2002

No. 265, $2 — Bears from Britain: a, Palace Guard bear. b, Bear with crown. c, Bear with bowler hat. d, Beefeater bear.
No. 266, $2 — Bears from Holland: a, Artist bear. b, Bear with black hat. c, Bears in wagon. d, Bear with overalls and checked shirt.

2003, Jan. 27 ***Perf. 13½x13¼***

Sheets of 4, #a-d

265-266 A519 Set of 2 15.00 15.00

Year of the Ram Type of 2003

No. 267 — Color of ram: a, Red violet. b, Red. c, Yellow green. d, Violet. e, Brown. f, Blue green.

2003, Jan. 27 ***Perf. 14¼x13¾***
267 A526 $1 Sheet of 6, #a-f 4.75 4.75

Princess Diana Type of 2003

No. 268: a, Wearing pink hat, holding roses. b, Wearing lilac dress and necklace. c, Wearing red hat. d, With hand on chin. e, Wearing pink blouse, holding flowers. d, Wearing blue dress.
No. 269, horiz.: a, Children's Cancer Hospital. b, Meeting with AIDS patients. c, Conference on eating disorders. d, Red Cross child feeding center.

2003, May 26 **Litho.** ***Perf. 14***
268 A536 $1.40 Sheet of 6, #a-f 6.75 6.75
269 A536 $2 Sheet of 4, #a-d 6.50 6.50

Kennedy Type of Bequia

No. 270: a, Denomination at UL, name at right. b, Denomination at UL, name at left. c, Denomination at UR, name at left. d, Denomination at UR, name at right.

2003, Aug. 25
270 B14 $2 Sheet of 4, #a-d 6.50 6.50

Elvis Presley Type of Bequia

No. 271 — Color of illustration: a, Brown. b, Dark blue. c, Green. d, Purple. e, Yellow brown. f, Red violet. g, Sepia. h, Bright blue. i, Red brown.

2003, Dec. 1 ***Perf. 13½***
271 B15 90c Sheet of 9, #a-i 6.50 6.50

Fish — U10

Designs: 90c, Great barracuda. $1, French angelfish. $1.40, Reef shark. $2, Tarpon.
$5, Queen angelfish.

2003, Dec. 1 ***Perf. 13¼***
272-275 U10 Set of 4 4.25 4.25

Souvenir Sheet

276 U10 $5 multi 4.25 4.25

Detail from Monkey and Cat, by Yi Yuan-Chi — U11

2004, Jan. 15 ***Perf. 13½***
277 U11 $1.40 shown 1.60 1.60

Souvenir Sheet

Perf. 13¾

278 U11 $3 Entire painting 5.75 5.75

New Year 2004 (Year of the Monkey). No. 277 printed in sheets of 4. No. 278 contains one 58x35mm stamp.

Marilyn Monroe Type of 2004

Monroe and: No. 279, 75c, Denomination in blue. No. 280, 75c, Denomination in red.

2004, May 3 **Litho.** ***Perf. 13½***
279-280 A558 Set of 2 1.40 1.40

Each stamp printed in sheets of 10.

Ronald Reagan Type of 2004

Reagan and denomination color of: a, Red. b, White. c, Blue.

2004, Oct. 13
281 Vert. strip of 3 3.75 3.75
a.-c. A564 $1.40 Any single 1.10 1.10

Printed in sheets containing two strips.

Babe Ruth Type of 2004

2004, Nov. 25 ***Perf. 14***
282 A561 75c multi .70 .70

Printed in sheets of 10.

Miniature Sheet

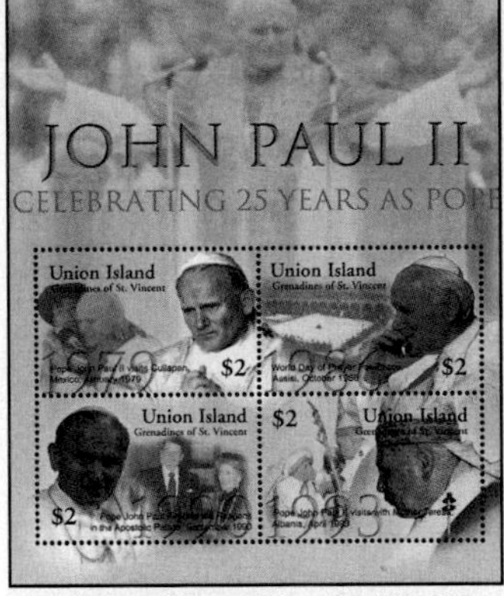

Election of Pope John Paul II, 25th Anniv. (in 2003) — U12

Pope John Paul II: a, With child, Cuilapan, Mexico, 1979. b, At World Day of Prayer for Peace, Assisi, Italy, 1986. c, With Ronald and Nancy Reagan, 1990. d, Visiting Mother Teresa, 1993.

2005, Jan. 26 ***Perf. 14***
283 U12 $2 Sheet of 4, #a-d 6.50 6.50

Basketball Players Type of 2004-05

Designs: No. 284, 90c, Mike Bibby, Sacramento Kings. No. 285, 90c, Reggie Miller, Indiana Pacers. No. 286, 90c, Alonzo Mourning, Miami Heat. No. 287, 90c, Paul Pierce, Boston Celtics. No. 288, 90c, Jim Jackson, Phoenix Suns.
No. 289: a, New Jersey Nets emblem. b, Jason Kidd, New Jersey Nets.

2005, Feb. 10 **Litho.** ***Perf. 14***
284-288 A572 Set of 5 4.00 4.00

Miniature Sheet

289 A572 90c Sheet of 12, 2 #289a, 10 #289b 8.75 8.75

Nos. 284-288 each printed in sheets of 12.

Vatican Stamp and Pope John Paul II Types of 2005

Designs: 70c, Vatican #64. $3, Pope holding Bible, horiz.

2005, June 1 ***Perf. 13x13¼***
290 A584 70c multi .60 .60

Perf. 13¼x13½

291 A585 $3 multi 2.50 2.50

No. 290 printed in sheets of 12; No. 291, in sheets of 6.

Railroads Type of 2004

No. 292, $1: a, British Rail intercity high-speed train. b, British-built Edwardian Mogul, Paraguay. c, Fireless locomotive, Ludlow jute mill, Calcutta. d, Welders working on Wisconsin Central. e, Serving breakfast on British intercity train. f, Pacific locomotive, Pulgaon-Avri line, India. g, Locomotive shed laborers, Wankaner, India. h, British Rail train driver with head out of window. i, British Rail train driver at controls.
No. 293, $1: a, Southern Pacific Bullied Pacific "Blackmore Vale." b, Bagnall 0-4-0ST on Assam coalfield. c, Orenstein & Koppel 0-8-0T, Java. d, Baldwin 0-6-6-0 Compound Mallet, Philippines. e, Coal loads on C&I sub, Illinois. f, Class 37 on China Clay, Cornwall. g, BNSF stack train, New Mexico. h, China Railways QJ 2-10-2 near Anshan. i, Kitson 0-6-2 at Suraya Sugar Mill, India.
No. 294, $5, Amtrak Coast Starlight, California. No. 295, $5, Glacier Express.

2005, June 7 ***Perf. 12¾***

Sheets of 9, #a-i

292-293 A565 Set of 2 14.50 14.50

Souvenir Sheets

294-295 A565 Set of 2 7.50 7.50

U14

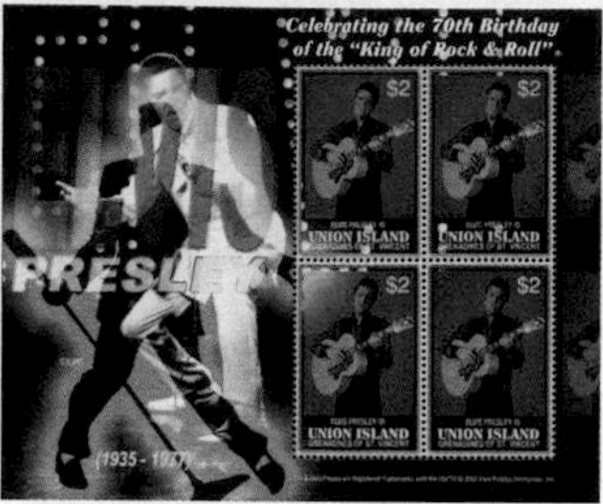
Elvis Presley (1935-77) — U15

No. 297 — Location of spotlights: a, Four spotlights along frame edge at LL, spotlights above and below "S" in "Island." b, Spotlights in top frame near UL corner and above head, spotlights above and below "U" in "Union," spotlight above "S" in "Island." c, Four spotlights in top frame at left, two faint spotlights in left frame at UL. d, Faint spotlight in top frame at UL.

2005, Nov. 21 Litho. *Perf. 13¼*
296 U14 $2 multi 1.75 1.75
297 U15 $2 Sheet of 4, #a-d 6.50 6.50

No. 296 printed in sheets of 4.

Queen Elizabeth II 80th Birthday Type of 2006

Queen Elizabeth II: No. 298, $2, Riding in coach at Trooping the Color parade, 1987. No. 299, $2, With fireman, 1992. No. 300, $2, At Queen Mother's 100th birthday celebration, 2000. No. 301, $2, Riding in coach in Golden Jubilee parade, 2002.

2006, Jan. 31 *Perf. 13½*
298-301 A603 Set of 4 6.25 6.25

Nos. 298-301 each printed in sheets of 8 + label.

Christopher Columbus Type of 2006

Designs: 10c, Arrival in Hispaniola, 1492. 90c, Columbus and ships. $2, Ships, vert. $3, Ships, diff., vert.
$5, Santa Maria, vert.

2006, July 21 *Perf. 12¾*
302-305 A611 Set of 4 4.75 4.75

Souvenir Sheet

306 A611 $5 multi 4.00 4.00

Space Achievements Type of 2006

No. 307, vert. — Venus Express: a, Denomination in white at LL. b, Denomination in white at UL. c, Denomination in black at LL. d, Denomination in black at UL.
No. 308 — First Flight of Space Shuttle Columbia: a, Lift-off. b, Columbia on launch pad. c, Astronaut John W. Young, Columbia. d, Astronaut Robert L. Crippen, Columbia. e, Columbia in space. f, Flight emblem.
$5, Luna 9.

2006, Dec. 22 *Perf. 13¼*
307 A612 $2 Sheet of 4, #a-d 6.50 6.50
308 A612 $3 Sheet of 6, #a-f 14.00 14.00

Souvenir Sheet

309 A612 $5 multi 4.00 4.00

Rembrandt Type of 2006

Self-portraits from: 50c, C. 1632-39. 75c, 1635. $1, 1629. $2, 1634.
No. 314, $2 — Drawings: a, Two Tramps, a Man and a Woman. b, Beggar Leaning on a Stick. c, Ragged Peasant with His Hands Behind Him, Holding a Stick. d, Beggar Man and Beggar Woman Conversing.
No. 315, $2 — Drawings: a, Study for the Drunkenness of Lot. b, A Girl Sleeping. c, Saskia at a Window. d, Old Man with Arms Extended.
No. 316, $5, The Apostle Simon (70x100mm). No. 317, $5, Winter Landscape, horiz. (100x70mm).

2006, Dec. 22 *Perf. 13¼*
310-313 A617 Set of 4 3.50 3.50

Sheets of 4, #a-d

314-315 A617 Set of 2 13.50 13.50

Imperf

316-317 A617 Set of 2 8.00 8.00

John F. Kennedy Type of 2007
Miniature Sheets

No. 318, $2, horiz. — Inauguration: a, Kennedy shaking hands with Father Richard J. Casey. b, Kennedy and State Department Seal. c, Medal of Kennedy, U.S. flag. d, Portrait of Kennedy, Kennedy with son.
No. 319, $2, horiz. — Cuban Missile Crisis: a, Kennedy, Soviet Premier Nikita Khrushchev, photographer. b, Cuban President Fidel Castro, Soviet trucks at Cuban port. c, Kennedy and map of plan to invade Cuba. d, KA-18A stereo strip camera, map of Cuba.

2006, Dec. 22 *Perf. 13¼*

Sheets of 4, #a-d

318-319 A622 Set of 2 13.00 13.00

Scouting, Cent. Type of Bequia of 2007

Designs: $4, Scouting emblem, doves and figure-eight knots. $6, Scouting emblem.

2007, Jan. 3
320 B30 $4 blue & green 3.75 3.75

Souvenir Sheet

321 B30 $6 multi 5.75 5.75

No. 320 printed in sheets of 3. No. 321 contains one 37x51mm stamp.

Wedding of Queen Elizabeth II and Prince Philip, 60th Anniv. Type of 2007

No. 322 — Couple with Queen wearing: a, Gray hat with black feather. b, Red and lilac hat. c, Black and white hat. d, Light blue jacket, no hat. e, Light blue jacket and hat. f, Light green jacket, red and light green hat.
$6, Couple under umbrella, vert.

2007, July 5 *Perf. 12¾*
322 A629 $1.40 Sheet of 6, #a-f 7.25 7.25

Souvenir Sheet

323 A629 $6 multi 4.75 4.75

Princess Diana Type of 2007

No. 324: a, Seated in chair. b, Reclining, wearing white dress. c, Wearing blue dress. d, Wearing white blouse and jeans. e, Wearing black dress. f, Wearing black sweater, pants and shoes.
No. 325: a, As Red Cross volunteer. b, Touring minefield in Angola. c, With Mother Teresa. d, Holding child at Shri Swaminarayan Mandir, London.
$6, Wearing headphones.

2007, July 5 *Perf. 12¾*
324 A630 $1.40 Sheet of 6, #a-f 7.00 7.00
325 A630 $2 Sheet of 4, #a-d 6.50 6.50

Souvenir Sheet

326 A630 $6 multi 5.00 5.00

Pope Benedict XVI Type of 2007

2007, July 5 *Perf. 13¼*
327 A632 $1.50 multi 1.25 1.25

Printed in sheets of 8.

Elvis Presley Type of 2007

No. 328 — Photographs of Presley from: a, 1946. b, 1956. c, 1962. d, 1970.

2007, Oct. 24
328 A633 $3 Sheet of 4, #a-d 9.50 9.50

First Helicopter Flight, Cent. — U16

Designs: 10c, Benson autogyro. 25c, Agusta-Sikorsky AS-61. 90c, Bell UH-1B/C Iroquois, horiz. $5, Bell UH-1 Iroquois, vert.
No. 333, horiz.: a, Eurocopter/Kawasaki BK 117, denomination at UR. b, Bell UH-1B/C Iroquois, denomination at LL. c, Bell UH-1B/C Iroquois, denomination at UR. d, Eurocopter/Kawasaki BK 117, denomination at UL.
$5, NH 90, horiz.

2007, Oct. 24
329-332 U16 Set of 4 7.00 7.00
333 U16 $2 Sheet of 4, #a-d 8.50 8.50

Souvenir Sheet

334 U16 $5 multi 4.50 4.50

The editors would like to examine any commercial covers mailed during 2000-2008 from Union Island, which are franked only with the island's stamps.

Stamps inscribed "Palm Island," "Tobago Cays," and "Young Island" are not listed as they do not meet Scott listing criteria.

SALVADOR, EL

'el-sal-və-ˌdor

LOCATION — On the Pacific coast of Central America, between Guatemala, Honduras and the Gulf of Fonseca
GOVT. — Republic
AREA — 8,236 sq. mi.
POP. — 5,839,079 (1999 est.)
CAPITAL — San Salvador

8 Reales = 100 Centavos = 1 Peso
100 Centavos = 1 Colón
100 Cents = 1 Dollar (2003)

Catalogue values for unused stamps in this country are for Never Hinged items, beginning with Scott 589 in the regular postage section, Scott C85 in the airpost section, and Scott O362 in the official section.

Watermarks

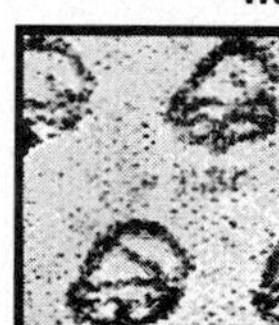
Wmk. 117 — Liberty Cap

Position of wmk. on reprints

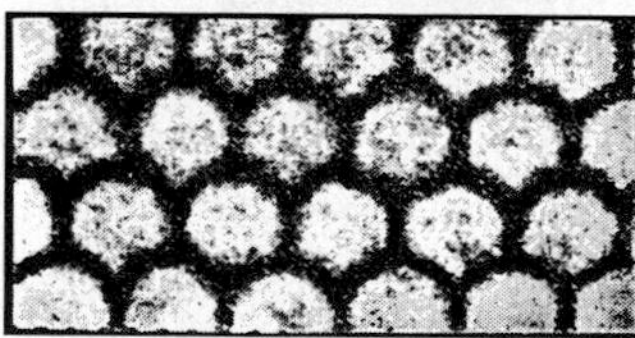
Wmk. 172 — Honeycomb

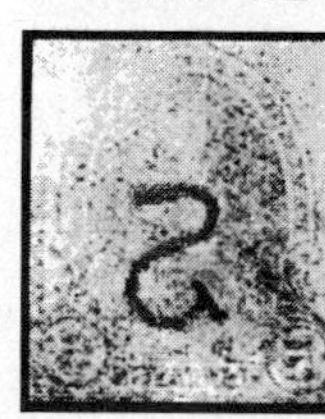
Wmk. 173 — S

Wmk. 240 — REPUBLICA DE EL SALVADOR in Sheet

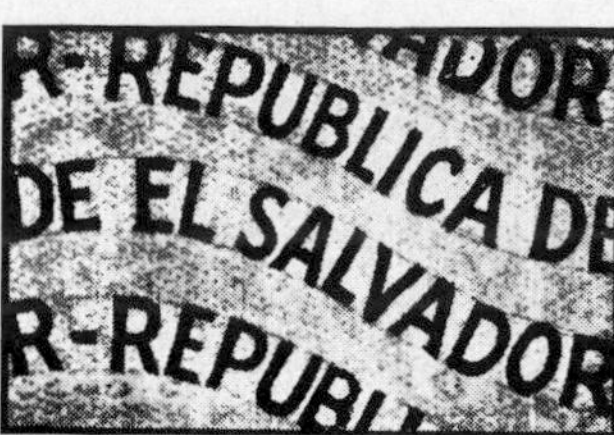
Wmk. 269 — REPUBLICA DE EL SALVADOR

Volcano San Miguel — A1

1867 Unwmk. Engr. *Perf. 12*
1 A1 ½r dk gray blue 7.00 *4.00*
2 A1 1r dark red 7.00 4.00
3 A1 2r dark green 8.50 4.50
4 A1 4r dp ol brn 32.50 17.50
Nos. 1-4 (4) 55.00 30.00

There were at least two printings of Nos. 1-4. Stamps from the second printing are lighter in color. See the *1840-1940 Classic Specialized Catalogue* for detailed listings.
Nos. 1-4 when overprinted "Contra Sello" and shield with 14 stars, are telegraph stamps. For similar overprint see Nos. 5-12.
Counterfeits exist.

Nos. 1-4 Handstamped Either Type I or Type II in Black

Type I

Type II

Type II

1874
5 A1 ½r blue 30.00 10.00
6 A1 1r red 20.00 10.00
7 A1 2r green 30.00 10.00
8 A1 4r bister 40.00 20.00
Nos. 5-8 (4) 120.00 50.00

Nos. 1-4 Handstamped Type III in Black

Type III

9 A1 ½r blue 8.00 6.00
10 A1 1r red 8.00 3.00
11 A1 2r green 10.00 3.00
12 A1 4r bister 12.00 10.00
Nos. 9-12 (4) 38.00 22.00

The overprints on Nos. 5-12 exist double. Counterfeits are plentiful.

Coat of Arms
A2 A3

A4

A5

A6

1879 Litho. *Perf. 12½*

13 A2 1c green 3.00 1.75
a. Invtd. "V" for 2nd "A" in "SALVADOR" 6.00 3.00
b. Invtd. "V" for "A" in "REPUBLICA" 6.00 3.00
c. Invtd. "V" for "A" in "UNIVERSAL" 6.00 3.00
d. Thin paper — —
14 A3 2c rose 4.25 2.25
a. Invtd. scroll in upper left corner 12.00 7.50
15 A4 5c blue 7.50 1.90
a. 5c ultra 12.00 6.00
16 A5 10c black 15.00 5.25
17 A6 20c violet 24.00 15.00
Nos. 13-17 (5) 53.75 26.15

There are fifteen varieties of the 1c and 2c, twenty-five of the 5c and five each of the 10 and 20c.

In 1881 the 1c, 2c and 5c were redrawn, the 1c in fifteen varieties and the 2c and 5c in five varieties each.

No. 15 comes in a number of shades from light to dark blue.

These stamps, when overprinted "Contra sello" and arms, are telegraph stamps.

Counterfeits of No. 14 exist.

For overprints see Nos. 25D-25E, 28A-28C.

Allegorical Figure of El Salvador — A7

Volcano — A8

1887 Engr. *Perf. 12*

18 A7 3c brown 2.00 2.00
a. Imperf., pair 10.00 10.00
19 A8 10c orange 30.00 3.00

For surcharges and overprints see Nos. 25, 26C-28, 30-32.

A9

1888 *Rouletted*

20 A9 5c deep blue 1.50 1.50

For overprints see Nos. 35-36.

A10

1889 *Perf. 12*

21 A10 1c green .40
22 A10 2c scarlet .40

Nos. 21-22 Overprinted in Black

23 A10 1c green .40 3.00
24 A10 2c scarlet .40

Nos. 21, 22 and 24 were never placed in use.

For overprints see Nos. 26, 29.

No. 18 Surcharged

Type I

Type II

Type I — thick numerals, heavy serifs.
Type II — thin numerals, straight serifs.

25 A7 1c on 3c brn, type II 4.00 *7.00*
a. Double surcharge 1.50
b. Triple surcharge 3.50
c. Type I .65

The 1c on 2c scarlet is bogus.

Handstamped

1889 Violet Handstamp

25D A2 1c green 19.00 19.00
25E A6 20c violet 45.00 45.00
26 A10 1c green, #23 10.50 *15.00*
26C A7 1c on 3c, #25 50.00 50.00
27 A7 3c brown 7.50 *15.00*
28 A8 10c orange 10.00 *12.50*

Black Handstamp

28A A2 1c green 22.50 21.00
28B A3 2c rose 26.00 26.00
28C A6 20c violet 45.00 45.00
29 A10 1c green, #23 10.50 *15.00*
30 A7 3c brown 10.50 *15.00*
31 A7 1c on 3c, #25 40.00 40.00
32 A8 10c orange 15.00 12.50

Rouletted

Black Handstamp

35 A9 5c deep blue 9.00 *15.00*

Violet Handstamp

36 A9 5c deep blue 9.00 *15.00*

The 1889 handstamps as usual, are found double, inverted, etc. Counterfeits are plentiful.

A13

1890 Engr. *Perf. 12*

38 A13 1c green .50 .50
39 A13 2c bister brown .50 .50
40 A13 3c yellow .50 .50
41 A13 5c blue .50 .50
42 A13 10c violet .50 .50
43 A13 20c orange .75 *3.00*
44 A13 25c red 1.50 *5.00*
45 A13 50c claret 2.00 *7.50*
46 A13 1p carmine 5.00 *30.00*
Nos. 38-46 (9) 11.75 *48.00*

The issues of 1890 to 1899 inclusive were printed by the Hamilton Bank Note Co., New York, to the order of N. F. Seebeck, who held a contract for stamps with the government of El Salvador. This contract gave the right to make reprints of the stamps and such were subsequently made in some instances, as will be found noted in italic type.

Used values of 1890-1899 issues are for stamps with genuine cancellations applied while the stamps were valid. Various counterfeit cancellations exist.

A14

1891

47 A14 1c vermilion .50 .50
48 A14 2c yellow green .50 .50
49 A14 3c violet .50 .50
50 A14 5c carmine lake 2.00 .50
51 A14 10c blue .50 .50
52 A14 11c violet .50 .50
53 A14 20c green .50 *.50*
54 A14 25c yellow brown .50 *2.50*
55 A14 50c dark blue 2.00 *7.50*
56 A14 1p dark brown .75 *25.00*
Nos. 47-56 (10) 8.25 *38.50*

For surcharges see Nos. 57-59.

Nos. 47 and 56 have been reprinted in thick toned paper with dark gum.

A15

Nos. 48, 49 Surcharged in Black or Violet

b

c

1891

57 A15 1c on 2c yellow grn 2.25 2.00
a. Inverted surcharge 8.00
b. Surcharge reading up 12.00
58 A14 (b) 1c on 2c yellow grn 1.60 1.40
59 A14 (c) 5c on 3c violet 4.00 3.25
Nos. 57-59 (3) 7.85 6.65

Landing of Columbus — A18

1892 Engr.

60 A18 1c blue green .50 .50
61 A18 2c orange brown .50 .50
62 A18 3c ultra .50 .50
63 A18 5c gray .50 .50
64 A18 10c vermilion .50 .50
65 A18 11c brown .50 .50
66 A18 20c orange .50 *.75*
67 A18 25c maroon .50 *2.00*
68 A18 50c yellow .50 *7.00*
69 A18 1p carmine lake .50 *25.00*
Nos. 60-69 (10) 5.00 *37.75*

400th anniversary of the discovery of America by Columbus.

Nos. 63, 66-67 Surcharged

Nos. 70, 72

Nos. 73-75

Surcharged in Black, Red or Yellow

1892

70 A18 1c on 5c gray (Bk) (down) 3.00 .75
a. Surcharge reading up 5.00 2.00
72 A18 1c on 5c gray (R) (up) 1.00 *3.00*
a. Surcharge reading down

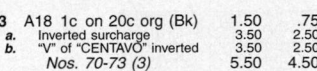

73 A18 1c on 20c org (Bk) 1.50 .75
a. Inverted surcharge 3.50 2.50
b. "V" of "CENTAVO" inverted 3.50 2.50
Nos. 70-73 (3) 5.50 4.50

Similar Surcharge in Yellow or Blue, "centavo" in lower case letters

74 A18 1c on 25c mar (Y) 1.50 1.25
a. Inverted surcharge 2.50 2.50
75 A18 1c on 25c mar (Bl) *250.00 250.00*
a. Double surcharge (Bl + Bk) *275.00 275.00*

Counterfeits exist of Nos. 75 and 75a. Nos. 75, 75a have been questioned.

Pres. Carlos Ezeta — A21

1893 Engr.

76 A21 1c blue .50 .50
77 A21 2c brown red .50 .50
78 A21 3c purple .50 .50
79 A21 5c deep brown .50 .50
80 A21 10c orange brown .50 .50
81 A21 11c vermilion .50 .50
82 A21 20c green .50 *1.00*
83 A21 25c dk olive gray .50 *2.25*
84 A21 50c red orange .50 *5.00*
85 A21 1p black .50 *20.00*
Nos. 76-85 (10) 5.00 *31.25*

For surcharge see No. 89.

Founding City of Isabela — A22

Columbus Statue, Genoa — A23

Departure from Palos — A24

1893

86 A22 2p green .75 —
87 A23 5p violet .75
88 A24 10p orange .75
Nos. 86-88 (3) 2.25

Discoveries by Columbus. No. 86 is known on cover, but experts are not positive that Nos. 87 and 88 were postally used.

No. 77 Surcharged "UN CENTAVO"

1893

89 A21 1c on 2c brown red 1.00 *1.25*
a. "CENTNVO" 6.00 5.00

Liberty — A26

Columbus before Council of Salamanca — A27

Columbus Protecting Indian Hostages A28

Columbus Received by Ferdinand and Isabella A29

1894, Jan.

No.	Type	Description	Unused	Used
91	A26	1c brown	.75	.50
92	A26	2c blue	.75	.50
93	A26	3c maroon	.75	.50
94	A26	5c orange brn	.75	.50
95	A26	10c violet	.75	*.75*
96	A26	11c vermilion	.75	*.75*
97	A26	20c dark blue	.75	*1.00*
98	A26	25c orange	.75	*5.00*
99	A26	50c black	.75	*10.00*
100	A26	1p slate blue	1.10	*20.00*
101	A27	2p deep blue	1.10	
102	A28	5p carmine lake	1.10	
103	A29	10p deep brown	1.10	
		Nos. 91-103 (13)	11.15	
		Nos. 91-100 (10)		*39.50*

Nos. 101-103 for the discoveries by Columbus. Experts are not positive that these were postally used.

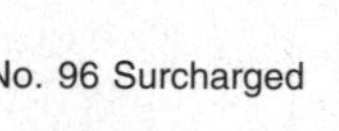
No. 96 Surcharged

1894, Dec.

No.	Type	Description	Unused	Used
104	A26	1c on 11c vermilion	4.50	.65
a.		"Ccntavo"	*40.00*	*40.00*
b.		Double surcharge		

Coat of Arms — A31

Arms Overprint in Second Color Various Frames

1895, Jan. 1

No.	Type	Description	Unused	Used
105	A31	1c olive & green	.50	.25
106	A31	2c dk green & bl	.25	—
a.		2c dark green & green	.50	.85
107	A31	3c brown & brown	.50	—
108	A31	5c blue & brown	.50	—
109	A31	10c orange & brn	.50	—
110	A31	12c magenta & brn	.50	—
111	A31	15c ver & ver	.50	—
112	A31	20c yellow & brn	.50	—
a.		Inverted overprint	2.00	
113	A31	24c violet & brn	.50	—
114	A31	30c dp blue & blue	.50	—
115	A31	50c carmine & brn	.50	—
116	A31	1p black & brn	.50	—
		Nos. 105-116 (12)	5.75	

As printed, Nos. 105-116 portrayed Gen. Antonio Ezeta, brother of Pres. Carlos Ezeta. Before issuance, Ezeta's overthrow caused the government to obliterate his features with the national arms overprint. The 3c, 10c, 30c exist without overprint. Value $1 each.

All values have been reprinted. Reprints of 2c are in dark yellow green on thick paper. Value, 25c each.

Coat of Arms — A32

Various Frames

1895 Engr. *Perf. 12*

No.	Type	Description	Unused	Used
117	A32	1c olive	7.25	.50
118	A32	2c dk blue grn	7.25	.50
119	A32	3c brown	10.00	.75
120	A32	5c blue	2.00	.75
121	A32	10c orange	5.00	.75
122	A32	12c claret	17.50	1.00
123	A32	15c vermilion	22.00	1.00
124	A32	20c deep green	30.00	2.00
125	A32	24c violet	22.50	4.00
126	A32	30c deep blue	30.00	5.00
127	A32	50c carmine lake	3.00	35.00
128	A32	1p gray black	10.00	*35.00*
		Nos. 117-128 (12)	166.50	*86.25*

The reprints are on thicker paper than the originals, and many of the shades differ. Value 25c each.

Nos. 122, 124-126 Surcharged in Black or Red

1895

No.	Type	Description	Unused	Used
129	A32	1c on 12c claret (Bk)	2.00	1.75
130	A32	1c on 24c violet	2.00	1.75
131	A32	1c on 30c dp blue	2.00	1.75
132	A32	2c on 20c dp grn	2.00	1.75
133	A32	3c on 30c dp blue	3.00	2.75
a.		Double surcharge	9.00	
		Nos. 129-133 (5)	11.00	9.75

"Peace" — A45

1896, Jan. 1 Engr. Unwmk.

No.	Type	Description	Unused	Used
134	A45	1c blue	2.00	.50
135	A45	2c dark brown	.50	.50
136	A45	3c blue green	.50	.50
137	A45	5c brown olive	2.00	.50
138	A45	10c yellow	.50	.50
139	A45	12c dark blue	4.00	*1.00*
140	A45	15c brt ultra	.25	—
a.		15c light violet	1.10	*2.00*
141	A45	20c magenta	4.00	*3.00*
142	A45	24c vermilion	1.50	*5.00*
143	A45	30c orange	1.50	*5.00*
144	A45	50c black brn	3.00	*7.50*
145	A45	1p rose lake	6.00	*20.00*
		Nos. 134-145 (12)	25.75	*44.00*

The frames of Nos. 134-145 differ slightly on each denomination.

For overprints see Nos. O1-O12, O37-O48.

Wmk. 117

No.	Type	Description	Unused	Used
145B	A45	2c dark brown	.25	.25

All values have been reprinted. The paper is thicker than that of the originals and the shades are different. The watermark is always upright on original stamps of Salvador, sideways on the reprints. Value 25c each.

Coat of Arms — A46

"White House" — A47

Locomotive A48

Mt. San Miguel A49

Ocean Steamship A50 A51

Post Office A52

Lake Ilopango A53

Atehausillas Waterfall A54

Coat of Arms A55

Coat of Arms A56

Columbus A57

1896

No.	Type	Description	Unused	Used
146	A46	1c emerald	.50	*1.50*
147	A47	2c lake	.50	*.90*
148	A48	3c yellow brn	.75	.75
149	A49	5c deep blue	.90	.50
150	A50	10c brown	2.00	.90
151	A51	12c slate	2.00	.90
152	A52	15c blue green	1.75	.75
153	A53	20c carmine rose	2.00	1.25
154	A54	24c violet	*8.00*	1.25
155	A55	30c deep green	5.00	2.00
156	A56	50c orange	10.00	5.00
157	A57	100c dark blue	15.00	*12.50*
		Nos. 146-157 (12)	48.40	*28.20*

Nos. 146-157 exist imperf.

Unwmk.

No.	Type	Description	Unused	Used
157B	A46	1c emerald	3.75	.90
157C	A47	2c lake	3.75	.50
157D	A48	3c yellow brn	6.00	.50
157E	A49	5c deep blue	4.00	.75
157F	A50	10c brown	7.50	.75
157G	A51	12c slate	10.00	1.00
157I	A52	15c blue green	20.00	1.75
157J	A53	20c carmine rose	7.50	1.00
157K	A54	24c violet	10.00	1.25
157M	A55	30c deep green	10.00	2.50
157N	A56	50c orange	15.00	7.00
157O	A57	100c dark blue	20.00	15.00
		Nos. 157B-157O (12)	117.50	*32.90*

See Nos. 159-170L. For surcharges and overprints see Nos. 158, 158D, 171-174C, O13-O36, O49-O72, O79-O126.

All values have been reprinted, the 15c, 30c, 50c and 100c on watermarked and the 1c, 2c, 3c, 5c, 12c, 20c, 24c and 100c on unwatermarked paper. The papers of the reprints are thicker than those of the originals and the shades are different. Value, 25c each.

Black Surcharge on Nos. 154, 157K

1896 Wmk. 117

No.	Type	Description	Unused	Used
158	A54	15c on 24c violet	4.00	4.00
a.		Double surcharge	20.00	*30.00*
b.		Inverted surcharge	15.00	

Unwmk.

No.	Type	Description	Unused	Used
158D	A54	15c on 24c violet	4.00	3.00

Exist spelled "Qnince."

Types of 1896

1897 Engr. Wmk. 117

No.	Type	Description	Unused	Used
159	A46	1c scarlet	2.75	.90
160	A47	2c yellow grn	2.75	.50
161	A48	3c bister brn	2.50	.50
162	A49	5c orange	2.50	.75
163	A50	10c blue grn	3.00	.75
164	A51	12c blue	8.00	1.00
165	A52	15c black	20.00	10.00
166	A53	20c slate	8.00	2.00
167	A54	24c yellow	20.00	20.00
168	A55	30c rose	15.00	5.00
169	A56	50c violet	15.00	5.00
170	A57	100c brown lake	30.00	15.00
		Nos. 159-170 (12)	129.50	61.40

Unwmk.

No.	Type	Description	Unused	Used
170A	A46	1c scarlet	2.00	*1.50*
170B	A47	2c yellow grn	1.00	*.90*
170C	A48	3c bister brn	.75	.75
170D	A49	5c orange	.90	.50
170E	A50	10c blue grn	5.00	.90
170F	A51	12c blue	1.00	2.00
170G	A52	15c black	10.00	10.00
170H	A53	20c slate	10.00	10.00
170I	A54	24c yellow	20.00	20.00
170J	A55	30c rose	10.00	10.00
170K	A56	50c violet	9.50	10.00
170L	A57	100c brown lake	50.00	*50.00*
		Nos. 170A-170L (12)	120.15	116.55

The 1c, 2c, 3c, 5c, 12c, 15c, 50c and 100c have been reprinted on watermarked and the entire issue on unwatermarked paper. The papers of the reprints are thicker than those of the originals. Value, set of 20, $5.

Surcharged in Red or Black

1897 Wmk. 117

No.	Type	Description	Unused	Used
171	A54	13c on 24c yel (R)	2.50	2.50
172	A55	13c on 30c rose (Bk)	2.50	2.50
173	A56	13c on 50c vio (Bk)	2.50	2.50
174	A57	13c on 100c brn lake (Bk)	2.50	2.50

Unwmk.

No.	Type	Description	Unused	Used
174A	A54	13c on 24c yel (R)	2.50	2.50
174B	A55	13c on 30c rose (Bk)	2.50	2.50
174C	A56	13c on 50c vio (Bk)	2.50	2.50
		Nos. 171-174C (7)	17.50	17.50

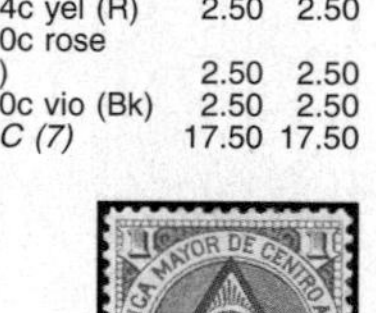

Coat of Arms of "Republic of Central America" — A59

ONE CENTAVO:

Originals: The mountains are outlined in red and blue. The sea is represented by short red and dark blue lines on a light blue background.

Reprints: The mountains are outlined in red only. The sea is printed in green and dark blue, much blurred.

FIVE CENTAVOS:

Originals: The sea is represented by horizontal and diagonal lines of dark blue on a light blue background.

Reprints: The sea is printed in green and dark blue, much blurred. The inscription in gold is in thicker letters.

1897 Litho.

No.	Type	Description	Unused	Used
175	A59	1c bl, gold, rose & grn	1.00	—
176	A59	5c rose, gold, bl & grn	2.00	—

Forming of the "Republic of Central America."

For overprints see Nos. O73-O76.

Stamps of type A59 formerly listed as "Type II" are now known to be reprints.

Allegory of Central American Union — A60

1898 Engr. Wmk. 117

No.	Type	Description	Unused	Used
177	A60	1c orange ver	2.25	.50
178	A60	2c rose	2.25	.50
179	A60	3c pale yel grn	2.00	.50
180	A60	5c blue green	2.00	.75
181	A60	10c gray blue	7.50	.75
182	A60	12c violet	8.50	1.00
183	A60	13c brown lake	8.50	1.00
184	A60	20c deep blue	9.50	2.00
185	A60	24c deep ultra	7.50	5.25
186	A60	26c bister brn	10.00	5.00
187	A60	50c orange	10.00	5.00
188	A60	1p yellow	25.00	15.00
		Nos. 177-188 (12)	95.00	*37.25*

For overprints and surcharges see Nos. 189-198A, 224-241, 269A-269B, O129-O142.

The entire set has been reprinted on unwatermarked paper and all but the 12c and 20c on watermarked paper. The shades of the reprints are not the same as those of the originals, and the paper is thicker. Value, set of 22, $5.50.

No. 180 Overprinted Vertically, up or down in Black, Violet, Red, Magenta and Yellow

1899

189	A60 5c blue grn (Bk)	7.50	6.25
a.	Italic 3rd "r" in "Territorial"	12.50	12.50
b.	Double ovpt. (Bk + Y)	37.50	37.50
190	A60 5c blue grn (V)	*82.50*	*82.50*
191	A60 5c blue grn (R)	*70.00*	*70.00*
191A	A60 5c blue grn (M)	*70.00*	*70.00*
191B	A60 5c blue grn (Y)	*75.00*	*75.00*
	Nos. 189-191B (5)	*305.00*	*303.75*

Counterfeits exist.

Nos. 177-184 Overprinted in Black

1899

192	A60 1c orange ver	2.00	.50
193	A60 2c rose	2.50	1.00
194	A60 3c pale yel grn	2.50	.50
195	A60 5c blue green	2.50	.50
196	A60 10c gray blue	4.00	1.25
197	A60 12c violet	6.50	2.50
198	A60 13c brown lake	6.50	2.00
198A	A60 20c deep blue	*75.00*	*75.00*
	Nos. 192-198 (7)	26.50	8.25

The overprint on No. 198A is only seen on the reprints.

Counterfeits exist of the "wheel" overprint used in 1899-1900.

Ceres ("Estado") — A61

Inscribed: "Estado de El Salvador"

1899 Unwmk. Litho. *Perf. 12*

199	A61 1c brown	.25
200	A61 2c gray green	.25
201	A61 3c blue	.25
202	A61 5c brown org	.25
203	A61 10c chocolate	.25
204	A61 12c dark green	.25
205	A61 13c deep rose	.25
206	A61 24c light blue	.25
207	A61 26c carmine rose	.25
208	A61 50c orange red	.25
209	A61 100c violet	.25
	Nos. 199-209 (11)	2.75

Nos. 208-209 were probably not placed in use.

For overprints and surcharges see Nos. 210-223, 242-252D, O143-O185.

Same, Overprinted

Red Overprint

210	A61 1c brown	60.00	40.00

Blue Overprint

211	A61 1c brown	2.00	1.50
212	A61 5c brown org	2.00	1.50
212A	A61 10c chocolate	15.00	10.00

Black Overprint

213	A61 1c brown	1.50	.75
214	A61 2c gray grn	2.00	.40
215	A61 3c blue	2.25	1.00
216	A61 5c brown org	1.50	.65
217	A61 10c chocolate	1.50	.80
218	A61 12c dark green	4.00	4.00
219	A61 13c deep rose	3.50	3.50
220	A61 24c light blue	30.00	27.50
221	A61 26c car rose	7.50	5.00
222	A61 50c orange red	9.00	7.50
223	A61 100c violet	10.00	9.00
	Nos. 213-223 (11)	72.75	60.10

"Wheel" overprint exists double and triple.

No. 177 Handstamped

1900 Wmk. 117

224	A60 1c orange ver	1.00	1.00

No. 177 Overprinted

225	A60 1c orange ver	15.00	15.00

Stamps of 1898 Surcharged in Black

1900

226	A60 1c on 10c gray blue	15.00	15.00
a.	Inverted surcharge	15.00	15.00
227	A60 1c on 13c brn lake	*100.00*	
228	A60 2c on 12c vio	50.00	50.00
a.	"eentavo"		
b.	Inverted surcharge		
c.	"centavos"	90.00	
d.	As "c," double surcharge		
e.	Vertical surcharge		
229	A60 2c on 13c brn lake	5.00	5.00
a.	"eentavo"	8.00	7.00
b.	Inverted surcharge	12.50	10.00
c.	"1900" omitted	7.50	7.50
230	A60 2c on 20c dp blue	5.00	5.00
a.	Inverted surcharge	8.00	8.00
230B	A60 2c on 26c bis brn	—	—
231	A60 3c on 12c vio	*90.00*	—
a.	"eentavo"		
b.	Inverted surcharge	—	—
c.	Double surcharge		
232	A60 3c on 50c org	35.00	35.00
a.	Inverted surcharge	35.00	35.00
233	A60 5c on 12c vio	—	—
234	A60 5c on 24c ultra	50.00	50.00
a.	"eentavo"		
b.	"centavos"	70.00	
235	A60 5c on 26c bis brn	*150.00*	*150.00*
a.	Inverted surcharge	*35.00*	*35.00*
236	A60 5c on 1p yel	50.00	35.00
a.	Inverted surcharge	60.00	60.00

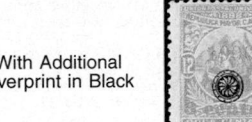

With Additional Overprint in Black

237	A60 2c on 12c vio	2.50	2.50
a.	Inverted surcharge	2.50	2.50
b.	"eentavo"	8.00	
c.	"centavos" (plural)	75.00	
d.	"1900" omitted		
237H	A60 2c on 13c brn lake		
238	A60 3c on 12c vio	125.00	125.00
a.	"eentavo"	75.00	75.00
239	A60 5c on 26c bis brn	150.00	150.00
a.	Inverted surcharge		

Vertical Surcharge "Centavos" in the Plural

240	A60 2c on 12c vio	125.00	125.00
b.	Without wheel		
240A	A60 5c on 24c dp ultra	125.00	125.00

With Additional Overprint in Black

241	A60 5c on 12c vio	50.00	50.00
a.	Surcharge reading downward		

Counterfeits exist of the surcharges on Nos. 226-241 and the "wheel" overprint on Nos. 237-239, 241.

Same Surcharge on Stamps of 1899 Without Wheel

1900 Unwmk.

242	A61 1c on 13c dp rose	1.50	1.50
a.	Inverted surcharge	4.00	3.00
b.	"eentavo"	4.00	3.00
c.	"ecntavo"	5.00	3.00
d.	"1 centavo 1"	15.00	10.00
e.	Double surcharge		
243	A61 2c on 12c dk grn	8.00	8.00
a.	Inverted surcharge	15.00	15.00
b.	"eentavo"		
244	A61 2c on 13c dp rose	3.00	2.50
a.	"eentavo"	3.00	4.00
b.	"ecntavo"	6.00	2.50
c.	Inverted surcharge	9.00	
245	A61 3c on 12c dk grn	3.00	2.50
a.	Inverted surcharge	9.00	5.00
b.	"eentavo"	12.00	12.00
c.	Double surcharge	9.00	
	Nos. 242-245 (4)	15.50	14.50

With Additional Overprint in Black

246	A61 1c on 2c gray grn	1.00	1.00
a.	"eentavo"	4.00	3.00
b.	Inverted surcharge	10.00	9.00
247	A61 1c on 13c dp rose	4.00	4.00
a.	"eentavo"	15.00	
b.	"1 centavo 1"		
248	A61 2c on 12c dk grn	5.00	4.00
a.	"eentavo"	15.00	
b.	Inverted surcharge	4.00	4.00
c.	Double surcharge		
249	A61 2c on 13c dp rose	100.00	100.00
a.	"eentavo"		
b.	Double surcharge	150.00	150.00
250	A61 3c on 12c dk grn	5.00	3.00
a.	Inverted surcharge	5.50	4.00
b.	"eentavo"	8.00	7.00
c.	Date double	15.00	
251	A61 5c on 24c lt bl	12.00	5.00
a.	"eentavo"	20.00	20.00
252	A61 5c on 26c car rose	4.00	4.00
a.	Inverted surcharge	12.00	9.00
b.	"eentavo"	6.00	5.00
252D	A61 5c on 1c on 26c car rose		
	Nos. 246-248,250-252 (6)	31.00	21.00

Counterfeits exist of the surcharges on Nos. 242-252D and the "wheel" overprint on Nos. 246-252D.

Ceres ("Republica") — A63

There are two varieties of the 1c, type A63, one with the word "centavo" in the middle of the label (#253, 263, 270, 299, 305, 326), the other with "centavo" nearer the left end than the right (#270, 299, 305, 326).

The stamps of type A63 are found in a great variety of shades. Stamps of type A63 without handstamp were not regularly issued.

Handstamped in Violet or Black

Inscribed: "Republica de El Salvador"

1900

253	A63 1c blue green	.90	.90
a.	1c yellow green	.90	.90
254	A63 2c rose	1.50	1.00
255	A63 3c gray black	1.25	1.00
256	A63 5c pale blue	1.00	.60
a.	5c deep blue	5.00	.60
257	A63 10c deep blue	2.00	.60
258	A63 12c yel green	5.00	3.50
259	A63 13c yel brown	4.00	3.00
260	A63 24c gray	15.00	15.00
261	A63 26c yel brown	7.00	7.00
262	A63 50c rose red	2.00	2.00
	Nos. 253-262 (10)	39.65	34.60

For overprints and surcharges see Nos. 263-269, 270-282, 293A-311B, 317, 326-335, O223-O242, O258-O262, O305-O312.

Handstamped in Violet or Black

263	A63 1c lt green	10.00	4.00
264	A63 2c pale rose	10.00	3.00
265	A63 3c gray black	10.00	3.00
266	A63 5c slate blue	14.00	3.00
267	A63 10c deep blue	—	—
268	A63 13c yellow brn	35.00	35.00
269	A63 50c dull rose	15.00	15.00
	Nos. 263-266,268-269 (6)	94.00	63.00

Handstamped on 1898 Stamps

Wmk. 117

269A	A60 2c rose	30.00	30.00
269B	A60 10c gray blue	30.00	30.00

The overprints on Nos. 253 to 269B are handstamped and, as usual with that style of overprint, are to be found double, inverted, omitted, etc.

Specialists have questioned the existence of No. 267. The editors would like to see authenticated evidence of the existence of a genuine example.

Stamps of Type A63 Overprinted in Black

1900 Unwmk.

270	A63 1c light green	1.50	1.00
271	A63 2c rose	7.50	2.00
272	A63 3c gray black	1.50	1.00
273	A63 5c pale blue	7.50	2.00
a.	5c dark blue	6.00	1.00
274	A63 10c deep blue	7.50	2.00
a.	10c pale blue	7.50	2.00
275	A63 12c light green	2.25	1.50
276	A63 13c yellow brown	1.50	1.00
277	A63 24c gray	1.75	1.25
278	A63 26c yellow brown	3.00	2.00
	Nos. 270-278 (9)	34.00	13.75

This overprint is known double, inverted, etc.

Nos. 271-273 Surcharged in Black

1902

280	A63 1c on 2c rose	8.25	6.75
281	A63 1c on 3c black	6.00	4.25
282	A63 1c on 5c blue	3.75	3.00
	Nos. 280-282 (3)	18.00	14.00

Morazán Monument — A64

Perf. 14, 14½

1903 Engr. Wmk. 173

283	A64 1c green	1.00	.60
284	A64 2c carmine	1.00	.60
285	A64 3c orange	10.00	2.00
286	A64 5c dark blue	1.00	.60
287	A64 10c dull violet	1.00	.60
288	A64 12c slate	1.25	.60
289	A64 13c red brown	1.25	.60
290	A64 24c scarlet	7.50	3.75
291	A64 26c yellow brn	7.50	3.75
292	A64 50c bister	3.75	2.25
293	A64 100c grnsh blue	11.00	7.50
	Nos. 283-293 (11)	46.25	22.85

For surcharges and overprint see Nos. 312-316, 318-325, O253.

Stamps of 1900 with Shield in Black Overprinted

(5¾x13½mm) — a

1905

(5x14¾mm) — b

(4½x16mm) — c

1905

(4½x13½mm) — d

(5x14½mm) — e **1905**

1905-06 Unwmk. *Perf. 12*

Blue Overprint

293A A63 (a) 2c rose — —
294 A63 (a) 3c gray blk 8.00 6.00
a. Without shield
295 A63 (a) 5c blue 10.00 7.50

Purple Overprint

296 A63 (b) 3c gray blk (Shield in pur) — —
296A A63 (b) 5c bl (Shield in pue) — —
297 A63 (b) 3c gray blk — —
298 A63 (b) 5c blue — —

Black Overprint

298A A63 (b) 5c blue — —

Blue Overprint

299 A63 (c) 1c green 10.00 5.00
299B A63 (c) 2c rose .50 .40
c. "1905" vert. 1.00
300 A63 (c) 5c blue 6.00 4.00
301 A63 (c) 10c deep blue 2.00 1.00

Black Overprint

302 A63 (c) 2c rose 10.00 5.00
303 A63 (c) 5c blue 25.00 25.00
304 A63 (c) 10c deep blue 12.00 7.00

Blue Overprint

305 A63 (d) 1c green 15.00 10.00
306 A63 (d) 2c rose, ovpt. vert. 9.00 5.00
a. Overprint horiz.
306B A63 (d) 3c gray black 8.00 4.00
307 A63 (d) 5c blue 3.00 1.50

Blue Overprint

311 A63 (e) 2c rose 10.00 8.00
a. Without shield 15.00 12.00

Black Overprint

311B A63 (e) 5c blue 30.00 20.00
Nos. 294-295,299-311B (15) 158.50 109.40

These overprints are found double, inverted, omitted, etc. Counterfeits exist.

Regular Issue of 1903 Surcharged

f

g

h

1905-06 Wmk. 173 *Perf. 14, 14½*

Black Surcharge

312 A64 (f) 1c on 2c car 4.00 2.00
a. Double surcharge 20.00 20.00

Red Surcharge

312B A64 (g) 5c on 12c slate 5.00 4.00
c. Double surcharge
d. Black surcharge 15.00 15.00
e. As "d," double surcharge

Blue Handstamped Surcharge

313 A64 (h) 1c on 2c car 2.00 2.00
314 A64 (h) 1c on 10c vio 2.00 2.00
315 A64 (h) 1c on 12c sl ('06) 2.00 2.00
316 A64 (h) 1c on 13c red brn 22.50 15.00

No. 271 with Handstamped Surcharge in Blue

Unwmk.

317 A63 (h) 1c on 2c rose — —
Nos. 312-316 (6) 37.50 27.00

The "h" is handstamped in strips of four stamps each differing from the others in the size of the upper figures of value and in the letters of the word "CENTAVO," particularly in the size of the "N" and the "O" of that word. The surcharge is known inverted, double, etc.

Regular Issue of 1903 with Handstamped Surcharge

i

j

k

Wmk. 173

Red Handstamped Surcharge

318 A64 (i) 5c on 12c slate 4.00 3.00
319 A64 (j) 5c on 12c slate 6.00 5.00
a. Blue surcharge

Blue Handstamped Surcharge

320 A64 (k) 5c on 12c slate 3.50 2.50
Nos. 318-320 (3) 13.50 10.50

One or more of the numerals in the handstamped surcharges on Nos. 318, 319 and 320 are frequently omitted, inverted, etc.

Regular Issue of 1903 Surcharged

l

m

Blue Handstamped Surcharge

321 A64 (l) 6c on 12c slate .75 .50
322 A64 (l) 6c on 13c red brn 1.50 .60

Red Handstamped Surcharge

323 A64 (l) 6c on 12c slate 27.50 15.00

Type "l" is handstamped in strips of four varieties, differing in the size of the numerals and letters. The surcharge is known double and inverted.

Black Surcharge

324 A64 (m) 1c on 13c red brn 2.25 1.50
a. Double surcharge 6.00 4.50
b. Right "1" & dot omitted
c. Both numerals omitted
325 A64 (m) 3c on 13c red brn .75 .60

Stamps of 1900, with Shield in Black, Overprinted — n

1905 Unwmk. *Perf. 12*

Blue Overprint

326 A63 (n) 1c green 9.00 6.00
a. Inverted overprint
327 A63 (n) 2c rose 5.00 5.00
a. Vertical overprint 12.50 12.50
b. Imperforate 9.00 6.00
327B A63 (n) 3c black 50.00 30.00
327C A63 (n) 5c blue 25.00 20.00
328 A63 (n) 10c deep blue 15.00 9.00

Black Overprint

328A A63 (n) 10c deep blue 20.00 15.00
Nos. 326-328A (6) 124.00 85.00

Counterfeits of Nos. 326-335 abound.

Stamps of 1900, with Shield in Black Surcharged or Overprinted

o

1906
p

q

1906 Blue and Black Surcharge

329 A63 (o) 2c on 26c brn org 1.00 .80
a. "2" & dot double 15.00 15.00
330 A63 (o) 3c on 26c brn org 8.00 6.50
a. "3" & dot double

Black Surcharge or Overprint

331 A63 (o) 3c on 26c brn org 9.00 7.00
a. Disks & numerals omitted
b. "3" and disks double
c. "1906" omitted
333 A63 (p) 10c deep blue 6.00 4.00
334 A63 (q) 10c deep blue 6.00 4.00
334A A63 (q) 26c brown org 50.00 45.00
b. "1906" in blue

No. 257 Overprinted in Black

335 A63 (q) 10c dp bl (Shield in violet) — —
a. Overprint type "p"
Nos. 329-334A (6) 80.00 67.30

There are numerous varieties of these surcharges and overprints.

Pres. Pedro José Escalón — A65

1906 Engr. *Perf. 11½*

Glazed Paper

336 A65 1c green & blk .25 .25
a. Thin paper .75 .25
337 A65 2c red & blk .25 .25
338 A65 3c yellow & blk .25 .25
339 A65 5c ultra & blk .25 .25
a. 5c dark blue & black .25 .25
340 A65 6c carmine & blk .25 .25
341 A65 10c violet & blk .25 .25
342 A65 12c violet & blk .25 .25
343 A65 13c dk brn & blk .25 .25
345 A65 24c carmine & blk .35 .35
346 A65 26c choc & blk .35 .35
347 A65 50c yellow & blk .35 .45
348 A65 100c blue & blk *3.00 3.00*
Nos. 336-348 (12) *6.05 6.15*

All values of this set are known imperforate but are not believed to have been issued in this condition.

See Nos. O263-O272. For overprints and surcharges see Nos. 349-354.

The entire set has been reprinted, perforated 11.8. Value, set of 12, $1.20.

Nos. 336-338 Overprinted in Black

1907

349 A65 1c green & blk .25 .25
a. Shield in red 3.50
350 A65 2c red & blk .25 .25
a. Shield in red 3.50
351 A65 3c yellow & blk .25 .25
Nos. 349-351 (3) .75 .75

Reprints of Nos. 349 to 351 have the same characteristics as the reprints of the preceding issue. Value, set of 3, 15c.

Stamps of 1906 Surcharged with Shield and

352 A65 1c on 5c ultra & blk .25 .25
a. 1c on 5c dark blue & black .25 .25
b. Inverted surcharge .35 .35
c. Double surcharge .45 .45
352D A65 1c on 6c rose & blk .25 .25
e. Double surcharge 1.25 1.25
353 A65 2c on 6c rose & blk 2.00 1.00
354 A65 10c on 6c rose & blk .50 .35
Nos. 352-354 (4) 3.00 1.85

The above surcharges are frequently found with the shield double, inverted, or otherwise misplaced.

National Palace — A66

Overprinted with Shield in Black

1907 Engr. Unwmk.

Paper with or without colored dots

355 A66 1c green & blk .25 .25
356 A66 2c red & blk .25 .25
357 A66 3c yellow & blk .25 .25
358 A66 5c blue & blk .25 .25
a. 5c ultramarine & black .25 .25
359 A66 6c ver & blk .25 .25
a. Shield in red 3.25
360 A66 10c violet & blk .25 .25
361 A66 12c violet & blk .25 .25
362 A66 13c sepia & blk .25 .25
363 A66 24c rose & blk .25 .25
364 A66 26c yel brn & blk .30 .25
365 A66 50c orange & blk .50 .35
a. 50c yellow & black 3.50
366 A66 100c turq bl & blk 1.00 .50
Nos. 355-366 (12) 4.05 3.35

Most values exist without shield, also with shield inverted, double, and otherwise misprinted. Many of these were never sold to the public.

See 2nd footnote following No. 421.

See Nos. 369-373, 397-401. For surcharges and overprints see Nos. 367-368A, 374-77, 414-421, 443-444, J71-J74, J76-J80, O329-O331.

No. 356 With Additional Surcharge in Black

1908

367 A66 1c on 2c red & blk .25 .25
a. Double surcharge 1.00 1.00
b. Inverted surcharge .50 .50
c. Double surcharge, one inverted .50 .50
d. Red surcharge

Same Surcharged in Black or Red

368 A66 1c on 2c *19.00 17.50*
368A A66 1c on 2c (R) *27.50 25.00*

Counterfeits exist of the surcharges on Nos. 368-368A.

Type of 1907

1909 Engr. Wmk. 172

369 A66 1c green & blk .25 .25
370 A66 2c rose & blk .25 .25
371 A66 3c yellow & blk .25 .25

372 A66 5c blue & blk .25 .25
373 A66 10c violet & blk .30 .25
Nos. 369-373 (5) 1.30 1.25

The note after No. 366 will apply here also.

Nos. 355, 369 Overprinted in Red

1909, Sept. **Unwmk.**

374 A66 1c green & blk 2.25 1.10
a. Inverted overprint 10.00

Wmk. 172

375 A66 1c green & blk 1.75 1.40
a. Inverted overprint

88th anniv. of El Salvador's independence.

Nos. 362, 364 Surcharged

1909 **Unwmk.**

376 A66 2c on 13c sep & blk 1.50 1.25
a. Inverted surcharge
377 A66 3c on 26c yel brn & blk 1.75 1.40
a. Inverted surcharge

A67

Design: Pres. Fernando Figueroa.

1910 **Engr.** **Wmk. 172**

378 A67 1c sepia & blk .25 .25
379 A67 2c dk grn & blk .25 .25
380 A67 3c orange & blk .25 .25
381 A67 4c carmine & blk .25 .25
a. 4c scarlet & black .25 .25
382 A67 5c purple & blk .25 .25
383 A67 6c scarlet & blk .25 .25
384 A67 10c purple & blk .25 .25
385 A67 12c dp bl & blk .25 .25
386 A67 17c ol grn & blk .25 .25
387 A67 19c brn red & blk .25 .25
388 A67 29c choc & blk .25 .25
389 A67 50c yellow & blk .25 .25
390 A67 100c turq bl & blk .25 .25
Nos. 378-390 (13) 3.25 3.25

A68

5c, José Matías Delgado. 6c, Manuel José Arce. 12c, Centenary Monument.

Paper with colored dots

1911 **Unwmk.**

391 A68 5c dp blue & brn .25 .25
392 A68 6c orange & brn .25 .25
393 A68 12c violet & brn .25 .25

Wmk. 172

394 A68 5c dp blue & brn .25 .25
395 A68 6c orange & brn .25 .25
396 A68 12c violet & brn .25 .25
Nos. 391-396 (6) 1.50 1.50

Centenary of the insurrection of 1811.

Palace Type of 1907 without Shield

1911 **Paper without colored dots**

397 A66 1c scarlet .25 .25
398 A66 2c chocolate .30 .30
a. Paper with brown dots

399 A66 13c deep green .25 .25
400 A66 24c yellow .25 .25
401 A66 50c dark brown .25 .25
Nos. 397-401 (5) 1.30 1.30

José Matías Delgado — A71

Manuel José Arce — A72

Francisco Morazán — A73

Rafael Campo — A74

Trinidad Cabañas A75

Monument of Gerardo Barrios A76

Centenary Monument A77

National Palace A78

Rosales Hospital — A79

Coat of Arms — A80

1912 **Unwmk.** ***Perf. 12***

402 A71 1c dp bl & blk 1.00 .25
403 A72 2c bis brn & blk 1.00 .25
404 A73 5c scarlet & blk 1.00 .25
405 A74 6c dk grn & blk 1.00 .25
406 A75 12c ol grn & blk 3.00 .25
407 A76 17c violet & slate 10.00 .25
408 A77 19c scar & slate 3.00 .30
409 A78 29c org & slate 5.00 .30
410 A79 50c blue & slate 5.00 .45
411 A80 1col black & slate 10.00 1.00
Nos. 402-411 (10) 40.00 3.55

Juan Manuel Rodríguez A81

Pres. Manuel E. Araujo A82

1914 ***Perf. 11½***

412 A81 10c orange & brn 5.00 1.50
413 A82 25c purple & brn 5.00 1.50

Type of 1907 without Shield Overprinted in Black

1915

Paper overlaid with colored dots

414 A66 1c gray green .25 .25
415 A66 2c red .25 .25
416 A66 5c ultra .25 .25
417 A66 6c pale blue .25 .25
418 A66 10c yellow .60 .30
419 A66 12c brown .50 .25
420 A66 50c violet .25 .25
421 A66 100c black brn 1.40 1.40
Nos. 414-421 (8) 3.75 3.20

Varieties such as center omitted, center double, center inverted, imperforate exist with or without date, date inverted, date double, etc., but are believed to be entirely unofficial.

Preceding the stamps with the "1915" overprint a quantity of stamps of this type was overprinted with the letter "S." Evidence is lacking that they were ever placed in use. The issue was demonetized in 1916.

National Theater — A83

Various frames.

1916 **Engr.** ***Perf. 12***

431 A83 1c deep green .25 .25
432 A83 2c vermilion .25 .25
433 A83 5c deep blue .25 .25
434 A83 6c gray violet .25 .25
435 A83 10c black brn .25 .25
436 A83 12c violet 2.50 .50
437 A83 17c orange .35 .25
438 A83 25c dk brown .80 .25
439 A83 29c black 5.00 .75
440 A83 50c slate 20.00 10.00
Nos. 431-440 (10) 29.90 13.00

Watermarked letters which occasionally appear are from the papermaker's name.

For surcharges and overprints see Nos. 450-455, 457-466, O332-O341.

Nos. O324-O325 with "OFICIAL" Barred out in Black

1917

441 O3 2c red .90 .90
a. Double bar
442 O3 5c ultramarine 1.00 .70
a. Double bar

Regular Issue of 1915 Overprinted "OFICIAL" and Re-overprinted In Red

443 A66 6c pale blue 1.25 1.00
a. Double bar
444 A66 12c brown 1.75 1.25
a. Double bar
b. "CORRIENTE" inverted

Same Overprint in Red On Nos. O323-O327

445 O3 1c gray green 3.50 2.50
a. "CORRIENTE" inverted
b. Double bar
c. "CORRIENTE" omitted
446 O3 2c red 3.50 2.50
a. Double bar
447 O3 5c ultra 18.00 12.00
a. Double bar, both in black
448 O3 10c yellow 2.00 1.00
a. Double bar
b. "OFICIAL" and bar omitted
449 O3 50c violet 1.00 1.00
a. Double bar
Nos. 443-449 (7) 31.00 21.25

Nos. O334-O335 Overprinted or Surcharged in Red

a

b

450 A83 (a) 5c deep blue 3.00 2.00
a. "CORRIENTE" double
451 A83 (b) 1c on 6c gray vio 2.00 1.50
a. "CORRIERTE"
b. "CORRIENRE" 5.00
c. "CORRIENTE" double

No. 434 Surcharged in Black

1918

452 A83 1c on 6c gray vio 1.75 1.00
a. Double surcharge
b. Inverted surcharge

No. 434 Surcharged in Black

1918

453 A83 1c on 6c gray vio 1.50 .75
a. "Centado" 2.25 1.50
b. Double surcharge 2.50 1.75
c. Inverted surcharge

No. 434 Surcharged in Black or Red

454 A83 1c on 6c gray vio 10.00 6.00
a. Double surcharge
b. Inverted surcharge 5.00 5.00
455 A83 1c on 6c gray vio (R) 10.00 6.00
a. Double surcharge
b. Inverted surcharge 5.00 5.00
Nos. 454-455 (2) 20.00 12.00

Counterfeits exist of Nos. 454-455.

Pres. Carlos Meléndez — A85

1919 **Engr.**

456 A85 1col dk blue & blk .50 .50

For surcharge see No. 467.

No. 437 Surcharged in Black

1919

457 A83 1c on 17c orange .25 .25
a. Inverted surcharge 1.00 1.00
b. Double surcharge 1.00 1.00

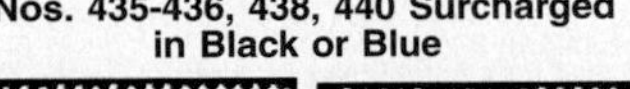

Nos. 435-436, 438, 440 Surcharged in Black or Blue

1920-21

458 A83 1c on 12c violet .25 .25
a. Double surcharge 1.00 1.00
459 A83 2c on 10c dk brn .25 .25
460 A83 5c on 50c slate ('21) .40 .25
461 A83 6c on 25c dk brn (Bl) ('21) 2.00 1.00

Same Srch. in Black on No. O337

462 A83 1c on 12c violet 1.00 1.00
a. Double surcharge
Nos. 458-462 (5) 3.90 2.75

No. 460 surcharged in yellow and 461 surcharged in red are essays.

No. 462 is due to some sheets of Official Stamps being mixed with the ordinary 12c stamps at the time of surcharging. The error stamps were sold to the public and used for ordinary postage.

Surcharged in Red, Blue or Black

15c Types:

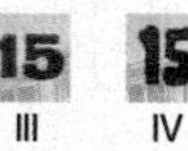

I II III IV

463 A83 15c on 29c blk (III) ('21) 1.00 .40
a. Double surcharge 2.00
b. Type I 1.50 1.00
c. Type II 1.00 .75
d. Type IV 2.50
464 A83 26c on 29c blk (Bl) 1.00 .60
a. Double surcharge
466 A83 35c on 50c slate (Bk) 1.00 .60
467 A85 60c on 1col dk bl & blk (R) .30 .25
Nos. 463-467 (4) 3.30 1.85

Surcharge on No. 464 differs from 15c illustration in that bar at bottom extends across stamp and denomination includes "cts." One stamp in each row of ten of No. 464 has the "t" of "cts" inverted and one stamp in each row of No. 466 has the letters "c" in "cinco" larger than the normal.

Setting for No. 467 includes three types of numerals and "CENTAVOS" measuring from 16mm to 20mm wide.

No. 464 surcharged in green or yellow and the 35c on 29c black are essays.

A93

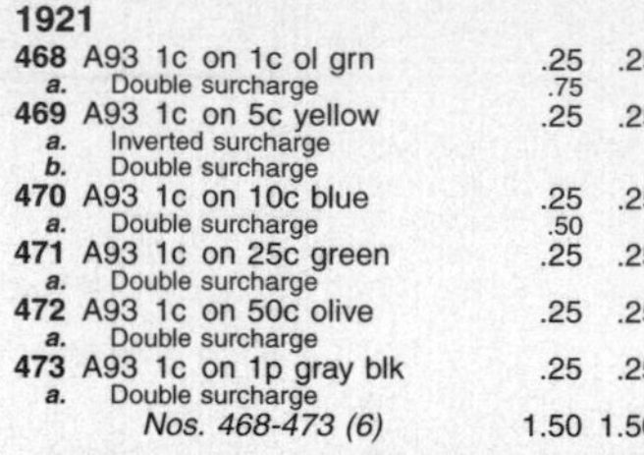

1921

468 A93 1c on 1c ol grn .25 .25
a. Double surcharge .75
469 A93 1c on 5c yellow .25 .25
a. Inverted surcharge
b. Double surcharge
470 A93 1c on 10c blue .25 .25
a. Double surcharge .50
471 A93 1c on 25c green .25 .25
a. Double surcharge
472 A93 1c on 50c olive .25 .25
a. Double surcharge
473 A93 1c on 1p gray blk .25 .25
a. Double surcharge
Nos. 468-473 (6) 1.50 1.50

The frame of No. 473 differs slightly from the illustration.

Setting includes many wrong font letters and numerals.

Francisco Menéndez
A94

Manuel José Arce
A95

Confederation Coin — A96

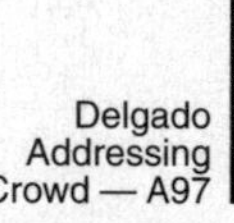

Delgado Addressing Crowd — A97

Coat of Arms of Confederation
A98

Francisco Morazán
A99

Independence Monument
A100

Columbus
A101

1921 **Engr.** ***Perf. 12***

474 A94 1c green 2.50 .25
475 A95 2c black 5.00 .25
476 A96 5c orange 2.00 .25
477 A97 6c carmine rose 2.00 .25
478 A98 10c deep blue 2.00 .25
479 A99 25c olive grn 4.00 .25
480 A100 60c violet 9.00 .50
481 A101 1col black brn 15.00 .75
Nos. 474-481 (8) 41.50 2.75

For overprints and surcharges see Nos. 481A-485, 487-494, 506, O342-O349.

Nos. 474-477 Overprinted in Red, Black or Blue

a

b

1921

481A A94 (a) 1c green (R) 5.00 4.00
481B A95 (a) 2c black (R) 5.00 4.00
481C A96 (b) 5c orange (Bk) 5.00 4.00
481D A97 (b) 6c car rose (Bl) 5.00 4.00
Nos. 481A-481D (4) 20.00 16.00

Centenary of independence.

No. 477 Surcharged

a

b

1923

482 A97 (a) 5c on 6c 4.00 .25
483 A97 (b) 5c on 6c 4.00 .25
484 A97 (b) 20c on 6c 4.00 .25
Nos. 482-484 (3) 12.00 .75

Nos. 482-484 exist with double surcharge.

No. 475 Surcharged in Red

1923

485 A95 10c on 2c black 4.00 .25

José Simeón Cañas y Villacorta — A102

1923 **Engr.** ***Perf. 11½***

486 A102 5c blue .60 .30

Centenary of abolition of slavery.
For surcharge see No. 571.

Nos. 479, 481 Surcharged in Red or Black

1924 ***Perf. 12***

487 A99 1c on 25c ol grn (R) .30 .25
a. Numeral at right inverted
b. Double surcharge
488 A99 6c on 25c ol grn (R) .25 .25
489 A99 20c on 25c ol grn (R) .60 .25
490 A100 20c on 1col blk brn (Bk) .75 .35
Nos. 487-490 (4) 1.90 1.10

Nos. 476, 478 Surcharged

1924

491 A96 1c on 5c orange (Bk) .40 .25
492 A98 6c on 10c dp bl (R) .40 .25

Nos. 491-492 exist with double surcharge.

A stamp similar to No. 492 but with surcharge "6 centavos 6" is an essay.

No. 476 Surcharged

493 A96 2c on 5c orange .40 .40
a. Top ornament omitted 2.00 2.00
Nos. 491-493 (3) 1.20 .90

No. 480 Surcharged

1924 **Red Surcharge**

494 A100 5c on 60c violet 6.00 5.00
a. "1781" for "1874" 13.00 12.00
b. "1934" for "1924" 13.00 12.00

Universal Postal Union, 50th anniversary.

This stamp with black surcharge is an essay. Examples have been passed through the post.

Daniel Hernández Monument
A106

National Gymnasium
A107

Atlacatl — A108

Conspiracy of 1811 — A109

Bridge over Lempa River — A110

Map of Central America — A111

Balsam Tree — A112

Tulla Serra — A114

Columbus at La Rábida — A115

Coat of Arms — A116

Photogravure; Engraved (35c, 1col)

1924-25 ***Perf. 12½; 14 (35c, 1col)***

495 A106 1c red violet .25 .25
496 A107 2c dark red .40 .25
497 A108 3c chocolate .30 .25
498 A109 5c olive blk .30 .25
499 A110 6c grnsh blue .40 .25
500 A111 10c orange .85 .25
a. "ATLANT CO" 8.00 8.00
501 A112 20c deep green 1.50 .40
502 A114 35c scar & grn 3.50 .50

503 A115 50c orange brown 2.75 .35
504 A116 1col grn & vio ('25) 4.00 .50
Nos. 495-504 (10) 14.25 3.25

For overprints and surcharges see Nos. 510-511, 520-534, 585, C1-C10, C19, O350-O361, RA1-RA4.

No. 480 Surcharged in Red

1925, Aug. ***Perf. 12***
506 A100 2c on 60c violet 1.50 1.25

City of San Salvador, 400th anniv.
The variety with dates in black is an essay.

View of San Salvador — A118

1925 **Photo.** ***Perf. 12½***
507 A118 1c blue 1.10 1.00
508 A118 2c deep green 1.10 1.00
509 A118 3c Mahogany red 1.10 1.00
Nos. 507-509 (3) 3.30 3.00

#506-509 for the 4th centenary of the founding of the City of San Salvador.

Black Surcharge

1928, July 17
510 A111 3c on 10c orange 1.25 .75
a. "ATLANT CO" 20.00 20.00

Industrial Exhibition, Santa Ana, July 1928.

Red Surcharge

1928
511 A109 1c on 5c olive black .45 .25
a. Bar instead of top left "1" .60 .25

Pres. Pío Romero Bosque, Salvador, and Pres. Lázaro Chacón, Guatemala A121

1929 **Litho.** ***Perf. 11½***

Portraits in Dark Brown

512 A121 1c dull violet .60 .45
a. Center inverted 11.50 11.50
513 A121 3c bister brn .60 .45
a. Center inverted 35.00 35.00
514 A121 5c gray grn .60 .45
515 A121 10c orange .60 .45
Nos. 512-515 (4) 2.40 1.80

Opening of the international railroad connecting El Salvador and Guatemala.
Nos. 512-515 exist imperforate. No. 512 in the colors of No. 515.

Tomb of Menéndez A122

1930, Dec. 3
516 A122 1c violet 4.50 3.50
517 A122 3c brown 4.50 3.50
518 A122 5c dark green 4.50 3.50
519 A122 10c yellow brn 4.50 3.50
Nos. 516-519 (4) 18.00 14.00

Centenary of the birth of General Francisco Menéndez.

Stamps of 1924-25 Issue Overprinted

1932 ***Perf. 12½, 14***
520 A106 1c deep violet .30 .25
521 A107 2c dark red .30 .25
522 A108 3c chocolate .45 .25
523 A109 5c olive blk .45 .25
524 A110 6c deep blue .60 .25
525 A111 10c orange 1.50 .25
a. "ATLANT CO" 12.00 9.00
526 A112 20c deep green 2.40 .75
527 A114 35c scar & grn 3.25 1.00
528 A115 50c orange brown 4.50 1.50
529 A116 1col green & vio 7.50 3.25
Nos. 520-529 (10) 21.25 8.00

Values are for the overprint measuring 7½x3mm. It is found in two other sizes: 7½x3¼mm and 8x3mm.

Types of 1924-25
Surcharged with New Values in Red or Black

1934 ***Perf. 12½***
530 A109 2(c) on 5c grnsh blk .25 .25
a. Double surcharge
531 A111 3(c) on 10c org (Bk) .45 .25
a. "ATLANT CO" 6.00 6.00

Nos. 503, 504, 502 Surcharged with New Values in Black

Perf. 12½, 14½
532 A115 2(c) on 50c .45 .25
a. Double surcharge 3.00
533 A116 8(c) on 1col .25 .25
534 A114 15(c) on 35c .45 .45
Nos. 530-534 (5) 1.85 1.45

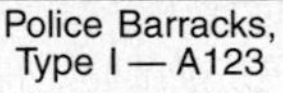

Police Barracks, Type I — A123

Type II

Two types of the 2c:
Type I — The clouds have heavy lines of shading.
Type II — The lines of shading have been removed from the clouds.

Wmk. 240

1934-35 **Litho.** ***Perf. 12½***
535 A123 2c gray brn, type I .25 .25
a. 2c brown, type II .25 .25
536 A123 5c car, type II .25 .25
537 A123 8c lt ultra, type II .25 .25
Nos. 535-537,C33-C35 (6) 4.70 2.45

Discus Thrower A124

1935, Mar. 16 **Engr.** **Unwmk.**
538 A124 5c carmine 3.00 2.25
539 A124 8c blue 3.25 2.75
540 A124 10c orange yel 4.50 3.00
541 A124 15c bister 4.50 3.25
542 A124 37c green 6.00 4.50
Nos. 538-542,C36-C40 (10) 64.75 38.50

3rd Central American Games.

Same Overprinted in Black

1935, June 27
543 A124 5c carmine 5.00 3.00
544 A124 8c blue 7.00 3.00
545 A124 10c orange yel 7.00 3.50
546 A124 15c bister 7.00 3.50
547 A124 37c green 12.00 5.50
Nos. 543-547,C41-C45 (10) 71.50 42.70

Flag of El Salvador — A125

1935, Oct. 26 **Litho.** **Wmk. 240**
548 A125 1c gray blue .30 .25
549 A125 2c black brn .30 .25
550 A125 3c plum .30 .25
551 A125 5c rose carmine .45 .25
552 A125 8c ultra .45 .25
553 A125 15c fawn .60 .45
Nos. 548-553,C46 (7) 2.80 2.05

Tree of San Vicente — A126

Numerals in Black, Tree in Yellow Green

1935, Dec. 26
554 A126 2c black brn .85 .45
555 A126 3c dk blue grn .85 .45
556 A126 5c rose red .85 .45
557 A126 8c dark blue .85 .55
558 A126 15c brown .60 .45
Nos. 554-558,C47-C51 (10) 7.75 5.35

Tercentenary of San Vicente.

Volcano of Izalco — A127

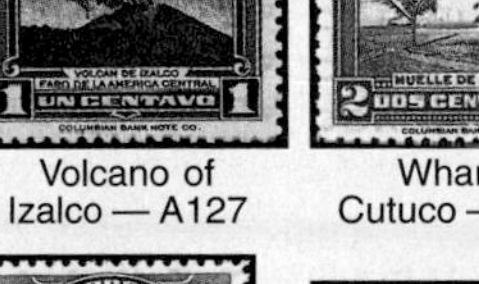

Wharf at Cutuco — A128

Doroteo Vasconcelos A129

Parade Ground A130

Dr. Tomás G. Palomo — A131

Sugar Mill — A132

Coffee at Pier — A133

Gathering Balsam — A134

Pres. Manuel E. Araujo — A135

1935, Dec. **Engr.** **Unwmk.**
559 A127 1c deep violet .25 .25
560 A128 2c chestnut .25 .25
561 A129 3c green .25 .25
562 A130 5c carmine .60 .25
563 A131 8c dull blue .25 .25
564 A132 10c orange .60 .25
565 A133 15c dk olive bis .60 .25
566 A134 50c indigo 3.00 1.75
567 A135 1col black 7.50 4.50
Nos. 559-567 (9) 13.30 8.00

Paper has faint imprint "El Salvador" on face.
For surcharges and overprint see Nos. 568-570, 573, 583-584, C52.

Stamps of 1935 Surcharged with New Value in Black

1938 ***Perf. 12½***
568 A130 1c on 5c carmine .25 .25
569 A132 3c on 10c orange .25 .25
570 A133 8c on 15c dk ol bis .30 .25
Nos. 568-570 (3) .80 .75

No. 486 Surcharged with New Value in Red

1938 ***Perf. 11½***
571 A102 3c on 5c blue .30 .25

Centenary of the death of José Simeón Cañas, liberator of slaves in Latin America.

Map and Flags of US and El Salvador — A136

Engraved and Lithographed

1938, Apr. 21 ***Perf. 12***
572 A136 8c multicolored .95 .70

US Constitution, 150th anniv. See #C61.

No. 560 Surcharged with New Value in Black

1938 ***Perf. 12½***
573 A128 1c on 2c chestnut .25 .25

Indian Sugar Mill — A137

Designs: 2c, Indian women washing. 3c, Indian girl at spring. 5c, Indian plowing. 8c, Izote flower. 10c, Champion cow. 20c,

Extracting balsam. 50c, Maquilishuat in bloom. 1col, Post Office, San Salvador.

1938-39 Engr. *Perf. 12*

No.	Type	Description	Unused	Used
574	A137	1c dark violet	.25	.25
575	A137	2c dark green	.25	.25
576	A137	3c dark brown	.30	.25
577	A137	5c scarlet	.30	.25
578	A137	8c dark blue	2.00	.25
579	A137	10c yel org ('39)	3.00	.25
580	A137	20c bis brn ('39)	2.75	.25
581	A137	50c dull blk ('39)	3.25	.70
582	A137	1col black ('39)	3.00	1.00
		Nos. 574-582 (9)	15.10	3.45

For surcharges & overprints see Nos. 591-592, C96.

Nos. 566-567, 504 Surcharged in Red

1939, Sept. 25 *Perf. 12½, 14*

No.	Type	Description	Unused	Used
583	A134	8c on 50c indigo	.45	.25
584	A135	10c on 1col blk	.80	.25
585	A116	50c on 1col grn & vio	4.50	3.25
		Nos. 583-585 (3)	5.75	3.75

Battle of San Pedro Perulapán, 100th anniv.

Sir Rowland Hill — A146

1940, Mar. 1 *Perf. 12½*

No.	Type	Description	Unused	Used
586	A146	8c dk bl, lt bl & blk	6.00	2.00
		Nos. 586,C69-C70 (3)	36.50	22.00

Postage stamp centenary.

Statue of Christ and San Salvador Cathedral — A147

A148

Wmk. 269

1942, Nov. 23 Engr. *Perf. 14*

No.	Type	Description	Unused	Used
587	A147	8c deep blue	.80	.25

Souvenir Sheet

Imperf

Without Gum

Lilac Tinted Paper

No.	Type	Description	Unused	Used
588	A148	Sheet of 4	25.00	22.00
a.		8c deep blue	10.00	10.00
b.		30c red orange	10.00	10.00

Nos. 587-588 commemorate the first Eucharistic Congress of Salvador. See No. C85.

No. 588 contains two No. 587 and two No. C85, imperf.

Catalogue values for unused stamps in this section, from this point to the end of the section, are for Never Hinged items.

Cuscatlán Bridge, Pan-American Highway — A149

Arms Overprint at Right in Carmine

Perf. 12½

1944, Nov. 24 Unwmk. Engr.

No.	Type	Description	Unused	Used
589	A149	8c dk blue & blk	.40	.25

See No. C92.

Gen. Juan José Canas — A150

1945, June 9

No.	Type	Description	Unused	Used
590	A150	8c blue	.60	.25

No. 575 Surcharged in Black

a

b

1944-46

No.	Type	Description	Unused	Used
591	A137(a)	1(c) on 2c dk grn	.30	.25
592	A137(b)	1(c) on 2c dk grn ('46)	.30	.25

Lake of Ilopango A151

Ceiba Tree A152

Water Carriers — A153

1946-47 Litho. Wmk. 240

No.	Type	Description	Unused	Used
593	A151	1c blue ('47)	.40	.25
594	A152	2c lt bl grn ('47)	.45	.25
595	A153	5c carmine	.40	.25
		Nos. 593-595 (3)	1.25	.75

Isidro Menéndez A154

2c, Cristano Salazar. 3c, Juan Bertis. 5c, Francisco Duenas. 8c, Ramon Belloso. 10c, Jose Presentacion Trigueros. 20c, Salvador Rodriguez Gonzalez. 50c, Francisco Castaneda. 1col, David Castro.

1947 Unwmk. Engr. *Perf. 12*

No.	Type	Description	Unused	Used
596	A154	1c car rose	.25	.25
597	A154	2c dp org	.25	.25
598	A154	3c violet	.25	.25
599	A154	5c slate gray	.25	.25
600	A154	8c dp bl	.25	.25
601	A154	10c bis brn	.25	.25
602	A154	20c green	.45	.25
603	A154	50c black	1.10	.35
604	A154	1col scarlet	2.25	.50
		Nos. 596-604 (9)	5.30	2.60

For surcharges and overprints see Nos. 621-626, 634, C118-C120, O362-O368.

Manuel José Arce — A163

1948, Feb. 25 *Perf. 12½*

No.	Type	Description	Unused	Used
605	A163	8c deep blue	.45	.25
		Nos. 605,C108-C110 (4)	4.40	2.75

President Roosevelt Presenting Awards for Distinguished Service — A164

President Franklin D. Roosevelt A165

A166

Designs: 8c, Pres. and Mrs. Roosevelt. 15c, Mackenzie King, Roosevelt and Winston Churchill. 20c, Roosevelt and Cordell Hull. 50c, Funeral of Pres. Roosevelt.

1948, Apr. 12

Various Frames; Center in Black

No.	Type	Description	Unused	Used
606	A164	5c dk bl	.25	.25
607	A164	8c green	.25	.25
608	A165	12c violet	.25	.25
609	A164	15c vermilion	.45	.25
610	A164	20c car lake	.45	.25
611	A164	50c gray	1.10	.70
		Nos. 606-611,C111-C116 (12)	10.65	6.60

Souvenir Sheet

Perf. 13½

No.	Type	Description	Unused	Used
612	A166	1col ol grn & brn	4.00	2.25

3rd anniv. of the death of F. D. Roosevelt.

Torch and Winged Letter A167

Perf. 12½

1949, Oct. 9 Unwmk. Engr.

No.	Type	Description	Unused	Used
613	A167	8c blue	1.10	.55
		Nos. 613,C122-C124 (4)	26.55	18.55

75th anniv. of the UPU.

Workman and Soldier Holding Torch — A168

1949, Dec. 15 Litho. *Perf. 10½*

No.	Type	Description	Unused	Used
614	A168	8c blue	.45	.45
		Nos. 614,C125-C129 (6)	9.85	7.25

Revolution of Dec. 14, 1948, 1st anniv.

Wreath and Open Book — A169

Wreath in Dark Green

Perf. 11½

1952, Feb. 14 Photo. Unwmk.

No.	Type	Description	Unused	Used
615	A169	1c yel grn	.25	.25
616	A169	2c magenta	.25	.25
617	A169	5c brn red	.25	.25
618	A169	10c yellow	.25	.25
619	A169	20c gray grn	.25	.25
620	A169	1col dp car	1.50	1.00
		Nos. 615-620,C134-C141 (14)	11.75	8.00

Constitution of 1950.

Nos. 598, 600 and 603 Surcharged with New Values in Various Colors

1952-53 *Perf. 12½*

No.	Type	Description	Unused	Used
621	A154	2c on 3c vio (C)	.25	.25
622	A154	2c on 8c dp bl (C)	.25	.25
623	A154	3c on 8c dp bl (G)	.25	.25
624	A154	5c on 8c dp bl (O)	.25	.25
625	A154	7c on 8c dp bl (Bk)	.25	.25
626	A154	10c on 50c blk (O) ('53)	.25	.25
		Nos. 621-626 (6)	1.50	1.50

Nos. C106 and C107 Surcharged in Various Colors

1952-53 Wmk. 240

No.	Type	Description	Unused	Used
627	AP31	2c on 12c choc (Bl)	.25	.25
628	AP32	2c on 14c dk bl (R) ('53)	.25	.25
629	AP31	5c on 12c choc (Bl)	.25	.25
630	AP32	10c on 14c dk bl (C)	.25	.25
		Nos. 627-630 (4)	1.00	1.00

José Marti — A170

Perf. 10½

1953, Feb. 27 Litho. Unwmk.

631 A170 1c rose red .25 .25
632 A170 2c bl grn .25 .25
633 A170 10c dk vio .30 .25
Nos. 631-633,C142-C144 (6) 3.05 1.85

José Marti, Cuban patriot, birth cent.

No. 598 Overprinted in Carmine

1953, June 19 *Perf. 12½*

634 A154 3c violet .25 .25

4th Pan-American Congress of Social Medicine, San Salvador, April 16-19, 1953. See #C146.

Signing of Act of Independence A171

1953, Sept. 15 Litho. *Perf. 11½*

635 A171 1c rose pink .25 .25
636 A171 2c dp bl grn .25 .25
637 A171 3c purple .25 .25
638 A171 5c dp bl .25 .25
639 A171 7c lt brn .25 .25
640 A171 10c ocher .25 .25
641 A171 20c dp org .70 .25
642 A171 50c green .95 .30
643 A171 1col gray 1.90 1.25
Nos. 635-643,C147-C150 (13) 7.10 4.75

Act of Independence, Sept. 15, 1821.

A172

Portrait: 1c, 2c, 5c, 20c: Capt. Gen. Gerardo Barrios. 3c, 7c, 10c, 22c: Francisco Morazan, (facing left).

Overprinted in Black

1953, Dec. 1 *Perf. 11½*

644 A172 1c green .25 .25
645 A172 2c blue .25 .25
646 A172 3c green .25 .25
647 A172 5c carmine .25 .25
648 A172 7c blue .25 .25
649 A172 10c carmine .30 .25
650 A172 20c violet .40 .25
651 A172 22c violet .60 .25
Nos. 644-651 (8) 2.55 2.00

The overprint "C de C" is a control indicating "Tribunal of Accounts." A double entry of this overprint occurs twice in each sheet of each denomination.
For overprint see No. 729.

Coastal Bridge A173

Motherland and Liberty A174

Census Allegory — A175

Balboa Park — A176

Designs: Nos. 654, 655, National Palace. Nos. 659, 665, Izalco Volcano. Nos. 660, 661, Guayabo dam. No. 666, Lake Ilopango. No. 669, Housing development. Nos. 670, 673, Coast guard boat. No. 671, Modern highway.

Perf. 11½

1954, June 1 Unwmk. Photo.

652 A173 1c car rose & brn .25 .25
653 AP43 1c ol & bl gray .25 .25
654 A173 1c pur & pale lil .25 .25
655 A173 2c yel grn & lt gray .25 .25
656 A174 2c car lake .25 .25
657 A175 2c org red .25 .25
658 AP44 3c maroon .25 .25
659 A173 3c bl grn & bl .25 .25
660 A174 3c dk gray & vio .25 .25
661 A174 5c red vio & vio .25 .25
662 AP44 5c emerald .25 .25
663 A176 7c magenta & buff .25 .25
664 AP43 7c bl grn & gray bl .25 .25
665 A173 7c org brn & org .25 .25
666 A173 10c car lake .25 .25
667 AP46 10c red, dk brn & bl .25 .25
668 A174 10c dk bl grn .25 .25
669 A174 20c org & cr .30 .25
670 A173 22c gray vio .30 .25
671 A176 50c dk gray & brn .85 .35
672 AP46 1col brn org, dk brn & bl 1.50 .90
673 A173 1col brt bl 1.50 .90
Nos. 652-673 (22) 8.70 6.90
Nos. 652-673,C151-C165 (37) 22.10 13.75

For surcharges & overprints see #692-693, 736, C193.

Capt. Gen. Gerardo Barrios — A177

Wmk. 269

1955, Dec. 20 Engr. *Perf. 12½*

674 A177 1c red .25 .25
675 A177 2c yel grn .35 .30
676 A177 3c vio bl .35 .30
677 A177 20c violet .50 .30
Nos. 674-677,C166-C167 (6) 2.15 1.80

Coffee Picker — A178

Perf. 13½

1956, June 20 Litho. Unwmk.

678 A178 3c bis brn .25 .25
679 A178 5c red org .25 .25
680 A178 10c dk bl .25 .25
681 A178 2col dk red 1.90 1.25
Nos. 678-681,C168-C172 (9) 8.85 5.80

Centenary of Santa Ana Department.
For overprint see No. C187.

Map of Chalatenango — A179

1956, Sept. 14

682 A179 2c blue .25 .25
683 A179 7c rose red .45 .30
684 A179 50c yel brn .70 .45
Nos. 682-684,C173-C178 (9) 4.30 3.35

Centenary of Chalatenango Department (in 1955).
For surcharge see No. 694.

Coat of Arms of Nueva San Salvador — A180

Wmk. 269

1957, Jan. 3 Engr. *Perf. 12½*

685 A180 1c rose red .25 .25
686 A180 2c green .25 .25
687 A180 3c violet .25 .25
688 A180 7c red org .45 .25
689 A180 10c ultra .25 .25
690 A180 50c pale brn .55 .25
691 A180 1col dl red .80 .75
Nos. 685-691,C179-C183 (12) 7.10 4.75

Centenary of the founding of the city of Nueva San Salvador (Santa Tecla).
For surcharges and overprints see Nos. 695-696, 706, 713, C194-C195, C197-C199.

Nos. 664-665, 683 and 688 Surcharged with New Value in Black

1957 Unwmk. Photo. *Perf. 11½*

692 A173 6c on 7c bl grn & gray bl .30 .30
693 A173 6c on 7c org brn & org .30 .30

1957 Litho. *Perf. 13½*

694 A179 6c on 7c rose red .25 .25

Wmk. 269

1957-58 Engr. *Perf. 12½*

695 A180 5c on 7c red org ('58) .25 .25
696 A180 6c on 7c red org .30 .25
Nos. 692-696 (5) 1.40 1.35

El Salvador Intercontinental Hotel — A181

Perf. 11½

1958, June 28 Unwmk. Photo.

Granite Paper

Vignette in Green, Dark Blue & Red

697 A181 3c brown .25 .25
698 A181 6c crim rose .25 .25
699 A181 10c brt bl .25 .25
700 A181 15c brt grn .25 .25
701 A181 20c lilac .30 .25
702 A181 30c brt yel grn .40 .25
Nos. 697-702 (6) 1.70 1.50

Presidents Eisenhower and Lemus and Flags — A182

1959, Dec. 14 Granite Paper

Design in Ultramarine, Dark Brown, Light Brown and Red

703 A182 3c pink .25 .25
704 A182 6c green .25 .25
705 A182 10c crimson .30 .25
Nos. 703-705,C184-C186 (6) 1.60 1.50

Visit of Pres. José M. Lemus of El Salvador to the US, Mar. 9-21.

No. 686 Ovptd.: "5 Enero 1960 XX Aniversario Fundacion Sociedad Filatelica de El Salvador"

1960 Wmk. 269 Engr. *Perf. 12½*

706 A180 2c green .25 .25

Philatelic Association of El Salvador, 20th anniv.

Apartment Houses A183

1960 Unwmk. Photo. *Perf. 11½*

Multicolored Centers; Granite Paper

707 A183 10c scarlet .25 .25
708 A183 15c brt pur .25 .25
709 A183 25c brt yel grn .30 .25
710 A183 30c Prus bl .35 .25
711 A183 40c olive .55 .40
712 A183 80c dk bl .95 .90
Nos. 707-712 (6) 2.65 2.30

Issued to publicize the erection of multifamily housing projects in 1958.
For surcharges see Nos. 730, 733.

No. 686 Surcharged with New Value

1960 Wmk. 269 Engr. *Perf. 12½*

713 A180 1c on 2c grn .25 .25

Poinsettia — A184

Perf. 11½

1960, Dec. Unwmk. Photo.

Granite Paper

Design in Slate Green, Red and Yellow

714 A184 3c yellow .25 .25
715 A184 6c salmon .25 .25
716 A184 10c grnsh bl .30 .25
717 A184 15c pale vio bl .30 .25
Nos. 714-717,C188-C191 (8) 3.40 2.30

Miniature Sheet

718 A184 40c silver 8.00 8.00
a. Ovptd. in sheet margin ('61) *16.00 16.00*
b. Ovptd. in sheet margin ('61) *16.00 16.00*
c. Ovptd. in sheet margin ('62) *16.00 16.00*
d. Ovptd. in sheet margin ('63) *16.00 16.00*
e. Ovptd. in sheet margin ('63) *16.00 16.00*
f. Ovptd. in sheet margin ('63) *16.00 16.00*

Overprints in sheet margin of No. 718:
a, PRIMERA CONVENCION FILATELICA / CENTRO-AMERICANA / SAN SALVADOR, JULIO DE 1961.
b, in purple, Portrait, dates and text commemorating the Death of General Barrios, 96th anniv.
c, in green, Arms of city of Ahuachapan and PRIMER CENTENARIO / Ciudad de Ahuachapan / 1862 22 de Febrero 1962.
d, in blue, Soccer players and text commemorating the 1st North & Central American Soccer Championships 24 March - 2 April, 1963.
e, in blue and green, emblem of Alliance for Progress and text commemorating the 2nd anniversary of the organization.
f, in green, Portrait of Dr. Manuel Araujo and College Arms with text commemorating the 4th Latin American Cong. of Pathological Anatomy and 10th Central American Medical Cong., Dec., 1963.
For surcharge see No. C196.

Fathers Nicolas, Vicente and Manuel Aguilar A185

Parish Church, San Salvador, 1808
A186

Designs: 5c, 6c, Manuel José Arce, José Matias Delgado and Juan Manuel Rodriguez. 10c, 20c, Pedro Pablo Castillo, Domingo Antonio de Lara and Santiago José Celis. 50c, 80c, Monument to the Fathers, Plaza Libertad.

Perf. 11½

1961, Nov. 5 Unwmk. Photo.

719 A185 1c gray & dk brn .25 .25
720 A185 2c rose & dk brn .25 .25
721 A185 5c pale brn & dk ol grn .25 .25
722 A185 6c brt pink & dk brn .25 .25
723 A185 10c bl & dk brn .25 .25
724 A185 20c vio & dk brn .30 .25
725 A186 30c brt bl & vio .40 .25
726 A186 40c brn org & sep .50 .25
727 A186 50c bl grn & sep .75 .40
728 A186 80c gray & ultra 1.25 .75
Nos. 719-728 (10) 4.45 3.15

Sesquicentennial of the first cry for Independence in Central America.

For surcharges and overprints see Nos. 731-732, 734-735, 737, 760, 769, 776.

No. 651 Ovptd.: "III Exposición Industrial Centroamericana Diciembre de 1962"

1962, Dec. 21 Litho. ***Perf. 11½***

729 A172 22c violet .40 .25
Nos. 729,C193-C195 (4) 4.15 2.65

3rd Central American Industrial Exposition.

Nos. 708, 726-728 and 673 Surcharged

1962-63 Photo.

730 A183 6c on 15c ('63) .30 .25
731 A186 6c on 40c ('63) .30 .25
732 A186 6c on 50c ('63) .30 .25
733 A183 10c on 15c .40 .25
734 A186 10c on 50c ('63) .40 .25
735 A186 10c on 80c ('63) .40 .25
736 A173 10c on 1col ('63) .40 .25
Nos. 730-736 (7) 2.50 1.75

Surcharge includes bars on Nos. 731-734, 736; dot on Nos. 730, 735.

No. 726 Ovptd. in Arc: "CAMPAÑA MUNDIAL CONTRA EL HAMBRE"

1963, Mar. 21

737 A186 40c brn org & sepia .95 .50

FAO "Freedom from Hunger" campaign.

Coyote
A187

2c, Spider monkey, vert. 3c, Raccoon. 5c, King vulture, vert. 6c, Brown coati. 10c, Kinkajou.

1963 Photo. ***Perf. 11½***

738 A187 1c lil, blk, ocher & brn .75 .25
739 A187 2c lt grn & blk .75 .25
740 A187 3c fawn, dk brn & buff .75 .25
741 A187 5c gray grn, ind, red & buff .75 .25
742 A187 6c rose lil, blk, brn & buff .75 .25
743 A187 10c lt bl, brn & buff .75 .25
Nos. 738-743,C200-C207 (14) 35.50 9.45

Christ on Globe — A188

1964-65 ***Perf. 12x11½***

744 A188 6c bl & brn .25 .25
745 A188 10c bl & bis .25 .25
Nos. 744-745,C208-C209 (4) 1.00 1.00

Miniature Sheets

Imperf

746 A188 60c bl & brt pur 1.60 1.25
a. Marginal ovpt. La Union 1.25 1.25
b. Marginal ovpt. Usulutan 1.25 1.25
c. Marginal ovpt. La Libertad 2.50 2.50

2nd Natl. Eucharistic Cong., San Salvador, Apr. 16-19.

Nos. 746a, 746b and 746c commemorate the centenaries of the Departments of La Union, Usulután and La Libertad.

Issued: #744-746, Apr. 16, 1964; #746a-746b, June 22, 1965; #746c, Jan. 28, 1965.

See #C210. For overprints see #C232, C238.

Pres. John F. Kennedy
A189

Perf. 11½x12

1964, Nov. 22 Unwmk.

747 A189 6c buff & blk .25 .25
748 A189 10c tan & blk .25 .25
749 A189 50c pink & blk .50 .25
Nos. 747-749,C211-C213 (6) 1.80 1.50

For overprints & surcharge see #798, 843.

Miniature Sheet

Imperf

750 A189 70c dp grn & blk 1.60 1.25
a. Overprinted in sheet margin in red brown ('69) 4.50 4.50

President John F. Kennedy (1917-1963).

Overprint on No. 750a reads: "Alunizaja / Apolo-11 / 21 Julio / 1969" and includes pictures of the landing module and astronauts.

Water Lily — A190

1965, Jan. 6 Photo. ***Perf. 12x11½***

751 A190 3c shown .30 .25
752 A190 5c Maquilishuat .30 .25
753 A190 6c Cinco negritos .40 .25
754 A190 30c Hortensia 1.25 .25
755 A190 50c Maguey 1.60 .25
756 A190 60c Geranium 1.60 .25
Nos. 751-756,C215-C220 (12) 12.60 3.05

For overprints and surcharges see Nos. 779, C243, C348-C349.

ICY Emblem
A191

1965, Apr. 27 Photo. ***Perf. 11½x12***

Design in Brown and Gold

757 A191 5c dp yel .25 .25
758 A191 6c dp rose .25 .25
759 A191 10c gray .25 .25
Nos. 757-759,C221-C223 (6) 1.55 1.50

International Cooperation Year.

For overprints see #764, 780, C227, C244, C312.

No. 728 Ovptd. in Red: "Ier. Centenario Muerte / Cap. Gral. Gerardo Barrios / 1865 1965 / 29 de Agosto"

1965 Unwmk. ***Perf. 11½***

760 A186 80c gray & ultra .65 .50
a. "Garl." instead of "Gral." 1.00 1.00

Capt. Gen. Gerardo Barrios, death cent.

Gavidia
A192

Perf. 11½x12

1965, Sept. 24 Photo. Unwmk.

Portrait in Natural Colors

761 A192 2c blk & rose vio .25 .25
762 A192 3c blk & org .25 .25
763 A192 6c blk & lt ultra .25 .25
Nos. 761-763,C224-C226 (6) 2.40 1.65

Francisco Antonio Gavidia, philosopher.

For surcharges see Nos. 852-853.

No. 759 Ovptd. in Carmine: "1865 / 12 de Octubre / 1965 / Dr. Manuel Enrique Araujo"

1965, Oct. 12

764 A191 10c brn, gray & gold .25 .25

Centenary of the birth of Manuel Enrique Araujo, president of Salvador, 1911-1913. See No. C227.

Fair Emblem — A193

1965, Nov. 5 Photo. ***Perf. 12x11½***

765 A193 6c yel & multi .25 .25
766 A193 10c multi .25 .25
767 A193 20c pink & multi .25 .25
Nos. 765-767,C228-C230 (6) 4.30 3.20

Intl. Fair of El Salvador, Nov. 5-Dec. 4.

For overprints and surcharge see Nos. 784, C246, C311, C323.

WHO Headquarters, Geneva — A194

1966, May 20 Photo. Unwmk.

768 A194 15c beige & multi .25 .25

Inauguration of WHO Headquarters, Geneva. See No. C231. For overprints and surcharges see Nos. 778, 783, 864, C242, C245, C322.

No. 728 Ovptd. in Red: "Mes de Conmemoracion / Civica de la Independencia / Centroamericana / 19 Sept. / 1821 1966"

1966, Sept. 19 Photo. ***Perf. 11½***

769 A186 80c gray & ultra .40 .40

Month of civic commemoration of Central American independence.

UNESCO Emblem
A195

1966, Nov. 4 Unwmk. ***Perf. 12***

770 A195 20c gray, blk & vio bl .25 .25
771 A195 1col emer, blk & vio bl .80 .30
Nos. 770-771,C233-C234 (4) 2.90 1.80

20th anniv. of UNESCO.

For surcharges see Nos. 853A, C352.

Map of Central America, Flags and Cogwheels
A196

1966, Nov. 27 Litho. ***Perf. 12***

772 A196 6c multi .25 .25
773 A196 10c multi .25 .25
Nos. 772-773,C235-C237 (5) 1.50 1.35

2nd Intl. Fair of El Salvador, Nov. 5-27.

José Simeon Cañas Pleading for Indian Slaves — A197

1967, Feb. 18 Litho. ***Perf. 11½***

774 A197 6c yel & multi .25 .25
775 A197 10c lil rose & multi .25 .25
Nos. 774-775,C239-C240 (4) 1.30 1.10

Father José Simeon Cañas y Villacorta, D.D. (1767-1838), emancipator of the Central American slaves.

For surcharges see #841A-842, 891, C403-C405.

No. 726 Ovptd. in Red: "XV Convención de Clubes / de Leones, Región de / El Salvador-11 y 12 / de Marzo de 1967"

1967 Photo.

776 A186 40c brn org & sepia .40 .25

Issued to publicize the 15th Convention of Lions Clubs of El Salvador, March 11-12.

Volcano San Miguel
A198

1967, Apr. 14 Photo. ***Perf. 13***

777 A198 70c lt rose lilac & brn 1.00 .60

Centenary of stamps of El Salvador.

See No. C241. For surcharges see Nos. 841, C320, C350.

No. 768 Ovptd. in Red: "VIII CONGRESO / CENTROAMERICANO DE / FARMACIA Y BIOQUIMICA / 5 di 11 Noviembre de 1967"

1967, Oct. 26 Photo. ***Perf. 12x11½***

778 A194 15c multi .25 .25

8th Central American Congress for Pharmacy and Biochemistry. See No. C242.

No. 751 Ovptd. in Red: "I Juegos / Centroamericanos y del / Caribe de Basquetbol / 25 Nov. al 3 Dic. 1967"

1967, Nov. 15

779 A190 3c dl grn, brn, yel & org .25 .25

First Central American and Caribbean Basketball Games, 11/25-12/3. See #C243.

No. 757 Ovptd. in Carmine: "1968 / AÑO INTERNACIONAL DE / LOS DERECHOS HUMANOS"

1968, Jan. 2 Photo. ***Perf. 11½x12***

780 A191 5c dp yel, brn & gold .25 .25

Intl. Human Rights Year. See #C244.

Weather Map, Satellite and WMO Emblem
A199

1968, Mar. 25 Photo. ***Perf. 11½x12***

781 A199 1c multi .25 .25
782 A199 30c multi .30 .25

World Meteorological Day, Mar. 25.

No. 768 Ovptd. in Red: "1968 / XX ANIVERSARIO DE LA / ORGANIZACION MUNDIAL / DE LA SALUD"

1968, Apr. 7 *Perf. 12x11½*
783 A194 15c multi .25 .25

20th anniv. of WHO. See No. C245.

No. 765 Ovptd. in Red: "1968 / Año / del Sistema / del Crédito / Rural"

1968, May 6 Photo. *Perf. 12x11½*
784 A193 6c yellow & multi .25 .25

Rural credit system. See No. C246.

Alberto Masferrer A200

1968, June 22 Litho. *Perf. 12x11½*
785 A200 2c multi .25 .25
786 A200 6c multi .25 .25
787 A200 25c vio & multi .30 .25
Nos. 785-787,C247-C248 (5) 1.30 1.25

Centenary of the birth of Alberto Masferrer, philosopher and scholar.
For surcharges and overprints see Nos. 819, 843A, 890, C297.

Scouts Helping to Build — A201

1968, July 26 Litho. *Perf. 12*
788 A201 25c multi .25 .25

Issued to publicize the 7th Inter-American Boy Scout Conference, July-Aug., 1968.
See No. C249.

Map of Central America, Flags and Presidents of US, Costa Rica, Salvador, Guatemala, Honduras and Nicaragua — A202

1968, Dec. 5 Litho. *Perf. 14½*
789 A202 10c tan & multi .25 .25
790 A202 15c multi .25 .25
Nos. 789-790,C250-C251 (4) 1.50 1.25

Meeting of Pres. Lyndon B. Johnson with the presidents of the Central American republics (J. J. Trejos, Costa Rica; Fidel Sanchez Hernandez, Salvador; J. C. Mendez Montenegro, Guatemala; Osvaldo López Arellano, Honduras; Anastasio Somoza Debayle, Nicaragua), San Salvador, July 5-8, 1968.

Heliconius Charithonius — A203

Various Butterflies.

1969 Litho. *Perf. 12*
791 A203 5c bluish lil, blk & yel 7.25 .25
792 A203 10c beige & multi 7.25 .25
793 A203 30c lt grn & multi 7.25 .35
794 A203 50c tan & multi 7.25 .55
Nos. 791-794,C252-C255 (8) 78.25 9.65

For surcharge see No. C353.

Red Cross Activities A204

1969 Litho. *Perf. 12*
795 A204 10c lt bl & multi .25 .25
796 A204 20c pink & multi .25 .25
797 A204 40c lil & multi .35 .25
Nos. 795-797,C256-C258 (6) 6.60 4.00

50th anniv. of the League of Red Cross Societies.

No. 749 Ovptd. in Green "Alunizaje / Apolo-11 / 21 Julio / 1969"

1969, Sept. Photo. *Perf. 11½x12*
798 A189 50c pink & blk .55 .30

Man's first landing on the moon, July 20, 1969. See note after US No. C76.
See No. C259.

Social Security Hospital A205

1969, Oct. 24 Litho. *Perf. 11½*
799 A205 6c multi .25 .25
800 A205 10c multi, diff. .25 .25
801 A205 30c multi, diff. .30 .25
Nos. 799-801,C260-C262 (6) 7.50 4.75

For surcharges see Nos. 857, C355.

ILO Emblem — A206

1969 Litho. *Perf. 13*
802 A206 10c yel & multi .25 .25

50th anniv. of the ILO. See No. C263.

Chorros Spa A207

Views: 40c, Jaltepeque Bay. 80c, Fountains, Amapulapa Spa.

1969, Dec. 19 Photo. *Perf. 12x11½*
803 A207 10c blk & multi .25 .25
804 A207 40c blk & multi .25 .25
805 A207 80c blk & multi .55 .40
Nos. 803-805,C264-C266 (6) 1.95 1.70

Tourism.

Euchroma Gigantea — A208

Insects: 25c, Grasshopper. 30c, Digger wasp.

1970, Feb. 24 Litho. *Perf. 11½x11*
806 A208 5c lt bl & multi .40 .25
807 A208 25c dl yel & multi .75 .25
808 A208 30c dl rose & multi .75 .25
Nos. 806-808,C267-C269 (6) 14.40 5.50

For surcharges see Nos. C371-C373.

Map and Arms of Salvador, National Unity Emblem A209

1970, Apr. 14 Litho. *Perf. 14*
809 A209 10c yel & multi .25 .25
810 A209 40c pink & multi .40 .25
Nos. 809-810,C270-C271 (4) 1.70 1.05

Salvador's support of universal human rights. For overprints and surcharge see Nos. 823, C301, C402.

Soldiers with Flag A210

Design: 30c, Anti-aircraft gun.

1970, May 7 *Perf. 12*
811 A210 10c green & multi .25 .25
812 A210 30c lemon & multi .25 .25
Nos. 811-812,C272-C274 (5) 1.50 1.25

Issued for Army Day, May 7.
For overprints see Nos. 836, C310.

National Lottery Headquarters A211

1970, July 15 Litho. *Perf. 12*
813 A211 20c lt vio & multi .25 .25

National Lottery centenary. See No. C291.

UN and Education Year Emblems A212

1970, Sept. 11 Litho. *Perf. 12*
814 A212 50c multi .40 .25
815 A212 1col multi .80 .40
Nos. 814-815,C292-C293 (4) 3.05 1.70

Issued for International Education Year.

Map of Salvador, Globe and Cogwheels A213

1970, Oct. 28 Litho. *Perf. 12*
816 A213 5c pink & multi .25 .25
817 A213 10c buff & multi .25 .25
Nos. 816-817,C294-C295 (4) 1.05 1.00

4th International Fair, San Salvador.

Beethoven — A214

1971, Feb. 22 Litho. *Perf. 13½*
818 A214 50c ol, brn & yel .85 .25

Second International Music Festival. See No. C296. For overprint see No. 833.

No. 787 Ovptd. "Año / del Centenario de la / Biblioteca Nacional / 1970"

1970, Nov. 25 *Perf. 12x11½*
819 A200 25c vio & multi .25 .25

Cent. of the National Library. See No. C297.

Maria Elena Sol — A215

1971, Apr. 1 Litho. *Perf. 14*
820 A215 10c lt grn & multi .25 .25
821 A215 30c multi .30 .25
Nos. 820-821,C298-C299 (4) 1.35 1.05

Maria Elena Sol, Miss World Tourism, 1970-71. For overprint see No. 832.

Pietà, by Michelangelo A216

1971, May 10
822 A216 10c salmon & vio brn .25 .25

Mother's Day, 1971. See No. C300.

No. 810 Overprinted in Red

1971, July 6 Litho. *Perf. 14*
823 A209 40c pink & multi .60 .25

National Police, 104th anniv. See #C301.

Tiger Sharks — A217

1971, July 28

824 A217 10c shown 1.40 .30
825 A217 40c Swordfish 1.75 .35
Nos. 824-825,C302-C303 (4) 8.75 2.10

Declaration of Independence — A218

Designs: Various sections of Declaration of Independence of Central America.

1971 ***Perf. 13½x13***

826 A218 5c yel grn & blk .25 .25
827 A218 10c brt rose & blk .25 .25
828 A218 15c dp org & blk .25 .25
829 A218 20c dp red lil & blk .25 .25
Nos. 826-829,C304-C307 (8) 2.40 2.10

Sesquicentennial of independence of Central America.
For overprints see Nos. C321, C347.

Izalco Church A219

Design: 30c, Sonsonate Church.

1971, Aug. 21 **Litho.** ***Perf. 13x13½***

830 A219 20c blk & multi .25 .25
831 A219 30c pur & multi .30 .25
Nos. 830-831,C308-C309 (4) 1.35 1.10

No. 821 Ovptd. in Carmine: "1972 Año de Turismo / de las Américas"

1972, Nov. 15 **Litho.** ***Perf. 14***

832 A215 30c multi .35 .25

Tourist Year of the Americas, 1972.

No. 818 Overprinted in Red

1973, Feb. 5 **Litho.** ***Perf. 13½***

833 A214 50c ol, brn & yel .35 .25

3rd Intl. Music Festival, Feb. 9-25. See No. C313.

Lions International Emblem A220

1973, Feb. 20 **Litho.** ***Perf. 13***

834 A220 10c pink & multi .25 .25
835 A220 25c lt bl & multi .25 .25
Nos. 834-835,C314-C315 (4) 1.05 1.00

31st Lions International District "D" Convention, San Salvador, May 1972.

No. 812 Ovptd. "1923 1973 / 50 AÑOS FUNDACION / FUERZA AEREA"

1973, Mar. 20 **Litho.** ***Perf. 12***

836 A210 30c lem & multi .35 .25

50th anniversary of Salvadorian Air Force.

Hurdling A221

1973, May 21 **Litho.** ***Perf. 13***

837 A221 5c shown .25 .25
838 A221 10c High jump .25 .25
839 A221 25c Running .25 .25
840 A221 60c Pole vault .30 .25
Nos. 837-840,C316-C319 (8) 6.50 3.05

20th Olympic Games, Munich, Aug. 26-Sept. 11, 1972.

No. 777 Surcharged

1973, Dec. **Photo.** ***Perf. 13***

841 A198 10c on 70c multi .30 .25

See No. C320.

Nos. 774, C240 Srchd. with New Value and Ovptd. "1823-1973 / 150 Aniversario Liberación / Esclavos en Centroamérica"

1973-74 **Litho.** ***Perf. 11½***

841A A197 5c on 6c multi ('74) .25 .25
842 A197 10c on 45c multi .45 .25

Sesquicentennial of the liberation of the slaves in Central America. On No. 841A two bars cover old denomination. On No. 842 "Aereo" is obliterated with a bar and old denomination with two bars.

Nos. 747 and 786 Surcharged

1974 **Photo.** ***Perf. 11½x12***

843 A189 5c on 6c buff & blk .30 .25

Litho. ***Perf. 12x11½***

843A A200 5c on 6c multi .75 .25

No. 843A has one obliterating rectangle and sans-serif "5."
Issued: #843, Apr. 22; #843A, June 21.

Rehabilitation Institute Emblem A222

1974, Apr. 30 **Litho.** ***Perf. 13***

844 A222 10c multi .25 .25

10th anniversary of the Salvador Rehabilitation Institute. See No. C324.

INTERPOL Headquarters, Saint-Cloud, France — A223

1974, Sept. 2 **Litho.** ***Perf. 12½***

845 A223 10c multi .25 .25

50th anniv. of Intl. Criminal Police Organization (INTERPOL). See No. C341.

UN and FAO Emblems A224

1974, Sept. 2 **Litho.** ***Perf. 12½***

846 A224 10c bl, dk bl & gold .25 .25

World Food Program, 10th anniv. See #C342.

25c Silver Coin, 1914 A225

1974, Nov. 19 **Litho.** ***Perf. 12½x13***

848 A225 10c shown .25 .25
849 A225 15c 50c silver, 1953 .25 .25
850 A225 25c 25c silver, 1943 .25 .25
851 A225 30c 1c copper, 1892 .25 .25
Nos. 848-851,C343-C346 (8) 2.55 2.10

No. 763 Surcharged

1974, Oct. 14 **Photo.** ***Perf. 11½x12***

852 A192 5c on 6c multi .75 .25

12th Central American and Caribbean Chess Tournament, Oct. 1974.

No. 762 and 771 Surcharged

1974-75 ***Perf. 11½x12, 12***

853 A192 10c on 3c multi .35 .25
853A A195 25c on 1col multi ('75) .35 .25

Bar and surcharge on one line on No. 853A.
Issued: #853, Dec. 19; #853A, Jan. 13.

UPU Emblem A226

1975, Jan. 22 **Litho.** ***Perf. 13***

854 A226 10c bl & multi .25 .25
855 A226 60c bl & multi .35 .30
Nos. 854-855,C356-C357 (4) 1.10 1.05

Cent. of UPU.

Acajutla Harbor A227

1975, Feb. 17

856 A227 10c blue & multi .25 .25

See No. C358.

No. 799 Surcharged

1975 **Litho.** ***Perf. 11½***

857 A205 5c on 6c multi .35 .25

Central Post Office, San Salvador A228

1975, Apr. 25 **Litho.** ***Perf. 13***

858 A228 10c bl & multi .25 .25

See No. C359.

Map of Americas and El Salvador, Trophy A229

1975, June 25 **Litho.** ***Perf. 12½***

859 A229 10c red org & multi .25 .25
860 A229 40c yel & multi .30 .25
Nos. 859-860,C360-C361 (4) 1.35 1.15

El Salvador, site of 1975 Miss Universe Contest.

Claudia Lars, Poet, and IWY Emblem — A230

1975, Sept. 4 **Litho.** ***Perf. 12½***

861 A230 10c yel & bl blk .25 .25
Nos. 861,C362-C363 (3) .80 .75

Intl. Women's Year 1975.

Nurses Attending Patient A231

1975, Oct. 24 **Litho.** ***Perf. 12½***

862 A231 10c lt grn & multi .25 .25

Nurses' Day. See No. C364. For overprint see No. 868.

Congress Emblem — A232

1975, Nov. 19 **Litho.** ***Perf. 12½***

863 A232 10c yel & multi .25 .25

15th Conference of Inter-American Federation of Securities Enterprises, San Salvador, Nov. 16-20. See No. C365.

No. 768 Ovptd. in Red "XVI / CONGRESO MEDICO / CENTROAMERICANO / SAN SALVADOR, / EL SALVADOR, / DIC. 10-13, 1975"

1975, Nov. 26 Photo. ***Perf. 12x11½***

864 A194 15c beige & multi .35 .25

16th Central American Medical Congress, San Salvador, Dec. 10-13.

Flags of Participants, Arms of Salvador A233

1975, Nov. 28 Litho. ***Perf. 12½***

865 A233 15c blk & multi .25 .25
866 A233 50c brn & multi .30 .25
Nos. 865-866,C366-C367 (4) 1.05 1.00

8th Ibero-Latin-American Dermatological Congress, San Salvador, Nov. 28-Dec. 3.

Jesus and Caritas Emblem — A234

1975, Dec. 18 Litho. ***Perf. 13½***

867 A234 10c dull red & maroon .25 .25

7th Latin American Charity Congress, San Salvador, Nov. 1971. See No. C368.

No. 862 Ovptd. "III CONGRESO / ENFERMERIA / CENCAMEX 76"

1976, May 10 Litho. ***Perf. 12½***

868 A231 10c lt grn & multi .35 .25

CENCAMEX 76, 3rd Nurses' Congress.

Map of El Salvador A235

1976, May 18

869 A235 10c vio bl & multi .25 .25

10th Congress of Revenue Collectors (Centro Interamericano de Administradores Tributarios, CIAT), San Salvador, May 16-22. See No. C382.

Flags of Salvador and US, Torch, Map of Americas A236

The Spirit of '76, by Archibald M. Willard — A237

1976, June 30 Litho. ***Perf. 12½***

870 A236 10c yel & multi .25 .25
871 A237 40c multi .25 .25
Nos. 870-871,C383-C384 (4) 4.50 3.25

American Bicentennial.

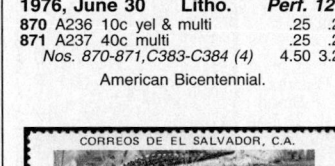

American Crocodile — A238

1976, Sept. 23 Litho. ***Perf. 12½***

872 A238 10c shown .30 .25
873 A238 20c Green iguana .65 .25
874 A238 30c Iguana .95 .25
Nos. 872-874,C385-C387 (6) 5.20 1.65

Post-classical Vase, San Salvador A239

Pre-Columbian Art: 15c, Brazier with classical head, Tazumal. 40c, Vase with classical head, Tazumal.

1976, Oct. 11 Litho. ***Perf. 12½***

875 A239 10c multi .25 .25
876 A239 15c multi .25 .25
877 A239 40c multi .30 .25
Nos. 875-877,C388-C390 (6) 2.10 1.65

For overprint see No. C429.

Fair Emblem A240

1976, Oct. 25 Litho. ***Perf. 12½***

878 A240 10c multi .25 .25
879 A240 30c gray & multi .25 .25
Nos. 878-879,C391-C392 (4) 1.30 1.15

7th Intl. Fair, Nov. 5-22.

Child under Christmas Tree — A241

1976, Dec. 16 Litho. ***Perf. 11***

880 A241 10c yel & multi .25 .25
881 A241 15c buff & multi .25 .25
882 A241 30c vio & multi .25 .25
883 A241 40c pink & multi .30 .30
Nos. 880-883,C393-C396 (8) 2.80 2.25

Christmas 1976.

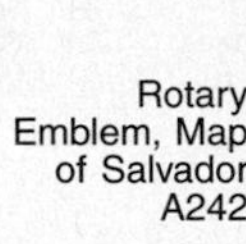

Rotary Emblem, Map of Salvador A242

1977, June 20 Litho. ***Perf. 11***

884 A242 10c multi .25 .25
885 A242 15c multi .25 .25
Nos. 884-885,C397-C398 (4) 1.55 1.25

San Salvador Rotary Club, 50th anniversary.

Cerron Grande Hydroelectric Station — A243

Designs: No. 887, 15c, Central sugar refinery, Jiboa. 30c, Izalco satellite earth station, vert.

1977, June 29 ***Perf. 12½***

886 A243 10c multi .25 .25
887 A243 10c multi .25 .25
888 A243 15c multi .25 .25
889 A243 30c multi .25 .25
Nos. 886-889,C399-C401 (7) 2.25 1.90

Industrial development. Nos. 886-889 have colorless overprint in multiple rows: GOBIERNO DEL SALVADOR.

Nos. 785 and 774 Srchd. with New Value and Bar

1977, June 30 ***Perf. 12x11½, 11½***

890 A200 15c on 2c multi .25 .25
891 A197 25c on 6c multi .30 .25

Microphone, ASDER Emblem — A244

1977, Sept. 14 Litho. ***Perf. 14***

892 A244 10c multi .25 .25
893 A244 15c multi .25 .25
Nos. 892-893,C406-C407 (4) 1.00 1.00

Broadcasting in El Salvador, 50th anniversary (Asociacion Salvadoreño de Empresa Radio).

Wooden Drum A245

Design: 10c, Flute and recorder.

1978, Aug. 29 Litho. ***Perf. 12½***

894 A245 5c multi .25 .25
895 A245 10c multi .25 .25
Nos. 894-895,C433-C435 (5) 1.85 1.40

For surcharge see No. C492.

"Man and Engineering" A246

1978, Sept. 12 Litho. ***Perf. 13½***

896 A246 10c multi .25 .25

4th National Engineers' Congress, San Salvador, Sept. 18-23. See No. C436.

Izalco Station A247

1978, Sept. 14 ***Perf. 12½***

897 A247 10c multi .25 .25

Inauguration of Izalco satellite earth station, Sept. 15, 1978. See No. C437.

Fair Emblem A248

1978, Oct. 30 Litho. ***Perf. 12½***

898 A248 10c multi .25 .25
899 A248 20c multi .25 .25
Nos. 898-899,C440-C441 (4) 1.00 1.00

8th Intl. Fair, Nov. 3-20.

Henri Dunant, Red Cross Emblem A249

1978, Oct. 30 ***Perf. 11***

900 A249 10c multi .25 .25

Henri Dunant (1828-1910), founder of the Red Cross. See No. C442.

World Map and Cotton Boll A250

1978, Nov. 22 ***Perf. 12½***

901 A250 15c multi .25 .25

Intl. Cotton Consulting Committee, 37th Meeting, San Salvador, 11/27-12/2. See #C443.

Nativity, Stained-glass Window A251

1978, Dec. 5 Litho. ***Perf. 12½***

902 A251 10c multi .25 .25
903 A251 15c multi .25 .25
Nos. 902-903,C444-C445 (4) 1.55 1.25

Christmas 1978.

Athenaeum Coat of Arms — A252

1978, Dec. 20 **Litho.** ***Perf. 14***

904 A252 5c multi .25 .25

Millennium of Castilian language. See No. C446.

Postal Service and UPU Emblems A253

1979, Apr. 2 **Litho.** ***Perf. 14***

905 A253 10c multi .25 .25

Centenary of Salvador's membership in Universal Postal Union. See No. C447.

"75," Health Organization and WHO Emblems — A254

1979, Apr. 7 ***Perf. 14x14½***

906 A254 10c multi .25 .25

Pan-American Health Organization, 75th anniversary. See No. C448.

Flame and Pillars — A255

1979, May 25 **Litho.** ***Perf. 12½***

907 A255 10c multi .25 .25

908 A255 15c multi .25 .25

Nos. 907-908,C449-C450 (4) 1.55 1.25

Social Security 5-year plan, 1978-1982.

Pope John Paul II, Map of Americas A256

1979, July 12 **Litho.** ***Perf. 14½x14***

909 A256 10c multi .25 .25

910 A256 20c multi .25 .25

Nos. 909-910,C454-C455 (4) 5.00 3.30

Mastodon A257

1979, Sept. 7 **Litho.** ***Perf. 14***

911 A257 10c shown .30 .25

912 A257 20c Saber-toothed tiger .30 .25

913 A257 30c Toxodon .50 .30

Nos. 911-913,C458-C460 (6) 4.70 2.40

Salvador Flag, José Aberiz and Proclamation A258

1979, Sept. 14 ***Perf. 14½x14***

914 A258 10c multi .25 .25

National anthem centenary. See No. C461.

Cogwheel around Map of Americas A259

1979, Oct. 19 **Litho.** ***Perf. 14½x14***

915 A259 10c multi .25 .25

8th COPIMERA Congress (Mechanical, Electrical and Allied Trade Engineers), San Salvador, Oct. 22-27. See No. C462.

Children of Various Races, IYC Emblem A260

Children and Nurses, IYC Emblem A261

1979, Oct. 29 ***Perf. 14x14½, 14½x14***

916 A260 10c multi .25 .25

917 A261 15c multi .25 .25

International Year of the Child.

Map of Central and South America, Congress Emblem — A262

1979, Nov. 1 **Litho.** ***Perf. 14½x14***

918 A262 10c multi .25 .25

5th Latin American Clinical Biochemistry Cong., San Salvador, 11/5-10. See #C465.

Coffee Bushes in Bloom, Coffee Association Emblem A263

Salvador Coffee Assoc., 50th Anniv.: 30c, Planting coffee bushes, vert. 40c, Coffee berries.

1979, Dec. 18 ***Perf. 14x14½, 14½x14***

919 A263 10c multi .25 .25

920 A263 30c multi .25 .25

921 A263 40c multi .30 .30

Nos. 919-921,C466-C468 (6) 2.60 2.00

Children, Dove and Star — A264

1979, Dec. 18 ***Perf. 14½x14***

922 A264 10c multi .35 .25

Christmas 1979.

Hoof and Mouth Disease Prevention A265

1980, June 3 **Litho.** ***Perf. 14½x14***

923 A265 10c multi .25 .25

See No. C469.

Anadara Grandis A266

1980, Aug. 12 ***Perf. 14x14½***

924 A266 10c shown .40 .25

925 A266 30c Ostrea iridescens .80 .25

926 A266 40c Turitello leucostoma 1.25 .25

Nos. 924-926,C470-C473 (7) 8.40 2.05

Quetzal (Pharomachrus mocino) — A267

1980, Sept. 10 **Litho.** ***Perf. 14x14½***

927 A267 10c shown 1.25 .30

928 A267 20c Penelopina nigra 1.25 .30

Nos. 927-928,C474-C476 (5) 11.60 1.60

Local Snakes A268

1980, Nov. 12 **Litho.** ***Perf. 14x14½***

929 A268 10c Tree snake 1.60 .30

930 A268 20c Water snake 1.75 .30

Nos. 929-930,C477-C478 (4) 9.25 1.15

Corporation of Auditors, 50th Anniv. — A269

1980, Nov. 26 **Litho.** ***Perf. 14***

931 A269 15c multi .25 .25

932 A269 20c multi .25 .25

Nos. 931-932,C479-C480 (4) 1.50 1.15

Christmas A270

1980, Dec. 5 **Litho.** ***Perf. 14***

933 A270 5c multi .25 .25

934 A270 10c multi .25 .25

Nos. 933-934,C481-C482 (4) 1.35 1.05

Dental Assoc. Emblems — A271

1981, June 18 **Litho.** ***Perf. 14***

935 A271 15c lt yel grn & blk .25 .25

Dental Society of Salvador, 50th anniv.; Odontological Federation of Central America and Panama, 25th anniv. See No. C494.

Hands Reading Braille Book — A272

1981, Aug. 14 **Litho.** ***Perf. 14x14½***

936 A272 10c multi .25 .25

Nos. 936,C495-C498 (5) 2.30 1.70

Intl. Year of the Disabled.

EL SALVADOR C.A.
XXV ANIVERSARIO
ROBERTO QUIÑONEZ
CORREOS
10c.

A273

1981, Aug. 28 **Litho.** ***Perf. 14x14½***

937 A273 10c multi .25 .25

Roberto Quinonez Natl. Agriculture College, 25th anniv. See No. C499.

World Food Day — A274

1981, Sept. 16 Litho. ***Perf. 14x14½***
938 A274 10c multi .25 .25

See No. C500.

1981 World Cup Preliminaries — A275

40c, Cup soccer ball, flags.

1981, Nov. 27 Litho. ***Perf. 14x14½***
939 A275 10c shown .25 .25
940 A275 40c multicolored .45 .25
Nos. 939-940,C505-C506 (4) 1.60 1.15

Salvador Lyceum (High School), 100th Anniv. — A276

1981, Dec. 17 Litho. ***Perf. 14***
941 A276 10c multi .25 .25

See No. C507.

Pre-Columbian Stone Sculptures A277

10c, Axe with bird's head. 20c, Sun disc. 40c, Stele Carving with effigy.

1982, Jan. 22 Litho. ***Perf. 14***
942 A277 10c multicolored .25 .25
943 A277 20c multicolored .25 .25
944 A277 40c multicolored .30 .30
Nos. 942-944,C508-C510 (6) 2.00 1.75

Scouting Year — A278

30c, Girl Scout helping woman.

1982, Mar. 17 Litho. ***Perf. 14½x14***
945 A278 10c shown .25 .25
946 A278 30c multicolored .25 .25
Nos. 945-946,C511-C512 (4) 1.15 1.00

Armed Forces A279

1982, May 7 Litho. ***Perf. 14x13½***
947 A279 10c multi .25 .25

See No. C514.

1982 World Cup A280

1982, July 14 ***Perf. 14x14½***
948 A280 10c Team, emblem .25 .25
Nos. 948,C518-C520 (4) 2.60 1.85

10th International Fair — A281

1982, Oct. 14 Litho. ***Perf. 14***
949 A281 10c multi .25 .25

See No. C524.

Christmas 1982 — A282

1982, Dec. 14 Litho. ***Perf. 14***
950 A282 5c multi .25 .25

See No. C528.

Dancers, Pre-Colombian Ceramic Design — A283

1983, Feb. 18 Litho. ***Perf. 14***
951 A283 10c shown .25 .25
952 A283 20c Sower .25 .25
953 A283 25c Flying Man .30 .25
954 A283 60c Hunters .55 .50
955 A283 60c Hunters, diff. .55 .50
a. Pair, #954-955 1.10 1.10
956 A283 1col Procession .75 .60
957 A283 1col Procession, diff. .75 .60
a. Pair, #956-957 1.75 1.75
Nos. 951-957 (7) 3.40 2.95

Nos. 953-957 airmail. #955a, 957a have continuous designs.

Visit of Pope John Paul II — A284

60c, Monument to the Divine Savior, Pope.

1983, Mar. 4 Litho. ***Perf. 14***
958 A284 25c shown .25 .25
959 A284 60c multicolored .55 .30

Salvadoran Air Force, 60th Anniv. A285

1983, Mar. 24 Litho. ***Perf. 14***
960 A285 10c Ricardo Aberle .25 .25
961 A285 10c Air Force Emblem .25 .25
962 A285 10c Enrico Massi .25 .25
a. Strip of 3, #960-962 .75 .75
963 A285 10c Juan Ramon Munes .25 .25
964 A285 10c American Air Force Cooperation Emblem .25 .25
965 A285 10c Belisario Salazar .25 .25
a. Strip of 3, #963-965 .75 .75

Arranged se-tenant horizontally with two Nos. 960 or 963 at left and two Nos. 962 or 965 at right.

Local butterflies — A286

1983, May 31 Litho. ***Perf. 14***
966 A286 Pair 1.40 1.40
a. 5c Papilio torquatus .35 .35
b. 5c Metamorpha steneles .35 .35
967 A286 Pair 1.75 1.75
a. 10c Papilio torquatus, diff. .75 .75
b. 10c Anaea marthesia .75 .75
968 A286 Pair 2.25 2.25
a. 15c Prepona brooksiana 1.10 1.10
b. 15c Caligo atreus 1.10 1.10
969 A286 Pair 3.50 3.50
a. 25c Morpho peleides 1.90 1.90
b. 25c Dismorphia praxinoe 1.90 1.90
970 A286 Pair 7.00 7.00
a. 50c Morpho polyphemus 2.25 2.25
b. 50c Metamorphia epaphus 2.25 2.25
Nos. 966-970 (5) 15.90 15.90

Simon Bolivar, 200th Birth Anniv. — A287

1983, June 23 Litho. ***Perf. 14***
971 A287 75c multi .70 .50

Dr. Jose Mendoza, College Emblem. A288

1983, July 21 Litho. ***Perf. 14***
972 A288 10c multicolored .40 .25

Salvador Medical College, 40th anniv.

A289

Perf. 13½x14, 14x13½
1983, Oct. 30 Litho.
973 A289 10c multi .25 .25
974 A289 50c multi, horiz. .40 .40

Centenary of David J. Guzman national museum. 50c airmail.

World Communications Year — A290

10c, Gen. Juan Jose Canas, Francisco Duenas (organizers of 1st natl. telegraph service), Morse key, 1870. 25c, Mailman delivering letters. 50c, Post Office sorting center, San Salvador. 25c, 50c airmail.

Perf. 14x13½, 13½x14
1983, Nov. 23 Litho.
975 A290 10c multi .25 .25
976 A290 25c multi, vert. .25 .25
977 A290 50c multi .40 .30
Nos. 975-977 (3) .90 .80

Dove Over Globe — A291

25c, Creche figures, horiz.

Perf. 13½x14, 14x13½
1983, Nov. 30
978 A291 10c shown .25 .25
979 A291 25c multicolored .30 .25

Christmas. 25c is airmail.

Environmental Protection A292

1983, Dec. 13
980 A292 10c Vehicle exhaust .40 .25
981 A292 15c Fig tree .50 .25
982 A292 25c Rodent .80 .25
Nos. 980-982 (3) 1.70 .75

15c, 25c airmail.

Philatelists' Day A293

1984, Jan. 5 ***Perf. 14x13½***
983 A293 10c No. 1 .40 .25

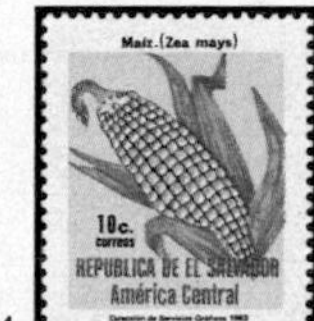

Corn — A294

1984, Feb. 21 Litho. ***Perf. 14½x14***

984 A294 10c shown .25 .25
985 A294 15c Cotton .25 .25
986 A294 25c Coffee beans .30 .25
987 A294 50c Sugar cane .50 .25
988 A294 75c Beans .80 .25
989 A294 1col Agave .30 .50
990 A294 5col Balsam 1.25 2.40
Nos. 984-990 (7) 3.65 4.15

See Nos. 1047-1051.

Caluco Church, Sonsonate A295

10c, Salcoatitan, Sonsonate. 15c, Huizucar, La Libertad. 25c, Santo Domingo, Sonsonate. 50c, Pilar, Sonsonate. 75c, Nahuizalco, Sonsonate.

1984, Mar. 30 ***Perf. 14x13½***

991 A295 5c multicolored .25 .25
992 A295 10c multicolored .25 .25
993 A295 15c multicolored .25 .25
994 A295 25c multicolored .25 .25
995 A295 50c multicolored .30 .25
996 A295 75c multicolored .40 .25
Nos. 991-996 (6) 1.70 1.50

Nos. 993-996 airmail.

Central Reserve Bank of Salvador, 50th Anniv. A296

1984, July 17 Litho. ***Perf. 14x14½***

997 A296 10c First reserve note .25 .25
998 A296 25c Bank, 1959 .25 .25

25c airmail.

1984 Summer Olympics A297

1984, July 20 ***Perf. 14x13½, 13½x14***

999 A297 10c Boxing .30 .25
1000 A297 25c Running, vert. .30 .25
1001 A297 40c Bicycling .40 .25
1002 A297 50c Swimming .50 .25
1003 A297 75c Judo, vert. .75 .30
1004 A297 1col Pierre de Coubertin 1.00 .30
Nos. 999-1004 (6) 3.25 1.60

Nos. 1000-1004 airmail.
For surcharge see No. C536A.

Govt. Printing Office Building Opening A298

1984, July 27 ***Perf. 14x13½***

1005 A298 10c multi .40 .25

5th of November Hydroelectric Plant — A299

Designs: 55c, Cerron Grande Plant. 70c, Ahuachapan Geothermal Plant. 90c, Mural. 2col, 15th of September Plant. 70c, 90c, 2 col airmail.

1984, Sept. 13 Litho. ***Perf. 14x14½***

1006 A299 20c multi .30 .25
1007 A299 55c multi .50 .25
1008 A299 70c multi .65 .25
1009 A299 90c multi .80 .30
1010 A299 2col multi 1.75 .50
Nos. 1006-1010 (5) 4.00 1.55

Boys Playing Marbles A300

1984, Oct. 16 ***Perf. 14½x14***

1011 A300 55c shown .25 .25
1012 A300 70c Spinning top .30 .25
1013 A300 90c Flying kite .40 .30
1014 A300 2col Top, diff. .80 .50
Nos. 1011-1014 (4) 1.75 1.30

11th International Fair — A301

1984, Oct. 31 Litho. ***Perf. 14x14½***

1015 A301 25c shown .25 .25
1016 A301 70c Fairgrounds .40 .30

70c airmail.

Los Chorros Tourist Center A302

25c, Plaza las Americas. 70c, El Salvador International Airport. 90c, El Tunco Beach. 2col, Sihuatehuacan Tourist Center.

1984, Nov. 23 Litho. ***Perf. 14x14½***

1017 A302 15c multicolored .25 .25
1018 A302 25c multicolored .40 .25
1019 A302 70c multicolored .55 .25
1020 A302 90c multicolored .65 .25
1021 A302 2col multicolored 1.40 .50
Nos. 1017-1021 (5) 3.25 1.50

The Paper of Papers, 1979, by Roberto A. Galicia (b. 1945) A302a

Paintings by natl. artists: 20c, The White Nun, 1939, by Salvador Salazar Arrue (b. 1899), vert. 70c, Supreme Elegy to Masferrer, 1968, by Antonio G. Ponce (b. 1938), vert. 90c, Transmutation, 1979, by Armando Solis (b. 1940). 2 col, Figures at Theater, 1959, by Carlos Canas (b. 1924), vert.

1984, Dec. 10 Litho. ***Perf. 14***

1021A A302a 20c multi .25 .25
1021B A302a 55c multi .30 .25
1021C A302a 70c multi .50 .30
1021D A302a 90c multi .50 .30
1021E A302a 2col multi 1.25 .50
Nos. 1021A-1021E (5) 2.80 1.60

Nos. 1021B-1021E are airmail. 70c and 2col issued with overprinted silver bar and corrected inscription in black; copies exist without overprint.

Christmas 1984 — A303

1984, Dec. 19 **Litho.**

1022 A303 25c Glass ornament .25 .25
1023 A303 70c Ornaments, dove .45 .25

No. 1023 airmail.

Birds — A304

15c, Lepidocolaptes affinis. 25c, Spodiornis rusticus barriliensis. 55c, Claravis mondetoura. 70c, Hylomanes momotula. 90c, Xenotriccus calizonus. 1col, Cardellina rubrifrons.

1984, Dec. 21 Litho. ***Perf. 14½x14***

1024 A304 15c multicolored .55 .30
1025 A304 25c multicolored .90 .30
1026 A304 55c multicolored 2.25 .50
1027 A304 70c multicolored 2.60 .65
1028 A304 90c multicolored 2.25 .70
1029 A304 1col multicolored 3.50 .80
Nos. 1024-1029 (6) 12.05 3.25

Nos. 1026-1029 airmail.

Salvador Bank Centenary A305

1985, Feb. 6 Litho. ***Perf. 14***

1030 A305 25c Stock certificate .45 .25

Mortgage Bank, 50th Anniv. — A306

1985, Feb. 20 Litho. ***Perf. 14***

1031 A306 25c Mortgage .45 .25

Intl. Youth Year A307

25c, IYY emblem. 55c, Woodcrafting. 70c, Professions symbolized. 1.50col, Youths marching.

1985, Feb. 28 Litho. ***Perf. 14***

1032 A307 25c multicolored .30 .25
1033 A307 55c multicolored .50 .30
1034 A307 70c multicolored .60 .30
1035 A307 1.50col multicolored .90 .55
Nos. 1032-1035 (4) 2.30 1.40

Nos. 1033-1035 airmail.

Archaeology A308

15c, Pre-classical figure. 20c, Engraved vase. 25c, Post-classical ceramic. 55c, Post-classical figure. 70c, Late post-classical deity. 1col, Late post-classical figure.
2col, Tazumal ruins, horiz.

1985, Mar. 6 Litho. ***Perf. 14½x14***

1036 A308 15c multicolored .35 .25
1037 A308 20c multicolored .40 .25
1038 A308 25c multicolored .50 .25
1039 A308 55c multicolored .90 .30
1040 A308 70c multicolored 1.10 .30
1041 A308 1col multicolored 1.25 .40
Nos. 1036-1041 (6) 4.50 1.75

Souvenir Sheet

Rouletted 13½

1042 A308 2col multicolored 2.00 .75

Nos. 1039-1041 airmail. No. 1042 has enlargement of stamp design in margin.

Natl. Red Cross, Cent. A309

25c, Anniv. emblem vert. 55c, Sea rescue. 70c, Blood donation service. 90c, First aid, ambulance, vert.

1985, Mar. 13 Litho. ***Perf. 14***

1043 A309 25c multicolored .25 .25
1044 A309 55c multicolored .45 .25
1045 A309 70c multicolored .55 .30
1046 A309 90c multicolored .75 .35
Nos. 1043-1046 (4) 2.00 1.15

Nos. 1044-1046 are airmail.

Agriculture Type of 1984

1985 ***Perf. 14½x14***

1047 A294 55c Cotton .55 .25
1048 A294 70c Corn .60 .25
1049 A294 90c Sugar cane .80 .30
1050 A294 2col Beans 1.90 .75
1051 A294 10col Agave 6.00 3.50
Nos. 1047-1051 (5) 9.85 5.05

Issued: 55c, 70c, 90c, 4/4; 2col, 10col, 9/4.

Child Survival A310

Children's drawings.

1985, May 3 Litho. ***Perf. 14x14½***

1052 A310 25c Hand, houses .25 .25
1053 A310 55c House, children .40 .25
1054 A310 70c Boy, girl holding hands .50 .25
1055 A310 90c Oral vaccination .70 .40
Nos. 1052-1055 (4) 1.85 1.15

Nos. 1053-1055 are airmail.

Salvador Army A311

1985, May 17 ***Perf. 14***

1056	A311	25c Map	.25	.25
1057	A311	70c Recruit, natl. flag	.40	.25

No. 1057 is airmail.

Inauguration of Pres. Duarte, 1st Anniv. — A312

1985, June 28 ***Perf. 14½x14***

1058	A312	25c Flag, laurel, book	.25	.25
1059	A312	70c Article I, Constitution	.35	.25

Inter-American Development Bank, 25th Anniv. — A313

25c, Central Hydro-electric Dam, power station. 70c, Map of Salvador. 1col, Natl. arms.

1985, July 5 ***Perf. 14x13½***

1060	A313	25c multi	.25	.25
1061	A313	70c multi	.55	.25
1062	A313	1col multi	.70	.40
		Nos. 1060-1062 (3)	1.50	.90

Nos. 1061-1062 are airmail.

Fish A314

25c, Cichlasoma trimaculatum. 55c, Rhamdia guatemalenis. 70c, Poecilia sphenops. 90c, Cichlasoma nigrofasciatum. 1col, Astyanax fasciatus. 1.50col, Dormitator latifrons.

1985, Sept. 30 ***Perf. 14x14½***

1064	A314	25c multi	.45	.25
1065	A314	55c multi	.65	.25
1066	A314	70c multi	.75	.25
1067	A314	90c multi	.85	.30
1068	A314	1col multi	1.00	.30
1069	A314	1.50col multi	1.50	.40
		Nos. 1064-1069 (6)	5.20	1.75

Nos. 1065-1069 are airmail.

UNFAO, 40th Anniv. — A315

1985, Oct. 16 ***Perf. 14½x14***

1070	A315	20c Cornucopia	.30	.25
1071	A315	40c Centeotl, Nahuat god of corn	.40	.25

Dragonflies A316

25c, Cordulegaster godmani mclachlan. 55c, Libellula herculea karsch. 70c, Cora marina selys. 90c, Aeshna cornigera braver. 1col, Mecistogaster ornata rambur. 1.50col, Hetaerina smaragdalis de marmels.

1985, Dec. 9 ***Perf. 14x14½***

1072	A316	25c multi	.40	.25
1073	A316	55c multi	.60	.25
1074	A316	70c multi	.75	.25
1075	A316	90c multi	.85	.30
1076	A316	1col multi	1.00	.30
1077	A316	1.50col multi	1.50	.40
		Nos. 1072-1077 (6)	5.10	1.75

Nos. 1073-1077 are airmail.
For surcharge see No. C544.

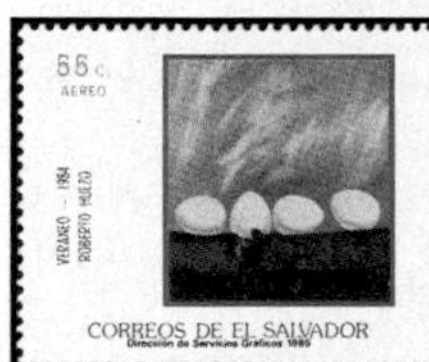

Summer, 1984, by Roberto Huezo (b.1947) A317

Paintings by natl. artists: 25c, Profiles, 1978, by Rosa Mena Valenzuela (b. 1924), vert. 70c, The Deliverance, 1984, by Fernando Llort (b. 1949). 90c, Making Tamale, 1975, by Pedro A. Garcia (b. 1930). 1col, Warm Presence, 1984, by Miguel A. Orellana (b. 1929), vert. Nos. 1079-1082 are airmail.

1985, Dec. 18 ***Perf. 14***

1078	A317	25c multi	.25	.25
1079	A317	55c multi	.25	.25
1080	A317	70c multi	.35	.25
1081	A317	90c multi	.45	.30
1082	A317	1col multi	.55	.35
		Nos. 1078-1082 (5)	1.85	1.40

San Vicente de Austria y Lorenzana City, 350th Anniv. A318

1985, Dec. 20

1083	A318	15c Tower, vert.	.25	.25
1084	A318	20c Cathedral	.30	.25

Intl. Peace Year 1986 — A319

70c, Dove over people's outstretched arms.

1986, Feb. 21 **Litho.** ***Perf. 14***

1085	A319	15c multi	.30	.25
1086	A319	70c multi	.70	.50

No. 1086 is airmail.

Postal Code Inauguration — A320

1986, Mar. 14 **Litho.** ***Perf. 14x14½***

1087	A320	20c Domestic mail	.25	.25
1088	A320	25c Intl. mail	.25	.25

Radio El Salvador, 60th Anniv. A321

1986, Mar. 21

1089	A321	25c Microphone	.25	.25
1090	A321	70c Map	.50	.40

No. 1090 is airmail.

Mammals A322

15c, Felis wiedii. 20c, Tamandua tetradactyla. 1col, Dasypus novemcinctus. 2col, Pecarii tajacu.

1986, May 30 **Litho.** ***Perf. 14x14½***

1091	A322	15c multicolored	.25	.25
1092	A322	20c multicolored	.30	.25
1093	A322	1col multicolored	1.40	.60
1094	A322	2col multicolored	2.75	1.25
		Nos. 1091-1094 (4)	4.70	2.35

Nos. 1093-1094 are airmail.

1986 World Cup Soccer Championships, Mexico — A323

Designs: 70c, Flags, mascot. 1col, Players, Soccer Cup, vert. 2col, Natl. flag, player dribbling, vert. 5col, Goal, emblem.

1986, June 6 ***Perf. 14x14½, 14½x14***

1095	A323	70c multi	.65	.45
1096	A323	1col multi	1.00	.65
1097	A323	2col multi	1.90	1.40
1098	A323	5col multi	4.50	3.25
		Nos. 1095-1098 (4)	8.05	5.75

Teachers — A324

1986, June 30 **Litho.** ***Perf. 14½x14***

1099		20c Dario Gonzalez	.25	.25
1100		20c Valero Lecha	.25	.25
a.	A324	Pair, #1099-1100	.35	.35
1101		40c Marcelino G. Flamenco	.25	.25
1102		40c Camilo Campos	.25	.25
a.	A324	Pair, #1101-1102	.70	.70
1103		70c Saul Flores	.35	.25
1104		70c Jorge Larde	.35	.25
a.	A324	Pair, #1103-1104	1.10	1.10
1105		1col Francisco Moran	.50	.35
1106		1col Mercedes M. De Luarca	.50	.35
a.	A324	Pair, #1105-1106	1.75	1.75
		Nos. 1099-1106 (8)	2.70	2.20

Nos. 1103-1106 are airmail.

Pre-Hispanic Ceramic Seal, Cara Sucia, Ahuachapan, Tlaloc Culture (300 B.C.-A.D. 1200) — A325

1986, July 23 **Litho.** ***Perf. 13½***

1107	A325	25c org & brn	.30	.25
1108	A325	55c grn, org & brn	.45	.25
1109	A325	70c pale gray, org & brn	.55	.25
1110	A325	90c pale yel, org & brn	.80	.30
1111	A325	1col pale grn, org & brn	.90	.35
1112	A325	1.50col pale pink, org & brn	1.40	.50
		Nos. 1107-1112 (6)	4.40	1.90

Nos. 1108-1112 are airmail.

World Food Day A326

1986, Oct. 30 **Litho.** ***Perf. 14x14½***

1113	A326	20c multi	.40	.25

Flowers A327

20c, Spathiphyllum phryniifolium, vert. 25c, Asclepias curassavica. 70c, Tagetes tenuifolia. 1col, Ipomoea tiliacea, vert.

1986, Sept. 30 ***Perf. 14***

1114	A327	20c multi	.65	.25
1115	A327	25c multi	.65	.25
1116	A327	70c multi	1.60	.40
1117	A327	1col multi	2.00	.55
		Nos. 1114-1117 (4)	4.90	1.45

Nos. 1116-1117 are airmail.

Christmas A328

Perf. 14x14½, 14½x14

1986, Dec. 10 **Litho.**

1118	A328	25c Candles, vert.	.25	.25
1119	A328	70c Doves	.60	.25

No. 1119 is airmail.

Crafts A329

1986, Dec. 18

1120	A329	25c Basket-making	.35	.25
1121	A329	55c Ceramicware	.45	.25
1122	A329	70c Guitars, vert.	.55	.30
1123	A329	1col Baskets, diff.	.75	.45
		Nos. 1120-1123 (4)	2.10	1.25

Christmas A330

Paintings: 25c, Church, by Mario Araujo Rajo, vert. 70c, Landscape, by Francisco Reyes.

1986, Dec. 22

1124 A330 25c multi .25 .25
1125 A330 70c multi .40 .25

No. 1125 is airmail.

Promotion of Philately A331

1987, Mar. 10 Litho. *Perf. 14½x14*

1126 A331 25c multi .50 .25

Intl. Aid Following Earthquake, Oct. 10, 1986 — A332

1987, Mar. 25

1127 A332 15c multi .30 .25
1128 A332 70c multi .60 .25
1129 A332 1.50col multi 1.00 .50
1130 A332 5col multi 2.75 1.75
Nos. 1127-1130 (4) 4.65 2.75

Orchids — A333

No. 1131, Maxillaria tenuifolia. No. 1132, Ponthieva maculata. No. 1133, Meiracyllium trinasutum. No. 1134, Encyclia vagans. No. 1135, Encyclia cochleata. No. 1136, Maxillaria atrata. No. 1137, Sobrialia xantholeuca. No. 1138, Encyclia microcharis.

1987, June 8 Litho. *Perf. 14½x14*

1131 20c multi .90 .25
1132 20c multi .90 .25
a. A333 Pair, #1131-1132 1.25 1.25
1133 25c multi 1.10 .25
1134 25c multi 1.10 .25
a. A333 Pair, #1133-1134 1.40 1.40
1135 70c multi 1.50 .55
1136 70c multi 1.50 .55
a. A333 Pair, #1135-1136 3.50 3.50
1137 1.50col multi 3.50 1.10
1138 1.50col multi 3.50 1.10
a. A333 Pair, #1137-1138 3.50 8.50
Nos. 1131-1138 (8) 14.00 4.30

#1133-1138 horiz. #1135-1138 are airmail.

Teachers — A334

Designs: No. 1139, C. de Jesus Alas, music. No. 1140, Luis Edmundo Vasquez, medicine. No. 1141, David Rosales, law. No. 1142, Guillermo Trigueros, medicine. No. 1143, Manuel Farfan Castro, history. No. 1144, Iri Sol, voice. No. 1145, Carlos Arturo Imendia, primary education. No. 1146, Benjamin Orozco, chemistry.

1987, June 30 Litho. *Perf. 14½x14*

1139 15c greenish blue & blk .25 .25
1140 15c greenish blue & blk .25 .25
a. A334 Pair, #1139-1140 .40 .40
1141 20c beige & blk .25 .25
1142 20c beige & blk .25 .25
a. A334 Pair, #1141-1142 .40 .40
1143 70c yel org & blk .35 .25
1144 70c yel org & blk .35 .25
a. A334 Pair, #1143-1144 1.25 1.25
1145 1.50col lt blue grn & blk .70 .50
1146 1.50col lt blue grn & blk .70 .50
a. A334 Pair, #1145-1146 2.75 2.75
Nos. 1139-1146 (8) 3.10 2.50

Nos. 1143-1146 are airmail.

10th Pan American Games, Indianapolis — A335

1987, July 31 *Perf. 14½x14, 14x14½*

1147 20c Emblem, vert. .25 .25
1148 20c Table tennis, vert. .25 .25
a. A335 Pair, #1147-1148 .25 .25
1149 25c Wrestling .25 .25
1150 25c Fencing .25 .25
a. A335 Pair, #1149-1150 .30 .30
1151 70c Softball .35 .25
1152 70c Equestrian .35 .25
a. A335 Pair, #1151-1152 .80 .80
1153 5col Weight lifting, vert. 2.40 1.75
1154 5col Hurdling, vert. 2.40 1.75
a. A335 Pair, #1153-1154 6.00 6.00
Nos. 1147-1154 (8) 6.50 5.00

Nos. 1149-1153 are horizontal.
Nos. 1151-1154 are airmail.

Prior Nicolas Aguilar (1742-1818) A336

Famous men: 20c, Domingo Antonio de Lara (1783-1814), aviation pioneer. 70c, Juan Manuel Rodrigues (1771-1837), president who abolished slavery. 1.50col, Pedro Pablo Castillo (1780-1814), patriot.

1987, Sept. 11 Litho. *Perf. 14½x14*

1155 A336 15c multi .25 .25
1156 A336 20c multi .25 .25
1157 A336 70c multi .30 .25
1158 A336 1.50col multi .70 .50
Nos. 1155-1158 (4) 1.50 1.25

Nos. 1157-1158 are airmail.

World Food Day A337

1987, Oct. 16 *Perf. 14x14½*

1159 A337 50c multi .45 .25

Paintings by Salarrue A338

Perf. 14½x14, 14x14½

1987, Nov. 30

1160 A338 25c Self-portrait .35 .25
1161 A338 70c Lake .55 .25

#1161 is airmail. See #1186-1189.

Christmas 1987 A339

25c, Virgin of Perpetual Sorrow, stained-glass window. 70c, The Three Magi, figurines.

1987, Nov. 18 *Perf. 14x14½*

1162 A339 25c multi .35 .25
1163 A339 70c multi .55 .25

No. 1163 is airmail.

Pre-Columbian Musical Instruments — A340

Designs: 20c, Pottery drum worn around neck. No. 1165, Frieze picturing pre-Columbian musicians, from a Salua culture ceramic vase, c. 700-800 A.D. (left side), vert. No. 1166, Frieze (right side), vert. 1.50col, Conch shell trumpet.

Perf. 14x14½, 14½x14

1987, Dec. 14 Litho.

1164 A340 20c multi .25 .25
1165 A340 70c multi .55 .30
1166 A340 70c multi .55 .30
a. Pair, #1165-1166 1.25 1.25
1167 A340 1.50col multi .90 .60
Nos. 1164-1167 (4) 2.25 1.45

Nos. 1165-1167 are airmail. No. 1166a has a continuous design.

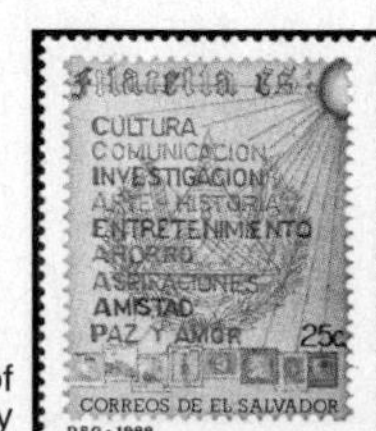

Promotion of Philately A341

1988, Jan. 20 Litho. *Perf. 14*

1168 A341 25c multi .35 .25

Young Entrepreneurs of El Salvador — A342

1988 *Perf. 14x14½*

1169 A342 25c multi .40 .25

St. John Bosco (1815-88) A343

1988, Mar. 15 Litho. *Perf. 14x14½*

1170 A343 20c multi .40 .25

Environmental Protection — A344

1988, June 3 Litho. *Perf. 14x14½*

1171 A344 20c Forests .75 .25
1172 A344 70c Forests and rivers 1.25 .40

No. 1172 is airmail.

1988-1992 Summer Olympics, Seoul and Barcelona A345

1988, Aug. 31 Litho. *Perf. 13½*

1173 A345 1col High jump .70 .30
1174 A345 1col Javelin .70 .30
1175 A345 1col Shooting .70 .30
1176 A345 1col Wrestling .70 .30
1177 A345 1col Basketball .70 .30
a. Strip of 5, Nos. 1173-1177
b. Min. sheets of 5 + 5 labels

Souvenir Sheets

1178 A345 2col Torch 16.00 —

Printed in sheets of 10 containing 2 each Nos. 1173-1177.

No. 1177b exists in 2 forms: 1st contains labels picturing 1988 Summer Games emblem or character trademark; 2nd contains labels picturing the 1992 Summer Games emblem or character trademark.

No. 1178 exists in 2 forms: 1st contains 1988 Games emblem; 2nd 1992 Games emblem.

Some, or all, of this issue seem not to have been available to the public.

World Food Day A346

1988, Oct. 11 Litho. *Perf. 14x14½*

1179 A346 20c multi .60 .25

13th Intl. Fair, Nov. 23-Dec. 11 — A347

1988, Oct. 25 ***Perf. 14½x14***

1180 A347 70c multi		.50	.30

Child Protection A348

1988, Nov. 10

1181 A348 15c Flying kite	.30	.25
1182 A348 20c Child hugging adult's leg	.45	.25

Christmas A349

Paintings by Titian: 25c, *Virgin and Child with the Young St. John and St. Anthony.* 70c, *Virgin and Child in Glory with St. Francis and St. Alvise,* vert.

Perf. 14x14½, 14½x14

1988, Nov. 15

1183 A349 25c multi	.40	.25
1184 A349 70c multi	.60	.30

70c is airmail.

Return to Moral Values A350

1988, Nov. 22 ***Perf. 14½x14***

1185 A350 25c multi	.60	.25

Art Type of 1987

Paintings by Salvadoran artists: 40c, *Esperanza de los Soles,* by Victor Rodriguez Preza. 1col, *Shepherd's Song,* by Luis Angel Salinas, horiz. 2col, *Children,* by Julio Hernandez Aleman, horiz. 5col, *El Nino de Las Alcancias,* by Camilo Minero. Nos. 1187-1189 are airmail.

Perf. 14½x14, 14x14½

1988, Nov. 30

1186 A338 40c multi	.30	.25
1187 A338 1col multi	.60	.40
1188 A338 2col multi	1.25	.75
1189 A338 5col multi	2.75	1.90
Nos. 1186-1189 (4)	4.90	3.30

A351

Discovery of America, 500th Anniv. (in 1992) — A352

Ruins and artifacts: a, El Tazumul. b, Multicolored footed bowl. c, San Andres. d, Two-color censer. e, Sihuatan. f, Carved head of the God of Lluvia. g, Cara Sucia. h, Man-shaped vase. i, San Lorenzo. j, Multicolored pear-shaped vase. 2col, Christopher Columbus.

1988, Dec. 21 ***Perf. 14x14½***

1190 Sheet of 10	6.50	6.50
a.-j. A351 1col any single	.40	.30

Souvenir Sheet

Roulette 13½

1191 A352 2col vermilion	2.00	1.25

UN Declaration of Human Rights, 40th Anniv. A353

1988, Dec. 9 ***Perf. 14½x14, 14x14½***

1192 A353 25c Family, map, emblem, vert.	.40	.25
1193 A353 70c shown	.70	.30

70c is airmail.

World Wildlife Fund — A354

Felines: a, Felis wiedii laying on tree branch. b, Felis wiedii sitting on branch. c, Felis pardalis laying in brush. d, Felis pardalis standing on tree branch.

1988 ***Perf. 14½x14***

1194 Strip of 4	12.00	12.00
a.-b. A354 25c any single	2.50	.25
c.-d. A354 55c any single	3.00	.25

World Meteorological Organization, 40th Anniv. — A355

1989, Feb. 3 Litho. ***Perf. 14½x14***

1195 A355 15c shown	.40	.25
1196 A355 20c Wind gauge	.40	.25

Meteorology in El Salvador, cent.

Promotion of Philately A356

1989, Mar. 15 Litho. ***Perf. 14½x14***

1197 A356 25c Philatelic Soc. emblem	.50	.25

See No. 1230.

Natl. Fire Brigade, 106th Anniv. A357

1989, June 19 Litho. ***Perf. 14x14½***

1198 A357 25c Fire truck	.40	.25
1199 A357 70c Firemen	.80	.30

French Revolution, Bicent. A358

1989, July 12

1200 A358 90c Anniv. emblem	.50	.35
1201 A358 1col Storming of the Bastille	.80	.40

Souvenir Sheets

Stamps on Stamps — A359

Statues of Queen Isabella and Christopher Columbus — A360

Designs: a, No. 88. b, No. 101. c, No. 86. d, No. 102. e, No. 87. f, No. 103.

1989, May 31 Litho. ***Perf. 14x14½***

Miniature Sheet

1202 A359 Sheet of 6	6.75	6.75
a.-f. 50c any single	.45	.25

Souvenir Sheet

Rouletted 13½

1203 A360 2col shown	3.00	3.00

Discovery of America, 500th anniv. (in 1992).

No. 1203 exists in two forms: margin pictures Natl. Palace with either 500th anniv. emblem or anniv. emblem and "92" at lower right.

Signing Act of Independence — A361

1989, Sept. 1 ***Perf. 14x14½***

1204 A361 25c shown	.30	.25
1205 A361 70c Flag, natl. seal, heroes	.50	.25

Natl. independence, 168th anniv. No. 1205 is airmail.

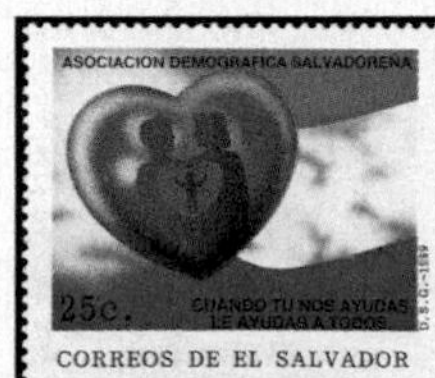

Demographic Assoc., 27th Anniv. — A362

1989, July 26

1206 A362 25c multi	.55	.25

1990 World Cup Soccer Championships, Italy — A363

Soccer ball, flags of Salvador and: No. 1207, US No. 1208, Guatemala. No. 1209, Costa Rica. No. 1210, Trinidad & Tobago. 55c, Trinidad & Tobago, Guatemala, US, Costa Rica. 1col, Soccer ball, Cuscatlan Stadium.

1989, Sept. 1 Litho. ***Perf. 14x14½***

1207 A363 20c multi	.30	.25
1208 A363 20c multicolored	.30	.25
a. Pair, #1207-1208	.60	.60
1209 A363 25c shown	.30	.25
1210 A363 25c multicolored	.30	.25
a. Pair, #1209-1210	.60	.60
1211 A363 55c multicolored	.30	.25
1212 A363 1col multicolored	.50	.35
Nos. 1207-1212 (6)	2.00	1.60

Beatification of Marcellin Champagnat, Founder of the Marist Brothers Order — A364

1989, Sept. 28

1213 A364 20c multicolored	.50	.25

America Issue A365

UPAE emblem and pre-Columbian artifacts: 25c, *The Cultivator,* rock painting. 70c, Ceramic urn.

1989, Oct. 12

1214 A365 25c multicolored	.75	.25
1215 A365 70c multicolored	1.50	.30

World Food Day A366

Perf. 14x14½, 14½x14

1989, Oct. 16 **Litho.**

1216 A366 15c shown .30 .25
1217 A366 55c Aspects of agriculture, vert. .50 .25

Children's Rights A367

1989, Oct. 26 **Litho.** ***Perf. 14½x14***

1218 A367 25c multicolored .55 .25

Creche Figures A368

1989, Dec. 1

1219 A368 25c shown .30 .25
1220 A368 70c Holy Family, diff. .65 .30

Christmas.

Birds of Prey A369

70c, Sarcoramphus papa. 1col, Polyborus plancus. 2col, Accipiter striatus. 10col, Glaucidium brasilianum.

1989, Dec. 20 ***Perf. 14½x14, 14x14½***

1221 A369 70c multicolored .65 .30
1222 A369 1col multicolored 1.10 .45
1223 A369 2col multicolored 1.75 .80
1224 A369 10col multicolored 7.50 4.00
Nos. 1221-1224 (4) 11.00 5.55

Nos. 1221 and 1223 vert.

Tax Court, 50th Anniv. A370

1990, Jan. 12 **Litho.** ***Perf. 14x14½***

1225 A370 50c multicolored .50 .25

Lord Baden-Powell, 133rd Birth Anniv. — A371

1990, Feb. 23 ***Perf. 14½x14***

1226 A371 25c multicolored 1.00 .25

Intl. Women's Day — A372

1990, Mar. 8 **Litho.** ***Perf. 14½x14***

1227 A372 25c multicolored .55 .25

Type of 1989 and

Hour Glass — A373

1990 ***Perf. 14½x14***

1228 A373 25c multicolored .25 .25
1229 A373 55c multicolored .35 .25

Souvenir Sheet

Rouletted 13½ with Simulated Perfs.

1230 A356 2col blk & pale blue 2.25 .95

Philatelic Soc., 50th anniv. Nos. 1229-1230 are airmail.

Fight Against Addictions A375

1990, Apr. 26 **Litho.** ***Perf. 14x14½***

1231 A375 20c Alcohol .30 .25
1232 A375 25c Smoking .40 .25
1233 A375 1.50col Drugs 1.00 .40
Nos. 1231-1233 (3) 1.70 .90

No. 1233 is airmail.

La Prensa, 75th Anniv. — A376

1990, May 14 **Litho.** ***Perf. 14½x14***

1234 A376 15c multicolored .30 .25
1235 A376 25c "75," newspaper .40 .25

A377

World Cup Soccer Championships, Italy — A378

Soccer player and flags of: No. 1236, Argentina, USSR, Cameroun, Romania. No. 1237, Italy, US, Austria, Czechoslovakia. No. 1238, Brazil, Costa Rica, Sweden, Scotland. No. 1239, Germany, United Arab Emirates, Yugoslavia, Colombia. No. 1240, Belgium, Spain, Korea, Uruguay. No. 1241, England, Netherlands, Ireland, Egypt.

1990, June 15 ***Perf. 14x14½***

1236 A377 55c multicolored .35 .25
1237 A377 55c multicolored .35 .25
1238 A377 70c multicolored .45 .25
1239 A377 70c multicolored .45 .25
1240 A377 1col multicolored .55 .35
1241 A377 1col multicolored .55 .35
1242 A378 1.50col multicolored .90 .50
Nos. 1236-1242 (7) 3.60 2.20

For surcharge see No. 1245.

Discovery of America Cent. — A379

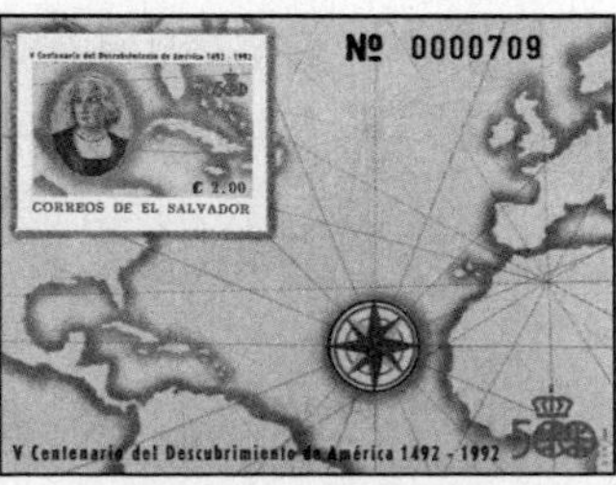

Columbus, Map — A380

Stained glass window: a, Christopher Columbus. b, Queen Isabella. c, Columbus' Arms. d, Discovery of America 500th anniv. emblem. e, One boat of Columbus' fleet. f, Two boats.

1990, July 30 **Litho.** ***Perf. 14***

Miniature Sheet

1243 A379 Sheet of 6 6.50 6.50
a.-f. 1col any single .50 .35

Souvenir Sheet

Rouletted 13 1/2

1244 A380 2col multicolored 3.00 3.00

See Nos. 1283-1284.

No. 1239 Surcharged in Black

1991, Feb. **Litho.** ***Perf. 14x14½***

1245 A377 90c on 70c multi 1.00 .30

World Summit for Children A381

1990, Sept. 25 ***Perf. 14½x14***

1246 A381 5col blk, gold & dk bl 2.75 2.00

First Postage Stamps, 150th Anniv. A382

a, Sir Rowland Hill. b, Penny Black. c, No. 21. d, Central Post Office. e, No. C124.

1990, Oct. 5 **Litho.** ***Perf. 14***

1247 Sheet of 5 + label 9.00 9.00
a.-e. A382 2col any single .95 .70

World Food Day — A383

1990, Oct. 16 **Litho.** ***Perf. 14***

1248 A383 5col multicolored 2.75 1.75

San Salvador Electric Light Co., Cent. A384

1990, Oct. 30

1249 A384 20c shown .40 .25
1250 A384 90c Lineman, power lines .70 .35

America Issue A385

1990, Oct. 11 **Litho.** ***Perf. 14x14½***

1251 A385 25c Chichontepec Volcano .50 .25
1252 A385 70c Lake Coatepeque .90 .25

Chamber of Commerce, 75th Anniv. A386

1990, Nov. 22

1253	A386	1 col blk, gold & bl	.70	.35

Traffic Safety — A387

Design: 40c, Intersection, horiz.

Perf. 14½x14, 14x14½

1990, Nov. 13

1254	A387	25c multicolored	.35	.25
1255	A387	40c multicolored	.55	.25

Butterflies A388

15c, Eurytides calliste. 20c, Papilio garamas amerias. 25c, Papilio garamas. 55c, Hypanartia godmani. 70c, Anaea excellens. 1col, Papilio pilumnus. 2col, Anaea proserpina.

Perf. 14x14½, 14½x14

1990, Nov. 28

1256	A388	15c multicolored	.80	.30
1257	A388	20c multicolored	.90	.30
1258	A388	25c multicolored	1.20	.30
1259	A388	55c multicolored	1.40	.40
1260	A388	70c multicolored	1.60	.55
1261	A388	1col multicolored	2.25	.70
		Nos. 1256-1261 (6)	8.15	2.55

Souvenir Sheet

Roulette 13½

1262	A388	2col multicolored	12.00	2.50

Nos. 1259-1261 are vert.

University of El Salvador, 150th Anniv. — A389

1991, Feb. 27 Litho. *Perf. 14½x14*

1263	A389	25c shown	.25	.25
1264	A389	70c Sun, footprints, hand	.45	.30
1265	A389	1.50col Dove, globe	1.00	.65
		Nos. 1263-1265 (3)	1.70	1.20

Christmas A390

Perf. 14x14½, 14½x14

1990, Dec. 7 Litho.

1266	A390	25c shown	.25	.25
1267	A390	70c Nativity, vert.	.50	.30

Month of the Elderly A391

1991, Jan. 31 *Perf. 14½x14*

1268	A391	15c purple & blk	.55	.25

Restoration of Santa Ana Theater A392

1991, Apr. 12 *Perf. 14*

1269	A392	20c Interior	.35	.25
1270	A392	70c Exterior	.65	.30

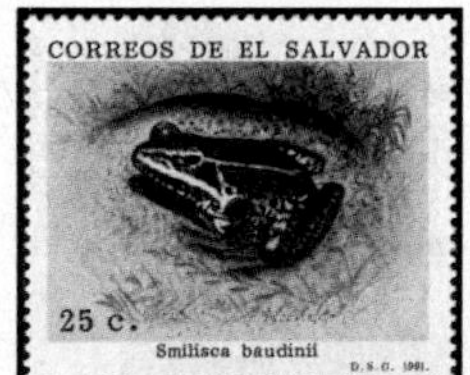
Amphibians — A393

Designs: 25c, Smilisca baudinii. 70c, Eleutherodactylus rugulosus. 1col, Plectrohyla guatemalensis. 1.50col, Agalychnis moreletii.

1991, May 29 Litho. *Perf. 14x14½*

1271	A393	25c multicolored	.75	.25
1272	A393	70c multicolored	1.20	.35
1273	A393	1col multicolored	1.90	.55
1274	A393	1.50col multicolored	2.90	.70
		Nos. 1271-1274 (4)	6.75	1.85

Aid for Children's Village A394

Designs: 90c, Children playing outdoors.

1991, June 21 Litho. *Perf. 14x14½*

1275	A394	20c multicolored	.30	.25
1276	A394	90c multicolored	.70	.35

United Family A395

1991, June 28 Litho. *Perf. 14½x14*

1277	A395	50c multicolored	.60	.25

Birds — A396

20c, Melanotis hypoleucus. 25c, Agelaius phoeniceus. 70c, Campylor-hynchus rufinucha. 1col, Cissilopha melanocyanea. 5col, Chiroxiphia linearis.

1991, Aug. 30

1278	A396	20c multicolored	.55	.25
1279	A396	25c multicolored	.65	.25
1280	A396	70c multicolored	1.00	.30
1281	A396	1col multicolored	1.10	.40
1282	A396	5col multicolored	4.00	1.75
		Nos. 1278-1282 (5)	7.30	2.95

Discovery of America, 500th Anniv. Type of 1990

No. 1283: a, Hourglass, chart. b, Chart, ship's sails. c, Sailing ship near Florida. d, Corner of chart, ships. e, Compass rose, Cuba, Yucatan Peninsula. f, South America, "500" emblem. No. 1284, Sail, landfall.

1991, Sept. 16 Litho. *Perf. 14*

Miniature Sheet

1283	A379	1col Sheet of 6, #a.-f.	6.50	6.50

Souvenir Sheet

Rouletted 6½

1284	A380	2col multicolored	3.00	3.00

America Issue A397

Designs: 25c, Battle of Acaxual. 70c, First missionaries in Cuzcatlan.

1991, Oct. 11 Litho. *Perf. 14x14½*

1285	A397	25c multicolored	.75	.25
1286	A397	70c multicolored	1.50	.30

World Food Day — A398

1991, Oct. 16 *Perf. 14½x14*

1287	A398	50c multicolored	.60	.25

Wolfgang Amadeus Mozart, Death Bicent. A399

1991, Oct. 23 *Perf. 14x14½*

1288	A399	1col multicolored	1.00	.40

Christmas A400

Perf. 14½x14, 14x14½

1991, Nov. 13 Litho.

1289	A400	25c Nativity scene, vert.	.30	.25
1290	A400	70c Children singing	.60	.30

Total Solar Eclipse, July 11 — A401

1991, Dec. 17 *Perf. 14x14½*

1291		70c shown	.60	.30
1292		70c Eastern El Salvador	.60	.30
a.		A401 Pair, #1291-1292	1.75	1.50

No. 1292a has continous design.

Red Cross Life Guards A402

1992, Feb. 28 Litho. *Perf. 14x14½*

1293	A402	3col Rescue	2.00	1.10
1294	A402	4.50col Swimming competition	2.75	1.70

Lions Clubs in El Salvador, 50th Anniv. — A403

1992, Mar. 13 *Perf. 14½x14*

1295	A403	90c multicolored	.85	.35

Protect the Environment A404

Designs: 60c, Man riding bicycle. 80c, Children walking outdoors. 1.60col, Sower in field. 3col, Clean water. 2.20col, Natural foods. 5col, Recycling center. 10col, Conservation of trees and nature. 25col, Wildlife protection.

1992, Apr. 6 Litho. *Perf. 14x14½*

1298	A404	60c multi	.35	.25
1299	A404	80c multi	.45	.25
1300	A404	1.60col multi	1.00	.50
1302	A404	2.20col multi	1.40	.75
1303	A404	3col multi	1.75	.90
1304	A404	5col multi	2.90	1.75
1305	A404	10col multi	5.50	3.25
1307	A404	25col multi	15.00	8.00
		Nos. 1298-1307 (8)	28.35	15.65

Physicians A405

80c, Dr. Roberto Orellana Valdes. 1col, Dr. Carlos Gonzalez Bonilla. 1.60col, Dr. Andres Gonzalo Funes. 2.20col, Dr. Joaquin Coto.

1992, Apr. 30 *Perf. 14½x14*

1308	A405	80c multicolored	.50	.30
1309	A405	1col multicolored	.60	.40
1310	A405	1.60col multicolored	.90	.60
1311	A405	2.20col multicolored	1.25	.85
		Nos. 1308-1311 (4)	3.25	2.15

Women's Auxiliary of St. Vincent de Paul Society, Cent. — A406

1992, Mar. 10 Litho. *Perf. 14½x14*
1312 A406 80c multicolored .75 .40

Population and Housing Census A407

80c, Globe showing location of El Salvador.

1992, June 29 Litho. *Perf. 14½x14*
1313 A407 60c multicolored .40 .30
1314 A407 80c multicolored .60 .40

1992 Summer Olympics, Barcelona A408

1992, July 17 Litho. *Perf. 14½x14*
1315 A408 60c Hammer throw .55 .30
1316 A408 80c Volleyball .65 .40
1317 A408 90c Shot put 1.00 .60
1318 A408 2.20col Long jump 1.75 .65
1319 A408 3col Vault 2.50 .85
1320 A408 5col Balance beam 4.00 1.50
Nos. 1315-1320 (6) 10.45 4.30

Simon Bolivar A409

1992, July 24
1321 A409 2.20col multicolored 1.50 .65

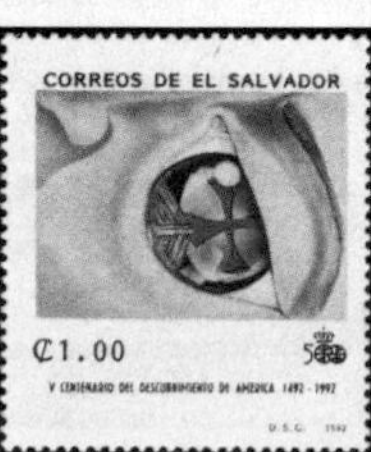

A410

Discovery of America, 500th Anniv. — A411

Designs: No. 1322, European and Amerindian faces. No. 1323, Ship in person's eye. No. 1324, Ship at sea. No. 1325, Ship, satellite over Earth. 3col, Cross, Indian pyramid.

1992, Aug. 28 Litho. *Perf. 14x14½*
1322 A410 1col multicolored 1.25 .30
1323 A410 1col multicolored 1.25 .30

Perf. 14½x14
1324 A410 1col multicolored 1.25 .30
1325 A410 1col multicolored 1.25 .30
a. Min. sheet, 2 each #1322-1325 10.00 4.00
Nos. 1322-1325 (4) 5.00 1.20

Souvenir Sheet
Rouletted 13½
1326 A411 3col multicolored 4.50 4.50

Immigrants to El Salvador A412

Designs: No. 1327, Feet walking over map. No. 1328, Footprints leading to map.

1992, Sept. 16 Litho. *Perf. 14x14½*
1327 A412 2.20col multicolored 1.50 .60
1328 A412 2.20col multicolored 1.50 .60
a. Pair, #1327-1328 4.00 4.00

General Francisco Morazan (1792-1842) A413

1992, Sept. 28 *Perf. 14½x14*
1329 A413 1col multicolored 1.00 .30

Association of Salvadoran Broadcasters A414

1992, Oct. 3
1330 A414 2.20col multicolored 1.50 .60

Salvadoran Radio Day, Intl. Radio Day.

Discovery of America, 500th Anniv. A415

1992, Oct. 13 Litho. *Perf. 14x14½*
1331 A415 80c Indian artifacts 2.40 .35
1332 A415 2.20col Map, ship 6.50 .75

Exfilna '92 — A416

1992, Oct. 22 *Perf. 14x14½*
1333 A416 5col multicolored 5.00 1.60

Discovery of America, 500th Anniv.

Peace in El Salvador A417

1992, Oct. 30
1334 A417 50c blk, blue & yel .70 .25

Christmas A418

Perf. 14x14½, 14½x14
1992, Nov. 23 Litho.
1335 A418 80c shown .80 .25
1336 A418 2.20col Nativity, vert. 1.75 .60

Wildlife A419

Designs: 50c, Tapirus bairdii. 70c, Chironectes minimus. 1col, Eira barbara. 3col, Felis yagouaroundi. 4.50col, Odocoileus virginianus.

1993, Jan. 15 Litho. *Perf. 14x14½*
1337 A419 50c multicolored .40 .25
1338 A419 70c multicolored .60 .25
1339 A419 1col multicolored 1.50 .30
1340 A419 3col multicolored 2.50 .85
1341 A419 4.50col multicolored 3.50 1.25
Nos. 1337-1341 (5) 8.50 2.90

Month of the Elderly A420

Design: 2.20col, Boy, old man holding tree.

1993, Jan. 27
1342 A420 80c black .60 .25
1343 A420 2.20col multicolored 1.60 .60

Agape Social Welfare Organization — A421

Designs: a, Divine Providence Church. b, People, symbols of love and peace.

1993, Mar. 4 Litho. *Perf. 14x14½*
1344 A421 1col Pair, #a.-b. 1.40 1.40

Secretary's Day A422

1993, Apr. 26 Litho. *Perf. 14x14½*
1345 A422 1col multicolored .60 .25

Benjamin Bloom Children's Hospital A423

1993, June 18 Litho. *Perf. 14x14½*
1346 A423 5col multicolored 3.00 1.10

Visit by Mexican President Carlos Salinas de Gortari A424

1993, July 14
1347 A424 2.20col multicolored 1.50 .50

Aquatic Birds A425

80c, Casmerodius albus. 1col, Mycteria americana. 2.20col, Ardea herodias. 5col, Ajaja ajaja.

1993, Sept. 28 Litho. *Perf. 14x14½*
1348 A425 80c multicolored .65 .25
1349 A425 1col multicolored .90 .25
1350 A425 2.20col multicolored 1.60 .25
1351 A425 5col multicolored 3.75 .60
Nos. 1348-1351 (4) 6.90 1.35

Pharmacy Review Commission, Cent. — A426

1993, Oct. 6
1352 A426 80c multicolored .55 .25

America Issue A427

Endangered species: 80c, Dasyprocta punctata. 2.20col, Procyon lotor.

1993, Oct. 11 Litho. *Perf. 14x14½*
1353 A427 80c multicolored 1.00 .25
1354 A427 2.20col multicolored 2.00 .35

Fifth Central America Games A428

50c, Mascot, torch. 1.60col, Emblem. 2.20col, Mascot, map of Central America. 4.50col, Map of El Salvador, mascot.

Perf. 14½x14, 14x14½
1993, Oct. 29 Litho.
1355 A428 50c multi .50 .25
1356 A428 1.60col multi 1.00 .35
1357 A428 2.20col multi, horiz. 1.25 .55
1358 A428 4.50col multi, horiz. 2.50 .70
Nos. 1355-1358 (4) 5.25 1.85

Miniature Sheet

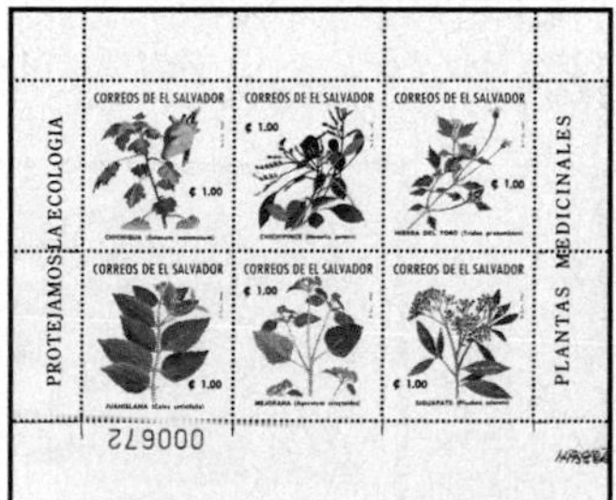

Medicinal Plants — A429

Designs: a, Solanum mammosum. b, Hamelia patens. c, Tridex procumbens. d, Calea urticifolia. e, Ageratum conyzoides. f, Pluchea odorata.

1993, Dec. 10 Litho. *Perf. 14½x14*
1359 A429 1col Sheet of 6, #a.-f. 5.00 2.50

Christmas A430

1993, Nov. 23 *Perf. 14x14½*
1360 A430 80c Holy Family .50 .25
1361 A430 2.20col Nativity Scene 1.00 .60

Alberto Masferrer (1868-1932), Writer — A431

1993, Nov. 30
1362 A431 2.20col multicolored 1.50 .60

Intl. Year of the Family — A432

1994, Feb. 28 Litho. *Perf. 14½x14*
1363 A432 2.20col multicolored 1.50 .60

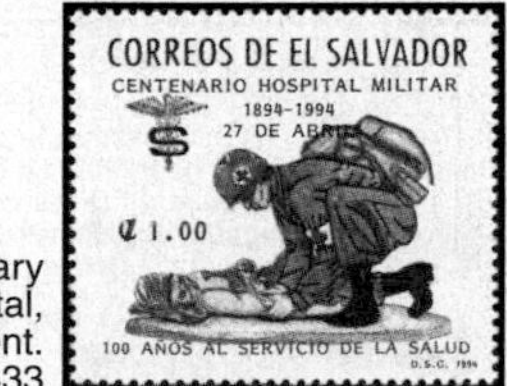

Military Hospital, Cent. A433

1994, Apr. 27 Litho. *Perf. 14*
1364 A433 1col shown .70 .30
1365 A433 1col Hospital building .70 .30

City of Santa Ana, Cent. — A434

Designs: 60c, Arms of Department of Santa Ana. 80c, Inscription honoring heroic deeds of 44 patriots.

1994, Apr. 29 Litho. *Perf. 14*
1366 A434 60c multicolored .45 .30
1367 A434 80c multicolored .55 .30

1994 World Cup Soccer Championships, US — A435

Soccer plays, flags from: 60c, Romania, Colombia, Switzerland, US. 80c, Sweden, Cameroun, Russia, Brazil. 1col, South Korea, Spain, Bolivia, Germany. 2.20col, Bulgaria, Nigeria, Greece, Argentina. 4.50col, Mexico, Norway, Ireland, Italy. 5col, Saudi Arabia, Netherlands, Morocco, Belgium.

1994, June 6 Litho. *Perf. 14*
1368 A435 60c multicolored .60 .25
1369 A435 80c multicolored .60 .25
1370 A435 1col multicolored .75 .30
1371 A435 2.20col multicolored 1.40 .45
1372 A435 4.50col multicolored 2.75 .75
1373 A435 5col multicolored 3.00 .85
Nos. 1368-1373 (6) 9.10 2.85

Plaza of Sovereign Military Order of Malta A436

1994, June 24 Litho. *Perf. 14*
1374 A436 2.20col multicolored 1.50 .40

Traditions A437

Designs: 1col, Tiger and deer dance. 2.20col, Spotted bull dance.

1994, June 30
1375 A437 1col multicolored .80 .30
1376 A437 2.20col multicolored 1.40 .40

Nutritional Plants — A438

70c, Capsicum annuum. 80c, Theobroma cacao. 1col, Ipomoea batatas. 5col, Chamaedorea tepejilote.

1994, Aug. 29 Litho. *Perf. 14*
1377 A438 70c multicolored .60 .25
1378 A438 80c multicolored .60 .25
1379 A438 1col multicolored .80 .25
1380 A438 5col multicolored 3.00 .55
Nos. 1377-1380 (4) 5.00 1.30

Postal Transport Vehicles A439

1994, Oct. 11 Litho. *Perf. 14*
1381 A439 80c Jeep .75 .25
1382 A439 2.20col Train 2.00 .55

America issue.

22nd Bicycle Race of El Salvador A440

1994, Oct. 26
1383 A440 80c multicolored .60 .25

16th Intl. Fair of El Salvador A441

1994, Oct. 31
1384 A441 5col multicolored 3.00 1.50

Christmas A442

1994, Nov. 16
1385 A442 80c shown .50 .25
1386 A442 2.20col Magi, Christ child 1.25 .55

Beetles A443

80c, Cotinis mutabilis. 1col, Phyllophaga. 2.20col, Galofa. 5col, Callipogon barbatus.

1994, Dec. 16 Litho. *Perf. 14*
1387 A443 80c multi .70 .25
1388 A443 1col multi .90 .30
1389 A443 2.20col multi 2.25 .40
1390 A443 5col multi 5.00 .75
Nos. 1387-1390 (4) 8.85 1.70

Salvadoran Culture Center, 40th Anniv. — A444

1995, Mar. 24 Litho. *Perf. 14½x14*
1391 A444 70c shown .45 .25
1392 A444 1col "40" emblem .60 .25

Ceramic Treasures Archeological Site — A445

Designs: 60c, Cup. 70c, Three-footed earthen dish. 80c, Two-handled jar. 2.20col, Long-necked jar. 4.50col, Excavation structure #3. 5col, Excavation structure #4.

1995, Apr. 26 Litho. *Perf. 14½x14*
1393 A445 60c multicolored .40 .25
1394 A445 70c multicolored .50 .25
1395 A445 80c multicolored .55 .25
1396 A445 2.20col multicolored 1.40 .55
1397 A445 4.50col multicolored 2.90 1.25
1398 A445 5col multicolored 3.25 1.25
Nos. 1393-1398 (6) 9.00 3.80

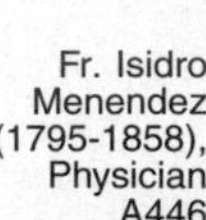

Fr. Isidro Menendez (1795-1858), Physician
A446

1995, May 19

1399 A446 80c multicolored .75 .30

La Centro Americana, SA, 80th Anniv. — A447

Designs: 80c, Insuring the future of children. 2.20col, Child wearing costume.

1995, July 7 **Litho.** ***Perf. 14***

1400 A447 80c multicolored .50 .25
1401 A447 2.20col multicolored 1.50 .65

Sacred Heart College, Cent.
A448

1995, July 26 ***Perf. 14x14½***

1402 A448 80c multicolored .80 .30

FAO, 50th Anniv. — A449

1995, Aug. 16 **Litho.** ***Perf. 14½x14***

1403 A449 2.20col multicolored 1.50 .65

Tourism
A450

Designs: 50c, Los Almendros Beach, Sonsonate. 60c, Green Lagoon, Apaneca. 2.20col, Guerrero Beach, La Union. 5col, Usulutan Volcano.

1995, Aug. 30 ***Perf. 14x14½***

1404 A450 50c multicolored .40 .25
1405 A450 60c multicolored .50 .25
1406 A450 2.20col multicolored 1.50 .55
1407 A450 5col multicolored 3.25 1.25
Nos. 1404-1407 (4) 5.65 2.30

Orchids
A451

#1408, Pleurothallis glandulosa. #1409, Pleurothallis grobyi. #1410, Pleurothallis fuegii. #1411, Lemboglossum stellatum. #1412, Lepanthes inaequalis. #1413, Pleurothallis hirsuta. #1414, Hexadesmia micrantha. #1415, Pleurothallis segoviense. #1416, Stelis aprica. #1417, Platystele stenostachya. #1418, Stelis barbata. #1419, Pleurothallis schiedeii.

1995, Sept. 28 **Litho.** ***Perf. 14½x14***

1408 A451 60c multicolored .50 .25
1409 A451 60c multicolored .50 .25
a. Pair, #1408-1409 1.00 .40
1410 A451 70c multicolored .70 .25
1411 A451 70c multicolored .70 .25
1412 A451 1col multicolored 1.00 .30
1413 A451 1col multicolored 1.00 .30
1414 A451 3col multicolored 2.75 .80
1415 A451 3col multicolored 2.75 .80
1416 A451 4.50col multicolored 4.00 1.25
1417 A451 4.50col multicolored 4.00 1.25
a. Pair, #1416-1417 8.00 3.00
1418 A451 5col multicolored 4.75 1.75
1419 A451 5col multicolored 4.75 1.75
Nos. 1408-1419 (12) 27.40 9.20

America Issue — A452

Martins: 80c, Chloroceryle aenea. 2.20col, Chloroceryle americana.

1995, Oct. 11

1420 A452 80c multicolored 1.25 .30
1421 A452 2.20col multicolored 3.50 .70

UN, 50th Anniv. — A453

Design: 2.20col, Hands of different races holding UN emblem, "50."

1995, Oct. 23

1422 A453 80c multicolored .60 .30
1423 A453 2.20col multicolored 1.75 .70

Christmas
A454

1995, Nov. 17 **Litho.** ***Perf. 14½x14***

1424 A454 80c shown .60 .30
1425 A454 2.20col Families, clock tower 1.75 .70

Miniature Sheet

Fauna — A455

Designs: a, Bubo virginianus. b, Potos flavus. c, Porthidium godmani. d, Felis pardalis (f). e, Dellathis bifurcata. f, Felis concolor (h). g, Mazama americana. h, Leptophobia aripa. i, Bolitoglossa salvinii. j, Eugenes fulgens (h, i).

1995, Nov. 24 ***Perf. 14x14½***

1426 A455 80c Sheet of 10, #a.-j. 10.00 10.00

Independence, 174th Anniv. — A456

Designs: 80c, Natl. arms, export products, money, textile workers, pharmaceuticals. 25col, Crates of products leaving El Salvador.

1995, Sept. 14 ***Perf. 14½x14***

1427 A456 80c shown .50 .25
1428 A456 25col multicolored 15.00 7.50

2nd Visit of Pope John Paul II — A457

5.40col, Pope John Paul II, Metropolitan Cathedral.

1996, Feb. 8 **Litho.** ***Perf. 14½x14***

1429 A457 1.50col multicolored 1.50 .45
1430 A457 5.40col multicolored 5.00 1.60

ANTEL, Telecommunications Workers' Day — A458

1.50col, Satellite dish, hand holding cable fibers. 5col, Three globes, telephone receiver.

Perf. 14x14½, 14½x14

1996, Apr. 27 **Litho.**

1431 A458 1.50col multi 1.00 .45
1432 A458 5col multi, vert. 3.50 1.50

City of San Salvador, 450th Anniv.
A459

Designs: 2.50col, Spanish meeting natives. 2.70col, Diego de Holguin, first mayor, mission. 3.30col, Old National Palace. 4col, Heroe's Boulevard, modern view of city.

1996, Mar. 27 ***Perf. 14x14½***

1433 A459 2.50col multicolored 1.75 .80
1434 A459 2.70col multicolored 2.00 .85
1435 A459 3.30col multicolored 2.25 1.00
1436 A459 4col multicolored 2.75 1.25
Nos. 1433-1436 (4) 8.75 3.90

Natl. Artists, Entertainers
A460

Designs: 1col, Rey Avila (1929-95). 1.50col, María Teresa Moreira (1934-95). 2.70col, Francisco Antonio Lara (1900-89). 4col, Carlos Alverez Pineda (1928-93).

1996, May 17 **Litho.** ***Perf. 14½x14***

1437 A460 1col multicolored .70 .35
1438 A460 1.50col multicolored 1.00 .50
1439 A460 2.70col multicolored 1.60 .85
1440 A460 4col multicolored 2.50 1.25
Nos. 1437-1440 (4) 5.80 2.95

YSKL Radio, 40th Anniv.
A461

1996, May 24 ***Perf. 14x14½***

1441 A461 1.40col multicolored 1.20 .60

1996 Summer Olympic Games, Atlanta
A462

Early Greek athletes: 1.50col, Discus thrower. 3col, Jumper. 4col, Wrestlers. 5col, Javelin thrower.

1996, July 3 **Litho.** ***Perf. 14***

1442 A462 1.50col multicolored 1.00 .50
1443 A462 3col multicolored 2.00 1.00
1444 A462 4col multicolored 2.75 1.40
1445 A462 5col multicolored 3.50 1.75
Nos. 1442-1445 (4) 9.25 4.65

Birds A463

Designs: a, Pheucticus ludovicianus. b, Tyrannus forficatus. c, Dendroica petechia. d, Falco sparverius. e, Icterus galbula.

1996, Aug. 9 Litho. *Perf. 14x14½*
1446 A463 1.50col Strip of 5, #a.-e. 18.00 9.00

Diaro de Hoy Newspaper, 60th Anniv. — A464

1996, Sept. 20
1447 A464 5.20col multicolored 3.50 2.00

Channel 2 Television Station, 30th Anniv. — A465

1996, Sept. 27 *Perf. 14½x14*
1448 A465 10col multicolored 6.00 3.75

UNICEF, 50th Anniv. A466

1996, Oct. 4 *Perf. 14x14½*
1449 A466 1col multicolored 1.00 .60

Traditional Costumes A467

America issue: 1.50col, Blouse, short flannel skirt, Nahuizalco. 4col, Blouse, long skirt, Panchimalco.

1996, Oct. 11 *Perf. 14½x14*
1450 A467 1.50col multicolored 5.00 .60
1451 A467 4col multicolored 12.00 1.40

Christmas A468

Designs: 2.50col, Night scene of homes, Christmas tree, church. 4col, Day scene of people celebrating outside homes, church.

1996, Nov. 28 Litho. *Perf. 14½x14*
1452 A468 2.50col multicolored 2.00 .85
1453 A468 4col multicolored 3.00 1.40

Constitution Day — A469

1996, Dec. 19 Litho. *Perf. 14½x14*
1454 A469 1col multicolored 1.10 .50

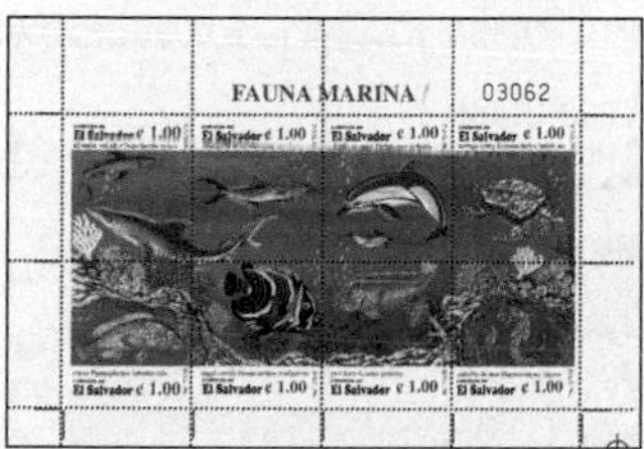
Marine Life — A470

a, Nasolamia velox. b, Scomberomorus sierra. c, Delphinus delphis. d, Eretmochelys imbricata. e, Epinephelus labriformis. f, Pomacanthus zonipectus. g, Scarus perrico. h, Hippocampus ingens.

1996, Dec. 17
1455 A470 1col Sheet of 8, #a.-h. 8.00 8.00

Jerusalem, 3000th Anniv. A471

1996, Dec. 5 Litho. *Perf. 14x14½*
1456 A471 1col multicolored .80 .40

El Mundo Newspaper, 30th Anniv. A472

1997, Feb. 6 Litho. *Perf. 14x14½*
1457 A472 10col multicolored 7.00 3.75

Exfilna '97 — A473

1997, Feb. 21
1458 A473 4col Baldwin 58441, 1925 4.25 1.50

Carmelite Order of San Jose, 80th Anniv. A474

Design: Mother Clara Maria of Jesus Quiros.

1997, Mar. 19
1459 A474 1col multicolored 1.10 .40

American School, 50th Anniv. — A475

1997, Apr. 10 *Perf. 14½x14*
1460 A475 25col multicolored 14.00 9.00

Tropical Fruit — A476

No. 1461: a, Annona diversifolia. b, Anacardium occidentale. c, Cucumis melo. d, Pouteria mammosa.
4col, Carica papaya.

1997, May 28 Litho. *Perf. 14x14½*
1461 A476 1.50col Sheet of 4, #a.-d. 6.00 6.00

Souvenir Sheet
Rouletted 13½
1462 A476 4col multicolored 3.50 3.50

Lions Club in El Salvador, 55th Anniv. A476a

1997, Aug. 15 Litho. *Perf. 14*
1463 A476a 4col multicolored 3.00 1.75

Montreal Protocol on Substances that Deplete Ozone Layer, 10th Anniv. — A477

1997, Aug. 28 Litho. *Perf. 14*
1464 A477 1.50col shown 1.75 .55
1465 A477 4col Boy drinking water 3.25 1.50

Inter-American Water Day (#1465).

Miguel de Cervantes Saavedra (1547-1616), Writer — A478

1997, Sept. 26 Litho. *Perf. 14*
1466 A478 4col multicolored 3.00 1.50

Independence Day — A479

1997, Sept. 10 Litho. *Perf. 14x14½*
1467 A479 2.50col shown 1.75 .85
1468 A479 5.20col Flag, children, dove 3.50 1.75

Scouting in El Salvador, 75th Anniv. — A480

1997, Oct. 3 *Perf. 14½x14*
1469 A480 1.50col multicolored 1.90 .75

Life of a Postman A481

America issue: 1col, Postman delivering mail. 4col, Postman on motor scooter, dog.

1997, Oct. 10 Litho. ***Perf. 14½x14***

1470 A481 1col multicolored 1.25 .40
1471 A481 4col multicolored 3.50 1.50

ACES (Automobile Club of El Salvador), 26th Anniv. A482

1997, Oct. 28 ***Perf. 14x14½***

1472 A482 10col multicolored 7.00 3.75

Christmas — A483

Children's paintings: No. 1473, Outdoor scene. No. 1474, Indoor scene.

1997, Nov. 20 Litho. ***Perf. 14***

1473 1.50col multicolored 1.50 .60
1474 1.50col multicolored 1.50 .60
a. A483 Pair, #1473-1474 3.00 3.00

Salesian Order in El Salvador, Cent. — A484

Designs: a, Map, St. John Bosco (1715-88). b, St. Cecilia College. c, San Jose College, priest. d, Ricaldone, students working with machinery. e, Maria Auxiliadora Church. f, City of St. John Bosco, students working with electronic equipment.

1997, Dec. 6

1475 A484 1.50col Sheet of 6, #a.-f. 6.00 6.00

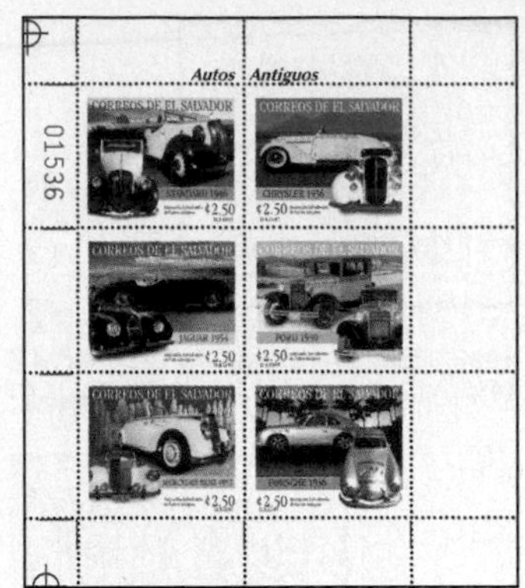
Antique Automobiles — A485

Designs: a, 1946 Standard. b, 1936 Chrysler. c, 1954 Jaguar. d, 1930 Ford. e, 1953 Mercedes Benz. f, 1956 Porsche.

1997, Dec. 17

1476 A485 2.50col Sheet of 6, #a.-f. 10.00 6.50

St. Joseph Missionaries, 125th Anniv. — A486

1col, Image, Church of St. Joseph, Ahuachapan. 4col, Jose M. Vilaseca, Cesarea Esparza.

1998, Jan. 23 Litho. ***Perf. 14***

1477 A486 1col multicolored .50 .25
1478 A486 4col multicolored 2.25 1.10

New Intl. Airport A487

1998, Mar. 17 Litho. ***Perf. 14***

1479 A487 10col multicolored 4.00 2.00

Organization of American States, 50th Anniv. — A488

1998, May 29 Litho. ***Perf. 14½x14***

1480 A488 4col multicolored 2.00 .90

1998 World Cup Soccer Championships, France — A489

Soccer player, Paris landmarks: a, Sacre Coeur. b, Eiffel Tower. c, Louvre. d, Notre Dame.

4col, Soccer ball, Arc d'Triumphe, horiz.

1998, May 13

1481 A489 1.50col Strip of 4, #a.-d. 4.00 3.00

Souvenir Sheet

Rouletted 13½

1482 A489 4col multicolored 9.00 9.00

El Salvador, 1997 Champions of the 6th Central American Games A490

Designs inside medals: No. 1483, Women's gymnastics, weight lifting, judo. No. 1484, Discus, volleyball, women's basketball. No. 1485, Swimming, tennis, water polo. No. 1486, Gymnastics, wrestling, shooting.

1998, July 17 Litho. ***Perf. 14***

1483 A490 1.50col multicolored .90 .50
1484 A490 1.50col multicolored .90 .50
1485 A490 1.50col multicolored .90 .50
1486 A490 1.50col multicolored .90 .50
Nos. 1483-1486 (4) 3.60 2.00

Dr. Jose Gustavo Guerrero (1876-1958), President of the World Court — A491

1998, July 22 Litho. ***Perf. 14***

1487 A491 1col multicolored .70 .30

18th International Fair — A492

1998, Aug. 28

1488 A492 4col multicolored 1.75 .85

Painting of the Death of Manuel José Arce, Soldier, Politician A493

1998, Sept. 1

1489 A493 4col multicolored 1.75 .85

Hummingbirds and Flowers — A494

a, Archilochus colubris. b, Amazilia rutila. c, Hylocharis eliciae. d, Colibri thalassinus. e, Campylopterus hemileucurus. f, Lampornis amethystinus.

1998, Sept. 7

1490 A494 1.50col Sheet of 6, #a.-f. 6.50 5.00

House Social Fund, 25th Anniv. — A495

1998, Sept. 29 Litho. ***Perf. 14***

1491 A495 10col multicolored 4.00 2.00

Natl. Archives, 50th Anniv. — A496

1998, Oct. 2

1492 A496 1.50col multicolored 1.00 .35

Famous Women A497

America issue: 1col, Alice Lardé de Venturino. 4col, Maria de Baratta.

1998, Oct. 12

1493 A497 1col multicolored .70 .30
1494 A497 4col multicolored 2.75 .85

Christmas A498

Children's drawings: 1col, Clock tower, nativity scene. 4col, Pageant players as angels, Holy Family parading to church, nativity scene.

1998, Nov. 24 Litho. ***Perf. 14***

1495 A498 1col multicolored .60 .30
1496 A498 4col multicolored 1.75 .90

World Stamp Day A499

1998, Nov. 27 Litho. ***Perf. 14***

1497 A499 1col multicolored .85 .30

Salvadoran Air Force, 75th Anniv. — A500

Designs: a, C47T transport plane. b, TH-300 helicopter. c, UH-1H helicopter. d, Dragonfly bomber.

1998, Dec. 1 Litho. *Perf. 14¼*
1498 A500 1.50col Strip of 4, #a.-d. 3.50 3.50

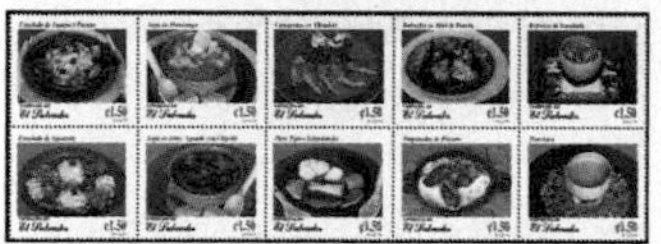

Traditional Foods — A501

Designs: a, Ensalada de papaya y pacaya. b, Sopa de mondongo. c, Camarones en alhuaiste. d, Buñuelos en miel de panela. e, Refresco de ensalada. f, Ensalada de aguacate. g, Sopa de arroz aguado con chipilín. h, Plato típico salvadoreño. i, Empanadas de plátano. j, Horchata.

1998, Dec. 9 Litho. *Perf. 14*
1499 A501 1.50col Block of 10, #a.-j. 10.00 10.00

Roberto D'Aubuisson Signing New Constitution, 1983 — A502

1998, Dec. 15 Litho. *Perf. 14x14¼*
1503 A502 25col multicolored 9.00 4.25

First Natl. Topical Philatelic Exhibition A503

Salvador Railway Company Steamship Service.

1999, Feb. 19 Litho. *Perf. 14*
1504 A503 2.50col multicolored 1.25 .50

Introduction of Television, 40th Anniv. — A504

1999, Feb. 24
1505 A504 4col multicolored 1.50 .75

European Union Cooperation with El Salvador — A505

1999, May 7 Litho. *Perf. 14x14¼*
1506 A505 5.20col shown 2.00 1.00
1507 A505 10col Hands clasped 3.50 1.75

Water Birds A506

No. 1508: a, Gallinula chlorupus. b, Porphyrula martinica. c, Pardirallus maculatus. d, Anas discors. e, Dendrocygna autumnalis. f, Fulica americana. g, Jacana spinosa. h, Perzana carolina. i, Aramus guarauna. j, Oxyura dominica.
4col, Aythya affinis.

1999, Apr. 22 *Perf. 14x14¼*
1508 A506 1col Block of 10, #a.-j. 8.00 8.00

Souvenir Sheet
Rouletted 8¾
1509 A506 4col multicolored 8.00 8.00

Bats A507

Designs: a, Glossophaga soricina. b, Desmodus rotundus. c, Noctilio leporinus. d, Vampyrum spectrum. e, Ectophilla alba. f, Myotis nigricans.

1999, June 30 Litho. *Perf. 14x14½*
1510 A507 1.50col Sheet of 6, #a.-f. 5.50 5.50

Visit of US Pres. William J. Clinton — A508

Designs: a, Seals, flags of El Salvador, US. b, Pres. Francisco Flores of El Salvador, Pres. Clinton.

1999, May 19 *Perf. 14¼*
1511 A508 5col Pair, #a.-b. 5.00 3.00

Quality Control Institute, 20th Anniv. — A509

1999, May 20 *Perf. 14¼*
1512 A509 5.40col multicolored 2.50 1.25

Geothermic Energy A510

1999, July 16 Litho. *Perf. 14x14½*
1513 A510 1col Drilling tower .50 .25
1514 A510 4col Power station 1.75 .85

Exports A511

1999, July 21 *Perf. 14½x14*
1515 A511 4col multicolored 2.00 1.00

Salvadoran Journalists' Association A512

1999, July 30 *Perf. 14x14½*
1516 A512 1.50col multicolored .80 .35

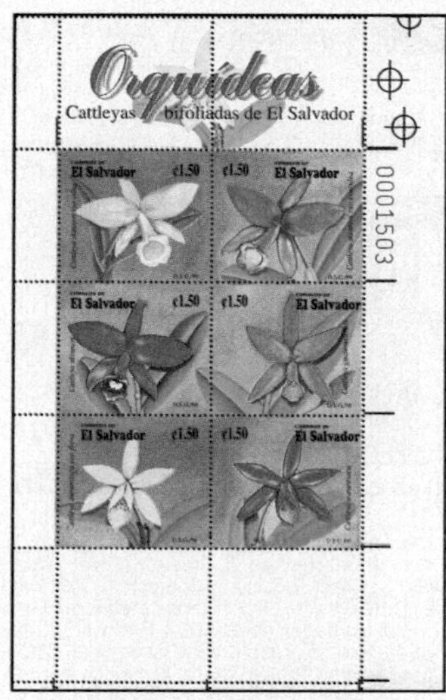

Cattleya Orchids — A513

Designs: a, Skinneri var. alba. b, Skinneri var. coerulea. c, Skinneri. d, Guatemalensis. e, Aurantiaca var. flava. f, Aurantiaca.

1999, Aug. 25
1517 A513 1.50col Sheet of 6, #a.-f. + 4 labels 6.00 6.00

Toño Salazar, Caricaturist A514

Designs: a, Self-portrait. b, Salarrué. c, Claudia Lars. d, Francisco Gavidia. e, Miguel Angel Asturias.

1999, Aug. 31
1518 A514 1.50col Strip of 5, #a.-e. 4.00 4.00

Central American Nutrition Institute A515

1999, Sept. 14 Litho. *Perf. 14x14½*
1519 A515 5.20col Children, food 2.00 1.10
1520 A515 5.40col Food 2.25 1.25

Armed Forces, 175th Anniv. — A516

1999, Sept. 24 *Perf. 14¼x14*
1521 A516 1col Gens. Arce & Barrios .60 .25
1522 A516 1.50col Soldier, flag .90 .40

Intl. Year of Older Persons A517

1999, Oct. 8
1523 A517 10col multicolored 3.50 2.00

America Issue, A New Millennium Without Arms — A518

1999, Oct. 12
1524 A518 1col Dove, children .65 .35
1525 A518 4col "No Guns" sign 2.25 1.25

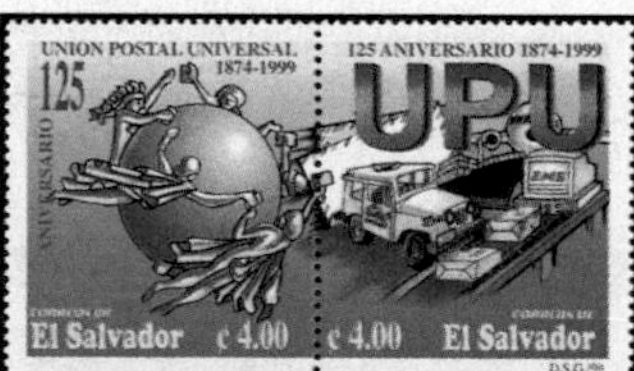

UPU, 125th Anniv. — A519

Designs: a, UPU emblem. b, Mail, jeep, ship, airplane, computer.

1999, Oct. 22
1526 A519 4col Pair, #a.-b. 4.00 4.00

Christmas — A520

Paintings by:
No. 1527: a, Delmy Guandique. b, Margarita Orellana.
No. 1528: a, Lolly Sandoval. b, José Francisco Guadrón.

1999, Nov. 4

1527	A520 1.50col Pair, #a.-b.		1.50	.60
1528	A520 4col Pair, #a.-b.		3.50	1.25

Inter-American Development Bank, 40th Anniv. — A521

1999, Nov. 24 Litho. *Perf. 14¼x14*

1529 A521 25col multi	10.00	5.00

Woodpeckers A522

Designs: a, Melanerpes aurifrons. b, Piculus rubiginosus. c, Sphyrapicus varius. d, Dryocopus lineatus. e, Melanerpes formicivorus.

1999, Dec. 3

1530 A522 1.50col Vert. strip of 5, #a.-e.	4.50	4.50

Salvadoran Coffee Assoc., 70th Anniv. A523

1999, Dec. 7 *Perf. 14x14¼*

1531 A523 10col multi	4.50	2.10

Millennium A524

2000, Jan. 6 *Perf. 14¼x14*

1532 A524 1.50col multi	1.10	.50

Fireman's Foundation, 25th Anniv. — A525

Designs: 2.50col, Fireman rescuing child. 25col, Emblem.

2000, Jan. 17 Litho. *Perf. 14¼x14*

1533 A525 2.50col multi	1.50	.60
1534 A525 25col multi	9.50	4.75

Faith and Happiness Foundation, 30th Anniv. — A526

2000, Feb. 10

1535 A526 1col multi	.70	.30

Millennium A527

No. 1536, Serie I: a, El Tazumal Mayan pyramid. b, Christopher Columbus and ships. c, Spanish soldier, native. d, Independence.

No. 1537, Serie II: a, Salvadoran White House, 1890. b, Shoppers at street market, 1920. c, Trolley and Nuevo Mundo Hotel, 1924. d, Automobiles on South 2nd Avenue, San Salvador, 1924.

2000 Sheets of 4 *Perf. 14x14¼*

1536 A527 1.50col #a.-d.	4.50	4.50
1537 A527 1.50col #a.-d.	4.50	4.50

Issued: No. 1536, 3/16; No. 1537, 6/16.

Nos. 1536 & 1537 includes two labels.

El Imposible Natl. Park — A528

No. 1538: a, Gate. b, Ocelot (tigrillo). c, Paca (tepezcuintle). d, Venado River waterfalls. e, Black curassow (pajuil). f, Tree with yellow leaves. g, Orchid (flor de encarnación). h, Honeycreeper (torogoz). i, Bird with purple head (siete colores). j, Vegetation near cliff. k, Interpretation center. l, Bird with black and yellow plumage (payasito). m, Frog. n, Mushrooms (hongos). o, Red flower (guaco de tierra). p, Green toucan. q, Hillside foliage. r, Agouti (cotuza). s, Ant bear (oso hormiguero). t, Cascaddes of El Imposible.

2000, Apr. 28 *Perf. 14¼x14*

1538	Sheet of 20	12.00	6.00
a.-t.	A528 1col Any single	.60	.30

La Prensa Grafica, 85th Anniv. — A529

2000, May 9

1539 A529 5col multi	2.25	1.00

Canonization of Marcelino Champagnat (1789-1840) A530

2000, June 2

1540 A530 10col multi	4.00	1.50

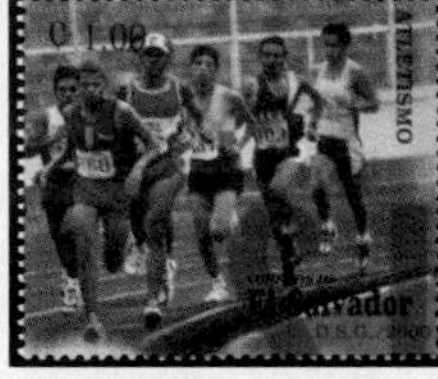

2000 Summer Olympics, Sydney A531

No. 1541: a, Runners. b, Gymnast. c, High jumper. d, Weight lifter. e, Fencer. f, Cyclist. g, Swimmer. h, Shooter. i, Archer. j, Judo.

2000, July 20 *Perf. 14x14¼*

1541	Sheet of 10	6.00	6.00
a.-j.	A531 1col Any single	.45	.25

Trains A532

No. 1542: a, Baldwin locomotive Philadelphia 58441. b, General Electric locomotive series 65k-15. c, Train car. d, Presidential coach car.

2000, Aug. 3

1542	Vert. strip of 4	6.00	6.00
a.-d.	A532 1.50col Any single	1.00	.50

World Post Day — A533

2000, Oct. 9 Litho. *Perf. 14¼x14*

1543 A533 5col multi	2.25	1.25

Christmas Tree Ornaments A534

No. 1544: a, Snowman. b, Bells. c, Striped pendants. d, Candy cane. e, Candles. f, Sleigh. g, Gifts. h, Santa Claus. i, Santa's hat. j, Santa's boot.

2000, Nov. 9

1544	Block of 10	7.00	7.00
a.-j.	A534 1col Any single	.65	.30

Art by Expatriates A535

Art by: a, Roberto Mejía Ruíz. b, Alex Cuchilla. c, Nicolas Fredy Shi Quán. d, José Bernardo Pacheco. e, Oscar Soles.

2000, Dec. 4 *Perf. 14x14¼*

1545	Horiz. strip of 5	15.00	15.00
a.-e.	A535 4col Any single	2.25	1.50

Pets A536

No. 1546: a, 1.50col, Dogs. b, 1.50col, Dog and cat.

No. 1547: a, 2.50col, Parakeets. b, 2.50col, Dogs, diff.

2001, Feb. 28 Litho. *Perf. 14x14¼*
Vert. Pairs, #a-b

1546-1547 A536 Set of 2	6.00	6.00

Nos. 1546-1662 show denominations in colons and US dollars.

Saburo Hirao Park, 25th Anniv. A537

Designs: 5col, Playground. 25col, Bridge in gardens.

2001, Mar. 14

1548-1549 A537 Set of 2	17.00	17.00

Claudia Lars (1899-1974), Salvadoran Writer, and Federico Proaño (1848-94), Ecuadoran Writer — A538

2001, Aug. 28 Litho. *Perf. 14x14¼*

1550 A538 10col multi	4.50	2.25

St. Vincent de Paul Children's Home, 125th Anniv. A539

2001, Oct. 26

1551 A539 4col multi	1.75	.90

Mushrooms A540

No. 1552: a, Lactaius indigo. b, Pleurotus ostreatus. c, Ramaria sp. d, Clavaria vermicularis.

No. 1553: a, Amanita muscaria. b, Phillipsia sp. c, Russula emetica. d, Geastrum triplex.

2001, Dec. 20 *Perf. 14¼x14*

1552	Horiz. strip of 4	5.00	5.00
a.-d.	A540 1.50col Any single	1.00	.60
1553	Horiz. strip of 4	14.00	14.00
a.-d.	A540 4col Any single	2.75	1.60

St. Josemaria Escrivá de Balaguer (1902-75), Founder of Opus Dei — A541

Balaguer and: 1col, Plowed field. 5col, People and computers.

2002, Apr. 26 **Litho.** *Perf. 14¼x14*

1554-1555	A541 Set of 2	5.00	2.50

San Miguel Lions Club, 51st Anniv. — A542

2002, July 31

1556	A542 5col multi	4.00	2.00

Rosales National Hospital, Cent. — A543

2002, June 28

1557	A543 10col multi	8.00	4.00

Peace Accords, 10th Anniv. — A544

Designs: No. 1558, 2.50col, Dove and sun. No. 1559, 2.50col, UN emblem and handshake.

No. 1560: a, 2.50col, Dove with olive branch flying over village. b, 2.50col, Dove, flag.

2002, May 15 *Perf. 14¼x14*

1558-1559	A544 Set of 2	4.00	2.00

Souvenir Sheet

Rouletted Irregularly

1560	A544 Sheet of 2, #a-b	4.00	4.00

19th Central American and Caribbean Games A545

No. 1561: a, Montage of athletes. b, Bicycle race. c, Children's drawing of various athletes. d, Gymnast.

4col, Mascots.

2002, June 13 *Perf. 14x14¼*

1561	Vert. strip of 4	3.50	3.50
a.-d.	A545 1col Any single	.65	.40

Souvenir Sheet

Rouletted Irregularly

1562	A545 4col multi	3.50	3.50

A546

2002 World Cup Soccer Championships, Japan and Korea — A547

No. 1563 — Various Korean World Cup stadia and flags of countries in Group: a, A. b, B. c, C. d, D.

No. 1564 — Various Japanese World Cup stadia and flags of countries in Group: a, E. b, F. c, G. d, H.

4col, Flag of winning team, Brazil.

2002, July 11 *Perf. 14x14¼*

1563	Vert. strip of 4	2.75	2.75
a.-d.	A546 1col Any single	.65	.40
1564	Vert. strip of 4	5.25	5.25
a.-d.	A546 1.50col Any single	1.00	.60

Souvenir Sheet

Rouletted Irregularly

1565	A547 4col multi	3.50	3.50

Natl. Academy of Public Security, 10th Anniv. — A548

2002, Sep. 6 **Litho.** *Perf. 14¼x14*

1566	A548 1col multi	1.00	.60

Central American Parliament, 10th Anniv. (in 2001) A549

2002, Sep. 13 *Perf. 14x14¼*

1567	A549 25col multi	17.00	10.00

Pan-American Health Organization, Cent. — A550

No. 1568: a, Headquarters, Washington, DC. b, Emblem and "100."

2002, Oct. 18 **Litho.** *Perf. 14¼x14*

1568	A550 2.70col Horiz. pair, #a-b	4.50	2.25

Tourism A551

No. 1569, 1col: a, Forest, Picacho Volcano. b, Jiquilisco Bay.

No. 1570, 4col: a, Joya de Cerén Archaeological Site. b, Juayua, Sonsonate Department.

2002, Dec. 6 *Perf. 14x14¼*

Vert. Pairs, #a-b

1569-1570	A551 Set of 2	8.50	4.25

America Issue — Youth, Education, and Literacy A552

Designs: 1col, Stylized person, book, block. 1.50col, Teacher and students.

2002, Nov. 26

1571-1572	A552 Set of 2	2.25	1.10

Scouting in El Salvador, 80th Anniv. — A553

2002, Dec. 16 *Perf. 14¼x14*

1573	A553 2.70col multi	2.25	1.10

Christmas A554

Infant Jesus and: 1.50col, Mary. 2.50col, Joseph.

2002, Nov. 29

1574-1575	A554 Set of 2	3.50	1.60

Daughters of Our Lady Help of Christians (Salesian Sisters) in Central America, Cent. — A555

Designs: 70c, Girls, nun in classroom. 1.50col, Statue of Madonna and Child.

2003, May 26 **Litho.** *Perf. 14¼x14*

1576-1577	A555 Set of 2	2.00	1.00

Town of Sonsonate, 450th Anniv. — A556

2003, May 28

1578	A556 1.60col multi	1.50	.75

Grupo Roble, 40th Anniv. A557

No. 1579: a, Tree without leaves. b, Cherries on branch.

4col, Bird and nest.

2003, July 18 *Perf. 14x14¼*

1579	A557 1.50col Vert. pair, #a-b	2.50	1.25

Souvenir Sheet

Rouletted 12¾x13½

1580	A557 4col multi	3.50	3.50

Regional Sanitary Agricultural Organization, 50th Anniv. — A558

2003, July 25 *Perf. 14x14¼*

1581	A558 25col multi	17.00	10.00

Agape Ministries in El Salvador, 25th Anniv. — A559

2003, Aug. 25 *Perf. 14¼x14*

1582	A559 1.50col multi	1.25	.65

A560

Independence, 182nd Anniv. — A561

No. 1583: a, 2.50col, Maria Felipa Aranzamendi y Aguiar. b, 2.70col, Manuela Antonia Arce de Lara.
4col, Cry for Independence, Nov. 5, 1811.

2003, Sept. 30 ***Perf. 14¼x14***
1583 A560 Horiz. pair, #a-b 4.00 4.00

Souvenir Sheet
Rouletted 13½x13¼

1584 A561 4col multi 3.00 3.00

FAO in El Salvador, 25th Anniv. — A562

Designs: 1.50col, Children, farmers.
4col, Child, farmer, food preparation workers.

2003, Oct. 8 ***Perf. 14¼x14***
1585 A562 1.50col multi 1.25 .60

Souvenir Sheet
Rouletted 13¼x13¾

1586 A562 4col multi 3.50 3.50

Insects and Flowers A563

No. 1587: a, Abejorro sp. b, Chrysina quetzalcoatli. c, Anartia fatima. d, Manduca sp. e, Manduca sexta. f, Tabebuia chrysantha. g, Alpinia purpurata. h, Tecoma stans. i, Tabebuia rosea. j, Passiflora edulis.
4col, Anartia fatima, Tabebuia rosea, vert.

2003, Oct. 23 ***Perf. 14x14¼***
1587 Block of 10 13.00 13.00
a.-j. A563 1.50col Any single 1.10 .65

Souvenir Sheet
Rouletted 13¼x13¾

1588 A563 4col multi 4.00 4.00

Christmas A564

Designs: 1.50col, Madonna and Child. 4col, Holy Family.

2003, Nov. 7 ***Perf. 14¼x14***
1589-1590 A564 Set of 2 4.50 2.25

Churches A565

No. 1591: a, Church of the Immaculate Conception, Citalá. b, St. James the Apostle Church, Chalchuapa. c, St. Peter the Apostle Church, Metapán. d, Our Lady of Santa Ana Church, Chapeltique. e, St. James the Apostle Church, Conchagua.
5col, Calvary Church, San Salvador, vert.

2003, Nov. 14 ***Perf. 14x14¼***
1591 Horiz. strip of 5 12.00 12.00
a.-e. A565 4col Any single 2.25 1.25

Souvenir Sheet
Rouletted 13¼x13¾

1592 A565 5col multi 3.00 3.00

Tourism A566

No. 1593: a, Brotherhood of Panchimalco. b, Church cupola, Juayúa. c, Shalpa Beach, La Libertad. d, Tazumal Ruins.

2003, Dec. 10 ***Perf. 14x14¼***
1593 Vert. strip of 4 4.75 4.75
a.-d. A566 1.50col Any single 1.00 .60

America Issue - Flora and Fauna A567

Designs: 1.50col, Fernaldia pandurata. 4col, Lepidophyma smithii.

2003, Dec. 19
1594-1595 A567 Set of 2 4.50 2.25

El Salvador — Panama Diplomatic Relations, Cent. A568

Designs: 10col, Flags of El Salvador and Panama. 25col, Flags, ship in lock.

2004, Feb. 17 **Litho.** ***Perf. 14x14¼***
1596-1597 A568 Set of 2 17.00 8.50

Salvadoran Cooperation With European Union — A569

Stars and map of: 2.70col, Central America. 5col, Europe.

2004, May 13 ***Perf. 14¼x14***
1598-1599 A569 Set of 2 3.75 1.90

Legends A570

No. 1600, 1col: a, La Carreta Chillona. b, La Siguanaba.
No. 1601, 1.60col: a, Justo Juez de la Noche. b, El Cipitío.

2004, June 30 ***Perf. 14x14¼***
Vert. Tete-beche Pairs, #a-b

1600-1601 A570 Set of 2 2.50 1.25

El Salvador College of Chemistry and Pharmaceuticals, Cent. — A571

2004, Sept. 17
1602 A571 10col multi 3.75 1.90

Santa Tecla (Nueva San Salvador), 150th Anniv. A572

Designs: 1.50col, Adalberto Guirola Children's Home. 4col, Second Avenue.

2004, Oct. 14
1603-1604 A572 Set of 2 2.25 1.10

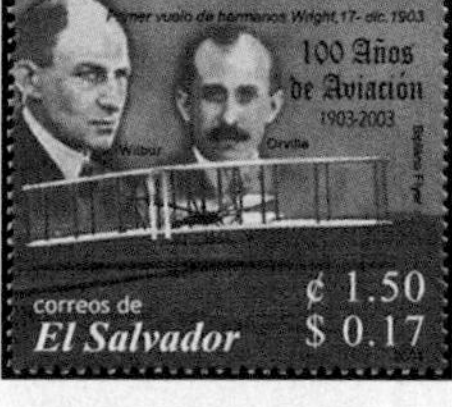

Powered Flight, Cent. (in 2003) A573

No. 1605: a, Wilbur and Orville Wright, Wright Flyer. b, Alberto Santos-Dumont, 14-Bis. c, Louis Blériot, Blériot XI. d, Glenn Curtiss, Curtiss JN-4D Jenny. e, Hugo Junkers, Junkers J.1.
No. 1606: a, Charles Lindbergh, Spirit of St. Louis. b, Amelia Earhart, Lockheed Vega. c, Chuck Yeager, Bell X-1. d, Robert Withe, X-15. e, Dick Rutan and Jeana Yeager, Voyager.
No. 1607, Wilbur and Orville Wright, Wright Flyer, vert.

2004, Nov. 5 ***Perf. 14x14¼***
1605 Horiz. strip of 5 3.00 1.40
a.-e. A573 1.50col Any single .55 .30
1606 Horiz. strip of 5 8.00 3.75
a.-e. A573 4col Any single 1.60 .75

Souvenir Sheet
Rouletted Irregularly

1607 A573 4col multi 3.00 1.50

Christmas A574

Designs: 1.50col, Holy Family. 2.50col, Shepherd and sheep. 4col, Magi. 5col, Flight into Egypt.

2004, Dec. 7 **Litho.** ***Perf. 14x14¼***
1608-1611 A574 Set of 4 5.00 2.25

America Issue - Environmental Protection — A575

Marine life: 1.40col, Akko rossi. 2.20col, Chromodoris sphoni.

2004, Dec. 17
1612-1613 A575 Set of 2 1.60 .75
1613a Tete-beche pair, #1612-1613 2.25 2.25

La Prensa Newspaper, 90th Anniv. A576

2005, Apr. 7
1614 A576 25col multi 8.00 4.00

Assassination of Archbishop Oscar Romero, 25th Anniv. — A577

Designs: 2.50col, Metropolitan Cathedral, San Salvador. 5col, Romero (1917-80).

2005, Apr. 23 ***Perf. 14¼x14***
1615-1616 A577 Set of 2 2.75 1.25

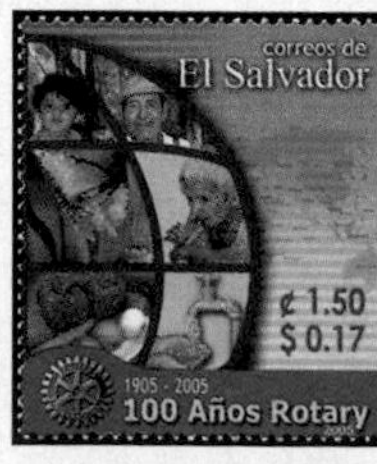

Rotary International, Cent. — A578

2005, June 15 ***Perf. 14¼x14***
1617 A578 1.50col shown 1.75 .70

Souvenir Sheet
Rouletted Irregularly

1618 A578 4col Children 5.00 1.75

Puerto de San Carlos de la Unión, 150th Anniv. A579

2005, July 27 *Perf. 14x14¼*
1619 A579 10col shown 4.00 2.00

Souvenir Sheet
Rouletted Irregularly

1620 A579 4col Pirigallo Island 2.00 1.00

Tenth Central American Students' Games A580

Designs: 1.60col, Wrestling. 2.20col, High jump. 2.70col, Karate. No. 1624, 4col, Rollerblading.

No. 1625, 4col, Karate, high jump and wrestling.

2005, Sept. 14 Litho. *Perf. 14¼x14*
1621-1624 A580 Set of 4 5.00 2.50

Souvenir Sheet
Rouletted 11x10¾x10x10½

1625 A580 4col multi 1.75 .85

Latin American Musicians — A581

No. 1626: a, Agustín Lara (1897-1970), composer, Mexico. b, Pedro Infante (1917-57), singer, Mexico. c, Libertad Lamarque (1906-2000), singer, Argentina. d, Carlos Gardel (1890-1936), singer, Argentina. e, Celia Cruz (1924-2003), singer, Cuba. f, Damaso Pérez Prado (1916-89), composer, Cuba. g, Daniel Santos (1916-92), song writer, Puerto Rico. h, Pedro Vargas (1908-89), singer, Mexico. i, Beny Moré (1919-63), singer, Cuba. j, Jorge Negrete (1911-53), singer, Mexico.

4col, Singer, microphone and guitar.

2005, Oct. 11 *Perf. 14¼x14*
1626 A581 1.50col Sheet of 10, #a-j 6.00 3.00

Souvenir Sheet
Rouletted 11x10¾

1627 A581 4col multi 2.40 1.10

Writers A582

Designs: No. 1628, 1col, Lilian Serpas (1905-85), poet. No. 1629, 1col, Oswaldo Escobar Velado (1919-61), poet. No. 1630, 4col, Alvaro Menendez Leal (1931-2000), dramatist. No. 1631, 4col, Roque Dalton (1935-75), poet. No. 1632, 5col, Pedro Geoffroy Rivas (1908-79), poet. No. 1633, 5col, Italo Lopez Vallecillos (1932-86), poet.

2005, Oct. 20 *Perf. 14¼x14*
1628-1633 A582 Set of 6 8.00 4.00

America Issue - Fight Against Poverty A583

Designs: 1.50col, Man holding food. 4col, Children and shack.

2005, Nov. 25 *Perf. 14x14¼*
1634-1635 A583 Set of 2 2.25 1.10

Christmas — A584

No. 1636 — Creche figures: a, Praying angel. b, Chicken and left half of star. c, Rooster and right half of star. d, Angel with horn. e, Donkey. f, Mary and Jesus. g, Joseph and two sheep. h, Cow. i, Camel with red saddle cloth and Magus. j, Camel without saddle and Magus. k, Camel with blue saddle cloth and Magus. l, Shepherd and three sheep. m, Woman, table and pot. n, Man and oxcart. o, Musicians. p, Bride, groom and church. q, Dog and kneeling woman. r, Sheep and shepherd holding lamb. s, Women with water jugs. t, Birds.

2005, Nov. 30 *Perf. 14¼x14*
1636 A584 Sheet of 20 8.00 8.00
a.-t. 1col Any single .40 .25

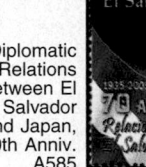

Diplomatic Relations Between El Salvador and Japan, 70th Anniv. A585

Designs: 2.50col, Flags of El Salvador and Japan, flowers, men shaking hands. 9col, Airport, medical worker and highway.

2005, Dec. 20 *Perf. 14x14¼*
1637-1638 A585 Set of 2 4.50 2.25

2006 Elections A586

Ballot box, flag and: 10col, José Mariano Calderón y San Martín. 25col, Miguel José de Castro y Lara.

2006, Feb. 28
1639-1640 A586 Set of 2 12.00 6.00

TACA Airlines, 75th Anniv. A587

No. 1641 — Anniversary emblem, parrot and: a, Stinson airplane, Northern hemisphere. b, Airbus A-319, Southern hemisphere.

2006, Mar. 31 Litho. *Perf. 14x14¼*
1641 A587 5col Vert. pair, #a-b 4.00 2.00

Laying of Cornerstone of Santa Ana Cathedral, Cent. — A588

Designs: 1.50col, Religious statues. 2.50col, Santa Ana Cathedral.

2006, Apr. 28 *Perf. 14¼x14*
1642-1643 A588 Set of 2 1.75 .85

Flora and Fauna A589

No. 1644: a, Pteroglossus torquatus. b, Smyrna blonfildia. c, Hypanartia dione. d, Sciurus variegatoides. e, Ceiba pentandra. f, Ramphastos sulfuratus. g, Eunica tatila. h, Catonephele numilia. i, Mephitis macroura. j, Enterolobium cyclocarpum.

2006, May 31 *Perf. 14x14¼*
1644 Block of 10 6.00 3.00
a.-j. A589 1col Any single .60 .25

2006 World Cup Soccer Championships, Germany — A590

No. 1645 — Flags, landmarks and people from World Cup host nations: a, Argentina, 1978. b, Spain, 1982. c, Mexico, 1986. d, Italy, 1990.

No. 1646: a, United States, 1994. b, France, 1998. c, Korea and Japan, 2002. d, Germany, 2006.

4col, Soccer ball showing German flags, horiz.

2006, June 29 *Perf. 14¼x14*
1645 Horiz. strip of 4 3.50 1.90
a.-d. A590 2.20col Any single .85 .40
1646 Horiz. strip of 4 4.25 2.10
a.-d. A590 2.70col Any single 1.00 .45

Souvenir Sheet
Rouletted 13¼

1647 A590 4col multi 2.50 1.25

Fossils A591

Designs: 1.50col, Mastodon skull. 1.60col, Vertebra of giant sloth. 5col, Mandible of giant sloth. 10col, Paw bones of giant sloth.

2006, July 26 *Perf. 14¼x14*
1648-1651 A591 Set of 4 7.25 3.50

Disaster Reduction A592

Intl. Year of Deserts and Desertification A593

2006, Aug. 31
1652 A592 1.50col multi .50 .25
1653 A593 4col multi 1.10 .60

America Issue, Energy Conservation A594

Designs: 1.50col, Woman in kitchen. 4col, Light bulb and socket.

2006, Sept. 29
1654-1655 A594 Set of 2 1.60 .80

Republic of China National Day — A595

Designs: 9col, Taipei 101 Building. 10col, President's Mansion, Taipei.

2006, Oct. 9
1656-1657 A595 Set of 2 7.50 3.75

La Constancia Industries, Cent. A596

2006, Oct. 25 *Perf. 14x14¼*
1658 A596 25col multi 10.00 5.25

Christmas A597

Designs: 1col, Our Lady of Candelaria. 1.50col, Our Lady of Carmen. 5col, Maria Auxiliadora. 10col, Our Lady of Peace.

2006 ***Perf. 14¼x14***
1659-1662 A597 Set of 4 7.00 3.25

2007 Census A598

2007, Mar. 26 Litho. ***Perf. 14¼x14***
1663 A598 1c multi .25 .25

Social Peace Year — A599

2007, May 3
1664 A599 $10 multi 35.00 17.50

Scouting, Cent. A600

Designs: No. 1665, 10c, Lord Robert Baden-Powell blowing kudu horn. No. 1666, 10c, Salvadoran Scouts.

2007, June 21 Litho. ***Perf. 14x14¼***
1665-1666 A600 Set of 2 .80 .80

Miniature Sheet

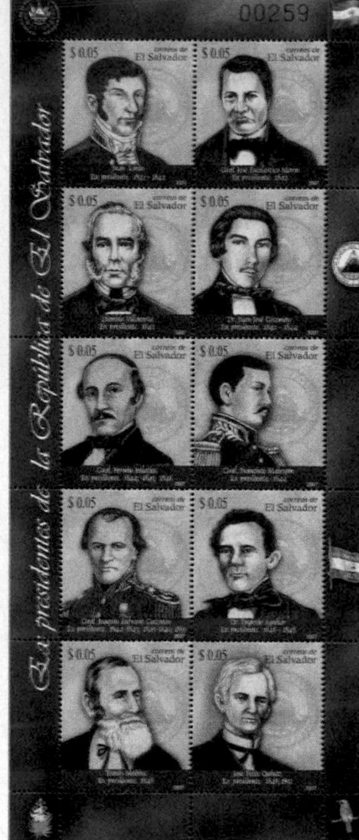

Salvadoran Presidents — A601

No. 1667: a, Juan Lindo, 1841-42. b, Gen. José Escolastico Marin, 1842. c, Dionisio Villacorta, 1842. d, Dr. Juan José Guzmán, 1842-44. e, Gen. Fermin Palacios, 1844, 1845, 1846. f, Gen. Francisco Malespin, 1844. g, Gen. Joaquin Eufrasio Guzmán, 1844-45, 1845-46, 1859. h, Dr. Eugenio Aguilar, 1846-48. i, Tomás Medina, 1848. j, José Felix Quiroz, 1848, 1851.

2007, June 29 ***Perf. 14¼x14***
1667 A601 5c Sheet of 10, #a-j 2.00 2.00

Miniature Sheet

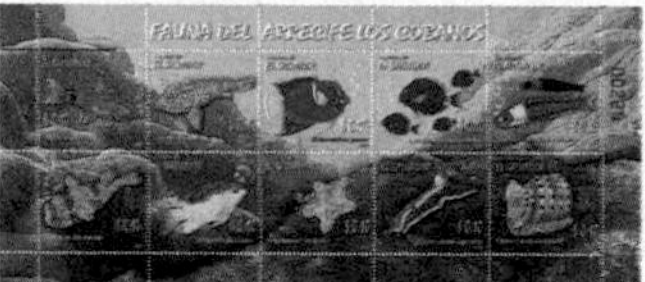
Fauna of Cobanos Reef — A602

No. 1668: a, Apogon dovii. b, Cirrhitus rivulatus. c, Holacanthus passer. d, Acanthurus xanthopterus. e, Thalassoma lucasanum. f, Diodon holocantus. g, Stegastes flavilatus. h, Amphiaster insignis. i, Hypselodoris agassizzi. j, Cypraecassis coarctata.

2007, Aug. 9 Litho. ***Perf. 14x14¼***
1668 A602 10c Sheet of 10, #a-j 4.00 4.00

El Mundo Newspaper, 40th Anniv. — A603

2007, Sept. 12
1669 A603 $5 multi 17.50 17.50

Archaeology — A604

No. 1670: a, Terracotta figurine. b, Tazumal archaeological site. c, Joya de Cerén. d, San Andres Acropolis.

2007, Oct. 5
1670 A604 25c Block or strip of 4, #a-d 3.50 3.50

America Issue, Education For All — A605

No. 1671 — Novels: a, El Cristo Negro, by Salarrué. b, Don Quixote de La Mancha, by Miguel de Cervantes.

2007, Oct. 31
1671 A605 $1 Vert. pair, #a-b 7.00 7.00

Christmas — A606

No. 1672: a, Stars on ears of corn. b, Teddy bear and gifts under Christmas tree. c, People touching stars on Christmas tree. d, Candles.

2007, Nov. 14
1672 A606 10c Block or strip of 4, #a-d 1.50 1.50

Popes A607

Designs: 1c, Pope John Paul II (1920-2005). 10c, Pope Benedict XVI.

2007, Nov. 22 ***Perf. 14x14¼***
1673-1674 A607 Set of 2 .50 .50

Birds — A608

No. 1675: a, Bombycilla cedrorum. b, Colaptes auratus. c, Anas clypeata. d, Falco peregrinus.
50c, Passerina ciris, horiz.

2007, Dec. 17 ***Perf. 14¼x14***
1675 A608 10c Block or strip of 4, #a-d 1.60 1.60

Souvenir Sheet

Rouletted 10½

1676 A608 50c multi 2.00 2.00

Fire Fighting Corps in El Salvador, 125th Anniv. A609

No. 1677: a, Firemen and truck. b, Fire truck, cab facing right. c, Fire truck, cab facing left. d, Ambulance.

2008, Feb. 15 ***Perf. 14x14¼***
1677 Vert. strip of 4 2.40 2.40
a.-d. A609 15c Any single .60 .60

37th Lions International Latin America and Caribbean Forum — A610

2008, Mar. 7
1678 A610 1c multi .25 .25

Miniature Sheets

Salvadoran Presidents — A611

No. 1679: a, Francisco Dueñas, 1851-52, 1852-54, 1856, 1863-71. b, Col. José María San Martín, 1852, 1854-56. c, Rafael Campo, 1856-58. d, Gen. Gerardo Barrios, 1858, 1859-60, 1861-63. e, Dr. Rafael Zaldívar,

1876-84, 1884-85. f, Gen. Fernando Figueroa, 1885, 1907-11. g, Gen. Francisco Menéndez, 1885-90. h, Gen. Carlos Ezeta, 1890-94. i, Gen. Rafael Antonio Gutiérrez, 1894-98. j, Gen. Tomás Regalado, 1898-1903. k, Pedro José Escalón, 1903-07. l, Dr. Manuel Enrique Araujo, 1911-13. m, Carlos Meléndez, 1913-14, 1915-18. n, Dr. Alfonso Quiñones Molina, 1914-15, 1918-19, 1923-27. o, Jorge Meléndez, 1919-23. p, Dr. Pío Romero Bosque, 1927-31. q, Arturo Araujo, 1931. r, Gen. Maximiliano Hernández Martínez, 1931-34, 1935-44. s, Gen. Salvador Castaneda Castro, 1945-48. t, Col. Oscar Osorio, 1950-56.

2008, Apr. 30 ***Perf. 14¼x14***
1679 A611 10c Sheet of 20, #a-t 4.00 4.00

Friendship Between Israel and El Salvador, 60th Anniv. A612

2008, May 29 ***Perf. 14x14¼***
1680 A612 10c multi .25 .25

2008 Summer Olympics, Beijing A613

No. 1681 — Salvadoran Olympic Committee emblem and: a, Cycling. b, Tennis. c, Weight lifting. d, Running.
50c, Judo, women's basketball, horiz.

2008, July 3 ***Perf. 14¼x14***
1681 Horiz. strip of 4 1.60 1.60
a.-d. A613 20c Any single .40 .40

Souvenir Sheet
Rouletted 10½
1682 A613 50c multi 1.00 1.00

Radio El Salvador, 82nd Anniv. A614

Designs: 25c, Engineer and radio control board. 65c, Radio equipment.

2008, July 31 ***Perf. 14¼x14***
1683-1684 A614 Set of 2 1.90 1.90

Central American Integration System A615

2008, Sept. 3 ***Perf. 14x14¼***
1685 A615 $5 multi 10.00 10.00

Villa Palestina A616

2008, Sept. 4 ***Perf. 14¼x14***
1686 A616 5c multi .25 .25

Miniature Sheet

Art of Fernando Llort — A617

No. 1687 — Details: a, Man waving. b, Man and animal. c, House and trees. d, Woman with basket on head holding child. e, Turkey and sun. f, Rooster and path. g, Man on horse on path. h, Short and tall women on path. i, Woman with jug on head, houses. j, Woman at well.

2008, Sept. 19 ***Perf. 14x14¼***
1687 A617 20c Sheet of 10, #a-j 4.00 4.00

Salvadoran Foundation for Economic Development, 25th Anniv. A618

2008, Oct. 22 ***Perf. 14¼x14***
1688 A618 $1 multi 2.00 2.00

18th Iberoamerican Summit, El Salvador — A619

2008, Oct. 27 ***Perf. 14x14¼***
1689 A619 $1 multi 2.00 2.00

America Issue, Festivals A620

Designs: 20c, Feria de las Palmas. 75c, Fiestas del Divino Salvador del Mundo.

2008, Nov. 7
1690-1691 A620 Set of 2 1.90 1.90

Ministry of Exterior Relations, 150th Anniv. A621

2009, Apr. 3 **Litho.** ***Perf. 14x14¼***
1692 A621 10c multi .25 .25

2009 Presidential Elections A622

2009, May 4 ***Perf. 14¼x14***
1693 A622 10c multi .25 .25

Intl. Year of Astronomy A623

No. 1694: a, Galileo Galilei (1564-1642), astronomer. b, Planetary moons discovered by Galileo. c, San Jan Talpa Astronomical Observatory. d, Meade Schmidt-Cassegrain telescope.

2009, May 27
1694 Horiz. strip of 4 2.00 2.00
a.-d. A623 25c Any single .50 .50

Miniature Sheets

National Symbols and Departmental Arms — A624

No. 1695, 10c: a, Eumomota superciliosa (national bird). b, Arms of Ahuachapan. c, Arms of Santa Ana. d, Arms of Sonsonate. e, Arms of La Libertad. f, Arms of Chalatenango. g, Arms of San Salvador. h, Arms of Cuscatlan.
No. 1696, 10c: a, Yucca elephantipes (national flower). b, Arms of La Paz. c, Arms of Cabañas. d, Arms of San Vicente. e, Arms of Usulutan. f, Arms of San Miguel. g, Arms of Morazan. h, Arms of La Union.

2009, July 22 ***Perf. 14¼x14***
Sheets of 8, #a-h
1695-1696 A624 Set of 2 3.25 3.25

Tourism A625

No. 1697: a, Butterfly, flower, Sapo River. b, Cranes, Jaltepeque Estuary. c, Butterfly, flowers, San Vicente Volcano. d, Butterfly, flowers, La Unión shoreline.
No. 1698: a, Pottery vendor, building, Guatajiagua. b, Man in costume, street in Izalco. c, Orchids, El Caracol Waterfall, Arambala. d, Native American sculpture, building, Ilobasco.

2009, Sept. 4 **Litho.** ***Perf. 14x14¼***
1697 Vert. strip of 4 .80 .80
a.-d. A625 5c Any single .25 .25
1698 Vert. strip of 4 .80 .80
a.-d. A625 5c Any single .25 .25
e. Block of 8, ##1697a-1697d, 1698a-1698d 1.60 1.60

America Issue A626

No. 1699 — Children's games: a, Jump rope. b, Hopscotch.

2009, Oct. 15
1699 A626 $1 Vert. pair, #a-b 4.00 4.00

Christmas A627

No. 1700: a, Candles, Bible passage, ornament. b, Madonna and child, star of Bethlehem, poinsettia. c, St. Joseph, lamb, dove, poinsettia. d, Magi, poinsettias, ornament.

2009, Nov. 30 ***Perf. 14¼x14***
1700 Horiz. strip of 4 .80 .80
a.-d. A627 10c Any single .25 .25

A628

A629

Oscar A. Romero (1917-80), Assassinated Archbishop of San Salvador — A630

No. 1701: a, Romero with hand raised. b, Romero and silhouette.
No. 1702: a, Romero touching person's head. b, Romero over church.
No. 1703: a, Romero. b, Romero and Salvadoran people.

2010, Mar. 19

1701	A628 $1 Horiz. pair, #a-b		4.00	4.00
1702	A629 $1 Horiz. pair, #a-b		4.00	4.00
1703	A630 $1 Horiz. pair, #a-b		4.00	4.00
	Nos. 1701-1703 (3)		12.00	12.00

City of San Vicente, 375th Anniv. — A631

No. 1704 — Arms and: a, Tempisque tree. b, Our Lady of Pilar Basilica.

50c, Cathedral and Tower of San Vicente.

2010, Dec. 15 ***Perf. 14¼x14***

1704 A631 $1 Horiz. pair, #a-b 4.00 4.00

Souvenir Sheet

Rouletted 10x10½

1705 A631 50c multi 1.00 1.00

America Issue A632

No. 1706 — National symbols: a, Coat of arms. b, Flag.

2010 ***Perf. 14x14¼***

1706 A632 $1 Vert. pair, #a-b 4.00 4.00

Children's Day and Missing Children's Day — A633

Denominations: 10c, $1.

2011, Mar. 25 ***Perf. 14¼x14***

1707-1708 A633 Set of 2 2.25 2.25

First Call for Independence, Bicent. — A634

No. 1709: a, Bell and doves. b, José Matías Delgado (1767-1832), independence leader, with hand on book. c, Gen. Manuel José Arce (1787-1847), holding paper. d, Crowd of people.

No. 1710: a, Monument. b, Delgado and bell. c, Delgado and wreath. d, Arce and wreath.

2011, June 7

1709	Horiz. strip of 4	4.00	4.00
a.-d.	A634 50c Any single	1.00	1.00
1710	Horiz. strip of 4	4.00	4.00
a.-d.	A634 50c Any single	1.00	1.00

Salvadoran Anniversaries — A635

No. 1711: a, Dr. Sun Yat-sen (1866-1925), President of Republic of China. b, José Matías Delgado (1767-1832), Salvadoran independence leader.

2011, Nov. 14

1711 A635 $1 Horiz. pair, #a-b 4.00 4.00

Diplomatic relations between El Salvador and Republic of China, cent. (#1711a), First call for Salvadoran independence, bicent. (#1711b).

America Issue — A636

No. 1712 — Mailbox with: a, Rounded top. b, Flat top.

2011, Nov. 14

1712 A636 $1 Horiz. pair, #a-b 4.00 4.00

Diplomatic Relations Between El Salvador and Canada, 50th Anniv. — A637

No. 1713: a, Maple leaf, "50," map of El Salvador. b, Canada highlighted on map of North America with Canadian flag, arrows.

2011, Dec. 7

1713 A637 $1 Horiz. pair, #a-b 4.00 4.00

Campaign Against Corruption A638

No. 1714: a, United Nations emblem in eye. b, Exchange of bribe money, emblem of Organization of American States. c, Magnifying glass over map of El Salvador, arms and flag of El Salvador.

2011, Dec. 9

1714	Horiz. strip of 3	6.00	6.00
a.-c.	A638 $1 Any single	2.00	2.00

2012 Elections A639

No. 1715: a, Stylized dove. b, House as ballot box.

2012, Mar. 6 ***Perf. 14x14¼***

1715 A639 $1 Vert. pair, #a-b 4.00 4.00

Statues of St. John the Baptist — A640

No. 1716 — Statue in: a, Chalatenango Cathedral. b, Monte San Juan Church, Cuscatlán.

2012, June 18 ***Perf. 14¼x14***

1716 A640 $1 Horiz. pair, #a-b 4.00 4.00

Signing of Chapultapec Peace Accords, 20th Anniv. — A641

"XX" and: No. 1717, $1, Dove. No. 1718, $1, Doves, book, pen, hands with olive branch.

2012, Sept. 14

1717-1718 A641 Set of 2 4.00 4.00

Cuscatlán Masonic Lodge, Cent. — A642

2012, Sept. 18

1719 A642 $5 multi 10.00 10.00

America Issue — A643

No. 1720 — Myths and legends of: a, The White Dog. b, The Headless Priest.

2012, Oct. 30

1720 A643 $1 Horiz. pair, #a-b 4.00 4.00

Animals and Their Pre-Columbian Ceramic Depictions — A644

No. 1721, 65c: a, Didelphis marsupialis. b, Pots depicting opossom, c. 900-1524.

No. 1722, $1: a, Panthera onca. b, Figurines depicting jaguars, c. 900-1524.

No. 1723, $5: Sylvilagus floridanus. b, Vessels depicting rabbits, c. 250-900.

No. 1724, $10: a, Ateles geoffroyi. b, Vessels depicting spider monkeys, c. 250-900.

2013, May 14 Litho. ***Perf. 14¼x14***

Horiz. pairs, #a-b

1721-1724 A644 Set of 4 67.00 67.00

Salvadoran Air Force, 90th Anniv. — A645

Frame color: 65c, Purple. $1, Red brown.

2013, Dec. 9 Litho. ***Perf. 14¼x14***

1725-1726 A645 Set of 2 3.50 3.50

Ciudad Mujer Women's Services Program A646

2014, June 12 Litho. ***Perf. 11***

1727 A646 $1 multi 2.00 2.00

Archbishop Oscar Arnulfo Romero (1917-80) A647

2014, June 23 Litho. ***Perf. 11***

1728 A647 65c multi 1.40 1.40

Renaming of El Salvador International Airport to honor Archbishop Romero.

National Association of the Sovereign Military of Malta, 40th Anniv. — A648

No. 1729: a, Rosales Hospital, San Salvador. b, Embassy of the Sovereign Military Order of Malta, Santa Elena.

2014, June 25 Litho. ***Perf. 11***

1729 A648 20c Horiz. pair, #a-b .80 .80

AIR POST STAMPS

Regular Issue of 1924-25 Overprinted in Black or Red

Back of No. C1

First Printing.
15c on 10c: "15 QUINCE 15" measures 22½mm.
20c: Shows on the back of the stamp an albino impression of the 50c surcharge.
25c on 35c: Original value canceled by a long and short bar.
40c on 50c: Only one printing.
50c on 1col: Surcharge in dull orange red.

Perf. 12½, 14

1929, Dec. 28 Unwmk.

C1 A112 20c dp green (Bk) 6.00 5.00
a. Red overprint 850.00 850.00

Counterfeits exist of No. C1a.

Additional Surcharge of New Values and Bars in Black or Red

No. C3

No. C4

No. C5

C3 A111 15c on 10c org 1.10 1.10
a. "ALTANT CO" 37.50 35.00
C4 A114 25c on 35c scar & grn 2.50 2.25
a. Bars inverted 10.00 10.00
C5 A115 40c on 50c org brn .85 .55
C6 A116 50c on 1col grn & bl vio (R) 15.00 10.00
Nos. C1-C6 (5) 25.45 18.90

Back of No. C7

No. C7

No. C9

No. C10

Second Printing.
15c on 10c: "15 QUINCE 15" measures 20½mm.
20c: Has not the albino impression on the back of the stamp.
25c on 35c: Original value cancelled by two bars of equal length.
50c on 1col: Surcharge in carmine rose.

1930, Jan. 10

C7 A112 20c deep green 1.00 1.00
C8 A111 15c on 10c org .75 .75
a. "ATLANT CO" 37.50 35.00
b. Double surcharge 20.00
c. As "a," double surcharge 75.00
d. Pair, one without surcharge 175.00
C9 A114 25c on 35c scar & grn .90 .90
C10 A116 50c on 1col grn & bl vio (C) 2.00 2.00
a. Without bars over "UN COLON" 4.50
b. As "a," without block over "1" 4.50
Nos. C7-C10 (4) 4.65 4.65

Numerous wrong font and defective letters exist in both printings of the surcharges.
No. C10 with black surcharge is bogus.

Mail Plane over San Salvador AP1

1930, Sept. 15 Engr. *Perf. 12½*

C11 AP1 15c deep red .40 .25
C12 AP1 20c emerald .40 .25
C13 AP1 25c brown violet .40 .25
C14 AP1 40c ultra .60 .25
Nos. C11-C14 (4) 1.80 1.00

Simón Bolivar — AP2

1930, Dec. 17 Litho. *Perf. 11½*

C15 AP2 15c deep red 6.00 5.00
a. "15" double 82.50
C16 AP2 20c emerald 6.00 5.00
C17 AP2 25c brown violet 6.00 5.00
a. Vert. pair, imperf. btwn. 175.00
b. Imperf., pair
C18 AP2 40c dp ultra 6.00 5.00
Nos. C15-C18 (4) 24.00 20.00

Centenary of death of Simón Bolivar. Counterfeits of Nos. C15-C18 exist.

No. 504 Overprinted in Red

1931, June 29 Engr. *Perf. 14*

C19 A116 1col green & vio 4.50 3.00

Tower of La Merced Church — AP3

1931, Nov. 5 Litho. *Perf. 11½*

C20 AP3 15c dark red 4.50 3.25
a. Imperf., pair 50.00
C21 AP3 20c blue green 4.50 3.25
C22 AP3 25c dull violet 4.50 3.25
a. Vert. pair, imperf. btwn. 110.00
C23 AP3 40c ultra 4.50 3.25
a. Imperf., pair 60.00
Nos. C20-C23 (4) 18.00 13.00

120th anniv. of the 1st movement toward the political independence of El Salvador. In the tower of La Merced Church (AP3) hangs the bell which José Matias Delgado-called the Father of his Country-rang to initiate the movement for liberty.

José Matias Delgado — AP4

1932, Nov. 12 Wmk. 271 *Perf. 12½*

C24 AP4 15c dull red & vio 1.25 1.10
C25 AP4 20c blue grn & bl 1.60 1.40
C26 AP4 25c dull vio & brn 1.60 1.40
C27 AP4 40c ultra & grn 1.90 1.75
Nos. C24-C27 (4) 6.35 5.65

1st centenary of the death of Father José Matías Delgado, who is known as the Father of El Salvadoran Political Emancipation.
Nos. C24-C27 show cheek without shading in the 72nd stamp of each sheet.

Airplane and Caravels of Columbus — AP5

1933, Oct. 12 Wmk. 240 *Perf. 13*

C28 AP5 15c red orange 2.00 1.75
C29 AP5 20c blue green 3.00 2.50
C30 AP5 25c lilac 3.00 2.50
C31 AP5 40c ultra 3.00 2.50
C32 AP5 1col black 3.00 2.50
Nos. C28-C32 (5) 14.00 11.75

Saling of Chistopher Columbus from Palos, Spain, for the New World, 441st anniv.

Police Barracks Type

1934, Dec. 16 *Perf. 12½*

C33 A123 25c lilac .60 .25
C34 A123 30c brown .95 .45
a. Imperf., pair 80.00
C35 A123 1col black 2.40 1.00
Nos. C33-C35 (3) 3.95 1.70

Runner AP7

1935, Mar. 16 Engr. Unwmk.

C36 AP7 15c carmine 3.75 2.25
C37 AP7 25c violet 3.75 2.25
C38 AP7 30c brown 3.00 1.75
C39 AP7 55c blue 20.00 8.50
C40 AP7 1col black 13.00 8.00
Nos. C36-C40 (5) 43.50 22.75

Third Central American Games.
For overprints and surcharge see Nos. C41-C45, C53.

Nos. C36-C40 Overprinted in Black

1935, June 27

C41 AP7 15c carmine 3.00 1.40
C42 AP7 25c violet 3.00 1.40
C43 AP7 30c brown 3.00 1.40
C44 AP7 55c blue 17.00 14.00
C45 AP7 1col black 7.50 6.00
Nos. C41-C45 (5) 33.50 24.20

Flag of El Salvador Type

1935, Oct. 26 Litho. Wmk. 240

C46 A125 30c black brown .40 .35

Tree of San Vicente Type

1935, Dec. 26 *Perf. 12½*

Numerals in Black, Tree in Yellow Green

C47 A126 10c orange .75 .60
C48 A126 15c brown .75 .60
C49 A126 20c dk blue grn .75 .60
C50 A126 25c dark purple .75 .60
C51 A126 30c black brown .75 .60
Nos. C47-C51 (5) 3.75 3.00

Tercentenary of San Vicente.

No. 565 Overprinted in Red

1937 Engr. Unwmk.

C52 A133 15c dk olive bis .35 .25
a. Double overprint 25.00

No. C44 Surcharged in Red

C53 AP7 30c on 55c blue 1.50 .60

Panchimalco Church — AP10

1937, Dec. 3 Engr. *Perf. 12*

C54 AP10 15c orange yel .30 .25
C55 AP10 20c green .30 .25
C56 AP10 25c violet .30 .25
C57 AP10 30c brown .30 .25
C58 AP10 40c blue .30 .25
C59 AP10 1col black 1.40 .45
C60 AP10 5col rose carmine 4.50 3.25
Nos. C54-C60 (7) 7.40 4.95

US Constitution Type of Regular Issue

1938, Apr. 22 Engr. & Litho.

C61 A136 30c multicolored .95 .70

José Simeón Cañas y Villacorta — AP12

1938, Aug. 18 Engr.

C62 AP12 15c orange 1.40 1.25
C63 AP12 20c brt green 1.75 1.25
C64 AP12 30c redsh brown 1.90 1.25
C65 AP12 1col black 6.00 4.50
Nos. C62-C65 (4) 11.05 8.25

José Simeón Cañas y Villacorta (1767-1838), liberator of slaves in Central America.

Golden Gate Bridge, San Francisco Bay — AP13

1939, Apr. 14 *Perf. 12½*

C66 AP13 15c dull yel & blk	.45	.25
C67 AP13 30c dk brown & blk	.45	.25
C68 AP13 40c dk blue & blk	.60	.45
Nos. C66-C68 (3)	1.50	.95

Golden Gate Intl. Exposition, San Francisco. For surcharges see Nos. C86-C91.

Sir Rowland Hill Type

1940, Mar. 1 **Engr.**

C69 A146 30c dk brn, buff & blk	8.00	2.50
C70 A146 80c org red & blk	22.50	17.50

Centenary of the postage stamp. Covers postmarked Feb. 29 were predated. Actual first day was Mar. 1.

Map of the Americas, Figure of Peace, Plane — AP15

1940, May 22 *Perf. 12*

C71 AP15 30c brown & blue	.45	.25
C72 AP15 80c dk rose & blk	.85	.55

Pan American Union, 50th anniversary.

Coffee Tree in Bloom — AP16

Coffee Tree with Ripe Berries — AP17

1940, Nov. 27

C73 AP16 15c yellow orange	1.60	.45
C74 AP16 20c deep green	2.25	.45
C75 AP16 25c dark violet	2.50	.55
C76 AP17 30c copper brown	3.00	.25
C77 AP17 1col black	9.00	.70
Nos. C73-C77 (5)	18.35	2.40

Juan Lindo, Gen. Francisco Malespin and New National University of El Salvador — AP18

Designs (portraits changed): 40c, 80c, Narciso Monterey and Antonio José Canas. 60c, 1col, Isidro Menéndez and Chrisanto Salazar.

1941, Feb. 16 *Perf. 12½*

C78 AP18 20c dk grn & rose lake	1.25	.70
C79 AP18 40c ind & brn org	1.25	.70
C80 AP18 60c dl pur & brn	1.40	.70
C81 AP18 80c hn brn & dk bl grn	3.00	2.00
C82 AP18 1col black & org	3.00	2.00
C83 AP18 2col yel org & rose vio	3.00	2.00
a. Min. sheet of 6, #C78-C83, perf. 11½	15.00	15.00
Nos. C78-C83 (6)	12.90	8.10

Centenary of University of El Salvador.

Stamps from No. C83a, perf. 11½, sell for about the same values as the perf. 12½ stamps.

Catalogue values for unused stamps in this section, from this point to the end of the section, are for Never Hinged items.

Map of El Salvador AP20

Wmk. 269

1942, Nov. 25 **Engr.** *Perf. 14*

C85 AP20 30c red orange	.80	.45
a. Horiz. pair, imperf. between	100.00	

1st Eucharistic Cong. of El Salvador. See #588.

Nos. C66-C68 Surcharged in Dark Carmine

1943 **Unwmk.** *Perf. 12½*

C86 AP13 15c on 15c dl yel & blk	.45	.25
C87 AP13 20c on 30c dk brn & blk	.60	.45
C88 AP13 25c on 40c dk bl & blk	1.25	.75
Nos. C86-C88 (3)	2.30	1.45

Nos. C66-C68 Surcharged in Dark Carmine

1944

C89 AP13 15c on 15c dl yel & blk	.45	.25
C90 AP13 20c on 30c dk brn & blk	.75	.45
C91 AP13 25c on 40c dk bl & blk	1.25	.45
Nos. C89-C91 (3)	2.45	1.15

Bridge Type of Regular Issue Arms Overprint at Right in Blue Violet

1944, Nov. 24 **Engr.**

C92 A149 30c crim rose & blk	.45	.25

No. C92 exists without overprint, but was not issued in that form.

Presidential Palace AP22

National Theater AP23

National Palace AP24

1944, Dec. 22 *Perf. 12½*

C93 AP22 15c red violet	.25	.25
C94 AP23 20c dk blue grn	.25	.25
C95 AP24 25c dull violet	.25	.25
Nos. C93-C95 (3)	.75	.75

For surcharge and overprint see Nos. C145-C146.

No. 582 Overprinted in Red

1945, Aug. 23 *Perf. 12*

C96 A137 1col black	1.00	.25

Juan Ramon Uriarte — AP25

Wmk. 240

1946, Jan. 1 **Typo.** *Perf. 12½*

C97 AP25 12c dark blue	.45	.25
C98 AP25 14c deep orange	.45	.25

Mayan Pyramid, St. Andrés Plantation AP26

Municipal Children's Garden, San Salvador AP27

Civil Aeronautics School, Ilopango Airport AP28

1946, May 1 **Unwmk.**

C99 AP26 30c rose carmine	.45	.25
C100 AP27 40c deep ultra	.45	.45
C101 AP28 1col black	1.50	.45
Nos. C99-C101 (3)	2.40	1.15

For surcharge see No. C121.

Alberto Masferrer — AP29

1946, July 19 **Litho.** **Wmk. 240**

C102 AP29 12c carmine	.45	.25
C103 AP29 14c dull green	.45	.25
a. Imperf., pair	12.50	

Souvenir Sheets

AP30

Designs: 40c, Charles I of Spain. 60c, Juan Manuel Rodriguez. 1col, Arms of San Salvador. 2col, Flag of El Salvador.

Perf. 12, Imperf.

1946, Nov. 8 **Engr.** **Unwmk.**

C104 AP30 Sheet of 4	4.50	4.50
a. 40c brown	1.00	1.00
b. 60c carmine	1.00	1.00
c. 1col green	1.00	1.00
d. 2col ultramarine	1.00	1.00

4th cent. of San Salvador's city charter. The imperf. sheets are without gum.

Felipe Soto — AP31

Alfredo Espino — AP32

Wmk. 240

1947, Sept. 11 **Litho.** *Perf. 12½*

C106 AP31 12c chocolate	.25	.25
C107 AP32 14c dark blue	.25	.25

For surcharges see Nos. 627-630.

Arce Type of Regular Issue

1948, Feb. 26 **Engr.** **Unwmk.**

C108 A163 12c green	.25	.25
C109 A163 14c rose carmine	.45	.25
C110 A163 1col violet	3.25	2.00
Nos. C108-C110 (3)	3.95	2.50

Cent. of the death of Manuel José Arce (1783-1847). "Father of Independence" and 1st pres. of the Federation of Central America.

Roosevelt Types of Regular Issue

Designs: 12c, Pres. Franklin D. Roosevelt. 14c, Pres. Roosevelt presenting awards for distinguished service. 20c, Roosevelt and Cordell Hull. 25c, Pres. and Mrs. Roosevelt. 1col, Mackenzie King, Roosevelt and Winston Churchill. 2col, Funeral of Pres. Roosevelt. 4col, Pres. and Mrs. Roosevelt.

1948, Apr. 12 **Engr.** *Perf. 12½*

Various Frames, Center in Black

C111 A165 12c green	.60	.45
C112 A164 14c olive	.60	.45
C113 A164 20c chocolate	.60	.45
C114 A164 25c carmine	.60	.45
C115 A164 1col violet brn	2.25	1.10
C116 A164 2col blue violet	3.25	1.75
Nos. C111-C116 (6)	7.90	4.65

Souvenir Sheet

Perf. 13½

C117 A166 4col gray & brn	5.50	3.75

Nos. 599, 601 and 604 Overprinted in Carmine or Black

1948, Sept. 7 *Perf. 12½*
C118 A154 5c slate gray .25 .25
C119 A154 10c bister brown .25 .25
C120 A154 1col scarlet (Bk) 1.90 .60
Nos. C118-C120 (3) 2.40 1.10

No. C99 Surcharged in Black

1949, July 23
C121 AP26 10(c) on 30c rose car .25 .25

UPU Type of Regular Issue

1949, Oct. 9 **Engr.** *Perf. 12½*
C122 A167 5c brown .60 .25
C123 A167 10c black .85 .25
C124 A167 1col purple 24.00 17.50
Nos. C122-C124 (3) 25.45 18.00

Flag and Arms of El Salvador — AP38

1949, Dec. 15 *Perf. 10½*

Flag and Arms in Blue, Yellow and Green

C125 AP38 5c ocher .25 .25
C126 AP38 10c dk green .25 .25
a. Yellow omitted 25.00
C127 AP38 15c violet .45 .25
C128 AP38 1col rose .95 .55
C129 AP38 5col red violet 7.50 5.50
Nos. C125-C129 (5) 9.40 6.80

1st anniv. of the Revolution of 12/14/48.

Isabella I of Spain — AP39

1951, Apr. 28 **Litho.** **Unwmk.**

Background in Ultramarine, Red and Yellow

C130 AP39 10c green .40 .25
C131 AP39 20c purple .40 .25
a. Horiz. pair, imperf. between 25.00
C132 AP39 40c rose carmine .55 .25
C133 AP39 1col black brown 1.75 .65
Nos. C130-C133 (4) 3.10 1.40

500th anniv. of the birth of Queen Isabella I of Spain. Nos. C130-C133 exist imperforate.

Flag, Torch and Scroll — AP40

1952, Feb. 14 **Photo.** *Perf. 11½*

Flag in Blue

C134 AP40 10c brt blue .25 .25
C135 AP40 15c chocolate .25 .25
C136 AP40 20c deep blue .25 .25
C137 AP40 25c gray .25 .25
C138 AP40 40c purple .40 .25
C139 AP40 1col red orange 1.10 .60
C140 AP40 2col orange brn 3.25 2.50
C141 AP40 5col violet blue 3.25 1.40
Nos. C134-C141 (8) 9.00 5.75

Constitution of 1950.

Marti Type of Regular Issue Inscribed "Aereo"

1953, Feb. 27 **Litho.** *Perf. 10½*
C142 A170 10c dk purple .30 .25
C143 A170 20c dull brown .45 .25
C144 A170 1col dull orange 1.50 .60
Nos. C142-C144 (3) 2.25 1.10

No. C95 Surcharged "C 0.20" and Obliterations in Red

1953, Mar. 20 *Perf. 12½*
C145 AP24 20c on 25c dl vio .30 .25

No. C95 Overprinted in Carmine

1953, June 19
C146 AP24 25c dull violet .55 .25

See note after No. 634.

Bell Tower, La Merced Church AP42

1953, Sept. 15 *Perf. 11½*
C147 AP42 5c rose pink .25 .25
C148 AP42 10c dp blue grn .25 .25
C149 AP42 20c blue .30 .30
C150 AP42 1col purple 1.25 .65
Nos. C147-C150 (4) 2.05 1.45

132nd anniv. of the Act of Independence, Sept. 15, 1821.

Postage Types and

Fishing Boats — AP43

Gen. Manuel José Arce — AP44

ODECA Officials and Flag AP46

No. C155, National Palace. No. C157, Coast guard boat. No. C158, Lake Ilopango. No. C160, Guayabo dam. No. C161, Housing development. No. C162, Modern highway. No. C164, Izalco volcano.

Perf. 11½

1954, June 1 **Unwmk.** **Photo.**
C151 AP43 5c org brn & cr .25 .25
C152 A175 5c brt carmine .25 .25
C153 AP44 10c gray blue .40 .25
C154 A176 10c pur & lt brn .40 .25
C155 AP43 10c ol & bl gray .40 .25
C156 AP46 10c bl grn, dk grn & bl .40 .25
C157 A173 10c rose carmine .40 .25
C158 A173 15c dk gray .55 .25
C159 A173 20c pur & gray .55 .25
C160 AP46 25c bl grn & bl .60 .25
C161 AP46 30c mag & sal .60 .25
C162 A176 40c brt org & brn .85 .35
C163 A174 80c red brown 1.75 1.25
C164 AP43 1col magenta & sal 2.00 1.25
C165 A174 2col orange 4.00 1.25
Nos. C151-C165 (15) 13.40 6.85

Barrios Type of Regular Issue

Wmk. 269

1955, Dec. 20 **Engr.** *Perf. 12½*
C166 A177 20c brown .35 .30
C167 A177 30c dp red lilac .35 .35

Santa Ana Type of Regular Issue

Perf. 13½

1956, June 20 **Unwmk.** **Litho.**
C168 A178 5c orange brown .25 .25
C169 A178 10c green .25 .25
C170 A178 40c red lilac .30 .25
C171 A178 80c emerald .90 .55
C172 A178 5col gray blue 4.50 2.50
Nos. C168-C172 (5) 6.20 3.80

For overprint see No. C187.

Chalatenango Type of Regular Issue

1956, Sept. 14
C173 A179 10c brt rose .25 .25
C174 A179 15c orange .25 .25
C175 A179 20c lt olive grn .25 .25
C176 A179 25c dull purple .45 .25
C177 A179 50c orange brn .70 .45
C178 A179 1col brt vio bl 1.00 .90
Nos. C173-C178 (6) 2.90 2.35

Nueva San Salvador Type

Wmk. 269

1957, Jan. 3 **Engr.** *Perf. 12½*
C179 A180 10c pink .25 .25
C180 A180 20c dull red .25 .25
C181 A180 50c pale org red .40 .25
C182 A180 1col lt green .90 .50
C183 A180 2col orange red 2.50 1.25
Nos. C179-C183 (5) 4.30 2.50

For overprints see Nos. C195, C198.

Lemus' Visit Type of Regular Issue

Perf. 11½

1959, Dec. 14 **Unwmk.** **Photo.**

Granite Paper

Design in Ultramarine, Dark Brown Light Brown and Red

C184 A182 15c red .25 .25
C185 A182 20c green .30 .25
C186 A182 30c carmine .25 .25
Nos. C184-C186 (3) .80 .75

No. C169 Overprinted in Red: "ANO MUNDIAL DE LOS REFUGIADOS 1959-1960"

1960, Apr. 7 **Litho.** *Perf. 13½*
C187 A178 10c green .35 .25

World Refugee Year, 7/1/59-6/30/60.

Poinsettia Type of Regular Issue

Perf. 11½

1960, Dec. 17 **Unwmk.** **Photo.**

Granite Paper

Design in Slate Green, Red and Yellow

C188 A184 20c rose lilac .35 .25
C189 A184 30c gray .40 .35
C190 A184 40c light gray .60 .25
C191 A184 50c salmon pink .95 .45
Nos. C188-C191 (4) 2.30 1.30

Miniature Sheet

Imperf

C192 A184 60c gold 8.00 8.00
a. Ovptd. in sheet margin ('61) *16.00 16.00*
b. Ovptd. in sheet margin ('61) *16.00 16.00*
c. Ovptd. in sheet margin ('62) *16.00 16.00*
d. Ovptd. in sheet margin ('63) *16.00 16.00*
e. Ovptd. in sheet margin ('63) *16.00 16.00*
f. Ovptd. in sheet margin ('63) *16.00 16.00*

Overprints in sheet margin of No. C192:
a, PRIMERA CONVENCION FILATELICA / CENTRO-AMERICANA / SAN SALVADOR, JULIO DE 1961.
b, in purple, Portrait, dates and text commemorating the Death of General Barrios, 96th anniv.
c, in green, Arms of city of Ahuachapan and PRIMER CENTENARIO / Ciudad de Ahuachapan / 1862 22 de Febrero 1962.
d, in blue, Soccer players and text commemorating the 1st North & Central American Soccer Championships 24 March - 2 April, 1963.
e, in blue and green, emblem of Alliance for Progress and text commemorating the 2nd anniversary of the organization.
f, in blue, Portrait of Dr. Manuel Araujo and College Arms with text commemorating the 4th Latin American Cong. of Pathological Anatomy and 10th Central American Medical Cong., Dec., 1963.
For surcharge see No. C196.

Nos. 672, 691 and C183 Ovptd. "III Exposición Industrial Centroamericana Diciembre de 1962" with "AEREO" Added on Nos. 672, 691

1962, Dec. 21 *Perf. 11½, 12½*
C193 A174 1col brn org, dk brn & bl 1.50 1.00
C194 A180 1col dull red .75 .50
C195 A180 2col orange red 1.50 .90
Nos. C193-C195 (3) 3.75 2.40

3rd Central American Industrial Exposition.
For surcharges see Nos. C197, C199.

Nos. C189, C194, C182 and C195 Surcharged

1963
C196 A184 10c on 30c multi .35 .25
C197 A180 10c on 1col dl red .35 .25
C198 A180 10c on 1col lt grn 1.25 .25
C199 A180 10c on 2col org red 1.10 .25
Nos. C196-C199 (4) 3.05 1.00

Surcharges include: "X" on No. C196; two dots and bar at bottom on No. C197. Heavy bar at bottom on No. C198. On No. C199, the four-line "Exposition" overprint is lower than on No. C195.

Turquoise-browed Motmot — AP49

Birds: 5c, King vulture (vert., like No. 741). 6c, Yellow-headed parrot, vert. 10c, Spotted-breasted oriole. 30c, Greattailed grackle. 40c, Great curassow, vert. 50c, Magpie-jay. 80c, Golden-fronted woodpecker, vert.

1963 **Unwmk.** **Photo.** *Perf. 11½*

Birds in Natural Colors

C200 AP49 5c gray grn & blk 1.50 .25
C201 AP49 6c tan & blue 1.50 .25
C202 AP49 10c lt bl & blk 1.75 .75
C203 AP49 20c gray & brn 3.00 .90
C204 AP49 30c ol bis & blk 3.75 .90
C205 AP49 40c pale & dk vio 4.50 1.25
C206 AP49 50c lt grn & blk 6.00 1.40
C207 AP49 80c vio bl & blk 9.00 2.25
Nos. C200-C207 (8) 31.00 7.95

Eucharistic Congress Type

1964-65 *Perf. 12x11½*
C208 A188 10c slate grn & bl .25 .25
C209 A188 25c red & blue .25 .25

Miniature Sheets

Imperf

C210 A188 80c blue & green 1.50 1.00
a. Marginal ovpt. La Union 1.50 1.00
b. Marginal ovpt. Usulutan 1.50 1.00
c. Marginal ovpt. La Libertad 1.00 .85

See note after No. 746.
Issued: #C208-C210, Apr. 16, 1964; #C210a-C210b, June 22, 1965; #210c, Jan. 28, 1965.
For overprints see Nos. C232, C238.

Kennedy Type of Regular Issue

1964, Nov. 22 *Perf. 11½x12*
C211 A189 15c gray & blk .25 .25
C212 A189 20c sage grn & blk .25 .25
C213 A189 40c yellow & blk .30 .25
Nos. C211-C213 (3) .80 .75

For overprint see No. C259.

Miniature Sheet

Imperf

C214 A189 80c grnsh bl & blk 1.75 1.75
a. Overprinted in sheet margin in red brown ('69)

Overprint on No. C214a reads: "Alunizaje / Apolo-11 / 21 Julio / 1969" and includes pictures of the landing module and astronauts.

Flower Type of Regular Issue

1965, Jan. 6 **Photo.** *Perf. 12x11½*
C215 A190 10c Rose .65 .25
C216 A190 15c Platanillo .65 .25
C217 A190 25c San Jose 1.25 .25
C218 A190 40c Hibiscus 1.50 .25
C219 A190 45c Veranera 1.50 .25
C220 A190 70c Fire flower 1.60 .30
Nos. C215-C220 (6) 7.15 1.55

For overprint and surcharges see Nos. C243, C348-C349.

ICY Type of Regular Issue

Perf. 11½x12

1965, Apr. 27 Photo. Unwmk.

Design in Brown and Gold

C221 A191 15c light blue .25 .25
C222 A191 30c dull lilac .25 .25
C223 A191 50c ocher .30 .25
Nos. C221-C223 (3) .80 .75

For overprints see Nos. C227, C244, C312.

Gavidia Type of Regular Issue

1965, Sept. 24 Photo. Unwmk.

Portraits in Natural Colors

C224 A192 10c black & green .25 .25
C225 A192 20c black & bister .30 .25
C226 A192 1col black & rose 1.10 .40
Nos. C224-C226 (3) 1.65 .90

No. C223 Ovptd. in Green "1865 / 12 de Octubre / 1965 / Dr. Manuel Enrique Araujo"

1965, Oct. 12 ***Perf. 11½x12***

C227 A191 50c brn, ocher & gold .40 .30

See note after No. 764.

Fair Type of Regular Issue

1965, Nov. 5 ***Perf. 12x11½***

C228 A193 20c blue & multi .25 .25
C229 A193 80c multi .55 .30
C230 A193 5col multi 2.75 1.90
Nos. C228-C230 (3) 3.55 2.45

For overprint see No. C311.

WHO Type of Regular Issue

1966, May 20 Photo. Unwmk.

C231 A194 50c multicolored .40 .25

For overprints see Nos. C242, C245.

No. C209 Ovptd. in Dark Green "1816 1966 / 150 años / Nacimiento / San Juan Bosco"

1966, Sept. 3 Photo. ***Perf. 12x11½***

C232 A188 25c red & blue .35 .25

150th anniv. of the birth of St. John Bosco (1815-88), Italian priest, founder of the Salesian Fathers and Daughters of Mary.

UNESCO Type of Regular Issue

1966, Nov. 4 Photo. ***Perf. 12***

C233 A195 30c tan, blk & vio bl .25 .25
C234 A195 2col emer, blk & vio bl 1.60 1.00

For surcharge see No. C352.

Fair Type of Regular Issue

1966, Nov. 27 Litho. ***Perf. 12***

C235 A196 15c multicolored .25 .25
C236 A196 20c multicolored .25 .25
C237 A196 60c multicolored .50 .35
Nos. C235-C237 (3) 1.00 .85

No. C209 Ovptd. "IX-Congreso / Interamericano / de Educacion / Católica / 4 Enero 1967"

1967, Jan. 4 Photo. ***Perf. 12x11½***

C238 A188 25c red & blue .35 .25

Issued to publicize the 9th Inter-American Congress for Catholic Education.

Cañas Type of Regular Issue

1967, Feb. 18 Litho. ***Perf. 11½***

C239 A197 5c multicolored .25 .25
C240 A197 45c lt bl & multi .55 .35

For surcharges see Nos. C403-C405.

Volcano Type of Regular Issue

1967, Apr. 14 Photo. ***Perf. 13***

C241 A198 50c ol gray & brn .60 .25

For surcharges see Nos. C320, C350

No. C231 Ovptd. in Red "VIII CONGRESO / CENTROAMERICANO DE / FARMACIA & B10QUIMICA / 5 di 11 Noviembre de 1967"

1967, Oct. 26 Photo. ***Perf. 12x11½***

C242 A194 50c multicolored .45 .40

Issued to publicize the 8th Central American Congress for Pharmacy and Biochemistry.

No. C217 Ovptd. in Red "I Juegos / Centroamericanos y del / Caribe de Basquetbol / 25 Nov. al 3 Dic. 1967"

1967, Nov. 15

C243 A190 25c bl, yel & grn .30 .25

First Central American and Caribbean Basketball Games, Nov. 25-Dec. 3.

No. C222 Ovptd. in Carmine "1968 / AÑO INTERNACIONAL DE / LOS DERECHOS HUMANOS"

1968, Jan. 2 Photo. ***Perf. 11½x12***

C244 A191 30c dl lil, brn & gold .40 .30

International Human Rights Year 1968.

No. C231 Ovptd. in Red "1968 / XX ANIVERSARIO DE LA / ORGANIZACION MUNDIAL / DE LA SALUD"

1968, Apr. 7 ***Perf. 12x11½***

C245 A194 50c multicolored .50 .50

20th anniv. of WHO.

No. C229 Ovptd. in Red "1968 / Año / del Sistema / del Crédito / Rural"

1968, May 6 Photo. ***Perf. 12x11½***

C246 A193 80c multicolored .65 .50

Rural credit system.

Masferrer Type of Regular Issue

1968, June 22 Litho. ***Perf. 12x11½***

C247 A200 5c brown & multi .25 .25
C248 A200 15c green & multi .25 .25

For overprint see No. C297.

Scouts Hiking AP50

1968, July 26 Litho. ***Perf. 12***

C249 AP50 10c multicolored .30 .25

Issued to publicize the 7th Inter-American Boy Scout Conference, July-Aug., 1968.

Presidents' Meeting Type

1968, Dec. 5 Litho. ***Perf. 14½***

C250 A202 20c salmon & multi .25 .25
C251 A202 1col lt blue & multi .75 .50

Butterfly Type of Regular Issue

Designs: Various butterflies.

1969 Litho. ***Perf. 12***

C252 A203 20c multi 7.25 .30
C253 A203 1col multi 12.00 .70
C254 A203 2col multi 12.00 1.25
C255 A203 10col gray & multi 18.00 6.00
Nos. C252-C255 (4) 49.25 8.25

For surcharge see No. C353.

Red Cross, Crescent and Lion and Sun Emblems AP51

1969 Litho. ***Perf. 11***

C256 AP51 30c yellow & multi .50 .25
C257 AP51 1col multicolored 1.50 .50
C258 AP51 4col multicolored 3.75 2.50
Nos. C256-C258 (3) 5.75 3.25

League of Red Cross Societies, 50th anniv.
For surcharges see Nos. C351, C354.

No. C213 Ovptd. in Green "Alunizaje / Apolo-11 / 21 Julio / 1969"

1969, Sept. Photo. ***Perf. 11½x12***

C259 A189 40c yellow & blk .35 .30

Man's 1st landing on the moon, July 20, 1969. See note after US No. C76.

Hospital Type of Regular Issue

Benjamin Bloom Children's Hospital.

1969, Oct. 24 Litho. ***Perf. 11½***

C260 A205 1col multi .85 .50
C261 A205 2col multi 1.60 1.00
C262 A205 5col multi 4.25 2.50
Nos. C260-C262 (3) 6.70 4.00

For surcharge see No. C355.

ILO Type of Regular Issue

1969 Litho. ***Perf. 13***

C263 A206 50c lt bl & multi .40 .25

Tourist Type of Regular Issue

Views: 20c, Devil's Gate. 35c, Ichanmichen Spa. 60c, Aerial view of Acajutla Harbor.

1969, Dec. 19 Photo. ***Perf. 12x11½***

C264 A207 20c black & multi .25 .25
C265 A207 35c black & multi .25 .25
C266 A207 60c black & multi .40 .30
Nos. C264-C266 (3) .90 .80

Insect Type of Regular Issue, 1970

1970, Feb. 24 Litho. ***Perf. 11½x11***

C267 A208 2col Bee 2.50 1.00
C268 A208 3col Elaterida 4.00 1.75
C269 A208 4col Praying mantis 6.00 2.00
Nos. C267-C269 (3) 12.50 4.75

For surcharges see Nos. C371-C373.

Human Rights Type of Regular Issue

20c, 80c, Map and arms of Salvador and National Unity emblem similar to A209, but vert.

1970, Apr. 14 Litho. ***Perf. 14***

C270 A209 20c blue & multi .25 .25
C271 A209 80c blue & multi .80 .30

For overprint & surcharge see #C301, C402.

Army Type of Regular Issue

Designs: 20c, Fighter plane. 40c, Gun and crew. 50c, Patrol boat.

1970, May 7 ***Perf. 12***

C272 A210 20c gray & multi .25 .25
C273 A210 40c green & multi .35 .25
C274 A210 50c blue & multi .40 .25
Nos. C272-C274 (3) 1.00 .75

For overprint see No. C310.

Brazilian Team, Jules Rimet Cup — AP52

Soccer teams and Jules Rimet Cup.

1970, May 25 Litho. ***Perf. 12***

C275 AP52 1col Belgium 1.10 .65
C276 AP52 1col Brazil 1.10 .65
C277 AP52 1col Bulgaria 1.10 .65
C278 AP52 1col Czechoslovakia 1.10 .65
C279 AP52 1col Germany (Fed. Rep.) 1.10 .65
C280 AP52 1col Britain 1.10 .65
C281 AP52 1col Israel 1.10 .65
C282 AP52 1col Italy 1.10 .65
C283 AP52 1col Mexico 1.10 .65
C284 AP52 1col Morocco 1.10 .65
C285 AP52 1col Peru 1.10 .65
C286 AP52 1col Romania 1.10 .65
C287 AP52 1col Russia 1.10 .65
C288 AP52 1col Salvador 1.10 .65
C289 AP52 1col Sweden 1.10 .65
C290 AP52 1col Uruguay 1.10 .65
Nos. C275-C290 (16) 17.60 10.40

9th World Soccer Championships for the Jules Rimet Cup, Mexico City, 5/30-6/21/70.
For overprints see Nos. C325-C340.

Lottery Type of Regular Issue

1970, July 15 Litho. ***Perf. 12***

C291 A211 80c multi .65 .25

Education Year Type of Regular Issue

1970, Sept. 11 Litho. ***Perf. 12***

C292 A212 20c pink & multi .25 .25
C293 A212 2col buff & multi 1.60 .80

Fair Type of Regular Issue

1970, Oct. 28 Litho. ***Perf. 12***

C294 A213 20c multi .25 .25
C295 A213 30c yel & multi .30 .25

Music Type of Regular Issue

Johann Sebastian Bach, harp, horn, music.

1971, Feb. 22 Litho. ***Perf. 13½***

C296 A214 40c gray & multi .75 .25

For overprint see No. C313.

No. C247 Ovptd. "Año / del Centenario de la / Biblioteca Nacional / 1970"

1970, Nov. 25 ***Perf. 12x11½***

C297 A200 5c brn & multi .25 .25

Miss Tourism Type of Regular Issue

1971, Apr. 1 Litho. ***Perf. 14***

C298 A215 20c lil & multi .25 .25
C299 A215 60c gray & multi .55 .30

Pietà Type of Regular Issue

1971, May 10

C300 A216 40c lt yel grn & vio brn .35 .25

No. C270 Overprinted in Red Like No. 823

1971, July 6 Litho. ***Perf. 14***

C301 A209 20c bl & multi .30 .25

Fish Type of Regular Issue

30c, Smalltooth sawfish. 1col, Atlantic sailfish.

1971, July 28

C302 A217 30c lilac & multi 2.10 .35
C303 A217 1col multi 3.50 1.10

Independence Type of Regular Issue

Designs: Various sections of Declaration of Independence of Central America.

1971 Litho. ***Perf. 13½x13***

C304 A218 30c bl & blk .25 .25
C305 A218 40c brn & blk .30 .25
C306 A218 50c yel & blk .35 .25
C307 A218 60c gray & blk .50 .35
a. Souvenir sheet of 8 2.25 1.60
Nos. C304-C307 (4) 1.40 1.10

No. C307a contains 8 stamps with simulated perforations similar to Nos. 826-829, C304-C307.
For overprints see Nos. C321, C347.

Church Type of Regular Issue

15c, Metapan Church. 70c, Panchimalco Church.

1971, Aug. 21 Litho. ***Perf. 13x13½***

C308 A219 15c ol & multi .25 .25
C309 A219 70c multi .55 .35

No. C274 Overprinted in Red

1971, Oct. 12 Litho. ***Perf. 12***

C310 A210 50c bl & multi .45 .30

National Navy, 20th anniversary.

No. C229 Ovptd. "V Feria / Internacional / 3-20 Noviembre / de 1972"

1972, Nov. 3 Photo. ***Perf. 12x11½***

C311 A193 80c multi .90 .50

5th Intl. Fair, El Salvador, Nov. 3-20.

No. C223 Overprinted in Red

1972, Nov. 30 Photo. ***Perf. 11½x12***
C312 A191 50c ocher, brn & gold .45 .30

30th anniversary of the Inter-American institute for Agricultural Sciences.

No. C296 Overprinted

1973, Feb. 5 Litho. ***Perf. 13½***
C313 A214 40c gray & multi 1.00 .25

3rd International Music Festival, Feb. 9-29.

Lions Type of Regular Issue

Designs: 20c, 40c, Map of El Salvador and Lions International Emblem.

1973, Feb. 20 Litho. ***Perf. 13***
C314 A220 20c gray & multi .25 .25
C315 A220 40c multi .30 .25

Olympic Type of Regular Issue

Designs: 20c, Javelin, women's. 80c, Discus, women's. 1col, Hammer throw. 2col, Shot put.

1973, May 21 Litho. ***Perf. 13***
C316 A221 20c lt grn & multi .45 .25
C317 A221 80c sal & multi 1.00 .35
C318 A221 1col ultra & multi 1.25 .55
C319 A221 2col multi 2.75 .90
Nos. C316-C319 (4) 5.45 2.05

No. C241 Surcharged Like No. 841

1973, Dec. Photo. ***Perf. 13***
C320 A198 25c on 50c multi .45 .25

No. C307a Ovptd. "Centenario / Cuidad / Santiago de Maria / 1874 1974"

Souvenir Sheet

1974, Mar. 7 Litho. ***Imperf.***
C321 A218 Sheet of 8 1.90 1.10

Centenary of the City Santiago de Maria. The overprint is so arranged that each line appears on a different pair of stamps.

No. C231 Surcharged in Red

1974, Apr. 22 Photo. ***Perf. 12x11½***
C322 A194 25c on 50c multi .35 .25

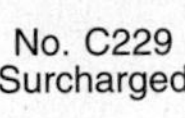

No. C229 Surcharged

1974, Apr. 24
C323 A193 10c on 80c multi .45 .25

Rehabilitation Type

1974, Apr. 30 Litho. ***Perf. 13***
C324 A222 25c multi .30 .25

Nos. C275-C290 Overprinted

1974, June 4 Litho. ***Perf. 12***
C325 AP52 1col Belgium .90 .50
C326 AP52 1col Brazil .90 .50
C327 AP52 1col Bulgaria .90 .50
C328 AP52 1col Czech. .90 .50
C329 AP52 1col Germany .90 .50
C330 AP52 1col Britain .90 .50
C331 AP52 1col Israel .90 .50
C332 AP52 1col Italy .90 .50
C333 AP52 1col Mexico .90 .50
C334 AP52 1col Morocco .90 .50
C335 AP52 1col Peru .90 .50
C336 AP52 1col Romania .90 .50
C337 AP52 1col Russia .90 .50
C338 AP52 1col Salvador .90 .50
C339 AP52 1col Sweden .90 .50
C340 AP52 1col Uruguay .90 .50
Nos. C325-C340 (16) 14.40 8.00

World Cup Soccer Championship, Munich, June 13-July 7.

INTERPOL Type of 1974

1974, Sept. 2 Litho. ***Perf. 12½***
C341 A223 25c multi .25 .25

FAO Type of 1974

1974, Sept. 2 Litho. ***Perf. 12½***
C342 A224 25c bl, dk bl & gold .25 .25

Coin Type of 1974

1974, Nov. 19 Litho. ***Perf. 12½x13***
C343 A225 20c 1p silver, 1892 .25 .25
C344 A225 40c 20c silver, 1828 .30 .25
C345 A225 50c 20p gold, 1892 .50 .25
C346 A225 60c 20col gold, 1925 .50 .35
Nos. C343-C346 (4) 1.55 1.10

No. C307a Ovptd. "X ASAMBLEA GENERAL DE LA CONFERENCIA / INTERAMERICANA DE SEGURIDAD SOCIAL Y XX / REUNION DEL COMITE PERMANENTE INTERAMERICANO / DE SEGURIDAD SOCIAL, 24 — 30 NOVIEMBRE 1974"

1974, Nov. 18 Litho. ***Imperf.***

Souvenir Sheet

C347 A218 Sheet of 8 2.50 1.75

Social Security Conference, El Salvador, Nov. 24-30. The overprint is so arranged that each line appears on a different pair of stamps.

Issues of 1965-69 Surcharged

a

b

c

d

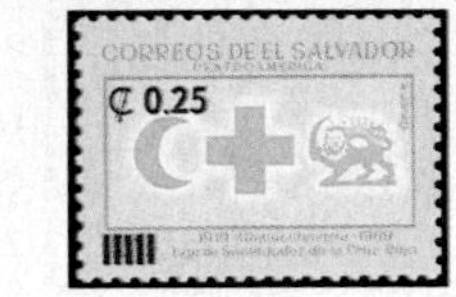

1974-75
C348 A190(a) 10c on 45c #C219 .60 .25
C349 A190(a) 10c on 70c #C220 .60 .25
C350 A198(b) 10c on 50c #C241 .75 .25
C351 AP51(d) 25c on 1col #C257 .35 .25
C352 A195(c) 25c on 2col #C234 ('75) .75 .25
C353 A203(d) 25c on 2col #C254 ('75) 50.00 .25
C354 AP51(d) 25c on 4col #C258 .45 .25
C355 A205(d) 25c on 5col #C262 .35 .25
Nos. C348-C355 (8) 53.85 2.00

No. C353 has new value at left and 6 vertical bars. No. C355 has 7 vertical bars.

UPU Type of 1975

1975, Jan. 22 Litho. ***Perf. 13***
C356 A226 25c bl & multi .25 .25
C357 A226 30c bl & multi .25 .25

Acajutla Harbor Type of 1975

1975, Feb. 17
C358 A227 15c bl & multi .25 .25

Post Office Type of 1975

1975, Apr. 25 Litho. ***Perf. 13***
C359 A228 25c bl & multi .35 .25

Miss Universe Type of 1975

1975, June 25 ***Perf. 12½***
C360 A229 25c multi .25 .25
C361 A229 60c lil & multi .55 .40

Women's Year Type and

IWY Emblem — AP53

1975, Sept. 4 Litho. ***Perf. 12½***
C362 A230 15c bl & bl blk .25 .25
C363 AP53 25c yel grn & blk .30 .25

International Women's Year 1975.

Nurse Type of 1975

1975, Oct. 24 Litho. ***Perf. 12½***
C364 A231 25c lt blue & multi .25 .25

Printers' Congress Type

1975, Nov. 19 Litho. ***Perf. 12½***
C365 A232 30c green & multi .25 .25

Dermatologists' Congress Type

1975, Nov. 28
C366 A233 20c blue & multi .25 .25
C367 A233 30c red & multi .25 .25

Caritas Type of 1975

1975, Dec. 18 Litho. ***Perf. 13½***
C368 A234 20c bl & vio bl .25 .25

UNICEF Emblem — AP54

1975, Dec. 18
C369 AP54 15c lt grn & sil .25 .25
C370 AP54 20c dl rose & sil .30 .25

UNICEF, 25th anniv. (in 1971).

Nos. C267-C269 Surcharged

1976, Jan. 14 ***Perf. 11½x11***
C371 A208 25c on 2col multi 2.40 .25
C372 A208 25c on 3col multi 2.40 .25
C373 A208 25c on 4col multi 2.40 .25
Nos. C371-C373 (3) 7.20 .75

Caularthron Bilamellatum AP55

Designs: Orchids — No. C375, Oncidium oliganthum. No. C376, Epidendrum radicans. No. C377, Epidendrum vitellinum. No. C378, Cyrtopodium punctatum. No. C379, Pleurothallis schiedei. No. C380, Lycaste cruenta. No. C381, Spiranthes speciosa.

1976, Feb. 19 Litho. ***Perf. 12½***
C374 AP55 25c multi 1.00 .35
C375 AP55 25c multi 1.00 .35
C376 AP55 25c multi 1.00 .35
C377 AP55 25c multi 1.00 .35
C378 AP55 25c multi 1.00 .35
C379 AP55 25c multi 1.00 .35
C380 AP55 25c multi 1.00 .35
C381 AP55 25c multi 1.00 .35
Nos. C374-C381 (8) 8.00 2.80

CIAT Type of 1976

1976, May 18 Litho. ***Perf. 12½***
C382 A235 50c org & multi .55 .25

Bicentennial Types of 1976

1976, June 30 Litho. ***Perf. 12½***
C383 A236 25c multi .25 .25
C384 A237 5col multi 3.75 2.50

Reptile Type of 1976

Reptiles: 15c, Green fence lizard. 25c, Basilisk. 60c, Star lizard.

1976, Sept. 23 Litho. ***Perf. 12½***
C385 A238 15c multi .50 .25
C386 A238 25c multi .80 .25
C387 A238 60c multi 2.00 .40
Nos. C385-C387 (3) 3.30 .90

Archaeology Type of 1976

Pre-Columbian Art: 25c, Brazier with pre-classical head, El Trapiche. 50c, Kettle with pre-classical head, Atiquizaya. 70c, Classical whistling vase, Tazumal.

1976, Oct. 11 Litho. ***Perf. 12½***
C388 A239 25c multi .25 .25
C389 A239 50c multi .45 .25
C390 A239 70c multi .60 .40
Nos. C388-C390 (3) 1.30 .90

For overprint see No. C429.

Fair Type of 1976

1976, Oct. 25 Litho. ***Perf. 12½***
C391 A240 25c multi .25 .25
C392 A240 70c yel & multi .55 .40

Christmas Type of 1976

1976, Dec. 16 Litho. ***Perf. 11***
C393 A241 25c bl & multi .25 .25
C394 A241 50c multi .40 .25
C395 A241 60c multi .50 .30
C396 A241 75c red & multi .60 .40
Nos. C393-C396 (4) 1.75 1.20

Rotary Type of 1977

1977, June 20 Litho. *Perf. 11*

C397 A242 25c multi .25 .25
C398 A242 1col multi .80 .50

Industrial Type of 1977

Designs: 25c, Radar station, Izalco (vert.). 50c, Central sugar refinery, Jiboa. 75c, Cerron Grande hydroelectric station.

1977, June 29 *Perf. 12½*

C399 A243 25c multi .25 .25
C400 A243 50c multi .40 .25
C401 A243 75c multi .60 .40
Nos. C399-C401 (3) 1.25 .90

Nos. C399-C401 have colorless overprint in multiple rows: GOBIERNO DEL SALVADOR.

Nos. C271 and C239 Surcharged with New Value and Bar

1977 *Perf. 14, 11½*

C402 A209 25c on 80c multi .30 .25
C403 A197 30c on 5c multi .25 .25
C404 A197 40c on 5c multi .30 .25
C405 A197 50c on 5c multi .40 .25
Nos. C402-C405 (4) 1.25 1.00

Broadcasting Type of 1977

1977, Sept. 14 Litho. *Perf. 14*

C406 A244 20c multi .25 .25
C407 A244 25c multi .25 .25

Symbolic Chessboard and Emblem — AP56

1977, Oct. 20 Litho. *Perf. 11*

C408 AP56 25c multi .25 .25
C409 AP56 50c multi .40 .25

El Salvador's victory in International Chess Olympiad, Tripoli, Libya, Oct. 24-Nov. 15, 1976.

Soccer AP57

Boxing AP58

1977, Nov. 16 Litho. *Perf. 16*

C410 AP57 10c shown .25 .25
C411 AP57 10c Basketball .25 .25
C412 AP57 15c Javelin .25 .25
C413 AP57 15c Weight lifting .25 .25
C414 AP57 20c Volleyball .25 .25
C415 AP58 20c shown .25 .25
C416 AP57 25c Baseball .25 .25
C417 AP58 25c Softball .25 .25
C418 AP58 30c Swimming .35 .25
C419 AP58 30c Fencing .35 .25
C420 AP58 40c Bicycling .45 .25
C421 AP58 50c Rifle shooting .55 .30
C422 AP58 50c Women's tennis .55 .30
C423 AP57 60c Judo .65 .35
C424 AP58 75c Wrestling .70 .40
C425 AP58 1col Equestrian hurdles .90 .50
C426 AP58 1col Woman gymnast .90 .50
C427 AP58 2col Table tennis 1.25 1.00
Nos. C410-C427 (18) 8.65 6.10

Size: 100x119mm

C428 AP57 5col Games' poster 4.00 4.00

2nd Central American Olympic Games, San Salvador, Nov. 25-Dec. 4.

No. C390 Ovptd. in Red "CENTENARIO / CIUDAD DE / CHALCHUAPA / 1878-1978"

1978, Feb. 13 Litho. *Perf. 12½*

C429 A239 70c multi .60 .55

Centenary of Chalchuapa.

Map of South America, Argentina '78 Emblem AP59

1978, Aug. 15 Litho. *Perf. 11*

C430 AP59 25c multi .30 .25
C431 AP59 60c multi .50 .40
C432 AP59 5col multi 4.00 3.00
Nos. C430-C432 (3) 4.80 3.65

11th World Cup Soccer Championship, Argentina, June 1-25.

Musical Instrument Type

Designs: 25c, Drum, vert. 50c, Hollow rattles. 80c, Xylophone.

1978, Aug. 29 *Perf. 12½*

C433 A245 25c multi .30 .25
C434 A245 50c multi .45 .25
C435 A245 80c multi .60 .40
Nos. C433-C435 (3) 1.35 .90

For surcharge see No. C492.

Engineering Type of 1978

1978, Sept. 12 Litho. *Perf. 13½*

C436 A246 25c multi .25 .25

Izalco Station Type of 1978

1978, Sept. 14 *Perf. 12½*

C437 A247 75c multi .60 .40

Softball, Bat and Globes AP60

1978, Oct. 17 Litho. *Perf. 12½*

C438 AP60 25c pink & multi .25 .25
C439 AP60 1col yel & multi .80 .50

4th World Softball Championship for Women, San Salvador, Oct. 13-22.

Fair Type, 1978

1978, Oct. 30 Litho. *Perf. 12½*

C440 A248 15c multi .25 .25
C441 A248 25c multi .25 .25

Red Cross Type, 1978

1978, Oct. 30 Litho. *Perf. 11*

C442 A249 25c multi .25 .25

Cotton Conference Type, 1978

1978, Nov. 22 *Perf. 12½*

C443 A250 40c multi .30 .25

Christmas Type, 1978

1978, Dec. 5 Litho. *Perf. 12½*

C444 A251 25c multi .25 .25
C445 A251 1col multi .80 .50

Athenaeum Type 1978

1978, Dec. 20 Litho. *Perf. 14*

C446 A252 25c multi .25 .25

UPU Type of 1979

1979, Apr. 2 Litho. *Perf. 14*

C447 A253 75c multi .60 .40

Health Organization Type

1979, Apr. 7 *Perf. 14x14½*

C448 A254 25c multi .25 .25

Social Security Type of 1979

1979, May 25 Litho. *Perf. 12½*

C449 A255 25c multi .25 .25
C450 A255 1col multi .80 .50

Games Emblem AP61

1979, July 12 Litho. *Perf. 14½x14*

C451 AP61 25c multi .25 .25
C452 AP61 40c multi .30 .25
C453 AP61 70c multi .50 .40
Nos. C451-C453 (3) 1.05 .90

8th Pan American Games, Puerto Rico, July 1-15.

For surcharge see No. C493.

Pope John Paul II Type of 1979

60c, 5col, Pope John Paul II & pyramid.

1979, July 12

C454 A256 60c multi, horiz. .50 .30
C455 A256 5col multi, horiz. 4.00 2.50

"25," Family and Map of Salvador — AP62

1979, May 14 Litho. *Perf. 14x14½*

C456 AP62 25c blk & bl .25 .25
C457 AP62 60c blk & lil rose .55 .35

Social Security, 25th anniversary.

Pre-Historic Animal Type

1979, Sept. 7 Litho. *Perf. 14*

C458 A257 15c Mammoth .35 .25
C459 A257 25c Giant anteater, vert. .50 .25
C460 A257 2col Hyenas 2.75 1.10
Nos. C458-C460 (3) 3.60 1.60

National Anthem Type, 1979

1979, Sept. 14 *Perf. 14½x14*

C461 A258 40c Jose Aberiz, score .30 .25

COPIMERA Type, 1979

1979, Oct. 19 Litho. *Perf. 14½x14*

C462 A259 50c multi .45 .25

Circle Dance, IYC Emblem AP63

Children's Village and IYC Emblems AP64

1979, Oct. 29 *Perf. 14½x14, 14x14½*

C463 AP63 25c multi .25 .25
C464 AP64 30c vio & blk .30 .25

International Year of the Child.

Biochemistry Type of 1979

1979, Nov. 1 Litho. *Perf. 14½x14*

C465 A262 25c multi .25 .25

Coffee Type of 1979

Designs: 50c, Picking coffee. 75, Drying coffee beans. 1col, Coffee export.

1979, Dec. 18 *Perf. 14x14½, 14½x14*

C466 A263 50c multi .40 .25
C467 A263 75c multi .60 .40
C468 A263 1 col multi .80 .55
Nos. C466-C468 (3) 1.80 1.20

Hoof and Mouth Disease Type

1980, June 3 Litho. *Perf. 14½x14*

C469 A265 60c multi .55 .30

Shell Type of 1980

15c, Hexaplex regius. 25c, Polinices helicoides. 75c, Jenneria pustulata. 1col, Pitar lupanaria.

1980, Aug. 12 *Perf. 14x14½*

C470 A266 15c multi .40 .25
C471 A266 25c multi .80 .25
C472 A266 75c multi 2.00 .30
C473 A266 1col multi 2.75 .50
Nos. C470-C473 (4) 5.95 1.30

Birds Type

25c, Aulacorhynchus prasinus. 50c, Strix varia fulvescens. 75c, Myadestes unicolor.

1980, Sept. 10 Litho. *Perf. 14x14½*

C474 A267 25c multi 1.60 .25
C475 A267 50c multi 3.00 .30
C476 A267 75c multi 4.50 .45
Nos. C474-C476 (3) 9.10 1.00

Snake Type of 1980

1980, Nov. 12 Litho. *Perf. 14x14½*

C477 A268 25c Rattlesnake 2.40 .25
C478 A268 50c Coral snake 3.50 .30

Auditors Type

1980, Nov. 26 Litho. *Perf. 14*

C479 A269 50c multi .40 .25
C480 A269 75c multi .60 .40

Christmas Type

1980, Dec. 5 Litho. *Perf. 14*

C481 A270 25c multi .25 .25
C482 A270 60c multi .60 .30

Intl. Women's Decade, 1976-85 — AP65

1981, Jan. 30 *Perf. 14½x14*

C483 AP65 25c ol grn & blk .25 .25
C484 AP65 1 col orange & black .80 .50

Protected Animals AP66

No. C485, Ateles geoffroyi. No. C486, Lepisosteus tropicus. No. C487, Iguana iguana. No. C488, Eretmochelys imbricata. No. C489, Spizaetus ornatus.

1981, Mar. 20 Litho. *Perf. 14x14½*

C485 AP66 25c multicolored .30 .25
C486 AP66 40c multicolored .35 .25
C487 AP66 50c multicolored .45 .25
C488 AP66 60c multicolored .55 .35
C489 AP66 75c multicolored .70 .40
Nos. C485-C489 (5) 2.35 1.50

Heinrich von Stephan, 150th Birth Anniv. — AP67

1981, May 18 Litho. *Perf. 14½x14*

C490 AP67 15c multi .35 .25
C491 AP67 2 col multi 1.60 1.00

Nos. C435, C453 Surcharged

Perf. 12½, 14½x14

1981, May 18 **Litho.**
C492 A245 50c on 80c, #C435 .40 .25
C493 AP61 1 col on 70c, #C453 .80 .55

Dental Associations Type

1981, June 18 Litho. ***Perf. 14***
C494 A271 5 col bl & blk 7.00 3.00

IYD Type of 1981

1981, Aug. 14 Litho. ***Perf. 14x14½***
C495 A272 25c like #936 .25 .25
C496 A272 50c Emblem .40 .25
C497 A272 75c like #936 .60 .40
C498 A272 1 col like # C496 .80 .55
Nos. C495-C498 (4) 2.05 1.45

Quinonez Type

1981, Aug. 28 Litho. ***Perf. 14x14½***
C499 A273 50c multi .40 .25

World Food Day Type

1981, Sept. 16 Litho. ***Perf. 14x14½***
C500 A274 25c multi .25 .25

Land Registry Office, 100th Anniv. — AP68

1981, Oct. 30 Litho. ***Perf. 14x14½***
C501 AP68 1 col multi .80 .55

TACA Airlines, 50th Anniv. AP69

1981, Nov. 10 Litho. ***Perf. 14***
C502 AP69 15c multi .25 .25
C503 AP69 25c multi .25 .25
C504 AP69 75c multi .60 .40
Nos. C502-C504 (3) 1.10 .90

World Cup Preliminaries Type

1981, Nov. 27 Litho. ***Perf. 14x14½***
C505 A275 25c Like No. 939 .30 .25
C506 A275 75c Like No. 940 .60 .40

Lyceum Type

1981, Dec. 17 Litho. ***Perf. 14***
C507 A276 25c multi .25 .25

Sculptures Type

1982, Jan. 22 Litho. ***Perf. 14***
C508 A277 25c Palm leaf with effigy .25 .25
C509 A277 30c Jaguar mask .30 .25
C510 A277 80c Mayan flint carving .65 .45
Nos. C508-C510 (3) 1.20 .95

Scouting Year Type of 1982

1982, Mar. 17 Litho. ***Perf. 14½x14***
C511 A278 25c Baden-Powell .25 .25
C512 A278 50c Girl Scout, emblem .40 .25

TB Bacillus Cent. — AP70

1982, Mar. 24 ***Perf. 14***
C513 AP70 50c multi 1.50 .25

Armed Forces Type of 1982

1982, May 7 Litho. ***Perf. 14x13½***
C514 A279 25c multi .25 .25

Symbolic Design — AP71

1982, May 14 ***Perf. 14***
C515 AP71 75c multi .60 .40

25th anniv. of Latin-American Tourist Org. Confederation (COTAL).

14th World Telecommunications Day — AP72

1982, May 17 ***Perf. 14x14½***
C516 AP72 15c multi .25 .25
C517 AP72 2col multi 1.60 1.00

World Cup Type of 1982

1982, July 14
C518 A280 25c Team, emblem .25 .25
C519 A280 60c Map, cup .50 .35

Size: 67x47mm

Perf. 11½

C520 A280 2col Team, emblem, diff. 1.60 1.00

1982 World Cup — AP73

Flags or Arms of Participating Countries; #C521a, C522a, Italy. #C521b, C522c, Germany. #C521c, C522e, Argentina. #C521d, C522m, England. #C521e, C522o, Spain. #C521f, C522q, Brazil. #C521g, C522b, Poland. #C521h, C522d, Algeria. #C521i, C522f, Belgium. #C521j, C522n, France. #C521k, C522p, Honduras. #C521l, C522r, Russia. #C521m, C522g, Peru. #C521n, C522i, Chile. #C521o, C522k, Hungary. #C521p, C522s, Czechoslovakia. #C521q, C522u, Yugoslavia. #C521r, C522w, Scotland. #C521s, C522h, Cameroun. #C521t, C522j, Austria. #C521u, C522l, Salvador. #C521v, C522t, Kuwait. #C521w, C522v, Ireland. #C521x, C522x, New Zealand.

1982, Aug. 26
C521 Sheet of 24 7.50
a.-x. AP73 15c Flags .25 .25
C522 Sheet of 24 7.50
a.-x. AP73 25c Arms .25 .25

Salvador Team, Cup, Flags — AP74

1982, Aug. 26 Litho. ***Perf. 11½***
C523 AP74 5col multi 6.00 2.50

International Fair Type

1982, Oct. 14 Litho. ***Perf. 14***
C524 A281 15c multi .25 .25

World Food Day — AP75

1982, Oct. 21 Litho. ***Perf. 14***
C525 AP75 25c multi .35 .25

St. Francis of Assisi, 800th Birth Anniv. — AP76

1982, Nov. 10 Litho. ***Perf. 14***
C526 AP76 1col multi .80 .60

Natl. Labor Campaign — AP77

1982, Nov. 30 Litho. ***Perf. 14x14½***
C527 AP77 50c multi .40 .25

Christmas Type

1982, Dec. 14 Litho. ***Perf. 14***
C528 A282 25c multi, horiz. .25 .25

Salvadoran Paintings AP78

#C529, The Pottery of Paleca, by Miguel Ortiz Villacorta. #C530, The Rural School, by Luis Caceres Madrid. #C531, To the Wash, by Julia Diaz. #C532, "La Pancha" by Jose Mejia Vides. #C533, Boats Near The Beach, by Raul Elas Reyes. #C534, The Muleteers, by Canjura.

Perf. 14x13½, 13½x14

1983, Oct. 18 **Litho.**
C529 AP78 25c multi .25 .25
C530 AP78 25c multi .25 .25
a. Pair, #C529-C530 .65 .65
C531 AP78 75c multi, vert. .60 .40
C532 AP78 75c multi, vert. .60 .40
a. Pair, #C531-C532 1.75 1.75
C533 AP78 1col multi, vert. .80 .55
C534 AP78 1col multi, vert. .80 .55
a. Pair, #C533-C534 2.50 2.50
Nos. C529-C534 (6) 3.30 2.40

Fishing Industry AP79

1983, Dec. 20 Litho. ***Perf. 14½x14***
C535 AP79 25c Fisherman .40 .25
C536 AP79 75c Feeding fish 1.50 .45

No. 999 Surcharged

1985, Apr. 10 Litho. ***Perf. 14***
C536A A297 1col on 10c multi .90 .50

Natl. Constitution, Cent. — AP80

1986, Aug. 29 Litho. ***Perf. 14***
C537 AP80 1col multi .50 .35

Hugo Lindo (1917-1985), Writer — AP81

1986, Nov. 10 Litho. ***Perf. 14½x14***
C538 AP81 1col multi .50 .35

Central American Economic Integration Bank, 25th Anniv. AP82

1986, Nov. 20
C539 AP82 1.50col multi .70 .50

12th Intl. Fair, Feb. 14-Mar. 1 AP83

1987, Jan. 20 Litho. ***Perf. 14½x14***
C540 AP83 70c multi .35 .25

Intl. Year of Shelter for the Homeless AP84

Perf. 14x14½, 14½x14

1987, July 15 **Litho.**
C541 AP84 70c shown .40 .25
C542 AP84 1col Emblem, vert. .50 .35

Miniature Sheet

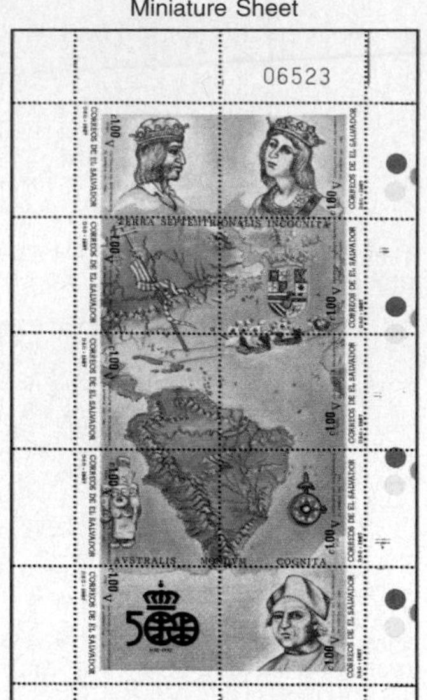

Discovery of America, 500th Anniv. (in 1992) — AP85

15th cent. map of the Americas (details) and: a, Ferdinand. b, Isabella. c, Caribbean. d, Ships, coat of arms. e, Base of flagstaff. f, Ships. g, Pre-Columbian statue. h, Compass. i, Anniv. emblem. j, Columbus rose.

1987, Dec. 21 Litho. *Perf. 14*

C543 AP85 Sheet of 10 8.50 8.50
a.-j. 1col any single .45 .35

No. 1075 Surcharged

1988, Oct. 28 Litho. *Perf. 14x14½*

C544 A316 5col on 90c multi 2.50 1.75

PRENFIL '88, Nov. 25-Dec. 2, Buenos Aire.

Organization of American States 18th General Assembly, Nov. 14-19 — AP86

1988, Nov. 19

C545 AP86 70c multi .40 .30

Handicapped Soccer Championships — AP87

1990, May 2 Litho. *Perf. 14½x14*

C546 AP87 70c multicolored .45 .25

REGISTRATION STAMPS

Gen. Rafael Antonio Gutiérrez — R1

1897 Engr. Wmk. 117 *Perf. 12*

F1 R1 10c dark blue *125.00*
F2 R1 10c brown lake .25

Unwmk.

F3 R1 10c dark blue .25
F4 R1 10c brown lake .25

Nos. F1 and F3 were probably not placed in use without the overprint "FRANQUEO OFICIAL" (Nos. O127-O128).

The reprints are on thick unwatermarked paper. Value, set of 2, 16c.

ACKNOWLEDGMENT OF RECEIPT STAMPS

AR1

1897 Engr. Wmk. 117 *Perf. 12*

H1 AR1 5c dark green .25

Unwmk.

H2 AR1 5c dark green .25

No. H2 has been reprinted on thick paper. Value 20c.

POSTAGE DUE STAMPS

D1

1895 Unwmk. Engr. *Perf. 12*

J1 D1 1c olive green .40 —
J2 D1 2c olive green .40 —
J3 D1 3c olive green .40 —
J4 D1 5c olive green .40 —
J5 D1 10c olive green .40 —
J6 D1 15c olive green .40 —
J7 D1 25c olive green .40 —
J8 D1 50c olive green .90 —
Nos. J1-J8 (8) 3.70

See Nos. J9-J56. For overprints see Nos. J57-J64, O186-O214.

1896 Wmk. 117

J9 D1 1c red .60 —
J10 D1 2c red .60 —
J11 D1 3c red .90 —
J12 D1 5c red 1.10 —
J13 D1 10c red 1.10 —
J14 D1 15c red 1.25 —
J15 D1 25c red 1.25 —
J16 D1 50c red 1.25 —
Nos. J9-J16 (8) 8.05

Unwmk.

J17 D1 1c red .40 —
J18 D1 2c red .40 —
J19 D1 3c red .40 —
J20 D1 5c red .40 —
J21 D1 10c red .40 —
J22 D1 15c red .50 —
J23 D1 25c red .50 —
J24 D1 50c red .50 —
Nos. J17-J24 (8) 3.50

Nos. J17-J24 exist imperforate.

1897

J25 D1 1c deep blue .40 —
J26 D1 2c deep blue .40 —
J27 D1 3c deep blue .40 —
J28 D1 5c deep blue .40 —
J29 D1 10c deep blue .50 —
J30 D1 15c deep blue .50 —
J31 D1 25c deep blue .40 —
J32 D1 50c deep blue .40 —
Nos. J25-J32 (8) 3.40

1898

J33 D1 1c violet 3.00
J34 D1 2c violet 1.00
J35 D1 3c violet 1.00
J36 D1 5c violet 5.00
J37 D1 10c violet 1.00
J38 D1 15c violet 1.00
J39 D1 25c violet 1.00
J40 D1 50c violet 1.00
Nos. J33-J40 (8) 14.00

Reprints of Nos. J1 to J40 are on thick paper, often in the wrong shades and usually with the impression somewhat blurred. Value, set of 40, $2, watermarked or unwatermarked.

1899 Wmk. 117 Sideways

J41 D1 1c orange .40
J42 D1 2c orange .40
J43 D1 3c orange .40
J44 D1 5c orange .40
J45 D1 10c orange .40
J46 D1 15c orange .40
J47 D1 25c orange .40
J48 D1 50c orange .40
Nos. J41-J48 (8) 3.20

Unwmk.

Thick Porous Paper

J49 D1 1c orange .40
J50 D1 2c orange .40
J51 D1 3c orange .40
J52 D1 5c orange .40
J53 D1 10c orange .40
J54 D1 15c orange .40
J55 D1 25c orange .40
J56 D1 50c orange .40
Nos. J49-J56 (8) 3.20

Nos. J41-J56 were probably not put in use without the wheel overprint.

Nos. J49-J56 Overprinted in Black

1900

J57 D1 1c orange 2.00
J58 D1 2c orange 2.00
J59 D1 3c orange 2.00
J60 D1 5c orange 3.00
J61 D1 10c orange 4.00
J62 D1 15c orange 4.00
J63 D1 25c orange 5.00
J64 D1 50c orange 6.00
Nos. J57-J64 (8) 28.00

See note after No. 198A.

Morazán Monument — D2

Perf. 14, 14½

1903 Engr. Wmk. 173

J65 D2 1c yellow green 1.75 1.25
J66 D2 2c carmine 2.75 1.75
J67 D2 3c orange 2.75 1.75
J68 D2 5c dark blue 2.75 1.75
J69 D2 10c dull violet 2.75 1.75
J70 D2 25c blue green 2.75 1.75
Nos. J65-J70 (6) 15.50 10.00

Nos. 355, 356, 358 and 360 Overprinted

1908 Unwmk. *Perf. 11½*

J71 A66 1c green & blk .80 .70
J72 A66 2c red & blk .60 .25
J73 A66 5c blue & blk 1.50 1.00
J74 A66 10c violet & blk 2.25 2.00

Same Overprint on No. O275

J75 O3 3c yellow & blk 1.50 1.25
Nos. J71-J75 (5) 6.65 5.20

Nos. 355-358, 360 Overprinted

J76 A66 1c green & blk .50 .50
J77 A66 2c red & blk .60 .60
J78 A66 3c yellow & blk .70 .70
J79 A66 5c blue & blk 1.00 1.00
J80 A66 10c violet & blk 2.00 2.00
Nos. J76-J80 (5) 4.80 4.80

It is now believed that stamps of type A66, on paper with Honeycomb watermark, do not exist with genuine overprints of the types used for Nos. J71-J80.

Pres. Fernando Figueroa — D3

1910 Engr. Wmk. 172

J81 D3 1c sepia & blk .30 .30
J82 D3 2c dk grn & blk .30 .30
J83 D3 3c orange & blk .30 .30
J84 D3 4c scarlet & blk .30 .30
J85 D3 5c purple & blk .30 .30
J86 D3 12c deep blue & blk .30 .30
J87 D3 24c brown red & blk .30 .30
Nos. J81-J87 (7) 2.10 2.10

OFFICIAL STAMPS

Nos. 134-157O Overprinted — a

Type a

1896 Unwmk. *Perf. 12*

O1 A45 1c blue .25
O2 A45 2c dk brown .25
a. Double overprint
O3 A45 3c blue grn 1.00
O4 A45 5c brown ol .25
O5 A45 10c yellow .25
O6 A45 12c dk blue .30
O7 A45 15c blue vio .25
O8 A45 20c magenta 1.00
O9 A45 24c vermilion .25
O10 A45 30c orange 1.00
O11 A45 50c black brn .45
O12 A45 1p rose lake .30
Nos. O1-O12 (12) 5.55

Nos. O1-O12 were not issued.

The 1c has been reprinted on thick unwatermarked paper. Value 25c.

Wmk. 117

O13 A46 1c emerald 4.75 3.00
O14 A47 2c lake 4.75 3.50
O15 A48 3c yellow brn 6.00 4.00
a. Inverted overprint —
O16 A49 5c dp blue 5.00 5.00
O17 A50 10c brown 7.00 3.75
a. Inverted overprint —
O18 A51 12c slate 10.50 8.00
O19 A52 15c blue grn 12.50 8.75
O20 A53 20c car rose 12.50 8.00
a. Inverted overprint
O21 A54 24c violet 12.50 9.00
O22 A55 30c dp green 15.00 12.50
O23 A56 50c orange 25.00 17.00
O24 A57 100c dk blue 40.00 25.00
Nos. O13-O24 (12) 155.50 107.50

Unwmk.

O25 A46 1c emerald 2.50 *3.50*
a. Double overprint — —
O26 A47 2c lake 2.75 *175.00*
O27 A48 3c yellow brn 3.00 *2.50*
O28 A49 5c dp blue 3.00 .90
O29 A50 10c brown 2.50 2.50
a. Inverted overprint
O30 A51 12c slate 10.00 7.00
O31 A52 15c blue grn 12.00 7.75
O32 A53 20c car rose 20.00 11.00
a. Inverted overprint
O33 A54 24c violet 20.00 11.00
O34 A55 30c dp green — —

O35 A56 50c orange — —
O36 A57 100c dk blue — —
Nos. O25-O36 (12) 75.75 221.15

All values have been reprinted. Value 25c each.

Nos. 134-145 Handstamped in Black or Violet — b

1896 **Type b**

O37 A45 1c blue 11.00
O38 A45 2c dk brown 11.00
O39 A45 3c blue green 11.00
O40 A45 5c brown olive 11.00
O41 A45 10c yellow 13.00
O42 A45 12c dk blue 16.00
O43 A45 15c blue violet 16.00
O44 A45 20c magenta 16.00
O45 A45 24c vermilion 16.00
O46 A45 30c orange 16.00
O47 A45 50c black brown 22.50
O48 A45 1p rose lake 22.50
Nos. O37-O48 (12) 182.00

Reprints of the 1c and 2c on thick paper exist with this handstamp. Value, 25c each.

The legitimacy of the "De Officio" handstamp has been questioned. The editors would like to see evidence regarding the authorized use of this handstamp.

Forged overprints exist of Nos. O37-O76, O103-O126 and of the higher valued stamps of O141-O214.

Nos. 146-157F, 157I-157O, 158D Handstamped Type b in Black or Violet

1896 **Wmk. 117**

O49 A46 1c emerald 9.00
O50 A47 2c lake 9.00
O51 A48 3c yellow brn 9.00
O52 A49 5c deep blue 9.00
O53 A50 10c brown 9.00
O54 A51 12c slate 16.00
O55 A52 15c blue green 16.00
O56 A53 20c carmine rose 16.00
O57 A54 24c violet 16.00
O58 A55 30c deep green 16.00
O59 A56 50c orange 16.00
O60 A57 100c dark blue 16.00
Nos. O49-O60 (12) 157.00

Unwmk.

O61 A46 1c emerald 9.00
O62 A47 2c lake 9.00
O63 A48 3c yellow brn 9.00
O64 A49 5c deep blue 9.00
O65 A50 10c brown 13.50
O66 A52 15c blue green 16.00
O67 A58 15c on 24c vio 11.50
O68 A53 20c carmine rose 16.00
O69 A54 24c violet 16.00
O70 A55 30c deep green 16.00
O71 A56 50c orange 19.00
O72 A57 100c dark blue 19.00
Nos. O61-O72 (12) 163.00

Nos. 175-176 Overprinted Type a in Black

1897

O73 A59 1c bl, gold, rose & grn .30
O74 A59 5c rose, gold, bl & grn .30

These stamps were probably not officially issued.

Nos. 175-176 Handstamped Type b in Black or Violet

1900

O75 A59 1c bl, gold, rose & grn 22.50
O76 A59 5c rose, gold, bl & grn 22.50

Nos. 159-170L Overprinted Type a in Black

1897 **Wmk. 117**

O79 A46 1c scarlet 8.00 8.00
O80 A47 2c yellow green 8.00 8.00
O81 A48 3c bister brown 7.00 7.00
O82 A49 5c orange 7.00 7.00
O83 A50 10c blue green 9.00 9.00
O84 A51 12c blue 20.00 20.00
O85 A52 15c black 40.00 40.00
O86 A53 20c slate 20.00 20.00
O87 A54 24c yellow 40.00 40.00
a. Inverted overprint
O88 A55 30c rose 40.00 40.00
O89 A56 50c violet 40.00 40.00
O90 A57 100c brown lake 100.00 100.00
Nos. O79-O90 (12) 339.00

Unwmk.

O91 A46 1c scarlet 5.00 5.00
O92 A47 2c yellow green 3.00 3.00
O93 A48 3c bister brown 2.00 2.00
O94 A49 5c orange 3.00 3.00
O95 A50 10c blue green 10.00 10.00
O96 A51 12c blue 3.00 3.00
O97 A52 15c black 30.00 30.00
O98 A53 20c slate 20.00 20.00
O99 A54 24c yellow 30.00 30.00
O100 A55 30c rose 30.00 30.00
O101 A56 50c violet 20.00 20.00
O102 A57 100c brown lake 50.00 50.00
Nos. O91-O102 (12) 206.00

All values have been reprinted. Value 25c each.

Nos. 159-170L Handstamped Type b in Violet or Black

1897 **Wmk. 117**

O103 A46 1c scarlet 7.50
O104 A47 2c yellow green 7.50
O105 A48 3c bister brown 7.50
O106 A49 5c orange 7.50
O107 A50 10c blue green 8.75
O108 A51 12c blue
O109 A52 15c black
O110 A53 20c slate 15.00
O111 A54 24c yellow 17.50
O112 A55 30c rose
O113 A56 50c violet
O114 A57 100c brown lake

Unwmk.

O115 A46 1c scarlet 7.50
O116 A47 2c yellow grn 7.50
O117 A48 3c bister brn 7.50
O118 A49 5c orange 7.50
O119 A50 10c blue green 7.50
O120 A51 12c blue
O121 A52 15c black
O122 A53 20c slate
O123 A54 24c yellow
O124 A55 30c rose 15.00
O125 A56 50c violet
O126 A57 100c brown lake 17.50

Reprints of the 1 and 15c on thick watermarked paper and the 12, 30, 50 and 100c on thick unwatermarked paper are known with this overprint. Value, 25c each.

Nos. F1, F3 Overprinted Type a in Red

Wmk. 117

O127 R1 10c dark blue .30

Unwmk.

O128 R1 10c dark blue .30

The reprints are on thick paper. Value 15c.

Originals of the 10c brown lake Registration Stamp and the 5c Acknowledgment of Receipt stamp are believed not to have been issued with the "FRANQUEO OFICIAL" overprint. They are believed to exist only as reprints.

Nos. 177-188 Overprinted Type a

1898 **Wmk. 117**

O129 A60 1c orange ver 4.50 4.50
O130 A60 2c rose 4.50 4.50
O131 A60 3c pale yel grn 4.00 4.00
O132 A60 5c blue green 4.00 4.00
O133 A60 10c gray blue 15.00 15.00
O134 A60 12c violet 17.00 17.00
O135 A60 13c brown lake 17.00 17.00
O136 A60 20c deep blue 19.00 19.00
O137 A60 24c ultra 15.00 15.00
O138 A60 26c bister brn 20.00 20.00
O139 A60 50c orange 20.00 20.00
O140 A60 1p yellow 50.00 50.00
Nos. O129-O140 (12) 190.00 190.00

Reprints of the above set are on thick paper. Value, 25c each.

No. 177 Handstamped Type b in Violet

O141 A60 1c orange ver 35.00 —

No. O141 with Additional Overprint Type c in Black

c

Type "c" is called the "wheel" overprint.

O142 A60 1c orange ver — —

Counterfeits exist of the "wheel" overprint.

Nos. 204-205, 207 and 209 Overprinted

1899 **Unwmk.**

O143 A61 12c dark green — 50.00
O144 A61 13c deep rose 50.00 —
O145 A61 26c carmine rose 50.00 —
O146 A61 100c violet 100.00 —

Nos. O143-O144 Punched With Twelve Small Holes

O147 A61 12c dark green
O148 A61 13c deep rose

Official stamps punched with twelve small holes were issued and used for ordinary postage.

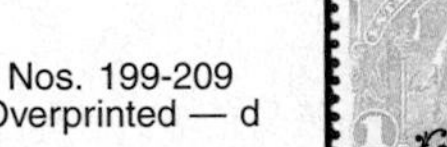

Nos. 199-209 Overprinted — d

1899 **Blue Overprint**

O149 A61 1c brown .30
O150 A61 2c gray green .30
O151 A61 3c blue .30
O152 A61 5c brown orange .30
O153 A61 10c chocolate .30
O154 A61 13c deep rose .30
O155 A61 26c carmine rose .30
O156 A61 50c orange red .30
O157 A61 100c violet .30

Black Overprint

O158 A61 3c blue .30
O159 A61 12c dark green .30
O160 A61 24c lt blue .30
Nos. O149-O160 (12) 3.60

Nos. O149-O160 were probably not placed in use.

With Additional Overprint Type c in Black

O161 A61 1c brown .60 .60
O162 A61 2c gray green 1.10 1.10
O163 A61 3c blue .60 .60
O164 A61 5c brown org .60 .60
O165 A61 10c chocolate .75 .75
O166 A61 12c dark green — —
O167 A61 13c deep rose 1.50 1.50
O168 A61 24c lt blue 30.00 30.00
O169 A61 26c carmine rose .75 .75
O170 A61 50c orange red 1.50 1.50
O171 A61 100c violet 1.50 1.50
Nos. O161-O165,O167-O171 (10) 38.90 38.90

Nos. O149-O155, O159-O160 Punched With Twelve Small Holes

Blue Overprint

O172 A61 1c brown 5.00 1.00
O173 A61 2c gray green 3.25 5.00
O174 A61 3c blue 8.00 3.75
O175 A61 5c brown org 10.00 3.00
O176 A61 10c chocolate 15.00 5.00
O177 A61 13c deep rose 7.50 7.00
O177A A61 24c lt blue
O178 A61 26c car rose 100.00 35.00

Black Overprint

O179 A61 12c dark green 6.00 4.50
Nos. O172-O177,O178-O179 (8) 154.75 64.25

It is stated that Nos. O172-O214 inclusive were issued for ordinary postage and not for use as Official stamps.

Nos. O161-O167, O169 Punched With Twelve Small Holes

O180 A61 1c brown 1.25 1.10
O180A A61 2c gray green
O181 A61 3c blue
O182 A61 5c brown orange 1.25
O182A A61 10c chocolate
O182B A61 12c dark green
O183 A61 13c deep rose 4.00 *5.00*
O184 A61 26c carmine rose

No. 209 Ovptd. Types a and e in Black

e

O185 A61 100c violet

Nos. J49-J56 Overprinted in Black

1900

O186 D1 1c orange 27.50
O187 D1 2c orange 27.50
O188 D1 3c orange 27.50
O189 D1 5c orange 27.50
O190 D1 10c orange 27.50
O191 D1 15c orange 62.50
O192 D1 25c orange 62.50
O193 D1 50c orange 62.50
Nos. O186-O193 (8) 325.00

Nos. O186-O189, O191-O193 Overprinted Type c in Black

O194 D1 1c orange *25.00*
O195 D1 2c orange *25.00*
O196 D1 3c orange *25.00*
O197 D1 5c orange *25.00*
O198 D1 15c orange 16.00 *25.00*
O199 D1 25c orange 19.00 *25.00*
O200 D1 50c orange 160.00 —

Nos. O186-O189 Punched With Twelve Small Holes

O201 D1 1c orange 45.00
O202 D1 2c orange 45.00
O203 D1 3c orange 45.00
O204 D1 5c orange 45.00
Nos. O201-O204 (4) 180.00

Nos. O201-O204 Overprinted Type c in Black

O205 D1 1c orange 9.00 6.50
O206 D1 2c orange 6.50
O207 D1 3c orange 6.50
O208 D1 5c orange 20.00 6.50

Overprinted Type a in Violet and Type c in Black

O209 D1 2c orange *25.00*
a. Inverted overprint *25.00*
O210 D1 3c orange *25.00*
O211 D1 10c orange 3.00

Nos. O186-O188 Handstamped Type e in Violet

O212 D1 1c orange 9.00 7.50
O213 D1 2c orange 9.00 7.50
O214 D1 3c orange 9.00 9.00
Nos. O212-O214 (3) 27.00 24.00

See note after No. O48.

Type of Regular Issue of 1900 Overprinted Type a in Black

O223 A63 1c lt green 22.50 —
a. Inverted overprint
O224 A63 2c rose 27.50 —
a. Inverted overprint
O225 A63 3c gray black 17.50 —
a. Overprint vertical
O226 A63 5c blue 17.50 —
O227 A63 10c blue 45.00 —
a. Inverted overprint
O228 A63 12c yellow grn 45.00 —
O229 A63 13c yellow brn 45.00 —
O230 A63 24c gray black 32.50 —
O231 A63 26c yellow brn 30.00 —
a. Inverted overprint
O232 A63 50c dull rose
a. Inverted overprint
Nos. O223-O231 (9) 282.50

Nos. O223-O224, O231-O232 Overprinted in Violet — f

O233 A63 1c lt green 4.75 4.00
O234 A63 2c rose 25.00
a. "FRANQUEO OFICIAL" invtd.
O235 A63 26c yellow brown .50 .50
O236 A63 50c dull rose .75 .55

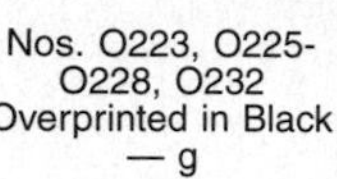
Nos. O223, O225-O228, O232 Overprinted in Black — g

O237 A63 1c lt green 5.00 5.00
O238 A63 3c gray black
O239 A63 5c blue 40.00
O240 A63 10c blue
O241 A63 12c yellow green

Violet Overprint

O242 A63 50c dull rose 10.00

The shield overprinted on No. O242 is of the type on No. O212.

O1

1903 Wmk. 173 *Perf. 14, 14½*

O243 O1 1c yellow green .45 .25
O244 O1 2c carmine .45 .25
O245 O1 3c orange 5.00 .85
O246 O1 5c dark blue 5.00 .25
O247 O1 10c dull violet .70 .35
O248 O1 13c red brown .70 .35
O249 O1 15c yellow brown 5.00 1.75
O250 O1 24c scarlet .45 .35
O251 O1 50c bister .70 .35
O252 O1 100c grnsh blue .70 .75
Nos. O243-O252 (10) 19.15 5.50

For surcharges see Nos. O254-O257.

No. 285 Handstamped Type b in Black

1904

O253 A64 3c orange 35.00

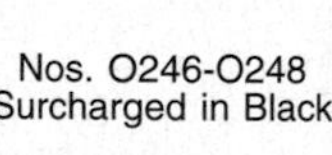
Nos. O246-O248 Surcharged in Black

1905

O254 O1 2c on 5c dark blue 6.50 5.50
O255 O1 3c on 5c dark blue
a. Double surcharge
O256 O1 3c on 10c dl vio 18.00 12.00
O257 O1 3c on 13c red brn 1.75 1.40

A 2c surcharge of this type exists on No. O247.

No. O225 Overprinted in Blue

a

b

1905 Unwmk.

O258 A63(a) 3c gray black 4.00 3.50
O259 A63(b) 3c gray black 3.50 3.00

Nos. O224-O225 Overprinted in Blue

c

d

1906

O260 A63(c) 2c rose 22.50 20.00
O261 A63(c) 3c gray black 2.50 2.00
a. Overprint "1906" in blk
O262 A63(d) 3c gray black 2.75 2.50
Nos. O260-O262 (3) 27.75 24.50

Escalón — O2

1906 Engr. *Perf. 11½*

O263 O2 1c green & blk .40 .25
O264 O2 2c carmine & blk .40 .25
O265 O2 3c yellow & blk .40 .25
O266 O2 5c blue & blk .40 *.75*
O267 O2 10c violet & blk .40 .25
O268 O2 13c dk brown & blk .40 .25
O269 O2 15c red org & blk .50 .25
O270 O2 24c carmine & blk .60 *.35*
O271 O2 50c orange & blk .60 *1.50*
O272 O2 100c dk blue & blk .70 *4.50*
Nos. O263-O272 (10) 4.80 *8.60*

The centers of these stamps are also found in blue black.

Nos. O263 to O272 have been reprinted, perforated 11.8. Value, set of 10, $2.50.

National Palace — O3

1908

O273 O3 1c green & blk .25 .25
O274 O3 2c red & blk .25 .25
O275 O3 3c yellow & blk .25 .25
O276 O3 5c blue & blk .25 .25
O277 O3 10c violet & blk .25 .25
O278 O3 13c violet & blk .25 .25
O279 O3 15c pale brn & blk .25 .25
O280 O3 24c rose & blk .25 .25
O281 O3 50c yellow & blk .25 .25
O282 O3 100c turq blue & blk .35 .35
Nos. O273-O282 (10) 2.60 2.60

For overprints see Nos. 441-442, 445-449, J75, O283-O292, O323-O328.

Nos. O273-O282 Overprinted Type g in Black

O283 O3 1c green & blk 3.00
O284 O3 2c red & blk 4.00
O285 O3 3c yellow & blk 4.00
O286 O3 5c blue & blk 5.00
O287 O3 10c violet & blk 5.00
O288 O3 13c violet & blk 6.00
O289 O3 15c pale brn & blk 6.00
O290 O3 24c rose & blk 8.00
O291 O3 50c yellow & blk 9.00
O292 O3 100c turq & blk 10.00
Nos. O283-O292 (10) 60.00

Pres. Figueroa — O4

1910 Engr. Wmk. 172

O293 O4 2c dk green & blk .30 .25
O294 O4 3c orange & blk .30 .25
O295 O4 4c scarlet & blk .30 .25
a. 4c carmine & black
O296 O4 5c purple & blk .30 .25
O297 O4 6c scarlet & blk .30 .25
O298 O4 10c purple & blk .30 .25
O299 O4 12c dp blue & blk .30 .25
O300 O4 17c olive grn & blk .30 .25
O301 O4 19c brn red & blk .30 .25
O302 O4 29c choc & blk .30 .25
O303 O4 50c yellow & blk .30 .25
O304 O4 100c turq & blk .30 .25
Nos. O293-O304 (12) 3.60 3.00

Regular Issue, Type A63, Overprinted or Surcharged

a

b

c

1911 Unwmk.

O305 A63(a) 1c lt green .25 .25
O306 A63(b) 3c on 13c yel brn .25 .25
O307 A63(b) 5c on 10c dp bl .25 .25
O308 A63(a) 10c deep blue .25 .25
O309 A63(a) 12c lt green .25 .25
O310 A63(a) 13c yellow brn .25 .25
O311 A63(b) 50c on 10c dp bl .25 .25
O312 A63(c) 1col on 13c yel brn .25 .25
Nos. O305-O312 (8) 2.00 2.00

O5

1914 Typo. *Perf. 12*

Background in Green, Shield and "Provisional" in Black

O313 O5 2c yellow brn .50 .25
O314 O5 3c yellow .50 .25
O315 O5 5c dark blue .50 .25
O316 O5 10c red .50 .25
O317 O5 12c green .50 .25
O318 O5 17c violet .50 .25
O319 O5 50c brown .50 .25
O320 O5 100c dull rose .50 .25
Nos. O313-O320 (8) 4.00 2.00

Stamps of this issue are known imperforate or with parts of the design omitted or misplaced. These varieties were not regularly issued.

O6

1914 Typo.

O321 O6 2c blue green .50 .25
O322 O6 3c orange .50 .25

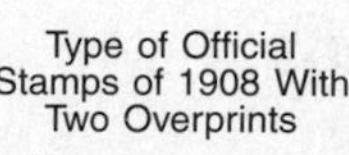
Type of Official Stamps of 1908 With Two Overprints

1915

O323 O3 1c gray green 1.00 .60
a. "1915" double
b. "OFICIAL" inverted
O324 O3 2c red 1.00 .60
O325 O3 5c ultra .35 *.70*
O326 O3 10c yellow .35 *.60*
a. Date omitted
O327 O3 50c violet .90 *1.50*
O328 O3 100c black brown 1.90 *3.25*
Nos. O323-O328 (6) 5.50 7.25

Same Overprint on #414, 417, 429

O329 A66 1c gray green 10.00 1.60
O330 A66 6c pale blue 1.00 .45
a. 6c ultramarine
O331 A66 12c brown 1.00 .75
Nos. O329-O331 (3) 12.00 2.80

O323-O327, O329-O331 exist imperf.

Nos. O329-O331 exist with "OFICIAL" inverted and double. See note after No. 421.

Nos. 431-440 Overprinted in Blue or Red

1916

O332 A83 1c deep green .45 .75
O333 A83 2c vermilion 1.60 1.60
O334 A83 5c dp blue (R) 1.25 1.60
O335 A83 6c gray vio (R) .45 .75
O336 A83 10c black brown .45 .75
O337 A83 12c violet 2.00 3.25
O338 A83 17c orange .45 .75
O339 A83 25c dark brown .45 .75
O340 A83 29c black (R) .45 .75
O341 A83 50c slate (R) 2.00 .75
Nos. O332-O341 (10) 9.55 11.70

Nos. 474-481 Overprinted

a

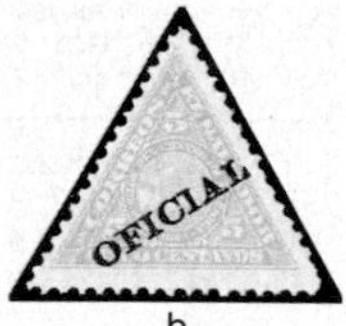

b

1921

O342 A94(a) 1c green .25 .25
O343 A95(a) 2c black .25 .25
a. Inverted overprint
O344 A96(b) 5c orange .25 .25
O345 A97(a) 6c carmine rose .25 .25
O346 A98(a) 10c deep blue .30 .25
O347 A99(a) 25c olive green .75 .35
O348 A100(a) 60c violet 1.00 .60
O349 A101(a) 1col black brown 1.10 .70
Nos. O342-O349 (8) 4.15 2.90

Nos. 498 and 500 Overprinted in Black or Red

1925

O350 A109 5c olive black .45 .25
O351 A111 10c orange (R) .85 .25
a. "ATLANT CO" 13.00 11.00

Inverted overprints exist.

Regular Issue of 1924-25 Overprinted in Black or Red

1927

O352 A106 1c red violet .25 .25
O353 A107 2c dark red .45 .25
O354 A109 5c olive blk (R) .45 .25
O355 A110 6c dp blue (R) 5.25 4.50
O356 A111 10c orange .50 .30
a. "ATLANT CO" 22.50 19.00
O357 A116 1col grn & vio (R) 2.25 1.40
Nos. O352-O357 (6) 9.15 6.95

Inverted overprints exist on 1c, 2c, 5c, 10c.

Regular Issue of 1924-25 Overprinted in Black

1932 *Perf. 12½*

O358	A106	1c deep violet	.25	.25
O359	A107	2c dark red	.45	.25
O360	A109	5c olive black	.25	.25
O361	A111	10c orange	.85	.35
a.		"ATLANT CO"	22.50	19.00
		Nos. O358-O361 (4)	1.80	1.10

Catalogue values for unused stamps in this section, from this point to the end of the section, are for Never Hinged items.

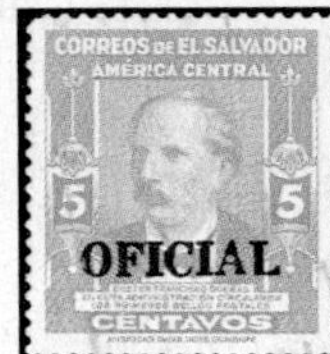

Regular Issue of 1947 Overprinted in Black or Red

1948 Unwmk. Engr. *Perf. 12*

O362	A154	1c car rose	65.00	32.50
O363	A154	2c deep org	65.00	32.50
O364	A154	5c slate gray (R)	65.00	32.50
O365	A154	10c bis brn (R)	65.00	32.50
O366	A154	20c green (R)	65.00	32.50
O367	A154	50c black (R)	65.00	32.50
		Nos. O362-O367 (6)	390.00	195.00

No. 602 Surcharged in Carmine and Black

1964(?)

O368 A154 1c on 20c green *90.00* —

The X's are black, the rest carmine.

PARCEL POST STAMPS

Mercury PP1

1895 Unwmk. Engr. *Perf. 12*

Q1	PP1	5c brown orange	.45
Q2	PP1	10c dark blue	.45
Q3	PP1	15c red	.45
Q4	PP1	20c orange	.45
Q5	PP1	50c blue green	.45
		Nos. Q1-Q5 (5)	2.25

POSTAL TAX STAMPS

PT1

Overprinted "REVISADO" in Violet, Black or Red

1900-04 Typo. *Perf. 11½*

RA1 PT1 1c black
RA2 PT1 1c black, dated "1903"
RA3 PT1 1c black, dated "1904"

Use of these stamps was obligatory on all domestic letters. The funds raised were used to maintain the public schools.

Nos. 503, 501 Surcharged

1931 Unwmk. *Perf. 12½*

RA4	A115	1c on 50c org brn	.50	.40
a.		Double surcharge	5.00	5.00
RA5	A112	2c on 20c dp grn	.50	.40

Nos. 501, 503 Surcharged

RA6	A112	1c on 20c dp grn	.50	.40
RA7	A115	2c on 50c org brn	.50	.40
a.		Without period in "0.02"	3.00	

The use of these stamps was obligatory, in addition to the regular postage, on letters and other postal matter. The money obtained from their sale was to be used to erect a new post office in San Salvador.

SAMOA

sə-'mō-ə

(Western Samoa)

LOCATION — Archipelago in the south Pacific Ocean, east of Fiji
GOVT. — Independent state; former territory mandated by New Zealand
AREA — 1,093 sq. mi.
POP. — 161,298 (1991)
CAPITAL — Apia

In 1861-99, Samoa was an independent kingdom under the influence of the US, to which the harbor of Pago Pago had been ceded, and that of Great Britain and Germany. In 1898 a disturbance arose, resulting in the withdrawal of Great Britain, and the partitioning of the islands between Germany and the US. Early in World War I the islands under German domination were occupied by New Zealand troops and in 1920 the League of Nations declared them a mandate to New Zealand. Western Samoa became independent Jan. 1, 1962.

12 Pence = 1 Shilling
20 Shillings = 1 Pound
100 Pfennig = 1 Mark (1900)
100 Sene (Cents) = 1 Tala (Dollar) (1967)

Catalogue values for unused stamps in this country are for Never Hinged items, beginning with Scott 191 in the regular postage section, Scott B1 in the semi-postal section and Scott C1 in the air post section.

Watermarks

Wmk. 61 — N Z and Star Close Together

Wmk. 62 — N Z and Star Wide Apart

On watermark 61 the margins of the sheets are watermarked "NEW ZEALAND POSTAGE" and parts of the double-lined letters of these words are frequently found on the stamps. It occasionally happens that a stamp shows no watermark whatever.

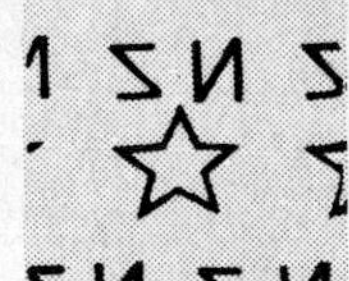

Wmk. 253 — Multiple N Z and Star

Wmk. 355 — Kava Bowl and WS, Multiple

Issues of the Kingdom

A1

Type I

Type II

Type III

Type IV

Type I — Line above "X" is usually unbroken. Dots over "SAMOA" are uniform and evenly spaced. Upper right serif of "M" is horizontal.

Type II — Line above "X" is usually broken. Small dot near upper right serif of "M."

Type III — Line above "X" roughly retouched. Upper right serif of "M" bends down (joined to dot).

Type IV — Speck of color on curved line below center of "M."

Perf. 11¾, 12½

1877-82 Litho. Unwmk.

1	A1	1p	Blue (III), Perf. 11¾ ('79)	37.50	*1,000.*
1a	A1	1p	sky blue (III), Perf. 12½ ('79)	260.00	125.00
2	A1	2p	lilac rose (IV), ('82)	25.00	—
3c	A1	3p	vermilion (I)	450.00	*250.00*
3d	A1	3p	vermilion, rough perfs (III), Perf. 11¾	65.00	—
4	A1	6p	lilac (III), Perf. 12½ ('79)	550.00	135.00
4e	A1	6p	dull lilac (III), Perf. 11¾ ('79)	55.00	*100.00*
5	A1	9p	pale chestnut (IV) ('80)	80.00	*425.00*
6	A1	1sh	orange yellow (II), Perf. 12½ ('78)	325.00	135.00
6c	A1	1sh	golden yellow (II), Perf 11¾ ('79)	110.00	*260.00*
7	A1	2sh	Deep brown (III), Perf. 11¾ ('79)	370.00	*500.00*
7d	A1	2sh	dp brn, Perf. 11¾ ('79)	275.00	—
8	A1	5sh	emerald green (III), Perf. 12½ ('79)	1,875.	850.00
8a	A1	5sh	yellow green (III), Perf. 11¾ ('79)	725.00	

Values are for the least expensive varieties. For detailed listings, see the *Scott Classic Specialized Catalogue.*

The 1p often has a period after "PENNY." The 2p was never placed in use since the Samoa Express service was discontinued late in 1881.

Imperforates of this issue are proofs.

Sheets of the first issue were not perforated around the outer sides. All values except the 2p were printed in sheets of 10 (2x5). The 1p, 3p and 6p type I and the 1p type III were also printed in sheets of 20 (4x5), and six stamps on each of these sheets were perforated all around. These are the only varieties of the original stamps which have not one or two imperforate edges. The 2p was printed in sheets of 21 (3x7) and five stamps in the second row were perforated all around. The 2p was also reprinted in sheets of 40, which are much more common than the sheets of 21.

Reprints are of type IV and nearly always perforated on all sides. They have a spot of color at the edge of the panel below the "M." This spot is not on any originals except the 9p, the original of which may be distinguished by having a rough blind perf. 12. The 2p does show a spot of color.

Forgeries exist.

Palms — A2

Perf. 11, 12x11½ (#14, 17a), 12½ (#16, 18)

1886-1900 Typo. Wmk. 62

9d	A2	½p	purple brown	5.75	*2.10*
10	A2	½p	dl bl grn ('99)	4.00	*4.50*
11f	A2	1p	bluish green ('97)	4.00	2.00
12	A2	1p	red brown	4.25	*20.00*
13g	A2	2p	bright yellow ('97)	16.00	10.00
14	A3	2½p	rose ('92)	80.00	6.00
14b	A3	2½p	rose	4.25	*10.50*
15	A3	2½p	black, perf 10x11 ('96)	2.25	*3.25*
16	A2	4p	blue	55.00	13.50
16f	A2	4p	deep blue ('00)	1.60	52.50
17a	A2	6p	maroon	325.00	12.50
17e	A2	6p	maroon ('00)	2.00	62.50
18	A2	1sh	rose carmine	67.50	13.50
a.			Perf 12½, diagonal half used on cover ('95)		375.00
18g	A2	1sh	carmine ('00)	1.80	—
19h	A2	2sh6p	deep purple ('98)	5.00	10.00
i.			Vert. pair, imperf. btw.	475.00	

The 2½p has only the 3rd form.

Nos. 9-19 exist in various printings, perf 11, 12½ and 12x11½. Values are for the least expensive varieties. For detailed listings, see the *Scott Classic Specialized Catalogue.*

For surcharges or overprints on stamps or types of design A2 see Nos. 20-22, 24-38.

Nos. 16b and 16c Handstamp Surcharged in Black or Red

a

b

c

1893 *Perf. 12x11½*

20	A2(a)	5p on 4p blue (#16c)	65.00	*100.00*
a.		On 4p deep blue (#16b)	100.00	100.00
21	A2(b)	5p on 4p blue (#16c)	75.00	—
a.		On 4p deep blue (#16b)	100.00	*110.00*
22	A2(c)	5p on 4p blue (#16c) (R)	42.50	*37.50*
a.		On 4p deep blue (#16b)	47.50	*50.00*
		Nos. 20-22 (3)	182.50	*137.50*

As the surcharges on Nos. 20-21 were handstamped in two steps and on No. 22 in three steps, various varieties exist.

Flag Design — A7

1894-95 Typo. *Perf. 11½x12*
23 A7 5p vermilion 35.00 7.50
a. Perf. 11 ('95) 70.00 15.00
b. As "a," deep red ('00) 5.00 *20.00*

Types of 1887-1895 Surcharged in Blue, Black, Red or Green

1½p, 2½p

3p

Handstamped Surcharges

1895 *Perf. 11*
24 A2 1½p on 2p org (Bl) 7.50 *10.00*
a. 1½p on 2p brn org, perf 12x11½ (Bl) 27.50 20.00
b. 1½p on 2p yellow, "2" ends with vertical stroke 5.00 *27.50*
c. As No. 24, pair, one without surcharge 650.00
25 A2 3p on 2p org (Bk) 10.00 *15.00*
a. 3p on 2p brn org, perf. 12x11½ (Bk) 60.00 25.00
b. 3p on 2p org yellow, narrow "R" (Bk) 6.00 *50.00*
c. Vert. pair, imperf. btwn. 650.00
d. As "b," pair, one without surcharge

Typographed Surcharges (#26 Handstamped)

1898-1900 *Perf. 11*
26 A2 2½p on 1sh rose (Bk), hstmpd. srch. 50.00 *50.00*
a. 2½p, typo surcharge 13.00 *15.00*
b. As "a," double surcharge 500.00 500.00
27 A2 2½p on 2sh6p vio (Bk) 13.00 *20.00*
28 A2 2½p on 1p bl grn (R) 1.75 *5.00*
a. Inverted surcharge 850.00 *425.00*
29 A2 2½p on 1sh rose car (R) 8.50 *20.00*
a. Double surcharge 400.00
30 A2 3p on 2p dp red org (G) 5.00 *130.00*
Nos. 26-30 (5) 78.25 *225.00*

No. 30 was a reissue, available for postage. The surcharge is not as tall as the 3p surcharge illustrated, which is the surcharge on No. 25. As Nos. 24-26 are handstamped, various varieties exist.

Stamps of 1886-99 Overprinted in Red or Blue

1899
31 A2 ½p dl bl grn (R) 3.50 *8.00*
32 A2 1p red brown (Bl) 4.25 *20.00*
33 A2 2p br orange (R) 2.50 *20.00*
a. 2p deep ocher 4.00 *20.00*
34 A2 4p blue (R) 1.00 *20.00*
35 A7 5p dp scarlet (Bl) 3.75 *20.00*
36 A2 6p maroon (Bl) 2.00 *20.00*
37 A2 1sh rose car (Bl) 2.00 *25.00*
38 A2 2sh6p mauve (R) 4.75 *40.00*
Nos. 31-38 (8) 23.75 *173.00*

In 1900 the Samoan islands were partitioned between the US and Germany. The part which became American has since used US stamps.

Issued under German Dominion

Stamps of Germany Overprinted

1900 Unwmk. *Perf. 13½x14½*
51 A9 3pf dark brown 11.00 *15.00*
52 A9 5pf green 14.00 *20.00*
53 A10 10pf carmine 11.00 *20.00*
54 A10 20pf ultra 21.00 *32.50*
55 A10 25pf orange 42.50 *85.00*
56 A10 50pf red brown 42.50 *80.00*
Nos. 51-56 (6) 142.00 *252.50*

Kaiser's Yacht "Hohenzollern"
A12 A13

1900 Typo. *Perf. 14*
57 A12 3pf brown 1.25 *1.40*
58 A12 5pf green 1.25 *1.40*
59 A12 10pf carmine 1.25 *1.40*
60 A12 20pf ultra 1.25 *2.75*
61 A12 25pf org & blk, *yel* 1.40 *14.00*
62 A12 30pf org & blk, *sal* 1.40 *13.00*
63 A12 40pf lake & blk 1.50 *14.00*
64 A12 50pf pur & blk, *sal* 1.50 *15.00*
65 A12 80pf lake & blk, *rose* 3.50 *37.50*

Perf. 14½x14
Engr.
66 A13 1m carmine 3.75 *70.00*
67 A13 2m blue 5.00 *120.00*
68 A13 3m black vio 9.00 *175.00*
69 A13 5m slate & car 140.00 *600.00*
Nos. 57-69 (13) 172.05

1915 Wmk. 125 Typo. *Perf. 14*
70 A12 3pf brown 1.25
71 A12 5pf green 1.50
72 A12 10pf carmine 1.50

Perf. 14½x14
Engr.
73 A13 5m slate & car 32.50

Nos. 70-73 were never put in use.

Issued under British Dominion

Nos. 57-69 Surcharged

On A12

On A13

G.R.I.
1 Shillings.

1914 Unwmk. *Perf. 14*
101 A12 ½p on 3pf brn 60.00 16.00
a. Double surcharge 800.00 625.00
b. Fraction bar omitted 90.00 42.50
c. Comma after "I" 750.00 450.00
102 A12 ½p on 5pf grn 65.00 20.00
a. Double surcharge 800.00 625.00
b. Fraction bar omitted 140.00 62.50
d. Comma after "I" 450.00 190.00
103 A12 1p on 10pf car 110.00 42.50
a. Double surcharge 850.00 675.00
104 A12 2½p on 20pf ultra 62.50 14.00
a. Fraction bar omitted 95.00 45.00
b. Inverted surcharge 1,150. 1,050.
c. Double surcharge 800.00 675.00
d. Commas after "I" 575.00 375.00
105 A12 3p on 25pf org & blk, *yel* 80.00 42.50
a. Double surcharge 1,150. 850.00
b. Comma after "I" 5,250. 1,150.
106 A12 4p on 30pf org & blk, *sal* 135.00 62.50
107 A12 5p on 40pf lake & blk 135.00 75.00
108 A12 6p on 50pf pur & blk, *sal* 67.50 37.50
a. Inverted "9" for "6" 190.00 110.00
b. Double surcharge 1,250. 1,150.
109 A12 9p on 80pf lake & blk, *rose* 210.00 110.00

Perf. 14½x14
110 A13 1sh on 1m car ("1 Shillings") 3,500. *3,750.*
a. "1 Shilling." *11,500.* *7,500.*
111 A13 2sh on 2m blue 4,000. 3,500.
112 A13 3sh on 3m blk vio 1,600. 1,500.
a. Double surcharge *10,500.* *11,500.*
113 A13 5sh on 5m slate & car 1,200. 1,100.
a. Double surcharge 15,000. 15,000.

G.R.I. stands for Georgius Rex Imperator.

The 3d on 30pf and 4d on 40pf were produced at a later time.

Unauthorized overprints, created as favors, exist on Nos. 101-113.

Stamps of New Zealand Overprinted in Red or Blue

k

m

Perf. 14, 14x13½, 14x14½
1914, Sept. 29 Wmk. 61
114 A41(k) ½p yel grn (R) 1.50 .35
115 A42(k) 1p carmine 1.40 .25
116 A41(k) 2p mauve (R) 1.40 1.10
117 A22(m) 2½p blue (R) 2.00 2.00
118 A41(k) 6p car rose, perf. 14x14½ 2.25 2.00
a. Perf. 14x13½ 19.00 26.00
119 A41(k) 1sh vermilion 11.00 *22.00*
Nos. 114-119 (6) 19.55 *27.70*

Overprinted Type "m"

1914-25 *Perf. 14, 14½x14*
120 PF1 2sh blue (R) 7.00 6.25
121 PF1 2sh6p brown (Bl) 6.25 *15.00*
122 PF1 3sh vio (R) ('22) 18.00 *65.00*
123 PF1 5sh green (R) 22.50 *11.00*
124 PF1 10sh red brn (Bl) 45.00 *42.50*
125 PF2 £1 rose (Bl) 100.00 85.00
126 PF2 £2 vio (R) ('25) 400.00
Nos. 120-126 (7) 598.75
Nos. 120-125 (6) *224.75*

Postal use of the £2 is questioned.

Overprinted Type "k"

Perf. 14x13½, 14x14½
1916-19 Typo.
127 A43 ½p yellow grn (R) 1.00 *1.40*
128 A47 1½p gray blk (R) ('17) .55 .25
129 A47 1½p brn org (R) ('19) .35 .50
130 A43 2p yellow (R) ('18) 2.00 .25
131 A43 3p chocolate (Bl) 3.50 *22.50*

Engr.
132 A44 2½p dull blue (R) 1.25 .60
133 A45 3p violet brn (Bl) .65 *1.10*
134 A45 6p carmine rose (Bl) 2.25 *2.50*
135 A45 1sh vermilion (Bl) 4.75 1.75
Nos. 127-135 (9) 16.30 30.85

New Zealand Victory Issue of 1919 Overprinted Type "k"

1920, June *Perf. 14*
136 A48 ½p yellow grn (R) 6.50 *16.00*
137 A49 1p carmine (Bl) 3.00 *20.00*
138 A50 1½p brown org (R) 2.00 *11.00*
139 A51 3p black brn (Bl) 9.25 *10.50*
140 A52 6p purple (R) 5.25 *8.00*
141 A53 1sh vermilion (Bl) 15.00 12.50
Nos. 136-141 (6) 41.00 78.00

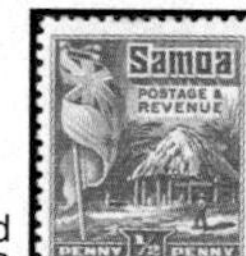

British Flag and Samoan House — A22

1921, Dec. 23 Engr. *Perf. 14x13½*
142 A22 ½p green 5.50 *2.00*
a. Perf. 14x14½ 5.50 *15.00*
143 A22 1p lake 6.50 .25
a. Perf. 14x14½ 9.00 1.75
144 A22 1½p org brn, perf. 14x14½ 1.50 *20.00*
a. Perf. 14x13½ 20.00 13.00
145 A22 2p yel, perf. 14x14½ 3.00 3.00
a. Perf. 14x13½ 15.00 .90
146 A22 2½p dull blue 2.00 *9.50*
147 A22 3p dark brown 2.00 *6.00*
148 A22 4p violet 2.00 *4.00*
149 A22 5p brt blue 2.00 *9.00*
150 A22 6p carmine rose 2.00 *8.00*
151 A22 8p red brown 2.25 *16.00*
152 A22 9p olive green 2.50 *40.00*
153 A22 1sh vermilion 2.25 *32.50*
Nos. 142-153 (12) 33.50 *150.25*

For overprints see Nos. 163-165.

New Zealand Nos. 182-183 Overprinted Type "m" in Red

1926-27 *Perf. 14½x14*
154 A56 2sh dark blue 5.75 *21.00*
a. 2sh blue ('27) 7.00 *50.00*
155 A56 3sh deep violet 25.00 *50.00*
a. 3sh violet ('27) 62.50 *110.00*

Issued: 2sh, Nov.; 3sh, Oct.; Nos. 154a, 155a, 11/10.

New Zealand Postal-Fiscal Stamps, Overprinted Type "m" in Blue or Red

1932, Aug. *Perf. 14*
156 PF5 2sh6p brown 18.00 *55.00*
157 PF5 5sh green (R) 30.00 *57.50*
158 PF5 10sh lake 55.00 *110.00*
159 PF5 £1 pink 80.00 *160.00*
160 PF5 £2 violet (R) *1,000.*
161 PF5 £5 dk bl (R) *2,600.*
Nos. 156-159 (4) 183.00 *382.50*

See Nos. 175-180, 195-202, 216-219.

Silver Jubilee Issue

Stamps of 1921 Overprinted in Black

1935, May 7 *Perf. 14x13½*
163 A22 1p lake .40 *.50*
a. Perf. 14x14½ *110.00* *200.00*
164 A22 2½p dull blue .75 *1.00*
165 A22 6p carmine rose 3.25 *4.00*
Nos. 163-165 (3) 4.40 5.50
Set, never hinged 9.00

25th anniv. of the reign of George V.

Western Samoa

Samoan Girl and Kava Bowl — A23

View of Apia — A24

River Scene — A25

Samoan Chief and Wife — A26

Samoan Canoe and House — A27

"Vailima," Stevenson's Home — A28

Stevenson's Tomb — A29

Lake Lanuto'o — A30

Falefa Falls — A31

Perf. 14x13½, 13½x14
1935, Aug. 7 Engr. Wmk. 61
166 A23 ½p yellow grn .25 .40
167 A24 1p car lake & blk .25 .25
168 A25 2p red org & blk, perf. 14 4.00 4.00
a. Perf. 13½x14 5.00 *4.25*
169 A26 2½p dp blue & blk .25 .25
170 A27 4p blk brn & dk gray .50 .35
171 A28 6p plum .70 .35
172 A29 1sh brown & violet .50 .50

173 A30 2sh red brn & yel grn 1.10 .80
174 A31 3sh org brn & brt bl 2.50 *3.50*
Nos. 166-174 (9) 10.05 *10.40*
Set, never hinged 20.00

See Nos. 186-188.

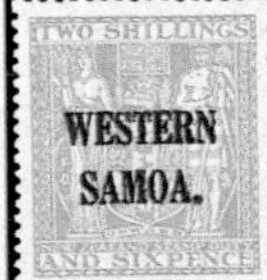

Postal-Fiscal Stamps of New Zealand Overprinted in Blue or Carmine

1935 ***Perf. 14***
175 PF5 2sh6p brown 11.00 *18.00*
176 PF5 5sh green 24.00 *32.50*
177 PF5 10sh dp car 70.00 *85.00*
178 PF5 £1 pink 62.50 *110.00*
179 PF5 £2 violet (C) 180.00 *400.00*
180 PF5 £5 dk bl (C) 260.00 *525.00*
Nos. 175-180 (6) 607.50 *1,170.*

See Nos. 195-202, 216-219.

Samoan Coastal Village — A32

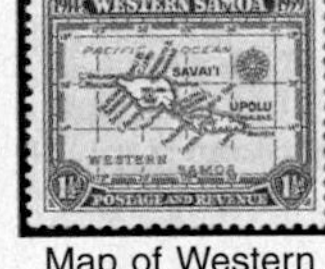

Map of Western Samoa — A33

Samoan Dancing Party A34

Robert Louis Stevenson A35

Perf. 13½x14

1939, Aug. 29 **Engr.** **Wmk. 253**
181 A32 1p scar & olive .60 .35
182 A33 1½p copper brn & bl 1.00 .90
183 A34 2½p dk blue & brn 1.10 1.00

Perf. 14x13½

184 A35 7p dp ol grn & vio 4.25 4.25
Nos. 181-184 (4) 6.95 6.50
Set, never hinged 12.00

25th anniv. of New Zealand's control of the mandated territory of Western Samoa.

Samoan Chief — A36

1940, Sept. 2 ***Perf. 14x13½***
185 A36 3p on 1½p brown .50 .35
Never hinged .85

Issued only with surcharge. Examples without surcharge are from printer's archives.

Types of 1935 and

Apia Post Office — A37

1944-49 **Wmk. 253** ***Perf. 14***
186 A23 ½p yellow green .30 *21.00*
187 A25 2p red orange & blk 2.00 *7.00*
188 A26 2½p dp blue & blk ('48) 5.00 *40.00*

Perf. 13½x14

189 A37 5p dp ultra & ol brn ('49) 1.40 1.00
Nos. 186-189 (4) 8.70 *69.00*
Set, never hinged 14.50

Issue date: 5p, June 8.

Catalogue values for unused stamps in this section, from this point to the end of the section, are for Never Hinged items.

Peace Issue

New Zealand Nos. 248, 250, 254, and 255 Overprinted in Black or Blue

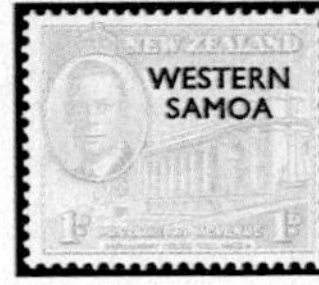

p

q

1946, June 1 ***Perf. 13x13½, 13½x13***
191 A94(p) 1p emerald .40 .25
192 A96(q) 2p rose violet (Bl) .40 .25
193 A100(p) 6p org red & red brn .80 .25
194 A101(p) 8p brn lake & blk (Bl) .45 .25
Nos. 191-194 (4) 2.05 1.00

Stamps and Type of New Zealand, 1931-50 Overprinted Like Nos. 175-180 in Blue or Carmine

1945-50 **Wmk. 253** ***Perf. 14***
195 PF5 2sh6p brown 15.00 *27.50*
196 PF5 5sh green 21.00 18.00
197 PF5 10sh car ('48) 23.00 19.00
198 PF5 £1 pink ('48) 130.00 *200.00*
199 PF5 30sh choc ('48) 200.00 *350.00*
200 PF5 £2 violet (C) 210.00 *310.00*
201 PF5 £3 lt grn ('50) 300.00 *425.00*
202 PF5 £5 dk bl (C) ('50) 425.00 *500.00*

Making Siapo Cloth — A38

Western Samoa and New Zealand Flags, Village A39

Thatching Hut A40

Samoan Chieftainess A41

Designs: 2p, Western Samoa seal. 3p, Aleisa Falls (actually Malifa Falls). 5p, Manumea (tooth-billed pigeon). 6p, Fishing canoe. 8p, Harvesting cacao. 2sh, Preparing copra.

Perf. 13, 13½x13

1952, Mar. 10 **Engr.** **Wmk. 253**
203 A38 ½p org brn & claret .25 *2.00*
204 A39 1p green & olive .25 .25
205 A38 2p deep carmine .25 .25
206 A39 3p indigo & blue .45 .25
207 A38 5p dk grn & org brn 9.00 .80
208 A39 6p dp rose pink & bl 1.00 .25
209 A39 8p rose carmine .35 .30
210 A40 1sh blue & brown .25 .25
211 A39 2sh yellow brown 1.10 .50
212 A41 3sh ol gray & vio brn 2.75 *2.75*
Nos. 203-212 (10) 15.65 7.60

Coronation Issue

Types of New Zealand 1953

1953, May 25 **Photo.** ***Perf. 14x14½***
214 A113 2p brown .85 .40
215 A114 6p slate black 1.25 .60

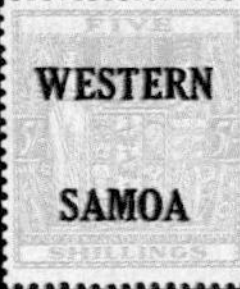

Type of New Zealand 1944-52 Overprinted in Blue or Carmine

Wmk. 253

1955, Nov. 14 **Typo.** ***Perf. 14***
216 PF5 5sh yellow green 11.00 *27.50*
217 PF5 10sh carmine rose 11.00 *50.00*
218 PF5 £1 dull rose 18.00 *57.50*
219 PF5 £2 violet (C) 100.00 *175.00*
Nos. 216-219 (4) 140.00 *310.00*

Redrawn Types of 1952 and

Map of Western Samoa and Mace A42

Designs: 4p, as 1p. 6p, as 2p.

Inscribed: "Fono Fou 1958" and "Samoa I Sisifo"

Perf. 13½x13, 13

1958, Mar. 21 **Engr.** **Wmk. 253**
220 A39 4p rose carmine .30 .25
221 A38 6p dull purple .30 .25
222 A42 1sh light violet blue .85 .45
Nos. 220-222 (3) 1.45 .95

Independent State

Samoa College A43

Designs: 1p, Woman holding ceremonial mat, vert. 3p, Public Library. 4p, Fono House (Parliament). 6p, Map of Western Samoa, ship and plane. 8p, Faleolo airport. 1sh, Talking chief with fly whisk, vert. 1sh3p, Government House, Vailima. 2sh6p, Flag of Western Samoa. 5sh, State Seal.

Wmk. 253

1962, July 2 **Litho.** ***Perf. 13½***
223 A43 1p car & brown .25 .25
224 A43 2p org, lt grn, red & brown .25 .25
225 A43 3p blue, grn & brn .25 .25
226 A43 4p dk grn, bl & car .35 .35
227 A43 6p yel, grn & ultra .80 .50
228 A43 8p blue & emerald .80 .55
229 A43 1sh brt grn & brn .35 .85
Complete booklet, 4 ea. #223-229
Complete booklet, 4 ea. #223, 225, 227-228
230 A43 1sh3p blue & emerald 1.25 .75
231 A43 2sh6p vio blue & red 2.75 1.75
232 A43 5sh olive gray, red & dk blue 3.00 2.75
Nos. 223-232 (10) 10.05 8.25

Western Samoa's independence.

The booklets described following No. 229 contain marginal blocks of stamps taken from sheets, with glassine interleaving, and stapled into the booklet cover.

See #242-247.

Tupua Tamasese Mea'ole, Malietoa Tanumafili II and Seal — A44

1963, Oct. 1 **Photo.** ***Perf. 14***
233 A44 1p green & blk .25 .25
234 A44 4p dull blue & blk .25 .25
235 A44 8p carmine rose & blk .25 .25
236 A44 2sh orange & blk .25 .25
Nos. 233-236 (4) 1.00 1.00

First anniversary of independence.

Signing of Western Samoa-New Zealand Friendship Treaty A45

1964, Sept. 1 **Unwmk.** ***Perf. 13½***
237 A45 1p multicolored .25 .25
238 A45 8p multicolored .25 .25
239 A45 2sh multicolored .25 .25
240 A45 3sh multicolored .25 *.35*
Nos. 237-240 (4) 1.00 1.10

2nd anniv. of the signing of the Treaty of Friendship between Western Samoa and New Zealand. Signers: J. B. Wright, N. Z. High Commissioner for Western Pacific, and Fiame Mata'afa, Prime Minister of Western Samoa.

Type of 1962

Wmk. 355

1965, Oct. 4 **Litho.** ***Perf. 13½***
242 A43 1p carmine & brn .40 *.75*
243 A43 3p blue, grn & brn 37.50 5.00
244 A43 4p dk grn, bl & car .40 *.75*
245 A43 6p yel, grn & ultra .50 .45
246 A43 8p blue & emerald .55 .25
247 A43 1sh brt green & brn .70 *.80*
Nos. 242-247 (6) 40.05 8.00

For surcharge see No. B1.

Aerial View of Deep-Sea Wharf A46

8p, 2sh, View of Apia harbor & deep-sea wharf.

1966, Mar. 2 **Photo.** ***Perf. 13½***
251 A46 1p multicolored .25 .25
252 A46 8p multicolored .25 .25
253 A46 2sh multicolored .30 .25
254 A46 3sh multicolored .50 .35
Nos. 251-254 (4) 1.30 1.10

Opening of Western Samoa's first deep-sea wharf at Apia.

Inauguration of WHO Headquarters, Geneva — A47

Design: 4p, 1sh, WHO building and flag.

1966, July 4 **Photo.** **Wmk. 355**
255 A47 3p gray, ultra & bister .35 .25
256 A47 4p multicolored .50 .35
257 A47 6p lt ol grn, pur & grn .60 .40
258 A47 1sh multicolored 1.50 .60
Nos. 255-258 (4) 2.95 1.60

Tuatagaloa L.S., Minister of Justice A48

Designs: 8p, F.C.F. Nelson, Minister of Works, Marine and Civil Aviation. 2sh, To'omata T. L., Minister of Lands. 3sh, Fa'alava'au Galu, Minister of Post Office, Radio and Broadcasting.

Perf. 14½x14

1967, Jan. 16 **Photo.** **Wmk. 355**
259 A48 3p violet & sepia .25 .25
260 A48 8p blue & sepia .25 .25
261 A48 2sh lt olive grn & sepia .30 .30
262 A48 3sh lilac rose & sepia .50 .50
Nos. 259-262 (4) 1.30 1.30

Fifth anniversary of Independence.

Samoan Fales, 1900, and Fly Whisk A49

1sh, Fono House (Parliament) and mace.

1967, May 16 *Perf. 14½*

263 A49 8p multicolored .30 .30
264 A49 1sh multicolored .40 .40

Centenary of Mulinu'u as Government Seat.

Wattled Honey-Eater — A50

Birds of Western Samoa: 2s, Pacific pigeon. 3s, Samoan starling. 5s, Samoan broadbill. 7s, Red-headed parrot finch. 10s, Purple swamp hen. 20s, Barn owl. 25s, Tooth-billed pigeon. 50s, Island thrush. $1, Samoan fantail. $2, Mao (gymnomyza samoensis). $4, Samoan white-eye (zosterops samoensis).

Perf. 14x14½

1967, July 10 Photo. Wmk. 355

Birds in Natural Colors

Size: 37x24mm

265 A50 1s black & lt brown .25 .25
266 A50 2s lt ultra, blk & brn org .25 .25
267 A50 3s blk, lt brn & emer .30 .25
268 A50 5s lilac, blk & vio bl .30 .25
269 A50 7s blk, vio bl & gray .75 .25
270 A50 10s Prus blue & blk .75 .25
271 A50 20s dk gray & blue 2.50 .50
272 A50 25s pink, blk & dk grn 1.00 .25
273 A50 50s brn, blk & lt ol grn 1.75 .40
274 A50 $1 yellow & black 4.00 *4.50*

1969 Size: 43x28mm *Perf. 13½*

274A A50 $2 blk & lt grnsh bl 3.00 *7.00*
274B A50 $4 dp orange & blk 35.00 17.50
Nos. 265-274B (12) 49.85 31.65

For surcharge see No. 294.

Child Care A51

Designs: 7s, Leprosarium. 20s, Mobile X-ray unit. 25s, Apia Hospital.

1967, Dec. 1 Litho. *Perf. 14*

275 A51 3s multicolored .25 .25
276 A51 7s multicolored .30 .25
277 A51 20s multicolored .55 .40
278 A51 25s multicolored .70 .55
Nos. 275-278 (4) 1.80 1.45

South Pacific Health Service.

Thomas Trood A52

Portraits: 7s, Dr. Wilhelm Solf. 20s, John C. Williams. 25s, Fritz Marquardt.

1968, Jan. 1 Unwmk. *Perf. 13½*

279 A52 2s multicolored .25 .25
280 A52 7s multicolored .25 .25
281 A52 20s multicolored .30 .25
282 A52 25s multicolored .35 .25
Nos. 279-282 (4) 1.15 1.00

Sixth anniversary of independence.

Samoan Agricultural Development A53

Perf. 13x12½

1968, Feb. 15 Photo. Wmk. 355

283 A53 3s Cocoa .25 .25
284 A53 5s Breadfruit .25 .25
285 A53 10s Copra .25 .25
286 A53 20s Bananas .35 .35
Nos. 283-286 (4) 1.10 1.10

Curio Vendors, Pago Pago A54

20s, Palm trees at the shore. 25s, A'Umi Beach.

Perf. 14½x14

1968, Apr. 22 Photo. Wmk. 355

287 A54 7s multicolored .25 .25
288 A54 20s multicolored .30 .25
289 A54 25s multicolored .35 .30
Nos. 287-289 (3) .90 .80

South Pacific Commission, 21st anniv.

Bougainville and Compass Rose — A55

Designs: 3s, Map showing Western Samoa Archipelago and Bougainville's route. 20s, Bougainvillea. 25s, Bougainville's ships La Boudeuse and L'Etoile.

1968, June 10 Litho. *Perf. 14*

290 A55 3s brt blue & blk .25 .25
291 A55 7s ocher & blk .30 .25
292 A55 20s grnsh blk, brt rose & grn .65 .40
293 A55 25s brt lil, vio, blk & org .90 .50
Nos. 290-293 (4) 2.10 1.40

200th anniv. of the visit of Louis Antoine de Bougainville (1729-1811) to Samoa.

No. 270 Surcharged with New Value, Three Bars and "1928-1968 / KINGSFORD-SMITH / TRANSPACIFIC FLIGHT"

1968, June 13 Photo. *Perf. 14x14½*

294 A50 20s on 10s multicolored .45 .45

40th anniv. of the 1st Transpacific flight under Capt. Charles Kingsford-Smith (Oakland, CA to Brisbane, Australia, via Honolulu and Fiji).

Human Rights Flame and Globe A56

Perf. 14½x14

1968, Aug. 26 Photo. Wmk. 355

295 A56 7s multicolored .25 .25
296 A56 20s multicolored .30 .25
297 A56 25s multicolored .40 .25
Nos. 295-297 (3) .95 .75

International Human Rights Year, 1968.

Martin Luther King, Jr. — A57

1968, Sept. 23 Litho. *Perf. 14*

298 A57 7s green & black .25 .25
299 A57 20s brt rose lil & blk .30 .25

Rev. Dr. Martin Luther King, Jr. (1929-68), American civil rights leader.

Polynesian Madonna — A58

1968, Oct. 12 Wmk. 355

300 A58 1s olive & multi .25 .25
301 A58 3s multicolored .25 .25
302 A58 20s crimson & multi .25 .25
303 A58 30s dp orange & multi .35 .25
Nos. 300-303 (4) 1.10 1.00

Christmas 1968.

Frangipani — A59

Flowers: 7s, Chinese hibiscus, vert. 20s, Red ginger, vert. 30s, Canangium odoratum.

1969, Jan. 20 Unwmk. *Perf. 14*

304 A59 2s brt blue & multi .35 .25
305 A59 7s multicolored .50 .35
306 A59 20s yellow & multi .90 .50
307 A59 30s multicolored 1.25 .75
Nos. 304-307 (4) 3.00 1.85

Seventh anniversary of independence.

R. L. Stevenson and Silver from "Treasure Island" — A60

Robert Louis Stevenson and: 7s, Stewart and Balfour on the moor from "Kidnapped," 20s, "Doctor Jekyll and Mr. Hyde." 22s, Archie Weir and Christiana Elliot from "Weir of Hermiston."

Perf. 14x13½

1969, Apr. 21 Litho. Wmk. 355

308 A60 3s gray & multi .30 .30
309 A60 7s gray & multi .40 .30
310 A60 20s gray & multi .40 .40
311 A60 22s gray & multi .40 *.55*
Nos. 308-311 (4) 1.50 1.55

75th anniv. of the death of Robert Louis Stevenson, who is buried in Samoa.

Weight Lifting — A61

Perf. 13½x13

1969, July 21 Photo. Unwmk.

312 A61 3s shown .25 .25
313 A61 20s Sailing .25 .25
314 A61 22s Boxing .35 .30
Nos. 312-314 (3) .85 .80

3rd Pacific Games, Port Moresby, Papua and New Guinea, Aug. 13-23.

American Astronaut on Moon, Splashdown and Map of Samoan Islands — A62

1969, July 24 Photo.

315 A62 7s red, blk, silver & grn .25 .25
316 A62 20s car, blk, sil & ultra .35 .25

US astronauts. See note after US No. C76.

Holy Family by El Greco A63

Christmas (Paintings): 1s, Virgin and Child, by Murillo. 20s, Nativity, by El Greco. 30s, Virgin and Child (from Adoration of the Kings), by Velazquez.

1969, Oct. 13 Unwmk. *Perf. 14*

317 A63 1s gold, red & multi .25 .25
318 A63 3s gold, red & multi .25 .25
319 A63 20s gold, red & multi .25 .25
320 A63 30s gold, red & multi .35 .25
a. Souvenir sheet of 4, #317-320 1.75 1.75
Nos. 317-320 (4) 1.10 1.00

Seventh Day Adventists' Sanatorium, Apia — A64

7s, Father Louis Violette, R. C. Cathedral, Apia. 20s, Church of Latter Day Saints (Mormon), Tuasivi, Safotulafai, vert. 22s, John Williams, London Missionary Soc. Church, Sapapali'i.

1970, Jan. 19 Litho. Wmk. 355

321 A64 2s brown, blk & gray .25 .25
322 A64 7s violet, blk & bister .25 .25
323 A64 20s rose, blk & lt violet .25 .25
324 A64 22s olive, blk & bister .25 .25
Nos. 321-324 (4) 1.00 1.00

Eighth anniversary of independence.

U.S.S. Nipsic A65

Designs: 5s, Wreck of German ship Adler. 10s, British ship Calliope in storm. 20s, Apia after hurricane.

1970, Apr. 27 *Perf. 13½x14*

325 A65 5s multicolored .40 .25
326 A65 7s multicolored .45 .30
327 A65 10s multicolored .75 .40
328 A65 20s multicolored 1.50 .90
Nos. 325-328 (4) 3.10 1.85

The great Apia hurricane of 1889.

Cook Statue, Whitby, England — A66

Designs: 1s, Kendal's chronometer and Cook's sextant. 20s, Capt. Cook bust, in profile. 30s, Capt. Cook, island scene and "Endeavour," horiz.

Perf. 14x14½

1970, Sept. 14 Litho. Wmk. 355

Size: 25x41mm

329 A66 1s silver, dp car & blk .35 .25
330 A66 2s multicolored .45 .35
331 A66 20s gold, black & ultra 1.50 .50

Perf. 14½x14

Size: 83x25mm

332 A66 30s multicolored 3.00 1.75
Nos. 329-332 (4) 5.30 2.85

Bicentenary of Capt. James Cook's exploration of South Pacific.

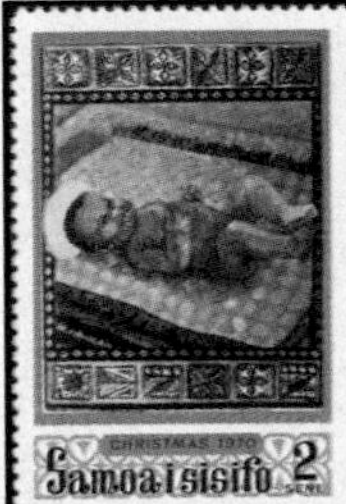

"Peace for the World" by Frances B. Eccles — A67

Christmas: 3s, Samoan coat of arms and Holy Family, by Werner Erich Jahnke. 20s, Samoan Mother and Child, by F. B. Eccles. 30s, Prince of Peace, by Sister Melane Fe'ao.

Perf. 13½

1970, Oct. 26 Photo. Unwmk.

333 A67 2s gold & multi .25 .25
334 A67 3s gold & multi .25 .25
335 A67 20s gold & multi .35 .25
336 A67 30s gold & multi .45 .35
a. Souvenir sheet of 4, #333-336 2.00 2.00
Nos. 333-336 (4) 1.30 1.10

Pope Paul VI — A68

Wmk. 355

1970, Nov. 29 Litho. *Perf. 14*

337 A68 8s Prus blue & black .25 .25
338 A68 20s deep plum & black .45 .30

Visit of Pope Paul VI, Nov. 29, 1970.

Lumberjack A69

8s, Woman and tractor in clearing, horiz. 20s, Log and saw carrier, horiz. 22s, Logging and ship.

Perf. 14x13½, 13½x14

1971, Feb. 1 Litho. Unwmk.

339 A69 3s multicolored .25 .25
340 A69 8s multicolored .25 .25
341 A69 20s multicolored .45 .25
342 A69 22s multicolored .55 .30
Nos. 339-342 (4) 1.50 1.05

Development of the timber industry on Savaii Island by the American Timber Company of Potlatch.

Souvenir Sheet

Longboat in Apia Harbor; Samoa #3 and US #3 — A70

1971, Mar. 12 Photo. *Perf. 11½*

Granite Paper

343 A70 70s blue & multi 2.00 2.00

INTERPEX, 13th Intl. Stamp Exhib., NYC, Mar. 12-14.

Siva Dance A71

Tourist Publicity: 7s, Samoan cricket game. 8s, Hideaway Resort Hotel. 10s, Aggie Grey and Aggie's Hotel.

Wmk. 355

1971, Aug. 9 Litho. *Perf. 14*

344 A71 5s orange brn & multi .40 .25
345 A71 7s orange brn & multi 2.50 .70
346 A71 8s orange brn & multi .90 .50
347 A71 10s orange brn & multi .90 .70
Nos. 344-347 (4) 4.70 2.15

A72

Samoan Legends, carved by Sven Ortquist: 3s, Queen Salamasina. 8s, Lu and his sacred hens (Samoa). 10s, God Tagaloa fishing Samoan islands of Upolu and Savaii from the sea. 22s, Mt. Vaea and Pool of Tears.

1971, Sept. 20

348 A72 3s dark violet & multi .25 .25
349 A72 8s multicolored .25 .25
350 A72 10s dark blue & multi .25 .25
351 A72 22s dark blue & multi .40 .40
Nos. 348-351 (4) 1.15 1.15

See Nos. 399-402.

A73

Christmas: 2s, 3s, Virgin and Child, by Giovanni Bellini. 20c, 30c, Virgin and Child with St. Anne and St. John the Baptist, by Leonardo da Vinci.

1971, Oct. 4 *Perf. 14x13½*

352 A73 2s blue & multi .25 .25
353 A73 3s black & multi .25 .25
354 A73 20s yellow & multi .40 .25
355 A73 30s dark red & multi .55 .30
Nos. 352-355 (4) 1.45 1.05

Samoan Islands, Scales of Justice A74

1972, Jan. 10 Photo. *Perf. 11½x12*

356 A74 10s light blue & multi .35 .30

1st So. Pacific Judicial Conf., Samoa, Jan. 1972.

Asau Wharf, Savaii A75

Designs: 8s, Parliament Building. 10s, Mothers' Center. 22s, Portraits of Tupua Tamasese Mea'ole and Malietoa Tanumafili II, and view of Vailima.

Perf. 13x13½

1972, Jan. 10 Litho. Wmk. 355

357 A75 1s bright pink & multi .25 .25
358 A75 8s lilac & multi .25 .25
359 A75 10s green & multi .25 .25
360 A75 22s multicolored .35 .30
Nos. 357-360 (4) 1.10 1.05

10th anniversary of independence.

Commission Members' Flags — A76

Designs: 7s, Afoafouvale Misimoa, Secretary-General, 1970-71 and Commission flag. 8s, Headquarters Building, Noumea, New Caledonia, horiz. 10s, Flag of Samoa, flag and map of South Pacific Commission area, horiz.

1972, Mar. 17 *Perf. 14x13½, 13½x14*

361 A76 3s ultra & multi .25 .25
362 A76 7s yellow, black & ultra .25 .25
363 A76 8s multicolored .30 .25
364 A76 10s lt green & multi .30 .25
Nos. 361-364 (4) 1.10 1.00

South Pacific Commission, 25th anniv.

Sunset and Ships — A77

Designs: 8s, Sailing ships Arend, Thienhoven and Africaansche Galey in storm. 10s, Outrigger canoe and Roggeveen's ships. 30s, Hemispheres with exploration route and map of Samoan Islands. All horiz.

1972, June 14 *Perf. 14½*

365 A77 2s car rose & multi .25 .25
366 A77 8s violet blue & multi .55 .25
367 A77 10s ultra & multi .65 .25

Size: 85x25mm

368 A77 30s ocher & multi 1.90 1.90
Nos. 365-368 (4) 3.35 2.65

250th anniv. of Jacob Roggeveen's Pacific voyage and discovery of Samoa in June 1722.

Bull Conch A78

2s, Rhinoceros beetle. 3s, Skipjack (fish). 4s, Painted crab. 5s, Butterflyfish. 7s, Samoan monarch. 10s, Triton shell. 20s, Jewel beetle. 50s, Spiny lobster. $1, Hawk moth. $2, Green turtle. $4, Black marlin. $5, Green tree lizard.

1972-75 Litho. *Perf. 14½*

Size: 41x24mm

369 A78 1s shown .30 .25
370 A78 2s multicolored .30 .25
371 A78 3s multicolored .30 .90
372 A78 4s multicolored .30 .30
373 A78 5s multicolored .35 .30
374 A78 7s multicolored 1.75 .75
375 A78 10s multicolored 1.75 .75
376 A78 20s multicolored 1.10 .30
377 A78 50s multicolored 1.75 1.75

Perf. 14x13½

Size: 29x45mm

378 A78 $1 multicolored 6.00 4.25
378A A78 $2 multicolored 4.00 2.75
378B A78 $4 multicolored 6.00 *7.00*
378C A78 $5 multicolored 4.00 *10.00*
Nos. 369-378C (13) 27.90 29.55

Issued: 1s-$1, Oct. 18, 1972; $2, June 18, 1973; $4, Mar. 27, 1974; $5, June 30, 1975.

Ascension, Stained Glass Window — A79

Stained Glass Windows in Apia Churches: 4s, Virgin and Child. 10s, St. Andrew blessing Samoan canoe. 30s, The Good Shepherd.

Perf. 14x14½

1972, Nov. 1 Wmk. 355

379 A79 1s ocher & multi .25 .25
380 A79 4s gray & multi .25 .25
381 A79 10s dull green & multi .25 .25
382 A79 30s blue & multi .50 .35
a. Souvenir sheet of 4, #379-382 2.00 2.00
Nos. 379-382 (4) 1.25 1.10

Christmas.

Scouts Saluting Flag, Emblems
A80

1973, Jan. 29 *Perf. 14*

383 A80 2s shown .25 .25
384 A80 3s First aid .25 .25
385 A80 8s Pitching tent .30 .25
386 A80 20s Action song .60 .60
Nos. 383-386 (4) 1.40 1.35

Boy Scouts of Samoa.

Apia General Hospital — A81

WHO, 25th anniv.: 8s, Baby clinic. 20s, Filariasis research. 22s, Family welfare.

1973, Aug. 20 **Wmk. 355**

387 A81 2s green & multi .25 .25
388 A81 8s multicolored .25 .25
389 A81 20s brown & multi .35 .35
390 A81 22s vermilion & multi .45 .40
Nos. 387-390 (4) 1.30 1.25

"A Prince is Born," by Jahnke — A82

Christmas: 4s, "Star of Hope," by Fiasili Keil. 10s, "Mother and Child," by Ernesto Coter. 30s, "The Light of the World," by Coter.

1973, Oct. 15 **Litho.** *Perf. 14*

391 A82 3s blue & multi .25 .25
392 A82 4s purple & multi .25 .25
393 A82 10s red & multi .25 .25
394 A82 30s blue & multi .55 .50
a. Souvenir sheet of 4, #391-394 2.00 2.00
Nos. 391-394 (4) 1.30 1.25

Boxing and Games' Emblem
A83

1974, Jan. 24

395 A83 8s shown .25 .25
396 A83 10s Weight lifting .25 .25
397 A83 20s Lawn bowling .25 .25
398 A83 30s Stadium .65 .65
Nos. 395-398 (4) 1.40 1.40

10th British Commonwealth Games, Christchurch, New Zealand, Jan. 24-Feb. 2.

Legends Type of 1971

Samoan Legends, Wood Carvings by Sven Ortquist: 2s, Tigilau and dove. 8s, Pili with his sons and famous fish net. 20s, The girl Sina and the eel which became the coconut tree. 30s, Nafanua who returned from the spirit world to free her village.

1974, Aug. 13 **Wmk. 355** *Perf. 14*

399 A72 2s lemon & multi .25 .25
400 A72 8s rose red & multi .25 .25
401 A72 20s yellow grn & multi .40 .30
402 A72 30s lt violet & multi .70 .70
Nos. 399-402 (4) 1.60 1.50

Faleolo Airport — A84

Designs: 20s, Apia Wharf. 22s, Early post office, Apia. 50s, William Willis, raft "Age Unlimited" and route from Callao, Peru, to Tully, Western Samoa.

1974, Sept. 4 **Unwmk.** *Perf. 13½*

Size: 47x29mm

403 A84 8s multicolored .35 .25
404 A84 20s multicolored .55 .45
405 A84 22s multicolored .60 .60

Size: 86x29mm

406 A84 50s multicolored 1.00 1.50
a. Souvenir sheet of 1, perf. 13 1.25 1.25
Nos. 403-406 (4) 2.50 2.80

Cent. of UPU. The 8s is inscribed "Air Mail"; 20s, "Sea Mail"; 22s, "Raft Mail."

Holy Family, by Sebastiano — A85

Christmas: 4s, Virgin and Child with Saints, by Lotto. 10s, Virgin and Child with St. John, by Titian. 30s, Adoration of the Shepherds, by Rubens.

1974, Nov. 18 **Litho.** *Perf. 13x13½*

407 A85 3s ocher & multi .25 .25
408 A85 4s fawn & multi .25 .25
409 A85 10s dull green & multi .25 .25
410 A85 30s blue & multi .50 .50
a. Souvenir sheet of 4, #407-410 1.75 1.75
Nos. 407-410 (4) 1.25 1.25

Winged Passion Flower
A86

20s, Gardenias, vert. 22s, Lecythidaceae, vert. 30s, Malay apple.

Wmk. 355

1975, Jan. 17 **Litho.** *Perf. 14½*

411 A86 8s dull yellow & multi .25 .25
412 A86 20s pale pink & multi .35 .30
413 A86 22s pink & multi .40 .30
414 A86 30s lt green & multi .65 .65
Nos. 411-414 (4) 1.65 1.50

Joyita Loading at Apia
A87

Designs: 8s, Joyita, Samoa and Tokelau Islands. 20s, Joyita sinking, Oct. 1955. 22s, Rafts in storm. 50s, Plane discovering wreck.

1975, Mar. 14 **Photo.** *Perf. 13*

415 A87 1s multicolored .25 .25
416 A87 8s multicolored .30 .25
417 A87 20s multicolored .50 .45
418 A87 22s multicolored .60 .55
419 A87 50s multicolored 1.00 1.00
a. Souvenir sheet of 5, #415-419 2.75 2.75
Nos. 415-419 (5) 2.65 2.50

17th INTERPEX Phil. Exhib., NYC, 3/14-16.

Pate Drum — A88

1975, Sept. 30 **Litho.** *Perf. 14½x14*

420 A88 8s shown .25 .25
421 A88 20s Lali drum .25 .25
422 A88 22s Logo drum .30 .25
423 A88 30s Pu shell horn .45 .45
Nos. 420-423 (4) 1.25 1.20

Mother and Child, by Meleane Fe'ao — A89

Christmas (Paintings): 4s, Christ Child and Samoan flag, by Polataia Tuigamala. 10s, "A Star is Born," by Iosua Toafa. 30s, Mother and Child, by Ernesto Coter.

1975, Nov. 25 **Litho.** **Wmk. 355**

424 A89 3s multicolored .25 .25
425 A89 4s multicolored .25 .25
426 A89 10s multicolored .25 .25
427 A89 30s multicolored .35 .35
a. Souvenir sheet of 4, #424-427 1.00 1.00
Nos. 424-427 (4) 1.10 1.10

Boston Massacre, by Paul Revere — A90

8s, Declaration of Independence, by John Trumbull. 20s, The Ship That Sank in Victory, by J. L. G. Ferris. 22s, Wm. Pitt Addressing House of Commons, by R. A. Hickel. 50s, Battle of Princeton, by William Mercer.

Perf. 13½x14

1976, Jan. 20 **Litho.** **Wmk. 355**

428 A90 7s salmon & multi .25 .25
429 A90 8s green & multi .25 .25
430 A90 20s lilac & multi .55 .40
431 A90 22s blue & multi .60 .40
432 A90 50s yellow & multi 1.25 1.25
a. Souvenir sheet of 5, #428-432 + label 6.50 6.50
Nos. 428-432 (5) 2.90 2.55

Bicentenary of American Independence.

Mullet Fishing
A91

1976, Apr. 27 **Litho.** *Perf. 14½*

433 A91 10s shown .25 .25
434 A91 12s Fish traps .25 .25
435 A91 22s Fishermen .40 .30
436 A91 50s Net fishing .90 .90
Nos. 433-436 (4) 1.80 1.70

Souvenir Sheet

Samoan $100 Gold Coin with Paul Revere and US Map — A92

Unwmk.

1976, May 29 **Photo.** *Perf. 13*

437 A92 $1 green & gold 2.75 2.75

American Bicentennial and Interphil 76 Intl. Phil. Exhib., Philadelphia, PA, May 29-June 6.

Boxing
A93

12s, Wrestling. 22s, Javelin. 50s, Weight lifting.

Perf. 14½x14

1976, June 21 **Litho.** **Wmk. 355**

438 A93 10s black & multi .25 .25
439 A93 12s dark brown & multi .25 .25
440 A93 22s dark purple & multi .35 .25
441 A93 50s dark blue & multi .65 .65
Nos. 438-441 (4) 1.50 1.40

21st Olympic Games, Montreal, Canada, July 17-Aug. 1.

Mary and Joseph on Road to Bethlehem
A94

Christmas: 5s, Adoration of the Shepherds. 22s, Nativity. 50s, Adoration of the Kings.

1976, Oct. 18 **Litho.** *Perf. 14x13½*

442 A94 3s multicolored .25 .25
443 A94 5s multicolored .25 .25
444 A94 22s multicolored .35 .25
445 A94 50s multicolored .65 .65
a. Souvenir sheet of 4, #442-445 1.75 1.75
Nos. 442-445 (4) 1.50 1.40

Presentation of the Spurs of Chivalry — A95

Designs: 12s, Queen and view of Apia. 32s, Royal Yacht Britannia and Queen. 50s, Queen leaving Westminster Abbey.

Perf. 13½x14

1977, Feb. 11 **Wmk. 355**

446 A95 12s multicolored .25 .25
447 A95 26s multicolored .30 .30
448 A95 32s multicolored .70 .30
449 A95 50s multicolored .30 .30
Nos. 446-449 (4) 1.55 1.15

25th anniv. of the reign of Elizabeth II.

Lindbergh and Spirit of St. Louis A96

Designs: 22s, Map of transatlantic route and plane. 24s, Spirit of St. Louis in flight. 26s, Spirit of St. Louis taking off.

1977, May 20 Litho. *Perf. 14*

450	A96 22s multicolored	.30	.25
451	A96 24s multicolored	.40	.25
452	A96 26s multicolored	.45	.25
453	A96 50s multicolored	.90	.90
a.	Souvenir sheet of 4, #450-453	4.00	4.00
	Nos. 450-453 (4)	2.05	1.65

Charles A. Lindbergh's solo transatlantic flight from New York to Paris, 50th anniv.

Apia Automatic Telephone Exchange — A97

Designs: 13s, Mulinuu radio terminal. 26s, Old wall and new dial telephones. 50s, Global communications (2 telephones and globe).

1977, July 11 Litho. *Perf. 14*

454	A97 12s multicolored	.25	.25
455	A97 13s multicolored	.25	.25
456	A97 26s multicolored	.35	.30
457	A97 50s multicolored	.60	.60
	Nos. 454-457 (4)	1.45	1.40

Telecommunications.

Samoa No. 3 and First Mail Notice — A98

13s, Samoa #4 & 1881 cover. 26s, Samoa #1 & Chief Post Office, Apia. 50s, Samoa #4 7 schooner "Energy," which carried 1st mail.

1977, Aug. 29 Wmk. 355 *Perf. 13½*

458	A98 12s multicolored	.30	.25
459	A98 13s multicolored	.30	.25
460	A98 26s multicolored	.40	.30
461	A98 50s multicolored	.65	.65
	Nos. 458-461 (4)	1.65	1.45

Samoan postage stamp centenary.

Nativity — A99

Christmas: 6s, People bringing gifts to Holy Family in Samoan hut. 26s, Virgin and Child. 50s, Stars over Christ Child.

1977, Oct. 11 Litho. *Perf. 14*

462	A99 4s multicolored	.25	.25
463	A99 6s multicolored	.25	.25
464	A99 26s multicolored	.30	.25
465	A99 50s multicolored	.45	.45
a.	Souvenir sheet of 4, #462-465	1.25	1.25
	Nos. 462-465 (4)	1.25	1.20

Polynesian Airlines' Boeing 737 — A100

Aviation Progress: 24s, Kitty Hawk. 26s, Kingsford-Smith Fokker. 50s, Concorde.

Unwmk.

1978, Mar. 21 Litho. *Perf. 14*

466	A100 12s multicolored	.25	.25
467	A100 24s multicolored	.35	.30
468	A100 26s multicolored	.40	.30
469	A100 50s multicolored	.90	.90
a.	Souvenir sheet of 4, #466-469, perf. 13½	3.00	3.00
	Nos. 466-469 (4)	1.90	1.75

Turtle Hatchery, Aleipata — A101

$1, Hawksbill turtle & Wildlife Fund emblem.

1978, Apr. 14 Wmk. 355 *Perf. 14½*

470	A101 24s multicolored	*3.50*	*1.00*
471	A101 $1 multicolored	*9.00*	*3.75*

Project to replenish endangered hawksbill turtles.

Common Design Types pictured following the introduction.

Elizabeth II Coronation Anniversary Issue

Souvenir Sheet

Common Design Types

1978, Apr. 21 Unwmk. *Perf. 15*

472	Sheet of 6	2.00	2.00
a.	CD326 26s King's lion	.30	.30
b.	CD327 26s Elizabeth II	.30	.30
c.	CD328 26s Pacific pigeon	.30	.30

No. 472 contains 2 se-tenant strips of Nos. 472a-472c, separated by horizontal gutter with commemorative and descriptive inscriptions and showing central part of coronation procession with coach.

Souvenir Sheet

Canadian and Samoan Flags — A102

Wmk. 355

1978, June 9 Litho. *Perf. 14½*

473	A102 $1 multicolored	1.75	1.75

CAPEX Canadian Intl. Phil. Exhib., Toronto, June 9-18.

Capt. James Cook — A103

Designs: 24s, Cook's cottage, now in Melbourne, Australia. 26s, Old drawbridge over River Esk, Whitby, 1766-1833. 50s, Resolution and map of Hawaiian Islands.

1978, Aug. 28 Litho. *Perf. 14½x14*

474	A103 12s multicolored	.30	.25
475	A103 24s multicolored	.40	.35
476	A103 26s multicolored	.50	.45
477	A103 50s multicolored	1.40	1.40
	Nos. 474-477 (4)	2.60	2.45

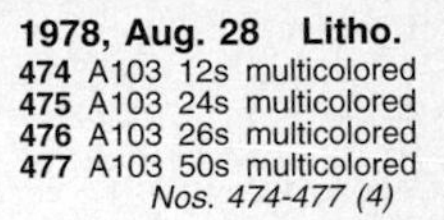

A104

Cowrie Shells: 1s, Thick-edged Cowrie. 2s, Isabella cowrie. 3s, Money cowrie. 4s, Eroded cowrie. 6s, Honey cowrie. 7s, Banded cowrie. 10s, Globe cowrie. 11s, Mole cowrie. 12s, Children's cowrie. 13s, Flag cone. 14s, Soldier cone. 24s, Cloth-of-gold cone. 26s, Lettered cone. 50s, Tiled cone. $1, Black marble cone. $2, Marlin-spike auger. $3, Scorpion spider conch. $5, Common harp.

1978-80 Photo. Unwmk. *Perf. 12½*

Size: 31x24mm

Granite Paper

478	A104	1s multicolored	.25	.25
479	A104	2s multicolored	.25	.25
480	A104	3s multicolored	.25	.25
481	A104	4s multicolored	.25	.25
482	A104	6s multicolored	.25	.25
483	A104	7s multicolored	.25	.25
484	A104	10s multicolored	.25	.25
485	A104	11s multicolored	.25	.25
486	A104	12s multicolored	.25	.25
487	A104	13s multicolored	.25	.25
488	A104	14s multicolored	.25	.25
489	A104	24s multicolored	.25	.25
490	A104	26s multicolored	.30	.25
491	A104	50s multicolored	.40	.30
492	A104	$1 multicolored	.90	.50

Perf. 11½

Size: 36x26mm

493	A104	$2 multi ('79)	1.50	.75
494	A104	$3 multi ('79)	2.25	1.50
494A	A104	$5 multi ('80)	3.75	2.25
		Nos. 478-494A (18)	12.10	8.55

Issue dates: 1s-12s, Sept. 15. 13s-$1, Nov. 20. $2, $3, July 18. $5, Aug. 26.

A105

Works by Dürer: 4s, The Virgin in Glory. 6s, Nativity. 26s, Adoration of the Kings. 50s, Annunciation.

Wmk. 355

1978, Nov. 6 Litho. *Perf. 14*

495	A105 4s lt brown & blk	.25	.25
496	A105 6s grnsh blue & blk	.25	.25
497	A105 26s violet blue & blk	.25	.25
498	A105 50s purple & blk	.45	.40
a.	Souvenir sheet of 4, #495-498	1.25	1.25
	Nos. 495-498 (4)	1.20	1.15

Christmas and for 450th death anniv. of Albrecht Dürer.

Boy Carrying Coconuts A106

Designs: 24s, Children leaving church on White Sunday. 26s, Children pumping water. 50s, Girl playing ukulele.

1979, Apr. 10 Litho. *Perf. 14*

499	A106 12s multicolored	.25	.25
500	A106 24s multicolored	.30	.25
501	A106 26s multicolored	.30	.25
502	A106 50s multicolored	.65	.65
	Nos. 499-502 (4)	1.50	1.40

International Year of the Child.

Charles W. Morgan A107

1979, May 29 Litho. *Perf. 13½*

503	A107 12s multicolored	.30	.25
504	A107 14s Lagoda	.40	.25
505	A107 24s James T. Arnold	.50	.35
506	A107 50s Splendid	.90	.90
	Nos. 503-506 (4)	2.10	1.75

See Nos. 521-524, 543-546.

Saturn V Launch — A108

Designs: 14s, Landing module and astronaut on moon, horiz. 24s, Earth seen from moon. 26s, Astronaut on moon, horiz. 50s, Lunar and command modules. $1, Command module after splashdown, horiz.

Perf. 14½x14, 14x14½

1979, June 20 Litho. Wmk. 355

507	A108 12s multicolored	.25	.25
508	A108 14s multicolored	.25	.25
509	A108 24s multicolored	.30	.25
510	A108 26s multicolored	.35	.25
511	A108 50s multicolored	.45	.45
512	A108 $1 multicolored	1.00	1.00
a.	Souvenir sheet	1.75	1.75
	Nos. 507-512 (6)	2.60	2.45

1st moon landing, 10th anniv.

Penny Black, Hill Statue — A109

24s, Great Britain #2 with Maltese Cross postmark. 26s, Penny Black and Rowland Hill. $1, Great Britain #2 and Hill statue.

1979, Aug. 27 *Perf. 14*

513	A109 12s multicolored	.25	.25
514	A109 24s multicolored	.25	.25
515	A109 26s multicolored	.25	.25
516	A109 $1 multicolored	.40	.40
a.	Souvenir sheet of 4, #513-516	1.50	1.50
	Nos. 513-516 (4)	1.15	1.15

Sir Rowland Hill (1795-1879), originator of penny postage.

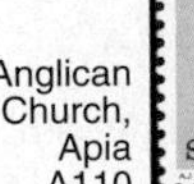

Anglican Church, Apia A110

Samoan Churches: 6s, Congregational Christian Church, Leulumoega. 26s, Methodist Church, Piula. 50s, Protestant Church, Apia.

1979, Oct. 22 Photo. *Perf. 12x11½*

517	A110 4s lt blue & blk	.25	.25
518	A110 6s lt yellow grn & blk	.25	.25
519	A110 26s dull yellow & blk	.25	.25
520	A110 50s lt lilac & blk	.60	.60
a.	Souvenir sheet of 4, #517-520	1.25	1.25
	Nos. 517-520 (4)	1.35	1.35

Christmas.

Ship Type of 1979

Wmk. 355

1980, Jan. 22 Litho. *Perf. 14*

521 A107 12s William Hamilton .30 .25
522 A107 14s California .30 .25
523 A107 24s Liverpool II .30 .25
524 A107 50s Two Brothers 1.00 1.00
Nos. 521-524 (4) 1.90 1.75

Map of Samoan Islands, Rotary Emblem A111

Missionary Flag, John Williams, Plaque — A112

Flag-raising Memorial — A113

14s, German flag, Dr. Wilhelm Solf, plaque. 26s, Williams Memorial, Savai'i. 50s, Emblem, Paul P. Harris, founder.

1980, Mar. 26 Photo. *Perf. 14*

525 A111 12s shown .50 .25
526 A112 13s shown .40 .60
527 A112 14s multicolored .90 .25
528 A113 24s shown .90 .40
529 A113 26s multicolored .75 .50
530 A111 50s multicolored 1.25 *1.50*
Nos. 525-530 (6) 4.70 3.50

Rotary Intl., 75th anniv. (A111); arrival of Williams, missionary in Samoa, 150th anniv. (13s, 26s); raising of the German flag, 80th anniv. (14s, 24s).

Souvenir Sheet

Village and Long Boat — A114

Wmk. 355

1980, May 6 Litho. *Perf. 14*

531 A114 $1 multicolored 1.50 1.50

London 80 Intl. Phil. Exhib., May 6-14.

Queen Mother Elizabeth Birthday Issue

Common Design Type

1980, Aug. 4 Litho.

532 CD330 50s multicolored .55 .55

Souvenir Sheet

Samoa No. 239, ZEAPEX Emblem — A115

Unwmk.

1980, Aug. 23 Litho. *Perf. 14*

533 A115 $1 multicolored 1.50 1.50

ZEAPEX '80, New Zealand International Stamp Exhibition, Auckland, Aug. 23-31.

Afiamalu Satellite Earth Station A116

14s, Station, diff. 24s, Station, map of Samoa. 50s, Satellite sending waves to earth. $2, Samoa #536, Sydpex '80 emblem.

1980, Sept. 17 Litho. *Perf. 11½*

Granite Paper

534 A116 12s multicolored .25 .25
535 A116 14s multicolored .25 .25
536 A116 24s multicolored .30 .25
537 A116 50s multicolored .60 .60
Nos. 534-537 (4) 1.40 1.35

Souvenir Sheet

1980, Sept. 29 *Imperf.*

538 A116 $2 multicolored 1.75 1.75

Sydpex '80 Natl. Phil. Exhib., Sydney.

The Savior, by John Poynton — A117

Christmas (Paintings by Local Artists): 14s, Madonna and Child, by Lealofi F. Siaopo. 27s, Nativity, by Pasila Feata. 50s, Yuletide, by R.P. Aiono.

Wmk. 355

1980, Oct. 28 Litho. *Perf. 14*

539 A117 8s multicolored .25 .25
540 A117 14s multicolored .25 .25
541 A117 27s multicolored .25 .25
542 A117 50s multicolored .40 .40
a. Souvenir sheet of 4, #539-542 1.25 1.25
Nos. 539-542 (4) 1.15 1.15

Ship Type of 1979

1981, Jan. 26 Litho. *Perf. 13½*

543 A107 12s Ocean .25 .25
544 A107 18s Horatio .40 .40
545 A107 27s Calliope .60 .60
546 A107 32s Calypso .70 .70
Nos. 543-546 (4) 1.95 1.95

Pres. Franklin Roosevelt and Hyde Park Home A118

IYD: Scenes of Franklin D. Roosevelt — 18s, Inauguration. 27s, Pres. & Mrs. Roosevelt. 32s, Atlantic convoy (Lend Lease Bill). 38s, With stamp collection. $1, Campobello House.

Wmk. 355

1981, Apr. 29 Litho. *Perf. 14*

547 A118 12s shown .25 .25
548 A118 18s multicolored .25 .25
549 A118 27s multicolored .25 .25
550 A118 32s multicolored .30 .30
551 A118 38s multicolored .30 .30
552 A118 $1 multicolored .50 .50
Nos. 547-552 (6) 1.85 1.85

Hotel Tusitala — A119

18s, Apia Harbor. 27s, Aggie Grey's Hotel. 32s, Ceremonial kava preparation. 54s, Piula Pool.

Perf. 14½x14

1981, June 29 Litho. Wmk. 355

553 A119 12s shown .25 .25
554 A119 18s multicolored .25 .25
555 A119 27s multicolored .30 .25
556 A119 32s multicolored .30 .25
557 A119 54s multicolored .50 .50
Nos. 553-557 (5) 1.60 1.50

Royal Wedding Issue

Common Design Type

Wmk. 355

1981, July 22 Litho. *Perf. 14*

558 CD331 18s Bouquet .25 .25
559 CD331 32s Charles .25 .25
560 CD331 $1 Couple .35 .35
Nos. 558-560 (3) .85 .85

Tattooing Instruments A120

1981, Sept. 29 Litho. *Perf. 13½x14*

561 Strip of 4 2.00 2.00
a. A120 12s shown .25 .25
b. A120 18s 1st stage .25 .25
c. A120 27s Later stage .35 .30
d. A120 $1 Tattooed man 1.00 1.00

Christmas — A121

1981, Nov. 30 Litho. *Perf. 13½*

562 A121 11s Milo tree blossom .25 .25
563 A121 15s Copper leaf .25 .25
564 A121 23s Yellow allamanda .25 .25
565 A121 $1 Mango blossom .85 .85
a. Souvenir sheet of 4, #562-565 2.00 2.00
Nos. 562-565 (4) 1.60 1.60

Souvenir Sheet

Philatokyo '81 Intl. Stamp Exhibition — A122

1981, Oct. 9 Litho. *Perf. 14x13½*

566 A122 $2 multicolored 2.00 *2.00*

250th Birth Anniv. of George Washington A123

1982, Feb. 26 Litho. *Perf. 14*

567 A123 23s Pistol .25 .25
568 A123 25s Mt. Vernon .30 .30
569 A123 34s Portrait .35 .35
Nos. 567-569 (3) .90 .90

Souvenir Sheet

570 A123 $1 Taking oath 1.00 1.00

20th Anniv. of Independence — A124

18s, Freighter Forum Samoa. 23s, Jet, routes. 25s, Natl. Provident Fund building. $1, Intl. subscriber dialing system.

1982, May 24 Litho. *Perf. 13½x14*

571 A124 18s multicolored 1.00 .30
572 A124 23s multicolored 1.25 .40
573 A124 25s multicolored .75 .40
574 A124 $1 multicolored 1.75 1.25
Nos. 571-574 (4) 4.75 2.35

Scouting Year A125

1982, July 20 Wmk. 355 *Perf. 14½*

575 A125 5s Map reading .25 .25
576 A125 38s Salute .45 .45
577 A125 44s Rope bridge .55 .55
578 A125 $1 Troop 1.25 1.25
a. Souvenir sheet 1.75 1.75
Nos. 575-578 (4) 2.50 2.50

No. 578a contains one stamp similar to No. 578, 48x36mm.

12th Commonwealth Games, Brisbane, Australia, Sept. 30-Oct. 9 — A126

Perf. 14x14½

1982, Sept. 20 Wmk. 373

579 A126 23s Boxing .25 .25
580 A126 25s Hurdles .30 .30
581 A126 34s Weightlifting .35 .35
582 A126 $1 Lawn bowling .85 .85
Nos. 579-582 (4) 1.75 1.75

Christmas A127

Children's Drawings: 11s, 15s, Flight into Egypt diff. 38s, $1, Virgin and Child, diff.

1982, Nov. 15 Litho. Wmk. 355

583 A127 11s multicolored .25 .25
584 A127 15s multicolored .25 .25
585 A127 38s multicolored .45 .45
586 A127 $1 multicolored .90 .90
a. Souvenir sheet of 4, #583-586 2.25 2.25
Nos. 583-586 (4) 1.85 1.85

Commonwealth Day — A128

Perf. 13½x14

1983, Feb. 23 Litho. Wmk. 373

587 A128 14s Map .25 .25
588 A128 29s Flag .35 .35
589 A128 43s Harvesting copra .35 .35
590 A128 $1 Malietoa Tanumafili II .85 .85
Nos. 587-590 (4) 1.80 1.80

Manned Flight Bicentenary and 50th Anniv. of Douglas Aircraft — A129

a, DC-1. b, DC-2. c, DC-3. d, DC-4. e, DC-5. f, DC-6. g, DC-7. h, DC-8. i, DC-9. j, DC-10.

Wmk. 373

1983, June 7 Litho. *Perf. 14*

591 A129 Sheet of 10 7.25 7.25
a.-j. 32s any single .60 .60

7th South Pacific Games, Apla — A130

1983, Aug. 29 Litho. *Perf. 14x14½*

592 A130 8s Pole vault .45 .45
593 A130 15s Basketball .55 .55
594 A130 25c Tennis .70 .60
595 A130 32s Weightlifting .90 .60
596 A130 35s Boxing .90 .90
597 A130 46s Soccer 1.10 1.10
598 A130 48s Golf 2.00 1.25
599 A130 56s Rugby 1.50 1.50
Nos. 592-599 (8) 8.10 6.95

Local Fruit — A131

Perf. 14x13½

1983-84 Litho. Wmk. 373

600 A131 1s Limes .35 .35
601 A131 2s Star fruit .35 .35
602 A131 3s Mangosteen .35 .35
603 A131 4s Lychee .35 .35
604 A131 7s Passion fruit .35 .35
605 A131 8s Mangoes .35 .35
606 A131 11s Papaya .35 .35
607 A131 13s Pineapple .35 .35
608 A131 14s Breadfruit .35 .35
609 A131 15s Bananas .35 .35
610 A131 21s Cashew nut .90 .90
611 A131 25s Guava 1.25 1.25
612 A131 32s Water Melon 1.50 1.50
613 A131 48s Sasalapa 1.75 1.75
614 A131 56s Avocado 2.00 2.00
615 A131 $1 Coconut 2.25 2.25

Perf. 13½

616 A131 $2 Apples ('84) 2.50 2.50
617 A131 $4 Grapefruit ('84) 5.00 5.00
618 A131 $5 Oranges ('84) 6.00 6.00
Nos. 600-618 (19) 26.65 26.65

Issued: 1s-15s, 9/28; 21s-$1, 11/30; $2-$5, 4/11.

For overprint see No. 628.

Miniature Sheet

Boys' Brigade Centenary — A132

1983, Oct. 10 *Perf. 14½*

619 A132 $1 multicolored 3.75 3.75

Togitogiga Falls, Upolu A133

32s, Lano Beach, Savai'i. 48s, Mulinu'u Point, Upolu. 56s, Nu'utele Island.

Wmk. 373

1984, Feb. 15 Litho. *Perf. 14*

620 A133 25s shown .45 .25
621 A133 32s multicolored .55 .55
622 A133 48s multicolored .75 .75
623 A133 56s multicolored .90 .90
Nos. 620-623 (4) 2.65 2.45

Lloyd's List Issue

Common Design Type

Perf. 14½x14

1984, May 24 Litho. Wmk. 373

624 CD335 32s Apia Harbor .35 .25
625 CD335 48s Apia hurricane, 1889 .65 .55
626 CD335 60s Forum Samoa .75 .75
627 CD335 $1 Matua 1.00 1.00
Nos. 624-627 (4) 2.75 2.55

No. 615 Ovptd. "19th U.P.U. CONGRESS / HAMBURG 1984"

1984, June 7 *Perf. 14x13½*

628 A131 $1 multicolored 1.75 1.75

Los Angeles Coliseum — A134

1984, June 26 Litho. *Perf. 14½*

629 A134 25s shown .25 .25
630 A134 32s Weightlifting .35 .35
631 A134 48s Boxing .45 .45
632 A134 $1 Running .85 .85
a. Souvenir sheet of 4, #629-632 2.00 2.00
Nos. 629-632 (4) 1.90 1.90

1984 Summer Olympics and Samoa's first Olympic participation.

Souvenir Sheet

Ausipex '84 — A135

1984, Sept. 21 Litho. *Perf. 14*

633 A135 $2.50 Nomad N24 6.75 6.75

Christmas — A136

The Three Virtues, by Raphael.

1984, Nov. 7 *Perf. 14½x14*

634 A136 25s Faith .45 .25
635 A136 35s Hope .55 .55
636 A136 $1 Charity 1.90 1.90
a. Souvenir sheet of 3, #634-636 4.00 4.00
Nos. 634-636 (3) 2.90 2.70

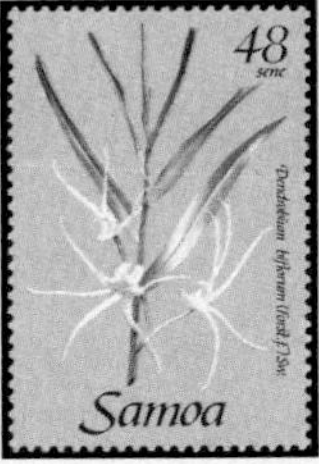

Orchids — A137

48s, Dendrobium biflorum. 56s, Dendrobium vaupelianum kraenzl. 67s, Glomera montana. $1, Spathoglottis plicata.

Unwmk.

1985, Jan. 23 Litho. *Perf. 14*

637 A137 48s multicolored .55 .45
638 A137 56s multicolored .90 .80
639 A137 67s multicolored 1.10 1.10
640 A137 $1 multicolored 1.60 1.60
Nos. 637-640 (4) 4.15 3.95

Vintage Automobiles — A138

48s, Ford Model A, 1903. 56s, Chevrolet Tourer, 1912. 67s, Morris Oxford, 1913. $1, Austin Seven, 1923.

Wmk. 373

1985, Mar. 26 Litho. *Perf. 14*

641 A138 48s multicolored 1.25 .75
642 A138 56s multicolored 1.60 1.00
643 A138 67s multicolored 2.00 2.00
644 A138 $1 multicolored 2.50 2.50
Nos. 641-644 (4) 7.35 6.25

Fungi — A139

48s, Dictyophora indusiata. 56s, Ganoderma tornatum. 67s, Mycena chlorophos. $1, Mycobonia flava.

1985, Apr. 17 Litho. *Perf. 14½*

645 A139 48s multicolored 1.50 .75
646 A139 56s multicolored 1.75 1.00
647 A139 67s multicolored 2.25 2.25
648 A139 $1 multicolored 3.25 3.25
Nos. 645-648 (4) 8.75 7.25

Queen Mother 85th Birthday

Common Design Type

32s, Photo., age 9. 48s, With Prince William at christening of Prince Henry. 56s, At Liverpool street station. $1, Holding Prince Henry. $2, Arriving at Tattenham corner station.

Perf. 14½x14

1985, June 7 Litho. Wmk. 384

649 CD336 32s multicolored .50 .35
650 CD336 48s multicolored .65 .45
651 CD336 56s multicolored 1.75 1.25
652 CD336 $1 multicolored 1.50 1.50
Nos. 649-652 (4) 4.40 3.55

Souvenir Sheet

653 CD336 $2 multicolored 4.25 4.25

Souvenir Sheet

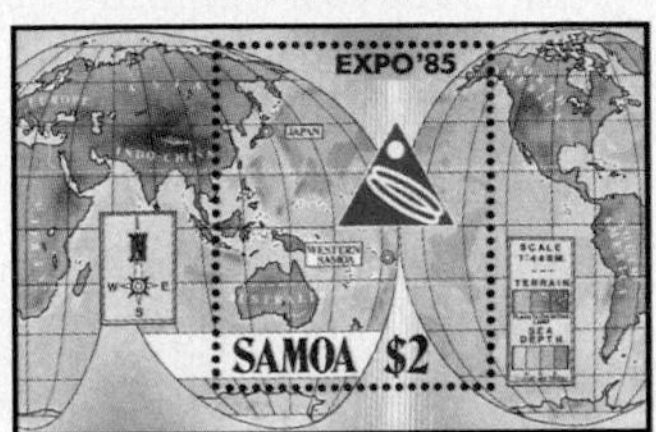

EXPO '85, Tsukuba, Japan — A140

Unwmk.

1985, Aug. 26 Litho. *Perf. 14*

654 A140 $2 Emblem, elevation map 2.50 2.50

Intl. Youth Year — A141

Portions of world map and: a, Emblem, map of No. America, Europe and Africa. b, Hands reaching high. c, Arms reaching, hands limp. d, Hands clenched. e, Emblem and map of Africa, Asia and Europe.

1985, Sept. 18 Wmk. 373

655 A141 Strip of 5 3.00 3.00
a.-e. 60s any single .50 .50

Christmas 1985 — A142

Illustrations by Millicent Sowerby from A Child's Garden of Verses, by Robert Louis Stevenson.

1985, Nov. 5 Unwmk. *Perf. 14x14½*

656 A142 32s System .30 .30
657 A142 48s Time to Rise .40 .40
658 A142 56s Auntie's skirts .45 .45
659 A142 $1 Good Children .80 .80
a. Souvenir sheet of 4, #656-659 2.50 2.50
Nos. 656-659 (4) 1.95 1.95

Butterflies A143

25s, Hypolimnas bolina inconstans. 32s, Anapheis java sparrman. 48s, Deudorix epijarbas doris. 56s, Badamia exclamationis. 60s, Tirumala hamata mellitula. $1, Catochrysops taitensis.

1986, Feb. 13 Wmk. 384 *Perf. 14½*

660 A143 25s multicolored .55 .35
661 A143 32s multicolored .65 .45
662 A143 48s multicolored .90 .75
663 A143 56s multicolored 1.00 1.00
664 A143 60s multicolored 1.10 1.10
665 A143 $1 multicolored 1.75 1.75
Nos. 660-665 (6) 5.95 5.40

Halley's Comet A144

Designs: 32s, Comet over Apia. 48s, Edmond Halley, astronomer. 60s, Comet orbiting the Earth. $2, Giotto space probe under construction at British Aerospace.

1986, Mar. 24

666 A144 32s multicolored .30 .30
667 A144 48s multicolored .40 .40
668 A144 60s multicolored .55 .55
669 A144 $2 multicolored 1.75 1.75
Nos. 666-669 (4) 3.00 3.00

Queen Elizabeth II 60th Birthday
Common Design Type

Designs: 32s, Engagement to the Duke of Edinburgh, 1947. 48s, State visit to US, 1976. 56s, Attending outdoor ceremony, Apia, 1977. 67s, At Badminton Horse Trials, 1978. $2, Visiting Crown Agents' offices, 1983.

1986, Apr. 21
670 CD337 32s scarlet, blk & sil .30 .30
671 CD337 48s ultra & multi .35 .35
672 CD337 56s green & multi .45 .45
673 CD337 67s violet & multi .55 .55
674 CD337 $2 rose violet & multi 1.25 1.25
Nos. 670-674 (5) 2.90 2.90

AMERIPEX '86, Chicago, May 22-June 1 — A145

1986, May 22 **Unwmk.**
675 A145 48s USS Vincennes .45 .45
676 A145 56s Sikorsky S-42 .55 .55
677 A145 60s USS Swan .60 .60
678 A145 $2 Apollo 10 splashdown 1.75 1.75
Nos. 675-678 (4) 3.35 3.35

Souvenir Sheet

Vailima, Estate of Novelist Robert Louis Stevenson, Upolu Is. — A146

1986, Aug. 4 **Litho.** ***Perf. 13½***
679 A146 $3 multicolored 6.00 6.00

STAMPEX '86, Adelaide, Aug. 4-10.

Fish A147

Unwmk.

1986, Aug. 13 **Litho.** ***Perf. 14***
680 A147 32s Spotted grouper .50 .50
681 A147 48s Sabel squirrelfish .70 .50
682 A147 60s Lunartail grouper .90 .90
683 A147 67s Longtail snapper .90 .90
684 A147 $1 Berndt's soldierfish 2.00 2.00
Nos. 680-684 (5) 5.00 4.80

US Peace Corps in Samoa, 25th Anniv. A148

Statesmen: Vaai Kolone of Samoa, Ronald Reagan of US and: 45s, Fiame Mata'afa, John F. Kennedy (1961) and Parliament House. 60s, Jules Grevy, Grover Cleveland (1886) and the Statue of Liberty.

1986, Dec. 1 ***Perf. 14½***
685 A148 45s multicolored .40 .40
686 A148 60s multicolored .45 .45
a. Souvenir sheet of 2, #685-686 4.00 4.00

Christmas, Statue of Liberty, cent.

Natl. Independence, 25th Anniv. — A149

Perf. 14x14½

1987, Feb. 16 **Litho.** **Unwmk.**
687 A149 15s Map, hibiscus .25 .25
688 A149 45s Parliament .45 .45
689 A149 60s Rowing race, 1987 .55 .55
690 A149 70s Dove .65 .65
691 A149 $2 Prime minister, flag 2.25 2.25
Nos. 687-691 (5) 4.15 4.15

Nos. 687-690 vert.

Marine Life A150

1987, Mar. 31
692 A150 45s Gulper .55 .35
693 A150 60s Hatchet-fish .65 .65
694 A150 70s Angler .85 .85
695 A150 $2 Gulper, diff. 2.00 2.00
Nos. 692-695 (4) 4.05 3.85

Souvenir Sheet

CAPEX '87 — A151

1987, June 13 ***Perf. 14½***
696 A151 $3 Logger, construction workers 3.25 3.25

Landscapes — A152

45s, Lefaga Beach, Upolu. 60s, Vaisala Beach, Savaii. 70s, Solosolo Beach, Upolu. $2, Neiafu Beach, Savaii.

1987, July 29 ***Perf. 14***
697 A152 45s multicolored .75 .40
698 A152 60s multicolored 1.00 .50
699 A152 70s multicolored 1.10 .90
700 A152 $2 multicolored 2.50 2.50
Nos. 697-700 (4) 5.35 4.30

Australia Bicentennial A153

Explorers of the Pacific: 40s, Abel Tasman (c. 1603-1659), Dutch navigator, discovered Tasmania, 1642. 45s, James Cook. 80s, Count Louis-Antoine de Bougainville (1729-1811), French navigator, discovered Bougainville Is., largest of the Solomon Isls., 1768. $2, Comte de La Perouse (1741-1788), French navigator, discovered La Perouse Strait.

1987, Sept. 30 **Litho.** ***Perf. 14½***
701 A153 40s multicolored .60 .35
702 A153 45s multicolored .75 .55
703 A153 80s multicolored 1.00 1.00
704 A153 $2 multicolored 2.25 2.25
a. Souvenir sheet of 1 3.00 3.00
Nos. 701-704 (4) 4.60 4.15

No. 704a Ovptd. with HAFNIA '87 Emblem in Scarlet

1987, Oct. 16
705 A153 $2 multicolored 3.25 3.25

Christmas 1987 — A154

1987, Nov. 30 ***Perf. 14***
706 A154 40s Christmas tree .40 .35
707 A154 45s Going to church .50 .40
708 A154 50s Bamboo fire-gun .60 .60
709 A154 80s Going home 1.00 1.00
Nos. 706-709 (4) 2.50 2.35

Australia Bicentennial — A155

a, Samoan natl. crest, Australia Post emblem. b, Two jets, postal van. c, Loading airmail. d, Jet, van, postman. e, Congratulatory aerogramme.

1988, Jan. 27 ***Perf. 14½***
710 A155 Strip of 5 5.75 5.75
a.-e. 45s any single 1.00 1.00

Faleolo Intl. Airport A156

40s, Terminal, Boeing 727. 45s, Boeing 727, Fuatino. 60s, So. Pacific Is. N43SP, terminal. 70s, Air New Zealand Boeing 737. 80s, Tower, jet. $1, Hawaiian Air DC-9, VIP house.

Perf. 13x13½

1988, Mar. 24 **Litho.** **Unwmk.**
711 A156 40s multicolored .65 .50
712 A156 45s multicolored .75 .50
713 A156 60s multicolored 1.00 .90
714 A156 70s multicolored 1.10 1.10
715 A156 80s multicolored 1.25 1.25
716 A156 $1 multicolored 1.60 1.60
Nos. 711-716 (6) 6.35 5.85

EXPO '88, Brisbane, Australia A157

45s, Island village display. 70s, EXPO complex, monorail and flags. $2, Map.

1988, Apr. 27 ***Perf. 14½***
717 A157 45s multicolored .65 .65
718 A157 70s multicolored 1.50 1.50
719 A157 $2 multicolored 2.25 2.25
Nos. 717-719 (3) 4.40 4.40

Souvenir Sheet

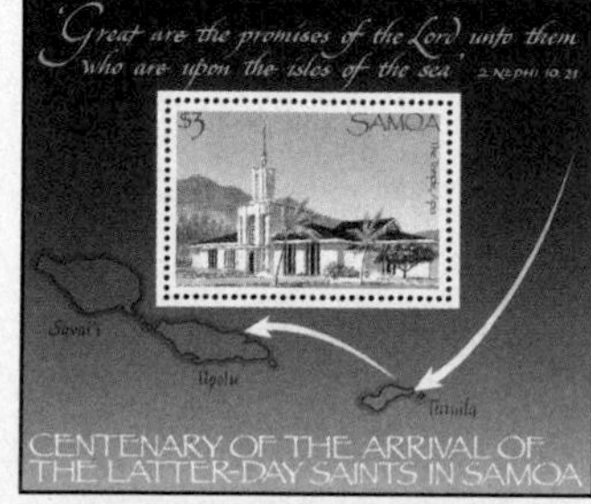

Arrival of the Latter Day Saints in Samoa, Cent. — A158

1988, June 9 **Litho.** ***Perf. 13½***
720 A158 $3 The Temple, Apia 3.00 3.00

1988 Summer Olympics, Seoul — A159

1988, Aug. 10 **Litho.** ***Perf. 14***
721 A159 15s Running .25 .25
722 A159 60s Weight lifting .50 .50
723 A159 80s Boxing 1.00 1.00
724 A159 $2 Olympic Stadium 1.50 1.50
a. Souvenir sheet of 4, #721-724 3.50 3.50
Nos. 721-724 (4) 3.25 3.25

Birds — A160

10c, Polynesian triller. 15s, Samoan wood rail. 20s, Flat-billed kingfisher. 25s, Samoan fantail. 35s, Scarlet robin. 40s, Mao. 50s, Cardinal honeyeater. 65s, Samoan whistler. No. 733, Many-colored fruit dove. No. 734, White-throated pigeon. No. 735, Silver gull. No. 736, Great frigatebird. 90s, Eastern reef heron. $3, Short-tailed albatross. $10, Common fairy tern. $20, Shy albatross.

1988-89 **Unwmk.** ***Perf. 13½***
725 A160 10s multicolored .30 *.45*
726 A160 15s multicolored .30 *.40*
727 A160 20s multicolored .30 *1.00*
728 A160 25s multicolored .40 *.50*
729 A160 35s multicolored .50 .50
730 A160 40s multicolored .75 .75
731 A160 50s multicolored .90 .90
732 A160 65s multicolored 1.10 1.10
733 A160 75s multicolored 1.25 1.25
734 A160 85s multicolored 1.40 1.40

Perf. 14

Size:45x39mm
735 A160 75s multicolored 1.50 1.50
736 A160 85s multicolored 1.50 1.50
737 A160 90s multicolored 2.40 1.90
738 A160 $3 multicolored 4.50 4.50
739 A160 $10 multicolored 12.00 12.00
740 A160 $20 multicolored 25.00 25.00
Nos. 725-740 (16) 54.10 54.65

Issue dates: #725-734, 8/17/88; #735-738, 2/28/89; #739-740, 7/31/89.

Conservation — A161

1988, Oct. 25 ***Perf. 14***
741 A161 15s Forests, vert. .85 .30
742 A161 40s Culture, vert. 1.00 .50
743 A161 45s Wildlife, vert. 2.00 .60
744 A161 50s Water 1.25 .75
745 A161 60s Marine resources 1.25 .90
746 A161 $1 Land and soil 1.50 1.50
Nos. 741-746 (6) 7.85 4.55

Christmas A162

Designs: 15s, 40s, Congregational Church of Jesus, Apia. 40s, Roman Catholic Church, Leauvaa. 45s, Congregational Christian Church, Moataa. $2, Baha'i Temple, Vailima.

Perf. 14x14½

1988, Nov. 14 Litho. Unwmk.

747 A162 15s multicolored .25 .25
748 A162 40s multicolored .50 .50
749 A162 45s multicolored .55 .55
750 A162 $2 multicolored 2.25 2.25
a. Souvenir sheet of 4, #747-750 3.75 3.75
Nos. 747-750 (4) 3.55 3.55

Orchids — A163

1989, Jan. 31 Litho. *Perf. 14*

751 A163 15s Phaius flavus .25 .25
752 A163 45s Calanthe triplicata .65 .65
753 A163 60s Luisia teretifolia .80 .60
754 A163 $3 Dendrobium moh-lianum 2.50 2.50
Nos. 751-754 (4) 4.20 4.00

Apia Hurricane, 1889 A164

1989, Mar. 16 Litho. Unwmk.

755 Strip of 4 9.00 9.00
a. A164 50s SMS Eber 1.25 1.25
b. A164 65s SMS Olga 1.50 1.50
c. A164 85s SMS Calliope 2.00 2.00
d. A164 $2 SMS Vandalia 2.50 2.50
e. Souv. sheet of 2, #c.-d., imperf. 7.50 7.50

World Stamp Expo '89.

#755e, issued Nov. 17, is wmk. 355.

Intl. Red Cross and Red Crescent Organizations, 125th Annivs. — A165

1989, May 15 *Perf. 14½x14*

756 A165 50s Youths in parade .40 .40
757 A165 65s Blood donation .55 .55
758 A165 75s First Aid .65 .65
759 A165 $3 Volunteers 2.50 2.50
Nos. 756-759 (4) 4.10 4.10

Moon Landing, 20th Anniv.

Common Design Type

Apollo 14: 18s, Saturn-Apollo vehicle and mobile launcher. 50s, Alan Shepard, Stuart Roosa and Edgar Mitchell. 65s, Mission emblem. $2, Tracks of the modularised equipment transporter. $3, Buzz Aldrin and American flag raised on the Moon, Apollo 11 mission.

1989, July 20 Wmk. 384 *Perf. 14*

Size of Nos. 761-762: 29x29mm

760 CD342 18s multicolored .35 .30
761 CD342 50s multicolored .75 .50
762 CD342 65s multicolored 1.00 .75
763 CD342 $2 multicolored 3.00 3.00
Nos. 760-763 (4) 5.10 4.55

Souvenir Sheet

764 CD342 $3 multicolored 4.50 4.50

Christmas A166

Perf. 13½x13

1989, Nov. 1 Litho. Unwmk.

765 A166 18s Joseph and Mary .40 .30
766 A166 50s Shepherds .90 .50
767 A166 55s Animals 1.00 .70
768 A166 $2 Three kings 3.50 3.50
Nos. 765-768 (4) 5.80 5.00

Local Transport — A167

Designs: 18s, Pao pao (outrigger canoe). 55s, Fautasi (longboat). 60s, Polynesian Airlines propeller plane. $3, Lady Samoa ferry.

1990, Jan. 31 Unwmk. *Perf. 14x15*

769 A167 18s multicolored .45 .35
770 A167 55s multicolored 1.10 .75
771 A167 60s multicolored 1.75 1.40
772 A167 $3 multicolored 5.50 5.50
Nos. 769-772 (4) 8.80 8.00

Otto von Bismarck, Brandenburg Gate — A168

1990, May 3 *Perf. 14x13½*

773 A168 75s shown 2.00 2.00
774 A168 $3 SMS Adler 6.75 6.75
a. Pair, #773-774 10.50 10.50

Opening of the Berlin Wall, 1989, and cent. of the Treaty of Berlin (in 1989). No. 774a has a continuous design.

Great Britain No. 1 and Alexandra Palace — A169

1990, May 3

775 A169 $3 multicolored 4.00 4.00

Stamp World London '90 and 150th anniv. of the Penny Black.

Tourism A170

1990, July 30 Litho. *Perf. 14*

776 A170 18s Visitors Bureau .25 .25
777 A170 50s Samoa Village Resorts .70 .40
778 A170 65s Aggies Hotel .90 .70
779 A170 $3 Tusitala Hotel 3.25 3.25
Nos. 776-779 (4) 5.10 4.60

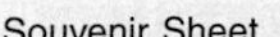

Souvenir Sheet

No. 240, Exhibition Emblem — A171

1990, Aug. 24 Litho. *Perf. 13*

780 A171 $3 multicolored 4.50 4.50

World Stamp Exhib., New Zealand 1990.

Christmas — A172

Paintings of Madonna and Child.

1990, Oct. 31 *Perf. 12½*

781 A172 18s Bellini .45 .25
782 A172 50s Bouts .90 .50
783 A172 55s Correggio 1.10 .60
784 A172 $3 Cima 4.75 4.75
Nos. 781-784 (4) 7.20 6.10

The 55s is "The School of Love," not "Madonna of the Basket."

UN Development Program, 40th Anniv. — A173

1990, Nov. 26 *Perf. 13½*

785 A173 $3 multicolored 3.50 3.50

Parrots A174

1991, Apr. 8 Litho. *Perf. 13½*

786 A174 18s Black-capped lory .75 .45
787 A174 50s Eclectus parrot 1.40 .70
788 A174 65s Scarlet macaw 1.75 1.00
789 A174 $3 Palm cockatoo 4.75 4.75
Nos. 786-789 (4) 8.65 6.90

Elizabeth & Philip, Birthdays

Common Design Types

Wmk. 384

1991, June 17 Litho. *Perf. 14½*

790 CD346 75s multicolored 1.10 1.10
791 CD345 $2 multicolored 2.50 2.50
a. Pair, #790-791 + label 4.25 4.25

Souvenir Sheet

1991 Rugby World Cup — A175

1991, Oct. 12 Litho. *Perf. 14½*

792 A175 $5 multicolored 11.00 11.00

Christmas A176

Orchids and Christmas carols: 20s, O Come All Ye Faithful. 60s, Joy to the World. 75s, Hark! the Herald Angels Sing. $4, We Wish You a Merry Christmas.

1991, Oct. 31 Litho. *Perf. 14½*

793 A176 20s multicolored .60 .25
794 A176 60s multicolored 1.10 .75
795 A176 75s multicolored 1.40 .90
796 A176 $4 multicolored 5.25 5.25
Nos. 793-796 (4) 8.35 7.15

See Nos. 815-818, 836-840.

Phila Nippon '91 — A177

Samoan hawkmoths: 60s, Herse convolvuli. 75s, Gnathothlibus erotus. 75s, Hippotion celerio. $3, Cephonodes armatus.

1991, Nov. 16 *Perf. 13½x14*

797 A177 60s multicolored 1.25 .85
798 A177 75s multicolored 1.50 1.00
799 A177 85s multicolored 1.75 1.40
800 A177 $3 multicolored 6.25 6.25
Nos. 797-800 (4) 10.75 9.50

Independence, 30th Anniv. — A178

1992, Jan. 8 Litho. *Perf. 14*

801 A178 50s Honor guard .70 .55
802 A178 65s Siva scene .90 .65
803 A178 $1 Parade float 1.50 1.50
804 A178 $3 Raising flag 4.75 4.75
Nos. 801-804 (4) 7.85 7.45

Queen Elizabeth II's Accession to the Throne, 40th Anniv.

Common Design Type

1992, Feb. 6 Wmk. 384

805 CD349 20s multicolored .70 .35
806 CD349 60s multicolored 1.25 .85
807 CD349 75s multicolored 1.40 .80
808 CD349 85s multicolored 1.50 .90

Wmk. 373

809 CD349 $3 multicolored 3.25 3.25
Nos. 805-809 (5) 8.10 6.15

Souvenir Sheet

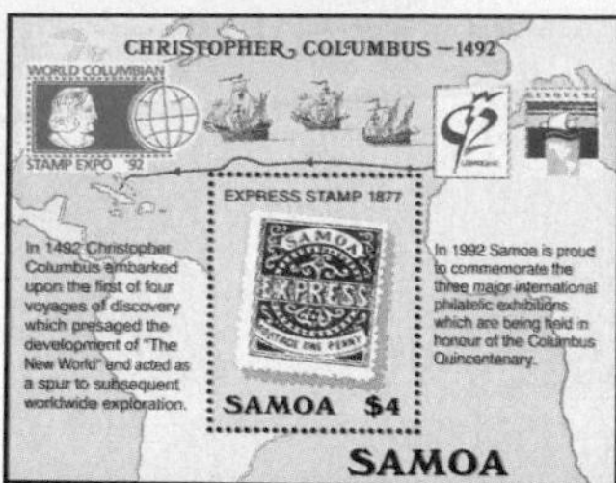

Discovery of America, 500th Anniv. — A179

1992, Apr. 17 Unwmk. *Perf. 14½*

810 A179 $4 No. 1	5.00	5.00

World Columbian Stamp Expo '92, Granada '92 and Genoa '92 Philatelic Exhibitions.

1992 Summer Olympics, Barcelona — A180

1992, July 28 Wmk. 373 *Perf. 14*

811 A180 60s Weight lifting	.90	.75
812 A180 75s Boxing	1.10	.95
813 A180 85s Running	1.40	1.25
814 A180 $3 Stadium, statue	4.75	4.75
Nos. 811-814 (4)	8.15	7.70

Christmas Type of 1991

Christmas carol, orchid: 50s, "God rest you, merry gentlemen...," liparis layardii. 60s, "While shepherds watched...," corymborkis veratrifolia. 75s, "Away in a manger...," phaius flavus. $4, "O little town...," bulbophyllum longifolium.

1992, Oct. 28 Litho. *Perf. 14½*

815 A176 50s multicolored	.65	.40
816 A176 60s multicolored	.75	.65
817 A176 75s multicolored	.90	.80
818 A176 $4 multicolored	4.75	4.75
Nos. 815-818 (4)	7.05	6.60

Fish A182

60s, Batfish. 75s, Lined surgeonfish. $1, Red-tail snapper. $3, Long-nosed emperor.

1993, Mar. 17 Litho. *Perf. 14*

819 A182 60s multicolored	.90	.65
820 A182 75s multicolored	1.10	1.10
821 A182 $1 multicolored	1.60	1.60
822 A182 $3 multicolored	4.50	4.50
Nos. 819-822 (4)	8.10	7.85

World Cup Seven-a-Side Rugby Championships, Scotland — A183

60s, Team performing traditional dance. 75c, Two players. 85c, Player. $3, Edinburgh Castle.

1993, May 12 *Perf. 13½x14*

823 A183 60s multi	1.40	.75
824 A183 75s multi, vert.	1.50	.85
825 A183 85s multi, vert.	2.00	1.25
826 A183 $3 multi	6.00	6.00
Nos. 823-826 (4)	10.90	8.85

Bats A184

1993, June 10 *Perf. 14x14½*

827 A184 20s Two hanging	*1.25*	*1.25*
828 A184 50s Two flying	*2.00*	*2.00*
829 A184 60s Three flying	*2.50*	*2.50*
830 A184 75s One on flower	*3.00*	*3.00*
Nos. 827-830 (4)	*8.75*	*8.75*

World Wildlife Fund.

Souvenir Sheet

Taipei '93, Asian Intl. Invitation Stamp Exhibition — A185

1993, Aug. 16 Litho. *Perf. 14*

831 A185 $5 multicolored	10.50	10.50

World Post Day A186

Designs: 60s, Globe, letter, flowers. 75s, Customers at Post Office. 85s, Black, white hands exchanging letter. $4, Globe, national flags, letter.

1993, Oct. 8 Litho. *Perf. 14*

832 A186 60s multicolored	.70	.45
833 A186 75s multicolored	.95	.55
834 A186 85s multicolored	1.25	1.00
835 A186 $4 multicolored	5.00	5.00
Nos. 832-835 (4)	7.90	7.00

Christmas Type of 1991

Flowers, Christmas carol: 20s, "Silent Night! Holy Night!..." 60s, "As with gladness men of old..." 75s, "Mary had a Baby, Yes Lord..." $1.50, "Once in Royal David's City..." $3, "Angels, from the realms of Glory..."

Perf. 14½

1993, Nov. 1 Litho. Unwmk.

836 A176 20s multicolored	.50	.40
837 A176 60s multicolored	1.00	.60
838 A176 75s multicolored	1.25	.75
839 A176 $1.50 multicolored	2.25	2.25
840 A176 $3 multicolored	4.50	4.50
Nos. 836-840 (5)	9.50	8.50

Corals A187

1994, Feb. 18 Litho. *Perf. 14*

841 A187 20s Alveropora allingi	.40	.30
842 A187 60s Acropora polystoma	.80	.60
843 A187 90s Acropora listeri	1.10	1.10
844 A187 $4 Acropora grandis	5.00	5.00
Nos. 841-844 (4)	7.30	7.00

Ovptd. with Hong Kong '94 Emblem

1994, Feb. 18

845 A187 20s on #841	.30	.30
846 A187 60s on #842	.80	.60
847 A187 90s on #843	1.10	1.10
848 A187 $4 on #844	5.00	5.00
Nos. 845-848 (4)	7.20	7.00

Manu Samoa Rugby Team A188

Designs: 70s, Management. 90s, Test match with Wales. 95s, Test match with New Zealand. $4, Apia Park Stadium.

1994, Apr. 11 Litho. *Perf. 14*

849 A188 70s multicolored	.80	.75
850 A188 90s multicolored	1.00	1.00
851 A188 95s multicolored	1.10	1.10
852 A188 $4 multicolored	5.00	5.00
Nos. 849-852 (4)	7.90	7.85

Souvenir Sheet

PHILAKOREA '94 — A189

Butterflies: $5, White caper, glasswing.

1994, Aug. 16 Litho. *Perf. 13*

853 A189 $5 multicolored	6.25	6.25

Teuila Tourism Festival A190

1994, Sept. 22 Litho. *Perf. 13½*

854 A190 70s Singers	1.10	.60
855 A190 90s Fire dancer	1.25	.85
856 A190 95s Parade float	1.40	1.00
857 A190 $4 Police band	6.50	6.50
Nos. 854-857 (4)	10.25	8.95

A191

70s, Schooner Equator. 90s, Portrait. $1.20, Tomb, Mount Vaea. $4, Vailima House, horiz.

1994, Nov. 21 *Perf. 14*

858 A191 70s multicolored	.85	.65
859 A191 90s multicolored	1.00	1.00
860 A191 $1.20 multicolored	1.40	1.40
861 A191 $4 multicolored	4.75	4.75
Nos. 858-861 (4)	8.00	7.80

Robert Louis Stevenson (1850-94), writer.

A192

Children's Christmas paintings: 70s, Father Christmas. 95s, Nativity. $1.20, Picnic. $4, Greetings.

1994, Nov. 30

862 A192 70s multicolored	.70	.60
863 A192 95s multicolored	1.10	1.10
864 A192 $1.20 multicolored	1.30	1.30
865 A192 $4 multicolored	4.25	4.25
Nos. 862-865 (4)	7.35	7.25

Scenic Views A193

Designs: 5s, Lotofaga Beach, Aleipata. 10s, Nuutele Island. 30s, Satuiatua, Savaii. 50s, Sinalele, Aleipata. 60s, Paradise Beach, Lefaga. 70s, Houses, Piula Cave. 80s, Taga blowholes. 90s, View from east coast road. 95s, Canoes, Leulumoega. $1, Parliament Building.

1995 Litho. *Perf. 14½x13*

866 A193 5s multicolored	.25	.25
867 A193 10s multicolored	.25	.25
871 A193 30s multicolored	.25	.25
874 A193 50s multicolored	.30	.30
875 A193 60s multicolored	.35	.35
876 A193 70s multicolored	.40	.40
877 A193 80s multicolored	.45	.45
878 A193 90s multicolored	.50	.50
879 A193 95s multicolored	.50	.50
880 A193 $1 multicolored	.55	.55
Nos. 866-880 (10)	3.80	3.80

Issued: Nos. 866-867, 871, 874-880, 3/29/95.

1995 World Rugby Cup Championships, South Africa — A194

Designs: 70s, Players under age 12. 90s, Secondary Schools' rugby teams. $1, Manu Samoa test match with New Zealand. $4, Ellis Park Stadium, Johannesburg.

1995, May 25 Litho. *Perf. 14x13½*

886 A194 70s multicolored	.65	.65
887 A194 90s multicolored	.90	.90
888 A194 $1 multicolored	1.10	1.10
889 A194 $4 multicolored	4.25	4.25
Nos. 886-889 (4)	6.90	6.90

End of World War II, 50th Anniv.

Common Design Types

Designs: 70s, OS2U Kingfisher over Faleolo Air Base. 90s, F4U Corsair, Faleolo Air Base. 95s, US troops in landing craft. $3, US Marines landing on Samoan beach. $4, Reverse of War Medal 1939-45.

1995, May 31 Litho. *Perf. 13½*

890 CD351 70s multicolored	1.00	.75
891 CD351 90s multicolored	1.25	1.00
892 CD351 95s multicolored	1.50	1.25
893 CD351 $3 multicolored	5.50	5.50
Nos. 890-893 (4)	9.25	8.50

Souvenir Sheet

Perf. 14

894 CD352 $4 multicolored	5.00	5.00

Year of the Sea Turtle — A195

1995, Aug. 24 Litho. *Perf. 13x13½*

895 A195 70s Leatherback	.75	.75
896 A195 90s Loggerhead	.95	.95
897 A195 $1 Green turtle	1.10	1.10
898 A195 $4 Pacific Ridley	4.25	4.25
Nos. 895-898 (4)	7.05	7.05

Souvenir Sheet

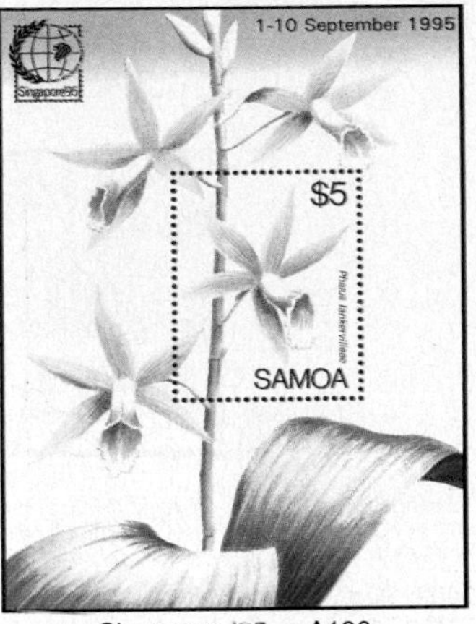

Singapore '95 — A196

1995, Sept. 1 *Perf. 14*
899 A196 $5 Phaius tankervilleae 6.00 6.00

See No. 935.

UN, 50th Anniv.

Common Design Type

70s, Mobile hospital. 90s, Bell Sioux helicopter. $1, Bell 212 helicopter. $4, RNZAF Andover.

Unwmk.

1995, Oct. 24 Litho. *Perf. 14*
900 CD353 70s multicolored 1.00 .70
901 CD353 90s multicolored 1.50 1.00
902 CD353 $1 multicolored 1.60 1.25
903 CD353 $4 multicolored 5.25 5.25
Nos. 900-903 (4) 9.35 8.20

A197

1995, Nov. 15 *Perf. 14½*
904 A197 25s Madonna & Child .40 .30
905 A197 70s Wise Man .85 .60
906 A197 90s Wise Man, diff. 1.00 .90
907 A197 $5 Wise Man, diff. 5.25 5.25
Nos. 904-907 (4) 7.50 7.05

Christmas.

A198

Importance of Water: 70s, Waterfall, bird, woman, hands. 90s, Girl standing under fountain, "WATER FOR LIFE." $2, Outline of person's head containing tree, birds, waterfall, girl. $4, Community receiving water from protected watersheds.

1996, Jan. 26 Litho. *Perf. 14*
908 A198 70s multicolored .60 .60
909 A198 90s multicolored .85 .85
910 A198 $2 multicolored 2.00 2.00
911 A198 $4 multicolored 3.75 3.75
Nos. 908-911 (4) 7.20 7.20

Queen Elizabeth II, 70th Birthday

Common Design Type

Various portraits of Queen, Samoan scenes: 70s, Apia, Main Street. 90s, Neiafu beach. $1, Official residence of Head of State. $3, Parliament Building.

$5, Queen wearing tiara, formal dress.

Perf. 14½

1996, Apr. 22 Litho. Unwmk.
912 CD354 70s multicolored .75 .75
913 CD354 90s multicolored 1.00 1.00
914 CD354 $1 multicolored 1.00 1.00
915 CD354 $3 multicolored 3.00 3.00
Nos. 912-915 (4) 5.75 5.75

Souvenir Sheet

916 CD354 $5 multicolored 5.75 5.75

Souvenir Sheet

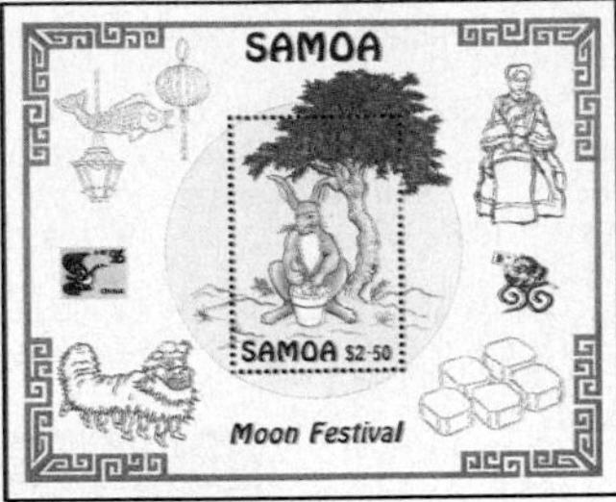

Moon Festival — A199

1996, May 18 Litho. *Perf. 14*
917 A199 $2.50 multicolored 4.00 4.00

CHINA '96.

Souvenir Sheet

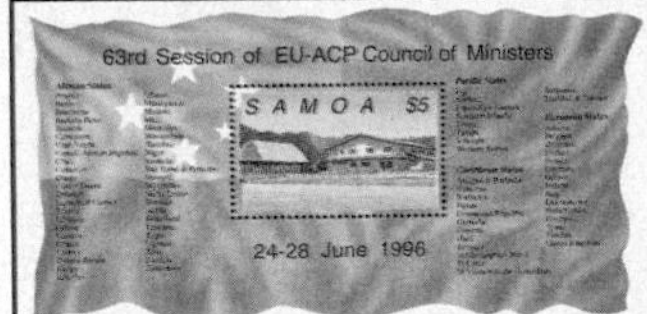

63rd Session of African-Carribean-Pacific-European Union Council of Ministers — A200

1996, June 19 Litho. *Perf. 13½*
918 A200 $5 multicolored 5.50 5.50

A201

1996, July 15 Litho. *Perf. 13½*
919 A201 70s Boxing .75 .75
920 A201 90s Running 1.10 1.10
921 A201 $1 Weight lifting 1.25 1.25
922 A201 $4 Javelin 4.25 4.25
Nos. 919-922 (4) 7.35 7.35

1996 Summer Olympic Games, Atlanta.

A202

1996, Sept. 13 Litho. *Perf. 14*
923 A202 60s Logo .65 .45
924 A202 70s Pottery .70 .55
925 A202 80s Stained glass .80 .80
926 A202 90s Dancing .90 .90
927 A202 $1 Wood carving .95 .95
928 A202 $4 Samoan chief 3.25 3.25
Nos. 923-928 (6) 7.25 6.90

7th Pacific Festival of Arts, Apia.

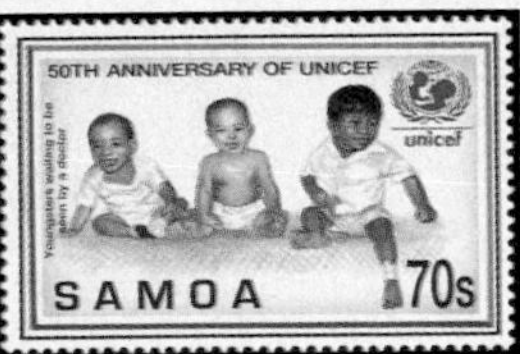

UNICEF, 50th Anniv. — A203

70s, Children in doctor's waiting room. 90s, Children in hospital undergoing treatment. $1, Child receiving injection. $4, Mothers, children playing.

1996, Oct. 24 Litho. *Perf. 14*
929 A203 70s multicolored .65 .55
930 A203 90s multicolored .75 .75
931 A203 $1 multicolored .85 .85
932 A203 $4 multicolored 3.50 3.50
Nos. 929-932 (4) 5.75 5.65

Souvenir Sheet

Many-Colored Fruit Dove — A204

1997, Feb. 3 Litho. *Perf. 14*
933 A204 $3 multicolored 3.25 3.25

Hong Kong '97. See No. 962.

Souvenir Sheet

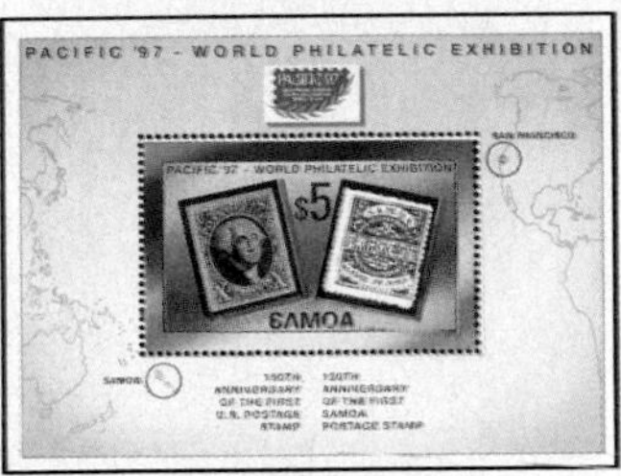

1st US Postage Stamps, 150th Anniv., 1st Samoan Postage Stamps, 120th Anniv. — A205

1997, May 29 Litho. *Perf. 14½*
934 A205 $5 US #2, Samoa #1 5.00 5.00

PACIFIC 97.

Phaius Tankervilleae Type of 1995

Souvenir Sheet

Wmk. 373

1997, June 20 Litho. *Perf. 14½*
935 A196 $2.50 multicolored 3.75 3.75

Return of Hong Kong to China, July 1, 1997.

Queen Elizabeth II & Prince Philip, 50th Wedding Anniv. — A206

No. 936, Queen. No. 937, Prince at reins of team, Royal Windsor Horse Show, 1996. No. 938, Queen, horse. No. 939, Prince laughing, horse show, 1995. No. 940, Zara Philips, Balmoral 1993, Prince Philip. No. 941, Queen, Prince William.

$5, Queen, Prince, Royal Ascot 1988.

1997, July 10 Unwmk. *Perf. 13*
936 A206 70s multicolored 1.25 1.25
937 A206 70s multicolored 1.25 1.25
a. Pair, #936-937 2.75 2.75
938 A206 90s multicolored 1.40 1.40
939 A206 90s multicolored 1.40 1.40
a. Pair, #938-939 3.00 3.00
940 A206 $1 multicolored 1.50 1.50
941 A206 $1 multicolored 1.50 1.50
a. Pair, #940-941 3.50 3.50
Nos. 936-941 (6) 8.30 8.30

Souvenir Sheet

942 A206 $5 multicolored 6.25 6.25

Greenpeace, 26th Anniv. — A207

Dolphins: 50s, #947a, Jumping out of water. 60s, #947b, Two swimming right. 70s, #947c, Two facing front. $1, #947d, With mouth open out of water.

1997, Sept. 17 Litho. *Perf. 13½x14*
943 A207 50s multicolored .55 .45
944 A207 60s multicolored .75 .65
945 A207 70s multicolored 1.00 1.00
946 A207 $1 multicolored 1.25 1.25
Nos. 943-946 (4) 3.55 3.35

Miniature Sheet

947 A207 $1.25 Sheet of 4, #a.-d. 4.50 4.50

Christmas A208

1997, Nov. 26 Litho. *Perf. 14*
948 A208 70s Bells .65 .55
949 A208 80s Ornament .75 .65
950 A208 $2 Candle 1.75 1.75
951 A208 $3 Star 2.75 2.75
Nos. 948-951 (4) 5.90 5.70

Mangroves A209

Bruguiera gymnorrhiza: 70s, Fruit on trees. 80s, Saplings. $2, Roots. $4, Tree at water's edge.

1998, Feb. 26 Litho. *Perf. 13½*
952 A209 70s multicolored .55 .50
953 A209 80s multicolored .65 .70
954 A209 $2 multicolored 1.50 1.50
955 A209 $4 multicolored 3.25 3.25
Nos. 952-955 (4) 5.95 5.95

Diana, Princess of Wales (1961-97)

Common Design Type

#956: a, Up close portrait. b, Wearing checkered jacket. c, In red dress. d, Holding flowers.

Perf. 14½x14

1998, Mar. 31 Litho. Unwmk.
955A CD355 50s like #956a 1.00 1.00

Sheet of 4

956 CD355 $1.40 #a.-d. 6.00 6.00

No. 956 sold for $5.60 + 75c, with surtax from international sales being donated to the Princess Diana Memorial Fund and surtax from national sales being donated to designated local charity.

Royal Air Force, 80th Anniversary

Common Design Type of 1993
Re-Inscribed

70s, Westland Wallace. 80s, Hawker Fury. $2, Vickers Varsity. $5, BAC Jet Provost.

No. 961: a, Norman-Thompson N.T.2b. b, Nieuport 27 Scout. c, Miles Magister. d, Bristol Bombay.

1998, Apr. 1 *Perf. 13½*
957 CD350 70s multicolored .80 .40
958 CD350 80s multicolored .90 .50

959 CD350 $2 multicolored 2.00 2.00
960 CD350 $5 multicolored 5.00 5.00
Nos. 957-960 (4) 8.70 7.90

Miniature Sheet

961 CD350 $2 Sheet of 4, #a.-d. 8.00 8.00

Many-Colored Fruit Dove Type of 1997

1998, Sept. 1 Litho. *Perf. 14*
962 A204 25s multicolored .60 .60

Christmas Ornaments — A210

1998, Nov. 16 Litho. *Perf. 14*
963 A210 70s Star .65 .55
964 A210 $1.05 Bell .95 .85
965 A210 $1.40 Ball 1.25 1.25
966 A210 $5 Cross 4.50 4.50
Nos. 963-966 (4) 7.35 7.15

Australia '99, World Stamp Expo A211

Boats: 70s, Dugout canoe. 90s, Tasman's ships Heemskerck & Zeehaen, 1642. $1.05, HMS Resolution, HMS Adventure, 1773. $6, New Zealand scow schooner, 1880.

1999, Mar. 19 Litho. *Perf. 14*
967 A211 70s multicolored .60 .40
968 A211 90s multicolored 1.00 .65
969 A211 $1.05 multicolored 1.25 1.00
970 A211 $6 multicolored 4.75 4.75
Nos. 967-970 (4) 7.60 6.80

Wedding of Prince Edward and Sophie Rhys-Jones
Common Design Type

1999, June 19 Litho. *Perf. 14*
971 CD356 $1.50 Separate portraits 1.00 1.00
972 CD356 $6 Couple 4.00 4.00

1st Manned Moon Landing, 30th Anniv.
Common Design Type

70s, Lift-off. 90s, Lunar module separates from Service module. $3, Aldrin deploys solar wind experiment. $5, Parachutes open.
$5, Earth as seen from moon.

Perf. 14x13¾
1999, July 20 Litho. Wmk. 384
973 CD357 70s multicolored .55 .45
974 CD357 90s multicolored .65 .60
975 CD357 $3 multicolored 2.00 2.00
976 CD357 $5 multicolored 3.50 3.50
Nos. 973-976 (4) 6.70 6.55

Souvenir Sheet
Perf. 14
977 CD357 $5 multicolored 6.75 6.75

No. 977 contains one 40mm circular stamp.

Queen Mother's Century
Common Design Type

Queen Mother: 70s, Talking to tenants of bombed apartments, 1940. 90s, At garden party, South Africa. $2, Reviewing scouts at Windsor. $6, With Princess Eugenie, 98th birthday.
$5, With film showing Charlie Chaplin.

Perf. 13½
1999, Aug. 24 Litho. Unwmk.
978 CD358 70s multicolored .70 .50
979 CD358 90s multicolored .80 .60
980 CD358 $2 multicolored 1.50 1.50
981 CD358 $6 multicolored 4.25 4.25
Nos. 978-981 (4) 7.25 6.85

Souvenir Sheet
982 CD358 $5 multicolored 5.25 5.25

Christmas and Millennium — A212

70s, Hibiscus. 90s, Poinsettia. $2, Christmas cactus. $6, Flag, Southern Cross.

Perf. 13½x13¼
1999, Nov. 30 Litho. Unwmk.
983 A212 70s multicolored .80 .60
984 A212 90s multicolored .95 .75
985 A212 $2 multicolored 1.50 1.50
986 A212 $6 multicolored 4.50 4.50
Nos. 983-986 (4) 7.75 7.35

Millennium — A213

Unwmk.
2000, Jan. 1 Litho. *Perf. 14*
987 A213 70s shown 1.60 1.60
988 A213 70s Rocks 1.60 1.60
a. Pair, #987-988 3.25 3.25

For surcharges, see Nos. 1235-1236.

Sesame Street — A214

No. 989: a, The Count. b, Ernie. c, Grover. d, Cookie Monster and Prairie Dawn. e, Elmo, Ernie and Zoe. f, Big Bird. g, Telly. h, Magician. i, Oscar the Grouch.
$3, Cookie Monster.

Perf. 14½x14¾
2000, Mar. 22 Litho.
989 A214 90s Sheet of 9, #a-i 6.00 6.00

Souvenir Sheet
990 A214 $3 multi 3.00 3.00

Fire Dancers — A215

Various dancers. Denominations: 25s, 50s, 90s, $1, $4.

2001, Sept. 3 Litho. *Perf. 13x13¼*
991-995 A215 Set of 5 6.00 6.00

For surcharge, see No. 1234.

Butterflies — A216

Serpentine Die Cut
2001, Dec. 12 Litho.
Self-Adhesive
996 Horiz. strip of 5 8.75 8.75
a. A216 70s Vagrans egista .75 .75
b. A216 $1.20 Jamides bochus 1.00 1.00
c. A216 $1.40 Papilio godeffroyi 1.10 1.10
d. A216 $2 Achraea andromacha 1.25 1.25
e. A216 $3 Eurema hecabe 1.75 1.75

Intl. Year of Ecotourism — A217

Designs: 60s, Snorkelers. 95s, Kayakers. $1.90, Village, children, craftsman. $3, Bird watchers.

2002, Feb. 27 *Perf. 13¼*
997-1000 A217 Set of 4 5.50 5.50
1000a Horiz strip of 4, #997-1000 + central label 6.50 6.50

Independence, 40th Anniv. — A218

Flag and: 25s, Buses, cricket player, huts. 70s, Natives. 95s, Flower, woman, ship, airplane, woman using telephone. $5, Flower, buildings, rugby player, inspection of troops.

Serpentine Die Cut
2002, June 1 Litho.
Self-Adhesive
1001-1004 A218 Set of 4 8.00 8.00
1004a Souvenir sheet of 1, #1004 8.00 8.00

People and Their Activities — A219

Designs: 5s, Woman holding fish. 10s, Family. 20s, Men carrying baskets. 25s, Two boys smiling. 35s, Woman, girl and flowers. 50s, Toddler and adult. 60s, Male dancer. 70s, Female dancer. 80s, Woman laughing. 90s, Group of women. 95s, Two women with flowers in hair. $1, Boy in stream of water. $1.20, Child smiling. $1.85, Man smiling. $10, People at church.

2002, Aug. 1 Litho. *Perf. 13x13¼*
1005 A219 5s multi .25 .25
1006 A219 10s multi .25 .25
1007 A219 20s multi .25 .25
1008 A219 25s multi .25 .25
1009 A219 35s multi .25 .25
1010 A219 50s multi .40 .40
1011 A219 60s multi .45 .45
1012 A219 70s multi .55 .55
1013 A219 80s multi .60 .60
1014 A219 90s multi .65 .65
1015 A219 95s multi .75 .75
1016 A219 $1 multi .80 .80
1017 A219 $1.20 multi .90 .90
1018 A219 $1.85 multi 1.40 1.40
1019 A219 $10 multi 7.50 7.50
Nos. 1005-1019 (15) 15.25 15.25

For surcharge, see No. 1239.

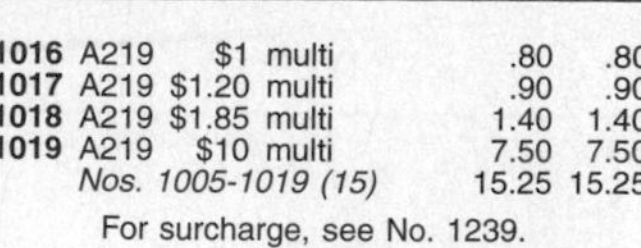

Scenic Views — A220

Designs: 95s, Family on rock. $1.20, Man and woman on beach. $1.40, Waterfall. $2, Woman in ocean.

2002, Sept. 18 *Perf. 14x14¾*
1020-1023 A220 Set of 4 5.75 5.75
1023a Souvenir sheet, #1021, 1023 3.50 3.50

For surcharge, see No. 1238.

Ginger Flowers A221

Designs: 25s, Alpinia purpurata. $1.05, Alpinia samoensis. $1.20, Etlingeria cevuga. $4, Hedychium flavescens.

2002, Nov. 20 *Perf. 13½*
1024-1027 A221 Set of 4 6.50 6.50

Decorated Buses — A222

Inscriptions on buses: 25s, Return to Paradise. 70s, Misileti Fatu. 90s, Jungle Boys. 95s, Sun Rise Transport. $4, Laifoni.

Serpentine Die Cut
2003, Jan. 22 Litho.
Self-Adhesive
1028-1032 A222 Set of 5 6.50 6.50

Marine Protected Areas A223

Designs: 25s, Aleipata. $5, Safata.

Perf. 13½x13¾
2003, Mar. 19 Litho.
1033-1034 A223 Set of 2 5.75 5.75

Artists and Their Works — A224

Artists: 25s, Vanya Taule'alo. 70s, Michel Tuffery. 90s, Momoe von Reiche. $1, Fatu Feu'u. $4, Lily Laita.

2003, May 7 **Litho.** ***Perf. 13***
1035-1039 A224 Set of 5 6.25 6.25

Sports Stars A225

Designs: 25s, David Tua, boxer. 70s, Beatrice Faumuina, discus. 90s, Michael Jones, rugby. 95s, Rita Fatialofa, netball. $4, Jesse Sapolu, football.

2003, July 16 ***Perf. 13½***
1040-1044 A225 Set of 5 6.50 6.50

For surcharge, see No. 1237.

Angelfish — A226

Designs: 25s, Centropyge bicolor. 60s, Centropyge loriculus. 90s, Pygoplites diacanthus. $5, Pomocanthus imperator.

2003, Sept. 10 ***Perf. 13x13¼***
1045-1048 A226 Set of 4 9.25 9.25
1048a Souvenir sheet of 1 7.00 7.00

Flowers — A227

Designs: 70s, Heliconia caribaea. 80s, Heliconia psittacorum. 90s, Hibiscus rosa-sinensis. $4, Plumeria rubra.

Perf. 12¾x13¼
2004, Mar. 26 **Litho.**
1049-1052 A227 Set of 4 7.00 7.00

Birds A228

Designs: 25s, Black-naped tern. 60s, Crested tern. 70s, Common noddy, vert. 90s, Lesser frigatebird, vert. $4, Reef heron.

2004, June 16 **Litho.** ***Perf. 13¼***
1053-1057 A228 Set of 5 8.00 8.00
1057a Souvenir sheet, #1053-1057 8.00 8.00

Butterflyfish — A229

Designs: 50s, Chaetodon meyeri. 90s, Chaetodon punctatofasciatus, horiz. $1, Chaetodon ephippium, horiz. $4, Chaetodon flavirostris.

Perf. 14¼x14, 14x14¼
2004, Sept. 29 **Litho.**
1058-1061 A229 Set of 4 8.00 8.00
1061a Souvenir sheet of 1 7.00 7.00

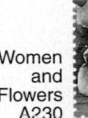

Women and Flowers A230

Various women and: 25s, Pink flower. 70s, Red flowers, vert. 90s, White flowers. $4, Orange flowers, vert.

2004, Dec. 15 **Litho.** ***Perf. 13¼***
1062-1065 A230 Set of 4 6.00 6.00

Scenes From Savaii Island A231

Designs: 25s, Children in small boat. 70s, Women, building. 90s, Women on rope bridge, vert. $4, Coastline, vert.

2005, Feb. 17 **Litho.** ***Perf. 13¼***
1066-1069 A231 Set of 4 7.50 7.50

Souvenir Sheet

Dolphins — A232

No. 1070: a, $1, Spinner dolphin. b, $1.75, Rough-toothed dolphin. c, $4, Bottlenose dolphin.

2005, Apr. 21 **Litho.** ***Perf. 13¼***
1070 A232 Sheet of 3, #a-c 8.00 8.00

Pacific Explorer 2005 World Stamp Expo, Sydney.

Legends — A233

Designs: 25s, Sau Sau, Dawn of the First Humans. 70s, Tuimanu'a and the Flying Fox. 90s, Fonuea and Salofa Escape Famine. $4, Patea, the Sea Demon.

2005, Sept. 28 **Litho.** ***Perf. 13¼***
1071-1074 A233 Set of 4 8.00 8.00

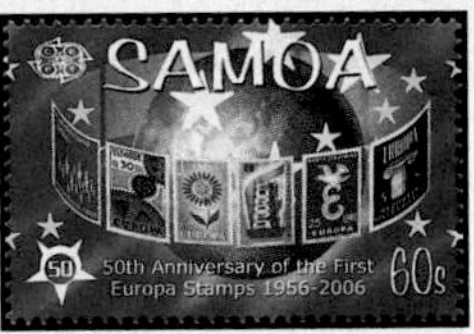

European Philatelic Cooperation, 50th Anniv. (in 2006) — A234

Globe, CEPT emblem, stars and various Europa stamps: 60s, $3, $4, $10.

2005, Dec. 7 ***Perf. 14***
1075-1078 A234 Set of 4 *19.00 19.00*
1078a Souvenir sheet, #1075-1078 *19.00 19.00*

Europa stamps, 50th anniv. (in 2006).

Diplomatic Relations Between Samoa and People's Republic of China, 30th Anniv. A235

Designs: 25s, Chinese and Samoan representatives and flags. 50s, Building. $1, Wooden bowl. $4, Chinese astronauts.

2005, Nov. 6 **Litho.** ***Perf. 13x13¼***
1079-1082 A235 Set of 4 *8.00 8.00*
1082a Souvenir sheet, #1079-1082, perf. 12 *8.00 8.00*

Sunsets A236

Various sunsets: 60s, 90s, $1, $4.

2006, Feb. 15 ***Perf. 13¼***
1083-1086 A236 Set of 4 *12.00 12.00*

Queen Elizabeth II, 80th Birthday A237

Queen Elizabeth II: $1, As young child. No. 1088, $1.75, Holding young Prince Charles. $4, Without hat. No. 1090, $5, Wearing hat.

No. 1091: a, $1.75, Like #1088. b, $5, Like #1089.

2006, Apr. 21 **Litho.** ***Perf. 14***
Stamps With White Frames
1087-1090 A237 Set of 4 13.00 13.00

Souvenir Sheet
Stamps Without White Frames
1091 A237 Sheet of 2, #a-b 8.00 8.00

Worldwide Fund for Nature (WWF) — A238

Various depictions of Humphead wrasses.

2006, Sept. 20 ***Perf. 13¼***
1092 Horiz. strip of 4 13.00 13.00
a. A238 $1.50 org red & multi 1.50 1.25
b. A238 $2.30 red & multi 2.50 1.90
c. A238 $2.50 yel org & multi 2.75 2.00
d. A238 $3.60 purple & multi 3.50 3.00

Issued in sheets of two strips.

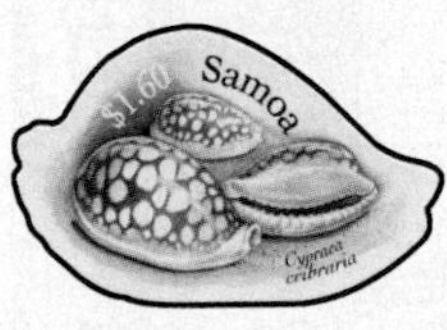

Shells A239

Designs: $1.60, Cypraea cribaria. $2.10, Cypraea aurantium. $2.40, Cypraea mauritiana. $3.10, Ovula ovum.

2006, Nov. 29 ***Die Cut***
1093-1096 A239 Set of 4 11.50 11.50

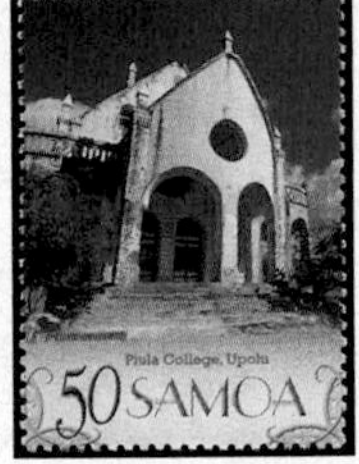

Houses of Worship — A240

Designs: No. 1097, 50s, Piula College Church, Upolu. No. 1098, 50s, Anglican Church, Apia. No. 1099, 50s, Protestant Church, Apia. No. 1100, 50s, SDA Church, Fusi Saoluafata. No. 1101, $1, Methodist Church, Matafele. No. 1102, $1, Mauga Church, Apia. No. 1103, $1, EFKS Church, Apia. No. 1104, $1, Malua Theological College. No. 1105, $2, Latter Day Saints Temple, Pesega. No. 1106, $2, Mulivai Cathedral, Apia. No. 1107, $2, EFKS Church, Sapapaii. No. 1108, $2, Bahai Temple, Apia.

2007, May 16 **Litho.** ***Perf. 13¼***
1097-1108 A240 Set of 12 16.00 16.00
1108a Miniature sheet, #1097-1108 19.00 19.00

South Pacific Games, Apia — A241

Designs: No. 1109, $1, Ele Opeloge, athlete. No. 1110, $1, Apia Park. No. 1111, $1, Aquatic Center. No. 1112, $1, Mana, Games mascot.

2007, Aug. 16
1109-1112 A241 Set of 4 5.00 5.00
1112a Souvenir sheet, 1 #1112 1.75 1.75

Tropical Fruit — A242

Designs: $1.60, Pineapples. $2.10, Coconuts. $2.40, Papayas. $3.10, Mangoes.

2007, Dec. 14 ***Die Cut***
Self-Adhesive
1113-1116 A242 Set of 4 11.50 11.50

2008 Summer Olympics, Beijing — A243

Designs: 50s, Cycling. $1, Boxing. $1.50, Wrestling. $2, Athletics.

2008, June 18 Litho. *Perf. 12*

1117-1120	A243 Set of 4		5.50	5.50
1120a	Souvenir sheet of 4, #1117-1120		5.50	5.50

Peonies, Statue and Temple A244

2009, Apr. 10 Litho. *Perf. 13¼*

1121	A244 $1 multi	.85	.85

Printed in sheets of 8.

Intl. Labor Organization, 90th Anniv. — A245

Color of top panel: $2, Green. $2.70, Blue. $3, Yellow brown. $3.90, Lilac.

2009, Apr. 27 Litho. *Perf. 13¼*

Granite Paper

1122-1125	A245 Set of 4	*9.50*	*9.50*

Worldwide Fund for Nature (WWF) — A246

No. 1126: a, Pacific robin. b, Polynesian triller. c, Polynesian starling. d, Wattled honeyeater.

2009, Sept. 2 *Perf. 13¼*

1126	Horiz. strip of 4	13.00	13.00
a.	A246 50s multi	.50	.50
b.	A246 $2 multi	2.00	2.00
c.	A246 $2.70 multi	2.50	2.50
d.	A246 $5 multi	4.75	4.75

No. 1126 was printed in sheets containing two strips.

Worldwide Fund for Nature (WWF) — A247

No. 1127 — Many-colored fruit dove: a, Two birds. b, Adult and chick in nest. c, Bird eating fruit. d, Two birds, diff.

2011, Apr. 25 *Perf. 14*

1127	Horiz. strip of 4	10.00	10.00
a.	A247 50s multi	.45	.45
b.	A247 $2 multi	1.75	1.75
c.	A247 $2.70 multi	2.40	2.40
d.	A247 $5 multi	4.50	4.50
e.	Souvenir sheet of 8, 2 each # 1127a-1127d	20.00	20.00

Samoa's Move Across International Date Line — A248

No. 1128: a, Map of Australia and New Zealand, flag and map of Samoa on jigsaw puzzle piece. b, Flag and map of Samoa on jigsaw puzzle piece.

2011, Dec. 15 *Perf. 14¼*

1128	A248 Horiz. pair + central label	5.00	5.00
a.	$2.50 multi	2.10	2.10
b.	$3 multi	2.50	2.50

Nos. 987-988 Surcharged

Methods and Perfs As Before

2011, Feb. 8

1129	A213 50s on 70s #987	—	—
a.	Inverted surcharge	—	—
1130	A213 50s on 70s #988	—	—
a.	Pair, #1129-1130	—	—
b.	Inverted surcharge	—	—
c.	Horiz. pair, #1129a, 1130b	—	—
1131	A213 $2 on 70s #987	—	—
1132	A213 $2 on 70s #988	—	—
a.	Pair, #1131-1132	—	—
1133	A213 $3 on 70s #987	—	—
1134	A213 $3 on 70s #988	—	—
a.	Pair, #1133-1134	—	—
1135	A213 $10 on 70s #987	—	—
1136	A213 $10 on 70s #988	—	—
a.	Pair, #1135-1136	—	—
	Nos. 1129-1136 (8)	125.00	—

Independence, 50th Anniv. — A249

Designs: $1, Longboats. $2, Palm tree and shore. $3, Dancers. $4, Dancer and audience.

2012, May 24 Litho. *Perf. 14¼*

1137	A249 $1 multi	.90	.90
1137A	A249 $2 multi	1.75	1.75
1137B	A249 $3 multi	2.60	2.60
1137C	A249 $4 multi	3.50	3.50
d.	Souvenir sheet of 4, #1137-1137C	8.75	8.75
	Nos. 1137-1137C (4)	8.75	8.75

Miniature Sheet

Christmas — A250

No. 1138: a, St. Joseph. b, Tree. c, Shepherd with flute. d, Madonna and Child. e, Heads of donkey and cow. f, Shepherd, body of cow. g, Sheep, body of shepherd. h, Sheep, hand of Mary. i, Feed trough and fence. j, Young shepherd holding lamb.

2012, Dec. 21 Litho. *Perf. 13¾*

1138	A250 50s Sheet of 10, #a-j	4.50	4.50

Miniature Sheet

New Year 2013 (Year of the Snake) — A251

No. 1139 — Background color: a, Yellow. b, Purple. c, Green. d, Orange.

Perf. 14¼x14¾

2013, Feb. 19 Litho.

1139	A251 $3 Sheet of 4, #a-d	10.50	10.50

Fuipisia Falls — A252

2013, Feb. 19 Litho. *Perf. 13¾*

1140	A252 $2.10 shown	1.90	1.90

Souvenir Sheet

Perf. 14¼x14¾

1141	A252 $10 multi	8.75	8.75

No. 1141 contains one 24x54mm stamp.

Endangered Bats and Birds — A253

Designs: $1, Emballonura semicaudata. $2.70, Gallinula pacifica. $3, Didunculus strigirostris. $3.90, Lalage sharpei. $4, Zosterops samoensis. $5, Nesofregetta fulginosa. $6, Numenius tahitiensis. $7.50, Pterodroma brevipes. $8, Pteropus samoensis. $10, Myiagra albiventris. $12.50, Gallicolumba stairi. $15, Gymnomyza samoensis.

2013, May 29 Litho. *Perf. 14*

1142	A253 $1 multi	.85	.85
1143	A253 $2.70 multi	2.40	2.40
1144	A253 $3 multi	2.60	2.60
1145	A253 $3.90 multi	3.50	3.50
1146	A253 $4 multi	3.50	3.50
1147	A253 $5 multi	4.25	4.25
1148	A253 $6 multi	5.25	5.25
1149	A253 $7.50 multi	6.50	6.50
1150	A253 $8 multi	7.00	7.00
1151	A253 $10 multi	8.75	8.75
1152	A253 $12.50 multi	11.00	11.00
1153	A253 $15 multi	13.00	13.00
	Nos. 1142-1153 (12)	68.60	68.60

Sopoaga Falls and Teuila Flower — A254

2013, Aug. 19 Litho. *Perf. 13¾*

1154	A254 $2.70 multi	2.25	2.25

Souvenir Sheet

Perf. 14x14¾

1155	A254 $20 multi	17.00	17.00

No. 1155 contains one 24x54mm stamp with an image similar to No. 1154 but which is erroneously inscribed "Fuipisia Falls Upolu Island."

Birth of Prince George of Cambridge A255

Designs: Nos. 1156, 1159a, $1, Duchess of Cambridge holding Prince George. Nos. 1157, 1159b, $5, Prince George. Nos. 1158, 1159c, $10, Duke of Cambridge holding Prince George.

2013, Aug. 26 Litho. *Perf. 14*

Stamps With Photograph 22mm Wide

1156-1158	A255 Set of 3	13.50	13.50

Souvenir Sheet

Stamps With Photograph 24mm Wide

1159	A255 Sheet of 3, #a-c	13.50	13.50

Photographs on Nos. 1159 extend to the tips of the perforations. A white frame is next to the outer sides of the photographs on Nos. 1156-1158.

Miniature Sheet

2013 Pacific Mini Games, Wallis & Futuna Islands — A256

No. 1160 — Inscriptions: a, Athletics. b, Beach volleyball. c, Rugby sevens. d, Sailing. e, Taekwondo. f, Va'a canoeing. g, Bodybuilding. h, Volleyball.

2013, Aug. 28 Litho. *Perf. 13¾*

1160	A256 $2.50 Sheet of 8, #a-h	17.00	17.00

A257

Teuila Festival — A258

No. 1162: a, Side view of pink teuila flower. b, Side view of red teuila flower. c, View of pink teuila flower from above.

2013, Sept. 17 Litho. *Perf. 13¾*

1161 A257 50s multi .45 .45

Souvenir Sheet

1162 A258 $10 Sheet of 3, #a-c 26.00 26.00

Souvenir Sheet

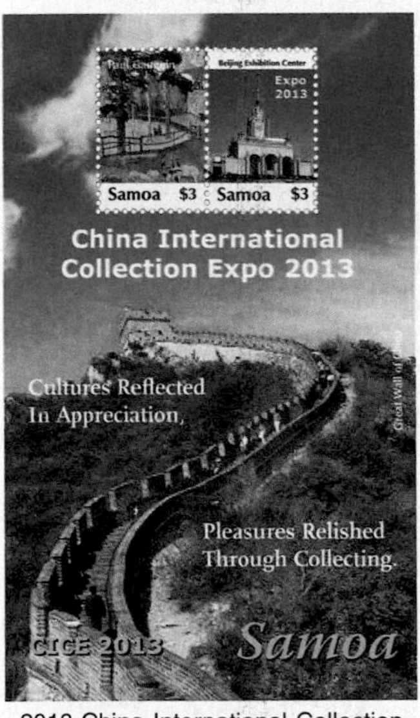

2013 China International Collection Expo, Beijing — A259

No. 1163: a, Painting by Paul Gauguin. b, Beijing Exhibition Center.

2013, Sept. 26 Litho. *Perf. 12*

1163 A259 $3 Sheet of 2, #a-b 5.25 5.25

Christmas A260

Details of paintings by: $1, Piero della Francesca. $3, Amerighi da Caravaggio.

2013, Nov. 26 Litho. *Perf. 13¼*

1164-1165 A260 Set of 2 3.50 3.50

Miniature Sheet

New Year 2014 (Year of the Horse) — A261

No. 1166 — Heads of various horses: a, 50s. b, 90s. c, $1.10. d, $2. e, $2.50. f, 3.

2014, Jan. 8 Litho. *Perf. 13¼*

1166 A261 Sheet of 6, #a-f 8.50 8.50

Endangered Marine Life and Reptiles — A262

Designs: 50s, Physeter macrocephalus. $1.50, Hippocampus histrix. $2, Bolbometopon muricatum. $2.25, Makaira nigricans. $2.50, Himantura gerrardi. $3.50, Cheilinus undulatus. $5.50, Isurus oxyrinchus. $6.60, Emoia samoensis. $7, Hippopus hippopus. $9, Eretmochelys imbricata. $20, Nebrius ferrugineus. $25, Carcharhinus longimanus.

2014, Jan. 10 Litho. *Perf. 14*

1167	A262	50s multi	.45	.45
1168	A262	$1.50 multi	1.25	1.25
1169	A262	$2 multi	1.75	1.75
1170	A262	$2.25 multi	1.90	1.90
1171	A262	$2.50 multi	2.10	2.10
1172	A262	$3.50 multi	3.00	3.00
1173	A262	$5.50 multi	4.75	4.75
1174	A262	$6.60 multi	5.75	5.75
1175	A262	$7 multi	6.00	6.00
1176	A262	$9 multi	7.75	7.75
1177	A262	$20 multi	17.00	17.00
1178	A262	$25 multi	21.50	21.50
		Nos. 1167-1178 (12)	73.20	73.20

Miniature Sheet

Easter — A263

No. 1179 — Various religious paintings by Giovanni Luteri: a, $2, Jesus. b, $2.70, Madonna and Child. c, $3, The Lamentation. d, $3.90, Ascension of Christ.

2014, Apr. 10 Litho. *Perf. 13¼*

1179 A263 Sheet of 4, #a-d 10.50 10.50

Souvenir Sheet

Nelson Mandela (1918-2013), President of South Africa — A264

No. 1180 — Various photographs of Mandela: a, $5. b, $10.

2014, May 9 Litho. *Perf. 14¼*

1180 A264 Sheet of 2, #a-b 13.00 13.00

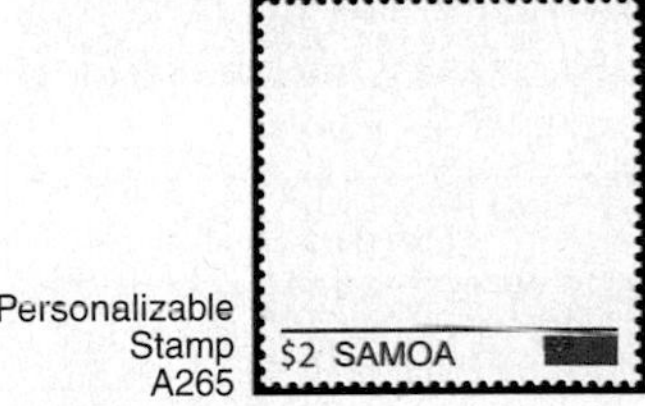

Personalizable Stamp A265

2014, Aug. 28 Litho. *Perf. 13¼*

1181 A265 $2 multi 1.75 1.75

Small Island Developing States — A266

No. 1182: a, Great barracuda. b, Loggerhead turtle. c, Barbour's seahorse. d, Cutthroat eels. e, Coral reef. f, Samoan coastline. g, Sunset at Fagamalo, Savaii Island. h, Sunset at Savaii. i, Lemafa Peak. j, Stone seawall, Lalomanu. k, Sailboat. l, Cruise ship. m, Tour boat. n, Man in canoe. o, Paddleboarding. p, Flag of Samoa.

No. 1183: a, Like #1182f. b, Like #1182p. c, Like #1182g. d, Like #1182h. e, Like #1182i. f, Like #1182j.

No. 1184: a, Like #1182a. b, Like #1182p. c, Like #1182b. d, Like #1182c. e, Like #1182d. f, Like #1182e.

No. 1185: a, Like #1182l. b, Like #1182p. c, Like #1182k. d, Like #1182m. e, Like #1182n. f, Like #1182o.

2014, Aug. 29 Litho. *Perf. 13¼*

1182 Block of 18, #1182a-1182o, 3 #1182p 8.25 8.25

a.-p. A266 50s Any single .45 .45

Miniature Sheets

1183	Sheet of 6	16.00	16.00
a.-f.	A266 $3 Any single	2.60	2.60
1184	Sheet of 6	21.00	21.00
a.-f.	A266 $3.90 Any single	3.50	3.50
1185	Sheet of 6	21.00	21.00
a.-f.	A266 $4 Any single	3.50	3.50
	Nos. 1183-1185 (3)	58.00	58.00

No. 1182 was printed in sheets containing 3 blocks of 18. The frame on each stamp in sheet, depicting a map of the Pacific Ocean, differs.

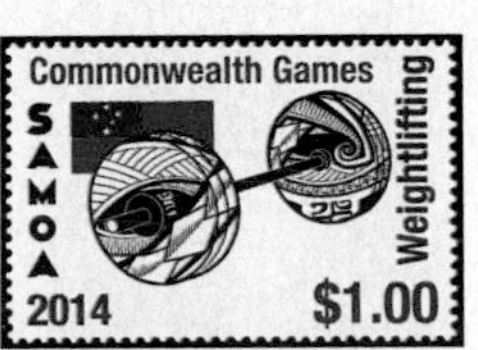

Samoan Participation in the Commonwealth Games, 40th Anniv. — A267

Samoan flag and: $1, Weight lifting. $2, Swimming. $3, Rugby sevens. $4, Boxing.

2014, Sept. 16 Litho. *Perf. 14*

1186-1189 A267 Set of 4 8.25 8.25

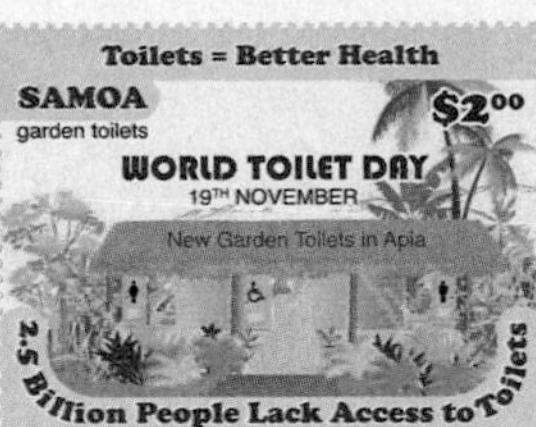

World Toilet Day — A268

No. 1190 — New garden toilets in Apia, with slogan at top: a, "Toilets = Better Health." b, "Toilets = Higher Income." c, "Toilets = Better Education." d, "Toilets = Higher Social Status."

2014, Nov. 19 Litho. *Perf. 13¼*

1190 Horiz. strip of 4 7.00 7.00

a.-d. A268 $2 Any single 1.75 1.75

World War I, Cent. A269

Designs: $2, New Zealand ships in Samoa. $2.70, New Zealand officers landing to demand German surrender, 1914. $3, New Zealand troops in Western Samoa, 1914. $3.90, New Zealand troops landing in Samoa, 1914.

No. 1195: a, New Zealand troops arriving in three boats to annex Samoa for Britain. b, New Zealand soldiers on board a troop ship en route to Samoa. c, New Zealand troops arriving in one boat to annex Samoa.

2014, Dec. 5 Litho. *Perf. 13¾*

1191-1194 A269 Set of 4 9.50 9.50

Souvenir Sheet

1195 A269 $2.50 Sheet of 3, #a-c 6.25 6.25

Miniature Sheet

Christmas — A270

No. 1196, a, Head of Santa Claus, Christmas tree, reindeer doll. b, Christmas ornament. c, Christmas stocking. d, Gift.

2014, Dec. 16 Litho. *Perf. 13¼*

1196 A270 $2 Sheet of 4, #a-d 6.75 6.75

Souvenir Sheet

New Year 2015 (Year of the Sheep) — A271

No. 1197 — Sheep with background color of: a, $5.50, Blue. b, $6.60, Red orange.

2015, Jan. 5 Litho. *Perf. 13¼*

1197 A271 Sheet of 2, #a-b 9.75 9.75

Worldwide Fund for Nature (WWF) — A272

Various photographs of Pacific tree boa: Nos. 1198, 1202, 50s, On tree. Nos. 1199, 1203, $2, On rock. Nos. 1200, 1204, $2.70, On ground. Nos. 1201, 1205, $5, On tree, diff.

2015, Feb. 24 Litho. *Perf. 14*

Stamps With White Frames

1198-1201 A272 Set of 4 8.25 8.25

Stamps Without White Frames

1202-1205 A272 Set of 4 8.25 8.25
1205a Souvenir sheet of 4, #1202-1205 8.25 8.25

Nos. 1202-1205 were each printed in sheets of 4.

Endangered Marine Life — A273

No. 1206: a, Brown-marbled grouper. b, Green sea turtle. c, Whale shark.

2015, Mar. 16 Litho. *Perf. 13¼*

1206 A273 Horiz. strip of 3 + 3 labels 50.00 50.00
a. $6.25 multi + label 5.00 5.00
b. $12.50 multi + label 10.00 10.00
c. $45 multi + label 35.00 35.00

Miniature Sheet

Easter — A274

No. 1207 — Pieta paintings by: a, Rogier van der Weyden. b, Enguerrand Quarton. c, Titian. d, Pietro Perugino.

2015, Apr. 2 Litho. *Perf. 14¼x14*

1207 A274 $2.70 Sheet of 4, #a-d 8.50 8.50

Souvenir Sheet

Birth of Princess Charlotte of Cambridge — A275

2015, June 24 Litho. *Perf. 13¾*

1208 A275 $12.90 multi 10.00 10.00

Magna Carta, 800th Anniv. — A276

Designs: $2, King John on coins. $2.70, Justice. $3, King John. $3.90, Arms of England and Samoa.

2015, July 21 Litho. *Perf. 14x14¾*

1209-1212 A276 Set of 4 9.00 9.00

Miniature Sheet

2015 Commonwealth Youth Games, Samoa — A277

No. 1213: a, Aquatics. b, Tennis. c, Track and field (athletics). d, Lawn bowls. e, Weight lifting. f, Boxing. g, Archery. h, Rugby 7s. i, Squash

2015, Sept. 2 Litho. *Perf. 13¼*

1213 A277 $2 Sheet of 9, #a-i 14.00 14.00

Miniature Sheet

Diplomatic Relations Between Samoa and People's Republic of China, 40th Anniv. — A278

No. 1214 — Flags of Samoa and People's Republic of China, handshake and: a, $2.50, Sua Trench. b, $3.70, Samoan government building. c, $4.70, Samoan Prime Minister Tuilaepa Lupesoliai Sailele Malielegaoi and Chinese President Xi Jinping. d, $5.40, 2015 Samoan Independence celebrations.

2015, Sept. 4 Litho. *Perf. 13¾*

1214 A278 Sheet of 4, #a-d 12.50 12.50

New Year 2016 (Year of the Monkey) A279

Designs: $3.90, Monkey holding peach. $4.70, Monkey scratching head.

No. 1217: a, $5.50, Monkey holding peach. b, $6.60, Monkey scratching head.

2015, Sept. 25 Litho. *Perf. 13¼*

1215-1216 A279 Set of 2 6.50 6.50

Souvenir Sheet

1217 A279 Sheet of 2, #a-b 9.25 9.25

No. 1217 contains two 50x50mm diamond-shaped stamps.

Oceania 21 Summit, New Caledonia — A280

No. 1218, $2.50: a, List of participating countries. b, Wind generator.

No. 1219, $3.70: a, Eiffel Tower. b, List of participating countries.

2015, Nov. 5 Litho. *Perf. 14*

Horiz. Pairs, #a-b

1218-1219 A280 Set of 2 9.50 9.50
1219c Souvenir sheet of 4, #1218a-1218b, 1219a-1219b 9.50 9.50

Miniature Sheet

Queen Elizabeth II, Longest-Reigning British Monarch — A281

No. 1220 — Queen Elizabeth II: a, $1, On telephone. b, $2, Wearing lime green wide-brimmed hat. c, $3, Wearing narrow-brimmed hat. d, $4, In car with Prince Philip.

2015, Nov. 16 Litho. *Perf. 14¼*

1220 A281 Sheet of 4, #a-d 7.75 7.75

Souvenir Sheet

Christmas — A282

No. 1221 — Nativity, by Lorenzo Lotto (details): a, Angels. b, St. Joseph and Virgin Mary. c, Infant Jesus.

2015, Dec, 4 Litho. *Perf. 13¾*

1221 A282 $1 Sheet of 3, #a-c 2.25 2.25

Nos. 987, 988, 993, 1018, 1020, and 1043 Surcharged

Methods and Perfs As Before

2016, Mar. 18

1234	A215	$2 on 90s #993	—	—
a.		Inverted surcharge	—	—
1235	A213	$2.70 on 70s #987	—	—
1236	A213	$2.70 on 70s #988	—	—
a.		Pair, #1235-1236	—	—
1237	A225	$5 on 95s #1043	—	—
a.		Double surcharge, one inverted	—	—
1238	A220	$15 on 95s #1020	—	—
a.		Inverted surcharge	—	—
1239	A219	$20 on $1.85 #1018	—	—
a.		Pair, one without surcharge	—	—

SEMI-POSTAL STAMP

Catalogue values for unused stamps in this section are for Never Hinged items.

No. 246 Surcharged "HURRICANE RELIEF / 6d"

Wmk. 355

1966, Sept. 1 Litho. *Perf. 13½*

B1	A43	8p + 6p blue & emerald	.30	.30

Surtax for aid to plantations destroyed by the hurricane of Jan. 29, 1966.

AIR POST STAMPS

Catalogue values for unused stamps in this section are for Never Hinged items.

Red-tailed Tropic Bird — AP1

Wmk. 355

1965, Dec. 29 Photo. *Perf. 14½*

C1	AP1	8p shown	.30	.25
C2	AP1	2sh Flying fish	.90	.50

Sir Gordon Taylor's Bermuda Flying Boat "Frigate Bird III" — AP2

Designs: 7s, Polynesian Airlines DC-3. 20s, Pan American Airways "Samoan Clipper." 30s, Air Samoa Britten-Norman "Islander."

Perf. 13½x13

1970, July 27 Photo. Unwmk.

C3	AP2	3s multicolored	.55	.25
C4	AP2	7s multicolored	.75	.25
C5	AP2	20s multicolored	1.10	.90
C6	AP2	30s multicolored	1.10	1.00
a.		Purple omitted	*250.00*	*250.00*
		Nos. C3-C6 (4)	3.50	2.40

Used value for No. C6a is for a stamp on a first day cover.

Hawker Siddeley 748 — AP3

Planes at Faleolo Airport: 10s, Hawker Siddeley 748 in the air. 12s, Hawker Siddeley 748 on ground. 22s, BAC 1-11 planes on ground.

1973, Mar. 9 *Perf. 11½*

Granite Paper

C7	AP3	8s multicolored	.50	.25
C8	AP3	10s multicolored	.70	.25
C9	AP3	12s multicolored	.75	.40
C10	AP3	22s multicolored	1.25	1.25
		Nos. C7-C10 (4)	3.20	2.15

Butterflies — AP4

Designs: $10, Glasswing butterfly. $12.50, Blue tiger butterfly. $56.25, Orange lacewing butterfly. $75, Brown pansy butterfly.

2015, Sept. 15 Litho. *Perf. 14¼*

Stamps With White Frames

C11	AP4	$10 multi	7.50	7.50
C12	AP4	$12.50 multi	9.50	9.50
C13	AP4	$56.25 multi	42.50	42.50
C14	AP4	$75 multi	55.00	55.00
a.		Souvenir sheet of 4, #C11-C14	115.00	115.00
		Nos. C11-C14 (4)	114.50	114.50

Stamps Without White Frame

C15	Strip of 4	115.00	115.00
a.	AP4 $10 multi	7.50	7.50
b.	AP4 $12.50 multi	9.50	9.50
c.	AP4 $56.25 multi	42.50	42.50
d.	AP4 $75 multi	55.00	55.00

Stamps on No. C14a have white frames on two adjacent sides.

OFFICIAL STAMPS

Nos. 1142-1153 Overprinted

2014, July 23 Litho. *Perf. 14*

O1	A253	$1 multi	.85	.85
O2	A253	$2.70 multi	2.40	2.40
O3	A253	$3 multi	2.60	2.60
O4	A253	$3.90 multi	3.50	3.50
O5	A253	$4 multi	3.50	3.50
O6	A253	$5 multi	4.25	4.25
O7	A253	$6 multi	5.25	5.25
O8	A253	$7.50 multi	6.50	6.50
O9	A253	$8 multi	7.00	7.00
O10	A253	$10 multi	8.75	8.75
O11	A253	$12.50 multi	11.00	11.00
O12	A253	$15 multi	13.00	13.00
		Nos. O1-O12 (12)	68.60	68.60

Nos. 1167-1178 Overprinted

2014, July 23 Litho. *Perf. 14*

O13	A262	50s multi	.45	.45
O14	A262	$1.50 multi	1.25	1.25
O15	A262	$2 multi	1.75	1.75
O16	A262	$2.25 multi	2.00	2.00
O17	A262	$2.50 multi	2.25	2.25
O18	A262	$3.50 multi	3.00	3.00
O19	A262	$5.50 multi	4.75	4.75
O20	A262	$6.60 multi	5.75	5.75
O21	A262	$7 multi	6.00	6.00
O22	A262	$9 multi	7.75	7.75
O23	A262	$20 multi	17.50	17.50
O24	A262	$25 multi	21.50	21.50
		Nos. O13-O24 (12)	73.95	73.95

GET YOUR COLLECTION IN ORDER WITH THE NEW SCOTT INTERNATIONAL ALBUM!

KEEP UP-TO-DATE WITH THE NEWEST INTERNATIONAL PAGES

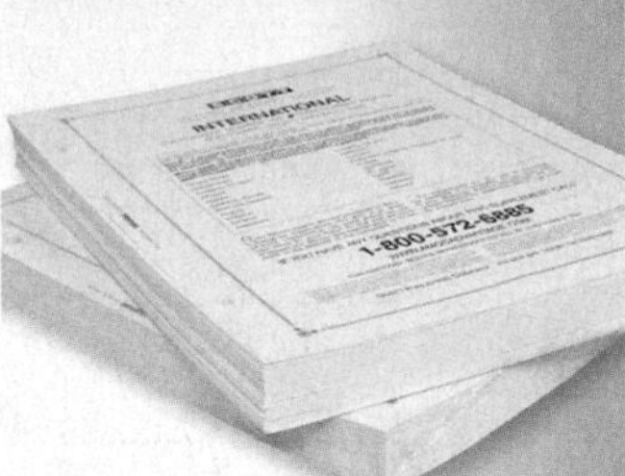

SCOTT INTERNATIONAL PART 50A: 2014

ITEM	RETAIL	AA
850P114	$135.00	$99.99

SCOTT INTERNATIONAL PART 50B: 2014

ITEM	RETAIL	AA
850P214	$135.00	$99.99

BINDERS & SLIPCASES

INTERNATIONAL SMALL BLUE BINDER (REGULAR)

ITEM	RETAIL	AA
800B001	$52.99	$40.99

INTERNATIONAL SMALL BLUE SLIPCASE (REGULAR)

ITEM	RETAIL	AA
800BC01	$32.99	$26.99

INTERNATIONAL LARGE BLUE BINDER (JUMBO)

ITEM	RETAIL	AA
800B002	$52.99	$40.99

INTERNATIONAL LARGE BLUE SLIPCASE (JUMBO)

ITEM	RETAIL	AA
800BC02	$32.99	$26.99

Get yours today by visiting
AmosAdvantage.com
Or call **1-800-572-6885**
Outside U.S. & Canada Call:
1-937-498-0800
P.O. Box 4129, Sidney, OH 45365

Vol. 5 Number Additions, Deletions & Changes

Number in 2016 Catalogue	Number in 2017 Catalogue
Niue	
new	55a
new	56a
North Borneo	
new	61b
Norway	
new	19c
Philippines	
deleted	173
Russia	
new	39b
new	41c
70c	70d
87e	87f
87f	87g
new	87e
326b	deleted
new	349c
new	349d
new	350b
new	350c
new	590A
new	591A
new	592A
new	593A
new	594A
new	590B
new	591B
new	592B
new	593B
new	594B
new	595B
new	590C
new	591C
new	592C
new	593C
new	594C
new	595C
new	590D
new	591D
Russia	
new	592D
new	590E
new	592E
new	729a
new	730a
new	753a
new	757a
new	758a
new	773b
new	B5b-8b
new	B18a-B23a
new	B18b
new	B19b
new	B21b
new	B22b
new	B24a-B29a
new	B25b-B29b
new	B30a-B33a
new	B30b-B33b
new	C18a
new	C69b
new	C70a
new	C71a
new	CO1a
St. Lucia	
new	50a
new	51a
new	52a
new	54a
new	J7a
new	J8a
new	J9a
new	J10a

SCOTT® Specialty Series

Embark on a new collecting journey. There are Specialty pages available for more than 140 countries with some of them back in print after many years thanks to on-demand printing technology. Start a new collecting adventure with countries featured in Volume 4 of the new Scott Standard Postage Stamp Catalogue!

Specialty Series pages are sold as page units only. Binders, labels and slipcases are sold separately.

ALBUM SETS

These money-saving album sets include pages, binders and self-adhesive binder labels. Some set contents may vary, please call or visit or web site for specific information.

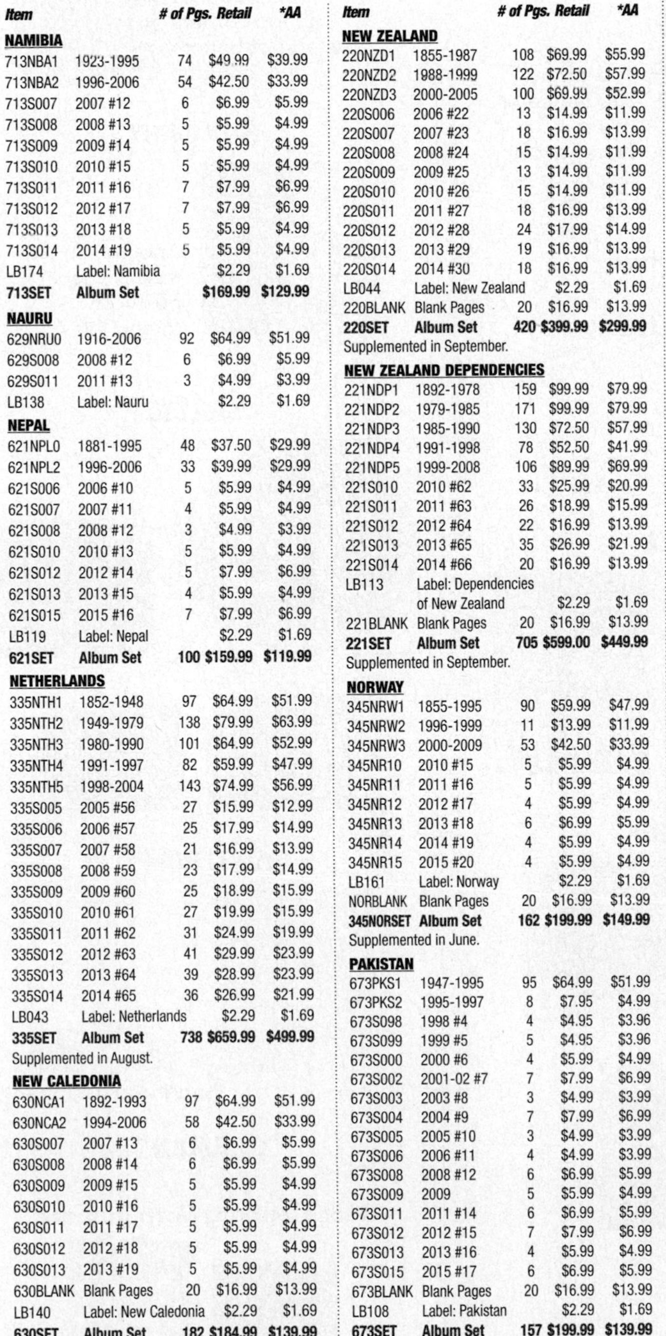

Item		# of Pgs.	Retail	*AA
NAMIBIA				
713NBA1	1923-1995	74	$49.99	$39.99
713NBA2	1996-2006	54	$42.50	$33.99
713S007	2007 #12	6	$6.99	$5.99
713S008	2008 #13	5	$5.99	$4.99
713S009	2009 #14	5	$5.99	$4.99
713S010	2010 #15	5	$5.99	$4.99
713S011	2011 #16	7	$7.99	$6.99
713S012	2012 #17	7	$7.99	$6.99
713S013	2013 #18	5	$5.99	$4.99
713S014	2014 #19	5	$5.99	$4.99
LB174	Label: Namibia		$2.29	$1.69
713SET	**Album Set**		**$169.99**	**$129.99**
NAURU				
629NRU0	1916-2006	92	$64.99	$51.99
629S008	2008 #12	6	$6.99	$5.99
629S011	2011 #13	3	$4.99	$3.99
LB138	Label: Nauru		$2.29	$1.69
NEPAL				
621NPL0	1881-1995	48	$37.50	$29.99
621NPL2	1996-2006	33	$39.99	$29.99
621S006	2006 #10	5	$5.99	$4.99
621S007	2007 #11	4	$5.99	$4.99
621S008	2008 #12	3	$4.99	$3.99
621S010	2010 #13	5	$5.99	$4.99
621S012	2012 #14	5	$7.99	$6.99
621S013	2013 #15	4	$5.99	$4.99
621S015	2015 #16	7	$7.99	$6.99
LB119	Label: Nepal		$2.29	$1.69
621SET	**Album Set**	**100**	**$159.99**	**$119.99**
NETHERLANDS				
335NTH1	1852-1948	97	$64.99	$51.99
335NTH2	1949-1979	138	$79.99	$63.99
335NTH3	1980-1990	101	$64.99	$52.99
335NTH4	1991-1997	82	$59.99	$47.99
335NTH5	1998-2004	143	$74.99	$56.99
335S005	2005 #56	27	$15.99	$12.99
335S006	2006 #57	25	$17.99	$14.99
335S007	2007 #58	21	$16.99	$13.99
335S008	2008 #59	23	$17.99	$14.99
335S009	2009 #60	25	$18.99	$15.99
335S010	2010 #61	27	$19.99	$15.99
335S011	2011 #62	31	$24.99	$19.99
335S012	2012 #63	41	$29.99	$23.99
335S013	2013 #64	39	$28.99	$23.99
335S014	2014 #65	36	$26.99	$21.99
LB043	Label: Netherlands		$2.29	$1.69
335SET	**Album Set**	**738**	**$659.99**	**$499.99**
Supplemented in August.				
NEW CALEDONIA				
630NCA1	1892-1993	97	$64.99	$51.99
630NCA2	1994-2006	58	$42.50	$33.99
630S007	2007 #13	6	$6.99	$5.99
630S008	2008 #14	6	$6.99	$5.99
630S009	2009 #15	5	$5.99	$4.99
630S010	2010 #16	5	$5.99	$4.99
630S011	2011 #17	5	$5.99	$4.99
630S012	2012 #18	5	$5.99	$4.99
630S013	2013 #19	5	$5.99	$4.99
630BLANK	Blank Pages	20	$16.99	$13.99
LB140	Label: New Caledonia		$2.29	$1.69
630SET	**Album Set**	**182**	**$184.99**	**$139.99**

Item		# of Pgs.	Retail	*AA
NEW ZEALAND				
220NZD1	1855-1987	108	$69.99	$55.99
220NZD2	1988-1999	122	$72.50	$57.99
220NZD3	2000-2005	100	$69.99	$52.99
220S006	2006 #22	13	$14.99	$11.99
220S007	2007 #23	18	$16.99	$13.99
220S008	2008 #24	15	$14.99	$11.99
220S009	2009 #25	13	$14.99	$11.99
220S010	2010 #26	15	$14.99	$11.99
220S011	2011 #27	18	$16.99	$13.99
220S012	2012 #28	24	$17.99	$14.99
220S013	2013 #29	19	$16.99	$13.99
220S014	2014 #30	18	$16.99	$13.99
LB044	Label: New Zealand		$2.29	$1.69
220BLANK	Blank Pages	20	$16.99	$13.99
220SET	**Album Set**	**420**	**$399.99**	**$299.99**
Supplemented in September.				
NEW ZEALAND DEPENDENCIES				
221NDP1	1892-1978	159	$99.99	$79.99
221NDP2	1979-1985	171	$99.99	$79.99
221NDP3	1985-1990	130	$72.50	$57.99
221NDP4	1991-1998	78	$52.50	$41.99
221NDP5	1999-2008	106	$89.99	$69.99
221S010	2010 #62	33	$25.99	$20.99
221S011	2011 #63	26	$18.99	$15.99
221S012	2012 #64	22	$16.99	$13.99
221S013	2013 #65	35	$26.99	$21.99
221S014	2014 #66	20	$16.99	$13.99
LB113	Label: Dependencies of New Zealand		$2.29	$1.69
221BLANK	Blank Pages	20	$16.99	$13.99
221SET	**Album Set**	**705**	**$599.00**	**$449.99**
Supplemented in September.				
NORWAY				
345NRW1	1855-1995	90	$59.99	$47.99
345NRW2	1996-1999	11	$13.99	$11.99
345NRW3	2000-2009	53	$42.50	$33.99
345NR10	2010 #15	5	$5.99	$4.99
345NR11	2011 #16	5	$5.99	$4.99
345NR12	2012 #17	4	$5.99	$4.99
345NR13	2013 #18	6	$6.99	$5.99
345NR14	2014 #19	4	$5.99	$4.99
345NR15	2015 #20	4	$5.99	$4.99
LB161	Label: Norway		$2.29	$1.69
NORBLANK	Blank Pages	20	$16.99	$13.99
345NORSET	**Album Set**	**162**	**$199.99**	**$149.99**
Supplemented in June.				
PAKISTAN				
673PKS1	1947-1995	95	$64.99	$51.99
673PKS2	1995-1997	8	$7.95	$4.99
673S098	1998 #4	4	$4.95	$3.96
673S099	1999 #5	5	$4.95	$3.96
673S000	2000 #6	4	$5.99	$4.99
673S002	2001-02 #7	7	$7.99	$6.99
673S003	2003 #8	3	$4.99	$3.99
673S004	2004 #9	7	$7.99	$6.99
673S005	2005 #10	3	$4.99	$3.99
673S006	2006 #11	4	$4.99	$3.99
673S008	2008 #12	6	$6.99	$5.99
673S009	2009	5	$5.99	$4.99
673S011	2011 #14	6	$6.99	$5.99
673S012	2012 #15	7	$7.99	$6.99
673S013	2013 #16	4	$5.99	$4.99
673S015	2015 #17	6	$6.99	$5.99
673BLANK	Blank Pages	20	$16.99	$13.99
LB108	Label: Pakistan		$2.29	$1.69
673SET	**Album Set**	**157**	**$199.99**	**$139.99**

Item		# of Pgs.	Retail	*AA
PITCAIRN ISLANDS				
632PNI1	1940-1993	52	$34.99	$26.99
632PNI2	1994-2002	27	$19.99	$15.99
632S003	2003 #10	5	$5.99	$4.99
632S004	2004 #11	5	$5.99	$4.99
632S005	2005 #12	4	$5.99	$4.99
632S006	2006 #13	5	$5.99	$4.99
632S007	2007 #14	4	$5.99	$4.99
632S008	2008 #15	5	$5.99	$4.99
632S009	2009 #16	5	$5.99	$4.99
632S010	2010 #17	5	$5.99	$4.99
632S011	2011 #18	4	$5.99	$4.99
632S012	2012 #19	6	$6.99	$5.99
632S013	2013 #20	5	$5.99	$4.99
632S014	2014 #21	4	$5.99	$4.99
LB133	Label: Pitcairn Islands		$2.29	$1.69
632SET	**Album Set**	**121**	**$169.99**	**$124.99**
Supplemented in August.				
POLAND				
338POL1	1860-1955	91	$59.99	$47.99
338POL2	1956-1970	100	$69.99	$55.99
338POL3	1971-1985	103	$69.99	$55.99
338POL4	1986-1999	81	$59.99	$47.99
338POL5	2000-2006	72	$49.99	$39.99
338S007	2007 #56	5	$5.99	$4.99
338S008	2008 #57	8	$8.99	$7.99
338S009	2009 #58	9	$9.99	$7.99
338S010	2010 #59	8	$8.99	$7.99
338S011	2011 #60	8	$8.99	$7.99
338S012	2012 #61	10	$10.99	$8.99
338S013	2013 #62	11	$13.99	$11.99
338S014	2014 #63	14	$14.99	$11.99
LB046	Label: Poland		$2.29	$1.69
338BLANK	Blank Pages	20	$16.99	$13.99
338SET	**Album Set**	**496**	**$449.99**	**$329.99**
Supplemented in August.				
PORTUGAL				
340PGL1	1853-1970	73	$49.99	$39.99
340PGL2	1971-1983	118	$69.99	$55.99
340PGL3	1984-1988	107	$69.99	$55.99
340PGL4	1989-1992	109	$69.95	$55.99
340PGL5	1993-1996	90	$59.99	$47.99
340PGL6	1997-1999	48	$29.95	$16.99
340PGL7	2000-2003	85	$52.50	$39.99
340PGL8	2004-2006	76	$49.99	$38.99
340S007	2007 #58	26	$18.99	$15.99
340S008	2008 #59	24	$17.99	$14.99
340S009	2009 #60	22	$16.99	$13.99
340S010	2010 #61	27	$19.99	$15.99
340S011	2011 #62	23	$17.99	$14.99
340S012	2012 #63	19	$16.99	$13.99
340S013	2013 #64	16	$15.99	$12.99
340S014	2014 #65	19	$16.99	$13.99
340S015	2015 #66	22	$16.99	$13.99
LB047	Label: Portugal		$2.29	$1.69
340SET	**Album Set**	**828**	**$799.99**	**$579.99**

Item		# of Pgs.	Retail	*AA
PORTUGUESE COLONIES				
341PGC1	1868-1977 A-L	102	$69.99	$55.99
341PGC2	1868-1977 M-N	98	$64.99	$51.99
341PGC3	1869-1973 P-Z	125	$72.50	$57.99
341S008	2008 #58	15	$14.99	$11.99
341S009	2009 #59	13	$14.99	$11.99
341S010	2010 #60	12	$14.99	$11.99
341S012	2012 #61	21	$16.99	$13.99
341S013	2013 #62	12	$14.99	$11.99
341S015	2015 #63	7	$14.99	$11.99
QATAR				
659QTR1	1957-94	95	$64.99	$51.99
659S009	2007-08 #10	8	$8.99	$7.99
659S011	2011 #11	11	$13.99	$11.99
659S013	2013 #12	4	$5.99	$4.99
659BLANK	Blank Pages	20	$16.99	$13.99
RUSSIA				
360RUS1	1857-1917	113	$69.99	$55.99
360RUS2	1918-1958	150	$92.50	$73.99
360RUS3	1958-1969	122	$79.99	$63.99
360RUS4	1969-1980	150	$92.50	$73.99
360RUS5	1980-1991	144	$92.50	$73.99
360RUS6	1992-1999	57	$42.50	$33.99
360RUS7	2000-2003	67	$44.99	$35.99
360RUS8	2004-2008	83	$63.99	$51.99
360S009	2009 #59	20	$16.99	$13.99
360S010	2010 #60	17	$15.99	$12.99
360S011	2011 #61	18	$16.99	$13.99
360S012	2012 #62	25	$18.99	$15.99
360S013	2013 #63	22	$16.99	$13.99
360S014	2014 #64	14	$14.99	$11.99
LB096	Label: Russia		$2.29	$1.69
360BLANK	Blank Pages	20	$16.99	$13.99
360SET	**Album Set**	**945**	**$839.99**	**$629.99**
Supplemented in August.				
SAMOA				
633SAM1	1877-1996	104	$69.99	$55.99
633SAM2	1996-2007	32	$24.99	$19.99
633S010	2008-2009	3	$4.99	$3.99
633S012	2012 #12	3	$4.99	$3.99
633S013	2013 #13	4	$5.99	$4.99
633S014	2014 #14	9	$9.99	$7.99
633SET	**Album Set**	**146**	**$189.99**	**$139.99**
SAN MARINO				
328SNM1	1877-1976	94	$64.99	$51.99
328SNM2	1977-1994	48	$37.50	$29.99
328SNM3	1995-2008	88	$79.99	$64.99
328S009	2009 #59	6	$6.99	$5.99
328S010	2010 #60	9	$9.99	$7.99
328S011	2011 #61	6	$6.99	$5.99
328S012	2012 #62	10	$10.99	$8.99
328S013	2013 #63	10	$10.99	$8.99
328S014	2014 #64	6	$6.99	$5.99
328S015	2015 #65	6	$6.99	$5.99
LB051	Label: San Marino		$2.29	$1.69
328BLANK	Blank Pages	20	$16.99	$13.99
328SET	**Album Set**	**230**	**$239.99**	**$179.99**

Call **1-800-572-6885**

Outside U.S. & Canada Call: (937) 498-0800

Visit **AmosAdvantage.com**

Mail to: P.O. Box 4129, Sidney, Ohio 45365-4129

Ordering Information: *AA prices apply to paid subscribers of Amos Media publications, or orders placed online. Prices, terms and product availability subject to change. Taxes will apply in CA, OH & IL. **Shipping & Handling: United States:** Orders under $10 are only $3.99; Orders over $10 are 10% of order total. Minimum charge $7.99; Maximum Charge $45.00. **Canada:** 20% of order total. Minimum charge $19.99; Maximum charge $200.00. Foreign orders are shipped via FedEx Intl. or USPS and billed actual freight.

Illustrated Identifier

This section pictures stamps or parts of stamp designs that will help identify postage stamps that do not have English words on them.

Many of the symbols that identify stamps of countries are shown here as well as typical examples of their stamps.

See the Index and Identifier for stamps with inscriptions such as "sen," "posta," "Baja Porto," "Helvetia," "K.S.A.", etc.

Linn's Stamp Identifier is now available. The 144 pages include more than 2,000 inscriptions and more than 500 large stamp illustrations. Available from Linn's Stamp News, P.O. Box 4129, Sidney, OH 45365-4129.

1. HEADS, PICTURES AND NUMERALS

GREAT BRITAIN

Great Britain stamps never show the country name, but, except for postage dues, show a picture of the reigning monarch.

Victoria

Edward VII George V Edward VIII

George VI

Elizabeth II

Some George VI and Elizabeth II stamps are surcharged in annas, new paisa or rupees. These are listed under Oman.

Silhouette (sometimes facing right, generally at the top of stamp)

The silhouette indicates this is a British stamp. It is not a U.S. stamp.

VICTORIA

Queen Victoria

INDIA

Other stamps of India show this portrait of Queen Victoria and the words "Service" (or "Postage") and "Annas."

AUSTRIA

YUGOSLAVIA

(Also BOSNIA & HERZEGOVINA if imperf.)

BOSNIA & HERZEGOVINA

Denominations also appear in top corners instead of bottom corners.

HUNGARY

Another stamp has posthorn facing left

BRAZIL

AUSTRALIA

Kangaroo and Emu

GERMANY

Mecklenburg-Vorpommern

SWITZERLAND

PALAU

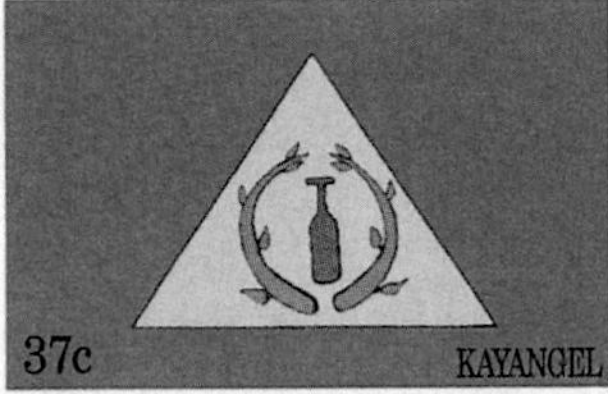

2. ORIENTAL INSCRIPTIONS

CHINA

Any stamp with this one character is from China (Imperial, Republic or People's Republic). This character appears in a four-character overprint on stamps of Manchukuo. These stamps are local provisionals, which are unlisted. Other overprinted Manchukuo stamps show this character, but have more than four characters in the overprints. These are listed in People's Republic of China.

Some Chinese stamps show the Sun.

Most stamps of Republic of China show this series of characters.

Stamps with the China character and this character are from People's Republic of China. 人

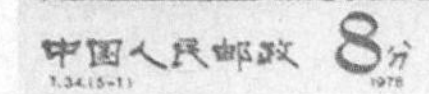

Calligraphic form of People's Republic of China

(一)	(二)	(三)	(四)	(五)	(六)
1	2	3	4	5	6
(七)	(八)	(九)	(十)	(一十)	(二十)
7	8	9	10	11	12

Chinese stamps without China character

REPUBLIC OF CHINA

PEOPLE'S REPUBLIC OF CHINA

Mao Tse-tung

MANCHUKUO

Temple

Emperor Pu-Yi

The first 3 characters are common to many Manchukuo stamps.

The last 3 characters are common to other Manchukuo stamps.

Orchid Crest

Manchukuo stamp without these elements

JAPAN

Chrysanthemum Crest

Country Name

Japanese stamps without these elements

The number of characters in the center and the design of dragons on the sides will vary.

RYUKYU ISLANDS

Country Name

PHILIPPINES (Japanese Occupation)

Country Name

NETHERLANDS INDIES (Japanese Occupation)

Indicates Japanese Occupation

Java

Sumatra

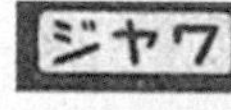

Country Name

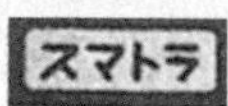

Country Name

Moluccas, Celebes and South Borneo

Country Name

NORTH BORNEO (Japanese Occupation)

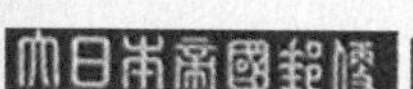

Indicates Japanese Occupation

Country Name

MALAYA (Japanese Occupation)

Indicates Japanese Occupation

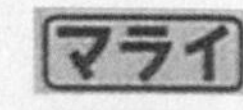

Country Name

BURMA

Union of Myanmar

ပြည်ထောင်စုမြန်မာနိုင်ငံတော်

Union of Myanmar

(Japanese Occupation)

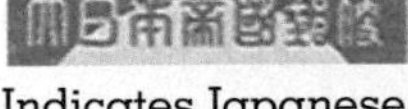

Indicates Japanese Occupation

シヤン

Country Name

Other Burma Japanese Occupation stamps without these elements

Burmese Script

KOREA

These two characters, in any order, are common to stamps from the Republic of Korea (South Korea) or of the People's Democratic Republic of Korea (North Korea).

This series of four characters can be found on the stamps of both Koreas. Most stamps of the Democratic People's Republic of Korea (North Korea) have just this inscription.

대한민국우표

Indicates Republic of Korea (South Korea)

South Korean postage stamps issed after 1952 do not show currency expressed in Latin letters. Stamps wiith " HW," "HWAN," "WON," "WN," "W" or "W" with two lines through it, if not illustrated in listings of stamps before this date, are revenues. North Korean postage stamps do not have currency expressed in Latin letters.

Yin Yang appears on some stamps.

South Korean stamps show Yin Yang and starting in 1966, 'KOREA" in Latin letters

Example of South Korean stamps lacking Latin text, Yin Yang and standard Korean text of country name. North Korean stamps never show Yin Yang and starting in 1976 are inscribed "DPRK" or "DPR KOREA" in Latin letters.

THAILAND

Country Name

King Chulalongkorn

King Prajadhipok and Chao P'ya Chakri

3. CENTRAL AND EASTERN ASIAN INSCRIPTIONS

INDIA - FEUDATORY STATES

Alwar

Bhor

Bundi

Similar stamps come with different designs in corners and differently drawn daggers (at center of circle).

Dhar

Duttia

Faridkot

Hyderabad

Similar stamps exist with different central design which is inscribed "Postage" or "Post & Receipt."

Indore

Jammu & Kashmir

Text varies.

Jasdan

Jhalawar

Kotah

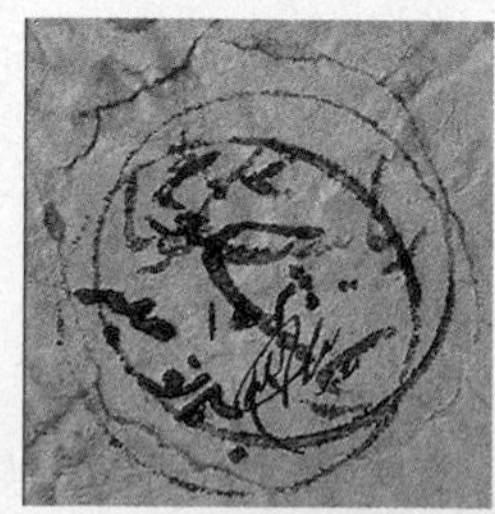

Size and text varies

Nandgaon

Nowanuggur

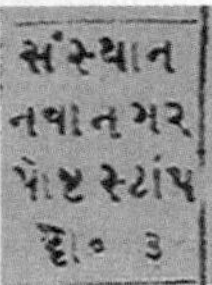

Poonch

Similar stamps exist in various sizes with different text

Rajasthan

Rajpeepla

Soruth

Tonk

BANGLADESH

Country Name

NEPAL

Similar stamps are smaller, have squares in upper corners and have five or nine characters in central bottom panel.

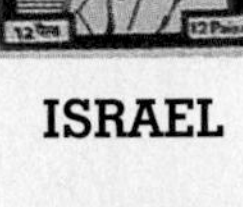

TANNU TUVA

ISRAEL

GEORGIA

This inscription is found on other pictorial stamps.

Country Name

ARMENIA

The four characters are found somewhere on pictorial stamps. On some stamps only the middle two are found.

4. AFRICAN INSCRIPTIONS

ETHIOPIA

5. ARABIC INSCRIPTIONS

١ ٢ ٣ ٤ ٥
1 2 3 4 5

٦ ٧ ٨ ٩ ٠
6 7 8 9 0

AFGHANISTAN

Many early Afghanistan stamps show Tiger's head, many of these have ornaments protruding from outer ring, others show inscriptions in black.

Arabic Script

Crest of King Amanullah

Mosque Gate & Crossed Cannons

The four characters are found somewhere on pictorial stamps. On some stamps only the middle two are found.

BAHRAIN

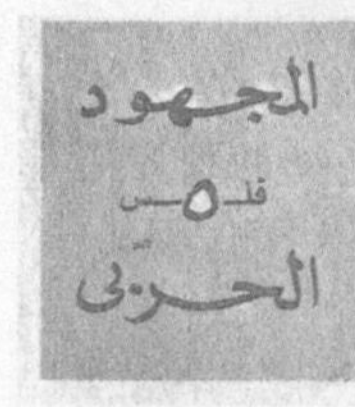

EGYPT

Postage

IRAN

Country Name

Royal Crown

Lion with Sword

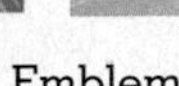

Symbol

Emblem

IRAQ

JORDAN

LEBANON

Similar types have denominations at top and slightly different design.

LIBYA

Country Name in various styles

Other Libya stamps show Eagle and Shield (head facing either direction) or Red, White and Black Shield (with or without eagle in center).

Without Country Name

SAUDI ARABIA

Tughra (Central design)

Palm Tree and Swords

SYRIA

Arab Government Issues

THRACE

YEMEN

PAKISTAN

PAKISTAN - BAHAWALPUR

Country Name in top panel, star and crescent

TURKEY

Star & Crescent is a device found on many Turkish stamps, but is also found on stamps from other Arabic areas (see Pakistan-Bahawalpur)

Tughra (similar tughras can be found on stamps of Turkey in Asia, Afghanistan and Saudi Arabia)

Mohammed V

Mustafa Kemal

Plane, Star and Crescent

TURKEY IN ASIA

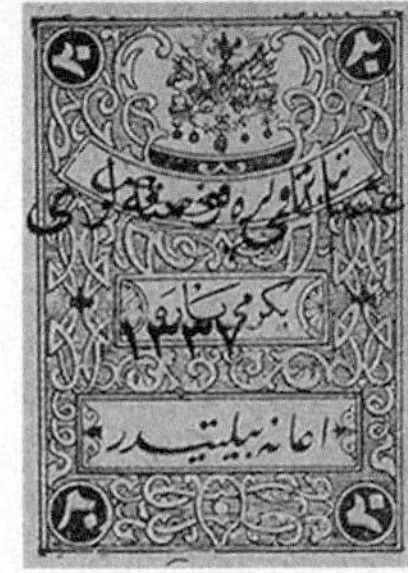

Other Turkey in Asia pictorials show star & crescent.
Other stamps show tughra shown under Turkey.

6. GREEK INSCRIPTIONS

GREECE

Country Name in various styles
(Some Crete stamps overprinted with the Greece country name are listed in Crete.)

Lepta

ΔΡΑΧΜΗ ΔΡΑΧΜΑΙ ΛΕΠΤΟΝ

Drachma Drachmas Lepton

Abbreviated Country Name ΕΛΛ

Other forms of Country Name

No country name

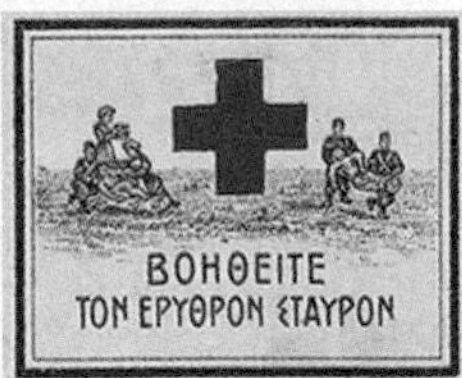

CRETE

Country Name

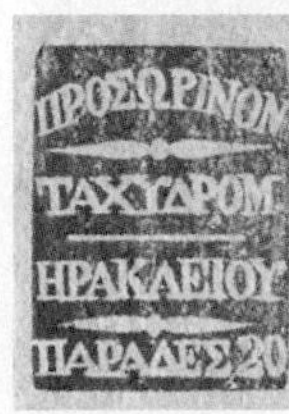

Crete stamps with a surcharge that have the year "1922" are listed under Greece.

EPIRUS

Similar stamps have text above the eagle.

IONIAN IS.

7. CYRILLIC INSCRIPTIONS

RUSSIA

Postage Stamp Imperial Eagle

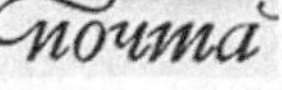

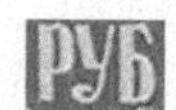

Postage in various styles

Abbreviation for Kopeck Abbreviation for Ruble Russia

Abbreviation for Russian Soviet Federated Socialist Republic RSFSR stamps were overprinted (see below)

Abbreviation for Union of Soviet Socialist Republics

This item is footnoted in Latvia

RUSSIA - Army of the North

"OKCA"

RUSSIA - Wenden

RUSSIAN OFFICES IN THE TURKISH EMPIRE

These letters appear on other stamps of the Russian offices.

The unoverprinted version of this stamp and a similar stamp were overprinted by various countries (see below).

ARMENIA

BELARUS

FAR EASTERN REPUBLIC

Country Name

FINLAND

Circles and Dots on stamps similar to Imperial Russia issues

SOUTH RUSSIA

Country Name

BATUM

Forms of Country Name

TRANSCAUCASIAN FEDERATED REPUBLICS

Abbreviation for Country Name

KAZAKHSTAN

ҚАЗАҚСТАН

Country Name

KYRGYZSTAN

КЫРГЫЗСТАН Country Name

ROMANIA

TAJIKISTAN

Country Name & Abbreviation

UKRAINE

Україні Україні

Country Name in various forms

The trident appears on many stamps, usually as an overprint.

Abbreviation for Ukrainian Soviet Socialist Republic

WESTERN UKRAINE

Abbreviation for Country Name

AZERBAIJAN

AZƏRBAYCAN

Country Name

Abbreviation for Azerbaijan Soviet Socialist Republic

MONTENEGRO

ЦРНЕГОРЕ

ЦРНА ГОРА

Country Name in various forms

ЦР.ГОРЕ

Abbreviation for country name

No country name (A similar Montenegro stamp without country name has same vignette.)

SERBIA

СРПСКА СРБИЈА

Country Name in various forms

СРП. К.С.

Abbreviation for country name

No country name

MACEDONIA

МАКЕДОНИЈА

Country Name

МАКЕДОНСКИ

Different form of Country Name

SERBIA & MONTENEGRO

YUGOSLAVIA

ЈУГОСЛАВИЈА

Showing country name

No Country Name

BOSNIA & HERZEGOVINA (Serb Administration)

РЕПУБЛИКА СРПСКА

Country Name

РЕПУБЛИКЕ СРПСКЕ

Different form of Country Name

No Country Name

BULGARIA

Country Name Postage

Stotinka

Stotinki (plural) Abbreviation for Stotinki

Country Name in various forms and styles

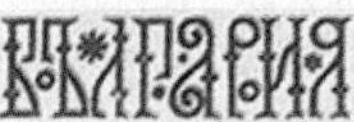

No country name

Abbreviation for Lev, leva

MONGOLIA

Country name in one word Tugrik in Cyrillic

Country name in two words Mung in Cyrillic

Mung in Mongolian

Tugrik in Mongolian

Arms

No Country Name

INDEX AND IDENTIFIER

All page numbers shown are those in this Volume 5.

Postage stamps that do not have English words on them are shown in the Illustrated Identifier.

INDEX TO ADVERTISERS
2017 VOLUME 5

2017
VOLUME 5
DEALER DIRECTORY YELLOW PAGE LISTINGS

This section of your Scott Catalogue contains advertisements to help you conveniently find what you need, when you need it...!

Accessories

BROOKLYN GALLERY COIN & STAMP, INC.
8725 4th Ave.
Brooklyn, NY 11209
PH: 718-745-5701
FAX: 718-745-2775
info@brooklyngallery.com
www.brooklyngallery.com

Appraisals

DR. ROBERT FRIEDMAN & SONS STAMP & COIN BUYING CENTER
2029 W. 75th St.
Woodridge, IL 60517
PH: 800-588-8100
FAX: 630-985-1588
drbobstamps@comcast.net
www.drbobfriedmanstamps.com

Argentina

GUILLERMO JALIL
Maipu 466,local 4
1006 Buenos Aires
Argentina
guillermo@jalilstamps.com
philatino@philatino.com
www.philatino.com
www.jalilstamps.com

Asia

THE STAMP ACT
PO Box 1136
Belmont, CA 94002
PH: 650-703-2342
PH: 650-592-3315
FAX: 650-508-8104
thestampact@sbcglobal.net

Auctions

DUTCH COUNTRY AUCTIONS
The Stamp Center
4115 Concord Pike
Wilmington, DE 19803
PH: 302-478-8740
FAX: 302-478-8779
auctions@dutchcountryauctions.com
www.dutchcountryauctions.com

R. MARESCH & SON LTD.
5th Floor - 6075 Yonge St.
Toronto, ON M2M 3W2
CANADA
PH: 416-363-7777
FAX: 416-363-6511
www.maresch.com

British Commonwealth

ARON R. HALBERSTAM PHILATELISTS, LTD.
PO Box 150168
Van Brunt Station
Brooklyn, NY 11215-0168
PH: 718-788-397
arh@arhstamps.com
www.arhstamps.com

THE STAMP ACT
PO Box 1136
Belmont, CA 94002
PH: 650-703-2342
PH: 650-592-3315
FAX: 650-508-8104
thestampact@sbcglobal.net

Buying

DR. ROBERT FRIEDMAN & SONS STAMP & COIN BUYING CENTER
2029 W. 75th St.
Woodridge, IL 60517
PH: 800-588-8100
FAX: 630-985-1588
drbobstamps@comcast.net
www.drbobfriedmanstamps.com

Canada

CANADA STAMP FINDER
54 Soccavo Crescent
Brampton, ON L6Y 0W3
PH: 905-488-6109
Toll Free in North America
PH: 877-412-3106
FAX: 323-215-2635
info@canadastampfinder.com
www.canadastampfinder.com

ROY'S STAMPS
PO Box 28001
600 Ontario Street
St. Catharines, ON
CANADA L2N 7P8
Phone: 905-934-8377
Email: roystamp@cogeco.ca

Collections

DR. ROBERT FRIEDMAN & SONS STAMP & COIN BUYING CENTER
2029 W. 75th St.
Woodridge, IL 60517
PH: 800-588-8100
FAX: 630-985-1588
drbobstamps@comcast.net
www.drbobfriedmanstamps.com

Ducks

MICHAEL JAFFE
PO Box 61484
Vancouver, WA 98666
PH: 360-695-6161
PH: 800-782-6770
FAX: 360-695-1616
mjaffe@brookmanstamps.com
www.brookmanstamps.com

German Colonies

COLONIAL STAMP COMPANY
5757 Wilshire Blvd. PH #8
Los Angeles, CA 90036
PH: 323-933-9435
FAX: 323-939-9930
Toll Free in North America
PH: 877-272-6693
FAX: 877-272-6694
info@colonialstampcompany.com
www.colonialstampcompany.com

Germany

JAMES F TAFF
PO Box 19549
Sacramento, CA 95819
PH: 916-454-9007
FAX: 916-454-9009

Great Britain

COLONIAL STAMP COMPANY
5757 Wilshire Blvd. PH #8
Los Angeles, CA 90036
PH: 323-933-9435
FAX: 323-939-9930
Toll Free in North America
PH: 877-272-6693
FAX: 877-272-6694
info@colonialstampcompany.com
www.colonialstampcompany.com

Latin America

GUY SHAW
PO Box 27138
San Diego, CA 92198
PH/FAX: 858-485-8269
guyshaw@guyshaw.com
www.guyshaw.com

New Issues

DAVIDSON'S STAMP SERVICE
Personalized Service since 1970
PO Box 36355
Indianapolis, IN 46236-0355
PH: 317-826-2620
ed-davidson@earthlink.net
www.newstampissues.com

British Commonwealth

THE BRITISH COMMONWEALTH
O•F N•A•T•I•O•N•S

We are active buyers and sellers of stamps and postal history of all areas of pre-1960 British Commonwealth, including individual items, collections or estates. Want lists from all reigns are accepted with references.

L. W. Martin, Jr.

CROWN COLONY STAMPS
P.O. Box 1198
BELLAIRE, TEXAS 77402
PH. (713) 781-6563 • FAX (713) 789-9998
E-mail: lwm@crowncolony.com

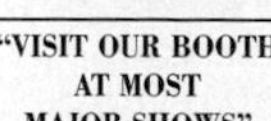

"VISIT OUR BOOTH AT MOST MAJOR SHOWS"

British Commonwealth

The British Empire 1840-1936

Aden to Zululand Mint & Used
Most complete stock in North America

For over 40 years we have helped our customers build some of the world's finest known collections. Our expert ***Want Lists Services*** can do the same for you. With over 50 volumes filled with singles, sets and rare stamps, I am sure we have what you need. We welcome your Want Lists in Scott or Gibbons numbers. Monthly payment plans available for larger purchases.

Put our expertise to work for you today!
You'll be glad you did!!

Colonial Stamp Company
5757 Wilshire Blvd., Penthouse 8
Los Angeles, CA 90036 USA
Tel: +1 (323) 933-9435 Fax: +1 (323) 939-9930
Toll Free in North America
Tel: 1 (877) 272-6693 Fax: 1 (877) 272-6694
E-Mail: *info@colonialstampcompany.com*
URL: *www.colonialstampcompany.com*

Ask for your free Public Auction Catalogue today!

CCNY, IFSDA, INTERNATIONAL SOCIETY OF APPRAISERS

Papua New Guinea

COLONIAL STAMP COMPANY
5757 Wilshire Blvd. PH #8
Los Angeles, CA 90036
PH: 323-933-9435
FAX: 323-939-9930
Toll Free in North America
PH: 877-272-6693
FAX: 877-272-6694
info@colonialstampcompany.com
www.colonialstampcompany.com

Proofs & Essays

HENRY GITNER PHILATELISTS, INC.
PO Box 3077-S
Middletown, NY 10940
PH: 845-343-5151
PH: 800-947-8267
FAX: 845-343-0068
hgitner@hgitner.com
www.hgitner.com

Rhodesia

COLONIAL STAMP COMPANY
5757 Wilshire Blvd. PH #8
Los Angeles, CA 90036
PH: 323-933-9435
FAX: 323-939-9930
Toll Free in North America
PH: 877-272-6693
FAX: 877-272-6694
info@colonialstampcompany.com
www.colonialstampcompany.com

St. Christopher

COLONIAL STAMP COMPANY
5757 Wilshire Blvd. PH #8
Los Angeles, CA 90036
PH: 323-933-9435
FAX: 323-939-9930
Toll Free in North America
PH: 877-272-6693
FAX: 877-272-6694
info@colonialstampcompany.com
www.colonialstampcompany.com

St. Helena

COLONIAL STAMP COMPANY
5757 Wilshire Blvd. PH #8
Los Angeles, CA 90036
PH: 323-933-9435
FAX: 323-939-9930
Toll Free in North America
PH: 877-272-6693
FAX: 877-272-6694
info@colonialstampcompany.com
www.colonialstampcompany.com

St. Kitts & Nevis

COLONIAL STAMP COMPANY
5757 Wilshire Blvd. PH #8
Los Angeles, CA 90036
PH: 323-933-9435
FAX: 323-939-9930
Toll Free in North America
PH: 877-272-6693
FAX: 877-272-6694
info@colonialstampcompany.com
www.colonialstampcompany.com

St. Lucia

COLONIAL STAMP COMPANY
5757 Wilshire Blvd. PH #8
Los Angeles, CA 90036
PH: 323-933-9435
FAX: 323-939-9930
Toll Free in North America
PH: 877-272-6693
FAX: 877-272-6694
info@colonialstampcompany.com
www.colonialstampcompany.com

St. Vincent

COLONIAL STAMP COMPANY
5757 Wilshire Blvd. PH #8
Los Angeles, CA 90036
PH: 323-933-9435
FAX: 323-939-9930
Toll Free in North America
PH: 877-272-6693
FAX: 877-272-6694
info@colonialstampcompany.com
www.colonialstampcompany.com

Samoa

COLONIAL STAMP COMPANY
5757 Wilshire Blvd. PH #8
Los Angeles, CA 90036
PH: 323-933-9435
FAX: 323-939-9930
Toll Free in North America
PH: 877-272-6693
FAX: 877-272-6694
info@colonialstampcompany.com
www.colonialstampcompany.com

Sarawak

COLONIAL STAMP COMPANY
5757 Wilshire Blvd. PH #8
Los Angeles, CA 90036
PH: 323-933-9435
FAX: 323-939-9930
Toll Free in North America
PH: 877-272-6693
FAX: 877-272-6694
info@colonialstampcompany.com
www.colonialstampcompany.com

Seychelles

COLONIAL STAMP COMPANY
5757 Wilshire Blvd. PH #8
Los Angeles, CA 90036
PH: 323-933-9435
FAX: 323-939-9930
Toll Free in North America
PH: 877-272-6693
FAX: 877-272-6694
info@colonialstampcompany.com
www.colonialstampcompany.com

Sierra Leone

COLONIAL STAMP COMPANY
5757 Wilshire Blvd. PH #8
Los Angeles, CA 90036
PH: 323-933-9435
FAX: 323-939-9930
Toll Free in North America
PH: 877-272-6693
FAX: 877-272-6694
info@colonialstampcompany.com
www.colonialstampcompany.com

Stamp Stores

California

BROSIUS STAMP, COIN & SUPPLIES
2105 Main St.
Santa Monica, CA 90405
PH: 310-396-7480
FAX: 310-396-7455
brosius.stamp.coin@hotmail.com

COLONIAL STAMP COMPANY
5757 Wilshire Blvd. PH #8
Los Angeles, CA 90036
PH: 323-933-9435
FAX: 323-939-9930
Toll Free in North America
PH: 877-272-6693
FAX: 877-272-6694
info@colonialstampcompany.com
www.colonialstampcompany.com

Stamp Stores

Delaware

DUTCH COUNTRY AUCTIONS
The Stamp Center
4115 Concord Pike
Wilmington, DE 19803
PH: 302-478-8740
FAX: 302-478-8779
auctions@dutchcountryauctions.com
www.dutchcountryauctions.com

Georgia

STAMPS UNLIMITED OF GEORGIA, INC.
Suite 1460
100 Peachtree St. NW
Atlanta, GA 30303
PH: 404-688-9161
tonyroozen@yahoo.com
www.stampsunlimitedofga.com

Illinois

DR. ROBERT FRIEDMAN & SONS STAMP & COIN BUYING CENTER
2029 W. 75th St.
Woodridge, IL 60517
PH: 800-588-8100
FAX: 630-985-1588
drbobstamps@comcast.net
www.drbobfriedmanstamps.com

Indiana

KNIGHT STAMP & COIN CO.
237 Main St.
Hobart, IN 46342
PH: 219-942-4341
PH: 800-634-2646
knight@knightcoin.com
www.knightcoin.com

New Jersey

BERGEN STAMPS & COLLECTIBLES
306 Queen Anne Rd.
Teaneck, NJ 07666
PH: 201-836-8987

TRENTON STAMP & COIN CO
Thomas DeLuca
Store: Forest Glen Plaza
1804 Highway 33
Hamilton Square, NJ 08690
Mail: PO Box 8574
Trenton, NJ 08650
PH: 609-584-8100
FAX: 609-587-8664
TOMD4TSC@aol.com

New York

CHAMPION STAMP CO., INC.
432 W. 54th St.
New York, NY 10019
PH: 212-489-8130
FAX: 212-581-8130
championstamp@aol.com
www.championstamp.com

CK STAMPS
42-14 Union St. # 2A
Flushing, NY 11355
PH: 917-667-6641
ckstampsllc@yahoo.com

Ohio

HILLTOP STAMP SERVICE
Richard A. Peterson
PO Box 626
Wooster, OH 44691
PH: 330-262-8907 (0)
PH: 330-262-5378 (H)
hilltop@bright.net
www.hilltopstamps.com

Supplies

BROOKLYN GALLERY COIN & STAMP, INC.
8725 4th Ave.
Brooklyn, NY 11209
PH: 718-745-5701
FAX: 718-745-2775
info@brooklyngallery.com
www.brooklyngallery.com

Topicals

E. JOSEPH McCONNELL, INC.
PO Box 683
Monroe, NY 10949
PH: 845-783-9791
FAX: 845-782-0347
ejstamps@gmail.com
www.EJMcConnell.com

Topicals-Columbus

MR. COLUMBUS
PO Box 1492
Fennville, MI 49408
PH: 269-543-4755
David@MrColumbus1492.com
MrColumbus1492.com

Topicals-Miscellaneous

HENRY GITNER PHILATELISTS, INC.
PO Box 3077-S
Middletown, NY 10940
PH: 845-343-5151
PH: 800-947-8267
FAX: 845-343-0068
hgitner@hgitner.com
www.hgitner.com

United Nations

BRUCE M. MOYER
Box 99
East Texas, PA 18046
PH: 610-395-8410
FAX: 610-395-8537
moyer@unstamps.com
www.unstamps.com

United States

BROOKMAN STAMP CO.
PO Box 90
Vancouver, WA 98666
PH: 360-695-1391
PH: 800-545-4871
FAX: 360-695-1616
info@brookmanstamps.com
www.brookmanstamps.com

KEITH WAGNER
ACS STAMP COMPANY
2914 W 135TH AVE
BROOMFIELD, COLORADO 80020
303-841-8666
WWW.ACSSTAMP.COM